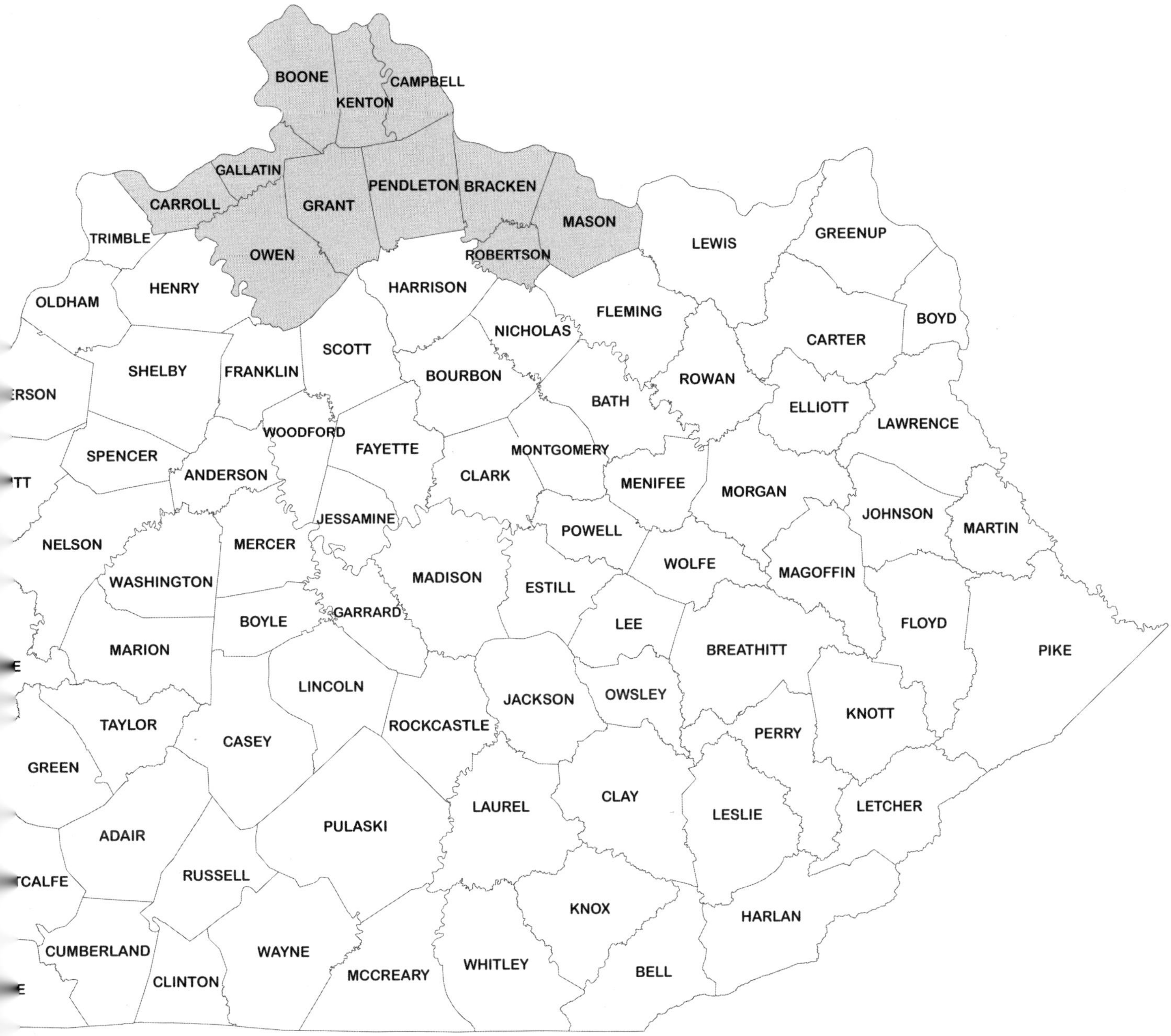

BOONE
KENTON
CAMPBELL
GALLATIN
CARROLL
GRANT
PENDLETON
BRACKEN
MASON
TRIMBLE
OWEN
ROBERTSON
LEWIS
GREENUP
OLDHAM
HENRY
HARRISON
FLEMING
NICHOLAS
BOYD
CARTER
SHELBY
FRANKLIN
SCOTT
BOURBON
ROWAN
ERSON
BATH
ELLIOTT
WOODFORD
LAWRENCE
SPENCER
FAYETTE
MONTGOMERY
ANDERSON
CLARK
MENIFEE
MORGAN
TT
JESSAMINE
JOHNSON
MARTIN
NELSON
MERCER
POWELL
WOLFE
MAGOFFIN
WASHINGTON
MADISON
ESTILL
GARRARD
BOYLE
LEE
FLOYD
MARION
BREATHITT
PIKE
E
LINCOLN
JACKSON
OWSLEY
KNOTT
TAYLOR
ROCKCASTLE
PERRY
CASEY
GREEN
LAUREL
CLAY
LESLIE
LETCHER
PULASKI
ADAIR
RUSSELL
TCALFE
KNOX
HARLAN
CUMBERLAND
WAYNE
WHITLEY
BELL
MCCREARY
CLINTON
E

The Encyclopedia *of* Northern Kentucky

A Project of the Thomas D. Clark Foundation, Inc.

The ENCYCLOPEDIA *of* NORTHERN KENTUCKY

Edited by
Paul A. Tenkotte
and
James C. Claypool

THE UNIVERSITY PRESS OF KENTUCKY

Scholarly publisher for the Commonwealth,
serving Bellarmine University, Berea College, Centre
College of Kentucky, Eastern Kentucky University,
The Filson Historical Society, Georgetown College,
Kentucky Historical Society, Kentucky State University,
Morehead State University, Murray State University,
Northern Kentucky University, Transylvania University,
University of Kentucky, University of Louisville,
and Western Kentucky University.

Editorial and Sales Offices: The University Press of Kentucky
663 South Limestone Street, Lexington, Kentucky 40508-4008
www.kentuckypress.com

13 12 11 10 09 5 4 3 2 1

Maps by Jeff Levy at the Gyula Pauer Center for Cartography & GIS, University of Kentucky

Library of Congress Cataloging-in-Publication Data

The encyclopedia of northern Kentucky / edited by Paul A. Tenkotte and James C. Claypool.
p. cm.
Includes bibliographical references and index.
ISBN 978-0-8131-2565-7 (hardcover : acid-free paper)
ISBN 978-0-8131-2585-5 (limited leather edition)
1. Kentucky, Northern—Encyclopedias. 2. Kentucky—Encyclopedias. I. Tenkotte, Paul A. II. Claypool, James C.
F451.E55 2009
976.9'3003—dc22
2009027969

This book is printed on acid-free recycled paper meeting
the requirements of the American National Standard
for Permanence in Paper for Printed Library Materials.

Manufactured in the United States of America.

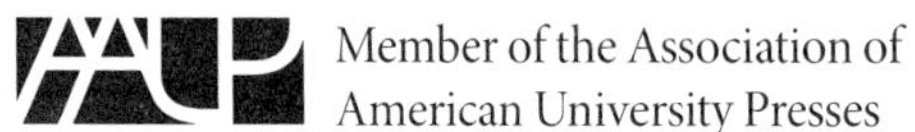

Editorial Staff

Editors in Chief

Paul A. Tenkotte
James C. Claypool

Associate Editors

David Hatter
John Schlipp
David E. Schroeder
Robert Stevie
Michael R. Sweeney
John W. Thieret (deceased)
Thomas S. Ward
Jack Wessling

Topical Editors

AGRICULTURE	Lynn David and James Wallace
ART	Rebecca Bilbo
BIOGRAPHY	Michael R. Sweeney
BUSINESS AND COMMERCE	John Boh
COUNTIES AND TOWNS	David E. Schroeder
ETHNOLOGY	Theodore H. H. Harris
GOVERNMENT, LAW, AND POLITICS	John Schlipp
LITERATURE	Danny Miller (deceased)
MEDICINE	Dennis B. Worthen
MILITARY	James A. Ramage
MUSIC, MEDIA, AND ENTERTAINMENT	John Schlipp
RELIGION	Thomas S. Ward and Alex Hyrcza
SPORTS AND RECREATION	James C. Claypool
TRANSPORTATION	Joseph F. Gastright (deceased)
WOMEN	Karen McDaniel

To Michael Hammons, and to the memory of his friend Thomas D. Clark, Kentucky's historian laureate, who both felt that Northern Kentucky deserved its own encyclopedia. Also to the memory of John W. Thieret, Danny Miller, and Joseph F. Gastright, members of our editorial staff who did not live to see the finished project.

Sponsors

Commonwealth of Kentucky, Governor's Office, Department for Local Government
Scripps Howard Foundation/The Kentucky Post
The Carol Ann and Ralph V. Haile Jr./U.S. Bank Foundation
Thomas More College
Gannett Foundation/Enquirer
Mark and Rosemary Schlachter
Alice Sparks
George and Ellen Rieveschl
Forward Quest Inc. dba Vision 2015
Fifth Third Bank Northern Kentucky
Bank of Kentucky
Eva and Oakley Farris
Louise Taft Semple Foundation
Bavarian Waste Services
Fidelity Investments
Libertas Technologies LLC
Toyota Motor Engineering and Manufacturing North America Inc.
Kenton County Public Library
Boone County Public Library
City of Florence
Great American Financial Resources Inc.
Greenebaum Doll and McDonald PLLC
J.J.B. Hilliard and W.L. Lyons Inc.
Kenton County Fiscal Court
Bruce Lunsford
National City Bank
Citigroup Business Services
City of Crestview Hills
Ruth M. Doering
Ray and Norma Mueller
City of Newport
PNC Bank
R.C. Durr Foundation Inc.
Northern Kentucky University
Robert E. Rich
Northern Kentucky Heritage League
Mountjoy and Bressler LLP
SSK Communities
City of Fort Wright
Clarence Lassetter
City of Erlanger
Michael and Kit Hammons
Northern Kentucky Chamber of Commerce
Victory Community Bank
Harold Brown Weldon
Kenneth and Kathleen Williams
BlueStar
Doug and Kate Hendrickson
William Terwort
Friends of Steely Library, Northern Kentucky University
Nancy J. Tretter
Sue Bogardus
Elissa May-Plattner
Chris Bolling
Heritage Bank
Dorothy and Harry Warmbier
Paul L. Whalen
George J. Budig
Nicholas J. and Nina Clooney
Bruce Ferguson
George E. Fern Co.
Northern Kentucky Medical Society
Col Owens
Leon Boothe
Ron and Linda Troxell

Authors

Marie Ackman
Al Alfaro
Fran Allen
Paul Anderson
Barbara Arrighi
Roger Auge II
Michael R. Averdick
William Baker
Sandy Banta
Sarah A. Barlage
Sabrina Alcorn Baron
Marja Barrett
Fred Bassett
Matthew E. Becher
Mildred Belew
Amber L. Benson
William H. Bergmann
Peggy Bertelsman
F. Keith Biddle
Rebecca Bilbo
Donna M. Bloemer
Nancy Due Bloemer
Terry Boehmker
Charles H. Bogart
John Boh
Vicki Bolden
Verna L. Bond-Broderick
William W. Bowdy
Jarrett Boyd
Perry Bratcher
John R. S. Brooking*
Barbara Loomis Brown
Lucinda Brown
Rick Brueggemann
Ruth Wade Cox Brunings
William S. Bryant
Millie Bush
Anne S. Butler
Vic Canfield
Michael Capek
Robin Caraway
Paul A. Carl Jr.
Sarah Caruso
Pamela Ciafardini Casebolt
Peggy Casey
James R. Cassidy
Garry A. Casson
Robert C. Cetrulo
Gail Chastang
Arden G. Christen
Judith G. Clabes
Karen Claiborne
Don Clare
Donald A. Clark
Kara Clark
James C. Claypool
Sharon Claypool
Nina Clooney
John B. Conrad*
Diane Perrine Coon
Kenneth Crawford
Deborah Diersen Crocker
Evelyn G. Cropper
Carol Culbertson
Steve Culbertson
Edna Marie Cummins
Mary Carmen Cupito
Jim Dady
Betty Maddox Daniels
Lynn David
Bill Davis
Don DeBats
Ronald Decker
Norbert F. DeJaco
Debbie Dennie
Eric Deters
Tom DiBello
D. W. Dills
Barbara Droege
Glenn Drummond
James R. Duvall
David J. Ebacher
Joyce Edmondson
Chuck Eilerman
Ron Ellis
William E. Ellis
Jim Embry
Mary Louis Evans
James Farrell
Rob Farrell
Joe Feiertag
Jim Feldman
Bruce Ferguson
Mary Fisher
Anne Moser Flannery
Patrick M. Flannery*
Deloris Foxworthy
Pat Frew
Anthony W. Frohlich
Kelly Fulmer
Jannes W. Garbett
Joseph F. Gastright*
Blanche Gaynor
Robert A. Genheimer
Robert Gioielli
Bill Goller
Sue Ellen Grannis
Jennifer Gregory
Jeanne Greiser
Matthew J. Grimes
Noelle Higdon Grimes
Donald E. Grosenbach
Barry Grossheim
Peter Grote
Heather Gulley
Patricia A. Hahn
Lori Haller
Robert Hans
Mary Jo Hardcorn
Fred C. Harmeyer
Lorna Petty Harrell
Theodore H. H. Harris
Dave Hatter
Brenda Hawkins
Raymond G. Hebert
Margaret Prentice Hecker
Jennifer Hedger
Ken Heil
Michelle Heil
Maggie Heran
Tim Herrmann
Dennis Hetzel
Joe Heving Jr.
Ann Hicks
Joy Higgins
Charles D. Hockensmith
Jennifer Holladay
Randolph Hollingsworth

Steve Huddleston
Barbara Huffman
Eric R. Hugo
Marc F. Hult
Laurel Humes
Alex Hyrcza
Eric R. Jackson
Steven D. Jaeger
Donald James
Sharon Jobert
Gary Lynwood Johnston
Coralie Runyon Jones
Judith Butler Jones
Bridget Kaiser
Denny Kelley-Warnick
Jerome L. Kendall
Amanda C. Kerley
Susan Claypool Kettles
Charles King
Peggy L. Kiser
John E. Kleber
John Klee
Larry Klein
Judy Lang Klosterman
James C. Klotter
Douglas Knerr
Jessica Knox-Perkins
Michael Kraus
Jeannine Kreinbrink
Deborah Kohl Kremer
Gretchen Landrum
Rob Langenderfer
Karen L. Leek
Terry W. Lehmann
Suzann Parker Leist
John E. Leming Jr.
John A. Lenox
Janet M. Lester
Karl Lietzenmayer
Thomas J. Lippert
Tony Llamas
Chris Lorentz
Hardin Lowe
Mary Ellen Lucas
Andrew O. Lutes
Julia Mace
Darrell Maines
James L. Mallory
Donn Manker
Kelly Marsh
MaryJoy Martin
Debian Marty
Ken Massey
Linda Maus
Mac McArthur
Mike McCormick
Karen McDaniel
James L. McDonald
Sharon McGee
Stephen T. McMurtry
Chris Meiman
Scott Merriman
Katherine Meyer
Rick Meyers
Caroline R. Miller
Danny Miller*
Orloff G. Miller
Carol Mitchell
Dan Moore
J. C. Morgan
Melinda G. Motley
Janice Mueller
Maggie Mulshine
Margaret A. Murphy
Jacquelene P. Mylor
Patricia Nagelkirk
Deborah R. Neace
Judy L. Neff
William C. Neuroth
Jon Nicholas
Betty Lee Nordheim
Jim O'Brien
Donna Oehler
Deborah Onkst
Wayne Onkst
Robin Rider Osborne
Col Owens
George Palmer
Connie Pangburn
Charles E. Parrish
Susan Patterson
Steven Pattie
Martha Pelfry
Greg Perkins
Mike Philipps
Elissa Plattner
Jenny Plemen
Bernie Poe
Michael J. Poehner
Daryl Polley
Marv Price
Frank X. Prudent
Jane D. Purdon
James A. Ramage
Thomas Rambo
Caroline Ransdell
Richard Rawe
Aprile Conrad Redden
Michael D. Redden
Johnna Reeder
Virginia Reeves
Jim Reis
Kenneth A. Reis
Carol Elsener Rekow
Robert M. Rennick
Jennifer Adkins Reynolds
Robert T. Rhode
J. Michael Rhyne
Doris Riley
Laurie Risch
Daniel Edgar Ritchie
Alice Kennelly Roberts
Stephen Rockenbach
Nicole Ropp
Michael D. Rouse
Richard M. Sacksteder
Kathryn Salyers
Brad Sayles
Laura Schaefer
Paul John Schewene
Thomas D. Schiffer
John Schlipp
Neil Schmidt
Craig Schneider
Robert Schrage
David E. Schroeder
Lydia Cushman Schurman
Melinda Senters
Lou Settle
Lois Ann Shannon
Pam Sheppard
Warren J. Shonert*
Mary Lou Simons
Kareem A. Simpson
Patrick Snadon
Robert B. Snow
David Sorrell
Sue Sorrell
J. T. Spence
Bernie Spencer
Sienna Spooner
Iris Spoor
Annemarie Springer

Ann Stanchina
Sherry Stanforth
Brenda Caldwell Stanley
William Michael Stanley
Steve Stevens
Robert W. Stevie
Bridget B. Striker
Michael D. Stull
Eric Summe
Gabrielle Summe
Michael R. Sweeney
Phil Taliaferro
Paul A. Tenkotte
William Terwort
Mary Texter
Bill Thomas
Sandra Thomas
Dan Tobergte
Don Heinrich Tolzmann
Nancy J. Tretter
Robert Trundle
Matthew Turner
Michael L. Turney
Rebecca Mitchell Turney
Dennis W. Van Houten*
Jane Van Ryan
George Vaughn
Robert Michael Venable
Stephen M. Vest
Dale E. Voelker
James Wallace
Laurie Walton
Thomas S. Ward
Margaret Warminski
Andrea Watkins
Robert D. Webster
Lee Shai Weissbach
Evelyn Welch
Alexandra K. Weldon
Rebecca Schaffer Wells
Suzanne C. Wendt
Jack Wessling
John West
Paul L. Whalen
John H. White
Robert White
Michael Whitehead
Mary Francis Whitson
Melissa J. Wickelhaus
Donald M. Wiedeman
Laurie Wilcox
Teresa Wilkins
Elizabeth Comer Williams
Mike Williams
Robert Joseph Williams
Brenda L. Wilson
Meg Winchell
Kathryn Witt
Ralph Wolff
Teresa Wolking
Pat Workman
Dennis B. Worthen
Carolyn Zink

* Deceased.

Contents

Foreword

The past 25 years have served as a bridge from one century to another. During this time, Northern Kentucky has truly come into its own. Now there is another sign of its maturity and cohesiveness—a regional encyclopedia.

I am a lifelong Kentuckian who was fortunate enough to have been given the assignment of a lifetime. In the early 1980s I came to Northern Kentucky as editor of its principal newspaper, the *Kentucky Post.* Old-timers were still calling it the *Post and Times-Star,* a sure sign of affection and regard. With this plum assignment, I had a front-row seat for the passing show that was the Renaissance of a region struggling to define and understand itself.

Northern Kentucky's identity crisis was endemic. Beset by a multiplicity of largely ineffective governmental silos, a speckled and colorful history, a collective stepchild mentality (not quite good enough for Cincinnati and not quite part of Kentucky), it was a region that embraced a "circle-the-wagons" mentality.

It was a bit of culture shock for me, too, having grown up in the breadbasket region of the state, having spent my college days in the inner Bluegrass region, and having started my professional career in Evansville, across the river from my hometown of Henderson. To me, Northern Kentucky was a vibrant, interesting place, one of the few truly urban areas of Kentucky, full of untapped potential and too much whining. Coming through the "Cut in the Hill" of I-75, what I saw was spectacular beauty that took my breath away; what I heard was a lot of complaining. As I traveled the area, I beheld lush fields and farms and met common-sense, down-to-earth people who belonged to the land. I discovered a region rich in diversity of experiences, lifestyles, and opportunities. Yet I heard little appreciation for the fullness of this largesse. To me Northern Kentucky was the truly "greater" part of Greater Cincinnati, though it called itself the "Southern side." We took for granted the advantages others envied: rivers, interstates, an airport, railroads, the architectural heritage of our urban cores, the livability of our suburbs and the vastness of our rural lands, and our citizenry, people who stay put. The rest of the state called us the third leg of the Golden Triangle, while we collectively limped along carrying the burden of our insecurities.

But the "Perfect Storm" was gathering, and things were about to change. Necessity being the mother of invention, economic good times drove much of the progress. A cohesive, though too short-lived, legislative caucus helped. The exponential growth of our regional university mattered. An effective newspaper that could build a "tribal fire" was crucial. The influx of new industry, well-paying jobs, and new, energetic human resources and perspective made a difference. The real catalyst, however, was a human resource of another kind: Northern Kentucky's own people. These were the men and women who had lived here all their lives, pulled themselves up by the bootstraps, become self-made successes in their businesses, built homes and roads and office buildings, started banks and created jobs, and generally changed the landscape of our perceptions, starting with our front door at the riverfront. They were ready to give back, and they did so with a vengeance. Superseding lazy political divisions, they mobilized an eager citizenry at its grass roots. Community-wide visioning created a road map for a purposeful journey into a promising future.

We began to embrace our regionalness. We started to do less whining and more strategizing. We got to know each other. We followed the road map in a parade to the greater good. We began to celebrate Northern Kentucky in its rich wholeness.

We are not finished, of course; there is still the future and much to do. But we embrace challenges as opportunities, and we have built a solid foundation for growth and prosperity, for a good place to live and put down deep roots. We have an abiding sense of place and belonging.

This encyclopedia adds bricks to the structure. It is yet another example of what can be done when leadership galvanizes the talent and energy of creative, caring people around an effort that matters. Its editors, writers, staff, volunteers, and funders are to be applauded for creating a remarkable resource that will serve us for decades to come.

Judith G. Clabes

Acknowledgments

The Editors in Chief wish to express their sincere gratitude to the individuals, institutions, and businesses that made this encyclopedia possible.

The following (listed alphabetically) assisted greatly in research or in the loan of pertinent materials such as photographs and documents, or in both ways: American Diversified Development Inc., Archdiocese of Cincinnati Archives, Roger Auge II, Michael R. Averdick, Matthew E. Becher, Behringer-Crawford Museum, Mildred Belew, Sue Bogardus, Charles Bogart, John Boh, Boone Co. Historical Society, Boone Co. Historic Preservation Review Board, Boone Co. Public Library, Bracken Co. Historical Society, Thomas B. Brackman, Cindy Brown, Ruth Brunings, Sharon Cahill, Campbell Co. Historical Society, Campbell Co. Public Library, Gene Carinci, Carroll Co. Public Library, Cincinnati/Northern Kentucky International Airport, City of Crestview Hills, Sharon Claypool, Nick and Nina Clooney, College Football Hall of Fame, Elizabeth Comer, Diane Perrine Coon, Dinsmore Homestead, Diocese of Dallas, Archives, M. Keith Dykes, Bob and Martha Hoppenjans Edwards, Ron and Christine Einhaus, C. Dale Elifrits, Ron Ellis, Evergreen Cemetery, Bill Finke, Flushing (NY) Cemetery, Gallatin Co. Historical Society, Gallatin Co. Public Library, Grant Co. Historical Society, Grant Co. Public Library, Jeanne Greiser, Don Grossenbach, Ray Hadorn Jr., Lori Haller, Larry Hanneken, Robert Hans, H. Edward Harber, Mary Jo Hardcorn, Theodore H. H. Harris, Hebrew Union College, Ken Heil, Maggie Heran, Dennis Hetzel, James Hill, Jill Hoefker, Dave Horn, Sharon Jobert, Bridget Kaiser, Kansas City (Mo.) Public Library, Kenton Co. Historical Society, Kenton Co. Public Library, Covington, Kentucky Department of Transportation, Kentucky Gateway Museum, Kentucky Historical Society, Charles King, John Kleber, John Klee, Larry Klein, Jeannine Kreinbrink, Fred Krome, Nichole Lainhart, Lakeview Cemetery, Cleveland, Walter E. Langsam, Lexington Public Library, Library of Congress, Karl Lietzenmayer, Lloyd Library, Andrew Lonneman Family, Los Angeles Public Library, Maysville Cemetery, Jim McHale, Randy McNutt, Paul Meier, Caroline Miller, Minnesota Historical Society, Roy J. Moser, Mountain View Cemetery, Oakland, Margaret Murphy, Newberry Library, Northern Kentucky University, Steely Library, Bonnie Lou and Milt Okum, Wayne Onkst, Owen Co. Historical Society, Owen Co. Public Library, Chris A. Papas & Son Company, Chuck Parrish, Greg Perkins, Eunice Rechtin, Jim Reis, Ken Reis, Carol Rekow, James C. Resing, Pete Rightmore, Doris Riley, Robertson Co. Historical Society, Robin Imaging, Joseph Ruh, John Schlipp, David Schroeder, Brandon Seiter, Marty Sheehan, Sisters of Divine Providence, Sisters of St. Benedict, Robert Snow, Dave Sorrell, Bernie Spencer, Spring Grove Cemetery, Jan Stanley, Steubenville Public Library, Robert W. Stevie, Ken Stone, Bridget Striker, Kelly Sutkamp, Michael R. Sweeney, Harry V. and Mary M. Tenkotte, Tennessee State University Library, Charles R. Tharp, Thomas More College Library and Archives, Don Tolzmann, Nancy Tretter, Thomas Ward, Margo Warminski, Jack Wessling, John White, Michael Whitehead, Laurie Wilcox, Kenneth & Kathleen Williams , Emmett Witham, Ralph Wolff, and Robert Yoder.

The following provided in-kind and/or academic support: Brad Bielski, Thomas More College; Raymond G. Hebert, Thomas More College; Peg Hancock, Thomas More College; Jon Draud; Katie Stein; and Jack Westwood.

The following (listed alphabetically) provided assistance with public relations: Cincinnati Business Courier, Grant Co. News, Kentucky Enquirer, Kentucky Monthly Magazine, Kentucky Post, Ledger-Independent (Maysville), Mike Philipps, WNKR, and WNKU.

David Cobb, Lois Crum, and Steve Wrinn provided assistance with editing. We offer special thanks also to our Web site designer and host, Dave Hatter. Finally, we offer our deepest appreciation to Alice Sparks for her tireless fundraising efforts and generosity to this project. Without her, it would not have been possible.

Introduction

Northern Kentucky is well represented by "Gateway" slogans and names—"Covington: Gateway to the South," "Maysville: Gateway to the Southland," "Williamstown: Gateway to the Bluegrass," Kentucky Gateway Museum, and Gateway Community and Technical College, to name but a sampling.[1] The popularity of the gateway terminology reflects Northern Kentucky's border status, lying across the Ohio River from the states of Ohio and Indiana. The 11 counties of Northern Kentucky—Boone, Bracken, Campbell, Carroll, Gallatin, Grant, Kenton, Mason, Owen, Pendleton, and Robertson—share a common history, bound together by links of transportation, commerce, and social patterns. The Ohio River, roads, and railroads have created a region featuring a heavily urbanized area and its surrounding suburbs and rural towns.

The term *gateway* evokes many images and helps to illustrate seven themes related to the border area of Northern Kentucky. First, a gateway is an opening, a passageway between two distinct places. Located along the Mason-Dixon line, Northern Kentucky (and Kentucky itself) began as part of the slaveholding Commonwealth of Virginia, while the Northwest Territory across the river prohibited slavery. Kentucky developed along the Virginia pattern, with large tracts of land granted to soldiers who served in the Colonial and Revolutionary wars. A haphazard, "shingled-over" pattern of conflicting land claims resulted. Counties and towns became the norm, connected by winding roads that followed the sometimes-difficult topography. Meanwhile, north of the Ohio River, the Northwest Territory was divided into tidy townships of 36 square miles each, with 1 square mile set aside for later resale to benefit the establishment of common schools. Roads were fairly straight, land claims more firmly established, and the terrain gentler, largely a result of prehistoric glaciers that stopped in the region. Even geologically, therefore, Northern Kentucky was at a border. Meteorologically, Northern Kentucky is a transition zone between two major climates, Humid Continental to its north and Humid Subtropical to its south. The old aphorism "If you don't like the weather here, wait five minutes" has a firm basis in science regionally.

Covington, "Dixie's Gateway."

Second, while North and South were seen as truly distinct, border areas were regarded as special places where a blend of cultures resulted. Hence, Northern Kentucky could "pick and choose" from the best of both worlds. In terms of 20th-century tourism, it chose southern hospitality, a theme echoed and reechoed from the 1930s through the 1960s in Northern Kentucky promotional brochures. In a 1950s Maysville brochure, entertainer Rosemary Clooney was featured bedecked in a southern belle dress, arms flung invitingly to her sides, in front of opening wrought-iron gates. Above her was the message "Maysville welcomes you to Kentucky, Gateway to the Southland." It reinforced the idea that Northern Kentucky was southern, hospitable, and a pleasant place to visit for tourists passing through the region.

The southernness of Northern Kentucky, however, has been exaggerated. For example, the presidential election of 1860 evidenced the divisions of Northern Kentucky as a border area that nevertheless overwhelmingly supported the preservation of the Union. Overall, the counties of Northern Kentucky cast 8,041 votes for Constitutional Unionist John Bell of Tennessee, 7,620 for Southern Democrat and Kentucky native John C. Breckinridge, 3,413 for Northern Democrat Stephen A. Douglas of Illinois, and 614 for native son and Republican Abraham Lincoln. Although Lincoln's vote seems low in relation to that of the North, his Northern Kentucky support was actually the highest in the state, with Campbell and Kenton ranking first and second among Kentucky counties

Maysville's *Gateway to the Southland* brochure, featuring Rosemary Clooney.

supporting Lincoln. Lincoln's Northern Kentucky votes accounted for 45 percent of his Kentucky total.[2]

While the gateway depiction of Northern Kentucky appealed to 20th-century tourists, it has also attracted investors and residents. The 1950s Maysville brochure, for instance, was sponsored by the Maysville–Mason County Development Association. In addition to points of interest and information about restaurants and "tourist facilities," the brochure included facts about banks, health, industry, and organizations. This third theme—the openness, innovation, and diversity of border areas like Northern Kentucky—proved enticing to settlers and investors alike. Beginning in the late 18th century, they included Daniel Boone, Simon Kenton, David Leitch, and James Taylor Jr. From earliest times, people have migrated back and forth between Kentucky, Ohio, and Indiana. Ferries crossed the Ohio River from the late 18th century onward, and bridges have graced its shores since the mid-to-late 19th century. Northerners and southerners; immigrants and natives; whites and blacks; Protestants, Catholics, and Jews all settled in Northern Kentucky. This mix produced an open and relatively peaceful culture that especially attracted Germans. The region became one of the three points (Milwaukee, St. Louis, and Cincinnati-Covington-Newport) of the "German Triangle," nationally recognized as a prime destination of German immigrants. Such an ethnic flowering of cultures produced artists Thomas P. Anshutz, James Beard, Frank Duveneck, Henry Farny, Johann Schmitt, and Dixie Selden. Innovations, for example the John A. Roebling Bridge, and inventors, such as Frederick McKinley Jones, abounded. Conservative and liberal ideas stood side-by-side. Social reformers Daniel Carter Beard, Lina and Adelia Beard, and Kate Trimble Woolsey championed causes ranging from boys' and girls' scouting to women's rights. Even socialism had a relative stronghold in places in Northern Kentucky in the early 20th century. Long before diversity became a politically correct term, Northern Kentucky was tolerant, and prosperity was its reward.

Fourth, the residents of Northern Kentucky sometimes experienced difficulties of self-identity. Were they the gateway to the south or to the north? Or were they merely Midwesterners? Were they citizens of Kentucky or suburbanites of Cincinnati? The pendulum has swung widely over the course of history. Before the mid-19th century, for instance, the residents of Covington and Newport regarded themselves as "rivals" to their counterparts in Cincinnati. By 1850, however, the citizens of Northern Kentucky realized that they would never catch up with Cincinnati in terms of population, commerce, or industry, so they settled into roles as suburban cities, that is, suburbs of Cincinnati, yet still important Kentucky cities. By 1850 Covington was the second-largest city in Kentucky, and by 1860 Newport ranked third-most-populous.[3]

Fifth, outsiders' viewpoints of border areas like Northern Kentucky often proved just as ambiguous as the residents' self-identity. Louisville, always a rival to Cincinnati, denigrated Covington as a mere tool of Cincinnati in an 1837 *Louisville Public Advertiser* editorial, calling the Northern Kentucky city a "fly perched on" the "coach wheel" of Cincinnati, exclaiming as it rolled down the road, "Gods! what a dust I make!"[4] Cincinnatians worried that the building of the John A. Roebling Bridge in the mid-19th century would serve to enrich Covington at the expense of Cincinnati. Once again, the pendulum swung back and forth, dependent upon the issue at hand and the goals of those who supported or opposed it.

Sixth, a gateway also triggers images of fences and walls. As implied, however, whereas rivers, roads, and railroads make excellent transportation routes, they make poor fences. Accordingly, the fences around and even within Northern Kentucky have been mental, not physical, constructs. They have been erected, torn down, and rebuilt throughout the years in service to whatever self-identity predominated at the time. It is said that we become what we espouse, and if the result is less than satisfactory or somewhat ambivalent, we can lapse into a tendency to blame others. Or we can build fences designed to protect ourselves from interaction with others. Perhaps the most profound example of this tactic in Northern Kentucky's history occurred during Prohibition (1919–1933). With a long tradition of an immigrant culture, which included the brewing of beer and the distilling of spirits, it was difficult for residents of Covington, Newport, and environs to embrace temperance. The end result was a culture of blatant lawlessness. First speakeasies, and then gambling, prostitution, and other vices led to an urban "Sin City" reputation. Before Prohibition, Northern Kentucky was respected regionally, statewide, and even nationally. It had produced four Kentucky governors—Joseph Desha (1824–1828), John White Stevenson (1867–1871), William Goebel (1900), and Augustus E .Willson (1907–1911)—and one additional Kentucky governor, James T. Morehead (1834–1836), moved to Covington after his tenure as governor. Northern Kentucky also claimed four lieutenant governors of Kentucky—John White Stevenson (1867), John G. Carlisle (1871–1875), James W. Bryan (1887–1891), and William H. Cox (1907–1911)—as well as numerous other state officials. National leaders from the region included William Orlando Butler, an 1848 presidential candidate; John G. Carlisle, who was Speaker of the U.S. House of Representatives three times and later U.S. secretary of the treasury; Horace Lurton, associate justice of the U.S. Supreme Court; and Green Clay Smith, an 1876 presidential candidate. During and after Prohibition, though, Northern Kentucky's reputation and its concomitant political influence suffered as the region distanced itself from others, sending a clear message to "stay out of our affairs." It was a double-edged sword. Vice was prosperous, but its costs were heavy. Northern Kentucky's "stepchild" image dated from this period, a symptom of the supposed "victim" who builds walls of blame to evade his own sense of responsibility. By the 1960s the cleanup of Northern Kentucky had proceeded to a point that permitted the region to turn its attention to reestablishing its reputation.

Seventh, border areas like Northern Kentucky sometimes tend to be fragmented in terms of local governance, perhaps because border residents hold ties to so many different affiliations and constituencies. By the end of the 20th century, the urbanized counties of Boone, Campbell, and Kenton evidenced this trend of fragmentation, as the landlocked cities of Covington and Newport lost population to the burgeoning suburbs. Metropolitan government, as pursued in Lexington and later in Louisville, never gained headway in Northern Kentucky. Instead, a "virtual metropolitan template" of special districts arose to deal with planning, zoning, water, sanitation, fire, police, education, economic development, mental health, and senior services.

Home to 454,000 residents,[5] Northern Kentucky is today one of the points of the "Golden Triangle" of Kentucky—the other two points are Lexington and Louisville—an economically prosperous area with high employment, investment, and job-creation rates. Attracted largely by the presence of the Cincinnati/Northern Kentucky International Airport in Boone Co., major corporations such as Ashland, Fidelity Investments, Omnicare, Toyota North America, and United States Playing Card dot its landscape. Northern Kentucky University, Thomas More College, and three community and technical colleges (Gateway, Maysville, and Jefferson) educate its citizens. The historic cities of Covington, Newport, Ludlow, Bellevue, and Dayton have experienced a renaissance and host office and condominium skyscrapers that line the southern shore of the Ohio River. And organizations like Forward Quest and its successor, Vision 2015, have led the way in planning the region's future and its quality of life.

In the 21st century, Northern Kentucky has also witnessed a renewed interest in its history. Kentucky Educational Television's three-hour documentary *Where the River Bends: A History of Northern Kentucky* premiered statewide in 2007, multi-million-dollar additions to the Behringer-Crawford Museum in Covington and to the Kentucky Gateway Museum in Maysville opened in 2007, and the last segment of the Roebling Murals at the Covington Riverfront debuted in 2008. As part of this enthusiasm to record the region's history, Michael Hammons, director of Forward Quest, approached this encyclopedia's coeditors in fall 2002 with the idea of compiling a comprehensive encyclopedia of Northern Kentucky. Made possible by hundreds of generous benefactors and dedicated volunteers, whose names are given elsewhere in this volume, *The Encyclopedia of Northern Kentucky* celebrates the people, places, and events of the border region's rich heritage. The editors grappled with defining the region as accurately as possible, basing their final inclusion of 11 counties upon both historical ties and contemporary commuting patterns. Eight of the counties lie along the Ohio River, and seven of them are included within the U.S. government's "Cincinnati-Middletown, OH-KY-IN Metropolitan Statistical Area." The definition of Northern Kentucky, of course, may change in the future. With that disclaimer, another should be added: The inclusion or absence of any entries is not intended, whatsoever, as a reflection of either approval or disapproval of particular topics. Rather, the editors have attempted to include, as objectively as possible, those people, places, and events that have fashioned Northern Kentucky. Their hopes are that this encyclopedia will help readers to appreciate the march of history and that it will promote an understanding of Northern Kentucky's role within the history of the Commonwealth of Kentucky and of the nation.

Paul A. Tenkotte and James C. Claypool

Notes

1. *Sesqui-Centennial Souvenir Program: 150th Anniversary, 1815–1965, City of Covington, Kentucky* (Covington, Ky.: T.&W., 1965). "Gateway to the Bluegrass" is painted on the Williamstown water tower, which is visible from I-75.
2. Jasper B. Shannon and Ruth McQuown, *Presidential Politics in Kentucky, 1824–1948* (Lexington, Ky.: Bureau of Government Research, Univ. of Kentucky, 1950). See also Paul A. Tenkotte, "A Note on Regional Allegiances during the Civil War: Kenton County, Kentucky, as a Test Case," *Register of the Kentucky Historical Society* 79, no. 3 (Summer 1981): 211–18.
3. See Paul A. Tenkotte, "Rival Cities to Suburbs: Covington and Newport, Kentucky, 1790–1890" (PhD diss., University of Cincinnati, 1989).
4. "Covington," *Louisville Public Advertiser,* February 3, 1837, 2.
5. Based upon population estimates of July 1, 2007, available at www.census.gov. (accessed July 29, 2008).

Guide for Readers

The following explanations are offered to assist the reader in using *The Encyclopedia of Northern Kentucky*.

Northern Kentucky

Northern Kentucky is defined as the 11 counties of Boone, Bracken, Campbell, Carroll, Gallatin, Grant, Kenton, Mason, Owen, Pendleton, and Robertson. These 11 were chosen based upon several criteria, including historical ties, past and present transportation links, and current commuting patterns. The editors have chosen to capitalize *Northern Kentucky* throughout, since it is a specific region of the state and its title is reflected in many area institutions, businesses, landmarks, and maps.

Types of Entries

The encyclopedia includes people, places, and events from earliest times to the present. The fifteen general entry categories include agriculture; art; biography; business and commerce; counties and towns; ethnology; government, law, and politics; literature; medicine; military persons and events; music, media, and entertainment; religion; sports and recreation; transportation; and women. Careful attempts have been made to include most high schools and towns (and their variant names in some cases) in the 11 counties. Individuals have been included based upon adherence to the criteria listed below. The inclusion or absence of any entries does not reflect approval or disapproval of particular topics. Rather, the editors have attempted to include, as objectively as possible, those people, places, and events that have fashioned Northern Kentucky. As much as possible, based on information available to the editors, the entries are up to date as of September 2008. Abbreviations have been used in order to save space. For example, *County* regularly appears as *Co.,* and many names of institutions are abbreviated after their first mention within individual entries.

The Index and Cross-Referencing

Within entries, names of people, places, and events that are also separate entries in this encyclopedia often appear in boldface type. (References to rivers, counties, and towns are too numerous to cross-reference.) The index should be checked for topics not readily found otherwise. For example, "Bridges" in the index will help the reader find the entry on the Covington and Cincinnati Suspension Bridge, also known as the Roebling Bridge, which appears under "John A. Roebling Bridge," in the "J" section.

Entries on Individuals

Entries on deceased individuals were included if one of the following facts was true of them:

They were born in Northern Kentucky or lived here in youth or adulthood, and made significant contributions to the region, the state, the nation, or the world.

If they were born elsewhere, they spent their most productive years in Northern Kentucky or launched their careers here; and they made significant contributions to the region, the nation, or the world.

If they never lived in Northern Kentucky, they had an important impact on the region by significantly representing Northern Kentucky and its interests in the U.S Congress or some other nationally or internationally important body.

For living individuals the same criteria were applied, except that regional contributions alone were deemed insufficient; these persons' contributions had to be at the state, national, or international level in order to merit an entry in the encyclopedia.

In all cases, for both deceased and living persons, consideration was carefully given to "pioneers," those who broke barriers such as those of race, gender, or ethnicity in making their contributions. For individuals featured in an encyclopedia entry, military titles, if any (and if discovered in our research), are indicated. The names of U.S. presidents and Kentucky governors are accompanied by their terms in office.

Many individuals, although they did not warrant separate entries according to our criteria, were members of Northern Kentucky families, businesses, or organizations that had or continue to have a significant impact on the region. Those persons may be mentioned within an entry dedicated to the family, the business, or the organization. Important visitors to the area are grouped in one general entry entitled "Visitors to Northern Kentucky."

Bibliographic Citations

An effort was made to include at least one bibliographic citation per entry, in order to entice readers to further their knowledge of the subject. The Select Bibliography serves the same purpose, listing all the major sources. Many of the resources are available at local libraries and museums, in particular the large Kentucky and Genealogy section of the Kenton Co. Public Library in Covington. The following abbreviations of frequently cited periodicals have been used in the entry source lists:

BCHS *Bulletin of the Cincinnati Historical Society*
CC *Cincinnati Commercial*
CDC *Cincinnati Daily Commercial*
CDE *Cincinnati Daily Enquirer*

CDG	*Cincinnati Daily Gazette*
CE	*Cincinnati Enquirer*
CJ	*Covington Journal*
CP	*Cincinnati Post*
CTS	*Cincinnati Times-Star*
DC	*Daily Commonwealth*
FCHQ	*Filson Club History Quarterly*
JKS	*Journal of Kentucky Studies*
KE	*Kentucky Enquirer*
KJ	*Kentucky Journal*
KP	*Kentucky Post*
KSJ	*Kentucky State Journal*
KTS	*Kentucky Times-Star*
LCJ	*Louisville Courier Journal*
LVR	*Licking Valley Register*
NKH	*Northern Kentucky Heritage*
NYT	*New York Times*
QCH	*Queen City Heritage*
RKHS	*Register of the Kentucky Historical Society*
SC	*Sunday Challenger*

AA HIGHWAY (the John Y. Brown Jr. AA Highway). Construction on the road commonly known as the AA Highway began in 1983 and was completed seven years later, at a cost of $428 million. The name of the 137-mile-long highway was taken from the names of Alexandria and Ashland, Ky. However, when completed, the AA Highway neither began nor ended in either city. The road starts at I-275 in Wilder then skirts east past Alexandria, Augusta, and Brooksville, through Maysville, and on to Vanceburg; east of Vanceburg it splits into two spurs. The northern leg crosses U.S. 23 north of Greenup, and the southern leg connects with I-64, near Grayson. The AA Highway provides an excellent economic corridor between Northern Kentucky and most of the northeastern part of Kentucky. Sections of the road have at times been known as Ky. Rts. 9, 10, 915, and 546, and, through Maysville, as the Martin Luther King Highway. In September 2002 the name of the AA Highway was officially changed to the John Y. Brown Jr. AA Highway, but people still usually call it the "Double A."

Former Kentucky governor John Y. Brown Jr. (1979–1983), for whom the highway is now named, was a successful partner in the Kentucky Fried Chicken Food Corporation. When elected governor, Brown was 45 years old and married to Phyllis George, a former Miss America who was also a successful network sports and news personality. Brown is the father of politician John Y. Brown III, who served as Kentucky secretary of state. The highway named for former governor Brown has taken much traffic away from **U.S. 27**, making that road less congested and safer to travel. The John Y. Brown AA Highway has brought a significant number of new businesses to areas such as Wilder, Cold Spring, and Maysville. In years to come, this roadway is expected also to bring about a development boom and add many much-needed jobs to Eastern Kentucky. Because it is not a limited-access highway and does not have four lanes throughout its length, it has had a relatively high accident rate. Strict enforcement of the 55-mph speed limit has failed to solve the problem. To become safer and to reach its full economic potential, the John Y. Brown AA Highway will eventually need to be widened to four lanes for its full length and to be changed to a limited-access road.

The Millennium Highway. www.millenniumhwy.net (accessed April 13, 2006).

"Take Your Pick: The AA, JYB, or Ky. 9," *KP*, July 23, 2003, 1K.

Jack Wessling

ABBOTT, DOROTHY (b. June 24, 1885, Covington, Ky.; d. April 13, 1937, Covington, Ky.). A Covington socialite and noted actress, Dorothea L. "Dorothy" Abbott was the daughter of George Morton and Eugenia Garland Abbott. She achieved popularity because of her performances in the plays *Within the Law* and *Under Fire.* Her father, known as Covington's traction magnate, was for 55 years the secretary-treasurer of the Cincinnati, Newport and Covington Railway Company in Covington.

Abbott received substantial training before embarking on her acting career. She completed one course at a college preparatory school in Cincinnati called Miss Doherty's School, studied at a local drama school, and later attended the Belasco Theater in New York City, where she was under the direction of theatrical manager and producer David Belasco. Belasco was also the mentor of Covington actor, playwright, and producer **Stuart Walker**.

In spring 1911 Abbott made her stage debut in New York, performing successfully in *Within the Law* in both Boston and New York. She also had considerable success in vaudeville. Abbott appeared in a two-act play in Covington during the week of February 27, 1912, and her Cincinnati debut took place during the week of March 2, 1912, at B. F. Keith's downtown theater. Her first part there was as the shoplifter in *A Romance of the Underworld.* Her friends attended every performance and thought her acting superb, so she was very popular in Northern Kentucky during the early 1900s.

Abbott's touring company traveled the northwestern, western, and eastern circuit of large cities in the United States. On these trips, she made friends with many famous people. For example, she once sailed with Jane Cowl, a noted American actress and playwright, who also attended the Belasco Theater and who achieved star billing in *Within the Law.* Abbott's travels brought some unpleasant adventure as well: in 1914 a German cruiser tried to capture the ship on which she was returning from a trip to Europe.

In 1937, at age 51, Abbott died of a heart attack at her home in Covington. Funeral services were held for her at the Swetnam Funeral Home, and the public schools were closed for two days to mourn her death. She was buried at Highland Cemetery in Fort Mitchell.

"Covington Girl Will Appear at Columbia," *KP*, February 23, 1912, 10.

"Covington's Society Belle Now Actress," *KP*, March 2, 1912, 8.

"Covington Woman Found Dead in Home," *KP*, April 13, 1937, 1.

"Dorothea L. Abbott," *KP*, April 14, 1937, 3.

Kentucky Death Certificate No. 11414, for the year 1937.

"Mrs. George M. Abbott of Covington Dead, " *KTS*, September 13, 1920, 16.

Sharon McGee

ABERT, JAMES W. (b. November 18, 1820, Mount Holly, N.J.; d. August 10, 1897, Newport, Ky.). James William Abert, a longtime military man, was the son of Col. John James Abert, who served as a topographical engineer during the **War of 1812**. James grew up in New Jersey, where he graduated from Princeton College in 1839. He then attended the U.S. Military Academy at West Point, N.Y., from which he graduated in 1842. His first military assignment was with his father's topographical unit, which surveyed the area around the Great Lakes in 1843–1844. His next assignment was under the command of Col. J. N. Macomb, to map the western prairies. On that mission he made contact with Indian tribes including the Kiowa and the Comanche. Late in 1844 he was promoted to lieutenant and served at Bent's Fort, Colo. The following year he participated in the exploration and mapping of New Mexico, which was then a part of Mexico.

During the **Mexican War**, Abert served under Gen. Stephen Watts Kearny in the invasion and occupation of what later became New Mexico. In the early 1850s, Abert was assigned the task of making repairs at the Falls of the Ohio at Louisville. During his stay there, he met and married Lucy Taylor, daughter of **James Taylor III** and granddaughter of **James Taylor Jr.**, founder of Newport. The Aberts had three daughters, Susan, Nellie, and Jennie. In 1856, when war broke out with the Seminole Indians in Florida, Abert was sent there and remained for three years. About 1860 he was sent to Europe to observe and be trained in the use of European military techniques. He returned to the United States at the beginning of the **Civil War** and saw service with the Union Army, building ferries across various rivers and streams and repairing damage done by Confederate forces. He was later transferred to Folly Island, S.C., where he was placed in charge of the engineering office. At the end of the war, he was transferred to the Southwest, under the command of Gen. **Edward Canby**.

Abert retired from the Union Army on June 25, 1864, with the rank of colonel. After leaving military service, he became a math professor at the University of Missouri at Columbia and also wrote numerous articles for scientific and historical publications. About 1890 Abert returned to Newport to live. In 1897 he died in his Newport home along Front St., at age 76. Funeral services were held at Newport's St. Paul Episcopal Church, and he was buried, with full military honors, in the Taylor section of Evergreen Cemetery in Southgate. His wife, Lucy Taylor Abert, died in 1916 and was buried next to him.

An Atlas of Boone, Kenton, and Campbell Counties, Kentucky. Philadelphia: D. J. Lake, 1883.

"James William Abert A.M., USA," *KJ*, December 6, 1892, 3.

"An Old Soldier," *KJ*, March 8, 1895, 8.

Reis, Jim. "Mark on Young Nation," *KP*, December 11, 2000, 4K.

———. "Wife Forged Newport Connection," *KP*, December 11, 2000, 4K.

ABOLITIONISTS. Abolitionists, emancipationists, and colonizationists lived in Northern Kentucky in the years before 1863. The term *abolitionists* refers to people in the antebellum United States who wished to abolish slavery completely. Abolitionists differed from other antislavery proponents such as emancipationists, who supported gradual emancipation of slaves with compensation to their owners, and colonizationists, who promoted sending freed slaves to Africa.

The religious basis for early abolitionism came directly from Quakers such as Arnold Buffin, Elihu Embree, and Charles Osborne and was well established by 1830. The evangelical basis for national abolitionism began in 1833 with the founding of the American Antislavery Society by William Lloyd Garrison, Lewis and Arthur Tappan, Thomas Weld, and many others. Disagreements emerged among these abolitionists relating to the constitutional framework of the United States and how it pertained to slavery. Garrison and others argued that the U.S. Constitution favored slavery and must be overthrown through civil disobedience; James G. Birney and many others countered that political action by amending the U.S. Constitution would achieve the purpose of eliminating slavery. Garrison was adamantly against political action, believing it would diffuse the religious and moral foundation of the antislavery movement. The Liberty Party ran Birney as an antislavery candidate for president in 1840 and 1844, and Gerrit Smith in 1848, but by then the emerging Free Soil Party had absorbed most of the antislavery abolitionists. Those abolitionists favoring direct action against slavery encouraged boycotting Southern goods and services, aiding runaway slaves through the Underground Railroad, and running antislavery candidates for state and national offices. The Tappan brothers were credited with much of the financing of the Underground Railroad and for helping to place its agents along the Ohio River. By the mid-1850s, the American Missionary Association had begun direct confrontation on the issue of slavery by placing colporteurs throughout the South, by giving Bibles to slaves, and by distributing antislavery tract materials to slave owners and yeoman farmers.

Southern slaveholders retaliated against abolitionists by employing their political power in the U.S. Congress and by direct action to mount posses, pay for detectives, extend the patroller system, and increase the rewards for returning runaway slaves. Once the 1850 Fugitive Slave Act was passed, Kentucky slave owners vigorously challenged Underground Railroad operators in federal courts, either winning large judgments or having large fines levied against these operators for the slave owner's lost slave properties. In 1849 slaveholders in Kentucky won a huge political battle: they sent an overwhelming majority of delegates to the Kentucky Constitutional Convention and to the Kentucky legislature, who rolled back whatever antislavery legislation and protection free blacks had achieved over the previous 50 years. The abolitionists in Kentucky were defeated, demoralized, and in disarray. **John G. Fee**'s autobiography cites many cases in which proslavery mobs targeted the remaining few white abolitionists in Kentucky and drove many of them out of the state.

By the 1850s it appeared to abolitionists in the North that their moderate tactics had not worked; slave states had aggressively expanded slavery into Texas, Arkansas, and Missouri and threatened to take it to Kansas. The 1854 Kansas-Nebraska Act repealed the Missouri Compromise of 1820, which had prohibited slavery north of latitude 36°30; thus all federal territories were opened up to the possibility of slavery. With the passage of the Kansas-Nebraska Act, abolitionists could no longer trust that the U.S. Congress would rectify the matter of slavery. Likewise, they lost hope in the U.S. Supreme Court, which, in the 1857 Dred Scott decision (*Scott v. Sandford*), declared the Missouri Compromise invalid, made any congressional attempts to prohibit slavery in the territories unconstitutional, and regarded slaves as property protected by the U.S. Constitution. With seemingly no recourse left to legislative or judicial action, the war of words erupted into armed aggression. John Brown's antislavery raids in Kansas and his attack on the federal arsenal at Harpers Ferry, Va., in October 1859 were the first large-scale overt abolitionist confrontations, and they helped to divide the nation's opinions on slavery into opposing camps.

Passive support to aid runaway slaves now became active tactics, emboldening even more slaves to escape from the South. From 1836 to 1840, antislavery societies espousing political, economic, and direct action against the institution of slavery spread throughout Ohio and Indiana. Slave losses from the river counties of Kentucky and the state's Bluegrass region mounted significantly during the late 1840s and 1850s. Each time a Kentucky posse went into Michigan, Indiana, or Ohio to retrieve runaway slaves, it was met by angry abolitionists determined to wrest the evil of slavery from the nation. Furthermore, abolitionist "agitators" from these and other Northern states began reaching down into Kentucky with greater frequency.

In his 2005 book *Bound for Canaan,* Fergus Bordewich points to the 1852 death of Isaac Tatum Hooper in New York City as the end of the early period of the abolitionist movement, a period characterized as one in which humble and religious friends of fugitives were simply aiding other human beings. In Northern Kentucky, one might mark the watershed of this change to 1847, when armed mobs rebuffed the slave-catcher Francis Troutman and his Carroll Co., Ky., posse at Marshall, Mich.; or when Rev. Benjamin Sebastian and George W. Brazier's posse from Boone Co., Ky., was confronted at Cass Co., Mich., and summarily dispatched from the state. The change was further displayed in the dramatic incursions of **Elijah Anderson** and John Fairfield into Boone Co., taking dozens of slaves out of the county.

Northern abolitionists who resorted to aggressive strategies sometimes used military terms and tactics. They also sent spies and colporteurs into the South deliberately to confront slaveholders, and they routinely accosted any "Southern kidnappers" coming into Northern antislavery states to capture runaway slaves. The new contemporary popular faces of the abolitionist movement included the talented black orator Frederick Douglass and the soon-notorious John Brown.

The continuous uproar from antagonistic abolitionist tactics was not received well in Kentucky. Conservative antislavery leaders, and even Cassius Clay, disavowed both the abolitionist leaders of this period and their tactics. The few abolitionists remaining in Kentucky were easily targeted for reprisal. John G. Fee and his tiny coterie living in Madison, Lewis, and Bracken counties during the 1850s were particularly vulnerable, because they acted openly and confronted deeply held local prejudices. Even across the Ohio River in Ripley, Ohio, a number of leading citizens were opposed to the overt abolitionist actives of such locals as Rev. John Rankin and John Parker.

According to an overwhelming majority of Kentucky's citizens, the despised abolitionists were agitators from the North who interfered with Kentucky's state's rights; who enticed and stole slaves from decent, law-abiding citizens; and who broke national, state, and local laws. In the view of most newspapers in Kentucky, it was these abolitionists who confronted Kentucky posses lawfully trying to retrieve "lost slave property" in Indiana, Michigan, and Ohio. It was also these zealot abolitionists who persisted in destroying the national unity of the Methodist Episcopal and the Presbyterian denominations by their activities. Moreover, it was these radical abolitionists who forced President Abraham Lincoln (1861–1865) to issue the Emancipation Proclamation in January 1863 and to accept Negro troops to fight for the Union. Kentuckians may not have been united on many issues during these difficult times, but they were, generally speaking, united in their abhorrence for the white abolitionists.

Kentucky's abolitionists who were white were easy to spot and few in number. Black abolitionists, in contrast, were numerous and were concentrated into the state's large urban areas—Louisville, Lexington, Frankfort, and Northern Kentucky—and across the river in Cincinnati. They also congregated in small separate rural slave churches and were spread out geographically as individuals still in bondage across the hundreds of plantations in the north central and Bluegrass regions of Kentucky. Although black preachers were suspected of abolitionist leanings, and isolated free blacks certainly were among the first to be accused of aiding fugitive slaves, few slave owners actually thought their own slaves might be abolitionists who were providing direct help to runaway slaves.

As their slave losses mounted, slave owners in Kentucky took action against the abolitionists in their midst and also crossed the Ohio River. Bounties were set for people like John Carr, John Fairfield, Rev. Charles Ide, and other white abolitionists active in the Underground Railroad. Author Ann Hagedorn tells of several attacks on abolitionists in Brown Co., Ohio, led by Mason Co., Ky., slave owner Col. Edward Towers. In late fall 1844, his posse inflicted more than 100 whiplashes on Harbor Hurley, a longtime free black at Sardinia, Ohio; attacked and killed Robert Miller; lynched a runaway slave; attacked Absalom King and several who were helping to defend him; and burned Miller's and King's homes. The Georgetown, Ohio, sheriff appeared unable to stop the marauding Kentuckians.

The most celebrated attacks by Kentucky slave owners were associated with a secretive organization of slave owners established in Covington in 1846, modeled after the Western Horsemen's Association set up in the western United States to deal with horse thieves. A spy calling himself Carpenter was hired and sent to Michigan to find runaway slaves from Northern Kentucky. He came back with detailed reports that supplied names, places where slaves were hiding, and the names of plantations where they had been enslaved. Based on this information, in December 1846 young Lexington attorney Francis Townsend, along with David Giltner, the son of a Central Kentucky slaveholding family; William Franklin Ford; James S. Lee; and several other Kentuckians, traveled to Marshall, Mich., to recapture the **Adam Crosswhite** family, slave runaways from the Giltner plantation. However, the invaders from Kentucky were turned away by an armed mob, arrested, and subsequently fined for having disturbed the peace. George W. Brazier, a slave jobber, and Benjamin Stevens from Boone Co., mounted a posse to Cass Co., Mich., to recapture as many as 50 runaway slaves, who had been identified by a spy calling himself Carpenter. This posse too was met by armed men, arrested, fined, and escorted out of the state.

Cassius M. Clay was a dramatic and significant figure in Kentucky's antislavery movement, not only for editing the *Lexington True American,* but also for his public speeches and frequent bouts with proslavery advocates in Kentucky. Although Clay was feted and applauded as an antislavery Southerner at Abolitionist Society meetings in New York City, he clearly favored gradual emancipation with monetary recompense to slave owners. Of all the colorful episodes in Clay's experiences, none was more lasting than his assigning 600 acres of land in Madison Co., Ky., to John G. Fee to start the Northern emigrant community of Berea. This community, along with Camp Nelson in Jessamine Co., became the nexus for true abolitionist sentiment and actions in Kentucky.

Clay and Fee could not remain united in their thinking for long; Fee was disappointed by Clay's political expediency, and Clay felt that Fee's radicalism mixing feminism and anticaste sentiments with antislavery beliefs actually damaged the antislavery cause in Kentucky. The break between the two Kentucky-born abolitionists was public and painful. Fee believed that Clay's denunciation of him led directly to harassment and mob actions to evict the abolitionists from Madison Co. in 1859. However, it is more likely that Berea College itself, which had teachers trained as Northern abolitionists at Oberlin, Ohio, and which educated white and black men and women together, was enough to create a proslavery furor in Berea, with or without Cassius Clay's approval or disapproval. After all, Fee's closest associates in Bracken and Lewis counties were driven out by proslavery mobs about the same time, and Clay had nothing to do with those cases. Simultaneously, abolitionist societies such as the American Missionary Association and particularly the Western Freedmen's Aid Commission at Cincinnati continued to provide immediate supplies and relief materials to former slaves. Clothing, building materials, and even garden tools and seeds were also being sent to assist free blacks who had remained in the South.

Also active in these sorts of activities were sectarian agencies such as the Baptist Home Missionary Society, the Episcopal Missionary Society, and the Methodist Home Missionary Society. In July 1864 a convention at Indianapolis, Ind., cited the following agencies as cooperating to provide direct aid to freedmen: the Cleveland Freedmen's Aid Commission, the Contraband Relief Commission at Cincinnati, the Friends' Aid Committee of Richmond, Ind., the Indiana Freemen's Aid Commission at Indianapolis, the North-Western Freedmen's Aid Commission at Chicago, the Western Freedmen's Aid Commission at Cincinnati, and the Western Sanitary Commission at St. Louis. Even after the Civil War, efforts were made to improve the lot of blacks remaining in the South, since many of the **Freedmen's Bureau Schools** became completely dependent on teachers recruited and paid by abolitionist groups such as these.

Activities of black abolitionists of Northern Kentucky on the Ohio River:

—In Madison, Ind., Elijah Anderson, a conductor and organizer, aided 200 slaves, 1838–1846.

—In Lawrenceburg, Ind., Anderson aided 800 slaves through conducting and organizing, 1846–1856.

—In Madison, George De Baptiste, a conductor and organizer, aided 108 slaves, 1838–1845.

—In Madison, John Carter was a conductor, organizer, and recruiter, 1838–1860.

—In Madison, Griffin Booth, George Evans, and John Lott were conductors and operated safe houses, 1830–1846.

—In Milton, Ky., Peter Scott was a local agent and organizer, 1840–1850.

—In Eagle Hollow, Ind., Rev. Chapman Harris was a conductor and a manager of river crossings, 1845–1860.

—In Hunters Bottom, Ky., **Richard Daly** made a river crossing to Eagle Hollow, 1845–1856.

—In S. Hanover, Ind., John R. Forcen, Simon Gray, and Mason Thompson were conductors, 1840–1860.

—In Coopers Bottom, Ky., Freeman Anderson and a slave made river crossings to S. Hanover, Ind., 1850s.

—In Carrollton, Ky., **Wheeling Gaunt** and Samuel Lightfoot operated safe houses, 1840s and 1850s.

—In Warsaw, Ky., John Brookings and Lewis Hamilton appeared before a Gallatin Co. grand jury, 1838–1861.

—In Rising Sun, Ind., and Rabbit Hash, Ky., Samuel Barkshire, Joseph Edington, and William Thompson operated safe houses.

—In Covington, **James Bradley** participated in the Lane Seminary debates.

—In Covington, **Jacob Price** helped slaves escape.

—In Cincinnati, John Malvin aided Susan Hall and eight children, 1830s.

—In Cincinnati, Henry Boyd operated a safe house and was an organizer, 1820–1860.

—In Cincinnati, Frances Scroggins, William Watson, and John Woodson operated a safe house and were conductors; Joseph Barber and James Williams were conductors; Nathan Brown, the Burgess family, Mrs. Amy Clark, Thomas and Jane "Kitty" Dorum, Ebenezer Elliott, the Hall family, and Mr. and Mrs. L. Lewis all operated safe houses; William Casey and Deacon John Hatfield were organizers and operated safe houses; 1830–1840s.

—In Cincinnati, Rev. Allen E. Graham of the Union Baptist Church in Cincinnati was a columnist for the *Palladium of Liberty,* 1840s.

—In Cincinnati, Joseph Carter Corbin, a graduate of Ohio University, was the editor of the *Colored Citizen* and later was president of the University of Arkansas at Pine Bluff, 1850–1860s.

—In Felicity, Ohio, Will Sleet was a leader of the free black community and a conductor; Mark Sims was a conductor; 1840–1850s.

—In Red Oak, Ohio, Harbor Hurley and George Williams received 100 lashes, unprovoked, given by Mason Co. posse in Indiana; Williams was jailed in Kentucky penitentiary and died after making a forced confession; 1844–1856.

—In Mason Co., Aunt Polly Jackson, Rhoda Jones, Uncle Billy Marshall, and John P. Parker made crossings to Ripley, 1840–1850s.

—In Bracken Co., Arnold Gragston was a conductor making a crossing to Ripley, Ohio; **Juliet Miles** was a woman jailed at Frankfort, Ky., for trying to get her children to freedom; she was visited by Fee; 1850s.

Activities of white abolitionists of Northern Kentucky on the Ohio River:

—In Eagle Hollow, Ind., Charles Almond, John Carr, John and Samuel Ledgerwood, Charlie Lutz, Jared Ryker, John Taylor, and William Woolen worked as organizers, conductors, and operators of safe houses, 1839–1861.

—In Carroll, Trimble, Gallatin, and Franklin counties, William Phelps and George Whitefield served as American Antislavery Society agents from Wheeling, W.Va.

—In Carrollton, Ky., Alex Fuller and the William Lee family were organizers and conductors, 1850s.

—In Lamb, Ind., George C. Ash, Captain Hildreth, William and John Shaw, and Thomas Wright were ferrymen and operated safe houses, 1840s–1861.

—In Vevay, Ind., Rev. James Duncan and Stephen Stevens were founders of the Liberty Party in Indiana, 1824–1830.

—In Vevay Ind., Stephen Girard and John and Stephen H. Pavy were organizers and conductors and operated a safe house, 1830–1861.

—Alex and Duncan Fuller and Daniel and Johnathan Howe made river crossings from Warsaw and Sugar Creek, Ky., to Patriot, Ind., and operated safe houses, 1840s and 1850s.

—In Florence and Quercus Grove, Ind., Rev. **Alexander Sebastian** made river crossings, operated safe houses, and established antislavery churches, 1840s–1861.

—In Switzerland and Dearborn counties, Ind., Rev. Charles Ide and Orthaniel H. Reed were organizers; a bounty was set for Ide by slave owners; 1840s.

—In Aurora, Ind., Daniel Bartholomew; Dr. Myron Harding; John Hope; John Milburn; the Harding, Shockley, and Shattuck families; and William Wymond, a station master, managed three major routes and operated safe houses; 1835–1861.

—In Manchester, Ind., John Angevin, John and Ralph Collier, Joseph Hall, Thomas and John Hansell, and Seth Platt were conductors and operated safe houses, 1835–1861.

—In Guilford and Lawrenceburg, Ind., Henry Beecher, Rev. John Clarke, Martin C. Ewbank, Benjamin Metcalf, and Thomas Smith were organizers, were cofounders of the Indiana Antislavery Society, operated safe houses, and were members of the Dearborn Co. Antislavery Society, 1835–1850.

—In Richwood in Boone Co., Rev. Joseph Cabell Harrison was an antislavery minister (see **Richwood Presbyterian Church**).

—In West Covington, **Henry Hathaway** was an abolitionist.

—In Campbell Co., Ira Root was an antislavery activist.

—In Newport, **William Shreve Bailey** was an antislavery newspaper editor, 1839–1850s.

—In Cincinnati, author Harriet Beecher Stowe operated a safe house; Salmon P. Chase was a political activist and organizer; Levi and Catherine Coffin operated a Free Store and a safe house; Calvin Stowe, a teacher, operated a safe house; Theodore Weld, a student, was an organizer and an agent of the American Antislavery Society; Samuel and Sally Wilson operated a safe house; and Zebulon Strong operated a safe house.

—In Cincinnati, James G. Birney and Cassius M. Clay were antislavery newspaper editors; John Jolliffe was an abolitionist attorney who represented Margaret Garner and others; Sarah Otis Ernst was the organizer of the Women's Sewing Society; Rev. Moncure Daniel Conway was a minister of the First Congregational Church; 1840s–1850s.

—In Cincinnati, in April 1854,abolitionist John G. Fee; William Hamilton, editor of the *Patriot*; and Thomas Metcalfe, a former Kentucky governor, were delegates to an antislavery convention that focused on repeal of the 1850 Fugitive Slave Act and repudiation of the Kansas-Nebraska bill.

—In Cincinnati, the Western Freedmen's Aid Commission provided relief materials (clothing, supplies, tools, school supplies) and teachers for industrial arts schools. These individuals were involved: Rev. D. H. Allen, Rev. C. B. Boynton, Levi Coffin, Edward Harwood, Rev. C. Kingsley, J. F. Larkin, James B. Lupton, Rev. G. M. Maxwell, William P. Nixon, Rev. Adam Poe, Rev. R. H. Pollock, Richard B. Pullan, M. Sawyer, Hon. Bellamy Storer, Rev. H. M. Storrs, Dr. J. Taft, Rev. M. L. P. Thompson, Rev. John M. Walden, and Dr. J. P. Walker, 1850–1860s.

—In operations between Pendleton Co., Ky., and Clermont Co., Ohio, Arthur Fee conducted a safe house in Felicity, Ohio; Oliver P. S. Fee was a station master at Felicity; Nelson Gibson, Dr. Mathew Gibson, Joseph Parrish, and Andrew Powell were all conductors of Felicity, Ohio; Rev. Silas Chase was an organizer in Bethel, Ohio; Richard Mace, Benjamin Rice, and Dr. William E. Thompson were all conductors from Bethel, Ohio; Rev. Amos Dresser and Dr. John Rogers were organizers from New Richmond, Ohio; Dr. L. T. Pease and Marcus Sims were conductors at Williamsburg, Ohio; and Charles B. Huber was a station master at Williamsburg.

—In Bracken Co., John G. Fee was a noted abolitionist and educator; James B. Cripps was a delegate to the Free Democratic convention in Pittsburgh, Pa.; he was arrested for aiding a fugitive slave falsely; John D. Gregg, Vincent Hamilton (John G. Fee's father-in-law), and John Humlong were active in antislavery churches and societies.

—In Germantown, Ky., J. M. Mallett, a teacher at a school at Bethesda, Ky., was driven out by proslavery forces, 1850s.

—In Augusta, Ky., **James A. Thome** was an agent of the American Antislavery Society.

—In Sardinia, Ohio, John B. Mahan was tricked by William Greathouse, tried in Mason Co., Ky., jailed in Washington, Ky., and died of tuberculosis contracted in jail; he was an organizer for the Liberty Party and *Philanthropist* subscriptions; 1840s.

—Between Maysville, Ky., and Ripley Ohio, Dr. Alfred Beasley, Dr. Alexander Campbell, Thomas Collins, Rev. James Gilliland, Archibald Leggett, Thomas McCaque, Dr. G. Norton, and Rev. John Rankin worked as organizers, conductors, and physicians and operated safe houses, 1840s–1861.

—In Washington, Ky., James A. Paxton operated a safe house, 1830–1861. (See **Paxton Inn**.)

—In Lewis Co., Ky., James S. Davis of Cabin Creek, Ky., had an antislavery church, 1850s.

Abolitionists from other regions and states who were active in Northern Kentucky:

—In Mason Co., Rev. Calvin Fairbanks and Delia Webster assisted in the escape of Lewis Hayden from Lexington, 1844.

—In Boone Co. and other parts of Northern Kentucky, John Fairfield, from Virginia and Michigan, brought 28 slaves out at one time and engaged in other daredevil exploits, late 1840s.

—In Bracken Co., Edward James "Patrick" Doyle, from Ireland and from Bardstown and Danville, Ky., assisted in the aborted escape of 40–75 runaway slaves from the Lexington area, 1848.

—Laura S. Haviland, from Adrian, Mich., disguised as free person of color, went into Boone Co. to get word to John White's wife.

—In Trimble, Carroll, Gallatin, and Franklin counties, William Phelps and George Whitefield, from Wheeling W.Va., agents of the American Antislavery Society, worked as organizers establishing routes and safe houses, 1840s.

—Rev. Daniel Worth, a Wesleyan minister from Ohio, active in the American Missionary Association (AMA), joined John G. Fee in preaching in Bracken Co., June 1853.

—Rev. Edward Matthews, an antislavery preacher from the Free Mission Baptists, preached with John G. Fee several times in Lewis and Bracken Co., 1850s.

—In Madison Co., Wiley Fisk was a controversial preacher with AMA, 1850s.

—A. G. W. Parker, from Rockcastle Co., a colporteur from the AMA, was arrested falsely and charged with aiding fugitive slaves, in order to break up a protracted meeting of John G. Fee, 1853.

—William Haines and James West, colporteurs from the AMA, distributed antislavery literature and Bibles to slaves in Northern Kentucky, 1850s.

—John Burnham, George Candee, Dr. Chase of New Hampshire, John G. Hanson, Roger Jones, Bro. Myers, Thomas E. Renfro, Bro. Richardson, John A. R. Rogers, Miss Tucker, and Otis B. Waters, from Berea, Camp Nelson, Pulaski, Jackson, and Garrard counties, were close allies, teachers, and companions of John G. Fee, 1850–1860s.

—Arnold Buffin, president of the American Antislavery Society and a Quaker, and Rev. Lewis Hicklin, a Methodist Protestant preacher and brother of Thomas Hicklin, a major Underground Railroad activist in Indiana, were associated with the early organization of the routes from the Ohio River north to Levi Coffin and other Wayne Co., Ind., safe houses, 1840.

—Francis Hawley, an antislavery Baptist minister, came from Syracuse, N.Y., to baptize John G. Fee and his wife in Cabin Creek, Lewis Co., Ky., 1852–1853.

Bordewich, Fergus M. *Bound for Canaan: The Underground Railroad and the War for the Soul of America.* New York: Amistad, 2005.

Coon, Diane Perrine. "Southeastern Indiana's Underground Railroad Routes and Operations," 1999, U.S. Park Service and Indiana DNR, unpublished technical report available at Indiana Department of Historic Preservation and Archaeology, Indianapolis, Ind.

Drummond, Dwight Lowell. *Antislavery: The Crusade for Freedom in America.* Ann Arbor: Univ. of Michigan Press, 1961.

Fee, John G. *Autobiography of John G. Fee.* Chicago: National Christian Association, 1891.

Griffler, Keith P. *Front Line of Freedom: African Americans and the Forging of the Underground Railroad in the Ohio Valley.* Lexington: Univ. Press of Kentucky, 2004.

Hagedorn, Ann. *Beyond the River.* New York: Simon and Schuster, 2002.

Harrison, Lowell H. *The Antislavery Movement in Kentucky.* Lexington: Univ. Press of Kentucky, 1978.

Howard, Victor B. *The Evangelical War against Slavery and Caste: The Life and Times of John G. Fee.* Selinsgrove, Pa.: Susquehanna Univ. Press, 1996.

Hudson, J. Blaine. *Fugitive Slaves and the Underground Railroad in the Kentucky Borderland.* Jefferson, N.C.: McFarland, 2002.

Kentucky Educational Television, Underground Railroad Educational Resources. "Westward Expansion and the Development of Abolitionist Thought." www.wcvn.org (accessed September 19, 2006).

LaRoche, Cheryl Jenifer. "On the Edge of Freedom: Free Black Communities, Archaeology, and the Underground Railroad," PhD diss., Univ. of Maryland, 2006.

Martin, Asa Earl. "Pioneer Antislavery Press," *Mississippi Valley Historical Review* 2 (March 1916): 510–28.
Rabb, Kate Milner, ed. *A Tour through Indiana in 1840: The Diary of John Parsons of Petersburg, Virginia.* New York: Robert M. McBride, 1920.
Ripley, C. Peter, ed. *The Black Abolitionist Papers.* Vols. 3–5. Chapel Hill: Univ. of North Carolina Press, 1991.
Tallant, Harold D. *Evil Necessity: Slavery and Political Culture in Antebellum Kentucky.* Lexington: Univ. Press of Kentucky, 2003.
Turner, Wallace B. "Abolitionism in Kentucky," *RKHS* 69 (October 1971): 319–38.

Diane Perrine Coon

ACTION MINISTRIES. Action Ministries is a faith-based food pantry, located at 4375 Boron Dr. in Latonia. Its purpose, according to its mission statement, is "to share the love of Jesus Christ by providing groceries, hope and encouragement to low-income families." Every day volunteers offer grocery items to low-income residents of southern Kenton Co. Clients are referred to the mission by the Family Resource Centers at schools, churches, and local government agencies, or they come without referral, having heard of the organization. The mission is supported by cash donations from individuals and churches, by product donations from local businesses that have damaged goods or excess perishable items, by grants, by the Federal Emergency Management Agency (FEMA), and by goods from government commodity programs. About 100 volunteers come from a variety of local congregations. There is no paid staff at Action Ministries.

The mission began in 1994 in Ryland Heights. Tom Dorman, now executive director, was asked by the town's mayor to begin a government commodity program for that community. The program operated out of a closet at Ryland Heights Elementary School and was available to families once a month. Needing more space, it moved in 1996 to a rented garage at the DeCoursey Baptist Church in Fairview in Kenton Co. and was open once a week. In 2003 Action Ministries moved into its own warehouse-office facility that it had built in Latonia and was able to be open daily. In 2004 it served 1,265 client families. Included were 3,456 people, one-third of them children and one-third senior citizens.

The philosophy of Action Ministries is to provide help for three months to people who come to them; it is expected that recipients will actively be seeking employment, will be in school or vocational training, or will be doing community service. The goal is to help families over rough times, not to enable a lifestyle of seeking assistance. However, the mission recognizes that there are people who will never be able to be self-sufficient because of age or disability, and those people are helped for as long as they wish to come.

Dorman, Tom. Interview by Sandy Banta, June 12, 2005, Latonia, Ky.
"Food Bank in Central Location," *CE,* May 2, 2003, 1B.
"Food Bank to Kick Off New Site," *CE,* 1B.
"Food Pantry to Break Ground," *KP,* September 13, 2002, 2K.
"Helpers Paid in Blessings," *CE,* December 26, 2004, C3.

Sandy Banta

ADAMS, SAMUEL W. (b. January 23, 1873, Boone Co., Ky.; d. September 19, 1954, Covington, Ky.). Lawyer and legislator Samuel William Adams was the son of William and Ida Adams of Boone Co., Ky. Samuel Adams attended the University of Chicago, and after graduating he moved to Covington, where he established a legal office. He was elected for a two-year term in the Kentucky House of Representatives as a Democrat in 1902. In about 1920, he was the Covington city solicitor. In 1922 he returned to the House of Representatives for another two-year term. During his final year in office, he was Speaker of the Kentucky House. In late 1924 he served for several months as a Kenton Co. Circuit Court judge. That same year, he was elected a state senator and held that office for the next eight years. He was a director of the Columbia Savings and Loan Association in Covington, a member of the Covington Elks Club (see **Civic Associations**), and also belonged to the lodge of the Masonic Order (see **Masons**) that met in Covington. Adams died at age 81 at St. Elizabeth Hospital in Covington. At the time of his death, he was living at 3172 Clifford Ave. in Latonia. Rev. Philip Wiggerman of the St. Paul Evangelical Church conducted the funeral service, and Adams was interred at the Odd Fellows Cemetery in Burlington, Ky. His only surviving relative was his wife, Ida.

Kentucky Death Certificate No. 18236, for the year 1954.
"Samuel W. Adams Rites Set Tuesday," *KP,* September 20, 1954, 1.

AFRICAN-AMERICAN BUSINESSMEN'S ASSOCIATION. This organization was begun in Covington during the late 1920s. Its first members included real estate agents, a funeral director, a grocer, an operator of a dry cleaning–tailor shop, and a restaurant-bar owner. Their businesses were located primarily on the east side of Covington, although they served the entire African American community. Each businessman was a member or leader in various other civic, patriotic, and fraternal organizations. For the youth of the community, they sponsored an annual picnic at the Shinkle Farm (see **Amos Shinkle**) in Crestview Hills. The model for this association was the National Negro Business League, developed by Booker T. Washington. The charter members of the local organization included Charles L. Deal, Clarence Frateman, Wallace Grubbs, Richard "Uncle Dick" Johnson, **Charles E. Jones**, **Gene Lacey**, William H. Martin, and **Horace S. Sudduth**. Their unofficial meeting place was the C. E. Jones Funeral Home at 635 Scott St.

Charles L. Deal was an agent for the Mutual Fire Insurance Company and also sold real estate. He was born in October 1877. His early years were spent in Latonia, along Winston Ave. and Main St., while he was working for the railroad. In 1928 he opened a real estate business at 1109 Russell St. in Covington. A few years later, he moved the business to his residence at 1421 Russell St. In the late 1930s, he established his office at 804 Greenup St., where it remained until the mid 1950s. After integration opened up the real estate market in Cincinnati, he moved to the Avondale neighborhood of that city and continued to work in real estate until his retirement in the 1960s. Deal died March 10, 1969.

Clarence Frateman was the nephew of Richard Johnson. No information is available about the type of business he operated in Covington.

Wallace Grubbs was a businessman who for a long time owned a restaurant and bar in Covington at 301 E. 11th St. Grubbs was born on February 2, 1894. He was a veteran of World War I, having served in the U.S. Army, Company A, 308 Labor Battalion, Quartermaster Corps, and was a member of the Charles L. Henderson American Legion Post No. 166. Grubbs died May 8, 1964.

Richard "Uncle Dick" Johnson was the consigliere of the association, and for years he owned property at 317 Scott St. Johnson was the grandfather of John "Jack" Price, whose other grandfather was **Jacob Price**. Johnson was also the uncle of fellow association member Clarence Frateman. Uncle Dick Johnson died October 9, 1957.

Charles E. Jones in 1913 purchased the funeral home owned by Wallace A. Gaines at 633–635 Scott St. Jones expanded the business and changed its name to C. E. Jones Funeral Home. It continued in business until 1972. Jones married Anna Watkins, daughter of Covington's first African American physician, Dr. **Simon J. Watkins**.

Eugene F. Lacey opened his first grocery store in Covington in 1918, at 508 Scott St., while residing at 839 Craig St. He opened his second Covington store at 205 E. Robbins St.; this one was called the Gene and Bess Store. He and his wife Bessie formed two companies, the Lacey Sausage Company and the Lacey Paper Company. In 1926 Lacey closed his store at 508 Scott St. He was a grade-school classmate of Horace Sudduth.

William H. Martin's dry cleaning and tailor business was first located at Athey Ave. and Craig St. in Cincinnati. He was a U.S. Army veteran of **World War I** and a member of Charles L. Henderson American Legion Post No. 166. In 1928 Martin moved his business to 508 Scott St., Covington, the site formerly occupied by Eugene Lacey's grocery. In 1932 Martin opened a second dry cleaning business, at 1015 Greenup St., near the corner of Clinton and Scott Sts. In the late 1930s, Martin closed the Greenup St. location to concentrate on his Scott St. business. In 1948 Martin moved from 508 Scott St. to 522 Scott St.

The leader and organizer of the group was Horace S. Sudduth, a native Covingtonian who was astute in the development of modern business practices. Sudduth founded the Horace Sudduth and Associates Real Estate Agency and owned the Manse Hotel in Cincinnati, the place where influential African American visitors stayed. He served as president of two national organizations, the National Negro Business League and the Industrial Federal Savings & Loan Association. Sudduth was married to Melvina Jones, the sister of Charles E. Jones, the funeral director.

These businessmen and the businesses they operated faced and overcame constant challenges such as the Great Depression and competition from emerging corporate business chains. The community activities they sponsored indicated their love of their community and benefited the people who participated. In 1941, at the beginning of **World War II**, a number of these activities, along with the African-American Businessmen's Association itself, ceased and were never reinstituted. Most of the African American businesses struggled on, until they disappeared in the 1950s because of the changing demographics in the community.

"Grubbs, Wallace," *KP*, May 9, 1964, 5K.
Harris, Ted. "Reader Recollection," *KP*, March 2, 1992, 4K.
"Johnson, Richard," *KTS*, October 12, 1957, 4A.
"Police Raids Bring 17 into Covington Court," *KP*, March 15, 1930, 1.

Theodore H. H. Harris

AFRICAN AMERICANS. African Americans arrived in Northern Kentucky during the 1750s–1770s with the first group of explorers and settlers, before the United States became a nation. When **Simon Kenton**, **Christopher Gist**, and others traveled down the Ohio River, enslaved blacks accompanied them. The African American presence in Northern Kentucky increased with Kentucky's statehood in 1792. As the counties in the region began to form, and as large tracts of land were subdivided into farms, the river cities of Maysville (then called Limestone) in Mason Co., Newport in Campbell Co., and Covington in Kenton Co. were organized. The numbers of African Americans in those counties increased proportionally with the general population. They played an important role in the development of each of these three northern river counties, adding to the fabric of society and contributing to economic development.

The **Civil War** was a major turning point for migration by African Americans into the urban centers of Northern Kentucky. Because of the Confederate threat to Northern Kentucky and the enlistment of blacks in the Union forces, many African Americans moved from the central Bluegrass region of Kentucky to the cities of Newport and Covington. They continued to do so throughout the 19th century, at first settling mostly in the counties along the Ohio River. At the beginning of the 20th century, another wave of African Americans began leaving the farms and migrating to the cities of Covington, Newport, and, to a lesser extent, Maysville. The following list gives an overview of how African Americans were distributed in the Northern Kentucky region, through 1900:

County (date est.)	*African American Population (year)*
Mason (1788)	4,391 slaves (1830); 3,772 slaves (1860); 4,392 (1880); 8,708 (1900)
Campbell (1794)	1,033 slaves (1830); 116 slaves (1860); 1,215 (1880); 1,258 (1900)
Bracken (1796)	833 slaves (1830); 750 slaves (1860); 816 (1880); 572 (1900)
Pendleton (1798)	428 slaves (1830); 424 slaves (1860); 780 (1880); 488 (1900)
Gallatin (1798)	1,184 slaves (1830); 708 slaves (1860); 617 (1880); 565 (1900)
Boone (1798)	1,820 slaves (1830); 1,745 slaves (1860); 1,232 (1880); 810 (1900)
Owen (1819)	790 slaves (1830); 1,660 slaves (1860); 1,508 (1880); 1,470 (1900)
Grant (1820)	266 slaves (1830); 696 slaves (1860); 733 (1880); 427 (1900)
Carroll (1838)	1,045 slaves (1860); 771 (1880); 804 (1900)
Kenton (1840)	567 slaves (1860); 2,528 (1880); 3,282 (1900)
Robertson (1867)	288 (1880); 128 (1900)

Mason Co.

Mason Co., Northern Kentucky's first county, initially encompassed most of the region. By the time Kentucky was admitted as a state in 1792, Mason Co. and its largest city, Limestone (Maysville), were well established. Maysville was the gateway to the central Bluegrass region and was its trading center, and a large black population resided in Mason Co. Three of the most notable members of this population were Rev. **Elisha W. Green** (1818–1893), enslaved at birth, who was allowed to minister throughout the Bluegrass and Northern Kentucky as the pastor of churches in Paris and Maysville; Col. **Charles Denton Young** (1864–1923), the first African American from Kentucky to graduate from the U.S. Military Academy at West Point; and **James A. Mundy** (1886–1978), who conducted and arranged for large choirs at Orchestra Hall in Chicago, thereby helping to revive black spirituals in the United States during the early 1900s. Another African American in the county was John Patty of Dover, who operated a coal and brick yard that furnished bricks for many of the houses built around that community. Blacks from Mason and surrounding counties attended the **John G. Fee Industrial High School** in Maysville. This school, which closed in the late 1950s with desegregation, was named for the Bracken Co.–born abolitionist John G. Fee, the founder of Berea College at Berea, Ky.

Campbell Co.

In Campbell Co. the African American population initially was not large. African Americans lived throughout the county at Alexandria, Cold Spring, Leitch's Station, and Newport. Enslaved blacks were brought to the county by early pioneers such as **David Leitch** and **James Taylor Jr.** Taylor, one of Campbell Co.'s wealthiest and most influential residents, freed his slaves upon his death in 1848. The Lumpkin brothers, along with other former slaves of Taylor, continued into the 1890s to fight in court for a property division from the Taylor estate. The Lumpkin family also helped to establish the **Southgate St. School** in 1873. One of the longest-lived persons in the United States was an African American woman named Aunt Hagar, who resided near Alexandria and was reportedly born March 21, 1751, in Virginia. She came to Kentucky in the days of early settlement with Lewis Wilcoxer, and when she died on July 6, 1873, she was supposedly age 122.

After the Civil War, black families retained the property they had acquired. In Cold Spring, the Jefferson family has resided on the six-acre farm off modern Bunning Ln. for more than 100 years. The father worked at the Newport rolling mills, and steel jobs became available to other members of his family living in Newport. Their children attended all-black schools in Newport and Covington.

Bracken Co.

In Bracken Co. an African American church, the Old Negro Church on "the Hill" near Augusta, was established in the 1830s; it was the first black church in the county. **Stephen Foster** reportedly based his song "My Old Kentucky Home" on the Negro spirituals sung there. Religiously, the city of Augusta was divided between the Methodist Norths, of antislavery persuasion, and the Methodist Souths, who were proslavery. Later, the St. Paul M.E. and the New Hope Baptist were the two African American churches in Augusta. The St. Paul church was founded on August 22, 1894, with a $200 down payment on the land, and Rev. McDade was its first pastor. At the beginning of the 20th century, blacks were attending the county's two integrated Methodist churches, one in Augusta and the other in Germantown. The African American church in Germantown was Reed's Chapel M.E. The elementary school for African Americans in Augusta was called the Augusta "B" school, and its counterpart in Germantown was called the Germantown "B" School. When the Germantown "B" school closed, its last commencement exercises, on May 21, 1953, were held in the sanctuary at Reed's Chapel M.E.

The local **Augusta College**, a Methodist institution, was a hotbed of antislavery thought. Abolitionism and slave escapes heavily dotted the landscape of Bracken Co. in its early history. The most noted abolitionist was **John G. Fee**, who spread the message through churches and public meetings that slavery was wrong. In 1848 a large group of slaves came through Brooksville headed toward Augusta on the Ohio River, in an escape attempt. Their route followed the natural corridors of terrain. Although all the fugitive slaves were captured, this event created great concern among slaveholders in the county.

Pendleton Co.

The Civil War had a great impact on Pendleton Co. Many of its young African American men went to

Covington to join the Union Army, including William Munday (1843–1899). His story is typical of many of the young blacks from Pendleton Co. who joined the Union's ranks. As a 20-year-old farmer, he enlisted for three years on May 23, 1864, at Covington and was assigned to Company D, 100th U.S. Colored Infantry (USCI). He saw action in Tennessee at the battle of Murfreesboro. Munday was buried in a field on the way to Hayes Station in the northern part of Pendleton Co.

Pendleton Co. had two black churches, located in Falmouth: the Ruth Temple A.M.E. Church and the First Baptist Church of Falmouth. There are a number of unnamed African American cemeteries in the county; two of them are on Miller's Ridge, where the dates of birth on tombstones range from 1828 to 1874 and the last burial recorded was in 1904. Harrison Miller was the owner of Miller's Ridge after the Civil War, and it is likely that his wife and children are buried there along with Miller. James Miller, who held the property containing this cemetery well into the 1930s, was the last Miller family member to own it. The other unnamed cemetery at Miller's Ridge is located off Ky. Rt. 22. Ben Munday (also spelled Monday), who died about 1939, owned the land. Daniel Monday, the father of Civil War soldier William Munday, is listed on the 1850 census as a free African American, born about 1795 in Kentucky. His occupation was given as farmer, and he had at least 10 children.

Two African American residents of Falmouth who rose to distinction were **John Merritt**, head football coach at Tennessee State University in Nashville, Tenn., and a member of the College Football Hall of Fame, and his cousin Dr. Harrison B. Wilson Jr. (b. 1925, Amsterdam, N.Y.), president of Norfolk State University (NSU) in Virginia from 1974 to 1997. Wilson's family was originally from Falmouth, and he attended school there. He received his BA from Kentucky State University in Frankfort and also taught at Jackson State University in Jackson, Miss., and at Tennessee State University.

Gallatin Co.

In Gallatin Co. abolitionists and **Underground Railroad** conductors Rev. **John Pavy** and Rev. **Alexander Sebastian** helped the steady flow of escaping slaves gain access to the Ohio River, using nearby Eagle Creek as the corridor to freedom. Blacks remaining in Gallatin Co. included members of the Consolidated Second Baptist Church in Warsaw, built in 1851 as a Presbyterian Church, which was later sold to the Colored Baptist Church. Trustees Oliver Hughes, Alexander Hamilton, and John Marshall purchased the building on August 15, 1881, for the sum of $500. It became the Consolidated Baptist Church in 1944, when it merged with another Warsaw African American Baptist church. The Second Baptist Church of Park Ridge had its beginning in the late 1890s. African Americans owned large tracts of land throughout Gallatin Co. In the 1880s blacks attended their own school at Park Ridge, near Sparta; that school was eventually replaced by a school funded by the Rosenwald Foundation of Chicago, which financed the construction of African American schools throughout the nation during the 1920s.

Boone Co.

African Americans in Boone Co. in the mid-19th century resided throughout the county. Near one of the county's oldest communities, Petersburg, blacks were present from the earliest days. They lived on the farms that supported the **Petersburg Distillery** and the river traffic on the Ohio River. Boone Co., with its wooded rural access to the Ohio River, also was an avenue of slave escapes during the 1850s. In January 1856 **Margaret Garner** made her famous attempt at freedom from the Gaines family farm in Boone Co.

By the 1870s African Americans had established several churches throughout Boone Co. The First Baptist Church of Florence at 21 Girard St. was started on November 27, 1870, and continued conducting services until 1976; the last pastor was Hershel Glenn of Covington. In 1977 the church's building was sold to the Church of God of Prophecy. In 1894 Richard Baker, George Clark, and Robert Sleet formed the Hopewell Baptist Church near Beaverlick, on land owned by G. W. Sleet.

Blacks operated their own schools in Boone Co. from 1883 until county schools were consolidated in 1954. In 1883 an African American school operated north of the present **Turfway Park Racecourse** near Florence. The property on which it stood, now owned by the Kenton Co. Airport Board, belonged to George Foster and Charles Cleaveland, two African Americans. Other black schools were at Idlewild and Burlington. In Walton an African American school began during the 1880s in a building behind today's **Zion Baptist Church** that also housed the church and an Odd Fellows Lodge. African Americans owned several sizable blocks of land in Boone Co. For instance, Rube Riley was a major landholder in the area known today as Big Bone. Members of his family attended Big Bone Baptist Church and are buried in that church's cemetery.

In Burlington, the county seat, numerous blacks resided on farms from the county's earliest beginnings. There were two Baptist churches in Burlington: one, located at the corner of Nicholas and Alley Sts. near Temperate St., currently is known as the First Baptist of Burlington; the second church is on the corner of Garrard and Alley near Orient St. These two churches later consolidated at the Nicholas and Alley Sts. location, where an elementary grade school was housed on the first floor. The second floor was rented to the Masonic Lodge for secondary education classes. During the 1920s, African American high school students from Boone Co. attended **Lincoln-Grant School** (William Grant High School) in Covington, either commuting or living with their Covington relatives. Beginning in 1955, Boone Co.'s black schools were shut down and their students began to attend integrated public schools within the county system.

Owen Co.

Owen Co. African Americans also lived throughout the county in the 1860s, in the communities at Cedar Hill, New Columbus, New Liberty, Owenton, and Pleasant Home. One of the oldest black churches in Northern Kentucky is the Second Baptist Church of New Liberty, which dates to 1846. The Second Baptist Church of Owenton was formed much later. African American **Teddy Vinegar** is a descendant of one of the first families to reside in the county. His family has maintained property holdings at **Mountain Island** in Owen Co. for more than 100 years. **Bill Livers**, a black born in Owen Co., was a well-known musician, a self-taught fiddle player. Several African American schools were established throughout the county. During the mid-20th century, a school financed by the Rosenwald Foundation replaced New Liberty's African American school, which was started in the late 1880s. At one time there was also a school for blacks at Pleasant Home.

Grant Co.

Grant Co.'s first church for blacks, at Williamstown, was built at the end of the 19th century. The current church, Ogg Chapel C.M.E., was named for Rev. Ogg, pastor of the **Williamstown United Methodist Church** on Paris St. Ogg came to help with the construction of the first church; then in 1950, when a replacement church was built, it was renamed in his honor. During the early 20th century, the Crittenden Christian Church on Olive Rd. in Grant Co. supported a large African American community. With the construction of I-75, most of that area's houses were removed, and for economic reasons their occupants moved to Covington. For more than 100 years, blacks have been buried in the Broadridge Cemetery near Dry Ridge. Many of the African Americans living in Grant Co. attended the Zion Baptist Church on U.S. 25 in Dry Ridge, until it closed in the late 1970s. African Americans attended a school in Dry Ridge until a new Rosenwald Foundation school replaced it in the 1920s.

Carroll Co.

Carroll Co. during the Civil War was the site of a skirmish between troops from the 117th USCI garrisoned in Covington and Col. George Jesse's Confederates at Gex Landing near Ghent (see **Gex Landing Incident**). The captured black troops later escaped, returning to duty in Covington. There are two African American churches in Carroll Co. that have been holding services since the 1870s; the **Second Baptist Church** of Carrollton, built in 1874, and the **Ghent Second Baptist Church**, founded in 1871. The Ghent church has a cemetery at the southeast end of Carroll St. Black children between the ages of 6 and 18 attended segregated schools at Carrollton and Worthville. There were 327 African American children living in the county in 1895. In 1921 the Worthville school closed and its students were transported via the **Carrollton and Worthville Railroad** to Carrollton's black school. These schools were supported by ad valorem taxes paid by African American taxpayers and continued operating until they were replaced by a new Rosenwald Foundation school. During the 1960s, this school was consolidated into the Carroll Co. system.

Kenton Co.

Kenton Co. was heavily influenced by the region's largest city, Covington. Covington had one of the longest service tunnel systems in the region, connecting the **Gano-Southgate House** on E. Second St. with the home of Kentucky governor **John White Stevenson** (1867–1871) at Garrard and E. Fourth Sts. The original intent of the tunnels was to convey supplies from the Ohio and Licking rivers to the main houses, but the tunnel under the Gano-Southgate House was used extensively for slave escapes when the owners were away. The grandmother of African American Annie Hargraves used the tunnel in her flight. The slaves of Governor Stevenson accompanied Margaret Garner in an escape using those tunnels. **Jacob Price**, a free person of color in 1860 who was living on Bremen St., a few doors from Main St., regularly helped slaves escape.

During the 1880s schools for black children were established in Erlanger, Independence, Kenton, Key West, Milldale, Morning View, and Scott. In 1896 the total enrollment of African Americans in the county schools was 313. High school students attended the **Lincoln-Grant School** (William Grant High School) in Covington, either commuting or living with relatives in town. The one-room school in Elsmere was named Dunbar. During the 1930s Thomas Lewis, a graduate of Lincoln-Grant High School who played on the school's undefeated football team in the late 1920s and was a graduate of Kentucky State University in Frankfort, became the Dunbar School's first teacher. In 1940 **Rosella Porterfield** was hired as the school's second teacher. In 1949 the Wilkins Heights School opened to replace the Dunbar School. It had two classrooms, a kitchen, and a gym that was also used as a cafeteria. As a part of desegregation during the 1950s, its students were transferred to another school within the Erlanger-Elsmere School District.

In the late 19th century, two black inventors with ties to Covington, **Granville T. Woods** and **Frederick M. Jones**, were receiving national attention. Woods incorporated the electrical manufacturing business he had founded in Newport while a resident of Covington. He later sold a number of his patents to Thomas Edison and Edison's General Electric Company and to the Westinghouse Corporation. Jones grew up in West Covington under the guidance of a Roman Catholic priest, Father William Ryan, and was known for his invention of air-cooling units for refrigerated trucks and trains.

Two events in the 20th century involving African American Covington residents gained the national spotlight and served as subtle reminders that freedom demands a heavy price. One, during the 1930s, concerned the John "Pete" Montjoy (1913–1937) case and was clearly a miscarriage of justice. Montjoy was charged with assaulting a white woman, found guilty, and sentenced to be hanged. The case has been termed a legal lynching that should have been reversed by Kentucky's "boy governor," A. B. "Happy" Chandler (1935–1939, 1955–1959), or by the U.S. Supreme Court. Montjoy's hanging in the Kenton Co. Courtyard on December 17, 1937, was one of the last public hangings in Kentucky.

The second incident is tied to the national **civil rights movement**. In 1970 a young civil rights worker from Covington, William Herman Payne (1943–1970), a member of the Student Non-Violent Coordinating Committee (SNCC), was in Maryland to support the organization's national chairman, Herbert "H. Rap" Brown, who was appearing in court there to face various charges. Payne and another passenger were killed when their car exploded on March 12, 1970. Brown was not in the car. Known as Ché in the civil rights movement, Payne had assisted in voter registration in Alabama and Mississippi. He was a 1963 graduate of Lincoln-Grant School (William Grant High School). This case brought national attention to Payne's hometown, the city of Covington, and remains a part of the history of violent incidents associated with the civil rights movement.

In 1971 **James Simpson Jr.** became the first black elected to office in Covington and Kenton Co. During the 1990s, **Pamela Mullins** was the first African American woman to be elected to the Covington Independent Board of Education; she later was elected to the Covington City Commission. In January 1999, when **Bill Bradford** became mayor of Elsmere, he was the first African American mayor of a city in the Northern Kentucky region. Bradford had been elected to the Elsmere City Council much earlier and also has served on various boards and commission in the region.

Robertson Co.

Robertson Co., the county with the smallest population in the state, was formed after the Civil War; therefore, any slave escapes or abolitionist activities in its territory are tied to the histories of the surrounding counties. During the late 1860s, two black schools, one at Mount Olivet and the other at Piqua, were established in what became Robertson Co. In 1927 the **Mount Zion Methodist Church** building was transferred (for the sum of one dollar) to be used for worship services by the African American community in Mount Olivet. According to recent U.S. censuses, very few blacks reside in the county now.

The forgotten masses of common, everyday African Americans must not be left out here. They need to be recognized in the aggregate even though their individual stories did not make it into the record. Just as the common white population is unnoticed by history, most blacks are unknown to historians. That is not to belittle their silent but important contribution to the history of the Northern Kentucky region.

African American Records: Bracken County, Kentucky, 1797–1999. Vol. 2. Brooksville, Ky.: Bracken Co. Historical Society, 1999.

"Another Suit by Col. Taylor's Old Slaves," *KJ,* April 12, 1892, 4.

An Atlas of Boone, Kenton, and Campbell Counties, Kentucky. Philadelphia: D. J. Lake, 1883.

Carey, Liz. "Black in N. Ky.: A History of Division," *Kenton County Community Recorder,* February 24, 2005, A1.

Harris, John. "Black Struggle Leader Buried," *KP,* March 16, 1970, 4K.

Hicks, Jack. "Show Tells of Ex-Slave Rev. Green," *KP,* November 25, 1991, 1K–2K.

"Maysville—Rev. Elisha Green," *KP,* November 2, 1893, 3.

"Newport–Resident," *CDC,* July 10, 1873, 3.

"An Outrage," *DC,* June 9, 1883, 3.

Reis, Jim. "Pioneers Opened Kentucky Frontier," *KP,* April 28, 1986, 4K.

Seibert, Herman R., Jr. "The Grave of a Forgotten Soldier," *NKH* 2, no. 1 (Fall–Winter 1994): 56–59.

"Services Held for Bomb Blast Victim," *KP,* March 17, 1970, 5K.

"Slaves in Kentucky," *CJ,* March 31, 1860, 1.

Turley-Adams, Alicestyne. *Rosenwald Schools in Kentucky, 1917–1932.* Frankfort: Kentucky Heritage Council, 1997.

Wright, George C. *Racial Violence in Kentucky, 1865–1940: Lynchings, Mob Rule, and "Legal Lynchings."* Baton Rouge: Louisiana State Univ. Press, 1990.

Theodore H. H. Harris

AFRICAN AMERICANS IN ELSMERE. African Americans began to migrate to Elsmere in Kenton Co. in the early 1900s. In 1900, 17 of the city's 137 residents were blacks; by 1910, there were 41 blacks out of a total city population of 331. By the late 1920s, partially in response to the labor needs of the **Southern Railway** (currently known as **Norfolk Southern**), the African American population of Kenton Co. had expanded to 1,390, but the number of blacks who lived in Elsmere remained about the same. Nevertheless, local African Americans began to create vibrant neighborhoods in Elsmere whose foundation rested on the construction of institutions such as churches and schools.

The creation of separate and exclusive black churches has helped to shape the lives of African Americans in the United States ever since the emergence of the independent African American church movement during the mid-1780s, led by Rev. Richard Allen and Rev. Absalom Jones. The people of African descent who lived in Elsmere were no different. In the winter of 1896, Rev. Daniel W. Ellison, along with several of his followers, established the first African Methodist Episcopal (A.M.E.) Church in the area at a railroad station on Woodside Ave. in Elsmere. The church moved several times before a permanent facility was established on Fox St., in 1905 or 1906. In 1934 a mysterious fire destroyed this building, but one year later, in 1935, a stone-fortified church replaced it. The following year, the cornerstone of the church was laid and the church was renamed the **Barnes Temple A.M.E. Church** of Elsmere, after Rev. H. L. Barnes. Between 1940 and 1948, the leaders of the church allowed the Erlanger-Elsmere Board of Education to use part of the building to teach first-, second-, and third-grade African American students from the local community. Over time, the Barnes Temple A.M.E. Church became one of the city's most prestigious black religious institutions.

Another black church, now named the First Baptist Church of Elsmere, was founded in 1891 by Deacon Matt Slaughter, Lucy Slaughter, and Soney

Slaughter. It originally held services and prayer meetings in an old school building along Spring St. A groundbreaking ceremony occurred in 1924 for the construction of a permanent facility on Garvey Ave. Several years later, the church was expanded, remodeled, and renamed Hanns Chapel in honor of Rev. Charles Hann. A new church was completed and renamed the First Baptist Church of Elsmere in 1934. Soon many local African Americans made it their spiritual home. From the late 1930s until today, the leadership of the First Baptist Church of Elsmere rested on the shoulders of four individuals, Rev. Edward Smith (1937–1966), Rev. Falvin Haygood (1971–1983), Rev. Jerome Norwood (1983–1991), and Rev. Norman Blankenship (1992–present). Each pastor brought stability and prosperity to the congregation and the larger local black community.

The public schools also helped to shape the development of the African American community of Elsmere. Local African Americans sought to use access to public education to expand their economic, political, and social opportunities. However, in Elsmere as elsewhere, racial segregation dominated all levels of public education until the 1954 *Brown v. Board of Education* U.S. Supreme Court decision. Nevertheless, the formal education of African Americans in the Erlanger-Elsmere area began as early as the late 1880s, when two black families, Thomas and Fanny Greene and the Slaughters, sponsored several local fundraising campaigns to build a local school for African American children. In 1896 this very small facility, located near the present-day Dixie Highway, in Erlanger, opened its doors and provided education for students from first through eighth grade, who were taught by one teacher. Several years later, fire destroyed the building; however, almost immediately the Dunbar School, named in honor of the famous black poet Paul Laurence Dunbar, was built on Spring St. in Elsmere. Here two African American teachers, Thomas Wood, the first instructor hired to teach at the school, and **Rosella French Porterfield**, a very influential community educator, librarian, and civil rights activist, taught African American students in grades one through eight.

Wilkins Heights School opened in 1949 and replaced the Dunbar School as the only all-black school in Elsmere. It was a much larger facility, containing two large classrooms, a kitchen, and a gym that also was used as a cafeteria. Most local African American elementary and middle school students attended Wilkins Heights School until it was closed with the movement toward school desegregation during the mid-1950s.

From the 1960s to the 1990s, Elsmere's black community gradually became more integrated into the larger society. For example, in 1974 **Bill "Billy" Bradford** became the first African American elected to the Elsmere City Council, where he remained until 1980, returning in 1982. He was elected the vice mayor of Elsmere in 1994 and in 1998 became mayor of Elsmere, the first black to hold such a position in Northern Kentucky. With the continuation of accomplishments such as these, over the past few decades Elsmere has become a very integrated community where all races and ethnicities can live, play, and work together harmoniously.

Barnes Temple A.M.E. Church pamphlet, Northern Kentucky African-American Heritage Task Force Collection, W. Frank Steely Library, Northern Kentucky Univ.

Bradford, Bill, mayor. Interviews by Eric R. Jackson, June 15, 19, 2006, Elsmere, Ky.

Bradford, Thomas, Mary Carneal, Bunt Hopkins, Wilma Porterfield, and Annie Wells. *Barnes Temple African Methodist Episcopal Church, Elsmere, Kentucky: African Methodism in Elsmere, Kentucky—Our Local History.* Elsmere, Ky.: Barnes Temple African Methodist Episcopal Church, 2006.

Elsmere Centennial Committee. *City of Elsmere Centennial Celebration Booklet, 1896–1996.* Elsmere, Ky.: City of Elsmere, 1996.

Jackson, Eric. *Black America Series: Northern Kentucky.* Charleston, S.C.: Arcadia, 2005.

Reis, Jim. "Schools of Distinction: Dunbar, Then Wilkins Educated Generations of Blacks in Elsmere," *KP*, January 19, 1998, 4K.

———. "Several Schools Taught Black Students," *KP*, February 17, 2003, 4K.

Eric R. Jackson

AFRICAN AMERICANS IN THE CIVIL WAR. In 1861, the first year of the **Civil War**, military service for African Americans living in Kentucky was not required. The Kentucky legislature, in fact, had declared in May 1861 that the state would take "no part" in the Civil War. The federal government ignored this declaration and immediately ordered county and state officials in Kentucky to supply troops for the Union Army. A whites-only draft was implemented in 1861 to fill the state quota.

Recruiters for the Union Army from Northern states, however, soon came into Kentucky seeking to sign up African Americans. Some of the earliest African Americans in the Union Army, including 13 members of the legendary 54th Massachusetts Regiment, were living in Kentucky in 1861. The requirements for induction into the Union Army included a complicated formula for African Americans, based on whether they were free or still in bondage.

Slaveholders in Kentucky trusted President Abraham Lincoln (1860–1865) to protect their property rights and took the stance that slavery would survive the war or, if it did not, they would be compensated once their slaves had been freed. During the war's first two years, 1861–1862, the large numbers of fugitive slaves who had sought asylum at federal army garrisons in Kentucky were returned to their masters while Lincoln's representatives tried unsuccessfully to broker a plan of compensatory emancipation with Kentucky's slaveholders.

Northern Kentucky was part of the 6th Military District, which consisted of Boone, Bracken, Campbell, Carroll, Gallatin, Grant, Harrison, Kenton, Pendleton, and Trimble counties. These 10 counties coincided with the 6th Congressional District. During the turbulent months of 1862, Northern Kentucky and Cincinnati braced for an invasion by Confederate troops. Forts were built on the hilltops of Kenton and Campbell counties to deter such an invasion, which never occurred on the scale that many expected. African American civilian laborers constructed the forts and breastwork necessary for defense, as bands of guerillas, bushwhackers, and secessionist sympathizers roamed the region.

The Emancipation Proclamation, issued by Lincoln on January 1, 1863, caused confusion in Kentucky since it freed slaves in states that had seceded, not in those, like Kentucky and several others, that had announced their neutrality. Caught in the middle of this issue, Kentucky's pro-Union governor, Thomas Bramlette (1863–1867), noted that because his state was neutral, the recruitment of African Americans into the Union Army should remain a point of contention. However, after the proclamation was issued, there was no turning back; thousands of former slaves and their families congregated at Union Army posts and recruitment stations throughout Kentucky. In February 1864, President Lincoln called for 500,000 additional men to join the Northern army; Bramlette then ended his opposition to the recruitment of African Americans in Kentucky for the Union Army.

The war came directly to Northern Kentucky's African Americans in early 1864, when President Lincoln, Secretary of War Edmund Stanton, and Kentucky governor Bramlette reached an agreement: whether African Americans were drafted or enlisted or served as substitutes, their inductions were considered to have contributed to the state's military quotas. Moreover, African Americans from Northern Kentucky were sent statewide to fill the ranks of other African American regiments. After the 72nd and 117th USCI Regiments were authorized, the majority of African Americans from the 6th Military District were assigned to these regiments.

The Union Army established two military facilities in Covington: Camp King, located along the Licking River, and, nearby, Webster Barracks, at the head of Greenup St. in the modern-day **Wallace Woods** neighborhood. Camp King served as headquarters for the district provost marshal and as a training post for new regiments. Two African American U.S. Colored Infantry (USCI) regiments were formed in Covington, the 72nd and the 117th. Col. Alexander Duncan commanded the 72nd, and Col. Lewis G. Brown led the 117th. Both commanders were white. In September 1861, Joseph Singer, the son of John Singer, became the first local African American civilian casualty of the war. Singer, who was working as a cook for the Union Army's Hawthorn Guards at Camp King, was shot while going for a bucket of water as he attempted to pass the sentinel without giving the password. Charles Singer, Joseph's brother, was drafted in May 1864; their father was a longtime African American businessman in Northern Kentucky and the future father-in-law of Rev. **Jacob Price**.

In March 1864, the enrollment of former slaves from Bracken, Campbell, Harrison, Kenton, and Pendleton counties for military service was progressing at a rapid pace. By April there were 1,192

African Americans (1,090 ex-slaves and 102 freemen) eligible for military duty in the 6th Military District. Some African Americans who enlisted came from outside of the 6th Military District (for example, from Bourbon and Owen counties) to join the war effort.

In May 1864, former slaves and other drafted African Americans from Kenton Co. were being sent to a general military rendezvous point at Louisville. In July 1864, Adj. Gen. Lorenzo Thomas, in charge of African American recruitment in Kentucky since 1863, ordered the establishment of a camp in Covington for organization, instruction, and training at Camp King, home to both the 72nd and 117th USCI Regiments. A Captain Webster, the 6th District's quartermaster, proclaimed that all enslaved African Americans not physically suited for military service were to be assigned to the quartermaster and employed at the government's stables at a pay rate of $30 per month. In August the quartermaster received an anonymous communication advising him to resign his commission "and stop hiring those African Americans unfit for military service."

By mid-August 1864, nearly 400 African American recruits were in Covington waiting assignment. Col. Lewis G. Brown and two other line officers were in charge of the enlistees and recruitment. Colonel Brown sent agents to Carroll, Gallatin, Harrison, and other nearby counties to enlist former slaves. A considerable force of both whites and African Americans was sent with each recruiting party to protect it from roaming rebel guerillas.

Some local people discouraged African American enlistments, while others tried to entice recruits away from Covington in order to sell them in Cincinnati as military substitutes. The penalty for being caught trafficking in substitute recruitments was imprisonment in Covington's military jails.

In late August, 60 soldiers from Company C, 117th USCI Regiment, under the command of Lt. Frederick D. Seward from the 72nd USCI Regiment, were attacked while camping at Ghent in Gallatin Co., by a force of 100 Confederates under the command of a Colonel Jessie. The majority of the Union troops were killed, and the remainder were taken captive. The Union soldiers were in Gallatin and Carroll counties on a recruiting mission. Lieutenant Seward and a number of these soldiers arrived in Covington after being released by Colonel Jessie. One of the men died and six were wounded. Two of the wounded were taken to the Seminary U.S. General Hospital, on the site of the former **Western Baptist Theological Institute**. Eight other African American soldiers taken as prisoners in the battle were seen leaving in the direction of Eagle Hills in Owen Co., accompanied by Colonel Jessie and his Confederate troops. Two weeks later, these eight soldiers escaped when Union soldiers garrisoned in Shelby Co. attacked Colonel Jessie and the troops he commanded while they were encamped.

On October 7, 1864, after having their ranks increased by 30 recruits from Owen Co. and 20 more from Bourbon Co., the 117th USCI Regiment, under Colonel Brown, was ordered to the field and departed for Louisville. Later, the regiment was ordered to Baltimore, Md., and arrived there on October 13. Maj. Gen. Lew Wallace (of *Ben Hur* novel fame) took over command of the regiment.

In January 1865 this regiment was transferred to the Union's 25th Army Corps and then moved to Camp Burnham near Richmond, Va. The regiment remained there until May 1865. In April they were stationed at Petersburg, Va., and by June the regiment had been moved to Brownsville, Tex., where it remained until the war's end in 1865.

In November 1864 Major Mitchell, the provost marshal for the 6th Military District, mustered into federal service 82 African Americans. They were to serve principally as teamsters but also to work in the engineering, quartermaster, and commissary departments. He was following orders issued by Adj. Gen. **George Thomas** (namesake of Fort Thomas) to have these men work in uniform, draw rations, and receive the same pay as any other Union soldier, not the $30 per month they had been earning.

In early 1865 Covington was receiving African American refugees primarily from the vicinity of the saltworks in southwestern Virginia. About 100 refugees were being housed in the Union Army's military barracks on Greenup St. Some of the most able-bodied men who had arrived indicated their desire to join the Union Army.

In April 1865, Company C, 72nd, proceeded to Taylorsville in Spencer Co. En route, they were attacked by about 20 Confederate guerrillas. After a brief skirmish, the company entered town without having sustained any loss of men. The company remained there until April 26, when they marched to Bloomfield in Nelson Co. In May the 72nd USCI Regiment, under Colonel Duncan, departed Covington eastward for Catlettsburg in Boyd Co. In June the company arrived at Camp Nelson, where it was discontinued and the soldiers were discharged. The troops remaining at Camp King were three companies of the 6th Colored Cavalry, two companies of the 124th, one company of the 24th Kentucky (state militia), and one or two companies of the 1st Ohio Heavy Artillery, the latter guarding fortifications. In September the 119th USCI Regiment left for Louisville. The 13th Colored Heavy Artillery arrived from Camp Nelson. About half the regiment proceeded up the Ohio River to Catlettsburg, and the remainder stayed at Camp King. Companies F and G, 24th Kentucky Infantry, which had been doing duty within the Quartermaster's Department, were relieved by Company A of that same regiment. The two former companies went to Camp Nelson. In October the troops garrisoned at the **Newport Barracks**, including the band, were ordered to New York City, as the barracks became the staging area for African American troops to be stationed in the West.

During April 1865, the drafting of African Americans ceased when the deputy provost marshals in some of the counties of the 6th Congressional District were discharged. Some of the African Americans still in the military service remained enrolled well into the mid-1860s, however. Deputy provost marshals from Boone, Bracken, Pendleton, and Trimble counties were notified of their discharge, once these soldiers were no longer needed. This action continued through May 1865 when other deputy provost marshals from Campbell, Carroll, and Gallatin counties were also discharged. Governor Bramlette maintained his resistance to what he considered federal occupation. Camp King was merged into Newport Barracks.

During the war, African American refugees flooded the southern part of Covington near Camp King, so the military had to provide them with means of survival. After the war, refugees from Central Kentucky came to Covington and Newport in large numbers, taxing the ability of those cities to provide education, medicine, employment, and housing for them. In December 1865, the Freedmen's Bureau was expanded into Kentucky and an office was opened in Covington. The Freedmen's Bureau, with assistance from the Freedmen's Aid Society and other groups, provided much of the medical and educational assistance for the African Americans who had migrated to Northern Kentucky.

"Agency of the Freedmen's Bureau for Covington, Kentucky and Vicinity," *CDG*, January 6, 1866, 2.
"Camp for Negro Troops," *CDG*, July 13, 1864, 2.
Gladstone, William A. *United States Colored Troops, 1863–1867.* Gettysburg, Pa.: Thomas, 1990.
"Homicide at Camp King," *CJ*, September 28, 1861, 3.
Howard, Victor B. *Black Liberation in Kentucky: Emancipation and Freedom, 1862–1884.* Lexington: Univ. Press of Kentucky, 1983.
"Movements of Troops," *CDE*, September 21, 1865, 2.
Reis, Jim. "Blacks Made Diverse Contributions," *KP*, January 18, 1988, 4K.
Ross, Joseph B., comp. *Tabular Analysis of the Records of the U.S. Colored Troops and Their Predecessor Units in the National Archives of the United States.* Special List No. 33, Washington, D.C.: NARS, 1973.
Simon, Jack. "The Civil War Military Hospitals of Covington, Kentucky," *NKH* 11, no. 1 (Fall–Winter 2003): 38–43.
"Slaves and Free-Colored Persons Liable for Military Duty," *CDE*, April 9, 1864, 3.
Wimberg, Robert J. *Cincinnati and the Civil War: Under Attack.* Cincinnati: Ohio Book Store, 1999.

Theodore H. H. Harris

AFRICAN AMERICANS IN WORLD WAR II (EUROPEAN THEATER). During **World War II** all able-bodied men who were U.S. citizens, including members of the African American community of Northern Kentucky, were required to serve in the military. Those who did not enlist were conscripted. The exact number of black Northern Kentuckians who served in the armed forces is not known. Official U.S. Army policy generally restricted African Americans to service units; only a few were assigned to combat units.

The largest concentration of African American soldiers from Northern Kentucky serving in Europe served with the 92nd "Fighting Buffaloes" Infantry Division in Italy, part of the 5th Army, commanded by Lt. Gen. Mark Clark. The 3rd Army, which was commanded by Lt. Gen. George S. Patton Jr., had the next-largest number of African Americans from the region.

The arrival of black soldiers in England was a matter of curiosity for the local population and a new experience for these soldiers. The British saw them not as Negroes or colored but simply as those "Tan Yanks" who had arrived to help in the war effort. Most African American soldiers regarded service in World War II as an opportunity to prove their patriotism and to visit other parts of the United States and of the world.

In General Patton's command, all troops, regardless of skin color, were utilized, whether in service or combat units. After the Normandy invasion, both types of units played a vital role when Patton made his famous dash across Europe. In late July 1944, once Patton had established his headquarters in France, a number of African Americans from Northern Kentucky joined the 3rd Army. During the fighting in Italy, the predominantly black 92nd Infantry Division was assigned to General Clark's 5th Army; the 92nd is distinguished as having been the only predominantly African American combat division to serve in Europe.

Lt. **Melvin W. Walker** entered the U.S. Army in March 1941. He trained at Camp Benning, Ga., and arrived in Italy as a member of the 366th Infantry Regiment, 92nd Infantry Division, in July 1944. He was awarded several service medals, including the Purple Heart Medal.

Following the Normandy invasion, U.S. secretary of war Henry L. Stimson applauded the African American soldiers who had fought during the Normandy invasion. A contemporary newspaper stated, "Military observers here pointed out that the Negro engineer and quartermaster detachments were bound to have suffered even heavier casualties than infantry troops, the reason being that their work had to be carried on under fire and without foxhole cover available to infantrymen engaged in combat operations."

George Frank Nutter and Albert Nutter Jr., the sons of Mrs. Minnie Nutter of Covington, were both drafted following their graduation from **Lincoln-Grant School**. During the Normandy invasion, Pfc. Albert Nutter Jr. was a demolition specialist and a member of Company D, 374th Engineer General Service Regiment. His brother, Frank Nutter, arrived in Italy in late July 1944 and was a member of Company E, 370th Infantry Regiment, and the 92nd Infantry Division. On December 27, 1944, Pfc. Frank Nutter was wounded in action in Italy. He was awarded numerous medals, including the Purple Heart and the Combat Infantry Badge.

Henry C. Lowe, a graduate of Newport's **Southgate St. School**, was drafted in February 1943. Private Lowe went to movie projector school at Camp Bowie, Tex., and ordnance detachment school at Aberdeen, Md. He arrived in England in July 1944 and not long thereafter joined Patton's 3rd Army, fighting in France. Lowe described his stay in England as very enjoyable, adding that "the English people were nice to me." As a member of the 657th Ordnance Company—Ammo ASP, Lowe had to establish ammunition sites for the ever-advancing U.S. 3rd Army. He established an ammo dump just outside Paris, serving as a master records stock clerk for all ordnance received. In France he learned to speak French "by listening to the people talk." By late September, Lowe had been promoted to sergeant. A German army officer who was a prisoner of war taught him how to speak German, although fraternizing with the prisoners was discouraged.

James Jennings of Covington attended Lincoln-Grant School and was drafted into the U.S. Army in November 1942. He served in Italy with the 92nd Signal Company. Jennings was awarded numerous ribbons and medals, including the American Theater Ribbon and the European African Middle Eastern Theater Ribbon. A sergeant, Jennings was the field wire chief for the 92nd Infantry Division. In later years, he formed and led the Covington African American veterans drill team that performed during the annual Memorial Day parade held in Covington. Jennings was also a charter member of Hurry-Berry-Smith, Veterans of Foreign Wars (**VFW**) Post 7453, organized in Covington in 1976.

James H. Robinson from Covington was killed in action on August 17, 1944, while serving in France. His wife, Ardella, who lived in Covington on Sanford St., was notified of his death on November 13, 1944. Private Robinson, a member of the 3918th Gasoline Supply Company, was buried in the Brittany American Cemetery, St. James, France. He received the Purple Heart.

World War II ended in Europe in May 1945, and U.S. troops began to return in December. For Northern Kentucky's African Americans, most discharges took place in and around the region in 1946 upon their return. These returning veterans saw a new beginning. Most had at least an eighth-grade education received from the Southgate St. School in Newport or the Lincoln-Grant School in Covington. Some had completed high school before the war at William Grant High School, the only high school serving blacks in Boone, Campbell, and Kenton counties. Before the war, their only educational experience had been in segregated school systems. Their army service in Europe, though also segregated, offered experiences that helped them later in civilian life. The vast majority of African American veterans found improved employment opportunities, usually within the federal government. Many made use of the GI Bill of Rights and continued their education. In addition, the postwar veteran saw a need for change in Northern Kentucky. When change was slow in coming, many veterans moved to Cincinnati or other locations, returning only for visits.

"Citations, Awards for Servicemen," *KTS*, January 19, 1945, 2.

Harris, Ted. "Stories of Africans Americans in WWII Went Untold," *KP*, February 28, 2002, 4K.

"Pvt. James H. Robinson," *KP*, November 13, 1944, 1.

"Three North Kentuckians Are Reported as Killed in Action," *KTS*, November 13, 1944, 1.

"Wounded in Action—PFC George Frank Nutter," *KTS*, January 10, 1945, 1.

Theodore H. H. Harris

AFRICAN AMERICANS IN WORLD WAR II (PACIFIC THEATER). African Americans of Northern Kentucky served with distinction in World War II. **World War II** in Europe ended in May 1945 (see **African Americans in World War II [European Theater]**), but the war against Japan in the Pacific Theater still had to be fought. African Americans serving in the Pacific and Asia were under the command of Gen. Douglas MacArthur of the Army and Gen. Henry "Hap" Arnold of the Army Air Force. African Americans serving in the Navy were commanded by admirals Chester W. Nimitz and William F. "Bull" Halsey. Nimitz was the commander in charge of all U.S. forces in the central and north Pacific and also was responsible for coordinating naval and land operations with MacArthur in the southwest Pacific.

The first major campaign in the Pacific Theater, the battle for New Guinea, began in March 1942. Once taken, New Guinea served as MacArthur's headquarters for most of the war. The key (though inadequate) facilities of the island were located at Port Moresby on the Gulf of Papua near the southern tip. Port Moresby, the principal base on the island, had to be rebuilt once the land fighting had ended. The African American soldiers stationed on New Guinea were put to work building airstrips, barracks, and port facilities, and soon, as a result of their efforts, the damage to the port had been repaired. Later, African American engineering, ordnance, and quartermaster units serving with the American Expeditionary Forces in the Bona-Gona area were commended highly by Lt. Gen. E. F. Herring of the Australian Army, for bravery during a battle fought in March 1943.

In June 1942, William Bannister of Covington, one of the many Northern Kentucky African Americans who served, was inducted into the Army Air Force and assigned to the 1060th Base Unit. He was a graduate of the William Grant High School (see **Lincoln-Grant School**) class of 1939. Bannister's unit saw combat in the battles of New Guinea and the southern Philippines at Leyte and the Ormac corridor. He earned the Army Good Conduct Medal, the Asiatic-Pacific Campaign Medal with two bronze stars, the World War II Victory Medal, and the Philippine Liberation Ribbon. Bannister rose to the rank of staff sergeant. He was discharged at AAF ORD, Greensboro, N.C., on October 31, 1945.

Henry B. Brown Jr., the son of Ada Brown and a 1942 graduate of William Grant High School, was inducted into the U.S. Army on March 26, 1943. Brown was a member of the 437th Aviation Squadron, 27th Air Depot Group, during the battle for New Guinea. He earned the marksman badges using both the 30-caliber carbine and the M-1 rifle. His awards included the Army Good Conduct Medal, the American Campaign Medal, the Asiatic-Pacific Campaign Medal with one bronze star, and the World War II Victory Medal. Before his discharge, Brown was a member of the military occupation force stationed in Japan. He was discharged from military service at Camp Atterbury, Ind., on July 2, 1946.

Also fighting in New Guinea and Luzon (Philippines) was James E. Talley of Covington. The son of Anna B. Talley, he was a 1943 graduate of William Grant High School. Talley was inducted into the army in June 1943, just after his high school graduation. He served in the 428th Port Company with the rank of tech 5. He earned the marksman badge using the SS carbine as well as the Army Good Conduct Medal, the American Campaign Medal, the Asiatic-Pacific Campaign Medal with two bronze stars, the World War II Victory Medal, and the Philippine Liberation Ribbon. Talley was discharged at Camp Atterbury, Ind., on February 24, 1946.

In June 1943, John Louis Herndon enlisted in the navy's Construction Battalion (Seabees) and served in the South Pacific at Tontouta, the most important air base on New Caledonia. Tontouta was one of the most highly developed facilities in the entire theater and was built from ground up by the Seabees. Herndon, the son of Emanuel and Mary Herndon of W. Ninth St. in Covington and a graduate of William Grant High School, was one of the few African Americans to serve in the Seabees during the war, earning the American Campaign Medal, the Asiatic-Pacific Campaign Medal with one Bronze Star, and the World War II Victory Medal. He was discharged in December 1945 with the rank of coxswain at the Great Lakes Naval Station in Illinois.

In June 1944, George R. Offutt, a resident of Covington, was inducted into the army and served with the 3064th Dump Truck Company. He earned the Army Good Conduct Medal, the Asiatic-Pacific Campaign Medal, and the World War II Victory Medal. While serving in Okinawa, Japan, Offutt recorded his experiences with photographs of Japanese Army officers who were prisoners of war in the camp as well as snapshots of local villagers. Offutt attained the rank of sergeant and was discharged at Fort Knox, Ky., on January 18, 1946.

In July 1944, Navy Seaman Leroy Ingram, a resident of Covington and the son of Gladys Ingram, was killed in an explosion at Port Chicago near San Francisco, Calif. Ingram attended Burlington, Ky., schools and then was employed in the CCC (Civilian Conservation Corps) for several years before his enlistment in the navy. The explosion that took his life cost the lives of over 300 sailors. Ingram was the sole Covingtonian to be killed in the blast.

In September 1944 Navy Stewart Mate 1st Class James M. Williams from Covington returned home from 23 months of duty in the Pacific Theater to visit his mother and stepfather, Mr. and Mrs. Edward Fender. Williams was a veteran of the Marshall Island and Gilbert Island invasions.

The U.S. Army arrived in the Burma, India, and China Theater during 1942, under the command of MacArthur. Sixty percent of the troops serving in India and Burma were African American. African Americans were not permitted in China until 1945. However, beginning in early 1943, while visiting Washington, D.C., and New York City, Madame Chiang Kai-shek, the wife of China's head of state, proclaimed that the Chinese people abhorred all racial bias. In a meeting during her visit with Walter White, **NAACP** secretary, she was assured of the deep interest of African Americans in the struggle of the Chinese people.

From 1942 to 1944, Lt. Gen. Joseph Stilwell was in command of the Burma, India, and China Theater. In October 1944, Lt. Gen. Albert C. Wedemeyer replaced Stilwell. Military operations in Burma and India, under Lt. Gen. Daniel Sultan, were separated from those in China. During this period, Maj. Gen. Claire Chennault was in command of the 14th Army Air Force. In the China Theater, Generalissimo Chiang Kai-shek, who was both China's head of state and the commander of the Chinese Army, began to permit African American troops to move freely about the country in small numbers. The first African American troops in China were members of the 858th Aviation Engineer Battalion.

LeRoy Waller, a resident of Covington, joined the 858th Aviation Engineer Battalion stationed in the Burma, India, and China Theater and helped build the Burma Rd. through some of the densest vegetation in the Asiatic Theater. In May 1945, the battalion, as part of the 14th Army Air Force (Flying Tigers), was assigned to the Burma Rd. in the China Theater, becoming the only African American unit to serve under Maj. Gen. Claire Chennault and Chiang Kai-shek.

Starting in October 1945, the African Americans who had served in the Burma, India, and China Theater began making their way home from the Far East. Most left the service and were mustered out at the various military processing installations throughout the United States before returning to Northern Kentucky. Some, however, never returned to Northern Kentucky, settling instead in other U.S. locations.

"Missing after Blast on Coast," *KTS*, July 20, 1944, 4.
"Navy Lists Negro Victims in Big California Disaster," *Pittsburgh Courier*, July 29, 1944, 18.
"Soldier Lauds Folks at Home in Letters to Parents," *KTS*, September 1, 1944, 2.
"S/Sgt. William F. Bannister," *KTS*, June 1, 1945, 2.

Theodore H. H. Harris

AGRICULTURE. From prehistoric times to the present, farming has played a vital role in Northern Kentucky, economically, politically, and culturally. The story of agriculture in Northern Kentucky is a complicated one, replete with paradoxes. Among the 11 counties, both density of population and size in area vary widely. Kenton Co. is one of the most urbanized counties in the state, and Robertson Co. is one of the least populated; in square miles, Owen Co. is one of the largest, and Gallatin Co. is one of the smallest. No single plot line seems adequate to describe the region's diversity. Proximity and geography have been both a blessing and a curse. **Tobacco**, with its rise and fall, has also been a central theme. Finally, the enduring and evolving agrarian heritage of the region is, ironically, counterpoised by a decline in farming as a way of life.

First, to consider Northern Kentucky agriculture as a unified, monolithic whole is incorrect. There are subregions with distinctive attributes. The uppermost tier of counties—Boone, Campbell, and Kenton—depend less than the others on tobacco, corn, hay, and cattle, which are Kentucky farmers' traditional recipe for success. Truck farming, vegetable production, fruit and nut orchards, wood crops, horse sales, and revenues from nurseries reflect a more diverse mix of commodities produced in these counties than in other sections; thus, most recently, the average per farm market value of production has tended to be higher than in counties more dependent upon tobacco. In these three counties, Northern Kentucky's most populous, the average farm size ranges between 87 acres (Campbell Co.) and 101 acres (Boone Co.), well below the 142-acre average for the rest of the Northern Kentucky region. The arrival of numerous German and other immigrant farmers during the 19th century also shaped Boone, Campbell, and Kenton counties' farming communities in distinctive ways; one is the early emphasis on **viniculture**. And farmers living in the three-county tier share the unfortunate distinction of being at risk from commercial and residential development pressures as suburbia metastasizes ever southward. During the latter 1990s, approximately 20 acres of Northern Kentucky farmland in Boone, Campbell, and Kenton counties were lost each day to development—an exceptionally fast pace. In the last decade of the 20th century, Boone Co.'s population increased by 49 percent, from 57,589 to 85,991. Between 1997 and 2002, more than 10 percent, some 8,300 acres, of the entire county's farmland was lost to development as the orchards and produce stands gave way to planned communities that featured polo fields, marinas, and high-priced residences. County planning commission projections indicate that if the present rate of development continues unabated, by 2030 the county's population will be more than 188,000 and only 2 percent of the land will be used for agriculture.

In contrast to Boone, Campbell, and Kenton counties stand the region's lower tier of counties: Bracken, Carroll, Gallatin, Grant, Mason, Owen, Pendleton, and Robertson. Tobacco revenues for 2002 show that Mason, Owen, Bracken, and Grant ranked 17th, 18th, 29th, and 36th, respectively, in Kentucky in value of tobacco sales, with Carroll and Pendleton counties not far behind. The rate of population increase, with the exception of Gallatin and Grant counties, has been nowhere near that of Boone Co., and consequently development pressures have been less severe. Between 67 percent (Robertson Co.) and more than 80 percent (Mason Co.) of the total acreage in the southern tier of counties remains in farms, compared to less than 50 percent for Boone, Campbell, and Kenton counties. Given their dependence upon tobacco and its declining production between 1997 and 2002, the average per farm market value of production fell for every county in the southern section, in some cases disastrously so: Robertson Co. had a 56 percent decline and Pendleton a 44 percent decline.

Despite the existence of distinctive subregions, there are strong unifying themes that provide a basis for shared experience among area farmers. The forces of geography and proximity are universal elements. Tilling the soil, which is predominantly Eden Shale formation (see **Eden Shale**

Farm), presents unique problems throughout Northern Kentucky. Steep slopes associated with Eden Shale terrain and the soil's tendency to shed, rather than store, water make it particularly difficult to farm. An emphasis on crops adaptable to the terrain and on those that can be grown profitably on small acreage has resulted. Production of grasses and woodlot management also reflect strategies designed to address the twin challenges of soil conditions and topography. Being near major markets such as Cincinnati and Louisville somewhat alleviated the transportation problems that historically confounded farmers in more remote regions. Ready access to the Ohio, Kentucky, and Licking Rivers—the highways of pioneer and antebellum Kentucky—traditionally have given Northern Kentucky farmers a distinct advantage in transporting crops and livestock to distant markets.

During the pioneer and antebellum eras, agriculture was Kentucky's primary economic activity. Settlers homesteading the state's northernmost region initially practiced subsistence farming by raising beans, corn, and squash and by free-range grazing of cattle, hogs, and other livestock. Typical surplus commodities produced for sale or trade included bacon, flour, livestock, pork, tobacco, and whiskey. Corn and hog production proved central to early Northern Kentucky agriculture throughout most of the 19th and early 20th centuries. Yet commercial agriculture during the settlement period faced numerous obstacles: security from American Indians, the time-consuming necessity of clearing forests to make large-scale crop production possible, and limited transportation networks. Developing an adequate transportation system ranks among the most important factors in any region's economic development. The first roads were little more than crude trails. For example, in early-19th-century Northern Kentucky, roads were so poor that a wagon loaded with goods could take as long as two days to travel roundtrip from Florence, Ky., to Covington, a distance of approximately 20 miles. Farmers in sections of the region found it more profitable to drive their stock to Maysville for shipment by river to Cincinnati than to take the Georgetown Rd., a more direct route but virtually impassable during certain seasons owing to its poor condition. Early trail drives did occur as Northern Kentucky farmers and stock raisers herded cattle, hogs, horses, sheep, and other livestock over routes such as the Wilderness Trail and through the Cumberland Gap to southern and eastern markets. The costly, time-consuming drives led to lost time and reduced profits from animals weakened by the lengthy journey. When good roads did eventually emerge, such as the **Covington and Lexington Turnpike**, Northern Kentucky farmers readily took advantage of them. One-half of all the pork packed in Cincinnati in 1839 came up the Covington and Lexington Turnpike from Kentucky farmers. Yet the farmers' dilemma of inadequate roads continued well into the 20th century. In 1900 Boone Co. possessed only 83 miles of hard-surface roads and more than 1,000 miles of mud ones. As late as 1940, four out of every five rural Kentucky dwellings lacked direct access to improved roads.

The importance of streams and rivers to pioneer and antebellum Northern Kentucky farmers cannot be overstated. Agricultural commodities traveled via flatboats, keelboats, rafts, and eventually steamboats down the Kentucky, Licking, and Ohio rivers. Shallow-draft vessels could moor at numerous points, and farmers with riverfront acreage often had their own private landings. Along the banks of the Ohio River between Rabbit Hash, in Boone Co., and the mouth of the Kentucky River, a distance of some 40 miles, 38 landings and 11 villages dotted both sides of the river. River-based communities such as Augusta, Carrollton, and Warsaw flourished as local agricultural distribution and transportation centers for area farmers, while Covington, Newport, and Maysville became major regional processing and shipping centers for flour, hemp, pork, tobacco, and whiskey. After the **Civil War**, as steamboat and other river-based shipping gradually gave way in importance to the railroads, many smaller Northern Kentucky river towns saw their status and their economic importance diminish.

Agriculture flourished in the antebellum era, particularly the 1850s. Kentucky ranked as a national leader in a wide array of commodities—corn, hemp, oats, rye, tobacco, and wheat, as well as production of draft animals and livestock. Emerging rail lines such as the **Covington and Lexington Railroad** facilitated the shipment of hogs and wheat to Covington and on to Cincinnati (by 1857 an estimated 45% of the wheat and 35% of the hogs entering Cincinnati were transported by the Covington and Lexington Railroad). Cincinnati's role as a primary consumer and processor of Northern Kentucky's agricultural products expanded throughout the era and was further solidified by the opening of the **John A. Roebling Bridge** in 1867 and the **Chesapeake and Ohio Railroad Bridge** in 1888.

Antebellum Northern Kentuckians, gentlemen farmers and essayists, played key leadership roles. James Dinsmore acquired approximately 700 acres of Boone Co. land and established the **Dinsmore Homestead**, where he cultivated grapes and raised corn, tobacco, wheat, and sheep. **Lewis Sanders**, master of Grasslands, his Carroll Co. estate, promoted an emphasis upon blooded livestock by importing Durham shorthorn cattle from England in 1817. Organizations such as the Northern Kentucky Cattle Importing Association later followed Sanders's example and began improving bloodstock through introducing European animals. Sanders also helped organize the State Agricultural Society to disseminate information on scientific agricultural methods and provide a forum for farmers. Men such as **Laban J. Bradford** of Bracken Co. who was president of the State Agricultural Society and the National Tobacco Association and initiated a tobacco exposition in Louisville. During that period the agricultural fairs, precursors to Kentucky's ubiquitous county fairs, began; they led to enduring community traditions in Northern Kentucky, such as the **Germantown** Fair. Farmer essayists, like Adam Beatty of Maysville, authored works such as *Essays on Practical Agriculture.* Both Beatty and Sanders were also important advocates for Kentucky's hemp industry, a major antebellum-era cash crop, of which Mason Co. farmers were Northern Kentucky's major producers.

One might not typically associate the southern planter class with Northern Kentucky, but large-scale, slave-based plantations operated alongside the small farms of yeoman landowners and landless tenant farmers. In the Timberlake district, now Erlanger, in Kenton Co., **Bartlett Graves** owned Walnut Grove plantation. Graves and other prominent citizens such as Thomas Buckner and William Timberlake played leading roles in the Kenton Co. Association, which was organized in the early 1840s to capture runaway slaves and return them to their masters. While the planter class represented only a small percentage of the farmers in the region, it did exist. In 1860 leading slaveholding counties included Mason (3,772 slaves), Boone (1,745 slaves), Owen (1,660 slaves), and Carroll (1,045 slaves). The fewest bondsmen resided in Campbell, Kenton, and Pendleton counties. After the Civil War, many newly emancipated blacks left rural areas and moved to urban centers to seek employment and better living conditions. By 1870 Kenton Co., home to only 652 blacks a decade earlier, had more than 1,657 black residents. The more rural areas, such as Carroll and Boone counties, experienced net out-migrations. Carroll Co.'s black population, slave and free, dropped from 1,087 in 1860 to 540 freedmen in 1870. Blacks were drawn to the cities, such as Maysville. Mason Co. today has the highest number of African Americans working in agriculture of all 11 counties.

The Civil War proved both harmful and beneficial to the district's farmers. The loss of laborers, both slave and free; the disruption of traditional, lower-South markets; government-mandated transportation restrictions; and political shenanigans such as the Great Hog Swindle all led to financial losses and reduced production levels in almost every category of agricultural commodity. In many instances, production did not return to preconflict levels until 20 years after the end of the war. As traditional southern markets reopened, some Kentucky farmers could supply draft animals, crops, and livestock to their southern neighbors.

The Reconstruction era in Kentucky is synonymous with the rise of tobacco as the major cash crop and the decline of the diversified crop and livestock mix that had characterized antebellum Kentucky. While long grown within the state, tobacco did not dominate farmers' interest and energy until after the Civil War. An increasing demand for Kentucky-grown tobacco resulted from the war's devastation of Virginia and North Carolina. Between 1865 and 1928, Kentucky led the nation in tobacco production. Northern Kentuckians stood at the forefront in raising tobacco, a crop that, while labor intensive, required little in the way of land and equipment. Increasingly, the region's farmers became hostage to the boom-bust cycle of tobacco prices.

According to some accounts, **white burley tobacco** originated in Bracken Co. in the mid-1860s, and a type of leaf known as Mason Co. tobacco ranked among the most sought-after varieties. Towns such as Covington and Maysville became regional tobacco warehousing and manufacturing centers. Yet almost every county seat had its share of drying houses and warehouses, "prizing" houses, and manufacturing facilities. Cincinnati, Lexington, and Louisville were the major markets, but throughout the 20th century, Carrollton and Maysville also ranked as important loose-leaf auction and warehousing centers until the recent reemergence of the contract system. During the Black Patch Wars of the first decade of the 20th century, many Northern Kentucky tobacco farmers allied themselves with the Burley Tobacco Society and the American Society of Equity to fight for higher prices from the American Tobacco Company. In the spring of 1908, violence raged throughout Northern Kentucky, but particularly in Bracken and Mason counties. There **Night Riders** burned tobacco barns and warehouses, terrorized entire communities, and held mass rallies. Farmers who refused to join were beaten or had their crops destroyed. Eight Grant Co. farmers were convicted under the criminal section of the Sherman Antitrust Act, reputedly the only such case in Kentucky, and fined $4,500 for their support of the Burley Tobacco Society and the American Society of Equity. Despite the violence of the early 20th century, burley tobacco continued to increase its hold on the state's agricultural production. In 1919 it represented 50 percent of Kentucky's total crop revenues, and by 1943 the figure had increased to 85 percent. Production peaked in the early 1980s.

Twentieth-century Northern Kentucky farmers experienced some of the most dramatic changes to occur in agriculture. In the 1880s, two-thirds of Kentucky's labor force worked on farms. By the beginning of the 21st century, less than 2 percent of Northern Kentuckians made their living working the land. Increasingly, farmers have employed migrant workers for labor-intensive work that many native Kentuckians hesitate to do. From 1870 to 1940, the total number of farms kept increasing as individual farms' acreage became smaller and smaller. Since **World War II**, the pattern has reversed: the overall number of farms has dropped continuously, while the size of the remaining ones has increased. Mechanization and the application of science have reshaped how work gets done on the farm. Consider Boone Co., where between 1940 and 1970, the number of tractors increased from 170 to 1,595 and the number of horses and mules declined from 3,770 to slightly more than 1,000. Livestock and crop patterns have seen fundamental shifts as the role of dairy cattle, hogs and sheep, and tobacco has declined and fruit and vegetable production, forage crops, horticulture, purebred cattle and horses, soybeans, and vineyards have become more important. Federal programs, regulation, and price supports have become intertwined with, and have reshaped, almost every facet of farming. In some instances, farmers have become dependent upon federal subsidy payments just to continue operation. In 2005 government payments totaled $828 million, or 40 percent of Kentucky's net farm income. Increasingly, Northern Kentucky farmers are producing for a highly competitive global market. The most dramatic and alarming trend has been the diminishing number of full-time farmers during the past few decades. In most Northern Kentucky counties, fewer than half of the principal operators farm on a full-time basis. The alarming decrease in the agricultural workforce—an ever-dwindling number of older farmers—when coupled with the rapid decline in the number of small, family farms, bodes ill for preserving Northern Kentucky's rural farming heritage. Perhaps the most important crop to be raised is a new generation of young Northern Kentuckians willing to experience the joys and frustrations of the farming life.

In the early 21st century, a statistical comparison of the region's farms to the rest of the state indicates that on average, Northern Kentucky farmers cultivate fewer acres for less profit (though, on the whole, the value of their land is considerable greater) than do farmers outside the bluegrass region. Eight percent, or 6,779 out of Kentucky's 86,541 farms, can be found in Northern Kentucky. While the average per acre value of the commonwealth's farmland stands at $1,824, farms in 7 of the region's 11 counties have a greater average value. In the case of Boone, Campbell, and Kenton counties, the value of good cropland is more than twice the average market value. Profitability remains a challenge for all Kentucky farmers, but more so for those in Northern Kentucky. In 2002 the typical net cash income from farm operation was approximately $9,800 for most of the commonwealth's farmers. Yet Northern Kentucky farmers earned on average only one-third to one-half of that figure. Producers in no single Northern Kentucky county reached the $9,800 figure, and farmers in four counties had a negative cash flow. Ranking Northern Kentucky farms by the value of sales shows that more than 70 percent of the region's farms realized less than $10,000 in total sales in 2002, compared to 67 percent for Kentucky as a whole. As farmers' profits dwindle, more and more of them are turning to part-time, nonfarm employment.

The picture that emerges is one of fewer and fewer full-time farmers cultivating larger and larger farms, while smaller production units consolidate. Small-farm owners, once buoyed by the stability and predictability of the federal tobacco program, are abandoning production of burley as the marketing and sale of tobacco come full circle. Tobacco farming has gone from the quota and price-support arrangement initiated during the **Great Depression** to a less predictable, free-market, contract system. In 1982, at its peak, more than 589 million pounds of tobacco were harvested from Kentucky fields; in comparison, only 143.5 million pounds were raised in 2005, the lowest production on record since 1927. In 2001 Northern Kentuckians grew 25.9 million pounds of leaf; by 2005 crop production had fallen to 17.2 million pounds, a 33 percent drop. Burley's demise has been so great that since 2004 (the end of the federal government's price support program) the U.S. Department of Agriculture no longer even tracks the number of acres raised. In Bracken Co. approximately half the burley growers ceased production by 2005. Those most likely to quit are the region's small-farm owners who raise 10 acres or less. Today as many as 60 percent of the Northern Kentuckians who continue working the land are scrambling to find options to replace tobacco, a crop that regularly generated as much as $4,000 to $5,000 per acre in revenue before expenses.

Many different strategies are being employed in the quest for profitable alternatives to burley tobacco. Farmers' markets, including large-scale regional ones, are being established throughout the district as Cincinnati-area residents and Northern Kentuckians seek out fresh, locally grown produce, organically raised foods, Kentucky-crafted items, and opportunities to socialize with neighbors in personal settings. In 2005 the Kentucky Agricultural Development Board granted $1.5 million to local and regional farmers' markets throughout the state to conduct feasibility studies. Out of 98 farmers' markets in Kentucky in 2005, 5 could be found in Northern Kentucky, with the Boone Co. Agricultural Extension's market on Ky. Rt. 18 having the highest gross sales of all markets in the state. During 2006, 107 farmers' markets had opened with a total of more than 1,800 vendors. Agricultural tourism, supported by area farmers in Bracken, Fleming, Lewis, Mason, and Robertson counties, has resulted in the River Valley Agritourism Alliance, an effort to promote collaborative marketing of area farms as tourist destinations. Other diverse approaches to replacing tobacco income include raising goats for an ever-increasing ethnic consumer market; growing and marketing increased amounts of alfalfa hay, grass, and vegetables, thereby strengthening and improving the quality of cattle herds; and returning to viniculture, a traditional strength of Northern Kentucky. In the mid-19th century, Kentucky ranked as the third-largest producer of wine in the nation. Some credit German immigrants in Northern Kentucky as establishing America's first commercial winery. Campbell and Bracken counties led in grape production during the era; in the 1950s and 1960s the Schwerin family's Campbell Vineyard and Orchards turned out 36 tons of grapes annually, with much of the fruit going to the Meier's Winery in Ohio. Currently, gross income from grapes can range from $6,000 to $11,000 per acre; increasing numbers of wineries and vineyards operate in the region.

The region's agricultural tradition, heritage, and identity stand at a crossroads. Only a conscious, deliberate alignment of business, farming, and governmental-sector resources and energy will prevent the scenario that has engulfed Boone Co. from spreading throughout all the counties of the region.

Bishop, Keenan. "Predicting Kentucky Agricultural Future Difficult," *Frankfort State Journal,* December 3, 2006, C4.

Clark, Thomas D. *Agrarian Kentucky.* Lexington: Univ. of Kentucky Press, 1977.

Eigelbach, Kevin. "It's Bye-bye Burley–As Profits Go Up in Smoke, More Farmers Are Not Planting Tobacco," *KP,* July 18, 2005, 2K.

Flynn, Terry. "At 93, Rooted in Land: Farmer Invented Vineyard Tool," *KE*, June 13, 1993, 3B.

Heithaus, Harriet Howard. "Grape Expectations: New Vineyards Test Kentucky Potential," *KP*, January 5, 2000, 8K.

Kleber, John E., ed. *The Kentucky Encyclopedia.* Lexington: Univ. Press of Kentucky, 1992.

Klotter, James C., and Lowell H. Harrison. *A New History of Kentucky.* Lexington: Univ. Press of Kentucky, 1997.

Kreimer, Peggy. "Tobacco Growers Consider Alternatives," *KP*, April 13, 2001, 1K.

Long, Paul A. "Farmers Go Part Time: 83 Percent Drop in 10 Years," *KP*, June 12, 2002, 1K.

Meiman, Karen. "Vanishing Farmland—As Suburbs Push Out More and More, Farms Are Giving Way to Development," *KP*, March 10, 2004, 10K.

Moores, Lew. "Healthy Growth . . . or Suburban Sprawl? Housing Spurt Creates Issues for NKY, Boone," *SC*, February 12, 2006, 1A.

Steitzer, Stephenie. "Boone County's Past Meets Its Present—Suburbs Pressing Closer and Closer to Fewer and Fewer Farms," *KP*, May 20, 2005, 1K.

U.S. Bureau of Economic Analysis. "Regional Accounts Data, Local Area Personal Income." www.bea.gov/bea/regional/reis/ (accessed November 30, 2006).

U.S. Census Bureau, Foreign Trade Division. "Total US Exports via Kentucky, Kentucky Exports—Top 25 Commodities, 2005." www.census.gov/foreign trade/statistics/state/data/ky.html (accessed November 30, 2006).

U.S. Department of Agriculture, National Agricultural Statistics Service. "2002 Census of Agriculture—County Data." www.nass.usda.gov/ky/ (accessed November 30, 2006).

James Wallace

AHLERING, GEORGE H. (b. August 1, 1845, Newport, Ky.; d. July 2, 1928, Newport, Ky.). Born in the same town that he would later run as mayor, George Hamilton Ahlering grew up to become a successful politician. He was the first of the nine children of Henry and Mary Ahlering, who had emigrated from Hanover, Germany, but met in Newport. Henry worked hard to become a successful contractor and even laid some of the earliest streets in Newport.

George attended Newport public schools for his primary education, and later the Commercial Business College in Cincinnati. During the **Civil War**, he was active with the Kentucky state troops, the Mississippi fleet, and the mounted volunteer infantry. After the war he moved to Cold Spring, Ky., where he started a grocery and later became postmaster. Ahlering met his first wife, Nannie Niles, in 1868; they had two children. In 1878 he began to study law in the offices of Judge James MacKibben in Newport. Only one year later, he opened a law office of his own in Newport, and because of his success, he was able to open another in Cincinnati. In 1883 Ahlering married again; his second wife was Mary Moore of Lexington. A Republican, Ahlering served as mayor of Newport from 1891 to 1893. During his term, the first brick paved streets were laid and the city's main sewer systems were installed. Two years after his term, he married his third wife, Minnie Perry. From 1895 to 1900, he worked in Kentucky state government under governors William O. Bradley and William S. Taylor. George Ahlering died July 2, 1928, at the age of 82.

"Ahlering Funeral," *KP*, July 3, 1928, 3.

Johnson, E. Polk. *History of Kentucky and Kentuckians.* Vol. 3. New York: Lewis, 1912.

Kentucky Death Certificate No. 16651, for the year 1928.

Jon Nicholas

AIRPORTS. The Northern Kentucky region is dominated by one major world-class airport, the **Cincinnati/Northern Kentucky International Airport** (CVG). Developed and owned by the Kenton Co. Airport Board, but located within Boone Co., CVG is ranked among the top 30 busiest U.S. airports in number of operations (one operation equals one takeoff or one landing). From its humble beginnings during the early 1940s as a practice field for military bombers, it has evolved to become the second-largest hub in the United States for Delta Airlines.

There are a few small, general aviation airports, landing strips, and heliports in the Northern Kentucky region (*general aviation* means not served by airlines). However, it is from CVG that Federal Aviation Administration air traffic controllers provide the radar separation for most of the Northern Kentucky region's airspace. Instrument flights taking off from any airport within the region talk to "Cincinnati, Ohio, radar" before being handed off to the Indianapolis center and being "established on course." The same goes for the converse, as radar in Cincinnati participates in vectoring (directing and separating aircrafts via radar vectors) the approach paths of airports within the region for landing.

On the east side of the region, Mason, Robertson, and Bracken counties, there is the Fleming-Mason Airport (with a 5,000-foot paved runway) in Mason Co. along the Fleming Co. line near Lewisburg. After **World War II**, when the Civil Aeronautics Board divided up landing rights to the commercial airlines, Piedmont Airlines (purchased by US Airways during the 1980s), based in Winston-Salem, N.C., was awarded the highly regulated flight franchise to Maysville. At that time there was no airport in or near Maysville that could handle Piedmont's DC3's, and as result Piedmont never served the Maysville area. Over the years, airline travelers from the Maysville area have had to drive to Cincinnati; Lexington; Ashland; Portsmouth, Ohio; or Huntington, W.Va., to catch a scheduled flight. Until the arrival of the Fleming-Mason Airport, the nearest general aviation field was at Aberdeen, Ohio—a grass strip (no longer existing) just across the **Simon Kenton Memorial Bridge** from Maysville. Other general aviation fields prior to Fleming-Mason's construction were at Flemingsburg in Fleming Co. (Cheap's Airport, owned by a local automobile dealer) and at Cynthiana in Harrison Co., both outside of the Northern Kentucky region but close to Maysville.

The airline-dominated CVG facility is near to the central part of the Northern Kentucky region (Campbell, Kenton, Pendleton, Grant, and Boone counties). Before 1947 Lunken Airport, on Cincinnati's east side, was home to the airlines. (It was known among pilots as "Sunken Lunken" because of the fog-prone Little Miami River Valley in which it sits.) These counties had access at Lunken and, to a smaller extent, at CVG (Boone Co. Aviation was the fixed-based operator at CVG for many years); in recent years the M. Gene Snyder Airport (with a 4,000-foot east-west runway), between Falmouth and Williamstown along Ky. Rt. 22W, has served the southern part of the region. The crosswinds around Snyder Field are tricky for pilots, as accident statistics reveal. Grant Co. has an airport two miles north of Williamstown, with a 2,200-foot north-south runway; and at Florence, Ky., in Boone Co., the Estes Airport surprisingly has a 1,500-foot north-south runway near the approaches to both Runway 36 Left and Runway 36 Right at CVG. Obviously, such short runway lengths suggest single-engine equipment operations. There have been proposals to build a general-aviation reliever airport in southern Campbell Co. near A. J. Jolly Park, but neighboring residents have successfully fought that suggestion. Similar proposals for a reliever field in Boone Co. east of Richwood have failed. Over time there have been several small airports in various local counties: Campbell Co.'s first airport was Boyer Field at Martz's Grove in Ross, where a twin-engine U.S. Army Air Force bomber made a successful emergency landing on April 30, 1946; Kenton Co. had an airport, the **Lionel Flying Field**, where President's Park is today in Edgewood. During the 1920s there was an airport at Crescent Springs, the Crescent Air Field, long closed and now a housing development. For Pendleton Co., during World War II there was a proposed military aircraft factory with a runway, to be situated on top of the hill south of Falmouth, along the east side of **U.S. 27**, but plans for both the factory and the runway were scrapped; and in the 1970s there was a small grass strip near Butler. Aircraft have landed along Taylor's Creek in Newport's **Taylor's Bottoms** and along Willow Run in Covington; both dirigibles and airplanes have set down at the original **Latonia Racecourse**.

The remainder of the Northern Kentucky region (Owen, Gallatin, and Carroll counties) has had occasional general-aviation airports over time. The **Perry Park** Resort in Owen Co. has a landing strip, the Glenwood Hall Airport. There is a 2,300-foot runway (northwest-southeast) at Owenton (the Owen Air Park), and Schroder Field has a 1,900-foot north-south runway four miles east of Owenton. In Gallatin Co. there was the Warsaw Airport, and in Carroll Co. there was a landing strip along U.S. 42 near Carrollton. Today the Craw Daddy Landing Airport, with its 2,400-foot north-south runway, is also near Carrollton. Residents of these three counties are required to drive some distance in Kentucky to CVG, Louisville (SDF), or Lexington (LEX) to catch airliners. During the 1960s for a few years, Owensboro-based Air Kentucky provided commuter airline service at the Frankfort Airport (FFT) in Frankfort, not very far from these counties. Recently there has been a proposal for an airport near where Carroll, Gallatin, and Owen counties meet, which would serve the new **Kentucky Speedway** at Sparta and the residents of those counties, while hopefully aiding the economic development of that part of the region.

For helicopters, there are heliports at most of the hospitals in the region for the sake of air ambulance flights (**St. Luke Hospital** East, **St. Elizabeth Medical Center**, and St Elizabeth Grant Co.). Otherwise, helicopters have been known to use the wide-open spaces of a park or a parking lot to set down, or even the grassy area between the lanes of an interstate to serve victims of an automobile accident. And on some occasions in the past, helicopters ferrying governors of Kentucky have been known to set down in the parking lot of the old Isle of Capri Restaurant in Southgate.

A few private businesses, for example Fidelity Investments in Covington and Midwest Communications in Highland Heights, have small heliports. There have been several places along the Ohio River where small seaplanes (float planes) have dipped their pontoons, and as long as there are farmers with an interest in aviation, there will be grass strips in places like Flagg Springs in Campbell Co. The number of farm strips is simply unknown, for they come and go quickly and are, more often than not, unannounced.

Perhaps because of the rolling terrain, or a population not interested in general aviation, or even a lack of population in the more rural parts of the area, the region has not seen the development of many airports.

Aircraft Charter World. "International Air Charters Worldwide." www. aircraft-charter-world.com.

Cincinnati/Northern Kentucky International Airport. cvgairport.com.

"Four Unhurt as Army Plane Crashes," *KTS*, May 1, 1946, 1.

Michael R. Sweeney

A. J. JOLLY ELEMENTARY AND HIGH SCHOOL. The A. J. Jolly Elementary and High School was just east of the community of California, in eastern Campbell Co., between the **Chesapeake and Ohio Railroad** tracks and Ky. Rt. 8 (the **Mary Ingles Highway**). Its origins are linked to two previous schools in the area, the private **Beech Grove Academy** on Smith Rd., a 12-year school, and the California Elementary School, a public school in the town of California.

Residents of Beech Grove and California wanted a newer, larger, more modern school building. They formed the California and Beech Grove Welfare Association, for the purpose of building a new school. In 1926 five acres were donated for the school building project, and a special tax was passed to fund it. The school was to be named for A. J. Jolly (1882–1925), a respected local educator and legislator. Architect E. C. Landberg of Newport designed the building, which consisted of a basement area containing a gym and two floors for classrooms. For some unknown reason, the new school was referred to as School District No. 17 in the Campbell Co. Board of Education minutes (see **Campbell Co. Public Schools**).

The school was dedicated on January 2, 1928, and its first principal was J. Lockhart. A large parade was held when the new school opened, and the old California Elementary School, having served as a combined school from 1925 to 1928, was closed and then sold in 1929. The area schools whose student bodies were redirected to the A. J. Jolly Elementary and High School were the Mentor, the Carthage, and the Flagg Springs schools.

During the **flood of 1937**, water rose to the ceilings of the first-floor rooms of the new school and damaged the building, but repairs were made quickly. Additions to the building were built during the 1950s, the 1960s, and the 1980s. The school's entrance was in the center at the front of the original building, but subsequent changes to the building moved it to the left side. The high school continued operating until 1946, when the state ruled that there were not enough students and that students of A. J. Jolly High School must attend the **Campbell Co. High School**. The last high school graduation at A. J. Jolly High School was held on May 22, 1946. Eventually, students in grades six through eight were transferred to new county middle schools: to the Cline Middle School in 1976 and to the South Middle School in 1979. A. J. Jolly Elementary remained a kindergarten-through-fifth-grade school until 2005, when a new consolidated elementary school, Campbell Ridge, was opened in Campbell Co. At that time both the A. J. Jolly Elementary and the Alexandria Elementary schools were shut down.

"Jolly Graduating Exercises Are Slated," *KP*, May 20, 1946, 1.

Reis, Jim. "State Legislator Jolly Honored after His Death," *KP*, August 26, 1986, 4K.

———. "20 Years of Education," *KP*, August 26, 1986, 4K.

Kenneth A. Reis

ALCOHOLICS ANONYMOUS. See **Substance Abuse Treatment**; **Transitions Inc.**

ALERDING, HERMAN J. (b. April 13, 1845, Ibbenbüren, Westfalen, Prussia; d. December 6, 1924, Fort Wayne, Ind.). The Right Reverend Herman Joseph Alerding, fourth Roman Catholic bishop of Fort Wayne, was born in the Diocese of Münster, the son of Bernard Herman Alerding and Maria Anna Theresia Schrameier. Maria Alerding died soon after her son's birth, and Bernard Alerding married his second wife, Anna Catharina Windoffer, on September 22, 1847. The family moved to the United States in 1850. In 1857 they resided at the southwest corner of Lowell and Walnut Sts. in Newport. Herman Alerding attended **Corpus Christi** School in Newport's **West End**. Recognizing the young Alerding's keen intelligence and early calling to the priesthood, the church's pastor, Rev. John Voll, instructed the boy in Latin. From 1858 to 1859, Alerding attended the Prepatory Seminary at Vincennes, Ind., and after his graduation was accepted as a seminary student of the Diocese of Vincennes. At the end of his first year, he returned to Kentucky for his second year of studies, which he completed at the St. Thomas Seminary near Bardstown. In fall 1860, at age 15, Alerding returned to Indiana to complete his education. He studied under the Benedictine fathers at St. Meinrad's College and Seminary in Spencer Co. and was ordained to the priesthood at St. Meinrad on September 22, 1868, by Bishop de St. Palais. On October 11 Alerding returned to his home parish of Corpus Christi in Newport to celebrate his first mass. From 1868 to 1900, Alerding served in the following positions: assistant to Rev. John Chasse at St. Joseph Parish in Terre Haute, Ind.; pastor of Cambridge City (formerly Pershing), Ind.; and pastor of St. Joseph Parish in Indianapolis and procurator of its short-lived seminary.

In 1883 Alerding, demonstrating his passion for history and scholarship, published *A History of the Catholic Church in the Diocese of Vincennes*. In 1886 the address he gave to St. Joseph's Young Men's Union on March 11 of the same year was published under the title *Plymouth Rock and Maryland*. In 1900 the death of Bishop Joseph Rademacher left the seat of Fort Wayne vacant. To Alerding's surprise, he was appointed as fourth bishop of Fort Wayne on August 30, 1900. The new prelate was consecrated three months later on the feast of St. Andrew, November 30, at the Cathedral of Fort Wayne by Archbishop Henry Elder of Cincinnati. In 1907, in celebration of the Diocese of Fort Wayne's Golden Jubilee, Bishop Alerding published a comprehensive history of the diocese, entitled *The Diocese of Fort Wayne*, covering the period from 1669 to 1907. Throughout his 24-year administration, Bishop Alerding's abiding faith, administrative competence, and steadfast dedication to parochial education were exemplified by his establishment of new churches, completion of improvements to both of the diocesan orphanages as well as to existing churches and parochial schools, and, in 1909, founding the Central Catholic High School for Boys in Fort Wayne, which remained in operation until June 1972. The bishop's prolific life came to an unexpected and tragic end on Thanksgiving Day 1924. The car in which the 79-year-old prelate was traveling was struck by a trolley car; severely injured, Bishop Alerding was transported to the hospital, where his condition worsened because of diabetic complications. He died the next month and was laid to rest in the crypt beneath the sanctuary at the Cathedral of the Immaculate Conception in Fort Wayne.

Alerding, Herman Joseph. *A History of the Catholic Church in the Diocese of Vincennes*. Indianapolis: Carlon and Hollenbeck, 1883.

Archives of the Archdiocese of Indianapolis, Indianapolis, Ind.

Archives of the Diocese of Fort Wayne–South Bend, Fort Wayne, Ind.

Corpus Christi Church. *The First Century of Corpus Christi Church, Respectfully Dedicated to Pastors and the People of the Parish*. Newport, Ky.: Vesper, 1944.

Ryan, Paul E. *History of the Diocese of Covington, Kentucky*. Covington, Ky.: Diocese of Covington, 1954.

Janice Mueller

ALEXANDER, SHAUN (b. August 30, 1977, Fort Thomas, Ky.). Shaun Alexander, who shattered athletic records at every stop in becoming one of the top running backs in football history, was born to Curtis and Carol A. Jackson Alexander. Because **Boone Co. High School** coach Owen Hauck had a policy of not playing freshmen on the varsity team, Alexander did not debut until his sophomore season with the Boone Co. High School Rebels, when he rushed for 1,099 yards and 13 touchdowns (TDs). Then he took off in performance, rushing for 2,401 yards and 42 TDs as a junior and 3,166 yards and 54 scores as a senior. In his final high school season, 1995, he led Boone Co. High School to Kentucky's Class AAAA championship game, he was named Gatorade Player of the Year in the state, and he earned *USA Today* and *Parade* All-American honors. When he finished his high school football career, he ranked fifth on the prep national career-record list, with 110 TDs, and ninth, with 6,657 yards (though his totals are no longer in the top 10 of either list).

After graduating from Boone Co. High School in 1996, Alexander went to the University of Alabama at Tuscaloosa, Ala., where he set 15 school records, including finishing as the Alabama Crimson Tide's all-time leading rusher (3,565 yards) and scorer (50 TDs). As a freshman he set the school's single-game rushing record with 291 yards against Louisiana State University. Although he earned all–Southeastern Conference honors in football, he was not named an All-American, and in the 2000 National Football League (NFL) draft, three other running backs were taken ahead of him before the Seattle Seahawks picked Alexander at number 19 in the first round. Alexander had spot duty as a rookie and then became a starter in 2001, his second professional season. At the beginning of the 2006 season, Alexander had amassed five consecutive 1,000-yard seasons and had become the first player in NFL history to score 15 TDs in five consecutive seasons. He already owns the Seattle Seahawk franchise record for career rushing yards (7,817 through 2005) and several other team marks. After his 1,696 yards in the 2004 season fell just 1 yard shy of the NFL rushing title, Alexander attained nearly every goal possible in 2005: he led the NFL in rushing (1,880 yards), set a league record for single-season TDs (28), and became the first Seattle Seahawk ever named the NFL's Most Valuable Player. Alexander concluded the season by leading his team to its first National Football Conference championship, but the Seattle Seahawks lost the Super Bowl XL to the Pittsburgh Steelers, 21-10. Alexander was released by Seattle in 2007; he played for the Washington Redskins in 2008.

Alexander published an autobiography, *Touchdown Alexander: My Story of Faith, Football, and Pursuing the Dream,* in August 2006. He has shown great compassion off the field, establishing the Shaun Alexander Foundation, which aims to empower fatherless young men. He married his wife, Valerie, in 2002; they live in Kirkland, Wash., with their daughters Heaven and Trinity.

Alexander, Shaun, with Cecil Murphey. *Touchdown Alexander: My Story of Faith, Football, and Pursuing the Dream.* Eugene, Ore.: Harvest House, 2006.

Demasio, Nunyo. "Must-See Seahawk," *Sports Illustrated,* December 19, 2005, 46–51.

O'Neil, Danny. "Alexander's Final Goal Has Ring to It," *Seattle Post-Intelligencer,* December 26, 2005, D1.

Schmidt, Neil. "Alexander Conquers Ego, Too," *CE,* November 24, 1994, C1.

Neil Schmidt

ALEXANDRIA. Alexandria in Campbell Co. is a city situated in the geographical center of the county, about 15 miles south of Newport. Settlers began arriving in the Alexandria area during the 1790s. The name Alexandria is said to have originated from Alexandria, Va., the former home of **Frank Spilman**, who is generally credited with laying out the town, around 1818, on 12 acres. Some other family names of people settling in the area at the time were Baker, Beal, Movin, Reiley, Shaw, Steven, Thatcher, and White. Alexandria, founded in 1819 and incorporated in 1834, is one of two county seats in Campbell Co., the other one being Newport, and each of the cities has a courthouse. People who live south of a line that passes through Cold Spring are supposed to do their courthouse business in Alexandria, and those who live north of the line are to go to the courthouse in Newport. Most of the county business ends up being transacted in Newport, however. The courthouse in Alexandria was built between 1840 and 1842 and was remodeled by the addition of a jail in the 1920s.

A road, not more than a trail, was built from Newport through Alexandria to Winchester in 1836; residents wanted something better, so they organized the Alexandria Turnpike Association in 1856, which established tollgates to pay for the road. The tollgates remained in use until 1922. Present-day Alexandria Pike (**U.S. 27**) bypassed the original town site.

The local 1883 Lake atlas shows Alexandria as having a Meister Brewery that was founded in 1860, a public school, various churches, a courthouse and a jail, tollgate houses, a sawmill-gristmill, and fairgrounds. The Alexandria Fairgrounds, dating to 1856, is operated by the Campbell Co. Agricultural Society (see **Alexandria Fair**). Campbell Co. Public Schools' first high school was constructed in Alexandria in 1909 on Washington St. Several of the early doctors in town, including Drs. Howe, Orr, Shaw, Todd, and Zinn, had offices located near the courthouse. Across the street from the courthouse were a bank, a hotel, a saloon, and the Hess and Racke Hardware Store. Six religious denominations, Assembly of God, Baptist, Catholic (see **St. Mary of the Assumption Catholic Church**), Church of Christ, United Church of Christ, and United Methodist, currently hold church services in town. At one time there was a Lutheran church in Alexandria as well. The **First Baptist Church** of Alexandria, one of the earliest churches in the county, dates back to 1820 and was built on land donated by Frank Spilman. There were several notable restaurants located in and around the town, for example Betsy Ann, Brass Key, Maple Lawn, and Palm Gardens. The Youtsey Brothers' General Store, later called Carmack's General Store, was also a well-known business in town.

At one time, the town had its own phone system and its own water reservoirs on Broadview Rd. In 1937 a town fire department was established, and the police department began in 1965. In 1970 a city building was completed on E. Main St. to consolidate city offices in one location; recently the city acquired the Main St. Baptist Church's complex and moved into those buildings in 2005. The main shopping area of the city is now located along U.S. 27, north of the original center of town. This is where the Village Green Shopping Center has sprouted up, along with restaurants and car dealerships. Alexandria seems poised to grow more than any other city in the county as the county's rapid business and population growth continues spreading southward. The population of Alexandria in the 2000 census was 8,286.

An Atlas of Boone, Kenton, and Campbell Counties, Kentucky. Philadelphia: D. J. Lake, 1883.

Campbell Co. Historical and Genealogical Society. *Images of America: Alexandria.* Charleston, S.C.: Arcadia, 2008.

Campbell Co. Historical Society. *Campbell County, Kentucky, 200 Years, 1794–1994.* Alexandria, Ky.: Campbell Co. Historical Society, 1994.

"Predict Record Attendance at Alexandria Fair," *KP,* August 30, 1978, 13K.

U.S. Census Bureau. "American Fact Finder. Data Set. Census 2000 Summary File 1 (SF1) 100-Percent Data. Custom Table." www.census.gov (accessed March 21, 2006).

Kenneth A. Reis

ALEXANDRIA FAIR. The Alexandria Fair of Alexandria, Ky., originated in 1856, when the Campbell Co. Agricultural Society, a corporation, was formed. Many men of distinction from the area volunteered to get the project under way, including **Thomas Laurens Jones**, later a state senator; **Frank Spilman**, the founder of Alexandria; Benjamin Beall, a landowner and surveyor; **James Taylor Jr.**, the founder of Newport; James Berry, the founder of Jamestown, Ky.; and H. K. Rachford, a distinguished Alexandria physician. The Campbell Co. Agricultural Society and the Alexandria Fair were established as separate nonprofit, all-volunteer private organizations. Unlike most other fairs, this one is not a governmental venture. To begin the project, 10 acres of land were purchased for $500 from John Stevens. Hemlock lumber was purchased (about 25,000 square feet), shipped up the Ohio River to Twelve Mile Creek, and hauled overland to the fairgrounds. Benjamin Smith, Joseph Shaw, and Frank Spilman built the arena at a cost of $1,000. A grandstand was then erected, along with exhibition barns having 75 stalls to house cattle, horses, and other animals. The first fair was held October 14–16, 1856. In 1868 an exhibition hall was added.

The fair was viewed as an opportunity for local farmers to display their crops, livestock, domestic talents, horses, and riding ability. Cash prizes and award ribbons were given to the winners in each category. The fair seemed to instill in all the participants a sense of pride that often translated into better farming practices. Some of the attractions that were early crowd favorites were the horse show, harness racing, music by local performers, and lively square dancing. A small herd of bison was brought in one year and caused quite a sensation. During the **Great Depression**, the fair remained popular and proved to be an inexpensive escape from life's problems. What contributed most to the fair's success seemed to be the festive community atmosphere that prevailed. The fair was so successful that it became an annual event, except that it was not held during the Civil War. In 1972 calamity struck when fire destroyed the grandstands, but larger and better facilities were built. Beginning in 1956 the fair extended its operation so that it ran from the Friday before Labor Day through Labor Day; today it runs from the Wednesday evening before Labor Day through Labor Day. The Alexandria Fair is one of the longest-running fairs within the state and is perhaps the best example of the important summer fairs occurring in most counties of the Northern Kentucky region.

Campbell Co. Historical Society. *Campbell County, Kentucky, 200 Years, 1794–1994*. Alexandria, Ky.: The Campbell Co. Historical Society, 1994.

ALLEN, ROBERT S., COLONEL (b. July 14, 1900, Latonia, Ky.; d. February 23, 1981, Washington, D.C.). Journalist and author Robert Sharon Allen was the son of Harry and Elizabeth Sharon Allen and a veteran of both world wars. He was nicknamed "Colonel" for his army rank as intelligence officer during World War II. Between the wars and before the days of Watergate, investigative journalists like Woodward & Bernstein and Allen and his journalist partner Drew Pearson reported what other newspapers rarely revealed about the Washington scene in their cofounded, highly controversial, popular New Deal–era column *Washington Merry-Go-Round* (1932–1941). The column was based on their best-selling books *Washington Merry-Go-Round* (1931) and *More Washington Merry-Go-Round* (1932), each of which sold nearly 200,000 copies.

Allen's family moved to Louisville during his early school years. At age 13, he was a copyboy at the Louisville *Courier-Journal*. Shortly thereafter, he began reporting local events in the newspaper. At age 16 he enrolled at the University of Kentucky at Lexington, but after one year he left to serve in the U.S. Army Cavalry during the Mexican border campaign, 1916–1917. He also served in France during **World War I**. Resuming his higher education at the University of Wisconsin at Madison, he earned a BA in the early 1920s. He was a reporter for the *Capital Times*, the *Wisconsin State Journal*, and the *Milwaukee Journal* during his Wisconsin years.

In 1923–1924, Allen studied at the University of Munich (Germany) on a fellowship award, while reporting as a European correspondent for the *Christian Science Monitor* and the United Press Association. During this period some claimed that he was the first American to attack Hitler and his Beer Hall Putsch, about which he reported for several American newspapers.

In 1925 Allen moved to Washington, D.C., to continue his career with the *Christian Science Monitor*. He was chief of its Washington bureau until 1931, when he first met journalist colleague Drew Pearson. During this time Allen began writing personality profiles of government figures for the *American Mercury* magazine. Allen and Pearson coauthored their two politically colorful books and then inaugurated their investigative journalistic column *Washington Merry-Go-Round*, based on them. While Drew Pearson's interview style was pleasant and yet to the point, Allen's approach was more emotional and offensive. His beat included congressmen and Supreme Court judges, whereas Pearson spoke with administration heads, diplomats, and military officials. By the late 1930s, their column was carried by more newspapers than any other syndicated political news columns. Allen and Pearson also coauthored *Nine Old Men* (1936) and *Nine Old Men at the Crossroads* (1937), exposing and demystifying the judges of the U.S. Supreme Court.

On December 7, 1941, at 6:30 p.m. EST, on the NBC Blue Radio Network, Pearson and Allen were among the first national reporters to discuss at length the Japanese attack on Pearl Harbor, which had occurred only hours earlier. For fifteen minutes they summarized the events and made predictions about the future. They were followed by Eleanor Roosevelt's regularly scheduled program at 6:45.

Allen reenlisted in the army near the start of **World War II** in 1942, leaving Pearson alone to handle the *Washington Merry-Go-Round* column. The renowned Jack Anderson later teamed with Pearson in reporting the "Merry-Go-Round" for many years to follow. Allen served in Gen. George Patton's intelligence unit on a reconnaissance mission during which Allen lost an arm; he received multiple military decorations. He later published *Lucky Forward: The History of Patton's Third U.S. Army* (1947), chronicling Patton's push into France and Germany.

After the war, in 1949, Allen began writing his own syndicated column, *Inside Washington*, which had a more nationalistic conservative view; it ran until 1980, shortly before his death. He also wrote several other governmental and political books during the postwar era, such as *Our Fair City* (1947), *Our Sovereign State* (1949), and *The Truman Merry-Go-Round* (1950).

Robert S. Allen.

Poor health beset him, and he committed suicide in 1981; he was buried at Arlington National Cemetery. His wife, Ruth Finney, whom he married on March 30, 1929, was a Scripps-Howard Washington newspaper correspondent and preceded him in death in 1979. Allen had no immediate survivors.

Block, Maxine, ed. *Current Biography: Who's News and Why, 1941*. New York: H. W. Wilson, 1941.

Contemporary Authors Online. Detroit: Gale Research, 2006. Reproduced in *Biography Resource Center* (Farmington Hills, Mich.: Thomson Gale. 2006). Available at http://galenet.galegroup.com/servlet/BioRC (accessed January 6, 2006).

Downs, Robert, and Jane Downs. *Journalists of the United States*. Jefferson, N.C.: McFarland, 1991.

Eisen, Jack. "Robert S. Allen, Colorful Newsman in Washington," *Washington Post*, February 25, 1981, C4.

Riley, Sam. *Biographical Dictionary of American Newspaper Columnists*. Westport, Conn.: Greenwood Press, 1995.

John Schlipp

ALLENDER HOMESTEAD. The Allender homestead had its beginning in 1811, when William and Elizabeth Ellis negotiated a trade of 80 acres in Fleming Co., plus 100 British pounds sterling, for 588 acres near Lenoxburg in northern Pendleton Co. The land had been owned by Samuel Christy. The Ellises never saw the land they purchased because William died in 1812. Some years later their grandson, James Allender, moved to the parcel that his grandparents had acquired, with his new wife, Mary Stout, of Rome, Ohio. He built a log home on Blair Fork Creek and later decided to build a larger log house on the ridge above the creek. It was a two-story log house of very fine workmanship, considering the tools of that era, and was completed in 1856. The house stands today; it has survived storms, tornadoes, and its use once as a barn. James Allender died of smallpox in 1866 at age 55, having lived in his new home only 10 years. It is reported that after his death his body was carried along Hickory Grove Rd. in a jolt wagon and buried in the first cemetery the funeral procession encountered, which was the Fisher Cemetery on Highway 10. When people saw the wagon coming with his body, they hid in fear of the dreaded disease.

The Allender land remained in the family from 1811 until 1941, when it was sold to the Miller family. Ronald and Billy Jo Woods returned the land to the Allender family in 1979. Ronald was raised by his grandmother, Mary Allender Carnes, granddaughter of James Allender. Mary was born in the log house, which the Woodses have restored. Because the restoration was carried out in memory of Mary, the structure is now known as the Mary Allender House. The Allender homestead was part of an original land grant of 4,400 acres, on the headwaters of the Licking River, to Reuben Taylor in 1788.

Falmouth Outlook, July 7, 1992, 5.

Mildred Belew

ALL SAINTS CATHOLIC CHURCH. Located in southeastern Boone Co. at Walton, the new All

Saints Catholic Church (formerly St. Patrick Church) stands above the Mary C. Grubbs Hwy., not far from the Walton-Verona exit off I-75.

As early as 1854, priests of the Diocese of Covington (see **Roman Catholics**) served the Verona area. In 1865 John Dempsey donated a lot for the St. Patrick Church. The Powers family donated land on Ky. Rt. 14 for the St. Patrick Cemetery. Among the names of persons buried at the St. Patrick Cemetery are Carr, Dempsey, Dwyer, Flynn, Madden, McCabe, Poole, Powers, and Ryan. Father Joseph Quinn became St. Patrick Church's first resident pastor in 1878. By 1886 the Verona church was offering Mass twice a month for more than 40 families. In 1891, indicating that 61 families were being served, Rev. Bernard J. Kolb sought to combine the parish with the one at Walton.

In 1927 the St Patrick Church acquired nine acres in Walton on Needmore St., and in the same year Pastor Oscar L. Poole erected a one-room frame building for summer religious and vocational training and offered the first mass on All Saints Day. In 1950 organizers held fundraisers; enlarged the little frame structure to serve as a church, a school, and a convent; and built a brick rectory. By November 1, 1950, the pastor of the St. Patrick Church, Father Henry A. Busemeyer, had moved to Walton. The new parish hosted its first mass on that day. On May 6, 1951, Bishop William T. Mulloy blessed the new building, administered Confirmation, and oversaw inaugural First Communion ceremonies. The church was now named All Saints Catholic Church. In 1951 the rectory at Verona was sold; masses were offered at the old St. Patrick's until 1964.

In 1950 Sisters Mary Adelgunda, Immaculata, and Paula, O.S.B. (**Sisters of St. Benedict**) opened All Saints Church's small school, thereby giving local Catholics the opportunity to provide their children with a parochial education. On May 16, 1966, Bishop Richard H. Ackerman dedicated a new brick elementary school building with four classrooms and a cafeteria. In 1970 the school's 52 students were taught by the Sisters of Charity of Nazareth and one lay teacher. The loss of the familiar Benedictine sisters at the end of 1968–1969 and the introduction of a post–Vatican II catechism had caused dissent, and enrollment dropped to 32 students. All Saints Catholic Church closed its elementary school after the 1971–1972 school year.

In 1976 the Sisters of St. Joseph, who had established a convent in Walton in 1974, leased the school building and re-opened the school as St. Joseph Academy, with about 45 students enrolled. During the 1980s, the parish enlarged the school by adding six more classrooms, a library, faculty space, and a parish hall. In 1987 St. Joseph Academy had 136 pupils in its eight elementary grades. In 2006, 201 students were enrolled in kindergarten through grade eight at the academy.

During the 1970s the All Saints parish undertook a major church renovation and rededication in order to accommodate its membership, which had grown to 74 families; by 1981 the parish had paid off the debt incurred from the renovations. When the Kentucky Department of Highways acquired more than four acres from the parish for the new Mary C. Grubbs highway, moneys from the sale helped fund the purchase of adjoining real estate. The parish continued to grow, reaching 280 households in 1985. In 1997, with 350 families on its rolls, the parish completed a feasibility study for a new church. Rob Zwick served as Building Committee chair. Architect Duncan Stroik, a professor of architecture at the University of Notre Dame at South Bend, Ind., designed the building, which was begun in 2001. Terry Frank, of the Cincinnati firm of Clarisey Frank, was the local architect. A local sculptor created four new decorative religious pieces out of limestone for the new church, including *All Saints in Heaven,* a re-creation of a 15th-century painting; it is mounted over the main entry. Under Pastor John Schulte, Father Heile's successor, the parish dedicated the new facility on May 31, 2003. The new church, with a capacity of approximately 600, is built along traditional lines and has a 102-foot-tall campanile (bell tower), a 60-foot-high nave, stained-glass windows, a 3,700-pound marble altar fashioned in Italy, and a 21-foot-high baldachin (canopy over the altar), as well as historic religious objects (statues, baptismal font, etc.) rescued from Catholic churches closed in the area. The edifice is described as old-world and the work of craftsmen. In 2003 the parish had 400 families as members.

All Saints Catholic Church: A House for the Lord. Walton, Ky.: All Saints, 2003.

Boone County Recorder, historical ed., September 4, 1930.

"The New School Building," *Messenger,* April 24, 1966, 5A.

John Boh

ALTAMONT SPRINGS HOTEL AND MINERAL BATHS. Samuel Bigstaff (1845–1912), who successfully developed subdivisions in northern Campbell Co. in the late 19th and early 20th centuries, had observed the popularity of the **Avenel Hotel** in the District of the Highlands (later Fort Thomas, Ky.) and concluded that the region could support a second resort hotel. Along with other investors, he bought property near Bivouac Pl. for the proposed hotel. On what is now Crown Point, Bigstaff built a 150-room resort hotel with grand verandas overlooking the Ohio River Valley and surrounding hills at a cost of $100,000. The Cincinnati architectural firm of **Samuel Hannaford** designed the buildings. Access from the streetcar line, just a few blocks away, made it a popular destination for guests living in the Greater Cincinnati area to come for days or weeks. It was most popular in the summer. A carriage road was constructed to lead down the back hillside to a stop on the **Chesapeake and Ohio Railroad** for guests coming by train. A grand opening of the Altamont Resort Hotel was held on August 1, 1905. A smaller hotel, the **Shelly Arms Hotel**, was opened in 1908, just southwest of the larger building.

Upon the death of Bigstaff in 1912, several of the investors sold their interests to a local group, headed by L. J. Crawford, a prominent attorney who had developed property around the nearby **Fort Thomas Military Reservation**. Soon afterward it was reported that mineral springs had been found near the Ohio River adjacent to the Altamont property. (Some scholars claim that this discovery had no foundation and was merely a clever marketing ploy; they believe that minerals were simply added to area spring water.) Thus, a public stock offering was made for the Altamont Springs Hotel Company Inc. A news item on June 24, 1916, described the two-story brick bottling plant and powerhouse costing $250,000, built near the railroad, and the new concrete road leading to it from the hotel. Advertisements appearing in the *Williams' City Directory for 1916* read: "The Altamont Springs Hotel and Mineral Baths, 150 rooms, mostly with private baths. Satisfactory cuisine, American Plan (includes 3 meals daily)." As World War I sent casualties back to the Fort Thomas Army Hospital, it became overloaded, and patients were cared for in the Altamont Hotel and the Shelly Arms Hotel, both of which became Medical Corps Convalescent Wards. Nurses

Altamont Springs Hotel.

were housed nearby in the Avenel Hotel. Both the resort hotel and the Altamont water ventures were sold at public auction in the spring of 1920. After the area was cleared, Crown Point, Crown Ave., and Altamont Ct. were developed. The remnants of the old roadway leading to the former bottling plant are faintly visible, and occasionally adventurers search for bottles near the site of the plant. The C&O Railroad station no longer stands.

Knapp, Paul T. *Fort Thomas, Kentucky: Its History, Its Heritage.* Fort Thomas, Ky.: Fort Thomas Centennial Committee, 1967.

Stegeman, A. Vinton. "The Legend of the Highlands' Mineral Springs," *Fort Thomas Living,* February 1987, 20–21.

Betty Maddox Daniels

AMERICA. The steamboat *America,* owned by the U.S. Mail Line, was built in 1867 by Morton and Startzman, Cincinnati. It was 302 feet long and had a 44-foot beam and a 7-foot-deep hold. The *America* was operated on the Ohio River between Louisville and Cincinnati, along with its sister boat, the ***United States,*** with which it collided in one of the most fiery steamboat disasters on record. The collision occurred shortly after 11:00 p.m., December 4, 1868, near Bryants Creek, at mile 527, between the communities of Florence, Ind., and Warsaw, Ky. Eyewitness accounts agree that the night was extremely dark with a strong upriver wind. Capt. **Richard M. Wade** of the *United States* attributed to those conditions watch pilot Jacob Remlein's failure to hear a whistle signal from the *America.* However, findings of the steamboat inspectors at Cincinnati placed the blame for the collision squarely on the *America's* pilot, Napoleon Jenkins, who was substituting for pilot Charles Dufour; Dufour had disembarked at Ghent, Ky., to visit family. In all fairness, Jenkins was unfamiliar with company practice when meeting the other boat: the up-bound vessel was supposed to cling to the Kentucky side of the river, allowing for a port-to-port pass. He may also have been unfamiliar with the relatively new rules of passage created by a treaty between Great Britain and France in 1863 and adopted by the United States in 1864. Ironically, those rules had been updated only two years before the accident, when regulations to prevent collisions were introduced. In violation of these rules, which state that the down-bound vessel shall dictate passing conditions, Jenkins, on the up-bound *America,* had signaled first with a two-whistle blast, indicating a starboard-to-starboard pass upon meeting. Remlein, aboard the *United States,* answered after hearing only one whistle from the *America,* his whistle thus overlapping the second blast from the latter vessel; the single whistle heard indicated a port-to-port pass, confirming company practice. Several contemporary accounts also state that visibility was hampered by a blind bend in the river; however, period charts show a straight reach of river where the two boats met. The *America* struck the *United States* on her port side abreast of the baggage room, sending the latter's deck cargo of several barrels of petroleum into its furnaces and immediately engulfing the vessel in flames. Many passengers aboard the *United States* jumped to safety aboard the *America.* The boats broke away from each other and headed toward the Indiana side, colliding for a second time when the current swept the *United States* against the *America* as they neared shore. Official loss of life stood at 70 on the *United States* (31 cabin and 5 deck passengers, plus 34 officers and crew) and 4 on the *America.* Both vessels burned to the waterline. It is often mentioned in connection with the collision that famous Norwegian violinist Ole Bull managed to save his violin. The *America's* timbers remained visible at low water for several decades. The hull of the *United States* was towed to Cincinnati and used in building a second vessel of the same name. Owen Co., Ky., native author **Alfred Cobb** was on board the *United States* that fateful night; he survived and wrote about it in his 1890 work *Liffy Leman or Thirty Years in the Wilderness.*

Certificate of Enrollment, Str. *America,* April 27, 1867, Life on the Ohio River History Museum, Vevay, Ind.

SIS Casualties, Inspection of Vessels, and Safety of Life at Sea: Index to Collisions, Wrecks, Fires, Founderings, and Explosions. SIS Annual Reports, 1852–1910, Record Group 41, Entry 7, National Archives and Records Administration, Washington, D.C.

"Steamboat Disaster on the Ohio River," *Harper's Weekly,* December 26, 1868, 1.

Tilford, Mark A., and William D. Kline. *Mariner's Guide to the Inland Rules.* Memphis, Tenn.: River School, 1998.

Barbara Huffman

AMERICAN INDIANS. American Indians arrived in the Northern Kentucky region as long as 12,000 years ago and remained until at least the 1500s. By the 18th century, they were using Northern Kentucky as a resource area rather than as a home. Hunting, salt-making, and trapping were important activities conducted in the area by regional tribes. The occupation of Northern Kentucky by American Indians during prehistory (before A.D. 1492) is divided into four major time periods: Paleo-Indian, Archaic, Woodland, and Late Prehistoric or Fort Ancient. These are arbitrary divisions but are based in general on changes in lifestyle, technology, and culture among the region's tribes.

The Paleo Period (before 8000 B.C.)

Paleo-Indian peoples entered the eastern United States after the Wisconsin glacial retreat, during a time of rapid shifting of the environment. Extensive climate change altered the Northern Kentucky environment as the glaciers retreated and the weather moderated. The first recognized Paleo-Indian tradition in this region is the Clovis period, characterized by projectile points and tools. Clovis points are long blades with a particular type of flute, or narrow channel flake, removed from the base. The Clovis tool kit includes a variety of utensils besides the points, such as scrapers and knives. Within 1,000 years, Clovis-point technology appeared across the continental United States. Whether the technology itself spread or the American Indians dispersed this quickly is still debated. Indians of the Paleo period hunted the last of the large Pleistocene mammals such as mammoth and mastodon, but evidence also exists that they had a varied diet based on both plants and animals.

Archaeology has identified both intensive and small isolated sites from the Paleo period throughout the United States, although no habitation sites have yet been documented in Northern Kentucky. The Paleo-Indian people moved around during the year. Some larger habitation sites in the central Ohio River Valley are known from stream valleys that indicate intensive occupations. Families may have lived at these sites off and on for years, returning to the same area periodically. Many of these are associated with chert quarries or game trails. Smaller camp or activity sites have also been found.

Locally, little is known about how the Paleo-Indians made use of the resources of Northern Kentucky. A few Clovis and late Paleo points have been collected, from the Big Bone Creek valley in Boone Co., for example. One site in Gallatin Co., located in an upland setting, may contain evidence of habitation, but no large, intensive sites are known yet. A review of the region's counties finds eight Paleo sites documented for Boone Co., two for Mason Co., and one each for Bracken, Gallatin, and Owen counties. No Paleo-period sites are documented for Campbell, Carroll, Grant, Kenton, Pendleton, or Robertson counties. The presence of the salt and mineral springs in Boone Co. on Big Bone Creek may account for the focus of Paleo-period sites in that county, although most of the eight Boone sites are based on the presence of Paleo points only. The lack of Paleo sites in Northern Kentucky in Carroll Co., where the Kentucky River enters the Ohio River, and the absence of documented sites in Northern Kentucky's Pendleton Co., which has the second-highest concentration of Early Archaic–period sites, are surprising.

After approximately 10,800–10,000 years ago, regional complexity increased, as documented through archaeological studies. Regionally specific projectile-point styles such as Quad, Dalton, and Hardaway-Dalton replaced the Clovis type. Most of these are long blades similar to the Clovis point but lack the distinctive flute at the base. What most archaeologists agree upon is that the late Paleo-Indian sites included evidence of a shift toward hunting smaller game with greater regional specialization of the stone tools used by these American Indians. The Archaic period, which followed, continued the shift in emphasis from larger game pursued in a migratory pattern to more locally available plant and animal resources.

The Archaic Period (ca. 8000–1500 B.C.)

The Archaic period continued the development of region-specific adaptations to local environments that had begun in the late Paleo period. The late Paleo people adapted to the changing climate and the greater variety of animals and plants, but essentially the same people remained. New groups may have moved into the area as populations increased, but for the most part, already-present groups of people began to settle into smaller territories.

Projectile-point types changed dramatically through the Early Archaic period. Kirk- and LeCroy-type projectile points are found over much of the eastern United States. They indicate continued exploitation of large territories by small hunting bands during the Early Archaic period but are very different from the preceding Paleo-period blades. Kirk points include a variety of side- and corner-notched types, while LeCroy and other similar points are generally small and have distinctive notches on the base (hafting area) of the point.

Site investigations indicate that American Indians living in this period had seasonal camps, often resorting to a base camp with outlying activity camps, and extractive sites such as chert quarries, periodically throughout the year. The addition of sandstone abraders and mortars to the Early Archaic period tool kit indicates that vegetable foods were becoming a substantial part of the Indians' diet. Throughout the Archaic period, the types and quantities of processing tools of all types increased in variety and form.

The Northern Kentucky counties have produced a range of Early Archaic–period sites, ranging from isolated projectile points found in fields to intensive sites located on river terraces. Boone Co. has at least 20 such sites. The presence of **Big Bone Lick** in the southern part of the county may account for the high number of Early Archaic–period sites: Boone Co. has more than twice as many sites of this period as the next county (Pendleton), which has 10 sites. Grant Co. has no documented Early Archaic–period sites, and Kenton Co. has only 1 with diagnostic artifacts from this period. The other Northern Kentucky counties have between 2 and 7 sites each, for a total of 59 sites, an increase over the number of Paleo-period sites.

A drier, possibly warmer climate known as the Hypothermal interval prevailed in the United States and reached its maximum impact around 4500 B.C. Culturally, this period is called the Middle Archaic, and it is generally given a date range of 6000–3000 B.C. Overall, the variety of plant and animal resources increased as the weather moderated and began to appear much as it did when Europeans began settling in Northern Kentucky during the late 18th century. The common occurrence of ground stone mortars, pestles, nutting stones, grooved axes, and celts at Middle Archaic–period sites suggests an increased involvement in plant foraging and woodworking by the region's tribes.

The quantity of sites with Middle Archaic–period projectile points in Northern Kentucky drops dramatically, from 59 Early Archaic sites to 23 Middle Archaic sites. None of the Middle Archaic–period sites have been excavated, so this dramatic difference is difficult to characterize. It may be that during the Middle Archaic period the inhabitants did not move around to different sites as much; because of the milder climate, they may have been able to stay in one place longer. Alternatively, some archaeologists believe that at least some of the Middle Archaic–period American Indians may have temporarily left the region.

The Late Archaic period was marked by increasing population, local complexity, and specialization among the various regional tribal groups. Evidence includes expanded trade networks, signs of status differentiation, and possible horticultural activities. Imported copper, marine shell, and mica demonstrate trade networks, and the presence of burial goods in some graves may indicate status differentiation. Plant-processing tools, including ground-stone items, increased again during the Late Archaic period. Evidence of domestication of plants such as gourds and sunflowers has been found on excavated sites in the central Ohio River Valley. Projectile-point types increase in quantity and stylistic variation, but there is a decrease in workmanship quality.

The earliest Late Archaic–period manifestations occur about 2600 B.C. in southwestern Ohio, and related diagnostic artifacts appear in Northern Kentucky during the same time. One regional manifestation is called the Central Ohio Valley Archaic (generally dated to 2750–1750 B.C.). Diagnostic artifacts include McWhinney points, atlatl or bell-pestle parts, hafted-end scrapers, and grooved axes. Projectile-point types associated with the overall Late Archaic period include a variety of point types: stemmed points such as the McWhinney Heavy Stemmed points, notched points such as Brewerton points, and very small points known as Merom or Trimble.

Excavations at the Glacken site, near Big Bone Lick, revealed a Late Archaic–period occupation by American Indians that included hearths and food-preparation features. Artifacts included Merom/Trimble points, and the site resembles those associated with the Maple Creek phase of the Late Archaic. Defined from sites in southwestern Ohio, artifacts diagnostic of this cultural expression have also been recovered from sites in several Northern Kentucky counties. Radiocarbon dating of the Glacken site reveals a date range of 2200–900 B.C., with a fall-winter occupation, based on analysis of faunal remains recovered from features at the site.

Late Archaic–period sites increase dramatically in the Northern Kentucky counties compared to the Middle Archaic period. At least 94 sites (versus 23 in the Middle Archaic period) in the 11-county region contain Late Archaic–period artifacts. This almost-fourfold increase remains unexplained due to lack of excavations in this area. Almost half (43) of these sites are documented in Boone Co., the most studied of the 11 counties, so some of the increase may be the result of survey intensity rather than site density. However, all the counties except Pendleton and Robertson see a dramatic upswing in site quantity during this period.

The transitional period between the Archaic period and the ensuing Woodland period ranges from before 1000 B.C. up to about 500 B.C., depending on location and settlement patterns. The shift becomes evident in Northern Kentucky during the 1000–500 B.C. range, when site quantity decreases again and pottery appears for the first time.

The Woodland Period (ca. 1000 B.C.–A.D. 1000)

The Woodland period was marked by significant shifts for regional tribes in subsistence strategy and changes in technology and settlement, although these did not appear instantly. The period is divided traditionally into the Early Woodland, Middle Woodland, and Late Woodland periods, and those time frames have been assigned varying date ranges. As for Kentucky, archaeologists generally designate the approximate date ranges of 1000–200 B.C., 200 B.C.–A.D. 500, and A.D. 500–1000, respectively, for the three periods; however, these date ranges are arbitrary. Cultures assigned to the Early Woodland period in Ohio (Adena, for example) span the Early Woodland–Middle Woodland periods in Kentucky. Adena is assigned a date range of 500 B.C.–A.D. 200 by many Kentucky archaeologists.

Three important differences in Northern Kentucky mark the separation of Late Archaic and Early Woodland periods. The first is the presence of pottery, which appears for the first time in this region by at least 700 B.C. Second, the quantity of sites again decreases across Northern Kentucky. Third, and a bit later in time, burial mounds begin to appear. In general, continuity from the Late Archaic into the Woodland period is seen for stone tools such as scrapers, knives, drills, nutting stones, and so forth. Bone tools also continue to be an important component of the American Indian tool kit. Technological changes are seen primarily in projectile-point form and in the introduction of pottery.

A total of 51 sites in the 11 counties in Northern Kentucky contain Early Woodland–period diagnostic artifacts. Some of them are open sites that have produced diagnostic projectile points and conical burial mounds (mostly in Boone Co.). No intensive village sites have been documented in any of the region's 11 counties. The open sites are primarily artifact concentrations that include at least one Adena-type point such as ovate stemmed, Robbins (square stemmed with a broad blade), or other similar point types.

Other sites have Early Woodland–period diagnostic artifacts that appear to predate the Adena phenomenon, including straight-contracting stemmed points such as Kramer. The West Runway site, located at the **Cincinnati/Northern Kentucky International Airport** in Boone Co., was excavated and provides information on pre-Adena, Early Woodland–period activities in the Northern Kentucky area. Radiocarbon dates that were taken for this site bracket the 770–450 B.C. range. The site produced Kramer points and Fayette Thick pottery together in shallow pit features, the first regional site with pottery of this type outside of a burial-mound context.

Numerous burial mounds and other earthworks have been documented at this site. The University of Kentucky at Lexington, in cooperation with the Works Progress Administration, excavated numerous mounds in Boone Co. from the 1930s until the early 1940s that date to the Adena period (500 B.C.–A.D. 200), among them the Robbins Mound, the Hartman Mound, and the Crigler Mounds. The Robbins Mound was a large burial mound containing projectile points that became a type point for the Adena period (Robbins points).

At least 40 mounds have been documented in Boone Co. that may date from this period. No fewer than 26 are known in Mason Co. Most of the other counties have only a few documented mounds that may be from the Early-to-Middle Woodland periods: 9 in Owen Co. and 2 each in Bracken, Campbell, Kenton, and Robinson counties. Gallatin and Pendleton counties each have only 1 earth mound that is likely to be from this period.

Researchers have found evidence of settlements by these American Indians, referred to as the Adena culture in the Ohio River Valley, on river and stream terraces, with possible winter upland resource extraction. The Adena tribal tradition is considered the most widely known Early Woodland–period culture in this region; yet it is poorly understood, partly because it is usually discussed only in terms of its elaborate burial ceremonialism. Some burial mounds provide significant evidence of social status differentiation. The presence of copper and shell ornaments in burial contexts is evidence of extensive trade networks among the eastern woodlands and the Southeast. The Adena sphere of influence was quite far-reaching. Encompassing not only Kentucky, its heartland, and surrounding states, it extended to some degree eastward through New England and the mid-Atlantic area and northward through the Upper Great Lakes.

Ceramics associated with the Adena include the following: Fayette thick (both plain and cordmarked), Adena plain, Montgomery incised, and Vinette I, each defined by differences in decoration and form. Finely made leaf-shaped blades and a variety of stemmed projectile points such as the Cresap, the Robbins, and the Adena types were manufactured. Copper was used to fashion ornaments such as beads, bracelets, rings, gorgets, and reels. Other typical artifacts include tubular pipes, quadraconcave gorgets, pendants of banded slate, fully grooved axes, hematite celts, and incised stone tablets. Adena may have been a cross-cultural tradition or a group of related tribes or cultures. However, the associated artifacts and the burial-mound tradition disappear from the archaeological record by early in this era, and certainly by about A.D 200.

During the Middle Woodland period, ca. 200 B.C–A.D. 500, trade networks in the Ohio River Valley produced complex sociocultural integration across regional boundaries. The Hopewell complex, centered near Chillicothe, Ohio, on the Scioto River, typically defines the Middle Woodland period. Another focus of development was in Illinois. Extensive Hopewell earthworks are known and exist in southwestern Ohio in Hamilton Co., for example. Elaborate geometric earthworks, enclosures, mounds that are often associated with multiple burials, and a wide array of exotic ceremonial goods characterize Hopewell culture. Ceremonially, the Hopewell culture appears to represent a continuation of Adena culture, but on an expanded and more elaborate scale. Hopewellian trade networks, for example, were more extensive.

Little evidence, however, has been found in Northern Kentucky that connects regional tribes intensively to the Hopewell complex. A few habitation sites, such as the Rogers Lower Village in Boone Co., have produced bladelets (long, narrow chert flakes) that are diagnostic of the Hopewell period. However, this site dates to the latter part of the date range (at least after A.D. 300–400). No Hopewell geometric earthworks or hilltop enclosures have been documented in Northern Kentucky. The Ohio River seems to have marked some type of cultural boundary, although Hopewell-associated sites have been documented farther south in Kentucky.

The Hopewell culture was the climax of the Middle Woodland period in the Ohio River Valley. It lasted only a few hundred years, and its influence waned after about A.D. 450. Ceremonial centers were abandoned, trade networks dissipated, and less emphasis was placed on burial ceremonialism. The ensuing period is called the Late Woodland period and lasted from approximately A.D. 500 to 1000, although some local cultures, such as the Newtown tradition, seem to have begun a bit earlier, perhaps as early as A.D. 300.

During the Late Woodland period, there was an increasing emphasis on domesticated plants, supplemented by hunting and intensive gathering. Regional variants of this pattern became focused within major drainages, where semipermanent horticultural villages were located on broad terraces. Additional fall and winter hunting stations also occur along smaller tributaries. Owen Co. has produced one rock shelter site that contains Late Woodland–period diagnostic artifacts. Other archaeological resources of the Late Woodland period are stone mounds and petroglyphs. Owen Co. and Carroll Co. each have one petroglyph site, although only the Owen Co. site has been assigned to the Woodland period.

Mound-building as a mortuary custom did continue during at least the early part of the Late Woodland period. Seasonal, and in some cases year-round, occupation of village sites located on terraces overlooking major stream valleys is seen in the Newtown phase. The Newtown phase was an early Late Woodland cultural period defined for southwestern Ohio and Northern Kentucky. Characteristic artifacts include distinctive pottery rims and pottery shoulder traits, Chesser or Lowe projectile points (corner-notched points), groundstone celts, and other unique tool types. The Rogers site, located along the Ohio River in Boone Co., is one Newtown-phase site in Northern Kentucky. The site included two villages and a mound situated close to each other. Many of the mounds associated with this period are covered, or layered, with limestone slabs. Owen Co. has eight sites that either have a stone mound or are village sites associated with low stone or earth mounds. Boone Co. has at least seven. Mason Co. has four sites, while the remaining counties have one or no mounds from this period.

In subsistence strategies an increasing reliance on domesticated plants is seen, including squash, seed plants, and maize agriculture, by the end of the Late Woodland period. Toward the end of the Late Woodland period, however, a decrease in plant diversity is found, as maize increased in importance. Technological changes were also introduced during this period. The Late Woodland people began to rely on agricultural crops instead of gathering nuts and wild plants. Archaeological sites contain many large storage pits dug deep into the ground for storage of plant harvests. Evidence is also found of houses built from wood framing with mud-and-stick (wattle-and-daub) walls.

The Late Prehistoric or Fort Ancient Period (A.D. 1000–beyond 1600)

By A.D. 800–900, the bow and arrow may have been introduced into the Ohio River Valley. Other changes in settlement and subsistence soon changed the character of the Late Woodland–period archaeological record. About 1000 the American Indian inhabitants of Northern Kentucky practiced maize agriculture, used the bow and arrow, and tempered their pottery with shell instead of grit or limestone. Social and political changes may have also accompanied these technological changes.

The Mississippian period, as seen in the Mississippi River Valley, included large town and mound complexes that influenced and controlled many of their neighbors. That influence reached the Ohio River Valley in terms of technological change as mentioned above, and perhaps social changes as well, although those are not as well documented.

In the central Ohio River Valley, including Northern Kentucky, this time frame is known as the Fort Ancient period. Permanently occupied villages have been documented as existing during the Fort Ancient period along most of the major streams and rivers in Northern Kentucky. Divided into at least three cultural time frames by many researchers, the Fort Ancient period saw changes in pottery styles and village layout through the more-than-600-year period. The Fort Ancient period reaches into the historic period, well into the 1600s.

Northern Kentucky has quite a few Fort Ancient–period villages, including documented sites in all 11 counties. The sites are concentrated along the Ohio River Valley and major streams. Generally they are village sites that include houses and, in some cases, stockade walls. The inhabitants usually built their houses in a circular pattern, with the doors facing in toward the center of the village. The center of the village was a plaza, or open-space area, used for ceremonies and other community activities.

The Northern Kentucky Fort Ancient peoples farmed corn, beans, and squash or pumpkins. They also hunted deer and many smaller mammals and birds and caught fish. Their farmlands were the fertile stream valleys that surrounded their village sites. They collected mussels from the local streams and rivers in large quantities. They ate the mussel animals and used the shells to temper their pottery and as hoes and other tools.

They buried their dead either in mounds located near their village or, later, in small cemeteries located within the village itself. Each village contained at least one community building or meeting place. Other buildings in the village included sweat lodges and houses. The Fort Ancient people usually had a surplus of food at the end of each growing season. They excavated very large storage pits, similar to small cellars, in which to store corn and other foods for the winter. The American Indians of the Fort Ancient period used a variety of tools and raw materials. Pottery vessels include shell-tempered pottery, bowls, shallow pans, larger storage vessels, and decorative containers. Triangular arrow points are characteristic of the Fort Ancient period. Stone tools include knives, drills, scrapers, and celts. The Indians manufactured hoes, fishhooks, and other implements from freshwater mussel shell or bone.

Some sites that date after the 16th century may also contain fragments of brass or copper trade items, glass beads, iron kettles, and axes. These artifacts, including some items found at Petersburg in Boone Co., indicate contact with European explorers. These may have been acquired through direct contact with French missionaries or trappers who had entered the region by the early 17th century. Local American Indian tribes may have received trade goods even earlier by trading with more coastal tribes, especially those in eastern Canada who had direct contact with French explorers and missionaries.

"Ancient Burial Site," *KE,* July 24, 2004, C3.
"Building on the Past," *SC,* August 1, 2004, 1.
Lewis, R. Barry. *Kentucky Archaeology.* Lexington: Univ. Press of Kentucky, 1996.
"Petersburg Dig Reveals Daily Life of Prehistoric People," *SC,* August 1, 2004, 3A.
"Petersburg's Treasury of History—Bone May Be Those of Ancient Indians," *KP,* July 20, 2004, 1K.
Pollack, David, ed. *The Archaeology of Kentucky: Past Accomplishments and Future Directions.* 2 vols. State Historic Preservation Comprehensive Plan Report, no. 1. Frankfort: Kentucky Heritage Council, 1990.
Rafferty, Janet Elizabeth. "The Development of the Ft. Ancient Tradition in Northern Kentucky," PhD diss., Univ. of Washington, 1974.

Jeannine Kreinbrink

AMERICAN LEGION. The American Legion, an organization of veterans from all the branches of the U.S. armed forces, is represented in Northern Kentucky by eight posts. Veterans returning from Europe after **World War I** established the organization in 1919. Today its nearly 3 million members include veterans from World War I and every U.S. conflict since.

During the **flood of 1937** in Campbell Co., the American Legion and the **Red Cross** were the major players in providing flood relief to the heavily flooded communities along the Ohio River. The Legion's volunteers were there to help in whatever way they could.

In addition to organizing commemorative events and volunteer activities, the American Legion is active in U.S. politics, especially with regard to issues such as veterans' pensions and medical care. Each state's American Legion organization sponsors an annual civic-training event for high school juniors called Boys State. Two members from each state's Boys State are selected for Boys Nation. The Boys State and Boys Nation programs were established in 1935 to counter the fascist-inspired Young Pioneer Camps. These programs teach youth about government and how it works, allowing participants to experience what it is like to hold various offices at the local, state, and national level. President William Jefferson Clinton (1993–2001) was a Boys State participant as a high school student.

All states have American Legion Ladies Auxiliary and Sons of the American Legion Squadrons, which support Legion activities and are connected to active legion posts. A Girls State and a Girls Nation program similar to the boys' programs function through the ladies auxiliary. Kentucky has always had an active American Legion program. The following Northern Kentucky counties have active American Legion squadrons:

Boone Co.: Post 4, Florence, and Post 277, Walton

Campbell Co.: Posts 11 and 327, Newport

Carroll Co.: Post 41, Carrollton

Grant Co.: Post 137, Williamstown

Kenton Co.: Post 203, Latonia, and Post 275, Independence.

American Legion. www.legion.org (accessed April 24, 2007).
American Legion Post Locator—Kentucky. http://members.tripod.com/~Post_119_Gulfport_MS/ky.html (accessed April 24, 2007).
Kreimer, Peggy. "The 1937 Flood Our Katrina," *KP,* January 13, 2007, A1.

Robert B. Snow

AMERICAN RED CROSS. The first Red Cross chapters in Northern Kentucky were organized in response to **World War I**, but the organization had a presence in the region much earlier.

The American Red Cross movement goes back to the battlefields of the **Civil War**, where Clara H. Barton (1821–1912), a Massachusetts-born schoolteacher, tended to the needs of the injured. After the war she went to Switzerland and in 1879 became familiar with the work of Henry Dunant and his International Red Cross and the Red Crescent Movement. When she returned to the United States, she established the American Red Cross in 1881. During the **flood of 1884**, Barton herself dispensed relief supplies from the steamboat *Josh V. Throop,* which was tied up at the Cincinnati Public Landing. The Red Cross considers this action its entry into disaster relief.

In 1905, with the encouragement of William Howard Taft, a Red Cross chapter was begun in Cincinnati; it was followed by Kentucky branches in Campbell Co. April 20, 1917; in Kenton Co. May 30, 1917; and in Boone Co. June 28, 1917. Each was the result of the U.S. entry into World War I. A war fund campaign was launched to raise money so that Red Cross personnel and supplies could be sent to Europe to care for U.S. soldiers. Several prominent Northern Kentuckians were involved in fundraising that took place during June 1917: A. Clifford Shinkle, a member of the influential Covington Shinkle family, was the treasurer for the fundraising effort; **Polk Laffoon Jr.**, a Covington utility official, was the Kenton Co. committee chairman; and A. M. Larkin, a Newport banker, was committee chairman in Campbell Co. He was assisted by Mrs. Albert H. Morrill, wife of a future **Kroger** Company president. Covington lawyer-banker **Richard P. Ernst** was a member of the overall executive committee for the successful drive. Bandages and surgical wraps made by volunteers at places such as St. Elizabeth Hospital (see **St. Elizabeth Medical Center**) were readied and sent to field hospitals in Europe. During **World War II**, the Kentucky counties ran their own separate but similar fundraising campaigns; in Campbell Co., Roger Littleford headed up the drive.

The Red Cross has done more than to help U.S. military personnel and families overseas and at home. In Northern Kentucky the Red Cross has provided swimming lessons, first aid training, and lifesaving classes; flood relief was given during the **floods of 1913**, 1937, 1948, 1964, and 1997; in 1944 the Red Cross Gray Lady Corps, a special unit of older female volunteers, was established in Fort Thomas; Red Cross workers assisted the victims of the April 1974 tornado; in 1977 the Red Cross in Southgate was at the site of the **Beverly Hills Supper Club** fire; the organization supported people affected by the **blizzard** of 1978; in 1986 Red Cross volunteers helped families who sustained storm damage in Boone Co.; and in 1993 the Red Cross helped Evangelos Kontos of Covington and his son become reunited after 45 years of separation. The Red Cross was also on-site for the three major airline crashes that have taken place at the **Cincinnati/Northern Kentucky International Airport**. The largest disaster in the region for the Red Cross clearly was the flood of 1937. The organization set up its flood headquarters within the Union Central Life Insurance Building in downtown Cincinnati, directing relief efforts from Pittsburgh, Pa., to Cairo, Ill.

In 1980, when an earthquake occurred near Maysville, the Mason Co. Red Cross chapter responded to the 200-plus affected families in the county; in the mid-1990s, Maysville area volunteers sheltered and fed 272 individuals who were evacuated from their homes as a result of the Cargill Fertilizer Plant's chemical discharge. In 2005 191 volunteers helped the Mason Co. chapter to carry out its activities.

In 1956 the Boone, Campbell, and Kenton Co. chapters of the Red Cross merged with the Hamilton Co., Ohio, chapter to create the Cincinnati Area Chapter, with headquarters in downtown Cincinnati at Seventh and Sycamore Sts. That chapter today maintains an office in Florence, Ky. It is also responsible for the administration of Red Cross activities in the following Northern Kentucky counties: Bracken, Gallatin, Grant, Mason, Owen, and Pendleton. Of those, both Bracken and Mason have Red Cross chapters of their own. Carroll Co., Ky., is under the auspices of the Oldham Co., Ky., office. In 2005 the American Red Cross celebrated a century of services in this region.

American Red Cross. *The Cincinnati Area Chapter Red Cross.* Cincinnati: Red Cross, 1989.
——. *A History of the Red Cross War Fund Campaign in Metropolitan Cincinnati.* Cincinnati: Red Cross, 1917.
——. *The Ohio–Mississippi Valley Flood Disaster of 1937.* Washington, D.C.: American Red Cross, 1937.
——. www.redcross.org (accessed January 21, 2007).
Reis, Jim. "Winning the War in 1943 Part Glamour, Part Grease," *KP,* October 5, 1998, 4K.
Union Central Life Insurance Company. *The Union Central and the 1937 Flood.* Cincinnati: Union Central Life Insurance Company, 1937.

AMERICAN REVOLUTION. See **Revolutionary War**.

AMTRAK. Amtrak, which has provided passenger train service to Northern Kentucky for nearly 40 years, was born on October 30, 1970, when President Richard Nixon (1969–1974) signed into law the Rail Passenger Service Act, transferring rail passenger service from the operating railroads to the U.S. National Railroad Corporation. The corporation name was soon changed to Amtrak for promotional purposes. Amtrak began its rail passenger service on May 1, 1971. The only rail route it maintained through Northern Kentucky was a Chicago-Cincinnati-Washington-Boston run that utilized the **Chesapeake and Ohio Railroad** from Covington to Ashland, Ky. The train was named the James Whitcomb Riley running east and the George Washington running west, but because of bad track conditions in Indiana and to the northwest, neither train could maintain its schedule. The train was cut back in 1972 to a Chicago–New York City trip and in 1973 modified to a Chicago–Washington, D.C., route. On May 19, 1974, Amtrak dropped the train name the George Washington; in a new marketing ploy, it called the train the Riley/Mountaineer. The Riley/Mountaineer was split into two sections at Ashland: the Riley continued to run to Washington and back, but the Mountaineer ran to Norfolk, Va., via Norfolk and Western Railroad track and then returned to Ashland to connect to the Riley. This short-lived experiment ended on October 30, 1977, when the Mountaineer was discontinued and the Riley was renamed the Cardinal. The Cardinal today links Chicago to Washington via Cincinnati, making three trips east from Chicago and three trips west from Washington each week. The only Amtrak stop for the Cardinal in Northern Kentucky is at the former C&O Depot in Maysville. The unique sound of the 6,000-horsepower, modern General Electric Genesis engines can be heard by attentive listeners as Amtrak passes through Newport and Covington early in the morning.

Bradley, Rodger P. *Amtrak: The US National Railroad Passenger Corporation.* New York: Blandford Press, 1985.
Sanders, Craig. *Amtrak in the Heartland.* Bloomington: Indiana Univ. Press, 2006.

Charles H. Bogart

AMUSEMENT PARKS. See **Lagoon Amusement Park**; **Tacoma Park**.

ANDERSON, ELIJAH (b. ca. 1808, Fluvanna Co., Va.; d. March 4, 1861, Frankfort, Ky.). Dubbed the "General Superintendent" of the Underground Railroad (UGRR) by Rush R. Sloane, an abolitionist in northwestern Ohio, Elijah Anderson became a major conductor, bringing hundreds of runaway slaves to freedom from Northern Kentucky counties.

Born a free person of color in Virginia, Anderson was forced from his native state by restrictive black laws passed after the 1831 Nat Turner Rebellion. Sometime before 1835, he relocated to Cincinnati. Because he was trained as a blacksmith and skilled in making wrought iron undercarriages and decorative fences, he found ready employment as a laborer fixing metal and steam fittings on Ohio River steamboats. He developed strong friendships with other free blacks: George De Baptiste, Chapman Harris, John Lott, and John Carter, a Lexington native who had settled in Cincinnati among the large free black community. Carter fled to Canada during the 1830 riots and then returned when things calmed down.

Both De Baptiste, a barber, and Carter, a grocer, worked as stewards; the position of steward was a high-ranking one for free blacks. According to Lott, these men were introduced to Ohio Underground Railroad leaders through Rev. Henry Ward Beecher, who, during the 1830s, was at Cincinnati's Lane Seminary and also was serving his first pastorate, the Lawrenceburg (Ind.) Presbyterian Church. Between December 1837 and early 1840, all five of these free blacks relocated to Madison, Ind., and soon provided energy and impetus to the UGRR's operations there. Anderson met and married Mary J., a native of Ohio 10 years his junior. Their only child, Martha, was born in 1840 at Madison. Elijah Anderson established his blacksmith shop on the southeast corner of Third and Walnut Sts. He prospered and, before early 1842, had purchased a brick town home valued at $800 and taxed at $3.00. It was in the Georgetown section of Madison on Walnut St. near Fifth St. He was listed as the owner and taxpayer on that property through 1847.

Soon Anderson attained leadership in the Madison UGRR. He excelled at opening and developing secure routes. Often he went over into Kentucky, particularly along the Kentucky River artery, contacting free blacks and slaves on plantations. He developed a solid relationship with free blacks at Carrollton and Frankfort, Ky., and Lawrenceburg, Ind., and also worked well with white abolitionists. By 1845 the black conductors at Madison managed most of the Ohio River crossing points. These free blacks shifted Madison's UGRR operations from a passive to an active state. De Baptiste claimed to have aided 108 runaways before 1846; Anderson said that he brought 200 through before 1850.

In 1845 two top agents of the American Anti-Slavery League, William Phelps and George Whitefield, who were originally from Wheeling, Va. (W. Va. today), but had most recently worked out of Cincinnati, came to Madison and over the next three years developed routes on Kentucky soil, giving recruited plantation slaves information on safe routes and pick-up times and places. Later that year a wealthy black abolitionist, John Simmons, was welcomed to Madison. Shortly thereafter, major routes were compromised and near captures occurred. Anderson, Harris, Lott, and a number of other activists believed that Simmons had betrayed their cause for monetary reward; they beat Simmons severely and threatened him with death. Simmons sued in Indiana's Jefferson Co. court, and the legal fees over six years caused Anderson to lose his property at Madison.

A 100-man posse of Kentuckians and local sympathizers marauded through Madison targeting the UGRR leadership. Free black activists, charged with inciting a riot, were fined sums of $50 and $25. De Baptiste fled to Detroit, Mich., and became active there. Lott headed for Canada. Harris hunkered down in Eagle Hollow, Ind., three miles east of Madison, and became a major leader during the 1850s. Griffin Booth was nearly drowned in the Ohio River by a mob. Amos Phillips was shot several times; he recuperated at Lancaster, Ind., and then moved to the Little Africa settlement south of Vernon, Ind. It took Harris and Carter three to five years to rebuild the UGRR base back to its original capabilities.

As a result of increased danger, the fines levied against him, and the Madison riots, Anderson moved his operations base to Lawrenceburg, Ind. Both Elijah and his wife were fair-skinned, and in the 1850 Dearborn Co., Ind., census, they both apparently passed as white. Since he spent months on the road away from his blacksmith business, it seems quite likely that at this time Anderson became an agent of the American Anti-Slavery League or was funded in part from Detroit's African American leadership. His Madison experience was helpful because Lawrenceburg, Ind., was hostile to free blacks and, by 1861, was trying to evict them from the city. During the early 1850s, Anderson was frequently linked to Cincinnati and to routes to Cleveland and Sandusky, Ohio.

As an experienced conductor, Anderson realized that bringing fugitives across by ones and twos was inefficient and likely to run afoul of the runaway-slave patrollers. Working with William Wyman, station master at Aurora, Ind.; with American Anti-Slavery League peddlers and ferrymen agents; and with his own local free black recruits, Anderson soon was able to bring large groups of fugitives out through Boone Co., Ky. Results showed almost immediately. In 1847 the David Powell family of six vanished from the John Norris plantation between the Lawrenceburg and Aurora, Ind., ferry landings. In May 1848 eight slaves owned by Benjamin Stevens opposite Rising Sun, Ind., made their escape. Gabriel Smith, an aged free black from Brookville, Ind., participated in helping Anderson bring 50 slaves north to Sandusky, Ohio. Boone Co. slave owners reported that 29 slaves had escaped between September 1 and November 17, 1852; in April 1853, they lost another 40 slaves.

During summer 1856, after Elijah took a group of fugitives to Cleveland via the railroad's network, he sought work to earn money before returning to Lawrenceburg. An abolitionist gave him the name of a person in Detroit, and Elijah worked in Detroit through fall 1856, then returned through Cincinnati and boarded a steamboat there. In a case of mistaken identity, a Madison UGRR activist, William J. Anderson, was arrested at Carrollton, Ky., and accused of pirating hundreds of runaway slaves and carrying incendiary abolitionist materials into Kentucky. William J. Anderson, who claimed in his defensive autobiography that he had never worked south of the Ohio River and only had loaned his carriage to the UGRR, was defended by antislavery lawyers from Madison and released. Within a day or so, Elijah Anderson was recognized at Cincinnati or turned in, and Delos Blythe of the Alan Pinkerton Detective Agency at Louisville came up to arrest him once the steamboat that he was on had set off. The free black community at Madison was certain that William J. Anderson had bought his way out of jail by turning in Elijah Anderson, and Elijah was forced to flee to safer ground at Indianapolis, Ind.

At Carrollton, Ky., Elijah Anderson was accused of enticing a slave owned by Gen. **William O. Butler**. It was a peculiar charge since Butler had emancipated some of his slaves when he returned from the **Mexican War** in the late 1840s. It was among Butler's freed slaves living near the mouth of the Kentucky River that Elijah Anderson likely had established a solid base for UGRR routes from the Bluegrass State. One of those freed slaves, Sandy Duncan, moved to Madison. James T. Allison, an antislavery attorney from Madison, represented Elijah at Carrollton and won acquittal. But on the steps of the courthouse at Bedford, Ky., the Trimble Co. sheriff arrested Elijah and incarcerated him. At Bedford, Elijah was accused of assisting and abetting a Negro boy named George to run away from his master, who lived in Henry Co., Ky. Elijah claimed to have gone north for work. Found upon his person was a chatty letter he had written but not mailed to his wife, Mary J., that gave the names of several abolitionist friends in Cleveland and Detroit. Sensationalist newspaper accounts in Louisville claimed that finding the letter broke the back of a ring of abolitionists that had been stealing slaves in Kentucky. Depositions from G. W. Burrows of Cleveland stated that Elijah Anderson was in Cleveland on September 1, 1856, and had sought employment from him, and that he had referred Elijah to a friend in Watertown, Wis. A second deposition from John P. Clark stated that he had hired Elijah from November 1 to December 13, 1856, at his blacksmith shop at a Springwell, Mich., dry dock.

But it was the eyewitness testimony of Right Ray, who headed a ring of slave-catchers operating in southeastern Indiana, that led to Elijah Anderson's 10-year sentence at the Kentucky State Penitentiary in Frankfort. Ray testified that he had seen Anderson in Madison on May 11, 1856, ascending the Texas deck of a mail boat headed to Cincinnati. Anderson had a carpetbag and was in company of a boy answering the description of George, a runaway slave owned by John Scott of Henry Co. The boy had escaped on May 8, and Scott had come to seek the services of Ray at Madison on May 12, 1856.

During the next few months, Chapman Harris, then a leader of the free blacks and slaves active in the Madison UGRR, attempted twice to mount a posse to free Anderson from the penitentiary. Meanwhile the antislavery attorneys at Madison tried to negotiate an interstate gubernatorial pardon. When Anderson's daughter, Martha, came to Frankfort to pick him up in April 1861, he was found dead in his cell of unexplained causes. The body was released to his family for burial. According to Wilbur Siebert and the *Firelands Pioneer*, Elijah Anderson claimed in 1855 to have brought out more than 1,000 runaway slaves, 800 of them after passage of the 1850 Fugitive Slave Act.

Annotated plat C., 1848–1850, Madison, Ind.
Bordewich, Fergus M. *Bound for Canaan: The Underground Railroad and the War for the Soul of America.* New York: Amistad, 2005.
Commonwealth of Kentucky vs. Elijah Anderson. Trimble Co. Circuit Court, Governors Papers, Kentucky Libraries and Archives, Frankfort, Ky.
Deed Book 6: 320, Jefferson Co., Madison, Ind.
Griffler, Keith P. *Front Line of Freedom: African Americans and the Forging of the Underground Railroad in the Ohio Valley.* Lexington: Univ. Press of Kentucky, 2004.
Hudson, J. Blaine. *Fugitive Slaves and the Underground Railroad in the Kentucky Borderland.* Jefferson, N.C.: McFarland, 2002.
Israel Moody vs. The Trustees of the African Methodist Episcopal Church. January 1, 1853, Dearborn Co. Civil Cases, Lawrenceburg, Ind.
Lawrenceburg Register, May 11, 1848; November 17, 1852; November 14, 1853.
Siebert, Wilbur H. *The Underground Railroad from Slavery to Freedom.* New York: Macmillan, 1898.
Tax Assessment Book 2: 1838–1847, Madison, Ind.

Diane Perrine Coon

ANDERSON, JOE E. (b. October 18, 1905, Banklick Station, Kenton Co., Ky.; d. May 8, 1975, Covington, Ky.). Kentucky Joe Anderson, as he was billed in the **boxing** world, attended Covington's **Holmes High School**. As a senior, the five-foot-nine athlete defeated world light-middleweight boxing champion Pinky Mitchell. Anderson then quit high school and fought professionally at **Tacoma Park**, the **Fort Thomas Military Reservation**, and the Covington Arena. Expanding to the national sphere, he boxed in California and Chicago and at New York City's Madison Square Gardens, appearing on fight cards together with other pugilists from the Cincinnati–Northern Kentucky area such as Tony LaRosa and Joe Sweeney. On October 10, 1927, Anderson was stabbed just below the heart while trying to detain a motorist who had collided with a fire truck in Covington. Anderson recovered and continued to fight. In 1928 and 1929, he was the number one light-middle-weight boxer in the world; he defeated three world champions during his career. His last fight was on September 22, 1931, against Dandy Harry Smith, where Anderson broke his arm in the second round but continued boxing into the fifth round. In his 10-year career, with a total of 98 professional fights, Anderson won 56 fights, tied 22, and lost 20; he had earnings totaling a half million dollars. Regarded as a speedy boxer, Anderson was trained by Elmer Cavanaugh and managed by Jim Dougherty.

During the early 1930s, Anderson and his wife, the former Cleora E. Sheriff, operated the Bluegrass Gym at Fifth St. and Madison Ave. in Covington. In 1935 the couple opened the Joe Anderson Café in Erlanger, a site long remembered for its big neon sign that featured a boxer moving his arms. In 1947 the restaurant was sold and the Andersons bought a Wiedemann Beer distributorship (see **Wiedemann Brewing Company**), which they operated for some 25 years. Cleora Anderson died in 1972, and Joe died in 1975, of a cerebral hemorrhage, a common cause of death for boxers, as a result of the pounding their heads sustain. Anderson was buried at Forest Lawn Cemetery in Erlanger and was survived by four grandchildren. During the 1920s, boxing was a popular sport and a means of both financial support and social mobility, and Joe E. Anderson used it wisely; he was the premier boxer ever to have come out of the Northern Kentucky region.

BoxRec. "Joe Anderson." http://boxrec.com (accessed March 5, 2006).
Kreimer, Peggy. "Joe E. Anderson . . . Boxer, Defeated Three World Champs," *KP,* May 9, 1975, 10.
Stein, Tim. "Joe Fought the Best," *KP,* March 31, 1973, 12K.

Michael R. Sweeney

ANDERSON, KEN (b. February 15, 1949, Batavia, Ill.). Football player Kenneth Allan Anderson, born in a western suburb of Chicago, attended high school in Batavia and then Augustana College, a Lutheran liberal arts school in Rock Island, Ill., where he had a half scholarship and worked summer jobs. He majored in mathematics, accumulating a 3.7 grade point average while also playing basketball and football, the latter as a safety and, most importantly, as a quarterback. In July 1981 he obtained a law degree from **Chase College of Law** of **Northern Kentucky University**.

Anderson was the third-round choice of the Cincinnati Bengals in the 1971 National Football League (NFL) players draft. He played as a quarterback for the Bengals from 1971 until 1986 and was an assistant coach (quarterbacks coach) for the Bengals from 1993 until 1996. His assistant-coach status was upgraded when he was named the offensive coordinator for the Bengals on October 21, 1996.

Anderson beat Virgil Carter out of a starting job in his second season with the Bengals and guided the Bengals to a division title in 1973. In 1974 and 1975 he led the NFL in passing, and he played in the Pro Bowl at the end of the 1975 and 1976 seasons.

On the night of August 26, 1978, the Bengals were playing a preseason game with the Green Bay Packers. During the game, Anderson broke his right hand on one of the Packers pass rushers as he released the ball. In surgery by Dr. Herbert Kleinert, a Louisville surgeon who specializes in such procedures, a pin was inserted into the hand, and it was announced that Anderson would be sidelined for six to eight weeks.

In 1981 Anderson led the Bengals to the Super Bowl. During the season, he once again led the NFL in passing and was also named the league's most valuable player. For that season, he threw for 3,754 yards and 29 touchdowns in winning the NFL passing title.

Anderson is the career leader for the Bengals in pass completions (2,654), passing yards (32,838), and touchdown passes (197). He owns the NFL record for the highest completion percentage among quarterbacks in a season, with 70.55 in 1982. He holds four NFL passing titles, was named to four Pro Bowls, led the league three times in lowest interception percentage, and twice has been among 15 finalists for election to the Pro Football Hall of Fame. His most memorable game was the AFC (American Football Conference) Championship game (the Freezer Bowl) played at the old Riverfront Stadium in Cincinnati on January 10, 1982. The outside temperature was −9 degrees Fahrenheit, with a wind chill of −59 degrees. The Bengals beat the San Diego Chargers that day 27-7 and advanced to the Super Bowl.

In December 2002 Anderson ended his 32-- year affiliation with the Bengals as a player, an assistant coach, and a broadcaster, and became an assistant coach for the Jacksonville Jaguars. His hobby is golf. Anderson has a wife, Cristy, a son, Matt, and two daughters, Megan and Molly. For many years, he lived in Lakeside Park in Northern Kentucky. He also was an owner in a Northern Kentucky Coors beer distributorship and in a replacement door company. He has done many commercial segments for local television.

Collett, Ritter. *Super Stripes PB and the Super Bowl Bengals.* Dayton, Ohio: Landfall Press, 1982.

Ludwig, Chick. *The Legends, Cincinnati Bengals: The Men, The Deeds, The Consequences.* Wilmington, Ohio: Orange Frazer Press, 2004.

Snyder, John, and Floyd Conner. *Day by Day in Cincinnati Bengals History.* New York: Leisure Press, 1984.

Michelle Heil

ANDERSON FERRY. The Anderson Ferry, located on the Ohio River in northeastern Boone Co. between Constance, Ky., and the western part of Cincinnati, has been in continuous operation since 1817. George Anderson, born in Maryland in 1765, lived near the mouth of Dry Creek in Boone Co., beginning about 1800. In July 1802 the Boone Co. Court ordered a group of men including Anderson to mark the most convenient path for a road from the Burlington courthouse to Dry Run, or Dry Creek as it is called today, the current location of the Anderson ferry. Thus, apparently at this very early date, Dry Creek was already a prominent point for crossing the river.

In 1817 Anderson bought 103 acres and a ferryboat from Raleigh Colston (see **Colston Family**) for $351 and was granted a license to operate. Traffic

Anderson Ferry.

in the early 1800s consisted of foot passengers, horse-drawn wagons, and livestock. The first ferryboat was propelled by men poling and was steered by using a wooden sweep with a long tiller arm. Around 1820 the Anderson family built a stone house overlooking the ferry landing and opened a tavern there. The stone house was torn down during the late 1960s. George and his wife operated the businesses until 1836, when the property was transferred within the Anderson family. George Anderson died in Boone Co. in 1839; his wife, Sarah Brooks Anderson, a native of North Carolina, died in 1841. In February 1841 Evan Anderson, a son of George and Sarah, sold the ferry to Montague McClure. The Anderson family had operated the ferry business for 24 years.

From 1841 to 1865, the ferry changed hands 10 times. Charles Kottmyer bought it from John Wilson in March 1865. Kottmyer had been a canal boatman and a stagecoach driver. At that time the ferry was driven by two paddlewheels, turned by two blindfolded horses walking on a treadmill. In 1867 Kottmyer built a new steam-powered boat, the *Boone # 1,* named after **Daniel Boone**. From then on, every new boat the Kottmyer family put into service was named for Daniel Boone and had a sequential number.

In 1937 Henry Kottmyer contracted to have an all-steel, steam-powered boat, the *Boone # 7,* built by the Stanwood Corporation of Covington (see **Houston, Stanwood & Gamble**). A sidewheeler converted to diesel in 1947, it can carry a maximum of eight cars. In 1964 Richard Kottmyer and his brother-in-law Duncan Huey bought a passenger barge, placing a second ferry into service as the *Boone # 8.* It is capable of carrying 10 cars, and its push boat is named the *Little Boone.* Four generations of Kottmyers owned and operated the Anderson Ferry for a total of 121 years. Under their ownership it survived the building of bridges over the Ohio River and the creation of the interstate highway system. Richard Kottmyer, a fourth-generation owner, retired in 1986, after selling the business to Paul and Deborah Anderson (their relationship to the original owner is unknown).

Paul Anderson worked for the Kottmyers for 25 years before he bought the Anderson Ferry. He began working on the ferry in 1961 and received his pilot's license at age 18 in 1965. With a staff of 12 and three boats in service, the Anderson Ferry now carries an average of 450 cars per day. Following the tradition set by Charles Kottmyer, in 1992 the Andersons, having purchased the excursion barge the *City of Parkersburg,* renamed it *Boone # 9.* It holds 15 automobiles and its push boat is called the *Deborah A.*

The Anderson Ferry is the only privately owned and operated ferry business on the 981-mile length of the Ohio River. It was placed on the National Register of Historic Places in 1982; in 1996 it was designated a Centennial Business by the Kentucky Historical Society. Almost 200 years after George Anderson took his first boatload of passengers and livestock across the river, the ferry continues to provide not only a cost-efficient and time-saving service but also a historic, scenic, and relaxing boat ride for families and tourists. Today the business is fueled by its proximity to the **Cincinnati/Northern Kentucky International Airport** and the faithful customers who use the ferry to commute.

Fitzgerald, William. "One of Boone County's Oldest Business Institutions," *Boone County Recorder,* March 14, 1968, 12.

Gordon, Richard L. "Namesake Back at the Helm of Ferry," *KP,* May 14, 1986, 1B.

Hale, Harry L. "Suburbs of Cincinnati: Anderson Ferry Was Laid Out as the Town of South Bend in 1789," *CE,* November 20, 1960, 6C.

O'Rear, Sherrie. "Ferry Tale: Ferry in Constance Family for 119 Years," *Boone County Recorder,* October 20, 1983, 6.

Paul Anderson and Laurie Wilcox

ANDERSON SLAVE PEN. The Anderson slave pen is a full two-story structure built of hewn logs that has one large, rectangular room on each floor and a 10-foot-wide chimney. Now located at the National Underground Freedom Museum in Cincinnati, it was first constructed and used in Mason Co. Its history began when Moses Frazee bought 100 acres of land from Lewis Craig in 1804. Frazee may have built the log building, or he may have taken over an existing log building on the 100-acre tract. At this time, the slave pen contained a 10-foot-wide chimney with a cooking fireplace at the north end of the building. On the east side, off-center, the structure had a single doorway with a rectangular transom over the door, and the door had a small brass doorknob, probably mounted with a surface lock to facilitate access. The doorway may have been constructed to reflect the Federal stylistic conventions that were popular at the time. The original building had at least one window with glass panes. Internally, the building exhibits evidence of shelves and division of the second floor.

Frazee sold the 100 acres to John W. Anderson in 1825, and Anderson bought additional land over the next nine years that totaled more than 900 acres. He apparently built himself a house, referred to as a mansion, in the adjacent field sometime between 1825 and 1834. He was certainly living there by the time of his death in 1834, because his widow, Susan S. Anderson, claimed the 100 acres as her "home farm" when she filed her claim for dower rights in early 1835. After Anderson constructed his mansion, the slave-pen building would not have been needed as a residence for his family. When he ceased using the slave-pen building as a house, he converted it to a very different purpose. The addition of the iron rings, chains, and barred windows altered the building and its history forever. Its original purpose was obscured. It became a prison for the slaves he bought from friends and neighbors. He had made it into a commercial building, a nonpersonal structure that became a hidden part of the local landscape.

Anderson built up his slave-export business through the late 1820s and early 1830s. He became a major local dealer and exporter of humans from Kentucky to the Deep South, making yearly trips to either Natchez, Miss., or New Orleans between 1830 and 1833. Enslaved persons, horses, and produce such as wheat were the "products" he transported. In three sales between November 1832 and May 1833, Anderson sold more than $38,000 worth of persons. In 2005 dollars, that is at least $800,000. Major Lexington slave dealers of the same period only claimed sales in the $5,000–$8,000 range. Anderson was a major player in the Kentucky-to-Natchez slave trade during his lifetime.

After Anderson died suddenly in July 1834, his widow, Susan Anderson, claimed dower rights over the 100 acres on which the slave pen was situated. She apparently lived there until her death in 1851 and was buried in the adjacent cemetery next to John W. Anderson and several of their daughters.

"Log 'Slave Pen' Won't Let Us Forget," *CE*, February 8, 2004, A1.

"Slave Pen Battles Continue," *KP*, January 17, 2000, 2K.

Jeannine Kreinbrink

ANDREWS (ANDRIOLA), FRANK J. "SCREW" (b. April 22, 1911, Cincinnati, Ohio; d. December 21, 1973, Fort Thomas, Ky.). Reputed underworld crime figure Frank Joseph "Screw" Andrews was born in the Little Italy section of the Cincinnati suburb of Walnut Hills. This neighborhood was home to many recently arrived Italian families, including the Martinellis, the LeDonnes, the Paulos, and the Andriolas. Frank got his start selling moonshine whiskey and beer illegally to the African American population of Cincinnati's West End, but it was in the illegal numbers game there that he made the most profits. Eventually, the Andriola family owned Spider's Italian Restaurant (Spider was Frank's brother), at the southeast corner of Boone and Burbank Sts. in the Little Italy neighborhood. Life in Little Italy was centered on Our Lady of Mount Carmel Roman Catholic Church along May St., where Frank Andrews spent his youth. By the 1940s Andrews had earned the less-than-honorable moniker "Screw" for his activities on the streets and in the clubs of nearby Newport. Fights, threats, intimidation, and other violent acts were commonplace for Andrews in his work "as a soldier" for the Cleveland crime syndicate (the Mayfield Road Gang) that controlled vice and corruption in Newport. In 1953 Andrews shot fellow numbers racketeer Melvin Clark in the parking lot of the Sportsman Club that Andrews operated on Central Ave. in Newport; Andrews was acquitted on the grounds of self-defense. Illegal gambling and the pandering of prostitution were two of Andrews's particular fortes. Later he moved the Sportsman Club to Second and York Sts., almost beneath the southern end of Newport's old **Central Bridge**, where his illicit activities catered especially to Ohioans who were seeking "action" 24 hours a day. For many years, Newport city officials did nothing to curtail any of these coming and goings.

Frank "Screw" Andrews, 1962.

Andrews and his family lived in a one-floor ranch in Cold Spring, on the west side of **U.S. 27** just south of Murnan Rd. That home contained a state-of-the-art security system and reportedly had secret hiding rooms like those discovered later at the clubs he operated in Newport. Andrews's career came to an abrupt halt in 1973 at **St. Luke Hospital** East in Fort Thomas. He was there for heart problems, and reportedly his wife, Eleanor Plunkett Andrews, paid him an evening visit. After she had departed, some still-unidentified men arrived and told the nurses on duty "to take a break." Andrews, whose room was on the fourth floor, was later found dead on a second-floor roof directly below his room's open window. The speculation has always been that Andrews was the victim of "a mob hit" to silence him because he knew so much about the syndicate's crime activities in Newport. Frank Andrews died at age 62, and his funeral mass was held at St. Therese Church in Southgate. He was buried at St. Stephen Cemetery in Fort Thomas.

Kentucky Death Certificate No. 32953, for the year 1973.

Michael R. Sweeney

ANDREWS, LORIN. (b. April 29, 1795, East Windsor [Vernon], Conn.; d. September 29, 1868, Honolulu, Hawaii). By age 10, New England–born Lorin Andrews, who later became a linguist, an educator, and a minister, was living in Portage Co., Ohio. He attended art school at Jefferson College in Pennsylvania and studied theology at Princeton University in New Jersey. As a young man, he moved to Maysville and worked in the printing office of a newspaper operated by his friend Judge **Lewis Collins**, the famed Kentucky historian. Andrews also taught school in both Maysville and "up the hill" in nearby Washington, Ky. On August 15, 1827, he married Mary Ann Wilson, daughter of a former Mason Co. Presbyterian minister. Andrews was also ordained a Presbyterian minister and became a missionary assigned to the Sandwich Islands (Hawaii). He and his bride set sail November 17, 1827, from Boston, Mass., and arrived, via Cape Horn, at Honolulu, Hawaii, March 30, 1828.

In 1831 Andrews founded the Lahainaluna Academy— the first college in Hawaii—on the Hawaiian island of Maui. This school evolved into what is now the University of Hawaii at Honolulu. Early on, Andrews recognized the need to provide the natives he was trying to convert to Christianity with a written language of their own. He wrote two very important books on the subject of the Hawaiian language: *A Vocabulary of Words in the Hawaiian Language* (1836) and *A Dictionary of the Hawaiian Language* (1865). In 1845 Hawaii's King Kamehameha III appointed Andrews a judge of the island in recognition of his valuable contributions to Hawaiian culture. Subsequently, Andrews held the office of secretary in the king's privy council for several different Hawaiian monarchs. He translated the Bible from English into the Hawaiian language, a language Andrews essentially had created. He also edited and published the first newspaper in the Hawaiian Islansds.

Lorin Andrews died in 1868 in Honolulu, at age 73. He was survived by his wife and several children and grandchildren. His son, also named Lorin Andrews, had died of consumption in August 1858, and his obituary appeared in the December 5, 1858, *Covington Journal,* indicating that the elder Lorin Andrews continued to have a following, years after leaving Maysville. Rev. Lorin Andrews, educator, linguist, minister, newspaperman, and judge, was buried at that most sacred of all Hawaiian burying grounds, the Kawaiahao Church Cemetery along S. King St. in downtown Honolulu. Countless Kentucky visitors to the island of Oahu each year drive past his grave on their way to the beautiful beaches of Waikiki, not knowing that the body of a former Northern Kentuckian, who gave the islands their written language, rests there.

Collins, Richard H. *History of Kentucky.* Vol. 1. Covington, Ky.: Collins, 1882.
"Lorin Andrews," *CJ,* December 5, 1858, 2.

Michael R. Sweeney

ANDREWS STEEL MILL. The company that became the Andrews Steel Mill began in 1858 when Alexander Swift incorporated the Swift Iron & Steel Works in Newport, which produced armor plates and castings. Over the next four decades, the company was sold four times. In 1890 Joseph and Albert L. Andrews, owners of Globe Iron Roofing & Corrugating Company of Cincinnati, bought the iron- and steelworks at a sheriff's auction for $249,000. The brothers relocated the corrugating operations of their company to the Newport mill, which would supply steel sheets for galvanizing and corrugating, but managed each half of their company as separate firms. After a Pittsburgh, Pa., supplier of iron bars raised its prices, the brothers organized the Andrews Steel Company in 1908 to smelt iron bars themselves at a new plant. The mill, located near Newport in Wilder, along the Licking River, featured three open-hearth furnaces. The Andrews brothers also founded the Newport Culvert Company in 1915 to make rust-resistant sewer pipes. The Andrews Steel Company later diversified into forging billets and oil-well tools. The vertically and horizontally integrated Andrews business empire also included the Hardy Burlington Coal Mine at Hazard, thus ensuring that the Andrews businesses would have a steady supply of inexpensive fuel.

The Andrews brothers were the leading industrialists in Campbell Co. at the turn of the 20th century. They succeeded despite the competitive nature of the steel industry, the Panic of 1893, and the depression that followed. In 1920 Newport and adjoining Wilder boasted Kentucky's second-largest concentration of heavy industry, in large part due to the efforts of the Andrews brothers. They eventually expanded the local steelworks from a 2-mill operation to 20 hot-mill stands, and their products found a global market. According to local historian Thomas L. Purvis, "It was through their efforts, that Newport remained a major center of steel production in the 20th century, when the industry withered in Cincinnati and disappeared from Covington." Joseph Andrews also built the West Side Hotel at 11th and Brighton Sts. in Newport, as well as plain but sturdy worker housing nearby.

In 1921 and 1922, the Andrews Steel Mill was the scene of a prolonged and violent labor strike. In November 1921 the owners cut wages in an increasingly competitive environment, and the union called for a strike. The owners vowed to fire any worker who rejected the new wage and insisted on a non-union ("open") shop. The union and the city were bitterly torn by the strike, which ended in a defeat for the union in April 1922. In 1943 the Andrews family sold their holdings to the Lehman Brothers brokerage firm of New York City. Over the next two decades, the company changed hands several times. It was reorganized as **Newport Steel** in 1980.

Purvis, Thomas L., ed. *Newport, Kentucky: A Bicentennial History.* Newport, Ky.: Otto Zimmerman, 1996.

Margaret Warminski

ANGEL, VERA (b. October 7, 1928, Covington, Ky.; d. January 4, 1997, Cincinnati, Ohio). Vera Angel paved the way for women to assume positions of leadership in Northern Kentucky business and politics through her successful real estate career and by chairing significant professional boards and educational campaigns, as well as by her city governmental service.

Vera Fay Rusk was the daughter of Loren J. and Clara McNay Rusk. She graduated from **Holmes High School** in Covington in 1946 and married her teenage sweetheart, James Bird Angel, on June 14, 1947.

Vera Angel knew the value of hard work. She worked as a bookkeeper for a Covington jeweler and at the Hudepohl Brewing Company before she began selling real estate from her home in Taylor Mill, Ky. In 1957 she hung out the first sign for Vera Angel Realty at Ritte's Corner in Latonia and operated a successful business there for 35 years. She was Realtor of the Year in 1973, 1975, and 1980 and served in many positions on the Kenton-Boone Board of Realtors, eventually becoming its president in 1979.

Angel also blazed a trail for women in Northern Kentucky politics. In 1968 she became the first woman elected to the Covington City Commission, where she served two terms. In 1971 she made an unsuccessful bid for mayor. In 1981 Angel became the first woman president of the **Northern Kentucky Chamber of Commerce**. In 1994 she received the Chamber's prestigious Frontiersman award for her lifetime of service to the community. The award is given to individuals with long histories of outstanding service to their professions and the Northern Kentucky community.

In the civic arena, she was on many boards and campaigns, especially for **Thomas More College**, **Northern Kentucky University**, Georgetown College, United Appeal, **Goodwill Industries**, and the **Diocesan Catholic Children's Home**. She was especially active as a member, state director, and president of the Northern Kentucky chapter of the American Cancer Society, long before being diagnosed with cancer herself in 1988.

Even when ill health forced the closure of her own business in 1991, Angel continued to sell real estate locally through Jim Huff Realty and remained a million-dollar salesperson each year until just before her death in 1997 at University Hospital in Cincinnati. She was buried in Floral Hills Memorial Gardens in Taylor Mill.

Kreimer, Peggy. "Political, Business Pioneer Vera Angel Dies," *KP,* January 6, 1997, 1K.
"Riverside Plan Fate's in Balance," *KP,* November 5, 1968, 1K.
Thorsen, Nancy. "Vera Angel Was Community Leader," *KE,* January 10, 1997, B6.
Wing, Paula Angel. Telephone interview by Rebecca Mitchell Turney, February 19, 2006, Park Hills, Ky.

Rebecca Mitchell Turney

ANN'S ICE BALLS AND ICEHOUSE. Bob and Ann Wolburn Bezold were the original owners of the establishment that became known as Ann's Ice Balls and Icehouse. Ann Bezold began selling her creations from her home on Park Ave. in Newport before **World War I**. When her husband opened a tavern on Ninth St., where the **Green Derby Restaurant** is currently located, Ann sold ice balls from the rear of the building. Bob Bezold sold his business in 1940, and Ann moved her ice-ball stand one block east to the current building at 28 E. Ninth St., between Orchard and John Sts. The price of an ice ball in 1919 was three cents. In the 1950s and 1960s, it cost a nickel; a dime bought two scoops of syrup in addition, and for 15 cents one could purchase an ice ball with a scoop of ice cream in the middle. The ice ball came in a tapered paper cup, and a small wooden spoon was provided. Currently, the price of an ice ball is $1.50. Rick Sacksteder, a relative of Ann Bezold, who worked at the ice-ball stand during the late 1950s and early 1960s, stated that Ann made all her own syrups from extracts. The flavors were cherry, grape, lime, nectar, orange, peach, raspberry, root beer, strawberry, and sometimes pineapple.

Ann's Ice Balls also sold crushed ice. Gusswin Buddy Sacksteder operated the icehouse from 1946 until his death in 1963. He usually picked up three 800-pound blocks of ice each day from icehouses in Newport, Covington, and Cincinnati and crushed them into 8-pound and 25-pound bags to be sold.

Since Ann Bezold began Ann's Ice Balls, the business has had several owners, and over the years additional syrups have been added and other foods have been sold. Bertha Caudill, who worked in the store, leased the business after Ann Bezold's death. Caudill, the owner for 21 years, sold it to Chuck Coffman of Bellevue. In 1988 it was bought by Ernie Pretot. In 1996 Tom Bush and his wife, Sylvia, purchased the business.

Franzen, Gene. "Ann's Ice Balls a Sweet Newport Tradition," *KE,* June 17, 2001, 1B.
Harper, Molly. "Ice Balls Still the Favorites at Ann's," *KE,* July 13, 1999, 1B.
Rosencrans, Joyce. "Summer's Best Slurp: Couple Carries on Ice Ball Tradition," *CP,* July 27, 1988, 1C.
Sacksteder, Rick. Interview by Michael Stull, December 8, 2004, Covington, Ky.

"7 Spots You Won't Want to Miss," *CE,* July 29, 2003, 4E.
Tortora, Andrea. "Summer's Always a Treat for Ice Ball Customers at Ann's," *KE,* July 7, 1996, 1B, 1C.

Michael D. Stull

ANSHUTZ, THOMAS P. (b. October 5, 1851, Newport, Ky.; d. June 16, 1912, Fort Washington, Pa.). Thomas Pollock Anshutz, one of the most influential American painters and art instructors of the 19th century, was a descendant of the German religious painter Hermann Anshutz. Thomas was one of four children born to Jacob and Abigail Jane Pollock Anshutz, who lived near the Ohio River, along what is now Third St. in Newport. In later life, Anshutz said that as a youth he showed no artistic bent but remembered being impressed tremendously by a storefront display of artwork in Cincinnati, pointed out to him by his mother. When he was about 12 years old, his family moved from Newport to Wheeling, W.Va., and he lived there with his aunts until 1871. Then he moved to Brooklyn, N.Y., where he lived with his uncle and aunt Peters for about two years. His uncle, who worked for the *Brooklyn Times,* suggested that Anshutz train to be an artist, after seeing his paintings of boats along the Ohio River.

In Brooklyn Anshutz attended the National Academy of Design. Although he was not impressed with either the instructors or the curriculum, he stayed at that school for about two years, under the tutelage of Lemuel Everett Wilmarth. He then transferred to the Philadelphia Sketch Club, where he studied under famous American artist Thomas Eakins. When his mentor left to teach at the Pennsylvania Academy of Fine Arts, Anshutz followed him. Thomas Eakins had a major impact on both the artwork and the life of Thomas Anshutz. From Eakins, Anshutz learned to observe carefully the form, anatomy, and movement of the human body, enabling him to depict realistically the people in his paintings.

In 1883 Anshutz was appointed Eakins's assistant and helped with his anatomy, painting, and drawing classes. In his new position, Anshutz worked in Eakins's shadow and became increasingly dissatisfied with his mentor's teaching style and philosophy. Three years later, when Eakins was charged with the "libertarian handling" of a nude model in his life class, Eakins resigned and Anshutz was named his successor.

Anshutz married Effie Shriver Russell on September 1, 1892, and they had one child, Edward Russell. Shortly after his marriage, Anshutz enrolled in the Académie Julian in Paris, France, where he studied for about three months. In spring 1893 he toured through France, Switzerland, and England, studying various painting styles. That fall he returned to his teaching position at the Pennsylvania Academy. Anshutz was a patient teacher, always open to new ideas, and was known to lavish praise on his pupils, rather than criticism.

At the 1904 St. Louis World Fair, Thomas Anshutz was awarded a silver medal for his portrait of John Trask. In 1909 he replaced famous American artist William Merritt Chase as director of the Academy of Fine Arts and later that year was awarded the academy's gold medal of honor. He also won the Walter Lippincott Award that year, for his painting *The Tanagra.* Anshutz was a gifted artist who produced numerous exceptional paintings; however, his artwork was never fully appreciated, because it was often overshadowed by his reputation as a teacher. Many experts considered him a one-picture artist, because they felt that his 1880 painting *The Ironworkers at Noontime* was far superior to anything else he had ever done. Harry Procter of the Procter and Gamble Company used an adaptation of that painting on an Ivory Soap advertising sign that he displayed in Fountain Square in Cincinnati. This display is reputed to be the first example of large-scale outdoor advertising in the United States. Anshutz won a gold medal for his artwork at the Buenos Aires International Exposition in 1910. That same year, he was named president of the Philadelphia Sketch Club.

At the height of his career, Anshutz developed a serious heart condition and traveled to Bermuda in an effort to regain his health. He attempted to return to teaching in fall 1911, but his heart condition worsened, and he was hospitalized for about a month. Anshutz died in his Fort Washington, Pa., home at age 60 and was buried in Hillside Cemetery in Hillside, Pa.

Thomas Pollock Anshutz has been called Newport's Duveneck, because of the similarity of their careers. Two of Anshutz's paintings, *On the Ohio River* (ca. 1880) and *Steamboat on the Ohio* (1896), are clearly linked to memories of his Newport childhood. A number of Anshutz's students were among the best American artists of the 20th century. They include renowned landscape painter Edward Redfield, Cincinnati-born impressionist Robert Henri (Robert Henry Cozad), illustrator John Sloan, photographer-painter Charles Sheller, and watercolor seascape specialist John Marin.

Claypool, James C. "An Unassuming Painter," *Enquirer Magazine,* August 4, 1985, 8–10.
Griffin, Randall C. *Thomas Anshutz, Artist and Teacher.* Huntington, N.Y.: Heckscher Museum, 1994.

Jack Wessling

ANSWERS IN GENESIS–USA (AiG-USA). This organization has established its headquarters in Northern Kentucky and has founded the Creation Museum. In 1979 Australian educator Ken Ham realized that most Christians were not equipped to provide answers to a "doubting world" in the age of science. So Ham left his position as a public school science teacher in Queensland, Australia, and began speaking full-time on creation/evolution and biblical-authority issues.

At the invitation of the Institute for Creation Research in San Diego, Calif., Ham and his family moved to the United States in January 1987. In late 1993 Ham and two colleagues, Mark Looy and Mike Zovath, founded a nonprofit organization initially called Creation Science Ministries. Within a year, the board renamed it Answers in Genesis (AiG).

In 1994 Ham, Looy, and Zovath moved their families to Northern Kentucky to establish the new headquarters of the organization, renting offices in Florence. The location was considered strategic because almost two-thirds of America's population lives within 650 miles of the region and because there were plans for a creation museum.

In the mid-1990s, AiG-USA was searching for land in Northern Kentucky on which to build a creation museum and new headquarters for its speaking ministry, radio program, and World Wide Web outreach. The organization was constantly in the local news as it received strident opposition from evolutionists and others opposed to rezoning efforts. The controversy soon made national and even international headlines (it was reported in the London *Times*). One local newspaper reader, even though he was not well acquainted with AiG-USA, became so concerned about the way the organization was being attacked that his family gave a $1 million gift for the museum.

In 2004 AiG-USA had grown to nearly 100 staff working out of four rented offices in Northern Kentucky. In September of that year, all employees moved into one building (next to the Creation Museum) that AiG-USA now owns, on 49 acres along I-275, just west of the Cincinnati/Northern Kentucky International Airport.

By 2008 AiG-USA and its Creation Museum had more than 300 staff and more to be hired, making it the world's largest apologetics organization. The $27 million Creation Museum, with an anticipated opening-year attendance of more than 250,000, actually drew over 200,000 museum guests in fewer than four months, attracting national and international visitors. This "walk through biblical history," from Genesis to the present, includes 70,000 square feet of 150 one-of-a-kind exhibits, animatronic dinosaurs, a state-of-the-art digital planetarium, a special-effects theater, a children's area, a plaza with a coffee bar, a Noah's Ark–themed café, a dragon-themed bookstore, beautiful nature trails that circle a three-acre lake, and a petting zoo. The museum opened Memorial Day, May 28, 2007.

Other aspects of the AiG-USA ministry include speeches (numerous speakers presented as many as a dozen illustrated talks at 300 events in various cities in 2006); the *Answers with Ken Ham* radio program (broadcast on more than 1,000 radio stations worldwide every weekday); the Answers in Genesis Web site, which received the Website of the Year award from the National Religious Broadcasters (NRB) for 2006 (it had nearly 1.6 million visits each month); the *Answers* magazine (over 50,000 subscribers) and other teaching resources; and distribution of hundreds of faith-building and evangelistic materials through its online bookstore.

Answers in Genesis. www.answersingenesis.org (accessed April 8, 2006).
"Creation Museum Is Taking Shape in Boone County," *KP,* September 26, 2005, 1K.
"Creation Museum Raises $20 Million," *KE,* January 15, 2006, 3B.
"Evolution of a Creation Museum," *SC,* July 11, 2004, 5A.

Pam Sheppard

ANTI-GERMAN HYSTERIA, 1917–1920. Throughout the United States, including Northern Kentucky, there was a climate of anti-German hysteria during **World War I** and shortly thereafter. Although the federal and state governments validated the anti-German mind-set with new discriminatory laws and by discriminatory actions, it was often private organizations that encouraged the view. In Covington the Citizens' Patriotic League (CPL), a vigilante-type organization with more than 1,000 members, had that effect. One of its actions was to force reluctant citizens (most often of German descent) to buy Liberty Bonds.

The CPL was also involved in attempts to promote patriotism. It warned of punishments if people were found to be pro-German, posted signs in the windows of residents who it believed were subscribing to German newspapers, and successfully protested the distribution of two Cincinnati German-language papers in Covington. Mobs of up to 200 participants traveled around posting signs and encouraging contributions to the war effort. The CPL alone was directly involved in bringing about 17 indictments against perceived German supporters, and these self-styled vigilantes helped create an atmosphere that contributed to many more indictments.

Among the CPL strategies were direct physical attacks and spying on individuals it believed to be disloyal. This hate organization rarely suffered legal repercussions for its actions, for a variety of reasons; one was that at least some of the officials in the state judicial apparatus were members of the CPL. The CPL's best-known member was **Stephens Blakely**, who was the commonwealth attorney for Kenton Co. He was directly involved in two infamous CPL incidents.

In the first episode, Blakely assaulted Joseph Grote on June 5, 1918. Blakely entered a bar, called Grote a series of names, accused him of being pro-German, and then hit him repeatedly. The occurrence did not come to light until 1919, when Grote sued Blakely and some others in civil court for assault and conspiracy. The trial began in December 1920, more than two years after the war had ended. Blakely's attorneys tried to tar Grote with a brush of anti-Americanism, while Grote's attorneys tried to keep individuals who had been members of the CPL off the jury.

Blakely's five codefendants all denied the charges. Blakely took a more direct route, admitting the assault but attempting to justify it. He claimed that he had been threatened for his patriotism and that German newspapers had been found in the bar where the assault happened. He admitted slapping Grote but denied cursing him. In the course of the trial, other assaults and threats by members of the CPL were disclosed, and witnesses also told of forced contributions by people targeted by the CPL.

The judge instructed the jurors that they must find Blakely guilty, because Blakely had admitted to the assault, and that damages of at least one cent had to be awarded. The jury deliberated for four and a half hours, freed all six defendants of the charge of conspiracy, and found only Blakely guilty on the charge of assault, awarding exactly one cent in damages. The deliberations had taken so long because several of the jurors did not want to give Grote anything; two of the jurors, even after the long deliberations, did not sign the verdict. The jury also donated one cent to Blakely, so that he could pay Grote. Many citizens in the community showed their agreement, sending pennies to Blakely to help him pay the fine.

The second well-known incident resulted in a series of legal cases that ultimately reached the U.S. Supreme Court. It began in the shoe shop of Charles Schoberg at Ritte's Corner in Latonia. Schoberg was an American citizen who by all accounts had been very supportive of his community for years. He had served in a variety of positions, including town marshal and city council member. At age 66, he was far past draft age. During the war some people suspected that Schoberg, who had German ancestry (he had immigrated with his parents at the age of five), was pro-German. However, whenever anyone entered his shop, the conversation was unrelated to the war. The CPL hired a detective agency to monitor the conversations via a listening device placed inside the shop. The group was able to gain access to plant the device on a pretext that the wiring in the shop needed repair. The bug did not record voices; it merely amplified them. Someone always had to be present to listen to the device and write down notes on what was said that was antiwar. Only antiwar comments were recorded. Based on these notes, seven people, including Schoberg, were indicted, and the CPL had them arrested on July 4, 1918, in a wartime circuslike atmosphere. About 400 people packed the courthouse to hear the evidence read.

Besides Schoberg, the leading defendants were J. Henry Kruse, a brewer and city leader in Latonia who had a street named after him, and Henry Feltman, a wealthy tobacco merchant. Kruse street in Latonia was renamed James Ave. after the indictments were handed down. The cases were tried in August 1918, and Schoberg's was heard first. The 32 counts against Schoberg charged him with saying things like "According to newspaper reports, the Allies had Germany whipped four years ago, if we believe them, but they haven't and never will" and "This is a damn war for money. If it were not for the damn Bonds and Thrift Stamps we would not be in this war. Somebody is getting rich. Not me that is a cinch." Schoberg hired two prominent attorneys, who tried to argue that private speech was protected under the First Amendment and that Schoberg had been patriotic. But Schoberg was convicted in a four-day trial and sentenced to 10 years in prison. Feltman was tried for using similar language and was convicted quickly as well, being sentenced to 7 years and a $40,000 fine (approximately equivalent to a half million dollars today). Kruse was tried, convicted, and sentenced to 5 years in jail. Besides the private nature of the conversations, it was also brought out that these men had purchased varying but significant amounts of war bonds; Feltman had contributed $45,000 to the purchasing of bonds.

All three men appealed their convictions to the Sixth Circuit Court of Appeals, which upheld their convictions. It was not illegal at the time to use a wiretap to convict a person without approval of the tap by any court, and the way the evidence was gathered was not even an issue. The appeals court held that these men constituted a clear and present danger and so could be constrained. The court also held that the private conversations would inevitably spread beyond the shoe shop (even though they had not yet done so, which was what necessitated the electronic surveillance) and so could be restricted. An appeal was made to the U.S. Supreme Court, but that Court declined to hear the case. The three men served about six months in a prison in West Virginia before being pardoned. Schoberg and Feltman returned to Covington and lived out their lives there, being accepted back into society. Kruse, however, was apparently bankrupted by the ordeal and moved to Florida. It should be noted that the only proof of unpatriotic speech was the notes of the detectives, who could have written down anything they pleased. These cases demonstrate the havoc that wartime hysteria caused in Northern Kentucky, even within the legal system.

Many small towns also had waves of anti-German prejudice. It will never be known how many people of Germanic heritage were painted with yellow paint, ridden out of town on rails, tarred and feathered, or had oil thrown into their wells. Sometimes such activities would merit a short mention in the local paper, but rarely if ever did the reporter disagree with the actions taken or comment negatively about the perpetrators of the crimes.

Anti-German hysteria was prevalent from 1917 to 1920 throughout much of the United States, especially in those regions that had high German populations. One positive note in Kentucky was that when the Kentucky legislature passed a bill forbidding the teaching of German as a language in the schools, Governor Augustus Stanley (1915–1919) vetoed the bill.

Charles B. Schoberg v. U.S. Records and Briefs, Case 3273, Records and Briefs, 1897–1962, Records of the U.S. Courts of Appeals for the Sixth Circuit, Record Group 276, National Archives, Atlanta, Ga.

Kennedy, David M. *Over Here: The First World War and American Society.* New York: Oxford Univ. Press, 1980.

Merriman, Scott Allen. "Ordinary People in Extraordinary Times? Defendants, Attorneys, and the Federal Government's Policy under the Espionage Acts during World War I in the Sixth Circuit Court of Appeals District," PhD diss., Univ. of Kentucky, 2003.

Murphy, Paul L. *World War I and the Origin of Civil Liberties in the United States.* New York: Norton, 1979.

Peterson, H. C., and Gilbert C. Fite. *Opponents of War, 1917–1918.* Madison: Univ. of Wisconsin Press, 1957.

Scott Merriman

ANTISLAVERY. In the 19th century, the term *antislavery* was applied to anyone who held the belief that the institution of slavery should be ended, either immediately or gradually. *Antislavery* was an umbrella term that included **abolitionists**, gradual emancipationists, and colonizationists.

Antislavery movements in Kentucky have been characterized by historians of slavery as Caucasian experiences, each new intellectual concept capturing attention, galvanizing sporadic actions, and then running out of steam. Biographies of Henry Clay, Cassius Marcellus Clay, **John G. Fee**, Robert J. and William L. Breckinridge, and even John Speed champion the antislavery credentials of each of these prominent Kentuckians. Yet in spite of nearly continuous antislavery activity from 1830 to 1860 by some of Kentucky's leading social and political figures, slavery as an institution was stronger and more widely fixed in the state in 1860 than it was in 1830.

Several recent histories recall free people of color, including **Elijah Anderson**, John P. Parker, George De Baptiste, Sheldon Morris, and Washington Spradling, who provided aid to fugitive slaves. It has even been reported that a few slaves living in Kentucky aided other slaves during escapes: Arnold Gragston in Bracken Co., Richard Daly at Hunters Bottom, Uncle Simon and Ben Swain at Henderson, and Uncle Elias at Catlettsburg.

The only continuous antislavery activities from 1780 to 1860 in Kentucky involved free people of color and slaves themselves. The black antislavery position required direct action—to purchase the slave's freedom, to escape to freedom or aid others in their escape to freedom, and to resist slavery in place. These actions alone did not overturn the institution of slavery, but they gave hundreds of slaves a free life and helped to injure slave owners economically. Neither the white antislavery pamphlets and conventions nor the pinpricks of black activism, however, were successful in removing slavery from Kentucky's soil. That required a bloody **Civil War**, the defeat of the Confederacy, and passage of the 13th Amendment to the U.S. Constitution.

When Rev. David Rice stormed out of the 1792 State Constitutional Convention at Danville, the first antislavery movement in Kentucky involving whites had already reached its political zenith. Rice was among the early white Presbyterian, Baptist, and Methodist preachers and elders attempting to keep a perpetual slavery system out of Kentucky. For the early settlement in Kentucky, there were two models, that of the Northwest Territory just to the north across the Ohio River, which was established free of slavery in 1787, and the Virginia model, which institutionalized slavery for people of African descent.

The passage of Article 9 in the 1792 Kentucky Constitution, over the objections of sixteen white preachers and lay leaders, permitted slave owners to bring their slaves into Kentucky and gave local jurisdictions authority to regulate slavery. Rev. John Rankin's short *Memoir of Samuel Donnell* describes some of the efforts to defeat Article 9's passage in the activities, during the 1790s, of leaders of the Concord Presbyterian Church, located in Bourbon (later Harrison) Co.

During the first three decades of the 19th century, the Virginia planter system that had been brought to Kentucky by the children of the Virginia gentry solidified through landholdings and political power. And the number of slaves imported into Kentucky rose from 40,843 in 1800 to 126,742 in 1820. In those twenty years, the slave system won out in Kentucky through overt political power of the landed gentry and failure of the yeoman farmers to perceive that slavery was detrimental to their own welfare. The state's planter class took control as magistrates, as judges, and as elected legislators, senators, and governors; and large sections of middle Kentucky became Whig in their political leanings, Henry Clay territory. Most significantly, property rights, that is, over land and slaves, acquired the significance of a religious dogma standing above justice, mercy, and equality under God.

Yet in those same twenty years, the Second Great Awakening in religion sent evangelistic tremors through and around mainstream Protestant denominations in Kentucky. Religiosity spread chiefly through the yeoman classes into the state. This religious awakening originated with the Separate and Freewill Baptist denominations that sprang from George Whitfield and Stubal Stearns; with the Pentecostal experience of Presbyterians, Methodists, and Reformed Baptists at Cane Run in Kentucky in 1801 and subsequent tent revivals; with the peeling away from the Presbyterians by the Associate Reformed and the Cumberland Presbyterians and by the Rankinites; and with the separation from the Methodists of the Methodist Protestants and later the Wesleyans. In all this turmoil, many Kentuckians found slavery incompatible with their new heightened sense of divine purpose; they decided that slavery was evil and was bringing harm to the new nation. The contemporary question, therefore, was what to do about the problem.

Between 1800 and 1827, a number of second-generation Baptist, Methodist, Presbyterian, and Reformed preachers advocated moral persuasion to convince slaveholders that they should free their slaves in their wills and leave sufficient land or financial resources so that the slaves could make a living in Kentucky or go to the North. A few of these ministers advocated educating slaves for future freedom, baptizing slaves, and identifying trustworthy slaves who could function as elders and deacons for separate black congregations.

For the Baptists the issue came to a head at Mount Sterling, between 1803 and 1806, in the person of David Barrow, a minister in the Separate Baptist tradition who served the Mount Sterling, Goshen, and Lulbegrud churches. Through political pressure from the Regular Baptists of the Elkhorn Baptist Association and their fledgling Bracken Baptist Association, David Barrow was expelled from the North District Baptist Association in 1806 for advocating the gradual emancipation of slaves and the eventual abolition of slavery itself.

Barrow not only preached continuously against slavery, but he also published British Baptist Thomas Clarkson's *Essay on Slavery and Commerce of the Human Species,* a 1785 treatise that greatly influenced U.S. abolitionists. Barrow himself wrote *Involuntary, Unmerited, Perpetual, Absolute, Hereditary Slavery Examined on the Principles of Nature, Reason, Justice, Policy, and Scripture,* which was printed in 1808 by John Bradford at Lexington. That same year, Barrow joined Carter Tarrant and founded the Baptized Licking-Locust Association, Friends of Humanity, also known as the Emancipation Baptists. The Baptized Licking-Locust Association, Friends of Humanity, included the Licking Locust, Gilgal, and Bracken Baptist churches from the Bracken Baptist Association and Lawrence Creek Baptist Church from Mason Co.

Some slave owners in Kentucky decided to manumit their slaves because of religious convictions. However, since the average number of slaves per owner in Kentucky was generally not large, these separate individual actions by white slaveholders did not significantly reduce the number of slaves held statewide. In the entire period from 1799 to 1868 in Bracken Co. in Northern Kentucky, for example, slaveholders filed only 156 emancipation records in the courthouse, 14 of them in 1834–1836 by Arthur Thome of Augusta. In Owen Co. in 1847, Susan Herndon Rogers freed 10 slaves, the Locust family, and gave them 403 acres known as Free Station, or **Mountain Island**. Her brother James Herndon executed a bond in 1853 for \$21,000 in order to have his 22 slaves manumitted. The Vinegar, Smith, and Carroll families divided 125 acres at Mountain Island (see **Theodore Vinegar**). By 1827 the emancipation movement in Kentucky that had been spurred on by the Great Awakening ran out of steam; as the movement's leaders died or moved away, the impact of moral persuasion proved anemic.

It was Kentuckian Henry Clay, long an advocate of gradual emancipation, who in 1817 stimulated the founding of the national American Colonization Society, an idea originally floated in 1800 by Thomas Jefferson and James Monroe. But not until 1823 were the first of the local colonization societies created in Kentucky. Even though there were few free people of color in the state in those early years, white slaveholders continuously tried to get them to leave, fearing that these freedmen would inspire blacks who were in bondage to seek freedom. Colonization was fundamentally an answer to the reality that if slavery ended, the South would have hundreds of thousands of freed slaves, a nightmare scenario to the whites who dominated and controlled the slave system. Colonization as an antislavery concept built on the underlying racism and fear within the white power structure.

Many historians described the reaction of slaveholders to the Nat Turner Rebellion in Virginia in 1831 as a near hysteria that swept through the entire South, producing far more stringent controls on slaves and heightening fears that free blacks might become agitators. In step with these times, contemporary newspapers in Kentucky, including some in Northern Kentucky, regularly published sensationalized accounts of all slave revolts in the United States and in the Caribbean.

Colonization, then, had more to do with white fear of freed blacks than it did with ending slavery. Through Clay's legislative skills and support from many of the Southern delegations, the federal government was persuaded to purchase land in Africa. Kentucky's colonization leaders—Henry Clay, Robert J. Breckinridge, William L. Breckinridge, John C. Underwood, some Old School Presbyterian congregations, and some Methodist Episcopal Church congregations—embraced the colonization concepts, because colonization would rid Kentucky of two perceived evils: perpetual slavery and the fact that the nation had 250,000 freed blacks. By sending all blacks back to Africa, Kentucky and the nation would be able to eliminate their race problem. Moreover, by supporting gradual emancipation, Kentucky slaveholders would continue to benefit from their slaves economically until properly compensated for their "loss of property." The only problem with the often-debated scenarios of the colonization movement was that the free people of color living in Kentucky did not want to go to Africa. In the thirty years of colonization activity, Kentucky sent only 658 freed blacks to Africa, and some of them returned. Maysville had an active colonization society. In May 1827 it met at the Presbyterian Meeting House and elected the following officers: Adam Beatty, John Chambers, Rev. John T. Edgar, William Huston Jr., and Andrew M. January. In addition, Johnston Armstrong, **Lewis Collins**, Peter Grant, James Morris, Capt. Thomas Nicholson, Isaac Outten, Maj. Valentine Peers, James M. Runyon, Francis Taylor, and Rev. Walter Warder were chosen as managers.

Many, if not most, of the early antislavery people left Kentucky as soon as the land title offices opened in Indiana and Illinois. They found themselves neighbors to fiercely antislavery farmers from Maine, New Hampshire, Vermont, and upstate New York, and among these antislavery people in Indiana and Illinois, early runaway slaves found individuals willing to give them food, rough shelter, and directions to another safe place. By mid-1824 several friendly communities aiding runaway slaves dotted the shoreline across from Kentucky on the north side of the Ohio River—Vevay and Pleasant Township in Switzerland Co., Ind.; the Free Will Baptists, the Methodist Protestants, and the Universalists of Aurora and of Dearborn Co., Indiana; and the Seceder and Associate Reformed Presbyterians of South Hanover, Carmel, and Rykers Ridge outside Madison, Ind. In Ohio, major assisting communities for runaway slaves were forming in Clermont and Brown counties.

As people migrated from North Carolina and eastern Tennessee into and through Kentucky, information about the Quaker- and Separate Baptist–inspired manumission societies filtered into Kentucky. A total of 89 manumission societies had been established by 1830 in the Virginia and Carolina tidewater cities and in Tennessee. There were 50 manumission societies in North Carolina, and 25 societies, totaling 1,000 members, were formed in eastern Tennessee, particularly in the area around Jonesboro. Quaker abolitionists transported hundreds of former slaves, purchased as intact families or manumitted by slave owners under the proviso that these freedmen would be taken out of the South. Soon free black agricultural communities emerged all along the southern regions of Ohio, Indiana, and Illinois. Each of these communities became a haven for runaway slaves.

Runaways found shelter among Kentucky's free blacks who had been brought or sent or who had migrated naturally into the Northwest Territory. In 1821 E. S. Abdy, a British scholar, found runaway slaves hiding among formerly enslaved Kentuckians at Graysville, near Hanover, Ind. Whites and free blacks who migrated to Kentucky were often guided by evangelistic religious denominations, were natural adherents of antislavery societies of the late 1830s, were often activists in the emerging **Underground Railroad**, and became promoters of antislavery political parties.

In the river counties north of the Ohio River, Universalists, Free Will Baptists, and Seceder and Associate Reformed Presbyterians—all denominations that promoted true equality and declared that slavery was the root of evil in the American political system—had only a modest influence as religious denominations on both sides of the Ohio River, but they clearly had a major impact on those individuals choosing to aid fugitive slaves.

Prior to 1838, when local and statewide antislavery societies were formed in Indiana and Ohio, aid to fugitive slaves was handled informally by small cells of antislavery black and white families who had relatives or trusted friends farther north. Even with regular meetings and attempts to create secure routes to handle increasing numbers of runaway slaves, the so-called Underground Railroad was never very well organized and continued to rely on experienced free black conductors such as Elijah Anderson and John P. Parker to bring large numbers of runaway slaves out of Kentucky to freedom.

Cheryl LaRoche's recent work comparing and contrasting free black agricultural communities in southern Illinois, Indiana, and Ohio concluded that harboring and aiding runaway slaves was a natural activity, an extension of the blacks' own experiences as former slaves and now freedmen. She also points out the significance of Bishop William Paul Quinn's evangelism on behalf of the African Methodist Episcopal (A.M.E.) Church, of the founding of aggressive antislavery churches, and of Prince Hall Masonic orders as components in establishing successful Underground Railroad routes. A.M.E. congregations in Kentucky—Quinn Chapel in Louisville, St. James in Lexington, St. John in Frankfort, and Bethel in Shelbyville—as well as the Mill Creek A.M.E. Church in Cincinnati, were all associated with black abolitionist and Underground Railroad activities.

Alarmed by the large free black community at Cincinnati and the economic loss of slaves along the Ohio River, Northern Kentucky newspapers maintained a steady drumbeat over the 1840s and 1850s portraying abolitionists and free people of color with extreme proslavery prejudice. The 1829 and 1841 race riots at Cincinnati were offered as proof that blacks could not make good citizens, while ignoring that Kentucky invaders and white troublemakers had brought about this violence, even to the point of employing cannons against the black community of Cincinnati. The 1834 Lane Seminary debates in Cincinnati by Theodore Weld, **James Bradley**, and others were not reported as being challenges to slavery as an institution but rather as examples of unruly and disruptive elements among the seminary's students. To Kentucky newspapers, the 1836 mob violence against James Gillespie Birney's antislavery newspaper press in Cincinnati was not an infringement of U.S. constitutional rights, but rather showed that even in Ohio the vast majority of citizens objected to formation of the *Philanthropist*, an avowed antislavery newspaper. Underground Railroad agents; John G. Fee's Kentucky congregations in Bracken, Madison, and Lewis counties; Berea College in Kentucky; the Liberty Party; and the Indiana and Ohio Anti-Slavery societies all, in turn, were portrayed by these newspapers as irresponsible agitation by outsiders interfering in Kentucky's affairs. Were the newspapers representing prevailing sentiment among Kentucky's citizens or goading latent prejudices into action? The arguments cut both ways, according to recent historians.

In the debates leading up to the 1849 Kentucky Constitutional Convention, 475 supporters of constitutional emancipation met in 1848 at Maysville in Mason Co. However, the antislavery resolution they drafted at this meeting was in reality a principal plank of the colonizationists—a plan for gradual emancipation and immediate colonization rather than the outright repeal of slavery that the early antislavery adherents desired.

During the 1850s, abolitionists in Indiana and Ohio concluded it was time to press hard for an end to slavery in the United States. The "Slave Power" of Southern states had broken the Missouri Compromise and was in the process of extending slavery beyond the Mississippi River; no Southern state seemed likely to abandon institutional slavery on its own, a point driven home further when the institution of slavery was reaffirmed by Kentucky's new state constitution in 1850.

Immediatists in Indiana and Ohio split, however, on the means. Boycotting Southern products, actively supporting the Underground Railroad, political action through the Liberty and Free Soil Parties, and creating communities sympathetic to Northern views on slavery—such as John G. Fee had done at Berea—in the midst of Southerners were some of the concepts followed. On the national level, abolitionist William Lloyd Garrison disapproved of any action other than moral persuasion. Although Fee's Berea plan was attractive to the Garrisonites, many Northern abolitionists believed that only through political action would slavery ever be overturned. James G. Birney turned from gradualism to outright abolition in what he advocated as a leader of the Liberty Party. Salmon P. Chase of Ohio and many of the Indiana leaders pushed the Free Soil Party's agenda to prevent further encroachment of slavery in the western territories. Infuriated by passage of the 1850 Fugitive Slave Act, these abolitionists helped to influence the nomination of Abraham Lincoln for U.S. president by the new Republican Party in 1860.

Direct political action to overturn slavery took many forms. Levi Coffin championed a boycott system whereby Northerners and others who were against slavery would refuse to buy Southern products made from slave labor. His store in Cincinnati sold goods made by free labor and eliminated cotton products, among many other agricultural products tied to the economy of the South. The

American Missionary Society tried to distribute thousands of Bibles and antislavery tracts in the South through colporteurs, religious men and women who traveled with suitcases and satchels full of what proslavery forces in the South termed "incendiary literature." John G. Fee was very much associated with colporteurs in Central Kentucky.

Eli Thayer and John C. Underwood are credited with pushing the American Missionary Society's activity beyond colporteurs to promote and finance the concept of "northern emigrant communities." This direct action placed Northern abolitionist Christians in the middle South and in the disputed western territories to model egalitarian societies so that slave owners could be shown how freedmen might act if they were educated and treated as citizens. The emigrant community established in Kansas in the 1850s, so much associated with John Brown and the Missouri raids, was the first attempt to test these ideas. The emigrant community established at Ceredo, W.Va., near Ashland, Ky., was a far more successful venture, focusing on mining and milling as a profit center. But in Kentucky the most famous and controversial of these abolitionist efforts was the failed community John G. Fee tried to establish in 1859 at Berea that also included a coeducational, integrated college. Located on lands granted by Cassius M. Clay, both the planned abolitionist colony and the college were immediately targeted by proslavery forces angered by John Brown's October 1859 violent raid on Harpers Ferry, Va., and Fee and his colleagues were forced to flee across the Ohio River.

Typical of the reaction in Kentucky to the expulsion of Fee and his associates was a resolution on January 21, 1860, at a meeting at Orangeburg in Mason Co., declaring: "No Abolitionist has the right to establish himself in the slaveholding community and disseminate opinions and principles destructive of the tranquility and safety." Northerners, therefore, should look to their own salvation and leave Kentuckians alone.

Antebellum newspapers in Northern Kentucky aligned with either the **Whig Party** or the Democratic Party and treated news about runaway slaves, slave uprisings, and Underground Railroad activities as crime stories. They also reported legislative acts of Congress concerning slavery and foreign news about the African slave trade and announced local meetings of abolition, proslavery, or colonization society meetings. In the 1840s and 1850s, Democratic newspapers took a decidedly antiblack position, running alarmist news stories about the Patrick Doyle slave revolt, **Margaret Garner**'s trial in Cincinnati for murdering her child, the Henderson slave revolt, runaway slave recaptures, and, whenever possible, examples of escaped slaves who returned to their masters voluntarily. The villains in these articles were always Northern agitator abolitionists. Free blacks were characterized as buffoons, criminals, or puffed up by self-importance and by "trying to imitate their betters."

In 1835 James Gillespie Birney, a slave owner who emancipated his slaves that year, and 40 others founded the Kentucky chapter of the American Anti-Slavery Society and announced plans for two ventures: their newspaper, the *Philanthropist,* to be printed at Danville, and a postal campaign to send 1 million pieces of antislavery literature throughout the South. Danville literally ran Birney and his antislavery publication out of town. Ironically, Birney's father had supported Rev. David Rice, a Presbyterian minister, in attempting to keep slavery out of Kentucky at the state's 1792 constitutional convention.

Undaunted, Birney published the first issue of the *Philanthropist* on January 1, 1836, at New Richmond, Ohio, opposite Campbell Co. He later moved the paper to Cincinnati, where an angry mob destroyed the press on July 30, 1836. Birney continued publication of a paper with widespread support among antislavery people in the northwest states. Editorially, the *Philanthropist* broke with William Lloyd Garrison's emphasis on moral persuasion and actively encouraged political action. Birney founded the Liberty Party and ran for president in 1840 and again in 1844. Most of the leading antislavery people in the nation contributed articles to the *Philanthropist.*

Northern Kentucky made its own contribution to the establishment and printing of an antislavery newspaper through **William S. Bailey**'s *Newport News,* which began publication in 1839 at Newport in Campbell Co. Editorially, Bailey was a one-man show, championing the economic interests of working-class people and claiming that slavery diminished their chances to earn decent wages. He was not at all interested in religious motivations to end slavery. As a result, abolitionists such as John G. Fee prevented the American Missionary Society from sending funds to Bailey after his newspaper press was burned out by arson. Bailey later traveled to New England and England seeking funds to restart his presses.

Some of the national antislavery newspapers found a few subscribers in Kentucky, especially in the cities; most of their influence, though, was through the antislavery societies in Ohio and Indiana. The truth was that the Kentucky educational system was so poor in quality that few yeomen could read or write. Ironically, it was the landed gentry, the slaveholders, who educated their children.

Even though Abraham Lincoln had been born in Kentucky, his candidacy for president in 1860, seen by his critics as being antislavery and anti-Southern, was immensely unpopular in Northern Kentucky. All three of the other candidates outpolled the Republican Lincoln in Kentucky. The old-line Whig constituencies tended to favor John Bell, the Constitutional Unionist from Tennessee, while the Democratic vote split in Kentucky: native-son John C. Breckinridge, the Southern Democrat, picked up the old Andrew Jacksonites, and Stephen Douglas of Illinois, the Northern Democrat, captured the national Democratic vote. Only in the urban communities of Covington and Newport did Lincoln poll respectable numbers in Northern Kentucky in the 1860 election. Just across the Ohio River, both Ohio and Indiana gave major support to the election of Abraham Lincoln and the new Republican Party ticket. Four years later in 1864, with Kentucky under military occupation, with rumors afloat that the Union Army was proposing enlistment of black slaves and freedmen, and with many Kentuckians serving in Confederate Army units, the total vote in the state was suppressed significantly. Differences within the region were exaggerated in the 1864 election. Although McClelland won Kentucky, Lincoln actually won in Kenton and Campbell counties, albeit with a suspicious and remarkable 107% of eligible voters in Campbell Co. By 1864 the overwhelming issues centered on the individual voter's support for the Union or the Confederacy as well as resentment about Kentucky's continued treatment as a hostile region under military rule. A vote in Kentucky for or against Abraham Lincoln now had more to do with current political issues; the importance of the antislavery movement in Kentucky had been eclipsed.

Bryant, James C. *Mountain Island in Owen County, Kentucky: The Settlers and Their Churches.* Owenton, Ky.: Owen Co. Historical Society, 1986.

Drummond, Dwight Lowell. *Antislavery: The Crusade for Freedom in America.* Ann Arbor: Univ. of Michigan Press, 1961.

Harrison, Lowell H. *The Antislavery Movement in Kentucky.* Lexington: Univ. of Kentucky Press, 1978.

Howard, Victor B. *The Evangelical War against Slavery and Caste: The Life and Times of John G. Fee.* Selinsgrove, Pa.: Susquehanna Univ. Press, 1996.

LaRoche, Cheryl Jenifer. "On the Edge of Freedom: Free Black Communities, Archaeology, and the Underground Railroad," PhD diss., Univ. of Maryland, 2006.

Martin, Asa Earl. "Pioneer Antislavery Press," *Missouri Valley Historical Review* 2 (March 1916): 510–28.

Nowlin, William Dudley. *Kentucky Baptist History, 1790–1922.* Louisville, Ky.: Baptist Book Concern, 1922.

Ripley, C. Peter, ed. *The Black Abolitionist Papers.* Vols. 3, 4, 5. Chapel Hill: Univ. of North Carolina Press, 1991.

Shannon, Jasper B., and Ruth McQuown. *Presidential Politics in Kentucky, 1824–1948.* Lexington: Bureau of Government Research, College of Arts and Sciences, Univ. of Kentucky, 1930.

Sparks, Elder John. *The Roots of Appalachian Christianity.* Lexington: Univ. Press of Kentucky, 2001.

Spencer, J. H. *History of Kentucky Baptists from 1769 to 1865.* Lafayette, Tenn.: Church History Research and Archives, 1976.

Tallant, Harold D. *Evil Necessity: Slavery and Political Culture in Antebellum Kentucky.* Lexington: Univ. Press of Kentucky, 2003.

Turner, Wallace B. "Abolitionism in Kentucky," *RKHS* 69 (October 1971): 319–38.

Diane Perrine Coon

APPALACHIANS. Appalachians are people from Appalachia, which is currently defined by the federal Appalachian Regional Commission (ARC) as a 200,000-square-mile region that includes 23 million people in 410 counties, encompassing all of West Virginia and parts of 12 other states: Alabama, Georgia, Kentucky, Maryland, Mississippi, New York, North Carolina, Ohio, Pennsylvania, South Carolina, Tennessee, and Virginia. The ARC definition does not include any of the 11 counties of Northern Kentucky; however, Northern Kentucky has been an important recipient of Appalachian migrants, who have enriched its cultural landscape.

Many Appalachians are descended from Scotch-Irish immigrants who came to America during the mid-1700s, mostly to the southern colonies. The Scotch-Irish were markedly different from the English lowlanders who had settled New England. They were a fierce, warlike people of traditional Norse-Gaelic society who, for generations, had populated the private armies of border lords in the northern and western sections of the British Isles. By English standards, they were considered uncouth and barbaric; the Scotch-Irish, for their part, had despised the English for centuries. Therefore, English colonists reasoned that the Scotch-Irish would make excellent buffers between the settled eastern-seaboard colonies and the **American Indians** to the west on the Appalachian frontier. The Colonial governments did whatever was necessary to induce the Scotch-Irish to settle along the Appalachian frontier.

By the 18th century, Appalachians were already a culturally and racially diverse population, as German immigrants and African Americans settled alongside American Indians and the Scotch-Irish. In the late 19th and early 20th centuries, Appalachia became even more diverse, with influxes of Mediterranean and eastern Europeans who immigrated to work in the lumber camps and the coal mines.

The Industrial Revolution of the late 19th century spurred demand for the extensive lumber, coal, and iron resources of Appalachia. Increasingly, speculators from outside the region purchased timber and mineral rights from its residents, often paying substantially less than their true value. This new absentee-owned, sometimes called neocolonial, economy subjected Appalachians to market conditions beyond their control, reduced many to the status of wage-earners, endangered coal miners by unsafe working conditions, led to erosion and defacement of the land, and fueled the development of dire poverty, now stereotypically associated with Appalachia.

Large numbers of Appalachians joined the U.S. military to fight in both world wars, and this exposure to the larger world emboldened many of them to move to industrial cities, including Covington, Newport, and Cincinnati, in search of employment. During **World War II**, the war industries of Northern Kentucky, including Newport's massive steel mills (see **Andrews Steel Mill**; **Newport Steel**), recruited workers. After the war, as oil, natural gas, and other forms of energy became more popular and as coal mining became more mechanized, unemployed miners joined their relatives in cities to take up manufacturing jobs. In the 20-year period 1940–1960, more than 7 million Appalachians left home to find jobs in industrial centers.

Initially, Appalachians took their place at the bottom of the socioeconomic ladder in Northern Kentucky. Lack of education and marketable skills prompted many to accept low-paying jobs. Housing was found in crowded, decaying inner-city neighborhoods where they lived in extended family groups, attempting to recreate the stability of their Appalachian communities. Previously established ethnic groups in Northern Kentucky did not always accept the new migrants with open arms and often failed to understand their customs. They referred to the newcomers by pejorative epithets such as "hillbilly," "cracker," "briar," or the anagram "P.I.W.A.T." (Poor, Inbred, White, Appalachian Trash).

Within the Northern Kentucky region, Appalachians settled primarily in Covington and Newport and to a lesser extent in Ludlow and Bromley in Kenton Co. and Bellevue and Dayton in Campbell Co. Since the U.S. Census does not categorize persons of Appalachian heritage, precise numbers are impossible to attain. Nonetheless, Frank J. Traina's *The Assimilation of Appalachian Migrants in Northern Kentucky*, utilizing a sample population of the 1977–1978 Northern Kentucky Quality of Life Survey, furnishes important statistics: at that time over 23 percent of the population of Boone, Campbell, and Kenton counties were either Appalachian migrants or children of Appalachian migrants, that is, second-generation Appalachians. This figure is consistent with other percentage estimates of people with generational ties to Appalachia, which range from 25–30 percent of the populations of Campbell and Kenton counties to more than 50 percent within the cities of Covington and Newport. In-migration studies of various Miami Valley towns, such as Hamilton and Middletown, Ohio, extrapolate numbers based upon employee records from companies, but there appear to be no similar studies for Northern Kentucky. In general, in-state migration has not been tracked as closely as out-of-state migration. Not surprisingly, Appalachians have been called "the Invisible Minority."

As longer-established ethnic groups, such as German Americans and Irish Americans, departed the cities of Covington and Newport for outlying suburbs, Appalachian migrants took their place. For example, after World War I, the **West End** of Newport changed demographically, as German and Irish families moved to Fort Thomas and beyond and were replaced by migrants from Appalachian Kentucky, who accepted jobs at the steel mills of Newport. Surnames like Turner from Breathitt Co. and Faulkner from Clay Co. began to dominate the area. Author **Ruth Wolff**, in her fictional account *A Crack in the Sidewalk* (1965), disguised her hometown of Newport as Brockton, while depicting a life of assimilation for her second-generation-Appalachian narrator, Linsey Templeton. Newport-born Wolff, a former schoolteacher, personally witnessed the vast extent of this migration. Since the mid-1960s, with Rev. William Neuroth's founding of the **Brighton Center**, there has been an attempt to address issues commonly confronting Newport's Appalachian migrants.

In Kenton Co., Covington's central area and West Side were neighborhoods where arriving Appalachians settled. The former Covington Community Center, now the **Center for Great Neighborhoods of Covington**, has been an important agency for the migrants. Founded in 1976, it was a merger of the outreach programs of two Covington churches, **Mother of God Catholic Church** and **Trinity Episcopal Church**.

Many Appalachians in the region say that they stopped in Northern Kentucky rather than continuing farther north because they wanted to retain their residency in the state of their birth. Some worked in Ohio, at places like the former General Motors plant in Norwood or at industries as far away as Hamilton and Middletown. They gradually acculturated into the mainstream of Northern Kentucky life.

Northern Kentuckians have also reached out to the Appalachian region itself. Over the years, churches have sent food, clothing, and volunteer laborers into Eastern Kentucky. Clothing drives were a major outreach mission of the **St. John the Evangelist Anglican Catholic Church** in Dayton, Ky., during the 1960s and 1970s, under the leadership of parishioner Joseph H. Phirman. The **Roman Catholic** Diocese of Covington was also very active in Appalachia, especially because the diocese took in 38 counties in Appalachian Kentucky until 1988, when, with the establishment of the new Diocese of Lexington, it retained only 2 counties in Appalachia. The diocese sent Newport-born Rev. **Ralph Beiting** into Appalachia, where he formed the Christian Appalachian Project, incorporated in 1964.

Since acculturation is, by definition, a two-way process, urban life has shaped Appalachian migrants as much as Appalachians have enriched the culture of Cincinnati and Northern Kentucky. The Urban Appalachian Council, founded in Cincinnati in 1974, has played an integral role in retaining and strengthening an Appalachian identity. In addition, Appalachian musicians are prominent in the local performing arts scene (see **Bluegrass**; **Country Music**).

Appalachian Regional Commission. www.arc.gov (accessed October 24, 2005).

Berlowitz, Marvin, comp. *Appalachian Migrants in Schools*. Cincinnati: DuBois Book Store, 2002.

Blethen, H. Tyler, and Curtis W. Wood Jr., eds. *Ulster and North America Transatlantic Perspectives on the Scotch-Irish*. Tuscaloosa: Univ. of Alabama Press, 1997.

Bokkon, Pauline. *Footprints in the Coal Dust*. Charleston, W.Va.: Printing Press, 1993.

Costanzo, Tina, et al., comps. *Appalachian Idea Book*. Cincinnati: Urban Appalachian Council, 1990.

Drake, Richard B. *A History of Appalachia*. Lexington: Univ. Press of Kentucky, 2001.

McWhiney, Grady. *Cracker Culture Celtic Ways in the Old South*. Tuscaloosa: Univ. of Alabama Press, 1989.

Moore, Arthur K. *The Frontier Mind*. Lexington: Univ. of Kentucky Press, 1957.

Obermiller, Phillip J., ed. *Down Home Down Town: Urban Appalachians Today*. Dubuque, Iowa: Kendall/Hunt, 1996.

Pudup, Mary Beth, Dwight B. Billings, and Altina L. Waller, eds. *Appalachia in the Making: The Mountain South in the Nineteenth Century*. Chapel Hill: Univ. of North Carolina Press, 1995.

Shackelford, Laurel, and Bill Weinberg, eds. *Our Appalachia: An Oral History*. New York: Hill and Wang, 1977.

Traina, Frank J. *The Assimilation of Appalachian Migrants in Northern Kentucky.* Cincinnati: Urban Appalachian Council, 2000.

Wagner, Thomas E., and Phillip J. Obermiller. *Valuing Our Past, Creating Our Future: The Founding of the Urban Appalachian Council.* Berea, Ky.: Berea College Press, 1999.

Karen Claiborne

ARCARO, GEORGE EDWARD "EDDIE" (b. February 16, 1916, Cincinnati, Ohio; d. November 14, 1997, Miami, Fla.). One of the most successful American jockeys of all time and one of the most famous athletes of Northern Kentucky, George Edward "Eddie" Arcaro was known as "The Master," "Old Banana Nose," and "The Greatest Rider since Paul Revere"—these were just a few of the terms of jest and admiration. He was the son of Italian immigrants Pasquale and Josephine Giancola Arcaro and was raised in both Newport and Covington, as his father frequently changed professions. Eventually, Arcaro's family owned an Italian restaurant in Erlanger. While the slender five-foot-three Arcaro was caddying golf at Highland Country Club in Fort Thomas, a horseman suggested that he should try to become a jockey. Dropping out of school at age 13, Eddie began galloping horses at the original **Latonia Racecourse** in Covington, earning 20 dollars a month and receiving little encouragement from trainers. At age 15, he rode his first race, illegally, at Bainbridge Park near Cleveland and rode in a few other races at Latonia; then he stowed away on a freight train headed to Agua Caliente Racecourse in Tijuana, Mexico, where there were few rules and a rider's age did not matter.

Arcaro lost 45 races before riding his first winner, a claiming-level (lower-level) horse named Eagle Bird, at Agua Caliente on January 14, 1932. Now 16 years old and finally able to ride legally, Eddie returned to the United States and quickly became the top apprentice at the Fair Grounds Racecourse in New Orleans. He moved to Chicago, where he was signed to his first contract by Warren Wright, owner of the powerful Calumet Farm racing stable. A contract rider for either Calumet or Greentree Stables throughout his career, Arcaro compiled an astounding riding record. In his 30-year career, from 1931 until his retirement in November 1961, Arcaro had 24,092 mounts, won 4,779 races at a winning clip of 19.8 percent, and won a record 17 Triple Crown Races (5 Kentucky Derbies, 6 Preakness Stakes, and 6 Belmonts), as well as 10 Jockey Club Gold Cups, 4 Metropolitan Handicaps, and 8 Suburban Handicaps. The only two-time winner of American horse racing's Triple Crown, first on Whirlaway in 1941 and then aboard Citation in 1948, Arcaro was the nation's leading money winner six times, received the prestigious George Woolf Memorial Jockey Award in 1953, and retired with what was, at the time, record purse earnings of $30,039,543. He was inducted into the Racing Hall of Fame in 1958.

Eddie Arcaro entering the winner's circle aboard Citation, 1948.

There were not many jockeys tougher than Eddie Arcaro. He was fearless and often fiery. In 1942, in an incident in which Arcaro knocked jockey Vincent Nodase over the racetrack's inside rail, Arcaro was called before the stewards to explain what had happened. He could have gotten off with a light suspension, since Nodase had committed the first foul. But instead of apologizing, Arcaro responded, "What I really meant to do was kill that Cuban SOB." Arcaro was suspended from riding for a year. After his retirement in 1961, Arcaro frequently served as a race expert and commentator on television. He retired to Miami, Fla., and played golf daily, sometimes joining a foursome that included baseball great Joe DiMaggio. Eddie's wife of 50 years, Ruth, died in 1988, and he remarried two years later. Arcaro died in 1997 of liver cancer; he was buried at Our Lady of Mercy Cemetery in Miami.

Arcaro, Eddie. *I Ride to Win!* New York: Greenberg, 1951.

"Man on a Horse," *Time,* May 17, 1948, 78–87.

James C. Claypool

ARCHAEOLOGY. The archaeology of Northern Kentucky involves mostly a search for information regarding the **American Indians** who lived in the region long ago. However, archaeologists also study artifacts from more recent centuries, to learn how people lived then.

Archaeology is the study of human culture through the analysis of the material remains left behind by past peoples. For virtually all of human history, most persons had no way to write down their genealogy, their religion, their history, or their culture. Archaeologists studying these aspects of life in the past must therefore rely on the interpretation of people's material remains, or material culture. Material culture includes all physical evidence, the actual things made or used by people in the past. It can take the form of artifacts, ecofacts, or features. Artifacts are items manufactured or altered by human beings, usually portable things, for example spearpoints, pottery, and clothing. Ecofacts are the items found in an archaeological context that were not manufactured by people but do indicate human activity, such as burned wood in a hearth or charred nuts or seeds. Features are complex, nonportable, artifacts such as hearths, pits, house foundations, burials, activity areas, or middens (garbage dumps). Features also include buried human remains that are found at archaeological sites; these form an important subgroup of features. They could be in burials or tombs, or the remains may have become buried in some other way after death from accidents or war or natural processes.

Archaeologists look for these kinds of material evidence at archaeological sites: places where people lived or worked and left behind physical evidence of their presence. For Indians in Northern Kentucky, the sites may have included small camps, villages, quarries, or burial mounds. For the historical period, there are rural sites such as the **Dinsmore Homestead** in Boone Co., urban sites such as the **Hemingray Glass Company** in Covington, and military sites such as those found in the **Civil War fortifications** that depict Northern Kentucky's part in the **Civil War**.

In Northern Kentucky, the documentation of archaeological sites began in the 19th century, although at that time it was not based on a systematic survey. Constantine Rafinesque, a naturalist who taught at Transylvania University in Lexington, traveled through Northern Kentucky and noted burial mounds or other Indian sites in several counties in this region, including Boone, Carroll, Gallatin, Kenton, and Pendleton. He also visited **Big Bone Lick** in Boone Co. Big Bone Lick, along Big Bone Creek, had many visitors, including noted explorers William Clark and Meriwether Lewis, Dr. **William Goforth**, and others who came to collect the famous Pleistocene fossils found there. Noted for its paleontological collections, Big Bone Lick also had attracted Indians, as had many of the other archaeological sites in the valley. **Lewis Collins** mentioned a few well-known archaeological sites in Northern Kentucky in his popular *Historical Sketches of Kentucky* (1847), including the town of Petersburg in Boone Co., which was well recognized in the 19th century as a location of Indian burials and artifacts (the town is situated over a **Fort Ancient**–period village).

Between 1928 and 1932, William S. Webb and W. D. Funkhouser of the University of Kentucky in Lexington (UK), published several books about the archaeology of the state that included significant passages on archaeological sites in Northern Kentucky. They relied heavily on reports from local artifact collectors, farmers, and other residents to document archaeological locations and types, such as mounds or village sites. By 1932 the two men had noted 75 archaeological sites in Northern Kentucky counties: 12 in Boone, 1 in Bracken, 8 in Carroll, 7 in Gallatin, 2 in Grant, 1 in Kenton, 26 in Mason, 5 in Owen, 2 in Pendleton, and 11 in Robertson. They found none in Campbell Co. Their knowledge of Mason Co., which at that time had the most known mound and village sites, was based on the work of Joseph Bernard Hoeing, who had been the state geologist of Kentucky.

Formal archaeological research in Northern Kentucky began during the **Great Depression**, as federal programs such as the Works Progress Administration (WPA) administered make-work projects, including archaeological investigations. The UK participated in this program under the direction of Webb and Funkhouser. Large-scale excavations at several important Indian mounds in Boone Co. were conducted during the late 1930s and early 1940s. Excavations in Boone Co. included the Robbins Mound, the Riley and Landing Mounds, the Hartman Mound, and the Crigler Mound. One participant in this program was a Mason Co. native named **Ellis Crawford**. Excavation of these mounds provided important information on the Adena culture, one of the Indian cultures that existed in Northern Kentucky about 500 B.C.–A.D. 200.

During the late 1940s, Crawford worked with the City of Covington to open the William Behringer Memorial Museum (now the **Behringer-Crawford Museum**) in **Devou Park**. At first, the museum housed the eclectic collections of **William Behringer**, a local builder who traveled extensively and collected curious items. His collection contained archaeological and paleontological artifacts from Northern Kentucky and southwestern Ohio. Crawford added to Behringer's collections through excavation of several Indian sites in Boone Co., including the Rogers Mound and village sites and the Gaines Mound. He documented dozens of archaeological sites, noted their locations, and obtained Kentucky site numbers for them. He accepted donations of collections from places such as the Bintz site, an important Fort Ancient village in eastern Campbell Co. that had been excavated by Howard McCord, a former army officer from Virginia.

The Behringer-Crawford Museum has continued archaeological research in Northern Kentucky but has switched its focus to historical-period sites under the supervision of archaeologist Jeannine Kreinbrink. The museum has operated archaeological field schools for junior high school students since 1981 at many Northern Kentucky sites: the Kenton Co. Courthouse, Piatts Landing, **Big Bone Lick** State Park, the Dinsmore Homestead, Maplewood Farm (see **Maplewood Children's Home**), and several private pioneer homesteads in Boone, Kenton, and Campbell counties. Ongoing Civil War research and archaeology has focused on Battery Bates in Devou Park and **Battery Hooper** in Fort Wright, both in Kenton Co.

UK has conducted several archaeological research studies in Northern Kentucky, focusing on Boone and Mason counties. They have worked at the Fort Ancient village in the town of Petersburg and at Big Bone Lick State Park and have also conducted several surveys to document additional archaeological sites in Boone Co. Other UK research projects have been conducted in Carroll and Mason counties at well-known archaeological sites such as Fox Field and the Pyles site. The University of Nebraska at Lincoln also dug at Big Bone Lick between 1962 and 1966. **Northern Kentucky University** at Highland Heights has conducted archaeological field schools in Boone and Campbell counties since the early 1970s, including digs at such sites as the Arrasmith site in Boone Co. and the Dunn Village in Campbell Co., both prehistoric Indian sites.

Cultural resource management projects have been conducted in all the Northern Kentucky counties, although some counties have seen more projects than others. These projects are conducted when federal involvement in a development project triggers compliance with the National Historic Preservation Act of 1966, a law that requires federal agencies to take into account what effect their project will have on cultural resources, whether from prehistoric Indian cultures or from the historical period. More cultural resource management projects have been undertaken in Mason and Boone counties than in the others. These projects survey, document, and investigate archaeological sites and historic buildings that may be located within their boundaries. They have provided important information on Indian lifeways and settlement patterns and on the historical settlement and development of Northern Kentucky.

One important local project was conducted in Kenton Co. in 1986. Known as the Covington Project, this urban archaeology project was supervised by Robert Genheimer, a local professional archaeologist, before the development of Second St. in Covington (see **Covington Urban Archaeology**). Urban archaeology is a special subfield of archaeology that focuses on city life and development. Studies of features such as outhouses, backyards, cellars, and cisterns provide important information about urban culture, ethnic groups, gender questions, and changes in urban life over time. This project studied and compared the archaeology of private residences, saloons, rental housing, and important industrial sites such as the **Hemingray Glass Company** and the **Bromley Pottery**, both located north of Second St. in the 19th century.

"Ancient Burial Site," *KE*, July 24, 2004, C3.
"Building on the Past," *SC*, August 1, 2004, 1.
Lewis, R. Barry. *Kentucky Archaeology*. Lexington: Univ. Press of Kentucky, 1996.
Pollack, David, ed. "The Archaeology of Kentucky: Past Accomplishments and Future Directions." Vols. 1 and 2. In *State Historic Preservation Comprehensive Plan Report No. 1*. Frankfort: Kentucky Heritage Council, 1990.
Rafferty, Janet Elizabeth. "The Development of the Ft. Ancient Tradition in Northern Kentucky," PhD diss., Univ. of Washington, 1974.

Jeannine Kreinbrink

ARCHITECTURE. See names of specific buildings, neighborhoods, cities, and architects.

ARION MÄNNERCHOR. This Newport men's singing group, named after the Greek mythological musician and poet Arion, was founded in 1883. In its time it was one of the leading German singing choirs in Northern Kentucky and Cincinnati. Other such groups included the Good Fellow Sängerchor, the Covington Leiderkranz, and the Bellevue Männerchor. The Arion Männerchor sang at many church and civic functions throughout Greater Cincinnati, but they performed mainly in Campbell Co. Over the years, they rehearsed at Phoenix Hall, Turner Hall, Eclipse Hall, Schneider's Hall, and the **Independent Order of Odd Fellows** Hall, which was at the northwest corner of Sixth and York Sts. in Newport. The organization's membership varied but usually numbered around 35. Numerous local politicians and businessmen were associate members. In 1907 the group elected Germany's Kaiser Wilhelm II as an honorary member, and in return they received a collection of music from the German consul Dr. Lettenbauer of Cincinnati.

World War I saw a reduction in the group's membership to 13. Those who remained kept the organization intact during the ensuing period of anti-German sentiment by meeting and continuing to sing together at their homes until the war ended. The membership then increased again, so that at the Arion Männerchor's golden jubilee in 1933, it had about 40 members. When **World War II** came, some of the men in the group were called into military service, and the organization gradually faded away.

"Articles of Incorporation and List of Incorporators," *KSJ*, April 27, 1886, 3.
"Sangerfest to Be Held in Newport," *KP*, January 8, 1915, 1.

Robert W. Stevie

ARNOLD, JAMES G. (b. December 10, 1792, near Paris, Ky.; d. November 16, 1876, Covington, Ky.). James Grimsley Arnold, who became a schoolteacher, a public official, a county sheriff, and a wealthy businessman, moved as young man to Washington in Mason Co., where he and his brother Willis established and conducted a school. James Arnold married Margaret Strain Daulton, sister of a mayor of Maysville. In 1817 Arnold moved to Covington, became a hotel keeper and dry-goods merchant, and taught at the public square in the town's log schoolhouse, used also for religious, court, and town trustee gatherings. In the 1840s he helped start the Covington Female Academy, one of his many educational initiatives. He served as justice of the peace in Campbell Co., as Covington tax collector, as town clerk, as postmaster (1824–1826), as city councilman, and as council president. Although he had expressed opposition to the 1840 creation of Kenton Co. out of Campbell Co., he served as Kenton Co.'s second sheriff (1842–1844). His earnings in the tobacco business grew into large real estate holdings. By 1844 Arnold had acquired one of the city's venerable mansions, at the end of W. Seventh St. The 1851 Covington map shows Arnold's name on six and one-half acres between Philadelphia St. and Willow Run Creek. After Arnold's death, the property was developed as the Arnold Homestead subdivision, which included the new Daulton (Dalton) St. As banker William Ernst had done for the Presbyterian Church, Arnold underwrote the First Christian Church and was its first elder. In 1844 he donated a lot for a new church. The present church site, dating back to 1865, honors him with a bronze plaque at the parsonage entrance. Arnold died at the home of a daughter in 1876 and was buried in Linden Grove Cemetery in Covington.

"Arnold Estate," *KP*, February 23, 1895, 4.
"The Death of James G. Arnold," *Covington Ticket*, November 17, 1876, 3.
Kenton Co. Deed Book 68, May 17, 1888, 95, 96.
Kenton Co. Property Tax Records, 1841, 1848, 1858.
Kenton Co. Will Book 2, February 5, 1867, 424.
Map of the City of Covington from Actual Survey. Rickey, Kennedy, and Clark, 1851.
Smith, Allen Webb. *Beginning at "the Point," a Documented History of Northern Kentucky and Environs, the Town of Covington in Particular, 1751–1834*. Park Hills, Ky.: Smith, 1977.

John Boh

ARNOLD, RICHARD C. (b. May 4, 1906, Squiresville, Ky.; d. October 17, 1992, Columbia, Mo.). Physician Richard C. Arnold was the son of Calvin W. and Margaret Morgan Arnold. In 1931 Arnold graduated from the University of Louisville Medical School in Louisville and was commissioned an officer in the U.S. Public Health Service (USPHS) the next year. His specialty was urology with a particular interest in venereal diseases. In 1943 he and fellow researchers Drs. John Mahoney and A. Harris demonstrated that syphilis could be successfully treated with penicillin, a discovery that brought them acclaim worldwide. Then Arnold became involved in heart research. He was an assistant surgeon general of the United States for three years. He spent 31 years with the USPHS before retiring in 1961 and moving to Columbia, Mo. He served as consultant to the United Nations and was the medical director of the Missouri Crippled Children's Service. Arnold died at his Missouri home, survived by his wife, the former Caroline Hitt, and three children.

Hobby, Gladys L. *Penicillin: Meeting the Challenge*. New Haven, Conn.: Yale Univ. Press, 1985.
Houchens, Mariam Sidebottom. *History of Owen County: "Sweet Owen."* Louisville, Ky.: Standard, 1976.
Columbia (Mo.) Daily Tribune. Obituary. October 19, 1992, 2A.

ARNOLD, WILLIAM, AND THE ARNOLD LOG HOUSE. William Arnold was the first sheriff of Grant Co. and the founder of Williamstown, the county's seat. The log house that he erected in Williamstown during the early 19th century is now a museum and a memorial to him. Arnold was born in East Jersey (now part of New Jersey) during the late 1750s. At age 16 he moved to Virginia and volunteered for service in the Virginia line during the Revolutionary War. According to family tradition, he held the rank of captain and was a personal friend of the French general the Marquis de LaFayette. Afterward, Arnold settled in Kentucky. He was commissioned a lieutenant in the Kentucky Militia and fought in the militia's Indian campaigns in northern Ohio. He married Lucy Pryor, a native Virginian, sometime after 1783, and they became the parents of at least six children.

William Arnold owned land in Bourbon, Campbell, Fayette, Mason, and Pendleton counties of Kentucky. When Pendleton Co. was formed from parts of Bracken and Campbell counties in 1798, Arnold was chosen as justice of the peace in the third district. In 1820 that district became Grant Co., and Arnold was sworn in as the county's first sheriff. The new county seat was established on two and one-half acres of land donated by Arnold, and he also donated the timber to erect the county's first building. He was instrumental in organizing the first educational facility in Williamstown, the Grant Seminary. Arnold built the county's first courthouse in Williamstown in 1822 and also set up a sawmill on his farm on High Street there. It is believed that Arnold erected his home on this farm sometime between 1799 and 1811. He used logs from huge yellow poplar trees and other hardwoods to construct a large two-story house, with a connecting kitchen. In 1824, when General Lafayette visited Kentucky, he stopped at Williamstown and had breakfast with his old friend Arnold. By the 1830s Arnold had watched the town that was named for him grow into a thriving village. He died there on November 18, 1836.

Arnold's High St. plantation was divided and passed along to several subsequent owners. In 1853 a number of rooms were added to the log house. The exterior was covered with wood siding, and plaster was used to cover the logs inside. In 1985 local historian Virgil Chandler Sr. learned of plans to remove the building. He uncovered the huge logs that make up the building's structure and determined that the house scheduled for demolition had been a part of the Arnold estate. Chandler enlisted the aid of the City of Williamstown and the Grant Co. Historical Society in a joint effort to save the house. It was carefully dismantled; each log was numbered; and then the structure was reassembled on city-owned property on Cunningham St., at the site of the Old Grant Seminary. In 1990 a memorial monument was dedicated there to the memory of William Arnold and his contributions to Grant Co. The house contains pioneer-era photographs, furniture, maps, and memorabilia of Grant Co.'s early history. It is open to the public on selected days and by appointment. The Grant Co. Historical Society coordinates the care and maintenance of the property. In spring 2007 the log house was moved again to a location on Main St. in Williamstown.

Chandler, Virgil, Sr. "William Arnold, First Sheriff of Grant County and Founder of Williamstown, Grant County, Kentucky," *NKH* 2, no. 2 (Spring–Summer 1995): 55–62.
Conrad, John B., ed. *History of Grant County*. Williamstown, Ky.: Grant Co. Historical Society, 1992.

Barbara Loomis Brown

ARNOW, HARRIETTE SIMPSON (b. July 7, 1907, Wayne Co., Ky.; d. March 21, 1986, Washtenaw Co., Mich.). Author Harriette Louise Simpson Arnow was the daughter of Elias T. and Mary Jane "Molly" Denney Simpson. She attended Berea College at Berea, Ky., for two years, taught for two years in rural Pulaski Co., and afterward graduated from the University of Louisville. She then taught for two years in the public schools of Louisville. In 1934 Harriette moved to Cincinnati and lived there and in Northern Kentucky for the next six years. These were very formative and important years for her: she gave herself to reading the classics of American and world literature (Dostoyevsky, Hardy, Tolstoy, Undset, and Zola, among others) from the Cincinnati Public Library while working at odd jobs such as waitressing and typing. She eventually began to work for the Works Progress Administration, where she met her husband, Harold B. Arnow. Before her marriage, Harriette lived for a time in Covington. At the publication of her first novel, *Mountain Path* (1936), for example, she was living at 1528 Greenup St. in Covington. She may have taken comfort in living in her native Kentucky among a large group of rural migrants like herself. Cincinnati as a destination of **Appalachians** throughout the first half of the 20th century was well known to Arnow and was surely relevant to her great migration novel, *The Dollmaker* (1954). In *Hunter's Horn* (1944), Cincinnati figures as part of Lureenie's dream of escape from the confines of the hill country. The difficulties of life for country migrants to the city are dramatically presented in these novels. Arnow is best known for her "Appalachian trilogy," *Mountain Path*, *Hunter's Horn*, and *The Dollmaker*. She is also the author of several exceptional social histories of Kentucky's Cumberland River area, including *Seedtime on the Cumberland* (1960) and *Flowering of the Cumberland* (1963). Harriette Arnow died in 1986 on her farm outside of Ann Arbor, Mich., and was buried beside her husband in the John Casada Cemetery, at Keno in Pulaski Co., Ky.

Chung, Haeja K., ed. *Harriette Simpson Arnow: Critical Essays on Her Work*. East Lansing: Michigan State Univ. Press, 1995.
"Harriette S. Arnow, 78, Author of *The Dollmaker*," *CP*, March 25, 1986, 3D.
Kleber, John E. ed. *The Kentucky Encyclopedia*. Lexington: Univ. Press of Kentucky, 1992.
Miller, Danny L. "Harriette Simpson and Harold Arnow in Cincinnati: 1934–1939," *QCH* 47, no. 2 (Summer 1989): 41–48.
Obermiller, Phillip, ed. *Down Home, Downtown: Urban Appalachians Today*. Chicago: Kent/Hunt, 1996.

Danny Miller

ART AND ARTISTS. Northern Kentucky has produced a range of artists representing nearly every major art genre, including several who attained national and international acclaim. Part of the region's success in artistic circles is due to the presence of the Art Academy of Cincinnati, which opened in 1869 as the McMicken School of Design. Northern Kentucky artists associated with the academy included **Frank Duveneck** and **Henry Farny**, both nationally acclaimed artists whose works can be found today in major collections worldwide. Others, including **Charles J. Dibowski** and **Charles McLaughlin**, trained at the Art Academy and went to work in the area as designers and decorators at places such as the Rookwood Pottery. **Clement Barnhorn**, first a student and later a sculpture instructor at the academy, never resided in Northern Kentucky, but his sculptural figures for the **Cathedral Basilica of the Assumption** in Covington became an integral part of the architecture of this important structure.

From Northern Kentucky emerged two artists-teachers who had a significant impact on the education of artists at the national level. **Thomas Anshutz**, the realist painter who followed Thomas Eakins as director of the Pennsylvania Academy, was born in Newport and lived along the Ohio River for his first 12 years. Duveneck, whose home is now a historic site, left the region as a young artist to seek training in Munich and returned after the death of his wife to an illustrious career of teaching at the Art Academy of Cincinnati. Among his students were Northern Kentuckians **Ira Cassidy**, best remembered for his works of the American Southwest, and **Dixie Selden**, a landscapist and portraitist.

Not until the mid-20th century did Northern Kentucky have its own institutions to provide arts education for its residents. The **Baker-Hunt Foundation** was formed in the 1930s by Margaretta and William Hunt, prominent Covington residents, who were left without an heir. Established to serve the region in both science and arts education, the foundation was the recipient of their collection of natural history objects, and it offered music and art classes for children. Art instruction eventually became the primary focus of the foundation. The **Carnegie Visual and Performing Arts Center** serves the community today as an art gallery, an auditorium, and a program center. The building was constructed in the early 20th century as part of the massive library project envisioned and endowed by Andrew Carnegie to build free community libraries throughout the country. In 1974, when Covington built a new library, the Carnegie was turned over to the Northern Kentucky Arts Council for conversion to an arts center.

Two of Cincinnati's major portraitists were actually Northern Kentuckians. **Frederick Eckstein** studied at the Berlin Academy of Arts and Sciences before moving to Northern Kentucky by way of Philadelphia, where he assisted in organizing the first major arts organization in the United States. He created plaster busts of early American leaders such as Henry Clay, Gen. Andrew Jackson, and William Henry Harrison. Among U.S. portraitists, in the 1830s **Aaron Corwine** of Northern Kentucky was considered second to Thomas Sully of Philadelphia. **John Wesley Venable**, also an active portraitist in Kentucky during the mid-19th century, recorded the faces of many of the local gentry and is credited as the first drawing teacher of Thomas Satterwhite Noble, the first director of the Art Academy of Cincinnati.

Much of the art activity in 19th-century Covington was centered around the growing influence of the Roman Catholic Church. With the organization of the first St. Mary's parish in 1834 and **Mother of God Catholic Church** in 1841, the need was great for altarpieces, murals, and church adornment. Thus the German Benedictine religious order under **Brother Cosmas Wolf** formed the **Covington Altar Stock Building Company** to supply the new churches with paintings and sculpture. Artists such as **Johann Schmitt**, **Wilhelm Lamprecht**, and **Wenceslaus Thien** came to Covington to work in the growing industry. This firm was active for about 10 years, beginning in 1862. The interest in church decoration continued, and the **DeJaco Brothers Company** began filling the needs of the Northern Kentucky churches in 1887. Many Northern Kentucky artists, for example Duveneck and **Leon Lippert**, started their careers with these companies or with church commissions. Two major Roman Catholic churches, one serving English-speaking Catholics (St. Mary's) and one for the German-speaking (Mother of God), brought to Covington impressive examples of revivalist architecture. These structures towered above all else in the city with their Gothic and Italian Renaissance Revival styles.

In 1852, when the **Hemingray Glass Company** was founded, the Cincinnati–Northern Kentucky area was one of the fastest-growing regions in the United States, and much of the impetus for growth can be attributed to the enormous increase in industries both large and small to serve the communities. In 1880 the Rookwood Pottery was founded by Maria Longworth Nichols in Cincinnati. It produced fine art pottery until the 1920s, when the firm shifted to producing mostly commercial ware. At this time former Rookwood employee Harold Bopp moved across the river and started **Kenton Hills Porcelains Inc.**, which made pottery sold in large department stores across the country. The 1930s brought the formation of Advertising Displays Inc., which designed and built commercial dioramas. Joseph and John Carl, skilled stone-carvers, came from their native Germany and joined the Covington Stone and Marble Company, which was responsible for much of the facade and for the gargoyles of the new **Cathedral Basilica of the Assumption**, as well as for its baptistery. The **Carl brothers** also were the major stonemasons for **St. Joseph Catholic Church**. From the demand for fine enameled art objects for the churches, as well as the market for home appliances, emerged the Woodrow Carpenter Co. in 1950. Northern Kentucky retains its prominence in the **enameling** industry today; classes are taught at the Baker–Hunt Foundation for children and adults.

Northern Kentucky's representative in the arts and crafts movement was **Kate Mosher**. Studying first under Benn Pitman, who helped to bring the craft of woodcarving to the region, Mosher exhibited her carved furniture pieces at the Philadelphia Centennial in 1876 and in the Chicago Columbian Exposition in 1893. The art pottery business was well established in the region before Maria Longworth Nichols formed the Rookwood Pottery in Cincinnati 1880. William Bromley (see **Bromley Pottery**), who operated the Brighton Pottery on Hamilton Rd. (today McMicken Ave.) in Cincinnati, expanded his pottery operation across the river and produced sanitary and kitchen wares at his Covington Pottery until 1864. **Mary Nourse** studied at the Art Academy of Cincinnati and then went to work at the Rookwood Pottery. She, like other students at the academy, learned both wood carving and pottery decoration. Northern Kentucky continues to be active in the area of ceramics with Owen Co.'s Greg Seigel, who shares his craft as a visiting artist at area schools and maintains a production studio. His wife Rebekka carries on the craft tradition by making exquisite storytelling quilts, some of which hang in national folk art collections (see **Greg and Rebekka Seigel**).

A sense of nostalgia runs through the work of Northern Kentucky artists like **Harlan Hubbard** and **Mary Bruce Sharon**. Hubbard's steamboat and river-life paintings recall an era that had long disappeared by the time he began to paint in 1929. Sharon's primitive-style paintings evoke the old South of her youth in Covington. The Beard family also played a significant role in presenting works that tell of a former era. **James Henry Beard**, the father of **Daniel Carter Beard** and **Lina and Adelia Beard**, was the best-known artist of the clan. His mid-19th-century portraits and genre paintings tell stories of immigrant families and storekeepers. His work was shown in New York City and won him a full membership at the National Academy of Design. All three of his children made contributions as book illustrators, in addition to founding girls' and boys' scouting organizations. **John James Audubon**, the famed bird painter, spent a short time in Northern Kentucky painting the cliff swallows that lived along the Licking River. Nostalgia for the past also enters the work of two artists whose reputations were made in journalism and in lithographed reproductions of their work. **Caroline Williams** made illustrations of locations around Cincinnati and Northern Kentucky for the *Cincinnati Enquirer*/***Kentucky Enquirer***, infusing her pictures with a sense of an earlier, more idealistic time. **Thomas Gaither**, a contemporary artist, found success in painting original watercolors of local subjects and locales; his works are often made into limited-edition prints.

The range of artwork from the last half of the 20th century is broad and reflects the major trends in American art during this time. **Aileen McCarthy**'s career spanned the century, first as a student of Duveneck and Barnhorn and then as an educator at **Thomas More College** in the 1950s and 1960s. **Jack Meanwell**'s abstractions are strongly influenced by the art of the abstract expressionists after **World War II**, while **Joseph Manning**'s watercolors resemble the superrealist painting of the 1980s. **Thomas Bluemlein**'s scenes of American and European landscapes also reflect a continuing interest in realism. The renewed art of quiltmaking can be seen in the work of **Jane Cochran**, who has quilts in many international collections, as well as at the National Underground Railroad Freedom Center in Cincinnati. Pop culture is also represented in our region. Comic illustrator **David Mack** has a worldwide following, especially in Japan, where his Kabuki works are highly prized.

Northern Kentucky artists of the 21st century continue to produce artwork, serve the art needs of growing businesses, and provide art education. African American artist **David Brean** began his career and training in Northern Kentucky, but his greatest contribution has been as director and teacher at the Harlem School of the Arts in New York. Northern Kentucky's educational institutions have expanded and new ones have emerged. The Baker-Hunt Foundation now serves the community with art classes for all ages, and the Carnegie Visual and Performing Arts Center also offers various community-based classes. **Darrell Brothers**, from Thomas More College's art program, taught painting and drawing to many Northern Kentucky college students for more than 27 years. **Northern Kentucky University** (NKU) and **Gateway Community and Technical College** have also developed opportunities for art education: they bring fine artist-instructors such as Barbara Houghton (NKU, photography) to the area and also offer programs in the arts that specialize in training designers in all areas of production.

Claypool, James C. "An Unassuming Painter," *Enquirer Magazine,* August 4, 1985, 8–10.
Neuhaus, Robert. *Unsuspected Genius: The Art and Life of Frank Duveneck.* San Francisco: Bedford Press, 1987.
Tenkotte, Paul A. *A Heritage of Art and Faith: Downtown Covington Churches.* Covington, Ky.: Kenton Co. Historical Society, 1986.

Rebecca Bilbo

ARTHUR, WILLIAM EVANS (b. March 3, 1825, Cincinnati, Ohio; d. May 18, 1897, Covington, Ky.). Politician and lawyer William E. Arthur was the son of William and Eliza Parsons Arthur. When he was seven years old, his family moved to Covington. He received his early education in area private schools and by a private tutor, then apprenticed law under attorneys **John White Stevenson** and **James T. Morehead** and was admitted to the bar in 1850. Arthur's first law office was set up in Covington. In 1855 he married Adeliza Southgate, daughter of **William Wright Southgate**. Adeliza died in 1858, and William married her younger sister Ethlinda in 1861. No children were born to his first wife, but a son and a daughter were born to his second one. William's son followed in his father's footsteps and became a lawyer. In 1856 William Arthur entered politics and was elected commonwealth attorney for Kentucky's Ninth District, a position he held for six years. In 1866 he was appointed a criminal judge of Kentucky's Ninth Judicial District and served in that position for two years. He served two terms as a Democrat in the U.S. House of Representatives, from 1871 until 1875, winning reelection in November 1872 in a race against **Harvey Myers Sr.** Afterward, he returned to local politics and in 1886 was elected to a six-year term as circuit court judge of Kentucky's 12th District. He then retired from politics and devoted his time to his legal practice. In 1897 he died in his Covington home at age 72 and was buried in Linden Grove Cemetery in Covington.

Biographical Encyclopedia of Kentucky. Cincinnati: J. M. Armstrong, 1878. Gov: Legislative Branch. "Arthur, William Evans (1825–1897)." www.bioguide.congress.com (accessed December 31, 2005).
The Political Graveyard. "Arthur, William Evans (1825–1897)." www.politicalgraveyard.com (accessed December 31, 2005).
Reis, Jim. "Celebrating 100 Years," *KP,* June 28, 2004, 4K.

ASBURY, FRANCIS (b. August 26, 1745, near Birmingham, England; d. March 31, 1816, Spotsylvania, Co., Va.). Francis Asbury, one of the founders of the Methodist Church in the United States, and specifically in Northern Kentucky, was the son of Joseph and Elizabeth Rogers Asbury. At age 18 Asbury was called to preach by John Wesley, the founder of Methodism. In 1771 Asbury he sailed from England to North America as a missionary, and by 1784 he was a bishop of the Methodist Episcopal Church, whose circuit or area of responsibility included Kentucky. As a Methodist bishop and circuit rider, he was directly responsible for assisting in the founding of at least two Methodist Churches in Northern Kentucky and contributing to the growth of Methodism in the state; until the mid-to-late 19th century, the Methodist denomination was the largest denomination in the commonwealth of Kentucky.

During the 1802 Great Revival, which swept Kentucky, Francis Asbury, who was nearly 58 years old at the time, stopped at Elizabeth Miles's log farmhouse on Winters Ln. in what is now Cold Spring, near the present site of the **Disabled American Veterans** national headquarters in Campbell Co. During his visit, Asbury conducted religious services. The group that worshipped at the Miles home formed the beginnings of the Asbury Methodist Episcopal Church, now the Asbury United Methodist Church in Cold Spring. In Carroll Co., Asbury held services in 1808 at the home of the widow Sarah Masterson, two miles east of present-day Carrollton. Methodists continued to meet at the **Masterson House** until 1810, when a brick church was built.

Asbury first traveled beyond the Allegheny Mountains in 1784 and rode on horseback along the Ohio River to present-day Northern Kentucky. This was a trip he made annually until 1815, the year before his death at age 71. Asbury's three-volume diary contains numerous entries relating to his adventures in early Kentucky.

As a Methodist circuit rider, Asbury was responsible not only for the spread of Christianity into the West but also for the spread of education. Asbury and other circuit riders carried books and gave them to the people to whom they preached. In addition to Bibles, riders such as Asbury were known to give families books that would help them learn to read and write. Often the homes and the churches doubled as schools during the week. For example, in 1802 the log schoolhouse in Newport was also used as a Methodist Church. Other denominations, including the Presbyterians, followed the example of Asbury and other Methodists in using circuit riders on horseback to spread Christianity. In 1816 Asbury died in Virginia and was buried at the Mount Olivet Cemetery in Baltimore, Md.

"Asbury Visited Cold Spring in 1802," *KP,* April 8, 2002, 4K.
Posey, Walter B., ed. "Kentucky as Seen by Bishop Francis Asbury," *FCHQ* 31 (1957): 333–48.
"Two Centuries of Faith—Asbury Methodist Served Cold Spring Beginning in 1802," *KP,* April 8, 2002, 4K.
Whitehouse, Jack. "Asbury United Methodist Church History," 2002, Asbury United Methodist Church, Cold Spring, Ky.

Paul L. Whalen

ASBURY UNITED METHODIST CHURCH. Campbell Co.'s Asbury United Methodist Church is the oldest Methodist church in continuous operation in Northern Kentucky and one of the oldest Methodist churches in Kentucky. During spring 1802, pioneer Methodist bishop **Francis Asbury** preached at the log home of the Miles family on what is now Winters Ln. in Cold Spring. It was after this visit by Asbury that a new Methodist church was organized under the leadership of Rev. Jarvis Taylor, along with Mrs. John Harrison, Elizabeth Miles, Stacey Reeves, and Delilah Travers. After meeting in the Miles home for a time, the church met in a nearby schoolhouse, and in 1812 a log church was built on the Miles property, later known as the Ed Payne Farm and now the national headquarters of the **Disabled American Veterans**. By 1837 the log church had begun to decay. With the generosity of James Dickerson, a new church was built on the present-day site of the Asbury Church in Cold Spring on Alexandria Pk. (**U.S. 27**) and John's Hill Rd. In 1838 a Sunday school was established. In 1846 the church built its first parsonage. The present parsonage located at 19 Orchard Ln. in Cold Spring was built on land donated by Melvin and Thelma Boden. The cemetery behind the present sanctuary of the church does not belong to the church. In March 1854, Charles W. Horner, Elijah Pierce, and Benjamin Smith incorporated the Asbury Chapel Cemetery Association. It is believed that these men were members of the church.

During the **Civil War**, raiding parties from both sides of the war passed by the church along Alexandria Pk., but none of the raiding parties caused any damage to the church building. In 1861 the church membership was 220. In 1862 an Annual Conference of the Methodist Church was held at the church, with Bishop Levi Scott officiating. At that time the local church commissioned its first missionaries, who were sent to Ohio. On Tuesdays during the 1860s, the Baptists allowed the Methodists from Asbury Methodist Episcopal Church to use their brick meeting house on the fourth Tuesday of the month. In 1877 the Cold Spring Baptist Church met at the Asbury Methodist Church until the Baptist congregation finalized plans for their building.

In 1883 a beautiful new church building was built to replace the log church built in 1837. It was constructed on the site where the present (2006) education building now stands. This land had been donated to the church in 1842 by Samuel and Mary Winston. The new Asbury Methodist Chapel was dedicated on November 11, 1883, during three services in which the featured speaker was Rev. E. T. Curnick of Grace Methodist Church in Newport (see **Grace United Methodist Church**). The new structure, costing $2,800, was described as Gothic in style. It was 30 feet wide, rose 22 feet from floor to ceiling, and had a classroom in the rear of the church. This building served as the church for 72 years and then as the Sunday school building for 17 years, until 1972.

On September 4, 1911, the Asbury Methodist Episcopal Church celebrated the Centennial Anniversary of its first permanent church building, built in 1812.

Around the turn of the 20th century, the membership of the Asbury Methodist Episcopal Church had fallen below 100 members. As a result, the church had to share a minister with the Southgate Methodist Church until 1927, since it could not support a minister by itself.

The Asbury Methodist Church held a Homecoming Celebration on September 10, 1934, that featured the unveiling of a bronze plaque honoring Methodist bishop Francis Asbury and commemorating the sesquicentennial of Methodism in America. Plaques like this were presented only to churches founded by Asbury. The plaque, which hangs in the vestibule of the sanctuary, has a raised surface depicting Asbury on horseback and represents the Asbury statue unveiled earlier in Washington, D.C., by President Calvin Coolidge (1923–1929).

After 118 years in existence, the Asbury Methodist Episcopal Church acquired its first organ, which was built by Johann Heinrich Köhnken and Gallus Grimm in 1930. The organ was rebuilt in 1972 after being stored for 17 years and today is used every Sunday.

On Sunday, April 5, 1936, Asbury Chapel (as the church was then known) dedicated its education building. The featured speaker at the dedication celebration was Kentucky governor A. B. "Happy" Chandler (1935–1939 and 1955–1959).

The construction of the present sanctuary began in January 1955, next to the existing church, while Rev. Thomas Ditto was the pastor. The cornerstone was laid on July 10, 1955, and the sanctuary formally opened on November 13, 1955. On July 22, 1973, the cornerstone was laid for a new education building, which was built on the site of the 1883 Asbury Chapel. The bell from the old church building is installed on top of that education building. Glass from the old church building was also preserved and installed in various windows throughout the church complex.

Asbury United Methodist Church celebrated 200 years of holding Sunday school on July 20, 1980. The church's Sunday school program was nominated as one of the 12 best in Kentucky that year. In 1999 the church embarked upon a major improvement program that included the purchase of property along John's Hill Rd. for parking and future expansion. Beginning the week of April 21, 2002, the Asbury United Methodist Church had its 200th Anniversary Celebration. Bishop James King preached at the Sunday services. During the week, many former ministers preached, including Rev. Don McKinney, Rev. Ron Berry, Rev. Paul Stoneking, Rev. Tom Ditto, and Rev. Robert Pugh.

Asbury United Methodist Church has engaged in interdenominational outreach in Northern Kentucky. It is currently a host church for the Interfaith Hospitality Network (see **Northern Kentucky Interfaith Commission**). The church presently has more than 600 members.

"Two Centuries of Faith—Asbury Methodist Served Cold Spring Beginning in 1802," *KP*, April 8, 2002, 4K.

Whitehouse, Jack. "Asbury United Methodist Church History," 2002, Asbury United Methodist Church, Cold Spring, Ky.

Paul L. Whalen

ASHLAND INC. Ashland Inc. celebrated its 75th anniversary in 1999, the same year it established its new headquarters in Covington. This Fortune 500 company's relocation to Northern Kentucky allowed it to maintain its roots in the state while moving closer to the company's operations in Cincinnati. Ashland Inc., founded in 1924 as Ashland Refining Company, has operations throughout the United States and in 120 countries. These include the four wholly owned divisions: Ashland Paving and Construction, Valvoline, and the two new divisions formed in 1999, Ashland Distributions Company and Ashland Specialty Chemical Company. In 2005 the worldwide, multi-industry company had operating sales of $9.3 billion.

As a regional refiner and marketer of petroleum products for the Swiss Oil Company of Lexington, Ashland Refining Company quickly became a success under the direction of general manager Paul Blazer. By 1930 the Swiss Oil Company had acquired Tri-State Refining Company and increased the production capacity of its refinery in Catlettsburg to 5,500 barrels per day. Under Blazer's leadership, Ashland Refining Company merged with its parent company, Swiss Oil, in 1936 to form Ashland Oil and Refining Company. During **World War II** the company built an aviation gasoline plant near the Catlettsburg refinery that became Ashland's number two refinery. In 1946 products were sold for the first time under the brand name Ashland. Over the years, the company expanded its product capacity and broadened its marketing base through a series of acquisitions and mergers. The 1949 purchase of Valvoline brought Ashland Inc. its third refinery. In 1966 the acquisition of Warren Brothers, one of the nation's largest paving contractors, brought expansion into highway construction and construction materials. In 1967, with the purchase of ADM Chemical Group, Ashland created Ashland Chemical and consolidated its chemical manufacturing and sales operations; the following year the company's sales surpassed $1 billion. The company name was changed to Ashland Oil Inc. in 1970. In that same year, SuperAmerica, a retail chain of gas stations, was acquired. Ashland Oil Inc. continued to expand through acquisitions and mergers, and in 1991 it tripled its crude-oil collection capacity when it merged with the Scurlock Oil Company and purchased the Permian Corporation. The company changed its name again in 1995 to Ashland Inc., to reflect the diverse nature of its business. As a global company, Ashland Inc. began construction of its first manufacturing plan in China in February 1999. With the move of the company's headquarters to Northern Kentucky, Ashland Inc. donated a portion of its 160-acre office campus in Ashland, Ky., to a charitable foundation, dedicated to community development in attracting new job growth. In 2005 the company sold its interest in Marathon Ashland Petroleum LLC to Marathon. Subsequently, Ashland's 81-year history of petroleum refining ended, and now it concentrates in the areas of chemicals and transportation construction.

Ashland. www.ashland.com (accessed April 14, 2006).

"Ashland to Move HQ to Covington," *Business Courier Journal*, July 20, 1998, 1, available at www.bizjournals.com (accessed April 14, 2006).

Massie, Joseph L. *Blazer and Ashland Oil: A Study in Management*. Lexington: Univ. of Kentucky Press, 1960.

Rodengen, Jeffrey L. *New Horizons: The Story of Ashland, Inc.* Lexington, Ky.: Write Stuff Enterprises, 1998.

Scott, Otto J. *The Exception: The Story of Ashland Oil and Refining Company*. Lexington, Ky.: McGraw-Hill, 1968.

Gabrielle Summe

ASIAN AMERICANS. In contrast to the thousands of European immigrants who arrived in Northern Kentucky in the 19th and early 20th centuries, immigrants from Asia were few in number and during that period were often viewed as curiosities by local residents. In the latter part of the 19th century, Chinese immigrants began arriving in the region. Many of them found homes and opened small businesses in Covington, and some others settled in Newport. Covington once had the largest Chinese population in the commonwealth of Kentucky. Another group of Asians came much later: after the fall of Saigon, Vietnam, in 1975, a small number of Vietnamese immigrants made Northern Kentucky their home.

Chinese people first began immigrating to the United States in large numbers in the middle of the 19th century. They came to this country primarily for economic reasons, and most of them settled in the western states, where jobs, especially in the building of railroads, were plentiful. By 1880, 25 percent of California's workforce was of Chinese descent. The overwhelming majority of these immigrants were male laborers.

Chinese Americans faced racial prejudice in this country. Their different styles of clothing, food, language, and customs set them apart from other Americans. In 1882 the U.S. Congress passed the Chinese Exclusion Act, preventing citizens of China from entering the country. The Chinese Americans who were already in the country were not forced to leave; however, they were forbidden to apply for naturalization. The Chinese Exclusion Act was the first legislation in U.S. history that barred an entire ethnic group from immigrating to this country.

The earliest mention of Chinese in Covington appears in the *Ticket* newspaper in 1877 in an article about the marriage of John Naw Lin, a Chinese American, and Mary Ann Morgan, who was of African American descent. Chinese Americans rarely received any attention in the local press, except for the celebration of the Chinese New Year. Reporters often covered the celebrations using stereotypical language.

In 1913 the 14-year-old Pong Dock, an American-born citizen of Chinese descent, registered to attend the Covington Public Schools, causing a minor furor in the city. Some Covington residents claimed that the boy should attend the African American School in Covington because he was not of European ancestry. The *Kentucky Post* and the *Kentucky Times-Star* both ran articles about the boy and the controversy concerning his education. Eventually, the issue was turned over to the Kentucky attorney general, M. Logan, who determined that the superintendent of the Covington Public Schools could choose which school the boy should attend. Pong Dock was permitted to attend Covington's First District School on Scott St. He began the first grade in September 1913. Other Chinese American children attended classes at a special Chinese-language program at St. Xavier Catholic School in Cincinnati. One of these children was Lily Wong, who was five years old in 1929. Her father operated a Chinese restaurant in Covington at the corner of Madison Ave. and Pike St. Lily was bilingual and thus was able to act as an interpreter at her father's restaurant. Another educational opportunity available to Chinese Americans was Bible lessons offered by the Covington **YMCA**.

Most Chinese Americans in Covington operated laundries. By 1880 one Chinese laundry had already been established at 519 Madison Ave. By 1897, 6 of the 11 laundries in Covington were operated by Chinese Americans. In 1910, 8 Chinese laundries were in operation, 1 on Pike St. and 7 along Madison Ave. The number of Chinese laundries remained stable in the years between 1900 and 1945, ranging between five and eight. The last Chinese laundries appear in the Covington City Directory in the late 1940s.

The U.S. Censuses for 1900 and 1910 shed much light on the lives of Chinese Americans in Covington. All were males and most were single (if they were married, their spouses were not living in Covington). The average age was between 35 and 40. A majority of the Chinese Americans had been born in China; all who were natives of the United States had been born in California. A significant number were able to speak English.

Vietnamese immigrants began arriving in Northern Kentucky during the 1970s. At the time of the fall of Saigon in 1975, the Diocese of Covington's Catholic Social Service Bureau began the Vietnamese Refugee Resettlement Program, which brought 30 Vietnamese refugees to Northern Kentucky. These individuals were all part of the extended family of Rev. Thomas Vu Minh Thai. Initially, the group was housed in **Mount St. Martin** in Newport. Mount St. Martin was owned by the **Sisters of Divine Providence** and was the religious order's original motherhouse. Rev. Raymond Nieman of the Covington Diocese spearheaded the relocation efforts in cooperation with Catholic Social Services.

In recent years, an increasing number of Japanese people have arrived in Northern Kentucky, since the **Toyota North America** headquarters has been located in Boone Co. and the company's manufacturing plant is just south of the Northern Kentucky region in Georgetown. As a result, new Asian-cuisine restaurants are appearing, as are English-language classes for Japanese children and adults.

"Covington Chinaman Is Waiting for Centennial," *KP*, August 19, 1914, 4.
Covington City Directories, 1880–1948.
"Enters Now a Chinese Beauty to Be Haled as World's Perfect Woman," *KP*, September 13, 1913, 1.
"Great Joy among Chinese," *KP*, April 21, 1905, 1.
"Little Chinese Boy Is Given Chance in Covington School; How to Teach Him Is a Puzzle," *KTS*, September 19, 1913, 20.
"Little Lilly Entertains Papa's Customers," *KP*, October 28, 1929, 1.
"A Novel Marriage," *Covington Ticket*, September 18, 1877, 3.
"Play Ping Pong with Pong Case," *KP*, September 24, 1914, 1.
"Queer," *KP*, February 16, 1904, 1.

David E. Schroeder

ASMAN, HENRY BERNARD, JR., "BUB" (b. August 17, 1949, Louisville, Ky.). Henry Bernard Asman Jr., an award-winning sound editor, is the son of Harriet McIntyre and Dr. Henry Bernard Asman Sr. He graduated from St. Xavier High School in Louisville in 1967 and received a BA in telecommunications from the University of Kentucky in Lexington in 1971, then relocated to Los Angeles to begin a career in sound editing.

Asman won an Oscar in 2007 at the 79th Academy Awards ceremony for his work as a sound editor on Clint Eastwood's movie *Letters from Iwo Jima;* he was also nominated in the same category for Eastwood's *Flags of Our Fathers.* Previous Oscar nominations by the Academy acknowledged Asman's sound editing for Arnold Schwarzenegger's film *Eraser* in 1997 and for Eastwood's *Space Cowboys* in 2001. Asman has served as a sound editor and supervising sound editor for more than 50 motion pictures. His credits include *The Legend of Zorro, Million Dollar Baby, Mystic River, Lara Croft: Tomb Raider, Midnight in the Garden of Good and Evil, The Bridges of Madison County, Die Hard 2, Lethal Weapon 2,* and *The Postman Always Rings Twice.*

Asman and his wife, the former Jacquelyn Chism, moved to Northern Kentucky in 1984 to begin raising their two sons in Fort Wright. Asman now lives in Union. Both of his brothers, William L. Asman and John B. Asman, pursued careers in the television and motion picture industry, William as a camera operator and cinematographer and John as a sound rerecording mixer.

Asman, Henry Bernard "Bub," Jr. Telephone interview by Ron Ellis, March 8, 2007.

Ron Ellis

ASPEN GROVE/SUN VALLEY. The two small towns of Aspen Grove and Sun Valley are adjacent in south-central Campbell Co. along **U.S. 27**. Aspen Grove is a small rural community of family farms and a few buildings. The Aspen Grove Elementary School, which operated from 1871 to 1936, was a one-room structure and the source of the community's name. The local 1883 Lake atlas shows the school, at that time called the Flatwoods School, and a cooper shop and a few residences. Today, Aspen Grove is home to the Aspen Grove Ministries (also known as the Aspen Grove Pilgrim Holiness Church), which dates back to about 1900. There are also three other organizations with buildings at Aspen Grove: Lake Clariola, the Campbell Co. Game and Fish Sportsmen's Club building, and a clubhouse and a lake owned by the **Knights of Columbus**. All are located on Licking Pk., just west of U.S. 27. The John W. Reiley School, formerly South School, is also there along U.S. 27.

Sun Valley, also known as Slopptown, is at the intersection of Licking Pk., U.S. 27, and Race Track Rd. The nickname Slopptown is a reference to the many pig farms earlier found there. Legend has it that a county official, wanting to buy land and build a home nearby, wanted a better name for the community. This person reportedly used his influence to change the name to Sun Valley. Always a city dwellers' retreat area, Sun Valley has had stores, roadside motels, campgrounds, and fishing lakes (such as Bartlett's Lake) since long before expressways were built in the vicinity.

One of these former motel sites is where Main St. Baptist Church of Alexandria has recently moved. Several subdivisions have started, and the Southern Campbell Fire Department has a new facility on Race Track Rd. The Fire Department began in a building along U.S. 27, but this firehouse was taken by the highway expansion. Race Track Rd. derives its name from a short-lived horse-racing track that was once on the grounds of **A. J. Jolly** County Park. The park began in 1961 as the Campbell Co. Park and was renamed for a former county judge executive. At 600 acres, it is one of the largest county-owned parks in the state. Sun Valley has the potential for much growth and quite likely will become more of a bedroom community in the near future.

An Atlas of Boone, Kenton, and Campbell Counties, Kentucky. Philadelphia: D. J. Lake, 1883.
Campbell Co. Historical Society. *Campbell County, Kentucky, 200 Years, 1794–1994.* Alexandria, Ky.: Campbell Co. Historical Society, 1994.

Kenneth A. Reis

ASSUMPTION OF THE BLESSED VIRGIN MARY CATHOLIC CHURCH. The small village of Mullins Station, along the **Kentucky Central Railroad**, was home to the first Catholic church in the Morning View area of southern Kenton Co. The small log church was built by the Benedictine Fathers of the St. Joseph Priory (see **St. Joseph Catholic Church**) in Covington in the late 1860s and named St. Benedict. The Benedictines relinquished care of the church in 1873, at which time a priest of the Diocese of Covington (see **Roman Catholics**), Rev. Charles Excel, was appointed its first resident pastor. In the early 1880s, the parish started a small school that operated until 1901. It closed because it was never able to establish a viable enrollment. The original log church was replaced in 1886 by a new structure, and the parish was renamed Assumption of the Blessed Virgin Mary. The church is usually referred to as St. Mary.

The parish acquired new property near Morning View Station and built a frame church and a priest's house on a hilltop. This church, complete with a mural by local artist **Johann Schmitt**, remains, but the house, along with many parish records, burned in 1917. In 1908 Covington bishop **Camillus P. Maes** created St. Matthew Catholic Church in White Villa (now known as Kenton) as a mission to St. Mary. By the 1950s, St. Matthew Church had grown enough that parishioners constructed a school, which was staffed by the **Sisters of Divine Providence**, who resided in a convent within the same building. With the new school and with population growing more in Kenton than in Morning View, the status of the two churches was reversed in 1955: St. Matthew Church was made the parish and St. Mary its mission. St. Matthew Church's school closed in 1969 because the sisters could no long staff it.

After the school closed, the building was no longer needed for classrooms or living quarters for the sisters. St. Matthew Church's pastor, Rev. Henry Haacke, turned the former convent into a rectory and in 1975 took up residence at St. Matthew Church instead of St. Mary. In 1975 he decided to close and demolish the old St. Matthew Church and convert the former classrooms into a place of worship. St. Mary has remained open as a mission of St. Matthew Church, though it is used only in the summer; it lacks heating, and the road up the hill is sometimes icy in winter. Some parishioners attempted in the 1970s and 1980s to place St. Mary on the National Register of Historic Places, hoping that this designation would prevent future destruction of the church, but their efforts were unsuccessful.

Bach, Jean. "Families Keep 125-Year-Old Parish Alive," *Messenger*, August 5, 1994, 20.

Beaver, Susan. "Holy Cause: Man, 18, and Woman, 83, Are Working to Preserve Their Church," *KP*, July 2, 1983, 6K.

Messenger, May 29, 1955, 13A.

Ryan, Paul E. *History of the Diocese of Covington, Kentucky*. Covington, Ky.: Diocese of Covington, 1954.

Shroeder, David E. "Jubilee Cross Visits St. Matthew and St. Mary," *Messenger*, July 28, 2000, 7.

Thomas S. Ward

ATHEY, ROBERT (b. December 19, 1825, Lexington, Ky.; d. April 17, 1901, Covington, Ky.). Robert A. Athey was born and raised in Lexington, where, after studying law at Transylvania University, he was admitted to the Fayette Co. Bar Association. In 1850, he was elected to the Kentucky House of Representatives. He moved to Covington in about 1855 and became a prominent figure in local politics. In 1862 he was elected U.S. commissioner; his duties were to serve as paymaster for local Home Guard troops during the **Civil War** and to act as a federal judge. Athey secured nomination as Kenton Co. attorney following his attendance at an **antislavery** convention in Independence in 1864. After the war he was elected a Kenton Co. commissioner, a position he held for two years. Athey formed a legal partnership with **John Finnell**, and they set up offices in Covington at 323 Scott St. He was Covington city attorney (1866, 1867, and 1871). He served as mayor of Covington from 1874 to 1890. Near the end of his mayoral term, a street in Covington was named in his honor. Athey married twice and had a daughter by his first wife and three daughters and one son by his second wife, Kate Stephens Athey. His only son, Paul, died unexpectedly at age three.

A group of Athey's friends in 1883 presented to him a handmade walking cane that was carved from an oak tree located near the courthouse in Lexington. In 1890 he was elected Covington police judge, and he held that position until 1897. Athey died in 1901 at age 75, while living at the Woodford Flats in Covington and was buried in the Highland Cemetery in Fort Mitchell.

Biographical Encyclopedia of Kentucky. Cincinnati: J. M. Armstrong, 1878.

Johnson, W. A. "Judge Athey Is Dead," *KP*, April 18, 1901, 1.

Reis, Jim. "Street Honors Popular Mayor," *KP*, June 7, 1999, 4K.

ATWOOD, LEE (b. October 6, 1904, Walton, Ky.; d. March 5, 1999, Santa Monica, Calif.). Aeronautical engineer and CEO John Leland "Lee" Atwood left Northern Kentucky at a young age. He attended Wayland College in Plainview, Tex., and studied engineering at the University of Texas at Austin. He worked for the Douglas Aircraft Company in Santa Monica, Calif., before joining North American Aviation in 1934 as chief engineer; he became a vice president the following year. He was associated with North American until 1967, serving as president, CEO, and chairman of the board; after merging the company with Rockwell Standard, he served North American Rockwell as president and CEO until his retirement in 1971.

Under his leadership the following aircraft were developed: T-6 Texan, B-25 Mitchell, P-51 Mustang, F-86 Sabre, F-100 Super Sabre, X-15, XB-70, and the B-1 Bomber. He also led North American Rockwell into the manufacturing of space capsules. Upon his death in 1999, a British aviation and space writer wrote that no one individual had shaped the face of the British air force more than Lee Atwood. In 1954 Atwood was elected president of the Institute of Aeronautical Sciences, and in 1984 he was named to the International Aerospace Hall of Fame.

"Boone Man Is Honored," *KTS*, January 12, 1954, 3A.

Gunston, Bill. "Obituary," *Independent (London)*, April 3, 1999, available at http://FindArticles.com (accessed November 9, 2007).

AUDUBON, JOHN JAMES (b. April 26, 1785, Les Cayes, Haiti; d. January 27, 1851, New York City). America's foremost ornithologist and illustrator of birds, John James Audubon, was the illegitimate son of Jeanne Rabbine, a Santo Domingo chambermaid and mistress to the French sea captain and slave trader Jean Audubon. John's mother died when he was about six months old, and his father and his father's wife, Anne Moynette Audubon, adopted John. The name John James Audubon is a later Americanized version of the name, Jean-Jacques Fougère Audubon, that the Audubons gave him. Audubon grew up in France, where he received little formal education; he attended a military academy, however, and briefly studied art under Jacques-Louis David in Paris. Audubon immigrated to the United States in 1803, to manage his father's estate, Mill Grove, at Norristown, Pa.

In 1808 Audubon married Lucy Green Bakewell (see **Bakewell Family**), who lived on an adjoining Norristown farm. Historian John Burns reports that Audubon and his wife lived in Covington, Ky., for a short time with her brother, Thomas Woodhouse Bakewell. The Audubons and the Bakewells moved to Louisville later in 1808, where they operated a mercantile business for about two years. The partners moved the business to Henderson in 1810, but it eventually failed. One of the reasons the business failed was that Audubon spent too much time with his avocation, birdwatching. Audubon served time in a debtor's prison but was freed after filing for bankruptcy. In 1819 he moved to Cincinnati and was employed as a taxidermist with the new **Daniel Drake** Western Museum. While there, Audubon studied and painted cliff swallows living in the Licking River valley. He kept his taxidermist position for about a year and then traveled down the Ohio and Mississippi rivers to New Orleans, studying birds along the way. From 1823 to 1828, he and his wife supported themselves by operating a private school for girls at West Feliciana Parish, La.

In his later years, Audubon compiled several books of his nature studies: a five-volume set, *The Birds of America* (1827–1838); *Synopsis of Birds of North America* (1839), which cataloged all his birds; and a three-volume set, *The Viviparous Quadrupeds of America* (1846–1854). These books and the tales he told about his adventures in the American frontier brought him worldwide fame and prosperity.

He lived his later years in his New York City home called Minnie's Land, along the Hudson River, where Audubon Park is now located. Audubon died at age 65 and was buried in the Trinity Church Cemetery in Manhattan, N.Y.

The Audubon name is carried by four streets in Northern Kentucky: Audubon Rd. and Audubon Ln. in Park Hills, near **Devou Park**; Audubon Pl. in Fort Thomas; and Audubon Ct. in Florence. There is also a statue honoring Audubon, along Riverside Dr. near downtown Covington.

Answers.com. "John J. Audubon." www.answers.com (accessed March 27, 2007).

Burns, John E. *A History of Covington, Kentucky, through 1865*. 6 vols. Covington, Ky.: Self-published, 1986.

Keating, L. Clark. *Audubon: The Kentucky Years.* Lexington: Univ. of Kentucky Press, 1976.

Kleber, John E. ed. *The Kentucky Encyclopedia.* Lexington: Univ. Press of Kentucky, 1992.

Jack Wessling

AUGUSTA. Augusta, the former county seat of Bracken Co., is situated at the convergence of the Ohio River and Bracken Creek at the intersection of Ky. Rt. 8 (**Mary Ingles Highway**) and Ky. Rt. 19, about 42 miles east of Cincinnati. The Ohio River flows along the north city limit, with no bends for nine miles and without the obstruction of a floodwall, creating a truly outstanding view, one that has been used in several Hollywood movies. The name of the town may have originated with its founder, Capt. **Philip Buckner**, in honor of his former home, Augusta Co., Va. At Buckner's behest, a meeting was held and town trustees were chosen, and then Buckner deeded over to them the 600 acres on which the city is located. Parts of this land were then parceled and sold as lots in 1795. Two years later, on October 2, 1797, the Kentucky legislature issued the town its charter.

Augusta was the seat of government in Bracken Co.; a courthouse was constructed in 1803 on the public square at Third and Park Sts. This site served as the county's seat until the late 1830s, when the county government was moved to Brooksville. Between 1840 and 1904, the county's first courthouse served as the Augusta community hall, hosting many amateur plays and providing the town with a forum site for speeches delivered by several noted orators.

The first school in Augusta was a private one begun in 1795 by Robert Schoolfield. It met in a two-story log cabin at 211 Riverside Dr. that remains in excellent condition. Later, private schools were operated by a Professor Bricket, a Mr. Henderson, Richard Keene, Richard Mitchell, and Z. Harmon; Harmon advertised a school for ladies and gentlemen in Buckner's home. The town's leaders established Bracken Academy in 1798, and the state awarded it a charter and a grant of land in 1799. The academy built several buildings, including a classroom on the southeast corner of Third and Elizabeth Sts.; the brick dormitory remains standing today and is used as a private residence. The trustees of the academy were named Armstrong, Blanchard, Boude, Brooks, Buckner, Davis, Fee, Logan, Marshall, Patterson, Patti, and Wells. Bracken Academy merged in 1822 with **Augusta College**, which received its charter from the Kentucky legislature that year and was fully operational by 1825. The conferences of the Methodist Church of Ohio and of Kentucky sponsored Augusta College. Governed overall by America's Methodist Episcopal Church, Augusta College was the first Methodist college in Kentucky and only the third in the United States. The original building was 80 by 40 feet, three stories high, and had 15 rooms, including a chapel, a lecture hall, and the library.

The Presbyterian congregation in Augusta began in 1803. Arthur Thome built its first church building in 1815–1818 on land at E. Main at Third that he had donated. The current **Augusta Presbyterian Church** on Fourth St. was built in 1879. The second church in Augusta was the Methodist Episcopal Church, initially a log structure built by James Armstrong around 1817 at Riverside and Bracken Sts.; that building was replaced in the 1830s by the current stucco-covered structure at 222 Riverside. The **Augusta Christian Church** was organized on March 14, 1840, and its original brick meetinghouse was at 311 Bracken; in 1888 the current church on Fourth St. was erected. The old church building on the corner of southeast Third and Bracken Sts. was used for the first Baptist Church established in Augusta, which was pastored at its beginning by J. F. Felix. The present Baptist church building was erected on Fourth St. in 1893. Augusta's **St. Augustine Catholic Church** was formed in 1859. The St. Paul Methodist Episcopal Church, formerly known as the Methodist Episcopal Church, was moved to its new location on Frankfort and Second Sts. on September 11, 1894. Its first pastor was Rev. McDade. The Nazarene Church began in 1924, with O. E. Shelton as its pastor. In June 1925 the Nazarene Church began holding services in a new building on Park St.; the current site of this church is on W. Fourth St.

The family archives of **Stephen Collins Foster**, who composed the song "My Old Kentucky Home" and many others, indicate that Foster visited Augusta and stayed with his uncles, Dr. John Tomlinson and Dr. Joseph S. Tomlinson, president of Augusta College. A historical highway marker located in the city notes the town's influence upon Foster's later compositions. In particular, the "old Negro church on the hill," in Augusta's west side, was said to have been where Foster heard the harmonious sounds that later inspired him to incorporate similar melody lines into his famous spirituals.

The publishing of newspapers in Augusta was an excellent funding supplement to the academies, the churches, and even the college in Augusta. The earliest newspapers printed in Augusta were the *Augusta Whig* and the *Colonizationist and Literary Journal,* published by J. S. Power in 1818, and the *Bracken Sentinel,* printed in 1820, copies of which are contained in files at the Bracken Co. Historical Society. The next paper to serve Augusta was the *Western Watchman,* edited by H. H. Kavanaugh and published by James Armstrong in 1822. In 1825 the *Augusta Chronicle* appeared in print; the *Augusta Herald* was next, in 1827, printed by John Wood. Both of these papers were supported directly by Augusta College. Later, the *Bracken Chronicle,* the *Augusta Independent,* and the *Augusta Times* were printed and circulated in town.

Ferries have provided service from Augusta across the Ohio River continuously since April 2, 1798. The land used by the first ferry was initially owned by John Jenkins. On April 3, 1798, John Blanchard and John Boude paid 50 pounds for the right to have a ferry at Augusta, under John Boude's management. At one time Augusta College operated this ferry service and received a large portion of the revenues from it. Several different ferry services have been conducted over the years, and currently two ferry boats, the *Ole Augusta* and the *Jenny Ann,* remain in daily operation under the auspices of the Augusta Ferry Authority Inc. In former times there were palatial steamboats docking at Augusta with many hogsheads of New Orleans sugar cane, molasses, and sorghum in barrels to be purchased for resale by local merchants.

In its early history, Augusta was a popular port where settlers brought products such as hemp, livestock, tobacco, and wine for shipment on the river. Between 1820 and 1850, settlers from the Rhineland

The Beehive Tavern, W. Riverside Dr., Augusta.

of Germany arrived in Augusta and helped to establish a thriving **viniculture** and wine industry. Sometime before 1860, three German craftsmen, named Federer, Stievater, and Schweitzer, constructed for Abraham Baker an imposing stone winery 40 by 100 feet. This edifice remains at the junction of Ky. Rt. 19 and Ky. Rt. 8 and is currently being renovated. There was a time when the wine production of the Baker and Bradford wineries rivaled that of the larger wineries in Cincinnati, but eventually most of the region's vineyards were destroyed by blight.

Before the **Civil War**, Augusta was a noted center of **abolitionists** (see **Underground Railroad, Bracken Co.**). Debates among the students at Augusta College concerning the "peculiar institution" of slavery were held regularly. Among the college's noted students opposing slavery were Rev. **John G. Fee**, founder of Berea College, and Rev. **James Armstrong Thome**, who became a professor of belles lettres at Oberlin College in Oberlin, Ohio.

On September 27, 1862, Confederate lieutenant colonel Basil Duke led seven companies of Morgan's Raiders (see **John Hunt Morgan**), with two pieces of artillery, onto the cemetery hill overlooking Augusta (see **Augusta Civil War Raid**).

Augusta's greatest period of growth began in the second half of the 19th century, when the town became a center of shipping for north central Kentucky and had a commodious 20-by-45-foot market house. With the addition of a wharf boat, the town was able to export large quantities of the products grown and produced in the area. Bracken Co. became the nation's top producer of **white burley tobacco**, which was used in the manufacture of fine cut, plug, and snuff tobacco, and the white burley that was produced in the county commanded the highest prices offered on the market. Great quantities of this tobacco were bought by local dealers in Augusta and shipped off to commission houses for sale in other markets. In some years, these shipments amounted to more than 4 million pounds.

During the last quarter of the 20th century, Augusta has been known best as the site of three major films: James Michener's *Centennial,* PBS's *Huckleberry Finn,* and Neil Simon's *Lost in Yonkers.* Augusta is also home of **Nick Clooney**'s family, the former home of **Rosemary Clooney**, and currently the home of the family of Miss America 2000, **Heather Renee French** Henry, whose husband, Dr. Steve Henry, was a two-term Kentucky lieutenant governor (1995–2003). Noted playwright **Stuart Walker**, who patented the portable stage and introduced the individual spotlight system used in theaters today, was raised on Augusta's Riverside Dr. The town's foremost artist was Stephan Alke, who painted in oil and chose area landscapes and portraits as his central themes. Alke later became a student of the nationally known Kentucky artist **Frank Duveneck**.

In the last half of the 20th century, some businesses in town closed their doors, but two factories continue to thrive in Augusta. Clopay Plastic Products Company, which opened in August 1955, initially produced plastic covers, then later switched to making window blinds and blackout covers. This company continues to manufacture barrier film for health-care and hygienic use; it is a division of the Griffon Corporation, which has corporate headquarters in Jericho, N.Y. The oldest manufacturing firm now operating in Augusta was established in 1883 as the Excelsior Handle Company. Today it is operated as the F. A. Neider Auto-Fastener Group, which currently is a part of AUVECO, a division of the Auto Vehicle Parts Company. F. A. Neider, who initially patented and manufactured hardware and trimmings for fine horse-drawn carriages, founded the original company. The Neider plant now manufactures add-ons for the automotive aftermarket and boat industries.

The river has been both a hindrance and a benefit as the city of Augusta has advanced into the 21st century. The devastating **flood of 1997** led to the removal of several homes, but it also provided an opportunity for the town to develop green spaces and parks for its visitors. The U.S. Army Corps of Engineers is responsible for maintenance of the boat-dock facilities and was instrumental in constructing the O'Neill River Walk, which makes it possible for large pleasure and passenger entertainment boats to dock adjacent to the town's center. Local restaurants and an inn continue to thrive, offering fine dining and overnight facilities for tourists. In 2000, according to the U.S. Census, 1,204 people lived in the city of Augusta; in 2005 it estimated the city's population at 1,257.

Algier, Keith. *Ante-Bellum Augusta: The Life and Times of a Kentucky River Town.* Maysville, Ky.: Standard Quick Print, 2002.

Bracken Co. Extension Homemakers. *History of Bracken County.* Bicentennial ed. Brooksville, Ky.: Bracken Co. Extension Homemakers, 2002.

Rankins, Walter H. *Augusta College, Augusta, Kentucky: First Established Methodist College, 1822–1849.* Frankfort, Ky.: Roberts, 1957.

Caroline R. Miller

AUGUSTA BAPTIST CHURCH. Although the Augusta Baptist Church in Bracken Co. was organized in 1818, the church's first service was not held until 1819. The congregation met in several buildings and member homes in Augusta until a permanent building was erected in the town in 1843 at the southeast corner of Third and Bracken Sts. The church's chandelier, which used kerosene, was lighted by means of a weight-and-pulley system that raised and lowered it. That meetinghouse lasted more than 100 years before the current building was opened in 1948. This lovely building has had various additions, including a new bell tower that replaced the first church's well-used wooden one. Today, electricity has replaced the kerosene lighting system; however, some of the first church's fixtures are still being utilized at the new church.

Bracken Co. Extension Homemakers. *History of Bracken County.* Bicentennial ed. Brooksville, Ky.: Bracken Co. Extension Homemakers, 2002.

Caroline R. Miller

AUGUSTA CHRISTIAN CHURCH. The Augusta Christian Church in Bracken Co. was organized March 15, 1840, as this newly formed denomination of independent Christian churches spread throughout Kentucky. The Augusta Christian Church, located on Bracken St., was closed shortly afterward and then reorganized on January 1, 1854. In 1888 a new church building was erected on a lot offered by Amanda Perrine, who also contributed $1,000 for its construction. The church building is brick with a stone foundation and has a seating capacity of 200. Later, two rooms and a baptistery were added to the building. In 1982 Fred and Ida Mae Schweitzer left funds for the erection of a back addition to the church for additional Sunday school rooms.

Bracken Co. Extension Homemakers. *History of Bracken County.* Bicentennial ed. Brooksville, Ky.: Bracken Co. Extension Homemakers, 2002.

Caroline R. Miller

AUGUSTA CHURCH OF THE NAZARENE. The Augusta Church of the Nazarene in Bracken Co. had its origins in 1924 in a tent pitched for religious services at the City Park of Augusta. The church's next meeting place was a spacious Riverside Dr. home in town that could accommodate about 100 worshippers. In 1925 the church erected a building on Park Ave. close to the City Park, but this structure suffered great losses over the years from intermittent flooding. Under the leadership of Rev. Shelby Mathews, the church's current building was constructed on W. Fourth St. in town; weekly attendance there numbers about 300. There have been several additions to the church during the last 20 years, and the church still strives to serve the community.

Bracken Co. Extension Homemakers. *History of Bracken County.* Bicentennial ed. Brooksville, Ky.: Bracken Co. Extension Homemakers, 2002.

Caroline R. Miller

AUGUSTA CIVIL WAR RAID. The Confederate raid of Augusta on September 27, 1862, during the Civil War, culminated in 20 minutes of intense hand-to-hand combat demonstrating that when Union militia were well commanded, they could effectively fight regular Confederate soldiers. The raid occurred during the Confederate invasion of Kentucky when Lt. Col. Basil W. Duke, screening Confederate general Edmund Kirby Smith's northern flank in Falmouth, decided to raid Cincinnati. Leading 450 men of Col. John Hunt Morgan's cavalry brigade, Duke was determined to capture the home guard force recently organized in Augusta, cross the Ohio River, and threaten Cincinnati, causing Union troops to withdraw from Walton in order to relieve the threat.

In Augusta, Col. **Joshua T. Bradford** had been drilling a new home guard unit of 125 men, and when his scouts reported the approach of Duke's column that morning, Bradford called them out and organized a very effective interservice defensive plan. He went to the Ohio River landing and ordered the captains of the gunboats *Belfast* and *Florence Miller,* each vessel with one 12-pound cannon, to fire grape and canister shot at Duke's men when they advanced toward the river along Upper St., Augusta's main street. He had his men drawn up in ranks in a vacant lot, and he told them they were to move into the second stories of brick houses on each side of Upper St. near the river landing. They would win, he said, by overwhelming the Rebels with infantry crossfire and grape and canister shot from the gunboats. "Now, my gallant boys," he shouted, "all who are willing to stand by me, and by our arms, hold up your right hand." They all raised their hands and gave a cheer.

Duke and his raiders arrived with two howitzers and occupied the hill that runs parallel to the river and overlooks the town. He had a clear view of the gunboats, and they were well within range of his artillery. He ordered a detachment of 100 men to move to the right, enter the town from the east, and occupy a sandbar upriver a short distance from the landing. When the cannons began firing, they were to open on the gunboats with their rifles. Bradford had ordered the gunboat captains to shell Duke's men on the hill, and the crew of the *Belfast* fired three cannon shots. But after the first shot, Duke's cannons commenced firing and splashed water on the boats, making one direct hit on the *Belfast.* At the same time, Duke's men on the sandbar fired their rifles, riddling both boats with bullet holes. This was too much punishment for the gunboat captains; they hoisted anchors and fled upriver at full steam.

Expecting the outnumbered "green" home guards to quickly give up as well, Duke ordered most of his men to charge dismounted toward the river on Upper St. and capture the men he had seen entering houses when he first arrived. The attack was easy until the Confederates reached the last town square toward the river. Suddenly, they were caught in crossfire by home guards firing down from second-story windows. Duke ordered his men to one side of the street and brought up his two cannons. He had them double-shotted with canister and elevated to fire just below the windows from which the militiamen were firing. Duke's men set fire to a few houses, and white flags appeared from a few windows. The Confederates incorrectly assumed that this was a general surrender, and when firing continued from other houses, the attackers were infuriated. They broke down doors and closed on home guards inside in hand-to-hand fighting. "I never saw them fight with such ferocity," Duke recalled.

After about 20 minutes, all of the surviving militia men surrendered. Bradford had 9 dead and 15 wounded. Two and one-half squares of the town were burning, and the damage was estimated at $100,000. Duke had 21 men killed and 18 wounded, one of whom was Lt. Col. William Courtland Prentice, son of George Prentice, editor of the *Louisville Journal.* Prentice was shot through the lungs and died two days later. Duke withdrew and remembered that night in Augusta as "the gloomiest and saddest that any man among us had ever known." Bradford blamed his surrender on the gunboats and in a letter to the *Cincinnati Commercial* commended both sides. "In some instances," he wrote, "'Greek met Greek,' and in some instances of a hand to hand fight, where the doors were broken in, some of our young men displayed a heroism, and traces of cool, manly courage, worthy of regulars on any battlefield."

Augusta College. This original 1825 building was destroyed by fire in 1856.

Duke, Basil W. *A History of Morgan's Cavalry.* 1867. Reprint, West Jefferson, Ohio: Genesis, 1997.

Matthews, Gary Robert. *Basil Wilson Duke, CSA: The Right Man in the Right Place.* Lexington: Univ. Press of Kentucky, 2005.

James A. Ramage

AUGUSTA COLLEGE. The first school in Augusta, Augusta College, was begun by Robert Schoolfield in 1795 in a simple log structure that, remarkably well preserved, still stands at 211 W. Riverside Dr. The second school in Augusta was Bracken Academy, started in 1798 at 301 Elizabeth St. There was a series of buildings at this site with wooden dormitory rooms attached to the main two-story brick classroom building.

In 1822 Bracken Academy merged with Augusta College, which had just received a charter from the Kentucky legislature that year. The new Augusta College, which was the first Methodist College in Kentucky and the third in the nation, was sponsored by the Methodist Church conferences of Ohio and Kentucky. Each state had appointed a committee to consider establishing a Methodist school in the region. The committee members representing Ohio were John Collins, **Martin Ruter**, and David Young, and those representing Kentucky were **Henry Bascom**, Alexander Cummins, and Charles Holliday. One of the factors that led to choosing Augusta as the site for the new college was the town's location along the Ohio River and the Ohio-Kentucky border.

By 1825 Augusta College was completely operational, and the trustees began to disseminate information about the curriculum and the faculty in newspapers published in Ohio and Kentucky. John Armstrong was president of the college. At this time tuition for Latin and Greek languages was $3.00 per quarter, tuition for "high branches" of English was also $3.00, and boarding at the college for each term ranged from $1.00 to $1.50. The college campus began at Third St. and extended to Riverside Dr. It had two dormitories, one at Second and Bracken Sts., and the other at Second and Frankfort Sts. The brick classroom structure was 80 by 40 feet, three stories high, and had a basement. The campus included a chapel, recitation and lecture rooms, literary society halls, the library, mineral and geological storage cabinets, and a chemistry laboratory.

The collegiate year was divided into two terms, the first commencing on the fourth Monday in September and the second on the third Monday in March, with the second term closing on the first Friday in August. The public commencement ceremonies were held on the third Friday in August. Instruction in the modern languages, fine arts, and lectures on chemistry all required an additional fee to be paid to the professors of those courses.

Students came from several states, arriving by stagecoach, horseback, steamboat, and other means. From 1825 until 1849, when it closed, the college's enrollment ranged between 130 students and a high of almost 200. There were two literary societies, the Union and the Jefferson Societies, each of which played a major role in student activities. Students had personal libraries, and the 2,500-volume college library was available to them as well.

Aside from the properties and general resources available to the institution, a plan was made to establish a permanent endowment fund in order to create endowed teaching posts that paid either $10,000 or $14,000 per year. It was further stipulated that these endowment funds were to be applied to the McKendree Professorship of Moral Science and the Roberts Professorship of Mathematics. Some progress was made toward establishing another $10,000 endowed teaching seat to honor Bishop Soule of Ohio, who was president of the Board of Trustees. Additional sources of revenue for the college came from its publication of the *Augusta Herald* and from operating the Augusta ferry.

Rev. John P. Finley of Ohio had been appointed to the Kentucky Methodist Conference in order to found the Augusta College's preparatory department. He became president of the college for a short while before he died in 1825. The next president was Martin Ruter, from Massachusetts, who also became the college's professor of oriental languages and belles-lettres. Ruter later founded Southwestern University in Texas. About this same time, construction of the Methodist church on the corner of Riverside and Bracken Sts. began, paid for by funds donated by James Armstrong.

After Martin Ruter left, Joseph S. Tomlinson, a professor of natural philosophy and chemistry and composer **Stephen Collins Foster**'s uncle, became the president of the college. Some regarded Tomlinson as the "ablest debater in America." It turned out that he was Augusta College's last president; by the 1840s, the college was experiencing a declining enrollment and severe financial difficulties, some of which came about because in 1842 the Kentucky Methodist Conference transferred its support from Augusta College to Transylvania University in Lexington. Two years later, in 1844, the Ohio Methodist Conference terminated funding for Augusta College, leaving the institution in dire financial straits. Both of these decisions had geographical and social-political underpinnings. In the case of the Ohio Methodist Conference, the decision was based on a desire to charter a Methodist school in Ohio and the fact that Kentucky was a slave state. In the case of the Kentucky Methodist Conference, its desire to have a more centrally located school and the fact that many of the professors at Augusta College had expressed **antislavery** sentiments were prominent factors. Abandoned by both Methodist conferences, Augusta College was doomed. The college's charter was revoked by the Kentucky legislature on February 26, 1849, and the college ceased to function on June 1, 1849.

Two of the most prominent local families whose sons attended the college were the Marshalls and Doniphans. Gen. George Catlett Marshall's grandfather, William Champe Marshall, and many in his family studied there. **Alexander Doniphan** graduated from Augusta College before becoming a general in the U. S. Army. Often, too, the college's trustees were from well-known local families with names such as Bradford, Key, Payne, Savage, Shropshire, Thome, and Weldon.

Several of Augusta College's faculty, for example Henry Bascom, who became president of Transylvania University, and **John P. Durbin** and Herman Johnson, both of whom served as president of Dickinson College (Pa.), achieved high levels of professional achievement. The college also had many distinguished alumni, some of the most prominent being **Randolph S. Foster**, president of Northwestern University in Illinois; Governor Robert Wickliffe of Louisiana; U.S. general William Preston; **John G. Fee**, cofounder of Berea College, Berea, Ky.; George Robertson, honorary chief justice of the Kentucky court of appeals; and William S. Groesbeck, an independent candidate for president of the United States in 1872.

To some, paradoxically, the greatest glory of Augusta College was in its demise. Operating from 1822 until 1849, it was a center of the antislavery movement in Kentucky, and the feeling against the college became so intense that the Kentucky legislature decided to revoke the college's charter. Thus closed an institution with great prospect and future. However, the achievements of Augusta College graduates brought high honor to both its community and the state where it stood.

Algier, Keith. *Ante-Bellum Augusta: The Life and Times of a Kentucky River Town.* Maysville, Ky.: Standard Quick Print, 2002.

Rankins, Walter H. *Augusta College, Augusta, Kentucky: First Established Methodist College, 1822–1849.* Frankfort, Ky.: Roberts, 1957.

Caroline R. Miller

AUGUSTA FERRY. The licensing of ferry operations in Augusta, which continue today, began when John Jenkins and Hugh Marshall established boat landings on the Kentucky and Ohio shores of the Ohio River on April 2, 1798. One day later, John Blanchard pledged financing, in the sum of 50 pounds, for John Boude to operate a ferry between Augusta and the Ohio shore. Over the next century, numerous individuals operated a ferry in roughly this location.

During the early 1800s, ferry usage fees were established by local courts, beginning at 25 cents for two-wheel carriages and 66 cents for four-wheel vehicles. The charge for passengers riding a horse on a ferry was a nickel, and free-standing cattle cost 13 cents per head. Farmers paid 25 cents for each hogshead of tobacco they transported on a ferry.

On February 12, 1900, J. W. Bowman and T. S. Bradford, owners of the Augusta Ferry, reported to the town court that they had sold their rights to operate a ferry to the Commercial Club of Augusta. Later Roy Edgington, John O'Neill, and Charles Smith served as operators of this ferry. In 1926 Kline O'Neill purchased the operational rights, and his son Robert O'Neill ran the ferry businesses using the tug *Mr. Hanes,* which had two wheels underneath on each side.

The next tugboat put into use as a ferry was the *Ole Augusta;* this ferry service was owned by a group of Augusta businesspeople. The group sold their operating rights to the City of Augusta, which ran the ferry service for a few years. David Cartmell of Maysville bought the ferry and operated it for a few more years before a group of local citizens bought it back in order to enhance tourism in Augusta.

Having obtained grant moneys from the state, the Augusta Ferry Authority purchased a new tugboat, the *Jenny Ann,* which currently is used as the power unit to transport a barge that, when full, can carry eight cars or trucks for a fee of five dollars each. The *Ole Augusta* tug is kept ready to use whenever there are repairs and scheduled drydock inspections of the larger tug. In 2005 the ferry was operating between Augusta and Boude's Landing in Ohio from 8:00 a.m. to 8:00 p.m. daily.

Algier, Keith. *Ante-Bellum Augusta: The Life and Times of a Kentucky River Town.* Maysville, Ky.: Standard Quick Print, 2002.

Miller, Caroline, ed. *Augusta, Kentucky: Old Timer Talks by J. W. Crumbaugh.* Maysville, Ky.: Standard Quick Print, 2003.

Caroline R. Miller

AUGUSTA HIGH SCHOOL. Augusta High School, on Bracken St. in Augusta (Bracken Co.), operates under the auspices of Augusta Independent Schools, one of the smallest systems in Kentucky, with an enrollment of 280 students from prekindergarten through grade 12. Augusta High School dates back to 1887, when Augusta Independent Schools moved to the site once occupied by **Augusta College**. Formal class instruction began in fall 1889. The third building on the lot, the Augusta Free Grade School, was completed in October 1899 and burned in December 1899. A gymnasium with a 500-person capacity was built at Augusta High School and dedicated in December 1926; that structure contained eight feet of water during the **flood of 1937**. Before integration in the 1950s, African American elementary students attended a separate Augusta grade school, and high school students were transported to the **John G. Fee Industrial High School** in Maysville.

The most famous graduate of Augusta High School is Hollywood idol **George Clooney** (1979), and the carillon at the high school is dedicated to his aunt, the "girl singer" **Rosemary Clooney**.

Bracken Co. Extension Homemakers. *History of Bracken County*. Bicentennial ed. Brooksville, Ky.: Bracken Co. Extension Homemakers, 2002.

"Schools Show Strong Improvement," *KP*, August 14, 2004, 1K.

AUGUSTA JAIL. The historic 1811 jail in Augusta is located on the south side of the town's public square. It served as the Bracken Co. jail until the late 1830s and then was used as the city jail until the latter half of the 1900s. The lower level, which housed the inmates, was constructed of limestone rock, with three-foot-thick outer walls. The second level was brick and was the jailor's living quarters.

The jail is believed to be the oldest jail in the state still remaining on its original foundation. The inmates' section had two rooms; one served as a debtors' prison, while the other housed common criminals. The criminals' room featured a "jail within a jail," a dungeonlike room of solid log construction. A replica of the secure room has been constructed, providing visitors with an understanding of how prisoners were commonly treated in a 19th-century rural county jail. The debtors' prison, which was later altered by the addition of two holding cells, contains fascinating examples of prisoners' graffiti.

Bracken Co. Extension Homemakers. *History of Bracken County*. Bicentennial ed. Brooksville, Ky.: Bracken Co. Extension Homemakers, 2002.

Caroline R. Miller

AUGUSTA PRESBYTERIAN CHURCH. The Augusta Presbyterian Church, presently on Fourth St. in Augusta, can trace its roots to 1803, when the first Presbyterian Church in Bracken Co. was established. By June 1812 the congregation was meeting at the Augusta courthouse with Rev. Robert Wilson as the regular minister, and by 1815 the group had the name Augusta Presbyterian Church.

The first church building was constructed on Upper St. in Augusta in 1818. By 1820 the Augusta Presbyterian Church had become a charter member of the newly formed Ebenezer Presbytery and had two commissioners serving on its General Assembly. Over the next 40 years, the social and political turbulence that engulfed the nation was also felt by the church. Rev. John Rankin, a famous abolitionist (see **Abolitionists**), baptized several children of the congregation, the church's members witnessed a Confederate attack on Augusta (see **Augusta Civil War Raid**), and the congregation suffered a split within its membership. The resulting two congregations (First Presbyterian and Second Presbyterian) met in the same building on alternate Sundays, and it was not until 1873 that the two churches began to settle their differences.

In 1879 the Fourth St. Presbyterian Church was built. The building was described as a "modern building with a beautiful round stained glass window in the front and an iron fence and a grassy plot between the two entrance doors," and it boasted a pipe organ. In 1894, at the urging of the General Assembly of the Presbyterian Church, the two Augusta Presbyterian churches reunited and became known, once again, as the Augusta Presbyterian Church. The church grew over the next several years, and its women's group became more dynamic. In 1929 a Sunday School building–fellowship hall was built. As more years passed, the church installed its first female elder and deacon, and in 2003 it celebrated its 200th anniversary. Today the Augusta Presbyterian Church, led by commissioned lay pastor Les Grooms, continues to play an active role in the life of the Augusta community.

Augusta Presbyterian Church. *One Hundred and Fiftieth Anniversary, 1803–1953*. Augusta, Ky.: Augusta Presbyterian Church, 1953.

Davidson, Robert. *History of the Presbyterian Church in the State of Kentucky*. 1847. Reprint, Greenwood, S.C.: Attic Press, 1974.

Millie Bush

AUGUSTA TRINITY UNITED METHODIST CHURCH. About 1799 John Benton organized a Methodist group in Bracken Co. in a log church at Sharon, near Chatham. Five years later, Ferdinand Dora convened a Methodist society in Augusta and later constructed Dora's Meeting House and School, located near Gertrude. The Gertrude school and church meetinghouse became the Mount Zion United Methodist Church of today, and the Sharon Presbyterian Church was later built on the site of Benton's log church. The Sharon Methodist band of worshippers, a separate body, continued in Augusta and occupied a new building on Riverside and Bracken Sts. until persistent flooding made it unsafe. Many members of this church's original congregation were supporters of **Augusta College**, which was sponsored by the Ohio and Kentucky conferences of the Methodist denomination. In 1885 property at Fourth and Frankfort Sts. in Augusta was purchased, and the current church was erected; additional Sunday school rooms were built later. The Mount Zion United Methodist Church is now closed, and only occasional services are still held for special events.

Bracken Co. Extension Homemakers. *History of Bracken County*. Bicentennial ed. Brooksville, Ky.: Bracken Co. Extension Homemakers, 2002.

Caroline R. Miller

AUSTINBURG. The neighborhood of Austinburg, located on the southeast side of Covington, was founded in 1850 by Seneca Austin. He had purchased an 80-acre farm along the Licking River in January 1844 from S. C. Parkhurst. His farm encompassed an area that now includes 16th and 17th Sts. from the Licking River west to Greenup St. and, in the north-south direction, Water, Glenway, Oakland, and Eastern Sts. and Maryland Ave.

Austin and his wife Julia built a beautiful home along a creek that led to the Licking River. Their house (now gone) was just south of the present 17th St. and about where a floodwall is located today. Access to the farm was by a gated private road, which was entered from Madison Ave., near 15th St. Austin built several greenhouses on his land and also grew fruits and vegetables for sale on the Covington and Cincinnati markets. He planted a beautiful formal flower garden along a walkway leading from the house to the Licking River.

About 1850 Austin subdivided his land and began selling building lots to mostly German Catholic settlers, who were interested in moving outside Covington city limits to avoid city taxes. However, the City of Covington annexed Austinburg in 1851. In the late 1880s, the first public utilities came to the area; water, sewer, and gas lines were installed, brick sidewalks were laid, and the streets were paved.

Within Austinburg, the Fourth Street Public School, designed by Covington architect **Lyman Walker**, opened about 1870, and the **St. Benedict Catholic Church** and school (see **Samuel Hannaford and Sons**), opened in 1884. The church and the schools have been important to the community ever since.

The **Covington and Lexington Railroad** ran north and south along the western edge of Austinburg and contributed greatly to the growth of the community. In the late 1880s, the **Chesapeake and Ohio Railroad** ran tracks east and west through northern Austinburg, to connect with the **Kentucky Central Railroad** (the former Covington and Lexington) at 17th St. and Madison Ave. (the KC Junction) in Peaselburg. Good jobs were plentiful with both the railroads and the large number of businesses in or near Austinburg. Among the businesses were the Bogenschutz Foundry and the Welsh and Craig Packing Company, both built along the Licking River, and the Jasper Distillery, at Burnet and Water Sts. In later years, the Rice Packing Company operated a plant at Patton and Eastern Aves. In 1903 the **Stewart Iron Works** opened a plant along Madison Ave. and soon became Covington's largest employer. In 1912 **R.A. Jones & Company** came to the southeast corner of 15th and Garrard Sts.

Entertainment was available to the citizens at the Covington Blues baseball park in nearby Peaselburg and at a skating rink and a public playground (Stewart Park) at 17th St. and Madison Ave. During the 1920s three open-air silent movie theaters were in business, one at 17th St. and Eastern Ave., another at 18th and Garrard Sts., and another at Patton and Eastern Aves. The Warneford family operated the private Glenway Swimming Pool at the southeast corner of 15th St. and Oakland Ave. until the late 1950s.

During the late 1890s and early 1900s, Austinburg was one of Covington's most desirable and fastest-growing areas. Jobs were plentiful, churches were full, and businesses were prospering. Then came **World War I**, the **Great Depression**, and the **flood of 1937**, all of which had devastating effects on the community of Austinburg and its citizens. However, with the end of the Great Depression, prosperity returned, and the ensuing boom period lasted through the 1940s and into the 1950s. By the 1960s the area had begun to decline, due to many citizens' flight to the suburbs. Churches, schools, businesses, and residents began to experience problems. St. Benedict School, which had more than 400 pupils in the mid-1920s, dropped to about 100 by the late 1970s and was eventually merged with Bishop Howard School to become Holy Family Elementary School. Individuals and businesses continued to move from Austinburg to the suburbs, where taxes were lower and larger tracts of land were available.

One of Austinburg's greatest assets was the St. Elizabeth Hospital, which was built in 1912, at 20th St. and Eastern Ave. (see **St. Elizabeth Medical Center**). It provided both employment and superior medical care. However, the hospital business also changed as the exodus to the suburbs persisted. Inpatient admissions decreased dramatically, and as a result, St. Elizabeth built a new larger, better-equipped facility off Thomas More Dr. in Edgewood.

Austinburg today is considerably larger than when it was founded in 1850. It now includes all of the east-west streets from 16th St. through 21st St. and the north-south streets of Water, Glenway, Oakland, Eastern, and Maryland, south as far as Wallace Woods. Mostly lower-income, working-class people live in Austinburg now. The quality of construction and condition of area homes vary widely, from fully restored historic structures to poorly maintained substandard buildings. The Austinburg Neighborhood Association has been formed, with the goal of encouraging residents to restore the historic structures and to upgrade or raze substandard structures. With reasonable real estate prices, close proximity to major highways, and easy access to major restaurants and shopping areas, Austinburg may someday return to its past prominence. Most of Austinburg is listed on the National Register of Historic Districts (1987). It has buildings of various styles, including Colonial Revival, Greek Revival, Italianate, Neoclassical, and Queen Anne. Some well-known residents of Austinburg have been **John G. Carlisle**, U.S. congressman and lieutenant governor of Kentucky, Covington mayor Butch Callery, Covington councilman Bernie Moorman, Kenton Co. judge executive Robert Aldemeyer, and Boone Co. judge Charles Moore.

"Austinburg Historic District," National Register of Historic Places Nomination, 1986, Kentucky Heritage Council, Frankfort, Ky.

Gastright, Joseph F. *Gentleman Farmers to City Folks.* Cincinnati: Cincinnati Historical Society, 1980.

Reis, Jim. *Pieces of the Past.* Vol. 1. Covington: Kentucky Post, 1988.

Jack Wessling

AUTON, JESSE, BRIGADIER GENERAL (b. December 1, 1904, DeMossville, Ky.; d. March 30, 1952, Offutt Air Force Base, Neb.). U.S Air Force pilot and commander Jesse Auton was the son of Robert Wesley and Julia E. Bagby Auton. He graduated from **Piner High School** in 1923 and was named class valedictorian. During his high school years, Auton was on the debating team and played basketball. He attended Georgetown College in Georgetown, graduating in 1927 with a BA in education, and then returned to Piner High School to teach and serve as assistant principal for the 1927–1928 academic year. It was at this time that he became interested in aviation. In 1928 he left teaching and enlisted in the U.S Army Air Service to become a pilot.

Gen. Jesse Auton, ca. fall 1945.

Auton received pilot training in Texas and was commissioned as a 2nd lieutenant in January 1930. From 1930 until 1936, he was given a number of assignments: he was a pursuit pilot with the 94th Pursuit Squadron based at Selfridge Field, Mich.; commander of the Civilian Conservation Corps Camp at Ludington, Mich.; and group adjutant for the First Pursuit Group in California. He also served as an Army Air Mail Service pilot in 1934 and was assigned as aide and pilot for Maj. Gen. Preston Brown, commander of the 2nd Army Corps. During his service under General Brown, Auton commanded the Air Service color guard for the funeral of Will Rogers. In early 1936 Auton was ordered to Washington, D.C., where he served as a White House Aide under President Franklin D. Roosevelt (1933–1945) and as aide and pilot for Assistant Secretary of War Louis Johnson.

In January 1941 Auton commanded the 79th Pursuit Squadron in California, and by March he had been promoted to executive officer of the 20th Pursuit Group. He took command of the group in October 1941 and led the unit through the Louisiana War Maneuvers of that year. Following the outbreak of **World War II**, he was sent as an observer to England and Ireland to survey sites for potential U.S air bases for the newly formed 8th Air Force. Upon returning to the United States, he was assigned as plans and training officer for the 3rd Fighter Command in Tampa, Fla., and in January 1943 he was given command of the San Francisco Air Defense Wing. During this time he authored a fighter training guide for squadron and flight commanders, which was used through the end of the war. By April 1943 he had transformed his command into an overseas fighter wing and deployed it to England. The unit was designated the 65th Fighter Wing of the 8th Air Force when it arrived in England, and it became the first operational U.S. fighter wing in Europe. As wing commander, Auton had overall control of five fighter groups and one emergency rescue squadron. He and his staff, along with others, developed a strategic fighter control and communications system, which helped protect bomber formations more effectively. In March 1944 he was given the temporary rank of brigadier general; he commanded the wing through November 1945, flying 12 combat missions.

After the war, Auton reverted to the rank of colonel, and from 1946 to 1950 he held a number of positions, including base commander of Lowery Field, Denver; director of operations for the Air Transport Command; wing commander of the 313th Troop Carrier Wing, which hauled coal into Berlin during the Berlin Airlift; and commander of the U.S. Air Force Station at Goose Bay, Labrador. In April 1950 he was assigned to Strategic Air Command Headquarters (SAC) in Omaha, serving in operations under Gen. Curtis Lemay. General Lemay sent him to Korea in 1950 to carry out a limited assessment of air operations in the **Korean War**, and during his time in Korea, he flew nine combat missions using various types of aircraft. Auton returned to the United States in early 1951 and gave public talks regarding the air war in Korea for SAC. In October 1951 he was promoted to the rank of brigadier general, with the position of director of Fighter Support operations. He was killed in a plane crash at Offutt Air Force Base on March 20, 1952, while returning from California, and was buried at Arlington National Cemetery with full military honors. He was never married. Upon his death he left a bequest to Piner High School (now Piner Elementary), funds that have continued to help the school pay for various projects, including the recent construction of a new library dedicated in his name.

Auton's decorations and honors include two Legion of Merit medals, the Distinguished Flying Cross, the Air Medal, the Bronze Star, two Army Commendation Ribbons, the Order of the British Empire (Military), the French Legion of Honor, the French Croix de Guerre with palm, and the Belgian Croix de Guerre with palm. He was the only American to receive the award of the Freedom of the Borough of Saffron Walden, England. Auton also received an honorary doctorate of military science from Georgetown University in 1951. For many years a street was also named in his honor at March Air Force Base, Calif.

"Artifacts Tell General's Story," *KE,* June 3, 1994, C1.

"Kenton General Killed in Air Crash," *KTS,* March 31, 1952, 1.

Who's Who in America. Vol. 24 (1946–1947), "Latest Listings and Data" section, p. 15. Chicago: A. N. Marquis, 1946.

"Wins Honor," *KTS,* April 5, 1945, 1K.

Robert B. Snow

AVENEL HOTEL. In 1870 James M. and Mary Southgate sold a 50-acre tract in the District of the Highlands (now Fort Thomas) to St. Xavier College of Cincinnati, for $18,000. The land included present-day Avenel Pl., Manor Ln., Glenway Ave., and lots on Chalfonte Pl. The Jesuit fathers of St. Xavier College used the property for a summer villa and as a retreat for the faculty of the college. A small farmhouse on the grounds accommodated 8 to 10 men. There were also a refectory and a private chapel, where the first mass was held in what became **St. Thomas Catholic Church**. Legend contends that there were vineyards on the property and that wine was made and bottled for sacramental use in local parishes; both full and broken wine bottles have been found on the hillside. In 1886 Crescentia C. Schriver purchased from the college the land between Avenel Pl. and Manor Ln. on S. Fort Thomas Ave. for the building that became the Avenel, a resort hotel. Crescentia's husband was Henry Ahart Schriver (1829–1908), a successful contractor from Newport and the construction manager of the Fort Thomas Military Reservation.

When originally planned, the building was to be a private residence for the Schriver family, but after a fire destroyed their home, a hotel was erected on the site in 1894 and a new home for the family was constructed at the end of Manor Ln. The hotel, at 39 Fort Thomas Ave., was built in only three months out of red bricks; it had wide wooden porches facing both Manor Ln. and the Ohio River. Because the hotel was on the **streetcar** line connecting to Cincinnati, Covington, and Newport, guests used the streetcar to come for a few days or the entire summer. Some families stayed at the hotel while their homes were being built in the growing town of Fort Thomas. Two large stone pillars marked a lane leading up a slight grade to the hotel. Two cottages in the pear orchard at the rear of the structure were rented to special guests. The main floor of the hotel had an entrance hall with a wide staircase and balustrade. Large parlors on each side, carpeted in red, featured crystal chandeliers and large, gold-framed mirrors. At the rear of the entrance hall was the public dining room, which had a large fireplace flanked by two windows. On the back wall a large bay window offered a view of the orchard. Also on the main floor were a small family-and-staff dining room, a big kitchen, and an office. There were 30–40 rooms on the upper floors. No cooking was done at the hotel on Sundays; food prepared on Saturdays was served buffet style on Sundays. Dancing and card-playing were prohibited on Sunday. Cincinnatian Nicholas Longworth and his bride Alice Roosevelt, the daughter of U.S. president Teddy Roosevelt, were once guests. The couple were startled when one of the Schriver daughters, Miss Jessie, informed them that they would no longer be welcome because of "their frivolities."

The Schriver children were employed at the hotel all summer tending to the gardens, orchards, and livestock that provided the food for the dining room. A pond at the end of Glenway Ave. was the source of ice in the winter, which was stored in sawdust for summer use. A long meadow stretched down the back hillside, allowing wide views of the Ohio River. Near the end of Manor Ln. there was also an open pavilion for the guests.

Dr. James A. Averdick, ca. 1927.

The business venture known as the Avenel Hotel ended when the property was sold in 1918 and became a residence for nurses caring for **World War I** army patients convalescing at the Altamont and Shelly Arms hotels nearby. By this time, the District of the Highlands had become Fort Thomas. Afterward, the property's new owner lived alone in the building until 1928. The structure was torn down in the 1930s.

Reis, Jim. "Runaway Faced Fair Winds and Foul," *KP*, November 19, 1990, 4K.

Betty Maddox Daniels

AVERDICK, JAMES ANDREW (b. December 25, 1852, Cincinnati, Ohio; d. August 1, 1931, Covington, Ky.). James A. Averdick was a popular and prominent physician in Covington, where he was also known as a forthright politician and a patriarch of the local Democratic Party. He was the eldest son of Henry G. and Joanna D. Eagen Averdick, both immigrants, who had arrived in the United States in 1847 and 1848, respectively. Henry was born in Germany; Joanna was from Ireland. The Averdieck (the German spelling of the name) farm in Germany has been held by the family since early in the ninth century. Joanna D. Eagen had been a governess for a merchant family in Cincinnati, and Henry G. Averdick worked as a druggist, reading medicine with Dr. Israel Wilson as his preceptor in preparation for his graduation from Cincinnati's Eclectic College of Medicine in 1854. Dr. Henry G. Averdick practiced briefly in Cincinnati before moving to Oldenburg, Ind., in 1855 at the request of Father F. J. Rudolf of the Franciscan (see **Roman Catholics**) religious community there.

As a boy, James A. Averdick wished to be a physician like his father, so he prepared for his career by attending St. Mary's Institute (later the University of Dayton) in Dayton, Ohio, prior to entering Cincinnati's Ohio College of Medicine in 1871. With his father as his preceptor, he graduated in 1874 and received the Dawson Prize for rendering the finest surgical drawings in his class. The Dawson Prize consisted of a fitted wooden presentation case of fine surgical instruments; it was awarded by Dr. W. W. Dawson of the Good Samaritan Hospital. After graduation, Averdick returned to Indiana, where he married Clara J. Ertel and assisted in the practice of Dr. Douglas Harding in Batesville, Ind. In 1875 Averdick moved to Covington, where he settled in the **West Side**, presently known as **Main Strasse**. The doctor was a convivial gentleman who enjoyed hosting gatherings in his home and at places such as Covington's Arbeiter Halle. Averdick's abilities and popularity won him election as Kenton Co. coroner in 1877, at age 24. In 1878 he was appointed to the county Board of Health and in 1879 was elected to the Covington School Board. In the early years of his medical practice, Averdick was active in the Covington Medical Society and often served as one of the city's district physicians. He was instrumental in the development of the Kentucky Publishing Company, which issued the city's weekly and daily German-language newspaper, *Der Kentucky Demokrat*. In 1891 it was reported that this new newspaper was the first in Kentucky to be printed on an electric press. Averdick initially served as vice president of the publishing company and by 1896 was listed as its president.

Averdick was elected in 1901 to serve in the Kentucky House of Representatives. He was not shy about proposing legislation in the session of 1902. Of particular interest was the welfare of prisoners at the state penitentiary in Frankfort. He proposed improvements in sanitation, cold storage, and hospital conditions. The doctor successfully supported the State Federation of Labor's proposed child labor law. He presented and saw adopted a set of resolutions denouncing British warfare and oppression in South Africa. They were drafted by artist **Henry F. Farny**'s committee and signed by more than 300 citizens, including artist **Frank Duveneck**. Elected again in 1903, Averdick proposed fewer bills in the 1904 session. His sense of history obliged him to present a petition of the **Daughters of the American Revolution** (DAR) to preserve the former capitol building in Danville, where the state's first constitution was drafted in 1792.

After serving in Frankfort, Averdick again focused on his foremost civic interest, the public schools of Covington. He served for nearly a half century on the school system's governing board. During his tenure many advancements were made: kindergartens were begun, indoor restrooms were provided, truancy officers were appointed, and many fine school buildings were built, including **Holmes High School** and the new **Lincoln-Grant School**. Through the years, Averdick served on almost every school board committee and as president of the board. His goal was to develop the school system's facilities and programs in a fiscally responsible manner.

Averdick was honored in 1912 by St. John's Orphanage (see **Diocesan Catholic Children's Home**) for his 25 years of service as that institution's house physician. In **World War I**, Averdick assisted the local Council of National Defense by enrolling needed mechanics during his regular evening office hours. He was elected by his peers in 1920 to serve as chief of staff at the new St. Elizabeth Hospital (later **St. Elizabeth Medical Center**) in Covington. Testimonial dinners were held in 1924 to celebrate Averdick's 50th anniversary as a physician. The first was at Tom Cody's farm (see **Gourmet Strip**); the second, an elaborate affair, was at the Industrial Club of Covington.

Dr. and Mrs. Averdick took in and raised several orphans, including George Weindel, Mary Ertel, and Robert J. Ertel; Robert Ertel became a physician and partner with Averdick in the practice of Averdick and Ertel. Averdick's siblings, Nell and Henry G. Jr., were among those who boarded for extended periods at the doctor's longtime residence and office on the northeast corner of Eighth and Bakewell Sts. Averdick was widowed in 1922; he later married Ella Stearns Ventner, who died in 1926. The elderly physician was fortunate in his later years to have present in his home Mrs. Emma Schwegman, his housekeeper, and her sons Cletus and Marcellus, both of whom later became physicians.

Averdick enjoyed fraternal organizations, and over the years he belonged to the **Knights of Columbus**, the Elks, the Eagles, the Knights of Honor, and the Catholic Federation of Societies. He served as surgeon for the Sons of Union Veterans–Ohio Division and as supreme medical examiner for the Catholic Knights of America. He also belonged to several medical societies. The University of Dayton conferred an honorary JD degree upon Averdick in 1928, having also given him its first honorary degree, a BA, in 1901. In keeping with the Kentucky Education Association's contemporary campaign of Equal Educational Opportunities for Every Kentucky Child, Averdick in 1928 pushed for the passage of the bond issue that built the new Lincoln-Grant School. The bond issue passed, but various school board issues delayed the project. Averdick proudly attended the groundbreaking ceremonies in 1931 but did not live to see the school building completed.

Averdick died at his commodious, well-appointed Covington home. Survivors included his sister, Nell Averdick, and his brother, Henry G. Averdick Jr., and family. Accounts of his passing appeared in numerous newspapers, including the *New York Times*. The *Kentucky Times-Star*'s lead editorial, entitled "James A. Averdick," noted: "The physician was known to every man, woman and child in the western section of the city. He was genial and companionable and his passing adds to the list of colorful personages who were prominent in public life in this city." Services by the Knights of Columbus were held in Covington on August 4, 1931. The following morning, after services at **St. Aloysius Church**, the funeral procession began the long journey to Oldenburg, Ind., by way of Brookville, Ind. In Oldenburg, the late physician lay in state for several hours prior to final services and burial in his father's lot in the Holy Family Cemetery. The flags on the schools in Covington remained at half-mast for 30 days in honor of Dr. J. A. Averdick and his contributions to the public schools of his adopted city.

Averdick, Michael R. *The Averdick Family of Oldenburg, Indiana.* Forthcoming.
"Duty to Provide New School Building for Negro Children," *KTS*, November 1, 1928, 5.
"James A. Averdick," *KTS*, August 3, 1931, 4.
"Laud Averdick in Resolution," *KP*, August 29, 1931, 2.
"Nestor of School Board Is Dead," *KTS*, August 3, 1931, 1.

Michael R. Averdick

AVIATION ACCIDENTS. Just as aviation has been a very important part of Northern Kentucky's history, unfortunately accidents have also gained a place. Many early aviation accidents were unreported; however, even among those early ones, a few made the headlines. Today most aviation accidents are covered by national news and investigated by the National Transportation Safety Board. Recorded aviation accidents in the Northern Kentucky region include the following.

Falmouth. On July 20, 1928, Albert Boyer, an early aviation pioneer in Campbell Co., made an unsuccessful landing in his biplane at Falmouth, crashing through two fences and hitting a five-foot embankment. Boyer was able to walk away from the accident.

Ross. On October 11, 1929, Boyer Field at Ross was the scene of another accident when Albert J. Rutterer took Reynolds Faber of Fort Thomas for a plane ride. Apparently, the engine failed while they were over the airport, and the plane crashed between hangars at the edge of the field. Both men were seriously injured and required medical attention at Speers Hospital in Dayton, Ky. (see **Speers Memorial Hospital**).

Fort Thomas. In 1931 a mail carrier departed Cincinnati's Lunken Airport en route to Louisville, and when he experienced engine problems, he made a forced landing in Kentucky at the **Highland Country Club**'s golf course. The pilot, Julius Johannpeter, was not seriously injured; the plane received minor damage, and the mail was safe.

Fiskburg. At Fiskburg in 1944, two U.S. Army pilots parachuted from their twin-engine plane after experiencing engine failure. The plane crashed in Pendleton Co., but the crew landed on the ground without injuries.

Brooksville. One of the first early fatalities in the Northern Kentucky region occurred in Bracken Co. at Brooksville in 1946 when a military Lockheed P-80 Shooting Star jet fighter caught fire and crashed on the farm of H. C. Poe. The pilot, Brig. Gen. Melvin E. Gross, was killed instantly and the plane was scattered in the field of nearly 40 acres. Gross was stationed with the U.S. Army Air Corps and was flying out of Dayton, Ohio.

Fort Thomas. On September 12, 1947, Charles Davis took a friend, Fred Lense, for a plane ride from Lunken Airport in Cincinnati. The plane developed engine trouble and, as Davis attempted to return to the airfield, crashed into a tree near the residence of R. C. Reeves along N. Fort Thomas Ave. in Fort Thomas. Both men were injured and were taken to Speers Hospital.

Limaburg. On May 8, 1948, two Tulsa, Okla., men were killed when their twin-engine Beechcraft aircraft crashed on takeoff in a pasture one-half mile south of Limaburg. The men were Noble T. Rush and Daniel Crowley.

Hebron. On January 12, 1955, the first commercial air crash in the region occurred. A TWA Martin 202 departed the Greater Cincinnati Airport (see **Cincinnati/Northern Kentucky International Airport**) and struck the wing of a privately operated Douglas DC-3. The right propeller of the Martin cut across the top of the DC-3 and then through the vertical fin and rudder (tail). Both planes crashed as a result, killing all occupants. On board the TWA flight were 10 passengers and a crew of 3; the DC-3 was carrying 2 crew members. The accident was later blamed on the operation of the DC-3 in the control zone as unknown traffic, without clearance, very close to or in the base of the overcast, which at the time was 700–900 feet above the ground.

Florence, Ky. On September 6, 1957, a single-engine plane had taken off from a private strip and soon developed what witnesses described as an engine problem. The plane attempted a return to the field and crashed in a field one and one-half miles south of Florence. Both occupants, Leroy Abbott and James E. Rhodes, were killed.

Constance. On November 14, 1961, a four-engine Douglas DC-4, owned by cargo operator Zantop Air Transport, crashed on approach to Greater Cincinnati Airport. The airplane broke in half, skidded about 400 feet, and broke into flames. The two occupants, Calvin Goutier and Richard Brethren, escaped with only minor injuries.

Constance. On the evening of November 8, 1965, American Airlines Flight 383 was making an approach in light snow when it crashed into the hillside along the Ohio River, killing 58 and severely injuring 4. The plane, a three-engine Boeing 727 Astrojet, was en route from New York City to the Greater Cincinnati Airport, and the cause of the accident was determined to be the pilot's failure to monitor altimeters during the approach. Survivors of the crash were Captain Elmer Weekley, an American Airlines employee but not the captain of the flight, stewardess Toni Ketchell, Israel Horowitz, and Norman Specter. Since the crash, Toni Ketchell has devoted her life working as an advocate for airline safety.

Greater Cincinnati Airport. On November 6, 1967, Flight 159, a TWA Boeing 707, ran off the end of the runway while attempting to abort a takeoff. The 29 passengers and 7 crew members escaped; 11 were treated for injuries, and 1 passenger died four days later. The crew had performed a routine takeoff roll but thought that they had contacted a part of a **Delta Air Lines** DC-9 that was stuck in the mud near the runway and therefore aborted the takeoff. It was later determined that the aircraft did not strike the DC-9.

Constance. On November 20, 1967, TWA Flight 128, a four-engine Convair 880, crashed on approach to the Greater Cincinnati Airport, killing 70 and injuring 12. The flight originated in Los Angeles and was making a stop in Cincinnati before proceeding to Pittsburgh and Boston. The airplane struck trees before making several additional impacts with the ground, finally coming to a stop 6,878 feet from the end of the intended runway. The cause of the accident was later determined to be the attempt of the crew to make a nighttime visual approach during deteriorating weather conditions, without adequate altimeter cross-reference. This accident remains the worst in terms of total fatalities in Northern Kentucky's history.

Hebron. On February 7, 1970, three people were killed when their Beechcraft aircraft crashed while attempting to land at Greater Cincinnati Airport. The plane had previously tried to land at Lunken Airport, where fog prevented the approach. The cause of the crash was pilot error, blamed on deficiencies in the pilot's training for that type of weather.

Cold Spring. In 1975 a single-engine Piper Comanche heading for Lunken Airport ran out of fuel and crashed while attempting to make an emergency landing. The plane struck a hill off Old State Rd. 1 and came to rest on the edge of another hill. All three passengers were injured but survived.

Greater Cincinnati Airport. On October 8, 1979, a Piper PA31-310 Navajo (twin-engine aircraft) operated by **Comair** lost an engine on takeoff and crashed, killing all seven passengers and the pilot. The cause of the crash was later determined to be loss of control, following a partial loss of power immediately after liftoff from the runway.

Falmouth. On April 20, 1980, a Piper PA-28 Warrior (single-engine plane) crashed at the airport in Falmouth while attempting to take off without flaps. The four occupants were killed and the plane was consumed by fire. The cause of the crash was pilot error.

Cincinnati/Northern Kentucky International Airport. On June 2, 1983, a routine flight turned deadly when smoke was discovered coming from the rear lavatory of Air Canada Flight 797 over Indianapolis, at 35,000 feet. The plane was carrying 41 passengers and 5 crew members from Dallas, Tex., to Toronto. As the smoke spread, the crew declared an emergency and Cincinnati/Northern Kentucky International Airport, 100 miles distant, was chosen as the site for an emergency landing; the aircraft could not lose altitude quickly from that height. In the final few minutes of the flight, the smoke was so intense that the pilot could not see his own controls and was guided to the runway by a Piedmont Airlines pilot. The landing was made without incident; however, the fire spread and it was later discovered that many of the passengers had died from inhalation of deadly chemicals produced by the burning material in the cabin. This accident resulted in many debates on cabin safety and is somewhat responsible for the floor lighting found in airliners today and a reduction in the use of materials that cause toxic fumes when ignited. Canadian television manufacturer Curtis Mathis was one of the 23 persons who died in this incident.

Florence, Ky. In 2004 a DHL Convair 580 twin-engine cargo plane, operated under contract to DHL and owned by Air Tahoma of Columbus, Ohio, crashed on approach to Cincinnati/Northern Kentucky International Airport after apparently running out of fuel. The plane crashed short of Runway 36R on a green at World of Golf, killing the copilot and injuring the captain.

National Transportation Safety Board. "Accident Database and Synopses." www.ntsb.gov/ntsb/query.asp (accessed May 25, 2007).

Newspaper articles, 1925–2006. Collection of John E. Leming Jr.

Reis, Jim. "70 Years of Air Crashes," *KP*, July 25, 1998, 4K.

John E. Leming Jr.

AYERS, RHODA MAE "RHONNIE" (b. July 26, 1931, Rock Island, Ill.; d. February 21, 1984, Fort Thomas, Ky.). Rhoda Mae Ayers, the first African American to be elected in Newport and in Campbell Co., was the daughter of George and Lauretta Reynolds. Ayers moved to Newport, Ky., from Rock Island, Ill., in 1972, following the death of her husband, to live with her mother. Upon arriving in Newport, Ayers got involved in youth and other community activities; her service in those areas gave her the name recognition necessary for her first attempt at the Newport Board of Education. In the 1976 election, she ran on a "poor people's" platform. She won the election, placing third among the candidates, and served for four years on the board. During her tenure on the Board of Education, she strived to ensure fairness for students and teachers alike. When she ran for reelection in 1980, the Newport Teachers Association endorsed her, but despite that support, Ayers lost. Afterward, she was appointed to the Newport Recreation Commission and served as a member of the Community Action Commission advisory board. Ayers also was a board member of the **Brighton Center**. Employed at the U.S. Postal Service Annex in Cincinnati, she became the Postal Union's recording secretary. Ayers died in 1984 at St. Luke Hospital in Fort Thomas and was buried in the New St. Joseph Cemetery, Cincinnati.

Freeman, Dick. "Tax Stands Help Elect Newport 4," *KP*, November 3, 1976, 4.

Hicks, Jack. "Election Brings No Surprises, No Mixup," *KE*, November 4, 1976, C1.

Kentucky Deaths. "Rhoda Ayers, Active in Community," *KP*, February 24, 1984, 12A.

"School Board Reactions Run Hot in Ludlow; Others Cool," *KP*, November 5, 1980, 3K.

Theodore H. H. Harris

B

BACCHUS, PERCIVAL L. (b. May 2, 1902, Virgin Islands, West Indies; d. June 3, 1962, Cincinnati, Ohio). Percival L. Bacchus was an African American medical doctor who practiced in Newport for more than three decades. He was born in the Virgin Islands, but when he was young his family moved to New Jersey. Bacchus attended Meharry Medical School in Nashville, Tenn., and graduated in the late 1920s. He practiced for a short time in Nashville before coming to Kentucky, where he passed the Kentucky State Medical Examination and, on August 10, 1931, was licensed to practice.

Bacchus was instrumental in revitalizing the long-dormant Newport Masonic Lodge PHA No. 120 (see **African Americans**). He served as master of the Newport Lodge No. 120 for many years. Meetings were held in the basement of his office at 341 Central Ave. The practice of medicine and the Masonic lodge were the two greatest passions of his life.

In December 1955 Bacchus was tried in the Campbell Co. Circuit Court on a charge of performing an illegal abortion (see **Birth Control**). The jury failed to reach a verdict, and a second trial took place in April 1956. The second jury also failed to return a decision. In August 1956 the State Board of Health revoked Bacchus's medical license on the grounds that he had "committed an unlawful abortion."

Bacchus was a 33rd Degree Mason, a Shriner, and the Illustrious Potentate of Aleikum Temple No. 96 in Covington. He died at General Hospital in Cincinnati in 1962 and was buried at Mary E. Smith Cemetery in Elsmere.

"Bacchus, Dr. Percival L.," Death Notices, *CTS,* June 6, 1962, 40.

"Journey's End, Bacchus, Dr. Percival L.," *CE,* June 6, 1962, 24.

Kentucky Board of Medical License Records, Louisville, Ky., March 25, 2004.

Theodore H. H. Harris

BAILEY, CLAY WADE (b. September 22, 1905, Little Sandy, Elliot Co., Ky.; d. February 19, 1974, Lexington, Ky.). Clay Wade Bailey, who has been called the dean of Kentucky journalists, was the son of George W. and Rebecca Weddington Bailey. Clay's father was a Sandy Hook (Elliot Co.) lawyer and schoolteacher; he died of tuberculosis in 1912. The family's children, three boys and a girl, were placed in the Louisville Masonic Widows and Orphans Home. Clay Wade attended grade school at the orphanage and then lived with relatives in Kansas during his high school years. He later graduated from Sue Bennett Junior College in London, Ky.

Clay Wade Bailey (*left*) and Governor Ned Breathitt, 1965.

Howard J. Henderson, bureau chief of the *Courier Journal* in Louisville, told of how he first met Bailey. It seems that at a campaign rally for Kentucky governor John C. W. Beckham (1900–1903, 1903–1907), Henderson saw the diminutive (five-foot-two) Bailey approach the candidate and engage him in deep conversation about current events. Henderson was so impressed by the young man's knowledge that he immediately gave him a job with his newspaper. In the 1930s, Bailey took a position with the United Press. He left that organization in 1938 to become a reporter in Covington for the ***Kentucky Post***. He also wrote columns for the *Lexington Herald* and for the *Evansville Press* in Indiana. On May 12, 1939, Bailey married Ann Robison, who died eight years later of a cerebral hemorrhage. The couple had one child, a son Logan.

Clay Wade Bailey covered Kentucky state government for the *Kentucky Post* and was said to have access to everyone there, so that he was able to write articles that no one else could even attempt. He called at least 150 people each morning, before making his rounds of Frankfort offices, where he exchanged stories and gathered the latest gossip. Bailey was a friend of everyone in state government, from the governor to the clerks and janitors. He had a photographic memory and also an encyclopedic knowledge of Kentucky history. He also possessed ithe uncanny ability to read upside down, namely government documents that were lying on officials' desks.

In 1970 Bailey received three of the greatest honors of his life. A Clay Wade Bailey Day was proclaimed at the capitol in Frankfort, he was asked to address all three branches of government (an unprecedented honor), and Kentucky governor Louie B. Nunn (1967–1971) named an Ohio River bridge after him. When learning of the bridge's naming, Bailey quipped, "I just hope that with a name like that, it won't fall into the Ohio River." Bailey did not live to see that bridge dedicated. He died at the age of 68, at St. Joseph's Hospital in Lexington, about a week after suffering a stroke. He was buried next to his wife, Ann, in the Frankfort Cemetery.

Reis, Jim. "Honoring Clay Wade Bailey," *KP,* August 23, 2004.

——. "Omniscient Bailey Was Friend to All," *KP,* February 27, 1984.

Univ. of Kentucky. "Clay Wade Bailey." www.uky.edu.

Jack Wessling

BAILEY, WILLIAM S. (b. February 10, 1806, Centerville, Ohio; d. February 20, 1886, Nashville, Tenn.). William Shreve Bailey, an abolitionist, an editor, and a proprietor of several antislavery newspapers, was the son of John and Rebekah Shreve Bailey. He married Caroline A. Withnall in Wheeling, Va. (now W.Va.), on December 13, 1827. Bailey was trained as a mechanic; in 1839 he moved his family to Newport, where he opened a machine shop. He wrote numerous articles in the *Newport News* that advocated abolition (see **Abolitionists**; **Antislaver**y), thereby causing difficulties for the newspaper's owner, a man named Ryan. Bailey was encouraged to purchase the newspaper and its press.

Besides the *Newport News,* Bailey also published several other newspapers dedicated to antislavery, such as the *Kentucky Weekly News,* the *Newport & Covington Daily News,* and the *Free South.* Bailey's sentiments gained the attention of other abolitionists, but in contrast to most of them, who were concerned about religious and moral issues, Bailey's opposition to slavery was based on economic principles. He believed that all workers should be paid for their efforts. Prominent abolitionist **John G. Fee** thought Bailey lacked the intelligence and correct principles for abolition work, and Fee communicated his opinion to the American Missionary Association. Fee even refused to associate with Bailey.

Bailey's newspapers were constantly in need of financial help. In 1851 his office and presses where destroyed by fire. Proslavery Kentuckians also were pressuring his supporters in Cincinnati. Although Fee did not agree with Bailey's efforts, he believed that the newspaper would be a useful tool in the antislavery efforts in Kentucky. In a rare instance of communication with Bailey, Fee recommended William Goodell, a Northern antislavery minister and writer, as a possible editor.

In 1858 Bailey requested and received financial help for his *Free South.* In 1859, a few days after the John Brown raid at Harper's Ferry, Va., a mob entered Bailey's office and destroyed his presses and type. Bailey had the advantage of being in Newport, just across the Ohio River from Cincinnati, so in 1860 he brought suit in a Cincinnati court against some Campbell Co. residents for the destruction of his printing office. He was then warned to leave the state, but, ignoring the warnings, he continued to publish his paper. Bailey was arrested after the reappearance of the *Free South,* charged with incendiarism, and jailed. He was granted bail and departed for England. He later returned to Kentucky, but his trial never took place because the **Civil War** had begun.

During the war Bailey continued publishing the *Free South,* reporting on the activities of the Lincoln administration and pertinent antislavery actions. In 1867 he was arrested and sued for libel in Campbell Co. Circuit Court by J. R. Hallam. Bailey agreed to print a retraction and to pay Hallam's attorney fees. He moved to Nashville, where he died in 1886; he was buried in Nashville.

"Aid for 'The Free South,'" *Free South,* September 3, 1858, 2.
Allen, L. P. *The Genealogy and History of the Shreve Family from 1641.* Greenfield, Ill.: Privately published, 1901.
Aptheker, Herbert. *Anti-Racism in U.S. History.* New York: Greenwood Press, 1992.
"Fire in Newport," *CJ,* October 11, 1851, 2.
"Married," *Free South,* January 7, 1859, 3.
"Newport," *CDE,* April 1, 1867, 1.
Steely, Will Frank. "William Shreve Bailey; Kentucky Abolitionist," *FCHQ* 31 (1957): 274–81.
"The Title of Our Paper," *Free South,* September 3, 1858, 2.
"William S. Bailey," *CJ,* February 4, 1860, 2.

Theodore H. H. Harris

BAIRD, HANNAH HUME (b. April 8, 1939, Stearns, Ky.; d. March 31, 2004, Florence, Ky.). Hannah Hume Baird, a political activist, a community leader, and a women's rights champion, was the daughter of Clarence Whitman and Hattie P. Hume. Her father, who was the editor of the *McCreary County (Ky.) Record* and the principal of Stearns High School, was a descendant of the Hand family that had once owned large amounts of land around the town of Morgan, in Pendleton Co., Ky. Hannah graduated from Sullins Junior College for Women, Bristol, Va., and later from the University of Kentucky at Lexington. In 1958 she married Glenn F. Baird, who had been a fellow university student. While Glenn attended medical school at the University of Louisville, Hannah taught in the Jefferson Co., Ky., schools. The couple became the parents of two children. The Baird family moved to Florence, Ky., in 1964, where Hannah was involved in Democratic politics and with women's and children's issues. She was also a great lover of history and helped establish the **Dinsmore Homestead** Foundation, which was responsible for saving the Dinsmore Farm, near Burlington, Ky. She served as a board member for the **American Red Cross**, the Community Chest, **Northern Kentucky University**, and several other institutions.

During President Jimmy Carter's administration (1977–1981), Hannah was appointed to the National Advisory Council on Economic Opportunity. The *Cincinnati Enquirer* named her Woman of the Year in 1978, and her portrait was added to the Women Remembered Collection, on display at the Kentucky state capitol in Frankfort.

Hannah Hume Baird died in her Florence home of esophageal cancer at age 64. She was cremated and her ashes were buried in the Hume family section of the Morgan Cemetery, in Pendleton Co. She was survived by her husband, her son, Glenn W, and her daughter, Hannah E. In March 2004 the *Kentucky Post* recognized her as one of Northern Kentucky's Most Outstanding Women. She was also posthumously awarded a Lifetime Advocate Award, by a panel from the Outstanding Women of Kentucky.

"Doer, Achiever, Risk-Taker, Hannah Hume Baird," *KP,* April 1, 2004, 1.
"Hannah Baird, Community Leader," *CE,* April 2, 2004, 4B.
"Hannah Hume Baird," *KP,* April 1, 2004, 11A.

BAKER, JOSHUA, COLONEL (b. 1762, Virginia; d. 1816, Owen Co., Ky.). Joshua Baker, an Owen Co. Indian fighter and pioneer, came to Kentucky from Virginia and in 1775 married Mary Callaway, a relative of Richard Callaway, one of the leaders at the Kentucky Fort Boonesborough. In 1776 two of Callaway's daughters, Betsy and Francis, along with Daniel Boone's daughter, Jemima, were kidnapped outside the fort by Indians. The three girls were later dramatically rescued.

Baker, who was a colonel in the Virginia Militia, scouted on the north side of the Ohio River in 1787 when that area was still filled with bands of hostile Indians. His fellow scout on this mission was his friend **Simon Kenton**. In 1792 he and Kenton tried unsuccessfully to capture the Shawnee Indian chief Tecumseh. Baker was an officer in Kentucky's Cornstalk Militia (so called because Kentucky's citizen soldiers carried an assortment of arms) from 1792 until 1811. During that time he also served as a delegate to the state convention that wrote the second Kentucky Constitution in 1799. Baker died in 1816; his former home and his grave are two miles south of the junction of Ky. Rt. 227 and Highway 330, south of Owenton.

KYHistorical Society. "Kentucky Historical Marker Database." http://kentucky.gov/kyhs/hmdb/MarkerSearch.aspx.
Lee, Lloyd G. *A Brief History of Kentucky.* Berea: Kentucky Imprints, 1981.

BAKER, RICHARD TARVIN (b. September 13, 1816, Alexandria, Ky.; d. 1891, Alexandria, Ky.). Lawyer and legislator Richard Tarvin Baker was the fifth of the 13 children of Samuel Baker, a native of Westmoreland Co., Pa., and the former Elizabeth Armstrong of Mason Co. In 1797 Samuel Baker had come to Northern Kentucky and settled on a farm on Pond Creek Road, near the Licking River. Richard Baker's early education was in Campbell Co. schools, and in March 1843 he graduated from the Cincinnati Law School. He was elected Campbell Co. clerk in 1844 and became county attorney in 1846. In 1849 he was elected to the Kentucky House of Representatives, and in 1860 he became a state senator. In 1863, and again in 1867, he was the Republican candidate for governor but was defeated both times. When embattled Governor Beriah Magoffin was forced out of office during the Civil War because of his Confederate loyalty, Baker served for a short time as acting governor. The next in line of succession was Lieutenant Governor Linn Boyd, but he had recently died, so while a permanent replacement for the governor was being sought, Baker held the position.

In 1841 Baker married Sarah B. Beall, the daughter of Benjamin Duke Beall. They built a magnificent home next to the courthouse in Alexandria. Tragically, she died less than three years later. On February 9, 1854, he married Maria J. Orr, daughter of John Orr, a prominent physician in Alexandria. Richard had no children by his first wife and five by his second. He died in 1891 and was buried in the Alexandria Cemetery. According to local legend, the celebrated author **Samuel Clemens** (Mark Twain) was Baker's friend and occasionally visited him at his Alexandria home.

Kleber, John E., ed. *The Kentucky Encyclopedia,* s.v. "Distinguished Men of Kentucky." Lexington: Univ. Press of Kentucky, 1992.

Jack Wessling

BAKER-HUNT FOUNDATION. Baker-Hunt, an educational foundation, is located at 620 Greenup St., within the **Licking-Riverside National Historic District** of Covington. Its headquarters is a lovely Victorian home. Throughout the year classes in drawing, painting, photography, pottery, quilting, and other topics are offered at this center for both children and adults. The beautifully landscaped garden campus also contains a second 19th-century house, an auditorium building, and a classroom building. This gift to the community was made possible in 1922 when Margaretta Wager Baker-Hunt set up a trust fund at a Cincinnati bank to establish the Baker-Hunt Foundation with her holdings of stock investments and property. The purposes of the foundation were to promote the study of art, education, and science and to support the religious and spiritual development of Covington and the vicinity. Since Margaretta Hunt's death in 1930, board members and executive directors have carried out her intentions with a wide range of programs. The goals she established reflected the values and spirit of her family. Her parents, John and Henrietta Baker, had moved in 1839 from Philadelphia to Cincinnati, where John and his friend Henry Von Phul started an oil lamp business. It was a time of growth and prosperity for the region, and in the following years the young partners were quick to adopt new and innovative products to meet the changing needs of their customers. As a result, both men became very wealthy.

In 1854 John Baker purchased the house along Greenup St., which became home for him, Henrietta, and their children, William and Margaretta. The family's active membership in the community included involvement with **Trinity Episcopal Church**. Their home became a center of social and cultural events, and they were generous in their philanthropic gifts. They contributed in meaningful ways to the region that had helped foster their wealth. As the years passed, there were many happy times for the family, but they also experienced significant losses. One such loss occurred in 1866, when William Baker died at the young age of 22. A happier occasion was the marriage of Margaretta

Baker to Dr. William Hunt of Covington in 1872 and their decision to make their home at 620 Greenup St. with John and Henrietta. Misfortune struck again when Margaretta and William Hunt's only child, daughter Katie, died of spinal meningitis on her 15th birthday. These two family deaths meant that the Baker and Hunt families were left with no heirs, and Margaretta Hunt wanted to establish the foundation so that the proud traditions of the families would continue.

To ensure a good beginning for the kind of programs Margaretta envisioned, a two-part plan was launched. The first was to construct a building that would house an excellent natural-history collection owned by Archie Williams of Covington. He later became the curator when the museum opened in October 1930. The museum provided education classes for Covington schoolchildren and a variety of other programs that were recognized for excellence. The museum operated until the late 1940s. The second phase of the plan stipulated that Margaretta's personal secretary and confidante, Virginia Reed, be named executive secretary of the foundation when it became operational. Reed worked with the board of directors to recruit talented and trained staff members. By 1932 art and music classes for children were begun, and they became very popular. Later, craft classes for boys and sewing and knitting classes for girls were added. The Six-Twenty Club for young businesswomen was organized to provide educational, social, and service activities for them. The need for such a program became evident when it grew so rapidly that membership limits had to be set. Other adult classes included training in art, music, drama, and leadership. The drama and choral groups offered public performances for the community.

The variety of programs offered to the public by the Baker-Hunt Foundation during the troubling years of the **Great Depression** and **World War II** became significant for the people of Covington and Northern Kentucky. The art and cultural activities gave them time away from personal and world problems to participate in uplifting cultural experiences. Designing programs to meet changing times has continued to be a challenge for the Baker-Hunt Foundation's board and the executive program directors. The foundation's success continues, as evidenced by the increasing number of people enrolled in class offerings through the years. Until 1995 there were no fees for the children's classes. In addition to the ongoing emphasis on drawing, painting, and ceramics, there has been expansion into other cultural areas with classes in dance, languages, and music. A recent innovative class called WORMS (We're Organically Re-cycling Mulchers) has been offered for children of ages 5 to 11. This program celebrates nature through art, gardening, and community projects. Many art classes offered at the Baker-Hunt Foundation's facility also benefit children who are homeschooled or otherwise lack public school art instruction.

Outreach to the community has also been enhanced with scholarship programs for youth and seniors. The Baker-Hunt Foundation has supplied art teachers for senior centers and other organizations requiring on-site art lessons; these offerings have been supported by the Friends of Baker-Hunt, a volunteer organization. The Friends of Baker-Hunt has established a house museum in part of the original mansion, consisting of a unique collection of clothing, furniture, letters, paintings, photographs, and journals belonging to the Baker and Hunt families. This collection not only features the artifacts of bygone generations but also documents a valuable component of the history of Covington. The legacy of Margaretta Baker Hunt has favorably impacted the community. The Baker-Hunt Foundation prides itself in making this contribution and being a part of the rich historical and cultural fabric of Covington and Northern Kentucky.

Archives of the Baker-Hunt Foundation, Baker-Hunt Foundation, Covington, Ky.

"Baker-Hunt to Begin Classes," *KP,* December 30, 1931, 1.

Franzen, Gene. "Now & Then—Covington's Baker Hunt Foundation," *KE,* October 8, 2000, B1.

"Garden of Mrs. Hunt Described," *KP,* August 15, 1914, 1.

"Natural History Museum Planned," *KTS,* May 14, 1929, 1.

Stevens, Harry R. ***Six Twenty: Margaretta Hunt and the Baker-Hunt Foundation.*** Covington, Ky.: Baker-Hunt, 1942.

Whitson, Frances, and Margaret Jacobs. "If These Walls Could Talk: Covington's Baker-Hunt Foundation," *NKH* 12, no. 1 (Fall–Winter 2004): 2–10.

Mary Frances Whitson

BAKEWELL FAMILY. In 1832 developer and businessman Thomas Woodhouse Bakewell (1778–1874), of the firm of Bakewell, Page, and Bakewell, acquired substantial property in Covington, which by the mid-1830s had become the Johnson-Bakewell subdivision, a part of the **West Side** (see also **Main Strasse**). Thomas Woodhouse Bakewell began his business career working as an importer in New York for his uncle Benjamin Bakewell of Pittsburgh, Pa., "the father" of flint glass-making.

Back in England, William Bakewell, the father of Thomas Bakewell, had known the grandfather of Charles Darwin. William Bakewell immigrated and settled in 1802 near Valley Forge, Pa., where he became a gentleman farmer. A neighbor, famed naturalist **John James Audubon**, married William Bakewell's daughter Lucy. In 1819 Audubon moved to Cincinnati and sketched cliff swallows near the Licking River. William Bakewell's sister Ann married Alexander Gordon, a well-to-do New Orleans businessman whose father, Maj. William Gordon, owned a sugar plantation and was a part owner of a mercantile house at Natchez, Miss. Thomas Bakewell learned the southern cotton business from the Gordons. By about 1820, Thomas Bakewell had become involved in foundry and shipbuilding enterprises in Louisville.

Having moved to Cincinnati in 1824, Thomas Bakewell set up two businesses, to build steam engines and to build sugar mills. He operated a shipyard that produced three steamboats each year until 1830. While living in Cincinnati, Bakewell was a director of the Mechanics Institute and of the Cincinnati branch of the Bank of the United States, a director and president of the Ohio Insurance Company, and a member of a special three-man committee seeking to build a railroad between Cincinnati and Charleston, S.C. (see **Cincinnati and Charleston Railroad**). Another business partnership, the Bakewell-Cartwright foundry, lasted until 1844.

The panic and economic depression of 1837 caused Bakewell, who by this time had expanded into a number of business enterprises in Covington, to divest himself of some of his businesses. He sold off his interest in Covington's Johnston-Bakewell housing subdivision and also lost the title to his large Covington burlap-bagging factory. In the mid-1830s, that factory had produced $25,000 worth of finished hemp per year. It manufactured bags and ropes for transporting 400-pound bales of cotton. After another depression in 1857 closed his business career, Bakewell resided with one of his 12 children near Pittsburgh until his 1874 death and burial in Spring Grove Cemetery, in Cincinnati.

According to Mrs. **Stephens Blakely**, a descendant of Thomas Bakewell, his daughters attended a fashionable female academy as residents of a venerable family mansion built by Bakewell, located at 653–655 Dalton St. in Covington. Demolished in 1970, the estate was said by a local newspaper society columnist in 1929 to be "a home of great interest, the lawns being covered with statuary . . . the meeting place of artists and literary men of the day." In Bakewell's day, men with dreams and with economic motives such as **Thomas D. Carneal**, **William Bullock**, and Thomas Bakewell viewed the area west of Covington as potentially a pristine retreat from the bustling activities taking place across the Ohio River in Cincinnati. Inventors, developers, and entrepreneurs in the steamboat era were often teachers, artists, and people of culture, and the Bakewells were members of that class of society.

Blakely, Mrs. Stephens L. "The Covington I Remember." ***Papers of the Christopher Gist Historical Society,*** vol. 1, paper read March 28, 1950.

Laidley, Mary. "This Was Meeting Place of Artists and Teachers," *KP,* October 27, 1929, 8.

Sinclair, Bruce, ed. "Thomas Woodhouse Bakewell's Autobiographical Sketch and Its Relation to Early Steamboat Engineering on the Ohio," *FCHQ* 40, no. 3 (July 1966): 235–48.

Tenkotte, Paul A. "Rival Cities to Suburbs: Covington and Newport, Kentucky, 1790–1890," PhD diss., Univ. of Cincinnati, 1989.

John Boh

BALL FAMILY SINGERS. The Ball Family Gospel Singing Group of Covington began in 1969, when Herbert Ball, his son Nelson Ball, his daughter Peggy Ball Arnold, Carole Hill, and Ruby Williams decided to "make a difference." Since then they have traveled all around the country in a tour bus that once belonged to magician David Copperfield. Previously, gospel singer Herbert Ball often had sung on radio station WLW-AM Cincinnati and on early local television. The group has performed at churches, auditoriums, camp meetings, prisons, and community events across the nation. They mix music, humor, and real-life testimonies on stage, usually starting with their version of the classic "Amazing Grace." The Balls do about 250 concerts annually.

Although Herbert Ball died in September 1981, the group has stayed much the same over the years. It has added three new members: Sarina Ball, Glen Steely, and Paul Shelton. The Balls have published 35 albums and have won several awards for their work. One such recognition was from the City of Covington, which proclaimed them Goodwill Ambassadors. They were also the first gospel group ever to sing in the Roman Catholic **Cathedral Basilica of the Assumption** in Covington, where they have an open invitation to return every year. In 1996 the **Wilmington Baptist Church** in southern Kenton Co. hosted a Ball family homecoming. Today the group is led by Nelson Ball, who does the bookings, and Arnold Ball, who handles the administration.

"Ball Family Singers," *KP*, June 12, 2003, 5K.
"Gospel Music to Fill the Air at Ball Family Homecoming," *KP*, August 31, 1996, 6K.
"Herbert P. Ball," *KE*, September 24, 1981, D5.

Elizabeth Comer Williams

BANKEMPER, CARL (b. October 23, 1917, Bellevue, Ky.; d. November 29, 1984, Park Hills, Ky.). Carl Cyril Anthony Bankemper was one of the most influential designers of Northern Kentucky's architectural landscape for more than 30 years. He graduated from the **Covington Latin School** in 1935. From 1943 to 1946 he served overseas in the 6th U.S. Naval Construction Battalion, attached to the 1st Marine Division, and participated in the invasion of Guadalcanal and Okinawa. After his discharge, Bankemper married Dorothy Kathryn Beiser on September 28, 1946. They resided in Park Hills and raised a family of six daughters and a son. Bankemper received his degrees in architecture from the University of Cincinnati and the University of Illinois and was a member emeritus of the American Institute of Architects.

Before his military service, Carl Bankemper worked as a draftsman in Cincinnati. When he returned from the navy, he restarted his career. Around 1952 he and an associate, Fred E. Betz, formed the architectural firm of Betz, Bankemper & Associates in Covington. In 1961 Betz left the firm, and Carl C. Bankemper & Associates was established. Bankemper designed several churches, schools, convents, and other buildings for the Diocese of Covington (see **Roman Catholics**), including the **Covington Catholic High School**, Park Hills (1953); the **Newport Central Catholic High School**, Newport (1953); the St. Agnes Elementary School and Rectory, Fort Wright (1955); the St. Francis Xavier Elementary School, Falmouth (1956); the **Marydale** Retreat House, Boone Co. (1955–1966); the St. Pius X Elementary School and Rectory, Kenton Co. (1956–1957); the St. Pius X Seminary Building (1956–1957) and Gymnasium (1961–1962), Boone Co.; the St. John the Evangelist Parish School and Convent, Carrollton (1958); the **St. Vincent de Paul Catholic Church**, Newport (1958); the **St. Joseph Catholic Church** and Rectory (1959) and Convent (1964), Cold Spring; the St. Mary Elementary School, Alexandria (1960–1961); the **St. Catherine of Siena Catholic Church**, Fort Thomas (1962); the Immaculate Heart of Mary Elementary School, Hebron; the **Diocesan Catholic Children's Home,** Fort Mitchell; and the **St. Charles Care Center**, Covington. Bankemper was the designer and architect of many other church projects throughout the Midwest, such as the St. William Church and Community Hall, Lancaster, Ky. (1960), and the St. Edward Church and Rectory, Cynthiana (1966).

His firm designed government, municipal and commercial structures, including four Internal Revenue Service Centers, in Memphis; in Washington, D.C.; in Kansas City, Mo.; and in Covington. The firm also designed the Boone Co. Courthouse; the Hall of Justice, the Courthouse Annex, the Administration Building, the jail, and the Health Clinic for Burlington; the City-County Building for Covington and Kenton Co., Covington; the Panorama Apartments, East and West Units, Covington; the Golden Tower, Covington; the Woodspoint Nursing Home, Florence; the Rosedale Manor, Covington; the Glenn O. Swing Elementary School, Covington; the Latonia Elementary School, Latonia; **Peoples-Liberty Bank** locations in Northern Kentucky; the Columbia Federal Savings & Loan, Covington; the Kentucky Executive Building, Fort Mitchell; and the Town & Country Restaurant, Park Hills. Bankemper also designed a parking garage in downtown Indianapolis.

Bankemper retired in 1983 and was honored by his many friends and colleagues with a surprise dinner party to celebrate his retirement and his career of over three decades. He died in 1984 and was interred in the St. Mary Cemetery mausoleum in Fort Mitchell.

"Architect Carl Bankemper, Designed Kenton, Boone Municipal Buildings," *KP*, November 30, 1984, 12C.
"He Left His Mark," *KP*, December 5, 1984, 4K.

Norbert F. DeJaco

BANKLICK CREEK AND WATERSHED. Banklick Creek drains 58 square miles of northern Kenton and eastern Boone counties. It discharges into the Licking River some 4.7 miles upstream from the confluence of the Licking and the Ohio rivers. The main stem is approximately 19 miles long. Tributaries in the Banklick watershed include Brushy Fork, Bullock Pen Creek, Fowler Creek, Holds Branch, Mosers Branch, Thompson Branch, and Wolf Pen Branch.

The Banklick watershed includes unincorporated areas and 10 cities and towns that had a combined population of about 65,000 in 2000. Early settlement in the watershed included the city of Taylor Mill, founded near a **sawmill** and **gristmill** business built in 1795 about one-fourth mile upstream from the Licking River.

Since settlement, agriculture has been the traditional land use in the headwaters and upland areas of the Banklick watershed. During the **Civil War** land was cleared more quickly than before, for construction of fortifications. In 2004 approximately 33 percent of the watershed, primarily in the northern part, was forested. Almost 75 percent of the watershed can be classified as riparian (near-stream) areas owing to the dense distribution of small streams. As the water flows downstream (northward), the watershed becomes increasingly urbanized; its streams enter Covington in the residential and light-industrial neighborhood of Latonia.

Natural flooding and droughts are cyclical natural conditions exacerbated by human activities. Major flooding in 1997 and 1998 in the Banklick watershed was followed by extreme drought in 1999. In 1973 the U.S. Department of Agriculture, in cooperation with the Kenton Co. Conservation District, published a plan to control flooding using three dams. Only one dam was built, however. The filling of the impoundment in 1982 created the 51-acre Doe Run Lake, which is the largest body of water in the county (excluding the Licking and Ohio rivers). Continued urbanization has increased surface-water runoff, leading to additional flooding. In response, the U.S. Army Corps of Engineers and Kenton Co. have developed a plan to buy out the most seriously affected properties.

Sources of pollution include overflows by sanitary and combined sewers, failing septic systems, illegal discharges, urban and agricultural runoff, and industrial "Superfund" sites. Steep topography, deforestation, and land disturbance during development, combined with readily eroded, poorly permeable soils, also result in excess sediment in the stream. Efforts to reduce the impact of pollution date at least as far back as 1958, when barriers to odors were built along the upstream banks. In 1998 the stream was placed on the list of impaired waters reported to the U.S. Environmental Protection Agency by the Commonwealth of Kentucky. Problems listed in 2002 included pathogens (fecal coliform), siltation (sediment deposition), excess nutrients (nitrogen and phosphorus), excess organic substances and a low level of dissolved oxygen, stream-channel changes, , and a poor habitat for organisms. A study completed in 2004 for Sanitation District No. 1 (see **Sanitation**) also indicated pollution by heavy metals.

Through an interagency prioritization process completed in 2000, the Kentucky Division of Water listed Banklick as one of the three highest-priority watersheds in the Licking River region. The Banklick Watershed Council was incorporated in 2001 to address the issues identified, and in November 2005 the council published a comprehensive watershed action plan to (1) clean the water, (2) reduce flooding, (3) restore the banks, and (4) honor the creek's heritage.

In October 2005 Sanitation District No. 1 entered into a consent decree with the U.S. Department of Justice, the U.S. Environmental Protection Agency, and the Commonwealth of Kentucky to deal with sewer overflows and water quality in Northern Kentucky, including all of the Banklick watershed. The effort is expected to take approximately 20 years.

Banklick Watershed Council. "Introducing the Banklick Watershed Action Plan." www.banklick.org (accessed December 27, 2006).

Kentucky Water Science Center. "Water Resources Data for Kentucky." U.S. Geological Survey. http://ky.water.usgs.gov/ (accessed December 27, 2006).

Sanitation District No. 1. www.sd1.org (accessed December 27, 2006).

Marc F. Hult

BANKLICK TURNPIKE COMPANY. The Banklick Turnpike Company, chartered by an act of the Kentucky legislature in 1839, was to build a road that followed a much older **buffalo trace** from Covington to the central Bluegrass region. The capital stock of the corporation was $40,000, sold at $50 a share, and stock sales began on the second Monday of May 1839. In Covington the stock sales were under the direction of John B. Casey, Frederick Gedge, A. P. Howell, John Perry, and Robert Wallace, who were appointed commissioners.

Farther out in Kenton Co., stock was sold at the store of Elijah Williams in the Bagby Precinct, where Thomas Corgan, Ezra K. Fisk, Robert Perry, and Williams were appointed commissioners. When 150 shares had been sold, the stockholders met and elected a president and four directors. A. W. Gilbert, city engineer for the City of Cincinnati, made the original road survey.

In February 1844 the corporation was reincorporated to build a turnpike from the Covington city limits stretching 12 miles to the south. Additional stock sales were held at Colmansville, Crittenden, Cynthiana, Falmouth, and Williamstown. Construction probably began in 1845. The actual road was 30 to 40 feet wide, and the artificial, or macadamized, portion was at least 16 feet wide. The road was lengthened to 17 miles and then extended to the Pendleton Co. line. After 1900 the road became known as the **Three-L Highway** to emphasize the connection with Latonia, Lexington, and Louisville, or with the names of the three racetracks in those cities, the Three-L Racetracks, each of which also began with the letter *L*. At the turn of the 20th century, the turnpike was taken over by the fiscal courts of the counties through which it passed, and the tollgates were removed.

Truesdale, C. B. "Early Turnpikes Which Led to and from the Newport-Covington Area," a paper delivered at the October 28, 1952, meeting of the Christopher Gist Historical Society, Covington, Ky.

Joseph F. Gastright

BANK OF KENTUCKY (MODERN). The Bank of Kentucky, a full-service commercial bank, was formed in 1990 by a group of local investors with strong ties to the Northern Kentucky community, including **Rodney "Biz" Cain**, **R. C. Durr**, and Robert Zapp. The bank was originally called the Bank of Boone County, but in 1995 it acquired Burnett Federal Savings Bank (see **Savings and Loan Associations**). The name was then changed to the Bank of Kentucky. Soon thereafter, the Fort Thomas Savings Bank was acquired, giving the Bank of Kentucky locations in Boone, Campbell, Grant, and Kenton counties. By 2002 the Bank of Kentucky, headquartered in Crestview Hills, had purchased the assets of the local Peoples Bank of Northern Kentucky, thereby becoming the area's fastest-growing bank. The Bank of Kentucky plays a major leadership role in the Northern Kentucky community, with more than 270 employees, $900 million in assets, 27 branches, and 41 ATM locations. Its latest branch is near **Newport-on-the-Levee** at Fifth and Monmouth Sts. in Newport. The bank has given major gifts to **Thomas More College** for its Bank of Kentucky Observatory and also its Bank of Kentucky Field (an athletic field) and to **Northern Kentucky University** for its Bank of Kentucky Arena.

The Bank of Kentucky. www.bankofkyhb.com (accessed March 27, 2006).

"Bank of Kentucky to Buy Fort Thomas Financial," *CE*, December 22, 1999, B12.

"Bank of Ky Branches Out—Small-Bank Service, Big-Bank Profits," *SC*, September 19, 2004, 5B.

Gabrielle Summe

BANK OF KENTUCKY (19TH CENTURY). This bank operated a branch in Washington, Ky. (1806), and later in Maysville (1835). At the beginning of the 19th century, Kentucky was rich in land but poor in dollars. Only small amounts of money circulated within the state, and much of what did was debased currency. Paper money, of dubious value, was the accepted medium of exchange, since gold or silver coins were so rare. An economy without a stable currency cannot prosper; it usually stagnates and declines. In order to provide stability for its businesses and commerce, the Commonwealth of Kentucky chartered the Bank of Kentucky in 1806. The bank was modeled after the Bank of the United States.

A president and a 12-member board governed the Bank of Kentucky. The president and six members of the board were elected by the state legislature, while private shareholders elected the other six members. Robert Alexandria served as president of the bank from 1807 to 1821. He administered the bank in a conservative manner and developed it into a sound and profitable institution.

From 1819 to 1823, the Kentucky economy and that of the nation were shaken by a depression, in which bank loans were recalled and payment of bills was demanded. The demand for payment in gold and silver became so great that the Bank of Kentucky had to suspend specie payments in 1820. With businesses closing, farms being sold to settle debts, and citizens fleeing the state to avoid creditors, the Kentucky legislature insisted that the Bank of Kentucky adopt an inflationary fiscal policy. When the bank refused to do so, the legislature in 1820 chartered a new bank called the Bank of the Commonwealth, which flooded the state with paper currency, destroying whatever faith citizens had in paper money. Paper currency bills drawn on both the Bank of Kentucky and the Bank of the Commonwealth were soon being heavily discounted.

The runaway inflation, caused in large part by the creation of the Bank of the Commonwealth, brought economic ruin to the state. Many people who survived the depression were wiped out by the inflation. In 1822 a new legislature revoked the charters of both the Bank of Kentucky and the Bank of the Commonwealth. The Bank of the Commonwealth was without assets at the time of its demise, but the Bank of Kentucky was able to recover its capital. The Bank of Kentucky was rechartered in 1841, and then again in 1858. The repercussions from the destruction of the state's banking system adversely affected the development of Kentucky through the first half of the 20th century.

Within the Northern Kentucky region, the Bank of Kentucky operated a branch at Maysville. It was to that branch that Virgil McKnight, the long-time president of the Bank of Kentucky, sent **James Barbour** in 1852 to serve as its cashier. Barbour founded the **Bank of Maysville** in 1871, while helping to finance the completion of the **Maysville and Lexington Railroad** into Maysville in the early 1870s. In Covington the predominant state-chartered bank was the Northern Bank of Kentucky, which was organized in the mid-1830s and moved into its newly completed Covington Branch at Third and Scott Sts. in 1836. The Covington Branch of the Northern Bank of Kentucky, with headquarters in Lexington, later on was most closely associated with Northern Kentucky's **Ernst** family. It is often confused with the Bank of Kentucky, which had little impact around Covington or Newport. Covington developed later than Newport and before 1840 was part of Campbell Co., the fiscal terrain of **James Taylor Jr.**, Newport's founder, who controlled banking in the area.

The modern **Bank of Kentucky**, which just happens to occupy the original home of the Covington Branch of the Northern Bank of Kentucky, has no corporate lineage connecting it to any of these earlier banking entities.

Barlow, Don W. "How the Buck Happened to Stop Here: The Development of Banking in Covington Prior to 1880," *Colonel Covington's Chronicle*, November 1979, 11.

Barrett, Lisa V. "Banking in Kentucky," *NKH* 7, no. 2 (Spring–Summer 2000): 29–30.

Beauchamp, C. D. "Banking in Kentucky," *Kentucky Banker* (1986): 34–47.

Royalty, Dale. "Banking and the Commonwealth Ideal," *RKH* 77, no. 2 (Spring 1979): 91–107.

Charles H. Bogart

BANK OF MAYSVILLE. The Bank of Maysville is Kentucky's oldest independent bank. It began in 1835 as the Maysville branch of the Bank of Kentucky, on the site of the current **Kentucky Gateway Museum Center** on Sutton St. Its first deposit was $5,000 from James N. Morrison. In 1871 the Kentucky legislature outlawed branch banking, and at that time the bank became the Bank of Maysville. It joined the national banking system in 1916, when it absorbed the Union Trust and Savings Company of

Maysville and became the Bank of Maysville, National Banking Association. In 1919 the name reverted to the Bank of Maysville, when the institution merged with the First Standard Bank and Trust Company. In 1920 it completed its architecturally stunning headquarters at 20 W. Second St. in downtown Maysville, designed by the **Weber Brothers**, noted architects. The beautiful interior murals, completed in about 1960, were executed by Marsh and Company of Cincinnati.

This independent institution has enjoyed a stable financial history. The Bank of Maysville has had seven presidents. Its first president was Andrew M. January (see **January and Wood**), who held the position from 1835 until 1877; he was followed as president by **James Barbour** (1877–1896), J. Foster Barbour (1896–1919), and **James N. Kehoe** (1919–1945). Since 1945 the bank has been presided over by Finch family members, James M. Finch Sr. (1945–1958), James M. Finch Jr. (1958–1995), and James A. Finch (1995–present). James Kehoe was the maternal grandfather of James A. Finch. These forward-looking leaders kept the institution solvent during the **Great Depression** and continually kept pace with banking industry changes such as the introduction of drive-through banking in 1957. The bank's reputation as a regional banking pacesetter has continued. The Bank of Maysville was the first local bank in its service region to offer automated teller machine (ATM) banking in 1977, the first to install a satellite office in a local Kroger grocery store, and, in 1993, the first to offer seven-day-a-week banking. The bank has also kept pace with new banking technologies by offering on-line Internet banking services. The bank's "People caring about people" philosophy is credited for much of its success.

Throughout its history, the Bank of Maysville has taken an active role in the educational and economic health of individuals and businesses in the communities it serves. Its markets include the Kentucky counties of Bracken, Mason, and Robertson and extend 20 miles into the Ohio counties of Adams and Brown. The Bank of Maysville has supported the University of Kentucky College of Agriculture's Extension Program in Mason Co. by donating office space and telephone service. The bank strongly backed the development of the John Y. Brown Jr. **AA Highway** (Alexandria to Ashland), just as it helped to finance the completion of the **Maysville and Lexington Railroad** under James Barbour back in the early 1870s. The completion of the AA Highway has had a significant impact on the local economy: a wide variety of businesses have located in Maysville, including Mitsubishi Electric Automotive America (a car radio and automotive parts manufacturer), Green ToKai (a manufacturer of weather stripping and auto trim), and new businesses and homes.

Bank of Maysville. *125th Anniversary Bank of Maysville.* Brochure.

Bank of Maysville Collection. Vertical files, Kentucky Gateway Museum Center, Maysville, Ky.

Finch, James A. Interview by Blanche Gaynor, May 19, 2005, Maysville, Ky.

Robinson, Ella D. *Annual Report 1999: 1912–1999 Supervising Kentucky's Financial Industry for 87 Years.* Kentucky Department of Financial Institutions.

The Spirit of a Greater Maysville and Mason County. Maysville, Ky.: Daily Independent, 1929.

Blanche Gaynor

BAPTIST CONVALESCENT CENTER. The 167-bed Baptist Convalescent Center (now called Baptist Life Communities), a ministry of the Northern Kentucky Baptist Association, is affiliated with both the Kentucky Baptist Convention and the Southern Baptist Convention. In 1952 this nursing center was established as the Baptist Home of Northern Kentucky in Newport. The original building, at 120 Main St., was purchased from the **Campbell Co. Protestant Orphan's Home**. It was once the estate of former Newport mayor George Fearon. Frederick W. Winkler, a longtime Campbell Co. veterinarian and local history buff, was the president of the Baptist Home of Northern Kentucky in its early years. The center has experienced tremendous growth since that time. It was expanded in 1954, 1957, 1960, and 1967. A replacement wing was built in 1989, and an assisted-living unit was added in the late 1990s.

Beginning in the mid-1990s, this ministry extended its boundaries beyond Newport into three other locations in Northern Kentucky. One is the Baptist Village complex in Erlanger, which currently consists of four distinct units: the Long House (48 beds), the Munro House (58 beds), the Village Care Center (100 beds), and the Baptist Commons (32 condominiums). These units offer a variety of levels of care, from skilled nursing care to independent living. The second new location is the multistory St. John Nursing Health Care Center along Highland Ave. in Covington, which was purchased in the late 1990s and renamed Baptist Towers; currently it houses more than 100 residents. The third new location is the Greisser Farm Retirement Village in Burlington, a facility designed for senior independent living. The development of this retirement home was made possible by a 1998 gift of land from Dorotha Griesser.

These acquisitions led the original umbrella organization to change its corporate name from the Baptist Convalescent Center to Baptist Life Communities, a name more in tune with the agency's broadened, nonsectarian mission. Administrators for the center and the other communities have been Mr. and Mrs. W. N. Carnes (1952–1959), Rev. Leo Drake (1959–1969), Robert Ronald Wilson (1969–1970), George Jones (interim), Arnold Caddell (1971–1978), Rev. Lee Hopkins (1978–1991), Gary Parker (1991–2001), John Hutchinson (interim), and Dr. Robert Long, (2003–present). This nonprofit care-giving organization has earned and retains its excellent reputation for serving people.

"Baptists Purchase Old Orphans' Home," *KP,* June 22, 1951, 1.

"Home for Aged Has Anniversary," *KP,* September 26, 1955, 1.

Lynch, Iardella. *The History of the Baptist Convalescent Center, 1952–1983.* Newport, Ky., 1983.

Northern Kentucky Baptist Association. *Annual of the Northern Kentucky Baptist Association.* Erlanger, Ky.: The Association, 1984–2004.

Perry Bratcher

BAPTISTS. John Tanner was the first known Baptist minister to come to Northern Kentucky. He and his family, originally from Virginia, first came to Central Kentucky; they settled near what is now Petersburg in Boone Co. during the 1780s (see **Tanner's Station**), built a cabin, and began raising crops. American Indians kidnapped Tanner's nine-year-old son, also named John Tanner, in 1789. The Tanner family is reported to have lost a second son to the Indians also, and they soon moved back to Central Kentucky. John Tanner held some religious services locally but never established a church in Northern Kentucky. In August 1791 a Baptist congregation was established (see **Old Baptist Church on the Dry Ridge**) near **Campbell's Blockhouse** in what later became Grant Co. In June 1794 a small group of Baptists moved to what is now Boone Co. from Central Kentucky and organized a Baptist church of seven members in the North Bend area of the Ohio River. That church, called the **Bullittsburg Baptist Church**, retains its original records from early 1795 to the present. Soon other Baptist churches were established in Northern Kentucky: Mouth of the Licking (now **First Baptist Church, Cold Spring**) in 1794, Forks of the Licking Baptist Church (now Falmouth Baptist Church) in 1795, Dry Creek Baptist Church in 1800, Bank Lick Baptist Church in 1801, and Middle Creek Baptist Church (now **Belleview Baptist Church**) in 1803. The **Ten Mile Baptist Church**, in what is today Gallatin Co., was established in 1804. David Lillard became pastor there in 1817 and served for 42 years. When Lillard began his ministry, the church had about 50 members; when he retired, it had nearly 400.

In the 19th century, Baptist churches met only one Sunday of the month; usually they conducted any business that was necessary on the Saturday just before their Sunday worship service. Churchgoers would travel by horseback or in a horse-drawn carriage or wagon, and most of the early church meetinghouses were located near a water source, so that people's animals could be watered properly. Often a preacher would pastor as many as three or four churches at the same time. Ministers received very little financial compensation throughout the 19th century and generally were bivocational. Not until near the end of the century did many of the churches begin meeting on a weekly basis. If evening services were held, light was supplied by lanterns in the days before electricity became available.

The great frontier revival of 1800–1801 occurred in Northern Kentucky as in other areas of the state. Rev. **John Taylor** was a frontier Baptist preacher who came to Northern Kentucky and preached at the Bullittsburg Baptist Church. He described in his book, *A History of Ten Baptist Churches* (1823), how the revival he conducted in Northern Kentucky began in a service in the Corn

Creek community of Gallatin (now Trimble) Co. Soon the revival spread to Boone Co. and to other parts of Northern Kentucky. There were many unusual activities (the falling-down experience, the barking experience, the swooning experience) described at Cane Ridge Campground in Bourbon Co. and other Central Kentucky communities, but these were not reported in Northern Kentucky. In 1800 more than 122 persons professed faith in Christ and were baptized in the four churches that existed in Northern Kentucky, and as a result some new Baptist churches were organized. More revival activity followed in 1801. Revivals among the Baptist churches in Northern Kentucky were also recorded in 1811, when 277 were baptized; in 1817–1818, with 728 baptisms; and in 1828–1829, with 228 immersions. These events led to the organization of more new churches in the region's outlying areas.

The first Baptist churches of the Northern Kentucky area became members of the Elkhorn Association of Central Kentucky, which was organized in 1785. The North Bend Baptist Association (named after the northernmost curve in the Ohio River) was established in 1803 with 9 churches. It grew to 25 churches by 1827, but then 8 churches from Campbell Co. withdrew and established another association, which they named Campbell Co. Baptist Association. These two associations merged in 1967 and became the Northern Kentucky Baptist Association; the year after they merged, 61 churches and 22,199 members belonged to the association. In 2005 the association had 70 churches with 34,600 members reported, the third-largest number for any association in the state. But this is not the only Baptist association in the region.

The Bracken Association was established in 1799. Lewis Craig, leader of the famed "Traveling Church" that came to Kentucky from Virginia, was regarded as the father of this association. In the Bracken Association during the years 1827–1828, there were 1,116 persons baptized. Some members in the Bracken Association were adamantly opposed to slavery. For example, a church near Mayslick, pastored by Donald Holmes, adopted emancipation principles. Some of the churches separated from the Bracken Association and formed an association that emphasized the abolition of slavery. The Bracken Association presently extends along the Ohio River from Augusta eastward to beyond Vanceburg and as far south as Morehead.

The Ten Mile Association was constituted in 1831 from 9 churches, with 4 churches from the North Bend Association and others from Gallatin Co. This association presently has 15 churches in its membership. The Crittenden Association includes 29 churches in Grant, Pendleton, and Harrison counties. The Union Association has 15 churches from Falmouth, Brooksville, and Cynthiana. The Owen Co. Association has a total of 24 churches, and the White's Run Association has 10 churches in Carroll Co. and the surrounding area.

For most of the 19th century, the various associations annually sent out a circular letter to member churches, according to a custom that began among Baptists in early 17th-century England. The letter was written by a local pastor or church leader and usually emphasized a doctrinal theme or an exhortation to the churches.

Baptists are noted for their doctrinal beliefs that salvation is by grace through faith in Jesus Christ and that there are two symbolic ordinances of the church, baptism and the Lord's Supper, or Communion. Baptism is for believers only, by immersion of the believer in water, and the Lord's Supper is administered by a church to its members. The two offices, or official positions, in the Baptist church are pastors and deacons. There are some Baptists who believe that foot-washing is also a church ordinance, and some hold that elders are a third type of official in the church. Individual churches are autonomous bodies and are self-governed.

Alexander Campbell was a religious leader from Virginia who came into Kentucky in the 1820s and edited a newspaper called *The Christian Baptist*. He opposed missions and taught that baptism by immersion was not merely symbolic but was necessary for salvation. Following the revivals, Alexander Campbell's doctrine, which deviated from Baptist doctrine, created agitation and unrest among many attenders at Baptist churches in Northern Kentucky. William Vaughan, an able theologian, strengthened the Baptist churches of the Bracken Association in their doctrine; in those churches Campbell's influence had been strongly felt. Some churches in the region split and a group of members went with the Campbell faction, though Campbell did not have the impact in Northern Kentucky that he had in other areas of the state, where as many as one-third of the Baptist churches were divided or joined his movement. However, one prominent Northern Kentucky Baptist pastor, William Montague, left his church and joined the Campbell faction. Campbell's followers identified themselves as members of either the Churches of Christ or the Disciples of Christ, which are two separate denominations.

In 1840 the Salem Association of Predestinarian Baptists was formed by 6 churches that withdrew from the Regular Baptists of the North Bend and Campbell Co. Associations. This group grew to 14 churches and had 413 members by 1845. Known as Primitive (or Old-School) Baptists by some, they held to extreme Calvinistic views and did not practice any evangelizing. They opposed missions, Bible societies (distributing agencies), and the formal education of ministers. Lewis Conner and John Underhill were prominent pastors at Gunpowder Baptist Church and leaders among these churches. Many of the churches died out by the end of the century, but there are presently a few Primitive Baptist churches still holding services in Northern Kentucky.

In 1845 the **Western Baptist Theological Institute** was established at Covington. It was to be a cooperative educational effort between Baptists in the northern and the southern states, but the issue of slavery became a dominant factor, and the school closed after 10 turbulent years. The building was used as a hospital during the **Civil War**, and later part of its campus became St. Elizabeth Hospital (see **St. Elizabeth Medical Center**).

In antebellum times, **slavery** proved a contentious issue among Baptists. Many of the early settlers came from Virginia and brought their slaves with them. Slaves became members at local Baptist churches when they made a profession of their personal faith and were immersed in baptism. They were not required to support their church; neither were they allowed to vote or participate in any church business. There was a gallery (balcony) in most Baptist meetinghouses where the slaves were to sit during the worship services. Church records mention two African American Baptist preachers, Asa and Barnabas, who became influential preachers and held separate services for the slaves living in their communities. Asa and his wife were purchased in 1839 by a Baptist pastor in southern Indiana, where they were subsequently freed.

During the Civil War men could obtain a waiver from serving in the military by paying $300 for a substitute. James A. Kirtley, who pastored three churches during the war, paid for a substitute so he could continue his pastoral work. The Campbell Co. Association issued a circular letter to its churches during the war, deploring slavery and urging church members not to participate in the war. There were men in some of the churches who volunteered for the Confederate army as well as the Union army.

After the Civil War, African Americans began to establish churches of their own. For instance, the Bracken Association had 26 churches with 2,523 members in 1862; about 1,000 of these were African Americans who left the church rolls after the Civil War. There are now black Baptist churches in Northern Kentucky in Covington, Burlington, Walton, and other towns.

In the 19th century, local Baptists began an effort to evangelize the German population of Covington, and a German-speaking church was established in the town for a short period. Today, there is a Spanish-speaking Baptist congregation in Covington.

There are more than 170 Baptist churches in Northern Kentucky, with nearly 63,000 members associated with the Kentucky Baptist Convention; these churches also align themselves with the Southern Baptist Convention and voluntarily support mission projects through these conventions. Some Baptist churches choose not to join an association. Approximately 20 unaffiliated (sometimes referred to as independent) Baptist churches are extant in Northern Kentucky, the largest being **Calvary Baptist Church** in Covington. In addition, some Baptists who refer to themselves as Reformed Baptists operate a few churches in this region.

Northern Kentucky Baptists became involved in various outreach ministries in the 20th century. The **Baptist Convalescent Center** in Newport opened in 1952. The Baptist Village in Erlanger provides a continuum of care for its residents and also provides care for young children. Baptist Towers in Covington offers housing and nursing care for the elderly. The Baptist Student Union, located at **Northern Kentucky University** at Highland Heights, ministers to college students.

Some prominent Baptist leaders of the past are Rev. Robert Kirtley and his two sons, Rev. James A. and Rev. R. E. Kirtley, who were the most influential pastors in Boone Co. throughout the 19th century; Rev. W. A. M. Wood, an associational missionary of Campbell Co., and later of North Bend, who started many preaching points between 1915 and 1942 that later became churches; Rev. Chase Jennings Sr., the North Bend Association director from 1948 to 1969; Dr. George Jones, who served as the association's director for the following 15 years; Rev. Roy A. Johnson, pastor of Big Bone, Burlington, and Florence churches from the 1930s through the 1950s; and Rev. D. B. Eastep, the pastor of Calvary Baptist Church in Covington from 1927 to 1962.

Dickens, William Earl. *United on Mission: A History of the Northern Kentucky Baptist Association (1803–1995).* Erlanger, Ky.: Northern Kentucky Baptist Association, 1996.

Spencer, John H. *A History of Kentucky Baptists from 1769 to 1885.* Lafayette, Tenn.: Church History Research and Archives, 1976.

Taylor, John. *A History of Ten Baptist Churches.* Frankfort, Ky.: J. H. Holeman, 1823.

James R. Duvall

BARBOUR, JAMES FOSTER (b. May 27, 1820, Danville, Ky.; d. September 17, 1896, Maysville, Ky.). James Barbour, a state auditor, was the son of Maj. James and Letitia Green Barbour. He graduated from Centre College at age 17 and from Transylvania Law School three years later. He practiced law in Danville. In 1850, Kentucky governor John L. Helm (1850–1851; 1867) appointed Barbour the ninth Kentucky state auditor of public accounts. While in Frankfort, he became acquainted with Virgil McKnight, the president of the **Bank of Kentucky**, a bank with which the state was heavily involved, and Barbour was able to obtain concessions on behalf of the state from the bank. He was later hired as a cashier at the Bank of Kentucky branch in Maysville, where he moved in 1852. In 1871 Barbour founded the **Bank of Maysville** and ran it, with his children, until his death. While he lived in Maysville, Barbour was influential in financing the completion of the **Maysville and Lexington Railroad**; he was also involved with the Union Coal & Oil Company and the waterworks. In 1844 James Barbour married Elizabeth Graham Foster in Danville. He died in 1896 and was buried next to his wife at the Danville Cemetery. His son replaced him at the Bank of Maysville, and Barbour family members have been community leaders in Mason Co. since.

Kerr, Charles. *History of Kentucky.* 5 vols. Chicago: American Historical Society, 1922.

Lewin, H., ed. *The Lawyers and Lawmakers of Kentucky.* Chicago: Lewis, 1897.

BARLEYCORN'S FIVE MILE HOUSE, LAKESIDE PARK. The Five Mile House, so named because it is located five miles from Covington, is a historic tavern located at 2642 Dixie Highway. It dates from the mid-19th century and may have been a toll house along the old **Covington and Lexington Turnpike**. In early 1867, Capt. John Tennis, one of the founding citizens of Kenton Co. and longtime owner of the land, died. In April of the same year, after his death, the original frame building was completely destroyed by fire, and the tavern was subsequently rebuilt. In 1873 the heirs of John Tennis sold the property to John Gries. It passed to Joseph Rusche in 1877, to John Henry Freulker in 1888, to John Martin Freulker in 1904, and to Jacob Dennis in 1910. Dennis was proprietor of the tavern for two years and sold it in June 1912 to Charles and Anna Retschulte. The Restchultes converted it into a restaurant, complete with an adjoining shady grove available for family picnics. When the old turnpike became the **Dixie Highway**, Retschulte changed the restaurant's name to Dixie Inn. He provided free transportation to and from the "end-of-the-line" (the electric streetcar line; see **Green Line**) in Fort Mitchell to his restaurant and also installed street lights along the route. During **Prohibition**, Retschulte was twice accused of possessing liquor at his roadhouse. In 1923 he was fined $100; and in April 1925, when he was again convicted of possession of liquor, he refused to take the stand and to name the seller of his 11 barrels of beer; the judge fined him $5,000 and sentenced him to 18 months in prison. The restaurant was closed, and a lien was placed against it for fines owed. In 1926 Retschulte, then age 60, began serving his prison sentence in Atlanta. After his release, he apparently reopened the restaurant. In the early 1940s, Elmer and Stella Bruce Price leased Retschulte's Inn, making it one of the gambling establishments along the **Gourmet Strip**. Elmer Price died in 1954, and Stella subsequently relinquished operation of the restaurant to Florence R. Cahill, Charles Retschulte's granddaughter, who operated it until 1962. After being closed for nine years, it was restored and reopened by Arthur List in 1971, serving pan-fried chicken, roast beef, Kentucky ham and red-eye gravy, steaks, seafood, and hot slaw. Ken Heil reopened the restaurant in February 1984 as Barleycorn's Five Mile House. In 2008 Heil oversaw a major renovation.

Retschulte's Five Mile House, Lakeside Park.

"Covington: Fire in the Country," *Cincinnati Daily Gazette,* April 29, 1867, 1.

Deed books 30, pp. 41–42; 37, pp. 22–23; 61, pp. 220–21; 119, pp. 103–4; 138, p. 229; 145, pp. 614–15; 299, pp. 52–54, Kenton Co. Clerk's Office, Covington, Ky.

"John Tennis Estate," plat map 319, Kenton Co. Clerk's Office, Covington, Ky.

Kreimer, Peggy. "Mrs. Stella Price: Owned Retschulte's Inn 11 Years," *KP,* January 26, 1974, 13.

Schneider, Craig. "Retschulte's Five Mile House," *Bulletin of the Kenton County Historical Society,* March–April 2005: 2–3.

Ken Heil and Paul A. Tenkotte

BARNES TEMPLE A.M.E. CHURCH. The Barnes Temple A.M.E. Church of Elsmere was established in the late 19th century by Rev. Daniel W. Ellison, an evangelical minister who had stopped in nearby Florence to deliver one of many sermons in the area. During his visit, Ellison envisioned the establishment of a small Methodist church. As a result, during the Christmas holiday season of 1896, he and several followers, while traveling house to house sponsoring prayer meetings, decided to hold services regularly at the local railroad station depot on Woodside Ave. Because the city of Elsmere was incorporated that same year, the new church became the African Methodist Episcopal Church (A.M.E.) of Elsmere.

Ellison served as pastor for only two years, until 1898; however, even though it had no permanent spiritual leader for several years, the church continued to grow and prosper. During this period the church moved to a building in Elsmere on Spring St. and later to a facility in town along Shaw St. From there the church was relocated to the Brittle House on Fox St. and then to a small building at the end of Palace Ave. While they met at this location, the congregation made plans to construct a permanent building along Fox St. on land donated by the Carneal family, who were well known throughout the community.

Over the next half century, several worship facilities were built at the Fox St. site. In 1905 or 1906, under the leadership of Rev. C. E. Carson, a small wood-frame building was constructed; in 1934, a "suspicious" fire destroyed it. The next year, under the direction of Rev. H. L. Barnes, a stone church building was begun. One year later, the cornerstone of the facility was laid, and the church was renamed the Barnes Temple African Methodist Episcopal (A.M.E.) Church of Elsmere. From 1940 to 1948, the Barnes Temple A.M.E. allowed the Erlanger-Elsmere Board of Education to use part of the building to educate first- through third-grade African American students from the local community.

After several years, some church leaders decided that a new facility was needed. During the 1950s and 1960s, under the pastorates of Rev. Robert E. Mitchell and Rev. **Edgar L. Mack**, another church building was constructed at the Fox St. location. Modifications and additions to this facility, such as a remodeled sanctuary and a larger parking lot, were built during the late 1990s and early 2000s. Today, under the leadership of Rev. William Robert Thomas Hale, the Barnes Temple A.M.E. Church continues to serve the citizens of Elsmere, both black and white, with a strong emphasis on spirituality, inclusiveness, and social justice.

Barnes Temple African Methodist Episcopal Church. www.barnestemple.com/ (accessed November 26, 2007).
"Barnes Temple A.M.E." *KP,* August 19, 2004, 4K.
"Barnes Temple A.M.E. Church Pamphlet," Northern Kentucky African American Heritage Task Force Collection, W. Frank Steely Library, Northern Kentucky Univ.
Bradford, Bill "Billy," mayor. Interview by Eric R. Jackson, June 15, 2006, Elsmere, Ky.
Elsmere Centennial Committee. *City of Elsmere—Centennial Celebration Booklet, 1896–1996.* Elsmere, Ky.: City of Elsmere, 1996.
"Park to Be Rededicated," *KP,* July 23, 2002, 2K.
Ries, James. "Black Churches Offered Stability in Troubled Times," *KP,* January 20, 1997, 4K.

Eric R. Jackson

BARNHORN, CLEMENT J. (b. January 8, 1857, Cincinnati, Ohio; d. August 2, 1935, Cincinnati, Ohio). Although he never resided in Northern Kentucky, Clement Barnhorn has been closely linked with the region, especially through his architectural sculpture on the facade of the **Cathedral Basilica of the Assumption** in Covington. Barnhorn was the son of Clemens and Agnes Garmmers Barnhorn. He attended Xavier University in Cincinnati and studied at the Art Academy of Cincinnati from 1880 to 1891, attending evening classes under Louis Rebisso, the first sculpture instructor at the academy. He later assisted Rebisso in the execution of the monument to William Henry Harrison for Piatt Park in downtown Cincinnati, and he assumed Rebisso's position as instructor at the academy after Rebisso's death in 1901. As a student, Barnhorn was selected for the Art Academy's prestigious annual scholarship award for study in Italy and Paris in 1891.

Bishop **Camillus Paul Maes** of the Diocese of Covington chose Barnhorn to design and create a statue for the pedestal between the two central doors of the front entrance to the new cathedral in Covington. The subject selected was the Madonna and Child. Made from Bedford limestone, the five-foot tall sculpture, which has remained on the facade since 1912, took two years to complete. Barnhorn later replicated the work for the Barnhorn Memorial for St. John Cemetery in St. Bernard, Ohio. In 1914 Bishop Maes commissioned Barnhorn to execute a tympanum carving above the central doors of Covington's cathedral. The subject this time was the Assumption of Mary into heaven. Completed in 1917, this Bedford stone carving is 18 feet, 7 inches wide and 13 feet, 3 inches high.

While at the Art Academy, Barnhorn established a close friendship with artist **Frank Duveneck.** Barnhorn first sculpted the sepulchral effigy of Elizabeth Boott Duveneck, Duveneck's deceased wife, as a grave memorial in clay, and then he cast it in bronze. The original plaster model remains on display at the Cincinnati Art Museum. Barnhorn and Duveneck collaborated on a sculpture of Ralph Waldo Emerson. Barnhorn was also called upon to sculpture the memorial for Frank Duveneck's grave in **Mother of God Cemetery** in Latonia. Carved from Red Warsaw stone, this monument is 10 feet long and has four winged figures in bronze at the corners representing the virtues of Faith, Hope, Charity, and Resurrection. Also in Mother of God Cemetery are the figures for the Crucifixion Group that was carved by Barnhorn. The depiction of Christ on the cross, St. John the Evangelist, Mary the Mother of Jesus, and Mary Magdalene was cast in bronze and completed in 1915. The entire group, base to top, is 24 feet high.

Other works by Barnhorn include a bronze plaque on the water tower at the **Fort Thomas Military Reservation**, honoring the deceased of the 6th Regiment U.S. Infantry of the Spanish-American War; a piano case that he carved for the Baldwin Piano Company, which won awards at the Paris Exposition in 1900; and bronze reliefs for the Queen City Club in Cincinnati. He was also responsible for creating the Galbraith Memorial in Cincinnati's Eden Park, a monument to **World War I** military and nursing personnel from Cincinnati. He worked with the Rookwood Pottery Company in Cincinnati, carving several fountains in clay that Rookwood covered with their famous faience glazes. One of the fountains, formerly installed in the Losantiville Lanes in Ohio, can be seen today in the Cincinnati Wing of the Cincinnati Art Museum.

Barnhorn died in 1935 at Good Samaritan Hospital in Cincinnati and was buried at St. Mary Cemetery in St. Bernard, Ohio.

Archives, Art Academy of Cincinnati Library, Cincinnati.
Frieberg, Walter A. *A Guide to the Cathedral.* Covington, Ky.: Messenger, 1947.
Ohio Death Certificate No. 48548, for the year 1935.
Reis, Jim. "Barnhorn's Legacy," *KP,* October 3, 2005, 4K.
——. "Sculptor's Reputation Equals His Work," *KP,* May 14, 1984, 8K.

Rebecca Bilbo

BARTLE, JOHN, COLONEL (b. April 2, 1745, New York City; d. December 9, 1839, Cincinnati, Ohio). A merchant and a **Revolutionary War** militia captain and prisoner of war, John Bartle spent five years as a captive of the Indian allies of the British during the Revolution. After his release in 1789, he traveled to Maysville and Lexington, Ky., and then moved to Cincinnati the following year, where he built a house and operated a store. Bartle purchased a large farm near Leitch's Station (see **David Leitch**), 17 lots in Newport, and several more in Cincinnati. He was married three times, first to Elizabeth Mold, then to her sister Lydia Mold, and lastly to Rachel Writtenhouse, a widow. He had a daughter (Eliza, b. 1791 or 1792, who is said to be the first child born in Newport) by his first wife and a son and a daughter by his second. By 1794 Bartle was operating a ferry between Cincinnati and Newport, but this license was revoked in 1798 because his property did not extend to the riverbank. He served as one of the first justices of the peace of Campbell Co. and also as a sheriff there. In 1807 Bartle was forced to sell his properties and declare himself insolvent. He applied for a military pension, which was ultimately denied because the army was unable to locate his service records. He spent the rest of his life in poverty, living with his son, John James Flourney Bartle, in Newport, or his daughter Eliza Bartle Pierce, near the city. He died at the age of 94 and was buried in the Old Presbyterian Burying Grounds in downtown Cincinnati.

Campbell County Kentucky History and Genealogy. Falmouth, Ky.: Falmouth Outlook, 1978.
"John Bartle, Pension." Roots.web. www.rootsweb.com/~kycampbe/johnbartlepension.htm (accessed November 26, 2007).
Purvis, Thomas L., ed. *Newport, Kentucky: A Bicentennial History.* Newport, Ky.: Otto Zimmerman, 1996.
Tenkotte, Paul A. "Rival Cities to Suburbs: Covington and Newport, Kentucky, 1790–1890," PhD diss., Univ. of Cincinnati, 1989.

Jack Wessling

BARTON, EDWARD E. (b. July 29, 1870, Pendleton Co., Ky.; d. November 11, 1951, Falmouth, Ky.). A lawyer, a historian, and a politician, Edward Barton was the son of Thomas M. and Mary Beckett Barton. He was one of Pendleton Co.'s leading citizens for more than 60 years, becoming the dean of the Pendleton Co. legal community and a prominent historian. Throughout his life, he collected histories of most of the families of Pendleton Co. as well as many historical facts concerning the county. Upon his death, his family gave this vast collection to the University of Kentucky, where it was organized and microfilmed. Today the collection is known as the Barton Papers and consists of 200-plus microfilm rolls available in historical and genealogical libraries as far away as Los Angeles.

Barton was an active Democrat and served in 1898 as a representative in the Kentucky legislature. He was a successful candidate for Speaker of the House during both **World War I** and **World War II**. Barton was also a member of the Pendleton Co. draft board during World War II. He obtained a law degree from George Washington University in Washington, D.C. For a time, he worked for the Pendleton Bureau and later moved west to work for the federal government. He was an excellent land surveyor and did much surveying in New Mexico; in those days a lawyer-surveyor combination was common. After he returned to Falmouth, he became a farmer, at one time owning 1,550 acres of land in Bracken and Pendleton counties. Barton pioneered in the development of sweet clover seed, for which Pendleton Co. is noted. He engaged in many civic affairs and served as city attorney. Barton married Louise Brandt, and they had two children, Mary Jackson and Charles Barton. In 1951 Barton died of a heart attack at his home in Falmouth and was buried in Riverside Cemetery. At the time of his death he was the master commissioner of Pendleton Co.

Kentucky Death Certificate No. 23435, for the year 1951.

Mildred Belew

BASCOM, HENRY BIDLEMAN (b. May 27, 1796, Hancock, Delaware Co., N.Y.; d. September 8, 1850, Louisville, Ky.). Bishop Henry Bidleman Bascom's paternal forebears were French Huguenots. With little education but great determination, Bascom began his life of religion at age 12 and converted to the Methodist faith on August 18, 1810. His father moved west and the family settled near Maysville in 1812. In 1813 they moved to Ohio in the direction of Ripley, not far from Maysville. In February 1813, near New Market in Highland Co., Ohio, Bascom was licensed to preach as a Methodist minister in the Brush Creek Circuit, which extended throughout the Ohio counties of Adams, Highland, and Scioto. He was admitted to the church's Ohio Conference on a trial basis and began to preach on the frontier for the yearly salary of $12. His style was sometimes too florid for his congregations, who thought that he did not dress or look like a Methodist minister. In 1816 he was transferred to the Tennessee Conference, which covered most of the state of Kentucky, and was appointed to the Danville and Madison circuits in Kentucky. In the same year, he became acquainted with Kentucky statesman Henry Clay.

In 1822 Bascom returned to Ohio and was appointed to a committee to negotiate between the trustees of Bracken Academy in Augusta, Ky., and the Methodist Church of Ohio and Kentucky to create **Augusta College**. In 1823 Henry Clay arranged an appointment for him to become the chaplain to the U.S. Congress. Bascom continued as the congressional chaplain until 1827, when he was appointed to chair a committee to establish a college at Uniontown, Pa. He accepted a position as president of that school, which became Madison College. In 1829 he resigned to accept a ministerial post as an agent for the American Colonization Society. In 1832 he returned to Northern Kentucky, where he became a professor of moral science at Augusta College. Soon the presidency of the college was offered to Bascom, but he declined. He remained in Bracken Co. for several years before resigning from his teaching post at the college in December 1837. The trustees did not accept his resignation but offered him time to travel and lecture. At that time, leaders of Cincinnati were concerned about the problem of marital infidelity and invited Bascom to deliver a series of lectures on the subject of Christianity and infidelity.

During the next few years, Bascom traveled and lectured, and in 1838 a DD degree was conferred upon him by Wesleyan University at Middletown, Conn. He married Eliza Van Antwerp in New York in 1839. In 1840 he was elected president of Louisiana College, but because he wanted to retain his relationship with the trustees at Augusta College, he rejected the position; within the same year, he rejected a similar offer from the University of Missouri at Columbia. At the annual Methodist Conference of 1840, a message was sent from the trustees of Transylvania University in Lexington that control of the university was being offered to the Methodist Episcopal Church. Bascom was elected as chairman of a commission to investigate, and in the spring of 1842, with the institution under Methodist control, the commissioners asked Bascom to assume the presidency of Transylvania University. Bascom declined the offer; however, he agreed to serve as president pro tem. He then resigned his teaching position at Augusta College.

In 1844 Bascom was a delegate to the Methodist Church's General Conference; in 1845 he was a member of the Southern Methodist Convention, which organized the Methodist Church South, and he both authored the report of those proceedings and chaired the commission appointed to settle the differences between the two branches of the church. In 1848 Bascom attended his church's Southern General Conference and became editor of the *Southern Methodist Quarterly Review*. At his church's General Conference at St. Louis in May 1850, Bascom was elected bishop of the Methodist Episcopal Church South. He authored several books, including *Methodism and Slavery* (1845), *Sermons from the Pulpit* (1850), and *Lectures on Infidelity: Lectures on Moral and Mental Science*. In July 1850 he preached his last sermon, in St. Louis, and on September 8, 1850, he died at Louisville and was buried in the Eastern Cemetery in that city.

Henkle, M. M. *Life of Henry Bidleman Bascom, D.D., LLD.* Nashville, Tenn.: Methodist Church South, 1851.

Wright, John D. *Transylvania: Tutor to the West.* Lexington, Ky.: Transylvania Univ., 1975.

John E. Leming Jr.

BASEBALL. Baseball in the Northern Kentucky region has been both a popular activity and a spectator sport. From the early days of following the Red Stockings in Cincinnati to the modern era when youngsters begin with tee ball, baseball has been a sport of summer for almost 140 years. Northern Kentucky soldiers returned from the **Civil War** having seen the rudiments of the game demonstrated, however primitively, during lulls in the fighting. In one incident more than 10,000 soldiers witnessed an Easter Sunday contest between two New York military units near Hilton Head Island, S.C.; it was said to be the sports gathering of the 19th century with the largest attendance. The Civil War helped to spread baseball throughout the nation.

It was soon afterward that the sport's first professional baseball team, the Red Stockings, was organized in Cincinnati and its 1869 team played through an undefeated season. The *Cincinnati Commercial* thought enough of the interest in the new game that a full-time reporter was assigned to travel with "the Reds"; it was the first newspaper in the country to make such an assignment. Being part of the Cincinnati media market, Northern Kentuckians became aware of baseball and have been ever since. In Covington the Ernst family supported baseball, and its teams were known to play against the Red Stockings at various ball fields on each side of the Ohio River. **James C. Ernst**, a first baseman for Princeton College in New Jersey during the early 1870s who was sought after by several major league teams, was a member of those Kentucky teams. The Red Stockings challenged Northern Kentucky squads in Ludlow during the 1870s, long before the advent of spring training in the South. A look at the few surviving rosters of the Covington teams the Kentons and the Stars (see **Baseball, Early Professional**; **Kenton Base Ball Association**) reveals the names of several future community leaders, and their Ohio opponents sometimes included Billy Howard Taft, later the 27th president of the United States (1908–1912).

At the minor league level, there have been a number of teams in the region. Maysville had a team called the Bears as early as 1905. In 1910 Casey Stengel roamed the outfield for the Blue Grass League team in Maysville (see **Baseball, Maysville**). For the 1913 season, Covington industrialist Richard C. Stewart of the **Stewart Iron Works** organized a squad in the incipient Federal League, the **Covington Blue Sox**. In Newport the success of the **Wiedemann Brewing Company**'s semipro team prompted several businessmen to field a minor league team. The Newport Brewers, for the 1914 season, played in the OKI (Ohio, Kentucky, Indiana) League. Neither the Blue Sox nor the Brewers remained in the area very long. In Boone Co. during the first years of the 21st century, there has been an attempt to capitalize on the resurgent interest in minor league baseball in the form of a team called the **Florence Freedom**.

The region has supplied a number of players who have made it to the major leagues, even if for only a few games. The most famous Northern Kentuckian to play in the "bigs" is clearly **Jim Bunning** of Southgate, a Hall of Fame right-handed pitcher and a U.S. senator. He pitched 17 from 1955 through 1971, almost unheard of by today's standards, playing in 591 games with a 224-184 win-loss record and becoming the first pitcher to win more than 100 games in both leagues. Bunning played for the Detroit Tigers in the American League (AL) and for the Philadelphia Phillies, the Pittsburgh Pirates, and the Los Angeles Dodgers in the National League (NL). He also holds the rare distinction of having pitched no-hitters in both leagues, with the second one being a perfect game as well. The other successful modern-era professional ball player connected with the region is **David Justice**. Justice played under legendary coach **Jim Connor** at **Thomas More College** in Crestview Hills before beginning his pro career in 1989 with the Atlanta Braves. He went on to play with the Cleveland Indians, the New York Yankees, and Oakland Athletics through 14 seasons and 1,610 games.

Numerous lesser-known major leaguers (players who made an appearance in a major league game) also are connected with the region. Covington has given rise to the largest number of professional players. Arranged chronologically according to their participation in the major league, the following players have Covington ties. Amos Booth, who lived in Covington, played in 110 games over 4 seasons, mostly as an infielder with the Reds, beginning in 1876. Jack Shoupe played 3 seasons starting in 1879 as an infielder in 55 games, with three teams. Also beginning in 1879 was George Strief, an infielder for 5 seasons with Pittsburgh, Cleveland, the St. Louis Browns, and the Philadelphia Phillies over 362 games. Prior to the major league, Strief had played for the Covington Stars. Mox McQuery played first base in both leagues for several teams from 1884 for 5 years, appearing in 417 games. After his playing days, McQuery became a Covington policeman in 1896 and was killed in the line of duty in 1900. Bob Clark played 7 years, beginning in 1886, mostly as a catcher for the Brooklyn Trolley-Dodgers in the American Association, a major league at the time, and appeared in 288 games. Joe Sommer spent 10 seasons with the Reds and the Baltimore Orioles, beginning in 1890, mainly as an outfielder, appearing in 713 games. **Hank Gastright**, a right-handed pitcher, threw in the AL in the 1890s for several teams, appearing in 173 games; he had a record of 72-63 over 7 seasons. Later, he became a Newport policeman. Bill Niles was an infielder for 11 games in the NL with St. Louis and Pittsburgh in the 1895 season. John Farrell played second base with the St. Louis Cardinals for 5 years and 541 games beginning in 1901. Harry Berte appeared in 3 games for the St. Louis Cardinals in 1903 at second base. **Howie Camnitz** was a right-handed pitcher for 11 years, beginning in 1904, mainly for the Pittsburgh Pirates. He appeared in 326 games and had a 133-105 record. Bill Sweeney played 8 seasons, beginning in 1907, appearing in 1,031 games, mainly at second base for the Boston Braves of the NL.

Eddie Hohnhorst, the son of a Covington brewery agent, played first base in 21 games for Cleveland in 1910 and later played in the fleeting Federal League. Hohnhorst, who became a Covington policeman in 1914, committed suicide in Latonia in March 1916, while on duty. Jack Black appeared in 54 games at first base for the St. Louis Browns in 1911. Dick Niehaus was a left-handed pitcher for the St. Louis Cardinals for 4 seasons beginning in 1913, seeing action in 45 games with a 4-5 record. John Heving (see **Heving Brothers**) was a catcher for 8 seasons at Boston in the AL starting in 1920, appearing in 399 games; his brother Joe Heving was a right-handed pitcher mostly at Cleveland for 13 seasons starting in 1930, playing in 430 games, with a 76-48 record. Bob Barton, a 1959 graduate of **Holmes High School**, who turned down an invitation to play basketball for Adolph Rupp at the University of Kentucky, began his 10 years in the majors in 1965 with the San Francisco Giants and later played with the San Diego Padres as a catcher, playing in 393 games. Joeff Long was a first baseman with the Chicago White Sox and the Boston Red Sox for 2 years beginning in 1964, appearing in 56 games. Leo Foster, from Holmes (1969), played 5 years as an infielder for Atlanta and the New York Mets in the mid-1970s, participating in 144 games. Jim Minshall, born in Covington but raised in Campbell Co., played baseball and basketball at **Newport Central Catholic High School** (1966) under Jim Connor. Minshall was a right-handed pitcher and played for Pittsburgh during the mid-1970s for 2 seasons, seeing action in 6 games, with a 0-1 record. Joel McKeon was a left-handed pitcher for 2 years with the Chicago White Sox in the AL, starting in 1986. He saw action in 43 games with a record of 4-3. The last players from Covington were the Thobe brothers: J. J. was a right-handed pitcher for the Montreal Expos in 1995, where he appeared in 4 games, with no decisions; Tom was a left-handed pitcher and played for 2 seasons with Atlanta beginning in 1995, where he pitched in 7 games, with a 0-1 record.

Other players from Kenton Co. include Ludlow's Dale Williams, a right-handed pitcher who played for Cincinnati in 1876 for 9 games, where he went 1-8. From the same city came Neal Brady, a right-handed pitcher, who played for 24 games with the New York Yankees and the Reds between 1915 and 1925, going 2-3. Brady later managed local semipro teams. Also connected with Kenton Co. was Jimmy Viox, a 5-season second baseman mainly with the Pittsburgh Pirates beginning in 1916, appearing in 506 games. After his playing days, Viox lived in Erlanger. Brian Drahman, out of Kenton, in the southern part of the county, and from Miami-Dade Community College in Florida, a right-handed pitcher, was a 4-season player for the Chicago White Sox during the early 1990s, seeing action in 47 games, with a 3-2 record. Chris Hook, who attended **Lloyd Memorial High School** in Erlanger and **Northern Kentucky University** in Highland Heights, a right-handed pitcher, pitched at San Francisco for 2 seasons, 1995–1996, where he threw in 55 games, going 5-2. Brandon Berger, out of Beechwood High School (see **Beechwood Public Schools**) and Eastern Kentucky University in Richmond, a right-hand-hitting outfielder, was drafted in the 16th round in 1996 by the Kansas City Royals; through the end of the 2004 season, Berger had appeared in 81 games in 3 seasons.

Several players arose from Newport. George Miller was a catcher with Cincinnati teams for 2 seasons, in 1877 with the Red Stockings of the NL, and in 1884 with the Outlaw Reds of the American Association, for a total of 17 games. Clarence "Kid" Baldwin played every position, but mostly shortstop, with the Reds for 7 years beginning in the early 1880s. John Dolan pitched in 35 games as a right-hander in the NL for the Cincinnati Reds, the St. Louis Cardinals, and the Chicago Cubs during the 1880s, with a record of 15-16. Rudy Hulswitt played in 644 games as an infielder for Philadelphia, Cincinnati, and St. Louis in the NL for 7 years beginning in 1891. Orlie Weaver, a right-handed pitcher, saw action in 40 games in 1910–1911 with the Chicago Cubs and the Boston Braves in the NL, going 6-15. George Textor was a catcher for 2 seasons in the Federal League (1914–1915), with the Newark Peppers and with the Indianapolis Hoosiers, appearing in 24 games. Tommy Reis, from **Newport High School** (1933), a right-handed pitcher, in 1938 played with Philadelphia and Boston in the NL for 8 games, with a record of 0-1.

Other Campbell Co. players include Bellevue's Ed Kennedy, who played third base for Cincinnati in the one year that city had two major league teams, 1884, seeing action in 13 games; Kennedy was with the Union Association team that played near the intersection of Kellogg and Delta Aves. on Cincinnati's East Side. St. Louis native Harry Al Steinfeldt, who grew up in Bellevue, was an infielder with the Chicago Cubs of the NL during the club's heydays. He spent 14 seasons there and with Cincinnati, mostly at third base beginning in 1898. Bellevue's Eddie Hunter played in 1 game in 1933 with the Reds at third base. Bill Kissinger, of Dayton, was a right-handed pitcher and played for 3 seasons, beginning in 1895, mostly for St. Louis in the NL, seeing action in 53 games, with a record of 7-25. Dayton also produced the **Tannehill brothers**: Jesse spent 15 years, beginning in 1894, as a left-handed pitcher with the Pittsburgh Pirates of the NL and the Boston Red Sox in the AL, seeing 506 games with a record of 197-116; brother Lee was on third base for the Chicago Sox of the AL for 10 seasons starting in 1903 for 1,090 games. Lee Tannehill saw action in the 1905 World Series. Chick Smith, a left-handed pitcher also from Dayton, played for Cincinnati in 1913 in 5 games with a record of 0-1. The marble-shooting champion of Dayton in the early 1920s was Lloyd "Dutch" Dietz, who became a football and baseball star at Dayton High School (1932) (see **Dayton Public Schools**) and a baseball player at Western Michigan University at Kalamazoo. He pitched as a right-hander in 106 games, mainly for the Pittsburgh Pirates during the early 1940s, over 4 seasons with a record of 14-16. After baseball, Dutch became the recreation director of the City of Beaumont, Tex. Dayton-born Todd Benzinger, a descendant of a Northern Kentucky family of barristers, spent 7 years in both leagues in the 1980s and early 1990s. He made the last putout at first base for the champion Reds in the final game of the 1990 World Series. Benzinger ended his career having played in 924 games for several teams. Fort Thomas has produced four major leaguers: Jack Thoney, who had 6 major league seasons between 1902 and 1911, mostly as an outfielder with the Boston Red

Sox of the AL over 264 games; Walt Terrell, a right-handed pitcher mostly for Detroit for 11 seasons, 1982 to 1992, who went 111-124 (he once hit two home runs in the same game, a somewhat rare occurrence among pitchers); Chris Peters, a left-hander who pitched at Indiana University in Bloomington and played 2 seasons for the Pittsburgh Pirates (1996–1997), appearing in 47 games with a record of 4-6; and in 2002 Scott Wiggins, a left-handed pitcher who attended Newport Central Catholic High School and Northern Kentucky University and played for the Toronto Blue Jays, appearing in 3 games with no decisions. Grants Lick native Bill Hobbs, a 2-season second baseman, appeared in 2 games, in 1913 and 1916, with Cincinnati.

Other parts of the region also have produced major league players: Ed Merrill, of Maysville, saw action in 57 games for Worcester Ruby Legs (when that Massachusetts city had a major league team) in 1882 as a second baseman. Barry McCormick played the infield for the Chicago Cubs in the NL for 10 years and 989 games, beginning in 1895. Don Hurst guarded first base for the Philadelphia Phillies in the NL for 7 years beginning in 1928, appearing in 905 games. Although born at Ewing, on the region's edge in Fleming Co., Woodie Fryman prepared heavily for his major league career on the ball fields of Maysville. A left-handed pitcher, he stayed 18 seasons mostly in the NL with five teams from 1966 through 1983, with a record of 141-155 in 625 games. Also from Mason Co. hailed Dave Tomlin, a left-handed pitcher who participated in 409 games over 13 seasons (1972–1986), mainly for the Cincinnati Reds and the San Diego Padres of the NL, with a record of 25-12. Herb Moford, from Brooksville, a right-handed pitcher, played for 4 seasons during the late 1950s and early 1960s with four teams: the St. Louis Cardinals, the Detroit Tigers, the Boston Red Sox, and the New York Mets. He compiled a 5-13 record in 50 games. Carl Bouldin came from Germantown. He played at Norwood (Ohio) High School and the University of Cincinnati (and also played basketball with Oscar Robertson). Bouldin was with the Washington Senators during the early 1960s over 4 seasons and 29 games as a right-handed pitcher, with a record of 3-8. Falmouth produced Frank Browning, a right-handed pitcher who appeared in 11 games with Detroit in 1910, with a record of 2-2. Owenton reared Dale Roberts, who had a "cup of coffee" (a brief career) as a New York Yankee, pitching in 2 games as a left-hander at the end of the 1967 season, with no decisions. Union, in Boone Co., was home for Larry Luebbers Jr., who attended **St. Henry District High School** and the University of Kentucky. As a right-handed pitcher, Luebbers saw action in 36 games over 3 seasons between 1993 and 2000 with the Reds and the St. Louis Cardinals; his record was 5-10. **Conner High School**'s Jason Johnson (1992) has pitched 9 seasons, mainly with the Baltimore Orioles and the Detroit Tigers, appearing in 215 games with a 52-86 record through the 2005 season. Warsaw, in Gallatin Co., produced Jim Blackburn, who pitched as a right-hander in a total of 18 games for the Reds in 2 seasons, 1948 and 1951, with a 0-2 record.

During the mid-1990s, when a prospect signed his first major league contract, the scout would often inform the wide-eyed kid that seeing action in a major league game was only a distant possibility. At that time, the odds of making it into a major league game were 1 in 35. Prior to the major league expansion, which began in the 1960s, there were not 30-plus teams being fielded, but a total of 16, 8 in the NL, the "Senior Circuit," and 8 in the AL, the "Junior Circuit." Statistically, it was even more difficult then to "smell the grass" of a big-league park. It is simply a tribute to any person from the region who had enough talent, skill, dexterity, and patience to make it into any major league game, in any era.

There have been a few individuals involved in professional baseball from Northern Kentucky who have not been players. Three have held ownership or management positions in the Cincinnati Reds. **Nelson Lloyd**, a pharmacist and one of the Lloyd brothers from Florence, along with John T. Brush, owned the Reds before selling the team to Gerry Herrmann, the Fleischman brothers, and George B. "Boss" Cox in 1902; after the sale, Lloyd went on to own the New York Giants baseball team. Edwin C. Widrig, another pharmacist (see **Pharmacy**), who worked in Newport for 40 years, became the treasurer of the Cincinnati team in the early part of the 20th century; and William "Bill" Reik, a Fort Thomas investment banker, holds limited partnership shares in the present team. Since the early 1980s, Covington native and Holmes High School graduate Randy Marsh has been a major league umpire.

Boehmker, Terry. *Northern Kentucky High School Sports Guide.* Terry Boehmker, n.d.

James, Bill, et al., eds. *Stats All-Time Major League Handbook.* Skokie, Ill.: Stats, 1998.

BASEBALL, EARLY PROFESSIONAL. Two Northern Kentucky teams revived professional baseball in the Cincinnati region five years after the 1870 breakup of the famous Cincinnati Red Stockings. In Kentucky the Star Base Ball Club of Covington and the Ludlow Base Ball Club of Ludlow were organized as professional teams for the 1875 season. Both clubs had commenced play the previous year as crack amateur squads, with the Star team, led by Covington native and former Princeton University baseball standout **James C. Ernst**, emerging as the region's best team. Some of Covington's foremost politicians operated the Star Base Ball Club, including James B. Casey, **William L. Grant**, and **Smith N. Hawes**. George W. McCoy, proprietor of the Ludlow ferry, was the Ludlow club's primary owner.

Though the teams represented distinct Northern Kentucky cities, both the Stars and the Ludlows sought the same metropolitan fan base that had supported the Cincinnati Red Stockings. Each team built an enclosed ballpark with access to mass transit (see **Streetcars**). They also advertised their games in Cincinnati newspapers to attract patrons beyond their respective communities. The spacious Star Base Ball Grounds, which took up an entire city block, were located on Covington's periphery at Madison Ave. and 17th St. Horse-drawn streetcars made the ballpark accessible locally to downtown Covington, Newport, and Cincinnati. The cozier Ludlow Base Ball Grounds were situated along the Ohio River near Elm St. in Ludlow—reachable by ferry (see **Ferries**) from Cincinnati and by omnibus from Covington.

The two Northern Kentucky teams received national attention for their superior play. The Stars and the Ludlows each defeated every prominent baseball club in Northern Kentucky and southwestern Ohio. A much-anticipated showdown between the two Kentucky clubs generated tremendous excitement throughout the Cincinnati area. The Stars emerged victorious in a pair of close games played before capacity crowds in Covington and Ludlow. Newspapers in major urban areas and national sporting periodicals, such as the *New York Clipper,* chronicled the exploits of the Stars and the Ludlows.

The Stars and the Ludlows competed against the game's best players, among them several future members of the Baseball Hall of Fame. Fledgling major league teams, including the powerhouse Boston Red Stockings, came to Northern Kentucky to play the Stars and the Ludlows. Michael "King" Kelly, an early baseball superstar, recalled playing against the Covington Stars as one of his career's highlights.

During the 1875 season, the cities of Covington and Ludlow hosted the only two major league baseball games ever played in Northern Kentucky. In the days before set schedules, baseball teams in transit sometimes met at neutral sites to save travel expenses. Northern Kentucky hosted two such meetings. On September 21, 1875, the Philadelphia White Stockings defeated the Hartford Dark Blues at the Star Base Ball Grounds in Covington. The next day, the Philadelphia team lost to the St. Louis Browns locally at the Ludlow baseball grounds.

Encouraged by the success of both the Stars and the Ludlows, several Cincinnati businessmen revived the Cincinnati Red Stockings as an independent professional team late in the 1875 season. These three area teams became instant rivals. Their games against each other thrilled fans and again made Cincinnati a hotbed of professional baseball. The Reds and the Stars became the primary foes among the three teams. Streetcars and wagons clogged Madison Ave. in Covington as fans packed the Star Base Ball Grounds for the opening game between the team from Covington and the Cincinnati Reds. The teams did not disappoint the crowd, as the game ended in a 5-5 tie after 12 innings of play. The Stars won the next two games against the Reds before the Cincinnati club revamped its roster and took the next four contests.

Although intense, the rivalry between the Cincinnati area's professional baseball teams proved fleeting. The underfinanced Ludlow Base Ball Club folded late in the 1875 season. In 1876 the newly formed National League, with the Cincinnati Reds as a charter member, sought to monopolize the Cincinnati baseball market. The National League took dead aim at the Covington Stars by prohibiting its teams from playing non-League clubs based within a five-mile radius of any National League city. Without access to top teams, the Stars could no longer deliver elite baseball entertainment to their fans. Management instability, exacerbated by a Covington municipal embezzlement scandal involving Star Base Ball Club president Smith N. Hawes, also plagued the team. A month-long eastern tour drained the baseball club's treasury and forced it to disband in July 1876.

The Ludlow Base Ball Club briefly reemerged as an independent professional team for the 1877 season; however, the team quickly folded after the City of Ludlow prohibited it from having home games on Sundays. Baseball pioneer Dickey Pearce was the team's shortstop.

Despite their brief existence, the local Stars and Ludlows left an imprint on professional baseball. Several players from both teams enjoyed long major league careers, including Frank "Silver" Flint of the Stars and Charley Jones, captain of the Ludlows. Jones, a slugging outfielder who later played for the Cincinnati Reds, once held major league baseball's single-season and career home-run records. Flint became one of baseball's best fielding and most durable catchers in an era when players did not yet wear gloves. Several Northern Kentuckians played for the Stars and the Ludlows: Frank Boughner of Maysville, Andy Cummings and John Shoupe of Covington, Isaac F. Van Burkalow of Newport, and Elisha "Dale" Williams of Ludlow.

Beyond baseball, the Stars and the Ludlows represent another chapter in Northern Kentucky's continuing search for identity. By the 1870s many observers viewed Northern Kentucky's river cities not as urban centers in their own right, but as Cincinnati suburbs, an image that for some persists today. Its proximity to Cincinnati, however, did not keep Covington from having its own interests to protect and expand. After all, Covington ranked second only to Louisville in population among Kentucky cities. Even tiny Ludlow, a village of a few hundred inhabitants, had urban aspirations spurred by the construction of the **Cincinnati Southern Railroad Bridge** connecting it to Cincinnati and points beyond. For ambitious cities like Covington and Ludlow, sponsoring "first-class baseball nines" provided greater visibility within an emerging urban America.

"Base Ball," *CDE,* May 27, 1875, 8.
"Base Ball—the Covington Stars," *CDE,* May 26, 1875, 4.
"Covington, the Return of the Stars," *CC,* July 24, 1876, 7.
"Ludlow Base Ball Club," *Ludlow Reporter,* April 17, 1875, 3.
"Notice of Incorporation, Star Base-Ball Club," *Covington Ticket,* June 22, 1875, 1.

Greg Perkins

BASEBALL, MAYSVILLE. Maysville has long been a bastion of baseball in Northern Kentucky. Like many other Ohio Valley river cities, Maysville supported both cricket and **townball** clubs before the **Civil War**; baseball emerged during the late 1860s. By 1875 the Maysville Eckfords played professional and amateur baseball clubs throughout Kentucky and Ohio. The Chicago White Stockings made a memorable visit to Maysville that season. An overflow crowd at the Maysville Trotting Park spilled over to surrounding trees and adjoining houses, only to see the White Stockings give the Eckfords a 31-to-3 drubbing.

By 1895 Maysville had assembled a baseball team that could compete at a high level. The Maysville club made national headlines that season, with three victories against major league teams. Two wins were against a Cincinnati Reds team that featured Baseball Hall of Famers Buck Ewing and Bid McPhee. The Washington Senators also fell to the crack Maysville squad, which was led by Shelbyville, Ky., native Dan McGann. McGann later had a successful major league career, primarily with the New York Giants.

After years of fielding teams in independent leagues, Maysville joined "organized" baseball in 1910, securing a Blue Grass League franchise. Established in 1908, the Kentucky-based Blue Grass League was designated Class D, the lowest minor league level. A group of Maysville businessmen bought the struggling Shelbyville team and transferred it to Maysville in August 1910. Thomas Russell served as the team's president. Future Baseball Hall of Famer Casey Stengel played centerfield for the 1910 Maysville Rivermen. Always the showman, Stengel would amuse Maysville fans with antics such as sliding into second base on his way to and from the outfield.

Through the second and third decades of the 20th century, Maysville was Northern Kentucky's main link to what many historians consider a golden age of minor league baseball. Northern Kentucky's proximity to Cincinnati made it difficult for professional baseball to make inroads in the region. The rules governing organized baseball gave the Cincinnati Reds territorial rights for a five-mile radius surrounding Cincinnati. For a long time, this limitation prevented Covington and Newport from having professional baseball teams. The Maysville Rivermen remained a Blue Grass League franchise until 1913, when the entire circuit was expelled from organized baseball for violating the five-mile rule. The Blue Grass League had tried to place a team in Covington without securing permission from the Cincinnati Reds. The *Sporting News* criticized the National Commission, which governed organized baseball, for its despotic handling of the situation. Only the Lexington and Maysville franchises, which joined the Ohio State League for the 1913 season, survived the Blue Grass League's demise.

In the fluid world of pre–World War II minor league baseball, Maysville teams struggled to find a home. Maysville continued its affiliation with the Ohio State League until the league folded after the 1916 season. In 1922 minor league baseball returned to Maysville with the revival of the Blue Grass League. The Maysville Cardinals edged Cynthiana for the pennant that season. Unfortunately, the Blue Grass League's collapse after the 1924 season marked the end of minor league baseball in Maysville. For many years, however, Maysville remained an active participant in the amateur and semipro leagues that thrived in Northern Kentucky throughout the 1950s.

Over the years, Maysville has contributed several players to the major leagues. Maysville natives Barry McCormick, Don Hurst, and Dave Tomlin all had long major league careers. McCormick played 10 seasons, mostly as an infielder for the Chicago Cubs during the 1890s. Hurst, a slugging first baseman for the Philadelphia Phillies, had a career batting average of .298 and led the National League in runs batted during the 1932 season. Reliever Dave Tomlin pitched for 13 seasons, most notably with the Cincinnati Reds during the late 1970s. The late Herb Moford, from neighboring Brooksville, pitched for Casey Stengel's New York Mets in 1962.

Maysville can also claim some notable amateur baseball achievements. The **Maysville High School** baseball team won a state championship in 1958. Noah Welte, a 2000 **St. Patrick High School** graduate, set Kentucky high school baseball records for highest single-season batting average and career stolen bases. At **Thomas More College**, Welte was an Academic All American and finished his collegiate baseball career as the Saints' all-time leader in hits and runs scored.

"Amateurs Who Can Play Ball," *National Police Gazette* 66, no. 941 (September 14, 1895): 6.
Creamer, Robert. *Stengel: His Life and Times.* Lincoln: Univ. of Nebraska Press, 1984.
Hamilton, Chuck. "Casey at the Bat in Maysville," *Maysville Ledger Independent,* July 8, 2005.
———. "Maysville's Early Years of Professional Baseball," *Maysville Ledger Independent,* July 8, 2005.
———. "Re-Visiting Maysville's Baseball History," *Maysville Ledger Independent,* July 2, 2005.
"A Lesson to Be Found," *Sporting News* 55, no. 5 (April 3, 1913): 4.
Spalding's Official Base Ball Guide. New York: American Sports, 1911.

Greg Perkins

BASEBALL AND SOFTBALL, AMATEUR. Northern Kentuckians have played a major role in making the Ohio Valley a baseball and softball center. Modern baseball originated in New York City during the early 1840s. By summer 1858 the New York version of baseball had reached Cincinnati, where, for a time, it coexisted with cricket and **townball** as fledgling team sports. Several early Cincinnati-area baseball milestones have Northern Kentucky connections. Northern Kentucky likely hosted the first baseball game played in Greater Cincinnati between organized teams. On September 8, 1866, the Eagles of Dayton, Ky., "crossed bats" with the Live Oaks of Cincinnati at the Dayton team's home field. The next month, Florence, Ky., hosted the Cincinnati area's first baseball tournament as part of the annual Florence Fair. Early baseball promoters in Greater Cincinnati include Northern Kentuckians Henry Pudder of Dayton, Newport's William Holt, and the Grant and Ernst families of Covington.

Baseball soon emerged as a favorite pastime throughout Northern Kentucky. Neighborhood

Covington Ballpark.

teams flourished in Covington, Ludlow, Newport, and Dayton. The completion of the **John A. Roebling Bridge** and the expansion of omnibus and streetcar lines helped baseball become a neighborhood phenomenon. As smaller communities vanished into the growing Greater Cincinnati metropolis, baseball helped promote neighborhood cohesion. Moreover, baseball provided a new lens through which people viewed the city and themselves. The "rowdies" who broke the Sabbath and played baseball on Sundays in South Covington only added to the neighborhood's wild reputation. Baseball teams comprised of young gentlemen, teams like the Newport Holts or Covington's Copecs, played on Saturday afternoons in more refined locations like the Newport Trotting Park or Covington's College Square. Outside the urban core, Burlington, Independence, and Maysville also reported outbreaks of "baseball fever" in the decade following the **Civil War**.

Though popular, baseball in Northern Kentucky was no more inclusive than society at large. Teams comprised of African American men formed as early as the 1870s; however, interactions between white and black clubs were infrequent. When such encounters did occur, racial tensions sometimes flared. In 1919 the City of Newport threatened to ban baseball games between black and white teams when fans nearly rioted during one heated contest. Integrated teams also met bigotry. The Covington High School baseball team left the field in protest during a 1923 game when its opponent sent an African American player in to pinch-hit. Northern Kentucky's African American teams persevered despite pervasive racism and segregation. The Newport Excelsiors played some of Negro League baseball's best teams; for example, there was a 1932 home game with the powerhouse Homestead Grays and Baseball Hall of Fame pitcher Smokey Joe Williams. Eventually, baseball, along with other aspects of Northern Kentucky life, became more integrated after **World War II**.

Women also played baseball in Northern Kentucky, despite receiving little initial encouragement from men. An 1883 *Daily Commonwealth* article about a game in Covington between two women's teams reflected prevailing attitudes about women playing baseball. The reporter ridiculed the women's baseball skills and declared it fortunate that "female ball players do not call more than once in a lifetime." Women's participation in baseball received a boost in 1933 when Covington softball legend **Bill Cappel** organized women's softball teams in Covington. In the early 1960s, Cappel also founded the Covington Major Girl's League, an endeavor that produced three national-championship teams.

By the early 1900s, baseball, aided by widening automobile ownership, brought Northern Kentucky communities together as never before. From about 1910 through 1939, amateur and semipro leagues attracted teams from all over the region. The Kentucky, Indiana, and Ohio League (KIO); the Northern Kentucky Amateur League; and the Sunday League, to name a few, featured such legendary Northern Kentucky baseball teams as the Covington Golden Rods, the Newport Wiedemanns, and the Ludlow White Stockings.

Starting in the 1930s, Northern Kentuckians began putting their imprint on softball. Nick Carr's Covington Boosters, led by second baseman Bill Cappel and ace pitcher Norb Warken, won the American Softball Association fast-pitch world championship at Chicago's Soldier Field in 1939. Covington welcomed the champions back home with a parade. In slow-pitch softball, Northern Kentucky produced several men's national-champion teams during the 1950s. Myron Reinhardt, Walt Wherry, Alex Burkhart, and Doc Morris were standout players from this era. In 1956 the Joe Gatliff Auto Sales of Newport sponsored a slow-pitch team that captured another world championship.

The region's high school baseball and softball teams have also brought laurels home to Northern Kentucky. In baseball, **Newport High School** captured the first two Kentucky state baseball crowns in 1940 and 1941, with legendary coach **Jim Connor** as a player. **Newport Central Catholic** has won four state titles, the most by any Northern Kentucky school, under that same Jim Connor. **Holmes**, **Covington Catholic**, and **Maysville** high schools have won one state championship apiece. Northern Kentucky schools have dominated women's slow-pitch softball, winning every state title from 1997 through 2006. Newport Central Catholic has won five slow-pitch softball titles, three of them consecutive. Erlanger **Lloyd Memorial** and Covington **Holy Cross** won two straight, and **Bishop Brossart** and **Campbell Co.** won one each. **Larry A. Ryle High School** won the 2006 state fast-pitch softball championship.

On the collegiate level, **Northern Kentucky University** (NKU) and **Thomas More College** both have thriving men's baseball and women's fast-pitch softball programs. Longtime NKU baseball coach Bill Aker's career victory total ranks among the highest in NCAA Division II history. The 2005 NKU women's fast-pitch softball team had a record-setting year. Led by pitching ace Krystal Lewallen, the NKU Norse had a collegiate record of 55 consecutive victories and set a new NCAA Division II standard for winning percentage. Lewallen's stellar season earned her the women's award as NCAA Division II Athlete of the Year. The Thomas More College baseball program produced **David Justice**, a former All-Star major league outfielder, again coached by Jim Connor.

Northern Kentucky's renowned baseball and softball players have performed in some memorable local venues. In Covington, townball and then baseball were played at Willow Run beginning at least in the 1850s. The first organized baseball game played in Covington also took place there in 1866. The Covington Ballpark, now memorialized by a mural on Covington's floodwall, opened in 1895 at Ninth and Philadelphia Sts. at Willow Run. The construction of I-75 through Willow Run forced the Covington Ballpark's demolition in 1958. Other notable baseball fields in Northern Kentucky include Wiedemann Field, Rough Riders Park, and **Taylor's Bottoms** in Newport, and Spinks Park in Bellevue.

"Ballpark to Close for Road August 20," *KE,* August 9, 1958, 1K.

"Base Ball," *Ludlow Reporter,* August 15, 1874, 2.

"Base Ball Tournament at Florence, Kentucky, Yesterday," *CDG*, October 18, 1866, 2.
Boehmker, Terry, comp. *Northern Kentucky High School Sports Guide*. Self-published, 1995.
"Complex Named for Cappel," *KE*, November 13, 2002, C1.
Reis, Jim. "Sports Complex Gave Boost to Newport's Image and Pride," *KP*, October 10, 1994, 4K.
——. "World Champs of 1939: Covington Team No. 1 in Softball," *KP*, July 24, 1990, 4K.
"World Softball Champs Honored," *KTS*, October 4, 1956, 13A.

Greg Perkins

BASKETBALL. Basketball has long been a popular athletic endeavor in the schools of Northern Kentucky. An affordable sport, it requires neither the expenditure for equipment and a playing field that is needed for football or baseball, nor as many participants; and most schools have a gymnasium, used for many purposes such as physical education, recess, lunch, and assemblies. Because the hanging of rims and backboards inside a building is not costly, small rural schools can play and enjoy the game. Even today, many schools that do not field football teams participate in basketball.

Clearly the foremost basketball player to emerge from Northern Kentucky is Newport native **Dave Cowens** of Newport Catholic High School (see **Newport Central Catholic High School**). He is the region's first player to be inducted into the Naismith National Basketball Hall of Fame in Springfield, Mass. (1990). His 10-year-plus professional career includes two National Basketball Association (NBA) championships with the Boston Celtics and Most Valuable Player, All-Star teams, and Rookie of the Year awards. He set rebounding records at Florida State University at Tallahassee, Fla. (1970), and led his Newport Catholic team (1966) into the state tournament. Since he retired from playing, he has coached several professional teams. He played the center position even though many people believed he was too small to do so at six feet eight inches.

The other person from Northern Kentucky to enter the Naismith Hall is **Arnie Risen** of Williamstown (1998). A graduate of the old Williamstown High School (1942), Risen played the forward position in the NBA during the league's formative years. After playing college ball at Eastern Kentucky University at Richmond and Ohio State at Columbus, he began his professional career in 1946 with the Indianapolis Kautskys; later he played with the Rochester Royals (N.Y.), helping that team win the 1951 NBA championship. Risen ended his professional career with the Boston Celtics in 1958, in an age when the sport was different from today's game.

Behind Cowens and Risen are a few other Northern Kentuckians who made it into the NBA. One is **Larry Staverman** of Newport Catholic (1954) and Villa Madonna College (**Thomas More College**) (1958), who played five years in the professional ranks. He began with the Cincinnati Royals and went on to Chicago and Detroit, then held a couple of professional coaching positions. Another Cincinnati Royal from the area is guard Dan Tieman from **Covington Catholic High School** (1958) and Villa Madonna (Thomas More) (1962). John Turner from **Newport High School** (1957) gained All American status at the University of Louisville (UL) (1961) and played a couple of seasons with Chicago in the NBA; George Stone, who graduated from Covington's William Grant High School (see **Lincoln-Grant School**) (1964) and Marshall University at Huntington, W.Va. (1968), enjoyed five seasons in the American Basketball Association (ABA); **Thomas Thacker**, also from William Grant High School (1959), who went to the University of Cincinnati (UC) (1963), is the only basketball player to play on teams that won an NCAA (National Collegiate Athletic Association), an ABA, and an NBA championship. One of his championship rings was from the Boston Celtics. At six feet two, Thacker was short to play the forward position. Bob Arnzen from Fort Thomas attended St. Xavier High School (1965) in Cincinnati and played two sports at Notre Dame University at South Bend, Ind. (1969), before playing four professional seasons in the ABA and the NBA, including seasons with the Cincinnati Royals and the Indiana Pacers. He also pitched in minor league baseball for several seasons.

The most famous basketball coach ever associated with Northern Kentucky went on to become the person some regard as being the greatest NCAA coach of all time, **John Wooden**. Following his graduation from Purdue University at West Lafayette, Ind. (1932), Wooden began his coaching career at Dayton (Ky.) High School (see **Dayton Public Schools**). He was there only two years, before moving back to Indiana on the way to his 10 NCAA championships at UCLA in the 1960s and 1970s. He became the legendary "Wizard of Westwood" and lives today near the UCLA campus. Some other coaches deserve to be mentioned. **Jim Connor**, who mentored both Cowens and Staverman, earned more than 560 basketball victories while coaching at Newport Catholic, Bellarmine College in Louisville, **Boone Co. High School**, and Thomas More College. Charlie Wolf coached at Thomas More and for the Cincinnati Royals and two other NBA teams. Mote Hils finished his coaching career at **Northern Kentucky University** (NKU) with 119 victories. Hils's protégé Kenny Shields, from Covington Catholic (1960) and the University of Dayton in Ohio (1964), went from coaching the old **St. Thomas High School** in Fort Thomas to **Highlands High School**, and then to NKU, where he retired with 306 victories in 16 seasons at the college rank. Shields's daughter married Hils's son. Coach Steve Ridder, who starred at Bellevue High School (1977) (see **Bellevue Public Schools**) and Berea College in Kentucky (1981), has built a highly successful basketball program since 1989 at Embry-Riddle Aeronautical University in Daytona Beach, Fla., winning the National Association of Intercollegiate Athletics (NAIA) championship in the 1999–2000 season.

Players from Northern Kentucky whose careers stopped after the collegiate level include Howard Stacey, who played at **Dixie Heights High School** (1957) and at UL (1961), and Scott Draud from Highlands High School (1986), who played at Vanderbilt University in Nashville, Tenn. (1990). Draud is considered the best natural shooter to come out of the region and remains the Ninth Region's all-time scorer. Dickie Beal went from Covington's **Holmes High School** (1980) to play at the UK (1984); also from Holmes came Doug Schloemer (1978), Kentucky's Mr. Basketball in 1978, who played at UC (1982). Jack Thobe from Ludlow played at St. Xavier High School (1958) in Cincinnati and Xavier University in Ohio (XU) (1962); Carl Foster from Newport Catholic (1963) also played at XU (1967); Dick Maile went from Covington Catholic (1961) to earn All American status at Louisiana State University at Baton Rouge (1965), before becoming a high school coach and teacher in Northern Kentucky. Roger Tieman, Dan's brother, also came out of Covington Catholic (1956) to play at UL (1960). John "Frenchy" Demoisey from Walton High School (see **Walton-Verona Independent Schools**) (1930) played at UK (1934), where he became Adolph Rupp's first All American, and later worked as the longtime personal driver for Kentucky governor A. B. "Happy" Chandler (1935–1939, 1955–1959); Cincinnatian Dan Doellman played at NKU from 1975 to 1979, and his son Justin, from **Larry A. Ryle High School** (2003), played at XU (2007); Brian O'Connor played on the first **Covington Latin School** varsity basketball team before going to Thomas More College (1981) and afterward playing in Europe for a while; Sean Dineen played at Covington Catholic (1987) and for the University of Pennsylvania at Philadelphia (1991); Fort Thomas's Charlie Wolf played at St. Xavier High School (1944) and XU before becoming the coach at Villa Madonna College and later coaching for the Cincinnati Royals.

Early on, many high schools in the area offered women's basketball. Tiny Corinth High School in Grant Co. won a girls' state championship during the 1920s. That sport then disappeared until gender equity brought it back in the 1970s. **Pam Browning** of **Carroll Co. High School** (1974) played at UK (1978) and then professionally for the New Jersey Gems of the Women's Basketball League, before her tragic death in 1989. Donna Murphy of Newport High School (1976) set records there and then attended Morehead State University in Kentucky (1980). She has coached at various places since. Melissa Stone of Highlands (1987) and NKU (1991) coached at the college level (Montana State University at Billings) before returning to Northern Kentucky to coach at Newport High School. Celeste Hill from Holmes (1990) had an excellent college career at Old Dominion University at Norfolk, Va. (1994), and played in Europe (including Greece) and Israel before returning to Holmes as its women's coach. Jamie Walz from Highlands (1996), the first Miss Kentucky Basketball, attended Western Kentucky University at Bowling Green (2000) and today coaches at her high school back in Fort Thomas.

The foremost collegiate women's basketball coach in the area is Nancy Winstel of NKU, who since 1982 has amassed more than 500 victories and one NCAA Division II National Championship in 2000. Thomas More College also plays women's basketball.

In terms of high school boys' basketball, six teams from the Northern Kentucky region have won state championships: Corinth (1930); Brooksville (1939); Maysville (1947); Simon Kenton (1981); Mason Co. (2003); and Holmes (2009). **Simon Kenton High School**'s championship in 1981 came one year after a science laboratory explosion had seriously damaged the school (see **Simon Kenton High School Explosion**). That championship team was led by Troy McKinley (1981), who went on to play at UK (1984) and was a member of UK's national championship team in 1984. **Mason Co. High School**'s state champion team (2003) was led by Chris Lofton, who played on the University of Tennessee's 2008 basketball team. That team reached the third round of the NCAA Men's Division I Basketball Championship but lost to the University of Louisville. Lofton was also a Mr. Kentucky Basketball. Several Northern Kentucky teams have made it to the state basketball tournament's final game, only to lose: Newport High School lost in 1954 to Inez High School, Covington Catholic lost to Earlington in 1967, and Holmes, in overtime, lost in 1978 to Shelby Co.

College basketball fans in Northern Kentucky, despite proximity to UC and XU, are loyal to the UK Wildcats in Lexington. Over the years, UK, with 7 national basketball titles, is second only to UCLA's total of 11 national championships. Although UC has two such championships from the early 1960s, Northern Kentucky follows its Wildcats; and from mid-November through the end of both high school and college seasons, basketball fans in Northern Kentucky, as in the rest of the state, can be found somewhere glued to a television watching a sport they affectionately refer to as "roundball."

Douchant, Mike. *Encyclopedia of College Basketball.* New York: Gale Research, 1994.

Grace, Kevin. *Cincinnati Hoops.* Charleston, S.C.: Arcadia, 2003.

Sachare, Alex, ed. *The Official NBA Basketball Encyclopedia.* New York: Villard Books, 1994.

BATTERY HOOPER. Battery Hooper, located in Fort Wright, was a gun battery constructed during the **Civil War** as part of a strategy to defend Cincinnati using the hills of Northern Kentucky. The construction of Battery Hooper was begun by Col. **Charles Whittlesey**, who was responsible for surveying and establishing the defenses for Cincinnati until November 1, 1861. The battery was finished and armed by Col. James Simpson, who was assigned to the defenses around Cincinnati for the duration of the war. Battery Hooper was present, but not armed, when, in September 1862, Gen. Henry Heth made a military feint against Cincinnati during the Confederates' fall invasion of Kentucky. The battery probably served as a command post or communications point during the Heth incident, owing to the commanding view of the Licking River it afforded. Battery Hooper, significant in that it is one of the few surviving relics of the defense of Cincinnati, is being restored and preserved as a site the public may visit.

The battery was named for William Hooper, a prominent Cincinnati businessman, who provided monetary aid for defense of the city. Hooper was an active, patriotic citizen who was appointed assistant quartermaster, as well as paymaster, during the 1862 Cincinnati invasion crisis. He also helped to purchase steamboats and equip them as gunboats to be used against the Confederate fleet on the Mississippi River.

Archaeological investigation of the Battery Hooper site has uncovered a stone foundation of what was probably a powder magazine, as well as a circular cistern made of brick. The battery was probably armed with two smoothbore 18-pound guns. Information concerning the cannon is purely conjectural, since the guns were sent to Pittsburgh at war's end.

The remains of Battery Hooper are currently part of a restoration project undertaken by **Northern Kentucky University** (NKU) and the City of Fort Wright. Funding for this project has been provided by the City of Fort Wright and the Community Partnership Program of NKU, sponsored by the Scripps Howard Foundation for Civic Engagement. The James A. Ramage Civil War Museum, honoring the NKU professor and Civil War scholar and author who helped to initiate the battery's restoration project, is operated by the City of Fort Wright. The restoration of Battery Hooper is also significant in that it is a model of a university-community partnership to preserve a historical site that might have been lost to a housing development.

"Battery Park Moves Closer—Fort Wright Structure Built during the Civil War," *KE,* March 11, 2004, C2.

"14 Acres Eyed as Site for a Park," *KP,* June 3, 2003, 1K–7K.

"Homeland Security 1860s Style—Civil War Site to Be Restored as Museum," *KP,* February 17, 2005, 1K–7K.

Kenneth Crawford

BAUER, GARY LEE (b. May 4, 1946, Covington, Ky.). Gary Bauer, a player in Republican politics, grew up on the East End of Newport, at 807 Park Ave. He is the son of Stanley "Spike" Rynolds Bauer and Elizabeth Gossett Bauer. Bauer graduated from **Newport High School** in 1964 and Georgetown College (in Kentucky) in 1968. He earned his law degree from the Georgetown University Law School at Washington, D.C., in 1973. He also received a certificate from the John F. Kennedy School of Government at Harvard University in Cambridge, Mass.

Bauer was director of research for the Republican National Committee (1972–1973); he assisted in the Reagan-Bush campaign (1980) and then spent eight years in the Reagan administration (1981–1989) as an undersecretary of education and a domestic issues adviser. His areas of expertise have been education and family policy. In 1988 he became president of the Family Research Council. In 1999 he was for a short time a Republican candidate for president, but he did not survive the primaries and withdrew in February 2000. On April 21, 1999, the day that he announced his candidacy at his alma mater, Newport High School, he took his campaign entourage with him to lunch at the **Dixie Chili** parlor in Newport. In recent years Bauer has championed conservative causes on many political television talk shows; and since his presidential run, he has been president of the American Values interest group and chairman of the Campaign for Working Families. Today he lives with his family in Fairfax, Va.

Bauer, Gary Lee. *Doing Things Right.* Nashville, Tenn.: W Publishing Group, 2001.

——. *Our Hopes, Our Dreams: A Vision for America.* Washington, D.C.: Focus on the Family, 1996.

——. *Our Journey Home: What Parents Are Doing to Preserve Family Values.* Nashville, Tenn.: W Publishing Group, 1994.

"Bauer Returns Home to Announce," *KP,* April 15, 1999, 2K.

"Bauer Waits, Watches, Builds His Conservative War Chest," *CP,* July 3, 1998, 1A.

Dobson, James, and Gary Lee Bauer. *Children at Risk: The Battle for the Hearts and Minds of Our Kids.* Nashville, Tenn.: W Publishing Group, 1992.

BAVARIAN BREWING COMPANY. The Bavarian Brewing Company of Covington was at 528 W. 12th St., on the north side of the street near the eastern edge of **Willow Run** Creek. Its original owners and founders, Julius H. DeGlow and Charles L. Best, were making beer on that site before the end of 1867. The man who built Bavarian into a major brewery, German-born Wilhelm Riedlin, purchased control of the firm in 1884, after it had gone through a succession of other owners. It was Riedlin who built the plant structures that remain today. The complex covered some 2.5 acres. By 1893 the brewery's malt house had a 30,000-bushel capacity, and its 31-ton refrigeration plant could produce 100 tons of ice a week. The company sold its excess ice to neighborhood customers for public use and supplied many saloons with ice in exchange for the selling of Bavarian products. With the help of the the Ruh family, Covington's well-known brewmasters, the years just before **Prohibition** saw Bavarian ascend to second place in production among Northern Kentucky breweries, behind Newport's **Wiedemann Brewing Company**; like the Wiedemann Brewing Company, the Bavarian Brewing Company had been making inroads into the Cincinnati beer market. Riedlin died in 1919, just before Prohibition stopped the making of beer; the company bottled soft drinks until Prohibition ended in 1933.

The Bavarian Brewing Company reopened after Prohibition, with new competition in Covington from the startup Heidelberg Brewing Company (see **Brewing Industry**). For almost 15

Bavarian Brewing Company offices, Covington, ca. 1911.

years, the two companies fought for the local Covington beer market. Finally, Bavarian was able to purchase Heidelberg in 1949, and Bavarian used Heidelberg's W. Fourth St. facility in Covington as plant two for its operations until 1955, when production was consolidated on 12th St. and the former Heidelberg building was sold to C. Rice Packing (see **Meatpacking**). Between 1945 and 1952, employees at the Bavarian brewery worked 24 hours each day, seven days each week, to keep up with the demand for the company's products: Bavarian, Bavarian Bock, Bavarian's Old Style, Schott's Ale, and, for the Florida market, Silver Bar. The company employed 200 and had a $1.7 million payroll under company president William R. Schott, Riedlin's son-in-law.

In the mid-1950s, the plight that plagued brewers who did not, for whatever reason, go national, began to beset both the Bavarian and the Wiedemann breweries. All the local advertising and the Nordic beauty of Bavarian Girl Brenda Cotter could not compete with the national television promotions of rival brewers Budweiser and Miller. International Breweries of Buffalo, N.Y., purchased the Bavarian Brewing Company in 1959. In 1962 Bavarian won first prize in a taste test at the Brussels Beer Festival in Belgium. However, the market decline could not be stopped, and by 1965 the company was losing about $1,400 each day. The company was closed, and the Bavarian brand was licensed to the Associated Brewery of Detroit, Mich. The plant's equipment was auctioned off to a Tampa, Fla., concern, and the building was sold to Justin Schneider, who moved his Central Sales general merchandise store there. During the 1990s, the Party Source nightclub-microbrewery operated in the former Bavarian building; later it was occupied by Jillian's, a restaurant-entertainment center, which closed in 2006. In 2008, Bill Yung (see **Columbia Sussex Corporation**) purchased the property.

Holian, Timothy J. *Over the Barrel: The Brewing History and Beer Culture of Cincinnati, 1800 to the Present.* 2 vols. St. Joseph, Mo.: Sudhaus Press, 2000.

Reis, Jim. "Even Prohibition Didn't Stop Bavarian Brewmaster Family," *KP*, August 16, 1999, 4K.

——. "Memory of Bavarian Beer Fades: Brew Was Popular for Some 100 Years," *KP*, August 25, 1986, 4K.

——. "Turning Barley into Big Bucks," *KP*, October 20, 2003, 5K.

Wimberg, Robert J. *Cincinnati Breweries.* Cincinnati: Ohio Book Store, 1989.

BAVARIAN TRUCKING COMPANY. The Bavarian Trucking Company Inc., founded by Lawrence Brueggemann and incorporated in 1934, developed from a horse dray-line that was established by Lawrence's father, Ben Brueggemann, in 1901. The dray-line eventually became known as the Brueggemann Trucking Company. When Ben died of influenza during the epidemic of 1917, he left the business to his wife, Mary Ann, and their 11 young children. Lawrence was the oldest of the children and, although only 16 years of age, the head teamster in the ongoing transport of 40-foot lathes from a Covington manufacturing concern to the city's rail depot.

Lawrence Brueggemann managed the family business for his mother until the 1930s, when he founded his own separate business, the Lawrence Brueggemann Trucking Company. He nevertheless maintained a close relationship with his siblings, who continued the Brueggemann Trucking Company into the 1970s. The Great Depression of the 1930s was hard on Lawrence's company, and after a significant account defaulted on its payment, he was counseled to file bankruptcy. He rejected the suggestion and insisted on repaying all of his debts.

Brueggemann sold all but the oldest of his trucks in the fleet and continued to serve his Covington clients. He made up for his shortage of equipment by expanding his services to offer the mining, hauling, and sale of sand; he also added a repair garage and a truck-parts business. His operation was housed in part of the old Bavarian Brewery complex on Pike St. in Covington. Brueggemann used its name when he incorporated as the Bavarian Trucking Company Inc. in 1934.

During the 1950s the Bavarian Trucking Company expanded its excavating and hauling services and began providing residential and industrial waste disposal. In 1969 the company was rechartered and Bernard Brueggemann became president, although Lawrence continued to work at the company until his death in 1989. Bernard governed the company until 1998, when he passed control to his son James.

In 2003 the Bavarian Trucking Company became the first refuse hauler in Kentucky to generate electricity from methane gas created by the waste in its landfill. The electricity is produced from landfill gas in a generating plant owned by East Kentucky Power that is located at the trucking company's facility in Boone Co. A form of green power, the electricity is marketed as EnviroWatts by the **Owen Electric Cooperative**.

In 1999 and 2000, *Waste Age* and *Waste News* both ranked the Bavarian Trucking Company among the top 100 waste companies in the United States and Canada. In 2004 the University of Cincinnati's Goering Center for Family and Private Business in Ohio selected the company as a finalist in the 2004 Tri-State Family Business of the Year competition.

"Garbage Goes Green at Bavarian," *SC*, September 18, 2005, 2A.

"Landfill May Recover Gas," *KE*, March 25, 2001, B1–B2.

Rick Brueggemann

BAWAC INC. BAWAC Community Rehabilitation Center began in March 1973 as a unit of the Northern Kentucky Mental Health–Mental Retardation Regional Board, with support and assistance from the Boone Co. Association for Retarded Citizens. The center is a private 501(c)(3) nonprofit corporation. A separate volunteer board of directors assumed responsibility for the program from the regional board in 1975. At the same time, the center moved to its present location at 7970 Kentucky Dr. in Florence, in the Northern Kentucky Industrial Park. In response to its clients' needs, BAWAC expanded this facility in 1985 with funding from the Northern Kentucky Association for the Retarded. Another expansion in 1989 was made possible by a grant from the Kentucky Department of Vocational Rehabilitation. Through the years BAWAC has developed new programs to meet the needs of people with disabilities or barriers to employment, or both.

BAWAC's policies and goals are determined by its board, whose members represent an active cross-section of the community. The organization receives funding through fees for services, ultimately paid by various state and county agencies. It is also supported by United Way and Community Chest of Greater Cincinnati; by contributions from community groups, organizations, and individuals; by memorial gifts; and by revenue from its production activities.

BAWAC's mission is to help its clients improve their vocational potential and quality of life by offering counseling, evaluation, training in life and work skills, job placement, support services, and remunerative employment in a therapeutic or community setting. The organization's purpose is to provide, for its service population, a socially accepted pattern for daily living, the opportunity to develop personal skills that are needed in order to adapt to adult life, and an opportunity to develop vocational skills through work. BAWAC provides a "normal" model of living and working for clients as an alternative to institutionalization; clients can also advance to other training programs or move out into competitive industry. For individuals who need continuing job-related services, a work facility is provided. The minimum age for participation in the center's programs is 16, and applicants must be disabled as a result of developmental disability, injury, or illness or be experiencing significant barriers to employment, or both.

BAWAC. "About BAWAC." www.bawac.org/ (accessed January 2, 2006).

Gail Chastang

BB RIVERBOATS. Founded in 1976 by restaurateurs **Benjamin Bernstein** and his wife Shirley, BB Riverboats has operated from Newport since December 2005. Before that, its docking facilities were located just downriver of what was once called Covington Landing, at the foot of Madison Ave. along the Ohio River in Covington. The firm, which is an adjunct of Benson's Catering and the **Mike Fink Floating Restaurant** situated at the foot of Greenup St., provides both scheduled and chartered cruises on the river, giving riders a sense of what mid-19th-century steamboat life was in its heyday. Sometimes meals are available as part of the passengers' cruise tickets. BB Riverboats also provides riverboat ferry service to both Cincinnati Reds and Bengals home games in Ohio just across the water. A trip on a BB Riverboat is a favorite activity of visitors to Northern Kentucky and Cincinnati. With the removal of Covington Landing, the fleet has moved upriver to Newport. The size of the fleet has varied over the years; the present flagship of the line is the new *Belle of Cincinnati.*

Founder Ben Bernstein died in 1992, and the operation is now managed by his son Alan; continuity is assured because Alan's son Ben recently obtained his river pilot's license to command the company's boats on the open water. This family and company has also been a heavy promoter of the Tall Stacks Celebrations held along the Cincinnati riverfront. Tall Stacks attracts 20 or so excursion steamboats from throughout the Ohio and Mississippi river valleys, along with thousands of international visitors, for a week of re-creating and reenacting the days of Cincinnati's steamboat era.

"Fink Owner Bernstein Is Dead," *KP,* January 21, 1992, 1K.

Saladin, Luke. "Newport, BB Sign 1-Year Lease," *KP,* March 7, 2006, A5.

BEAGLE, RON (b. February 7, 1934, Hartford, Conn.). College Hall of Fame football player Ronald G. Beagle is the son of Joseph C. and Marie R. Bernaducci Beagle. The family moved from the Bond Hill area of Cincinnati to the Winston Park neighborhood (Taylor Mill) during Ron's freshman year of high school, 1947–1948. His father played basketball at **Holmes High School** and worked for Procter and Gamble, and his mother was a nurse. Ron attended Purcell High School in Cincinnati and became a star football player there, graduating in 1951. Legend has it that he rode his bicycle to and from school every day. At that time, nonresident students were allowed to play high school sports in Ohio, but today they are not. For the 1951 football season, Ron attended Wyoming Prep School in Pennsylvania; then he received a scholarship to the U.S. Naval Academy at Annapolis, where he played end. He is the only Northern Kentuckian to be named the nation's outstanding college football player of the year (1954). He was an All-American in 1954 and 1955, receiving the coveted Maxwell Trophy in 1954. He is one of only a few linemen to win that award and one of a few underclassmen to do so. In 1956 the City of Covington and mayor John J. Maloney presented him with a key to the city. Upon graduating from Annapolis, Ron was commissioned an officer in the U.S. Marine Corps. After completing his military obligation in 1960, he tried out for the Oakland Raiders of the defunct American Football League. A football trading card for him was printed that year, but a knee injury ended his football career. Ron Beagle is one of the most famous collegiate football players to come from the Northern Kentucky region. He is a member of the College Football Hall of Fame. Today he lives with his family in Sacramento, Calif.

Arnim, Margaret. "Mother of Nation's Top Grid Star Could Pass for His Date," *KP,* December 3, 1954, 1.

"Beagle, Navy Team's End, Named to Receive Maxwell Club Trophy," *NYT,* November 30, 1954, 37.

Beagle, Ronald G., to Michael R. Sweeney, various dates, 2005.

"Navy League Unit to Fete Ron Beagle," *KP,* December 14, 1954, 8.

Sports Biographies. "Beagle, Ronald," Hickok Sports .com. www.hickoksports.com/biograph/beaglero .shtml (accessed May 24, 2005).

Michael R. Sweeney

BEALL, BENJAMIN (b. ca. 1750, Prince George Co., Md.; d. January 5, 1809, Mentor, Ky.). The Beall "clan" immigrated to America from Scotland in 1621 and settled in Maryland, where Benjamin Beall, later a surveyor, was born. After he moved to Northern Kentucky in 1790, he married Jeannette Hamilton Kennedy, daughter of **William Kennedy** and Mary Lindsey Kennedy. Benjamin worked with his father-in-law and his brother-in-law James Kennedy to survey thousands of acres in Campbell Co., including the vast landholdings of **David Leitch**. For their services, surveyors were typically given one-third of the land surveyed, and by this means Beall and his in-laws acquired much real estate.

Benjamin Beall's family made their home on a large farm called Beallmont at Mentor, Ky., along the Ohio River. Beall served as an ensign in the 21st Kentucky Militia during the Tripolitan War (1801–1805). Kentucky governor Christopher Greenup (1804–1808) appointed him a Campbell Circuit Court judge in 1807, and he held that position for the rest of his life. Benjamin and his wife had nine children; one son, Benjamin Duke Beall, became a Campbell Circuit Court judge, like his father before him. Benjamin Duke Beall built a two-story frame home, which stands today just east of the Campbell Co. Courthouse, on Main St. in Alexandria. Benjamin Duke Beal's daughter Sarah married **Richard Tarvin Baker**, a well-known Alexandria lawyer and a Kentucky state senator.

Benjamin Beall died in 1809, and Jeannette in 1812. Both were buried in unmarked graves in a small family cemetery along Smith Rd. near Flagg Springs. Following the death of Jeannette Beall, her children had to sell many of the family's lands to pay off debts. Jeannette willed the family home to her mother, Mary Lindsey Kennedy. **Francis Spilman**, who, along with his wife Rebecca, founded the City of Alexandria, agreed to raise the Beall's two minor children, Samuel and James, after Jeannette's death.

Wessling, Jack. *Early History of Campbell County, Kentucky.* Alexandria, Ky.: Self-published, 1997.

Jack Wessling

BEAN, ROY "JUDGE" (b. ca. 1825, Mason Co., Ky.; d. March 16, 1903, Del Rio, Tex.). Roy Bean, who later became a notorious western justice of the peace, moved in 1840 from the Maysville area to the New Mexico Territory, where he operated a series of trading posts and began a lifelong habit of heavy drinking. After killing a man in a fight, he moved to San Diego, where his brother Joshua was mayor. There, Bean worked as a bartender in his brother's saloon and served as a lieutenant in the California militia. In 1852 Bean wounded a man in a duel, and his brother was killed in another duel. Bean then returned to New Mexico.

During the next 20 years, Bean held a number of jobs, generally as a bartender, in New Mexico and Texas. In the 1860s he settled in San Antonio, where he tried to support his wife and five children by both legal and illegal methods. He became the leader of a disreputable section of town, which was named Beanville in his honor.

In 1882 Bean deserted his wife and family and set up a saloon near Del Rio, Tex. That year, he was appointed justice of the peace in the nearby town of Langtry. Langtry had been named for a Southern Pacific official, although Bean always insisted he had named the town for the actress Lillie Langtry. He called his saloon the Jersey Lilly, which was Lillie Langtry's stage name. Above the saloon's door were two signs: "Ice Cold Beer" and "Law West of the Pecos."

With no legal training whatsoever, Judge Roy Bean began to dispense justice in a manner that the local lawless element would accept. His rulings were colorful and became part of American folklore.

In one case he ruled, "Gentlemen, I find the law very explicit on murdering your fellow man but there is nothing on killing a Chinaman. Case dismissed." In another case, when presented with the body of a dead man who had a gun and $40 in his pocket, Bean fined the dead man $40 for carrying a concealed weapon.

The local citizens liked Bean, and between 1884 and 1902 he won every election for justice of the peace. In 1896 he built a new saloon and an opera house for Langtry's performances. In 1898 he staged an illegal boxing match near Langtry between Bob Fitzsimmons and Peter Maher. The fight resulted in international publicity for Bean and the town of Langtry.

In 1903 Bean visited Del Rio, where he went on a drunken binge and died after consuming too much alcohol. He was buried at what later became the Whitehead Museum in that city. Judge Roy Bean became a larger-than-life folk hero during the 20th century and the subject of several books and movies and a weekly television series.

Lloyd, Everett. *Law West of the Pecos: The Story of Judge Roy Bean.* San Antonio, Tex.: Naylor, 1936.
Sonnichsen, C. L. *The Story of Roy Bean: Law West of the Pecos.* Greenwich, Conn.: Fawcett, 1972.

Charles H. Bogart

BEARD, DANIEL CARTER (b. June 21, 1850, Cincinnati, Ohio; d. June 11, 1941, Suffern, N.Y.). One of the founders of the Boy Scouts of America, Daniel Carter Beard, or "Uncle Dan," as he was affectionately known, became one of America's most beloved public figures. He was one of six children of James Henry and Mary Caroline Carter Beard. His father, a professional painter (**James Henry Beard**), served as a Union captain during the Civil War. Dan was 11 years old and the Civil War had just begun when his family moved to 322 E. Third St., in Covington. He lived in this home until he was 21. In 1965 the home was designated a landmark by an act of Congress through the U.S. Department of the Interior.

Dan's room was the only room on the third floor, and he wrote in his autobiography about the pets that lived with him: a squirrel named Cudjo, a raccoon, and a quail. When Dan was growing up, the Civil War was on everyone's mind. Dan and his friends often played "cowboys and Indians." They poured buckets of water down the banks of the Licking River to create waterslides, and Union soldiers joined Dan and his friends in sliding down into the river.

Beard's experience on the banks of the Licking River helped to shape his life's vision. He became an acclaimed artist whose work was featured in several of Mark Twain's books, including *A Connecticut Yankee in King Arthur's Court.* Beard was also a writer for *Recreation* magazine and *Woman's Home Companion.*

"Uncle Dan's" life passion lay in his work with young boys and his love of nature. He worked daily to expose boys to nature and teach them how to use, respect, and live off the land. The organization he founded, the Sons of Daniel Boone, later became the Boy Scouts of America.

Beard's influence within the Boy Scouts of America was dramatic. In addition to his intimate involvement as founder, he designed the organization's uniforms, patches, and awards. He also created the hand sign now used by Cub Scouts. Beard's book *The American Boy's Handy Book* was used by both the Sons of Daniel Boone and the Boy Scouts of America.

Beard served for decades as a vital link between the men in charge of the Boy Scouts of America and the boys themselves. In 1934 he returned to his childhood hometown, where he visited with 2,000 scouts camping at **Devou Park** in Covington. He was the national scout commissioner from 1910 until his death in 1941. Ten days before his 91st birthday, he died of myocarditis at Brooklands, his New York estate. He was buried nearby at the Brick Church Cemetery in Rockland Co., N.Y.

The Beard Home was later acquired by the adjacent **Booth Memorial Hospital** and fell into disrepair during the 1970s. The home was purchased in 1983 and renovated by Phil and Diana Taliaferro. In 1987 the Dan Beard Plaza was created next to his home. The plaza features a bronze statue of Dan Beard with a Boy Scout, along with hundreds of inscribed bricks.

Beard, Dan. *Hardly a Man Is Now Alive: The Autobiography of Dan Beard.* New York: Doubleday, Doran, 1939.
"Dan Beard to Return to Childhood Home . . . ," *KP,* August 18, 1934, 1.
"No. Ky. Council Plans to Honor Father of Scouting," *KP,* October 13, 1933, 9.
Reis, Jim. "Where the Daniel Carter Beard Bridge Got Its Name," *KP,* May 9, 2005, 4K.

Phil Taliaferro

BEARD, JAMES HENRY (b. May 1812, Black Rock [now Buffalo], N.Y.; d. April 4, 1893, Flushing, N.Y.). James Beard, a noted American artist, was the father of **Daniel Carter Beard**, as well as **Lina and Adelia Beard**; three other sons (James Carter, William Henry "Harry," and Thomas Francis "Frank") also became artists. Beard was born near Buffalo, N.Y., where his father transported supplies to military posts along the Great Lakes during the War of 1812. In 1819 James Beard moved with his family to northern Ohio; his father's death several years later left James's mother with five children. James, the oldest of them, secured employment as a store clerk in Painesville, Ohio, to contribute to the family's finances; he later worked in a watchmaking firm in Detroit, Mich. In 1825 Beard left Detroit and returned to northern Ohio, where his mother sent him to study at a school in Burton. Eventually, he began to work as an artist, painting portraits in nearby towns. Moving to Pittsburgh with few resources, he found little opportunity there, so in October 1830 he boarded a keelboat as a hired hand and sailed for Cincinnati. In Cincinnati, he became a painter at a chair factory, while also painting portraits as a sideline. While he stayed at a hotel owned by Col. Thomas Carter, Beard met the colonel's daughter, Mary Caroline Carter, whom he married. In 1833 Beard began accompanying his father-in-law on occasional flatboat trips to New Orleans to sell whiskey, pork, flour, and other products. On his return trips to Cincinnati, he painted portraits for a living.

Beard also traveled throughout the neighboring region, including Kentucky cities such as Danville, Frankfort, Georgetown, Lexington, and Versailles, painting portraits. He sometimes traveled by steamboat to other river cities in the region and painted while aboard. At times he would lay over in one of these cities, rent rooms for a studio, and distribute broadsides at local art stores and studios announcing his availability for art commissions. Over the next 30 years, he became one of Cincinnati's favorite artists.

Beard, who was very active in politics, started out as a **Whig**, but the issue of slavery made him a Republican.

In 1846 he entered one of his paintings, the *Carolina Emigrants*, in the National Academy Show in New York City; the painting sold for $750, considered a large sum for the period. By 1848 he was an honorary member of the National Academy. In the 1840s, he painted portraits of John Quincy Adams, Lyman Beecher, Henry Clay, William Henry Harrison, William Tecumseh Sherman, and Zachary Taylor. He continued painting portraits occasionally until the end of his life, but his moneymakers were portraits of young children, often with their pet dogs. He painted historical subjects now and then; if the works proved popular, he would paint multiple copies. His animal portraits, most commonly of dogs and horses, were his most valuable genre. He also created humorous paintings of anthropomorphic dogs. A typical one might have a pair of dogs eating a fancy meal with a bottle of champagne and what looked like a bit of flirtation.

In about 1861 Beard moved to Covington, apparently renting a house that has since been called the Daniel Carter Beard Home, at 322 E. Third St. With the outbreak of the **Civil War**, he sponsored a corps of volunteer nurses for the Union Army composed of artists, writers, and poets who were beyond military age. He raised enough money by personal subscriptions to charter and equip three steamers to return injured soldiers from Fort Donaldson in Tennessee to the military hospitals in Cincinnati. Beard became ill on the trip, but not a single man was lost. The Beard house became the unofficial meeting place and dormitory for the staff of Gen. Lew Wallace, commander of the Union forces in Northern Kentucky; it was a remarkable staff made up of poets; artists, including Beard; and literary men, including Thomas Buchanan Read, the author of *Sheridan's Ride.* All of the adult members of Beard's family joined the military in some capacity. Beard's painting *The Night before the Battle* was said to show the interior of the parapet of Fort Mitchel.

From 1863 until 1866, Beard lived mostly in New York City. He then resided in several places, including St. Louis and Chicago, before returning to New York in 1870. He died of chronic nephritis in Flushing, Queens, N.Y., in 1893. After a Swedenborgian Church funeral from his home at 87 Bonne

Ave. in Flushing, Long Island, N.Y., he was buried at the Flushing Cemetery.

Alexander, Mary L. "James H. Beard Achieved Fame with Early Portrait Paintings; Cincinnatian for Several Years," *CE*, August 9, 1953, sec. 4, p. 8.
Beard, Daniel Carter. *Hardly A Man Is Now Alive: The Autobiography of Dan Beard.* New York: Doubleday, 1939.
Flushing Cemetery Records, Flushing, N.Y.
"Funeral of James H. Beard," *NYT*, April 8, 1893, 5.
James H. Beard autobiography, Papers of Daniel C. Beard, box 15, Library of Congress, Washington, D.C.
Vitz, Robert. *The Queen and the Arts: Cultural Life in Nineteenth-Century Cincinnati.* Kent, Ohio: Kent State Univ. Press, 1989.
"Western Artists. Original. James H. Beard," *Cincinnati Mirror and Chronicle*, April 25, 1835, 208–9.
Wilson, James Grant, and John Fiske, eds. *Appleton's Cyclopedia of American Biography.* New York: D. Appleton, 1894.

Joseph F. Gastright and Paul A. Tenkotte

BEARD, LINA AND ADELIA (Lina: b. July 20, 1852, Cincinnati, Ohio; d. August 13, 1933, Flushing, N.Y.; Adelia: b. April 1, 1857, Painesville, Ohio; d. February 16, 1920, Flushing, N.Y.). Mary Caroline "Lina" and Adelia Belle Beard, the founders of Camp Fire Girls, were the daughters of artist **James Henry Beard** and Mary Caroline Carter Beard; they were sisters of **Daniel Carter Beard**, founder of the **Boy Scouts of America**. By 1866 the Beard sisters were living in New York City, where their father had moved to further his portrait-painting career.

Lina, the better known of the two girls, attended Mrs. Collin's Private School in Covington and then studied art at Cooper Union in New York City. In the early 1880s, she and Adelia founded the nation's first girls' scouting group, first known as the Girl Scout Society, later as the Girl Pioneers, and finally as the Camp Fire Girls. For many years, Lina was the treasurer of the group. In 1907 Lina Beard founded the Good Citizenship League in Flushing, N.Y., and was a delegate to the First Arbitration and Peace Conference. She was also one of the founders of the Equal Franchise Association of Flushing, N.Y.

Adelia Beard provided the funds to get the Good Citizenship League started. Both sisters, like the rest of their talented family members, illustrated books. Together, they wrote several books; the most famous was *The American Girls Handy Book* (1887), which over the years has gone through at least 12 printings. The book is a veritable encyclopedia of projects, devices, toys, gifts, dolls, recipes, decorations, perfumes, wax and clay modeling, painting, and games, with explanations telling, for example, how to make the toys and how to play the games. It was only natural that these two educated and talented sisters of Dan Beard, given their belief in women's equality, should endeavor to do for girls what their brother did for boys. Neither sister married; both were buried at the Flushing Cemetery in Flushing, N.Y.

Beard, Lina, and Adelia Belle Beard. *The American Girls Handy Book.* New York: Scribner's, 1887.
"Lina Beard Dies; Began Girl Scouts," *NYT*, August 14, 1933, 13.
"Miss Adelia Belle Beard, Author," *NYT*, February 17, 1920, 9.

Michael R. Sweeney

BEATTY, CLARE ELSIE (b. October 28, 1915, Dayton, Ohio; d. August 11, 1989, Warsaw, Ky.). The daughter of Albert and Louise Hosket Kinzeler, Elsie, as she preferred to be called, ran a marine business with her husband and was active in Ohio River affairs. She went to St. Anthony's Elementary School and Stivers High School in Dayton, Ohio, and graduated magna cum laude in 1937 from Western College in Oxford, Ohio. She taught school and was dean of girls at Franklin High School, Franklin, Ohio, from 1937 to 1943. Classically trained in Latin and Greek and fluent in French, she was employed by the Air Service Command at Patterson Field (now Wright-Patterson Air Force Base) in Fairborn, Ohio, during summer 1943. She was officially a clerk in the data maintenance section, but there is some evidence that she served as a French translator. She enrolled at Northwestern University in Evanston, Ill., in September 1943, where she was a resident adviser in a freshman girls' dormitory. She married Capt. **John L. Beatty** in January 1944 and was his partner in all his marine operations from that time until her death. She became a fixture on the Cincinnati Public Landing immediately after **World War II**, entering a male-dominated work world when most women were returning to home and hearth from wartime factory jobs. She took an active role in Columbia Harbor, the river service she and her husband opened after the war along Eastern Ave. in Cincinnati, and in the operations of their Cincinnati Marine Service and the Port of Cincinnati Terminal at the former Fernbank Repair Station (Dam 39) at Sayler Park, Cincinnati. Well regarded by all who knew her, she was a formidable force in the inland river industry, standing her ground equally well with marine insurance surveyors, towing company officials, admiralty attorneys, the U.S. Coast Guard, and the U.S. Army Corps of Engineers. She was a prolific writer, producing a running commentary on her husband's political campaigns in 1965 and 1967 and writing letters to the editors of major area newspapers for decades.

A teacher by profession, she worked tirelessly to educate the public about the Ohio River and its history, conducting hundreds of student tours aboard the Beattys' **Mike Fink Floating Restaurant** in Covington. She led the battle to move the restaurant to the Covington riverfront along Riverside Dr. The floating restaurant was moved to Covington shortly afterward, where it opened for business in May 1967. Besides attracting the best regional clientele there, it was frequented by international celebrities, including Raymond Burr, Perry Como, Bob Hope, David Frost, Peter Graves, and Mickey Rooney. Her own name exploded onto the international scene in January 1978 when the flagship of her husband's fleet, and her namesake, the towboat *Clare E. Beatty*, sank at Markland Dam (see **Blizzards and Severe Winter Weather**). News of the vessel's sinking was reported as far away as Rome, Italy, and attracted hundreds of letters from persons throughout the United States who expressed their sympathy and offered encouragement for the vessel's recovery. Husband John and his crew did raise the vessel and restore it. She was listed in the 1966–1967 edition of *Who's Who among American Women.* Clare E. Beatty died in 1989 at her home in Warsaw and was buried at Spring Grove Cemetery in Cincinnati.

Huffman, Barbara. *Beatty's Navy: The Life and Times of Capt. John L. and Clare E. Beatty.* Vevay, Ind.: Spancil Hill, 2004.

Barbara Huffman

BEATTY, JOHN L. (b. February 25, 1914, Ironton, Ohio; d. August 20, 1994, Cincinnati, Ohio). Third-generation river man John Beatty was the son of Captain William Campbell and Bertha Ellen Baker Beatty. His father and his paternal grandfather, W. S. C. Beatty, were engaged in marine construction and demolition before **World War I**. In 1918 John accompanied his father to a marine salvage operation to raise the steam towboat *J.R. Ware.* Although only four years old, John stayed occupied during the salvage operation constructing his first vessel, a canoe made of scrap tin roofing that he caulked with blue clay from the riverbank. He attended grades one through eight at Central School in Ironton, Ohio. When his family moved to Cincinnati in 1929, he enrolled at an electrical trade school there, but he was expelled because of an altercation with a staff member. Because of the domestic steel shortage during **World War II**, John and his father pursued marine salvage operations on a large scale, retrieving sunken vessels, barges, and pipelines and removing abandoned bridges, recycling for the war effort. John began working for marine insurance giant Neare, Gibbs & Company of Cincinnati in July 1944 as salvage engineer and later started his own company, Beatty Inc.

From the 1950s through the 1970s, Beatty was regarded as the foremost salvage engineer on the Ohio River and was often the first operator called upon by the U.S. Army Corps of Engineers when a marine accident required emergency cleanup. He and his wife, **Clare E. Beatty**, started one of the first postwar harbor services along the Northern Kentucky waterfront, called Columbia Harbor. In 1955 they greatly diversified their holdings by purchasing the former U.S. Corps of Engineers repair station at Fernbank, Ohio (Dam 39). The property included marine ways and other facilities that allowed for construction and repair of towboats, barges, pleasure boats, and ferries. Railroad tracks running through the property facilitated river-to-rail service, making the operation competitive with Cincinnati Sheet Metal's Rookwood Terminal, where his father had been employed as yard superintendent beginning in 1929. Beatty remodeled two steam towboats into floating restaurants, *Captain Hook's,* which opened on Cincinnati's public landing in May 1964, and the *Mike Fink,* which opened as the **Mike Fink Floating Restaurant** in May 1967 and is still operating on the Covington waterfront. Embroiled in a rezoning dispute with the City of Cincinnati regarding his Fernbank holdings, Beatty ran for Cincinnati City Council twice, as a Republican in 1965 and as an Independent in 1967, losing both times. He designed and constructed his own home below Warsaw in Gallatin Co. in 1976. During the blizzard of January 1978, he was engaged in rescuing runaway barges at Markland Dam when his towboat, the *Clare E. Beatty,* was caught in an ice floe and trapped above the dam (see **Blizzards and Severe Winter Weather**). The boat subsequently sank but was raised and returned to service by Beatty and his crew. Beatty died in 1994 and was buried next to his beloved Clare at Spring Grove Cemetery in Cincinnati. In August 1995 the *Clare E. Beatty,* along with the remainder of the Beatty salvage, sank again below Maysville.

Huffman, Barbara. *Beatty's Navy: The Life and Times of Capt. John L. and Clare E. Beatty.* Vevay, Ind.: Spancil Hill, 2004.

Ironton (Ohio) City Directories, 1882–1922, 1928, Briggs/Lawrence Co., Ohio, Public Library.

Barbara Huffman

BEAVERLICK. Beaverlick, a town in western Boone Co., was founded during the early 1800s. It may have received its name from the local fur trade, which included beaver pelts. Now, Beaverlick is best known as the intersection of Ky. Rt. 338 and U.S. 42, at the turn-off in Boone Co. to **Big Bone Lick** State Park. Beaverlick was once a busy center with three churches, a hotel, a millinery shop, a flour mill, two blacksmiths, a carriage maker, a general store, and two physicians, but the population has decreased along with the number of businesses.

A post office was established in 1854 at the community, which at that time was called Beaver Lick; in 1895 it became one word, Beaverlick. The post office remained active until 1944. Rev. George Buffington organized the Hughes Chapel Methodist Church at Beaverlick in 1878, and in 1883 a new church was constructed. The Hughes Chapel Cemetery remains, though the church is long gone. The Beaverlick Baptist Church was organized in 1883 with 130 members. The original building on Beaver Rd. still stands, but in 1979 the congregation built a new church along U.S. 42.

In 1932 an emergency landing field for aircraft was constructed at Beaverlick along the Cincinnati-to-Louisville airmail route, and a 23-inch rotating beacon light was placed along U.S. 42 to aid pilots flying at night. The searchlight became a landmark, and later the Beacon Light Motel was built on that site.

Not much is left of this small village that had 50 residents at the end of the 19th century, except historic houses, churches, and cemeteries. The completion of I-71 to Louisville during the late 1960s removed most of the traffic that had previously passed through Beaverlick.

Boone County Recorder, historical ed., September 4, 1930. Available at Boone Co. Public Library, Burlington, Ky.

Lutes, Ann. *A Brief History of Boone County.* Florence, Ky.: Boone Co. Historical Society, 1954.

Reis, Jim. "Tiny Unincorporated Towns Abound in Boone," *KP,* December 9, 1985, 4K.

Warminski, Margo. *Historic Structures of Boone County.* Burlington, Ky.: Boone Co. Historic Preservation Board, 2002.

Nancy J. Tretter

BE CONCERNED INC. This nonprofit organization is dedicated to helping low-income families in Northern Kentucky obtain basic necessities, such as food and clothing. Now located at 714 Washington St. in Covington, the organization began as the Christmas Store in 1968 and has since grown into an organization that helps families year-round. Be Concerned assists more than 1,200 families each month through its Food Program, its Clothing Store, its Housewares Store, and the Christmas Store.

The mission of Be Concerned was formulated by Sister Donna Kinney, the organization's founder: to help low-income clients preserve their dignity as they shop for food and clothing at a discount. In 1968 the Diocese of Covington (see **Roman Catholics**) Social Services director, Rev. Msgr. Thomas Finn, asked Sister Donna to take charge of the Christmas Bureau, which had over past years provided baskets of food and gifts to the poor. Sister Donna felt that it would be more meaningful to serve the poor by enabling them to buy toys and clothing of their own choosing for a nominal fee. In that way, recipients would not be receiving a simple handout but would be maintaining their dignity and individuality.

During the first year, the Christmas Store was located at the then-closed **St. Patrick Catholic Church** in Covington, and by soliciting donations of gently used toys and clothing from parishes in the Diocese of Covington, the Christmas Store served about 30 families. The following year, Sister Donna worked with Sister Anita Hagen and a network of Catholic nuns and priests to obtain more donations from the local Catholic schools. The Christmas Store operated this way out of various locations in Covington for the next four years. As the volume of donations increased and the need for storage grew, it became apparent that the organization needed a permanent home.

In 1973 Betty Zimmer assumed leadership of the Christmas Store, and it was through her efforts that the organization incorporated in 1975 as Be Concerned Inc. With the help of a handful of dedicated volunteers, including Ray and Peggy Smith and Betty and Dick Schieman, the organization was able to solicit greater financial support with which to purchase new Christmas toys and clothing.

Throughout the 1970s and early 1980s, Be Concerned served greater numbers of low-income families at the Christmas Store. However, the organization was still without a much-needed permanent home. In 1985 Bill Butler, the president of Corporex and a well-known Northern Kentucky philanthropist, formed a foundation in honor of his father, Robert M. Butler, and this foundation purchased a building for Be Concerned at 714 Washington St. in Covington. A team of volunteers turned the building into a facility that could accommodate an ongoing food program, which began in 1987.

The Food Program allows families to shop on a rotating basis for food, housewares, and toiletries. Families are assigned to volunteers, who often get to know the family's personal preferences and help them meet their individual needs. Food is obtained through donations from individuals, produce companies, and stores.

It became apparent in 1988, particularly after the development of the year-round Food Program, that the organization would need a full-time paid director. Once again through the generosity of Bill Butler, funds were provided to support a salary. Initially, Sister Anita Hagen served in the position, but she became ill after only six months as organizational director and was forced to resign. Thereafter, Karen Smith and Mary Jo Boerger became codirectors. Through the dedication of these women, Be Concerned continued to increase its services as well as the number of clients served. In 1989 the Clothing Program began. Gently worn donated clothing is laundered and mended if necessary, categorized, and displayed neatly for clients to shop year-round, purchasing garments for a nominal fee. The program currently distributes more than 100,000 items annually; it emphasizes school clothing and winter coats.

The services offered by Be Concerned continued to grow as the organization receives increasing financial support from individuals, families, churches, and businesses in the Northern Kentucky community. Be Concerned holds one major fundraiser annually, a midsummer golf outing, which has a loyal group of supporters and is always popular. The organization receives funding only from private sources. Donations of food, housewares, and clothing are an essential part of the programs.

Be Concerned also sponsors an Easter Program, through which schools, churches, and businesses donate more than 1,000 Easter baskets annually for children and also cleaning, health, and hygiene products for the families who participate in the Food Program. In summer, the Fan Club is active, donating some 800 box fans each year, which are available to Be Concerned clients for a small contribution.

During its 28-year history, Be Concerned has grown from helping a few dozen families at Christmastime to providing supplemental ongoing help to thousands of families year-round. A team of more than 150 volunteers is the mainstay of the organization's workforce. Be Concerned is operated by a board of directors, a board of advisers, director Sister Mary Jennings, and assistant director Brenda Young. Be Concerned remains true to Sister Donna Kinney's underlying philosophy that enhancing the pride and self-esteem of the poor is just as important as providing relief from poverty.

Be Concerned, Inc. "Sister Mary Jennings, Be Connected." www.beconcerned.org (accessed July 1, 2006).

Jennings, Sr. Mary, Be Concerned Inc. director. Interview by Sarah A. Barlage, June 12, 2006, Covington, Ky.

Sarah A. Barlage

BEDINGER, BENJAMIN FRANKLIN (b. 1797, Blue Licks, Ky.; d. 1871, Erlanger, Ky.). Benjamin Franklin Bedinger (called Franklin), the son of Maj. George Michael and Henrietta Clay Bedinger, was a Northern Kentucky physician and businessman. He studied medicine at the Surgeons College in Philadelphia. After graduating in 1818, he practiced medicine under the famous physician **Daniel Drake** in Cincinnati. In 1820, Bedinger married Sarah Everett Wade, daughter of David Everett Wade, a prominent Cincinnati businessman. The couple lived in Covington, Erlanger, and Cincinnati; then in 1845 they bought Forest Home on Richwood Rd. in Boone Co., where they lived for 16 years. Bedinger, carrying on a family tradition, provided each of his six children a farm and a newly built home at the time of their marriage. When his son David Wade Bedinger married, Franklin Bedinger gave him the remaining 300 of the original 2,100 acres of Forest Home and the house, and Franklin and his wife moved back to Erlanger. He later bought the Bartlett Graves's farm, Walnut Grove, and renamed it the Elms; Franklin and Sarah Bedinger then lived in Erlanger the remainder of their lives.

Bedinger eventually gave up the practice of medicine and invested in real estate and toll roads. He was president of the **Covington and Lexington Turnpike** for many years and remained a director throughout his life. U.S. President Zachary Taylor (1849–1850), who knew Bedinger, asked him to be governor of the Oregon Territory. Because he had promised his wife that he would never enter the dangerous world of politics, Bedinger declined and suggested instead appointing Maj. **John Pollard Gaines** to the post. Although Bedinger was active in politics, he rejected opportunities for public office, on both the national and the state levels. He was a member of the **Whig Party** before the **Civil War** and after the war became a **Democrat**; he opposed both the **Mexican War** and the Civil War. Bedinger's antislavery position was a defining aspect of his character. An emancipationist, he freed his own slaves, giving each one money and a horse.

Bedinger regularly attended church services at the **Richwood Presbyterian Church**; he and Sarah donated money for the purchase of the land for the Richwood Presbyterian Church Cemetery, and the first burial there was Bedinger's brother, George Michael, who died in 1833. They also donated money for the rebuilding of Richwood Church after a fire.

The Bedingers hired Irish immigrants as farm laborers and household domestics and then helped them buy farms; they also gave the immigrants, who were Catholics, the use of a horse and buggy so they could attend Sunday mass in Florence. The Bedingers built neighborhood schools for children in the Richwood area. Bedinger died in 1871 and was buried at the Richwood Presbyterian Church Cemetery.

Bedinger, Everett Wade, *A History of the Yale Class of 1851, Autobiography.* New Haven, Conn.: Yale Univ., 1891.

Boone Co. Deed Books, Burlington, Ky.

Brunings, Ruth Wade Cox. "Slavery and the Tragic Story of Two Families—Gaines and Garner," *NKH* 12, no. 2 (Fall–Winter 2004): 37–45.

Dandridge, Dansk. *George Michael Bedinger: A Kentucky Pioneer.* Charlottesville, Va.: Michie, 1909. Reprint, Frankfort: Kentucky Historical Society, 1974.

Onkst, Wayne, ed. *From Buffalo Trails to the Twenty-First Century: A Centennial History of Erlanger, Kentucky.* Erlanger, Ky.: Erlanger Historical Society, 1996.

Ruth Wade Cox Brunings

BEDINGER, GEORGE MICHAEL, MAJOR (b. 1756; d. 1843, Blue Licks, Ky.). George Michael Bedinger (called Michael) was one of the first pioneers in Kentucky. He was the son of a German emigrant, Henry Budingen, who came to America in 1737 at age eight with his parents. The Budingens anglicized their name to Bedinger.

Bedinger and a friend, inspired by Patrick Henry, were the first two men from Shepherdstown, Va. (now W.Va.), to volunteer for service in **Lord Dunmore's War**. When the **Revolutionary War** started, Michael and his brother Henry were among the first recruits to join a Virginia rifle company. Michael Bedinger served several tours of duty during the Revolutionary War and fought the **American Indian** allies of the British in Kentucky with **Daniel Boone**. In 1779 he joined a party of 12 men from Shepherdstown and traveled to Boonesborough, Ky., arriving in time to help defend it from a fierce Indian attack. He remained there for seven months, serving as a spy, a scout, a hunter, a surveyor, and a soldier. He participated in raids on Indian villages as far away as modern-day Illinois as the pioneers took an offensive position in their battles with the Indians. Bedinger returned to the war to take command as a captain of a company of militia and served until the surrender of Cornwallis at Yorktown in 1781. He eventually was promoted to the rank of major.

Not long after the war, Bedinger returned to Kentucky as a surveyor and an explorer and accumulated a great deal of land for himself. During this time he bought property in Maryland, built a saw- and gristmill, married, and had a daughter. Both he and his wife had a serious illness, which she did not survive. When Bedinger recovered, he left his infant daughter with his mother-in-law and returned to his frontier life in Kentucky to survey land. Later, he married Henrietta Clay, a cousin of the statesman Henry Clay and the emancipationist Cassius Clay; they settled on a farm in Blue Licks, along the Licking River. He built three houses on "The Bedinger Place" there, first a log cabin, then a stone house, and finally a large 30-room white frame structure. He donated two acres of land for the first school and church at Blue Licks.

Bedinger was a member of the convention that wrote the first constitution for Kentucky. He was in the minority on the issue of slavery, voting for Kentucky to be a free state. He was elected to the Kentucky legislature and served as an elector for the first governor. He was the first judge of the Court of Quarter Session. Elected to the U.S. Congress, he chaired the Committee for the Suppression of Slavery and successfully worked for passage of the law that abolished the Atlantic slave trade in 1808. His publicly stated views on slavery cost him reelection to the U.S. Congress, when he ran again in his later life. Bedinger never sold any slaves, but instead prepared them for freedom and self-support at around age 30, teaching them to "read, write and cipher." He called his slaves "servants," paid them wages, and built a wing on his house for them.

Michael outlived all of his brothers and sisters and half of his 10 children. He was buried on his farm in the Bedinger family cemetery, on the Licking River in Blue Licks. He had set aside this parcel of land for the burial of his family and his servants (former slaves).

Belue, Ted Franklin. *The Hunters of Kentucky: A Narrative History of America's First Far West, 1750–1792.* Mechanicsburg, Pa.: Stackpole Books, 2003.

Dandridge, Danske. *George Michael Bedinger: A Kentucky Pioneer.* Charlottesville, Va.: Michie, 1909. Reprint, Frankfort: Kentucky Historical Society, 1974.

Levin, Alexandra Lee. *For Brave America: The Bedinger Brothers in War and Peace.* John Day, Ore.: Shamrock Hollow, 1995.

Ruth Wade Cox Brunings

BEECH GROVE ACADEMY. This historic southeastern Campbell Co. school was established about 1858, along Smith Rd. between Flagg Spring (also known as Flagg Springs) and Mentor, Ky. It was located near where the Flagg Springs Golf Course and the Beech Grove Celebration Grounds are today. In 1869 **James Monroe Jolly**, a minister and a contractor, built a two-story brick structure for the school. Jolly was an ancestor of **A. J. Jolly**, the later well-known Campbell Co. judge. James Jolly constructed many buildings in the southern part of Campbell Co., including the courthouse in Alexandria. Beech Grove Academy had begun as both an elementary and a high school and was sometimes called the Flagg Spring School. In 1911, after the public county school system consolidated, the Beech Grove Academy was closed and its building demolished. Afterward, students in the area attended the California Common School. Beech Grove Academy was one of several private schools that filled a need when the public education system (see **Campbell Co. Public Schools**) was not yet ready to properly serve lightly populated areas. The Beech Grove Academy and the California Common School were predecessors of the **A. J. Jolly Elementary and High School**, which closed in 2005. The Beech Grove Reunion, now past its 130th year, continues to be held across the road from the school's site.

Campbell County Kentucky: 200 Years, 1794–1994. Alexandria, Ky.: Campbell Co. Historical Society, 1994.

BEECHWOOD. Beechwood in Owen Co., is located along Ky. Rt. 227, 14 miles south of Owenton, near the Scott Co. line. Large numbers of beech trees once grew in this area. It is in the northwestern part of the Harmony Precinct. At one time Beechwood had a hotel that treated people with mineral water from its well, reportedly of therapeutic value. One of Owen Co.'s first one-room schools was in Beechwood. In 1964 the community made national news with the report and photograph of its 104-year-old resident Mrs. Mary Alice Webster Porter, shown smoking a cigarette. She died two years later. The hotel has been destroyed by fire, and today the Beechwod community consists of the Bethany Baptist Church plus some residences.

An Atlas of Owen County, Kentucky. Philadelphia: Lake, 1883.

Houchens, Mariam Sidebottom. *History of Owen County: "Sweet Owen."* Louisville, Ky.: Standard, 1976.

BEECHWOOD PUBLIC SCHOOLS. The Beechwood Independent School District is a unique K-12, one-building public school district in Fort Mitchell. The elementary school (grades K–6) and the high school (grades 7–12) each have enrollments of approximately 500 students. Throughout their history, the Beechwood schools have been noted for their sense of tradition and academic excellence. Both Beechwood Elementary School and Beechwood High School have received numerous awards and honors for their outstanding accomplishments. The exemplary level of performance exhibited by Beechwood students over the years has been directly related to the high expectations set by the schools for achievement and the consistently strong parental involvement and support. A demonstration of the district's remarkable level of student performance is that an average of 90 percent or more of Beechwood High School graduates go to college.

Beechwood began in 1858 when area residents decided to found a school for the local children. Alfred Pope Sandford provided land to erect a two-room gray clapboard frame building, and the school was chartered in 1860. In 1912 Beechwood School dissociated itself from the county school system and became an independent district grade school. Beechwood's first board of education was composed of F. A. Hilker, president; John Hoffman, secretary; J. G. Heileman, treasurer; G. N. Hobbs; Charles H. Meyers; and G. V. Wert. At that time there were 34 students enrolled in the school. Eric M. Martin was the principal and taught grades five through eight; Alma Holmes taught grades one through four. Potbellied stoves heated the two-room building, and a cistern in the side yard provided water. There was no running water in the building or bathroom facilities inside. School hours were 8:30 a.m. to 3:30 p.m. There was a one-hour lunch period when students could eat lunches brought from home or go home to eat. Two 15-minute recess periods broke up the morning and afternoon lessons.

In 1915, after an increase in enrollment, the school building was remodeled, and a furnace and two new rooms were added. The building then had four rooms, two on each side of a central hallway. The two rooms on one side could be joined together by opening the folding doors that separated them to make an auditorium space with a stage. As enrollment continued to increase, a new brick building was constructed in 1927 and later expanded in 1930, 1934, and 1937. High school classes were added in 1930, and the first class graduated from Beechwood High School in 1935. Since that time Beechwood has continued to expand its facilities and course offerings. More recently, a state-of-the-art science addition was constructed in 2000, a community-funded artificial-surface football field was completed in 2003, and a high-tech foreign-language lab was added in 2006.

Because the elementary school and the high school share a single building at Beechwood, interaction among students and teachers at all grade levels, kindergarten through grade 12, occurs regularly. This has resulted in an exceptional learning environment that encourages a strong sense of school spirit and a very supportive and effective academic program. In 2008 the district announced a $9.3 million construction project that will include a three-story addition to the elementary school, scheduled to begin in June 2009.

The Beechwood. Fort Mitchell, Ky.: Beechwood High School, 1935.

Beechwood Independent School District. www.beechwood.k12.ky.us (accessed June 25, 2006).

"Beechwood School Then," *Fort Mitchell Living,* July 1985, 16–19.

Bravo, Betty. "What's in the Name of a Street? Onward to Beechwood Road," *Fort Mitchell Living,* July 1985, 12–14.

"Great Neighborhood Series—Fort Mitchell, Fort Wright, and Park Hills," *CE,* June 15, 2004, G2.

Fred Bassett

BEHRINGER, WILLIAM J. (b. January 10, 1884, Covington, Ky.; d. December 10, 1948, Covington, Ky.). William Jacob Behringer, the son of Theodore and Sophie Behringer, both born in Germany, was a builder, a diarist, a self-educated naturalist, a taxidermist, and a world traveler. An avid hunter, Behringer traveled the world, gathering animals and geologic specimens. A prolific diarist, Behringer filled several thick volumes, which not only record his adventures but also report local weather conditions and include hundreds of clippings from Northern Kentucky and Cincinnati newspapers.

Today, Behringer is best remembered for the collection of curiosities and memorabilia that became the foundation for the **Behringer-Crawford Museum** in **Devou Park** in Covington. The large, eclectic collection Behringer amassed during his travels and displayed in his home along Forest Ave. in West Covington featured, for example, large mounted mammal specimens, glass replicas of the world's largest diamond, and even a shrunken head from the Amazon Basin. At the time of his death, the value of Behringer's collection was estimated at from $25,000 to $50,000.

One of William Behringer's closest friends and admirers, **Ellis Crawford**, encouraged Behringer's heirs to give his entire collection to the City of Covington, and they did so. Crawford understood the value of the collection and persuaded Covington officials to house the collection in the former Devou family homestead, owned by the City of Covington and sitting empty in the heart of Devou Park. July 5, 1950, marked the grand opening of the William J. Behringer Memorial Museum; Ellis Crawford was its first director. The museum was later renamed the Behringer-Crawford Museum to honor the creative and progressive work of both of these Northern Kentuckians. The oil portraits and stories of the museum's founders can be seen in the lobby of the museum, along with some of the stranger items in Behringer's original collection.

Although Behringer traveled widely, he continued to reside in Northern Kentucky. He was buried in Highland Cemetery in Fort Mitchell.

Harrell, Lorna Petty. "The Legacy of Ellis Crawford and the Behringer-Crawford Museum," *NKH* 8, no. 1 (Fall–Winter 2000): 15–20.

Highland Cemetery Records, Fort Mitchell, Ky.

Kentucky Death Certificate No. 26094, for the year 1948.

"Picturesque Devou Home to Be Museum," *KP,* September 9, 1949, 1.

"$25,000 Gift Starts Devou Park Museum," *KTS,* September 9, 1949, 1.

Lorna Petty Harrell

BEHRINGER-CRAWFORD MUSEUM. Covington's Behringer-Crawford Museum (BCM), a nonprofit organization, collects, exhibits, and interprets the culture of Northern Kentucky. The museum is located in the historic Devou family home, within the 700-acre **Devou Park**. Formed by the City of Covington, BCM opened to the public in 1950 as a natural history museum based on the collections of **William Behringer**, including many curios and oddities from his world travels. The shrunken head, the hairball from a cow's stomach, and the two-headed calf have been visitor favorites for many decades. The museum expanded between 1950 and 1970 through the archaeological excavations of its first curator, **Ellis Crawford**, and from 1979 to 1992 under an autonomous board of trustees, who hired Greg Harper as executive director. Laurie Risch has served as executive director since 1993 and continues to manage the museum's growth. The trustees initiated several changes at the museum, including the restoration of the Devou family home in 1984 and the construction of an outdoor amphitheater in 1994. They also initiated a budget based on community donations and made the initial plans for the current expansion project.

BCM is a community-focused organization committed to bringing the region's prosperous development to life by providing educational, entertaining, interactive, and historically accurate hands-on exhibits and programs in an accessible and creative history-museum environment. Attendance at and usage of the museum's educational programs, events, and rotating exhibits have increased annually.

The successes of the museum's efforts and response from the community dictated the current growth plan, which includes a 15,000-square-foot building addition to the 5,000-square-foot historic home of BCM. The addition, completed and opened in December 2007, includes expanded exhibition areas that feature regional history through the unique lens of transportation. The exhibits act as anchors for the museum to advance its mission with a full range of educational programming, rotating exhibits, civic activities, and gatherings. The museum has become a gathering place that hosts meetings, provides rental space, and attracts tourists through the displays and through professionally interpreted authentic artifacts and scenic views.

BCM offers a variety of opportunities for area schools and learning centers either on-site at the museum or off-site at community locations. Interactive educational programs provided for residents, schools, and civic groups include hands-on art workshops, archaeological digs, living-history events, fossil hunts, summer camps, and concert series. All activities are linked to the conviction that this region's history provides an educational opportunity for personal enrichment. Some examples of BCM activities are these:

Educational Programs. The museum presently provides 17 interactive local-history programs embracing paleontology, American Indian prehistory, archaeology, the **Civil War**, home life, wildlife, river heritage, folk and fine art, politics, industry, and agriculture.

Suitcase Exhibits. These portable displays of some of the museum's artifacts allow for off-site outreach programs for schools, senior citizen homes, business organizations, and service clubs.

Grand Discovery Camps. These camps are designed for grandparents and their grandchildren, ages four to six. Crafts, games, skits, songs, and snacks complement special museum tours for first-time campers.

Junior Curator Program in Archaeology. This program, begun in 1981, allows students ages 11 to 16 to participate in and assist with every aspect of an actual archaeological dig, from working in the field, to researching and documenting their finds in the lab, to preparing a museum exhibit. Through this hands-on summer camp, students learn about local history and prehistory as well as responsible archaeology, including the necessity of sharing their found information and making it available to the public.

Music@BCM. Since 1999, the museum has embraced Kentucky's musical heritage by offering family-friendly concerts that include the popular Coffee Cup Concert Series, held weekly during the summer. Performers, through a combination of local, regional, and national acts, present a variety of music, including Celtic, **bluegrass**, gospel, **jazz**, **blues**, and classical.

Since the formation of an independent board of trustees in 1979, the museum has operated annually with help from the community. Individuals and businesses support the museum through donations of money, time, professional services, and collection items. Approximately 99 percent of the 200,000-plus-item collection has been donated by local families or uncovered through museum-sponsored archaeological excavations.

Community volunteers supply the manpower necessary to help conduct the business of the museum, from greeting visitors and answering the telephone, to planning and fundraising, to gardening and maintenance duties. Annually, volunteers put in close to 6,750 hours for the museum, at a value of $121,770. Professional services rendered by CPAs, computer technicians, attorneys, historians, architects, and engineers total about 805 hours annually, at a value of $140,875.

"Museum Makeover—Behringer-Crawford's New Theme is 'History in Motion,'" *KP*, November 29, 2007, 1A.

"Museum Receives Facelift," *Kenton County Recorder*, March 21, 1984, 1.

"Picturesque Devou Home to Be Museum," *KP*, September 9, 1949, 1K.

Laurie Risch

BEITING, RALPH W. (b. January 1, 1924, Covington, Ky.). Ralph W. Beiting was the first of 11 children of Ralph T. and Martha Hianre Beiting. His family's struggles during the **Great Depression** made an impact on Ralph Beiting's life, giving him an abiding concern for people living in poverty. He had a strong Catholic upbringing, attending St. Joseph School in Cold Spring and **Newport Central Catholic High School** in Newport. With the priesthood as his goal, he entered St. Gregory Seminary in Mount Washington (Cincinnati) in 1941. As a seminarian, Beiting participated during the summer of 1946 in mission work at St. Michael Mission Center at Paintsville in the mountains of Eastern Kentucky. Following his ordination by Bishop **William Mulloy** on June 4, 1949, Beiting spent one year as an associate pastor at **St. Bernard Catholic Church** in Dayton, Ky., before being assigned to work in the mountains. Mulloy had an interest in furthering the mission work in Appalachia (see **Appalachians**), and in 1950 Mulloy sent Beiting to Berea to start a Catholic church there.

The area in and around Berea offered Beiting few opportunities as he began what became his lifelong mission. The declining coal-mining industry, enduring poverty, and pervasive anti-Catholicism made the assignment a difficult undertaking. But he threw himself into the work of building a mission center and winning over the populace with his generosity in meeting their physical needs. St. Clare Catholic Church in Berea, named for its famous benefactor Clare Booth Luce, was established in 1951. Beiting also started Cliffview Lodge on Herrington Lake as a camp for children and invited seminarians to spend summers with him "street preaching," using a manner of spreading faith familiar to people in the area.

Beiting did more than try to meet the immediate physical needs of the mountain people; in 1962 he established the Christian Appalachian Project (CAP) as a nonprofit, nondenominational organization to help the poor to help themselves. To preserve CAP's independence and a Christian outlook, Beiting relied on donations rather than accepting federal funding. The organization was incorporated in 1964. He hoped that CAP could get to the root causes of poverty. According to his plan, CAP would focus on creating opportunities for people in the region to start self-sustaining businesses that would provide a living for the owners and workers. It also provided family and educational services for young and old, as well as summer camps and Bible schools. Volunteers of all faiths from around the country supplied much of the labor to build various centers and carry on CAP's many ministries, though Beiting also tried to involve many local people in its operations.

While overseeing CAP, Beiting, who was made a monsignor in 1971, continued his priestly service to the Diocese of Covington (see **Roman Catholics**) as pastor of St. William Parish in Lancaster. Many other priests of the diocese assisted him in the parish and with services to the poor. In the 1970s and 1980s, Beiting brought his street preaching to parishes in Northern Kentucky, by cruising the Ohio River in a large houseboat and making stops along the way on both sides of the river to preach to people who gathered to listen.

CAP grew in magnitude over the decades. Thousands of volunteers assisted in the work being done by CAP in the mountains, and many millions of dollars were donated and spent to help alleviate poverty in the area. In 1982 Beiting turned CAP over to a management team of laypeople so that he could devote himself to fundraising. Even after being injured in a serious car accident in 1990, he continued both his efforts for CAP and his ministry in his new Diocese of Lexington, which was formed in 1988. The new diocese, split from the Diocese of Covington, encompassed the Bluegrass and mountain areas of Eastern Kentucky. Beiting has been the recipient of numerous awards and has written a number of books about his experiences in the mountains. He ended his ties to CAP in 1999, leaving it the hands of lay directors. Beiting remains an active priest for the Diocese of Lexington as pastor of St. Jude Parish in Louisa, a parish he helped to establish in 1992.

Beiting, Ralph W. *Called to the Mountains: The Autobiography of Reverend Ralph W. Beiting and the Christian Appalachian Project.* Lancaster, Ky.: Christian Appalachian Project, 1993.

"Beiting Steps Down as Chairman," *KE*, September 1, 1999, B1.

Salatino, Anthony J. *A True Man of God: A Biography of Father Ralph William Beiting, Founder of the Christian Appalachian Project.* Ashland, Ky.: Jesse Stuart Foundation, 2001.

Thomas S. Ward

BELEW, ADRIAN (b. Robert Steven Belew, December 23, 1949, Covington, Ky.). Adrian Belew, a guitarist, singer, and songwriter, is the son of Chester E. and Louise Frost Belew. His family lived in Florence, Ky., and he graduated from **Boone Co. High School** in 1967. One day his parents took him to a neighborhood bar, where he heard Elvis

Presley's "Hound Dog" playing on a jukebox; the boy decided then and there that he wanted to become a rock musician. He first learned to play the drums and later switched to the electric guitar. As a teenager he started a band called the Denims, which played mostly songs performed by the Beatles. In 1979, while performing in Nashville, Tenn., with a band called Sweetheart, he was discovered by musician Frank Zappa. That encounter thrust him into the big-time performance circuit, and Belew played electric guitar with notable entertainers such as Zappa, Paul Simon, David Bowie, Laurie Anderson, the Talking Heads, the Nine-Inch Nails, and King Crimson. Today, he is considered one of rock music's greatest and most prolific guitarists. The physical features that make Belew instantly recognizable are his receding hairline and his signature ponytail. Belew and his wife, Margaret, have three children, Ernie, Iris, and Audie. When Audie was 12 years old, she recorded, with her father, a song called "Oh Daddy, When Are You Going to Write That Big Hit?" The song became a number-one seller, and its video became a smash hit on the MTV television network. Owing to the success of the record, father and daughter were featured in a *People Magazine* article. The family now lives at Lake Geneva, Wis. Belew was recently quoted as saying, "My only regret is that my folks didn't live to see that I didn't turn out to be such a bad egg. I could die tomorrow, a happy man."

"Adrian Belew." *All Music Guide*. www.allmusic.com (accessed November 23, 2007).

"Adventurous Belew Wows Home Crowd," *CE*, June 29, 1999, C7.

"Belew Shares Rock-Star Fame with Family," *CE*, June 17, 1990, E1.

Bird, Rick. "Adrian Belew: Rock's Renaissance Man," *CP*, February 18, 2005, 1B.

Jack Wessling

BELLEVIEW. Laid out as Mount Vernon in 1815 by Col. Edward Meeks, and officially named Grant in 1869, this town in the East Bend Bottoms changed to its present name of Belleview in 1883. Situated between the hills of western Boone Co. and the Ohio River, Belleview once was a prosperous steamboat town and farming community. Some of the county's best farmland is in the Belleview area, where the larger farms had their own river landings. Silas Dinsmoor settled there, and his descendants farmed the land and built a homestead that is now a living-history site where visitors learn what life was like in the 19th and early 20th centuries (see **Dinsmore Homestead**).

J. J. Huey & Company established a general store at this settlement in 1800. In 1864, the Corbin & Son General Store opened, dealing in lumber, coal, and shingles. Later, the Farmers Cooperative Store was started by farmers who pooled their resources to buy and sell agricultural goods in quantity. This store was affiliated with the national men's club, made up of farmers, called the Grange. The Grant Post Office, which adjoins the Jonas Clore House, built in 1878, is the only surviving example of a 19th-century single-function post office in Boone Co. An original privy and coal shed still stand in the backyard. In the early 1880s, Belleview had a hotel, two tobacco warehouses, three general stores, and a blacksmith. A major business was a basket factory, which made baskets from riverfront willows. The baskets, used to carry luggage and goods, were shipped out by boat, along with tons of willow switches. Farm produce from the area was shipped by steamboat. The population at that time was 713. The Belleview Christian Church was founded in 1883, dedicated a new church in 1884, and continues to hold services today.

One of Boone Co.'s early consolidated schools was the Belleview School, built in 1909, which offered grades 1 through 12. By 1914 a high school had been added. During the 1980s, the Boone Co. Board of Education built Kelly Elementary School at Belleview, replacing the Belleview School, and the old school building, across from the new school, is now a private business.

Within the Belleview Precinct is the historically important village of Middle Creek, which, in the 19th century, laid claim to a distillery, a carding mill, a shingle mill, two grist mills and a saw mill, a store, a post office, and a church. In 1876 Middle Creek Baptist Church (constituted March 12, 1803) was destroyed by a windstorm and two years later was rebuilt on an acre of bottomland donated by Michael Clore. In 1885 the church was renamed **Belleview Baptist Church**, and 12 years later 5.5 additional acres were purchased to lay out a cemetery, which today contains the graves of many important people from Boone Co.'s past. In 1903 a new, larger church was built. In 1949 a baptistery was added, and the church no longer conducted baptisms in the Ohio River and Middle Creek. One renowned Middle Creek citizen, an inventor named **Thomas Zane Roberts**, built a solar clock after he had lost track of the days of the week. The eight-foot-tall cabinet clock, based on celestial observations calculated in his backyard observatory, continues to keep perfect time. Swiss clockmakers and other visitors came to Boone Co. to see this amazing clock, which was completed in 1913. The clock, which has never failed to indicate the correct date, is housed today in the Heritage Bank in Burlington.

The Ohio River **flood of 1937** inundated the area. The tree line was shoved into the riverbed and families were evacuated when the banks of sand and gravel collapsed. Property loss in Boone Co. from this flooding was estimated at $250,000.

Today, the town of Belleview has a school, two churches, a bank, a taxidermy business, two cemeteries, a volunteer fire department, and a grocery store. Though no longer a farming nor a riverboat community, Belleview's history and quaintness are still being preserved.

Boone Co. Historic Preservation Review Board. *Historic Structures of Boone County, Kentucky*. Burlington, Ky.: Boone Co. Historic Preservation Review Board, 2002.

Boone County Recorder, illustrated historical ed., September 4, 1930.

Cabot, Susan M., and Michael D. Rouse. *Boone County*. Charleston, S.C.: Arcadia, 1998.

Lutes, Ann. *A Brief History of Boone County*. Florence, Ky.: Boone Co. Historical Society, 1954.

Schrage, Robert. *Boone County*. Charleston, S.C.: Arcadia, 2005.

Wilson, Noel. "Life in Boone County 100 Years Ago," *Boone County Recorder*, March 2, 1978, 10.

Nancy J. Tretter

BELLEVIEW BAPTIST CHURCH. The Belleview Baptist Church grew out of the Middle Creek Baptist Church in western Boone Co., which was constituted in 1803 after 23 members of the **Bullittsburg Baptist Church** requested assistance from the North Bend Association of Baptists in forming a new congregation. The group in Boone Co. occupied a log building on the bank of Middle Creek in 1804. Eight years later, they moved to a site overlooking the Middle Creek Valley and erected the brick church in which they worshipped for the next 64 years. During this time, the congregation was led by pastors Christopher Wilson, Lewis DeWeese, Chichester Matthews, Robert Garnett, Charles Carter, James Vickers, Robert Kirtley, James A. Kirtley, and Robert E. Kirtley.

Before the **Civil War**, a number of slaves, including several from the nearby **Dinsmore Homestead**, were members of the Middle Creek Baptist Church congregation. During and after the war, however, the church fell upon hard times. By 1875 the old building was in disrepair and the dwindling congregation considered disbanding.

In 1876 a wind storm destroyed the church building, and the remnants of the congregation worshipped for a short time in the Locust Grove schoolhouse. That same year, a decision was made to start over in the then-bustling river village of Belleview, two miles away. Led by Pastor A. M. Vardiman, the members built a new church and parsonage there on donated property in 1878 and changed the name of their church from Middle Creek Baptist Church to Belleview Baptist Church.

The church flourished in its new location and the membership quickly grew. A new church building was erected in 1903, and the congregation hosted the North Bend Association of Baptists gathering that year. That church building, which is listed in the National Register of Historic Places, has undergone several modifications over the years but continues to retain much of its original form and charm, including its striking steeple. Among the pastors who served the congregation during the first five decades of the 20th century were E. N. Dicken, J. H. Fullilove, Tandy Lee Utz, Elmer Atwood, Howell B. Hensley, Clarence Baker, Raymond Smith, Walter C. Guth, Forest Taylor, Bill Burkett, Richard Carlton, and Otis Brooks.

Under Pastor Bill Garrison, a large educational wing was added to the church building in 1966, supplying space much needed by the church's expanding membership. Pastors Howard Roberts, Gary Light, Roy Bennett, Bill Stith, and Gary Mitchell ably guided the church through the 1970s and 1980s.

Rev. Steve Alford was called as pastor in 1991 and led the small church through the most vital period in its long history, when its membership rose from less than 400 in 1990 to more than 800 in 2006. In 2003 the congregation initiated a bold program to purchase surrounding property with a view toward building a new worship center sometime in the future. Plans are in place to incorporate parts of the existing historic building into the new one.

Alford resigned the Belleview pastorate in January 2006, and the congregation began a search for a new pastor.

Capek, Michael. *Lively Stones: A Narrative History of Belleview Baptist Church, 1803–2003*. Knoxville: Tennessee Valley, 2003.

Michael Capek

BELLEVUE. The city of Bellevue in Campbell Co. was established in 1866 on the banks of the Ohio River. Its somewhat higher elevation and shorter riverfront helped preserve it from much of the periodic flooding that ravaged the neighboring communities of Dayton, Ky., to the east, and Newport, to the west. Bellevue was named after the Newport estate of **Revolutionary War** hero Gen. **James Taylor**, a property said to have been named Belleview, that formerly occupied much of the vicinity. The town was incorporated by the Kentucky legislature on March 15, 1870, with a population of 381. Bellevue's original town plat was limited to what is now the northwest corner of the city. Subdivisions were later added by **Albert Seaton Berry**, by Henry Timberlake, and by the heirs to the **John Williamson** estate. Many of the street names had Taylor family associations: Berry, Foote, Washington, Ward, and Van Voast, as well as Taylor. Unlike its two neighboring cities to the east and west, Bellevue developed as a quiet residential community rather than a manufacturing town.

Over the next two decades, the town grew slowly, "owing to a stagnant condition caused by limited powers." Nonetheless, it soon took steps toward permanence. A Methodist Church congregation was founded in 1870 and was followed by the **Sacred Heart Catholic Church** in 1873. Also in 1873, the city bought a fire engine and built a firehouse. Bellevue became a fourth-class city in 1884 and in the same year annexed the Harris Heirs Addition, which extended its boundary eastward from Washington Ave. to the Dayton city corporation line, O'Fallon Ave. From 1885 to 1891, the total value of Bellevue's real estate increased from $534,300 to $1,051,850. News accounts praised the city's "rapid but not hot-bed growth . . . the result of a beautiful and healthful location, and honest management by building owners."

During the late 1880s, St. Anthony Catholic Church was founded, as well as several Protestant church congregations. An 1890s Bellevue city directory listed 56 local businesses: 15 groceries, 4 bakeries, 6 boot makers, 7 confectioneries, 2 livery stables, a blacksmith, 3 millineries, 6 doctors, 7 saloons, a hotel, a gas company, 2 undertakers, and a wagon manufacturer. As Bellevue grew, dozens of narrow, two- or three-story dwellings, most of frame construction, were built along its narrow streets. Ideally suited to the city's small lots, they provided middle-class families with the most house for the least cost. Popular housing styles of the 1800s and early 1900s included the Italianate, the Queen Anne, the Colonial Revival, the Craftsman, and the bungalow. Local lumberyards, planing mills, brickyards, and stone yards kept Bellevue's builders well supplied with a wide range of quality materials.

The prosperous late 1800s also brought high-style architecture to the city, some of it designed by Cincinnati architects. In 1884 Balke's Opera House (demolished in the early 1960s), a handsome commercial Queen Anne edifice designed by George W. Rapp, was opened along Fairfield and Berry Aves. It housed three storefronts, city offices, an auditorium, and lodge rooms; its last days were spent as home to an Eagles hall. In 1885 Buddemeyer, Plympton & Trowbridge designed a one-of-a-kind Fairfield Ave. residence for Edward Johnston, a draftsman for the firm. Built of brick and structural timber framing, it featured a stucco skin, casement windows, and a slate gambrel roof. In 1889 S. E. Desjardins designed a monumental Queen Anne style residence, with Roman arches and chateauesque gables, along Lake St. for distiller George W. Robson.

In the early 1890s, a newly formed streetcar company linked Bellevue to Covington, Newport, and Dayton, making it an even more convenient place of residence. By this time, Bellevue's population had more than doubled and had reached 3,200.

Like its neighbor Dayton, Bellevue capitalized on its river location by becoming a recreation center for the Greater Cincinnati area. Three public beaches (see **Ohio River Beaches**)—the Bellevue Bathing, Primrose, and Riviera beaches—opened by the 1890s, followed in 1902 by the Queen City Beach. Sewage contamination and rising river levels, due to flood control and navigation improvements, eventually brought an end to these popular public attractions; but in 1898, because of its proximity to the beaches, Cincinnati was able to attract the Grand Army of the Republic national convention.

During the 1920s, Bellevue expanded in size and population by annexing hilly land to the south. The Bonnie Leslie neighborhood, first developed in the late 19th century, filled with comfortable homes from the 1920s through the 1940s. Bungalow, Tudor Revival, and Colonial Revival styles predominated in this suburban neighborhood. Covert Run Pk., which follows the creek of the same name, saw a bungalow-building boom, with "scores of neat homes" constructed. Flooding, however, proved a vexing problem for the low-lying homes in the picturesque valley. A promotional brochure extolled the city of Bellevue as a "healthy, convenient and attractive place to live," and the Federal Writers' Guide to Cincinnati described midcentury Bellevue as being "almost entirely a middle-class suburb." Beginning in the 1920s, and continuing for more than 40 years, the **Grote Manufacturing Company** built cabinets and automotive parts at its three-story factory at the corner of Lafayette and Grandview Aves. in Bellevue. For a long time, Grote was the city's largest employer.

The **flood of 1937** on the Ohio River inundated the Bellevue riverfront and cut the city in two. Sixty years later another flood, which exceeded the river's 64.7-foot crest, again turned lower Bellevue into a lake. Following construction of I-471 along the eastern border of Newport, the swampy bottomland along Donnermeyer Dr.—known as the "Sixth Street Fill"—was filled in to create a strip shopping center called Bellevue Plaza and a small commercial center along Riviera Dr. (see **Taylor's Bottoms**). The center serves shoppers from the surrounding area as well as from Cincinnati.

By the 1980s Bellevue was in economic decline. The city's housing stock was deteriorating from deferred maintenance; there was a decline in owner-occupied homes and an increase in low-cost rental housing. Marginal businesses and vacancies were proliferating in the Fairfield Ave. business district. Under the leadership of Mayor Thomas J. Wiethorn, a strong supporter of historic preservation, the city used preservation as a revitalization tool, working in partnership with the Kentucky Heritage Council and the state historic preservation office. Jointly, they fought blight with stronger building-code enforcement, sought grant funds for revitalization, and made ambitious plans for riverfront development; the latter were realized more slowly than the other efforts.

One of the city's first preservation projects was the conversion of the old Bellevue High School, later renamed the Center Street School, into apartments for senior citizens. The complex, which opened in 1986, utilized federal tax credits for the rehabilitation of historic buildings. Preservation tax credits were also used to convert the former St. Anthony School at Poplar and Washington Sts. to elderly housing in 1993. In 1988 two Bellevue historic districts were listed in the National Register of Historic Places. The adjacent Fairfield Ave. and Taylor's Daughters historic districts took in the city's historic business district and the residential neighborhood south of "The Avenue." Over the next three decades, dozens of residential and commercial buildings throughout Bellevue were renovated and restored. The city's decline was reversed as new residents and businesses were attracted to the city, and the outflow of longtime residents slowed. Property values began climbing steadily.

In 1987 the city passed a historic preservation ordinance that regulated exterior alterations and new construction in the overlay zone. The city joined the Kentucky Heritage Council's Certified Local Government program in 1988 and became a Kentucky Renaissance community in 2001, with grant funds and infrastructure improvements targeted to the Fairfield Ave. business district. In 2004 Bellevue was designated a Preserve America community.

Bellevue also sought to enhance its quality of life by creating new parks. The city used a federal Transportation Efficiency Act for the 21st century (TEA-21) grant to create Bellevue Beach Park on the riverfront between Foote and Ward Aves. The park featured a small amphitheater and a ball field, as well as benches where visitors could sit and enjoy the panoramic Ohio River view. Smaller green spaces included Nagel Park, home to the city's Christmas crèche, and Swope Playground, both along Taylor Ave. Across the city, small garden plots were planted and tended by the Bellevue Garden Club.

Facing fiscal necessity and seeking to maintain high levels of service, the Bellevue and Dayton fire departments merged in 2002. In the same year, Bellevue built a new community center, named for longtime state representative Jim Callahan, behind the City Building. The historic iron pedestrian bridge spanning the **CSX** railroad tracks at Van Voast Ave. was restored and returned to functionality in 2004, with a transportation grant.

Beginning in the 1990s, Bellevue shared in Northern Kentucky's riverfront-development boom. Luxury riverfront housing came to the city in 2006, when construction began on two multistory condominium developments. "Trophy" homes and condos began to be built on choice waterfront lots and on hillsides with city views. "Teardowns" came to Bellevue as well, resulting in the destruction of historic buildings and mature trees. Commercial development included waterfront restaurants, a small office building, and a convenience store with front parking, east of Riviera Dr. along Fairfield Ave. Downtown Bellevue attracted new businesses and investment as well, although some storefronts remained vacant. In 2003 the city secured a grant from the Kentucky Heritage Council to reilluminate the brilliant neon marquee of the Marianne Theater, an Art Deco landmark (see **Movie Theaters**).

From 1987 to 2006, $7 million was invested in Bellevue and more than 200 jobs were created. In the 21st century, the city faced the challenge of preserving its historic character in the face of new development pressures. In 2000 Bellevue had a population of 6,480.

"Bellevue," *KSJ*, November 13, 1891, 3.
Federal Writers' Project in Ohio. *Cincinnati: A Guide to the Queen City and Its Neighbors.* Cincinnati: City of Cincinnati, 1943.
Giglierano, Geoffrey J., and Deborah A. Overmyer. *The Bicentennial Guide to Greater Cincinnati: A Portrait of Two Hundred Years.* Cincinnati: Cincinnati Historical Society, 1988.
"Newport News," *CDE*, May 28, 1866, 4.
Pictorial and Industrial Review of Northern Kentucky. Newport, Ky.: Fennell, 1923.
U.S. Census Bureau. "American Fact Finder. Data Set. Census 2000 Summary File 1 (SF1) 100-Percent Data. Custom Table." www.census.gov (accessed July 18, 2006).
Warminski, Margo. "Fairfield Avenue Commercial Historic District," National Register of Historic Places Nomination, 1986, Kentucky Heritage Council, Frankfort, Ky.
———. "Taylor's Daughters Residential Historic District," National Register of Historic Places Nomination, 1986, Kentucky Heritage Council, Frankfort, Ky.

Margaret Warminski

BELLEVUE PUBLIC SCHOOLS. When the City of Bellevue incorporated in 1870, the students in the Bellevue area were attending public schools in Newport. Bellevue soon turned its attention to providing public education for its children, and from 1871, when Bellevue became an independent school district, until the early 1890s, a special committee of the Bellevue city council managed the city's school system. In May 1871, the city had 119 school-aged children. A one-room wood frame schoolhouse was constructed at the corner of Center St. and Lafayette Ave. in Bellevue during that summer, and Miss Eva Harpold was hired at $40 per month to teach the 67 enrolled students. The following year the school's enrollment numbered 83 students.

In 1873 a four-room brick schoolhouse was built on the same lot, replacing the original schoolhouse. By 1881, 279 students attended the school, and a night school for boys over 12 years old was offered. A four-room addition was built onto the building in 1882, and by 1885, the school system had elementary students in all eight grades.

An additional six-room brick school was constructed in Bellevue at Poplar St. and Vanvoast Ave. and opened in September 1887, for both elementary and secondary students. The first high school graduation ceremony was in 1888, but the program was only a two-year course at the time; it did not expand into a four-year program until 1907. A formal board of education took over operation of the Bellevue schools beginning in the early 1890s.

By 1900 Bellevue was operating an eight-room school in town at Center St. and Lafayette Ave. and a nine-room school on Poplar St. and Van Voast Ave., but the system again was running out of space. A one-room school known as Union St. Primary School opened in the city in 1900 at the foot of Union St. In 1901 a two-room building at Eden and Washington Aves. was purchased as a temporary school, and in 1902, two rooms were added as a second story of the Eden Ave. school building. The primary-grade students from the Poplar St. School were moved to the school on Eden Ave.

In March 1905 the school board purchased a lot at Center St. and Washington Ave. for a new high school. The cornerstone was laid on October 21, 1905, and the new building, containing 15 classrooms, two offices, and a combination gymnasium and auditorium on the third floor, was dedicated on October 19, 1907. High school students were moved from the Poplar St. School into the new Center St. and Washington Ave. School, and the elementary students from the Eden Ave. School were moved back into the Poplar St. School. The Eden Ave. School building was sold in 1907. By 1909, the Bellevue public school system enrolled 858 students.

As the city's school system continued to expand to meet the needs of local students, kindergarten classes were added around 1924. An additional lot was purchased adjacent to the Center St. and Lafayette Ave. school; the cornerstone of a new school building was laid on August 2, 1930, and the school was dedicated on March 20, 1931. By 1936 the school board once again found that they needed more space and that the Poplar St. School needed to be modernized. It was decided to build an addition onto the new school at Lafayette Ave., renovate the 1905 high school at Center St. and Washington Ave., and close the Poplar St. School. Students in grades 1 through 6 were removed to the old high school building at Center St. and Washington Ave., while grades 7 through 12 were moved into the newly expanded school at Center St. and Lafayette Ave., which later became known as Bellevue High School. The Poplar St. School was sold in 1938 to the city for use as the Bellevue City Building.

The Bellevue School System also obtained a new football field in 1936, thanks to the Works Progress Administration. The facility is called Gilligan Stadium and was named for Leo Gilligan, a longtime Bellevue teacher, principal, and superintendent. The first football game at Gilligan Stadium was played October 23, 1936, and more than 5,000 fans watched Bellevue defeat rival Dayton High School by a score of 31-0. In the early 1970s, a new gymnasium was built next to the stadium and named in honor of Ben Flora, a longtime coach, principal, and superintendent at Bellevue.

Grandview Elementary School opened on Grandview Ave. in 1966, providing 23 classrooms. Grades one through six transferred to Grandview Elementary School, and the Center St. Elementary School closed, only to be reopened again a few years later for grades six through eight to relieve overcrowding. The Center St. Elementary School closed once again because an addition had been built onto the high school in the early 1970s, allowing more students to be placed there. The Center St. Elementary School building was sold to the city for use as a recreation center and was later converted into apartments. Grandview Elementary School and Bellevue High School continue to serve the needs of Bellevue students.

Campbell Co. Historical Society. *Campbell County, Kentucky, 200 Years, 1794–1994.* Alexandria, Ky.: Campbell Co. Historical Society, 1994.
Campbell County Recorder, June 1, 2004.
Reis, Jim. "Bellevue Schools Celebrate 100th Class of Graduates," *KP*, August 2, 1988, 10K.
———. "School Bells Once Rang at Bellevue City Building," *KP*, August 6, 2001, 4K.
Tully, James Robert. "History of the Public Schools of Bellevue, Ky." master's thesis, Univ. of Cincinnati, 1942.

Daryl Polley

BELLEVUE VETS. In 1945 the Bellevue Veterans Club was organized by a group of seven returning veterans of **World War II**, who met for the first time at Resch's Café on Fairfield Ave. The club was formed to provide social and recreational activities for members, but also for the overall community. The group elected Bill Frede as its first president and began to recruit members. As membership increased, the club started meeting at the Bellevue City Building. By 1948 the Bellevue Vets were gathering at the Avenue Night Club & Restaurant. When they saw that a permanent meeting space was needed, they held various fundraising events, such as dances and raffles, and purchased a nine-acre lot on Fairfield Ave. (Ky. Rt. 8), near the Bellevue-Newport border, for $1,400. Architect

Leonard Smoot drew plans for a building, members skilled in the various trades undertook the construction, and the new meeting hall, with a baseball diamond on the grounds, was dedicated in May 1955. The club intended to offer sports and recreation for the youth of the area. The original field was enlarged with the help of the U.S. Army Reserves, allowing for the placement of additional baseball diamonds. In 1955 members organized their first baseball league; softball and knothole baseball were added later. In 1967 several horseshoe courts were installed and a league was formed; horseshoes proved to be very popular, so more courts were added in 1980. Three years later, lights were installed for night ball games. A volleyball league was established in 1970, and the club developed three volleyball courts, which drew participants from all over Campbell Co. By 1977, when the Bellevue Vets became a nonprofit entity, it had become one of the largest private veterans organizations in the state. In 2000 members built an addition to their clubhouse, enhancing the bar and grill.

The Vets raise money to operate the club through a variety of fundraisers. Their annual summer carnival, which began in 1951, remains a popular and widely anticipated event. They promote civic pride and community improvement and conduct several programs, such as the Christmas Relief Fund, blood drives, and Stand Down, which offers help and support to homeless veterans. Today more than 1,000 children are involved in the Bellevue Vets' youth sports; the club has more than 450 members and is growing while many similar organizations are closing.

"Bellevue Vets Club Dedicated," *KTS,* May 31, 1955, 1.

Roberts, Alice Kennelly. "Decades of Memories: Bellevue Vets Club Celebrates 45th Anniversary," *KP,* January 31, 1990, 5KK.

Robin Caraway

BENHAM, JOSEPH SHALER (b. ca. 1795, Newport; Ky.; d. July 15, 1840, Cincinnati, Ohio). Joseph Shaler Benham, an attorney, was the 10th child born to Captain **Robert Benham** and his wife, Elizabeth. In about 1802 Robert Benham moved his family to a farm in Lebanon, Ohio. Joseph attended one of the best schools in the area, the **Newport Academy**, operated by Rev. Robert Stubbs, and in about 1819 became a lawyer, opening his office in Cincinnati. About that time he married Isabella Greer. When the French general the Marquis de Lafayette, a **Revolutionary War** hero, visited the region in 1825, local leaders chose Joseph Benham to deliver the main welcoming speech. In September 1826 he entered into partnership with another attorney, Jefferson Phelps, and they opened an office in downtown Covington. Benham was considered one of the finest attorneys in the Ohio Valley. In the late 1830s, he served as editor of a patriotic weekly newspaper, the *Kentucky and Ohio Journal.* Benham died at the age of 45 and was buried at the Old Presbyterian Burying Grounds in Cincinnati; in 1858 his remains were moved to Spring Grove Cemetery in Cincinnati.

Cooley, Elizabeth M. "The Benham Brothers—Robert, Peter and Richard," *BCHS* 10, no. 1 (January 1952): 69–78.

"Joseph S. Benham and Jefferson Phelps Practice Law in Partnership," *North Kentuckian,* September 10, 1836, 2.

Spring Grove Cemetery Records, Cincinnati, Ohio.

BENHAM, ROBERT, CAPTAIN (b. November 7, 1750, Monmouth Co., N.J.; d. 1809, Lebanon, Ohio). A **Revolutionary War** hero, an Indian fighter, and an adventurer, Robert Benham was the most daring and colorful of the six sons and daughters of Peter and Anna James Benham. After his mother died in 1758, his father married Catherine Wessel, and the couple moved to Loudon Co., Va. The Benham children were left behind to be raised by their maternal grandparents. Robert Benham was a captain in the Revolutionary War, serving as a government contract Indian fighter. He participated in the Harmar, Wilkinson, St. Clair, and Wayne campaigns into Indian Territory north of the Ohio River in the 1780s and 1790s. However, his most harrowing experience occurred earlier, during the Battle of Dayton, Ky. (**Rogers' Defeat**). He had been sent with 30 soldiers from Fort Pitt to Kaskaskia, Ill., to deliver a message to Gen. **George Rogers Clark**. At Louisville on the return trip, his party joined Col. David Rogers and his party of 40 soldiers, who were returning from New Orleans after buying munitions from the Spanish. On October 4, 1779, the combined party landed their keelboats on the sandbar at what is now Dayton to prepare breakfast. Seeing several Indians approaching in canoes, they prepared for a fight. Without warning, 200 Indians and British soldiers led by the white renegade Simon Girty suddenly overwhelmed the group. The attackers had been hidden among the many willow trees that covered the sandbar. Only a few of the 70 men with Benham and Rogers were able to avoid death or capture. Rogers was killed, and Benham was shot through both legs but managed to remain undetected in a sand pit under a fallen tree. Shortly after the massacre, the Indians left, but they returned the next morning to strip the dead and steal their keelboats. After they left the second time, Benham shot at a raccoon in a nearby tree. Following the gunshot, Robert Benham heard a man's voice and called out to him. It turned out to be a fellow soldier, who had been shot through both arms. Despite their wounds, the two men eventually made it to the mouth of the Licking River. Some nineteen days later, they were rescued by men in a small boat moving down the Ohio River. They were taken to Louisville, where both fully recovered and were returned to their units.

After leaving the army, Benham visited family in New Jersey, then moved to western Pennsylvania and later to Newport, Ky., and Losantiville (Cincinnati), owning property in both towns. In February 1792 he was granted the right to operate a ferry between Cincinnati and both banks of the Licking River on the Kentucky side. Benham became one of the first three justices of Campbell Co. (1794). In 1797 he sold his land in Campbell Co. and moved to Cincinnati, and then about 1802 he and his wife Elizabeth relocated to Lebanon, Ohio, where he died and was buried. Forty years later, James Berry, the founder of Jamestown (now Dayton) named a street near that fateful sandbar Benham St. in Robert Benham's honor.

Collins, Richard H. *History of Kentucky.* Vol. 2. Covington, Ky.: Collins, 1882.

Cooley, Elizabeth M. "The Benham Brothers—Robert, Peter and Richard," *BCHS* 10, no. 1 (January 1952): 69–78.

Ford, Henry A., and Kate B. Ford. *History of Hamilton County, Ohio, with Illustrations and Biographical Sketches.* Cleveland, Ohio: W. W. Williams, 1881.

Greve, Charles Theodore. *Centennial History of Cincinnati and Representative Citizens.* Vol. 1. Chicago: Biographical Publishing, 1904.

Purvis, Thomas L., ed. *Newport, Kentucky: A Bicentennial History.* Newport, Ky.: Otto Zimmerman, 1996.

Wessling, Jack. *Early History of Campbell County.* Alexandria, Ky.: Self-published, 1997.

Jack Wessling

BENNETT, VIRGINIA (b. May 16, 1924, Dayton, Ky.). Ohio River folklore historian Virginia Bennett comes from a family of river people. The only child of Elmer and Alene Dugray Bennett, she grew up in Newport. On her father's side of the family, her great-grandfather Capt. Edward Jackson Smith worked on the river for 50 years. Captain Smith was born in Maysville February 27, 1827. His grandfather was frontiersman Daniel Boone's brother, Edwin Boone. Captain Smith was a master pilot on the Ohio, Mississippi, and Tennessee rivers. Virginia's father was paymaster, from 1933 until his death in 1944, on the wharf boat of the Greene Line Steamboat Company at the foot of Broadway in Cincinnati.

Virginia Bennett's first trip on the river occurred with her parents when she was two and a half years old. Little Virginia liked the boat trip so much that she hid on the boat because she did not want to leave it. When she was in grade school, Virginia would go to work on Sundays with her father and help him tear off freight bills. She continued to help her father after she graduated from **Newport High School**. "I used to ride riverboats many days after high school," she recalls. Bennett officially began her career on the river after her father died. It was then that she took over his job as a pay clerk for the Greene Line Steamboat Company. This was the beginning of a 24-year career, from 1944 to 1968, with the company. In 1946 the Greene Line bought the *Steamer Delta Queen* and brought the steamboat to Cincinnati from California. For three years, 1953–1955, Bennett worked onboard the *Steamer Delta Queen* as an assistant purser. From 1969 to 1976 she took a break from the river to help an ailing relative.

From 1977 to 1982 Bennett was an office clerk, dispatcher, and paymaster for the Columbia Marine Services, a Cincinnati-based harbor service located in Ludlow. At the time she was the only woman working at Columbia Marine Services. Previously, her knowledge had been mostly related to packet boats. This job increased her knowledge of the towboat industry as well as of river people. Her work at Columbia Marine Services was what first earned her the nickname of "Harbor Mother." Virginia Bennett is still known as Harbor Mother to the riverboat and towboat pilots and captains plying their trade up and down the Ohio River.

In 1955 Bennett obtained a Hallicrafter radio from the widow of Harry Reardon, a river pilot. With her radio she could hear the boats broadcast crew changes and the daily log of tows to be picked up on the river. She would listen to these broadcasts and then contact families by telephone to tell them of their husbands' shift changes. It was in this way that Bennett became acquainted with many people. In 1985 she received her first two-way, hand-held marine radio, which enabled her to talk with towboat pilots, tourist boats, and excursion boats from her Covington apartment along the Ohio River. Over the years, Bennett has become known up and down the Ohio River and its tributaries. Her river career shifted in 1983 to **BB Riverboats** in Covington, where she worked until her retirement in 1991. For three years before she retired, Bennett was a weekly contributor to the *Waterways Journal* in a column called *Cincinnati News.*

In 1999 the *Chicago Tribune* reported that "a crew from the Coast Guard cutter *Obion,* based in Owensboro, Ky., presented Bennett in October with a mile marker: 471.5." The article went on to explain that such recognition is usually given to "people who are special to the river community. Bennett qualifies in part because of her work in historic preservation."

Over the years, many towboat operators and others with private collections offered river memorabilia to Bennett or sought her help in directing such items to the proper places. These significant items would have been lost without her guiding them to river collections in the area where the items would be most appreciated. Much of her acclaim is for her contributions of river memorabilia to many institutions that preserve river history. She has helped establish river collections at the **Behringer-Crawford Museum**, Covington; the Howard Steamboat Museum, Jeffersonville, Ind.; the River Museum, Point Pleasant, W.Va.; the Cincinnati and Kentucky historical societies; the Inland Rivers collection in Ohio at the Public Library of Cincinnati and Hamilton County; and the Seamen's Church Institute's library in New York City. On April 22, 2000, a rare honor was bestowed on Virginia Bennett. The U.S. Coast Guard erected the Virginia Bennett light on the south bank of the Ohio River immediately below her apartment in Covington. Capt. David Smith commented that "few living people have been so honored by the Coast Guard."

Cincinnati Tall Stacks is a grand event celebrating the steamboat era and heritage in Cincinnati and Northern Kentucky. Bennett was involved in the planning of the first Tall Stacks in 1988 and continues to participate in each of the Tall Stacks celebrations. In 2003 she was honored by being designated the Grand Marshall of the Tall Stacks parade of boats.

Because of her extensive knowledge and service to the river, Bennett is listed as a resource for towboat pilots in training at the Paducah Center for Maritime Education in Paducah.

Bennett, Virginia. Interview by Victor Canfield, June 24, 2006, Covington, Ky.

Cornwell, Lisa. "Harbor Mistress: To Boat Captains, Ohio River Maven Is Just 'Mom,'" *Chicago Tribune,* March 12, 2000, sec. 12, p. 3.

———. "Love for Ohio River Shapes Life of 'Harbor Mother.'" MSNBC Breaking News. www.msnbc.com/local/RTCIN/3229.asp (accessed August 7, 2006).

Friedman, Roslyn. "Virginia Bennett a Part of Tall Stacks since the Beginning," *Cincinnati Senior Monthly,* October 1995, 3.

"'Harbor Mother' Has Helm at Columbia," *KP,* May 24, 1980, 2K.

Hicks, Jack. "Memories Breathe Life into River Exhibit," *KP,* July 11, 1994, 1K–2K.

Kinney, Courtney. "River-Watcher's Vigilance Honored by Navigation Light," *KP,* April 25, 2000, 2K.

Smith, Captain David. "Coast Guard Installs 'Virginia Bennett Light,'" *Waterways Journal,* June 5, 2000, 6.

"Virginia Bennett . . . Mother of the Harbor." *Inside Fort Thomas,* July 2006, 1.

Wecker, David. "Civil War Letters Tell of Man's Love for Family," *KP,* March 24, 1982, 2K.

Vic Canfield

BENTEL HOTEL/MILLER'S INN. Augustus Miller, an 1852 immigrant from Bavaria, Germany, was trained as a blacksmith in Newport. At age 21, he opened a combination hotel, tavern, blacksmith shop, and grocery in Brent in 1861. He served travelers along the Ohio River trail, which was part of the route covered by Mary Ingles in 1775 on her trek back home to Virginia (see **Mary Ingles Highway**). Brent, then known variously as Coney Island Station and as part of Cold Spring Precinct, was served by neither road nor railroad. For packet boats going downriver, and for pack trains on the trail, the inn was a welcome sight, signaling that Newport and Cincinnati were near. The first floor of the two-story portion of the brick structure served as a dining room. Hotel guests and the extended Miller family occupied rooms on the second floor. The east side of the building was the tavern. On the west side was a wooden kitchen and next to it a large stable, where Miller did his blacksmithing. The business had just opened when the **Civil War** erupted. On November 28, 1861, Augustus Miller joined the 4th Ohio Cavalry at Camp Dennison, Ohio, as a blacksmith, for a term of three years, and while he was away, his sister, Augusta Eva Miller Bentel, and her husband, Adam Bentel, ran the business. Augustus returned to Brent after he was discharged from the service on November 30, 1864.

By the late 1860s, the **Twelve Mile Turnpike** was being built where only a trail had previously existed, and the inn was strategically located near the road's bridge over Four Mile Creek. Business was good, as traffic going past the inn was dramatically increased by the turnpike. After Augustus Miller died of gunshot wounds suffered in an altercation near Newport on December 30, 1875, management of the inn reverted once again to Adam and Augusta Bentel, and they called it the Bentel Hotel. The blacksmith shop ceased to operate, but a second floor was added over the tavern side of the building. A pond was built on the property and, when it froze, the ice was harvested and stored in a large icehouse, where the supply lasted throughout the year (see **Icehouses**). The hotel quickly became a gathering place for town meetings, parties, celebrations, and other occasions. The Bentels' hotel was *the* place to be in Brent. But Adam Bentel died in 1889, and in 1895 Augusta sold the business to Augustus Miller's oldest son, Gustav V. "Gus" Miller and his wife, Margaret Weisman Miller. The name was changed to Miller's Inn. Workers building the locks and dams on the Ohio River began to frequent the establishment, as did railroad men from the **Chesapeake and Ohio Railroad**'s company town, Silver Grove, built in 1914 just southeast of Brent. Margaret Miller became sole owner of the inn when Gus died in 1921. She added a screened-in porch to the east side of the building for outdoor dining. When the 18th Amendment to the U.S. Constitution ushered in **Prohibition** in 1919, Margaret turned to her specialty, fried chicken dinners, to retain her clientele, apparently with much success. At the end of Prohibition in December 1933, Margaret turned over operation of the business, but not the ownership, to one of her sons, Edward, and his wife, Hazel Blades Miller. They discontinued the hotel business around **World War II**, and meals ceased to be served when Hazel died in 1951. Only the tavern survived, under the name Miller's Inn. But it had slot machines, and perhaps other gambling occurred there in the "wide open" days of midcentury Campbell Co.

In 1960 the State of Kentucky, which had purchased the Twelve Mile Turnpike in 1916, widened the road on which Miller's Inn was located, Ky. Rt. 8, and the 100-year-old inn had to be demolished. It was burned in a controlled fire on August 10, 1960. Ed Miller built a new, smaller Miller's Inn tavern farther back from the highway. After his death in 1968, his sister, Florence Miller, operated the tavern until she died in 1979. Her death marked the end of the business begun by Augustus Miller in 1861. The "new" Miller's Inn building now serves as the office of an electric contractor.

"Century-Old Tavern Makes Way for Road," *KP,* August 11, 1960, 27K.

"Historic Miller's Inn Burned, Intentionally," *KE,* August 11, 1960, 3.

Roster Commission, comp. *Official Roster of the Soldiers of the State of Ohio in the War of the Rebellion, 1861–1866.* Vol. 11. Akron, Ohio: Werner, 1891.

Venable, Robert Michael. *Will and Gus.* Fort Thomas, Ky.: Privately published, 2002.

Robert Michael Venable

BENTON, MORTIMER M. (b. January 21, 1807, Benton, Ontario Co., N.Y.; d. March 5, 1885, Covington, Ky.) Mortimer Murray Benton, the first mayor of Covington, was the son of Joseph and Amy Reynolds Benton. His birthplace was named for an ancestor, Levi Benton. Benton's fa-

Mortimer Murray Benton.

ther, Joseph, was a surveyor. When Mortimer Benton was nine years old, his family moved to Franklin Co., Ind., where he grew up and began the study of law. He then moved to Cincinnati, where he worked as a store clerk and completed his education in 1828. He became a law partner in the Covington firm of Jefferson Phelps in 1831.

As an attorney, Benton gained local stature, and when Covington was incorporated on February 24, 1834, he became the mayor. He served until October 2, 1835, when he resigned; but he remained active in Covington city government: his name appeared on city records as clerk, and he was council president from 1849 to 1853. Benton was president of the Covington Literary Association and is credited with helping the **Covington and Lexington Railroad** obtain a state charter; he became the railroad's president in 1850. Because of his work with the railroad, when a new steam locomotive was made by the Kentucky Locomotive and Machine Works for the Covington and Lexington Railroad, it was christened the *M. M. Benton* in May 1857. Benton served in the Kentucky House of Representatives in 1863 and the Kentucky Senate in 1865.

This 1865 senate election was contested by **John G. Carlisle**, on the grounds that the military had interfered. Benton had strong pro-Union feelings during the **Civil War**, and election officials were accused of prohibiting supporters of the South from voting in the race. In the new election that was held, Benton lost. His opponent termed Benton a radical Republican and an abolitionist; Benton referred to himself as simply a Union man.

Physically, Benton was an imposing figure, standing six feet tall. He married Angeline Clemons on March 10, 1832. He was active in the Episcopal Church, and one of his sons, Mortimer Benton Jr., became a minister in Maysville. Two of his other sons, John C. Benton and William K. Benton, became attorneys and worked in their father's law firm.

Mortimer Benton died in 1885. One local newspaper called him a pioneer of the state, and his funeral drew Kentucky's most prominent citizens. He was buried in Highland Cemetery in Fort Mitchell.

Collins, Richard H. *History of Kentucky.* Vol. 1. Covington, Ky.: Collins, 1882.
"Funeral Notice," *KSJ,* March 7, 1885, 2.
Reis, Jim. "Covington's First Mayor Was Man of Solid Values," *KP,* June 24, 2002, 4K.
——. "Past Vip's," *KP,* October 20, 1986, 4K.

Jim Reis

BENTON STATION. In August 1853 the **Covington and Lexington Railroad** opened its rail link between Covington and DeMossville, as it built its way toward Lexington. By 1879 there were 11 train stations along this route, to serve towns along the way. The wealthy businessman Samuel T. Roberts started a village around the fourth rail stop from Covington, which was called Benton Station. It was near the Licking River, between Visalia and Morning View. An early plat shows 36 building lots along five streets: Washington, Benton, Main, Casey, and Water. A small, bustling community developed, with a church, a school, several stores, a tobacco warehouse, and a town hall. Later, Benton was granted a post office, and W. W. Spillman was the postmaster. Spillman also served as ticket agent at the Benton railway station.

An 1878 newspaper article described Benton as one of the most delightful places for the location of a town in the entire Licking River valley. When Decoursey Pk., the **Three-L Highway** (Ky. Rt. 177) was built through the area, the railroad became less important, and the train station closed. Over the years, fire destroyed several commercial buildings in Benton, many people moved away, and the town lost its identity. Today, little remains of what was once the town of Benton. Two of the original streets no longer exist, and another is used for access to the **Thorn Hill Drag Strip**. Several years ago, a developer attempted to revive the area by building a subdivision, but financial problems caused the project to fail. Presently there are only five or six widely scattered homes where the proud little town once stood. The area is now a part of the city of Kenton, which is located just to the south along Ky. Rt. 177.

An Atlas of Boone, Kenton, and Campbell Counties, Kentucky. Philadelphia: D. J. Lake, 1883.
"Benton," *Newport Local,* March 28, 1878, 1.
"Former Postmaster," *Newport Local,* October 31, 1878, 1.
"Kenton County–Benton," *Newport Local,* April 25, 1878, 1.
"Noon News," *DC,* September 25, 1883, 1.

BERKSHIRE. In the southwestern part of Boone Co. is the area known as Berkshire, formerly called South Fork because of its proximity to the South Fork Creek (modern Big South Fork Creek), which empties into Big Bone Creek nearby. The Gallatin Co. boundary line is less than a mile to the west. A post office operated at South Fork in 1853–1854 under the name Slusher, and it reopened as Berkshire for the period 1881–1882 and again from 1888 to 1919. Ky. Rt. 1925 (the Old Louisville Rd.) skirts the settlement, which was once home to the South Fork Christian Church, a blacksmith, a general store, a steam sawmill, and public scales. Today there is a boat ramp along the creek, providing easy recreational access to the Ohio River. The area has been bypassed at least twice: first by the opening of U.S. 42 to Louisville, and more recently by I-71 .

An Atlas of Boone, Kenton, and Campbell Counties, Kentucky. Philadelphia: D. J. Lake, 1883.
Warner, Jennifer S. *Boone County: From Mastodons to the Millennium.* Burlington, Ky.: Boone Co. Bicentennial Book Committee, 1998.

BERLIN. Berlin (also spelled Burlin), a small community that was once incorporated in the western half of Bracken Co., is located along Ky. Rt. 10 (the Willow-Lenoxburg Road). In times past it was a rest stop on the **buffalo trace** for travelers on their way to Falmouth. Originally known as Pleasant Ridge, by 1859 it was called Hagensville. After an influx of German settlers, it became Berlin. When the community was incorporated, court was conducted there. Berlin had a post office until 1913. The 1871 Barretts map of Bracken Co. indicated that leaf tobacco was grown there and that Berlin had a medical doctor and wheelwright, blacksmith, dry goods, and grocery businesses. As of September 2004, two businesses remained: an automotive garage and Figgins Market, which is a combination grocery, deli, gas station, and pizza parlor. Tobacco continues to be grown in the immediate area. Two churches in the community take care of the spiritual needs of the local residents: Berlin Baptist Church and Forest Hills Baptist Church. Blackerby Cemetery, named for an early prominent family of Berlin, is nearby at the intersection of Haley Ridge Rd. and Ky. Rt. 10.

An Atlas of Bracken and Pendleton Counties, Ky. Philadelphia: D. J. Lake, 1884.
Bracken Co. Extension Homemakers. *History of Bracken County.* Bicentennial ed. Brooksville, Ky.: Bracken Co. Extension Homemakers, 2002.
Brooksville Centennial Celebration, 1839–1939. Brooksville, Ky.: Brooksville and Bracken Fire Department, n.d. [ca. 1940].
Rennick, Robert M. *Kentucky Place Names.* Lexington: Univ. Press of Kentucky, 1984.

Paul John Schewene

BERNSTEIN, BENJAMIN L. (b. January 25, 1921, Cincinnati, Ohio; d. January 27, 1992, Cincinnati, Ohio). Ben Bernstein, a prominent Northern Kentucky restaurateur, was the son of Arron and Dora Handelsman Bernstein. He graduated from Walnut Hills High School and the University of Cincinnati in Ohio. During **World War II** Bernstein served in the U.S. Army for four years, seeing combat in Africa, France, and Italy. Upon his return to the United States, he joined his family's dress-manufacturing business in downtown Cincinnati. In 1961 he started his first restaurant, Gregory's Steak House, a business that later expanded into four locations. In 1963 he joined the U.S. State Department's USAID program under President John Kennedy (1960–1963) and, along with his wife, Shirley, and their children, Linda, Jim, and Alan, moved to Quito, Ecuador, where Bernstein worked until 1968. When he returned to Kentucky, he opened the El Greco (formerly the Isle of Capri) restaurant in Southgate.

An inspired entrepreneur, Bernstein bought the *Mike Fink* riverboat in 1976 from Captain **John Beatty**, who had turned it into Northern Kentucky's first floating restaurant. The vessel remains anchored at a site parallel to Covington's scenic Riverside Dr. Along with his family and a friend, **Betty Blake**, Bernstein started a business known as **BB Riverboats**. The business's first riverboat, the *Betty Blake,* was the official riverboat at the 1982 World Fair in Knoxville, Tenn. BB Riverboats then bought another riverboat, the *Chaperon,* and today the fleet consists of the *Belle of Cincinnati,* the *Mark Twain,* the *River Queen,* the *River Raft,* the *Shirley B,* and other floating units. In 1982 the Bernstein family started a catering company as an offshoot of BB Riverboats. In 1984 they opened a Chuck E Cheese franchise unit in Florence, Ky. During the mid-1980s, the family opened four additional restaurant operations: Benjamin's, Covington Landing, Crocket's River Café, and Shirley's. Bernstein died at his Cincinnati home in late January 1992 and was buried at Spring Grove Cemetery in that city. His children and grandchildren continue to operate the family businesses.

Bernstein, Alan. Interview by Nancy J. Tretter, January 7, 2005, Covington, Ky.
"Fink Owner Bernstein Is Dead," *KP,* January 21, 1992, 1K.

Nancy J. Tretter

BERRY, ALBERT S., CAPTAIN (b. May 13, 1837, Dayton, Ky.; d. January 6, 1908, Newport, Ky.). Albert Seaton Berry, a Confederate officer, a politician, and a judge, was the son of **James T. Berry** (founder of Jamestown, now part of Dayton, Ky.) and Virginia Wise Berry. He was a grandson of **Washington Berry** and Alice Thornton Taylor Berry, who was a sister of **James Taylor Jr.**, founder of Newport. Albert's early education was in Newport schools, and he attended Miami University at Oxford, Ohio, graduating in 1856, and went on to the Cincinnati Law School. After graduation he was admitted to the bar. He was named Newport city attorney in 1858 and served for two years. In 1861 he joined the Kentucky 5th Cavalry Unit of the Confederate Army as a private, serving until the end of the war, when he was discharged as a captain. Three days before Gen. Robert E. Lee's surrender at Appomattox, Berry was captured by Union Forces and imprisoned for two months at Johnson's Island, Ohio. After being released, he returned to his legal practice in Newport. In 1867 he married Ann Shaler, daughter of **Nathaniel Burger Shaler** and Ann Southgate Shaler (daughter of **Richard Southgate**). The couple had five children. Berry served as mayor of Newport from 1870 to 1876 and then purchased the Newport and Cincinnati Ferry Company (see **Ferries**) in 1879. He was a state senator from 1878 to 1883 and was the Democratic candidate for Kentucky governor in 1887, but

Albert S. Berry.

he was defeated in the election. He served in the U.S. House of Representatives from 1892 until 1902. Berry was appointed Campbell Co. Circuit Court judge in 1904, a position he held until his death in 1908. He died in Newport at age 70 and was buried in Evergreen Cemetery in Southgate.

Biographical Encyclopedia of Kentucky. Cincinnati: J. M. Armstrong, 1878.
"Hon. A.S. Berry," *DC,* July 21, 1881, 1.
RootsWeb.com. "Albert S. Berry," Campbell County, Kentucky Biographies. www.rootsweb.com (accessed November 22, 2005).

Jack Wessling

BERRY, ANNA SHALER (b. 1845, Newport, Ky.; d. February 8, 1908, Newport, Ky.). Women's rights activist Anna Shaler Berry was the daughter of **Nathaniel Burger Shaler**, a medical doctor and surgeon at the **Newport Barracks**. Her mother was the former Ann Southgate, daughter of **Richard Southgate**, a wealthy landholder and owner of the Southgate Mineral Wells health resort in Southgate, Ky.

In 1867 Shaler married **Albert Seaton Berry**, son of **James T. Berry**, founder of Jamestown (Dayton, Ky.), and grandson of **Washington Berry** and Alice Taylor Berry, sister of **James Taylor Jr.**, founder of Newport. Anna Shaler and Albert Seaton Berry became the parents of five children, Albert Seaton Jr., Alice, Anna, Robert, and Shaler. During the **Civil War**, Albert Seaton Berry Sr. fought with the Kentucky 5th Cavalry of the Confederate Army for more than four years. He later served as mayor of Newport, as state senator, as U.S. congressman, and as Campbell Co. Circuit Court judge. Albert is also credited with the founding of Bellevue, Ky.

Anna Shaler Berry became a dedicated women's rights activist. She was a close friend of **Mary Barlow Trimble** and Susan B. Anthony. The three women campaigned tirelessly for the legal rights of women, especially the right to vote (see **Women's Suffrage**). In October 1879, when Anthony came to Newport to speak at the **Independent Order of Odd Fellows** Hall at Sixth and York Sts., she stayed in the home of Anna Shaler Berry, at Third and York Sts.

Albert Seaton Berry died of pneumonia on January 6, 1908, in his home. Grief over her husband's death apparently contributed to Anna's death, one month later. Both were interred in a vault at Evergreen Cemetery in Southgate.

"Death Again Invades Berry Home," *KP,* February 8, 1908, 5.
"Funeral Services at Berry Home," *KP,* February 10, 1908, 5.
Reis, Jim. "They Fought to Secure Equal Rights for Women," *KP,* August 4, 2003, 4K.
RootsWeb.com. "Albert Seaton Berry, 1836–1908." www.rootsweb.com (accessed October 14, 2006).
"To Perfect Deeds," *KP,* April 23, 1907, 5.

BERRY, JAMES T. (b. March 17, 1806, Dayton, Ky.; d. January 29, 1864, Dayton, Ky.). James Thomas Berry, the cofounder of Jamestown, was one of the 12 children born to **Washington Berry** and Alice Thornton Taylor, a sister of Gen. **James Taylor Jr.**, founder of Newport. In 1792, on the advice of his brother-in-law, Washington Berry purchased the 1,000 acres where Dayton, Ky., now stands from Katie and Caroline Muse, daughters of **George Muse**. The following year, Washington Berry and his family moved onto their new land. He farmed the site and also operated a ferry service across the Ohio River, to Fulton, Ohio. When he died in 1813, he left the western portion of the farm (known as Fairfield) to his wife; the eastern portion was divided among his nine surviving children. Over the next several years, James bought out the interests of his brothers and sisters and acquired sole ownership of the eastern portion of the farm.

James Berry married Virginia Wise of Alexandria, Ky., on December 16, 1832, and the couple had two children, **Albert Seaton Berry** and Virginia Berry. Berry and his family continued to work the farm and operate the ferry service begun by his father. In 1848 Berry entered into a partnership with **James McArthur** and Henry Walker to found the city of Jamestown (in Campbell Co.). Berry died in 1864 and was buried in the family plot in Evergreen Cemetery, Southgate, Ky. He was survived by his wife Virginia and their two children, Albert Seaton Berry and Virginia Berry Spence, who became the mother of well-known congressman **Brent Spence**. Several years after Berry's death, Jamestown was merged with Brooklyn to form the present City of Dayton. James T. Berry is an important link between Newport's founding Taylor family and its 20th-century descendants.

"Berry Family," vertical file, Kenton Co. Public Library.
"The Late Major James T. Berry," *CDE,* March 9, 1864, 3.
Reis, Jim. "Union Gave Birth to Today's Dayton," *KP,* March 23, 1992, 4K.

BERRY, THEODORE MOODY (b. November 8, 1905, Maysville, Ky.; d. October 15, 2000, Cincinnati, Ohio). Ted Berry, the first African American to serve as mayor of Cincinnati, was the son of Cora Berry. With his mother and his siblings, he moved from Mason Co., Ky., to Cincinnati at a young age and attended public schools there. In 1924 Berry graduated from Woodward High School, where he was the first African American valedictorian. While attending the University of Cincinnati, he worked at the Newport steel mills. He later went to law school, and in 1932 he passed the bar and began practicing law in Cincinnati. Berry was appointed the first African American assistant prosecuting attorney for Ohio's Hamilton Co. In 1938 he married Johnnie Mae Elaine Newton of Cincinnati.

In 1935, while serving as an attorney for the Cincinnati branch of the **NAACP**, Berry became actively involved in a capital murder case in Covington that concerned the death sentence of a Covington African American resident, John "Pete" Montjoy. The case had been brought to the attention of Berry and the NAACP because of the numerous constitutional questions involved.

In 1956, when Berry was vice mayor and a councilman in Cincinnati, he spoke on the topic "Our Responsibility for World Understanding" for a Woman's Society of Christian Service workshop held at the Covington Ninth St. Methodist Episcopal Church. It was an integrated gathering. In 1957 Berry made his next appearance in Covington as the guest speaker at the dedication of the renovated **L. B. Fouse** Civic Center. Berry commended the civic league for its efforts in the community and encouraged the adults to take the lead in youth guidance. Having served as vice mayor of Cincinnati in the mid-1950s, in 1972 Berry was elected the first African American mayor of Cincinnati and served until 1975.

Berry died in 2000 and was buried in Spring Grove Cemetery, Cincinnati. The Theodore M. Berry International Friendship Park, along Cincinnati's Eastern Ave., was dedicated in his honor in May 2003. The Theodore M. Berry Way connects Paul Brown Stadium with the National Underground Freedom Center.

"Berry Speaks at Dedication," *CE,* December 16, 1957, 54.

"Churchwomen Plan Workshop," *KTS,* March 7, 1956, 2A.

Pulfer, Laura. "It Shows We Can Do Better—Ted Berry's Park," *CE,* May 20, 2003, B1.

Wright, George C. *Racial Violence in Kentucky: 1865–1940.* Baton Rouge: Louisiana State Univ. Press, 1990.

Theodore H. H. Harris

BERRY, WASHINGTON (b. ca. 1764, Stafford Co., Va.; d. May 4, 1813, Campbell Co., Ky.). Washington Berry, a landowner and a city and county officeholder, was the son of Thomas and Elizabeth Washington Berry. In 1791 he married Alice Thornton Taylor, the sister of Gen. **James Taylor Jr.**, founder of Newport; Washington and Alice Berry had nine children. In 1792, on the advice of his brother-in-law Taylor, Berry purchased from Katie and Caroline Muse the 1,000 acres where Dayton, Ky., now stands. Berry held several positions in Campbell Co. He was Newport city trustee, county commissioner, county treasurer, and board chairman of the Newport Academy, the first school in Northern Kentucky. He also operated a ferry service across the Ohio River at Dayton.

Washington Berry died in 1813. When his son James died on January 29, 1864, Washington Berry's remains were exhumed and reburied next to his son's in Southgate's Evergreen Cemetery. Washington Berry left the western part of the farm to his wife and the eastern portion to his children. His son James bought out the interests of his siblings and became sole owner of the eastern portion, where, in 1848, he established a new settlement, Jamestown. Washington's wife sold her part of the farm in 1849 to two Cincinnati steamboat builders, Burton and Lewis Hazen, and they began another town, Brooklyn. In 1867 the two towns merged to form the present city of Dayton.

Hartman, Margaret Strebel, and W. Rus Stevens. *Campbell County Kentucky History and Genealogy.* Campbell Co., Ky.: W. R. Stevens, 1984.

"The James Taylor Narrative, 1840," Kenton Co. Public Library, Covington, Ky.

Wessling, Jack. *Early History of Campbell County, Kentucky.* Alexandria, Ky.: Privately published, 1997.

Jack Wessling

BERTELSMAN, ODIS W. (b. May 14, 1900, Newport, Ky.; d. July 13, 1991, Fort Thomas, Ky.). This lawyer and Campbell Co. judge was educated in local schools. He served in **World War I** and was one of the youngest soldiers to have served from Campbell Co. After leaving the Army, Bertelsman attended the **YMCA** Law School in Cincinnati (later the **Chase College of Law**). He set up his legal practice in Newport, where he was admitted to the American and the Campbell Co. bar associations. He married Dorothy Gegan and the couple had a son, William. Bertelsman was elected as a Republican to be Campbell Co. judge in 1936 and served in that capacity until 1948, when he retired to resume his legal practice. He practiced law then with his son **William Bertelsman**, who later became a federal district judge.

Odis Bertelsman served locally as a director of the Bellevue Commercial Bank and was on the advisory board of the Kentucky Enterprise Bank. He was also a member of the **American Legion** and the Masonic Order (see **Masons**). He practiced with the Newport law firm of Bertelsman, Kaufman, Seidenfaden, and Kolentse from 1979 until shortly before his death. Bertelsman was 91 when he died at St. Luke Hospital East in Fort Thomas. He was survived by his wife, Dorothy, his son William, and a sister, Wilma Hoess. Private funeral services were held at the Dobbling Funeral Home in Fort Thomas, and burial was in the Evergreen Cemetery Mausoleum in Southgate.

"Bertelsman," *KP,* July 15, 1991, 12.

"Judge Odis W. Bertelsman, 70 Years of Law," *KP,* July 15, 1991, 12.

"Odis Bertelsman, Ft. Thomas," *CE,* July 7, 1991, A7.

BERTELSMAN, WILLIAM O. (b. January 31, 1936). William Odis Bertelsman, Northern Kentucky's first resident federal judge, is the son of Odis W. and Dorothy Gegan Bertelsman. Both parents' families were residents of Northern Kentucky for several generations. **Odis W. Bertelsman** was the county judge of Campbell Co. from 1936 to 1948. William Bertelsman attended **St. Thomas** Grade School in Fort Thomas; his high school and higher education was obtained in Cincinnati, where he graduated from St. Xavier High School (1954), Xavier University (with a BA in 1958, summa cum laude), and the University of Cincinnati College of Law (1961). In law school he was associate editor of the law review and a member of the Order of the Coif. He graduated first in his class. Bertelsman has resided in Fort Thomas all his life, with the exception of military service in 1963–1964. In 1959 he married Margaret Ann "Peggy" Martin, also a lifelong resident of Fort Thomas. They have three daughters.

Bertelsman was commissioned as a second lieutenant in the Army Artillery upon graduation from Xavier University. He was a member of an Ohio National Guard unit and a Kentucky National Guard unit during law school and until 1963, when he was called to active duty. He held the rank of captain when his military service was completed in 1964.

Bertelsman practiced with his father in the Newport law firm Bertelsman & Bertelsman and served during that period as city attorney of Highland Heights. He was active in professional civic organizations during those years, as a member of the American, Kentucky, and Campbell Co. bar associations. (The Campbell Co. Bar Association later merged into the **Northern Kentucky Bar Association**.) He served on the Board of Governors of the Kentucky Bar Association from 1976 until his appointment to the federal bench in 1979. He was a member of the Newport Optimists and the **Northern Kentucky Chamber of Commerce**, serving on the board of directors of the latter for several years. He was president of the Northern Kentucky Chamber of Commerce in 1974.

Bertelsman had a wide general and civil practice. The firm's clients included several insurance companies, two railroads, two banks, a savings and loan firm, and a school district. Bertelsman also represented plaintiffs in various kinds of cases. He was on the plaintiffs' lead counsel committee for the **Beverly Hills Supper Club** fire litigation from the time of the Beverly Hills tragedy in 1977 until his appointment as judge. He wrote several law review and law periodical articles and was commissioned by the West Publishing Company to prepare a new edition of West's treatise on *Kentucky Civil Procedure* (completed in 1984 with coauthor Kurt Philipps). He also taught courses in civil procedure, equity, legal ethics, and corporations at the University of Cincinnati College of Law.

In 1979 President Jimmy Carter (1977–1981), through U.S. attorney general Griffin Bell, established nonpartisan commissions to screen candidates for federal judgeships. At the same time, Kentucky received three new district judgeships because of the huge backlog of black lung, social security, and other civil cases that had accumulated. The crisis was especially acute with regard to black lung cases; there were several thousand that had been pending for years. The nonpartisan commission nominated three attorneys for each of the three judgeships. One was to be stationed at Covington, which had never had a resident judge. The other panels of nominees were designated for Lexington and Pikeville. Bertelsman was one of those nominated by the commission for the Covington seat. Although a Republican, he was appointed as U.S. district judge by Carter in November 1979. The U.S. Senate confirmed the appointment on November 27, 1979, and Judge Bertelsman was sworn into office on December 10, 1979.

Until these appointments were made, the Covington Division of the U.S. District Court for the Eastern District of Kentucky was essentially a rural court. The judge came to town twice a year to hold terms of court. At those times the judge would empanel a grand jury, try all the criminal cases that had been docketed in the past six months, qualify a civil jury panel, call the entire civil docket, rule on all pending motions, and try all civil cases that were ready for trial. In earlier times, these tasks would usually be accomplished in two weeks; the types of cases were much less complex than cases later became. In the preceding 10 years, however, there had been a litigation explosion of both civil and criminal cases, so that the docket at Covington, as elsewhere in the Eastern District, had more than tripled, while the number of judges had remained the same. Trials of civil cases were suspended since criminal cases had priority. At Covington there were several hundred civil cases ready for trial that still needed to have their trials set.

Bertelsman had promised the bar and the public that he would bring the Covington docket current and keep it current, disposing of as many cases each year as were filed, and he has kept the promise. Doing so required implementing several management devices that were new to this area, such as serious treatment of summary judgment motions, bifurcation of issues for trial, the use of pretrial conferences and proceedings to narrow the issues, and settlement conferences. Bertelsman introduced the summary jury trial—a type of mock trial used for settlement—to Northern Kentucky.

During his years on the bench, Bertelsman has served as chief judge of the U.S. District Court for the Eastern District of Kentucky (1991–1998) and chair of the district's Judicial Reform Act Committee, which was mandated by the Judicial Reform Act passed by Congress in 1991 (the "Biden Bill"). He was also a member of the Judicial Council of the Sixth Circuit for seven years. He was appointed by the chief justice of the United States to serve on the U.S. Judicial Conference's Standing Committee on Practice and Procedure (1989–1995), a committee that is responsible for continually updating and revising all of the sets of federal procedure rules: civil, criminal, appellate, and bankruptcy. As part of his service on the Standing Committee, he was designated by the chair as a liaison member of the Advisory Committee on Civil Rules. In 1999 he was also a member of a committee appointed by the chief justice to revise the Bench Book for Federal Judges. During 2005–2006 he served as a member of the Judicial Conference of the United States, the primary administrative body of the U.S. judiciary. For many years, he wrote a quarterly informal column for *Bench and Bar,* the official magazine of the Kentucky Bar Association. He is a frequent speaker at local and national seminars and has also taught federal procedure and federal practice classes at the Salmon P. **Chase College of Law** of **Northern Kentucky University** in Highland Heights from 1989 until the present.

As a federal district judge, Bertelsman is invited, as are other district judges from the circuit, to sit by designation with the Sixth Circuit Court of Appeals, usually once a year for two to four days per sitting. Therefore, he has had the opportunity to write several opinions for that court. Some of these, such as *Street v. J.C. Bradford Co.,* 886 F.2d 1472 (6th Cir. 1989) (a new approach to summary judgments) and *Pearson v. City of Grand Blanc,* 961 F.2d 1211 (1992) (setting federal standards for reviewing zoning cases), established the law of the circuit on various subjects.

In February 2001 Judge Bertelsman took senior status, a form of semiretirement afforded to federal judges, allowing them to continue in service with a reduced caseload. Senior federal judges may sit by designation on any federal court in the nation. Under this program, Bertelsman has sat with the U.S. Court of Appeals for the Second Circuit in N.Y., the U.S. Court of Appeals for the Ninth Circuit in Seattle and San Francisco, the U.S. District Court in Albuquerque, the U.S. District Court for South Carolina in Charleston, and the U.S. District Court for the Southern District of Ohio in Cincinnati and Dayton, Ohio. He has also continued his annual service with the Sixth Circuit. He continues to serve as a trial judge at Covington and throughout the Eastern District of Kentucky.

Bertelsman's most significant opinions include *American Civil Liberties Union v. Wilkinson,* 701 F. Supp. 1296 (E.D. Ky. 1988) (the constitutionality of Christmas display), *aff'd,* 895 F. 2d 1098 (6th Cir. 1990); *Granzeier v. Middleton,* 955 F. Supp. 741 (E.D. Ky. 1997) (the Good Friday closing of Kenton Co. Courthouse), *aff'd,* 173 F.3d 568 (6th Cir. 1999); *Kagin v. Kopowski,* 10 F. Supp.2d 756 (E.D. Ky. 1998) (the Establishment Clause of the First Amendment to the U.S. Constitution; mandatory counseling for divorcing parents); and *Planned Parenthood of South Carolina, Inc. v. Rose,* 236 F. Supp.2d 564 (D.S.C. 2002) (sitting by designation) (the "Choose Life" license plate case), *aff'd,* 361 F.3d 786 (4th Cir. 2004).

Bertelsman, William O. "What You Think You Know (but Probably Don't) about the Federal Rules of Evidence—A Little Knowledge Can Be a Dangerous Thing," *Northern Kentucky Law Review* 8 (1981): 81.

Peggy Bertelsman

BETHANY CHURCH OF CHRIST. At Berlin in southern Bracken Co., the county's first nondenominational church was erected in 1861 to serve as a New Testament Meetinghouse. Initially, circuit riders came and performed ministerial duties there; a nearby pond was used for baptisms. A full-time minister was later hired and the church became known as the Bethany Church of Christ. A tornado destroyed the church building in 1936 and a new one, still in use, was erected and completed in 1939. Additions to supply classrooms and a choir loft were added in 1973. Behind the church is a cemetery, which has not been used since 1916; it includes monuments to several **Civil War** veterans who are interred there.

Bracken Co. Extension Homemakers. *History of Bracken County.* Bicentennial ed. Brooksville, Ky.: Bracken Co. Extension Homemakers, 2002.

Caroline R. Miller

BETHANY LUTHERAN CHURCH. On Sunday, November 28, 1937, Pastor O. H. Schmidt delivered the dedication sermon to an overflow audience in the new Bethany Lutheran Church on Madison Ave. in Covington. Schmidt, the pastor at the Concordia Lutheran Church in Cincinnati, had petitioned the Central District Mission Board of the Missouri Synod in 1931 about surveying Northern Kentucky with the prospect of starting a church. The fledgling church was officially sanctioned at the Missouri Synod's Convention of the Central District in 1933, with $1,100 budgeted for an 11-month period to accomplish this mission.

Victor M. Selle, a candidate for ministry, secured space in rooms above an "undertaker's parlor," for $20 per month in rent, and the first worship service was held there on September 24, 1933. The name Bethany was adopted, the neighborhood was canvassed to invite people to worship, and the church quickly grew. Bethany Lutheran Church was officially organized on April 12, 1934, with 24 communing members. By June that year, Selle was ordained at the Concordia Lutheran Church in Cincinnati and called as full-time pastor to the new church. The congregation's membership in the Central District of the Missouri Synod was also acknowledged at this time. By fall 1935 the church was incorporated with a charter from the Commonwealth of Kentucky and the congregation was advised to make plans to acquire property on which to build a permanent home.

The church purchased property at 2214 Madison Ave., opposite Wallace Ave., on June 17, 1937. Architect J. Adam Fichter of Akron, Ohio, designed the new building, and Harry Beckmann was the general contractor. A cornerstone was laid August 29, 1937, for the church building constructed of modified Gothic brick, cinder block, and cut Bedford stone. It included a 16-square-foot chancel, with altar, lectern, and pulpit all made from Appalachian white oak. The building was financed by gifts of the Women's Missionary Endeavor, offerings from members and friends, contributions to the building fund, and a loan from the Church Extension Board.

In 1974 the Bethany Lutheran Church felt the effects of the changing urban community and suburban growth in Kenton Co., and the Madison Ave. property was sold so that a new church could be built on Turkeyfoot Rd. in developing Erlanger.

After the move, about 50 percent of the membership was lost, partly because of transportation issues. There was no parking lot in Covington, and those who had walked to church there experienced problems with a commute to Erlanger, about eight miles south of their Covington homes.

The new Bethany Lutheran Church's building at 3501 Turkeyfoot Rd., was dedicated in December 1974; an addition was dedicated on September 15, 2007. This location suffered from road-widening between 2003 and 2006, and several members were lost over this interruption. The Bethany Lutheran Church had 110 members at the most recent count.

"Bethany Church to Build Home," *KP,* August 31, 1936, 1.

"A Big Day in Covington, Kentucky," *Lutheran Women's Missionary Endeavor Quarterly,* Central District Missouri Synod, 10 (First Quarter, January 1938): 2.

"Congregation Files into New Bethany Church," *KP,* November 29, 1937, 3.

Dedication Day Program, Bethany Evangelical Lutheran Church, November 28, 1937. Covington, Ky., Bethany Evangelical Lutheran Church, 1937.

Etter, Rev. Mark. Interview by Melinda Motley, Erlanger, Ky., October 4, 2006.

Melinda G. Motley

BETHEL BAPTIST CHURCH. Maysville's Bethel Baptist Church is the oldest continuing church organization founded for an African American congregation in Mason Co. Its early history is linked with history of its founder, Rev. **Elisha Green**. Green was a former slave who established the church in 1844 to serve the slave and free black populations of the town. He was granted official permission to preach on May 10, 1845, 18 years before the abolition of slavery in 1863. There were 385 free blacks and 4,000 slaves living in Mason Co. in 1850. For some 50 years, Green pastored the congregation; it first met in homes and then in a frame building that also served as the African American school in Maysville. Baptisms were conducted in the Ohio River. On May 17, 1875, an impressive brick meetinghouse, built by the members, was dedicated on Fourth St. in Maysville, along what was once part of the original **buffalo trace** followed by pioneers traveling in and out of the area. Donnard Morrison helped lay the foundation for the building, and while the men primarily did the construction work, the ladies helped and prepared food. Sunday School was organized in 1845, under the management of such leaders as Beatrice Jackson Lewis; she and other leaders at the church stressed serious study, with exercises, and gave diplomas for the completion of the course of study. Lizzie Mundy was the first to be married in the church; her wedding took place on December 8, 1875. Her son, **James Mundy**, who left Maysville in 1912 and became a nationally renowned choir director in Chicago, was an organist for the church. Bethel Baptist Church supported him in his education at Simmons University in Louisville.

After Green's death, a succession of pastors served the church for brief periods until Robert Jackson arrived in 1911 and stayed until 1925. During this time the church held two revivals each year, and a baptistery, new windows, pews, and an organ were added to the church. The 1925 revival, led by Dr. W. H. Moses of New York City and organized by the new pastor, A. F. Martin, was so popular that it was moved to the county courthouse. The church's parsonage was destroyed by fire on February 6, 1940, and a new parsonage was built and dedicated on September 12, 1940, at a cost of $2,800. The church sponsored many organizations, including the Baptist Training Union, the Bethel Missionary Society, the Church Aide, the Fidelis Club, the Lily of the Valley Club, the May Flower Club, and the Sewing Circle. The Church Aide is still in operation.

Bethel Baptist Church was a strong supporter of the African American schools in Maysville. The principal of the **John G. Fee Industrial High School** in the 1940s, Professor **W. H. Humphrey**, was a deacon of the church, and the Fidelis Club gave assistance to needy children of the school. From the late 1950s until his death in 1964, Rev. M. L. Jackson was the pastor of the church. His community activism and outreach work was important to the church and community during the changing racial climate of the times.

The church building that had served the congregation for a century was destroyed by arson on January 19, 1977, along with all the church records. The congregation purchased the Forest Avenue School building in Maysville and, after remodeling was completed, dedicated the new facility in 1978. Bethel Baptist Church is affiliated with the Consolidated District and the Kentucky General Association.

Centennial Celebration of Bethel Baptist Church. Booklet. Maysville, Ky., Bethel Baptist Church, 1945.

Vicki Bolden and John Klee

BETHEL CHURCH. Bethel Church was located roughly four miles north of Falmouth along modern **U.S. 27** in Pendleton Co. According to William Bradford's 1876 will, his estate was to be divided between his wife and his children except for one and one-half acres, which were to be used by the Bethel community for a church and a graveyard. Two Baptists and two Methodists supervised the construction; the building was built by them with donated help from both men and women. The Bethel Church was dedicated in 1881 and named by Mrs. T. J. Campbell. Rev. Spillman, a Baptist minister, preached the first sermon. The first regular minister was Gabriel C. Mullins, a Baptist. The first Methodist minister was S. A. Day. Both denominations jointly used the church for several years. The cemetery was plotted for one acre on the west side of the church. At first no one paid for grave sites, but in 1895, after Alex Emerich fenced off the graveyard, graves were sold, and church members and families of the deceased were expected to help keep the cemetery in good shape. When the new Mount Moriah Christian Church was built in 1911, many Bethel Church members joined it. No list of charter members of Bethel Church is available, since the church and cemetery papers were all destroyed in a fire some years ago.

Belew, Mildred Boden. *The First 200 Years of Pendleton County.* Falmouth, Ky.: M. B. Belew, n.d. [ca. 1994].

Mildred Belew

BETTS, MARY E. WILSON (b. January 1824, Maysville, Ky.; d. September 16, 1854, Maysville, Ky.). Poet Mary E. Wilson Betts was the daughter of Isaiah and Hannah Wilson. Educated in Maysville schools, Betts grew up to be a prolific writer whose poems were widely published in newspapers across Kentucky, as well as in *Moore's Western Magazine,* published in Cincinnati, where she was affectionately nicknamed by the editor "our Up River Pet." In William Coggeshall's book *The Poets and Poetry of the West,* he called her "one of the most popular of the younger writers of the State [Kentucky]."

Betts's best-known poem, the four-stanza "A Kentuckian Kneels to None but God," published originally in the *Maysville Flag,* was inspired by the last words of Col. William Logan Crittenden, a graduate of West Point, who grew up in Shelbyville, Ky., and had fought with distinction in the **Mexican War**. In 1851 Crittenden joined a force led by Narcisco Lopez to free Cuba from Spain, but on August 16 of that year, Crittenden was captured with 50 of his men and marched to Castle Altares in Havana to be executed. The men were forced to kneel, five at a time, with their backs to the firing squads, but Crittenden refused to kneel when his turn came. Instead, he spoke the now-famous words "A Kentuckian kneels to none except his God, and he always dies facing the enemy" and then was executed. In introducing Betts's poem, the editor of the *Maysville Flag* wrote, "The lines which follow are from one of Kentucky's most gifted daughters of song." The poem was reprinted widely and in various forms. Fifty years later, during the Spanish-American War (see **National Guard, Spanish-American War**) in 1898, it was revived as a morale booster.

The **Kentucky Gateway Museum Center** in Maysville has in its permanent collection a scrapbook of Betts's handwritten poems, donated by Bess Lindsay Bell Barnes, Betts's great-grandniece. Included are many poems composed during the 1840s and published in a variety of newspapers and in "New York publications" other than newspapers; the book also contains a collection of sonnets and writings that may never have appeared in print.

In the summer of 1854, Mary Wilson was married to Morgan L. Betts, editor of the *Detroit News.* That same fall, she died at age 30 of congestion of the brain. Her husband died several weeks later, in October.

Calvert, Jean. "Museum Musings," *Maysville Ledger Independent,* January 25, 1978.

Coggeshall, William T. *The Poets and Poetry of the West.* Columbus, Ohio: Follett, Foster, 1860.

Collins, Richard H. *History of Kentucky.* Vol. 1. Covington, Ky.: Collins, 1882.

Townsend, John Wilson. *Kentucky in American Letters.* Cedar Rapids, Iowa: Torch Press, 1913.

Ward, William S. *A Literary History of Kentucky.* Knoxville: Univ. of Tennessee Press, 1988.

Kathryn Witt

BEVERLY HILLS SUPPER CLUB. The Beverly Hills Supper Club, the site of one of the nation's most tragic fires ever, was a popular nightspot in Southgate, located on a hill above and on the west side of **U.S. 27**. The club began in the 1930s as an upscale restaurant and gambling casino. Over the years, it featured entertainers ranging from the Andrews Sisters to Liberace, and its guest list regularly included famous athletes and movie stars. Although **gambling** was illegal in Kentucky, a mob syndicate controlled local operations in Campbell Co., protecting establishments such as the Beverly Hills. All of that ended in 1961 with the election of reform candidate **George W. Ratterman** to the post of sheriff of the county. Ratterman and the reform-minded Committee of 500 (see **Newport Reform Groups**; **Cleveland Syndicate**) set out to clean up the local towns. Facing organized resistance for the first time, the mob left the area. Without the money from its gambling operation, the Beverly Hills, like many other such clubs in the region, could not remain open.

The building was sold and another entrepreneur reopened it as a supper club in 1969. That club lasted only two months before folding from lack of business. At this point the property was sold again, to Dick Schilling and his sons. Schilling had already purchased the **Lookout House** in Fort Wright and was looking for an opportunity to build something larger and grander, an establishment that he could pass on to his sons. Beverly Hills gave him that opportunity.

Schilling immediately began to remodel the old club, adding on to the ground floor of the existing structure and renovating the second story. While the main bar remained in place, the kitchen was converted into the main dining room. A new kitchen was added behind it. The casino area was transformed into the elegant Viennese Room, which could be divided for smaller parties. The second-floor offices became the Crystal Rooms, two large banquet rooms that could also be divided. The renamed Empire Room continued as the showroom for the time being, though Schilling already had plans to build a new, larger showroom onto the back of the structure. The interior decor was first class: a hall of mirrors, plush red carpeting, original oil paintings, a grand spiral staircase to the second floor, and crystal chandeliers ordered from Europe.

Schilling was nearly ready to open his new club when fire broke out on June 21, 1970. This, the second fire at the Beverly Hills, destroyed the entire interior. Firefighters were only able to save the outer walls of the building. Arson, believed to have also been the cause of the first fire, on February 3, 1936, was immediately suspected. The Kentucky State Police investigated but never determined an exact cause for the fire.

Although he already had his entire life savings and more invested in the club, Dick Schilling managed to raise the money to rebuild. Demolition work began almost immediately. With the rubble cleared, Schilling was ready to go to work. When the club opened to the public on February 21 of the following year, it had been rebuilt and decorated in the opulent style Schilling had planned originally. A new showroom, the Cabaret Room, had been added onto the back, allowing the Empire Room to be devoted to large banquets.

The new Beverly Hills Supper Club was an immediate success. Hosting receptions, banquets, and parties of all kinds, the club also provided top-notch entertainment and elegant dining. In the summer of 1972, Schilling redesigned the front facade, one feature that had remained unchanged from the original building. In 1974 Schilling set out to remodel the Cabaret Room, substantially enlarging it in order to seat more people.

The Beverly Hills was so popular that Schilling was constantly in need of more floor space at the club. In 1975 the storage space behind the spiral staircase became the Zebra Room. Small and elegantly decorated, it was a popular room for wedding receptions. The supper club later received its final change with the addition of the Garden Room, a large dining area built onto the back of the club with a glass wall looking out over the club's formal gardens.

Despite its sometimes-colorful history, the Beverly Hills Supper Club will be remembered most for the tragic fire that destroyed the building, taking 167 lives (165 plus 2 unborn children) with it. Saturday, May 28, 1977, was a beautiful spring evening in Northern Kentucky, the middle of the Memorial Day weekend. The club was in full swing on the biggest night of the year with every room booked for the evening. Popular entertainer John Davidson was performing two shows in the Cabaret Room that evening, wrapping up a full week of performances.

Approximately 200 people were attending banquets on the second floor, 100–125 were scheduled for a party in the Viennese Room, an awards banquet had filled the Empire Room, and the crowds seated for dinner overflowed the dining areas. The Cabaret Room, which had been intended to seat 900 people, contained many more than that number, as favorable reports throughout the week had increased attendance at the final Davidson show. In an effort to seat every person who entered the room, the showroom manager had lined chairs along the ramps to the stage and crowded tables so closely that waitresses were reportedly unable to thread their way through certain parts of the room. Estimates for the total number of people in the building that night run between 2,400 and 2,800.

At 8:15 p.m. a wedding party in the Zebra Room began complaining about the heat, asking that the air conditioning be adjusted. At 8:35 the wedding reception broke up early because of the increasing heat. The first recognized sign of trouble was at 8:50, when a reservations clerk smelled smoke. Opening the door to the Zebra Room, she found it already in flames. By 9:00 the fire had blocked off the spiral staircase, forcing Wayne Dammert, the banquet captain upstairs, to lead the second-floor customers down the service stairs and to a safe exit through the kitchen.

By this time, word had reached busboy Walter Bailey. Knowing that the Cabaret Room was relatively isolated from the rest of the club and that no one there was aware of the danger, he took matters into his own hands. Taking the microphone from the opening act currently on stage, he calmly informed the audience that there was a fire at the front of the building and directed them to the exits.

Meanwhile, an employee at the front called the fire department. The dispatch center logged the

Beverly Hills Supper Club, Southgate.

first call at 9:01 p.m. Minutes later, smoke was pouring through ventilation ducts into previously unaffected portions of the building, hindering attempts to escape. Employees all over the club continued to evacuate the building despite the rapidly deteriorating conditions. Customers from all parts of the building escaped through both the Garden Room and the kitchen until all but the Cabaret Room was empty.

Once the fire reached the main corridor, it raced to the Cabaret Room, cutting off an avenue of escape for the customers trapped inside. The room quickly filled with smoke, which confused those still trying to find their way out through the service bar or past the stage. People in the Cabaret Room managed to stay calm for a long period of time while they evacuated. It was not until the smoke and flames reached the main doors to the room that many began to panic, fighting their way toward the exits. In the ensuing rush, some people fell, tripping those behind them. This eventually created a bottleneck at the door into the service bar, and many people were trapped in the Cabaret Room.

Firemen were on the scene, with more local departments on the way, and units were coming from Cincinnati. Having been informed that the fire was at the front of the building, they were unaware of the deadly situation in the Cabaret Room. In one of the few strokes of luck that evening, an officer with the Cincinnati Fire Department had been dining with his wife there. After seeing his wife to safety, he looked for a place where he could help. He found it at the exit of the Cabaret Room service bar. Organizing several of the club's employees, he joined the rescue efforts, pulling people from the smoke-filled room.

Despite the heroic efforts of the club employees, the firefighters, and many customers of the club, 167 people (165 adults and teens and 2 unborn children) died in the fire. It remains one of the worst nightclub fires in U.S. history. Two victims were found on the second floor. They had earlier escaped the fire but, not realizing the seriousness of the situation, had returned to the building for possessions they had left behind. The other victims died in the Cabaret Room, many of them within a few yards of the exit doors. It was later determined that a considerable number of these had been overwhelmed by toxic fumes emanating from the building materials and club furnishings. Nevertheless, the tragedy could have been much worse; there was a party of physicians in the Viennese Room. Doctors were therefore on the scene even before the fire department.

As is often the case with tragedies of this magnitude, no one factor can be blamed for the disaster. The building was a firetrap from the beginning. The city building inspector, otherwise very conscientious in his duties, was untrained for his job and unacquainted with fire safety codes. He missed the dangers in the building's construction. One member of the state fire marshal's office did recognize the danger, but his warning was lost in the office's bureaucratic paperwork.

What these officials did not see was flame-accelerant rather than flame-retardant building materials, an open staircase in direct violation of state law, inadequate and unmarked exits, faulty wiring (the direct cause of the blaze), and employees who were not trained in safety procedures. Some blamed the fire marshal, some blamed the City of Southgate, and others blamed the Schillings. In the end the state determined that the fire represented a systemic failure, for which no one person could be held responsible.

As a result of the tragedy at the Beverly Hills, the aluminum wiring that caused the fire was taken off the market, and furniture manufacturers now make furnishings out of materials that do not release toxic gases when they burn. The state fire marshal's office was reorganized, with a separate department created specifically to oversee construction projects and regulations; programs were put in place to ensure that building inspectors had the knowledge and tools they needed to do their jobs effectively; and fire codes were tightened. Still considered some of the toughest fire codes in the nation, Kentucky's codes became a model for other states anxious to prevent a similar tragedy. The site of the Beverly Hills Supper Club remains vacant today, overlooking the intersection of U.S. 27 and I-471. In 2008 a group called the Beverly Hills Supper Club Survivors for Justice, with the help of professional fire investigators, asked that the state files concerning the 1977 fire be reopened based on the belief that the original report was flawed. In 2009, the state reaffirmed its stance that no arson had taken place.

"The Beverly Hills Tragedy," *CP*, May 24, 1997 (13 news articles following the story and its results, available at www.cincypost.com/bhfire/ [accessed July 26, 2006]).

Elliott, Ron. *Inside the Beverly Hills Supper Club Fire*. Paducah, Ky.: Turner, 1996.

Kleber, John E., ed. *The Kentucky Encyclopedia*. Lexington: Univ. Press of Kentucky, 1992.

Lawson, Robert G. *Beverly Hills: The Anatomy of a Nightclub Fire*. Athens: Ohio Univ. Press, 1984.

Jennifer Gregory

BIG BAND MUSIC. See **Jazz**.

BIG BONE LICK During the Pleistocene Epoch, 15,000 to 20,000 years ago, a great ice sheet stretched from northern Canada to the Ohio River. South of the sheet, elephant-like woolly mammoths and mastodons, giant ground sloths, giant bison, and other animals came to a salt lick about 12 miles from the present town of Burlington in Boone Co. Many were trapped in the surrounding bogs and died, their bones buried and preserved around the salt lick that came to be named Big Bone Lick.

Big Bone Lick was discovered by white Europeans in either 1729 or 1739, when Charles Lemoyne de Longueil, commanding an expedition out of French Canada against hostile Indians, happened on the site. Longueil's expedition was military, however, and the French failed to exploit his discovery. In 1744 Robert Smith, a British trader living on the Big Miami River (Ohio) visited the lick. At the time, ownership of the vast territories comprising the Ohio and Mississippi river valleys was disputed between France and England. In 1749 Pierre-Joseph Céloron de Bienville led another French expedition out of Canada, but it turned back at the mouth of the Big Miami River, stopping short of the lick. The Ohio Land Company, chartered by American colonials in 1748, sent Christopher Gist into the region in 1751 (including a stop at Big Bone Lick) to survey and prepare the area for settlement. A year later, John Finley, the frontier trader who later talked Daniel Boone into exploring Kentucky, visited Big Bone Lick on a trading expedition with the Ohio Indians.

The British victory in the **French and Indian War** (1754–1763) and the ceding by the French of all territories in the Ohio River Valley made Big Bone Lick a British Crown possession. During the war, in 1755, **Mary Draper Ingles** made a daring escape from her Shawnee Indian captors back to her home in Virginia while they were on a salt-making expedition to Big Bone Lick. Word of her harrowing escape and her return from the salt lick in Kentucky circulated and assumed legendary status throughout the American colonies.

The first attempt by the English to harvest Big Bone Lick's prehistoric treasures, however, ended in disaster when Col. George Croghan was attacked by Shawnee Indians in 1765. Fleeing for his life, he abandoned the bones that had been collected. But Croghan returned to the Lick in 1766 with two English scientists, and together they gathered a comprehensive collection of bones and teeth, some of which were sent for study by Lord Shelbourne and Benjamin Franklin in England.

Franklin's involvement with the fossils brought one of America's foremost scientists into play. He corresponded with Croghan, asking for more details about the "elephant's tusks and grinders." Later he presented several specimens to the Royal Society of London, thus establishing a collection there that soon attracted international notice. Meanwhile, in the early 1770s, several Virginians had laid claim to various tracts of land at the lick; the foremost of them was William Christian, a friend of Thomas Jefferson, who claimed 3,000 acres, 1,000 of which he later sold. However, Christian's plans to exploit the lick ended in 1786 when he was killed by Indians.

The **Revolutionary War** (1776–1783) had held back settlement in Kentucky, but with the war's conclusion, many new settlers entered Kentucky. By 1792 much of Kentucky, including the area around Big Bone Lick, was settled, and Kentucky had become a state . Even though England and America had just fought a major war, scientists on both sides of the Atlantic continued to collaborate on identification of Big Bone Lick's fossil bones. The recording of Big Bone Lick on a series of maps published in Europe between 1744 and 1784 spurred international interest in the discoveries at the site.

Another of America's great scientists, Thomas Jefferson (Virginia governor 1779–1783 and U.S president 1801–1809), had become increasingly interested in Big Bone Lick and had even written to a friend in 1782: "your letter has given me hopes of being able to procure for me some of the big bones." In 1795 another future president, William Henry Harrison, gathered a massive collection of bones from Big Bone Lick, filling 13 hogsheads, all of which were lost when the boat transporting them capsized and sank on the Ohio River just below Pittsburgh.

Jefferson had better luck. In 1797 he was given a fine collection of bones by a French general named Colland, and Jefferson later sent some of the bones to Georges Cuvier, the noted French anatomist and paleontologist. By 1803, David Ross, who now owned the land at Big Bone Lick, had forbidden further digs on his property. Undaunted, Jefferson instructed his former personal secretary, Capt. Meriwether Lewis, who was journeying down the Ohio River, to visit Big Bone Lick on his way to meet Capt. William Clark at Louisville and report what he found (see **Lewis and Clark in Northern Kentucky**). Lewis and a renowned naturalist, Dr. William Goforth, who had joined him in Cincinnati, were able to visit the lick, thanks to an arrangement Jefferson had made with Ross. Lewis afterward dispatched a nine-page report to Jefferson detailing his observations. Unfortunately, the bones collected by Lewis on this visit and shipped to Jefferson were lost in Natchez, Tenn., when another boat sank.

In 1807 Jefferson renewed his efforts to obtain bones from the lick by persuading Ross to allow William Clark, just back from his historic expedition, and his famous brother, George Rogers Clark, to dig up specimens for the collection of the American Philosophical Society and for Jefferson's own collection. The Clarks were able to gather more than 300 specimens, most of which are still accounted for in the Museum of Natural History in Paris, France; at the Academy of Natural Sciences in Philadelphia; and at Jefferson's home in Monticello, Va. This expedition to Big Bone Lick also unearthed three Clovis spear points, which provided the evidence that Paleo-Indians were contemporaneous with the huge beasts that had died there. The Clark expedition's bone specimens arrived in Washington, D.C., in 1808, and the bones were laid out on the floor of the unfinished East Wing of the White House for examination by Jefferson's guests and members of the scientific community. The publication in 1812 and subsequent translation of Georges Cuvier's *Researches on the Bone Fossils* chronicled the discoveries at Big Bone Lick and helped to spread their fame among the members of the international scientific community.

Since pioneer days, settlers had been engaged in salt-making, and the activity had developed into a commercial enterprise. Now, in 1815, an even richer source of revenue, exploiting the salt mineral springs, was established when Clay House, a resort named for the fiery Kentucky statesman Henry Clay, opened. It featured a fine hotel, a medicinal spring, a long row of bathhouses, and a large pavilion. From 1815 until it closed in 1830, Clay House was one of the most popular health resorts west of the Allegheny Mountains. Although most of the visitors to Big Bone Lick during this era were attracted by the hotel's health and recreation facilities, there remained a steady parade of scientists visiting the Lick. Some of them came to gather bones for museum or private collections, others to study the relics, and still others to do research for publication in scholarly journals, thereby keeping the scientific world apprised about what was happening at the now famous prehistoric bone site. From Europe came the noted English geologist Sir Charles Lyell, from Yale University came the distinguished scientist and professor Benjamin Silliman, and from Transylvania University in Lexington, Ky., came the odd and eccentric professor of natural history Constantine Rafinesque. During these times, bones were gathered and dispersed, specimens were tested and cataloged, and learned conclusions were rendered as to the importance of the various finds.

Big Bone Lick was, by the mid-19th century, internationally renowned as one of the most important repositories of prehistoric animal bones on earth, but slowly the site was being looted and its contents carried to other locations; the tombs of Egypt later suffered the same fate. Compounding the problem was that no one seemed to be concerned. For example, none other than the official geologist of Kentucky, Harvard professor **Nathaniel Southgate Shaler**, announced in 1868 that he had come to Big Bone Lick "to make certain that the licks be worked to their very bottom in search of contents."

Shaler's dictum was rigorously followed, and it seems likely that today there is no substantial number of bones remaining to unearth. In more recent times, scientific interest in the site at Big Bone Lick has been limited to occasional scholarly observations such as those in a 1925 book, *Ancient Life in Kentucky,* by W. D. Funkhouser, professor of zoology at the University of Kentucky, in which he discusses the prehistoric animals found at the lick. There was one final thorough dig that took place from 1962 to 1966. Those excavations were connected to the State Museum at the University of Nebraska, and the finds unearthed are housed there. Earlier bone specimens from Big Bone Lick are dispersed throughout America and Europe, either in private collections or in museums.

In 1935 articles of incorporation for a Big Bone Lick Association were signed, complete with a statement of objectives for the organization. The foremost objective was to protect and develop the site. Although the association soon disbanded, it did sponsor one important work. Willard Rouse Jillson, former Kentucky state geologist, published in 1936 for the association *Big Bone Lick: An Outline of Its History, Geology, and Paleontology,* the association's only book. That publication remains the premier authoritative history and annotated bibliography of Big Bone Lick.

In 1950, when the Boone Co. Historical Association was organized, the lost opportunities to develop an understanding of Big Bone Lick and its history soon became regular topics for discussion. Out of these discussions came plans and action. In December 1953, with support from the Boone Co. Historical Association, a Big Bone Lick Historical Association was founded. Among the topics most often discussed by both organizations was an idea to develop a state park at Big Bone Lick. The first step toward that end came in 1956 when the historical association purchased 16.66 acres and deeded the tract to the acting Kentucky state commissioner for conservation, for the purpose of establishing a state park.

In December 1960, the Kentucky Department of Parks announced plans to develop picnic areas, a shelter, and roads and parking areas. During the next two years, the Boone Co. Historical Association, the Boone Co. Fiscal Court, and the State of Kentucky together acquired several additional land parcels, thereby expanding the size of the park to 175 acres. By 1971 about 80 acres at Big Bone Lick had been listed on the National Register of Historic Places, and one year later the master plan for the park was completed.

It was fair to say that attention to Big Bone Lick was at best serendipitous during this period, as evidenced by the fact that the year 1979, suggested by Jillson as being the 250th anniversary of Longueil's discovery, passed without recognition or mention. The archaeological work at Big Bone Lick, initiated in the early 1980s by scientists from universities in Kentucky and Cincinnati, had by now shifted its focus to studying the presence of prehistoric humans. A handful of civic-minded locals attempted to spark interest in having the dispersed bones from the lick returned on permanent loan for display at the park. But their initiative, termed Big Bones Come Home, failed miserably owing to lack of interest and participation, and thus 1989, the second 250th anniversary date ascribed to Longueil's discovery, also passed without recognition or mention.

The 1990s produced a number of promising developments concerning Big Bone Lick and its future. The Kentucky General Assembly in 1990 appropriated money for a museum master plan that outlined exhibits, themes, and concepts for a $4 million museum, contingent upon funds being raised. This has led to a number of other studies and proposals aimed at building a consensus and finding ways to fund the museum project. One of the ideas still being considered is a proposal submitted in 1994 to make Big Bone Lick a Paleo-Indian National Historic Landmark.

While discussions continue regarding how to make the museum project work, a series of ideas have been implemented to help build the case for its construction. On December 17, 1998, groundbreaking ceremonies for the Big Bone Discovery Trail were held. The trail, which winds around a diorama portraying prehistoric animals being trapped in a bog, opened August 30, 1999. A month before, on July 12, 1999, the Articles of Incorporation and By-Laws of Friends of Big Bone Inc. were filed with the State of Kentucky. Since it was founded, this organization has actively sought to "identify, locate, gather, review, evaluate, and summarize" all extant scientific literature concerning Big Bone Lick. Using moneys provided by the Boone Co. Fiscal Court, the Friends of Big Bone Inc. are also researching the geology, the stratigraphy, the climate, and the hydrology of Big Bone Lick, as well as cultural aspects of the lick's history.

For the first time in its history, Big Bone Lick seems to have momentum on its side. Since the Friends were organized, Big Bone Lick has been designated as one of only four official Lewis and Clark Heritage Sites east of the Mississippi and Missouri rivers. UNESCO has been approached as a funding source for making Big Bone Lick a World Heritage Site, and Nancy Jordan Blackmore published in 1998 a popular children's book, *The Story of Big Bone Lick,* meant to spark the interest and imagination of readers, young and old alike. In 2009, Big Bone Lick was designated a National Natural Landmark by the National Park Service. The museum has attracted an important sponsor in the influential and longtime Kentucky representative Paul Marcotte, who has pledged to push for state funding for the museum. Big Bone Lick, which has no rival, is truly a treasure unique to the Northern Kentucky region.

Blackmore, Nancy J. *The Story of Big Bone Lick.* Florence, Ky.: Thoroughbred, 1998.

Jillson, Willard Rouse. *Big Bone Lick: An Outline of Its History, Geology, and Paleontology.* Louisville, Ky.: Big Bone Lick Association Publications, 1936.

James C. Claypool and Don Clare

BIG BONE METHODIST CHURCH. The Big Bone Methodist Church is located on Beaver Rd. just outside the entrance to **Big Bone Lick** State Park. The salt springs of the area made it a popular destination; many people believed the springs provided relief for various physical ailments. As a result, the community grew and included the old Henry Clay Hotel and other businesses. In 1888 the minister George Froh founded the Big Bone Methodist Church and built its house of worship. At the time, he was preaching in an old tavern. Froh, a veteran of the **Civil War**, served the church for 45 years. In July 1894 the Big Bone Ladies Aid Society was formed with 10 members. In 1930 the society had 17 members and the church 30. The oldest member of the church was John L. Jones Sr., who had been with the church from its beginning. It is believed that he hauled the first load of stone for the foundation. The church building is an excellent example of Gothic Revival architecture with Queen Anne features. When constructed, the first and second floors were deeded separately, a unique occurrence; the church was on the first floor and a social lodge upstairs. In 1988 the building was listed on the National Registry of Historic Places. Closed as a church, the building has since been purchased and restored by the Commonwealth of Kentucky.

Boone County Recorder, historical ed., September 4, 1930.

Robert Schrage

BIGSTAFF, SAMUEL (b. 1845, Flat Creek, Bath Co., Ky.; d. August 18, 1912, Fort Thomas, Ky.). Samuel Bigstaff, a lawyer and a real estate developer, was the youngest child of Samuel "O.S." and Fenton Bean Bigstaff. When the **Civil War** began, 16-year-old Samuel was eager to participate. De-

Samuel Bigstaff.

spite his mother's objections, he joined the Confederate Army's 2nd Kentucky Cavalry, commanded by Kentucky-born Gen., Basil W. Duke. While Duke's cavalrymen were attached to Gen. John Hunt Morgan's command at a battle in Versailles, Ky., Bigstaff was captured and taken to Tennessee. He escaped and returned to his unit, then was shot in the leg in battle. Taken to a Union prison camp in Nashville, Tenn., the young soldier was sent to Louisville and then to the **Newport Barracks** as one of its few political prisoners. Soon he made friends with his jailers and was allowed to receive frequent visitors from Newport. After the war, in 1868, Bigstaff married Alice Webster, the oldest daughter of F. M. Webster, a New York native and a prominent Newport attorney. The couple lived in Newport and had a son, Frank, and a daughter, Nazzie. Bigstaff, who called himself a major, went into the iron business but was forced out by the 1873 economic panic. Campbell Co. judge **Charles J. Helm** helped him get into law school in Cincinnati and then in 1875 took him into his firm.

After the Ohio River severely damaged the Newport Barracks during the **flood of 1884**, Bigstaff visited Washington, D.C., to seek a new site so that the military post could be moved to higher ground. Gen. Phillip Henry Sheridan came to inspect the situation, and Bigstaff showed him adequate property high above the river in the District of the Highlands (Fort Thomas). Bigstaff, who owned part of the 111 acres proposed as the site, was able to make all necessary arrangements for the sale. Unfazed by the lack of roadways to the new site, he encouraged the extension of the electric **streetcar** line along what is now Memorial Pkwy. through the District of the Highlands, extending to the new post. The Grand Ave. Turnpike, running from E. 10th St. in Newport to S. Fort Thomas Ave., within three blocks of the site, was developed in 1888 with Bigstaff as a backer. As a director of the **Chesapeake and Ohio Railroad**, which runs along the Ohio River east of the proposed site, Bigstaff arranged for the building of a siding to bring building materials to the post.

With the new Covington Waterworks in the Highlands providing service and the streetcar line running through the length of the Highlands, development in the area boomed. Bigstaff was the principal owner of the Highland Land Company, which owned 250 acres in the area. He developed the nine-hole Inverness Golf Club, which served 400 members from Cincinnati, Covington, and Newport via the streetcar line. His **golf** course was the first in Northern Kentucky and the second in Greater Cincinnati. After a fire destroyed the clubhouse in 1913, the golf club lasted just two more years. Its lands, in which Bigstaff had a substantial interests, were turned into housing sites along streets with Scottish names: Dumphries, Dundee, Rob Roy , Sterling, Stewart, and Strathmore. In 1905, in another section of the growing town, Bigstaff developed a resort hotel, the **Altamont**. A smaller hotel nearby, the **Shelly Arms**, was another of his projects. At this time, his family lived in the former Samuel Shaw house near the intersection of Highland and S. Fort Thomas Aves. (now 25 Audubon Pl.). Bigstaff shared his law office there with his son, Frank, who much preferred to write poetry.

When the James Taylor estate was divided under executor Samuel Bigstaff's guidance, he created the Mansion Hill area of Newport and began development there. In addition to the development of the Highlands, Bigstaff created two neighborhoods in Newport: the city of **Cote Brilliante** and the adjacent subdivision, Ingalls Park. In Bellevue, he promoted the Bonnie Leslie subdivision on the hill south of town, conveniently along the streetcar line to the Highlands. Bigstaff was also a founding trustee of **St. Andrew's Episcopal Church** in Fort Thomas. He died at his home in 1912 and was buried at Evergreen Cemetery, in Southgate.

Goss, Charles Frederick, ed. *Cincinnati: The Queen City, 1788–1912.* 4 vols. Chicago: S. J. Clarke, 1912.

Johnson, E. Polk. *A History of Kentucky and Kentuckians.* Vol. 2. Chicago: Lewis, 1912.

Stegeman, A. Vinton, "The Legend of the Highlands' Mineral Springs," *Fort Thomas Living,* February 1887, 20–21.

Betty Maddox Daniels

BIRD'S (BYRD'S) WAR ROAD. In early June 1780, during the **Revolutionary War**, about 150 British soldiers and 100 Indians of various tribes left Detroit, Mich., to attack white settlements in Kentucky. En route, they were joined by an additional 700 Indians. The raid was said to be in retaliation for attacks made the previous summer, by John Bowman and 300 Kentuckians, against Indians living near present-day Xenia, Ohio. In the 1780 attack, Capt. Henry Bird (also spelled Byrd) served as commander of the British force and was accompanied by **Simon Girty**. The army moved south from Detroit to the Maumee River, then overland to the Great Miami River, which they followed to the Ohio River. They then went up the Ohio River to the mouth of the Licking River (this spot was known as **the Point** and later as Covington, Ky.). They traversed the Licking River to its south fork (present-day Falmouth). Bird's army followed the south fork to a point about one mile south of the abandoned Boyd Station. From there they cleared a wagon road through the wooded countryside until they reached a place near present-day Cynthiana, where they crossed the Licking River. On June 20, 1780, Bird's army attacked Ruddle's Station (on the South Licking River near Lair and about midway between Cynthiana and Paris), in modern Harrison Co. Being completely outnumbered, Captain Ruddle agreed to surrender the station, if the women and children were promised safe passage to another station. However, when the gates were opened, the Indians broke their promise and savagely attacked the people, killing 27 and taking the remainder prisoner. Bird's army then advanced to Martin's Station (on Stoner Creek, about five miles south of Ruddle's), where again residents surrendered without resistance. On that occasion, however, the people were not harmed but were all taken prisoner. John Filson, in his book *The Discovery, Settlement, and Present State of Kentucke* (1784), gave the name Bird's War Road to the route taken by Bird's army from the Point to Ruddle's and Martin's Stations.

The army had intended to continue on to the Falls of the Ohio (later Louisville), where they planned to attack Gen. **George Rogers Clark**'s army. However, Bird's Indian allies decided to take their spoils and return to Ohio. Colonel Bird and his depleted army had no choice but to return to Detroit, without attacking their final target. Bird's troops captured 350 Kentuckians, some of whom were marched to Detroit by Bird, while others were kept captive by the Indians. In retaliation for the attacks on Ruddle's and Martin's Stations, General Clark, accompanied by **Daniel Boone** and **Simon Kenton**, raised an army of about 1,000 men, who gathered at the Point and attacked the Ohio Shawnee Indian towns of Chillicothe and Piqua. Captain Bird continued to live around Detroit for many years after the raids and even married one of the captives. In 1796 he returned to England. Several years later he participated in a British expedition to Egypt, where he died in 1801.

Talbert, Charles G. "Kentucky Invades Ohio—1780," *RKHS* 52, no. 181 (October 1954): 291–300.

Jack Wessling

BIRTH CONTROL. Birth control during the modern era, in Northern Kentucky as elsewhere, has involved various douches, suppositories, diaphragms, the hit-or-miss rhythm method, vulcanized prophylactics, pills of various sorts, and abortion. Short of abstinence, no method of birth control has been found to be foolproof.

It appears that one of the first dispensers of birth control in Northern Kentucky was also one of the region's first women medical doctors, Dr. **Louise Southgate**. Southgate, a descendant of two of the leading families of the region, the Southgates and the Kennedys, practiced medicine in Covington during the first three decades of the 20th century. As a suffragette and a women's rights activist, she became involved in 1914 in the **Salvation Army** home for girls in her neighborhood on E. Second St. in Covington (the former **Amos Shinkle** mansion). When that facility became the **Booth Memorial Hospital**, an all-purpose general hospital, Southgate joined the medical staff, helping young girls in sexual matters and family planning. It has been suggested that she participated in some terminations of pregnancy; her relationship with the hospital's management was not always amicable.

During the early 1940s, the activist Roman Catholic priest Rev. Henry Haake founded the Catholic Druggists Guild in Covington. Members pledged not to dispense contraceptives of any type, in accord with their religion's teachings. Almost 30 years later, Haake was encouraging his parishioners at **St. John the Evangelist Catholic Church** in Carrollton and Catholics throughout the Diocese of Covington (see **Roman Catholics**) to cancel their Blue Cross–Blue Shield health insurance because the company paid for abortions.

Sometimes abortion has been used as a means of birth control. Local medical practitioners performed abortions even before the U.S. Supreme Court's decision in *Roe v. Wade* (1973), which legalized abortion. There were physicians' offices in both Newport and Dayton, Ky., where neighbors often saw taxicabs arrive with young ladies inside and, four or five hours later, return to pick them up. Rumors circulated that these one-visit patients came to have their pregnancies terminated. Illegal abortions were carried out as discreetly as possible by members of the Northern Kentucky medical community, who also served at nearby hospitals in the general practice of medicine. On occasion, however, these physicians were prosecuted by the courts.

Dr. **Charles E. Horner**, an African American doctor in Newport who delivered most of the African American children in Covington and Newport of his time, was charged in August 1940 with performing an illegal operation (abortion) on a 17-year-old Cincinnati girl. His office was at 212 W. Fifth St. in Newport. Horner pled not guilty; how the Newport City Court judge ruled in the case is not known. Horner retired from medical practice in 1943 and died in 1948. In December 1955, Dr. **Percival L. Bacchus**, another African American, was tried in the Campbell Co. Circuit Court on the charge of performing an illegal abortion, and juries twice failed to reach a verdict. Nevertheless, Bacchus's medical license was revoked in August 1956 on the grounds that he had "committed an unlawful abortion." In 1969 a Newport physician who was an Idaho native, Dr. Yasug Sasaki, was charged with performing an abortion on a 21-year-old Cincinnati woman in his office at 506 Central Ave. Sasaki's warrant, dated August 24, 1969, read that he "prepared or administered to or used means upon [name of the woman] who was then pregnant . . . miscarriage being not necessary to preserve her life."

Between January and July 1973, following *Roe v. Wade,* the Women's Center operated at the southeast corner of Third and Greenup Sts. in Covington. Its existence raised quite a stir in heavily Roman Catholic Northern Kentucky, and the building was often surrounded by protesters. The facility was owned by Dr. William Wagner and his partner, Dr. Phillip Crossen of Lexington. The publicity that arose after a botched abortion performed on a Cincinnati girl did not help matters for the clinic's operators, nor did the public comments on the matter made by Roman Catholic bishop Richard H. Ackerman. The clinic conducted as many as 40 abortions per day, priced at $175 each. By 1990 some 1.6 million abortions were performed in the United States; that was the peak year. By 2000, 1.3 million abortions were recorded, as public support seemingly declined somewhat just after 1990.

Almost 100 years ago, Margaret Higgins Sanger (1870–1966) founded the American Birth Control League, which by 1921 had evolved into an organization known as Planned Parenthood. An atheist, a Socialist, and a eugenicist, Sanger opened the first family planning and birth control clinic in the United States in Brooklyn, N.Y. No Planned Parenthood has existed in Northern Kentucky, but the Planned Parenthood facility along Auburn Ave. in the Mount Auburn neighborhood of Cincinnati has served the region. Its presence has been a source of protests and picketing by the prolife movement over the years (see **Northern Kentucky Right to Life**). In recent years the Northern Kentucky Independent Health District has walked a precarious path in dealing with birth control.

In 1960 the birth control pill for women was introduced in the United States; by 1970 it had driven down the national birth rate. In 2006 the FDA (Food and Drug Administration) approved over-the-counter sales of the morning-after pill. Today, legislatures debate whether pharmacists can be required to sell contraceptives when they have moral objections to doing so, whether federal and state funds should be used for family planning and related counseling, and exactly what information should be made available and taught in the schools.

Byrd, Sigman. "Priest Fights Blue Cross on Abortions," *KP,* July 1, 1970, 8K.
Gordon, Linda. *The Moral Property of Woman.* Urbana: Univ. of Illinois Press, 2002.
Moncrief, Nancye. "Charge Physician with Abortion," *KP,* October 7, 1969, 2K.
Mueller, Jan. "Dr. Louise Southgate," *JKS* 21 (September 2004): 144–54.
Murdoch, Norman H. "A Protestant Hospital for Covington: Booth Memorial Hospital," *JKS* 3 (October 1986): 107–49.
———. *The Salvation Army in Cincinnati: 1885–1985.* Cincinnati: Salvation Army, 1985.

BISHOP BROSSART HIGH SCHOOL. The beginnings of Bishop Brossart High School can be traced back to 1949, when the parishioners of **St. Mary of the Assumption Catholic Church** in Alexandria purchased the old Campbell Co. public school building at Grove and Jefferson Sts. Following a complete renovation, the building began its new life as the home of St. Mary Elementary

School and the new St. Mary High School. The coeducational St. Mary High School opened its doors to 32 freshmen in September 1950, and Bishop **William T. Mulloy** dedicated the remodeled building on October 22, 1950. The high school faculty for that first year consisted of Rev. Louis Brinker and a **sister of Notre Dame**. In each succeeding year, an additional grade was added, until all four grades of high school were offered. At the first high school graduation, in 1954, 25 students received diplomas.

St. Mary High School grew quickly, and by 1961 an addition to the original building was necessary. That same year, Bishop Richard H. Ackerman named St. Mary High School a district school serving the parishes of St. Mary in Alexandria, **St. Joseph** in Cold Spring, **St. Joseph** in Camp Springs, Saints Peter and Paul in the town of California, and **St. Philip** in Melbourne. To reflect this change from a parish to a district school, St. Mary High School was officially renamed Bishop Brossart High School in 1962. Bishop Ferdinand Brossart had been the fourth bishop of the Diocese of Covington (see **Roman Catholics**) and a resident of rural Campbell Co.

By the 1980s the building that served Bishop Brossart High School had become inadequate. Planning and fundraising for a new facility began under the direction of principal Tom Seither, who had been appointed to that post in 1978, and a new campus was constructed on the same site as the old building and dedicated as Hegenauer Hall and the Seither Center in 1986. Nine years later, in 1995, the original building was demolished to make way for the Crouch Center, the academic wing of the school. In 2006, in response to growth of both the school and the population of southern Campbell Co., Bishop Brossart High School's athletic department initiated a football program.

The Church of St. Mary of the Assumption, Alexandria, Kentucky 1860–1960—A Story of Faith. Alexandria, Ky.: Church of St. Mary of the Assumption, 1960.

Reis, Jim. "Native Son, Man of God—Bishop Brossart Touched Many Lives in Early 20th Century," *KP*, April 13, 1998, 4K.

Ryan, Paul E. *History of the Diocese of Covington, Kentucky.* Covington, Ky.: Diocese of Covington, 1954.

Tenkotte, Paul A., David E. Schroeder, and Thomas S. Ward. *To Be Catholic and American in Northern, Central, and Appalachian Kentucky: The Diocese of Covington, 1853–2003.* Forthcoming.

David E. Schroeder

BLACK, BRADY F. (b. July 31, 1908, Lawrence Co., Ky.; d. October 9, 1991, Edgewood, Ky.). For more than 64 years, journalism played the defining role in the life of Brady Black, the son of Fred Nixon and Melissa Cornwell Black. His newspaper career—from sports editor to vice president and editor—was followed by a teaching career in journalism.

Departing their native Lawrence Co., Ky., the Black family moved to Ashland, Ky., when Brady was a teenager, and he graduated from Ashland High School. In 1927 he joined the *Ashland Independent* as sports editor and later served as city editor. Black moved to Northern Kentucky, with his wife, Edra Dailey Black, and their children, to take a job as a copy editor with the *Cincinnati Enquirer.* Over the years from 1940 through 1956, Black worked his way up through the ranks. He covered the state government in Kentucky and worked as a correspondent; after he moved to Ohio, he served as the newspaper's Columbus bureau chief, as managing editor, as the local political reporter, and as assistant city editor. In 1957 Black was appointed editor of the editorial page, and in 1959 he became executive editor. On January 22, 1964, he was promoted to editor and vice president and elected to the *Enquirer*'s board of directors. He continued in those roles until his retirement on September 1, 1975.

During his years at the *Enquirer,* Black traveled extensively, chasing stories of international interest to five Latin countries in 1962; El Salvador, Panama, and Costa Rica in 1966; and Europe, South Africa, and South America in 1974. Black loved political conventions, public-affairs reporting, and telling humorous stories about his newspaper work.

From 1963 to 1965, Black was a Pulitzer Prize juror. He was on the board of trustees of the Citizens Conference on State Legislatures, and in 1968 his remarks on the role of state legislatures in the federal systems were presented before the Mid-Atlantic Regional Conference on Strengthening the Legislature. His address, "State Government at the Crossroads," was printed in the *Congressional Record.* In 1971 **Northern Kentucky University** in Highland Heights hired Black to help in its public relations. In 1979 he served on the inaugural board of trustees for the **Behringer-Crawford Museum** in Covington. He also was vice president of the Ohio Chamber of Commerce and served on its board of directors.

After his retirement from the *Enquirer,* Black became the Kiplinger professor of public affairs reporting at the Ohio State University School of Journalism in Columbus. Ohio State University Press later published a book of his writings, *Fighters, Lovers, and Others.*

Black died in 1991 at age 83 at **St. Elizabeth Medical Center** South in Edgewood, Ky., and was buried at Highland Cemetery in Fort Mitchell. A mailbox marked with his name stood at the drive to his stately home in Fort Wright, along the west side of the **Dixie Highway** (U.S. 25), for at least two decades.

"Black Is Hired to Polish NKU Image," *KP,* November 10, 1971, 6K.

"Brady F. Black," *KP,* October 11, 1991, 8A.

Elkins, Robert. "Enquirer's Brady Black Dies at 83," *CE,* October 10, 1991, B1.

Highland Cemetery Records, Fort Mitchell, Ky.

"Retired Editor Brady Black Dead at 83," *KP,* October 9, 1991, 6K.

Nancy J. Tretter

BLACK, ISAAC E. (b. June 1848, Kentucky; d. April 18, 1914, Louisville, Ky.). The African American lawyer Isaac Black was born in Kentucky and lived his early years in Covington. In 1869 he resided at the Old Hotel Building across from the Kenton Co. Courthouse in Covington, where he served as janitor and law librarian. One day in the early 1870s, while Black was working at the law library, **John G. Carlisle**, an eminent attorney and politician, sparked in him an interest in legal matters. Carlisle noticed the young man reading paperback novels and suggested that he instead devote his time to reading law. According to Robert S. Tate's biographical sketch of Carlisle, Black engaged in some law study under Carlisle's direction and, furthermore, was the only African American who had that privilege.

Black's community activism embraced many areas, from education and voter rights to civil rights and politics. These challenges in Covington, an arena of conflict between the heavily Democratic majority and an influential Republican minority, demanded much of him. Yet, he rose above the circumstances. As long as he remained in Northern Kentucky, even during the segregation of the Reconstruction era, the former slave was able to develop both personal and professional relationships with Kentuckians of both races.

In 1869 Black, **Jacob Price**, and Rev. **William Blackburn** were members of a delegation representing Covington at the Freedmen's Bureau for Education convention in Louisville. After the convention, Black and the other Covington delegates took the initiative and began to organize a board of trustees for the city's proposed black schools.

On February 25, 1870, the first statewide African American political convention was scheduled for Frankfort. Some of the newly enfranchised African Americans wanted to vote the straight Republican ticket. However, Black, Price, and Blackburn favored voting for anyone who supported policies that were in the best interest of Covington's African American community. This political position later benefited the community by giving it a voice with politicians from both major parties. For example, **William Grant**, an influential businessman and a Covington City Council member, asked Black and other African American community leaders for their support. He said that if the African American voters supported him in his attempt to gain the Democratic nomination for the Kenton Co. district's seat in the Kentucky General Assembly, he would have the city charter of Covington amended to provide for an African American public school. Grant won the election, and as he had promised, the new Covington city charter soon provided for an African American school. Black's political wisdom had been demonstrated.

In August 1870 Black took a break from the rigors of politics and education to become president of the Starlight baseball club. The club remained organized for only a short period and was the last organized African American amateur baseball club formed in Covington until the turn of the century.

In early 1875, during the Easter holidays, a significant incident occurred when Black tried to attend Covington's **Trinity Episcopal Church**. He was denied a seat downstairs among the "quality" people. Black walked out of the church in disgust, but although the church had anticipated a lawsuit because of the incident, no suit was filed. Black moved to Atlanta, Ga., where he studied theology. Thereafter, he established a law practice in Louisville and returned to Covington only for short visits. In 1914 Black died at age 66 in Louisville and was buried in the Louisville Cemetery.

Harris, Theodore H. "Creating Windows of Opportunity: Isaac E. Black and the African American Experience in Kentucky, 1848–1914," *RKHS* 98, no. 2 (Spring 2000): 155–77.

Tate, Robert S. "John G. Carlisle—Truly a Mental Giant," *Papers of the Christopher Gist Historical Society* 2 (1950–1951): 147–67.

Tenkotte, Paul A. "Rival Cities to Suburbs: Covington and Newport, Kentucky, 1790–1890," PhD diss., Univ. of Cincinnati, 1989.

Theodore H. H. Harris

BLACKBURN, WILLIAM B. (b. 1848, Kentucky; d. April 2, 1880, Covington, Ky.). Kentucky native William Blackburn arrived in Covington in 1869 and became pastor of the First Baptist Church (see **First Baptist Church, Covington [African American]**) in 1870, replacing **Jacob Price**, the church's first pastor. The First Baptist Church had been actively involved in providing space for one of the city's private African American schools, and the practice continued with Blackburn as pastor. In 1869 Blackburn, **Isaac Black**, and Jacob Price were members of a delegation representing Covington at the Freedmen's Bureau for Education convention in Louisville. In October 1872 Blackburn and the other Covington delegates drew upon what they had heard at the convention and began to organize a board of trustees for the city's proposed public African American schools. The result was a board that eventually oversaw the city's two African American public schools, one at First Baptist Church and the other at the Methodist Church.

Blackburn was apparently a **Civil War** Union Army veteran, and if so he may have been one of the large number of African American Civil War veterans living in Covington who filed claims against the government for back pay and bounty. In December 1869 an effort was made to organize Covington's African American soldiers into a post under the banner of the Grand Army of the Republic (GAR). In September 1875 Blackburn was installed as the Past Noble Grand in the Grand Lodge of the United Order of Odd Fellows, No. 1650. The installation took place at Greer's Block in Covington, opposite the site of John G. Carlisle School. In 1880 Blackburn died and was buried at the Linden Grove Cemetery in Covington. On January 3, 1898, the William B. Blackburn Post 43 of the GAR, named in his honor, opened and the first officers were installed.

"Grand Army Officers," *KP*, January 4, 1898, 1.

Theodore H. H. Harris

BLAKE, BETTY (b. September 20, 1930, Lexington, Ky.; d. April 13, 1982, Georgetown, Ky.). Betty Blake's father, Stanley, was a popular state politician whose brand of populist politics served Betty well in her public-relations career. Her mother was Ada L. Donnell Blake. Young Betty accompanied her father as he campaigned; at his knee she learned how to sway a crowd of hundreds or earn a vote from one person.

After graduating from the University of Kentucky in Lexington (1952) with a degree in business administration, Blake went to work for WLW Radio, Cincinnati's radio station powerhouse, selling airtime. At WLW she was able to hone her sales and marketing skills while gaining an important new one, dealing with the media. Soon Ernst Meyer, the president of the Cincinnati corporation that owned the steamer *Avalon* (today the *Belle of Louisville*) asked Blake to come to work for him. Her job was to be the excursion boat's advance person. She traveled to the various towns along the Mississippi River system that the *Avalon* was going to visit soon, and successfully interested local groups in chartering the boat for an excursion. Unfortunately, after an accident in which several people were injured while moving through a lock near Pittsburgh, the company owning the *Avalon* was forced into bankruptcy.

Blake was then offered a job at the upper end of the Cincinnati wharf boat where the *Avalon* tied up. This job was serving as the first public-relations executive of Greene Line Steamers Inc., the owners of the *Delta Queen*. Beginning in 1962, Blake remained there for the next 17 years. Using her media and marketing skills, she made the *Delta Queen* an institution known around the world and kept the romanticism of the river and steamboats alive. Blake and a group of Louisville civic boosters orchestrated the first publicized passenger steamboat race in more than 30 years on the Ohio River. The *Delta Queen* and the *Belle of Louisville* squared off in "The Great Steamboat Race," which turned out to be the forerunner of one of the major events of the annual Kentucky Derby Festival.

The *Delta Queen* entered a very prosperous time. The future was bright until 1968, when the U.S. Congress passed the Safety of Life at Sea Law. This law would have ended the *Delta Queen*'s very existence because of its wooden superstructure. The steamboat's owners gave Blake a new job, which required all of the political savvy that she had learned stumping with her father on the campaign trail. She was charged with leading the fight in Washington, D.C., to save the *Delta Queen* from extinction. She lobbied Congress and created a nationwide letter-writing and signature-petition campaign that became known as "Save the Delta Queen."

Blake succeeded, winning the boat a temporary exemption from the Safety of Life at Sea Law. Soon after her success in saving the *Delta Queen,* Blake's attention was turned to the design, construction, and introduction of the *Mississippi Queen,* which made its maiden voyage in 1976. Blake was promoted to president of what was then known as the Delta Queen Steamboat Company; she was the first woman president of a major American cruise line.

She continued as president until 1979. Afterward, she started her own public-relations firm, Betty Blake and Associates. It was during this period that she moved to a rented townhouse on E. Third St. in Covington. Also at this time, Blake encouraged local restaurateur **Ben Bernstein** to begin the excursion boat business **BB Riverboats**. Bernstein honored her by naming his first boat the *Betty Blake.* Shortly thereafter, Blake was diagnosed with stomach cancer She died at her sister's home in Georgetown. Her tombstone in the family plot at the Carlisle Cemetery in Carlisle simply reads, "Hi There."

Bates, Alan, and Clarke C. Hawley. *The Excursion Boat Story: Moonlight at 8:30.* Louisville, Ky.: Art-Print and Publishing, 1994.

"Betty Blake, Ex-Officer of the Delta Queen Co.," *NYT,* April 14, 1982, D21.

Keating, Bern. *The Legend of the Delta Queen.* New Orleans: Delta Queen Steamboat, 1986.

Mayfield, Frank H., Jr. "The Big Exemption," paper delivered at the Literary Club of Cincinnati, Cincinnati, May 17, 1982.

Obituary. *S and D Reflector* 19, no. 2 (June 1982): 3.

"River Mourning for Betty Blake," *KP,* April 14, 1982, 1K.

Frank X. Prudent

BLAKE, TONI (b. October 16, 1965, Covington, Ky.). Author Toni Blake is the daughter of Talc and Rita Blevins Brewsbaugh. When she was about seven years old, her family moved to rural Grant Co. After a successful high school experience at **Grant Co. High School**, where she excelled as editor of the yearbook and the newspaper, she spent a year at **Northern Kentucky University** before taking a job as a secretary and a mutual funds accountant in Cincinnati. Blake has published more than 40 short stories and articles and was nominated for the Pushcart Prize in 1996. She also received the Kentucky Women Writers' Fellowship. Blake has reached many readers through her contemporary romance novels, including *Tempt Me Tonight* and *Swept Away.* In 2007 she traveled the country in the Blondes Have More Fun Book Tour. Toni and her husband, Clifford Blair Herzog, live in Northern Kentucky.

"Writers Open Their Hearts," *CE*, February 3, 2005, E1.

Danny Miller

BLAKELY, STEPHENS L. (b. April 23, 1878, Covington, Ky.; d. February 24, 1959, Covington, Ky.). Stephens L. Blakely, a prominent Kenton Co. attorney and an historian, was the son of Laurie J. and Lily Landrum Blakely. Laurie J. Blakely fought with the Confederate Army during the **Civil War**. After the war he became editor of the *Newport Journal* and also taught journalism at St. Xavier College in Cincinnati.

Stephens Blakely was educated at **La Salette Academy** in Covington and later graduated from Cincinnati's St. Xavier High School and St. Xavier

College. He earned his law degree from the McDonald Institute in Cincinnati, which later became part of the **Chase College of Law**. Blakely had a lifelong interest in history and was one of the founders of the local **Christopher Gist Historical Society**. He entered politics in 1910, serving six years as Covington city solicitor and later another six years as Kenton Co. commonwealth attorney. He also served as legal counsel for the Union Light, Heat and Power Company and the **Green Line Company**. He personally designed and built his home in Fort Mitchell, which he called Beechwood. He practiced law in the Greater Cincinnati area for more than 55 years. After a short illness, Blakely died at age 80 at St. Elizabeth Hospital in Covington. Funeral services were held at the Blessed Sacrament Catholic Church in Fort Mitchell, and he was buried in that city's St. Mary Cemetery. He was survived by his wife Margaret, three daughters, and two sons. Two of his children later established the Stephens L. and Margaret J. Blakely Annual Scholarship Fund, at what is now Xavier University in Cincinnati. His son John R. Blakely became, like Stephens Blakely, a prominent Northern Kentucky attorney.

"Gist Society to Beat Clay Shrine," *KTS*, April 10, 1950, 1.

"Heads Bar Association," *KTS*, December 4, 1916, 13.

"John R. Blakely, Ft. Mitchell Attorney," *KP*, April 5, 1999, 8A.

Reis, Jim. "Three Trial Lawyers Were Prominent," *KP*, September 23, 1996, 4K.

"Stephens Blakely Dies; Lawyer for 55 Years," *KP*, February 25, 1959, 1.

BLANCHET. An area in southern Grant Co., first identified about 1873 as a station on the **Cincinnati Southern Railroad**, Blanchet was named for H. L. D. Blanchet, who was a prominent landowner of French descent residing in the area. Two other French-speaking families, the Bouscarens (see **Gustave Bouscaren**) and the Simons, also owned large amounts of land in the area.

Before 1871 there were no stores, schools, or churches in the area. When the St. Joseph Church and cemetery were organized about that time, St. Joseph was the only Catholic Church in the county. The church was closed in the 1940s. In 1890 the Grant Co. White School District No. 18 was established on Long Ridge (Keefer) Rd., about one mile by road from Blanchet. African American students continued to walk three miles or so to their segregated school district in Corinth. A post office was established at Blanchet in 1891 and discontinued in 1907.

Today there is not much left to identify Blanchet. The curbing around the railroad station can be found, and so can the cemetery, which is still maintained.

Conrad, John B., ed. *History of Grant County*. Williamstown, Ky.: Grant Co. Historical Society, 1992.

John B. Conrad

BLANKET CREEK BAPTIST CHURCH. The beautiful Blanket Creek Baptist Church along Broadford Rd. in south central Pendleton Co., about two miles southeast of Morgan, was founded before 1850. The first meetinghouse was a log building erected in 1847. An old Methodist Church previously occupied the site. When the Baptist denomination took over the site, they built a log house for the church. The present church was built in 1916. A frame church building existed on the site before the present building was erected.

Belew, Mildred Boden. *The First 200 Years of Pendleton County*. Falmouth, Ky.: M. B. Belew, n.d. [ca. 1994].

Mildred Belew

BLESSED SACRAMENT CATHOLIC CHURCH. The origins of Blessed Sacrament Parish and School in Fort Mitchell, Kenton Co., can be traced back to the 1871 establishment of the St. John Orphanage (see **Diocesan Catholic Children's Home**) in Fort Mitchell. The few Catholic families living in that part of the county began attending Mass at the orphanage chapel. In 1885 the chaplain of the orphanage, Father Bernard Hillebrand, formally organized those Catholics into a congregation named St. John Parish. The new community met in the orphanage chapel for services, and many of their children attended the orphanage school before a separate school for the parish children was constructed on the orphanage grounds in 1889. By 1905 the St. John congregation numbered 50 families, and 38 students were enrolled in the parish school.

The growing suburban Fort Mitchell area attracted many Catholic residents in the years before **World War I**, and a larger church and school were needed. Plans for the congregation progressed rapidly under the direction of Rev. William Blees, who became pastor of the St. John Parish and chaplain of St. John Orphanage in 1916. Blees acquired property along the old **Covington and Lexington Turnpike** (see **Dixie Highway**), where a combination church and school building was constructed in 1920. The new building contained classrooms, a temporary chapel, and living quarters for the pastor. At this time the name of the congregation was officially changed to Blessed Sacrament Church. Blessed Sacrament School was placed under the care of the **Sisters of St. Benedict** of the St. Walburg Monastery in Covington.

Blessed Sacrament Parish and School thrived from the start. In 1920 the parish consisted of 114 families, and 42 children were enrolled in the school. By 1930 there were 475 families in the parish and 346 children in its school, making Blessed Sacrament Parish the sixth-largest in the Diocese of Covington (see **Roman Catholics**). A flurry of building activity resulted from this growth. In 1922 a temporary rectory was constructed. This building was later utilized as a convent and eventually as a residence for the parish custodian. A permanent rectory was completed in 1928, and a spacious convent was built in 1935. The present Blessed Sacrament Church was constructed in 1938–1939 and dedicated by Bishop **Francis Howard** on September 24, 1939. This beautiful Lombardy-Romanesque-style edifice was designed by parishioner and noted regional architect Howard McClorey. The highlight of the new church was the hand-carved marble high altar, designed in the shape of a medieval city gate. Other features included stained-glass windows executed by the G. C. Riordan Firm of Cincinnati and bronze doors fabricated by the **Michaels Art Bronze Company** of Covington.

In 1924 the growing Blessed Sacrament School was enlarged to include eight classrooms. When the new church was completed, the former chapel was converted into additional classrooms. Further additions that included classrooms and a large gymnasium were made during the 1950s and 1960s. Msgr. Leo Streck served the parish as pastor from 1948 until 1971. In 1953 about 480 students were enrolled in the parish school, and by 1968 enrollment had reached 915. Blessed Sacrament School was named a Blue Ribbon School by the U.S. Department of Education in 1994.

"Blessed Sacrament Celebrates 50 Years," *News Enterprise*, June 28, 1989, 11.

Ryan, Paul E. *History of the Diocese of Covington, Kentucky*. Covington, Ky.: Diocese of Covington, 1954.

Tenkotte, Paul A., David E. Schroeder, and Thomas S. Ward. *To Be Catholic and American in Northern, Central, and Appalachian Kentucky: The Diocese of Covington, 1853–2003*. Forthcoming.

David E. Schroeder

BLIND AND VISUALLY IMPAIRED. During the 19th and early 20th centuries, the only state-supported school where blind Northern Kentucky children could receive an education was the Kentucky School for the Blind (KSB) in Louisville. The third state-supported school for the blind established in the United States, it was founded by Bryce McLellan Patten, who began teaching a class of six blind students in summer 1839. On February 5, 1842, the school was chartered and received an appropriation from the state of $10,000. It opened in May 1842 in downtown Louisville and today is situated on Frankfort Ave. in Louisville. The mission of KSB is to provide comprehensive educational services to all Kentucky students who are blind and visually impaired, from birth to age 21.

In the decade of 1910–1920, a leader in blind advocacy in Northern Kentucky was Newport minister Carl Scheben. At least since the 1940s, the local **Lions Clubs** have participated in the annual Mile-of-Dime campaigns, and they were later joined by the *Kentucky Post*. On February 1, 1955, the Lions Clubs sponsored a sight-saving classroom that opened in Covington's 10th District School for students with low vision residing in Boone, Campbell, and Kenton counties. It was the first class for children with low vision in any school system in this region. The classroom had special lighting, and the students used no-glare paper and large type to complete assignments, in order to keep up with their peers who had normal vision.

In 1975 the U.S. Congress passed Public Law 94-142, now called IDEA (Individuals with

Disabilities Education Act), which stipulates that in order to receive federal funds, states must develop and implement policies that assure a free appropriate public education to all children with disabilities. At present Northern Kentucky schools have integrated many visually impaired children into the regular classroom to learn along with their peers. Each school district has a teacher of the visually impaired to instruct students in Braille and other skills that they need in order to be successful in the classroom.

The Kentucky Office for the Blind provides opportunities for employment and independence to individuals with visual disabilities. The agency offers services to help consumers become more independent and productive in the workplace, the community, the school, and the home. Its office in Florence assists students transitioning from high school to college, performs job placement, and makes arrangements for rehabilitation and vocational training. Independent living specialists assist people in gaining independence in the home and the community. Residents of Kentucky with vision loss also avail themselves of services from Ohio such as training for employment and independent living. The Cincinnati Association for the Blind and Visually Impaired and the Clovernook Center for the Blind and Visually Impaired provide services such as computer training, orientation, and mobility and rehabilitation services.

The Kentucky Talking Book Library in Frankfort was established in 1968 as the Kentucky Regional Library for the Blind and Physically Handicapped. Its mission is to provide library services to individuals who have a visual or physical disability that prevents them from using standard print materials. The library has more than 50,000 titles in Braille and on cassette tapes that are selected to appeal to people of all ages and with a wide range of interests. The library sends books on tape and in Braille through the mail at no cost to the patrons and participates in a nationwide network of cooperative libraries headed by the National Library Service for the Blind and Physically Handicapped, a division of the U.S. Library of Congress that was established in 1931. The Northern Kentucky Talking Book Library in Kenton Co. serves residents in Boone, Campbell, Carroll, Gallatin, Grant, Kenton, Owen, and Pendleton counties with talking-book services only.

The Northern Kentucky Council of the Blind, a chapter of the consumer organization Kentucky Council of the Blind, received its charter on November 9, 2005. It gives people who are visually impaired a chance to meet, network, and solve problems. This chapter has worked diligently to ensure that the **Transit Authority of Northern Kentucky** (TANK) continues to provide much-needed door-to-door services for its riders with disabilities.

Northern Kentucky has made much progress in both attitudes and services to allow people who are blind and visually impaired to live productively and independently. Visual impairment does not mean that life must be over. With knowledge and resources, people who are visually impaired can live active and fulfilling lives in Northern Kentucky.

"Blind Men Will Appeal to Assembly—Association Formed," *KTS*, April 14, 1917, 11.

"Blind People Push to Keep TANK Going," *KP*, June 6, 1978, 7K.

"Lavish Classroom Has 4 Students; It's Covington Sight-Saving Setup," *KP*, December 19, 1955, 1.

"Lest We Forget School for Blind," *KP*, November 12, 1955, 2.

"Lion Clubs of Northern Kentucky Launch Annual Mile-of-Dimes Campaign," *KP*, December 5, 1945, 1.

Jennifer Holladay

BLIZZARDS AND SEVERE WINTER WEATHER. Northern Kentucky has had plenty of bad weather, but some winter storms that have passed through the region have been memorable. From snowdrifts to frozen rivers, Northern Kentuckians have seen it all and have managed to plow through it.

One particularly bad winter was that of 1909–1910, when the area was covered in snow and ice for months. A blizzard struck on November 22, 1909: strong winds and heavy rains turned to ice, and the temperature dropped below 0° Fahrenheit. By December 30 the Ohio River had frozen. In January the weather began to warm and then seven inches of new snow fell the night of January 5, 1910, and some roads in Bromley, in Kenton Co., were under two-foot snowdrifts. Once again the weather started to warm up, and more snow fell on February 16–17, a total of 11 inches. Two days later, the temperature was below 0°. After three months of snow and ice, warmer temperatures moved in, and a thaw caused the river to rise. Flooding was not as bad as was expected, however, except for those who lived on boats or close to the shore.

The winter of 1917 was a two-month roller-coaster ride of weather for Northern Kentucky. On December 8 an 11-inch snowfall set a new record in the region for the greatest accumulation within a 24-hour period. Floods occurred in places when all of the snow melted; then below-zero temperatures followed. (A month later −16° at Cincinnati was recorded on January 12, 1918—the record low for Cincinnati was −17° on February 9, 1899.) The Ohio River froze, and many boats were crushed along the public landing at Cincinnati. The worst result of the bad weather was the coal shortage in both Newport and Covington. Some 1,500 railroad cars laden with coal were frozen onto the tracks at the **Chesapeake and Ohio Railroad** Yard in Silver Grove. Finally the ice began to break around December 30, and much-needed coal was delivered to households. The rivers began to rise in the early part of 1918 and flooded once again by February 11, but fortunately they started subsiding by February 13, and the harsh winter episode was over.

The year 1937 is remembered for the great **flood of 1937**, but in 1936 a blizzard arrived in Northern Kentucky around 8:45 a.m. on January 22. Temperatures fell, visibility was poor, and lights flickered throughout the area. The winds aloft from the northwest at the 4,000-foot level were measured at 62 miles per hour; temperatures in Canada had already reached −40°, and in Minnesota, −32°. The following day the temperature in Northern Kentucky dipped to −16° (−17° according to some measurements), the coldest since January 12, 1918, and was not expected to rise above 0°. The Licking River froze over in many places, and a four-inch water main at Emma and Main Sts. in Covington burst. Men were housed overnight in both the Covington and the Newport jails, rural schools were closed, and all accommodations at Williamstown were occupied by stranded U.S. 25 tourists. Firemen were kept busy in Covington, Newport, Dayton, Ludlow, and S. Fort Mitchell, Ky. The temperature during the day rose to −9°. Some relief came on January 24, but that did not prevent the Licking River from freezing solid. In Kenton Co. only the Covington city schools remained open. The 25th of January brought a new blanket of snow, and the temperature was near 0°. By January 28 the temperature hovered around 0°, as people were being found frozen to death throughout the state of Kentucky. By January 30 trees' survival was threatened, livestock were endangered by the lack of water. But by February 1, the temperature was in the 10°-to-20° range, and life began to return to normal.

The winter of 1963 witnessed snow, freezing rain, and below-zero temperatures in January. On January 24 the temperature plunged to −19°, setting a new record low for the Cincinnati region. Large ice floes made the rivers, including the Ohio, treacherous. In Dayton, Ky., the Harrison Boat Dock broke away and nearly crashed into Newport's **Central Bridge**. By March the Ohio River flooded.

The early part of 1977 was particularly harsh in Northern Kentucky. Freezing rain and snow arrived by January 14, and ice was showing up on the Ohio River. Conditions only worsened as new snowstorms kept coming and the temperature remained below freezing. All-time records for the region were set on January 16 (−21°), January 17 (−24°), and January 18 (−25°), accompanied by blizzard conditions. By January 20 the Ohio River had frozen; Captain **John Beatty** could be found trying to keep ice from gouging his **Mike Fink Floating Restaurant** along Riverside Dr. in Covington; and at Columbia Marine in Ludlow, the barges were frozen in place. City water lines and fire hydrants in both Covington and Newport began to freeze and leak, while brave (or foolhardy) residents ventured across the Ohio on foot. The high for January 27 was 13°. By the end of January, the supply of natural gas to industrial and commercial users was being restricted, schools remained closed, and the **Florence Mall** operated under shortened hours. Business at the **Latonia Racecourse** was greatly diminished. On February 4, the temperature rose into the 40s, and the river began to open for traffic.

The most notorious of all winters soon followed in 1978. On the night of January 5, 5 inches of snow were on the ground when the rain started and temperatures dropped 23 degrees in just four hours. By morning, there were 11 inches of snow and temperatures were below zero. Salt does not work on ice and snow at such low temperatures, so sand and cinders were used to improve the roads; however, wind gusts of 50 miles per hour blew these substances off as soon as they were laid. Roads were closed and motorists were stranded everywhere. Chunks of ice were floating on the Ohio River, and on January 30 the *Clare E. Beatty* towboat (owned by Captain John Beatty) sank. Temperatures finally returned to normal, and after a month of snow, the region was able to recover. Overall, the Cincinnati and Northern Kentucky region had approximately 53 inches of snow on the ground; 35 people died in this blizzard.

In the ensuing years, Northern Kentucky has been hit by blizzards several times. In 1994 a foot of snow fell in Cincinnati. Although Northern Kentucky was expected to get between 6 and 9 inches, some areas to the southeast, such as Maysville and Augusta, received as much as 14 inches. On January 6–7, 1996, the National Weather Service at **Cincinnati/Northern Kentucky International Airport** measured 12.8 inches of snow, a new 24-hour record. Again in 1999 the region was covered in snow. Many people compared that storm to the 1978 blizzard. Snow and ice had just stopped falling and the roads were starting to clear when more snow and ice began to fall. The airport was kept especially busy trying to clear its runways.

"Hundreds Risk Lives on River Ice," *KP,* January 24, 1977, 1K.
Johnson, Omer W. "It Was a Day Like Today, and Outside . . ." *KP,* January 25, 1983, 1K.
McNeil, Samuel. Telephone interview by Paul A. Tenkotte, January 19, 2007, National Weather Service Forecast Office, Wilmington, Ohio.
National Weather Service Forecast Office, Wilmington, Ohio. "Unique Local Climate Data." www.weather.gov/climate/local_data.php?wfo=iln (accessed January 19, 2007).
Reis, Jim. "Welcome to North Pole," *KP,* December 14, 1998, 4K.
———. "A Winter Northern Kentucky Didn't Forget," *KP,* December 26, 1983, 10K.
U.S. Department of Agriculture, Weather Bureau. "Monthly Meteorological Survey with Comparative Data, Cincinnati, Ohio," 1906–, Public Library of Cincinnati and Hamilton Co., Cincinnati, Ohio.

Elizabeth Comer Williams

BLUEGRASS. Bluegrass has been nurtured in Northern Kentucky for more than a half century by performers and audiences both live and broadcast.

Bluegrass music is derived mainly from traditional folk ballads and old-time music that arrived in the Appalachian Mountains with the earliest Scots-Irish settlers. It is an amalgamation of early mountain music and ballad singing, square-dance fiddling, **blues**, **jazz**, gospel music, and Tin Pan Alley song style. Bluegrass performance technique is patterned after jazz, in which instrumental soloists alternate playing improvisational variations on the melody. Bill Monroe of Rosine, Ky. (1911–1996), the "Father of Bluegrass," introduced this unique approach, which relies mostly on acoustic stringed instruments accompanied by high-pitched, "lonesome" tenor vocals. The music has a fast tempo, generally in duple meter, highlighting the offbeats. Folklorist and music collector Alan Lomax labeled it "folk music with overdrive."

The name of this distinctive country musical style originates from Bill Monroe's band, *The Blue Grass Boys.* His first band in 1939 consisted of banjo, bass, fiddle, guitar, and mandolin players. However, the definitive bluegrass sound was introduced in 1945 when Lester Flatt and Earl Scruggs joined Monroe's band. Scruggs played the banjo with a three-finger roll. Flatt and Scruggs soon left to form their own act, which rivaled Monroe's, and both groups were highly successful for decades.

Cincinnati's King Records supported bluegrass artists such as the Delmore Brothers, **Pop Eckler**, Grandpa Jones, Bob Osborne and Jimmy Martin, Don Reno and Red Smiley's Tennessee Cutups, and the Stanley Brothers (Ralph and Carter). Covington's **WCKY** radio cultivated the bluegrass sound over its 50,000-watt station, with country disc jockeys such as Nelson King.

In the late 1970s, Ricky Skaggs of Cordell brought a new fresh sound of bluegrass to mainstream country music that was reminiscent of the traditional bluegrass sound of Bill Monroe. In his youth, Skaggs performed on television with Flatt and Scruggs and began his professional career as a member of Ralph Stanley's legendary bluegrass band.

The International Bluegrass Music Association was established in 1985 in Owensboro. In 1997 the association moved its annual convention and fanfest to Louisville. The event draws bluegrass fans and musicians from around the world. The music has also encouraged the development of hundreds of bluegrass festivals nationwide, including the annual Northern Kentucky Bluegrass Festival (founded 1984), located first in Burlington, later in Independence, and now in Alexandria; and the Northern Kentucky Bluegrass Music Association's "Pickin' for Memory" festival in Sparta, newly organized for the Alzheimer's Association of Greater Cincinnati. In addition to local bands, nationally known artists such as Melvin Goins, Ralph Stanley, IIIrd Tyme Out, and Windy Mountain perform at these festivals.

For more than 20 years, local bluegrass artists have met at the Hebron Masonic Lodge in Hebron for Friday-night jam sessions sponsored by Gene Thompson (founder and coordinator of the Northern Kentucky Bluegrass Festival). Bobby Mackey, owner of **Bobby Mackey's Music World**, the region's oldest country night spot, released a bluegrass compact disc entitled *Ten Shades of Green* (2004) with Rhonda Vincent. Mackey has also formed the Pine Hill Pickers to play at bluegrass festivals.

A newer bluegrass performer, Alison Krauss, is one of the few women to become successful in bluegrass music, traditionally dominated by male musicians. She has won more Grammy awards than any other female artist and is featured with other old-time-music artists such as the renowned Ralph Stanley on a multi-platinum-selling soundtrack recording of the popular movie *O Brother, Where Art Thou?* (2000), starring **George Clooney**, a Northern Kentucky native. The soundtrack recording introduced old-time music and the traditional bluegrass acoustic sound to a new generation of fans.

John Harrod of Owen Co. is a performer and a scholar of traditional Kentucky folk music. He has produced collections for the bluegrass independent-label Rounder records and has performed with old-time string bands in the region. Harrod rediscovered "Mountain Girl" **Blanche Coldiron** of Grant Co. and recorded her for Rounder records. Coldiron started her career with the *Kentucky Hillbillies* in 1937. After raising her family, she made a comeback during the 1990s, playing banjo and other stringed instruments in the traditional Appalachian style.

It has become a common belief that bluegrass music is one of Kentucky's most famous cultural exports to the world, since it can be found on both major and independent record labels. According to Neil Rosenberg, author and researcher of *Bluegrass: A History,* the tri-state region remains one of the most active bluegrass areas of the nation because of the nurturing of the music by Covington radio station **WCKY** between 1946 and 1964. **WNKU** (the radio station at **Northern Kentucky University** in Highland Heights) continued the tradition of playing Kentucky folk music, including bluegrass, for many years when it first went on the air in 1985.

Cohen, Ronald D., ed. *Alan Lomax: Selected Writings, 1934–1997.* New York: Routledge, 2003.
Hitchcock, H. Wiley, and Stanley Sadie, eds. *The New Grove Dictionary of American Music.* New York: Macmillan, 1986.
Kingsbury, Paul, ed. *The Encyclopedia of Country Music: The Ultimate Guide to the Music.* New York: Oxford Univ. Press, 1998.
Rosenberg, Neil V. *Bluegrass: A History.* Urbana: Univ. of Illinois Press, 1985.
Wolfe, Charles K. *Kentucky Country.* Lexington: Univ. Press of Kentucky, 1996.

John Schlipp

BLUE LICKS. Along the Licking River in Kentucky, on the Robertson-Nicholas county line, the Lower Blue Licks is the site of prehistoric fossils, a battle of the **Revolutionary War** that was Kentucky's worst defeat in its conflicts with Indians, and a 19th-century health resort that rivaled the best health spas in the country. There were once two salt springs active along the Licking River, called by pioneers the Upper and Lower Blue Licks. Their names were derived from the salt springs near the river whose oozing waters gave the mud a bluish tint. The Lower Blue Licks, the larger of the two health springs areas, is commonly known as Blue Licks.

The salt at Blue Licks was important over the centuries for animals and more recently for humans. The trail that opened up Central Kentucky from the Ohio River, called the Buffalo Trace (see **Buffalo Traces**), was determined partially by people and animals visiting Blue Licks for its salt. The highway route to Blue Licks that is in use today follows essentially the same path. The muck from the salt spring was also a trap for many animals. The remains of prehistoric animals such as mammoths, mastodons, and sloths were discovered in the 1800s, and some are on display in the museum that is part of the **Blue Licks Battlefield State Resort Park**.

American Indians, and later the pioneers who settled Kentucky, also used the salt spring regularly. Maj. John Finley was one of the explorers from Pennsylvania who surveyed the area in 1773 and then moved there to live; his family continued to reside in the region until the mid-19th century. In January 1778 **Daniel Boone** was captured by a party of more than 100 American Indians and 2 Frenchmen while he was hunting and on a salt-making expedition at Blue Licks. He persuaded the other 30 Kentuckians in the salt-making party to surrender. This event led to one of Boone's most famous adventures, living with the Shawnee Indians and, later, after escaping his captivity, being tried for treason by the settlers at Fort Boonesborough when he returned to the fort.

Blue Licks soon became infamous for its role in the Revolutionary War (see **Battle of Blue Licks**). Although the colonists and the British had negotiated peace after the Battle of Yorktown, the disposition of the lands west of the Appalachian Mountains was uncertain. Lands throughout the trans-Appalachian region were still being fought over by some of the tribes of American Indians, aided by the British, and the colonials trying to settle them. On August 19, 1782, a small party of British regulars and a band of American Indians killed more than 60 settlers at the Battle of Blue Licks.

Blue Licks again reached prominence from 1840 through 1870 because a large spa was constructed there and water from the region's springs, purported to have healing qualities, was bottled and sold. A label from one of the Blue Licks bottles boasts: "A glass or two before breakfast for disorder of stomach, liver, kidneys, render greates [*sic*], satisfaction." The water's reputation was enhanced when the spa, known as the Arlington Hotel, experienced no outbreaks of cholera while the surrounding counties in Kentucky were all struck with the disease. Blue Licks water was sold around the country until the springs ran dry in 1896. In 1845 the hotel was often filled with 400 to 600 guests, the structure was three stories tall, and it ran 670 feet in length. It was during the same time period (in 1847) that the Western Military Institute was chartered at Blue Licks. Advertisements from 1848 heralded the institute's merits and proclaimed that it had space for up to 300 students. James G. Blaine, a future U.S. presidential candidate, taught there. He had, however, left his position at the school sometime before the institute moved to Nashville, Tenn., in 1854. The large hotel at Blue Licks burned on April 7, 1862, but was rebuilt. The Robert Hemingray family (see **Hemingray Glass Company**) of Covington enjoyed vacationing at the site. The rebuilt hotel and spa operated until the early 1900s, by which time the spa period in the United States had faded and the waters at the Blue Licks were gone.

The community of Blue Licks, formerly the site of the grand hotel, currently consists of a few houses along the Licking River and is a part of Nicholas Co. The area is subject to flooding from the Licking River. The battlefield and burial site, located in Robertson Co., are now the Blue Licks Battlefield State Resort, which has recreational facilities, a lodge, campsites, and a museum.

Collins, Richard H. *History of Kentucky*. Vol. 1. Covington, Ky.: Collins, 1882.
Conley, Joan Weissinger, comp. and ed. *History of Nicholas County*. Carlisle, Ky.: Nicholas Co. Historical Society, 1976.
Kentucky Gateway Museum Center, vertical files, Maysville, Ky.

John Klee

BLUE LICKS, BATTLE OF. Blue Licks, one of Kentucky's most important historical sites, is today maintained and preserved within the **Blue Licks Battlefield State Resort Park**. Located just north of the Licking River in Robertson Co., Blue Licks was the location of a battle on August 19, 1782. Although characterized even today by some historians as "the last battle of the American Revolution," this event was only one of a series of frontier skirmishes that took place between the 1781 defeat of the main British army at Yorktown, N.Y., and the 1783 conclusion of the final peace agreement.

It is fortunate that the battle at Blue Licks had little impact on the war itself, since it ended in a disastrous defeat for the frontier colonials. A force of about 300 Indians, mainly Wyandots, and a contingent of 60 Canadian Rangers led by the British captain William Caldwell attacked the Kentuckians at the Bryants Station stockade outside Lexington on August 15, 1781. After a couple of days, the Indians tired of the fight, and the attackers retreated northward toward the Ohio territories. Word of the attack spread quickly, and a force of about 180 Kentucky militiamen, under the command of Col. John Todd, arrived at Bryants Station on August 18, only to discover that the enemy had left.

Instead of waiting to join with a larger force of militia being assembled by Col. Benjamin Logan, Todd led his forces northward on a trail the enemy had made no efforts to conceal. **Daniel Boone**, a militia officer and one of those in pursuit, warned of a possible ambush, but Todd ignored his warning and pressed recklessly on to the Lower Blue Licks ford. Divided roughly into three divisions commanded by Todd, Boone, and Col. Stephen Trigg, the Kentuckians crossed to the north shore of the Licking River and assumed an attack formation. As they began their advance up the hill that overlooked the river, the enemy struck. In the sharp exchanges that followed, the Kentuckians could do no more than fight holding actions as those who survived fled southward back across the Licking River. Both Trigg and Todd were among those killed; Boone's son Israel was also killed. The Indians, momentarily held back by covering fire from a group organized by militiaman Benjamin Netherland, pursued for a couple of miles and then gave up the chase. While the stunned colonials limped back to Bryants Station, the Indians returned to the battlefield to strip, scalp, and mutilate bodies. More than 70 Kentuckians died, whereas the Canadians and Indians are said to have suffered only two dozen casualties—14 wounded and perhaps 10 killed.

Logan, meantime, had assembled his forces at Bryants Station and started north to join up with Todd's forces. Within five miles they met the fleeing survivors and turned back. On August 24, Logan finally arrived at the battle site with a command of 500 men, but all that could be done was to bury the remains of their comrades. The bloody defeat stunned the residents of the Kentucky frontier, and a period of both fear and mourning followed. Many communities had lost leaders, and Brig. Gen. **George Rogers Clark** soon was receiving blame for not preparing to defend the Kentucky forts properly. Clark responded decisively: before long he mounted a successful retaliatory attack into the Indian homelands in Ohio.

In retrospect, the battle of Blue Licks was but one of many episodes that pitted an Indian raiding party against settlers in Kentucky, part of a half-century struggle over land and territories that in the end saw the Indians driven out of the state. The sounds of the fighting that took place at the Blue Licks are gone; in their place are a beautiful state park and a metal historical marker commemorating the great battle fought there so many years ago.

"The Disastrous Battle of Blue Licks," *DC*, August 19, 1882, 2.
"Historic Battleground," *KP*, August 17, 1998, 1K.
"The Slaughter at Blue Licks—Boone's Account of Battle," *KSJ*, August 22, 1882, 1.

James C. Claypool

BLUE LICKS BATTLEFIELD STATE RESORT PARK. This Robertson Co. historical and recreational gathering spot along the old **Maysville and Lexington** Turnpike (U.S. 68), south of Maysville and 48 miles north of Lexington, has been known to Kentuckians from the earliest days of Kentucky's settlement. Now one of the four state parks within the Northern Kentucky region, this is where the 1782 **Revolutionary War** Battle of Blue Licks (see **Blue Licks, Battle of**) took place. It is also where the famous 19th-century Blue Licks Springs hotel catered to the carriage trade who could afford to stay there, enjoying the benefits of the salt spring's waters (see **Blue Licks**). As early as the 1860s, families such as the **Robert Hemingrays** of Covington were guests at the hotel. Small steamboats successfully navigated their way up the North Forth of the Licking River, bringing passengers to Blue Licks. Memorial ceremonies celebrating the historic Battle of Blue Licks—known to generations of Kentuckians as the last battle of the American Revolution—are a staple at the site.

The state park opened in 1926 and operated seasonally (April 1–October 31) until the lodge was completed during the 1990s. At that time the state park formally became a state resort park. The park's cedar-and-fieldstone museum housing the Indian artifacts excavated by archaeologist W. J. Curtis was opened in 1926. Also at the park is a large stone monument that commemorates the early pioneers who died in the famous battle and are buried at its base, including **Daniel Boone**'s son Israel. Today's visitors find shaded picnic and camping areas, hiking trails, a large outdoor swimming pool, a 32-room lodge with cottages, a restaurant, and a gift shop. Several large events are scheduled throughout the year. The annual August reenactment of the battle attracts a large crowd. In recent years the park has provided jobs to a part of the Northern Kentucky region in need of employment opportunities.

Landers, Arthur B., Jr. "Blue Licks Battlefield State Park: Commemorates Last Kentucky Battle of American Revolution," *American Motorist,* October 1976, 10–11.

BLUEMLEIN, THOMAS (b. February 13, 1948, Cincinnati, Ohio). Tom Bluemlein was first trained and employed in commercial art, but he is best known for his impressionist-style landscapes of regional locales, European city scenes, intimate wooded interiors, still life, portraits, and seascapes. Even though his subjects range from the local to international, Bluemlein resides in Northern Kentucky, where he presently paints in his Fort Mitchell loft studio. After graduating from **Lloyd Memorial High School** in Erlanger, he married his high school sweetheart, Jonna House; they had two children. He entered the Central Academy of Commercial Art of Cincinnati in 1967, and upon completion of the two-year program, he worked as a designer for Quell Sign Co. For 13 years he was employed by the **Kroger** Company in Cincinnati as a photographer and illustrator, and then he started his own design firm, Creative Services. Bluemlein's interest and work in creative arts, particularly oil painting, has run a parallel course with his career as a designer. While doing commercial art, he began to study life painting at the Art Academy of Cincinnati in the late 1970s. He continued to be involved in both fields until 2000, when he began painting and teaching full-time. He studied with Paul Chidlaw and attended workshops with nationally known illustrator N. C. Wyeth. He has taught in numerous community art classes and has been active in the Northern Kentucky Watercolor Society. Bluemlein holds memberships in the Cincinnati Art Club and in Oil Painters of America. He is interested currently in the legacy art concept, creating commissioned oil paintings that are metaphoric in nature and reflect a sense of legacy. His paintings can be found in galleries in Jackson Hole, Wyo.; Highlands and Myrtle Beach, S.C.; Santa Fe, N.Mex.; and Carmel, Calif., in addition to local private collections.

Blumlein, Thomas. Interview by Rebecca Bilbo, fall 2006, Fort Mitchell, Ky.

"Colorful Cottage Makeover," *CE,* March 6, 1999, C1.

"Lloyd Inducts Hall of Famers," *Erlanger Dixie News,* July 7, 1994, 11.

"St. Luke Festival of the Arts," *KP,* November 1, 1995, 3KK.

Rebecca Bilbo

BLUES. Blues, always popular in Northern Kentucky, is an African American folk music based on a simple, repetitive musical structure consisting of a three-line, AAB, poetic form. It is a musical predecessor to **jazz**. The vocal technique of blues comes from the field-holler, call-and-response pattern found in the work songs of former slaves and poor laborers of the South, mixed with contrasting European influence. The term *blues* is also associated with a frame of mind, with conveying a personal feeling in a harmonic progression, typically via a 12-bar musical structure. The blues notes are commonly bent or slurred by way of a slight drop of pitch on the third, fifth, or seventh tone of the major scale.

Blues styles are usually based on their geographic origin. There are Mississippi Delta blues, Chicago blues, New Orleans blues, Texas blues, West Coast blues, and so forth. In *Going to Cincinnati,* author Steven Tracy asserts that the Cincinnati region does not have a specific style associated with its early blues music, as the region's **African Americans** migrated from many different parts of the South, via the Ohio River and various southern railroads. Ohio's free-state status in antebellum days, along with its proximity to the South, further attracted African Americans. Although no specific homegrown style developed for the region, a burgeoning blues landscape emerged that leaned toward the southern jugbands style of the blues. Some of the minstrel and **ragtime** musical styles, preceding the birth of the blues, lingered in the early Cincinnati blues sound.

Cincinnati had a place in early blues, however. W. C. Handy's first blues song, "Memphis Blues," was printed by Otto Zimmerman & Son in Cincinnati in 1912 (later, Zimmerman moved to Newport). Cincinnati-born Mamie Smith (1883–1946) was one of the first singers to record the revolutionary "Crazy Blues" in 1920, in a vaudeville blues style.

An early-recorded song, "Newport Blues," performed by the Cincinnati Jug Band, referred to Kentucky's "wide-open" city of Newport, where the band frequently performed at parties. Brothers Bob and Walter Coleman, along with Sam Jones "Stovepipe No. 1," were the early members of the band. In 1936 the Cincinnati Jug Band recorded "I'm Going to Cincinnati," which was a blues account of the local red-light district, which centered on George St. in Cincinnati during the early blues era. Sam Jones and David Crocket paired as King David's Jug Band in another example of this early Cincinnati blues style.

Blues was performed during the early days in Cincinnati by local pianist Jesse James (later, in the 1950s, a Northern Kentucky resident) and pianist Leroy Carr of Indianapolis. Blues pianists Walter Davis and Roosevelt Sykes, both of St. Louis, recorded at Cincinnati's Sinton Hotel in 1930. During this period, the Cincinnati blues street musicians were songsters attempting to please both white and black crowds, with a mixture of rural and urban musical styles.

The modern blues sound emerged in the 1940s with the rise of independent recording studios such as King Records in Cincinnati, and with the use of the electric guitar. The accelerated migration of African Americans from the South to the North resulted in the blending of an urban blues sound with its down-home roots. Known as the Boogie Man, renowned blues singer, guitarist, and Grammy award winner John Lee Hooker (1917–2001) worked in a Walnut Hills, Ohio, factory while performing at tri-state house parties and blues dances in the 1940s. He also sang with gospel groups in Cincinnati and, between 1949 and 1953, recorded for the innovative King Records. Hooker integrated boogie-woogie and swing rhythms into his raw, percussive riff-based guitar technique and passionate singing approach. Hooker's recording of "Boogie Chillun" in the 1950s influenced the new rhythm-and-blues era.

An electric-guitar blues specialist and vocalist with a more refined, smooth style, Lonnie Johnson (1889–1970), performed locally in the late 1940s and early 1950s and recorded hits such as "Pleasing You" and "Tomorrow Night" for King Records. Johnson also played the piano, the violin, the harmonica, and the kazoo. He backed jazz artists such as Duke Ellington and Louis Armstrong before arriving at King Records. He performed on a regular basis at the 333 Club in Newport.

During the early 1950s, radio and the major record companies began to support blues along with rhythm and blues, which soon gave way to rock and roll. The growing popularity of amplified guitars and harmonicas, as evidenced by artists such as Muddy Waters and B. B. King, drastically changed the blues style. The unique sound of these artists modernized popular music, providing the essentials for subsequent genres such as Soul and Rock in the 1960s.

Randy McNutt's *Guitar Towns* identifies an evolving Cincinnati sound that emerged in the late 1950s from the tri-state musical mixture of blues, rhythm and blues, country, and pop to create a unique blues-rock. Nationally during the 1960s, blues influenced both soul music and psychedelic blues. Legendary James Brown's million-seller "Papa's Got a Brand New Bag" (1965) was an example of the soul sound recorded at King Records in Cincinnati.

Because popular music of the 1970s was significantly influenced by the blues, an increased interest in the roots of the genre and its older blues musicians ensued. Examples included Northern Kentucky blues artists such as Albert Washington (a Newport resident in his youth), a blues singer and instrumentalist; James "Pigmeat" Jarrett (also a Newport resident in his youth), a pianist; and Covington-born Ed Conley, a backup bassist. Washington recorded for local King Records and Fraternity Records and performed regularly for local tri-state audiences in the 1960s, 1970s, and 1980s. Jarrett grew up in Newport and Cincinnati hearing blues and ragtime. He played the piano on the *Island Queen* steamer and later performed blues locally in the 1980s, after recording for Cincinnati blues scholar and musician Steven C. Tracy. Conley backed many famous artists at King Records, including James Brown.

Another Cincinnati blues artist specializing in boogie-woogie piano was Big Joe Duskin, who learned from the earlier blues pianists performing in Cincinnati, such as Leroy Carr, Roosevelt Sykes, Fats Waller, and the local pianist Jesse James. Duskin performed locally during the blues renaissance of the early 1970s at clubs in Cincinnati's Mount Adams and for university crowds in the Clifton neighborhood, and also later with Albert Washington. Duskin appeared on local television broadcasts with hosts such as **Nick Clooney**. He found international fame traveling and performing in Europe in the 1980s. In 2004 Duskin performed at the Southgate House in Newport.

Longtime area resident Bob "H-Bomb" Ferguson, attracted to Cincinnati to record for King Records in the late 1950s, performed at tri-state venues such as Covington's Winter Blues Fest at **Main Strasse** in 2006. Known for his flamboyant shouting "rhythm and blues" performances in which he wore different-colored wild wigs, Ferguson also became internationally known; he performed in Holland at Blues Estaffette '88 in 1988. He played the piano for some of his performances but usually was backed by a "rhythm and blues" band. He died in November 2006.

Lucille's Blues Club at 3715 Winston Ave., in the Latonia section of Covington, opened in 1994, dedicated exclusively to blues. Local, regional, and national blues artists performed there, including legendary Carl Weathersby. Although Lucille's Blues Club closed circa 2002, the Southgate House in Newport and Chez Nora in Covington offer an eclectic blend of music including blues. Both "H-Bomb" Ferguson and James "Pigmeat" Jarrett have played at the Mansion Hill Tavern in Newport, a well-known blues spot for 20 years.

A century after its creation, the blues still reflects a down-home cultural feel, despite its urbanized development and growing international popularity. Blues remains essentially folk songs that tell stories focusing on intimate personal relationships, usually sung solo in a first-person style. Loyal audiences of all cultural backgrounds are often emotionally inspired with a sense of life-affirming unity. Blues has influenced not only jazz, but also country, rhythm and blues, rock, and hip hop (rap) musical styles.

Cohen, Ronald D., ed. *Alan Lomax: Selected Writings, 1934–1997.* New York: Routledge, 2003.

Cohn, Lawrence. *Nothing but the Blues.* New York: Abbeville Press, 1993.

McNutt, Randy. *Guitar Towns: A Journey to the Crossroads of Rock 'n' Roll.* Bloomington: Indiana Univ. Press, 2002.

Ruppli, Michael. *The King Labels: A Discography.* Westport, Conn.: Greenwood Press, 1985.

Russell, Tony. *The Blues—From Robert Johnson to Robert Cray.* New York: Schirmer Books, 1997.

Sonnier, Austin, Jr. *Guide to the Blues: History, Who's Who, Research Sources.* Westport, Conn.: Greenwood Press, 1994.

Tracy, Steven C. *Going to Cincinnati: A History of the Blues in the Queen City.* Urbana: Univ. of Illinois Press, 1993.

John Schlipp

BOATYARDS. Riverboat building was once a large industry in the Greater Cincinnati region. Small and large yards were located along the banks of the Ohio River, with the greatest concentration in Cincinnati's East End. This area (part of the City of Cincinnati today, along Eastern Ave.) was called Fulton, Ohio, in honor of the popular, if not the actual, inventor of the steamboat. The sounds of industry were heard by anyone who ventured near one of these yards. The ringing of the anvil, the roar of the forge, and the hum of the circular saw were noticeable blocks away as dozens of workers labored to fabricate new steamers and barges. Production rose and fell with the economy. Between 1817 and 1880, some 1,374 boats were built in yards near Cincinnati, according to the U.S. Census of 1880.

Some of these boats were built in Northern Kentucky. One of the first was the ***Missouri,*** launched in March 1819 at T. J. Palmer's yard in Newport. The *General Putnam* was launched from a boatyard near the mouth of the Licking River two months later. During the early 1850s, three ferryboats were completed in Newport for local service. Covington was active in the boat business as well. In 1853 the packet *Franklin Pierce* was completed for Red River trade. Some 20 years later, the hull for the U.S. snagboat *E.A. Woodruff* was completed in Covington, but the machinery was made and installed in Pittsburgh. Other boats built in these yards are listed in Captain Fred Way's *Packet Directory.*

The Covington Dry Dock, operated by S. W. Coflin, was likely the best equipped of the various Northern Kentucky yards. It was located along Second St., near the foot of Philadelphia St., in the West Side of Covington (see **West Side [Covington]**). It was particularly active in the 1880s and advertised that it would build steamboats and barges and repair and caulk them. Coflin used a stern-wheel towboat, the *Alex Montgomery,* as a harbor tug. This same boat also towed coal barges downriver from the Kanawha River in West Virginia.

Some Cincinnati boat builders lived in Kentucky. Burton Hazen (1807–1883) established a yard at Fulton in about 1838 but resided in Dayton, Ky., along the opposite shore of the Ohio River. He began to develop real estate near his house while managing his boat building business. Hazen eventually lost his boatyard, but he managed to keep his Kentucky home and lived in the Dayton-Bellevue community until his last days.

One of Hazen's sons-in-law, Charles Barnes, led a similar existence. He operated a riverboat engine-building business in downtown Cincinnati near the river but had a home in Dayton, Ky. Barnes was born in Louisville in 1836 and raised and educated in Cincinnati, attending St. John's School and Xavier College. He ran a bookstore in Newport from 1857 to 1870 but found steam engines more attractive and likely more profitable than the book trade. He had a machine shop on Second St. in Cincinnati and by 1910 moved it to Main St., also in Cincinnati. His firm built engines for many river steamers, including the second *Island Queen* (1925).

"Burton Hazen, an Early Cincinnati Steamboat Builder," *S and D Reflector* 38, no. 1 (March 2001): 12–13.

Way, Frederick Jr. *Way's Packet Directory, 1848–1994.* Athens: Ohio Univ. Press, 1994.

White, Robert J. "The Cincinnati Marine Railway," *QCH* 57, nos. 2–3 (Summer–Fall 1999): 69–83.

John H. White

BOBBY MACKEY'S MUSIC WORLD. The noted **country music** entertainment center Bobby Mackey's Music World is located at 44 Licking Pike in Wilder. The current building was preceded by one constructed about 1850, which served as a slaughterhouse and **meatpacking** plant in what was then called Finchtown. A well was dug in the basement of the building to collect the animal blood that accumulated during slaughtering. The packing plant closed down in the late 1800s. Local legend has it that occult groups began using the abandoned building and its well during their rituals. In 1896 the building became involved in one of the state's most spectacular murder trials. A young woman named **Pearl Bryan** was murdered by two young men. Her decapitated body was found less than two miles from the former slaughterhouse. Both men were hanged for their crime but refused to reveal the whereabouts of Bryan's head. Speculation abounded that the head had been used in an occult ritual and disposed of in the well of the old slaughterhouse. After the trial ended, the building remained empty for several years. It was eventually torn down and replaced with a roadhouse. During the 1920s the building became known as a speakeasy and a **gambling** joint.

In 1933 Ernest "Buck" Brady purchased the building and turned it into a popular nightclub called the Primrose. It had a restaurant and a casino that thrived during the 1930s and 1940s. The success of the club caught the attention of the **Cleveland Syndicate**, which at the time controlled activities in adjacent Newport. Individuals from the syndicate pressured Brady to sell the club, even threatening to end his life. Brady sold it, and it was renamed the Latin Quarter. It quickly became an entertainment hot spot in Northern Kentucky. The nightclub offered dining, dancing, floor shows, and a casino. During the early 1950s, the new club owners, including **Frank "Screw" Andrews**, were arrested several times on gambling charges. The club continued to flourish until 1961, when the citizens of Campbell Co. began a drive to rid the area of organized crime (see **Newport Reform Groups**). In the 1970s the building housed another nightclub, known as the Hard Rock Café. After several fatal shootings on the premises, the club was closed by police in 1977. In 1978 a well-known aspiring local country singer named Bobby Mackey purchased the building. He renovated it and turned it into a country western bar, equipped with a mechanical bucking bull and a stage for live performances. The bar began attracting a large crowd. Several strange occurrences were reported, and some people claimed that the club was haunted. The claim attracted national attention, with segments about the club appearing on television shows such as *Hard Copy, Geraldo, Sightings, Jerry Springer,* and *A Current Affair,* as well as on the Lifetime Channel (cable). The media attention influenced Bobby Mackey to make plans to tear down the building and construct a new club on adjacent property. The property that he purchased was rendered useless, however, by the sudden appearance of a six-inch-wide and 60-foot-deep fissure extending from the old slaughterhouse well to the middle of the adjacent property. Bobby Mackey's Music World continues to operate in its original building.

Franzen, Gene. "Country Western Club Spent Time as a Casino," *KE*, September 30, 2001, B1.

Hensley, Douglas. *Hell's Gate: Terror at Bobby Mackey's Music World.* Jacksonville, Fla.: Audio Books Plus, 1993.

Taylor, Troy. *No Rest for the Wicked: History and Hauntings of American Crime and Unsolved Mysteries.* Alton, Ill.: Whitechapel Productions Press, 2001.

Robin Caraway

BOGARDUS, CARL R., SR. (b. May 1, 1906, Warsaw, Ky.; d. December 16, 1992, Warsaw, Ky.). Physician, historian, and genealogist Carl Bogardus Sr. was the son of Oren Arthur and Nancy Ballard Bogardus. Arthur Bogardus operated the noted Bogardus Furniture Company in Warsaw, where Carl worked when he was a boy. Carl Bogardus attended public schools in Warsaw, graduating from Warsaw High School in 1924. He received his premedical education at Hanover College in Madison, Ind., and his MD degree from the University of Louisville School of Medicine in 1930. Bogardus served a 15-month general rotating internship at Gorgas Hospital in Ancon, Panama Canal Zone, and then was employed for three years as a full-time county health officer at Hyden in Leslie Co. Bogardus's work as Leslie Co.'s health officer took him by horseback to some of the most remote regions of the state. He soon became associated with the county's famed Frontier Nursing Service, and together he and the agency helped to improve dramatically the health conditions of the citizens they served.

In 1934 Bogardus left his work in the mountains and opened a general practice of medicine at Glencoe in Gallatin Co. One year later, in 1935, he moved to his hometown of Warsaw, where he engaged in the general practice of medicine for three years. In 1938 Dr. Bogardus moved to Austin, Ind., where he practiced general medicine for the next 39 years, 1938–1977. While in Indiana he continued working at his hobby of local and family history and found time to write and publish many books, booklets, and newspaper articles. In the early 1970s, he began limiting his medical practice to office work and spent much time traveling the world and researching the history of his hometown of Warsaw and the genealogy associated with the town. Bogardus retired to Warsaw in 1977 and in 1978 built a stately home overlooking the Ohio River. Since the days of his youth, when he had gazed with awe out the windows of his father's furniture factory at the comings and goings of the traffic on the Ohio River, Bogardus had had a deep fascination and love for rivers and their lore. His return to Warsaw allowed him to pursue this attraction, and he plunged headlong into chronicling the history of the Ohio River and its system of waterways and collecting memorabilia about it. He continued his local historical and genealogical writings and became the founder and president of the Gallatin Co. Historical Society. As its president he oversaw the restoration of the historic Hawkins-Kirby House, the site of the society's meetings. Bogardus was a member of the Warsaw Lions Club, the Warsaw chapter of the Sons of the American Revolution, and many other historical and genealogical societies. During the final years of his life, he was blind, but he continued to write by dictating into a tape recorder, from which his wife, Sue McDarment Bogardus, transcribed his writings to paper. Bogardus's extensive collection of books, photographs, genealogical research, and articles about rivers, along with his own publications, were donated in 1991 to **Northern Kentucky University** at Highland Heights and are housed in the university's archives. Researchers of local history and genealogy also still use the materials that remain at his home in Warsaw. Bogardus died after a brief illness in 1992, at age 86. His body was cremated and his ashes were buried in the Warsaw Cemetery. His wife Sue, who faithfully cared for him after he became blind, survived him. A manuscript entitled "The Story of Gallatin County," which Bogardus had nearly completed, was organized, edited, and published as a book in 2003.

Bogardus, Carl R., Sr. *The Story of Gallatin County.* Ed. James C. Claypool. Privately printed, 2003.

"Dr. Carl R. Bogardus." *S and D Reflector* 30, no. 4 (March 1993): 6.

James C. Claypool

BOONE, DANIEL (b. November 2, 1734, Berks Co., Pa.; d. September 26, 1820, Missouri.). Daniel Boone, Indian fighter and pioneer settler, was the sixth of 11 children born to Quakers Squire and Sarah Morgan Boone. The family moved to the Yadkin Valley of North Carolina in 1751 or 1752. Boone married Rebecca Bryan on August 14, 1756, and they lived in the Yadkin Valley along Sugar Tree Creek for 10 years. He first entered what later became Kentucky in fall 1767 as part of a hunting expedition with his brother Squire and another hunter. On Daniel Boone's next visit to the region in 1769, he caught sight of the Bluegrass region from Pilot Knob or Pilot View.

The first trip Boone made into the Northern Kentucky region was not by choice. He and his brother-in-law, John Stuart, were captured by a group of Shawnee warriors in December 1769 after ignoring a warning from the Shawnee leader, Captain Will, to leave Kentucky and return home. The Shawnees took Boone and Stuart north from Station Camp Creek along the Kentucky River toward the Shawnee towns across the Ohio River. One night, as the group made camp near present-day Maysville, both captives acquired guns and ran to a nearby cane break to hide. After the Shawnees gave up on finding the two men, Boone and Stuart rejoined their hunting party.

During summer 1770 Boone explored the central and northern portion of Kentucky alone. **Buffalo traces** served as his trails much of the time, and he made a stop at **Big Bone Lick** in modern-day Boone Co., where he saw many large fossils of mammoths. He also visited the Upper and Lower Blue Licks. In January 1778 Boone, along with 30 other men, made a trip to **Blue Licks** in order to procure salt for the settlers' survival at Fort Boonesborough. Again Boone was captured by Shawnee warriors, this time under the command of Blackfish and two Frenchmen working as agents of the British in the **Revolutionary War**. In February 1778 Boone, who was a captain in the colonial forces, and the other captives were marched across the Ohio River to the Shawnee towns at Chillicothe on the Little Miami River. Boone had negotiated the postponement of an attack on Boonesborough as well as the survival of the men in his party. After the adoption of many of the men, including Boone, and the transfer of others to the British at Detroit, Boone managed to escape, four and a half months into his captivity. He returned to Kentucky as quickly as he could to warn the settlers at Boonesborough of an impending attack. His actions throughout his capture and the later siege of Fort Boonesborough led to a court-martial, but he was acquitted of all charges and promoted to major.

After the Virginia legislature divided Kentucky into three counties in 1780, Boone served as sheriff, coroner, and county lieutenant-colonel for Fayette Co. which included Northern Kentucky. He was also a county representative to the Virginia State Assembly, lieutenant-colonel in the militia, and deputy surveyor. When an allied force of British and American Indians attacked Bryants Station in August 1782, Boone commanded one of the three divisions that followed the retreating attackers toward Blue Licks. As the group approached the ravines Boone knew so well, he sensed a trap. He counseled the officer in charge to wait for reinforcements to arrive, but a hasty decision led the settlers across the river and into the anticipated ambush. The Americans suffered heavy casualties before their retreat, and among those killed was Boone's son Israel.

In 1783 Boone moved his family to Limestone (now Maysville), where he opened a store and a tavern. His tavern provided meals and boarding for travelers, and he sold supplies to new immigrants from his store. Limestone was an important port along the Ohio River during the settlement period. Boone owned a warehouse and wharf along the river where goods could be loaded and unloaded. He also worked for the Virginia government, supplying Indian prisoners transferred through the area. Much of his trade involved locally produced whiskey, skins, furs, and ginseng roots. He also earned a reputation as a good horse trader; he made a steady profit from selling horses raised in Kentucky to customers east of the mountains. At Limestone, Boone was a community leader: he directed the layout of a road to Lexington in 1783, and he was made a trustee when Limestone was incorporated as Maysville in 1786. This period of his life was the most prosperous. He owned several slaves who were used as servants in the tavern.

Boone also worked as a surveyor and had a good business, but because he did not regularly follow through with the legal process of land registration, many of the claims he surveyed later ended up in court. Much of the land Boone acquired in Kentucky was lost through lawsuits. In 1789 he moved his family to Point Pleasant, Va., but the family returned in 1795, and Boone spent a period of time as a hunter and farmer on land owned by his son Daniel Morgan Boone near Blue Licks. In 1798, the year Boone was honored by the naming of a Kentucky county for him, he moved again, to the mouth of the Little Sandy River. He also lost more than 10,000 acres of land, when the sheriffs of Mason and Clark counties sold it for unpaid back taxes.

Boone left Kentucky for Missouri in September 1799. It is reported that when someone in Cincinnati asked him why he was leaving Kentucky, Boone responded, "Too crowded—I want more elbow-room." He died in Missouri in 1820 and was buried in the Marysville Cemetery at Defiance, Mo. His and Rebecca Boone's remains were reinterred at Frankfort Cemetery in Frankfort, Ky., on September 13, 1845.

Faragher, John Mack. *Daniel Boone: The Life and Legend of an American Pioneer.* New York: Henry Holt, 1992.

Kleber, John E. ed. *The Kentucky Encyclopedia.* Lexington: Univ. Press of Kentucky, 1992.

Lofaro, Michael A. *Daniel Boone: An American Life.* Lexington: Univ. Press of Kentucky, 2003.

Andrea Watkins

BOONE, JACOB (b. August 15, 1754, Berks Co., Pa.; d. May 4, 1827, Maysville. Ky.). Jacob Boone, an early settler and official of Maysville, was the son of Joseph Boone II and Elizabeth Warren Boone. During the **Revolutionary War**, he fought in Capt. John Bishop's Company, the 5th Battalion of the Pennsylvania Militia, from 1777 to 1778. Perhaps the reason he left the militia after one year was to be with his wife, Mary DeHart, whom he married at the time of the Revolution. It is clear that his loyalty to the colonies did not waver, since Pennsylvania records show that he paid a supply tax on behalf of the militia in 1782.

Several sources suggest that by fall 1785 **Daniel Boone**, Jacob's second cousin, visited his Pennsylvania relatives and persuaded Jacob and his brothers Thomas and Ovid to try their fortunes in Kentucky. The brothers sold their Pennsylvania property that fall and made their way down the Monongahela River to the mouth of the Sewickley River, downriver but northwest of Fort Pitt, where they stopped for the winter and built a boat. In spring 1786 they continued toward Limestone (Maysville), Ky., where the group arrived without incident on May 11.

Jacob soon put himself to good use within the community. He served as the interpreter between Col. Benjamin Logan and Indian warriors and chiefs during a conference on prisoner exchange on August 20, 1787. At that summit, Logan instructed the Indians to turn over any white prisoners in the future directly to Jacob Boone. As quartermaster of the militia throughout the conflict with the Indians, Jacob also provided grain for Gen. Anthony Wayne's and Gen. Arthur St. Clair's troops.

Concurrent with their negotiations and struggles with the Indian population, the people of Limestone were trying to persuade the Virginia General Assembly to create a separate county (which became Mason Co.) from Bourbon Co. After the first petition was rejected, second and third petitions were sent, and Jacob's signature appears on the latter two. On December 11, 1787, the Virginia assembly officially recognized the town of Limestone (still in Bourbon Co.) and named Jacob Boone, Daniel Boone, Henry Lee, Arthur Fox, Thomas Brooks, and George Mefford as its first trustees. As part of their mandate, the trustees (or their appointees) were to lay out the town into lots to be sold at public auction, and the Boones—Jacob, Thomas, Ovid, and Daniel—had the honor of so doing.

In addition to his official duties, Jacob Boone ran a tavern on Front St. in Maysville, which Daniel Boone allegedly helped to construct. In 1820 Maysville's first jail was built as an annex to the tavern. From 1808 onward, Jacob also operated one of the many **ferries** on the Ohio River at Maysville. In 1827 Jacob Boone died and was buried at the Pioneer Cemetery in Maysville. His headstone remains intact.

Clift, G. Glenn. *History of Maysville and Mason County.* Lexington, Ky.: Transylvania Publishing, 1936.

Spraker, Hazel Atterbury. *The Boone Family: A Genealogical History of George and Mary Boone Who Came to America in 1717.* Baltimore: Genealogical Publishing, 1974.

Amber L. Benson

BOONE BLOCK. The historic three-story brick building known as the Boone Block is located on the east side of Scott St., between Fourth and Fifth Sts., in Covington. It does not occupy the entire city block, as its name suggests. Anthony D. Bullock had the structure built in 1872, and his initials (ADB) are intertwined on a stone tablet above the original entrance. Bullock also had built the Vernon Manor Hotel in Cincinnati. His family owned and operated the Bullock Electric Company in Norwood, Ohio. For many years the Boone Block held the offices of some of Kenton Co.'s most successful lawyers, judges, and politicians. Included were governors **John White Stevenson** (1867–1871) and **William Goebel** (1900); Lieutenant Governor **James W. Bryan**; judges **William E. Arthur**, **Walter W. Cleary**, **John Menzies**, **James J. O'Hara**, **Michael T. Shine**, and **James Pryor Tarvin**; and politician **John G. Carlisle**. The Kenton Co. **Democratic Party** also had its headquarters in the building, along with the fraternal organizations the Knights of Pythias and the Bull Moose Club. In the early 1900s, many of the building's tenants moved to more convenient locations in Covington along Madison Ave. and Pike St., and vacancies resulted. In 1914 the Boone Block was extensively remodeled into commercial space on the first floor and apartments on the second and third. The remodeling had only limited success in filling the vacancies; further remodeling was done in 1926, but the problem persisted. Today, several businesses are located on the first floor, but the upper floors are unoccupied.

"A. D. Bullock has Completed Building on Scott St., between Fourth and Fifth Sts." *CJ*, November 9, 1872, 3.

"Building Notes," *KP*, November 3, 1914, 4.

"Covington K. of P. to Have New Home," *KP*, January 18, 1911, 3.

"Historic Boone Block Soon to Change," *KP*, July 29, 1914, 4.

Jack Wessling

BOONE CO. Long before recorded history, prehistoric cultures of **American Indians**, dating back to 10,000 B.C., lived in the area that is now Boone Co. All along the county's 39-mile Ohio River shoreline, from the mouth of Dry Creek, which separates Boone Co. from Kenton Co., to Big Bone Creek, which separates Boone Co. from Gallatin Co., there is documented archaeological evidence of all four of the major temporal prehistoric native traditions: Paleo Indian, Archaic, Woodland, and Late Prehistoric. It was a logical and practical choice for American Indians to settle in the region. The Ohio River provided water and game and afforded a means for transportation, and the fertile bottomlands offered native vegetation for food, basket-making, weaving, bedding, attracting game, and later, farming opportunities. Eons of glacial events had left behind creek and river cobbles that provided materials for stone tools and other implements. The upper and inland hardwood forests above the separate riverine terraces provided nuts, berries, forage, fuel, and cover. The later American Indians utilized the abundant shell, limestone, and clay for the manufacture of pottery and other ceramic items. The lush grazing and browsing resources and the presence of mineral springs and salt licks in the area guaranteed an ever-available meat source.

As far back as prehistoric times, there were three major navigational landmarks on the Ohio River in the region, and each was identified long before the river was named by whites or the Commonwealth of Kentucky was created. Of these three, the Falls of the Ohio, **Big Bone Lick**, and Split Rock (see **Split Rock Conservation Park**), the latter two are in present Boone Co. Split Rock is located along the bank at the Ohio River's 500-mile marker and is a unique natural history feature. It is a rare freestanding glacial conglomerate formation, which was well known to prehistoric and historical travelers alike. Big Bone Lick is the most famous depository of Pleistocene vertebrate megafauna fossil remains in North America. President Thomas Jefferson (1801–1809) is considered the father of vertebrate paleontology, and Big Bone Lick is regarded as its home. Six separate once-unknown Pleistocene species have been discovered there. In the late 1700s, and throughout the 20th century, world-renowned naturalists and scientists arrived to study specimens from Big Bone Lick. Early Kentucky explorers, frontiersmen, and military leaders such as George Rogers Clark, **Daniel Boone**, **Simon Kenton**, and others went to the Big Bone Lick area during the course of their adventures, not necessarily collecting specimens, but knowing and noting what was there. The first doc-

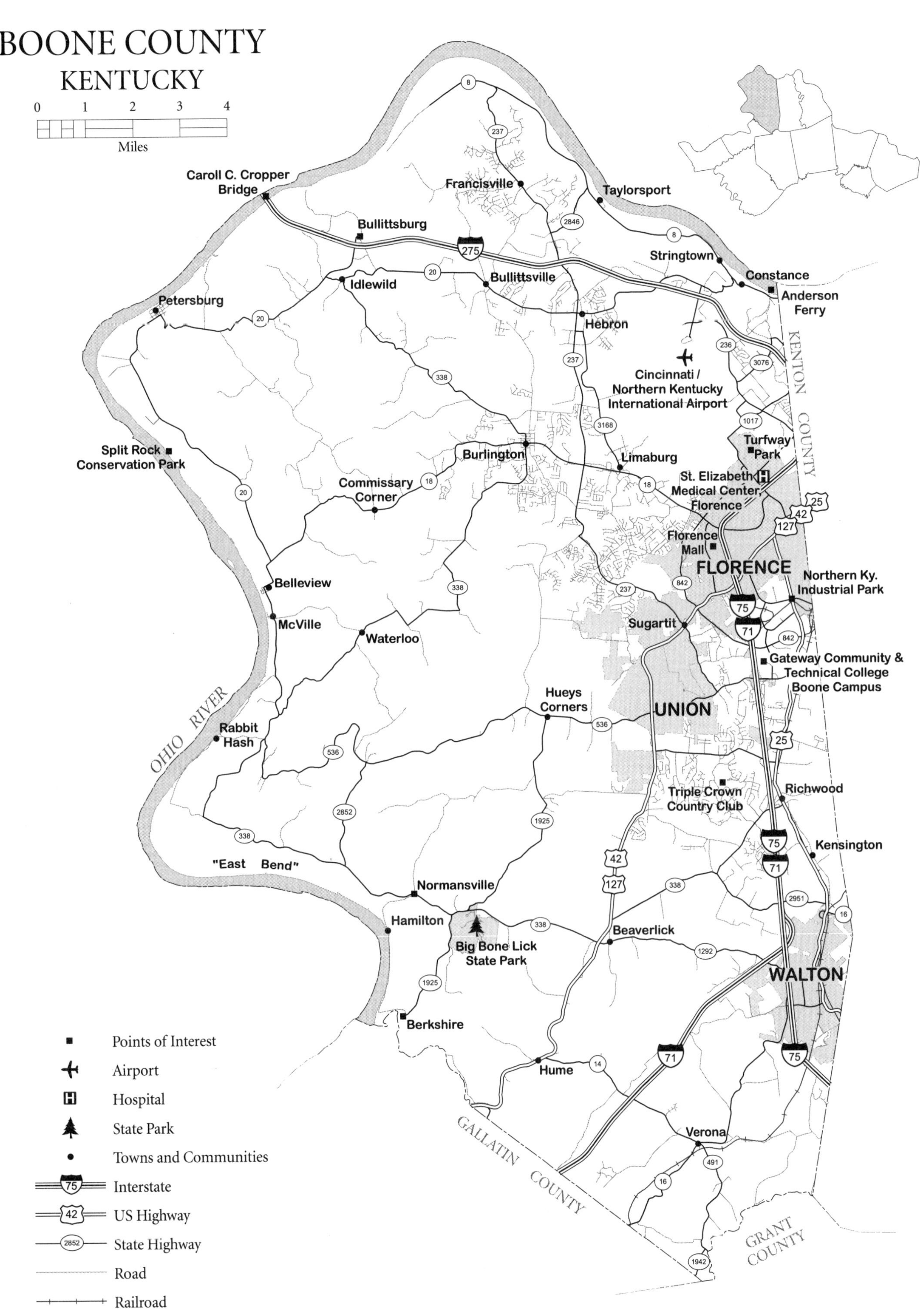
BOONE COUNTY
KENTUCKY
0 1 2 3 4
Miles
Caroll C. Cropper Bridge
Francisville
Taylorsport
Bullittsburg
Stringtown
Constance
Anderson Ferry
Idlewild
Bullittsville
Petersburg
Hebron
Cincinnati / Northern Kentucky International Airport
KENTON COUNTY
Turfway Park
Limaburg
Split Rock Conservation Park
Burlington
St. Elizabeth Medical Center, Florence
Commissary Corner
Florence Mall
FLORENCE
Northern Ky. Industrial Park
Belleview
Sugartit
McVille
Waterloo
Gateway Community & Technical College Boone Campus
Hueys Corners
UNION
OHIO RIVER
Rabbit Hash
Richwood
Triple Crown Country Club
Kensington
"East Bend"
Normansville
Hamilton
Beaverlick
Big Bone Lick State Park
WALTON
Berkshire
Hume
Verona
GALLATIN COUNTY
GRANT COUNTY
8
237
2846
275
20
236
3076
338
1017
3168
18
25
42
127
842
75
71
536
2852
1925
2951
16
1292
14
491
1942
Points of Interest
Airport
Hospital
State Park
Towns and Communities
Interstate
US Highway
State Highway
Road
Railroad

umented visit to Boone Co. was in 1739 by Charles Le Moyne, the second Baron de Longueuil, who was the commander of a French Canadian military expedition in the Mississippi River Valley. It was this expedition that gave credit to Longueuil for the formal discovery of Big Bone Lick.

The Kentucky legislature established Boone Co. on December 13, 1798, by an act stating "that from and after the first day of June next . . . [there] shall be one distinct county, and called and known by the name of Boone." Named in honor of Daniel Boone, Boone Co. officially became the 13th of Kentucky's 120 counties on June 1, 1799. The total population in the county at the time was 1,500.

The first permanent settlement in Boone Co. was Tanner's Station, located on a high terrace above the Ohio River. It was founded in 1789 by John Tanner, a Baptist preacher from North Carolina. Renamed Petersburg in 1814, the settlement was established right on top of two separate prehistoric Fort Ancient American Indian village cultural sites. The site was chosen wisely by all those who settled there: Petersburg has never flooded, unlike many of the other Boone Co. river communities. Numbered among those who arrived during the pioneer settlement era in Boone Co. was a group of German Lutheran pioneers from Madison Co., Va., who settled in the east-central portion of the county in 1805. They established the **Hopeful Lutheran Church** as the centerpiece of their settlement. Other persons of German heritage followed and settled nearby in the present-day area of Florence.

On June 17, 1799, the first Boone Co. court officially met in a private home. The justices, duly sworn in by the county sheriff, attended to their first order of business, to qualify and appoint a clerk and determine a location for the county seat of government and a place to hold court and erect public buildings. The currently unincorporated town of Burlington was chosen for the county seat. It was originally named Craig's Camp; its name was later changed to Wilmington, and then in 1816 to Burlington. The first courthouse was a log structure built in 1801. A more stately and formal-looking seat of county government was built in 1817, replacing the first courthouse. After undergoing several renovations over the following 80 years, the 1817 courthouse was replaced by the 1889 structure, which is in use today and is affectionately known as "the Old Courthouse." It is flanked by the newer Boone Co. Administration Building and the recently completed Federal-style Justice Center, while still holding on to its historic place of honor as the focal point of government in Boone Co.

The Ohio River, as the main transportation corridor into the area, determined the settlement patterns of Boone Co. Families with all their possessions on a flatboat migrated downriver to their intended destinations. However, unintended destinations with unplanned and unexpected outcomes also account for some of Boone Co.'s pioneer population. Most of the early arrivals settled along the river and up its many tributaries, seeking out the most suitable sites for their subsistence needs. Just as the American Indians had done before them, they looked for fertile cropland, water sources, plentiful game, and good hunting and fishing. They avoided unhealthy swampy ground and its accompanying miasma that was believed to cause the malarial symptoms of the ague. The desirable real estate on which to erect buildings was the high and dry land with good air circulation.

Early pioneers also arrived in Boone Co. from the southern regions of Kentucky via the Cumberland Gap and the Wilderness Trail. Many of the early roads in the county were merely old buffalo traces or trails following creeks, rivers, and ridges, and contemporary roads throughout the county tend to follow the same routes.

Boone Co.'s early settlers were generally yeoman farmers. They improved their land and raised enough crops to sustain their family; they also usually had some left over for sale or barter. Farm produce was transported to the river, where it was loaded onto flatboats and later steamboats or ferried across the river to the markets to the North awaiting it. Manufactured goods came to the settlements in reverse manner. Boone Co. remained predominately agricultural and rural for a century and a half; beginning before the **Civil War**, tobacco was the main cash crop sustaining the county's farm families. Even commercial operations such as sawmills, gristmills, or blacksmith shops basically served the agricultural community. It was not until the mid-20th century that the focus in the county shifted from agriculture to manufacturing, industrial, and service-based businesses. The metamorphosis of the county's economic base began during the 1940s with the opening of the **Cincinnati/Northern Kentucky International Airport** and continued with the building of the major highway systems (I-75, I-71, and I-275), which started in the early 1960s. **Florence Mall**, opened in 1976, shifted the region's commercial center to Boone Co., which also became home to many industries.

During the Civil War, families in the county often held split allegiances. Boone Co. proudly claimed military leaders and enlistees in each of the two armies. There were, however, only two minor military skirmishes in the county, one in the town of Florence and one at **Snow's Pond** in Walton. The Confederate general **John Hunt Morgan**'s escape route through Boone Co. from a federal penitentiary in Columbus, Ohio, has remained a very proud topic among county residents over the years, revealing that loyalties to the South were quite strong in the county.

After the war, Boone Co. continued its agrarian tradition. Family farms and farming endeavors predominated, and tobacco continued to be the main cash crop. But when the automobile made transportation less time-consuming and more practical, people began to migrate from the farm to the city, for hourly-wage jobs and regular employment. The turn of the 20th century witnessed a larger percentage of Boone Countians finding their employment outside the family farm, and there was a resulting loss of next-generation farmers. Until the **Great Depression**, the elders continued the agricultural tradition as long as they were physically able. But by the 1930s , poverty and a subsistence strategy prevailed. Those who could do so depended on the farm for a livelihood. Others took advantage of the various New Deal opportunities and social programs in order to get by. At the onset of **World War II**, the rural landscape changed forever. The men went to war and the women went to work in factories for the war effort. The exodus from the family farm began and was never reversed.

The second half of the 20th century continued in this vein as Boone Co. became less and less agricultural. Today, only a handful of family farms are operating in the county, and the tobacco settlement to end tobacco production is threatening the existence of the part-time farmers. The only lucrative return on farmers' land now is gained by selling it to developers. Every day, Boone Co. farms are purchased, subdivided, and developed. That is why Boone Co.'s current claim to fame is its status as one of the two fastest-growing counties in the state, in terms of population. In 2000 Boone Co. had a population of 85,991; in 2006 the population was estimated at 110,080, making it the second-most-populous county in Northern Kentucky.

Boone Co. Historic Preservation Review Board. *Historic Structures of Boone County, Kentucky*. Burlington, Ky.: Boone Co. Historic Preservation Review Board, 2002.

U.S. Census Bureau. www.census.gov/ (accessed December 31, 2007).

Warner, Jennifer S. *Boone County: From Mastodons to the Millennium*. Burlington, Ky.: Boone Co. Bicentennial Book Committee, 1998.

Don Clare

BOONE CO. HIGH SCHOOL. The campus of Boone Co. High School (BCHS) in Florence was constructed in 1954 along Ky. Rt. 18, the Burlington Pk., to consolidate the districts of **Hebron High School**, **Burlington High School**, New Haven High School, and **Florence High School**. The mascot selected by the first senior class at BCHS was Rebels, from the movie *Rebel without a Cause,* starring James Dean.

The 1980s and 1990s were significant years for the school's student body, as they became competitive and recognized across the state for their developing athletic teams, for their outstanding bands, and for exceeding state and national test scores. The school was also noted for producing numerous Commonwealth Diploma recipients (24 in one year); for advanced programs in calculus, Spanish, French, history, chemistry, and English; and for a professional staff who exhibited pride and loyalty toward their school.

BCHS has produced three professional football players. Irv Goode (1958) played for the St. Louis Cardinals and the Super Bowl champion Miami Dolphins; John Shannon (1983) was a University of Kentucky lineman who played for the Super Bowl champion Chicago Bears and the San Francisco 49ers; and All-Pro Most Valuable Player **Shaun Alexander** (1996) was University of Alabama All-American running back, currently plays for the Washington Redskins, and was designated the NFL's Most Valuable Player in 2005. In addition, three baseball players were drafted by major league baseball teams. In the early 1970s, the Pittsburgh Pirates signed Scott Johnson, who had pitched for BCHS for three years before graduating from Millersburg Military Institute (1970); Tony Runion (1990) was drafted by the Cleveland Indians from Duke University; and the San Francisco Giants signed Chad Dillion (1994). Songwriter and entertainer **Adrian Belew** graduated from BCHS in 1967.

The staff and students of BCHS will long remember the terrible band-room fire during the 1980s. They can also reminisce about when the Rebel wrestling team won the state championship, when John Alford was featured in *Sports Illustrated,* and when the undefeated (14-0) football team was ranked in the nation's top 20 by *USA Today.*

The rich tradition of the school's influence continues. BCHS was the first high school in the state to offer computer classes and to initiate use of walkie-talkies for custodial and administrative staff members. The landscaping at BCHS was developed and maintained by the vocational agriculture classes, making for a strong sense of pride and loyalty among those associated with the high school as it became a well-manicured and beautifully landscaped campus. BCHS was renovated in 1983–1984.

"Adrian Belew Rediscovers Boone High Roots," *CP,* June 26, 1997, Timeout sec., 31.
Boone Co. High School Records, Boone Co. High School, Florence, Ky.
"Boone to Dedicate Addition," *KP,* November 23, 1985, 2K.
"Reporter Reviews New Boone School and Program," *Northern Kentucky News,* September 17, 1954, 7.

William Baker

BOONE CONSERVANCY. The Boone Conservancy in Boone Co. is a nonprofit organization dedicated to the creation of parks and the protection of land with unique or significant recreational, natural, scenic, historical, or cultural value. The conservancy is dedicated to the belief that planning for appropriate land conservation improves the quality of life and increases economic prosperity in Boone Co. An executive director and a board of directors that meet regularly govern the Boone Conservancy. It accepts property through various means, including donations, bargain sales, charitable remainder interest, and conservation easement. Established in 1999, the Boone Conservancy was the first such land-trust program in Northern Kentucky, but other local conservancies soon developed in Kenton and Campbell counties.

"Founder Now Leads Boone Conservancy," *KP,* February 24, 2005, 16A.
"Scarred Land to Be Reclaimed," *KE,* February 3, 2006, B3.
"Stewarts of the Land," *KP,* October 7, 2003, 4K.

William S. Bryant

BOONE CO. PUBLIC LIBRARY. Before 1974 residents of Boone Co. traveled to Covington or Cincinnati for library services. Beginning in the early 1940s, citizen groups tried to build public support to establish a full-service county public library. Each attempt met with failure until 1973, when a citizen's organization called ABLE (Association for Boone Library Encouragement) collected enough signatures to place the issue of a library tax on the ballot. On November 6, 1973, the voters of Boone Co. chose to support the tax and thereby established the Boone Co. Public Library District.

Ted Bushelman presided over the first meeting of the Boone Co. Public Library Board of Trustees on December 17, 1973. Central to the business of that meeting was discussion of how to build a facility for the new library; the first official action of the board was to apply for a state construction grant. By July 1974 temporary quarters had been found, negotiations for the site of the new library building were under way, and the first staff members were at work. On October 14, 1974, under the direction of Jane Smith, librarian, the Boone Co. Public Library opened its doors at 2 Girard St. in Florence, Ky. That day more than 180 patrons visited the library.

Work on the new library building proceeded according to schedule. After several months of meetings with architect Robert Ehmet Hayes, a final design was accepted, and ground was broken on July 17, 1975. Eleven months later, in June 1976, the temporary facility was closed and the Boone Co. Public Library moved to its new, permanent location at 7425 U.S. 42 in Florence.

In its first year at the new location, the library circulated more than 100,000 items. Children's programs filled quickly and waiting lists for the programs were long. By the early 1980s, circulation figures had doubled. The library provided full reference services, a full-time children's librarian, and expanding local history and genealogy collections. Popular new formats such as videos and audio books were also added to the offerings. In 1983 the library joined the Greater Cincinnati Library Consortium, providing Boone Co. residents with free access to about 30 area academic, public, and special libraries.

Like the rest of its rapidly growing county, the library struggled to keep pace with the needs created by the expanding population. The board began planning for additional facilities and services that would bring convenient library service to all county residents. With funds from a generous bequest provided by Mr. and Mrs. R. V. Lents, who were long-time library supporters, a site was purchased and plans were drawn for a branch library to serve the northern section of the county. On April 23, 1989, the Lents Branch Library opened in Hebron.

Soon thereafter, the library acquired a location in Walton to serve southern Boone Co. and construction of a second branch library began. At the same time, staff was busy converting the library's records into a computer-readable format in preparation for the planned automation of library services. Both projects reached their conclusion in the first half of 1994. On April 15 computers replaced the card catalog, and on June 25 county residents and officials dedicated the Walton Branch Library. In 1996 public Internet stations were added at all locations, thus updating and modernizing services and giving all library customers access to the worldwide information highway. A library Web page made it possible for patrons to "visit" the library via remote technology.

The Scheben Branch, dedicated on March 4, 2000, and the new Main Library in Burlington, dedicated on January 5, 2008, placed a new emphasis on the public library as a cultural and community center. From large multipurpose rooms to individual study rooms, toddler play areas to teen centers, Wi-Fi hotspots to art galleries, specially designed spaces invited patrons to visit often and stay longer. In a unique partnership, the library participated in the construction of a community center in Petersburg that included space for a small library. The Chapin Memorial Library, named for the local benefactor who endowed it, reopened in that space under the management of the library district on October 22, 2006.

Today the Boone Co. Public Library District serves a population of more than 100,000 residents from its six locations in Florence, Hebron, Union, Walton, Petersburg, and Burlington. Library collections offer more than 400,000 books, videos, DVDs, audiotapes, and CDs. Professional librarians answer hundreds of reference questions each day, and programs for children and adults attract thousands of participants each year. New information technologies offer improved access to greater stores of information. The Boone Co. Public Library District continues to grow in order to meet the needs of the fastest-growing county in the Northern Kentucky region.

"Annual Report of Public Libraries," Boone County Public Library District, 1974–2004.
Board of Trustees. Minutes. Boone Co. Public Library District, 1973–2005.
"Boone Library Looks Back on a Booming First Decade," *KP,* October 26, 1984, 9K.
"Celebrating an Anniversary—Boone County Library System Expands to Four Branches in Its 30 Years," *KP,* March 1, 2004, 4K.
"Library System Grows with Boone County," *KE,* December 26, 1998, B1.

Lucinda Brown

BOONE CO. SCHOOLS. Education in Boone Co. has come a long way since the county's first school was established at the foot of Banklick St. in Florence. That school's location was called Squirrel Hollow, because of the number of gray squirrels inhabiting it, according to the late A. M. Yealey, an educator and historian in Boone Co. during the first half of the 20th century.

Today the Boone Co. School District (BCSD), with an enrollment of 18,000 students, is the third-largest school district in Kentucky. With 4 high schools, 5 middle schools, 12 elementary schools, an Alternative Center, and a Day Treatment Care Unit, the BCSD is the fastest-growing school system in Kentucky; the county itself, with a population exceeding 100,000, is in the top 100 fastest-growing counties in the United States. The BCSD grew by 2,400 students over three years recently and is one of the largest employers in Boone Co., with more than 2,600 employees. The county has three major cities—Florence, Union, and Walton—and growth areas in Hebron and Burlington. The changing demographics in Boone Co., home to the **Cincinnati/Northern Kentucky International Airport** and several industrial parks, have included the transition from rural to suburban-urban, the influx of a diverse population, and an increase in industry and business.

Harvard University and the Wallace Foundation selected the BCSD along with other cutting-edge districts to participate in the Executive Leadership Program for Educators. Boone Co. school superintendent Bryan Blavatt and his dedicated leadership team focus on building knowledge and skills in three essential categories: systematic thinking and alignment; adaptive leadership and team building; and leadership for instructional improvement.

Dedication to a strong tradition of "Achieving Excellence Together" motivates faculty and staff to help students become lifelong learners, effective communicators, creative thinkers, and collaborative citizens. In partnership with all stakeholders, the leaders of the BCSD believe that all children can learn, and the district's leaders are dedicated to providing a challenging educational environment that allows each student to achieve his or her highest potential as a learner and a citizen.

The BCSD's standardized test scores are among the highest in the state and in the nation. Its schools have made gradual progress with academic performance as measured by the state accountability system, but they also want to be able to meet effectively the needs of the population as it increases in both size and diversity. To assure that academic progress does not stall, the district is proactively seeking new ways to enhance and assure success for all students. That goal is driven by excellent instructional staff, school personnel, students, and facilities and by strong parental involvement.

The BCSD is among only 16 percent of the nation's 15,573 public school districts recognized for demonstrating commitment to meet the needs and desires of both students and parents, and the district has also been recognized for the past 10 years with the prestigious public education award What Parents Want. The district was chosen by the Scientific Learning Corporation (SLC) as its first SLC Leadership Center. An SLC representative called the BCSD "a visionary educational center" and an "example for all others to follow."

The BCSD has instituted a variety of support programs to develop well-rounded young adults. With a strong districtwide emphasis on state-of-the-art technology/media labs, the BCSD incorporates extensive use of technology in and outside of the classroom and in all school and district data areas. Enrichment programs are offered for students at all levels, including advanced-placement courses in language arts, science, history, and mathematics. Career-oriented educational programs and vocational offerings are also available to students within the system. In addition to academics, strongly emphasized by the school system, students participate in extracurricular activities that include many sports, as well as a marching band, a jazz ensemble, a show choir, a student broadcasting system, a yearbook, language clubs, student government, academic and social clubs, and intramural and conference athletic competitions.

Boone Co. Schools Records, Boone Co. Schools, Florence, Ky.

Boone County Schools. www.boone.kyschools.us (accessed October 2, 2006).

"Boone County Schools—Trying to Keep Up with the Growth," *KP*, May 16, 2006, 1A, 8A.

Conrad, William. *The History of Boone County Schools*. Boone Co., Ky.: Boone Co. Community Education Council, 1982.

Laurie Walton

BOONE COUNTY JAMBOREE. The *Boone County Jamboree* (see **Country Music**) was a "barn dance" Saturday night radio series that originated in 1938 on Cincinnati's radio station WLW. It was later known as *Midwestern Hayride* and was broadcast on the NBC and ABC television networks in the 1950s. In the 1960s and the early 1970s, the series was syndicated on 41 television stations, in addition to the WLW regional television network (WLWT Cincinnati; WLWC Columbus, Ohio; WLWD Dayton, Ohio; and WLWI Indianapolis).

The *Boone County Jamboree* was patterned after the *Renfro Valley Barn Dance* in Kentucky, another WLW radio broadcast, which premiered in 1937. The *Boone County Jamboree* borrowed the name of Boone Co., in the 1930s a rural area just across the river from Cincinnati, where farming was a countywide career and way of life. A *Boone County Jamboree* music folio published in 1941 noted that the program's intent was to "radiate sincere friendliness; feature the simple, tuneful melodies of rural communities, southern mountains and the western plains—a program which would lighten the workaday cares of the great mass of people, both old and young, to many of whom modern dance did not appeal."

At the *Boone County Jamboree*'s peak, WLW claimed it had up to 100 performers to call on for the show. Merle Travis, Grandpa Jones, and the Delmore Brothers were among the most prominent of them. Other acts included the Boone County Buccaneers, Pa and Ma McCormick, Sunshine Sue and her Rangers, the Happy Valley Girls, Lulu Belle and Scotty, Curly Fox and Texas Ruby, and the Girls of the Golden West. Bonnie Lou (later known for her support on Ruth Lyon's *Fifty/Fifty Club* and the *Paul Dixon Show*, also on WLW television) joined the *Boone County Jamboree* in 1945, before it transitioned to television with the new name *Midwestern Hayride*. Northern Kentuckian **Kenny Price** (1931–1987) performed on the *Midwestern Hayride* from the late 1950s through its final days in the early 1970s.

During *Boone County Jamboree*'s early years, the "nation's station," WLW, broadcast the country music program to virtually all of rural North America via its 500,000-watt transmitter. It is no wonder, then, that, according to former *Billboard* staff member Bill Sachs, the *Boone County Jamboree* most likely achieved one of the longest successive runs of live performance bookings ever held by a single attraction by playing at 72 fairs during the late 1930s and early 1940s throughout Kentucky, Ohio, Indiana, West Virginia, Tennessee, Virginia, North Carolina, and Pennsylvania. By 1941 WLW reported that members of the *Boone County Jamboree* cast had made personal appearances at theaters, auditoriums, picnics, and state and county fairs before 1 million fans.

The WLW radio and television countrified broadcasts, such as the *Boone County Jamboree*, were probably the most effectual cultural introduction of Appalachian and country music to the world. They performed a mission similar to that of the later television shows *Grand Ole Opry* and *Hee Haw*. In 1941 WLW received the Peabody Award in recognition of its efforts in delivering country-targeted programming to rural listeners nationwide.

More than 50 years later, the image of this WLW program was revitalized with a 1997 alternative country recording entitled *Straight Outta Boone County: Cowboy Songs, Home Songs, Western Songs, Mountain Songs*. Contemporary musicians and singers not only pay homage to songs performed originally on one of country music's all-time great radio shows, but also include some tunes that were originally recorded by *Boone County Jamboree* artists at Cincinnati's legendary King Records.

"Before C&W and Bluegrass—In the '20s and '30s, Radio Discovers the Folksingers—The Mountain Tradition," *KP*, November 14, 2005, 4K.

Cincinnati Radio: The Nation Station (1921–1941). XSTAR Radio Network, 2002. A compact disc and booklet set.

Favorite Songs of the WLW Boone County Jamboree: Cowboy Songs, Home Songs, Western Songs, Mountain Songs. Chicago: M. M. Cole, 1941. A music score folio.

Kinsgbury, Paul, ed. *The Encyclopedia of Country Music*. New York: Oxford Univ. Press, 1998.

Perry, Dick. *Not Just a Sound: The Story of WLW*. Englewood Cliffs, N.J.: Prentice-Hall, 1971.

Sies, Luther F. *Encyclopedia of American Radio, 1920–1960*. Jefferson, N.C.: Jefferson, 2000.

John Schlipp

BOONE CO. WATER RESCUE. Boone Co. Water Rescue (BCWR), established in 1967 under the direction of the Boone Co. Civil Defense program, is a group of dedicated volunteers who work more than 12,000 hours annually in water-rescue activities. Currently a branch of the Boone Co. Emergency Management Services and administered on a not-for-profit basis by the Boone Co. Fiscal Court, the BCWR team is available 24 hours a day and 7 days a week to all governmental agencies. Founder Dale Appel started the squad after his best friend drowned in the Ohio River. Appel said he did not want other people to suffer through anything like he had—days of waiting for a drowned body to surface before it could be recovered.

Since its origin, the team has been based on members' diving abilities. Countless hours are spent training new divers and sharpening the skills of accomplished ones. Each diver not only earns the general diver certification but is trained under a public-safety diver program and as a search-and-rescue diver. The team also has ice-rescue capabilities. Basic ice-rescue classes are taught in the winter months by three certified dive and ice-rescue instructors to fire departments, police departments, and other rescue agencies. Kentucky-certified EMTs have been added to give emergency prehospital care and provide medical and trauma services on water and land. These professionals are crucial in maintaining a medically safe environment for divers during rescue, recovery, and training operations.

The most visible part of the team is its water-rescue units. General-purpose work and rescue boats are used for lakes and rivers. These boats are easily transported and can be dispersed throughout Northern Kentucky and beyond. But the pride of the water rescue units are boats 218 and 219 (boat 219 is essentially a floating ambulance, complete with a defibrillator). These two boats are fully equipped with state-of-the-art sonar, radar, and communications, dramatically increasing their capability and efficiency for any type of water rescue or recovery. On board every boat are an EMT, fire personnel, and rescue divers.

BCWR offers many services to the surrounding geographic area and to other states: water safety programs; boat patrols; evidence collection; vehicle, bus, and aircraft recovery; and victim recovery. No other governmental body in the region provides such an array of services for boaters. The team's capabilities include the use of the most sophisticated electronic equipment on the market, the side-scan sonar (from Marine Sonic Technology) and underwater cameras (from Fisher). The side-scan sonar not only reduces the risk to divers but has made recovery efforts faster. Systems include the ability to transmit (by wireless means) the video image and side-scan sonar imaging to other boats and land-based operations. Of course, after the object of the search is found in the water, the mission turns to recovery. BCWR divers use Exo-26s and SuperLites 17 (supplying surface air) with full communication and dive cameras that also transmit to the command center, boats, and dive supervisors for review. The primary goal continues to be the recovery of drowning victims as quickly as possible to bring closure to families suffering from the loss of a loved one.

Eigelbach, Kevin. "Funding of Water Rescue May End," *KP*, June 5, 2003, 1K.

Nancy J. Tretter

BOOTH MEMORIAL HOSPITAL. The William Booth Memorial Hospital began in 1914 at 165 E. Second St. (323 E. Second St. today) in what is now Covington's **Licking-Riverside and Ohio Riverside National Historic Districts**. It was owned and operated by the **Salvation Army** and was that international organization's first general hospital in the United States. This was the second general hospital in Northern Kentucky's leading city and the third in Kenton and Campbell counties (after St. Elizabeth Hospital [see **St. Elizabeth Medical Center**] and **Speers Memorial Hospital**). The Shinkle family donated its three-story, 33-room Gothic Revival mansion, built in 1869 of white stone, to the Salvation Army for use as a rest home for its officer corps. At that time the property, valued at $150,000, was the largest bequest to the Salvation Army in its U.S. history. The proposed use of the building was changed to make it a rescue home for unwed women; and then the plan was quickly changed again, to use it as a general Protestant hospital—the suggestion of local physician Dr. John Risk Meek. Meek's idea was approved by the Shinkle family, given support locally, and sanctioned by Salvation Army leaders in Ohio, New York City, and London. The new general hospital hosted its first birth on October 30, 1914, that of Wilma Boehmer, whose parents came across the Ohio River from Cincinnati. During the hospital's first year, 465 patients were treated; that year there were 54 births and 27 deaths.

A new $500,000, 100-bed hospital was dedicated on October 24, 1926, replacing the Shinkle mansion, which was then demolished. Renowned Northern Kentucky physician Dr. **Louise Southgate** practiced at the new hospital. From May 1, 1932, through January 20, 1937, the Salvation Army experienced persistent deficits, and the hospital was temporarily closed. It reopened just in time for the devastating flood of 1937. Afterward the hospital grew, added beds and departments, and served the Northern Kentucky community well. Its school of nursing trained local nurses as well as Salvation Army staff nurses. Its many well-attended auxiliaries provided support in many areas of care.

By the early 1970s, competition from St. Elizabeth Hospital South and suburbanization began shifting patients away from the inner city and undermining Booth's popularity. A move to another location was recommended by hospital consultants, and in late summer 1979, after an amazing series of regulatory approvals, a new Booth Hospital opened at the intersection of Turfway Rd. and I-75 in Florence, Boone Co. This site was the former Scott farm, whose 48 acres allowed for future expansion. The Covington physical plant was vacated except for the cafeteria, which continued for a few more years serving good food at more-than-reasonable prices.

The Florence location was ideal for attracting what the industry terms "unreferred trauma." Booth's new position easily captured emergency visits, because it was the first hospital people would come to on their way north from a large section of Kentucky. Fewer of its new patients were uninsured than those from the urban Covington area. Nevertheless, competition from the St. Elizabeth Medical Center and the St. Luke Hospital proved too much, and St. Luke purchased the 161-bed Booth Hospital in Florence for $23.9 million and named it St. Luke Hospital West. Ownership changed hands on June 30, 1989, ending the Salvation Army's 75-year hospital presence in Northern Kentucky. With St. Luke Hospital West, the new owner has been able to compete in the marketplace. The Salvation Army, a freestanding entity in a turbulent sea of hospital alliances and in the age of governmental reimbursement games, simply could not do this.

On the original Covington site, once home to that great industrialist-benefactor **Amos Shinkle** and later to the beloved Booth Hospital, now sits the Governors Point Condominiums, 49 units in the remodeled hospital building. Today's quiet residential setting belies the busy atmosphere that once surrounded the William Booth Memorial Hospital.

Murdoch, Norman H. "A Protestant Hospital for Covington: Booth Memorial Hospital," *JKS* 3 (October 1986): 107–49.

———. *The Salvation Army in Cincinnati: 1885–1985*. Cincinnati: Salvation Army, 1985.

BOSTON STATION. Boston Station in Pendleton Co. was originally known as Lynn. It was founded by the Licking River Lumber and Mining Company, whose stockholders lived in Boston, Mass. The company bought large tracts of timberland on the headwaters of the Licking River and floated loose logs down the river. The logs were caught at Boston by a series of booms in the river and landed on the west side of the river at a 30-acre mill lot. The logging and milling were done by men from Maine, who settled and raised their families at Boston Station; over time the families intermarried with Kentuckians.

The post office for this area was Merediana until Boston Station was started, at which time the Merediana office was discontinued. Gabriel Mullins, a **Revolutionary War** soldier who arrived in the 1790s, was one of the residents of Boston Station. He had a family of 10 sons and daughters, all of whom settled in Pendleton Co. His grave in the Bonar Cemetery was marked by the Daughters of American Revolution in 1937. Other families who came early to Boston Station were the Becketts, the Bonars, the Duckers, and the Shoemakers. The Harris School, one of the first schools in Pendleton Co., was at Boston Station. One of the first churches in the county, the United Boston Church, was also there. Several denominations used the church as a meeting place. A small Methodist chapel was built at the end of Ball Rd. shortly after Boston Station became a stop on the **Covington and Lexington Railroad**. The chapel was officially dedicated in 1859.

Serious flooding eventually caused the sawmill to be moved to Butler, an event that marked the beginning of the end for this once-vibrant area, which declined rapidly after 1900. Its cemetery, however, received burials as late as 1961.

Belew, Mildred Boden. *The First 200 Years of Pendleton County*. Falmouth, Ky.: M. B. Belew, n.d. [ca. 1994].

Mildred Belew

BOUSCAREN, LOUIS FREDERIC GUSTAVE (b. August 26, 1840, Guadeloupe, French West Indies; d. November 6, 1904, Cincinnati, Ohio). Engineer Gustave Bouscaren was the son of Victor Gabriel Gustave and Lise Cecelia Segond Bouscaren. In May 1850 the Bouscarens immigrated to the United States, after an earthquake and financial and political unrest made their plantation on the island of Guadeloupe unprofitable. They settled on 400 acres at Blanchet, just south of Williamstown in Grant Co. at the recommendation of a family friend. Ten-year-old Gustave dubbed their new home the family's "Caribbean Farm." Gustave attended school in Georgetown and in Cincinnati (St. Xavier School) until he was awarded the opportunity to study at the Lycée St. Louis in Paris, France, in 1854. After five years of studies there, he entered the École Centrale des Arts et Manufactures, where he trained as a mechanical engineer for three years.

At the end of the **Civil War**, Bouscaren returned to the Northern Kentucky region and eventually was hired as a draftsman for the Cincinnati architectural firm **Samuel Hannaford and Sons**. He designed a bridge across the Great Miami River in Ohio, setting his career in motion. In 1865 he began an eight-year stint of building a network of railroads across Indiana and Illinois, all leading to St. Louis, where he worked. Two of his first bosses from his draftsman days were later hired by the **Cincinnati Southern Railroad** to build that railroad system's roadbed to the South in 1873. They, in turn, hired Bouscaren. Then in December 1876, when his superior Thomas D. Lovett resigned, Bouscaren became the consulting and principal engineer of the Cincinnati Southern Railway. He is credited with the design of the first **Cincinnati Southern Railway Bridge** across the Ohio River at Ludlow (completed in 1877), thought to be the longest truss bridge in the world at that time. As principal engineer of the railroad's construction, he obviously played an integral role in Charles Shaler Smith's design of the world-famous High Bridge across the Kentucky River south of Wilmore in Jessamine Co., supposedly the first cantilever bridge on the North American continent. Later, Bouscaren was a consultant for New York City's Brooklyn Bridge, for the **Central Bridge** connecting Cincinnati to Newport (financed by **John A. Williamson**), and for the Panama Canal as well. In 1881 Bouscaren became the chief engineer for the Cincinnati, New Orleans, and Texas Pacific Railroad, leaseholder of the Cincinnati Southern Railway's route to Chattanooga. In 1897 his railroad career ended when he was appointed chief engineer of the Cincinnati Waterworks. Bouscaren designed the public utility's new water plant located at California, Ohio, a few miles upriver from Cincinnati. It was his idea to collect water for the city of Cincinnati at a pump house along the Kentucky side of the Ohio River between Dayton and Brent in Campbell Co. and pump it via a tunnel deep beneath the river to the plant on the Ohio shore. He did not live to see his unique plans completed. He died in August 1904 at his home on Josephine St. in the Mount Auburn section of Cincinnati. After a funeral mass at Cincinnati's St. Peter-in-Chains Cathedral said by Archbishop Elder, Bouscaren was laid to rest next to his wife Helen (whom he had married in 1876) at the New St. Joseph Cemetery on the west side of Cincinnati. Several engineering marvels throughout Ohio, Kentucky, and the upper South survive and remain as tributes to the genius of Gustave Bouscaren.

Bouscaren, Gabrielle. *My Communion of Saints.* Privately published, n.d.

Bouscaren, Louis Henri Gustave. *The Bridge Builder.* Privately published, 1964.

"Bouscaren," November 7, 1904, *CE*, 10.

Hall, Charles G. *The Cincinnati Southern Railway, a History: A Complete and Concise History of the Events Attending the Building and Operation of the Road.* Cincinnati: Railway, 1902.

"Obituary: Mrs. Helen L. Bouscaren," *Commercial Times,* July 26, 1901, 2.

Michael R. Sweeney

BOXING. In the 19th century, boxing in the United States was secretive, normally occurred in remote locations, and was sometimes illegal. Derived from the English form of prizefighting, it was akin to **duels** and cockfighting. Boxing matches were held on the edge of town and quickly arranged; there were no Marquis of Queensberry rules, nor were there boxing gloves—it was simply fisticuffs. In Kentucky varying amounts of fighting took place, depending on the exact location and the extent to which local reform movements had rendered the sport illegal; boxing had an appeal for all levels of male society, although the wealthy seldom scuffed their own knuckles. Fighters were often local criminals looking for work. Newspapers reported on the results of a match but often were reluctant to announce upcoming bouts, lest they be accused of promoting unlawful activities. Furthermore, beyond the brutality of the sport, reformers associated boxing with the evils of gambling.

Some of the early boxers became the first sports heroes in the nation. The famed John L. Sullivan defeated Dominic McCaffrey at the Chester Park amusement grounds in nearby Cincinnati in August 1885. Fought before a crowd of some 15,000, it was the first modern heavyweight championship match using gloves. Sixteen-year-old John Sweeney, a resident of the Mount Adams neighborhood of Cincinnati, witnessed the bout and afterward shook Sullivan's hand. Even about 75 years later, Sweeney greeted people by saying, "Shake the hand that shook the hand of John L. Sullivan." The Boston Strong Boy, as Sullivan was called, was an imposing figure not easily forgotten, and by his travels throughout the nation, including his appearance at Chester Park and his 1893 boxing demonstration in Maysville at the **Washington Opera House**, he became one of the first nationally known sports celebrities, capturing the public's fascination without the aid of radio or television.

At first, lawmakers did not seem to know how to deal with boxing. Prizefighting was made illegal throughout Kentucky in 1869, but that law seems to have been enforced unevenly. In 1873 it was repealed and boxing was made legal. Then in 1896 boxing became a felony statewide, but again local authorities usually looked the other way. Cincinnatians sometimes came to Northern Kentucky to circumvent Ohio's boxing law. Covington ministers by 1901 were openly opposing fights and were known to have stopped a few bouts. In 1902 Mayor William A. Johnson proclaimed that fighting was no longer allowed in Covington.

In September 1919 Sammy Sandow beat Pete Herman at the old Newport baseball grounds at Second and Washington Sts., just off the end of the **L&N Bridge**, a site that was geographically as close as one could get to downtown Cincinnati without having to abide by Ohio law. Thousands of boxing fans crossed the bridge to view the spectacle. It was not long after the Sandow-Herman bout that Kentucky representative Rodney Bryson of Covington submitted legislation in 1920, successfully creating the Kentucky Boxing Commission, a government regulatory body now named the Boxing and Wrestling Authority.

There were several venues in Northern Kentucky where boxing took place. One was Dayton's **Tacoma Park**, where upwards of 12,000 fans enjoyed summer evening boxing bouts during the late 1920s. Tacoma was the occasional scene of important fights. It was located at the end of the Dayton **streetcar** line, and because of the other attractions there, such as wrestling, dog races, and marathon dances, almost everyone knew how to find the so-called Tacoma Bowl (boxing ring). Tacoma later added an indoor arena. The other major place in Campbell Co. where boxing occurred was the armory at the **Fort Thomas Military Reservation**. Reportedly, boxing matches were held for the entertainment of the soldiers, as Army officers got involved in the fighting—placing their candidates on the evening's card and betting among themselves. Few soldiers participated in the actual fighting, but in 1927 even an officer, Lt. R. S. Henderson, got into the ring. In 1928 Cincinnati's world champion, Freddy Miller, fought at the fort. Extra streetcars along the Fort Thomas line were scheduled to accommodate the crowds attending Fort Thomas fights during the 1920s and 1930s. Other boxing sites included Taylors Grove in Silver Grove, as early as 1858; the Clifton Club in South Newport; the Newport Turners Gym; and the Newport Gym (the Costigan American Legion Post at Sixth and Orchard). Boxing also occurred at an undetermined remote spot in Cold Spring. In 1931 fights took place at the **Newport High School** gymnasium.

In Kenton Co., favorite boxing locations included the Riverside Boxing Arena at Second St. and Madison Ave. in Covington, next to the old Federal League Park, home of the **Covington Blue Sox** baseball team. A contingent of African American boxers boxed at the Riverside in the 1920s. The **Latonia Springs** Resort is where Joe Coburn and Mike McCoole trained in 1868; Feeney's Gym, at Third and Bakewell Sts. in Covington, was the starting point for many pugilists between 1910 and 1920, under the sponsorship of Jack Feeney and his nephew Charley Feeney; the Admiral Athletics Club headquartered at Feeney's was a noted boxing site around 1915 and also promoted the sport; Heidel Hall in Peaselburg, a town that was well known for boxing and cockfighting, held bouts in the second decade of the century; an old **Civil War** parade grounds named Foley's Common was the scene of many bouts; and young men from Covington fought brutally on Sundays in the **Willow Run** Bottoms during the 1920s. The Dixie Park Arena in Florence opened for boxing in 1928. Both the Moose and the Eagles clubs in Covington scheduled occasional bouts. In the 1940s in Covington, a bar called the Step Inn, located near 12th and Johnson Sts., had, in addition to a typical drinking decor, a small boxing ring, with a training area and lockers for anyone willing to go a few rounds as the patrons drank.

Two well-known pugilists who lived in Kenton Co. were **Walter Wyk** and **Joe Anderson**. Wyk, a Buffalo, N.Y., native who moved to Covington around 1920, won 98 of his 182 bouts by knockouts. In 1922 he knocked out a respected fighter named Perry Nelson in a fight in Covington. For many years Wyk was associated with the **YMCA** in that city. Anderson, hailing from Banklick, during his 10-year career defeated three world champs. His record was 56 wins, 22 ties, and 20 defeats. He parlayed his fight winnings into successful business careers after boxing; he operated the Bluegrass Gym in Covington, ran a successful restaurant along the **Dixie Highway**, and became a distributor for the **Wiedemann Brewing Company**.

Perhaps the finest professional boxer to come out of Campbell Co. was Frank "Midget" Guerrea (1907–1992), the son of Italian immigrants. He spent his entire life in Newport and credited boxing as his stepping-stone to success. He began fighting at age 15 in bouts held before the soldiers at the Fort Thomas Military Reservation, earning between 55 and 95 cents per match. In his first big fight, he earned $30 for knocking his opponent out in the first round. He was a lightweight, fighting at 112 pounds, and many of his followers called him "Midget Gary." In Guerrea's 10-year career, he won 73 fights, lost 10, and fought to a draw 12 times. In a World Lightweight Title Fight, he lost to Sammy Mandrell at Tacoma Park on Labor Day 1927. He also fought at Redlands Field (Crosley Field) in Cincinnati. During the 1930s he staged boxing demonstrations at summer church festivals throughout Northern Kentucky. In the late 1940s and early 1950s, he visited neighborhood playgrounds around Newport on behalf of the city recreation department, teaching boxing techniques. In the 1950s, he owned a bar, the Midge Guerrea Tavern along Fifth St. in Dayton, and was a board member of the Newport Housing Authority. Guerrea also served as a Newport city commissioner and as vice mayor from 1948 to 1950. He was well respected throughout Newport.

Other Campbell Co. fighters included Frank Dean of Dayton; Ray Steigerwald of Bellevue, who won the Southern Golden Gloves flyweight championship in Nashville in 1941; and Fort Thomas native Ray D'Amico, who began his fighting career in the late 1940s at the Fenwick Club in Cincinnati. D'Amico has run a tailor shop along Scott St. for two decades and in recent years has done some training and referee work in Northern Kentucky.

At least two other Northern Kentuckians who held political office took their turns in the fight ring. **Thomas P.** "Timmy" **Fitzpatrick**, Covington's Democratic mayor during the mid-1940s and Kentucky Speaker of the House in the 1950s, received several poundings in the boxing ring in the 1920s before entering politics. He was a part owner, with "Biddy" Bishop, of Riverside Arena (the Riverside Boxing Club), where both men promoted fights and served as matchmakers, bringing many national star boxers into Northern Kentucky. In Campbell Co., A. J. "Tony" Warndorf boxed at the old Fenwick Club in Cincinnati and refereed three important championship fights during the 1950s, before he entered politics. The editor of *Ring* magazine once said that Warndorf ran a tight fight as a referee. Warndorf became a Newport city commissioner (two terms, 15 years apart), and he loved nothing better than a good old political donnybrook. In the 1950s, Joe Seta, a multiterm judge in Hamilton Co., Ohio, was matchmaking at the Covington Athletic Club.

Over the years, Catholic organizations often scheduled boxing for entertainment. A major boxing center in Cincinnati was the Fenwick Club, which operated from 1915 until 1982, when the Procter and Gamble company headquarters took its site. The Archdiocese of Cincinnati developed the Fenwick as a young men's club, and many pugilists trained and fought in its gymnasium. A number of Northern Kentucky boxers practiced there, such as Covington's Art "the Flying Dutchman" Schultz. In Northern Kentucky, the Catholic Order of Foresters, a fraternal benefit group, staged fights at various places locally. **St. Patrick Catholic Church, Covington**, often had boxing on its program of events; in 1929 the **Sisters of Notre Dame** added four boxing bouts to the activities at their annual July 4th festival at St. Joseph Heights in Parks Hills; in 1940 the **Knights of Columbus** were backing boxing; also in the 1940s, Newport Catholic High School (**Newport Central Catholic High School**) had a boxing team; and in the 1950s, Covington's African American champion Eddie Thompson was fighting at **St. Joseph Catholic Church**'s gym in Cold Spring. In 1956 Thompson was a local Golden Gloves champion. He was so good that few locals would fight him; he had to go to New York City to find bouts. Both Anderson and Guerrea mentored Thompson in Amateur Athletic Union (AAU) boxing.

Other organizations sponsoring boxing included the Fort Thomas Woman's Club, which raised funds at the fort's ring in 1921; the Newport Elks at Tacoma Park; the GOHI Athletic Club in Newport's **West End**; the **Campbell Co. Protestant Orphans Home** summer festival (1931); the Moose Club in Covington; Speers Hospital in Dayton (see **Speers Memorial Hospital**); the **Red Cross** in 1932; and even the Young Democrats (see **Democratic Party**), who became involved in boxing as a fundraising technique in 1933.

In more recent years, Covington's Terry O'Brien was a successful Golden Gloves boxer during the 1960s. He had a brief professional career regionally in Chicago; Cleveland; Indianapolis; Columbus, Ohio; and Fort Wayne, Ind., until injuries ended it. In the late 1970s, O'Brien started the Northern Kentucky Boxing Club on Pike St. in Covington, where he became the mentor for another Covington pugilist, Steve Woods. Woods had a short-lived regional professional run. In the 1980s and 1990s, the Vegas Convention Hall in Erlanger and Peel's Palace in that same city staged boxing events, and **Holmes High School** was the site of a few fights. In 1990 O'Brien opened the Shamrock Gym at Eighth St. and Madison Ave. in Covington, and it continues in operation today. Most boxing in the area today occurs at the Belterra Casino down the Ohio River near Vevay, Ind., where events are staged to help bring customers into the gambling area, sometimes in association with nationally known promoter Don King. Of late, the Drawbridge Convention Center in Fort Mitchell has been holding Saturday night fights.

Rinzi Nocero of Lee St. in Covington, a friend of Ray D'Amico, never fought in this region but ascended to within the top 10 nationwide for middleweights. Larry Mullins, a Covington native, does matchmaking and promotion for local events in Las Vegas. Living in Covington today is Larry Hodge, who has the distinction of being one of eight amateur fighters to defeat Cassius Clay (Muhammad Ali). In a bout in Louisville in 1957, when both boxers were in their teens, Hodge defeated Clay by a TKO in the first round. Today, Hodge and Clay are friends.

"Feeney's Gym In Covington: Many Stars Started There," *KP*, July 10, 1914, 6.

"Frank 'Midge' Guerrea, Pro Boxer," *KP*, November 9, 1992, 4A.

Grace, Kevin. *Cincinnati Boxing*. Charleston, S.C.: Arcadia, 2006.

"The Greatest," *KP*, February 3, 2007, 10A.

Harmon, Rick. "Fracture Put O'Brien's Comeback in Limbo," *KP*, June 22, 1978, 8K.

Reis, Jim. "Covington Riot Roiled from Clash That Dashed 'Great White Hope,'" *KP*, May 27, 1991, 4K.

——. "Despite Efforts to Stop It, Boxing Proved a Popular Sport," *KP*, March 18, 1996, 4K.

——. "Riverside Club a Boxing Mecca," *KP*, February 8, 1999, 4K.

——. "When Boxing Was Champ," *KP*, April 22, 2002, 4K.

Michael R. Sweeney

BOYD CATTLE COMPANY. The Boyd Cattle Company, known locally as Boyd Beef Cattle, is a family-owned farming operation that began almost 100 years ago. Eugene Boyd's father, Frank Boyd, was the first county agent in Mason Co. Eugene, who grew up on a farm, continued the tradition as a diversified farmer. When his son Ward Boyd joined 4H, he bought the boy a heifer to raise as his project, and this was the start of a cattle operation that has now spanned five generations. Ward's son Charlie, who saw the potential in raising superior cattle, today heads the seven-family farm operation that is known internationally for its superior Hereford and Angus yearling bulls.

Charlie Boyd graduated from the University of Kentucky in Lexington in 1964 with a degree in animal science. He returned to Mason Co., and in 1973 he and his wife, Martha Donovan Boyd, bought a farm near Mayslick. Within nine years they had paid off the farm and had started to build a superior herd of beef cattle. Charlie judges shows throughout the United States and is considered the finest breeder of Hereford and Angus bulls in the nation. He is one of only two full-time beef breeders east of the Mississippi River. Boyd Heavy Hitter and Boyd New Day are the two champion bulls that have cemented the Boyd Beef Farm and Charlie's reputation.

Using modern tools, his knowledge of genetics, and business acumen, Charlie has been able to develop strains with the traits sought by his customers. The fertility rates of these strains are closely monitored, and the farm's bulls are sought by commercial and local farmers for their ability to deliver superior offspring that bring good returns on the buyer's money. The Boyds also sell semen and fertilized eggs from the herds. Some of the semen and eggs from their cattle have been shipped to Africa, Australia, Canada, and New Zealand.

Today the seven farms that are home to the Boyd Cattle Company's herds are managed and run by Charlie, his son Charles II, Charles II's wife Paula, Charlie's son-in-law Andrew Matheny, and Andrew's wife Suzanne. The family recently built its own sales barn in Mayslick, where spring and fall yearling bulls are sold to buyers from around the world. Charlie Boyd's grandchildren are also now very much involved in the operation.

Boyd, Charlie. Interview by Lynn David, October 3, 2006, Mayslick, Ky.

Mitchell, Clifford. "Resources and Environment Build Bull Power," *Cattle Today,* April 2005, www.cattletoday.com/archive/2005/April/CT387.shtml (accessed October 11, 2006).

Lynn David

BOYS & GIRLS CLUB. The Boys & Girls Clubs of Greater Cincinnati includes two units in Northern Kentucky. The first of the two was the Kenton Co. Club, now known as Marge Schott-Unnewehr Boys & Girls Club. Discussions about the creation of a Kenton Co. club began during the early 1950s, and by 1955 the Kenton Co. Boys Club was housed above a drugstore at the corner of Fourth and Scott Sts. in Covington. Initially, it had a membership of about 100 boys, who were given academic assistance, athletics, and life skills training. On August 11, 1957, the club broke ground for a day-camp facility on the Bromley–Crescent Springs Pk. In 1970 the Kenton Co. Club was required by the Boys Clubs of America (BCA) to merge with the Boys Clubs of Greater Cincinnati (BCGC). Just two years later, the club was moved into a newly constructed building in Covington at 26th St. and Madison Ave., which it continues to use today. On November 15, 1982, the BCGC began accepting girls as members and officially became the Boys & Girls Clubs of Greater Cincinnati (BGCGC).

In 1984 the Campbell Co. Boys & Girls Club began meeting in Newport, in the basement of the York Street Congregational Church. The club in Campbell Co. received its charter from the Boys and Girls Clubs of America on May 17, 1985, and it became the fifth unit in the BGCGC group. In 1996 the Campbell Co. club moved to its current location at 10th and Orchard Sts. in Newport. It was renamed the Clem and Ann Buenger Unit in honor of the former president of the **Fifth Third Bank** and his wife, both longtime advocates for children in Northern Kentucky.

Today the BGCGC serves more than 3,000 youths per year in Northern Kentucky and attendance averages more than 300 children per day. Children from age 6 to age 18 are welcome to join for a nominal annual fee. Members receive a hot meal each day in addition to access to athletic teams and equipment, homework assistance and tutoring, and a variety of small-group activities that encourage personal development. A dedicated staff and volunteers support the children. Together, the employees and volunteers hope to create an environment that is fun, nurturing, and empowering for each child who walks through the door. Supported through private donations and funding from the United Way, the BGCGC provides an after-school environment that keeps at-risk children off the streets and gives them an exciting alternative.

"Boys Club Dedication," *KTS,* August 5, 1957, 1A.

"Club Is Named for Donor Schott," *KP,* July 5, 2001, 2K.

Jennifer Hedger

BOY SCOUTS OF AMERICA, DAN BEARD COUNCIL. It seems only appropriate that the local chapter of the Boy Scouts of America began in the boyhood home of one of the scouting organization's founders, **Daniel Carter Beard**, who resided in Covington. From 1918 through 1923, the Dan Beard Council (the home office of the various local scout troops) was called the Covington Council and served only that city. In January 1925 the council reorganized as the Northern Kentucky Council, serving Boone, Campbell, and Kenton counties from its headquarters in Covington. Bracken, Grant, and Pendleton counties joined the council in February 1931 as the popularity of scouting grew. A year later Mason, Owen, and Robertson counties were added. The council's headquarters was moved to Newport in 1941, and in 1944 Gallatin Co. joined the council. In 1951 Bracken, Mason, and Robertson counties transferred to a scout group based in Portsmouth, Ohio. In 1952 the council's headquarters returned to Covington as its name was changed to the Dan Beard Council. In October 1956 the Dan Beard Council consolidated with the Cincinnati Area Council to form the Dan Beard Council, No. 438. Since that time some Ohio counties have been added to the council; its headquarters is located along Victory Parkway in Cincinnati. The United Way agency partially funds the scouts in this region.

The scouts in the Northern Kentucky–Cincinnati region operate campgrounds at Camp Edgar Friedlander in Clermont Co., Ohio, and Camp Michaels (formerly Camp Powderhorn) in Union, Ky., where members of each of the three divisions of scouting, the Cub Scouts, the Boy Scouts, and Venturing (formerly the Explorers), gather for events. Scouting has changed in recent years as the organization has returned to the inner city, providing counseling and self-improvement for boys along with the traditional activities of camping, crafts, hobbies, and civic involvement. For many years in Northern Kentucky, most Boy Scout troops were neighborhood- and church-based, generally directed by male volunteers from the church membership who led the troops in all sorts of prescribed scouting activities.

The first scout troop in Northern Kentucky was organized in 1911 by Rev. Harlan C. Runyan at the Latonia Christian Church. During the next decade, prominent Covington civic leaders such as **Richard P. Ernst** and **J. T. Hatfield** were active in the scouting movement, as was the **Baker-Hunt Foundation**. Local places where scouts gathered during those years included Camp Hill and Camp Hatfield in Morning View, the **Latonia Racecourse**, and Goebel Park in Covington; out-of-town trips were often made to Mammoth Cave National Park and to the Kentucky State Capitol in Frankfort.

Boy Scouts of America. "Dan Beard Council." www.danbeard.org (accessed October 28, 2006).

Covington Troop 6. "Adventure in Scouting: Covington Troop 6, 1911–1936," Kenton Co. Public Library, Covington, Ky.

"Dan Beard to Return to Childhood Home . . ." *KP,* August 18, 1934, 1.

Franzen, Gene. "Daniel Carter Beard Statue," *KE,* July 30, 2000, B2.

BRACHT. Never incorporated, this community in southwestern Kenton Co. appears on maps today at U.S. 25 (the **Dixie Highway**) and Ky. Rt. 14, on the Bracht-Piner Rd. Before 1840, when this area was a part of Campbell Co., it was called Key West and was the childhood home of Kentucky statesman **John G. Carlisle**. The **Covington and Lexington Turnpike** (the Dixie Highway) ran along a natural dry ridge from Central Kentucky to the Ohio River. Drovers guided cattle, hogs, mules, and even turkeys up the dirt pike, stopping to water them at a natural spring near Key West. In the late 1870s, the **Cincinnati Southern** opened its railway along this ridge. By 1883, from a depot with stockyards called Bracht Station (named for Maj. F. B. Bracht of Grant Co.), trains transported farm produce and animals, tobacco, fresh milk, passengers, and mail. A post office operated at Key West from May 1877 until February 1910 and afterward at Bracht Station, a half mile north. Businesses sprang up: general stores, a blacksmith, one-room schools, a trotting course, and taverns, but no churches. After labor shortages created by **World War I**, the paving of U.S. 25, and the Great Depression, rural commerce declined, and the railroad depot and post office at Bracht closed.

An Atlas of Boone, Kenton, and Campbell Counties, Kentucky. Philadelphia: D. J. Lake, 1883.

Kleber, John E., ed. *The Kentucky Encyclopedia.* Lexington: Univ. Press of Kentucky, 1992.

Rennick, Robert M. *The Post Offices of Northern Kentucky.* Lake Grove, Ore.: Depot, 2004.

Suzann Parker Leist

BRACKEN, WILLIAM (date of birth unknown; d. after 1773, Bracken Co., Ky.). Pioneer William Bracken, an early explorer in Kentucky, helped to chart the territory as a prelude to settlement. In 1773 he accompanied a party headed by the McAfee brothers (George, James, and Robert) as they canoed down the Kentucky River surveying what became Frankfort and Harrodsburg. At the Falls of the Ohio (Louisville), the group met up with another party of surveyors headed by Capt. Thomas Bullitt. Bullitt's group had been sent by the governor of Virginia to survey the land in Kentucky promised to Virginia soldiers as bounty for having fought in the **French and Indian War**. The two groups joined and proceeded to plot sections of town lots in the vicinity of Limestone Creek (modern-day Maysville).

The combined group then headed down the Ohio River. Along the way, they discovered two creeks and named them after Bracken. The 10-member team arrived on July 4, 1773, at **Big Bone Lick** (located in modern-day Boone Co.), a site they had heard about from both Indians and white men. The group reported "making seats and tent poles of the enormous backbones and ribs of the mastodon found there in large quantities."

Bracken left the surveying party and settled near the two creeks that had been named for him, the Big Bracken and Little Bracken creeks, which converge and empty into the Ohio River at what today is Augusta. Indians later killed him, and his burial place is unknown. Bracken Co., established in 1796, was named in honor of this early Kentucky pioneer and settler in the area.

Collins, Richard H. *History of Kentucky.* Vol. 1. Covington, Ky.: Collins, 1882.
Cotterill, R. S. *History of Pioneer Kentucky.* Berea, Ky.: Kentucke Imprints, 1917.
Foster, Judith Ann. *History of Bracken County Bicentennial Edition.* Brooksville, Ky.: Bracken Co. Extension Homemakers, 1996.
Kleber, John E., ed. *The Kentucky Encyclopedia.* Lexington: Univ. Press of Kentucky, 1992.

Rebecca Mitchell Turney

BRACKEN BAPTIST CHURCH (LEWIS CRAIG MEMORIAL BAPTIST CHURCH). This church, located in Minerva in Mason Co., was built in 1793 and has been restored in recent years by the Friends of Minerva. The church was founded by the famous Baptist preacher and evangelist Rev. Lewis Craig, who had been persecuted for his Baptist beliefs in Virginia. Craig and a group of Baptist families left Spotsylvania, Va., in 1781 and organized churches in southern Kentucky and at South Elkhorn, near Lexington. In 1792 Craig moved from South Elkhorn to Mason Co., and the following year, the Bracken Baptist Church was constructed. Craig served as pastor until the early 1800s. In 1795, the congregation joined the South Elkhorn Association of Baptists. In 1796 the church had 156 members. In 1799 it was the site of the formation of the Bracken Association of Baptists, which the congregation joined.

Like many other churches and denominations of the time, the congregation divided over the issue of slavery in 1805. Anti- and proslavery groups took turns worshipping in the same building until about 1815, when the split was healed. In 1829 there was a division regarding doctrine in the Baptist movement; a majority of the congregation joined the Campbell movement, begun by **Alexander Campbell**, which called for biblical literalism. The Campbellites controlled the congregation and the building until 1842, when the Baptists regained control.

The size of the congregation began to decrease around 1850, and by 1900 the building was no longer used for worship. It was a community center until 1930, when it was sold for $280; the proceeds were used to erect a marker at Craig's grave. From 1930 to 1996, the structure was used as a tobacco barn. The Friends of Minerva began restoring the building in 1996 and completed the process in 2006. The church today is home to community functions, including the annual interdenominational Minerva Community Thanksgiving in the fall.

"Pioneer Baptist Honored," *KP*, October 31, 1930, 11.

Paul L. Whalen

BRACKEN CO. Bracken Co. in Northern Kentucky, bounded on the north by the Ohio River, was formed from Mason and Campbell counties in 1796 and chartered in 1797. Bracken Co.'s southern boundary is at the North Fork of the Licking River. Topographically, the county is rolling and hilly. Brooksville is the county seat, and Augusta, with proximity to the railroad and the Ohio River, is the county's principal town.

The Court of Quarter Sessions was created in Augusta on June 12, 1797, and John Blanchard, John Pattie, and Francis Wells were named the court's gentlemen justices of the peace. Rueben Young was appointed sheriff, and Francis Wells was Augusta's first surveyor. The county was 23rd in order of formation in Kentucky and currently covers an area of 203 square miles. Its name comes from two creeks, Big Bracken and Little Bracken, which may have been named after an early explorer, **William Bracken**, who was reportedly killed by American Indians.

Early inhabitants of the county recorded that Augusta was built over an Indian burying ground, thought by archeologists to be one of the **Fort Ancient Indian Sites**. Many skeletons were removed when the cellars of homes in the town were dug. When early pioneer **Philip Buckner** brought numerous families to the region, many of them settled in Bracken Co. and became the founding fathers of several Bracken Co. communities. Also, two traveling Baptist ministers, Lewis and Elijah Craig, came into adjoining Mason Co., and some of their followers entered Bracken Co.

Bracken Co. was the home of several stonemasons who quarried stone, faced it, and used it to build their homes, structures that have stood for nearly two centuries. In the Augusta area, the stone houses remaining are the Chalfont house, three miles west of Augusta on Ky. Rt. 8 (currently being preserved by the Bracken Historical Society); the Boothe family's two-story home, three miles south of Augusta on Ky. Rt. 435 (Augusta-Minerva Rd.); and the Stroube house, built during the early 1820s along Ky. Rt. 2370 (Dutch Ridge Rd.), which is in pristine condition and occupied by the Charles Schweitzer Sr. family.

Log structures that were built in the county have continued to fascinate residents. Records state that the first log home in the county, near Minerva, belonged to John Winter and dated to 1792. It is no longer standing. The oldest remaining log house, protected by an overhanging tobacco barn on Mount Zion Rd. near Chatham, is the two-story home erected by Thomas Heaverin in 1793. On Third St. in Augusta is the Dickerson log building, which housed the first court of the county in 1796. Also in Augusta at 209 W. Riverside Dr. are a two-story log structure attached to Tom Broshear's Tavern, the oldest three-story brick structure in Northern Kentucky, and the Mohrfield cabin, which was relocated from the Augusta-Minerva Rd. to the Parkview Inn property.

The first pike chartered through the county in the early 1800s is currently known as Ky. Rt. 19; its original name was the Augusta-Georgetown Pk. The Ohio Valley Pk. followed, along the Ohio River shoreline, but the lower bank has been obliterated and there is no trace of the old road. The road between Germantown and Brooksville in the county was formerly known as Woodward's Cross Rd. in honor of the early Woodward brothers, settlers of Brooksville.

Augusta, the first county seat, was the port of call for flat and keelboat packets in use on the river and quickly became the county's largest city. Flatboats constructed in Harrison Co. at Claysville, near the southern part of Bracken Co., floated surplus farm products from Bracken Co. down the Licking, Ohio, and Mississippi rivers to markets at Natchez, Miss., and New Orleans.

In the late 1880s, the **Chesapeake and Ohio Railroad** was built across the northern part of the county, along the Ohio River. Although the packet boat industry was still serving residents, providing a source of income and commerce, the rail line brought an increase of shipments of goods and passengers. As early as 1875 in the Bracken Co. town or Germantown, a railway was proposed, the **Covington, Flemingsburg, and Pound Gap Railroad**. A branch railroad, the Brooksville Railroad (see **Brooksville and Ohio Railroad**), was constructed in the county from Wellsburg to Brooksville and hauled a large amount of freight, thereby enhancing the economy of the central portion of the county. The Brooksville-to-Wellsburg Railroad was discontinued in 1931 and the rails were removed.

Phillip Buckner donated the 600 acres on which the city of Augusta was founded and also

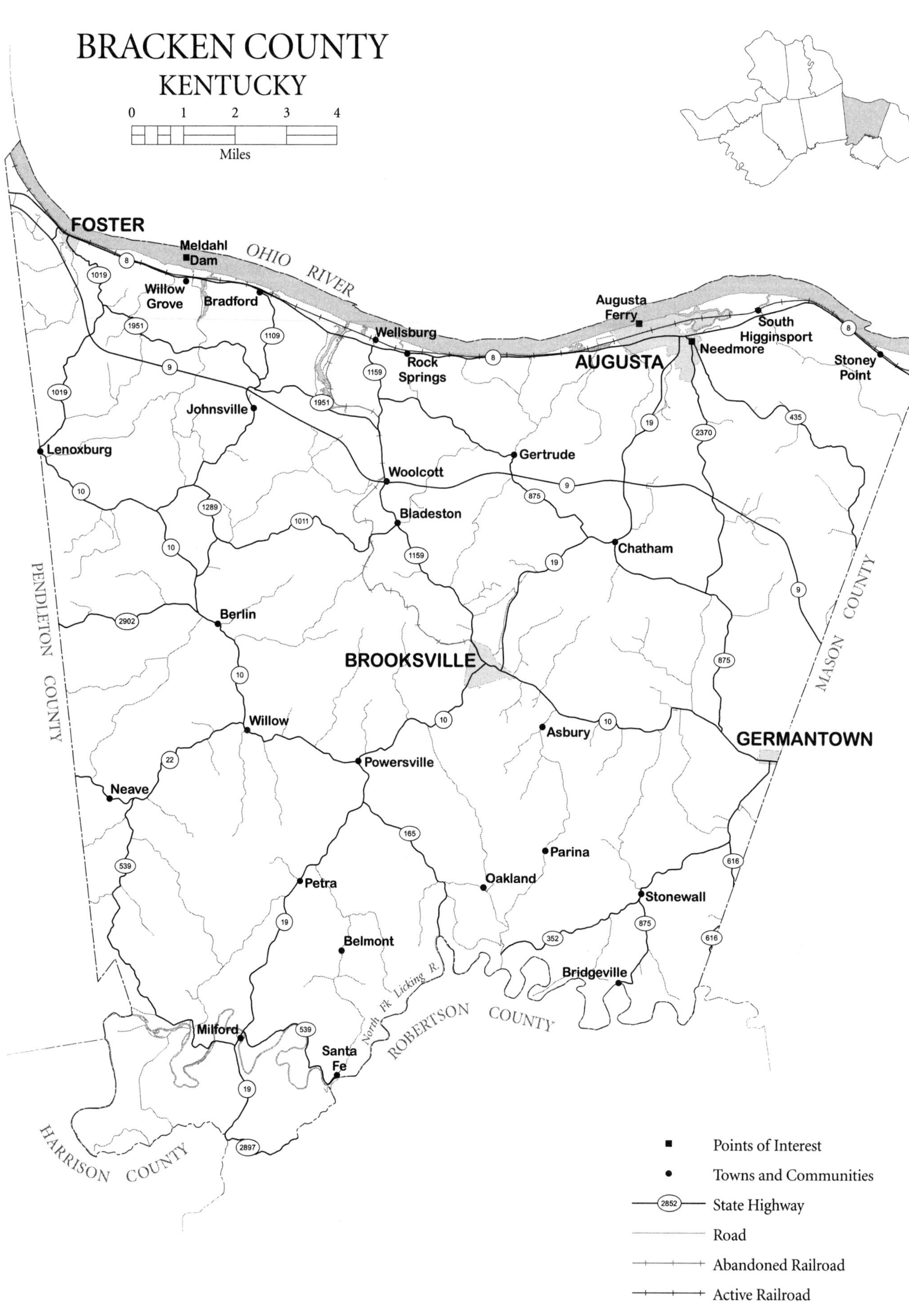

BRACKEN COUNTY
KENTUCKY
0 1 2 3 4
Miles
FOSTER
Meldahl Dam
OHIO RIVER
Willow Grove
Bradford
Augusta Ferry
South Higginsport
Wellsburg
Rock Springs
Needmore
AUGUSTA
Stoney Point
Johnsville
Lenoxburg
Gertrude
Woolcott
Bladeston
Chatham
Berlin
BROOKSVILLE
PENDLETON COUNTY
MASON COUNTY
Asbury
GERMANTOWN
Willow
Powersville
Neave
Parina
Oakland
Petra
Stonewall
Belmont
Bridgeville
North Fk Licking R.
ROBERTSON COUNTY
Milford
Santa Fe
HARRISON COUNTY
Points of Interest
Towns and Communities
State Highway
Road
Abandoned Railroad
Active Railroad

plotted these acres into in-lots and out-lots, which were divided and sold by Augusta's trustees. Because the Augusta riverfront was a good site for a port between Maysville and Cincinnati, the new town of Augusta quickly flourished. Bracken Academy (see **Augusta College**) was established two years after Augusta was chartered, elevating the reputation of the town.

Brooksville was selected as the seat of Bracken Co. on February 16, 1839, by the Kentucky legislature, which also approved a bill to change the name of the town from Woodward's Cross Roads to Brooksville in honor of David Brooks, a public-spirited state legislator who had guided the county-seat bill through to passage.

Several small villages have survived since the formation of the county. Berlin, located in west-central Bracken Co., was settled in 1844 as Pleasant Ridge and later became Hagensville, before being officially named Berlin in 1869. The village was a convenient stopover on the journey between Mason Co. and Falmouth. The hamlet of Bradford, just west of Augusta, once had a prosperous river landing, originally called Metcalf's Landing. In 1866 the name was changed in honor of **Laban J. Bradford**, a merchant and tobacco dealer who owned much land locally. There were once three tobacco warehouses in Bradford.

Chatham lies in the fertile rolling hills of the northeastern section of the county, and plantation farms and mansions still remain from earlier years. The county infirmary at Chatham, which served the ill and the destitute of the county, was the town's largest employer until it burned in the early 1980s. Foster, located in the western part of the county near the **Meldahl Dam**, was once a thriving and populous town. It was named for an early settler, Israel Foster. A Kentucky State Historical Marker stands to the west of the town, marking the site of a 1793 ambush of American Indians by **Simon Kenton**. Flatboats, and later steamboats, brought people and supplies to the town and transported farm surplus goods to markets.

Germantown, laid out by Whitfield Craig in 1794, is the second-oldest settlement in the county. It was built just east of Buckhanan Station, which is at the junction of Ky. Rt. 10 and Ky. Rt. 875 (Asbury Rd.). The town was long known for its sizable tannery, consisting of several large production vats that sat on Tanyard Hill. Johnsville, or Fairview as it is often called, was an early settlement in the northwestern section of the county on a long, high ridge well suited for homesites. The town was named for two men named John who operated the store where the post office was to be located. Another small town in the county, Lenoxburg, was named for Samuel B. Lenox, who owned the town's general store and was its postmaster. Most of Lenoxburg's economy depended on the transport of tobacco to larger markets. In 1887 the E. C. Gosney broom factory also operated there.

Milford, on the North Fork of the Licking River, was established in 1831 by John Ogdon, who took the name from the mill located near the ford in the river. Milford was almost destroyed by a disastrous fire in 1889, and in 1956 a portion of the town was once again engulfed in flames. Neave, named for one of its first settlers, is a small hamlet in the southern portion of the county that was first called Holton's Corner. Most of its commercial buildings were destroyed by tornadoes in the 1920s.

Needmore is located at the intersection of the Dutch Ridge Rd. and the Augusta-Minerva Rd., just east of Augusta. It originally was the location of a tollhouse for the upkeep of the road. Over the years, several large Victorian-style homes were constructed near the Frolicher windmill, which supplied well water to the area. A winery at the west end of Needmore is a massive and impressive structure. The vaulted limestone cellar is 100 feet long, 40 feet wide, and 37 feet high. The entrances are keystone arches built of one-foot-square timbers. Oakland is a rural farm community in the southern portion of the county probably named for the massive oak trees that grew there. On nearby Marshall Rd. is an old Indian burial ground, which represents a time when native peoples hunted in the rich bottomlands. Abner Haley, who settled on Willow Creek, along Bull Skin Rd., named the county's small community of Petra. A descendant of Haley was the founder of the Porter Haley Distillery, which was located on the Haley family's farm. He distributed his whiskey in stores in Kentucky and eventually as far away as New York.

The Bracken Co. community of Powersville was named after its first postmaster, John F. Power, in 1833. This hamlet's hotel became known as a stopover for travel between Cynthiana and Augusta. Walcott, another small community in the county, was so named by its first postmaster, who used the spelling Walcott because he had learned that another town named Walcot already existed. Its location by Locust Creek made it a natural spot for a flourmill, and portions of the millrace of the old Murray Mill remain visible. Walcott's famous "White" covered bridge was assembled in 1824 and reconstructed in 1881.

Other communities in the county were destroyed by floods or other means. Several of those were located along the Ohio River: Rock Springs, South Higginsport, Stoney Point, Tietzville, Wellsburg, and Willow Grove. For some early settlements, such as Bladeston, Bridgeville, Browningsville, Cumminsville, Gertrude, Mount Hor, and Stonewall, their location away from the main transportation routes may have resulted in their downfall.

In the early history of the county, **white burley tobacco** was a prime crop, whose economical importance was second only to the production of wine; both enterprises had their origins in the northern portion of the county on the hills bordering Big and Little Bracken creeks. White burley tobacco was first cultivated in 1864 on the river farm of G. W. Barkley, east of Augusta. Tobacco growers and warehouse managers disagreed over tobacco prices in 1907 and 1908 so sharply that those who refused to join the tobacco association, also called the pool equity, suffered barn burnings and beatings. Masked riders in groups traveled the county at night and lighted the sky with burning crops and timbers; the Noah Johnson farm at Willow was one of the sites of such activity.

Before 1860, Abraham Baker and his son built a wine cellar on the Baker farm near Augusta. A number of immigrants from Baden, Germany, who worked for Baker oversaw the quarrying of stones for the farm's buildings from the nearby hill. Slaves dug out the stones, sometimes taking two or three days to get one loose. Some of these stones when dressed measured three feet wide by two feet high and 12–14 inches thick. Stonemasons working for Baker at the time were Mike Constantine, C. S. Federer, Dominick Federer, George Schweitzer, Joseph Schweitzer, Constantine Stiefvater, and Mike Weitlauf.

Bracken Co.'s involvement in the **War of 1812** was in large part due to the efforts of Gen. John Payne of Augusta, who raised a company of mounted infantrymen that became a part of Kentuckian Richard Johnson's regiment at the Battle of the Thames in October 1813. Payne's father, Maj. Duval Payne, also served in the war. Four men had earlier volunteered to go with Oliver Hazard Perry's fleet and took part in Perry's victory at Lake Erie on September 10, 1813. These men, James Artus, John Norris, William T. Taliaferro, and John Tucker, were awarded medals by the Kentucky legislature for their courage and valor at the Battle of Lake Erie. In 1848 the young soldiers of the county again went to war, this time to Texas and Mexico to fight in the **Mexican War**.

Bracken Co. was as divided as the nation was over the question of states' rights and slavery, and Kentucky's participation on both sides in the **Civil War** was reflected in the county. Many men served the Confederacy, and many fought for the Union, while the larger towns instituted home guard units to protect their citizens from attack. Company D of the Union Army's 16th Kentucky Infantry fought gallantly in the war. This unit comprised men from Bracken Co. and was commanded by Capt. Henry Clay Weaver of Brooksville. In September 1862, Augusta was the site of a Confederate raid (see **Augusta Civil War Raid**).

Francis M. McMillen of Bracken Co. received the Medal of Honor, the nation's highest military honor, for capturing a Confederate flag in battle at Petersburg, Va., on April 2, 1865 (see **Medal of Honor**). A military unit's battle flag served both as a symbol of honor and for communications while directing a unit in combat, and the capture of a flag was both a difficult and a significant achievement. McMillen was issued his medal on May 10, 1865.

Orlan Arnold, Hobart Lee Free, Arthur P. Lytle, and John J. Pepper were some of the men in Bracken Co. who served in the Spanish-American War. The significance of this war and the sinking of the U.S. battleship *Maine* in Havana harbor in Cuba on February 15, 1898, was the subject of several poems written by county citizens.

A *Bracken County News* article of May 2, 1940, related that more than 300 men had enlisted from the county for military service in **World War I**. The same article stated that 29 of these soldiers had been killed and 35 wounded. Several of them remain interred in France and Belgium. Bracken Co.'s contribution of men and women to **World War II** was similar to that of many other counties in Kentucky. Men enlisted by the hundreds, and women volunteered to serve as well. The county lost more than 20 men fighting on foreign soils, while others were stationed in the United States. Bracken Co. men and women also served in the military during the **Korean War**, the **Vietnam War**, and subsequent Middle East wars, and fortunately, there have been few losses.

The only manufacturing facilities in Bracken Co. are located in Augusta; Clopay Inc. is a plastics manufacturer, and F. A. Neider Company Inc. is an auto-parts supplier. Together, they employ close to 400 skilled workers. Before these companies opened for business in Augusta, there was a shoe factory, L. V. Marks, on the current Clopay company site, as well as various tobacco warehouses in the town that employed many seasonal workers.

The following sites and districts in Bracken Co. are listed on the National Register of Historic Places: the Augusta College Historic Buildings, the Augusta Historic District, the Brothers-O'Neil House, the Chalfant Rock House, Evan Griffith's Grocery, the James Weldon House, the John Gregg Fee House, the J. R. Minor House, the Rock Spring Warehouse, the Snag Creek Site, the Stone House on Bracken Creek, the Stone House on old Ky. Rts. 19 and 8, the Stroube Rock House, a Turtle Creek Site, the **Walcott Covered Bridge**, the Water St. Historic District, the Wells-Keith House, and the Wine Cellar. There are also 22 historic sites in the county that have received Kentucky Landmark Certificates.

In 2000 the U.S. Census Bureau reported that Bracken Co. had a population of 8,279.

Bracken Co. Extension Homemakers. *History of Bracken County.* Bicentennial ed. Brooksville, Ky.: Bracken Co. Extension Homemakers, 2002.

Bracken Co. Historical Society. *Walter Crumbaugh—Old Timer Speaks.* Maysville, Ky.: Standard Quick Print, 2004.

Caroline R. Miller

BRACKEN CO. PUBLIC LIBRARY. In 1983 the Town and Country Women's Club of Brooksville applied to the Kentucky Department for Libraries and Archives (KDLA) for a grant to start a library in Bracken Co. The club was awarded $250,000 and given a bookmobile to begin a demonstration library.

The Bracken Co. Public Library opened its doors on July 20, 1984, in a building donated by the Continental Telephone Company. The library ran successfully until September 1987, when it closed because the county fiscal court had not approved a tax levy. Petitions from taxpayers, a heated public hearing, and subsequent lawsuits failed to keep the library open.

In 1990 the process to develop a library began again. Petitions were signed, public hearings were held, and the fiscal court subsequently passed a .05 mill tax levy to support the library. The fiscal court's action did not stop the opposition, though: three suits were brought against levying a tax for the library. The suits claimed double taxation by the city and its fiscal court and also attempted to prevent reappointment of the library board's president. The library initiative survived all three lawsuits. The reconstituted library opened in the old jail building in the courthouse yard, which had been rented from the fiscal court for $200 a month.

Libraries across the state sent shelving, books, and supplies to help; no grant moneys for new libraries were available at this time. The other libraries that helped knew the value of a library in a county. Mary Lou Simons (who had served as librarian earlier) was rehired as head librarian on June 10, 1991, and a grand opening of the library's new facility was held on September 9, 1991.

In 1994 the library board applied for a grant to build a new building and was awarded $250,000 for the building project, a sum that had to be matched. The Bracken Co. Public Library Public Properties Inc., formed to raise the needed additional moneys, accomplished its goal through a loan from the First National Bank of Brooksville. As a result, on April 9, 1995, the Bracken Co. Public Library opened its new 5,000-square-foot building at 310 W. Miami St. in Brooksville.

In 1998 the library made its third application to the state for a new bookmobile; the library's application was approved and a new 1998 bookmobile was sent to replace the outdated model. In 2004 a new 1,000-square-foot children's wing was opened at the library. This wing had been in the library's long-range plans and became a reality through a bequest from Richard A. Hause. The new wing bears his name.

The Bracken Co. Public Library continues to grow. It has 12 computers with Internet connection for public use, of which three are in the Hause Children's Wing, available for game-playing. Each afternoon after school, the library fills with children enjoying the services offered in the library's Children's Wing.

"Augusta, Others Sue Fledgling Library," *KP,* April 1, 1992, 7A.

"Bracken Library Closes," *KP,* September 30, 1987, 1K.

"Bracken Library to Move," *KP,* May 7, 1994, 12K.

Mary Lou Simons

BRACKEN CO. PUBLIC SCHOOLS. There are two public school districts in Bracken Co., Ky., the Augusta Independent Schools (see **Augusta High School**) and the Bracken Co. Public Schools. The modern Bracken system is the result of consolidation over the years, as economies of scale were recognized as a way to improve education within the county. The improvement of roads and highways also allowed for shorter commuting times to and from school.

The Bracken Independent–Graded School district existed from 1899 until 1925, serving the area within the city of Brooksville with two schools, the Brooksville Graded School and the Brooksville High School. They became part of the Bracken Co. School district in 1925, and the high school was renamed the Bracken Co. High School in 1946. In the eastern part of the county, there was the Germantown Independent School from 1899 until 1960; the Germantown High School then became part of the Bracken Co. system. In the southern part of the county, Milford ran a graded school and a high school from 1899 until 1956, when they became part of the Bracken Co. system. In the Western Hill (western) area of the county, the Western Hills Elementary School and, beginning in 1959, the Western Hills High School, gradually merged into the Bracken Co. system; the elementary school finally joined in 1987. Bracken Co.'s history of school consolidation is similar to that of most rural counties in Kentucky. At times even a merger with the smaller Robertson Co. School System to the southeast has been considered. The spillover of population growth from Campbell Co., the result of the new **AA Highway**, makes it likely that more students will attend Bracken Co. schools in the future.

The Bracken Co. Public School district consists of three schools today, at three different locations around the county seat of Brooksville: the Taylor Elementary School, on Gibson Dr., with 430 students and 29 teachers; the Bracken Co. Middle School, on Parsley Dr., with 360 students and 23 teachers; and the Bracken Co. High School, which opened in 1997, on W. Miami St., with 400 students and 23 teachers.

Perhaps the most famous graduate of the Bracken Co. Public Schools was Hollywood actor **Don Galloway**, who appeared with Raymond Burr on the television series *Ironside*.

Bracken Co. Extension Homemakers. *History of Bracken County.* Bicentennial ed. Brooksville, Ky.: Bracken Co. Extension Homemakers, 2002.

Bracken Co. School District. www.bracken.k12.ky.us (accessed January 24, 2007).

"Bracken Schools to Merge," *KP,* November 10, 1972, 1K.

"Counties Consider Merged School," *KP,* March 22, 1991, 5K.

BRADFORD, BILL "BILLY" (b. March 4, 1935; Covington, Ky.). Billy Bradford is the son of Thomas and Sarah White Bradford. His father worked at a factory in Newport for many years. Billy spent most of his days laboring on a dairy and tobacco farm in Boone Co. owned by his maternal grandparents, John W. and Sarah Fisher. During those years he attended one of Boone Co.'s colored schools through the eighth grade and then was transferred to the **Lincoln-Grant School** in Covington; he left school after completing the 10th grade.

As a youth, Bradford did not foresee a life in public service. However, as a church steward at **Barnes Temple A.M.E. Church** in Elsmere and an admirer of Dr. Martin Luther King's integration and nonviolent philosophies, young Bradford began to take on more leadership roles within his community. (Bradford was able to meet King in 1964 at an A.M.E. church convention at the Cincinnati Gardens, in Cincinnati.) For example, in 1974 he became the first African American elected to the Elsmere City Council; he held that office until 1980. Bradford returned to the council in 1982 and in 1994 was elected as the vice mayor of

Elsmere. At that time he also was one of the founding members of the Elsmere Fire District Board, a group that helped to acquire much-needed equipment for the local Fire Department. Bradford also was elected to the Elsmere Housing Authority Board. When asked about these accomplishments, Bradford replied, "As a farm kid from Boone County . . . I never imagined a life in politics. I have always enjoyed helping people."

In 1998 Billy Bradford was elected mayor of Elsmere, the first African American to hold such a position in Northern Kentucky. He lists the completion of the Garvey Rd. connector and the Industrial Rd. project, as well as the construction of the Elsmere Senior Center, as some of the important ventures of his tenure as mayor. More importantly, however, Mayor Bradford has proclaimed that his spirituality, a dedicated staff, and a diligent city council are the main reasons for his success as mayor; he is also proud that he has been able to help foster a community where African Americans and whites can work and live together harmoniously.

Bradford, Bill "Billy." Interviews by Eric R. Jackson, June 15, 19, 2006, Elsmere, Ky.

"First Annual Northern Kentucky African-American Heritage Festival—1995," Northern Kentucky African American Heritage Task Force Collection, W. Frank Steely Library, Northern Kentucky Univ.

Fisher, John C. K. "Folks View Bradford as Listener, Leader," *KP,* October 24, 1998, 7K.

——. "Northern Kentucky's First Black Mayor," *KP,* October 24, 1998, 1K.

Eric R. Jackson

BRADFORD, JOSHUA TAYLOR (b. December 9, 1818, Bracken Co., Ky.; d. October 31, 1871, Bracken Co., Ky.). The celebrated ovarian surgeon Joshua Bradford was the seventh son of William and Elizabeth Johnson Bradford, pioneer settlers of Bracken Co. Bradford attended the local **Augusta College**, studied under his brother Dr. Jonathan J. Bradford (1806–1878), and graduated from the Transylvania University Medical School in Lexington in February 1839, after completing a dissertation on Asiatic cholera. Joshua Bradford established a large general practice at Augusta. He married Sarah Emily Armstrong on February 4, 1845.

As a doctor, Bradford undertook the very dangerous practice of ovarian surgery, and in two spectacular cases, he removed a 22-pound tumor and a 41-pound tumor. He employed careful selection and diagnosis and used boiled water and other sanitary practices to achieve a record of only 3 deaths in 30 operations—an unparalleled accomplishment that brought accolades from observers both in Europe and in the United States. Bradford also achieved great success in other areas of medicine. He developed an effective treatment for skin cancer, and when confronted with a carious heel bone (the os calcis and the cuboid), Bradford extracted the calculus and restored the limb to full usefulness. In the case of a woman who suffered from complete rupture of the perineum, his knowledge and skills returned her to normal.

Outside of his medical practice, Bradford maintained a successful vineyard and wine cellar. He engaged in various business ventures with his brother Col. **Laban J. Bradford** (1815–1891), judged agricultural contests, and served as president of the Mason and Bracken Co. Agricultural Society. Bradford also loved to hunt, participated in **Whig** politics, and served on the Augusta city council. By mid-October 1861, he felt duty-bound to help preserve the Union and volunteered to be a brigade surgeon and personal physician to his friend Maj. Gen. **William "Bull" Nelson** (1824–1862), a Maysville native. Bradford served in the Union Army's Big Sandy Expedition in Kentucky and went to Camp Wickliffe in Larue Co., Ky., where he served as 10th Brigade Surgeon in Nelson's 4th Division. That division became the first to enter Nashville, Tenn., and it led the advance to Savannah, Tenn. On April 4, 1862, Bradford received a commission as a major in the U.S. Medical Corps., and two days later he became involved in the Battle of Pittsburg Landing (Shiloh, Tenn.). During the fight to retain control of the landing on Sunday evening, April 6, 1862, Bradford led retreating troops back to the front line and fought beside them. Once the situation stabilized, he treated wounded persons from both sides. Just before the 4th Division entered Corinth, Miss., Bradford became severely ill and returned home. While he recuperated in July and August 1862, the Confederates invaded Kentucky, and it became impossible for Bradford to rejoin Nelson in Tennessee. Kentucky governor James F. Robinson (1862–1863) recommended to President Abraham Lincoln (1861–1865) that Bradford become a colonel, authorizing Bradford to raise a regiment to protect the Maysville region. Confederate general Basil Duke, who wanted to stop that effort, attacked Augusta on September 27, 1862. Duke gained nothing from the bloody fight, and later Bradford had to explain to the medical corps just why he had acted in the capacity of an infantry officer. Much to his dismay, that misunderstanding led to his being mustered out of service as a Union medical officer in February 1863.

Bradford returned to family practice and on two occasions declined offers to accept the Dr. George C. Blackman chair of surgery at the Medical College of Cincinnati. Bradford died in 1871 from a hepatic abscess of the liver.

Anderson, W. W. "Dr. Joshua Taylor Bradford," *Kentucky Medical Journal* 15 (1917): 140–42.

Biographical Encyclopedia of Kentucky. Cincinnati: J. M. Armstrong, 1878.

Collins, Richard H. *History of Kentucky.* Vol. 1. Covington, Ky.: Collins, 1882.

"Diary of Joshua Taylor Bradford, 1862," Library of Congress Manuscript Division, Washington, D.C.; National Archives and Records Administration, Medical Officer Files, 7W2/23/8/1 box no. 64; 2916, ACP 1887, 9W3/19/33/5 box no. 1091, CMSR, 7W3/1/22/5 box no. 9.

Schachner, August. "Joshua Taylor Bradford." In *Dictionary of American Medical Biography.* New York: Appleton, 1928.

Transactions of the American Medical Association. Vol. 23. Philadelphia: Collins, 1872.

"W. G. Bradford Statement," Special Collections and Archives, Transylvania Univ.

Donald A. Clark

BRADFORD, LABAN JOHNSON "COLONEL" (b. June 26, 1815, Augusta, Ky.; d. September 11, 1891, Covington, Ky.). Laban J. "Colonel" Bradford, an agriculturalist and a promoter of education, was the son of William and Elizabeth Johnson Bradford. His father, who came from Fort Jackson, Pa., to Irish Station in Nicholas Co. in 1791, became the sheriff of Bracken Co. and acquired more than 1,900 acres of land and 11 slaves. Laban worked on the family farm, received a basic education, and briefly took up medical training with his brother, Jonathan J. Bradford. Laban Bradford started a general merchandise business that shipped goods from New Orleans to Augusta and Maysville. He lived at St. Martinsville, La., on Bayou Teche, for several years and in 1844 married Jane Marie Jewell of Pointe Coupee Parish in Louisiana.

Bradford, who went by the nickname of "Colonel," enjoyed hunting, a good cigar, and a sip of bourbon. In 1855 he served as a member of the Kentucky House of Representatives. He helped to start an institute for feeble-minded individuals, served as chairman of the Committee on Penitentiaries, and promoted a two-year $5,000 appropriation that established the first state agricultural society. In 1857 he persuaded officials in Kentucky to hold the National Tobacco Fair in conjunction with the second State Agricultural Fair. For 7 of the 10 years the Tobacco Fair existed, Bradford served as its president. About this time, he noticed that a particular mutated tobacco plant on his farm appeared superior to the common red burley. He later gave seeds for that mutation to a tobacco grower in Brown Co., Ohio. In a few years, the project to grow this new strain of tobacco proved successful, and over the next decade, the new **white burley tobacco** variety became an economic boon to the region.

In August 1860 Bradford, a slave owner, led a meeting of Democrats at Brooksville who supported John Bell, the 1860 presidential candidate of the Constitutional Unionists. Two years later many of these same men, including Laban Bradford, continuing to regard the Constitution as inviolate, were promoting peace and sought to restore the Union "as it was." As president of the Kentucky State Agricultural Society in 1862–1863, Bradford participated in discussions that led to the February 22, 1865, establishment of the Agricultural and Mechanical (A&M) College at Lexington. From the college's inception, he served as president of the Board of Visitors. When the National Tobacco Convention elected him president, Bradford appealed to the U.S. Revenue Commission not to tax leaf tobacco, and he succeeded in getting existing laws modified. He served as a delegate to the U.S. Fair at Philadelphia and represented the National Tobacco Convention at the Universal Exposition at Paris, France, in 1866. He moved to Covington in 1874 and worked with A&M president James K. Patterson to help ensure the success of the school. In 1878 the A&M College in Lexington became Kentucky State College, and from then on Bradford served as a member of its Board of Trustees. In 1887 his only son, Alexander Jewell Bradford, died from a ruptured appendix while campaigning for state representative. The loss of his son sent Bradford into a steady decline, and he died at his home at 58 W. 11th St. in Covington in 1891. His remains were placed in the family plot at Linden Grove Cemetery in Covington, and in 1892 his home became the new Democratic headquarters. He left behind his widow, Jane Marie, and three children. In 1908 Kentucky State College became the Kentucky State University, and in 1916, fulfilling a cherished dream of Laban Bradford, the school became the University of Kentucky, the flagship educational institution of the commonwealth of Kentucky.

Biographical Encyclopedia of Kentucky of the Dead and Living Men of the Nineteenth Century. Cincinnati: J. M. Armstrong, 1878.

Clowes, Jack. "'My Lady Nicotine' Becomes Cash Crop with Aid of Frankfort's Founder," *Lexington Herald-Leader,* August 10, 1969.

Kenton Co. (Covington) Death Certificate No. 492, for the year 1891.

Laban J. Bradford, Biographical File, Univ. of Kentucky Special Collections.

Perrin, William Henry, J. H. Battle, and G. C. Kniffin. *Kentucky: A History of the State.* Louisville, Ky.: F.A. Battey, 1888.

Donald A. Clark

BRADLEY, JAMES (b. ca. 1800, Africa; date of death unknown). James Bradley, a slave who became an abolitionist, was born into slavery in Africa and as an infant was taken to South Carolina. He was sold to a slave trader, who sold him to the owner of the Bradley Plantation in Pendleton Co., Ky., from which Bradley derived his surname. As a teenager he moved to Arkansas with his owner, performing normal duties by day. By night, with permission from his master, he did odd jobs for other plantation owners and received wages. There were many days when Bradley was only able to muster a few hours of sleep. After five years he had saved $700, which he used to purchase his freedom.

Once free, he briefly returned to Northern Kentucky before entering into free territory in Ohio, crossing the Ohio River at Covington. Soon afterward, Bradley was admitted to the Lane Theological Seminary in Cincinnati. As the first African American student there, he joined in the seminary's abolitionist movement, participating in the famous Lane Debates of 1834. He later attended the Sheffield Manual Labor Institute, a branch of Oberlin College in northern Ohio, for one year. From then on, Bradley appears to be lost to history.

A statue of Bradley was placed along Riverside Dr. in Covington, marking roughly where he crossed the Ohio River into Ohio. Created by sculptor George Danhires, the bronze statue has the dimensions 49 by 29 by 53 inches, with a base of 28 by 8 by 17 inches. Bradley is depicted sitting on a park bench reading a book, a tribute to a man who, in difficult circumstances, taught himself to read.

Lesick, Lawrence Thomas. *The Lane Rebels: Evangelicalism and Antislavery in Antebellum America.* Metuchen, N.J.: Scarecrow Press, 1980.

Weaver, Randall. "Confronting the Soul Destroyers: James Bradley and the Abolitionist Movement's Origin," *Journal of Unconventional History* 11, no. 2 (Winter 2000): 1–13.

Wolff, Christine. "Former Slave Receives Honor 153 Years Late," *CE,* November 2, 1987, D1.

Kareem A. Simpson

BRAMLETTE BAPTIST CHURCH. The Bramlette Baptist Church in Gallatin Co., originally called Lick Creek Baptist Church, was sent out as a colony from the New Liberty Baptist Church and established before 1827. Records show that Bramlette helped to organize another church that year, known as Poplar Grove Church. In 1831 the Lick Creek church was listed as a charter member of the Ten Mile Association. In 1849 the first church building, located on Lick Creek, was constructed of logs cut from nearby woods and hewn by hand. A small window behind the pulpit provided light for the preacher to read by. Only daytime services were held, sometimes just once a month. The preacher came on horseback and stayed with families of the church. His pay was usually yarn socks, knitted by hand, or jeans cloth woven by the women, since each family did its own knitting and weaving in those days. The church was admitted to the Concord Association at its 1859 annual meeting. At a much later date, when a torrential rain caused Lick Creek to rush out of its banks, the church building was washed away and one person drowned. A brave gentleman waded into the church's remains and saved the pulpit Bible. The members reconstructed their church where the creek crossed Ghent-Sanders Rd. in a community called Bramlette, which provided the church's name. When the post office was established there, it was discovered that there was another community in Kentucky named Bramlett, so Carson was chosen as the name for the community.

In 1900 the Bramlette Baptist Church and seven other churches withdrew from the Concord Association to form the White's Run Baptist Association, the first annual meeting of which was held at Bramlette in October 1901. During the **Great Depression** of the 1930s, the pastor was paid five dollars a week, or sometimes he was given a chicken or some other item. During 1940 and 1941, the members built a new building at Carson. In 1965 I-71 was created, passing right through the Carson community, so the church was moved to Lick Creek on Ky. Rt. 465S, near the site of the first church building. Five Sunday school rooms were added and the building was encased in red brick.

Bogardus, Carl R., Sr. *The Story of Gallatin County.* Ed. James C. Claypool. Cincinnati: John S. Swift, 2003.

Ken Massey

BRASHEAR. In northeast Gallatin Co., at the mouth of Steele's Creek, is an area once known as Brashear. The town site is opposite Patriot, Ind., along the Ohio River, and roughly two miles west of the Boone Co. boundary line. A post office operated at Brashear from 1881 until 1887; it was reestablished in 1895 and continued until 1931. The first postmaster was appropriately named John T. Brashear, but the post office reportedly was named for Captain Henry C. Brashear, a noted steamboat pilot of the Cincinnati & Louisville U.S. Mail Line Company. Once the steamboat traffic disappeared, the area was bypassed with the construction of Cincinnati-to-Louisville roads to the south: U.S. 42 (the Old Louisville Rd.) and I-71.

Bogardus, Carl R., Sr. *The Story of Gallatin County.* Ed. James C. Claypool. Cincinnati: John S. Swift, 2003.

BRATTON (PINHOOK; BRATTON'S MILL). Originally within Bracken Co., this Robertson Co. village was founded by the brothers Aaron H. and George Washington "Wash" Bratton in the 1840s. It is five miles north of Mount Olivet, near the North Fork of the Licking River. The name Pinhook is said to come from a story about a small boy who fished in nearby streams with a bent pin as his hook. Others say the name arose from the term for a person who is involved in the buying and selling of tobacco. The Bratton brothers operated a stationary sawmill at Pinhook, which afterward also became a gristmill. Later, a general store, a tobacco warehouse, a post office (1865), and an undertaker appeared in town. One of the original schools in the county was located at Bratton's Mill, before the community's name changed to Pinhook. In 1875, in a three-story building at Pinhook, Wash Bratton opened a normal school. He recognized the need to train teachers and hoped that the school would become a great academy, but it operated for only a few years. For many years, there was a tollgate in town where fees were collected from persons traveling along the Pinhook and Santa Fe turnpikes. Bratton is where Dr. Mark Insko and his partner in the early 1900s, Dr. Clarence Swinford, practiced medicine. Because of the area's remoteness, it was common for medical operations to take place in homes on kitchen tables. The first telephone was installed at the Bratton store in 1908. Bratton is also where residents of that part of the county cast their votes on Election Day. For most of its existence, Bratton has had a population numbering about 20. With the consolidation of schools within Robertson Co. and the improvements in roads, this little village slowly has lost its importance as a gathering place.

Walton, Alma Mae. "Bratton's Mill or Pinhook and Its People," *Mt. Olivet Robertson County Review,* July 1971 (1871–1971 centennial ed.), p. 1.

BRAUN, BOB (b. April 20, 1929, Ludlow; Ky.: d. January 15, 2001, Cincinnati, Ohio). Bob Braun, popular host of radio and television shows, singer, and actor, was raised during the **Great Depression** by hard-working parents John and Thelma Hunnicutt Braun. Braun developed an early interest in entertaining and at age 13 made his debut on WSAI-AM radio as the host of a Saturday-morning knothole baseball show. During his years at Ludlow High School, he did impersonations locally with an amateur act, "Braun and Miller," that he

Bob Braun.

had created. After he graduated from high school, he worked as a lifeguard at Coney Island Amusement Park and sometimes sang at Coney's Moonlight Gardens. His first television appearance, singing with the amateur Harris Rosedale group, was on Crosley Broadcasting's experimental W8XCT, the forerunner of WLWT (Cincinnati). WCPO-TV hired Braun in 1949, and there he ran cameras for the *Paul Dixon Show,* directed the *Uncle Al Show,* and became a regular on the nationally telecast *Dottie Mack Show,* pantomiming songs. His became one of the region's most popular stars. In 1957 Braun won first prize on *Arthur Godfrey's Talent Scouts* on CBS. He then joined WLWT-TV in Cincinnati as a regular cohost on Ruth Lyons's *50-50 Club* and hosted his own *Bandstand* television show. His recording of "Till Death Do Us Part," on the Decca label, peaked at 26 on *Billboard*'s chart in 1962 and led to appearances on Dick Clark's nationally broadcast *American Bandstand* television show. He also had hit singles with "Red Roses for a Blue Lady" and "Sweet Violets." In total, Braun recorded 20 albums and more than 100 singles.

While cohosting the *50-50 Club* with Ruth Lyons, Braun also hosted, between 1963 and 1966, the *Good Morning Show,* a live one-hour weekday-morning radio broadcast from the McAlpin's Department Store Tea Room in downtown Cincinnati. His support cast included **Kenny Price** and later **Nick Clooney**. Clooney eventually took over as host of the *Good Morning Show,* as Braun's duties at the *50-50 Club* increased.

When Ruth Lyons retired in 1967, Braun took over as host of her very popular show, and it became the *Bob Braun Show,* which ran from 1967 until 1984. The show was the number-one-rated live entertainment–information program in the Midwest. The syndicated 90-minute show included live performances and many special guests, including the top entertainers in the nation and politicians. Changing times led to the cancellation of the *Bob Braun Show* in 1984. It was the last locally produced variety show in the Cincinnati region. Braun was also instrumental in maintaining the success of the Ruth Lyons Christmas Fund.

After the demise of the *Bob Braun Show,* Braun moved to California and continued his successful entertainment career. He appeared in four films: *La Pelle* (1981), *Die Hard II (Die Harder)* (1990), *Defending Your Life* (1991), and *Christmas in Connecticut* (1992) . He cohosted the show *Everybody's Money Matters,* hosted KTTV's *Good Day LA* for two years, and served as master of ceremonies on such shows as the *Miss California Pageant* and the *Festival of Roses Parade* for Fox TV. He twice cohosted the Los Angeles *Jerry Lewis Telethon.* He closed out his career back in Cincinnati as host of a morning radio show on WSAI-AM. In 1954 Braun married Wray Jean Wilkinson, and together they had two sons, Rob and Doug, and a daughter, Melissa. For years they lived in Cincinnati. Bob Braun died in 2001, having battled Parkinson's disease, and was buried at Spring Grove Cemetery in Cincinnati. His son Rob Braun is a news anchor for WKRC-TV in Cincinnati.

Bird, Rick. "Goodbye, Bob Braun," *KP,* January 16, 2001, 1C.
Braun, Bob. *Here's Bob.* Garden City, N.Y.: Doubleday, 1969.
Perry, Dick. *Not Just a Sound: The Story of WLW.* Englewood Cliffs, N.J.: Prentice-Hall, 1971.

Robert Schrage

BREAN, DAVID (b. April 12, 1925, Neptune, N.J.; d. October 12, 2004, New York City). David Brean, the son of Rev. William L. and Bessie E. Brean, was a renowned African American artist and educator. Brean graduated from William Grant High School (see **Lincoln-Grant School**) in Covington in 1943. During his senior year, he prepared an art piece that was part of an exhibit at the Cincinnati Art Museum in September 1943. He enlisted in the U.S. Army June 19, 1943, to serve in **World War II**. After the war Brean earned a BA and a BS in education from the University of Cincinnati in 1955. In September 1956 he was enrolled in Columbia University, New York City, pursuing a master of fine arts degree. That same year, he was one of 51 students from throughout the nation to receive a John Hay Whitney Foundation scholarship. He graduated with an MFA on June 4, 1957.

Brean became a director and later director emeritus of the Visual Arts Department of the Harlem School of the Arts in New York and a friend of its founder, Dorothy Maynor. He began teaching at the school from its very beginning. Brean exhibited at the Cincinnati Art Museum, the Cincinnati Modern Art Society, and the Alms Gallery at the University of Cincinnati. His other shows were in New York City, at the Art Students League Gallery and at the Macy Art Gallery at the Teachers College and East Hall Gallery, both at Columbia University.

The Brean family attended the **Ninth St. Methodist Episcopal Church** in Covington. Brean crafted and donated several pieces of art to the church. Brean died in October 2004 in New York City and was cremated. His ashes were returned to Covington and buried with his mother in Linden Grove Cemetery.

"Gets Fellowship," *KTS,* June 12, 1956, 2A.
Murray, Wendy. "Kids' Art Brings Poems to Life—Harlem School of the Arts Students," *Instructor,* January–February 1995.
"Scholarship," *KTS,* October 11, 1956, 4A.

Theodore H. H. Harris

BRECK. The community of Breck in Owen Co. is within the Lusby's Mill Precinct at the intersection of county roads 845 and 1883. It is just east of the **Elk Lake Shores** development, 10 miles southeast of Owenton, and 2 miles west of **Lusby's Mill**. One of the county's original one-room schools was located at Breck. Before the settlement of the county, there were several Indian camps and two Indian burial grounds nearby, and one of the camps was called Breck. Owen Co. resident Bill Booth built the Breck–Elk Ridge Turnpike, improving access to Breck. This is also where the Smith family's cemetery is found. The geography and roadways of the immediate area have changed markedly since the creation of the adjacent Elk Lake Shores development during the early 1960s.

An Atlas of Owen County, Kentucky. Philadelphia: Lake, 1883.
Houchens, Mariam Sidebottom. *History of Owen County: "Sweet Owen."* Louisville, Ky.: Standard, 1976.

BRENT. Settled in the mid-19th century by German immigrants, Brent was an unincorporated Campbell Co. farming community along the Ohio River between two of its tributaries, Three Mile Creek on the west and Four Mile Creek on the east. Brent was originally named Coney Island Station, since it was directly across the river from Ohio's Coney Island amusement park. To avoid confusion in mail delivery, in 1885 the Post Office Department renamed the area Brent after Newport postmaster Philip Brent Spence, father of the future U.S. congressman Brent Spence. Access to Brent was via the **Twelve Mile Turnpike** (today's Ky. Rt. 8/**Mary Ingles Highway**) and later also by railroad. Successive owners operated a ferryboat between Brent and Coney Island beginning as early as 1861. By 1891 Brent boasted many businesses, including lumber sales, coal- and brickyards, a saw and planing mill, a grocery store, a cobbler's shop, a carpenter's enterprise, barber shops, a hotel, an athletic club, and a hauling business. Farming, however, remained the primary occupation. Planners of a resort in Brent were going to market summer-home lots, but that project did not mature. The Brent Public School opened a new schoolhouse on September 14, 1891, raising needed capital through various talent performances by staff and students. By 1898 it had 40 students; it was closed and sold in 1940. Private telephone service came to Brent in a connection with nearby Cold Spring in 1894. Meanwhile, the Brent Tigers baseball team competed against other area squads.

During the first half of the 20th century, construction crews on Lock and Dam No. 36 on the Ohio River and railroad workers from Silver Grove, the C&O Railroad's company town to the southeast, patronized many of Brent's businesses, but economic expansion ceased owing to Silver Grove's emergence. Nonetheless, Brent's small population increased 20-fold on summer Sunday evenings as motorists stopped to view the Coney Island fireworks display over the Ohio River. Eventually, businesses began to leave Brent when the railroad abandoned Silver Grove in 1981. John Laughead, the last area ferryboat operator, stopped making river crossings in 1978, two years after the **Combs-Hehl Bridge** opened and made the automobile the preferred means of access to Coney Island. By a series of annexations between 1982 and 1992, Silver Grove acquired the part of Brent from the south edge of the Mary Ingles Highway north to the Ohio River and several parcels on the south side, including the local fishing lake. The rest of the area south of the highway remains in county jurisdiction. While some small businesses linger, Brent's existence as an independent entity is now history.

"Brent," *KJ*, July 2, 1891, 7. A brief history of Brent.
"Brent—Fundraiser for the New School House," *KJ*, August 13, 1891, 1.
"Cold Spring—To Be Connected by Telephone to Brent," *KJ*, May 4, 1894, 5.
Hubbard, Harlan. *Shanty Boat.* Lexington: Univ. of Kentucky Press, 1977.
Reis, Jim. "Small Brent Once Boomed, but Lost Out to Silver Grove," *KP*, November 29, 1999, 4K.
Sayers, John, police chief, Silver Grove, Ky. Interview by Robert M. Venable, June 24, 2004, Silver Grove, Ky.
Wright, Kay, city clerk, Silver Grove, Ky. Interview by Robert M. Venable, June 24, 2004, Silver Grove, Ky.

Robert Michael Venable

BRENT SPENCE BRIDGE. The Brent Spence Bridge at Covington opened in 1963 as a vital link in the Interstate Highway System (see **Expressways**). The bridge, named for longtime congressman **Brent Spence**, opened with little ceremony on November 25, 1963, the day President John F. Kennedy (1961–1963) was buried. Tolls ceased to be charged on the **John A. Roebling Bridge** in conjunction with the opening of the new structure. Motorcades formed in each direction at the tollbooths of the older bridge and proceeded to break ribbons at 3:30 p.m., signifying the end of the toll requirements, then crossed the bridge and returned to their respective states by way of the new Brent Spence Bridge. Dinners had been scheduled for that evening at three restaurants on the **Gourmet Strip**, to be followed by dedication ceremonies culminating with a fireworks display. The dinners were rescheduled for the following week with Governor Bert Combs (1959–1963) and Lieutenant Governor Wilson Wyatt in attendance. The fireworks were replaced by a 21-gun salute to the slain president. There was sentiment to rename the local structure for Kennedy, but it was announced that instead, the I-65 bridge nearing completion at Louisville would bear his name.

The Brent Spence Bridge, which serves as the Ohio River crossing for both I-75 and I-71, is a three-span double-deck steel cantilever truss structure. The main span is 830.5 feet long, and each side span is 453 feet. Northbound traffic uses the lower deck, southbound traffic the upper deck. Modjeski & Masters, Engineers, of Harrisburg, Pa., designed the bridge, and Charlie B. White, of Alexandria, was the resident engineer for the Kentucky Department of Highways on the bridge construction project. The superstructure was erected by the American Bridge Division of U.S. Steel Corp. of Pittsburgh. A newspaper report at the time noted that the four coats of paint alone weighed 36 tons. The total expenditure for the structure was approximately $10 million, not including the costly approach spans on both sides of the river. Two workmen were killed during the construction.

The bridge has long been a bottleneck in the Interstate System because of its heavy use by local commuter traffic. It was originally designed and built with a 42-foot roadway between the curbs, carrying three 12-foot lanes in each direction. However, the approaches to the bridge narrowed to two lanes, meaning that traffic bottlenecked at the approaches as vehicles fed from three lanes into two. Northbound, the highway dropped a lane at Fifth St. in Covington, and picked up a lane from Fourth St. Southbound traffic in Ohio had two lanes each from I-75 and from the Fort Washington Way segment of I-71 with a merge to the center lane of the bridge. In an attempt to correct the bottleneck, the Kentucky approaches to the bridge were widened to three lanes in the mid-1980s. The curbs and handrails were replaced with barrier walls, providing adequate roadway width to accommodate four substandard 11-foot lanes in each direction. The northbound lanes were restriped to provide these lanes in 1986. The southbound roadway continued to carry just three lanes until after the completion of the Covington Hill reconstruction project in the early 1990s. As a result of these changes, no emergency lanes remain on the bridge, for use when accidents occur.

The Brent Spence Bridge was reportedly designed to carry 80,000 vehicles per day, but it exceeded that traffic volume by 1968, and in 2007 the average traffic count was 156,000 vehicles per day. Trucks constitute roughly 20 percent of this volume. With the heavy increase in traffic on I-71 and I-75, the structure's reconfiguration to carry 4 substandard-width lanes of traffic in each direction, and the absence of emergency shoulders, concerns about the future use of the structure began to arise in the mid-1990s. In 1998 the Ohio-Kentucky-Indiana Regional Council of Governments (**OKI**) commissioned a Major Investment Study (MIS) for the I-71 corridor, which extended from the Cincinnati/Northern Kentucky International Airport to Kings Island. One part of the MIS was to explore various strategies for improving congestion on the Brent Spence Bridge and to analyze its fatigue life (useful safe structural life). As part of the analysis, a rudimentary calculation indicated a structural fatigue life of 16 years for the structure.

In 2000 OKI and the Miami Valley Regional Planning Commission, the metropolitan planning organization for the Dayton, Ohio, area, formed a partnership to undertake an MIS of the section of the I-75 corridor from northern Kentucky to Piqua, Ohio. This analysis, known as the North-South Transportation Initiative, made several recommendations for replacement or rehabilitation projects along the I-75 corridor. One key recommendation was the replacement or rehabilitation of the Brent Spence Bridge in order to improve capacity, access, and safety along the corridor.

Because limited engineering had been performed in both studies, and because the Brent Spence Bridge is located in a very complex urban setting, the Kentucky Transportation Cabinet (KYTC) and the Ohio Department of Transportation (ODOT) decided to explore the feasibility of replacing the Brent Spence Bridge. A detailed engineering analysis of the fatigue life was also determined to be necessary. This 30-month study, known as the Engineering Feasibility Study (EFS), began in 2003. The results of the study indicated that a replacement or rehabilitation of the Brent Spence Bridge was possible and, more importantly, that the previous fatigue-life calculations were inaccurate. Provided that the structure is properly maintained, the actual fatigue life is infinite. The Brent Spence Bridge is determined to be functionally obsolete, as noted in the Federal Highway Administration's (FHWA) National Bridge Inventory, but not structurally deficient.

Based on the recommendations of the EFS, KYTC and ODOT started planning and development of conceptual alternatives for the Brent Spence Bridge Replacement/Rehabilitation project. This phase of the project began in July 2005 and includes the improvement of I-71–I-75 from the Dixie Highway interchange in Kentucky to the Western Hills Viaduct interchange in Ohio. At the time of this writing, four different alternatives are being evaluated. All of them utilize the existing Brent Spence Bridge in conjunction with the addition of a new river crossing. The two structures will carry a combined total of 12–14 lanes, depending on the alternative selected. The selection of a preferred alternative is anticipated in 2009. The current project schedule indicates that construction on the improved I-71–I-75 corridor, including the Brent Spence Bridge and a new river crossing, could begin in 2015. At an estimated cost of $2.09 to $3.03 billion, this project will be the most costly transportation infrastructure project to occur in the Greater Cincinnati area.

Bridge maintenance files, Kentucky Transportation Cabinet, District Six, Fort Mitchell, Ky.
Feasibility and Constructability Study of the Replacement/Rehabilitation of the Brent Spence Bridge, May 2005, Kentucky Transportation Cabinet, District Six, Fort Mitchell, Ky.
"New Bridge Opens; Suspension Freed of Toll," *CE*, November 26, 1963, 1.
Planning Study Report, Brent Spence Bridge Replacement/Rehabilitation Project, September 2006, Kentucky Transportation Cabinet, District Six, Fort Mitchell, Ky.

Ralph Wolff and Robert Hans

BREWING INDUSTRY. The brewing industry followed the migration patterns of the Alsatian, German, and Swiss populations into Northern Kentucky in the mid-19th century. According to the earliest records, the first brewery in Kentucky was in Louisville, an operation that opened in 1808 and closed a few years later. Breweries appeared in the larger cities on both sides of the Ohio River and made beverages including ales, bock, lagers, malt tonics, and porter/stout. These products were sold locally in glassware and on tap in local saloons. They were also served in the saloons that the breweries maintained on their premises. Both the **Bavarian Brewing Company** in Covington and the **Wiedemann Brewing Company** in Newport maintained on-site "tap" rooms for many years; these beer halls were often the venue for important political, social, sports-related, and civic gatherings. Consumers could also bring a container to a brewery or a saloon to carry home beer; many times they used a galvanized tin bucket that had been greased with lard, thus lessening the foaming of the beer as it came from the tap.

Beer was kept chilled in root cellars with blocks of ice or in ice ponds. Bavarian maintained several such ponds on its grounds fronting on Pike St. in Covington. The invention of refrigeration and ice machines in the 1880s made it easier to keep the product cold. Beer had a short shelf life requiring speedy delivery, and frequently it was delivered in horse-drawn wagons. Some older citizens in Newport today can still recall seeing the Wiedemann horse wagons deliver large barrels to local taverns.

Brewing methods were brought from the brewmaster's home country in Europe. George Wiedemann sent his son **Charles Wiedemann** to Germany to learn to become a brewmaster. The breweries were often small, owned and operated by a family, sometimes doubling as the family's residence.

In Northern Kentucky, brewing began as early as the 1830s. Brewmasters moved with their skills from Cincinnati to Newport and Covington and established many smaller breweries during this era, including the Newport Brewery and the Jefferson Street and Lewisburg breweries (both in Covington). Throughout Northern Kentucky other smaller breweries opened, such as the Meister Brewery in Alexandria and the Star, Best, and Brenner breweries in Covington. These operations were either bought out by larger companies or eventually ceased production.

In Kenton Co. by 1838, transplanted Cincinnati brewer Peter Jonte, a native of France, was making beer in Covington at Sixth and Scott Sts. In 1845 Jonte sold the operation to Charles Geisbauer, who sold it to John Brenner and John Seiler in 1881. Three years later, Brenner was the sole owner of the brewery and the malt house, each four stories tall; in 1886 he employed 50 workers and produced 30,000 barrels of beer. It was the home of "IXL Lager Beer," advertised as "Always cool and fresh and sold everywhere." Brenner's business, known as the Covington Lager Beer Brewery, was at 601–629 Scott St. Brenner died in 1895, and Charles Fink became the company president of what was then known as the Covington Brewery. In 1917 Philipp Jung assumed control of the brewery, which closed in 1918 and never reopened. One of the brewery's buildings remains today at the southwest corner of Pike and Scott and is home to a tailor shop, a graphic artist, and apartments.

The largest brewery in Covington was the Bavarian Brewing Company, at 528 W. 12th St., which operated from 1867 until it closed in 1919 because of **Prohibition**. It reopened in 1933 and then closed finally in 1966. In recent years the Party Source, and later Jillian's nightclub, operated in the restored Bavarian Brewing Company building. Jillian's restaurant–entertainment center closed in 2006, and the brewery's former buildings are vacant at this writing.

The Heidelberg Brewing Company, which was located along W. Fourth St. in Covington, opened in 1934. Its new building was designed by Chicago architects Richard Greisser and Son. Heidelberg's president was George H. Meyerratken, and the brewery employed longtime former Bavarian brewmaster Joseph A. "Sep" Ruh and his son Carl Ruh, later a sheriff and politician. Soon it was selling its excellent Student Prince brand as well as its basic Heidelberg product and its Heirloom label, which captured a French Grand Prix Gold Medal in 1939 and was named one of the world's finest. However, the **flood of 1937** and shortages during **World War II** (of both grain and metal for bottle caps) caused the company woes. Bavarian purchased the company in 1949, operating it as Plant Two for the making of Bavarian's own brew. That operation closed in 1955, and the building was sold to the C. Rice Packing Company (meatpackers).

Northern Kentucky's largest and most popular brewer, the Wiedemann Brewing Company, was located in Newport at Sixth and Columbia Sts. It opened in 1870 as the John Butcher Brewery and ceased producing high-alcohol-content beer during Prohibition, when it turned to manufacturing rubbing alcohol. The Wiedemann brewery reopened in 1933. In 1902 the Wiedemann Brewing Company was a financial backer of Kettenackers Bar, a predecessor of **Pompilio's Restaurant** in Newport. Kettenackers Bar was a "kept house," meaning that only Wiedemann brewery products could be sold there in exchange for Wiedemann's financial involvement in the venture. The Wiedemann Brewing Company also supplied the wooden bar used in the business. At the time the Wiedemann Brewing Company closed, it was one of the area's largest industries and clearly had been the largest employer in Newport for many years. In 1967 the G. Heileman Brewing Company of La Crosse, Wis., makers of Old Style and Special Export labels, purchased the Wiedemann Brewing Company for $5 million; the brewing plant in Newport was closed in 1983 and 400 employees were laid off.

Both Wiedemann and Bavarian were players in the Cincinnati beer market, competing in later years with major brewers in that town such as Burger, Hudepohl, Schoenling, and Red Top.

Due to state tax regulations and the need to produce 3.2 percent beer for the younger Ohio market, Wiedemann operated a warehouse along Paddock Rd. in the Bond Hill section of Cincinnati for many years. Northern Kentucky brewers were not allowed simply to deliver beer directly from their plants. In turn, several Northern Kentucky families, such as the Brannens, the Crowes, the Links, the Dennerts, the Snodgrasses, the Doerings, the Pharos, and the Seligmans, plus former Cincinnati Bengal quarterback **Ken Anderson**, owned and operated beer distributorships in Northern Kentucky, selling products brewed outside of the area.

In recent years the microbrewery has appeared in Northern Kentucky. The Oldenberg Brewing Company, located in Fort Mitchell, opened in 1987 as a microbrewery and closed in 2000. The Party Source, a local spirits specialty store, was making its own brew when it was located in the former Bavarian building in Covington. Since 2003 the Hofbrauhaus, a restaurant and beer hall patterned after the famous establishment of the same name in Munich, has operated successfully in Newport at Third and Washington Sts.; it not only offers food and German entertainment but has its own microbrewery on-site.

Some of the first celebrations of German heritage in Kentucky were held in Northern Kentucky. In Covington an annual "Volksfest" parade included the police and fire departments. Other parade participants celebrating ties to their German heritage included the Shooting (see **Schuetzen Clubs**), Pioneer, **Arion Männerchor**, and Turner societies and the German Workers' Club, named Arbeiter-Verein. Some events during these local celebrations of the area's German heritage included beer, while others were more religious in nature, concluding with a church service. Today there are at least four different German heritage organizations in the Greater Cincinnati area that hold annual Oktoberfest celebrations. At each of these events traditional beer kegs are tapped and German food is served. During the summer many Northern Kentucky churches stage weekend fundraising festivals, where beer and German bratwurst are the standard fare.

Harper, Laurel. "Rumors Brewing at Wiedemann," *Campbell County News*, January 17, 1980, 1.

Holian, Timothy J. *Over the Barrel: The Brewing History and Beer Culture of Cincinnati, 1800 to the Present.* 2 vols. St. Joseph, Mo.: Sudhaus Press, 2000.

Reis, Jim. "Even Prohibition Didn't Stop Bavarian Brewmaster Family," *KP*, August 16, 1999, 4K.

———. "Heidelberg Brewery Tasted Fame Early, Fizzled in 15 Years," *KP*, June 17, 1985, 4K.

———. "Memory of Bavarian Beer Fades: Brew Was Popular for Some 100 Years," *KP*, August 25, 1986, 4K.

———. "Turning Barley into Big Bucks," *KP*, October 20, 2003, 5K.

Sweeney, Michael R. "Pompilio's Restaurant, a Centennial History: 70 Years of Spaghetti and More," *NKH* 11, no. 2 (Spring–Summer 2004): 2–20.

Wimberg, Robert J. *Cincinnati Breweries.* Cincinnati: Ohio Book Store, 1989.

Jeanne Greiser

BRICKYARDS. Shortly after settlement of the region, families in Northern Kentucky began living in brick homes rather than in primitive log cabins. Skilled brick-makers were needed to fashion the bricks used to build the new homes. Early newspapers suggest that traveling brick-makers often manufactured bricks from clay excavated at the building site. Many of these itinerant brick workers also laid the bricks for the structures. In the larger communities, there arose small primitive brickyards, where handmade bricks were fired in kilns constructed of the green (unfired) bricks. The finished bricks were transported to building sites in heavy-duty wagons. The tradition of making bricks by hand continued in Northern Kentucky until the 1870s or 1880s.

By the 1880s many brickyards had acquired machines that allowed them to produce large quantities of bricks. Most of the machines replicated the hand-making technology: they mixed the clay, filled trays with clay, removed the excess clay, and then dumped the green bricks. This is known as the soft-mud method. The molds that were used allowed companies often to add their brand name to each brick. Brickyards of this period employed drying sheds to protect the unfired bricks from the elements until they were sufficiently dried. The firing of the bricks removed the remaining moisture and hardened the clay into nearly indestructible building material. Permanent updraft kilns were also utilized during this period. Some of these late-19th-century brickyards were able to produce tremendous quantities of bricks, as many as 3.5 million during a production season.

During the early 20th century, additional innovations were introduced into the brick industry. Some brickyards used machines that pressed low-moisture clay into bricks inside steel molds. Many brickyards shifted to stiff-mud brick machines, which produced a continuous column of clay that was cut into bricks by wires attached to a revolving wheel. Initially, stiff-mud bricks were solid, but later they were made with holes to reduce their weight and shipping costs. They evolved into the 10-hole bricks that are common today. Updraft kilns continued to be used, but more efficient downdraft (beehive-shaped) kilns were added to many brickyards. Large quantities of bricks were mass-produced by these modern brick-making facilities. Some of the soft-mud brick machines could produce 40,000 bricks per day, while some stiff-mud machines could produce 30,000 to 45,000. In spite of great productivity, the Northern Kentucky brick industry was in decline by the 1930s and 1940s and had disappeared by the middle of the century.

The brick industry was concentrated near urban areas, where there was a great demand for new bricks. Often several brickyards operated within one of the larger communities, whereas the more rural counties might have a single brickyard. Abundant clay resources and cheap transportation were important considerations in the placement of these yards. Brickyards located near a major river or rail line could ship bricks to more distant markets.

Few details are available about the early brickyards of Northern Kentucky. Starting in 1859, local gazetteers and business directories listed various industries, including brickyards. Also, city directories for Covington contained business directories for several other communities in the vicinity. No brickyards were listed for either Gallatin or Robertson Co. in these directories. The primary production centers for bricks in Northern Kentucky were in Campbell, Kenton, and Mason counties. The list below gives company names, dates of operation and brick production statistics if available, and some additional notes.

Boone Co.

Walton: J. J. Craven, ca. 1895–1906.

Bracken Co.

Augusta: A. J. Ritter, 1883–1884; Woods & Keene, 1896.

Foster: Unnamed brickyard, 120,000 bricks in 1880.

Campbell Co.

Bellevue: Brickyards were concentrated in the Fairfield Ave. area.

Dayton: J. C. Ramsey, 1884–1885; Ryall & Otters, 1886–1887. Dayton had eight brickyards in all.

Fort Thomas: One brickyard.

Mentor: One brickyard.

Newport: Abbott & Morten, 1869; Marion M. Allen Supply Company; Co-Operative Manufacturing & Home Company; Frank Derrick, 1898 (or earlier) to 1929; Adam Ebert, 1878 (or earlier) to 1882; James Ebert, 2,150,000 bricks in 1880; F. W. Tippenhauer, 2,730,000 bricks in 1880.

Carroll Co.

Carrollton: Carrollton Brick Company; Thomas Diston; H. Grobmeyer; J. E. Grobmyer & Company; George Meier; Gary Mercer.

Grant Co.

Williamstown: W. T. James, 1883–1884.

Kenton Co.

Bromley: Foley & Aspey, 1895–1899; N. W & J. W. Foley, 1892–1901.

Covington: Benhoff & Samping, 600,000 bricks in 1880; Henry Berte; Clemens Bramlage; Broering and Meier; John J. Brown; Anthony Bruegge; Brumlager & Arkanna Brick Company; Busse & Bramlage, 1878–1879; Busse & Company, 1876–1877; Busse Brick Company, 1904–1932; Busse-Heidecker Brick Company, 1894–1903; J. J. Busse & Sons and Henry Binz partnership, 1888–1889, produced enameled bricks; J. J. Busse Sons, 1882–1892; John J. Busse, 1876–1887; Joseph J. Busse, 1,200,000 bricks in 1870, 2,250,000 bricks in 1880; B. Haring Company; Haven & Brinke; Hefkers & Brocke; H. H. Heidecker, 800,000 bricks in 1880; Bernard Heving; B. Heving & Company, 1,200,000 bricks in 1870, 1,400,000 bricks in 1880; Herman Hoefkers; A. W. Keen; Kenton Brick Company; Kroger & Gerhauser; Frank Lamping (also spelled Lampeng); August Meier & Company; J. Henry Meier; Clemens Schweinefuss, 700,000 bricks in 1880; Henry Schweinefuss (also spelled Schweinefus); Speiler & Meihaus; Ignatz Speller; Staggenborg & Kreimborg; Tate Builders Supply Company; Venholf & Company; John Volkering; John Waldron; Wehebrink & Meier; Joseph Wieghaus & Brother, 1,500,000 bricks in 1880; J. C. Wilde Company, successor to the T. W. Spinks Company; **St. Augustine Catholic Church**, two brickyards.

Erlanger: Fred Ficke & Company; Herman Ficke; T. W. Spinks (branch office), 1938–1941.

Ludlow: Several brickyards.

Unspecified locations: Pickens Broaddus, 800,000 bricks in 1850; Haggermain (?) & Brother, 2,000,000 bricks in 1870; William Hopkins, 800,000 bricks in 1850; Herman Hyncker, 700,000 bricks in 1870; I. Keene, 3,552,000 bricks in 1850; Hiram and T. (or I.) Martin, 3,000,000 bricks in 1850; Southgate Stample (?), 2,500,000 bricks in 1850.

Mason Co.

Maysville: Newton Cooper & Company; Holiday & Hutchinson; **Maysville Brick Company**, 1894–1956; **Sphar Brick Company**, 1878–1960.

Unspecified locations: Garislaw Mertchell, 1,200,000 bricks in 1850; Thomas Iquatine Mertchell, 430,000 bricks in 1850; Harrison B. Niellelson, 800,000 bricks in 1850.

Owen Co.

Owenton: J. N. Beck, 1906

Pendleton Co.

Aspen Grove and Falmouth had brickyards.

Covington and Newport city directories, various years, 1861–1929.

Haddock, T. M. *Haddock's General and Business Directory of Covington, Newport, 1878–1879.* Cincinnati: T. J. Smith; Wrightson, 1879.

Hawes, George W. *George Hawes' Kentucky State Gazetteer and Business Directory for 1859 and 1860.* Louisville, Ky.: George W. Hawes, 1859.

Ries, Heinrich. *The Clay Deposits of Kentucky: An Economic Consideration of the Pottery, Brick, and Tile Clays, Fire Clays, and Shales of Kentucky, with Notes on Their Industrial Development.* Series 6, vol. 2. Frankfort: Kentucky Geological Survey, 1922.

R. L. Polk Company. *Kentucky State Gazetteer and Business Directory.* Detroit: R. L. Polk, 1876–1896.

Ryan, Paul E. *History of the Diocese of Covington, Kentucky.* Covington, Ky.: Diocese of Covington, 1954.

Seiller, Edward F. *Kentucky Natural Resources, Industrial Statistics, Industrial Directory Descriptions by Counties.* Bureau of Agriculture, Labor, and Statistics, Bulletin 34. Frankfort, Ky.: State Journal, 1929.

Young & Company. *Business Professional Directory of the Cities and Towns of Kentucky.* Atlanta, Ga.: Young, 1906.

Charles D. Hockensmith

BRIGHT, JESSE D. (b. December 18, 1812, Norwich, N.Y.; d. May 20, 1875, Baltimore, Md.). Jesse David Bright, a U.S. senator and a Kentucky legislator, moved with his family in 1820 to Madison, Ind., after a brief stay along the way in Shelbyville, Ky. Although he is generally associated with Hoosier politics, Bright had and maintained ties with the Bluegrass State. As a young man, Bright made frequent trips into Kentucky, where he met his wife, Mary E. Turpin. They were married in 1835 and had seven children. Bright practiced law in Madison and eventually became an influential member of the Democratic Party in Indiana. His reputation earned him an appointment as U.S. marshal in 1840, and in 1843 he began a term as Indiana's lieutenant governor. Although he was not an eloquent speaker, his charisma and shrewd personality allowed him to enter the realm of national politics. Indiana Democrats rewarded Bright's service to the party by choosing him in 1845 to occupy a seat in the U.S. Senate, which he held until 1862.

Bright's most enduring legacy during his leadership of the Indiana Democratic Party was his participation in the intense national debate over slavery in the 1850s. As the Indiana Democratic champion in the Senate, Bright advocated compromise on the issue of slavery's expansion into the territories, vehemently contesting the Free-Soil Party's stance against tying the issues of slavery and westward expansion together. Between 1853 and 1857, while he was president of the Senate, Bright used his position to frustrate the efforts of antislavery politicians, including some of the founding members of the Republican Party. Throughout this period, Bright maintained his strong Kentucky connections, which included owning a farm and 20 slaves in the state.

Bright's career as a U.S. senator ended with his expulsion in 1862, a result of the bitter partisanship that characterized **Civil War** politics. Republicans seized on the discovery of a letter of introduction Bright wrote to Jefferson Davis, president of the Confederacy, on behalf of Thomas B. Lincoln, an arms dealer, as an opportunity to eliminate one of their most vocal critics. Although Bright wrote the letter in March 1861, before the war began, Republicans pointed to Bright's deference toward Davis as evidence of disloyalty. In February 1862 the mostly Republican Senate voted 32 to 14 to expel him. After several unsuccessful attempts to regain his seat, Bright moved to Carrollton, Ky., and eventually settled in Covington. Bright's opposition to the Republican Party did not hamper his political aspirations in Kentucky. He represented Trimble and Carroll counties in the state legislature from 1866 to 1874. Bright moved to Baltimore, Md., in 1874 to pursue business interests; he died one year later of heart disease and was buried at Greenmount Cemetery in Baltimore.

Biographical Directory of the United States Congress. "Bright, Jesse David (1812–1875)." http://bioguide.congress.gov/scripts/biodisplay.pl?index=b000835 (accessed April 3, 2007).

Lewis, Ethan M. "The Expulsion of Senator Jesse Bright," 1994. www.ethanlewis.org/jessebright (accessed March 19, 2005).

Murphy, Charles B. "The Political Career of Jesse D. Bright," *Indiana Historical Society Publications* 10, no. 3 (1931): 101–45.

Van Der Weele, Wayne J. "Jesse David Bright, Master Politician from the Old Northwest," PhD diss., Indiana Univ., 1958.

Volpe, Vernon L. "Jesse David Bright." In *American National Biography*, ed. John A Garraty and Mark C. Carnes, 3:550–51. New York: Oxford Univ. Press, 1999.

Stephen Rockenbach

BRIGHTON CENTER. The Brighton Center is a social-service agency based in Newport and serving more than 40,000 families in Northern Kentucky with low to moderate incomes. The center operates child-care programs and a shelter for runaways and offers employment counseling, housing assistance counseling, and housing for needy families and single, married, and widowed (or displaced) senior citizens. It is also involved in development and networking activities with the Appalachian Regional Commission (see **Appalachians**).

The center was established to provide religious instruction to Roman Catholic children living in Newport's **West End**, but its mission quickly expanded. Founder Rev. William Neuroth soon recognized that that part of the city was going through a profound transition. The West End, which had been a largely homogeneous Catholic community, was experiencing an influx of families who had left impoverished communities in Appalachia. Neuroth, influenced by his work at the Bible Center in Cincinnati's Over-the-Rhine neighborhood, where young seminarians and other volunteers brought the church to the people of that poverty-stricken community, concluded that a center in Newport's West End would best serve the needs of the people if it offered a combination of Christian witness, educational activities, recreation, and social services. He rented an abandoned storefront at Eighth and Brighton Sts., and the organization's original name, Brighton Street Center, was coined when it opened on June 15, 1966.

The Brighton Street Center helped pioneer an ecumenical movement in the area by bringing together volunteers from churches throughout the Greater Cincinnati area. The organization became a United Way agency in 1970; that same year, Robert Brewster became the center's executive director, a position he continues to hold. In 1985 the organization changed its name to the Brighton Center; its headquarters is currently located at 799 Ann St. in Newport.

Since its inception, the Brighton Center has sought to address the needs of people of all ages. One of its earliest programs, the Clothing Closet, is still in existence. Its preschool program, begun in 1985, was followed a year later by the Family Day Care program, to provide families with child-care in private homes. Other programs include Every Child Succeeds, a youth strategies program, the Family Development Program, and Project Safe Place, which assists young people in crisis. Since 1983 the Brighton Center's Homeward Bound Runaway Shelter has provided emergency care for runaway teenagers and homeless young people. Two family centers provide food, clothing, and emergency assistance.

Brighton Center has long been active in generating housing for low- and moderate-income families. Its Two Rivers apartments, opened in 1983, were followed by the Austinburg Apartments in 1994 and two years later by the Brighton Row II housing development. The center has since joined the City of Newport in projects to encourage home ownership.

The center operates on an annual budget of approximately $6.4 million dollars. Resources come from the United Way Fund, contributions, and state and private grants. The center has a staff of 50 full-time and part-time workers as well as more than 1,000 volunteers.

"A Bright Spot in Newport," *SC*, February 18, 2005, 6C.

Rutledge, Mike. "Brighton Family Center Begins to Take Shape," *KP*, December 13, 2002, 2K.

Welcome to Brighton Center. www.brightoncenter.com (accessed March 18, 2006).

Jeanne Greiser

BROMLEY (KENTON CO.). The history of the city of Bromley, located along the Ohio River in Kenton Co., can be traced to the year 1784, when Prettyman Merry received a land grant of 2,000 acres in the area from the U.S. government. Soon afterward the Merry family began constructing a home on this property. Called the Landmark, the house stands today in Bromley on Shelby St.

The need for a suitable road to link the western section of Kenton Co. to Ludlow began to be discussed in 1846. In that year George Anderson, who lived at the mouth of the Dry Creek between Ludlow and Bromley, held a meeting of interested residents, and they established a corporation to build the new road. Funds were raised and construction on the Dry Creek Turnpike (Ky. Rt. 8) began. The easy access to employment opportunities in Ludlow and Covington that the turnpike provided resulted in a population boom for Bromley. Initially, the tollgate for the turnpike was located on the east side of Pleasant Run Creek in Ludlow, but in 1872 the tollgate was moved to the Bromley side of the creek.

In 1848 Charles Collins acquired a portion of the original Merry estate and immediately commissioned the design of a small town on his property. He named the town Bromley after his hometown in England. As the village of Bromley grew, residents began discussing the need for street and other improvements. At town meetings in 1890, the residents decided to incorporate, and the State of Kentucky officially approved the incorporation of the city of Bromley on May 23, 1890.

By the 1860s a public school was in operation. In 1893 the citizens of the town financed the construction of a permanent schoolhouse, a brick building constructed on Shelby St. Bromley did not sponsor a high school program; Bromley students attended nearby Ludlow High School, paying tuition for the privilege. In 1920 a number of residents filed suit to force the county school district to offer high school courses, but the suit was struck down by the Kenton Co. Circuit Court. The issue of a high school in Bromley was again raised in 1936. State officials mandated that every school district in Kentucky provide a high school curriculum. Because tax revenues in Bromley were not sufficient to finance the operation of a high school, the Bromley Independent School District merged with the Kenton Co. Public Schools (see **Kenton Co. School District**) in September 1936. Now Bromley residents could attend grades K–12 without paying tuition. The Kenton Co. School System constructed a new Bromley elementary school in 1950, and it was replaced according to county plans that began during the late 1980s. The new school was built in the neighboring community of Villa Hills, and in 1992 the Bromley Elementary School closed; the building was eventually remodeled for use as an apartment building. Bromley students now attend River Ridge School in Villa Hills, Turkey Foot Middle School, and **Dixie Heights High School** in Edgewood.

Beginning in the 1890s, several churches appeared in the community. In 1892 the **Bromley Christian Church** was established on Kenton St. In 1894 the First German Reformed Church (the **Immanuel United Church of Christ**) was established and acquired property at the northeast corner of Boone and Harris Sts. On this site a small frame church was constructed. The cornerstone of the building was set in place on July 15, 1894, and the building was dedicated on September 30, 1894. During the early 1980s, the Pleasant View Baptist Church of Constance relocated to Pike St. in Bromley. The congregation sponsored a private school offering grades K–12. In 1999 the congregation constructed a new worship space.

A town volunteer fire department was established in 1895, after a fire destroyed the local Highhouse and Hilker Grocery. Residents soon lost interest, however, and the department dissolved. Another tragic fire in 1900, which destroyed eight homes and businesses, clearly demonstrated the city's need for a fire department, so the citizens met on October 4, 1900, and established the Bromley Volunteer Fire Department.

The exact date of construction for Bromley's first city hall has been lost to history. By 1910, however, a city hall is mentioned in local newspapers. The structure was built on the north side of Boone St. west of Harris St. (Steve Tanner St.), and a 25-by-30-foot addition, including a large meeting hall, was constructed in 1939. In 1961 Bromley voters approved a bond issue of $40,000 to remodel the city hall–firehouse, by a vote of 145 to 53. The exterior of the building was remodeled in the Colonial Revival style, and the interior of the structure was also extensively modernized. A new bay for fire apparatus was added to the building in 2001.

The issue of sanitation services brought controversy to the small community of Bromley. In 1954 **Sanitation District No. 1** (see also **Sanitation**) constructed a large sewage treatment plant in town along Pike St. Bromley residents opposed the facility from the beginning, arguing that it should have been built in a more rural setting. The relationship between the sanitation district and the city remained tense for decades; then finally, the district closed the plant in 1979. Since then, the site has served as a fish restaurant and later as a Chinese restaurant, both unsuccessfully.

Bromley has suffered from periodic flooding throughout its history, since much of the city was built on low ground near the Ohio River. Early floods, including the **flood of 1913**, did severe damage to the town, but the **flood of 1937** clearly was the greatest catastrophe in the history of the city. Floodwaters began rising in mid-January and cut off the natural gas supply on January 23. By that time, a ferry was in operation between Ludlow and Bromley, which supplied the city with coal and food. On Black Sunday, January 25, 1937, the Ohio River reached 79.9 feet, and 70 percent of Bromley was under water. The Bromley City Hall became a relief headquarters, where food was served and a number of people found temporary shelter. By January 26, some 600 Bromley residents had been driven from their homes. Many were living with friends and relatives on high ground. Relief activities were under the direction of Bromley fire chief Walter Scheid, and Herman Bogenschutz, a Bromley grocer, was put in charge of food rationing. As the floodwaters receded, cleanup work began. Nearly 20 homes in the city had been shifted from their foundations during the flood; seven homes had simply disappeared downriver. Although the federal government sent 165 Works Progress Administration (WPA) workers to Bromley and Ludlow to aid in the cleanup, it took the city of Bromley months to recover from the devastation. The 1937 flood gave the residents of Bromley the impetus to construct Highwater Rd., which linked the city to Crescent Springs and provided a needed exit route for Bromley during floods.

The **flood of 1997** caused considerable damage to Bromley. On March 3, 1997, the Ohio River spilled over its banks, blocking Ky. Rt. 8 between Bromley and Ludlow. By March 5, the only way in and out of Bromley was by Highwater Rd. As the floodwaters continued to rise, members of the Bromley Fire Department patrolled the city in a small boat dubbed the "minnow." Almost 100 families in Bromley were driven from their homes; many residents fled the city. Three families who had been forced from their homes took up residence in the city hall, and many others were given shelter by the **Sisters of St. Benedict** at St. Walburg Convent in Villa Hills. Several hundred meals were served at the Bromley Firehouse under the guidance of the Salvation Army. When the Ohio River finally crested at 64.7 feet on March 7, 1997, 133 structures in Bromley were located in the flood zone. Cleanup began as soon as the water receded and lasted well into April 1997.

In 2000 the city of Bromley had a population of 838.

"Extended Vacation Is Prospect Faced by Bromley Children," *KTS,* September 10, 1936, 1.

Kenton Co. Public Library Local History Files, Covington, Ky.

Reis, Jim. "Growing from Civil War Fort to Major Suburb." In *Pieces of the Past,* vol. 1. Covington: Kentucky Post, 1988.

"School Merger Being Urged," *KTS,* September 9, 1936, 1.

U.S. Census Bureau. "American Fact Finder. Data Set. Census 2000 Summary File 1 (SF1) 100-Percent Data. Custom Table." www.census.gov (accessed July 14, 2006).

David E. Schroeder

BROMLEY (OWEN CO.). Bromley in Owen Co., not to be confused with the Kenton Co. city of the same name, is located on Ky. Rt. 35, north of its junction with U.S. 127, eight miles north of Owenton. It is within the Poplar Grove Precinct. Bromley was named for the Bromley brothers, Al and Robert, and it had a post office from 1861 until 1906. There was once a one-room school at Bromley also. In recent years a farm implement store and a beauty shop have operated in the town.

An Atlas of Owen County, Kentucky. Philadelphia: Lake, 1883.

Rennick, Robert M. *Kentucky Place Names.* Lexington: Univ. Press of Kentucky, 1984.

Houchens, Mariam Sidebottom. *History of Owen County: "Sweet Owen."* Louisville, Ky.: Standard, 1976.

BROMLEY CHRISTIAN CHURCH. There were no churches in Bromley when it was first chartered as a city in 1890. Therefore, some individuals, most of whom had been attending worship services in Scott's Chapel, on the river road below Bromley, decided they would build a church of their own. Bromley Christian Church was soon established with the construction of a small wooden building and dedicated on Sunday, September 25, 1892. Among the founders were J. W. Foley, George Gardiner, John J. Gardiner, Mr. and Mrs. John Heist, Mrs. J. Jones, Mollie Jones, William Underwood, and Mrs. Mary Weber. The 1892 minute book further states that the cost of the church, not including paint, was $841.42.

Early ministers include Louis Koehler, who served from 1912 until 1919, W. L. Richards, John Ricketts, and Elwood C. Nance. In 1925, during Nance's tenure, a building committee consisting of Charles Brown, John J. Gardiner, Henry Haberle, Louis Penick, and Albert Smith was appointed to design a new house of worship. During the construction, services were held at the Bromley School on Shelby St. Many church members were experienced in the trades and participated in the building of the church, which was dedicated on April 8, 1928, and continues to be used. The plain block exterior belies the beautiful oak hardwood furniture and pews of the interior, illuminated by many stained glass windows.

On January 2, 1927, Walter E. Mill was called and served as minister until his death on December 22, 1952. Subsequent ministers included Charles Gilliam (1953–1954), Stuart Mill (son of Walter, 1954–1958), Frank Reese (1958–1959), Ira R. Harris (1960–1964), Nobel Lucas (interim, 1964–1965), Bill Sale (1965–1972), Milton Butler Jr. (1973–1978), Roy Bentley (1978–1997) and Marion (Pete) Gosney, (1997–present).

Although Bromley is a "river" town and plagued by many spring floods, the church sits high on Kenton St. and was not affected even by the great **flood**

of 1937. In fact, many displaced persons were housed in the church basement during the flood. The building has undergone two major renovations over the years. In 1955 the kitchen was remodeled and the basement partitioned with movable walls for Sunday school classes. In 1975 the sanctuary was redesigned and a new organ purchased. It was dedicated to the church's young organist, Tim Pace, who tragically drowned at Cumberland Falls at age 18. The church has owned three parsonages; one on Deverill St. in Ludlow, one on Old State Rd. in Park Hills, and one on Moore St. in Bromley. Even with a declining membership, the church maintains a strong presence with community events, social gatherings, and support of world missions. The church is associated with the Disciples of Christ.

Rouse, James W., and Edward A. Voelker. Bromley Christian Church scrapbook, Bromley Christian Church, Bromley, Ky.

Dale E. Voelker

BROMLEY POTTERY. This early Northern Kentucky pottery can be traced to the flood of British immigrants that began in the mid-1830s. Some of them were highly skilled potters from the Staffordshire district of west-central England who were coming to the United States to work in existing potteries or to establish their own businesses. William Bromley and his brother Thomas left Stoke-upon-Trent in England during the 1830s. They may have worked briefly at the pottery center of East Liverpool, Ohio, before settling in Cincinnati sometime in the late 1830s. William operated or worked at the Brighton Pottery near Hamilton Rd. and Freeman Ave. in the northwest part of Cincinnati from at least the mid-1840s through the mid-1860s. Kenton Co. property deeds indicate that he began to acquire parcels of land at the northwest corner of Second St. and Madison Ave. in Covington beginning in 1839. By 1859 William Bromley had assembled a rectangular parcel measuring 109 by 125 feet, upon which he constructed a two-kiln yellow-ware pottery plant. He apparently operated both the Covington Pottery and the Brighton Pottery until approximately 1864. Bromley's Covington operation was well described in the 1860 Manufacturing Schedule of the U.S. Census. He produced domestic queensware (yellow ware), many of the items in large quantities. Listed were 2,500 dozen pitchers, 3,000 dozen bowls, and 1,000 dozen fruit jars. Bromley invested $5,000 capital in the pottery and had receipts of $7,800 for 1860. All 10 employees were males, and an average of $300 was paid in monthly wages for all 10. Historical and archaeological data indicate that Bromley was manufacturing mostly sanitary ware and kitchenware in Covington. The majority of his high-end products, including hound-handled pitchers and tobacco jars, most with elaborate appliquéd hallmarks, were produced at his Brighton facility. The end of Bromley's Covington operation was heralded by the transfer of a portion of his property to the **Hemingray Glass Company** in 1864 and was finalized by the sale of all remaining parcels to the Hemingray firm in 1865 for $10,000. That 1865 deed indicates that William Bromley and his wife Susannah lived in a small house at the former pottery site.

In 1986 the former site of Bromley's Covington Pottery was excavated pursuant to a proposed development at the Covington Nineteenth Century Riverfront District (see **Covington Urban Archaeology**; **Hemingray Glass Company Archaeology**). During a testing phase, no structural elements of the pottery facility were located, but large quantities of wasters (e.g., unglazed and undecorated shards; annular, dendrite, and Rockingham-decorated shards; fragments of the containers used to fire delicate pieces; and various kiln furniture) were recovered. During the final mitigation phase, the most notable pottery features were a pair of updraft bottle-type kiln bases. Only the bases remained; the chambers, stacks, and accessory structures had been removed during expansion of the Hemingray Company's plant during the late 1860s. The first of the kiln chambers measured 18.5 feet in diameter, while the second, largely destroyed by Hemingray construction, was between 18.4 and 21.7 feet in diameter. Kitchenware at the site was represented by canning jars, small bowls, mixing bowls, pie plates, pitchers, crocks, tea or coffee pots, mugs, and bottles. Sanitary ware included chamber pots, spittoons, and urinals. Annular-decorated wares were wheel-thrown and turned, some pitchers were likely slip-cast, and other wares were either slip-cast or jigger-molded.

Genheimer, Robert A. "Archaeological Testing, Evaluation, and Final Mitigation Excavations at Covington's Riverfront Redevelopment Phase 2 Site, Kenton County, Kentucky," prepared by R. G. Archaeological Services, Covington, Ky., and submitted to the City of Covington, 1987.

——. "Bromley's Covington Pottery: A Study in Mid-19th Century Utilitarian Ware Production," *Ohio Valley Historical Archaeology* 6 (1988): 55–64.

Robert A. Genheimer

BROOKSVILLE. Brooksville, the county seat of Bracken Co., is in the geographic center of the county and on a natural watershed. The city is along the old State Road, which stretched from Augusta to Cynthiana and on to Georgetown, intersecting the buffalo trace (see **Buffalo Traces**) on the high ground in the central ridge of the county. When the Woodward brothers, William and Joel, ventured to this part of Kentucky, they built their cabins and brick homes at this juncture. The large brick house in Brooksville on the corner of Miami St. and Ky. Rt. 19 remains to remind citizens of the settlers and their legacy when the town was known as Woodward's Cross Road.

The Frazee family was also well known in the early days of the town. Many of the town's citizens bought property from the Frazees. Without a river port or manufacturing facility, the settlement grew slowly, even though it was on the route of travel to Central Kentucky. What served as an impetus for growth was the transfer of the county courthouse from Augusta to Woodward's Cross Road. In 1839 Representative David Brooks of Woodward's Cross Road successfully maneuvered a bill through the Kentucky legislature to move the county court's proceedings to his more centrally located hometown. In honor of him, the town was renamed Brooksville.

The normal growth accompanying the relocation of the courthouse ensued, and Brooksville seemed to be set for the future. However, four major fires swept the business section, each nearly destroying the small town. On February 12, 1899, the *Brooksville Review* reported that the central business section was destroyed even though the fire alarms, the B&W whistle, and the courthouse bell had all been sounded. Fighting the fire was difficult because it was said to be eight degrees below zero that day, with snow covering the ground. The fire began in the Hackett block (Downard building) and spread to the Pope Hotel, the Barrett Drugstore, the *Brooksville Review* office, the Wallen block, Spark's grocery, Zeitz's barbershop, and several houses. Six weeks later, on March 27, another fire worked its way through the town, beginning at Commonwealth Attorney Eginhard Daum's home. This fire spread quickly owing to the supply of coal oil stored in the affected buildings. Several homes and businesses were destroyed that had been spared in the February blaze.

Since the majority of structures had to be replaced, many owners decided to rebuild using brick. Fires burned near some of these new brick buildings in 1919 and 1921, when more of the clapboard buildings were destroyed. Slowly, Miami and Locust Sts. in Brooksville were rebuilt, and several businesses reopened on these streets. In 1934 Works Progress Administration workers constructed the City Building, where city court was held on the second floor.

Brooksville has been home to several doctors, who have occupied the fine buildings constructed between and after the fires. The Wallin men were most faithful to the town, beginning with Dr. David Jackson Wallin (1840–1924) and his sons Dr. Will Wallin (1870–1959) and Dr. Carly Wallin (1872–1945); they became long-term medical practitioners in town. Dr. David Wallin had come to Brooksville after the **Civil War** from Mount Sterling, where his father, Dr. John Wallin, practiced medicine. Along with the Wallins was Dr. Benjamin Workman (1888–1967), who graduated from the Louisville School of Medicine before opening an office near Brooksville in the hamlet of Powersville. Dr. C. R. Haley moved his practice to Brooksville on Locust St. It was reported that he delivered nearly 4,000 babies in his 50 years of medical practice. Coming to Brooksville next were Dr. J. M. Stevenson and Dr. Dewey E. Cummins. Cummins remained in Brooksville from 1961 until his retirement in 1989.

Something that promised to be a boon to the town was the drilling for oil and natural gas in the surrounding area. John Brown became known locally as the "oil man," since he would often light the gas well and citizens would gather to watch the displays. The first oil and gas line drilled was near the bottom of Depot Hill, where the old railroad had its center. However, the line was destroyed by fire. A few months later, Brown tried, with little success, to find oil and natural gas near Augusta. What did bring success for several decades was the **Brooksville and Ohio Railroad**, which operated from May 21, 1897, until June 6, 1931.

Brooksville High School won the state **basketball** championship in 1939 by defeating Hindman. Brooksville was the home of a Hollywood actor and director, **Don Galloway** (1937), of the *Ironsides* television series. A well-known writer, **Ed McClanahan**, was also born in Brooksville. McClanahan has authored several books, including *The Natural Man*, as well as contributing articles to nationally recognized magazines.

Bracken Co. Extension Homemakers. *History of Bracken County*. Bicentennial ed. Brooksville, Ky.: Bracken Co. Extension Homemakers, 2002.

Caroline R. Miller

BROOKSVILLE AND OHIO RAILROAD. The Brooksville Railroad (BRR) was built in 1897 to connect Brooksville with the **Chesapeake and Ohio Railroad** at Wellsburg Junction, along the Ohio River in Bracken Co. The rail line began at Wellsburg, followed Locust Creek upstream to Goose Creek, and then proceeded southward to Brooksville, for a total distance of 10 miles. The BRR carried farm goods and lumber from Brooksville to the outside world and acted as a funnel for the movement of finished goods into Brooksville, the county seat. From its beginning, the BRR was barely profitable, and it quickly proved unable to generate sufficient money to keep the roadbed and equipment in compliance with state and federal regulations.

In 1918 the BRR went into receivership, and formal passenger service was discontinued. In 1919 it was sold to a group of local businessmen and renamed the Brooksville and Ohio River Railroad (B&OR). The B&OR lingered until 1931, using a motorized section handcar with a trailer to move goods. Having lost its local business to trucks, and its rail bed having been condemned as unsafe by the Interstate Commerce Commission (ICC) on April 11, 1931, the B&OR received permission from the ICC to abandon its line. Two road tank cars (not owned by BBR) were left landlocked at Brooksville by the abandonment and were later removed by trucks. During its life, the BRR-B&OR owned six locomotives, but only two were on the property at any one time. Recorded passenger equipment consisted of one combination coach.

Leming, John E., Jr. "Bracken County and the Brooksville Railroad Company," *NKH* 3, no. 2 (Spring–Summer 1996): 52–56.

Sulzer, Elmer G. *Ghost Railroads of Kentucky*. Bloomington: Indiana Univ. Press, 1967.

Charles H. Bogart

BROOKSVILLE ASSEMBLY OF GOD. The Brooksville Assembly of God began at the home of Mrs. Russell Mattox on Parina Rd. in Bracken Co. in 1935. During that year, revival services were held in the Asbury Schoolhouse until the congregation was able to have a permanent church building built on a lot donated by William Butler. In the early 1940s, the church was relocated to the corner of Miami and Frankfort Sts. in Brooksville. After holding services at several more locations, the Brooksville Assembly of God moved in 1952 to a site on Frankfort St. in Brooksville, where it remains today.

Bracken Co. Extension Homemakers. *History of Bracken County*. Bicentennial ed. Brooksville, Ky.: Bracken Co. Extension Homemakers, 2002.

Caroline R. Miller

BROOKSVILLE CHRISTIAN CHURCH. The Brooksville Christian Church, located on Miami St., was the first church within the city of Brooksville and the second Christian Church organized in Bracken Co. The congregation dates to 1842, when 190 persons voiced their support for this nondenominational church. The congregation stayed intact until 1873, when 60 members left to establish the Christian Church in Powersville. The congregation of the Brooksville Christian Church worshipped in the city's courthouse until 1859; then a lot was purchased for the construction of a house of worship that was completed in 1860. This structure was of wood, measuring 40 by 60 feet; its area was extended significantly in 1916. The building was destroyed by fire in 1923, with only a few items escaping unscathed. The next church was constructed of brick and dedicated on June 15, 1924; two minor additions, a baptistery and an entrance accessible to the handicapped, have since been made. The congregation of the Brooksville Christian Church remains large, just as it was in 1842; many of this church's worshippers travel from distant parts of the county to attend services.

Bracken Co. Extension Homemakers. *History of Bracken County*. Bicentennial ed. Brooksville, Ky.: Bracken Co. Extension Homemakers, 2002.

Caroline R. Miller

BROOKSVILLE METHODIST CHURCH. The Brooksville Methodist Church was assembled in 1866 at Brooksville in Bracken Co., after a trying number of years during the **Civil War**. The earliest congregation worshipped in the open under a tree at the home of Caleb Tarleton and was led by Methodist circuit riders who had come into Kentucky from Virginia. Among the charter members of the Brooksville Methodist Church in 1866 were Judge Adamson, Anderson Field, H. A. Lee, and Caleb Tarleton. Church services were for a time held in the carpenter's shop on Church St. in Brooksville, before the group started purchasing brick and other building supplies with which to build a church building. However, the Civil War halted the building's construction, and most of the bricks had to be used for other purposes. In 1866 timbers were cut and the Brooksville Methodist Church's first and only permanent building was erected on Woodward Ave. in town. The church bell was a gift from Henry Ferber, who had purchased it from the owners of the *Magnolia* excursion boat, which had sunk in the Ohio River. The stained-glass windows were installed in 1913, under the leadership of Rev. Price Smith. In 1944 a major remodeling of the structure was undertaken, in the course of which an organ and chimes were installed. The current worshippers have maintained an active membership, and the Brooksville Methodist Church continues to serve them with updated facilities and services.

Bracken Co. Extension Homemakers. *History of Bracken County*. Bicentennial ed. Brooksville, Ky.: Bracken Co. Extension Homemakers, 2002.

Caroline R. Miller

BROSSART, FERDINAND (b. October 19, 1849, Buchelberg, Bavaria; d. August 6, 1930, Melbourne, Ky.). Ferdinand Brossart, who became a bishop of the Diocese of Covington, was the son of Ferdinand and Catherine Dissel Brossart. The family immigrated to the United States in 1851 and lived in New Orleans until an outbreak of yellow fever prompted them to move to Cincinnati. There they became members of St. Michael Parish. In 1861 the Brossarts moved to the Gubser's Mill area of Campbell Co., Ky. Ferdinand Brossart received a good classical education at St. Francis Gymnasium in Cincinnati and began his studies for the priesthood at Mount St. Mary Seminary in Price Hill. In 1868 George A. Carrell, bishop of Covington, sent him to Louvain University in Belgium to complete his studies. On September 1, 1872, Bishop Augustus M. Toebbe of Covington ordained him a priest at St. Mary Cathedral (see **Cathedral Basilica of the Assumption**).

Brossart began his service as a priest of the Diocese of Covington in the Bluegrass area of Kentucky, first in Cynthiana, then in Georgetown. After being made pastor of St. Paul Parish in Lexington in 1878, he distinguished himself in the early 1880s by ministering to victims of a smallpox epidemic in that city. His courageous service to the sick when other clergymen had refused to serve earned him the admiration of Protestants and Catholics alike. Bishop Camillus P. Maes appointed him pastor of the Cathedral Parish in Covington and vicar general of the diocese in 1888. Brossart's efficiency and competence in this prominent role as assistant to the bishop made him a good candidate to succeed Bishop Maes when he died in 1915. On November 29 of that year, he received word that Pope Benedict XV had appointed him the fourth Bishop of Covington. Archbishop Henry Moeller of Cincinnati consecrated him bishop at St. Mary Cathedral on January 25, 1916. He remains to this day the only priest of the Diocese of Covington who became its bishop.

As head of the diocese, Bishop Brossart introduced new regulations for its administration, created the Board of Charities, established the **Society of St. Vincent de Paul** and **Boy Scout** troops in diocesan parishes, and implemented the new 1917 Code of Canon Law of the Roman Catholic Church. After America's entry into World War I in 1917, the governor of Kentucky appointed Brossart to the District Committee of the State Defense Council; apparently the anti-German sentiment of the time had not adversely affected the reputation of the German-born bishop. In 1920 Bishop Brossart reorganized the boundaries of the parishes of the diocese on a geographical basis, rather than maintain the "national parishes" in use since the 19th century, which were based on whether congregations were English-speaking or German-speaking. Ill health led to his resignation as bishop in March 1923, ending his brief but eventful episcopacy. Brossart spent his remaining years in residence at the **Sisters of Divine Providence**'s St. Anne Convent in Melbourne. He died on August 6, 1930, and was buried in the cemetery at St. Anne. He is the only deceased bishop of the Diocese of Covington not interred at St. Mary Cemetery.

Diocese of Covington Archives, Erlanger, Ky.
Ryan, Paul E. *History of the Diocese of Covington, Kentucky.* Covington, Ky.: Diocese of Covington, 1954.

Thomas S. Ward

BROTHERS, DARRELL (b. September 18, 1931, Tecumseh, Ala.; d. October 4, 1993, Covington, Ky.). Darrell Brothers began his art career in 1959 teaching high school art in the Cincinnati Public Schools, primarily at Taft High School. Also during this time, he taught evening painting classes at the University of Kentucky Northern Community College (now **Northern Kentucky University**). In 1966 he began a long and fruitful career as a painting and printmaking instructor at **Thomas More College** in Crestview Hills, where he remained until his death in 1993.

It was at the Herron School of Art in Indianapolis, Ind., that he first received art training, beginning in 1949. The next year he transferred to Ball State University at Muncie, Ind., where he earned a BA in art education in 1953. He continued in the area of art education for the next three years, earning a MAT in art in 1956 from Indiana University in Bloomington, where he met his wife, artist Betty Brothers. Under the leadership of Henry Radford Hope, the art program at Indiana University was rapidly expanding, and Brothers remained in Bloomington until 1959, earning his MFA in painting under Hope. During his years with Cincinnati Public Schools, he spent one summer at Iowa State University in Ames, pursuing his interest in printmaking.

Although painting was his primary medium, Brothers's work also includes large- and small-scale drawings, etchings, and prints. His art school training in the 1950s coincided with the rapid rise of the abstract expressionist school. Nevertheless, Brothers concentrated his studies on the human figure, and his early works reflect this emphasis. By 1968 Brothers began to explore geometric abstraction and minimalism, in both painting and collage. His work through the 1970s is primarily geometric. By 1979 he had returned to focus on the figure, with a growing interest in historical methods of perspective. His renewed interest in the figure and in mathematically ordered composition is reflected in his mature style in the 1980s. During this period Brothers's work was part of an academic revival occurring nationally. He thus pays allegiance to the academic painters that preceded him while incorporating experience with mid-20th-century art movements.

In addition to his illustrious teaching career, Darrell Brothers continued to be an exhibiting artist. His works can be found in the Kentucky State Fair Collection (Louisville) and the Ball State University (Ind.) Art Collection and in collections at the following institutions: Grinnell College (Iowa); Western College at Oxford, Ohio (now part of Miami University); the J. B. Speed Museum (Louisville); the Norfolk (Va.) Museum of Arts and Sciences; the Montgomery (Ala.) Museum of Fine Arts; the College of Mount St. Joseph (Cincinnati); Indiana University; the University of Kentucky (Lexington); and Thomas More College. Brothers died in 1993 at his home in Covington and was cremated.

"Darrell Brothers, 62, Art Professor at TMC," *KP*, October 5, 1993, 8A.
Findsen, Owen. "Darrell W. Brothers Painted Human Form," *KE*, October 5, 1993, B4.
"Our Culture Strings Tied to Cincinnati," *KP*, January 25, 1969, 1K.

Rebecca Bilbo

BROWN, CAROLE WHEELER (b. January 9, 1951, Mount Sterling, Ky.) Glenda Carole Wheeler, who became Gallatin Co. sheriff, is the daughter of Virgil and Mayme Walters. The family moved to Gallatin Co. in 1952, settling on a farm along Ky. Rt. 35, two miles south of Warsaw. Wheeler graduated from Gallatin Co. High School in 1969 and then became an active member of the county's life squad.

In 1982 Gallatin Co. sheriff Delmar "Buck" Alexander, appointed her deputy sheriff. After Alexander died barely a year into his term, Wheeler became a candidate for the office of sheriff. In the special election to fill out the remainder of Alexander's term, Wheeler defeated five other candidates in the Democratic primary. She won the general election of November 1983 by a large margin and was installed as Gallatin Co. sheriff. Wheeler served as sheriff for the remainder of Alexander's term, ending January 1986.

At the time of Wheeler's election, it was reported that she was the first woman in Kentucky to be elected county sheriff, and the assertion remains unrefuted. Unable to succeed herself as sheriff because of a state law prohibiting it, Wheeler ran unsuccessfully for the office of Gallatin Co. judge-executive in 1985.

Gallatin County News, November 3, 11, 2003.
Records of the Gallatin Co. Clerk, Warsaw, Ky.

Steve Huddleston

BROWN, CRAIG M. (b. October 2, 1933, Fort Thomas, Ky.; d. January 1, 2002, Mentor, Ky.). Freelance writer Craig M. Brown grew up in Fort Thomas, where he graduated from **Highlands High School** in 1951. He entered Northwestern University at Evanston, Ill., and eventually earned an MA from that school's prestigious Medill School of Journalism. Brown spent most of his professional career in the fields of television advertising and freelance writing. He wrote a number of television scripts for the soap opera *The Catlins*. Brown also wrote scripts for corporate and industrial films and advertising copy for television. He wrote numerous guest columns for the local newspaper, the *Kentucky Post,* and submitted frequent letters to its editor. Brown wrote and self-published a controversial book, *Caketown, U.S.A.*, which he said was inspired by Garrison Keillor's book *Lake Woebegon.* Brown's book, subtitled "An Almost Factual Compendium of Remembrances," was an irreverent look at the citizens of his hometown of Fort Thomas. Brown was an ardent football fan, especially of the Cincinnati Bengals. He also crusaded relentlessly against Kentucky's tailpipe emissions testing program. He did not live to see the program end in 2005, however. Craig Brown died of lung cancer at the age of 68 on New Years Day 2002. He was survived by his wife, Debbie, and the couple's sons, Michael and Mitchell.

"Bill Would Let Counties End Emissions Testing," *KP*, December 1, 1999, 2K.
Brown, Craig M. *Caketown, U.S.A.: An Almost Factual Compendium of Remembrances.* Alexandria, Ky.: Caketown, n.d. [ca. 1991].
"Craig M. Brown," *KP*, January 3, 2002, 8A.
Hicks, Jack. "Writer (Craig Brown) Takes Sharp Look at 'Caketown' of Yesterday," *KP*, April 14, 1993, 1K–2K.

BROWN, PARIS C. (b. May 5, 1838, Concord, Ky.; d. September 7, 1911, Newport, Ky.). Paris Brown, a poor boy who grew rich in the steamboat trade, was the son of Thomas L. and Mary Brown. He was a longtime resident of Newport and served as mayor of that city (1894–1897). He was born in Concord, a small river town about 12 miles east of Maysville in Lewis Co. At the age of 16, he began his river career as a cook on a flatboat bound for New Orleans. Between flatboat sojourns, he studied bookkeeping at a Cincinnati business school. In 1859 he was back on the Ohio River as a steamboat clerk but advanced to a position as a captain in a few years. Soon after the **Civil War**, he left the river to become a bookkeeper for a boat supply store along Front St. in Cincinnati. This firm sold lamps, rope, steering wheels, and other items required by boat operators. He soon became associated with James D. Parker and J. S. Wise, both steamboat captains and major players in the steamboat supply trade. He became a partner in Parker, Wise & Company and was also president of the Consolidated Boat Store. In 1890 he served as president of the city's largest boatyard, the Cincinnati Marine Railway and Dry Dock Company, after it was forced into bankruptcy. Because of his activity in the local economy, the Cincinnati Chamber of Commerce made him an honorary member. He served on its board as well. Yet Brown's reputation suffered somewhat when it was revealed, late in 1900, that his son Frank had embezzled more than $200,000 while employed as a cashier at the German National Bank of Newport. Paris Brown was a director of the same institution, but no connection could be made between the actions of the son and the father in this incident.

Brown's health was never robust, but he was strong-willed enough to soldier on even when ill.

He appeared small and frail, yet on one occasion he pulled a drowning boy from the Ohio River at the foot of Broadway St. in Cincinnati.

Brown worked to benefit the national economy by improving navigation on the Ohio River through a series of locks and dams so that boats could move even during periods of low water. He became a charter member of the Ohio Valley Improvement Association in 1895 (see **Ohio River Navigation**; **Ohio River Locks and Dams**). This group, which included civic and political leaders of the region, lobbied the U.S. Congress to fund a huge public works project to create a river with a nine-foot-deep channel year-round. Congress was a reluctant partner but became more generous under the prodding of President William Howard Taft (1909–1913). Shortly before Brown's death in Newport, the Fernbank Dam, just downriver from Cincinnati, opened to traffic; it was in effect a memorial to his good work. He was buried at Evergreen Cemetery, Southgate.

"About the Late Paris C. Brown," *Waterway's Journal*, September 30, 1911, 10.
"Former Mayor of Newport," *KP*, September 8, 1911, 10.
Kentucky Death Certificate No. 22743, for the year 1911.
"Shortage of $201,000 in Kentucky Bank," *NYT*, November 19, 1900, 1.

John H. White

BROWNFIELD, BRUCE O. (b. Covington, Ky., September 26, 1921; d. Cincinnati, Ohio, February 17, 2004). Musician and educator Bruce Brownfield was the son of a well-known riverboat musician and vaudevillian, Harvey Alan Brownfield Sr., and Eleanor "Nora" Stephenson Brownfield. Bruce was raised in Covington at 309 Wright St., formerly the home of actor **Edwin Forrest**. He became a prominent band leader and musician for WLW television programs, best known for his band on the highly popular *Paul Dixon Show* on the Crosley/AVCO regional television chain.

One of Brownfield's notable early public performances was as an accordionist at a benefit show at the **Fort Thomas Military Reservation** in 1941. After serving as a U.S. Navy pilot during **World War II**, he began playing music professionally.

While studying at the Cincinnati Conservatory of Music, Brownfield performed on the accordion with the Dell Staton Trio and won a competition in New York City on the national *Arthur Godfrey's Talent Scouts* television show in 1950. CBS television hired Brownfield as a network staff musician. Soon, he was touring the United States as a backup musician for the 1950s popular singer Vic Damone.

Weary of traveling and homesick, Brownfield returned to Northern Kentucky and took a position as a WLWT (Cincinnati) staff musician. Later he became the band leader for the weekday *Paul Dixon Show*, where he remained for nearly 20 years. After Dixon's untimely death in 1974, the show ceased and Brownfield began a new career in education as an assistant to David Lusk, superintendent of **Covington Independent Schools**. He also taught music classes at **Northern Kentucky University** and performed with the Bruce Brownfield Trio at regional social events.

Bruce and his wife Mildred "Millie" Edmonds Brownfield were married for 60 years and had three children, Dinah Martin, Bruce E. Brownfield, and Steve A. Brownfield. Bruce O. Brownfield died in 2004 and was buried in Highland Cemetery in Fort Mitchell.

"Bruce Brownfield Sr., Band Leader for 'Paul Dixon Show,'" *KP*, February 19, 2004, A12.
Goodman, Rebecca. "B. Brownfield Musician for WLW Shows: Pianist, 82, Was Also Educator," *CE*, February 20, 2004, B4.
"Millie Brownfield, Flamboyant, Born Organizer," *KP*, January 22, 2005, A11.
"Whatever Happened to . . . ? TV 5 Musician Is Still Enjoying Making Melodies," *KP*, August 5, 1992, 10S.

John Schlipp

BROWNING, PAM (b. August 20, 1956, Carrollton, Ky.; d. December 30, 1989, near White Sulphur Springs, W.Va.). Athlete Pamela Kay Browning was the daughter of Taylor and Laura Smith Browning of Ghent. After her parents both died, she was raised in Ghent by an older sister, Mary Jean Hulvey. A tall, blond, athletic tomboy, Browning was a star of the **Carroll Co. High School** girls' **basketball** team during the early 1970s. No Kentucky colleges offered scholarships for women's sports when Browning was considering colleges, but the University of Kentucky at Lexington (UK) was reviving Women's Inter-Collegiate Basketball after a 50-year hiatus and recruited the talented six-foot-tall Browning to be the center for the women's basketball team, known as the LadyKats.

Playing from 1974 to 1978, Browning set a number of UK women's basketball performance records that have not been surpassed; in other team records, she is second only to Valerie Still. Browning was team captain, an All American, and toured Europe with Athletes in Action. She and a teammate became the first women to receive full UK athletic scholarships once they were made available, and Browning was the first woman from a UK women's basketball team to play professionally, spending two seasons with the New Jersey Gems of the Women's Basketball League. She had been working for five years with the United Parcel Service in Lexington when she was killed in a jeep accident in 1989 at age 33, while on a skiing vacation in West Virginia. She was buried in the Ghent Cemetery next to her parents. On June 24, 2000, Pam Browning was inducted into the Gallery of All Americans at the UK Basketball Museum in Lexington.

"Ex-UK Lady Kats Star Killed in Accident," *KP*, January 1, 1990, 6K.
UKathletics.com. "University of Kentucky Lady Kats." www.ukathletics.com (accessed January 10, 2006).

Bill Davis

BROWNING MANUFACTURING/OHIO VALLEY PULLEY WORKS. Browning Manufacturing in Maysville (formerly Ohio Valley Pulley Works) was a family-run business established in 1911 by Edward Parry Browning, LeWright Browning, and Edward's nephew Samuel Pearce Browning. It is now known as Emerson Power Transmission Company.

In 1886 M. K. "Otto" Sprinkle launched a company in Wheeling, W.Va., that produced split-wood pulleys. By 1895 Sprinkle's company was failing, so, taking his machinery along with him, he boarded a steamboat bound for Cincinnati in search of better opportunities. While stopping overnight in Maysville, Ky., Sprinkle met with local businessmen, one of whom was Edward Parry Browning. These businessmen, when they learned Sprinkle's intention to begin a pulley manufacturing company in Cincinnati, convinced Sprinkle that he should open his business in Maysville instead. Sprinkle agreed, the businessmen became investors, and the Ohio Valley Pulley Works was born; the new firm was incorporated in 1896.

The Ohio Valley Pulley Works produced split pulley drive shafts that held flat leather belts connected to smaller pulleys. The pulley rotation and movement of the belts transmitted power to the machines. Known unofficially as the Pulley Works, the company earned $15,626 in 1897 and continued to grow despite numerous difficulties facing it. On July 2, 1899, a fire in the plant destroyed almost everything and nearly forced the investors into bankruptcy. The owners agreed to rebuild, and that year the company reported $45,861 in earnings, even though it had closed for three months to rebuild.

After the fire, the Pulley Works continued to manufacture wooden pulleys while competitors were using new technology to develop steel pulleys. Seeing the potential in this new steel product, the investors secured a contract with the Oneida Steel Company in 1911. According to their contract, the Ohio Valley Pulley Works would sell the steel pulleys made by the Oneida Steel Company throughout the territory south of the Ohio River and west of the Mississippi River. Added income from this contract allowed the pulley company to continue expanding. On December 29, 1911, Edward Parry Browning, nephew Samuel Pearce Browning, and LeWright Browning bought out the other shareholders of the Pulley Works and changed the company's incorporation, converting it to a family-run business.

In 1918 the Oneida Steel Company refused to renew the contract, leaving the Pulley Works without any means to market steel pulleys. The Pulley Works filed suit and lost. At this point, the family was uncertain how to save this portion of their business. During this time, the limestone wooden pulley, a new version of the original pulley system, had been created. This newly designed wooden pulley was the salvation of the company. The **Great Depression** of the 1930s hit Mason Co. as severely as the rest of the country. Nonetheless, the Browning family, who now owned the Pulley Works, were able to keep their workers employed, and the company's high volume of sales of its limestone wooden pulleys during **World War II** (1941–1945) helped the company to prosper and continue to grow.

The Pulley Works continued to succeed. In 1969, under the direction of Edward Parry Browning's grandnephew John Nelson Browning and three great-grandnephews–Robert E. Browning, Louis Nulton Browning, and Laurance LeWright Browning Jr., this family-owned business, which started in Maysville in 1897, was sold to Emerson Electric of St. Louis. Now called the Emerson Power Transmission Company, the plant remains in Maysville and employs approximately 1,000 people, making it the largest employer in Mason Co.

Comer, Elizabeth. "The Brownings: An Unwavering Maysville Family," *NKH* 11, no. 2 (Spring–Summer 2004): 21–27.

Comer, Martha. "Browning Family Influence Felt throughout Maysville," *Maysville Ledger Independent*, August 18, 1986, 10.

Mason Co. Deed Book 96, 1896, p. 458; Book 114, 1911, p. 367.

Elizabeth Comer Williams

BROWNING MEDICAL ARTS CENTER. The Browning Medical Arts Center, at 1 W. McDonald Pkwy., in the center of downtown Maysville, was named for John Nelson Browning, a member of a prominent Maysville family. His father, Samuel Pearce Browning, was known for having begun the Ohio Valley Pulley Works, along with John Browning's granduncle Edward Parry Browning.

Born in 1898, John Nelson Browning worked with his family at the Ohio Valley Pulley Works. He married Carlisle Chenault in 1923, and together they had four children. Their youngest child, Thomas Chenault Browning, died in 1951 at age 17 in a car accident. Their loss affected them greatly, but they were determined to help others, and they made donations to many charitable causes in the area. One such cause was the Tom Browning Boys and Girls Club, which opened in 1953 and continues today. Another was the John Nelson Browning Medical Center.

During the early 1970s, the City of Maysville wanted to find a way to draw new doctors to the downtown area and away from the region's newer suburbs. It started a search committee to attract doctors. To aid this effort, John and Carlisle Browning donated funds for the construction of a new three-story office building that could be rented at reasonable cost by new doctors. It was built downtown just off Main St. in a convenient location. The John Nelson Browning Medical Building opened in 1975, before the closure of the local **Hayswood Hospital**. It is currently home to five medical businesses, including pharmacies and doctors' offices, and a certified public accounting firm. Until 1994 the Hayswood Foundation owned the building. The Browning Medical Arts Center continues today with its original purpose, to provide medical access and affordable health care to families in Mason Co.

Comer, Elizabeth. "The Brownings: An Unwavering Maysville Family," *NKH* 11, no. 2 (Spring–Summer 2004): 21–27.

"Maysville Men Buy Browning Medical Building," *Maysville Independent Ledger*, March 2, 1994, 1.

Elizabeth Comer Williams

BRUCE, ELI METCALF (b. February 22, 1828, Flemingsburg, Ky.; d. December 15, 1866, New York City). Eli M. Bruce, the son of George Stubblefield and Sabina Metcalf Bruce, became an important financier of the Army of the Confederacy and, after its defeat, a philanthropist assisting destitute Confederate soldiers. He was a member of the Council of Ten, which met at Bowling Green, Ky., and planned Kentucky's entry into the Confederacy. Bruce represented the Ninth District in the First Provisional Congress of Kentucky, which met at Russellville and later, in exile, at Macon, Ga. He also represented the Provisional Government of Kentucky in the Confederate Congress at Richmond, Va. Bruce served on the staff of Gen. John C. Breckinridge as a noncombatant and was a close friend of Gen. John Hunt Morgan. On January 30, 1865, Secretary of War James E. Seddon appointed Bruce acting commissary general of the Confederacy, so that he could rectify previous mismanagement in that office.

In 1847 Bruce had worked as a clerk in a Maysville store before moving to Covington to work for his uncle, John S. Morgan, a Cincinnati pork-packing industrialist (see **Meatpacking**). He married Elizabeth Sally Withers of Covington, sister of Charles Albert Withers (see **Withers Family**), who was later adjutant general to General Morgan. Bruce made his fortune before the **Civil War** by establishing a chain of pork and beef packing plants along the Wabash, Missouri, and Mississippi rivers, with headquarters at St. Louis. Recognizing that Lincoln's election meant war, Bruce moved his operations to Chattanooga, Tenn., shipping great quantities of salt down the Mississippi River before it was blockaded, to be stored at strategic locations in the South in anticipation of extended hostilities and the need for cured meat. Bruce and his partners, the Crenshaw Brothers of Liverpool and New York millionaire R. T. Wilson, the father of Mrs. Cornelius Vanderbilt, purchased 24 blockade-runners to penetrate the Union blockade of the South's Atlantic ports in order to trade cotton for war munitions. Bruce's favorite task was supplying the First Kentucky Brigade, known as the Orphan Brigade, following the death of its leader Gen. Ben Hardin Helm of Elizabethtown, the brother-in-law of Abraham Lincoln.

After the fall of Richmond and the surrender of generals Joseph E. Johnson and Robert E. Lee, Bruce opened an office in Augusta, Ga., supplying gold to returning Kentucky soldiers and urging them both to respect the Union and to work for reconciliation. He offered school tuition to every Kentuckian who was disabled fighting for the Confederacy, and he recommended that they study English, mathematics, grammar, and penmanship.

After the war Bruce obtained a pardon from President Johnson and moved to New York City, where, with his uncle **Henry Bruce Jr.**, he operated the grand Southern Hotel and founded the private banking firm of W. L. Lyons and Company, now the financial services firm Hilliard Lyons, still in operation in Louisville. Bruce died in 1866, at age 38, in New York City and was buried in the Linden Grove Cemetery in Covington, then later (1917) moved to the Highland Cemetery, Fort Mitchell, Ky., to be buried beside his wife.

Bruce Family Papers, Northern Kentucky Univ. Library Archives, Highland Heights, Ky.

Rankin, Frank G. "Eli Metcalf Bruce," a signed, unpublished article, in possession of the author.

Reis, Jim. "Eli Bruce's Wealth Aided Penniless Soldiers," *KP*, July 2, 1984, 10K.

Stephen T. McMurtry

BRUCE, HENRY, JR. (b. 1817, Fleming Co., Ky.; d. December 31, 1891, Kansas City, Mo.). Henry Bruce Jr., a hotel owner, was a descendant of George Stubblefield, member of the Virginia House of Burgesses, and Charles Bruce, an overseer in Virginia appointed by Governor Alexander Spotswood. Bruce's parents were Henry Bruce Sr. and Mary Stubblefield. Henry Sr., a prosperous Kentucky farmer, nurtured his namesake, one of 10 children, by sending him on successful hog drives and trading trips throughout Georgia and northern Florida during 1830 and 1831.

In 1853 Henry Jr. purchased the **Orr Academy/Rugby School** at 630 Sanford St., Covington, where he lived with his wife, Mary Bruce, who was also his first cousin. The couple raised four daughters. One of them was Pauline Duke, who married a cousin of Col. Basil W. Duke of Morgan's Raiders (see **John Hunt Morgan**), and another was Henrietta Green, mother of the acclaimed primitive artist **Mary Bruce Sharon**. Henry Bruce Jr. fled his Covington home in December 1863, ahead of a contingent of Yankee troops who came to arrest him for allegedly financing the escape of Gen. John Hunt Morgan from the Ohio State Penitentiary at Columbus. Bruce escaped to Canada; after the **Civil War**, in 1866, he established himself in New York City. He became the proprietor of the Southern Hotel on Broadway, a venture he shared with his nephew, Confederate Army financier **Eli Metcalf Bruce**. Henry Bruce Jr. also operated the Maltby House, fronting Lafayette Pl. in New York City, and the Hart House and the St. James Hotel in Kansas City, Mo. During the 1870s Henry Jr. maintained an office in Cincinnati, from which he launched his son-in-law Richard Lashbrook Green, of Maysville, a Centre College graduate, into a successful tobacco warehouse business. Green was the father of artist Mary Bruce Sharon, in whose paintings Henry Jr., "Grandpa," is depicted in scenes of fishing on the Licking River, holiday feasting at 630 Sanford St., and fleeing Yankee troops from that same address.

Henry Bruce Jr. is remembered as one of the founders and the president pro tempore of the Covington and Cincinnati Bridge Company, which contracted with **John Roebling** to design and construct what was then the longest suspension bridge in the world, the **John A. Roebling Bridge** across the Ohio River. Roebling lived with Bruce on Sanford St. while designing the bridge.

In 1872 Bruce moved to Kansas City and lived in the St. James Hotel. He died there in 1891 of kidney disease. After a funeral in the hotel parlor, his body was returned to Covington for burial next to his wife in the Bruce family lot at Linden Grove Cemetery.

Aument, Shary. "The Food of Love: Recollections and Recipes," an unpublished work given to the author by the Bruce Family of Dallas, Tex.
Bruce Family Papers, Northern Kentucky Univ. Library Archives, Highland Heights, Ky.
"Death of Henry Bruce," *Kansas City Star,* December 31, 1891, 1.
"Funeral Notice," *Kansas City Star,* January 2, 1892, 7.
Linden Grove Cemetery Records, Burial No. 4419, Covington, Ky.
Ludwig, Charles. "They Said It Was Impossible," *CTS,* January 13, 1953, magazine sec., 7.

Stephen T. McMurtry

BRYAN, JAMES W. (b. June 9, 1852, Millersburg, Ky.; d. April 7, 1903, Covington, Ky.). James William Bryan, a Democrat and a Kentucky lieutenant governor, graduated from Millersburg High School in Millersburg. He attended Kentucky Wesleyan College (then in Millersburg) on a full scholarship, graduating in 1873, and moved to Covington the following year. He later paid back the total cost of his education, plus interest. Bryan studied law under former governor **John White Stevenson** and Judge **James O'Hara** in Covington and was admitted to the bar in 1875. He married Virginia Ellis Martin, daughter of Judge J. B. Martin, in 1880. The couple had two daughters, Mattie and Katherine. He served as a state senator from 1885 to 1887 and as lieutenant governor under Governor Simon G. Buckner from 1887 to 1891. At that time he was the youngest person ever elected lieutenant governor. He also served as a director of the **First National Bank** of Covington. Bryan died of pneumonia at age 50 at his Garrard St. home. Funeral services were held at St. Mary Cathedral in Covington and burial was in Highland Cemetery.

"Brief-Reviewed Life and Character of Attorney, James Wm. Bryan," *KP,* April 11, 1903, 1.
Death Certificate No. 3947, Kenton Co., Ky., for the year 1903, available on microfilm at the Kenton Co. Public Library, Covington, Ky.
"Death of Gov. Bryan," *CC,* April 10, 1903, 1.
Perrin, William Henry, J. H. Battle, and G. C. Kniffin. *Kentucky: A History of the State.* Louisville, Ky.: F.A. Battey, 1888.
"Sudden Demise of Bryan," *KP,* April 8, 1903, 1.
"Tribute of Tears," *KP,* April 10, 1903, 1.
"Tribute to Bryan by Bar," *KP,* April 9, 1903, 1.

BRYAN, MARY BOONE (b. ca. November 10, 1736, North Carolina; d. July 6, 1819, Grants Lick, Ky.). Mary Boone Bryan was a daughter of Squire and Sarah Morgan Boone and the sister of Daniel Boone. In 1755 she married William Bryan, who was one of the founders of Bryants Station, near Lexington. While she and her family lived there, four members of her family met tragic deaths. Her husband and their son William Jr. were killed by Indians, and sons John and Abner died of disease. Shortly after the tragedies, Mary moved with her remaining family back to North Carolina but later returned to Kentucky and settled on a farm near the Licking River close to Grants Lick, in southern Campbell Co. She lived with her son Samuel Bryan and his family. Mary died there in 1819, at age 82, and was buried in the Bryan Family Cemetery on the family farm. In 1929 the Daughters of the American Revolution (DAR) had her reburied in the Oakland Cemetery on Clay Ridge Road in Grants Lick. It was felt that a grave in that cemetery would be better maintained and more accessible. One of the diggers later gave his account of her exhumation. He said they had found about four feet of stone slabs near the surface, evidently placed there to prevent wild animals from disturbing her grave. About three feet below the slabs, they found what they described as her complete, well-preserved skeleton. All that remained of her wooden coffin were 16 square nails that had been used in its construction. The diggers were surprised to see a coil of her gray hair still neatly combed in a bun. They placed her remains in a small box and reburied them at Oakland, behind the old Grants Lick Baptist Church. The DAR also placed a beautiful small monument on the new grave.

"Campbell County History and Genealogy," *Falmouth Outlook,* supplement, December 15, 1978.
Wessling, Jack. *Early History of Campbell County, Kentucky.* Alexandria, Ky.: Self-published, 1997.

Jack Wessling

BRYAN, PEARL (b. ca. 1874, Greencastle, Ind.; d. late January, 1896, near Fort Thomas, Ky.). Arguably the most sensational crime in the history of Northern Kentucky was the murder and beheading of a young woman in 1896, in what is today Fort Thomas in Campbell Co. Pearl Bryan was a 22-year-old country girl from Greencastle, Ind.; she was the youngest of 12 children and had graduated in 1892 from Greencastle High School with the highest honors and special awards in her class. She was the daughter of Alex and Jane Bryan.

Bryan was described as a Sunday school and church worker, sprightly, vivacious, and a social favorite in her home. She had bright blue eyes, blond hair that shaded to auburn, a pretty face, and an almost flawless complexion. In 1893 she met a young dental student, Scott Jackson, through her second cousin William Woods. Bryan and Jackson became friends, meeting whenever Jackson visited Greencastle. The relationship changed in the summer of 1895, when Bryan discovered that she was pregnant. She confided her situation to Woods, who in turn wrote Jackson. Jackson told Woods, in his response, to have Bryan travel to Cincinnati. She arrived by train at Cincinnati's Grand Central Station on Tuesday January 28, 1896.

Two days later, on a cold and foggy morning, John Hewling was walking across a field along Alexandria Pike (**U.S. 27**) on property owned by Col. John Lock, for whom he worked. He noticed a woman on the ground. He later said that he did not know whether she was drunk or dead. The body was found in an isolated spot that young women and soldiers from the nearby **Fort Thomas Military Reservation** sometimes used as a trysting place. Hewling said they often had to run women out of the field.

The county deputy sheriff and other law enforcement investigators, including coroner Bob Tingley, were summoned and found what appeared to be signs of a struggle and a pool of blood at the woman's feet. When Tingley turned the body over, he pulled her dress down, revealing that the woman's head was missing. Officials searched the surrounding area for it. Bloodhounds were called out and trailed the scent to the nearby Covington water reservoir in Fort Thomas. The reservoir was drained, but no head was found.

The body, meanwhile, was shipped to Newport, where an autopsy was performed by a team led by Dr. **Robert Carothers**. The woman was discovered to have been pregnant, and cocaine was found in her stomach. It took several days to discover her identity. The identification occurred when police traced the manufacturer of her shoes to Greencastle, Ind., and from there to her family.

Jackson was arrested that same evening, after police had learned of a letter that referred to Jackson's part in the pregnancy. A friend of Jackson, Alonzo Walling, who appeared to be mentally challenged, was arrested the next day as an accessory. Jackson and Walling had become friends in dental school.

Walling told police that Jackson had wanted to perform an abortion on Pearl Bryan but decided instead to poison her, trying to make her death appear to be a suicide. A Campbell Co. grand jury indicted Walling and Jackson on February 13, 1896, for murder. Most of the police effort concentrated on trying to persuade the men to confess and to reveal the location of Bryan's missing head.

Police even took Jackson and Walling to the funeral home where the woman's headless body had been laid out in her high school graduation dress. Pearl's sister begged the two men to disclose what happened to her head, but they showed no emotion and declared their innocence.

Scott Jackson was the first to be tried. His trial lasted from April 21 to May 14, 1896. Part of the sensational medical testimony was the belief that Bryan had been alive during part of the decapitation. Jackson insisted on his innocence, saying he was involved only after she was dead. The jury, however, found Jackson guilty.

Walling's trial was scheduled and ran from May 29 to June 18, 1896, with the prosecution citing the same basic information used in convicting Jackson. Walling was found guilty and sentenced to death. The police at the Newport jail had to place special guards on duty to handle threats of lynching.

In an ironic twist, Jackson and Walling became local celebrities, attracting curious visitors to the jail cell. They spent the Christmas holidays in the Newport jail with visitors, especially young women, bringing cakes, cookies, and other presents. The jail eventually had to restrict visitors to prevent interference with regular jail activities.

The execution date was set for May 20, 1897; the men were scheduled to die by hanging in the jail's courtyard. Since the local authorities had limited experience with hangings, an expert from Lexington was brought in, along with the Bracken Co. sheriff, who had overseen a recent hanging. The execution was set for 9:00 a.m., and it was only a little later than that when Jackson and Walling were brought out, having been delayed a few minutes for final talks with religious advisers. Jackson is said to have commented that Walling was not guilty of murder, causing local authorities to telegraph Kentucky governor William Bradley (1895–1899) to ask whether the executions should be delayed. That inquiry put off the execution for only a few minutes, however, as local officials continued to demand the whereabouts of Pearl Bryan's head.

The execution resumed. Jackson was asked if he had any final comments. Witnesses reported that Jackson hesitated for a moment and then said that he was not guilty of a crime for which he was about to pay with his life. Walling also was asked for any final comments and continued to maintain his innocence. The final preparations were made, and at 11:40 a.m. the trapdoors were sprung and the two men were hanged. For the many people involved in the police work, medical duties, and legal matters, the Pearl Bryan case became the major event in their careers. Soon after the execution, a ballad known by assorted titles, including "The Ballad of Pearl Bryan" and "The Death of Pearl Bryan," became a popular folk song.

Campbell Co. Historical Society. *Campbell County, Kentucky, 200 Years, 1794–1994.* Alexandria, Ky.: Campbell Co. Historical Society, 1994.
"Head Cut Off," *KP,* February 1, 1896, 1.
Kuhnheim, Anthony W. *The Pearl Bryan Murder Story.* Alexandria, Ky.: Campbell Co. Historical and Genealogical Society, 1996.
The Mysterious Murder of Pearl Bryan. Cincinnati, Ohio: Barclay, 1896.
Reis, Jim. "Infamy Followed Killers of Young Pregnant Woman," *KP,* June 6, 2005, 4K.
———. "A Particularly Foul Murder—Shoe Key Piece of Evidence in Case," *KP,* January 29, 1996, 4K.

Jim Reis

BUCKNER, PHILIP (b. 1747, Caroline Co., Va.; d. 1830, Powersville, Ky.). The generosity of Philip Buckner, a **Revolutionary War** soldier, was primarily responsible for the December 1797 founding of Augusta in Bracken Co. Buckner donated 600 acres in Bracken Co. and posted a $1,000 bond for the purpose of organizing a frontier town. Much of the land he owned in Kentucky had originated in land grants for his service during the Revolutionary War as a commissary officer in Virginia. In 1781 more than 7,000 acres of land were granted to him in Lincoln, Jefferson, and Bracken counties of Kentucky, as recorded in the Virginia land office at Richmond. A portion of this land formed a corridor from Germantown through Brooksville and past Powersville. When Buckner decided to come to Kentucky and make the Ohio River town of Augusta his permanent home, he reportedly brought with him 40 families from Virginia, by way of the Midland Trail, also known as the **Warrior Trail**. Not all the families traveling with Buckner entered Bracken Co., as some chose to remain in adjacent Mason Co. or other places along their route.

Buckner was a member of the Second Kentucky Constitutional Convention in 1799 and a member of the state legislature. He lived in Augusta with his wife Tabitha Daniel of Port Royal, Va. According to local tradition, Buckner disliked the influx of settlers into Augusta and soon moved farther inland in Bracken Co. to Powersville. At Powersville he constructed a hunting lodge for fox hunts, and he lived at the lodge until his death. Buckner was buried about one-half mile from the center of the village of Powersville on Goose Ln. He was the grandfather of **Buckner Stith Morris**, who became the second mayor of Chicago during the 1830s.

Bracken Co. Extension Homemakers. *History of Bracken County.* Bicentennial ed. Brooksville, Ky.: Bracken Co. Extension Homemakers, 2002.

Caroline R. Miller

BUDDHISTS. The introduction of the worldwide religion known as Buddhism into Northern Kentucky began with William Dometrich and his wife Barbra. Teachers and practitioners of U.S. Chito Ryu Karate, the Dometriches operate the Yoseikan So-Honbu at 22 Martin St. in Covington. Their dojo (karate school) was begun in 1963. In the late 1980s a zendo was added to the dojo, since William Dometrich is an ordained Zen Buddhist priest. The following and tending of the zendo was sporadic during the 1980s, and although the zendo still exists, it is no longer in use. The karate school and the karate organization remain strong today, however.

In April 2002 Heesoon Choi opened the Gomang Meditation and Dharma Center Inc., as a Dharma Center of the Gelug Tradition of Tibetan Buddhism. Heesoon was inspired to open the center after the death of her husband, who left her with an inheritance. Both had been followers of Buddhism. It was this inheritance that partially funded the creation of the center. The Gomang Meditation and Dharma Center was housed in an old schoolhouse in Independence that was renovated and rezoned for the center. The resident teacher, Geshe Jinpa Sonam, was a Tibetan philosophy scholar who officiated at services, gave talks, and guided meditations. The center remained active until 2004, when Geshe Jinpa Sonam left. Since then services have no longer been held. A Zen center operates in Cincinnati.

"The Sensei—Boone County Deputy Is Zen Buddhist Leader," *KP,* May 1, 2003, 5K.

David J. Ebacher

BUECKER IRON WORKS. Few businesses in Kentucky can claim the longevity of Buecker Iron Works. Even fewer have been continuously owned and operated by a single family. The founder of this business, German immigrant Ernst Buecker, first obtained employment in a Cincinnati machine shop but subsequently established his own ironworking business in Newport in 1858. He handcrafted the lathe and two steam engines utilized at the steam-powered ironworks, once located in Newport along W. Sixth St. The ornamental iron gates and fences that Buecker manufactured adorned many Newport properties, as well as others in adjacent counties and cities. Through the years, the firm also made sewing machines for tailor shops and industrial items such as grates, catwalks, handrails, and ladder racks. War-related ironwork was performed by Buecker Iron Works during the **Civil War**, the Spanish-American War, and both **World Wars**.

Henry F. Buecker was the family member in the next generation who led the business. The sheriff of Newport, Jule Plummer, drew upon Buecker's expertise in iron-working in 1897. During the construction of an unusual gallows being built to facilitate an unprecedented double hanging at Newport, a special release mechanism was needed to ensure that both trapdoors opened simultaneously. Buecker fabricated this item for the sheriff. The subsequent legendary double execution of **Alonzo Walling and Scott Jackson** in May 1897, after they were convicted in the murder of **Pearl Bryan**, was the last public hanging in Campbell Co.

The Buecker Iron Works then passed to third-generation family member Ernst V. Buecker; fourth-generation brothers Robert V. and Ernst H. Buecker subsequently continued the trade. Robert is credited with introducing modern hydraulic machinery to the business, and he also received a patent for the steel joist system he invented. Extensive property damage to the ironworks resulted from a fire in 1964, yet the family business endured.

Fifth-generation siblings David Buecker and Linda Buecker Velten then carried on the family tradition. Their talents as graphic artists benefited the company as they created new products: custom-designed furniture, including tables, chairs, and headboards; and artistic home and garden accessories. These Buecker artisans sustained the personalized craftsmanship of their predecessors. The business also housed the Robert V. Buecker Gallery, which opened in 2003, showcasing Buecker products and the work of other local artists.

Buecker Iron Works reached a milestone in 2008, celebrating a century and a half of commerce in Newport. However, that same year proved bittersweet as declining sales led to closure of the historic establishment. Many of the quality loop-and-spear-style gates crafted by Buecker Iron Works more than a century ago still remain throughout the region. The skilled work of this family is often recognized by the signature cast-iron medallion bearing the Buecker name.

"Fire Hits 106-Year-Old Plant; Loss May Reach $75,000," *KP,* February 12, 1964, 1.
Kreimer, Peggy. "Honoring Tireless Trades," *KP,* July 31, 2001, 1K.
Moores, Lew. "Iron Family Ties in Newport," *SC,* April 17, 2005, 1C.

Judy L. Neff

BUENA VISTA. One of Newport's nine neighborhoods, Buena Vista is located in the city's heavily populated **West End**. In 1846 Gen. **James Taylor Jr.** surveyed this addition to Newport's residential area, naming the neighborhood after the climactic **Mexican War** battle in which his cousin Zachary Taylor's outnumbered troops soundly defeated Santa Anna's forces. With the exception of the four blocks laid out as house lots along the south side of Mayo (Seventh) St. west of Isabella St., the city's residential area had not been extended beyond its original limits of Jefferson (Sixth) St. and the east side of Columbia St.

Newport's rapid industrialization during the 1840s called for more housing lots to accommodate the city's recent growth. Trustees annexed the 31-acre Licking River factory row in 1845, then 27 acres known as the Ohio River factory row in 1846, and an additional 10-acre, three-block area between Saratoga St. and Washington Ave. from Sixth to Ninth Sts. in 1849. Annexed by the city in 1850, the Buena Vista addition encompassed an 80-acre area that included 750 lots between Monmouth and Cabot St. (Central Ave.) from Ringgold (Eighth St.) south to Liberty St. (12th St.). Because many of the lots General Taylor surveyed measured just one-fourteenth of an acre, his Buena Vista addition was destined to have a dense population, capable of housing 4,125 new residents (at 5.5 persons per family).

Along with the rather small lots, General Taylor apportioned more spacious lots between Eighth and Ninth Sts. on Monmouth, York, and Columbia Sts. The 20 quarter-acre lots and 2 half-acre lots attracted some of the area's most prominent citizens and public servants. During the 1860s notable residents who had constructed their elegant homes on York St. between Eighth and Ninth Sts. included Newport's 12th mayor, Edward W. Hawkins; Newport Brewery owner August Constans; and Col. William Whistler, a retired army veteran from the **War of 1812** who was also painter James Abbott McNeill Whistler's uncle. James Taylor's cousin **Washington J. Berry**, who had also served as attorney on the Buena Vista addition, was another distinguished resident of the neighborhood.

James Taylor died on November 7, 1848. In his will he designated that another 120 acres owned by him along the Licking River be set aside to allow for Newport's future growth. Because this acreage bordered Buena Vista, it became known by the same name. Taylor's will also stipulated that the tract not be partitioned immediately or hastily sold, thus allowing for its unhurried development during the late 19th century as part of Newport's West End.

In the late 1970s, the Buena Vista Neighborhood Association was established to represent its citizens' interests as part of a larger grassroots organization founded in 1976, the **Newport Citizens Advisory Council** (NCAC). This coalition allowed citizens from each of Newport's neighborhoods to voice their concerns and provide input on the city government's decisions on planning, zoning, code enforcement, and other relevant topics. The Buena Vista Neighborhood Association not only takes its name from James Taylor's 1846 survey, and later addition to the city, but also encompasses most of that original tract. The neighborhood's current boundaries run from Monmouth St. to the Licking River and from 12th St. to the south side of Ninth St. Representing the citizens of Newport's largest neighborhood, the group maintains an active role in the NCAC, though the West End's considerable population is also represented by a recently formed independent group known as the West Side Citizens Coalition.

City of Newport. "Comprehensive Plan for the City of Newport." www.newportky.gov (accessed July 26, 2006).

Fenhoff, Verna. Telephone interview by Jan Mueller, July 27, 2006.

Purvis, Thomas L., ed. *Newport, Kentucky: A Bicentennial History*. Newport, Ky.: Otto Zimmerman, 1996.

Remlinger, Connie. "Council Marks Birthday—Newport Group Remains Strong," *KP*, April 11, 1986, 3K.

Janice Mueller

BUFFALO TRACES. American buffalo, bison, which later made their way to Northern Kentucky, are believed to have first crossed the Mississippi River in the 15th century. As the buffalo moved east, they created a system of paths, roads, traces, and trails that described their annual movements. In prehistoric times mammoths and mastodons used similar trails, and in later times, elk and even deer utilized the trails.

Northern Kentucky was on the buffalo's path as they moved south in late winter and early spring from their winter range on the prairies of central Ohio to their grazing sites in Central Kentucky. The Indians called this trail the Alanant-O-wamiowee, or Great Buffalo Path (see **Warrior Trail**). It funneled herds from the Little Miami River and the Great Miami River in Ohio across the ford at the mouth of the Licking River at Covington, from which it followed the high ground along modern Banklick St. in Covington south to the Banklick Creek. Five miles from the river, this Little Miami–Big Bone Trace passed through a large salt lick in Kentucky later called Latonia Springs. The trace continued on 15 miles to **Big Bone Lick**, where it was joined by two traces from the Great Miami River that crossed the Ohio River at Petersburg and at the mouth of Gunpowder Creek.

Access to salt was a major attraction of the portion of the Alanant-O-wamiowee that followed a crescent-shaped outcrop of salt springs from Big Bone Lick southwest to Drennon Licks on the Kentucky River. It then crossed the ford at Leestown, near Frankfort, and continued east through Stamping Ground, Great Crossing, and Georgetown and on to Paris. The eastern section of the Alanant-O-wamiowee followed a geologic fault that produced a variety of salt springs from the Upper Blue Licks to the Lower Blue Licks (see **Blue Licks**) and then on to Mayslick, Washington, and the Ohio River at Limestone (Maysville).

The eastern portion of the buffalo trail provided the best early road to the Bluegrass region and was known as the Limestone Trace. A buffalo trace was converted to a wagon road by cutting the small trees to axle height; the Limestone Trace became the Limestone Pike, the first improved section of road in the state. Virtually all of the major highways follow buffalo traces for all or part of their length. Towns and cities often developed where two or more traces crossed.

The Licking River route was particularly popular with the American Indians, who used it to transport game from their annual hunts in Central Kentucky to their villages in Ohio along the two Miami rivers. A buffalo trace ascended the west side of the Licking River to Falmouth, where it crossed the river and continued on to Paris, intersecting the Alanant-O-wamiowee.

In 1780 Capt. Henry Bird used the Licking route to attack Ruddle's (Harrison Co.) and Martin's (Bourbon Co.) stations in Kentucky (see **Bird's [Byrd's] War Road**). His party of Canadians and Indians traveled down the Great Miami River using rafts, canoes, and horses. At Falmouth Bird left his canoes and proceeded on foot. It took 11 days to cut a wagon road to Ruddle's Station from Falmouth along the Licking trace.

The **Dry Ridge Trace** followed the drainage divide between the Licking River to the east and the Kentucky River to the west. It provided the shortest route from Lexington and the central bluegrass to the mouth of the Licking River. It was little used until the white population began to increase just before 1780. Cincinnati was surveyed by a troop of pioneers from Lexington who traveled up the Dry Ridge Trace and then down Banklick Creek to the mouth of the Licking. In time, a turnpike and a railroad shared the Dry Ridge.

The Big Bone Lick–Blue Lick trail followed the Dry Ridge Trace to Williamstown, where it moved east down Lick Creek and then crossed the South Fork of the Licking River in southern Pendleton Co. It continued on to the Great Buffalo Path near Carlisle, which gave access to both the upper and lower Blue Licks. This trail was quite old and was used mostly by game and by hunters because it was very rugged.

The Washington Trace was mentioned in the 1790s. It connected Washington in Mason Co. with the mouth of the Little Miami River across from Campbell Co. It was developed rather quickly into a wagon road (see **Washington Trace Rd.**).

The buffalo and the civilizations living in the region did not coexist for very long. The buffalo were killed off in a short period after the arrival of settlers and the growth of towns. The use of the buffalo roads by other game ended about the same time. The last buffalo in Pennsylvania was reported in 1801, in Ohio in 1808, and in Kentucky in 1820. It is estimated that buffalo were extinct east of the Mississippi River by 1830. The waves of immigrants who later used the buffalo traces never saw a buffalo.

Belue, Ted Franklin. *The Long Hunt—Death of the Buffalo East of the Mississippi*. Mechanicsburg, Pa.: Stackpole Books, 1996.

Jillson, Willard Rouse. *Pioneer Kentucky*. Frankfort, Ky.: Standard, 1934.

Joseph F. Gastright

BUFFINGTON SPRINGS. American Indians from Kentucky and Ohio are believed to have come to what later was known as Buffington Springs in central Kenton Co. possibly centuries before Europeans arrived. The Indians attributed miraculous healing properties to the waters there. The early European settlers also promoted the medical benefits of these springs. C. F. Reid, a missionary to China, named the springs Ke-o-me-zu, which supposedly means in Chinese "sparkling waters." The springs were renamed Buffington Springs by the later owner Rev. George Nicholas Buffington, a West Virginia–born Methodist minister. His family was also a partner in the Lovell & Buffington Tobacco Company of Covington, and when Buffington died in 1917, he was the president of the Citizens Bank of Erlanger. He owned much of the valuable land in Kenton and Boone counties.

The three Buffington springs were named Alpha, Bonanza, and Climax, and Buffington advertised different healing benefits for each. Claims were made that the waters were effective against almost every ailment known to man. Similar mineral springs located throughout the country became popular medical vacation sites, until their claims were proved false by scientific research. The Buffington Springs were located beside the Queen and Crescent Railroad (see **Cincinnati Southern Railroad**), along what is today Garvey Ave. in Elsmere. In 1910 the hotel at the springs was destroyed by fire, never to reopen. As late as 1950, the three springs still existed but were capped with zinc plates. Other popular Northern Kentucky health resorts were the Southgate Mineral Wells, south of Newport, owned and operated by the Southgate family; **Latonia Springs**, south of Covington; and **Blue Licks**, south of Maysville.

"Erlanger—Funeral," *KTS*, November 21, 1917, 20.
Kentucky Death Certificate No. 39823, for the year 1917.
Where Cooling Breezes Blow: Summer Tourist Spots on the Queen and Crescent Route and Its Connection Lines. Cincinnati: General Passenger Department, Queen and Crescent Route, 1894.

Jack Wessling

BUILDING, COMMERCIAL. Commercial building in the counties of Boone, Campbell, and Kenton expanded greatly after **World War II**, with a special impetus due to the location in Northern Kentucky of the **Cincinnati/Northern Kentucky International Airport**. The airport was founded during World War II as a training field for military pilots but soon became a powerful economic engine for the region. Near the airport there are now high-end industrial parks, notably those built by the Corporex and Paul Hemmer companies, that are free-standing multitenant industrial buildings. Built in recent years, they accommodate foreign and domestic firms that require convenient access to an airport and to the interstate highways that crisscross the region. Commercial construction also produced suburban shopping centers and malls, including the **Newport Shopping Center**, **Florence Mall**, and **Crestview Hills Town Center**.

The development of the Covington-Newport-Bellevue riverfront has also stimulated investment in office, entertainment, and residential venues (see **Covington, Downtown**). Developments at both the riverfront and the airport have included commercial ventures; shopping and service facilities have sprung up along the riverfront in particular. Prominent among the local commercial contractors involved in this boom in commercial building are Ashley Development; Century Construction; the EGC Corp.; Klenco, Milay, and Company; and Pilot Construction. There are also many local contractors providing light commercial and office construction in Northern Kentucky.

Available statistics estimate that commercial/industrial construction in Northern Kentucky from 1985 to 2004 reached values of $8 billion for new construction and $2 billion for remodeling. The ripple effect in providing local jobs, local taxes, and income is, of course, significant, and additional continuing economic benefits derive from the operation of these new industrial/commercial facilities.

Home Builders Association of Northern Kentucky. *Industry Standard.* Fort Mitchell: Home Builders Association of Northern Kentucky, 2001.
Wiedeman, Donald M. *Milestones and Memories: The Heartbeat of Housing in Northern Kentucky.* Fort Mitchell: Home Builders Association of Northern Kentucky, 2001.

Donald M. Wiedeman

BUILDING, RESIDENTIAL. Although home building had always been an important industry, it became especially significant economically after **World War II** (1941–1945). Two decades of economic depression and war, the 1930s and 1940s, had stymied development and construction, but now in Northern Kentucky, as well as nationwide, new homes were being built in increasing numbers. Many returning veterans bought homes with government loans and moved with their families to suburbs.

While the Greater Cincinnati Airport was in the initial planning stage, there was always concern that the impetus of the ongoing building boom in Northern Kentucky might shift northward to Cincinnati if the airport was built in Ohio instead of Kentucky. It was clear that if opponents to locating the airport in Kentucky were successful, the prospects for home building in Northern Kentucky would be dimmed. In 1947, however, the airport (later named **Cincinnati/Northern Kentucky International Airport**) was completed in Boone Co.

Originally, Northern Kentucky builders were home grown; that is, they were small-volume builders who grew up and lived in the area. A few came from Germany, though, including George and Nick Kreutzjans, Anthony Erpenbeck, and Matthew Toebben. The first large-volume builder was a Cincinnati company owned by Marvin Warner and named Liberty Construction. It began operations in Northern Kentucky in 1964, causing concern about its impact on the industry and on the traditional small builder. However, as demand for housing increased, some of the once-small builders grew larger themselves and opened subdivisions in the suburbs, a number of them in multiple locations. Some of these builders, such as the Drees Company (see **Ralph Drees**), Fischer Homes, Arlinghaus Builders, and Finke Homes, have now produced a large number of homes in the region. The Drees Company and Fischer Homes have also become major national home builders. Others have become custom builders with fewer units but very large homes, while some remain small both in volume and in the size of the homes they erect.

The tight-money building depression of 1974–1975 slowed the construction industry's output of new homes. Interest rates soared to 10.5 percent, and unemployment hit the industry. Recovery came at the close of the 1970s with the advent of double-digit inflation. Home values increased faster than inflation: the average home that sold for $25,000 in 1970 was selling for $68,000 or more by 1979.

In the early 1980s, the bad news was the combination of tight money, skyrocketing interest rates of 16–18 percent, continuing double-digit inflation (but this time making a negative impact through higher interest rates for construction loans), and a rise in the cost of energy. These factors together helped bring the industry to its knees. Housing starts plummeted; some builders stopped building, others turned to remodeling, and some went out of business. Northern Kentucky's savings and loan associations, prime sources for home loans, were under duress. While Kentucky's usury laws limited loan rates, the federal government entered the money markets with Treasury bills paying higher rates of interest than the savings and loans were permitted to offer. Thus, the source of money for mortgage loans dried up, and what loans were available came at rates as high as 18 percent. Calls went out to the federal government to cut spending, including entitlement programs and Social Security cost-of-living increases, which contributed to the federal debt by tapping money once available for housing. In an initiative termed "Call to Action," builders expressed support for the campaign by mailing to members of Congress two-by-four-inch pieces of lumber inscribed with appropriate messages. Their actions also caught the attention of the media. The nation and the building industry began to change their way of doing business as politicians now were pressured to help the building industry through legislation.

Fundamental changes in the building business were evident. The recession had put some builders and suppliers out of business; others simply stopped building new homes. Soon, the survival word in the industry was "diversify," and many builders, because of the severe recession in the single-family housing market, went into new areas of building. They expanded their business activity in home improvement and invested in light commercial, apartment, and duplex projects. Some established other businesses, such as car washes or furniture stores. Builders previously had employed their own crews for carpentry, bricklaying, drywall, painting, concrete finishing, and other tasks, but now subcontracting became the norm rather than the exception. With new policies governing overtime, benefits, and overhead, builders could control their costs better by the use of subcontractors.

Another significant change in the housing industry was in the types of financing used to purchase homes. Whereas the fixed mortgage had been the traditional method of financing a home, creative financing now introduced such concepts as buydowns and down-payment escrow accounts. Then came ARMs (adjustable rate mortgages), renegotiable mortgage rates, points, balloons, and many other new ways to finance homes. Home mortgages were made exempt from state usury laws that set a limit on interest, and the federal government changed the structure and functions of financial institutions. No longer were savings and loans the primary source of mortgages. Mortgage bankers, banks, and others took a more prominent role in the home mortgage market. Thus, savings and loans (see **Savings and Loan Associations**) entered the consumer market and competition determined the rates. The merging of banks and savings and loan institutions followed.

The typical home buyer was in a better financial position than before. Home owners, who had benefited from increased equity values in older homes due to inflation in the late 1970s, found themselves with cash for a variety of needs and wants. The "trade up" home market resulted in sustained high levels of sales as well as mortgage borrowing that reached astronomical proportions. The benefits of home ownership included the mortgage interest tax deduction (which later came under attack in the U.S. Congress), the increase in equity, and the appreciation of value due to inflation. All of these influences fueled additional spending for consumer luxuries, including newer and more expensive housing.

Home building generates substantial local economic activity, including income, jobs, and revenue for local governments. The economic impact of construction in Northern Kentucky has been measured in terms of its influence on jobs, wages, local taxes, and user charges and fees generated by the actual development, construction, and sale of the home during the year of construction. The ripple effect includes wages and profits distributed during the construction period and spent by local workers and business owners on locally supplied goods and services; the recycling of those business owners' income back into the community, producing more jobs, wages, and taxes to the community; the money the new home occupant spends on items produced by local businesses; and so on.

The construction of 100 single-family homes typically produces more than $10 million in local income, approximately $850,000 in local taxes, and 253 local jobs. Additional recurring, less direct impacts of building these homes include nearly $2.4 million in local income, $393,000 in local taxes, and 476 local jobs.

Home Builders Association of Northern Kentucky. *Industry Standard.* Fort Mitchell: Home Builders Association of Northern Kentucky, 2001.

Wiedeman, Donald M. *Milestones and Memories: The Heartbeat of Housing in Northern Kentucky.* Fort Mitchell: Home Builders Association of Northern Kentucky, 2001.

Donald M. Wiedeman

BULLITTSBURG BAPTIST CHURCH. One of the few scattered settlements on the Ohio River in Boone Co. during the pioneer era was located at Bullitt's Bottom, where the Bullittsburg Baptist Church, the first organized church of any kind in Northern Kentucky, was constituted in June 1794. The area was still vulnerable to Indian attacks at the time. John Taylor, who was a frontier Baptist preacher–farmer, was present at the church's founding. A few months later, his family moved to the area so that he could become the first preacher for the church. Taylor remained at the church for seven years, though he never became the official pastor. In his 1823 *A History of Ten Baptist Churches,* he describes frontier Baptist churches in Virginia and Kentucky; his text is especially detailed in its portrayal of the Bullittsburg Baptist Church and many of its early members.

The congregation erected its first house of worship in 1797. During the great religious revival referred to as the Second Great Awakening, which began in 1800, more than 100 persons made professions of faith, were baptized, and became members of the Baptist church at Bullittsburg. Following the revival, the Bullittsburg Baptist Church helped start churches in various communities throughout the county. The church held revivals frequently during the 19th century. At the start of 1811, 21 persons were received for baptism; by the first of November of that year, 170 members had been added. During the latter part of 1817 and the first part of 1818, 165 persons were baptized at the church. Through the joint labors of James Dicken, Absalom Graves, and Robert Kirtley, in 1823 and 1824, 118 persons were baptized and joined the church. In 1853, 54 individuals became members, mainly through the preaching of James A. Kirtley.

The Bullittsburg Baptist Church admitted its first African American member in 1797. It received many slaves into its membership over the years, as did many other local churches. At one time, the Bullittsburg Baptist Church had more than 100 African American members. In 1829, according to the church's record book, the congregation consisted of 190 whites and 89 blacks. This practice of nondiscrimination at the Bullittsburg Baptist Church continued until after the **Civil War**, when separate churches for whites and African Americans were organized.

For the first century of the church's existence, a local family, the Kirtleys, were its main leaders. Jeremiah Kirtley came to the area from Virginia. His son Robert, when he died at age 86, had been a member of the church for 61 years and had served as the church's pastor for half a century. Robert's son James A. Kirtley aided his father and later pastored at the Bullittsburg Baptist Church for many years. James also pastored the Big Bone Baptist Church in Boone Co. for many years; he was able to do so because the churches at that time usually met for worship only once a month. The church at Bullittsburg was the largest and most influential Baptist church in Northern Kentucky during the early 19th century. Three pastors, Robert and James A. Kirtley and J. W. Campbell, led the church for more than 100 years.

Church records show that during the 19th century, 1,170 individuals joined the church; the Bullittsburg church helped constitute eight other Baptist churches; the Bullittsburg church licensed 27 of its members to preach; and it ordained 16 ministers and 21 deacons and appointed 14 church clerks. In 1873 the Bullittsburg Baptist Church built an outdoor baptismal pool by the side of an overflowing spring at the entrance of the church property. It is made of stone in the shape of a keyhole, and its steps descend at the small end of the keyhole. The church members refer to it as "the Pool," and it continues in use today.

In 1944 the Bullittsburg Baptist Church began having services every Sunday, both morning and evening, for the first time in its history. It was also in the 1940s that electricity became available for the church meetinghouse. Between 1945 and 1955, more than 75 members were added to the congregation.

Among the other Baptist churches in Northern Kentucky that the Bullittsburg Baptist Church helped start are the Dry Creek Baptist Church in Kenton Co. (1800), the Wolper's Creek Baptist Church (1801), the Middle Creek Baptist Church, now Belleview (1803), the Sand Run Baptist Church (1819), and the Petersburg Baptist Church (1915).

"Bullittsburg Celebrates 185 Years of Service," *KP*, June 2, 1979, 4K.

Kirtley, James A. *History of Bullittsburg Church with Biographies.* Covington, Ky.: Davis, 1872.

"180th Homecoming in Bullittsburg," *KP,* June 1, 1974, 14K.

"174-Year Old Bullittsburg Congregation Still Building," *KP,* November 30, 1968, 4K.

James R. Duvall

BULLITTSBURG/NORTH BEND BOTTOMS. Bullittsburg and Bullittsville, two villages located in northern Boone Co., just three miles apart, can easily be confused: Bullittsville is three miles east of Idlewild; and Bullittsburg, on Garrison Creek, is one mile north of Idlewild. Bullittsburg, once a part of Virginia, was named in honor of the land's first claimant, Capt. Thomas Bullitt (1734–1782). In 1773, Bullitt, a veteran of the **French and Indian War**, was surveying the land in the north bend of the Ohio River that he had received in a land grant. He selected a site near the mouth of Sand Run Creek as a likely location for a town. Shortly thereafter, Bullitt left the area and never returned to Kentucky. Twenty-four years later, **Revolutionary War** colonel Cave Johnson (1760–1850) platted a 100-acre site, originally called Bullitt's Bottom (now North Bend Bottoms), but the town of Bullittsburg was never built (see **Cave Johnson House**). The name Bullittsburg survives, however, in the still-functioning **Bullittsburg Baptist Church**, founded here in 1794. The little settlement in that bend on the Ohio River was one of the few early scattered settlements in Northern Kentucky, and at first the threat of Indian attacks was constant.

In 1799, when Boone Co. was established, Johnson was appointed clerk of the County Court, and the county's first court was held at his home. Later, he was commissioned a colonel of the militia and subsequently a justice of the peace. In 1833 he became sheriff of Boone Co. He built a brick house in Boone Co. overlooking the Ohio River in about 1797 (a structure listed on the National Register of Historic Places in 1988) and spent time visiting a friend, future U.S. president William Henry Harrison (1841), who lived directly across the river.

Gen. John Brown (1752–1824), also a Revolutionary War veteran, built the **Sugar Grove Plantation** on land obtained from a land grant in North Bend Bottoms near Garrison Creek. **Zebulon Montgomery Pike** (1779–1834), the discoverer of Pike's Peak, was visiting his maternal uncle here when he met and married Clara Brown in 1801.

Even though books were scarce at North Bend Bottoms, one of the first one-room schoolhouses in Boone Co. was built there as early as 1808. It was called, in succession, the Balsly School, the Crisler School, and the North Bend School before it was consolidated as a part of the Hebron School. In October 1812, Elder James Hamilton Goss, from Virginia, taught school in the original schoolhouse at North Bend Bottoms.

A gristmill, where farmers ground their oats, corn, and wheat, was located nearby on Garrison Creek; two huge millstones were later found in the creek, which had been dammed for a mill pool. A millstone was reportedly seen there in the 1960s, but now there is nothing left to determine the gristmill's site.

Cabot, Susan M., and Michael D. Rouse. *Boone County.* Charleston, S.C.: Arcadia, 1998.

Conrad, William, comp. *The History of Boone County Schools.* Boone Co., Ky.: Boone Co. Community Educational Council, 1982.

Johnson, Cave. "The Early Days of Kentucky: Some Reminiscences from the Life of Col. Cave Johnson, Together with an Obituary Written at the Time of His Death," *Boone County Recorder,* February 1, 1877, 1.

Lutes, Ann. *A Brief History of Boone County.* Florence, Ky.: Boone Co. Historical Society, 1954.

Wilson, Noel. "Life in Boone County 100 Years Ago," *Boone County Recorder,* March 2, 1978, 10.

Nancy J. Tretter

BULLITTSVILLE. Bullittsville, located along Ky. Rt. 20 in Boone Co., near Hebron, was settled before 1794 and at the time called Corneliusville. The town's name later became Mitchellsville, and in 1853 it was changed to Bullittsville, in honor of Capt. Thomas Bullitt, a veteran of the **French and Indian War** who received a land grant in the area. Considered one of the principal points of trade in Boone Co., the community rapidly built up with stores, churches, physicians' offices, a post office (1853–1918), schools, a sawmill and a gristmill, and the Masonic (see **Masons**) and Grange Hall. The **Bullittsville Christian Church** met for nearly one year in the Masonic and Grange Hall before dedicating a new $4,000 church building in 1879.

There was a private school located next to the Christian Church, on the second floor of the Grange Hall, a two-story frame building that was torn down in 1955. A current resident of Bullittsville has the Grange door, with its original peephole, as well as the yellow poplar and yellow pine beams that held up the suspended ceiling. In 1883 there was a one-room schoolhouse located on the hill toward Burlington. One of the teachers was Anna Engle. When the school burned down in 1941, the students began attending a consolidated school in Burlington.

In 1878 C. S. Basley opened a general store in town. His grandfather was the first Democrat from Boone Co. elected to the state legislature. Another store in town, the Marshall store, also served as the post office. In the mid-1900s, the Engle Grocery operated in a long building that still sits by the bridge at Graves Rd. and is now a private residence. A blacksmith shop was nearby. With the decline of agriculture in the rural community, Bullittsville lost its commercial importance, and its residents began leaving the farm to work in the city.

At 5:37 p.m. on April 3, 1974, a three-square-mile section of Bullittsville was damaged by a strong **tornado** that took off awnings and shingles and tore the roofs off buildings. Penningon's store and its attached residence were completely destroyed. The tornado moved over the hill down toward the Ohio River, stripping all trees in its path. Two electric towers were topped. When the funnel hit a lake, a waterspout pulled all the water out until the bottom was visible. This tornado injured 20 people and damaged 50 homes and 20 barns in Boone Co.

Cabot, Susan M., and Michael D. Rouse. *Boone County.* Charleston, S.C.: Arcadia, 1998.

Reis, Jim. "Tiny Unincorporated Towns Abound in Boone," *KP,* December 9, 1985, 4K.

Warner, Jennifer S. *Boone County: From Mastodons to the Millennium.* Burlington, Ky.: Boone Co. Bicentennial Book Committee, 1998.

Nancy J. Tretter

BULLITTSVILLE CHRISTIAN CHURCH. The Bullittsville Christian Church, which was organized in 1879, is associated with the **Disciples of Christ** denomination. Elder W. S. Keene of Lexington arranged the first meetings to discuss creating a Christian Church in the Bullittsville area of Boone Co. The site he proposed is located on the Petersburg Pk. (Ky. Rt. 20). At the organizational meeting on November 27, 1879, Keene preached and conducted services and then led discussions of his proposal to create a new church. By the end of the meeting, the church was founded with 19 members. A total of $1,205 was pledged to construct a "meeting house." J. C. Jenkins of Petersburg was selected as chairman of the elders and James A. Davis of Hebron was chosen as secretary. A few weeks later, on December 12, the meeting was continued and 43 new members joined. In 1880 the first church building was constructed at a cost of $4,000. The sizable new frame structure could accommodate seating for up to 400. W. S. Keene served for four years as the first pastor of the church.

Like many Protestant churches of the time, the Bullittsville Christian Church prohibited dancing, gambling, and playing cards. In early days, services were held about once a month, but the schedule often changed when a new minister began serving. The second minister was R. L. Howe, who was later followed in the post by his brother W. J. Howe. By 1910, the Bullittsville Christian Church consisted of about 100 members. The pastor was Edger Riley of Burlington. During this year, the original structure, insured for about $2,200, was struck by lightening and destroyed. At the next meeting of the church, held at the nearby Mount Pleasant Church, it was decided to rebuild the Bullittsville church on the original site. According to the original deed of the church, if the "lot ever ceases to be used for a church, the lot shall be sold and the money given to Midway Orphans School [today, Midway College, Midway, Ky.]." The church still conducts its services at the original site. A new church was built debt-free and dedicated on December 11, 1910. In 1921 the first parsonage was built in Hebron. It was later sold, and the money was used to buy a lot for a new parsonage.

In 1929 a missionary society was formed at the church. Subsequent years saw the expansion of the church building to accommodate Sunday school and various fellowship activities including youth camps and Boy Scout Troop sponsorships. By the mid-1950s, the church averaged about 170 in Sunday school and expansion was taking place. On June 14, 1963, ground was broken for a new education building, and in late January 1974 the last service was held in the 1910 building. A new church was built on that site and dedicated on February 2, 1975. In March 2003 the church called its first female minister, Trisch Standifur.

Furnish, Emily, comp. *A History of Bullittsville Christian Church,* 1979. Available at the Boone Co. Public Library, Burlington, Ky.

Robert Schrage

BULLOCK, WILLIAM (b. ca. 1773, Birmingham, England; d. March 7, 1849, London, England). William Bullock, a renowned naturalist, collector, museum curator, and businessman who was born in Birmingham, England, resided in Northern Kentucky during the late 1820s and the 1830s and proposed building a speculative town to be called **Hygeia**. Although never built, Hygeia was one of the most interesting new-town plans of the period, either in America or Europe.

Bullock began as a silversmith and jeweler but learned showmanship from his mother, who created displays of wax figures. His brother was George Bullock, a noted Regency cabinetmaker, sculptor, and designer. The brothers were occasional artistic and business partners. William Bullock began collecting objects of art, natural science, and history, which he exhibited in England in

Bath, Birmingham, Leeds, Liverpool, Sheffield, and elsewhere. In 1809 he moved to London, England, where in 1812 he built the famous Egyptian Hall museum in London's Piccadilly entertainment district. Bullock's London Museum (its formal name), designed by P. F. Robinson, underwent interior remodeling in 1819 by architect John Buonarotti Papworth. Exotic Egyptian Revival architecture was utilized for novelty and commercial appeal, but the museum also represented one of the earliest attempts to arrange collections by scientific and educational principles and to exhibit international plant and animal specimens in re-created vignettes, or habitats.

Bullock purchased Napoleon Bonaparte's traveling carriage (captured by the British in 1815, after the Battle of Waterloo) and displayed it in his museum and around Britain. In 1822–1823, Bullock visited Mexico and returned to London to exhibit his discoveries. On a second Mexican trip in 1826, he and his wife returned via the United States. They traveled up the Ohio River and, in 1827, visited Cincinnati. The beauty and fertility of the region, the ease of travel to it by steamboat, and the rapid growth of Cincinnati greatly impressed Bullock. The religious toleration of the country also appealed to the Bullocks, who were Roman Catholics. Bullock purchased the nearly 1,000-acre **Elmwood** estate of Northern Kentucky businessman **Thomas D. Carneal** and planned to build Hygeia, a "small town of retirement," on the site, just downriver and across from Cincinnati (the location of present-day Ludlow). Returning briefly to London, Bullock retained J. B. Papworth to design the elegant town plan and promoted it in his publication *Sketch of a Journey through the Western States of North America*.

Bullock made a declaration of intent to become a U.S. citizen, a move that argues for his intent to remain; yet the Hygeia plan insensitively proposed a row of houses to be built between the existing house at Elmwood and its river view, a plan that perhaps calls Bullock's long-term motives into question. Bullock also planned a museum for Hygeia. While promoting Hygeia, Bullock and his wife lived at Elmwood and filled the house with art. Their visitors included English author Frances Trollope, who left an account of the estate in her book *The Domestic Manners of the Americans*. Bullock may have influenced her ill-starred Cincinnati bazaar, whose exotic architecture echoed his Egyptian Hall (which itself briefly contained a bazaar in 1819). Bullock may also have encouraged Trollope in her creation of exhibitions, such as the famous "Pandemonium" (or view of hell) that she and her artist friend Auguste Hervieu created for the Western Museum in Cincinnati.

Given his ability to attract crowds, Bullock surely felt he could lure investors and residents to Hygeia from both Great Britain and the United States. In the end, however, his town failed to materialize. In 1831 he sold 710 acres and the house at Elmwood to Israel Ludlow Jr. and moved to a cottage on the remaining, eastern portion of his estate. In 1836 he sold the rest of the property. He may have resided in the Cincinnati area until the late 1830s but eventually returned to England. He received little notice thereafter; perhaps the failed Hygeia scheme and his long absence from London had checked his momentum.

Altick, Richard D. *The Shows of London*. Cambridge: Harvard Univ. Press, 1978.

Bullock, William. *Sketch of a Journey through the Western States of North America*. London, 1827.

Costeloe, Michael P. *William Bullock, Connoisseur and Virtuoso of the Egyptian Hall: Piccadilly to Mexico (1773–1849)*. Bristol, UK: Univ. of Bristol, 2008.

——. "William Bullock and the Mexican Connection," *Mexican Studies/Estudios Mexicanos* 22 (Summer 2006): 275–309.

Shepperson, Wilbur S. "William Bullock—An American Failure," *Bulletin of the Historical and Philosophical Society of Ohio* 19 (April 1961): 144–52.

Tenkotte, Paul A. "Rival Cities to Suburbs: Covington and Newport, Kentucky, 1790–1890," PhD diss., Univ. of Cincinnati, 1989.

Patrick Snadon

BUNNING, DAVID L. (b. July 14, 1966, Fort Thomas, Ky.). Federal district judge David Louis Bunning is the son of U.S. Senator James P. **"Jim" Bunning** and Mary C. Theis Bunning. David Bunning grew up in Fort Thomas and graduated from **Newport Central Catholic High School** in 1984. Both his undergraduate (1988) and law (1991) degrees are from the University of Kentucky in Lexington. He was admitted to the Kentucky bar in 1991. Also in 1991 he served as a law clerk for the U.S. Attorney's Office for the Eastern District of Kentucky and began his tenure in that office as an assistant U.S. attorney. In August 2001, it was announced that he was a presidential selection as a judge in the U.S. Sixth District Court; in September 2001, his nomination was sent to the U.S. Senate; and the Senate confirmed his appointment in February 2002. Based in Covington, he holds court about one week each month at the federal courthouse in Pikeville.

Harden, Crystal. "Bunning Begins Federal Judgeship," *KP*, March 28, 2002, 2K.

United States Department of Justice. "Office of Legal Policy." www.usdoj.gov (accessed November 8, 2006).

The White House. "Presidential Nomination." www.whitehouse.gov/news/nominations/72.html (accessed November 8, 2006).

BUNNING, JIM (b. October 23, 1931, Covington, Ky.). James Paul David "Jim" Bunning, a baseball player and a U.S. senator, grew up in Southgate. In 1949 he graduated from St. Xavier High School in Cincinnati, where he played football, basketball, and baseball. After he completed his first year at Xavier University in Cincinnati, on a basketball scholarship, the Detroit Tigers signed him to a baseball contract. He graduated from Xavier University with a degree in economics in 1953 and spent six years in the minor leagues as an intimidating right-handed side-arm pitcher. In 1955 he made his major league debut and began a remarkable 17-year career, during which he played with four teams: Detroit (AL), Philadelphia (NL), Pittsburgh (NL), and Los Angeles (NL). His career record was 224 wins and 184 losses, and he struck out 2,855 batters. Seven times Bunning was selected to the All-Star Baseball Team. He became only the second player in major league history to record 1,000 strikeouts and attain 100 wins in both leagues. Bunning pitched a no-hitter against the Boston Red Sox on July 20, 1958, while with the Detroit Tigers; and then, as a Philadelphia Philly, he threw a perfect game (27 batters retired in a row) against the New York Mets on June 21, 1964. Upon his retirement from baseball in 1971, Bunning was second on the all-time pitching strikeout list. After his playing days, Bunning became a key figure in the creation of the Major League Players Association. In 1996 he was elected to the Baseball Hall of Fame.

He began his political career in 1977 by being elected to the City Council of Fort Thomas, and two years later he was elected to the Kentucky State Senate as a Republican. In 1983 he ran for governor of Kentucky, losing to Martha Layne Collins. However, three years later, Bunning was elected to the U.S. House of Representatives from the Fourth District of Kentucky, succeeding longtime Republican congressman Gene Snyder. Bunning held his congressional seat for 12 years and served on various committees, including Banking and Ways and Means. He was chair of the Social Security Subcommittee. As a member of the U.S. House, Bunning voted for the impeachment of Democratic president William Clinton (1993–2001); and just a month later, having been elected a U.S. senator from Kentucky in 1998, he also voted on the charges in Clinton's U.S. Senate trial. After his election to the U.S. Senate in 1998, he immediately won a seat on the Finance Committee, becoming the first Kentuckian to serve on this important committee in 40 years. Bunning has also served on the U.S. Senate's Budget and Energy committees. In 2004 he won reelection to the U.S. Senate in a close election. He married Mary Catherine Theis, and they have 9 children, one of whom is U.S. District Judge **David Bunning**, and 35 grandchildren.

Jim Bunning, U.S. Senator for Kentucky. http://bunning.senate.gov (accessed March 6, 2006).

Kleber, John E., ed. *The Kentucky Encyclopedia*. Lexington: Univ. Press of Kentucky, 1992.

The National Baseball Hall of Fame and Museum. "Bunning, Jim." www.baseballhalloffame.org (accessed March 6, 2006).

Robert Schrage

BURLEIGH, WILLIAM R. "BILL" (b. September 6, 1935, Evansville, Ind.). Editor and media businessman Bill Burleigh is the son of Joseph Charles and Emma Bertha Wittgen Burleigh. He earned a BS in education from the University of Wisconsin at Milwaukee in 1957. During the late 1970s Burleigh moved to suburban Cincinnati to become the editor of the *Cincinnati Post*. When it came time to build his retirement home, he bought a farm in Boone Co., near Rabbit Hash, that overlooks the Ohio River.

Until 2009 Burleigh was chairman of the board of the E. W. Scripps Company, a Cincinnati-based media company that he joined as a reporter while still attending high school. During his 50 years with this media giant, he helped the company evolve from its traditional newspaper roots into one of the nation's leaders in cable network programming. He began his career with the Evansville Press in 1951 and retired as the company's president and CEO in 2000. He has been honored with some of the media industry's highest awards, including induction into the Indiana and Cincinnati Journalism halls of fame.

Burleigh is also well known in the Indiana-Ohio-Kentucky tri-state business community for his volunteer work and leadership. His service as chairman of the Greater Cincinnati Chamber of Commerce was so much appreciated that the organization created an annual award in his name to honor business leadership. Likewise, the Scripps Howard Foundation created an annual award in Burleigh's name to honor individuals for their distinguished community service.

Devoted to the Catholic Church, Burleigh has taken leadership roles in church matters, locally and nationally. In 2002 he was named to the U.S. Conference of Catholic Bishops National Review Board. Locally he was instrumental in the building of a new All Saints Church in Walton. Burleigh married Catherine Anne Husted on November 28, 1964. He and his wife have three children, David; Sister Anne Catherine, O.P.; and Margaret Brecount, plus six grandchildren.

Burleigh, Bill. Interview by Nancy J. Tretter, February 22, 2005, Burlington, Ky.

"William Robert Burleigh." In *Marquis Who's Who, 2006.* http://galenet.galegroup.com (accessed June 9, 2006).

Nancy J. Tretter

BURLESQUE AND EXOTIC DANCING. In Northern Kentucky burlesque was represented by occasional events and a few well-known performers, but exotic dancing, a later form, could be found in established clubs.

To burlesque is to satirize, spoof, or mock; thus, any stage performance that does so may be called a burlesque. Since the **Civil War**, however, the term *burlesque* has related more specifically to the art of striptease, in theatrical venues that emphasize the scantily clothed, or fully unclothed, live female figure. Burlesque, much like its more highbrow cousin vaudeville, was performed by troupes that traveled nationally for 40 weeks or more each year, mainly visiting towns for only one week. The system assured an almost endless supply of new and—dare it be said—raw talent to cycle through the classic "burlyque" theaters in the sordid and seedy sections of downtown urban America, supplying new blood for newspaper ads, marquee writers, and, of course, devotees of the art form. Ohio had more of these burlesque palaces than any other state.

Outside the burlesque theater stood the barker, attracting males with promises of gorgeous women with great figures performing acts of unbelievable contortion; inside, between acts, hawkers prowled the aisles selling saltwater taffy and popcorn to the crowd of gawkers, who knew that their purchase might contain a valuable hidden prize of some sort. Onstage were the eagerly anticipated performers. Mabel Saintley became the country's first native-born burlesque star, appearing in Mme. Rintz's Female Minstrels after 1880; the biggest star of the early 20th century was Millie DeLeon, described as an attractive brunette who brazenly tossed her garters into the audience while occasionally neglecting to wear tights. Her raunchy behavior helped fill seats nationwide, as did the news of her countless arrests, many of which were planned in advance.

The burlesque performers considered themselves comedians, it must be noted. After all, several male comics, wearing large top hats, were on stage with them. The head comic was known as the "top banana," and the others were ranked in order—second banana, third banana, and so forth. The higher the number, the more cream pies in the face a comic received, and the more he was required to slip on banana peels. Furthermore, the girls could deliver funny lines as well as the men could. Burlesque was a training ground, for this is where people like George M. Cohan, W. C. Fields, Al Jolson, Bert Lahr, Phil Silvers, and even Bob Hope got their start. Acts were accompanied by an orchestra pit full of union musicians. Once air-conditioning became available and was installed, these emporiums advertised cool comfort along with their other attractions.

Within the Northern Kentucky region, there were no formal classic burlesque houses. However, men and boys easily escaped across the Ohio River to the Gayety Theater (an 1848-era church building) in Cincinnati on Vine St. near Ninth St. (where part of the main library stands today), just up the street from another burlesque house, the Standard Theater at Vine St. and Central Pkwy. The other similar establishment in Cincinnati was the Imperial Follies (once called the Mohawk) on W. McMicken Ave. Twenty-five cents got a person inside, with little regard for the patron's age. Today, many mature Northern Kentucky men boast of how they skipped school to take in the latest show at the Gayety: Virginia Bell, Rose Larose, Gypsy Rose Lee, Virginia Lee, the famous fan dance of Sally Rand and her feathers, and Blaze Storm. The Gayety went from vaudeville to burlesque in 1909, became a strip joint in 1937, and closed in spring 1970.

Occasionally, respectable burlesque transpired in Northern Kentucky. One evening in September 1941, Sally Rand performed at the **Twin Oaks Golf Course** in Latonia. The event was an orphans' benefit, courtesy of Jimmy Brink's **Lookout House**, where she was appearing for a brief run. Gypsy Rose Lee and her entourage once considered staying overnight at the old Flannery Hotel at Fourth and Garrard St. in Covington, but for some reason they chose to go elsewhere. She played at the **Beverly Hills Supper Club** that evening. Rand's and Lee's immense success allowed them an occasional one-night stand at mainstream entertainment outlets such as the Beverly Hills Supper Club. The seemingly ageless Rand returned to play in Newport during the 1950s at the Glenn Rendezvous Club and in the 1960s at the Silver Slipper and the Stardust clubs.

There were at least two statuesque women from Northern Kentucky who entered the trade of stripping. By 1905 Covington native Rose Sydell (born about 1870) had been an established national star for some 14 years, and by 1910 she had her own burlesque troupe. She began as a ballet dancer at Robinson's Opera House in Cincinnati and gradually worked her way into burlesque. Sydell thoroughly enjoyed playing at Cincinnati's Standard Theater, because it gave her the opportunity to spend the week with her family along Athey St. in Covington. The Standard Theater knew how to promote, for when Sydell was in town, the theater held special Covington days to give Northern Kentucky boys a chance to see some local talent. She married William Campbell and retired to her new home in Brooklyn, N.Y.

Another Covington girl, Carrie Lee Finnell, who was born at the turn of the century, traveled the world, practicing the art. As "the girl with the $100,000 legs," Finnell became known as the originator of the routine of twirling tassels in opposite directions simultaneously. By 1916 she was listed as an actress in the Covington city directory. She began her career in theatrical groups in Covington and Newport before heading off to Chicago. Later she danced at the Winter Garden Theater in New York City as part of the famous Minsky's Burlesque, in Europe, and in her favorite town, New Orleans. As late as 1963, she played at Newport's Galaxie Club, called "Newport's only adult night club," as a singer. It was difficult to do without the adulation heaped on her for so many years, so she resorted to singing just to get on the stage again. Soon after the performance, she died of a heart attack at her farm in Ohio.

For Northern Kentucky, Finnell represents the transition between the burlesque of the 1930s, which took place mostly in Cincinnati, and exotic dancing, which was on the bill that night when she sang at the Galaxie. Burlesque was of the 19th century, urban, and vaudevillian in origin, and it had waned by the end of the 1960s. The origins of exotic dancing were in the 20th century: it was modern go-go dancing brought to fruition, with full frontal nudity sans comedy as a required sideshow. The sexual revolution and performers such as San Francisco's Carol Doda popularized exotic dancing in the early 1960s. Burlesque was not common in Northern Kentucky, but exotic dancing was a product ideally suited for the nature of Newport's nightclubs.

Perhaps the most famous exotic dancer was the beautiful and bodacious Morganna Roberts Cottrell, born in 1946. Beginning in 1965 or so, Morganna graced the runway of Newport's Galaxie Club along Monmouth St. for upwards of three months each year, appearing at two- and three-week intervals, giving three and sometimes four shows per night. Conventioneers from Cincinnati, old men from Campbell and Kenton counties, and pubescent boys populated the place night after night, shoulder to shoulder, at a minimum cover charge of $5. Originally dubbed "The Wild One," she transitioned into "Baseball's Kissing Bandit," traveling to most ballparks around the country, where she would run onto the field scantily dressed and plant kisses on baseball's best players, beginning with the Cincinnati Red Pete Rose. Morganna promoted herself by occasionally taking barely clothed walks through the town in which she was playing. The unusual was her specialty, but anyone who ever had a drink with her found her a real person full of humor, as were parts of her act. She clearly understood the origins of burlesque, although by her day the art form had become exotic dancing. After 35 years of such antics, Morganna retired in 2000, having been a star of the stage, of film, and of magazines.

Lesser houses of exotic dancing existed in Newport and Covington, but the Galaxie was the best known. Elsewhere around the region at some of the county fairs, performances in tents occasionally would occur, involving dancing girls and sometimes becoming very risqué. In the mid-1960s, the long-running Germantown Fair in Bracken Co. had such a place, which admitted underage young men. Whether the Germantown activities should be labeled burlesque or exotic dancing, their quality was poor. The fair girls could not compare in talent or beauty with the queens on the circuit.

Burlesque houses had vanished from the national landscape by 1970, yielding to slick girlie magazines, movies (see **Cinema X**), and recently the Internet. If there is a modern equivalent, it is the new, suburban gentlemen's club, a further refinement of exotic dancing, found in areas where local mores and zoning regulations permit. The reform movement that cleaned up Newport eventually drove the dance parlors out of town (see **Newport Second Cleanup**).

"Burlesque Star Is a Covingtonian," *KP*, September 7, 1905, 3.
"Galaxie Club Burned in '70," *KP*, February 22, 1999, 4K.
"Gayety Theater Took Final Bow in '70," *CP*, December 29, 1987, 2B.
"Miss Sydell Spends Her Holiday with Mother," *KP*, September 28, 1910, 3.
Reis, Jim. "'$100,000 Legs' Carried Carrie to Striptease Fame," *KP*, February 22, 1999, 4K.
——."Sally Rand Brought Her Act to Town," *KP*, March 28, 1905, 4K.
"Wild One Caught," *KP*, January 11, 1972, 2K.

Michael R. Sweeney

BURLINGTON. Burlington, under its earliest name, Craig's Camp, was planned as a capital city. It has been the seat of Boone Co. government since 1799, when the county court located the center of government in the north-central part of the county on 74 acres of land donated by Robert Johnson and John Hawkins Craig. The second name the town was known by in its early years was Wilmington. It was renamed Burlington in 1816 at the request of the U.S. Post Office. Burlington was incorporated in 1824, and the corporation was annulled in 1923. Today, Burlington is one of only two unincorporated county seats in Kentucky.

Burlington's town plat, drawn in about 1805 by county surveyor Moses Scott, is a fine example of formal town planning. As originally conceived, it called for 12 squares grouped around two intersecting roads, with a central "Publick Square." The plan was later modified to allow the two principal roads, Washington St. (Burlington Pk.) and Jefferson St. (Idlewild–East Bend Rd.) to cross the square rather than travel around it. The central square was divided into four rectangular plots, and the western plots were sold for commercial development. The courthouse has always occupied the northeast plot, while the clerk's building and the jail occupied the southeast plot.

Some of Burlington's quaint street names reflect geographical orientation: Temperate St. forms the north side of the town plan, Torrid St. borders the south, and Orient St. borders the east. Other streets were named after founding fathers such as George Washington and Thomas Jefferson or Kentucky politicians like Garrard, Gallatin, and Nicholson.

From 1799 to 1801, county functions were conducted at homes in and around Burlington. The county's first log courthouse was completed by January 1801. Its presence is noted in the County Court Order Book, which states simply that "Court [was] held for the County of Boone at the Courthouse." In 1817 the log building was replaced by a large brick structure facing Jefferson St. In 1833 the first brick jail was built; it was replaced by a more substantial brick jail in 1853. Also in 1853, the county constructed a Greek Revival temple-style building to house the office of the county clerk. The 1817 courthouse was remodeled several times and then replaced in 1889 by a building designed by the McDonald Brothers architects of Louisville, who designed numerous courthouses in Kentucky and Indiana in the late 19th century. The present courthouse cupola was designed by the renowned Cincinnati architectural firm of **Samuel Hannaford and Sons** and built in 1898.

By 1840, stylish brick houses, taverns, and commercial buildings began to crowd the center of town. The Central House Hotel (now the County Seat Restaurant) stood opposite the courthouse at the corner of Jefferson and Washington Sts. The Boone House Hotel (now known as the Renaker House) on Union Square, built about 1830, was a tavern and inn for most of the 19th century. Along Jefferson St. stood stately brick residences in the Federal and Greek Revival styles, some of which were used as commercial buildings at various times. One of the finest of these homes is the Erastus Tousey House, a brick Federal-style residence dating from about 1822, which was rehabilitated and opened as the Tousey House Restaurant in 2002.

By 1850 Burlington had 200 residents, stores, taverns, three hotels, and a wool factory. Four religious congregations were organized: Baptist, Methodist, Presbyterian, and Universalist. Two African American Baptist congregations were formed after the **Civil War**, including the First Baptist, which continues to hold regular Sunday services. Turnpikes led to Florence and later to the bustling river town of Petersburg.

Two newspapers have operated out of Burlington. The first was the *Burlington Advertiser*, a weekly paper founded in 1849 by W. H. Nelson. The paper was published for just one year. In 1875 the *Boone County Recorder* began publication in Burlington as a weekly paper; it continues to operate today as a Community Press publication, and the organization has been recognized as a Centennial Business.

A 1903 publication entitled *The Commercial History of the Southern States*, by A. B. Lipscomb, describes Burlington as follows: "Burlington, the county seat, is situated near the center of the county. . . . The town has about 300 inhabitants, two general merchandise stores, one drug store, one bank, one good hotel, a printing office, which is owned by W. L. Riddell, editor of the Boone County Recorder, one of the best papers in the state outside Louisville, also four nice church buildings. The town is laid off in a square, with a beautiful courthouse at the center."

One of the most important institutions of early Burlington was the Morgan Academy, established in 1814 and originally funded by the sale of seminary lands that had been set aside by the Commonwealth after it became a state. The school remained open until the 1890s. The first high school in Boone Co. was established in Burlington in 1910 and served both local students and those from surrounding areas, some of whom boarded in town. African American students attended a small school on Nicholas St. next to the First Baptist Church that operated from 1891 to 1956, when schools were integrated.

The Boone Co. fair was established at Burlington in 1942. That year, the 4-H and Utopia Club Council established permanent fairgrounds on Idlewild Rd. north of town. The first building constructed was a cattle barn. The three-acre lake at the entrance was constructed in 1942. While many of the fair buildings are of recent construction, the grounds retain a core of historic structures, including the entrance gate, which was rebuilt in 1995.

In 1979 Burlington was listed in the National Register of Historic Places as a historic district, primarily owing to the historic significance of the 1805 town plan. Burlington merchants have successfully capitalized on their town's heritage. Historic buildings have been renovated to house specialty shops, restaurants, and a bed-and-breakfast inn. The Burlington Antiques Show is one of the largest of its kind, drawing tourists to the fairgrounds one Sunday a month from April to October.

Becher, Matthew E., Michael A. Rouse, Robert Schrage, and Laurie Wilcox. *Images of America: Burlington.* Charleston, S.C.: Arcadia, 2004.
Boone Co. Historic Preservation Review Board. *Historic Structures of Boone County, Kentucky.* Burlington, Ky.: Boone Co. Historic Preservation Review Board, 2002.

Matthew E. Becher and Margaret Warminski

BURLINGTON BAPTIST CHURCH. Founded in 1842, Burlington Baptist Church has had a long and active presence in the town of Burlington. In late 1842 other churches in Boone Co. were consulted for their opinions concerning the creation of a Baptist church in Burlington. **Bullitttsburg Baptist Church** and Middle Creek Baptist Church had no objections, and so on December 13, 1842, the new church was founded. Robert Kirtley, the moderator of the original meetings resulting in the creation of Burlington Baptist Church, was also selected as the first pastor, a sign of respect for his long religious service. Approximately 20 individuals made up the church at the time, including 5 blacks and 15 members transferred from the Middle Creek Baptist Church. The growth of Burlington Baptist Church paralleled that of Burlington itself. Originally known as Craig's Camp, the town was established in October of 1800. Around the time Burlington Baptist Church was constituted, the town had about 200 residents, three other churches, and many businesses.

Robert Kirtley served until 1845, when James Kirtley became the second pastor. In May 1844 the congregation met for the first time in a new building that they had built. Their longest-serving house of worship was constructed in 1892 in a unique Stick Style and served the congregation until 1979, when the current church building was completed. Today the Burlington Baptist Church continues to be a major part of life in the unincorporated town of Burlington and spiritually serves much of the surrounding rural and suburban community. One of the most active churches in the county, it has strong programs in student and youth ministry, athletic ministry, community activities, and Bible study.

Kirtley, Elizabeth. *Burlington Baptist Church, 150 Years, 1842–1992.* Burlington, Ky.: Burlington Baptist Church, 1992.

Robert Schrage

BURLINGTON HIGH SCHOOL. A 1908 state law required each county in Kentucky to have at least one public high school, located in the county seat. Burlington High School, at Burlington, the county seat of Boone Co., was built as a result and opened in September 1910. It was located where the present Burlington Elementary School is. **Carroll L. Cropper**, later a Boone Co. judge, graduated from Burlington High in 1916. The PTA began serving lunches at the school in 1927, and in 1939 a new building was constructed. The school was heated with coal until 1943. In 1949 Burlington High School won the state championship in six-man football. In 1954 the high schools of Burlington, Florence, Hebron, and New Haven were consolidated into the new **Boone Co. High School** at Florence.

"Burlington on Firing Line as Progressive City," *KP*, February 22, 1912, 2.
Conrad, William, comp. *The History of Boone County Schools.* Boone Co., Ky.: Boone Co. Community Educational Council, 1982.
Warner, Jennifer S. *Boone County: From Mastodons to the Millennium.* Burlington, Ky.: Boone Co. Bicentennial Book Committee, 1998.

Gail Chastang

BURMAN, BEN LUCIEN (b. December 12, 1895, Covington, Ky.; d. November 12, 1984, New York City). Ben Lucien Burman is one of the best-known and most prolific authors born in Northern Kentucky. His parents, Samuel N. and Minnie Hurwitz Behrman, were Jewish immigrants, and there was a Jewish community (see **Jews**) in Covington when Burman was young. The family lived at 15 E. Eighth St. in Covington. Ben attended the old Covington High School and, from 1913 to 1915, Miami University, in Oxford, Ohio. **World War I** found him in the U.S. Army fighting in France. He was wounded (gassed) at Soissons in 1918 and returned home 20 percent disabled. He finished college in 1920 at Harvard University in Cambridge, Mass. Returning to Covington, he taught at **Holmes High School**, where he was charged with teaching Bolshevism. Burman eventually worked in Cincinnati as an editor for the *Cincinnati Times-Star* and wrote for newspapers in Boston and in New York City. He contributed writings to such periodicals as *Nation, Reader's Digest,* and *Saturday Review.* His best-known writings, though, are his books about life on the Ohio and Mississippi rivers.

The 1929 *Mississippi,* Burman's first book concerning a river, was the first of his 22 novels. *Steamboat Round the Bend,* published in 1933, became famed actor-humorist Will Roger's last and most successful movie; it was released under the title *Heaven on Earth.* Burman befriended Rogers on the set of that movie. The novel *Blow for a Landing* followed in 1938, the same year that Burman won the Southern Authors Award and was nominated for a Pulitzer Prize. Yet another successful river tale, *Big River to Cross,* appeared in 1940. Burman came to be regarded as the "new Mark Twain" because of his affection for the river and the characters he created in his writings, such as Captain Lilly, Doctor Jim, Willow Joe, and a cast of other steamboat owners, roustabouts, and shanty-boat people. Alice Caddy, whom Burman married in 1927, illustrated his books so adeptly that people bought the books both for his writing and for her drawings.

Ben Lucien Burman, 1913.

Burman changed professions during **World War II**: he became a war correspondent reporting on the Vichy government in France from his base of operations in North Africa. For that work he was awarded the French Legion of Honor in 1946. After the war he returned to writing about the river, now in the satirical Catfish Bend stories. The 1952 *High Water at Catfish Bend* was followed by six other mythical fables of animal folks, set along the Mississippi River in Louisiana. Based on the themes he developed in the Catfish Bend novels, Burman was likened to a modern-day Aesop. Alice Caddy, his artistic wife, drew the images of the animals that Burman conjured up. Through his writings, Burman captured the spirit of river life in the Midwest in much the same spirit as had the hit musical *Show Boat.*

The sales of Burman's books numbered in the millions. Most of his river novels have been translated into several foreign languages. Burman also contributed more than 60 articles to the *Reader's Digest;* in his later years that company pensioned him, even though he had never been its employee. Burman occasionally returned to Covington to visit his old haunts, but as his local friends gradually died off, he found such trips difficult and made them less often. Alice Caddy died in 1977; Burman died in New York City seven years later and was cremated. His ashes were mixed with those of his wife and were spread by his friends from the bow of a steamboat in the lower Mississippi River near New Orleans, as a Dixieland band played music. There is a fitting tribute to Ben Lucien Burman today along Riverside Dr. in Covington: a Kentucky State Highway Marker reminding passers-by of that bygone steamboat era and of the world-renowned writer from Covington who did so much to popularize it. Burman's collected works and letters are archived in the special collections department of the Tulane University library in New Orleans.

"Author Ben Lucien Burman," *CP*, November 13, 1984, 10A.
"Ben Lucien Burman, 88, Author of 22 Books," *NYT*, November 13, 1984, B6.
King, Charles D. "Burman, Ben Lucien." In *The Kentucky Encyclopedia*, ed. John E. Kleber. Lexington: Univ. Press of Kentucky, 1992.
Tulane Manuscripts Department. "Ben Lucien Burman and Alice Caddy Burman Papers." www.tulane.edu/~lmiller/BurmanFamily.html.

Michael R. Sweeney

BURTON, NELSON (b. September 12, 1922, Covington, Ky.). Nelson Burton, a musician, jazz historian, speaker, and author, is the son of James R. and Ardell Coleman Burton. He graduated from Lincoln-Grant High School in 1939 and attended Kentucky State College (now Kentucky State

University) in Frankfort, receiving a football scholarship. He was not able to serve in **World War II** because of a medical condition (a double hernia) that caused him to be classified 4F. Like many young African American men at the time, Burton believed that serving his country would be a way to become accepted as a full citizen of the United States, thereby helping to break down segregation laws. Because he was not able to become a soldier, he chose to work at the foundry of the Wright Aeronautical factory, just north of Cincinnati in Evendale, Ohio. He also volunteered to play drums for the U.S.O. groups that entertained the troops, thus beginning his 50-year career as a rhythm drummer. Burton was a house musician for Cincinnati's famed black Cotton Club in the 1940s and 1950s and a studio musician in the 1950s for the legendary King Records of Cincinnati. During his career Burton has backed up or has had jam sessions with some of the most popular entertainers in the United States: Pearl Bailey, Count Basie, Cab Calloway, Nate King Cole, Duke Ellington, Harry James, and Maybelle Smith.

In the 1970s, with Lisa Ledin, a public radio announcer and producer, Burton started recording his memoirs, which were published in 2000 as *Nelson Burton: My Life In Jazz.* He is in his 80s but still willing to perform on his drums or speak to young people about jazz music. He believes that jazz music is an important element of American culture that must be kept alive.

Burton, Nelson. *Nelson Burton: My Life In Jazz.* Cincinnati: Clifton Hills Press, 2000.

Jessica Knox-Perkins

BUSINESS AND COMMERCE. See names of specific businesses.

BUTLER. Butler, a city in Pendleton Co., was first called Fourth Lock, because it was near the proposed fourth lock and dam on the Licking River. After the town grew in importance, a more graceful name than Fourth Lock seemed appropriate, so in 1852 the name was changed to Clayton. Then in 1853, after the **Covington and Lexington Railroad** had been completed, the townspeople attempted to obtain a post office. Because there was another post office in Kentucky named Clayton, another name had to be selected. Joel Ham, a contractor working on the dam, named the town Butler in honor of W. D. Butler, a member of Congress from the district.

One of the first settlers in Butler was Pope Williams, who owned and cultivated land there. The town's first store, opened about 1837 by the Ham brothers, prospered as long as work on the lock and dam continued. When work ended, the Hams closed their store and moved to Cincinnati. William L. Barton was the first blacksmith in Butler. His blacksmith shop also served as the first school, continuing until shortly before 1860, when the town opened its first schoolhouse. It was a one-story, one-room, frame building that closed in 1882 or 1883, after a new, graded school opened. The new school's principal was Thomas M. Barton, a respected educator. Although the new building provided more space, it was not all used by the school at the time; the three rooms in the upper story of the school building were rented out for purposes other than education.

The Covington and Lexington Railroad, with its rail line through town, was completed in 1853, the same year the Butler post office opened. The renamed town was incorporated in 1856. Butler achieved considerable attention and fame when the **Butler Covered Bridge** over the Licking River opened in 1871. It was said to be the longest covered cantilever bridge in the nation. In that same year, 1871, Butler's town hall, the Masonic Hall, and a church congregation all moved into a new multipurpose building. Previously, there had been no church organizations in Butler except for a few Methodists who held meetings in the town's schoolhouse. On January 10, 1884, 18 Baptists who attended the Union Church (a nondenominational congregation that at the time was the only church in Butler) met to form the Butler Baptist Church. Dr. J. M. Blades was elected church moderator in 1921, an office he held for many years while he also served as deacon. Rev. D. P. Dehart became pastor in 1937 and served for 16 years. In 1953 when the Baptists built a new church on Peoples St., the historic bell was removed from the old church and hung in the new structure. An attempt in Butler's early history to utilize the area for commercial river navigation failed because of shallow water as well as obstructions at the mouth of the Licking in Covington. The idea to develop the area for commercial traffic frequently resurfaces but has been held back by high cost estimates.

Belew, Mildred Boden. *The First 200 Years of Pendleton County.* Falmouth, Ky.: M. B. Belew, n.d. [ca. 1994].

Mildred Belew

BUTLER, DOROTHY E. S. (b. December 17, 1912, Cincinnati, Ohio). Pharmacist Dorothy E. Schmied Butler is the daughter of Christopher and Hilma Anderson Schmied. Her mother had emigrated from Sweden in 1892, and her father was born in Switzerland Co., Ind. Dorothy married William Albert Butler in Covington in 1932. They had a daughter born in 1933. In 1940, at age 28, Dorothy Butler entered the Cincinnati College of Pharmacy, graduated in spring 1944, passed the pharmacy board exams, and was licensed by the State of Ohio. Subsequently, she operated a drugstore in Cincinnati.

Reciprocity of licensure was easily obtained in Kentucky, so Butler was able to move her operation to Warsaw, Ky., in 1958. Roy Prill, not a pharmacist but a businessman who had an interest in the **Warsaw Furniture Factory**, became her partner, and they opened Bailey's Corner Drug Store, Butler and Prill Sts. The B. K. Bailey Drug Store, where Nettie Weldon had been a pharmacist for 30 years, was their predecessor at the same site. After six months, Prill developed a brain tumor and died. Butler then sold her drug store to a former pharmacy classmate, Grandville "Bill" Beverly, who operated it until it was sold to the current owner, Thomas Barringer.

After working for some years as a pharmacist in both Kentucky and Ohio, Butler returned to college in 1969 and earned an MLS from the University of Kentucky. Afterward, she was employed at the Lloyd Library, a pharmaceutical library in Cincinnati, and was influential in moving it to its present location at 917 Plum St. The Lloyd brothers (**John Uri Lloyd** and **Curtis Gates Lloyd**), successful manufacturers of patent medicines, had established the library. Later, Butler returned to practicing pharmacy in hospital and retail settings. She is now retired and lives in Gallatin Co., just outside of Warsaw.

Judith Butler Jones

BUTLER, PERCIVAL P., ADJUTANT GENERAL (b. April 4, 1760, Carlisle, Pa.; d. September 9, 1821, Carrollton, Ky.). A soldier, a patriot, and the first adjutant general of Kentucky, Percival Pierce Butler was the 7th of 11 children of Thomas and Eleanor Parker Butler of Ireland, who had come to America in 1748. He and his brothers were known as the "Fighting Butlers" of the American Revolution. On September 1, 1777, at age 17, Butler began his service in the **Revolutionary War** as a 1st lieutenant in the 3rd Pennsylvania Regiment, fighting at Brandywine and Germantown. He served under the command of Gen. George Washington at Valley Forge, Pa., and Monmouth, N.J., and then under Gen. Marquis de Lafayette at the taking of Yorktown, N.Y., in October 1782. Butler went on to fight with Gen. Anthony Wayne in the southern theater of war until January 1, 1783; he then transferred to the 2nd Pennsylvania and on September 23 joined the 1st Pennsylvania, remaining with that unit until the end of the war, at which time he was brevetted a captain. Lafayette presented a sword to Butler for his service.

Butler moved to the mouth of Hickman Creek in what later became Jessamine Co., Ky., in 1784. He married Mildred Hawkins of Lexington, a descendant of Sir John Hawkins, on May 30, 1786; they had 11 children. In 1792, Kentucky's two-term governor Isaac Shelby (1792–1796 and 1812–1816) appointed Butler the new state's first adjutant general. In 1796 Butler moved his family to the confluence of the Kentucky and Ohio Rivers, to Port William Settlement (now Carrollton). He and his wife built a two-story log home approximately three miles from the Kentucky River, on land they purchased from John McKinley on April 12, 1797. Butler held the office of adjutant general for 24 years, resigning September 19, 1817, when a new law required the adjutant general to reside in Frankfort. He was unanimously elected as clerk of Gallatin Co. on May 17, 1799, and served in this position until his death in 1821, at Carrollton. He was buried in the Butler Family Cemetery. The Butler-Turpin State Historic House, at General Butler State Resort Park in Carrollton, is a second-generation home built on the estate originally owned by Percival Butler.

Butler, William D., John C. Butler, and Joseph M. Butler. *The Butler Family in America.* St. Louis, Mo.: Shallcross, 1909.

Heitman, Francis B. *Historical Register of the Officers of the Continental Army during the War of the Revolution, April 1775, to December, 1783.* Washington, D.C.: Government Printing Office, 1914.
Idzerda, Stanley J., Anne C. Loveland, Marc H. Miller, and the Queen's Museum. *LaFayette, Hero of Two Wars: Queen's Museum.* Lebanon, N.H.: Univ. Press of New England, 1989.
Pozar, Stephen M. *Richard Butler.* Butler, Pa.: Mechling, 2001.
Trussell, John B. B. *The Pennsylvania Line.* Harrisburg, Pa.: Historical and Museum Commission, 1983.

Evelyn Welch

BUTLER, WILLIAM ORLANDO, GENERAL (b. April 19, 1791, Carrollton, Ky.; d. August 6, 1880, Carrollton, Ky.). William Orlando Butler, a soldier, a politician, and a poet, was the son of Percival and Mildred Hawkins Butler. William received his bachelor's and law degrees from Transylvania College in Lexington. When the War of 1812 began, he joined the 5th Regiment of Kentucky Volunteers. In December 1812 he was made an officer and served in the Raisin River Campaign in Michigan, where he was wounded and captured. Released in 1814, he was made an aide to future president Gen. Andrew Jackson. Butler returned to Carrollton in 1817, where he set up his law practice and was elected to the U.S. House of Representatives. In April 1817 he married Eliza Todd, daughter of Gen. Robert Todd of Lexington. Butler became a poet of some renown; in the 1820s he received national recognition for his poem "The Boatman's Horn." When the **Mexican War** began, he was again called into military service and was made a major general of the Volunteers. During that war he was sent to Mexico in support of Gen. Zachary Taylor's troops. While leading his men in battle, Butler received a leg wound. In 1848 he ran for vice president on the Democratic ticket with Lewis Cass of Michigan. Butler supported the North during the **Civil War**, even though he was a slaveholder. He favored the gradual emancipation of slaves. He died in Carrollton in 1880 at age 89 and was buried in a private cemetery. In recent years, the Commonwealth of Kentucky honored Butler by naming a state park for him at Carrollton (see **General Butler State Resort Park**).

William Orlando Butler.

Kleber, John E., ed. *The Kentucky Encyclopedia.* Lexington: Univ. Press of Kentucky, 1992.
Roberts, Gerald F. "William O. Butler, Kentucky Cavalier," MA thesis, Univ. of Kentucky.

BUTLER COVERED BRIDGE. The longest covered bridge in Kentucky was the one across the Licking River at Butler in Pendleton Co. According to the Historic American Buildings Survey of 1934, the bridge was built in 1870 by J. J. Newman and F. B. Erwin, was about 460 feet long, consisted of three spans, and was of double Burr truss construction. The county appointed a committee to oversee the bridge project. Its first duty was to select a location, so they retained B. R. Morton, an engineer and bridge builder from Newport, to survey and render an opinion concerning the best location. Of the three sites Morton recommended, the committee chose the one just above the mouth of Willow Creek. However, the State of Kentucky induced the committee to change their minds by offering instead the stoneworks still in place from an old lock started in the 1830s. This new site was just below the mouth of Willow Creek. The uncompleted lock's stoneworks were to be utilized as part of the western abutment on the Butler side.

On May 15, 1870, the partnership of J. J. Newman and F. B. Erwin, bridge builders from Middletown, Ohio, submitted the winning bid to the Pendleton Co. commissioners. Their contract, dated May 31, 1870, called for the structure to be a double-truss Burr bridge, with a single track 18 feet wide, an independent arch, and three 152-foot spans. The chords were to be made of white pine, and the braces were to be pine or poplar. The contract specified oak floor beams covered by 2-inch-thick oak flooring, 8 to 12 inches wide. The rafters and sheeting were to be pine or poplar, with pine or poplar siding no more than 12 inches wide, along with 3-inch battens and shingles of number one pine, 18 inches long. The stonework for the piers and abutments was to be laid in regular courses, rubble dressed and bedded and not less than 8 inches in thickness, with a 24-by-36-inch bed. The entire project, costing $18,450, was to be completed and ready for use by January 1, 1871.

Some problems arose during construction. When the contractor had nearly finished the stonework, the bridge committee decided to extend the wing walls into the banks of the river. However, after the work on the wing walls had been completed, the lower wall on the Butler side began to fall. This was evidently a result of backfilling during the winter season, when the soil was not as easily compacted because of freezing and thawing. The committee attempted to stabilize the wall by inserting iron anchor rods in the fill and through the walls on each side, but to no avail. The wall fell. The bridge problems were corrected by J. Gray, an engineer, and the covered bridge at Butler carried traffic for 66 years, standing as a landmark and a popular postcard subject.

The high waters of the **flood of 1937** and the accompanying wind destroyed one of the spans, and for several months the bridge was used in its open condition. It was torn down in September 1937. Today, a steel-truss bridge stands in its place, but some of the stoneworks of the Butler Covered Bridge still can be seen nearby.

Belew, Mildred Boden. *The First 200 Years of Pendleton County.* Falmouth, Ky.: M. B. Belew, n.d. [ca. 1994].
Reis, Jim. "Covered Bridges Becoming a Rarity," *KP*, December 1, 1986, 4K.
U.S. Library of Congress. "Covered Bridges Recorded by Historic American Buildings Survey (HABS) and the Historic American Engineering Record (HAER)." www.loc.gov/rr/print/list/088_covb.html (accessed December 31, 2007).

BUTLER HIGH SCHOOL. Butler's first school, which included multiple grades, operated in three rented rooms on the upper story of the Armstrong Store. The first schoolhouse in town was constructed around 1856, from an old blacksmith's shop. This one-room structure housed all grades, including high school. Twenty years later, the Butler School was one of nearly 70 schools for whites in Pendleton Co. (there were also 3 schools for African Americans in the county). In 1898 the school's trustees awarded Butler High School's first graduation certificate to Ernest M. Rouse.

By 1909 there were three high schools in the county, one of which was located in Butler. Around this time, the school was relocated to Matilda St. and housed in a two-story frame building. In 1927 a larger, multistory brick building was constructed on the same site. By 1940, because the district had outgrown this building, 12 rooms were added.

Until 1930 the school was independently run as the Butler Graded High School. Soon afterward, the school's name was changed to Butler Consolidated School, to reflect its inclusion in the Pendleton Co. School System. Bus transportation for students began during this period. Also the high school changed to a nine-month term, while the lower grades continued with an eight-month school year. Until the lower grades' year was extended, high school students were required to furnish their own transportation during the extra month.

Butler High School held commencement exercises every year from 1901 until 1959, graduating 1,216 students. The class of 1901 consisted of 4 members; the final class of 1959 included 47. The school's largest graduating class, with 50 members, was in 1958. The school's colors were blue and white and its mascot was the Bobcat. During the 1936–1937 academic year, Butler High School began publishing a newspaper, called the *Bugle.* This same year, the school's first yearbook was published; its name changed annually.

During Butler High School's final year, 26 courses were included in the curriculum and at least seven extracurricular activities in addition to cheerleading and basketball were also offered. The school employed 24 teachers; a librarian; a principal; 8 cafeteria, custodial, and mechanical workers; and 11 bus drivers.

In the fall of 1959, the Pendleton Co. Board of Education consolidated the upper grades from Butler and Morgan high schools into the newly constructed **Pendleton Co. Memorial High School**, and Butler High School ceased to exist. Throughout the history of Butler High School, at least 22 principals served the school. Nobel Prize winner Dr. **Philip A. Sharp** was attending the Butler High School when it closed and was transferred to the new county high school.

From fall 1959 until the early 1970s, the Butler High School building served as a county elementary school, offering grades one through eight. For many years afterward, the building contained apartments, primarily for low-income persons. Around 2005 the building was damaged by fire and now remains vacant.

Belew, Mildred Bowen. "History of Pendleton County Schools." www.rootsweb.com/~kypendle/schoolhistory.htm (accessed September 29, 2006).

Butler Woman's Club, comp. *As I Remember Butler.* Butler, Ky.: Butler Women's Club, 1975.

Dennie, Debbie, and Patty Jenkins, comps. *Forks of the Licking, Bicentennial Edition, 1798–1998.* Falmouth, Ky.: Falmouth Outlook, 1998.

Hornbeek, Carolyn Pape. Interview by Aprile Conrad Redden, September 23, 2006, Butler, Ky.

Hornbeek, Carolyn Pape, and Bobby Nordheim, eds. *The Farewell, 1959.* Butler, Ky.: Butler High School, 1959.

Moore, Virginia Stevenson, ed. *School Daze, 1937.* Butler, Ky.: Butler High School, 1937.

Morris, Linda S. Thornton. Interview by Aprile Conrad Redden, September 23, 2006, Butler, Ky.

———, ed. *The Pendleton Echo, 1960.* Falmouth, Kentucky: Pendleton High School, 1960.

Michael D. Redden and Aprile Conrad Redden

BUTLER ROSS, TRACEY (b. June 5, 1966, Kittery, Maine). Tracey Butler Ross, the first woman African American dentist in Northern Kentucky, is the daughter of George T. Butler and Beverly Dickerson Butler. As a U.S. Air Force "brat," Butler lived in California, North Carolina, and Florida, before moving in 1975 to Covington, Ky., the childhood home of her parents. She attended the Covington public schools, graduating at the age of 16 from **Holmes High School** in 1983.

Two teachers at the Sixth District Elementary School in Covington provided the support that launched her onto the road of success. At age 9, she was encouraged by her fourth-grade teacher, Mrs. Gebhart, to be an obstetrician-gynecologist instead of an obstetric nurse. At age 11, at the insistence of Mr. William Gray, she was promoted into the eighth grade, thus enabling her to enter Holmes High School the next year, where she later graduated with honors. During those early years, she already had the goal of becoming a medical doctor, and she excelled scholastically as a result of her mentors.

Butler attended Kentucky State University (KSU) in Frankfort on a full four-year presidential scholarship. In 1987 she graduated from KSU with a BS degree in biology; but while at KSU, she had inadvertently missed the application deadline for entry into the University of Louisville (UL) Medical School. On the advice of her mentor, Dr. Kathy Peale, a local Frankfort attorney, Butler decided to apply to the UL Dental School for her first year, intending to apply to the Medical School to begin her second year. It was this pivotal decision that introduced Butler to her lifelong calling as a dentist. She obtained her DMD in 1991.

Wanting to give back to her community, Dr. Butler returned to Covington immediately after graduation. She began employment with the Northern Kentucky Family Health Center and stayed there for more than 12 years. Butler married Covington resident Richard Ross in 1996, and they reside in the **Main Strasse** neighborhood of Covington. In 2001 she and her husband cofounded New Horizons Christian Ministries Inc., and currently they serve as its pastors. With the ever-present desire to bring excellence to a waning community, Dr. Butler Ross began her private practice in 2003 at 1044 Scott St. in Covington. At the close of her first year in practice, she proudly boasted a clientele of more than 1,000 patients, a number that continues to grow. She continues with her desire of "changing lives, one smile at a time."

Butler Ross, Tracy. Interview by Ted Harris, July 2006, Covington, Ky.

Devroomen, Sacha. "Dentist to Serve Hometown," *KP*, April 20, 1991, 25K.

Theodore H. H. Harris

BUTLER-TURPIN STATE HISTORIC HOUSE. The Butler-Turpin State Historic House belonged to one of Kentucky's foremost military families from Colonial times through the **Revolutionary War**, the **War of 1812**, the **Mexican War**, and the **Civil War**. The estate, which was originally owned by Kentucky's first adjutant general, Revolutionary War hero **Percival Butler**, is located at **General Butler State Resort Park**, Carrollton. Butler and his wife, Mildred Hawkins, settled at the confluence of the Kentucky and Ohio rivers in 1796 at what was then known as Port William Settlement in Gallatin Co. On April 12, 1797, Butler purchased land from John McKinley to farm and build a home. Today, a portion of that farm makes up the western side of the General Butler State Resort Park. The Butlers built a two-story log house, barns, and other outbuildings. Gen. **William Orlando Butler**, the man for whom the park is named, and Maj. Thomas Langford Butler, who resided at the Butler-Turpin State Historic House, were among the 10 children raised in this log house. The house was destroyed by fire in 1863 but has been preserved as an archaeological site.

In 1859 Thomas Langford Butler, the eldest son of Percival Butler, along with Thomas's daughter Mary Ellen and her husband Philip Turpin, built the second-generation home, now the Butler-Turpin State Historic House. Thomas was aide-de-camp to Gen. Andrew Jackson and commanded the city of New Orleans, La., during the famous battle fought there on January 8, 1815. Butler was given a military officer's commission of brevet major for his service. President James Madison (1809–1817) later appointed him surveyor and inspector of the Port of New Orleans. Thomas Butler resided at the home in Gallatin Co. with his son-in-law Philip Turpin, an influential farmer and state legislator, until Thomas's death in 1880.

Built of native masonry construction laid in common bond with a stone foundation, the Butler-Turpin State Historic House is in the Greek Revival style. It is a three-bay, two-story structure commanding a view of the Kentucky River valley. The house is a traditional four over four with central hallways and paired interior brick chimneys located at the north and south ends of the block. The entryway, a one-story porch on substantial square posts, is located in the center bay. Ornamental brackets and dentils are used on the porch and throughout the cornice-work. Stone sills and lintels frame the six-over-six sash openings. Smaller four-over-four pane sash windows are located at the peak of the gable ends.

The original interior floor plan and details remain intact along with the stairway dogleg plan on the north side of the central hall, the Greek "ear" door and window moldings on the first floor, and the segmental arches on the second floor as well as on the fireplace mantels in all the rooms and the high baseboards. The historic items displayed in the house include original military documents along with family furniture and other objects. The house was first opened to the public as the Butler Mansion, Butler Memorial Park, in 1933. The house, the detached kitchen, the family cemetery, and the site of the first-generation Butler log house were placed on the National Register of Historic Places in 1977.

Biographical Encyclopedia of Kentucky. Cincinnati: J. M. Armstrong, 1878.

Carroll Co. Deed Book 2, p. 385; Book 3, p. 43; Book 6, pp. 439–40.

Gallatin Co. Deed Book D, p. 431.

Evelyn Welch

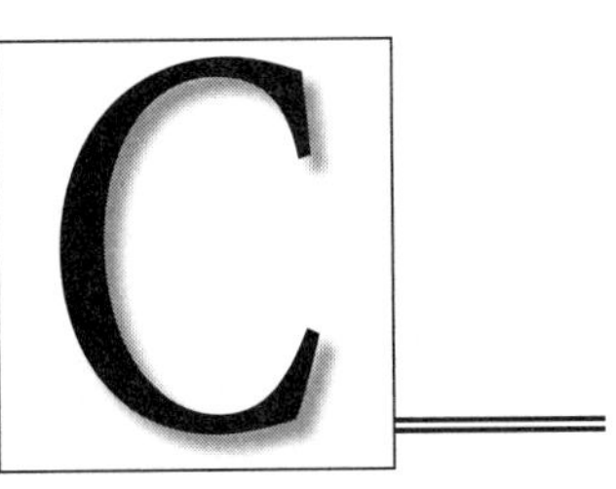

CABLE TELEVISION. The earliest cable television systems were in the form of community antenna television, which was created to bring distant television broadcasts to rural areas and smaller communities with reception problems during the early 1950s. The Maysville Community Television Tower Company first offered broadcasts from Cincinnati to its customers in 1953. In 1960 the Cable-Vision Company, owned and operated by Maysville radio station WFTM, expanded cable television in the Maysville region by carrying TV stations from both Cincinnati and Lexington. The name changed to Limestone Cablevision in the late 1970s, and the service area expanded to include neighboring Bracken and Robertson counties.

Some suburban cities in Kenton Co. awarded cable franchises in the early 1970s, but owing to federal regulations, these systems were never installed, and the franchises were revoked. Cable television in the urban and suburban cities of Northern Kentucky became a reality with the Storer Cable franchise in the early 1980s. MetroVision cable served the city of Newport exclusively for a short period of time before Storer obtained its franchise. Premium movie services such as Home Box Office (HBO) and an added number of television channels not available over off-air broadcasting were draws for cable television customers in Northern Kentucky. Between 1993 and 1999, reorganization and acquisitions brought name changes and new ownerships to Storer, which eventually led to the present Northern Kentucky cable franchise, Insight Communications Company. Insight enhanced cable reception and expanded programming with digital cable service. In 2003 high definition television (HDTV) channels arrived as an option for customers, offering both local HDTV broadcasts and HDTV cable programming. Cable television features a number of public access programs such as *Northern Kentucky Magazine,* which was initially hosted by **Richard "Dick" Von Hoene**, then by Twana Thomas, and later by **Nancy James**.

D&N Cable served Owen Co. until 2007, when an engineer living in Lexington purchased the franchise and renamed it Kentucky Ridge Country Communications (KRCC) to reflect the rolling landscape of the community. KRCC supports neighboring Liberty Communications for the rural cable customers in Gallatin Co. Insight Communications Company covers cable services in Warsaw as well as Carrollton in Carroll Co.

Personal cable systems became an alternative choice available to Northern Kentuckians in the early 1980s as large satellite television dishes were installed on private properties of many rural homes in the region. These early systems were known as Television Receive Only (TVRO), or earth station receivers of satellite television broadcasts. The home TVRO systems were an alternative to community cable providers. By the mid-1990s, home satellite dish systems were digital and received higher-powered satellite television signals; therefore the size of the satellite dishes could be reduced to that of smaller off-air television antennas. Today it is common to see the smaller dishes mounted on homes in Northern Kentucky communities where cable television is also available.

Allen, Randy. "Panel Picks Storer for Cable TV in Kenton, Boone," *KE*, November 18, 1980, A1.

Coffman, Joshua. "Cable Company Gets New Ownership, Looks to Go Digital," *Owenton News-Herald*, January 24, 2007, 1–2.

Get with the Show! Storer Cable promotional flyer. Covington, Ky.: Storer Communications of Northern Kentucky, 1981.

Hackett, Rosemary. "Cable TV Turned On in Newport," *KP*, September 2, 1981, 10K.

Kentucky Gateway Museum Center, vertical files, Maysville, Ky.

Kreimer, Peggy. "InterMedia Cable Has New Owner," *KP*, April 20, 1999, 7A.

Nash, Francis M. *Towers over Kentucky: A History of Radio and TV in the Bluegrass State.* Lexington, Ky.: Host Communications, 1995.

Reiter, John. "Cable TV Just 'Flirting' Now but Very Soon . . ." *KP*, January 27, 1979, 9K.

"Storer to Have New Name," *KP*, January 14, 1993, 3K.

John Schlipp

CADY, MARY L. MITCHELL (b. ca. 1834, Maysville, Ky.; d. September 27, 1888, Maysville, Ky.). Mason Co. native Mary Louise Mitchell, a poet, was the great-granddaughter of **Jacob Boone**, a cousin of **Daniel Boone**, who settled in Maysville in the late 1780s. The daughter of Andrew and Lavinia Degman Mitchell, she was well educated and by age 15 had developed a love for poetry. She contributed several pieces to the *Louisville Journal,* the *Saturday Evening Post, Willis' Home Journal,* and her hometown newspapers, the *Maysville Bulletin* and the *Maysville Eagle.* On November 23, 1854, Mary wedded Jarvis Gladden Cady in Mason Co. In 1869 she published the poem "The Fabric of Life" in the *Maysville Bulletin,* extolling life's good works as the key to salvation. In another poem, "Resignation," she suggested that man simply place himself in God's plan without resistance.

The family moved to Covington during the early 1870s. Jarvis Cady died on July 31, 1875, at Maysville's Central Hotel, from what appeared to be an overdose of opium. Between 1876 and 1882, Mary lived in Covington as the widowed mother of four children at 70 W. 10th St. Mary died in 1888 and was buried at the Maysville and Mason Co. Cemetery.

Covington City Directories, 1876–1882.

"Mary L. Mitchell Cady," Biography Files, Kentucky Department of Libraries and Archives, Frankfort, Ky.

"Mr. J. G. Cady . . ." *CJ*, July 31, 1875, 3.

CAIN, RODNEY "BIZ" (b. November 17, 1938, Independence, Ky.). Rodney "Biz" Cain is a businessman, a farmer, and an active community member. He graduated from Simon Kenton High School and the University of Kentucky. Cain married Jacqueline Malone, of Smiths Grove, in 1963, and they have three sons. He worked in the agricultural chemical industry for International Mineral and Chemicals until 1970. In the early 1970s, Cain founded Wiseway Plumbing, which sells light fixtures, cabinets, and plumbing supplies; it grew from one store in Independence to six over the years. During this time he was a leader in the Homebuilders' Association of Northern Kentucky and the Master Plumbers' Association. He officially retired from Wiseway in the early 1990s and handed over control to his two eldest sons.

Cain became chairman of the **Northern Kentucky Chamber of Commerce** in 1988. He was also active for many years in the Tri County Economic Development Corporation (**Northern Kentucky Tri-ED**), the **Northern Kentucky Convention and Visitors Bureau**, and Kentucky's Pritchard Committee for Education. Cain served as a director of Boone State Bank beginning in the 1970s. After Fifth-Third Bank purchased this bank, he remained a member of the board until 1998. In 1990 he was one of the cofounders of the new Boone State Bank, which has moved into Kenton, Campbell, and Grant counties and is now known as the **Bank of Kentucky**. Cain is still a member of its board of directors.

Cain began his political career by supporting several local Democratic candidates. He ran for a seat in the Kentucky senate in 1994 but was defeated by Gex Williams. In 1996 Governor Paul Patton chose Cain to be secretary of workforce development. He was at the forefront of the move to combine state technical schools with the University of Kentucky system of community colleges. In 1998 he was chosen by Patton to complete the term of Kenton Co. Republican judge-executive Clyde Middleton. His accomplishments included changing the process of appointing airport board members: they are now selected by the county judge. Cain lives on the farm where he was raised, Caintuckee Acres in Independence.

"Cabinet Position for Cain," *KP*, December 7, 1995, 1K.

Cain, Charles. Interview by Deborah Kremer, January 25, 2005, Florence, Ky.

Cain, Rodney "Biz." Interview via email by Deborah Kremer, February 3, 2005.

"Cain Pledges to Clean Up Bid Mess," *KP*, March 9, 1998, 1K.

"Cain's Agenda," *KP*, March 5, 1998, 4K.

"A Job Well Done," *KP*, January 1, 1999, 4K.

Deborah Kohl Kremer

CALDWELL, ALFRED M. (b. May 16, 1872, LeSage, W.Va.; d. August 7, 1948, Dayton, Ky.). Judge Alfred M. Caldwell was the son of Robert and Elizabeth Schlaegel Caldwell. He married Beulah Rich in 1897, and the couple had two children, a daughter and a son. In 1901 Alfred Caldwell entered politics and was elected Bellevue's city attorney. As a private attorney, he incorporated many small communities in Campbell Co., such as

Highland Heights and Woodlawn. He later served as Campbell Co. attorney and county judge, before being elected to the circuit court bench in 1922. He served in that capacity for 18 years and was replaced by Roger Neff Jr. Caldwell was an active member of the Newport Elks Club and the Masonic Order (see **Masons**). He also served as a director of the Campbell Co. Bank and the Citizens Building and Loan Association. He died in 1948 at Speers Hospital in Dayton, Ky., after suffering a stroke at home the night before. At the time of his death, he was living at 452 Ward Ave. in Bellevue. Funeral services were held at the Dobbling Funeral Home, and he was buried in the Highland Cemetery in Fort Mitchell.

Explore NKY. "Highland Heights Kentucky." www.Northern-Kentucky.com (accessed December 10, 2005).

"Former Judge Taken by Death," *CE*, August 8, 1948, 26.

"Judge Caldwell Dies at Age of 78," *KP*, August 7, 1948, 1K.

Kentucky Death Certificate No. 15826, for the year 1948.

CALDWELL, CHARLES H. (b. December 2, 1915, Williamstown, Ky.; d. December 22, 1989, Williamstown, Ky.). Charles Herbert "Herb" Caldwell, longtime mayor of Williamstown, was the youngest of seven children born on a farm outside Williamstown to Ezra Clarence and Laura Belle Works Caldwell. Caldwell graduated from Williamstown High School (see **Williamstown Independent Schools**) in 1935 and began working as a clerk in a dry goods store for $1 a day. He married Della Bennett in 1938.

After taking a correspondence course from the National Radio Institute in Washington, D.C., he fulfilled a childhood dream by opening his own business in town, Caldwell Electric, in March 1941. He operated that concern successfully for 47 years. Because of his ability in repairing refrigeration, he was not drafted into World War II.

Caldwell's involvement in the local business community led him to become a member of the Williamstown Volunteer Fire Department, and he continued as a member for 35 years. He was a charter member of the Grant Co. Hospital Board and the Williamstown Kiwanis as well as helping to found Williamstown's Grant Manor nursing home and Parkview Manor senior housing community (see **Nursing Homes and Retirement Housing**). He was an active member of the **Williamstown Baptist Church**, Gideons International, Grant Lodge No. 85 Free & Accepted **Masons**, Oleika Shrine Temple of Lexington, the Grant Co. Shrine Club, and the Indra Consistory of the Scottish Rite.

After being elected to the Williamstown City Council, he became actively involved in the construction of Lake Williamstown. He was elected town mayor in 1964, a position he held until his death. During Caldwell's 26-year term as the mayor, the city's assets increased dramatically as it received a total of $8 million in grants. At the time of his death, the city owned its own water and sewer, electrical distribution, and **cable television** systems.

Locally, he was selected as Grant Countian of the Year in 1987, an award sponsored by the Grant Co. Chamber of Commerce, and he also received the Distinguished Alumni Award from Williamstown High School. On the state level, Caldwell was a charter member and two-time chairman of the **Northern Kentucky Area Development District**. He was president of the Kentucky Municipal League, which represented more than 400 cities in the state, and chairman of the board of directors of the Kentucky Association of Counties–Kentucky Municipal League Workman's Compensation Insurance Board. On the national level, Herb served for 12 years either as a member or as chairman of the advisory board for Small Cities of the National League of Cities. The Small Cities organization represented more than 800 cities nationwide with populations of 50,000 or fewer.

During the last four years of his life, Caldwell suffered a major heart attack and battled cancer. He died at the Grant Co. Hospital in 1989 and was buried at the Williamstown Cemetery.

Baker-Nantz, Jamie. "Memorial Dedicated for Former Mayor," *Grant County News*, November 1, 1990, 1.

———. "Williamstown Mayor Dies after Extended Illness," *Grant County Express*, December 26, 1989, 1.

Jasper, Debra. "Williamstown Mayor Decides Not to Seek Re-election," *Grant County News*, August 24, 1989, 1.

Johnson, Omer W. "Faith, Prayer, and Hope Toppled Cancer," *KP*, June 21, 1984, 1.

———. "Williamstown Mourns the Loss of Its Mayor and Best Friend," *KP*, December 27, 1989, 7A.

———. "Williamstown's Driving Force Dies of Cancer," *KP*, December 22, 1989, 1.

Rouse, Ann. "Williamstown's Biggest Booster, Its Mayor," *CE*, January 17, 1972, 21.

Turmell, Mike. "Mayor Herbert Caldwell, 74," *CE*, December 23, 1989, C4.

Brenda Caldwell Stanley

CALDWELL ACADEMY. The H. C. Smith Academy, which became the Caldwell Academy in 1900, was located in Owenton, the county seat of Owen Co. Caldwell Academy itself operated for two years, 1900–1902. The school was owned and run by Dr. Jesse Caldwell, the pastor of the Christian Church in Owenton from 1897 until 1902. The academy was closed after Owenton High School opened in 1902. Rev. Caldwell moved away from town; there was no reason to remain, since students desiring secondary education could attend the new Owenton High School tuition-free. Such transitions were common throughout the region as public education was expanded to the high school levels. After serving as the dean of the Bible college at Drake University in Des Moines, Iowa, and occasionally returning to Owenton to visit his wife's family, the Settles, Caldwell died in March 1941.

Houchens, Mariam Sidebottom. *History of Owen County: "Sweet Owen."* Louisville, Ky.: Standard, 1976.

CALDWELL STATION. Caldwell Station in Pendleton Co. was between DeMossville and Butler, adjacent to the Licking River and the **Covington and Lexington Railroad**. It was named for William Caldwell, on whose land it was located, and it was mainly used by Caldwell for shipping.

Mildred Belew

CALEB MANLEY HOUSE. The Manley mansion in Erlanger, one of the oldest structures in suburban Kenton Co., was built on a 68.5-acre site purchased by Caleb Stone Manley from Hubbard T. Buckner in 1851. The Commonwealth of Virginia originally granted the property to Robert Johnson and Robert D. Watkins, who sold it to **Revolutionary War** soldier Thomas Buckner. Buckner built his home, Beechwood, on the east side of the tract, and the Manley property was located on the west side, fronting on the **Covington and Lexington Turnpike**. The property was inherited by Hubbard Buckner upon the death of Thomas Buckner.

Manley had moved to the Cincinnati area from the Deep South to be near his daughter, who was attending school in Cincinnati. The family's mansion was constructed of bricks made on-site by slave laborers. Originally built as a rectangle with an ornate French colonial wrought-iron porch on the front, the house included nine fireplaces. All floor joists were poplar, and all exterior walls, as well as major interior walls, were three bricks thick to the roofline. The foundation was constructed of fieldstones at least two feet thick. A rear wing that lacked such high-quality workmanship was added at a later date. Other buildings were built on the property as needed for the operation of a small plantation.

Because Manley had a strong interest in botany, he introduced many new trees and plants on his farm. The cypress trees around the lake in front of the home serve as reminders of his work. He sold the property to William H. Wilson in 1858. Manley died in 1869 and was buried in the Timberlake Family Cemetery near the mansion. His body was removed to Highland Cemetery in Fort Mitchell in 1925. The mansion and grounds were purchased by Asahel Hathaway in 1862 and then sold in 1864 to Cincinnati businessman James P. Garvey for use as a summer home. After the **Cincinnati Southern Railroad** was built in 1877, Garvey opened a lumberyard nearby and became one of the developers of the city of Erlanger. Miss Anna Bedinger purchased the property from Garvey's widow in 1900 and lived there until it was sold in 1913 to restaurateur Thomas R. Cody, who converted the mansion into a restaurant and used the surrounding grounds for various types of social activities. He was noted for his mint juleps and Kentucky burgoo. **Prohibition** severely inhibited his business, and Cody was forced to close the restaurant. Heavily in debt, he sold the property to Marguerite Stetter in 1935. She led a group of investors who established **Forest Lawn Cemetery** on the property. The mansion was converted for use as offices for the cemetery.

Manley's beautiful mansion, with its small lake in front surrounded by the cypress trees he planted, forms one of the most picturesque settings in the area. The City of Erlanger, Forest Lawn Cemetery, and the Kentucky Highway Department have worked together to preserve the property as development has occurred on all sides.

Campbell Co. Deed Book D2, 301, Alexandria, Ky.
Kenton Co. Deed Books, Covington, Ky.
Onkst, Wayne, ed. *From Buffalo Trails to the Twenty-First Century: A Centennial History of Erlanger, Kentucky.* Erlanger, Ky.: Erlanger Historical Society, 1996.

Wayne Onkst

CALIFORNIA (CAMPBELL CO.). The small city of California, Ky., is located along the Ohio River in eastern Campbell Co. Over the years, floods have inundated this community and some public records have been destroyed, but the earliest surviving ones date from 1849. Since that was the year of the much-publicized California Gold Rush, it is believed that the city's name may have been derived from that event. John H. Nelson and E. P. Dameron, credited with laying out the town into lots, made the first land transactions. The earliest extant map, drawn in 1871, shows eight streets. In 1852 California received its first post office, with John H. Nelson as postmaster. The town was incorporated on February 7, 1874. In the early days, the town was isolated; overland it was necessary to reach it from Alexandria Pk. (**U.S. 27**) via **Washington Trace Rd.** and California Crossroads. Much early transportation was done by steamboat, but in 1888 the **Chesapeake and Ohio Railroad** came through town and built a depot, providing quick and easy access to towns such as Augusta, Maysville, Dayton, Bellevue, Newport, and Cincinnati. In 1948 the **Mary Ingles Highway** was completed through California, linking the community by roadway with other communities along the Ohio River. According to the 2000 U.S. census, the city has 86 residents; it is the smallest incorporated community in Campbell, Kenton, and Boone counties. California was home to the Jolly family, which included the church-building minister Rev. **James M. Jolly** and his son, the educator A. J. Jolly Sr., and to the Carnegie Hall diva **Mary Hissem DeMoss**.

Collins, Lewis. *History of Kentucky.* Reprint. Frankfort: Kentucky Historical Society, 1966.
Reis, Jim. "California (Ky.) in 1890s Bustled as Rail, River Hub," *KP,* March 8, 1999, 4K.
U.S. Census Bureau. "American Fact Finder. Data Set. Census 2000 Summary File 1 (SF1) 100-Percent Data. Custom Table." www.census.gov. (accessed August 8, 2007).

CALIFORNIA CHRISTIAN CHURCH. The California, Ky., Christian Church (**Disciples of Christ**) was founded in 1851 by Rev. Benjamin Franklin, an itinerant minister, while he was on a preaching mission through Ohio, Indiana, and Kentucky. The original edifice was located near the riverbank in the village, which at the time was a thriving steamboat port. The building was plagued by flood and fire and was so badly damaged by a storm in 1860 that it no longer could be used as a place of worship. Without a place in which to meet, the congregation all but disbanded until 1879, when William Pepper Houston reorganized the church and made it into one of the leading churches in Campbell Co.

Although the Ohio River flooded the church many times during the last half of the 19th century, the congregation continued to worship until 1892, when its building, including the church records, was completely destroyed by fire. Again the church was rebuilt, but the Ohio River **flood of 1937** and another damaging flood a few years later took their toll on the small congregation (by then down to 21 members), and it was decided to move to higher ground. Rev. Robert Matheny reorganized the church at that time. In 1945 a log cabin on the farm of Bill France was dedicated as the congregation's meeting place. This was later sold to pay for the material to build a more permanent structure on land given by Karl Iles, who also did the stonework that set the church apart from so many other buildings of its period. The first service was held in the new church in 1947, but the congregation waited until 1951 to dedicate the structure so that a dual centennial and dedication celebration might be held. This building had stained-glass windows made by James Taylor, a member of the church who was a stained-glass designer and artisan with Riordan Glass of Covington.

Although small, the church had a significant ministry. The large number of people who returned to annual "homecoming" celebrations testify to the importance of the support and Christian foundation the church provided. Ultimately, the size of the congregation dwindled so much that continuation of the church was beyond their strength. The final service was celebrated on Sunday, April 30, 2006. The last minister of the church was lay minister Thomas Rambo, who had served throughout the final 25 years of the church's existence.

"California—Dedication of New Christian Church," *KJ,* May 18, 1894, 4.
"Call Is Accepted by Rev. Severns—Bellevue Pastor to Go to California," *KP,* July 17, 1940, 1.
"Minister Gets Scholarship," *KTS,* April 3, 1956, 4A.

Thomas Rambo

CALIFORNIA ELEMENTARY AND HIGH SCHOOL. A two-story frame school was built on a 2.45-acre parcel in the town of California, located along the Ohio River in southeastern Campbell Co., sometime between 1890 and 1900. Apparently, this school began as an elementary school and added a high school curriculum in 1925; at that time the elementary grades met on the first floor and the high school on the second floor. It was called a seminary or a high school in some records. The building was improved, closed, and reopened several times because of disrepair or low enrollment. It had a capacity of 80 students and was referred to as common school district 17 in the Campbell Co. School Board's minutes. It remained open until 1928, when a neighboring school on Smith Rd., the **Beech Grove Academy**, initiated discussions to combine the two schools. A special vote was held on a proposed tax that would supply funds to build a new school, located about halfway between the two schools. The vote passed, and on September 12, 1925, the combined school opened, but it met in the old building until the new **A. J. Jolly School** was completed in 1928. The A. J. Jolly School, with its elementary and high school curricula, replaced the two original schools. The old California building was sold in 1929 for $850. The A. J. Jolly School remained open until 2005, but the high school portion closed in 1946. The old California school structure, which still stands, is used as a private residence.

Campbell County Recorder, January 1983.
Campbell Co. School Board Minutes, from the John W. Reiley era, Campbell Co. Board of Education, Alexandria, Ky.

Kenneth A. Reis

CALLENSVILLE. Callensville, once a vibrant town, was located across the South Licking River from Morgan in Pendleton Co. The town was first known as Littell's Station, after William Littell, and was renamed for Jonathan Callen, who came to the area in the early 1800s. Callen ran a hog-slaughtering house and a tavern near his residence. In the wide South Licking Valley adjacent to the town, there was a racetrack, owned by James Hand, where Kentucky thoroughbreds were trained for the racing circuits in Philadelphia and in Baltimore. A physician named Dr. Minturn was raised in Callensville and later practiced there.

In 1900, Callensville was still a town, with six houses, two barns, a tollgate, a grain mill, a slave cemetery, and one large building run by a Mr. Makemson, which housed a saloon, a dance hall, the post office, and a general store. In 1923 all that remained was six houses; in 1929 three of those were condemned and torn down. Another house burned the following year. On the night of February 29, 1952, the last house in Callensville burned. Today nothing remains of Callensville except memories.

Beckner, Peggie. "A Reach into the Past," 1973, vertical file, History, Pendleton Co. Public Library, Falmouth, Ky.
Belew, Mildred Bowen. *The First 200 Years of Pendleton County.* Falmouth, Ky.: Privately published, 1994.
Cossaboom, Ewing O. "More Reminiscences of Morgan Kentucky," *Falmouth Outlook,* January 20, 1984, 6.
"Morgan," vertical file, Pendleton Co. Public Library, Falmouth, Ky.

Melissa J. Wickelhaus

CALVARY BAPTIST CHURCH. The Calvary Baptist Church was organized in Latonia (a part of Covington) on November 3, 1920, with 52 charter members present. Articles of faith and the church covenant were adopted and church officers were elected. The church voted to call Harry O. Fry as its beginning pastor, and the first service took place on November 7, 1920, in Bird's Hall at Ritte's Corner in Latonia, where the church remained for two years. Services were then moved to the old Latonia Christian Church on 36th St. Pastor Fry resigned, and in December 1922 Kitley Johnson was called as the second pastor. He stayed until April 1925 and was followed by Pastor L. A. Byrd, who served from June 1925 until January 1927. D. B. Eastep replaced Byrd and continued as the Calvary Baptist Church pastor for 35 years. In 1927, on Christmas Day, the first church bulletin was published. One of Pastor Eastep's early innovations was to place offering boxes in the rear of the church instead of passing offering plates. In July 1931 he began a program called the Whole Bible Study Course. The first course booklet was published in 1937. The popularity of the course, along with other writings by Eastep, led to creation of the Calvary Baptist Church Book Room, where religious books and related items were sold, with the stipulation that all profits be used to support missions. Dr. Harry Ironside, who donated a complete set of his books to the Calvary Baptist Church's library, was the guest speaker at the first Bible Conference in March 1933. On Anniversary Sunday, February 24, 1934, Eastep asked everyone to take one building fund envelope and put seven pennies in it, one for each year of his service. Thus began the Calvary Baptist Church's Building Program.

In 1938 the church initiated local broadcasting over radio station WCPO. That year also marked the purchase of property at W. Southern and Tibbatts Sts. in Latonia. On January 4, 1939, the cornerstone of the chapel was laid there, and on September 17, 1939, the first service was held in the new building. The total cost of the building was only $20,000 because church members did much of the work. The church's first Vacation Bible School was held in 1942. The church voted in 1944 to build a larger auditorium, which was completed and opened on April 30, 1950. When the city of Covington ended its kindergarten program, Calvary Baptist Church, in 1959, built a building to house its own kindergarten program.

That same year Warren Wiersbe spoke for the first time at Calvary Baptist Church; in 1960 he returned for a fall Bible Conference. Wiersbe was called as an associate pastor on June 14, 1961. Upon Eastep's death, March 19, 1962, Wiersbe assumed leadership of the church. During his tenure Wiersbe refined the Whole Bible Study Course, and his published booklets were distributed worldwide. The church broke ground for a new auditorium in 1967, and the building opened on October 2, 1968. Wiersbe resigned on August 8, 1971, to become the pastor of the Moody Church in Chicago.

Galen Call, Calvary Baptist Church's assistant pastor, was called to become the church's senior pastor on January 12, 1972. Six months later, Call led the church to approve the creation of **Calvary Christian School**. On October 21, 1979, Call resigned and Randall Faulkner was named interim pastor. On May 14, 1980, the church called Faulkner as Calvary's next senior pastor. In 1985 Calvary began participating in the Awana program, a ministry to children ages 3–12. On September 6, 1987, Robert Montgomery, the minister of music, resigned from that position and began a new program for senior adults called Young at Heart. Pastor Faulkner resigned in late 1989, and in February 1991 Dr. Charles U. Wagner became the senior pastor. Wagner placed special emphasis on missions and also implemented a visitation program called Organized Obedience. In August 1995 the church began a year-long 75th-anniversary celebration, during which many former pastors returned as guest speakers. One highlight of the year was visits to the church's former meeting sites. In 1999 the church built the Calvary Center addition. The church purchased the adjoining eight-acre property, formerly Liberty Cherry's processing plant, to be used for future expansion and additional parking. Wagner retired as pastor in 2003 to give his full time to conference speaking. The church called Dr. Curtis DeGraaff to become the new senior pastor in May of that year. Currently, Calvary Baptist Church, with a membership of about 1,800, is one of the largest Baptist churches in Northern Kentucky.

"Calvary Baptist to Break Ground for Fifth Building Project," *KP*, March 21, 1998, 8K.
"Church Is Sold," *KP*, December 1, 1921, 1.
"This Sunday, We Welcome Our New Senior Pastor—Dr. Curtis deGraaff," *KE*, May 10, 2003, B4.

Marv Price

CALVARY CHRISTIAN SCHOOL. Calvary Baptist Church in Latonia started the Calvary Christian School in 1973 as a ministry in which religious education would be central and primary to every aspect of the curriculum and every extended program. With the strong pastoral leadership of Senior Pastor Galen Call, the church congregation committed to a two-phase building program, designed for a maximum enrollment of 700. The Calvary Christian School operates solely on the basis of tuition and gifts; the school and church leadership have chosen not to receive any federal or local government funding. Beginning in 1973, with 64 students enrolled through grade four, classes were held for the first two years in the facilities of the Calvary Baptist Church. During that period, Phase I of construction of the school was under way at 5955 Taylor Mill Rd. in Independence. Students first began using the new facility in fall 1975. The following year Phase II was completed.

Thirty years later, during the 2003–2004 academic year, 673 students were enrolled in preschool and kindergarten through grade 12. In 1979 the Calvary Christian School celebrated its first graduating class with 19 students. In 1994 the school was awarded its first accreditation by the Association of Christian Schools International. The Southern Association of Colleges and Schools granted accreditation to the school in 2001. The school's executive committee approved joining the Kentucky High School Athletic Association beginning with the 2000 academic year.

Calvary Christian School Records, Calvary Christian School, Independence, Ky.
"Placing Faith in Private Schools," *KE*, February 12, 1995, A1.
"School Marks 30 Years of Growth," *KE*, August 23, 2003, 61.

Donald James

CALVERT, JAMES W. "J. W." (b. July 2, 1817, Lexington, Ky.; d. August 18, 1889, Burlington, Ky.). James Williamson Calvert, a Boone Co. attorney, was known to friends and family as J. W. He was the son of Willis and Elizabeth Ewing Calvert. The family moved to Boone Co. and J. W. attended the **Morgan Academy** (known then as the Boone Academy). His mother died November 13, 1827, and his father married Rebecca Ragsdale. After his father's death in 1849, J. W., who never married, lived in the same household as Rebecca Calvert and several of his siblings.

Calvert was instructed in the profession of law by attorney James M. Preston of Burlington. In 1841 Calvert was admitted to the bar in Boone Co. and practiced law until his retirement at age 61. He was also active in the Masonic Order (see **Masons**) in Burlington and was a member of the Christian Church. By 1860 Calvert was living in Foster's Hotel in Burlington, where **Fountain Riddell**, another Boone Co. attorney and former student of Morgan Academy, also lived. Calvert was a mentor to Riddell.

The 1870 census listed Calvert's assets as real estate holdings of $2,000 and a personal estate valued at $4,500. A portion of his personal holdings no doubt included his collection of antique coins and paper money; some pieces in his collection were 200 years old.

In 1889 Calvert contracted malarial fever and died. The body was initially interred in a vault in the Burlington **Independent Order of Odd Fellows** cemetery (the New Burlington Cemetery) and soon afterward moved to the Old Burlington Cemetery on Bullittsville Rd.

Boone County Recorder, July 1, 1885, 3; August 21, 1889, 2; August 28, 1889, 3; September 4, 1889, 3.
Worrel, Stephen A., and Anne W. Fitzgerald. *Boone County, Kentucky Marriages: 1798–1850*. Falls Church, Va.: S. Worrel, 1991.

Jannes W. Garbett

CAMMACK, ALLEN B. (b. January 6, 1899, Owenton, Ky.; d. July 10, 1985, Chapel Hill, N.C.). Allen Berriman Cammack, a legislator and a businessman, was the eldest of eight children born to Judge **James W. Cammack Sr.** and Nell Allen Cammack. He graduated from Owenton High School and, on May 1, 1917, volunteered to serve in **World War I**. Cammack went into the U.S. Navy and was trained at the Navy Radio School at Harvard University in Cambridge, Mass. After the war, he entered law school at the University of Kentucky at Lexington, where he graduated in 1923. Allen Cammack practiced intermittently in his father's Owenton law firm from 1924 through 1942. He was the state representative from Owen Co. between 1923 and 1925 and was Owen Co. attorney from 1930 to 1932. He was also in charge of the National Youth Administration's Industrial Work Shop Training program for Kentucky from 1936 through 1942.

In 1942 Cammack moved to Burlington, N.C., to work for the Fairchild Aircraft Company. Eventually, he owned the Cammack Office Supply Company. He also became involved in politics and civic service projects in Burlington, serving on that city's council from 1955 to 1959 and at one time acting as mayor pro tem. Cammack, who was especially interested in environmental issues and water resources, planned and implemented the development of Lake Burlington, an 850-acre reservoir and recreational lake near Burlington. In 1979 the lake was renamed Lake Cammack, in recognition of Allen Cammack's part in creating it. After three years of failing health, he died in 1985 while staying at his daughter's home in nearby Chapel Hill, N.C. His wife, the former Louella Arnold, and a son and a daughter survived him. Cammack was cremated and his ashes were spread over Lake Cammack.

"Allen Berriman Cammack Sr." *Burlington (N.C.) Times-News*, July 10, 1985, 2D.
Cammack, Allen, Jr., to Michael R. Sweeney, May 2005.
Houchens, Mariam Sidebottom. *History of Owen County: "Sweet Owen."* Louisville, Ky.: Standard, 1976.
"Lake Cammack Offers Nice Mixture," *Burlington (N.C.) Times-News*, May 12, 2002.

CAMMACK, JAMES WILLIAM, JR. (b. 1902, Owenton, Ky.; d. July 30, 1958, New York, N.Y.). Judge James W. Cammack Jr. was born in Owenton in 1902 to James W. and Nell Allen Cammack. He graduated from Castle Height Military Academy, Lebanon, Tenn., in 1919 and attended Owenton High School for his senior year. He earned an LLB from the University of Kentucky (UK), where he also played guard on the football team. He passed the state bar in 1924. He taught high school and coached football for a few years before returning to UK to earn a BA in 1927 and an MA in education in 1929. After further study at Peabody College in Nashville and at the University of Chicago, he received a PhD from UK in 1937. Cammack held various state government positions in the interim. In 1938 Governor A. B. Chandler (1935–1939, 1955–1959) appointed him to the Kentucky Court of Appeals. In 1944, having run as a candidate from both major parties, he was elected judge in that same court. In 1951 he became the chief justice of the court and was reelected for a second eight-year term. In 1958, while he was in New York City to attend an annual seminar for appellate judges, he died at St. Vincent Hospital following emergency surgery for an ulcer condition. He was buried at the Lexington Cemetery in Lexington, in the lot with his parents.

Houchens, Mariam Sidebottom. *History of Owen County: "Sweet Owen."* Louisville, Ky.: Standard, 1976.
The Lexington Cemetery. www.lexcem.com.

CAMMACK, JAMES WILLIAM, SR. (b. July 15, 1869, Crawford Co., Ind.; d. February 5, 1939, Louisville, Ky.). Judge James Cammack was the eldest son of William Butler and Elizabeth Jane Franks Cammack. The family moved to Grant Co., Ky., along Eagle Creek, in 1872. James attended school in Grant Co. and also studied at the **Cedar Grove College** at Gratz. He taught school from 1884 until 1889 in Grant Co. and then entered the National Normal University at Lebanon, Ohio, where he studied law; he passed the Kentucky examination to practice law in 1892. Afterward, he set up a law practice in Owenton and quickly was recognized as a talented and able lawyer. Cammack married Nell Allen of Lexington in 1898; future U.S. Congressman **June W. Gayle** was one of his groomsmen. Cammack and his wife lived in Owenton and raised eight children, and Cammack practiced law there. From 1904 until 1907, he served as a Kentucky state senator for Owen and Grant counties. He sponsored legislation on temperance and legislation that provided the initial funding of the institutions that became Eastern Kentucky University at Richmond and Western Kentucky University at Bowling Green. Cammack was a member of the Board of Regents at Eastern Kentucky University for many years. In 1907 he became a circuit judge for the 15th Judicial District (Boone, Carroll, Gallatin, Grant, and Owen counties) and continued in the position until 1916. In 1927 he was elected attorney general of Kentucky. While in that office, he sponsored legislation that improved laws governing commercial shipping; he joined with fellow Northern Kentuckians **Charles B. Truesdell** and **Ellsworth Regenstein** in a successful fight to save Cumberland Falls State Park from destruction by an upstream dam; he spoke out against gambling and prostitution in Northern Kentucky; and he promoted the building of the bridge at Gratz across the Kentucky River, eliminating the antiquated ferry service located there. In 1932 Cammack returned to his law practice in Owenton. Following abdominal surgery, he contracted pneumonia and died in 1939 at St. Joseph Infirmary in Louisville. He was buried at the Lexington Cemetery in Lexington.

Houchens, Mariam Sidebottom. *History of Owen County: "Sweet Owen."* Louisville, Ky.: Standard, 1976.
Kentucky Death Certificate No. 4021, for the year 1939.
Lexington Cemetery Records. www.lexcem.com.

CAMNITZ, HOWIE (b. August 22, 1881, Covington, Ky.; d. March 2, 1960, Louisville Ky.). Major league baseball player Samuel Howard "Howie" Camnitz was the son of Henry Camnitz, a printer, and Elizabeth Camnitz (see **Baseball**). Howie began his major league career in 1904, as a right-handed pitcher with the National League's Pittsburgh Pirates. He was nicknamed "Red" or "Rosebud" because of his bright red hair. Howie's younger brother Harry also attempted to become a major leaguer, but he only managed to pitch four innings for the Pirates and two for the National League's St. Louis Cardinals, winning just one game. Howie's best pitch was a curveball, but he used it so often that opposing players soon caught on and he was sent back to the minors to develop other pitches and learn to disguise his curveball. There, he compiled a win-loss record of 14-5, with 151 strikeouts. He returned to the Pirates in September 1906, and it soon became apparent that he had corrected his problems. In 1907 he compiled a pitching record of 13-8, with four shutouts and an earned run average (ERA) of 2.15. During the 1908 season, his pitching improved, giving him a 16-9 record, and he lowered his ERA to a microscopic 1.56. He saved his best pitching for 1909, when on opening day he pitched a shutout against the National League's Cincinnati Reds. That year he became the ace of the Pittsburgh Pirates team and led them to the National League pennant. However, during the World Series, Camnitz apparently developed arm problems and pitched poorly. Some claimed that he was just out of shape, while others said that perhaps he had developed a drinking problem. He again pitched poorly during the 1910 season, posting a record of 12-13 with an ERA of 3.22. He rebounded the next year and pitched two 20-win seasons in a row. In 1913 he mysteriously developed control problems and walked a career-high of 107 batters, while compiling a record of 6-17.

In August 1913 Camnitz was traded to the National League's Philadelphia Phillies, where he continued his subpar pitching. Between the two clubs that year, he lost a total of 20 games. Although he was under contract with Philadelphia for the 1914 season, he jumped to the newly formed Federal League. In that much-less-competitive environment, Camnitz compiled a record of 14-18, with an ERA of 3.23. Early in the 1915 season, he was accused of violating club rules and was given an unconditional release.

Camnitz returned to Louisville, where he took a job as an automobile salesman, a position he held for the next 40 years. He worked until about a month before his death at age 78. He was buried in the family plot at Cave Hill Cemetery, Louisville.

Cave Hill Cemetery Records, Louisville, Ky.
The Library of Congress: American Memory. "Howie Camnitz." http://memory.loc.gov (accessed January 7, 2007).
Reis, Jim. "Bluegrass Players Left Mark," *KP*, December 20, 1993, 4K.
SABR. "Howie Camnitz." http://bioproj.sabr.org (accessed January 7, 2007).

CAMPBELL, ALEXANDER (b. September 12, 1788, near Ballymena, County Antrim, Ireland; d. March 4, 1866, Bethany, W.Va.). Alexander Campbell, an influential preacher, was the oldest of the seven children of Thomas and Jane Corneigle Campbell. His minister father was a Scottish Presbyterian; his mother was a French Huguenot. By 1809 the family had arrived in the United States; in Pennsylvania they organized the Christian Association of Washington. Alexander, who had trained for the Presbyterian ministry at the University of Glasgow in Scotland, delivered his first sermon in 1810 while living in Pennsylvania. The following year, he wed Margaret Brown, and they made their home in Bethany, Va.

An educator, debater, and reformer, Alexander Campbell arrived in Kentucky in 1823 to debate Presbyterian minister William L. McCalla of Augusta. The debate, which concerned the issue of baptism, was staged in Washington, Ky., on October 15 of that year. Campbell's reputation had preceded him, and he was in Maysville one month before, meeting with influential church and civic leaders. Preachers, lawyers, and people interested in such matters attended the debate, and many were favorably impressed by Campbell's arguments. Judge Walker Reed, previously an Episcopalian, was one of the individuals who joined Campbell's Christian Church (Disciples of Christ). During several later tours to Kentucky, Campbell preached at other locations in Mason Co., including the **Germantown Christian Church**, the Beasley Church, and Orangeburg. His influence spurred the creation of the **Mayslick Christian Church**. The Maysville Christian Church was founded in 1828 as a direct result of Campbell's presence in the city, despite the church's Baptist origins (see **First Christian Church, Maysville**). In January 1832 Campbell's group, the Campbellites, also called the New Lights, merged with the followers of Barton Stone, from the Lexington area. Much has been written about Alexander Campbell in the histories of religion in America, as Campbell's influence was felt across the young nation.

Theologically, Campbell was part of the second Great Awakening of religion that spread across the American frontier, as he championed the supreme authority of scripture, weekly Communion, baptism by immersion for adults, and independence for each congregation. In 1840 Campbell founded Bethany College in his hometown of Bethany in western Virginia. He added the distinctive flavors of the American frontier to his theology, and by the time of the **Civil War**, his church counted 225,000 members. During the war, Campbell remained neutral. Since scripture did not condemn slavery, he did not view it as wrong, just inexpedient. He freed the slaves that he owned, however. Campbell died in 1866 at his home in Bethany, Va. (today, West Virginia), and was buried in a family cemetery nearby.

Braden, Gayle Anderson, and Coralie Jones Runyon. *A History of the Christian Church, Maysville, Kentucky.* Maysville, Ky.: Maysville Christian Church, 1948.
Calvert, Jean, and John Klee. *Maysville, Kentucky: From Past to Present in Pictures.* Maysville, Ky.: Mason Co. Museum, 1983.
——. *The Towns of Mason County: Their Past in Pictures.* Maysville, Ky.: Maysville and Mason Co. Library Historical and Scientific Association, ca. 1986.
Kleber, John E., ed. *The Kentucky Encyclopedia.* Lexington: Univ. Press of Kentucky, 1992.

CAMPBELL, JOHN, COLONEL (b. ca. 1735, Ulster, Northern Ireland; d. October 1799, Frankfort, Ky.). Col. John Campbell came to Pennsylvania in 1755 with British general Edward Braddock's troops, to fight in the **French and Indian War**. For their services in that war, Campbell and Dr. John Connelly were each given a land grant of 2,000 acres at the Falls of Ohio (Louisville). Connelly sold 1,000 acres of his land to Campbell. During the **Revolutionary War**, Campbell was one of the soldiers sent from Pittsburgh to New Orleans in 1779 to buy munitions from the Spanish. On their return trip, his company of soldiers was attacked at Dayton, Ky., by a band of Indians and British soldiers, led by the infamous Simon Girty (see **Rogers' Defeat**). Most of the soldiers with him were either killed or captured. Campbell was one of those captured and was taken by the British to Montreal, where he remained a prisoner for three years. After his release in late 1782, he settled on the land that he owned at Louisville. There, he opened a tobacco warehouse and operated a ferry. In that same year he entered politics and was elected a representative in the Virginia legislature. In 1784 and 1785, he served as a delegate to Kentucky statehood conventions in Danville. In 1795 he moved to a farm near Lexington, where he was elected a Kentucky state senator from Fayette Co. Campbell and Connelly are credited with founding the cities of Pittsburgh and Louisville, and Campbell Co. was named after Campbell. Campbell died of an apparent heart attack while at work in his senate office in 1799. He was buried in an unmarked grave, on land he owned near Nicholasville Pk. in Lexington. He had never married.

Hartman, Margaret Strebel. "Campbell County Kentucky History and Genealogy," supplement to *Falmouth Outlook*, December 15, 1978.
Kleber, John, E., ed. *The Kentucky Encyclopedia.* Lexington: Univ. Press of Kentucky, 1992.
Watlington, Patricia. *The Partisan Spirit: Kentucky Politics, 1779–1792.* New York: Atheneum, 1972.
Wessling, Jack. *Early History of Campbell County, Ky.* Alexandria, Ky.: Self-published, 1997.

CAMPBELL CO. Campbell Co. was formed on December 17, 1794, becoming the 19th county in Kentucky. It was cut from Harrison, Madison, and Scott counties and named for Col. **John Campbell**, an Irish-born **Revolutionary War** officer. The county's borders are the Ohio River on the north and east, the Licking River on the west, and Pendleton Co. on the south. Campbell is one of two counties in the commonwealth of Kentucky with two county seats, Alexandria and Newport.

Nine early Campbell Co. settlers founded communities in the county: **James Taylor Jr.** founded Newport; **David Leitch**, Wilder; **James T. Berry**, Dayton; **Albert Seaton Berry**, Bellevue; **Richard Southgate**, Southgate; **John Bartle**, Cold Spring; John Grant, Grants Lick (see **Grant Family**); **William Kennedy**, Flagg Springs/Mentor; and **Frank Spilman**, Alexandria.

There are three major events in Campbell Co. history that have garnered nationwide attention: the **Pearl Bryan** murder case in 1897, the **George W. Ratterman** trial of 1961, and the **Beverly Hills Supper Club** fire in 1977. Several Campbell Countians have earned national reputations. **Horace Lurton** became a member of the U.S. Supreme Court; **James P. "Jim" Bunning** entered the Baseball Hall of Fame and was also a U.S. senator; **Dave Cowens** was named to the National Basketball Hall of Fame after his career as a Boston Celtic; and **Gary Lee Bauer** of Newport ran for president of the United States in the Republican primary of 2000.

The largest city in the county is Newport, founded at the confluence of the Licking and Ohio rivers in 1795 by James Taylor Jr. Its first major employer was the military, home from 1808 to 1895 to the **Newport Barracks**, which was important enough in its early days to be considered in 1819 as a potential site for a second U.S. military academy. Born in Newport were **Nathaniel Southgate Shaler**, the state geologist of Kentucky and the most popular professor at Harvard University in the 19th century, and Gen. **John Taliaferro Thompson**, the inventor of the Thompson submachine gun, which helped change the face of modern combat; Newport was home for a while to **Barney Kroger**, the originator of the modern one-stop grocery store concept. Other industries in Newport have included steel (see **Newport Steel**), watchcases made by the **Dueber Watchcase Company**, silk (see **Newport Silk Manufacturing Company**), and ropemaking. In later years, the largest employer was the **Wiedemann Brewing Company**, until the consolidation of the beer industry caused the plant to close in the 1980s. For many years Newport was known as "Sin City"; however, improvements in its reputation in recent years have attracted new developments such as **Newport-on-the-Levee** and riverfront and hillside condominiums.

Campbell Co. has also been the home of many war heroes, including **Sidney Sherman**, Squire Grant (see **Grant Family**), **William Horsfall**, **William Corbin**, **T. J. McGraw**, **John Bartle**, William Steinmetz (see **Medal of Honor [Congressional]**), **Samuel Woodfill**, and Donald C. Faith Jr.

Campbell Co. is served by two waterways, the Ohio and Licking rivers; and two railroads originally served the county, the **Louisville and Nashville** from the southwest to Newport and the **Chesapeake and Ohio** along the Ohio River from the east.

In recent years, there has been little population growth in the northern Campbell Co. cities of Newport, Bellevue, and Dayton. However, considerable growth has occurred in the cities of Wilder, Highland Heights, Cold Spring, and Alexandria, primarily due to the founding of **Northern Kentucky University** and the construction of I-275, I-471, and the **AA Highway**.

From 1950 to 2000, the population of Campbell Co. increased about 16 percent, from 76,000 to 89,000. That percentage is somewhat misleading in that the northern tier of the county actually lost population, while the southern portion increased dramatically. With stable local government, quality schools, good fire and police protection, modern medical facilities, and a growing economy, the future of Campbell Co. appears bright.

Campbell Co. Historical Society. *Campbell County, Kentucky, 200 Years, 1794–1994.* Alexandria, Ky.: Campbell Co. Historical Society, 1994.
Kleber, John E., ed. *The Kentucky Encyclopedia.* Lexington: Univ. Press of Kentucky, 1992.
Wessling, Jack. *Early History of Campbell County, Kentucky.* Alexandria, Ky.: Privately published, 1997.

Jack Wessling

CAMPBELL CO. HIGH SCHOOL. Campbell Co.'s system of secondary education was created by a state law in 1909 mandating each county to have a high school in place that fall. Previously four high schools functioned in the county: one in Newport; one in Cold Spring, the **Walnut Hills Academy**; and two in the California vicinity, the **A. J. Jolly School** and the **Beechgrove Academy**.

CAMPBELL COUNTY
KENTUCKY

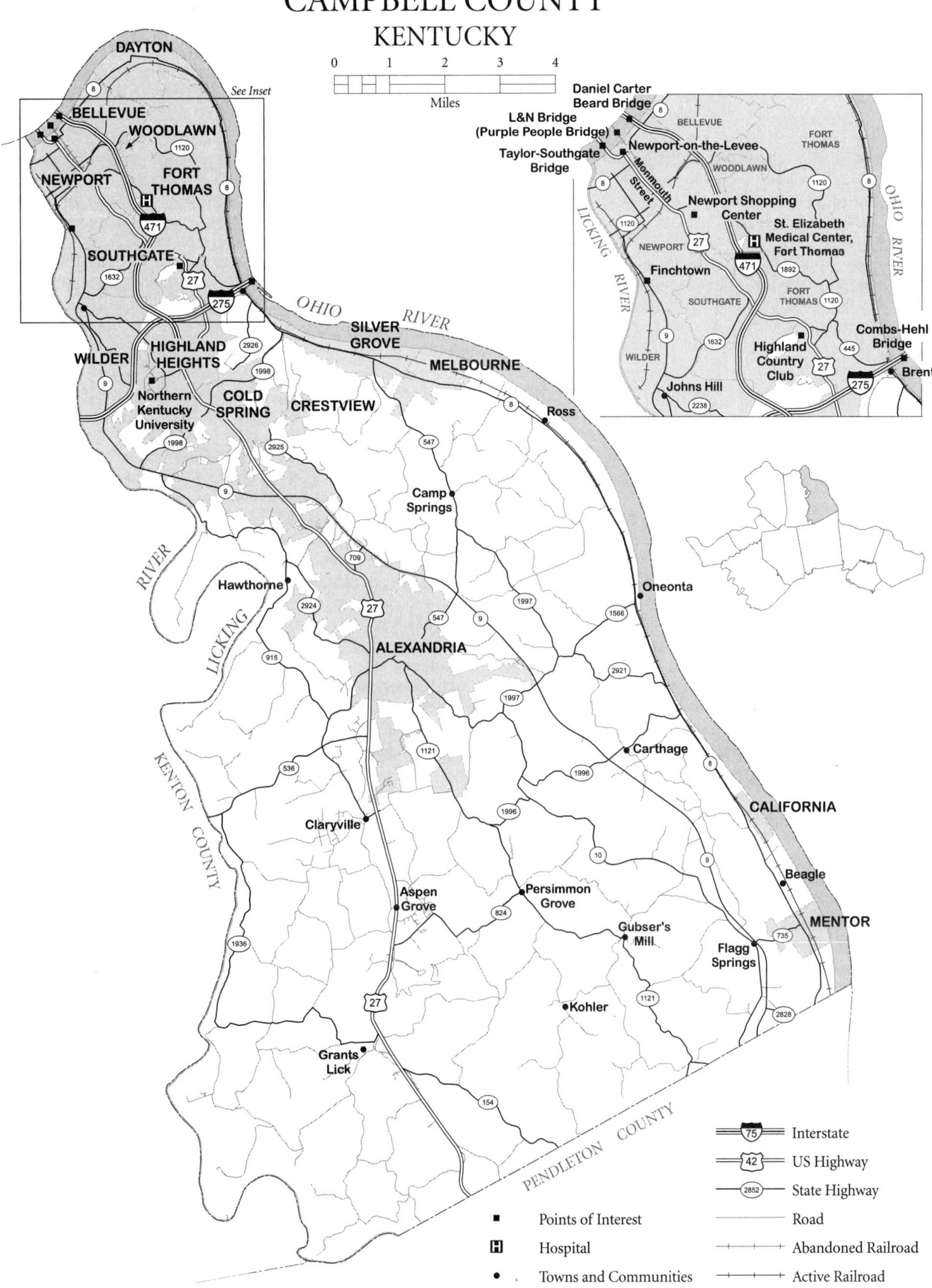

The first Campbell Co. High School operated in two rented rooms along Washington Ave. in Alexandria. The Knights of Pythias owned the building, an old brick structure known as the Meister Brewery. School sessions were begun there on October 4, 1909. H. W. Barr was the first principal. By 1911 all four years of high school were offered, and the first class graduated in 1912: three boys and one girl. The rented space in Alexandria was utilized until 1922, when overcrowding led the board of education to purchase land behind the building and adjacent to the Alexandria Elementary School, a one-room brick school building. A new two-story brick building, attached to the old Alexandria Elementary School, was built to serve as an elementary and high school; it was opened in 1922. The high school remained at this location until 1939, when a new building was built on a 19-acre parcel along **U.S. 27**, known as Alexandria Pk., about a half mile north of the old school. In 1946, both the Jolly High School in California and the Cold Spring High School closed and were consolidated into Campbell Co. High School. Between 1939 and 1995, Campbell Co. High School graduated more than 11,550 students. Changes were made in those years. In 1948 a new Alexandria Elementary School was constructed several yards south of the high school on the same lot. This elementary school became overcrowded and was replaced in 1960. That year, the 1948 building became part of the high school's program. In 1962 a large gym was built between these two buildings, connecting them. Another addition to the high school was made in 1969. Over the years, a large stadium, metal stands for seating, a track, tennis courts, and a baseball field were added at the rear of the property.

In 1995 Campbell Co. High School moved into a new two-story brick building along U.S. 27 at Lickert Rd. in southern Campbell Co. High-tech computer labs and access to the Internet are among the up-to-date facilities provided. Of the 90-member faculty at the school in 2005, 85 were classroom teachers. That year the enrollment was nearly 1,500. Growth has continued, and already an addition has been built onto the new 1995 building.

Campbell Co. School Board Minutes, from the John W. Reiley era, Campbell Co. Board of Education, Alexandria, Ky.

Isles, Ray. "Basic Characteristics of Campbell County, Kentucky as a Community," master's thesis, Univ. of Tennessee, 1970.

Satterlee, Frank. "A History of the Campbell County, Kentucky High School," master's thesis, Univ. of Cincinnati, 1948.

Kenneth A. Reis

CAMPBELL CO. PROTESTANT ORPHANS HOME. In 1884 a group of ministers determined that a Protestant orphan's home was needed in Campbell Co., and they appointed a committee to find a suitable location. The first site selected and purchased was a six-acre tract on Alexandria Pk. in Fort Thomas (now the location of the **YMCA**). In view of complaints that this site was too remote, the committee began a new search. George R. Fearons, a former mayor of Newport, offered to sell his 20-room mansion, on five and a half acres, just south of Newport. The sale was completed in July 1886, minor alterations to the building were made, and the home began accepting orphans on August 1. In 1890 the board named the new facility the Campbell Co. Protestant Orphans Home. Though it was intended to shelter only orphans, many of the children housed had one or both parents, who were either unable or unwilling to support them.

One of the residents was Walter Koch, who came to live at the home in 1914, after both of his parents died. He appreciated the shelter but wished that the atmosphere there could better reflect the warmth of a normal home. After eight years, he left the facility and married. In 1946 Koch returned with his wife, to accept the position of superintendent, and the couple then faithfully served as surrogate parents to the children until 1973.

To help support the work, several fundraisers were held each year, and the annual Orphans Feast became a popular Northern Kentucky event. Boys older than 10 were prepared for adult life by being sent to work as apprentices on local farms or in businesses. In the first 65 years of operation, 624 children lived at the Campbell Co. Protestant Orphans Home, staying 11 years, on average. Because of overcrowding and safety concerns, the Orphanage Board began in 1947 to look for a new location. Subsequently, a 25-acre site along modern E. Alexandria Pk. in Cold Spring was purchased for $15,000, and in 1951 the Newport facility was sold for $75,000 to the Campbell Co. Baptist Association. It is currently used as part of the **Baptist Convalescent Center**. Three modern buildings were erected on the Cold Spring site, and the name of the home was changed to Holly Hill Protestant Children's Home. The group moved into its new home in January 1952. Most Campbell Co. Catholic orphans were housed nearby at the St. Joseph Orphanage, on Alexandria Pk. in Cold Spring (now the site of the **Disabled American Veterans** National Headquarters). Since Holly Hill had ceased being restricted to Protestants, the name was shortened in 1971 to the Holly Hill Children's Home. After about 20 years of operation in Cold Spring, a new facility was built on **Washington Trace Rd.** in rural Campbell Co. The Cold Spring property was sold to the City of Cold Spring, to be used as its city building.

"Charitable Work for Little Orphans," *KP*, May 28, 1902, 5K.

Reis, Jim. "Hilltop Location of Baptist Convalescent Center," *KP*, August 9, 1993, 4K.

——. *Pieces of the Past.* Vol. 2. Covington: Kentucky Post, 1991.

——. *Pieces of the Past.* Vol. 3. Covington: Kentucky Post, 1994.

CAMPBELL CO. PUBLIC LIBRARY. Before the Campbell Co. Public Library District was established, library service in Campbell Co. was available in the city of Newport through the **Newport Public Library** on Monmouth at Fourth St. This building, opened in 1902 with funds from the Carnegie Foundation, provided free public library service to the citizens of Newport. Residents of other cities in Campbell Co. could use the facility for a fee. In 1971 Betty Daniels and a group of volunteers established a subscription library in Fort Thomas. This library operated in the former Erschell Funeral Home, on N. Fort Thomas Ave. Attempts to create a countywide library system began in 1968. At that time a petition was circulated by the Campbell Co. Chamber of Commerce requesting voter approval for the establishment of a special local taxing district for a county library system. The petition failed.

After that disappointing vote, the Chamber of Commerce and the Campbell Co. Fiscal Court made arrangements for the citizens of Campbell Co. to use the Public Library of Cincinnati and Hamilton County for an annual fee of $15. The Fiscal Court paid half of this cost and the user paid the other half. Betty Daniels became the driving force behind establishing countywide library services after 1968. In 1975 Daniels and the Northern Kentucky regional librarian, Philip N. Carrico, obtained a grant for a demonstration library system. During the demonstration period, the Kentucky State Library and the Campbell Co. Fiscal Court cooperated to provide countywide library services.

Three facilities and two bookmobiles (serving the north and south ends of the county) were maintained. A mobile home was leased and moved to the **Newport Shopping Center** for use as a branch library. In Fort Thomas, the library on N. Fort Thomas Ave. was used as the demonstration's headquarters. The basement of the Alexandria City Building was renovated to accommodate a library. During the demonstration period, books were donated from libraries across the state, and the Kentucky State Library purchased some new materials for the library.

Daniels and a team of volunteers were successful in placing on the November 1977 ballot a voter referendum calling for a countywide library system, but by a margin of 136 votes, the effort failed. Undaunted, Daniels and her group of supporters circulated another petition for a special taxing district for library services in 1978. The petition effort proved successful, yielding 12,352 signatures. Campbell Co. Judge-Executive **Lambert Hehl Jr.** signed the resolution establishing the library system and appointing its first board of trustees on October 13, 1978.

On October 17, 1978, the first meeting of the board of the Campbell Co. Public Library was held. Betty Daniels was named its president, and the first director was Beverly Bury. The demonstration facilities in Alexandria and Fort Thomas became parts of the county system. Within months the new organization purchased and took over the operation of the Newport Public Library. One bookmobile continued making its rounds.

The Friends of the Library group was organized in 1977 as a support and fundraising arm of the libraries. Always dependent on staff support, the organization was dissolved in 1989. In 1991 the Friends of the Library was reestablished as a self-supporting volunteer organization.

Since its beginning, the county library system has provided attractive facilities for its patrons and materials. The library opened an 8,000-square-foot facility in 1984 in Cold Spring. With its completion, the branch in the Alexandria City Building was closed. An additional 6,500 square feet were added to the Cold Spring facility in 1996. The Philip N. Carrico Branch, on Highland Ave. in Fort Thomas, opened in 1995 with 8,800 square feet. At that time the library on N. Fort Thomas Ave. closed. An additional 6,200 square feet were added to the Carrico Branch in 2001.

The Newport building on Monmouth St. was remodeled in 1987, and the children's services department was moved to the second floor. This building was sold to the City of Newport in 2004, ending 102 years of library services in that location. In 2004 the library system opened a new 27,000-square-foot facility on E. Sixth St. in Newport, convenient to Bellevue, Dayton, and Woodlawn.

The library system has always sought to provide service to its patrons through improved access to materials. In 1988 the system's catalog became available on microfiche. In 1991 the county's libraries entered into a cooperative agreement with other southeastern libraries to offer computerized access to interlibrary loan materials. At present materials can be borrowed from libraries nationwide. Library circulation became fully computerized in 1996 as access to its catalog via a modem began.

In 1997 the libraries in the county began offering full Internet access. The Internet has proved to be very popular. With this service demand, the library system's provision of public-access computers has also increased dramatically. More than 70,000 patrons used the county libraries' computers in 2005. The library system's first Web site was created in 1998, making information available through the Internet on programs and services. Soon the library system's catalog became accessible via the Internet. An upgrade to its automation system in 2005 brought the notification of overdue and held materials via e-mail. The library system has also kept pace with the formats for new materials. It began circulating videocassettes in 1986, DVD-format items in 2000, and computer software in 2001.

The citizens of Campbell Co. have responded warmly to the services offered by their libraries. From 1985 to 2005, registered borrowers increased from 2,625 to 56,000. More than 500,000 people visited the libraries in 2005. Programs include book discussions, children's story times, computer classes, and craft-making. More than 25,000 patrons attended these programs in 2005.

Directors administer the daily operations of the libraries. The following persons have served as directors in the past: Beverly Bury (1978–1984), Rebecca Callendar (1984–1989), Paul Wright (1989–1990), Philip N. Carrico (1990–1999), and Michael Doellman (1999–2002). J. C. Morgan is presently the director. Long-range plans in 2005 included opening an additional branch near Alexandria, making more electronic formats available, establishing children's outreach services, and adding wireless Internet connections at all facilities.

Carrico, Philip N. "A History of Public Library Service in Campbell County." Presented to the Campbell Co. Historical Society, Cold Spring, Ky., March 9, 1995.

Carrico, Philip N. Interview by J. C. Morgan, October 5, 2005, Cold Spring, Ky.

Minutes of Meetings, Campbell Co. Public Library Board of Trustees, 1978–2005.

Mueller, Jan. *Soul of the City: A Centennial History of the Newport, Kentucky Public Library.* Newport, Ky.: Jan Mueller, 2004.

J. C. Morgan

CAMPBELL CO. PUBLIC SCHOOLS. In Campbell Co., as elsewhere, private schools generally preceded the development of public ones. Public education in Campbell Co. was sporadic at best for some time. In 1838 the State of Kentucky set up districts, and the schools in each district were governed by five trustees. By 1856 the Campbell Co. government, specifically the county school commissioners, oversaw these districts, while trustees at each school handled local issues. By 1878 the number of trustees at each school was set at three and each teacher was required to hold a state teaching certificate. Beginning in 1869, such certificates could be earned by teachers at county-sponsored teacher institutes (comparable to the modern-day professional development days). Campbell Co. offered many of these institutes. In 1884 the system of county school commissioners was abolished and replaced by an elected superintendent. Trustees continued to run individual schools.

The actual number of "common" or public schools before 1884 is open to question. In 1885, when B. K. Rachford was elected the first county school superintendent, 50 or so one- or two-room schools were operating in the system. A one-room school typically contained grades 1 thru 8. The teachers were generally female, some barely older than their students. Female teachers had to be unmarried, and they would often live with the parents of one of their students, usually at a trustee's home. The teacher had to clean her own classroom, carry in firewood, and start and maintain a fire to heat the building. Pay was minimal and supplies and materials were scarce. One-room schools were located throughout the county. By law, schools were to be located within three miles of each student's home. Students often walked or rode horses to their schools. School buildings were built of logs, stone, wood clapboard, frame, or brick. The Campbell Co. School Board minutes for 1890 indicate an interest in purchasing McGuffey's readers for students at a cost of 17 cents for each book.

Perhaps the most important figure in the system's history was John W. Reiley, who was elected county school superintendent in 1906. No one person has shaped the school system more than he. Reiley served from 1906 until 1942, longer than any other superintendent in Kentucky at that time. During the early 1920s, after the state changed the way superintendents were hired, Reiley was appointed by a county school board rather than being elected as previously had been the case. Reiley oversaw the administration of all the county's 50 one-room schools. After the 1920 School Consolidation Act, which eventually combined and closed the smaller schools in Kentucky, Reiley implemented the present system, in which the county's local community schools serve geographic districts. He met great resistance in closing the one-room schools but forever changed the school system through his leadership.

Reiley oversaw the building of **Campbell Co. High School** in 1909, Alexandria Elementary and Campbell Co. High School in 1922, **A. J. Jolly Elementary and High School** in 1926, Dale Elementary (later renamed Highland Heights Elementary) School in 1930, Grants Lick Elementary School in 1935, and a new Campbell Co. High School in 1939. Cold Spring was an independent school system until 1944, when it became part of the county school system. Alexandria Elementary School underwent additions and renovations, but much at the school did not change until school superintendent Charles E. McCormick put all the county schools on double sessions because of overcrowding. Some children attended school in the morning and early afternoon, and others attended during late afternoon and evening. These double sessions ended with the completion of the new Cline Middle School in 1976. In 1979 another new middle school, originally named South Middle School but renamed John W. Reiley Middle School, was built. The middle schools removed the sixth-, seventh-, and eighth-grade students from the overcrowded elementary schools. The school board decided to replace the high school with a new building that was built on Lickert Rd. and opened filled to capacity in 1995. In 1997, a very controversial decision was made to close Cline and Reiley middle schools and combine them into the current 1,200-student Campbell Co. Middle School. This combined school was put into the old, but completely renovated, high school building located on **U.S. 27** in Alexandria.

Recently the school board has decided to combine and redistrict its schools. The Alexandria and A. J. Jolly elementary schools were closed and their students combined into a brand new elementary school, Campbell Ridge Elementary School, opened in 2005. Crossroads Elementary School in Cold Spring was completed in 2007.

Campbell Co. Historical Society. *Campbell County, Kentucky, 200 Years, 1794–1994.* Alexandria, Ky.: Campbell Co. Historical Society, 1994.

Kenneth A. Reis

CAMPBELL LODGE. Campbell Lodge, a boys' home at 5161 Skyline Dr. in Cold Spring, Campbell Co., began because of the inspiration of Rev. Raymond Nieman, a priest of the Diocese of Covington. As chaplain for the Kenton Co. Juvenile Court, Nieman saw firsthand the need for helping troubled teenage boys. His goal was to prevent delinquency before it started by creating a stable, decent home environment for boys ages 14 through 18 who were products of broken homes. Bishop **William T. Mulloy** gave his approval of the plan and appointed Nieman as director of Campbell Lodge. College students served as counselors. Nieman envisioned his nondenominational program as a smaller, somewhat modified, version of Father Edward Flanagan's Boys Town in Omaha, Neb.

Campbell Lodge's first location was the home of Dr. James Ogden in Cold Spring, purchased in 1958 for that purpose. The following year, work began on a new structure that would hold up to 100 boys. According to the 25-year plan that was established, a new wing was to be built every five years. A gymnasium and swimming pool were included in the plan. Through the 1960s to the mid-1970s, three halls were built: Ponte Hall, Guild Hall, and Moriarty Hall. The various programs of Campbell Lodge are carried out in these halls.

Today Campbell Lodge offers residential treatment for boys 10 to 18 years old for periods of six months to two years. The boys, most of whom have been neglected or abused before their arrival, are admitted to Campbell Lodge from psychiatric hospitals, state custody, or the care of their parents. Campbell Lodge started the unique Equine-Assisted Counseling, which offers residents the therapeutic experience of caring for the two horses that are kept on the premises.

"Boys' Home Planned on Campbell County Site," *Messenger*, June 22, 1958, 1.

Campbell Lodge Boys' Home. www.clbh.org (accessed May 12, 2007).

"First Anniversary: Campbell Lodge Cites Future Plans, History," *Messenger*, November 1, 1959, 1.

Thomas S. Ward

CAMPBELL'S BLOCKHOUSE. Campbell's Blockhouse is believed to be the first building erected on the lands that became Grant Co. John Campbell, after whom Campbell Co. was named, may have built this blockhouse as early as 1784. Campbell resided at the Falls of the Ohio (Louisville) but frequently made trips to the Northern Kentucky region. He bought and traded furs and skins with the Shawnees and other Indians from north of the Ohio River who were hunting and trapping in the area. The crude blockhouse, surrounded by virgin forest and ordinarily unoccupied, was a safe place to "hole up" after trading in the area to keep unscrupulous Indians or trappers from stealing back the skins and furs Campbell had bought. The blockhouse is said to have been located where the small cemetery known as the Old Cemetery on the Dry Ridge is today, on Conrad Ln. in northern Williamstown, adjoining the southern Dry Ridge corporation line.

Conrad, John B., ed. *History of Grant County*. Williamstown, Ky.: Grant Co. Historical Society, 1992.

John B. Conrad

CAMP KING. Camp King, a Civil War camp, was situated on one of Northern Kentucky's premier antebellum amusement areas. In May 1849, Professor Ormsby MacKnight Mitchel (1809–1862) reported on the proposed **Covington and Lexington Railroad**, which would run through Sunnyside, past Cole's Gardens (three miles south of Covington), and through Taylor's flats. The gardens had become a favorite site for summer picnics, swimming, and fishing, and from May through September, the Licking River Packet Company took boatloads of eager Cincinnatians upriver to enjoy the site's numerous refreshment stands.

In early September 1861, Confederate forces occupied Columbus, Ky., prompting Brig. Gen. U. S. Grant (1822–1885) to move forward from Cairo, Ill. On September 18, the pro-Union majority of the Kentucky legislature passed a resolution ordering Confederate troops to withdraw from the state. The next day, Mitchel received command of the Department of the Ohio, an area that embraced Indiana and Ohio and extended fifteen miles into Kentucky. Maj. John Haskell King (1820–1888) commanded the Newport Barracks, and it appears that he started Camp King about that time. Col. Marcellus Mundy began recruiting volunteers for the 10th Kentucky Regiment, and on September 23 Col. Leonard A. Harris (1824–1890) moved the 2nd Ohio Infantry across the Ohio River to Camp King. Three days later, when Mitchel met with the mayors of Cincinnati, Covington, and Newport, they agreed to "employ a large force of laborers to dig intrenchments or redoubts on the hills back of Covington and Newport, four in number, and two flanking redoubts on the hills back of the city [Covington]" (see **Civil War Fortifications**).

The plan called for a line that would extend from Bromley up through Fort Mitchel (now Fort Mitchell), then across Kyles Ln. and down the ridgeline to Buena Vista Hill. At Ridge Rd. and 26th St., soldiers began work on what became a battery named for Larz Anderson (1803–1878), the brother of Brig. Gen. Robert Anderson (1805–1871). It overlooked Madison Pk. (Ky. Rt. 17) and Decoursey Pk. (Ky. Rt. 177). This battery and Camp King represented the center of a 14-mile defensive line that was later connected to Campbell Co. by a pontoon bridge. A 700-foot railroad tunnel (for the Covington and Lexington Railroad) ran through Buena Vista Hill, passed under Madison Pk., and came out on the northern edge of Camp King. On September 28, 1861, Camp King had more than 1,100 troops. The 10th and 23rd Kentucky Infantry Regiments remained there until February 1862. At that time, the federal army began a major campaign into western Tennessee, which caused all work on fortifications and installations around Covington and Newport to languish until Confederate general John Hunt Morgan (1825–1864) raced into Kentucky. Morgan's July 17 raid on Cynthiana, and the rout of federal recruits at Richmond, Ky., on August 30, led to renewed work on the fortifications. Those efforts picked up in earnest when Confederate general Henry Heth (1825–1899) brought his 3rd Division forward northward on September 6. One Union soldier remarked that the year-old Camp King had nothing but a few sutlers that supplied "the hungry soldiers with bologna sausages and very bad cheese." The Confederates left Kentucky in October, and by December 18, 1862, Cole Bealer, the owner of Cole's Gardens, brought civil suits against 46 neighboring residents for vandalizing his property.

During the course of the war, Camp King also served as headquarters for the district provost marshal and as a training post for new regiments. Two African American U.S. Colored Infantry (USCI) regiments were formed at Camp King, the 72nd and the 117th (see **African Americans in the Civil War**). During and after the war, the Camp King area was where African American refugees from Central Kentucky and West Virginia gathered, requiring the military to provide a means of survival. Today, the former beer garden and military camp is home to Meinken baseball field and Marathon Oil tanks.

Cincinnati Gazette, September 12, 28, 1861.

CJ, May 11, 1849; September 28, 1861; December 18, 1862; October 26, 1872.

Heitman, Francis B. *Historical Register and Dictionary of the United States Army, 1789–1903*. 2 vols. Washington, D.C.: Government Printing Office, 1903.

Wimberg, Robert J. *Cincinnati and the Civil War: Off to Battle*. Cincinnati: Ohio Book Store, 1992.

———. *Cincinnati and the Civil War: Under Attack*. Cincinnati: Ohio Book Store, 1999.

Donald A. Clark

CAMP KYSOC. In the period after **World War II**, most polio victims and children with multiple physical disabilities were institutionalized or kept indoors. Two Jefferson Co. residents associated with the Kentucky Easter Seals program, Dr. Sharp and Sidney Rosenblum, established the first residential summer camp program in the United States for children with such disabilities. Camp KYSOC was created from 124 acres of wooded land adjacent to the **General Butler State Resort Park** along U.S. 227, just outside of Carrollton. Today, **Cardinal Hill** Healthcare System manages Camp KYSOC.

There were only three buildings on the campgrounds during the summer of 1960. Several counselors who were experienced in working with disabled children at day camp were invited to spend three days at Camp KYSOC and develop the residential program. The first summer camping program was held in 1961, and Jim Watkins, now assistant camp director, recalls that many of the early counselors were recruited from Dr. Polk's special education classes at Peabody College, Nashville, Tenn. The University of Kentucky at Lexington developed a practicum that combined physical therapy and special education and over the years sent many students to Camp KYSOC as counselors. As a result of the tremendous growth of interest in research and careers in special education, Camp KYSOC today offers opportunities for children with a variety of disabilities, eating or behavioral disorders, autism, spina bifida, and other conditions that make it difficult for them to attend other camps.

The ratio of camper to counselor is 2:1, and Camp KYSOC operates as a decentralized group of villages, each designated by an authentic Indian phrase. Within each village are four counselors and eight campers. The children determine what kind of activities they want to participate in during their six-to-eight-day adventure. A master schedule is then set for the nine villages. Among the most popular activities are swimming, boating, fishing, arts and crafts, and campfires. A specially designed climbing tower with four progressively more difficult levels was added a few years ago, and it has become one of the most popular features of the camp. The final level includes a zip line.

Therapeutic swimming was a major feature of Camp KYSOC from the beginning. A state-of-the-art heated swimming pool was added in 1963, with two ramps and rails at one end for wheelchairs to descend into the water. At the opposite end of the pool, children who can leave their wheelchairs enter the water via steps and handrails. In 2002 a new enclosed heated pool, funded in part with a $50,000 grant from Louisville's WHAS-TV Crusade for Children, was opened. This also is a state-of-the-art facility; it has a Hoyer lift on one side and a ramping system that continues the length of the pool to a five-foot depth.

Also quite popular is the 12-acre lake, complete with a fishing dock and an area for canoeing. The Kentucky State Fish and Game Department keeps the lake stocked with game fish, and KYSOC shares the lake with General Butler State Park. Fields for various sports activities and blacktopped nature trails, plus an arts and crafts area, see plenty of use each summer.

The dining lodge is designed for family-style eating, with round tables that seat four campers and two counselors. Each village takes turns "hopping" to set the tables for breakfast, lunch, and dinner. The entire camp sings grace and also sings camp songs after breakfast and dinner. The whole village also participates in the flag ceremony and color-guard activity in the morning and evening.

Today, Camp KYSOC provides eight summer sessions, each six to eight days in length. The maximum number of campers per session is 72; however, the maximum for a particular session depends on staffing and program limits. Students come from all counties in Kentucky and from southern Indiana, Ohio, Georgia, and Missouri. Two weekends in the spring and the final weekend in the summer are reserved for family camp. The spring weekends permit parents of first-time campers to investigate the facilities and the program, and the final weekend permits parents to catch up with the experience their child has just encountered.

Camp KYSOC's pioneering effort in bringing a summer camp experience to severely disabled children has been recognized and duplicated by camps and sports programs throughout the United States and internationally. The staff's dream for the future is to add therapeutic horseback riding to the program. The camp has a barn, but horses have been too expensive to contemplate to date.

The relationship between KYSOC and the local Carroll Co. community has been excellent over the years. Although a nurse and a nurse assistant are always members of the camp staff, the Carroll Co. Emergency Management Services, the **Carroll Co. Memorial Hospital**, and physicians on call have been important contributors to the success of Camp KYSOC. Also, children of local townspeople attend summer day camp that runs concurrently with the regular residential program.

The KYSOC facilities are open for the community to book conferences and meetings during the fall and winter, and these rentals provide an important stream of income for the camp. In addition to the grants from the WHAS Crusade for Children, from the local **Rotary Club**, and from several corporations, KYSOC is supported by hundreds of individuals who "adopt a child" by paying for all or part of the child's summer camping experience. The Cardinal Hill Healthcare System has also been most supportive of the KYSOC program.

Camp KYSOC. Produced by David Shuffett. KET Video.

Cardinal Hill Healthcare System. "Camp KYSOC." www.cardinalhill.org (accessed May 7, 2006).

Gentry, Mary Ann. *A History of Carroll County.* Madison, Ind.: Coleman, 1984.

Watkins, James. Interview by Diane Perrine Coon, April 4, 2006, Carroll Co., Ky.

Diane Perrine Coon

CAMP SPRINGS. The community of Camp Springs in southern Campbell Co. is situated in a valley served by Four Mile Rd. (Ky. Rt. 547), about three miles from Alexandria. The first people who are known to have lived in the area were American Indians of the **Fort Ancient** period, A.D. 1000–1600. Archaeologists exploring near Camp Springs have found that these Indians, forerunners of the Shawnees, lived in the Twelve Mile Creek watershed. In the 1820s–1830s, settlers arrived in the valley from the region of Alsace-Lorraine, Austria, various German states (see **German Americans**), and other parts of Europe and began farming and organizing a community, which was called Indian Springs and Hayfield before it gained the name Camp Springs. In those developing years, wine-making was the strongest agricultural interest in the valley. Kentucky was once the nation's third-largest wine producer, and Campbell Co. was responsible for almost one-half of the state's production. The high hopes for a local thriving wine industry faded away, however, when a destructive blight annihilated the grape-growing industry of the Camp Springs valley in the post–**Civil War** years (see **Viniculture**). Other crops then came to fill the farmlands.

What became the distinctive architectural heritage of the community was its handcrafted stone homes, barns, smokehouses, and other outbuildings. They were not like the stone buildings constructed in Central Kentucky but followed a more definitive European design with German roots: the stone was not finely hand-hewn but considered to be rubble stone; nonetheless, builders who were artisans fit the stones into intricate patterns. Stone barns were built into hillsides and often housed milking parlors on the cooler lower level; they sometimes also served as wine, fruit, and garden-produce storage cellars.

Sentiments in Camp Springs were strongly pro-Union during the period of the Civil War; yet because the area was rural and somewhat remote, it was not deeply affected by the war. Records show, however, that many people living in Camp Springs, as well throughout all of Campbell Co., who were not yet U.S. citizens, served in the Union forces. At the end of the war, these soldiers received their citizenship papers, some signed by Gen. Ulysses S. Grant. It is said that during the war a squad of Union soldiers camped beside Four Mile Creek in the valley, and the name Camp Springs came into being at that time.

The Four Mile Baptist Church of Jesus Christ, established in the late 1790s, was the earliest congregation in Camp Springs. It was founded by Beutel Riggs on the farm of Israel Ware. **St. John Lutheran Church** was organized at Camp Springs in 1850, and its original building was built of stone. **St. Joseph Catholic Church** dates from 1854, when Peter Steffen held, on his farm, the first service of what later became the church. The Camp Springs Post Office operated from 1871 until 1907. A tavern also operated in town.

At the end of the 19th century, the **Sisters of Divine Providence** of Newport, a Roman Catholic order of nuns who had immigrated from Alsace-Lorraine to the Ohio River Valley, came to staff the school at St. Joseph Church. The school began in 1840 in a log cabin and, after passing through numerous transitions, remains in operation today. The sisters later established their motherhouse nearby. Some other schools that once operated in the valley were the Four Mile School, Tug Fork Elementary, and the school at St. John Lutheran Church, which continued for 11 years.

Today, a 19th-century traveler would find Camp Springs much as it was 150 years ago. Farming, including the raising of livestock, has continued in the area, and grape-growers have returned. Conservation of the land remains essential to the fabric of the community. Some of the preserved stone homes, barns, and outbuildings are now on the National Register of Historic Places. The city is not incorporated.

"Camp Springs," vertical file, Campbell Co. Public Library, Cold Spring, Ky.

Heck, Pat. "History Abounds in Community of Camp Springs," *Campbell County News*, August 6, 1981, 1.

Reis, Jim. "Campbell County's Southern Half Has a Rich Heritage and Character," *KP*, April 14, 1986, 4K.

Rennick, Robert M. *The Post Offices of Northern Kentucky.* Lake Grove, Ore.: Depot, 2004.

Elissa Plattner

CANBY. Canby, a community on the eastern edge of Owen Co. near the Grant Co. border, is 15 miles east of Owenton. One of Owen Co.'s original one-room schools was at Canby. The community of Canby is within the Lusby's Mill Precinct, along Ky. Rt. 330, the Hallam-Corinth Rd. There are a few homes in the area.

An Atlas of Owen County, Kentucky. Philadelphia: Lake, 1883.

Houchens, Mariam Sidebottom. *History of Owen County: "Sweet Owen."* Louisville, Ky.: Standard, 1976.

CANBY, EDWARD RICHARD SPRIGG, BRIGADIER GENERAL (b. November 9, 1817, Piatt's Landing, Boone Co., Ky.; d. April 11, 1873, Mount Shasta, Calif.). **Civil War** veteran Edward Canby was the oldest son of Dr. Israel and Elizabeth Piatt Canby. He became known as the general who accepted the last two surrenders of the Civil War. After graduating from West Point Military Academy in 1839, Canby married Louisa Hawkins of Crawfordsville, Ind. He served in the Seminole War (1835), in the 1838 relocation of American Indians termed the Trail of Tears, and in the Mexican War (1846–1848). As a colonel commanding the Military Department of New Mexico during the Civil War, he ably thwarted an 1862 Confederate invasion at Glorieta Pass, N.Mex., a battle called the Gettysburg of the West. After serving in a staff position with the War Department in Washington, D.C., he was sent to New York City to command Union troops following draft riots in July 1863. In 1864 he was appointed major general and commander of the Military Division of West Mississippi, where he masterminded the campaign leading to the capture of Mobile, Ala., in April 1865. Wounded by guerrillas at White River, Ark., on November 16, 1864, he returned to action and accepted the surrenders of Confederate generals Richard Taylor (early May 1865) and Edmund Kirby Smith (May 26, 1865), more than six weeks after Robert E. Lee's surrender at Appomattox, Va.

In 1866 he was given the permanent rank of brigadier general. After being posted during Reconstruction to military administrative positions in Louisiana and the Carolinas, and earning a reputation as one of the most fair-minded army officers serving in the South, the politically independent Canby was reassigned to Texas. He was credited with supervising the process that led to the ratification of that state's constitution in 1869, guaranteeing blacks the right to vote. Canby made sure that the state's constitutional convention records were preserved and published. He carefully protected the rights of freedmen without suppressing the rights of southern Democrats.

During the 1870s, Canby was named commander of the Department of the Pacific and served in the West until he was murdered in 1873. Despite being warned by Winema, the female subchief of the Modoc Indians, Canby and two civilians went unarmed to negotiate a treaty with Chief Kintpuash "Captain Jack" and a group of Modocs near the Tule Lake lava beds, east of Mount Shasta, Calif. During these talks, an argument broke out and Canby was shot by Captain Jack and stabbed. Canby was the only regular army general killed in the Trans-Mississippi Indian Wars. Canby's Cross, a monument erected in his honor, stands in the Lava Beds National Monument. Cities in California and Oregon and Fort Canby State Park (now Cape Disappointment) in the state of Washington, were named in his honor. He was buried at Crown Hill Cemetery in Indianapolis, Ind.

Boatner, Mark Mayo, III. *The Civil War Dictionary.* New York: David McKay, 1959.

Hall, Martin Hardwick. *Sibley's New Mexico Campaign.* Austin: Univ. of Texas Press, 1960.

The Handbook of Texas Online. www.tsha.utexas.edu.

Heyman, Max L., Jr. *Prudent Soldier: A Biography of Major General E. R. S. Canby.* Glendale, Calif.: Clark, 1959.

Reis, Jim. "Canby Killed Pursuing Peace," *KP,* December 8, 2003, 5K.

Stephen M. Vest

CANCER AND CANCER RESEARCH. The incidence of most forms of cancer in Northern Kentucky closely parallels state data and, with slightly less correlation, national data. Lung cancer rates are higher than the national average for the region and the state, probably owing to higher-than-average tobacco use. The most commonly occurring forms of cancer in the area are cancers of the prostate, the breast, the lung, the colon, the bladder, and the uterus.

Cancer is not a single disease, but rather a collection of more than 200 different diseases that share some common features. The disease is characterized by uncontrolled growth of cells originating from normal cells. Once formed, cancer cells often acquire the ability to migrate or metastasize to new locations in the body. The disease is the result of multiple random genetic changes caused by exposure to DNA-damaging chemicals, radiation, or certain viruses. Generally, a single genetic change will not result in the creation of a cancer cell.

Cancer therapy is widely available in Northern Kentucky. **St. Luke Hospitals Inc.** (Health Alliance) and **St. Elizabeth Medical Center** offer state-of-the-art treatment options for cancer patients. The region also has several hospices providing end-of-life care. Experimental cancer therapies are available at the University of Cincinnati's Barrett Cancer Center.

Cancer research is performed at several locations in Northern Kentucky. **Northern Kentucky University** and **Thomas More College** both have faculty engaged in cancer research, in which undergraduate students are also involved. Unique to Northern Kentucky is the Wood Hudson Cancer Research Laboratory (WHCRL), located on Isabella St. in Newport in the former elementary school of the **Corpus Christi Catholic Church**. The laboratory is a publicly funded, nonprofit research facility directed by Dr. Julia H. Carter, one of its founders. WHCRL is engaged in collaborative cancer research with the U.S. Environmental Protection Agency, local universities, and the pharmaceutical industry. The laboratory is notable in that it possesses a human-tissue-sample bank consisting of more than 250,000 paraffin-embedded specimens of normal and cancerous human tissue. The tissue bank is an invaluable resource in evaluation of new cancer diagnostic methods and in identification of candidate target molecules for cancer chemotherapy. WHCRL also operates an undergraduate research education program, which has helped to train some 125 local college students in biomedical research methods. In 2009 it broke ground for a new $600,000 wing.

Bonfield, Tim. "Medicine's Cutting Edge at Home in Small Places," *CE,* February 13, 2004, 2B.

Kentucky Cancer Registry—Incidence. http://cancer-rates.info/ky/ (accessed March 18, 2005).

Listerman, Mary Lu. "Grant Promotes Cancer Research," *CE,* February 13, 2005, 3C.

National Cancer Institute. "State Cancer Profiles." http://statecancerprofiles.cancer.gov/incidencerates/incidencerates.html (accessed March 18, 2005).

Starr, Cindy. "Soldiers in the War on Cancer," *KP,* March 27, 2002, 1K.

Vela, S. 1999. "Expert Says Cancer Blame Misplaced," *CE,* July 1, 1999, www.enquirer.com/editions/1999/07/01/loc_expert_says_cancer.html (accessed March 12, 2005).

Eric R. Hugo

CANDY AND ICE CREAM. The making and selling of candy and ice cream go hand in hand, since they are sometimes produced and often sold by the same entrepreneurs. Although in general candy was available earlier than ice cream, the latter was being sold in Covington before 1850. One proprietor, A. Clark, was operating an ice cream saloon and making root beer along Madison Ave. between Fifth and Sixth Sts. in 1845. However, until the improvements in refrigeration of the late 19th century, most of these stores, called confectionaries, sold mainly homemade penny candy. It was called "penny" candy because the price matched its small size. Newspapers of the day were full of both purchased ads and news stories announcing that certain stores were making special batches of candy products for holidays such as Valentine's Day. T. F. Brickley opened his Superior Candy wholesale business in late 1856 along Scott St. between Fourth and Fifth Sts. in Covington. By the 1890s there were about 40 similar confectionaries in the city; and by that time, more of the stores were adding homemade ice cream to their offerings. Confectionaries that ventured into the ice cream business had the problem that they often had to buy ice to make their ice cream from ice manufacturers with whom they were competing in the making of ice cream. Businesses such as Coston Brothers, at the northeast corner of Sixth St. and Madison Ave. in Covington, served candy and ice cream. Soterios Droganes, the Costons' cousin, acquired their store and moved it to 205 W. Pike St. in 1911. In 1918 he built a new parlor at 207 W. Pike St. called Sam's Ice Cream and Candy. In Maysville, Traxel's Bakery, Confectionery, and Soda Fountain had been established in 1878 and usually did a brisk business, particularly during the 1940s. There was not much difference between the making of candy and the making of ice cream, once the freezing problem of the latter was solved. These small candy and ice cream shops tended to be operated by families.

The best-known candy manufacturer in Kenton Co. is the Chris A. Papas & Son Company. In

Hand-dipping candy in the basement of 830 Madison Ave. (next door to the Lily Candy Shop at 832 Madison), 1947. *Left to right*: unknown woman, Katherine Papas Hartmann (*seated*), Chris Papas, Alex Papas, Norb Hartmann.

1909 Christus (Chris) Papas (1894–1984) of Macedonia immigrated to the United States at age 15. After learning to make candy at a friend's shop in Cincinnati, he started making candy in Covington in the late 1920s. By 1935 Papas was making and selling both candy and ice cream; he and his wife Lillian opened their new store, the Lily Chocolate Shop, that same year at 830 Madison Ave. in Covington. In 1948 they moved the candy and ice cream shop next door, to 832 Madison (the northeast corner of Ninth and Madison Aves.). In August 1951, Chris Papas retired from the candy and ice cream business, leaving the Lily Chocolate Shop in the hands of his daughter, Katherine Hartmann, and her husband, Norbert. Together, they served ice cream and specialty handmade candies under the Lily brand name until they retired in 1987. Chris's son Alex took over the manufacturing production of the Papas candy brand at 6 E. Ninth St., above the store, and later at the factory at 921 Baker St. in the Lewisburg neighborhood of Covington, a plant built there by the family in 1957. They made only candy, of which their Papas Easter eggs are the most popular today. The family's third generation, Chris and Carl Papas, continue to operate the candy plant. The factory has the capacity to produce as many as 80,000 candy eggs per day, and they are sold across six states.

Robert Schneider Sr. opened his sweet shop (ice cream and candy store) in Bellevue in 1939 at the southwest corner of Fairfield and Foote Aves. Schneider's is famous not only for its opera cream and other candies, and its homemade ice cream (400 gallons per week), but also for ice balls and ice cream ice balls. In the fall of each year, once the apples are ready, thousands of caramel and candy apples are made and sold by Schneider's. Robert Schneider Sr. retired in 1986, and the Bellevue store is today owned and operated by his son Jack Schneider. The Bellevue store expanded into the East Side of Cincinnati with a store at the former Beechmont Mall and into Alexandria, but both of those outlets are now closed. Robert Schneider Jr. has operated a similar store, the Sweet Tooth, at 125 W. 11th St. in Newport for the past 35 years. The Sweet Tooth has its candy kitchen at 1020 Saratoga St. in Newport, and it once had a branch in the former Crestview Hills Mall in Kenton Co. The Sweet Tooth makes caramel apples for its own sales and also contracts some 10,000 of these for sale locally by the **Remke Markets** grocery chain. The queen of England has eaten the Sweet Tooth product.

At one time both Newport and Covington had many small candy operations. Some lasted a long time, such as the Sweet Shop at the northwest corner of E. 10th and Monroe Sts. in Newport, which sold candy to local children until at least 1960. That store eventually had to diversify to other products. On Fridays in 1958, one could buy fried fish sandwiches there for 25 cents each. During the 1940s through the 1960s, Mary and Walter C. Wallace made Christmas and Easter candies, and fruitcakes, in a specially constructed factory in their backyard at 32 W. Crescent Ave. in Woodlawn, just southeast of Newport.

Once the commercial **dairies** began making ice cream, as a way to utilize the excess raw milk that they obtained from their supply relationships with local farmers, some began to operate ice cream stores, and chains of ice cream shops appeared. The making of cheese was another method of dealing with excess milk supplies. The Clover Leaf Dairy in Campbell Co. in the 1940s ran several stores where they also sold their dairy products (milk and cottage cheese) and also scoops of flavored ice cream, sodas, malts, and shakes. Clover Leaf had three outlets in Fort Thomas alone, one near their ice cream plant on S. Fort Thomas Ave., across from the old Summit Gardens. The dairy had two outlets in Newport, including one across 11th St. from the **Trauth Dairy**. In 1940 the Monarch Ice Cream Company (associated with the Summe Dairy) had stores in both Campbell and Kenton counties: one in Ludlow, four in Covington, one in Latonia, two in Newport, and one in Bellevue. Monarch later sold to Clover Leaf. Other similar operations included the Delicious Dairy along Waterworks Rd. in E. Newport, next to the site of the former Maple Grove playground (recently Bellwood Bowling Lanes); Jersey Farm; Meadow Lane; and the Newport Dairy (owned by the Feldman Dairy). Such shops became havens of temporary relief on hot summer evenings and places for students to go after completing a hard day at school. The Trauth Dairy in Newport acquired the former Niser Ice Cream Company in 1968 but did not begin its own label until 1990. By 1991 Trauth was making some 43 new ice cream products. Trauth Ice Cream was made at the company's Newport dairy until recently; but Trauth's new corporate owner, Suiza Foods Corporation, has now shifted the making of the award-winning Trauth Ice Cream brand to one of its Tennessee subsidiaries.

Lily Candy Shop, July 1948.

At one time many pharmacies had soda stands on their premises where ice cream was sold, mainly sodas, malts, and shakes, besides fruity parfaits. One such place was Albert Bathiany's Drug Store at 601 Monmouth St. in Newport; one could stop there for a refreshing respite while shopping in the **Monmouth St. Business District**. Not far from the Sweet Tooth stood **Ann's Ice Balls** at 28 E. Ninth St. in Newport, which sold ice, ice cream, and ice cream ice balls through a window along the sidewalk, at the site the shop had occupied since 1940. In the early 1950s on hot summer nights, it was common to find a half-block-long line of Ann's customers outside, waiting their turn.

For many years during the summer, roving ice cream trucks—less often seen today—traveled the urban neighborhoods of Northern Kentucky peddling their ice cream. Customers knew when an ice cream truck was in the vicinity because they heard the repetitious music emanating from a public address system on the truck's roof. Perhaps the most famous of such moving operators was the franchise known as Mister Softee, named for the soft-serve ice cream it sold. The major Mister Softee distributor in Campbell Co. was Gene Thomas, son of the founders and owners of the **F&N Steakhouse**.

Since 1979 the Italian confectionary company Perfetti Van Melle USA has been located in Erlanger, along Turfway Rd., and it has manufactured candy since 1982. Home of the Air Heads brand of candy and a cotton candy bubble gum, the 120,000-square-foot plant employs nearly 200 workers. Erlanger is also home to the recently arrived ice cream manufacturing facility United Dairy Farmers (UDF), situated along Crescent Springs Pk. UDF, a large Cincinnati concern, has nine retail store locations throughout Northern Kentucky today, at sites seemingly selected for reasons of gasoline sales, not ice cream. Graeter's Ice Cream, the long-standing favorite of Cincinnati ice cream lovers, presently operates four stores in Northern Kentucky.

Day, Michelle. "Kentucky's Sweet Tooth," *KP*, December 14, 1984, 13K.
Gallagher, Janice. "The Candy Maker," *KP*, February 2, 2003, 5K.
Hicks, Jack. "Autumn's Sweet Treats," *KP*, October 5, 2005, 10K.
Newberry, Jon. "Candy Plant Will Add Jobs," *KP*, February 18, 2005, 1K.
"New Candy Plant for Covington," *KP*, March 7, 1957, 1.
"New Wholesale Candy Manufactory," *CJ*, December 27, 1856, 4.
Paeth, Greg. "Age Catches up with Lily's," *KP*, February 4, 1987, 1K.
Reis, Jim. "Dairies Added a Daily Personal Touch," *KP*, May 14, 1990, 4K.
——. "Ice Cream Soda Brought Magnolia Building Fame," *KP*, May 17, 2004, 4K.
Van Sant, Rick. "Candy Is Dandy at Easter," *CP*, April 10, 1998, 1A.
Yelton, Kim. "Alex Papas Has a Sweet Deal," *KP*, January 27, 1977, 15K.

Michael R. Sweeney

CAPPEL, WILLIAM F. "BILL" (b. November 12, 1912, Covington, Ky.; d. December 16, 2003, Covington, Ky.). Baseball player and promoter Bill Cappel was a living embodiment of baseball in Covington for more than 60 years, lived all of his life along Perry St. in Covington (not far from the old Covington Ball Park), and never married. He was a lifelong member of **St. John Catholic Church** on nearby Pike St. Cappel, the son of Anthony and Katherine Volphenheim Cappel (both born in Germany), and was a member of the first graduating class of the **Covington Latin School** (1927). In September 1939 he was both the captain and second baseman for Nick Carr's Covington Boosters baseball team—a team that some have said produced Covington's greatest moment in sports when it won the World's Amateur Softball Championship (fast pitch) at Soldier's Field in Chicago. Cappel served in **World War II** in the army, earning the Legion of Merit, the Bronze Star, and five other service-related medals. From 1948 thorough 1958, he was the general manager of Covington's city ballparks: he worked seven days a week, from 5:30 p.m. until midnight, without compensation. He was involved with promoting women's softball as early as 1935 and started the Covington Major Girls League at Covington's Meinken Field. He was a cofounder of both the Northern Kentucky Umpire's Association and the Northern Kentucky Sports Hall of Fame, into which he was later inducted. He never learned to drive, instead riding with friends or walking wherever he went. He first worked for the Union Pacific Railroad and later for the Cincinnati Terminal Warehouse. In August 2003, at age 91, Cappel fell and broke his hip twice and went to a nursing home. He remained there until his death. He was buried at St. John Cemetery in Fort Mitchell. Countless residents of Covington remember him at the ballpark; they routinely paid him the utmost respect, intuitively knowing that he had forgotten more about baseball than most people would ever learn, while he effortlessly made certain that everything and everyone was ready for the next pitch. Many who are knowledgeable about sports in Northern Kentucky consider Bill Cappel, the player, manager, umpire, and groundskeeper, as having been the region's Sportsman of the Past Century.

"60 Years Is Enough for Cappel," *KP*, December 13, 1985, 6K.
"Sportsman of the Century Dies at 91," *KE*, December 19, 2003, B1.
"William F. Cappel, 91, on World Champion Team," *KP*, December 17, 2003, A15.

CAPRONI'S RESTAURANT. Caproni's has been a Maysville dining tradition since 1945. Leo Caproni bought the restaurant that year and operated it with his brother and sister-in-law, Alfred and Lea Caproni. The restaurant is located beside the Amtrak railroad station and along the **CSX** tracks, overlooking the Ohio River, at the base of what is now **Rosemary Clooney** St. The town floodwall is immediately south of the restaurant, which is a prime place in Maysville to view the river, the **Simon Kenton Memorial Bridge**, and the new **William H. Harsha Bridge**. A fast freight train roars by within feet of diners. In the early years, the railroad station was a source of customers for the restaurant. Locals from all over frequented Caproni's. The site of countless receptions, club meetings, and retirement dinners, it was also the place to go for lunch. Alfred and Lea Caproni bought the business in 1953. Alfred died in 1966, and Lea remodeled the building in the summer of 1967, so that a wall of windows on the north side brought the Ohio River vista to nearly all the diners.

In 1975 *Louisville Courier-Journal* writer Billy Reed named Caproni's one of the 10 best places to eat in Kentucky. Many diners were regulars, including John Skillman, who was involved in the construction of the floodwall. In 1970 he married the owner, Lea Caproni, and together they ran "Cap's" until his death in 1987. Lea gave up the business in 1990, and the namesake family was no longer associated with the restaurant. It went through a succession of owners and was closed when Jerry Lundergan, a Maysville native and nationally known caterer, bought the business in 1999. After extensive remodeling, Caproni's reopened in December 2000. Over the years many dignitaries dined there, including governors of Kentucky John Y. Brown Jr. (1979–1983) and Wallace Wilkinson (1987–1991). Caproni's has been a longtime favorite of the Clooney family and in recent years has been the reception site for the headliners of the local Rosemary Clooney Music Festival, such as singers Linda Rondstadt and Roberta Flack.

Caproni's features fine dining with a casual atmosphere and honors its heritage with both Italian dishes and other choices. It continues to attract customers from all walks of life; locals often entertain their guests there. The Capronis of Cincinnati, cousins to the Maysville family, operated their Caproni's Italian Restaurant in downtown Cincinnati on Court St., and later along Main St.; after 89 years of business, it closed in 1975. Many old photographs of Crosley Field, home until 1970 of the Cincinnati Reds baseball team, show a billboard for the local Caprioni's painted on the outfield wall.

Caproni's file, Kentucky Gateway Museum Collection, Maysville, Ky.
Clooney, Nick. "A Dining Institution Is Reborn," *KP*, March 9, 2001, 1B.
"Maysville Eatery for Sale," *KP*, February 24, 1990, 6K.

John Klee

CARDINAL HILL OF NORTHERN KENTUCKY. Founded in Covington in 1923 as Kentucky Easter Seals, Cardinal Hill today is a nonprofit organization and an outpatient facility specializing in various areas of health care. In Northern Kentucky these include speech-language therapy, audiology, early intervention, adult day health care and respite care, and the operation of the Cardinal Hill Specialty Hospital.

Cardinal Hill has achieved many firsts within the commonwealth of Kentucky. It offered the first special education classes for children and the only classes for children with physical disabilities (in the Opportunity School) in Northern Kentucky. It was the first facility in Northern Kentucky to provide (in the 1950s) audiology (hearing) services to children, adults, and newborn infants. Cardinal Hill provided the first orthopedic care and the first physical, occupational, and speech therapy for children and adults; its adult day care center was the first to offer daily care and nursing services for young adults as well as persons older than 60; and it established the first preschool for special-needs children.

The Cardinal Hill Specialty Hospital is a 33-bed long-term acute-care hospital located on the third floor of St. Luke Hospital East in Fort Thomas, Ky. (see **St. Luke Hospitals Inc.**). A "hospital within a hospital," the Cardinal Hill unit is recognized by Medicare as a facility providing specialized acute hospital care for patients who are critically ill, have multisystem complications or failure (or both), or other conditions requiring a stay of 25 or more days. Typically, patients at this facility are unable to be discharged to a nursing home or a rehabilitation facility or to go home. Examples are ventilator-dependent patients, brain injury or stroke patients, or people with postsurgical complications of many types. The relationship between the Cardinal Hill Specialty Hospital and St. Luke Hospital is one of synergy.

Cardinal Hill of Northern Kentucky is a part of the Cardinal Hill Healthcare System, which includes its 108-bed postacute rehabilitation hospital in Lexington, four outpatient centers (one is in Covington, and one in Florence, Ky.), and a camp for adults and children in Carrollton, **Camp KYSOC**.

Kreimer, Peggy. "Balancing Act," *KP,* July 25, 2003, 1K.

———. "A Hospital within a Hospital," *KP,* August 26, 2003, 1K.

Sarah Caruso

CARINCI, TITO (b. December 15, 1928, Steubenville, Ohio; d. November 12, 2006, Torrance, Calif.). Mayfield Road Gang member Peter Tito Carinci was born in the bustling southeastern Ohio steel-mill town of Steubenville. He was the son of August and Mary Porreca Carinci. His mother's family had family ties with the family of entertainer Dean Martin, Steubenville's most famous prodigy. He was educated in that city's Catholic school system, graduating in 1947 from Steubenville Central Catholic High School, where he was a star football player. The Roman Catholic bishop of Steubenville during the late 1940s was John King Mussio, who often sent his top athletes to his alma mater, Xavier University in Cincinnati. Tito Carinci was one of these. Carinci excelled in football at Xavier University, and Xavier paid him its highest honor, inducting him into the institution's Legion of Honor. He was a "little All-American" linebacker, playing in Xavier's victory over Arizona State in the 1951 Salad Bowl (the predecessor to today's Fiesta Bowl). While living in Cincinnati, Carinci frequently enjoyed the nightlife of Newport. After graduation in 1951, and following a brief stay in the Green Bay Packers training camp and a stint in the U.S. Army,, he returned to Northern Kentucky in 1957 and went to work for the Cleveland, Ohio, crime syndicate (the Mayfield Road Gang) that was operating in Newport. By 1960 Carinci had attained essentially the general managership of the Levinson Brothers' Glenn Rendezvous Hotel at 928 Monmouth St in Newport. It was at that location, within its bar, the Tropicana Club, in the early morning hours of May 9, 1961, where Carinci and his 26-year-old stripper friend April Flowers (Juanita Hodges) tried to frame Campbell Co. sheriff candidate and Committee of 500 (see **Newport Reform Groups**) member **George W. Ratterman**, another former football player. The future sheriff had been slipped a "mickey" by Carinci earlier that evening in Cincinnati, and later at the Glenn Rendezvous Hotel was found in bed partially unclothed lying next to Carinci's stripper friend. The subsequent trial and proceedings made national headlines, as Carinci's name was intimately and forever linked to Newport's sordid past. In 1963 Carinci unsuccessfully ran for mayor of Newport; he then moved to Miami, Fla., where he served two prison terms for tax evasion and bookmaking. Carinci spent another period in New York City, dressed like a hippie and running a credit card scam. He died at age 77 in 2006 in Torrance, Calif., near where he had operated a nightclub, the Pitcher House. He was cremated and was survived by his wife Barbara.

Obituary. *Steubenville (Ohio) Herald-Star,* November 19, 2006, 3B.

Wecker, David. "Old Newport—New Twist," *KP,* October 2, 2002, 1K.

Michael R. Sweeney

CARL BROTHERS. The stonemasons Joseph Carl (1862–1937) and John Carl (1865–1942) emigrated from their native Alsace, France, during the 1880s to escape the economic instability brought on by the German occupation of the province following the Franco-Prussian War of 1870–1871. Alsace, once described by Joseph's wife, Mary "Marie" Schmitt (1863–1939), to her sons as having one farm better than the other and one stone house on top of another, provided these German-speaking immigrants with their special vocational calling, stonemasonry.

Upon arrival in the United States, Joseph and John Carl immediately made their way to Covington, settling in the **Lewisburg** neighborhood. They found instant opportunity in the stone trade in and around the burgeoning city of Covington. The brothers quickly developed a reputation for skilled masonry craftsmanship, a strong work ethic, and perfection down to the finest detail.

Working as stonemasons in conjunction with the Covington Stone and Marble Company, Joseph and John Carl contributed their talents during the construction of Covington's **Cathedral Basilica of the Assumption**. The Carl Brothers firm subsequently was selected as the contractor in charge and orchestrated the second phase of the cathedral's construction, its facade, from 1908 to 1910. Upon completion of that phase, Joseph Carl, on behalf of the Carl Brothers firm, presented the gargoyles and akroteria that adorn the top of the cathedral. In 1934 Carl Brothers constructed the Cathedral's baptistery, a small chapel located in the south transept under the organ balcony.

The Carls formed Carl Brothers, also known as the Carl Construction Company, around the beginning of the 20th century. For many years Carl Brothers was the pioneer firm of its kind in Northern Kentucky. Originally the firm's office was located on the second floor of Joseph Carl's residence, a yellow brick house that still stands at the northwest corner of Lewis and Baker Sts. in Covington. The horses and the construction carriages used by the firm were kept along Baker St., behind the office-residence. Eventually, trucks replaced the horses and carriages. The firm maintained a large stone yard on the north side of the Fedders Feed and Seed lot along Russell St. in Covington. The stone yard kept a stock of the various types of materials and construction equipment. Upon the death of Joseph Carl in 1937, at age 74, the office moved to the Russell St. site. During **World War II** the company relocated the stone yard and office to the opposite side of Fedders Feed and Seed, where it remained until the stone company's closing in August 1982.

The sons of Joseph and John Carl began working with the firm during the building of the Cathedral Basilica. Each of the sons subsequently participated in **World War I**. Joseph's sons, Joseph G. (1891–1930) and John W. (1896–1973), encountered front-line action in France. Both men were injured during the war, Joseph critically. Neither returned to the Carl Brothers firm after their military service. John's son, Al Carl (1896–1964), who also briefly participated in World War I, returned to the company.

During the 1920s and 1930s, Joseph Carl handled the firm's primary business affairs, bidding on jobs, negotiating, and visiting job sites. John Carl conducted the skilled operations of the business and oversaw on-site construction. With the deaths of Joseph in 1937 and John in 1942, Al Carl took over the full operation of the company. Al's only son, Paul Carl Sr. (b. 1923), joined the firm permanently following his return from service in the Pacific during World War II. Al and Paul Carl jointly operated the company until Al's death in June 1964. Paul Carl continued the business until his retirement in August 1982, and the assets of the firm were sold to the Tate Building Supply Company in Erlanger.

In addition to the Cathedral Basilica, noted churches built, renovated, or reconstructed by Carl

Brothers include **St. Joseph Catholic Church** and School at 12th and Greenup Sts. (Covington), **Mother of God Catholic Church** (Covington), **St. John Catholic Church** and School (Covington), **St. Augustine Church** and School (Covington), St. Stephens Church, now **Holy Spirit Catholic Church** (Newport), **St. Thomas Catholic Church** (Fort Thomas), **St. Henry Catholic Church** (Erlanger), **Holy Cross Catholic Church** (Latonia), St. John Church (Newport), St. Paul United Church of Christ (Fort Thomas), Our Lady of Lourdes Church (Cincinnati), St. Vivian Church (Finneytown, Ohio), Holy Trinity–St. Nicholas Greek Orthodox Church (Finneytown), and others in Kentucky, Ohio, and Indiana.

In addition to work on churches, Carl Brothers constructed the exterior or supplied the stone, or both, for the limestone and granite exteriors of local bank buildings including **First National**, **People's-Liberty Bank and Trust Company**, Covington Savings Bank and Trust Company (see **Huntington Bank**), Security Bank, Latonia First National, and the Latonia Deposit Company. Carl Brothers also laid the stone on other noteworthy buildings: **Covington Latin School**; what was most recently the Northern Kentucky Community Center on Greenup St. (Covington); the Cincinnati Bell building (Lakeside Park); **Notre Dame Academy** (Park Hills); St. Joseph Heights Convent (Park Hills); the first **Covington Catholic High School** (Park Hills); the Masonic Order Temple (Covington) (see **Masons**); Bellevue High School (see **Bellevue Public Schools**); **Campbell Co. High School**, now the Campbell Co. Middle School (Alexandria); Glenmary Home Mission (Sharonville, Ohio); the Cincinnati Police Headquarters; the former Carousel Inn complex (Sycamore Township in Ohio); Johnson Elementary School (Fort Thomas); and the Logan Building on the campus of Xavier University (Cincinnati). Through the years, the firm was involved in additions and renovations for LaSalle High School (Monfort Heights, Ohio), St. Anne Convent (Melbourne), **St. Luke Hospital** East (Fort Thomas), and **St. Elizabeth Medical Center** North (Covington).

Mainly noted for commercial work, Carl Brothers also constructed foundations, piers, shelters, and walls still standing in and around Northern Kentucky for public structures and for residential use. Several architecturally appealing stone houses were also built by Carl Brothers, including at least three in Park Hills (1002, 1005, and 1009 Park Dr.), two in Fort Mitchell (4 Sunnymede Ave. and 30 Orphanage Rd.), and two in Lakeside Park (35 W. Lakeside and 44 Locust). They also built mausoleums, such as the Maloney Mausoleum in **St. Mary Cemetery**, Fort Mitchell.

"Carl Company's Part," *KP,* September 5, 1923, 5.
"Carl Firm," *KP,* May 20, 1924, 6.
"Cathedral Gargoyles Not Apostles or Devils," *KP,* May 2, 1910, 2.
"Father Hopes Sons Will Drive Huns from Alsace," *KP,* June 3, 1918, 4.
"Prominent in Corner Stone Laying," *KP,* September 5, 1927, 1.

Paul A. Carl Jr.

CARLISLE, JOHN G. (b. September 5, 1834, Key West, Campbell Co. [now Kenton Co.]; d. July 31, 1910, New York City). Secretary of the treasury and legislator John Griffin Carlisle was the eldest of 11 children of Lilborn and Mary Reynolds Griffin. John was educated at the best schools of his day. Intelligent and well read, he was hired as a teacher in Covington schools slightly before his 16th birthday. His father died in 1853, leaving him the sole support of his large family. In 1856 he gave up teaching to study law under **John White Stevenson**, a prominent Covington attorney who served later as Kentucky governor (1867–1871). At the age of 23, Carlisle joined the Covington law firm of William Kinkead. He married Mary Jane Goodson in 1857, and they had five children, all of whom died before their parents did.

Carlisle, a Democrat, served in the state House of Representatives from 1859 to 1861 and in the state Senate from 1867 to 1871, before becoming lieutenant governor in the administration of Governor Preston H. Leslie (1871–1875). He served in the U.S. House of Representatives for six consecutive terms, from March 4, 1877, until May 26, 1890, and as Speaker of the House from 1883 until 1889. He served in the U.S. Senate from May 26, 1890, until February 4, 1893, resigning when President Grover Cleveland named him secretary of the treasury, a position he held from 1893 to 1897. He returned to Covington in 1896 to make a speech at the Odd Fellows Hall at Fifth and Madison and was driven from the stage by protestors who disagreed with his policy concerning the government's remaining on the gold standard. Carlisle suffered much personal tragedy in his life, and after being rejected in his hometown, he retired from public life. He sold his Garrard St. home in Covington and moved to New York City, where he died in 1910. He was returned to Covington to be buried at the Linden Grove Cemetery. John G. Carlisle Elementary School at 910 Holman Ave. in Covington was named in his honor.

John G. Carlisle.

Barnes, James A. *John G. Carlisle: Financial Statesman.* 1931. Reprint, Gloucester, Mass: Peter Smith, 1967.
Biographical Directory of the United States Congress. www.bioguide.congress.gov (accessed October 5, 2005).
Collins, Richard H. *History of Kentucky.* Vol. 1. Covington, Ky.: Collins, 1882.

CARLSBAD SPRINGS HOTEL. J. B. Sanders, operator of a large general mercantile business in Dry Ridge, developed plans for building the Carlsbad Springs Hotel in 1911. He had purchased from the Dry Ridge Creamery Company a property fronting on Broadway where a deep well yielded mineral water instead of the fresh water needed to operate a creamery. On the east side of Main St. in Dry Ridge, Sanders purchased or owned several pieces of property, including the Dry Ridge Roller Mill, which totaled about three acres. There he established his hotel, sanitarium, and bath houses. He also bottled and sold mineral waters. The name of his business, the Carlsbad Springs Hotel Company, formed in 1912, was chosen to capitalize on the reputation of mineral resorts located in Carlsbad, Germany. The mineral water, pumped on Broadway, was piped to the hotel on the east side of Main St. Hotel guests suffering from rheumatic or arthritic problems would take hot mineral-water baths, and guests who had digestive or intestinal problems would drink the mineral water.

Although there were usually plenty of guests at the hotel, it changed hands and reorganized several times, each time with new investors. In 1927 a large part of Dry Ridge was destroyed by fire, including the hotel. The hotel lot was sold again and again, and various attempts were made to rebuild the hotel. These efforts were not successful until 1937, when E. C. Holliday and others started construction on a new hotel facility. The walls, the floors, and the roof of a two-story building were in place, but the group lacked the necessary funds to install doors and windows. After going through receivership twice more, the partially completed hotel and the land were sold to Ralph L. Taylor, a real estate developer. In 1947 Taylor sold the Carlsbad site (a 40-room hotel along with furnishings, fixtures, baths, and the Carlsbad pump house) to Carlsbad Mineral Well and Sanitarium Inc., a company incorporated by Clarence M. Hook, Robert M. Lucas, and Taylor.

In 1955 the property was sold to Nell Tully Bradford, who sold it to Stewart Realty Company. It was then sold to the Carlsbad Commerce Center. In 1973 Catherine P. Smith bought the property and operated it as a residential hotel; it still operates as such. However, the mineral-water wells and health spas that dominated the Dry Ridge business community from about 1910 to 1960 are now long gone.

Conrad, John B., ed. *History of Grant County.* Williamstown, Ky.: Grant Co. Historical Society, 1992.

John B. Conrad

CARMEL MANOR. Carmel Manor nursing home is located in Fort Thomas in the mansion of

Carlsbad Springs Hotel, ca. 1912.

Cincinnati banker Eli Kinney. Kinney built his mansion overlooking the Ohio River in 1877 on a 44-acre site. Later, the **Fort Thomas Military Reservation** was developed adjacent to this property.

In 1949 Roman Catholic bishop William Mulloy invited the Carmelite Sisters for the Aged and Infirm to the Diocese of Covington (see **Roman Catholics**), asking them to operate a home for the aged in Northern Kentucky. Mother Mary Teresa, a Carmelite sister, became the first superior-administrator of the nursing home. Carmel Manor was originally home to 35 residents, who were housed in the three-story mansion. Until 1953 the facility was owned by the diocese and operated by the Carmelite Sisters; at that time the Carmelite Sisters purchased the property and built a larger home to meet the growing needs of the elderly. A new building dedicated in 1956 was licensed to accommodate 99 residents.

During the administration of Bishop Richard Ackerman, it was decided that there was a need in the area for a home for retired priests. To serve that purpose, the Regina Cleri house was completed in 1969 on the grounds of Carmel Manor, with a connection to the personal-care wing of Carmel Manor.

From the 1940s to the 1980s, Carmel Manor functioned solely as a personal-care residence. A certificate-of-need to add a nursing wing was granted to Carmel Manor in 1987. This wing, with 65 nursing-facility beds, was built and occupied by July 4, 1990. It was named St. Joseph Terrace and was dedicated by Bishop William Hughes on October 13, 1990. The personal-care wing license of Carmel Manor was decreased to 80 beds, resulting in a total capacity of 145 residents. Today, the facility provides 24-hour nursing care and is Medicare and Medicaid certified. Residents are offered daily religious services, rehabilitation services, and beauty and barber services, and they take part in numerous activities and outings.

"Historic Home Became Carmel Manor," *KP*, October 11, 1999, 4K.

Ryan, Paul E. *History of the Diocese of Covington, Kentucky*. Covington, Ky.: Diocese of Covington, 1954.

Tenkotte, Paul A., David E. Schroeder, and Thomas S. Ward. *To Be Catholic and American in Northern, Central, and Appalachian Kentucky: The Diocese of Covington, 1853–2003*. Forthcoming.

Bill Thomas

CARNEAL, THOMAS DAVIS (b. January 31, 1786, Alexandria, Va.; d. November 3, 1860, Cincinnati, Ohio). Thomas D. Carneal, a founder and a prominent booster of the city of Covington, moved to Franklin Co., Ky., from Virginia with his parents, Thomas and Alice Davis Carneal, in about 1792. In 1800 the family relocated to Big Bone in Boone Co. In 1806, while his parents returned to Franklin Co., Thomas D. Carneal remained to establish himself in the Cincinnati area. By 1812 he was involved in a military supplies business with Newport's founder, **James Taylor Jr.** In 1815 Campbell Co. appointed Carneal to survey the streets, "ways," and roads of Newport. In that same year, Carneal married Sally Howell Stanley, a widow and the sister of the first wife of wealthy Cincinnati businessman Nicholas Longworth. After 1818, when the Kentucky legislature established state banks in 45 towns, Carneal and four others, including Taylor, organized the "first legal bank" in Campbell Co. Carneal also officiated in the early development of some of that county's major roads.

Earlier, in 1814, Richard Gano and Carneal, with **John S. Gano** and James W. Bryson, had purchased 200 acres in Covington for $50,000 from **Thomas Kennedy**, one of that town's early settlers. In the same year, R. M. Gano sold his one-fourth interest to Bakewell, Page, and Bakewell of Pittsburgh, Pa. (see **Bakewell Family**). In 1815 proprietors Carneal, John Gano, and Richard Gano requested that the Kentucky legislature incorporate Covington, appoint trustees, and plat the new town. Before the year's end, Carneal sold his part of the land holdings purchased in Covington to his partners, John and Richard Gano, for $4,000 and a certain 9.5 acres within town limits at the east end of Fourth St. in Covington, valued at $5,000. About 1818 Carneal acquired land, including a portion of present-day Ludlow, where in 1820 he built one of Northern Kentucky's landmarks, **Elmwood Hall**, overlooking the Ohio River.

Thomas Carneal's name is still well remembered locally because of the stately mansion on E. Second St. in Covington that is known as the Carneal House (see **Gano-Southgate House**). Deed records and old newspapers indicate that John Gano's son Aaron owned the lots during the mansion's construction, about 1820–1822. Over the years, newspaper accounts erroneously claimed that Carneal had built the house and that the famed French general the Marquis de Lafayette had been entertained there. The Kentucky Historical Highway Marker for the home also claims that the house was an **Underground Railroad** site. None of these claims are verifiable, and the details of Carneal's exact connection to the home are lost.

According to 1820 tax records from Kenton Co., Carneal owned land in Boone, Davies, Gallatin, Hardin, Henderson, Henry, Kenton, Pulaski, and other Kentucky counties. Besides his business dealings in Covington and Cincinnati, Carneal engaged in land-development ventures around Louisville with a brother-in-law, James Breckinridge.

By 1828 Covington was competing with nearby Newport to attract private investments. Carneal offered seven lots he owned in the name of the City of Covington, which he sold for $5 to developers of a cotton factory that became Covington's first large industry. In 1831 Carneal and his wife Sarah sold their residence in Covington, on the south side of Second St. between Scott St. and Madison Ave., and other lots for $6,200 to the developer of the Covington Rolling Mill. Carneal and his family then moved to a new house on Broadway Ave. in Cincinnati.

Anticipating Covington's expansion west along the river in 1830, Carneal purchased 42 acres for $2,000 between the Ohio River and Sixth St. in Covington that joined with Craig's Rd. (now Craig St.) to the west. In 1832 Carneal sold those 42 acres for $8,000 to Samuel Russell of Middletown, Conn. The parcel, which became the Johnston and Russell Subdivision, included Covington's pioneer burying grounds (on Craig St.) and the site of the St. Mary Church, the first Catholic church in Covington (now the U.S. Courthouse on Fifth and Montgomery Sts.). In 1847, after the death of his wife, Carneal moved to Frankfort. While still residing in Frankfort, he became ill during a visit to Cincinnati. He convalesced in the residence of Nicholas Longworth (home today of Cincinnati's Taft Museum) but soon died. He was buried in Cincinnati's Spring Grove Cemetery.

Smith, Allen Webb. *Beginning at "The Point": A Documented History of Northern Kentucky and Environs, the Town of Covington in Particular, 1751–1834*. Park Hills, Ky.: A. W. Smith, 1977.

Spring Grove Cemetery Records, Cincinnati.

Tenkotte, Paul A. "Rival Cities to Suburbs: Covington and Newport, Kentucky, 1790–1890," PhD diss., Univ. of Cincinnati, 1989.

John Boh and Karl Lietzenmayer

CARNEGIE VISUAL AND PERFORMING ARTS CENTER. The Carnegie Visual and Performing Arts Center is located at the southeast corner of Scott Blvd. and Robbins St. in Covington, inside the former home of the **Covington Public Library**. Construction at the site began in 1902, and the library opened on March 16, 1904, occupying the building until January 20, 1974. The Cincinnati architecture firm of Boll & Taylor designed the magnificent Beaux Arts structure. The arts center is named after industrialist-philanthropist Andrew Carnegie, who funded the library. The structure, placed on the Register of Historic Places in 1971, continues to be owned by the City of Covington; it was leased to the Northern Kentucky Arts Council and became an arts center in 1974.

Today the Carnegie Visual and Performing Arts Center has three components: education, galleries, and theater. The building has undergone a complete renovation; various additions were built, beginning in 2001. In 2003 the Eva G. Farris Education Center was added to the rear of the building, and a parking lot was constructed. The center's educational programming includes events for children and hands-on art sessions for adults. Its galleries have some 6,000 square feet of display space and are used for numerous exhibits each year. Its theater strives to be a venue for as many local and traveling performing groups as possible. Many important local meetings are also held in the newly renovated 475-seat theater, thanks to the generous patronage of the Otto M. Budig Jr. Family Foundation. Another restored item is the glass dome in the ceiling.

For almost 13 years, ending in August 1995, Arlene Gibeau was the executive director of the Carnegie Visual and Performing Arts Center. She has been credited with getting the arts center under way. Gibeau was succeeded by Jeff Baum. Mary Anne Wehrend took the reins of leadership beginning in 1999, and she was followed by Nancy Henry Chadwick in 2004. Chadwick resigned in early March 2007. Originally hired in 2004 as development director, Chadwick became the executive director shortly afterward. The center has an annual budget of $1.3 million and a staff of 13. More than 30,000 visitors pass through the center's doors yearly.

Doane, Kathleen. "The Glorious Rebirth of the Carnegie Theater," *Cincinnati Magazine*, April 2006, 92–99.

Martin, Neva. "Gibeau Leaves Carnegie Brimming with Art," *Kenton County Recorder*, August 31, 1995, 1.

Pearce, Sara. "Carnegie Arts Center Director Resigns," *CE*, March 10, 2007, B2.

——. "Restored Glass Dome Wows Carnegie Patrons," *KE*, March 5, 2005, A1.

Perry, Jan. "The Carnegie: A Second Century of Service," *CP*, November 11, 2004, 1C.

Wood, Roy. "Renovation of Arts Center Will Begin Soon," *KP*, May 30, 2001, 2K.

CAROTHERS, ROBERT (b. August 17, 1864, District of the Highlands [Fort Thomas], Ky.; d. September 23, 1954, Cincinnati, Ohio). The son of Robert Barr and Elizabeth Abbott Carothers, Dr. Robert Carothers received his medical degree from the Ohio Medical College in Cincinnati in 1890 and became a licensed surgeon a year later. In 1891 he served his internship at the Soldiers' Home (now the Veterans Administration Hospital) in Dayton, Ohio. He then set up his medical practice in Newport. In 1900 he moved his office to 409 Broadway in Cincinnati, where it remained for the next 45 years and where he treated patients from both Cincinnati and Northern Kentucky. For a long time, he was on the staff of **Speers Memorial Hospital** in Dayton, Ky. Carothers was married to Clara Cole, and they had three sons and a daughter. After **World War I**, his son Dr. Ralph G. Carothers (also a surgeon) joined his medical practice, and a grandson, Dr. Charles O. Carothers, joined them in 1954. Later, Robert Carothers served as a consultant in orthopedic surgery at the University of Cincinnati College of Medicine. In 1896, during the nationally publicized **Pearl Bryan** murder case, he performed the autopsy on Bryan's headless body and testified in court. A diversion from his high-profile medical practice was his love of circuses. Carothers was known to spend weeks traveling with circus performers. He became a close friend of the owners of several **circuses,** including the Ringling Brothers. His wife died on June 11, 1945; his son Thomas drowned at Lake Walloon, Mich., on July 21, 1947. After a lengthy illness, Robert Carothers died at Good Samaritan Hospital in Cincinnati in 1954, at the age of 90. He and his wife are buried in Evergreen Cemetery in Southgate. In 1956 a new road in South Newport was named in honor of the Carothers family. Robert was a brother of the well-known Newport attorney Thomas P. Carothers.

"Dr. Carothers Succumbs at 90," *KTS*, September 24, 1954, 7.

CAROTHERS, THOMAS PATRICK (b. March 30, 1857, District of the Highlands [Fort Thomas], Ky.; d. May 5, 1924, Newport, Ky.). Attorney, businessman, orator, historian, and politician Thomas Carothers was the son of Robert Barr and Elizabeth Abbott Carothers. Educated first in the public schools of Newport and Cincinnati, he received his law degree from the Cincinnati Law School in 1878. He married Caroline Butler in 1876, and they had two daughters. Caroline was a member of the distinguished Butler family of Carrollton, for whom **General Butler State Resort Park** was named. Carothers served in the Kentucky legislature in 1883 and 1884 as a Democrat. He became city attorney for Newport in 1891 and served through 1895. He died in 1924 at age 67 at his home and was buried in Evergreen Cemetery in Southgate. In 1956 the Carothers family was honored by having a road in South Newport named after them. Thomas was a brother of the well-known Northern Kentucky surgeon Dr. **Robert Carothers**.

Biographical Encyclopedia of Commonwealth of Kentucky. Chicago: John M. Grisham, 1896.

"Col. Carothers Is Dead," *KP*, May 5, 1924, 1.

CARROLL, CHARLES (b. September 1737, Annapolis, Md.; d. November 14, 1832, Elliott City, Md.). Carroll Co., Ky., established on February 9, 1837, was named in honor of Charles Carroll of Carrollton, an estate located in the colony of Maryland. The town of Port William, formerly a part of Gallatin Co., became Carrollton in 1838 when that portion of Gallatin Co. was incorporated into Carroll Co.

Charles Carroll was born into a Catholic family of English and Irish descent. Educated in Europe and in England, he returned to the colonies in 1765. He was aghast at the injustices he witnessed in Colonial America and began to protest by writing articles and debating. He represented Maryland in the Provincial Convention that the colonies established in 1774 and was often called on for other public service. He served on a committee that visited Canada to seek support there in gaining independence for the colonies; he was elected a delegate to the Continental Congress and as such signed the Declaration of Independence on August 2, 1776; he served as a Maryland state senator and was on the committee that settled the boundary between Maryland and Virginia (the **Mason-Dixon Line**); and he served as a U.S. senator from Maryland. Carroll also presided over the dedication ceremonies for the opening of the Baltimore and Ohio Railroad. He married his cousin, Mary Darnell, on June 5, 1768, and the couple had seven children. Charles Carroll died in 1832 at Doughoregan Manor, near Ellicott City, Md.

Biographical Directory of the United States Congress. "Carroll, Charles (of Carrollton)." http://bioguide.congress.gov.

Maryland State Archives. "Charles Carroll." http://query.mdarchives.state.md.us/.

Wexler, Robert I., ed. *Chronology and Documentary Handbook of the State of Kentucky*. Dobbs Ferry, N.Y.: Oceana Publications, 1978.

Paul John Schewene

CARROLL CROPPER BRIDGE. Named for the longtime former Boone Co. judge **Carroll L. Cropper**, this continuous-span arch, a four-lane interstate bridge, was completed in late 1977. It carries I-275, the expressway that circles Cincinnati and Northern Kentucky, across the Ohio River on the west, connecting the Greendale, Ind., area with Boone Co., Ky. (see **Expressways**). The bridge is 10 miles downstream from the **Anderson Ferry**, 20 miles downstream from Cincinnati, and 40 miles upriver from the **Markland Dam** Bridge. The second of the four interstate bridges across the Ohio River to be finished in Northern Kentucky, it has improved access to the **Cincinnati/Northern Kentucky International Airport** from southeastern Indiana and the western parts of Hamilton Co., Ohio., while providing a northwest-southeast bypass around metropolitan Cincinnati.

In 1970 the Nashville Bridge Company was awarded a $9.6 million contract for 11 dry-land piers (part of the project). However, because of construction delays on the Indiana side of the river, the bridge was not completed and ready to be dedicated until December 6, 1977; but there were problems even then, as a snowstorm closed the bridge before it could be opened, so its dedication ceremony was moved to the River Queen Restaurant at the Cincinnati/Northern Kentucky International Airport. Since that time, although this bridge has been a somewhat removed and silent link, it constitutes a very important part of the interstate system in Northern Kentucky. Carroll C. Cropper, who served as Boone Co. judge from the 1940s into the 1960s, died in 1976, before the bridge named for him was completed.

Cincinnati-Transit.net. "Carroll C. Cropper Bridge." www.cincinnati-transit.net (accessed October 31, 2006).

Hicks, Jack. "Name the Bridge," *KP*, May 18, 1999, 8K.

Reis, Jim. "Gold and Silver Anniversaries," *KP*, May 24, 1993, 4K.

CARROLL CHIMES BELL TOWER. Dedicated on September 8, 1979, the Carroll Chimes Bell Tower, located in the **Main Strasse** village area of Covington, was erected for the cultural benefit and enjoyment of the people of the region, in honor of Governor Julian M. Carroll (1975–1979). The large, red-brick structure was designed to be the feature attraction of the new Main Strasse area, a German-style village of shops and eateries. Near the top of the tower are 43 bells, ranging in weight from 20 to 1,000 pounds, which play a variety of short melodies that begin every 15 minutes. Another feature is a mechanical puppet show added in 1980. Based on the famous German tale "The Pied Piper of Hamelin," this tower's version of the story is portrayed by various mechanical figures, including the piper, the mayor, weeping women, nine children, and nine rats. In fall 1995, a lightning strike halted the piper and silenced his music for nearly two years. At a cost of just over $30,000, the Verdin Company of Cincinnati repaired the metal marionettes, which were rededicated in August 1997. In 2004 the mechanism once again stopped working because of mechanical problems. A $245,000 renovation was completed and the chimes were rededicated in September 2007.

"Chiming In," *KP*, May 4, 1995, 1.

"Going Up," *Col. Covington's Chronicle*, June 1978, 5.

"Main Strasse Pipers Still Silent," *KP*, November 4, 1996, 2K.

"Main Strasse Schedule of Events," *Col. Covington's Chronicle*, September 1979, 12.

"The Tale of the Tower," *KP*, April 10, 1997, 6K.

Robert D. Webster

CARROLL CO. Carroll Co., with an area of 130 square miles, was established in 1838 as the 87th Kentucky county; it was formed from sections of Gallatin, Trimble, and Henry counties. **Christopher Gist** and **James McBride** were the first explorers to come to this area of Kentucky. Carroll Co. is named for **Charles Carroll** of Maryland, the last surviving signer of the Declaration of Independence. Carrollton, the county seat, is situated along the Ohio River at the mouth of the Kentucky River, midway between Louisville and Cincinnati. Established in 1794, the town was originally named Port William when it was part of Gallatin Co. During the days of settlement, the Kentucky and Ohio rivers were routes of commerce for this small community. Gen. Charles Scott built a fortified blockhouse in the vicinity for defense against American Indians in 1789. There have been four courthouses in the history of the area, built in 1798 and 1808 at Port William in Gallatin Co. and in 1840 and 1884 at Carrollton in Carroll Co. River trade on both the Kentucky River and the Ohio River continued to nourish the growth of Carroll Co. well into the 19th century. The *Hattie Brown*, the *Island Queen*, the *Carrollton*, the *Kentucky*, the *Delta Queen*, and the *Belle of Louisville* were among the commercial and passenger boats familiar to the citizens of Carroll Co. Ferryboats (see **Ferries**) included the *Leon*, the *Mary Jo*, the *Ohio*, and the *Martha A. Graham*. A pictorial exhibit of these and other riverboats and ferries can be seen, along with early pictures of Carroll Co., at the Two Rivers Restaurant in the **General Butler State Resort Park**.

U.S. 42 in the northern part of Carroll Co. passes through Ghent and the historic portion of Carrollton, following along the Ohio River. Lock No. 1 on the Kentucky River in Carroll Co., four miles above the river's mouth, was completed in 1844. The lock was partially destroyed and disabled by Confederate guerrillas on August 29, 1864, during the **Civil War**, but was repaired and continues in operation. The fertile farmland known as the Ohio River Valley has a rich agricultural history that led to the growth of Carroll Co. The quantity of tobacco produced in the county, for a time, helped to make Carroll Co. the third-largest Burley tobacco market in the world.

In 1867 the **Louisville, Cincinnati, and Lexington Railroad**, later the short-line division of the **Louisville and Nashville Railroad** (L&N), was built across the southern part of the county, which included Worthville, originally known as Coonskin. The town was renamed when the railroad was built, to honor Gen. William Worth. The railroad brought prosperity to the farmers and businesses of Carroll Co. by transporting farm produce, tobacco, whiskey, and coal. The **Carrollton and Worthville Railroad** operated a passenger train that ran from Worthville to Carrollton; the train was known by the nicknames "Careworn and Worthless" and "See and Wonder." The railroad currently is used for the industry it serves along the Ohio River.

Located on the west side of the confluence of the Kentucky and Ohio Rivers across from Carrollton is Prestonville, once a successful shipping port, named for Col. William Preston of **Revolutionary War** fame. From Prestonville, flatboats and keelboats shipped merchandise up the Kentucky River. Further upriver was a site of **Underground Railroad** activity, the Hunter's Bottom Locust area, a stretch of nine miles along the Ohio River.

English, established in the 1850s six miles southwest of Carrollton, was named for Capt. James Wharton English. The L&N runs through the middle of English, serving as a shipping point in Carroll Co. and for the surrounding counties, including Trimble and Henry counties.

During the early 1800s, Sanders, located in Carroll Co. 10 miles east-southeast from Carrollton, had two passenger stagecoaches that made two round trips daily, carrying mail and freight to Ghent and, by ferry, on to Vevay, Ind. As the railroad made its way through the heart of Sanders, this community too became known as a resort town and had two thriving hotels.

Originally known as McCool's Creek, the town of Ghent was laid out by Samuel Sanders in 1816, along the Ohio River eight miles above Carrollton. **Lewis Sanders** of Grass Hills received fame as a shorthorn cattle entrepreneur. Ghent is also known as the location of an important meeting on November 1843 that was organized by **George N. Sanders**. A resolution proposing the annexation of Texas, which had become independent of Mexico, was drafted on that occasion and then mailed to prospective candidates for president of the United States, including William O. Butler, Lewis Cass, Henry Clay, James K. Polk, and Martin Van Buren. Polk was the only candidate who replied to Sanders; Polk endorsed the proposition, campaigned on this issue, and won the election. Sanders called another meeting in November 1859 to discuss state's rights. He then went to Frankfort, where the Kentucky legislature was in session, to try to persuade the legislators that it would be in the best interest of the Commonwealth of Kentucky to unite with the South. Carroll Co. was much divided during the Civil War; a skirmish took place on the Craig farm outside of Ghent on the Ohio River, and the soldiers who died there are buried on the farm. **James Tandy Ellis**, poet, columnist, and Kentucky's adjutant general (1914–1919), was known for creating the fictional character Uncle Rambo and for his newspaper column *Tang of the South*.

Carroll Co.'s most prominent citizen is Gen. **William Orlando Butler**, the namesake of General Butler State Resort Park, located just outside of Carrollton. The park features the **Butler-Turpin State Historic House**, which belonged to the illustrious Butler family, known for their exploits in the Revolutionary War, the **War of 1812**, the **Mexican War**, and the Civil War. The park that bears Butler's name offers lodging, a restaurant, camping, fishing, golfing, and other recreational activities and is home to the Carrollton Veterans Memorial. The Butler Family Cemetery is also located inside the park, on the west side near the Butler-Turpin State Historic House. Near Butler Lake is **Camp KYSOC**, a rustic recreational setting for children and adults who have physical and developmental disabilities. A variety of traditional activities, including camping, hiking, swimming, and crafts, in addition to other programs, are offered there throughout the year.

In 2000 the population of Carroll Co. was 10,155; the county's industry base includes Arkema

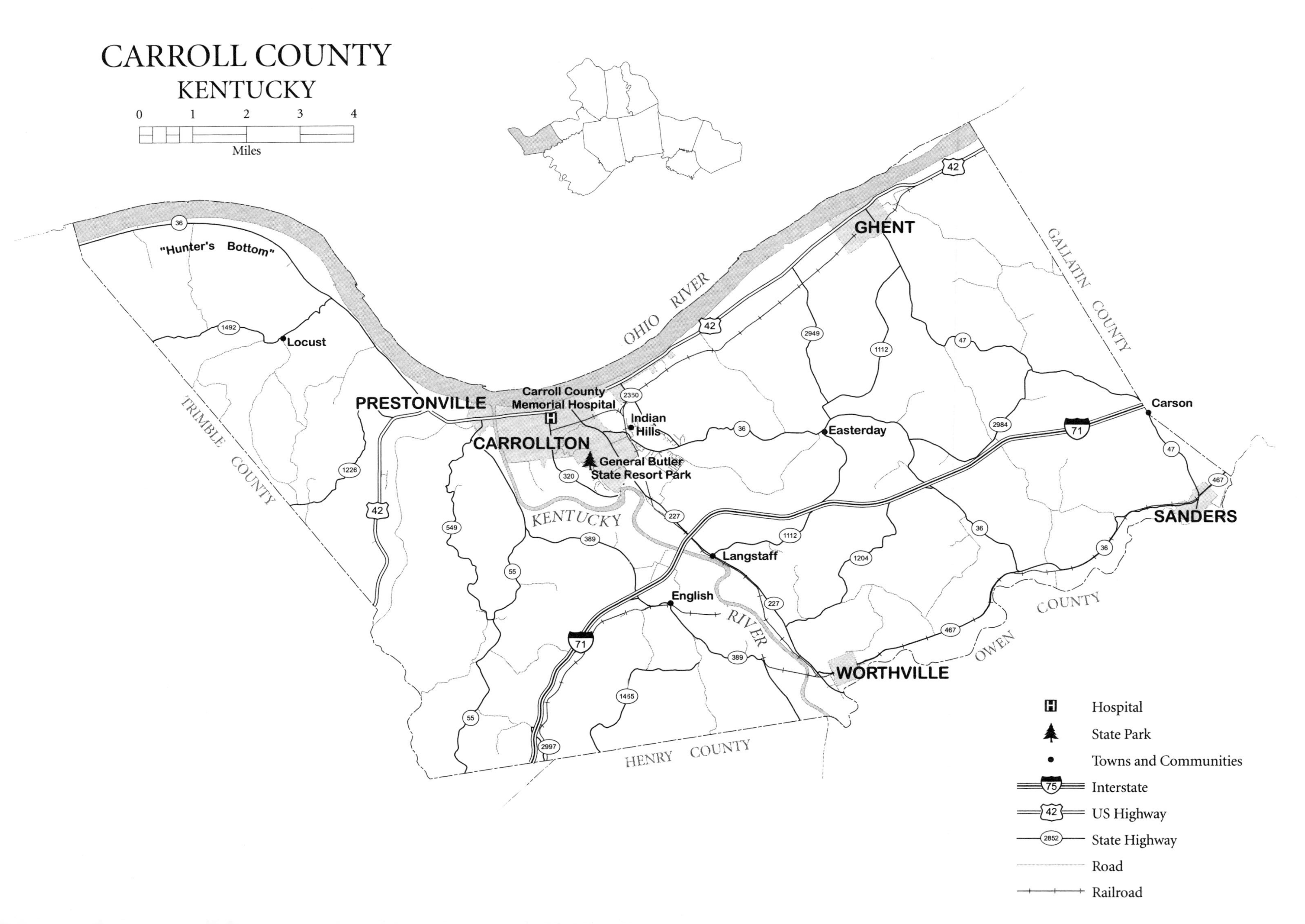

CARROLL COUNTY
KENTUCKY
0 1 2 3 4
Miles
"Hunter's Bottom"
Locust
PRESTONVILLE
Carroll County Memorial Hospital
CARROLLTON
Indian Hills
General Butler State Resort Park
Easterday
Carson
GHENT
OHIO RIVER
GALLATIN COUNTY
TRIMBLE COUNTY
KENTUCKY RIVER
Langstaff
English
SANDERS
WORTHVILLE
OWEN COUNTY
HENRY COUNTY
Hospital
State Park
Towns and Communities
Interstate
US Highway
State Highway
Road
Railroad

Inc., Arvin Meritor, Dow Corning Corporation, Kentucky Utilities, and North American Stainless.

Carroll Co. Deed Books 7, 10, 17.
Collins, Richard H. *History of Kentucky.* Vol. 1. Covington, Ky.: Collins, 1882.
Johnson, Leland R. *The Falls City Engineers: A History of the Louisville District Corps of Engineers United States Army.* Louisville, Ky.: Louisville District, 1984.
National Registry of Historic Places, Carroll Co., State Preservation Office, Frankfort, Ky.
Parker, Anna V. *The Sanders Family of Grass Hills.* Madison, Ind.: Coleman, 1966.
U.S. Census Bureau. "American Fact Finder. Data Set. Census 2000 Summary File 1 (SF1) 100-Percent Data. Custom Table." www.census.gov (accessed July 19, 2006).

Evelyn Welch

CARROLL CO. HIGH SCHOOL. The dedication of the Carroll Co. High School and the Carroll Co. Vocational School on October 12, 1969, culminated years of planning to consolidate city and county high schools and upgrade the quality of educational programs and facilities in Carroll Co. The $2 million educational complex was built on land in Carrollton that had been used as the Carroll Co. Fairgrounds since 1946; the high school is immediately south of the Cartmell Elementary School on U.S. 42. The combined complex of the high school and the vocational school was designed by Louisville architects Luckett & Farley. Rogers Construction of Madison, Ind., served as general contractor for the high school, and Dick Construction of Louisville built the vocational school. Both contractors completed the facilities in time for fall 1969 classes.

The school superintendent in 1969 was Robert B. Ison, and the Carroll Co. High School principal was Palmore Lyles. In its first year, the high school housed 540 high school students and 175 eighth-graders until the next year, when the new Carroll Co. Middle School was completed on the site of the obsolete 1917 **Carrollton High School** building that had been razed. In addition to 28 classrooms and laboratories, the high school contained a sizable central office, a band room, a gym, a library, a cafeteria, and home economics and music rooms, all air conditioned. The outdoor sports facilities included baseball and football fields, a track, and three tennis courts.

The vocational school opened in 1969 under director Don Garner with 191 students from Carroll, Gallatin, Trimble, Oldham, and Owen counties and initially offered commercial, air conditioning, auto mechanics, welding, and woodworking classes. In January 1970 Garner announced a major extension of the vocational school, adult education evening classes. The first set of adult evening programs offered were commercial and trades, with nurses training and blueprint-reading added once the curricula had been approved by the Commonwealth of Kentucky.

The new high school's basketball program was a noteworthy success. In 1972, under Coach T. K. Stone, the Carrollton Panthers reached the state basketball tournament for the first time in 34 years. They posted an 85-55 win over Bullitt Central, and all-state Carrollton High School star David Miller scored 38 points, Greg Schepman 15, Coty Hill 12, Grad Mefford 7, and Dennis Clifton 4. The team then lost to Elizabethtown, 89-68, even though David Miller again scored well.

Although some refurbishing and maintenance has occurred, the 1969 Carroll Co. High School building remains essentially the same facility as when it was built.

Bevarly, R. W. "History of Education in Carroll County," master's thesis, Univ. of Kentucky, 1936.
Campbell, Justine Tandy. "History of the Carroll County Schools," 1976, Carroll Co. Public Library, Carrollton, Ky.
Carrollton News-Democrat, August 21, September 17, 1969.
Gentry, Mary Ann. *A History of Carroll County.* Madison, Ind.: Coleman, 1984.

Diane Perrine Coon

CARROLL CO. MEMORIAL HOSPITAL INC. The Carroll Co. Memorial Hospital, on 11th St. in Carrollton, was built by the county in 1954 as a 54-bed facility and opened in 1955. Like many small rural hospitals, it has experienced financial difficulties. In 1978, the Alliant Management Group of Louisville, a division of the Norton Hospital Group of Louisville, assumed management of the Carroll Co. Memorial Hospital. In 1995, the county created a nonprofit corporation, the Carroll Co. Memorial Hospital Inc., to which the county deeded the assets of the hospital. In turn, the nonprofit entity leased the hospital plant to the Alliant Management Group of Louisville. Afterward, this group not only managed the hospital but also controlled all business transpiring at the hospital. The hospital has been expanded three times, in 1972, in 1990, and in 1995. The Carroll Co. Memorial Hospital Inc. has been forced to compete with the larger hospitals located in Louisville and Northern Kentucky. The local facility has added several new departments and items of equipment in its struggle to keep its beds full. The hospital's occupancy rate in 1983 was 57 percent; by 1988, occupancy had dropped to 26.9 percent. The Norton Hospital Group's involvement helped to stave off a threat that the hospital in Carroll Co. might close, and the Norton group benefited, in turn, since the Carroll Co. operation referred its more difficult cases to Norton's hospital services in Louisville. Today, there are 150 employees at the hospital in Carroll Co. The facility serves the 4,440 residents of Carrollton, along with the 30,000 who reside close by in Carroll, Gallatin, Owen, and Trimble counties. On July 1, 2004, the Carroll Co. Memorial Hospital Inc. ended its relationship with the Norton group, as Associated Healthcare Systems of Brentwood, Tenn., specialists in small rural hospitals, became the new management team at the hospital in Carroll Co.

"Carrollton Hospital Projects Seeks to Boost Occupancy," *KP,* March 26, 1990, 1–2.
"Hospital Operations to Transfer July 1," *Carroll County News-Democrat,* June 2004.
"Rural Hospitals Adapting to Change," *KP,* December 20, 1985, 1K–2K.

CARROLL CO. PUBLIC LIBRARY. Today's successful public library program in Carroll Co. had its beginnings in the Carrollton Woman's Club on Sycamore St. during the late 1940s. Shortly after the clubwomen purchased the building that became their meeting place, using bonds they had bought during World War II to finance the venture, they turned a part of it into a reading room filled with donated books and opened their facility to the public. Volunteers spent weekday afternoons acting as hostesses for users. Mrs. Mary Pearce, a longtime library board member and a past president of the Woman's Club, recalled that some of the early reading-room hostesses were Mrs. John Bond, Velma Cochran, Mrs. Gier, Mrs. Casper Hill, Gen Howe, and Jane Stringfellow.

In July 1952 the Library Commission of Carroll Co., appointed by Judge Luther Fothergill, applied for two grants totaling $5,000 under the Hays-McLain Act of the 1952 Kentucky legislature. According to the grant application, the only library of a public nature in the county was the one owned and operated by the Carrollton Woman's Club; it offered only limited service and had never served the entire county. The Carrollton Woman's Club promised that the club would donate its collection of 347 adult books and 150 children's books to the new library, if the state funds were provided. The club would also make available to the commission a building 30 feet by 60 feet in size for use as a library. Members of the first library commission who submitted this grant were Mary Broberg, Martha Meng, Mr. J. H. Newman, Mary Pearce, and Mrs. H. V. Stewart. In addition to the state grant, the commission would rely upon a yearly appropriation from the Carroll Co. Fiscal Court of $250, with the City of Carrollton making a like appropriation. The grant was approved, and the commission hired Helen Morgan in 1952 to run the library day by day. She stayed with the library for 30 years, retiring in 1982.

Eventually the building on Sycamore St. in Carrollton, the one donated by the Carrollton Woman's Club, began to need more repairs than the club could manage, and the library was moved to the Hodges Building on Main St. In 1974 a move was made to larger quarters, just across the street at 407 Main. At this time the library occupied about 3,000 square feet and operated as a demonstration library on a grant from the Kentucky Department for Libraries and Archives (KDLA). November of 1975 was the turning point for the Carroll Co. Public Library; the voters approved a tax creating the Carroll Co. Library District. The tax was three cents per $100 of assessed valuation of property. The final vote was 1,302-471 in favor of supporting the county library with tax funds.

The modern history of the library began in September 1981, when the library was moved from Main St. to a well-equipped 6,000-square-foot facility at 136 Court St. in Carrollton. The property was purchased and the new quarters built with the help of a $235,000 grant from the KDLA. Jarrett Boyd was hired as library director in June 1982. The Library Board of Trustees, looking to the future, created a foundation, which in 1994 purchased the adjacent property (about 10,000 square feet) from the Dorothy M. Buckner Remainder Trust for $100,000. Mrs. Buckner subsequently named the foundation as the beneficiary of the trust. In 2005 the foundation set about raising funds for the renovation and expansion of the library. The architectural firm Brandstetter Carroll of Lexington was the successful applicant to draw the plans. The foundation, led by local attorney Ruth Baxter, and the many dedicated library supporters in the county raised $500,000 for the project. Carroll Co. Fiscal Court, under Judge Harold Tomlinson; North American Stainless Steel; and Dow Corning each contributed $100,000. Rural Development, of the U.S. Department of Agriculture, loaned the foundation $1.5 million dollars. The KDLA once again came through with a grant for $64,000 per year for 20 years to assist in repaying the debt. The newly expanded $2 million library opened on July 28, 2007, increasing the space from 6,000 to 13,250 square feet. It includes a community room seating 60, a children's activity room opening into a reading garden, and a local history and genealogy room.

"Books on Wheels," *KP*, July 8, 1977, 4K.
"New Library," *KP*, September 14, 1978, 14K.

Jarrett Boyd

CARROLL CO. PUBLIC SCHOOLS. The first public schools opened in Carroll Co. around 1838, as soon as the state legislature permitted local cities and townships to start three-month schools supported by local property taxes. Before the **Civil War**, schoolhouses had been built in the county at Hunters Bottom in 1846; in Mount Ogburn east of Carrollton in 1850; in Ghent in 1850; in Boneyard in 1850; in White's Run east of the Carrollton-Worthville Turnpike, in Centerville on the New Castle Turnpike, and on the west branch of Mill Creek, in the 1850s; and in Beech Grove north of Liberty Station in 1860.

In 1867 the Kentucky legislature directed each county to appoint a commissioner to establish public school districts. W. B. Gullion and L. B. Wilson set the school boundaries for Carroll Co., and T. J. McElrath was the county's first education commissioner. Thirty-two districts for white children were identified, each to have a one-room school, and five districts for black pupils were created. In addition, the school term was extended to five months and the property tax rate was raised from 5 to 20 cents per 100 dollars. In the next five years, under the leadership of J. J. Orr, one-room schools were opened throughout the county.

In 1891 E. A. Gullion, Carroll Co. school superintendent, submitted the following census report to the state superintendent of public instruction: the county had 2,751 white children in 31 districts, with 1,821 of them enrolled in school; 24 teachers, 9 of them male; 28 frame schools; 3 brick schools; and $5,346 raised in local tax levies. Gullion also reported a census of 318 black children in 5 districts, with 202 children enrolled in school; 5 teachers, 1 of them male; 4 frame schools; 1 brick school; and $24 raised in local tax levies.

In this era children were taught basic grammar, mathematics, geography, and reading in three-to-five-month school terms. In the rural districts, the superintendents faced an uphill struggle over extending the school term from three months (usually January–April) to four or five months, because the children were needed to work on the farms. And it was difficult to get increased tax levies passed to buy slate blackboards, books, and maps. Often the young schoolteachers had up to 60 students in six or eight classes; by 1895, to keep up with the growing enrollments, some of the schoolhouses in the county had been enlarged. To have an outdoor privy was considered modern. Most schoolhouses by the end of the 19th century had a potbellied stove, kept going in cold months by the boys who cut, stacked, and carried the wood.

Encouraged strongly by the Kentucky State Board of Public Instruction, Carroll Co. in 1911–1912 organized a set of high schools at strategic locations. Two-year high schools were established at Locust and English and four-year high schools at Carrollton, under the city school system, and at Worthville, Sanders, and Ghent. In the mid-1930s, the impact of the **Great Depression** led to consolidation of all high school students into Carrollton High School. The addition of the Works Progress Administration wing to this high school in 1936 provided enough room for all county high school students to attend the one facility.

At the turn of the century, there were 25 rural schools in Carroll Co. Many of the schoolhouses had been damaged by floods or fires or simply were poorly constructed. During the 1920s and 1930s, most of these one-room schools were closed and students were transported to five large consolidated schools: Sanders, Ghent, Worthville, Locust, and English. By 1936 all white high school students in the county had been moved to Carrollton High School; African American high school students, however, continued as boarding students at the Lincoln Institute in Shelby Co. until schools were integrated in 1961.

The educational facilities for the county's elementary students were consolidated in 1963, when all students from Sanders, Worthville, English, and Locust, and the seventh and eighth grades from Ghent, were transported to the new U.S. 42 Elementary School, now Cartmell Elementary. The Ninth St. Elementary School, now the Kathryn Winn Elementary School, was completed at Carrollton and became the second new consolidated elementary school in the county. In 1969, while Robert B. Ison was county school superintendent, the new Carroll Co. High School and Vocational Schools were completed in East Carrollton. The middle school was then constructed at the old Seminary St. location and opened for the fall term the next year. Also, plans were under way to build a regional community college at Carrollton (see **Jefferson Community and Technical College, Carrollton Campus**).

Bevarly, R. W. "History of Education in Carroll County," master's thesis, Univ. of Kentucky, 1936.
Campbell, Justine Tandy. "History of the Carroll County Schools," 1976, Carroll Co. Public Library, Carrollton, Ky.
Gentry, Mary Ann. *A History of Carroll County*. Madison, Ind.: Coleman, 1984.
Parker, Anna V. "A Short History of Carroll County," 1958, Carroll Co. Public Library, Carrollton, Ky.

Diane Perrine Coon

CARROLLTON. Carrollton, the county seat of Carroll Co., is located at the confluence of the Kentucky and Ohio rivers, on Ky. Rt. 227 and U.S. 42, off exit 44 of I-71. The town's name was changed from Port William to Carrollton in 1838, honoring **Charles Carroll** of Maryland, the last surviving signer of the Declaration of Independence, whose Maryland estate likewise was named Carrollton. Before 1838, when Carroll Co. was formed from parts of Gallatin, Henry, and Trimble counties, Carrollton was known as Port William and was the county seat of Gallatin Co. Because of Carrollton's location, it was a community known for river commerce during the early 1800s. Picturesque

Downtown Carrollton, mid-20th century.

scenes of large boats on the Kentucky and Ohio rivers were commonplace. The town's early years as Port William brought political leaders, educators, lawyers, tradesmen, farmers, doctors, and inventors who helped the town prosper.

Carrollton's most prominent citizen, Gen. **William Orlando Butler**, was known for his service in the **War of 1812** and the **Mexican War**. The first newspaper in Carrollton was the *Carrollton Eagle,* published in 1848. During the Civil War, on September 6, 1863, Confederate renegades and three local citizens robbed the Southern Bank of Kentucky at Carrollton, and the Union Army Cavalry pursuing them used the First Presbyterian Church in town as a horse stable. Confederate soldiers took from the home of General Butler a gold sword that had been presented to him for service in the Mexican War by President James K. Polk (1845–1849). When Butler returned home and learned that his sword had been stolen, he mounted a horse, caught up with the Confederate soldiers, and retrieved the sword.

The railroads came to the area around Carrollton during the 1860s, causing a decline in river traffic; however, Carrollton's agricultural production was on the rise, especially burley **tobacco**. At one time, Carrollton was ranked as the third-largest burley sales center in the world. John Howe, owner of the Carrollton Woolen Mills and the **Carrollton Furniture Manufacturing Company**, made good use of the railroads to ship products outside the county. Howe Furniture Company is remembered for furnishing a bedroom at the White House during the second administration of Grover Cleveland (1893–1897).

Storefronts and houses in the historic district of Carrollton still display the Federal, Georgian, Greek Revival, and Italianate architectural styles of the 19th century. Some of the finest buildings in that district include the 1870s Italianate Seppenfeld Butcher's building on Main St. and the Art & George Leep's Pioneer Grocery Store, built in 1882, whose original ironwork is intact. The three-story Carrollton Post Office, a masonry structure of Neoclassical Revival style built in 1901, is one of the town's most prominent buildings. The earliest courthouse in the community was built when Carrollton was Port William; the present courthouse, a two-story brick building built in an eclectic style, was erected in 1884. The National Register of Historic Places lists Carrollton as having 334 buildings, covering 920 acres.

The **flood of 1937** devastated Carrollton, the water level in town reaching 79.9 feet. A plaque in the courthouse marks the height of these floodwaters. It is recorded that small boats could be rowed through the open doors of the courthouse.

Although Carrollton today is view somewhat as an industrial community, it still retains its small-town lifestyle. The town is attracting commuter residents because of its proximity to two major cities: it is 46 miles north of Louisville and 50 miles south of Cincinnati. The population of the fourth-class city of Carrollton in 2000 was 3,846. During a visit in 2004, hosted by Ann Deatherage, Carrollton's first woman mayor, First Lady Laura Bush declared Carrollton a Preserve America Community.

Carroll Co. Deed Books 1, 2, 3, 7, 17.

Collins, Richard H. *History of Kentucky.* Vol. 1. Covington, Ky.: Collins, 1882.

National Register of Historic Places, Carroll Co., State Preservation Office, Frankfort, Ky.

U.S. Census Bureau. "American Fact Finder. Data Set. Census 2000 Summary File 1 (SF1) 100-Percent Data. Custom Table." www.census.gov (accessed July 15, 2006).

Evelyn Welch

CARROLLTON AND WORTHVILLE RAILROAD. When the city of Carrollton developed at the confluence of the Kentucky River and the Ohio River, the city's commercial activity depended upon the use of river steam packets to move goods. In 1869 the **Louisville, Cincinnati, and Lexington Railroad** (LC&L) built a rail line from Louisville to Newport (and eventually Cincinnati) that passed through Carroll Co. The LC&L, instead of following the Ohio River floodplain, built inland and south of the river; its approach to the Kentucky River was thus via Eagle Creek from the east and Mill Creek from the west. The result was that the tracks of the LC&L bypassed Carrollton some eight miles to the south, and the only connection to this rail line from Carrollton was by wagon road to the LC&L's refueling point at Worthville.

At the beginning of the 20th century, packet boat service on the Ohio and Kentucky rivers was in decline. Railroads claimed most of the freight and passenger service formally moved by riverboats. Carrollton, with its river connections, was in jeopardy, and therefore its leaders moved to build a railroad connection from their city to the former LC&L, then the **Louisville and Nashville** (L&N) track at Worthville (the L&N acquired the bankrupt LC&L in 1881).

Construction of the Carrollton and Worthville Railroad (C&W) began in 1906, with the L&N as the principal holder of the bonds sold to finance construction. The line "as built" was 10 miles long and used 58-pound rail. The road ran from Fourth and Polk Sts. in Carrollton to Worthville via bridges over White Run and Goose creeks. Amazingly, for a line built through the hilly Kentucky River valley, it had a ruling grade of 2 percent. The only passenger depots on the line were at Carrollton and Worthville. Passenger service on the C&W continued until 1926, and in its last years this service was operated with a gasoline-powered rail motorcar. This motorcar, two engines, one passenger car, one combination car, and some maintenance equipment were apparently the only rolling stock ever owned by the C&W.

The C&W failed to generate the revenue expected by its backers, and money for track maintenance and retirement of the road's bonds was not forthcoming. By 1920 the C&W's customers teasingly referred to it as the "Careworn & Worthless." The C&W went into receivership in 1926 and in 1930 was sold at a foreclosure sale to the L&N. The C&W was then reorganized by the L&N as a new corporation, the Carrollton Railroad (CARR), which was maintained as a separate corporation by the L&N. CARR employees did not enjoy the same benefits as employees of the L&N.

Under direct L&N control, the CARR track was rebuilt with 100-pound rail, and new locomotive power was provided under lease from the L&N. The length of the line in L&N service was reported as 8.8 miles. Freight service was supplied by the CARR to the Nugent Sand Company, the Carrollton Furniture Manufacturing Company, the Carrollton Canning Company, the George T. Stagg Distillery, and several other industries and tobacco warehouses. CARR operated under steam power, using leased L&N power, until January 28, 1957, when locomotive number 1882 returned to the L&N DeCoursey Yard. This was the last L&N steam engine to operate over L&N track. Since then, CARR has used diesel power leased from the L&N and from **CSX**. In 1982 the L&N merged with the **Seaboard Coast Line** to form the Seaboard System Railroad. In 1986 the Seaboard System was merged into CSX Transportation. CARR continues to operate as a separate corporation with its own work agreements and employees.

During the 1960s and 1970s, the industrial base of Carrollton and Carroll Co. changed; old industries closed and new ones opened on the outskirts of Carrollton. The result has been that the CARR track was extended eastward to Dow Corning in 1964, to Kentucky Utilities in 1971, and to Queen Coal in 1976. The track within the city of Carrollton was taken up in 1994. In 2004 the length of the CARR was 15.3 miles of company-owned track. The railroad operates over additional private rights-of-way of the industries it serves.

Herr, Kincaid A. *The Louisville & Nashville Railroad.* 1943. Reprint, Lexington: Univ. Press of Kentucky, 2000.

Lewis, Edward A. *American Short Line Railway Guide.* Strasburg, Pa.: Baggage Car, 1957; 4th ed., Waukesha, Wis.: Kalmbach Books, 1991.

Charles H. Bogart

CARROLLTON BUS CRASH. After working a double shift at a chemical plant on May 14, 1988, a 35-year-old factory worker, Larry Wayne Mahoney, stopped by Tubby's Tavern on the outskirts of Carrollton and had a beer. Then he drove to a friend's house and shared a dinner of pizza and beers. At his next stop, he drank more beers with friends, and one friend took his truck keys away from him. Later that night the friend gave Larry his keys back—after Mahoney promised to drive straight to his home, a short distance away in rural Owen Co. On the seat beside him in his small pickup truck was a cold pack of beer. Mahoney was observed driving erratically on I-71 north near English, a small town in Carroll Co. Soon afterward, he crossed the highway and drove at high speed the wrong way in the southbound lane. He hit an automobile and then collided with a school bus full of children accompanied by adult chaperones. The school bus was returning to Radcliff, Ky., after a day's outing at the King's Island Amusement Park, near Cincinnati. The bus's gas tank exploded and its occupants were trapped inside the burning bus. That night, 27 died, 24 of them children. Another 34 passengers were injured; 6 passengers escaped with no injuries. Mahoney survived but suffered knee and lung injuries.

Trooper Sonny Cease, of the Kentucky State Police, Post No. 5, LaGrange, responded to the accident call and immediately summoned more help. State and local police, fire departments, and ambulances responded to the accident. The injured and the dead were taken to the National Guard Armory on Ky. Rt. 227, near Tubby's Tavern. From there the injured were transported to hospitals. A temporary morgue was set up in the armory. Kentucky governor Wallace Wilkinson (1987–1991) called Carroll Co. coroner James Dunn and promised to provide him with whatever support he needed. One of Dunn's first requests was for air conditioners, since the armory was not air-conditioned. Clerks from the Kentucky Department of Vital Statistics in Frankfort were sent to help Dunn with the massive amounts of documentation, including death certificates.

The general manager of the nearby Holiday Inn, Lila Shelton, received an early-morning call concerning the accident and drove to the Inn to set up facilities for the **American Red Cross,** whose job it was to inform parents of their children's deaths. Coroners and emergency workers from all over Kentucky came to help. Members of various communications media were cordoned off in the motel's parking lot in order to allow victims' families and disaster workers easier access to the motel.

On May 16, 1988, Carroll Co. District Court judge Stanley M. Billingsley issued an arrest warrant for Larry Mahoney. The warrant allowed sufficient time for Mahoney to recover from his injuries before appearing in court, and it denied bail because of the 27 counts of manslaughter listed in the complaint. The court case of *Commonwealth of Kentucky v. Larry Mahoney* began in 1989, with Judge Charles Satterwhite presiding, and lasted many months. Mahoney was convicted of a long list of crimes, the harshest of which were 27 counts of second-degree manslaughter. Although his sentence was for 16 years, he served less than 11, earning nearly 6 years off for good behavior. Mahoney was considered a model prisoner.

In financial terms, the high cost of the trial strained the resources of Carroll Co. The toll the bus crash took in terms of human life and suffering, though it may have been figured up using insurance actuarial tables, was beyond calculation.

As a result of the accident, and the subsequent trial disclosures, the National Transportation Safety Board called for changes in Driving under the Influence (DUI) laws and asked for the number of school bus safety exits to be increased, along with other specified engineering changes in the buses. Efforts were made to retire school buses manufactured before 1977 after these vehicles were found to have defects similar to those found in the school bus involved in the Carrollton bus crash.

Crowley, Patrick. "Drunken Driver Lives in Obscurity," *KE*, May 14, 2003, 1.

Dunn, James. Interview by Karen F. Claiborne, May 5, 2004, Carrollton, Ky.

Dunn, James, Carroll Co. coroner. Archives of the Carrollton Bus Crash, May 1988, Coroner's Office, Carrollton, Ky.

National Transportation Safety Board Publications. "Highway Accident Report." www.ntsb.gov/publictn/1989/HAR8901.htm.

The Pulitzer Prize Winners, 1989. "Journalism: General News Reporting." www.pulitzer.org/cyear/1989w.html.

Shelton, Lila. Interviews by Karen F. Claiborne, October 30, 2004; June 21, 2005, Carrollton, Ky.

Karen Claiborne

CARROLLTON CHRISTIAN CHURCH. The Carrollton Christian Church began shortly after the followers of Alexander Campbell and those of Barton Stone merged their movements at Lexington in 1841 and founded the Christian Church (Disciples of Christ). Carrollton Christian was one of several house churches that joined the Reform movement in Carroll and Gallatin counties. The others were at White's Run (1825), New Liberty (1833), Warsaw (1836), and Ghent (1837). Three letters appearing in the *Millennial Harbinger* in 1850 provide evidence of a lively and growing congregation at Carrollton.

The first services were held at the homes of Robert Darling and Amelia Lampson Salyers. As the congregation grew, it met at the courthouse in Carrollton. In February 1855 trustees Allen Hanks, J. T. Guthrie, and O. W. Coburn signed a deed for lot 198 on the west side of Fifth St. Mary Corn, Daisy Rankin, and Kathryn Fothergill took up the shovels and broke ground for the first church building, which was completed in 1870. It consisted of one room and a gallery.

There were several early preachers, but Joseph Taylor was the first permanent resident pastor; he came in 1879 and moved to Carrollton in 1881. Among the many subsequent preachers were H. V. Elliott, "the boy preacher"; Charles Trout, "the hand shaking preacher"; George Nutter, "the nervous preacher"; George Anderson, "the Englishman"; W. J. Loos, "the encyclopedia preacher"; and Lawrence Williams, "the determined preacher."

The current church building, at 310 Fifth St. in Carrollton, has been renovated over the years. Between 1902 and 1906, stained glass windows were added to the sanctuary and a baptistery was completed. Sunday School rooms and the bell tower were added between 1915 and 1917. In 1950 an addition with Sunday School rooms, a fellowship hall, and restrooms brought much-needed space, and in 1967 a sanctuary redecoration included the addition of colonial-style pews.

The Carrollton Christian Church has been active in the development of the local ministerial association, through which pastors provide community-wide worship services and aid to families facing emergencies. During the late 1960s, under Pastor James Hazelrigg, a day school for mentally challenged children was sponsored, and the church's meetinghouse also became an active center for **American Red Cross** Bloodmobile drives. The congregation has had a strong relationship with Transylvania University at Lexington and the Lexington Theological Seminary, an association that has provided the church with several student ministerial interns over the years.

Christian churches were founded in other parts of Carroll and Gallatin counties: in South Fork, 1844; in Sugar Creek, 1863; in Sparta, 1875; in Sanders, 1880; in English, 1892; and in Worthville, 1895.

Bogardus, Carl R., Sr. *The Story of Gallatin County.* Ed. James C. Claypool. Cincinnati: John S. Swift, 2003.

Deed Books 3:116, 9:3329, 11:312, 14:452, 21:205, 23:21, 35:324, Carroll Co., Carrollton, Ky.

Fisher, W. R., and Kathryn Salyers. Untitled manuscript histories, last updated in 2003, Carrollton Christian Church, Carrollton, Ky.

Fortune, Alonzo Willard. *The Disciples in Kentucky,* Lexington: Convention of the Christian Churches of Kentucky, 1932.

Gentry, Mary Ann. *A History of Carroll County.* Madison, Ind.: Coleman, 1984.

Diane Perrine Coon

CARROLLTON FIRST BAPTIST CHURCH. The Cane Run (Port Royal), Corn Creek, Ghent, New Liberty, Sharon (now extinct), and White's Run Baptist churches helped to organize the Carrollton First Baptist Church with 13 founding members at a meeting held in the old Carroll Co. Courthouse on June 30, 1849. On the following day, eight more new members were received into the church. On July 22 there were two baptisms; in addition a black woman named Rose, belonging to Daniel Brown, joined by letter from the **New Liberty Baptist Church**. A lot at the corner of Highland Ave. and Fourth St. in Carrollton was purchased, and in March 1852 the congregation met in their newly constructed church. During 1852 James Eblin and his sisters Malinda and Catherine joined the church. They lived behind the church, and their house came into the possession of the church after they died.

In the 1860s, the question of using music in church services was hotly debated. On February 4, 1866, the church voted not to buy and use a melodeon in the church. In the beginning, blacks and whites worshipped together; but later **African Americans** were asked to secure a separate meeting place. In 1875 the church permitted African Americans to worship in the back room of the basement for six months. On October 23, 1900, the new White's Run Baptist Association was organized in a meeting held at this church. In 1905 the first pipe organ was purchased; it remained in use until 1954. In 1932 the Eblin house was torn down and the three-story Bible School Annex built. In 1937 the church's basement was flooded (see **Flood of 1937**), and for the first time in the history of the church, the doors were closed for several weeks.

In 1940 the interior of the church was redecorated, and in 1946 new chimes were donated and installed. During **World War II**, the church was left unlocked, so that people could come and pray at any time. In 1954 the church built a three-story addition and acquired a new Wicks pipe organ. A garage on Highland and Court Sts. was purchased and torn down in 1963 to provide additional parking space. In 1980 the pews were upholstered and a new steeple added, and in 1989 carillons were presented to the church and installed. In 1989 and 1990, the church sponsored organization of the Prestonville Baptist Mission and also sent volunteer missionaries to Argentina, Canada, Kenya, Maine, and Wisconsin. In 1999 the church built an addition containing an elevator and classrooms.

Carrollton First Baptist Church Centennial Service Booklet. Carrollton, Ky.: Carrollton First Baptist Church, 1949.

Rice, Eloise, and Christopher White. *Carrollton First Baptist Church: 150th Anniversary Booklet*. Carrollton, Ky.: Carrollton First Baptist Church, 1999.

Ken Massey

CARROLLTON FURNITURE MANUFACTURING COMPANY. The Carrollton Furniture Manufacturing Company (CFMC) was established in Carrollton in 1884 and developed into a major business in Carroll Co. In 1886 its owners, H. M. Winslow, Henry Schuerman, and L. H. and W. F. Schuerman, purchased an in-lot in Carrollton from W. B. Winslow and a year later purchased an additional lot from D. K. Vance. By 1900 the CFMC had built and was operating in two large five-story brick buildings connected by elevated causeways; they were located on Fourth St. in Carrollton. The company employed 75 skilled workmen and shipped fine furniture all over the eastern United States. The mortgage on the buildings, held by Kentucky's Louisville Trust Company, was paid in full by 1891.

The CFMC payroll of around $36,000 annually in the early 1900s was one of the highest in the region. Some raw materials were purchased locally, and their freight bill amounted to thousands of dollars yearly. Using a highly successful marketing strategy, the CFMC offered a very narrow product line. For several years their only output was high-class bedroom furniture suites. They won a blue ribbon at the exposition in New Orleans around the turn of the century, and when Grover Cleveland was president (1893–1897), one bedroom at the White House was furnished with furniture made at the Carrollton factory.

The Carrollton-based manufacturer maintained an extensive auxiliary sample room in Grand Rapids, Mich., and was closely connected with the furniture industry of that city. Catalog photographs of bedroom furniture produced at the CFMC, saved by F. G. Hill, superintendent of the furnishing department from 1915 to 1940, were given to the **Carroll Co. Public Library**. One photo of a complete bedroom ensemble carries this description: "'French 18th Century Suite No. 253' Combination Stippled Bone Lacquer with Hand Painted Decorations, Five-Ply Panels, Mahogany Interiors." The set consisted of two beds, a four-drawer highboy, a three-drawer chest with mirror, a ladies' dressing table with mirror, a side table, a straight-backed side chair, and a bench, both of the latter with upholstered seats in a striped material.

In 1947 the CFMC was sold to the Crosley Corporation of Cincinnati and was operated under the name of Avco. John G. Hamburg was named manager of the Carrollton manufacturing plant. For the first 10 years after the Crosley Corporation's purchase, only television cabinets were manufactured, and during that time 1 million cabinets were built. After April 1957 the line expanded to include occasional tables, cabinets, and other wood furniture.

In 1961 the Carrollton Cabinet Company purchased the assets of Avco and a lot on the east side of Fifth St. in Carrollton and two years later expanded its holdings by acquiring the old school property at English, Ky.

Local History Files, Carroll Co. Public Library, Carrollton, Ky.

Parker, Anna V. "A Short History of Carroll County," 1958, Carroll Co. Public Library, Carrollton, Ky.

Diane Perrine Coon

CARROLLTON HIGH SCHOOL. Before 1886 some high-school-level courses were taught at private schools in Carrollton, one as early as 1813 at the Gallatin Academy and another by 1872 at Professor Pritchard's school in the basement of the Carrollton Baptist Church. The first free public high school was completed in 1887. This large two-story Victorian brick schoolhouse stood on Sixth and Polk Sts. and was constructed under the direction of Carrollton Independent School trustees J. V. Blessing, W. A. Fishback, A. F. Kipping, T. J. McElrath, C. D. Salyers, and D. N. Vance. It housed both the high school and the other upper grades. The school began with E. W. Weaver as principal, and it had a 500-book library and a sizable "geographical" or map cabinet. In 1888 the school graduated its first class.

The Carroll Co. and the City of Carrollton school boards were unified in 1911 under Superintendent G. H. Wells, who was followed by W. F. O'Donnell, and plans were made to bring high school students from the English, Ghent, and Locust schools into the Carrollton High School the following fall term. By 1916 the Carrollton High School had 81 students, four full-time teachers, and three part-time teachers. In 1917 a $25,000 bond was issued to erect a new school building that would house all 12 grades at Carrollton High School, to be located on the old Seminary St. property. With the sale of the school district's Sixth St. property, plus prior receipts, the School Board and the Fiscal Court authorized spending a total of $40,000 on the new facilities. The three-story brick building had 16 classrooms, cloakrooms, offices, restrooms, and an auditorium.

During the 1920s, Carrollton High School was graduating about 20 students per year and had a faculty totaling 11 teachers. The Great Depression of the 1930s had a devastating impact on the cost structure of the other smaller rural high school programs in Carroll Co., and by 1939 all of these had been consolidated into the Carrollton High School. Under Superintendent Ted Sanford, a large addition to the Carrollton City School was completed in 1935 by the Works Progress Administration (WPA). The school's new wing housed a cafeteria, 12 classrooms, a laboratory, a library, and a large gymnasium. A fire in 1941 destroyed the gym in the old part of the building, and a new 600-seat auditorium was constructed in its place.

As 12 years of education became the standard during the 1940s and 1950s, graduating classes at Carrollton High School increased in numbers. The 1917 building was used exclusively for high school students. School integration for high school students began at Carrollton High School in the fall of 1961; Shirley Reed, who had boarded for two years at Lincoln Institute in Shelby Co., transferred into Carrollton High School in spring 1963 and became the first African American student to graduate from the school. Carrollton High School's last class, graduating in 1969, had 83 students. All high school students and faculty were then transferred

Carrollton High School.

to the new **Carroll Co. High School** in East Carrollton. The 1917 school building was razed to make room for a new middle school.

Bevarly, R. W. "History of Education in Carroll County," master's thesis, Univ. of Kentucky, 1936.
Campbell, Justine Tandy. "History of the Carroll County Schools," 1976, Carroll Co. Public Library, Carrollton, Ky.
Carrollton News-Democrat, August 25, 1949.
Gentry, Mary Ann. *A History of Carroll County*. Madison, Ind.: Coleman, 1984.
Parker, Anna V. "A Short History of Carroll County," 1958, Carroll Co. Public Library, Carrollton, Ky.

Diane Perrine Coon

CARROLLTON NEWSPAPERS. The *News-Democrat,* a weekly newspaper published at Carrollton, is now the only local newspaper in Carroll Co. Since 1975 the paper, one of 20 in communities surrounding Louisville, has been owned by Landmark Communications Inc., a privately held communications company headquartered in Norfolk, Va. Jeff Moore became publisher of the *News-Democrat* in October 2003; it had a paid circulation of 3,480 as of September 2004. Moore presided over the first move of the newspaper's headquarters in 21 years, from 422 Main St. to 122 Sixth St. in Carrollton in March 2005. In keeping with tradition, the *News-Democrat* remains in the downtown business district of Carrollton, where its offices overlook the Ohio River.

Today's paper is a composite of three newspapers. The oldest one was the *Carrollton Democrat,* which dated its first issue March 25, 1868. It was published by Lemuel R. Harris and Joseph B. Rucker. Harris, the senior partner, was a native of Carroll Co. and was a financial backer, along with W. F. Howe. In October 1868 Harris sold his interest to Capt. Thomas P. McElrath. Rucker remained as junior partner and assistant editor until 1869.

Sometime between 1872 and 1878, the *Carrollton Democrat* changed hands. The new owners were educators, ministers, and local businessmen whose primary activity was not the newspaper business. E. A. Gullion, who became sole proprietor in 1878, published the paper for 20 years. Ernest Carol Smith became publisher-editor in 1903 and remained in that post until 1920. He sold to a group of farmers and businessmen, some of whose names were lost when the newspaper's archives were destroyed in the Ohio River **flood of 1937**. Three members of this group, Perry Gaines, I. O. Harris, and C. M. Dean, managed the *Carrollton Democrat* until its consolidation with the *Carrollton News.*

The *Carrollton News,* begun in 1892, was published by George Somers Lee and T. Sanders. Lee continued to be involved by writing a column long after he relinquished his role as publisher. In 1926 Nellie M. Lee became the first woman editor of a newspaper in Carrollton. By 1930 she and her husband, Jake Lee, had controlling interest in the paper, which was next sold to Mr. and Mrs. Norvin A. Perry. The Perrys also bought the *Carroll Republican* from Oscar Kipping and combined the three newspapers to create the *News-Democrat* in April 1930.

Throughout the remainder of the 20th century, the *News-Democrat* reported on local people, businesses, and economic events shaping the community. The construction of I-71 (see **Expressways**) adversely affected the city, converting its once bustling downtown business center into a sleepy river town bypassed by progress. Weathering consolidations and changes in ownership, the *News-Democrat* has maintained its position as a newspaper that focuses on coverage of local news. The most widely distributed story ever to be reported on and printed by the paper was the tragic **Carrollton Bus Crash**, which occurred in May 1988.

Ford, Joyce. Telephone interview by Karen F. Claiborne, March 29, 2004, LCNI Central Office, Shelbyville, Ky.
"History of News-Democrat and Editors of Paper," *News-Democrat,* October 12, 1967, 1.
Kentucky Combo Network Rate Card. Landmark Community Newspapers, 2005. www.lcni.com.
"Moore Named N-D publisher," *News-Democrat,* October 15, 2003, 3.
"Newspaper Preparing to Move to Sixth Street Location," *News-Democrat,* March 2, 2005, 1.

Karen Claiborne

CARROLLTON UNITED METHODIST CHURCH. The oldest religious gatherings in Carrollton were meetings held in the home of Richard and Sarah Masterson in 1790; the first preacher, Henry Ogburn, settled nearby, and services alternated between the Masterson and the Ogburn homes. In 1799 Ogburn performed the first marriage service conducted in Carrollton when he married Nicholas Lantz and Mary Pickett.

In 1810 the local Methodist congregation built a log cabin and held services there for eight years. A larger building was erected in Carrollton on Sixth St. but was sold as a residence in 1830. In 1842 Joseph Myrick donated land to the Methodist Episcopal Church; it later was used by an African American congregation. In 1870 W. B. Winslow deeded lots 140 and 141 to the Methodist Episcopal Church–South, and the large brick building was completed in 1871 facing High Street (now 310 Highland Ave.).

A Pilcher organ was installed in the sanctuary in 1885, and a major renovation of the sanctuary was completed in 1939, including restoration of the cherry stairways by F. G. Hill. Bishop Darlington spoke at the church's rededication service, which was conducted by Rev. H. L. Moore. On October 16, 1938, members of the Carrollton Methodist Episcopal Church–South gathered at the Milton-Madison bridge over the Ohio River with members of the Methodist Protestant Church and the Methodist Episcopal Church of Madison, Ind., for a daylong celebration of the creation of the United Methodist Church denomination.

In 1943 the sanctuary's high steeple came down in high winds and was never replaced. In 1957 an education building and fellowship hall was added, and a new parsonage was completed in 1961. The congregation remains active today.

Carrollton News Democrat, October 13, 1938, 1.
Gentry, Mary Ann. *A History of Carroll County.* Madison, Ind., 1984.

Diane Perrine Coon

CARTER'S CHAPEL. On October 18, 1861, Lilburn and Sarah Elizabeth Crail deeded land in the northwest corner of Pendleton Co. for the Carter's Chapel Methodist Church. The property was transferred to the church trustees, George Rouse, Richard Simpson, and George Spegal. The church was named after Rev. Carter, its first pastor, and the original log church building was built by George Spegal and Jefferson Oliver. That building was replaced by the present frame structure, built by Arthur Yelton and Doc Golden, in 1901, but the new building was not officially completed and dedicated until the summer of 1902. The rafters of the building were twisted by a storm when the church was under construction and had to be reinforced. Carter's Chapel is just across the county lines of Kenton and Grant counties, on the Fiskburg, Carter's Chapel, and Gardnersville Rds. It is bounded on three sides by a cemetery with graves dating back to the cholera epidemic of the mid-1800s. One tombstone is marked 1854; many inscriptions on other tombstones are no longer legible. Today, only the church and a few houses remain in the community, which was named Carter's Chapel for the church. The road is sometimes referred to as the Carter's Chapel Rd.

Belew, Mildred Boden. *The First 200 Years of Pendleton County.* Falmouth, Ky.: M. B. Belew, n.d. [ca. 1994].

Mildred Belew

CARTERSVILLE. Cartersville is an area within central Grant Co. bounded by Barnes Rd., the Baton Rouge Rd., and U.S. 25 (the **Dixie Highway**). Early on, many members of the Barnes family lived on Barnes Rd., also known as Steammill Rd. The road was also home to the Ridge Meeting House (1791), a tannery (1817), and the Cartersville School, (1856), named for B. N. Carter, a leader in the early county schools. Today, this area is booming with new development. Along Barnes Rd. at the Clay Graveyard, a tombstone notes the arrival of Capt. John Clay in colonial Jamestown in 1613 and also bears the names of descendants of his, including Charles Thomas Clay, who died in 1898.

Conrad, John B., ed. *History of Grant County, Kentucky.* Williamstown, Ky.: Grant Co. Historical Society, 1992.
Pease, Janet K., comp. *Kentucky County Court Records: Grant, Harrison, Pendleton.* Williamstown, Ky.: Grant Co. Historical Society, 1985.
Rutledge, Mike. "Jump Start for Project Saves Bucks," *CE,* April 21, 2005, 1.

CARTHAGE. Carthage, located along the **Washington Trace Rd**. (once a horse path to Washington, Ky.) and the **AA Highway**, is a small rural community in the southeastern part of Campbell Co. It was settled early in Campbell Co.'s history. Carthage had a post office from 1828 to 1907. The local 1883 Lake atlas shows Carthage as having a store, a post office, a blacksmith shop, a Grange hall, and a Methodist church, and the community had a one-room school that closed in 1935. Today, with the opening of the AA Highway, the Carthage area is growing. There are several churches and cemeteries in the community, as well as many new homes. From the homes built on the eastern side of the town, there is a commanding view of the Ohio River Valley below.

An Atlas of Boone, Kenton, and Campbell Counties, Kentucky. Philadelphia: D. J. Lake, 1883.
Campbell Co. Historical Society. *Campbell County, Kentucky, 200 Years, 1794–1994.* Alexandria, Ky.: Campbell Co. Historical Society, 1994.

Kenneth A. Reis

CARTMELL, HARRIET H. (b. April 26, 1921, Maysville, Ky.; d. August 9, 1992, Cincinnati, Ohio). Harriet Cartmell was the daughter of Winn E. and **Rebekah Hechinger Hord**. Her mother was a former mayor of Maysville and the wife of Dr. William Cartmell. Harriet entered politics and, like her mother, ran for mayor of Maysville. She won election in 1986 and served one term, deciding not to run again in 1990 because of injuries she suffered from a 1988 auto accident. As mayor, she was known for always wearing a hat. Her most controversial position was advocating the legalization of marijuana for medicinal purposes. She proposed the sale of marijuana as a means of tax revenue and as a cash crop for Mason Co., which was once a major producer of hemp. Some of Cartmell's accomplishments as mayor were having decorative lights installed on the **Simon Kenton Memorial Bridge** over the Ohio River and bringing in a trolley bus that gave tours of Maysville. She was also instrumental in attracting to Maysville Technotrim, a company that produces plastic seat covers. Her other interests included work with Kentucky Educational Television and the **American Red Cross**. She died at the University of Cincinnati Medical Center in Cincinnati in 1992, after suffering a fall at her Maysville home. She was buried at the Maysville and Mason Co. Cemetery.

DeVroomen, Sacha. "Maysville's Mayor Cartmell Dies at Age 71," *KP*, August 11, 1992, 1K–2K.
Johnson, Omer W. "Former Mayor Left Her Mark on Maysville," *KP*, August 12, 1992, 6A.

Thomas S. Ward

CASSIDY, IRA DIAMOND GERALD (b. November 10, 1879, Covington, Ky.; d. February 12, 1934, Santa Fe, N.Mex.). As a child Cassidy, later a well-known painter, took classes from **Frank Duveneck** at the Institute of Mechanical Arts in Cincinnati. At age 20, the precocious Cassidy was an art director for a New York City lithographer. About that same time, having contracted pneumonia, he moved to Albuquerque, N.Mex., and entered a tuberculosis sanitarium. As his health improved, he began to paint scenes of the American Southwest. Later, he spent time in Denver and in Santa Fe. Perhaps his most famous work is *The Cliff Dwellers of the Southwest.* He married the sculptor Ina Sizer Davis on January 5, 1912. At the Panama Pacific Exposition in San Diego (1915–1916), Cassidy was awarded grand prize and a gold medal for a series of murals in the Indian Arts Building, depicting native American symbols and the cliff dwellers. In 1934, while painting in a temporary studio, he was overcome by a combination of turpentine fumes and carbon monoxide generated by a faulty gas heater. He had been working there on a large mural for the Santa Fe Federal Building. He died shortly thereafter and his funeral was at the Masonic Order Temple (see **Masons**) in Santa Fe, with burial at the Fairview Cemetery in that same city. Ina, his wife, lived until at least 1959.

Fineoldart.com. "Ira Diamond Gerald Cassidy (1879–1934)." Lawrence J. Cantor and Company. www.fineoldart.com/ (accessed January 13, 2006).
"Gerald Cassidy," *Santa Fe New Mexican*, February 13, 1934.
Samuels, Peggy. *Samuels' Encyclopedia of Artists of the American West.* Secaucus, N.J.: Castle, 1985.
William A. Karges Fine Art. "Gerald Cassidy (1879–1934)." http://store.kargesfineartgallery.com/ (accessed January 13, 2006).

CASTO-METCALFE DUEL. Union colonel Leonidas Metcalfe (1819–1868) and Southern sympathizer William T. Casto (ca. 1824–1862), a former mayor of Maysville, became involved in a duel under Kentucky's "code duello" (the printed rules established for the conduct of a duel) on May 8, 1862. The duel occurred near Dover, along the Ohio River, at the border of Mason and Bracken counties.

What precipitated this event was Union brigadier general **William "Bull" Nelson**'s ordering the arrest of William T. Casto, a well-known Maysville lawyer who was termed an "active secessionist," and six others. They were initially sent to Camp Chase, a Union prison in Columbus, Ohio, and later transferred to Fort Lafayette, a federal prison in New York. Each was asked to sign an oath of allegiance to the United States in order to be released. However, Casto refused to sign and remained imprisoned for three months. Edwin M. Stanton, the U.S. secretary of war, then asked that Casto state that he would not render aid or comfort to the enemies of the United States, and Casto soon made this statement.

Some of the Southern sympathizers in Maysville were convinced that Metcalfe, who was the son of Kentucky governor Thomas Metcalfe (1828–1832), was the person responsible for Casto's arrest. When Metcalfe attended a judicial convention in Maysville in May 1862, he was given a note from Casto challenging him to a duel. Although Metcalfe was not under any obligation to duel, he unreservedly accepted the challenge. The terms of the duel stipulated that Casto and Metcalfe would meet at the "fishing shore" near Stony Point Creek in Bracken Co., just downstream from Dover, at 5:00 p.m. on May 8, 1862. The location was sheltered and ideal for the "affair of honor." Casto and Metcalfe traded chilly acknowledgments as their seconds continued to make their preparations. Colt .56 caliber revolving (five-shot cap and ball) rifles were the weapons, loaded in one chamber only as the men took their dueling positions at 60 yards. At the end of the exchange of shots, Casto fell, with the bullet from Metcalfe's rifle lodging near his heart. Metcalfe, who was unscathed, asked his physicians to attend to the stricken Casto. Their heroic labors were not successful, as Casto lived only 15 minutes after being wounded. Metcalfe soon announced that he took Casto's fire before discharging his rifle.

The next day, Casto was buried in the Maysville Cemetery. The funeral was attended by great numbers of relatives and Southern supporters. This Casto-Metcalfe duel caused a deepening rift within the community, and the news of it spread quickly across the state of Kentucky.

Later during the war, Metcalfe was in command at the disastrous battle at Big Hill in Kentucky, where his regiment deserted him. Overcome with disappointment, Metcalfe resigned his commission and settled in Cincinnati, where he was associated with Metcalfe & Evans, commission merchants, at 312 Sycamore St. He died on June 7, 1868, and was buried at Spring Grove Cemetery in Cincinnati.

Coleman, J. Winston, Jr. *The Casto-Metcalfe Duel.* Lexington, Ky.: Winburn Press, 1950.
Metcalfe, William. "Hard Feelings during Civil War Caused Metcalfe-Casto Duel," *Kentucky Explorer* 15, no. 8 (February 2001): 63.

Caroline R. Miller

CATAWBA. Catawba, located along the **Covington and Lexington Railroad** (later the Louisville and Nashville Railroad) and the Licking River, four miles north of Falmouth in north-central Pendleton Co., is an example of a town that once flourished and then faded from existence. It was the arrival of the Covington and Lexington Railroad in 1854, with its connections to both Lexington and Covington, that spawned Catawba's beginnings. On September 22, 1858, the town was organized. Fifty acres were laid out for a town site with streets, a city park, and a public square. A college and a bridge across the Licking River were planned. The bridge would have provided a shorter route to Foster, which then was a steamboat landing on the Ohio River in Bracken Co. From Foster, oxen or horse teams hauled supplies overland to Falmouth and other points. In 1858 Richard Pettit became Catawba's first postmaster. Lots sold quickly: lots 9–12 were sold to James H. Casey for $50; lots 13–16 to J. W. Stevens for the same amount; and lots 57, 58, 70, and 71 to Hiram Thornton for $30. In all, 112 lots were transferred. Catawba soon was thriving. It had homes, a railroad passenger and freight depot, a school, a church, a railroad section with section houses, and many businesses, including a sawmill, a large cooper shop, and numerous stores. By the early 1900s, however, the town had begun to decline. During the 1920s the school closed and the children of the community began attending the Oak Grove School. The last store closed about the same time. The cattle pens, no longer occupied, fell down, the depot disappeared, and the church had only an occasional service. Now this once-thriving small community is a mere memory.

Belew, Mildred Boden. *The First 200 Years of Pendleton County.* Falmouth, Ky.: M. B. Belew, n.d. [ca. 1994].

Mildred Belew

CATHEDRAL BASILICA OF THE ASSUMPTION. The Cathedral Basilica of the Assumption, 1140 Madison Ave., Covington, is the cathedral church of the Roman Catholic Diocese of Covington (see **Roman Catholics**). It is one of Covington's architectural and artistic treasures. Founded as a mission church in 1833 and originally called St. Mary, it is the oldest Catholic congregation in Northern Kentucky. The original church, located on the southeast corner of W. Fifth and Montgomery Sts. in Covington, was dedicated in 1834 by Bishop John Baptist Purcell of Cincinnati, at the request of Bishop Benedict Joseph Flaget of Bardstown, Ky., in whose diocese Covington was then located. Covington's proximity to Cincinnati also occasioned the assignment of Rev. Stephen H. Montgomery, a Dominican priest stationed at the cathedral in Cincinnati, to attend to the needs of Covington's Catholics, both Irish and German. In 1837 the mission church of St. Mary was made a parish, with Rev. Montgomery as the first resident pastor. In 1841, with the establishment of **Mother of God Catholic Church** for Covington's German immigrant population (see **German Americans**), St. Mary turned its attention to the English-speaking Catholics (mainly Irish) of the city (see **Irish Americans**). In the same year, 1841, the Diocese of Bardstown was transferred to the new metropolis of Louisville, and Covington and Northern Kentucky Catholics remained under the Diocese of Louisville until 1847, when the three-mile radius around Cincinnati, including the area south of the Ohio River, was assigned to the Diocese of Cincinnati. In 1848, under the leadership of Rev. **John Lamy** (1814–1888), St. Mary parish purchased part of three lots in Foote's 1st Subdivision of Covington on the north side of E. Eighth St. for the site of a new church. In 1850 the Diocese of Cincinnati was elevated to an Archdiocese, and Lamy bought 10 acres outside the city limits for a Catholic cemetery, within the confines of Covington's later **Devou Park** (sold to the Devou family in 1900; the graves were transferred to **St. Mary Cemetery** in Fort Mitchell). Lamy was subsequently appointed the first bishop of Santa Fe, N.Mex., and in 1852 his successor, Rev. Thomas R. Butler, began the delivery of bricks and materials to the building site. Then, hearing that a new diocese was to be formed in Covington, he temporarily postponed construction. The following year, in 1853, the Diocese of Covington was officially established.

Cathedral Basilica of the Assumption; construction of the west facade, ca. 1909–1910.

Covington's first bishop, George Aloysius Carroll (1803–1868), was familiar with the city. As a Jesuit priest, he had served as president of St. Xavier College (now Xavier University) in Cincinnati before his appointment as bishop. Carroll decided to continue the construction of St. Mary Church and to make it his new cathedral. He laid the cornerstone of the new Gothic Revival style St. Mary Cathedral, built and likely designed by Richard Wasser, in October 1853. By December 1853, the congregation attended their first mass in the structure, which was formally dedicated in June 1854. Measuring 126 feet in length and 66 feet in width, this modest church featured painted windows and ornamental paintings by artist U. C. Tandrop of Cincinnati and a pipe organ by Mathias Schwab of Cincinnati (see **Pipe Organs**). The church served as the cathedral until 1901 and was demolished in March 1904.

When **Camillus Paul Maes** (1846–1915) became bishop of Covington in 1885, he found the old cathedral too small and in need of repair. Having trained in an architect's office in Belgium before becoming a priest, Maes had a profound appreciation for fine art and architecture. He purchased the Delaney and McVeigh properties on Madison Ave., in 1890 and 1893, respectively, and hired Leon Coquard (1860–1923) of Detroit as the architect of his new cathedral. Coquard had designed the magnificent St. Anne Church in Detroit and later was the architect of the Immaculate Conception Cathedral in Denver, Colo. Irish American distillery owners James N. Walsh (1818–1890) (see **Walsh Distillery**) and **Peter O'Shaughnessy** (1843–1926) provided donations of nearly $100,000 for the project, and ground was broken in April 1894. On September 8, 1895, Maes laid the cornerstone of the building. The Covington Stone and Marble Company constructed the walls of brick, facing them with limestone on both the exterior and the interior. The interior columns of Bedford limestone were segmented and connected by metal pins. The Corning Brick and Terra Cotta Company of Utica, N.Y., cast the terra cotta work used in the ceiling vaults, the window tracery, and other ornamental pieces. Built to imitate Europe's great Gothic cathedrals, but scaled down to fit the property and the available finances, the cathedral was nonetheless of impressive size—with an exterior length of 190 feet and exterior widths of 77 feet at the nave and 148 feet at the transepts; the interior ceiling was 81 feet high.

Like European cathedrals, it was situated so that the congregation faced the liturgical east, toward the Holy Land, during services. Coquard's plans for St. Mary Cathedral drew upon the Abbey Church of St. Denis in Paris, France, for its interior inspiration, and upon Reims Cathedral for the proposed front facade. Further funding came from **Ignatius Droege** (1828–1910), who gave $10,000 in 1899. In January 1901 the building was opened for services and dedicated, but it was still incomplete in decoration. Plain glass in the windows temporarily substituted for stained glass, and the simple brick entrance facade was to be replaced when additional funding became available.

The construction of the cathedral's elaborate front elevation was made possible by a substantial donation of government bonds worth $100,800 by Nicholas Walsh (1855–1915), son of James Walsh. Nevertheless, there were still financial constraints, so Coquard scaled back his plans for the facade, choosing the Notre Dame of Paris facade as a pattern instead of the more ornate facade at Reims. In the end, Coquard's somewhat difficult personality probably persuaded Maes to hire **David Davis** (1865–1932) as architect of the entrance facade. Construction on the cathedral began anew in 1908 and included the installation of 82 stained-glass windows, 78 of which were by the Munich, Germany, studios of Mayer and Company. **Carl Brothers** of Covington acted as the contractor and stonemason for this phase, donating the gargoyles and acroteria surmounting the cathedral. Because of unstable soil and mounting costs, the twin bell towers that had been planned were not built. On June 29, 1910, the feast day of St. Paul (Maes's personal patron saint, as well as that the diocese), the new facade was opened in grand style; its opening coincided with the celebration of Maes's silver jubilee as bishop.

The cathedral building adheres closely to the form of Europe's great cathedrals. The nave features the three distinctive levels of arcade, triforium, and clerestory; however, in Covington's cathedral these are interrupted in the transepts to allow placement of a choir loft on the south and one of the world's largest stained-glass windows on the north, the latter measuring 67 feet in height and 24 feet in width. Significant artwork includes four murals in the Blessed Sacrament Chapel by artist **Frank Duveneck** (1848–1919), completed in 1910; a statue of the Madonna and Child, carved in Bedford limestone by artist **Clement Barnhorn** (1857–1935) and placed in a niche between the center doors on the front facade in 1912; a marble altar in the Blessed Sacrament Chapel with a gold tabernacle and surround by Edward Bourdon of Ghent, Belgium, installed in 1913; a bas-relief limestone sculpture of the Assumption of the Blessed Virgin Mary in the tympanum over the central doors of the main entrance by Clement Barnhorn, executed in 1914; 14 mosaic Stations of the Cross, each containing some 70,000 separate pieces, ordered through the Frederick Pustet Company of Cincinnati and executed at the Venice, Italy, studio of the Ellrich Brothers, installed in 1915; marble side altars and statues of Our Lady of Lourdes, St. Joseph, and the Sacred Heart of Jesus, designed and imported by the Frederick Pustet Company and finished in 1921; and a baptistery located in the south transept under the choir loft, designed by H. H. Heisand, an architect of Eaton, Ohio, and built and completed by Carl Brothers in 1934. The cathedral has two **pipe organs**, a 1982 Aultz-Kersting organ in the main (south transept) choir loft, and an 1859 Mathias Schwab tracker organ in the rear (west) choir loft; the 1859 organ was removed from the demolished **St. Joseph Catholic Church** in Covington.

The cathedral has been altered throughout the years. The first massive renovation, 1946–1950, was overseen by architect Edward J. Schulte of Cincinnati and included the construction of a north entrance, as well as substantial changes to the sanctuary. The original white marble altar, which was based upon Coquard's drawings, inspired by the altar of Cologne Cathedral in Germany and executed in Italy, was removed. It was replaced by a verde marble altar and an impressive 69-foot-tall hand-carved Appalachian oak baldachin, surmounted by an oak statue of Mary. Hand-carved oak choir stalls were placed in a semicircle surrounding the baldachin. The baldachin, the choir stalls, the lectern, and other carved works were executed by the internationally renowned Irving and Casson Company of Boston and cost nearly $150,000. In recognition of its artistic significance, the cathedral was designated a Minor Basilica by Pope Pius XII in 1953, the centenary of the diocese.

In 1958 August Schmidt, originally of Cologne, Germany, and later of Hyattsville, Md., completed installation of his ornate hand-carved oak screen surrounding the cathedral's Our Lady of Lourdes altar, and in 1959 he executed the splendid oak surround of the St. Joseph Altar. Also in 1959, Schmidt's hand-carved multiethnic nativity set was completed. In 1971 a hand-carved oak screen for the Sacred Heart Altar was installed; a gift of **Helen Theissen**, it was created by Ferdinando Stuflesser, Ortisei, Italy.

In 2001 the cathedral underwent a massive $4.7 million renovation, overseen by liturgical designer and architect Bill Brown of Colorado Springs, Colo., that included repairs and cleaning, new lighting and sound systems, installation of air conditioning, handicap accessibility, and a new bronze statue and shrine to Our Lady of Guadalupe, executed by sculptor Huberto Maestas of San Luis, Colo. The old marble altar, communion rail, and sanctuary floor were dismantled and elements reincorporated into a new marble altar, baptismal pool, and ambry, all by the Botti Studio of Architectural Arts of Evanston, Ill. The sanctuary floor was lowered 30 inches, and the sanctuary itself was moved to the crossing of the nave with the transepts. The Appalachian oak baldachin was retained, but the hand-carved choir stalls were removed.

St. Mary Church conducted a school for many years. The sacristy of the first church (1834) was used as a school. Throughout the mid-19th century there were separate schools for boys and girls of the parish, and then in 1875 a new school for both male and female students opened on the south side of E. Seventh St., between Scott and Greenup Sts. The Shine (see **Michael T. Shine**) homestead on Madison Ave., across from the cathedral, was purchased in 1910 and retrofitted as a school. In 1915 a beautiful new Collegiate Gothic style school building was dedicated on Madison Ave. It operated through the 1966–1967 academic year, and in autumn 1967 a nongraded elementary school called Bishop Howard, a merger of St. Mary Cathedral School and St. Joseph School, opened at St. Joseph's. The cathedral school building was later home to the Cathedral Child Development Center, operated by the nonprofit organization **Children Inc.**, and, as of 2008, served as an extension of Covington Latin School while its building across the street was undergoing remodeling.

Archives of the Diocese of Covington, Ky., St. Mary Cathedral files, Erlanger, Ky.

"Cathedral School Notes Centennial," *Messenger*, April 8, 1956, 7A.

"The Cathedral's New Parochial School," *Christian Year*, July 18, 1914, 7.

"Celestial City into the Millennium," *Messenger* (suppl.), December 14, 2001.

"Dedication of St. Mary's Cathedral," *CJ*, June 17, 1854, 3.

Deed Book 13, p. 483; Book 14, p. 405, Kenton Co. Courthouse, Independence, Ky.

Deed Book 65, p. 437; Book 81, p. 206, Kenton Co. Courthouse, Covington, Ky.

Durkin, Mary-Cabrini. *St. Mary's Cathedral Basilica of the Assumption: Full of Grace*. Strasbourg, France: Éditions du Signe, 2002.

"Fine Gift: Bishop Maes Gets Ten Thousand Dollars," *KP*, November 18, 1899, 1.

Freiberg, Walter A. *A Guide to the Cathedral*. Covington, Ky.: Messenger, 1947.

"Ground Broken," *KP*, April 18, 1894, 4.

Krebs, Robert T. *The Celestial City: A History of the Cathedral Basilica of the Assumption*. Covington, Ky.: Diocese of Covington, 1991.

Kreimer, Peggy. "New Life: Cathedral Organ Breathes Again," *KP*, October 16, 1982, 1K.

Kroger, John. "History of St. Mary's Cathedral," Archives of the Diocese of Covington, Covington, Ky.

Ryan, Paul E. *History of the Diocese of Covington, Kentucky*. Covington, Ky.: Diocese of Covington, 1954.

"St. Mary's Cathedral, Covington," *Catholic Telegraph and Advocate*, June 17, 1854, 4.

"Silver Anniversary of Bishopric of Rt. Rev. Camillus Maes and Completion of Cathedral Will Be Celebrated Wednesday," *CTS* (Ky. ed.), June 28, 1910, 8.

"Six North Kentucky Schools in Mergers," *Messenger*, March 5, 1967, 1A.

Tenkotte, Paul A., David E. Schroeder, and Thomas S. Ward. *To Be Catholic and American in Northern, Central, and Appalachian Kentucky: The Diocese of Covington, 1853–2003*. Forthcoming.

Withey, Henry F., and Elsie Rathburn Withey. *Biographical Dictionary of American Architects (Deceased)*. Los Angeles: New Age, 1956.

Paul A. Tenkotte

CATHEDRAL BASILICA OF THE ASSUMPTION CHORAL MUSIC. The musicians who worked at the **Cathedral Basilica of the Assumption** in Covington before **World War II**

were rarely included in written accounts. Most newspaper reports of the major events at the cathedral note the name of the bishop or bishops and sometimes the priests present. All describe the physical structure in some way, but the music directors, the organists, the vocal soloists, and the choir singers are not usually mentioned. Perhaps after cathedral parish records are consolidated and organized into archives, some of the forgotten musicians will come to light.

In 1934, one year after the installation of the Wicks **pipe organ** in the south transept, Professor Francis D. Schmidt was already well established as the cathedral's organist and choir director. The choir at that time was exclusively men (tenors and basses) and boys (sopranos and altos), in the European tradition of all-male choirs. The boys were students at the Cathedral Lyceum (the cathedral parish elementary school, located across Madison Ave. from the cathedral) and the **Covington Latin School**. This tradition had its roots in the early view that women should not be allowed in the sanctuary. Schmidt trained many young boys and men in the cathedral choir. In the 1930s there were four or five paid men singers along with volunteer singers. The boys were not paid regularly but sometimes received fees for special occasions. For instance, weddings were often held on Wednesdays, and the boys who sang at those might receive payment. During summers, Schmidt might use his car to pick up several boy singers, who would sing six to eight masses during the day. For that service they would probably be paid. Schmidt was highly regarded by his singers, who in most instances remained devoted to the cathedral choir for many years.

After Schmidt left the post of music director, James "Jim" McKeever replaced him and continued Schmidt's practices; the main role of the choir in those days was singing the parts of the mass, usually set in Gregorian chant. This was the Ordinary of the mass parts of the liturgy, portions of the mass that did not change from week to week, such as the *Kyrie* ("Lord have mercy"), the *Gloria*, the *Credo* ("We believe in one God . . ."), the *Sanctus* and the *Benedictus* (now both part of the "Holy, Holy, Holy, Lord God / Blessed are You . . ."), and the *Agnus Dei* ("Lamb of God"). There were many settings of the Ordinary available in the *Liber Usualis*, or "usual book," which was used at many churches worldwide. The editions of the *Liber* currently used were published mostly in 1956, some in 1923. There are not major distinctions between editions of the *Liber Usualis*, because of the unchanging nature of the Roman Catholic liturgy before the Second Vatican Council (1962–1965). In those days the choir was the sole source of sung music, aside from the presider (the priest or the bishop). Currently, post–Vatican II, the congregation sings many parts of the mass, accompanied solely by organ and choir or in antiphonal response to the choir. McKeever continued a high standard of vocal music and adept organ literature.

Leonard "Leo" Grote became the choir director around the beginning of World War II and remained until 1955. He was already well established as the director at **Mother of God Catholic Church** in Covington and held both positions for many years. He trained and worked with many singers, including noted parishioner Bernard Brungs, as well as several singers who are still regular touring members of the Cathedral Choir. Brungs's accomplishments as an adult spanned music, community service, and historical writing, and the parish founded the Brungs Award in the 1980s for outstanding service in the parish and the Covington community.

Puerto Rican organist Miguel Mullert moved his family to the United States for about 25 years of study and work. He resided in Latonia, east of Church St., while working as organ accompanist under Grote. In the early 1950s, the Mullerts returned to Puerto Rico, but when Miguel observed what he called a "noted decrease in sincerity of devotion" in Puerto Rico, he was sorry he had left the Covington cathedral.

Bishop **William Mulloy** wrote to Msgr. Francis R. Mielech on June 3, 1955, telling of Grote's resignation letter and of the need for a new music director. Names of other fine church musicians were put forth for the job, but a music degree was required, and that alone left some out of the running. The remaining candidates were Omer Westendorf and the organ accompanist, **Robert Schaffer**. The job description at the time included the music duties at the cathedral as well as directing the Mother of God Choral Club and teaching at the **Covington Latin School** (CLS). At this juncture, Bishop Mulloy and his advisers decided that the work at Mother of God and the cathedral should become separate jobs. The responsibilities of each church had grown enough that the director's presence at both could become problematic.

In September 1955, Omer Westendorf (1916–1997) was hired as the new music director for the cathedral, while he remained at his post at St. Bonaventure parish in Cincinnati. Westendorf held a master of music degree from the College of Music in Cincinnati and has since been recognized both for introducing fine music that he brought from Europe after World War II and for the publishing house he founded in 1950, World Library of Sacred Music. The World Library was originally located in Cincinnati on Central Pkwy. in the Mohawk Building. Its well-known *People's Mass Book* was a crucial source of hymnody and of the Ordinary after the Second Vatican Council and is used in innumerable parishes throughout the United States. In 1971 the World Library was purchased by the J. S. Paluch Co. of Franklin Park, Ill., and it continues as World Library Publications. The CLS speech and chant teaching duties, as well as Lyceum teaching, remained part of the job. According to Mielech, Westendorf was "extremely guarded" in fulfilling the CLS speech class requirement. Mielech said, "We concluded that we might be asking for too large a package" to expect an artist in both music and speech. The CLS faculty had seen a direct connection between the technique of effective speech and impressive choral work, which, in the end, was not mastered by most musicians. Accordingly, the ability to teach Gregorian chant was considered to be a more important qualification, and the speech teaching was dropped from the music director's job description.

In September 1958 Westendorf felt compelled to resign the post in order to devote more time to his publishing firm. Bishop Mulloy and Msgr. Mielech approached the former organist, Robert Joseph Schaffer, who had worked with Leo Grote (1949–1951). Having earned the masters of music degree in musicology, Schaffer happily took the position he holds today—with some very important changes to the job description.

Schaffer has overseen many major liturgies at the cathedral, including the ordination or installation of four bishops and the visit of Jozsef Cardinal Mindszenty of Hungary in the 1970s. Gregorian chant is still a regular part of the liturgy (after the Second Vatican Council, the congregation is encouraged to sing along with the choir). Several organists, including Paul Zappa and Mark Schaffer, have worked with Schaffer as accompanists; the current associate organist and choral assistant, Gregory Schaffer, is noted as an accomplished organ improviser. He has regularly made use of the synthesizer and prepared tapes in concerts and main liturgies each year.

In the 1980s, because many Covington residents had moved to the new suburban areas, the number of boys who could participate regularly in the choir diminished. Women replaced the boys' sections of soprano and alto, and that is how the Covington Cathedral Basilica of the Assumption Bishop's Choir remains. Singers have joined the choir who formerly sang at other churches with Grote, and members of his extended family are currently choir members. This choir has made European tours, singing in St. Peter's Basilica (Vatican City), Westminster Cathedral (London), Canterbury Cathedral (Canterbury, England), Notre Dame cathedrals (Paris and Chartres, France), and many other churches in Austria, Belgium, Germany, and Switzerland. The choir also tours in the United States and Canada.

After the 1970 dismantling, moving, maintenance, and reinstallation of the historic Matthias Schwab pipe organ (ca. 1858) from **St. Joseph Catholic Church** in Covington to the cathedral, Schaffer, with his wife Rita as organist, presented a concert at the 1974 rededication of the Schwab organ. The concert alternated between motets sung by the choir in the south transept and solo organ works played on the Schwab organ. The success of the concert, combined with the remembered excitement of standing-room-only concerts in the great cathedrals and churches of Europe during family tours, sparked the idea of a concert series that would be set in the cathedral's notable environment of stained glass windows, pure Gothic architecture, and rare acoustics. The resulting Cathedral Concert Series, with the mission of presenting instrumental and choral music from the rich traditions of Western liturgy and inspired classical music, completed its 31st annual season in 2006–2007.

Many people, Roman Catholics and others, visit the cathedral each year specifically to hear the music at liturgies and concerts. The many singers, organists, and music directors of the Cathedral Basilica of the Assumption have invested innumerable hours for decades to offer excellent, worshipful, and inspiring music.

Brungs, Clifford. Interview by Rebecca Schaffer Wells, Covington, Ky., March 2006.

Business letters of Msgr. Francis Mielech and Bishop William Mulloy, June 1955–September 1958, Archives of the Diocese of Covington, Erlanger, Ky.

"Choir Show to Preview European Tour," *KP*, May 31, 1989, 1KK.

"Plan Concerts," *KP*, April 22, 1931, 2.

Schaffer, Robert J., address upon his 50th anniversary as music director at the Cathedral Basilica of the Assumption, at the Brungs award ceremonies, December 1999.

Schaffer, Robert J. Interviews by Rebecca Schaffer Wells, June 2005, January and March 2006, Covington, Ky.

Schmaedecke, William. Interview by Rebecca Schaffer Wells, March 2006, Covington, Ky.

Timbrel Home Page. "Cathedral Concert Series." http://home.fuse.net/timbrel/ (accessed April 7, 2006).

Rebecca Schaffer Wells

CATHOLIC CHARITIES. In response to the devastating effects of the **Great Depression**, the bishop of Covington, **Francis W. Howard**, created the Diocesan Bureau of Catholic Charities in 1931 and appointed Msgr. Edward Klosterman, spiritual director of the charitable Society of St. Vincent de Paul and pastor of **Mother of God Catholic Church**, to be director of the new bureau. The purpose of the new organization was to coordinate the various diocesan activities that were taking place to assist the needy. Its early emphasis was on meeting the immediate crises facing people who were unemployed and hungry.

Following **World War II**, the Diocesan Bureau of Catholic Charities was reorganized under Bishop **William T. Mulloy** to serve a variety of needs on a more permanent basis. In 1948 the agency assumed a dual purpose as Klosterman remained the overall director and oversaw the continued efforts to give direct assistance to the poor, while **Mary Moser**, a professional social worker, was hired to offer a new service to unwed mothers and to find adoptive homes for children; in this aspect, the agency was primarily a child welfare agency, licensed by the Kentucky State Welfare Department in 1949. Previously, Moser had done social casework for that same department. At this time, the Catholic Charities agency had its quarters above a St. Vincent de Paul store in Covington. Under Moser's leadership, the agency succeeded in finding adoptive homes for nearly 300 children between 1948 and 1959. Klosterman was able to bring Catholic Charities within the funding purview of the United Way Campaign of Cincinnati in 1955.

Catholic Charities made an important advance in the early 1960s. After Bishop Richard H. Ackerman conducted an evaluation of the agency, the Daughters of Charity of St. Vincent de Paul, an order of Catholic nuns, was invited to participate in expanding the agency's services. The sisters who arrived had extensive experience in nursing and social work; as they carried out various new multidisciplinary family services, they adopted a more clinical approach to meeting the needs of the agency's clients. In 1961 the agency's name was changed to Catholic Social Service Bureau.

In 1964 Bishop Ackerman appointed Msgr. Thomas B. Finn as the bureau's director. Under Finn's leadership, the Catholic Social Service Bureau added an emphasis on social justice. The bureau was instrumental in bringing a number of Vietnamese refugees to be expatriated in the Diocese of Covington following the fall of Saigon, Vietnam, in 1975. A bureau branch office in Lexington was established in 1978, and the main Covington office was relocated the following year to the former convent of the Benedictine Sisters at Holy Cross School in Latonia (see **Sisters of St. Benedict**). This building underwent extensive renovation and expansion in 2004. During the short tenure of William H. Mertes as director in the early 1980s, the Catholic Social Services Bureau extended its direct service to the poor by helping to organize and finance the **Welcome House** (a shelter for homeless women and children) and the **Parish Kitchen** in Covington.

Bishop William A. Hughes departed from tradition in 1985 by naming a noncleric as bureau director. Sister Joan M. Boberg, C.D.P., the former provincial superior of the **Sisters of Divine Providence**, began a 20-year term in office that brought a new focus on prevention of child abuse and substance abuse and the formulation of a long-range plan in cooperation with other community groups. In 1993 the agency's name was changed to Catholic Social Services. Catholic Social Services received accreditation from the Council on Accreditation for Services to Families and Children in 1995. William G. Jones was appointed director in 2005. In 2008 the agency returned to the name Catholic Charities.

Archives, Diocese of Covington, Catholic Social Services, Erlanger, Ky.

"Mary Moser Goes Beyond Call of Duty for Others," *KE*, September 22, 1980, A2.

Tenkotte, Paul A., David E. Schroeder, and Thomas S. Ward. *To Be Catholic and American in Northern, Central, and Appalachian Kentucky: The Diocese of Covington, 1853–2003*. Forthcoming.

Thomas S. Ward

CAUTHEN, STEVEN MARK (b. May 1, 1960, Covington, Ky.). International jockey champion Steve Cauthen is the eldest of three sons born to horse owner and trainer Myra Bischoff and horse trainer, breeder, and blacksmith Ronald "Tex" Cauthen. Steve, who grew up on a farm at Walton, Ky., began galloping horses at age 5 and soon decided he would become a jockey. At age 16 he obtained his jockey license and immediately began to ride at Churchill Downs in Louisville. His first ride, in which his mount finished last, was on a horse named King of Swat. Cauthen rode his first winner, Red Pipe (trained by his uncle Tommy Bischoff), on May, 17, 1976, at River Downs Racecourse in Ohio. He ended as River Downs's leading

Steve Cauthen in his jockey silks in England, 1980s.

rider in 1976 with a record-setting 120 wins. Cauthen, a natural athlete, was eager to learn and benefited from the guidance given to him by his father, a knowledgeable and experienced horseman. After River Downs, Steve rode successfully at two tracks in Chicago and then in the Fall Meet of 1976 at Churchill Downs.

Cauthen next moved his tack to New York, where he boarded with friends of his parents. He rode in Aqueduct's Winter Meet of 1976–1977, flying off on weekends to Los Angeles to ride at Santa Anita. In 1977 Cauthen became the first jockey in the world to win $6 million with 299 wins, a new riding record in New York. By then, "Stevie" Cauthen ("The Kid") was the darling of New York's ever-demanding race fans and a media sensation.

When 1977 ended, Steve had been selected *Sports Illustrated*'s Sportsman of the Year and was featured on the magazine's cover. He was named the Eclipse Award winner as the nation's top jockey, was the Associated Press male athlete of the year, and won the Seagram Seven Crowns of Sports Award as the year's top athlete.

In 1978 Cauthen became the youngest jockey to win thoroughbred racing's Triple Crown when he guided his mount Affirmed to three exciting victories. All three races saw Affirmed defeat Calumet Farm's Alydar, and the combined margin of victory in these races was the closest ever in Triple Crown racing. The Belmont, in particular, is remembered as a classic. In the Belmont, Affirmed and Alydar raced heads apart for the final six furlongs (three-quarters of a mile), and about 150 yards from the finish, Cauthen boldly switched his whip and engaged in left-handed whipping for the first time. The maneuver, now recalled as "the whip switch," gave him both fame for his skill as a jockey and the victory.

Difficult and trying times were soon to follow. When Cauthen shifted to riding in California, he lost 110 straight races in 1979, prompting California turf writers to say it was beginning to look like "The

Kid" was just another flash-in-the-pan rider. Cauthen ended the losing streak on a horse named Father Duffy. Soon thereafter, it was announced that Cauthen had accepted from Robert Sangster, the British soccer and horseracing maven, a $l million offer to ride in England. Cauthen commenced his high-profile 14-year riding career in England (1979–1992) by winning his first ride on April 7, 1979. He soon demonstrated that he was up to the many new challenges English racing posed and worked hard to succeed. Cauthen went on to become leading English Jockey three times (1984, 1985, and 1987) and the only jockey to win all five major derbies (the Kentucky, 1978; the Epsom, 1985; the Irish, 1989; the French, 1989; and the Italian, 1991). He is remembered internationally as a gentleman sportsman who captured the imagination of the race fans on both sides of the Atlantic Ocean. Cauthen married Amy Rothfuss from Bellevue, Ky., in 1992 and retired after the 1992 racing season. In August 1994 he was inducted into the Racing Hall of Fame at Saratoga Springs, N.Y. He does public-relations work at **Turfway Park** in Florence, Ky., and lives with his wife and three daughters on their farm Dreamfields at Verona, where he breeds thoroughbreds that he sells or races. He also operates a horse training and boarding facility nearby.

Axthelm, Pete. *The Kid.* New York: Bantam Books, 1978.

Cauthen, Steve. Video interview by James C. Claypool, August 7, 1994.

Northern Kentucky Univ. Archives, Highland Heights, Ky.

James C. Claypool

CAVE JOHNSON HOUSE. The imposing main block of Boone Co.'s northernmost home, the Cave Johnson House, was built in about 1797 by Cave Johnson soon after his arrival in Boone Co. Johnson settled in North Bend Bottoms and became involved in county public affairs. In 1798 he was appointed the first Boone Co. clerk. In 1811 he was named colonel of the militia and justice of the peace. Later, he also served as sheriff. The Cave Johnson House, which is listed in the National Register of Historic Places, incorporates a monumental portico and veranda overlooking the Ohio River. The house is arguably the oldest brick building in the county and is also one of the county's finest examples of Federal period architecture. The Federal style is apparent in the building's Flemish bond brickwork and jack arch openings. The brick slave quarters, dating from about 1800, still stand on the property. It is a story and a half, four-bay building with a standing-seam roof; it was converted to a garage in the 20th century. Originally fronting on the Ohio River, the house was remodeled in the mid-19th century to create a formal entrance facing River Rd. The tree-lined drive was developed in the early 20th century. Johnson's friend William Henry Harrison lived on the opposite shore of the river in North Bend, Ohio, and the two men frequently crossed the river to visit.

BCPL. "Local History and Genealogy." www.bcpl.org/lhg/.

Boone Co. Historic Preservation Review Board. *Historic Structures of Boone County, Kentucky.* Burlington, Ky.: Boone Co. Historic Preservation Review Board, 2002.

"Survey of Historic Sites in Boone County," 1979, Kentucky Heritage Commission, Frankfort, Kentucky.

Gail Chastang

CEDAR GROVE COLLEGE. Cedar Grove College was located in Gratz, in western Owen Co. It was an academy and is generally considered to have been the first graded school in the county. Cedar Gove College appears to have operated during the last 30 years of the 19th century. Land for the school was donated by Knox Brown, with a stipulation that if the property was not used as a school for any period of five years, its ownership would revert to the Brown family. Such an agreement clearly demonstrates how risky private education ventures were at that time. Eventually the property did return to the Brown family, and Cedar Grove College has become only a vague memory in the history of education in Owen Co. Among Cedar Grove's former students was Judge **James W. Cammack Sr.**, the Kentucky state attorney general from 1928 to 1932.

Houchens, Mariam Sidebottom. *History of Owen County: "Sweet Owen."* Louisville, Ky.: Standard, 1976.

CEDAR HILL. Community life in Cedar Hill, Owen Co., has centered on the Cedar Hill Baptist Church, which dates back to 1876. Cedar Hill is three miles south of Owenton along the east side of U.S. 127. One of the early one-room schools of the county, the Kenny School, was located there on Old Monterey Rd. James M. Clark built the largest home in the area at the close of the **Civil War**, not far from the church. Several African American families living close by are descendants of the slaves who worked the farms around Cedar Hill.

An Atlas of Owen County, Kentucky. Philadelphia: Lake, 1883.

Houchens, Mariam Sidebottom. *History of Owen County: "Sweet Owen."* Louisville, Ky.: Standard, 1976.

CEMETERIES, RURAL. Early cemeteries in Northern Kentucky, as elsewhere in the United States, were developed by local churches, communities, or individual families or groups of neighbors. Commercial public and privately owned, and often not-for-profit, cemeteries became more common during the late 19th century. In the 20th century, privately owned for-profit cemeteries and cemeteries owned or operated (or both) by churches were the two major types in the Northern Kentucky region. However, the hundreds of rural cemeteries documented in Northern Kentucky belong to one of three categories: small church cemeteries, family cemeteries, and customary cemeteries.

When the first settlers arrived in Northern Kentucky during the late 18th and early 19th centuries, they had few choices regarding where to bury their deceased loved ones. Few churchyards existed, and no community cemeteries had been established. Most families set up small graveyards on their property. They informally set aside a plot of land but seldom went on to plat the site legally or describe the cemetery in a deed. These became family cemeteries. Children, cousins, in-laws, and other descendants were commonly buried together either chronologically in rows or grouped by relationships. In some cases, the space was shared with neighbors and these became customary cemeteries. If the families involved were slave owners, their slaves were often buried in one section of the small graveyard.

Customary cemeteries are burying grounds used by more than one family. They may be located along a road, near a property boundary, or between two properties. They often began as family cemeteries but expanded through generosity and local custom. Generally, neighbors shared the use and care of the cemetery although the land was owned by one family. These cemeteries are rarely platted or otherwise legally set aside as cemeteries, although some may hold more than 100 interments. Once they fell out of use, they often became abandoned and overgrown.

Some of the forgotten cemeteries found along roads or in the woods of Northern Kentucky belong to long-ago-defunct small churches that closed when their membership dwindled. After dissolution of the associated church, many of these cemeteries were abandoned.

The abandoned cemeteries that belonged to a family, a neighborhood, or a church range in size from a single interment to those that contain more than 100 graves. Many of these cemeteries share at least several of the following common characteristics. Many have some type of fence, wall, or plantings that mark traditional boundaries. Most include some type of domestic vegetation with symbolic meaning, such as evergreens or spring-flowering plants. These may be yucca, evergreen ground cover such as periwinkle, bulb flowers such as daffodil or narcissus, small flowering trees such as dogwood, or especially Eastern red cedar trees. Other large trees including oak, walnut, and other hardwoods were often allowed to grow in or adjacent to the cemetery. The plantings help to set apart the cemetery from the surrounding farmland.

Most of the family and customary cemeteries are located near a fencerow or a property boundary or on marginal areas at the edge of a ridge or a hill slope. They are rarely found in the center of prime agricultural land. Some are situated at the edge of the house yard, usually to the rear or the side of the main house. Church cemeteries are generally near the old location of the church, typically to the side or at the rear, and are usually found closer to a road than many family cemeteries.

Within each cemetery, the graves are organized by one of two main methods. Some cemeteries have parallel rows of graves. The earliest burials may be at the center of the row, or the earliest may begin at one end of the row. In most Northern Kentucky cemeteries, the graves are laid out with the feet toward the east and the head toward the west, so the rows are oriented north-south. Christians of many denominations in the 19th century preferred this orientation in the belief that when Jesus Christ returned on Judgment Day, their bodies would stand up and face him as he arrived in the East.

In other cemeteries, families are grouped into separate sections. Within those sections, the graves are usually organized by row as mentioned above, but spaces are left between the groups to more easily distinguish one family from another. Some church cemeteries were organized into lots, squares of varying size, that contained individual burial plots. Later in the 19th century, many of these family groups had a central family monument with individual names engraved on different sides. Smaller markers indicating "Mother," "Father," or first names were then placed at the head of the individual graves that surrounded the monument.

Formal grave markers, made of marble, sandstone, limestone, or other carved materials, were used in most small cemeteries in Northern Kentucky. Early on they were handmade by local stonemasons, but mass-produced markers were available by late in the 19th century. The local mason had only to engrave the name of the deceased and other relevant information. The style of the formal marker provides information on the deceased's religious beliefs, economic status, and other associations such as the person's Masonic Order (see **Masons**) and other affiliations. Military service was often noted on grave markers.

Formally carved markers are not the only type of grave marker documented in Northern Kentucky cemeteries, however. Rough limestone markers are very common in many local graveyards. They were usually rectangular limestone slabs, sometimes with the shape enhanced by some chipping. These markers served a variety of purposes in local cemeteries. They might mark the grave of a child or other relative when the family could not afford a formal marker. Perhaps relatives intended to come back at a later date and install a formal marker but never did. Sometimes, a rough marker is found with a formal marker next to it, showing that they did return later. In other cases, the rough limestone markers may indicate that the family was too poor to buy a marker at all. This category may include servants, tenants, poor landowners, and, before the end of the **Civil War**, slaves. During those years, many slave owners set aside a portion of their family or customary cemetery as a burial ground for African American slaves. These sections may contain rows of rough markers that delineate their graves. Other small graveyards found along fencerows or on marginal land that contain only rough markers may represent isolated slave or tenant-farmer burials.

Each Northern Kentucky county has a variety of small cemeteries, some well cared for and others hidden in woods and on farms where they have become run down. Boone, Bracken, Mason, and Owen counties have documented at least several hundred each. The other counties have at least several dozen each that have been recorded. Many cemeteries have been lost forever to time or development. Efforts to record cemeteries began with the **Daughters of the American Revolution** (DAR) and with a federal Works Progress Administration program during the **Great Depression** of the 1930s. The DAR first worked to find the graves of **Revolutionary War** soldiers. Along the way they expanded their focus and documented any small graveyard. The WPA program found work for historians and geographers and mapped graveyards that were already hidden and forgotten. Since the 1960s, all Northern Kentucky counties maintain a list of cemeteries at the county library. Local historians and researchers add to these lists when possible. Many cemeteries have been endangered by development; in some such cases, burials have been moved to safety in formal cemeteries, and some others remain in place and are protected.

"Forgotten Cemeteries Need Care," *KE*, July 25, 2004, C3.

"Forgotten Cemetery Conjures Family's Past," *KP*, October 25, 1985, 2B.

"Neighbors Question Cemetery Upkeep," *KP*, October 10, 1986, 4K.

"39 Tombstones and a Lot of Questions," *KP*, April 17, 1995, 1K.

Jeannine Kreinbrink

CENTER FOR GREAT NEIGHBORHOODS OF COVINGTON. The Center for Great Neighborhoods of Covington, formerly known as the Covington Community Center, was founded in 1976 as a neighborhood center serving residents on the west side of Covington. For more than 30 years, the center has helped people improve their lives by improving conditions in Covington's urban neighborhoods. The center was the product of a merger of two small community centers begun in the late 1960s and early 1970s, the Downtown Neighborhood Center, founded by the **Mother of God Catholic Church**, and the Fourth Street Community Center, founded by the **Trinity Episcopal Church**. Volunteers committed to responding to the needs of local residents created both organizations. When, in the 1970s, a consultant hired by the United Way and Community Chest recommended a merger of the two centers to increase their effectiveness, the groups came together to form the Covington Community Center. For its first 25 years, that center was located in a storefront property at 1008 Lee St. in Covington.

Throughout its history, the center has reflected a belief that the Covington community's future depends on identifying and utilizing the strengths of all its members. Initially, services were provided for low-income residents, including emergency assistance, family support, and youth programs, as well as community organizing to address the causes and effects of poverty. Most notably, the organizing efforts resulted in the passage of uniform landlord-tenant laws in some Northern Kentucky cities and in statewide welfare reform, adopted in 1988, that removed provisions in state law penalizing welfare recipients who attempted to work their way off welfare.

Over the years, the center's work evolved to focus on community-based strategies to improve quality of life. Its certification by the United Way as a "Family Resource Center" in 1996 and as a "Neighborhood Support Organization" in 2002 reflected this shift in focus. The center has helped start or has strengthened neighborhood civic organizations in 13 Covington neighborhoods. Its "self-help" community development model, emphasizing leadership development for both youth and adults, supplies residents with the skills and resources needed to improve their neighborhoods.

In 2001 the center moved to a new Covington location at 1650 Russell St. and, soon after, launched a capital campaign to purchase, renovate, and expand the facility. In 2005 the center celebrated the opening of its new community-building campus, as well as the introduction of its new name: the Center for Great Neighborhoods of Covington.

Today the Center for Great Neighborhoods acts as a catalyst for positive community change by bringing people together to resolve some of their city's toughest issues. With the center's assistance, residents have combated crime, developed parks and playgrounds, expanded educational opportunities, removed litter and blight, and built community pride. Some of the center's significant recent initiatives include forming the Covington Neighborhood Collaborative, a citywide network of neighborhood associations; coordinating the annual citywide Great American Clean-up; leading the **Austinburg** Neighborhood Revitalization Initiative, a multiyear collaborative effort bringing together public and private resources to help revitalize the Austinburg neighborhood by decreasing crime, increasing home ownership, and stimulating economic activity; transforming public schools into community learning centers through the Community Schools Initiative, in partnership with the **Covington Independent Schools** and other local organizations; providing leadership development programs that empower at-risk youth with the tools to identify and address important community issues; and proliferating a model of "community-built" public art projects, including several outdoor murals, neighborhood gateway signs, oral history projects, and the award-winning city Millennium Mosaic project. In the latter project, hundreds of residents worked with artists to create five glass-tiled mosaic benches depicting Covington, which were installed at Seventh St. and Madison Ave.

In addition, the Center for Great Neighborhoods has worked to increase home ownership opportunities for families of low and moderate income through the rehabilitation of housing and associated support services. Since 2001 the center has increased its capacity in real estate development. Future plans include both new housing construction and rehabilitation to promote revitalization in targeted neighborhoods. Executive directors of the center have included Jim Schenk (1976–1978), Angela Casanova (1978–1994), and Tom DiBello (1995–present). For its excellence in community building, the Center for Great Neighborhoods has received recognition locally and at the state level, including the Kentucky Department of Education's Community Partnership Award (2000), the Greater Cincinnati Inclusion Network's Community Leadership Award (2001), and the Kentucky Governor's Award for the Arts (2001).

"Center for Great Neighborhoods of Covington." www.greatneighborhoods.org (accessed March 26, 2006).
"Center Sees 20th Year of Empowering People," *KP*, May 13, 1996, 2K.
"Owning Means Helping—Program Provides Chance at Home Buyer," *KE*, February 1, 1995, C3.

Tom DiBello

CENTER FOR OHIO RIVER RESEARCH AND EDUCATION. The center is located at the **Thomas More College** Biology Station, the previous site of U.S. Government Lock and Dam No. 35 along the **Mary Ingles Highway** in eastern Campbell Co. Thomas More College acquired the 25-acre site in 1967 from the federal government and has been using the facility for research and educational purposes. In 1997, through a grant from the James Graham Brown Foundation of Louisville, the field station underwent a major renovation and now includes a state-of-the-art research facility with two laboratories, a museum, and a classroom. In addition there are eight residential structures, a maintenance building, a nature trail, and a fleet of research boats on the site. In 1998 the Center for Ohio River Research and Education was established. The faculty and staff at the center offer students, faculty, and staff of Thomas More College an opportunity to enhance their knowledge of the natural world through field courses, research projects, and outreach programs that focus on the ecology of the Ohio River. The center welcomes students of all ages, from grade school to graduate school, and visitors from the general public. It provides scientific equipment, supplies, and expertise in the areas of aquatic biology. This center functions within the Biology Department at Thomas More College and works to enhance the academic careers of Thomas More College undergraduate students and encourage them to progress toward graduate programs.

Beginning in 1971, and continuing through the present, faculty and students at the field station have conducted research projects in the areas of bioassessments, fisheries, limnology, microbiology, and toxicology. Since the establishment of the Center for Ohio River Research and Education in 1998, the number of course offerings and related outreach programs has increased significantly. Courses are offered in aquatic biology, ichthyology, environmental ethics, and other topics. Day-long field trips for grade schools, weeklong science camps for high schools, and teacher workshops are scheduled at the center. More than 1,000 visitors annually participate in the programs. The center at the field station offers an interactive setting where students become involved in doing science. The Center for Ohio River Research and Education also invites other colleges and universities, as well as regulatory agencies such as the Ohio River Valley Water Sanitation Commission and the U.S. Environmental Protection Agency, to use the facilities for both research and teaching. Hanover College at Madison, Ind., **Northern Kentucky University** at Highland Heights, Ky., and the University of Cincinnati are partners with the Center for Ohio River Research and Education at Thomas More College.

"River Station Open," *KE*, October 16, 1997, B2.
"Students Monitor the Ohio River—Waterway Is a Classroom," *KP*, December 24, 2005, 1K–5K.
"Thomas More Crew Keeps Eye on Habitat in and around Ohio River," *KE*, June 3, 2006, B3.
"Thomas More Joins River Research," *KE*, November 4, 2003, B1–B2.

Chris Lorentz

CENTRAL BRIDGE. Some contemporary observers hailed August 29, 1891, as the most important date in the history of Newport, because it marked the opening of the new Central Railway Bridge, or the Newport-Cincinnati Bridge, better known to generations of locals as the Central Bridge.

Built to carry people on foot, by trolley, and by wagon, the Central Bridge was a vital link in the growing City of Newport's transit system. Although the existing L&N Bridge (for the **Louisville and Nashville Railroad**) included a single streetcar track, most passengers traveled to Cincinnati by first crossing the Fourth Street Bridge to Covington and then completing their trip via the **John A. Roebling Bridge**. Newport boosters clamored for an improved "street railway" that would speed commuters over the Ohio River to Cincinnati on low-fare electric streetcars.

The champion of the new bridge was Captain **John A. Williamson**, a river man who rose from poverty to become a successful business owner. Although he had opposed construction of the L&N Bridge, because he leased the Taylor family's ferry operation in Newport, he later invested in Newport's street railroads, among other enterprises. Williamson and Newport attorney **Robert W. Nelson** became the leaders of the Newport & Cincinnati Bridge Company. After Newport's bankers spurned the bridge venture as too risky, Nelson and Williamson persuaded New York City financiers to invest in the project.

L. F. G. Bouscaren (1840–1904), the chief engineer for the **Cincinnati Southern Railroad**, prepared the preliminary surveys and general layout for the Central Bridge. He had supervised the construction of the first cantilever bridge in the country, the famed "High" Bridge over the Kentucky River at Dixville. The bridge at Dixville was constructed by the King Iron Bridge & Manufacturing Company of Cleveland, Ohio, one of the nation's leading bridge-builders; King also built the Central Bridge. In April 1890 Williamson promised that the bridge in Newport would be finished in two years. During the winter of 1890–1891, work was suspended, for the most part owing to high water, but it was resumed vigorously in the spring. Manmade trouble also came from lawsuits, strikes, and the like. Despite these setbacks, construction took only 16 months. But some Newporters could not wait for the official opening. On August 12, hardware merchant M. M. Ware became the first person to use the bridge by crossing it with a horse and wagon. After delivering a load of nails to the Cincinnati side, he decided to shorten his return trip by taking the new bridge, to the delight of spectators. On August 25, fog grounded the ferry and prevented some workers from reaching their jobs across the river. Ignoring warnings from security guards, they removed barricades and marched across the unfinished span from Newport to Cincinnati free of charge, as a watching crowd cheered.

The Central Bridge's official opening was perhaps the biggest party in Newport's history. The city council declared August 29 a legal holiday. To ensure the proper festive atmosphere, appointed committees supervised the decorating of homes and brought citizens out in large numbers. A 25-foot model of the bridge, crafted of evergreens and flags, hung across York St. in town. The celebration climaxed that night with a great parade and a fireworks display on the riverfront. Over the next few decades, the new bridge, an improved transit network, a pure water system, and attractive new housing in the East End helped make Newport a thriving bedroom community as well as a manufacturing town.

In addition to its historical importance, the Central Bridge was one of Kentucky's pioneering examples of a new bridge type: the cantilever truss. The new bridge consisted of a three-span cantilever "through" (above-deck) truss, two Pennsylvania Petit trusses, a Pratt truss and viaduct, and viaduct and girder approach spans. It was built of Carnegie steel, with some tension members of wrought iron. The foundation piers were Ohio River freestone with Bedford limestone copings. The structure was designed to accommodate two lines of trolley tracks and two sidewalks, as well as the main roadway. It was 2,342 feet long and 18.3 feet wide, arcing in a gentle S curve from bank to bank.

As the proud symbol of Newport, the bridge was also a thing of beauty. Its graceful design, with distinctive curved top chords, was copied widely for long-span bridges for subsequent decades. Like many King-built bridges, it was profusely ornamented. The end spans were decorated with wrought-iron crown finials (a King symbol), lacy filigree work, portal struts, and decorative cutouts. In addition, King's initials were displayed in many places to catch the pedestrian's eye. Upon completion, the Central Bridge reigned briefly as the longest span of its kind in the nation. Eighty years later, it was hailed by a Kentucky historic bridge survey as the state's longest and most decorative highway span, the state's earliest highway cantilever bridge, and one of the nation's longest King bridges.

Motorists continued to pay tolls to cross the Central Bridge until the Kentucky Transportation Cabinet, having purchased it on October 30, 1947, for about $2 million, made it toll-free on August 27, 1953. By the late 20th century, the bridge was in a deteriorated condition and suffering from deferred maintenance, its weight limit reduced to only three tons. Stopgap repairs made in 1983 were designed to add only a few years to its life.

The 101-year-old bridge was imploded in 1992. Because the Central Bridge was determined eligible for listing in the National Register of Historic Places, the Historic American Buildings Survey recorded it for posterity. The Central Bridge's replacement, the **Taylor-Southgate Bridge**, opened to traffic in 1995.

"Across the Ohio," *KJ*, August 29, 1891, 1.
"All the News," *KJ*, August 29, 1891, 3.
"Central Bridge Becomes Free Span as Kentucky Takes Over Suspension," *KP*, August 27, 1953, 1.
Fiegel, Jayne Henderson. "US 27 Central Bridge, Historic American Buildings Survey No. KY-28," Kentucky Heritage Council, Frankfort, Ky.
Purvis, Thomas L., ed. *Newport, Kentucky: A Bicentennial History.* Newport, Ky.: Otto Zimmerman, 1996.
Warminski, Margo. "'Gala Day for Newport': The Grand Opening of the Central Bridge, 1891," *JKS* 3 (1986): 161–68.

Margaret Warminski

CENTRO DE AMISTAD. The Centro de Amistad, Spanish for "Center of Friendship," is a Roman Catholic agency that has served Hispanic immigrants in Boone, Kenton, and Campbell counties with social assistance and classes since 2001 (see **Latinos**). It offers classes in English as a second language, the Spanish language, citizenship, basic education toward obtaining a GED, carpentry, and home buying. The center also serves as a cultural bridge where **Catholic Charities** assists with many social services. Volunteers at the center help with tax preparation, banking services, and job placement. Together with the Area Health Education Center, the Centro de Amistad sponsors a health program in Spanish that guides interested persons toward careers in the health and medical fields. The center's bilingual story time at nearby libraries, readings done by student volunteers from **Northern Kentucky University**, is popular with persons of all ages.

The Centro de Amistad is an outreach program of **Cristo Rey Parish**, the only Spanish-speaking Roman Catholic parish in Northern Kentucky. As a church-sponsored program, Centro de Amistad receives no public or tax money; it is fully funded by grants, donations, the Diocesan Annual Appeal, fundraisers, and an annual festival held the first weekend of June at the Catholic Center in Erlanger. The center's director is Sister Juana Mendez of the Catholic order Sisters of Charity. She was born in Puerto Rico but has lived in the continental United States for more than 40 years; thus she has an understanding of both cultures. She is well known by immigration lawyers and social services throughout Northern Kentucky. The Centro de Amistad is temporarily located at the Diocese of Covington's Catholic Center in Erlanger but will move together with the Cristo Rey parish when a permanent location is found.

Tony Llamas

CHAMBERS, JOHN, MAJOR (b. October 6, 1780, Bromley Bridges, Somerset Co., N.J.; d. September 21, 1852, Paris, Ky.). John Chambers, who became the second territorial governor of Iowa, was one of the 14 children of Col. Rowland Chambers, a **Revolutionary War** veteran. John Chambers was age 14 when he moved with his family to Kentucky. He attended local schools and later enrolled at Transylvania Seminary in Lexington, Ky. After the Chambers family settled in the historic community of Washington in Mason Co., John Chambers worked in a store. He began to study law in Mason Co., and after being admitted to the bar in 1800, he became an attorney and served as deputy court clerk in Mason Co. With the outbreak of the **War of 1812**, John Chambers joined the staff of Gen. William Henry Harrison and later attained the rank of major. Reports say he distinguished himself several times, including at the Battle of Thames in 1813 in Canada, where Kentuckians played key roles in the U.S. victory. Chambers was elected to the Kentucky legislature in 1812 and 1815. He was appointed to the Kentucky Court of Appeals in 1825. In 1828 he was elected to the U.S. Congress; he was reelected in 1835 and served four years.

In those days territorial governors were appointed by the U.S. president, and in 1841 Chambers was selected as the second territorial governor of Iowa. He was appointed by his former military commander, William Henry Harrison. Chambers found politics in Iowa interesting especially because he was a member of the **Whig Party**, while Iowa at the time was heavily Democratic. Nevertheless, Chambers gained much respect when he helped to negotiate a treaty with the Sauk and Fox American Indians, under which the tribes terminated their land claims in Iowa. Chambers was reappointed Iowa governor by President John Tyler (1841–1845), a Whig, in 1844, but he was removed as governor the next year when a Democrat, James Polk (1845–1849), was elected president. In poor health, Chambers remained in Iowa and was called out of retirement in 1849 to help negotiate a treaty with the Sioux Indians in Minnesota. Chambers was married twice and had 12 children. He died in 1852, while visiting a daughter in Paris, Ky., and was buried in Mason Co. at the family cemetery at Washington.

Biographical Directory of the United States Congress, 1774–1989. Washington, D.C.: Government Printing Office, 1985.
Reis, Jim. "Kentuckians Led Territories," *KP*, December 1, 2003, 5K.
———. "They Governed U.S. Territories," *KP*, November 28, 1988, 4K.
———. "Trusted by Presidents—Greatest Fame Came in Iowa Territory for Chambers," *KP*, November 11, 2004, 4K.

Jim Reis

CHAMBERS, ROBERT, HOUSE. See **Robert Chambers House**.

CHAMBERS, VACTOR T. (b. August 6, 1830, Burlington, Ky.; d. August 7, 1883, Covington, Ky.). Lawyer, scientist, and author Vactor Tousey Chambers was the son of Charles Chambers, a wealthy and cultured lawyer. Vactor's mother died when he was 11 years old, and his father endeavored to become both a father and a mother to his son as he raised the boy in Burlington. For his early education, Vactor attended the prestigious **Morgan Academy** in Burlington. He apprenticed law for several years under Judge James Pryor and then attended the Louisville Law School, from which he graduated in 1852. After practicing in Burlington for about two years, Chambers moved to Covington, where he spent the remainder of his life. In 1857 he married Nannie Pryor, daughter of his mentor, Judge Pryor. The couple had three sons, John, James, and Charles. Vactor Chambers entered into a partnership with lawyer **John W. Finnell** but left that partnership after several years and began a partnership with his father-in-law. Although Chambers was an excellent lawyer, he never fully embraced his profession. He loathed courtroom battles between attorneys and often advised his clients to drop their suits or settle out of court rather than face the pain and anguish of a public trial. A voracious reader, especially of scientific material, Chambers developed a consuming passion for the fields of entomology and botany. He was particularly interested in the life cycles of metamorphic insects, such as moths and butterflies, and became one of the world's foremost authorities on the subject. He wrote many articles that appeared in scientific journals and periodicals. He was fond of children and encouraged them to ask questions on any subject, which he patiently answered. Chambers was a member of the Presbyterian Church but was not conspicuous in his religious beliefs. However, he adhered scrupulously to biblical teachings; he wholeheartedly believed in the ethical treatment of his fellow man, showing honor to his parents, and being a considerate husband and father. Friends and acquaintances referred to him as a kind and gentle person, honest and conscientious in his dealings, and one whose word could be implicitly believed. He suffered a cerebral hemorrhage on his 53rd birthday and died early the next morning, in his Stevens St. home. His remains were placed in a vault at the Highland Cemetery in Fort Mitchell.

"Biographical Sketch," *Covington Courier*, August 26, 1904, 1.
"Death of Vactor T. Chambers," *DC*, August 7, 1883, 1.
"The Funeral of the Late Vactor T. Chambers," *DC*, August 10, 1883, 1.
Hall, J. W., Jr. "In Memoriam—Vactor T. Chambers," *Journal of the Cincinnati Society of Natural History* 6, no. 4 (December 1883): 239–44.
"The Late Vactor T. Chambers," *DC*, August 9, 1883, 4.

CHASE COLLEGE OF LAW. On September 13, 1893, the *Cincinnati Commercial Gazette* announced that a night law school had been set up as a branch of the Cincinnati and Hamilton Co. **YMCA**. Seventeen students came to the first class that October, and within weeks 39 students had enrolled. The YMCA, then located at Seventh and Walnut Sts. in Cincinnati, had been active in the field of education; its leaders wanted to help young people develop job skills and improve their financial status by studying in their spare time. The YMCA was able to accomplish this purpose at an affordable cost by enlisting able teachers who taught in their own spare time for little or no salary.

The person who established the YMCA Night Law School, Robert M. Ochiltree, an Indiana native, became its first dean and continued as dean until 1916. During this period, he helped to make part-time legal education a viable educational pathway. His strategy was to use the same curriculum and study materials as full-time day law schools and employ outstanding members of the bench and the bar as instructors. The student body was eager for the opportunity to study law. The first commencement conferred LLB degrees to 65 candidates in June 1900. During the next 50 years, the YMCA Night Law School was able to operate at a profit, upgrade its curriculum, and establish and improve its library's holdings. Alumni of the school gradually gained prestige within the Cincinnati legal community.

In 1943 the school celebrated its 50th anniversary. When the students and faculty proposed changing the school's name, the name chosen was the Salmon P. Chase College of Law, after U.S. Supreme Court justice Salmon P. Chase. Chase was born in Cornish, N.H., on January 13, 1808, graduated from Dartmouth College at Hanover, N.H., in 1826, and was admitted to the bar in 1829. By 1830 Chase had settled in Cincinnati and had begun his political career. In 1849 he was elected to the U.S. Senate from Ohio and became a prominent speaker against the extension of slavery in the territories. He was the first Republican governor of Ohio, serving a term of four years, and later rendered a valued service as U.S. secretary of the treasury during the first years of the **Civil War**. His establishment of a national banking system contributed to U.S. economic development and the issuing of U.S. Treasury notes (greenbacks) as legal tender. The now retired $10,000 U.S currency note featured Chase's portrait. President Abraham Lin coln appointed Chase to the U.S. Supreme Court in 1864, and he served there until he died in New York City on May 7, 1873. Chase's political wisdom in handling constitutional problems brought on by the Civil War and Reconstruction helped to safeguard the Supreme Court and restore its prestige. The Chase College of Law had chosen a distinguished jurist as its namesake.

The post–**World War II** years witnessed many changes for the evening law school. The newly enacted G.I. Bill of Rights guaranteed millions of veterans a tuition-free college education. Chase experienced significant increases in enrollment. This meant a larger faculty was required, but the school's physical space was limited. In 1947 the Ohio State University at Columbus inspected the law school and recommended that it become independent of the YMCA. It did become organizationally independent in 1951, as Chase set up its own board of regents to govern the college. However, some ties with the YMCA remained until 1968, particularly in the area of physical plant.

During the 1960s, Chase began contemplating a possible association with the University of Cincinnati. In time, the school attempted to negotiate affiliation with Xavier University in Cincinnati; Miami University at Oxford, Ohio; and Wright State University in Dayton, Ohio, but none of these discussions bore fruit. In 1962 the graduating class was awarded juris doctor (JD) degrees instead of bachelor of law (LLB) degrees; later, in 1987, the school offered JD degrees to all Chase alumni holding the LLB.

Chase College of Law did not have to go very far to find an institution with which to affiliate. It was only a few miles away, just across the Ohio River in Kentucky. In 1968 the Northern Kentucky State College (NKSC) was created by an act of the Kentucky legislature, upgrading the former University of Kentucky Northern Community College to a new four-year school. In March 1971 NKSC approached Chase College of Law to ask if there could be informal discussions regarding a merger of the two schools. In its attempt to meet the educational needs of Northern Kentucky and Greater Cincinnati, NKSC had planned for a law school, but importing an established school of law had definite advantages over creating a new entity. Dr. Will Frank Steely, founding president of NKSC, was often heard to say, "Lawyers are involved in politics and Chase graduates in the legislature in Frankfort, Ky., would be a great base of support for the future of Northern Kentucky State College and Northern Kentucky in general." After much discussion and opposition, some support for the merger began to coalesce. Some of the first seeds of merger were planted by Ben Stoner, a member of the Chase board of regents; Harold J. Siebenthaler, chairman of the Chase board of regents; and **Ken Lucas**, a member of NKSC's board of regents. Other early advocates were Kentucky state senator Clyde Middleton, a student and later a graduate of the law school; John DeMarcus, of Governor Louie Nunn's office; Governor Nunn (1967–1971) himself; local businessman Peter Kappas; NKSC president Dr. W. Frank Steely; and W. Jack Grosse, dean of the Chase law school.

On July 1, 1971, an agreement was signed by both colleges, and in August 1971 the Kentucky Council on Public Higher Education approved the merger. In the fall semester of 1972, the Chase College of Law moved to the former site of the University of Kentucky Northern Community College in Park Hills. By that time, NKSC had moved to its new campus in Highland Heights. In 1976 NKSC achieved university status, and its named changed to **Northern Kentucky University**, with the Chase College of Law as a prestigious part of that institution of higher learning.

Blue, Frederick J. *Salmon P. Chase: A Life in Politics*. Kent, Ohio: Kent State Univ. Press, 1987.

Dieffenbach, C. Maxwell, Stanley E. Harper Jr., and W. Jack Grosse. *The Lawyers' School: A Centennial History of Salmon P. Chase College of Law*. Cincinnati: Gateway, 1995.

"NKSC-Chase Sow Unity Seeds," *KP*, July 3, 1972, 1K.

Steely, Will Frank. *Northern: Birth of a University*. Cincinnati: Gateway, 1993.

"Suit Challenges Merger for KNSC," *KP*, September 10, 1971, 1K.

Martha Pelfrey

CHERRY GROVE (HARDSCRABBLE). This Grant Co. community was first referred to as Thomas Clark's, after a tavern that he established on the **Dry Ridge Trace** (later, U.S. 25; see **Dixie Highway**) in 1795, about halfway between Lexington and Covington. In 1834, with the incorporation of Leesburg Rd. from the southeast and its completion more than a decade later, more travelers began arriving at the tavern. In the late 1870s the Cincinnati, New Orleans, and Texas Pacific Railroad (**Cincinnati Southern Railroad**) came through the area, improving freight and passenger connections.

Hardscrabble, the second name for the community, suggested the many skills once required to live in the immediate area. Over the years, there have been several groceries and general stores at Cherry Grove. In June 1860, George Mozze operated a post office in his general store; the post office closed in 1861. In 1863 George W. Hill opened a general merchandise store and called the area Cherry Grove for its trees. George W. Hill & Co. opened a Covington store in 1865, becoming one of the largest feed and seed stores in Northern Kentucky. James L. Atkinson reopened the post office as Cherry Grove in April 1891, and it closed in October 1906. Other stores included a grocery-appliance store and gas station opened by the Edmonsons in the 1930s, with its landmark tepee. In the late 19th and early 20th centuries, a Cherry Grove school operated. There are also several churches in the area. The most recent development centers around the veterans' cemetery planned by the Veterans Administration; land has been purchased for it west of U.S. 25.

Conrad, John B., ed. *History of Grant County, Kentucky*. Williamstown, Ky.: Grant Co. Historical Society, 1992.

Rennick, Robert M. *The Post Offices of Northern Kentucky*. Lake Grove, Ore.: Depot, 2004.

Westover, John H. "Souvenir Edition," *Williamstown Courier*, May 30, 1901, 48.

CHERRY GROVE CEMETERY. This Grant Co. cemetery has had various names since its first burial, that of tavern owner Thomas Clark, husband of Sarah Bryan Clark, in 1803. It was first called the Clark Burying Ground. Because it contains the graves of some of the first inhabitants of the county, it also is regarded as a pioneer cemetery. This is where John Ferguson (1789–1877), a man who arrived in Grant Co. in 1793, was buried. Thomas Clark, son of Thomas and Sarah Bryan Clark, and the person who took over the license of the tavern upon the death of his mother, was buried here. This Thomas Clark, like his father, was heavily involved in the early county government. The Clark Burying Ground remained in the family until 1893, when Eliza Clark Gouge deeded the property to three trustees, who allowed burial of any relative of a person already buried there. At that time, it became the Gouge Cemetery. In 1961 it had the name Eibeck Cemetery, because a trust fund was left by Sadie Eibeck to care for the grounds. In 1991, when a new trustee agreement was drawn up, it became the Cherry Grove Cemetery. Located two miles south of Williamstown along US 25 (**Dixie Highway**), at the "Hill Top," where the **Norfolk Southern Railway** tracks cut across the old Clark property, the well-kept Cherry Grove Cemetery contains 40 or so burials. It is clearly a link with the early days of Grant Co., but it also reflects what can happen to a cemetery as a result of the passing of time and of families. In addition to its other names, the cemetery has at times been known as the George Elliston Cemetery.

Conrad, John B., ed. *History of Grant County, Kentucky.* Williamstown, Ky.: Grant Co. Historical Society, 1992.

Reis, Jim. "Gunplay, Crime Made Lively Reading in 1874," *KP,* July 30, 2001, 4K.

USGenWeb Archives. www.rootsweb.com/~usgenweb/newsearch.htm.

CHESAPEAKE AND OHIO RAILROAD. The Chesapeake and Ohio Railroad (C&O) in the 1970s ran from Newport News, Va., across Virginia and West Virginia to Ashland, Ky. From Ashland it hugged the south bank of the Ohio River to Covington, where it crossed the Ohio River into Cincinnati and continued on to Chicago. The C&O sent out numerous branch lines into the West Virginia and Eastern Kentucky coal fields; a branch also ran from Ashland to Lexington and Louisville, and another mainline track crossed the Ohio River at South Shore in Lewis Co. and ran north through Ohio into Michigan.

The C&O began as the Louisa Railroad in 1847; its builders hoped to make it stretch from the Virginia Tidewater to the Ohio River. In 1850 the Louisa Railroad was renamed the Virginia Central (VC), and during the **Civil War** the VC controlled track from Richmond to Charlottesville, Va. The VC was badly damaged in the war. In 1865 the VC and the Covington and Ohio Railroad were merged into the Chesapeake and Ohio Railroad. In 1869 the C&O came under the control of Collis P. Huntington, who set out to complete its track to the Ohio River. On January 29, 1873, the C&O reached the Ohio River at what became Huntington, W.Va.

In 1875 the C&O went into receivership and was reorganized as the Chesapeake and Ohio Railway. Huntington's vision was to connect it with the Chesapeake, Ohio, and Southwestern (CO&SW), which ran from Louisville to Memphis. This road, in turn, would connect with the Huntington-owned Southern Pacific Railroad to create the first route to extend from the Atlantic Ocean to the Pacific Ocean. To accomplish this goal, Huntington needed to tie the C&O to the CO&SW. He planned to reach Lexington with his own track and then use track rightage purchased from the **Louisville and Nashville Railroad** (L&N) to reach Louisville and the CO&SW. In order to reach Lexington, Huntington first had to build across the Big Sandy River to Ashland, Ky. Once this was accomplished, he undertook two projects. The first was to build west from Ashland along the southern bank of the Ohio River to connect with the **Kentucky Central Railroad** (KC), which had existing track from both Maysville and Covington to Lexington. The second was to gain control of the Lexington and Big Sandy Railroad (L&BS). The L&BS provided a route from Ashland to Lexington via Mount Sterling.

In order to build west along the Ohio River, Huntington purchased the charters of the Maysville and Big Sandy Railroad (M&BS) and the Kentucky and Great Eastern Railroad. He used these two railroad charters to build the track to tie Ashland to the KC. The C&O reached Covington in 1886 and established a rail yard there west of Madison Ave. The C&O also organized the Covington & Cincinnati Elevated Railroad & Transfer & Bridge Company in order to build a bridge across the Ohio River from Covington into Cincinnati. The bridge opened for use on December 25, 1888, and was rebuilt in 1929. The C&O Ohio River line also connected with the **Brooksville and Ohio Railroad** (B&OR) at Wellsburg in Bracken Co.

In 1897 Huntington lost control of the CO&SW to the Illinois Central Railroad, and the dream of merging the CO&SW and the C&O to create a railroad extending from the Atlantic Ocean to the Mississippi River came to an end. In 1910 the C&O acquired the Chicago, Cincinnati and Louisville Railroad and renamed it the Chesapeake and Ohio Railway of Indiana (C&OI). That line was often called a railroad that ran from somewhere, Cincinnati, to somewhere, Chicago, but in between went nowhere.

The extension of the C&O to Chicago saw an increase in traffic through Cincinnati that was beyond the capability of the Covington Rail Yard to process. The result was the building of the Stevens Hump Yard at Silver Grove in Campbell Co. between 1911 and 1912 to sort and marshal incoming and outgoing C&O trains. The rail yard was named for George W. Stevens, president of the C&O from 1900 to 1920. The C&O experienced a growth in coal traffic through Cincinnati during the next three decades. In response, the rail line undertook a program to eliminate highway rail grade crossings in Campbell and Kenton counties. Among these works were highway underpasses built for Monmouth St. in Newport and Madison Ave. in Covington. The new Ohio River **Chesapeake and Ohio Railroad Bridge** built in 1929 led to a new C&O depot for Covington. In the early 1980s, the Stevens Yard was phased out with the opening of the **Chessie System**'s Queensgate Yard in Cincinnati.

The C&O operated some named passenger trains, the *George Washington,* the *Fast Flying Virginian,* and the *Sportsman,* from Cincinnati to Washington, D.C., and Newport News, Va., through Northern Kentucky, plus a host of local numbered trains. The C&O's last passenger train to serve Northern Kentucky was the *George Washington*; its last day under the C&O was April 30, 1971. The next day the *George Washington* continued to operate, but as an **Amtrak** train. However, the most famous of the C&O passenger trains to operate in Northern Kentucky was the *Chippee.* The *Chippee* ran back and forth between the Covington Yard and the Stevens Yard carrying C&O workers to and from work. This train was operated by the C&O according to an agreement with the railroad unions, for when the Stevens Yard opened, there was no public transportation between Covington or Newport and Silver Grove. At first the *Chippee* consisted of an engine and a passenger car, but as workers began driving their own cars, it turned into just an engine and a caboose.

In the 1960s the C&O gained control of the Baltimore and Ohio Railroad (B&O), the Western Maryland Railway (WM), and the Chicago, South Shore and South Bend Railroad (CSS&SB). In 1973 the C&O, the B&O, and the WM were brought under the umbrella of the Chessie System holding company, which later merged with the **Seaboard Coast Line** to form the **CSX**. Because of legal constraints, the C&O continued to exist as a nonoperating railroad company well into the 1980s, when its charter was finally surrendered.

The C&O had depots in the following Northern Kentucky locations: in Bracken Co.: Augusta, Carntown, and Wellsburg (shared with the B&OR); in Campbell Co.: Bellevue, Dayton, Melbourne, New Richmond Station, Newport (shared with the L&N), and Ross; in Kenton Co.: Covington (shared with the L&N); and in Mason Co.: Dover and Maysville.

Toothman, Fred Rees. *Working for the Chessie System.* Huntington, W.Va.: Vandalia, 1993.

Turner, Charles W. *Chessie's Road.* Clifton Forge, Va.: Chesapeake & Ohio Historical Society, 1986.

Charles H. Bogart

CHESAPEAKE AND OHIO RAILROAD BRIDGE. In 1886, when the **Chesapeake and Ohio Railroad** (C&O) began to build a railroad bridge across the Ohio River between Covington and Cincinnati, the firm organized the Covington & Cincinnati Elevated Railroad & Transfer & Bridge Company (C&CER&T&B) as the successor to the Covington & Cincinnati Bridge Pier Company. The C&CER&T&B finished the bridge, located at the foot of Main St. in Covington, on December 25, 1888. The structure was designed by William Burr and erected by the Philadelphia Bridge Company of Pennsylvania. In 1888 the noted Covington reformer **William Goebel**, then a Kentucky state senator, made the bridge a political football. His distrust of big business made him fight for free pedestrian tolls on both the **John A. Roebling Bridge** and the new C&O Bridge. The Kentucky legislature subsequently passed some restrictions on what the owners of the bridges could charge for passage.

The C&CER&T&B provided switching service between the C&O Covington Freight Yard and various railroad yards in Cincinnati. In 1929 the present C&O Railroad Bridge, now used by **CSX**, was built and the C&CER&T&B Bridge was deeded to the Commonwealth of Kentucky for use as a highway bridge. The C&CER&T&B Bridge was torn down in 1974 and replaced by the Clay Wade Bailey Bridge. The C&O Railroad was not the only user of the railroad bridge; the **Louisville and Nashville Railroad** for many years, when it was not corporately a part of CSX, leased track rightage across it.

Reis, Jim. "C&O Bridge Carried the Freight," *KP,* October 21, 2002, 4K.

Tenkotte, Paul A. "Rival Cities to Suburbs: Covington and Newport, Kentucky, 1790–1890," PhD diss., Univ. of Cincinnati, 1989.

Turner, Charles W. *Chessie's Road.* Clifton Forge, Va.: Chesapeake & Ohio Historical Society, 1986.

Charles H. Bogart

CHESSIE SYSTEM. The Chessie System was formed in 1973 as a holding company to control the Baltimore and Ohio Railroad, the **Chesapeake and Ohio Railroad**, and the Western Maryland Railroad. In 1977 the Chessie System started construction of the Queensgate Hump Yard in Cincinnati. Queensgate, opened in 1981, replaced the DeCoursey Hump Yard at Latonia, Kenton Co., and the Stevens Hump Yard at Silver Grove, Campbell Co. In 1980 the Chessie System and Seaboard Coast Line Industries merged to form the **CSX** Corporation.

Doyle, Jerry. *Chessie System Diesel Locomotives.* Lynchburg, Va.: TLC, 1999.
Rhodes, Michael. *North American Railyards.* St. Paul, Minn.: MBI, 2003.
Turner, Charles W., Thomas W. Dixon, and Eugene L. Huddleston. *Chessie's Road.* 2nd ed. Parsons, W. Va.: McClain, 1993.

Charles H. Bogart

CHEVALIER, ELIZABETH PICKETT (b. March 25, 1896, Chicago, Ill.; d. January 3, 1984, Brentwood, Calif.). Author and movie director Elizabeth Pickett Chevalier, the daughter of Montgomery and Alma Osborne Pickett, grew up in River Forest, Ill., where in 1914 she graduated from Oak Park High School. While a student there, she took a dance class, in which the young Ernest Hemingway was her reluctant partner. At Wellesley College, in Wellesley, Mass., she became a close friend of the future Madam Chiang Kai-shek of China. Elizabeth received her BA degree from Wellesley College in 1918 and went to live on her grandfather's farm at Tuckahoe Ridge, Mason Co., Ky. Both sets of grandparents lived there, on land that had once been owned by Virginia statesman Patrick Henry. Growing up, Elizabeth had spent her summers on the farm, with her mother and sister. Her grandfather, Joseph DeSha Pickett, had been a chaplain with Kentucky's famed Confederate Orphan Brigade during the **Civil War**. After the conflict, he served in Lexington as president of Transylvania College and later as president of the school that became the University of Kentucky.

In August 1918 Elizabeth took a job as a publicity agent with the **American Red Cross**. She wrote two books while she worked there, *History of Red Cross Nursing* and *The American National Red Cross: Its Origin, Purposes and Service.* She also wrote and directed a short film for the organization; it was designed to encourage young girls to become U.S. Army nurses. In 1924 Elizabeth began her professional movie career by signing a contract with Winfield Sheehan Studios, in New York City. She later worked for Fox Studios in both New York and Hollywood, on such films as *What Price Glory, Seventh Heaven,* and *Sunrise Serenade.* She left Fox Studios in 1928 and began writing and directing movies for Paramount Pictures. That same year, she wrote a book entitled *Redskin,* which was subsequently made into one of Hollywood's first epic color movies.

In 1929 she returned to the farm at Tuckahoe Ridge in Mason Co., which she had recently inherited from her grandfather, and began writing *Drivin' Woman.* The idea for the novel came from reading the diary of her grandmother, Sallie Bouldin. Her book covers the 50 years after the Civil War and is somewhat autobiographical; activities around her grandfather's farm play an important part. In 1936 Elizabeth married corporate tax attorney Stuart M. Chevalier, whose firm, Miller and Chevalier, had offices in New York City, Washington, D.C., Chicago, and Los Angeles. Over the next few years, the couple lived in each of those cities. Stuart had been a professor at Jefferson School of Law in Louisville and later at Washington and Lee University, Lexington, Va., where he received his law degree. He was also an author; he wrote a book entitled *A Window on Broadway.*

In 1940, after working on *Drivin' Woman* for 11 years, Elizabeth presented the manuscript to literary agent Maxwell Aley. He persuaded the Macmillan book company to publish the work in 1942, and it was an instant success, selling more than 300,000 copies in six months. Aley sold the movie rights to Metro Goldwyn Mayer Studios for $105,000, a larger sum than was paid for the *Gone with the Wind* script. The heroine of *Drivin' Woman* was America Moncure, whose first name Elizabeth had borrowed from her mother-in-law, America Chevalier.

In 1943 the Chevaliers began spending a considerable amount of time at Warm Springs, Ga. While Stuart received treatment there (he was a polio victim), the couple developed a close friendship with President Franklin D. Roosevelt (1933–1945). In the early 1960s, President John F. Kennedy (1960–1963) considered Elizabeth for the position of treasurer of the United States. Although Elizabeth Pickett Chevalier lived in many different states, including California, she always considered herself a Kentuckian. After a long and illustrious career, she died in Brentwood, Calif., at age 87, and was buried next to her husband at the Mountain View Cemetery in Altadena, Calif.

Browning, Mary Carmel, O.S.U. *Kentucky Authors.* Evansville, Ind.: Keller-Crescent, 1968.
"Elizabeth Chevalier: Writer, Film Scenarist, Producer," *Los Angeles Times,* January 13, 1984, D19.
"Farm Once Scene of Novel, Sold," *KTS,* March 1, 1957, 2A.
"Novelist Arrives on Bond-Selling Tour," *LCJ,* November 30, 1942, 2.
Wilson, Bess M. "Author Hews to Line and Lets Chips Fly: Pasadenan Recounts Editing Feat on *Drivin' Woman* for Publishers," *Los Angeles Times,* March 29, 1942, D11.

Jack Wessling

CHILDREN INC. Beginning in 1977 with the Cathedral Child Development Center in Covington, Children Inc. has developed into one of the largest and highest-quality child care agencies in Kentucky. It offers nationally accredited child care and early childhood education programs in a variety of settings throughout Northern Kentucky for infants through the school-age child. The agency's corporate office is at 333 Madison Ave., Covington.

The newest project of Children Inc. is Service Learning NKY. Sponsored by **Ashland Inc.**, the Gap Foundation, the Mayerson Foundation, and Toyota, it has more than 200 teachers who are involved at 35 different schools, guiding teachers in implementing service learning projects.

Each day Children Inc. programs serve about 3,500 children, who are cared for, nurtured, and taught by skilled staff. Families of the children are encouraged to participate also in the goal of creating a world that understands young children and their needs.

Children Inc. Centers

Montessori and Early Learning Academy, 419 Altamont Rd., Covington

Campbell Child Development Center, 909 Camel Crossing, Alexandria

Gardens at Greenup Child Development Center, 133 E. 11th St., Covington

Imagine Tomorrow Child Development Center, 1260 Pacific Ave., Erlanger

Kenton Child Development Center, 11096 Madison Pike, Independence

Newport Preschool Center, 30 W. 8th St., Newport

Park Hills Child Development Center, 1030 Old State Rd., Park Hills

Treasure House Child Development Center, 203 W. Rivercenter Blvd., Covington

"Agencies to Share Location?" *KE,* March 27, 2000, B1.
Children, Inc. www.childreninc.org (accessed June 30, 2006).
"How Parents and Schools Work Together," *KP,* November 2, 1994, 4KK.
Mayerson Northern Kentucky Service Learning Initiative. www.servicelearningnky.org (accessed June 30, 2006).

Robin Rider Osborne

CHILDREN'S HOME OF NORTHERN KENTUCKY. The Covington Protestant Children's Home was established in 1882 by Col. **Amos Shinkle**, who was also its chief benefactor. A coal merchant on the Ohio River, Shinkle saw great poverty and need, especially among children living in shantyboats along the riverbanks. As a result, he began sometime in 1879 to work toward founding a home for children. By 1880 a charter was drawn, setting out the purpose, plan, operation, and maintenance of the corporation, and boards of directors and managers were selected. Unable to find a suitable building for the home, Shinkle, president of the Board of Directors, proposed, at a meeting on March 14, 1881, that the board purchase an $8,000 lot at 14th and Madison Ave. in Covington. There, as stated in the board's bylaws, a building would be erected to house and instruct children under the age of 12 "whose parents are sick or at work, or from any cause unable for the time being to care for them." The Building Committee employed **Samuel Hannaford** as the architect, and after his plans were reviewed, the committee was instructed to let contracts and begin construction. The first donation, $10, was presented by four little girls who had held a fair to raise the money. It was the beginning of a long series of local charitable efforts by children. The remainder of the cost of the building and lot, $53,500, was a gift from Shinkle. On December 19, 1882, dedication of the home took place. The day after, four children were admitted to the state-of-the-art facility, which included a kindergarten schoolroom, an infirmary, a parlor and reception rooms, a spacious dining room, and double-deadened floors for noise reduction. The building was heated by steam.

Years passed, and the neighborhood, once ideal for the home, became too industrial for the safety of the children. In February 1914 five acres, the Bird property in Latonia, were purchased as the site for a new home. Shinkle's heirs issued a quitclaim deed relinquishing all claim to the property at 14th and Madison. However, **World War I** began, and plans for the new home were delayed for 10 years. At a Board of Managers meeting in February 1924, plans for a new home were revived. Several sites were considered, including the property in Latonia. Eventually, the Board of Trustees purchased, at a cost of $19,537, some 26 acres of the Helen Bryant estate in Devou Park. Located on a hill, the property provided a magnificent view of the Ohio River. An intensive 10-day fundraising campaign began on May 15, 1925; it was possibly the best-planned and -conducted campaign of its kind ever carried out in Kenton Co. On May 26, 1925, the amount raised by the campaign, $225,439.02, was announced at a Victory Dinner held at the Masonic Temple in Covington. On December 14, 1925, representatives from both boards were present to break ground for the new home. The children were thereby ensured a new start in more comfortable quarters, safer and healthier surroundings, and better recreational facilities.

In 1935 the Junior Board was created to alleviate the fundraising burden that had previously rested on the Board of Managers. Over the years, the Junior Board has raised substantial sums of money for the home, the most successful venture being the Annual Charity Ball held each November.

As the need for orphanages decreased in the 1970s and the need for long-term treatment for children with emotional, behavioral, and social issues increased, the home adjusted its services to meet these demands. In 1980 the Children's Home developed a residential treatment program for abused, neglected, and troubled boys of ages 7 through 17. Today the home, now known as the Children's Home of Northern Kentucky, has emerged as a community leader offering comprehensive services designed to strengthen families. It operates the Residential Treatment Program, Community Based Family Services, Adoption Home Studies, and the After School program. In 2000 the home passed yet another milestone and became an accredited facility after the Council on Accreditation for Children and Family Services in the United States and Canada performed an extensive study.

Caywood, J. A. "History of the Covington Protestant Children's Home," 1964, Children's Home of Northern Kentucky, Covington, Ky.
Children's Home of Northern Kentucky. www.chnk.org.

Susan Claypool Kettles

CHILDREN'S HOMES. See **Campbell Co. Protestant Orphans Home**; **Campbell Lodge**; **Children's Home of Northern Kentucky**; **Diocesan Catholic Children's Home**; **Maplewood Children's Home**.

CHILDREN'S LAW CENTER INC. The Children's Law Center Inc., at 1002 Russell St. in Covington, was established in 1989 to protect and enhance the legal rights and entitlements of children through quality legal representation, research and policy development, and training and education for attorneys and others regarding the rights of children. The priorities of the Children's Law Center Inc. include juvenile justice, child welfare, and education issues generally, as well as an emphasis on making legal representation for children more accessible.

The Children's Law Center developed out of the need to provide legal representation and services for children who were falling through the "cracks" of the juvenile and family court systems. Since its inception, it has provided free legal representation for thousands of children in the areas of juvenile justice, child protection, and education. The center has established other nonlitigious strategies to accomplish its goals and has become a nationally recognized children's advocacy organization. Although direct services remain at the core of the center's activities, it has joined efforts through the years with such national organizations as the Youth Law Center Inc. in San Francisco, the Southern Poverty Law Center, the Justice Policy Institute in Washington, D.C., and the National Juvenile Defender Center, as well as numerous state and local organizations that provide advocacy to children.

In 2002 the Children's Law Center Inc. expanded its services to Ohio. The center emphasizes especially these objectives:

—to promote the rights of children to a safe, permanent home, using a continuation of services and the least restrictive alternative;

—to reduce the unnecessary incarceration of children in lieu of appropriate alternatives and eliminate the use of adult jails to detain children;

—to protect the rights of children to effective treatment reasonably calculated to bring about an improvement in condition, including those youth who are incarcerated or are being transitioned back into the community after incarceration;

—to reduce unnecessary government intervention into the lives of children and families, so that family autonomy can be preserved;

—to promote and protect the rights of children to have access to counsel where statutorily required or otherwise necessary to protect their vital interests;

—to improve the quality of legal representation to children;

—to ensure that children's right to a free, appropriate public education is protected;

—to promote effective judicial policies to protect the rights of children in the judicial system; and

—to promote equitable treatment of all youth without regard to race, ethnicity, gender, or handicapping condition.

The Children's Law Center Inc. provides legal representation to more than 200 children and youth each year and assists more than 1,000 callers each year with information and referrals regarding issues involving children's rights.

"Children's Law Center Making Mark," *KP*, January 18, 2000, 1K.
Crowley, Patrick. "Study Reveals 'Juvenile Injustice,'" *KE*, April 26, 2000, B1.
"A Voice for Our Children—Law Center Founded by Ex-Social Worker," *SC*, January 2, 2005, 1B.

Mary Fisher

CHRISTOPHER GIST HISTORICAL SOCIETY. The Christopher Gist Historical Society was organized on May 24, 1949, through the efforts of **Stephens L. Blakely**, a Northern Kentucky attorney who enjoyed local history and wanted to see it preserved. He gathered 19 individuals from Kenton, Boone, and Campbell counties, among them Russell Clark, a Covington school principal and teacher; Sherwood Gunk, pastor of the Shinkle Methodist Church in Covington; physician Charles W. Reynolds, an ear, nose, and throat specialist; Joe Dressman, a newspaper editor; **Charles B. Truesdell**, an employee of Cincinnati Gas & Electric; and Blakely's son John Blakely. Shortly thereafter, the elder Blakely was joined by his legal associate, W. Baxter Harrison. Stephens L. Blakely was elected the first president. When the subject of a name for the society came up, Dressman suggested naming it after Christopher Gist, the first surveyor to work in the Northern Kentucky region, representing the Ohio Land Company. Gist was also a close friend of George Washington and had once saved the future president's life by pulling him from a frozen stream in the wilderness. Strict requirements for membership in the society were established. Each member was required to research and write an original paper on local history, to be presented before the organization. Also, there was a ballot box containing white and black marbles, to be used when members voted on new applicants. Anyone receiving a black marble (a negative vote) was not accepted into the group. Both of these requirements were later discontinued. The presentation of a paper frightened some prospective members and became an obstacle in attracting members. The ballot box caused dissension if a prospect was rejected.

The first meetings were held in various locations: the Covington Public Library, the Covington YMCA, the Education Building of the Madison Ave. Christian Church in Covington, and the Union Light, Heat, and Power Auditorium. Finally, in 1960, Charles Adams, a lawyer and a member of the group, announced that one of his clients, Mrs. Robert deValcourt Carroll, was bequeathing to the society a three-story brick building at 216 E. Fourth St., Covington. Monthly meetings were held there until 1975, when the building and its contents became a target of vandals. The building was sold to attorney Patrick M. Flannery, and the proceeds were used to set up a scholarship fund for college-bound high school students.

The first awards, $200 each, were given in 1976 in recognition of the 200th anniversary of Kenton Co. The scholarships have continued to be awarded and have increased in size. At one ceremony, as many as seven awards were presented. A dinner is also held to honor recipients and their parents. The Christopher Gist Historical Society also provides support to the Kentucky Humanities Council, the Dinsmore Foundation (see **Dinsmore Homestead**), and other worthy projects. Fred A. Stine IV of Fort Thomas, a retired pediatrician and coroner, served as president for many years.

"Christopher Gist Society Has Home," *KP*, May 25, 1960, 11K.

"Gist Society Gets Wealth of Local Historical Materials," *KTS*, November 22, 1956, 14A.

"Historical Society Chooses Gist Name," *KP*, June 8, 1949, 1.

"Historical Society May Be Organized," *KP*, April 30, 1942, 5.

Roberts, Alice Kennelly. "Gist Society Celebrates 50 Years," *KP*, August 28, 1999, 22K.

———. "Gist Society Helps Scholars," *KP*, June 26, 1999, 22K.

Alice Kennelly Roberts

CHURCH OF JESUS CHRIST OF LATTER-DAY SAINTS. The Church of Jesus Christ of Latter-day Saints, known also as the Mormon Church, organized in 1830 in Fayette, N.Y., with six members, soon sent missionaries to the Ohio River Valley. Early prominent church leaders Joseph and Hyrum Smith, Oliver Cowdery, and Parley P. and Orson Pratt also visited the Greater Cincinnati area. Missionaries traveled in pairs in Northern Kentucky to teach and preach in public places.

The first branch of the Mormon Church in Cincinnati consisted of 100 members. Another local branch, led by Robert Culbertson, was established at the mouth of the Licking River in Campbell Co. In January 1835 there were 11 members in this small congregation. Elders Orson Pratt and Lorenzo Barnes exerted their missionary efforts in the region, and by February they had baptized 7 more into the Mormon Church.

As resistance to the Mormons began and increased, the congregation in Northern Kentucky lingered but did not flourish until the 20th century. Many members joined the westward movement of the church in the mid-1800s. It was not until 1953 that the Northern Kentucky branch of the Mormon Church began to experience significant growth.

Early Mormons with ties to Northern Kentucky include Charles Coulson Rich and Martha Jane Knowlton. Rich was born August 21, 1809, near Big Bone Lick. By 1810 the Rich family had resettled in Indiana. It was there, in 1832, that Mormon missionaries baptized Charles Rich. He farmed and also served a mission for the church. By 1838 Rich and his wife, Sarah DeArmon Pea, had settled in Missouri. When the Mormons were driven from Missouri, the couple moved to Nauvoo, Ill. Charles was appointed as the major general of the Nauvoo Legion and helped lead the Mormons from Nauvoo into the Salt Lake Valley in Utah in 1846–1847. At age 39 Charles Rich was named to the Quorum of the Twelve Apostles. Later, he was called to help establish a settlement at San Bernardino, Calif., and served as that town's mayor. Eventually, Rich and his family served the Mormon Church in Bear Creek Valley, Idaho, where he remained until his death on November 17, 1883. A roadside marker at Beaver Rd. and Gum Branch near Big Bone Lick stands as a memorial to Charles Rich and his Boone Co. heritage.

The family of Martha Jane Knowlton had moved from Boone Co. to Kenton Co. before her birth in 1822 in Covington. When she was five years old, the Knowltons moved to Cumminsville, Ohio, just north of Cincinnati. In 1835 this family, who were Campbellites, moved on to Hancock Co., Ill. As the persecuted Mormons poured into Nauvoo, Martha's family took pity on the homeless people. The Knowltons listened to the Mormon message and were baptized in the icy Mississippi River in winter 1840.

The seeds of faith that were sown locally more than 170 years ago in the tiny congregation at the mouth of the Licking River took root in Northern Kentucky. In 1953 the Northern Kentucky branch of the Mormon Church, led by branch president Alvin Gilliam, made plans for a new building, for which construction began in 1959 at 1806 Scott St. in Covington. The congregation quickly developed into the Northern Kentucky Ward, with Victor Bang as the first bishop. Among Bang's successors were Robert Ginn (deceased) and Grant Chapin of Florence.

By 1986 the Mormons had outgrown the Scott St. chapel and moved to new quarters at 144 Buttermilk Pk., Lakeside Park. This building continues to serve as a stake center and also houses a family history center. The newest Northern Kentucky chapel, dedicated in June 2004 in Hebron, provides meeting space for three local congregations: the Hebron and Northern Kentucky wards and the Crittenden Branch.

The Mormon Church in Northern Kentucky has a membership of 1,900, divided among four wards and two branches: the Hebron and Northern Kentucky wards in Boone Co.; the Highland Heights and Lakeside Park wards for members in Campbell and Kenton counties; and two smaller congregations, the Crittenden and the Ohio River branches. These wards and branches are part of the Cincinnati Ohio Stake.

The Mormon Church today is the fourth-largest religious body in the United States. Membership worldwide approaches 13 million members, more than half of whom are outside the United States. More than 50,000 missionaries serve around the world. Church buildings include 27,000 ward meetinghouses, 2,700 stake centers, and 122 temples. For Mormons in Northern Kentucky, the Louisville Temple is a quick trip down I-71 to Crestwood, just east of Louisville.

Arrington, Leonard J. *Charles C. Rich Mormon: General and Western Frontiersman.* Provo, Utah: BYU Press, 1974.

Evans, John Henry. *Charles Coulson Rich: Pioneer Builder of the West.* New York: Macmillan, 1936.

Fish, Stanley L., Bradley J. Kramer, and William Budge Wallis. *History of the Mormon Church in Cincinnati, 1830–1985.* Cincinnati, 1997.

Jannes W. Garbett

CINCINNATI AND CHARLESTON RAILROAD. This proposed link between Cincinnati and Charleston was expected to be of great benefit to Northern Kentucky.

The period between 1830 and 1860 witnessed an explosion of economic expansion and development within the nation. Railroads were one of the major instruments for accomplishing both tasks. Railroads were viewed as the conquerors of both distance and time, and proposals to connect various destinations became a topic of everyday conversation. Some of the proposals led to state-granted charters to build; in a few cases, the promoters of these ventures raised enough cash to begin construction. Eventually, many of these railroads failed miserably because they were impractical. Theoretical lines drawn on flat maps failed to demonstrate the difficult topography they had to cross in reality. The engineering capability to build through certain types of mountainous terrain simply did not exist.

Among the railroads proposed for construction during this period was the Cincinnati and Charleston Railroad (C&C). This railroad, as envisioned, would have diverted to the eastern port of Charleston, S.C., slow-moving goods that had been traveling down the Ohio River toward the southern port of New Orleans, thus shortening delivery times to the end users. The technical challenge of building this railroad was immense, since the track would cut through the Appalachian Mountains at an acute angle; the resulting problems would have pushed costs ever skyward. The promoters with their line drawn on the map, however, made light of such difficulties.

During the 1830s numerous mass meetings were held in Tennessee and South Carolina to encourage the construction of the C&C. In 1836 the governors of Tennessee, South Carolina, and North Carolina, requesting that an officer of the Army Corps of Engineers be assigned to survey a route for the C&C, presented a joint petition to the U.S. Congress. The proposal foundered when Congress asked the states to supply $3,000 to cover part of the survey cost. Only South Carolina offered $1,000 toward the survey.

Several influential leaders in Cincinnati and Northern Kentucky supported the proposed railroad. Dr. **Daniel Drake**, the foremost medical practitioner in Cincinnati, who grew up in Mason Co., Ky., believed that a rail link with Charleston would unite the cities not only economically but also culturally. Gen. **James Taylor Jr.**, Newport's founder, and **William Wright Southgate**, a member of Congress from Covington, supported the plan, as did Covington's T. W. Bakewell (see **Bakewell Family**), an industrialist. William Henry Harrison, the future president, and Nicholas Longworth, the wealthiest man in the West at the time, also backed the C&C.

The promoters of the C&C were not deterred by the failure of the congressional petition, and they continued to publish maps depicting its planned path. The route would run westward from Charleston to Columbia, S.C. (124 miles), on to the junction of the Thicketty and Broad rivers (65 miles), and thence to a confluence of the Green River with the Broad River (52 miles), to Asheville, N.C. From there it would pass down the valley of the French River to the mouth of the Nolichucky River (60 miles), to the junction of the Elk River with the Clear Folk of the Elk (90 miles), and west to Cincinnati (190 miles). The cost was estimated at $10,084,326, or an optimistic $17,214 per mile. Within the Northern Kentucky region, the railroad would follow the path of the present-day **CSX** from Maysville along the southern shore of the Ohio River into Newport and Covington, before crossing somehow into Cincinnati. Later, the route of arrival changed so that it would proceed north from Paris or Lexington.

The C&C concept went through a number of modifications. One of them was the chartering of a new company in 1836, the Louisville, Cincinnati and Charleston Railroad (LC&C). The LC&C plan was to run from Charleston to Lexington, Ky. (proposed once before by Daniel Drake), where it would split into three lines bound for Louisville, Cincinnati, and Maysville. In 1837 the LC&C purchased South Carolina's Charleston and Hamburg Railroad with the intention of using it as its launching road. By 1842 stockholder expectations were lower, and the LC&C was renamed the South Carolina Railroad (SCRR). When the **Civil War** occurred, the SCRR track extended only from Charleston to Columbia, wholly within South Carolina.

What killed the C&C for Kentucky was politics and the attempt at compromise within Kentucky (the plan to split the railroad into three branches), plus the fact that the Kentucky legislature made the granting of its charter contingent upon the building of the three branches from Lexington to the Ohio River simultaneously, thus making the project economically unfeasible. The rivalry among Louisville, Maysville, and Cincinnati–Northern Kentucky precluded the project's success for all involved. Lexington was linked with those cities later, by other trunk railroads.

The investors in the C&C never fully comprehended the costs and engineering challenges involved in completing its roadbed. It was one thing to lay track in the eastern Tidewater, but to use that same cost per mile as a basis for estimating the cost of tracks through the mountains was sheer folly. The projected wealth that the C&C was projected to generate for Charleston blinded its backers to the actual costs.

The dream of the promoters of the C&C finally came true in 1894, when the **Southern Railway** pieced together rails to provide a one-owner connection serving both Charleston and Cincinnati. Today the **Norfolk Southern** operates that route. The impact on Northern Kentucky, had the C&C been built when first proposed, will never be known.

Davis, Burke. *The Southern Railway.* Chapel Hill: Univ. of North Carolina Press, 1985.

Ellis, Coulter M. *The Railroad and the City.* Columbus: Ohio State Univ. Press, 1977.

Phillips, Ulrich B. *History of Transportation in the Eastern Cotton Belt.* New York: Octagon Books, 1968.

Tenkotte, Paul A. "Rival Cities to Suburbs: Covington and Newport, Kentucky, 1790–1890," PhD diss., Univ. of Cincinnati, 1989.

Charles H. Bogart

CINCINNATI/NORTHERN KENTUCKY INTERNATIONAL AIRPORT. Located in Hebron, in Boone Co., the Cincinnati/Northern Kentucky International Airport (CVG) is the child of both **World War II** and the **flood of 1937** on the Ohio River. The flood left Cincinnati's eastside Cincinnati Municipal Lunken Airport under water, proving it ill suited for the region's growing aviation demands. In the days leading up to World War II, the U.S. Army Air Corps was caught with virtually no paved runways except at civilian airports. An airbase program was started, called Development of Landing Areas for National Defense. Under this program, more than 300 airports were built or improved with federal funds; the land, however, had to be provided by local governments or organizations. CVG turned out to be a solution for both problems.

O. G. Loomis, a prominent Covington and Newport civil engineer, in his role as a civil engineer, began tramping through fields and over hills in Kentucky, searching for a large, fog-free tract of land. Loomis was initially a volunteer but was later paid $8,100 for his work by the Kenton Co. Fiscal Court. Early in 1941, Loomis went to see Judge **Nathaniel E. Riddell** of the Boone Co. Fiscal Court. A local sponsor was needed. The judge agreed to be the sponsor, as long as local funding came from neighboring Kenton Co. In spring 1941 Loomis; Phil Vondersmith, head of the Covington-Kenton Co. Industrial Association (a predecessor of the **Northern Kentucky Chamber of Commerce**); and V. H. Logan, editor of the *Kentucky Enquirer* selected a site in Boone Co. that offered several advantages: land was selling for $40 to $50 per acre; the area, at a higher elevation than Lunken Airport, was nearly fog-free; it was only 13 miles from downtown Cincinnati; and there was plenty of room for expansion. Elected officials in Campbell, Kenton, and Boone counties supported the project. So did civic organizations, most of which sent letters to U.S. senator Alben W. Barkley and U.S. representative **Brent Spence** urging their support. Meanwhile, Vondersmith persuaded top executives from American, Delta, and TWA airlines to commit to using the airport, if it was built.

President Franklin D. Roosevelt (1933–1945) on February 11, 1942, approved preliminary funds for airport site development. The formal approval of the four runways and $2 million came on October 1, 1942. Kenton Co. attorney William Wherman instituted condemnation proceedings against several parcels of land so that sufficient land could be acquired. The Kenton Co. Fiscal Court created the six-member Kenton Co. Airport Board in June 1943 to function as a board of directors. The board has been augmented over the years to give Ohio, Boone Co., and Campbell Co. a voice in airport affairs.

On March 29, 1943, the airport board selected Frank Mashuda and Associates to build four runways with connecting taxiways in 150 days. Construction began after the May 3 groundbreaking, which was attended by Kentucky governor Keen Johnson (1939–1943). The runways were completed on August 12, 1944, and three days later U.S. Army Air Corps B-17 bombers, mostly out of Lockbourne Army Air Base in Columbus, Ohio, began making practice landings and takeoffs. The U.S. Army Air Corps used the field until September 1945. In December 1945 Senator Barkley informed the board that the U.S. Army had declared the airport surplus property, meaning the government would surrender its lease.

Boone Co. Airline was the first air carrier at the airport, operating out of a wood-frame building. The three-story brick administration building, part of which remains in use as Terminal 1, was dedicated on October 27, 1946. A crowd estimated at between 35,000 and 50,000 clogged roads to

The Cincinnati/Northern Kentucky International Airport in 1947, when it was still named the Greater Cincinnati Airport.

attend the ceremony. The *Times Star* newspaper reported, "The Boone County Airport is a first-rate field. It is larger, more up to date and better from an aeronautical standpoint than Lunken. Cincinnati owes a lot to the energy of Northern Kentucky interests." American, Delta, and TWA airlines had signed 20-year operating leases. An American Airlines DC-3 inbound from Cleveland, Ohio, touched down at the Greater Cincinnati Airport (its name at first) at 9:23 a.m. on January 10, 1947. A Delta Airlines DC-4 landed close behind it, followed minutes later by a TWA flight. Scheduled passenger service began with 24 flights daily. The airport's identifier code, CVG, comes from the abbreviation of the nearest major city at the time of its opening, Covington. The airport's first official name reflected the metropolitan area it served. Later it became the Greater Cincinnati International Airport, and finally, the Cincinnati/Northern Kentucky International Airport.

The commercial jet era changed the face of aviation. On December 16, 1960, a Delta Convair 880 jet began the first scheduled jet service at CVG. To accommodate jets better, as well as the rapid passenger growth that came with them, the airport expanded the original terminal by 85,000 square feet. "The more powerful jet engines meant aircraft could be much larger," said William Whitson, a longtime airport board member. "Jets also needed longer runways. That's why we built a new 7,800-foot east-west runway. Most jets have no integral stairway, so we had to build jetways as part of the terminal building."

On November 8, 1965, an accident focused national attention on the airport for a brief period (see **Aviation Accidents**). An American Airlines Boeing 727 jet, inbound from New York City, crashed into the hillside as it crossed the Ohio River on approach to Runway 18 (today's Runway 18 Center) in Constance. Fifty-eight people died; four survived. The new and safer 7,800-foot east-west runway opened on April 1, 1967. The airport then proceeded with plans for a $1.2 million extension of the only north-south runway at the time (Runway 18/36) to a total of 9,500 feet. The new runway system was able to handle any type of aircraft. On November 6, 1967, a TWA Boeing 707 jet, attempting to abort a takeoff, skidded to a fiery crash on a hill at the end of the east-west runway (Runway 27/9). All on board survived. The plane, however, was destroyed. The worst airplane crash in Cincinnati's history was on November 20, 1967. TWA flight 128 from Los Angeles, a Convair 880 jet, crashed into an orchard a mile and a half from the airport, on approach to Runway 18 (today's Runway 18 Center), very near to the previous American Airlines incident. Seventy passengers and crew died; 17 survived.

The Federal Aviation Administration (FAA) dedicated a new 128-foot control tower on the south side of the airfield on May 9, 1970. It remained in use until 1998, when the FAA dedicated a new 256-foot tower. The airport reached a major milestone on November 17, 1971, when the airport board signed agreements with seven airlines for the largest expansion to date. Up to that time, there had been calls among some tri-state leaders to build a bigger airport elsewhere. "This pressure had existed for many years," said Wilbert L. Ziegler, the airport's longtime general counsel. "The financial commitment made by the air carriers in 1971 showed that they were committed to keeping the airport here in Boone Co. The discussion to move the airport ceased." The $38 million expansion was completed in 1974—updating Terminal 1 and adding two additional terminals. The functional design earned recognition in aviation circles as "the Cincinnati concept." The airport board hosted a two-day grand opening on September 14 and 15, 1974. More than 35,000 people gathered on the second day to hear former astronaut Neil Armstrong deliver the principal address. He was appointed to the advisory board of the airport the following year. During his speech, Armstrong came up with the airport's oft-used marketing slogan: "CVG—Cincinnati Very Good." As part of the renovation and expansion, the airport installed 14 huge murals, which had been removed from the concourse at Cincinnati's Union Terminal (train station) before it was razed. Tri-state citizens, businesses, and the airport contributed more than $500,000 to relocate the 20-ton murals to their new home.

On June 15, 1975, fire swept through the airport offices and the weather bureau in Terminal 1. Two airport firefighters died fighting the blaze (see **Fires**), which caused heavy damage and consumed many historic records. Its origin was never determined.

Comair began at CVG in 1977 with two twin-engine commuter aircraft flying to Evansville, Ind. Tragedy struck on October 8, 1979, when flight 444, a Piper Navajo Aircraft, crashed during takeoff, killing eight people. After becoming a feeder carrier for Delta Airlines in 1984, Comair grew to become one of the largest commuter airlines in the United States by the mid-1990s.

Air Canada flight 797, a DC-9 jet, made an emergency landing on June 2, 1983. Fire broke out on the aircraft en route from Dallas, Tex., to Toronto, Canada, over Indianapolis. The aircraft required the 100 miles from Indianapolis to CVG to descend from its 35,000-foot cruising altitude. After evacuation on the ground at CVG, it was found that 23 of the 41 passengers aboard had died of smoke inhalation, including Canadian television entrepreneur Curtis Mathis.

President Jimmy Carter (1977–1981) deregulated the airlines in 1977. As the 1980s brought deregulation into full swing, CVG began to experience growth unparalleled in its history. From the early 1980s to 2005, CVG grew from an origin-and-destination airport to a major transfer center, transitioning from 35 nonstop cities to more than 120 nonstop destinations, including Europe and Canada.

Delta Airlines established a hub and doubled its number of gates to 10 in 1981. On December 16, 1986, Delta added 60 flights, bringing its daily total to 105. No other U.S. airline had ever orchestrated that type of increase in a single day. Six months later, on June 1, Delta added 21 more daily flights, pushing its total to 126.

By 1987 Delta Airlines had expanded its number of gates to 40 with the $45 million addition to Concourse A. In June of that year, Delta added nonstop service from CVG to London, England, marking the first of many nonstop flights to Europe. Three years later, Delta added a $20 million maintenance hangar large enough to accommodate MD-11s. "The thing I have enjoyed the most and felt the best about in my many years at CVG was the inauguration of our first international flight [to London]. I've always felt that opened up our community to being a player in the global marketplace," said Robert Holscher, director of aviation since 1975.

CVG dedicated a new north-south runway in January 1991 (Runway 18 Left). In the decade that followed, CVG became one of the nation's fastest-growing airports as the number of annual passengers doubled to more than 20 million. To minimize any negative impact of noise on the airport's neighbors, CVG spent more than $100 million on airfield modifications, sound insulation, and voluntary property acquisitions.

A $500 million expansion completed in 1994 added a new Delta Airlines terminal, a new road system, and an underground transportation system connecting Delta's facilities. The addition of Concourse B increased the number of Delta gates to 50. At the same time, Comair added a new concourse that could accommodate more than 50 planes, making it the largest regional airline facility in the world.

The hub established by Delta Airlines was not the only one to be established at CVG in the 1980s. DHL Worldwide Express, a package and freight overnight carrier, opened a 50,000-square-foot package-sorting facility in 1984, making Cincinnati its primary North American hub. DHL eventually enlarged its CVG hub to 355,000 square feet, with a capacity of 2 million pounds nightly. CVG would operate as DHL's primary North American hub until 2005, when DHL merged operations with Airborne Express in Wilmington, Ohio.

The new millennium brought many challenges to the aviation industry. The events of September 11, 2001, preceded by a Comair pilot strike several months earlier, prompted a decline in passengers for the first time in CVG's history. CVG handled 17.3 million passengers in 2001. Activity eventually rebounded, peaking at a record 22.8 million passengers in 2005, with as many as 670 daily departures. Delta Airline's bankruptcy and subsequent hub realignment in December 2005 led to an approximately 25 percent decrease in flights at CVG, foreshadowing an overall decrease in passengers for 2006.

Even with these changes, the Delta Airline hub remains strong. Today, CVG offers nonstop service to 120 cities—nearly three times the number of destinations served by the five surrounding airports combined. Delta has continued to strengthen its international network at CVG with flights to Amsterdam, Frankfurt, London, Paris, and Rome. In the Midwest, only airports in Chicago and Detroit offer more service to Europe.

In addition to providing a gateway to the world, CVG supports tens of thousands of jobs in the region and remains one of the region's primary economic drivers. The opening of a third north-south runway (Runway 18 Right) in December 2005 placed CVG among the most efficient airports in the world.

"The quality of the airport board membership—the forward thinking they have brought to the board—has been crucial to the airport's growth," Holscher said. "You can see this clearly in our infrastructure, with CVG being one of only six airports in the world to enjoy triple simultaneous landings."

Passenger Statistics

1947, 302,707; 1957, 1,174,377; 1967, 2,307,561; 1977, 2,741,500; 1987, 7,259,085; 1997, 19,898,187; 2005, 22,778,785; 2007, 15,700,000.

Directors of Aviation

Oscar R. Parks (1944–1948); Robert M. Isenberg (1948–1953); Byron R. Dickey (1953–1960, 1963–1971); Arven Saunders (1960–1963); Barry S. Craig (1971–1975); Robert F. Holscher (1975–present).

Board Chairmen

V. H. Logan (1943); C. Lisle Kays (1943–1950, 1965, 1967); Fred T. Macklin (1950–1962, 1966); Bernard H. Eilerman (1962); Bernard Rutemiller (1963); Maurice Walsh (1964, 1972); Clemens B. Deters (1968, 1973, 1979, 1983, 1987–1988); William C. Whitson (1969, 1974, 1980, 1984, 1988–1989); Clifford E. Kohlhepp (1970–1971); Joseph L. Scanlon (1975, 1982); Walter L. Pieschel (1976); Ted R. Richardson (1977); James Simpson Jr. (1978); Peter Burris (1981, 1985, 1989–1990, 1992–1993); Jerome A. Stricker (1986); Paul F. Michels (1986–1987, 1990–1991); Frank Schleper (1991–1992); Ralph A. Drees (1993–1995); Michael J. Gibbons (1995–1997); Bert M. Huff (1997–1999); Gary R. Bockelman (1999–2001); Arylyn T. Easton (2001–2002); John S. Domaschko (2004); William T. Robinson III (2004–2006); Richard D. Crist (2006-present).

Bushelman, Ted J., Robert F. Holscher, and Wilbert L. Ziegler. Interviews by Joe Feiertag, Nicole Ropp, and Richard Rawe, August 2006, Cincinnati/Northern Kentucky International Airport.

Keefe, Robert A. *Chronological History of the Greater Cincinnati International Airport.* Self-published, 1991.

Kenton Co. Airport Board. Minutes of the Board of Directors Meetings, Cincinnati/Northern Kentucky International Airport.

Rawe, Richard L. *Creating a World Class Airport: Cincinnati/Northern Kentucky International, 1947–1997.* Encino, Calif.: Cherbo, 1997.

Joe Feiertag, Nicole Ropp, and Richard Rawe

CINCINNATI SOUTHERN RAILROAD. The leaders of Cincinnati had been planning since the 1840s to build a railroad south from the Ohio River to Georgia and Alabama. Such a rail line would allow Cincinnati merchants to sell their goods in the developing southern states. In 1850 Cincinnati investors helped to fund the **Covington and Lexington Railroad** (C&L), which was to have reached Chattanooga, Tenn., via connecting tracks. The proposed route began with the C&L to Paris, Ky., the **Maysville and Lexington** (M&L) to Lexington, and the Lexington and Danville (L&D) to Danville, Ky. The plan foundered south of Nicholasville in Jessamine Co., when the L&D was unable to bridge the Kentucky River. In the late 1860s, Cincinnati's leaders proposed a rail line to the South via Louisville, but the resultant **Louisville, Cincinnati, and Lexington Railroad** was of a different gauge than the L&N, requiring transshipment of goods at Louisville.

In 1869 the City of Cincinnati set out to build its own railroad into the southern heartland. That same year, the Ohio legislature passed the Ferguson Bill, allowing Cincinnati to circumvent a provision in the 1851 Ohio constitution that forbade cities to lend money to railroads for construction. The legislation permitted a city to build a railroad if the city owned it. Under the provisions of this law, Cincinnati organized the Cincinnati Southern Railroad (CSRR). The CSRR had to fight the L&N in the Tennessee (1872) and Kentucky (1874) legislatures before securing charters to build.

The route chosen for the CSRR lay west of the existing **Kentucky Central** line, which ran from Covington to Paris, Ky. The CSRR rail line crossed the Ohio River at Ludlow and ran south through Kenton, Grant, Scott, and Fayette counties into Lexington. At Walton, the CSRR and the Louisville, Cincinnati, and Lexington (LC&L) track from Covington to Louisville met. The CSRR right-of-way was an elevated track that crossed over the LC&L track on a trestle.

In 1877 the CSRR bridged the Ohio River with a single-track span containing a section that pivoted horizontally to allow steamboats to pass in high water. Owing to the increased weight of carloads and engines at the beginning of the 20th century, the bridge was replaced in 1922 with the current double-track version. The circular pivot pier of the original CSRR bridge remains near the southern shore beneath the bridge.

At Lexington the CSRR connected with the Lexington and Danville (L&D). Using portions of a survey originally undertaken by Union troops during the **Civil War** to extend the L&D south to Burnside, the CSRR built southward. It crossed the Kentucky River near Wilmore in Jessamine Co., on what became known as High Bridge. This bridge, opened in 1877 (see **Gustave Bouscaren**), soared 275 feet above the river. In 1929 it was replaced with the current structure.

From Danville, Ky., south to Oakdale, Tenn., the CSRR passed through the foothills of the Appalachian Mountains, requiring the construction of 27 tunnels and 105 bridges; the longest tunnel, at Kings Mountain, Ky., was 3,984 feet long. This portion of the route became known as the Rathole. Engineers and firemen running their coal-fired locomotives here were subjected to extreme heat and poisonous fumes inside the tunnels. Lung disease was high among these train crews. During the first three decades of the 20th century, the tunnels of the Rathole were enlarged, daylighted, or bypassed, so that by 1930 only 16 remained. In the 1940s the CSRR began converting its means of locomotive engine power from steam to diesel. The arrival of piggyback loads, jumbo hoppers, autoracks, and container shipments in the 1950s found the surviving tunnels again too small to handle the new types of equipment. In 1961 the City of Cincinnati issued $35 million in bonds to daylight or further enlarge these tunnels. Huge cuts, as deep as 160 feet, were made through the hillsides to daylight the tunnels and provide the necessary overhead clearance for the new rolling stock. The tunnels left in place were enlarged to give them a height of 30 feet and a width of 20 feet.

From Oakdale to Chattanooga in Tennessee, the CSRR had to build through continuing rough terrain, but simple fills, cuts, and bridges were able to overcome the elevation changes along this section. Except for Erlanger Hill in Kenton Co., Ky., only at Kings Mountain, Ky., and Sunbright, Tenn., did grades exceed 1 percent. The 336-mile CSRR rail line from Cincinnati to Chattanooga was opened in early 1880 at a cost of $59,000 per mile.

The steep climb up the 1.2 percent grade from Ludlow to Erlanger necessitated then, and today, that a helper engine be stationed at the bottom of the hill. The CSRR developed a locomotive and passenger car service yard at Ludlow. This service yard became the major employer in Ludlow during the era of steam locomotive engines.

Because the operation of a railroad was beyond the scope of a city government, the CSRR was leased in 1881 to the Cincinnati, New Orleans, and Texas Pacific Railway Company (CNO&TP). The CNO&TP was controlled by Baron Frederick Emile d'Erlanger, who owned an interest in several railroads. Control of the CNO&TP allowed d'Erlanger to put together a rail line that stretched 1,165 miles from Cincinnati, the Queen City, to the Crescent City, New Orleans. The rail line was then marketed as the Queen and Crescent route.

In 1890 the Richmond and West Point Terminal Railroad Company (R&WP), a holding company, gained control of the CNO&TP. The R&WP, having overextended itself, went into receivership. In 1894 East Coast banker J. P. Morgan reorganized the R&WP as the **Southern Railway** Company (SR). The SR shed part of the rail lines held by the R&WP, but the CSRR was retained as the crown jewel. In that same year, the SR acquired the Louisville Southern Railroad, which linked Louisville to Danville. This acquisition allowed the SR to compete head-on with the L&N for goods moving south through both Cincinnati and Louisville. In 1982 the SR merged with the Norfolk and Western Railroad to form the **Norfolk Southern Railroad** (NS).

During the 20th century, the SR ran a few noted passenger trains south out of Cincinnati. The most famous were the *Queen and Crescent,* the *Royal Palm,* the *Ponce de Leon,* and the *Florida Sunbeam.* Passenger service over the line ceased in 1971.

The CSRR's original lease to the CNO&TP was extended in 1901 for 60 years, or until 1961. In 1928 the terms of the lease were amended so that the lease extended until 2026. Since the CSRR lease is with the CNO&TP, this corporation continues to exist as a legal entity within the NS empire.

Butler, Tod Jordan. "The Cincinnati Southern Railway: A City's Response to Relative Commercial Decline," PhD diss., Ohio State Univ., 1971.
Hall, Charles G., ed. *The Cincinnati Southern Railway, a History.* Cincinnati: Ault & Wiborg, 1902.
Tenkotte, Paul A. "The 'Chronic Want' of Cincinnati: A Southern Railroad," *NKH* 6, no. 1 (Fall–Winter 1998): 24–33.
White, John H. *On the Right Track—Some Historic Cincinnati Railroads.* Cincinnati: Cincinnati Railroad Club, 2003.

Charles H. Bogart

CINCINNATI SOUTHERN RAILROAD BRIDGE. Built to serve the **Cincinnati Southern Railroad**, now the **Norfolk Southern Railway**, the Cincinnati Southern Railroad Bridge spans the Ohio River, connecting Cincinnati and Ludlow. The original bridge, opened in 1877, consisted of a single track with a circular pivot pier that enabled a 369-foot draw span to be moved horizontally to allow the passage of steamboats during high water. The 1877 bridge was replaced by a new double-track span in 1922 to allow for heavier engines and loads, but the old pivot pier still remains visible near the Ludlow shore. For many years after 1922, the former pivot section of the bridge could be raised and lowered by a vertical lift, not rotated. It was used once on October 6, 1922, for demonstration purposes.

"Complete New Bridge," *KP*, August 26, 1922, 1.
"New 'Vertical Lift' of the Southern Bridge, Costing Thousands, May Never Have to Be Raised," *KTS*, October 7, 1922, 1.
"Tests of the Cincinnati Southern Railway Bridge," *Engineering News*, November 24, 1877, 332.

Paul A. Tenkotte

CINCINNATI SOUTHERN RAILROAD YARD. This railroad yard starts at the top of the hill about one-eighth of a mile from the southern shore of the Ohio River and extends southward for about one-half mile over a relatively flat plateau within Ludlow. The yard has parallel tracks that interconnect through switches at both ends. Here, incoming trains were broken up, their cars were sorted, and outgoing trains were assembled. The yard worked mostly with freight cars. Passenger trains to and from Cincinnati passed through the yard without stopping, except for a few locals. A locomotive roundhouse and repair shops were located on the west side of the yard. The Ludlow yard dates back to the mid-1870s, when the **Cincinnati Southern** was building toward Chattanooga, Tenn. An incline plane brought rail and other track supplies up the hillside from a river landing. After the **Cincinnati Southern Railroad Bridge** was finished in 1877, the incline was abandoned. The yard trackage and adjacent service building had developed in a generally unplanned manner.

A major fire in November 1887 reduced the old plant to ruins. The railroad's master mechanic, **James Meehan** (1834–1908), rebuilt the shops on a grand plan that included a brick repair shop 668 feet long. It had machine, blacksmith, and boiler shops. The smokestack stood 84 feet high. A brick roundhouse was erected with ample space for 16 locomotives. Among the auxiliary buildings were an office, a sand house, and a coaling station. This facility became a major employer in Ludlow.

Even before the new plant opened, Meehan had fabricated several new locomotives and repaired hundreds of locomotives and cars. An even bigger job was undertaken in May 1886, when the railroad converted from the old southern railroad gauge of five feet to the national standard of four feet eight and one-half inches. Locomotives and cars were converted in stages, starting in 1884. Much of this work was planned and staged at Ludlow.

This yard and repair shop facility remained very active during the steam-locomotive era. When the final steamers on the system were retired in 1953, Ludlow and many other such facilities went into an eclipse. Only routine repairs are made at Ludlow today, in an engine shed. The yard itself sees little use, since so few trains originate on the **Norfolk Southern** in the Cincinnati area. Even so, the railroad carries more freight tonnage than ever before. Passenger trains disappeared in about 1970, but around 30 freight trains operate over the line presently.

White, John H. *On the Right Track: Some Historic Cincinnati Railroads.* Cincinnati: Cincinnati Railroad Club, 2003.

John H. White

CINEMA X. An adult "XXX" movie theater operated in Newport during the 1970s. The theater closed its doors in early 1982, after being prosecuted and convicted of state obscenity charges on seven occasions in approximately 24 months, beginning in April 1980.

Located at 716 Monmouth St., in the building of the former State Theater, Cinema X opened in 1970. Michigan pornography entrepreneur Floyd Bloss had purchased the property. An owner of several porn businesses and a veteran of several obscenity-related litigations in Michigan, Bloss was not the "real owner" or "the money" behind the venture. That distinction belonged to Harry Virgil Mohney, of Durand, Mich. Mohney was a projectionist in an adult-film theater during the early 1960s, opened an adult drive-in theater known locally in Flint, Mich., as the "Durand Dirties," and expanded from there. His financial worth was between $5 million and $10 million in 1970, when he put his money into adult enterprises in Cincinnati and into Newport's Cinema X. Over the next decade, Mohney built a complex network of corporations, estimated to number at least six to eight dozen, which often existed in name only, to avoid taxes and criminal liability. Films shown and peep-show booths located in the Cinema X in Newport were marketed to the theater from companies that had connections with some of the major U.S. crime families. By the mid-1970s, Mohney's porn-distribution empire was exceeded in scope by only a few international porn-distribution networks.

In early 1971 Newport and Campbell Co. authorities began investigations and raids of the theater and the theater's associated adult bookstore, then managed and operated by "front men" working for Mohney. One was Stanley Marks, a Greater Cincinnati pornography retailer who became involved in obscenity litigation on both sides of the Ohio River during the 1970s. Newport Police and Campbell Co. commonwealth attorney Frank Benton conducted a raid and seizure at the Cinema X in 1971, and over the next year several more were conducted, despite at least two separate federal and state suits filed by Marks against Benton and Newport authorities. In the mid-1970s, local federal prosecutors brought obscenity-related charges against Marks and other corporate entities associated with the Cinema X, including Harry V. Mohney and a corporation that still contained his name on record, a situation Mohney shortly corrected. The criminal actions were brought over the showing of the movie *Deep Throat.* After two lengthy trials, convictions, and judicial findings that the film was obscene, the cases against Mohney and Marks and most of the other defendants were dismissed. Twice the matters went to the U.S. Supreme Court, once because the standard for determining obscenity changed, and another time because of evidentiary issues. In the early 1980s, charges against Marks were officially dismissed. By then, Marks had left the Greater Cincinnati area to work in other parts of Mohney's far-flung empire.

Mohney's theaters and bookstores had successfully defended themselves against obscenity civil and criminal litigation again and again in Indiana, Michigan, and elsewhere since the late 1960s. His attorneys included Robert Eugene Smith, from Maryland and Georgia, whose litigation credentials in porn defense were as impressive as they were numerous around the country; however, in 1978 Campbell Co. voters elected Paul Twehues as Campbell Co. attorney, and Smith's fortunes changed dramatically.

New to politics, and having never in his brief legal career handled an obscenity case, Twehues hired three assistants, Bill Schoettelkotte, Justin Verst, and Bill Wehr, who also had no experience in obscenity litigation. Apparently believing they had nothing to fear from the new prosecutors in Newport, the operators of Cinema X continued to show "XXX" film fare, and the theater's prominent marquee encouraged all those who passed to visit and view films that surely violated Kentucky's obscenity laws because of the films' graphic sexual content. In early 1980 a three-member majority of the Newport City Commission rejected the entreaties of citizen groups and ministerial associations urging them to act against the Cinema X and the negative "Sin City" image that the theater seemingly projected. The two minority commission members found themselves powerless in the issue.

To the surprise of the Cinema X operators, the theater's corporate owners, and the Newport City Commission's majority, the Kentucky State Police and the Campbell Co. Attorney's Office initiated an antivice campaign in early 1980 that included the Cinema X. In April 1980 and on six other occasions over the next 19 months, Twehues's staff and the state police conducted raids and seizures at the Cinema X (the Newport Police were not able to assist because of the City Commission's stance). Seven separate obscenity jury cases were tried, and seven separate convictions were obtained against three corporations involved in the ownership and management of the Cinema X. Fines for convictions and contempt-of-court assessments came to hundreds of thousands of dollars. There were no acquittals of the corporate defendants.

In early 1982 the Cinema X was closed and title to the property was transferred to the City of Newport. After the closing, the 1982 Newport city attorney, Wil Schroder, and Newport city manager **Ralph Mussman** conducted a walk-through at the Cinema X. During the inspection, Schroder and Mussman made a startling discovery. A "pile" of photos were found that had obviously been taken with some special film and by cameras specially mounted behind and to the sides of the Cinema X screen. The Cinema X operators had been photographing their audiences. Schroder, new to Newport at the time, did not know any of the individuals photographed; however, Mussman remarked that "he knew a bunch of the people in the pictures." Before the prosecution, none of the police investigators or prosecutors knew anything about the photographing of audiences.

Mohney eventually served some federal prison time for tax evasion, and the federal witnesses included his former mistress and wife, who had produced a few of the movies seized in a July 1980 Cinema X raid. Mohney invested some of his extensive fortune in the national chain of Deja Vu gentlemen's clubs. His enterprises are found almost everywhere in the United States, but not where Paul Twehues and Justin Verst prosecuted. Mohney and his great wealth have not returned to Campbell Co., Ky.

Newport's Cinema X was not the only adult cinema in Northern Kentucky during the 1970s. The Ludlow Cinema opened for "adult films" in March 1970; Kenton Co. authorities soon brought charges, a settlement was reached in court, and the Ludlow Cinema ceased presenting pornographic movies.

Diaz, Kevin, and Rachel Reynolds. "Porn Merchant Gets Prison," *Detroit News,* May 3, 1990, B2.

"Peepshow Operator Appeals Tax Conviction," *Cleveland Plain Dealer,* July 19, 1991, A1.

United States v. Harry Mohney, et al., 723 F. Supp. 1197 (E. D. Mich. 1989).

U.S. Department of Justice, Attorney General Edwin Meese, *Attorney General's Commission on Pornography–Final Report: July 1986,* vol. 2. Washington, D.C., 1986.

Webb, Gary. "Who Is Behind the Cinema X," *KP,* November 22, 1980, 1K.

Mike Williams

CIRCUSES. Circuses have appeared locally in Bellevue, Covington, Latonia, Ludlow, and Newport. One such circus advertised three Zulu tribesmen, a band of Sioux Indians, Mexican warriors, cowboys, Australian cannibals, 13 Nubians, and an eight-foot-tall man.

The modern circus evolved from ancient Roman and Greek festivals, English horse shows, and other festive celebrations. *Circus* is the Latin word for "circle" and is used because the action usually occurs in rings, the best example being the three-ring circus. An Englishman, Philip Astley, is generally considered the father of the circus. About 1777 Astley began operating a riding school in London, where he presented open-air horse shows. His exhibitions combined horsemanship with comedy and some elements of theater. Another resident of London, Charles Diblin, built a ring of houses around a horse exercise area, which he called "The Circus." Similar circular public areas were later built in London and were named the Oxford and the Piccadilly circuses. Today these are popular shopping and meeting places and no longer have anything to do with performing circuses.

Over the years, circuses added wild and exotic animals to their shows to increase crowd appeal. P. T. Barnum introduced various curiosities, such as the smallest man on earth, the fattest woman, the bearded lady, and other similar peculiarities. The ultimate showman and promoter, Barnum became wealthy by exploiting gullible people. It was he who coined the phrase "there's a sucker born every minute." Early circuses came to town via wagon or in their own brightly colored railroad trains, parading their animals and sequined performers down main streets to the sound of loud music en route to the circus grounds. Barnum brought his circus to Northern Kentucky in 1883. Newspaper accounts heralded the arrival of ferocious animals, beautiful young ladies, and lovable clowns.

During the early 1900s, the Gentry Brothers, the Norris and Rowe, and the Hagenbeck-Wallace circuses all appeared in Northern Kentucky. Some of these performed at Third and Philadelphia Sts. in Covington, the Covington Ball Park, the Rough Rider Park in Newport (W. Fifth and the Licking River), and later the **Twin Oaks Golf Course** in Latonia. Circus trains would park on the **Louisville and Nashville Railroad** siding along Lowell St. in the **West End** of Newport. The famous Gentry Brothers brought the first motorized circus to Northern Kentucky in late summer 1930. It arrived in six trucks and set up on the polo grounds of the **Fort Thomas Military Reservation**; it was sponsored by the Fort Thomas Men's Club. One of the early crowd favorites was the famed animal trainer Clyde Beatty, who later formed his own circus. Many circuses in the United States featured wild-west shows with real American Indians, wild buffalo, rugged cowboys, entertaining clowns, high-wire acts, and people being shot from cannons. At the height of circuses' popularity, the appearance of a circus in any town was one of the highlights of the year.

Newport physician Dr. **Robert Carothers** was so enamored with circuses that he would often close his medical practice for extended periods and travel from town to town with them. World-renowned geologist, paleontologist, and Harvard professor Dr. **Nathaniel Southgate Shaler** tells in his autobiography about caring for a circus elephant on his father's Southgate farm (modern **Evergreen Cemetery**). In the mid-20th century, Bellevue was home base for the **Sherman Brothers** Clown Act. Chester Sherman, who grew up in Bellevue, and his partner Joe Vani appeared in circuses internationally from 1932 through 1975 and were inducted into the International Clown Hall of Fame in 1995.

With citizens less easily astounded and with permanent zoos and television and movies now in the picture, circuses have lost much of their appeal. The most popular circus to appear in Greater Cincinnati in recent years is the Ringling Brothers, Barnum & Bailey Circus, a result of the merger of three separate circus operations. The future of circuses appears bleak in view of dwindling attendance figures, high arena rental fees, soaring transportation costs, and increased salaries, coupled with pressure from animal-rights advocates regarding treatment of animals.

"First Motorized Circus Will Play in Fort Thomas," *KP,* September 18, 1930, 3.

"Old Circus Grounds Soon to Be Playfield," *KP,* April 25, 1941, 1.

Reis, Jim. "Under the Big Top," *KP,* May 10, 2004, 4K.

Speaight, George. *A History of the Circus.* New York: A. S. Barnes, 1980.

CITIGROUP. Citigroup, the preeminent global financial services company, is a major employer in Northern Kentucky. Citigroup has locations and services worldwide, involving some 200 million customer accounts in more than 100 countries, and provides consumers, corporations, governments, and institutions with a broad range of financial products and services: consumer banking and credit, corporate and investment banking, insurance, securities brokerage, and asset management. Major brand names under Citigroup's trademark red umbrella include Banamex, Citi, Citibank, CitiFinancial, Primerica, and Smith Barney.

Citigroup's Northern Kentucky operations opened in Erlanger with 50 employees in 1989. Eight years later, the ribbon was cut and the doors were opened to the company's new facility on Houston Rd. in Florence, Ky., not far from the **Cincinnati/Northern Kentucky International Airport**. In 1997 Citigroup moved into this new credit-card-processing center on 81 acres west of I-75. The property, formerly a part of Camp **Marydale**, was purchased in 1996 from the Diocese of Covington (see **Roman Catholics**). Today, after a $44 million expansion in 2001, the facility has 344,000 square feet, and 2,800 employees work there. Citigroup views this location, which still has enough space for another building, as a premier site for future expansion.

Citigroup doubled the size of its facility to meet the growing demands of its call-center operations for Citi Cards Customer Service and Sales, Citi Cards Collections, Retail Banking Sales and Customer Service, Primerica Shareholder Services, and Smith Barney (formerly Salomon Smith Barney) businesses. Employees benefit from the on-site National Wildlife Habitat, a complete wellness center, and tuition assistance at any accredited college or university. Citigroup added express bus service from downtown Cincinnati, Covington, and Newport in 2004. The Florence location granted almost $900,000 in financial support to philanthropic causes and more than 3,500 hours in community impact giving in 2006, winning numerous awards for its philanthropic giving through such organizations as the United Way, the March of Dimes, and the P-16 Council on Education.

Citigroup promotes education for its employees and for the people of the region. In 2003 the company formed the Gateway Center, a collaborative partnership between Citigroup and the **Gateway Community and Technical College**, with linkage to entities such as the **Northern Kentucky Chamber of Commerce**, **Northern Kentucky University**, and the Kentucky Department for Employment Services One-Stop Center. Gateway Community and Technical College has established a comprehensive education and training center on the Citigroup Kentucky campus to assist Citigroup with student assessment, educational and training services, and career development. The on-site center is expected to increase the number of individuals who pursue postsecondary education and career opportunities. One of many current classes being offered to Citigroup team members is "Career Discovery," a class through which the company hopes to recognize, groom, and retain the most qualified professional candidates, while employees gain tangible career plans and goals for success. The success of this class has become apparent, as a number of employees have been promoted into management upon completion.

Citigroup expects to fill an additional 1,000-plus positions over the next few years to support its ongoing growth. The firm has traditionally hired from within Boone, Campbell, and Kenton counties but is expanding its target area to include Indiana, Greater Cincinnati, and the other counties in the Northern Kentucky Area Development District.

Citi. www.citigroup.com (accessed on November 11, 2006).
Crowley, Patrick. "Citibank Begins Expansion," *CE*, June 28, 2001, 1D.
Newberry, Jon. "Citibank Chooses Blue Ash," *CE*, June 20, 2005, 1A.

Johnna Reeder

CITIZENS NATIONAL BANK, COVINGTON. Founded in Covington in 1890, Citizens National Bank opened in March of that year on the southwest corner of Madison Ave. and Pike St. in rented quarters. Its first president was Henry Feltman. By 1894 **William Goebel** was serving on the bank's board. In 1896 the bank (in conjunction with jeweler Fred Pieper) built a three-story building across the street, at the southeast corner of Pike and Madison, designed by architect **Daniel Seger**. The third floor was rented by the Knights of Pythias, a fraternal organization. During the **Great Depression**, the bank remained solvent, earning the nickname "the Little Stone Jug." Citizens remodeled its Covington home in 1962, removing the two-story turret and enveloping the exterior with a metal grill. In 1983 the bank moved its headquarters to Fort Wright. At the time of its acquisition by Central Bancorporation of Cincinnati in 1986, Citizens National was the fourth-largest bank in Kenton Co.

1890–1940: 50th Anniversary, Citizens National Bank, Covington, Ky. Booklet available in the vertical files at Kenton Co. Public Library, Covington, Ky.
"Central Trust to Purchase Citizens National," *KP*, January 17, 1986, 1K.
"New Structure. The Citizens' Bank Pieper Block," *KP*, January 31, 1896, 4.

Paul A. Tenkotte

CITY MARKETS. Markets were necessary fixtures in the lives of 19th-century urban residents. Because the lack of refrigeration made food storage difficult, people needed to shop for food on a daily basis. Within Northern Kentucky, one of the earliest market spaces was in downtown Covington, near the city hall and the county courthouse. Another market existed in the **Eastside** neighborhood at 11th St. between Scott and Greenup Sts. in Covington. This 11th St. market space has since been converted into a small city park. Two larger market houses also served the residents of Covington for many years. One was located on Seventh St., between Madison Ave. and Washington St. and the other on Sixth St. in **Main Strasse.**

The Seventh St. site had been used as an open market for many years before the **Civil War**. In June 1845 a number of interested citizens, including **James G. Arnold**, H. C. Ashbrook, Hiram Bond, W. H. Burgess, C. Carpenter, F. G. Gedge, H. C. Watkins, and John Wolf, met to discuss the construction of a market house there. A market house was constructed soon thereafter and replaced by a new structure in 1889.

City Market House, Seventh St., Covington.

In 1921 the Covington City Commission began plans for the construction of a modern Seventh St. Market House. That year, the commission granted an option to the Market Finance Corporation of Louisville; the firm was given 60 days to secure the necessary financing and begin construction on a new building. The company hired Covington architect **Bernard T. Wisenall** to develop the plans for the new market. Wisenall's plans called for a two-story California Mission style building (40 by 400 feet). The first floor was planned to house 38 stalls and space for a drugstore, a cigar shop, and a candy shop. The balcony level was designed to house a full-service cafeteria and restrooms. The total construction costs were estimated at $140,000. Controversy soon erupted over the proposed new Seventh St. Market House. In August 1921 a group of hucksters presented to the Covington City Commission a petition to halt the demolition of the old market house. These persons believed the market house should remain under public ownership and control and not be operated privately. Their efforts led to the abandonment of the proposed new market.

The supporters of a new Seventh St. Market House tried again to gain public support in 1922. In May of that year, two competing proposals were submitted to the Covington City Commission for approval, which was not granted. The major opponents of the measures were area farmers and hucksters, who rented stalls in the old building for very small amounts. In fact, the *Kentucky Post* noted that the market house usually lost money for the city.

The issue of a new market house was again raised in 1928. A petition, this time with 700 signatures, was again presented to the Covington City Commission resisting the plans. In 1929 the question of removing the market and replacing it with a modern building was placed on the ballot. The issue failed, with 5,671 voting in favor of the bond and 5,933 opposed.

Finally, in March 1930, a resolution for a new market house was passed by the Covington City Commission. At that time, city commissioner Louis Meyer agreed to lease his automobile storeroom to the city for use as a market house. Meyer's building was located on the east side of the 600 block of Scott St. The city commissioners agreed to the plan, and the new market house was officially opened for business along Scott St. in May 1930. At about that time, the old Seventh St. Market House was demolished.

The Sixth St. market dates from 1860, when the Covington City Council appointed a special committee to investigate the construction of a market house there, in Covington's growing **West Side**. Dr. J. E. Stevenson was appointed chairman of the committee. A site on Sixth St. was acquired between Main and Bakewell Sts., and construction of the Sixth St. Market House began in 1861. Legend holds that Union general Lew Wallace used the completed building for his headquarters during the **Civil War**. Covington city records indicate payments of $25 per month from the federal government for rent; for about a one-month period, the structure did serve as a Civil War hospital (see **Civil War Hospitals**). By 1875 business at the Sixth St. Market House was booming. The market housed 16 butchers, stalls for 28 rural farmers, and space for 30 area hucksters. By 1900, however, the market house had fallen into disrepair and West Side shoppers went elsewhere. In 1906 the members of the newly established Covington Parks Board approached the city council for permission to take over the market house as a site for a park. City officials agreed to the plan, and on May 2, 1907, the market house was razed. At this time, the strip of land between eastbound and westbound W. Sixth St. was turned over to the park board.

Upriver, other market houses operated for many years in the 19th century at Maysville. From the early days until 1829, a two-story market house stood on Sutton St. between Second and Third Sts. The upstairs served as city council chambers before the city hall was built. Two days per week, the market was open, and it was the place where Mason Co. people met and greeted each other. That building was torn down in 1829, to be replaced by a market house on Market St. between Second and Third Sts. The second structure served as a morgue during the great cholera epidemics of 1832 and 1833. It also functioned as the opera house, until an opera house was built. In spite of much protest, the second Maysville market house was demolished in 1863, and its customers shopped for meat and produce in the stores of town. There are no records of city markets operating in Newport or any other urban center of Northern Kentucky.

In the late twentieth century, farmers' markets developed throughout the Northern Kentucky region. These new farmers' markets usually are open-air, held on particular days, and feature fresh produce sold from vendors' tables and farmers' trucks. For example, an open farmers' market began operation in Covington in 2005 on a parking lot in the 600 block of Scott Blvd., on the east side of the street near the site of the old Meyer building. The Northern Kentucky Regional Farmers' Market, as this new organization is known, relocated to Main Strasse in 2006. Other markets include the Boone County Farmers' Market in Burlington; the Bracken County Farmers' Market in Brooksville; the Campbell County Farmers' Market in Alexandria, Highland Heights, and Newport; the Dry Ridge Farmers' Market in Grant Co.; the Family Roadside Farmers' Market in Williamstown; the Grant Co. Farmers' market in Williamstown, Crittenden, Dry Ridge, and Edgewood; the Dixie Farmers' Market in Erlanger; the Simon Kenton Farmers' Market in Independence; the Mason County Farmers' Market in Maysville; and the Pendleton County Farmers' Market in Falmouth.

"Awards at Market," *KP*, May 7, 1930, 1.
"Doom of City Markethouse Is Sealed," *KP*, April 3, 1930, 1.
"Here's the New and Old Markethouse for Covington Housewives," *KP*, May 3, 1930, 1.
"Market House in Sight," *KP*, July 14, 1921, 1.
"Market House Razing Put Up to People," *KP*, May 4, 1926, 1.
Maysville Centennial Exposition Commission. *As We Look Back: Maysville, 1833–1933.* Maysville, Ky.: Daily Independent, 1933.
"Move to Raze Markethouse," *KP*, March 11, 1930, 1.
"Officials Pass Markethouse Ordinance," *KP*, April 17, 1930, 1.
"See Change in Market Place," *KP*, April 14, 1930, 1.
"Sixth St. Market House Torn Down," *KP*, May 3, 1907, 2.
"Will Begin Work on Park," *KP*, March 10, 1905, 2.

David E. Schroeder

CIVIC ASSOCIATIONS. A wide variety of nonprofit, nongovernmental civic associations, other than **historical societies**, **hospitals**, **nursing homes**, schools, and museums, have been established over the years throughout Northern Kentucky to serve broad-based constituencies. One of the largest categories of civic associations has been that of fraternal organizations, which have provided sickness, death, and other benefits to their dues-paying members, as well as generous contributions to charities in the region. They include the **American Legion**, the **Bellevue Vets**, the **Jaycees**, the **Knights of Columbus**, the **Lions Clubs**, the **Masons**, the **Odd Fellows**, the **Rotary Clubs**, and the **VFW** (Veterans of Foreign Wars). Likewise, the Elks, Eagles, Kiwanis, and Optimist clubs have long-standing traditions in Northern Kentucky. The Benevolent and Protective Order of Elks (BPOE) opened its first Northern Kentucky lodge (No. 273) in Newport in 1893. In 1906 the lodge purchased the former home of **Oliver W. Root** at 312 York St., remodeled it, and built an addition. The Bellevue Lodge (No. 585), chartered in 1900, merged with the Newport Lodge in 1908. In November 1965, the Elks moved to a new facility on Alexandria Pk. (**U.S. 27**) in Cold Spring. Currently, this lodge sponsors many charitable events and distributes various scholarships each year. The Covington Elks lodge (No. 314) was chartered in 1895. In 1905 its members remodeled an old residence on W. Fifth St. as their headquarters, adding an annex to the back; on the same site, they dedicated a new building in 1937, designed by architect Ray Hayes. In 1994 Lodge No. 314 relocated to Boone Co., and it currently meets in a building on the **Dixie Highway** in Florence. The lodge participates in numerous philanthropic events, including food drives at Thanksgiving; it also works with the Special Olympics and hosts appreciation receptions for police and firefighters. Women have been accepted as members since 1995. Covington also has an African American Elks lodge (see **Benjamin Franklin Howard**), called Ira Chapter No. 37, established in 1916. It meets in a building on E. 11th St. In the past, Maysville had an Elks lodge (No. 704).

Newport's Fraternal Order of Eagles (No. 280), established in 1902, was the first in the state. By 1923 it had 750 members and met in the upper floors of the Widrig's Pharmacy Building on the northwest corner of Eighth and York Sts., which is still standing (see **Widrig Family**). Covington's Eagles lodge (No. 329) was chartered in 1903. After occupying several halls, the group moved to a renovated house at 16 E. Eighth St. It had a Glee Club and a Drill Team. Dayton's lodge (No. 1285) was organized in 1906 and in 1916 purchased a large home on the northwest corner of Fifth and Berry Sts. as its meeting hall, which is still used. Today there are lodges in Bellevue, Dayton, Maysville, and Newport.

Covington's Kiwanis club, chartered in 1928, originally met at the **Trinity Episcopal Church**. Currently there are two Kiwanis chapters in Northern Kentucky, Covington–Kenton Co. and Williamstown. Optimist International is represented by three chapters in Northern Kentucky, located in Covington, Newport, and Southgate.

Among other civic associations are those providing specialized services to youth, seniors, families, and women:

Boys & Girls Club
Boy Scouts of America
Campbell Lodge
Children's Home of Northern Kentucky
Children's Law Center
Covington Ladies Home
Diocesan Catholic Children's Home
Family Nurturing Center
Girl Scouts
Maplewood Children's Home
Northern Kentucky Right to Life
Northern Kentucky Transit
Senior Services of Northern Kentucky
Warsaw Woman's Club
Welcome House of Northern Kentucky
Williamstown Women's Club
Women's Crisis Center
YMCA

Others are concerned with emotional, mental and physical issues (see **BAWAC Inc.**; **Blind and Visually Impaired**; **Camp KYSOC**; **Comprehend Inc.**; **Deaf and Hearing-Impaired**; **Kentucky Consumers Advocate Network**; **New Perceptions Inc.**; **Northern Kentucky Services for the Deaf**; **NorthKey Community Care**; **Point/Arc of Northern Kentucky**; **Protection and Advocacy**; **Recovery Network**; **Substance Abuse Treatment**; and **Transitions Inc.**). Some focus on addressing poverty, hunger, homelessness and emergency crises, including

Action Ministries
American Red Cross
Be Concerned Inc.
Brighton Center
Catholic Charities
Goodwill Industries
Hosea House
Northern Kentucky Community Action Commission
Parish Kitchen
Salvation Army
Society of St. Vincent de Paul

Still other organizations provide opportunities for leaders to address community problems:

Center for Great Neighborhoods of Covington
Forward Quest/Vision 2015
Leadership Northern Kentucky
Northern Kentucky Chamber of Commerce

The attainment of **civil rights** for minorities has been espoused by the **Northern Kentucky African-American Task Force**, the **African-American Businessmen's Association**, the **NAACP**, and groups dedicated to **gays and gay rights**. Residents of Northern Kentucky cities, towns and subdivisions have also formed municipal civic associations, country clubs, and swim clubs throughout the region.

"Big Time for Elks: New Home to Be Dedicated March 7," *KP*, February 14, 1905, 3.

Chavez, Elizabeth J. "The Covington Elks," *Papers of the Kenton County Historical Society* 2 (1990): 132–38.

"Covington Elks: Organize and Install Officers at Hermes Hall," *KP*, February 1, 1895, 4.

"Kiwanis Club Is Given Charter," *KP*, January 14, 1928, 1.

Kiwanis International. www.kiwanis.org (accessed August 17, 2008).

"New Home for Elks Planned in Covington," *KP*, April 28, 1937, 1.

Pictorial and Industrial Review of Northern Kentucky. Newport: Northern Kentucky Review, 1923.

Elizabeth Comer Williams and Paul A. Tenkotte

CIVIL DEFENSE. Civil defense, which is the protection of the nonmilitary population during war, consists of two basic options, providing shelter in place or evacuating the area that is at risk. Both options were represented when settlers of Northern Kentucky during the late 1700s built fortified stations that at first defended residents living at the stations and later served as places to which the surrounding population could retreat during threats of Indian raids.

Civil defense as a function of the U.S. government came into existence in 1917, during **World War I**, when the federal government promoted the formation of a Council of National Defense within each local government, to support regulations and laws issued by the federal government. Such councils existed in many of the counties and cities of Northern Kentucky, but they were little more than propaganda organizations, and they quickly disbanded after the war.

In 1941 the federal government created the Office of Civilian Defense. With the Allies and the Axis bombing each other's cities, it was deemed prudent to prepare American cities to withstand such attacks. The Commonwealth of Kentucky created its own Office of Civilian Defense and encouraged all counties and cities to form civilian defense units also. The Cincinnati Metropolitan Area Civil Defense organization, encompassing the cities within Boone, Campbell, and Kenton counties, was created. The other counties of Northern Kentucky also formed civil defense units, which were trained to fight fires, conduct rescues in collapsed buildings, provide basic first aid, assist in law enforcement, perform expedient shelter construction, and feed displaced citizens. Many Northern Kentucky fire departments were established on the basis of the training and equipment provided under this **World War II** program. The major contribution of local civilian defense organizations to the war effort was to make the people feel that they were part of the global battle. The national Office of Civilian Defense, along with the local organizations, closed in late 1945.

In 1950, after the explosion of an atomic bomb by the Soviet Union, the federal government established the Office of Civil Defense (OCD) to prepare plans to protect the citizens of the United States from nuclear war. Responding to natural disasters was not part of the OCD mission. The Commonwealth of Kentucky in December 1950 created the Kentucky Division of Civil Defense (KYDCD) under the state's adjutant general. Each county and city in the state was encouraged to set up its own civil defense organization under the direction of the county judge or mayor. Within the next two years, civil defense organizations sprang up in all the counties of Northern Kentucky. The federal civil defense concept then in vogue was to evacuate the major cities of nonessential people as soon as war broke out. The citizens of Boone, Campbell, and Kenton counties were to go into the other counties of Northern Kentucky. The plans developed under this scenario were mostly paper concepts with no formal plans for execution.

In the aftermath of the Cuban Missile Crisis of October 1962, the federal government set out to fund the development of executable civil defense plans. Owing to the threat offered by missiles, which could arrive without warning, the federal government began to develop a fallout-shelter program to protect citizens from nuclear fallout, though not from the direct blast of a nuclear weapon. Fallout shelters were identified in all of the Northern Kentucky counties. The shelters were marked and supplied with food, water, and medical kits. Amateur radio operators were mobilized to provide communication; citizens were trained to take radiological readings; first-aid and shelter-management courses were taught; hospitals of the mobile army surgical type were stored in counties outside Boone, Campbell, and Kenton counties; sirens were mounted in various locations to give warning of an attack; and the Emergency Alert System was put in place using local radio and television stations. Many of the warning sirens were mounted at volunteer fire department stations and were also used to call their volunteer firemen to respond to an emergency. Emergency operations plans and community shelter plans were written for each county, indicating how to prepare for, respond to, and recover from an attack.

In 1972 the federal government reorganized the Office of Civil Defense as the Defense Civil Protection Agency (DCPA) and gave the new organization two tasks: its primary mission was to prepare the United States to survive a nuclear attack, and its secondary mission was to respond to natural disasters that a state could not handle by itself. With this change in the federal civil defense posture, Kentucky in 1974 changed the name of KYDCD to Kentucky Disaster and Emergency Services (KYDES). Over the next year, each Northern Kentucky county changed the name of its civil defense organization accordingly. This name change reflected the heavy involvement of local civil defense organizations in response to manmade and natural disasters. In 1977 DCPA was abolished and the Federal Emergency Management Agency (FEMA) was established and given a dual mission of preparing to protect the U.S. population from the effects of natural disasters and nuclear war.

The 1980s saw a shift in the federal civil defense program for preparedness in case of war. The development of shelters that protected only against fallout within a blast area was recognized as being not viable. The new U.S. civil defense plan, which mirrored the Soviet Union's civil defense plan, called for the evacuation of key communities during periods of increased international tension. Among the local areas to be evacuated, designated as risk counties under this scenario, were Boone, Campbell, and Kenton counties. Plans were developed specifying how these counties would be evacuated and where the citizens would go. In the host counties, the other counties of Northern Kentucky, plans were developed to house and feed the evacuees. These plans, ridiculed by certain segments of the population, were declared obsolete by the federal government in 1990 with the collapse of the Soviet Union.

Civil defense during the 1990s, if defined as protecting citizens from an enemy attack, was no longer a federal program. FEMA during the 1990s rescinded all federal civil defense war guidance documents. In 1998 KYDES was reorganized as the Division of Emergency Management, and all the counties of Northern Kentucky adopted this name.

In 2001, after the terrorist attack on the World Trade Center in New York City, civil defense again became part of the mission of county emergency management organizations. Civil defense was revitalized by the federal government and, in 2003, was made part of the Department of Homeland Security. Local emergency operation plans were updated to include the response to a terrorist incident. Civil defense continues to exist, though not in name, in each Northern Kentucky county, within the county's emergency management agency. These agencies serve under the direction of the county judge executive. All of the counties have built structures or modified existing ones to serve as emergency operation centers in time of disaster, and they are recruiting citizens to undertake training in various areas of preparedness, response, and recovery.

Blanchard, Boyce W. *American Civil Defense*. Charlottesville: Univ. of Virginia Press, 1980.

Federal Emergency Management Agency. *An Introduction to Emergency Management, 1950–1992*. Emmitsburg, Md.: Federal Emergency Management Agency, 1993.

Kentucky Department of Military Affairs Annual Reports, 1950–2002, Kentucky Department of Military Affairs, Frankfort, Ky.

Charles H. Bogart

CIVIL RIGHTS MOVEMENT. The civil rights movement in Northern Kentucky was an important part of the larger national movement that brought about the fall of Jim Crow in the South. The most visible forms of racial discrimination and inequality were protested and removed, only to expose the need for even more radical changes in the social, economic, political, and cultural fabric of the nation.

The struggle of African Americans in their quest for freedom and against white supremacy has been part of the U.S. experience since the times of enslavement. " "The civil rights movement had its beginnings in the constitutional amendments enacted during the post–**Civil War** Reconstruction era. The 13th Amendment to the U.S. Constitution (1865) abolished enslavement, the 14th Amendment (1868) provided citizenship rights, and the 15th Amendment (1870) guaranteed the right to vote. These amendments served as a second Bill of Rights and gave recently freed African Americans the hope that they would be treated as full citizens. The gains in the exercise of civil rights made during this period were short-lived, however, and collapsed under a variety of U.S. Supreme Court decisions, congressional compromises, Jim Crow laws, and mob violence that created a kind of pseudo-slavery. African Americans and progressive whites immediately formed pockets of resistance to this restoration of white supremacy and laid foundations for the U.S. civil rights movement. The resistance and protest movement involved the work of many different organizations, court decisions, and countless acts of individual courage.

Kentucky's African Americans understood very clearly that they would have to stand up against the Jim Crow laws, the racial violence, and the entire system of white supremacy if they hoped to have a better life in this society. They were also aware that acting solely as individuals was not effective against the policies dictated by the white majority. They knew, as in slavery days, that they had to organize themselves into well-structured organizations that cooperated together and were linked both locally and nationally, in order to protest successfully against restrictions on their rights.

Beginning in 1866, African Americans in Kentucky formed numerous organizations, for example, the State Convention of Colored Citizens, which was active through the 1890s. The state convention presented resolutions to the state legislature supporting such initiatives as a new state constitution, compulsory education, normal schools, the right to serve on any jury, equal access to public accommodations, and full civil rights. Statewide county meetings preceded the annual state convention, and delegates were allocated by population. At the 1885 convention, Northern Kentucky was represented by three delegates from Boone Co., seven from Kenton Co., and one from Campbell Co. J. W. Hawkins, from Newport, Ky., served on the state convention executive committee.

The Kentucky Negro Educational Association (KNEA) was founded in 1877. It comprised principals and teachers working to provide equal education for each Kentucky child, challenging segregated and inferior education, making the case for equal pay for teachers, and supporting other social and economic initiatives. The KNEA cooperated with many other organizations over the years and served as an important advocate for full civil rights until 1955. William Fouse, principal at William Grant High School (see **Lincoln-Grant School**) in Covington, served as the KNEA president for many years. Other local educators at William Grant, **Southgate**, and Elsmere schools were also active members. Professor **William Humphrey**, principal of the **John G. Fee Industrial High School** in Maysville, also served as president of the KNEA in 1930.

The modern movement for civil rights began in 1909, with the formation of the National Association for the Advancement of Colored People (**NAACP**). In 1919 the NAACP national office sent Walter White around Kentucky to establish branches. The Covington branch was formed and immediately began a campaign to protest lynching and mob violence; it also worked with other organizations to oppose Jim Crow laws. Over the next 40 years, the branch went through periods of activity and inactivity. Legal counsel provided by the NAACP proved beneficial in a number of cases, helping African Americans avoid unjust jail sentences and the death penalty. In 1930 Anderson McPerkins was charged with raping a white woman, was found guilty, and was sentenced to death. The local NAACP, inactive at the time, was soon reinvigorated by the case. Collaborating with the Cincinnati International Labor Defense, the Cincinnati American Civil Liberties Union, and the Commission on Interracial Cooperation, the Covington branch of the NAACP intervened in the case, brought forward new information, and subsequently obtained McPerkins's release from prison. From 1931 to 1948, the Covington branch was again inactive. It was revived in 1948, when the national NAACP received a letter from Louis Brown of Covington, expressing a desire to reorganize the Covington branch. In 1949 Jack Delaney of Covington was elected as a board member of the state conference of the NAACP. In April 1959 the branch was again rechartered, and Mrs. E. Conley was elected president of the Covington group.

In 1903 the National Association of Colored Women (NACW) organized local chapters around the state and also founded the Kentucky Association of Colored Women's Clubs, which created life-enrichment programs especially for children and women. The Covington chapter, through the leadership over the years of such women as **Lizzie Fouse**, **Elizabeth B. Delaney**, and Bertha Moore, provided leadership locally, within the state organization, and on the national board of NACW. Using their motto "lifting as we climb," these club women worked to "uplift the race" by providing college scholarships, setting up programs on health and sanitary education, organizing antilynching campaigns, and developing recreational facilities. This network of women's clubs laid the foundation stones for the emerging civil rights movement of the 1950s and 1960s. The L. B. Fouse Civic Center, the home of the NACW Covington chapter, also provided meeting and training space for the NAACP and CORE.

Organized in 1931, the Association of Southern Women for the Prevention of Lynching had an active chapter in Northern Kentucky. Mrs. Don Griffin of Fort Thomas, local chapter president, was also vice president of the state organization. The women of this organization repudiated the lie that lynchings were justified as a defense of white women in the South. They proclaimed that the mob spirit was a greater threat to democracy than any other form of crime in the United States. They led a campaign to contact the sheriff's office in every county, asking sheriffs to sign pledges of cooperation in the prevention of lynching. Louis Vogt, the Kenton Co. sheriff, signed such a letter.

In response to the racial violence following **World War I**, the Commission on Interracial Cooperation (CIC) of Kentucky was formed in 1921 to find more effective means of interracial communication and collaboration. The CIC soon grew into 63 county interracial committees, including a very active Northern Kentucky chapter, in which many Kentuckians experienced their first opportunity to discuss and act on community problems with an interracial membership. While not a protest organization, the CIC provided educational programs and worked on issues pertaining to health, education, recreation, law and order, court justice, and the improvement of transportation facilities for African Americans. In 1935 Covington CIC members, along with the local KNEA, petitioned the school board regarding unequal pay for black and white teachers in Kenton Co.

In 1954, with the *Brown v. Board of Education* decision, the Supreme Court overturned their "separate but equal" doctrine of *Plessey v. Ferguson* (1896) and declared that segregated education was inherently unequal and therefore unconstitutional. This case was the culmination of a long-deliberated strategy of the NAACP Legal Defense team and was the legal foundation of the civil rights movement of the 1960s. Desegregation of public schools was not immediate, however, and *Brown v. Board of Education* was followed by *Brown II* (1955), which created guidelines for public school desegregation in local communities.

The outlawing of racial segregation in public schools presented for the Northern Kentucky school districts different challenges, which were met peacefully. Separate but equal had been for some a financial burden. Districts with small black populations that were forced to send their black students to schools in neighboring larger districts to attend segregated schools suddenly took them back. The Newport and Boone Co. school districts, which had been paying Covington to accept its African American students at William Grant High School, quickly developed integration policies for the 1955–1956 school year. In 1956 African American students in Covington were offered the opportunity to attend John G. Carlisle elementary school, **Holmes High School**, and other public schools in the city. In Newport, the Southgate School was closed and students enrolled in other city public schools. In Northern Kentucky, as well as around the country, the formerly all-white schools were integrated and the formerly all-black schools were torn down or turned into neighborhood community centers. Integration of public schools was clearly an unequal burden for the African American community.

Integration of schools also had a negative effect on the employment status of African American teachers, principals, and staff members. Most of their jobs were eliminated, and the few who were given positions at the now integrated schools were forced to accept a much lower rank and pay. With the closing of the all-black schools such as William Grant and Southgate, the African American communities also lost profoundly important educational and cultural centers that had served and inspired many generations of families.

The civil rights movement victory in the Brown decision and other inspirations, such as Rosa Parks and the Montgomery (Ala.) Bus Boycott, sparked renewed anger, courage, and activism among African Americans, encouraging them to accept second-class citizenship no longer. In Covington, African Americans who had tolerated a "white only" bathroom sign at **Coppin's Department Store** for more than 45 years decided in late 1960 that "Jim Crow must go." The NAACP and the L. B. Fouse Civic Center, led by **Alice Shimfessel** and Bertha Moore, organized community protest meetings around this issue. The protest meetings moved into direct action when the **Congress of Racial Equality** (CORE) decided in December 1960 to organize a chapter in Northern Kentucky. Over the next three years, CORE galvanized the local movement and successfully desegregated public accommodations in Northern Kentucky even before the Civil Rights Act of 1964. In addition, CORE worked to eradicate discrimination in employment, housing, and educational access faced by African Americans during this era. Its collaboration with the NAACP and the Young Catholic Workers and its successful negotiations with local officials and business people enabled CORE in a relatively short and peaceful period of time to dismantle most of the remaining vestiges of segregation that had colored race relations in this community for more than 100 years.

CORE closed its chapter in Northern Kentucky in 1963, and the NAACP reemerged as the primary civil rights organization in the region. Guided by the leadership of **Fermon Knox**, the local branch and state president of NAACP, and Rev. **Edgar L. Mack**, the state youth organizer, the Northern Kentucky NAACP continued the fight against all forms of discrimination and inequality. These groups worked closely with the Cincinnati chapter of the NAACP, the Greater Cincinnati Commission on Religion and Race, the Human Rights Commission, and the Catholic Interracial Council on issues such as education, employment, and housing.

The Northern Kentucky chapter of the NAACP was an active participant in the Allied Organizations for Civil Rights in Kentucky, which sponsored the Freedom March on Frankfort, held March 5, 1964. This demonstration, which included a large contingent from Northern Kentucky and involved more than 10,000 people, was called to show support for a public-accommodations bill being considered by the Kentucky legislature. The speakers at the march included Dr. Martin Luther King Jr., Jackie Robinson, Rev. Ralph Abernathy, artists, and other prominent civil rights activists. Although the public-accommodations bill was not passed, two years later, in 1966, the state legislature passed the Kentucky Civil Rights Act, which was even more comprehensive. In the meantime, Fermon Knox and other Kentucky civil rights leaders were invited to address the U.S. Congress in support of the 1964 Federal Civil Rights Act.

After Dr. King was assassinated in 1968, a call for Black Power challenged the integrationist thrust of the early 1960s, focusing renewed attention on black political and economic empowerment, while black consciousness and racial pride found expression in the cultural renaissance of the black arts movement. Years later, African Americans began demanding affirmative action as a way to more effectively gain economic and educational access.

Kentucky Commission of Human Rights. *Kentucky's Black Heritage*. Frankfort: Kentucky Commission of Human Rights, 1971.

Lucas, Marion. *A History of Blacks in Kentucky*. Vol. 1. Frankfort: Kentucky Historical Society, 1992.

The Papers of the Congress of Racial Equality, 1941–1967. Microform. Frederick, Md.: Univ. Publications of America, 1983.

The Papers of the NAACP. Microform. Frederick, Md.: Univ. Publications of America, 1982.

Wright, George C. *A History of Blacks in Kentucky*. Vol. 2. *In Pursuit of Equality, 1890–1980*. Frankfort: Kentucky Historical Society, 1992.

Jim Embry

CIVIL WAR. When the Civil War began, many Northern Kentucky citizens were German and Irish immigrants who had moved across the Ohio River from Cincinnati during the previous two decades. They tended to oppose slavery and support President Abraham Lincoln (1861–1865), emancipation, and the Union war effort. Northern Kentucky had slaves, but slave-owning was less prevalent than across the commonwealth of Kentucky in general. While slaves accounted for 19.5 percent of the state population in 1860, Campbell Co. had 116 slaves among a population of 20,909, or about 0.5 percent. Kenton Co. had 567 slaves in its population of 25,467, about 2 percent. In the presidential election of 1860, Campbell and Kenton counties were the only two in Kentucky that gave Lincoln more than 200 votes. Campbell Co. provided him with 314 votes, 11.9 percent of its votes, and Kenton Co. cast 267 votes for him, 7.5 percent. In the presidential election of 1864, when almost 70 percent of Kentuckians voted for Democrat George McClellan, Lincoln carried Kenton Co. by 55.5 percent, with 1,716 votes. Campbell Co. gave Lincoln 53.9 percent, with 1,504 votes.

Men of Northern Kentucky volunteered for both armies; official records probably fail to reflect the level of Union enlistment because some Northern Kentuckians enlisted in Union regiments in southern Ohio. The records show that 1,166 men joined the Union army from Kenton Co., 1,013 from Campbell Co., and 462 from Boone Co. These figures, only somewhat more than 4 percent of the white population in each county in 1860, rank below the numbers of Union volunteers in most Kentucky counties. However, when enrolling in the home guards and in Ohio regiments is considered, participation in the Union war effort appears more significant.

Northern Kentucky also had an outspoken minority of Confederate supporters, especially in Boone Co., where in 1860 there were 1,745 slaves, 15.5 percent of the population. In the election of 1860, Lincoln received only 1 of Boone Co.'s 1,849 votes. In 1864, McClellan carried Boone Co. with 84.2 percent of the vote. Boone Co's. citizens showed their sentiment when enthusiastic crowds in Walton and Florence welcomed Confederate troops during Confederate general Henry Heth's invasion. At that time, Cincinnati reporters considered Florence a pestilential center of Rebel sympathy. Union authorities, who were in command of Kentucky, arrested and imprisoned several Southern sympathizers in the region. During Gen. John Hunt Morgan's First Kentucky Raid (July 4–28, 1862), pro-Southern families in Covington held secessionist rallies in their homes until the Union provost marshal ordered the gatherings halted.

During the preparation for defense against Heth's invasion, Union general Lew Wallace took into account the presence of pro-Southerners. He believed that Confederates in houses on the riverfront in Cincinnati were communicating with their friends across the Ohio River by means of heliographic lamps flashing in windows. Undeterred, he ordered the arrest of anyone who refused to fight or work on the fortifications. One day during the crisis, two men were arrested on Fifth St. in Covington for shouting "Hurrah for Jeff Davis!" Several prominent Confederates were from Northern Kentucky, including **Charles John Helm**, the Newport attorney who served as Confederate consul to Cuba. **Eli Metcalfe Bruce**, of Covington, was one of the most prominent members of the Confederate Congress. Charles Albert Withers (see **Withers Family**), John Hunt Morgan's adjutant, was also from Covington. A small group of men from Pendleton Co. enlisted in Morgan's 4th Kentucky Cavalry. Their admiration for Morgan led to the local legend after the war that their small Pendleton Co. town of Morgan was named for the famous general. Actually, the city of Morgan was named before the war and before John Hunt Morgan became famous. Nevertheless, before Morgan High School closed with consolidation in 1959, the men's basketball team played as the Morgan Raiders.

When Union officials in charge of the defense of Newport, Covington, and Cincinnati asked the mayors of Newport and Covington to call out the home guards during emergencies, they responded immediately, and pro-Union men in both communities volunteered. Twice this response was needed against John Hunt Morgan, during his First Kentucky Raid and his Last Kentucky Raid (June 1–12, 1864), and both times men shouldered their arms. But the greatest test of the sentiment of Northern Kentucky residents was during Heth's invasion of Boone and Kenton counties, a coordinated part of Confederate general Braxton Bragg's full-scale invasion of Kentucky in 1862. On August 30, 1862, Gen. Edmund Kirby Smith's Confederate army, which had come from Tennessee and was planning to link up with Bragg's force, routed the Union army defending Kentucky and on September 2 occupied Lexington. Kirby Smith could have attacked Louisville, but instead he sent General Heth and 8,000 men to threaten Northern Kentucky and Cincinnati.

"Are we threatened?" people asked, and the *Cincinnati Commercial* answered that the threat was very serious: "Remember that your firesides, your wives, and little ones, your honor, are in danger." It was true; Northern Kentucky and Cincinnati—one of the top five industrial cities in the North—lay open to attack, with only a few regiments and independent companies for defense. Kirby Smith and Heth knew this, and, receiving reports of panic in Cincinnati, Heth started on September 6 and marched slowly, moving only 20 to 25 miles per day.

Gen. **Horatio G. Wright**, commander of the Department of Ohio, and his staff escorted Kentucky governor James Robinson (1862–1863) and the state legislature from Frankfort to Louisville. Wright hastily appointed General Wallace to organize the militia to defend Cincinnati. Wallace met with the mayors of Cincinnati, Newport, and Covington and secured their full support. He declared martial law on September 2 and, with the slogan "Citizens for Labor, Soldiers for Battle," rallied the community to restore and construct the eight-mile defensive line of entrenchments south of Newport and Covington. Business was suspended and men, women, and children united in a great effort of homeland security. Women in Newport furnished the temporary military hospital on York St. and served as nurses. At one point 34 soldiers were treated for illness. The Cincinnati Black Brigade cleared forests and built military roads, erecting batteries and rifle pits (see **Civil War Fortifications**).

Wallace told his aides that if the Confederates gave him one week, he would be ready. They did, and he was prepared. Kirby Smith should have ordered the offensive on September 2, the day he occupied Lexington, and Heth should have marched more speedily. By the time his scouts arrived south of Fort Mitchel (modern-day Fort Mitchell) on September 9, Wallace's fortification line was complete. Wright had returned from Louisville to his headquarters in Cincinnati on September 4 and had gathered about 22,000 regular Union soldiers. Wallace and Governor David Tod of Ohio and Governor Oliver P. Morton of Indiana had called out about 50,000 state militia troops.

Heth and his staff arrived on the morning of September 10 and halted before a farmhouse on the Lexington Pk., a short distance south of Fort Mitchel. They dismounted, and Heth climbed to the top of the house and with his field glasses reconnoitered Wallace's defensive line while his staff lounged around in the front yard, reading the Cincinnati newspapers. On the parapet of Fort Mitchel, below the American flag, stood a small officer with a broad-brimmed hat, looking back at Heth with his field glasses. It was General Wallace, and he observed his adversary at such close range that Wallace's artillery officer requested permission to fire. "I forbade it," Wallace recalled. "There were women and children under the roof; but, if that were not enough, good policy, as it appeared to me, demanded that the enemy should be allowed to see from a distance all he could of what he had to go against."

Heth left the house and rode back and forth in front of Fort Mitchel. As far as he could see, the hills bristled with heavy artillery and rifle pits connected with newly thrown up breastworks of dirt and logs. All along the line the trees were newly cut in a swath of about 2,000 yards. Among the stumps were tangled limbs and tops designed as abatis to deter enemy infantry. The ground was streaked where the logs had been dragged to the trenches. Heth disguised scouts as farmers with produce and sent them into Newport and Covington to investigate whether the Union defenses were as real as they appeared. The scouts reported that Wallace had an ideal defensive position connected with military roads and pontoon bridges across the Ohio River and the Licking River. After the war, Whitelaw Reid, an astute and famous war correspondent, wrote that the fortifications made Cincinnati "one of the strongest fortified cities in the Union." Reid's evaluation took into account additional construction and armament that occurred after September 1862, but Heth's scouts reported that Wallace's position was very strong.

Heth dispatched a courier on a fast horse to Lexington with the report that the enemy was in force behind breastworks with heavy artillery. Kirby Smith attempted to reinforce Heth but, finding it impossible, ordered Heth to withdraw without attacking. In picket skirmishing, which went on all day on September 11, 4 Union men were killed and 3 wounded. On the Confederate side, 2 soldiers were wounded and 16 captured. While a forest was being cleared in Campbell Co., a falling tree had killed Joseph Johns, a member of the Black Brigade. During the night of September 11, Heth withdrew toward Lexington. Correspondence between Kirby Smith and Heth in the *Official Records* indicates that they meant to capture Covington, Newport, and Cincinnati. In a conversation in Cincinnati a few years after the war, Heth hinted to Wallace that he had intended to take Cincinnati and threaten to allow his men to sack it unless city officials paid a ransom of $15 million. As soon as Kirby Smith called off the attack, he ordered John Hunt Morgan to "proceed without delay with all of your cavalry that can be collected" and march toward Northern Kentucky to meet with Heth on his withdrawal and discuss "the advisability of making an expedition into the State of Ohio with your command." Morgan sent six companies under John Hutcheson, and they marched to Walton and united with Heth's division, screening the Confederate retreat. Ohio Governor David Tod sent a message to U.S. secretary of war William Stanton commending the militia and crediting the civilians with the decisive role. "This uprising of the people is the cause of the retreat," he wrote. "You should acknowledge publicly their gallant conduct."

Northern Kentucky citizens celebrated the end of the war with enthusiasm on Friday, April 14, 1865. Mayor R. B. McCrackin of Newport requested that all citizens suspend business and decorate homes and businesses with flags "in honor of the glorious victories of the Federal arms over the enemy." In Covington and Newport, all the bells rang and cannons fired at morning, noon, and night. Covington had a general illumination after dark and bonfires in the streets. Both cities sponsored worship services in all churches at 10:30 a.m. Nothing was scheduled in the afternoon so that Northern Kentuckians could attend the grand procession of veterans in Cincinnati at 2:00 p.m. The Covington Fire Department participated in the parade with its elaborately decorated steam fire engine, named U. S. Grant.

The next day news came of Lincoln's assassination. Covington and Newport prepared public commemorations for Wednesday, April 19, the day of Lincoln's funeral in the White House. Both cities cooperated with the request of Kentucky governor Thomas Bramlette (1863–1867) to suspend business. The bells were tolled and Covington held a worship service at noon at the First Baptist Church on Fourth St. Newport had a very large meeting at the courthouse square at 2:00 p.m. Following an opening prayer, the **Newport Barracks** band played a sorrowful dirge and several dignitaries spoke, including Judge William Dickson, former colonel of the Black Brigade. In victory and in mourning, most Northern Kentuckians identified with Lincoln and his goals as they had during the war.

Crawford, Kenneth. "Defense of Cincinnati and the Legacy of William Hooper," *NKH* 12 (Spring–Summer 2005): 20–36.

Ramage, James A. "Panic in Cincinnati," *Blue and Gray* 3 (April–May 1986): 12–15.

Reid, Whitelaw. *Ohio in the War*. Cincinnati: Wilstach, Baldwin, 1868.

Tenkotte, Paul A. "A Note on Regional Allegiances during the Civil War: Kenton County, Kentucky, as a Test Case," *RKHS* 79 (Summer 1981): 211–18.

Wallace, Lew. *Lew Wallace: An Autobiography*. New York: Harper, 1906.

The War of the Rebellion: A Compilation of the Official Records of the Union and Confederate Armies. Washington, D.C.: Government Printing Office, 1880.

James A. Ramage

CIVIL WAR, CARROLL CO. Alarms, rumors, and anxiety swept through the Ohio River counties of Northern Kentucky in the months leading up to the **Civil War**. In late 1860 a local militia of about 50 men and boys, calling themselves the Invincibles, was created at **Hunter's Bottom** in Carroll Co. These young men included Capt. W. J. Hoagland, 1st Lt. William H. Bradley, 2nd Lt. Henry Spillman, and 3rd Lt. Jarrett Banks. They were organized as part of Simon Bolivar Buckner's Kentucky State Guards. Brothers Harvey, George, and Clinton Conway were among the privates. Within months, Buckner, who rejected a commission in the Union Army to become a Confederate brigadier general, had taken most of the Kentucky Guards and their arms and equipment into the Confederacy. From the Invincibles, 8 men went into the Union Army and 16 to the Confederates. Many of the boys from Hunter's Bottom eventually joined Col. Henry L. Giltner's 4th Kentucky Cavalry, CSA. In September 1861 a number of men from Carroll Co., including Moses T. Pryor and his brothers-in-law Gideon B. Giltner and Henry Liter Giltner, rendezvoused with General Buckner and the Confederates at Camp Boone. Almost immediately, Gen. Humphrey Marshall appointed Henry L. Giltner as his aide-de-camp.

In summer 1862, as Maj. Gen. Don Carlos Buell of the Union chased Gen. Braxton Bragg of the Confederacy from Tennessee into Kentucky, the Confederates were mounting a major recruiting drive in Central Kentucky. Col. (later Gen.) John Hunt Morgan, commander of the 2nd Kentucky Cavalry, CSA, and Gen. Kirby Smith, among others, were convinced that thousands of Kentuckians around the bluegrass would swarm to the Confederate cause.

Meanwhile, Union troops were being deployed and trained in Kentucky, and Union Home Guards were being equipped. This development led to a number of skirmishes in the lower regions of the Kentucky River. From June 20 to 23, 1862, Confederates were sighted in Owen Co., and on August 31 a skirmish took place near Monterey along the Kentucky River. Carroll Co. was full of news and rumors.

In July 1862 Henry L. Giltner, previously the sheriff of Carroll Co. and now a CSA colonel, and captains Moses T. Pryor, Nathan Parker of Bedford, Peter Everett of Montgomery, and 16 other officers sought additional Confederate troops, especially for the cavalry. Although the overwhelming sentiment in rural Carroll Co. was in favor of the Confederacy, the CSA recruiters found a substantial number of entrenched Union forces in the region. They were part of the Union troop positioned along the Ohio River in defense of General Bragg's incursion.

On September 17 Giltner, astride his dapple-gray warhorse Billy, led about 100 Confederate cavalrymen into Carrollton. In an act of retaliation for the recent arrest of rebel leaders "[Thomas] Dugan, Southgate [probably William, John, or James Southard], and Barnum [Edwin Burnham]," the Confederate cavalrymen seized the courthouse; tore down Union flags and hoisted the Confederate flag; arrested a number of citizens, including Charles Emery, R. H. Jett, and Monticue T. McClure; and hunted unsuccessfully for the provost marshal, Benjamin E. Archer. A number of Union supporters had already fled across the Ohio River to Indiana. The *Cincinnati Daily Commercial* claimed that the Carrollton raid was backed up by 1,200 CSA troops nearby, but that assertion may have referred to CSA cavalry activities relating to the sweep across to Lawrenceburg, Ind., and back to Perryville in Central Kentucky that culminated October 8, 1862.

Between October 15 and October 20, Union forces swept through the Northern Kentucky region, and the newly recruited Confederates headed inland to join with Gen. Humphrey Marshall in preparation for the Battle of Perryville. According to the muster lists, the 4th Kentucky Cavalry, CSA, began with 900 men in total. Many of the Carroll Co. men were in Company F and came from Carrollton, Eagle Station, Ghent, Hunter's Bottom, Jordan, Mill Creek, Worthville, Prestonville, Sanders, and White's Run.

The new cavalry unit was placed under the Department of East Tennessee; later the 4th Kentucky Cavalry, CSA, was placed under the Department of Western Virginia and East Tennessee. The field officers were Col. Henry L. Giltner, Lt. Col. Moses T. Pryor, and Maj. Nathan Parker. The unit saw substantial action in eastern Tennessee and participated in various raids into Eastern Kentucky. One of the high points of the unit's combat occurred November 10, 1863, when Confederate cavalry units under Col. Henry L. Giltner, as commander of the Confederate 2nd Cavalry Brigade, captured 550 prisoners, 30 wagons of military and commissary equipment, four brass 6-pounder James guns, and a large number of horses and arms belonging to the 2nd East Tennessee Mounted Infantry, the 7th Ohio Cavalry, and Phillips's battery at Big Creek in Tennessee. Among the Confederate officers singled out and complimented in Giltner's field report on the engagement were Lt. Col. Trimble of the 10th Kentucky Cavalry and Major Parker of the 4th Kentucky Cavalry.

In June 1864 Giltner's forces participated in Gen. John Hunt Morgan's "Last Raid" through Kentucky, including the battles at Mount Sterling and Cynthiana, and they proved themselves battle-hardened campaigners in spite of the Confederate losses. The death of General Morgan (September 4, 1864, at Greeneville, Tenn.) affected many of the men in the 4th Kentucky Cavalry, CSA.

Had the war ended in the summer of 1864, Giltner and his cavalry regiments would have achieved high praise. However, in October 1864 Col. Henry Giltner, as commanding officer of the 7th Battalion Confederate Cavalry, was ordered to defend the salt and lead mines and the East Tennessee and Virginia Railroad. Thus, the Kentuckians became enmeshed in one of the most despicable acts of the Civil War, the deliberate massacre of wounded and captured Negro troops of the 5th U.S. Colored Cavalry (USCC) at Saltville, Va. Although chiefly undisciplined cavalrymen conducted the atrocities, several Kentucky officers, including Capt. Edward O. Guerrant, failed to halt the killings. At one point **George Dallas Mosgrove**, of Carroll Co., who wrote the Kentucky 4th Cavalry's regimental history, although present, failed to prevent the murder of captured black soldiers inside a cabin. Eyewitnesses from the Union 12th Ohio and the 11th Michigan attested to the massacres. Reports of the number of black soldiers slaughtered vary wildly, from New South historian William Marvel's estimate that only 5 were killed and certainly no more than a dozen, to the National Park Service claim that 35 members of the 5th USCC were killed in action. A more recent study by Thomas Mays and other researchers concluded that upwards of 50 of the 400 men of the 5th USCC were killed. After the Civil War, CSA guerilla leader Champ Ferguson was hanged for a series of murders of Union soldiers and civilians during 1861–1865, including his taking five wounded USCC soldiers from the Union surgeon at Saltville and murdering them.

In the fading days of the Civil War, Colonel Giltner was given supreme command of CSA forces in Lee, Scott, Russell and Wise counties in Virginia on February 16, 1865; the surrender at Appomattox Courthouse in Virginia took place on April 9, 1865, and the 4th Kentucky Cavalry, CSA, returned to Kentucky and surrendered at Mount Sterling on April 30, 1865. Most of the men from Carroll Co. returned home. Henry Giltner became a merchant at Milton, Ky., but by 1880 he had moved to Tennessee. During the next few decades, the legend of Gen. John Hunt Morgan's 2nd Kentucky Cavalry, CSA, and Henry Giltner's 4th Kentucky Cavalry, CSA, merged somewhat and became much romanticized.

Several strong Unionist families lived in Carrollton. In an interesting dispatch dated September 14, 1862, a letter from Unionists in Carrollton to Capt. Joseph H. Williams, commander of the gunboat *Cottage* was quoted in the *Cincinnati Daily Commercial:* "Respected Sir—Please accept these refreshments from the undersigned Union ladies, with our many thanks to you and your command for your timely protection; and we remain, respectfully, your obliged friends, Mrs. Mary D. Nely, Mrs. H. Hamilton, Mrs. F. Rabb, Mrs. S. McClure."

Among the merchants at Carrollton were a number of Northerners: Theoderick Fisher from New Hampshire; Peter C. Adams, B. B. Bennett, Henry Gilbert, W. H. Swain, and John W. White from Massachusetts; Lyman Martin, James T. Root, and William Root from Connecticut; John D. Ames, Samuel Ball, and John W. Root from New York; Theophilus Reed and Joseph Vance from New Jersey; and James Robb and his son David Robb, who was a cadet at West Point Military Academy in New York.

In addition, a number of Carroll Co. men served in the 13th Kentucky Volunteer Infantry, Union. Officers from Carroll Co. in that regiment included Capt. Albert M. Jett; 2nd Lt. Charles McCracken; Capt. P. Gilbert Fisher, who was dismissed January 5, 1863; and 1st Lt. William L. Lee, who was killed in action on April 28, 1862. All of these officers were from Carrollton. Carroll Co. men also served in Louisville-raised and southern Indiana Union units as well, but the muster lists are inconclusive.

Throughout the war, small detachments of Union naval forces patrolled the Ohio River and stopped at Carrollton occasionally. Once the western Ohio and Mississippi river campaigns began, most of the inland Union Navy was engaged around Vicksburg, Miss., and New Orleans. The

Union received most of the news and information along the Ohio River from friendly steamboat captains such as Captain Hildreth of Switzerland Co., Ind., who manned the *Florence* and reported regularly in Cincinnati. It has been claimed that Abraham Lincoln stopped at Hildreth's house between Lamb and Vevay, Ind., during his 1864 presidential campaign.

The Union Army posted troops at Carrollton during the Civil War. Many residents, particularly in the surrounding rural area, saw these troops as enemies occupying their land. The Union officers and men, in turn, felt that enemies and spies surrounded them. At Carrollton in 1862 the officers irritated local legend Gen. **William O. Butler**, who had declared neutrality before the war began. Men and horses from the Union Army were posted in the Presbyterian Church, Butler's home congregation, and the local lore claims that much damage was done to the building and grounds.

Whatever neutrality or pro-Union sentiment was apparent among the white citizens of Carroll Co. disintegrated quickly with the Emancipation Proclamation in January 1863 and the subsequent arrival of African American troops in Kentucky. Around August 22, 1864, a U.S. Colored Troop (USCT) squad, posted at Ghent, Ky., to protect recruiters for the 5th U.S. Colored Cavalry, arrested James Southard, a leading Confederate advocate and local ferryman. He owned land along the Ohio River that formed the Ghent landing. Southard's brother notified Col. George Jesse in Henry Co., Ky., that James Southard had been taken by USCT troops. Jesse's hardened remnants of Morgan's last Kentucky raid quickly routed the raw recruits of the 117th USCT (see **Gex Landing Incident**). There were rumors, fed by Louisville-based Union officers and a Union-friendly newspaper, that another Saltville-like incident had occurred, a massacre of Negro troops. The record was set straight only after Colonel Jesse released the captured USCT officer and men at Owenton the next month.

With few exceptions, after the war the Confederate soldiers returned to Carroll Co. and gradually took positions of political power and civic responsibility. By 1880 most leadership positions in church and state were held by former CSA soldiers. Each funeral of a Confederate veteran called forth marches or honor guards in full regalia, prominently chronicled in the *Carrollton Democrat.* A succession of former CSA officers were elected Kentucky governors, including Simon Bolivar Buckner (1887–1891).

A Grand Army of the Republic (GAR) Post (No. 78) was established at Carrollton and named the William L. Lee post after the Carrollton native who had died in 1862 with the Union's 13th Kentucky Infantry at Bowling Green. The Carrollton GAR Post had five members who attended the 1895 state GAR convention: W. M. Bowling, J. G. Bunton, A. C. Jones, J. T. Lewis, and A. N. Jett, who was listed as commander. In 1889 the Carrollton post had 17 members, and in 1906, 13.

Carrollton Democrat, May 24, 1884.
CDC, September 14, 19, 1862.
Gentry, Mary Ann. *A History of Carroll County.* Madison, Ind.: Coleman Printing Co., 1984.
Marvel, William. "The Battle of Saltville: Massacre or Myth?" *Blue and Gray Magazine,* August 1991, 10.
Mosgrove, George Dallas. *Kentucky Cavaliers in Dixie: The Reminiscences of a Confederate Cavalryman.* 1895. Reprint, Lincoln: Univ. of Nebraska Press, 1999.
Report of Colonel Henry L. Giltner. http://home.cinci.rr.com/secondtennessee/giltner.html (accessed May 7, 2006).
Report of the Adjutant General of the State of Kentucky. Confederate Kentucky Volunteers, War of 1861–1865. Frankfort, Ky.: State Journal, 1915.
Report of the Adjutant General of the State of Kentucky. 2 vols. Frankfort: Kentucky Yeoman Office, 1866.

Diane Perrine Coon

CIVIL WAR, GALLATIN CO. The **Civil War** in Gallatin Co. was marked by divided loyalties and bitterness within the local population, punctuated by outbreaks of bloody violence. Early in the war, the county was occupied by rival bands of Union Home Guards and Secessionists, who were known as the Eagle Home Guards.

On the night of September 25, 1861, a band of about 50 mounted Confederate guerillas invaded Warsaw, breaking into the armory on the courthouse square. While in the process of plundering the arsenal, they were surprised by Union Army regulars. In the ensuing firefight, one Union soldier was wounded and one Confederate raider (George McCandlass, a Gallatin Co. native) was killed. In October 1861, it was reported by the *Frankfort Commonwealth* that Union men in the Warsaw area had recently been subjected to attacks by an aggressive group of Secessionists led by one Luther Green. A Union volunteer company of some 20 men organized by Capt. Jonathon Howe, who operated a store at the mouth of Sugar Creek in Gallatin Co., made contact with the Confederate party, which numbered close to 40, routing them and killing two of the Confederate soldiers. Green was captured and sent by steamboat into internment at Cincinnati.

In December 1861 a delegation of Warsaw Union loyalists called upon Union general Melancthon Smith Wade at Camp Dennison just east of Cincinnati, seeking protection. They reported that there had been three recent attacks on the town by armed Confederates resulting in civilian deaths and that the local situation approached anarchy. As they related it, the general populace favored the Union by a narrow margin, but the Confederates were more organized and aggressive.

In response, Col. **Charles Whittlesey** was dispatched to the area with four companies of the 20th Ohio Mounted Cavalry. He arrived on Christmas Day 1861, establishing headquarters in the Christian Church (later the United Methodist Church) at First and Main Sts. in Warsaw. This site was dubbed Camp Burbank. Until the war ended, federal troops were stationed periodically there. Warsaw became the headquarters for counterguerrilla activity in Boone, Carroll, Gallatin, Grant, and Owen counties.

Colonel Whittlesey appears to have gone straight to work with good effect. A few days after his arrival, Whittlesey learned that a company of Confederate Eagle Home Guards was camped along Eagle Creek near Sanders. He dispatched Company B of the 20th Ohio Mounted Cavalry to take the Confederate Guards into custody. The Confederates eluded the Union cavalry, but the Union forces captured a substantial cache of armaments, including a six-pound cannon that had been taken from the British during the Battle of Thames (see **War of 1812**). The Confederates had been camped on the property of Capt. G. Washington Sanders, a prominent local landholder and mill operator. Captain Sanders later presented himself in Warsaw and swore an oath of allegiance to the United States, thus absolving himself of support for the Confederate cause.

The *Louisville Journal,* under the headline "The Affairs in Warsaw," reported later that four prominent elected officials from Gallatin Co. had been taken prisoner by Whittlesey's command and incarcerated in Cincinnati. The prisoners included Lorenzo Graves, judge of the County Court; Hiram Baldwin, clerk of the court; Dr. A. B. Chambers, a member of the state legislature; and an unnamed fourth citizen. It was reported that Chambers took particular umbrage at "the invasion of the sacred soil of Warsaw" by the Union Army and threatened to burn the town unless the "Lincoln hirelings" immediately evacuated it.

Despite these and other efforts, in late 1862 Whittlesey asked to be relieved of his assignment in Warsaw. In an article entitled "An Episode in the Rebellion," printed in 1885 in the *Magazine of Western History,* Whittlesey was quoted as saying, "My position was becoming so ineffectual to protect Union men, and uncomfortable to myself, that I applied to be relieved from that duty." He attributed this decline in civil decorum to the softening of his orders by his new commander, Gen. Don Carlos Buell. He believed Buell to be overly sympathetic toward the Confederates. Whittlesey's request was granted and his command was transferred to the Southern Theater. The 45th Kentucky Mounted Cavalry replaced the unit from Ohio.

In 1863 a local physician and druggist, Cyrus W. Farris, was appointed assistant provost marshal for the county and charged with the maintenance of law and order. He was given the assistance of the federal troops stationed locally. Farris's efforts spawned considerable animosity. A bitter feud with the Southern-sympathizing Morrow family ensued when John J. Morrow and an associate were killed in a firefight with men under Farris's command. Following the war, Farris removed himself from his threatened situation locally by procuring a position as U.S. mail agent aboard the Ohio River steamer the *General Buell.* On September 20, 1866, while delivering mail, he was arrested at gunpoint in Ghent by one of the Morrows and two others, all former members of **John Hunt Morgan**'s Confederate Raiders. Farris was charged with the murder of John J. Morrow. Crewmen of the steamer armed themselves and extricated Farris from his difficulty. However, after the *General*

Buell put in upriver at its next stop, Warsaw, it was met by the Gallatin Co. sheriff and three deputies who had a warrant for Farris's arrest. The warrant was executed and Farris was incarcerated in the Gallatin Co. jail. Col. John J. Landrum (a renowned local attorney, a state legislator, and a Union military officer during the **Mexican War** and the **Civil War**) and Henry J. Abbett had the case transferred to federal court, where Farris was exonerated. The sheriff and the deputies who arrested him later were indicted by a federal grand jury for interfering with the U.S. mail. In 1868 Farris was killed in the calamitous collision of the steamers the *United States* and the *America* on the Ohio River near Warsaw.

Other bloody skirmishes during the war were reported in eastern Gallatin Co. near Sugar Creek and in the far western region of the county in the area once known as Gex, on property later occupied by the Gallatin Steel Company. The event at Gex occurred in August 1864 and involved the 117th Colored Regiment, which had come to Ghent to recruit local African Americans (see **Gex Landing Incident**).

There was also a report in the *Warsaw Independent* that a blacksmith living on Sugar Creek named John Edwards, age 47, was murdered by Confederate guerillas in 1863, leaving a widow and eight children. Anticipating trouble, he had buried all of his paper money ($75) in a bottle. In 1885 rooting hogs unearthed the bottle. The cork had rotted out and the currency was so wet and decomposed as to be worthless.

Contemporaneous letters and memoirs also indicate that locals believed that Confederate general Morgan had "spies" and agents at work in the county during each of the raids he conducted into Kentucky.

Bogardus, Carl R., Sr. *The Story of Gallatin County,* Ed. James C. Claypool. Cincinnati: John S. Swift, 2003.

Louisville Journal, January 1, July 30, December 30, 1862; October 13, 1866.

Warsaw Independent, April 21, 1888, 3.

Whittlesey, Charles. "An Episode in the Rebellion," *Magazine of Western History*, April 2, 1885.

Steve Huddleston

CIVIL WAR FORTIFICATIONS. The Union Army's interest in protecting Cincinnati as a vital river port, transportation hub, and manufacturing center began early in the **Civil War**. Gen. George McClellan sent Lt. Orlando M. Poe, of the topographical engineers, to Cincinnati during May and June 1861 to map the area for defensive purposes. By September, Brig. Gen. **Ormsby M. Mitchel** assigned Col. **Charles W. Whittlesey** to organize and construct a fortification system in Northern Kentucky to protect the southern approaches to Cincinnati. When Whittlesey arrived in the region on September 23, 1861, he carefully chose the locations of his first series of fortifications. They were spaced across the ridgetops from what is today Ludlow on the west to Fort Thomas on the east, focusing on vulnerable roads and valleys. Whittlesey successfully built nine fortifications in Kentucky (eight cannon batteries and Fort Mitchel) during the fall and winter of 1861. On the Cincinnati side of the Ohio River, he used the natural setting of steep-sided hills to place several gun platforms on Price Hill and Mount Adams. Whittlesey's original plan called for the construction of 17 military fortifications. However, because action on other military fronts required the attention of the engineers, only the first 9 installations were completed initially: Fort Mitchel, Battery Coombs (called Ludlow Hill Battery in 1861), Battery Riggs (not used after 1862), Battery Hooper (called Battery Kyle in 1861; name changed later to Battery Hooper), Battery Burnet (called Quarry Battery in 1861), Battery Larz Anderson (called Tunnel Battery in 1861), Battery Holt (called Three-Mile Creek or Stuart Battery in 1861), Battery Shaler, and Battery Phil Kearny (called Beechwoods Battery in 1861). Holt, Shaler, and Kearny Batteries are in Campbell Co.; the remaining ones are in Kenton Co. A small allotment of artillery and a detachment of regular soldiers were stationed at **Camp King** (the site of modern Menken Field, between Latonia and Covington along the Licking River). They kept the cannons in repair, drilled, and visited the fortifications daily. A separate detachment camped at Fort Mitchel until late summer of 1862.

In the summer of 1862, Confederate forces had marched into Kentucky intending to take over the state and possibly capture Cincinnati and Louisville. By late August, after the Confederates won at the battle of Richmond, the Kentucky state government fled to Louisville. Gen. Horatio G. Wright, commander of the Union Department of the Ohio, ordered Gen. Lew Wallace to Cincinnati in late August 1862 to organize a defense against the anticipated Confederate attack from inside Kentucky. Within a week, Wallace declared martial law in Cincinnati, Covington, and Newport.

Wallace placed Capt. James H. Simpson, of the U.S. Engineers, in charge of preparing the defensive fortifications. Simpson requested the assistance of Colonel Whittlesey. Whittlesey had recently retired from military service but returned to aid Simpson. In a few weeks, work brigades added to the original eight defensive fortifications, building a series of cannon batteries, rifle trenches, and connecting roads, just outside the city limits of Covington and Newport. Construction crews included the Black Brigade, the first organized use of free **African Americans in the Civil War**.

Manned by a large number of volunteer regiments, the defensive line deterred a Confederate advance into Northern Kentucky long enough for other Union forces to threaten the invaders from the south. At least 8,000 Confederate troops, under the direction of Gen. Henry Heth, advanced to within sight of Fort Mitchel in Kenton Co. Proceeding north along U.S. 25 (the **Dixie Highway**, or the **Covington and Lexington Turnpike**), they then stopped and waited. Scouting reports told Heth of the impressive string of fortifications, artillery, over 50,000 inexperienced militia and home guard troops, and at least 20,000 veteran soldiers ahead. The standoff took place September 10–12, 1862. On September 10, near Fort Mitchel, a skirmish between the 104th Ohio Infantry and the Confederates resulted in the death of four Union soldiers. The Confederate command soon realized they were vastly outnumbered. Union troop movements in Central Kentucky hastened their withdrawal. Harassed by Union cavalry, Heth and his troops withdrew southward, ending up at the Battle of Perryville in early October 1862. As a result of that battle, the Confederate army withdrew from Kentucky. Confederate general John Hunt Morgan continued to conduct cavalry raids throughout the state into 1864, but the Confederates never returned in force, and Kentucky remained a Union-controlled state.

After the end of the invasion emergency, Captain Simpson worked through the winter of 1862 and through the summer of 1863 to complete the fortification system, bringing it up to military specifications. General Morgan and a number of smaller renegade bands of rebel soldiers continued to ride through Kentucky for the rest of the war, necessitating the manning of the forts.

Several major forts, such as Fort Wright, were not constructed until 1863. However, all were upgraded or finished by the fall of 1863. The fortifi-

Fort Mitchel.

cations were periodically visited and upgraded throughout the remainder of the war. By then a colonel, Simpson remained in command of the fortifications. During 1864 he tried repeatedly to get additional troops to help guard the earthworks. He had more than 80 large guns at 25 locations but less than 120 men under his command. Local citizens wrote letters to him requesting more troops, as renegades and small groups of pro-Southern soldiers were occasionally looting in the area. The citizens felt that the presence of more Union troops would make the forts more of a deterrent. Because of war efforts in the East, no artillery troops could be sent to the region. Simpson was only able to find some convalescent soldiers to support his small garrison.

Simpson's final report on the forts was in May 1865. He found the forts to be in fair condition, except for Fort Whittlesey (in modern Fort Thomas), but he did not explain further. The full complement of artillery guns was still on hand, apparently not needed elsewhere during the winter of 1864–1865. Later, Simpson sent the artillery pieces to Pittsburgh and turned the land where the fortifications had been erected back to the landowners. The only compensation offered to these owners was the right to salvage any usable items left behind. After 1865 the fortification line became part of local war legends or fell into obscurity. Many of the forts and batteries endured relatively intact into the 20th century until building development began to move outward in the counties involved. Older citizens have reported that, as children during the first two decades of the 20th century, they played on many of these military earthworks. Residential development quickly claimed the fortifications situated on broad hilltops, while some smaller features of the fortifications have remained hidden. In the early 21st century, remnants of only six or seven of the forts or batteries exist.

Each battery or fort is briefly described below. All the fortifications were officially named in a Union Army order dated in 1864. Before that, many were known by informal names based on the names of landowners, topographic, or other local features. Name changes were common.

Battery J. L. K. Smith was located somewhere in the Ludlow-Bromley area. An earthwork, with two sides and an open rear, it was built in early 1862 as part of the emergency construction undertaken. Later, the Union Army named this battery for Col. J. L. Kirby Smith, of the 43rd Ohio Volunteers, who died at the Battle of Corinth, Miss. Its approximate vicinity is now in a residential development, and no trace of any artificial landforms remains.

Battery Coombs, one of the eight fortifications built in 1861, was originally known as the Ludlow Hill Battery. The Union officially named it after Gen. Leslie Coombs, a Kentucky native who fought in the **War of 1812**. It is an irregular ditch-and-bank earthwork on the northwest side of a hill above Ludlow, now part of **Devou Park**. Evidence still visible in the park includes rifle trenches, segments of the old military road, traces of the ditch, and the bank portion of the battery.

Battery Bates is a large epaulement situated on a hilltop in Devou Park. (An epaulement is an open, three-sided earthwork with one long and two short sides.) In 1864 the Union Army named the battery for Brig. Gen. Joshua H. Bates, retired, who organized Ohio Volunteers for the September 1862 invasion crisis. The informal name of the battery is unknown. The battery is in fair condition and may be the most intact of the remaining earthworks. Excavations by the **Behringer-Crawford Museum** during the 1980s and 1990s documented a remnant of the interior revetment, or wood facing, that lined the interior of the earthwork. The investigation determined that Battery Bates was constructed solely of earth. The powder magazine contained no stone foundations or other permanent structural elements. Physical traces that survive include the earthwork itself, the collapsed powder magazine, rifle trenches, military road segments, and an outer breastwork near the base of the hill.

Battery Riggs (called "old battery" on 1862 maps) was another of the 1861 batteries. However, during the 1862 emergency, Battery Bates and Battery Perry replaced Battery Riggs, which was located between them. Its form and size are unknown, and its site off Sleepy Hollow Rd. (in modern-day Fort Wright) was destroyed by construction by the early 1980s.

Battery Perry was an epaulement with a powder magazine centered behind the battery. It was named for A. F. Perry of Cincinnati, an agent who helped organized the local labor force in 1862. In the early 1980s, the Battery Perry site included a low embankment wall and the remains of an earth-covered powder magazine. Rifle trenches were visible to the north along the ridgetop. Battery Perry was very similar to Battery Bates in size and layout, except that the powder magazine was centered behind the earthwork at the Perry site. Battery Perry was destroyed by Fischer Homes for its Glengarry subdivision development in 2003.

Fort Mitchel was a fully bastioned fort, situated on a hilltop just west of the Covington and Lexington Turnpike. Construction began in 1861, but the fort did not reach its final form until 1863. It was named for Gen. Ormsby M. Mitchel, who was in command when construction began in 1861. Mitchel died October 30, 1862, at Beaufort, S.C. The fort sat forward (to the south) of the main line of cannon batteries. Designed to protect the approach from the south along the turnpike, the fort lay west of a curve in the turnpike, providing an unobstructed view over a wide expanse of farmland. It was built of a combination of earthen walls and wood revetment and contained at least 17 artillery pieces, including 24- and 32-pound cannon. Fort Mitchel was the site of the only skirmish along the fortification line during the September 10–12, 1862, standoff between the Union defenders and the Confederate general Heth's forces. The fort was abandoned by the Union Army at the end of the war, as were all of the other local fortifications. The Fort Mitchel site was destroyed during the early 20th century by the construction of a large house on the property. No oral history survives describing the condition of this major fort during the latter part of the 19th or early 20th century. The only trace of the Fort Mitchel installation remains in the sweeping driveway that curves up the hill from the Dixie Highway to the house. The driveway follows the same path as the military road access to the fort.

Battery Kyle (not to be confused with the original name of Battery Hooper), a two-sided earthwork with small additional embankments and a powder magazine, had been constructed in the yard of the Kyle family home, on the south side of Kyle's Ln., near its intersection with the Covington and Lexington Turnpike. In recent times, landowners and highway construction destroyed the battery. Residents in Fort Wright reported that one owner had leveled part of the earthwork because it stood between the owner's house and Kyle's Ln. Final destruction occurred during construction of I-75 in the early 1960s, as it stood directly in the road's path.

Battery McCrae was designed as an earthwork with one long and one short side. The Union Army named it for Capt. Alexander McCrae, of the 3rd U.S. Cavalry, who was killed February 21, 1862, at the Battle of Valberde, N.M. The engineering maps of the time placed the battery east of the turnpike and north of Battery Kyle. Conflicting stories about its location exist and have not been resolved owing to residential development and the construction of I-75. Reports that the battery was on the grounds of St. Joseph Heights, the convent of the **Sisters of Notre Dame**, were tested in the 1980s by the Behringer-Crawford Museum. The site near St. Joseph Heights is situated approximately 2,100 feet east of the intersection of Kyle's Ln. and the Dixie Highway, on the east side of the highway. Research in the 1980s documented an earthwork in a wooded area just south of St. Joseph Heights and not actually on the property. The location was destroyed during commercial development, but it may have been the site of Battery McCrae. Other reports placed the battery in a housing subdivision along Kyle's Ln., a location that was destroyed earlier by the housing subdivisions built during the post–**World War II** building boom.

Fort Wright was a hexagonal redoubt, its interior crest approximately 619 feet in diameter. This large fortification was planned and built in 1863, after the 1862 emergency had ended. It sat forward of the main line of the fortification system and looked over two access roads (modern Highland Pk. and Kyle's Ln.) that led down to what became Ky. Rt. 17. The Union Army named the fort in honor of Maj. Gen. Horatio G. Wright of the U.S. Engineers, who was in command of the Union Army Department of the Ohio. Fort Wright was situated near the original intersection of Kyle's Ln. and Highland Pk. Both roads at this spot have been altered by modern construction. The fortification site stood vacant until the 1980s. Older residents remembered playing at the site as children. Time and earthmoving activities over the years have obscured the actual location of the walls. The Fort Wright city building stands nearby today.

Battery Hooper, situated at the edge of a ridge that overlooks Highland Pk. and a gap in the hills that overlooks the Licking River valley, was built in 1861.

Battery Carlisle was located on a ridgetop east of Highland Pk. and north of Kyle's Ln., on property now owned by the **St. Charles Care Center**. The battery, an epaulement with three sides, was named after George Carlisle, a resident of Cincinnati who gave money for construction of the fortifications. No evidence of the earthwork was found during a walkover and survey of the property. An older area resident claimed that the earthwork had been destroyed during construction of additional buildings at the care center in recent years.

Battery Burbank was situated on a hilltop that overlooks the Licking valley and the **Three-L Highway** (Ky. Rt. 17). It is a large earthwork with an additional third wall at a right angle to the long side. It was named after Lt. Col. Sidney Burbank, 2nd U.S. Infantry, who was commandant of Cincinnati during September 1862. A senior citizen retirement community now stands there. Construction has lowered the hilltop by at least eight feet.

Battery Hatch is on a narrow ridgetop that extends northward, parallel to Ky. Rt. 17 and the Licking River valley, north of Battery Burbank. The ridge is very narrow and the battery is found at the north end overlooking the Licking River valley. Battery Hatch was named after George H. Hatch, the mayor of Cincinnati in September 1862. The area between the earth mound (the magazine) and the oblique V-shaped embankment was lined with flagstones. Its configuration closely matches the military drawings of other fortifications.

Fort Henry was not a fortification but a Covington headquarters used by Maj. Gen. Lew Wallace. Wallace's headquarters, referred to as Fort Henry, were situated in the Thompson Winery (later known as the Benedictine Brothers **Monte Casino** Monastery). This site is now a residential development.

Battery Buford was on a ridge that extends from Fort Henry northward to a sharp bend in Ky. Rt. 17, where it becomes Madison Ave. in Covington. The Union Army named this battery after Maj. Gen. John Buford, assistant inspector general of the United States. A housing development now stands there. Battery Buford was built in 1863 during the upgrade of the area's fortification line. It was a three-sided epaulement closed at its opening with a stockade fence.

Battery Burnet: Battery Burnet was north of Battery Buford on the same ridgeline overlooking the Licking River valley. First constructed during 1861, it was then known as the Quarry Battery. It reportedly had a powder magazine with a stone foundation, probably similar to the one found at Battery Hooper. The Union Army named this battery after Robert W. Burnet, president of the Cincinnati Branch of the U.S. Sanitary Commission during 1862. The battery, repaired in 1863, no longer exists.

Battery Larz Anderson's actual location is disputed, but it apparently was near a sharp bend in Madison Pk. that proceeded around the base of a large hill and southbound out of Covington. This battery was first built in 1861, and at that time it was known as the Tunnel Battery. This would put it close to the old railroad tunnel along Madison Pk. In any case, the battery no longer exists. It had a lunette-shaped earthwork and was named after Larz Anderson of Cincinnati, who gave money to the Union Army for construction of these fortifications.

Battery Wiggins was situated on the Campbell Co. side of the Licking River on a hilltop that overlooks the Ohio River Valley. Today, the hilltop appears as an isolated knoll because construction of Ky. Rt. 9 cut through the ridge. Preparation of the hilltop for development in the 1970s destroyed the earthwork. Built in 1862, it may not have been used again after the invasion emergency, as no official drawing of this earthwork has been found. It was officially named for Samuel Wiggins of Cincinnati, who gave money for the fortification system's construction in early September 1862.

Battery Holt is situated on a hilltop in Wilder in Campbell Co. that overlooks the intersection of Moock Rd. and Ky. Rt. 9. Battery Holt was first constructed in 1861 and was known variously as Three-Mile Creek Battery and Stuart Battery. Later, in 1864, it was officially named for Col. Joseph Holt, judge advocate general of the U.S. Army. Construction of a recent apartment complex has impacted the site. The apartment complex's owner reached an agreement with local officials to preserve the battery and its immediate setting, so the fortification was isolated in a small area of woods located near the manager's office. The remainder of the ridgetop has been lowered at least 10 feet below the level of the battery, effectively removing any evidence of activities to the rear of the earthwork. In its shape, the battery is unique among the fortifications. It is circular in form, with an opening to the rear where a powder magazine was constructed.

Battery McLean, located on the long ridge parallel to the Licking River in Campbell Co., was destroyed in 1994–1995 by residential development. This was a lunette-shaped fortification built in 1862 and finished in 1863. The Union Army officially named it for Maj. Nathaniel H. McLean, assistant adjutant general of the U.S. Army.

Battery Harrison was a redan-shaped earthwork located on the hill overlooking the Licking River valley, although its exact location has not been determined. Today, these hills contain residential subdivisions. It was built in 1862 and finished in 1863 and was officially named for Lt. Montgomery Pike Harrison, of the 5th U.S. Infantry.

Battery Shaler is located in **Evergreen Cemetery** off **U.S. 27**, in Campbell Co. Battery Shaler was built in 1861 and apparently has been known as Battery Shaler ever since. It included a three-sided epaulement and a redan-shaped advance breastwork. Dr. **Nathaniel B. Shaler** was the property owner and the physician in charge at **Newport Barracks**. The earthwork, which is in good condition, was probably reconstructed in the early 20th century. At that time, the powder magazine was replaced with a large gazebo commemorating war dead. A family mausoleum replaced the small forward rampart. The larger earthwork is planted in lawn grass and well maintained.

Battery Groesbeck, no longer in existence, may have served as an advance outwork of nearby Fort Burnside; it was located south of that location on the same ridge. The earthwork was built in 1862 and completed in 1863. The battery was named for William S. Groesbeck of Cincinnati, who gave money for construction of the fortification system in September 1862. It was on the site of the **Beverly Hills Supper Club**, which burned in 1977. It is unknown whether any remnant of the earthwork was left when the nightclub was built. The site has not been field checked. Although the property has not been developed or improved since the fire, access to the property is restricted.

Fort Burnside was an enclosed redoubt begun in 1862 and completed in 1863. Located on high ground overlooking U.S. 27, the redoubt was hexagonal in shape and was reportedly 684 feet in diameter along the interior crest. It was named after Maj. Gen. Ambrose E. Burnside, the previous commander of the Department of the Ohio, Union Army. The site was reported as destroyed as early as 1972.

Battery Phil Kearny, which dates to 1861, when it was known as the Beechwoods Battery, was upgraded in 1863. This battery, a modified redan with three sides, was situated on the former property of the Sisters of the Good Shepherd in Campbell Co. The site is on top of a steep hill overlooking U.S. 27. A subdivision now occupies the top of the hill, which has been severely graded and altered. The entrance road from U.S. 27 is named Canon Ridge. No trace of Battery Phil Kearny remains. It was named for Maj. Gen. Philip Kearny, who was killed at the battle of Chantilly, Va., on September 1, 1862.

Fort Whittlesey (15Cp55) was situated on the west side of present-day Fort Thomas Ave. It was located to protect this road as it intersected with U.S. 27 south of the site, which connected northern Campbell Co. with Falmouth and Lexington. Construction was begun in 1862 and completed in 1863. This was a double redoubt. Each section was square, and these were connected by a wood stockade. The Union Army named the fort after Col. Charles Whittlesey, who had designed the first set of fortifications in 1861 and who contributed to the 1862 emergency as a skilled engineer. An early-20th-century subdivision sits on the site; however, small remnants of the earthwork are still extant in the yards of these houses.

Battery Lee was a small earthwork located on a hilltop overlooking the Ohio River. Its location became part of the **Fort Thomas Military Reservation**. It was built in 1863 and provided an overlook to the Ohio River approach from upriver. The Union Army named Battery Lee after R. W. Lee of Covington, who, according to the official name list, had "ever by his hospitality shown himself the Union soldier's friend."

Adams, Roger C. "Panic on the Ohio: The Defense of Cincinnati, Covington, and Newport, September 1862," *JKS* 9 (September 1992): 80–98.

Crawford, Kenneth. "Defense of Cincinnati and the Legacy of William Hooper," *NKH* 12, no. 2 (Spring–Summer 2005): 20–36.

Geaslen, Chester F. *Our Moment of Glory in the Civil War, When Cincinnati, "The Queen City of the West," and the Sixth Largest City Was Defended from the Hills of Northern Kentucky.* Newport, Ky.: Otto, 1972.

Ramage, James A. "Panic in Cincinnati," *Blue and Gray* 3 (April–May 1986): 12–15.

Roth, David E. "'Squirrel Hunters' to the Rescue," *Blue and Gray* 3 (April–May 1986): 16–18.

Stern, Joseph S., Jr. "The Siege of Cincinnati," *BCHS* 18 (July 1960): 163–86.
Walden, Geoffrey R. "The Defenses of Cincinnati," *Blue and Gray* 3 (April–May 1986): 19–33.

Jeannine Kreinbrink

CIVIL WAR HOSPITALS. During the **Civil War**, military hospitals were opened in Northern Kentucky to care for the wounded and sick. Located along the Ohio River's steamboat connections and at the terminus of the railroad line from Lexington, Covington had about five military hospital facilities, and adjoining Newport, for a short time, had one. These hospitals were often located in hotel buildings leased to the federal government on a short-term basis and staffed by local volunteer women. During the first year of the war, the Union Army failed to deal seriously with the issue of military hospitals, for its commanders believed that the war would be short and local medical practitioners would be able to care for the wounded. Not only did the war continue longer than ever imagined, but it was fought mainly in the rural South, where there were fewer local medical practitioners. Hence, Union soldiers needing care were transported north to border areas such as Cincinnati and Northern Kentucky.

In Covington the largest and longest-operating military hospital was the Main Street U.S. General Hospital. It opened just before the Battle of Shiloh in April 1862, and when it closed, in June 1865, it was the last of its kind still operating. Situated on the west side of Main St., between Third and Fourth Sts., in the former Ellison House Hotel (not the Elliston House, which was on Russell St.), it had at one point some 300 beds. The second in size in Covington was the 218-bed Seminary U.S. General Hospital, on 11th St. near Madison Ave., in a building once part of the **Western Baptist Theological Institute**; it began in September 1862 and closed in late April 1865. In 1867 that site became **St. Elizabeth Medical Center**. A third hospital in Covington was located in the former Bridge Hotel, at the foot of Greenup St.; it operated from September 1862 to May 1863 and had 53 beds.

An attempt was made to convert Covington's Sixth St. market house, near Sixth and Main Sts. in modern **Main Strasse**, into a hospital. It failed within a month, as patients there were moved to other facilities. The care facility on Sixth St. was more of a convalescent home than a general hospital. Another convalescent facility was at Cole's Garden, a beer garden and amusement park near **Camp King**, south of Covington along the Licking River. The Cole's Garden facility, leased from Cole Bealer, had about 50 beds and opened in August 1863; it operated under the name Licking Branch of the Seminary U.S. General Hospital. As the war wound down and war-related injuries and illnesses diminished, the hospitals were consolidated and the government leases were not renewed.

"Covington Hospitals Have the Reputation of Being the Best Managed Institutions of Their Kind," *CDE*, May 13, 1863, 2.
Reis, Jim. "Wounded Soldiers, Prisoners Brought Reality of Civil War to the Home Front," *KP*, September 9, 1991, 4K.
Simon, Jack. "The Civil War Military Hospitals of Covington, Kentucky," *NKH* 9, no. 1 (Fall–Winter 2003): 38–43.
"There Are 325 Patients in Covington's Military Hospitals," *CDE*, November 19, 1862, 3.

CIVIL WAR ORGANIZATIONS. In 1866 Union veterans of the **Civil War** organized into the Grand Army of the Republic (GAR). Local GAR groups were called posts. The Northern Kentucky post of the GAR was organized March 23, 1882, as Post 195, Department of Ohio. On June 20, 1882, it adopted the name James A. Garfield Post 2 and was assigned to the Department of Kentucky.

In 1881 the GAR formed the Sons of Veterans of the United States of America for sons of GAR members. In 1925 the name of this organization was changed to Sons of Union Veterans of the Civil War (SUVCW). Local SUVCV groups are called camps. On May 31, 1998, the Nelson-Garfield Memorial Camp No. 3 was chartered and was assigned to the Department of Kentucky. It was named after **William "Bull" Nelson**, a Civil War Union general who commanded the Army of Kentucky, and James A. Garfield, a Union general who served in Eastern Kentucky and later became president of the United States.

Hampton, Jeffrey. *History of Nelson Garfield Memorial Camp # 3*. Self-published, 2006.
Sons of Union Veterans of the Civil War. *Sons of Union Veterans of the Civil War*. Paducah, Ky.: Turner, 1996.

Andrew O. Lutes

CLABES, JUDY (b. Judith A. Grisham, May 24, 1945, Henderson). Newspaper editor and civic leader Judy Grisham Clabes is the daughter of Jesse Robert and Virginia Louis Kenney Grisham. She received her BA from the University of Kentucky in 1967 and an MPA from Indiana State University in 1984. Before her newspaper career began, she taught at both Henderson (Ky.) High School and Henderson Co. (Ky.) High School. She joined the *Evansville Press* in 1972, launching her career in journalism.

In 1983, when Judy Clabes arrived in Northern Kentucky as editor of the *Kentucky Post,* she quickly began taking an active role in her new community. Her high level of participation in community affairs did not end once she became president and CEO of the Scripps Howard Foundation in 1996. Clabes has a long list of involvements in civic matters. She has been one of the founding board members for **Forward Quest** Northern Kentucky; a member of the Governor's Task Force on the Economic Status of Kentucky's Women; a member of the board of the Huntington Banks and the Northern Kentucky Convention Center; one of the founding board governors for the Metropolitan Club; a founder of the Northern Kentucky Fund of the Greater Cincinnati Foundation and a major fundraiser to encourage a philanthropic endowment to meet quality-of-life needs in Northern Kentucky; a permanent cochair of **Northern Kentucky University**'s Capital Campaign; a member of the advisory board and a fundraiser for the **Urban Learning Center**, which takes entry-level college courses to inner-city neighborhoods, providing the opportunity for a college education to people who never thought it possible; a member of the Dean's Council with the University of Kentucky's School of Communications; and a University of Kentucky Fellow.

The Northern Kentucky region was enriched when Clabes and her husband, Gene, and their two boys, Joe and Jake, moved into it. Judy Clabes's voice and energies continue to be devoted to important civic causes, among which are support for funding for universities, attending to the needs of children, gathering community support for the arts, promoting cooperation between business and government, advocating protection for free speech, and, more than any other cause, obtaining resources for public education.

Clabes, Judy. Interview by Nancy J. Tretter, January 20, 2005, Covington, Ky.
"Clabeses Honored as Outstanding Alumni by UK," *KP*, December 6, 2004, 2K.
"Judith Grisham Clabes." *Marquis Who's Who, 2006*. http://galegroup.com (accessed June 8, 2006).

Nancy J. Tretter

CLAIR, MATTHEW WESLEY (b. October 21, 1865, Union, W.Va.; d. June 28, 1943, Washington, D.C). Matthew Wesley Clair, who became a Methodist Episcopal bishop, was the son of Anthony and Ollie Green Clair. He graduated from Morgan College (now Morgan State University) in Baltimore, Md., and earned a doctorate from Bennett College in North Carolina, a divinity degree from Howard University in Washington, D.C., and another degree from Wilberforce College in Ohio. In 1889 he was ordained a minister in the Methodist Episcopal Church. He served churches at Harper's Ferry, W.Va., and Staunton, Va., eventually being assigned to the Ebenezer and then the Asbury Methodist Church, both in Washington, D.C. He worked several years in Washington for various Methodist national organizations. In 1920 he was one of the two first African Americans elected as bishops within the Methodist Episcopal Church; he was made the Bishop of Africa and assigned to Monrovia, Republic of Liberia. His missionary groups took motion-picture equipment and films to Africa to use in teaching morality and religion. In 1924 Clair was assigned to Covington, Ky., in charge of a territory including the states of Kentucky and Tennessee. In Covington, he and his wife, Eva Wilson Clair, resided at 1040 Russell St. It is believed that he was stationed in Covington because there were three African American Methodist Episcopal churches in Covington and one in Newport. His preaching often included examples from, and discussions about, his experiences in Africa. In 1926 he was selected as one of eight Northern Kentuckians to appear in that year's *Who Who*. In 1936 he retired and remained in Covington. On June 28, 1943, Clair died while he was in Washington, D.C., to conduct funeral services for his brother-in-law Edward Gray, a Cincinnati medical doctor. Clair's funeral was conducted at the Asbury Methodist Church in Washington, and he was buried at the Harmony Cemetery on the east side of Washington. Bishop Clair's oldest son, Matthew Wesley Clair Jr., became the Methodist bishop of St. Louis and in 1964 participated in protests against the segregation of congregations within his denomination.

"Bishop Is Dead," *KTS*, June 28, 1943, 1.
"Death Notice," *KP*, June 29, 1943, 4.
"Eight Northern Kentuckians in 1926 Edition of *Who's Who*," *KP*, October 8, 1926, 5.
"Methodists Raise Six to Episcopate," *NYT*, May 18, 1936, 15.
Reis, Jim. "Matthew Clair a Link to History," *KP*, January 16, 1995, 4K.
"Taking Films to Heathens: Eighty-Six Methodist Missionaries to Sail This Week," *NYT*, January 27, 1926, 21.

Michael R. Sweeney

CLARK, DORIS V., CAPTAIN (b. January 11, 1912, Sherman, Grant Co., Ky.; d. August 13, 1976, Cincinnati, Ohio). Chemist Doris Vest Clark was the daughter of Thomas Webb and Clarabelle Vest Clark and a descendant of early Grant Co. pioneer Sarah Bryan Clark. Doris Clark graduated from Williamstown High School (see **Williamstown Independent Schools**) in Grant Co. in 1927, and her training in chemistry was from Randolph-Macon Woman's College, Ashland, Va. (BA, 1931); Washington University, St. Louis, Mo. (MS, 1932); and postgraduate studies at the University of Cincinnati (1933–1935). Before **World War II**, Clark worked as a chemist for Indo-Vin Inc., Cincinnati (1936–1937); Century Chemists, Williamstown (1937–1941); and DuBois Company, Cincinnati (1941–1942). During the war, while serving in the Woman's Air Corps (WAC), she rose to the rank of captain, commanding officer, 151st Company WAC (Experimental Gun and Searchlight Battery). She was discharged honorably in 1946.

Clark came home and returned to work for the DuBois Chemical Company in Cincinnati, where she served as plant and production manager, director of research and development, and senior vice president; she held the latter position at the time of her death. She was one of the first women to serve as a high-ranking officer of a chemical company. She was also on the board of governors of the Chemical Specialist Manufacturing Association of New York City and a member of the American Oil Chemist Society. In 1967 she was selected to be included in *Who's Who of American Women.*

Clark served on the board of the Grant Co. Chamber of Commerce and the Grant Co. Hospital (see **St. Elizabeth Medical Center**). She was actively involved with the **American Red Cross**, and the **Williamstown Women's Club**. She died in 1976 at Christ Hospital in Cincinnati and was buried in the Williamstown Cemetery.

"Doris Clark Dies," *KP*, August 14, 1976, 11.
"Ladies, a Formula for Success!" *CE*, July 15, 1973, 14C.
"Services Held for Miss Clark," *Grant County News*, August 19, 1976, 3.
Stringfield, Leonard H. "Doris Clark: At the Top in a Man's World," *Detergents and Specialties*, May 1969.
Who's Who of American Women: A Biographical Dictionary of Notable Women, 1968–1969. Chicago: Marquis, 1969.

CLARK, GEORGE ROGERS, LIEUTENANT COLONEL (b. November 19, 1752, near Monticello, Albemarle Co., Va.; d. February 13, 1818, near Louisville, Ky.). George Rogers Clark, a surveyor and an Indian fighter, was the son of John and Ann Rogers Clark. His father's farm was near Charlottesville, Va. He received a typical pioneer education and may have studied for a year or two with his uncle Donald Robinson, a renowned educator and a graduate of the University of Edinburgh, Scotland. As a youth, Clark heard Virginian Patrick Henry give his famous speech on liberty. Clark lived next door to George Mason, another prominent Virginia political leader, and often stayed overnight with the Mason family. At age 19, Clark purchased a copy of Euclid and a set of surveying tools. Soon afterward, on June 9, 1772, he set out from Pittsburgh, Pa., to explore the new unsettled territories to the west. He spent a couple of years surveying for himself and his neighbors on the Ohio River about 30 miles south of Wheeling, W.Va. Clark was given a captain's commission in the Virginia militia by Lord John Murray, Earl of Dunmore, the last royal governor of Virginia (see **Lord Dunmore's War**). After peace, the flood of immigrants moving westward resumed. Clark then worked for the Ohio Company as a surveyor. He was a deputy to Hancock Lee, who had replaced George Washington (president 1789–1797) as the Ohio Company's head surveyor. Lee and Clark laid out the Leestown settlement on the Kentucky River in 1775. Later, at a meeting held at the settlers' fort at Harrodsburg, Ky., Clark was chosen to return to Williamsburg, Va., and assist in promoting the establishment of Kentucky Co., a new entity that Virginia would have to help defend. So in 1776 he traveled to Virginia through the Cumberland Gap and presented the idea to Virginia governor Patrick Henry. During these talks, Clark also requested that money be allocated to raise a force to attack the British line of defensive forts north of the Ohio River. Kaskaskia, Ill.; Vincennes, Ind.; and later Detroit, Mich. were to be attacked to relieve the threat of British attacks on the settlements in Kentucky. Virginia supplied 500 pounds of gunpowder to help the settlers in Kentucky defend themselves. Clark recruited some troops at Pittsburgh and picked up the gunpowder, which he delivered to Limestone (modern Maysville, Ky.), where it was hidden to protect it from Indians. Later, this gunpowder was recovered and distributed to settlers at the forts in Kentucky. Clark, who had been promoted to lieutenant colonel in the Virginia militia, soon took over command of the Kentucky Co. militia. He appointed Joseph Bowman to recruit militiamen from the settlers in Kentucky to serve with him on his attack on the British. Louisville, located strategically along the Ohio River and at the midpoint of Kentucky, became Clark's home and command center. The Indians of the region respected Clark (whom they called the "long knife" because he wore a sword) because troops under his command performed so well in the field. The Indians' respect for Clark served him well in 1780, when an Indian raiding party, serving with British captain Henry Bird, set out to attack Louisville; the party turned back after reaching Cincinnati because it was rumored that Clark had just returned to Louisville.

Clark was ordered by officials in Virginia to build forts at the mouth of the Licking River and the mouth of the Kentucky River to protect the central Bluegrass. He responded that he lacked the manpower to build and man the forts. Instead he built an oared galley that cruised the Ohio River from Louisville to **Big Bone Lick** in Kentucky. Then, when calls for militia to defend the settlements in Kentucky resulted in few recruits, Clark simply closed the land office so that no new patents could be filed. Moreover, it was circulated quietly that the Kentucky militia would not defend settlers north of the Licking River, thus leaving those in Northern Kentucky and southern Ohio in a precarious position until the threat of Indian attacks died in 1815 at the conclusion of the War of 1812.

Clark's expeditions against the British in the Illinois Territory were miracles of good planning and audacious activity. They were uniformly successful until the target became the British fort and garrison at Detroit, which could be supplied and reinforced by ship. Clark's health had begun to deteriorate by 1798, and the rumors of his problems with alcoholism were confirmed. He eventually moved to Clark's Point in Clarksville, Ind., where he operated a gristmill and farmed. In 1809 he suffered a stroke and fell unconscious in front of his fireplace, burning one of his legs so badly it had to be amputated. He then moved to Locust Grove, his sister's home near Louisville, where he lived for nine years. Clark died of a second stroke on February 18, 1818, at Locust Grove. He was buried on at the Croghan Family Cemetery there; on November 4, 1869, he was reburied at Cave Hill Cemetery in Louisville .

Bodley, Temple. *George Rogers Clark*. Boston: Houghton Mifflin, 1926.
Butterfield, Consul Wilshire. *History of George Rogers Clark's Conquest of the Illinois*. Columbus, Ohio: F. J. Heer, 1904.
Palmer, Frederick. *Clark of the Ohio*. New York: Dodd, Mead, 1930.
Thwaites, Reuben Gold, ed. *Chronicles of Border Warfare*. Cincinnati: Stewart, Kidd, 1895.

Joseph F. Gastright

CLARKE, ERNEST SWOPE (b. November 25, 1872, Falmouth, Ky.; d. September 22, 1948, Cincinnati, Ohio). Ernest Swope Clarke was a prominent Democratic politician from Pendleton Co. who rose to become the chief justice of the Kentucky Court of Appeals. He was the second of five children of Asahel Rawlings Clarke and Martha

Ann Swope. His father had fought for the Confederacy under Gen. John Hunt Morgan and moved to Falmouth after being released from a Union prison in Chicago at the end of the **Civil War**. Ernest Clarke graduated from Bethany College in West Virginia in 1892, studied law under Leslie T. Applegate, and passed the bar exam in 1894. That same year, Clarke began practicing law in Falmouth with Applegate. Clarke was involved in the community as a member of the Beta Theta Pi social fraternity and of the Disciples of Christ Church and in other ways as well. He also served as the captain of Company C of the Kentucky State Guard from 1898 to 1899. On June 12, 1900, Clarke married Mary Virginia Oldham; they had two sons. He quickly became a successful lawyer in Falmouth and practiced privately there for six years. Between 1900 and 1915, he was elected Pendleton Co. attorney, county treasurer, and county judge. Clarke served as president of the Citizens Bank of Falmouth from 1911 to 1919.

In 1915 Clarke was elected as a judge on the Kentucky Court of Appeals. He served in that position until September 1, 1925, when he was appointed chief justice of the court. He resigned a year later and moved to Louisville, where he became the vice president and trust officer of the First National Bank and Kentucky Title Trust Company. In Louisville, Clarke became highly involved in civic matters. He was a trustee of the University of Louisville from 1928 to 1948 and of the American Printing House for the Blind from 1927 to 1948. He retired in 1945 and died in 1948. He was buried in Louisville's Cave Hill Cemetery.

Cave Hill. "Clarke Sr., Ernest S." www.cavehillcemetery.com (accessed March 3, 2005).

Kerr, Charles. *History of Kentucky.* 5 vols. Chicago: American Historical Society, 1922.

The National Cyclopedia of American Biography. Vol. 37. New York: James T. White, 1951.

Reis, Jim. "Little Known Figures Worthy of Note," *KP,* November 29, 1993, 4K.

Southard, Mary Young, and Ernest C. Miller, eds. *Who's Who in Kentucky: A Biographical Assembly of Notable Kentuckians.* Louisville, Ky.: Standard, 1936.

Elizabeth Comer Williams

CLARKE, JOHN B. (April 14, 1833, Brooksville, Ky.; d. May 23, 1911, Brooksville, Ky.). Legislator John Blades Clarke was the son of John and Mary Blades Clarke, both native Kentuckians. He attended schools in Augusta, including **Augusta College**. After his college graduation, Clarke briefly taught school before reading law with Judge **Joseph Doniphan** of Augusta. He was admitted to the bar in 1854 and set up his first law practice in Rockport, Ind. When his wife, Cordelia A. Robertson, became ill at the end of 1855, he moved back to Brooksville. There, Clarke continued to practice law and began his political career when he was elected Bracken Co. attorney in 1857, a post he held until 1862. As a member of the Democratic Party, he was elected to the Kentucky state senate in 1867 and served there until 1870. The Democrats of the Ninth Congressional District made Clarke their candidate for the U.S. House of Representatives in 1874. He was elected to the 44th Congress and reelected two years later to the 45th Congress. He declined to run again in 1878, choosing instead to return to the practice of law. Clarke died of throat cancer in 1911 and was buried in Mount Zion Cemetery, near Brooksville.

Biographical Cyclopedia of the Commonwealth of Kentucky. Chicago: John M. Gresham, 1896.

Biographical Directory of the United States Congress, 1774–1989. Washington, D.C.: Government Printing Office, 1989.

Biographical Encyclopedia of Kentucky. Cincinnati: J. M. Armstrong, 1878.

Thomas S. Ward

CLARYVILLE. Claryville, located just south of Alexandria in Campbell Co. along **U.S. 27** and the Licking Pk., is a rural community that today is experiencing rapid growth. In its long history, the small town of Claryville, named for the Clary family who settled there, was never incorporated, but it has always been a hub of activity for the immediate area. The 1883 Lake atlas shows several stores, a shoemaker, a post office, two blacksmith shops, a school, two cooper or basket shops, and several taverns situated at Claryville. At one time there was a local "bus" service provided by means of a horse-drawn carriage service to Newport. The Rackes, a prominent family in Claryville, operated a general store, a hardware store, and a lumberyard in town. The Claryville Inn has also been a popular spot for years. The Bob White Sportsman's Club opened in town in 1933 on 85 acres. There are mobile home parks in Claryville as well as the new **Campbell Co. High School**, which opened in 1995. The Kahns meatpacking plant relocated to Claryville from Cincinnati in 1983, supplying many jobs to local residents. This company and its plant are now a part of the Sara Lee Foods Corporation. Many new homes are being built at Claryville, and the relatively flat terrain lends itself to a bright future of community growth.

An Atlas of Boone, Kenton, and Campbell Counties, Kentucky. Philadelphia: D. J. Lake, 1883.

Kenneth A. Reis

CLAXON, JOSEPH LUCAS, JR. (b. May 31, 1918, Monterey, Owen Co., Ky.; d. January 18, 1999, Florence, Ky.). Extension agent Joseph Claxon was the son of Joe Lucas and Mary Kemper Claxon. He spent his youth on a farm at Claxon Ridge in Owen Co., then graduated from the University of Kentucky in Lexington with a degree in agriculture and also served in **World War II**. He married Elizabeth Trueheart in 1946 and they became the parents of two children. He and his family settled in Florence, Ky., where he served as the Boone Co. Extension Agent for 28 years. A room at the Ellis Cooperative Extension Center in the county was named in his honor. Claxon was a member of the Boone Co. Fair Board for 40 years, president and chairman of the Kentucky State Fair Board, director and president of the Boone Co. Farm Bureau, twice president of the Florence Rotary Club, and a member of the **Florence Baptist Church**. He died in 1999 and was buried at the Hebron Lutheran Cemetery in Boone Co.

"Agriculture Agent Joseph Claxon Jr. Led Fairs, Farm Bureau, 'Loved People,'" *KP,* January 21, 1999, 2.

Murphy, Margaret Alice, and Lela Maude Hawkins. *The History of Historic Old Cedar Baptist Church and Community, 1816–2004.* Frankfort, Ky.: Lynn, 2004.

Margaret A. Murphy

CLAYTON, RICHARD (b. ca. 1807, England; date and place of death unknown). Balloonist Richard Clayton came to the United States in the early 1830s and set up a clock-making and silversmith shop, called Clayton's Wholesale House, on the southeast corner of Second and Sycamore Sts. in Cincinnati. In 1854, after purchasing Somerset Hall in Ludlow, Ky., Clayton moved there. Somerset Hall was the former summer home of William Butler Kenner (d. 1853) (see **Kenner Family**), a New Orleans plantation owner and the brother of George Kenner, who had owned Ludlow's nearby **Elmwood Hall**.

While living in England, Clayton had witnessed several balloon flights and developed a keen interest in the activity. At the time he arrived in Cincinnati, a number of both professional and amateur balloonists were making flights in various northeastern cities. Clayton decided to become a balloonist and constructed a 50-foot-tall airship from 4,500 square feet of silk cloth. When filled with hydrogen gas, the balloon, named *The Star of the West,* could carry a payload of about 1,000 pounds. Clayton made his first flight on April 8, 1835, from an amphitheater in Cincinnati on Court St, between Race and Elm Sts. He ran newspaper advertisements, saying that he would be "making a grand aerial voyage, in the most splendid balloon in the U.S." Clayton's flights were not merely for entertainment or for thrilling personal experiences; he also had a profit motive. He arranged for several hotels in the city to sell tickets to view his balloon flights for 50 cents each. Clayton took off in his balloon at 5:00 p.m., accompanied by a 20-pound dog, which he dropped by parachute from an altitude of about one mile. The dog landed safely near the city. Clayton's flight ended on a 3,000-foot-high mountaintop in Monroe Co., Va. (now W.Va.). On that flight, Clayton set a world record for the longest balloon flight. He succeeded in traveling 350 miles in nine and one-half hours. As a result of that feat, Clayton became a national hero. Within a week after landing, he was back in town preparing for his next flight. On May 13, 1835, he flew again from the Court St. site. On the day of the flight, there were strong, gusty winds, which caused the balloon to crash into a nearby building shortly after takeoff. The basket was torn free from the balloon, and Clayton was fortunate to land safely on a rooftop. His balloon was destroyed in the mishap, but friends and neighbors donated money to help pay for a replacement.

He made another flight on July 4, 1835, on which he predicted that he would reach the Atlantic seaboard. He took with him several letters, which were later called the country's first airmail. The balloon ascended to an altitude of several miles, where the temperature was about 10 degrees. Ice collected on the balloon and leaks in the fabric occurred, which caused Clayton to abort the flight at Waverly, Ohio, just 100 miles from Cincinnati. He walked to a nearby house for help and deposited the mail he had been transporting in the Waverly post office. Clayton narrowly escaped disaster on another flight in late summer 1835. On that trip, his balloon exploded in flight, but he was able to descend safely, with the silk fabric acting as a parachute. Clayton made a successful flight from New Orleans, with a much smaller balloon, on Christmas Day 1835. He also made several flights from both Louisville and Lexington, Ky.

Clayton is clearly the first person to have observed the Northern Kentucky region from the air. After more than a dozen flights, he retired from ballooning and returned to his clock-making business, which he thereafter called Clayton's Balloon Shop. Cincinnati's city directories had a listing for the business through 1859. In the 1860 census, Richard Clayton was listed as a retired clockmaker, living in Ludlow. He was not listed in the 1870 census, so possibly he either died or moved away sometime during that 10-year period.

"Aerial Navigation," *Western Monthly Magazine*, June 1835, 305–6.

Cunningham, Paul. "Air Mail Pioneer," *CP*, May 12, 1943.

Maurer, Maurer. "Richard Clayton—Aeronaut," *Bulletin of the Historical and Philosophical Society of Ohio* 13 (April 1955): 143–50.

Pence, Henry. "First Airmail Flight Made from Cincinnati," *CE*, October 1, 1944, 20.

Tenkotte, Paul A. "Rival Cities to Suburbs: Covington and Newport, Kentucky, 1790–1890," PhD diss., Univ. of Cincinnati, 1989.

CLAYTON-BULLOCK HOUSE. In 1839 John W. Clayton built a two-story frame house at 528 Greenup St. in Covington. The name of the house comes from the first two owners of the home, John Clayton and his daughter Mary Clayton Bullock. Over the years, the house has been altered many times. Part of it was even torn down several years ago, owing to termite infestation. It is rumored that timbers from a ship that came up the Ohio River to Cincinnati were used in construction of the house. John W. Clayton died in this house on August 28, 1865. During the **Civil War**, Gen. Ulysses S. Grant sent his wife and children to Covington to live near his father, **Jesse Root Grant**, where he felt they would be safe. The historic house where Jesse Grant, who was Covington's postmaster, and his wife resided is just a few doors north of the Clayton-Bullock House on Greenup St. John Clayton's daughter Mary ran a private school in the Clayton family's home, when other schools were closed during the war. One of Ulysses Grant's sons, Frederick Grant, was a pupil in Mary's school. Mary married W. R. Bullock on February 28, 1867, and they had eight children. Mary Clayton Bullock lived in the house from the time she was six months old until her death on October 13, 1907, at age 68. Mary, her husband, and her mother and father are all buried in Highland Cemetery in Fort Mitchell.

"Bullock Rites," *KP*, November 12, 1930, 1.

"Death Notice—John W. Clayton," *CDE*, August 29, 1865, 7.

"Home Makes Its Mark," *KE*, March 25, 1999, 1B.

"Mrs. Mary C. Bullock of Covington, Dead," *KTS*, October 14, 1907, 7.

Jack Wessling

CLEARY, EDWIN (b. Cynthiana, Ky., 1857; d. London, England, August 3, 1922). World traveler Edwin Cleary was the son of Judge W. W. Cleary and the brother of Kenton Co. judge **Walter Cleary**. Born in Harrison Co., by 1876 he had already studied briefly for the priesthood (to honor his Irish Catholic father's request) and had also studied law for a time in the office of **John G. Carlisle**. He soon found himself acting in the Old Bowery Theater in New York City, and by 1887 he had traveled to London with the great actor Edwin Booth to perform there. He became a producer and took theatrical companies throughout South Africa and South America.

In the 1890s Cleary was a builder of African railroads (from Cairo to Cape Town) with Cecil Rhodes, and eventually he founded an English newspaper in Cairo. During World War I, he served as a war correspondent for the London *Daily Express*. He recounted the siege of Antwerp for his readers as well as interviewing the German Kaiser. Much of his reporting was wired back to Covington for Northern Kentucky readers. Cleary became involved with the beginnings of aviation in France, tried to introduce the world to the playing of football at night under the lights, and invented the Cleary oil burner (a wickless oil burner that converted petroleum into gas); his oil burner was taken over by the British Petroleum Company. In 1922, while at a London railway station buying a ticket for Birmingham, he collapsed and died from heart failure. Over the course of his life, he both amassed and lost fortunes.

"Edwin Cleary Dies Abroad," *NYT*, August 4, 1922, 12.

"Veteran Actor, Formerly of Covington, Dies," *KTS*, August 4, 1922, 20.

White, F. M. "A Real Covington Soldier of Fortune," *KP*, July 20, 1910, 8; July 21, 1910, 8; July 22, 1910, 5.

CLEARY, WALTER W. (b. August 31, 1854, Harrison Co., Ky.; d. March 20, 1916, Covington, Ky.). Judge Walter W. Cleary was the son of W. W. Cleary, a native of Ireland. Little is known about Walter's early life, but by 1880 he was living on Greenup St. in Covington. When the **Latonia Racecourse** was being built in 1882, Walter Cleary served as vice president of the Latonia Agricultural and Stock Association, the group that developed the track. In addition, he was the publisher and editor of the *Kentucky Turfguide* magazine. Cleary was an active member of the Eagles and Elks Clubs in Covington. As a Democrat, he was elected a circuit court judge in 1908. He was known as "the people's judge" because he typically backed projects that helped the average citizen. Judge Cleary played an active role in the abolishment of toll roads in Northern Kentucky. He also endorsed legislation that required the pasteurization of milk, and he was instrumental in having a new courthouse built at Independence and in establishing the first modern high school in Boone Co. In 1912 he was elected to his second four-year term as circuit court judge but was unable to complete it, as he suffered from a severe case of diabetes. In an attempt to improve his health, he took a month-long cruise from New York City to Galveston, Tex., in August 1915, during which the ship encountered a hurricane while rounding Florida. His condition continued to deteriorate, and in March 1916 doctors amputated a leg. Cleary died several days later at age 61, in St. Elizabeth Hospital in Covington. At the time of his death, he was a widower. Funeral services were held at the St. Mary Cathedral, and he was buried at St. Mary Cemetery in Fort Mitchell.

"Body of Late Judge Cleary Lies in State," *KP*, March 21, 1916, 1K.

"Hundreds Attend Two Funerals," *KP*, March 22, 1916, 1K.

Reis, Jim. "John B. Read Led Kenton with Foresight and Compassion," *KP*, October 19, 1998, 4K.

——. "Writer, Gadfly, and Earl," *KP*, July 7, 1999, 4K.

CLEMENS, SAMUEL (author Mark Twain), in Campbell Co. There is a persistent local tradition that Samuel Clemens, a.k.a. Mark Twain, occasionally visited in the home of **Richard Tarvin Baker**, next to the courthouse in Alexandria. In recent years, attempts have been made to determine whether that actually happened. Newspaper stories of the day have been checked for references to a visit, in the belief that if Clemens actually came to Alexandria, it should have been front-page news. Many of the books by or about the man who wrote as Mark Twain have also been checked for clues. Andrew Hoffman's *Inventing Mark Twain,* Justin Kaplan's *Mark Twain and His World,* and Margaret Sanborn's *Mark Twain: The Bachelor Years* all state that Twain moved to the Greater Cincinnati area in November 1856 and lived there until April 1857. In one of the "Keokuk Letters" from Cincinnati, dated November 29, 1856, Clemens tells of his train trip from Keokuk, Ill., through Quincy, Ill., Chicago, and Indianapolis, and on to Cincinnati. When he arrived in Cincinnati, he would have been just 20 years old, unknown in the region and certainly not yet worthy of newspaper headlines. Clemens did not become nationally known as a writer, humorist, and novelist until years later. While living in the region, he was employed as a typesetter by the Thomas Wrightson Printing Company. Contemporary city directories list two addresses for the company: 167 Walnut St. in Cincinnati, and the southwest corner of Taylor (modern Third) and Monmouth Sts. in Newport. No home address for a Samuel Clemens was found. However, one of his biographies indicates that he lived in a boardinghouse close to the print shop. In his autobiography, Clemens tells of spending many evenings visiting with a 40-year-old fellow boardinghouse resident named Macfarlane, who knew the spelling and definition of every word in the dictionary. The Wrightson Printing Company had an employee named John J. McFarland, who Clemens may well have thought knew everything about the printing business and whom he possibly later glamorized as "Macfarlane." The owner of the printing company was Thomas Wrightson, a Kentucky state senator, listed as living in Newport on Jefferson St. (modern Sixth St.) between Monmouth and Saratoga Sts. Whether Samuel Clemens worked at the Newport location or the Cincinnati site could not be determined.

The owner of the Alexandria house that Clemens is said to have visited was Richard Tarvin Baker, also a Kentucky state senator, and a director of the Alexandria Fair Board. Copies of the 1865 brochures for the Alexandria Fair show that the Thomas Wrightson Printing Company printed them. While no direct evidence was found that Clemens actually visited in the Baker home, it can at least be proved that he lived and worked in the region and that his employer, Thomas Wrightson, and Richard Tarvin Baker were both Kentucky state senators. Another indication that the stories about his visiting Alexandria may have some validity is found in the names he gave to some of the characters in *Tom Sawyer.* Clemens had a habit of using the names of his friends and acquaintances in his books. In *Tom Sawyer* he talks about Johnny Baker, which was the name of one of the sons of Richard Tarvin Baker. He also gives several characters the last name of Thatcher, including Tom Sawyer's girlfriend Becky, and that happens to have been the surname of Alexandria's most prominent family at the time. The name of Clemens's most recognizable character, Tom Sawyer, is said to have been borrowed from Tom Sawyer Spivey, a young boy he met in Cincinnati. Spivey indicated that he first met Clemens (then a riverboat pilot) when Spivey was just 12 years old. Spivey's wife said that Spivey often traveled to New York City, where he and Clemens would enjoy a drink together and reminisce about life on the river. Clemens also refers to Dick (Richard) Baker's pet cat in *Mark Twain's Short Stories.* The Baker name occurs as well in *Baker's Blue Jay Yarn.*

Further evidence of Clemens's Northern Kentucky connections is found in the "Keokuk Letters," sent from Cincinnati and written under the pseudonym Thomas Jefferson Snodgrass. Richard Tarvin Baker's cousin Thomas Jefferson Baker was the same age as Clemens, and there was also a Snodgrass family living in the area at the time. One additional possible connection between Clemens and the city of Alexandria was found. A descendant of the Baker family indicated that, according to family tradition, Samuel Clemens occasionally crossed the Ohio River to New Richmond, Ohio, by rowboat to visit a lawyer named Lucien M. Dawson. A *Covington Journal* article of the time states that Dawson married Richard Tarvin Baker's daughter Sarah Bina Baker on July 11, 1888, and that the couple moved to New Richmond. Could those trips have possibly been made while Clemens was visiting in Baker's Alexandria home, and perhaps even in the company of Richard Tarvin Baker? Alexandria is but a short distance from Oneonta, Ky., which is across the Ohio River from New Richmond.

Clemens may have intended to live permanently in the region; however, the winter that he stayed there was exceptionally cold. The Ohio River froze over; river traffic was impossible and there were severe shortages of needed supplies. In April 1857, when departing for New Orleans on the steamer *Paul Jones,* Clemens said that he did not care for Cincinnati's severe winters.

Hoffman, Andrew J. *Inventing Mark Twain.* New York: William Morrow, 1997.
Kaplan, Justin. *Mark Twain and His World.* London: Crown, 1974.
"Licensed to Wed," *CJ,* July 12, 1888, 5.
Sanborn, Margaret. *Mark Twain: The Bachelor Years.* New York: Doubleday, 1990.
"Spivey, Friend of Twain, Dies," *CP,* November 8, 1938, 1.
"Tom Sawyer, Dead; Inspired Mark Twain," *CE,* November 9, 1938, 1.
"Tom Sawyer of Mark Twain's Famous Book Dies in Hospital," *CTS,* November 8, 1938, 1.

Jack Wessling

CLEVELAND, HENRIETTA ESTHER SCOTT (b. October 3, 1817, Covington, Ky.; d. May 12, 1907, Covington, Ky.). Catholic charity worker Henrietta Scott Cleveland was the daughter of Maj. Chasteen and Abigail Fowler Scott and the granddaughter of Maj. **Jacob Fowler**, one of the pioneer settlers of Northern Kentucky. In November 1834 Henrietta married George P. Cleveland (1808–1839), a seventh-generation descendant of an old New England family. The couple's first child, Charles Holmes Cleveland, died at age two in 1838. In January 1839 tragedy struck again when 31-year-old George Cleveland died; Henrietta was barely one month pregnant with their son George Putnam (1839–1851) at the time. According to the 1850 U.S. Census, Henrietta lived at her father's home in Boone Co., and her son George attended St. Xavier College, a Jesuit preparatory school in Cincinnati. One year later, in July 1851, her son died at age 11.

Although records of her baptism cannot be found, Henrietta Cleveland became a convert to the Roman Catholic Church (see **Roman Catholics**). Sometime before 1860 she moved to Covington and became involved in a ladies' society that dedicated itself to works of charity among the poor. Cleveland's friendship with Cincinnati's wealthy Catholic convert Sarah Worthington King Peter (1800–1877) was cemented by both widows' interest in charitable enterprises. Sarah Peter's benevolent activities included establishment of the Ladies' Academy of Fine Art in Cincinnati and the recruitment of two orders of nuns to Cincinnati, the Sisters of Mercy of Kinsale, Ireland, and the Sisters of the Poor of St. Francis of Aix-la-Chapelle (Aachen), then a part of Germany. With Peter's help, the Sisters of the Poor of St. Francis opened St. Mary Hospital in Cincinnati in 1859. Both Cleveland and Peter influenced Covington's first Catholic bishop, George Aloysius Carrell (bishop 1853–1868), to invite the Sisters of the Poor of St. Francis to open St. Elizabeth Hospital (see **St. Elizabeth Medical Center**) in Covington in 1861. Cleveland and Peter raised funds for the purchase of the hospital's first building in 1861, as well as for an additional building where the nuns cared for the children of working mothers during the **Civil War** and later accepted foundlings. Throughout the Civil War, the two women continued their work of visiting the sick, the poor, and prisoners, without regard to anyone's religious or political affiliations. Together, they nursed back to health **Thomas Major**, an escaped prisoner of war and private in Gen. **John Hunt Morgan**'s 2nd Kentucky Cavalry (Confederate). Later, Thomas Major converted to Catholicism and became a Catholic priest, the only known member of Morgan's Raiders to do so. Following the Civil War, Cleveland raised funds for the purchase of a much larger facility for St. Elizabeth Hospital on W. 11th St. in Covington, part of the former home of the **Western Baptist Theological Institute**. In 1907 she died at age 90 at her home on E. Fourth St. in Covington. Her funeral mass was held at Covington's Cathedral Basilica of the Assumption, and she was buried in St. Mary Cemetery in Fort Mitchell.

Cleveland, Edmund Janes, and Horace Gillette Cleveland. *The Genealogy of the Cleveland and Cleaveland Families.* 3 vols. Hartford, Conn.: Case, Lockwood, and Brainard, 1899.
"Mrs. Cleveland Dead," *CE,* May 13, 1907, 11.
Tenkotte, Paul A., David E. Schroeder, and Thomas S. Ward. *To Be Catholic and American in Northern, Central, and Appalachian Kentucky: The Diocese of Covington, 1853–2003.* Forthcoming.

Paul A. Tenkotte

CLEVELAND SYNDICATE ("Mayfield Road Gang"). By 1950 Newport and some of its suburbs were firmly entrenched as Cincinnati's entertainment district, broadly speaking; for some of the visitors from Ohio, Newport served, more specifically, as Cincinnati's vice district. But what made Newport different, what made it a regional **gambling** center, was the presence of the Cleveland Syndicate, the so-called Mayfield Road Gang.

Over the first half of the 20th century, many smaller municipalities in major metropolitan areas developed significant economies related to gambling, **prostitution**, and general vice; Newport was one of the most notorious of these. As large cities reformed their governments and attempted to clean up their image, vice and criminal interests moved to peripheral municipalities, where they could control local officials more easily. Thus, many of the progressive reform efforts of the first decades of the 1900s had the effect not of cleaning up metropolitan areas but rather of driving the undesirable elements to the outer edges. Newport was firmly controlled by the interests of vice and gambling as early as the 1920s. It was also home to local innovators, such as Peter Schmidt, whose success in a well-run, "honest" casino gained the attention of the Cleveland Syndicate.

The Cleveland Syndicate is often remembered, or mythologized, as the tough-minded mob group that "controlled" Newport after **World War II**. The reality of the syndicate's involvement in Newport is, of course, far more complicated. The principals in the Cleveland Syndicate were Morris Kleinman, Thomas McGinty, Samuel Miller, Louis Rothkopf, Samuel Tucker, and especially Moe Dalitz. This syndicate took shape during the 1920s as Dalitz and others consolidated their bootlegging efforts in and around Ann Arbor and Detroit, Mich., and in Cleveland. Running alcohol into the United States from Canada during the 15 years of **Prohibition** had left syndicate members and bootleggers across the country with enormous stockpiles of capital. Some successful bootleggers, most notably Joseph Kennedy, subsequently channeled these profits into more legitimate businesses. Others branched out into diversified criminal operations.

The Cleveland Syndicate specialized in gambling operations—but not just any gambling operations. It was one of the pioneers of the modern form of the casino. This was a gambling operation in which the odds may have always been with the house, but the games were honest. They made their profits not by swindling their patrons but by the margins accrued over time. Simply put, patrons lost more than they won. To lure patrons, casinos offered gourmet meals and elaborate shows often featuring national acts.

The syndicate's casinos were first located in Cleveland proper, and then in towns around Cleveland, but Ohio governor Frank Lausche successfully shut down organized gambling in Ohio in the late 1940s. Forced out of Ohio, the Cleveland Syndicate decided to move its operations across the Ohio River to Northern Kentucky, where it already had active interests. It was also putting money into casinos in Miami; Havana, Cuba; and eventually Las Vegas.

The most famous Cleveland Syndicate casino, the **Beverly Hills Supper Club**, was actually founded by Cincinnatian Pete Schmidt, a former bootlegger. Seeing the kind of money he was making, the Cleveland Syndicate moved in on Schmidt during the early 1940s. Beverly Hills was the model for the type of "honest" casino that the syndicate knew was a better source of long-term profits. Gamblers from across the Midwest would drive or fly into town to take in a show, have a gourmet meal, and gamble all night at the blackjack or poker tables. Conventioneers from Cincinnati would hire cabs to drive them down **U.S. 27** so they could enjoy amenities not available north of the Ohio River. Although technically illegal, Beverly Hills operated essentially as a legal club. One could go there for dinner and a show and perhaps never notice that there was a casino. But all it took was a simple request and one would be shown into the club's lavish gambling room.

By the time the cleanup of vice in Northern Kentucky began, the syndicate's members were already divesting themselves of their other, "illegal" gambling holdings. Led by Dalitz, Cleveland Syndicate members were investing in Nevada casinos, most notably the Desert Inn in Las Vegas. Nevada offered the opportunity for casino owners not only to operate legally, but also to make their businesses legitimate.

By the time the Committee of 500 (see **Newport Reform Groups**) shut down most of the vice operations in Newport and Campbell Co., the Beverly Hills Club already had closed. The club would usually shut its doors whenever it looked as if local authorities were on one of their periodic reform kicks. After such a closure in 1961, the club remained closed, because it became apparent that the Committee of 500 was there to stay. Dalitz and other Cleveland Syndicate members had shifted most of their investments to Las Vegas. They had no interest in fighting the reform committee or in drawing attention to themselves. They were too busy establishing legal operations in the Nevada desert. Thus, by the time the Committee of 500 engaged in its legendary fight to rid Newport of gambling, the Cleveland Syndicate was largely absent from the scene. The era's most prominent episode, the attempted framing of Campbell Co. sheriff candidate **George W. Ratterman**, was engineered by Newport's small-time casino operators, who at the time had a lot more to lose.

But a discussion of the Cleveland Syndicate helps one understand fully the place of Newport within the history of modern casino gambling. Newport was one of the few regional gambling centers to survive into the early 1960s. The Englishman Ian Fleming, author of the many James Bond novels, recognized Newport's stature in the gambling world with a passing reference to the town in the early pages of his 1961 work *Diamonds Are Forever*. And it was in Newport that the Cleveland Syndicate helped to pioneer the type of large-scale casino gambling that has flourished in Las Vegas ever since. With lavish shows, gourmet restaurants, and finely appointed gambling halls, Beverly Hills was one of the prototypes for the newer casinos that made Las Vegas an international center for gambling. More importantly, the money that Dalitz and others made at Beverly Hills helped fund the modern Las Vegas with the construction of casinos like the Desert Inn.

Gioielli, Robert. "Suburbs v. Slot Machines: The Committee of 500 and the Battle over Gambling in Northern Kentucky," *Ohio Valley History* 5, no. 2 (Summer 2005): 61–84.

Shearer, Jason G. "Urban Reform in Sin City: The George Ratterman Trial and the Election of 1961 in Northern Kentucky," *RKHS* 98, no. 4 (Autumn 2000): 343–65.

Robert Gioielli

CLIFT, G. GLENN (b. October 2, 1909, Newton, Kans.; d. November 9, 1970, Frankfort, Ky.). Garrett Glenn Clift, who became a librarian and an author, was the son of Charles L. and Mary Ethel Tomlin Clift. When Glenn was almost four, his family returned to Mason Co., Ky., having moved away around the turn of the century. Glenn Clift grew up on a farm near Maysville and graduated from Washington High School, in Mason Co. He entered the University of Kentucky in Lexington in 1929 and began his first library job at the Lexington Public Library that same year. By 1935 he had become the assistant librarian. He continued working at this library until 1942 and then moved to New York City. He worked briefly at the New York Public Library and married Virginia Diller Gilmore, of New York City. Clift entered the army and served during **World War II** in the 36th "Texas" Infantry Division in North Africa, Italy, France, and the German Rhineland. In the final year of the war, he was transferred to Allied Force Headquarters at Caserta, Italy. While stationed there, he wrote a one-volume unpublished history about the U.S. Army Medical Department of the Mediterranean Theater during World War II. Before leaving the army, he was commissioned a 2nd lieutenant and was awarded several medals and ribbons, including the Bronze Arrowhead. Back in the United States, Clift rejoined the staff of the New York Public Library. In 1948 he moved to the University of Miami Library in Miami, Fla., after earning a degree from the Pratt Institute Library School in New York. In 1950 he returned to Kentucky as a staff member of the Kentucky Historical Society and began contributing to its journal, *The Register*. Clift became assistant director of the Kentucky Historical Society and editor of its journal, the *Register*, in 1960. Beginning in the early 1930s, Clift wrote about the history of Kentucky, in works such as *History of Maysville and Mason County, The Governors of Kentucky, 1792–1942, The "Corn Stalk" Militia of Kentucky, 1792–1811,* and *Remember the Raisin*. He also wrote several guides to historical records. Clift died in 1970 in Frankfort, Ky., and was buried in the Washington Cemetery in Mason Co.

Browning, M. Carmel, OSB. *Kentucky Authors*. Evansville, Ind.: Keller-Crescent, 1968.

"G. Glenn Clift, 1909–1970," *RKHS* 69, no. 2 (January 1971): i–viii.

Thomas S. Ward

CLIFTON. Clifton in Campbell Co., a town established in 1888, is located on a hill south of Newport, which annexed Clifton in 1935. At its peak, Clifton had a population of 3,080. It was bounded by Newport along the railroad tracks to the north, Licking Pk. (Ky. Rt. 9) to the west, Southgate to the south, and U.S. 27 to the east. Clifton's name was inspired by its location on the top of a hill overlooking the northern part of Campbell Co. and Cincinnati. The location was considered desirable for residential development during the late 19th and early 20th centuries because its country atmosphere contrasted sharply with the turmoil associated with life in the more established urban neighborhoods of Newport and Bellevue.

Although Clifton's reputation as the center of Northern Kentucky's Italian community is today well entrenched (see **Italian Americans**), the first founders of the town were of Irish and German heritage. The community experienced its first building boom between 1888 and 1897, with as many as four different construction companies selling lots and building homes there. One of the first buildings constructed in 1888 after Clifton was incorporated was Fearon's Mansion, later known as the **Campbell Co. Protestant Orphans Home**. It is the current site of the **Baptist Convalescent Center**, which provides senior citizen housing and nursing home care. Dr. Shaler Berry was a prime developer of residential construction in the Clifton area during the early years. A bank collapse temporarily halted construction in Clifton, but home-building resumed in 1900 when Newport built on a Clifton hilltop a 300,000-gallon water tank that remains in use.

Early political leaders in the Clifton community included Mayor George Fewlass and councilmen Peter Enslen, Jacob Hahn, and E. C. Remme. The first town meeting was held in 1888. Clifton became informally known as Spaghetti Knob because of an influx of Italian immigrants during the early 1900s and the influence they had on the social and political institutions of the city. By 1910 the Catholic population of Clifton had grown enough that they petitioned the bishop of Covington for their own church. The new church, **St. Vincent de Paul Catholic Church**, built in 1916, began with 86 families evenly divided between German and Italian immigrants and their descendants. The church and its school became one of the gathering places for Italian immigrants. In the latter part of the 20th century, a general decline in the number of Catholics in Newport made it necessary to merge the four Catholic churches in the city, and the St. Vincent de Paul Church was closed in 1999, although the building still stands.

Beginning in 1906, Clifton was the target of an aggressive annexation campaign by the larger City of Newport. Newport was beginning to lose population to the suburbs, mostly because of the advent of the automobile. Because of its desirable location and tax base, Clifton was considered a prize. After the 1906 annexation attempt failed, Newport's city leaders tried again without success in 1912. Then Newport filed a lawsuit challenging Clifton's legal status as a fifth-class city. The suit was temporarily successful, as Clifton was downgraded to a district status that affected its ability to raise taxes and sell bonds. However, Clifton was reinstated as a city in 1916. Newport continued aggressively pursuing annexation, but Clifton voters rejected attempts made in 1920, 1925, and 1930. The issue sparked intense controversy. Citizens on both sides wrote opposing articles published by area newspapers. Even local school children were given homework assignments to write papers on whether Clifton should become part of Newport.

Although Clifton was a growing community, it lacked many city services that were coming into vogue, such as paved streets, indoor plumbing, and sewage disposal. The City of Clifton had jeopardized its tax base with a heavy bonded indebtedness to finance these civic improvements. When the Great Depression left the town's government strapped for funds, the prospect of financial relief from a Newport takeover became more tempting. In 1935 a new annexation proposal succeeded by a Clifton vote of 627 to 539, and the City of Clifton ceased to exist on November 26, 1935, after 47 years as an independent city.

By annexing Clifton, Newport added about 3,000 residents, many of whom worked at the Andrews Steel Mill in Wilder. At the time of annexation, Clifton consisted of its residents, a brick manufacturer, a cigar maker, seven building contractors, seven small groceries, and a Kroger grocery store. Some remnants of the original town remain. The old Clifton firehouse is still maintained by the City of Newport as a substation to serve the southern parts of the city.

Clifton resurfaced as a distinct community during the 1970s when the residents, who were organizing the neighborhood to become part of the **Newport Citizens Advisory Council**, chose the name of Clifton. Since the 1990s, parts of the Clifton district have seen the first residential developments in Newport in many years; these projects take advantage of the district's scenic views of the Licking River valley and the Cincinnati skyline.

Casebolt, Pamela Ciafardini, and Philip G. Ciafardini. *Images of America: Italians of Newport and Northern Kentucky*. Charleston, S.C.: Arcadia, 2007.

"Once a Mere Hamlet Clifton Heights Now a Beautiful Suburb," *KP*, July 25, 1910, 2.

Purvis, Thomas L., ed. *Newport, Kentucky: A Bicentennial History*. Newport, Ky.: Otto Zimmerman, 1996.

Reis, Jim. "Festival Imported Flavor of Old Italy," *KP*, May 25, 1992, 4K.

"Why Clifton Doesn't Want to Be Annexed," *KP*, July 11, 1916, 1.

Michael Whitehead

CLINE, THOMAS H., COLONEL (b. September 19, 1920, Campbell Co., Ky.). Thomas H. Cline, who became a **World War II** test pilot, is the son of Thomas E. and Vivian Schwartz Cline. He attended the University of Kentucky College of Engineering in Lexington before enlisting in the U.S. Army Air Force in 1940. When World War II was declared, he was trained to fly the B-18 Douglass aircraft. Then in 1942 he was reassigned to test aircraft taking off from the aircraft carrier *Hornet*, before General Jimmy Doolittle's famous bombing raid on Tokyo on April 18, 1942 . Under conditions of optimum wind and carrier speed, Cline and his crewman, Oscar Wertz, lifted their aircraft off the carrier's deck, about 300 feet long, using only 183 feet of the deck. The tests Cline conducted demonstrated the feasibility of Doolittle's plan to launch his B-25 bombers off an aircraft carrier's deck. Cline was relocated to fly missions with copilot Gen. Richard H. Ellis over the Bismarck Sea, and both men earned DFC (Distinguished Flying Cross) medals. After the war, Cline remained in the Air Force reserves and was activated again during the **Korean War**. He also operated an airport in Rio Grande, Ohio, and taught mathematics. He and his wife, Betty, reside in their 1795-era home on Riverside Dr. in Augusta in Bracken Co.

"Capt. Tommy Cline Helps Bomb Japs in Bismarck Sea Battle Early in March," *Bracken Chronicle*, April 22, 1943, 1.

Cline, Thomas. Interview by Caroline Miller, November 2, 2004, Augusta, Ky.

Caroline R. Miller

CLOONEY, BETTY (b. April 12, 1931, Maysville, Ky.; d. August 5, 1976, Las Vegas, Nev.). Betty Clooney, a popular singer and a female television pioneer, was the sister of **Rosemary Clooney** and **Nick Clooney** and an aunt of **George Clooney**. Her parents were Andrew and Frances Guilfoyle Clooney. Betty spent most of her childhood years with her sister Rosemary and their grandmother Guilfoyle in Maysville, Ky. The sisters moved to Cincinnati to live with other relatives while teenagers. They partnered in an act known as the Clooney Sisters, first singing on WLW radio in Cincinnati in 1945. Betty and Rosemary toured nationally with the Tony Pastor Orchestra, making most of their commercial recordings together between 1946 and 1949.

After the two had toured with Pastor for three years, Betty altruistically resigned, allowing Rosemary to record as a solo performer for Columbia Records in New York City. Betty returned to Cincinnati during the formative years of the Crosley Broadcasting Company and its regional television programs. As a pioneering female television personality, Betty was one of WLWT's busiest full-time television employees, performing on multiple programs each week. She was a singer for the *Ruth Lyons 50 Club* (later renamed the *50-50 Club*), simulcast on both WLW radio and the Crosley television chain. She hosted her own television programs, such as *Boy Meets Girl* and *Teen Canteen*, as well as other shows at WLWT. She also recorded a few songs on the legendary King Records (Cincinnati) label and made some local appearances backed by many regional tri-state "territory bands," such as Clyde Trask.

Betty went to New York City as a solo act at the Starlight Roof of the Waldorf-Astoria Hotel in the early 1950s. She was a guest on several national television programs, including the highly popular *Gary Moore Show* on the CBS network, and was a regular cast member (along with journalist Charles

Betty and Rosemary Clooney.

Collingwood) on Jack Paar's *Morning Show,* also on CBS. At the *Morning Show,* a rival to NBC's groundbreaking news format of the *Today* show, she met and worked with Pupi Campo, the *Morning Show* Latin bandleader and her husband-to-be. Rosemary and Betty were together in New York City as separate acts, but the sisters remained close, always encouraging each other professionally. They made a few more recordings together, including the somewhat autobiographical Irving Berlin tune "Sisters," from *White Christmas* (1954), on the Columbia label. Betty also recorded songs for RCA and for Coral, a subsidiary of Decca.

During the mid-1950s, Betty spent a few years as a regular on the *Robert Q. Lewis Show,* a CBS daytime television variety series. She guest starred on the prime-time *Lux Show Starring Rosemary Clooney* in 1957 on NBC and made a string of other guest television appearances, before she retired from show business to raise a family a few years after her marriage to Pupi Campo in 1955. Campo and his band performed as a feature act for many years in Miami, Fla., and later in Las Vegas.

Betty returned to network television news briefly on NBC's *Today.* She supported John Chancellor as one of the *Today* Girls in 1961 and later as a guest sponsor performer for Hugh Downs in 1962 and 1963. Betty also worked with Barbara Walters, who had just started as a news researcher, writer, and reporter on *Today.*

The Clooney sisters remained close and supported each other in challenges, usually related to their husbands' infidelities. After a few guest co-host performances on brother Nick Clooney's WCPO and WKRC variety television shows in Cincinnati, the sisters discussed comeback plans for a reunion tour in the mid-1970s. It never came to pass, because Betty died of a brain aneurysm at age 45 in 1976. Her funeral mass was at St. Viator's Catholic Church in Las Vegas. In Betty's honor, Rosemary and Nick established the Betty Clooney Foundation in 1983 and the Betty Clooney Center in Long Beach, Calif. (opened in 1988), which treats persons with traumatic brain injury. Beginning in 1986, major Hollywood performers, including Tony Bennett, Carol Burnett, Bob Hope, Linda Ronstadt, and Frank Sinatra, participated in Rosemary and Nick's fundraiser for the foundation, entitled "Singers' Salute to the Songwriter," at the Dorothy Chandler Pavilion in Los Angeles. The fundraiser continued into the early 1990s.

Betty's four children, listed by birth chronology, are Rosemary Cari Leary, Cathi Campo Muckle, Carlos Campo, and Christina Stretz. Cathi performed with Rosemary Clooney in the 1990s at live concerts and made a popular recording of the "Coffee Song," which the Clooney Sisters had performed.

"Betty Clooney Dead at Age 45," *CE,* August 6, 1976, B2.

"Betty Clooney Dies at 45 in Las Vegas," *NYT,* August 8, 1976, 41.

Bliss, Edward. *Now the News: The Story of Broadcast Journalism.* New York: Columbia Univ. Press, 1991.

Clooney, Nick. "Betty's Legacy in Song," *KP,* July 19, 2006, B1.

———. Faxes to Paul A. Tenkotte, January 28, 2007, and February 8, 2007.

Clooney, Rosemary. *Girl Singer: An Autobiography.* New York: Doubleday, 1999.

Hyatt, Wesley. *The Encyclopedia of Daytime Television.* New York: Billboard Books, 1997.

Kinkle, Roger. *The Complete Encyclopedia of Popular Music and Jazz, 1900–1950.* Vol. 2. New Rochelle, N.Y.: Arlington House, 1974.

Records of Betty Clooney's NBC television appearances between 1949 and 1963, NBC News Archives, New York City.

Wood, Carlyle. *TV Personalities: Biographical Sketch Book.* Vol. 1. St. Louis, Mo.: Carlyle Wood, 1954.

John Schlipp

CLOONEY, GEORGE (b. May 6, 1961, Lexington, Ky.). Writer, director, and actor George Timothy Clooney is the son of **Nick Clooney** and Nina Warren Clooney and the nephew of **Rosemary Clooney**. George has a sister, Ada, who is one year older than he.

George Clooney at his 1979 graduation from Augusta High School.

Due to the peripatetic nature of the radio and television broadcast business, in which Nick Clooney made his living, there were many moves during George's formative years that taught him what would be needed to succeed in show business. He began first grade at **Blessed Sacrament** School in Fort Mitchell and later attended St. Michael's School in Columbus, Ohio, and the Western Row and St. Susanna schools in Mason, Ohio, before the family moved to Augusta, Ky., for his high school education. Always a sports fan, George had hoped to play football, but **Augusta High School**, from which he graduated in 1979, offered only basketball and baseball. He participated in both, eventually trying out, unsuccessfully, to play professional baseball with the Cincinnati Reds.

Although his career took several years to develop, George's livelihood turned out to be in television and motion pictures. He attended **Northern Kentucky University** at Highland Heights and, very briefly, the University of Cincinnati. In spring 1981 his cousins Miguel and Rafi Ferrer (two of his Aunt Rosemary's sons) and their father, José Ferrer, went to Lexington to do a movie. They invited George to the set. For George, this exposure to acting was love at first sight, and he never looked back. When his father, Nick, tried to persuade George to stay in school by saying, "At least with a diploma, you'll have something to fall back on," George replied, "If I have something to fall back on, I'll fall back."

George cut tobacco, sold lemonade at the Labor Day festival in Augusta, and drew caricatures of people to get enough money together for his trip to Los Angeles to become an actor. In fall 1981 he climbed into an old Monte Carlo automobile, and three days later he had arrived in his newly adopted hometown of Los Angeles, ready to do what was necessary to become an actor. Odd jobs, "cattle calls" (highly competitive acting auditions), trading work for acting lessons, auditioning, dashed hopes, showcases, readings, and new friends all followed, but no acting jobs materialized for George for almost two years.

Slowly, small television appearances that he made led to several unsuccessful television pilots. Then in 1984 George was cast in a role for a new television program called *ER* that was soon canceled. Ironically, George's great TV success came with a second show also named *ER*. His engaging portrayal of Dr. Doug Ross, *ER*'s handsome children's medical specialist, quickly transformed George Clooney into a household name.

George had appeared in a half dozen small films before his portrayal of Dr. Ross on television brought him to the attention of major movie producers and directors. Never one to shrink from an opportunity or from his responsibility, George lived up to his five-year contract with Warner Bros. for *ER* while, with the company's help in scheduling, he also made six movies. Half of them were filmed during *ER*'s summer hiatus, and the others during regular tapings of the successful hospital drama. Clooney was Dr. Doug Ross in scrubs in the mornings; then in the afternoons, he would jump on his bicycle and pedal across the Warner production lot to various sound stages where he made *From Dusk to Dawn* (1996), *Batman & Robin* (1997), and *The Peacemaker* (1997). George has proved his versatility with success in far-ranging movies that include *Three Kings* (1999); *O Brother, Where Art Thou?* (2000); *The Perfect Storm* (2000); *Ocean's Eleven* (2001); *Confessions of a Dangerous Mind* (2002); *Intolerable Cruelty* (2003); *Ocean's Twelve* (2004); *Good Night, and Good Luck* (2005); *Syriana* (2005); *Michael Clayton* (2006); and *The Good German* (2006).

In 1998 George Clooney and Steven Soderbergh formed the Section Eight Production Company, which drew upon the combination of Clooney's acting and directing talents in the production of *Out of Sight* (1998), *Solaris* (2002), *Ocean's Eleven* (2001), *Ocean's Twelve (2004), Syriana* (2005), and the highly acclaimed *Good Night, and Good Luck* (2005), as well as two television series for HBO. During this time Clooney also served as executive producer of several "small" movies.

In 2005 George won an Academy Award for best supporting actor as Bob Barnes in *Syriana.* He set an Academy first by also being nominated for best director and best writer for *Good Night, and Good Luck.* No one had ever before been nominated for two different movies in two different categories.

Beginning in 2000 George has split his time between his residences in Los Angeles and in Italy. He was married to Talia Balsam from 1989 until 1991. The success of his career has made possible George's philanthropic activities, including efforts for the victims of the New York City terrorist attack 9/11 (2001) and of hurricane Katrina (2005). In 2006 he and his father, Nick, traveled to the Sudan, bringing attention to the plight of civil war refugees in Darfur. In January 2008 he was designated a "Messenger of Peace" by the United Nations. Clooney was pictured on the cover of *Time* magazine of March 3, 2008, which also included a feature article.

Clooney, George. *Good Night, and Good Luck: The Screenplay and History behind the Landmark Movie.* New York: Newmark Press, 2006.
"Is Superstar Status Ahead for Clooney?" *CE,* July 10, 2000, C2.
"The 100—Clooney among World's Most Influential," *KP,* May 1, 2006, 14C.
Stein, Joel. "Guess Who Came to Dinner?" *Time,* March 3, 2008, 46–52.

Nina Clooney

CLOONEY, NICK (b. January 13, 1934, Maysville, Ky.). Nicholas Joseph Clooney, a radio and television broadcaster and an author, was a son of Andrew and Frances Guilfoyle Clooney. Nick's parents divorced when Nick was four years old. He and his sisters **Rosemary Clooney** and **Betty Clooney** stayed in Maysville with their grandmother Guilfoyle most of the time, because their mother needed to find work in Cincinnati. The children listened to radio broadcasts on Cincinnati station WLW, as well as other radio stations, and fell in love with the wonderful radio voices that spoke and sang to them. In their teens, they followed their dreams: Rosemary and Betty left Maysville to pursue successful singing careers, and Nick took a job at age 16 at Maysville radio station WFTM that launched a long and distinguished career in broadcasting.

The consistent thread in the career of Nick Clooney is communication. As a television newsman, Nick has been a reporter, an anchor, a managing editor, and a news director in Cincinnati; Salt Lake City; Buffalo, N.Y.; and Los Angeles. In journalism, another of his pursuits, Nick has, since 1989, contributed three columns each week to the *Cincinnati Post* and the *Kentucky Post* dealing with current politics, travel, and American history. Many of his articles and op-ed pieces have appeared in newspapers around the country, including the

Nick Clooney, host of American Movie Classics.

Los Angeles Times and the *Salt Lake Tribune.* As an author, Nick has published three books, including *The Movies That Changed Us* in November 2002. As a TV host, he was for five years a daily on-air spokesman and writer for the American Movie Classics cable channel (AMC). He has made scores of personal appearances coast-to-coast on AMC's behalf, with a special focus on film preservation. Earlier he hosted talk variety programs in Cincinnati and Columbus, Ohio, and was a guest host on programs in New York City, Washington, D.C., Atlanta, and Indianapolis. He also hosted for the American Life TV cable channel.

Nick has accumulated a number of awards, including one that named him one of the "best in business of television news," given by the *Washington Review of Journalism.* He has received a regional Emmy for commentary, was nominated three times for national Emmys for his work on AMC, and has received nearly 300 other awards. In December 1998 Nick was presented an honorary doctorate of fine arts from **Northern Kentucky University** at Highland Heights. In 2000 Nick received the President's Medal from **Thomas More College** in Crestview Hills, was inducted into the Cincinnati Journalism Hall of Fame by the Society of Professional Journalists, and received the Distinguished Kentuckian award from the Kentucky Broadcasters Association. In April 2001 Nick was inducted into the Kentucky Journalism Hall of Fame. In October 2005 he was inducted into the Ohio Television Hall of Fame.

Nick is married to Nina Warren of Perryville, who is a writer, inventor, and television host. Their older child, Ada, also a writer, is the mother of Allison and Nick. The Clooneys' younger child, son **George Clooney**, is a high-profile, Oscar-winning actor and a successful producer and director in film and television.

In the early 1970s, after several moves, Nick and Nina decided to establish a permanent home. It was clear that their work would continue to take them far afield, but they wanted to have a stable home base. At that time Nick was hosting in Cincinnati both a daily television talk-variety show and a daily morning radio show. On weekends he flew to New York City to tape *The Money Maze,* a daily network game show on ABC-TV. Within two years, Nick returned to his great love: news, anchoring, and serving as managing editor for WKRC-TV news in Cincinnati. Three years later, his newscast became the city's most successful one. Nick also was principal anchor on Channel 13 in Salt Lake City, Channel 4 in Buffalo, and Channel 4 in Los Angeles, KNBC-TV. In the midst of this itinerant lifestyle, Nick and Nina found their home. After much searching, they chose Augusta, not only for its beauty but also to enable their children to experience the small-town life they had known, Nick in Maysville and Nina in Perryville. The move was everything they had hoped. Both children excelled in school and gained confidence in their own abilities in many aspects of real life. In time other family members followed the lure of Augusta. In addition to aunts, uncles, and cousins who came to the region, Nick's sister Rosemary had a home on Riverside Dr. in Augusta for 20 years. More recently, Nick's younger sister Gail built a home overlooking the Ohio River in Augusta.

Clooney, Nick. *Cincinnati—City of Charm: A Love Story.* Memphis, Tenn.: Towery, 1991.
——. *The Movies That Changed Us: Reflections on the Screen.* New York: Alta Books, 2002.
——. *Nick: Collected Columns of Nick Clooney.* Cincinnati: WVUX/Xavier Univ., 1995.
"Clooney's Ease Sets His Style," February 11, 1975, *KP,* 4K.
"I Believe in Myself," *KP,* April 26, 1974, 4K.

Nina Clooney

CLOONEY, ROSEMARY, HOUSE. See **Rosemary Clooney House**.

CLOONEY, ROSEMARY "ROSIE" (b. May 23, 1928, Maysville, Ky.; d. June 29, 2002, Beverly Hills, Calif.). Rosemary Clooney was one of America's premiere pop and jazz singers and was an excellent lyric interpreter. The daughter of Andrew and Frances Guilfoyle Clooney, Rosemary was raised in her grandmother's house on W. Third St., Maysville. The street where she spent her childhood days is now named Rosemary Clooney St., and her grandmother's house is listed on the National Register of Historic Places. Rosemary noted in her memoir, *Girl Singer,* that as a child she sat on her grandmother's porch looking at the Ohio River and thought of it as a promise of better times ahead and faraway places to be seen. During Rosemary's early years, her family life was unstable and she was shuffled among different relatives. Her siblings included brother **Nick Clooney** and sister **Betty Clooney**. There was also a half-sister, Gail, and a half-brother, Andrew; Andrew died young in a drowning accident. Rosemary's mother worked as a saleslady and managed retail shops, and her father was a house painter. The two sisters spent much of their time with their maternal grandmother, who later moved to Ironton, Ohio, and eventually settled in Cincinnati when Rosemary was in her early teens. During this time, her mother remarried, taking son Nick to California. Later, her father came to Cincinnati to work during **World War II** at a defense plant and to take care of the two girls, but he disappeared at war's end. Finally, Rosemary and Betty stayed with their Aunt Jean in the Greenhills area of Cincinnati. Rosemary attended St. Patrick Grade School in Maysville and Our Lady of Mercy Academy in Cincinnati.

In 1945 Rosemary and Betty auditioned and were hired to appear on WLW radio in Cincinnati. WLW was known as "the nation's station," reaching all corners of North America. The radio spotlight led to bookings by Cincinnati bandleader Barney Rapp, who acted as their agent. Singing engagements included regional clubs such as the **Beverly Hills**, the **Lookout House**, Moonlight Gardens at Cincinnati's Coney Island, Glenn Rendezvous in Newport, and Castle Farms in Cincinnati, as well as remote radio broadcasts from the Netherland Plaza Hotel in Cincinnati. In 1946 the sisters joined the nationally known traveling big band of Tony Pastor. Their uncle George Guilfoyle became their legal guardian and accompanied the two teenage singers; Rosemary was 17 and Betty was 15. The girls made numerous recordings with the Pastor band. After touring with the band for three years, they left in 1949 for separate careers. Rosemary pursued a solo career in New York City, where she established her own recording contract with Columbia Records. Betty returned to WLW in Cincinnati and later became a cohost of CBS's *Morning Show* in New York City with Jack Paar.

Rosemary recorded numerous songs at Columbia that topped the charts; four became million-sellers. She also made several nightclub and television appearances in New York. During one of these television broadcasts, she met her future husband, actor José Ferrer. In 1951 Rosemary recorded one of her biggest hits for Columbia, "Come On-A My House." Although she initially refused to sing the tune, her record producer, Mitch Miller, insisted that she record it, and it became her first million-seller. But it was the million-selling recording of "Tenderly" that was associated with her throughout her career and eventually became her theme song. Her other million-selling titles included the Hank Williams composition "Half as Much" and the Italian novelty piece "Botch a Me." During this period at Columbia, Rosemary also recorded with bandleader Harry James.

In 1953 Rosemary debuted in her first motion picture, *The Stars Are Singing*, which premiered at the now historic **Russell Theater** in Maysville. The following year she participated in what has become a perennial holiday classic film, *White Christmas*, costarring with Bing Crosby, Danny Kaye, and Vera-Ellen.

In 1955 Rosemary was released from her Paramount movie contract to spend more time with her family. During this period she made many guest appearances on popular variety television. In 1956 *The Rosemary Clooney Show* debuted as a syndicated half-hour series featuring Nelson Riddle's orchestra, the popular male vocal group the Hi Lo's, and various guest stars.

Rosemary married actor-producer-director José Ferrer on July 13, 1953, in Durant, Okla. After a stormy relationship, they divorced. In 1968 Rosemary suffered a nervous breakdown related to family challenges and to witnessing the assassination of her close friend Robert F. Kennedy. She continued therapy for many years, singing occasionally at small supper clubs such as the Lookout House. She also promoted a paper towel product in television commercials during her recovery period.

In 1976 sister Betty died suddenly from a brain aneurysm. In the same year, Rosemary joined Bing Crosby on his 50th-anniversary concert tour. The following year she signed a recording contract with the Concord Jazz label, officially launching her second career. She recorded some two dozen albums with Concord, mostly showcasing American popular standards from the likes of Irving Berlin, George Gershwin, Cole Porter, and Richard Rodgers. Critics praised her new, more mature singing style as she joined forces at different performances with Rose Marie, Helen O'Connell, Barbara McNair, Kay Starr, and Margaret Whiting to create "4 Girls 4." The success of this tour produced the concept of the oldies nostalgia tour. She later sang on the road with Michael Feinstein but principally continued to sing solo up to her last concert, December 15, 2001, at the County Basie Theatre in Red Bank, N.J.

Since 1999 the Rosemary Clooney Music Festival has been held in her honor annually in Maysville to raise funds for renovation and maintenance of the historic Russell Theater. As one of Kentucky's most popular festivals, this event draws thousands of people from all over the nation.

In 1997 Rosemary married her longtime companion, Dante DiPaolo, at **St. Patrick Catholic Church, Maysville**. As a dancer, he appeared in classic movie musicals such as MGM's *Seven Brides for Seven Brothers* (1954).

Although Rosemary spent her adult years at her Beverly Hills home, she admitted that her historic Augusta home on Riverside Dr. always remained her haven, providing a feeling of community. Her home in Augusta now offers public tours and features memorabilia from her legendary musical career.

Rosemary was honored with a Grammy lifetime achievement award a few months before she died of lung cancer on June 29, 2002, and was buried in St. Patrick Cemetery in Maysville. In 2002 she was inducted into the Kentucky Music Hall of Fame. Rosemary's children include Miguel Ferrer, Maria Ferrer Murdock, Gabriel Ferrer, Monsita Ferrer Botwick, and Rafael Ferrer. Rosemary's nephew is the world-famous actor **George Clooney** (son of Nick and Nina Clooney).

Clooney, Nick, and Nina Clooney to Paul A. Tenkotte, fax, June 17, 2006.

Clooney, Rosemary. *Girl Singer: An Autobiography.* New York: Doubleday, 1999.

——. *This for Remembrance.* New York: Playboy Press, 1977.

Kreimer, Peggy. "For Rosie, Marriage Sealed Love and Faith," *KP*, November 11, 1997, 1K.

Moores, Lew. "Memories of Rosie: Festival Helps Save a Landmark," *SC*, September 19, 2004, 1C.

The Rosemary Clooney House Inc. "The Rosemary Clooney House, Augusta, Ky." www.rosemaryclooney.com/house/ (accessed August 6, 2006).

"The Rosemary Clooney Palladium." www.rosemaryclooney.com (accessed August 6, 2006).

Severo, Richard. "Rosemary Clooney, Legendary Pop Singer, Dies at 74," *NYT*, July 1, 2002, B7.

John Schlipp

CLOSSON, ASA BURTON, JR. (b. June 27, 1837, Norwich, Vt.; d. August 7, 1910, Ludlow, Ky.). The parents of banker and entrepreneur Asa Burton Closson Jr. were Asa Burton and Carolyn Taylor Closson. When Asa Jr. was two years old, his family moved to Franklin, N.H. Because he was a sickly child, he received his entire education with private tutors. In 1865 the family moved to Cincinnati. Asa Jr. married Julia Payne on June 2, 1866, and they had four children, Helen, Henry, Fannie, and Walter. That same year, Asa Jr. opened an art gallery in Cincinnati at 140 W. Fourth St., which he named Clossons. The associated store initially sold only art supplies, maps, charts, and pictures of military heroes. The family lived in Cincinnati until about 1870, when they moved across the Ohio River to Ludlow, Ky. There, Asa Jr. served on the Ludlow School Board for 10 years and was a founder and president of the Farmers and Mechanics Bank. In 1885 he purchased a Ludlow mansion, known as Somerset Hall, which had been built by George Kenner about 1845. Kenner, a wealthy Louisiana landowner, had the house built as a retreat so his family could escape the hot Louisiana summers. Asa Burton Closson Jr. retired in 1895 and turned his business over to his sons, Henry and Walter. In 1907 Walter, who was then president of Clossons, was diagnosed with an incurable disease, and he traveled to Europe to enjoy one last vacation. During the trip he learned that the diagnosis he had been given was incorrect, so to celebrate, he went on a shopping spree. He purchased china, antiques, and tapestries, which he sent back to the Clossons store. He continued to make European buying trips each year, through 1929. Asa Burton Closson Jr. died on August 7, 1910, after a long illness, and was buried in Spring Grove Cemetery in Cincinnati. In the 1920s Clossons expanded its product line by offering housewares, decorative items, and interior design services. In 1933 the company moved into a six-story building in Cincinnati at 421 Race St., which had formerly been used as a schoolhouse. In 1966 Clossons held a 100th anniversary celebration at which they displayed works by local artists such as **Frank Duveneck**, **Henry Farny**, Robert Henri, and John Ruthven. In 1967 Clossons moved its store to Fourth and Race Sts., where it began to sell furniture, giftware, and rugs in addition to its usual product line; the downtown Cincinnati store closed in 2003. In 1993, the company was sold to a native Cincinnatian, Stuart P. Sutphin III, whose father had started the Hudson Department Stores.

Alltucker, Ken. "Closson's Leaving Deprives Downtown of Marquee Name," *CE*, January 5, 2003, 1.

Demaline, Jackie. "Closson's Gallery Was a Foundation of City Arts Scene," *CE,* January 5, 2003, A11.
Goss, Charles. *Cincinnati the Queen City, 1788–1912.* Vol. 4. Cincinnati: S. J. Clarke, 1912.

COAL COMPANIES. Most of the coal used in Northern Kentucky came from the mountains of Appalachia and arrived by rail or coal barge. People used the coal to heat their homes, at first in fireplaces and small coal-burning stoves and later in large cast-iron furnaces that could heat an entire home. Homes with coal furnaces had a special room in the basement called a coal bin, where the coal was kept. Because of the dirt, this room was always completely contained; it had a small window to the outside so that coal could be put in. A load of coal was sometimes delivered to a home and dumped in a pile near the street, and the homeowner would use a wheelbarrow or a wagon to move the coal to the window and dump it into the coal bin. For an extra charge, the company would move the coal directly from the truck into the coal bin by using conveyor belts. Central heating was an improvement over fireplaces and small coal stoves, but heating a home with coal was a very dirty method. As the heat rose to heat the rooms, black soot also rose and settled on the walls and furnishings in the rooms. When cleaner-burning sources of heat became available, many people were happy to switch from coal heat.

J. T. Hatfield started one of the oldest coal companies in the Northern Kentucky region, when he opened a small coal yard on 15th St. in Covington in 1882. He delivered kindling wood and coal to homes in the immediate neighborhood, using a small wagon he pulled by hand. He later purchased a mule and a larger cart for his deliveries. Five years later, he acquired Bond Brothers Coal Company and renamed it the J. T. Hatfield Coal Company. Other coal concerns that Hatfield acquired included Blick and Philips, the largest company in Covington; D. H. Steine & Brother; August Kultzer, at Ninth and Pike Sts., Covington; Tighe and Berger, 10th and Greenup Sts., Covington; Uriah Shinkle, Second and Scott Sts., Covington; Von Voken and Gobel; and the Hignite Coal Company.

One of the largest coal companies in Covington was the Montgomery Coal Company, on 19th St. adjacent to the railroad tracks. In Latonia there were two coal companies: Economy Coal Company, located at about 33rd St. between Church St. and Decoursey Ave., and Latonia Ice & Fuel (see **Icehouses**), which was adjacent to the **Louisville and Nashville Railroad** (L&N) on Eugenia Ave. Latonia Ice & Fuel's complex took up an entire city block and was unusual because it sold ice as well as coal. The company was started by two brothers, Joe and Phil Mueller, around 1902 and incorporated in 1908. Most of the coal at Latonia Ice & Fuel was purchased from the Blue Diamond Coal Company, arrived by railcar, and was stored in the Latonia Ice & Fuel coal yard, either on the ground or in one of five concrete silos. Each silo was 90 to 95 feet tall. By use of a winch, a railcar was pulled into place over an open pit beneath the tracks, and the four hopper doors in the bottom of the car were opened so that the coal fell into the pit. In the pit an electrically operated gate would open, allowing the coal to fall into a large steel bucket, which would then proceed on a set of rails partway up the silos and then go straight to the top of the silos, run sideways to the proper silo, and then move down into the silo until it touched the coal. Touching the coal tripped a latch so that the coal was deposited into the silo. The bucket would then return to the top of the silo and descend for another load. Each bucket-load was about three-fourths of a ton of coal. Each of the five silos had a chute in front that could be opened to allow the coal to be loaded onto a waiting coal truck and taken away for delivery. Besides delivering to homes, Latonia Ice & Fuel had contracts with the City of Covington to supply coal to some of its housing projects. At the projects, the coal was dumped through manholes into underground bins that held approximately 20 tons of coal.

Other areas within Northern Kentucky had similar coal operations. Along the **Chesapeake and Ohio Railroad**, at Brent in Campbell Co. was the Grimm Coal and Lumber Company; in Dayton there was the Breitenstein & Son Coal Company; Bellevue was home to Peters Coal; and Newport had the Newport Coal Company at 12th and Columbia Sts., near the Wagon Bridge leading to Clifton, and the Bell Coal Company, at Sixth and Saratoga Sts., along the L&N Railroad. Each of these companies had a rail siding, where coal was unloaded from hopper cars into bins for distribution to customers. In recent years, Maysville has become a coal port city as Eastern Kentucky coal is being brought there via the refurbished **Trans-Kentucky Transportation Railroad** for loading onto Ohio River coal barges.

Loading coal at the Latonia Ice and Fuel Company.

Boh, John. "The J. T. Hatfield Company (1882–1950)," *Kenton County Historical Society Newsletter,* November 1992.
——. "The Pioneer, Montgomery, Rusk Coal Companies," *Kenton County Historical Society Newsletter,* October 1992.
"Latonia Ice & Fuel," *KP,* August 26, 1908, 2.
"Phil Mueller Rites Set for Thursday," *KP,* June 1, 1954, 1.

Mary Jo Hardcorn

COBB, ALFRED (b. 1833, near Lusby's Mill, Ky.; d. January 25, 1904, place of death unknown). The surname Cobb is common throughout Owen Co., and a member of that family has provided a quasi-autobiographical insight into life during the 19th century in the Kentucky county nicknamed Sweet Owen. In his *Liffy Leman; or, Thirty Years in the Wilderness,* Alfred Cobb says that he was born in the hill country of Eagle Creek, and he refers to his environs as the "wilderness." In 1830 Owenton had, at most, 50 houses; Georgetown in Scott Co. had sophistication not found in Cobb's backwoods wilderness: he notes that Georgetown had log homes chinked with mortar. Cobb recounted his **Civil War** experiences as a Confederate under Gen. Braxton Bragg. He went to war with his own horse, and later, after some Southern defeats, returned home starved after an 11-day ride from Tennessee. He described a famous hanging in Owenton that was attended by 5,000 people. Throughout his book, he supported temperance in consumption of alcohol, as demonstrated by the exemplary behavior of his character Aunt Milly. Simply put, Cobb warned about what could happen if a person overindulged in alcohol. At 11:00 on the night of December 4, 1869, Cobb was aboard the Ohio River steamboat ***United States,*** headed downriver from Cincinnati near Warsaw, when his boat collided with the upriver-bound ***America.*** It was one of the more famous collisions in steamboat history. Somehow Cobb made it to safety. Naturally, in his book he indicated his suspicion that the pilots of the *United States* had been consuming alcoholic beverages. Cobb's writings were favorites among the temperance-movement crowd.

Cobb, Alfred. *Liffy Leman; or, Thirty Years in the Wilderness.* Louisville, Ky.: H. A. Kunnecke, 1890.
Houchens, Mariam Sidebottom. *History of Owen County: "Sweet Owen."* Louisville, Ky.: Standard, 1976.

COBURN, JOHN (b. 1763, Philadelphia, Pa.; d. February 1823, Maysville, Ky.). Businessman and judge John Coburn was educated in Philadelphia.

He came to Kentucky in 1780 and settled, along with **Daniel Boone**, at Boonesboro. He moved to Lexington in 1784, where he entered into a business partnership with George Gordon; in the same year Coburn was elected a Lexington town trustee. In 1785 he was a delegate to Kentucky's first Constitutional Convention, at Danville. He studied law at Transylvania University in Lexington and was admitted to the bar in 1788. He moved to Washington, Ky., in 1794, where he operated a mercantile partnership with physician Dr. **Basil Duke**. In 1796 Coburn was nominated, along with Robert Johnson, to mark the official boundary lines between Kentucky and Virginia.

About that same time, Coburn married Mary Ann Moss, sister of **Keturah Moss Leitch Taylor**, the widow of **David Leitch** and later the wife of Newport's founder, **James Taylor Jr.** Another of Mary Ann's sisters was Sally, who was married to Dr. George Gordon, the physician from Fort Washington (Cincinnati) who treated David Leitch as he was dying of pneumonia. After David Leitch's death, Keturah lived for a short while with John Coburn's family. One of the children of John and Mary Ann Moss Coburn was Dr. James Wynn Coburn, who later came to Newport in 1850, at the request of his Aunt Keturah, to treat some of her family members who were ill.

President James Madison (1809–1817) appointed John Coburn superior court judge of the Louisiana Territory, a position he held from 1806 to 1809. He resigned after being appointed revenue collector for Kentucky's Fourth District, again by President Madison. During the **War of 1812**, Coburn served on the military staff of Kentucky governor Isaac Shelby (1792–1976 and 1812–1816). Coburn died at the age of 60 and was buried in Maysville.

Biographical Encyclopedia of Kentucky. Cincinnati: J. M. Armstrong, 1878.

Reis, Jim. "A Killer Named Cholera Stalked Victims Rich and Poor," *KP*, October 4, 1999, 4K.

COCHRAN, ANDREW McCONNELL JANUARY (b. February 4, 1854, Maysville, Ky.; d. June 14, 1934, Maysville, Ky.). Andrew Cochran, a federal district judge, was the son of Robert and Harriett January Cochran. His grandfather McConnell was killed at the **Battle of Blue Licks**. Part of Andrew Cochran's education in Maysville was at the **Maysville Academy**, whose primary educator was W. W. Richeson, a noted scholar throughout the region. Cochran attended Centre College in Danville, Ky., and graduated with honors from the Harvard Law School at Cambridge, Mass., in 1874. Returning to Maysville, he became president of three companies, the Maysville Street and Transfer Company, the Cotton Mills, and the Maysville Gas Company. He also was director of the **January and Wood** Company for 30 years and director of the water company. In 1882 he married Lucy McElroy of Marion Co., and they had three children.

On April 24, 1901, President William McKinley (1897–1901) appointed Cochran the first district judge for the eastern federal court district of Kentucky, following the 1901 split of the state into two districts. President Theodore Roosevelt (1901–1909) renominated Cochran, and the U.S. Senate confirmed him on December 17, 1901. Cochran faced a variety of challenges during his 30 years on the bench. Sessions of the federal district court that he presided over were held in Covington, Lexington, Frankfort, London, and Richmond. Local tradition holds that he was strict on moonshiners except in the case of women, who often appeared in court with a baby in tow. Cochran presided at a series of espionage trials in Covington in 1918 in the midst of anti-German sentiment during **World War I** (see **Anti-German Hysteria**). He died in 1934 and was buried in the Maysville Cemetery.

Kentucky Death Certificate No. 15186, for the year 1934.

Reis, Jim. "Americanism Triumphed in Espionage Trials of 1918," *KP*, March 31, 1997, 4K.

The Spirit of a Greater Maysville and Mason County. Maysville, Ky.: Daily Independent, 1930.

John Klee

COCHRAN, JANE BURCH (b. October 11, 1943, Louisville, Ky.). Artist Jane Hill Burch Cochran is the daughter of Judson Kerfoot Burch of Clover, Halifax Co., Va., and Mildred James Burch of Leitchfield, Grayson Co., Ky. Growing up, Jane migrated from Louisville to Michigan and New Jersey, where she received her primary and secondary education. She then returned to Kentucky and earned a BA degree from Centre College in Danville in 1965, the same year her parents and her only brother moved back to Louisville.

In 1966 Cochran moved to Cincinnati, where she held various full-time jobs while preparing for her formal art training at the Cincinnati Art Academy, which extended from 1967 through 1970. It took her until 1980 finally to localize her artistic expression to the medium of fabric, in the form of art quilts. She has produced 135 such quilts and is recognized internationally for her work. Her works have been displayed in England, Ireland, Finland, the Netherlands, the American Embassy in Uruguay, and many additional European venues. She was one of 30 distinguished quilt artists of the world whose quilts were exhibited at the 2002 Tokyo International Great Quilt Festival. Her works have appeared in Japanese, British, and German publications, and she has lectured and taught across the United States. Her art quilts have traveled in exhibits to almost every state of the United States, including Alaska, and are included in the collections of the National Underground Railroad Freedom Center in Cincinnati, the Kentucky History Center in Frankfort, the University of Kentucky Art Museum in Lexington, the **Delta Air Lines** International Concourse in Atlanta, Ga., the Federal Reserve Bank in Cincinnati, and myriad national business corporate headquarters throughout the Midwest. Her most prestigious Kentucky recognition was her inclusion in the 1997 edition of *Kentucky Women: Two Centuries of Indomitable Spirit and Vision,* a literary tribute to the social impacts resulting from the actions and influences of the historically most formidable and influential women in the state. She has been featured in more than 100 selected exhibitions, more than 50 art trade books and catalogs, and more than 50 periodical and newspaper articles. Because Cochran wants to be the most critical judge of her own works, she critiques them by hanging them outside her Rabbit Hash studio window on the side of the barn, to give her the proper perspective.

Cochran's very feminine expression of the subject matter treated in her art, coupled with her preferred medium of fabric, recalls the strong but gentle matriarchal influences of her roots and upbringing. Her mother, grandmothers, and aunts all played a part in formulating her artistic styles and her method of delivery. Cochran began painting at an early age under the tutelage of her maternal grandmother, and thus she learned something of the patience and determination required to teach grade school art in the Erlanger-Elsmere school system as she continued her art studies and career. To execute the abstract expressionistic style of painting that she preferred, she soon forsook the canvas for the fabric medium that has defined her role as a celebrated leader in the international circles of the art quilt.

Heilerman, Diana. "Stitch Wizardry," *LCJ*, January 14, 2001.

Mitchell, Rebecca. "Kentucky Women," *KP*, February 4, 1998, 2KK.

Potter, Eugenia K., ed. *Kentucky Women: Two Centuries of Indomitable Spirit and Vision.* Louisville, Ky.: Four Colour Imports (Big Tree Press), 1997.

Don Clare

COHEN SHOE STORES. Dan Cohen, the founder of this company, which was also known as the Dan Cohen Shoe Company, was born on April 22, 1840, in Oldenzaal, Netherlands. He immigrated to the United States in 1878 and came to Covington, Ky., in 1887. There he opened a general-merchandise store, which he operated until 1893. At that time he decided to specialize in shoe sales and opened a small shoe store in Covington at 124 Pike St. He later opened a second store at 833 Monmouth St. in Newport and a third at Fifth and Central in Cincinnati. The distinctive wrapping paper Cohen used in his stores had anchors printed on it, and his many friends and customers knew him as Anchor Dan. Dan Cohen died on August 2, 1903, at age 62 and was buried in the Judah Torah Burial Grounds in Price Hill, Cincinnati. Shortly before his death, he had turned the business over to his three sons, Abraham, Moses, and Daniel. By 1910 the Covington store had grown enough that larger quarters were needed, so a new store was built at 22–24–26 Pike St. The brick building measured 93 x 120 feet and was designed by noted Covington architect **Lyman Walker**. It was the largest shoe store in Kentucky. Over the next few years, Cohen's sons opened a chain of Dan Cohen Shoe Stores throughout the Midwest. At the height of their business success, they were operating 38 stores and had more than 500 employees. They were also wholesaling shoes to many other companies. Distribution was made from a large warehouse on Vine St. in Cincinnati. The Dan Cohen Shoe Company survived the **Great Depression** years and the shortages of **World War II**, but it faced increased competition after the war. Its market share gradually declined, and the company ceased operations in 1957.

"Cohen Building Completed," *KP*, August 15, 1910, 3.
"Dan Cohen Dead," *KP*, August 3, 1903, 1.
"40th Anniversary of the Cohen Company," *KP*, October 19, 1933, 1.
"New Penny's Store in Covington," *KP*, October 29, 1941, 1.
St. Mary, Franklin J., and James W. Brown, comps. *Covington Centennial: Official Book and Program*. Covington, Ky.: Semple and Schram, 1914.

COLDIRON, BLANCHE (b. April 22, 1922, Pine Ridge, Wolfe Co., Ky.; d. November 20, 2005, Crittenden, Grant Co., Ky.). Blanche Coldiron, prominently known as "Blanche the Mountain Girl," played the banjo with the Kentucky Hillbillies, an Appalachian traditional music group that performed during the **Great Depression**. Born to parents Harlan and Betty Sparks Hurt in 1922, she moved with her family to Powell Co., Ky., when she was six years old. After listening to entertainer Uncle Dave Macon play banjo on the *Grand Old Opry* radio show from Nashville, Tenn., Blanche, who was only age nine, taught herself to play the instrument. She could play the banjo using five different picking styles, including the core old-time down-stroke picking style known as "claw hammer," which was her customary style. She also played the bass, the guitar, the fiddle, and the mandolin. In 1937 Blanche joined her older brother, Oasa Hurt, to play for Asa Martin's *Kentucky Hillbillies* on WHAS (Louisville) and WLAP (Lexington) radio broadcasts, as well as public shows in the region. According to her son Jim Coldiron, Blanche's parents were quite concerned about having their 15-year-old daughter go on the road with a band of boys. But since her older brother was part of the band, her parents allowed her to participate. Blanche's association with the band was short-lived, however, because her family moved to Grant Co. when she was 17 years old. She was hospitalized with pneumonia for a year and afterward married Earl Coldiron at age 21 and began to raise a family. She resumed her music career, performing locally at dances, fairs, and family gatherings.

Blanche's public performances were postponed when her first child, daughter Carolyn, developed encephalitis at three years old. Most of Blanche's time was spent as a dedicated caregiver for Carolyn. Nevertheless, her son Jim remembers that Blanche's heart was always in music; she taught him how to play the banjo, the fiddle, the guitar, and the mandolin. Her other daughter, Sandra Coldiron Good, occasionally sang along with Jim and Blanche.

After Carolyn died in 1996, Blanche wrote songs, mentored other musicians, and returned to perform on the banjo in public while in her 70s. At this time she was rediscovered by traditional Appalachian music expert **John Harrod** of Owenton. He recorded her banjo performances as part of a collection released in 1999 by Rounder Records, entitled *Kentucky Old-Time Banjo*, showcasing a sampling of traditional banjo performers from the Bluegrass State. In addition to playing the banjo, Blanche was a natural storyteller with a pleasant personality and loved to talk about her experiences with the Kentucky Hillbillies act that traveled to remote schoolhouses throughout Jackson and Clay counties in Eastern Kentucky.

In June 2005 Blanche was honored with Morehead State University's Appalachian Treasure Award for her lifelong contribution to the cultural heritage of Appalachia. A special display in her honor is exhibited at the Kentucky Music Hall of Fame and Museum in Renfro Valley. The museum's current codirector, Robert Lawson, affirms Blanche as one of the finest banjo players from Kentucky, as well as a great influence on younger generations of new banjo players. She died in late 2005 and was buried at the Hill Crest Cemetery in Dry Ridge.

"Blanche the Mountain Girl," *Kentucky Life*, program 313, aired February 3, 1997. Kentucky Educational Television, Lexington, Ky.
Coldiron, Jim. Telephone interview by John Schlipp, Fort Wright, Ky., January 20, 2007.
Collinsworth, Matt. E-mail to John Schlipp, January 22, 2007.
Goodman, Rebecca. "B. Coldiron, Extraordinary Banjo Player," *KE*, November 26, 2005, B9.
Harrod, John, and Mark Wilson, producers. *Kentucky Old-Time Banjo*. Program notes. Cambridge, Mass.: Rounder Records Corp., 1999.

John Schlipp

COLD SPRING. Cold Spring in Campbell Co. dates back to about 1790, when Col. **David Leitch** settled Leitch's Station nearby in Wilder and first traveled through what is now the Cold Spring community. The Mouth of the Licking Baptist Church was established at Cold Spring in 1794. Today, this congregation is called the **First Baptist Church** of Cold Spring. The name Cold Spring comes from the many springs found in the environs of the city. Two springs in particular are referred to as "the cold springs." One spring is behind the Ameristop corporate offices on the east side of Alexandria Pk. (**U.S. 27**); the other is beside the townhouse condominiums off Bunning Ln., west of U.S. 27. Either one could be the original "cold spring."

The city of Cold Spring was incorporated in 1941, after being threatened with annexation by nearby Highland Heights. The local 1883 Lake atlas shows commercial activity in the Cold Spring district: the Six Mile House tavern, a blacksmith shop, stores, a tollhouse, and a post office; also listed are a Catholic church, a cemetery, and an orphans' asylum. **St. Joseph Catholic Church** in Cold Spring was begun during the 1870s. Next door to it was the St. Joseph Orphanage (see **Diocesan Catholic Children's Home**), which opened in 1866. The St. Joseph Catholic Church moved south on U.S. 27 into a new building in 1960. After the orphanage merged with another orphanage and moved to Kenton Co., the **Disabled American Veterans** built its national headquarters on the former orphanage's site in 1966.

One of the first schools in Cold Spring was the **Walnut Hills Academy**. Established by Rev. N. C. Pettitt before the **Civil War** as a private school, it became a Union Army Headquarters during the war. Afterward, it reopened but struggled. In 1876 the Cold Spring Independent School District was established and took over the academy's building for its use. Eventually, during the 1940s, the **Campbell Co. Public Schools** became responsible for the schools in Cold Spring. At the intersection of E. Alexandria Pk. and U.S. 27 there were several other important buildings besides the Walnut Hills Academy/the Cold Spring School. This is where the home of Dr. **George W. Ragan** was located; today the property is the location of the offices for **Griffin Industries**. Directly across the street, where there was once a post office, sat the Pike 27 Auto Theatre (see **Drive-Ins**) and a number of popular restaurants, including Buckskin Bev's, the Frontier Cattle Company, Guys and Dolls (a dance club), and the Plantation. A palm reader (see **Gypsies**) was also located nearby for a while. Just down the road to the south was a mansion called Twelve Maples, and a short way off E. Alexandria Pk. and Dodsworth Ln. was Holly Hill Orphanage. This orphanage, originally named the Campbell Co. Protestant Home (see **Campbell Co. Protestant Orphans Home**), had been moved to Cold Spring from Newport in 1952. In 1990 the Holly Hill Orphanage moved to **Washington Trace Rd.** in Campbell Co., and its property was sold to the City of Cold Spring for offices and a park. Also along Dodsworth Ln. in Cold Spring is the **Campbell Lodge** boys' home, opened in 1958. The institution, run by the Diocese of Covington (see **Roman Catholics**), is in the former home of **Henry Farny**, a world-renowned artist.

In the 1960s, Industrial Rd. (Ky. Rt. 1998) was built connecting U.S. 27 with the **Mary Ingles Highway** (Ky. Rt. 8). Along this road, the Grimm family opened a lumberyard (now Barleycorn's). US. 27 was straightened in 1940 and completely rebuilt in 1974. On the outskirts of Cold Spring to the north, the Lakeside Place Nursing Home (see **Nursing Homes**) was built, and later the Campbell Co. Extension Office relocated there. Many new homes, condominiums, and businesses have appeared recently. The **AA Highway** opened in 1990, and in 2004 Cold Spring was recognized as the fastest-growing city in Kentucky. Two shopping centers have opened at the intersection of U.S. 27 and the AA Highway. With the planned developments of more than 1,000 new homes and condominiums, Cold Spring's further growth is assured. In the 2000 U.S. census, Cold Spring had a population of 3,806.

An Atlas of Boone, Kenton, and Campbell Counties, Kentucky. Philadelphia: D. J. Lake, 1883.
Campbell Co. Historical Society. *Campbell County, Kentucky, 200 Years, 1794–1994.* Alexandria, Ky.: Campbell Co. Historical Society, 1994.
U.S. Census Bureau. "American Fact Finder. Data Set. Census 2000 Summary File 1 (SF1) 100-Percent Data. Custom Table." www.census.gov (accessed March 21, 2006).

Kenneth A. Reis

COLD WAR. The cold war, which lasted from 1946 until 1990, was a conflict between the Soviet Union, along with its allies of the Warsaw Pact, and the United States, with its allies in the North American Treaty Organization (NATO). It was a battle over restricted private property rights as well as for ideological world domination. The cold war had little direct impact on the daily life of the general population living in Northern Kentucky, but many individuals within the region were directly affected by it. Northern Kentucky had no major military base considered essential to the overall military defense of the United States. The **Fort Thomas Military Reservation**, during this period, was limited to providing space for a U.S. Army Reserve unit, offering housing either to officers assigned to the Cincinnati District of the Corps of Engineers or to the Veterans Administration, and conducting medical examinations for recruits entering the armed forces.

The U.S. government during the cold war identified numerous possible targets within the country that the Soviet Union might strike with nuclear weapons delivered by aircraft or missiles. Among these possible Soviet targets were sites within Northern Kentucky such as the steel mill in Newport, the Greater Cincinnati International Airport (CVG) in Boone Co. (today the **Cincinnati/Northern Kentucky International Airport**), the power plants along the Ohio River in Mason and Gallatin counties, the railroad yards in Kenton and Campbell counties, and the phone switching station in Grant Co. The most prominent target listed by the U.S. government within the immediate area was the General Electric jet engine plant at Evendale, Ohio. A consequence of this possible-Soviet-target designation for portions of Northern Kentucky was the development of a civil defense program. Many local chambers of commerce lobbied to get their city or county added to the list of possible Soviet targets; apparently they wanted their community to be recognized as worthy of such status.

The national Selective Service System, which drafted selected males into the armed forces for two years of service, individually affected all males over age 18 between 1946 and 1973. Many young men, realizing that they could be drafted, joined one of the branches of the armed forces for four-year enlistments. Military recruiting stations were located in all county seats on a full-time or part-time basis. A four-year volunteer for military duty could count on going to a military technical school to learn a trade, whereas technical schooling was denied to military draftees, since such schooling might take between one and two years to complete. This technical or vocational training provided by the armed services to its people is one of the overlooked cold war benefits to the American economy during the 1950s and 1960s. Each year, a steady stream of men and women left the military trained in skills needed by business and industry.

Northern Kentucky during this period also had various National Guard, Army, Navy, and Coast Guard reserve units meeting in the area. Covington was home to U.S. Naval and Coast Guard reserve units from the late 1940s until the early 1970s. Two U.S. Army Reserve units were based at Fort Thomas, the 478th Engineer Battalion and the 15th Psychological Operations Battalion. Kentucky National Guard units were the 118th Maintenance Company (Light Equipment) at Walton; Company A, 206th Engineer Battalion, 35th Infantry Division, at Maysville; and Battery A, 2nd Howitzer Battalion, 138th Field Artillery, at Carrollton. At various times during national alerts and exercises, Strategic Air Command (SAC) bombers and Air Defense Command (ADC) interceptors were based at the Greater Cincinnati International Airport. A Coast Guard Auxiliary unit, some of whose members were Northern Kentucky residents, was located in Cincinnati, and a U.S. Air Force Civil Air Patrol unit operated in the Greater Cincinnati area. In addition, a number of local high schools were home to Junior Reserve Officer Training Corps (ROTC) units.

The counties of Boone, Campbell, and Kenton, as part of the Greater Cincinnati Area, were protected by four Nile Hercules surface-to-air missile sites manned by U.S. Army or National Guard units from 1960 to 1970. These sites, all armed with 4 launch rails and 12 missiles housed in underground storage, were located at Dillsboro, Ind. (Nile missile site Cincinnati-Dayton No. 63, or CD-63); Oxford, Ohio (CD-78); Wilmington, Ohio (CD-27); and Felicity, Ohio (CD-46).

Northern Kentucky's closest direct encounters with the cold war, as a community, were during the Berlin Wall confrontation of 1961 and during the Cuban Missile Crisis in October 1962, when there arose a short-term interest in home fallout shelters and the development of local fully staffed civil defense organizations. Another time the cold war became part of the fabric of the community was during the debates over the Vietnam War in the late 1960s.

The drawdown of the military and of the U.S. war industrial base during the 1990s had little visual impact on the region. The end of the cold war did, however, affect the area both directly and indirectly whenever military equipment contracts were canceled or modified. The trickle-down effect caused some industries and services to go out of business or switch to other products. The physical landscape of Northern Kentucky, however, holds no structure that can be linked with the cold war except for the Interstate Highway System (see **Expressways**).

The Interstate Highway System was conceived and enacted under the administration of President Dwight D. Eisenhower in the 1950s as a means to move the military rapidly throughout the country and to serve as emergency runways for aircraft operations. It led to the building of I-71, I-75, I-275, and I-471 in the Northern Kentucky region, plus four modern bridges across the Ohio River: the **Brent Spence Bridge** (I-75–I-71), the **Daniel Carter Beard Bridge** (I-471), and the two I-275 bridges, the **Carroll C. Cropper Bridge** to Indiana and the **Combs-Hehl Bridge** to eastern Cincinnati.

Commonwealth of Kentucky. Annual Reports, Kentucky Department of Military Affairs—1950 to 1992. Kentucky Department of Military Affairs, Frankfort, Ky.
Friedman, Norman. *The Fifty-Year War—Conflict and Strategy in the Cold War.* Annapolis, Md.: U.S. Naval Institute, 1999.
Gregory, Richard, ed. *Cold War America—1950 to 1990.* New York: Facts on File, 2003.

Charles H. Bogart

COLEMAN, JOHN (b. January 31, 1868, Covington, Ky.; d. September 14, 1943, Cincinnati, Ohio). Black businessman John Coleman, the son of David and Mary C. Coleman, moved to Cincinnati in 1882 and in 1884 took a position as the head bellman at the Palace Hotel, where he continued working for 12 years. He resided at 730 Barr St. in the city's West End. In 1911 Coleman became an elevator operator at the Methodist Book Concern, a position he held for 30 years. While there, he began pursuing a career in real estate sales. In 1918 he moved from the Barr St. address to 1214 Lincoln Ave. in the Walnut Hills neighborhood of Cincinnati, where he opened the Coleman Real Estate Company, the first African American real estate firm in the area. Later, he moved his real estate office to Richmond St. in Cincinnati's West End.

Coleman was a 32nd degree **Mason**; politically, he was a Republican. Coleman was also active in the Methodist Episcopal Church. He served as president of the United Order of Good Shepherds, for 10 years was a member of the Walnut Hills Welfare Association, and belonged to both the Negro Protective Association and the Queen City Fountain No. 853. In the 1940s, Coleman served as secretary of the Colored Waiter Alliance Local No. 541 of the American Federation of Labor, located in downtown Cincinnati on Plum St. He died at his home in Walnut Hills in 1943 and was buried in Union Baptist Cemetery in Cincinnati.

Dabney, W. P. *Cincinnati's Colored Citizens.* Cincinnati: Dabney, 1926.
"Death Notices," *CTS*, September 15, 1943, 26.
Obituary. *CTS*, September 16, 1943, 36.
William's Cincinnati city directories, 1884–1944.

Theodore H. H. Harris

COLEMAN'S SPRINGS. A few hundred yards above the mouth of the South Licking River in Pendleton Co., near Falmouth, is where the crystal-clear water of Coleman's Springs bubbles forth. This water source had been long known to **American Indians** when British captain Henry Byrd (see **Bird's [Byrd's] War Road**) and the irascible **Simon Girty** reportedly drank from it on their way to the Ruddells Mills massacre in 1780. Close by was the home of the legendary Simon the Trapper, who lived there for years before moving westward to avoid the onslaught of civilization. Coleman's Springs is where Pendleton Countians came during droughts and hauled off wagons loaded with barrels of water. In recent years, there has been talk of using the water to manufacture ice.

Belew, Mildred Boden. *The First 200 Years of Pendleton County.* Falmouth, Ky.: M. B. Belew, n.d. [ca. 1994].

Mildred Belew

COLLINS, LEWIS (b. December 25, 1797, near Bryants Station, Ky., d. January 29, 1870, Lexington, Ky.). Kentucky historian Lewis Collins was born in Fayette Co., Ky. He was the third son of Richard Collins of Virginia, who had served during the **Revolutionary War**. Lewis Collins had no formal education. Orphaned at age 13, he became a printer's apprentice for the *Paris Citizen* newspaper in Paris, Ky., at age 16. He helped found the *Washington Union* newspaper at Washington, Ky., and became its associate publisher in 1818. In 1820 he was the editor and publisher of the *Maysville Eagle.* He held that post for more than 20 years.

In 1823 Collins married Mary Eleanor Peers, daughter of Maj. Valentine Peers, a Virginian who served during the Revolutionary War and was with George Washington at Valley Forge in Pennsylvania. In 1847 Collins published the book that made him famous, *Historical Sketches of Kentucky.* Its contents ranged from early explorations in Kentucky and the surrounding regions to events of his own period. The book was a collective effort based largely on research begun by Collins's brother-in-law, Henry Peers, who died before it was published. It was revised and substantially expanded in a second version published by Lewis's son **Richard Collins** in 1874.

Lewis Collins became the first judge of the Mason Co. Court in 1851 and served until 1855. He was also a school commissioner for 20 years; served as president, secretary, and treasurer of several Kentucky turnpike companies; was a deacon in the Presbyterian Church; and owned a book business.

Politically, Collins was a **Whig** and a supporter of Henry Clay. In 1844 he served as secretary to a citizens' committee seeking changes in laws that discouraged abolitionists from inciting slaves to flee. Yet in 1845 he denounced Cassius Clay's antislavery newspaper the *True American* as "reckless" and "incendiary." In 1860 Collins served as vice president of a committee of Kentucky and Ohio citizens devoted to the Union and committed to standing by it regardless of developments.

Collins died in January 1870 in Lexington and was buried in Maysville Cemetery. The Kentucky legislature passed a resolution noting his achievements and also contracted for copies of his book to be provided to public school libraries throughout the state. Richard Collins spoke before the General Assembly urging its members to adopt *Historical Sketches of Kentucky* as official state history and require every schoolchild to read it.

Collins, Richard H. "Memorial to the General Assembly of Kentucky of 1871–2," 1871, Kentucky Gateway Museum, Maysville, Ky.

"It Was Century Ago That Lewis Collins Died," *Maysville Ledger Independent,* June 16, 1970, 1.

Kleber, John E., ed. *The Kentucky Encyclopedia.* Lexington: Univ. Press of Kentucky, 1992.

"Lewis Collins' Kentucky History Soon Available," *Maysville Daily Independent,* February 12, 1960, 3.

"Peers Compiled History of Kentucky; Credit Was Due His Brother-in-Law," *Murray (Ky.) Ledger and Times,* March 30, 1976, 12.

Col Owens

COLLINS, RICHARD HENRY (b. May 4, 1824, Maysville, Ky.; d. January 1, 1888, Maryville, Mo.). Richard Henry Collins, a famous Kentucky historian, was the son of Judge **Lewis Collins**, historian, journalist, and public servant, and Mary Eleanor Peers, daughter of Maj. Valentine Peers, a Virginian who served during the **Revolutionary War** and was with George Washington at Valley Forge in Pennsylvania.

Richard Collins graduated from Centre College at Danville, Ky., in 1842 and from Transylvania Law School at Lexington in 1846. He received an LLD degree from Austin College in Texas in 1880. Collins followed his father as editor of the *Maysville Eagle,* serving from 1845 to 1850 and again from 1853 to 1857. He practiced law from 1851 to 1853 in Maysville and later in Cincinnati from 1862 to 1871, while residing in Covington. It was said that he often gave legal advice without charging a fee. He founded the *Danville Review* in 1861 and served as its publisher for a time.

Collins married Mary Cox, daughter of Edward Cox of Maysville, in 1846. They had six children. Following his father's death in 1870, Collins moved back to Maysville. The Kentucky legislature contracted to provide copies of his father's *Historical Sketches of Kentucky* to all public school libraries in the state. Collins attempted to persuade the legislature to adopt the work as the official history of Kentucky and to require every schoolchild to read it. However, the measure proved controversial and Collins's attempt was unsuccessful.

In 1874 Collins published a revised and substantially expanded version of the work, called *Collins' History of Kentucky.* Included in its two volumes were annals, historical sketches, a short history of the commonwealth of Kentucky, a history of each county, and a wealth of statistical and biographical information. This work was acknowledged as the most inclusive history of the period.

In 1877 Collins moved to Louisville and lived there for the remainder of his life. He died in 1888 in Missouri while visiting a daughter and was buried in Maysville Cemetery. Shortly after his death, the Kentucky legislature purchased his library, which is housed at the Kentucky Historical Society in Frankfort. A state historical marker noting Richard Collins's achievements stands today along Scott St. near the **Kenton Co. Public Library** in Covington.

"Collins, Richard H." *Lexington Gazette,* May 22, 1886.

Collins, Richard H. "Memorial to the General Assembly of Kentucky of 1871–2," 1871, Kentucky Gateway Museum, Maysville, Ky.

Kleber, John E., ed. *The Kentucky Encyclopedia.* Lexington: Univ. Press of Kentucky, 1992.

Morton, Jennie C. "Sketch and Picture of Richard H. Collins, Historian," *RKHS* 7, no. 19 (May 1909): 10–16.

Col Owens

COLONIAL COTTAGE. In 1933 Clara Rich opened a restaurant in a small white cottage in Erlanger to feed the local tobacco warehouse workers. Known as the Colonial Cottage, the restaurant served basic home-cooked meals, including fried chicken, meatloaf, and the cream pies that soon became popular. It was not long before locals and **Dixie Highway** travelers discovered this cozy dining gem and joined the tobacco men at the Colonial Cottage. Rumor has it that Elvis Presley once ate at the restaurant on his way home to Tennessee, following his stint in the U.S. Army.

Clara Rich operated the restaurant for 37 years and then sold it to Verne Epperson. Epperson, a native of Dry Ridge, had eaten at the restaurant only a few times when he decided to purchase the business. The purchase deal was struck in 1970 and the restaurant changed hands. In 1987 Epperson and his wife, Bonnie, took the restaurant into a new era by moving it from the old tiny cottage to a newly constructed building less than one block away, where the seating capacity was nearly doubled. The relocated restaurant thrived.

In July 1999 the Eppersons sold the Colonial Cottage to the next generation of owners, Matthew and Noelle Higdon Grimes. The Grimeses, both graduates of Centre College in Danville, Ky., have strong ties throughout Kentucky, stretching from Ashland to Danville and from Louisville to Northern Kentucky. Their innate love for both Kentucky history and Kentucky food made the purchase of the Colonial Cottage a good fit for this young couple. Under their guidance, a small banquet room was added, the restaurant's floor plan was redesigned, and a catering business was established. Throughout these changes, the food quality and offerings at the restaurant have remained consistent with the original high standards established decades earlier. Fried chicken dinners are still served on Tuesday nights, salmon croquettes are a staple on Friday nights, and a variety of cream pies are always on the menu. Breakfast is served all day, and **goetta** is a hot menu item for the local dining crowd.

On August 2, 2005, the Colonial Cottage gained national attention for its quality products and unique dishes. The television Travel Channel's *Taste of America* devoted an episode to the phenomenon of goetta and featured the Colonial Cottage on the show. As a part of the episode, the restaurant put together a minifestival to show just how much Northern Kentuckians love their goetta.

The Colonial Cottage has seen a lot of changes since its opening in 1933: recessions, wars, bull markets, weddings, and births. Through them all, the quaint restaurant has remained an integral part of the Erlanger business community and provides a constant reminder of home, family, and friends. The restaurant continues to have a loyal following, and its owners and staff develop personal relationships with customers. In 2006 it became one of Northern Kentucky's first restaurants to implement a nonsmoking policy.

"Regulars Go for Food, Family—Colonial Cottage Offers Home-Style Cooking, Ambience," *KE*, September 20, 2003, B1.

"Taste Treats," *SC*, August 22, 2004, 2C.

"'We Plan to Be Here for Next Half-Century,' Says Restaurateur," *KP*, August 31, 2004, 3B.

Noelle Higdon Grimes and Matthew J. Grimes

COLSTON FAMILY. In the late 18th century, Raleigh Colston, who was born in Virginia on May 11, 1747, purchased from his brother-in-law William Peachy a 5,000-acre tract along the Ohio River that today is included in the western suburbs of Covington. Several members of the Colston family had immigrated to the United States during the mid-1600s and settled in Northumberland Co., Va., and Raleigh was a descendant of those early immigrants.

Raleigh's father was a friend of James Taylor Sr., whose son **James Taylor Jr**. was the founder of Newport. The Colstons intermarried with the Bealls, whose descendants were early settlers of eastern Campbell Co. (see **Benjamin Beall**). About 1750 Raleigh Colston and his brother William inherited a large plantation estate along the Rappahannock River from their uncle Daniel Hornby.

Eventually, Raleigh Colston became an attorney. He married Elizabeth Marshall, a sister of U.S. chief justice John Marshall, and the couple had several children, including a son Edward. Raleigh and his brother-in-law William Peachy soon began buying up military warrants in the west from veterans of both the **French and Indian War** and the **Revolutionary War**. In 1789 Peachy was given several tracts of land for his military service; part of that land was the Northern Kentucky tract sold to Raleigh Colston. As native Virginian James Taylor Sr. had done, Colston, the patriarch of the Colston family, sent his son to manage his Northern Kentucky lands while he, the father, stayed on in Virginia. Raleigh Colston later moved to Northern Kentucky to be close to his son.

Edward Colston married twice, and his family made their home in downtown Covington. One of Edward's children, Edward Jr., married Sally Coles Stevenson, a daughter of future Kentucky governor **John White Stevenson** (1867–1871). When Sally Colston died in 1890, Edward Jr. married her sister, Mary White Stevenson. Mary died in 1917 and Edward Jr. died in 1928. Many members of the Colston family were buried in Spring Grove Cemetery in Cincinnati.

Edward Colston Papers, box 2, folder 11, Cincinnati Historical Society, Cincinnati.

"Raleigh Colston Resurvey, Campbell Co," Court Order Book B, Courthouse, Alexandria, Ky.

Tenkotte, Paul A. "Rival Cities to Suburbs: Covington and Newport, Kentucky, 1790–1890," PhD diss., Univ. of Cincinnati, 1989.

COLTER, JOHN (b. ca. 1774, Staunton, Va.; d. May 7, 1812, near New Haven, Mo.). Explorer John Colter was of Ulster-Scottish descent. The Colter family moved to Limestone (present-day Maysville), and there Colter met Capt. Meriwether Lewis in 1803 as Lewis descended the Ohio River. Colter enlisted in the Corps of Northwest Discovery on October 15, 1803, at Maysville. He later became the first white man to see what is today Yellowstone Park.

After spending the difficult winter of 1803–1804 at Camp River Dubois, across from the mouth of the Missouri River, the expedition headed west, and Colter soon proved to be one of the group's most dependable hunters. Because of his skills as a woodsman, he was selected to search for missing expedition member George Shannon in 1804 and to take part in the 1805 reconnaissance of the Salmon River in Idaho. As the expedition neared Fort Mandan in present-day North Dakota in August 1806, they met two trappers, Forest Hancock and Joseph Dickson, who were going up the Missouri River. Hancock and Dickson persuaded Colter, with little difficulty, to leave the expedition and to return to the beaver-trapping country he had just left. History does not record the fate of Hancock and Dickson, but in spring 1807, at the mouth of the Platte River, Colter met St. Louis, Mo., entrepreneur Manuel Lisa with a trapping party headed for the Yellowstone River. Former expedition members George Drouillard, John Potts, and Peter Wiser were in the group. John Colter was urged a second time to return to the beaver-trapping country, and he did so. In October 1807, at the confluence of the Bighorn and Yellowstone Rivers in present-day Montana, Lisa and the party built Fort Raymond, more popularly called Manuel's Fort. In November, Lisa sent Colter with a supply of trade items to let the Crow Indians know that the fort was open for trade. Colter's 1807–1808 tour through the thermal region, which later became Yellowstone National Park, is shown on William Clark's 1814 map. Although no map drawn by Colter or journal written by him has been found, his route of travel was recounted to William Clark by George Drouillard in 1808 and by Colter himself in 1810. "Colter's Hell," as the region was known, is reminiscent of the trapper's yarns attributed to Colter after the 1807 tour.

Colter's legend grew further with his escape from captivity by the Blackfeet Indians at the Three Forks of the Missouri River in 1808: With former expedition member John Potts, Colter traversed the route followed by William Clark and his party in 1806 from the Three Forks to the Yellowstone River. Colter and Potts had been trapping in the Three Forks area, and they were discovered by the Blackfeet. Potts was killed immediately, and Colter was stripped of all his clothes before a chase began. Colter outran all the pursuing Blackfeet except one and killed that Blackfoot with the Indian's own spear. Taking the spear and the blanket of the pursuer, Colter traveled 11 days before arriving at Manuel's Fort. Later that winter, he was retracing his trail to the Gallatin Fork to retrieve the traps dropped in the water, where he and Potts had been caught, and Colter was attacked by the Blackfeet a second time. His escape this time persuaded him to leave the mountains and the beaver-trapping country and never return.

Colter was back in the St. Louis area in May 1810 and married a woman named Nancy Hooker; the couple had one son, Hiram. John Colter sued the estate of Meriwether Lewis for $599, his expedition pay, but later settled for $377. Colter joined a group of Mounted Rangers, led by Nathan Boone, son of **Daniel Boone**, to defend the region around St. Louis from Indian attacks during the **War of 1812**. He served with Boone from March until May 1812. In May 1812 Colter died. His burial place is unknown but is believed to be near New Haven, Mo.

Harris, Burton. *John Colter: His Years in the Rockies*. Lincoln: Univ. of Nebraska Press, 1993.

Holmerg, James J. *Exploring with Lewis and Clark: The 1804 Journal of Charles Floyd*. Norman: Univ. of Oklahoma Press, 2004.

Morris, Larry E. *The Fate of the Corps*. New Haven, Conn.: Yale Univ. Press, 2004.

Moulton, Gary E. *The Journals of the Lewis and Clark Expedition*. Lincoln: Univ. of Nebraska Press, 1993.

James L. Mallory

COLUMBIA SUSSEX CORPORATION. Columbia Sussex, a Fort Mitchell–based hotel management and development company, in recent years has made notable inroads into the U.S. gaming industry. Founded by William J. "Bill" Yung in 1972, the firm owns, leases, and manages hotels, most of them in the major franchise hotel chains. Its first property was the Days Inn in Richwood. Today, it owns 83 hotels and casinos. Columbia Sussex conducts business in 25 states and is wholly owned by the Yung family. It is one of the largest privately held hotel companies in the United States. The company's first gaming license was acquired in 1990. The firm moved in October 2007 into its new $15-million, eight-story office building on a 40-acre site in Crestview Hills. Columbia-Sussex and its affiliates ranked number two on the Cincinnati USA–Deloitte 2006 list of the largest privately held businesses in Greater Cincinnati and Northern Kentucky, with 2005 revenues of $1.04 billion. In January 2008, the company purchased the former **Bavarian Brewing Company** in Covington for $7 million, with the intention of building a casino and restaurants should casino gambling become legal in Kentucky.

Columbia Sussex Corporation. www.columbiasussex.com (accessed November 15, 2006).

"$8M Office Building Planned," *KP*, November 14, 2006, A2.

Newberry, Jon. "Bill Yung and Columbia Sussex: Building a Casino Empire," *KP*, June 10, 2006, A1.

"Yung on Grand Victoria: No Thanks," *KE*, May 11, 2007, 1A.

COMAIR. Comair is an airline company maintaining a significant presence at the **Cincinnati/**

Northern Kentucky International Airport and employing many Northern Kentuckians. Raymond Mueller and son David Mueller founded Comair in April 1977. The airline consisted of three Piper Navajo aircraft, which provided scheduled service from Cincinnati to Akron, Cleveland, and Detroit. In 1981 Comair added a Piper Chieftain and began negotiations to purchase Embrare Bandeirante turboprop aircraft. This increase resulted from the company's going public, as Comair Holdings Inc., with an initial offer of common stock in July 1981. Then in December 1981 Comair became part of the computer reservation system of **Delta Airlines**.

In 1984 Comair became a Delta Connection regional carrier and was able to participate in code-sharing: Comair flights were listed in the airline reservation system with a Delta Airlines flight code. In 1986 Delta Airlines infused Comair with capital by purchasing 20 percent of Comair's stock. Subsequently, Comair expanded its fleet by adding 30-seat Saab 340 turboprop aircraft.

In 1987 Comair, in cooperation with Delta Airlines, began marketing the Cincinnati/Northern Kentucky International Airport (CVG) and the Orlando International Airport (MCO) as its two major hubs. This arrangement allowed Delta Airlines to provide connecting flights with ticket code-sharing to cities not generating sufficient passengers for Delta's large aircraft. Comair benefited from the arrangement by being funneled a steady supply of passengers who needed connecting jet service but lived in smaller markets.

With increased demand as a result of development of the Cincinnati and Orlando hubs, Comair began to purchase 30-seat Embrare Brasilia turboprop aircraft in 1988. The next year Comair established Comair Aviation Academy at Orlando, an airline-owned school providing flight training. In 1993, with the purchase of 50-seat Canadair Regional Jets, Comair began to convert from propeller-driven planes to an all-jet fleet.

In 1994 Comair's freestanding Concourse C at CVG was opened. By 1997 Comair carried 5.4 million passengers, and almost half of them passed through Concourse C. This increase in passenger load resulted in further expansion of Concourse C in 1998. In 2000 Comair operated more than 100 Canadair Regional Jets, announced its eighth three-for-two stock split since 1981, carried more than 8 million passengers, moved into its new headquarters building at CVG, and was purchased by Delta Airlines for $1.8 billion.

Delta Airlines retained Comair as a separately owned company providing service in competition with similar regional carriers then being organized. In 2001 Concourse C was again expanded to keep up with demand. That year was also marked by a strike by Comair pilots. Lasting 38 days, the strike cost the airline an estimated $70 million in lost revenues. The following year Comair took delivery of its first 70-seat Bombardier CRJ Regional Jet and retired its last propeller-driven aircraft, becoming the first all-jet regional airline. In 2003 Comair employed more than 6,000 persons, carried more than 10 million passengers, and operated 1,050 flights daily to 115 cities. Comair remains an all-jet operation, flying a fleet of 31 40-seat, 106 50-seat, and 27 70-seat Bombardier CRJ Regional Jets.

By 2004 Comair was the second-largest regional airline in the United States, providing service to 115 cities in 37 states, Canada, and the Bahamas, with a fleet of 164 Bombardier CRT Regional Jets. In 2005 Comair was the largest employer in Northern Kentucky, with 4,400 employees.

Boulton, Guy. "Cooperative Relationship Helps Delta, Comair Dominate Locally," *CE,* June 22, 1997, I1.

Crowley, Patrick. "Fidelity to Add Up to 2,000 Jobs," *KE,* May 29, 2005, A1.

Dias, Monica. "Comair's $45 Million Facility Nearly Done," *KP,* August 16, 1994, 3K.

Miller, Nick. "Delta Buying Comair for $1.8B," *KP,* October 18, 1999, 1K.

Mueller, Ray. *Pedals to Planes.* Cincinnati: Custom Editorial Productions, 1995.

"Northern Kentucky Cincinnati International Airport into the 21 Century." Press Release. Cincinnati/Northern Kentucky International Airport, 2000.

Rawe, Richard L. *Creating a World-Class Airport: Cincinnati/Northern Kentucky International, 1947–1997.* Encino, Calif.: Cherbo, 1997.

Charles H. Bogart

COMBS-HEHL BRIDGE. The $30.5 million Combs-Hehl Bridge along I-275 (see **Expressways**), the roadway circling Cincinnati and Northern Kentucky, crosses the Ohio River between Brent in Campbell Co., Ky., and California in eastern Hamilton Co., Ohio. The bridge is five miles upriver from the **Daniel Carter Beard Bridge**. The Combs-Hehl Bridge is the east-side connection of the interstate highway circle and has twin spans, each with three automobile lanes. It is sometimes referred to as the Brent Bridge or as the Coney Island Bridge, a reference to Brent, Ky., and to the popular Coney Island amusement park at the Ohio end of the structure. The cantilevered-truss bridge is 1,509 feet long, with a 720-foot main span. It has a single central pier in the center of the river. The bridge was dedicated on December 19, 1979, and was named in honor of former Kentucky governor Bert T. Combs (1959–1963) and longtime Campbell Co. judge **Lambert Hehl Jr.** About 72,000 cars cross this bridge daily, including commuters; patrons of Coney Island, the Riverbend entertainment center, and the River Downs Racecourse; and bypass traffic off I-75 and I-71.

The opening of the Combs-Hehl Bridge spelled the end of the Coney Island Ferry, also known as the Brent Ferry (see **Ferries**). It was a small passenger ferry holding maybe 20 or so customers for each river crossing between Brent and the boat landing at Coney Island. The Kentucky Department of Transportation made a one-time payment to John Laughead, the owner of the ferry, when the Combs-Hehl Bridge opened, as compensation for putting him out of business. Because the Combs-Hehl Bridge completed the last link in the circle freeway around the Greater Cincinnati area, it has expanded the suburban development of Northern Kentucky.

Cincinnati-Transit.net. "Combs-Hehl Bridge." www.cincinnati-transit.net (accessed on October 31, 2006).

"Ferry Owner Loses Appeal," *KE,* September 4, 1982, C1.

"Hehl, at 55, a 'Million-Dollar Baby,'" *KP,* December 19, 1979, 1.

McNutt, Randy. "I-275 Bridge Seen as Business Boom," *CE,* December 16, 1979, B1.

Wiegand, Rolf. "I-275 Bridge Will Open New Tristate Area Link," *CE,* December 16, 1979, B1.

COMER, MARTHA PURDON (b. September 8, 1906, Maysville, Ky.; d. March 5, 2003, Maysville, Ky.). Newspaper editor Martha Purdon Comer, one of Maysville's most distinguished citizens, was the daughter of James and Elizabeth Brown Purdon. Martha's early education was at St. Patrick Grade School; in 1924 she graduated from Maysville High School, where she was the class salutatorian. She attended Brenau College in Gainesville, Ga., and later received her degree from **Maysville Community and Technical College**. After leaving school, she worked for the Maysville *Daily Independent* newspaper, which had been founded in 1906 by her father. Martha's brother, J. Clifford Purdon, was editor of the paper, and when he died in 1935, she assumed that position. She married her hometown boyfriend, Patrick W. Comer, whom she had known from the age of 14. The couple became the parents of two daughters, Mary Pat Comer Latham and Barbara Comer Thornhill. The family home, called Woodlawn, was of gothic revival design. The *Daily Independent* merged with the *Ledger* newspaper in 1968, to form the *Ledger Independent*, and Martha Comer was named editor of the combined paper. She retired as editor in 1977 but continued to write a daily column called *Do You Know?*

Comer was a strong advocate for the completion of the **Mary Ingles Highway**, the building of the Maysville Floodwall, and the establishment of Maysville Community College. She retired completely in the 1990s but continued to serve as an editorial consultant for the remainder of her life. She had the honor of being invited to the White House to meet with President John F. Kennedy. During her career she was named Maysville's Most Distinguished Citizen, 1956 Woman of the Year, and the Most Distinguished Alumna of Maysville High School. She was inducted into the Kentucky Journalism Hall of Fame. Comer campaigned tirelessly for many organizations and causes, including the Cancer Drive, the Heart Fund, the Red Cross Blood Bank, public housing, and civil rights legislation. She was also a lifetime member of the Mason Co. Historical Society. She died in the Maysville Nursing and Rehabilitation Center at age 96 and was buried in Maysville's St. Patrick Cemetery. In December 2002 the City of Maysville renamed the access road into Maysville Community College Martha Purdon Dr. in honor of this distinguished lady.

"Martha Comer, Legendary Editor," *KP,* March 7, 2003, 11A.

"Martha Comer Led Maysville Paper," *CE,* March 7, 2003, B4.

COMMISSARY CORNER. Commissary Corner, a historic landmark in Boone Co., is found on current maps, but today thickets and brambles cover the site of the area's late-19th-century foot-stomping entertainment center. The popular picnic grounds and dance pavilion, located at the junction of the Woolper and Burlington-Bellevue (Belleview) turnpikes, drew crowds of people from Belleview, Burlington, and Petersburg for weekend dances. Woolper Turnpike ended with the Commissary picnic site at Rocky Springs Rd., an old country path that wound its way to Boone Cliffs at Middle Creek. Longtime local residents continue to refer to Woolper Rd. as Commissary Rd.

Commissary Corner was shown on the local 1883 Lake atlas as simply a "picnic ground." It sat in a grove of beech trees, surrounded by the farms of John E. Walton and William Walton. The picnic grounds, complete with a restaurant (the commissary) at William Walton's grove, were dedicated June 4, 1881. The *Boone County Recorder* reported that there was quite a crowd in attendance. Within the grove, on a dance floor that had been built for $70, ladies and gentlemen danced to the music of the Burlington Band. Everett Walton, the restaurant owner, hoped for a booming start, but the weather that June was too cool for much business. Foot-tappers in attendance included Squire Early, Pink Rice, C. W. Saxton, and Claude Walton. Harry Blythe, N. W. Botts, R. A. Brady, Dr. Piatt, Scott Rice, W. I. Rouse, W. T. Ryle, and William Walton watched. Dr. Smith was there but did not bring his family. The crowd danced until sundown, when they had to abandon their amusement for the night.

John Brady Walton remembers traveling up and down Rocky Springs Rd. with his father, taking cornmeal to be ground at the Middle Creek mill. When they passed the once-lively place, the shady grove was quiet, the dancers long gone. The Walton family continues to own land adjacent to Commissary Corner.

An Atlas of Boone, Kenton, and Campbell Counties, Kentucky. Philadelphia: D. J. Lake, 1883.

Boone Co. Historic Preservation Review Board. *Historic Structures of Boone County, Kentucky.* Ann Arbor, Mich.: Cushing-Malloy, 2002.

Boone County Recorder, June 8, 1881, 3.

Walton, John B., Jr. Telephone interview by Jannes Garbett, December 27, 2004, Burlington, Ky.

Jannes W. Garbett

COMMITTEE FOR COVINGTON–KENTON CO. While the **Kefauver Committee** hearings on criminal activities in the United States were being viewed on television during early 1951, Northern Kentucky groups in both Campbell and Kenton counties formed to address organized crime locally. The Campbell Co. group was called the Newport Social Action Committee; the organization in Kenton Co. was the Committee for Covington–Kenton Co. (CCKC).

After some preliminary organizational meetings, the CCKC went public in May 1951. Its purpose was to rid Kenton Co., and particularly Covington, of **gambling**, **prostitution**, and other related activities. It began with the tenets that the heart of democracy lies in the local community; that each individual citizen must act to ensure honest and capable elected officials; that the committee's goal was to help elect those officials; that the committee was not affiliated with any political group; and that the organization should include representatives of all religious faiths. Its primary objective was to eliminate all forms of syndicate and commercialized gambling and to have good government thereafter. The only way that this could be accomplished was to build a political coalition to elect government officials who agreed with the group and who would not tolerate illegal behavior.

The CCKC consisted of some 25 founding members, primarily led by two men, Andrew W. Clark and Larry C. Wilson. The chairman of the group was Wilson, a wounded **World War II** veteran and a business professor at the University of Kentucky Northern Community College in Covington (see **Northern Kentucky University**). He lived in Erlanger. Clark, a native of Versailles in Woodford Co., held a law degree from the University of Kentucky in Lexington (1937) and was a member of a successful Covington law firm. He and his family were Methodists and resided in Park Hills. He was a well-respected member of the Chamber of Commerce, from which much of the reform activities originated (see **Northern Kentucky Chamber of Commerce**). Years later, in November 1967, Clark died in a Trans World Airlines crash on approach to the **Cincinnati/Northern Kentucky International Airport**. Clark began as president of the group but resigned that position in June 1951 to run against James E. Quill in the August Democratic primary for the office of commonwealth attorney in Kenton Co. Also involved in the CCKC was Chester Disque, a local architect, who was its treasurer.

The initial plan of the CCKC was to solicit the support of community clubs and service organizations: the Chamber of Commerce, the Kiwanis (see **Civic Associations**), the Optimists, and **Rotary**. Not all of these groups bought into the CCKC "creed" entirely. Since these clubs and organizations cut across both of the major political parties of the day, they could ill afford to back candidates selected by the CCKC and risk losing members on the other side politically.

The Roman Catholic Diocese of Covington (see **Roman Catholics**) was somewhat ambivalent toward the CCKC. For whatever reason, whether it was not initially consulted by the committee, or whether it thought its parishes might lose their weekly gaming nights, where bingo was played, or whether the gambling that transpired at many Catholic charitable fundraising events and at all important summer festivals was a concern, the diocese openly questioned in its weekly newspaper, *Messenger,* what could be the ultimate effects of the proposed CCKC agenda. That publication's editor, Rev. Henry Haacke, in November 1951 signed an affidavit claiming to have seen 1949 gambling receipts from slot machines present at the White Horse Tavern along the **Dixie Highway** in Park Hills; later, he recanted, claiming that he had been confused at the time, and the issue died as quickly as it arose. Haacke's reversal was suspiciously timed just before the elections held that month.

On the Protestant side of the issue, W. Sharon Florer, the antigambling editor of *Protestant Action*, an area newsletter distributed to Protestant churches, commented that noncommittal citizens "must be counted with the opponents." He called it "fence-straddling" defeatism. He also distanced himself from the term "reformer," believing that it was used derogatorily as a smear technique.

Two area radio stations, **WCKY** and **WZIP**, provided live airtime or campaign speeches made in advance of the elections. Clark, in his formal opening campaign volley, promised that he had the will to crush gambling interests: "No group of individuals should be bigger than the law," he declared. Referring to the **Cleveland Syndicate**, which controlled illegal activities locally, he suggested that his opponent, James E. Quill, was "deaf, dumb and blind" to the conditions pointed out by the Kefauver Committee. Another reform candidate was Elmer P. Ware, who ran against Judge Daniel P. Goodenough.

In 1951 there were three elections that determined the fate of the CCKC. In the August 4 Democratic primary election, despite a heavy registration drive run out of the CCKC's Covington headquarters and a large voter turnout, both Clark and Ware were handily defeated by Goodenough and Quill. In a *Kentucky Post* editorial, the editors proclaimed that the "voters had made known their wishes." Meanwhile, the CCKC vowed to continue its efforts. In September, in the Covington primary city election, held on a rainy Saturday, John J. Maloney, backed by the CCKC, won the Democratic mayoral race against several candidates; his four running mates for city commission on the Peoples Ticket, also backed by CCKC, were also elected. In November of that year, Maloney defeated state senator Sylvester J. Wagner and Goodenough was reelected. Maloney and a few of his Peoples Ticket running mates were the only CCKC-backed people to win. Quill continued on as commonwealth attorney in the county. The CCKC simply did not gain enough political clout to enact its agenda.

In the end, the *Kentucky Post* suggested that the people of Kenton Co. were not yet ready for the reform that was needed. During the course of the year, gambling at various establishments throughout the county continued unabated, except when the grand jury was in session. There were several announcements of gambling activities taking place, but nothing seemed strong enough to motivate voters to throw out the gaming interests. Although the CCKC promised to continue its antigambling stance, several years passed before the cleanup in Kenton Co. materialized.

"Clark Will Oppose Quill in Primary," *KP,* June 11, 1951, 1.

"Covington-Kenton Committee Elects," *KP,* June 5, 1951, 1.

"Dispelling Defeatism by Votes, Editor Says," *KP*, October 8, 1951, 1.
"Maloney Wins Top Spot over State Senator," *KP*, September 24, 1951, 1.
"Policy Plan Is Drawn Up by Committee," *KP*, June 12, 1951, 1.
"Priest Seeks Tavern Warrant," *KP*, November 3, 1951, 1.
"Voters Made Known Their Wishes," *KP*, August 6, 1951, 2.
"Will Crush Gaming, Says Clark in Talk," *KP*, July 3, 1951, 1.

COMMITTEE OF 500. See **Newport Reform Groups**.

COMMUNITY OF FAITH PRESBYTERIAN CHURCH. In 2000 two churches, the First Presbyterian Church of Covington and the First Presbyterian Church of Ludlow, united to form the Community of Faith Presbyterian Church, which meets at 1400 Highland Pk. in Covington, near the Fort Wright city limits. Both churches have extensive histories dating back into the 1800s.

The First Presbyterian Church of Covington began in May 1841 when Rev. William Orr moved his school for girls from Charleston, Ind., to Covington. He offered to preach to the Presbyterians of Northern Kentucky who were making the difficult ferry trip across the Ohio River to worship in Cincinnati. By November of that year, there was enough interest that the Presbytery appointed a committee to organize a Covington church. A few months later, the First Presbyterian Church of Covington moved from two rented rooms to a building on Madison Ave. between Fourth and Fifth Sts. The next year, a larger church building on Fourth St. between Scott and Greenup Sts. was dedicated. In 1854 the church "colonized" by forming a second church in the southern portion of the city, at Ninth St. and Madison Ave. The pastor of the First Presbyterian Church at the time, John M. Worrall, achieved much during his 23-year tenure. He built a new church building with a 185-foot steeple at 34 W. Fourth St. (dedicated in 1870 and designed by the architectural firm of **Walter and Stewart**) and established churches in Florence, Visalia, and Ludlow. By 1932, three years into the **Great Depression**, the steeple was removed because it was too costly to keep it in good repair. Another blow came with **flood of 1937**. Five feet of water did considerable damage to the first floor of the church. "This sudden emergency was met with courage and sacrifice, and tended to increase interest among the membership," according to a centennial history of the church. By the 1950s, members were moving away from Covington; when the **Lakeside Presbyterian Church** in Lakeside opened in 1955, 23 members from the Covington church joined. On January 9, 1957, the First Presbyterian Church congregation relocated to a 17-acre site along Highland Pk. The Fourth St. property was sold to the U.S Internal Revenue Service and torn down in March 1963. Because it was close to Fort Wright, the church was often called the First Presbyterian Church of Covington–Fort Wright, but that never was its official name. The building was designed so that an education building could easily be added, and a second building was completed by March 1968. One annual tradition of the church continues at the Community of Faith Presbyterian Church: a community ice cream social. Initiated by the church's faith circle in the side yard of the Fourth St. church, it now takes place every summer at Highland Pk.

First Presbyterian Church, W. Fourth St., Covington.

The First Presbyterian Church of Ludlow was begun in summer 1867, when Worrall rented a meeting room at the Odd Fellows Hall (see **Independent Order of Odd Fellows**), 306 Elm St., for a Sabbath school. In October of that year, a congregation was formed. By 1871, when membership had increased from 6 to 35, the congregation had outgrown their space in the hall and moved to a site on Elm St. Two years later, fire destroyed their building one week after the insurance on the structure had lapsed. When enough money had been raised, a new church was built at 429 Oak St. and dedicated in May 1873. The **A. B. Closson** family, residents of Ludlow for many years, gave the church a parsonage at 421 Closson Ct. On the morning of October 20, 1959, a fire broke out in the education building at the rear of the church that damaged the sanctuary as well. State inspectors determined the fire was arson, but no one was ever charged. A new education building was dedicated in 1961. In 1964 a malfunctioning heating system caused water damage. Attendance was declining, and by the end of the century, only about 25 worshippers remained. In 2000 the Ludlow church merged with the Covington church to become the Community of Faith Presbyterian Church, with services taking place in Covington. The Ludlow facility is used for the Campus Ludlow After School Program (CLASP), the pride and joy of the congregation. It has become the glue that made the merger work, according to pastor Donald H. Smith.

"Celebrating 150 Years/Rooted in the Past—Growing into the Future: A Brief History of First Presbyterian Church, 1841–1991," Community of Faith Presbyterian Church, Covington, Ky.
"Community of Faith Presbyterian," *KP*, March 11, 2004, 10K.
Eigelbach, Kevin. "Flocks Move Away from City Churches," *KP*, September 10, 2002, 1K.
Reis, Jim. *Pieces of the Past*. Vol. 3. Covington: Kentucky Post, 1994.

Ann Hicks

COMPREHEND INC. Comprehend Inc. is a private nonprofit corporation based in Maysville that provides planning, prevention, treatment, and support in the areas of mental health, alcohol and drug abuse, and mental retardation and other developmental disabilities. It operates within Bracken, Fleming, Lewis, Mason, and Robertson counties; the organization is similar to **NorthKey**, which operates in counties to the west of these. Founded in 1967 under the leadership of **Harriet Cartmell**, Comprehend Inc. began functioning in 1969 as a licensed community mental health center. A board of directors, with members selected from each of its counties, directs the policy, planning, and governing of the organization, and the Comprehend services are carried out under the leadership of an executive director and a staff of 180. Outpatient counseling, day treatment, emergency services, psychosocial rehabilitation, residential services, and consultation and educational services are the main areas of its program. In the counties that it covers, Comprehend Inc. has service offices in Brooksville (Bracken), Maysville (Mason), Mount Olivet (Robertson), Flemingsburg (Fleming), and Vanceburg (Lewis).

"Comprehend, Inc." www.comprehendinc.com (accessed December 5, 2005).
Kreimer, Peggy. "Treatment Agency Seeks State Money, New Home," *KP*, August 5, 2005, 3K.

CONCORD. Concord, located four miles east of Falmouth on Ky. Rt. 159, was once known as Penhurst. It was a small town, with several businesses, a post office (opened in 1887), a sawmill, a telephone switchboard service, a blacksmith shop, and a church. Raymond Fields was the postmaster. The post office became a general store when the post office in Falmouth began rural route deliveries and the Concord post office was no longer needed. After the post office closed in 1903, the town became known as Concord. During the Great Depression, the town's general store closed. A sulfur spring well in Concord that is over 200 years old and more than 100 feet deep was known for its smell of rotten eggs. When a new bridge on Ky. Rt. 609 was constructed over the creek in 1982, the well was capped. The blacksmith shop in Concord had a great deal of business in its day. Sometimes the blacksmith also made wagon wheels and cutter plows. The business closed in 1934, but the building remains. The sawmill began about 200 years ago with a sash saw pulled by waterpower.

The Concord telephone exchange, one of the first in this part of the county, had 24 plugs. Users rang the operator, who then rang the desired party. The exchange operated for about 40 years, until a fire destroyed it in 1944. Afterward, the Bell System assumed management. The **Concord Methodist Church**, more than 100 years old, was used by both the Methodists and the Presbyterians until the Presbyterians moved to Falmouth in 1928. All that remains of Concord now is a church and a graveyard and a few homes.

Belew, Mildred Boden. *The First 200 Years of Pendleton County.* Falmouth, Ky.: M. B. Belew, n.d. [ca. 1994].

Rennick, Robert M. *The Post Offices of Northern Kentucky.* Lake Grove, Ore.: Depot, 2004.

Mildred Belew

CONCORD BAPTIST CHURCH. The Concord Baptist Church is in eastern Gallatin Co. on Ky. Rt. 16, Concord Rd., between Napoleon to the west and Verona to the east. It is built in the style commonly referred to as a white country church, with a cupola housing a traditional bell. There is a cemetery in the side and rear yards of the church. The grounds contain approximately two acres of land. Organized on September 4, 1856, the church first held services in the Lachere log school that was on the east side of Concord Rd. Soon needing more room, the congregation purchased a site across the road. The first building was completed in 1859 but burned down two years later, and another church meetinghouse was erected on the same foundation. In 1905 this building was considered unsafe and razed. The present building was built on the same site and dedicated October 22, 1905. In May 2003, the church was remodeled using the original woodwork and windows from the 1905 building, and a basement was dug under the building. There is a small addition in the rear that is used as Sunday school rooms, constructed sometime during the 1950s. The bell still rings calling members to the services.

Bogardus, Carl R., Sr. *The Story of Gallatin County.* Ed. James C. Claypool. Cincinnati: John S. Swift, 2003.

"Eye-Catcher of the Week," *KP*, January 7, 1994, 4K.

"Revival in Gallatin," *KP*, August 5, 1930, 6.

Judith Butler Jones

CONCORD COLLEGE. Concord College, located in New Liberty in northern Owen Co., was established in 1867 for male and female students. In 1869 it had an enrollment of 60 students from Owen and surrounding counties. Professor James Rice taught music there. Congressman and long-time Owen Co. politician and businessman **June Gayle** studied at Concord. By 1904 Concord College had closed, and its building became the home of the Stoute School.

Houchens, Mariam Sidebottom. *History of Owen County: "Sweet Owen."* Louisville, Ky.: Standard, 1976.

CONCORD METHODIST CHURCH. In 1800 some Pendleton Co. Methodists organized a church at Concord, four miles northeast of Falmouth along Ky. Rt. 159 in Pendleton Co. The families making up this group were the Harts, the Hendricks, the Hitches, the Lockwoods, the Mountjoys, the Steeles, and the Tulls. Before they had a church building, the people met in their homes or at the local school. There were no roads; worshippers arrived on foot or on horseback.

In 1844 Thomas Rush set land aside for the Concord Methodist Church building and cemetery. When he died in 1850, he was the first person buried there. In 1867 his land was deeded over to the church. Carpenter Henry Waggerman, for a cost of $100, took charge of construction of the church. Others assisted him, including Jeremiah Trankler, who sawed the lumber free of charge. There are no records stating that the church was a part of the Methodist Church's Falmouth Circuit in the beginning. The date of the dedication of the first church building and the name of its pastor are unknown. The first date in extant written accounts of the church's pastors is 1869.

In 1885, during the ministry of T. F. Taliaferro, the decision was made to construct a new building. Lee Hasrcuin and George L. Myers were the contractors. This church was a frame structure with its pulpit situated in the back, two aisles, and two front doors. In 1904 that building, its furnishings, and the church records were destroyed by fire, leaving the people of the Concord area without a place to worship. Church leaders soon called a meeting to plan a new church. Since the Presbyterians in the vicinity had been holding services in the same building for several years, the members of both congregations decided to build a union church. A tract of land across the road from the old church was purchased from John Kidwell, and the new church, constructed by both denominations, became known as the Concord Methodist and Presbyterian Union Church. The officials at that time for the Methodists were the Rev. E. L. Griffy, pastor, and Hayden Ellis and John Houchen, trustees; the Presbyterian pastor was Rev. T. C. Kerr, and N. J. Fields and Daniel Rush were elders. Edward Houston served as the head contractor for the project. Volunteers did most of the work, and the building was ready for use in fall 1905. This third church was a frame building, 38 feet by 44 feet, having a side entrance and vestibule, with an alcove at the rear where the pulpit was situated. The two groups held their own individual services at different times, usually on alternate Sundays. The shared use of the church continued until 1928, when the Presbyterians discontinued their worship services at Concord and disbanded. In 1953 the Methodists dug out a basement and made other improvements.

Belew, Mildred Boden. *The First 200 Years of Pendleton County.* Falmouth, Ky.: M. B. Belew, n.d. [ca. 1994].

Mildred Belew

CONFEDERATE RECRUITING IN OWEN CO. During the **Civil War**, Confederate troops were recruited at two locations in Owen Co., clearly demonstrating that there was sympathy for the Southern cause in the county. One of the recruitment sites was known as Vanlandingham's barn, a building only a mile and a half or so from Owenton on the Georgetown Rd. The 4th Kentucky Cavalry, CSA, was formed and trained at the farm where this barn was located. Each of the 10 companies in this Confederate military unit had Owen Co. men on its roster, but Companies C and F had the most local men. Confederate recruiting also occurred at a place called Camp Marshall. Named for the Southern general Humphrey Marshall, who established the camp in 1861, it was located atop a precipice near Lusby's Mill. From this height one could see the surrounding land in all directions. Locals who were recruited into the Confederate ranks here laughed, many years later, about how they struggled down the steep hill into Lusby's Mill for Owen Co. whiskey and afterward stumbled back to camp. The very existence of both of these recruiting stations not only reveals the Southern leanings of some of the residents of Owen Co. but also points to the county's remoteness, since the Union Army never sought to eliminate these Southern billets.

Houchens, Mariam Sidebottom. *History of Owen County: "Sweet Owen."* Louisville, Ky.: Standard, 1976.

CONGRESSIONAL DISTRICTS. Throughout the years, Northern Kentucky has been divided between a number of changing U.S. congressional districts, the result of redistricting. The population size of a congressional district is based on the U.S. Census. The census is taken at the beginning of each decade, and the Census Bureau takes a year to determine how many representatives a state will have; then in Kentucky, the state legislature, which holds its regular sessions in even years, has just enough time to redistrict for the congressional elections, which also occur in even years. The number of Kentucky representatives was 13 at its peak during the decade of the 1830s; the smallest number was 2, immediately after Kentucky became a state. Until 1933, Kentucky's congressional delegation was equal to or larger than California's. The number of representatives from Kentucky has declined with the westward population shift. The latest loss was in 1993, when it was reduced from 7 to 6. California's delegation now has more than 8 times Kentucky's total. See "Congressional Districts" table.

Many Northern Kentucky landmarks are named after congressmen. The most prominent is the **Brent Spence Bridge**.

Martis, Kenneth C., Clifford Lee Lord, Ruth Anderson Rowles, et al. *The Historical Atlas of United States Congressional Districts, 1789–1983.* New York: Free Press, 1982.

Robert W. Stevie

CONGRESSIONAL DISTRICTS

Congress	*Years*	*District Nos.*	*Representatives*	*Northern Kentucky Counties*
1788: Mason Co. (Va.) established				
1st	1789–1791	Second District of Virginia	John Brown	Mason
2nd	1791–1792	Second District of Virginia	John Brown	Mason
1792: Kentucky became a state				
2nd	1792–1793	Second	**Alexander D. Orr**	Mason
3rd	1793–1795	Second	Alexander D. Orr	Campbell, Mason
1794: Campbell Co. established; 1796: Bracken Co. established				
4th	1795–1797	Second	Alexander D. Orr	Bracken, Campbell, Mason
1798: Boone, Gallatin, and Pendleton counties established				
5th	1797–1799	Second	John Fowler	Boone, Bracken, Campbell, Gallatin, Mason, Pendleton
6th	1799–1801	Second	John Fowler	"
7th	1801–1803	Second	John Fowler	"
8th	1803–1805	Fourth Sixth	Thomas Sanford **George M. Bedinger**	Boone, Bracken, Campbell, Gallatin, Pendleton Mason
9th	1805–1807	Fourth Sixth	**Thomas Sandford** George M. Bedinger	"
10th	1807–1809	Fourth Sixth	Richard M. Johnson **Joseph Desha**	"
11th	1809–1811	Fourth Sixth	Richard M. Johnson Joseph Desha	"
12th	1811–1813	Fourth Sixth	Richard M. Johnson Joseph Desha	"
13th	1813–1815	Third Fourth	Richard M. Johnson Joseph Desha	Boone, Campbell, Gallatin, Pendleton Mason
14th	1815–1817	Third Fourth	Richard M. Johnson Joseph Desha	"
15th	1817–1819	Third Fourth	Richard M. Johnson Joseph Desha	"
1819: Owen Co. established; 1820: Grant Co. established				
16th	1819–1820	Third Fourth	William Brown Thomas Metcalfe	"
17th	1821–1823	Third Fourth	John T. Johnson Thomas Metcalfe	"
18th	1823–1825	Second Fifth Sixth	Thomas Metcalfe John T. Johnson David White	Bracken, Mason Boone, Campbell, Grant, Pendleton Owen
19th	1825–1827	Second Fifth Sixth	Thomas Metcalfe James Johnson Joseph LeCompte	"
20th	1827–1829	Second Fifth Sixth	Thomas Metcalfe Robert McHatton Joseph LeCompte	"
21st	1829–1831	Second Fifth Sixth	Nicholas D. Coleman Richard M. Johnson Joseph LeCompte	"

(*Continued*)

CONGRESSIONAL DISTRICTS

Congress	*Years*	*District Nos.*	*Representatives*	*Northern Kentucky Counties*
22nd	1831–1833	Second	Thomas A. Marshall	"
		Fifth	Richard M. Johnson	
		Sixth	Joseph LeCompte	
23rd	1833–1835	Twelfth	Thomas A. Marshall	Bracken, Mason, Pendleton
		Thirteenth	Richard M. Johnson	Boone, Campbell, Gallatin, Grant, Owen
24th	1835–1837	Twelfth	**John Chambers**	"
		Thirteenth	Richard M. Johnson	
1838: Carroll Co. established				
25th	1837–1839	Twelfth	John Chambers	"
		Thirteenth	**William Southgate**	
1840: Kenton Co. established				
26th	1839–1841	Twelfth	Garrett Davis	"
		Thirteenth	**William O. Butler**	
27th	1841–1843	Twelfth	Garrett Davis	"
		Thirteenth	William O. Butler	
28th	1843–1845	Seventh	William Thomasson	Carroll
		Eighth	Garrett Davis	Owen
		Tenth	**John W. Tibbatts**	Boone, Bracken, Campbell, Gallatin, Grant, Kenton, Mason, Pendleton
29th	1845–1847	Seventh	William Thomasson	"
		Eighth	Garrett Davis	
		Tenth	John W. Tibbatts	
30th	1847–1849	Seventh	W. Garnett Duncan	"
		Eighth	Charles S. Morehead	
		Tenth	**John P. Gaines**	
31st	1849–1851	Seventh	Humphrey Marshall	"
		Eighth	Charles S. Morehead	
		Tenth	**Richard H. Stanton**	
32nd	1851–1853	Seventh	Humphrey Marshall (resigned August 4, 1852), **William Preston**	"
		Eighth	John Breckinridge	
		Tenth	Richard H. Stanton	
33rd	1853–1855	Seventh	William Preston	"
		Eighth	John Breckinridge	
		Tenth	Richard H. Stanton	
34th	1855–1857	Ninth	Leander M. Cox	Mason
		Tenth	**Samuel F. Swope**	Boone, Bracken, Campbell, Carroll, Gallatin, Grant, Kenton, Owen, Pendleton
35th	1857–1859	Ninth	John C. Mason	"
		Tenth	**John W. Stevenson**	
36th	1859–1861	Ninth	Laban T. More	"
		Tenth	John W. Stevenson	
37th	1861–1863	Ninth	**William Wadsworth**	"
		Tenth	**John W. Menzies**	
38th	1863–1865	Fifth	Robert Mallory	Owen
		Sixth	**Green C. Smith**	Boone, Bracken, Campbell, Carroll, Gallatin, Grant, Kenton, Pendleton
		Ninth	William Wadsworth	Mason
1867: Robertson Co. established				
39th	1865–1867	Fifth	Lovell H. Rousseau	"
		Sixth	Green C. Smith	
		Ninth	Samuel McKee	
40th	1867–1869	Fifth	**Asa P. Grover**	"
		Sixth	**Thomas L. Jones**	
		Ninth	Samuel McKee	
41st	1869–1871	Fifth	Boyd Winchester	"
		Sixth	Thomas L. Jones	
		Ninth	John M. Rice	

CONGRESSIONAL DISTRICTS

Congress	*Years*	*District Nos.*	*Representatives*	*Northern Kentucky Counties*
42nd	1871–1873	Fifth	Boyd Winchester	"
		Sixth	**William E. Arthur**	
		Ninth	John M. Rice	
43rd	1873–1875	Sixth	William E. Arthur	Boone, Campbell, Carroll, Gallatin, Grant, Kenton, Pendleton
		Seventh	James B. Beck	Owen
		Tenth	John D. Young	Bracken, Mason, Robertson
44th	1875–1877	Sixth	Thomas L. Jones	"
		Seventh	Joseph Blackburn	
		Tenth	**John B. Clarke**	
45th	1877–1879	Sixth	**John G. Carlisle**	"
		Seventh	Joseph Blackburn	
		Tenth	John B. Clarke	
46th	1879–1881	Sixth	John G. Carlisle	"
		Seventh	Joseph Blackburn	
		Tenth	**Elijah C. Phister**	
47th	1881–1883	Sixth	John G. Carlisle	"
		Seventh	Joseph Blackburn	
		Tenth	Elijah C. Phister	
48th	1883–1885	Sixth	John G. Carlisle	Boone, Campbell, Carroll, Gallatin, Grant, Kenton, Pendleton
		Seventh	Joseph Blackburn	Owen
		Ninth	William Culbertson	Bracken, Mason, Robertson
49th	1885–1887	Sixth	John G. Carlisle	"
		Seventh	William Breckinridge	
		Ninth	William Wadsworth	
50th	1887–1889	Sixth	John G. Carlisle	"
		Seventh	William Breckinridge	
		Ninth	George M. Thomas	
51st	1889–1891	Sixth	John G. Carlisle (resigned May 26, 1890), **William Dickerson**	"
		Seventh	William Breckinridge	
		Ninth	Thomas W. Paynter	
52nd	1891–1893	Sixth	William Dickerson	Boone, Campbell, Carroll, Gallatin, Grant, Kenton, Pendleton
		Seventh	William Breckinridge	Owen
		Ninth	Thomas W. Paynter	Bracken, Mason, Robertson
53rd	1893–1895	Sixth	**Albert S. Berry**	"
		Seventh	William Breckinridge	
		Ninth	Thomas W. Paynter	
54th	1895–1897	Sixth	Albert S. Berry	"
		Seventh	William C. Owens	
		Ninth	Samuel J. Pugh	
55th	1897–1899	Sixth	Albert S. Berry	"
		Seventh	**Evan E. Settle**	
		Ninth	Samuel J. Pugh	
56th	1899–1901	Sixth	Albert S. Berry	"
		Seventh	Evan E. Settle (died November 16, 1899), **June W. Gayle**	
		Ninth	Samuel J. Pugh	
57th	1901–1903	Sixth	**Daniel L. Gooch**	"
		Seventh	South Trimble	
		Ninth	**James N. Kehoe**	
58th	1903–1905	Sixth	Daniel L. Gooch	"
		Seventh	South Trimble	
		Ninth	James N. Kehoe	
59th	1905–1907	Sixth	**Joseph L. Rhinock**	"
		Seventh	South Trimble	
		Ninth	Joseph B. Bennett	
60th	1907–1909	Sixth	Joseph L. Rhinock	"
		Seventh	William P. Kimball	
		Ninth	Joseph B. Bennett	

(Continued)

CONGRESSIONAL DISTRICTS

Congress	*Years*	*District Nos.*	*Representatives*	*Northern Kentucky Counties*
61st	1909–1911	Sixth	Joseph L. Rhinock	"
		Seventh	James C. Cantrill	
		Ninth	Joseph B. Bennett	
62nd	1911–1913	Sixth	**Arthur B. Rouse**	"
		Seventh	James C. Cantrill	
		Ninth	William J. Fields	
63rd	1913–1915	Sixth	Arthur B. Rouse	"
		Seventh	James C. Cantrill	
		Ninth	William J. Fields	
64th	1915–1917	Sixth	Arthur B. Rouse	"
		Seventh	James C. Cantrill	
		Ninth	William J. Fields	
65th	1917–1919	Sixth	Arthur B. Rouse	"
		Seventh	James C. Cantrill	
		Ninth	William J. Fields	
66th	1919–1921	Sixth	Arthur B. Rouse	"
		Seventh	James C. Cantrill	
		Ninth	William J. Fields	
67th	1921–1923	Sixth	Arthur B. Rouse	"
		Seventh	James C. Cantrill	
		Ninth	William J. Fields	
68th	1923–1925	Sixth	Arthur B. Rouse	"
		Seventh	James C. Cantrill	
		Ninth	William J. Fields; vacancy filled by Fred M. Vinson, 1924	
69th	1925–1927	Sixth	Arthur B. Rouse	"
		Seventh	Virgil Chapman	
		Ninth	**Fred M. Vinson**	
70th	1927–1929	Sixth	**Orie S. Ware**	"
		Seventh	Virgil Chapman	
		Ninth	Fred M. Vinson	
71st	1929–1931	Sixth	**Judson L. Newhall**	"
		Seventh	Robert Blackburn	
		Ninth	Elva R. Kendall	
72nd	1931–1933	Sixth	**Brent Spence**	"
		Seventh	Virgil Chapman	
		Ninth	Fred M. Vinson	
73rd	1933–1935	Sixth	Brent Spence	9 General Ticket Representatives
		Seventh	Virgil Chapman	
		Ninth	Fred M. Vinson	
74th	1935–1937	Fifth	Brent Spence	Boone, Campbell, Carroll, Gallatin, Grant, Kenton, Pendleton
		Sixth	Virgil Chapman	Owen
		Eighth	Fred M. Vinson	Bracken, Mason, Robertson
75th	1937–1939	Fifth	Brent Spence	"
		Sixth	Virgil Chapman	
		Eighth	Fred M. Vinson	
76th	1939–1941	Fifth	Brent Spence	"
		Sixth	Virgil Chapman	
		Eighth	Joe B. Bates	
77th	1941–1943	Fifth	Brent Spence	"
		Sixth	Virgil Chapman	
		Eighth	Joe B. Bates	
78th	1943–1945	Fifth	Brent Spence	"
		Sixth	Virgil Chapman	
		Eighth	Joe B. Bates	
79th	1945–1947	Fifth	Brent Spence	"
		Sixth	Virgil Chapman	
		Eighth	Joe B. Bates	

CONGRESSIONAL DISTRICTS

Congress	*Years*	*District Nos.*	*Representatives*	*Northern Kentucky Counties*
80th	1947–1949	Fifth	Brent Spence	"
		Sixth	Virgil Chapman	
		Eighth	Joe B. Bates	
81st	1949–1951	Fifth	Brent Spence	"
		Sixth	Thomas Underwood	
		Eighth	Joe B. Bates	
82nd	1951–1953	Fifth	Brent Spence	"
		Sixth	Thomas Underwood (resigned March 17, 1951), John C. Watts	
		Eighth	Joe B. Bates	
83rd	1953–1955	Fifth	Brent Spence	Boone, Bracken, Campbell, Carroll, Gallatin, Grant, Kenton, Mason, Pendleton
		Sixth	John C. Watts	Owen, Robertson
84th	1955–1957	Fifth	Brent Spence	"
		Sixth	John C. Watts	
85th	1957–1959	Fifth	Brent Spence	"
		Sixth	John C. Watts	
86th	1959–1961	Fifth	Brent Spence	"
		Sixth	John C. Watts	
87th	1961–1963	Fifth	Brent Spence	"
		Sixth	John C. Watts	
88th	1963–1965	Fourth	Frank Chelf	Boone, Campbell, Carroll, Gallatin, Kenton
		Sixth	John C. Watts	Bracken, Grant, Owen, Pendleton, Robertson
		Seventh	Carl D. Perkins	Mason
89th	1965–1967	Fourth	Frank Chelf	"
		Sixth	John C. Watts	
		Seventh	Carl D. Perkins	
90th	1967–1969	Fourth	**Marion G. Snyder**	Boone, Campbell, Carroll, Gallatin, Grant, Kenton, Pendleton
		Sixth	John C. Watts	Bracken, Mason, Owen, Robertson
91st	1969–1971	Fourth	Marion G. Snyder	"
		Sixth	John C. Watts	
92nd	1971–1973	Fourth	Marion G. Snyder	"
		Sixth	John C. Watts	
93rd	1973–1975	Fourth	Marion G. Snyder	Boone, Carroll, Gallatin, parts of Campbell and Kenton
		Sixth	John B. Breckinridge	Grant, Owen, Pendleton, and portions of Campbell and Carroll not in the Fourth
		Seventh	Carl D. Perkins	Bracken, Mason, Robertson
94th	1975–1977	Fourth	Marion G. Snyder	Boone, Campbell, Carroll, Gallatin, Kenton
		Sixth	John B. Breckinridge	Grant, Owen, Pendleton
		Seventh	Carl D. Perkins	Bracken, Mason, Robertson
95th	1977–1979	Fourth	Marion G. Snyder	"
		Sixth	John B. Breckinridge	
		Seventh	Carl D. Perkins	
96th	1979–1981	Fourth	Marion G. Snyder	"
		Sixth	Larry J. Hopkins	
		Seventh	Carl D. Perkins	
97th	1981–1983	Fourth	Marion G. Snyder	"
		Sixth	Larry J. Hopkins	
		Seventh	Carl D. Perkins	
98th	1983–1985	Fourth	Marion G. Snyder	Boone, Campbell, Carroll, Gallatin, Grant, Kenton, Owen, Pendleton
		Sixth	Larry J. Hopkins	Bracken, Robertson
		Seventh	Carl D. Perkins (died August 3, 1984), Carl C. Perkins	Mason

(*Continued*)

CONGRESSIONAL DISTRICTS

Congress	Years	District Nos.	Representatives	Northern Kentucky Counties
99th	1985–1987	Fourth Sixth Seventh	Marion G. Snyder Larry J. Hopkins Carl C. Perkins	"
100th	1987–1989	Fourth	**Jim Bunning**	Boone, Bracken, Campbell, Carroll, Gallatin, Grant, Kenton, Mason, Owen, Pendleton, Robertson
101st	1989–1991	Fourth	Jim Bunning	"
102nd	1991–1993	Fourth	Jim Bunning	"
103rd	1993–1995	Fourth	Jim Bunning	"
104th	1995–1997	Fourth	Jim Bunning	"
105th	1997–1999	Fourth	Jim Bunning	"
106th	1999–2001	Fourth	**Ken Lucas**	"
107th	2001–2003	Fourth	Ken Lucas	"
108th	2003–2005	Fourth	Ken Lucas	"
109th	2005–2007	Fourth	**Geoffrey C. "Geoff" Davis**	"
110th	2007–2009	Fourth	Geoffrey C. "Geoff" Davis	"

CONGRESS OF RACIAL EQUALITY, NORTHERN KENTUCKY CHAPTER. The Congress of Racial Equality (CORE), the national civil rights organization formed in 1942 that initiated nonviolent direct-action campaigns, organized four chapters in Kentucky (Lexington, Louisville, Richmond, and Northern Kentucky) during the 1960s. Through the use of negotiations, picketing, sit-ins, and other forms of nonviolent direct action, the Northern Kentucky CORE was successful in integrating all of the segregated businesses and facilities in the region.

In July 1960 the local chapter of the NAACP (National Association for the Advancement of Colored People) called a community meeting, held at the L. B. Fouse Civic Center in Covington (see **Elizabeth Fouse**), to voice objections to a "white only" sign still present in Coppin's department store at Seventh St. and Madison Ave. in the city. This sign hanging over the women's restroom had been in place more than 45 years, but the African American community, inspired by the emerging civil rights movement, now wanted to take action. At this meeting the group talked about organizing a picket line to protest the blatant racial segregation, but the NAACP, not having a tradition of leading picketing efforts, could not guide this community outrage into direct action.

CORE, invited by local residents to help lead a direct-action campaign, sent Joseph Perkins, the CORE regional field secretary, to organize a chapter in Covington. Forty community residents, 6 whites and 34 blacks, from Covington, Highland Heights, Newport, and Park Hills, Ky., and Cincinnati, met on November 29, 1960, with Joseph Perkins at the Fouse Center in Covington and organized the Northern Kentucky CORE chapter, which included Boone, Campbell, and Kenton counties. The first officers were Lucille Barrett, chairman; Janet Greis, vice chairman; Jean Embry, recording secretary; Barbara Cantrill, corresponding secretary; and Joseph Garr, treasurer.

The support of the L. B. Fouse Civic Center was critical to CORE's success. The Fouse Center officers, **Alice Shimfessel** and Bertha Moore, were members of the NAACP and also joined the local CORE chapter. All CORE chapter meetings and nonviolent direct-action training sessions were held at the Fouse Center at 309 Bush St. Another important ally for CORE was the Young Christian Workers (YCW), which had six members who joined CORE. YCW offices, located at 5 W. Fifth St. in Covington, were used as the staging ground for the CORE negotiations, pickets, and sit-ins in the downtown Covington area.

CORE Northern Kentucky members picketing the Liberty Theater, Covington, in December 1960.

CORE members were expected to attend meetings, share responsibilities, and most importantly, take part in direct-action projects. Proper training was a prerequisite before any direct action could take place, so that members would be able to handle themselves under any circumstance. Joseph Perkins conducted training sessions on nonviolent philosophy, negotiating, picketing, sit-ins, and other forms of direct action. CORE members were taught that the movement was a life-and-death struggle and that they could be jailed, beaten, or killed while acting for justice.

When CORE's first pickets began on December 3, 1960, Covington's police chief, John Bornhorn, allowed CORE to have six to eight persons on the picket line and to pass out leaflets. Later, the police department ruled that only two picketers would be allowed at any one time and forbade them to pass out leaflets because the leaflets constituted a litter hazard. The initial targets of CORE's direct action in Covington were the Woolworth and Kresge dime stores (see **Five-and-Dime Stores**), **Lang's Cafeteria**, McClure's Restaurant, the Mergard's and Dixie Lanes bowling alleys, the **YMCA**, and the Madison and Liberty movie theaters. By March 1961 CORE was able to integrate most of these businesses, plus the Coach & Four and Lloyd's restaurants. The YMCA and the Madison and Liberty movie theaters were the most difficult of all; these places required several months of picketing before they finally agreed to integrate.

In May 1961, when the Freedom Rides began, the local CORE chapter raised money for the Freedom Rides and picketed the Greyhound Bus Terminal in Covington in sympathy with the Freedom Riders. During the next year, CORE continued its direct-action campaign and was successful at integrating the facilities at the Gateway and Lamplighter motels, the Rosedale Pool, Devou Park, Pasquale's and Newport Bowling Lanes, and Wiggs and Robertson's restaurants. CORE negotiated to get African Americans hired by Sears and Roebuck department store; Albers, A&P, and **Kroger** grocery stores; the city government; JCPenney; Robert Hall; **Coppin's**; Goldsmith's; and the **Green Line** bus company. CORE joined with the Cincinnati NAACP to boycott the Coca Cola Company and the **Wiedemann Brewing Company** for employment discrimination. CORE also succeeded in getting the Northern Kentucky Dental and Medical associations to admit African American members.

The Northern Kentucky CORE was a small group of dedicated civil rights activists who received little support from the local black community, black ministers, and black business owners. The organization's work, however, benefited the entire community. CORE closed its chapter in Northern Kentucky in early 1963.

"Core to Meet," *KP*, January 5, 1961, 14K.
Embry, Gilbert. Interview by Jim Embry, May 15, 2004, Covington, Ky.
"Local CORE Unit in National Setup," *KP*, February 18, 1961, 2K.
Lonnemann, Joann, Ruth and George Miner, and Mary Paolucci. Interview by Jim Embry, June 10, 2004, Covington, Ky.
"New Integration Testing Planned," *KP*, December 5, 1960, 2.
"Officers Named for CORE Here," *KP*, December 13, 1960, 7K.
The Papers of the Congress of Racial Equality, 1941–1967, microform, Frederick, Md.: University Publications of America, 1983. Available at the Univ. of Kentucky, Lexington, and the Univ. of Louisville, as well as the Univ. of Cincinnati.
"Two Theaters to Be Picketed," *KP*, December 2, 1960, 1.

Jim Embry

CONNOR, JAMES "JIM" (b. November 14, 1922, Newport, Ky.; d. March 23, 1996, Fort Thomas, Ky.). James Robert Connor, who spent more than four decades coaching men's high school and college teams, winning roughly 1,300 games, was the son of Charles and Esther Sullivan Connor. He gained renown first as an athlete, playing baseball and basketball at **Newport High School** and helping the baseball team claim the Kentucky state championship in 1940, the year he graduated. His education was interrupted by service in **World War II** as a U.S. Army photographer; he landed in Normandy six days after D-Day. He played basketball at Villa Madonna College in Covington (which later became **Thomas More College**), completing his education degree in 1950. He received an ME (master of education) degree from Xavier University in 1955. Connor married Mary Meinken of Latonia in 1951.

Connor made his greatest mark as a baseball and basketball coach at **Newport Central Catholic High School**, where he began as an assistant coach in 1948. As head baseball coach from 1950 until 1966, he coached the Newport Catholic Thoroughbreds to Kentucky state titles in 1950, 1954, and 1956. His record was 322-113-3, not counting the 1955 season, for which no record is available. He also became the school's most successful basketball coach, compiling a 318-142 record. One of his basketball players, **Dave Cowens**, was inducted into the National Basketball Hall of Fame and in 1996 was named one of the 50 greatest players in the history of the National Basketball Association (NBA). Two other Newport Catholic professional athletes coached by Connor were Larry Staverman, who played for several NBA (including the Cincinnati Royals) and ABA basketball teams, and Jim Minshall, who pitched, though briefly, for the old Seattle Mariners. Toward the end of his tenure at Newport Catholic, Connor was assistant principal.

He next served as athletic director, head baseball coach (with a 71-65 record), and assistant basketball coach at Bellarmine College in Louisville, from 1966 until 1970. Then he coached baseball (achieving a 166-98 record, not including unavailable totals from 1972) and basketball (113-107) at **Boone Co. High School** in Florence, from 1970 until 1978. From 1978 until 1990, he served as athletic director, baseball coach (a 156-303 record), and basketball coach (133-235) at Thomas More College in Crestview Hills. One of his baseball players at Thomas More, **David Justice**, became a three-time All-Star in a 14-year major league career. Connor was also a part-time scout for several major league baseball teams. He was instrumental in the building of Thomas More's convocation center, which is named for him. Moreover, Connor built baseball fields at all four of the schools where he coached. His career totals, counting high school and college, were 564-484 in basketball and 699-568-4 in baseball, not including three baseball seasons for which records are not available. His younger brother, Neal, was the basketball coach at Purcell High School in Cincinnati for many years.

Jim Connor raised his family along Saratoga St. in Newport. He died in 1996 of congestive heart failure at St. Luke Hospital in Fort Thomas and was buried at Mother of God Cemetery in Covington. One of his sons, Terry Connor, followed in Jim Connor's footsteps by becoming Thomas More College men's basketball coach in 1998, adding athletic director duties in 2000. The elder Connor is a member of Newport Central Catholic's, Thomas More's, and Bellarmine's halls of fame and of the Northern Kentucky Sports Hall of Fame. The Kentucky High School Athletic Association, the Kentucky Association of Basketball Coaches, and the Kentucky Baseball Coaches Association have also inducted Connor into their respective halls of fame. In 2001 he was given a posthumous Lifetime Achievement Award from the Greater Cincinnati Basketball Hall of Fame. Newport Central Catholic High School presents an annual Jim Connor Award based on distinguished community service, and Thomas More College established the Jim Connor Scholarship Fund upon Connor's retirement in 1990.

"Funeral Today for Coaching Great Jim Connor," *KE*, March 26, 1996, B1A.
Kaiser, Rob. "Coach Connor Showed Way for So Many," *KE*, March 29, 1996, C1.

Neil Schmidt

CONNER HIGH SCHOOL. This Boone Co. high school was named in honor of the Conner family, who donated the land along Cougar Path in Hebron on which the school was built. Previously, the Conner family had operated a farm there for many years. Conner High School opened in 1970 with 32 faculty members, under the direction of principal Paul Hogan and vice principal Hillard Collins. That first year the school had 498 students enrolled in grades 10 through 12: 131 seniors, 173 juniors, and 194 sophomores. The new school offered many programs allowing for student involvement, including the Beta Club, Future Teachers of America, Men and Women of Conner, the *Capers* newspaper, the Health Careers Club, Future Farmers of America, Future Homemakers of America, Senior and Junior Tri Hi Y, the Language Club, the Pep Club, staff for the yearbook, and Student Council. A wide range of sports and extracurricular programs also were initiated: football, basketball, wrestling, baseball, boys' and girls' track, boys' and girls' tennis, golf, cheerleading, and a dance team. For the students who were musically inclined, both a concert band and a chorus were formed.

Since the Conner High School building was not completely finished at the start of the school year, classes were held for the first three months at the adjacent Conner Middle School. When the high school officially opened, it was necessary for the students to walk to and from many of the activities, including sports programs. The athletic facilities were not completed until February 1971; however, Conner High School, remarkably, won the district championship in basketball that first year. Jason Johnson, a 1992 graduate of the school, is now pitching in his 10th season of major league baseball. The right-hander has played mainly with the Baltimore Orioles and the Detroit Tigers and appeared in 215 games with a 52-86 record through the 2005 season.

Conner High School has grown considerably over the years and now has one of the largest high school enrollments in Northern Kentucky. It presently has 120 faculty members and a student body of about 1,600, in grades 9 through 12. Many improvements have been made to the campus, including the addition of two classroom wings, a new gymnasium, and an auditorium. The current principal is Mike Blevins, assisted by Todd Shupe, Mary Sargent, and Jason Shearer. Many of the same clubs exist as in the beginning, and the following activities have been added: speech teams, the art society, a Hispanic honor society, the Calculus Club, a media club, and the Technology Club. The girls' sports program has been greatly expanded by the addition of volleyball, basketball, softball, bowling, swimming, and soccer. Conner High School has won many athletic and academic awards and has produced numerous outstanding graduates. The school is also an innovative partner with the region's business and industrial communities.

Conner High School records, Hebron, Ky.

"Major League Talent—Hebron Native Jason Johnson at Home on the Mound," *SC*, September 11, 2005, 1D.

Yearbooks, 1970–2005, Conner High School, Hebron, Ky.

Sue Sorrell

CONRAD, CHARLES LAMONT. (b. April 24, 1888, Falmouth, Ky.; d. January 4, 1984, Louisville, Ky.). Charles L. Conrad was one of 15 children born to Frank W. and Emma Monroe Conrad. He entered the Academy of Carson-Newman College, Jefferson City, Tenn., in 1909 and graduated in 1911. He received his BA in 1915 and went on to Newton Theological Institution, Newton Centre, Mass., where he received a BD degree in 1919. He did a year of postgraduate work in the Divinity School of the University of Chicago in 1925–1926. Conrad was licensed to preach in 1906 at the little Short Creek Baptist Church near Falmouth and ordained on July 20, 1911. He pastored small churches during his high school and college years. While he attended Newton College, Conrad was assistant pastor of the Warren Ave. Baptist Church, Boston, Mass. In 1917 and 1918, he served with the French Army under the International Committee of the YMCA and was given a Bronze Medal by the French government. In 1919 he was appointed by the American Baptist Foreign Mission Society to serve in Jamshedpur, India, and then in 1921 was transferred to work among the tribal Pwo Karen in Bassein, Burma. On December 2, 1921, he married Ruth Zachery of Louisville, in the high school chapel in Bassein. They had five children.

Conrad's service in the Pwo Karen villages of the Bassein-Myaungmya Districts of Burma included evangelism, education, and health and welfare work. Between 1921 and 1949, when Conrad and his wife were forced to leave Burma because of civil war, the churches he supervised grew in number from 63 to 94 and in membership from 4,120 to 9,525. For several of those years, Conrad served as superintendent of a 500-pupil high school.

In order to deal with the multiple health needs of the children he served, Conrad also became a self-trained doctor. In 1938, while on furlough, he purchased two medical books and large amounts of medicine. Back in Burma, he examined villagers with medical problems, and his wife assisted by keeping records of all the patients he saw. Those who had ailments Conrad could not diagnose were sent to the nearest hospital. After examining 1,587 people, he returned to Bassein. He carefully studied the records, selected 21 diseases and ailments that could be cured without the aid of a doctor, and published a booklet, *Diseases Common to Our Pwo Karen Villages and How to Cure Them*. This publication was adopted by the Burma Christian Council in 1948 for nationwide use.

In 1937 the Police Department of Burma presented to Conrad a silver Swiss watch, chain, and medallion for arresting single-handedly two criminals who had murdered a Burmese man in front of Conrad's home in Bassein. In March 1942, during **World War II**, he was forced to evacuate Burma. His wife had already left for Calcutta, India, but Conrad remained as acting field secretary for the mission. When he had to leave in order to avoid being captured by the Japanese Army, he walked 171 miles out of Burma to India over mountains 8,000 feet high. He contracted malaria during this march but finally, after stopping at a hospital for treatment, rejoined his wife in Calcutta.

They proceeded to Karachi, India (now Pakistan), where U. S. Army officials begged them to undertake welfare work for both white and African American U.S. troops in the Karachi area. The Conrads organized two clubs for the soldiers, and Charles Conrad was made director of the troops in the African American club. He continued there until he was asked to open the U.S. Office of War Information and was appointed director of that office, with his wife as his assistant. The couple served in that capacity until they returned to the United States in 1945 on furlough. While in the United States, Conrad took a special course in New York City in government finance and administration and at the end of his training was to have been posted in Rangoon, Burma, as an administrative officer with the Information Service Office. But after he received letters from the Pwo Karens he had served, urging him to return to help them, he and his wife resigned from government service and went back to Bassein.

After his return to the United States in 1949, Conrad spent four years traveling throughout the nation as a representative of the American Baptist Foreign Mission Society; he then retired in 1953 to Falmouth. In fall 1953 he was hired by the Falmouth Farm Supply Store, a branch of Southern States Co-operative, and he remained in that position until the end of 1955. The people of his district asked him to run for state representative, and he was elected. In the legislature he took the lead in securing a lake and a state park for Pendleton Co. and the Northern Kentucky region. He had help in this endeavor from the directors of the Kincaid Park Development Association, an organization he helped organize.

Conrad chaired a committee that was successful in securing a new library building for Pendleton Co. Conrad was listed in *Marquis Who's Who* of 1959–1960, was made a member of the Honorable Order of Kentucky Colonels in 1959, and was treasurer and vice president of the Kincaid Park Development Association. He was a king in the Hauser Chapter of the Royal Arch Masons and was a member of the Falmouth Rotary Club, the Pendleton Co. Chamber of Commerce, and the Pendleton Co. Farm Bureau; he was also active in the Falmouth Baptist Church. After Conrad's first wife died, he married Emmaline Arnold Galloway in 1963. The last four years of Conrad's life were spent at the Baptist Home East in Louisville, where he died in 1984.

Belew, Mildred Boden. *The First 200 Years of Pendleton County*. Falmouth, Ky.: M. B. Belew, n.d. [ca. 1994].

Mildred Belew

CONRAIL. Conrail (the Consolidated Rail Corporation) began in 1976 as a result of the 1970 bill passed by the U.S. Congress that created the United States Railway Association (USRA) to plan the reorganization of the northeastern railroads. Because of the duplication in existing rail lines; an unfriendly Interstate Commerce Commission, which refused to allow railroads to consolidate and abandon unproductive railroad service; and the shift from railroad movement of goods to truck transport, all of the railroads in the Northeast by 1970 had filed for bankruptcy or were in the process of doing so. The New York Central Railroad (NYC) and the Pennsylvania Railroad (PRR) had merged in 1968 to form the Penn Central Railroad, but the reorganization did not save these two major railroads from bankruptcy in 1970.

The USRA recommended to Congress that northeastern rail lines be merged into one company and that the federal government finance its startup. Congress then created Conrail, which absorbed the Penn Central, the Erie Lackawanna, the Lehigh and Hudson River Railroad, the Lehigh Valley Railroad, the Reading Company, and the New York, New Haven and Hartford Railroad.

In 1987 Conrail became a private company, with its stock trading on the New York Stock Exchange. Then in 1997, following hostile takeover bids, Conrail was split into two parts: 60 percent of the assets went to the **Norfolk Southern Railway** (NS) and 40 percent to the **CSX** Corporation. All the former Conrail lines in the Cincinnati area were assigned to NS. Although Conrail had no lines into Northern Kentucky, its engines often were seen performing transfer runs between Conrail yards and the L&N DeCoursey Yard and **Chessie System** Stevens Yard, before the building of Queensgate Yard in Cincinnati.

Daughen, Joseph R., and Peter Binzen. *The Wreck of The Penn Central*. Boston: Little, Brown, 1971.

Drury, George H. *The Train-Watcher's Guide to North American Railroads*. Waukesha, Wis.: Kalmbach Books, 1992.

Withers, Paul K. *Conrail: The Final Years—1992 to 1997*. Halifax, Pa.: Withers, 1997.

Charles H. Bogart

CONSERVATION. Concerted efforts to protect and conserve Northern Kentucky's natural resources began in the 1930s, after the natural disaster in the panhandles of Texas and Oklahoma known as the Dust Bowl forced people to recognize a long history of abuse of the land. Programs to protect natural resources arose as part of the New Deal under President Franklin D. Roosevelt (1933–1945). The Soil Conservation Service (SCS), formed under the leadership of Dr. Hugh H. Bennett, began the task of educating landowners about the proper use of soils and other resources. By the early 1940s, each of the 11 Northern Kentucky counties had established a conservation district overseen by a local board of elected residents, and these boards were provided technical assistance by the SCS (now renamed the Natural Resources Conservation Service). The Kentucky Division of Conservation also works with each district, and the Boone, Campbell, and Kenton Co. conservation districts work closely with conservation programs of the Ohio-Kentucky-Indiana Council of Governments (**OKI**).

The Kentucky Department of Fish and Wildlife Resources maintains more than 8,000 acres in Wildlife Management Areas (WMA) in the Northern Kentucky region: the Lloyd Wildlife Center (see **Curtis Gates Lloyd Wildlife Area**) in Grant Co.; the Mullins WMA in Kenton Co.; the Dr. Norman and Martha Adair WMA in Boone Co.; and the John A. Kleber WMA, the Dr. James R. Rich WMA, the Kentucky River WMA, and the Twin Eagle WMA, all either entirely or partially in Owen Co. (see **Wildlife Areas in Owen Co.**).

The Kentucky Chapter of the Nature Conservancy purchased and preserved two unique areas, both in Boone Co.: the Boone Co. Cliffs Nature Preserve, approximately 75 acres of forest and conglomerate cliffs of Kansan glacial outwash; and the 107-acre Dinsmore Woods Nature Preserve (see **Dinsmore Homestead**), an old-growth forest on glacial slopes. These two preserves were brought into the Kentucky Nature Preserve System and thereby given further protection.

The four Kentucky State Parks in the region include the **General Butler State Resort Park** in Carroll Co.; the **Blue Licks Battlefield State Resort Park** in Robertson Co.; the **Big Bone Lick** State Park in Boone Co.; and the **Kincaid Lake State Park** in Pendleton Co. These parks maintain hiking trails, support passive recreation, and often host conservation meetings.

The Ohio River Sanitation Commission (ORSANCO) monitors water quality in the Ohio River and its tributaries. Various aspects of the river are monitored by the U.S. Environmental Protection Agency, by ORSANCO, and by local colleges and universities (see **Center for Ohio River Research**). The Hillside Trust is active in protecting the highly erodible hillsides of Cincinnati and Northern Kentucky. Other local organizations, such as the Banklick Watershed Council (see **Banklick Creek and Watershed**), work with local, state, and federal agencies to promote all aspects of watershed management.

During the late 1990s and early 2000s, a number of local conservancies (land trusts) were formed to preserve and protect lands that were significant locally but not of state or national interest.

Garner, M. M. *Conservation Districts: Their Origin, Development, and Functions.* Washington, D.C.: National Association of Conservation Districts, 1990.

William S. Bryant

CONSTANCE. Constance is a small town located along the Ohio River in the northeastern corner of Boone Co., opposite the outskirts of Cincinnati. Settled by people of German origins, Constance is named after the Rhine River city of Konstanz in Germany. Dolwick, Hempfling, and Kottmeyer are German family names still common in Constance. Popular farmers' markets, selling locally grown produce and flowers along scenic Ky. Rt. 8 near Constance in Boone Co., still carry these family names.

In 1817 George Anderson began the Anderson Ferry near Constance. It is today one of the few remaining **ferries** operating along the Ohio River. The post office at Constance was established in 1853 and closed in 1997. In 1868 a school was opened in a one-room building in town. In the 1920s, the school moved into a two-room schoolhouse, and in 1930 a three-room school was built. The Constance Elementary School closed in the 1970s, but the old school building still stands. In 1870 the Constance Christian Church was established; the congregation built a new building in the 1920s. In 1880, the town's population of 133 included four steam engineers, three shoemakers, two blacksmiths, a retail merchant, a butcher, a gardener, a wagon maker, a stone mason, a painter, a stock trader, and a rolling-mill worker. During the **flood of 1937**, floodwaters were 15 feet deep in the city and covered all the houses near the river. Most of the population moved to a shelter at the school because the school building sat above the flood's waters.

During the 1960s, owing to its location on the landing-path approach to the **Cincinnati/Northern Kentucky International Airport**, Constance was the site of three airline crashes: a Zantop Airlines cargo plane in 1961; an American Airlines flight arriving from New York City in 1965; and a Trans World Airlines arrival from Los Angeles in 1967 (see **Aviation Accidents**). These crashes led to construction of an elaborate approach lighting system at the beginning of the airport's Runway 18C, which connects to the air landing pathway above Constance.

For a brief time during the 1960s, it was believed that Constance would become a site for heavy industry following the completion and dedication of **Markland Dam** (October 12, 1963). It was rumored that entrepreneurs from Cincinnati were taking options in Boone Co. on lands in this "second bottoms" area with the idea of drilling for natural gas. The consensus was that because several small gas wells existed around Constance, deep test borings would locate an extensive natural gas field. Such speculations proved to be false, however, and Constance, no longer the busy river town it once was, has become a town one passes through on the way to other destinations. Nevertheless, hundreds of vehicles and passengers still utilize the **Anderson Ferry** daily.

In 1999, both the City of Florence and the Fiscal Court of Boone Co. contracted for water service with the Cincinnati Water Works. To deliver the water from Anderson Ferry, Ohio, to Constance, a 42-inch river tunnel was drilled and 3,000 feet of 36-inch pipe were installed. The Ohio River, which runs over a boulder-packed glacial plain, was a daunting crossing site for this project. Luckily, an area was located where glacial sand outwash (dense sand, gravel, and silt) overlaid the bedrock, and that layer could support the directional drilling process. Horizontal directional drilling began in September 2001 on the Ohio side of the river, and once the rig's reaming drill head had emerged at Constance, the steel water main was attached to the head and the drill rig then dragged the 3,000-foot pipe into the tunnel. A 2.5-million-gallon storage reservoir and a pump station were constructed at nearby Dry Creek to complete the project. The pipe pumps 30 million gallons of water a day and is the largest interstate water-transfer system in the United States.

Boone County Recorder, historical ed., September 4, 1930.

"Pipe Will Bring Water under River to Boone," *KP*, August 28, 2001, 1K.

Reis, Jim. "The Town the Ferry Built," *KP*, November 17, 1997, 4K.

Nancy J. Tretter

CONWAY, MILES WITHERS (b. March 2, 1753, Stafford Co, Va.; d. February 28, 1822, Mason Co., Ky.). Sometime before 1786, surveyor and sheriff Miles Withers Conway and his brother John (1757–1842) settled in Mason Co. Miles W. and John Conway were the sons of Capt. Withers Conway and Dulcibella Bunbury of Stafford Co., Va. Captain Withers Conway, having served as a captain in the Virginia Militia during the **French and Indian War**, was entitled to land warrants in Kentucky. The DAR lists Miles Conway and his brother John Conway as **Revolutionary War** soldiers from Spottsylvania, Va. Somehow the Conway brothers became friendly with the sizable Berry family clan in Frederick Co., Va. John Conway married Mary "Mollie" Berry, and Miles married Susannah, who was probably Mary Berry's sister. The Conway brothers' father-in-law was Joseph Berry, who was married to Mary Fairfax Berry, from the well-connected Fairfax family of Virginia. In 1787 Miles Conway filed a survey and patent in his name, using a 1785 Fincastle Co., Va., treasury warrant from Joseph Berry, for 637.5 acres along the Kentucky River in what was then Fayette Co. From the transaction sequence on these lands, it appears that this might have been a dowry or a wedding gift from Joseph Berry to his son-in-law Miles Conway. That land was not sold until after the Miles Withers Conway estate was settled in 1831, and by then at least 30 acres from the original tract was located in Owen Co.

In 1786 Miles Conway purchased several in-lots and became a trustee of the town of Washington in Mason Co. His house adjoined the courthouse lot, and Joseph Berry settled two houses down the street. Miles soon began work as a surveyor. Miles's brother John had purchased land along the Mill Creek southeast of Washington along with two of the six Berry families then residing in Mason Co.

Miles Conway fit easily into the class of people who became magistrates in Mason Co. He served on the first court as a gentleman justice and in August 1786 became district commissioner of the western side of Mason Co. Conway platted the town of Mayslick and was called upon by the

Virginia courts to resurvey disputed earlier land claims. He was elected sheriff of Mason Co. in 1790. In that capacity he had the dubious distinction of serving a warrant issued in Bourbon Co. for breach of contract and nonpayment of debt on Simon Kenton, the famed pioneer and Indian fighter, who was at the time a major in the local militia. Using uncommon judicial restraint, Conway, as the arresting sheriff, set a parole perimeter within which Kenton was to stay. The 10-mile diameter of the parole area took in the taverns located in Limestone (Maysville), Kenton's house, and Kenton's favorite hunting and fishing spots. Having shown such good and popular judgment, Conway was reelected sheriff in 1792 and, in the same year, was elected a delegate from Mason Co. to the state constitutional convention at Danville. At Danville Conway did a surprising thing. Although he was slaveholder from a slaveholding Virginia family, he voted with the seven preachers present to strike Article 9 of the proposed constitution. Article 9 did not go so far as to institutionalize slavery in Kentucky, but it permitted slaves to be brought into the state with their masters, and it provided for local governments to regulate slaves within their jurisdictions. The article passed over the objections raised, however, and Miles, in the end, signed the first Kentucky Constitution. The 1795 Mason Co. tax list showed Miles owning 6 slaves, 7 horses, and 20 cattle.

In December 1802 Conway and Henry Lee were appointed associate judges to the circuit court in Kentucky. Both men were well acquainted with the land-interference and criminal-mischief cases that dominated early Kentucky court dockets; thus they were uniquely qualified to assess the many overlapping claims brought into their respective courts.

Unlike most of the early surveyors in Kentucky, Conway was familiar with the use of new surveyors' instruments, such as quadrants and transits—that is, with the mathematical underpinnings of professional surveying. Sometime between 1802 and 1805, Conway wrote his *Geodosia; or, A Treatise on Practical Surveying,* which was based on Robert Gibson's *Treatise on Surveying,* a two-volume text that took its worked examples from English land claims in Northern Ireland; the second volume was entirely given over to log tables and to sine, cosine, and tangent tables. In May 1805 Conway took a simplified version of his work to Thomas Tunstall, clerk of the U.S. District Court, where Conway cited his publication as being "an act for the encouraging of learning by securing the copies of Maps, Charts and Books to the authors and proprietors or such copies during the time therein mentioned." By this action Conway applied a very early copyright protection for his surveying book. Daniel Bradford, the son of John Bradford, the pioneering editor of Kentucky's first newspaper, the *Kentucky Gazette,* published Conway's book in 1807 at Lexington. Recognizing that few frontiersmen in America had a sufficient knowledge of mathematics or owned the proper surveying instruments to apply Gibson's more exacting scientific surveying principles directly, Conway emphasized in his treatise a method called latitude and departures. Applicable chiefly to plane surfaces, this method required a compass reading of latitude and then establishing a grid of measurements of deviations from that latitude, by use of a compass ring and simple calculations. Obviously written as a guide for basic surveying in wilderness areas, Conway's book had only 64 pages and was smaller than five by eight inches in size, easily carried in a saddlebag or in the inside pocket of a greatcoat or hunting jacket. All examples given in the book were very practical and taken directly from Conway's experiences surveying in Kentucky. Conway died in 1822 and was buried in Mason Co.

Conway, Miles W. *Geodosia; or, A Treatise of Practical Surveying.* Lexington, Ky.: Daniel Bradford, 1807.

"A Few Facts and Events Surrounding the Town of Washington in 1786." In personal collection of Ben Lane, Richmond, Ky.

Journal of the First Constitutional Convention of Kentucky, Held in Danville, Kentucky, April 2 to 19, 1792. Lexington, Ky.: State Bar Association, 1942.

Kentucky Gazette, January 2, 1790; May 17, 1792; May 25, 1793; June 4, November 5, May 17, 1796; August 15, 1798; September 15, 1800; December 28, 1802; and March 22, 1808.

King, George H. S., to Rev. Melvin Lee Steadman, January 20, 1962. In personal collection of Ben Lane, Richmond, Ky.

Reed, Mrs. Stanley, to George H. S. King, January 15, 1962. In personal collection of Ben Lane, Richmond, Ky.; original in "Stations and Settlements and Preemptions in and around Washington," Virginia State Archives.

"Surveyor's Measurers," vertical files, Kentucky Historical Society, Frankfort, Ky.

Diane Perrine Coon

COOPER HIGH SCHOOL. Randall K. Cooper High School, part of **Boone Co. Schools**, is located at 2855 Longbranch Rd. in Union. The $42-million high school opened in August 2008 with 850 students, a response to Boone Co.'s burgeoning population. The high school is named for Randall K. Cooper, who served as the first principal of **Ryle High School** in Boone Co. from 1992 until 2006, when he died of a heart attack. Cooper High School, situated on 80 acres, can accommodate 1,000 students and includes 32 classrooms, computer labs, a media center, a band room, a choral room, a 400-seat auditorium, a gymnasium, a cafeteria, a football stadium, a football practice field, baseball and softball fields, tennis courts, and soccer fields. Its mascot is the Jaguar and its colors are maroon and gold.

Croyle, William. "Students 'Pumped' for Cooper High," *KE,* August 12, 2008, B1.

COPPIN, JOHN R. (b. December 24, 1848, Cincinnati, Ohio; d. December 21, 1913, Independence, Ky.). John Roberts Coppin was the second-oldest of the seven children of William and Mary Roberts Coppin, who were both of English parentage. Young John attended Cincinnati public schools, working summers as a bundle boy for the H. & S. Pogue Company. Aggressive and attentive to his work, Coppin became a department store head by age 24. Confident that he had sufficient background, he decided to establish his own dry goods business. The opening of the **John A. Roebling Bridge** in 1867, connecting Cincinnati to Covington, had spurred growth in Covington and prompted Coppin to move there. After pondering several locations, he leased space in a new building at 607 Madison Ave. on March 1, 1873, and opened The California Dry Goods Company (see **Coppin's Department Store**). Coppin weathered the financial panic of 1873 by arranging deferred payments with suppliers. Eventually, he became a depositor and stockholder in the German National Bank (see **People's-Liberty Bank and Trust Company, Covington**) and, finally, a director.

In Covington Coppin purchased a house at 115 (now 215) W. Fifth St. He married Elizabeth R. Egolf in 1875 and the couple moved into the Fifth St. home. They had four children. By 1880 Coppin's business had outgrown the small rented space at 607 Madison, and he moved it to larger quarters at 538 Madison. He found this a favorable location and in 1884 negotiated a seven-year lease with M. C. Motch, its owner, with an option to purchase. A few years later, he became owner of the property. When electric lights began to replace gaslights, Coppin had his store wired, becoming the first Covington merchant with electric lighting. By 1890 he purchased a lot behind Covington Savings Bank and Trust and erected a large two-story addition, which was connected to his Madison location. This gave his enterprise an additional entrance off Sixth St. After just 13 years of operation, Coppin employed 25 clerks.

Soon Coppin began buying acreage in Milldale (Latonia), then an unincorporated suburb of Covington. He acquired 52 acres and by 1891 had developed most of it into a subdivision called Lake View Park (now west Latonia). He built a large Queen Anne Victorian home on a hill (now 28th and Rogers Sts.) overlooking woods and lakes (presently the site of the Ninth District School).

Coppin's highly successful business made additional expansion a necessity. Several new locations were considered, but the property at Seventh and Madison proved most desirable. Coppin purchased that lot in July 1906 with $33,000 obtained with money he had won at **Latonia Racecourse** on a very rainy day; he had bet on a "mudder" with 100-to-1 odds. The California Dry Goods name had long since vanished, and in September 1907 Coppin incorporated his business as the John R. Coppin Company. The seven-story Coppin Building was completed in 1910, becoming the first reinforced concrete structure in Kentucky. Profits, however, were somewhat meager in the new facility, due partially to the tremendous building debt and the 1907 panic.

On December 21, 1913, while he was enjoying an automobile ride in the country with his daughter and son-in-law, Mr. and Mrs. C. C. Herrick, Coppin died of a cerebral hemorrhage. He was buried at Spring Grove Cemetery in Cincinnati.

"John R. Coppin, Sr., Pioneer Merchant, Died in Automobile," *KTS,* December 22, 1913, 1.

"John R. Coppin, Trade Prince, Dies Suddenly," *KP,* December 22, 1913, 15.

Coppin's Department Store, Seventh St. and Madison Ave., Covington.

Kentucky Death Certificate No. 32739, for the year 1913.

Lietzenmayer, Karl J. "John Roberts Coppin: The Family and the Company," *NKH* 5, no. 2 (Spring–Summer 1998): 1–15.

Karl Lietzenmayer

COPPIN'S DEPARTMENT STORE. After working for the H. & S. Pogue Department Store in Cincinnati, 24-year-old **John Roberts Coppin** moved to Covington to open a dry goods business. In 1873 he leased space in a new building at 607 Madison Ave. and named his new store the California Dry Goods Company. The store weathered the financial panic of that year and by 1880 had outgrown its limited space. Coppin rented a larger space nearby at 538 Madison Ave. from M. C. Motch (see **Motch Jewelers**). In 1884 Coppin negotiated a seven-year lease on this site with an option to purchase. By 1886 he owned the building. About that time, he purchased the lot behind the Covington Trust Bank (now **Huntington Bank**) facing on Sixth St. and erected a two-story building that connected with the rear of his Madison Ave. store, giving the dry goods store 13,000 square feet of space and allowing for $45,000 of stock. After 13 years in business, the company was employing 25 clerks. By 1903 the company's growth demanded more room, and it expanded into a rear alley, increasing the store's commercial space to 18,000 square feet; there was now room for $70,000 of merchandise. As continued growth required searching for a new location nearby, in 1906 Coppin purchased an available lot at the northeast corner of Seventh St. and Madison Ave. in Covington and began planning for construction of the first reinforced concrete skyscraper in Kentucky. The building was designed by architect James Gilmore.

The name California Dry Goods had long since disappeared, and the firm was officially incorporated on September 21, 1907, as the John R. Coppin Company. The officers were John R. Coppin, president; his brother William Coppin, vice president; and John's son J. Roberts Coppin Jr. and H. A. Schroetter, stockholders. Charles Clifford Coppin joined the firm in 1915, after the death of his father, John Roberts Coppin Sr. The 1907 panic delayed construction of the new building for two years, but by 1910 the seven-story Coppin building in Covington was completed. The store suffered with debt during this time, especially after 1913. In 1915 Frank Thorpe and Henry Sterne purchased 51 percent of the outstanding capital stock of the corporation. The company's officers in 1915 were Frank Thorpe, president; William Coppin, vice president; William Macklin (Thorpe's brother-in-law), secretary; and Harry Sterne, treasurer. Clifford Coppin resigned his position with the store in 1919, and William Coppin died while working at his company desk in 1923. Thorpe bought the outstanding stock of these two men as well as that of J. Roberts Coppin. This was the last year any Coppin family member was connected with the department store.

In 1920 the John R. Coppin Company joined Arkwright Merchandise Corp., a New York–based buying group. Arkwright was a merchandising service, which pooled the buying power of 125 stores by the 1960s, and the association enabled Coppin's buyers to keep abreast of fashion and market trends. In 1936 the entire store was remodeled. However, the **Great Depression** was a lean time for the company. Thorpe died in 1932 and management passed to William and Fred Macklin. Under the Macklins, the business became quite successful during the 1940s, 1950s, and 1960s. Aldens Inc., of Chicago, a leading retail merchandiser, bought the Coppin's Department Store in June 1964. Bryce J. Frankin, a Whitesburg, Ky., native, was sent to Covington to be store manager. By the early 1970s, Coppin's was sold again to the Gambles Department Store chain, also of Chicago. The 1976 erection of the **Florence Mall** in Boone Co. was an immediate commercial threat to downtown Covington businesses. One year after the inauguration of the Florence Mall, Coppin's Department Store closed permanently; eventually, other downtown Covington stores closed as well (see **Covington, downtown**).

"Coppin Store Buys 627 Site for Parking Lot," *KP*, December 22, 1955, 1.

"Coppin Store Remodeled in Modern Style," *KP*, September 22, 1936, 3.

"Covington's Downtown Business Is Slipping," *KP*, December 8, 1977, 1K.

"Era Ends as Coppins Winds Down after 104-Year History," *KP*, December 15, 1977, 23K.

Lietzenmayer, Karl. "John Roberts Coppin: The Family and the Store," *NKH* 5 no. 2 (Spring–Summer 1998): 1–15.

Karl Lietzenmayer

CORBIN, WILLIAM FRANCIS (b. 1833, Campbell Co., Ky.; d. May 15, 1863, Johnson's Island, Ohio). The friends of Will Corbin, who was executed during the **Civil War**, described him as a brave, noble, generous young man, enjoying a reputation of good morals and citizenship. He grew up on **Washington Trace Rd.**, near Carthage, in the southern part of Campbell Co., attended school in Alexandria, and, after graduation, taught school at California, Ky. With the Civil War on the horizon, Corbin told friends that he deplored war and the effect that divided loyalties would have on his family and friends. However, as Union Homeguard troops began patrolling Northern Kentucky, his thinking changed. When an informal company of men was being formed, Corbin joined. An election of officers was held, and he was elected a 1st lieutenant. On September 25, 1862, Corbin's company was sworn into the 4th Cavalry Unit of the Confederate Army. On February 20, 1863, Gen. Humphrey Marshall ordered Corbin and his friend **T. J. McGraw** to recruit a company of men from Northern Kentucky. While doing so, they were captured by a squad of Union Homeguard troops and taken to Cincinnati. Eventually they were placed in a military prison at Johnson's Island on Lake Erie, near Sandusky, Ohio. They were tried by a military court and sentenced to die. Upon hearing the news, Will's family was horrified. His sister Melissa traveled to Cincinnati to plead her brother's case before General Ambrose Burnside, who had ordered the executions, but he refused to stay his order. Undeterred, she traveled to Washington in an attempt to persuade President Abraham Lincoln (1861–1865) to spare her brother's life. The president refused to see her, but an aide said that the request needed to be in writing. She went to the pastor of Lincoln's church in Washington and asked for his help. A Rev. Sutherland was sympathetic to her cause and helped her compose a written request for clemency. The next day the pastor went to the Capitol and met with Lincoln, but the president refused to intervene. Heartbroken, Melissa returned home the next day, to await her brother's fate. In May Corbin and McGraw were executed by a firing squad. Their bodies were returned to Campbell Co., where they were laid out at the Corbin home. Will Corbin was buried in the family plot on their farm; Jeff McGraw was buried about a mile south, in the **Flagg Springs Baptist Church** Cemetery. Will's mother, grief-stricken, died within months.

DeMoss, J. C. *The Short Story of William Francis Corbin*. Privately published, 1897.

Dicken, Absolom Columbus. "Civil War Diary of Absolom Columbus Dicken, 1862–1865." Kenton Co. Public Library, Covington, Ky.; Campbell Co. Historical Society, Alexandria, Ky. Also available at the National Archives, Washington, D.C.

Wessling, Jack. *Early History of Campbell County*. Alexandria, Ky.: Privately published, 1997.

Jack Wessling

CORDOVA. Cordova, a community in the southern part of Grant Co., at the intersection of Ky. Rt. 36 (Old Leesburg Pk.) and Ky. Rt. 330 (Crooked Creek Rd.), became part of Grant Co. in 1827, when the Harrison-Grant county line was moved father south. One of the earliest families in the area was that of Jeremiah Morgan, who operated a general store there in 1858. He was the overseer of the

Leesburg Pk. and later served as justice of the peace and sheriff of Grant Co. The two-story Morgan home stands today, on a hilltop south of Cordova. The post office was established shortly after the **Mexican War**. It is said a soldier of that war suggested the Spanish name Cordova. The post office remained until around 1900, when rural routes were established.

Cordova became a thriving community with a schoolhouse and several businesses, including a sawmill, a harness shop, an icehouse, and a blacksmith shop. In 1846 Layton's Chapel Methodist Episcopal Church was established at Cordova, and in 1866 the Mount Pleasant Church of Christ appeared in town; it has moved since then and today is located along Ky. Rt. 36. Currently there is one business in Cordova, Henry's Grocery, which was started in 1900 by Edward L. Dunn. Owned and operated by Charles and Rita Henry since 1973, this grocery is one of the few remaining country stores in the county. The restored home of the Cordova physician Dr. Robert E. Limerick also survives. After graduation from the Cincinnati Medical College in 1885, Limerick served the area until his death in 1912.

Conrad, John B., ed. *History of Grant County*. Williamstown, Ky.: Grant Co. Historical Society, 1992.

Dunn, Shirley Limerick. "Morgans Settled Cordova Community about 1827." In *The Grant County Sesqui-Centennial Bulletin, 1820–1970*, Williamstown, Ky.: Grant Co. Sesquicentennial Publications Committee, 1970.

Barbara Loomis Brown

CORINTH. This settlement developed during the 1820s on the Dry Ridge Trace (now U.S. 25) at the southern tip of Grant Co. It was first called Mullinexville, after the first postmaster who received the weekly mail by stagecoach delivery in town. It was later identified as Corinth because the Corinth Christian Church had built a log church there in 1825. The church's meetinghouse was located in what today is the Corinth Cemetery, on the north side of Cordova Rd. between U.S. 25 (**Dixie Highway**) and the **Norfolk Southern Railway**. In 1869 a post office named Corinth was established, and David Williams served as the first postmaster. In 1873–1874, the Corinth Christian Church built a new meetinghouse on New Columbus Rd., on a lot donated by W. A. Million, where the present church building stands; at that time, the church's lot was partly in Owen Co. and partly in Grant Co.

In 1876 the Kentucky legislature transferred into Grant Co. a substantial section of Owen Co., which was identified as the Corinth and Keefer voting precincts. Until then, residents on the Grant Co. side of Corinth voted in the Cordova precinct. In 1878 Corinth was incorporated by an enactment of the Kentucky legislature stating "that a town by the name of Corinth . . . is hereby established . . . including the present village of Corinth to be known . . . as the Town of Corinth." The charter is unusual in that the corporate boundaries extended beyond one county, in this case into the northern tip of Scott Co.

Also in 1878, the Kentucky legislature chartered the Corinth Academy to educate children through the first eight grades and offer continuing education for a fee to persons seeking a teacher's certificate or proficiency in bookkeeping, foreign languages, higher math, music, or telegraphy. In 1906, when the Corinth Academy was separated from the common school district, losing the common school tax funds, the academy was closed.

Additional churches were established in town. The Methodist Episcopal Church South was deeded land in June 1881 by C. W. Hutchinson. It did well until the 1950s but, owing to loss of membership, closed its doors in 1970. The Baptist Church in Corinth was organized in July 1878 with 26 charter members, and a new church building was dedicated in 1895. The present church, large enough for a growing membership, was built in 1959. There were two churches, one Baptist and one Methodist, organized by slaves in the area, but no records exist today other than that the churches were operated by ex-slaves and their families until both closed before 1940.

Corinth has survived four disastrous fires, in 1890, 1904, 1914, and 1933. A positive step was taken in 1986 to minimize future damage when the Corinth Water District was created. Pipelines were laid serving the town and others in the southern end of the county with water from Williamstown's Water Purification Plant. Corinth has extended its corporate limits to include its I-75 interchange area, the existing tourist and traveler facilities, and the additional facilities that are being constructed there. In 2000, the population was 181.

Conrad, John B., ed. *History of Grant County*. Williamstown, Ky.: Grant Co. Historical Society, 1992.

John B. Conrad

CORINTH HIGH SCHOOL. Corinth High School in Corinth was one of the four high schools operated by the Grant Co. Board of Education in the early part of the 20th century. The school began in 1915 as the Corinth Graded Common School, an independent district that extended into Scott Co. and drew pupils and tax support from both counties. High school subjects were added each year, as needed. The Corinth High School's first graduating class was that of 1918, composed of Zelma McCord, Carl Northcutt, and Marshall Wright.

In the 1920s a new elementary and high school building was built in Corinth. The first students to graduate from the new facility were the class of 1926. The fame and memory of tiny Corinth High School was assured when, in 1930, its team won the Kentucky state basketball title. The last class graduated from Corinth High School in 1953. Thereafter, students were transferred to the new Grant Co. Intermediate School and **Grant Co. High School** at Dry Ridge.

The Corinth Elementary School continued to conduct classes at the Corinth school for students in grades one through six until the new Mason-Corinth Elementary School, along U.S. 25 (Dixie Highway) between Corinth and Mason, opened in 1991.

Conrad, John B., ed. *History of Grant County*. Williamstown, Ky.: Grant Co. Historical Society, 1992.

"State Cage Title Won by Corinth," *KP*, March 23, 1930, 6.

John B. Conrad

CORINTHIAN BAPTIST CHURCH. The Corinthian Baptist Church is the oldest African American church in Campbell Co. On February 24, 1869, the African American community in Newport, having established what was at the time known as Zion Baptist Church, was meeting on Eglantine St. near Cabot St. (see **Newport Barracks**). In July the congregation purchased a house for their worship services. They attempted to raise $1,000 by requesting donations from area Christians. In November 1872, Zion Baptist Church changed its name to Corinthian Baptist Church and Mr. B. Jones became its first pastor. In 1873 the church moved to a location on Roberts St. in Newport, with Dennis S. Lightfoot as pastor.

On October 24, 1882, the Corinthian Baptist Church purchased the First German Baptist Church building at Columbia and Jefferson Sts. In 1885 Lightfoot was replaced as pastor by J. W. Hawkins, and in February 1892, John W. Clark became pastor. After the George Wiedemann Brewery (see **Wiedemann Brewing Company**) purchased the property of Corinthian Baptist Church on Columbia St. for the sum of $2,000 in 1892, the congregation bought the church building formerly belonging to the **First Presbyterian Church** on Columbia St. near Fifth St. From July 1899 until 1902, C. P. M. Bigbee served as pastor. During that period, the District Convention of Kentucky Baptists and the National Baptist Convention were both convened at the church. A traditionalist, Bigbee regularly took new converts to the nearby Ohio River to be baptized, sometimes even when the river's waters were icy.

The **flood of 1937** did extensive damage to the Corinthian Baptist Church's building, which was later restored by the church members. In 1956 the Newport Board of Education sought to purchase the church's property in order to build a new school. The church fought against the proposed purchase but lost the subsequent law case, in which the court decided that the church had to sell the property to the Newport Board of Education for $23,000 and that the premises must be vacated immediately. The church eventually found a suitable new location at the northwest corner of Seventh and Saratoga Sts., and on April 2, 1958, the Corinthian Baptist Church's new building was dedicated.

CDG, February 25, July 1, 1869; November 25, 29, 1872; May 2, 1873.

KTS, December 19, 1956, 4A.

Theodore H. H. Harris

CORNELL, ANNETTE (b. December 8, 1897, Knoxville, Tenn.; d. July 9, 1986, Cincinnati, Ohio). Annette Patton Cornell, the daughter of James Patton, published her first poem at age 15. She began college at the University of Tennessee in Knoxville, Tenn., but completed her degree at the University of Cincinnati. After **World War I**, she married Dr. Josiah H. Cornell Sr., and they had four children. For many years the family lived on Virginia Ave. in Fort Mitchell.

Annette Cornell began her working career as a librarian at the East End Library in Cincinnati and soon began to write. Her poems and other writings, which appeared in several newspapers and national magazines, were known for their diverse themes, their versatility, their metrical arrangement, and their skillful use of language. She also had a program on WLW radio in Cincinnati during the 1930s, in which her pleasant voice was heard reading poems to families huddled around their radio receivers. She won a Best Writer award from the National Society of American Pen Women, and a governor of Ohio once tried to make her Ohio's poet laureate. She refused, remarking that she was "a Kentucky lady." She wrote society news for the region's *Kentucky Post* during the 1940s and for a time published a quarterly magazine of poetry. In all, she published five books of poetry. Cornell's varied works have contributed to the cultural history of Northern Kentucky, in both quantity and quality. In 1986, at age 88, Cornell died at Bethesda Hospital in Cincinnati. Her funeral was held at the Trinity Episcopal Church in Covington, and she was interred at Highland Cemetery in Fort Mitchell. She was the mother of Joseph H. "Si" Cornell, who wrote for the *Cincinnati Post* for some 44 years.

"Annette Cornell, 88, Poet, Writer," *KP,* July 10, 1986, 2C.
"Girl Writer Gets First Interview with a Poet and Her Notions Are Upset," *KP,* December 25, 1928, 1.

CORPOREX. Corporex, the largest locally owned commercial real estate developer in Greater Cincinnati, began in 1965 when William P. Butler, then age 22, started a construction company. From humble beginnings in Covington to offices in Cincinnati, Denver, Boston, and Orlando, Corporex, whose headquarters is in Covington, has developed more than 17 million square feet of Class A office and industrial space and numerous hotels. The company offers architecture, engineering, and construction in one guaranteed design-build service. Corporex is also the first to introduce the concept of the year-round family country club. The success of the Four Seasons Country Club in Crestview Hills has led to the development of the Five Seasons Country Clubs in Indianapolis and Chicago and in Cleveland and Dayton, Ohio, and there is a five-year plan to build as many as 30 clubs in the United States. Once the Five Seasons Country Club division reaches its development goal, Corporex will sell it at a public offering, just as in 2004 the firm sold the Eagle Hospitality Trust, a full-service hotel operation. With the development of the RiverCenter (see **Covington, Downtown**), Corporex changed the landscape of Covington and encouraged other local regional developments, including the **Northern Kentucky Convention Center**, the Metropolitan Growth Alliance, and **Forward Quest**. Corporex's other management properties and developments include hotels, the Baldwin office buildings in Cincinnati, and the 650-acre CirclePort Business Park located near the **Cincinnati/Northern Kentucky International Airport**. The CirclePort Business Park was built in phases and includes the Center for Corporate Learning, built by Corporex for **Northern Kentucky University**'s Metropolitan Education Training Services (METS). CirclePort Business Park is also the headquarters for such companies as G.E. Capital IT Solutions, the National Underwriter, **Toyota** Motor Manufacturing USA, and Wild Flavors. In recognition of extraordinary success in financial performance and personal commitment to business and community developments, president and CEO William Butler was awarded the National Entrepreneur of the Year Award in 1996. In 2004 Corporex launched the Corporex Select Hotel Company, intending to build as many as 40 select service hotels throughout the nation over five years. On November 16, 2005, Corporex broke ground on its newest project, the Ascent, designed by architect Daniel Libeskind, who also was the architect of Corporex's Museum Residences, located next to the Denver Art Museum. The Ascent was completed in 2008.

Corporex. www.corporex.com (accessed March 31, 2006).
"Corporex Reveals Plans for Covington Riverfront," *CE,* March 30, 1995, C13.
"Tuesday a Day of Celebration in N. Ky." *SC,* March 20, 2005, 5A.

Gabrielle Summe

CORPUS CHRISTI CATHOLIC CHURCH. Corpus Christi (Latin for "Body of Christ") was the first Catholic church in the city of Newport and in Campbell Co. While Northern Kentucky was still part of the Diocese of Louisville, priests from both Cincinnati and Covington occasionally ministered to the Catholic population on the east side of the Licking River. When Father Charles Boeswald was appointed in 1844 to care for Newport's small number of Catholics, he was offered land by a Catholic man on which to build a church. Both Catholics and non-Catholics assisted in the construction of a church, which was ready for use by June 1845, and Boeswald was the first pastor of Corpus Christi parish. In spite of having to struggle to pay off the debt for the church building, the parish managed to build a small school and a pastor's residence in 1848.

By 1853, when the Diocese of Covington was created by Pope Pius IX, Corpus Christi had increased in size, due primarily to a large influx of immigrants. During the pastorate of Father John Voll, the need for a more spacious church was obvious. A new Gothic style church was erected in 1854 and dedicated by Covington's first bishop, George A. Carrell, on Christmas Eve. A larger school was built in the 1860s. Corpus Christi and the St. Stephen Church, erected in 1854, were the two German American Catholic churches in Newport.

Damage to the Corpus Christi Church building during several floods in the 1880s prompted Pastor Paul Kolopp to relocate the church to a site farther from the river, and he purchased the property on the northwest corner of Ninth and Isabella Sts., where the current church stands. Bishop Camillus Paul Maes dedicated the new edifice, a combination church, school, and rectory, on October 4, 1903. The Sisters of Divine Providence took charge of the school from the Ursuline Sisters of Louisville, who had taught at the old school. In 1927 the parish constructed a high school. The high school was changed to a two-year commercial high school for boys in 1931 and then closed in 1933; the parochial elementary program then used the former high school structure. Newport Catholic High School (see **Newport Central Catholic High School**) used the building for a time in the 1940s and early 1950s, until its own building was completed.

With the Catholic urban population dwindling throughout the 1960s and 1970s, the Newport parishes found it difficult to maintain their own separate schools. The Diocese of Covington began in 1981 to study merging the schools, and in 1984, under the direction of Bishop William A. Hughes and the Diocesan School Board, the four Newport parishes (which included the St. Francis de Sales parish, established in 1915, and the St. Vincent de Paul parish, established in 1916) merged their school systems into one, renamed Holy Spirit School. In the shift of properties, the Corpus Christi School was abandoned and adapted to serve as a thrift store and food pantry.

The church itself, remodeled after a fire in 1974, continued to serve the parish as a house of worship. But because of a shortage of priests, as the pastors of the four Newport parishes neared retirement age, the Diocese of Covington decided it would no longer be possible to staff them all. In 1997 the four churches were merged into a single parish called Holy Spirit, headed by a single pastor, but with each of the four churches remaining as "missions." Then in 2000 the four missions were merged. Of the four buildings, St. Stephen Church was designated as the one to be used for the Holy Spirit parish, with Father Richard Bolte as pastor. The other three churches, including Corpus Christi, were relegated to secular uses. The Corpus Christi church has since been renovated into apartments for senior citizens.

"Fire Cripples Newport Parish," *Messenger,* January 27, 1974, 1A.
The First Century of Corpus Christi Church, Newport, Kentucky. Newport, Ky.: Vesper Print, 1944.
"Newport to Become One Parish, Four Missions," *Messenger,* April 25, 1997, 1.
Ryan, Paul E. *History of the Diocese of Covington, Kentucky.* Covington, Ky.: Diocese of Covington, 1954.
Tenkotte, Paul A., David E. Schroeder, and Thomas S. Ward. *To Be Catholic and American in Northern, Central, and Appalachian Kentucky: The Diocese of Covington, 1853–2003.* Forthcoming.

Thomas S. Ward

CORWINE, AARON H. (b. August 31, 1802, Maysville, Ky.; d. July 4, 1830, Philadelphia, Pa.). Aaron Houghton Corwine, a renowned Romantic-period portraitist, was the youngest of six children born to Amos and Sarah Brook Corwine. Aaron

Corwine's fame grew after he died at age 28, at the peak of his decade-long career as an artist. Historian **Lewis Collins** said of Corwine that he had much "character" and would have reached the "head of his profession," had he lived longer. At age 10 Aaron painted his father's farm fence with "grotesque figures of men, beasts, and fowls." His father was impressed with the artistic display and decided his son would make a better artist than a farmer. Corwine was first tutored in Kentucky by an itinerant artist named J. T. Turner and then went to Cincinnati in 1818, with a letter of introduction to another former Mason Co. resident, famed Cincinnati surgeon Dr. **Daniel Drake**. Corwine pursued his craft as an artist and subsequently was sent by Drake and some other sponsors to Philadelphia, Pa., to study under the renowned American painter Thomas Sully. When Corwine returned to Cincinnati in 1820, he was the city's premier portraitist; only portrait artist Matthew Jouett had a similar reputation in what was then considered the West. Among Corwine's subjects were **Simon Kenton**, Andrew Jackson, and the general Marquis de Lafayette, who, because he did not have time to sit for a portrait, had to be painted by Corwine while the general was a passenger aboard the Ohio River steamboat the *Herald*. Successful commissions and exhibitions allowed Corwine to travel to London, England, for further studies and for his health. His moneys were lost when a trusted banker went bankrupt, but Corwine was able to continue his studies by visiting art galleries. He applied what he learned, and a self-portrait in the collection of the **Kentucky Gateway Museum Center** in Maysville, painted in 1829, demonstrates his ever-improving skill. It shows a handsome young man with tousled hair, wearing a coat with a fur lining; the artist bears a thoughtful expression and seems as if he is looking over the viewer's shoulder. Corwine's energy, youth, and promise were a metaphor for the expanding West. The 1829 self-portrait has those same combined features, although Corwine was ill at the time from the tuberculosis that killed him the next year. He died in Philadelphia on July 4, 1830, at the home of his cousins, as he was making his way home to Maysville from England. His place of burial is unknown.

AskArt. "Aaron Corwine." www.askart.com (accessed September 22, 2006).

Collins, Richard H. *History of Kentucky*. Vol. 1. Covington, Ky.: Collins, 1882.

Dwight, Edward. "A Cincinnati Artist: Aaron H. Corwine," *Bulletin of the Philosophical and Historical Society of Ohio* 17, no. 2 (April 1959): 103–8.

The Golden Age: Cincinnati Painters of the Nineteenth Century Represented in the Cincinnati Art Museum. Cincinnati: Cincinnati Art Museum, 1979.

Vitz, Robert C. *The Queen and the Arts: Cultural Life in Nineteenth-Century Cincinnati*. Kent, Ohio: Kent State Univ. Press, 1989.

John Klee

COTE BRILLIANTE. This southeastern Newport neighborhood was incorporated as a fifth-class city by the Kentucky legislature in July 1888. The area was developed by **Samuel Bigstaff** and his cartel of investors and named Cote Brilliante ("shining hill" in French) after a topographically similar section of St. Louis, Mo. Cote Brilliante and the adjacent subdivision of Ingalls Park were annexed into the city of Newport during the mid-1920s with the standard promise of city services. Originally, both were planned as commuter suburbs with convenient access to the **Chesapeake and Ohio Railroad** trains to Cincinnati. Small building lots (40 by 175 feet) sold for $300 with payments of $1 per week and no interest. Cote Brilliante generally consisted of Park Ave. and Vine St., south of E. 10th St. up and over the hill to Grand Ave. Ingalls Park was mainly E. 10th St. (east of Vine St.) and Grand, Chesapeake, and Ohio Aves. Ingalls Park derived its name from Melville Ezra Ingalls, the subdivision's financial backer and longtime president of the C&O Railroad. Ingalls Park has generally been thought of as part of Cote Brilliante.

Grand Ave., the major thoroughfare, was named for the Grand Army of the Republic even though Bigstaff was a Confederate. In 1888 it began as the Grand Ave. Turnpike, a toll road until 1922 (see **Turnpikes, Campbell Co.**), built to provide quick travel to the U.S. Army installation in the District of the Highlands (Fort Thomas). With its 50-foot-wide right-of-way through Cote Brilliante, the turnpike when new was a very modern road. Not all of the potential home sites in these two subdivisions were built on, as evidenced by the wooded areas that remained among the established homes. In the 1890s, when the lots first went on sale, the impact of the automobile and streetcars on people's lifestyle could not have been foreseen. Home seekers soon found that they could easily leapfrog over Cote Brilliante for properties in the higher elevations farther south.

The two focal points of the neighborhood were the Cote Brilliante School, built in 1896 at the corner of Park and Grand Aves. (see **Campbell Co. Public Schools**), and the **St. Francis de Sales Catholic Church**, built in 1912 at the corner of Chesapeake and Grand Aves. The neighborhood had a few saloons and small food stores, and later a city playground was laid out in the bottoms of Duck Creek. Early on there were brickyards, one on Vine St. at Center St. and another on Reservoir Rd. (Water Works Rd.) near the beginning of Grand. In recent years, the Raaker Tire Company has stood its ground at the entrance to Cote Brilliante at the railroad bridge at E. 10th and Park. That bridge, which clearly needed to be replaced as early as the mid-1950s, finally was rebuilt in 2004.

In 1895 Newport brewer George Wiedemann's widow Alice and son Charles moved into their new mansion, designed by **Samuel Hannaford**, at 1102 Park Ave. This was the most impressive structure in Cote Brilliante, and the Wiedemanns were its most affluent and influential residents. Lavish parties took place at their home during the first three decades of the 20th century. The grounds often overflowed with partygoers enjoying the first private in-ground swimming pool in Northern Kentucky as well as the shuffleboard and tennis courts. This was the boyhood home of Charles Wiedemann's son Carl, a football letterman at Yale, a felon, a horseman, and a general all-around bon vivant. In spring 1951 the Wiedemann heirs sold the 15-room, six-acre estate to the Diocese of Covington, and Bishop **William T. Mulloy** lived there for a time beginning in summer 1951.

Once annexed, the neighborhood lingered as an isolated, neglected, and forgotten outpost of Newport. After the **flood of 1937**, the Newport School Board tried to close the Cote Brilliante School. The strong protest of residents succeeded in keeping its doors open until 1961, when it was replaced by the new Mildred Dean School located farther south on Grand Ave.

The 1940s saw several Cote Brilliante boys go off to war; a few never returned, and their lives were commemorated on the monument in front of the St. Francis de Sales Church. During **World War II**, the St. Francis community published the *Hot Dawg*, a newsletter for the entire population of the area, keeping residents informed about the comings and goings of their military personnel.

The 1950s witnessed other changes to the landscape. The hilltop between Vine St. and Grand Ave. was leveled in 1954 in preparation for the proposed construction of the **WXIX**-TV (Channel 19) studio and tower. The station was not built, but today about 50 posh townhomes occupy the site, capturing its spectacular view. A Cleveland developer in 1956 opened the **Newport Shopping Center**, the first of its type in Northern Kentucky, just to the southwest. **Newport Central Catholic High School** moved into its new building on the hill behind the Wiedemann estate in 1955. In the late 1950s, one of the last major public improvements was made to Cote Brilliante, when the state rebuilt Grand Ave. south beginning at Carothers Rd. The new four-lane highway straightened Grand Ave. while providing easier access to the new **St. Luke Hospital** along the road at the Newport–Fort Thomas boundary. Harper Construction built the highway, using new concrete paving equipment that greatly expedited the project.

The most famous day in the history of Cote Brilliante was Thursday, October 6, 1960, when John F. Kennedy, a Massachusetts senator, came to 1168 Park Ave., the home of Mrs. Alvin Steil. His presidential campaign had brought him to Cincinnati, and he took time to visit this **World War II** Gold Star mother. Students from both grade schools were dismissed early to see the candidate for president, and some shook his hand. Afterward, his entourage traveled down Park Ave. to the Cote Brilliante School, where he met with its Mothers' Club. The visit ended as quickly as it began, and Kennedy rode off into the afternoon sun in his black Lincoln Town Car convertible, waving to an enthusiastic crowd.

In the 1980s, the long-awaited I-471 was completed, taking out some of the best housing stock in Newport along Lorain Ct., Water Works Rd., and Chesapeake, Ohio, and Grand Aves. This only isolated Cote Brilliante even more. Cote Brilliante continued to lose population as more owner-occupied dwellings turned into rental units and as the demographic shift to southern Campbell and Kenton counties contributed to what the city of

Newport referred to as "blight." The St. Francis de Sales Catholic Church closed in 1997. By spring 2004, the City of Newport had bought and torn down some 90 homes in the southern half of the area, and in April of that year the city purchased the St.Francis property, hoping to attract high-end developers desiring to capitalize on the highly visible open area along the west side of I-471 for commercial development. Some residents chose to fight the city's heavy-handed plans, and in return, the city threatened to use eminent domain. In spring 2007 the St. Francis buildings were torn down, as were the homes of the five hold-out owners who fought the city's plans; in the summer of 2007, construction began on the new Pavilion shopping development (still under construction in 2008).

Long gone are the Cote Brilliante School, the city park, and the St. Francis de Sales Catholic Church. The Wiedemann house, now short-term executive housing, is surrounded by trendy condominiums with skyline views. The "woods" where young boys once played are the sites of luxurious housing communities. It has taken almost 110 years for Bigstaff's shining hill to be noticed, and few remain who remember what a solid and substantial neighborhood it once was.

"Bishop Mulloy to Move Home to Newport Estate," *KTS*, June 15, 1951, 1.

"Cote Brilliante Church Dedicated," *KP*, October 14, 1912, 2.

"Ky House Passes Bill Incorporating Village," *KSJ*, March 15, 1888, 4.

"$1 Million Grand-Av. Work Near," *KP*, October 13, 1958, 1.

"Transferred Pike," *KP*, July 22, 1922, 1.

Michael R. Sweeney

COTTON MILLS. By the mid-19th century, Northern Kentucky had several cotton mills, to which cotton grown in the southern states was shipped on steamboats via the Ohio River. The cotton companies, which included substantial mills, spun cotton into yarns, twine, and small cordage and wove it into cloth. These mills helped furnish the Northern Kentucky market with needed goods.

Kentucky historian **Lewis Collins** reported one cotton factory in Campbell Co. in 1847. Benjamin Clifford Jr., Darius B. Holbrook, S. R. M. Holbrook, **James Taylor Jr.**, James Taylor Sr., Isaiah Thomas, John W. Tibbatts, and William M. Walker incorporated the Newport Manufacturing Company on November 26, 1831. By 1836 this company's extensive operations included a cotton factory, a woolen factory, a hemp mill, and other endeavors; the company employed 329 individuals. A story in the January 9, 1836, edition of the local *Daily Evening Post* reported that the company had "fifty power looms for the manufacture of Kentucky jeans, linseys, and cotton plains . . . and the necessary auxiliary machinery for the manufacture of cotton bagging, by steam power."

The June 17, 1854, edition of the *Covington Journal* carried a story that Thomas O'Shaughnessy's Newport Cotton Mill was destroyed by fire. It is not known whether O'Shaughnessy's mill was a successor to the Newport Manufacturing Company or whether he established a later cotton mill. Also, Robert Warring operated a cotton batting factory located at the northwest corner of Eglantine and E. Row Sts. in Newport.

In 1829 the Covington Cotton Manufacturing Company was incorporated. The new company manufactured cloth out of wool, cotton, silk, flax, and hemp. The incorporators were listed as Robert Buckhannon, Charles MacAlister Jr., Edward MacAlister, William Whitehead, Edward Yorke, and William Yorke. By 1831, their four-story structure was equipped with 2,288 spindles (1,600 in use with plans for operating the others in a few weeks), and 60 hands were employed to produce 4,000 pounds of cotton yarn daily. Plans were under way in 1831 to add 20 additional employees to enable the company to produce 6,000 yards of cloth per week. In 1872 Brooks, Kellogg, and Walsh of Cincinnati bought the old cotton-mill property and planned to build a distillery on the riverfront (see **Walsh Distillery**).

The Argonaut Cotton Mill Company was located at the southeast corner of Second St. and Madison Ave., in Covington. By late 1915, the mill had closed.

Some additional references to the cotton industry in Covington were found for the period between 1872 and 1929. In 1894 a new cotton mill (Putnam, Hooker & Company) was opened in Ludlow. The R. T. Pearce Company in Covington operated at 16 E. Pike St. between 1920 and 1923 and at 515 Scott St. between 1923 and 1929.

The December 19, 1827, issue of the *Maysville Eagle* contained an ad placed by J. C. DeWees for his new Cotton Factory in Maysville. His cotton-spinning business, it was said, was equipped with new machinery that could produce yarns "equal to any made in the country." These yarns were available through William Tinker of Maysville at factory prices. The firm of Duke & Davis had formerly used the cotton factory.

The best-documented and longest-surviving cotton mill in Northern Kentucky is **January and Wood** in Maysville. William Shotwell built the cotton mill in 1834, and in 1851 Andrew January and Benjamin W. Wood bought the company, renaming it January and Wood.

The Acts of Kentucky for 1837 included the articles of incorporation for the Mason County Hemp Manufacturing Company. This company processed cotton as well as other raw materials. The incorporators included Robert Blanchard, Thomas Forman, Richard Lee, Isaac Lewis, William Mackey, John M. Morton, Christian Shultz, and Andrew Woods. Collins also reported two steam cotton factories in Mason Co.

Another Maysville company that processed some cotton was the Maysville Linen Company. R. T. Blanchard, John Chambers, Richard Collins, Henry Cutter, Thomas Foreman, James Jacobs, Charles A. Marshall, H. R. Reader, A. C. Respass, Dudley Richardson, James Robinson, R. H. Stanton, William Stillwell, and W. R. Wood incorporated the company.

Bodley, Temple. *History of Kentucky: The Blue Grass State.* Vol. 4. Chicago: S. J. Clarke, 1928.

Collins, Richard H. *History of Kentucky.* Vol. 1. Covington, Ky.: Collins, 1882.

Connelley, William Elsey, and E. M. Coulter. *History of Kentucky.* 5 vols. Chicago: American Historical Society, 1922.

Daily Independent. *The Spirit of a Greater Maysville and Mason County.* Maysville, Ky.: Daily Independent, 1935.

Smith, Allen Webb. *Beginning at "the Point": A Documented History of Northern Kentucky and Environs, the Town of Covington in Particular, 1751–1834.* Park Hills, Ky.: Smith, 1977.

Tenkotte, Paul A. "Rival Cities to Suburbs: Covington and Newport, Kentucky, 1790–1890," PhD diss., Univ. of Cincinnati, 1989.

Thompson, Charles. *Going on 200: Century-Old Businesses in Kentucky.* Prospect, Ky.: Harmony House, 2003.

Charles D. Hockensmith

COUNTRY MUSIC. Country music is a popular folk music of the rural South originally called hillbilly music. Derived from traditional folk music brought by English and Scots-Irish settlers to the American South, it evolved upon contact with **blues**, cajon, Celtic, gospel, minstrel, and old-time music; sentimental ballads; and other ethnic musical types. It eventually blended with urban music, such as vaudeville and Tin Pan Alley, as country music rapidly became popular in the 1920s via commercial recordings and **radio** broadcasts. The term *country and western music* was introduced during the 1940s when the earlier name *hillbilly music* came to be considered demeaning. By the 1970s, the simpler title *country* alone was applied as the genre gained a mainstream international following. Although there are many kinds of country music, the more traditional folk, old-time, and **bluegrass** sounds are most often associated with the tri-state region of Indiana, Kentucky, and Ohio, owing to its proximity to the South.

Beginning in the late 1930s, residents of Northern Kentucky tuned in to live radio broadcasts originating from Cincinnati's "Nation's Station," WLW, such as the *Renfro Valley Barn Dance* and the long-running ***Boone County Jamboree*** (later renamed *Midwestern Hayride* as it transitioned to television in the late 1940s). At the same time, a significant number of rural Kentuckians and **Appalachians** were migrating to Covington and Newport and to Cincinnati and Norwood, Ohio, seeking high-paying factory jobs. These migrants created storefront churches and honky-tonks, which, along with the *Boone County Jamboree* and King Records, helped Cincinnati and Northern Kentucky become a capital of country music and bluegrass, even surpassing Nashville during this period.

The legendary King Records of Cincinnati, as well as other independent labels dedicated to the country sound, targeted this music genre very effectively to record buyers, jukebox owners, and radio station disc jockeys. King Records' first commercial recordings in the early 1940s included artists such as the Delmore Brothers, Grandpa Jones, and Merle Travis, all harking back to WLW's stable of stars featured on the *Boone County Jamboree*. Later, other WLW country talent, such as Bonnie Lou, Jerry Byrd, **Pop Eckler**, Louis Innis, Tommy Jackson, and Zeke and Zeb Turner, recorded at King Records. One of the last country recordings made at King Records was "Lonesome 7-7203," sung by Hawkshaw Hawkins immediately before his untimely death in the tragic 1963 plane crash that also killed Patsy Cline and Cowboy Copas.

Covington's 50,000-watt radio station **WCKY** was one of the nation's leading broadcasters of country music recordings, featuring a disc-jockey evening program called the *WCKY Jamboree* that ran from 1946 through 1964. WCKY radio personality Nelson King contributed significantly to country music's popularity during the postwar era by playing records that preserved much of the music's down-home uniqueness while also promoting its commercial appeal. He was named "America's number one Hillbilly disc jockey" in many national radio listeners' polls and was elected as the first president of the Country Music Disc Jockey Association (forerunner of the Country Music Association), formed in 1953. Fans throughout the eastern half of North America were listening to King. Two other WCKY disc jockeys, Jimmie Logsdon and Wayne Raney, were also country artists who recorded at King Records. After WCKY dropped its country music format, a new Covington daytime radio station, WCLU (established in 1965), featured modern county music and identified itself as "Big CLU Country." WCLU played country music exclusively through 1981. Then, changing its call letters to **WCVG**, it featured a variety of formats, including country, for 25 years. In 2006 it switched to Mexican Latino music, responding to a new generation of migrants to Northern Kentucky.

Since 1978 **Bobby Mackey's Music World** in Wilder has been one of the longest continuously operating county nightclubs in the tri-state region. Much of its longevity can be credited to the popularity of the contemporary country culture in the 1980s, after the release of the motion picture *Urban Cowboy* (1980), starring John Travolta. Mackey's country and western bar features a mechanical bucking bull and a stage for live performances. The owner, Bobby Mackey, is himself a musician who performs and records both country and bluegrass music regionally.

Northern Kentucky's most prominent country artists include **Skeeter Davis** (Mary Frances Penick, 1931–2004), born in Dry Ridge, an early female country-to-popular crossover artist known best for her 1962 sentimental ballad "The End of the World"; **Pure Prairie League**, a country-rock band formed in the early 1970s, many of whose group members are from Northern Kentucky; **Gerry House** (born in 1948 in Covington and raised in Independence), award-winning country music radio personality, comedian, and country songwriter heard on WSIX (Nashville); and **Kenny Price** (1931–1987) a native of Boone Co. and host of the WLW *Midwestern Hayride* as well as a cast member of the nationally syndicated television series *Hee Haw*.

Charles Wolfe, author of *Kentucky Country*, maintains that Kentucky has contributed more stars to country music than any other state except Texas. Perhaps that explains why Northern Kentucky has such a close relationship with the legacy of country music, ranging from WLW's *Boone County Jamboree* (*Midwestern Hayride*) to WCKY's nationally famous country disc jockeys of the 1940s through the early 1960s and the innovative country recordings of King Records.

Hitchcock, H. Wiley, and Stanley Sadie, eds. *The New Grove Dictionary of American Music*. New York: Macmillan, 1986.

Kingsbury, Paul, ed. *The Encyclopedia of Country Music: The Ultimate Guide to the Music*. New York: Oxford Univ. Press, 1998.

Malone, Bill C. *Country Music, U.S.A.* Austin: Univ. of Texas Press, 1985.

Wolfe, Charles K. *Kentucky Country*. Lexington: Univ. Press of Kentucky, 1996.

John Schlipp

COUNTRY STORES. For more than 100 years, the country store stood in villages and hamlets of Northern Kentucky and elsewhere as the social center of the community. The country store was where the mail was delivered and where the farmers and townspeople discussed upcoming births and weddings, planting times, the weather, village gossip, and politics. It was in country stores throughout Kentucky that some of the most colorful tall tales of feuds, duels, fracases, murders, and mayhem were told again and again along with the scores earned in horseshoe and checkers tournaments and the play-by-play of the latest Blue Grass League baseball game.

Among the wildest tales associated with Northern Kentucky country stores were two shootings in Bracken Co. that ended in death: Louis Jacobs killed his best friend Harry Jett over a long-festering slight at the country store at Oakland, and Ronnie Weisbrodt, on guard at his father's store in Bradford Landing, accidentally shot and killed a would-be robber; he was merely aiming at the robber's lantern.

The country store developed from frontier trading posts, those rough settler cabins where backwoodsmen traded furs and pelts for butter, flour, fresh eggs, and sugar. Many of the early country stores in Northern Kentucky counties were located at the junction of a **buffalo trace** or along a settler route from the Ohio River. For example, such stores followed at 10- to 12-mile intervals along the old State Rd. from Augusta in Bracken Co. to Cynthiana in Harrison Co.

Generally, the smaller villages of Northern Kentucky grew up around a country store or stores and a gristmill, or both. Most staples came in barrels, kegs, and half kegs, or in large wooden flour bins. Fresh produce was sold from baskets or from the top of the counter; cracker barrels and pickles in glass jars or stoneware crocks came later. From the beginning, the country store sold hats and caps and shoes and boots, along with groceries and dry goods. By the 1830s village stores no longer carried bearskins but featured lace curtains, bolts of calico, leather boots and shoes, and useful furniture, as well as the local butter, eggs, fresh corn, and corn whiskey. The words *cassimere, queensware,* and *bombazine* had entered the language of even small villages. By 1840 the local post office often was housed in or next to the country store. The few store ledgers that remain record the changing demands of farm families over time, from a bartering system to one of cash and credit. Only a few of the larger stores, usually only those that bought merchandise in Cincinnati, kept separate records of purchases.

One famous country store in Northern Kentucky, the Rabbit Hash General Store in Boone Co., has maintained continuous operation since 1831. Built by James A. Wilson when Rabbit Hash was called Carlton, the store was operated by two best friends, Benjamin Wilson and Calvin Riddell, from 1883 to 1900. Riddell continued to run the store until 1920. The Rabbit Hash General Store was described in Reuben Gold Thwaites's famous travelogue *On the Storied Ohio*, about a journey down the Ohio River. The store at Rabbit Hash sits on a slight knoll overlooking this tiny hamlet's one street, two houses, and feed store. People in this section of Boone Co. know that when the Ohio River reaches a depth of 60 feet, the water covers the Rabbit Hash General Store's porch. In 1884, 1913, and 1937, the river's floodwaters covered the entire store (see **Floods of 1884**, **1913**, and **1937**). How did the store survive? Iron rods driven into the ground anchor the building. Each time a major flood occurred, the townspeople loaded wagons with the store's goods and drove the wagons to high ground. However, the 1937 flood did take the back porch away and leave a 20-foot ravine where the porch had been. Describing the significance of the Rabbit Hash General Store, Robert Hayden Wilson once said, "Why, on Saturdays, they'd all gather here and talk religion, and Sundays, they'd gather outside church and talk politics." The store was the center of communications but also the post office, the voting poll, and the site of continuous checkers and horseshoe games.

Many women helped their husbands run the country stores, but only a few women owned and operated stores of their own. Among them were Miss Lou Allen, who ran a combined dry-goods store and millinery shop about 1890 at Petersburg in Boone Co., next to the community's Christian Church; and Mrs. K. Willey, who in 1883 had a combined millinery and dry-goods store at Morning View in southern Kenton Co. Before the **Civil War**, Irene Eggleston was a storekeeper at Glencoe, and Nancy Bryan ran a store at Fredericksburg (now Warsaw), both in Gallatin Co. In 1883 Mrs. R. Hopkins ran the general store at Bramlette in Carroll Co. In 1897 Melissa Gayle sold the Piqua country store to Lucius and Sally Robinson. During the 20th century, Jewell and Pete Overbey replaced Frank and Mary Curtis in the Piqua store. In 1883 Mrs. Emily I. Corley had a full-line country store four miles southwest of Union in Boone Co. Bracken Co. had several women storekeepers. At Neave, Mary Cain Perkins was listed as a storekeeper, and Jewell Morehead was also listed with her husband Wilbur. Katherine Holleran was a storekeeper along with her husband at Needmore in Bracken Co. Well into the 20th century, Gussie Tietz Murray was the last to operate her family's store at Tietzville, also in Bracken Co.; Gussie also kept the navigation light on the Ohio River. Just after **World War II**, Ethel Moore purchased the old country store and grocery at Prestonville in Carroll Co. and operated it successfully until 1984.

In rural areas slaves and free people of color purchased goods from country stores owned by whites, and if the customers were freedmen, they were often listed on the store ledgers only by their first names. In Covington and Newport, where sufficient numbers of African Americans resided in the early 20th century, one or more local grocery stores were owned by local African American families. They gradually added items to their shelves until these stores resembled small country stores. One such store, the Gene and Bess Grocery Store at 205 E. Robbins St. in Covington, became a regular casual gathering place for African Americans living in the community (see **Gene Lacey**).

Larger towns, such as Port William (now Carrollton), Covington, and Limestone (now Maysville), lost their country stores soon after they were settled. These Ohio River towns established an open market square where farmers and traders bartered goods and produce. Port William's market square began about 1810. The frontier vanished rather quickly in Northern Kentucky, because steamboats launched a vast mercantile trade on the Ohio River; Kentucky's flour, hemp, lumber, tobacco, and whiskey were traded for eastern manufactured and crafted goods, and oysters from Louisiana were shipped directly to the wharfs.

The port cities of Cincinnati and Louisville quickly moved into a complex merchandising system of wholesalers, distributors, and clusters of specialty stores. In the 1850–1870 period, bakeries, corner grocers, hardware stores, lumber and coal yards, and taverns displaced multipurpose stores. Carrollton, Covington, Newport, and Maysville were not far behind. By the time of the Civil War, these smaller river cities had already lost their country stores in favor of the vigorous new specializations: bakeries, boot and shoe shops, butchers, grocers, hardware stores, pharmacies, and, by 1900, ice cream parlors and confectioners, often called sweet shops. Notions became a popular concept in the 1850s. Manufactured hardware and ready-made clothing advertised widely became available. During the 1880s patent medicines of every conceivable composition were stocked on the shelves. Along with medicines came wines and liquors for medicinal purposes.

Unlike stores located in Southern and Eastern Kentucky, which often depended on traveling peddlers to bring tinware and hardware from New England, most country stores in Northern Kentucky were close enough to the Ohio River that proprietors could obtain their wares from the river towns. By the 1840s most major river towns had a wharf boat with an entrepreneur engaged in wholesale and merchant warehouse operations. Local country store proprietors picked up the products handled through these river towns usually by horse-drawn wagon. In this manner, tiny hamlets such as Needmore in Bracken Co. and Helena and Fern Leaf in Mason Co. could boast queensware, china, ready-made clothing, patent medicines, and notions of all kinds. If a railroad passed through town, the storeowner picked up larger items such as plows, harrows, and milk cans at the local depot. In the late 1880s, several stores in railroad towns began to offer farm implements in lean-tos or sheds attached to the main store.

The larger country stores, such as the ones in Mason Co. at Sardis, bought directly from Cincinnati wholesalers and specialty stores. Joe Mendoza operated a large store at Williamstown in Grant Co. His partner had a sizable dry-goods store in downtown Cincinnati that supplied the Kentucky operation. In 1891 the Mendoza store was earning $40,000 in revenue a year and had hired a full-time head clerk and a junior clerk.

As immigrants moved into Northern Kentucky counties just before and after the Civil War, competing Bracken Co. stores opened in Germantown, Milford, Lenoxville, and Neave. With competition, some country stores added blacksmith shops, some sold grain and agricultural implements, and others started sideline lumbering or tobacco operations that eventually, for many of them, became their main business. Still others added harnesses, saddles and bridles. The S. C. Pinkard store at Germantown offered coffins for prices from $1.50 to $8.00.

By the 1870s villages in Northern Kentucky hosted more than 200 country stores. Most of these enterprises were small family-owned operations that carried small quantities of a great many items. A few stores were operated by widows or by sons of the original merchant. Printed advertisements in the 1870s clarified which stores had cash-only policies and which ones continued the old barter system of fresh produce for store-bought items. The first cigar advertisements also made their appearances about this time. With the emergence of public school systems in the 1880s, the country store stocked writing slates, McGuffey's Readers, and pencils needed by pupils and teachers. A southern Kenton Co. merchant, C. E. Fisk at Fiskburg, and stationery store specialists J. T. Strode and James Smith at Maysville were among the first storekeepers to promote the merchandising of schoolbooks and family Bibles.

In 1884 the Conway brothers, John and Harvey, owned the Locust Store in Carroll Co., which received most of its wares from Cincinnati. The store was 32 feet wide by 20 feet deep with a half story above. The Locust Store's post office had an area inside the store and an outside window. Upon entering, a clerk or one of the owners greeted the customer. Four glass showcases that displayed notions, dry goods, groceries, and millinery goods, including the latest city bonnets, filled the rest of the first floor. Upstairs were boots and shoes, hats and caps, and clothing. The produce section was large; the store sold 350 dozen eggs per month. A creamery was added in a side building, and farm implements were sold from a shed built at the rear.

Huckstering was always a sideline competitor to the country store business. As soon as roads were constructed in the early settlement period, New England peddlers supplied tinware, copper pots, tools, and notions from their horse-drawn wagons as they meandered on annual circuits often hundreds of miles long. Clarence Austin began his regular huckster route in Kentucky through Bracken, Pendleton and Robertson counties in 1910; he stopped the runs in 1962. By 1930 Ford or Chevy trucks, outfitted with an aisle, had replaced hucksters' horses and side counters and even external kerosene tanks. A small piece of lath attached to the edges of shelves kept the goods from falling off the side of the truck. Herbert Sandifer drove routes in six Kentucky counties, showing up at set places, often at county schools, about once a week. W. A. Sparks told of selling eggs to the hucksters and also selling culled-out laying hens. Hucksters operating in Robertson Co. fastened chicken coops on the sides of their trucks and collected fresh chickens as barter during their weekly routes. Occasionally, they would accept country hams in payment.

During World War II, gasoline was in such short supply that huckster wagons drawn by mules or horses reemerged as "the Country Store on Wheels." By the 1950s and 1960s, many farm families purchased automobiles and trucks and began shopping at the department stores, supermarkets, and malls in larger towns and cities. The rural country store became a grocery, a local restaurant, or a gas station. For example, Pete and Jewell Overbey offered home cooking to about 25 customers each day at Piqua, their barbershop and creamery. Ralph and Jane Sims installed a gas pump in front of their Burika store in remote southeastern Robertson Co. Until the 1950s, the Yocums at Locust did a good business in ice cream cones, stick candy, and Nehi soft drinks as the schoolchildren rushed out of class at the end of each day; but then the small schools closed in the sweep of consolidation, and the store eked out an existence as a grocery until it finally closed.

Today most country stores have fallen into disrepair, have been abandoned, or have changed beyond recognition. Some of them still offer sandwiches and pickles, but because of modernization, they often seem more like gasoline convenience stores. One of the few to retain its original style, the Mitchell's Store at Piqua is open in the summer and by appointment; with its 1925 cash register, ceiling-mounted twine ball, narrow shelves, and 1930s cooler, the Piqua Store maintains tradition and has added local crafts as well.

Bogardus, Carl R., Sr. *The Story of Gallatin County.* Ed. James C. Claypool. Cincinnati: John S. Swift, 2003.

Boone Co. Historic Preservation Review Board. *Historic Structures of Boone County, Kentucky.* Burlington, Ky.: Boone Co. Historic Preservation Review Board, 2002.

Bracken Co. Extension Homemakers. *History of Bracken County.* Bicentennial ed. Brooksville, Ky., 2002.

Carrollton Democrat, May 8, 1884.
Clark, Thomas D. *Pills, Petticoats, and Plows: The Southern Country Store.* Norman: Univ. of Oklahoma Press, 1964.
Collins, Richard H. *History of Kentucky.* Vol. 1. Covington, Ky.: Collins, 1882.
Gentry, Mary Ann. *A History of Carroll County.* Madison, Ind.: Coleman, 1984.
Jackson, Eric R. *Northern Kentucky.* Charleston, S.C.: Arcadia, 2005.
Robertson Review, centennial ed., 1971.
Thwaites, Reuben Gold. *On the Storied Ohio.* Chicago: A. C. McClurg, 1903.
Thwaites, Reuben Gold, Robert L. Reid, and Dan Hughes Fuller. *Pilgrims on the Ohio: The River Journey and Photographs of Reuben Gold Thwaites.* Bloomington: Indiana Univ. Press, 1997.
Williamstown Courier, souvenir ed., May 30, 1901.
Willigen, John Van. "Rolling Huckster Trucks," *Robertson County Historical Society Newsletter,* October 2002.

Diane Perrine Coon

COURT SYSTEMS. Like the rest of the nation, Northern Kentucky has multiple levels of law and court systems. To the U.S. Supreme Court this area has contributed both justices and a few noteworthy cases for decision. **Horace Lurton**, born in Newport in 1844, was appointed to the Supreme Court by President William Howard Taft (1909–1913) in 1910; he served four years before his death in 1914. The other U.S. Supreme Court Justice from Northern Kentucky was Maysville's **Stanley Reed**, who was appointed in 1938 by President Franklin Roosevelt (1933–1945) and served until 1957. One local court case that reached the U.S. Supreme Court involved the rates and tariff structure of the **Green Line** bus company, which operated in two states. In the early 1950s, *Perlman v. Feldman* concerned the valuation of stock prices at the **Newport Steel** Corporation just before a large stock sale and the distribution of money to minority stockholders. In recent years, a Boone Co. attorney brought before the Court a case related to the issue of search and seizure.

Since the early days of Kentucky statehood, Covington has been an important area for the federal court system. Judge **William W. Trimble** sat on the federal bench in Covington, as have his successors Mac Swinford, Eugene Seiler, **David Bunning**, and **William Bertelsman**. The federal courtroom in Pike Co. operates one week of each month as a branch of the Covington-based U.S. District Court for the Eastern District of Kentucky. Like U.S. Supreme Court justices, the federal judges are appointed for life by the federal executive branch.

For many years, the top court within the Kentucky state court system was the Court of Appeals. In November 1975, as a result of the Judicial Article, a Kentucky constitutional amendment, the high court changed its name to the Kentucky Supreme Court. It is made up of seven judges, who serve eight-year elected terms. Judge **James Milliken**, who grew up in Bellevue, was a member of the Court of Appeals from 1951 until 1975 and was the chief justice of that body three times during that period. In recent years Judge **Donald Wintersheimer** from Covington has served on the Kentucky Supreme Court through several terms. From 1969 until his death in 1981, **Robert Lukowsky**, also from Covington, served on the Court of Appeals before and after its transition to the Kentucky Supreme Court. A new lower court of appeals was created when the old Court of Appeals was renamed the Kentucky Supreme Court.

Before the early 1980s, each city in Kentucky had its own jail, and untrained judges held what critics derisively termed "kangaroo courts." In some cities these were called mayor's courts, and the speeding tickets dealt with in them were frequently sources of substantial revenues. Starting in the early 1980s, each county has consolidated its courts into a district court (handling misdemeanors) and a circuit court (handling felonies and divorce matters). At the same time, county government took responsibility for the jails, thereby bringing prisoners into one setting. Where in the county to locate the jail remains a burning issue in several Northern Kentucky counties today.

Circuit courts in Kentucky do not have to be contained within one county. For example, in the 1940s, Northern Kentuckian **Ward Yager** was the circuit court judge for a territory consisting of Boone, Carroll, Gallatin, Grant, and Owen counties. It was within the Campbell Co. Circuit Court that the 1896 **Pearl Bryan** murder trial took place under Judge Charles John Helm Jr. In that same courtroom, in 1961, **Tito Carinci** and codefendant exotic dancer April Flowers were tried and convicted for plotting to drug **George W. Ratterman** and have him arrested. Those were two of Northern Kentucky's most famous trials.

A trend in court structure at the local level includes the formation of specialized courts. In Campbell Co. today, Judge D. Michael "Mickey" Foellger heads up the county's new family court, dealing with juvenile justice. In the 1920s, during **Prohibition**, Covington was home to a special federal court dealing with the offenders of the 18th Amendment; federal commissioner Oscar H. Roetkin meted out the punishment for such violators.

Perhaps the most famous judge to come from Northern Kentucky was Judge **Roy Bean**, who was born in Mason Co., but earned his reputation in Texas.

Bridges, G. Wayne. "A Recent History of Kentucky's Courts and Judges," *KP,* October 21, 1998, 4K.
Kleber, John E., ed. *The Kentucky Encyclopedia.* Lexington: Univ. Press of Kentucky, 1992.

COVE HILL BAPTIST CHURCH. Cove Hill Baptist Church, located at the junction of Ky. Rts. 55 and 549 in Carroll Co., dates its origin to a revival in summer 1873 that was held in a log schoolhouse near the present church lot. In the early part of the 1870s, three Christian groups in the Cove and Mound Hill neighborhoods, Methodists, Baptists, and Disciples of Christ, united and built a building known as the Union Church at Cove Hill. Before long, the Disciples of Christ group erected their own separate church down the road on Mound Hill, and the Methodists built a church across Ky. Rt. 55, leaving the property to the Baptists. The Baptists held services in this original building until a new house of worship was built in 1951.

Levi Chilton preached the first sermon for the Cove Hill Baptist Church in November 1873. At the time, the church met once a month, conducting worship services on Saturday and Sunday and holding business meetings on Saturday after worship. Pastors were selected "in proportion to the number of *male* members of the church," because women were not allowed to speak in the meetings. In the early years, the church had the custom of calling a pastor for one year only; each year there was a vote to decide whether to renew the pastor for another year. This practice continued into the 1960s.

In 1874 the Cove Hill Baptist Church was accepted into the Sulphur Fork Baptist Association. J. V. Riley, pastor in 1975, led a 10-day revival meeting, in which five new members joined the church. The White's Run Baptist Association was formed in October 1900, with Cove Hill as a charter member. J. F. Jones, the pastor in 1901, was listed also as the pastor of the Locust and Union Grove churches, as well as a church clerk of the **Carrollton First Baptist Church**.

The Cove Hill Baptist Church's first musical instrument was an organ obtained in 1904. In 1909 it was replaced with a new organ that cost $70. In 1911 the church began to meet twice a month but later returned to one service a month. Not until 1944 did they begin having services every Sunday. A new building was erected in 1951 to replace the old log one, and an aggressive bus ministry was begun. In 1956 the Sunday School enrollment was 128. In 1972 restrooms were installed in the building, replacing the old outhouses. Cove Hill Baptist Church celebrated its 100th anniversary on Sunday August 19, 1973. In 1993 a woman preached at a revival service at the church for the first time.

Fundraising began in 1996 for a new church building, to be built on adjacent land at the corner of Ky. Rt. 55 and Mound Hill Rd. (Ky. Rt. 549). Pastor Larry Smith pledged to shave his handsome beard if the church raised $5,000 and to shave his head if they raised $10,000. The congregation responded by raising a total of $15,000, and Smith submitted to the scissors and the razor. On December 2, 2000, the new church building was dedicated. In 2003 the church elected two women as deacons.

Gentry, Mary Ann. *A History of Carroll County.* Madison, Ind.: Coleman, 1984.
Wright, Bryant. "History of Cove Hill Baptist Church," 1978, Cove Hill Baptist Church, Carroll Co., Ky.

Ken Massey

COVERED BRIDGES, MASON CO. Only two covered bridges remain in Mason Co., one at Dover and one, privately owned, on Valley Pk. Once a common sight, covered bridges were erected from the early 1800s up through the **Civil War** to replace earlier structures. Covering the bridges protected both the wooden floors and the truss systems that gave these bridges their strength. It was the trusses, more than the abutments or the floor

Dover Covered Bridge.

beams, that carried the loads of the bridges. Mason Co.'s remaining bridges' trusses represent the two most common types: the **Dover Covered Bridge** features a queenpost truss system, and the Valley Pike Bridge has a kingpost construction.

After the Civil War, iron and later steel bridges were built to replace the covered bridges. Many of the covered bridges succumbed to fire, neglect, or other forms of destruction, making way for bigger, wider bridges. Some ended more spectacularly: the covered bridge over the North Fork of the Licking River on the Lexington Turnpike was destroyed by Gen. John Hunt Morgan's Confederate cavalry during a raid on June 8, 1864. The covered bridges that remained were on the less-traveled roads and thus lasted long enough to become the subject of preservation.

The Dover bridge, in the northwestern part of the county, is one of the oldest in Kentucky; the date of construction is given as 1835. However, since the streams they spanned were prone to flooding, covered bridges commonly had to be rebuilt several times. Stockton Bower, a third-generation craftsman of covered-bridge repair, remembered that the Bower Bridge Company repaired the covered bridge at Dover during the 1920s. He also supervised repairs done on it in 1966. Later the Kentucky Transportation Department placed steel beams under the bridge, and these now carry the weight of the loads. The bridge crosses Lees Creek on Tuckahoe Rd. near Dover, a short distance off Ky. Rt. 8, the **Mary Ingles Highway**. A new concrete bridge was constructed nearby in 2004, but the Dover Covered Bridge is still open to lower-load traffic.

The Valley Pike Bridge is the only privately owned original covered bridge in Kentucky. Bower also worked on this bridge, in 1972, and he calculates that it was built in 1864. The bridge is only 23 feet long but is 14 feet tall and 15 feet wide. It crosses the Frasure Branch of Lees Creek in northwestern Mason Co. on Valley Pk. off Ky. Rt. 435.

Brandenburg, Phyllis, and David Brandenburg. *Kentucky's Covered Bridges.* Cincinnati: Harvest Press, 1968.

Powell, Robert A. *Kentucky's Covered Wooden Bridges.* Lexington: Kentucky Images, 1984.

White, Vernon. *Focus on Kentucky: Covered Bridges.* Berea, Ky.: Berea Imprints, 1985.

John Klee

COVINGTON. Covington is located on the west bank of the Licking River at its mouth opposite Cincinnati, along the Ohio River. The "Mouth of Licking" described where it was, for people traveling north to the Ohio River. From the river itself, the same place was known as **the Point**. The Point was much higher than the opposite bank and stood out, from the perspective of someone in a flatboat or canoe. The buffalo road that led away from the Point was one of the entry points to the Great Buffalo Rd. leading to the salt licks and pastures that surrounded the central Bluegrass region. Because the Ohio River was very shallow at the mouth of the Licking, it provided a convenient crossing for both buffalo and humans (see Buffalo Traces). In late winter, the buffalo gathered into herds on the prairies of central Ohio and traveled south along the Miami River to a river crossing. The Indians would follow the buffalo and the Licking River trails that were popular with the hunters. The Kentucky land north of Falmouth and west of Maysville was largely unsettled before 1790, because Indian predation continued until after the turn of the century. A census carried out in the winter of 1804–1805 in conjunction with a widespread smallpox epidemic found only 76 people living in the 30 square miles centered on the mouth of the Licking.

Thomas Kennedy, a justice of the Campbell Co. Court, purchased 200 acres of land at the mouth of the Licking and established a ferry and a tavern (see **Ferries**). His ferry drew much of its business from the old road to Lexington, which ran down the dry ridge to Walton. In 1789 seed corn for the settlers at Cincinnati was so scarce that it was obtained from Lexington and Georgetown, via the Licking River and the buffalo trace. This unimproved road was used by pack trains of horses and mules. By 1789 the new soldiers and settlers around Fort Washington in Ohio, located directly across the Ohio River from the mouth of the Licking, had interrupted the flow of buffalo. The army was forced to send out hunting parties to bring back meat to feed the soldiers from more distant localities. A defensive station had been set up with a small number of soldiers to protect the pack trains bringing food up the dry ridge to Fort Washington.

In 1814 Kennedy sold 150 acres of his farm to the Covington Company, which was made up of **Thomas D. Carneal**, Gen. **John Stites Gano**, and Richard M. Gano, for $50,000. On August 31, 1815, the Kentucky legislature recorded the plat of the town of Covington, named after Gen. Leonard Wales Covington of Maryland, who died in November 1813 at the Battle of Chrysler's Field. This battle was fought in western New York, just east of the Niagara River. The American defeat was so profound that the bodies of the losers remained on the field for months. The battlefield is now flooded by the Intercoastal Waterway. Onerias Powell surveyed the plat of Covington. The western boundary of the plat was the east line of Washington St., and the southern boundary was the north line of Sixth St. The plat included a 20-acre apple orchard, in which some of the trees were still alive 30 years later.

The first industry in Covington was developed with money from Cincinnati and Philadelphia. Investors built the Covington Cotton Factory (see **Cotton Mills**) in 1828 on the east half of the square, bounded by Front, Scott, Second, and Greenup Sts. The factory was run very successfully by a Mr. Whitehead and, after his tragic death, by his son-in-law John T. Levis. In 1831 the next block west was covered by the McNickle Rolling Mill and a pottery factory. A tobacco-grading warehouse was opened during the 1830s, and a home-based industry in **tobacco** products thrived during the 19th century.

The 1832 cholera epidemic put a damper on Covington's semicentennial celebration of the largest pioneer raid into Ohio. It was a raid to punish the Shawnee Indians for their part in the **Battle of Blue Licks**. Gen. **George Rogers Clark**, who commanded the raid, had called the Kentucky militia to meet at the "Mouth of Licking" to attack the Indian town of Piqua on the Little Miami River. **Simon Kenton** was the pathfinder for the group, which was said to have included every able-bodied pioneer available. In the successful attack, the Indian town and crops were destroyed. As the troops were returning to Cincinnati, Capt. V. McCracken, who had fought at Kenton's side and lay dying, suggested that survivors of the battle meet 50 years later to discuss the affairs of the campaign and the hardships and dangers of the past. Col John Floyd of Louisville brought forth a resolution in support of the idea, it passed, and it was agreed that a reunion meeting would be held 50 years hence. McCracken's body was carried to the Kentucky shore and buried near the blockhouse on the Point. As the 50th anniversary approached, Simon Kenton was chosen to remind the survivors of the meeting. Addressing his reminder to the "Citizens to the Western Country," Kenton said, "I wish to see once more before I die my few surviving friends. May heaven grant us a clear sky, fair and pleasant weather—a fair journey and a happy meeting." The reunion date fell on November 4, 1832, a Sunday. The pioneers were asked to meet at the Point in Covington in November to make their final adieus. The event drew only a few of the surviving pioneers. Simon Kenton fell ill at the house of a Mr. Doniphan in Ohio and was prevented from attending.

The city charter of Covington was granted on February 24, 1834. In an April 1834 election, **Mortimer M. Benton**, a native of New York, was chosen as the town's first mayor. On February 22, 1834, a company was incorporated to construct a turnpike road from Covington through Williamstown and Georgetown to Lexington. In 1835 the **Cincinnati and Charleston Railroad** was proposed, and the proposal prompted much discussion, both positive and negative. The citizens of Louisville and Maysville, as could be expected, were opposed. The residents of Lexington, however, were largely positive. Over the next 30 years, the turnpike was slowly finished. The **Covington and Lexington Railroad** (C&L) was chartered in February 1849 and served to make up for the lost Cincinnati and Charleston Railroad. Support for the C&L was high in Falmouth and in Cynthiana. The railroad followed the Licking River to Paris. In 1854 connection was made with the **Maysville and Lexington Railroad** at Paris and an arrangement was made to lease the Paris-to-Lexington section to complete the C&L. The C&L was quite successful: in 1855 alone, it transported 256,000 bushels of wheat to Covington. Many of the products delivered to Covington were soon transferred to Cincinnati. Increases in the quantity of livestock carried on the C&L led to significant growth of the meatpacking industry in Covington and increases in the number of pigs taken through the streets of Covington to the ferries to Cincinnati. After New Year's Day 1867, the newly opened **John A. Roebling Bridge** was used to move many of the animals to Cincinnati. The Licking River Suspension Bridge served to transfer a regular amount of livestock to the butchers in Campbell Co., who made regular pleas for the toll charges to be reduced.

The **Civil War** increased the military use of the railroad by the Union Army, which used it to maintain control of the eastern half of Kentucky, including Lexington. Confederate general John Hunt Morgan and local irregulars made regular attacks on the bridges and the rights-of-way along the **Kentucky Central Railroad**, as the C&L was known after its emergence from bankruptcy in 1858. Covington was heavily used as a Union training center both before and after the unsuccessful Confederate invasion of Northern Kentucky in September 1862. On that occasion, thousands of regular troops and militia personnel gathered in Covington to man the 14-mile ring of rifle pits and forts set up to defend against invasion. After a two-week standoff, Confederate general Henry Heth decided that these defenses were too formidable for his force of 8,000 troops, so he retreated down the turnpike toward Lexington.

Between 1840 and 1860, the population of Covington increased dramatically, rising from 2,026 to 16,471. Irish and German immigrants made up a large proportion of the increase. By 1850 Covington was the second-largest city in the state. The increase in population was directly related to its prosperity and the number of jobs available. The city annexed largely unoccupied land to the south in 1840 and again in 1850. The **Western Baptist Theological Institute** voluntarily included its land within the city limits. In a census publication on the nation's 100 largest cities, published in 1880, Covington was described as the most densely populated city in the country.

Covington's influence in the eastern half of the state increased with the expansion of the federal courts into Covington and the creation of the **Roman Catholic** Diocese of Covington in 1853. Covington banks also did an increasing business in Eastern Kentucky. The **Chesapeake and Ohio Railroad** (C&O) was designed to cover the same ground as the much earlier Cincinnati and Charleston Railroad. The C&O began in Norfolk, Va., and entered Kentucky at Ashland. It followed the Ohio River to Maysville, where the C&O leased the **Kentucky Central Railroad** via Paris, Ky., and used the track to Covington while the riverside track from Maysville to Covington was laid down. The C&O bridge at the end of Main St. in Covington was built in 1888 to carry the C&O rail traffic across to a connection with the Big Four Railroad in Cincinnati. When the C&O mainline reached Covington across the Licking River bridge at 15th St., it connected to the Kentucky Central Railroad at 17th St. and Madison Ave. For many years this section of track, known as KC Junction, was the busiest in the country. The bridge at Main St. in Covington was the heaviest and the longest truss bridge in the nation at the time. An even heavier bridge replaced the C&O bridge in 1928, the old railroad bridge was converted into a toll-free automobile bridge, and the track was elevated through Covington.

Covington increased its size further by annexing the bordering communities of Central Covington (1906), Latonia (1909), and West Covington (1909). By 1910 the city's population had risen to 53,000. The Roman Catholic Church finished a Gothic cathedral in midtown in 1910 as the Diocesan church (see **Cathedral Basilica of the Assumption**). At about the same time, the new church-affiliated St. Elizabeth Hospital (see **St. Elizabeth Medical Center**) was built in the Austinburg section of town. In 1930 the population reached its all-time high of 65,252. The new concrete **Dixie Highway** (U.S. 25) spurred suburban growth to the southwest, which eventually caused a reduction in Covington's population. The development of the **streetcar** line to Fort Mitchell reinforced the same suburban growth. The completion in 1963 of the **Brent Spence Bridge** on I-75 provided high-speed access to suburban subdivisions and shopping. Covington's downtown reached its zenith in the 1960s (see **Covington, Downtown**), before the opening of the **Florence Mall** in 1976. An urban renaissance, featuring restorations of historic properties (see **Main Strasse**; **Licking-Riverside and Ohio Riverside National Historic Districts**) and the construction of new skyscrapers and the **Northern Kentucky Convention Center**, has helped to revive the city. Today, Covington is home to some of the largest employers in Northern Kentucky, including **Fidelity Investments**, the **Internal Revenue Service Center**, and Fortune 500 companies like **Omnicare Inc.** and **Ashland Inc.** Covington's population was 52,535 in 1970, 49,585 in 1980, 43,264 in 1990, and 43,370 in 2000.

Burns, John. *A History of Covington, Kentucky, 1861–1990*. Covington, Ky.: John Burns, 1990. Available on microfilm at the Kenton Co. Public Library, Covington, Ky.

Collins, Richard H. *History of Kentucky*. Vol. 1. Covington, Ky.: Collins, 1882.

Kleber, John E., ed. *The Kentucky Encyclopedia*. Lexington: Univ. Press of Kentucky, 1992.

Tenkotte, Paul A. "Rival Cities to Suburbs: Covington and Newport, Kentucky, 1790–1890," PhD diss., Univ. of Cincinnati, 1989.

Tolzmann, Don Heinrich. *Covington's German Heritage*. Bowie, Md.: Heritage Books, 1998.

U.S. Census Bureau. "American Fact Finder. Data Set. Census 2000 Summary File 1 (SF1) 100-Percent Data. Custom Table." www.census.gov (accessed October 18, 2006).

Joseph F. Gastright

COVINGTON, DOWNTOWN. The largest shopping and business district in Northern Kentucky from the mid-19th century until the 1970s, downtown Covington featured **department stores**, **five-and-dime stores**, and specialty shops selling men's, women's, and children's wear; appliances; bicycles; **candy and ice cream**; draperies; drugs (see **Pharmacy**); fabrics; flowers; furniture; gifts; greeting cards; groceries; hardware; hats; jewelry; music; seed and feed; paint; plumbing supplies; **toys**; school and office supplies; shoes; and sporting goods. **Movie theaters**, cafeterias (see **Lang's Cafeteria**), and doctor's offices also abounded. Most major businesses stretched along Madison Ave. from Fourth to Ninth Sts. and along Pike St. between Madison Ave. and Russell St. Before the late 1980s, the area north of Fourth St. stretching to the Ohio River was largely composed of factories and warehouses. Since 1990, however, this industrial and warehousing district has been replaced by new office, commercial, and residential developments, anchored by RiverCenter. Accordingly, the focus of downtown has shifted from south to north of Fourth St., a reality recognized in the 2007 preliminary draft of a collaborative plan entitled "Building Covington's Future," which defines downtown's northern boundary as the Ohio River.

Downtown Covington, Pike and Madison Sts., World War II era.

Following the opening of suburban retail stores in the 1950s and 1960s, and of the **Florence Mall** in 1976, downtown Covington began a slow business decline. Since the 1990s, however, it has experienced a steady renaissance, with the opening of art galleries, wedding shops, loft apartments, and offices. Today, the area contains the **Northern Kentucky Convention Center** and many offices, restaurants, churches, and small shops, such as historic **Motch Jewelers**, which was founded in 1857 and has been at its present location, 613 Madison Ave., since the 1870s. Downtown is home to two Fortune 500 companies, **Ashland Inc.** and **Omnicare**. In addition, the federal government's **Internal Revenue Service** (IRS) employs thousands at its downtown Covington service center, which opened in 1967. The federal and county courthouses are also major employers.

In 1965 downtown Covington was a flourishing central business district, encompassing a variety of stores and services. In October of that year, a research firm conducted a random survey of 914 pedestrians. Of those interviewed, 38.4% indicated that their main reason for coming downtown was to shop. Other main reasons were work (26.3%); business, financial, or legal matters (11.5%); recreation, amusement or eating (9.3%); education or culture (6.2%); medical or dental visits (5.8%); and meeting friends or business associates (2.5%). The pedestrians were also asked their place of residence, and it was found that 47.3% were from Covington, 21% from Kenton and Boone Co. suburbs, 4.8% from Newport and Fort Thomas, and 4.3% from Cincinnati. Even more important, 85% of those interviewed said they visited downtown Covington once or more per week. The vitality of downtown Covington in 1965 was still due largely to forms of transportation other than the private automobile. In fact, nearly 54.5% of the respondents had arrived downtown via bus or taxi or by walking.

Throughout the 1950s and 1960s, the Covington Retail Merchants' Association and the City of Covington studied proposals suggesting ways to compete with the growing number of suburban shopping alternatives. Additional parking lots were built, improved street lighting was installed, and special sales days were held. Proposals for a new five-story multiuse facility, to include stores, offices, a hotel, convention space, and parking for 1,223 automobiles, failed to materialize, as did a proposed Twin Fair discount store and later a Kmart. Old Town Plaza, a pedestrian mall closed to vehicular traffic, was opened on W. Pike St. between Madison Ave. and Washington St. in July 1977. Merchants in Old Town agreed to restore their buildings to reflect a 1890s-era theme, in a setting enhanced by trees, shrubs, and a fountain. Like many pedestrian malls in downtowns across the United States, however, Old Town Plaza was not successful, and in 1993 it was reopened to vehicular traffic and on-street parking. Covington's downtown was listed on the National Register of Historic Places in 1983.

The principal department stores of the downtown area were the **Coppin Department Store**, Sears and Roebuck, JCPenney, and Montgomery Ward, while the five-and-dime stores included F. W. Woolworth on the southeast corner of Madison Ave. and E. Seventh St. (closed in 1990) and S. S. Kresge at 624 Madison Ave. (closed in 1966). Coppin's, founded in 1873 and closed in 1977, was the largest department store in Covington, occupying a basement, a balcony, and three floors of the seven-story Coppin Building on the northeast corner of Madison Ave. and E. Seventh St. (now the Covington City Hall). Montgomery Ward, a major national retailer at 727–741 Madison Ave., opened its Covington store, comprising a basement, a balcony, and two floors, in 1929; it closed the retail store in about 1961–1962 but continued to operate a catalog outlet until the mid-1960s. Sears and Roebuck opened its Covington store in a new, leased building at 13 W. Seventh St. in February 1935. Despite the **Great Depression**, Sears and Roebuck's Covington location performed so well that the company expanded its square footage the following year with the construction of a second floor, thus occupying a basement, a balcony, and two floors. Sears closed in 1976 when it opened its new store in the Florence Mall. In 1941 JCPenney opened in the Dan Cohen building at 18–22 W. Pike St. (see **Cohen Shoe Stores**), eventually occupying a basement, a balcony, and two floors; it closed in early 1984.

Major apparel stores, now closed, included **Eilerman & Sons, Men's Clothiers**, whose 1896 four-story building still stands on the northeast corner of Pike and Madison Ave. (closed in 1973); the Parisian of Covington, at 40 W. Pike St. (opened in 1913 and closed in 1996); Dalton's Women's Wear, at 620 Madison Ave. (opened in 1936); and Goldsmith's Ladies' and Children's Wear, at 630–636 Madison Ave. (closed 1966). Among the furniture stores were Modern Furniture, at 513 Madison Ave. (closed 1987), and Louis Marx and Brothers Furniture, which opened its Covington store in the mid-1890s, eventually moving to 520 Madison. A. J. Ostrow opened a radio store at 711 Madison Ave. in 1926, later expanded into furniture and other appliance lines, and moved to 717–719 Madison Ave. in 1940. Edward P. Cooper's furniture and appliance store began in West Covington in 1913, selling RCA Victor victrolas and records. Later, it expanded its line to include some of the first crystal radios, as well as some of the first television sets, in Northern Kentucky; it long occupied the southwest corner of Fifth St. and Madison Ave. William J. Tillman began selling radios and appliances in the 1920s and expanded into furniture in 1939, with a store on the northeast corner of Eighth St. and Madison Ave.

Major Developments in Downtown Covington since 1990

- The first phase of RiverCenter on Rivercenter Blvd., consisting of the 19-story office tower RiverCenter I, a companion parking garage accommodating 1,000 cars, and a 7-story Embassy Suites Hotel (1990)
- The 10-story office tower Gateway Center on Scott St., home of the IRS, with a 500-car parking garage (1993)
- The 11-story Gateway Center West (2001)
- The 4-level City Center Parking Garage on E. Seventh St. (1993)
- The $30.5 million Northern Kentucky Convention Center on Rivercenter Blvd. (1998)
- The 16-story office tower RiverCenter II (1997–1998)

- The 8-story Kenton Co. Justice Center on the northeast corner of E. Third St. and Madison Ave., with the accompanying **Transit Authority of Northern Kentucky** Riverfront Transit Center and Parking Garage (1999)
- The 5-story Federal Courthouse on W. Fifth St. (1999)
- The 14-story Marriott Hotel on Rivercenter Blvd. (1999)
- Madison Place on Rivercenter Blvd., a 15-story office and condominium project with a parking garage (garage, 1995; other structures, 2000–2001)
- The 6-level, 364-space Mid-Town parking garage on the southwest corner of Fifth and Scott Sts. (2002)
- The restoration of the old F. W. Woolworth building into The Madison, a banquet hall (1990–1991), and its companion, the Madison South, in the old Tillman Furniture Store (2002)
- The restoration of the historic **Northern Bank of Kentucky** building on Scott St., into offices and the **Bank of Kentucky** (1999)
- The Northern Kentucky E-Zone, a nonprofit incubator to promote high-technology businesses (2001)
- A $3 million renovation of the historic Madison Theater (2001)
- Odd Fellows Hall, Covington's first example of saving a historic facade and rebuilding a new 5-story commercial and office structure inside (built, 1856; damaged by fire, 2002; rebuilt, 2005)
- The reconstruction of the old Goldsmith's store into the Wedding Mall (2006)
- Pulse, a 64-unit condominium development in the block bounded by Banklick, Russell, Eighth, and Ninth Sts. (2007)
- The 22-story condominium development Ascent at Roebling's Bridge at the corner of Rivercenter Blvd. and Scott St., designed by internationally renowned architect Daniel Libeskind, master planner of the new World Trade Center in New York City (2007)

City of Covington, Ky., et al. "Building Covington's Future: A Community Visioning and Strategic Planning Process," preliminary draft, 2007. www.covingtonky.com/documents/Strategic_Plan_FINAL_FINAL_VERSION-5-22-07_.pdf.

Collins, Michael. "Ashland Picks Covington," *KP*, July 20, 1998, 1K.

"Covington Becoming Wedding Central," *CP*, February 3, 2006, 1B.

"Covington Merchants Told Trade Will Falter Unless Town Builds," *CE* (Ky. ed.), July 31, 1966, 6A.

"Covington Parking Plan Bared: Off-Street Sites in Downtown Area Outlined in Report," *KP*, November 29, 1955, 1.

"Covington's Downtown on Historic List," *KP*, June 18, 1983, 3K.

"Covington Unveils City Hall," *KP*, August 17, 1991, 3K.

Economic Development Department, City of Covington, Annual Reports, 1989–1999, Kenton Co. Public Library, Covington, Ky.

Hartel, Greg. "Covington's F. W. Woolworth to Close Down," *KP*, July 28, 1989, 3K.

Kreimer, Peggy. "Saving the Mosler Building," *KP*, June 26, 1999, 1K.

"Men's Store Ends Family Tradition," *KE*, April 10, 1996, B1.

"Montgomery Ward Is 83 Years of Age," *KP*, September 14, 1935, 5.

"Music and Speeches Mark Opening of Plaza," *KP*, July 15, 1977, 1.

"New Dalton Store Will Be Opened in Covington Saturday," *KP*, October 1, 1936, 1.

"New Tillman Store Is Opened in Covington," *KP*, September 29, 1939, 4.

"Old Town Plaza Dismantled," *CP*, March 30, 1993, 6D.

"Penney's to Close Covington Store," *KP*, December 28, 1983, 5K.

"Property Leased in Covington for New Store of J. C. Penney Company," *CE* (Ky. ed.), January 23, 1941, 1.

Real Estate Research Corporation. "Economic Feasibility and Strategy Study, Downtown Covington, Kentucky," prepared for the City of Covington, Ky., May 1966, Kenton Co. Public Library, Covington, Ky.

"River Center: We Have Ignition," *KP*, February 25, 1988, 1K.

"Sears Store in Covington to Open Doors on Thursday," *KP*, February 13, 1935, 1.

"29th Anniversary for Ostrow Store," *KP*, September 29, 1955, 16.

"Wide Line of Goods to Be Sold by Ward Store," *KP*, August 15, 1929, 5.

"Will Remodel Sears Store," *KP*, September 25, 1936, 4.

Paul A. Tenkotte

COVINGTON, FLEMINGSBURG, AND POUND GAP RAILROAD. A Northern Kentucky example of the popularity of narrow-gauge railroads in the late 19th century, the Covington, Flemingsburg, and Pound Gap Railroad suffered financial difficulties during the course of its operation. During the 1870s and 1880s, a backlash against what was perceived as over-charging by the railroads led to the concept of building "People's Railroads," or narrow-gauge railroads. The idea gained political and economic support, and money was raised to start such lines. The People's Railroads were built with the rails only 3 feet apart; the rails of standard-gauge railroads, in contrast, were 4 feet 8.5 inches apart. The theory was that the construction and operation costs for narrow-gauge roads would be less and that the savings could be passed on to shippers in the form of lower rates. The following three arguments were made by the promoters of the narrow gauge: less money would have to be spent acquiring right-of-ways, since each right-of-way would be narrower; the engines, rolling stock, and equipment would be smaller, and thus less expensive to build and operate; and since the equipment would be smaller, the rails could be lighter, and thus less expensive. Promoters claimed that narrow-gauge railroads could be built at half the cost of standard-gauge railroads and that their operating costs would be significantly lower. Narrow-gauge railroads would run at moderate speed, moving items to market with reasonable rates. Ohio became a hotbed of such development during the 1870s and 1880s, particularly the area around Van Wert, in the northwestern part of the state. Among the narrow-gauge railroads built during this period, the Cincinnati area hosted the Cincinnati Northern; the Cincinnati and Eastern; the Cincinnati, Georgetown, and Portsmouth; the College Hill Railroad; and James Gamble's ward, the Cincinnati and Westwood.

The belief that narrow was less costly than standard gauge proved fallacious. Little or no savings were achieved in the acquisition of narrower right-of-ways. Narrow-gauge engines and cars, while smaller than standard, were only slightly less expensive, because such equipment still required the same parts. The lighter narrow-gauge rail wore out more quickly. In addition, a narrow-gauge car could carry only two-thirds of the load of a standard-gauge car, so more cars were needed to move the same amount of material, eliminating the anticipated savings. Finally, the real cost of operating a railroad, labor, was not reduced; the same number of laborers were necessary to operate either gauge. Operating costs for narrow-gauge lines actually proved to be higher than costs for standard-gauge lines, as only two-thirds of the tonnage of a standard-gauge railroad could be transported for the same labor cost. There was also the cost of transferring loads to or from standard-gauge railroads at connections; no easy or inexpensive way was found to accomplish this task.

The Covington, Flemingsburg, and Pound Gap (CF&PG) was one of the narrow-gauge enterprises conceived during this frenzy of narrow-gauge promotion. As its title implies, it proposed to run eastward from Covington to Flemingsburg in Fleming Co., into the eastern coalfields, and on to Pound Gap, Va. Its promoters believed that the CF&PG would allow coal, then the major fuel supply for factories, businesses, and homes, to be delivered more cheaply to the Northern Kentucky region than via the **Kentucky Central Railroad**. The CF&PG intended to connect with the Ohio narrow-gauge railroads by ferry until such time as a railroad bridge could be built to span the Ohio River. The Cincinnati Northern Railroad would have provided connections with other narrow-gauge railroads extending into northern Ohio. Nothing was ever said about how these Ohio narrow roads would connect into Covington, one of the line's endpoints.

Construction of the CF&PG began in 1876 in Fleming Co. The CF&PG started at its connection with the L&N, along the former **Maysville and Lexington Railroad** at Flemingsburg Junction, and built eastward to Flemingsburg and Hillsboro in southern Fleming Co., a distance of 17 miles. As much as the narrow gauges wanted to be separate and different, they always seemed to begin at some easy interchange point with a standard-gauge operation such as at Flemingsburg Junction. The line never laid track beyond Hillsboro, Ky., and after a wreck in 1907 at Weaver's Ford, just south of Flemingsburg, which destroyed a trestle, the railroad was cut back to Flemingsburg. In 1909, during the course of one day, the extant six miles of CF&PG track was converted to standard gauge, a fate common to many narrow-gauge railroads. Never a moneymaker, the CF&PG, then operating as the Flemingsburg and Northern (F&N), ceased operations on December 6, 1956; it was unable to compete with the modern trucking industry. Its depots at Flemingsburg Junction and Flemingsburg still stand.

The CF&PG during its life span carried seven names. The name changes took place as the road went into and came out of receivership. In 1880 the CF&PG became the Licking Valley Railroad Company, but later that year it was renamed Covington, Flemingsburg, and Southeastern Railroad. In 1881 the name was changed to Cincinnati and Southeastern Railway. Then in 1887 the line was renamed as the Covington, Flemingsburg, and Ashland Railroad. That name lasted until 1905, when the road became the Cincinnati, Flemingsburg, and Southeastern Railroad. In 1920 the CF&PG received its final name, Flemingsburg and Northern Railroad (F&N), and it was as the F&N that it ceased operations in 1956.

"The Pound Gap R.R." *DC*, November 29, 1879, 1.
Reis, Jim. "Dark Month for Trains," *KP*, May 19, 1991, 4K.
"State News," *Covington Ticket*, December 4, 1876, 1.
Sulzer, Elmer G. *Ghost Railroads of Kentucky*. Indianapolis, Ind.: V. A. Jones, 1967.

Charles H. Bogart

COVINGTON ALTAR STOCK BUILDING COMPANY (Institute of Catholic Art). Covington was home to a unique center for the creation of religious art during the 1860s. Altars, altar and mural paintings, baptismal fonts, confessionals, and pulpits originated at the Covington Altar Stock Building Company, also known as the Institute of Catholic Art. The establishment enriched places of worship nationwide as churches and monastic institutions commissioned religious art from the Covington studio and workshop.

The company was founded by the Benedictine religious order, which came to the United States from Germany to establish missions and to minister to the spiritual needs of a growing German Catholic immigrant population. In 1846 the German-born priest Rev. Boniface Wimmer led a small group of Benedictine monks and lay brothers to Latrobe, Pa. They erected a monastery and the St. Vincent School for Boys with the financial support of King Ludwig I of Bavaria. Wimmer and the king shared a deep love for the visual arts and vowed to introduce German painting and sculpture into the United States. As new Benedictine missions were established and new churches built, their need for interior decoration became an important priority for Wimmer. In 1859 he sent two Benedictine priests to Covington's **St. Joseph** Parish, where a German Catholic congregation had been worshipping since 1854. St. Joseph Church was consecrated in 1859.

When the priests reported to the St. Vincent school that St. Joseph Church lacked altars, Wimmer asked the Benedictine Rev. Odilio von der Gruen to establish an altar-building company in Covington. Von der Gruen was an artistic man who immediately recognized the need of a great number of new churches for altars of beauty and quality. He appointed **"Brother Cosmas" Wolf**, a Benedictine lay brother from St. Vincent, as director and chief designer at the Institute of Catholic Art. Wolf had studied at the Munich Royal Academy of Art in Bavaria between 1857 and 1862. Beginning in fall 1862, Wolf assembled a group of competent painters, gilders, and woodworkers to create church art in Northern Kentucky. Working for Wolf were Claude Haeusler, Harry Gehrig, William Grawe, Philip Lohr, George Rose, and Louis Steiner. Wolf designed most of the altars and assisted in their construction.

In neighboring Cincinnati, several artists had founded the Society of Christian Art, which attracted many talented European immigrants who found employment at the Covington Institute of Catholic Art. Among these men were the Schroeder brothers and sculptors Johann Heinrich and Johann Friedrich, who had studied in Munich before they settled in Cincinnati. The Society of Christian Art also counted among its members several outstanding painters, such as **Wilhelm Lamprecht** and **Johann Schmitt,** both of whom had distinguished careers with the Covington Altar Building Company. Other altar and fresco painters who contributed to the fame of the company were H. Becker, M. Geiger, P. Gerstrein, E. Humbrecht, A. Kloser, and **Wenceslaus Thien**.

The company's workshop in Covington was located in a frame building at the corner of Bush and Greenup Sts., on a lot next to St. Joseph Church. There Wolf received commissions for church art from across the nation. Once he had designed the altars and decided on the basic outlines of the altar paintings, construction began. Most of the altars made in Covington resembled German Gothic prototypes, made of wood. Tripartite, with one central panel and two folding side panels, they had pointed arches and fancifully carved tracery and pinnacles. The altar pieces, decorative paintings above and behind the altars, portrayed biblical scenes from the Old and New Testaments, images of saints, and devotional depictions of the Madonna and the Christ Child. The Covington altars were painted white, and the altar paintings had a gold-leaf background.

Several Covington churches obtained altars constructed by the Covington Altar Stock Building Company. Among them were St. Joseph Catholic Church, **St. John Catholic Church**, and **Mother of God Catholic Church**. The main altar at St. Joseph Church was the most spectacular, measuring 40 feet in height and built at a total cost of $2,000; each side altar cost $500. The company also installed altars in Indiana, Maryland, New Jersey, Minnesota, Ohio, Pennsylvania, and Wisconsin. The first major commission the company received was for the altar at St. Mary's Church in Newark, N.J., in 1862. After 10 years of operation in Covington, Wolf moved the company to the St. Vincent School for Boys in Latrobe, Pa., where he continued the work of church decoration until his death in 1894.

Cochran, Nathan M., O.S.B. *Ora et Labora: The Saint Vincent Lay Brothers, 1846–1946*. Latrobe, Pa.: St. Vincent Archabbey Press, 1988.
Pohlkamp, Diomede, O.F.M. "A Franciscan Artist of Kentucky, Johann Schmitt, 1825–1898," *Franciscan Studies* 7 (June 1947): 147–70.
Souvenir, Diamond Jubilee, St. Joseph Church. Covington, Ky.: Acorn Press, 1934.
Springer, Annemarie. *Nineteenth Century German-American Church Artists*. www.ulib.iupui.edu/kade/springer/index.html (accessed November 16, 2005).
Tenkotte, Paul A. *A Heritage of Art and Faith: Downtown Covington Churches*. Covington, Ky.: Kenton Co. Historical Society, 1986.

Annemarie Springer

COVINGTON AND LEXINGTON RAILROAD. In 1850 the Covington and Lexington Railroad (C&L) began construction south from Covington toward Paris in Bourbon Co. Covington tobacco merchant Charles A. Withers (see **Withers Family**) financed the first 18 miles away from Covington and served as the railroad's superintendent. Other major financing was provided by subscriptions to the railroad's stock by the city of Covington ($300,000) and the counties of Fayette ($200,000), Bourbon ($100,000), and Pendleton ($50,000) and by a loan from the city of Cincinnati ($100,000). Two tunnels had to be carved out of the Kenton Co. landscape: one at 24th St. and Madison Ave. in Covington, and another farther south near Ryland Heights at Grant's Bend. By October 1853, the route was completed from Covington to Falmouth, by May 1854 to Cynthiana, and by September 1854 to Paris, Ky. The C&L made a connection with the **Maysville and Lexington Railroad** at Paris and ran over the latter's right-of-way into Lexington. Construction of the C&L effectively ended all steamboat operations on the Licking River, since the railroad generally paralleled the river. The C&L was utilized during the **Civil War** to transport troops and supplies between Covington and Central Kentucky. Later the C&L became part of the Kentucky Central Railroad, then the **Louisville and Nashville Railroad**, and today the **CSX**.

Herr, Kincaid A. *The Louisville & Nashville Railroad*. Lexington: Univ. Press of Kentucky, 2000.
Hunter, Louis C. *Steamboats on the Western Rivers*. 2nd ed. New York: Dover, 1993.
Klein, Maury. *History of the Louisville & Nashville Railroad*. New York: Macmillan, 1972.
Tenkotte, Paul A. "Rival Cities to Suburbs: Covington and Newport, Kentucky, 1790–1890," PhD diss., Univ. of Cincinnati, 1989.

Charles H. Bogart

COVINGTON AND LEXINGTON TURNPIKE. In 1834 the Kentucky legislature approved formation of the Lexington Turnpike Company, which was given the task of financing construction of the Covington and Lexington Turnpike (the road was to roughly follow today's U.S. 25). The company was capitalized with $300,000 of common stock, much of it purchased by Covington interests. Construction of the road began shortly thereafter, but progress was slow. On March 16, 1839, a group of civic-minded citizens of Lexington met, hoping to find a way to speed the road's construction and to have a bridge built across the Ohio River at Covington, giving Central Kentucky farmers access to the Cincinnati markets. Shortly thereafter, groups from Lexington and Covington met with Cincinnati officials to try to obtain their assistance in building a bridge and completing the turnpike. The three groups agreed that the project could be quite beneficial to both Kentucky and Ohio. Good roads already existed from Lexington to Louisville and Lexington to Maysville, but a new road was needed to connect Lexington with Northern Kentucky and Cincinnati. The officials knew that Kentucky farmers could play an important role in supplying the Cincinnati pork and beef packing industries. It was also clear that much of the money paid for the livestock would eventually be spent at Cincinnati businesses. The highway would also open up northern and eastern markets to Kentucky farmers, by permitting travel northward through Cincinnati to the Miami and Erie Canal. A *Licking Valley Register* article said, "Nothing is of more importance to the area than the proposed Covington and Lexington Turnpike."

By 1839 just 10 miles of the highway south from Covington had been completed, and on the southern end, a 12-mile portion between Lexington and Georgetown was finished. However, the unfinished 63-mile stretch was quite remote and sparsely populated. When considering the project, the Kentucky legislature pointed out that the central portion in Kentucky through Boone, Grant, and Scott counties would be difficult to build and a hardship on local farmers to maintain. The law required property owners to maintain the road, and all males 16 and over were ordered to assist in the work. Tollgates were allowed at sites along the road to help defray the cost of maintenance. The turnpike was to be 30 feet wide and to have a surface of gravel, rock, logs, or other suitable material. Tree stumps were not to protrude more than six inches above the ground, and the grade level was not to exceed five degrees (much of the road near Covington exceeded the five-degree limit). At least 10 feet of the width was to have a fairly good surface, which would permit safe travel by wagons and carriages. By 1849 a substantial portion of the road was finished. There had been monumental problems associated with its construction. After nearly 20 years, however, the turnpike was finally completed in the early 1850s. The road had cost the Commonwealth of Kentucky $213,000, or about $2,500 per mile, to construct. The final leg of the project, connecting the road with Cincinnati, was not completed until 1867, when the new **John A. Roebling Bridge** opened. In recent years I-75 has replaced U.S. 25 as the primary artery between Covington and Lexington.

"Covington Turnpike Road," *LVR*, May 13, 1843, 3.
"Sketch," *CJ*, August 30, 1873, 1.
Tenkotte, Paul A. "Rival Cities to Suburbs: Covington and Newport, Kentucky, 1790–1890," PhD diss., Univ. of Cincinnati, 1989.

COVINGTON ART CLUB. The Covington Art Club (CAC), founded March 14, 1877, celebrated its 130th anniversary in 2007; it may be the oldest women's club in the Greater Cincinnati–Northern Kentucky metropolitan area. The club was organized by a group of "eight young women as they sat on a front porch on Wallace Avenue" in Covington. Their interests centered on the areas of "art, embroidery, sculpture, wood carving, wood burning, and painting in all media, including china painting." At first called the Young Ladies Art Union, it was designed for the purpose "of inciting the members to greater effort in the various branches of Art." Programs were planned for meetings, scheduled every two weeks at members' homes, and special exhibitions occurred at six-month intervals. From the beginning, an effort was made to secure "outstanding musicians, artists and speakers." The multitalented members themselves were often presenters at these group meetings. The eight dedicated young women from Covington who formed the nucleus of the CAC were Clementine R. Abbott, Laura Charles, Carrie H. Gedge, Lillie B. Gedge, Edith M. Linn, Jeanie D. McKee, Mary B. Price, and Lulu M. Wright.

On January 3, 1887, the name Young Ladies Art Union was changed to Covington Art Club; in 1891 the club became a member of the General Federation of Women's Clubs; in 1894 it joined the Kentucky Federation of Women's Clubs as a charter member. Meetings were held at members' homes, in churches, at the **Covington Public Library**, or at the **Covington Ladies Home**. Then in 1923 the group purchased from Charles A. J. Walker the Hermes Building, at the corner of Court and Fourth Sts., to be their clubhouse. Walker's wife had been an active member of the CAC and had served as president. The club was officially incorporated in February 1926.

A month later, members voted to establish a clubhouse at 604 Greenup St., adjacent to the **Baker-Hunt Foundation**. The impressive three-story brick structure was built in the 1820s and enlarged in 1867 and 1870. The front door still bears the original leaded glass, and there are two stained-glass windows, a large wooden carved newel post, and elegant marble fireplaces. In addition to an auditorium, a kitchen, and an upstairs apartment, the building houses the Jeanie B. McKee Booklovers' Library, which is also the boardroom. The library was named as a memorial to McKee, who was a charter member of the CAC. Valuable books from her library were added to the club library as well as books from Mrs. A. E. Stricklett in memory of her husband, Kentucky state senator Alfred E. Stricklett. U.S. senator **Richard P. Ernst** donated a gift of Proctor and Gamble stock valued at $500, the income from which was to be used to maintain the library, and interest earned from this stock is still used toward the purchase of new library books annually.

In 1973 the CAC building was placed on the National Historic Register. In 1986 it was damaged by a heavy storm (see **Tornadoes**) and subsequently was restored by architect **George F. Roth Jr.** In 2000 the clubhouse was sold to the Baker-Hunt Foundation because of the tremendous costs of maintenance. The CAC has a 10-year lease agreement with 5-year renewal options, and the Baker-Hunt Foundation has the use of the club's complete facilities, other than the Jeanie B. McKee Library.

As the club grew in size, special departments were added. In April 1900 the bylaws were amended to include departments of music and civics, and in 1906 three more departments were added: the Garden Circle, Arts & Crafts, and Literacy and Music. The Dramatic Circle was founded in 1924, and in 1927 the Literature and Booklovers Department. Today the major departments are Arts and Crafts, Bridge, Home and Garden, Literature-Booklovers, Music and Drama, and Travel. Each department except the Bridge Department is responsible for providing the programs, teas, and lunches throughout the club's yearly seasons (September–December and February–May). New members are encouraged to join at least one department in order to become better acquainted with the inner workings of the club itself and to foster friendships.

Members of the CAC have also been actively involved in improving existing social conditions. For instance, the club established its first playground in July 1901 and continued managing it for 20 years. Along with learning to play, the children were given sewing instructions. Club members also created gardens at the schools. In conjunction with this project, the CAC worked with the City of Covington to gain cooperation from local residents in establishing public cleanup days.

The club's community involvement was far-reaching: it extended to the Hindman Settlement School in Knott Co, Ky., and several other Eastern Kentucky mountain schools. Besides clothing, books, and school supplies, the club sent "traveling libraries and traveling art galleries" to the schools. The members also worked with the Smoke League to eliminate the nuisance of smoke, and with the city council from 1915 until 1920 to demand pasteurization of milk and to promote sanitary conditions in all dairies. The CAC supported improved conditions in the jails and, in 1921, planted and presented to the City of Covington 50 scarlet oak trees in **Devou Park**. The club's Welfare Department was created in early 1930. Members sewed for the **Red Cross** and later made dressings for poor patients at the **Booth Memorial Hospital** cancer clinic.

In cooperation with the Society to Prevent Blindness, the Home Life Department instigated in 1972 an annual preschool visual screening in the Covington and Kenton Co. schools for approximately 1,800 children. The club is no longer involved in the screening, which is now overseen by the superintendent of Covington Schools. In 2001 the club began giving art scholarship awards to two deserving senior high school students from Boone, Campbell, or Kenton counties. In recent years the club has also awarded essay scholarships to two deserving high school senior students selected from the same three counties. Both of these awards were originally established by a $5,000 trust given to the club by **Vance Trimble** in memory of his wife Elzene, formerly an active member. Other monetary gifts are presented to deserving local charities, according to the availability of funds at year-end. The Finance Committee determines the recipients, but members may make suggestions.

Two well-respected artists were members of the club: **Dixie Selden** and Lela Cooney. Selden was a student of **Frank Duveneck.** Lela Cooney was a multitalented local artist who created oil paintings and sketches, fashioned creative decors, and taught at Baker-Hunt. Numerous other members had a long-lasting influence on the club. According to Mrs. Harold Brown Weldon, a longtime member, the "Three Powerhouses" who were prominent in the Kentucky State Federation of Women's Clubs were Mary Elizabeth Cobb, Mrs. James C. Layne, and Mrs. John E. Shepard. Cobb served three times as president and was governor of this district. Mrs. Layne, who filled the unexpired governor's term of her predecessor as well as additional terms, also was a first, second, third, and fourth vice president. The state federation recognized her as an honorary first vice president for life. Mrs. Layne also received a gold medal from the Federation of Women's Clubs at a federation meeting in Atlantic City, N.J., honoring her as a "pioneer Kentucky Club Woman." Mrs. Shepard was state recording secretary of the federation, fourth vice president, and governor of this district twice. Like Cobb, she also served three terms as president of the CAC. Member Miss **Mary Nourse** designed a new insignia in the early 1920s, consisting of a circle enclosing the initials C.A.C.; the insignia is found on the bimonthly bulletins and the yearbooks.

On March 10, 1952, the CAC received a 75th Anniversary Scroll from the General Federation of Women's Clubs, "in recognition and appreciation of distinguished service to the community and the nation." On March 14, 1977, at its 100th anniversary, Covington mayor George Wermeling proclaimed the special occasion "Covington Art Club Day." At the anniversary luncheon, a special congratulatory telegram from President Jimmy Carter (1977–1981) was read.

The ladies attending the CAC and its programs today no longer feel compelled to accessorize their outfits with hats and gloves, like the original members. Nevertheless, they still seek the same educational, spiritual, and educational fulfillment and enrichment through the variety of programs offered and by reaching out to the community.

"Art Center (604 Greenup)," *KP*, October 6, 1974, 6K.
"Art Club Celebrates Its 78th Year as Oldest Group," *KP*, March 15, 1955, 3.
"Art Club Will Celebrate 93rd Anniversary March 9," *KP*, February 26, 1970, 23K.
Bradley, Bertine J. Telephone interview by Lois Shannon, July 2006.
Flottman, Ardyth. Telephone interview by Lois Shannon, July 2006.
Hall, Lucille. Telephone interview by Lois Shannon, July 2006.
Harrison, Mrs. W. Baxter. "The Covington Art Club," a paper presented to the Christopher Gist Historical Society, June 23, 1953.
Weldon, Harold Brown. Telephone interview by Lois Shannon, July 2006.
"Work Never Done," *KP*, May 19, 1978, 8K.

Lois Ann Shannon

COVINGTON BLUE SOX. The Covington Blue Sox professional baseball team, a member of the short-lived Federal Baseball League, was Northern Kentucky's only attempt to establish a major league baseball team. In 1913 Richard C. Stewart Jr. of the **Stewart Iron Works**, Covington's largest employer, and other prominent businessmen financed the start-up team. The original intention was to play in the Bluegrass League, but Covington's proximity to the market of the Cincinnati Reds made it impossible to join that league. Like today's Independent League franchise in Florence, Ky., the **Florence Freedom**, the Federal League existed mainly to provide cities with major league baseball where Major League Inc. would not allow it. The newly formed Federal League was looking for an eighth team to complete the league, and Covington was quickly accepted in March 1913. In May 1913, the Blue Sox began the season in Cleveland; the game ended in a tie. Home games were played in a hastily constructed ballpark at Second and Scott on the site of the former River Breeze Park, renamed Federal Park. The **flood of 1913** delayed progress on assembling the ballpark, which seated 6,000. The best seats sold for a dollar and the least expensive for a quarter. Opening Day in Covington was Friday, May 9, 1913, as the season began with former major leaguer Sam Leever as manager and several past and future major leaguers on the Covington roster. The Sox beat St. Louis 4-0 before a capacity crowd. Reportedly, legendary baseball player Ty Cobb had been offered the job as manager. Just before the first pitch, carrier pigeons (see **Homing Pigeons**) were released to the mayors of the seven other cities in the league with the message "Covington now has a Federal League team." The team was obviously a matter of civic pride. But enthusiasm quickly waned, attendance plummeted, and the organization picked up its bats and moved to Kansas City before July 1, with a win-loss of record of 21-31. The Covington Blue Sox team was the pinnacle of professional baseball in the Northern Kentucky region for the short period of the team's existence. By the start of the 1916 baseball season, the entire Federal League had folded.

"Covington Blue Sox," *KP*, March 5, 1913, 1.
"Covington Team to Open in Cleveland," *KP*, April 14, 1913, 3.
Reis, Jim. "Big League Dreams in'13—Covington Lost Team as Early Crowds Faded," *KP*, April 14, 2003, 4K.
——. "Third League Fields Eight Teams," *KP*, April 14, 2003, 4K.
"Remembering the Covington Blue Sox," *KP*, July 11, 2003, 5K.

Michael R. Sweeney

COVINGTON CATHOLIC HIGH SCHOOL. The history of Covington Catholic High School can be traced back to the year 1885, when the Brothers of Mary of Dayton, Ohio, a Roman Catholic religious order, were invited to the Diocese of Covington (see **Roman Catholics**) by Bishop **Camillus P. Maes** to staff the St. Joseph Boys School on 12th St. in Covington. Eventually, the brothers expanded their work in Covington by establishing St. Joseph Commercial High School. This two-year program provided young men with business skills, offering courses in basic accounting, bookkeeping, civics, and typing. The school attracted students from many of the Northern Kentucky parishes. The first graduating class received diplomas in 1892, and the last class graduated in 1926.

When Bishop Francis Howard arrived in Covington in 1923, he became concerned about the lack of educational opportunities for high-school-aged young men. In 1925 he requested that the Brothers of Mary open a four-year academic high school for boys in Covington. The provincial of the Brothers of Mary agreed to the project and appointed Anthony Weber S.M. as the first principal of the new school, named Covington Catholic High School. Msgr. Edward Klosterman of the **Mother of God** parish in Covington provided classroom space in the parish elementary school building on W. Sixth St. The school began with a freshman class of 32. In each succeeding year, an additional grade level was added, until in 1928 a four-year curriculum was under way. At the first graduation, in 1929, 17 young men received diplomas. In that same year, the Southern Association of Colleges and Secondary Schools and the Commonwealth of Kentucky accredited Covington Catholic High School.

As a central Catholic high school for young men in Kenton Co., Covington Catholic was not the responsibility of a single parish. Instead, the school drew students from throughout the county. In the early years, most of the students were graduates of the parish elementary schools in Covington, Fort Mitchell, Fort Wright, and Ludlow. The pastors of these parishes served as an unofficial school board and finance committee for Covington Catholic High School.

Enrollment at Covington Catholic High School was limited because of the amount of physical space allocated at Mother of God School. Many prospective students were turned away. In the years following **World War II**, the number of young men in Kenton Co. wishing to attend a Catholic high school greatly increased. Additional space was found in the old school building on Sixth St. in Covington to ensure modest growth. In 1952 Bishop William T. Mulloy appointed a committee of pastors from the 13 parishes located in Covington, Fort Mitchell, Fort Wright, and Ludlow to make plans for the construction of a new Covington Catholic High School. A 14-acre parcel of property was acquired along the **Dixie Highway** in Park Hills as a new site. Each of the participating parishes contributed to the building fund in accordance with their size. Construction began in 1953, and the cornerstone was laid the following year. The last portion of the new building, the gymnasium, was dedicated on January 29, 1955. The total cost of construction and land amounted to $845,439.

Covington Catholic High School's enrollment and faculty grew rapidly in its new building in Park Hills. The faculty included Brothers of Mary, diocesan clergy, and a significant number of laypersons. The last Marianist to serve as principal of Covington Catholic was Rev. Richard K. Knuge (1969–1971).

By the mid-1990s, the 1955 high school building was showing its age. The need for a more modern facility was apparent. On November 17, 1997, Bishop Robert Muench gave the approval to the Covington Catholic School Board to begin plans for a new building. Ground was broken for the new structure on October 29, 2002, and the new facility was dedicated the following year on December 7, by Covington's new bishop, Roger Foys. The school has won numerous athletic championships and academic awards. In 2009, its new Schott Sports Center opened.

Messenger, December 12, 2003, special section.

Ryan, Paul E. *History of the Diocese of Covington, Kentucky*. Covington, Ky.: Diocese of Covington, 1954.

David E. Schroeder

COVINGTON HISTORIC BUILDINGS. As for any city, geography, history, ethnicity, and economics, as well as the friction of tradition, innovation, and creativity shaped Covington's built environment. Established in 1815 as a suburb of Cincinnati, Covington benefited from the development of its larger neighbor. People—developers, architects, business owners, and workers—and ideas moved freely back and forth across the Ohio River and, to a lesser extent, up and down the river. Travel to the interior of Kentucky was much more difficult. Therefore, it is not surprising that the architecture of Covington, like that of its neighboring Kentucky towns Bellevue, Dayton, Ludlow, and Newport, has much more in common with Cincinnati and other towns along the Ohio River than with the interior of the state. In fact, the grid system in which Covington was laid out was intended to coincide with Cincinnati's streets.

Because Covington remained much smaller than Cincinnati, it retained many types of buildings that in Cincinnati disappeared long ago as victims of the relentless march of urban growth. Such still-existing structures include smaller-scale commercial buildings, freestanding lodge halls, numerous downtown churches, and elegant residences close to the center of town.

There were talented local architects and craftsmen, some of whom worked on both sides of the Ohio River, who made their homes in Covington during the first half of the 19th century. Seneca Palmer, designer of the **Western Baptist Theological Institute**, was one of these, and Peleg Kidd, creator of the first Covington City Hall in the 1830s, was another. Downtown Covington boasts a series of key buildings by leading Cincinnati architects, as well designs by local architects, some of whom trained at major Cincinnati architectural firms. The material of choice for Covington buildings was brick, set off by carved and rough-cut stone, wood clapboards and shingles, cast and wrought iron, and terra cotta.

The city developed as a series of neighborhoods, many of them with a strong ethnic identification and sense of identity. These neighborhoods tended to be clustered around churches. The city was built densely, along a grid of narrow streets, reflecting high land prices and a desire to use space efficiently. To maximize garden space and privacy, houses were built abutting lot lines, with windows limited to the side facing the house's yard.

From about 1860 to 1920, hundreds of two- and three-story dwellings, many of brick, were built for working middle-class families. Much like freestanding row houses, these "Covington-Newport townhouses" are tall and narrow, with facades two bays wide. Often, the main entrance was located on the sidewall. These versatile buildings, with countless variations, could be "dressed" up or down according to the owner's desires and means. A substantial Covington-Newport house could be built for as little as $1,000. The origins of this distinctive and durable house type, not found anywhere else in the state, remain a mystery.

Complementing the city's everyday buildings are architect-designed landmarks and extraordinary buildings that serve as neighborhood focal points. The city's first high-style building, and its oldest brick structure, is the **Gano-Southgate House**, also known as the Carneal House, on E. Second St. in the Licking-Riverside Riverside Drive Historic District. Built around 1815, it is a refined Federal-style residence reminiscent of Palladio's Villa Pisani, with an inset two-tier porch.

Over the next century, successive European revival styles, like waves of immigrants, washed over the city. The classically inspired Greek Revival style reigned before the **Civil War**, followed by the Italianate mode, derived from the architecture of Renaissance Italy. One of the city's oldest high-style commercial buildings is the Greek Revival–style **Northern Bank of Kentucky** on Scott St.; it is a stately temple-front brick edifice built in 1836 and enlarged in the 1880s. The building was saved from demolition and renovated in the late 1990s. The Grecian style was used for elegant antebellum residences as well, including the **Richard Southgate** House on Garrard St. in Licking-Riverside and the Robert Patton House built in roughly 1855 in Austinburg, with a Victorian porch added around 1890.

Towering over the intersection of Fifth St. and Madison Ave. is the Odd Fellows Hall. Constructed in 1857 by Cincinnati builder Isaac Graveson, it features Greek Revival and Italianate elements. On the eve of its proposed renovation in 2002, a raging fire gutted the hall, leaving only three full walls. The still-elegant ruin was rebuilt and renovated to preservation guidelines and won local and statewide awards. In the building's shadow is the former African American Odd Fellows Hall, a modest brick structure two stories high. The juxtaposition of the two lodge halls in style, scale, and siting is a silent reminder of the challenges faced by African Americans in Covington during the 1800s.

Designed in stripped Italianate style, the **Motch Jewelers** building of 1871 on Madison Ave. features a severe incised facade of smooth stone with colonnettes framing the openings. The Motch store is one of the few surviving commercial buildings designed by the innovative Cincinnati architect James W. McLaughlin. Strategically located at the visual closure to E. Fifth St., the Jonathan David Hearne House on Garrard St., built in 1874, is an Italianate palazzo (large urban building) in brick.

The post–Civil War years saw the visually rich and complex French Second Empire and High Victorian Gothic styles come to the fore. The home of the **Baker-Hunt Foundation** on Greenup St. is a rare, fully developed example of the Second Empire style. All the openings of the facade are curved or arched, including the coupled dormers on the bell-cast (curved like a bell) Mansard roof. The most spectacular example of the High Victorian Gothic in downtown Covington is the Charles Donnelly & Company Undertaking and Livery Stable building on Madison Ave., dating from about 1880. Its "bravura" facade includes a carved horse's head over the former stable entrance. The former Park Hotel (now law offices), located at W. Sixth and Philadelphia Sts. in the West Side/ **Main Strasse** Historic District facing Goebel Park, also used the High Victorian Gothic successfully.

While relatively uncommon in the city, excellent examples of the fanciful and picturesque Queen Anne style were built during the late 1880s and 1890s. The James T. Earle House on Southern Ave. in Latonia was built in 1897 for the last mayor of that formerly independent town. Clad in clapboards and shingles with beaming sunbursts, an encircling veranda with gazebo, and an imbricated (patterned) slate roof, it is also one of the city's best-preserved frame houses. The more sedate Queen Anne Free Classic style, popular at the turn of the 20th century, is well represented by the home of saloonkeeper Slade Webb on Decoursey Ave. in Latonia.

The waning years of the century saw the beginnings of a revolt against Victorianism, with the rise of the Richardsonian Romanesque, Shingle, and Colonial Revival styles. Attributed to Cincinnati architect Henry A. Siter, the former German National Bank on Madison Ave., built around 1890, uses Richardsonian elements, for example rough-textured and checkerboard surfaces.

Around the turn of the 20th century, a variety of Neoclassical revivals arose as a reaction to Victorianism, emphasizing refinement of detail and high-quality craftsmanship. Civic landmarks in the monumental and monochromatic Beaux-Arts Classical style include three bank buildings at Sixth St. and Madison Ave., built between 1900 and the early 1920s: the former Farmers' and Traders' National Bank (later **First National Bank and Trust Company of Covington**; now Republic Bank), the **Peoples-Liberty Bank** (now **US Bank**), and the Covington Trust (now **Huntington Bank**) building. Both the Farmers' and Traders' National Bank—the first true high-rise office structure in Northern Kentucky—and the Peoples Liberty building were designed by Cincinnati architect Harry Hake. The Beaux-Arts style was also used effectively for the former **Covington Public Library** at 1028 Scott Blvd., built 1900–1903 and designed by Boll & Taylor architects, and for the 1923 Covington Telephone Building at 11th and Scott Sts., which was designed by Harry Hake.

Defining the early 20th century was the counterpoint of the conservative Colonial and Georgian revivals and the progressive Craftsman style, as well as the first stirrings of Modernism. The **Coppin** Building at Seventh St. and Madison Ave., built in 1906 by the Ferro Concrete Construction Company, combines Beaux-Arts Classical and progressive Chicago School elements. James Gilmore, a Cincinnati architect with Modernist leanings, was its designer.

One of Covington's exceptional early "modern" houses is the Sayers House at 435 Wallace Ave. in the Wallace Woods Historic District, built around 1907 for an automobile dealer. The Craftsman-style stucco dwelling features wooden beams, earth-toned tile bands, and "Germanic" clipped gables. The Northcutt House at 2126 Glenway Ave. in Wallace Woods, a Japanesque bungalow built about 1920, exhibits a combined front porch and porte cochere overlapping the gabled main block, as well as a matching garage.

A stripped Moderne aesthetic took hold in the 1930s, along with the last stand of Classicism in the form of Depression Modern. The U.S. Post Office and Court House, built in 1938 at Scott and Seventh Sts., is a monumental edifice of dressed limestone, with stone bas-reliefs. Architect T. H. Ellett won a rare national competition for the building's design.

The city's most celebrated house of worship is the **Cathedral Basilica of the Assumption**, built about 1895–1910 by Charles McDonald. The church was designed by Leon Cocquard and **David Davis** in the Gothic–Beaux Arts style, with a facade modeled on the Notre Dame Cathedral in Paris, France. Roman Catholic bishop **Camillus Maes**, a great patron of architecture, purposely chose the site near the railroad tracks so the stone would become stained by soot and assume a false veneer of antiquity. The Cathedral's German Catholic counterpart is the **Mother of God Catholic Church** on W. Sixth St., built in 1871. A monumental Renaissance Revival basilica-plan edifice with twin towers and dome, it was designed by the Cincinnati architectural firm of **Walter and Stewart**.

The former Second Presbyterian Church on E. Ninth St., designed by James W. McLaughlin and built by J. A. Walthall in the 1860s, is a Romanesque Revival brick edifice with arcaded corbel table and narrow, round-arched openings. Rebuilt after a fire in 1880, it was sold to an African American congregation in 1902 and renamed the Ninth St. Methodist Church (see **Ninth St. United Methodist Church**). The First Methodist Church (see **First United Methodist Church**), built 1866–1867 and designed by Walter & Stewart, on Greenup St. in Licking-Riverside, is a very sophisticated example of High Victorian Gothic design. Complementing the church building is the Victorian Gothic–style rectory next door, with grinning gargoyles. The **Madison Ave. Christian Church**, designed by the **Weber Brothers**, dates from 1912–1913. In the Neoclassical Revival style, it carries a stately, pedimented ionic portico and is crowned by a hemispherical dome.

Built of enduring materials, the city's public schools represent civic architecture at its best and reflect the value placed on education. The Holman St. or Fifth District School in Peaselburg is a late Richardsonian–Renaissance Revival work in red brick and limestone. A striking design of striated brick and stone, it features arcaded windows, boxed pediments with oculi, and an arcaded porch trimmed in rough stone.

Holmes High School is a monumental Collegiate Gothic–style edifice completed in 1919. Designed by the Weber Brothers, it was built on the grounds of Holmesdale, the 17-acre estate of New Orleans, La., dry goods merchant **Daniel Holmes**. The Holmes mansion was also used for cafeteria and classroom space until it was demolished to make way for a new administration building in 1936.

During the 1930s, Northern Kentucky's public schools adopted low, horizontal plans with minimal Art Moderne detailing. Lincoln Grant High School on Greenup St. was built in 1932 for Covington's African American students (see **Lincoln-Grant School**). Upon its completion, the yellow-brick structure was praised as the best equipped of all "colored schools" in Kentucky. E. C. and G. T. Landberg designed it.

The postwar decades saw the triumph of Modernist styles that had first appeared four decades before, as well as a new appreciation for the city's historic architecture.

Boh, John. "Ninth Street United Methodist Church, Covington, Kentucky, Part I," *Kenton County Historical Society Bulletin* 156 (May 2002): 2–3.

——. "Ninth Street United Methodist Church, Covington, Kentucky, Part II," *Kenton County Historical Society Bulletin* 157 (June 2002): 2–3.

Cabot, Susan. "Architecture of Lewisburg: Italianate," *Kenton County Historical Society Bulletin* 100 (March 1997): 4–5.

Gastright, Joseph S. "Austinburg, a Covington Neighborhood," *Kenton County Historical Society Bulletin* 91 (June 1996): 2–4.

Konicki, Leah. "Hearne House: A Treasure Repeatedly Threatened," *Kenton County Historical Society Bulletin* 145 (May 2001): 2–3.

Kornilowicz-Weldon, Alexandra. "Lewisburg Historic District," National Register of Historic Places nomination, 1983. Available at the Kenton Co. Public Library, Covington, Ky.

Langsam, Walter E. "Architectural Database," in the possession of Walter E. Langsam, Cincinnati.

——. *Biographical Dictionary of Cincinnati Architects.* www.architecturecincy.org/dictionary/index.html (accessed April 2009).

——. "Covington Downtown Commercial Historic District," National Register of Historic Places nomination, 1983. Available at the Kenton Co. Public Library, Covington, Ky.

——. "Licking Riverside Historic District," National Register of Historic Places nomination, 1975. Available at the Kenton Co. Public Library, Covington, Ky.

Reis, Jim. "A Home for Holmes: Covington High School Built on Tycoon's Estate," *KP*, January 5, 2004.

Schneider, Charlotte. "Mutter Gottes Historic District," National Register of Historic Places nomination, 1980. Available at the Kenton Co. Public Library, Covington, Ky.

"Wallace Woods Historic District," National Register of Historic Places nomination, 1983. Available at the Kenton Co. Public Library, Covington, Ky.

Walsh, Rita. "Northern Kentucky Townhouse Study," 1993, Kentucky Heritage Council, Frankfort, Ky.

Margaret Warminski

COVINGTON INDEPENDENT SCHOOLS. Public education, or nontuition schools, began in Covington in 1825, in a log-cabin school with an annual budget of $80, one teacher, and 20 students enrolled. Before that, education in Covington was available only in private schools and only to the people who could afford to pay for it. More schools, both public and private, followed as the population grew.

Once the public schools began operating, a controlling body was needed. This responsibility was handled by five men who had been appointed as "school visitors"; their major duties were to establish and administer the schools. At that time males and females were taught separately. However, girls have always been included in public education in Covington, and the enrollment numbers for boys and girls usually have been about equal.

The Covington City Charter of 1850 made several provisions for the city's public school system. A board of trustees was instituted to replace the "school visitors." The new governing body was composed of several men from each of the city wards, who were charged with operating the system's schools until a superintendent could be hired. An additional provision established a board of examiners to administer qualifying examinations to teachers. To become a teacher in the Covington school system, a person was required simply to pass an examination. A third provision gave the new trustees the duty of selecting a superintendent for the schools and stated that this person's pay would be no more than $300 per year. Another provision, probably the most important one, called for establishing a tax-supported, tuition-free secondary or high school. Until this time, after students completed the eighth grade, they were either finished with their education or were required to pay for the remainder at private academies. The new educational system in Covington included the first public high school established in Kentucky.

The Covington school system's first brick school opened in 1864. This three-story building had 12 rooms, 4 on each floor. The rooms were well lighted, heated by coal stoves, and had a means of ventilation—opening and closing the windows. Each room was equipped with blackboards and double desks that could seat 56 students. There were outhouses in the school yards and buckets of drinking water with dippers provided in each room. The fire escape was a long tube reaching from the top floor to the ground by which the children could slide down to safety. Three more elementary schools and a separate school for African American children were built on the same pattern (see **Lincoln-Grant School**).

Between 1901 and 1910, three additional elementary schools were erected, all in different architectural styles. These buildings were equipped with running water and bathrooms. By 1909 Covington had outgrown its boundaries, so it annexed two areas to the south known as Latonia and Rosedale and one to the west known as West Covington. There were schools already operating in those areas that were under their own school boards. The Covington Board of Education simply took over control of these schools and assumed any debts they had.

After 1922 construction at the elementary school level included additions to older schools, new buildings that were replacements for older buildings, and new buildings that consolidated two or more older district schools. During the early 1930s, the city of Covington benefited greatly from the federal government's WPA work programs. Several new buildings and additions, including some to the city's schools, were constructed by the WPA.

By 1892 the importance of kindergartens had been recognized, and classes at this level were started. These early kindergartens were not an integral part of the elementary school buildings but were located in nearby rented rooms. The women in charge of the kindergartens were not necessarily teachers and were paid lower salaries. As late as 1936, for example, Miss Daisy operated a kindergarten in a storefront at Pike and Hermes Sts. in Covington's **Lewisburg** neighborhood.

In 1853 Asa M. Drury started the first secondary classes at what was called the Covington High School. There were 11 boys and 9 girls who were taught in one room of an elementary building. This, the first public high school in the state, was coeducational. The high school's curriculum grew, and in 1869 the first graduate, Amelia Orr, received a high school diploma. There were six high school graduates in 1870 but none in 1871. In 1872 the first permanent high school building was constructed at the northeast corner of 12th and Russell Sts. Professor Drury, who was formerly on the faculty of the **Western Baptist Theological Institute** in Covington, became the high school's first superintendent. He was appointed in 1856 at a salary of $1,200 and served for three years but was dismissed for "making too much money." There was no other superintendent until the Covington City Charter was revised, after which, in 1865, the school superintendent's position was once again filled. This brief interlude was the only break in continuity for the office of superintendent.

By 1904 Covington had employed truant officers and was requiring children to attend school. It was not until 1908, however, that a law was passed making regular attendance compulsory in Kentucky. In 1912 several changes occurred. First, the current governing school board system was established. Under the new system, five citizens were elected by popular vote to serve on the school board for four-year terms. Second, two new junior high schools, consisting of grades seven and eight, were established. The junior high school setup continued until 2002, when a middle school format was adopted. Third, half-year classes were initiated, beginning each year in September and in February. This made it possible for children starting school to be placed with students of their own age, rather than waiting until the next fall to enroll in first grade. Also, students who did not pass a grade level now had only to repeat a half year of work instead of being held back an entire year. The half-year format continued until 1941.

The high school, which began in 1853 in one room and by 1872 had grown to a 12-room building, was, by 1915, crowded and in need of a larger, more modern facility. A site search committee selected the Holmesdale estate of the late **Daniel Henry Holmes Sr.** for the high school's new location. The new school opened in January 1919 with 40 rooms, a gymnasium, special-purpose rooms, and a student body numbering 500. It was renamed Covington **Holmes High School**. Additional classrooms were needed, and in 1927 a junior high school building was added to this campus. In 1936 the Holmes mansion was razed and an administration building was constructed. The David M. Evans Field House and Science Buildings were added in 1966. In 1980 the Chapman Academic and Technical Center was constructed as part of the Holmes educational complex. This center handles instruction in various trades and maintains the requisite high school curriculum. In 1987 a renovation was begun to make the entire Holmes High School campus accessible to the physically handicapped.

As the system grew, the need for better-qualified teachers also increased. Standards for teachers were established. In the early years, male teachers were paid higher salaries than female teachers. Since 1960 there has been a single salary schedule based solely on educational degrees attained and years of teaching experience.

By 1988 the Covington Independent School District was the largest independent district in the Commonwealth of Kentucky, with an enrollment of about 6,000 students. Since then, as the population of Covington has declined, the number of students has decreased and the need for some of the elementary schools has diminished. At one time the district had 12 elementary schools, 2 junior high schools, and 1 high school; now it has 6 elementary schools, 1 middle school, and 1 junior-senior high school.

The Civil Rights Act of 1964 ended segregation in the schools. At that time all of the African American students in Covington attended the Lincoln-Grant School on Greenup St., and none of the faculties in the Covington school system were integrated. Desegregation proceeded over the next 10 years and involved changing district boundaries to achieve racial balance.

Through the years many programs were tried. Some, including night school and German language training in the elementary schools, were abandoned. Homebound teaching, special education, Marine Corps Junior ROTC, advanced placement, International Baccalaureate classes, and adult high school classes were instituted and remain.

The new millennium has seen significant changes, including full-day kindergartens, further redistricting to achieve better racial and population balances, the founding of a Holmes High School Hall of Distinction, and most importantly, renewed efforts to ensure that all students learn to the best of their abilities.

Nordheim, Betty Lee. *Echoes of the Past: A History of the Covington Public School System*. Covington, Ky.: Covington Independent Public Schools, 2002.

Betty Lee Nordheim

COVINGTON LADIES HOME. Originally known as the Home for Aged and Indigent Women, this Covington institution, at the southeast corner of Seventh and Garrard Sts., has served women in Covington and Kenton Co. for more than 120 years. Founded by a group of philanthropically minded women in 1886, the home was the first local organization begun and operated by women to serve the needs of women.

The home's founder, Ellen B. Dietrich, who resided on W. Fifth St. in Covington, was acutely aware of the conditions of the poor in her own neighborhood, and her own home often served as a haven for women who had no other place to stay. With the help of 11 other Covington women, Dietrich formed an associated charity called the Women's Educational and Industrial Union, which sought to teach women marketable skills to foster their independence. This was a revolutionary concept for the time. The organization provided an employment bureau and a sewing school and offered housekeeping classes for women in need. The Home for Aged and Indigent Women is the only permanent outgrowth of the Union. Dietrich contacted several prominent Covington businessmen requesting donations for the purchase of a building and was able to raise the necessary funds to acquire the Hays home at 10th and Russell Sts. in Covington for $5,000. After a gracious outpouring of gifts and money, the home was quickly furnished. It opened November 1, 1886, and the first residents moved in on January 8, 1887. Among these was a woman of only 40 years of age, who was suffering from tuberculosis and had no means of financial support. It was because of her case that the word *indigent* was inserted into the home's name. The home was subsidized by the Educational and Industrial Union during its first year only; in 1887 the home became a separate organization, and the first Board of Lady Managers was formed. The board incorporated with the State of Kentucky in March 1888. According to the charter, three gentlemen, Joseph Chambers, Frank Ford, and **Jonathan Hearne**, were elected fiscal trustees to assist the managers in legal and corporate matters. It is in large part due to the financial generosity of these men that the home survived its first few years. As it became more established in the ensuing years, the Board of Lady Managers established standing committees and rules for the residents. The admissions committee formulated strict standards for admission to the home, including the requirements that each applicant submit "testimonials of the propriety of her conduct and respectability of her character," that no woman under age 60 be admitted unless she was deemed suffering from "premature old age," that each applicant pay the sum of $150 if she could afford it, and that each woman agree to accept the rules and to surrender all her real and personal property to the board's custody. The high standards set by the board have ensured the high quality of the institution since its inception.

By 1889 the home's population had grown too large for its location at 10th and Russell. Under the direction of board president Charity Warner, and with the strong encouragement of J. D. Hearne, the board began raising funds and ultimately purchased a lot at the corner of Seventh and Garrard Sts. in Covington. The lot, which was owned by the enterprising and wealthy Covington businessman **Amos Shinkle**, was the site of an old lawn-tennis court. Shinkle agreed to sell the property for $5,430 and donated $2,000 from the sale to the home. The board hired Cincinnati architect H. E. Seter to design the new residence, which was to have a basement, three floors, and an octagonal tower ascending on the northwest corner, at the main entrance. It was designed to accommodate 50 residents, and its estimated cost was $20,000. With Hearne's generous donation to the building fund, the residence was completed by spring 1894.

Near the turn of the 20th century, the board also established an endowment fund, which was fortified by a $10,000 bequest from Hearne that was collected after his death in 1905. The endowment fund continues to serve the home to this day. During the Great Depression, the Board of Lady Managers administered the home's finances so proficiently that no staff members were dismissed, furthermore, all of the workers received their regular Christmas bonuses. The home was also able to donate unused items to Kenton Co. Relief and even provide odd jobs for the unemployed.

The board has regularly authorized funds to modernize the structure at Seventh and Garrard Sts. to ensure the comfort of residents. In 1941 plumbing was installed in each room so that each resident had her own sink and mirror. In 1953 the dining room, the chapel, and the front room were redecorated and a sprinkler system was installed. In 1961 the home was expanded with a new addition, which allowed for an enlarged dining and sitting room and for each resident to have a private room. In 1975 the grand staircase was replaced with stairs encased in firewalls with steel doors. In May 1983 the official name of the residence was changed to the Covington Ladies Home.

Today the home accommodates 32 women, all in private rooms. It provides meals, personal care, laundry, housekeeping, and activities. There is a 24-hour on-site nursing staff. Although once financed almost completely by private donations, the home now accepts some state aid and charges monthly rent. The home is still operated by the Board of Lady Managers as well as three fiscal trustees nominated by the board. The success of the Covington Ladies Home over its 120 years is a direct result of superior management by the Board of Lady Managers, which takes a personal interest in the comfort, happiness, and general welfare of each resident.

Barlage, Sarah A. *The Covington Ladies Home: The First Hundred Years.* Covington, Ky.: Covington Ladies Home, 1997.

Covington Ladies Home Corporate Minutes and Treasury Reports, 1887–1987, Covington Ladies Home, 702 Garrard Street, Covington, Ky.

Reis, Jim. "Home Gives Women a Haven," *KP*, July 25, 1994, 4K.

Sarah A. Barlage

COVINGTON LATIN SCHOOL. The origins of the Covington Latin School in Covington can be traced to the appointment of Rev. **Francis W. Howard** as the fifth bishop of the Diocese of Covington (see **Roman Catholics**) in 1923. A longtime advocate of Catholic education and a founding member of the National Catholic Education Association, Bishop Howard quickly recognized the need for secondary schools in his new diocese. In September 1923 he established the Covington Latin School in a small brick residence near the cathedral at 12th St. and Madison Ave., the former residence of **Michael T. Shine**. Howard said the purpose of the school was "to provide intelligent young boys with the opportunities of a solid classical education that would develop them into scholarly, Catholic leaders." The first class consisted of 15 young men. The Covington Latin School accepted students who had completed the sixth grade, and the school offered a four-year classical curriculum preparing them for college. The first headmaster was Rev. John Kroger, a priest who had been ordained for one year. He was assisted by Sister Mary Grace Callahan, S.C.N., an instructor of mathematics. Eventually, many of the most talented clergy in the diocese were added to the Covington Latin School faculty, and talented lay teachers taught there as well.

In 1925 the program moved to three classrooms at the **Mother of God** School on Sixth St. in Covington. That same year, Howard initiated an examination for all sixth-grade male students in the diocese. Those who received high grades on this examination were invited to enroll at the school. The annual examination continued for many years. To establish the school in a separate building, in 1926 Howard purchased the former Knights of Columbus Hall on E. 11th St. Following a thorough renovation, the three-story building, dedicated on March 27, 1926, became the new home of the Covington Latin School. By the late 1930s, when the school had outgrown the facilities on 11th St., each parish in Northern Kentucky was assessed an amount to contribute for the construction of a new building. The old building was demolished, and the new one was begun in 1940. On December 7, 1941, Howard dedicated the current Covington Latin School building.

The Latin School continued to prosper under Bishop Howard's successors. Bishops **William T. Mulloy** and Richard H. Ackerman both carried on the tradition of Covington Latin School as the bishop's school. Both were frequent visitors in the classroom, and both assigned many of the most talented clergy to its faculty.

During the 1980s, Bishop William A. Hughes commissioned a comprehensive plan for the high schools in the Diocese of Covington. This plan, known as the Dayton Study, conducted by consultants from the University of Dayton in Ohio, recommended that the Covington Latin School and the **Villa Madonna Academy** in suburban Villa Hills be merged and use the suburban campus of Villa Madonna Academy. After opposition from Latin School faculty, students, parents, and alumni was expressed, and after unfruitful discussions by the officials at both schools, the plan to merge the two institutions was dropped. Both institutions have since become coeducational, Covington Latin School in 1992.

Over the years, numerous graduates of Covington Latin School have earned scholarships to prestigious colleges and universities. Alumni are counted in many fields, including the clergy, medicine, law, science, and engineering. The school attracts students from throughout Northern Kentucky and Greater Cincinnati.

Leader, January 1951, 2. Covington Latin School newspaper.

Messenger, Bishop Howard Memorial ed., 1944, 18.

Ryan, Paul E. *History of the Diocese of Covington, Kentucky.* Covington, Ky.: Diocese of Covington, 1954.

Tenkotte, Paul A., David E. Schroeder, and Thomas S. Ward. *To Be Catholic and American in Northern, Central, and Appalachian Kentucky: The Diocese of Covington, 1853–2003.* Forthcoming.

David E. Schroeder

COVINGTON LOCOMOTIVE AND MANUFACTURING WORKS. In April 1853 the *Covington Journal* described the Covington Locomotive and Manufacturing Works as "the most extensive" in the West. The newspaper said the firm would employ approximately 600 hands and planned to build four locomotives each month. Daniel H. Feger, a master machinist and draughtsman, had come to Covington from the railroad shops in Reading, Pa., to work for the Covington Locomotive and Manufacturing Works. By November, the new works in Covington, located at Third and Philadelphia Sts., were not yet at capacity and only about 150 workers were on the payroll. The company anticipated producing engines for the **Covington and Lexington Railroad** (C&L), a new rail line in Kentucky, much of which had yet to be constructed. The C&L had already bought two engines from the Portland, Maine, Locomotive Works: the *Bourbon*, a passenger locomotive,, and the *Falmouth*, a freight engine.

In February 1854, Covington Locomotive and Manufacturing Works was building four locomotives for the C&L, two engines for the Little Miami Rail Road, and four locomotives for a railroad company in Indiana. With 130 workers at the time, the factory in Covington was adding a shop for the manufacture of railroad cars. A special charter from the Kentucky legislature assured unencumbered production and expansion of the business.

On April 11, 1854, the first locomotive produced by the company, the *Covington*, was tested. The new engine replaced an earlier *Covington*, built in 1852 by Cincinnati's Harkness and Company. On April 29, 1854, the company christened its new locomotive, ornamented with flags and a wreath at the front of the boiler. That Saturday was a holiday for the employees. They marched to the depot in a parade behind a brass band. The *Covington* left the station at 8:00 a.m. and carried its 300 passengers a distance of 37 miles to Falmouth in only two hours. The engine continued to Boyd, located 55 miles from Covington, and then returned to Falmouth for a luncheon. By 5:00 p.m. the locomotive had returned to Covington. That night, 100 guests enjoyed a 10:00 p.m. dinner at the Magnolia House in Covington. The *Covington*'s maiden trip was proclaimed a triumph.

On June 8, 1854, the C&L rail line arrived at the village of Cynthiana, where a celebration took place to commemorate the event. The engine *Cynthiana*, built at the Covington Locomotive and Manufacturing Works, made its maiden trip that day. Although reporters called the locomotive "an admirable piece of workmanship," they stated that the *Covington* "wears the horns." The line was extended to Paris, Ky., by early August. On July 7, 1854, the engine named *Paris,* also made by the locomotive manufacturing firm in Covington, was added to the railroad, and on August 30, another creation of the firm, the locomotive *Lexington,* began service.

Scholar John H. White Jr. has found that, in September 1854, Feger sent to the Baldwin Locomotive Works an order for boiler tubes—a fact suggesting that the Covington Locomotive and Manufacturing Works was still in business. Notwithstanding Feger's order, the works apparently closed for an undetermined duration. On April 14, 1855, the *Covington Journal* reported that the works might reopen. On May 19, 1855, the *Covington Journal* announced that Cowles, Sickles & Company were reopening the factory with Feger as superintendent. The firm planned to cease production of railroad equipment and to manufacture oscillating-cylinder steam engines for riverboats instead. White believes that, for whatever reason, the plant was out of business completely by October of 1855.

The Covington Locomotive and Manufacturing Works may have expanded prematurely or it may have suffered from an eight-year slowdown in the U.S. economy that began in 1853. On December 15, 1855, a commissioner sold the firm at auction to A. D. Powell of Cincinnati for $100,000, but because the sale terms had not been met, a second auction became necessary. A commissioner's sale was listed for January 19, 1856. Finally, on April 4, partners Scott and Wolf bought for $70,000 the Covington Locomotive and Manufacturing Works, in which more than $250,000 had been invested. The new firm was named the Kentucky Locomotive and Machine Works.

By December 1856, the factory of the former Covington Locomotive and Manufacturing Works had been idle for a year. Planning to build steamboat machinery, Anchutz & Company of Cincinnati leased the property. By 1857 Scott and Wolf managed to establish their new business on the site, producing a freight locomotive named the *M. M. Benton* for **Mortimer M. Benton**, the first mayor of Covington. It was claimed that the engine gave the highest satisfaction while pulling 33 cars loaded with cattle. The Kentucky Locomotive and Machine Works also advertised stationary and marine engines.

In August 1857 the Kentucky Locomotive and Machine Works fell victim to a national financial panic. However, from the demise of the locomotive industry in Covington grew a vast and profitable firm, for in 1891 the **Houston, Stanwood & Gamble Company** occupied the property of the Covington Locomotive and Machine Works.

"A. L. Greer and Company Are Constructing Four Locomotives for the Covington & Lexington Rail," *CJ*, November 12, 1853, 3.

"A. L. Greer's Company Almost Ready to Commence Work," *CJ*, April 16, 1853, 3.

"Covington Locomotive Works," *CJ*, February 25, 1854, 2.

"The Locomotive 'Covington'—Excursion and Supper," *CJ*, May 6, 1854, 3.

"Locomotive Works in Covington," *DC*, January 4, 1882, 2.

White, John H. *Cincinnati Locomotive Builders*. 1965. 3rd ed., Cincinnati: Cincinnati Museum Center, 2004.

Robert T. Rhode

COVINGTON PUBLIC LIBRARY. Library service was first provided in Covington shortly after the founding of the city in 1815. The first library of which there is record was the Covington Social Library, which was established in 1824 and flourished for a brief time. Over the next 75 years, numerous libraries served the city. The *Covington Journal* reported in 1850 that the city had 27 libraries containing 11,755 volumes. Among the successors to the earliest library were the Covington Fireman's Library, opened in 1852, the Franklin Library, opened in 1868, and the West End Library, opened in 1877. Most of these libraries were subscription-based; the users paid minimal fees for the right to use books.

Heightened by the philanthropy of Andrew Carnegie, who was contributing to cities across the nation so that they could build libraries, interest in establishing a free public library in Covington intensified in the 1890s. The mayor of Covington appointed a board of prominent citizens, including Professor Melchor Abele, Dr. J. T. Dodd, Kentucky senator **William Goebel**, **Bradford Shinkle**, and Judge **James P. Tarvin**, to oversee the process. After Goebel and Dodd died, **Joseph L. Rhinock** became a member of the board and assumed leadership. Carnegie contributed $40,000 for the construction of the library, on the condition that the city agree to provide sustaining support. The Kentucky legislature assisted by passing legislation that required the city to support the library perpetually. As the library was being planned, it was determined that more money was needed, and Carnegie was persuaded to give an additional $35,000. The library board purchased property at the corner of Scott and Robbins Sts. and hired architects Boll and Taylor to design the building. Construction began in April 1902. While plans for the new library were being developed, a temporary location was found in Ideal Hall at the corner of Seventh St. and Madison Ave. The Covington Public Library first opened at this site in 1901, with Helen B. Landsdowne as the head librarian.

The completed Carnegie Library, built at a cost of $87,170, opened on March 16, 1904, boasting plenty of space for books, a rotunda resembling the one in the Library of Congress, and a grand auditorium. The first program in the auditorium that evening was a performance of the Polyphonic Choral Society. The first books were circulated from the new library on March 28, 1904. At the time, there were six employees, with Anne M. Spears serving as head librarian. Rules adopted for use of the library offered service for anyone in Covington, making the Covington Public Library the first public library in the South to offer racially integrated service. The services of the Covington Public Library were free for city residents, while other county residents could use the library for $2.00 per year.

During the library's first decade, the collection grew to 14,867 volumes and the number of users increased to more than 10,000. In 1906 head librarian Spears asked the library board to modify the rules to allow users to check out two books at a time, one fiction and one "solid reading." Shortly thereafter, Spears arranged for 150 books to be available for checkout at Pope's Drugstore in nearby Latonia, the first "library station" in Covington. Additional stations were opened at the Seventh District School and at **Lincoln-Grant School** in Covington and at the Latonia High School.

The Covington Public Library's auditorium turned out to be problematic from the beginning. As early as 1909, the library board retained an architect to develop plans for remodeling the auditorium,

Covington's Carnegie Library.

though no funds were available for the renovation. The city building officer inspected the auditorium and noted its inadequacies, citing a need for fireproof walls, modified steps, additional exits, red-lighted exit signs, rebuilt rails, and improved ventilation. In August 1914 the auditorium was ordered closed until repairs could be made. Following these repairs, the auditorium was reopened in June 1915. The cost of the repairs strained the library's finances so much that no funds were available to purchase books and the number of periodical subscriptions was reduced. Again in the late 1920s, city officials declared the auditorium "a disgrace to the city" and gave the library's board $200 for its repair.

In spite of the problems, the auditorium was in great demand for use by groups such as the Covington Board of Education and the Covington Lecture Club. During **World War I**, patriotic organizations frequently used the auditorium for programs. Other groups that used the auditorium included the Epworth League, the Friends of Irish Freedom, Kenton Co. Equal Rights, **La Salette Academy**, and the Woman's Suffrage League. In 1928 the auditorium was the site of a speech by Kentucky governor Flem Sampson (1927–1931).

The Covington Public Library's longtime head librarian Anne Spears retired in 1928 after 27 years of service and was succeeded by Alma L'Hommedieu. To obtain funds to purchase more popular books, L'Hommedieu created a system by which residents could "rent" popular books for three cents per day. In 1928 the Covington Public Library agreed to oversee the local Erlanger-Elsmere Library, which had been established by the Erlanger Woman's Club in 1914.

Throughout the 1930s and into the 1940s, a key staff member was Children's Librarian Eleanor McKenna, who worked tirelessly to ensure that every child knew about the library. She visited every classroom twice each year, made sure the Children's Room at the library was bright and inviting, and created dozens of new exciting programs to get children to come to the library. In 1931 McKenna organized the Library Vacation Reading Club, which has remained a tradition through the years.

The **Great Depression** resulted in increased usage of the Covington Public Library. The librarian's report dated February 5, 1931, states, "Many times not a single vacant chair can be found. These people always read. We find that many men are reading up along the line of their work, really putting this time to advantage." In December 1933, L'Hommedieu resigned as head librarian and Hilda Glaser was chosen as her replacement. In 1936 the popular circular desk at the Covington Public Library was moved under the building's dome to create more space. The Ohio River **flood of 1937** closed the Covington Public Library from January 25 to February 8; 53 books were reported lost in the flood, and many more were reported missing.

After head librarian Glaser resigned in October 1937, Catherine Lyons Towers took her place and served for the next three years. Library board member Rebecca Cox became head librarian in 1940. During 1940, 200 new books were added to the Covington Public Library's shelves each month. Between 300 and 400 new cardholders were added each month as well. The library's typists created, on average, 800 new catalog cards each month. The library's total book budget was $2,000 per year and the librarian's salary was $135 per month. Considerable expenditure was required for repairs and refurbishment of the library in the 1940s.

In 1942 the Covington Public Library Board determined it could no longer manage the Erlanger-Elsmere Library without additional contributions from the cities of Erlanger and Elsmere, so control was returned to the Erlanger Woman's Club.

Technology was introduced to the public library in Covington after **World War II**. In 1950 the first microfilm reader was purchased for $298, enabling the library to collect local history and genealogy materials on microfilm. Growth in the 1950s resulted in additional funds appropriated by the city. The year 1957 was the busiest year yet. Phonograph records were purchased and started circulating in 1959.

In 1958 Rebecca Cox retired after 18 years of service as head librarian. Mary Ann Mongan, a graduate of the University of Kentucky at Lexington and formerly a librarian in Newport, was hired to succeed Cox. Mongan directed the Covington Public Library and its successor, the **Kenton Co. Public Library**, for the next 41 years.

By the early 1960s, problems with the Carnegie building and the lack of funding for the library were making deficiencies in service apparent. An assessment by library consultants Galvin & Associates reported that the Covington Public Library was well below the minimum standards set by the American Library Association; it had only 11,000 square feet of space, whereas the proper amount to serve the population was 46,000 square feet. The local library, which seated only 78 people, had fewer books than the number of residents in the city, 60,326. The library had a staff of eight, while the American Library Association's standard was 48.

Discussions with the boards of the Erlanger-Elsmere Library, the Kenton Co. Bookmobile, the City of Covington, and the Kenton Co. Fiscal Court led to the creation of a countywide library district funded by a property tax. The campaign for the new library district began in April 1967. By the summer, more than 16,000 signatures were obtained. The Kenton Co. Fiscal Court accepted the petition creating the Kenton Co. Public Library from the Covington Public Library, the Erlanger-Elsmere Library, and the Kenton Co. Bookmobile.

Summer 1967 brought to the Covington Public Library, and later the Kenton Co. Public Library, a gallery for a collection of local artist **Frank Duveneck**'s paintings. The Frank Duveneck Art Museum Society and the artist's son and daughter-in-law, Frank and Josephine Duveneck, donated several paintings to the Covington Public Library. At the opening of the gallery, 250 people attended, including Kentucky governor Edward "Ned" T. Breathitt Jr. (1963–1967). The Duveneck Gallery was the first public art gallery established in Northern Kentucky.

By October 1967, the Covington City commissioners had approved the agreement to transfer the Covington Library to the Kenton Co. Library District. By January 1968, Mary Ann Mongan had been appointed the head librarian, and the Covington Public Library became the Kenton Co. Public Library.

The old Carnegie Library continued to serve the residents of Covington until 1974, when it was abandoned in favor of a new library in Covington at the corner of Fifth and Scott Sts. In disrepair, the Carnegie Library was rescued by a group of local citizens and reconstituted as the **Carnegie Visual and Performing Arts Center**.

"Circulating Library," *CJ*, November 2, 1850, 2.
CJ, April 19, 1845, 3.
"Covington Lay Library," *CJ*, April 8, 1871, 3.
"Covington Library for Young Ladies," *CJ*, January 31, 1846, 3.
"Firemen's Library—Reminiscences of Covington Fire Co. # 1," *CJ*, August 21, 1852, 3.
"Library," *LVR*, January 31, 1846, 2.

Wayne Onkst

COVINGTON URBAN ARCHAEOLOGY. In 1986 R. G. Archaeological Services was contracted by the City of Covington to perform archaeological testing and final mitigation excavations at a three-block area along the Ohio River known as Covington's Riverfront Redevelopment Phase II Site. Bounded on the north by the Ohio River, on the south by Second St., on the east by Court St. and the **John A. Roebling Bridge**, and on the west by the intersection of the floodwall and Second St., the redevelopment site contained a variety of industrial and commercial-residential components. The project area was slated for a hotel–office complex development partially funded by an Urban Development Action Grant in 1985. The development, known as RiverCenter (see **Covington, Downtown**), was completed in the late 1980s and early 1990s.

The roughly six-acre project area was subdivided into three blocks: Block A was the area nearest the Roebling Bridge, Block B was between Block A and Madison Ave., and Block C was west of Block B. At the time of the excavations, Block A contained numerous structures, including a commercial glass-manufacturing facility and a series of mixed residential-commercial structures facing Second St. The eastern half of Block B was covered by an abandoned ice factory, while the western half was an unpaved parking lot. No structures were present in Block C; however, it was covered with concrete and asphalt.

Much of the early history of Covington's riverfront was associated with industrial and commercial developments that relied on the Ohio River as a transportation corridor (for example, to obtain materials and fuel) and the proximity of the fast-growing city of Cincinnati, immediately to the north. By 1850, Cincinnati was the fifth-largest city in the United States, and Covington was a fledgling community poised to take full advantage of Cincinnati's and Northern Kentucky's expanding commercial markets. Within the project area were the Covington Cotton Factory, built in 1828, and the Covington Rolling Mill and a steam flour mill, both constructed in 1831. The A. J. Alexander and Company shipbuilding yard was added in 1850, the Gray and **Hemingray Glass Company** in 1853, **Bromley Pottery** in 1859, and the **Walsh Distillery** during the early 1870s. The Champion Ice Manufacturing Company replaced the rolling mill in 1884. By the second half of the 19th century, Covington's central riverfront was a vibrant industrial and commercial corridor. But by the end of the 19th century, the attributes that caused the industrial corridor to thrive were no longer as critical to continued industrial success. The Ohio River had ceased to be the most important transportation corridor after the introduction of railroads, and new fuels, such as natural gas, made other areas of the country more lucrative for operations. The result was a decline in industrial pursuits along the river in Covington; many of the earlier manufactories were utilized for smaller-scale commercial pursuits throughout the 20th century. At Block A, these commercial establishments, such as the Averbeck Boots and Shoe Shop and at least two saloons, operated with residential rooms above the businesses.

During a preliminary testing phase, both mechanical testing and hand excavations were undertaken to determine the extent of historic fill and the presence of significant archaeological features. Heavy equipment was utilized almost exclusively at Block C and the western half of Block B but was also used in the more open areas of Block A. The majority of hand testing was reserved for the more built-up areas of Block A, particularly in the rear of the commercial and residential structures along Second St. A total of 79 historic features (e.g., cisterns, foundations, privy shafts, and trash pits) were recorded within approximately 50 heavy-equipment trenches and 15 hand-excavated test units. During final mitigation excavations, 16 additional features were located, and 26 features were either partially or fully excavated. In addition, four areas within the Hemingray Glass Company complex were exposed and recorded. Excavated features included nine privy shafts, four cisterns, three glass ovens, two yellowware pottery kilns, and various historic refuse deposits (see **Hemingray Glass Company Archaeology**).

Privy-shaft excavations proved to be the most successful features for the recovery of well-dated historic materials within the project area. Privies are important features because they are deep, stratified (that is, older materials are found below newer materials), and easily tied to documentation such as census schedules and city directories identifying site occupants. The majority of privies encountered during the Covington excavations were wood-lined; however, one brick-lined and one stone-and-brick-lined privy were also investigated. While wood liners were typically shallow, ranging in depth from 0.55 to 3.16 meters (1.8 to 10.4 feet), stone and brick liners were deep, ranging from 3.44 to 5.60 meters (11.3 to 18.4 feet). At eight excavated privy shafts, nearly 90,000 artifacts were recovered from 45 cubic meters (1,590 cubic feet) of privy fill. The temporal range of deposits in these former toilets spanned the second half of the 19th century and occasionally reached into the first quarter of the 20th century. The introduction of indoor bathrooms in the last quarter of the 19th century meant that most privies were abandoned as toilets and came to serve as trash repositories.

The artifact assemblages within the privy shafts were dominated by what are referred to as "kitchen" items, objects associated with food preparation, food serving, or food storage. Most of the kitchen items consisted of plant and animal food remains such as animal bones, seeds, nuts, and pits. In addition, a variety of glass and ceramic items related to food, such as beer and wine bottles, food bottles, glasses, and kitchen dishes, were recovered. The majority of these items were thrown into the privy shafts during their use as toilets, indicating that the outhouse was a common waste point source for broken dishes, food scraps, and used bottles. Privy shafts were also utilized for the disposal of architectural items such as brick, nails, plaster, stone, and window glass. Identifiable layers of architectural items probably represent demolition or construction episodes at the residence. Other debris types, such as clothing and personal items, were less well represented, but buckles, buttons, cloth scraps, ink wells, leather shoe soles, lice combs, mirror glass, pencil lead, perfume bottles, picture frames, and writing slates were recovered. Residential-commercial activities were represented by a variety of items, including animal liniments, brooms, electric parts, horseshoes, lamp globes and lamp elements, marbles and toy fragments, phonograph and record parts, scrub brushes, shoe polish, and wooden buckets. Today, the artifacts from the Covington archaeological project are curated at the **Behringer-Crawford Museum**.

Genheimer, Robert A. "Archaeological Testing, Evaluation, and Final Mitigation Excavations at Covington's Riverfront Redevelopment Phase 2 Site, Kenton County, Kentucky," prepared by R. G. Archaeological Services, Covington and submitted to the City of Covington, 1987.

———. "Not All Are the Same: Pattern Recognition at Ohio Valley Urban Privies." In *Historical Archaeology in Kentucky*, ed. Kim A. McBride, W. Stephen McBride, and David Pollack, 296–314. Frankfort: Kentucky Heritage Council, 1995.

Robert A. Genheimer

COWENS, DAVE (b. October 25, 1948, Covington, Ky.). David William Cowens, who is considered by some to be the greatest basketball player to hail from Northern Kentucky, is the son of Jack and Ruth Atwood Cowens. Growing up in Newport, he attended Newport Catholic High School (now **Newport Central Catholic High School**) and graduated in 1966. He led his high school basketball team to the Kentucky state tournament in his senior year, where they lost to Glasgow High School in the first round. He attended Florida State University in Tallahassee. There he set rebounding records and averaged 19 points per game as a six-foot-eight-inch center. In 1970, the year he graduated, he was the fourth overall pick in the National Basketball Association (NBA) draft, chosen by the Boston Celtics.

Dave Cowens, 1966.

Although he was reportedly too small to play the center position in the professional ranks, Cowen's intensity never wavered during his 11-year career. He was NBA Rookie of the Year in 1970, overall NBA Most Valuable Player and Most Valuable Player in the All-Star game in 1973, all-NBA first and second team selection several times, and a member of the 1974 and 1976 Boston NBA Championship teams. His aggressive play, almost reckless and full of passion, gave fans their money's worth. During his days in Boston, his father would drive up to the hill on which Newport Catholic High School sat in order to receive better long-distance AM radio reception of the Boston station carrying Celtic games. During Dave Cowens's off-seasons since 1972, he has run the Dave Cowens Basketball Camp in various locations around the United States.

Cowens's coaching career has included stints as player and coach of the Celtics during the 1978–1979 season, head coach of the Bay State Bombadiers of the Continental Basketball Association in 1984–1985, an assistant coach for the San Antonio Spurs from 1994 to 1996, head coach of the Charlotte Hornets from 1996 to 1999, and head coach of the Golden State Warriors from 1999 to 2001. In 2005 he became the head coach of the Chicago Sky, that city's entry in the Women's National Basketball Association. In September 2006 he joined the coaching staff of the Detroit Pistons. In 1990 Cowen was inducted into the Naismith Memorial Basketball Hall of Fame at Springfield, Mass., the first person from Northern Kentucky to be so honored. Cowen is affectionately known as "Big Red," for the color of his hair, and as old number 18 (his Boston jersey number).

"Cowens Learned Lessons—Former Coach Was Inspiration," *CP*, February 22, 2001, 1C.

NBA. "Dave Cowens Summary." www.nba.com (accessed January 7, 2007).

"Newport's Own 'Big Red' in Basketball Hall of Fame," *KP*, May 14, 1991, 1K.

Michael R. Sweeney

COX, ATTILLA (b. August 16, 1843, Ghent, Ky.; d. July 7, 1909, Louisville, Ky.). Attilla Cox, a legislator and a businessman, was the son of James P. and Felicia O'Boussier Cox. He was educated in local schools at Ghent. In 1862 Attilla and his brother Florian opened the F&A Cox Dry Goods Store in Warsaw in Gallatin Co.; later they moved the store to Owenton. The Cox family owned the store until the early years of the 20th century, when it was sold. Attilla Cox was an excellent merchandiser, trader, and banker. He was a promoter and owner of stage lines and of telephone service connections in Gallatin Co. Cox was elected twice to the Kentucky Senate and represented the 23rd District for six years. He was a delegate to the 1884 Democratic National Convention in Chicago, where he was part of the committee that nominated Grover Cleveland for president. Cleveland later appointed him the collector of internal revenue at Louisville. In 1869 Cox married Katherine Martin of Owenton, and they had three children. His son Attilla Cox Jr. became a railroad president and an attorney. Attilla Cox Sr. died at St. Joseph Infirmary in Louisville in 1909 and was buried at Cave Hill Cemetery in that city.

Houchens, Mariam Sidebottom. *History of Owen County: "Sweet Owen."* Louisville, Ky.: Standard, 1976.

COX, WILLIAM H. (b. October 22, 1856, Maysville, Ky.; d. October 13, 1950, Maysville, Ky.). Politician and businessman William Hopkinson Cox Jr. was the son of William Hopkinson Cox Sr. and Elizabeth Newman Cox. He was educated in the best private schools of Mason Co. but quit at the age of 15 to take a job as a clerk in his father's dry-goods store. William Cox Jr. married Sue E. Farrow, of Mount Sterling, in 1880, and the couple had one child, a daughter, Roberta. The family lived at 228 W. Third St. in Maysville. When William Cox Sr. died in 1885, William Jr. and his brother inherited their father's business. During the next several years, William constructed numerous buildings in Maysville and also took a keen interest in city affairs. He built a large building on the front part of the Cox block, at Third and Market Sts., and 13 single-family homes to the rear. He served as president of the State National Bank and as a director of the Electric Light and Gas Co., and he owned a one-third interest in the Electric Street Railway in town. In politics, he served as a city councilman, as mayor, as state senator, and, from 1908 to 1912, as lieutenant governor of Kentucky under Governor **Augustus E. Willson** (1907–1911). Cox died at age 93 at Maysville's **Haywood Hospital**, of cerebral thrombosis, and was buried in the Maysville Cemetery.

Biographical Cyclopedia of the Commonwealth of Kentucky. Chicago: John M. Gresham, 1896.
Calvert, Jean, and John Klee. *Maysville, Kentucky: From Past to Present in Pictures.* Maysville, Ky.: Mason Co. Museum, 1983.
"Cox May Run for Governor," *KTS,* March 26, 1914, 14.
"Former State Official, 93, Dies at Maysville," *KP,* October 14, 1950, 1.
Kentucky Death Certificate No. 21276, for the year 1950.

CRAIG, BENJAMIN (b. March 30, 1751, near Cedar Run, Culpepper Co., Va.; d. December 5, 1822, Ghent, Ky.). Benjamin Craig, an influential early settler of Carroll Co., was the son of Taliaferro and Polly Hawkins Craig. Three of his brothers were Baptists ministers who had been jailed for preaching without being licensed by the Church of Virginia. Benjamin and his wife, Nancy Tureman (or Stuman), brought their family into Kentucky with "The Traveling Church," a large caravan of Baptist families led by his brother Rev. Lewis Craig.

Benjamin Craig and his brother John were Fayette Co. delegates to the First Kentucky Convention in 1784; Benjamin and his brother Jeremiah signed a bond for Kentucky's first statehouse in 1792. Benjamin lived at South Elkhorn and Frankfort before 1794, the year he moved to what is now Carroll Co. and established a settlement at McCool's Bottom (now Ghent). He and his cousin James Hawkins incorporated Port William (now Carrollton) on another tract, for which they had only partially paid. When Hawkins conveyed his interest in the property to his brother Martin Hawkins, Craig found himself saddled with a troublesome partner. The subsequent feuding and unsettled property situation may have hindered the development of a much larger city at the mouth of the Kentucky River.

In 1800 Craig called upon Rev. John Taylor to minister to a meeting of Baptists and Methodists at Port William, where the spirit of the "Great Awakening" first took hold among Kentucky Baptists. The church organized in the wake of that meeting consisted almost entirely of members of Craig's family and eventually became the **Ghent Baptist Church**, the "mother church" of the other Baptist churches in the region.

Benjamin Craig died in 1822 and was buried near his home. A Kentucky State Highway Historical Marker stands near his grave, two miles east of Carrollton.

Bogardus, Carl R., Sr. *The Story of Gallatin County.* Ed. James C. Claypool. Cincinnati: John S. Swift, 2003.
"Ghent Church to Celebrate 175th," *KP,* August 2, 1975, 6K.

Bill Davis

CRAIG, JOHN J., SR. (b. November 14, 1873, Covington, Ky.; d. September 23, 1930, Covington, Ky.). Politician, banker, and builder John J. Craig was the son of A. John and Anna June Davis Craig. He was educated in Covington public schools, graduating from Covington High School. After graduation, John went to work in his father's construction business. He served as Covington mayor from 1908 to 1911 and from 1916 to 1920. He ran for Covington mayor again in 1923 but was defeated. He had also been defeated in a run for Kentucky railroad commissioner in 1911. After his second mayoral term, he was appointed by Governor Edwin P. Morrow (1919–1923) as Kentucky state auditor, a position he held from 1920 to 1923. Craig's last public office was that of master commissioner of Kenton Co., from 1927 to 1930. He served as vice president of the Citizens Building Association and was on the board of directors of the **First National Bank of Covington** and the **Highland Cemetery** Association. Craig was married first to Ella Smith, and the couple had three children. His first wife died on November 26, 1915, and in 1918 John married his second wife, Mattie Laws, of Walton; they had one child. Craig died of a heart attack at his Covington home in 1930 and was buried in Highland Cemetery in Fort Mitchell.

Reis, Jim. "Persistent John J. Craig Beat the Odds to Earn Recognition and Respect in Northern Kentucky," *KP,* June 14, 1993, 4K.

CRAPSEY, CHARLES (b. November 25, 1849, Cincinnati, Ohio; d. July 26, 1909, Cincinnati, Ohio). Architect Charles C. Crapsey, the son of Jacob S. and Rachel Crapsey, was born and raised in Cincinnati. In July 1865 he began working for Cincinnati architect James Keys Wilson. Other area architects, including **Samuel Hannaford** and James W. McLaughlin, also honed their craft as apprentices of Wilson, who had been trained by important architects in the East. Crapsey stayed with Wilson for about 10 years before starting his own architectural firm. His early projects were the design of mostly Queen Anne style residences, in the growing suburbs of Cincinnati. In about 1889, Crapsey entered into partnership with W. R. Brown to create the firm of Crapsey and Brown. The partnership designed a wide range of building types but specialized in churches and church-related structures, including the First English Lutheran Church on Race St. in Cincinnati. During that period, the firm also designed several industrial buildings, including a carriage factory, two print shops, a stove foundry, and new pavilions for the Cincinnati Reds baseball team.

In the late 1890s, Crapsey and Brown planned several buildings in Winchester, Ky., including two churches, a hotel, and the main building at Kentucky Wesleyan College. In the late 1880s Crapsey and Brown designed the jail, the jailer's residence, and the workhouse for Newport. During the late 1890s and the early 1900s, the design of Protestant churches began to change from traditional styles; the newer styles de-emphasized the altar and emphasized the communal nature of the sanctuary. Some unusual church tower shapes emerged, such as the one the firm designed for the **First Baptist Church** of Maysville. Among the Covington churches that Crapsey and Brown designed were the Madison Avenue (Second) Presbyterian and the Scott Street Methodist Episcopal Church South. They also designed both the **First Presbyterian Church** and the Central Christian Church in Newport, in addition to the First Presbyterian Church in Dayton, Ky. Crapsey died in Cincinnati at age 59 and was buried at Spring Grove Cemetery in that city.

"American Architects and Building News," *American Architect and Building News,* May 27, 1882, 251; February 16, 1884, 75–76.
Biographical Dictionary of American Architects. Los Angeles: New Age, 1956.
Spring Grove Cemetery Records, Cincinnati, Ohio.
Tenkotte, Paul A. *A Heritage of Art and Faith: Downtown Covington Churches.* Covington, Ky.: Kenton Co. Historical Society, 1986.

CRAWFORD, ELLIS C. (b. May 21, 1905, Maysville, Ky.; d. October 4, 1972, Covington, Ky.). Ellis Cummins Crawford was a self-educated archaeologist, geologist, and naturalist, who during the mid-20th century became the foremost proponent of Northern Kentucky's prehistoric heritage. He was the second son of Harry and Mary Crawford. Around 1927 he moved to Kenton Co., married, and settled in Covington.

An event that changed Crawford's life was his introduction to William J. Behringer (1884–1948), a self-educated taxidermist and naturalist. Behringer traveled the world and assembled an extensive collection of animals, geologic specimens, and natural oddities. Upon his death, Behringer's family gave his entire eclectic collection to the City of Covington. His friend, Ellis Crawford, persuaded city officials to house the collection in the old Devou homestead at **Devou Park**. In that setting, the William J. Behringer Memorial Museum opened on July 5, 1950, with Crawford as its first director.

Like his mentor Behringer, Crawford enjoyed fieldwork and exploration, although most of his work kept him close to Northern Kentucky. Beginning in the 1950s, Crawford assembled a team that conducted a 20-year excavation of the Rogers archaeological site in Boone Co. He was described by students and co-workers as very methodical in his research and documentation. As this Woodland-period mound and village site became nationally known (see **Archaeology**), Crawford gained credibility as an archeologist, a reputation that paved the way for his later work at **Big Bone Lick**, also in Boone Co. One of Crawford's enduring legacies was his inspiration to young people in various fields of science. He involved as many young persons as feasible in his excavations. Indeed, some of his work would not have been accomplished without their eager labor. The Gaines farm in Boone Co. was another Northern Kentucky archaeological site first excavated by Crawford. About the same time, Crawford founded the Northern Kentucky Archaeological Society, which explored many **American Indian** sites along the Ohio River and its tributaries.

Ellis Crawford, 1969.

During the 1960s, Crawford's name became almost synonymous with Big Bone Lick, the first widely known locality for vertebrate paleontology in North America. Although Crawford began working at Big Bone Lick during the 1950s, the most intensive work occurred there during the summers of 1962 through 1966. He served as associate investigator of the excavation and helped coordinate the project's extensive partnership, which included the University of Nebraska State Museum, Lincoln, Neb.; the U.S. Geological Survey; the Commonwealth of Kentucky; the Behringer Memorial Museum; and others. The National Science Foundation was one of the primary sources of funding for the endeavor. After the excavation ended in 1966, Crawford continued to interpret and publish the project's findings. Crawford also was much involved in an important parallel development during the excavation, the plan to make Big Bone Lick into a state park.

When Crawford retired from directing the Behringer Memorial Museum in 1970, the city of Covington honored him by renaming it the **Behringer-Crawford Museum**. He died in 1972 at St. Elizabeth Hospital in Covington and was buried at St. John's Cemetery in Fort Mitchell.

Archives of the Behringer-Crawford Museum, Covington, Ky.
"Ellis Crawford," *KP*, October 5, 1972, 15.
Harrell, Lorna Petty. "The Legacy of Ellis Crawford and the Behringer-Crawford Museum," *NKH* 8 no. 1 (Fall–Winter 2000): 15–20.

Lorna Petty Harrell

CRAWFORD, LEONARD J., SR. (b. April 29, 1860, Newport, Ky.; d. July 25, 1925, Newport, Ky.). Leonard Jacob Crawford Sr., a distinguished lawyer and Republican politician, was the son of Jacob H. Crawford, who worked as a steamboat pilot on the Ohio River. Leonard Crawford Sr.'s mother was the former Mary Elizabeth Eckert, daughter of L. M. Eckert, who was president of the Newport city council. Leonard received his early education in Newport public schools and attended Hughes High School in Cincinnati, from which he graduated in 1880. He entered the Cincinnati Law School in 1880 and graduated in 1882. He then apprenticed under attorney Ben Butterworth. Crawford set up his legal office in Newport, where he practiced for the remainder of his life. He was active in Republican politics (see **Republican Party**), holding a number of party leadership roles, but never held elected office. He served as a director of the Newport National Bank and also of the Covington Trust Company. Crawford married Ella J. Horner in 1883, and the couple had two children, Leonard Jr. and Clay. Leonard Sr. became one of the best-known and most respected attorneys in Northern Kentucky. During the sensational **Pearl Bryan** murder trial, Crawford served as legal counsel for one of the defendants, Scott Jackson (see **Walling, Alonzo, and Scott Jackson**). Leonard Crawford Sr. died at age 65 and was buried in Evergreen Cemetery in Southgate. His son Leonard J. Crawford Jr. also became a well-known Northern Kentucky attorney.

Biographical Cyclopedia of the Commonwealth of Kentucky. Chicago: John M. Gresham, 1896.
"Crawford—President of Republican Club," *KP*, July 14, 1897, 5.
Evergreen Cemetery Records, Southgate, Ky.
"L. Crawford, Sr. Is Dead," *KP*, July 27, 1925, 1.

CRESCENT PARK. The Crescent Park area of Kenton Co. was settled in the late 1700s, by veterans of the **Revolutionary War**, but it remained a mostly rural farming community until the Queen and Crescent Railroad (later the **Southern Railway**) was built through the area in 1877. The name Crescent Park was taken from the railroad, whose name was in turn taken from the nicknames of Cincinnati (the Queen City) and New Orleans (the Crescent City), between which cities the railroad traveled. The town of Crescent Park was created in the late 1940s, as an FHA housing development for veterans of **World War II**. The site contained 64 acres on which the developer planned to build two-bedroom homes that would be sold only to veterans for about $7,000 each. Plans for the community did not fully materialize, so a private developer completed the development and sold to both veterans and nonveterans.

Crescent Park was incorporated as a sixth-class city in 1952 and was run by a marshal, his deputies, and four trustees, all of whom worked without pay. When completed, the town was less than a half mile square and had a population between 500 and 600. The area presently contains five streets: Avon Ct., Avon Dr., Clay Ct., Dale Ct., and Summit Ave. A sixth street, with 35 homes, was bought by the highway department when I-75 was being built through the city in the early 1960s.

Crescent Park's largest employer was the Northern Kentucky District Headquarters for the Kentucky Department of Transportation. Over the years many attempts were made to annex Crescent Park to a neighboring city, but residents kept voting down the attempts. Finally in 1998 Crescent Park, with a population of about 420, was annexed by Fort Mitchell. Today, the remnants of old Crescent Park can be found behind and to the south of the commercial development that has taken place along Buttermilk Pk.

"City Independent Now, but Future Merger Possible," *CE*, August 27, 1979, A2.
Hassart, Dan. "Cities under Pressure," *KP*, November 2, 2006, A1.
"Northern Kentucky Suburbs: Separate but Together," *KP*, May 9, 1983, A12.

CRESCENT SPRINGS. In the late 1700s, veterans of the **Revolutionary War**, nearly all of them farmers, settled the section of Kenton Co. where Crescent Springs is now located. By 1850 most of the land there was owned by four families, the Andersons, the Clevelands, the Griffins, and the Scotts. Later residents of Crescent Springs were the Eubanks, the Hons, the Niemeyers, the Ramblers, the Reinharts, and the Thirs. Many descendants of those early families still reside in Northern Kentucky. The name Crescent Springs is thought to have been taken from the **Cincinnati Southern Railroad** (called the Queen and Crescent Railroad) and the three natural springs located nearby. However, others say that the name referred to the crescent shape of the railroad tracks through the area. The main road in town was Buttermilk Pk., so called because of the three dairies operating there, the Echo, the List, and the Thirs. In those early days, Buttermilk Pk. was a one-lane dirt road, far different from the heavily traveled, five-lane state highway it is today.

In 1893 Cincinnatians James O. Gibson, H. H. Kingsbury, and Nathan R. Park incorporated the Crescent Springs Improvement Company, which bought up land in the area and began to develop the city of Crescent Springs. They built a train station in town and began advertising building lots for sale, in Cincinnati and Northern Kentucky newspapers. The ads touted a healthy elevation of 500 feet above Cincinnati, a fine new train station, graded streets, sidewalks, free schools, churches, and a post office. Lots measuring at least 25 feet wide and 100 to 200 feet deep were offered for as little as $9, with reasonable payment plans available. The company also promised no property taxes for two years and free train transportation to and from Cincinnati for one year, to anyone who built and occupied a home there. The first school was built on Anderson Rd. in 1892. The Crescent Springs Presbyterian Church was established in 1898, the Crescent Springs Baptist Church in 1913, and the **St. Joseph Catholic Church** in 1916. A major flood hit Northern Kentucky and Cincinnati in 1913, which made it impossible for residents to reach their places of employment via the railroad. Additional problems developed in the winter of 1917–1918, when the area experienced record-breaking temperatures and excessive snowfall (see **Blizzards and Severe Winter Weather**) and those disasters were followed by a major influenza outbreak.

In the early 1900s, Poage Park, with a bandstand, was built between Crescent Ave. and Swan Rd. for the enjoyment of city residents. In later years, a semipro baseball team was formed, and a ball field with grandstands was built near where Buttermilk Pk. presently crosses I-75. Just before **World War II**, railroad service to Crescent Springs was discontinued and was replaced by bus service from Crescent Springs to Fort Mitchell, where passengers could catch a **streetcar** to Covington and Cincinnati. That bus line later became a part of the **Green Line** system.

Crescent Springs formed a volunteer fire department in 1928–1929 (reorganized in 1932) and built its first firehouse at Poage Park in 1938. The town was incorporated as a sixth-class city in 1957, governed by a mayor and six council members. Construction of the **Cincinnati/Northern Kentucky International Airport** and building of the I-75 expressway through the area in the early 1960s contributed greatly to the rapid growth of all of Northern Kentucky, including Crescent Springs. Over the years, the city has grown from a once sleepy farming community to a bustling small city, with a population of 3,931 in 2000. In 2008 the city's police department merged with that of neighboring Erlanger.

Crescent Springs, Kentucky. www.crescent-springs.ky.us/City%20History.htm (accessed May 3, 2007).
Crescent-Villa Bicentennial Group. *The Bicentennial Celebration, 1776–1976: The Crescent-Villa Community.* Crescent Springs, Ky.: Crescent-Villa Bicentennial Group, 1976.
Reis, Jim. "Fresh Air, Clean Water, and Blackberries Were This City's Sales Pitch," *KP*, September 13, 1982, 4K.
Steitzer, Stephanie. "Shopping Center Faces Opposition," *KP*, March 2, 2004, 1K.
Tenkotte, Paul A. "Rival Cities to Suburbs: Covington and Newport, Kentucky, 1790–1890," PhD diss., Univ. of Cincinnati, 1989.
U.S. Census Bureau. "American Fact Finder. Data Set Census 2000 Summary File 1 (SF1) 100-Percent Data. Custom Table." www.census.gov (accessed May 3, 2007).

CRESCENT SPRINGS HIGH SCHOOL. Prior to consolidation, which began in the 1920s, most Kentucky counties had small local elementary schools that had replaced the earlier one- and two-room neighborhood schools. High schools, if they existed before 1910, were in urban areas. In the post–**World War I** era, with the recognition of the need for secondary education, these elementary schools simply began teaching classes at the high school level within the same buildings. The Crescent Springs High School in Kenton Co. developed according to that pattern. The first high school classes were offered in September 1916, the first graduating class was in 1920, and the first graduate that year is generally said to be Beulah Slayback. Classes were held in an old frame structure that had once been a church. The first years found high school graduating classes of fewer than 5; total high school enrollments were no more than 30. Nevertheless, the high school grew and participated in some competitive sports. Both boys and girls played high school basketball, and the girls' team made it to the state finals a few times.

A two-story, eight-room, fireproof red-brick building on Buttermilk Pike, containing an auditorium, a gymnasium, and a cafeteria with a kitchen, was opened in February 1925. Enrollment by that time had reached 350 students (grades 1 through 12), reflecting the population growth in the area and the desire of students to obtain high school diplomas. In the mid-1930s, the high school student population was such that a high school football team could be formed. As Crescent Springs grew and more school space was required, it was only logical that the consolidation that first took place on the elementary level would carry over to the secondary level. With the planned opening of the **Dixie Heights High School** in Erlanger by the **Kenton Co. School District** on September 13, 1937, the high school division at Crescent Springs ceased in May 1937. Only a six-grade elementary school remained. The Crescent Springs High School, like its counterparts **Piner High School** and **Independence High School**, belonged to an era that was passing as more modern and efficient consolidated centers of learning became viable and economically feasible.

Caywood, James A. "A Brief Sketch of the Development of the Kenton County School System." Address delivered to the Filson Society, Louisville, Ky., January 14, 1958.
"High School to Be Dedicated," *KP*, February 25, 1925, 1.
Reis, Jim. "Looking Back on Dixie High," *KP*, November 1, 1999, 4K.
"Two Buildings Are Alike in Inside Setup," *KP*, September 3, 1937, 9.
"2 County Schools to Open in Kenton," *KP*, September 3, 1937, 9.
"Two New High Schools Are Opened by County Director and Start Courses of Study for Two and Four Years," *KP*, September 11, 1916, 1.

CRESTVIEW. When the veterans of **World War II** returned home to Northern Kentucky, many appreciative people wondered what could be done to provide low-cost home ownership for them. Several sites were considered for a veterans' community, but the site finally chosen was a 52-acre parcel at the intersection of Dodsworth Ln. and Uhl Rd., near Cold Spring in Campbell Co. A group called the Vet Village Home Builders was formed and purchased the land on which to build 120 homes. The projected cost of each was $8,750, with a market value of $11,000. Construction began in spring 1948, and by August a few families were in their homes. The town was originally planned to have five streets; a sixth was added later. In 1950 residents organized a volunteer fire department, adding to the sense of community. In October of that year, the village's name was changed from Vets Village to Crestview, and Crestview was incorporated in November 1950. Campbell Circuit Court Judge **Ray Murphy** appointed the first officers, who included William Toner as the mayor and five trustees. Most of the original veterans are now gone from this sixth-class city, but tiny Crestview remains a friendly and close-knit community. In 2000 the population was 471.

Reis, Jim, *Pieces of the Past.* Vol. 3. Covington: Kentucky Post, 1994.

CRESTVIEW HILLS. The land on which the city of Crestview Hills now stands was originally part of a nearly 1,000-acre farm of John Leathers, the father of **John W. Leathers**. The Leathers home stood on the **Covington and Lexington Turnpike** (now the **Dixie Highway**). In September 1863, during the height of the **Civil War**, John W. Leathers sold 80 acres of the family farm to **Amos Shinkle**, a Covington banker, businessman, and civic leader. Shinkle built a summer home in about 1866 along what is now the Dixie Highway, and that house is today the sole remaining building in Crestview Hills from that era. The Shinkle house is located next to the entrance to the Lookout Farms subdivision. Various members of the family continued to live in the Leathers home until the late 1800s. In 1874, 575 acres of the farm became the property of John B. Casey, when he married the widow of Benjamin W. Leathers. Upon John Casey's death, the land

One of the original homes in the Crestview Hills subdivision, at 21 Winding Way, built by William and Emma Horstman Hoppenjans, ca. 1925. The photo dates from the mid-20th century.

was subdivided into 21 parcels ranging in size from 10 to 80 acres and sold at public auction. Elizabeth Bungener later acquired 120 acres of the original farm. When she died, the land was sold to the Kenton Development Corporation for creation of the stately Crestview Hills subdivision, which is located across the Dixie Highway from the present-day **Crestview Hills Town Center**. The company built a model home in the subdivision, paved several streets, installed underground utilities, and erected elaborate brick entrances at the heads of two streets leading into the development. Kenton Development Corporation began selling building sites in 1924, but during the **Great Depression** very few sales occurred. As a result, a subsidiary of the **Peoples-Liberty Bank and Trust Company** foreclosed on the property in 1943. The bank sold the remaining 62 acres in the Crestview Hills subdivision to William H. Hoppenjans. Upon his death, his heirs sold the land to the Crestview Hills Development Company, which upgraded the subdivision, added new streets and park areas, and began the sale of the remaining lots. In September 1975 the last building site was sold, and the subdivision soon became the center of wealth and culture in the area.

Crestview Hills had about 200 residents when it was incorporated as a sixth-class city in October 1951. A mayor and six council members were named to run the city. The Crestview Hills area remained a uniquely residential island in Northern Kentucky until construction of **Thomas More College** in the late 1960s. Subsequently, the city experienced a building boom, with construction of the Gieske Subdivision, the College Park Subdivision, I-275 (see **Expressways**), the Crestview Mall (later replaced by the Crestview Hills Town Center), the Thomas More Research Park, the Four Seasons Country Club, the Lookout Farm housing development, and the headquarters of the **Columbia Sussex Corporation**.

The city currently has about $400 million dollars of taxable real estate and is in excellent financial condition. Mayor Paul W. Meier and a six-member city council run the city. Crestview Hills has just four employees, since most city services are contracted out. The city shares police protection with Lakeside Park and fire and ambulance service with Fort Mitchell and Edgewood. In 2000, the U.S. Census Bureau listed the city with a population of 2,889.

Groth, Dan, Crestview Hills city administrator. Telephone interview by Jack Wessling, May 9, 2007.

Leathers, John W., III. Personal letter, Leathers family file, Kenton Co. Library, Covington, Ky.

Reis, Jim. "Crestview Hills Marks Half-Century of Growth," *KP*, September, 2001, 4K.

——. "Leathers Family Member Made Mark in State Politics and Real Estate Deals," *KP*, November, 4, 1991, 4K.

CRESTVIEW HILLS TOWN CENTER. The Crestview Hills Town Center, located along the east side of the **Dixie Highway** (U.S. 25), just south of I-275 in Crestview Hills, began its commercial life as the Crestview s Mall (later Crestview Hills Mall) in 1979. For many years before the mall opened, a real estate development sign promised passersby that a shopping mall was coming to the 49.5-acre site. Its original anchor store was McAlpin's, a department store chain based in Cincinnati. That firm wanted a share of the Northern Kentucky market, having seen the remarkable commercial success of its competitors nearby at the **Florence Mall**. Three anchor stores had been planned, but the adjacent I-275 interchange required more land than first expected, reducing the number of anchors to two; and the anticipated second anchor never arrived. The two-story shopping center had an area of about 475,000 square feet. Many different retailers attempted business at the location, but none of them had much success. At the end, Southwestern College, a small business college, operated out of the mainly vacant building. Dillard's Department Store remained in the former McAlpin's store. Over the years, the Crestview Hills Mall's interior hall space became a popular place for walkers to gather and exercise. At one time, the **Kenton Co. Public Library** wanted to build a branch library on the grounds, before finally deciding instead to build in Erlanger. One expert called the lackluster Crestview Hills Mall the most underutilized piece of commercial real estate in Northern Kentucky. In 2002, valued at almost $12 million for property tax reasons, the declining mall was owned 50-50 by Dillard's and Dreiseszun-Morgan, a shopping-center developer based in Shawnee Mission, Kansas.

During 2005 the Crestview Hills Town Center, a project of Jeffrey R. Anderson, of Jeffrey Anderson Real Estate of Norwood, Ohio, opened on the site. Anderson demolished the old building and replaced it with a 60-tenant, open-air lifestyle center that included almost 20 restaurants. The Anderson group mostly owns the new venture, but some shares are held by Dreiseszun-Morgan. Only Dillard's Department Store remained, with its new two-story building of 180,000 square feet; the total square footage of the new development is 514,000. The new center is patterned after Anderson's two successful Norwood, Ohio, ventures: Rookwood Commons and Rookwood Pavilion. From a marketing point of view, the successful new town center is aimed at women between ages 25 and 55.

Crowley, Patrick. "Outdoor Mall Could Bring Growth to Crestview Hills," *CE*, March 8, 2004, B5.

Eigelbach, Kevin. "Dillard's Set to Anchor a Rookwood-Type Center," *KP*, November 12, 2003, 1K.

Kreimer, Peggy. "Mall's Menu: Restaurants," *KP*, December 13, 2002, 1K.

——. "Walkers Lament Loss of Mall," *KP*, November 25, 2003, 1K.

Paeth, Greg. "Location, Location, Location," *KP*, June 28, 2003, 1K.

Steitzer, Stephennie. "Mall Redevelopment Includes Tax Deal," *KP*, March 9, 2004, 1K.

CRISTO REY PARISH. Cristo Rey parish, the only Spanish-speaking Roman Catholic parish in Northern Kentucky, was established on July 11, 2004, by Bishop Roger Foys. It was the first new parish in the 14-county Diocese of Covington since 1989. The name is Spanish for "Christ the King." The Cristo Rey parish serves the Hispanic community, which is made up of immigrants from Mexico, Guatemala, Honduras, Puerto Rico, the Dominican Republic, and Cuba.

The idea for the Cristo Rey parish originated in 1997 when Foys's predecessor, Bishop Robert

Muench, became aware of growing numbers of Hispanic parishioners and created the Hispanic Ministries outreach program for Covington's **Cathedral Basilica of the Assumption**. In 10 years **Latinos** in the diocese increased by 235 percent, from 1,665 in 1990 to 5,574 in 2000. Experts agree that the true number is much larger yet, since census numbers typically underrepresent immigrants.

Rev. John Cahill is the pastor of Cristo Rey's 400 parishioners. Masses are celebrated every day except Fridays in a 375-seat hall at the Covington Diocese's former Catholic Center in Erlanger, which is a temporary location. The permanent location will also be in Boone Co., because that is where Northern Kentucky's Hispanic population is growing most rapidly.

Programs offered by Cristo Rey include sacramental education, preparation for marriage, and parenting programs, as well as one-day retreats. Cristo Rey's comprehensive outreach program for immigrants, Centro de Amistad, brings together many common resources such as social workers, the Covington diocese's **Catholic Charities**, the Area Health Education Center, immigration lawyers, and volunteers. The program offers classes in English, Spanish, GED test preparation, citizenship, credit, carpentry, and home buying.

Diocese of Covington Archives, Erlanger, Ky.

Tony Llamas

CRITTENDEN. Crittenden, a city located on the border of Kenton and Grant counties along U.S. 25 (**Dixie Highway**), was preceded by a community on the Dry Ridge Trace, immediately to the south, known as The Wells. The focal point of this first community was Reed's Tavern, operated by Archibald Reed, who was a Campbell Co. magistrate in 1795 when the area was a part of that county. Just to the west of Reed's Tavern was the Lebanon Presbyterian Church, founded in 1796, the second church established in the area that became Grant Co. in 1820.

The Crittenden community started to develop in 1819. It was located a mile north of The Wells on land owned by William Sanders, who had opened a stagecoach stop on the newly developed **Covington and Lexington Turnpike** (on the crest of the dry ridge). By 1826 the community also included a tavern operated by Charles Sechrist, a carding mill owned by Henry Sayers, and a newly formed Christian Church. In 1829 John W. Finley bought 400 acres of Sanders's land that included all four of these sites. In 1831 Finley attempted to incorporate the area and name it Sanders, but he could not do so because another town in Kentucky already had that name. Instead, the community was incorporated under the name Crittenden in 1837; it was the second of the four towns in Grant Co. that remain incorporated. The new town's first trustees were George Buckner, Ephriam Carter, John W. Fenley, Gustavious Fisher, and James Hudson.

Today's Crittenden Presbyterian Church was begun in The Wells in 1842. Many of its members came from the Lebanon Presbyterian Church. In 1846 the Presbyterian Church located at The Wells moved into a new meetinghouse in Crittenden. Rev. Thomas Henderson started the Baptist Church at The Wells. After his death it was reorganized in Crittenden as the Crittenden Baptist Church. In 1881 ex-slaves established and built a Christian Church on a lot donated by the people of Crittenden. In 1895 two of this church's trustees, Willis Jones and Isaac Tone, deeded a part of a lot to open a school in what came to be known as Colored School District B. The church remained open until the early 1980s, when most of the members had died or moved.

Over a period of time, much of the area called The Wells became included in the town of Crittenden. Other than the Henderson-Rouse tavern, which became a private residence, all the businesses in The Wells appear to have closed by 1900. The Violet Ridge Church of Christ was organized in 1972 with 30 members. It has enjoyed a steady growth in membership and occupied a new building in 1980.

The Bullock Pen Water District and its 134-acre lake west of town supplies water to Crittenden and the northern part the county. A pipeline extending southward also supplies water to Dry Ridge's water system.

Among the most noted people from Crittenden are three brothers, **John Uri Lloyd**, **Nelson Ashley Lloyd**, and **Curtis Gates Lloyd**. The three were all highly respected pharmacists, involved in developing new medicines from plants and herbs, and attained international recognition for their work. John Uri Lloyd was also a famous author. The youngest of the brothers, Curtis Gates Lloyd (1859–1926), established the Lloyd Library in Cincinnati and the Botanical Park and Wildlife Refuge on the outskirts of Crittenden. A part of this area serves the public today as a Grant Co. park. Crittenden is enjoying unprecedented growth and development with the opening of new subdivisions and the associated residential construction. Businesses serving the increased population are being established as needed. In 2000 the city of Crittenden had a population of 2,401.

Conrad, John B., ed. *History of Grant County*. Williamstown, Ky.: Grant Co. Historical Society, 1992.

U.S. Census Bureau. "American Fact Finder. Data Set. Census 2000 Summary File 1 (SF1) 100-Percent Data. Custom Table." www.census.gov (accessed January 25, 2006).

John B. Conrad

CRITTENDEN HIGH SCHOOL. The Crittenden High School, one of the four original high schools in Grant Co., opened in fall 1908 in one room of the two-story frame public school building at Crittenden. A new two-story brick building, erected in front of the old frame building, had four rooms on the first floor for the elementary grades, and the second floor was used for the high school. The Crittenden High School graduated its first class in 1911, consisting of one student, Jessie Crutcher. Thereafter, increased enrollment required construction of an addition on the north end of the building to house vocational agriculture and home economics classes. In 1927 the graduating class totaled 12 students. The high school graduated its last class in 1953; beginning that fall, high school students attended the new **Grant Co. High School** at Dry Ridge. The first eight grades at the Crittenden School continued to use the old facilities until the seventh and eight grades were moved to the new Grant Co. Middle School, also at Dry Ridge. The first six grades were moved to the new Crittenden–Mount Zion Elementary School, built in 1973 on the Crittenden–Mount Zion Rd. south of Crittenden.

Conrad, John B., ed. *History of Grant County*. Williamstown, Ky.: Grant Co. Historical Society, 1992.

"Twelve Graduated by Crittenden High School," *KP*, June 6, 1927, 1.

John B. Conrad

CROPPER, CARROLL L. (b. May 19, 1897, near Burlington, Ky.; d. February 4, 1976, Burlington, Ky.). Carroll Lee Cropper, a Boone Co. judge, was the son of Woodford Lee and Anna "Birdie" G. Kirtley Cropper. He graduated from Burlington High School in 1916 and then attended the University of Kentucky School of Agriculture in Lexington. Following service in the army during **World War I**, he married Kathryn Brown of Burlington. Cropper worked as a bank cashier, eventually becoming vice president of the Peoples Deposit Bank in Boone Co. In 1934 he was elected to the state legislature representing Boone and Grant counties. In the 1930s, Cropper served as acting Boone Co. judge when Judge **Nathaniel E. Riddell** was unable to attend meetings. When Riddell died in September 1942 before completing his term, Cropper was appointed judge for the remainder of the term; he was then elected county judge in 1943 and served for the next 20 years, until 1962. From 1942 to 1950, with no court aides, Cropper handled all fiscal court matters and road complaints himself and presided over both domestic and juvenile courts. During his tenure, the population of Boone Co. increased from 10,000 to 25,000 and the development of the **Cincinnati/Northern Kentucky International Airport** began. Cropper was instrumental in the creation of **Big Bone Lick** State Park and the construction of I-275. He was one of only four men to hold the office of judge-executive in Boone Co. between 1901 and 1982. The **Carroll C. Cropper Bridge** in Boone Co. was dedicated in 1977, completing the vital interstate link between Kentucky and Indiana. Cropper died in 1976 and was buried in the Bullittsburg Baptist Church Cemetery.

Becher, Matthew E., Michael A. Rouse, Robert Schrage, and Laurie Wilcox. *Images of America: Burlington*. Charleston, S.C.: Arcadia, 2004.

Remlinger, Connie. "Judge Cropper: Million Dollars in Memories," *KP*, July 20, 1974, 9.

Matthew E. Becher

CROSSWHITE, ADAM (b. October 17, 1799, Bourbon Co., Ky.; d. January 23, 1878, Marshall, Mich.). Adam Crosswhite was a fair-skinned mulatto slave who successfully escaped from his owner in Bourbon Co. His father was a white slave owner named Powers, who was a half brother of Miss Frances Crosswhite. Ownership of Adam shifted to Frances Crosswhite through the will of her father, Isaac Crosthwaite (later spelled Crosswhite), on January 28, 1811. Frances married Ned Stone, who sold Adam Crosswhite for $200, and in 1819 Adam was traded to Francis Giltner, a planter in Bourbon Co. There, Adam married Sarah in a slave ceremony and raised four children, John Anthony, Benjamin Franklin, Cyrus Jackson, and Lucretia. Before 1830 Giltner moved the entire family and his slaves to Hunters Bottom in Carroll Co. along the Ohio River.

In August 1843 Adam Crosswhite learned that Giltner planned to sell part of Crosswhite's family. Crosswhite sought help from the Underground Railroad organization in Madison, Ind. As runaway slaves, and after having two narrow escapes using the newly organized safe routes through Indiana, the Crosswhites managed to escape to Marshall, a town in south central Michigan. There, Adam maintained a low profile. He worked, built a cabin, and became accepted in the village.

In response to the increased number of runaway slaves through the 1840s, slave owners in the north central river counties and the bluegrass of Kentucky sought to recover their financial investments. In 1846 a coalition of slave owners met in Covington and hired a spy to ferret out runaway slaves in southern Michigan. In late fall 1846, this spy, who called himself Carpenter, arrived in Marshall and in Cass Co. Masquerading as an abolitionist from Worcester, Mass., he visited the homes of free people of color. The information he gathered led to two major raids by Kentuckians, the earliest at Marshall in Calhoun Co., and the second in Cass Co.

In December 1846, acting on intelligence gathered by the spy, Francis Troutman, the grandson of a former owner of Adam Crosswhite and a nephew of Francis Giltner, went to Calhoun Co., Mich., posing as a schoolteacher seeking a place to settle. He hired local deputy sheriff Harvey Dixon to pose as a census taker to scout the Crosswhite family. On January 20, 1847, Troutman reappeared at Marshall with three other Kentuckians, William Franklin Ford, David Giltner, and James S. Lee, and, accompanied by Deputy Sheriff Dixon, went to the Crosswhite cabin. There they attempted to capture Adam, but he and his son Johnson fled through a cornfield; Crosswhite accompanied Deputy Sheriff Dixon to secure counsel, and Troutman stayed in the Crosswhite cabin with drawn pistol as several neighbors attempted to enter the house, one of whom, a Mr. Hackett, was assaulted by Troutman.

When Dixon returned, he charged Troutman with assault and battery on Hackett and with trespassing and housebreaking. Troutman paid $100 in fines the next day in the local court before Judge Randall Hobart. Meanwhile, the townspeople hid the Crosswhite family in the attic of George Ingersoll's mill. Isaac Jacobs, the hostler at the Marshall House, hired a team and covered wagon, and on the night of January 27, Ingersoll and Asa B. Cook drove the Crosswhite family to Jackson, where they boarded a train to Detroit. George De Baptiste, the former Underground Railroad leader at Madison, Ind., met the Crosswhites in Detroit and took them into Canada.

The Kentuckians were furious, and several slave-owner meetings were held. Citizens of Trimble and Carroll counties, led by Moses Hoagland of Hunters Bottom, met at Kings Tavern on February 10 and drew up three resolutions demanding that the Kentucky legislature call upon its U.S. senators and congressmen to pass federal legislation giving slave owners redress and imprisoning and fining those who enticed, harbored, or aided runaway slaves.

By June 1847, Michigan newspapers along the southern tier were equally outraged that Kentucky posses were seizing fugitives in a free state whose citizens detested slavery. In August 1847 a large Kentucky raid led by Boone Co., Ky., slave owners George W. Brazier and Benjamin Stevens was repulsed from Cass Co. after attempting to recapture several former slaves (see **Slavery—The Kentucky Raid**).

The legislative wheels were set in motion. Joseph Underwood's report and resolutions from the Kentucky legislature were sent to the U.S. Senate on December 20, 1847, and in May 1848 Senator Andrew P. Butler of South Carolina printed his report favoring strong federal sanctions against persons who aided runaway slaves; 10,000 copies were distributed. Momentum built for passage of the 1850 Fugitive Slave Act, which made it mandatory for U.S. marshals to seize runaway slaves, for representatives of the slave owner to identify the runaways, and for severe fines to be levied on all those aiding and harboring fugitive slaves. Henry Clay, a personal friend of Francis Giltner, proposed a clause mandating restitution of property to southerners reclaiming runaway slaves.

Attorney Francis Troutman returned to Michigan in May 1848 to gather evidence and press charges against those who aided the Crosswhite family. On June 1, 1848, in Detroit, Justice McLane of the federal bench heard *Giltner vs. Gorham et al.* McLane instructed the jury to ignore their attitudes toward slavery and decide the case based only on the plaintiffs' right to the services of the fugitives and therefore the right to obtain financial redress. The first trial jury hung and was discharged on June 12. A second trial was held, and the jury awarded Giltner $1,926 in damages and heavy court costs, for a total of about $4,500. Zachariah Chandler, a leading antislavery Whig in Detroit, paid the greater part of the fine. Juryman Philo Dibble, a resident of Marshall, was publicly chastised from the pulpit by his Presbyterian minister for his participation in the verdict.

Northern reaction to passage of the 1850 Fugitive Slave Act was swift. By 1854 Indiana, Michigan, and Ohio had formed significant Republican parties that were obtaining antislavery majorities in their state legislative bodies, sending antislavery congressmen and senators to Washington, and, by 1860, giving Abraham Lincoln the presidential candidacy.

The Crosswhite family, with a new daughter, Frances, born in 1848 in Canada, returned to Marshall, Mich., after the **Civil War**; in 1878 Adam Crosswhite died and was buried in the Oakridge Cemetery in Marshall. In 1923 Michigan erected a bronze marker set in a stone boulder near the old Crosswhite cabin. The marker commemorates the runaway slave from Carroll Co., Ky., and the role of the people of Marshall in repulsing the Kentucky posse.

Battle Creek (Mich.) Enquirer, July 14, 1907; January 28, 1929; July 3, 1930; April 1960.

Battle Creek (Mich.) Tribune, January 20, 1847.

Crosswhite File, Marshall District Public Library, Marshall, Mich.

Enquirer and Evening News of Battle Creek, Michigan, February 18, 1923; February 11, 1945; February 17, 1974.

Frankfort (Ky.) Weekly Commonwealth, February 23, 1847.

Fuller, George N., ed. *Michigan: A Centennial History of the State and Its People.* Chicago: Lewis, 1939.

Gara, Larry. *The Liberty Line.* Lexington: Univ. of Kentucky Press, 1961.

Gardner, Washington. *History of Calhoun County, Michigan.* Chicago: Lewis, 1913.

Giltner vs. Gorham et al. Case No. 5,453, Circuit Court D, Michigan (114 McLean 402: 6 West Law J, 491).

History, Arts, and Libraries. Adam Crosswhite Deposition (edited transcription). State of Michigan. www.michigan.gov/hal/0,7-160-17451_18670_44390-160647--,00.html (accessed March 26, 2007).

History of Calhoun County, Michigan. Philadelphia: L. H. Everts, 1877.

Isaac Crosthwaite's Will, Clark Co., Ky., Will Book 3:54.

Journal of the House of Representatives, Kentucky, February 13, 1847, pp. 338–41.

Diane Perrine Coon

CSX. CSX Transportation is the railroad-operating arm of CSX Corporation, a holding company created in 1980 to assume control of the **Chessie System** and the **Seaboard Coast Line** Industries. The Chessie System controlled railroads including the **Chesapeake and Ohio Railroad** (C&O), which passed through Northern Kentucky, and the Baltimore and Ohio Railroad (B&O), which did not. Seaboard Coast Line Industries controlled the **Louisville and Nashville Railroad** (L&N).

In 1997 the CSX and **Norfolk Southern** (NS) railroads, after each failed in their attempts at hostile takeovers of **Conrail** (the merged New York Central and Pennsylvania railroads), split Conrail into two parts. CSX took control of 40 percent and NS took the remainder. Both former components of Conrail had provided east-west service through Cincinnati.

CSX's major railroad yard in the Cincinnati area is Queensgate, which consolidated the L&N's DeCoursey Yard in Kenton Co. and the C&O's Stevens Yard in Campbell Co. CSX's corporate name was created by taking the C from Chessie and the S from Seaboard and adding an X to indicate improved multiplied service as a result of their merger. CSX is based in Jacksonville, Fla.; from there it controls the movement of each train throughout its system.

For legal reasons having to do with leasehold agreements, many of the component railroads that made up CSX continued in existence long after the 1980 merger. In 1980 CSX began to paint the engines and rolling stock of its component railroads in CSX colors and reporting marks, regardless of the equipment's particular corporate ownership. Today, some of the railroads merged into CSX continue to retain a separate legal corporate existence.

CSX Corporation. CSX Corporation Annual Reports for 1990 to 2004. CSX Corporation, Jacksonville, Fla.

Drury, George H. *The Train Watcher's Guide to North American Railroads.* Waukesha, Wis.: Kalmbach Books, 1992.

The Historical Guide to North American Railroads. 2nd ed. Waukesha, Wis.: Kalmbach Books, 2000.

Charles H. Bogart

CULL. Cull in Owen Co. is in New Liberty Precinct along Ky. Rt. 1761, five miles west of Owenton and three miles south of New Liberty, near where the waters of Panther Lick and Big Twin intersect. The community began as a grocery store and post office operated by Dave Cull and his sister Annie. Many persons in that area had the surname Cull. The Cull post office closed in 1907, and thereafter mail was trucked in from Sanders in adjoining Carroll Co.

An Atlas of Owen County, Kentucky. Philadelphia: Lake, 1883.

Houchens, Mariam Sidebottom. *History of Owen County: "Sweet Owen."* Louisville, Ky.: Standard, 1976.

CURTIS, DICK (b. Richard Dye, May 11, 1902, Newport, Ky.; d. January 2, 1952, Los Angeles, Calif.). Movie actor Richard Dye was the son of Frank and Elizabeth Faulkner Dye. At age 16 he made his film debut as an extra in the 1918 feature movie *The Unpardonable Sin.* Assuming the screen name of Dick Curtis, he became known for his heavily wrinkled face, high cheekbones, and shifty eyes. Curtis was cast as a sailor in the original *King Kong* (1933). He became a classic bad guy, appearing in more than 200 movies during his career. He was a familiar character in B westerns such as *The Lion's Den* (1935), *Wildcat Trooper* (1936), *Colorado Trail* (1938), and *Taming of the West* (1939). His most noted role was his portrayal of the cold-blooded, revenge-seeking Mitch Crew in producer's Bill Elliot's *Across the Sierras* (1941). Curtis also had a flair for slapstick, appearing in several Columbia Pictures comedy shorts, often with the Three Stooges. In the Stooges' 1946 short *Three Troubledoers,* a parody on B westerns, Curtis played the villain. His last film was *My Six Convicts* (1952), in which he played a prison guard; the film had not yet been released at the time of his death. He was also one of the founders of Pioneertown, a 32,000-acre movie ranch, home, resort, and dude ranch development two hours east of Los Angeles in Yucca Valley. Many westerns have been filmed there since the late 1940s. His partners in Pioneertown were Gene Autry and Roy Rogers. Curtis died of brain cancer in 1952 at Cedars of Lebanon Hospital in Los Angeles and was buried at Holy Cross Cemetery in Culver City, Calif. He was survived by his wife, Ruth Sullivan Curtis, an actress of the silent-film era.

"Dick Curtis," *NYT,* January 4, 1952, 40.

"Dick Curtis," *Variety,* January 9, 1952.

Michael R. Sweeney

CURTIS GATES LLOYD WILDLIFE AREA. This wildlife area, located on farmland outside Crittenden in Grant Co., had its beginning in 1910 when **Curtis Gates Lloyd** obtained the 324 acres of land. It was later named the Lloyd Library Botanical Gardens and Arboretum, and the expanded property is currently called the Curtis Gates Lloyd Wildlife Area. Lloyd loved the Crittenden area, and his love of the place showed in his farm. He planted flower gardens with many kinds of flowers and made the property's Woodland Grove a place for families to picnic and enjoy gatherings. It has been the site of many graduation parties. Also on the farm are two 20-acre tracts of virgin timber, known as the Old Growth Forest. Concerned about the property's upkeep, Lloyd drew up a 27-page document detailing specific points of maintenance.

After Lloyd's death, the land was put into a trust at Central Trust Bank in Cincinnati. On May 25, 1965, the land was deeded to the Kentucky Department of Fish and Wildlife to be developed as a wildlife refuge. After that department purchased additional land, today the area consists of 1,179 acres. A clubhouse was built and a fishing lake was created. The property was dedicated July 24, 1966.

There are skeet, trap, archery, and pistol ranges. The fishing lake's handicapped-accessible pier was the first in the state. There are also walking trails that go through the Old Growth Forest. In the Old Growth Forest stands the tombstone that Lloyd erected to himself before his death. After he died and was cremated, his ashes were scattered over the forest.

Curtis Gates Lloyd Collection, Lloyd Library, series 10, Crittenden Farm, boxes 23–26, folders 639–758, Cincinnati.

Grant Co. Deed Book, book 101, p. 318, Williamstown, Ky.

"Nature Lover Adopts Town of Crittenden," *Falmouth Outlook,* December 5, 1924, 1.

Rankin, Bob. "C.G. Lloyd Preserved the Outdoors He Loved," *KE,* July 25, 1966, 2.

Reis, Jim. "Younger Lloyd Brother an Eccentric Whose Love of Nature Lives in Legend," *KP,* September 10, 1990, 4K.

Edna Marie Cummins

CUTTER, GEORGE W. (b. ca. 1809, Massachusetts; d. December 25, 1865, Washington, D.C.). Covington lawyer and activist George W. Cutter was among the thousands of men who volunteered for military service when the **Mexican War** broke out in May 1846. Cutter organized a company of volunteers and was elected captain.

Cutter became well known in Covington after arriving there in 1840 with his new bride, Frances Ann Denny Drake (**Mrs. Alexander Drake**), the widow of nationally known actor Alexander Drake. Born in New England, Cutter moved to Indiana, where he learned law and was elected to the state legislature in 1838, serving two terms. While in the legislature, he met and courted Frances; their wedding on January 23, 1840, was conducted by Rev. Henry Ward Beecher. In the same year, Cutter published his first book of poetry, *Elskatawa; or, The Moving Fires, and Other Poems.* In Covington, the couple lived in the Drake house, subsequently known as the Cutter house; George Cutter practiced law and was involved in causes including temperance, public health, and politics.

Cutter's war record was mixed. The majority of his company mutinied and refused to serve under him because of his tyrannical conduct. The men returned to duty only through the intervention of Maj. **John P. Gaines** of Boone Co. Cutter apparently acquitted himself well on the battlefield. At the renowned Battle of Buena Vista in February 1847, he participated in an ill-timed charge by the Kentucky Volunteers. Fresh Mexican reserves mauled the attack, and among the casualties was the regiment's second in command, Lt. Col. Henry Clay Jr. The mortally wounded Clay entrusted his pistols to Cutter for return to Clay's father, the famed Henry Clay. After this battle Cutter penned one of his most famous poems, "Buena Vista."

Cutter petitioned newly elected president and fellow Kentuckian Zachary Taylor for a government appointment after the war, reportedly coveting a post as minister to Morocco. Taylor's untimely death spoiled this effort, though Cutter did receive an offer of a law clerkship in the Treasury Department. His acceptance of this position apparently led to estrangement from his wife and ultimately to divorce. While in Washington, D.C., he continued to publish poetry.

Cutter then disappeared from the historical record until December 1865, when an acquaintance discovered him in Providence Hospital in Washington, D.C., suffering from an unstated illness. Cutter died at the hospital later that month and was buried in Washington's Congressional Cemetery.

Throughout his life, George W. Cutter published numerous poems in newspapers and journals and collected many poems into volumes sold by subscription. His most famous poem was "The Song of Steam," a paean to the steam technology gains of the 1820s and 1830s. This poem ultimately proved so popular that it remained in publication into the 20th century.

Herrmann, R. Timothy, B. Michael McCormick, and Robert T. Rhode. "George W. Cutter: America's Poet Warrior," *JKS* 18 (September 2001): 74–82.

DAIRIES. Because Northern Kentucky has a strong agricultural tradition, it is not surprising that an estimated 500 dairies operated in the region before 1920. In addition, individual farms (see **Truck Farming**), working on a smaller scale, supplied dairies with dairy produce.

The regional daily demand for dairy products to be pasteurized, homogenized, and refrigerated is what sustained such a large number of dairies. As the region's population grew, and as milk production became more regulated and industrialized, many of the dairies—their names now lost—were bought out or merged with larger ones.

By the 1920s, 54 dairies operated in Northern Kentucky. No documented history indicates which one was the first to become an independent business. However, the **Trauth Dairy** in Newport can claim to be the only remaining milk plant in Northern Kentucky. It was established in 1920, when Louis Trauth and his wife Clara Stephany Trauth bought one milk route from Fred Schuerman's Dairy. Schuerman's farm was located where the **Newport Shopping Center** is today; and Trauth continues to expand its operations to this day around the intersection of 11th and Monmouth Sts. in Newport, just to the north of the shopping center.

Besides Trauth Dairy, Campbell Co. was home to companies such as Sealtest (Newport) and Clover Leaf Dairy. Clover Leaf, founded by Emmert J. Marschman in about 1915 on Johns Hill Rd. in Cold Spring, later opened its processing plant in Newport. Beginning with a store in Fort Thomas in 1937, Clover Leaf's "dairy bars" were precursors to modern convenience stores, selling milk and dairy products as well as deli and grocery items. Their popularity was evidenced in 1956 when the brand new Newport Shopping Center included a Clover Leaf Dairy Bar. Also in Campbell Co. were George B. Moock's dairy farm on Moock Rd. in Southgate and the associated processing plant called Hiland Dairy in Newport; Jansing Dairy in Wilder, at Licking Pk. and Three Mile Rd.; Feldmann Dairy on Licking Pk. (Feldmann's dairy barn later served as the Wilder police station); and Jersey Farms Dairy in Fort Thomas, purchased by Clover Leaf in 1952. The H. Meyer Dairy Company of Cincinnati purchased the Clover Leaf milk processing plant in Newport in the mid-1970s, and in 1984 Trauth Dairy bought Clover Leaf's ice cream facility.

In Kenton Co., Buttermilk Pk. in Crescent Springs and Villa Hills was lined with dairy farms, and they remained until I-75 was constructed during the 1960s. Local legend has it that Buttermilk Pk. was so named not only because of the large number of dairies but also because transporting milk over the bumpy dirt road on a humid day would churn the milk and turn it into buttermilk. In the 1880s this area had several dairies, including the Echo Dairy, run by Joseph Cleveland; the Thirs Dairy, operated by Amos Collins; and two dairies owned by Col. J. G. Anderson, one of which was known as the List Dairy.

The city of Edgewood was developed from lands acquired by the sale of dairy farms, including the Edgewood Dairy Farm, owned by the Requardt family. The **Summit Hills Golf and Country Club** in Edgewood was once the Hartke Dairy, and the country club's original clubhouse had previously been the dairy's two-story barn. The Foltz Dairy, located on Dudley Rd. in Edgewood, sold its milk to local producers and stayed in operation until 1987. The Rehkamp Dairy on the **Three-L Highway (LLL)**, which started as a distributor, eventually became a full-service dairy.

The Steenken family owned two dairies in Fort Mitchell. Their dairy on Highland Ave. produced milk that was sold to processing plants. The family also contracted to milk cows for other farms, since there were enough family members to provide the manual labor needed to milk cows twice daily.

A number of dairies were located in Covington. The Trenkamp Dairy operated on W. 11th St. until the 1950s, and the Hanneken Dairy, which bought out the Steffen Dairy, was headquartered at 624 Scott St. The Hanneken family partnered with the Rehkamps and relocated to 533 Pike St. (now 533 Goetta Pl.) in what is now Glier's **Goetta**, formerly part of the **Bavarian Brewing Company**. Clover Leaf Dairy bought the Hanneken Dairy in July 1964. Also in Covington was the French Bauer Dairy Products Company, a cooperative of farmers.

The Latonia Springs Dairy, named after the defunct **Latonia Springs** resort and located along the Three-L Highway (LLL) in what is now Fort Wright, was operated by the Ratermann family. According to Bob Ratermann, the Latonia Springs Dairy farm included as many as 113 head of cattle, which had to be milked twice daily (4:00 a.m. and 4:00 p.m.). The Ratermanns, along with their cousins the Summes, had a processing plant called Summe and Ratermann Company at 224 E. 20th St. in Covington; it later added the Latonia Springs brand name. Charles Summe, a descendant, recalled that most dairies had two kinds of cows, Holstein cows because they produced volume and Jersey cows because they produced more milk butterfat. Milk was bought based on the amount of butterfat and the weight of the milk. Often milk from the Jersey cows and the Holstein cows would be mixed to get the right percentage of fat. This was most important in the production of ice cream. Summe stated that the initial step in a purchase was to smell the milk, to make sure it did not smell like the wild onions that the cows often ate. Once it passed the "smell test," the milk would be tested for fat content and tasted for sweetness. Summe added that before the invention of dry ice and refrigeration, milk could be easily stored beyond daily usage in the winter, but in the summer milk was harder to store; it was often preserved by placing containers of it in the cool water of a well. The Summe and Ratermann Dairy closed in 1965, three years after selling its milk delivery routes to Clover Leaf Dairy.

In the twentieth century, many dairies were not full-service but carried out only a part of the larger production process. For instance, one dairy farm would raise cows and sell the milk to a local processing plant. That plant, after processing was completed, would either label and distribute the milk or sell it to another distributor. Some dairies only shipped milk under their labels, while other dairy farmers sometimes contracted with members of their families to do milking at a neighbor's dairy farm.

Theodore Joseph Hanneken of Hanneken Dairy (purchaser of the Steffen Dairy Company), 624 Scott St., Covington. To the right is the Packard automobile dealership of Louie Meyer.

In 1928 the Carnation Milk Company arrived in Maysville, and for several decades it canned milk there; and in Owenton the Kraft Company ran a cheese factory for several years. Canning milk and making cheese were efficient ways of making use of excess milk production, and the end product could be easily stored.

Historically, dairy farming was an important component of Northern Kentucky's **agriculture**, providing milk, cheese, and butter to a growing urban population. Horse-drawn milk wagons, and later mechanized trucks, delivered bottled milk and dairy products door-to-door to residences in cities and suburbs. Metal milk boxes could be seen on porches and stoops throughout the region. Suburbanization, the popularity of automobiles, and the building of grocery supermarkets spelled the end of an era in dairy farming and milk delivery. One truck farming family evidenced the trends. John Boh (1881–1975) operated a 49-acre truck farm on Buttermilk Pk. that, in the post–World War II era, was subdivided into one of Villa Hills's early subdivisions. His son George Boh (1912–2003), was born on the Bramlage dairy farm on Turkeyfoot Rd., where **Thomas More College** is now located. After his marriage, George Boh inherited a small farm on Highland Pk. in Fort Wright, which also became a post–World War II subdivision. Having grown up on a labor-intensive farm, he was ambitious to cultivate larger fields—with tractors and without horses. He moved his family to a farm of more than 100 acres on old Price Pk. (now Turfway Rd.) in Boone Co. and engaged in dairy, grain, and tobacco farming. The family milked some 30–40 cows by machine and shipped the milk to the Summe and Ratermann Dairy, originally in 10-gallon cans and later in tanks. Other families who moved from small operations to larger farms in Boone Co. included displaced and ambitious Kenton Co. truck and dairy farmers named Foltz, Brueggeman, Kunkel, and Gripshover. When the Cincinnati/Northern Kentucky International Airport bought the Boh farm in 1977, the farm had been enlarged to more than 200 acres, much of it used for grazing milk cows. Finally, the family bought a 500-acre farm along the Ohio River in Boone Co., not far from Rabbit Hash, where they raise soybeans and corn rather than dairy cows.

"As Other Dairies Vanish, Trauth Company Expands," *CP*, July 31, 1984, 11B.

Boh, John. Interview by Paul Tenkotte, December 26, 2008, Covington, Ky.

Campbell Co. Historical Society. *Campbell County, Kentucky, 200 Years, 1794–1994*. Alexandria, Ky.: Campbell Co. Historical Society, 1994.

Reis, Jim. *Pieces of the Past*. Vols. 2, 3. Covington: Kentucky Post, 1991, 1994.

Summe, Charles. Interview by Gabrielle Summe, May and June 2006, Covington, Ky.

Gabrielle Summe

DALY, RICHARD (dates and places of birth and death unknown). Although Richard Daly's birth and death dates, like those of many Kentucky slaves, are unknown, he was still alive in 1894 in Windsor, Canada, when interviewed by a reporter for a Detroit, Mich., newspaper. Daly's four children were born between 1840 and 1850 in Hunter's Bottom, Carroll Co., Ky. His oldest daughter, Mary, was listed as being age 17 in the 1860 Detroit census.

In the 1850s Richard Daly, his brother Joe Daly, and Tom Owen were slaves owned by Samuel Fearn Sr. at Hunter's Bottom. The **Fearn family** came to Kentucky from Buckingham Co., Va. Samuel Fearn (1766–1828) (the father of Samuel Sr.) and his oldest son, George (1796–1869), arrived in 1803 in Hunter's Bottom, a 10-mile stretch of Ohio River bottomland between Canip and Locust creeks. Samuel Fearn Sr., the family's fourth child, was born at Hunter's Bottom in 1806 and married Elizabeth Owen in 1826. George and Samuel Fearn together owned about 1,000 acres along the banks of the Ohio River, straddling the Carroll and Trimble county line, but Samuel Sr.'s main income came from his gristmill and packet steamship businesses in Milton, on the Kentucky side of the Ohio River opposite Madison, Ind. He also purchased timberland in Jackson Co., Ind., on the White River. George Fearn speculated in land along the wharf area in Madison and along the Indiana shoreline on the east side of Madison. The two Fearn brothers were quite wealthy. Samuel Fearn had three slaves; George, a bachelor, owned four or five slaves. The Fearn family history states that George Fearn had become an ardent Methodist and emancipated all of his slaves in his will. George was so pro-Union and so openly opposed to slavery that horses were stolen from his farm in a targeted attack by Confederate raiders during the **Civil War**.

In his 1894 interview, Richard Daly referred to Samuel and George Fearn as "kind," and it appeared that Daly had many advantages over other slaves in the region. He lived in a brick house behind the main Samuel Fearn homestead and was permitted to take produce to market in Madison, Ind., in order to earn money to purchase his freedom. Furthermore, Samuel Fearn had set an extremely low purchase price, $100, for Daly's freedom, although comparable prices for slaves of his age and ability were well above $800–$900. Daly claimed that by 1856 he had already saved $100 "in his pocket." Fearn, like many of the Hunter's Bottom slave owners, allowed frequent conjugal visits by Richard to his wife, Kitty, a house servant owned by Moses Hoagland (see **Hoagland Family**), who lived east of the Fearns along the Ohio River toward Carrollton. Richard and Kitty had four living children, who by law and custom were owned by Moses Hoagland.

But the most unusual fact about Richard Daly was that he had worked actively in the **Underground Railroad** (UGRR) for some years. He stated that he had ferried 30 fugitive slaves across the Ohio River before 1856. He would meet the slaves two miles above Milton and row them across in his small boat. During the 1850s this route through Eagle Hollow in Carroll Co., Ky., was one of the most active crossing points on the Ohio River between Cincinnati and Louisville. Daly's method of signaling his friend, a white leader of the UGRR (probably John Carr) was also highly unusual. Daly said that he would row into the middle of the Ohio River and shoot a revolver into the air. The UGRR agent would then shoot his revolver in response. By the time Daly arrived at the Indiana shore, his white friend would be ready and would take charge of the runaways.

It was well known that Samuel Fearn enjoyed hunting and had several hunting dogs always running through the house and farm. But for a slave to have access to a revolver and ammunition was remarkable. Moreover, the sound of gunshots in the middle of the Ohio River at night would have carried to both shores. If the Indiana UGRR agent heard it, the Fearns would have heard it also. Therefore, it has been suggested locally that the Fearn brothers tacitly, if not actively, approved of Daly's aiding runaway slaves.

Daly said that he was happy in his circumstances and had no plans to escape, but then his wife Kitty unexpectedly died. Richard was concerned about his children and asked Mrs. Hoagland (Sarah Payne of Lexington) to keep them in Hunter's Bottom, and she agreed. However, a short time later, the Hoagland daughter married a doctor and moved to Louisville. She asked for Mary, the oldest Daly daughter, to go with her permanently. When Richard Daly learned that his family was to be separated, he went to pick up all four children. They crossed the Ohio River and took the Madison UGRR route north through Indiana. Daly said that they rode horses northward, accompanied successively by two sets of UGRR agents, one from twilight to midnight and another from midnight to dawn. The family slept in various farmhouses until they reached Michigan. There, they boarded the Michigan Central Railroad to Detroit and crossed over the ferry to Windsor, Canada.

In Canada, Daly worked feeding cattle for a man named Hiram Walker, who exported livestock to Great Britain from a farm located along the Detroit River. Daly said that he had crossed the Atlantic Ocean several times with these shipments. At some point, he married a second time. In 1894 three of the children who escaped with him were living in Detroit, and one child had died in Windsor.

Apparently Joe Daly and Tom Owen continued to live with Samuel Fearn at Hunter's Bottom even after the 13th Amendment to the U.S. Constitution freed all slaves. When George Fearn died in 1869, he left Fearn Hill, his antebellum home, to his nephew, George Fearn. The emancipation clause was still in George's will, but it was moot since his slaves were already free by law.

Blassingame, John W., ed. *Slave Testimony*. Baton Rouge: Louisiana State Univ. Press, 1977.

Coon, Diane Perrine. "Southeastern Indiana's Underground Railroad Routes and Operations," 1999, U.S. Park Service and Indiana DNR, unpublished technical report, Indiana Dept. of Historic Preservation and Archaeology, Indianapolis, Ind.

Emma McClaran Fearn family Bible. In possession of Larry Douglas Smith, Louisville, Ky.

Smith, Larry Douglas. "The Fearns of Hunters Bottom, Kentucky," Kentucky Historical Society, Frankfort, Ky.

Diane Perrine Coon

DANIEL CARTER BEARD BRIDGE. The twin-span interstate structure known as the Daniel Carter Beard Bridge, which crosses the Ohio River and connects the east side of downtown Cincinnati and Newport, was completed in late 1975 and opened on January 1, 1976. Named for one-time Covington resident **Daniel Carter Beard**, the founder of the **Boy Scouts** of America, it is the northernmost section of I-471 (see **Expressways**) and has become an important means of travel to and from Cincinnati and beyond for commuters. Sometimes referred to as the "Big Mac" bridge because of its painted golden arches, it provides access to the new entertainment areas of Newport and Bellevue before heading into central Campbell Co. via I-471 southbound. The exit ramp southbound off the bridge onto Ky. Rt. 8 is being redesigned to avoid the dangerous traffic bottlenecks and backups onto the bridge that form there in the early evenings, as a result of the business traffic coming to **Newport-on-the-Levee**.

Cincinnati-Transit.net. "Daniel Carter Beard 'Big Mac' Bridge." www.cincinnati-transit.net (accessed October 31, 2006).

"I-471 Bridge Named for Daniel Beard," *KP*, October 19, 1976, 1.

"To Open I-471 Bridge Jan. 1," *KP*, December 15, 1975, 9K.

DAUGHTERS OF THE AMERICAN REVOLUTION. The Kentucky Daughters of the American Revolution (DAR) society, organized in 1891, has 83 chapters, nine of which are located in the Northern Kentucky region. The local chapters are in Augusta, Erlanger, Florence, Fort Thomas (two chapters), Ghent, Grant Co., Maysville, and Owenton. The DAR's motto is "God, Home, and Country," and the society's goals include historic preservation, the promotion of education, and patriotic service to veterans at home or overseas. The state headquarters are housed at the Duncan Tavern Historic Center in Paris, Ky.

The national society was founded in 1890. It has 50 state societies, plus one in the District of Columbia, with more than 2,900 local chapters, and many chapters overseas. The DAR's headquarters are at Constitution Hall in Washington, D.C. The DAR's objectives include working together to keep the public aware of educational opportunities for youth through programs in schools and providing many different kinds of scholarships for students. To become a member of the DAR, an applicant must be 18 years of age, and she must prove lineal bloodline descent from an ancestor who aided in achieving America's independence. Documentation for each ancestor is required, including birth, marriage, and death records. Each application is sent to the National DAR Headquarters to be researched and approved. Affiliated with the DAR are organizations for the Sons of the American Revolution (SAR), and the Children of the American Revolution (CAR). Women under age 30 who join the DAR have junior memberships. Some chapters are now scheduling, in addition to their regular monthly luncheon meetings, evening or Saturday meetings that generally feature speakers. Some of the chapters in Northern Kentucky assist in the bingo games held for the patients at the **Veterans Administration Medical Center** in Fort Thomas, and most chapters participate in the Fourth of July parades in their communities.

Kentucky Society Daughters of the American Revolution. www.kentuckydar.org (accessed January 15, 2006).

Robin Rider Osborne

DAVIS, DAVID (b. David Davies, September 12, 1865, Monmouthshire, Wales, U.K.; d. March 21, 1932, New York City). Architect David Davis was born in Wales to John B. and Mary Davies. When he was age two or three, his family immigrated to the United States, settling in Newport, where Davis graduated from **Newport High School**. The family name was originally Davies, but David changed his surname to Davis as a young man. He is reputed to have studied at both the Ohio Mechanics Institute in Cincinnati and the Massachusetts Institute of Technology (MIT) in Boston, although whether he actually matriculated at either institution is unknown at this time. By 1889 David Davis was practicing as a draftsman in the Johnston Building in Cincinnati, where a number of architects' offices were located. He lived in Newport.

By 1891 Davis had joined noted Cincinnati architect Alfred Oscar Elzner as a draftsman. Elzner had trained at MIT and also in the Boston office of the renowned American architect H. H. Richardson (1838–1886). It is probably through his connection to Elzner that Davis is presumed to have gone to MIT. In 1894 and 1895, Davis was listed as an architect in Newport. By 1899 he was a partner of William R. Brown and Matthew Burton in the architectural practice of Brown, Burton, and Davis in Cincinnati. By 1902 the firm had become Brown and Davis, and by 1906 it listed offices in both Cincinnati and Chicago. In late 1907, Davis set out on his own as an architect, remaining so until his association with Alexander W. Stewart in Cincinnati in 1923. Davis moved to New York City about 1926.

David Davis was a very prominent architect by the early 20th century, especially in ecclesiastical architecture. Bishop **Camillus Paul Maes** of the Diocese of Covington greatly respected his work and hired him to complete the west facade of Covington's magnificent **Cathedral Basilica of the Assumption** (1908–1910); the original plans for the cathedral had been drawn by Leon Coquard. The diocese also commissioned him to design plans for St. Mark Church in Richmond (1907–1908), **St. Philip Catholic Church** in Melbourne (1908), Holy Guardian Angels School in Sanfordtown (1909), an addition and new front elevation to the bishop's home at the northeast corner of 12th and Madison Ave. in Covington (1912), **St. Patrick** School in Covington (1913), **St. Augustine Catholic Church** in Covington (1914), and St. Camillus Academy in Corbin (1914–1915). He was also commissioned by the diocese to design a three-story addition to St. Joseph Orphanage in Cold Spring (1915) and to complete architect Leon Coquard's plans for **St. Patrick Catholic Church** in Maysville (1907–1909).

In addition to their work for Covington's Catholic bishop, in 1906 and 1907 the firm of Brown and Davis had commissions for churches in Ames, Iowa (First Methodist Episcopal [M.E.]); Kansas City, Mo. (First M.E. Church and also Swope Park Methodist); Auburn, N.Y. (Trinity M.E.); Ithaca, N.Y. (First M.E.); Atertown, N.Y. (M.E.); Williamsport, Pa. (M.E.); and Aberdeen, S.Dak. (First M.E.). Also, Burton and Davis designed administrative and dormitory buildings for Union College (Methodist) at Barbourville, Ky.; a building at Kansas City University (Kans.); a 150-foot tower for Kansas City University (in conjunction with architects Garber and Woodward of Cincinnati); and a two-story addition to the Ruffner Hotel in Charleston, W.Va.

After Burton and Davis dissolved their partnership in late 1907, Davis continued his career with an impressive series of commissions. His later works included a tower for St. Mary's Church, Auburn, N.Y.; an M.E. church in Greenfield, Ohio; a Chamber of Commerce building in Charleston, W.Va. (with Garber and Woodward); a bank at Charleston, W.Va.; and the **Latonia Christian Church**, Covington (1923).

David Davis died in New York City in 1932 and was buried in the family lot at Evergreen Cemetery in Southgate, Ky. He lived most of his life along E. Fourth St. in Newport.

"Add Dormitory for St. Joseph Orphans," *KP*, September 30, 1915, 1.

"The Addition to the Bishop's House," *Christian Year* (Covington), November 1, 1912, 1.

Cincinnati city directories, 1889–1925.

Evergreen Cemetery records, Southgate, Ky.

Freiberg, Walter A. *A Guide to the Cathedral*. Covington, Ky.: Messenger, 1947.

Painter, Sue Ann. *Architecture in Cincinnati*. Athens: Ohio Univ. Press, 2006.

"St. Patrick's New School," *Christian Year* (Covington), May 17, 1913, 7.

Tenkotte, Paul A., David E. Schroeder, and Thomas S. Ward. *To Be Catholic and American in Northern, Central, and Appalachian Kentucky: The Diocese of Covington, 1853–2003*. Forthcoming.

"Was Architect for Catholic Cathedral: Rites Arranged for Noted New York Resident," *CTS*, March 24, 1932, 1.

Western Architect and Builder, 1906–1910.

Paul A. Tenkotte

DAVIS, GEOFFREY C. "GEOFF" (b. October 26, 1958, Montreal, Quebec, Canada). Congressman Geoffrey Clark Davis is the son of Barbara Clark Davis. He is a graduate of Hampton High School, Pittsburgh, Pa. While on active duty in the U.S. Army, Davis successfully obtained a rare appointment to the U.S. Military Academy at West Point, N.Y., where he graduated in 1981. His active-duty military career extended from 1976 until 1987. He was an assault helicopter flight commander pilot with the 82nd Airborne Division, an Army Ranger, and a parachutist. In 1992 he started his own business, Capstone Inc., a manufacturing consulting firm. A naturalized U.S. citizen and a strong proponent of smaller government, Davis was first elected to the 109th U.S. Congress as a Republican in 2004, defeating Democrat **Nick Clooney**. Davis represents Northern Kentucky in the Fourth District. He was reelected in 2006, defeating three-term Democratic congressman **Ken Lucas** in a rematch, having lost previously to Lucas in 2002. In January 2007, Davis began service as a member of the 110th U.S Congress. Davis and his wife, Pat, and their six children live in Hebron in Boone Co.

"Candidate Biographies," *KP*, November 1, 2002, T3.
Collins, Michael. "Davis Candidacy Now Official," *KP*, October 10, 2001, 2K.
"Geoffrey C. Davis." http://bioguide.congress.gov (accessed November 11, 2006).

DAVIS, "SKEETER" (b. Mary Frances Penick, Glencoe, Ky., December 30, 1931; d. Nashville, Tenn., September 19, 2004). Skeeter's story resembles those of other famous female country singers and songwriters of her era. Born into a poor farming family faced with challenges of alcoholism, incest, and murder, Skeeter was able to rise above her background and become an internationally renowned country music artist. She was best known for her timeless popular recording "The End of the World."

Mary Frances was born in a two-room clapboard shack on the banks of Eagle Creek in Glencoe (Owen Co.), the first of seven children of William and Sarah Penick. She spent most of her childhood with her grandparents in rural Dry Ridge. During her early school years, she assumed the name Skeeter because of her energetic and quick-moving nature. Her harmonizing musical talent surfaced at school and at Dry Ridge Christian Church.

Skeeter Davis, 1957.

The Penick family moved to the outskirts of Covington during Skeeter's teenage years, and at **Dixie Heights High School** she befriended Betty Jack Davis (b. 1932, Corbin, Ky.). With the stage name of the Davis Sisters, they began singing duets at local events and on radio. Their unique harmonizing style set them apart from other country and rockabilly artists at the time. Both attended DeCoursey Baptist Church in Covington. They occasionally appeared with bluegrass performers Flatt and Skruggs on the *Kentucky Barn Dance*, broadcast by WLEX (Lexington). Performances on Cincinnati and Detroit radio led to a recording contract with RCA. There they recorded "I Forgot More Than You'll Ever Know," which became a number-one country hit in 1953. The rising star of the Davis Sisters ended in August 1953, when an automobile accident northeast of Cincinnati killed Betty Jack and seriously injured Skeeter. Davis was buried at Highland Cemetery in Fort Mitchell.

With the assistance of Betty Jack's mother, Skeeter performed briefly with Betty Jack's sister Georgia. The girls toured with other music artists, including Elvis Presley. In 1958 Ernest Tubb persuaded Skeeter to pursue a solo career. At this time she also developed a strong friendship with country singer June Carter. Skeeter's 1959 recording "Set Him Free" established her as a solo artist on the country charts and earned her the first of five Grammy nominations. Follow-up hits included "I'm Falling Too" (1960) and "My Last Date (with You)" (1961). In 1959 she garnered a contract with the Grand Ole Opry, where she remained a regular performer.

Under the professional guidance of renowned Nashville Sound producer-guitarist Chet Atkins, Skeeter's 1962 hit "The End of the World" earned her a gold record and brought her longtime international fame. Atkins utilized a "double-track" recording technique to recreate the popular harmony of the Davis Sisters. During this period, Skeeter crossed over to pop music, disappointing some die-hard country music fans. She defended her middle-of-the-road pop music style by anchoring her roots in country music as an ongoing Grand Ole Opry performer, while expanding her pop audience base in appearances with Duke Ellington, the Rolling Stones, and the contemporary rock band NRBQ. Subsequently she produced country gold and platinum records and performed with country music artists Bobby Bare, George Hamilton IV, and Porter Wagoner.

Known as a religious rebel and a social activist, Skeeter was suspended for a year by the Grand Ole Opry in December 1973 because she criticized the Nashville Police for its arrest of a young Christian demonstration group at a local shopping mall during the holidays. Skeeter was married three times. Most notable was her heartbreaking second marriage to Ralph Emery, host of the *Nashville Now* cable television show.

In addition to frequently appearing at the Grand Ole Opry, Skeeter was a guest star several times on television's *American Bandstand* and *Hee Haw*. She entertained loyal fans around the world, most notably in Austria, Barbados, Indonesia, Jamaica, Korea, Malaysia, Singapore, Thailand, and many countries in Africa. During her career, she recorded more than 60 singles and 30 long-play albums for RCA. In 1998 Dry Ridge literally placed Skeeter on the map by naming a section of Ky. Rt. 22, between I-75 and the **Dixie Highway** (U.S. 25), the Skeeter Davis Highway. She was buried in Williams Memorial Gardens at Franklin, Tenn.

Davis, Skeeter. *Bus Fare to Kentucky: The Autobiography of Skeeter Davis*. New York: Birch Lane Press, 1993.
Kingsbury, Paul, ed. *Encyclopedia of Country Music*. New York: Oxford Univ. Press, 1998.
Kreimer, Peggy. "Skeeter Davis Is Dead at 72," *KP*, September 20, 2004, 1K.
Wolf, Charles K. *Kentucky Country*. Lexington: Univ. Press of Kentucky, 1996.

John Schlipp

DAYTON. Long before the first Europeans set foot on what later became Dayton, Ky., American Indians from north of the Ohio River were known to frequent the site. Proof can be seen in the large numbers of arrowheads, relics, and pottery fragments that have been found there. Several Indian mounds were also located in the eastern part of the city, the most significant one being near Fourth and Benham Sts. None of the mounds were ever excavated, and they are no longer visible. The first Europeans known to have visited the site were the French explorer René-Robert Cavelier La Salle and two Jesuit priests, who came in 1669. The men landed on the sandbar at Dayton, where they met a group of friendly Miami and Iroquois Indians who were returning to Ohio from a hunting trip into Central Kentucky. The next significant event occurring at Dayton was the **Revolutionary War** battle known as **Rogers' Defeat**, which took place on that same sandbar in 1779.

The first owner of the land that is now Dayton was **George Muse**, a British Army officer during the **French and Indian War**. He gave the 1,000-acre site to his daughters Katy and Carolyn Muse, who later sold it to **Washington Berry**, a brother-in-law of **James Taylor Jr.**, founder of Newport. Berry's son James eventually acquired the eastern portion of the farm and, in partnership with **James McArthur** and Henry Walker, founded the city of Jamestown in 1848. The city apparently was named for **James T. Berry**. In 1849 two riverboat builders from Fulton, Ohio, Burton and Lewis Hazen, started a city called Brooklyn on the western part of the farm. Then in 1867 the two cities merged to form the present city of Dayton. The name Dayton is believed to have been taken from the Ohio city by that name, which was founded in 1803. The most popular lodging place in Dayton was the Jamestown Hotel, at the foot of Clay St., owned and operated by James T. Berry.

The shipbuilding industry across the Ohio River at Fulton dominated the early days of Dayton. Several wharfs were built along the riverfront to accommodate visitors to the region and to transport area workers to and from the shipyards. One of the first **ferries**, named the *John Hastings,* began operating in 1853 at the foot of Dayton St. In the mid-1800s, Dayton had nine rope-making companies, called **ropewalks**, which sold their products to area businesses, including the Fulton shipyards. In those early years, there were also several **sawmills** and brick-making companies (**brickyards**) in the city. In later years some of the city's largest employers were the **Wadsworth Watch Case Company**, **Speers Memorial Hospital**, the **Harvard Piano Company**, Perry and Derrick Paints, and the Mastercraft Metals Company. The Wadsworth Watch Case Company began in Newport but in 1900 moved to Fifth and Clay Sts. in Dayton. It was Dayton's largest employer by far, at its peak providing about 1,350 jobs. Well-known businesses in Dayton in subsequent years were the Dayton Chili Parlor, the **F&N Steakhouse**, **Harmeyer Paint Company**, Klingenberg's Hardware, Rifkin Shoes, and Wing's Delicatessen.

Early transportation to the area was mostly by water, but in 1873 a bridge was built across Newport's Taylor's Creek, which provided Bellevue and Dayton residents with convenient access to Newport. That bridge led to travel by horse-drawn carriages and, in 1893, by electric **streetcars**. Later on, the No. 12 Dayton **Green Line** became a popular route. In 1888 the **Chesapeake and Ohio Railroad** began service to Dayton and Bellevue. Public transportation contributed greatly to the rapid development of both cities, of their famous **Ohio River beaches**, and of Dayton's **Tacoma Park**.

Some of Dayton's more famous residents have been Dr. James Barnsfather, discoverer of the bacillus that causes tuberculosis and scarlet fever, and sports figures such as UCLA college basketball coach **John Wooden** and football players Bob "Twenty Grand" Davis, Bob DeMoss, and Johnnie "Deep" Wing. Professional baseball players include Lloyd "Dutch" Dietz, Bill Kissinger, Chick Smith, and Jesse and Lee Tannehill (see **Tannehill Brothers**).

Over the years, numerous floods have ravaged the city, the Ohio River **flood of 1937** being the worst; it put two-thirds of Dayton under water. To solve the flooding problem, a 1.5-mile-long floodwall was built in 1981, which led to revitalization of the once vulnerable city. Since then, several new businesses, such as the Radac Corporation and the Rivertown Marina, have located in Dayton. A new high school, single-family public housing, and a senior citizens complex have replaced many of the substandard buildings that were once located near the river, and recently a large condominium development has also been built on Prigge's Hill. Dayton was incorporated as a fourth-class city; its population peaked at 9,050 in 1960 but fell to 5,966 by 2000.

Dayton Centennial Committee, *Centennial, Dayton, Kentucky, 1849–1949: Keepsake Program.* Newport, Ky.: Michaels, 1949.

Kleber, John E., ed. *The Kentucky Encyclopedia.* Lexington: Univ. Press of Kentucky, 1992.

Northern Kentucky Views. "The City of Dayton, Kentucky." www.nkyviews.com (accessed September 23, 2006).

Reis, Jim. "Union Gave Birth to Today's Dayton," *KP,* March 23, 1992, 4K.

U.S. Census Bureau, "American Fact Finder. Data Set. Census 2000 Summary File 1 (SF1) 100-Percent Data. Custom Table." www.census.gov (accessed September 29, 2006).

Wessling, Jack. *Early History of Campbell County, Kentucky.* Alexandria, Ky.: Privately published, 1997.

Jack Wessling

DAYTON PUBLIC SCHOOLS. The Dayton (Ky.) Public Schools had their beginning in the town of Jamestown, before Jamestown and Brooklyn merged in 1867 to form the city of Dayton. One of the first acts of the Jamestown trustees was the establishment (ca. 1848) of the town's first public school, in a frame house that was erected at the head of Main St. at a cost of $324. George W. Legge became the first superintendent of Dayton schools in 1869 and served until 1872. A board of education was first organized in May 1871, with members Adelbert E. Doisy, William Hasson, Pleasant Stamper, Henry C. Tibbetts, and William Tiemann. The clerk was H. P. Brazee Jr. A former pretzel factory, built on Sixth St. about 1850, became the city's Sixth St. School. During the late 1920s, when the school system had no further use for this building, it was offered to the city, and in 1932 the city offices and the jail were moved into the building.

High school classes were added to the already existing Lincoln School in Dayton in 1888, and the school celebrated its first high school graduating class in 1891. The Lincoln School served as the town's high school until a new high school was built on W. Eighth St. in 1904. By 1923 plans had been formulated to build a new 15-room school at a cost of $75,000 that would serve as a combined elementary and high school. Those plans became important when fire broke out at the Eighth St. High School on the morning of January 21, 1924. The building was destroyed, all the school records inside were lost, and damage was estimated at $75,000. Some 193 high school students and 450 grade school students were displaced by this calamity, which was caused by an overheated furnace. Dayton school officials announced that students would attend school for half-day sessions. The high school students were to share the Junior High School building on Sixth St. Grade school students shared a grade school building on Fifth Ave. Several fraternal lodges in the city offered their meeting rooms for use as temporary school rooms. The plans for the new Dayton High School building were updated to include a three-story concrete and brick building to be built on the location of the burned high school. Groundbreaking for the new building occurred on June 2, 1924, and work progressed quickly, allowing the new high school to be dedicated on May 10, 1925.

In September 1932, **John Wooden**, a recent graduate of Purdue University at Lafayette, Ind., was hired to be athletic director, coach, and an English teacher at Dayton High School. Coach Wooden's basketball team had a losing season his first year, and he moved on to another job after his second season, eventually becoming head basketball coach at UCLA in Los Angeles, where his teams won a record 10 NCAA Championships. The football program at Dayton High School was aided in the 1930s as the federal government fought the **Great Depression** by funding building projects. The NRA (National Recovery Administration) and the Works Progress Administration came to Dayton to construct a stadium and football field, which were dedicated on October 26, 1934. The students voted to name the new stadium for Olin W. Davis, in honor of his service as superintendent of Dayton Schools.

The Lincoln School continued to serve as an elementary school, and additions to the building were completed in 1949. On February 7, 1952, a fire occurred at that school while approximately 300 students were in the building. All students escaped without injury, but the building was gutted and the loss was estimated at $100,000. Students attended classes in local churches for the next two years while a new school building was erected and opened in fall 1954.

The high school on Eighth St. in Dayton continued in use until a new school was built and dedicated in August 1983. The new school, on Jackson St., was dedicated to Dayton school superintendent Jack Moreland for his work to obtain financing for the new school. A fire broke out in the west wing of the vacated old high school building on December 12, 1983. Arson was suspected in the blaze, and damage was estimated at $25,000, but there was no damage to the building's exterior. Developers purchased this property and spent more than $1 million renovating; the property was reopened in January 1986 as an apartment complex.

Campbell Co. Historical Society. *Campbell County, Kentucky, 200 Years, 1794–1994.* Alexandria, Ky.: Campbell Co. Historical Society, 1994.

Dayton Centennial Committee. *Dayton Kentucky Centennial, 1849–1949.* Dayton, Ky.: Dayton Centennial Committee, n.d. [ca. 1949].

Dayton Kentucky Centennial Jubilee, 1849–1974. Kenton Co. Public Library, Covington, Ky. Microfilm.

"Dayton to Get New School," *KP,* February 28, 1923, 1.

"Dayton Will Get New School," *KP,* November 5, 1919, 1.

Reis, Jim. "Famous Fires of '50s," *KP,* January 28, 2002, 4K.

———. "Two Schools, Two Fires on Frozen Day in 1924," *KP,* November 16, 2000, 4K.

Remlinger, Connie. "School Dedicated to the Man Who Came Up with the Millions," *KP,* August 15, 1983, 1K.

"Time Capsule Lifting Marks End of Era," *KP,* November 23, 1985, 3K.

Daryl Polley

DEAF AND HEARING-IMPAIRED. According to the 2000 U.S. Census, the counties of Boone, Campbell, Grant, Kenton, and Pendleton had 36,284 persons classified as deaf or hard of hearing. The *Kentucky Revised Statutes* 163.500 (2004) defines this special population as "persons who have hearing disorders [such that they] cannot hear and understand speech clearly through the ear alone, with or without hearing aids." The Northern Kentucky–Greater Cincinnati area offers significant services for the deaf and hearing-impaired.

Originally established as the Cincinnati League for the Hard of Hearing in 1925, the Hearing, Speech & Deaf Center of Greater Cincinnati celebrated its 80th year in 2005 as a nonprofit organization providing state-of-the-art hearing aids, speech therapy, audiology management, and other services. Through its community services, the center also provides interpreter referral, lip-reading and sign-language classes, advocacy, and technology assistance. Dr. Jean W. Rothenberg, who became severely hearing-impaired during the 1937 flu epidemic and wore hearing aids thereafter, expanded the organization in the 1950s to become the Cincinnati Speech & Hearing Center. In 2000 the University of Cincinnati honored Rothenberg for a half century of service.

The **Northern Kentucky Services for the Deaf**, located at Florence, provides state-qualified sign-language interpreters for deaf clients in a variety of situations and offers sign-language classes and other information to employers who have deaf or hearing-impaired employees. The organization's Hearing Impaired and Audiology Clinics serve children diagnosed with significant sensorineural hearing losses at the Cincinnati Children's Hospital Medical Center. The Clovernook Center for the Blind and Visually Impaired, also in Cincinnati, provides innovative rehabilitation and vocational skill programs for the blind, including those who are deaf and blind.

The St. Rita School for the Deaf in Cincinnati is the region's only residential school for the deaf. Henry J. Waldhaus, a Catholic priest whose responsibility was the deaf parishioners of the Archdiocese of Cincinnati, raised funds to purchase the 237 acres that became the St. Rita School for the Deaf in 1915. Among St. Rita's recent graduates is Kevin Hall, the valedictorian of his class and the first deaf golfer competing in tournaments with the Professional Golf Association. As a toddler, Hall lost his hearing following a bout with meningitis. His parents enrolled him in the St. Rita School at age three. While there, Hall played golf at the nearby Winton Woods High School, where he became a four-year letter winner in the sport. After he graduated from the St. Rita School in 2000, Hall also became the first African American to receive a golf scholarship at Ohio State University in Columbus.

The first state-supported school for the deaf in the United States, the Kentucky School for the Deaf, provides outreach services in Northern Kentucky. Located at Danville, this school has a residential school on its campus and offers outreach consultation, curriculum evaluation, and program planning for deaf and hearing-impaired students in public schools. The Northern Kentucky/Kentucky School for the Deaf Regional Program, located at the River Ridge Elementary School in Villa Hills, serves the public schools in the counties of Boone, Campbell, Grant, Kenton, and Pendleton. The Kentucky School for the Deaf also administers an early childhood program in which hearing-impaired preschoolers and their families are locally served by home visits and classes.

Colleges and universities in Northern Kentucky are committed to educating their students who have hearing impairments. **Northern Kentucky University** (NKU), **Thomas More College**, and **Gateway Community and Technical College** provide interpreting and support services to such students. A Modern Language Association survey notes that the percentage of college students enrolling in American Sign Language courses increased 18 percent between 1998 and 2002. Cincinnati State Technical and Community College Xavier University in Cincinnati, and NKU embrace this trend, offering American Sign Language in their curriculums. Cincinnati State Technical and Community College also has an interpreter training program, through which students can become qualified sign-language interpreters. High schools in the region also offer American Sign Language as a foreign language.

Counseling services are available for persons with hearing losses in Northern Kentucky. In Erlanger, the Catholic Center of the Covington Diocese provides counseling services for hearing-impaired parishioners. Assistive or interpretive devices are available for religious services in certain churches, such as the Catholic Church's Pastoral Office for the Deaf and Hard of Hearing in Erlanger and the **Mother of God Catholic Church** in Covington. The **Erlanger Baptist Church** offers American Sign Language interpretation as part of its regular services.

Cecil L. Bennett, who became an advocate for the deaf following the diagnosis of deafness in his two-year old daughter in 1968, founded a spiritual outreach ministry, the Deaf Institute, in Cincinnati. In Bellevue, Ky., Betty Timon, who lost her hearing as an adult, recently served as a commissioner for the Kentucky Commission on the Deaf and Hard of Hearing. She founded the Greater Cincinnati Coalition for Deaf and Hard of Hearing and the Cincinnati group of the Self Help for Hard of Hearing People (SHHH). Timon was among a group of women selected in 2005 as the Outstanding Women of Northern Kentucky by the *Kentucky Post* in conjunction with NKU and Thomas More College. The former Independence police chief, Charles T. Donaldson, learned American Sign Language in order to communicate with deaf persons in his community. The nonprofit organization 4 Paws for Ability, based in Xenia, Ohio, has placed service dogs in Northern Kentucky homes of persons with disabilities, including those with hearing losses. The **Cincinnati/Northern Kentucky International Airport** has volunteer ambassadors who are trained to assist travelers with disabilities, including the deaf.

Technological advances have expanded the cultural and social life of the deaf. Alerting devices that use visual and motion techniques of flashing lights and vibrations make it possible for persons with hearing loss to become aware of wake-up times, fire or smoke alarms, doorbells, intercoms, and ringing telephones. Kentucky Educational Television and the local television stations incorporate closed captioning for the hearing-impaired into their regular programming. Beyond Hearing Aids Inc. of Florence and the Deaf Communications of Cincinnati have telecommunication devices available. The Resource Center of the Cincinnati Bell Telephone Company lists 30 area locations with deaf telecommunication devices on-site, such as the Cincinnati Zoo, the Greater Cincinnati Convention and Visitor Center, the I-75 Rest Areas in Boone Co., the Steely Library of NKU, and Remke's Market in Fort Mitchell. Within Kentucky, hearing or speech-impaired individuals are eligible to apply to the Kentucky Commission on the Deaf and Hard of Hearing for free specialized telecommunication equipment, allowing equal access to the telecommunication system via the Kentucky Telephone Relay Service or the Internet Relay service.

Bennett, Sara J. "Book Collection Dedicated: School Honors Jean Rothenberg," *CE*, May 17, 2000.

"Charles T. Donaldson, Former Police Chief," *KP*, October 14, 2002, 6A.

Cincinnati Bell. "Public TDD/TTY Telephone Locations." www.cincinnatibell.com/customerservice/resource center/specialneeds/tdd_tty_locs.asp (accessed August 28, 2005).

4 Paws for Ability. "Taking the 'dis' out of disAbility." www.4pawsforability.org/ (accessed December 4, 2005).

Howard, Allen. "Hearing, Speech & Deaf Center Turns 80 Innovatively," *CE*, July 7, 2005, 3C.

Kelly, Morgan. "Putting Is Deaf Hall's Biggest Worry in Tour Debut," *USA Today*, July 21, 2005, 3C.

Kentucky Commission on the Deaf and Hard of Hearing. *Directory of Services for Individuals Who Are Deaf and Hard of Hearing, 2005*. Frankfort, Ky.: KCDHH, 2005.

——. "Statistical Demographics: Deaf and Hard of Hearing Individuals in Kentucky," issued September 15, 2002, and received by E-mail from KCDHH on October 10, 2005.

Kentucky Educational Television. "Fast Facts." www.ket.org/about/glance/ (accessed December 4, 2005).

Kranz, Cindy. "Oh, Say Can You Sign?" Help Kids Hear.org. www.helpkidshear.org/news/media/2005/06-02-2005-enq.htm (accessed August 28, 2005). Also in *CE*, June 2, 2005, A1.

Kreimer, Peggy. "They Have Their Community at Heart," *KP*, April 16, 2005, 1K.

Pilcher, James. "Hearing Impaired Have a New Way of Conversing by Phone," *CE*, July 19, 2005, D1.

"Section 163.500 (2004). Definitions of 'Deaf' and 'Hard of Hearing,'" *Kentucky Revised Statutes Annotated*. LexisNexis. www.lexisnexis.com/ (accessed October 8, 2005).

Stakauskas, Betsy. "Determination Marked Cecil Bennett's Life: Advocate for the Deaf Had Ministry and Career," *CE*, September 10, 2001, 4B.

Wecker, David. "Need Help at the Airport? Hunt Grins," *CP*, September 7, 2000, 1B.

Wells, Elizabeth B. "Foreign Language Enrollments in United States Institutions of Higher Education, Fall 2002," *ADFL Bulletin* 35, nos. 2–3, (Winter–Spring 2004): 8–26.

Margaret Prentice Hecker

DeCOURSEY, ELBERT, MAJOR GENERAL (b. April 12, 1902, Ludlow, Ky.; d. December 4, 1994, San Antonio, Tex.). Elbert DeCoursey, a military general and a doctor, was the son of William Bedford and Mary Elizabeth Carter DeCoursey. He graduated from **Holmes High School** (1919), the University of Kentucky (1924), and the Johns Hopkins Medical School (1928), specializing in pathology. DeCoursey joined the U.S. Army on March 18, 1924, and as **World War II** began, he was stationed in Hawaii. He became a member of the team investigating the effects of the atomic bomb, first at Nagasaki and later at Bikini Atoll in the Pacific. In 1954 he attained his highest military rank, major general. His research areas, publications, honors, awards, and citations were extensive. DeCoursey retired from the Army on October 1, 1959, after 35 years of service to his country, and moved to San Antonio, Tex., where he died in 1994. He was buried with full military honors at Sam Houston National Cemetery in that city. At the time of his death, he was the only person who had commanded all three of the army's major medical institutions. He was survived by his wife of many years, Esther.

Reis, Jim. "Holmes Grad Became Doctor, General," *KP*, October 2, 2000, 4K.

Univ. of Kentucky Alumni Association. "Hall of Distinguished Alumni." www.uky.edu/Alumni/hoda/decourseyE.htm.

Michael R. Sweeney

DeCOURSEY AND CULBERTSON RAILWAY STATIONS. These two railway stations along the **Covington and Lexington Railroad** (now the **CSX** rail system) in southern Kenton Co. were named after early settlers in Northern Kentucky. One of the settlers was a **Revolutionary War** veteran, William DeCoursey Sr. (1756–1841), who arrived from Maryland about 1794. He lived near the site that became the former DeCoursey railroad yard of the **Louisville and Nashville Railroad**. DeCoursey was instrumental in the formation of the Mouth of the Licking Baptist Church in Northern Kentucky. The station that bears his name was nearly four miles south of the Ohio River. About 1813, four Culbertson brothers (James, 1781–1834; William, 1787–1871; Allen, 1790–1856; and Robert, 1793–1856) arrived in Northern Kentucky. The station bearing their name was approximately one mile south of the DeCoursey Station.

The Covington and Lexington Railroad began operations in 1853. Trains left Covington and stopped at South Covington, DeCoursey, Culbertson, and other stations, making their way south to Lexington. During the business year ending November 1, 1855, there were 395 passenger arrivals at the DeCoursey Railway Station and 298 departures; and the Culbertson Railway Station had 775 arrivals and 683 departures. The passenger and commuter trains that stopped at these stations are long gone, but freight continues to roll through these former stops along the rail line, often in the form of unit trains for the automotive industry.

An Atlas of Boone, Kenton, and Campbell Counties, Kentucky. Philadelphia: D. J. Lake, 1883.

"Covington and Lexington Railroad Was Opened to the Public as a Regular Daily Train," *CJ*, August 27, 1853, 2.

Culbertson, Stephen C., and Carol A. Culbertson. *Culbertson Family—County Tyrone, Ireland, to Campbell/Kenton County, Kentucky, United States of America.* Madison, Wis.: Self-published, 2002.

Rennick, Robert M. *Kentucky Place Names.* Lexington: Univ. of Kentucky Press, 1984.

Sixth Annual Report to the Stockholders of the Covington & Lexington Railroad, November 1, 1855. Covington, Ky.: Covington Journal, 1856.

Steve and Carol Culbertson

DeJACO BROTHERS COMPANY. The DeJaco Brothers painting and decorating firm of Newport was noted for its decorative interior designs, including decoration of church interiors; art object restoration; altar works; and fresco painting. The enterprise was founded by Franz DeJaco (1847–1928), a sculptor and artist trained in his homeland of Tyrol, Austria. He came to the United States in 1881 and established an art studio in Milwaukee, Wis. The enterprise, known as F. DeJaco & Company, relocated to Newport about 1887. In Newport Franz "Frank" DeJaco and his wife Antonia "Anna" Thoeny raised a family of eight sons and a daughter. Frank introduced to the decorating trade sons Fred F. DeJaco (1884–1962), Francis "Frank" J. DeJaco Jr. (1889–1976), Louis A. DeJaco (1891–1951), Charles A. DeJaco (1893–1956), George E. DeJaco (1895–1968), John Edward DeJaco (1897–1968), and Anthony E. DeJaco (1901–1943). Carrying on the family decorating tradition, the brothers formed the DeJaco Brothers Company in 1918. Two of the DeJaco brothers, Frank Jr. and Louis, became Roman Catholic priests of the Diocese of Covington (see **Roman Catholics**). Fred and Anthony DeJaco were talented artists specializing in religious themes.

About 1956 the DeJaco brothers Fred, Charles, George, and Edward retired, after completing their last major interior decorating project at St. Mary Catholic Church in Alexandria. Their brother Rev. Francis "Frank" DeJaco had been pastor of that parish since 1932, and the church was preparing to celebrate its centennial in 1960. The DeJaco Brothers also operated paint and hardware stores at 103 Sixth St. in Dayton, Ky., and at 908 Monmouth St. in Newport. They advertised as painters and decorators, skilled in interior decorating, graining, glazing, hardwood finishing, enameling, and gilding.

The firm decorated churches in Northern Kentucky and neighboring states. Some Northern Kentucky churches decorated by DeJaco Brothers Company artists include the following:

Alexandria: **St. Mary of the Assumption Catholic Church** (1917, 1934, and 1956)
Brooksville: **St. James Catholic Church** (1926)
Camp Springs: **St. Joseph Catholic Church**
Cold Spring:
St. Joseph Catholic Church (1939)
St. Joseph Orphanage Chapel
Dayton: **St. Bernard Catholic Church**
Falmouth: **St. Francis Xavier Catholic Church**
Florence: **Hopeful Lutheran Church** (1937)
Fort Mitchell: **Blessed Sacrament Catholic Church**
Fort Thomas: **Highland (United) Methodist Church** (1938)
St. Andrew's Episcopal Church (1928)
Melbourne: **St. Philip Catholic Church**
Mount Sterling: St. Patrick Catholic Church
Newport:
Corpus Christi Catholic Church
Immaculate Conception Catholic Church
Newport Baptist Church
Newport Methodist Church
Presbyterian Church (1937)
St. Francis de Sales Catholic Church
St. Mark Lutheran Church
York Street Congregational Church
Stepstone: **Immaculate Conception Catholic Church** (1935)
Taylor Mill: **St. Anthony Catholic Church** (1941)
Twelve Mile: Saints Peter and Paul Catholic Church (1938)
Wilder: **St. John the Baptist Catholic Church**

Ryan, Paul E. *History of the Diocese of Covington, Kentucky.* Covington, Ky.: Diocese of Covington, 1954.

"Sculptor Dies," *KP*, July 20, 1928, 1.

Tenkotte, Paul A., David E. Schroeder, and Thomas S. Ward. *To Be Catholic and American in Northern, Central, and Appalachian Kentucky: The Diocese of Covington, 1853–2003.* Forthcoming.

Norbert F. DeJaco

DELANEY, ELIZABETH B. (b. September 13, 1882, Fayette Co., Ky.; d. February 17, 1964, Cincinnati, Ohio). Elizabeth Berry Delaney, a funeral home owner and operator and an organization leader and clubwoman, was born in Fayette Co. on September 13, 1882. Orphaned at a young age, Elizabeth was raised by her grandmother in an environment that promoted self-reliance, religion, education, and community service. She attended public schools in Lexington and completed the normal course at Berea College in Berea. On April 28, 1898, she married John W. Delaney. They made their home in Covington, where John operated the Delaney Funeral Home. **John W. Delaney Jr.**, their only child, was born in 1912. Elizabeth acquired a mortician's license in 1919 and joined her husband in operating the family's funeral business. Following John Delaney's death eight years later, she became the sole owner of the establishment and continued its operation for nearly 40 years. When her son later joined in the business, the firm was renamed E. B. Delaney and Son Funeral Home and expanded to include a second funeral establishment in Cincinnati. As a businesswoman, Elizabeth was one of the first women to serve on the Board of Directors of the National Negro Business League, founded in 1900 by Booker T. Washington. Also, she was an active member of the National Association of Black Funeral Home Directors.

She was an active member of the **First Baptist Church (African American)** in Covington and served in many roles, including 12 years as the church's treasurer. Another area of commitment for Delaney was the State and Local Federation of Colored Women's Clubs. She was elected president of the Ladies Improvement Club in Covington and in 1926 became the 11th president of the Federation of Colored Women's Clubs in Kentucky. Delaney's interest in youths led her to promote the establishment of junior clubs for young girls in affiliation with the federation.

Delaney's executive ability and eloquence in public speaking, coupled with her interest in civic affairs and women's suffrage, positioned her for numerous leadership roles. She was the first African American Chairwoman of the Colored Women Voters of Kenton Co. and used her influence to stake a claim for African American women voters within the **Republican Party**. Moreover, she became a member of the Kentucky Commission on Interracial Cooperation and attended the first Southern Women and Race Cooperation Conference held in 1920 in Memphis, Tenn.

Delaney was instrumental in establishing several chapters of the Order of Eastern Star and other civic organizations throughout Northern Kentucky. She was an active member and served in multiple roles with each organization. Following a brief illness, Delaney died at age 82 in 1964 and was buried at the Mary E. Smith Cemetery in Elsmere.

"Colored Notes and News," *Lexington Leader*, February 18, 1964, 14.
"Elizabeth Delaney," *KP*, February 20, 1964, 14K.
"Our President," *Kentucky Club Woman* 8, no. 3 (July 1926), in the John and Elizabeth Delaney Collection, Center of Excellence for the Study of Kentucky African Americans, Kentucky State Univ.

Anne S. Butler

DELANEY, JOHN W., JR., "JACK" (b. September 5, 1912, Latonia; Ky.; d. May 17, 1991, Cincinnati, Ohio). Judge and businessman Jack Delaney was the only child of John W. and **Elizabeth B. Delaney**. He attended Covington's **Lincoln-Grant School**, commonly known as the Seventh St. School, and graduated from William Grant High School in 1929. He was a classmate of World War II hero Maj. **Melvin W. Walker**. Delaney became active in his mother's funeral business, Elizabeth B. Delaney & Son Funeral Home in Covington. Later he earned a bachelor's degree at the University of Cincinnati; he also graduated from the Salmon P. **Chase College of Law** in Cincinnati, from the Cincinnati College of Embalming, and from Cincinnati's Cosmopolitan School of Music.

In 1966 Delaney was named the first African American judge pro tem in Kenton Co. Seventeen years later, the job title was changed to deputy judge executive, making Delaney Kenton Co.'s second-highest-ranking official. He wrote the articles of incorporation of the Northern Kentucky Community Council, which evolved into the Northern Kentucky Community Center. In conjunction with the Macedonia Missionary Baptist Church and the **St. James A.M.E. Church**, both in Covington, he helped to develop the Geisler Garden apartments as low-income housing units.

Delaney was the historian of his Masonic Order lodge and later became a 33rd degree **Mason**, at which level he served as a member of the Supreme Council. He was a Grand Master of Prince Hall Masonic Grand Lodge, president of the National Funeral Directors Association, and eastern vice president of Epsilon Nu Delta Mortuary fraternity. He was a member of the **First Baptist Church (African American)** of Covington, where he served on the board of trustees as treasurer for many years and as organist for the senior choir. In 1991 Delaney died in Cincinnati and was buried in Mary E. Smith Cemetery, in Elsmere.

"John Delaney, Funeral Director, Public Servant," *CP*, May 18, 1991, 9A.
Neikirk, Mark. "Kenton County's No. 2 Man Shuns the Limelight," *KP*, February 7, 1983, 1K.
"New Attorneys," *KTS*, April 24, 1958, 15A.
"Pass Bar Examination," *KTS*, April 17, 1958, 1A.

Theodore H. H. Harris

DELIA. Delia was located in Grant Co. on Clark's Creek at the junction of Baton Rouge Rd. and the Dry Ridge–Owenton Rd., better known today as Ky. Rt. 22. An early road long since abandoned, known as the Withers (Weathers) Mill Rd., paralleled Clark's Creek past Delia to the mouth of Clark's Creek at Eagle Creek. A water-powered gristmill, first known as Ruddle's Mill, was located a few hundred feet upstream from Delia. An outline of the mill sluice on the west side of Clark's Creek may still be found. By 1832 the mill was called the Baton Rouge Mill. John A. D. Barrows and James C. Hall, the last-known operators of the mill, acquired the operation in 1840.

In 1868 the boundaries of the Smokey Road School, District 49, included white children at Delia on the east side of Clark's Creek. A post office was established at Delia in 1890 but discontinued in 1905. Will "Red Brush" Carter operated a smithy, and Frank and Lowe operated a general store in the community. John W. Gardner purchased and ran the store until he sold out in 1913. Bud and Harold Maines, brothers, operated the store until it was closed in 1930. By the 1950s, there were no longer any businesses or residences at Delia.

Conrad, John B., ed. *History of Grant County*. Williamstown, Ky.: Grant Co. Historical Society, 1992.

John B. Conrad

DELTA AIR LINES. Delta Air Lines was the first provider of jet air service to Northern Kentucky. If the boll weevil had not spread from Mexico in the early 1890s to devastate the cotton fields of the southern United States, Delta Air Lines might never have come to exist. Because the weevil's relentless destruction posed a serious economic threat to the southern economy, C. E. Woolman, an agricultural agent associated with Louisiana State University, sought to use a new technology—the airplane—as an effective way to eradicate this pesky insect. Thus began the story of Delta Air Lines. Started as a crop-dusting operation, Delta began passenger service in 1929, and by the end of that year, its route system extended from Alabama to Texas.

By 1941 new destinations had been added to Delta's growing network. Delta moved its corporate headquarters from Monroe, La. (MON), its birthplace, to Atlanta (ATL) that year. Cincinnati was a factor in the decision to move. The Civil Aeronautics Board had recently granted Delta the authority to fly from ATL north to Knoxville (TYS) and Cincinnati Lunken Airport (LUK) and south to Savannah (SAV). This made Atlanta a more desirable central location, a hub, for a general office and maintenance base.

Delta began serving Cincinnati on April 15, 1941, with twice-daily service to the city's eastside Lunken Airport (LUK), using twin-engine Douglas DC-3s. The flight to Atlanta took two hours and 45 minutes and cost $19.50 each way. With the completion of the Greater Cincinnati Airport (CVG) in Northern Kentucky in 1947 (see **Cincinnati/Northern Kentucky International Airport**), Delta offered service on the new and "fast" four-engine Douglas DC-4 equipment, which reduced flight time to ATL to less than two hours. Interchange agreements with other airlines at CVG connected Delta passengers with other parts of the country. In 1947 63,542 passengers flew Delta from CVG.

Delta brought Northern Kentucky its first jet service in 1960, with nonstop Convair 880 service to Miami (MIA) at a cruising speed of more than 600 miles per hour. CVG's first "night coach" service began in 1961, with Douglas DC-8 service to Miami (MIA) and Detroit (DTW). In 1969 Delta became the leading airline at CVG. Service continued to grow at a steady rate during the 1970s and 1980s, as a result of deregulation of the airline industry in 1977 during the Jimmy Carter administration. In 1984 **Comair**, a regional commuter airline headquartered at CVG, joined with Delta as one of its Delta Connection carriers. Comair became part of Delta's reservation system and shared flight numbers (codes) and terminal facilities at CVG. Passengers could conveniently and seamlessly connect between Delta and Comair flights. Later, Delta bought Comair.

On December 15, 1986, the "largest single-day expansion" in the company's 57-year history, Delta expanded its flight schedule at CVG to 104 daily departures and increased service to 15 new markets in the Northeast, Florida, the West Coast, and the Pacific Northwest. The merger with Western Airlines in 1987 opened up additional markets, including Alaska and Canada through Western's Salt Lake City hub (SLC). Delta created an international gateway at CVG on June 15, 1987, with the introduction of nonstop service to London's Gatwick Airport (LGW).

On May 1, 1995, Delta made CVG its second-largest hub. Its dramatic growth to 203 daily flights was made possible by the 1994 completion of Delta's $375 million expansion, which nearly doubled its facilities. Since then, Delta's Northern Kentucky hub has continued to expand its domestic and international flights. In February 2005 Delta, with its Delta Connection partners, operated more than 600 daily flights to 138 domestic and international destinations from CVG. Today, more than 8,500 persons work for Delta in the region, making it the region's largest employer. In 2008 Delta merged with Northwest Airlines.

"History Takes Flight," *KP*, September 21, 2000, 1K.

Lewis, W. David, and Wesley Phillips Newton. *Delta: The History of an Airline.* Athens: Univ. of Georgia Press, 1979.

Eric Summe

DEMING, OSMER SAGE (b. December 22, 1837, Otsego Co., N.Y.; d. July 10, 1917, Warren, Ohio). Osmer Sage Deming, the son of David W. and Almina Sage Deming, became a Robertson Co. attorney and judge. He came from Pennsylvania as a young man, after serving in the Union Army during the **Civil War**. He arrived in Mount Olivet, Ky., with a law degree from what is today Pennsylvania State University at University Park and was one of the driving forces in the formation of Robertson Co. in 1867. On October 27, 1868, Deming married Leona C. Rigg. Deming, who became the first county attorney in Robertson Co. in 1867, also planned and supervised the construction of the county's first courthouse, which is still in use. He took an active role in politics and was elected county judge, serving from 1872 to 1876. A staunch Republican, he unsuccessfully ran for the office of lieutenant governor of Kentucky with Judge Walter Evans in 1879. O. S. Deming, as he was commonly known, represented the Commonwealth of Kentucky at the Chicago World Fair in 1890, where he made the principal address on behalf of Kentucky. Deming continued to practice law in Robertson Co. through 1910. He was a Freemason and a strong supporter of the Grand Army of the Republic. Deming died in 1917 at Warren, Ohio, and was first buried at the Oak Lawn Mausoleum in that city, then re-interred at the Mount Olivet Cemetery in Robertson Co.

One of Deming's sons, William C. Deming, was the president of the Civil Service Commission in Washington, D.C., during **World War I**. During the summer of 1915, the Deming family's house in Mount Olivet was remodeled as a school and served as the county high school until 1928, when the structure was razed for a new school that had been built next door. William Deming and his brother Thomas contributed substantially to the funding of the proposed new county high school. The school was officially named Deming High School (see **Robertson Co. Public Schools**), as a memorial to their father.

Moore, T. Ross, ed. *Echoes from the Century, 1867–1967.* Mount Olivet, Ky.: Robertson Co. Historical Society, 2000.

Ohio Death Certificate No. 48695, for the year 1917.

Karl Lietzenmayer

DEMOCRATIC PARTY. From the early days of statehood in 1792 until the fairly recent past, Kentucky, including Northern Kentucky, has been predominantly a Democratic state. The commonwealth's population was rural until the 1970 census, and its rural citizens normally followed the agrarian political principles espoused by Thomas Jefferson: an emphasis on states' rights, a proslavery stance, and fear of big federal government. Initially named the Republican Party, Jefferson's party was later called the Democratic-Republican Party (with no relationship to the later **Republican Party** of Abraham Lincoln), and then at the 1828 election of Andrew Jackson, it became simply the Democratic Party. As in the rest of the "solid Democratic South," the planter class greatly influenced Kentucky politics, and for most of Northern Kentucky's history there have been more voters registered as Democrats than as Republicans.

Early prominent Democrats in Northern Kentucky included Col. **John G. Carlisle** from Covington, William DeCoursey, **John Leathers**, **James O'Hara**, George C. Tarvin, and Robert Wallace. During the **Civil War**, Democrats were labeled as rebel sympathizers. Newport's **Thomas Laurens Jones** overcame that stigma to win a seat in the U.S. Congress in 1871. **Albert Seaton Berry**, the "tall Sycamore of the Licking," later a mayor of Newport, fought for the South and was also elected to Congress. Other Democrats in the late 19th century were **William L. Grant**, a Covington city councilman who assisted in the development of schools in that city for African Americans; **Walter Cleary**, a Kenton Co. judge who helped to develop the **Latonia Racecourse** in the early 1880s; H. C. Hallam, an attorney, a former Kenton Co. Circuit Court clerk, and a foe of **William Goebel**; and John C. Droege, a rolling mill owner and another Goebel rival at century's end.

Drug merchant Daniel Linn Gooch served two terms in the U.S. Congress in the early 1900s, competing with fellow Democrat **Joseph L. Rhinock** for that seat. By 1904 **Brent Spence** had begun his long political career in Campbell Co. and the U.S. Congress. His contemporaries were Dr. Shaler Berry and **Robert W. Nelson**, both successful Democrats in Campbell Co. **Orie Ware** appeared on the scene in 1912 and was named the Sixth District Democratic chairman. From 1908 until 1940, **Theodore Kluemper** served Covington as a councilman and city manager. **Arthur Blythe Rouse** was a Democratic U.S. congressman from Boone Co. for 16 years, beginning in 1910. In 1931 Judge **James W. Cammack Sr.** of Owen Co.; James A. Diskin, a well-connected Irish powerbroker in Campbell Co.; and **Ulie Howard** of Kenton Co. were active in the party. **C. L. Cropper** of Boone Co., a banker, represented his county in the state legislature during the 1930s as a Democrat; during the 1940s Edward C. Kelley, a well-known Covington plumber, helped run Democratic politics in Covington.

Two U.S. Senate Democrats who visited the region during the 1940s were Alben Barkley of Kentucky, the man most responsible for putting the **Cincinnati/Northern Kentucky International Airport** in Northern Kentucky, and J. Strom Thurman of South Carolina, who came to Covington with his wife in October 1948 for a grand Democratic rally.

Covington has had a number of Irish Roman Catholic Democratic mayors: **Thomas F. Donnelly** (1920–1924 and 1928–1932); Daniel A. O'Donovan (1924–1928); **Thomas P. Fitzpatrick**, a former boxer (1944–1946) who went on to become Speaker of the House in Frankfort and served as mayor in the 1950s; John J. Maloney (1952–1956 and 1960–1964); and Thomas Beehan (1984–1987).

The 1950s witnessed the emergence of Democrats **Gus Sheehan** in Kenton Co. at the state level and **A. J. Jolly** of Campbell Co. on the local scene. In 1970 Democrat Charles W. Webster failed to unseat the district's Republican U.S. congressman, **Gene Snyder**; in 1991 Democrat Dr. **Floyd Poore**, of Boone Co., failed in his attempt to unseat **Jim Bunning**, Snyder's protégé and successor. In 1992 local attorney Eric Deters, who had been a GOP leader, defected to the Democratic Party, ironically at a time when Republican voter registration almost equaled that of the Democrats.

In 1995 the local Democratic Party, like local Republicans, proclaimed itself a prolife party. Also at about that time, Ruth Bauman, a loyal 30-year party worker for the Democrats from Bellevue, used her political influence to name the replacement of the **Shortway Bridge** (between Covington and Newport) the Licking Valley Girl Scout Bridge. In 1996 Joseph U. "Joe" Meyer, a Covington attorney, who as a state legislator played a leadership role in the passage of KERA (the Kentucky Education Reform Act), was considering a run for state senate, as was Michael E. Plummer, who later switched to the GOP. African American **Arnold Simpson** ran unopposed for the state house that year. John Stephenson, a Kenton Co. Democrat who campaigned statewide in a "Down Home" populist style in 1991, became the last elected Kentucky Education commissioner but was prevented from serving his term after the enactment of KERA abolished the office. Fort Thomas native Mark Guilfoyle, another Covington attorney, gained a position on the staff of Democratic governor Paul Patton (1995–2003) as his appointment secretary; Northern Kentuckian Mike Hammons, also a Covington attorney, had held a similar position with Governor Breton Jones (1991–1995). At that time the local Democrats were stepping back from any connections with President Bill Clinton (1993–2001), whose popularity in Northern Kentucky had fallen amid scandal. The district's U.S. congressman, moderate Democrat **Ken Lucas**, did not even attend the 1997 Democratic National Convention that renominated Clinton for president. Simultaneously, in Kenton Co., long a Democratic Party stronghold, the county's party chairman, Terry Mann, was stressing his party's centrist theme, hoping to offset rising Republican strength. A few years later, in 2006, and for the only time in the modern era, Kenton Co. briefly had more voters registered Republican than Democrat, a political condition that already existed in Northern Kentucky's two other heavily populated counties, Boone and Campbell. Two bright spots for Democrats at the time were Jack Snodgrass in Campbell Co. and Bill Aylor in Kenton; each had been reelected as county clerk. By 2002 there were even rumors that lifelong Democrat Lucas, who had announced his retirement after completing his congressional term in 2000, was considering a switch to the GOP; **Nick Clooney** agreed to run in 2004 as the Democratic candidate for the 4th District seat in Congress, but he was soundly defeated by a well-financed Republican incumbent, **Geoff Davis**, who had replaced Lucas.

In 2005 Jerry Stricker, a Democrat from the **West End** of Newport, won a seat on the Covington city commission in a nonpartisan race, as Democrats worked hard to hold onto control of Kenton Co. Campbell Co. has traditionally supported Republicans, while Boone Co., which has experienced significant demographic changes based on population growth and the flight to suburban living, has shifted from political balance between the two parties into a second Republican county stronghold. The eight other Northern Kentucky counties, Bracken, Carroll, Gallatin, Grant, Mason, Owen, Pendleton, and Robertson, usually favor Democrats, especially in local elections. In national elections, most of these counties tend to vote for the candidate rather than along straight party lines. Currently, Boone and Campbell counties are likely to vote Republican on the national level, while Kenton Co. might vote Democratic. In 2006, when Democrat Ken Lucas returned to challenge Republican incumbent Geoff Davis for the district's congressional seat, Davis won handily and carried Lucas's home county of Boone, as well as Campbell and Kenton counties. Republican president George W. Bush, both times he ran, also won in all three of those counties.

Several Northern Kentuckians have plied their political trade elsewhere as Democrats. Three former residents of Northern Kentucky have ascended to the mayoral position in Cincinnati: **Theodore M. Berry**, from Maysville, the first African American to be elected Cincinnati mayor (1972–1975); **David Mann**, from Fort Wright (1980–1982 and 1991); and **Roxanne Qualls**, from Erlanger (1993–1999). Other examples include progressive, anticapitalist Democrat William Goebel, a late-19th-century Kentucky state senator and reformer from Covington, the only governor ever to be assassinated in U.S. history. **Stanley F. Reed**, from Maysville, served as U.S. Supreme Court justice (1938–1954). Kentucky governor **John White Stevenson** (1867–1871), a Kenton Co. native, was the second Northern Kentuckian to serve as governor (Joseph Desha [1824–1828] of Mason Co. was the first). Another Democrat who become famous in politics elsewhere is Campbell Co.'s **John H. Whallen**. Whallen left Newport in the early 1870s for Louisville and built a group of theaters, the Empire Burlesque circuit, with his brother John. From 1880 or so until his death in 1913, he also organized Irish and German Catholics in Louisville into a strong voting block and functioned as the boss of that city's politics. He did not hold office, for there was no need; he picked the candidates he wanted and then orchestrated their election. **Isabella Greenway**, born at the **Dinsmore Homestead** in Boone Co., who was a Democrat, became the first woman U.S. representative from Arizona in the 1930s. She was a strong supporter of her close friend Franklin Delano Roosevelt.

A number of Democrats from the outlying and traditionally Democratic counties of Northern Kentucky played influential political roles during the first half of the 20th century. Among these were Benjamin F. Beall, one-time postmaster of Warsaw in Gallatin Co., and, in Carroll Co., capitalist Frank B. Adcock; educator Paul B. Boyd; county clerk C. S. Griffith; **J. Lyter Donaldson**, an unsuccessful candidate for governor in 1943; and attorney James Houston Newman. Robert Humphreys, a dentist in Maysville in Mason Co.; automobile dealer R. Larue Case and banker Chambers Perry from Mount Olivet in Robertson Co.; Edward Duvall, the county attorney in Owen Co.; and Elizabeth C. Bainum, once the postmaster of Germantown in Bracken Co., are also remembered as leaders within the Democratic Party.

Two other Democrats with significant local connections, Steve Henry and Bruce Lundsford, were unsuccessful candidates for Kentucky governor in the November 2007 election. Henry, who was Patton's two-term lieutenant governor, is married to **Heather French** Henry, a former Miss America from Mason Co. The Henrys reside in Louisville but own and have restored **Rosemary Clooney**'s former residence as a museum in Augusta (see **Rosemary Clooney House**) and visit there often. Lunsford, a Louisville businessman who was raised on a farm just outside Independence, spent millions in the 2003 Democratic primary for governor, then dropped out late in the race; he returned for a second try in 2007.

Horowitz, David. *The Shadow Party.* Nashville, Tenn.: Nelson Current, 2006.

Kleber, John E., ed. *The Kentucky Encyclopedia.* Lexington: Univ. Press of Kentucky, 1992.

Lewin, H., ed. *The Lawyers and Lawmakers of Kentucky.* Chicago: Lewis, 1897.

Willis, George Lee, Sr. *Kentucky Democracy: A History of the Party and Its Representative Members—Past and Present.* 3 vols. Louisville, Ky.: Democratic Historical Society, 1935.

DEMOSS, MARY HISSEM "MAMIE" (b. July 27, 1871, California, Ky.; d. August 22, 1960, Montclair, N.J.). This concert soprano soloist was the daughter of Captain Martin L. Hissem, owner and captain of the *Tacoma,* an Ohio River packet, and Rachel Galloway Hissem. Mary's brother, W. T. Hissem, was also a steamboat captain, and her uncle was the former Campbell Co. judge and state senator W. J. Hissem. Mary Hissem married Lacy M. DeMoss on March 29, 1894, at **Grace United Methodist Church** in Newport, the city each called home at that time. Mary, who had become a celebrated vocal soloist, often performed at important events, such as the dedication on July 29, 1900, of the **Highland United Methodist Church** in Mount Pleasant (Fort Thomas, Ky.). She had studied voice at the Cincinnati College of Music under Lino Mattioli. The conductor of the Cincinnati Symphony Orchestra, Frank van der Stucken, encouraged the gifted soprano to take her vocal talents to New York City. Reluctantly, she did so, only to find herself later in the year 1900 making her professional singing debut under the direction of Frank Damrosch at Carnegie Hall. Performing as Madame DeMoss, she was featured in performances at the Worcester (Mass.) Musical Festival, the Cincinnati May Festival, and the Boston, Mass., Handel and Haydn Society. She sang on the same stage with Mme. Schumann-Heinck and under the baton of Max Fiedler, Leopold Stowkowski, Victor Herbert, and Walter Damrosch. DeMoss was also associated with several mainline Protestant churches along the East Coast (New York City's Fifth Avenue Presbyterian, Washington Square Methodist, and East Orange Calvary Methodist in New Jersey), where she was a soprano soloist on Sunday mornings. She retired from the concert stage in 1933. After her husband, Lacy, who had graciously supported and encouraged her postgraduate vocal studies, died in 1936, she married singer Frederick D. Lyon. The couple lived at 274 Linden Ave. in Verona, N.J., where Frederick died in 1952. Mary Hissem DeMoss Lyon continued to give private voice lessons until a year before her death. She died in 1960, at age 89, in the Montclair Nursing Home and was buried next to Frederick Lyon at Woodlawn Cemetery in the Bronx, N.Y. She was a member of the Methodist Church.

"Capt. W.T. Hissem Died in Newport," *KP,* August 10, 1900, 5.

Cronin, John P. "Brilliant Career Recalled," *CE,* March 14, 1954, sec. 3, p. 1.

"Madame De Moss Dies," *NYT,* August 24, 1960, 29.

The National Cyclopedia of American Biography. Vol. 14. New York: James T. White, 1910.

Obituary. *Verona–Cedar Grove (N.J.) Times,* August 25, 1960.

"Successful Singer Is from Newport," *KP,* March 14, 1904, 5.

Michael R. Sweeney

DEMOSSVILLE. DeMossville, in northwestern Pendleton Co., was incorporated by the Kentucky legislature in 1860. It lay along the **Covington and Lexington Railroad**. Its boundary lines were established as follows: "beginning at the Licking

River and the mouth of Grassy Creek, up said creek to Wolf Pen branch; thence up said branch to the north side of same to include the Gardner farm . . . ; thence to the Licking River and same to include the Willett farm; thence to the said river to the beginning." The town trustees appointed were William Clark, B. F. Cummins, H. Hightower, Eli Mullins, and Aaron Thracher.

Early on, DeMossville had serviceable roads and highways, an assortment of businesses, farms nearby raising tobacco, a post office, schools, civic and fraternal organizations, churches, and even a band of counterfeiters who once operated nearby. During the 1890s the **Louisville and Nashville Railroad** ran a scheduled train through DeMossville, from Butler to Cincinnati, which returned the same day. DeMossville had two saloons that dated from the period 1850–1871; the proprietors were Pat Collins and James Oldhouse. A law was enacted in 1871 prohibiting the sale of spirituous liquor or malt beverages within two miles of DeMossville. Richard Mullins, who died in 1860, owned 6,000 acres adjacent to the waters of Grassy Creek. During the early 1800s, he built a large brick house on land located at the junction of Ky. Rt. 17 and the DeMossville Rd. When the Grassy Creek political precinct was established in 1835, its meetings were held in the Mullins's home; this house played a role in much of the early history of the community. The Mullins house was later torn down and replaced by another, smaller brick structure, which still stands. Bricks for these houses were made on Mullins's farm with slaves doing most of the labor.

The town's Masonic Lodge was chartered in 1851 as DeMoss Lodge No. 220, at Grassy Creek. The lodge's minutes of August 20, 1853, are the first time the name DeMossville appears in the Masonic records. It is believed, therefore, that the lodge and the town of DeMossville were both named to honor one of the lodge's founding fathers, Thomas DeMoss.

Early settlers in the area of DeMossville often operated mills; the rapid flow of the waters of Grassy Creek made a perfect setting for their gristmills. One of the better known of these mills was about 300 yards north of **Grassy Creek Christian Church** and 125 yards from the creek. (The church was at that time located a few feet from the junction of the middle, east, and north forks of Grassy Creek.) The millrace (the canal through which the water flowed to furnish power for the mill) started at the east fork and the middle fork of Grassy Creek. This once-noted gristmill had a large wooden dam to channel the water into the millrace, and the deep channel on the south side of the church was the starting point of the millrace. From there, the channel flowed through the flat land to the mill. A mill built by a man named Kanapke was located on the east prong of Grassy Creek. Hampton Knight was operating this mill in 1864. James Mullins operated a mill on the middle fork of Grassy Creek about three-fourths of a mile from the Grassy Creek Church. In 1867 the Kentucky legislature established two governmental stations in Pendleton Co. to inspect tobacco and flour. One station was on Lot 8 in Falmouth, and the other was on the north fork of the Wolf Pen branch. Because of the threat from flood waters and because more modern mills were being constructed elsewhere, the station on the Wolf Pen branch was discontinued and razed about 1905.

The two tobacco warehouses in DeMossville were located at the railroad station and on a lot now owned by Ray Reid. The one at the railway station, operated by George Otzel, was full of tobacco when it was destroyed by fire in about 1925. In 1884 the population of DeMossville was 141; in 1900 it was 113; and in 1961 it had decreased to 88.

Belew, Mildred Boden. *The First 200 Years of Pendleton County.* Falmouth, Ky.: M. B. Belew, n.d. [ca. 1994].

Mildred Belew

DENHAM, MITCHEL B. (b. November 12, 1912, Lewis Co., Ky.; d. July 12, 1983, Maysville, Ky.). Mitchel Denham, a physician and a Kentucky legislator, was the son of Harvey and Elizabeth Bertram Denham. At the age of 11, he was inspired to become a doctor by observing his mother's illness and death. After attending school at Vanceburg, he went to Berea College at Berea and Eastern State Teachers College at Richmond (now Eastern Kentucky University), where he received his BA. He returned to Lewis Co. and taught at a rural school and at the school at Garrison, saving money for a medical education. He completed his medical degree in 1940 at the University of Louisville Medical College. Afterward, he served an internship at the St. Louis (Mo.) City Hospital and was employed as a company doctor for the U.S. Coal and Coke Company at Lynch in Eastern Kentucky. In spring 1943 he was invited to join the practice of Dr. A. O. Taylor in Maysville, who died of a heart attack right after Denham arrived; Denham then took over the practice. In June of that year, he was appointed local physician and surgeon for the **Louisville and Nashville Railroad**. In November he was commissioned a 1st lieutenant in the U.S. Army Medical Corps; he was the fourth doctor taken from Mason Co.

After distinguished service during **World War II** in both the European and Pacific theaters, Denham returned to his practice and his family in Maysville. He had married Harriet Smith of Maceo on August 28, 1941, in Harlan, and they became the parents of eight children. In 1948 Denham provided the leadership that resulted in the establishment of the local health department, and he served on the county health board for many years. In 1955, with Dr. George Estill and his own brother Dr. Harry Denham, Mitchel Denham purchased the property on Forest Ave. where the Denham Clinic was established. In 1960 the two brothers provided half the cost of a health department building to be built in Lewis Co., dedicating it to their parents.

While seeing patients in the clinic, making house calls, and raising his children, Mitchel Denham joined several community organizations and ventured into business. He became a co-owner of the E. A. Robinson Company, formerly a cigar manufacturer that became a wholesaler of tobacco and related products. His concern for medical care and education led him to run for the state legislature as a Democrat from the 70th district. He was elected in 1959 and served from 1960 to 1970, then again from 1974 to 1978. In 1962 he was a leader in the effort to require immunizations for infants for polio, tetanus, whooping cough, and diphtheria. That successful effort led to his receipt of a distinguished service medal from the Kentucky Academy of General Practice. He had previously been honored, in 1958 and 1964, as Doctor of the Year by the same organization. He was the first doctor to be given that award twice.

Denham was recruited by Kentucky governor Edward T. "Ned" Breathitt Jr. (1963–1967) to be the Democratic house majority leader in 1964. During one session, Denham served on 11 house committees. When house members replaced Denham in 1966, the special post of speaker pro tem was created, and Denham was placed in it. Breathitt's support was also evident when the statewide University of Kentucky Community College System was created and debates were held regarding where to locate the colleges. Mitchel Denham went to Breathitt for his support, and Harry Denham, who was serving on the Board of Trustees of the University of Kentucky at Lexington, also worked for a Maysville site for a community college. The Denham brothers' efforts were successful, and the brothers were present at the dedication of **Maysville Community and Technical College** on September 12, 1969. Classes had started the year before, using downtown Maysville buildings. The first addition to the college was named the Denham Building, in honor of Mitchel Denham, when it was dedicated in 1983.

Mitchel Denham belonged to many service organizations and boards and received many honors. He was active in the **Rotary Club**, and that organization gave him its first Community Service Award in 1966 and later sponsored a Paul Harris Fellowship in his name. Eastern Kentucky University honored him twice, in 1947 with the Centennial Alumni Award and in 1964 as an outstanding alumnus. He was president of Hayswood Hospital and an elder of the **First Presbyterian Church** in Maysville, where his funeral was held following his death. He was buried at the Valley Cemetery, at Charters in Lewis Co.

Denham file, Kentucky Gateway Museum Center, Maysville, Ky.

"Maysvillan Named Doctor of Year," *KTS,* April 23, 1958, 2A.

"Maysville Physician Ran Clinic," *KP,* July 13, 1983, 3B.

John Klee

DEPARTMENT STORES. As small towns grew during the 19th century, itinerant peddlers settled in them and opened general stores, the forerunners of today's department stores. In the more populated areas of Northern Kentucky, such as Covington, Newport, and Maysville, there were enough potential customers for one such general store to carry a wide range of merchandise under one roof. The first use of the term *department store* occurred in 1887 when a New York City establishment advertised itself as H. H. Heyn's Department Store. The concept of individual departments within stores can be found in print at least 40 years earlier, however. The first large successful store of this type was Stewart's Department Store in New York City.

The city in Northern Kentucky with the most substantial department stores was Covington (see **Covington, Downtown**). There **Coppin's Department Store**, the largest department store in the region, occupied the tallest structure in Covington. **John R. Coppin**'s store operated from 1873 to December 1977 in the city, moving into its new large building, at the northeast corner of Seventh St. and Madison Ave., in December 1909. After the store closed, the building was remodeled and became the Covington Municipal Building.

The second department store to appear in Covington was owned by Montgomery Ward, a department store chain founded in Chicago in 1871. The Montgomery Ward store opened in Covington in 1929 at 727–741 Madison Ave. The store was remodeled in 1935 and expanded in 1940 but had closed by the early 1960s. Toward the end, Montgomery Ward ran a catalog store in Covington; Montgomery Ward himself had started in Chicago as the founder of the mail-order industry in the United States.

The third department store in Covington was Sears, Roebuck & Company, another Chicago-based enterprise. Sears built a one-story facility at 13 W. Seventh St. that opened in February 1935 and generated such a brisk business that a second floor was needed the following year. The building had been planned to allow for as many as four floors. Sears sold clothes, tools, appliances, rugs, farm equipment, and tires and did auto repairs. The company's store in Covington closed in 1976, just two days before the company opened the present Sears store in the **Florence Mall** at Florence.

In 1941, the JCPenney Company opened a department store in Covington in the former Dan Cohen Shoe Store building at 18–22 Pike St. (see **Cohen Shoe Stores**). That store closed in January 1984. JCPenney also has had a store at the Florence Mall since 1978. The W. T. Grant Company had an Expressway Plaza (Fort Mitchell) store that closed as the company filed bankruptcy in the 1970s.

In Campbell Co., a JCPenney department store was a tenant of the **Newport Shopping Center** from the day that center was dedicated in 1956 until 1999. The company opened a smaller department store at the Village Green Shopping Center in Alexandria in March 1993 and closed it in 2002. Sears has never operated a department store in Campbell Co.; it did, however, open a Sears Hardware Store in the lower level of the Newport Shopping Center during the mid-1990s, which remains in operation. The Montgomery Ward department store chain has not had an outlet in Campbell Co.

In Maysville, a few locally owned dry goods stores grew into full-service department stores. In 1901 the Merz brothers, Arthur L., Millard, and Eugene, purchased the Bee Hive, a 25-year-old dry goods store, from the Rossenau brothers. Within 10 years, the new operation grew to occupy a three-story building and was marketing both wholesale and retail merchandise. The Kline Stores chain purchased the Merz Department Store in 1973 but maintained the family name. Because of reduced retail traffic into downtown Maysville, the store closed in 1991. Maysville also had a department store known as the New York Store, originally founded in 1898 by Simon Straus. Straus sold it in about 1929 to the Litwack brothers, who retained the local store's name; the Litwack family owned a small chain of stores that included two stores in Hamilton, Ohio, one in Connersville, Ind., and another in Georgia. United Department Stores, a company with holdings in small and medium-sized towns (similar to the Kline department store chain), also operated in Maysville, from 1929 through 1983. Montgomery Ward's Maysville store, designed by the **Weber Brothers** architectural firm, operated from 1929 until 1972. JCPenney had a downtown store in Maysville from at least 1923 but much later relocated to a suburban shopping center, where it still operates. Dawahare's, with corporate offices in Lexington, opened a store in 2001 in the Maysville Bluegrass Center. Dawahare's attempted a branch store in the Florence Mall for a short time during the 1990s.

Because consumers demand easy parking and because of the growth of "big box" stores, the department stores in Northern Kentucky's inner cities have moved to the suburbs, along with their market.

Hendrickson, Robert. *Grand Emporiums: The Illustrated History of America's Great Department Stores.* New York: Stein and Day, 1979.

Leitzenmayer, Karl. "John R. Coppin Company: Then and Now Photographs," *NKH* 9, no.1 (Fall–Winter 2001): 47–49.

——. "John Robert Coppin: The Family and the Company," *NKH* 5, no. 2 (Spring–Summer 1998): 1–15.

"Montgomery Ward Is 83 Years of Age," *KP*, September 14, 1935, 5.

Public Ledger, Maysville, Ky., Kentucky Gateway Museum Center, Maysville, Ky.

"Sears Store in Covington to Open Doors on Thursday," *KP*, February 13, 1935, 1.

Karl Lietzenmayer

DESHA, JOSEPH (b. December 9, 1768, Monroe Co., Pa.; d. October 12, 1842, Harrison Co., Ky.). Joseph Desha, a Kentucky governor, was the son of Robert and Eleanor Wheeler Desha. He married Margaret Bledsoe on December 31, 1789, in Sumner, Tenn., and they moved to Mason Co. in 1792. In Mason Co. he farmed and was a slave owner. In 1794 he served with William Henry Harrison and Anthony Wayne in the wars with the American Indians. His growing public reputation led to election to the Kentucky House of Representatives in 1797 and 1799 and to the Kentucky Senate, where he served from 1803 through 1807. Politically, Desha was a Jeffersonian, elected on the Democratic-Republican ticket. He was elected to the U. S. House of Representatives and served there from 1807 to 1819, becoming chairman of the Committee on Public Expenditures in the 15th U.S. Congress. While serving in the U.S. House of Representatives, Desha fought in the Battle of the Thames (1813) during the **War of 1812**, along with Richard Johnson, also a U.S. Representative from Kentucky, and Kentucky governor Isaac Shelby (1792–1796 and 1812–1816). After failing in an 1820 bid for the Kentucky governorship, Desha won election to the office in 1824 by promising economic relief for the state's debtors. He served until 1828.

An economic boom in Kentucky during the first two decades of the 19th century and an expansion of banks, currency, and credit in the state had been followed, in 1819, by depression. A law passed in Kentucky during the early 1820s to relieve debtors from foreclosure by the banks was declared unconstitutional by the Kentucky Court of Appeals (later called the "Old Court"). Quickly, at Desha's urging, the state courts were reorganized. The "New Court" could not enact business, however, because the "Old Court" maintained its legitimacy and would not relinquish its records to the new body. This struggle continued into 1825 and 1826 until newly elected conservative majorities in the Kentucky legislature abolished the "New Court" over Desha's opposition.

Education was another issue in which Desha became involved as governor with a largely negative effect. In 1825 Desha categorized Transylvania University in Lexington as a "hotbed of aristocracy." Two forces were at work. Desha wanted to divert state funds that were supporting Transylvania University to turnpike construction, using a proposed common school system as a pretext. Also Desha, and various conservative religious and political figures, disliked Horace Holley, a Progressive, who had been the Transylvania president since 1818. Holley had transformed the institution with the addition of new medical and law colleges and increased enrollment and prestige for the school. Desha's opposition led to Holley's departure and the diversion of educational funds to turnpikes. Future dividends from the turnpikes were to benefit the common schools of the state, but no such dividends accrued.

A final personal crisis faced Desha in office. His son Isaac was tried and convicted of the murder in Fleming Co. of Francis Baker, a traveler who, in September 1824, was on a journey to be married in New Jersey. Young Desha cut his own throat after his conviction, and Governor Desha, believing his son close to death, pardoned him. This pardon was widely criticized. Desha retired to a farm in Harrison Co., died in 1842, and was buried in the Georgetown Cemetery in Georgetown.

Clark, Thomas D. *A History of Kentucky.* New York: Prentice-Hall, 1937.

Kentucky Gateway Museum Center Collections, Maysville, Ky.

John Klee

DETERS, CLEMENS BERNARD "BUD" (b. March 21, 1907, Cincinnati, Ohio; d. July 30, 1991, Edgewood, Ky.). Bud Deters was active in Northern Kentucky's political, business, and civic matters for his entire adult life. The Deters family immigrated from Oldenberg, Germany, in 1848 and settled in the German neighborhood of Over-the-Rhine in Cincinnati. Bud's grandfather, Heinrich Clemens, owned and operated a bar on Plum St. across from Cincinnati's City Hall. Deters began a news career as a newspaper boy for the ***Kentucky Times-Star*** and ended his news career as its editor. The *Times-Star* played a critical role in the cleanup of the prostitution and gambling syndicate operating out of Newport in the 1950s. When the *Times-Star* merged with the ***Kentucky Post***, Deters received a telegram discharging him from his employment. He responded by starting a real estate and insurance business under the name C. B. Deters. In 1963 Judge James Dressman Jr. of the Kenton Co. Fiscal Court appointed Deters to the county-owned Airport Board that today operates the **Cincinnati/Northern Kentucky International Airport**. Deters was on the board for 28 years and served as its chairman six times. He was active as a member of boards for his parish church, **Cathedral Basilica of the Assumption**, in Covington; the Redwood School (see **Redwood Rehabilitation Center**); the Northern Kentucky **Goodwill Industries**; and other civic organizations. Goodwill named its apartments on Russell St. in Covington in his honor. His marriage to Cedora Braunstein lasted 64 years and produced five children, Gerald, Charles, James, Joan, and Kathleen. Their son Gerald Deters followed in his father's civic footsteps by serving on countless boards; for example, he was one of the founders of the Northern Kentucky Homebuilders (see **Building, Residential**) and the **Northern Kentucky Convention and Visitors Bureau**. In 1970 Gerald built the popular Drawbridge Inn and Convention Center, and it remains a center for meetings, weddings, conventions, and parties to this day. Another son, Charles Deters, also became involved in civic endeavors of the community. His law firm, Deters, Benzinger & LaVelle, grew to become the largest Northern Kentucky–based law firm. **Thomas More College** and **St. Elizabeth Medical Center** are two of the boards Charles served on for many years. When Bud Deters died in 1991at the St. Elizabeth Medical Center in Edgewood at age 84, he was still the active chairman of the airport board. In his honor, the flags at the airport were flown at half-mast. He was buried at the Deters Family Cemetery along Green Rd. in southern Kenton Co.

Long, Paul A. "'Bud' Deters Leaves a Legacy of Service," *KP*, July 31, 1991, 1K.

Roberts, Alice Kennelly. "Goodwill Renames Apartments to Honor Bud Deters," *KP*, October 30, 1991, 2KK.

Stein, Tim. "Airport's on Move Again," *KP*, October 20, 1990, 1K.

Eric Deters

DEVOU, WILLIAM P., JR. (b. July 15, 1855, Cincinnati, Ohio; d. December 8, 1937, Cincinnati, Ohio). William P. Devou Jr., a noted owner and donor of property in Northern Kentucky, was the son of William and Sarah Ogden Devou. He was born in a home at Ninth and Race Sts. in Cincinnati. In 1860 the family moved to Northern Kentucky and took up residence in the Hillcrest House in Covington. The verdant grounds around the Hillcrest House provided ample opportunities for young William to acquire a great love of horses and nature. At age 15 William was sent away to a Moravian school near Heidelberg, Germany, for high school and college, having completed his elementary training at the Second Intermediate School on Ninth St. in Covington. When he returned home after college, he worked in his father's Cincinnati millinery shop, where he kept the firm's books. However, this work was not enough for him.

In conjunction with his elder brother Charles, William Jr. started to amass tenement properties shortly after he returned from Germany, and later he donated to the City of Covington property that became **Devou Park**. Regarding this early period of land acquisition, one account of his life stated, "It seems as if Covington's benefactor had only one obsession in life: that of owning property and making money." He eventually owned more than 250 properties and became the stereotypical miser landlord, renting his tenements out to all sorts of people, yet barely keeping the properties in livable condition. Devou was notorious for carrying around eviction notices with a receipt for rent payment stamped on the back. If individuals paid, they received the receipt, and if they did not pay, they received the eviction notice.

Over time, Devou became wealthy, from the will of his father and also at the expense of his tenants. The properties he managed were rundown, unsanitary, and some of them even unlivable. Devou, who did not believe in hiring people to do his work for him, would travel on one of his horses to make repairs in the Greater Cincinnati area. His personal efforts were obviously insufficient: in the 1920s the State of Ohio brought a lawsuit against him for violating state housing codes.

In 1912 Devou had been arrested and fined for failure to maintain the property where he lived, on George St. in Cincinnati. Because he refused to pay the fine, he was thrown into prison, where he stayed for approximately four hours and then paid the $50 fine. He purchased clothing a few sizes too large in order to be able to wear layers underneath during the winter. The single room that he stayed in in Cincinnati on George St. was both his office and his living space, packed with all of the equipment needed to make repairs in his tenements. His stinginess was merely one of the facets of the man, though. During the **Great Depression**, a softer side of Devou emerged, when he collected no rent from any of his tenants throughout the depression.

In 1937 Devou was found ill in his George St. room; he had pneumonia, yet he refused any care. Early in December, he was admitted to the St. Mary's Hospital in Cincinnati's West End, where he died of bronchial pneumonia. In April 1938, an appraisal of Devou's estate listed 240 pieces of property, valued at $963,630. He also had personal wealth of $105,961. His fortune went to the continuous upkeep and development of Devou Park in Covington.

Behringer-Crawford Museum, vertical files, Covington, Ky.

"Devou Tells Why He Gave Park to Covington," *KP*, August 29, 1910, 8.

"Find W.P. Devou Ill in Home and Alone," *KP*, November 17, 1937, 1.

Reis, Jim. "A Gruff, Grubby Old Man Left Us the Devou Park Land," *KP*, June 7, 1982, 4K.

Spoor, P. Andrew. "Devou Park," *NKH* 13, no. 1 (Fall–Winter 2005): 24–39.

Spring Grove Cemetery Records, Cincinnati, Ohio.

Bridget Kaiser

DEVOU PARK. The establishment of Devou Park, in the northwestern portion of the city of Covington, can be traced back to the year 1910. In that year William P. and Charles P. Devou donated 500 acres to the City of Covington for park purposes in memory of the brothers' parents, William P. and Sarah Ogden Devou. On November 28, 1910, the deed for the Devou property was officially transferred to the Covington Park Board. In 1911 the board hired engineer J. J. Weaver of Ludlow to create a topographical survey of the property and lay out the roads in the park. Weaver planned for two major roads, one to connect Amsterdam Pk. to Main St. in West Covington, and another to connect Western Ave. in Covington to Ludlow. The roads were completed in 1912. Devou Park became a favorite place for recreation among Covington residents and citizens from throughout Northern Kentucky. By 1913 use of the park had increased so much that a police officer became necessary. George Brady, hired by the city to fill this position, patrolled the park on horseback.

The City Commission of Covington passed a resolution in 1916 to establish a quarry in the park. City prisoners were to do most of the work at the quarry. On April 17, 1916, the first prisoners from the Covington jail were transported to the quarry in the park and put to work crushing stones, but the operation was not initially successful. Prisoners were typically escorted to the quarry by a single guard, and in the first few years of operation, a number of prisoners found working at the quarry to be a convenient opportunity to escape. Eventually, the quarry provided crushed rock that was used to construct streets in the city. Around 1920 the quarry was closed and a lake was formed on the site. Area residents christened the lake Prisoners Lake.

In 1922 Park Board officials began discussing the creation of a municipal golf course in the park. The City Commission hired John Brophy, a golf professional at the **Fort Mitchell Country Club**, to design a new course. In fall 1922 a committee was appointed by the Covington City Commission to raise the necessary funds to construct a nine-hole golf course and to set guidelines for its use. In about 1936 the original course was redesigned and graded for better play. Area residents established the Covington Tennis Club in 1923; its 75 members hoped to build five tennis courts in the park. The club rented the former Montague home and remodeled the building into a clubhouse. Plans to construct a new clubhouse near the golf course and tennis facility took shape in 1929, and architect Leslie S. Deglow designed the Colonial style structure to include locker rooms, shower facilities, bowling alleys, a billiards room, and a small lunch counter. A fire destroyed the building in 1933, and it quickly was replaced by a more modern structure.

The Covington **Rotary Club** began an effort to beautify the park in 1932. Rotarians started planting trees in memory of their deceased members, in an area that became known as Rotary Grove; it was dedicated on June 7, 1932. Additional trees were planted over the next decades, and by 1963, 50 trees had been planted in the grove.

Devou Park benefited greatly from the Works Progress Administration (WPA) during the **Great Depression**. In 1938 the WPA presented Covington with a $97,251 grant for park improvements. The three major projects planned for Devou Park were the construction of a shelter house, two swimming pools, and a large band shell (the **Devou Park Band Shell**). The shelter house, constructed of native fieldstone and containing a large fireplace, was ready for use by spring 1939. The band shell was completed in summer 1939, and in August of that year, a crowd of 40,000 attended a concert at the new band shell.

The post–World War II era brought additional activity to the park. In 1950 the **Behringer-Crawford Museum** was established in the old Devou homestead and placed under the direction of area archaeologist **Ellis Cummins Crawford**. The initial displays included many items from Crawford's own collection. The taxidermy collection of West Covington resident **William Behringer** also added much-needed color. Among Behringer's most unusual specimens was a two-headed calf, which in time became a veritable symbol of the museum. In 1979 the museum became an entity independent from the city, and the first official board of directors was appointed.

The 1950s also witnessed the construction of the park's Memorial Building. In October 1956 workers began demolishing the shelter house at the overlook on the eastern side of the park, a site that offered spectacular views of both Covington and Cincinnati. The new building was designed by the firm of Pepinsky, Grau & Schrand and featured an auditorium and a kitchen. Dedication ceremonies for the Memorial Building took place on August 10, 1958. The Memorial Building served the community well for many years as a gathering place for weddings, political rallies, and parties of all kinds. By the year 2000, the building was showing signs of age, so it was demolished and replaced in 2003 by the Drees Pavilion (see **Ralph Drees**), a large reception facility with sweeping views of the Ohio River Valley and Cincinnati.

In 1956, when the Kentucky legislature passed a bill that eliminated park boards in second-class cities, the Covington Park Board disbanded and the park facilities were placed under the jurisdiction of the City Commission. During the following year, a 44-acre portion of the park was turned over to the University of Kentucky in Lexington, as a site for the Northern Kentucky Extension Center (now **Northern Kentucky University**). At the same time, a 19-acre portion of park was given to the state for use as a site for a vocational school.

The recession of the 1970s hit the city of Covington hard. The city's population declined sharply, and few tax dollars were available for park upkeep. To help meet the need, the Friends of Devou was established in May 1977. This group dedicated itself to maintaining the park and promoting its use and improvement. Despite these efforts, the necessary funds for the proper upkeep of the park remained elusive. In 1978 a proposal was made to share the responsibility for the park between the City of Covington and Kenton Co., but city officials decided not relinquish any authority over the park to the county. Another proposal, which called for the park to be turned over to the Commonwealth of Kentucky for use as a state facility, was also rejected.

By the 1980s Covington city officials began discussing possible revenue-enhancement plans for the park. But hindering any such plans were the restrictions placed on the park by the Devou family when the property was transferred. When the city requested that the restrictions be struck down, the Kenton Co. Circuit Court ruled, in 1987, that the deed restrictions were burdensome and were no longer enforceable. Not everyone was pleased with the court's decision, however. The Devou heirs claimed that the park property should return to the family because the city was not following the requirements of original gift. The family acquired the services of a local attorney and in 1991 brought their case to the Kentucky Court of Appeals, which ruled that the 23 original restrictions placed on the deed were indeed valid. Covington officials would have to follow the restrictions unless it could be proved that they were unreasonable. The court also ruled that the Devou heirs were not entitled to reclaim the property.

In 1989 golf enthusiasts began discussing the expansion of the Devou Park golf course. Early plans, however, were not acceptable to city officials. In 1992 Covington hired the Gene Bates Gold Design Company of Palm Beach Garden, Fla., to prepare plans for a nine-hole expansion of the Devou Park course. Opposition to the proposed golf course expansion emerged quickly, and more than 6,000 area residents signed a petition against any golf course expansion. The Devou Park Advisory Board, the Hillside Trust, and many individual residents of nearby Park Hills formally opposed the plans. On July 2, 1993, these two groups filed suit against the City of Covington to halt any expansion activity, arguing, along with other individuals, that the expansion would destroy 100 acres of wooded land in the park. They also claimed that the expansion was in violation of the original 1910 deed restrictions placed on the park by the Devou family. When the lawsuit eventually reached the Kentucky Court of Appeals, the court ruled, in December 1994, that the expansion was legal. Construction on the nine-hole course proceeded rapidly, and it opened on May 1, 1995. In recent years, the formation of the Devou Park Rangers has enhanced the safety of the park. In addition, the City of Covington and the Devou Trust have invested heavily in aesthetic improvements.

"The Board of Park Commissions, 1902–1957," Local History File, Kenton Co. Public Library, Covington, Ky.

"Commission Named to Establish Devou Park Public Golf Links," *KP*, September 14, 1922, 1.

"Covington Concerts," *Newsweek*, September 8, 1941, 73–74.

"Devou Memorial Dedicated," *KTS*, August 11, 1958, 1.

"Golf Course Is Surveyed," *KP*, September 12, 1922, 1.

Houck, Jeanne. "City Must Abide by Devou Deed," *KP*, April 20, 1991, 1K.

——. "Decision Strengthens Hold of City, Deed on Devou Park," *KP*, October 19, 1991, 7K.

"Prisoners Will Quarry City's Rock," *KP*, March 7, 1916, 1.

"Public Golf Links Urged for Devou Park," *KP*, September 1, 1922, 1.

"Rotary Grove Is Dedicated," *KP*, June 8, 1932, 1.

"Sea of Humanity Greets Photographer at Concert in Devou Park," *KP*, August 18, 1939, 1.

"$300,000 Land Tract Given to Covington for Beautiful Park," *KP*, August 27, 1910, 1.

Whitehead, Shelly. "Devou Park Future Sitting in Limbo," *News Enterprise*, June 13, 1990. 1.

David E. Schroeder

DEVOU PARK BAND SHELL. Devou Park was established in Covington in 1910. From its inception, residents recognized the potential of a natural bowl-shaped slope near the center of the park for theatrical and other performances. Beginning in 1935, summer concerts began to be held there. The concerts included music and comedy acts and usually ended with an audience sing-a-long. Tens of thousands of spectators from Northern Kentucky, Cincinnati, and beyond attended each of the concerts.

The Devou summer concerts became so popular that the City of Covington began planning for the construction of a permanent bowl with a stage at the base of the slope. The project was advanced greatly in 1938 when the Works Progress Administration (WPA) agreed to provide $97,251 to the building fund. In order to accept the grant, the city was required to provide additional funds amounting to $43,000. The William P. Devou Trust provided $15,000 of this amount. Construction began immediately, and the bowl was ready for the 1939 summer concert series. The first concert in the bowl was held on June 28, 1939.

In August 1939 a crowd of 40,000, the largest ever recorded at a performance in the park, experienced a concert at the new band shell. John R. Walsh organized the concerts. Many of the acts that performed at the bowl were already in the area working at the **Lookout House** in Lookout Heights (now Fort Wright) or at the **Beverly Hills**

Supper Club in Southgate. A number of these entertainers were nationally known, including Ruth Best, Sophie Tucker, and Jimmy Durante.

Gas rationing during **World War II** brought the summer concerts to a temporary halt. Since that time, the bowl has been used for theatrical performances and other entertainments. More recently, the bowl has again hosted summer concerts, presented by the **Kentucky Symphony Orchestra**.

"Covington Concerts," *Newsweek*, September 8, 1941, 73–74.
Local History File: Park–Devou, Kenton Co. Public Library, Covington, Ky.
"Outstanding Program Prepared for Devou Park Concert Tonight," *KP*, August 9, 1939, 1.
"Work Pushed to Have New Band Shell Ready," *KP*, June 24, 1939, 1.

David E. Schroeder

DEYE, ANTHONY H. (b. August 28, 1912, John's Hill (Wilder), Ky.; d. January 21, 1988, Fort Thomas, Ky.). Anthony Henry Deye, a staunch advocate of racial equality, was the son of Anthony and Elizabeth Nieman Deye. He attended St. John the Baptist School in Wilder and **Covington Catholic High School** in Covington. After being accepted as a seminarian for the Diocese of Covington (see **Roman Catholics**), Deye studied at St. Gregory Seminary in Cincinnati and at the Gregorian University in Rome, Italy. He was ordained a priest there in 1937. He later did postgraduate work to obtain a PhD in history and taught history at Villa Madonna College (later **Thomas More College**) and at the **Seminary of St. Pius X** in Covington. He was academic dean at the college from 1956 to 1963.

As a seminarian in Rome, Deye observed the evil effects that Nazism had on Europe, and he later attributed to that experience his strong commitment to racial equality. He would even speak out against actions by the Catholic Church that he thought unjust and was often referred to by his fellow priests as the "conscience of the Diocese." Deye served as an assistant pastor in several inner-city parishes. In the early 1940s, he began a camping program for underprivileged boys, including boys from **Our Savior Catholic Church**, an African American parish in Covington. He was upset that black children were not allowed to attend some of the camps that the diocese utilized in Kentucky. Therefore, he sought a location for a camp that the Diocese of Covington itself might sponsor. Bishop **William T. Mulloy**, who had recently arrived, solved the problem by purchasing the Williamsdale farm in Erlanger in 1946. The bishop appointed Deye to start a diocesan camping program, which became Camp **Marydale**. Deye's plan was to put groups of boys and girls together from all the parishes of the diocese. When some white Catholic parents complained about having their children camp with black children, Deye insisted that the diocese not give in to demands for segregation at Camp Marydale. Bishop Mulloy agreed completely, and Camp Marydale conducted integrated camping programs from its beginning in 1947.

Deye carried his crusade for justice onto the national stage as well. He met Dr. Martin Luther King Jr. and was very well impressed by his oratorical skills and commitment to the nonviolent struggle against segregation and for the equality of the races (see **Civil Rights**). Deye joined in the second march for voting rights in 1965 that King led from Selma, Ala., to that state's capitol in Montgomery. As pastor of **Corpus Christi Catholic Church** in Newport, Deye took a leading role as head of the Newport Ministerial Association in helping to close down an adult bookstore and movie theater in Newport during the early 1980s. He also made efforts to assist the poor and tried to keep a separate Corpus Christi church and school open for the benefit of Newport's **West End**, though both eventually merged with the city's other parishes and schools.

Deye died of congestive heart failure on January 21, 1998, and was buried in the priests' cemetery on the grounds of the former St. Pius X Seminary in Erlanger.

"Father Deye, Former Academic Dean, Dies at 85," *Archivia* (Thomas More College Archives) 8, no. 2 (January 1988): 1.
"Father Tony Deye: Led life as 'a Humble, Genuine Servant of Jesus,'" *Messenger*, January 30, 1998, 3.
Fisher, John C. K. "Priest Carried Civil Rights Torch High: Rev. Anthony Deye, Now 80, Has Fought the Good Fight for 50 Years," *KP*, January 18, 1993, 1K.
Fisher, John C. K., and Peggy Kreimer, "Civil Rights Champion Deye Dies: Priest Was Activist for Over 50 years," *KP*, January 23, 1998, 1K.
Horstman, Barry M. *100 Who Made a Difference*. Cincinnati: Cincinnati Post, 1999.
"Obituary of Reverend Anthony Henry Deye," Archives of the Diocese of Covington, Covington, Ky.
Ryan, Paul E. *History of the Diocese of Covington, Kentucky*. Covington, Ky.: Diocese of Covington, 1954.
Tenkotte, Paul A., David E. Schroeder, and Thomas S. Ward. *To Be Catholic and American in Northern, Central, and Appalachian Kentucky: The Diocese of Covington, 1853–2003*. Forthcoming.
Workum, Bert. "Priest Tells Newport It's City Cleanup Time," *KP*, March 6, 1980, 1K.

Thomas S. Ward

DIBOWSKI, CHARLES J. (b. January 2, 1875, Cincinnati, Ohio; d. November 1, 1923, Cincinnati, Ohio). Charles John Dibowski, a noted ceramic tile artist and lithographer, was the son of Charles and Sophia Langlow Dibowski and a brother of Richard J. Dibowski, a Covington saloonkeeper and local **Boy Scout** leader, of the **Wallace Woods** neighborhood of Covington. The family moved from Cincinnati to Covington when Charles was a young boy. He studied at the Cincinnati Art Academy and worked for several regional companies, including the Rookwood Pottery of Cincinnati, Weller Pottery in Zanesville, Ohio, and Lonhuda Pottery in Steubenville, Ohio. He also worked as chief timekeeper for the Central Division during the construction of the Panama Canal, then for the Internal Revenue Service, and afterward as an artist at the Donaldson Lithographing Company in Newport. Dibowski married Henrietta Connell, and they became the parents of six children. Charles Dibowski lived in Covington for many years, and he was an active member of the Colonel Clay Masonic Order in Covington; however, at the time of his death, he was living at 6700 E. Ledge St. in the Cincinnati suburb of Madisonville. He died suddenly at age 49 from an intestinal obstruction. Funeral services were held at the George Rohde Funeral Home in Madisonville, and burial was in Spring Grove Cemetery in Cincinnati.

Cummins, Virginia Raymond. *Rookwood Pottery Potpourri*. Cincinnati: Cincinnati Art Galleries, 1991.
"Dibowski, Charles J." *KP*, November 2, 1923, 29.
Kentucky Death Certificate No. 1749, for the year 1923.
"Lithographic Artist Was Taken by Death," *KTS*, November 2, 1923, 29.
Spring Grove Cemetery Records, Cincinnati.

DICKEN, ABSOLOM COLUMBUS "LUM" (b. January 3, 1835, Campbell Co., Ky.; d. March 20, 1918, Campbell Co., Ky.). Absolom Columbus Dicken, a soldier and a meticulous diarist, was the son of Simeon and Elizabeth Herndon Dicken. During the **Civil War**, he joined the 4th Kentucky Cavalry of the Confederate Army. Over the next few years, he kept a detailed diary while seeing action in some 43 engagements against Union forces. Much of his time was spent cutting telegraph lines, destroying bridges, and ripping up railroad tracks to disrupt the flow of Union supplies. Many of his diary entries deal with visits to local homes, where he attempted to obtain needed supplies for his fellow soldiers. Although most supplies were purchased, some were acquired by fear or intimidation. The diary was written with homemade ink, using goose quill pens. At war's end, Dicken was stranded in Rich Valley, Va., 250 miles from home. He and his friend Bob Ellis, with whom he had joined the Confederate Army, began the long trek home after first having their shoes half-soled by a local cobbler. They walked to Paris, Ky., and from there they rode the train to Covington. Along the way, local citizens, who were glad to see the war end, gave them food and shelter. From Covington they crossed the Ohio River to Cincinnati, where they caught the *New Richmond Packet* to go upriver. Leaving the boat at California, Ky., they walked the final few miles home. When news of their return spread, friends and well-wishers came from far and wide to welcome them home. After the war Dicken returned to his life as a farmer; in later life he became a teacher in rural Campbell Co. He married Mary Lancaster on October 7, 1867, and they had five children. Dicken died in 1918, at age 83, and was buried in the Flagg Springs Baptist Church cemetery. His original diary is in the National Archives, but typewritten copies can be found at the Kenton Co. Public Library in Covington and at the Campbell Co. Historical Society office in Alexandria.

Dicken, Absolom Columbus. "Civil War Diary of Absolom Columbus Dicken, 1862–1865," Kenton Co. Public Library, Covington, Ky.; Campbell Co. Historical Society, Alexandria, Ky. Also available at the National Archives, Washington, D.C.
Kentucky Death Certificate No. 25361, for the year 1918.
Wessling, Jack. *Early History of Campbell County.* Alexandria, Ky.: Self-published, 1997.

Jack Wessling

DICKERSON, WILLIAM W. (b. November 29, 1851, Sherman, Grant Co., Ky.; d. January 31, 1923, Cincinnati, Ohio). Legislator William Worth Dickerson attended the local public schools and the private academy of N. M. Lloyd in Crittenden; after studying law, he was admitted to the bar in 1872 and opened a law practice in Williamstown. He served as a prosecuting attorney in Grant Co. from 1872 until 1876, in the Kentucky House of Representatives from 1885 to 1887, and in the Kentucky Senate from 1887 until 1890. Dickerson replaced **John G. Carlisle** in the U.S. House of Representatives, serving from June 21, 1890, until March 3, 1893. Unsuccessful at reelection, he resumed his law practice in Williamstown and then moved to Cincinnati in 1902, where he was a practicing attorney until his death. He was cremated, and his ashes were interred at the Williamstown Cemetery. He was survived by his widow, Cora Tunis Dickerson.

"Dickerson, W. W." http://bioguide.congress.gov (accessed December 4, 2005).
"Dickerson, Worth W." *CE*, February 2, 1923, 6.
"Tribute Paid to Memory of Congressman," *KTS*, March 5, 1923, 16.

DILLON, GEORGE HILL (b. November 12, 1906, Jacksonville, Fla.; d. May 9, 1968, Charleston, S.C.). At the age of five, poet and editor George Dillon moved to Covington with his father and mother, William S. Dillon and Adah Hill Dillon. His mother was a Kentucky native. George attended schools in Kentucky and in Cincinnati. After 1920 the family relocated from Covington to Chicago, where George initially worked with his father selling electrical equipment.

In 1923 Dillon began attending the University of Chicago. It was there that he began to pursue his interest in poetry. He joined the Poetry Club, and several magazines published poems of his. He and a group of students started a series of poets' readings and used the proceeds from this endeavor to publish a literary magazine, *The Forge.* While still an undergraduate, Dillon caught the attention of Harriet Monroe, the editor of *Poetry Magazine*, and she offered him a position as her associate editor. He accepted and spent his final two years in college working part-time with the magazine.

His first book of poems, *Boy in the Wind*, was published the year he graduated, 1927. For the next three years he also worked writing advertising copy, until the agency that employed him dissolved. His second poetry collection, *The Flowering Stone*, published in 1931, won Dillon the 1932 Pulitzer Prize for poetry. He also received a Guggenheim Fellowship, which allowed him to travel and study at length in Europe.

Dillon is also known not only for his own poetry but also for his work with the well-known poet Edna St. Vincent Millay, who also won a Pulitzer Prize. In 1936 the pair translated the French poet Charles-Pierre Baudelaire's *Flowers of Evil.* Although Millay was 14 years Dillon's senior and married, the two had a passionate love affair. She had a reputation for being a seductive woman who attracted many lovers, both male and female, but her relationship with Dillon lasted longer than her previous affairs. Millay even produced a book of 52 love sonnets, most of them addressed to Dillon, titled *Fatal Interview.*

After the death of Harriet Monroe in 1936, Dillon accepted an invitation to be the editor of *Poetry Magazine.* He spent a total of 24 years with the magazine before retiring in 1949. Dillon was a veteran of **World War II**, having served with the Army Signal Corps in Africa and Europe between 1942 and 1945. In addition to his degree from the University of Chicago, he received a BA from Yale and an MA and a PhD from the University of California at Berkley. He was married to Judith D. Dillon. He died in May 1968 and was buried in Jacksonville, Fla.

Brennand, Elizabeth A., and Elizabeth C. Clarase. *Who's Who of Pulitzer Prize Winners.* Phoenix, Ariz.: Oryx Press, 1999.
Case Western Reserve University. "Edna St. Vincent Millay: Poetry Collections and Plays." www.cwru.edu (accessed July 14, 2006).
"Funeral Rites for Dillon Will Be Today," *Charleston (S.C.) News and Courier*, May 11, 1968, 9A.
"George H. Dillon, Poet-Editor, Dies," *NYT*, May 12, 1968, 85.

Susan Patterson

DINSMORE, JULIA STOCKTON (b. March 6, 1833, Terrebonne Parrish, La.; d. April 19, 1926, Santa Barbara, Calif.). Poet Julia Dinsmore was born on Bayou Black plantation in southern Louisiana to James Dinsmore (1790–1872), a lawyer educated at Dartmouth College in Hanover, N.H., and Martha Macomb Dinsmore (1797–1859), daughter of Alexander Macomb, a land speculator from New York. Julia had an older sister, Isabella (1830–1867), and a younger sister, Susan (1835–1851). Julia loved to walk along the bayou listening to the birds and animals and finding wildflowers, and her interest in nature endured throughout her life. When Julia was six, her mother took the girls to Lexington, Ky., to attend school, but occasionally they returned to their home in Louisiana. Their friends the Gibson family also had homes in both Kentucky and Louisiana. When James's uncle Silas Dinsmore encouraged him to buy land in Northern Kentucky to grow grapes, James took his advice. In 1842 the Dinsmore family moved into a home James had built on the 371-acre family farm in Boone Co. Just one mile from the Ohio River, the farm offered ponds, woods, and hills to explore; Julia's love of nature continued to be nurtured. Her father's sister was the mother of B. F. Goodrich, and the Goodrich cousins often visited the Dinsmores.

Julia and her sisters were tutored at home by Eugenia Wadsworth, and at age 16 Isabella, then Julia, entered the Young Ladies' Seminary in Cincinnati. There Julia met Julia Resor, who became a lifelong friend. Julia Dinsmore, who was gifted in languages, later read books in French, German, Greek, Italian, and Latin. She also displayed considerable talent in singing and playing the piano. Julia's younger sister Susan never went to the seminary, because she and one of the Goodrich cousins were drowned in 1851 in a boating accident on Lake Erie; this was the first of many tragic losses for Julia.

After finishing her studies in Cincinnati, Julia returned to the Boone Co. farm to help her mother and continue her reading. Although the farm was not a large plantation, James Dinsmore owned 7 to 15 African American slaves between 1842 and 1865 and had white tenant farmers to help raise sheep, grapes, and willows for basket weaving. Julia came to believe that this was the proper order for society, that some people were destined to be in charge of others. But she also felt responsible for taking care of those in need, including the children of slaves and tenants, several of whom she personally educated. The farm became a retreat for friends and relatives and a forum for continuing education.

Julia's sister Isabella married her first cousin Charles Flandrau in 1859, and seven days later, Julia's mother died. During the **Civil War**, Julia often visited the Gibson family in Lexington and Woodford Co., and there were letters from two different men who were interested in Julia, but she never married. Just after the birth of Isabella's second daughter in 1867, Isabella died. Charles sent the daughters, Martha "Patty" and Sarah "Sally," to live with Aunt Julia. In 1872 James died, leaving Julia the farm, a large debt, and two nieces to educate. Her journal details her dealings with the tenants and the daily workings of the farm. It reveals the drudgery of all her responsibilities, tempered with occasional joy.

An inheritance of $10,000 left to Julia by a cousin in 1888 eased Julia's burdens, so that she was able to travel with her nieces and enjoy an easier life. She had begun to write poetry, and at Sally's encouragement, she submitted poems to the *New Orleans Times-Democrat;* they appeared with the pseudonym F.V. In 1910 a collection of her poetry, *Verses and Sonnets,* was published. It contained 83 poems describing the sights, smells, and memories of her life—the bayou, the farm, the Civil War, and her family and friends. It was believed that one of them, "Louisiana Buttons," was about a young soldier whom she had loved and who was killed in the war. Among the many letters of praise and thanks Julia received was one from Theodore Roosevelt, who had met her through her niece Patty Flandrau (1861–1923). Patty by this time was the wife of Tilden Selmes and the neighbor of the future U.S. president in Mandan, N.Dak. Sally Flandrau (1867–1947) married Frank Cutcheon and lived in New York City. Patty and her daughter

Isabella Dinsmore Selmes (1886–1953) also lived in New York City while Isabella attended finishing school. Julia visited her nieces in New York City, and there she met many of the friends of the Cutcheons and the Selmeses. She traveled to Europe several times with Sally, to Louisiana with Sarah Gibson Humphreys, and to West Palm Beach, Fla., with Julia Resor Foster. She was visiting Sally in Santa Barbara, Calif., when she fell and broke her hip. She died in 1926 of complications from the hip fracture. According to her request, she was cremated and her ashes were returned to the cemetery on the Dinsmore farm in Boone Co., where many of her family were buried. The **Dinsmore Homestead** properties are now held as a trust and operated as a museum.

Collopy, Catherine T. "Julia Stockton Dinsmore," on file at the Dinsmore Homestead, Burlington, Ky.

Dinsmore, Julia Stockton. *Verses and Sonnets.* New York: Doubleday, 1910.

Dinsmore Family Papers, Dinsmore Homestead, Burlington, Ky.

Miller, Kristie. *Isabella Greenway: An Enterprising Woman.* Tucson: Univ. of Arizona Press, 2004.

Sharon Claypool

DINSMORE HOMESTEAD. In 1842 James Dinsmore (1790–1872), a Dartmouth College–educated New Englander, after living in Terrebone Parrish, La., for a time, moved his family into a newly constructed house in northwestern Boone Co., Ky. This home where Dinsmore and his wife brought up their three daughters is now known as the Dinsmore Homestead. It displays documents and artifacts giving the history of the family over several generations and recounting family members' close associations with an array of individuals prominent on the national scene.

James Dinsmore had moved to Boone Co. at the urging of his uncle Silas Dinsmoor (Dinsmore) (1766–1847), who had told him that western Boone Co. at the head of the Belleview Bottoms was a good place to grow grapes. This was the same Silas Dinsmoor who, in 1812 while serving as a Choctow Indian agent in Alabama, attempted to enforce the rules against transporting slaves without papers across Indian Territory, thereby incurring the wrath of U.S. general Andrew Jackson. Silas also had previously been a Cherokee Indian agent. He was the first person buried in the family cemetery on James Dinsmore's Kentucky farm.

James Dinsmore's wife, Martha (1797–1859), was the daughter of merchant and land speculator Alexander Macomb (1748–1831). Macomb was a friend of Gen. George Washington and had rented a house that he owned in New York City to Washington during the general's term as president of the United States (1789–1797). In 1792 Macomb purchased about one-fourth of the state of New York from the federal government at a cost of about eight cents per acre. The transaction was known as Macomb's Purchase; unfortunately for Macomb, he was not able to make the payments scheduled.

Dinsmore's sister was the mother of B. F. Goodrich, the famous U.S. industrialist. The Dinsmore children and their Goodrich cousins often visited.

Only one of Dinsmore's three daughters married. Susan Bell (1835–1851) drowned in Lake Erie, along with a Goodrich cousin. Julia (1833–1926) remained on the farm unmarried until her death at age 93. Isabella (1830–1867) married Charles Flandrau (1828–1903), who was from Minnesota. Flandrau was an Indian agent, lawyer, judge, and politician who once ran for governor in Minnesota and also wrote a history of Minnesota. On August 23, 1862, Flandrau helped to repel an Indian attack at New Ulm, Minn. Shortly after the untimely death of his wife Isabella, Judge Flandrau sent his two daughters, Martha "Patty" and Sarah "Sally," to Boone Co. to be raised by their aunt, Julia Dinsmore. It was through those two girls that Julia Dinsmore traveled and saw the world outside of Boone Co.

Patty Flandrau (1861–1923) married a lawyer, Tilden Selmes (1853–1898), and the couple took up ranching near Mandan, N.Dak. A neighbor on an adjoining ranch was a young New Yorker who had come west to mourn the death of his wife. That neighbor, Theodore ("Teddy') Roosevelt (later U.S. president from 1901 to 1909), developed a long and fast friendship with the Selmeses and through them got to know Julia Dinsmore. Sally Flandrau married a young corporate lawyer, Frank Cutcheon (1864–1936), and spent much of her life in New York City.

Patty Selmes's only child, Isabella Dinsmore Selmes (1886–1953), was born at the Dinsmore farm. After Tilden Selmes's death, Patty and Isabella Selmes divided their time between Boone Co. and New York City, where they lived with Sally Cutcheon while Isabella attended finishing school. It was there that Isabella met Eleanor Roosevelt, who was a classmate of hers. Isabella Selmes and Eleanor Roosevelt began what became a lifelong friendship, and Isabella was a bridesmaid when Eleanor married Teddy's Roosevelt's cousin, future U.S. president Franklin D. Roosevelt (1933–1945).

Isabella Selmes married Robert M. Ferguson (1868–1922), a Scotsman 18 years her senior. Robert "Bob" Ferguson was a friend of Teddy Roosevelt and one of Roosevelt's famed Rough Riders. Ferguson was also one of the financial advisers to John Jacob Astor, who died when the Titanic sank in 1912. The Fergusons moved to the dry climate of the New Mexico territory after Bob developed tuberculosis. The Roosevelts, Franklin and Eleanor, visited the Fergusons in their tent home in the West. Following Bob Ferguson's death, Isabella married another former Rough Rider and friend of Teddy Roosevelt, the Arizona copper developer John Greenway (1872–1926). A few years after their marriage, John Greenway died of complications from gall bladder surgery.

Isabella F. Greenway, active in civic affairs, was the first congresswoman from Arizona who served two terms (1933–1936). She gave one of the nominating speeches in 1933 for Franklin D. Roosevelt in his first bid for the presidency, but when FDR ran for a third term, she did not support him. Isabella eventually established a hotel in Tucson, Ariz., the Arizona Inn.

Isabella had three children. Both of her sons, Robert Ferguson (1908–1984) and Jack Greenway (1924–1995), became lawyers. Her daughter, Martha Ferguson (1906–1994), married Charles Breasted, whose father was the famed University of Chicago Egyptologist James Henry Breasted.

The Dinsmore family, even with all of its contacts away from Boone Co., kept close ties to their home in Kentucky and returned to visit whenever possible. Julia Dinsmore managed the farm following her father's death in 1876 until her death in 1926. The Dinsmore heirs maintained the house and farm from 1926 through 1988 when the Dinsmore Homestead Foundation purchased the property. The story of the Dinsmore family is detailed in more than 90,000 documents (letters, day books, and slave records) that were preserved by the family and are now available on microfilm at the homestead. The little family cemetery on the hill overlooking the farm is the resting place of most of the Dinsmore family members.

A group of volunteers founded the Dinsmore Homestead Foundation as a nonprofit institution in 1986, with the intention of purchasing the historic home with its surrounding 30.7 acres of land, the furnishings, and the documents of the Dinsmore family and of opening a museum. Martha Ferguson Breasted and her half-brother John Selmes Greenway deeded the property and the home and its contents to the Dinsmore Homestead Foundation in June 1988; Martha Breasted donated her half of the estate and the foundation purchased Greenway's share. Volunteers who were instrumental at this early stage included John F. Caldwell, **Hannah Baird**, Dr. William Bryant, and **Judy Clabes**. Clabes chaired a $1 million capital campaign that exceeded its goal by September 1990. William "Sandy" Kreuger served as the first director of the museum, which opened in 1989. The following year the Dinsmore Homestead inaugurated its first educational programs for schoolchildren.

Baird, H. H. "Julia Dinsmore." In *Kentucky Women,* ed. E. K. Potter. Louisville, Ky.: Big Tree Press, 1997.

Chastang, Gail. "The Dinsmore Homestead, Boone County Treasure," *NKH* 5, no. 1 (Fall–Winter 1997): 15–31.

"Historic Homestead to Be Open," *KP,* August 5, 1989, 5K.

Miller, Kristie. *Isabella Greenway: An Enterprising Woman.* Tucson: Univ. of Arizona Press, 2004.

William S. Bryant

DIOCESAN CATHOLIC CHILDREN'S HOME. The Diocesan Catholic Children's Home began in the mid-1800s with the involvement of August M. Toebbe, second bishop of the **Roman Catholic** Diocese of Covington. Bishop Toebbe, concerned for the care and education of orphan children, labored to establish institutions in Northern Kentucky that would afford suitable housing, physical support, and education for these children. From the various parishes of the diocese, he urged the formation of branch orphan societies.

On June 4, 1848, the St. John's Orphan Society of Kenton Co. held its first meeting to organize a home for Catholic orphan girls. With an initial capital of $63, the society founded St. John's Orphanage. A property on Madison Ave. near 15th St. in Covington was the original site. In January 1868 the society purchased for $17,000 the 55-acre St. Aloysius Seminary property in Fort Mitchell, which was used for the orphanage and today is the site of the Diocesan Catholic Children's Home.

In 1866 Rev. Conrad Rotter, pastor of St. Stephen Parish, Newport, organized the St. Boniface Orphan Society of Campbell Co. for the purpose of founding an orphanage for boys within the Covington diocese. Three years later, on May 12, 1869, Bishop Toebbe opened the St. Joseph Orphanage Campbell Co. on the 125-acre former Walsh farm in Cold Spring. The orphanage consisted of an eight-room residence along with barns and other buildings. In 1871 a large building was erected at a cost of $15,000. Although the general contractor had been paid in full, he failed to settle with his subcontractors, and a court ordered the sale of the institution on December 13, 1875, to settle the claims. In 1876 the St. Joseph Orphanage became the property of the St. Boniface Orphan Society when three of its members (unnamed) purchased it in the name of the society.

Both orphanages encountered disastrous fires during their existence. On June 30, 1884, fire completely destroyed the St. Joseph Orphanage. Two months later, a new cornerstone was laid, and by December of that same year, the orphans moved into their newly built home. Four years later, fire again completely destroyed the orphanage. At this time the diocese and the societies governing both orphanages, at the instruction of Bishop **Camillus Maes**, investigated the possibility of combining the two orphanages, with St. John's Orphanage slated to survive. After the proposed terms of unification were rejected by the Committee of Directors of St. John's Orphanage, the St. Boniface Orphan Society resolved, on August 19, 1888, to rebuild its institution. The orphans had returned fully to the St. Joseph Orphanage by May 1, 1889. As for St. John's Orphanage, fire completely consumed the school and several other buildings in February 1926. A nonsectarian drive in Kenton Co. raised $100,000. By May 1927 construction of new buildings, including "one of the most imposing structures in Northern Kentucky," was under way. Included in the new construction were a school building and a central plant; in addition, baths were installed and a water line was scheduled to be brought in from **Dixie Highway** (U.S. 25). A fire in March 1935 damaged the chapel, the dining room, and the kitchen at St. John's Orphanage, and repairs to the facilities were completed by Thanksgiving.

For the first eight years of its existence, responsibility for the operation of the St. Joseph Orphanage fell to the Franciscan Brothers of Mount Alverno Protectory in Cincinnati. In 1877 the original agreement between the Franciscan Brothers and the St. Boniface Orphan Society was revised, so that the Brothers relinquished their responsibilities at the orphanage. The **Sisters of Notre Dame** immediately assumed charge. The St. John's Orphan Society of Kenton Co. initially operated St. John's Orphanage. In 1871 the **Sisters of St. Benedict** from St. Walburg Convent assumed the daily operational duties. Later, in 1957, the Sisters of Notre Dame assumed full authority over the institution. Today Jean Marie Hoffman, S.N.D., heads the Diocesan Catholic Children's Home as executive director.

At their peak, each overcrowded orphanage housed more than 100 children. Most children came to the orphanages as a result of illness in their families, marital separation, divorce, or a parent's lack of employment. Over time, particularly following **World War II**, improvements in the economy and advances in medicine brought about societal changes, so that very few traditional orphans were being served by either orphanage by the 1950s. A 1957 study on the needs of dependent children in the Diocese of Covington concluded that two institutions were no longer needed. In 1961 the governing boards of the two institutions voted to merge into one entity, with the surviving facility located on the property occupied by St. John's Orphanage. Shortly thereafter, the bishop of the Diocese of Covington, Richard H. Ackerman, announced the merger of the two institutions into a single home to be known as the Diocesan Catholic Children's Home.

Since the 1960s the Diocesan Catholic Children's Home has focused on the treatment of all children with serious emotional and behavioral problems. The home was the first institution of its kind in Northern Kentucky to receive state accreditation, and it is the only children's home in Northern Kentucky with an on-site educational facility, Guardian Angel School. This school helps to meet children's emotional and academic needs while preparing them to return to a less restricted, community-oriented educational setting. Today the Diocesan Catholic Children's Home serves children through a variety of services, including its Assessment/Crisis Stabilization/Treatment (ACT) Unit, which is a short-term placement for children with emotional and behavioral needs, and the Therapeutic Foster Care Program, which assists children in a home-based environment.

Children's Home. "Diocesan Catholic Children's Home." www.dcchome.org/ (accessed April 3, 2007).

"New Orphanage Is Planned; $100,000 Planned," *KP*, February 14, 1927, 1.

Ryan, Paul E. *History of the Diocese of Covington, Kentucky.* Covington, Ky.: Diocese of Covington, 1954.

Tenkotte, Paul A., David E. Schroeder, and Thomas S. Ward. *To Be Catholic and American in Northern, Central, and Appalachian Kentucky: The Diocese of Covington, 1853–2003.* Forthcoming.

Paul A. Carl Jr.

DISABILITIES. See **New Perceptions Inc.**; **Point/Arc of Northern Kentucky**; **NorthKey Community Care**; **Redwood Rehabilitation Center**; **Riverside–Good Counsel School**.

DISABLED AMERICAN VETERANS (DAV). The DAV, now headquartered in Cold Spring, was organized in 1920 at Cincinnati as the Disabled American Veterans of the World War (DAVWW), under the leadership of Judge Robert S. Marx. In 1932 the DAVWW was chartered by the U.S. Congress as a nonprofit organization meant to champion disabled veterans' rights. It was open to veterans who had been permanently injured, physically or mentally, during **World War I** and had received an honorable discharge. The U.S. government at the time did not have programs to assist disabled veterans once they were discharged. No matter how crippled veterans were as a result of a service-connected injury, once discharged they were left to fend for themselves or to be cared for by their family or community. The DAVWW lobbied the U.S. Congress during the 1920s and 1930s to fund training programs and benefits for disabled vets.

In 1941, at the outbreak of **World War II**, the DAVWW shortened its name to DAV and continued its programs of support for disabled veterans. It was a sponsor of the GI Bill of Rights. During World War II, the DAV broadened its scope to include all U.S. citizens who had become physically or mentally disabled as a result of a service-connected incident, within either the U.S. or Allied armed service, and had received an honorable discharge. Today the DAV continues to work with government and private organizations to ensure equal rights for the present 2.1 million U.S. veterans suffering from service-connected disabilities.

In 1966, as a result of a property tax issue with Ohio, the DAV moved its national headquarters from Cincinnati to a new building along **U.S. 27** in Cold Spring, Ky., the site of the former St. Joseph Orphanage (see **Diocesan Catholic Children's Home**). In 2004 DAV membership stood at 1 million and there were three chapters in the Northern Kentucky region: Chapter 19 in Cold Spring, Chapter 26 in Falmouth, and Chapter 148 in Alexandria.

Disabled American Veterans. *Wars and Scars—Compassion and Service.* Cold Spring, Ky.: DAV, 1995.

Charles H. Bogart

DISCIPLES OF CHRIST. The Christian Church (Disciples of Christ), strongly represented in Northern Kentucky, is a Protestant denomination that began in the Bourbon Co. community of Cane Ridge during the early 19th century. Today it is national in scope with some 3,800 congregations. Unlike the denominations from which its founders came, its churches are self-governing and call their own pastors; they worship both formally and informally and include lay women and men in leadership; open discussion of issues is encouraged, and diversity of opinion is common; and in recent years, the church has been growing in its racial and ethnic diversity. The plan was and is to build a united church organization of Jesus Christ modeled on the New Testament.

The Christian Church was founded by Maryland-born Barton W. Stone (1772–1844). A Presbyterian minister and schoolteacher by training, he hosted the historic Cane Ridge Revival in 1801 that was attended by as many as 25,000 during its five-or-six-day duration and from which the Christian Church (Disciples) ultimately arose. Other founders included Thomas and Alexander Campbell. Irish-born Thomas Campbell (1763–1854) attempted to reform the Presbyterian Church in Pennsylvania. He first aligned with the Baptists, but by 1830 that association was severed. **Alexander Campbell** (1788–1866), Thomas's son, who spent much time in the Maysville area, was a renowned public speaker, debater, author, and educator. It was said that he and his father were united in the attempt to reform the Presbyterians of their day, but by 1832 Barton W. Stone joined the Campbells to form the Campbell-Stone movement with a formal handshake in Lexington, creating a new American denomination, the Christian Church (Disciples of Christ).

In the years since, although in some ways the church has evolved, it has always adhered to its core beliefs. In the 20th century, American Asian, Hispanic, and African American Disciples congregations have multiplied. In 2005 the General Assembly of the church, meeting in Portland, Ore., voted Sharon Watkins in as the first woman general minister and president.

In Northern Kentucky there are at least 37 Disciples churches. From the **Mayslick Christian Church** and the **First Christian Church** in Mason Co. to the influential **Madison Ave. Christian Church** in Covington and the **Florence Christian Church** in Boone Co., they have provided religious and community leadership for many years as a Kentucky-bred church. Today these congregations are part of the Kentucky region of the church, with ministerial offices along Red Mile Rd. in Lexington.

"Christian Church Assembly to Emphasize Spirit of Unity," *KP*, March 8, 1986, 7K.

"Christian Church (Disciples of Christ)." www.disciples.org (accessed June 6, 2007).

Harrison, Richard, Jr. *From Camp Meeting to Church: A History of the Christian Church (Disciples of Christ) in Kentucky.* Lexington, Ky.: Richard Harrison Jr., 1992.

"Relevant Issues of Today Will Concern Disciples of Christ in Annual Assembly," *KE*, April 18, 1971, 6A.

DISKIN, JOHN A. (b. August 19, 1925, Newport, Ky.; d. March 28, 1994, Fort Thomas, Ky.). Judge John Diskin was born in Newport's **West End** to Thomas M. and Rosemary Tierney Diskin. The family moved to Fort Thomas, where John attended public schools, graduating from **Highlands High School** in 1943. His father died when John was 14 years old. Diskin received his law degree from the University of Kentucky in the early 1950s and was asked by Governor A. B. "Happy" Chandler (1935–1939, 1955–1959) to direct the Kentucky Commission of Aeronautics, where he served with distinction during a period of statewide airport expansion. Diskin later practiced law in Owensboro and served in the commonwealth attorney's office there. In the early 1960s he returned to his Northern Kentucky home and joined the law firm of Blakely, Moore & O'Hara in Covington. Later he practiced by himself and became an assistant commonwealth attorney in Campbell Co. under Frank Benton. Diskin was appointed to the Campbell Circuit Court bench in 1975 to replace the retiring judge, Fred Warren Jr. Later that year he was elected to a full term as circuit judge. An activist judge, Diskin was known for his professionalism and attention to detail in presiding over the massive and complicated civil litigation arising from the **Beverly Hills Supper Club** fire of 1977. In 1982 Judge Diskin suffered a stroke while presiding at the bench in a medical malpractice case. The physicians in the courtroom attended and supported him until he could be rushed to a hospital. He then retired from the bench, but he recuperated from his stroke with vigor and humor. After a two-year convalescence, some of which was spent with his brother Tom in Las Vegas, he returned home.

Diskin came from an illustrious political family. His father was post office inspector for Kentucky; an uncle, **Lawrence Diskin**, was Campbell Co. commonwealth attorney; and another uncle, James Diskin, was Kentucky Democratic Party chairman. John Diskin was a lifelong student of history and politics, bringing to them the same intellectual vigor and attention to detail that he dedicated to the bench. A lively and witty conversationalist, he could be counted on to contribute humor and energy to any gathering. He died at St. Luke Hospital and was buried at New St. Joseph Cemetery in Cincinnati.

"Diskin Resigns State Aero Post," *KTS*, February 11, 1956, 2A.

"Kentucky Deaths," *KP*, April 1, 1994, 10A.

"Those Who Died Touched Lives for Generations," *KP*, December 31, 1994, 1–3K.

Patrick M. Flannery

DISKIN, LAWRENCE J. (b. April 1876, Newport, Ky.; d. August 15, 1942, Cincinnati, Ohio). Attorney Lawrence J. Diskin, a well-known Campbell Co. commonwealth attorney, was a son of Thomas W. and Mary Mullaney Diskin. His father was the janitor at the Campbell Co. Courthouse in Newport, where the family lived on the third floor. Lawrence's early education was at Immaculate Conception School in Newport (see **Immaculate Conception Catholic Church, Newport**). He apprenticed under judges **John T. Hodge** and **Otto Wolff Sr.** and later graduated from the **YMCA** Law School (see **Chase College of Law**) in Cincinnati. Diskin was appointed Newport city clerk in 1912 and served for two years. In 1914 he was elected Campbell Co. commonwealth attorney, a position he held for the remainder of his life. Shortly after his election, he married Charlotte "Lottie" Williamson; they had one child, a daughter Elizabeth. Charlotte was the granddaughter of Captain **John Williamson**, the well-known steamboat operator and builder of the **Central Bridge**.

Diskin and his family moved to 114 Mayo Ave. in Fort Thomas, where he became an active member of the **St. Thomas Catholic Church**. He was also a member of many other religious and civic organizations, including the Catholic Order of Foresters, the Holy Name Society, the Knights of St. John, the St. Boniface Orphans Society, the **Knights of Columbus**, the Eagles, the Elks (see **Civic Associations**), and the Newport Moose Club.

Diskin suffered from leukemia for about the last two years of his life. He died of a cerebral hemorrhage at Good Samaritan Hospital, Cincinnati, at age 66. Funeral services were held at the Immaculate Conception Church in Newport. More than 3,000 people attended his funeral; this was the largest group ever to attend a funeral in Newport. Many state and local politicians were present, including J. Lyter Donaldson, Arthur B. Rouse, and Brent Spence. Diskin was buried at the New St. Joseph Cemetery, Price Hill, Cincinnati. His wife Charlotte preceded him in death in March 1931.

"Death Comes to Larry Diskin," *KE*, August 16, 1942, 18.

"Kentucky's Governor and Federal Officials to Attend Rites for Lawrence J. Diskin," *KTS*, August 17, 1942, 1.

"Respect Paid by Hundreds," *KE*, August 18, 1942, 1.

DISTILLERIES. In February 1935 the **New England Distillery** of Covington celebrated its 50th anniversary of continuous production, having operated throughout **Prohibition** by making rum to flavor cigarettes and for medicinal purposes. Previously, the firm was nationally known for its Red Star Straight Rum brand. The New England Distillery fared better than most liquor manufacturers in that it was one of the few remaining makers in Northern Kentucky, surviving into the 1960s at its 115 Pike St. location, next to an important **Louisville and Nashville Railroad** siding. Successful distilleries needed an adjacent railhead to on-load shipments of corn and off-load their products for distribution in distant markets. The fragrance of distilled spirits from the New England Distillery permeated downtown Covington until the company's last days of business; the distillery's buildings remain today.

For many years the Pogue family distilled spirits in the Maysville area. Later they had an interest in the New England Distillery's operation in Covington. From the 1880s to 1911, the Maddox-Hobart, Thorne, and Hazel Gap distilleries were located, successively, in Campbell Co. at the site that later became **Tacoma Park** in Dayton. In Finchtown, south of Newport along the Licking River, George Robson Sr.'s Old 76 Distillery made spirits from early in the 1900s until 1946, when Schenley Distillers Inc., took over and changed the name to the Pebbleford Distillery; in December of the same year, the plant burned in a whiskey-fueled conflagration. However, the company's $18 million stand of stored whiskey was saved. That was the third fire in the Finchtown operation's history, in addition to the explosion that took place there in 1888. After the fire of 1946, there was no further whiskey production on that site.

Between 1888 and 1913, Covington had at least 13 distilleries: Crigler and Crigler, 517 Scott St.; New England Distillery, Pike St.; Old Dexter, 27 Park Pl.; Sheldon Distillery, 14 E. Pike St.; Sunnyside Distillery, 61 Pike St.; **Walsh Distillery**, Front St.; Hanlon Distillery, 22 W. Seventh St.; Elk Horn Distillery, 12 E. Pike St.; Neal and Hoffman, Third and Main Sts.; Old Kentucky Distillery, Fourth and Court Sts.; Latonia Distillery, Milldale; Licking Valley Distilling Company, 67 Pike St.; and the Millbrook Distillery, Front and Scott Sts. The Walsh operation endured several major fires, much to the dismay of some Covington city officials who opposed whiskey-making. By 1910 Walsh had packed up and moved to Lawrenceburg, Ind., where it eventually became part of the Schenley Distillers Inc. empire.

Ancillary distillery businesses in Covington included both barrelhouses and whiskey wholesalers: Orene Parker, 12 Pike St.; Meyer and Company, Third and Scott Sts.; Henry Brinker, 640 Scott St.; J. H. Reinke, 64 Pike St.; Joseph Von Handorf, 609 Main St.; Chas. J. Wigger, Patton and Mary Sts.; Thomas Carr, Wallace St. and Madison Ave.; Tom Conry, 34 Pike St.; Tom Ruh, 509 Scott St.; Patty Carroll, Wallace and Madison Ave. John Boske, 11th and Greenup Sts.; William Bechtold, Fifth and Johnson Sts.; William Kranz, Pike and Russell Sts.; and Gus Staggenborg, 1922 Madison Ave.

In Boone Co. at Petersburg, from roughly 1836 to 1910, the **Petersburg Distillery** (Boone County Distilling Company) operated. It was founded by William T. Snyder but later went through many different owners.

Wars, Prohibition, the **Great Depression**, reform movements, the diminishing demand for bourbon beginning in the 1960s, and industry consolidation have contributed to the disappearance of distilleries in Northern Kentucky. There were several proposals for building new distilling plants during the mid-1930s, including one in Ludlow on the site of the former Pintscher Gas Company; another in Mentor, by Seagram-Distillers of New York; and a third in Wilder, by the Cave Springs Distilling Company. None of them developed further. The overall number of distillers in Kentucky has declined in recent years.

Becher, Matthew E. "The Distillery at Petersburg, Kentucky, Part 1: Snyder's Old Rye Whiskey," *NKH* 9, no. 2 (Spring–Summer 2002): 49–55.

———. "The Distillery at Petersburg, Kentucky, Part 2: A Kentucky Giant," *NKH* 10, no. 1 (Fall–Winter 2003): 35–47.

"Distilling Company Here 50 Years Old," *KP*, February 15, 1935, 2.

Geaslen, Chester. "There Ran a Distillery or Two in Covington," *KE*, December 15, 1966, 2.

"Old Whiskey to Be Made Here Again," *KP*, December 9, 1933, 1.

"Two Sites in Northern Kentucky Considered by Distilling Interests," *KP*, April 9, 1935, 1.

Covington City Building and Kenton Co. Courthouse, Third and Court Sts. Designed by Dittoe and Wisenall, it was completed in 1901 and demolished in 1970.

DITTOE AND WISENALL. This architectural firm and the two individuals who formed it made their mark on Northern Kentucky by designing many buildings in the region. Louis G. Dittoe was born in Covington in 1867, the son of real estate agent George M. Dittoe. The family moved to Newport, where George Dittoe took a position as editor of the *Kentucky State Journal* newspaper. Louis was educated in Newport public schools but left school at an early age to work for the Cincinnati architectural firm of **Samuel Hannaford and Sons**. He also began the formal study of architecture at the night school of the Ohio Mechanics Institute. He showed such aptitude in the field that he became a teacher of architectural courses at the school. Bernard T. Wisenall was born in Maysville on September 4, 1869, the son of John Bernard and Jane Eckmann Campbell Wisenall. In April 1893 Dittoe and Wisenall formed a partnership, creating the architectural firm that bore their names. The firm designed a number of buildings in Northern Kentucky, including the old Covington City Hall (northeast corner of Third and Court Sts., demolished), the **Kentucky Post** Building, the **First Christian Church**, and an addition to the **Citizens National Bank** Building. It also designed the Pugh Building (later called the Polk Building) in Cincinnati. The partnership of Dittoe and Wisenall was dissolved in 1910, and Dittoe returned to private practice. The only Northern Kentucky buildings Louis Dittoe is known to have designed in later life are the Alma Apartments in Fort Mitchell and a private residence in Fort Thomas. After the dissolution of the partnership, Wisenall continued to design buildings in the region. With architect Chester Disque, he drew the plans for the John G. Carlisle Junior High School and the Third District School in Covington. In 1924 he designed the Ben Adams Insurance Building located on the northwest corner of Fifth and Madison in Covington. Three years later, he designed the Girls Friendly building for the **Trinity Episcopal Church** in Covington. Wisenall died at his home on July 16, 1942 in Covington and was buried at Highland Cemetery, Fort Mitchell; Dittoe died at his home in Cincinnati on January 24, 1947, and was cremated.

"Covington Architect," *KP*, January 2, 1917, 1.

Goss, Charles Frederick, ed. *Cincinnati: The Queen City, 1788–1912*. Vol. 3. Chicago: S. J. Clarke, 1912.

"New Building on Way," *KP*, May 15, 1924, 1.

Tenkotte, Paul A. *A Heritage of Art and Faith: Downtown Covington Churches*. Covington, Ky.: Kenton Co. Historical Society, 1986.

DIUGUID, NANCY (b. October 18, 1948, Cincinnati, Ohio; d. May 21, 2003, Johannesburg, South Africa). Nancy Elizabeth Diuguid, a pioneering theater director in England and South Africa, was the daughter of prominent Carroll Co. tobacco farmer Gex Diuguid and Elizabeth Lineback Diuguid. She attended schools in Ghent and Carrollton, Ky., and Indiana University in Bloomington, Ind., before moving to London, England, to study at the Central School of Speech and Drama.

Openly homosexual, she broke new ground with gay and feminist themes (see **Gays and Gay Rights**) in her early efforts. She did street theater with alternative groups such as the Gay Sweatshop and then moved into more mainstream work, holding director's positions in a number of respected London theaters. She won awards in London; Munich, Germany; and Edinburgh, Scotland for her productions and garnered acclaim as a visionary in a staid English theater culture where gays, feminists, and Americans were considered suspect. In search of new challenges, she directed short films and operas, serving as staff director for the English National Opera. A believer in the arts as an agent for healing and social justice, she launched arts projects working with prisoners, traumatized children, and victims of illness, rape, and abuse.

In 1999 Diuguid moved to South Africa and was diagnosed with breast cancer the following year. She continued working until shortly before her death in 2003. Her companion of 17 years, South African filmmaker Melanie Chait, and their foster son, Desmond, survived her. She left instruction to spread her cremated remains in England, South Africa, and Kentucky. Diuguid was memorialized by a plaque in St. Michael's Church, Guiting Power, Gloucestershire, England, and with a cenotaph at the Ghent Cemetery in Carroll Co.

Woddis, Carole. "Nancy Diuguid—Visionary Actor and Director Who Used the Creative Arts, and Her Own Gay Identity, in a Lifelong Campaign for Justice and Healing," *Guardian (England),* May 28, 2003, 23.

Bill Davis

DIVIDING RIDGE. A small community in Pendleton Co., Dividing Ridge was located within the Grassy Creek Precinct and was the location of a U.S. Post Office from 1862 until 1896. Simpson School, a one-room schoolhouse, was located near there. The community is currently home to the historic **St. John Catholic Church**.

Belew, Mildred Bowen, comp. *The First 200 Years of Pendleton County.* Falmouth, Ky.: M. B. Belew, n.d. [ca. 1994].

Mildred Belew

DIXIE CHILI. Dixie Chili represents a young Greek immigrant's business dream come true in a regionally successful and lasting restaurant chain that began in Northern Kentucky. Papa Nick, Nicholas D. Sarakatsannis (1900–1984), arrived in the United States in 1915, and after working for years in several other ventures, including Cincinnati's Empress Chili, he founded Dixie Chili in 1929. He began ladling his famous chili recipe in Newport at 733 Monmouth St., in an 8-by-30-foot front room. He did everything from cooking to serving, often working 18-hour days. This was the first chili parlor in Northern Kentucky. On his first day of business, he made 9 gallons of chili, and today some 150 gallons are prepared daily at that same location in an expanded commissary. Dixie Chili remains family-owned and is now run by two of Nicholas's sons, Spiros and Panny. Especially popular with chili connoisseurs is the Dixie Chili coney, a hot dog in a bun with mustard, smothered in chili and perhaps enhanced by Bermuda onions or shredded cheddar cheese. Customers can also order one of the variations of chili served over spaghetti—with cheese, onions, beans, chopped garlic, or any combination of those ingredients. At one time the chain had a Cincinnati store in Clifton, one in Independence, and one on Mall Rd. in Florence. Currently there are three Dixie Chili locations in operation: in Newport, Covington, and Erlanger. In recent years the firm has begun canning and shipping its products throughout the world. Papa Nick died October 29, 1984, and was buried at Evergreen Cemetery in Southgate.

Dixie Chili and Deli. "History of Dixie Chili." www.dixiechili.com (accessed June 20, 2007).
Hicks, Jack. "Escape from Turks the First Ingredient for Chili," *KE,* June 12, 1979, A1.
"Nicholas Sarakatsannis," *KP,* October 30, 1984, 12C

Michael R. Sweeney

DIXIE HEIGHTS HIGH SCHOOL. The fall 1937 opening of Dixie Heights High School, located at 3010 **Dixie Highway** in Edgewood, provided northern Kenton Co. with a public high school facility comparable to the best in the region. Construction of the Dixie Heights High School and its companion school, the **Simon Kenton High School**, stemmed from a 1935 state review aimed at modernizing the Kenton Co. school system. At the time, Kenton Co. high schools suffered when compared to high schools with better facilities in Covington and South Fort Mitchell (Fort Mitchell). Dissatisfied Kenton Co. residents often enrolled their children out-of-district. The state's findings generated a plan that recommended, among other things, the construction of two high schools, one in southern Kenton Co. to replace the antiquated **Independence High School** and **Piner High School** buildings, and the other in northern Kenton Co. to relieve the overcrowded **Crescent Springs High School**. For the northern high school, the Kenton Co. School Board acquired 12 acres on the Dixie Highway opposite Dudley Pike. The two proposed high schools received federal funding through the Works Progress Administration, a New Deal agency. The Dixie Highway school's original name was Franklin D. Roosevelt High School; however, objections were raised to naming a school after a living person. Instead, the county school board chose the name Dixie Heights, a reference to the school's location on a rise overlooking the Dixie Highway. The school was completed at a cost of approximately $178,000; architect Howard McClorey's Art Deco–inspired design featured 18 classrooms, a cafeteria, and a gymnasium. James A. Caywood served as the school's first principal. Students at the school voted to name its athletic teams the Colonels. The enrollment of almost 1,000 students at the new Dixie Heights and Simon Kenton High Schools in 1937 represented a nearly 50 percent increase in high school enrollment in the Kenton Co. school system.

Since its opening, the Dixie Heights High School campus has undergone many expansions and renovations. During the 1950s and 1960s, more classrooms, a new cafeteria, and a football stadium were added. A 1980 renovation resulted in expanded gymnasium, music, and industrial education facilities. A multiphase $14 million major upgrade was commenced in 2001 that will result in essentially a new school building that preserves the facade of the original 1937 structure. Scheduled for completion in 2008, the project, designed by architects Piaskowy and Cooper, will feature a media center, expanded science and computer labs, an auditorium with stadium seating, central heating and air conditioning, and a new formal entrance. The removal of the Caywood Elementary and the Kenton Co. Board of Education offices from the Dixie Heights campus will permit new and expanded athletic facilities for the high school.

Over the years, Dixie Heights High School students, marching bands, and athletic teams have won several honors. Notable Dixie Heights High School alumni include **Ron Ziegler**, former press secretary for President Richard M. Nixon; former Cincinnati mayor **David Mann**; Kentucky secretary of state **Trey Grayson**; and Mark Pike, an NFL athlete.

Caywood, James A. "A Brief Sketch of the Development of the Kenton County School System." Address delivered to the Filson Society, Louisville, Ky., January 14, 1958.
"Tight Deadlines to Meet—As Summer of Construction Winds Down, Schools Rush to Opening Day," *KP,* July 24, 2003, 1K.

Greg Perkins

DIXIE HIGHWAY. The Dixie Highway was a system of roads that stretched more than 5,000 miles and encompassed two major routes and several spurs. Both divisions ended at Miami, Fla.; the eastern section started at Sault Ste. Marie, Mich., and the western part at Chicago. The highway was the brainchild of Carl G. Fisher, the creator of the Lincoln Highway, which connected San Francisco with New York City, and of the Indianapolis 500 motor race. One of Fisher's projects was a new resort on a sandbar that he had just purchased, called Miami Beach. Fisher used his political connections to push the idea of the Dixie Highway at a convention of governors in 1915. Construction started quickly thereafter, and many parts of the highway were operational by the end of 1916, including much in the Midwest and Florida. Delays hindered the process, especially in rough or swampy terrain, but the highway was rounding into shape by spring 1917.

Unlike interstate highways, which were built entirely new in almost all cases, the Dixie Highway was much more like the U.S. highway system that began in the 1920s as a series of previously connected roads, with some small construction connecting and upgrading the largely rural roadbeds. Because the Dixie Highway was primarily composed of previously existing routes, cities and towns anywhere near the proposed route petitioned the Dixie Highway Association to have their particular Main Street given the designation of Dixie Highway. While some people in Northern Kentucky lobbied for the **Three-L Highway** or Alexandria Pk. to receive the designation, the obvious choice was the **Covington and Lexington Turnpike**. Much of the roadway had to be reconstructed and paved with concrete to meet the standards of the Dixie Highway Association.

The Covington and Lexington Turnpike was rechristened the Dixie Highway in October 1915, after the association accepted the local bid. It was then up to local officials to raise the necessary funds to upgrade the old turnpike. The section from Covington to Erlanger was completed in July

Intersection of the Dixie Highway and U.S. 42 in Florence, with the Caintuckee Grill, in the 1960s.

1916 and celebrated with the planting of 400 trees along the route and plans for a statue of **Simon Kenton** to greet travelers after they crossed the **John A. Roebling Bridge**. The route from Erlanger to Florence, Ky., was completed in August 1921. It was celebrated by a parade and dance in Erlanger, which drew hundreds. The highway was opened to Williamstown in September 1924. The entire highway was not completed through Kentucky until a bridge spanning the Rockcastle River in Laurel Co. was finished in 1925.

Seeing the success of the highway and its impact on towns, boosters along the Three-L Highway wanted their road to be designated part of the highway as well. Pendleton Co. officials submitted petitions to the Dixie Highway Association in 1923 to have the Three-L Highway designated the Licking Valley Branch of the Dixie Highway. Although some began to call the Three-L Highway "Dixie Highway," the association never recognized any stretch of the Three-L Highway as part of its official highway system.

The net effect of the Dixie Highway was to place Northern Kentucky along one of the major north-south corridors connecting the industrial North with the rapidly growing Florida playgrounds. Tourist stops such the **Halfway House** in Williamstown that provided food, gasoline, and accommodations thrived on the tourist trade of families going to and from vacation spots in Florida.

Clark, Thomas D. *A History of Laurel County*. London, Ky.: Laurel Co. Historical Society, 1989.
"Covington Good Willers Celebrate Opening of Pike to Williamstown," *KP*, September 25, 1924, 1.
"Covington Plan Draws Praise from Forester," *KP*, January 24, 1917, 1.
"Double Track Highway," *KP*, May 29, 1923, 1.
"Erlanger Celebrates," *KP*, August 15, 1921, 1.
Foster, Mark S. *Castles in the Sand: The Life and Times of Carl Graham Fisher*. Tallahassee: Univ. of Florida Press, 2000.
Preston, Howard L. *Dirt Roads to Dixie: Accessibility and Modernization in the South, 1885–1935*. Knoxville: Univ. of Tennessee Press, 1991.
"State Will Not Give Pike Trees," *KP*, March 8, 1917, 2.

Chris Mieman

DIXIE TERMINAL. The Dixie Terminal in Cincinnati was used by Northern Kentucky streetcars and buses from 1921 until 1996.

In the second decade of the 1900s, area civic leaders Frank J. Jones, A. Clifford Shinkle, and Charles P. Taft formed a company to build, on the southwest corner of Fourth and Walnut, a commercial complex that became Cincinnati's largest indoor shopping arcade and office building. The first two floors of the building were to be devoted primarily to retail shopping, and the remaining eight floors were to be leased as commercial office space.

Shinkle, who was the president and one of the primary stockholders of the Covington and Cincinnati Bridge Company (see **John A. Roebling Bridge**), suggested to Taft that an annex to the south of the proposed Fourth & Walnut Building would be an ideal terminal location for the **Green Line Company**'s **streetcars** arriving from Northern Kentucky. Taft, who was a major stockholder in the Cincinnati Gas and Electric Company, a business owned by the Green Line's parent, the Columbia Gas & Electric Company, agreed. Taft had plans drawn for a four-story annex to the Fourth & Walnut Building, with the lower two floors for use as the transit company's streetcar terminal and the top two floors designed for additional office space.

The Green Line signed a long-term lease on the annex in 1917. Cincinnati's Planning Commission was delighted that as many as 70 Covington Division Green Line streetcars per hour would no longer run on Cincinnati city streets; they could go directly from the Suspension Bridge to the Dixie Terminal's proposed upper streetcar loop. Although Newport Division cars would travel on Cincinnati's Third St., they would avoid the very congested areas of Fourth and Fifth Sts. and would unload and load in a Dixie Terminal ground-level loop.

Since the Suspension Bridge linked Cincinnati to the South via Kentucky, the bridge company's president, Clifford Shinkle, proposed naming the whole project, including the annex, the Dixie Terminal, and his proposal was accepted. Shinkle was also responsible for getting the **Dixie Highway** project (U.S. 25) from Michigan to Florida routed over the Suspension Bridge from Cincinnati to Covington through Kenton Co., along the route of the Lexington Pike.

Construction on the Dixie Terminal was delayed by **World War I** and did not begin until 1919. The terminal was completed in 1921, at a cost of $3.5 million. The shopping arcade was designed in the Italian Renaissance architectural style, with a sky-blue vaulted ceiling over the main shopping area. Low-relief medallions decorating the ceiling were colored alternately brown and cream and blue and cream, with touches of gold. The arcade was furnished with warm cream–colored marble walls, and shops in it were framed with pilasters rising to the vaulted ceiling. The *Cincinnati Enquirer* labeled the Dixie Terminal the brightest jewel in Cincinnati's crown.

On Sunday, October 23, 1921, the Green Line's Covington Division cars began running directly into the upper terminal level through a viaduct from the Suspension Bridge above Second and Third Sts. A month later, on November 27, the Newport Division streetcars started using the Dixie Terminal's lower level via Third St. With the opening of the lower level of the Dixie Terminal, the Green Line discontinued its use of the **L&N Bridge**, and all of the Newport Division cars used the Central Bridge to and from Cincinnati.

The two levels within the Dixie Terminal were arranged similarly. The tracks in each level formed a horseshoe-shaped loop. The streetcars entered

Dixie Terminal, Cincinnati.

the eastern side of the horseshoe, discharged their passengers, and proceeded around to the western side to pick up passengers bound for Northern Kentucky. Each loop was 355 feet long, and four small or three large streetcars could be simultaneously unloaded on one side of the horseshoe curve, while up to five small or four large streetcars could board passengers at the same time on the other side.

When inbound passengers disembarked from streetcars at the Dixie Terminal, they left the terminal area via an exit-only passageway. Passengers bound for Northern Kentucky dropped their nickels or tokens into mechanical turnstiles or, if they needed change, went to a cashier's booth and then proceeded through the cashier-controlled barrier. Because streetcar conductors were not required to handle money at the Dixie Terminal, they could attend solely to the task of rapidly loading or unloading passengers.

The economic benefits of the Dixie Terminal to the Green Line were considerable. The Covington Division's streetcars saved an average of 10 minutes per round trip by avoiding Cincinnati's street traffic. Even the Newport Division's trips saved an average of 5 minutes simply by being able to unload and load off-street. These factors meant that the company could run fewer streetcars per route while maintaining the same service levels.

Even when the Green Line changed over from streetcars to buses, between 1935 and 1950, the Dixie Terminal continued to serve as the off-street terminal until the company ceased transit business in November 1972. The publicly owned successor to the Green Line, the **Transit Authority of Northern Kentucky** (TANK), continued to use the Dixie Terminal for another 24 years. However, in September 1996, TANK was notified that its lease at the Dixie Terminal would be terminated on October 18. At 12:45 a.m., October 18, 1996, the No. 1 Erlanger-Florence bus pulled out of Dixie Terminal; this was the last bus to make a service run emanating from the Dixie Terminal. Henceforth, buses with service routes to Northern Kentucky picked up their passengers on downtown streets in Cincinnati.

Lehmann, Terry W., and Earl W. Clark. *The Green Line.* Chicago: Central Electric Railfans' Association, 2000.

Terry W. Lehmann

DIXIE TRACTION COMPANY. The predecessor of the Dixie Traction Company was J. W. Bentler's motorbus operation in Northern Kentucky, which began in 1915. Bentler operated one 30-passenger bus from the end of the **Green Line** streetcar line in Fort Mitchell south along the **Covington and Lexington Turnpike** (later the **Dixie Highway**) to the adjoining communities of Erlanger and Elsmere. The combination of hard rubber tires, uncomfortable benchlike seats for passengers, and the crushed-gravel washboardlike surface of the pike, coupled with rising fuel prices and parts shortages, caused Bentler's operation to fold before the end of **World War I**.

When Bentler's operation ended, the residents of Erlanger and Elsmere were left without public transportation between their cities and the Fort Mitchell streetcar line, with its access to downtown Covington and Cincinnati. After the Dixie Highway was paved in August 1921, public bus services from Florence, Erlanger, and Elsmere to Covington and Cincinnati became feasible.

In 1922 a group of businessmen, led by Kenton Co. attorney **Stephens Blakely**, established the Dixie Traction Company, a corporation with an initial capitalization of $10,000. Beginning operations on August 15, 1922, the company used three buses and linked its roundtrip services from Florence, Elsmere, and Erlanger along the Dixie Highway to the streetcar line's termination point in Fort Mitchell. On August 18, 1925, the company extended its route further north along the Dixie Highway through downtown Covington to Cincinnati. The initial investors sold the company in 1927 to Erlanger businessmen F. Walton Dempsey and Arthur Rouse. In November 1929 the Dixie Traction Company established two additional routes, from Fort Thomas to Cincinnati. By 1930 the company had become a serious competitor of the Green Line Company wherever its routes closely paralleled the rival company's existing streetcar tracks. To house the Dixie Traction Company's growing fleet of 15 buses, a new garage with a 30-bus capacity was built on the southeast corner of Dixie and May in Elsmere in 1929. It was located just feet away from Erlanger's city boundary line and was always called the Erlanger Garage. By the end of 1937, the company owned 25 buses. It made 62 round trips daily, except on Sundays, between Florence and Cincinnati and 26 round trips daily, except on Sundays, on its two routes between Fort Thomas and Cincinnati. Sunday buses ran between Florence and Cincinnati at 30-minute intervals; no service was maintained on Sunday between Fort Thomas and Cincinnati.

In June 1939 news reports revealed that the Green Line Company had reached an agreement to purchase the Dixie Traction Company for the sum of $200,000. In October 1939 it was announced that the Dixie Traction Company had entered into side agreements to purchase the Cold Spring Bus Company and the Alexandria Bus Company at a cost of $25,000. In 1940 the Green Line Company was given clearance by the Interstate Commerce Commission (ICC) to complete its purchase of the Dixie Traction Company, but included was a mandate that the suburban routes to Erlanger, Cold Spring, and Alexandria be operated under the banner of the Dixie Traction Company as a separate operating subsidiary of the CN&C (the Green Line).

Beginning in 1943, the Dixie Traction Company ran a roundtrip bus shuttle service for construction workers from its Erlanger-Florence route at Commonwealth Ave. and the Dixie Highway to where the Greater Cincinnati Airport (**Cincinnati/Northern Kentucky International Airport**) was being built in Boone Co. The bus company was surprised to discover that many riders were using this service merely to view the ongoing progress of the airport's development. In September 1946 **David L. Ringo**, the assistant general manager of both the Dixie Traction Company and the CN&C, confirmed that the Dixie Traction Company had contracted with three major airlines and the Airport Board to carry passengers in a scheduled motor-coach service between downtown Cincinnati hotels and the new airport. In addition, the company had obtained exclusive rights from the Airport Board to provide incoming passengers with taxi-for-hire service to all points within a 20-mile radius of the airport. However, its taxi-for-hire authority to return to the airport was limited to picking up customers at the Gibson, Terrace Plaza, Netherland Plaza, and Sinton hotels in downtown Cincinnati. The company marketed the scheduled motor-coach service as Airporter Services and its taxi-for-hire service as Red Top Limousines (the company never referred to its limousines as cabs). The agreements were consummated following the move of American, Delta, and Trans World airlines from Lunken Airport in Cincinnati to the new Greater Cincinnati Airport in January 1947. The Dixie Traction Company, or its parent the Green Line, operated both scheduled motor-coach service and nonscheduled taxi service to and from the airport until 1973.

On March 16, 1950, the ICC approved the abandonment of CN&C's No. 1 Fort Mitchell streetcar service. Furthermore, the Dixie Traction Company was given permission to serve certain points of the old streetcar line with a new Erlanger-Florence bus route that commenced on July 3, 1950. The Dixie Traction Company's lines in Campbell Co. were merged with the parent Green Line Company's bus services as the No. 21 N. Fort Thomas and the No. 24 Cold Spring–Alexandria routes. In 1955 the Dixie Traction Company was given permission by the ICC to merge with the Cincinnati, Newport, and Covington Railway Company (CN&C). On March 15 Stephens Blakely, general counsel for both the CN&C (Green Line Company) and the Dixie Traction Company and one of the original bus company's founders, had the sorrowful duty of filing the Dixie Traction Company's dissolution papers with the Kentucky secretary of state. On June 27, 1955, the former Dixie Traction garage in Elsmere was destroyed by fire. The fire, which broke out during the late afternoon, quickly spread through the building, destroying three buses. One employee suffered a minor injury. Along with the building and the buses, valuable tools, company records, and fare boxes were destroyed. The total loss from this fire exceeded $100,000.

Lehmann, Terry W., and Earl W. Clark. *The Green Line.* Chicago: Central Electric Railfans' Association, 2000.

Terry W. Lehmann

DONAGHY, MARK F. (b. January 5, 1956, Philadelphia, Pa.). Mark F. Donaghy, the innovative general manager of the **Transit Authority of Northern Kentucky** (TANK) for almost 15 years (1990–2003), is the fifth of seven children born to

James W. and Justine Evans Donaghy. His father's employment with the parent company of the **Green Line** transit company caused the family to move often during Mark's childhood. Mark's father, James, received his initial managerial training in Newport and later managed transit companies in such diverse locations as Chester, Pa.; Youngstown, Ohio; Omaha and Lincoln, Neb.; and Worcester, Mass. James W. Donaghy was inducted into the American Public Transportation's Hall of Fame in 1993.

In 1979 Mark Donaghy married Dora Lee Booth; the couple raised three children.

Following in his father's footsteps, Donaghy accepted a management position in 1980 with First Transit Inc., a predecessor of his present employer. His first management position with a transit company was in Manchester, N.H., as director of operations. In 1981 First Transit Inc. assigned Mark to TANK to serve as assistant general manager and planning and grants administrator. Donaghy served the transit authority for six years and was the person responsible for researching, making applications for, and administering federal grants and for implementing TANK's equal opportunity and minority business enterprise programs. Most significantly, Donaghy served as project manager during the planning and construction of TANK's general offices, maintenance, and storage garage on Madison Pk. in Fort Wright, which opened on November 20, 1982. While assistant general manager at TANK, he earned his bachelor's degree in business administration from **Thomas More College** in December 1985, having previously garnered credits toward his degree from the University of Nebraska and Youngstown State University in Ohio.

In 1986 Donaghy was promoted to general manager of the Missoula Urban Transit District in Montana. There he was responsible for all the operational, maintenance, and administrative functions of that system. He was brought back to Newport by First Transit Inc. in 1990, to serve as the general manager of TANK. During the early years of Donaghy's second term at TANK, he recognized the needs of the underserved, but growing, southern portions of the three-county region (Boone, Kenton, and Campbell counties) that the transit system served. The decade saw expanded service to **Northern Kentucky University** and to the Cold Spring–Alexandria area of Campbell Co. as well as new services to the Boone Co. area centered on Empire Dr. Also, a new No. 2–Airport Express route was instituted between downtown Cincinnati and the **Cincinnati/Northern Kentucky International Airport**, with the schedule primarily aimed at shift-change times at the airport.

Also included in TANK expansion plans was service to the newly developing business districts (and new condominium construction) along the Northern Kentucky riverfront. On May 6, 1998, the Southbank Shuttle began; it was a new bus route developed by Donaghy to link the downtown business districts of Cincinnati, Covington, Newport, and Bellevue. The shuttle was designed to connect the downtown Cincinnati sports complexes and Cincinnati's retail and restaurant district with the rapidly expanding Newport, Bellevue, and Covington entertainment districts along the Ohio River and with Covington's Main Strasse Village. The shuttle was a complete success, so much so that TANK found it necessary to order new, larger buses in 2001.

Through Donaghy's leadership, TANK developed an alternative indoor transfer location after it was notified in September 1996 that its lease for the Dixie Terminal, its downtown Cincinnati terminal, would not be renewed. That development gave impetus to implementing TANK's long-range plan to operate a primary transfer facility in downtown Covington. A new indoor facility, located on the ground floor of the Kenton Co. parking garage on Madison Ave. between Second and Third streets in Covington, was opened on July 25, 1998. Named the Riverfront Transit Center, the facility was designed to serve as TANK's major transfer point in order to speed up operations, to replace the former main transfer locations in congested downtown Cincinnati (and at Third and Madison in Covington), and to provide TANK's transferring passengers a place to make connections under shelter.

Further initiatives by TANK under Donaghy's leadership included assisting employers and social service agencies by the institution of commuting service to outlying areas where abundant employment opportunities exist. Also during the 1990s TANK greatly expanded its Regional Area Mobility Program known as RAMP. By 2003 RAMP's door-to-door service for the mobility impaired assisted almost 4,000 individuals each month.

TANK received a Spirit of the ADA Award from the Kentucky Disabilities Coalition in 2001. Donaghy's leadership skills at TANK were also recognized by the Kentucky Transportation Cabinet when it named TANK the Outstanding Transit Operation in the Commonwealth in 1993. On the national level, Donaghy received the American Public Transportation Association's national award for the Advancement of Minorities and Women in the Workplace in 1997.

In September 2003 First Transit Inc. promoted Donaghy to vice president of its transit management services. In his new position, he assumed oversight responsibility for the further development of First Transit Inc.'s consulting business in North America. He also became the supervisor of all the managers of First Transit Inc.'s transit operations in Ohio, Michigan, Indiana, and Kentucky, including TANK.

Donaghy, Mark F. Interview by Terry W. Lehmann, April 20, 2005, Cincinnati.

Lehmann, Terry W., and Earl W. Clark. *The Green Line.* Chicago: Central Electric Railfans' Association, 2000.

Terry W. Lehmann

DONALDSON, J. LYTER (b. April 10, 1891, Carrollton, Ky.; d. March 27, 1960, Louisville, Ky.). Lawyer and politician J. Lyter Donaldson was the son of Joseph A. and Susie Giltner Donaldson. He graduated from **Carrollton High School** and entered Virginia Military Institute in Lexington, Va., then transferred to Centre College in Danville, Ky., where he earned his bachelor's degree. He received his law degree from Cumberland University in Lebanon, Tenn., in 1913. He returned to Carrollton and began his law practice. Friends described Donaldson as straight-spoken, honest, and sincere, reminding them of Abraham Lincoln. In December 1913 he married Jessie Rose Hill of Carrollton. He entered politics in 1921 and was elected Carroll Co. attorney, a position he held until 1930. His father died on August 1, 1930, and J. Lyter was chosen to succeed him as president of the First National Bank of Carrollton. In April 1935, Kentucky governor Ruby Laffoon (1931–1935) named Donaldson chairman of the Highway Commission; he served until 1939. In that same year, he managed Keen Johnson's campaign for governor and, after Johnson's victory (Johnson served from 1939 to 1943), was appointed state highway commissioner. In his new position, Donaldson became a major promoter of many Northern Kentucky highway projects, which contributed greatly to the growth of the area. Those projects included the widening of **U.S. 27** from Fort Thomas to Cold Spring, the widening of the **Dixie Highway** from south Covington through Fort Mitchell, and the construction of U.S. 42 in the direction of Louisville. He was also instrumental in the construction of Donaldson Rd., named in his honor, which became the main artery leading to the **Cincinnati/Northern Kentucky International Airport**. He resigned as Kentucky Highway Commission chairman in 1944 to run for governor on the Democratic ticket. In one of the closest elections in state history, Republican Simeon Willis defeated him. Donaldson served as chairman of the state Democratic Executive Committee from 1944 to 1948 and afterward returned to his legal practice in Carrollton. He died of a heart attack at age 68 in 1960 while visiting friends in Louisville. His body was returned to Carrollton for burial in the Odd Fellows Cemetery. At the time of his death, he was living in the same house in which he had been born. His wife had preceded him in death in June 1951. His only surviving close relative was a brother, Giltner A. Donaldson, who was executive secretary to U.S. Representative **Brent Spence**.

Kleber, John, ed. *The Kentucky Encyclopedia.* Lexington: Univ. Press of Kentucky, 1992.

Reis, Jim. "J. L. Donaldson Put Area on Fast Track for Growth," *KP*, March 27, 1960, 4K.

DONALDSON LITHOGRAPHIC COMPANY. By the turn of the 20th century, the Newport-based Donaldson Lithographic Company had become known internationally for its high-quality colorful **circus** posters. It operated out of a four-story building at the southeast corner of Sixth and Washington Sts., across from the site of the modern-day **Pompilio's Restaurant**, employing as many as 300 workers. Donaldson's art department provided jobs for many graduates of the Cincinnati Art Institute.

The company was founded by Cincinnati-born William Mills Donaldson (1840–1931), who lived most of his life in Campbell Co. He attended the Fourth St. Elementary School in Newport and Woodward High School in Cincinnati. He started a lithographic firm in Cincinnati in 1863. In 1890 the company was located at 11 W. Eighth St., and as it expanded, it moved to Newport in 1898 to a building once occupied by the **Dueber Watch Case Company**. By the time of the relocation, most of the firm's business consisted of circus posters for clients such as the Ringling Brothers, Buffalo Bill Cody, the Tom Mix Circus, and Annie Oakley. Donaldson became so deeply involved with the Gentry Brothers Circus, attempting to keep it operating, that he ultimately owned that organization. The lithographic firm also produced large posters for outdoor advertising billboards. In 1905 the Donaldson concern was merged with six other lithographic companies to form the Consolidated Lightographing Company, with William Donaldson remaining at the helm of the Newport operation. In addition to its circus accounts, the company printed theater marquee posters and advertising posters for florists, hardware associations, Plymouth automobiles, Florsheim Shoes, and Kuppenheimer Clothes.

In Covington, at the site of the former Central Covington Stock Yards (see **Meatpacking**) along the **Louisville and Nashville Railroad** and 22nd St., William Donaldson built the forerunner of the Donaldson Art Sign Company in 1914. It was a separate operation specializing in "tin ornamentation" for powder cans and the like. One of Donaldson's sons, also named William, became the founder of *Billboard* magazine, which continues to be the bible of the music business. William Mills Donaldson died at his home in Fort Thomas in 1931. The Newport company closed in 1936, and Hyde Park Clothes later occupied the building it had used. The Covington company operated until 1988 before it closed; its fire-damaged building was demolished in 2002.

"Newport Firm Goes into Merger," *KP*, May 27, 1905, 5.

Reis, Jim. "Posters Painted Company's Success," *KP*, September 22, 1987, 4K.

Michael R. Sweeney

DONIPHAN, ALEXANDER WILLIAM, BRIGADIER GENERAL (b. July 9, 1808, Mason Co., Ky.; d. August 8, 1887, Liberty, Mo.). Alexander Doniphan, a **Mexican War** commander, was the son of Joseph Doniphan of Virginia, who died early in Alexander's life. When Alexander was age nine, his elder brother was named as his guardian, and young Alexander joined him in Augusta in Bracken Co. Shortly after graduating from **Augusta College** at age 19, Doniphan began the study of law under the tutelage of Martin Marshall. He passed the bar in 1829 and subsequently decided to move to Missouri, first settling in Lexington and then in Liberty, Mo. Doniphan served three terms as a Missouri state legislator. As a brigadier general in the Missouri militia, in 1838 he was credited with bloodlessly quelling a threatened uprising by the Mormons.

When fighting commenced between the United States and Mexico in 1846, Doniphan organized a regiment of Missouri volunteers for military service. Elected as their commander, he led this contingent of troops during Gen. Stephen Kearny's invasion of New Mexico. After the seizure of the town of Santa Fe, Kearny left Doniphan in command, whereupon Doniphan forced peace upon a hostile Navajo people. Later ordered to join Gen. Zachary Taylor's army in northern Mexico, Doniphan led his men on one of the longest marches in U.S. military history. By the time the volunteers from Missouri reached Taylor's encampment at Saltillo, Mexico, they had covered more than 3,600 miles, a feat for which their commander, Doniphan, was lauded and hailed as an American "Xenophon."

After the Mexican War ended, Doniphan returned to Liberty, Mo., resuming his law practice and championing the cause of education. When secession threatened to tear the country apart in 1861, Doniphan, a slave-owning Unionist, sought to find compromise. He attended the 1861 Washington Peace Conference, but that meeting's effort to avert the war and strike a compromise failed. Afterward, Doniphan declined an offer of a command in the Union Army, preferring to continue working as a lawyer and assisting refugees displaced from western Missouri. He remained in Liberty as a prominent lawyer and respected member of his community until his death in 1887. He was buried at the Fairview Cemetery, Liberty, Mo.

Find A Grave. www.findagrave.com (accessed November 30, 2005).

Hughes, John T. *Doniphan's Expedition, Containing an Account of the Conquest of New Mexico.* New York: Arno Press, 1973.

Tim Herrmann

DONIPHAN, JOSEPH (b. August 19, 1823, Augusta, Ky.; d. May 2, 1873, Augusta, Ky.). Joseph Doniphan, a Bracken Co. lawyer, judge, and politician, was the son of local businessman George Doniphan, who ran grocery, tobacco, and leather-tanning businesses in Augusta. Joseph attended local schools and entered **Augusta College**, but he left during his senior year without graduating. From 1839 to 1842, Joseph worked as a clerk in his father's businesses. In 1844 he began the study of law and was admitted to the bar in 1848. Doniphan entered politics in 1849 and was elected to the Kentucky House of Representatives, representing Bracken Co. He married E. A. Ward on December 16, 1856, and they had three children. He served three terms as mayor of Augusta, 1852–1854, 1860–1862, and 1869–1871. In August 1862 he was elected circuit judge of the Kentucky Ninth Judicial District Court and served a term of six years. Doniphan was elected chancellor of the courts in Bracken, Campbell, Kenton, and Pendleton counties in May 1871 and held that position for the remainder of his life. He was 49 years old when he died in 1873 at his residence. He was buried at the Augusta Hillside Cemetery; his wife and three children survived him.

Biographical Encyclopedia of Kentucky. Cincinnati: J. M. Armstrong, 1878.

DONNELLY, THOMAS FRANCIS (b. October 27, 1870, Covington, Ky.; d. April 1, 1955, Covington, Ky.). Thomas F. Donnelly, Covington mayor, was the son of Irish parents, Lawrence and Mary Tierney Colleron Donnelly. His father died when he was six years old. He attended both the public and the parochial schools of Covington. At age 14 Thomas began work as a bookbinder in Cincinnati; later, in 1902, he became a car conductor with the Pullman Company. In 1915, at the age of 45, his political career began: he was elected to the Covington City Commission and reelected in 1917. In 1920 Donnelly became the mayor of Covington, serving until 1924. He promoted the city-manager form of government as a means to lessen corruption. In 1924 Donnelly returned to the City Commission for another term before becoming mayor a second time from 1928 to 1932. After his political career, he worked as a ticket-taker on the **Chesapeake and Ohio Railroad Bridge**. He was a popular stereotypical Irish Catholic Democratic politician of his era and a member of the **Cathedral Basilica of the Assumption** parish and several local fraternal benefit organizations. He never married. He spent the last 10 years of his life living in a boardinghouse at 1810 Greenup St., a structure that he had inherited from his brother. Donnelly died at St. Elizabeth Hospital in Covington and was buried at St. Mary Cemetery. Politics had provided the means of upward mobility for this second-generation Covington man, and until recent times, he was Covington's only two-term mayor.

Sacramental Records of St. Mary Cathedral Parish, Covington, Kenton Co. Public Library, Covington, Ky.

"Tom Donnelly, Former Covington Mayor, Dead," *KTS*, April 1, 1955, 1.

"Two-Time Mayor of Covington Dies," *KP*, April 1, 1955, 1.

DONNERMEYER, WILLIAM I. (b. September 19, 1924, Dayton, Ky.). William Irwin "Bill" Donnermeyer, a former Kentucky legislator, is the son of Frank John and Bertha Schlereth Donnermeyer. Bill was the youngest of eight children. He played football at Dayton High School in Dayton, Ky., but left before graduating and joined the U.S. Navy on December 11, 1942. He served as a radioman aboard the USS *Weber*, a destroyer escort in the Atlantic Ocean. After the Allied victory in Europe, he was being trained in multicommunications for the Army, the Navy, and the Marines in preparation for the invasion of Tokyo, when the war ended. He then served as part of the occupational forces in Japan for six months. After returning from Japan in February 1946, he completed his high school education, graduating from Dayton High School that same year.

After attending Villa Madonna College (**Thomas More College**) for a period of time, Donnermeyer joined the Pipe Fitters Union No. 392 in 1947. From 1958 to 1964 he served on the

Pipe Fitter's executive board. In 1964 he became a member of the Bellevue City Council and served until 1969. He won a close election for Kentucky state representative for the 68th District as a Democrat and remained in that office until he retired in 1994 (see **Democratic Party**). During his term in the Kentucky legislature, he was a member of the Labor and Industry Committee and, in 1972, the vice chairman of the Business, Organizations, and Professions Committee. In 1974 he became the chairman of that committee. From 1976 to 1986 he was majority caucus chairman. In this position he was able to place people on various committees. In 1990 he became the chairman of the Cities Committee and in 1992 the chairman of the Open Meetings and Open Records Committee; that same year he also served as chairman of the Statewide Information Committee, in which position he pushed for the greater use of computers in state government.

More than 200 bills were enacted into law in Kentucky that Bill Donnermeyer sponsored or cosponsored. He was the primary sponsor of 98 of them. The legislation that he sponsored or cosponsored is the subject of a 128-page booklet from the Kentucky Information Systems Commission. Among the bills was legislation concerning the automated registration and titling of automobiles, the state lottery, and the abolition of bail bondsmen. Donnermeyer was also involved in the establishment of the Community Action Agencies, funding for training of local firefighters and police, the adoption of a legislative code of ethics, and bills to legalize bingo and harness racing.

He has remained a steadfast member of the Democratic Party and has supported many Democrats in their campaigns for office. In 1972 he served as the Campbell Co. chairman for Walter Dee Huddleston's successful campaign as a Democrat for the U.S. Senate. Donnermeyer has always taken the position of those who needed help, including the homeless and the unborn, and is well known for his strong right-to-life advocacy.

In 1948 he married Shirley Snyder, who died in 1967. They had three boys, William, James, and Thomas. In 1970 he married Mary Ruth Hill, and they had one daughter, Teresa. Bill Donnermeyer resides with his family in Bellevue. Donnermeyer Blvd. in Bellevue is named after him. He is an honorary lifetime member of the Pipe Fitters Union and a member of the **Bellevue Vets**, the **American Legion**, and the **VFW**.

"Abortion Heats Up Primaries," *KP*, May 25, 1996, 1K.
Armstrong, Bryan. "A Man of the People," *KP*, January 3, 1995, 1K.

Robert W. Stevie

DOREMUS, ELIZABETH (b. May 22, 1853, Newport, Ky.; d. April 15, 1934, New York City). Elizabeth Johnson Ward Doremus, playwright and genealogist, was the daughter of George W. and Josephine Harris Ward. She was a granddaughter of **James Taylor Jr.**, founder of Newport, on her mother's side. Her father owned several plantations throughout the South. Educated in France, Germany, and Italy, she married noted chemist Charles Doremus in Washington, D.C., in 1880 and spent the remainder of her life in New York City. She was a respected social leader and genealogist, who traced the lineage of members of high society; she wrote three plays for the Broadway stage: *The Circus Rider* (1888), *The Fortunes of the King* (1890s), and *By Right of the Sword* (1905). Doremus was a friend of Lionel and John Barrymore. In the 1880s and 1890s she appeared in amateur performances. In 1934 she died from a stroke and was buried at the Woodlawn Cemetery in Bronx, N.Y.

Births Campbell County 1850–1910, available at Kenton Co. Public Library, Covington, Ky.
"Mrs. C.A. Doremus, Playwright, Dead," *NYT*, April 17, 1934, 21.

DOUGHERTY, WILLIAM AND ELIZABETH. In 1779 Elizabeth Conway and William Dougherty, accompanied by her father and mother, one child, brothers and sisters, and several other families, moved from Virginia to Kentucky. The families settled in Bourbon Co. about 10 miles north of Paris, in the neighborhood of what was then called Ruddell's Station. In 1780 British captain Henry Bird (see **Bird's (Byrd's) War Road**) attacked that settlement, and William and Elizabeth were captured with the rest of her family and taken to Detroit, Mich. After their release, William and Elizabeth Dougherty lived in Bourbon Co. for a few years before moving north to Pendleton Co. They settled on Grassy Creek, not far from the present town of Falmouth, and remained there until William died.

Belew, Mildred Boden. *The First 200 Years of Pendleton County*. Falmouth, Ky.: M. B. Belew, n.d. [ca. 1994].
Edward E. Barton Papers. Pendleton Co. Library, Falmouth, Ky.

Mildred Belew

DOVER. The town of Dover is situated on the Ohio River in Mason Co., about eight and a half miles northwest of Maysville, along Ky. Rt. 8, the **Mary Ingles Highway**. The area that is now Dover was in prehistoric times an abode of the American Indian mound-building Adena people (see **Mound Builders**), who erected a large mound there. With the arrival of white settlers, a town eventually emerged and thrived for a time. In 1786 Jeremiah Washburn and his family built the first house in Dover. Arthur Fox Jr. laid out the town in 1818, and they named it Dover for the town in England from which his father had immigrated. A post office was established in Dover in 1823, and the town was incorporated in 1836.

Dover had seen significant growth by the mid-19th century and became important as a shipping center. Several early businesses prepared the way. Gen. Anderson Lyon and Langhorn Tabb Sr. formed the Tabb and Lyon Company, which purchased tobacco for shipping to ports as far away as New Orleans and Boston. African American builder John Patty operated a coal- and brickyard that furnished bricks for many of the houses built around Dover. Several banks, factories, and newspapers provided an environment of prosperity and optimism. The town expanded after the **Civil War** to include nearby Frenchtown in 1874 and extended its boundaries further in the following decade. During the late 1880s, the **Chesapeake and Ohio Railroad** ran a service line through Dover, giving it better access to markets. The town managed to recoup after the great **flood of 1937**, and the Mary Ingles Highway was completed in the 1950s. But by that time, the population of Dover was in decline and some businesses had closed. In 1968 a devastating tornado was a calamity that the residents of Dover found difficult to overcome. The community remained, but its once-bright potential as a commercial center was gone. During the 1990s the completion of the **AA Highway** served to isolate Dover further. In the year 2000, the city of Dover had a population of 316.

Calvert, Jean, and John Klee. *The Towns of Mason County: Their Past in Pictures*. Maysville, Ky.: Maysville and Mason Co. Library Historical and Scientific Association, 1986.
Clift, G. Glenn. *History of Maysville and Mason County, Kentucky*. Lexington, Ky.: Transylvania, 1936.
Rennick, Robert. *Kentucky Place Names*. Lexington: Univ. Press of Kentucky, 1984.
U.S. Census Bureau. "American Fact Finder. Data Set. Census 2000 Summary File 1 (SF1) 100-Percent Data. Custom Table." www.census.gov (accessed April 3, 2007).

Thomas S. Ward

DOVER COVERED BRIDGE. The Dover Covered Bridge in northwestern Mason Co., the oldest surviving covered bridge in Kentucky, was first built in 1835 as a toll bridge to replace a bridge that burned. Only 13 covered bridges remained standing in Kentucky in 2007, of which only Dover Covered Bridge and three others continue to carry auto traffic. There were once hundreds of covered bridges in the state, but their numbers have been whittled down by many causes. Some were burned during the **Civil War**; the vehicles crossing them became heavier over the years; new bridges have been built to replace them; and floods, storms, neglect, arson, and vandalism have damaged them as well.

Covered bridges were built as an attempt to protect the wooden floor of a bridge from the ravages of weather. The sloped roof of the bridge protected the deck and main truss of the bridge from rain, snow, and the heat of the sun. Water remaining on the floor or on a truss of a wooden bridge hastens rot, while prolonged heat causes wood to shrink and warp. The long-term effects of both rain and sun will cause the eventual deterioration of a wooden bridge.

The Dover Bridge carries Ky. Rt. 3113 across Lee Creek, just south of Ky. Rt. 8 (the **Mary Ingles Highway**) and the city of Dover. The bridge, built of treated wood, is 63 feet long. It was rebuilt in 1928, 1966, and 2000. During the 2000 rebuilding, steel I-beams were inserted into the floor to help carry the heavier weight of vehicles. The original bridge construction used a double set of queenpost trusses on each side, much in the manner of barns built in that day. Each covered bridge, when built, expressed a unique construction method, based upon local building material and construction knowledge, to solve the problems relating to a stream's width and the height of its banks. Ky. Rt. 3113 has recently been routed around the covered bridge, although motorists can still drive over the bridge on a short bypass road. The Dover Covered Bridge is on the National Register of Historic Places.

Brandenburg, Phyllis, and David Brandenburg. *Kentucky's Covered Bridges.* Cincinnati: Harvest Press, 1968.
Powell, Robert A. *Kentucky's Covered Wooden Bridges.* Lexington: Kentucky Images, 1984.
White, Vernon. *Covered Bridges.* Berea: Kentucky Imprints, 1985.

Charles H. Bogart

DOW DRUG STORES. Cora Dow (1868–1915) graduated from the Cincinnati College of Pharmacy in 1888 and took over her father's small store on Fifth St. in Cincinnati. By 1915 Dow owned 11 drugstores, the second-largest pharmacy chain in the United States, larger than Walgreens at the time. In July 1916 Dow Drugs announced the purchase of the Gilmore Drug Company at the corner of Seventh and Madison Sts. in Covington, claiming that although Dow's home was in Cincinnati, once the bridge was crossed, a Dow Drug Store became Kentuckian in feeling and spirit. In December the company announced that it would soon open a store in Newport at Eighth and Monmouth Sts.

The Dow stores were cut raters, selling at below the normal retail price, an uncommon retail practice of the day. Some manufacturers refused to sell to Dow, but she challenged their pricing practices in court and won. Her firm was an early Rexall agency, an important pharmacy cooperative until the mid-1900s. Dow recognized the importance of women to her trade and furnished her stores so that they would be a welcoming place for them. She also hired women pharmacists and sales clerks.

Cora Dow's only interests outside the business were animals and music. She campaigned nationally for the idea that horses should have a two-week annual vacation. She loved music and wanted to be a musician, but there is no evidence that she ever received any formal training.

Before her death in 1915, Dow sold her drugstores to an investment group. She designated the Cincinnati Symphony Orchestra as her major beneficiary, leaving it more than $700,000 (the equivalent of $13 million in 2004).

The original staff at the Covington store included pharmacists Charles H. Wagner and Charles Bock, as well as Hildreth Green, Marie Herget, and Bessie Ferguson. The Newport store opened on March 24, 1917, with much fanfare. The first pharmacist there was H. S. Kendrick. The 21st store in the chain opened at Pike and Madison in Covington on April 13, 1918, with pharmacist Albert C. Wells in charge.

Henderson, M. L., and Dennis B. Worthen. "Cora Dow (1868–1915)—Pharmacist, Entrepreneur, Philanthropist," *Pharmacy in History* 46 (2004): 91–105.

Dennis B. Worthen

DOWNINGSVILLE. A milling and trade-route community, Downingsville, once existed in west-central Grant Co. where Ky. Rt. 36 crosses Eagle Creek. Downingsville was situated in a wide valley of fertile bottomland not far from Eagle Creek's Horseshoe Bend. The precise date of the village's founding is not known, but a post office was opened there in 1843 or 1844. This village may have been named for pioneer John Downing, who founded the Democratic election precinct of Downingsville. In the 1840s the village was reported to be 10 miles west of Williamstown and described as containing one tavern, one doctor, one lawyer, one store, a few mechanics, and 30 inhabitants.

Spanning Eagle Creek at Downingsville was an iron bridge, one of four built in the county by the King Iron Bridge Company of Cleveland, Ohio. It was the county's only double- span bridge, indicating a wider crossing at Downingsville. Completed around 1891, the bridge connected the turnpikes that linked the towns of Dry Ridge and Jonesville.

In 1901 Downingsville occupied both sides of Eagle Creek and had two stores, a blacksmith shop, and one saloon. New and improved roads bypassed the village, and the post office closed in the early 20th century. In 1956 a new road and a concrete bridge replaced the old iron bridge, which was torn down, leaving empty piers to mark its location.

Collins, Richard H. *History of Kentucky.* Vol. 1. Covington, Ky.: Collins, 1882.
Conrad, John B., ed. *History of Grant County.* Williamstown, Ky.: Grant Co. Historical Society, 1992.
Westover, John H. *Iron Bridges of Grant County.* Williamstown, Ky.: Williamstown Courier, 1901.

Barbara Loomis Brown

DRAKE, DANIEL (b. October 20, 1785, near Bound Brook, N.J.; d. November 5, 1852, Cincinnati, Ohio). Daniel Drake, a physician, a professor, an author, and a founder of medical institutions, was the son of Isaac and Elizabeth Shotwell Drake. In 1788 his family moved to Mayslick in Mason Co. In 1800 Daniel's father apprenticed him to Dr. **William Goforth**, a Cincinnati physician. Drake continued his studies in medicine at the prestigious University of Pennsylvania in Philadelphia in 1805–1806, studying under the noted physician Benjamin Rush. He returned to Northern Kentucky in 1806 and practiced medicine for one year in Mayslick, then moved to Cincinnati in 1807, where he assumed the practice of Dr. Goforth and married Harriet Sisson; they eventually had five children, three of whom survived past infancy. In 1810 he opened a general store and pharmacy with his brother Benjamin. Daniel sold the store to complete his medical degree at the University of Pennsylvania in 1815–1816.

Drake was one of the most influential men of his day: he founded the Medical College of Ohio (now the University of Cincinnati College of Medicine) in 1819–1820, the Commercial Hospital and Lunatic Asylum in Cincinnati (now University Hospital, Cincinnati) in 1820–1821, and the *Western Medical and Physical Journal* in 1827. He held medical professorships at Transylvania University in Lexington (1817–1818 and 1823–1827); Jefferson Medical College in Philadelphia (1830–1831); Cincinnati College (1835–1839); Louisville Medical Institute, later called the University of Louisville (1839–1849 and 1850–1852); and the Medical College of Ohio (1819–1822, 1831–1832, 1849–1850, and 1852).

A prolific author, Drake published, among other works, *Notices concerning Cincinnati* (1810–1811); *Natural and Statistical View, or Picture of Cincinnati and the Miami Country* (1815); *A Practical Treatise on the History, Prevention, and Treatment of Epidemic Cholera, Designed for both the Profession and the People* (1832); and *A Systematic Treatise, Historical, Etiological, and Practical, on the Principal Diseases of the Interior Valley of North America, as They Appear in the Caucasian, African, Indian, and Esquimaux Varieties of Its Population* (vol. 1, 1850; vol. 2, 1854 [published posthumously]). Drake's *Pioneer Life in Kentucky* (1870 [published posthumously]) is a source of much information about early Kentucky. He was also editor of the *Western Journal of Medicine and Physical Sciences* (1828–1838) and of the *Western Journal of Medicine and Surgery* (1840–1849).

Drake was also a civic activist, serving as an elected trustee of the City of Cincinnati. A strong supporter of building a railroad from Cincinnati to Charleston, S.C., he published a tract entitled *Rail-road from the Banks of the Ohio River to the Tide Waters of the Carolinas and Georgia* in 1835 (see **Cincinnati and Charleston Railroad**). Drake died in 1852 and was buried in Spring Grove Cemetery in Cincinnati.

Horine, Emmet Field. *Daniel Drake (1785–1852): Pioneer Physician of the Midwest.* Philadelphia: Univ. of Pennsylvania Press, 1961.
Shapiro, Henry D., and Zane L. Miller, eds. *Physician to the West: Selected Writings of Daniel Drake on Science and Society.* Lexington: Univ. of Kentucky Press, 1970.

Paul A. Tenkotte

DRAKE, MRS. ALEXANDER ("MRS. DRAKE") (b. Frances Ann Denny, November 6, 1797, Schenectady, N.Y.; d. September 1, 1875, Oldham Co., Ky.). Frances Ann Denny grew up in Albany, N.Y., and made her theatrical debut at age 14 in *Midnight Hour* at a small theater owned by Noble Luke Usher in nearby Cherry Valley. A respected East Coast thespian, Usher had built the first theater in Kentucky at Lexington in 1808. Because he was unable to persuade professional companies to travel to the west, he used amateur actors in his productions for several years. In 1814, though, he persuaded English-born stage manager Samuel Drake to organize a professional theater company in Albany to perform at Kentucky playhouses. Veteran actors rejected Drake's proposal, so he relied upon his children: Samuel, Alexander, James, Martha, and Julia. Frances Ann Denny was one of the five novices who joined them. By the time the Drake Theater Company reached Lexington in 1815, Denny was an experienced and proficient actress. In late 1819 Denny left the Drakes to make a North American stage tour to Quebec, Montreal, Boston, and New York City, where she was spectacular when she appeared at the Park Theater on April 17, 1820, in *Man and Wife.*

She reunited with the Drakes in 1823, marrying Alexander Drake and assuming the name Mrs. Drake, by which she is still remembered. The couple built an elegant home in Covington, where they raised their daughter Julia, but Frances, known as "America's finest tragedienne," "First American Lady of Stage," "Sarah Siddons of the West," and "Star of the West," often performed in the East. Then, on February 10, 1830, Alexander Drake died unexpectedly on a stage in Cincinnati, leaving Frances to raise Julia. On January 23, 1840, Frances wed lawyer **George W. Cutter**, an Indiana state legislator and an accomplished poet. The ceremony was performed by Rev. Henry Ward Beecher of Indianapolis. After a brief residency in Terre Haute, Ind., the couple moved to the Drake estate (the **Daniel Carter Beard** home) in Covington, Ky., where Cutter published poetry, headed a Kentucky military company during the **Mexican War**, and was active in **Whig** politics. When Zachary Taylor (1849–1850) was elected president in 1848, Cutter expected to be named U.S. ambassador to Morocco. However, Taylor died before making the appointment, and President Millard Fillmore (1850–1853) gave the sometimes-intemperate Cutter a job in the U.S. Treasury Department. The Cutters' marriage dissolved when Frances refused to relocate to Washington, D.C. After the divorce, Mrs. Drake appeared at theaters in Cincinnati and in St. Louis, Mo., and managed another venue, the Histrionic Temple, at the site of the old Louisville Theatre in Louisville. She eventually retired to Harmony Landing, the Drake farm along the Ohio River in Oldham Co., where she died on September 1, 1875. She was probably buried first on the farm next to her father, who had died in 1854; both were re-interred on the same day at Cave Hill Cemetery in Louisville in 1893.

Ford, George D. *These Were Actors: The Story of the Chapmans and the Drakes.* New York: Library, 1955.

Hill, West T., Jr. *The Theatre in Early Kentucky, 1790–1820.* Lexington: Univ. of Kentucky Press, 1971.

Odell, George C. D. *Annals of the New York Stage.* Vol. 3. New York: Columbia Univ. Press, 1927.

Mike McCormick

DREES, RALPH A. (b. April 7, 1934, Covington, Ky.). Ralph A. Drees, a humanitarian and the president of the Drees Company, was the second of three sons born to German immigrant Theodore Drees and Elizabeth Feldmann Drees. Growing up in Wilder in Campbell Co., Drees attended **Newport Central Catholic High School** and graduated with the class of 1952. He was then hired to work on the construction crew for his father's company, Theodore Drees Builder. In 1956 Ralph Drees was drafted into the U.S. military and served in the Army Corps of Engineers in Alexandria, Va. On June 22, 1957, he married Irma Schultz. After Drees was discharged in September 1958, he created a partnership with his father and his brother called Drees Builders and Developers. In the first subdivision the firm developed, Fairwood Hills, Drees moved into the second home he built, bought a van, and drove the subdivision's school bus for three years. On December 31, 1967, Drees and his brother dissolved their partnership (their father had retired earlier), and by August 27, 1968, Drees had formed a new corporation, Drees Builders and Developers Inc. He brought many innovations to the housing market. In 1974 he established the first planned unit development in Northern Kentucky—Prospect Point in Villa Hills. By the 1980s Drees Builders and Developers Inc. had moved into its first office building, on Royal Dr. in Fort Mitchell. As the firm became part of the larger national market, it was renamed the Drees Company. Drees built his organization into the largest privately held company in the Greater Cincinnati Area and one of the top 25 homebuilders in the United States. In 1994 Drees stepped down as president of the company but remained chairman of the board of directors. On January 14, 2004, he was sworn in as judge executive of Kenton Co. after being appointed by Kentucky governor Ernie Fletcher (2003–2007).

Over the years, Drees became involved in local government and business organizations, including the **Home Builder's Association of Northern Kentucky** (HBANK), for which he was secretary in 1963, vice president in 1964, and president in 1965. He served a second term as president of the HBANK in 1978 and was instrumental in establishing the HBANK's scholarship fund. Elected to the Erlanger City Council in November 1965, Drees was appointed by the mayor to the Erlanger Planning and Zoning Commission and the **Northern Kentucky Area Planning Commission** (NKAPC). Drees served on the NKAPC for 11 years. He was elected to the national board of directors for the Home Builders Association in 1973 and was appointed by Kentucky governor John Y. Brown (1979–1983) to a task force to analyze and prescribe solutions for Kentucky's depressed real estate economy. Drees's devotion to the housing industry earned him a position as president of the Home Builders Association of Kentucky in 1985.

As a businessman and community leader, Drees has received many awards, among them the Martin Conrad Memorial Award in 1987 and the 1990 Kentucky Entrepreneur of the Year Award in the Real Estate/Construction category. He was named Northern Kentucky Chamber of Commerce's Business Person of the Year in 1990, the National Builder of the Year (by *Professional Builder Magazine*) in 1991, and the Northern Kentuckian of the Year (by **Covington Catholic High School**) in 1993. He has served in various community organizations, including the Northern Kentucky Chamber of Commerce, where he was chairman of the board in 1991; for 13 years he was a member of the Kenton Co. Airport Board (see **Cincinnati/Northern Kentucky International Airport**). He was inducted into the Greater Cincinnati Business Hall of Fame in 2000.

In honor of his company's 75th anniversary in 2003, Drees donated the Drees Pavilion in Covington's Devou Park to the community. In 2006 Drees was honored with National Hearthstone/Builder Humanitarian Award for all his giving to charities, civic organizations, museums, schools, and social service groups. Drees and his wife have five children, and together they created a charitable trust with the Northern Kentucky Fund of the Greater Cincinnati Foundation.

"Celebrating Generosity," *KP*, April 30, 2004, A14.

Drees, Ralph. Interview by Gabrielle Summe, March 2005, Covington, Ky.

Drees Homes. www.dreeshomes.com (accessed April 2, 2006).

"High School to Honor Homebuilder Drees," *KP*, May 12, 1903, 2K.

Steinberg, Janice Burke, and Anne L. Mitchell. *A Solid Foundation: The History of the Drees Company.* Fort Mitchell, Ky.: Drees Homes, 2002.

Wilson, Dennis. "Ralph Drees Wins Honor for His Charity Work," *KP*, December 19, 2005, 2K.

Gabrielle Summe

DRIVE-INS. Drive-in movie theaters and restaurants, where customers stayed in their cars to eat a meal or watch a movie, operated in Northern Kentucky from the mid-20th century until 1992. The flourishing of such establishments was directly related to the post–**World War II** "car culture."

At a drive-in movie theater, customers simply purchased a ticket at the gate, pulled the car into an open spot, and attached the speaker inside a window on the car's left side. Having a meal at a drive-in restaurant was a bit more complex. Upon entering the parking lot, the driver would find a parking spot and study the menu, which was displayed either on one large sign or on a small sign next to each parking spot. Once a decision was made, the driver would turn on the car's headlights to attract a carhop. After taking the order, the carhop would deliver the food on a tray designed to fit onto the driver's-side window. Once the food was consumed, the driver would signal with the headlights again, and a carhop would come and remove the tray. Later drive-in restaurants were equipped with two-way speaker systems for communication between the driver and the carhop.

Drive-in restaurants in Northern Kentucky all took their cues from one franchise, Frisch's. The Greater Cincinnati area's first drive-in restaurant was the Frisch's Mainliner, which opened in 1939 in Fairfax, Ohio, along Wooster Pk. The first drive-in in Northern Kentucky, a Frisch's, was established in Newport in 1949, at 19th and Monmouth Sts. (**U.S. 27**). Eventually four more Frisch's drive-in restaurants opened in Northern Kentucky, in Covington, Erlanger, Fort Thomas, and Fort Mitchell. The last remaining drive-in restaurant in the region was the Erlanger Frisch's. An era ended when on April 1, 1988, carhops took their customers' final orders at the Frisch's in Erlanger at **Dixie Highway** and Forest Ave. The company was converting all of its drive-in restaurants to the use of drive-through windows instead.

Of course, other drive-in restaurants made their names known in Northern Kentucky. One of the most famous was Schilling's Drive-In in Fort Wright. Owned by the Schilling family who also owned the **Lookout House** and the **Beverly Hills Supper Club**, Schilling's Drive-In was a successful entry into the drive-in market. The establishment earned some publicity when it appeared in a 1955 *Popular Science* article that described its new audio system featuring walkie-talkies. The other drive-in chain in the region was Jerry's, a company based in Lexington that had outlets in front of the entrance to the Dixie Gardens Drive-In Theater and in Florence at Turfway Rd. and the Dixie Highway. Jerry's Restaurants, now the corporation Jerrico Inc., also established the successful Long John Silver's chain of restaurants.

Drive-In theaters were established in Northern Kentucky during the late 1940s. The first one, the Florence Drive-In, opened on the Dixie Highway near Main St. in Florence on May 22, 1947, at a cost of $143,000; it could accommodate 800 cars. Just a few weeks later, on July 3, 1947, Willis Vance opened the Dixie Gardens Drive-In Theater, which had a 700-car capacity, along the Dixie Highway in Lookout Heights (Fort Wright). Vance had also started the Strand Theater in Covington and theaters in Newport and Latonia. On the site of **Tacoma Park**'s failed dog track and speedway in Dayton, the Riverview Drive-In Theater opened on September 5, 1948. Southern Campbell Co. received its own drive-in when the Pike 27 Auto-Theater opened in October 1954. It was customary for the drive-ins to show two films per night; starting times varied with the time of sunset.

By 1960 both the Dixie Gardens and the Florence Drive-In theaters were owned by Redland Theaters, which also owned the Madison Theater and the Liberty Theater in Covington. Often the Madison Theater and the Dixie Gardens Drive-In Theater would show the same film; another film would be shown at both the Liberty Theater and the Florence Drive-In Theater. The Florence Drive-In Theater was open year-round, through the use of "in-car warmers." The Dixie Gardens Drive-In Theater had an accompanying building with a skating rink for winter amusement. Both of these drive-in theaters were sold to National Amusements in August 1969. While the heyday of the drive-in theaters was the 1950s and 1960s, both theaters survived into the 1970s, showing largely a combination of B-grade horror movies, oddities films, and soft-core pornography.

In December 1970 Kenton Co. commonwealth attorney John J. O'Hara began targeting the Dixie Gardens Drive-In Theater as what he called a public nuisance. O'Hara cited films such as *Love Object* and *The Seducers*, both rated X, and the R-rated *Barbarella* as examples of movies that should not be shown. Although he conceded that he could not shut down the theater on the content of the films, he did get a permanent injunction on the basis of a public nuisance, because its screen was visible to travelers on I-75.

The demise of drive-in theaters in Northern Kentucky in the 1980s occurred mostly because of two factors, rising land prices and competition from multiscreen cinemas. As development pushed farther and farther south, land values increased, making land-intensive businesses like drive-in theaters more expensive. At the same time, interstate highways made traveling to multiscreen cinemas a much more attractive option even for the reluctant driver. Cinemas in Florence and Erlanger claimed the clientele that drive-in theaters had retained.

The Riverview Drive-In Theater was severely damaged in the **flood of 1964** and never regained its earlier success. The theater limped on until it closed in 1982, to be replaced by the Watertown Yacht Club. The Florence Drive-In Theater closed in 1988 and was soon replaced by condominiums and retail business in the fast-developing area. The screen of the Dixie Gardens Drive-In Theater was destroyed by a fire in 1990; the site has been purchased and is being developed into luxury-car dealerships. Even the Pike 27 Auto-Theater in Cold Spring, threatened by no nearby multiscreen cinemas and serviced by no nearby interstate highways, closed in 1992, leaving the Boone-Kenton-Campbell Co. area without a drive-in theater. Other drive-in theaters in the outlying areas included the Riverview Drive-In Theater in Carrollton in Carroll Co., the Judy Drive-In Theater in Dry Ridge in Grant Co., and the Park Drive-In Theater in Maysville in Mason Co.

Most recently, the availability of movies that can be viewed at home, via purchase or rent or cable access, has made the trip to the drive-in theater seem even more a quaint fixture of the past.

Reis, Jim. "Big Screen Entertainment," *KP,* February 11, 2002, 4K.

Theoret, Nanci. "Curb Service Returns for This Weekend at Erlanger Landmark," *Dixie News,* July 30, 1992, 1.

Chris Meiman

DROEGE, IGNATIUS J. (b. January 30, 1828, Velmede, Germany; d. June 12, 1910, Covington, Ky.). Ignatius Joseph Droege, a Covington industrialist, was the seventh of 10 children of Frederick and Maria Franciscius Huecker Droege. In 1849 he immigrated to America in pursuit of financial opportunity. Trained as a blacksmith, he found employment in steel manufacturing at the Bush & Jordan Rolling Mill along the Licking River in Covington. He became a lifelong member of the German Pioneer Society (see **German Americans**) shortly after arriving. Five years later, on April 19, 1853, he married Maria Anna Schmidt, the stepdaughter of a German immigrant carpenter, and the couple had four sons and one daughter. They lived first on the north side of 12th St. between Greenup and Scott; then in 1863 the family moved to a larger home at 1217 Greenup. Ignatius handcrafted the cherry mantelpieces in the new home and the iron fencing surrounding it. Soon after their move, Maria Anna died of cholera, and her half sister, Antoinette Koran, moved into the Droege house to care for the five young children. Antoinette and Ignatius were married May 16, 1865, at **St. Joseph Catholic Church, Covington**. Antoinette gave birth to nine children.

In 1867 Droege joined Charles Bogenschutz as a partner in the Droege & Bogenschutz Stove Foundry Company, manufacturers of stoves, hollowware, and castings. In 1877 Droege secured a bank loan, enabling him to purchase the Phillips & Jordan Rolling Mill (formerly the Bush & Jordan Rolling Mill). His partnership in the Droege & Bogenschutz Foundry was dissolved that same year, and Bogenschutz retained the foundry. Droege changed the name of his company to the Licking Rolling Mill. Its output was 25,000 tons of bar iron annually, mainly for industrial use. At that time the mill was the largest employer in Covington, with 350 workers. Droege continued to be identified with the Licking Rolling Mill until his retirement in 1897, when he turned its management over to his sons. His wealth was estimated at $1 million. In 1899, when the Diocese of Covington (see **Roman Catholics**) was having financial difficulty funding the completion of its **Cathedral Basilica of the Assumption**, Droege presented Bishop **Camillus Paul Maes** with a check for $10,000. In 1910, at the age of 82, Droege died of a stroke at his home and was buried at St. Mary Cemetery in Fort Mitchell. He was preceded in death by three sons and three daughters. The Droege homestead, with the I. Droege brass nameplate on the front door, still stands. It remained in the family until Emily, his last surviving child, died in 1964.

"Fine Gift: Bishop Maes Gets Ten Thousand Dollars," *KP,* November 18, 1899, 1.

"The German Pioneer Society of Covington and Newport: History, Minutes, and Papers, 1877–ca. 1902," trans. Sr. Mary Romilda Bertsch, S.N.D., and Sr. Mary Edwin Paetzold, S.N.D., 1988, Kenton Co. Public Library, Covington, Ky.

"Ignatz Droege Dies," *KP,* June 6, 1910, 2.

Johnson, E. Polk. *History of Kentucky and Kentuckians.* New York: Lewis, 1912.

"Notice—Co-Partnership Dissolves," *Covington Ticket,* August 3, 1877, 2.

Reis, Jim. "Smoke Stacks Once a Familiar Sight," *KP,* July 14, 1986, 4K.

St. Mary Cemetery Records, Fort Mitchell, Ky.

Schroeder, David E. "Building a Celestial City," *Messenger,* December 14, 2001, 20A–29A.

Barbara Droege and Joyce Edmondson

DRUG ABUSE. See **Substance Abuse Treatment**; **Transitions Inc.**

DRURY CHAPEL METHODIST CHURCH. This lovely old southwestern Gallatin Co. church is located in a small community once known as

Hoggins. The church is on Drury Chapel Rd. about one mile off Walnut Valley Rd. It sits atop a hill next to a former one-room school, where there is a spectacular view of the valley. A circuit-riding Methodist preacher from Flemingsburg was the first pastor of the church. Early meetings were held in the homes of members, in the old log schoolhouse, or on the Fothergill farm at Campground Springs in Gallatin Co. The **Civil War** delayed the construction of the first church's building, which was dedicated on October 10, 1867. Members of the congregation provided building materials and the labor. The pastor at that time was Rev. E. L. Southgate of Newport. The Drury Chapel Methodist Church continues to function today in the community.

Bogardus, Carl R., Sr. *The Story of Gallatin County*. Ed. James C. Claypool. Cincinnati: John S. Swift, 2003.

Rennick, Robert M. *Kentucky Place Names*. Lexington: Univ. Press of Kentucky, 1984.

Darrell Maines

DRY RIDGE. The community established in Kentucky on the north-south **Dry Ridge Trace**, at its intersection with the northwest-southeast buffalo trail (see **Buffalo Traces**) between Big Bone Lick and the Blue Licks, became known as Dry Ridge. Early members of the **Old Baptist Church on the Dry Ridge**, organized in 1791 at **Campbell's Blockhouse**, settled in the vicinity. Another early resident was James Theobald, who served as justice of the peace in 1799 while the area was a part of Pendleton Co. As time passed, the Dry Ridge community grew and spread north of Campbell's Blockhouse.

The post office established in 1815 at Dry Ridge was the first in the area that became Grant Co. The first postmaster was G. P. Koulat, who was succeeded by William Hopkins in 1816, then by Griffin Theobald in 1818. In 1820, when Grant Co. was formed, some of the county's residents included the families of Lawrence Buskirk, Henry Childers, Joseph Childers, G. Childers, Major Childers, Thomas Childers, William Conrad, Jesse Conyers, Acklin DeHart, Martin Draper, Richard Landrum, John Lawless, Simon Nichols, Charles Norton, John Norton, Absolam Skirvin, Asa Tungate, and George F. Wheeler.

The community of Dry Ridge developed around two population centers, The largest of these was between the Big Bone Lick–Blue Licks Buffalo Trail (today's Warsaw Ave., Ky. Rt. 467) and Big Bone Lick, joined by the Dry Ridge Trace (today's U.S. 25). The second center, south of the first, was where the buffalo trail (Knoxville or Broadridge Rd.) to Blue Licks joined the Dry Ridge Trace. These two centers are still known by long-time residents as the Upper Ridge (Knoxville Rd.) and the Lower Ridge (Warsaw Rd.). The terms are in keeping with "up to Lexington" (higher elevation) and "down to Covington or Cincinnati" (lower elevation) but are confusing to visitors and new residents, who usually think of south as down and north as up.

Dry Ridge developed as a trading center for the surrounding farming area. Landowners established taverns or general stores to serve travelers as well as nearby residents. The first record of a sale of land in building-lot size (rather than by acres) was a piece of property acquired in April 1848 by trustees of the James Chapel Methodist Episcopal Church South in the Lower Ridge. Soon afterward, in September 1848, the trustees of the **Dry Ridge Baptist Church** on Broadway purchased a building site in the Upper Ridge. The Presbyterian Church in Dry Ridge, whose congregation traces its history to the Old Baptist Church on the Dry Ridge, occupies an 1892 meetinghouse on Warsaw Ave. The Christian Church (Disciples of Christ) in town, organized in 1896, built its church on School St. in 1900 and has added many improvements since. The Dry Ridge Colored Baptist Church, as it was first named, was organized in 1915 with 50 members. In 1918 it acquired a lot adjoining the Black School in the Upper Ridge from Arthur Thompson and his wife, and the church changed its name to the Second Baptist Church of Dry Ridge. It has been in continuous use over the years and is now named Zion Baptist Church.

Dry Ridge was incorporated in 1909, the last of the four towns in Grant Co. to incorporate. Also in 1909 a creamery company, drilling for fresh water, instead found mineral water believed to include medicinal qualities beneficial in treating arthritis and similar conditions. A hotel was built and named the **Carlsbad Springs Hotel**, after the famous health hotel in Carlsbad, Germany. The hotel in Dry Ridge was destroyed by fire in 1927, along with many other businesses in the area. Although later rebuilt, the hotel never regained its earlier prominence.

In 1937 Dry Ridge completed a water-distribution system supplied with water from Williamstown's municipal lake and water purification plant. Later, Dry Ridge signed a contract with the Bullock Pen Water District for supplemental water. By 1980 a sewage-collection system was completed by Dry Ridge. A contract with Williamstown was entered into for the processing and disposal of sewage through the Williamstown plant.

Today, with an increasing population; active retail and wholesale distributors, including an outlet center, modern restaurants, and motels for travelers and tourists; and a recently enlarged and expanded interchange with I-75, continued growth and development is to be expected for Dry Ridge.

Conrad, John B., ed. *History of Grant County*. Williamstown, Ky.: Grant Co. Historical Society, 1992.

John B. Conrad

DRY RIDGE, OLD BAPTIST CHURCH ON THE. See **Old Baptist Church on the Dry Ridge**.

DRY RIDGE BAPTIST CHURCH. The Dry Ridge Baptist Church was the fourth church to be organized in the part of Kentucky that became Grant Co. in 1820. Initially, to distinguish it from the congregation known as the **Old Baptist Church on the Dry Ridge**, the Dry Ridge Baptist Church was known as the Baptist Church at the Dry Ridge, Free Will. Elders Benjamin Lambert and Alexander Monroe founded this church on July 12, 1817, with 11 original members. The 12th member, and the first minister, was Elder Christian Tomlin, a native of Virginia who moved to the Dry Ridge from Ohio in 1817. Services were held in the meetinghouse that was built in 1799 and shared with the Old Baptist Church on the Dry Ridge, under an agreement reached in 1818. The latter church moved to Williamstown in 1826, leaving this meetinghouse to the Free Will Baptists, who had improved it with the purchase of a stove.

In 1843 the church's trustees reported that a building site had been obtained at the intersection of the **Covington and Lexington Turnpike** (U.S. 25) and the Broadridge (Knoxville) Rd. The meetinghouse that was built there was of frame construction, 50 feet by 30 feet. A deed for this property was not recorded until 1848; it is reported that church records for the period 1846 to 1877 were lost. In August 1875 the church's trustees purchased a building site on Warsaw Rd. (now Warsaw Ave. in Dry Ridge), and a new church was built. It was used until 1895, when it was found to be inadequate for the church's rapidly growing needs; a larger building was completed on the same site and dedicated July 28, 1901.

In 1924 the church constructed a new parsonage on Broadway in Dry Ridge, which was occupied by Rev. J. W. Black and his family. In August 1928 a lot was purchased on which to erect a new house of worship on the southwest corner of Broadway and Church Sts. On September 29, 1929, this church was dedicated; it remains the church building in use today. To support the church's needs, an annex was built in 1957. A new parsonage was constructed on Broadway near the church in 1960, and the old parsonage at 44 Broadway was sold. In 1988 the church refurbished the sanctuary. In 1992 this large and growing congregation celebrated its 175th anniversary.

Conrad, John B., ed. *History of Grant County*. Williamstown, Ky.: Grant Co. Historical Society, 1992.

John B. Conrad

DRY RIDGE HIGH SCHOOL. The Dry Ridge High School was one of four high schools established by the Grant Co. Board of Education during the early part of the 20th century. The school began in 1909 in one room of the existing four-room school building of the Dry Ridge Graded Free School. The school's principal (and its only teacher) was Bruce Franks. He was succeeded by Robert Sheriff for the school year 1910–1911, who had four students for whom he offered extra teaching time and classes after regular hours so that they might complete the regular four-year curriculum in three years. Orie P. Gruelle followed Sheriff at the school in the fall of 1911. The students' accelerated course of studies was completed, and the first class of four students graduated in the spring of 1912.

A new brick building was constructed, with four classrooms on the first floor for the first eight grades and three classrooms and an assembly room on the second floor for the high school. That building was destroyed by fire in 1914 and was replaced by another brick building that served as the school for many years.

Eighteen students graduated in the last class at Dry Ridge High School in the spring of 1953. The new consolidated **Grant Co. High School**, built on the south side of Dry Ridge, replaced the four county high schools. The new Grant Co. Middle School was built on the same property. Classes for the Dry Ridge Elementary School, grades one through six, were held in the building that had housed Dry Ridge High School until that building was destroyed by fire in 1973. A new building for the Dry Ridge Elementary School was built near the Grant Co. Middle School to replace the building that had burned.

Conrad, John B., ed. *History of Grant County.* Williamstown, Ky.: Grant Co. Historical Society, 1992.

John B. Conrad

DRY RIDGE TRACE. The Dry Ridge Trace, a north-south path between modern Lexington and the mouth of the Licking River, was an early animal and American Indian trail (see **Buffalo Traces**) used for decades before the European settlers arrived. The trace followed the crest of the dry ridge, the great drainage divide between the tributaries of the Licking River on the east and those of the Kentucky River on the west. For some 60 miles, from Georgetown in Scott. Co. north to the floodplains of the Ohio River, there are no streams to cross, so travel on foot or horseback is easy.

Col. John Bowman used this route in 1779, and again in 1780, to lead his pioneers to punish the Shawnee Indians north of the Ohio River for their interference with Kentucky settlers. In 1788 John Filson and two partners surveyed the Dry Ridge Trace on their way to the north side of the Ohio River, where they were going to develop a settlement for settlers who would move from Lexington. Originally called Losantiville, the settlement was later named Cincinnati. In 1790, when the area was a part of Woodford Co., Va., the county court adopted the Filson Survey of the Dry Ridge Trace, describing the path as "a tolerable good wagon road." As county formations took place in Kentucky, each succeeding county, Scott in 1792, Campbell in 1794, and Pendleton in 1798, adopted the road as a county road. These counties required landowners to maintain the portion of the road abutting their property; however, this requirement was not always enforced for absentee owners with large tracts of unsettled land.

In 1819 the Kentucky legislature made the Dry Ridge Trace a state turnpike, leading from Georgetown north, and established a commission to maintain the road with toll collections from tollgates (see **Covington and Lexington Turnpike**). After the **Civil War**, the Kentucky and Tennessee, legislatures chartered the **Cincinnati Southern Railroad** (now **Norfolk Southern**), granting it the power to acquire the necessary rights-of-way through both states. In the open country between built-up communities, the crest of the dry ridge from Erlanger to Georgetown was taken by the railroad for its tracks; with no streams to cross, the railroad had no bridges to build. The turnpike was rebuilt alongside the tracks and is now identified as the **Dixie Highway** (U.S. 25).

Conrad, John B., ed. *History of Grant County.* Williamstown, Ky.: Grant Co. Historical Society, 1992.
Jillson, Willard Rouse. *Pioneer Kentucky.* Frankfort, Ky.: State Journal, 1934.
"Your Town—Dry Ridge, Ancient Buffalo Trace Rides Crest of Kentucky Progress," *KTS,* March 5, 1957, 15.

John B. Conrad

DUEBER WATCH CASE COMPANY. In about 1863, in association with Francis Doll, John C. Dueber established an office and workshop to make watches in one room on the third floor of the Carlisle Building in Cincinnati. A year later, Dueber struck out on his own and established the Dueber Watch Case Company, utilizing various locations in Cincinnati and Newport. Around 1874, he moved the company into a new building at Washington and Jefferson (now Sixth St.) in Newport. He hired the best artisans available and began the manufacture of high-quality watchcases. To this day, Dueber watchcases rival those made anywhere else in the world, commanding prices in the hundreds or thousands of dollars. The firm's early cases were made of solid gold or coin-quality silver, but later gold-filled and -plated cases were also made. The company sold its product to many large companies, including Waltham and Elgin. Dueber soon became one of the largest manufacturers of watchcases in the United States. By 1880 its business had increased enough that it built a second factory, one block north, at Washington and Madison (now Fifth) Sts. A tunnel was dug under Sixth St., connecting the two buildings. One of Dueber's customers was the Mozart Watch Company of Providence, R.I., which also had begun business in 1864. Over the years, Mozart had several name changes and was eventually known as the Hampden Watch Company and was located in Springfield, Mass. About that time, the American Watch Trust was formed by some competing watchmakers, which led to a boycott of Dueber-made cases. To protect his company's interest, John Dueber purchased controlling interest in the Hampden Company in 1886. He named his new company the Dueber-Hampden Watch Company and began to manufacture complete watches. He found that operating two widely separated plants was impractical, so he built two new buildings on a site in Canton, Ohio, and closed the other factories, including the two in Newport.

The company's success was at its pinnacle about the time of John C. Dueber's death, in 1907. Dueber-Hampden had about 3,000 employees at that time. John's son Albert took over as president of the company and tried to continue his father's business practices. However, business conditions were changing and watch sales fell so much that the company was no longer profitable. In September 1925 Albert sold his interest in the company to a group of Cleveland businessmen for $1,551,000. The new owners had no experience in watchmaking, which led to further deterioration in sales, and eventually the company was forced into receivership. The Dueber-Hampden Watch Company ceased operations in 1930 and the following year sold its equipment to Armand Hammer, the well-known head of Occidental Petroleum Corp., who sent the equipment to Moscow, Russia. The company there was called the Amtorg Watch Company and became Russia's first watchmaker. That company later ceased operations, and the equipment was sold to a Swiss watchmaker.

Gibbs, James. W. *The Dueber-Hampden Story.* Philadelphia: National Association of Watch Case Companies, 1954.
Oldwatch.com. "Hampden Pocket Watches." www.oldwatch.com (accessed April 3, 2007).
The Watch Guy. "Hampden Watch Co. aka Dueber Watch Co." www.thewatchguy.homestead.com (accessed April 3, 2007).

DUELS. The two most famous duels that took place in Northern Kentucky were between future governor **William Goebel** (1890) and John L. Sandford in April 1895 in Covington and between Leonidas Metcalfe and William Casto in Maysville in May 1862, when Metcalfe killed Casto (see **Casto-Metcalfe Duel**). Some well-known duels involving Kentuckians from other parts of the state pitted future U.S. President Andrew Jackson (1829–1837) against Charles Dickinson in 1806, Henry Clay against political antagonist Humphrey Marshall in 1809, and aggrieved newspaperman George Trotter against Charles Wickliffe in 1829.

Kentuckians inherited the practice of dueling from their European forebears. In this elite societal ritual, only wealthy and middle-class gentlemen engaged in formal duels, and men challenged only other men of the same social rank. If a gentleman was insulted by a man of lower rank, the gentlemen would cane or beat the offending person. Among peers, a prescribed ritual guided the behavior of both the accuser and the aggrieved. It began when an accuser insulted the honor of another. Insults could take a variety of forms, but they were often derogatory statements regarding a man's character or that of his family. The aggrieved party returned the insult with a challenge, thereby questioning the honor of the accuser and necessitating that the honor of both principals be defended. The accuser established the place of the duel, the date and time, the distance, and the instruments (often pistols) to be used. Word of mouth or public notice then made the community aware of the impending event. Men called "seconds" were on hand to guarantee that neither principal violated the established rules. After firing, the men—dead or alive—were viewed as having restored or confirmed their honor, and the issue was resolved.

The ritual of dueling revolved around complex systems of honor. Although men typically described honor as a personal attribute, it was more accurately defined as a community consensus about a man's social status, based upon a set of ethical rules. Thus, the community, not the individual, determined honor. As a standard by which men judged other men, honor was considered important both on a personal level and in business relationships. For slave owners, honor and mastery were seen also as important tools needed to control their slaves. The duel sought to mollify tensions through a ritualistic bloodletting designed to purify the social status of both the accuser and the aggrieved party by demonstrating their courage and manhood in the face of fire.

By the beginning of the 19th century, several forces in Kentucky chafed against the ideals that had bolstered the tradition of dueling. Geographic and social mobility destabilized communities and disrupted clear class hierarchies. Important opposition came from religious leaders, as well as from members of the middle class who viewed dueling, death, and injury as threatening to business partnerships and contracts. Businessmen found an alternate arena in which to restore besmirched honor—the courtroom. Lawyers, not arms and bullets, became the preferred tool to fight slander and libel, a choice reflected in the law. In 1799 the Kentucky legislature prohibited dueling and established substantial fines for each offense. Later, it added jail terms to the list of punishments. By 1811 Kentucky law mandated that government officeholders take a nondueling oath. Finally, lawmakers added a provision to the 1849 state constitution that forbade anyone who participated in a duel to hold public office. By the last third of the 19th century, dueling had become anachronistic.

Coleman, J. Winston, Jr. *Famous Kentucky Duels.* Lexington, Ky.: Henry Clay Press, 1969.

"Tragedy, John L. Sandford, Director and Cashier, Killed by Senator Goebel," *KP,* April 11, 1895, 3.

Williams, Jack K. *Dueling in the Old South: Vignettes of Social History.* College Station: Texas A&M Univ. Press, 1980.

Wyatt-Brown, Bertram. *Southern Honor: Ethics and Behavior in the Old South.* Oxford: Oxford Univ. Press, 1982.

William H. Bergmann

DUKE, BASIL (b. 1766, Calvert Co., Md.; d. June 11, 1828, Washington, Ky.). Born to James and Mary Wilson Duke, Dr. Basil Duke studied medicine in Baltimore, Md. After briefly practicing medicine in his home state, he moved to Kentucky in 1791, locating initially in Lexington. In 1794 he married Charlotte Marshall, daughter of **Revolutionary War** veteran Col. **Thomas Marshall** and sister of U.S. Supreme Court chief justice John Marshall. The couple settled in Washington, Ky., in 1798, where Duke again established a medical practice and served residents of Mason Co. as well as surrounding areas. The two-story brick structure that once served as the Duke family residence still stands along Green St. in historic Washington, although it is now abandoned and dilapidated. Remembered as being one of Mason Co.'s pioneer doctors, Duke died in 1828; his burial place is unknown.

"Basil Duke House May Be Demolished: Building Was Once a Schoolhouse," *KP,* February 8, 2003, 7K.

Best, Edna Hunter. *The Historic Past of Washington, Mason County, Kentucky.* Cynthiana, Ky.: Hobson Book Press, 1944.

Collins, Richard H. *History of Kentucky.* Vol. 1. Covington, Ky.: Collins, 1882.

Judy L. Neff

DUKE ENERGY. In April 2006 Charlotte, N.C.–based Duke Energy, which now serves Northern Kentucky, merged with CINergy Inc. in a $9 billion deal, in which the Duke name was retained. This merger created a mega power-generation organization with 5.4 million customers, including 3.7 million electric consumers and 1.7 million gas users—one of the nation's largest utilities. Duke Energy has $27 billion in annual revenues, with 54,000 megawatts of electric generation capacity both domestically and internationally. CINergy was formed by the 1994 merger of the 157-year-old Cincinnati Gas and Electric Company (CG&E) with PSI Resources of Plainfield, Ind., in a $3.3 billion transaction.

Since 1945 Northern Kentucky's Union Light, Heat & Power Company (ULH&P) had been a wholly owned subsidiary of CG&E, serving some 145,000 residential customers in five counties: Boone, Campbell, Kenton, Grant, and Pendleton. For state-regulatory reasons, CG&E in Northern Kentucky was conducted as a separate corporation. Before 1945, the Columbia Gas System, the same holding company that held CG&E until September 1946, also owned ULH&P. Columbia had purchased ULH&P in 1907, operating CG&E and ULH&P as affiliated but separate entities until October 1945, when ULH&P became a subsidiary of CG&E. The Columbia group also owned the Cincinnati, Newport, and Covington Railway (the **Green Line**) from February 1907 until October 1944. A 1935 federal law required that gas and electric energy producers such as Columbia divest themselves of nonrelated business subsidiaries. It was Columbia that had brought the first natural gas transmission lines to Northern Kentucky and Cincinnati from the West Virginia gas fields via a 183-mile, 20-inch pipeline into and through Covington in 1909, replacing the locally produced artificial gas diffused from coal.

By 1902 the six or so gas and electric companies in Northern Kentucky had consolidated into the ULH&P organization. Two of the last survivors were the Suburban Electric Company and the old Covington Gas Light Company. Covington native **James C. Ernst** was the company's president and served in that capacity until his retirement in 1914. Another Northern Kentuckian who later was heavily involved in both ULH&P and the Green Line was **Polk Laffoon**.

Beckjord, Walter C. *The Queen City of the West—during 110 Years.* New York: Newcomen Society, 1951.

Cincinnati Gas & Electric Company. *The CG&E Story.* Cincinnati: Cincinnati Gas & Electric, 1959.

"Cinergy, Duke Merger Gets OK," *KP,* November 30, 2005, 3K.

"Columbia Corporation Closes Deal," *KP,* February 5, 1907, 1.

Dawson, Albert F. *Columbia System: A History.* New York: J. J. Little and Ives, 1937.

"Light Company Organized," *KP,* April 30, 1901, 1.

"Utility Seeks Control of ULH&P," *KP,* March 16, 1994, 8A.

DURBIN, JOHN PRICE (b. October 10, 1800, Bourbon Co., Ky.; d. October 18, 1876, New York City). John P. Durbin was an accomplished cabinetmaker when at age 18 he experienced a religious conversion and decided to become a minister. In 1821 he began preaching in Hamilton, Ohio, and also attending nearby Miami University at Oxford. Later, he resumed his studies at Cincinnati College, where he was awarded both a bachelor's and a master's degree in 1825. From 1825 to 1831, he was a professor of languages at **Augusta College** in Bracken Co., when that school was a flourishing center of learning. In 1831 he was named chaplain of the U.S. Senate. From 1833 to 1844 he was the president of Dickinson College in Pennsylvania, and after that he traveled abroad. He was a preacher and an author. His two most famous travel works are *Observations in Europe, Principally in France and Great Britain* (1844) and *Observations in the East, Chiefly in Egypt, Palestine, Syria, and Asia Minor* (1845). In 1849 he moved to Philadelphia, where he preached and was elected secretary of the Methodist Episcopal Church's Missionary Society, a position he held until 1872. In 1876 Durbin died in New York City and was buried in Philadelphia.

Chronicles. http://chronicles.dickinson.edu (accessed March 31, 2007).

Rankins, Walter H. *Augusta College.* Frankfort, Ky.: Roberts, 1955.

DURO BAG MANUFACTURING COMPANY. S. David Shor started the Duro Bag Manufacturing Company in 1953 in Ludlow. At this first location, it manufactured only paper grocery and shopping bags. During the 1970s the company expanded by opening new plants in Florida, Texas, Wisconsin, and Mexico. The company's Ludlow warehouse caught fire on May 28, 1977, the night of the horrific **Beverly Hills Supper Club** fire. The warehouse was rebuilt and full operations resumed. Duro added a plastic bag and designer division in the 1980s, and it acquired the S&G Packaging Company, which increased sales and allowed product line expansions. The Duro Bag Manufacturing Company now has 12 plants and employs more than 2,500 persons. Duro products are sold directly to customers or through distributors and brokers. The company, which remains privately held and family-owned and -operated, is now the largest bag manufacturer in North America. It operates plants at three Northern Kentucky locations, Covington, Florence, and Richwood. The corporate offices are in Ludlow. The current president and CEO of the Duro Bag Manufacturing Company is Charles Shor.

"Duro Bag Acquires Richmond Paper Plant," *KP,* January 24, 1995, 3K.

Duro Bag Mfg. Co. www.durobag.com (accessed April 3, 2007).

"Duro Bag Unit Plans Merger," *KE*, May 23, 1997, 12C.
"Duro Bag Warehouse Burns," *KP*, May 30, 1977, 15.

DURR, R. C. (b. May 14, 1919, Atwood, Ky.; d. May 21, 2007, Edgewood, Ky.). Construction entrepreneur and philanthropist Robert Charles Durr was the second son born to Steve and Carrie L. Stevens Durr. Durr was a member of the last graduating class of **Independence High School** at Independence in 1939; but instead of enrolling in college, he bought a car with the $500 his aunt gave him for college tuition and went to work at **Newport Steel** in Newport, making 50 cents an hour. Over the years, he ran a general store with his brother, drove a supply truck for $12 a week, served in the U.S. Army, sharpened tools at Wright Aeronautical, and worked at General Motors. In 1941 Durr met Katherine Ballinger at a skating rink in Falmouth, Ky., and they married in 1946. Having borrowed money in 1945 to buy three trucks, Durr hauled limestone to farmers and blacktopped driveways until 1949, when he became the successful bidder to build Frogtown Rd. in Boone Co., his first highway project. In 1950 Durr formed the R. C. Durr Company, which focused on grading and draining roads, mining coal, and building railroads. He successfully operated a coal mine for 10 years, and his company built more than 300 miles of road, including large portions of I-75. Durr's firm was awarded the initial contract for a segment of the Eastern Kentucky Turnpike (Mountain Pkwy.) in 1961. He built one of the first modern gravel pits in Northern Kentucky. In 1964 he acquired Eaton Asphalt and established it as Northern Kentucky's largest paving company. He was president of the Kentucky Association of Highway Contractors, the Kentucky Chapter of the American Road Builders Association, and the Kentucky Highway Division of the Associated General Contractors of America. He served on the board of the Boone Co. Water and Sewer District and the **Northern Kentucky University** Foundation. He also founded the **Northern Kentucky Industrial Foundation** in Florence.

Durr's interest in horses became a business interest by 1970; he bought, sold, and raced thoroughbreds. He served on the Kentucky State Racing Commission from 1980 to 1992. The R. C. Durr Company ceased construction operations in 1987, leaving Durr to pursue his interest in banking. He was a founder of Boone State Bank in Florence, which later was sold and became **Fifth Third Bank**. In 1990 Durr helped establish the Bank of Boone County, now the **Bank of Kentucky**, and he served on its board of directors. He also served on the local boards of the Covington Trust and Banking Company and Fifth Third Bank. After his wife Katherine died in 1992, Durr created the R. C. Durr Foundation. His generosity extended to small charities and nonprofit organizations. Self-effacing and modest, Durr shunned recognition, allowing only the YMCA on Burlington Pike in Boone Co., to be named for him. In 2003 he was inducted into the Kentucky Transportation Hall of Fame as one of the construction industry's visionaries. Durr married his second wife, Deborah Jo, in September 2002, and they lived on a 193-acre farm in Richwood, raising cattle and thoroughbred horses. R. C. Durr died in 2007 of complications related to cancer and was buried in Independence Cemetery.

Kreimer, Peggy. "Durr's Generosity Shaped the Region," *KP*, May 23, 2007, 1A.
"Millionaire Counts Blessing, Not Money," *CE*, August 10, 2003, B1.
"NKU Foundation Salutes Durr's Generosity," *KP*, November 8, 1991, 8A.
Univ. of Kentucky College of Engineering. "A Tribute to R.C. Durr." www.ktc.uky.edu (accessed March 27, 2006).

Gabrielle Summe

DUVENECK, FRANK (b. Francis Decker, October 9, 1848, Covington, Ky.; d. January 3, 1919, Cincinnati, Ohio). The renowned artist, sculptor, and teacher Frank Duveneck (Francis Decker) was born into the German Catholic working-class family of Bernard and Catherine Siemers Decker. Both the Decker and the Siemers families were originally from Damme, a small town near Oldenburg, Westphalia, Germany. According to family accounts, Frank's father died during the cholera epidemic of 1849. On February 27, 1851, Catherine Decker married Joseph Duveneck at St. John the Baptist Catholic Church on Green St. in Cincinnati. Joseph Duveneck, an 1847 immigrant from Germany, was a grocer and a justice of the peace in Cincinnati. After the marriage, the family moved to Covington, where Joseph operated a beer garden at 13th and Greenup Sts. (see **Duveneck House**). As a young boy, Frank earned money by running a sign-painting business. The Duvenecks attended **St. Joseph Catholic Church** in Covington, and the Benedictine brothers there encouraged Frank to become a serious painter and sculptor. By his teenage years, he was apprenticed at the **Covington Altar Stock Building Company** to **Johann Schmitt** and **Wilhelm Lamprecht**, German painters who were creating murals in Catholic churches throughout the northeastern United States. Early works by Duveneck include 14 paintings of *Stations of the Cross* for St. Joseph Catholic Church, Covington, Ky. (1866–1867), a few of which survive in private hands; *Madonna and Child* (1867), in the possession of the **Sisters of St. Benedict**, Villa Hills; and 2 paintings of angels (ca. 1868) at Holy Trinity Catholic Church, W. Fifth St., Cincinnati (demolished in 1953).

With financial help from his stepfather and the encouragement of the Benedictines, Frank sailed for Germany in 1869, to study art under Wilhelm Von Diez at the Royal Academy of Munich. German critics quickly recognized his exceptional artistic ability, and he was presented with several awards. In 1872, while still in Munich, Duveneck painted what many consider his finest picture, which he called *Whistling Boy* (now in the collection of the Cincinnati Art Museum). When an outbreak of cholera hit Germany in 1873, Duveneck returned to Covington. The following year, he began teaching art at the Ohio Mechanics Institute in Cincinnati, where his pupils were often referred to as "Duveneck's Boys." He also opened a studio in

Frank Duveneck.

Covington on Greenup St., where he painted portraits. Duveneck portraits often featured a strongly modeled face or figure emerging from a dark, shadowy background. During that period in Covington, he developed a close friendship with artist **Henry Farny** and sculptor **Clement Barnhorn**.

Duveneck missed the thrill and excitement of the European artist community, so he returned there in 1875, accompanied by Frank X. Dengler, Farny, and John H. Twachtman. Many of his paintings at that time were of the elderly, the working poor, and street urchins. After short stays in Paris and Venice, Duveneck returned to Munich and began to teach young aspiring artists. One of his students was Elizabeth Boott, the daughter of a socially prominent Boston, Mass., family. Elizabeth spoke fluent Italian and French, was an accomplished pianist, and was also a promising artist who had studied under Greek-born historic painter Giorgio Mignaty. A romance soon developed between Frank and Elizabeth, and they announced their engagement in December 1880. However, her father was not pleased with her choice of a future husband, a man from the working class who had little formal education. Tensions soon arose over money, manners, and class and eventually led to cancellation of the engagement. After several years of separation, however, the romance was rekindled, and Frank and Elizabeth were married in Paris on March 25, 1886. A magistrate performed the ceremony in the apartment of the bride's widowed father, and the impoverished groom borrowed the $200 needed to cover wedding expenses. During the ceremony, Elizabeth wore a brown dress, the same one she is seen wearing in a portrait of her that hangs today in the Cincinnati Art Museum. Their only child, Francis Boott Duveneck, was born about a year after the marriage. When the child was about one year old,

41-year-old Elizabeth died of pneumonia in 1888 and was buried in the Cemetery of the Laurels, in Florence, Italy.

Duveneck was devastated by his wife's death and returned to Covington. There, he renewed his acquaintance with friends and relatives and began teaching at the Cincinnati Art Academy. His old friend Clement Barnhorn encouraged Duveneck to create a sculpture in memory of his beloved wife, so Duveneck made a bronze monument of a prostrate Elizabeth. Francis Boott was so impressed with his daughter's memorial that he asked his son-in-law to create a marble copy. When completed, it was placed in the Boston Museum of Fine Arts, where her son, Francis Boott Duveneck, could easily visit and see it. According to the terms of a prenuptial agreement that Elizabeth's father had required Duveneck to sign, her half brother and his wife raised young Francis in their home at Waltham, Mass. Duveneck began spending his summers with the art colony at Gloucester, Mass., so he could be near his son. Francis Boott Duveneck's first visit to his father's home in Covington occurred after he had become an adult.

Duveneck received a gold medal for his portraits and paintings at the Panama-Pacific Exposition in San Francisco in 1915. In later life, painting became less important to Duveneck, and he concentrated on teaching his art to young people at the Cincinnati Art Academy. Three of his local students who gained national fame were Farny, **Dixie Selden**, and John Henry Twachtman. In 1967 **Vance Trimble**, editor of the *Kentucky Post* in Northern Kentucky, headed a drive to raise funds to buy some of Duveneck's paintings. Sufficient money was collected to purchase 4, and Duveneck descendants donated 6 others; all 10 are on display at the **Kenton Co. Public Library** in Covington. Other Duveneck paintings can be seen at the Cincinnati Art Museum and at various museums and galleries around the world. In 1919 Frank Duveneck died of cancer at age 71 in Cincinnati's Good Samaritan Hospital and was buried in Covington's Mother of God Cemetery.

"Duveneck Masterpeices. Famous Paintings to Perish When Historic Church Razed," *CTS*, June 23, 1953, 9.

Frank Duveneck Collection, microfilm, Kenton Co. Public Library, Covington, Ky.

Herbert, Jeffrey G. *Restored Hamilton County, Ohio Marriages, 1850–1859.* Cincinnati: Hamilton Co. Chapter, Ohio Genealogical Society, 1998.

Kleber, John E., ed. *The Kentucky Encyclopedia.* Lexington: Univ. Press of Kentucky, 1992.

Mother of God Catholic Church, sacramental records for 1848, microfilm, Kenton Co. Public Library, Covington, Ky.

Neuhaus, Robert. *Unsuspected Genius: The Art and Life of Frank Duveneck.* San Francisco: Bedford Press, 1987.

Reis, Jim. "From Sign Painter to Portrait Artist," *KP*, November 18, 1992, 4K.

Traditional Fine Arts Organization. "Frank Duveneck and Elizabeth Boott Duveneck: An American Romance." www.tfaoi.com (accessed November 30, 2006).

Jack Wessling

DUVENECK HOUSE. The Frank Duveneck House & Studio, located at 1232 Greenup St. in Covington, was built by Joseph Duveneck (1823–1883) about 1861. In 1851 Duveneck married the widowed Catherine Siemers Decker (1831–1905) and adopted her young son, **Frank Duveneck** (b. Frank Decker [1848–1919]). Joseph Duveneck purchased the 89-by-85-foot property at the southeast corner of 13th and Greenup Sts. in three separate transactions. The first two parcels were purchased in 1855 from Mary Behne of Cincinnati, and the third was purchased in 1858 from the Fairmont Theological Seminary, successor to one-half of the **Western Baptist Theological Institute**'s holdings. Even though by that time the family had grown to five children, the original house was probably a three room, one-story structure. The front room retains evidence of the original rounded Italianate wood trim, suggesting the room's importance; the remainder of the first floor has plain, flat wood trim.

By the time Frank Duveneck left to study art in Munich, Germany, in 1869, Joseph Duveneck was operating a beer garden on the premises. This venture may be what prompted the addition of two rooms on the first floor and of a three-room second floor, accessed by an exterior stair, to provide the family with separate living quarters; even with Frank gone, seven children remained. The Italianate front facade, with its distinctive ashlar-cut wood siding, was probably installed at the same time.

The beer garden continued in operation only until Joseph Duveneck's death in 1883; in 1885 his widow sold a 22-foot parcel on the corner, where a building was soon built enclosing the family garden. Between 1870 and 1900, Frank Duveneck often returned to the house, sometimes remaining for extended periods. In 1899 Catherine Duveneck purchased a 25-by-89-foot parcel east of the property, perhaps at the request of Frank, who had just accepted a permanent teaching position at the Cincinnati Art Academy, to begin in 1900. A one-story board-and-batten addition containing a modern bathroom and an art studio with a skylight was soon built at the rear of the house.

Frank Duveneck lived in the house until his death in January 1919. During that time he was apparently responsible for other changes to the home, including the installation of electricity and of gas heating stoves. After his death, his family sold the property. The house was eventually converted into a two-family dwelling, and by 1924 a hardware store was built on the south part of the property.

In the mid-1960s, an effort was launched to restore the house and studio; although unsuccessful, that campaign resulted in the formation of the **Northern Kentucky Heritage League** and the creation of the Duveneck Gallery at the **Kenton Co. Public Library**. Instead, the building was converted into a frame shop in 1967. At that time several major modifications to both the interior and the exterior were made.

In 2000 **Forward Quest**, an area planning and development organization based in Covington, purchased the property, including the former hardware store. With the aid of a Kentucky Heritage Council grant, the exterior restoration of the house and the studio was completed in 2002. This restoration substantially restored the exterior siding, the windows, the shutters, and the doors. Based on professional analysis, the house and the studio were painted in the colors chosen by Frank Duveneck when he first built the studio in 1900. In 2006 a Kentucky Preservation Grant was awarded to the Frank Duveneck Arts & Cultural Center to pursue the making of architectural drawings in preparation for the property's further restoration.

Bricking, Chuck. *Covington's Heritage: A Compilation of the City's Historical Houses and a Short Biography of the Inhabitants.* Covington, Ky.: Privately published, 1980.

Covington City Directory, numerous years.

Deed books, Kenton Co. Courthouses, Covington and Independence, Ky.

Duveneck, Joseph W. *Frank Duveneck: Painter-Teacher.* San Francisco: John Howell Books, 1970.

Hopkins, G. M. *City Atlas of Covington, Kentucky.* Philadelphia: G. M. Hopkins, 1877.

Inventory books, Kenton Co. Courthouse, Covington, Ky.

Sanborn Fire Insurance Company. *Map of Covington, Kentucky.* New York: Chadwick-Healey, various years.

Thomason, Philip. *Covington, Kentucky Eastside Multiple Resource Area National Register Nomination.* Nashville, Tenn.: Thomason, 1986.

Will Book 14, Kenton Co. Courthouse, Covington, Ky., pp. 103–4.

Alexandra K. Weldon

EAGLE BANK. Grant Co.'s first bank originated April 6, 1880, when it was chartered by the Kentucky legislature. The bank, initially named the Bank of Williamstown, opened its doors for business on July 6, 1880, with capital of $50,000. The incorporators were T. L. Clark, W. G. Frank, Tim Needham, E. H. Smith, and John H. Webb.

The main office of the Bank of Williamstown was on Main St. in Williamstown; however, over the years the bank has been housed in four separate buildings. After banks were given permission to establish countywide branches, additional branch banks were constructed in Corinth, Crittenden, Dry Ridge, and Williamstown. These branch locations continue a pattern of progressive participation by Eagle Bank in Grant Co.'s significant growth during the past two decades.

Throughout 126 years, only seven presidents have headed the bank. The first president was E. H. Smith, and he was followed by A. G. DeJarnette, James W. Webb, James L. Webb, Kenneth M. Juett, William C. Wilson, and Dennis W. Rich, the current president. With capital now in excess of $20 million and total assets exceeding $150 million, the bank is a conservative, progressive, well-capitalized, locally owned financial institution meeting the needs of the community. The fact that the bank has paid dividends to its shareholders continuously since 1884 indicates the soundness of the bank.

The bank's name was changed from the Bank of Williamstown to Eagle Bank in 1994, after a bank holding company, Eagle Fidelity Inc., was incorporated on January 4, 1988, to become Eagle Bank's sole stockholder. All the owners of the stock of the original bank became owners of stock in the holding company, with the same management of the newly formed organization. The name change reflects the bank's declaration that, through its various branch locations, it serves all of Grant Co. and the adjacent counties, not just the citizens of Williamstown.

Eagle Bank is overseen by a board of directors. Current board members are James J. Hale, Kenneth M. Juett, Dennis W. Rich, William K. Rich, William M. Stanley, William F. Threlkeld, William C. Wilson, and Rick W. Wood.

Conrad, John B., ed. *History of Grant County.* Williamstown, Ky.: Grant Co. Historical Society, 1992.
Williamstown Courier, May 30, 1901.

William Michael Stanley

EAGLE HILL. Located in the northeastern corner of Owen Co., near Eagle Creek and in Poplar Grove Precinct, the hamlet of Eagle Hill was home to one of the county's one-room schools. Eagle Hill is four miles from Glencoe in Gallatin Co. and four miles from Poplar Grove. The very active Pleasant Home Baptist Church is in Eagle Hill, and for many years there was only one occupied home in the immediate area. Lonnie Poland, who lived nearby, used to drive the mail from Glencoe to Jonesville in Owen Co. and on to Folsom in Grant Co., and even sometimes to Napoleon in Gallatin Co. Poland was better known for his famous sorghum and molasses, which he made at home. He was only able to produce a few gallons each day, as it was a slow process. People came from miles around for his product.

An Atlas of Owen County, Kentucky. Philadelphia: Lake, 1883.
Houchens, Mariam Sidebottom. *History of Owen County: "Sweet Owen."* Louisville, Ky.: Standard, 1976.

EAGLE PLOW WORKS. The city of Maysville had several companies that manufactured farm equipment; however, none of these were as successful as the company known as the Eagle Plow Works. This company was formed in January 1878, under the name of the James H. Hall Plow Works Inc., but it was commonly called the Eagle Plow Works. The principals of the firm were James H. Hall Sr., James H. Hall Jr., John H. Hall, Samuel Hall, and Robert F. Means. The firm's large brick factory building was located in Maysville on the south side of E. Second St., between Lexington and Walnut Sts. The company manufactured a number of different lines of plows, marketed as the Limestone, the Star, the Champion, the Copper, the Cotton, and the Lone Star; the first two types were the most successful. The plows sold extremely well in the southern United States and in Central and South America.

Calvert, Jean. *Maysville Kentucky—From Past to Present in Pictures.* Maysville, Ky.: Mason Co. Museum, 1983.

EAGLES. See **Civic Associations**.

EAGLE STATION. See **Jordan Baptist Church**.

EAGLE TAVERN. This structure in Maysville, built around 1800, was both a tavern and a hotel and was later known as the Goddard House. One of the earliest hotels in the city, it was located on the southeast corner of Market and Front Sts., opposite the city's steamboat landing. It was operated for many years by Col. Maurice Langhorne and his son John T. Langhorne, who died during the cholera epidemic of 1833. In 1825 the hotel was host to a dinner for Gen. Marquis de Lafayette and his son. It was also a frequent stopping point for Henry Clay. In the late 1830s, Judith Goddard, the former operator of Maysville's Washington Hotel, purchased the Eagle Tavern and renamed it the Goddard House. During the **flood of 1937**, the old hotel collapsed.

Calvert, Jean, and John Klee. *Maysville Kentucky—From Past to Present in Pictures.* Maysville, Ky.: Mason Co. Museum, 1983.
Clift, G. Glenn. *History of Maysville and Mason County.* Lexington, Ky.: Transylvania, 1936.
"Eagle Tavern," *Western Globe*, August 16, 1839, 4.
"The Goddard House, Maysville," *Weekly Kentucky Flag*, October 27, 1852, 3.
Kentucky Gateway Museum Center, vertical files, Maysville, Ky.

EARLE, JAMES T. (b. August 27, 1868, Berry, Ky.; d. April 3, 1943, Cincinnati, Ohio). James Thomas Earle, a banker and the mayor of Latonia, was the 6th of 13 children born to Jonathan R. and Araminta King Earle. By age 15, he was working as a railroad telegraph operator in Falmouth. A quick learner, Earle soon became both an agent and an operator at Falmouth and Berry, for the old **Kentucky Central Railroad** (now **CSX**). In 1885, armed with high recommendations from several rail executives, Earle moved to Texas and worked in various positions for the railroad in Galveston. By 1889 he had been promoted to secretary to the receiver of the International and Great Northern Railroad at Palestine, Tex. In August 1889 he married his childhood sweetheart, Katherine "Katie" Good. J. T. and Katie Earle settled in Covington in 1890, so that Katie could be closer to her family and J. T. could accept a better opportunity as secretary to the joint agent of the Big Four and **Chesapeake and Ohio** (C&O) railroads. Earle became freight agent for the C&O Railroad at Cincinnati and served in that position for 53 years, through several railroad mergers and dissolutions, until his retirement.

In 1897 the family purchased property and built a spacious home in a newly developing section of Milldale known as Dinmore Park. A small portion of Milldale had been incorporated in 1884 as a sixth-class city, South Covington. Latonia became the town's vernacular name. J. T. Earle quickly became involved in the town's politics and business, becoming president of both the Latonia Board of Education and the Latonia Commercial Club. A lifelong Republican, he was appointed by the governor of Kentucky in 1901 to the Kenton Co. Election Commission, representing the Republican Party.

Earle's friendships with wealthy and influential Northern Kentuckians enabled him to become a partner in the establishment of the First National Bank of Latonia, where he became president in 1902. He supervised the building of the bank's new headquarters in 1903, at Ritte's Corner in Latonia. The second floor served as the town hall and post office, and Earle also served as the unpaid postmaster of the growing community.

In 1905 Earle was elected mayor of Latonia, and by February 1906 he was embroiled in an annexation fight with the **Latonia Racecourse**. Even though half of the track was brought into the city limits, no city fees or taxes appear to have been levied on the track. Earle was a holder of temperance and antigambling convictions, which brought him into several conflicts with the racetrack and saloon interests in the town. His attempts to enforce local blue (morality) laws prompted heated arguments in council chambers.

Latonia's indebtedness for its infrastructure caused a financial crisis of sorts among the city fathers. Seeing that the small town could not provide the street improvements and other services demanded by the growing number of residents, the council petitioned for annexation to Covington in return for the assumption of Latonia's public debt. After much negotiation, Latonia was annexed into the City of Covington officially on July 22, 1909. Earle ran unsuccessfully for county commissioner after his Latonia mayor's job was eliminated through the annexation.

Meanwhile, Earle's bank was prospering, showing nothing but secure growth through the years until 1914, when a surprise visit from a federal bank examiner ordered it closed because of loan irregularities. The examiner felt that the bank's officers themselves were borrowing too much of the bank's assets. The bank was closed for about a month while it was reorganized. When it reopened in June 1914, only three of the former officers remained, and Earle was not among them. Earle may have borrowed excessively from his bank to finance his real estate development in Latonia. In 1914 he had begun building homes in Latonia; however, with the start of **World War I**, it was virtually impossible to obtain carpenters to finish the homes under construction. Earle's financial situation became quite tenuous, and in February 1918 he declared bankruptcy. The Earles sold their elegant home in Latonia and moved to Linwood Rd. in Cincinnati. J. T. Earle died there in 1943, two days after retiring as a Chesapeake and Ohio Railroad freight agent, and was buried in Highland Cemetery in Fort Mitchell.

Claypool, James C. *The Tradition Continues: The Story of Old Latonia, Latonia, and Turfway Racecourses.* Fort Mitchell, Ky.: T. I. Hayes, 1997.

"Earle, James T." *KP*, April 5, 1943, 4.

Lietzenmayer, Karl J. "James T. Earle: The Last Mayor of Latonia, Kentucky," *NKH* 2, no. 1 (Fall–Winter 1994): 42–55.

Karl Lietzenmayer

EARTHQUAKES. Although Northern Kentucky is not located near any of the major faults separating the earth's surface into a dozen or so large, moving tectonic plates, it is subject to earthquakes. Unlike California, with its earthquake-active San Andreas Fault (where the Pacific and North American plates are sliding past each other), Northern Kentucky lies above one immense, strong and relatively stable continental plate, the North American plate. But major tectonic activity has occurred within the North American plate as recently as 60 to 90 million years ago, causing faults throughout the Midwest and the Southeast that occasionally rock the area with earthquakes today.

Faults in the bedrock of the North American plate are, relative to the very stable crust around them, areas of weakness. Many lie buried deep beneath the sediments of the Mississippi and Wabash River valleys; therefore, unlike the San Andreas Fault, they are generally not visible, or "expressed" at the ground surface. Their existence is basically known and mapped from the occurrence of earthquakes in these fault zones, from surface deformations caused by seismic activity, from oil and gas exploration, and from more recent geologic mapping efforts and methods. Also in contrast to the San Andreas Fault, the faulting regionally is not between plates but is contained deep within the North American plate itself; hence earthquakes here are called intraplate earthquakes.

The faults of the North American plate, themselves, are not completely responsible for earthquakes in the region. The earthquakes are also related to activity in the middle of the Atlantic Ocean, where the North American and Eurasian tectonic plates are diverging, that is, moving apart. In the process, the North American plate is slowly being compressed westward. This compression, coupled with the weaknesses of ancient faults, causes earthquakes that occasionally shake Northern Kentucky and the surrounding region. Earthquakes felt in Northern Kentucky usually result from fault movement within one of three zones: the New Madrid Seismic Zone, the Wabash Valley Seismic Zone, and the Cincinnati Arch.

The magnitude of earthquakes, a measure of energy they release, is calculated by the Richter Scale, developed by Charles F. Richter in 1935 for use in evaluating earthquake activity in specific fault zones in the state of California. The Richter Scale is logarithmic, meaning that each increase of one point on the scale represents an earthquake ten times greater. Hence, a 6.0 earthquake is 10 times greater than a 5.0 quake, and a 7.0 one is 10 times greater than a 6.0 (or 100 times greater than a 5.0). The intensity of earthquakes, however, including levels of damage, is measured by the Modified Mercalli Scale. Preferred by professional seismologists, the Mercalli Scale uses 12 levels designated by Roman numerals, with XII designating earthquakes that cause the greatest destruction.

Near where the states of Kentucky, Missouri, and Tennessee intersect along the Mississippi River is the New Madrid Seismic Zone (NMSZ), named for the historic town of New Madrid, Mo. The Reelfoot Scarp, a graben or subsided area, is the centerpiece of this seismic area; nearby is Reelfoot Lake in Tennessee (and partly in Kentucky). Deep ancient faults that crisscross the area have been the epicenters of some of its major earthquakes. More than 200 earthquakes occur in the NMSZ each year, but only about 10 are large enough to be felt (3.0 or more on the Richter Scale). Scientists estimate that an earthquake with a magnitude of 6.0 to 7.0 can be expected along the NMSZ about every 75 years; the last one of this magnitude occurred in 1895.

By 1811 New Madrid, Mo., a Mississippi River city founded in 1783, was the second-largest city in its state. Unknown to its residents, it lay atop the NMSZ. In the winter of 1811–1812, the zone was the center of what remains to this day the longest sequence of major earthquakes and aftershocks in the United States. Occurring before the Richter Scale was invented, the tectonic activity was nevertheless reported in detail by numerous eyewitnesses. On December 16, 1811, the first major earthquake occurred. It was felt throughout Northern Kentucky and Cincinnati and as far away as the eastern seaboard and Ontario, Canada. Dr. **Daniel Drake** of Cincinnati recorded the occurrence in his journal. Modern geologists estimate that this earthquake was probably in the range of 7.2 to 8.1 in magnitude, although numerous studies have not led to any consensus on this matter among scientists. Actually, the issue of magnitude, though important, pales by comparison to the sheer number of tremors in 1811–1812. Jared Brooks, a Louisville resident at the time, listed more than 600 quakes that occurred between December 26, 1811, and January 23, 1812, alone; over a three-month period, he listed a total of 1,874 distinct tremors. On the morning of January 23, 1812, the second major New Madrid earthquake struck, followed by more than 200 aftershocks in the weeks following. Then, on February 7, 1812, the most powerful of the New Madrid earthquakes hit. Drake observed in Cincinnati that the tremor "threw down the tops of more chimnies [*sic*], made wider fissures in the brick walls, and produced vertigo and nausea in a greater number of people, than the earthquakes of either the 16th of December or the 23rd of January." Eyewitness accounts and geologic evidence demonstrate that the New Madrid earthquakes and aftershocks of 1811–1812 were so powerful as to cause liquefaction. In other words, sandy soil underground was so severely shaken that it lost its solidity and turned to liquid. In these instances, the overlying ground can subside, partially explaining events like the expansion of Reelfoot Lake in Tennessee. In other cases, the sand, under great pressure, was violently expelled through the clay surface in "sand blows." Furthermore, at least 221 landslides occurred along the Mississippi River's bluffs. Recent work of paleoseismologists, based upon paleoliquefaction sites, suggests that earthquakes of similar intensity to those of 1811–1812 have occurred in the NMSZ in about A.D. 900 and in the period A.D. 1400–1500. A NMSZ earthquake, with its epicenter at Charleston, Mo., struck on October 31, 1895. The largest in that area since 1811–1812, it was estimated at 6.6 magnitude and an intensity of VIII. It shook 1 million square miles, causing damage to the Odd Fellows Hall in Ludlow and knocking down chimneys in Covington.

The Wabash Valley seismic zone is the second epicenter of earthquakes felt in Northern Kentucky. A 5.4 magnitude earthquake of intensity VII, with its epicenter near Dale, Ill., occurred on November 9, 1968, shaking 580,000 square miles, including Northern Kentucky. On June 10, 1987, a 5.1 earthquake, centered near Olney, Ill., struck the region, ringing a church bell at **Mother of God Catholic Church** in Covington and shaking the 150-foot-tall scaffolding within the church itself. On April 18, 2008, a 5.2 quake (epicenter near West Salem, Ill., with a 4.6 aftershock occurring later that day) awoke Northern Kentuckians as beds knocked against walls and windows rattled. The shaking was preceded by a rumbling noise.

The Cincinnati Arch, of which Northern and Central Kentucky are part, is the third center of tectonic activity in the region. Stretching from Tennessee into Ontario, this geologic arch began to form during the Ordovician Period of the Paleozoic Era, about 470 million years ago (see **Geology**). It was uplifted as a result of continental collisions and was named by geologists for Cincinnati, which lies at the crest of the fold. Significant Cincinnati Arch quakes with epicenters in Kentucky affected Northern Kentucky on February 20, 1869 (Lexington, estimated intensity III–IV); October 23, 1909 (Staffordsburg [Kenton Co.], estimated intensity III); and May 28, 1933 (near Maysville, intensity V). Other quakes, whose epicenters are not specifically known but which were felt intensely in Northern Kentucky, occurred in 1779 (Northern Kentucky); April or May 1791 or 1792 (Northern and Eastern Kentucky); and November 20, 1834 (Northern Kentucky, estimated intensity V). The 1834 quake lasted 30 to 40 seconds, cracked plaster, and roared like thunder.

The strongest historical earthquake ever to originate within Kentucky itself and the second-largest North American quake to occur east of the Continental Divide in a twenty-year period preceding its occurrence, was that of Sharpsburg, Ky., July 27, 1980. This 5.1–5.3-magnitude, intensity VII quake had its epicenter near Sharpsburg (Bath Co., part of the Cincinnati Arch) and struck along a previously unknown intraplate fault. It shook 15 states and Ontario, Canada, and caused damage in Kentucky, Ohio, and Indiana. The worst losses occurred in Maysville, about 31 miles from the epicenter; there more than 300 buildings were damaged. The quake was also felt in Cincinnati, where a stone ornament atop Cincinnati's City Hall crashed to the front steps below.

Cities of Ohio, especially Anna, Jackson Center, Lima, and Sidney, all part of the Cincinnati Arch, have been epicenters of many earthquakes felt in the Northern Kentucky region. Major ones have occurred on June 18, 1875 (Urbana-Sidney, estimated intensity VII); September 20, 1931 (Anna, estimated intensity VII); and March 2 and 8, 1937 (Anna, both intensity VII [the latter was felt throughout an area of 200,000 square miles]). Earthquakes of lesser intensity with epicenters in the Cincinnati Arch have included those of April 22, 1873 (Dayton, Ohio); June 1876 (Anna); August 29, 1881 (Hillsboro, Ohio); September 19, 1884 (Lima); December 23, 1884 (Anna); September 1889 (Anna); summer 1892 (Anna); March 15, 1896 (Sidney); March 26, 1925 (southwestern Ohio); April 4, 1925 (Cincinnati); October 1925 (Anna); March 8, 1929 (Bellefontaine, Ohio); June 26 and 27, 1930 (Sidney and Lima); July 10, 1930 (Marion, Ohio); September 20, 29, and 30, 1930 (Anna); October 1930 (Anna); March 21 and 31, 1931 (Sidney and Jackson Center); October 8, 1931 (Anna); February 22, 1933 (Sidney); October 8, 1936 (Cincinnati-Middletown); December 25, 1936 (Cincinnati); April 23 and 27, 1937 (Anna); May 2, 1937 (Anna); October 16, 1937 (Cincinnati); March 18, 1939 (Jackson Center); June 17, 1939 (Anna); July 9, 1939 (Anna); November 13, 1944 (Anna); January 27, 1956 (Anna, Sidney, and Lima); and July 23, 1957 (Ripley, Ohio).

Central United States Earthquake Consortium. www.cusec.org/ (accessed July 17, 2008).

Coffman, Jerry L., and Carl A. von Hake, eds. *Earthquake History of the United States.* Publication 41-1, rev. ed. Washington, D.C.: U.S. Department of Commerce, 1973.

Collins, Richard H. *History of Kentucky.* Covington, Ky.: Collins, 1882.

Docekal, Jerry. "Earthquakes of the Stable Interior, with Emphasis on the Midcontinent," PhD diss., Univ. of Nebraska, 1970.

"Earthquake Damages Homes in Maysville," *KE,* July 28, 1980, 1.

"5.2 Magnitude Quake Jolts Midwest, Shaking Buildings but Injuring Few," *NYT,* April 19, 2008, A10.

Hanson, Robert D., et al. *Reconnaissance Report: Northern Kentucky Earthquake, July 27, 1980.* Berkeley, Calif.: Earthquake Engineering Research Institute, September 1980.

Herrmann, Robert B., Charles A. Langston, and James E. Zollweg. "The Sharpsburg, Kentucky, Earthquake of 27 July 1980," *Bulletin of the Seismological Society of America* 72, no. 4 (August 1982): 1219–39.

Hough, Susan Elizabeth. *Earthshaking Science: What We Know (and Don't Know) about Earthquakes.* Princeton, N.J.: Princeton Univ. Press, 2002.

Minsch, J. H., C. W. Stover, B. G. Reagor, and P. K. Smith. *Earthquakes in the United States, July–September 1980.* Circular 853-C. Alexandria, Va.: U.S. Geological Survey, 1981.

Nuttli, Otto W. *The Effects of Earthquakes on the Central United States.* 3rd ed. Marble Hill, Mo.: Gutenberg-Richter, 1995.

Stover, C. W., B. G. Reagor, and S. T. Algermissen. *Seismicity Map of the State of Kentucky.* Washington, D.C.: U.S. Department of the Interior, U.S. Geological Survey, 1987.

Street, R. "Ground Motion Values Obtained for the 27 July 1980 Sharpsburg, Kentucky, Earthquake," *Bulletin of the Seismological Society of America* 72, no. 4 (August 1982): 1295–1307.

U.S. Geological Service. "Kentucky Earthquake Information." http://earthquake.usgs.gov/regional/states/index.php?regionID=17 (accessed July 17, 2008).

Paul A. Tenkotte and Nancy J. Tretter

EAST BEND. The great East Bend of the Ohio River commences at mile marker 508.4 (measured from Pittsburgh). As the name implies, the river veers off its southwesterly course at this spot, about 2.5 miles southwest of Rabbit Hash, Ky., and flows east for about six miles until it resumes a southerly direction at Hamilton. Along the Kentucky bank at the bend is East Bend Bottoms, through which drain the watersheds of Lick Creek, Gunpowder Creek, and Landing Creek (also known as Little Gunpowder Creek); the creeks enter the Ohio River at miles 512, 513.6, and 514.6. This six-mile stretch in western Boone Co. is known simply as the neighborhood or community of East Bend. The site was occupied by **American Indians** during the Archaic and Woodland periods.

In the late 18th and early 19th centuries, some prestigious names were associated with the East Bend neighborhood. In 1782 Kentucky statesman-historian Humphrey Marshall came to the area as the official Fayette Co. surveyor. (Present-day Boone Co. was, until 1798, a part of that county.) Marshall had a land grant for 4,000 acres, which he used to acquire property at East Bend. Raised and educated in Virginia, Marshall was a cousin of John Marshall, who became chief justice of the U.S. Supreme Court. Humphrey Marshall eventually owned more land in Kentucky than any other contemporary Kentuckian, as he continued to purchase land warrants and military grants from others. He is most remembered as the man who wrote *The History of Kentucky* (1812), a controversial polemic supporting the doctrines of the Federalist political party, and as the man who challenged Henry Clay, leader of the Whig Party in Kentucky, to a duel.

In 1808 Humphrey Marshall sold his East Bend property to Thomas Carneal. Carneal's son Thomas D. Carneal eventually sold these holdings to Robert Piatt, who built Winfield Cottage and Piatt Landing and operated a ferry. The ferry was near where the East Bend Power Generating Station now stands. Winfield Cottage, the home of the Piatt family, was a unique river-oriented villa, with fancy architecture that was most unusual for the area. It continued to be a well-known landmark on the Ohio River long into the 20th century. Robert Piatt was part of a family originally from New Jersey, whose patriarch brothers had served as officers in the **Revolutionary War** and who later used their land grants to acquire lands in Ohio and in Northern Kentucky. In time, the Piatts became a very influential family in the mercantile, banking, and law sectors in Cincinnati.

Dr. Israel T. Canby established himself in Boone Co. about the same time as Robert Piatt. The two became neighbors and their families intermingled. Canby and Elizabeth Piatt (a daughter of Robert) married. Their son Edward Richard Sprigg Canby (see **Edward Canby**) became a military hero. He graduated from West Point Military Academy in 1839 at age 22 and subsequently served in the Florida Indian Wars, the **Mexican War**, and the **Civil War.** He also commanded troops on the frontier in the future states of Utah and New Mexico. In 1873, during peace talks on the frontier with leaders of a band of renegade Modoc Indians, he was attacked by one of their chiefs and murdered.

East Bend has always depended on agriculture and river commerce for its subsistence. **Piatt's Landing**, Piatt's Ferry across the river to North's Landing, and Kirtly Landing, at the mouth of Lick Creek, were all charted steamboat landings on early river charts and maps of the Ohio River. To this day, the rich bottomlands of Upper and Lower East Bend Bottoms produce some of the highest-quality agricultural products of Boone Co. And except for the East Bend Power Generating Station, this area remains solely agricultural, still farmed by many families with names such as Boh, Ogden, Schwenke, and Stephens, dating from generations past.

East Bend had no commercial center or general stores because of its proximity to the commercial enterprises at Rabbit Hash, Normansville,

Hamilton, and Big Bone. But it did have two churches with sizable congregations, the East Bend Baptist Church, established in 1819, and the East Bend Methodist Episcopal Church, established in 1860. The East Bend Baptist Church is active. The **East Bend Methodist Church** dissolved its congregation, but the building remains and is listed on the National Register of Historic Places. It is jointly maintained by the East Bend Cemetery Board and the Rabbit Hash Historical Society.

Schaffer, James F. *Piatt's Landing East Bend*. Cincinnati: Cincinnati Gas and Electric, 1978.

Don Clare

EAST BEND BOTTOMS PLANE CRASH. On Friday, August 11, 1944, Reuben Kirtley, a farmer at **East Bend** Bottoms in Boone Co., was working in his fields on his tractor when suddenly an odd, eerie noise overpowered the sound of his tractor's motor. Looking up, he saw a U.S. military C-47 aircraft (DC-3, "Gooney Bird") overhead about to crash land in the middle of his wheat field. After some expert maneuvering by the pilot, the plane finally came to rest; an abrupt 90-degree turn prevented it from going into either the Ohio River or nearby Lick Creek where it joins the river at mile marker 512. Kirtley stopped his tractor and watched as two uniformed men climbed out of the wreck, neither of whom was hurt. Both propellers were missing from the aircraft, one of them having punctured the plane's fuselage. It is not known where the plane was headed, or what its mission was. The mission was top secret and the crew members refused to provide any information. The accident, however, could not be kept secret; the crash scene drew many spectators over the next few days.

An unidentified local newspaper clipping reported that there were three men aboard, a pilot, a copilot, and a navigator. Armed with pistols, the occupants of the plane remained at the scene and carefully guarded the wreckage. It turned out that inside the nose cone of this aircraft was an experimental, newly developed, and very sophisticated radar device. Armed military guards soon arrived and guarded the scene while the plane's crew slept in the fuselage.

A five-man salvage team was deployed to the East Bend Bottoms site from Louisville's Bowman Field. They were there to dismantle and retrieve the plane and all its parts and haul everything back to Louisville. To accomplish their mission, the salvagers had to remove the aircraft's wings and put the plane, the wings, and all other component parts on trucks, after pumping out the remaining aviation fuel into barrels.

One member of the recovery crew was Roland Rogers, who now resides in California. He clearly remembers the recovery mission. He and the four other men drove the 100 miles from Bowman Field in a truck with a 60-foot trailer, a crane, and a jeep. They were supplied with all the necessary tools and equipment to complete the task. Rogers operated the jeep to knock down trees and other obstructions in their path. They brought provisions to last five to seven days, and they were ordered also to sleep in the fuselage of the plane with its crew.

Norman Schwenke, a neighboring East Bend farmer, also remembered the event vividly. He said that the armed guards, after completing a day's work, would drive to Elsmere and join the locals for beer and food while the aircraft's crew remained in the wreckage.

When the plane was loaded and ready to go, the recovery team cleared the roads of all trees, telephone poles, and mailboxes. Because the width of the loaded truck and trailer was 24 feet, and the roads were no more than 18 feet wide, the salvagers had to return to Louisville by a roundabout route through Frankfort. The task of replacing mailboxes and telephone poles was left to the locals; the military never returned.

To this day, Betty Kirtley, farmer Kirtley's wife, wonders why the plane was not loaded onto a barge and floated downriver. If handled that way, the salvage operation would have been easier on the utilities and infrastructure of East Bend Bottoms.

Don Clare

EAST BEND METHODIST CHURCH. "The red church" is how locals refer to the East Bend Methodist Church, in northwestern Boone Co. Close by is the East Bend Baptist Church, known locally as "the white church." Both in former years and today, one church is red on the outside, and the other is white. The East Bend Methodist Church, established in 1860, held regular Sunday services for more than 100 years. The congregation met in a building that was erected on land donated by John McConnell, a local landowner and farmer. Originally, it was a two-story brick structure, and on the second floor was a lodge hall that had its own entrance at the rear. A tornado in the early 1890s took off the church's roof and damaged the walls. It was rebuilt as a single-story structure with gable ends and high ceilings.

There are not many extant records from the East Bend Methodist Church, and only one surviving church register. The last entry, dated March 1, 1971, refers to a member's transfer to the Burlington Methodist Church. The absence of subsequent records agrees with the local perception that the East Bend Methodist Church closed "sometime in the early 1970s." Although the church itself is no longer active, the Methodist cemetery is still in use, governed by a separate administrative board, and this cemetery is the preferred final resting place for the inhabitants of the East Bend–Rabbit Hash community. When the church closed, a four-member cemetery board was created and endowed for the operation and upkeep of the cemetery. This board is now in its second generation of overseers. Until 1997 the cemetery board also maintained the church building; then the Rabbit Hash Historical Society assumed the stewardship of and management responsibilities for the building, which was listed on the National Register on February 6, 1989, by the Department of the Interior. The Cinergy–East Bend Power Station donated to the East Bend Cemetery Board two acres of land contiguous to the current cemetery, ensuring its continued use.

"Keeping the Faith in Rabbit Hash," *KP*, June 25, 1998, 1B.
"Resurrecting a Church," *KP*, November 4, 1997, 12A.
"Wanted: Best Mayor That Money Can Buy," *KE*, June 16, 1998, A1.

Don Clare

EAST NEWPORT NATIONAL HISTORIC DISTRICT. First listed in 1983 on the National Register of Historic Places, the East Newport National Historic District (or East Row as it is commonly known) is the second-largest federally sanctioned historic preservation area in the state. Containing some 1,070 homes, the district is bounded by Sixth St. on the north and 11th St. on the south, Saratoga St. on the west and Oak St. on the east. East Row reflects the late-19th-century Victorian ambience in which it was developed, with Italianate, American Four Square, and Queen Anne architectural home styles.

The East Row Historic District began as a suburban bedroom commuter community. It was once home to grocery store giant **Barney Kroger**, brewer George Wiedemann, and other successful merchants and wealthy families. This is where even today **Pompilio's Restaurant** continues to offer its Italian cuisine in a classic neighborhood setting to thousands of customers each year. Distiller **Peter O'Shaughnessy** invested in land in the district and developed many of its homes in the 1890s. **Green Line streetcars** (route 11) transported riders to and from jobs, school, and shopping in downtown Cincinnati. This streetcar line ran along Washington Ave. and E. 10th St. The St. Stephen Catholic Church (see **Holy Spirit Catholic Church**), along Washington Ave. near Ninth St., tended to the needs of its parishioners, while several Protestant churches (the **First Presbyterian Church**, **St. John's United Church of Christ**, and the **St. Mark Lutheran Church**) served other residents. The **Louisville and Nashville Railroad** ran down the middle of Saratoga St., on the western edge of the district, and slow freight trains often cut the city of Newport in two for a half hour at a time. The Park Ave. School, once one of the finest schools of the **Newport Independent Schools** system, provided quality primary education at Seventh and Park Sts. East Row was only a short walk to all that was happening, both good and bad, along Monmouth St. to the west.

Industry in the district included the **Dueber Watch Case Company** at the southeastern corner of Sixth and Washington Sts. and its successor in that building, the Hyde Park Clothes Company. The Penn family's Newport Ice Company was located at the end of E. Ninth St., near Oak St. and the **Chesapeake and Ohio Railroad**; and the Alhambra Tile Company had kilns at 10th and Monroe Sts. for many years. The Dreier Tool & Die Company operated on the east side of Saratoga near 11th St., and the City of Newport's stable (later garage) was along the north side of 11th St. between Washington and Saratoga Sts. for a long time.

After **World War II** families started moving south to the suburbs, such as Fort Thomas. Beautiful two- and three-story homes became rental property. Then, beginning in the early 1980s, East Newport was rediscovered. Revitalization set in, and new residents showed off their work with home and garden tours. Property values began to rise as homeowners replaced renters. The once proud East Row of Newport regained its former elegance and continues to renew itself.

Dube, Allen G., and Margaret Warminski. "East Newport Historic District," National Register nomination, 1983, available at Kentucky Heritage Council, Frankfort, Ky.

"Historic Newport Area," *KP*, September 14, 1983, 2K.

"Tristate Sketchbook—East Row Historic District," *CE*, June 21, 1988, B3.

EASTSIDE COVINGTON. The Eastside of Covington is bounded by 15th St. (see **Austinburg**) on the south, Eighth St. (see **Licking-Riverside**) on the north, Madison Ave. (the central business district) on the west, and the Licking River on the east. For many years it was known as "the East End." By the early 20th century, the neighborhood was racially mixed and economically diverse; there were churches, a **synagogue**, schools, playgrounds, and many small businesses.

The ethnic and racial makeup of the East End included Irish and German immigrants and African Americans. It was a religious mix of Protestants, **Jews**, and Catholics. In 1880 small numbers of **African Americans** began to concentrate in the area around Washington St. and the railroad and in homes along the alleys between Fifth and Sixth Sts. east of Madison Ave. Between 1880 and 1910, there was a population surge among the African Americans, and larger groups of blacks began living between Eighth and 11th Sts. near Greenup St. In 1880 the streets in this area were only partially completed, and the inhabitants were a mixture of African Americans, whites and German and Irish immigrants. In 1890 African Americans began to cluster on Washington St. and also settled in large numbers between Fifth and Sixth Sts. near Scott St. and Madison Ave. in the central business district.

The Germans and the Irish had established an athletic club, the Democratic Club, and a welfare association that by October 1916 was meeting regularly at the Sixth District School on Maryland Ave. These organizations sought to improve their communities. African Americans, who at the time resided on the fringes along 16th and Water Sts. (in the Austinburg neighborhood) and on Ninth and Scott Sts., did not belong to these groups.

In the 1920s the German-Irish organizations became influential in shaping events in the area. They had a city park at 15th St. and Eastern Ave., where football teams such as the semipro East-End Merchants played their games. The African American William Grant High School football team used that field to practice from 1927 to 1932, despite resistance from the German-Irish organizations. Symptomatic of the racial issues festering in the area was an attempt in 1929, by the German-Irish controlled East-End Property Owners' Development Association, to stop the construction of the African American **Lincoln-Grant School** at Ninth and Greenup Sts.

During the 1920s the East End was the center of Covington's African American community. About 90 percent of the African American churches were located in this area and served as stabilizing factors in the black community. Among them were the **First Baptist Church** (the oldest black church in town), the **Ninth St. United Methodist Church**, and the St. James A.M.E. Church Moreover, population shifting occurred as more African Americans migrated from the Deep South. A few businesses owned by African Americans moved away from the Fifth St. and Scott St. area, and some African American doctors from this neighborhood followed suit. Schoolteachers and other professionals continued to live on Russell St. and on the Westside of Covington. In the late 1930s, the Covington Housing Authority completed the Jacob Price Homes, a housing project built for black residents. Ever since, streets in the East End have been generally segregated, except for a few individual ones (Bush, Kendall, Pleasant, and Robbins Sts.).

Before the 1930s, African Americans were widely dispersed throughout the city of Covington. However, once they became concentrated in the city's East End, the neighborhood was transformed into a bedroom community; residents worked in other parts of Covington or in Cincinnati. Entertainment for resident African Americans was available in nearby taverns or in night spots they frequented in Newport. But the liveliest times were found in Cincinnati, where the big bands often appeared playing music popular with African Americans.

In 1921 **Villa Madonna College** was established as part of the St. Walburg Monastery at 116 E. 12th St. in the East End. In 1954 the college purchased land for a new campus in Crestview Hills. But in 1958, before moving to its new quarters, the college integrated its student body. On February 21, 1968, Villa Madonna College, fully integrated, left Covington's East End, moved to Crestview Hills, and became **Thomas More College**.

The **St. Joseph Catholic Church**, located on the corner of 12th and Greenup Sts. in Covington, was established in November 1853 to serve the German population of the East End. Like many urban churches, St. Joseph witnessed an exodus of members to the suburbs during the 1950s. After the church closed on July 5, 1970, its associated St. Joseph School was merged with the St. Mary School at the **Cathedral Basilica** in the East End to form the Bishop Howard School, which was closed in 1988.

In the 1930s the Jewish congregation moved from its synagogue at Seventh and Scott Sts. to make room for the new U.S. Post Office and the new courthouse. In 1938 the cornerstone for the new Temple of Israel was laid at Lynn and Scott Sts. This structure was used by the Jewish group until 1973, when the building was sold to the Church of God. In that same year, the nearby Covington Library (see **Kenton Co. Public Library**) moved from Robbins and Scott Sts. farther north to the corner of Fifth and Scott Sts.

The war years of the 1940s witnessed a major change in Covington social and economic demographics, especially in its East-End neighborhood. With men off to war, households were being maintained by women, who often took jobs outside the home. In the East End, new homes were not being built, and therefore returning servicemen and servicewomen who had grown up in this neighborhood had to find other places to live. Moreover, an increasing number of graduates of the William Grant High School were going to college and not returning to live in the neighborhood. As many of these younger African Americans moved away permanently, and as their parents grew older or died, economically deprived newcomers from the South moved into Covington's Eastside and filled up the only available housing, at the government housing project known as the Jacob Price Homes. Adding to this mix socially was the fact that many living in the government-built homes were on public assistance, which had not been so common in Covington's East End earlier.

In 1943 the Diocese of Covington formed the first Roman Catholic African American church in Northern Kentucky, as a mission of its cathedral in Covington. The **Our Savior Catholic Church**, located just east of the cathedral, became the only Roman Catholic parish for African Americans in the diocese. At one time this African American church and parish had both a grade school and a high school. The church's members were primarily from Covington and Newport.

For over three decades, African American leaders in the community operated businesses on Covington's Eastside. Charles L. Deal operated the Mutual Fire Insurance Company office at 804 Greenup St. **Gene Lacey** owned and operated a grocery store at 205 E. Robbins St. The E. B. Delaney and Son Funeral Home was on the southwest corner of Ninth and Greenup Sts. Jacob Crittenden's dry cleaning and tailor shop was across the street, on the southeast corner. Alberta Ellis's beauty salon was at 226 E. Robbins St. In 1972 the Jones & Simpson Funeral Home moved to 1129 Garrard St., where it remains today. (See **Funeral Homes**.) These firms were anchors of the black community, while others, including restaurants, barbershops, a record shop, and other funeral homes, came and went.

The Civil Rights era of the 1950s through the 1970s brought a change of focus in the neighborhood. The East End came to be known as the Eastside, and streets and homes once banned from African American occupancy became available to them. One of the changes during this period, however, was that a group of dwellings were demolished when the floodwall for the Ohio and Licking rivers was created in the 1950s. The homes, dating from the 1930s, were in an area called "the subdivision," abutted by Prospect St. (north- and southbound) and on two streets, 11th and Bush Sts. (east- and westbound), extending to the Licking River. Also in connection with the floodwall, the only African American neighborhood playground and swimming pool, at 13th St. and Maryland Ave., was demolished and reestablished at 12th and Wheeler Sts. In the early 1970s, the City of Covington passed an open-housing law, finally permitting African Americans to live anywhere in the city.

The two largest employers on the Eastside, the Blue Bird Laundry and the Hatfield Coal Company (see **James Tobias Hatfield**), did not employ African Americans. This period also saw a decrease in the number of African American businesses and doctors. In addition, the pastors of some of the leading churches had died, without sufficient replacements. A new type of community leadership was taking hold. Blacks who had been active in the political arena (such as in the Voters' League) began seeking elected office. The Lincoln-Grant School remained, for many, an icon.

With the addition of the L. B. Fouse Civic Center (see **Elizabeth House**) on Bush St., African Americans now had a place to gather. This center housed meetings for the **NAACP**, the **Congress of Racial Equality**, and the civil rights freedom riders. Dances for teenagers were also held there. Federal programs during the 1960s, such as the Urban Renewal and Model Cities programs, designed to provide housing and other infrastructure for the Eastside, were generally limited in their impact. Those programs provided only two new houses on E. 13th St., the first new homes constructed on the Eastside in nearly three decades. The Model Cities program funded Randolph Park, a multipurpose facility, including a deep-water swimming pool, surrounded by Eighth, Saratoga, and Greenup Sts. and named in honor of longtime East-End physician Dr. **James E. Randolph**. It replaced the outdated pool at 12th and Prospect Sts. In the 1970s, the Northern Kentucky Community Council was formed. Later, the council formed the Northern Kentucky Community Center (NKCC), which purchased the former Lincoln-Grant school building. The NKCC operated various community-based social programs and served as a neighborhood center, replacing the L. B. Fouse Civic Center as the community meeting place.

In the 1980s a watchdog organization was formed, called the Coalition of Black Organizations and Churches, which helped create two housing organizations, the Citizen Housing Action Program and the Eastside Neighborhood Development Corporation. These organizations sought to improve neighborhood living standards. With the guidance of the city, a neighborhood housing construction and rehabilitation effort was established under a federal Urban Development Action Grant and a Community Development Block Grant. A number of houses were rehabilitated, and new homes were built in the Dickie Beal Subdivision, named in honor of an area college basketball star. In 1988 growth continued as the Eastside Neighborhood Association was formed. Its goal was to continue the block-watch program, generate youth activities, stimulate economic development, and abolish substandard education.

After 2000 the diversity that marked the early years of the East End began to return. Young professionals began purchasing and remodeling the stately homes along the major streets of Scott, Garrard, and Greenup. The Frank Duveneck Arts and Cultural Center (see **Duveneck House**), adjacent to the former Klingenberg's Hardware on Greenup St., was purchased and opened as a center for community artists and youths. During that same period, the Eastside witnessed another shift in migration of African Americans, as blacks from the west end of Cincinnati began arriving.

In 2003, following years of inactivity, the neighborhood association was reestablished. The newly formed association targeted the NKCC building, which had been closed. The association is focusing on new community challenges while it also works to utilize community resources and to engender a new spirit of community involvement. One of its main concerns is that many of the community social services and youth activities once provided have been lost and need to be restored. The association has also questioned the decision to demolish and replace the more-than-60-year-old Jacob Price Homes. As an interim measure, until something is decided about reopening the NKCC, the **Carnegie Visual and Performing Arts Center** (housed in the former Covington Library) has been revitalized and now serves as a multipurpose facility and meeting place for the Eastside community.

Calhoun, Jim. "Covington Homes Revive 'Dream,'" *KE*, September 29, 1985, 1B–2B.

Collins, Michael. "Group Sees New Hope around Corner in Eastside," *KP*, April 21, 1988, 5K.

"East End Democrats," *KP*, February 25, 1903, 5.

"East End Merchants," *KP*, September 10, 1931, 2.

"Housing Boss Says Eastside Can Depend Only on Itself," *KP*, September 22, 1981, 2K.

Reis, Jim. "St. Joseph Church, Suburban Exodus Sealed Fate of Covington Landmark," *KP*, December 11, 1995, 4K.

———. "Temple Israel Served Covington Jews until '73," *KP*, December 10, 2001, 4K.

Weiss, Edwin T., Jr. "The Evolution of Covington's Black Residential Pattern, 1860–1980," Northern Kentucky Univ.

Theodore H. H. Harris

ECKLER, GARNER LEE "POP" (b. October 17, 1905, Dry Ridge, Ky.; d. March 20, 1970, Covington, Ky.). Garner Lee "Pop" Eckler, a country and western performer, bandleader, and composer, was the son of Samuel H. and Clara M. Eckler. Beginning in the late 1920s, after being laid off from his **Louisville and Nashville Railroad** job, he became a fairly well-known musician (see **Country Music**). He played the violin and the guitar and wrote several songs. In 1931, after appearances in the Dry Ridge and Grant Co. area, his group, the Grant County Entertainers, so impressed **L. B. Wilson** of **WCKY** in Covington that they were booked to sing over the station's airwaves on Saturday nights. The *Pop Eckler's Barn Dance* lasted two years. Locally, Eckler and his group also played at the Liberty Theater and the Broadway Theater (see **Movie Theaters**), both in Covington, and their act included the use of the mandolin, the Hawaiian guitar, and the Jew's harp. From there, Eckler's career moved to WLW radio in Cincinnati; WSB in Atlanta, where his group was billed as Pop Eckler and All the Young'uns on the station's *Cross Road Follies* show; and other places in the South and along the East Coast, where the country and western style of music was popular.

Eckler was involved in the formation of several groups, beginning with the Grant County Entertainers; others were the Mountain Rangers, the Yodeling Twins, and the Pine Ridge Boys. He had country radio programs in various cities: *Pop Eckler's Jamboree* performed on a station in Rome, Ga.; at WLW in Cincinnati his show was called *Happy Days in Dixie;* and at station WKRC in Cincinnati, he was the Mountain Ranger broadcasting from the Hotel Alms in the Cincinnati suburb of Walnut Hills. Eckler received literally tons of fan mail. His association with the Pine Ridge Boys led to the classic "You Are My Sunshine" in the early 1940s. His most popular written piece was "Money, Marbles, and Chalk," brought to the music hit charts in 1949 by singer Patti Page. He also wrote some bluegrass and pop songs. After his performing tours, Eckler returned to work on the railroad and resettled in Grant Co.

Eckler lived most of his life in Dry Ridge, but his last years were spent in Covington. In March 1970 a drunken driver struck and killed him in Covington at 16th and Scott Sts. as he crossed the street. He was buried in the Broad Ridge Cemetery in his native Grant Co. In 1988 entertainer Pop Eckler was inducted into the Atlanta Country Music Hall of Fame.

Answers.com. "Pop Eckler." www.answers.com (accessed November 1, 2006).

Eid, Mike. "Car Kills Former Music Man," *KP,* March 21, 1970, 1.

Hillbilly-Music.com. "Pop Eckler and All the Young'uns." www.hillbilly-music.com (accessed November 1, 2006).

"Old-Time Fiddlers Booked at Second Local Theater," *KP,* January 4, 1931, 11.

Michael R. Sweeney

ECKSTEIN, FREDERICK (b. 1776, Berlin, Germany; d. February 10, 1852, Cincinnati, Ohio). Frederick John Eckstein, scholar, painter, and sculptor, was the son of Johann Eckstein, who served as painter and sculptor to Frederick the Great of Prussia. Frederick Eckstein studied art under Johann Gottfried Shadow at the Berlin Academy of Arts and Sciences. In 1794 Johann Eckstein brought his family to the United States, and they settled in Philadelphia. There, he and his son helped to establish the short-lived Columbianum Society, a forerunner of the Pennsylvania Academy of Fine Arts. Later, when Frederick Eckstein moved to Cincinnati in 1823, he proposed the concept of a fine arts academy that would help educate and support artists.

Frederick Eckstein married Jane Bailey, and the couple had five children, Frederick Jr., Mary, Eleanor, Frances, and Frank. In the early years of their marriage, Frederick started a number of small businesses in Philadelphia and Lancaster, Pa., all financed by his father-in-law. Eckstein proved to be a poor businessman, and all his businesses eventually failed, so he decided to return to teaching. He moved his family to Cincinnati, where he established the Cincinnati Academy of Fine Arts in 1826, on a corner lot on Fourth St. near Gen. William Lytle's land. About that same time, a group of prominent citizens started the Ohio Mechanics Institute (OMI). The following year, the Cincinnati Academy of Fine Arts merged with OMI. Eckstein has often been called the father of Cincinnati art, because he was instrumental in convincing Cincinnatians of the need for an art school. Two of Eckstein's most famous pupils were sculptors Shubael Clevenger and Hiram Powers.

Eckstein always appeared to be searching for the ideal teaching position but never seemed to be happy with his choices. He and his family moved numerous times, as he sought various teaching positions. He taught at more than a dozen schools and in five states. Eckstein always had grandiose ideas; however, he apparently lacked the discipline and perseverance to make them successful. He was an accomplished sculptor and in the 1820s made plaster busts of a number of famous people, including Henry Clay, William Henry Harrison, Gen. Andrew Jackson, the Marquis de Lafayette, and Gen. Edmund Pendleton Gaines.

Eckstein's wife, Jane, died of cholera in July 1833. After her death, Eckstein took a teaching position at **Augusta College** in Augusta, where he taught until 1838. In his final years, he lived in Cincinnati with his widowed daughter, Mary Eckstein Kinmont, on Walnut St. just below Ninth St. He died while living there, at age 76, and was buried in Cincinnati's Presbyterian Cemetery; later he was re-interred at Cincinnati's Spring Grove Cemetery.

Rankins, Walter H. *Augusta College, Augusta, Kentucky: First Established Methodist College, 1822–1849.* Frankfort, Ky.: Roberts, 1957.

Smith, Ophia D. "Frederick Eckstein, the Father of Cincinnati Art," *BCHS* 9, no. 4 (October 1951): 266–82.

——. "A Survey of Artists in Cincinnati, 1789–1830," *BCHS* 25, no. 1 (January 1967): 2–20.

Vitz, Robert. *The Queen and the Arts.* Kent, Ohio: Kent State Univ. Press, 1989.

Wilson, John. "Cincinnati Artists and the Lure of Germany in the Nineteenth Century," *QCH* 57, no. 4 (Winter 1999): 3–6.

EDEN SHALE FARM. The Eden Shale Farm, in Owen Co., Ky., conducts research to aid farmers in the northern part of Kentucky, who have long felt that they encountered unique problems in tilling their land. Eden Shale itself is a soil formation that is predominantly found in 33 counties in the northern part of the commonwealth of Kentucky. Geologically, it is the second-oldest soil stratum in the state; the oldest is the stratum in the central bluegrass region (see **Geology**).

Steep slopes characterize Eden Shale terrain, the incline average being 27 percent. It has relatively high potash content, is low in organic matter, and has an underlying layer that prevents the proper storage of groundwater, causing the soil to dry quickly in the summer. Because of the lack of organic matter, during periods of drought the soil develops large cracks to a depth of 18 to 24 inches, which add to its dryness.

In 1953 a citizens' committee from the Eden Shale counties was formed to acquire a test demonstration (experimental) farm. It was to be operated by the University of Kentucky (UK) College of Agriculture for the primary purpose of studying problems peculiar to this region. Until then, little research had been done on the problems associated with Eden Shale farming. Farmers and their friends donated money for this venture, and by July 1955 the committee was ready to purchase a farm that would be deeded over to the UK. That same year, approval was given by the UK to purchase Kepple Roland's 660-acre farm, about four miles north of Owenton, between Owenton and Dry Ridge, along Ky. Rt. 22. Later, adjacent properties were added to the Eden Shale Farm.

Work was started on the Eden Shale Farm, which eventually encompassed 950 acres, in spring 1956. After completion of a plan specifying what tests and projects were needed, a rather intensive renovation program and a thorough study of the topography, the soils, the physical plant, and the water facilities were conducted. O. D. Hawkins, a former U.S. military officer in China and chairman of the fundraising and site-selection committee, became the farm's first manager and worked in that position for 23 years. In 1979 Joe Wyles became manager.

Over the years, research has focused on many phases of farming common to Eden Shale conditions. Because of the steepness of the land, row crops that require cultivation were not considered practical. Only level land can be cultivated successfully, and on many Eden Shale farms, level land makes up a small percentage of total acreage. Grasses and legumes grow and produce well in the region, require no cultivation, and are adaptable to the steep terrain. Work in agronomy has been an important aspect of the Eden Shale Farm's history. Approximately 600 acres were put into pastureland and meadows. Apples, strawberries, raspberries, and tomatoes proved to be profitable cash crops. These high-density crops can be grown profitably on a small acreage. Dwarf apple trees, which will grow on steep land, proved to be highly successful. Greenhouse work proved that tomatoes, lettuce, and potted plants could be produced successfully. Forestry studies, though a minor part of the farm's purpose, have utilized the many small tracts of timber scattered throughout its land. Research in woodlot management has been carried out, and Christmas tree production was pioneered, since the soil is adaptable to the growth of Scotch pine trees. Work on the farm has concentrated on small-acreage cash crops and on the development of pastures and meadows that can support a profitable livestock system.

Lakes have been created at the farm to supply water during any season. New barns and a new house have been built, along with a water-treatment plant and farm roads. Test-crop plots are planted throughout the farm. The farm's experimental research facilities have been of untold benefit to farmers of the Northern Kentucky region as well as the rest of the surrounding Eden Shale area. In 2005 the Eden Shale Farm celebrated its 50th anniversary.

"Eden Shale Farm Fund Is Growing," *KP,* January 6, 1955, 1.

"Eden Shale Project Supported in Boone County," *KP,* January 21, 1955, 1.

"Five 'Eden Shale' Farms Are Studied," *KP,* January 21, 1955, 1.

Houchens, Marian Sidebottom. *History of Owen County: "Sweet Owen."* Louisville, Ky.: Standard, 1976.

"Owen County Chosen for Test Farm Site," *KTS,* May 11, 1955, 3A.

Doris Riley

EDGEWOOD. The history of the city of Edgewood in Kenton Co. begins with the Sanford family. B. F. Sanford lived along Madison Pk. (Ky. Rt. 17), at the bottom of Florer Hill (now Dudley Pk.). He was one of the first settlers in this area, and as his estate grew, the location became known as Sanfordtown. Other settlers arrived throughout the late 1700s and early 1800s , attracted to the advantages of this location near the Licking River and the high-quality timber covering the land. Many of these families were the recipients of land grants.

Thomas Buckner, with the help of a grant of several thousand acres, purchased 55 acres in the area where Edgewood sits today. He and his wife, Mildred Washington, built the Beechwood House, which stands today in Edgewood's Twelve Trees subdivision. This founding family of Edgewood had a military connection to the **Civil War**. A relative and a Confederate general named Simon Bolivar Buckner surrendered Fort Donelson, Tenn., to Union general U. S. Grant. There are accounts of many other soldiers from early Edgewood families serving during this war as well.

Among the important farms in the area of Edgewood was that of the Foltz family. Carl and Marie Foltz raised 10 children in Northern Kentucky and, in the late 1920s, founded the Foltz Dairy (see **Dairies**). Later, they purchased a 30-acre farm along Dudley Pk. Carl Foltz sold some of his land to allow the creation of **Summit Hills Golf and Country Club** and the Sunoco gas station, both of which are located today at the corner of Dudley Pk. and Turkeyfoot Rd. Because the Foltz family wanted to give back to their community, they purchased a shrine from Italy for the new **St. Pius X Catholic Church** in Edgewood. Carl and Marie died in the 1970s, survived by their children and 52 grandchildren.

By the 1920s, Edgewood was being developed into subdivisions. In 1927 the ***Kentucky Post***, the Peoples Saving Bank and Trust Company, the Liberty National Bank, and the Liberty Theater funded a contest. The media devoted much attention to the grand prize, a newly built house in the area now commonly referred to as Old Edgewood. The *Kentucky Post* held a house-naming contest, in which the winning name was the "Dream-a-Way" house, suggested by Myrtle Flick. The newspaper carried a floor-by-floor description of the house, and it was opened for touring by the general public. Readers voted on the person they wanted to win the house. At the start of the contest, most people voted for themselves or family members. Soon, however, only a top few people among the vote-getters were left in the race, and on September 18, 1927, it was announced that Mrs. George Ficke had won the "Dream-a-Way" house, located at 2 Lyndale Rd. The Fickes had 12 children and lived in the house until Mr. Ficke's death in 1944.

A few years after the house contest, on May 4, 1930, **Lionel Flying Field** opened in Edgewood on an 11-acre tract of land along Dudley Pk. The field derived its name from Lionel Stephenson, a professional in aviation and aeronautics. Expectations were that this airport would be the largest in Northern Kentucky, owing to its proximity to Summit Hills Golf Course. The flying field played an important role in community celebrations and was used as an attraction to lure people into the city of Edgewood to live.

In 1948 Judge Rodney G. Bryson, Kenton Circuit Court, signed an order to create the new sixth-class City of Edgewood. About 375 people resided in Edgewood, an area of about one-half square mile, situated along Dudley Pk. Soon the Edgewood Police Department was created, mainly to help handle growing traffic problems. The Sanfordtown and Community Volunteer Fire Department was created in 1955. The original location of the station was on present-day Horsebranch Rd., but as the community grew, a new location was discussed for the station. On May 13, 1959, a new station opened on the top of Dudley Hill, on land that Carl Foltz donated. The name of the fire department was changed in 1961 to the Southern Hills Volunteer Fire Department, and a life squad division was added in 1970. A new addition was built in 1977, which allowed for the closure of the original Sanfordtown branch.

In 1962 Covington, a neighboring Kenton Co. city, proposed the annexation of Edgewood. Two other cities, Summit Hills Heights and Pius Heights, bordered the Edgewood area. To combat Covington's annexation attempt, the cities of Edgewood, Summit Hills Heights, and Pius Heights voted to merge into one city. In 1968 the new fourth-class City of Edgewood was formed through the merger of the three communities. However, Covington continued the battle for annexation. Finally, the annexation law of Kentucky was changed. The new law allowed the people to be affected by a proposed annexation to vote on the issue. In order to defeat an annexation, 75 percent of the voters would have to object to the proposal. When the Edgewood votes were counted, 89 percent of the voters opposed the annexation. Thus, after more than 17 years, the threat of annexation was put to rest. A park located off Timber Ridge Rd. in Edgewood still carries the name Victory Park, to celebrate the victory over Covington's annexation attempt.

As Edgewood's population increased, the citizens began to address community needs. Neighborhood watch programs against crime were established, and the potential for commercial development was explored. Edgewood wanted to make a land exchange with the City of Fort Wright: Edgewood would acquire from Fort Wright an area consisting of 40 homes in the Winding Trails Subdivision that were accessible only through Edgewood, and Edgewood would release territory along Old Horsebranch Rd. to Fort Wright. The swap was made. In 1981 plans were approved to address the needs for the expansion of the police force, better city maintenance, and a new city building. A new two-story city building was constructed adjacent to the Southern Hills Fire Department and contained the council chambers and the offices of the city administrator, the city clerk, the mayor, and the police department.

In October 1989 Edgewood residents were concerned about the proposed development of a new 20-acre city park that was going to be located along Dudley Pk. Their concerns related to increased traffic in the city and to the rear entrance to the park, near Poke Away Ln. Although the city tried to address the concerns, the park property was purchased for $900,000. Today, the park, known as President's Park, displays information about the presidents of the United States. Brief histories of the presidents line the walkway into the park. The shelters are named after U.S. presidents, and the smaller of the baseball fields is named Lincoln. The larger field was to be named Washington, but, as the mayor of the city explained, "a gentleman who lived in the city, Robert E. Snow, came to us and said that he would donate some money so that his grandchildren would have a place to play baseball, so we named it after him, Snow Field." The Millennium Clock at the park's entrance has become a landmark for the city.

The first school in the Edgewood area was started in Sanfordtown in 1843. As the Edgewood community grew, there was a need for more schools. Today, there are two public elementary schools, a public middle school, a public vocational school, a public high school, and a technical college in Edgewood. In addition, the **St. Pius X Catholic Church** parish campus along Dudley Pk. contains an elementary school, along with a convent, a rectory, and church buildings. The modern **St. Elizabeth Medical Center** South in Edgewood, a full-service hospital, offers many services in both inpatient and outpatient care. As the Edgewood community continued to grow, the city realized it needed a new city building and a new firehouse. On May 20, 2006, the city held a ribbon-cutting ceremony and offered public tours of the new facilities. As of the 2000 census, Edgewood had 9,400 residents.

City of Edgewood. www.edgewoodky.gov (accessed June 17, 2006).

"Died," *LVR*, June 22, 1844, 2.

"Mrs. George Ficke Winner of Dream-a-Way Home," *KP*, September 18, 1927, 1.

"New Buildings to Open for Inspection," *KP*, August 27, 1937, 2.

"Pius Heights 27th City in Kenton," *KP*, July 31, 1965, 6K.

Reis, Jim. "City Talks May Change Borders," *KP*, March 14, 1981, 4K.

——. "Promotion Was a Dream," *KP*, May 29, 1995, 4K.

U.S. Census Bureau. "American Fact Finder. Data Set. Census 2000 Summary File 1 (SF1) 100-Percent Data. Custom Table." www.census.gov (accessed June 17, 2006).

Weakley, Mrs. Calvin S. "A Drive out Madison Pike." *Papers of the Christopher Gist Historical Society* (1953–1954): 49–56.

Workum, Bert. "Annex Decision End of Beginning," *KP*, May 19, 1979, 1.

Steven D. Jaeger

EDWARDS, TRACEY DENISE (b. 1965). Singer and television host Tracey Edwards is the adopted daughter of Wilson Edwards, a Boone Co. jailer who lived with his family beneath the county jail. The family, including two girls and a boy, helped to cook for the inmates and clean at the jail. When Wilson was killed in an automobile accident in 1979, his wife, Ruth, became Boone Co.'s first female jailer. Tracey Edwards says her colorful personality is a direct result of her unconventional upbringing. She sang to the prisoners, calling them a captive audience. She liked the attention she received and moved into a television and singing career. A 1982 **Conner High School** graduate, Edwards attended **Northern Kentucky University** at Highland Heights, where she received a scholarship for her acting and singing abilities.

Edwards appeared regularly on cable television's Home Shopping Network's *America* store from 1998 to 2004. She also hosted on two other shopping networks' shows. She has performed in the *U.S. Comedy Arts Festival* sponsored by HBO and was a guest show host for *Pure Country* on the Oxygen Network. Edwards produced and was a cohost of *The Hunt USA,* which combined traveling and shopping, and co-hosted *Daytime,* a morning talk show on a Tampa, Fla., NBC affiliate. She also has released a Christmas compact disk and a disk entitled *Songs I Like to Sing.*

Warner, Jennifer S. *Boone County: From Mastodons to the Millennium.* Burlington, Ky.: Boone Co. Bicentennial Book Committee, 1998.

Nancy J. Tretter

EGBERT, HARRY, BRIGADIER GENERAL (b. 1839, Philadelphia, Pa.; d. March 26, 1899, Malinta, Philippines). As a lieutenant colonel during the Spanish-American War (see **National Guard, Spanish-American War**), Harry Egbert commanded the 6th Infantry Regiment, which was based at Fort Thomas. On the south face of the **Fort Thomas Military Reservation** water tower, there is a bronze plaque honoring him.

In 1861 Egbert was commissioned a 1st lieutenant in the 12th Infantry Regiment. He served with the Army of the Potomac during the **Civil War**; he was wounded twice and ended the war with the rank of captain. After the war, he served in South Carolina, Washington, D.C., and on the American western frontier. Between 1870 and 1890, he took part in the Indian wars of the West conducted against the Apaches, the Nez Percés, the Bannocks, and the Sioux. In 1890 he was promoted to major and assigned to the 17th Infantry Regiment. In 1893 he was promoted to lieutenant colonel and assigned to the 6th Infantry Regiment as its executive officer. When the 6th Infantry Regiment was mobilized for the Spanish-American War in 1898, he took command of the regiment after Col. Melville Cochran, the commander at Fort Thomas, was hospitalized. While leading the 6th Infantry up San Juan Hill in Santiago, Cuba, Egbert was shot in the chest and left for dead on the battlefield. Found alive that night, he was returned to the United States for hospitalization.

For his service in the Cuban Campaign, Egbert was promoted to full colonel, given command of the 22nd Infantry Regiment, and made a brigadier general of the Volunteers, without assignment. At the end of the Spanish-American War, Egbert's rank reverted to colonel in the regular army.

In early 1899 Colonel Egbert and his 22nd Infantry were ordered to the Philippines to take part in the army's efforts to pacify the islands. On March 26, 1899, while leading an attack against the Philippine Insurrection Army at Malinta, north of Manila, Egbert was shot and killed. His body was returned to the United States and buried in Arlington National Cemetery. A plaque, commissioned by the citizens of Northern Kentucky to honor Egbert, was placed on the Fort Thomas water tower, and the U.S. Army renamed a Signal Corps post in Alaska Fort Egbert.

Bogart, Charles H. "Harry Egbert, 1840 to 1899," Fort Thomas Historical Society, Fort Thomas, Ky.
"Egbert Memorial Will Likely Be Placed on Ft. Thomas Water Tower," *CE*, April 25, 1898, 5.
"Egbert—Sixth Infantry Officer Made Brigadier General," *KP*, October 10, 1899, 1.
"Harry Egbert Military Record File," Campbell Co. Historical Society, Alexandria, Ky.
Reis, Jim. "'98 Vets Few but Proud," *KP*, May 26, 1997, 4K.

Charles H. Bogart

EGELSTON, CHARLES (b. 1886, Covington, Ky.; d. October 31, 1958, New York City). Actor Charles P. Egelston was the son of Charles R. L. and Anna Havlin Egelston. The family lived along Scott St. in Covington. An uncle, John Havlin, was a Covington and Cincinnati theatrical agent and the owner of the Havlin Hotel in Cincinnati, and Charles Egelston grew up in an acting environment. In 1899 he appeared at the Odd Fellows Hall in Covington in a grand minstrel performance. By 1911 he was working for his uncle John Havlin in New York City, arranging acts for the Greater Cincinnati area. Egelston was part of the National Players group in Cincinnati. He eventually became a staff actor at WLW radio in Cincinnati, where he and Virginia Payne had roles on the daytime epic radio soap opera *Ma Perkins*. For 26 years (1933–1960), Egelston played Shuffle Shober in the drama. *Ma Perkins* quickly advanced from WLW to Chicago and the national network market. Egelston was also the first person to portray Scrooge in Dickens's *Christmas Carol*, which became an all-time radio classic. In the 1950s he made some early television appearances, such as on *The Hallmark Hall of Fame:* he appeared on August 3, 1952, in episode 31, "The World on a Wire," about Samuel Morse and his telegraph; and on April 19, 1953, in episode 65, Rod Serling's "The Carlson Legend." He died at age 72 at New York City's Park East Hospital in 1958. He was survived by his actress wife, Aileen Poe.

"Charles Egelston Dies," *NYT*, November 1, 1958, 19.
"Covington-Home Minstrel Company," *CE*, January 22, 1899, 3.
"Covington's Charlie Egelston to Pay Visit," *CP*, March 14, 1952, 2.
"Kentucky Deaths," *CP*, November 1, 1958, 5.

Michael R. Sweeney

EILERMAN, YVONNE "BONNIE," CAPTAIN (b. September 7, 1913, Foster, Ky.; d. June 6, 1976, Covington, Ky.). Yvonne D. Looney, a dancer and a model, was born in Bracken Co. to Michael F. and Hilda Jett Looney. She studied ballet at the Schuster-Martin School in Cincinnati and eventually danced with the famous Roxy Ballet at the Radio City Music Hall in New York City. She returned home to become one of the area's first high-fashion models. She married Richard D. Eilerman, a co-owner of the men's store **Eilerman & Sons, Men's Clothiers**. Yvonne Eilerman modeled for Mabley & Carew in Cincinnati, for other department stores, and for New York fur dealers; she modeled her last show at age 58 in 1971. She was a captain in the Kentucky state militia during **World War II**. She conducted charm classes for young teens at Pogue's (H. & S. Pogue Company) and later worked in fashion coordination. She died of a cerebral hemorrhage at St. Elizabeth Hospital in 1976 at age 62 and was buried at St. Mary Cemetery in Fort Mitchell.

"Yvonne Eilerman Dies at 62," *KP*, June 8, 1976, 5.

EILERMAN & SONS, MEN'S CLOTHIERS. Herman J. Eilermann (original German spelling of name) (1830–1913), a native of Schapen, Germany, opened his first store in 1886 at 610 Monmouth St. in Newport, and a replacement store was built there in 1889. His business expanded to Covington in 1892, and a four-story flagship store at the northeast corner of Pike and Madison (Eilerman's Corner) was built for the business in 1896. The Covington store, designed by architect **Daniel Seger**, featured a corner bay window that culminated in a tower and spire. Its 500-light electric sign was the first electric sign in the city. The third and final Newport location was built in 1898 at 808 Monmouth. Additional stores were opened in Xenia and Lima, Ohio; Milwaukee; and Minneapolis.

By the turn of the century, the company's proprietors called themselves "the Most Liberal and Progressive Retailers in the World." For many years their advertisements referred to the locations in Covington and Newport as the "Twin Cities."

In 1921 a fire devastated the Covington store, causing $80,000 in damages. The store was rebuilt but without its distinctive tower. The Eilermans were major stockholders of the Henry Geiershofer Clothing Company of Cincinnati. The 1923 *Northern Kentucky Review* stated that some 1,500 local tailors were employed in the making of Eilerman Celebrated Clothes.

The Kentucky stores eventually adopted the slogan "Kentucky's Best" and featured extravagant promotions, exterior displays, lavish windows, and musical entertainment. They were active in the community, promoting the downtown areas and acting as a lead sponsor of the Devou Park Summer Concerts in Covington.

Beyond their comprehensive men's and boys' offerings, the stores were noted for extensive hat and shoe departments, golf and tennis apparel, and fine tailoring. The Covington and Newport stores also featured complete selections of Boy Scout outfits and supplies. The Ohio, Wisconsin, and Minnesota stores had closed by the late 1930s. The Newport store closed in 1964; the Covington store, in 1973.

"Clothiers Celebrate 42nd Anniversary," *KP*, April 27, 1928, 1.
"Eilerman Store Swept by Flames," *KP*, October 6, 1921, 1.
"Five Hundred Electric Lamps in Eilerman & Sons Great Sign," *KP*, April 20, 1896, 8.
"Modern Throughout—Will Be New Building of Eilermans at a Cost of $60,000," *KP*, January 22, 1896, 5.
"Personals—Eilerman Store in Minneapolis," *Covington Courier*, September 20, 1902, 4.
Reis, Jim. "Devou Magic: Summer Concerts in the Park Attracted Thousands Weekly," *KP*, June 10, 1985, 4K.

Chuck Eilerman

EILERMAN FAMILY. The Eilerman family, who helped shape Northern Kentucky, prospered during the growth of mass production and merchandising in the United States and eventually became contributors to many areas of Kentucky civic life.

Herman Eilermann, a young immigrant from near Hanover, Germany, married Maria Anna "Mary" Barg, from Hamburg, Germany, at Old St. Mary's Church in Cincinnati's Over-the-Rhine district in 1861. The couple established a household on Dayton St. in Newport and had 13 children. Herman was a clothing salesman who opened his first clothing store in Newport in 1886 and was successful from the outset (see **Eilerman & Sons, Men's Clothiers**). He twice moved his store to larger quarters and in 1892 began a second store in Covington. It also prospered, and additional stores followed in Lima and Xenia, Ohio; in Milwaukee, Wis.; and, briefly, in Minneapolis, Minn. Eilerman (he had dropped the final *n* from the family name) made substantial investments in local clothing-manufacturing firms, which provided merchandise under the Eilerman brand name.

Herman and Mary's oldest son, George Herman, moved to San Diego, Calif., where he pursued his own business interests. The next son, Henry John, moved to Lima and ran a large clothing store until 1931. The children most active in the local stores were sons August, Benjamin, Herman J., and Edward. August succeeded his father as president of the company and was also president of the Newport Merchants Association. Benjamin and his sons Bernard, Robert, Arthur, and Richard acquired control of the business in September 1931.

The success of the stores enabled family members to branch out into other ventures. Benjamin and his son Robert established a real estate company and a construction firm in 1925 and were early builders in the Coral Gables community near Miami, Fla. August's son August Jr. was an owner of Atlas Cleaners in Newport and a banker, serving as the president of the American National Bank. Arthur was an original investor in the development of Crestview Hills. Leaving the family firm, he started radio station **WZIP** in Covington in 1947.

Benjamin participated during the early 1900s in the development of the White Villa resort community in southern Kenton Co. His family joined those of other leading businessmen, including the Coppins (see **Coppin's Department Store**), the Stevies, the Hugenbergs, and the Luhns. Benjamin Eilerman led the establishment of St. Matthew Roman Catholic Church Mission across the **Three-L Highway** to serve the summer residents at White Villa.

Eilerman family members were involved in many civic projects and organizations throughout the 20th century. August Jr. was chairman of the board of the Good Shepherd Orphanage in Fort Thomas and a trustee of the local **St. Luke Hospital**. He provided leadership in the construction of the hospital's campus on Grand Ave. in Fort Thomas. Bernard helped establish the Northern Kentucky Industrial Foundation, developer of the Northern Kentucky Industrial Park. He was an original member of the Kenton Co. Airport Board (see **Cincinnati/Northern Kentucky International Airport**), serving as both chairman and finance chair. He was also a trustee of Villa Madonna College (now **Thomas More College**). He was elected president of the Covington Chamber of Commerce in 1940 (see **Northern Kentucky Chamber of Commerce**) and was elected twice, in 1936 and 1955, as president of the Kentucky Merchants Association. On both occasions, he used his statewide prominence to support the gubernatorial campaigns of A. B. "Happy" Chandler (in 1935 and 1955). Arthur was active in business groups and in the Kiwanis Club. He was elected president of the Kentucky Broadcasters Association in 1956 and was the only Northern Kentuckian ever to hold the post. Arthur was particularly devoted to the **Boy Scouts** and served for years as a scoutmaster and as a commissioner of the Northern Kentucky Boy Scout Council. He was awarded the Silver Beaver Medal, scouting's highest honor.

Eilerman women were also active in local civic projects. Bernard's wife, Alma, was a founder of the Seminary Guild, which helped support **St. Pius X** Seminary. Arthur's wife, Carmen, was a pioneer woman radio broadcaster who had two popular programs on WZIP. She was an organizer of the Six-Twenty Woman's Club, supporting the **Baker-Hunt Foundation**, and was a founder of the Northern Kentucky Association for Retarded Children. Richard's wife, **Yvonne "Bonnie" Eilerman**, was an accomplished dancer; she performed with the Roxy Corps de Ballet at Radio City Music Hall in New York City and with national touring companies. Returning home, she operated a dance studio at Covington's Odd Fellows Hall (see **Independent Order of Odd Fellows**) and was a leading fashion model in Cincinnati.

Devou Park was a particular interest of the family. Bernard Eilerman helped establish the Covington Tennis Club, the Devou Fields Golf Course, and the local Park Hills Riding Club. WZIP broadcast music from the concert bowl at the park. Arthur organized large scout jamborees in its meadows, and Carmen led **Girl Scout** and **Boys Club** outings there. The Eilerman stores were also organizers and long-term sponsors of the Community Sing programs.

"Clothiers Celebrate 42nd Anniversary," *KP*, April 27, 1928, 1.

"Eilerman Store Was Pioneer," *KP*, November 8, 1925, 2.

"Eilerman Succumbs—Manager of Lima, Oh. Store, Was One of Founders of Concern," *KP*, January 27, 1931, 1.

"New Council for Retarded Children Planned: WZIP Series Will Assist," *KTS*, July 17, 1952, 1.

"President Elected President of Kentucky Broadcasters Association," *KTS*, October 12, 1956, 8A.

"Radio Grant Proposed for Airways Group, Is FCC Announcement," *KE*, April 11, 1947, 1K.

"To Open Course: Director of Devou Park Links to Lead Ceremonies," *KP*, May 22, 1928, 1.

"Veteran Store Head Resigns—Merchandise Firm Passes to Younger Members," *KP*, September 10, 1931, 1.

Chuck Eilerman

ELIZABETHVILLE. Elizabethville is west and a little north of Falmouth in Pendleton Co. along Ky. Rt. 22. At one time this little community had a school in addition to the **Turner Ridge Baptist Church** and Cemetery. It was named Elizabethville because there were so many women in the area named Elizabeth. Locally, the community was known as Modoc. It is reported that the first postmaster of Elizabethville spent so much of his time mowing dock that hardly a weed grew in the area. He decided to call the place Modoc and it remains so, informally, to this day. In 1950 the present Turner Ridge Baptist Church was dedicated in Elizabethville.

Belew, Mildred Boden. *The First 200 Years of Pendleton County.* Falmouth, Ky.: M. B. Belew, n.d. [ca. 1994].

Mildred Belew

ELK LAKE SHORES. Elk Lake Shores in Owen Co. is one of the many new combination housing and recreational developments that have appeared in Northern Kentucky since the 1960s. Elk Lake, which has 200 acres of water and 14 miles of shoreline, is located four miles southeast of Owenton, east of the Georgetown Rd. (once U.S. 227, the William Howard Taft Highway, now just Ky. Rt. 227) and west of Lusby's Mill. The American Realty Service Corporation developed Elk Lake Shores. In the beginning, the project was heavily advertised in the three television markets of Cincinnati, Louisville, and Lexington as vacation homesites with year-round-living potential. The development was heavily promoted. With the completion of I-75 and I-71, some Elk Lake residents commute to locations as far away as Cincinnati. There are more than 250 living units at the lake. There is a boating marina and a swimming beach, fishing is good, and security is provided. Given the topography of Owen Co., and the lack of an industrial base, Elk Lake Shores was welcomed by local residents.

Houchens, Mariam Sidebottom. *History of Owen County: "Sweet Owen."* Louisville, Ky.: Standard, 1976.

ELKINS, BOB (b. 1932, Mount Hope, W.Va.). Character actor Robert Grant Elkins was the son of a hard-working coal miner, George W. Elkins, and his wife Ellie. When Bob was five years old, the family moved to Muncie, Ind., where his father took a job with a lawnmower company. When Bob was 12 years old, his family moved to Covington, Ky., and shortly thereafter his father deserted the family. To support the family, Bob's mother took a job as a maid and his two sisters took part-time jobs. Bob continued his education and graduated from **Holmes High School** in 1950.

At the age of 18, Elkins enlisted in the U.S. Navy, where he was given an aptitude test and found to be quite intelligent but suffering from dyslexia. One of his best friends in the Navy, gunnery officer Lt. Jack Russell, worked with Elkins and helped him to read more effectively. The navy made a college education available to him, but he graciously declined the offer. However, he did take several courses taught by navy personnel and achieved the rank of petty officer. Elkins spent four years in the navy and said that the experience completely changed the course of his life.

After returning to Covington, Elkins studied acting at the Eyer Theater School. He won a small part as a navy shore patrol officer in a stage production of *Mr. Roberts,* and a year later was given the lead role. He acted in dozens of plays and television commercials, but with a family to feed, he took a job with the Magnus Chemical Company, where he had a more stable income. He worked his way up to the position of division assistant vice president of the company.

Elkins resigned from his position at Magnus when he was chosen to play the part of a disc jockey in the 1980 motion picture *Coal Miner's Daughter*, with Sissy Spacek and Tommy Lee Jones. That same year, Elkins and his wife of 23 years divorced. After his four children were grown, Elkins moved to Los Angeles, where he attended an acting seminar given by Jason Alexander (George on *Seinfeld*). He also acted in several plays and in a movie called *The Big Day*, with Sandra Seacat. However, he found the sporadic income from Hollywood projects difficult to exist on, so he returned to Northern Kentucky.

In Greater Cincinnati, Elkins fared much better, appearing in several plays and movies, including *This Train,* with Soupy Sales, and *Tattered Angel,* with Lynda Carter. He also played the part of a bar owner in the 2001 independent film *April's Fool.* Much of that film's action was shot in the former Trixie's Delight lounge at Ninth and Monmouth Sts. in Newport. Also shown in *April's Fool* were the **John A. Roebling Bridge** and various street scenes from Newport and Cincinnati. Elkins then appeared as the German admiral Günther Lütjens in the 2002 docudrama *James Cameron's Expedition: Bismarck,* on the Discovery Channel. One of his most recent acting roles was as the father of a trapped miner in the 2002 ABC Television movie *Pennsylvania Miner's Story.*

The Kentucky House of Representatives honored Bob Elkins in 2002 "for his many and significant achievements throughout nearly 50 years in the performing arts." Elkins also won the Best Actor Award at the Dublin Film and Music Festival in Ireland, for his portrayal of a homeless man in the 2003 movie *Homefree.* He now lives in West Chester, Ohio, and serves as an acting coach at the Cincinnati Actors Studio in the Essex Art Center, Walnut Hills.

"Bob Elkins: Hiding in the Spotlight." http://bobelkinsactor.com (accessed February 12, 2007).

Elkins, Bob. Telephone interview by Jack Wessling, February 12, 2007.

The Enquirer. "A Minute with Bob Elkins." Cincinnati.com. http://news.enquirer.com (accessed February 9, 2007.

Wikipedia. "Bob Elkins." http://en.wikipedia.org (accessed February 12, 2007).

ELKS. See **Civic Associations**.

ELLIS, ALSTON (b. January 26, 1847, Kenton Co., Ky.; d. November 14, 1920, Athens, Ohio). Alston Ellis, who became a college president, was born on a farm in Kenton Co. to Absalom and Mary Ellis Ellis (his father had married his first cousin, who had the same surname). In 1863 the family moved to Covington. Alston Ellis attended a private school in Covington operated by the noted teacher S. Mead. Ellis taught school for a short time near Carrollton and then enrolled at Miami University in Oxford, Ohio. He received a bachelor's degree in 1867 and an MA in 1872 from Miami University. Ellis served as a principal of schools in both Covington and Newport before taking a position with the Hamilton, Ohio, city schools. In 1879 he served with the Ohio state board of school examiners. From 1880 until 1887 he was superintendent of the Sandusky, Ohio, schools and afterward returned to his former job in Hamilton. From there Ellis went west in 1891 to become the president of the State Agricultural College of Colorado (which later became Colorado State University) in Fort Collins. As president there, Ellis doubled the enrollment of the school, added several new buildings, and added new departments. His strong personal and moral convictions often clashed with the academic and local communities, however, and in 1899 the board of trustees in Colorado terminated his contract at the end of that school year. In 1901 Ellis became the 10th president of Ohio University (OU) in Athens, Ohio, where he remained until his death. He brought many of the same kinds of improvements to the OU campus. He died suddenly of a heart attack in 1920 at his home in Athens, survived by his wife of 53 years, Katherine Ann Cox Ellis. He was awarded honorary PhD and LLD degrees by Wooster College and Ohio State University, for his accomplishments in the field of education.

"Alston Ellis." http://lib.colostate.edu/archives/presidents/ (accessed June 20, 2007).

"Alston Ellis." www.memoriallibrary.com/CO/1898DenverPB (accessed June 20, 2007).

Ohio Death Certificate # 67483, for the year 1920.

Michael R. Sweeney

ELLIS, JAMES TANDY (b. June 9, 1868, Ghent, Ky.; d. December 9, 1942, Ghent, Ky.). James Tandy Ellis, newspaper columnist, poet, humorist, entertainer, raconteur, and Kentucky adjutant general, was the son of Dr. Peter Clarkson and Drusilla Tandy Ellis. He took classes locally and at **Ghent College** until he was 18 and then attended classes at the Agricultural and Mechanical College (University of Kentucky) in Lexington, which included military training. Ellis had just published his first notable poem, "Back in Old Kentucky." He studied at the Cincinnati Conservatory of Music, returning to Ghent in 1889 to be a companion for his wealthy grandfather James Bledsoe Tandy, who died in 1895.

In 1898 a Louisville newspaper published Ellis's defense of a former Lexington girlfriend, Harriet Richardson, who was then in national headlines as Temperance forces assailed her for wanting to use Kentucky bourbon to christen the new U.S. battleship *Kentucky.* He had just published *Poems by Ellis,* and the romantic reunion and subsequent marriage of the defamed heroine and the young poet was reported throughout the country. Two children were born to this union; both died young. In 1900 Ellis joined the Kentucky Infantry, serving two years at Owensboro and attaining the rank of major. He returned to Owensboro in 1904 as manager for an embattled water company, placating the locals by writing and performing in local entertainments. He produced another book of poems, *Sprigs o' Mint,* in 1906. In 1908 Ellis was secretary for the Lexington Burley Society and published *Awhile in the Mountain.* He released *Kentucky Stories* in 1909 and *Shawn of Skarrow* in 1911.

Ellis entered the Kentucky Adjutant General's Office as a colonel in 1912, becoming adjutant general in 1914 and serving throughout **World War I** as Kentucky's highest-ranking officer. After the war, he made a career of traveling and performing, often as a banjo-playing blackface character, Uncle Rambo. In 1923 he published two songs and a novel, *Sycamore Bend,* and began his syndicated newspaper column, *Tang of the South. Tang of the South Stories,* the first of two anthologies of his columns, appeared in 1924 and was followed by a work called *Colonel Torkey Shabb* in 1925. Ellis, who fancied himself an authority on "camp cooking," published a booklet on the subject in 1923; he was known for his burgoo recipe, which can still be found in cookbooks.

Ellis's written evocation of the Kentucky dialect, of which he was considered a master, is somewhat dated and difficult for moderns to read, and a condescending view of "colored" citizens is expressed in his works. Further clouding the issue concerning race is the fact that Ellis went largely unpunished for shooting and maiming a disrespectful black servant in 1893, when he was 25 years of age.

At the height of Ellis's popularity, dramatizations of his columns were broadcast over WHAS radio in Louisville. *Flash of the Flintlock,* a movie of an Ellis story slated to be filmed in Somerset, however, was never made. In 1932 declining health compelled Ellis to end his touring. He settled into a home in Ghent and wrote his newspaper columns there until his death in 1942 from a heart ailment. His wife, Harriet Richardson Ellis, committed suicide 46 days later and was buried beside her husband in the Ghent Cemetery.

Jillson, Willard Rouse. *Rambo Flats: A Sketch of the Life, Military Service, and Literary Achievements of James Tandy Ellis (1868–1942).* Frankfort, Ky.: Perry, 1957.

Kentucky Death Certificate No. 25877, for the year 1942.

Noe, J. T. Cotton, ed. *A Brief Anthology of Kentucky Poetry: Selections of Poetry Written by Ninety-Three Persons Closely Identified with Kentucky, Most of Them Native Born.* Lexington: Univ. of Kentucky Department of Extension, 1936.

Bill Davis

ELLISTON. Elliston in northwestern Grant Co., located along Ky. Rt. 1942, was first known as Eagle Mills (not the same as New Eagle Mills). Benjamin Elliston settled there on Ten Mile Creek in 1813. His descendants owned much of the land when the **Louisville, Cincinnati, and Lexington Railroad**, the Short Line, later a part of the **Louisville and Nashville Railroad**, was opened after the **Civil War**, and the train station was named Elliston. Just west of town, along the railroad, is the site of the former Eagle Tunnel, more than 600 feet long, which took the track westward into the Eagle Creek valley. After one-third of the tunnel collapsed in January 2005, the tunnel was "daylighted" by the railroad; that is, it no longer exists.

There were taverns and a general store in Elliston even before the railroad came, but with the opening of a rail line through town, commercial activity soon increased. Farmers were shipping livestock by rail to market, a tobacco warehouse was built, several stores and blacksmith shops were opened, a physician moved to town, and a drug store and hotel appeared. The railroad built company homes for its section hands, who were employed to maintain the railroad. A post office was established in 1870 but discontinued in 1976. Today, Elliston no longer depends on the railroad for goods and services. Trucks and cars have taken the railroad's place for Elliston residents.

Conrad, John B., ed. *History of Grant County.* Williamstown, Ky.: Grant Co. Historical Society, 1992.

John B. Conrad

ELLISTON, GEORGE (b. 1883, Mount Sterling, Ky.; d. October 7, 1946, Cincinnati, Ohio). George Elliston, a poet and journalist, was a fourth-generation Kentuckian, daughter of Joseph Lillard and Ida Givens Elliston. When she was a child, the family moved to Covington. She was educated at the old Covington High School (see **Covington Independent Schools**), and while a student there, she began writing for the ***Kentucky Times-Star*** newspaper. As a young woman, Elliston wrote on cooking and weddings. In 1907 she married Augustus T. Coleman, a newspaper artist from St. Louis. In 1909 she became the society editor at the *Kentucky Times-Star.* Although she moved to St. Louis with her husband, Elliston returned to the Cincinnati area shortly afterward and bought real estate that eventually netted her a small fortune. She was considered a "brilliant" newspaper writer who "blazed new trails for women in journalism." Her writing career included work as a hard-news reporter for the former *Cincinnati-Times Star* (now *Cincinnati Post*), where she covered breaking news, including murders and other crimes. She was also the editor of the *Gypsy,* a poetry magazine.

Elliston was a well-known and highly regarded writer who traveled across the country and to Europe to report the news firsthand. She was also a poet who authored several volumes of poetry, including *Changing Moods, Through Many Windows, Bright World,* and *Cinderella Cargoes: Poems for Poets and for Those Who Love Poetry.* At one point in her career, Elliston had a twice-weekly radio broadcast on Cincinnati's WSAI, where she also recited her poetry. She was a member of the League of Amateur Poets, the Ohio Newspaper Women's Association, the Ohio Valley Poetry Club, and the Cincinnati MacDowell Society. In the 1926 edition of *Who's Who in America,* Elliston was cited for her literary achievements and contributions, one of eight Northern Kentuckians (and the only woman of the group) to be so honored.

Elliston bought a century-old log cabin at Morrow, Ohio, and lived there almost until her death. She bequeathed the bulk of her estate to the University of Cincinnati for the creation of the George Elliston Poetry Trust Fund. Its purpose was to "establish, as far as practicable, a chair of poetry to encourage and promote the study and composition of poetry." Today the George Elliston Poetry Foundation sponsors a yearly poet-in-residence and organizes programs to further the study and practice of poetry. In the Langsam Library at the university is the Elliston Poetry Room, which contains writings on poetry and a collection of 20th-century English-language poetry. In recalling Elliston's career, her former employer the *Times-Star* called her death "the passing of a great esteemed member of the family." Her funeral was held at her downtown Cincinnati home, along Broadway at Arch St., the former home of the Cincinnati Natural History Museum. She was cremated.

"Eight Northern Kentuckians in 1926 Edition of *Who's Who,*" *KP,* October 8, 1926, 5.

Elliston, George. *Cinderella Cargoes: Poems for Poets and for Those Who Love Poetry.* New York: George Sully, 1929.

"George Elliston Times Star Writer and Poet Dies after Long Illness," *CE,* October 8, 1946, 16.

Noe, J. T. C. *A Brief Anthology of Kentucky Poetry.* Lexington: Univ. of Kentucky, Department of Univ. Extension, 1936.

Reis, Jim. "Noteworthy Lives," *KP,* November 29, 1993, 4K.

The University Libraries Newsletter. "A Poet's Legacy." University Libraries, University of Cincinnati. www.libraries.uc.edu/source/volthree/elliston2.html (accessed February 25, 2007).

Kathryn Witt

ELLISTON-STANLEY FUNERAL HOME. The Elliston-Stanley Funeral Home of Williamstown is the second-oldest continuously operated business in Grant Co. The firm, established in 1881 by R. H. Elliston, his brother O. P. Elliston, and their father, Hiram Elliston, was organized as a lumber and hardware business with the mortician work as a sideline. Early in the 20th century, the mortician business became the major portion of the firm's business, under the direction of O. P. Elliston.

Beuford E. Stanley, a native of Grant Co., purchased the business in 1937 after returning to Williamstown the year before to become an employee of Elliston as a funeral director and embalmer. At that time much of the work, including embalming, visitations, and funerals, was accomplished in the homes of those they served. Stanley operated the funeral business with his wife, Frances Clinkscales Stanley, also a native of Williamstown, whom he married in 1937. She became a licensed funeral director in 1943, and they worked together in the business until his death in 1995 at age 81.

The business included invalid and emergency ambulance service for area residents until 1973. In 1955 the Stanleys moved their storefront business to a residential neighborhood where they had purchased and remodeled a former residence into a modern funeral home. Their service was expanded with the purchase of the Hamilton Funeral Home in Verona in 1982 and the addition of a branch facility in Crittenden in 1998.

Now in its 125th year of service to Northern Kentucky, the business continues to be owned and operated by Frances Stanley and her two sons, William Michael Stanley and Dennis E. Stanley, along with the assistance of her two grandsons, Patrick M. Stanley and Douglas R. Stanley, all of whom are licensed funeral directors and embalmers.

"Centennial Club," *KE,* November 8, 1996, B1C.

Conrad, John B., ed. *History of Grant County.* Williamstown, Ky.: Grant Co. Historical Society, 1992.

"Funeral Home Wins Trade Award," *KE,* November 8, 2003, B4.

Stanley, Frances Clinkscales. Interview by William Michael Stanley, June 24, 2006, Williamstown, Ky.

Williamstown Courier, May 30, 1901.

William Michael Stanley

ELMER DAVIS LAKE. On February 1, 1960, when the Kentucky Department of Fish and Wildlife Resources (KDFWR) in Frankfort announced that the new Elmer Davis Lake near Owenton was available for fishing, it was a milestone for the Owen Co. Sportsman's Club. For years, Owen Countians had been planning for a suitable lake for fishing and boating, since there was no large lake in the county. Having been stocked with black bass, black crappie, bluegill, channel catfish, large-mouth bass, long-ear sunfish, shell-crackers, walleye, warmouth, and white crappie, the new lake became a fisherman's dream come true.

The sportsman's club, which began in 1952, had built a modern brick lodge and in 1953 purchased the adjacent 110-acre Dunavent farm some three miles west of Owenton on the Dunavent Ridge (Lake Rd.). Elmer Davis Lake was built in 1958 by the KDFWR on land purchased from the Owen Co. Sportsman's Club. It has approximately 149 surface acres, 5.6 miles of shoreline, and a maximum depth of 59 feet and surrounds three sides of the club's property. Along with the boating and fishing, visitors can also enjoy a swimming pool and the club's beach. Homes for weekend living as well as for permanent living have been constructed along the shoreline.

The namesake of the lake, Elmer Davis, was a longtime area automobile dealer and the commissioner of the KDFWR under Kentucky governors Keen Johnson (1939–1943) and A. B. Chandler (1935–1939 and 1955–1959).

Owen Co. Historical Society Files, Owen Co. Library, Owenton, Ky.

Doris Riley

ELMWOOD HALL, LUDLOW. **Thomas Davis Carneal,** a local businessman, had by 1820 accumulated an estate he called Elmwood, which comprised more than 1,000 acres in Northern Kentucky along the Ohio River, across and slightly west (downriver) from Cincinnati, on what eventually became the site of the city of Ludlow. Carneal was a speculator, builder, and amateur architect. He and his partners, the brothers **John S. Gano** and Richard M. Gano, laid out Covington in 1815 (and John S. Gano built the Federal-style dwelling there, now known as the Gano-Southgate House, for Aaron Gano). Thomas Carneal served in the Kentucky legislature but also had business interests in Ohio and built several townhouses in Cincinnati. The Elmwood estate stretched for two and a half miles along the river and was virtually self-supporting, with picturesquely landscaped grounds, orchards, vineyards, ornamental and vegetable gardens, a coach house, an icehouse, a dairy, barns, and a sawmill. Although Carneal proposed a bill for the gradual eradication of

Elmwood Hall, Ludlow, ca. 1908.

slavery from Kentucky, Elmwood included houses for his own enslaved African American artisans and servants.

Between 1818 and 1820, Carneal and his wife Sarah Stanley Carneal, a renowned hostess, designed and built for themselves a villa—also called Elmwood—on the estate. They situated it on a gentle rise 150 yards from the river; although altered, it survives at 244 Forest Ave. in Ludlow. A square, one-story, neoclassical pavilion on a raised basement, it has a hipped roof capped by an observation deck. The deck is surrounded by a railing and is accessible via an interior corkscrew stair. The house originally had an elliptical-arched and fan-lighted entrance (later turned into a window) facing the river on the north front, with twin recessed porches screened by slender Tuscan columns on its east and west sides. An ell wing containing a kitchen protruded asymmetrically from the rear, or south facade. Except for the ell, the plan was perfectly symmetrical, consisting of eight square rooms arranged in an offset grid, with three rooms each across the north and south fronts and two large parlors at the center of the plan opening through jib-windows onto the recessed porches at the sides. The overall scheme resembles certain villas designed by 16th-century Italian architects Palladio and Scamozzi, whose published treatises the Carneals may have known and consulted. The ceilings of the house are 14 feet high, and the most elaborate room is the entrance hall, in the center of the north front. It has corner columns supporting curving plaster pendentives that form a circular disk ceiling with a recessed central panel, creating the effect of a flattened dome and oculus. Pilasters flank the symmetrical doorways, and a continuous frieze of ornamental leaves encircles the room above the columns and door heads, acting as a datum line for the springing of the pendentives. The composition of this room recalls spaces created by Federal-period architect Benjamin Henry Latrobe (1764–1820); he was briefly in Cincinnati in 1820 when Elmwood was nearing completion, and the Carneals may have consulted him for this room, or they may have known his designs through other sources. In the later 1820s, the second owner of the house likely enriched the room by adding cast plaster shells and rosettes. It is perhaps the most sophisticated Federal-period interior surviving in Kentucky. The other spaces of the house exhibit none of the same sculptural or ornamental character, being simple cubic volumes articulated only by carved mantelpieces and door and window frames in an elaborate but provincial Federal style.

In 1828 the Carneals sold the estate to Englishman William Bullock (founder of the renowned Egyptian Hall museum in London), who made plans to build an elaborate speculative town on the site, to be called **Hygeia**. While Bullock and his wife resided at Elmwood, English author Frances Trollope (1779–1863) visited them and left a description of the house in her book *The Domestic Manners of the Americans* (1832). She had little good to say about Cincinnati (or America, for that matter) but commented on the "exquisite beauty" of the Elmwood estate—though deploring its remoteness—and said of the Bullocks' house that "there is more taste and art lavished on one of their beautiful saloons, than all Western America can shew elsewhere" and that "the gems of art [Bullock] has brought with him, shew as strangely there, as would a bower of roses in Siberia." Bullock's art collection at Elmwood perhaps included furniture and sculpture by his brother George Bullock (d. 1818), one of the foremost cabinetmakers of Regency England.

Bullock's proposed town came to naught, and in two sales, of 1831 and 1836, he disposed of the estate to Israel Ludlow Jr. (son of Israel Ludlow Sr., who laid out Cincinnati in 1788). Ludlow and his heirs, along with their relatives the Kenners, gradually sold parcels of the estate and developed the town of Ludlow. Incorporated in 1864, the bucolic village became a booming industrial town after the 1877 completion of the **Cincinnati Southern Railroad** and the construction of its shops in Ludlow. This development hastened the subdivision of the Elmwood estate, the laying out of streets, and the building of hundreds of middle- and working-class Victorian houses. In the 1880s the Webster family, who then owned Elmwood, subdivided the final 40 acres around the villa and partitioned it into a double house, or duplex. They demolished its rear kitchen wing to accommodate the laying out of Forest Ave. and created a new street front on the south with Victorian hoodmolds over the doors and windows. The original riverfront on the north of the house became its rear facade.

In 1920 Elmwood became the factory for the Mrs. Thomas' Candies Company. The owners, Eda and Albert Thomas, hired local architect Chester H. Disque to do a partial restoration (contemporary with that of Colonial Williamsburg in Virginia and echoing some of its forms). Known throughout the 20th century as Elmwood Hall, the house gained a mythic local status and accumulated legends. It was said, for example, that Elmwood was a site on the **Underground Railroad** with a secret tunnel to the river. Contradicting that story was the rumor that the basement contained a "slave whipping post." Neither was true. The house was, however, recorded by the Historic American Buildings Survey in 1936 and entered in the National Register of Historic Places in 1972. Artists had their studios in Elmwood Hall during the 1970s–1990s, and the house is now gradually being restored as a residence.

Archive of miscellaneous notes, records, clippings, etc., collected by past owners. Elmwood Hall, Ludlow, Ky.

Bullock, William. *Sketch of a Journey through the Western States of North America.* London, 1827. Reprinted in *Early Western Travels, 1748–1846,* ed. Ruben G. Thwaites (Cleveland, 1905).

Costeloe, Michael P. *William Bullock, Connoisseur and Virtuoso of the Egyptian Hall: Piccadilly to Mexico (1773–1849).* Bristol, UK: Univ. of Bristol, 2008.

———. "William Bullock and the Mexican Connection," *Mexican Studies/Estudios Mexicanos* 22 (Summer 2006): 275–309.

Fazio, Michael, and Patrick Snadon. *The Domestic Architecture of Benjamin Henry Latrobe.* Baltimore: Johns Hopkins Univ. Press, 2006.

Lancaster, Clay. *Antebellum Architecture of Kentucky.* Lexington: Univ. Press of Kentucky, 1991.

Langsam, Walter E. *Great Houses of the Queen City: Two Hundred Years of Historic and Contemporary Architecture and Interiors in Cincinnati and Northern Kentucky.* Cincinnati: Cincinnati Historical Society, 1997.

Tenkotte, Paul A. "Rival Cities to Suburbs: Covington and Newport, Kentucky, 1790–1890," PhD diss., Univ. of Cincinnati, 1989.

Patrick Snadon

ELSMERE. The city of Elsmere is located on land originally granted by the commonwealth of Virginia to John D. Watkins and Robert Johnson in 1785. The Watkins-Johnson property was located on the **Dry Ridge Trace**, a natural high point that runs from near the Ohio River to Central Kentucky. The tract was divided by a buffalo trail used in 1793 to build the Georgetown Rd., which became the primary route to Central Kentucky. This road ran near the western boundary of today's city of Elsmere.

According to legend, the first settlers arrived at the site that became Elsmere about 1820. The first house was built near present-day Shaw Ave. In 1834 the Commonwealth of Kentucky legislated improvements to the Georgetown Rd. by chartering the **Covington and Lexington Turnpike** and requiring the use of stone, gravel, wood, and other materials in its construction. By 1839 the first 10 miles of the turnpike from Covington were finished, including the section that passes through present-day Elsmere. At a cost of $ 7,800 per mile, it was the most expensive highway built in Kentucky up to that time. Toll booths situated every five miles charged 10 cents for a horse and cart.

The end of the **Civil War** initiated an economic revitalization for Cincinnati and Northern Kentucky. As the urban areas grew, traffic on the turnpike increased. A railroad from Cincinnati into the South was needed to give the developing industries better access to agricultural products. In 1874 the City of Ludlow outbid Covington and Newport for the railroad bridge from Cincinnati. With the bridge at Ludlow, the most direct route to the South went through what later became Erlanger and Elsmere. To encourage selection of this route, property owners contributed funds and property for the railroad right-of-way. Laying of track began in 1876, and the first train rolled down the tracks on April 20, 1877, reaching Lexington in 2 hours and 45 minutes. Passenger service was inaugurated on July 23, 1877. A station was established south of Erlanger and named Woodside Station. With the opening of the railroad, a trip from that station to Covington or Cincinnati that took hours on the turnpike could be made in minutes on the train. Developers worked with the railroad company to hold Sunday excursions stopping at Woodside Park, in order to introduce potential residents to the area. Lots were sold by the Woodside Land Syndicate with such enticements as railroad passes.

Additional development in this area occurred rapidly during the 1890s. The first church, **St. Henry Catholic Church**, was built in 1890, and a volunteer fire department was organized. On May 11, 1896, the area that had become known as South Erlanger was incorporated as the city of Elsmere. The city was named by developer Lou Nolan for a street in Norwood, Ohio; the name was said to mean "by the lake." Less than a year later, on January 25, 1897, the neighboring city of Erlanger was also chartered. Elsmere's first government included a town marshal and a jail, built in 1903 at the corner of Garvey and Ash Aves. Elsmere built its first school in 1899 on Central Row.

One aspect of the growth that occurred during this period was the migration of black families to the area. By 1900 at least 17 black families had settled in Elsmere, and they had established Dunbar School for the education of their children. Although this school burned, the black families rebuilt; they continued to maintain the new school until the **Erlanger-Elsmere Schools** built Wilkins Heights Elementary School in 1951 on Capital St. Black residents also established the A.M.E. Church in Elsmere about 1905.

As usage of the railroad waned and automobiles became more prevalent, highway improvements assisted in the development of Elsmere. In 1913 Kenton Co. condemned and purchased the Covington-Lexington Turnpike so that tolls could be discontinued. Begun in 1915 and completed in 1921, the **Dixie Highway** was created by covering the old turnpike with concrete. The new highway encouraged development of the old farms around the cities, which resulted in a building boom in the Erlanger-Elsmere area in the 1920s. More than 400 homes were constructed in Erlanger and Elsmere in 1927 alone, and the population of both cities doubled. The Erlanger and Elsmere school systems were consolidated, and a new high school was completed in 1928. The first sewers in Elsmere were constructed in 1930; most of the work on the sewers was completed by the WPA in the late 1930s. The city's fire department was organized and a fire chief appointed. The center of the business district was Dixie Highway at Garvey Ave. This intersection became known as Shankers Corner, named for a dry-goods store there. Also located on Garvey was a movie house that doubled as a basketball floor. The Joyland Corner Building on Garvey hosted parties. For a time, the Erlanger-Elsmere Library was also located on Garvey near Dixie Highway.

In 1952 Elsmere had grown enough that it was declared a fourth-class city by the Kentucky legislature. The old board of trustees became the town council. Construction of I-75 nearby in 1961 changed traffic patterns. Most travelers now bypassed Elsmere; however, the new highway provided more opportunities for suburban growth, because it made Elsmere more convenient to residents of the larger cities.

In the 1970s, discussion of a merger between Erlanger and Elsmere resulted in a ballot initiative to merge the neighboring cities. The measure was soundly defeated in both cities. Following this decision, Elsmere undertook a major rebuilding of streets from 1971 to 1978 at a cost of $1 million. In the 1980s, under the leadership of longtime mayor Al Wermeling, Elsmere annexed land for industrial development and residential expansion, enabling development of an identity separate from that of Erlanger. Elsmere has benefited substantially from industrial development in the 1980s and 1990s.

Building on its tradition of diversity, Elsmere elected **Billy Bradford**, longtime councilman, as mayor in 1998. Mayor Bradford was the first African American to hold such a position in Northern Kentucky.

With its advantageous location, the excellent transportation to other cities, the availability of industrial land, a strong tax base, and the potential for residential expansion, Elsmere is in an excellent position for future growth. In 2000 Elsmere had a population of 8,139.

Blincoe, Caden. "Small Community Enjoys 'Mainstream of Progress,'" *CE*, February 5, 1979, 2K.

City of Elsmere Centennial Celebration, 1896–1996. Elsmere, Ky.: Centennial Committee of 1996, 1996.

Kathman, Janice. "Elsmere: A Tale of Two Cities," *Erlanger Dixie News*, May 5, 1988, 21.

Newman, Mary. *The Bicentennial Story of Elsmere, Kentucky, 1776–1976*. Elsmere, Ky.: Elsmere Volunteer Fire Department Ladies Auxiliary, 1976.

Wayne Onkst

EMANCIPATIONISTS. Northern Kentucky contributed to and took part in the two quite different concepts of how to abolish slavery that developed between 1790 and 1850: constitutional emancipation and gradual emancipation. During the first decades of Kentucky statehood, constitutional emancipation formed the conceptual basis for emancipationists' antislavery political actions. These early antislavery proponents tried to prevent Kentucky from becoming a slave state, and once the 1799 state constitution legalized slavery, they attempted to repeal that part of it. This movement was most closely identified with Rev. David Rice and several other Baptist, Methodist, and Presbyterian preachers and churchmen.

Constitutional emancipation was the path that Northern states chose for eliminating slavery. In some New England states, the abolition of slavery took place as outright bans. Vermont (1777), Massachusetts (1780), and New Hampshire (1784) followed this course. Rhode Island, New York, Pennsylvania, Connecticut, and eventually New Jersey, codified gradual emancipation in their state constitutions. The major unresolved issues in the North were the legal status of a slave who moved into a Northern state or fled from a slave state into a free state, and whether or not to grant full citizenship to free people of color. As settlers from New England and Pennsylvania flooded into Northern Kentucky, they brought their experience in states that had enacted constitutional emancipation.

In Southern states, where slavery had become embedded as an institution, and where slaves had the status of private property, emancipation took place through a legal process called manumission: the individual slave owner could free slaves from bondage through a will or through a declaration in a local court. The counties that were formed in Kentucky during the state's early years tended to enshrine the principle of private ownership of slaves. Many Kentucky counties required that, in the event of manumission, a slaveholder or the administrator of an estate post a bond or provide sufficient financial resources, such as land or money, to avoid making a freed black a pauper dependent on the county. The Quakers, some **Presbyterians**, and the Separate Baptists were active in North Carolina, Tennessee, and parts of Georgia in creating manumission societies dedicated to promoting manumission; these groups also purchased families of slaves in order to free them from bondage. As settlers from these regions came into and through Kentucky, a small number of such manumission societies were established.

Some slaveholders in Kentucky believed slavery to be evil but also regarded their slaves as prized private property. Generally, these slaveholders applauded the economic benefits of emancipation accruing to white landowners but also feared that emancipation might produce large numbers of freedmen living in Kentucky. Gradual emancipationists believed that slavery would be eliminated over time as slave owners of their own volition freed existing slaves through legal manumission. One form of gradual emancipation, publicized by James G. Birney and Cassius Clay, emphasized that slavery impeded economic development in Kentucky. They contrasted the booming economies of Ohio and Indiana with that of Kentucky to prove their point. These arguments were meant to persuade slave owners to emancipate their slaves. In any case, gradual emancipationists tended to believe that slaveholders should be compensated for the loss of their property if, at some point, slaves were freed by action of the state.

Abolitionists, by contrast, advocated eliminating the institution of slavery without compensation to slave owners. In early Kentucky, both constitutional and gradual emancipationists used the term *abolition* when advocating an end to slavery; however by 1850 abolition referred only to immediate emancipation in the South.

Slavery and emancipation proved difficult topics for a number of Christian denominations. For the **Baptists** in 1803–1806, the issue came to a head at Mount Sterling, Ky., in the person of David Barrow, a minister in the Separate Baptist tradition who served Goshen, Lulbegrud, and Mount Sterling churches. Through political pressure from the Regular Baptists of the Elkhorn Baptist Association and their fledgling Bracken Baptist Association, David Barrow was expelled from the North District Baptist Association in 1806 for advocating the gradual emancipation of slaves and the eventual abolition of slavery. Barrow not only preached continuously against slavery, but he published British Baptist Thomas Clarkson's *Essay on Slavery and Commerce of the Human Species,* a 1785 treatise that greatly influenced U.S. abolitionists. Barrow himself wrote *Involuntary, Unmerited, Perpetual, Absolute, Hereditary Slavery Examined on the Principles of Nature, Reason, Justice, Policy, and Scripture,* which was printed in 1808 by John Bradford at Lexington. That same year, Barrow joined Carter Tarrant and founded the Baptized Licking-Locust Association, Friends of Humanity, also known as the Emancipation Baptists.

The Baptized Licking-Locust Association, Friends of Humanity, included Bracken, Gilgal, and Licking-Locust Baptist churches from the Bracken Baptist Association; Lawrence Creek Baptist Church from Mason Co.; Bethel and Mount Sterling Baptist churches from the North District Baptist Association; New Hope Baptist Church from Woodford Co., with members from the original Clear Creek and Hillsboro Baptist churches; and Bullskin Baptist Church from Shelby Co.

The Emancipation Baptists acted chiefly in the traditional method of other Baptist associations, with messengers, queries, reports, and periodic meetings and preaching. They were not a political party. However, these same Kentuckians were influenced by the creation in 1814 of the Tennessee Manumission Society, which had Charles Osborn and John Rankin as charter members, and the creation of the American Emancipation Society. The Kentucky antislavery people began to think about political action to repeal the slavery clause in their constitution and moral-ethical action by individual slave owners to emancipate their slaves in their wills.

In 1821 Carter Tarrant and David Barrow formed the Kentucky Abolition Society. At that time, Tarrant was living in Carrollton. The Kentucky Abolition Society included the Baptist churches from the Emancipationist Baptists that Tarrant had helped to form and a few preachers and elders from the Methodist and Presbyterian denominations. Three of these were the Reverends Alexander, Moses Edwards, and John Mahan; 21 ordained members also belonged to the Kentucky Abolition Society. At its peak, however, the statewide organization never claimed more than 200 members.

The Maysville Abolition Society, led by Amos Corwine Jr., was active during this period. A small group was located at Shelbyville, and another at Frankfort hosted the statewide organizing meeting. Although there was clearly an antislavery group at Louisville, led chiefly by Presbyterian and Unitarian ministers, there is no indication that they were part of the Kentucky Abolition Society.

Lucien Rule cited Lyman Beecher, Gideon Blackburn, John Dickey, Henry Little, Samuel Shannon, and Parson John Todd as early influential antislavery Presbyterian preachers in Northern Kentucky and southern Indiana. The Scots Convenanter, Seceder, and Associate Reformed Presbyterians led by John Anderson, Andrew Fulton, and George Shannon settled on the Indiana side of the Ohio River, north and west of Madison. These Scots congregations began early to provide aid to fugitive slaves all along the Ohio River and up into central Indiana.

John Finley Crowe, a student at Transylvania University in Lexington, was asked to edit a flagship newspaper, the *Abolition and Intelligence Messenger,* for the Kentucky Abolition Society. Crowe began the publication in Lexington. He then moved to Shelbyville, where for a few months he published his paper advocating the repeal of Kentucky's slave laws. Crowe then proceeded to seminary and ordination, and in 1825 he began his first church assignment at Vernon, Ind. He later achieved prominence as the first president of Hanover College at Madison, Ind., and as head of the Indiana Old School Presbyterian Colonization Society.

The enthusiasm for emancipation of slaves soon began to spread through the mid-South. In 1823 Tennessee reported 25 manumission societies, mostly in the eastern part of the state. In the same year, North Carolina declared 50 societies active at the national Emancipation Society Meeting at Philadelphia. Between 1823 and 1828, representatives from Baltimore, New England, and Philadelphia met annually. The eastern Tennessee groups usually sent delegates, but there is no evidence that Kentucky was represented at the national level.

A number of slave owners manumitted their slaves. However, in the entire period from 1799 to 1868, slaveholders in Bracken Co., for instance, filed only 156 emancipation records in the courthouse. Fourteen of them were filed by Arthur Thome of Augusta in 1834–1836. In 1847, in Owen Co., Ky., Susan Herndon Rogers freed the 10 slaves of the Locust family and gave them 403 acres known as Free Station, or **Mountain Island**. Susan's brother James Herndon in 1853 executed a bond for $21,000 in order to have his 22 slaves manumitted. His manumitted slaves, the Carroll, Smith, and **Vinegar** families, divided 125 acres at Mountain Island. Yet, actions such as these hardly made a dent in the huge numbers of slaves pouring into Kentucky from the Carolinas, Maryland, and Virginia. By 1827 the emancipation movement had run out of steam as the leaders had died or moved away, and the impact of moral persuasion proved anemic.

Speaking into this intellectual vacuum, the faculty of the Danville Presbyterian Seminary, led by Rev. Dr. Robert J. Breckinridge, with the aid of his brother William J. Breckinridge, an influential Louisville minister, steered the antislavery movement toward a conservative approach that linked gradual emancipation with the concept of colonization, sending freed blacks to Africa. The American Colonization Society, founded in 1810, was developed chiefly as a method of ridding the nation of its free people of color and was not originally conceived as a tactic to eliminate slavery from the South. In fact, it was the opposite. The manumission movement, adopted by many Presbyterians and Methodists in the early years of Kentucky statehood, had been all too productive: hundreds of free blacks now populated Southern cities and Northern rural communities. To the slave owner, a free black living in a community where there were slaves caused an unnecessary tension, a temptation for slaves to become dissatisfied with their bondage. The Nat Turner Rebellion of 1831 in Virginia exacerbated fears of a slaveholding minority controlling the daily movements of millions of black slaves. One result was the immediate imposition of harsh laws against free people of color throughout the South and the Ohio River Valley. Another result was that the antislavery leaders of the Presbyterians, the Methodists, and many forms of Baptists vigorously adopted the tenets and the tactics of the colonization movement. Sending free blacks to Africa was considered the ultimate solution. Colonizationists, with Kentucky statesman Henry Clay as their leader and the federal government and wealthy individuals backing the movement, purchased large tracts of land on the coast of Africa, lined up ships to transport former slaves to Liberia, and persuaded some slave owners to follow their precepts in educating slaves to Christianize their new African homelands. By 1849, however, it became evident that free people of color did not want to go to Africa. Fewer than 650 former Kentucky slaves ever went to Liberia, and some of them later returned. The colonization-emancipationists were faced with 250,000 Kentucky slaves who intended to stay in the United States.

As the October 1849 Kentucky Constitutional Convention approached, the antislavery forces in the state made a determined assault on slavery. A statewide emancipation convention was scheduled for April 1849 in Frankfort. Leading up to this meeting, the abolitionists in Kentucky, led by **John G. Fee** from Lewis and Bracken counties, demanded nonimportation of slaves and called upon the Kentucky legislature to emancipate slaves and grant them status as free citizens. The colonizationists, led by Robert J. Breckinridge, William Breckinridge, Henry Clay, and John R. Young, backed a gradual-emancipation plan by which slave owners would pay the transportation costs to send freed slaves to Africa instead of paying county and state taxes on their slave property. The April showdown was a disaster. The abolitionist forces championed by Fee and the colonization forces championed by the Breckinridges could not find common ground, and a weakened plank highlighting gradual emancipation with immediate colonization of freed blacks was finally hammered out, to no one's satisfaction. Meanwhile the proslavery leaders John Breckinridge and Robert Wycliffe and others were courting delegates to the October convention and labeling all antislavery people as radical abolitionists. They reminded voters of the August 1848 Doyle armed slave revolt affecting Lexington and Bracken Co. in Kentucky and other slave revolts in the South. The scare tactics worked to perfection, and the antislavery people were routed badly. Statewide, only in Campbell Co., with the election of **Ira Root**, and in Knox and Harlan counties, with Silas Woodson's election, were emancipationists successful in electing delegates to the constitutional convention.

Emboldened by the political disarray among antislavery parties, the Kentucky legislature moved quickly to repeal the nonimportation-of-slaves act of 1833, and the 1850 Kentucky constitution squeezed the economic noose around free people of color and constricted emancipation requirements, demanding that any freed slave immediately leave the state, thereby clearly delineating Kentucky's status as a slave state.

During the early 1840s at Lane Seminary in Cincinnati, John G. Fee not only turned his back on his father's slaveholdings and his Bracken Co. neighbors' approval of the peculiar institution; he moved all the way to embrace the concept of the immediate abolition of slavery. Fee spent the next few years searching for a method to challenge slavery on Southern soil. At first he worked within the New School Presbyterians, founding churches in Lewis and Bracken counties; but the New School Synod disciplined him for his virulent antislavery activities. Fee had already moved toward an anticaste, antislavery position, and he gradually moved beyond any attachment to a denomination. In fact, he influenced the Bracken and Lewis Co. churches to become part of the Free Church movement.

Fee worked with Simeon S. Jocelyn, Amos Phelps, Lewis Tappan, and George Whipple of the American Missionary Association to develop a colporteur system, bringing Northern antislavery preachers and dedicated lay people to distribute Bibles, antislavery literature, and anticaste congregation development into the mid-South, particularly into Madison Co., Ky. Greatly influenced by Eli Thayer and John C. Underwood's concepts of northern emigrant communities in the upper South, Fee decided in 1858 to create a model egalitarian community at Berea, Ky., on lands donated by Cassius M. Clay. Fee recruited religious leaders and educators but never had the economic managerial expertise of the similar Ceredo community formed in West Virginia. Both as an educator and as a symbol, Fee stands alone in Kentucky's antislavery history.

Most historians acclaim Fee's courage at Berea, where former slaves and white men could form a community, and his work in educating men, women, and children at Camp Nelson in Garrard Co. and at Berea. But most historians also find Fee irrelevant to the attitudes and actions taken by the overwhelming numbers of Kentuckians during the 1860s. Fee, the last emancipationist, neither persuaded slave owners to give up their slaves nor persuaded yeomen to embrace blacks as fellow citizens. Consequently, Kentucky moved into and through the **Civil War** as a slave state.

Barrow, David. *Involuntary, Unmerited, Perpetual, Absolute, Hereditary Slavery Examined on the Principles of Nature, Reason, Justice, Policy, and Scripture.* Lexington, Ky.: Bradford, 1808.

Dumond, Dwight Lowell. *Antislavery: The Crusade for Freedom in America.* New York: W. W. Norton, 1961.

Howard, Victor B. *The Evangelical War against Slavery and Caste: The Life and Times of John G. Fee.* Selinsgrove, Pa.: Susquehanna Univ. Press, 1996.

Martin, Asa Earl. "Pioneer Antislavery Press," *Missouri Valley Historical Review* 2 (March 1916): 510–28.

Miller, Carolyn R., comp. *African American Bracken County Kentucky, 1797–1999.* Brooksville, Ky.: Bracken Co. Historical Society, 1999.

——. *Slavery in Newsprint: Central Ohio River Borderlands, 1840–1859.* Brooksville, Ky.: Bracken Co. Historical Society, 2003.

Tallant, Harold D. *Evil Necessity: Slavery and Political Culture in Antebellum Kentucky.* Lexington: Univ. Press of Kentucky, 2003.

Tenkotte, Paul A. "Rival Cities to Suburbs: Covington and Newport, Kentucky, 1790–1890," PhD diss., Univ. of Cincinnati, 1989.

Turner, Wallace B. "Abolitionism in Kentucky," *RKHS* 69 (October 1971): 319–38.

Diane Perrine Coon

ENAMELING. Enameled objects have been produced in Northern Kentucky since the mid-20th century; in addition, the region now has a museum devoted to enameling.

Enameling is fusing glass on metal by firing. Many commonly used metals can be utilized for enameling; especially popular are aluminum, copper, gold, silver, and steel. Enameling has industrial and functional applications in the manufacture of appliances, electric parts, pots, and sinks, and it is also used for artistic and craft purposes, as in jewelry, painting, and large wall sculptures. There are many types of artistic enameling, for instance, champlevé, cloisonné, grisaille, impasto, and plique-à-jour. Enameling has a long history, dating as far back as the 13th century B.C. in Cyprus.

Throughout the 19th and first half of the 20th centuries, Northern Kentucky's demand for enameled objects, such as appliances, chalices, and jewelry, was met by imports. Some examples include Msgr. Edward G. Klosterman's chalice at **Mother of God Catholic Church** and religious items in the collection of the **Cathedral Basilica of the Assumption**, both in Covington. Regarding the latter collection, Sr. Ernestine Ott, C.D.P., recollected, "I designed some of these religious objects for Bishop Mulloy, but the objects had to be sent abroad to be executed, including the enamel work. Some items were sent to Maria Laach Abbey in Germany."

The history of enameling production in Northern Kentucky began with Woodrow Carpenter, who was born in Snyder, Ill., September 11, 1915. His uncles raised him in West Union, Ill., because his mother died when he was 11 months old and his father was serving in **World War I**. Carpenter considered aviation as a career until the Illinois Clay Works Association offered him a scholarship to the University of Illinois at Champaign-Urbana. It was there that he decided to major in material science and engineering. He graduated in 1938 and settled in Frankfort, Ind., where he conducted research in the manufacture of vitreous enamel and founded the Woodrow W. Carpenter Company in 1950. The company produced art enamels and became a competitor of the Thomas C. Thompson Company in Chicago. In 1954 Carpenter moved his company to the basement of the Rookwood Company's facility in Cincinnati. In 1958 he founded the Ceramic Coating Company (CCC) at 1080 Waterworks Rd. in Newport.

Also in 1958, Woodrow met his future wife, Irmgard Toberg, originally of Krefeld, Germany. She had immigrated to Cincinnati with the help of her uncle, who worked with ceramic pigments at Shepherd Chemical in Norwood, Ohio. The couple married on September 3, 1960, in Cincinnati. In 1960 Woodrow Carpenter decided to merge his art enamel company in Cincinnati with CCC; he then moved CCC to Wilder by 1962. One of CCC's early customers was Tandy Leather, a division of American Handicraft.

The Ceramic Coating Company purchased its largest competitor, the 100-year-old enameling business of the Thomas C. Thompson Company of Chicago, on January 30, 1981, and made it the artistic enameling arm of CCC. The Thompson Company traced its enameling roots back to an ancestor, William Marlow, who enameled watches and clocks in Coventry, England, and immigrated to Illinois in 1882, at the urging of the Elgin Watch Company. The newly purchased division was moved to Kentucky in 1982. Art enamelists from all around the world order enamels from Thompson, because the company has streamlined the processes for students and teachers to examine and purchase enamels for artistic applications. Consequently, enameling has now become synonymous with the name of Woodrow Carpenter, at first in Northern Kentucky, then later in the United States, and finally in other parts of the world. The spread of Carpenter's reputation was assisted by the closing of other enamel companies, such as Schauer in Vienna, Austria. Since about 1985, Thompson Enamel has been the only manufacturer of jewelry enamel in the Western Hemisphere. It has become the driving force sparking many enameling activities in the Cincinnati–Northern Kentucky region, including numerous workshops and classes at its offices.

In 1982 the Ceramic Coating Company, in conjunction with the Thompson Enamel division, began publishing *Glass on Metal,* the enamelist's newsletter. By volume 6, number 6, the newsletter had grown into a 24-page magazine with color photos. This publication, one of the first of its kind, has made a monumental contribution to the education of enamelists. It has also played a significant role in promoting the science involved in the enameling process and in providing a forum for the exchange of ideas and information related to the process of enameling.

In 1986–1987, Thompson Enamel organized the Enamelist Society, which has grown to a membership of 900. "After a one-shot conference on enameling in Seattle, I wanted to start a society," Carpenter stated. "I thought there might be an opportunity to get people together on a regular basis." The Enamelist Society began with a conference, an invitational, a juried exhibition, and workshops in August 1987 in Cincinnati. Of the 10 conferences held thus far, the second and the third were in Covington at the Quality Hotel and the Carnegie Arts Center. Thompson Enamel, *Glass on Metal,* and the Enamelist Society and its conferences now serve an international population of artists. One of the most famous international enamelists, Valeri Timofeev of Russia, briefly took up residence in the Northern Kentucky region as a result of these conferences. The Enamelist Society eventually separated from Thompson Enameling.

The **Baker-Hunt Foundation** in Covington has sponsored additional enameling events in Northern Kentucky since at least 1970, when Tricia Kramer Noe of Northern Kentucky began teaching students there in the many techniques and styles of enameling. Her classes at the foundation continue, and her enameling students exhibit their artworks at Baker-Hunt shows and at Enamelist Society biennial conferences. According to Noe, some of the best enamellists in Northern Kentucky are Woodrow and Irmgard Carpenter, Charles Cleves of Cleves and Lonnemann Jewelers (Bellevue), Thompson artists-in-residence Tom Ellis and Harold Bill Helwig, and Rick Sacksteder. Bill Helwig is both a prolific artist and an extremely knowledgeable scientist regarding the physics of enameling.

On December 31, 1996, the Maehren family, relatives of Woodrow Carpenter, assumed control of the Thompson Enamel division of CCC, incorporating it as Thompson Enamel Inc. on January 2, 1997. Manufacturing was moved to nearby Bellevue, where the company has a current workforce of 22 employees. Research and development is a major focus. Thompson made a major advancement when it developed unleaded enamels, dropping its original line of enamels containing lead, for the safety of both employees and artists. In addition to art enamels, Thompson also sells many accessory products used by enamellists, such as furnaces, tools, and equipment. Highly valued for their durability and longevity, Thompson's enamels are used by manufacturers of badges, military insignia, and pins, as well as by producers of automotive emblems for trucks, special edition cars, and motorcycles such as Harley-Davidsons. For at least 10 years, Thompson enamel was used in Purple Heart medals.

In August 1991 Woodrow and Irmgard Carpenter established a small museum on their property along Winters Lane in Campbell Co. It exhibited enamels both historical, dating from as long ago as the third century, and contemporary. In 2004 the Bellevue City Council approved plans for the new W. W. Carpenter Enamel Foundation and Museum, located next to the Thompson plant. On Tuesday, September 19, 2006, the new museum opened to an international crowd of between 300 and 400. Participants were able to view an extensive permanent collection from the original museum, as well as a temporary exhibit of 98 enamels created by artists from seven nations.

Bates, Kenneth F. "The Enamelist Society Juried Exhibition," *Glass on Metal,* August 1989, 75–106.

Carpenter, Woodrow W. Interview by Rick Sacksteder, June 23, 2005, Bellevue, Ky.; telephone interview, December 29, 2006.

——. "Metals Suitable for Enameling," *Glass on Metal,* December 1986, 81–87, 96.

——. "Publisher's Column," *Glass on Metal,* December 2006, 99–101.

Eisman, Howard. "A Brief History of Enameling." www.archenamels.com (accessed December 27, 2006).

Friedenberg, Mary. "Made in Kentucky: Coating Hearts, Steel Ceramic Products Cover Medals, Pipes, Jewelry," *KP,* May 26, 1992, 10K.

Helwig, Harold Bill. Interview by Rick Sacksteder, June 23, 2005, Bellevue, Ky.

Noe, Tricia Kramer. Telephone interview by Rick Sacksteder, December 21, 2006.

Ott, Mary Ernestine, C.D.P. Telephone interview by Rick Sacksteder, December 31, 2006.

Stein, Jerry. "Carnegie Show Is a Rare Look at Enamel Art," *CP,* August 10, 1991, 1C.

Thompson Enamel. www.thompsonenamel.com (accessed December 27, 2006).

Wartman, Scott. "Museum Focuses on Art's Tiny Details," *CE,* September 15, 2006, 1B.

Richard M. Sacksteder

ENGLISH (ENGLISH STATION). English is six miles southwest of Carrollton in Carroll Co. The town was named for Capt. James Wharton English, who owned most of the land there. Captain English married Betsey DeMint, daughter of an early settler, and they lived in a log cabin along Mill Creek. The town of English grew somewhat after the completion of the **Louisville, Cincinnati, and Lexington Railroad** in 1867, connecting LaGrange with Newport. A tiny hamlet surrounding an early gristmill predated the railroad, and one of the earliest businesses there was the Green Brothers Country Store. The growth of English Station was due to the rail tracks that came through the center of the village. The station and siding served as a shipping point for the Mill Creek valley and large sections of the Kentucky River and the Little Kentucky River in Carroll, Trimble, and Henry counties.

Carroll Co.'s common schools were not organized comprehensively until 1867. At that time, English Station School was designated as District 15. Other early schools near English Station included Tomtown, District 17, on the West Fork of Mill Creek; and Malin's Branch, District 23, on the road to Cove Hill Union Church. These were one-room log buildings, generally about 20 by 30 feet in size. The rural schools were in session only during the three winter months. In 1903 land for a new graded schoolhouse in English was negotiated with M. A. Green. A large brick school building was built on that site and was used until 1943, when the local Board of Education consolidated all county pupils and transported them to the U.S. 42 school in Carrollton. The two-year high school at English (see **English High School**) served the community from 1915 until consolidation into **Carrollton High School** in 1938. In that year there were 225 pupils in the English School, 42 of whom were high school students being sent to the Carrollton High School. By 1959 the school at English was down to 183 students, and plans were being made to consolidate all county elementary schools into the new facility east of Carrollton that became the U.S. 42 Elementary School and later the Cartmell Elementary School.

The Baptist Church at English dates back to December 16, 1882, when delegates from several Baptist Churches in Carroll Co. gathered to constitute a new congregation. The congregation of **English Baptist Church** grew, and on September 29, 1907, a new house of worship was dedicated. The frame building seated 350 and was heated by a state-of-the-art furnace.

The Christian Church at English was founded in 1890 as the successor to a much older log church built on land donated in 1856 by T. C. Chilton along East Mill Creek. The log church gave way to a newer frame church that was known as the Old Mill Creek Christian Church. The decision to move the congregation to English was determined by whether more young people would attend at English than at the Old Mill Creek location, since the only method of transportation was horseback or walking. The Old Mill Creek Christian Church's building was torn down and moved to Worthville and used in the newly organized Christian Church there. The homemade benches from the Old Mill Creek Christian Church were also given to the Worthville Christian Church. The Old Mill Creek Christian Church's congregation split; some members went to Turners and some to English. Lafayette Hartman and several other members built the English Christian Church. The last service in the old church, a homecoming, was held on July 5, 1959; a large crowd turned out for the gathering. The next morning, workmen began tearing down the building. When the new brick church building was completed, the first service was held on Easter Sunday, April 17, 1960, with Rev. Thomas Mefford serving as pastor. Two of the chairs from the original 1890 church building remain in use.

A disastrous fire wiped out most of the section of English near the railroad tracks, and the buildings were never replaced. The population has declined slowly, and in 1984 English had only 300 people.

Bogardus, Carl R., Sr. *The Story of Gallatin County.* Ed. James C. Claypool. Cincinnati: John S. Swift, 2003.

Campbell, Justine Tandy. "History of the Carroll County Schools," 1976, Carroll Co. Public Library, Carrollton, Ky.

Gentry, Mary Ann. *A History of Carroll County.* Madison, Ind.: Coleman, 1984.

Diane Perrine Coon

ENGLISH BAPTIST CHURCH. The English Baptist Church, in Carroll Co. along Ky. Rt. 389, was constituted December 16, 1882, with 40 members. At this time they adopted a church covenant and articles of faith, and the church's rules of decorum were read and adopted. The naming of the church was postponed. It is unknown where the first house of worship was located, since the records of the English Baptist Church up to 1904 were destroyed.

In 1900 the English Baptist Church and seven other churches withdrew from the Concord Baptist Association to form the White's Run Baptist Association. These eight churches were joined by three churches from the Sulphur Fork Association for the organizational meeting at the Carrollton church. The English Baptist Church grew, and on September 29, 1907, a new house of worship was dedicated. The building was constructed of the best wooden material and had a seating capacity of 350. Churches in the White's Run Baptist Association donated $166 to help with the expense of the new building. Until at least 1915, the English Baptist Church held services only on the first Sunday of the month. By 1920 the church was gathering for worship twice a month, and on May 8, 1937, they decided to have services each week. In 1938 the church added classrooms for Sunday school. A mobile home was purchased in 1970 to serve as the parsonage. In 1979 the church built a fellowship hall. The construction of a new parsonage was started in 1988 by Kentucky Baptist Builders from the First Baptist Church of Richmond. Church members and people from other churches in the association assisted. Rev. Thomas Campbell moved into the new parsonage January 1989. A special relationship has existed between the English Baptist Church and the Southern Baptist Theological Seminary in Louisville. By 2005 membership of the church was 293, and 193 of the members lived close enough to attend regularly.

English Baptist Church Minutes, English Baptist Church, English, Ky.

Ken Massey

ENGLISH HIGH SCHOOL. Through a series of consolidations in Carroll Co. at the beginning of the 20th century, the one-room rural schools of the Mill Creek valley were closed, and students were transported into English. In 1903, when Margaret Schirmer was principal at the county's grade school at English, land for a new schoolhouse was acquired from M. A. Green. A large frame schoolhouse was built on that site.

In 1915 the local school district began planning a two-year high school. One room of the large two-story schoolhouse at English was assigned to the high school, and one full-time teacher was hired. In 1927 the English High School became part of the county school system in Carroll Co. John S. Forsee was the lone high school teacher, and 13 students attended the high school eight-month term that year. The next year J. L. Wilkington, a graduate of Kenyon College of Ohio with 25 years of teaching experience, was the teacher at the high school; while there, he tendered a report detailing the rundown condition of its frame building. It was also noted that the library contained only 10 books when he arrived. During his tenure at the high school at English, Wilkington added 150 books to the library, boosted the enrollment to 17 students, and expanded the school year to 155 days of instruction.

The townspeople raised $18,000 and erected a new brick school building for the grade and high school in 1929, and Woodford Davis, a graduate of Georgetown College in Kentucky, became the first teacher at the new high school. Davis soon had 19 students enrolled in the two-year high school. While Davis was the teacher, $100 worth of musical instruments were added to support the high school's music curriculum. In 1930 W. G. Lusby became principal at the high school, and Miss Lou Tandy taught the students. The following year, Roy McGee became principal, and he and Tandy built the high school enrollment to its peak of 25 students in 1933.

The community of English struggled with insufficient school funding and small numbers of students during the **Great Depression**. By 1938 English had closed its high school, and the school's upper-level pupils were transferred to the city high school at Carrollton.

Bevarly, R. W. "History of Education in Carroll County," master's thesis, Univ. of Kentucky, 1936.

Campbell, Justine Tandy. "History of the Carroll County Schools," 1976, Carroll Co. Public Library, Carrollton, Ky.

Carrollton News-Democrat, September 8, 1938.

Diane Perrine Coon

ENTERPRISE ZONES. The Kentucky Enterprise Zone Authority (KEZA), under which Campbell Co. and the City of Covington were named enterprise zones, was established in 1982 by the Kentucky legislature under Kentucky Revised Statute (KRS) 154.45-90. Modeled on a program begun in England, the enterprise zone concept was designed to renew economic vitality in economically depressed areas by concentrating governmental efforts through the use of incentives, for a dedicated period of time, that would attract private investment.

Ideally, zone designation would stimulate investment, thus creating jobs for "targeted" Kentucky residents who lived in the zone, who were unemployed for 90 days before being hired by an employer in the zone, or who had received public assistance for 90 days before being hired. Those businesses that were considered eligible to receive the benefits of the enterprise zone had to have at least 50 percent of their employees working in the zone.

Through KEZA 10 enterprise zones were created, each with a 20-year life span. The areas of the state receiving this designation (and dates) were Louisville (1983), Hickman (1983), Ashland (1984), Covington (1984), Owensboro (1985), Lexington (1985), Knox Co. (1986), Campbell Co. (1986), Paducah (1986), and Hopkinsville (1987).

Incentives for businesses associated with KEZA included exemption from state sales or use taxes for building materials utilized in remodeling, rehabilitation, or new construction of facilities located in the zone and for the purchasing or leasing of equipment; exemption from motor vehicle usage taxes for commercial vehicles purchased for the business; and exemption from taxes on the first $20,000 of the retail price of a noncommercial vehicle. Changes in the program instigated in the 1990s included granting businesses up to a $1,500 credit against local payroll taxes levied on "targeted" employees. Local governments were expected to add their own tax incentives to the program, thus creating an attractive tax incentive package to induce private investment.

The Kentucky Enterprise Zone Authority, under the state's Economic Development Cabinet, administered the program. Businesses wanting to take advantage of a zone's incentives were required to apply through a local zone administrator designated in each of the enterprise zones by local government. To be eligible to receive the program incentives, businesses had to meet specific thresholds associated with whether the business was considered "new" to the zone or "pre-existing," with different hiring and capital investment requirements associated with each. The Authority reviewed applications in league with an appointed board that then determined approval. Annual monitoring was meant to ensure that designated businesses stayed in compliance with zone requirements.

Northern Kentucky was approved to have two enterprise zones: Covington and Campbell Co. In Covington, approximately 90 businesses were participating in the enterprise zone program in its 20th year. Local incentives added to the KEZA program included an exemption for up to three years from the city's business license fee, a 40 percent rebate for up to five years on new payroll taxes collected by the city, a reduction of the Kenton Co. property tax up to .01 percent of every $1,000 of finished good inventory, and a five-year freeze on city property taxes collected on buildings rehabilitated by the business that were at least 25 years old.

Covington Enterprise Zone officials took the lead in pushing for the payroll tax credit to be added to the program. As originally designed, incentives were oriented toward attracting businesses that greatly benefited from property tax or sales tax incentives but may have employed only a few workers, such as warehouse operations. For urban areas, with a dependency upon increasing their payroll tax revenues, and with a limited availability of industrial acreage, the goal was to attract businesses that maximized the number of employees introduced to the community.

Payroll tax rebates provided the necessary stimulus to create opportunities for investments by companies that hired large numbers of employees. One such company was **Fidelity Investments** (a financial services company), which initially created more than 500 jobs with over $18 million in capital investment. Subsequent expansions of the company in Covington brought employment up over 2,500. Other companies that took advantage of the zone included Packaging Unlimited (a contract packaging and corrugated sheet plant), which was located on a vacant inner-city industrial property at the site of the former Ortner railroad freight car manufacturing facility. Several companies built new plants in the Pioneer Industrial Park, including White Castle (a food processor) and Atkins & Pearce (a manufacturer of braided hoses). Covington's zone also attracted new housing, such as Towne Properties' Roebling Row development, located in the city's riverfront area, which greatly benefited from the construction-material savings.

The Campbell Co. zone was unusual in that it originally covered a number of governmental units, including the cities of Bellevue, Dayton, Highland Heights, Newport, and Southgate, as well as county acreage. The Campbell Co. zone is credited for helping 190 businesses since its inception, 70 of which were still operating in 2006. Newport's riverfront development was stimulated when **Newport-on-the-Levee** developers took advantage of the program to create a major regional retail and tourist attraction that included the **Newport Aquarium** (which also took advantage of zone benefits). Development in the Levee project helped to bring other businesses to Newport, such as the world-famous Hofbrauhaus Restaurant.

Manufacturing in Campbell Co. also benefited from the program. **Newport Steel**, the last recipient of an Urban Development Action Grant given by the U.S. Department of Housing and Urban Development when it became employee-owned in the 1980s, won zone investment incentives. In the late 1990s, Campbell Co. received authorization to expand its zone south along the Ohio River to the city of Silver Grove as an inducement for the location of **LaFarge**, the largest wallboard manufacturer in the United States at the time of its development. Although no summary data exist for the 20 years of its program life, 2005 figures for the Campbell Co. zone show $4 million in new investment and the creation of 25 new jobs.

How well KEZA performed is an important question. Despite lobbying by state legislators and local government officials representing areas covered by KEZA, the program was not extended beyond its 20-year lifetime. Legislation submitted in 2003 and 2004 that would have extended the program failed to gain sufficient legislative support. Criticism of the program appears to have been primarily based upon its limitations; other parts of the state also were suffering from relatively high unemployment and low private investment and were not receiving the same level of state incentives. Essentially, KEZA covered only a small area of the state. Interest in expanding state incentives contributed to the impetus to replace KEZA with a program having a wider orientation.

Another criticism of the program was that it needed better oversight. For example, there are no summary figures for the years before 1997 to indicate how the enterprise zone program assisted in creating private investment or new jobs. Further, local enterprise zone coordinators were responsible for sending all paperwork to the state in order for companies to receive incentives, meaning that local pressure to assist development could result in exaggerations in the reporting of "targeted employee" hiring and other investment information, including what constituted a "business" vehicle.

In 2005 the Kentucky Enterprise Initiative Act (KEIA) was adopted by the Kentucky legislature as a replacement for KEZA. This program offers many of the same tax incentives; however, its emphasis is on manufacturing, service, or technology firms and tourism attraction projects. Under KEZA, a more diverse set of private investments was supported, including housing and small retail establishments. KEIA also differs from KEZA in that companies make application directly to the Kentucky Economic Development Finance Authority and receive reimbursements for expenditures from the Revenue Cabinet, not from local points-of-purchase. The new legislation gave preference (until January 2008) to companies locating in existing enterprise zones (referred to as "preference zones" under KEIA) that were willing to invest at least $100,000, while investment outside of those zones was at least $500,000. Once the last of the enterprise zones expire, KEIA legislation "preference zones" will no longer apply. KEIA was adopted under KRS 154.20-200 through 154.20-216.

While some analysis indicates that enterprise zones make a meaningful contribution to private investment, employment, and business growth, other research indicates that the zones do little to create "new" investment. In a U.S. Housing and Urban Development (HUD) study of eight enterprise zones located throughout the United States, Susan A. Jones, Allen Marshall, and Glenn Weisbrod found that the zones provided a great diversity in economic focus, strategies, and incentives. Although total business activity increased in the zones, the authors found that half of them declined in overall employment, a result that may be attributable to a change in business concentration away from manufacturing.

Several other studies indicated that, owing to the variability found in measuring investment, job creation, and retention, it is difficult to measure how successful enterprise zones have been; as an analysis of California's legislation to extend the lifespan of its enterprise zones illustrated, much of the investment in the zones likely would have occurred in the state anyway. Perhaps the most widely referenced study is that of Alan Peters and Peter Fisher, who found that most enterprise incentives are too small to greatly affect the investment and location decisions of most firms, that jobs in zones are often taken by nondisadvantaged individuals living far from the zone, and that employee tax rebates are usually not sufficient to significantly offset the cost of wages. Peters and Fisher concluded that most investments in the zones would have occurred in the state anyway, and while the zone may make a modest contribution to the local community, the incentive program becomes costly at the state level.

In another HUD study, 10 sites were examined, with findings indicating that the marketing associated with an enterprise zone may have been more important than the incentives offered in attracting new business. Northern Kentucky officials spoke of the zone as a "marketing angle" playing off of a national trend. KEZA was one in an array of incentives that local governments took advantage of to attract private investment. As one local official related, a community that had zone incentives had a better chance to attract investment.

Despite criticism of the enterprise zone program, local Kentucky communities saw the program as beneficial to attracting new investment and stimulating existing firms to expand. KEIA appears to acknowledge the desire to have such incentive programs and to address some of the issues raised by those in the state without access to the program and those concerned about greater programmatic oversight. In general KEIA appears to take into consideration the findings of Peters and Fisher and others as to the statewide costs associated with earmarking incentives only to limited areas of the state.

Adams, Brett. "Bill Would Replace State's Enterprise Zone Program," *Business First of Louisville*, January 21, 2005.

Bruning, Phyllis. Telephone interview by J. T. Spence, June 12, 2006.

Donovan, Kevin. Telephone interview by J. T. Spence, June 20, 2006.

Geisler, Bonnie. Telephone interview by J. T. Spence, June 19, 2006.

Jones, Susan A., Allen Marshall, and Glenn Weisbrod. "Business Impacts of Enterprise Zones, ACCN-4579," 1985, U.S. Department of Housing and Urban Development, Washington, D.C.

Kinney, Courtney. "Covington Faces Zone's Demise," *KP*, November 11, 2004, 1K.

"Officials Make Pitch for Enterprise Zones," *KP*, October 30, 2002, 1K.

Peters, Alan, and Peter Fisher. *State Enterprise Zone Programs: Have They Worked?* Kalamazoo, Mich.: W. E. Upjohn Institute for Employment Research, 2002.

"State Designated Enterprise Zones: Ten Case Studies, ACCN-4570," 1985, Office of the Assistant for Community Planning and Development, U.S. Department of Housing and Urban Development, Washington, D.C.

J. T. Spence

EP. A little settlement west of Hesler and near today's community of Greenup in Owen Co. was known as Ep. This community no longer exists except on old maps, but residents of Greenup still center their activities on the Baptist church located where Ep was. Ep has the distinction of being named after a woman, Penelope Wingate Sullivan, who was born February 9, 1832. She was the 12th of 14 children of **Cyrus Wingate** and his wife Emily Milly Spicer. Penelope married John Sullivan, and they were the parents of two daughters as well as rearing seven orphans. Because Penelope was a hard-to-pronounce name, everyone called her Ep for short. Along with her household work, Ep became well known for her knowledge of farming, especially the crop of tobacco. People stated that she had outstanding pioneer qualities for everyday living. When residents decided to name the community, the name that was suggested more than any other was Ep. A prominent resident of the community was **Lewis Henry Salin**. Today, a large number of descendants of Ep residents live where the community used to be.

Houchens, Mariam Sidebottom. *History of Owen County: "Sweet Owen."* Louisville, Ky.: Standard, 1976.

Doris Riley

EPISCOPALIANS. In this country, Episcopalians are members of the Episcopal Church of the United States, which has approximately 2 million members and is represented in Northern Kentucky by five congregations. The church is part of the worldwide Anglican Communion, with more than 80 million members, making it the second-largest Christian denomination in the world. Episcopalians are also sometimes called Anglicans to denote the spiritual traditions and bonds shared with overseas Anglican churches. The American Episcopal Church grew out of the Church of England, which became part of the Protestant movement in the 16th century when King Henry VIII broke with the Roman Catholic Church over his desire to divorce his wife, Catherine of Aragon. In the ensuing centuries, the Church of England spread throughout the British Empire, including the original 13 American colonies.

The Book of Common Prayer is the prayer book used in all Episcopal and Anglican churches. Thus, worship services in an Episcopal church in California will be identical in important aspects to worship services in an Episcopal church in Kentucky, as well as in overseas Anglican churches. Long regarded as one of the major works of English literature, the Book of Common Prayer traces its origins to the 16th century when the Protestant Church of England became the official church of England. The prayer book has been revised several times since, but the current version, adopted in 1979, retains some of the majestic cadences, phrases, and prayers of the original prayer book.

Episcopalians believe in the doctrine of apostolic succession, which holds that all members of the clergy—priests, deacons, and bishops—receive their spiritual orders and authority by the "laying on of hands," which continues an unbroken line of succession that reaches back to the Apostles.

Organizationally, the Episcopal Church is divided into dioceses, which generally are drawn within the geographic boundaries of a state. In Kentucky there are two Episcopal dioceses: the Diocese of Lexington, headquartered in Lexington and consisting of the counties in the eastern part of the state, and the Diocese of Kentucky, headquartered in Louisville, made up of the counties in the remainder of the state. Dioceses of the Episcopal Church are headed by bishops, selected by the church members within the dioceses and ordained by the presiding bishop of the Episcopal Church. There are presently 110 Episcopal dioceses in the United States.

Episcopalians meet every three years in the General Convention, where matters of governance, doctrine, and statements of the faith are debated and enacted. The convention is divided into the House of Bishops and the House of Deputies, composed of laity and clergy, which consider and report on matters to the convention as a whole.

St. Andrew's Episcopal Church in Fort Thomas, **Trinity Episcopal Church** in Covington, **St. Paul's Episcopal Church** in Newport, Grace Episcopal Church in Florence, and the **Church of the Nativity** in Maysville represent the Episcopal Church in Northern Kentucky. The **St. John the Evangelist Anglican Catholic Church** in Dayton, Ky., which began as a mission of St. Paul's in Newport, was a member of this group until severing its ties with the Episcopal Church in 1978. An additional church, the St. Stephen's Episcopal Church in the Latonia neighborhood of Covington, closed in 2005 after 95 years of service.

Swinford, Francis Keller, and Rebecca Smith Lee. *Great Elm Tree: Heritage of the Episcopal Diocese of Lexington*. Lexington, Ky.: Faith House Press, 1969.

John West

ERLANGER. The city of Erlanger in Kenton Co. was created in 1785 on 2,200 acres of land granted by the Commonwealth of Virginia to John D. Watkins and Robert Johnson. The Watkins-Johnson property was located on the Dry Ridge, a natural high point that runs from near the Ohio River into Central Kentucky. Huge herds of buffalo seeking salt licks in the area instinctively traveled the highest points to avoid climbing hills, and their use of the **Dry Ridge Trace** created an ancient highway that was used by the earliest travelers through the area. The Johnson-Watkins tract of land was divided by a buffalo trail that in 1793 served as the basis of the Georgetown Rd., which ran from the Ohio River to Georgetown and became the primary route to Central Kentucky.

Settlement began shortly after 1800, when Bartlett Graves and John Stansifer moved their families to the area and established plantations. William Thornton Timberlake, a major in the **War of 1812**, purchased Stansifer's property and in about 1826 built a home, which still stands in Erlanger (see **Timberlake House**). The George M. Bedinger and Thomas Buckner families joined these settlers during the 1820s. William and George Longmoor purchased property in the area in the 1830s, and David Riggs obtained property on the western side of later Erlanger.

These settlers saw increased traffic along the Georgetown Rd. as the Cincinnati meatpacking industry developed and as the stagecoach route was established in 1818, offering a 34-hour trip between Cincinnati and Lexington. In 1834 the Commonwealth of Kentucky legislated improvements to the road by chartering the **Covington and Lexington Turnpike** and providing for the construction of the turnpike; stone, gravel, wood, and other materials were used to build it. By 1839 the first 10 miles of the turnpike from Covington were finished, including the section through what became Erlanger. At a cost of $7,800 per mile, it was the most expensive highway built in Kentucky up to that time. Tollbooths, located every five miles, charged a toll of 10 cents for a horse and cart. When the road was finally finished in the 1850s, the travel time to Lexington was cut to 12 hours.

Settlers in the area were actively involved in development of the turnpike as well as other political affairs. Timberlake and Graves were leaders in the efforts to create Kenton Co. during the late 1830s. The farmers in the area were primarily slaveholders, and they were increasingly plagued by the loss of slaves who escaped across the nearby Ohio River. Buckner and Timberlake formed an organization to help prevent the escape of slaves, and Timberlake even led an expedition to Michigan, attempting, unsuccessfully, to recover escaped slaves from the area (see **Adam Crosswhite**).

During the early 1850s, Caleb Stone Manley purchased property in the growing community. Manley used bricks made by slaves on his property to build a mansion that fronted on the turnpike (see **Caleb Manley House**). He introduced many plants from the Deep South to adorn the property, which has served as a showplace for more than 150 years and now provides the final resting place for community residents as **Forest Lawn Cemetery**.

An agrarian economy continued to develop in the area, which by the 1850s was known as Timberlake in recognition of Timberlake's leadership. Many of the farms were large, were organized in plantation fashion, had large homes typical of those in the South, and were worked by slaves. Most of the settlers came from southern states. There was considerable sympathy with the South during the **Civil War**, and sons of the area fought primarily with the Confederate Army. In September 1862, when the Confederate Army made its only foray

Dixie Highway, Erlanger, showing the Erlanger Hardware store (*right*) and the Dempsey Motor Car Company, ca. 1920.

into Northern Kentucky, its soldiers marched up the turnpike through Timberlake before retreating after a few days.

The end of the Civil War initiated an economic revitalization for Cincinnati and Northern Kentucky. As the urban areas grew, traffic on the turnpike increased in Timberlake. The need for a railroad from Cincinnati into the South became apparent, since the developing industries needed better access to agricultural products. The State of Ohio approved the building of a railroad by the City of Cincinnati with Chattanooga, Tenn., as the terminus, but interests from Louisville blocked the plan until 1872, when the railroad was approved by a one-vote margin in the Kentucky Senate. In 1874 the City of Ludlow outbid Covington and Newport for the railroad bridge from Cincinnati. With the bridge located in Ludlow, the most direct route to the South went through Timberlake. To encourage selection of this route, property owners contributed funds and gave property for the railroad right-of-way. Building the railroad on this route required a six-mile climb up the hills surrounding Northern Kentucky. Steam engines that powered the trains required large amounts of water to climb the grade, and by the time the trains reached the top at Timberlake, additional water was needed. The location for a refilling station to meet this need was selected at the intersection of the railroad with the turnpike, where a depot could also be constructed for the loading of passengers and freight. This depot became the heart of the future city of Erlanger.

Laying of railroad track was begun in 1876, and the depot was built in 1877, along with a large reservoir, a wooden water tower, and stock pens, at a total cost of $3,879. The name Greenwood was chosen for the depot, in honor of Miles Greenwood, president of the Board of Trustees of the **Cincinnati Southern Railroad**. The lake soon became known as Silver Lake. The first train rolled down the tracks on April 20, 1877, and reached Lexington in two hours and 45 minutes. Passenger service was inaugurated on July 23, 1877.

With the opening of the railroad, the residents of Timberlake were much closer to the city. A trip to Covington or Cincinnati that could take hours on the turnpike was now possible in minutes on the train. Within a few years, new businesses including a saloon, an icehouse, a store, a hotel, a blacksmith, and a lumber company opened near the depot. Additional residents arrived also, and the need for a post office was felt by the early 1880s. The U.S. government rejected the name Greenwood because the name was so common. Proposed as an alternative was the name Erlanger, in honor of Baron Fréderick Émile d'Erlanger, whose banking firm owned the majority of the company holding the lease for the railroad. Erlanger was approved, and the post office was established on May 20, 1882, in George Bedinger's store, with Bedinger as the postmaster.

Developers soon recognized the value of the property around the depot. In 1887 a syndicate led by Cincinnati businessmen James P. Garvey and Charles P. Judkins persuaded others to join them in creating the Erlanger Land Syndicate, which laid out the streets of Erlanger basically as they exist today, constructing Commonwealth Ave. and improving Erlanger Rd. and removing its toll. The first sale of lots was conducted on June 18, 1887. Special excursions brought train carloads of prospective buyers to town; attractive financing options were offered, such as one-third down and $1 per week at 6 percent interest, along with free rail transportation for one year. The first home was completed in September 1887. The syndicate also provided lots for a Catholic church where **St. Henry Catholic Church** now stands and a Protestant church where the **Erlanger United Methodist Church** now stands. The Protestant church, known as the Erlanger Union Church, was built in 1888 and became the Erlanger Methodist Church, South, in 1889. The **Erlanger Baptist Church** was built in 1890, also on a lot donated by the Erlanger Land Syndicate.

As this development was taking place, Dr. Charles R. Slater collected $100 from residents to pay the fee to tap into the telephone line to Florence, Ky. The first telephone was installed in Slater's office in 1890. The first financial institution in Erlanger, the Erlanger Perpetual Building and Loan Association, was organized in 1890, and the first full-service bank, the Erlanger Deposit Bank, was established in 1892. Also in 1892, on the northwest corner of Commonwealth Ave. and the Lexington Turnpike, Robert J. Scott built a three-story building that became the center of activity in Erlanger and was known as the Town Hall.

Additional development occurred rapidly during the 1890s. In May 1896 the area that had been known as South Erlanger incorporated as the City of Elsmere. Less than a year later, on January 25, 1897, the City of Erlanger was incorporated. For the first 57 years, a board of trustees governed Erlanger. The city had its own court, presided over by a police judge; law enforcement was handled by the town marshal. The first town officers of Erlanger were Louis Morrelli, police judge; A. I. Wyss, town marshal; and George C. Bloss, Isadore Hagan, Mathew Huerkamp, Henry Mussman, and Larry Nusbaum, trustees.

The first federal census that included Erlanger as a city, conducted in 1900, reported that Erlanger had 453 residents along with three grocery stores, two livery stables, and a variety of other businesses. Because the dirt roads became quagmires after rains, the city began macadamizing, grading, curbing, and guttering the roads and also constructed concrete sidewalks. The first firefighting equipment was obtained in 1904, and the volunteer fire department was established with Andy Scheben Sr. as chief.

Always an issue, transportation again became a concern during the early 1900s. Just as the first automobile rolled down the turnpike, the railroad eliminated commuter service in 1907, greatly limiting options for Erlanger's residents. City leaders unsuccessfully lobbied the **Green Line** to extend service to Erlanger. As the city's population increased by 54 percent to 700 by 1910, only Kenton Co. and neighboring Boone Co. continued charging tolls on the turnpike. In 1913 Kenton Co. condemned and purchased the turnpike so that tolls could be discontinued. Beginning in 1915, the old turnpike was covered by concrete; the process was completed to the Boone Co. line in 1921. The **Dixie Highway** was the result.

Entertainment in Erlanger during this period was provided in several venues. The Erlanger Fairgrounds, located on 32 acres where the **Lloyd Memorial High School** now stands, offered horse and harness racing, fairs, circuses, and carnivals, as well as other attractions. A large theater opened, which used the icehouse located next door for air conditioning. Col. Thomas Cody operated a restaurant and various recreational activities at the mansion built by Caleb Manley and the surrounding farm that is now Forest Lawn Cemetery. The Erlanger Woman's Club opened the Erlanger Elsmere Library in 1914, in the Citizen's Bank Building on Dixie Highway. The first radio came to Erlanger in 1917 and could be heard at Dahlenberg's Drug Store, where residents could always find current baseball scores written on the sidewalk in front of the store.

With the completion of Dixie Highway and the installation of a public water system, development of the old farms around the city resulted in a building boom in Erlanger during the 1920s. More than 400 homes were constructed in Erlanger and Elsmere in 1927 alone, and the population of both cities doubled. There was so much growth that the city had difficulty constructing and maintaining the streets needed for development. To meet the educational needs of the city, the Erlanger and Elsmere school systems were consolidated (see **Erlanger-Elsmere Schools**), and a new high school was completed in 1929. Erlanger annexed additional territory in 1927 and 1929, extending the city's boundaries to the north and the west. According to the 1930 census, the population was 1,853, an increase of 260 percent in the previous 10 years.

Although the **Great Depression** resulted in the failure of the city's bank, improvements in the city continued, with the construction of a sewage system and the construction of the railroad underpass on Dixie Highway in 1936. The city's growth during the 1930s continued, as the 1940 census reported a population increase of 30 percent. City leaders adopted one of the first planning and zoning ordinances in Northern Kentucky in 1943, heralding a period of expansion. From 1946 until 1962, the city adopted 10 annexations.

One of the major factors in this development was the creation of the Greater **Cincinnati/Northern Kentucky International Airport**. Although the site was in Boone Co., Erlanger was the nearest town and provided much of the support for the construction and for transportation to the airport. To manage the ever-increasing population and need for city services, the government of Erlanger was changed in 1949 from the board-of-trustees system to a mayor-council system. Frank Dehner was elected Erlanger's first mayor. John Domaschko was employed to organize the city's finances in 1950; O. K. Price was elected as Erlanger's second mayor in 1953; and Mayo Taylor was chosen as the city's first coordinator in 1954. Clyde Rouse succeeded Taylor in 1958, as Erlanger moved up to third-class-city status and the city council increased to 12 members.

The 1950s were a golden era for dining and nightspots in Erlanger. All along Dixie Highway were establishments that attracted local residents along with famous out-of-towners who enjoyed the **Gourmet Strip**.

The city's population in 1960 was 7,072, which represented a 91 percent increase over 1950. This was also the year when the city's first McDonald's opened. In 1961 Erlanger joined the Northern Kentucky Area Planning Commission and elected a new mayor, Ray E. Price Jr. A new city building was constructed in 1962, consolidating city offices in one building. Another major improvement in transportation occurred in 1962, when I-75 was completed through Erlanger. The opening of I-275 in 1977 made the intersection of I-75 and I-275 in the city the center of transportation in the area once again.

Because of the rapid growth, the city government, recognizing the need for additional land for development, annexed land to the east of the city along Turkeyfoot Rd. This expansion was followed by another major annexation on Turkeyfoot and Narrows Rds. in 1972. The 1970 census counted 12,903 residents in Erlanger, an increase of 82 percent over the previous 10 years. The city acted to preserve its history by purchasing the old railroad property including the depot and Silver Lake. Silver Lake was drained and the area converted to Silver Lake Park. The old depot was moved away from the railroad tracks to be used as a museum of the city's history. It also serves as the centerpiece of Railroad Park. During the 1970s, mayors Austin Mann, James E. Ellis, and Orville Sorrell served Erlanger. The first woman council member, Carol Lainhart, was also elected.

Growth in the last quarter of the 20th century was seen in the 12 percent population increase reported in the 1980 census and the additional 10 percent increase in the 1990 census. Fred Thomas served as the city's mayor for 12 years and was succeeded by Mark Otto in 1993. Since the land for future residential expansion was located on the east side of the city, infrastructure including a fire station was built on Narrows Rd. The city successfully recruited major firms to its industrial parks on the west side of the city near the airport.

In 1997 Erlanger celebrated its centennial as a city with a yearlong schedule of events, including an ecumenical religious service and gala. In 2000 the U.S. Census Bureau reported that Erlanger had a population of 16,676.

Childress, Henry F. "The History of Erlanger," *KP*, February 16, 1924, 5.

Onkst, Wayne, ed. *From Buffalo Trails to the Twenty-First Century: A Centennial History of Erlanger, Kentucky.* Erlanger, Ky.: Erlanger Historical Society, 1996.

Records of the Cincinnati Southern Railroad, Cincinnati Historical Society, Cincinnati.

Wayne Onkst

ERLANGER BAPTIST CHURCH. The North Bend Association of Baptists established the first Erlanger Baptist Church in fall 1890 as a mission. On October 17, 1889, the Erlanger Land Syndicate had donated land along Commonwealth Ave. for the church, and the Erlanger Baptist Church met in an already-existing building there, which was set amid modest homes. The building could hold 350 people, and it included a baptistery and a dressing room. At the dedication of the new church, Sunday, November 30, 1890, Rev. W. H. Felix, DD, of Lexington, delivered the sermon. The charter members, according to church records, were Mrs. Robert Baker, Mr. and Mrs. Julius L. Bristow, Col. and Mrs. Hubbard T. Buckner, Miss Sophia Buckner, Miss Sativa B. Childress, and Mr. and Mrs. Ephraim E. Utz. A report of the executive board stated that the membership had increased to 19 by September 9, 1891. At the time, Erlanger and Elsmere had a combined population of 300.

On January 10, 1892, Oscar M. Huey was called to serve as pastor. In July 1892 the first church bell was purchased. In May 1900 the congregation decided to replace the coal oil lamps with gasoline lamps and to install a hot air furnace. In June 1926 a Sunday school annex was built, and by 1948 the Sunday school enrollment was 424. A new church building was dedicated on March 1, 1953. The church purchased a home in 1956 at 125 Erlanger Rd. for use as a parsonage. In May 1962 the congregation dedicated a new three-story educational building. In 1964 a kindergarten was opened, and Mrs. Pearl Silcox and Mrs. E. B. Yelton were hired as teachers. The kindergarten continued until 1978. In 1969 a radio ministry on Erlanger radio station WHKK was initiated. During the 1970s, several pieces of adjacent property were purchased, enlarging the complex to the size of a full city block and providing space for the ever-increasing needs of the growing church.

Dr. William E. Crosby Jr. became pastor in June 1983. "Brother Bill" served the church for 20 years and was also an active member of the Erlanger Rotary Club. In 1985 the church's choir, under the direction of Dr. Philip Quinn, gave the first performance of the "Living Christmas Tree," now an annual community holiday event. In January 1989 a multipurpose building with new offices, educational and fellowship halls, and recreational space was built. The Life Center, completed in 1997, included a day care center, a preschool, basketball and racquetball courts, an indoor track, and an exercise room with showers and lockers.

In June 2003 Crosby gave up his ministry, and Dr. Daniel Francis was elected pastor. The current membership of Erlanger Baptist Church is 1,500. The church now conducts a deaf ministry, dual Sunday schools, and a Saturday night worship service.

Bradshaw, Ortie E. *Erlanger Baptist Church, 1890–1990: "A Century of Ministry."* Erlanger, Ky.: Erlanger Baptist Church, 1990.

Erlanger Baptist Church records, Erlanger Baptist Church, Erlanger, Ky.

Kenton Co. Deed Book 64, p. 488.

Onkst, Wayne, ed. *From Buffalo Trials to the Twenty-First Century: A Centennial History of Erlanger, Kentucky.* Erlanger, Ky.: Erlanger Historical Society, 1996.

Patricia A. Hahn

ERLANGER-ELSMERE SCHOOLS. The first school in Erlanger and Elsmere, which began during the late 1860s, was in an old cabin behind Dr. **John Stevenson**'s house. The teacher was a college graduate and was paid by the citizens from the two towns who sent their children to the school. When the cabin could no longer be used, a drive was held to raise funds for a new school building, which was built in Elsmere opposite the Graves Pond in a locust grove at the corner of **Dixie Highway** and Erlanger St. (the current location of Dusing Brothers

Ice). The school was called the Locust Grove Academy. From 1871 to 1884, there were no schools in Erlanger or Elsmere. Students probably attended the nearby Florence or Turkeyfoot Rd. schools. For several years afterward, members of the Erlanger and Elsmere communities started many small private schools.

The Erlanger public school system began in a one-room frame building at what is today 46 Erlanger Rd. A state charter for the school district was obtained in 1888, and the school's first building was erected in 1889. The district served all the local children, including those from Elsmere and some from the surrounding areas. Only enough money was available to operate the school for five months a year, but parents could pay fees to keep the school open for an extra two to three months. It was then referred to as a pay school.

Around 1891, the first school for African American children in the area was built in North Erlanger along the **Covington and Lexington Turnpike**, far from where the black population of the two communities lived. Thomas Greene from Virginia led a group of citizens who raised money for this school. When the school burned, the same group renewed their efforts and purchased a lot on Spring St. that was located in the African American section of South Erlanger.

In 1896 South Erlanger was incorporated as Elsmere, and three years later, the city received its own school charter. A brick school was built at Central Row and Buckner Sts. (the present site of Dorothy Howell Elementary School) in 1903. In Erlanger, the Locust St. School was erected in 1907 and high school classes were started at that time. The first high school graduates received their diplomas in 1912.

During the late 1920s, it was decided to consolidate the Erlanger and Elsmere schools. However, Kentucky law at the time dictated that no new independent school districts could be formed. A group of citizens led by former U.S. congressman **A. B. Rouse** and J. C. Mills, a member of the state department of education, were able to get a rider attached to a bill that was certain to pass in the Kentucky legislature. The rider provided that a new district could be formed if it represented a community the size of the total population of Erlanger and Elsmere (about 5,000). The Erlanger-Elsmere Independent School System was then formed. The African American school in Elsmere, which had been operating independently, became part of the new school district, but the schools remained segregated.

Foeman A. Rudd, superintendent at the Locust St. School, was named the first superintendent of the Erlanger-Elsmere Schools. Edgar Arnett, the Elsmere school's superintendent, was named the principal of the high school. The new school board decided that a new high school was needed. About five acres of land near the Erlanger fairgrounds were purchased, and bonds were sold for the construction of the school, which was named **Lloyd Memorial High School** after **John Uri Lloyd**, a well-known local resident and author. The first graduating class celebrated commencement in the auditorium of the new high school in May 1929.

Foeman Rudd left the school district in 1929, and Edgar Arnett was named the second superintendent of the Erlanger-Elsmere Schools. In September 1945, black students held a strike because after the Erlanger-Elsmere Schools had announced plans to build two schools, one for white and one for black children, only the school for white children had been built. The school for black children was finally built on Capital Ave. in Elsmere in 1948 and was named the Wilkins Heights School after the Wilkins family, a prominent black family who owned the land on which the school was built.

In 1955 **Rosella French Porterfield**, the head teacher at the Wilkins Heights School, approached Superintendent Arnett about integrating the schools. She formulated a plan that would integrate a few grades at a time. The school district began implementing this plan in 1956, and the integration proceeded so smoothly that the school district was included in an article in the September 17, 1956, issue of *Life* magazine highlighting integration efforts across the country.

In late 1956 a new high school building was completed on the site of the old Erlanger Fairgrounds. The old high school building was converted to an elementary school and renamed Erlanger Elementary School. An addition was added to this elementary school in 1957, nearly doubling the classroom space for the growing population.

In 1965 Edgar Arnett retired after a long, successful career in the Erlanger-Elsmere Schools. His visionary leadership had helped form the new school district. James I. Tichenor, the high school principal, was named as his successor. In the late 1960s, the high school again became too small to accommodate the number of students enrolled. Seventh- and eighth-grade students were sent to the old Locust St. School until an addition could be added to Lloyd Memorial High School. The new expansion featured classrooms and a modern library, allowing the Locust St. School to be closed permanently. Growth in the district also created the need for a new elementary school, and Arnett Elementary (named after Edgar Arnett) opened in 1967. The school was already too small when it opened, however, and some students who were to attend the new school were sent to the Erlanger Elementary School instead.

In 1971 Superintendent James I. Tichenor retired after a long career in the Erlanger-Elsmere Schools. The school board changed the name of the Erlanger Elementary School to James I. Tichenor Elementary (later Middle) School. They also voted to change the name of Elsmere Elementary School to Dorothy Howell Elementary School to honor Dorothy Howell, who had been a teacher and the principal at that school for more than 30 years. John W. Miles was named as Tichenor's successor. Miles, a Lloyd Memorial High School alumnus, had been principal of Erlanger Elementary School. He was the youngest school superintendent in Kentucky at the time.

The rapid growth of the school district prompted the building of two new elementary schools, Sunset Elementary School and A. J. Lindeman Elementary School, in 1971. A. J. Lindeman was a longtime board member and supporter of education. A new cafeteria and a band room were added to Lloyd Memorial High School in 1971, and metal and wood shops, science laboratories, and a lecture room were added in 1973. Sunset Elementary School was renamed the John W. Miles Elementary School in 1975.

In 1979 the William J. Scheben Gymnasium was erected between the Tichenor Middle School and Lloyd Memorial High School. Scheben played basketball and football at Lloyd Memorial High School and was a great supporter of his alma mater.

John W. Miles resigned as superintendent in October 1982 and was succeeded by assistant superintendent Harold Ensor, who continued in the position until 1994. Because the school district was in a financial deficit, Ensor immediately had to draft a plan for the state detailing how the district would solve its money difficulties. During his tenure, sports facilities were upgraded, a maintenance building was completed, and computer labs were added at all schools in the Erlanger-Elsmere district. The schools continued their academic success and the district was once again operating in the black. James E. Molley was chosen to succeed Ensor as superintendent.

The Fred Dietz Jr. Auditorium, which seats 500 and is located inside the Scheben Gymnasium facility, was dedicated in 1996. It was named for board member Fred Dietz, at the time one of only two school board members in Kentucky with more than 25 years of continuous service. In 1999 a new wing was added to Tichenor Middle School. The old section of the building (the original high school building) was then renamed Ensor Educational Annex. The annex houses a meeting room, a teacher resource center, and offices.

James Molley retired in 2002 and was replaced by Michael D. Sander, who became the seventh superintendent of the Erlanger-Elsmere Schools. The gymnasium at Tichenor Middle School was renamed the James E. Molley Gymnasium. Today, the Erlanger-Elsmere Schools rank among the top schools in Kentucky. The district has been awarded the What Parents Want distinction. *Newsweek* magazine named Lloyd Memorial High School one of the nation's most innovative high schools in May 2006.

Archives of the Erlanger-Elsmere Independent Schools, Erlanger, Ky.

"Merger Is Urged: Consolidation of High Schools Is Suggested," *KP*, February 11, 1928, 1.

Onkst, Wayne, ed. *From Buffalo Trails to the Twenty-First Century: A Centennial History of Erlanger, Kentucky*. Erlanger, Ky.: Erlanger Historical Society, 1996.

Deborah Onkst

ERLANGER UNITED METHODIST CHURCH. The United Methodist Church is Erlanger's oldest church. The Erlanger Land Syndicate donated lots for a church to be called the Erlanger Union Church and to be shared by all Protestant denominations. It was located on the present site of the Erlanger United Methodist Church on Commonwealth Ave. By common consent the church became Erlanger Methodist Church South in 1889. Several Erlanger community services got their start in the Methodist Church. The original Erlanger Library was begun in the Erlanger Deposit Bank in 1914, but shortly afterward it moved to the Methodist Church and remained there until 1928. The Erlanger Elsmere United Ministries was located in a one-room office on the first floor of the Erlanger United Methodist Church in 1981 (see **United Ministries of Northern Kentucky**).

Methodist minister Merriman of Petersburg, Ky., came to Erlanger to hold services in 1894–1895. He had a pony and a light two-wheeled cart that he drove to Erlanger on Saturday evening; he spent the night at R. J. Cody's residence, then preached on Sunday morning. In 1897 the average attendance at the church was 47.

Just before daylight on January 4, 1948, a fire destroyed the Methodist Church building. The building was so damaged that it had to be demolished. However, the original pump organ, the pulpit, the pulpit Bible, and the altar were saved. A picture of Christ at Gethsemane painted by Mrs. Hayes Ketchum was destroyed, but Mrs. Ketchum repainted the picture, and it hangs in the sanctuary today. On December 18, 1955, the new building was dedicated.

On January 21, 1958, a house and lot on the corner of Commonwealth and Home Sts. were purchased, and the house was used for Sunday school. Property at 22 Graves Ave. was purchased on June 3, 1963, for a parsonage. In 1967 the property at 25 Commonwealth was acquired for additional Sunday school space, and additional property on Commonwealth and Home Sts. was purchased during the 1970s. Because this land was to be used for parking, the structures at 21 and 25 Commonwealth Ave. and 3509 and 3511 Home St. were torn down. The church now owned all the property along Home St. between Graves Ave. and Commonwealth Ave. except for one plot, so in 1981 the church bought the remaining parcel of land, 3513 Home St. In 1988 a large centennial celebration was held. Membership of the Erlanger United Methodist Church in 2005 was 397.

"Erlanger United Methodist Names Pastor," *KP*, June 20, 1992, 11K.

Reis, Jim. "Fire Raged in '47–'48," *KP*, April 28, 1997, 4K.

"Woman, 91, Leads Campaign to Rebuild Church," *KTS*, April 5, 1955, 2A.

Patricia A. Hahn

ERNST, JAMES C. (b. 1855, Covington, Ky.; d. September 20, 1917, Ashville, N.C.). Transportation executive James C. Ernst was one of five children of William and Sarah Butler Ernst. An outstanding student and athlete, Ernst graduated from Princeton University in Princeton, N.J., in 1873. He was named the best baseball player in the Ivy League and turned down a number of offers from professional **baseball** teams; instead, he returned to Covington. He accepted a position as head cashier with the **Northern Bank of Kentucky** and held that position until he was named the local general passenger agent of the **Kentucky Central Railroad**. He returned to banking thereafter as president of the German National Bank of Covington, a post he held for some 21 years.

Ernst also continued his interest in baseball and played for a number of local semiprofessional teams. In 1876 he formed a semiprofessional team, the Covington Stars, and eventually raised enough capital to purchase a parcel of property at Madison Ave. and Seventh St. in downtown Covington and erect a modest baseball park on the site.

In 1896 a group of local investors, which included his brother **Richard P. Ernst**, purchased the Cincinnati, Newport, and Covington Railway Company (CN&C, the **Green Line**) and its wholly owned subsidiary, the Rosedale Electric Company. The new owners installed James Ernst as president of both companies on January 11, 1897. Over the next five years, Ernst promoted the sale of excess electricity generated by the CN&C's Newport powerhouse on Lowell St. to local business and residential customers in Newport and Covington. He also introduced natural gas for use as a heating fuel. So successful was Ernst in promoting these enterprises that, by the turn of the century, a new subsidiary of the CN&C Railway Company was formed, the Union Light, Heat, and Power Company (ULH&P), and Ernst became its president. During the late 1890s, Ernst also oversaw expansion of the CN&C's electric **streetcar** line along Covington's 12th St. to Park Hills and out Holman Ave. to what was then the independent city of Central Covington.

In 1902 the CN&C and the ULH&P were sold to the Northern American Company, a large midwestern transit and energy company based in Milwaukee, Wis. Ernst was asked by the North American Company to remain as the chief executive of both local companies, a testament to his successful management of these companies under the former owners. In 1907 the North American Company sold both the CN&C Railway Co. and its subsidiary, the Union Light, Heat, and Power Company, to the Columbia Gas and Electric Company, another energy-producing conglomerate. The Columbia Gas and Electric Company's board of directors also asked Ernst to remain in charge of both of the companies they had purchased. During the period from 1907 to 1914, ULH&P became the dominant supplier of natural gas and electricity in Kenton, Campbell, and Boone counties and became more profitable than the Columbia Gas and Electric Company's multiple gas and electric holdings in New York, Ohio, Pennsylvania, and West Virginia. Also, Ernst presided over the last expansions of the Green Line Company's electric streetcar line to southern Bellevue in 1904 and to South Fort Mitchell in 1910.

Poor health forced Ernst into retirement in October 1914. Subsequently, he and his wife, the former Jennie Stites Early, moved to Asheville, N.C. There, on September 20, 1917, Ernst died of a chronic heart and respiratory disease. During the funeral services held in Covington, all the Green Line Company motormen stopped their electric streetcars for one minute in memory of their longtime president. James Ernst was buried at Highland Cemetery in Fort Mitchell.

"Ernst Dies in South, Funeral to Be Saturday," *KP*, September 21, 1917, 1.

Lehmann, Terry W., and Earl W. Clark. *The Green Line*. Chicago: Central Electric Railfans' Association, 2000.

Terry W. Lehmann

ERNST, RICHARD P., HOME. See **Richard P. Ernst Home**.

ERNST, RICHARD PRETLOW (b. February 28, 1858, Covington, Ky.; d. April 13, 1934, Baltimore, Md.). Lawyer and politician Richard Pretlow Ernst was a son of **William Ernst** and Sarah Butler Ernst. His early education was in Covington public schools, and he attended the Chickering Academy in Cincinnati. Ernst graduated from Centre College at Danville, Ky., in 1878 and received his JD degree from the University of Cincinnati in 1880. He married Susan Brent on September 28, 1886, and they had two children, William Ernst and Sarah Ernst Darnell. The family lived at 405 Garrard St., in Covington (see **Richard P. Ernst Home**). Richard Ernst practiced corporate law in both Cincinnati and Covington. He entered politics in 1920 and was elected to the U.S. Senate, where he served until 1927. When he ran for reelection, he was defeated by future U.S. vice president Alben W. Barkley. After the defeat, Ernst returned to his legal practice in Covington. There he served on the Covington City Council, was president of the Liberty National Bank, and served as a trustee of the University of Kentucky, Centre College, and Western College for Women. He was also an active member of the First Presbyterian Church of Covington (see **Community of Faith Presbyterian Church**). Ernst was a strong supporter of the **YMCA** and personally donated large sums to the organization while he was living; he also bequeathed a considerable amount to the YMCA. Ernst died at John Hopkins Hospital in Baltimore at age 76 and was buried in the Highland Cemetery in Fort Mitchell, Ky.

Bodley, Temple. *History of Kentucky: The Blue Grass State*. Vol. 4. Chicago: S. J. Clarke, 1928.

"Death Closes Long Career of Senator Richard P. Ernst," *KP*, April 13, 1934, 1.

Kleber, John E., ed. *The Kentucky Encyclopedia*. Lexington: Univ. Press of Kentucky, 1992.

Lewin, H., ed. *The Lawyers and Lawmakers of Kentucky*. Chicago: Lewis, 1897.

"R.P. Ernst Is Eulogized in Services," *KP*, May 14, 1934, 1.

St. Mary, Franklin J., and James W. Brown, comps. *Covington Centennial: Official Book and Program*. Covington, Ky.: Semple and Schram, 1914.

ERNST, WILLIAM (b. December 9, 1813, Bucks Co., Pa.; d. October 9, 1895, Covington, Ky.). Banker and politician William Ernst was born on a farm in Bucks Co., Pa. His parents were John C. and Amelia Steinman Ernst. At age 16 William took a job as a clerk at a store in Pottsville, Pa. In 1833 he moved to Lexington, Ky., where he was again employed as a clerk. In 1836 he took a position as a teller at the Lexington branch of the **Northern Bank of Kentucky**. Two years later he was transferred to the Covington branch of the bank. In 1839 he married Lydia A. Bush, who was an officer of the bank in Lexington. The couple had one daughter before Lydia Ernst died in 1841. Two years later, Ernst married a second time, to Sarah A. Butler, and they had nine children.

William Ernst worked as a teller until 1849, when he was made a junior officer of the bank. In 1867 he was promoted to president of the Covington branch of the Northern Bank of Kentucky. When he retired in 1888, his son John P. Ernst replaced him as the bank's president. At various times during his career, William also served as president of the Covington City Council, president of the **Covington and Lexington Turnpike** Company, and treasurer of the **Kentucky Central Railroad**. He was a founder of the First Presbyterian Church of Covington (see **Community of Faith Presbyterian**), where he served as an elder for more than 50 years. One of his sons was **Richard Pretlow Ernst**, who became a distinguished Covington lawyer and a U.S. senator; another son, **James C. Ernst**, besides being a well-known local baseball enthusiast, became president locally of both the **Green Line Company** and the **Union Light, Heat, and Power Company**. William Ernst died at age 81 at his Garrard St. home in Covington and was buried in the Highland Cemetery in Fort Mitchell.

"Death Notice Peacefully," *KP*, October 10, 1895, 8.
"Passing of Pioneer," *KP*, October 10, 1895, 4.
Rootsweb. "William Ernst." www.rootsweb.com (accessed December 31, 2005).
"Spirit of Past Invoked by Covingtonian," *KP*, August 24, 1914, 2.

ERPENBECK SCANDAL. Nearly 300 home purchasers in Northern Kentucky were victimized in this scheme. In 1924 Anthony Erpenbeck started the Erpenbeck Construction Company, and over the years many Erpenbeck family members worked for this respected home-building business in Northern Kentucky. In 1993 grandson Bill Erpenbeck incorporated his own enterprise, the Erpenbeck Company, as a separate entity to build homes; the original Erpenbeck Construction Company was no longer doing home construction.

In 2000 Bill Erpenbeck's construction company, based in Edgewood, had sales of $100 million and 75 employees. The company was known to take its employees on all-expense-paid Caribbean cruises and to offer other extraordinary benefits. When the facts came out, it was learned that the Erpenbeck Company had developed a cozy relationship with the local Peoples Bank of Kentucky. Checks that were tendered at Erpenbeck home closings made out to other parties involved in the transactions, which often took place at the bank itself, were deposited not into the proper account but into the Erpenbeck Company's account. Effectively, some $34 million was siphoned off into Erpenbeck coffers. Bill Erpenbeck and employees and friends at the bank were indicted in federal court in Cincinnati, after a 13-month investigation by the FBI and federal prosecutors.

In the end, after guilty pleas had been made, U.S. District Court judge S. Arthur Spiegel sentenced A. William "Bill" Erpenbeck, age 43, to 30 years in a federal facility at Coleman, Fla., for being the leader of the bank fraud scandal. He could be released in 2030; in 2006 an appeal to reduce his sentence time was unsuccessful. Bill's father, Tony Erpenbeck, age 70, was convicted of attempting to obstruct justice—conspiring with Bill to get Bill's sister, Lori Erpenbeck, to take the blame for the fraud scandal. It was also revealed that Tony Erpenbeck had attempted to hire a hit man to kill his daughter after she refused to help in the cover-up and had agreed to turn "state's evidence" for a reduced sentence. Tony Erpenbeck received a sentence of 10 years and 10 months, to be served at the Lexington Federal Medical Center. He is due for release in March 2009 and is appealing the sentence. Lori Erpenbeck, age 41, received a sentence of 1 year and 1 day at a Nashville, Tenn., federal lockup; she was released on June 15, 2005. Michelle Marksberry, age 35, the company's closing agent, received 2 years at Lexington for participating in the scandal. Her release date was April 28, 2006.

Two bankers were also given federal sentences. John Finnan, founder of the Peoples Bank of Kentucky, received 5 years and 3 months, for hiding $4 million in overdrafts, withholding information about the Erpenbeck Company's financial condition, and overstating the prices the bank paid for some 25 homes purchased from Bill Erpenbeck. These activities were designed to keep the Erpenbeck Company afloat. Finnan's associate at the Peoples Bank of Kentucky, Marc Menne, received 4 years and 6 months for his part.

Local attorney Brandon Voelker represented some 211 homeowners who had been harmed in the scandal, although almost 300 were affected in one way or another. Bill Erpenbeck lost his luxurious 19-room home in Crestview Hills, Ky. The Peoples Bank of Kentucky no longer exists. Liens on the homes were removed, and Erpenbeck homebuyers were made whole. A result of the Erpenbeck scandal was that in February 2003 Kentucky House Bill 251 was passed: proposed by local representative Jon Draud, it offered protection to home buyers and subcontractors by requiring that developers or builders show evidence that all debts have been paid at closing. The legislation died in the Kentucky Senate after passing in the Kentucky House.

Driehaus, Bob. "Erpenbeck Sentence Appealed: Tony Awaiting Trip to Permanent Jail," *KP*, July 15, 2004, 2K.
———. "Erpenbecks to Plead Guilty," *KP*, March 25, 2004, 1K.
———. "Tearful Erpenbeck Sentenced Thirty Years," *KP*, April 2, 2004, 1K.
"House Vote on Draud's Erpenbeck Bill: 93-2," *KP*, February 22, 2003, 7K.

ESTES, MARGARET (b. January 1908, Burnside, Ky.). Newport poet Margaret Estes, the daughter of George McCormick and Viva Jefferson Estes, was born in southern Kentucky, but by 1920 she was living with her family in **Clifton** (today South Newport). The family eventually moved to the east side of Newport along Monroe St. In 1926 Estes was residing at home and working as a stenographer. She attended the University of Kentucky, where she became a member of Phi Beta Kappa, graduating in 1938. Afterward she was an elementary teacher in the Newport school system. Her poems are often religious in tone, such as those titled "The Last Supper" and "Call to Worship," or they have themes drawn from nature, including birds and plants. Estes was raised as a Methodist and was the chairman of the local Methodist Epworth League in 1933. In September 1945, while living in Covington, she married Jennings Bryan Arvin, a farmer from Christian Co., at the **Grace United Methodist Church** in Newport, and she moved with her husband to Pembroke in that southern Kentucky county. She and her husband had no children of their own, but they reared a foster son, James Moss. Her husband died in June 1982. Margaret lives in an assisted-living retirement facility in Hopkinsville, and across the hall resides her sister Carolyn, also somewhat of a poet.

Campbell Co. Marriage Licenses, book 184, 1945, p. 846.
Christian Co. Genealogical Society. *Christian County, Kentucky*. Paducah, Ky.: Turner, 1986.
"League Union—to Hear Discussion," *KE*, January 7, 1933, 1.
Noe, J. T.C., ed. *A Brief Anthology of Kentucky Poetry*. Lexington: Univ. of Kentucky Extension Department, 1936.

ETHRIDGE. The Gallatin Co. community of Ethridge, located on the Ohio River west of Craig's Creek and east of Stephen's Creek, began in the early 19th century as North's Landing. Then the relatively narrow valley and surrounding lands became known as as Krutz's Landing, after Edward Krutz of Pennsylvania, who built a general store there. When a post office was established in town in 1886, it was named for Thomas B. Ethridge, the first postmaster. He was a merchant and stonemason who came to the community from Ohio around 1860. The town's name was then changed to Ethridge. The second postmaster at Ethridge was Augustus Bladen, and there were two other postmasters who served there before the town's post office closed on May 31, 1911. Most of the score of houses, the few businesses, a one-room school, a church, and a Masonic Home in Ethridge were located on the river side of the road that ran between Warsaw and Ghent along the Ohio River. Across the road, the land quickly rises to a steep hillside, through which one narrow, winding road runs up to Gridley Hill.

The community was narrowed even more in size when the U.S. Army Corps of Engineers built **Markland Dam** at the mouth of Stephens Creek to improve Ohio River navigation. When the dam was opened for operation, the Ohio River's pool stage above the dam went from 420 to 455 feet, flooding all of the bottomland of Ethridge and creating Craig's Creek Lake on the community's eastern border. The graves in the local cemetery were relocated to the Warsaw Cemetery, and several newcomers to Ethridge built riverside homes to enjoy the recreation provided on the deeper, widened river. The Pink House Restaurant, overlooking the dam at Ethridge, was a local landmark for several years. It closed as the river's erosion was causing homes and outbuildings to be perched even closer to the river's edge. US 42 is also subject to the effects of this erosion, since it runs 1.7 miles, the length of Ethridge, from the Craig's Creek Bridge to the bridge over Markland Dam. The community of Ethridge is now totally residential.

Bogardus, Carl R., Sr. *The Story of Gallatin County*. Ed. James C. Claypool. Cincinnati: John S. Swift, 2003.

Gray, Gypsy M. *History of Gallatin County, Kentucky*. Covington, Ky.: Self-published, 1968.

Jacquelene P. Mylor

EVERGREEN CEMETERY. The Evergreen Cemetery, founded as the Newport Cemetery in 1847, was one of many cemeteries in the United States established in the years following 1831. Earlier burials in the United States took place in church or family cemeteries, or people's remains were interred in a convenient plot with little or no thought of visiting the grave site. In 1831 Mount Auburn Cemetery opened at Cambridge, Mass.; it was the first of the privately owned garden cemeteries founded to provide burial in rural settings and to make profits for their owners. Mount Auburn Cemetery was imitated throughout the United States. The first garden cemetery in Kentucky was the Frankfort Cemetery, which was established in 1844. Before long the Spring Grove Cemetery in Cincinnati (1845), the Lexington Cemetery in Lexington (1847), and the Cave Hill Cemetery in Louisville (1850) were begun, in addition to the Evergreen Cemetery.

When the Evergreen Cemetery was founded, it consisted of 17 acres; today it covers some 300 acres. In 1847 it was on the extreme fringe of both Newport and Bellevue. Located four miles south of Newport's courthouse, on the Alexandria Pk. (**U.S. 27**), in what is now Southgate, the cemetery was not served by public transportation for many decades and therefore was initially difficult to reach.

In 1862, Evergreen Cemetery played a role in the **Civil War** when a military defensive work, known as the Shaler (artillery) Battery, was built there. Named for the family who owned the farm where the original cemetery had been established, this battery was constructed by the federal government as part of the defense line erected to withstand the advance of Confederate forces under generals Braxton Bragg and Edmund Kirby Smith against Cincinnati. The battery was part of a line of fortifications that stretched from Ludlow to Fort Thomas. The remnants of the Shaler Battery remain in the cemetery, and the site is now crowned by a bandstand. The cemetery was also used for interment of Union soldiers, in a section of the cemetery now surrounded by a stone fence and guarded by four cannons. The cannons were placed there in 1883, through the efforts of the Nelson Grand Army of the Republic (GAR) Post and of local congressman **John G. Carlisle**.

In 1894 a streetcar line known as Route 15 was established, with its terminus at Electric Ave. and Retreat St., and visits to Evergreen Cemetery became possible for all. Because there were no public parks for citizens to stroll and socialize in on holidays and Sundays, the cemetery became the place to visit, to take a walk in a rural setting, and to ponder the mortality of humans. Families began to have large memorial stones erected at their family members' grave sites, to affirm the family's wealth and prestige within the community. The use of the cemetery as a public park faded away after the streetcar line was discontinued in 1936. Even today, however, Evergreen Cemetery remains one of the few open spaces in northern Campbell Co. in which one can take a leisurely walk in a rural setting.

With the establishment of the **Fort Thomas Military Reservation** during the 1890s, a new military section was opened at Evergreen Cemetery. One person buried in the military section is Nicholas Pablo, of the 30th Company Philippine Scouts, who died in 1905 while on his way to Washington, D.C., with his unit to take part in the inauguration of President Theodore Roosevelt. At the beginning of the 20th century, the cemetery's acreage was increased, and a series of landmark buildings were constructed: a gatehouse, a chapel, and an annex. Other notable features in the cemetery are a sundial erected by the Dayton (Ky.) Woman's Relief Corps of the GAR, a monument to the **World War II** dead of Newport, and the Taylor and the Southgate family monuments.

Among other notables buried at Evergreen Cemetery are two holders of the Congressional **Medal of Honor**, Newport native **William Horsfall**, who won the medal at the Battle of Shiloh in the Civil War, and Thomas M. Doherty, who was awarded the medal for his heroic combat actions at San Juan Hill during the Spanish-American War. Also buried there are **James Taylor Jr.** and **Keturah Moss Leitch Taylor**, the founders of Newport; **George Baird Hodge**, a Civil War general and member of the Kentucky Confederate House of Representatives; and Kentucky congressmen **Brent Spence**, **Richard Southgate**, and **George Wiedemann**, along with Wiedemann's son Charles, who ran the **Wiedemann Brewing Company**.

National Park Service. *Mount Auburn Cemetery—A New American Landscape—A Study Guide*. Washington, D.C.: National Park Service, 2000.

Charles H. Bogart

Carroll "Hop" Ewing, 2005.

EWING, CARROLL MERLIN "HOP" (b. March 31, 1925, Lacey, Ky.; d. May 23, 2006, Florence, Ky.). The popular longtime mayor of Florence, Ky., Carroll Merlin Ewing, was born in Henry Co., Ky., one of six children of Christopher L. and Goldie Bird Ewing. He was educated in Henry Co. and graduated from Milton High School. He served in the U.S. Marine Corps during **World War II** and then was recalled to military service with the marines during the **Korean War**. Ewing attended the University of Kentucky (UK), where he earned a degree in education. In 1947 he married Sue Ann Houston, a fellow student at UK. After graduation, the couple settled in Erlanger, where Sue Ann had been raised. They had six children, Alan, Carol, Diane, Elizabeth, Emily, and Rebecca. In 1954 the family moved to a home in Boone Co., at the corner of U.S. 42 and New Uri Rd. Later, they also purchased and operated a 50-acre cattle and tobacco farm at Big Bone Lick, in rural Boone Co. Hop Ewing served as a principal and a teacher in schools in Trimble Co. and as a teacher and basketball coach in Boone Co. at Walton-Verona High School and later at Ockermann and R. A. Jones junior high schools.

Ewing was elected mayor of Florence in 1961, a position he held for 20 years. At the beginning of his tenure, Florence was a small rural town, but under his leadership it became Northern Kentucky's fastest-growing and most vibrant city. In the mid-1960s, Ewing and Florence councilman Ted Bushelman cohosted a locally popular talk radio show each morning, from the Burns Brothers Truck Stop in Florence. Ewing was a member of the Florence Volunteer Fire Department and also a strong supporter of the Florence Police Department. He was instrumental in bringing many commercial and industrial firms to the area, with the opening of the Northern Kentucky Industrial Park (see **Northern Kentucky Industrial Foundation**). Through his efforts the **Florence Mall** was built near the city's most recognizable landmark, the water tower. The name Florence Mall was painted on the tower before the construction of the mall.

The Commonwealth of Kentucky notified Florence officials that the name would have to be removed, because it advertised a business. In an effort to find an inexpensive solution to the problem, Ewing conceived the idea of changing the word "Mall" to "Y'all," a term that he said he often used. Of the myriad decisions he made during his years as mayor, none brought more fame to himself and his city than the changing of that one letter. The Florence Mall opened in 1976, and the now famous water tower still stands proudly along I-75–I-71. Mayor Ewing was also instrumental in the relocation of the **Booth Memorial Hospital** (later **St. Luke Hospital**, West) from Covington to Florence. He was proud of the street-paving program instituted during his tenure, which provided curbing and gutters on city streets. During Ewing's long and colorful career, he worked as a salesman and adjuster for the Jefferson National Insurance Company and owned a home repair business that specialized in the installation of continuous gutters, lawn mowing, and snow removal. His daughter Diane Ewing Whalen followed in her father's footsteps, being elected Florence mayor in 1999.

Ewing's wife Sue Ann died in February 1986, and in August 1987 he married Ruth Carroll. Ewing was an avid bowler, and his home contained many trophies that he had won. He was a member of the Florence Optimist Club and the Toastmasters, was the charter president of the Boone Co. **Jaycees**, and served on the County Planning and Zoning Commission. He was also a devout member of the Florence United Methodist Church, where he served for many years as a trustee, a teacher, and the Sunday school superintendent. At Christmas time he would purchase apples and oranges and personally pass them out to each child in attendance. He also brought candy every Sunday for the church's children and their parents.

On Monday, May 22, 2006, Ewing suffered a cardiac event during the night and was rushed to St. Luke Hospital West, where he died. His funeral, held at the Florence United Methodist Church, was attended by more than 500 of his relatives, friends, and fellow citizens. He was buried next to his first wife, Sue Ann, in the Hopeful Lutheran Cemetery in Florence.

"Florence's 'Y'all' Mayor Dies," *KE*, May 24, 2006, 1.

"'Hop' Ewing Put 'Y'all' in 'Mall,'" *KP*, May 24, 2006, 1A.

Whalen, Diane, Ewing's daughter. Telephone interview by Jack Wessling, May 31, 2006.

Construction of I-75 through Covington, looking north to Cincinnati and the Brent Spence Bridge, ca. 1962.

EXPRESSWAYS. The modern divided, limited-access highway of at least four lanes changed the face of Northern Kentucky in the last half of the 20th century. Population, housing, employment location, educational sites, and shopping have relocated as a result of these expressways. New federal expressways constructed since the early 1960s have made possible the recent growth of Cold Spring and Alexandria in Campbell Co. and of Crittenden and northern Grant Co., as well as other areas; the new subdivisions such as Triple Crown in Boone Co.; the industrial parks in Florence, Ky., and around the **Cincinnati/Northern Kentucky International Airport** (CVG); and the emergence of the **Florence Mall**. It must be recognized that the presence of these transportation arteries in Northern Kentucky, much like the arrival of the railroads in the 19th century, is a function of that larger population base to the north, Hamilton Co., Ohio (Cincinnati). The local expressways are descendants of the 1950s Eisenhower administration's cold war initiative, the National System of Interstate and Defense Highways, a $78 billion nationwide project.

As early as 1946, there was talk of building a limited-access highway from Florence to Covington, known as the Florence-Covington Highway. Although a bond issue was passed to fund the initial planning for the road, it never materialized as a local project. It was, instead, subsumed in a much greater project on the federal level and became the linchpin of the local expressway network. Designated I-75 and finished in 1962, it was the first portion of the system completed in Northern Kentucky. Its connecting bridge, the double-decked, multilane **Brent Spence Bridge**, which opened to traffic in November 1963, is now obsolete. I-75 carries traffic through Northern Kentucky from as far away as northern Michigan and southern Florida, while also accommodating local commuter traffic. A replacement for the Brent Spence Bridge is being planned. The bridge also carries into Northern Kentucky I-71, which comes from central and northeastern Ohio and continues south and west after traversing the region. Within Northern Kentucky, I-75 runs roughly 55 miles from Corinth in southern Grant Co. to the Ohio River at Covington on the north. Since its inception, at least four interchanges have been added to I-75 in Northern Kentucky: in 1985 the Turfway Rd. connection in Florence; in 1990 the Mall Road interchange in Florence; in 1994 the Pike St.–12th St. interchange in Covington; and in 2005 the Barnes Rd. connector in Grant Co. At least one off-ramp has been removed, the dangerously bent Jefferson Ave. northbound exit at the bottom of "Death Hill" in Covington (in 1982); the Jefferson Ave. entrance ramp to the south has also been eliminated. "Death Hill," the steep grade between Covington and Fort Wright, has been reconstructed several times over the years; it has been the scene of many accidents, often involving truck traffic. The same is true of the Fort Mitchell interchange with U.S. 25 and U.S. 42, where the roadbed was straightened. The multilevel intersection with I-275 in Erlanger, the likes of which is seldom seen outside of Los Angeles or Dallas, is an engineering marvel at the bottom of the circle freeway, the vehicular heart of Northern Kentucky. In many respects, I-75 is the spine of Northern Kentucky, running north-south roughly down the middle of the region, dividing it almost evenly.

I-71 is routed over I-75 from the Ohio River to Walton, where it branches off on its own to the southwest toward Louisville. I-71 has facilitated access to southern Boone, Owen, Gallatin, and Carroll counties and made these areas integral parts of Northern Kentucky. The portion of I-71 that serves these counties was ready for use in the late 1960s and was the second interstate to be completed. The opening of I-71 all the way to Louisville was delayed as a result of the deep pilings that had to be driven for its bridge over the Kentucky River near Frankfort—bedrock was found much deeper there than anticipated. That bridge is not far from Gallatin and Owen counties. In February 1968, I-71 opened from I-75 near Walton to U.S. 227 south of Carrollton; in July 1969, I-71 opened from U.S. 227 to Louisville. Both I-75 and I-71 have turned U.S. 25 and U.S. 42 into local traffic corridors.

I-471 is the shortest of the interstates in Northern Kentucky. It runs for only 3.5 miles southward from I-71 on the near east side of downtown Cincinnati, across the **Daniel Carter Beard Bridge** into Northern Kentucky, through **Taylor's Bottoms** between Newport and Bellevue in Campbell Co., and up the hill through Fort Thomas and

Southgate, connecting with I-275. I-471 fades into U.S. 27 in front of the NKU campus. Completed in late 1981, I-471 eliminated many of the nicer homes in Newport's East End and along Loraine Ct. and Grand Ave. farther south in the city. I-471 made access to the **St. Luke Hospital** in Fort Thomas much easier and quicker and has certainly eased commuting for the residents of eastern Hamilton and Clermont counties in Ohio to downtown Cincinnati via its connection with I-275. I-471 was talked about as early as 1957. Delays in the completion of the Daniel Carter Beard Bridge and homeowners' fighting eminent domain along Grand Ave. in Newport delayed the highway. This interstate was opened in late 1981, costing $85 million for the highway and the Daniel Carter Beard Bridge, and today its average use is a little more than 100,000 vehicles each day. The ramps at Ky. Rt. 8 are later additions to the highway. The road effectively destroyed the Newport neighborhood of **Cote Brilliante**, which subsequently lost some 90 homes to the bulldozer in preparation for the Newport Pavilion project—big box shopping and restaurants next to I-471 and to its west, between Memorial Pkwy. and Grand Ave.

I-275 is part of the Donald C. Rolf circle freeway (loop) around Greater Cincinnati, which goes through six counties in three states. Rolf was a major player in creating the highway project; construction on it began in Ohio in September 1958. In Northern Kentucky I-275 runs for 41 miles from the **Combs-Hehl Bridge** on the east at Brent in Campbell Co. to Petersburg in western Boone Co., where the road crosses the **Carroll C. Cropper Bridge** into southeastern Indiana. With a substantial bridge across the Licking River at Wilder (later named **Alvin C. Poweleit** Memorial Bridge), I-275 approached completion in December 1979, as the Combs-Hehl Bridge opened. I-275 made access to **Northern Kentucky University** (NKU), **Thomas More College**, and CVG easier, while uniting Northern Kentucky itself. No long were Northern Kentuckians required to pass through the urban areas of Covington and Newport to arrive at the airport or these colleges, or the Florence Mall. Convenience is one of the reasons why some 4,000 students from the east side of Hamilton Co., Ohio, attend NKU. A new interchange was added to I-275 at Mineola Pk. in Boone Co.; and on- and off-ramps were added at Three Mile Rd. in Highland Heights in Campbell Co., to ease access to and from NKU.

There have been several suggestions regarding what should be done, if anything, in future developments of the Northern Kentucky expressway system. The widening of I-75 to a minimum of three lanes all the way to Lexington is in progress. The continuation of I-471 south of the NKU campus and to the southwest, joining I-75 and I-71 where they split in Walton, has been proposed; the idea involves rerouting I-71 across the Daniel Carter Beard Bridge and over I-471 and changing the name of the present I-471 to I-71. An additional proposal calls for another outer loop, south of the existing I-275, through Northern Kentucky. Such a route would pass through Falmouth in Pendleton Co., Williamstown in Grant Co., and Owenton in Owen Co., turning north to perhaps Warsaw in Gallatin Co. or Carrollton in Carroll Co. Farther out in the region, there has been long discussion of a new interstate that would connect Lexington with Columbus, Ohio, cutting across the southeastern section of the Northern Kentucky region. The citizens of Robertson Co. would appreciate such a route, since they have been without good transportation links from the county's inception. Both Bracken and western Mason counties would also benefit. Such a road would cross the Ohio River over the new **William H. Harsha Bridge** just downriver from Maysville, en route to Columbus.

Cincinnati-Transit.net. "Local Expressways." www.cincinnati-transit.net (accessed November 13, 2006).

Dady, Jim. "Ready to Roll," *KP*, August 29, 1981, 1K.

Dias, Monica. "Gerald Lach Has a Dream," *KP*, April 5, 1997, 1.

"Florence-Covington Highway Issue Approved," *KP*, August 8, 1955, 1.

Gutsell, Jeff. "Interstate-471: More Than a Shortcut," *KE*, September 6, 1981, B1.

Johnson, John. "Circle Freeway Celebrates Milestone," *CE*, December 19, 1994, 1.

Lapides, Leslie. "Death Hill," *KP*, June 27, 1983, 1.

F&N STEAKHOUSE. George and Norma Schlueter Thomas opened their combination hot dog stand and sandwich shop just outside of Dayton, Ky., in 1929, even though the Great Depression was not the best economic time in which to start a new business. Once Prohibition laws were repealed in 1933, the Thomas family converted their food business into the F&N Steakhouse (named for the two Schlueter sisters, Florence, who died early in the venture, and Norma). The new steakhouse's building was carved into the hill on the south side of Ky. Rt. 8, the **Mary Ingles Highway**, just east of Dayton in Campbell Co. The restaurant quickly became a Northern Kentucky dining tradition. George and Norma Thomas learned to cut and age meat, and their menu featured delicious and high-quality prime ribs, charcoal steaks, and baby back ribs. The restaurant served large and tasty well-done baked potatoes, along with fresh salads with homemade dressings on chilled pewter plates, and German hot slaw. Diners gathered for late-night meals and after-hours drinks. The dark interior motif, soft lighting, and fireplaces contributed to a romantic mood.

Over the years, the F&N Steakhouse was remodeled and expanded. The restaurant suffered several fires. In 1968 a fire nearly destroyed the place, but it reopened within two months. The family later built the Thomasville Party House across the road along the Ohio River; this facility gave them a new line of business (large private gatherings) and the parking spaces they needed, along with a popular new boat landing. Before the many steakhouse restaurant chains of today made their appearance, gourmands generally agreed that there were two places in all of Greater Cincinnati and Northern Kentucky to find a good steak: Maury's Tiny Cove in Cheviot, Ohio, and the F&N Steakhouse in Dayton, Ky. Customers came from all over the Ohio River Valley region. Politicians, sports stars, entertainers, and disk jockeys all hobnobbed at the F&N Steakhouse. For a time, the restaurant had an old fire truck that was used to pick up boaters at the landing on the river and transport them to the restaurant, with the fire truck's sirens blaring. Waiting in line for up to two hours to be seated at the steakhouse was common in the F&N's heyday.

Norma Thomas died on August 21, 1971, at age 71, of a heart attack; Gene (Eugene) Thomas, the couple's exuberant son who became heavily involved in the business after his mother's death, died on December 21, 1986, at age 59; and on April 4, 1988, at age 85, George Thomas died. Third-generation family members continued the restaurant's tradition as best they could until beset by the long-term consequences of the new **AA Highway**, which diverted traffic away from Ky. Rt. 8, and the opening of several new restaurants at nearby Newport-on-the-Levee. The F&N Steakhouse had always been difficult to find, and the appearance of glamorous upscale dining alternatives just off the bridge into Newport did not help matters. The F&N Steakhouse's kitchen shut down for good at the close of business on Wednesday night, August 11, 2004, and shortly thereafter the owners filed for bankruptcy. The family sold the properties to David Hosea, a local businessman, who planned to restore what was once one of Northern Kentucky's great steakhouses.

"Death Notice—Norma Thomas," *KP*, August 23, 1971, 5.

"F&N Owner Thomas Dies," *KP*, December 22, 1986, 1–2.

"F&N Steakhouse Shuts Down, Files for Bankruptcy," *KP*, August 13, 2004, 4K.

"F&N Steakhouse's Thomas Dead," *KP*, April 5, 1988, 3K.

Michael R. Sweeney

FAIRBANKS. Fairbanks is a small community in southern Owen Co., along Ky. Rt. 607, where that road intersects the Owenton-Georgetown Rd. It is in the Hesler Precinct. Once there was a one-room school at Fairbanks.

An Atlas of Owen County, Kentucky. Philadelphia: Lake, 1883.

Houchens, Mariam Sidebottom. *History of Owen County: "Sweet Owen."* Louisville, Ky.: Standard, 1976.

FAIRS. Fairs have always been important celebrations for Northern Kentuckians. Their origin can be traced to religious celebrations in ancient times, usually held at harvest time. Ancient Greek fairs were held to honor the Greeks' many deities, but enterprising people soon learned to use fairs also as an opportunity to sell their wares, such as spices, cloth, glassware, and other items. Even the Olympic Games had their beginnings in such a setting. In the United States there have been world fairs, state fairs, and county fairs, but county fairs are the ones that have had the greatest impact on the lives of rural Americans. Many of today's sophisticated elite might describe such fairs as old-fashioned, obsolete, or even boring, but rural people continue to make them popular. The county fair as conceived in early Kentucky served a very useful purpose in that it encouraged friendly competition to develop among the participants. People wanted to see who could grow the best fruit, sew the prettiest dress, bake the tastiest pie, or raise the cow that produced the most milk. That intense competition resulted in a wide exchange of ideas, which led to better farming practices and to healthier farm animals and families. Life was difficult on early Kentucky farms, where most people had to work from dawn to dusk. Nothing could rejuvenate those individuals like a few days of fun and games at the end of the growing season. Commonly, fairs lasted for three days and most people attended for the duration. The longest-running Kentucky county fair started in 1856 at Alexandria, Campbell Co. The longest-running fairs in the Northern Kentucky region are Campbell Co.'s fair in Alexandria (see **Alexandria Fair**) and the Germantown Fair in Mason Co.

Campbell Co. Historical Society. *Campbell County, Kentucky, 200 Years, 1794–1994.* Alexandria, Ky.: Campbell Co. Historical Society, 1994.

FAIRVIEW. The Kenton Co. community of Fairview is located along Decoursey Pk., just south of Latonia. The town was first settled during the early 1800s. A lady who once lived there, who felt that the town had a pleasing, or "fair," view, is credited with naming it. A small group of German and Irish railroad workers moved to Fairview in the

Grandstand at the Fair Grounds, Erlanger, ca. 1908.

mid-1800s, shortly after the **Covington and Lexington Railroad** was built along the Licking River. To reach those workers, the St. Anthony Catholic Mission was built in 1877, at the intersection of Decoursey and Locust pikes. The mission also opened a school at Fairview in 1902. A large **Louisville and Nashville Railroad** rail yard was built near the city, and to escape the noise and pollution it created, the church and school were moved in 1928 to Grand and Harvard Sts. in what is today Taylor Mill.

In 1932 Ray Hansel opened a grocery store and gas station at Fairview. When **Prohibition** ended, he converted the store into a tavern, which became a popular gathering place for local residents. The business changed hands several times before it was destroyed by fire in the 1960s. The DeCoursey Baptist Church was organized in Fairview at 8276 Decoursey Pk., in 1950. Fairview was incorporated as a sixth-class city in 1957. The 2000 U.S. Census revealed that it had a population of 156, making it one of the smallest incorporated communities in Northern Kentucky. The median age of residents in that census was 41, and the per capita income was $20,737, with no one living below the poverty level.

"Fairview to Remain City," *KP*, November 8, 1989, 9K.
"Railroad to Speed Trap, Fairview Just a 'Little Town'—Everybody Helps Everybody Else," *CE*, December 1, 1998, A12.
Reis, Jim. "Tiny Towns," *KP*, June 30, 1986, 4K.
Wikipedia. "Fairview, Kenton County, Kentucky." http://wikipedia.org (accessed December 31, 2005).

FAITH, CARL CLIFTON (b. April 28, 1927, Covington, Ky.). Carl C. Faith, a world-renowned mathematician, is the son of Herbert and Vila Foster Faith. Growing up on W. Fifth St. in Covington, he attended Covington schools and graduated from **Holmes High School** (1945). He is a veteran of **World War II**, having served in the U.S. Navy as an Aviation Electronics Technician Mate (1945–1946). He graduated from the University of Kentucky at Lexington in 1951, cum laude, with honors in mathematics. His master's (1953) and doctoral (1955) degrees are both from Purdue University, West Lafayette, Ind. His academic career has included teaching at Purdue, Michigan State, Pennsylvania State, and Rutgers universities; at the latter institution he is an emeritus professor of mathematics. He served as a Fulbright-NATO Postdoctoral Fellow at Heidelberg, Germany, in 1959–1960. In 1960–1962 he held a two-year membership and an NSF Postdoctoral Fellowship at the Institute for Advanced Study at Princeton, N.J. He has studied and taught in Europe, the Middle East, and India and throughout the United States. Carl Faith's publications, awards, honors, and editorships in the special area of mathematics known as ring theory are numerous. In May 2003 he was awarded a bronze engraved plaque and inducted into Holmes High School's Hall of Distinction. Today, he and his family live in New Jersey.

Carl Faith, Professor Emeritus, Mathematics, Rutgers University. www.phoenix-designs.com/carlfaith/cv.htm (accessed June 20, 2007).
"Covington Man Named to MSU," *KTS*, August 3, 1956, 4A.

Michael R. Sweeney

FALMOUTH. The first permanent settlement in what is now Pendleton Co. was established in 1776 when pioneers arrived from Virginia, Pennsylvania, and other eastern states. They settled near springs, where they raised flax and a few sheep. The settlers' log cabins had clapboard roofs, slab doors hung on deerskin thongs, and earthen floors. Many of the early settlers of Kentucky (a place **American Indians** called "the dark and bloody ground") were **Revolutionary War** veterans.

Falmouth received a town charter on June 23, 1792, during the first session of the Kentucky legislature, six years before Pendleton Co. was created. However, there were citizens living at the Forks of the Licking River long before the city was chartered. **John Waller**, a Kentucky pioneer and the founder of Falmouth, who represented this area in the state legislature, brought Falmouth's charter home with him. The town is part of the 1,000 acres given to Col. Holt Richardson for military service in the Revolutionary War as a Virginia soldier. Falmouth was established on December 10, 1793. The town was laid out in lots of a quarter acre each, with streets included. Waller was a native of Stafford Co., Va., which had a town named Falmouth, and it is assumed this fact determined the name of the new town in Kentucky. The trustees held their first meeting on April 12, 1794, at the house of John Hume, near Morgan. On December 13, 1798, the Kentucky legislature approved an act to create from the counties of Campbell and Bracken a new county, to be called Pendleton Co., and Falmouth was chosen as the county seat. William C. Kennett was the first county clerk and James M. Wilson was elected the town's first mayor. The first courthouse was a stone building constructed on the present site in 1812. The land on which it was built had been acquired by Waller and Alvin Mountjoy (see **Mountjoy House**). Waller surveyed the town and gave the county the square surrounded by Main, Chapel, Main Cross (now Shelby), and Second Sts. for the courthouse. The present building was built in 1848. The first jail, built in 1800, was at Second and Maple Sts. It was replaced in 1854 by a new jail built behind the courthouse, facing Chapel St. One of the first roads was from Falmouth to the Harrison Co. line, marked out along the pathway used in 1780 by the English captain Henry Bird (see **Bird's [Byrd's] War Road**) in the attacks he led upon Ruddells and Martin's stations. In 1796 men were chosen to select the best route for a new road from John Sanders ferry on the South Licking River to intersect with Grassy Creek Rd., now **U.S. 27**, near the headwaters of Harris Creek.

The first house in Falmouth, a log cabin owned by Mountjoy, was built in the 1790s on Chapel St. Augustus Robbins owned the first mill in Falmouth, at the foot of Chapel St. It was both a sawmill and a grain mill, operating by water from a dam across the Licking River from a point near the north abutment of today's railroad bridge. This mill, later sold to Joseph Woodhead, became the **Falmouth Woolen Mill**. Henry Deglow was the proprietor of a tannery at the corner of Fourth and Maple Sts. There were no paved streets or sidewalks, but in a few places wooden planks had been laid down. Many times wagons sank up to their hubs and became stuck in the muddy streets, where livestock freely roamed. Mussel shells, along with a greasy rag or tallow dip, provided lighting indoors, and lanterns were used outside.

Dr. Jeremiah Monroe, who came to Falmouth in 1792, was the first physician. He had two brothers, one a lawyer and the other a Baptist minister, Alexander Monroe. Henry Gordon was the only shoemaker in town. He remained in Falmouth until the outbreak of the **Civil War**. There were two lawyers, S. F. Swoope and Samuel T. Hauser, both from North Carolina. Ansel Johnson was the village blacksmith. Major Wheeler operated a carding factory on Chapel St. In early days, the nearest bank was the Northern Bank of Covington, but it was patronized little by Falmouth residents, who usually carried their money in their pockets. Loans were made freely from one neighbor to another. The First National Bank of Falmouth was established in 1921.

The **Covington and Lexington Railroad** first came through town in 1854. In the mid-19th century, Falmouth had three hotels, the **Kennett Tavern**, the Lightfoot Hotel, and the Phoenix Hotel. The Oldham Plantation on Ky. Rt. 159 in Shoemakertown, just across the Licking River, was once a 1,000-acre tract purchased by Tyree Oldham and Samuel Hayden in 1816 from Henry Clay and James Hughes. Jesse Oldham, Tryee's father, brought his family here and built a stately house about 1825. The last Oldham occupant willed the property to the Northward Christian Assembly. There is a family graveyard on the property. Falmouth has two other cemeteries, Riverside Cemetery on U.S. 27 and St. Xavier Catholic Cemetery on Woodson St. At one time, there was an old burial ground along Mountjoy St., where the first settlers, their slaves, and American Indians were buried; the gravestones were removed during the Great Depression and crushed for use on roads. There is a memorial historical marker there today. A suspension bridge completed in 1854 spanned the Main Licking River until it collapsed into the river in 1868 (see **Falmouth Suspension Bridge**). Before 1854, people forded the river when it was low or crossed it on a ferry. The bridge that collapsed was replaced with a covered bridge, which burned in 1926 and was, in turn, replaced by the steel and concrete bridge standing today.

Falmouth has been subject to a number of devastating floods, including those in 1964 and 1997 (see **Flood of 1964, Licking River**; **Flood of 1997, Licking River**). In 2000 the city had a population of 2,058.

Belew, Mildred Boden. *The First 200 Years of Pendleton County.* Falmouth, Ky.: M. B. Belew, n.d. [ca. 1994].

U.S. Census Bureau. www.census.gov/ (accessed December 31, 2007).

Mildred Belew

FALMOUTH, BATTLE OF. In Pendleton Co., on a busy two-lane section of **U.S. 27**, a historical marker notes the location of a **Civil War** skirmish between 28 Confederate Cavalrymen and 11 Union Home Guardsmen. The marker states that the battle took place on September 18, 1862.

Col. George W. Berry led the Union Home Guards. He was the first postmaster of Berry in northwestern Harrison Co. and had donated land to be used for the establishment of the village of Berry. He was also a provost marshal during the Civil War. Provost marshals, stationed by the federal government in Kentucky counties, controlled all intrastate military affairs and were in charge of recruiting Home Guards. Because Colonel Berry was too old to volunteer for the army at the outbreak of the war, he organized a company of the Harrison Co. Home Guards. The Berry Home Guards fought side-by-side with the 18th Kentucky Volunteers under Col. John J. Landram, lending support to federal troops as they protected railroads, telegraph lines, and public properties. The primary responsibility of Berry's group, originally called Police Guard–**Kentucky Central Railroad**, was to guard railroad bridges. The early mission of the Kentucky State Guard was to provide neutral protection on the state's soil. The Home Guards were not compensated unless they became wounded. Today, the successor to that Civil War organization is the Kentucky Army National Guard.

According to a contemporary newspaper account, the Confederate Cavalrymen who fought at Falmouth were Texas Rangers, led by Capt. Charles Duncan. The Texas Rangers were scouts and guerrilla fighters originally organized before the Civil War to defend American settlers homesteading in Texas.

On September 18, 1862, Colonel Berry's Union Home Guard was traveling south toward Falmouth with 600 of Col. Joshua Tevis's 10th Kentucky Cavalry. Colonel Tevis, an attorney from Louisville, had organized the 10th Kentucky Cavalry. Accompanying the troops were a U.S. marshal from Bourbon Co. named Greenbury Reid and nine other men. They had traveled from Covington inspecting the roadbed of the Kentucky Central Railroad. Shortly before reaching Falmouth, the cavalry left the Home Guardsmen and returned to Covington. The guardsmen found the city of Falmouth evacuated. Not long thereafter, they came under fire from the Confederate Cavalry. During the attack, one Home Guard, A. McNees, was seriously wounded. On the Confederate side, two men were killed, four were wounded, and one was taken prisoner. The skirmish started at 3:30 p.m. and lasted about 40 minutes. As the Confederates retreated, they burned the railroad bridge over the south fork of the Licking River in Falmouth. Colonel Berry realized that his guardsmen did not have enough ammunition for another battle, so he repositioned his troops a few miles south of the city to wait for reinforcements and supplies. No further exchanges took place between the two factions.

Colonel Berry fought in the second battle of Cynthiana, on June 11, 1864, was wounded, and died on the day of the battle. U.S. marshal Reid joined the 18th Kentucky Volunteers as a captain and later earned the Distinguished Service Award. After the war, Reid returned to farming and continued that occupation until his death in 1882.

"Covington," *CDC*, September 20, 1862, 3.

McClanahan, Emma. "Influence of the War," 1934. www.rootsweb.com/~kypendle/civilinfluence.htm.

Reis, Jim. "Civil War Battle Fought in Falmouth," *KP*, May 9, 1988, 4K.

Jeanne Greiser

FALMOUTH BAPTIST CHURCH. This church in Falmouth, Pendleton Co., began as the Forks of the Licking Church. Its first pastor was Alexander Monroe, who served for some 30 years. He came to Kentucky from Virginia as early as 1789 and was initially associated with the Bryant's Baptist Church in Fayette Co. The church in Falmouth started with members dismissed from the Bryant's Baptist Church, and its constitution became effective on the fourth Saturday of June 1795. In August 1795, at the time when it united with Elkhorn Baptist Association, the Falmouth church reported having 18 members. In 1802 membership numbered 54, and the next year the church joined the North Bend Association of Baptists, just as the great religious revival that swept through Kentucky from 1800 to 1802 was winding down. Membership at the church in Falmouth declined in the years that followed, and by 1812 there were only 12 members. In 1817 the Falmouth Baptist Church joined the Union Association. In 1825 Pastor Monroe was succeeded by Blackstone L. Abernathy. In 1830 Abernathy joined the Campbellites (see **Disciples of Christ**), taking a large part of the membership with him. In 1831 William Vaughn took charge of those who remained in the Falmouth Baptist Church and ministered to them for one year. Since then, the church has had many pastors, including Robert Elrod.

As early as 1801, there were two places of worship under the same church leadership; one was in Falmouth, on the South Fork of the Licking River, and the other was at the Union schoolhouse in Falmouth, near the Main Licking River. The South Fork church was built of logs in 1802. In September 1830, a new brick church was constructed in Falmouth on Main St. That structure was torn down in 1854 and replaced with a new church building at the corner of Chapel and Church Sts. that opened in 1861. In 1872, the church changed its name to the Falmouth Baptist Church. The present church building in Falmouth was dedicated in 1930 at the corner of Maple and Fourth Sts. Another longtime pastor of the Falmouth Baptist Church was Carl Sears, who served there for 45 years.

Belew, Mildred Boden. *The First 200 Years of Pendleton County.* Falmouth, Ky.: M. B. Belew, n.d. [ca. 1994].

"100th Anniversary," *Falmouth Outlook*, December 25, 1942.

Spencer, John Henderson. *History of Kentucky Baptists from 1769 to 1885.* 2 Vols. Reprint, Lafayette, Tenn.: Church History and Archives, 1976.

Mildred Belew

FALMOUTH HIGH SCHOOL. The Falmouth Academy in Falmouth, later known as the Falmouth Graded School, and then as Falmouth High School, was opened between 1883 and 1900. As Falmouth High School, it provided instruction for grades 1 through 12 until 1968. There was a graduating class every year between 1900 and 1968. The school's colors were red and white, and its athletic teams were known as the Red Devils. Events were recorded in an intermittently published school newspaper, the *Falmouth Firecracker.* The yearbook's name changed from time to time, but most years it was *Retrospect.* School sports included baseball, basketball, cross-country, football, and softball. The school had a small band, and the music curriculum included flute-a-phone and accordion classes.

The Falmouth High School was located at first in a two-story brick structure with eight classrooms at Fourth and Broad Sts. The school was later moved to the site of the former Pendleton Academy, at 205 E. Fourth St. By the early 1930s, the school was in its final home, a multistory brick building at 500 Chapel St., on land donated by Joshua Woodhead. In the 1950s an addition was built, which consisted of two first-grade classrooms, a library, a biology room, and a home economics room. As late as 1963, a storage area in the basement still had a dirt floor.

Even though the high school operated a cafeteria, nearly all students either walked home for lunch or frequented a local diner, the 3L Restaurant. In fall 1968, Falmouth High School merged into the **Pendleton Co. Memorial High School**, which had opened in fall 1959. From the time of the merger until the early 1970s, the Falmouth High School's building served as one of the county's primary schools. In the early 1970s, the Falmouth High School building was converted into the countywide Pendleton Co. Middle School, for grades seven and eight. After January 1998, when the middle school was relocated to a new facility at 35 Wright Rd. and U.S. 27 North in Butler, the Falmouth High School building became the Falmouth School Center, offering GED, career placement, and other services. The Falmouth School Center is also the performance home of the Kincaid Regional Theatre Company. Falmouth High School has an active alumni association, which holds reunions every five years.

Belew, Mildred Bowen. "History of Pendleton County Schools." www.rootsweb.com/~kypendle/schoolhistory.htm (accessed September 29, 2006).

Bray, Nancy, transcriber. "Pendleton County Common School Directory." www.rootsweb.com/~kypendle/comschool.htm (accessed October 2, 2006).

Dennie, Debbie, and Patty Jenkins, comps. *Forks of the Licking, Bicentennial Edition, 1798–1998.* Falmouth, Ky.: Falmouth Outlook, 1998.

Michael D. Redden and Aprile Conrad Redden

FALMOUTH METHODIST CHURCH (MARY'S CHAPEL). When Paul C. Lair donated a lot in Falmouth, at the corner of Main Cross and Upper Mill Sts. (today Shelby St. and Maple Ave.), to the Falmouth Methodist Episcopal Church South, he helped start one of the leading churches in the city. Until then, the members of the Methodist Society, as the group was known in the early 1800s, did not have a regular meeting place; they met in the homes of members, for instance, in the home of Birkett Colvin Sr. of Mount Vernon in southeastern Pendleton Co., and later in the courthouse. This small group was included at first in the Cynthiana circuit, which extended from Cynthiana to Newport and included Harrison and Pendleton counties, as well as parts of Campbell, Grant, and Kenton counties. In 1832 the Methodist congregation at Falmouth left the Cynthiana circuit and became a member of the smaller Falmouth circuit, which included Mount Vernon and Boyd, a town in northwestern Harrison Co.

When the congregation erected a building on the land Lair had provided, Augustus Robbins named the new church Mary's Chapel in honor of his wife, Mary, who was a sister of Paul Lair. The original building had one entrance, facing Shelby St., with a small vestibule inside the entrance. A stove in the center of the room heated the church. The altar rail was in the same place where it is today, and an organ and the choir were on the side. This building was remodeled first in 1890. At that time the vestibule was replaced with three art-glass windows, and the other windows in the church were replaced with glass matching the front three. Two vestibules were then constructed, one on each side of the building, as they remain today. The building was remodeled for a second time in 1926. It was enlarged by several feet to make room for the seating of the choir behind the pulpit, and a small pastor's study was added. The pulpit and the altar rail have remained in the same locations where they were placed more than 125 years ago.

Belew, Mildred Boden. *The First 200 Years of Pendleton County.* Falmouth, Ky.: M. B. Belew, n.d. [ca. 1994].

Mildred Belew

FALMOUTH OUTLOOK. The *Falmouth Outlook* was founded by Warren Jeffrey Shonert Sr. and first published on June 21, 1907. Shonert, who had worked setting type and as a news editor in Cynthiana and Georgetown, started and printed the newspaper in a blacksmith shop owned by his father, Henry Shonert. Warren Shonert began with five subscribers. Several friends and his sister, Mayme McBride, helped him with finances.

Warren Shonert, a staunch Democrat, was not bashful about offering his opinion in weekly editorials titled, *Think about It.* The paper moved to its present location at 210 Main St. in 1922. Shonert's son Warren Jeffrey Shonert Jr. grew up around the newspaper's offices, watching and working with his father. In 1942, after graduating from college, Warren Shonert Jr. became the paper's editor. Publisher W. J. Shonert Sr. died in January 1953.

After his father's death, the younger Shonert became both editor and publisher. He married Genevieve Hancock, and the couple had twins, Jeffrey and Genevieve. The Shonert family spent most of their early life working in the newspaper business. Daughter Genevieve was editor from 1983 until 1985. Warren J. Shonert Jr. continued as editor and publisher until January 1986, when he sold the paper to Delphos Herald Inc.

The *Falmouth Outlook* was set with hot type until it went to offset printing in 1967. However, James Shelton and Warren J. Shonert continued to set type on the old linotype machines until 1985, printing auction flyers, business cards, and many other printing jobs. The old press stands in the back room of the business today. Gone, however, are the old linotype machines used to set type, along with the old headliner machines. The compugraphic machines that Shonert used to get the paper out in the early 1980s are also obsolete. In January 1986 Richard Fry became the newspaper's publisher and editor. In January 1987 the *Shopper's Outlook,* a supplement for shoppers, was born, with a subscription list of 9,090. For a short time, until August 1988, Sue Pullin edited the newspaper after Fry. In the following month, a native-born and lifelong Falmouth resident, Debbie Dennie, became publisher and editor. Dennie started working at the newspaper in 1981, where she learned much from Warren Shonert.

The modernization brought about by computers has taken a lot of the personal touch away from weekly **newspapers**. The Falmouth newspaper has never missed an issue of publication, and it has survived many hardships over the years since 1907, including the Great Depression, floods, blizzards, and tornados. In 1964, when a flood spread over the city of Falmouth, the newspaper had about three inches of water in its building. On March 1, 1997, when the great flood hit, the newspaper offices had five feet of water, which destroyed everything. Over 85 percent of the city of Falmouth was flooded. The newspaper that week was only two days late, though. The staff worked out of publisher Dennie's basement for 10 weeks until May, when the newspaper's building had been cleaned and was ready to occupy. Today, the newspaper is assembled by pagination on computers. There are nine employees, four of whom are full-time. Current circulation is 3,875 paid subscribers, with 1,400 copies placed in the newsstands and 9,000 *Shopper's Outlook*s mailed out each Tuesday.

Debbie Dennie

FALMOUTH RAILWAY DEPOT. The Falmouth Railway Depot in Falmouth was built along the **Louisville and Nashville Railroad** (L&N), 40 miles south of Cincinnati. The wood-frame structure was completed in 1912. It was originally designed with express and baggage rooms, three waiting rooms, and an agent's office. Later, new platforms and train sheds were added. In 1968 the L&N's last passenger train passed through Falmouth. One result of discontinuing service to Falmouth was that the railroad no longer needed most of the depot's space. On April 17, 1980, before the railroad was able to have the depot demolished, this 68-year-old railroad station burned to the ground.

"News Briefs," KP, April 18, 1980, 10K.

Mildred Belew

FALMOUTH SUSPENSION BRIDGE. One of the first wire suspension bridges in the United States was built across the Licking River at Falmouth in 1853. Falmouth, the county seat of Pendleton Co., is on the east side of the Licking River, some 60 miles south by river from the river's mouth at Covington.

Falmouth was to be the first major stop on the new Covington-to-Lexington railroad that was being built at the time. Moreover, a turnpike system connecting Falmouth to Alexandria, Ky., and Cincinnati was planned. After much discussion, a wire suspension bridge was selected for this site and a contract was executed with a firm from Pittsburgh, Pa. The best public road in Pendleton Co. at this time led to Foster's Landing, a steamboat stop on the Ohio River located about halfway between Newport and Maysville. The iron, the rolled iron wire, the anchors, the saddles, the anchor chains, and other supplies to build the new suspension bridge were transported to Foster's Landing from Pittsburgh and then moved on to Falmouth by ox-drawn wagons. The crew to build the bridge was also imported from Pittsburgh and was housed in shacks on the shore opposite the town. The constructor of the bridge was D. Griffith Smith, a civil engineer from Pittsburgh. The main span of the new bridge was 323 feet. The floor was supported on eight iron wires that were connected to anchor chains; the anchors were constructed of masonry. The 30-foot-high towers were described as wooden in one report, but it is unlikely that they were of wood construction. It is possible that stone towers were covered with wood for a more finished look. Another report says that the tollbooth was in one of the towers. The bridge never made money, since toll collection was lax. The bridge's greatest business was as a "kissing bridge." Its floor was occasionally damaged by flood-driven debris, but this span survived until 1868, when it collapsed for unknown reasons.

Belew, Mildred Boden. *The First 200 Years of Pendleton County.* Falmouth, Ky.: M. B. Belew, n.d. [ca. 1994].

Bridgemeister. "1853 (Suspension Bridge) Falmouth, Kentucky, USA." www.bridgemeister.com (accessed December 6, 2006).

Joseph F. Gastright

FALMOUTH WOOLEN MILL. Joshua Woodhead (1824–1886), later the owner of the well-known woolen mill in Falmouth, and his wife, Ann Bottomely (1828–1904), immigrated to the United States from England in 1854, along with their three sons. Upon arrival, they engaged in woolen manufacturing at Lowell, Mass., for two years. In 1866 the Woodhead family moved to Falmouth, where Joshua built the Falmouth Woolen Mill on Water St. There they created the now-famous Pendleton blankets. Joshua Woodhead continued in this business until his death, and eventually, two of his sons, Joseph and John, took over the operation of the mill.

Joseph Woodhead, who was born in 1854, married Elizabeth Kennett, and they had five sons who worked in the family's mill at various times. Joseph gave much of his time to civic endeavors for the city of Falmouth and founded the Woodhead Funeral Home, which celebrated its 100th anniversary in 2002.

Charles Kennett, a nephew of Joseph Woodhead, explained in a letter to the *Falmouth Outlook:* "The last ownership of the old Falmouth Woolen Mill, to my knowledge was my uncle Joseph Woodhead, for whom my two older brothers and I all worked in the mill at various times before we left Falmouth for other fields. I being the last to leave in 1905. During three summers I operated three of the machines in the preparation of making blankets, yarn and other woolen goods. My brothers wove blankets, some of which may still be in use in Pendleton Co. homes. Uncle Joseph ran the spinner and also worked in the mill."

Belew, Mildred Boden. *The First 200 Years of Pendleton County.* Falmouth, Ky.: M. B. Belew, n.d. [ca. 1994].

Woodhead family files, Pendleton Co. Public Library, Falmouth, Ky.

Mildred Belew

FAMILY NURTURING CENTER. The Family Nurturing Center in Florence, Ky., is a private non-profit agency, with a mission to end child abuse and promote individual well-being and healthy relationships within families and their communities. Services are provided primarily to residents of Boone, Campbell, Grant, Kenton, and Pendleton counties in Kentucky, but there are no geographic restrictions. Initial work to form the agency was begun as early as 1975 by a group of citizens and community leaders concerned about the problem of child abuse. The group shared a common concern for children, had a vision of the need to help build safe, nurturing families, and was willing to act on their beliefs. This visionary group learned that Northern Kentucky residents, unfamiliar with the law, were not reporting child abuse to the authorities. The very first program, Parents Anonymous, was established in September 1978 at the **YMCA** in Covington. Since then, the agency's services have evolved based on community needs and available funding.

The agency incorporated in 1979 and was known as Citizens Committee Against Child Abuse. Initially it operated from a volunteer's basement with an annual budget of $2,200. The two services first offered were Parents Anonymous and a 24-hour hotline. The first employee, hired in 1983, was housed at **Trinity Episcopal Church** in Covington. The organization's name changed to Committee for Kids in 1987 and then to Family Nurturing Center in 1993.

Today the Family Nurturing Center is one of the largest affiliates of Prevent Child Abuse Kentucky. The center became a United Way Member Agency in 1988 and later an affiliate of the National Family Nurturing Center, located in Park City, Utah. The local center's programs and services are rooted in the cross-cultural nurturing philosophy of Stephen Bavolek, PhD. In 1999 the Family Nurturing Center's board of directors reaffirmed the following philosophy as the guide for the agency's services: families are capable of incorporating love and respect for family members; the daily life of families requires structure and discipline that is balanced with open communication, laughter, and fun; families can learn the skills necessary to create a nurturing environment for members; alternatives exist to spanking as a form of discipline; children are entitled to be and to feel safe in a healthy, nurturing environment; and environments should be free of physical, sexual, emotional, and verbal abuse.

Pioneers involved with the Family Nurturing Center, such as Kathy Kunkel-Mains, Kathy Collins, and Mike Farrell, helped to form and shape the agency in response to the needs of the communities the agency serves. Literally thousands of individuals have contributed ideas, time, talent, and financial resources to make the Family Nurturing Center a leader in child abuse prevention, education, intervention, and treatment. Today the Family Nurturing Center has a budget of nearly $800,000 and provides a continuum of specialized service programs touching the lives of more than 20,000 people each year.

Agency archives: scrapbooks, annual reports, and news clippings, Family Nurturing Center, Florence, Ky.

"Center to Fight Child Abuse Has a New Name and Home," *KP,* April 24, 1993, 13K.

"Group Therapy to Begin," *KP,* August 14, 1997, 2B.

Herms, Jane, executive director, Family Nurturing Center. Interview by Patricia Nagelkirk, December 2005, Florence, Ky.

"New Director Named," *KP,* April 24, 1996, 2K.

"N. Ky Agencies Get $5.1 Million," *KP,* December 14, 1994, 11A.

Patricia Nagelkirk

FARNY, HENRY F. (b. July 15, 1847, Ribeauville, France; d. December 23, 1916, Cincinnati, Ohio). This artist of American Indian culture was born François Henri Farny but in later life anglicized his name to Henry Frank Farny. He was the third child of carpenter Charles Farny and Jeannette Weyband Farny. The family immigrated to the United States in September 1853, to escape religious and political persecution in their homeland, France. They landed in New York City, where they stayed for about three months, and then moved to a 165-acre farm that they purchased in Warren Co., Pa. To support his family, Charles Farny operated a sawmill on their farm; their home was a small log cabin. Charles and Jeannette home-schooled their children, with the help of a part-time tutor, who lived with the family for about three months each year. It was at the family's farm that Henry had his first contact with American Indians; they were members of the Onandaigua tribe, who lived on a nearby reservation.

In 1859 the family left the backwoods and sought a more comfortable life in a large city. They bought a 28-foot raft, on which they loaded their belongings, and floated down the Ohio River to Cincinnati. Henry attended Woodward High School in Cincinnati for about two years. In 1862, when Charles Farny became seriously ill, Henry had to leave school and support the family. Henry was age 16 when his father died on December 19, 1863. He held several different jobs, first as a bookkeeper, then as a decorator, and later as a lithographer in Cincinnati for Gibson & Company (see **Gibson Greeting Cards Inc.**). During the **Civil War**, Farny drew war-related sketches, which appeared in several publications. The sketches were not of exceptional quality but demonstrated that he had some artistic talent. In 1865 he took a position with *Harper's Weekly* as an engraver, illustrator, and cartoonist, and periodically worked for *Harper's* over the next 35 years. In 1867 the young artist traveled to New York City, then to Rome and later to the art centers of Germany. In Rome he studied art under the renowned painter Thomas Buchanan Read and the sculptor Randolph Rogers. When Read accepted him as a student, he invited Farny to live with him during his training. Farny worked as a secretary and studio assistant to Read but was never permitted to help with any of Read's paintings. Farny painted in his room at night but longed for the day when he could have his own studio. In July 1868 Farny left Read's employment and moved to Düsseldorf, Germany, for additional training. About that time Farny created one of his first significant paintings, which he called *Landscape.* At Düsseldorf Farny met an American artist, Albert Bierstadt, who painted mostly western American landscapes. Bierstadt was quite impressed with the young painter's talent and encouraged him to continue his education for at least another year. He also suggested that Farny visit the Rocky Mountains for inspiration. In 1868 Farny inherited 1,200 francs from an aunt, which he used for two additional years of training in Europe. While visiting Munich, he met the talented Kentucky artist **Frank Duveneck**.

Farny arrived in Northern Kentucky in 1874 but had a difficult time finding work as a painter. To support himself, he continued to do illustrations for *Harper's Weekly.* He also illustrated a local brochure for the Procter and Gamble Company, books printed by Van Antwerp and Company, and promotional material about the city's pork-packing industry for the Cincinnati Chamber of Commerce. The latter work won him a medal at the Vienna International Exposition in Vienna, Austria.

In summer 1874 Farny joined with a young *Cincinnati Enquirer* reporter, Lafcadio Hearn, to publish a humorous weekly magazine that they called *Ye Giglampz;* however, it failed after only nine issues. In May 1875 Farny and Duveneck worked together on a huge oil painting of Joan of Arc, called *Prayer on a Battlefield.* That August, Farny again traveled to Europe, this time with Duveneck and two other artists, Frank X. Dengler and John Henry Twachtman, remaining there for about a year.

Farny served as one of the major illustrators for a new version of the *McGuffey Readers,* published in 1879. By 1880 he had been a practicing painter for about 15 years and was also well known for his artwork in children's books. Between 1880 and 1892, he illustrated for *Harper's, Century,* and other similar publications but began spending more of his time painting western scenes in both oil and watercolor. He completely phased out his illustration work in the early 1890s, to concentrate on American Indian artwork. Farny began spending considerable time in the West, where he met future U.S. president Theodore Roosevelt and was adopted into the Sioux Indian tribe. During that time Farny collected Indian artifacts, relics, photographs, and other materials, which he used in later paintings.

From about 1890 to 1902, Farny lived in a Covington duplex at 1029 Banklick St. and had his studio in the other half of the building, 1031 Banklick St. In 1902 he moved his studio to Fourth and Race Sts. in Cincinnati. That same year, he bought a farm, which he named Umberville (Latin for "shady farm") along what is today Skyline Dr. in Cold Spring. Friends and associates of Farny considered him a confirmed bachelor, but in August 1906, at age 59, he married his 18-year-old ward, Anna Ray. The couple honeymooned in the Canadian wilderness and set up housekeeping at the Cold Spring farm, where they lived until 1910. Their only child, Daniel, was born in 1908 while the Farnys were living at Cold Spring. The house is presently owned and operated as the **Campbell Lodge**.

Hundreds of Farny's pencil sketches, watercolors, and oil paintings are held in museums around the world and in the homes of private collectors. His work ranks with such American masters as Frederick Remington, Charles Russell, John Singer Sargent, and James Whistler. Some of Farny's most famous paintings were *Hiawatha, Tellers of the Plain, The Last Vigil, Coming of the White Man,* and *Song of the Talking Wire.* In addition to his artwork, Farny also occasionally wrote short stories and acted in various plays. In Northern Kentucky he was a close friend and contemporary of two of Covington's most celebrated artists, Frank Duveneck and **Dixie Selden**.

After a short illness, Henry Farny died in the Deaconess Hospital, Cincinnati. He was cremated and his ashes were buried in Spring Grove Cemetery, Cincinnati. His wife, Anna, and his son, Daniel, survived him. At the time of his death, Farny was living at 424 Straight St. in Cincinnati.

Carter, Denny. *Henry Farny.* New York: Watson-Guptill Publications, in cooperation with Cincinnati Art Museum, 1978.

Cincinnati Art Museum. *The Golden Age: Cincinnati Painters of the Nineteenth Century Represented in the Cincinnati Art Museum.* Cincinnati: Cincinnati Art Museum, 1979.

"Farny, His Flitting to Ohio Is Kentucky's Loss," *KJ,* March 6, 1893, 4.

"Farny House Debate Is Settled Once and for All," *KP,* January 13, 1987, 1K.

"Farny Weds His 18 Year Old Ward," *KP,* August 16, 1906, 1.

Spring Grove Cemetery Records, Cincinnati.

Vitz, Carl. "Henry F. Farny and the McGuffey Readers," *Bulletin of the Historical and Philosophical Society of Ohio* 12, no. 2 (April 1954): 91–108.

Jack Wessling

FAUNA (VERTEBRATE). French explorers were the first Europeans to visit Boone Co.'s **Big Bone Lick**. They arrived in 1739 and collected bones and teeth from an extinct group of mammals that included the giant ground sloth (*Mylodon* sp.), the mastodon (*Mammut americanus*), the large bison (*Bison antiquus*), the musk ox (*Bootherium* sp.), a giant moose-like deer (*Cervalces scotti*), the mammoth (*Mammathus* sp.), the caribou (*Rangifer* sp.), and the horse (*Equus* cf. *compliatus*). Modern bison (*Bison bison*), American elk (*Cervus canadensis*), and white-tailed deer (*Odocoileus virginianus*), extant species, were also found in various excavations, most notably by a scientific team from the University of Nebraska during the 1960s. Time and land-use changes have altered most of the habitats in Northern Kentucky. Few pristine areas remain, and the species now present may not be the same as in earlier times. Some species that were nearly exterminated have made comebacks, alien species have been added, and some of the latter have replaced native species. The species listed below are regarded as representative of the Northern Kentucky vertebrate fauna today.

Fish

In 1820 Constantine Rafinesque, a scientist from Translvania University in Lexington, published *Ichthyologia Ohiensis,* in which he listed 111 species of fish for the Ohio River; approximately 90 percent of these were newly described. In the ensuing years, the Ohio River has experienced alterations due to siltation, pollution, alien introductions, and especially the effects of damming that have caused shifts in the population levels of native species. The gizzard shad (*Dorosoma cepedianum*) is perhaps the most abundant fish in the river, but other rough fish including various species of minnows, suckers, and catfish have been successful. The freshwater drum (*Aplodinotus grunniens*), gars (*Lepisosteus* spp.), and the introduced carp (*Cyprinus carpio*) are fairly abundant. The Licking and Kentucky rivers have undergone similar environmental and biotic changes.

Smaller streams and creeks, especially the less polluted ones, maintain strong populations of darters, especially greenside (*Etheostoma thalassimum*), johnny (*E. nigrum*), orangethroat (*E. spectable*), rainbow (*E. caeruleum*), and others. Creek chubs (*Semotilus atromaculatus*) and northern hogsuckers (*Hypentelium nigricans*) also are found in smaller streams.

Largemouth bass (*Micropterus salmoides*) and bluegill (*Lepomis macrochirus*) have been widely stocked in farm ponds across the area but also are abundant stream and river species.

Amphibians

The 24 species of amphibians (frogs, toads, and salamanders) that have been reported for Boone, Campbell, and Kenton counties perhaps are representative for the region. The redback salamander (*Plethodon cinereus*) is generally confined to the glacial areas of Boone and Kenton counties but is perhaps the most abundant salamander in the region. In spring-fed streams, dusky salamanders (*Desmognathus fuscus*) are common. Ambystomid salamanders are uncommon except locally.

Frogs, especially bullfrogs (*Rana catesbeiana*) and green frogs (*R. clamitans*), are commonly found; however, there appears to be a decline in the leopard frog (*R. pipiens*) numbers. The American toad (*Bufo americanus*) is more commonly encountered than the Fowler's toad (*B. woodhousii*).

Reptiles

The 24 species of reptiles (turtles, snakes, and lizards) reported for Boone, Campbell, and Kenton counties also seem to be representative for Northern Kentucky. Eastern box turtles (*Terrepene carolina*) are commonly encountered throughout much of the region. Distributions of other turtles are less well known. Lizard populations are not well known, however; native species such as the broadhead skink (*Eumeces laticeps*) and the fence swift (*Sceloporus undulatus*) may be less abundant than in the past. Populations of the introduced European wall lizard (*Podarcis muralis*) have expanded throughout the Cincinnati area, on both sides of the Ohio River.

The most commonly observed snakes in the region are the black rat snake (*Elaphe obsoleta*) and the garter snake (*Thamnophis sirtalis*) across the uplands and the northern water snake (*Nerodia sipedon*) and the queen snake (*Regina septemvittata*) along streams. The only poisonous snake found in the region is the copperhead (*Agkistrodon contortrix*), and its numbers appear to be declining because of loss of habitat. Other snakes are secretive in nature and their status is uncertain.

Birds

The status of breeding bird populations at the Boone Co. Cliffs Nature Preserve are as well documented as any in Kentucky. There, vireos, warblers, woodpeckers, wrens, and nuthatches appear to be abundant. Great horned owls are confined to older forest remnants. However, owing to fragmentation of forests, brown-headed cowbirds have increased. Introduced species, especially the starling, the house finch, the house sparrow, and the rock dove, are most noticeable around human habitations. Canada goose populations around suburban lakes and ponds have dramatically increased to nuisance levels.

The expansion of urban and suburban areas has allowed shifts in populations and species to occur. Northern cardinals, catbirds, mocking birds, and blue jays are common neighborhood residents. The widespread use of bird feeders has benefited such species as the ruby-throated hummingbird, the Carolina chickadee, and the tufted titmouse.

Christmas bird counts have revealed long- and short-term shifts in populations, especially those of the eastern bluebird and the Carolina wren. Some birds, especially the red-tailed hawk, appear to have taken advantage of open country along roadways.

Mammals

Although large mammals such as elk and buffalo disappeared from the region long ago, some large mammals, most notably white-tailed deer, have experienced great population increases. Reintroductions of beavers (*Castor canadensis*) and otters (*Lontra canadensis*) have also been successful. Coyotes (*Canis latrans*) have expanded their geographic range into the region and are now a problem.

The most abundant mammal species are small and secretive—white-footed mice (*Peromyscus leucopus*), short-tail shrews (*Blarina brevicauda*), and meadow voles (*Microtus pennsylvanicus*). Feral house mouse (*Mus musculus*) populations have expanded as human population has expanded across the region. Other native species that have adapted to human modifications of the environment are the opossum (*Didelphis virginiana*) and the raccoon (*Procyon lotor*). Bats, most notably big brown bats (*Eptesicus fuscus*) and little brown bats (*Myotis lucifugus*), are most successful around human settlements.

Woodchucks (*Marmota monax*) and eastern chipmunks (*Tamias striatus*) are often encountered throughout the region. Black squirrel (*Sciurus caroliniensis*) populations in the Fort Mitchell area are of local interest.

Barbour, R. W., and W. H. Davis. *Mammals of Kentucky.* Lexington: Univ. of Kentucky Press, 1974.

Ferner, J. W., P. J. Krusling, and M. Obermeyer. *A Survey of Reptile Populations in Boone, Kenton, and Campbell Counties, Kentucky.* Final Report. Cincinnati: Cincinnati Gas and Electric, 2000.

Krusling, P. J., and J. W. Ferner. *Distribution and Status of Amphibians in the Northern Tier Counties of Kentucky.* Final Report. Cincinnati: Cincinnati Gas and Electric, 1993.

Page, L M., and B. M. Burr. *Freshwater Fishes.* Boston: Houghton-Mifflin, 1991.

Palmer-Ball, B., Jr. *The Kentucky Breeding Bird Atlas.* Lexington: Univ. Press of Kentucky, 1996.

Schultz, C. B., L. G. Tanner, F. C. Whittmore Jr., L. L. Ray, and E. C. Crawford. "Big Bone Lick, Kentucky: A Pictorial Story of the Paleontological Excavations and the Fauna Found Locally from 1962 to 1966," *University of Nebraska News* 46 (1967).

William S. Bryant

FEARN FAMILY. In an age when land speculation was common and starting a family business was routine, the Fearn family of Hunter's Bottom in Carroll Co. was unique in the number and scope of their entrepreneurial activities. Over four generations, the Fearns built a substantial fortune based on utilization of 1,000 acres of prime Ohio River bottomland and of a large gristmill in Milton, in Trimble Co. Members of the Fearn family served as trustees of local turnpike toll roads and were owners of an Ohio River packet steamer business and a fruit company. In addition, family members speculated on timber tracts in Jackson Co., Ind., and owned mercantile locations near the wharf at Madison and at other locations along the Ohio River. The Fearns became the wealthiest family in Hunter's Bottom; yet by the end of the 19th century, many of the family members had died or moved away and their steamboats had been sold. But five of the antebellum mansions built by this family from profits made in the steamboat business still stand—reminders of the golden age of steamboats on the Ohio.

In 1803 the Fearn family started a financial empire when Samuel Fearn and his oldest son, George Fearn, purchased 1,000 acres of prime Gallatin Co. bottomlands along the Ohio River and moved their family from Bourbon Co. to Hunter's Bottom. A few years later Samuel Fearn Sr. (1807–1888), another son of Samuel Fearn, was born. The Fearns developed their farmland and, well before 1850, constructed a gristmill at Milton. Samuel Sr. had the major interest in the mill, while George Fearn began speculating in Indiana land at Madison and along the Ohio River on the Indiana side. Although a bachelor, George built a large home overlooking the river that he named Fearn Hill. It was one of the grandest homes of the period.

Samuel Fearn Sr. married Elizabeth Owen of Henry Co. in 1826 , and they had two sons, Samuel Jr. and George, and five daughters, all of whom had musical talent. The sprawling brick home Samuel Sr. built is still occupied. Samuel Sr.'s chief interest was the large flour mill at Milton, but, joining in business with his father, he became a trustee and head in 1877 of the Carrollton and Louisville Packet Company and in 1882 of the Milton and Hunters Bottom Turnpike Road Company.

Samuel Fearn Jr., who was born in Hunters Bottom in 1831, may have been the most enterprising of all the Fearns. He married Annie Hitt in 1856, and shortly thereafter he and his brother, George, moved to lands where there was a large timber tract along the Muscatatuck River in Jackson Co., Ind., southeast of Seymour, Ind. By the mid-1860s, the brothers had moved back to Hunter's Bottom and Samuel Fearn Jr. had become involved in both the flour mill and the family's packet steamboat business. He also became a trustee of the North View Fruit Company and the Madison and Bedford Turnpike Company. Samuel Jr. married three times, first to Annie Hitt, then to Emma McClaran, and then to Bettie P. Craig. He had one son, Samuel S. Fearn, known as Captain S. S. Fearn, and four daughters; all of the daughters died at relatively young ages. Meanwhile, his brother, George, inherited a family home, Fearn Hill, from his uncle in 1869 and married Maggie Porter. George was the major advocate of his family's packet business and in September 1877 launched the *Maggie Harper,* which became their main steamboat. George Fearn received his master's certificate as an Ohio River steamboat captain in 1880 and raised a family at Hunter's Bottom. At some point, he moved south to Georgia and later died there in 1930. The *Maggie Harper* was a 133-foot sternwheeler. Most of its trips involved routine triweekly round trips from Madison to Louisville, carrying passengers and freight. In 1880, when the Bay Brothers and the U.S. Mail Line brought a competitive 182-foot side-wheeler, the *Minnie Bay,* to make daily trips from Louisville to Madison, the Fearn family expanded their steamboat route and founded, on August 31, 1880, The Louisville, Madison, and Kentucky River Packet Company. As the steamboat competition increased on the Ohio River, the *Maggie Harper* entered upon the Kentucky River's commercial trade by running popular steamboat excursions for groups. A newer boat, the *Fannie Fearn,* was ordered by the Fearn steamboat company from the Howard Shipyards at Jeffersonville, Ind. The *Fannie Fearn,* using the machinery taken from the *Maggie Harper,* was delivered in 1886, and Captain S. S. Fearn was listed as captain. But by then it was too late; the Bay Brothers had absorbed the major and most lucrative part of the Fearn company's trade. The Fearns, forced to liquidate their packet business, sold the *Fannie Fearn* to an operator in Apalachicola, Fla., to be used in steamboat commerce on the Chattahoochee River.

With encouragement from Captain S. S. Fearn, the White Collar Packet Line brought the *Big Kanawha,* a 152-foot sternwheeler, to the Louisville-Madison trade, and Fearn served briefly as its captain. Shortly thereafter, Captain Sam Parsons brought the *Helen M. Gould,* a faster boat, to compete for commercial trade on the Ohio River. According to Frederick Way, "a swap was made in which Parsons acquired the *Big Kanawha* and the White Collar Line bought the *Helen M. Gould* with the proviso that Parsons would vamoose." Sometime before 1891, Captain S. S. Fearn moved to Cincinnati and worked as a steamboat inspector for 11 years before he died in 1905. By then, railroads crisscrossed Indiana, Kentucky, and Ohio. The steamboat era was fading into its twilight and was but a ghost of its former self.

Allen, Michael. *Western Rivermen, 1763–1861.* Baton Rouge: Louisiana State Univ. Press, 1990.

Hunter, Louis C. *Steamboats on the Western Rivers.* New York: Dover, 1993.

Smith, Larry Douglas. *The Fearns of Hunters Bottom, Kentucky.* Louisville, Ky.: L. D. Smith, 1992.

Way, Frederick, Jr. *Way's Packet Directory, 1848–1994.* Athens: Ohio Univ. Press, 1994.

Diane Perrine Coon

FEDDERS, EDWARD L. (b. December 14, 1913, Covington, Ky.; d. March 11, 1973, Pomato, Peru).

Edward Fedders, the son of Frank J. and Mary V. Schiffer Fedders, was one of two persons from the region to rise to the rank of bishop within the Roman Catholic Church. Four of his siblings also entered Catholic religious orders. Both Edward and his brother Albert became Maryknoll priests at the Catholic Foreign Mission Society, based at Maryknoll, N.Y.; three of their sisters joined the Benedictine order of nuns. Edward attended **St. John** Elementary School in Covington and St. Xavier High School in Cincinnati. He joined the Maryknoll order of missionaries in 1934 and, after his ordination in 1944, was assigned to Peru. He was one of the first Maryknoll priests assigned to South America. Fedders became a specialist in educational projects and his talents were quickly recognized. In 1963 he was made the bishop of Juli, Peru, and was consecrated at the **Cathedral Basilica of the Assumption** in Covington. In 1970 he suffered a heart attack and in 1973 died from a second attack, collapsing just as he finished saying Sunday Mass. He had funerals both in Covington and in Juli, Peru, where he was buried in a crypt at the Juli cathedral.

Raver, Howard. "Covington-Born Bishop of Peru Dies Saying Mass," *KP*, March 12, 1973, 1–2.

Reis, Jim. "Only Bishop Born Here Built Pastoral Career around World," *KP*, April 15, 2002, 4K.

Michael R. Sweeney

FEE, JOHN GREGG (b. September 9, 1816, Bracken Co., Ky.; d. January 11, 1901, Berea, Ky.). John Gregg Fee, a noted abolitionist and the founder of Berea College, in Berea, was the son of slaveholders John and Sarah Gregg Fee. He was born on the family farm along Hillsdale Rd. near Germantown, and Hillsdale was the location of his first church and school. Fee attended Miami University in Oxford, Ohio, and obtained a BA from **Augusta College** before entering the Presbyterian Lane Theological Seminary in Cincinnati in 1842. A personal epiphany initiated his antislavery convictions. When he returned home to Bracken Co., he was met with angry mobs who did not support his antislavery teachings. He was subjected to beatings, ridicule, and finally banishment. The American Missionary Society placed Fee in charge of 15 to 20 young ministers, and Fee and these associates were often accused of and charged with enticing slaves to escape. In September 1844, Fee married Matilda Hamilton, who shared his zeal for advancing the rights and education of the enslaved.

In 1854 Fee moved to Madison Co. at the inducement of his friend and fellow abolitionist Cassius Marcellus Clay, who had given Fee 10 acres of land. However, their relationship did not endure, since the two men took contrasting positions about how to end slavery. Clay favored a gradual approach, whereas Fee maintained the need for immediate emancipation.

Fee's belief in immediate emancipation prompted him to purchase a family slave, **Juliet Miles**, from his father to prevent her from being sold. A court action followed that resulted in the emancipation of Juliet and her son Henry. However, after a move to Clermont Co., Ohio, Juliet returned to Bracken Co. to attempt to rescue her other children. This daring action was unsuccessful; she and her family were arrested and she was remanded to the state penitentiary at Frankfort, where she died two years later.

John G. Fee.

By 1859 Fee had proposed an abolitionist colony at Berea in Madison Co., along with a coeducational, integrated college. Berea College, based on the New Testament principle of "open-mindedness," was intended to be similar to Oberlin College in Ohio. Just as he and his colleagues were preparing to open their new school, the abolitionist John Brown led his attack on Harper's Ferry in Virginia. Slaveholders from Madison Co. decided the abolitionist Fee represented a similar threat, and on December 23, 1859, a band of prominent citizens and slaveholders from nearby Richmond rode to Berea and told Fee and his associates they had 10 days to leave the state. When the governor of Kentucky, Beriah Magoffin (1859–1862), refused to help the Berea abolitionists, Fee and his associates fled to Ohio. Thus, the college at Berea failed to open as planned. It opened in 1866, one year after the **Civil War** (1860–1865) had ended. During the war, Fee kept in touch with the situation in Berea by occasionally visiting relatives and churches there.

Fee also returned to Kentucky during the war to offer food, shelter, and the promise of education to recently freed slaves reporting to Camp Nelson, a Union recruitment center in Jessamine Co. not far from Berea. While he was at Camp Nelson, Fee, now a Union Army chaplain, founded a trade school for former slaves, the Ariel Academy. Fee's work with freed slaves in Kentucky and his earlier plans to build an interracial college with biblical underpinnings delivered a hopeful message to Northern abolitionists: that the Berea and Camp Nelson experiences could serve as models for other such institutions in the South.

From 1866 until 1889 at Berea College, which began as both a college and a 13-grade (K-12) preparatory school, at least half of the students enrolled were African Americans. Thus, Fee's goal of demonstrating that education should be color blind was achieved. However, there developed a period of turmoil and disagreement among the trustees about sustaining this mission. The issue was settled when William Goodell Frost became Berea's new president in 1892. Fee, who had been concentrating for years on his work as a minister, no longer was in control, and the prevailing educational thought in America favored "separate but equal" education, Berea College was forced to segregate after its unsuccessful legal attempts to challenge the state's racist Day Law (1904). In 1950 the college was reintegrated. Fee, who saw his noble dreams for Berea College come to an end, died in 1901 and was buried in the Berea Cemetery.

"Abolitionism," *CJ*, May 1, 1852, 2.

"Bracken County Marker to Honor Abolitionist, Slave," *KP*, June 21, 2002, 3K.

Lucas, Marion. *A History of Blacks in Kentucky*. Vol. 1. Frankfort: Kentucky Historical Society, 1992.

Sears, Richard D. *The Day of Small Things: Abolitionism in the Midst of Slavery, Berea, Kentucky, 1854–1864*. Lanham, Md.: Univ. Press of America, 1986.

Caroline R. Miller

FERGUSON, BRUCE (b. March 21, 1929, Covington, Ky.). Bruce Ferguson, who became a Northern Kentucky judge, is the son of Walter and Shirley Rice Ferguson. Walter Ferguson was very active in the community and in the **Democratic Party**. Bruce married Elizabeth Reynolds in 1951, and they have five children. In 1967 he earned his BA in history and political science from **Thomas More College** in Crestview Hills. As a young man, Bruce Ferguson was involved in many organizations. During the early 1950s, he served as president of the Big Bone Lick Historical Association, a group that succeeded in establishing **Big Bone Lick** as a Kentucky state park in 1958.

Ferguson's political career spans more than 40 years. He first served on the Boone Co. Board of Education from 1955 to 1961 and then became the Boone Co. judge. He served as judge from 1963 to 1982 and again from 1986 to 1992. During this tenure, he opened the county's first hospital, started a county water system, and developed the Northern Kentucky Tri-County Economic Development Corporation, thereby helping to build Boone county into the thriving area it is today.

In 1992 he resigned as Boone Co. judge to accept the position of commissioner of the Department of Local Governments under Kentucky governor Brereton Jones (1991–1995). Ferguson retired in 1996 and returned to Boone Co. Although he retired from seeking public office in 2001, after serving on the Boone Co. Soil Conservation Board, he remains very active in the community, often delivering speeches to local civic groups. He lives at Glencairn Farm, which has been in his family for generations.

Ferguson, Bruce. Interview by Laurie Wilcox, September 14, 2005, Union, Ky.

Warner, Jennifer S. *Boone County: From Mastodons to the Millennium.* Burlington, Ky.: Boone Co. Bicentennial Book Committee, 1998.

Laurie Wilcox

FERGUSON, HUBBARD "HUB" (b. December 18, 1889, Gallatin Co., Ky.; d. June 18, 1954, Gallatin Co., Ky.). Gallatin Co. sheriff Hubbard Ferguson, the son of William and Julia Sanders Ferguson, disappeared on the night of June 18, 1954. He owned a farm that was located between Lick Creek and Park Ridge Rds. near Sparta, Ky., and had visited the farm's tenant at the farm earlier that evening. Ferguson's abandoned car was found on Park Ridge Rd. the next day, and his gun was missing from the car's glove compartment. His friends organized a search party, and hundreds responded; but it was not until two farmers noticed that their horses shied away every time they disked weeds near a certain section of Eagle Creek that the sheriff's dead body was found. Ferguson had been shot above the right ear, and a heavy railroad tie plate had been tied around his neck.

The motive was a mystery. County judge Earl Spencer said, "Hub just wasn't the type of man to get into trouble." Ferguson lived alone in an apartment in Warsaw. He had separated earlier from his wife of 30 years and had been divorced only a year before his death. The ***Gallatin Co. News*** described him as "not the most popular man in the county, but the least disliked." Various news reports characterized him as a loner, a nondrinker, and not a ladies' man.

More than 25 persons were given lie-detector tests, some as suspects, some merely to get good information, but none of those tested provided suitable leads. More than 200 people were questioned. The gun was never found. Former *Gallatin County News* editor Charles Adams argued that the death was a suicide, but most of the authorities and citizens in the community believed foul play was involved. The murder remains unsolved. Hub Ferguson was 64 years old at the time of his death and was survived by one son. He was buried at the Warsaw Cemetery.

Kentucky Death Certificate No. 11175, for the year 1954.

"Year-Old Slaying of Gallatin County Sheriff Still Unsolved," *KP,* June 26, 1955, 1.

Bernie Spencer

FERRIES. Ferries, among the first public utilities in the United States, played a major role in the history of Northern Kentucky, even before Kentucky became a state. They provided the link to Indiana and Ohio for westward expansion, economic development, and the growth of roads. Winthrop Sargent, the territorial secretary and sometimes governor of the Northwest Territory, signed many ferry licenses for Kentucky before it gained statehood, such as the license for a ferry at Limestone Landing (now Maysville).

American Indians crossed rivers with various types of ferries. Each Indian tribe had certain specific design features that suited its conditions for use. In general, though, if an individual or a small group needed a ferry, a collapsible skin boat was made. These boats could be constructed in about two hours by sewing three or four deerskins together over a frame. For larger groups, the birchbark canoe was the most popular, but dugout or elm-bark canoes were also used. The dugouts were made from oak, pine, or chestnut wood. The Indians would cut a tree down and then use fire, hot stones, and gouging to shape and hollow the log into a dugout canoe. Each dugout canoe took 10 to 12 days to complete and could hold from 3 to 40 people.

As the early white settlers moved into the Ohio River Valley, they used dugout canoes too, as well as pirogues and flat-bottomed boats, for river crossing. The first small ferries that carried passengers could be paddled, rowed, or poled in the shallow waters when the river was low. Sail-propelled scows were another type. However, sail ferries were notoriously unreliable, because the winds often did not blow when needed or in the right direction to push the ferry across the river.

At narrow crossings, many of the early ferries were flatboats, about 45 feet long; one man would pull the boat with a rope or wire stretched from bank to bank. The rope ferries worked very well, as long as the rope could be kept above the water. The cable was first stretched across the river, and the front of the ferry was attached with a sliding hitch. The current would exert force on the drifting back end and push the boat against the current. However, rope exposed to the weather over a period of time was likely to break. It snapped usually when the strain was heavy, such as when spring rains brought strong currents and floodwaters. At such times, passengers and ferryman could only hope that as the flatboat and all on board floated downstream, the boat would drift to either shore, not far below the landing place. In the 19th century, wire replaced the rope used for ferries. Wire ferries were inexpensive, easy to operate, and simple. Horses and buggies were able to make the trip in sufficient time, and the operation of these ferries was easier on the operator's back than using poles and oars.

By 1819 the horse ferry, also called a teamboat, was introduced on the Ohio River. In that year, a large boat propelled by eight horses was in service at Maysville. Gen. Ulysses S. Grant wrote about that ferry in his memoirs. Horse boats were long and wide enough that some were operated with as many as eight horses. The horses, usually blind (or wearing blinders), worked in a treadmill well in the back of the boat. The treadmill was attached to paddlewheels, one on either side of the ferry. Two horses, walking in place on opposite sides of the tread-wheel, generated enough power to turn the two side wheels. The driver sat in the back close to the horses but also near enough to the stern that he could control the direction of the boat with a long sweep or oar. If the pilot wanted to go faster, he would tell the deckhands to grab the horses' tails, causing them to walk faster and pull harder on the treads. Rowing the horse ferry was next to impossible on a windy day. Therefore, sails were used. However, if the current was swift and the wind in full force, sails could create a problem by diverting the ferry to a point far below the landing. It took several good horses per day to operate a busy ferry. The hulls of the horse ferries were usually made of oak. Some were framed with straight boards of oak that were cut across their width, steamed, and then bent on a mold to the proper shape. A Royal Navy shipwright in England, William Hookey, developed the technique of sawing, steaming, and bending timbers for frames.

As the number of travelers increased, steam ferries replaced the horse-propelled ferries. The original paddle side-wheeler steam ferries were built to accommodate a lighter volume of horse-drawn vehicles. Then when most of the ferry traffic consisted of larger and heavier vehicles, the side-loading boats were replaced with end-loading vessels and new causeways to make loading and off-loading easier. End-loading allowed the vehicles to load at one end of the vessel and unload at the other. Such ferries were double-ended and able to proceed equally well in either direction. Later, diesel electric propulsion became more efficient and replaced the steam ferries.

Early ferry licenses were granted to individuals, and licensees were directed to meet certain expectations, such as keeping a passable road leading from the ferry. Because there was little traffic in the early days, ferries did not run every day, but as settlements developed, ferries developed a schedule. The early ferries were called by the owner's name, such as Dufour's Ferry and George Ash's ferry. Later they were named for a family member or a location, such as the Martha A. Graham or the Ohio (River). In early years, the license was granted to run only one way across the river, so some ferry owners bought land on both sides of the river in order to have a more profitable business.

At first, the local county courts determined the toll rates. Gallatin Co. Order Book B described the change in ferry rate for a ferry on the Kentucky River near Carrollton on June 11, 1810: "The rate of Thomas Carraco's ferry will be nine pence for a man and horse and four pence and half penny for a single horse instead of rates established at the last court." Since the water could be treacherous with floating ice in the winter, the rate could be increased. For instance, Gallatin Co. Order Book B stated on January 13, 1812: "Ordered the owner of the ferry across the Ohio, opposite the mouth of Kentucky, be allowed 37 1/2 cents for taking a man and horse across the river during the three winter months." The Kentucky legislature later set the fees that could be charged. Ferrymen were not allowed to charge a toll for mail stages, funeral processions, or ministers.

The first ferries were spaced fairly close together when travel was by oxen, mules, or horses, and even after automobiles became fairly common, because of the number of miles people had to travel. Kentucky law required that ferries had to be at least one mile from each other. In the early days, the ferries quit running at sundown; rarely did people travel after dark, because dangers abounded. The overland trails were treacherous enough during the daytime, horses needed to rest, and the traveler sought a good place to sleep, many times at a tavern, a ferry-house, or an inn. Usually travelers stayed overnight in the vicinity of the ferry, since that is where the settlements were established. Ferries that operated at the end of a major route from Virginia or Tennessee or across the mountains of Kentucky that connected with another state were the most profitable, such as those at Maysville, Covington, Ghent, and Carrollton.

Before the building of the dams on the Ohio River, the water level was uncertain for navigation (see **Ohio River Navigation**). At times of drought, one could walk across the river in places. At other times, after a major rain, a ferry was a necessity. The U.S. Congress appropriated funds to build dams on the Ohio River in order to provide a channel at least nine feet deep between Pittsburgh, Pa., and Cairo, Ill. The Fernbank, Ohio, Dam opened in 1911; the McVille, Ky., Dam in 1921; and the Markland, Ind., Wicket Dam in 1921. Once the nine-foot channel was created, the use of the ferries increased.

Many stories accompany the history of the Northern Kentucky ferries. The Marquis de Lafayette, a hero of the **Revolutionary War**, was personally escorted across the Ohio River to Cincinnati on a small barge ferry at Covington during his tour of the United States in 1825. Beasley's ferry at Maysville was very popular in the 1800s, because Beasley had a large house on the Ohio side of the river where he married couples wanting to elope. It had a thriving business until the opening of the **Simon Kenton Memorial Bridge** at Maysville in 1931. The Augusta Ferry was involved during the Civil War in the escape of Confederate general John Hunt Morgan's Raiders.

The Brent Ferry in Campbell Co. catered to entertainment. Its sole mission was to transport persons to the Coney Island Amusement Park/River Downs Race Track in Ohio for a day of fun. It ceased with the completion of the nearby I-275 bridge; its last owner was John D. Laughead. George Ash's ferry at Carrollton (Port William) posed notable dangers for a time, since Ash was known for hiding along the riverbank and acting as a decoy to rob early settlers. His actions did not continue long, because he was converted to religion at an early tent revival. Captain William McCoy operated a ferry service between the Ludlow wharf and W. Fifth St. in Cincinnati. Ferry service was vital to this area, but McCoy refused to operate on a consistent schedule. In 1864, the town fathers of Ludlow petitioned the state for a city charter, thinking that an incorporated city could regulate McCoy's ferry. This strategy failed and the problem continued for another 20 years.

Northern Kentucky has two ferries still in operation on the Ohio River: the **Anderson Ferry** near Constance and Boude's **Augusta Ferry** at Augusta.

Cotterell, Harry, Jr. "Ohio River Crossings." *Steamboat Bill*, Spring 1976, 7–12.
Crisman, Kevin J., and Arthur B. Cohn. *When Horses Walked on Water: Horse-Powered Ferries in Nineteenth-Century America*. Washington, D.C.: Smithsonian Institution Press, 1998.
Fishbaugh, Charles Preston. *From Paddle Wheels to Propellers*. Indianapolis: Indiana Historical Society, 1970.
Reis, Jim. *Pieces of the Past*. Vols. 1 and 2. Covington: Kentucky Post, 1991.
——. "Small Brent Once Boomed, but Lost Out to Silver Grove," *KP*, November 29, 1999, 4.
Stivers, Eliese Bambach. *Ripley, Ohio: Its History and Families*. Self-published, 1965.
Way, Frederick, Jr. *Way's Packet Directory, 1848–1973*. Athens: Ohio Univ. Press, 1983.

Virginia Reeves

FIDELITY INVESTMENTS. One of the newer corporate residents of Covington is the Boston-

Northern Kentucky Ferries

In the following list, a single year indicates when the company or ferry was licensed. For some companies and ferries, no specific date is available; their placement in the list may be taken to indicate roughly when they operated. In the case of crossings listed with no further details, it is known only that a licensed ferry operated at those places. The crossing locations are arranged upstream to downstream for the Ohio River only.

OHIO RIVER FERRIES

Maysville, Ky. (Limestone Landing), to Aberdeen, Ohio	
Nathan Ellis Ferry	1795
William Brooks Ferry	1795
Benjamin Sutton Ferry	1795
Mr. York Ferry	
John Taylor's Ferry	1797
Edmund Martin's Ferry	1797–1827
Jacob Boone Ferry	1808
J. K. Ficklin's Ferry	1818
William B. Campbell	1820
Gleaner	
Shanghai	
Relief	1925
Laurance	1928
Kawanis	1931
South Ripley, Ky., to Ripley, Ohio	
Maggie May	1881
Proctor K. Smiley	ca. 1882–1921
Senate City	
New Richmond	
Relief	
Nora Belle	
W. S. Taylor Ferry	1935–1941
H & C Ferry	1951
Dover, Ky., to Levanna, Ohio	
Augusta, Ky., to Boude's Ferry, Ohio	
Edward Salts Ferry	1796
John Coburn Ferry	1796
James Bonwell Ferry	1796
John Boude Ferry	1798
Mr. Fleming Ferry	ca. 1798
John Taylor's Ferry	
Augusta College Ferry	1820–1822
Dr. Joshua T. Bradford Ferry	1822
Belle of Augusta	
Dr. George Mackay	1899
Whisper	1900
O'Neill	ca. 1930
Mister Haines	(shut down in 1973, back in service by City Fathers 1976)

(*Continued*)

based financial services company Fidelity Investments. Located atop Winston Hill south of Latonia, in the northwestern quadrant where Ky. Rt. 16 (Taylor Mill Rd.) crosses over I-275, the company's 188-acre campus has expanded Northern Kentucky's employment base.

In 1943 Edward C. Johnson II took over management of the Fidelity Fund (mutual fund) in Boston, which had been founded in 1930. In 1946 he started the Fidelity Management and Research Company as an adviser to the Fund. He believed that through research and active management of stocks, he could outperform the market in general. For many years, the company's successful Magellen Fund did exactly that. In 1972 Edward C. Johnson III succeeded his father as president of the privately held enterprise. He began his career with the growing company in 1957 as an analyst. Fidelity Management and Research started to invest in infrastructure and technology, allowing for growth in the retirement and outsourcing lines of business. In the early 21st century, the firm attained the milestone of having $1 trillion in assets under its management.

The firm became Fidelity Investments and opened in Northern Kentucky in 1994, after obtaining some lucrative tax breaks from local and state government. Its first building was designed by KZF Inc., of Cincinnati; its fourth building, completed in 2008, has 360,000 square feet and cost $144 million; at the same time, a 17,000-square-foot addition was added to Fidelity's main building. The Commonwealth of Kentucky recognized the importance of the firm when it agreed to construct a 1.7-mile connector highway from the west side of the Fidelity campus to Ky. Rt. 17. Completed in 2007, the Highland Pk. (Ky. Rt. 1072) extension spans the **CSX** railroad tracks and **Banklick Creek**, providing additional egress for Fidelity's campus and opening up another 100-plus acres for similar development along its path.

Fidelity Investments has been a good corporate citizen of the region. Its people are involved in many activities to improve life in Northern Kentucky, and the company has donated generously to causes within the region. Fidelity has joined with **Northern Kentucky University** (NKU) to create a Fidelity call center on campus, providing students with work experience on the NKU campus. In early 2005, Newport native Kevin Canafax, a 1982 graduate of **Newport Central Catholic High School**, was named the regional general manager of Fidelity Investments in Covington.

Twenty years ago, Fidelity Investments rose to prominence as a mutual fund company and became a financial services company; 10 years ago it got into insurance, brokerage, and retirement planning. With the knowledge of how large the demographic of the baby boomers will be, and all the discretionary investment income they will have available, Fidelity seeks to position itself to capture that market and the millions of financial transactions that will be made by that group. Fidelity Investments in Covington will be the home of that

Brent, Ky. (Campbell Co.), to Coney Island, Ohio (Ferry company closed with the opening of the I-275 bridge)	
James Bateman Ferry	1874
William Wilson	1899
Whoopee Girl	1933
John D	1934
Ferry Queen	1940–1949
Ferry Princess	1949–1968
Ferry Prince	1956–1978
Ferry Princess II	1968–1978
Bradford, Ky., to Chilo, Ohio	
Horse Ferry	1885–1895
Foster, Ky., to Neville, Ohio	
Ivory, Ky., to Moscow, Ohio	
New Richmond, Ky., to New Richmond, Ohio	
Dayton, Ky., to Cincinnati	
Newport, Ky., to Cincinnati	
Robert Benham Ferry	1792 (both banks of the Licking)
Lady Gay	1865–1870
City of Newport	1882–1890
Covington, Ky., to Cincinnati	
Francis Kennedy	1789
Thomas Kennedy Ferry (see **Thomas Kennedy**)	1791
Robert Benham Ferry	1792 (both banks of the Licking)
Samuel Kennedy	1815
Main St. (Covington) Ferry	19th century
Scott St. Ferry	19th century
Ludlow, Ky., to Cincinnati	
Ludlow Ferry	19th century
Constance, Ky., to Sedamsville, Ohio (see **Anderson Ferry**)	
Raleigh Colston Ferry	ca. 1817
George Anderson Ferry	1817–1841
John Wilson Ferry	1865
Boone	1867–1874
Boone 2	1874–1885
Boone 3	1881–1890
Boone 4	1891–1909
Boone 5	1900–1918
Boone 6	1920–1936
Boone 7	1937
Boone 8	1964
Bullittsville, Ky., to Lawrenceburg, Ind.	
Johnson Ferry	1804
Touseytown, Ky., to Lawrenceburg, Ind.	
Moses Tousey Ferry	1820
Samuel C. Vance	1826
Capt. Thomas Porter	1835
General A. Saunders Piatt Ferry	1842
Judge Jacob Piatt Ferry	1844
Charles Piatt Ferry	
Abram Piatt Sr.	1845

(Continued)

product line. In 2008 Fidelity Investments employed about 4,600 workers in Northern Kentucky, including 4,400 at its main Covington campus, 100 in downtown Covington (see **Covington, Downtown**), and 85 at Northern Kentucky University. It is the sixth-largest private-sector employer in Kentucky.

Driehaus, Bob. "Fidelity Names Canafax to Post," *KP*, January 14, 2005, 1K.
"Fidelity a Boon to Local Economy," *CP*, March 3, 1999, 7B.
"Fidelity Celebrates Its Newest Building," *KE*, May 22, 2008, B1.
Fidelity.com. www.fidelity.com (accessed on December 8, 2006).
"Fidelity Tapping NKU for Workers," *KP*, October 29, 1998, 6C.
"Firm Plans Scenic Campus," *KP*, April 24, 1992, 1K.
"High Fidelity in Covington," *SC*, December 18, 2005, 4B.
Mitsoff, Tom. "Highland Pike Connector on Schedule," *KP*, July 12, 2006, A2.
——. "Work Begins on Fidelity Connector," *KP*, June 14, 2006, A2.
Newberry, Jon. "Fidelity Will Be the No. 2 Employer," *KP*, June 3, 2005, 1K.
"Tax Break to Help Lure Brokerage," *KP*, March 20, 1992, 1.

FIELDS, GREG (b. June 11, 1955, Fort Thomas, Ky.; d. April 15, 2002, Woodland Hills, Calif.). Comedy writer Kenneth Gregory Fields was the son of Kenneth and Joann Derrick Fields. He grew up on the south side of Newport, on the hill behind the shopping center, where he attended Mildred Dean Grade School and **Newport High School**, graduating from the latter in 1973. Fields played quarterback on his high school football team and guard in basketball. He earned a basketball scholarship to Southwestern College (now Rhodes College) in Memphis, Tenn. By age 14, he knew what he wanted to do in life and worked during high school as a stand-up comedian at local nightclubs (see **Beverly Hills Supper Club**). While in college he opened for musical acts such as, Brook Benton, Chuck Berry, and Jerry Lee Lewis. In 1977 he moved to Los Angeles and took a job delivering liquor as he began writing material for other comedians. He eventually wrote for television shows such as *The Tonight Show, The Pat Sajak Show, Solid Gold, In Living Color, The Parenthood,* and *The New Smothers Brothers Show.* He went on to write for *Dean Martin's Roasts*, and he wrote the 1986 Rodney Dangerfield movie *Back to School.* Fields also scripted the 1998 movie *Garbage Picking, Football Kicking, Philadelphia Phenomenon.* He authored material for David Brenner, Jim Carey, Charo, former president Gerald Ford, Bob Hope, Jay Leno, Rich Little, Joan Rivers, and Slappy White. Fields was a personal friend of Disney's Michael Eisner, and he was known to financially help out other comedians with whom he had worked. At age 46, while working on two movies and a cartoon pilot about a dysfunctional family, Fields died of a heart attack at his home in California and was buried at Oakwood Memorial Cemetery

Touseytown, Ky., to Lawrenceburg, Ind. (*Continued*)	
Peter Hartman's Ferry	
Robert Terrill	
George Terrill	
Capt. William Huff	
Shirley T.	1897
Pearl	1927–1945
Petersburg, Ky., to Aurora, Ind.	
John Watts Ferry	1800–1815
John Grant	1806
John I. Flournoy	1806–1813
James Marshall	
Archibald Huston	
J. W. Loder Ferry	
Swing Ferry	
Buffington Ferry	
Appleman Ferry	
Frank Klopp Ferry	
Jacob Klopp	
Aurora	1937–1977
Everett Lee	1945–1958
Etta Belle	
C. J. Ferry	
Middle Creek, Ky., to Rice's Landing, Ind.	
McVille Ferry	
D. G. Rice Ferry	
J. W. Rice Ferry	
Rabbit Hash, Ky., to Rising Sun, Ind.	
Edward Meeks Ferry Flat	1830
James Alexander Wilson Ferry	1842–1850
James Carlton Ferry	1848
George Carlton Ferry	
James Calvert Ferry	1848–1861
John Q. A. Stephens	1852
Pembroke S. Ryle	1855
T. C. S. Ryle and William Rice Ferry	1856
William P. Ryle	1858
Leonard Clore	1859
Charles Craig	
James Perkins	1867
Jacob Piatt	
Robert Piatt	1872–1877
Richard S. Ryle	1874
John Huey	1888
Thomas Lumpkins	1890
Benjamin Wilson	1899
Josie Piatt and others	1899–1908
J. W. Whitlock	1906
Swan	
Katie Platt Ferry	1911–1918
Kittie Whitlock	1922
See Me Passenger	
Mildred	1922–1945
Rabbit Transit Company	1983
Gunpowder Creek, Ky. (just below Rabbit Hash), to Rising Sun, Ind.	
John Bush Ferry	1803–1810
Lott North	1807
Johnson Ferry	1807

(*Continued*)

in Woodland Hills. His wife, a son, and a daughter survived him.

"Greg Fields, Respected Hollywood TV, Film Writer," *KP,* April 22, 2002, 6A.
Obituary, *Variety,* May 16, 2002. www.variety.com.

Michael R. Sweeney

FIFTH THIRD BANK. The Fifth Third Bank of Cincinnati traces its origins to a bank founded in 1858, called the Bank of the Ohio Valley. That bank was later acquired by the Third National Bank of Cincinnati. Fifth Third Bank's present unique name comes from the 1908 merger of the Fifth National Bank of Cincinnati with the city's Third National Bank. Since that time, Fifth Third Bank has acquired numerous other financial institutions and is today a large regional bank with numerous branches in 10 states.

In the Northern Kentucky counties of Boone, Campbell, and Kenton, Fifth Third Bank acquired the American National Bank of Newport, the Boone State Bank, the First National Bank of Falmouth, the Kentucky Enterprise Bank of Newport, and the Security Bank of Covington.

One of Fifth Third Bank's important Northern Kentucky acquisitions was the **First National Bank of Covington,** located at the corner of Sixth St. and Madison Ave. That bank was established in 1864 by a group of prominent citizens, including members of the Shinkle family, who were also responsible for the building of the **John A. Roebling Bridge**. **Amos Shinkle**, one of Covington's leading citizens, served as the bank's first president. In later years the First National Bank absorbed the Merchants and Traders National Bank, the Farmers and Traders Bank, and the First National Bank of Latonia. The First National Bank's impact on the health and growth of the Northern Kentucky economy was considerable. With its financial assistance and guidance, many businesses flourished in the area; it also played an important role in the development of the **Cincinnati/Northern Kentucky International Airport**.

"Cincinnati Bank Backs Purchase of 1st National," *KP,* May 9, 1983, 1K.
Fifth Third Bank. "History and Expansion." www.53.com (accessed April 11, 2007).
"Our Hundredth Birthday," *KP* (suppl.), December 10, 1967.

FILMS AND FILMMAKING. Northern Kentucky has been the backdrop for several major motion pictures, filmed in locations from **Pompilio's** Italian restaurant and the **John A. Roebling Bridge** to Covington's historic railroad passenger station (see **Louisville and Nashville Railroad**) and the small-town charm of communities such as Augusta and Ludlow. High production costs and location licensing restrictions in Los Angeles and New York have made shooting movies elsewhere, such as in the Northern Kentucky–Cincinnati area, increasingly appealing to directors and producers. Filmmakers also look for new scenery to interest audiences who are tired of familiar landscapes. Since 1987 the his-

Steel's Creek, Brashear, Ky., to Patriot (Troy), Ind.	
Elisha Wade and James Hearick Ferry	1819
R & C Coffin and Sylvanus Howe Ferry	1836
Elijah H. Johnson Ferry	1852
Judge McClure Ferry	
Silas Howe Ferry	1881
Frank Emerson Ferry	1915
Warsaw, Ky., to Wiley's Landing/Florence, Ind.	
Henry Hampton Ferry	1814
William Campbell Ferry	1817
James Clancey Ferry	1821
John P. Lillard, William R. Wiley, and A. Hinman Ferry	1833
Samuel Howards Ferry	1836
Joseph Malin	1846
Elijah Wiley	
Kentucky Home	1864
Everett Lee	1930
Hazel S.	1947
Pearl	1950–1951
Warsaw	1960
Kelli	1961
Big Mamou, renamed *Troy D*	1977
Ethridge, Ky., to Markland, Ind.	
Taylor Beard	1882
A. Benedict & Sons	1883
Ghent (McCool's Creek), Ky., to Vevay, Ind.—two locations, a mile apart	
William Scott	1806
John Francois Dufour Ferry	1807
George Craig Ferry	1816
Samuel Sanders Ferry	1826
John Sheets Ferry	1830
Canary I	1848
Canary II	1872
Eva Everett I	1898
Eva Everett II	1900–1917
Robert T. Graham	1918–1942
Martha A. Graham	1942–1978
Carrollton, Ky., to Lamb (Erin), Ind.	
Charles Kilgore Ferry	1805
James McKay	1806
Capt. George Ash Ferry	1811
George Craig	1811
Edward McIntire	1816
Leeon	
Mary Jo	
Ohio	
Indiana	
Minnie	
David McKay	

LICKING RIVER FERRIES

Falmouth, Ky.	
Alvin Mountjoy	
John Sanders	1795
William Anderson	

(*Continued*)

toric architecture, the rolling hills, and the river ambience of Covington, Newport, and Cincinnati have provided the settings for many major motion pictures.

A large-scale motion picture production facility was considered for Northern Kentucky long before the heyday of Hollywood. In 1915 the newly formed Highland Film Company of New York investigated sites in the Highlands (Fort Thomas) and later in the **Lagoon Amusement Park** in Ludlow as a film studio. These were among the first film production sites considered in the Midwest. In 1924 the first Studio Mechanics Local union, representing entertainment industry workers, was chartered by the International Alliance of Theatrical Stage Employees in 1924 at the International Alliance Convention in Cincinnati.

Among the first films shot on location in Northern Kentucky was the high-profile, made-for-television movie-miniseries *Centennial* (1978), based on James Michener's best-selling 1974 novel. Augusta's splendid 18th- and 19th-century buildings on Riverside Dr. served as the background for the St. Louis waterfront scenes. Extras for these film takes included a local resident (then still in high school), **George Clooney**, who was making his motion picture debut.

The theatrical film *Eight Men Out* (1987) was the first major Hollywood film shot on location in Northern Kentucky. Covington's Railway Exposition Center in the **Latonia** neighborhood of Covington (see **Railway Museum of Greater Cincinnati**) provided backdrops. Fort Thomas native Lori Holliday influenced the producers of *Eight Men Out* to come to the region for the on-location filming. The success of *Eight Men Out* prompted Holliday to establish what became the Greater Cincinnati and Northern Kentucky Film Commission. The Kentucky Film Office (formerly the Kentucky Film Commission) has also been supportive in attracting films to the region.

On-location filming of *Rain Man* (1988) followed and featured many Northern Kentucky surroundings. This Oscar-winning movie, starring Dustin Hoffman and Tom Cruise, was the most noteworthy film shot in the region. Its legendary "dropped toothpicks" scene was filmed at Pompilio's Italian Restaurant in Newport. Other regional images in the movie included a drive across the John Roebling Bridge, interior scenes from the **Cincinnati/Northern Kentucky International Airport**, and shots from **Evergreen Cemetery** in Southgate and St. Anne's Convent (see **Sisters of Divine Providence**) in Melbourne. More than 55 million people in over 36 countries viewed *Rain Man* during its initial theatrical release.

The surrounding hills and the Hudson-like Ohio River, with neighborhoods reminiscent of the 1940s, attracted the production designer of *Lost in Yonkers* (1992) to shoot many of that film's scenes in Ludlow. The corner of Elm and Kenner Sts. at the west end of Ludlow's business district was transformed into Grandma's two-story apartment, with a candy storefront as the main set. Some other *Lost in Yonkers* scenes were filmed in Augusta.

Since the inception of the Greater Cincinnati and Northern Kentucky Film Commission, the region has become somewhat of a Hollywood on the Ohio River. Other films and Northern Kentucky locations include *Fresh Horses* (1987), Covington, Newport, and Union; *A Rage in Harlem* (1990), Covington; and *Airborne* (1993), Bellevue, Covington, and Newport. Northern Kentucky University student interns served as the support crew for *Crossing Field* (1998), for which some scenes were shot in Northern Kentucky, and local extras were used in *Seabiscuit* (2003), which was filmed in multiple Central Kentucky locations. *Rabbit Hash: The Center of the Universe* (2004), filmed in Rabbit Hash, Boone Co., was the latest movie shot on location in Northern Kentucky; it included Wynonna Judd in the cast.

Northern Kentucky natives who won Academy Awards include **Robert Surtees**, cinematography (1950, 1952, and 1959); **George Clooney**, acting (2005); and **Bub Asman**, editing (2006). George Clooney, **Rosemary Clooney**, **Dick Curtis**, and **Una Merkel** are among the most well-known Hollywood film stars from Northern Kentucky. Other motion picture stars from Northern Kentucky include **Bob Braun**, **Bob Elkins**, **Don Galloway**, **Josh Hutcherson**, and **Kathy Walsh**. In the 1940s **Anna Bell Ward** was a producer of western films. In the 1930s and 1940s, Covington-born photographer **George Hurrell** developed the glamour mode of photography stills, which helped immortalize the images of Hollywood luminaries.

DeBrosse, Jim. "Horray for Cinciwood," *CE*, October 1, 1987, D1.

DeChick, Joe. "Lost in Yonkers Film Finds 1942 Street of New York in Ludlow, Ky.: Time Travel," *CE*, July 22, 1992, C1.

Josten, Margaret. "Movie Makers Shoot Bright Economic Pictures in the Tristate: Scenes from the City," *CE*, October 12, 1992, D1.

Kings, John. *In Search of Centennial: A Journey with James A. Michener*. New York: Random House, 1978.

"Lagoon May Change Hands; May Become Highland Park," *KP*, March 17, 1915, 1.

"Made in Cincinnati: 'Traffic' Adds to Long List of Movies Filmed Here," *CP*, January 4, 2001, 3.

Wheeler, Lonnie. "John Sayles Finds His 'City of Hope' in Cincinnati," *NYT*, November 25, 1990, H6.

John Schlipp

KENTUCKY RIVER FERRIES

Carrollton, Ky., to Prestonville, Ky.	
James Coghill	1804
William Fauntleroy	1804
James Spoull	1809
Thomas Carraco	1808–1810
Abner Hanks	1809
Heath Ferry	1870–1900

FINCHTOWN. Today it is part of Wilder, but until 1938 Finchtown was a five-block-long area south of Newport along the Licking River, just north of Wilder. Ky. Rt. 9, the Licking Pk., runs through it. This was the location of the G. W. Robson Jr. and Company Distillery, later known as the "Old 76 Distillery." A large concrete shell of that plant remains and is used for storage. The former **Louisville, Cincinnati, and Lexington Railroad** (Short Line), which became the **Louisville and Nashville Railroad** and, of late, the **CSX**, passes through old Finchtown. It is not known how the town received its name. In addition to the distillery, Finchtown has had hotels, slaughterhouses, a soap factory, and coal companies. Buck Brady operated his famed Latin Quarters Night Club there in the supposedly haunted building of today's **Bobby Mackey's** place. In the last few years, a new gentlemen's club has appeared just up road along the Licking Pk., continuing the long tradition of wild bars. The town has had several major fires, and dogfighting was once popular there. Most of the streets of Finchtown are gone and forgotten, just as most of its history is.

An Atlas of Boone, Kenton, and Campbell Counties, Kentucky. Philadelphia: D.J. Luke, 1883.

Reis, Jim. "Fire Plagued Finchtown Finally Faded," *KP*, July 5, 1993, 4K.

FINNELL, JOHN WILLIAM, GENERAL (b. December 24, 1821, Winchester, Ky.; d. January 25, 1888, Helena, Mont.). John W. Finnell, a Kentucky adjutant general, was the son of Nimrod L. Finnell, a printer and newspaper editor. John Finnell graduated from Transylvania University in Lexington in 1837, at age 17, and immediately joined his father in the printing trade. He worked as an editor for a brief time before returning to Transylvania for a law degree, which he received in 1840. Shortly after starting his law practice, Finnell became involved in state politics. As a member of the **Whig Party**, he served in the Kentucky legislature as a representative of Nicholas Co. in 1845 and 1846 while also working as editor of the *Frankfort Commonwealth* in Frankfort. Impressed with Finnell's ability and potential, Governor John J. Crittenden (1849–1850) appointed the young lawyer secretary of state, a position Finnell held until 1852, when he moved to Covington to practice law. In 1856 he served as legal counsel for Archibald Gaines, whose slave **Margaret Garner** murdered her two-year-old daughter during a failed attempt to gain her family's freedom. During the fugitive slave trial for Garner held in Cincinnati, Finnell, also a slave owner, defended the institution of slavery and challenged local abolitionists' unsuccessful efforts to win Garner's freedom. Like many other Ohio Valley residents, Finnell, though holding proslavery ideas, was not pro-South. He objected to the secession of the Southern states and, during the **Civil War**, became an outspoken Unionist and member of the Republican Party. At the beginning of the Civil War, Kenton Co. Unionists elected Finnell to be their representative to the Kentucky legislature. Governor Beriah Magoffin (1859–1862) chose Finnell to assume the post of state adjutant general shortly after Kentucky abandoned the problematic policy of armed neutrality. He had the difficult task of organizing the pro-Union home guard in order to bolster the dwindled ranks of the state guard, which lost a number of its officers and men to the Confederate Army. Finnell was not able to completely reinvigorate Kentucky's military organization because many Kentuckians wished to remain uncommitted to either side. Additionally, Finnell worked diligently to fill the state's portion of the national government's military quota by raising volunteers for federal regiments, but he eventually accepted the necessity of a statewide draft. Finnell retired from his post as state adjutant general in 1863 and returned to his Covington law practice. In 1872 he moved to Louisville and spent two years there as editor of the *Louisville Commercial*. He then returned to his farm and orchard 20 miles south of Covington. During the 1880s he moved to Montana and died there of heart disease in 1888. He was buried in Linden Grove Cemetery in Covington.

Biographical Encyclopedia of Kentucky. Cincinnati: J. M. Armstrong, 1878.

Federal Writers Project. *Military History of Kentucky*. Frankfort, Ky.: State Journal, 1939.

John W. Finnell letter book, Kentucky Historical Society Archives, Frankfort, Ky.

Reis, Jim. "Surprise Eulogy for Lee," *KP*, August 18, 2003, 5K.

———. "They Served as Legislators When War Clouds Billowed," *KP*, January 27, 2003, 4K.

Stephen Rockenbach

FIRE DEPARTMENTS. The roots of modern fire departments in Northern Kentucky go back to the days when people settling the area first began collectively confronting the danger of fire. An early fire-extinguishing method was water buckets, constructed of shoe-sole leather, kept at each structure within a settlement and reserved for fighting fires. If a fire was discovered, a distinct alarm, often a drum, a rattle or clacker, or church bells, used only for fires, was sounded to alert citizens, who were required to respond and help fight the fire under penalty of a fine. The buckets were filled from the nearest source of water and passed to the fire from person to person, in what was called a bucket brigade.

As communities grew and homes and businesses were built closer together, better firefighting methods were developed to cope with the tendency of fire to spread from one wooden structure to another. A major improvement in firefighting, the fire pump, came into use in the early 1800s. It had a tank into which water was poured either from buckets or with a hose connected to a water pipe. Several men were needed to pull the heavy fire pump to the scene. It took six or more men to operate the pumping mechanism; they had to move bellows inside the tank by an action similar to rowing a boat or operating a railroad handcar. Around 1850, the hand-drawn and hand-operated fire pumps were replaced with steam-powered pumps drawn by horses.

Municipal water systems, when they were created, provided a more reliable water supply; fire hydrants were spaced to permit quick access. In the period when wooden water pipes were used, firefighters often had to dig to expose the pipe and then cut a hole to get water to fill their fire pumps. After the fire was extinguished, the hole was repaired with a wooden plug. The term "fire plug," which is still used to refer to a fire hydrant, stems from this practice. In rural areas, fire departments had to rely on water from farm ponds, wells, or creeks, and they continue to do so in some areas, although most localities have tanker trucks, which can carry more than 1,000 gallons. Most fire trucks now also have a built-in water tank of about 500 gallons, permitting instant fire attack even while connection to a water supply is being established. Flexible fire hoses and more dependable equipment make it possible for firefighters to enter the structure and extinguish the fire more quickly.

Alarm methods came to include fire alarm boxes placed at various intersecting streets in the larger Northern Kentucky cities like Covington and Newport; when activated, these alarms telegraphed an identifying number to fire headquarters and alarm bells tapped out the number at fire stations, which were quickly cross-checked on a list for the location. Firefighters soon memorized the numbers of the boxes in their district. As the telephone became available, citizens in less populated and rural areas had a means of direct contact with their fire departments. The street alarm boxes eventually were not needed, since nearly everyone had access to a telephone.

Until about 1920, firefighting equipment was drawn by horses. The trained horses would quickly back into their harnesses, ready to pull the equipment, when they heard the alarm bells. The precision movements of the two or more horse teams, the apparatus bell clanging, with smoke billowing from the steam pump, and the barking of the traditional Dalmatian dog mascot atop the fire engine often brought people out on the streets to watch. In Covington and Newport, such horses as Charley, Captain Jim, Dick, Pat, and Pete acquired almost as much local celebrity status as the best-known firefighters from those cities.

As the urban areas of Northern Kentucky grew, it became obvious that a force of full-time paid firefighters was needed to provide constant and

Theodore Joseph Hanneken driving an antique fire wagon to commemorate Covington's first paid fire department, ca. 1941.

adequate fire protection. Full-time paid firefighters in the region were hired in Covington in 1864 and in Newport in 1868, and later in Carrollton, Fort Thomas, and Maysville. For reasons of economy, some fire departments used volunteer firefighters to supplement the paid staff, especially during nights and weekends. Similar arrangements in several of the municipalities in Northern Kentucky continue today. Moreover, some rural areas still rely entirely on volunteer firefighters, though many are merging and forming fire districts with paid full-time staff to be on duty during the daytime when most volunteer firefighters are working at their regular jobs.

Women have always been involved in the firefighting endeavor, initially through the ladies' auxiliary. They prepared meals; brought dry clothing, hot drinks, and food to major fires; and raised funds for the purchase of equipment. As time went on, they often served as drivers or emergency medical technicians (EMTs) to free the men for firefighting tasks. Currently, women are employed as full-time paid firefighters and carry out all of the firefighting duties.

Personal protective gear enables a firefighter to enter a fire more safely and achieve better results. The familiar helmet is now constructed of high-impact fiberglass rather than metal, preventing electric shock. The rubber coat has been replaced with a coat, and usually pants, made of highly insulated water-resistant and flame-resistant materials. The suspenders are often brightly colored with reflective striping, for better visibility, rather than the traditional black. Firefighters wear knee-length rubber boots with steel toes, soles, and shin guards. The modern Self Contained Breathing Apparatus permits the firefighter to work in a toxic atmosphere, which is present in every fire situation. Thermal image cameras detect any image producing heat, even through heavy smoke and interior walls. As a result, search, rescue, and finding hidden fires can be completed quickly without subjecting the firefighter to the dangers of blind groping through dense smoke. Knox boxes for businesses or residences give firefighters access to locked buildings via a radio-controlled key release, permitting quick entry for investigation or fire attack without causing damage to doors or windows. Early firefighters had no such equipment and often lost their lives while attempting to extinguish fires and rescue people. Even today, with all the protective equipment, which might weigh 50 pounds or more, firefighting remains a dangerous job. Heart disease is a leading cause of disability or death for firefighters.

There was a time when a firefighter could succeed knowing "a little bit about everything," but that day is long past. Today's firefighter needs to be highly trained; often a person who intends to be a firefighter will specialize, in college, in a particular segment of the profession. The specific training and knowledge necessary to extinguish and prevent fires include such matters as building construction, materials, and contents; hazardous materials and chemicals; rescues of all kinds (high above ground, on the ground, under the ground, and under water); fire prevention and inspections; public education; and many kinds of medical emergencies and terrorist threats.

Fire vehicles, like firefighting teams, are often divided into specialty units. With costs exceeding $200,000 for each vehicle, fire departments plan carefully to achieve maximum value from their investment. The fire pumpers of today can produce 1,250, 1,500, or more gallons of water per minute. Water is still the most common extinguishing agent, although various additives may be used to produce foam or to enable more penetration or better "soaking" qualities of the water. The hoses used for supply from fire hydrants are commonly up to five inches in diameter. The handlines for fire attack are usually one and a half to three inches in diameter; each fire pumper carries several hundred feet of each hose size. Ladder trucks have an assortment of ground ladders in addition to elevating ladders, "cherry pickers," or a combination of both; some reach 135 feet, and new models are nearing a 150-foot height. Rescue trucks carry a vast array of tools, such as the "jaws of life," hazardous materials (HAZMAT) equipment, portable lighting equipment, and tarpaulins for covering storm-damaged roofs, furniture, or other items to prevent additional damage. Computers on many of the apparatuses can provide a complete description of the building or site where help is needed, including floor plans, contents, occupancy, where each apparatus should be placed in relation to the water connections, and many other details, to provide a quick setup and fire attack.

Establishment of Some Fire Companies and Fire Departments (Both Volunteer and Paid; Dates Given If Known)

Alexandria, 1937

Augusta, 1930

Belleview-McVille, 1966

Bellevue, ca. 1880

Bellevue/Dayton, 2002 (merger)

Bromley, 1895

Brooksville, 1927

Burlington, 1943

Butler

Camp Springs, 1949

Carrollton

Central Campbell Co. Fire District, 1999 (merger of the Cold Spring–Crestview and the Highland Heights Fire Departments)

Cold Spring–Crestview, 1943

Corinth

Covington, 1833

Crescent Springs, 1928–1929

Crittenden, 1949

Dayton, 1898

Dover

Dry Ridge, ca. 1909

Eastern Campbell Co., 1964

Edgewood (Sanfordtown, 1955; Southern Hills, 1961; Edgewood, 1996)

Elsmere, 1899

Erlanger, 1904, 1927–1928

Falmouth

Fernleaf Highland

Florence, 1936

Fort Mitchell, ca. 1927

Fort Thomas (District of the Highlands), 1904

Fort Wright, 1949

Germantown (Bracken Co.)

Ghent

Glencoe, 1964

Hebron, 1937

Independence, 1937

Jonesville, 1971

Kenton

Lewisburg (Mason Co.), organized 1970, operational 1972

Ludlow, 1884

Mayslick

Maysville, 1804 (bucket brigade); 1851

Melbourne, 1951

Monterey

Mount Olivet

New Liberty, 1972

Newport, 1840s

Northern Pendleton

Orangeburg

Owenton/Owen Co. (Owenton, 1893; reorganized as Owenton/Owen Co., 1954)

Park Hills, 1942

Petersburg, 1959

Piner-Fiskburg, 1964

Point Pleasant, 1956

Ryland Heights

Sanders

Sardis

Silver Grove

Southern Campbell

Southgate, 1909

South Owen

Sparta

Taylor Mill, 1957

Union, 1969

Verona, 1968

Walton, 1880 (bucket brigade), 1947

Warsaw/Gallatin Co., 1952

Washington-Maysville

Westside

Wilder, 1957

Williamstown, ca. 1890s

Woodlawn

Worthville, 1948

Annual Reports of City of Covington, Kentucky, Fire Department, 1864 to present, Office of the Chief, Covington, Ky.

Campbell Co. Historical Society. *Campbell County, Kentucky, 200 Years, 1794–1994*. Alexandria, Ky.: Campbell Co. Historical Society, 1994.

Campbell County Firefighter Educational Association. Campbell Co., Ky.: Campbell Co. Firefighter Educational Association, 2002.

Clift, G. Glenn. *History of Maysville and Mason County*. Lexington, Ky.: Transylvania Printing, 1936.

Conrad, John B., ed. *History of Grant County*. Williamstown, Ky.: Grant Co. Historical Society, 1992.

Conrad, William, ed. *Boone County: The Top of Kentucky, 1792–1992*. Fort Mitchell, Ky.: Picture This! Books, 1992.

A History of the Fort Mitchell Volunteer Fire Department, 1928–1980. Fort Mitchell, Ky.: Fort Mitchell Fire Dept, 1980.

Ludlow Volunteer Fire Dept. Records, 1884–1946, Ludlow Volunteer Fire Department, Ludlow, Ky.

Reis, Jim. "Big Blazes of '20s and '30s—in Rural Areas, Bucket Brigades Were Still Used," *KP*, January 6, 2003, 4K.

——. "Four-Legged Firefighters Once Raced to Blazes," *KP*, January 12, 2001, 4K.

Robert Joseph Williams and Nancy J. Tretter

FIRES. In the Northern Kentucky region, the urban areas of Covington, Maysville, and Newport were the first ones to develop fire departments. They started out using horse-drawn wagons to transport firemen carrying axes, picks, shovels, and ladders. Eventually, the departments had steam-engine pumpers with long hoses that they could dip into a nearby river, lake, well, or cistern and obtain water to spray onto the flames. Later, gasoline- or diesel-powered vehicles with pumpers replaced horse-drawn equipment, and the installation of citywide water systems provided fire hydrants as a source of water. As cities grew, fire departments could be summoned by means of a local alarm box or fire box. Until the early 1960s, one of these call boxes stood at the corner of Park and Grand Aves. in Newport. It was mainly a way for police and fire personnel to communicate with their counterparts in downtown Newport; yet there it remained, a relic from the past, long after its practical life had ended. At one time, when few households had telephones and VHF radio communications did not exist, Covington had 140 such fire call boxes, and Newport had half that number. Urban fire departments often were called to fight fires in adjacent areas. Newport's fire department, for example, responded to fires in **Cote Brilliante** even before that neighborhood was annexed to Newport during the 1920s. The promise of professional fire protection, along with lower home and fire insurance rates, was a major consideration in the vote that favored this annexation.

Ever since Mrs. O'Leary's cow purportedly kicked a lantern and started the fire that burned down most of Chicago in 1871, insurance companies have encouraged incorporation of fire-resistant features in the design of buildings. The Sanborn Map Company was developed to track the details of construction type, location, size, number of stories, and materials used in each structure in any given urban city, on a block-by-block grid basis. Those maps were and are continually updated to help underwriters set fire insurance rates. In the suburbs, volunteer fire departments sprang up, and as these appeared in the small cities and townships in Northern Kentucky, they helped foster the development of formal government; it turned out that local firehouses essentially became surrogate city halls. Woodlawn in Campbell Co. is one city where that occurred.

Over the years, there have been many nonresidential fires in the region that are worthy of note. Some of the most destructive ones are described in the following paragraphs. For fires associated with aviation accidents, see **Aviation Accidents**. Statistics on residential fires, including those involving loss of life, are kept separately by the individual fire departments in the region.

On September 21, 1880, the Ninth St. Presbyterian Church in Covington was totally destroyed by fire, as fire crews from Cincinnati assisted in the futile efforts to save the building. Also in Covington, on January 16, 1885, the David Keefer and Sons Flour Mill at Fifth and Craig Sts. was destroyed. Crews had just arrived when its north wall fell, covering much of the firefighting equipment with debris. Several neighboring buildings were also lost. Later that year, on March 24, 1885, Cook and Rich's Flour Feed store along Madison Ave. in Covington burned to the ground. Frozen hydrants delayed the response of the fire crews; about 12 buildings were lost during this incident. On March 5, 1893, the Fred J. Meyers Manufacturing Company on Madison Ave. in Covington, the Crawford Tobacco Warehouse, and the Central Christian Church were destroyed by fire, and three other businesses were damaged. This remained the largest fire in Covington's history for a long time. In Newport, on July 19, 1898, the Unnewehr Sawmill and Lumberyard on Lowell St. in the **West End** lost its mill, and 16 adjacent homes were destroyed. Both Cincinnati and Covington fire units responded to the call, and their firefighting efforts contained the fire, thereby saving the remainder of the city.

After the turn of the century there was no decrease in the frequency of major nonresidential fires. On December 9, 1909, a major blaze threatened the entire town of Butler in northern Pendleton Co. Six buildings were destroyed. On April 24, 1912, the Paris Dry Cleaning shop at 216 Pike in Covington caught fire. Several firefighters were injured when a gasoline tank inside exploded, and flying debris killed a bystander. In Boone Co. on June 7, 1921, at Burlington, an explosion was the cause of a fire that destroyed two businesses, two apartments, and the post office. Volunteers from Walton battled the flames until assistance from both Cincinnati and Covington arrived. In Dayton on January 20, 1924, the Dayton High School at Eighth and Walnut Sts. (see **Dayton Public Schools**) was destroyed as low water pressure and frozen hydrants handicapped firemen's efforts to contain the blaze. Bellevue, Cincinnati, Covington, and Newport provided help at the scene. There were no injuries, because the fire occurred in the early morning. In Grant Co., at Dry Ridge, on February 25, 1927, flames ripped through much of the business district, including the historic Carlsbad Hotel, destroying 11 businesses and several homes. Later that year in Williamstown, on July 23, 1927, three businesses and a home were destroyed. Dry Ridge's fire units assisted, preventing the flames from sweeping the town. Also in Grant Co., the Williamstown Lumber and Hardware was destroyed on June 5, 1930, as help from five cities arrived to try to contain this fire. Four adjacent buildings were lost, and a spectator was hit by a passing truck and died. On March 20, 1931, the Boone-Kenton Lumber Company on Crescent Ave. in Erlanger caught on fire; firefighters from four cities fought the blaze. The same site burned to the ground on June 20, 1966. On December 9, 1946, the huge, three-story Klaene Foundry at 16th and Russell Sts. in Covington was destroyed; on this occasion Fort Mitchell and Ludlow fire crews helped supplement Covington's crew. The First Methodist Church (see **First United Methodist Church**) at Fifth and Greenup Sts. in Covington burned on January 19, 1947. Covington's, Ludlow's, and Newport's fire departments fought the fire. The church was rebuilt, reopening on August 8, 1948. Another church, the Williamstown Methodist Church (see **Williamstown United Methodist Church**) was completely destroyed on April 5, 1948, in a fire fed by high winds. Fire crews from Williamstown, Dry Ridge, and Falmouth participated in extinguishing the blaze.

In the last half of the 20th century, there were numerous major fires in the region. On February 15, 1950, the Covington Paper and Woodenware Company at 212 Greenup erupted in flames. The blaze spread to adjacent businesses as firefighters fought the fire for 11 hours and several firemen received minor injuries. Exploding ammunition and paint housed in the store added to the inferno. On March 17, 1950, the two-story, 100-year-old Phoenix Hotel on Main St. in Walton was destroyed. Thirteen occupants of the hotel escaped unharmed. On February 7, 1952, in another Dayton school fire, the Lincoln Elementary at 715 Fifth Ave. caught fire with more than 300 students in their classrooms. All the children and the school's staff escaped uninjured; however, 27 emergency personnel sustained injuries. The W. W. Welch Company, a fan manufacturer at Second and Scott in Covington, burned on January 7, 1956. More than 200 firefighters from Covington, Ludlow, Newport, Park Hills, South Fort, and Mitchell were called to the scene. Five explosions rocked the neighborhood, slightly injuring three firemen. The fire spread throughout the adjacent buildings. On March 21, 1956, Milford, located along Ky. Rt. 19 in Bracken Co., almost was wiped off the map when a fire broke out in the town. Much of the city, including the post office and six businesses, was lost. Fire departments from Augusta, Brooksville, and Cynthiana responded to fight the blaze. On January 2, 1957, an explosion and fire destroyed the First Presbyterian Church in Dayton. Later that year, on September 2, 1957, the Perry and Derrick Paint Company on Lindsey St., also in Dayton, burned in dramatic fashion, fueled by exploding paint containers. Bellevue and Newport fire crews assisted. Many regard the Perry and Derrick fire as the worst in Campbell Co.'s history before the **Beverly Hills Supper Club** fire.

In Fort Thomas on January 6, 1962, fire destroyed the Highlands Junior High School building, causing more than $500,000 in damages. Departments from as far away as Park Hills responded. Nearly a dozen of the 118 firefighters at the scene were injured, two seriously. A favorite nightspot in Campbell Co. was lost on March 23, 1963, as the Avenue Nite Club and Restaurant in Bellevue burned. Two persons were killed. It was thought that a smoldering cigarette swept into a trash container started the blaze.

At least three fires have plagued the **Duro Bag Manufacturing Company** in Ludlow. The first was on November 21, 1959, when flames destroyed the Duro plant at Kenner and Poplar. The second occurred on March 1, 1964, when 200 firefighters from 10 cities fought a blaze that spread to 16 nearby homes, 7 of which were totally lost. It has been called the biggest fire in Kenton Co. during the last 100 years, and it resulted in $2 million in total damages. Finally, on the same night as the Beverly Hills Supper Club fire, May 28, 1977, Duro had another major fire at its plant, resulting in $300,000 in damages. Ten area fire departments fought that fire; Cincinnati fire units assisted at two different fires occurring in Northern Kentucky that evening.

On July 13, 1971, the Cabana Restaurant and the Kenton Bowling Lanes in Erlanger erupted in flames, resulting in $500,000 in damages. Firefighters from seven fire departments arrived on the scene, and four fighters received minor injuries. Ben Castleman's White Horse Tavern, along **Dixie Highway** in Park Hills, burned to the ground on January 26, 1972. On June 15, 1973, the administrative offices at the Greater Cincinnati Airport (later the **Cincinnati/Northern Kentucky International Airport**) burned. Crews from Hebron, Covington, and Fort Mitchell battled the fire, in which two firefighters, Donald Phillips and Thomas Zaferes, were killed. On August 14, 1973, the **Lookout House** supper club burned. Ten fire departments fought the fire for eight hours, but the famous landmark was totally lost. In Gallatin Co. the **Warsaw Baptist Church** was destroyed on November 20, 1973. Only a portion of the outer walls of the 91-year-old structure was left standing.

The worst fire in the history of the state was the May 28, 1977, Beverly Hills Supper Club fire in Southgate, which made national news. In that fire 167 persons died (165 adults and teens and 2 unborn children), and 500 fire and emergency personnel were on the scene of the disaster for days; ambulances came from as far away as Tennessee to help; a temporary morgue was set up at the Fort Thomas Armory. Many state laws and fire codes were changed or new ones implemented as a result of this fire.

On October 9, 1980, at the **Simon Kenton High School** in Independence, a gas line exploded, rocking the central building in the middle of a busy school day. Personnel from 14 fire districts responded. A second blast sent debris flying toward firefighters. One student was killed in the first blast, and more than 20 firefighters were injured in the second explosion. In one of two illegal fireworks explosions in the region, on April 2, 1981, at 938 John St. in Newport, a blast devastated a six-block area. Two persons were killed and 24 were injured as small fires burned throughout the area. Some 260 buildings in Newport received some damage. In Covington, at Second and Madison on November 2, 1981, approximately 120 firefighters from Covington, Fort Mitchell, and Ludlow responded to 70-foot-high flames at the Escue Datsun car dealership. The main building was destroyed, as well as 50 automobiles, adding up to a $2 million loss. On May 16, 1985, at **St. Aloysius Catholic Church** in Covington, a lightning strike caused a fire that destroyed the 118-year-old landmark. More than 100 Covington and Fort Mitchell fire personnel battled the blaze for several hours. On November 21, 1985, the Brown Hotel in Warsaw in Gallatin Co. burned to the ground. Previously, the building had been saved from fires on more than one occasion. On September 25, 1986, the dome of the historic **Mother of God Catholic Church** on W. Sixth St. in Covington caught fire. The fire was confined to the massive dome as two firefighters were slightly injured. The church was subsequently restored at a cost of $1.5 million. In Maysville, on January 4, 1998, the Cargill Fertilizer Warehouse exploded prior to a massive fire. Some 2,300 residents were evacuated for 13 hours, including many who lived across the river in Ohio. On August 11, 1999, a tremendous explosion occurred and flames and smoke rose from a three-story condominium building on Saddlebrook Lane in Florence. Sixty firemen from six different departments battled the blaze, which either destroyed or badly damaged about 24 apartment units. On October 9, 1999, also in Florence, the Garten Restaurant and the adjacent Bessler's Economy Market on Main St. burned to the ground. Fire crews from Erlanger, Elsmere, Hebron, Point Pleasant, and Walton assisted.

Thus far in the 21st century, there have been two noteworthy nonresidential fires. On May 21, 2002, a massive fire destroyed the historic 1856 Odd Fellows Hall (see **Independent Order of Odd Fellows**) at Fifth St. and Madison Ave. in Covington. Fire units from Fort Mitchell, Ludlow, Park Hills, and Newport helped extinguish the blaze. With the exception of the front wall, the building was a total loss, but it was rebuilt. On January 16, 2004, the **First Baptist Church** of Dayton was destroyed. Seventy firemen from five cities fought the fire. A firewall saved the gymnasium and the church office from destruction.

Earnest, Ernest. *The Volunteer Fire Company: Past and Present.* New York: Stein and Day, 1983.

Jewell, Simon, ed. *Campbell County Firefighters Educational Association.* Campbell Co., Ky.: Campbell Co. Firefighters Educational Association [ca. 2002–2003].

Reis, Jim. "Alarm Boxes Forerunner of 911 System," *KP,* May 20, 1996, 4K.

Webster, Robert D. *Northern Kentucky Fires: A Summary of the Most Memorable Fires of the Region.* Covington, Ky.: Kenton Co. Historical Society, 2006.

Robert D. Webster

FIRST BAPTIST CHURCH, ALEXANDRIA. A group of people met on April 17, 1820, and agreed to establish a Baptist church in Alexandria in Campbell Co. The meeting took place at the home of William DeCoursey, who in 1794 had been involved in the starting of the **First Baptist Church** of Cold Spring. Raymond Absalem Graves was appointed as the new church's first minister. Services were held in private homes in the area until a building could be constructed. The brick structure behind the courthouse on Main St. in Alexandria was the church's first permanent place of worship. This building was never fully completed, and services were moved to the courthouse. In 1864 the congregation moved to the Methodist Episcopal Church South, also on Main St. A new building was finally complete in 1870, 50 years after the founding of the church. This structure, at 104 Washington St. in Alexandria, remains in use today.

Several anniversaries have been celebrated over the years, and the church has also conducted several revivals. In 1995 a few problems arose when the community decided to clean up some tombstones that had been at the back of the church for years. Apparently, the tombstones had been moved from a graveyard to the church in 1949, and no one knew where the graves were. The church was planning to establish a memorial garden in which to place the tombstones, but the descendants of the deceased preferred that the original grave sites be found. The church worked with the descendants to correct the problem.

The First Baptist Church of Alexandria expanded in 2003. A zoning change was approved in August of that year, and plans called for addition of a youth center containing a gymnasium.

"Annexation OK'd," *KP,* August 22, 2003, 2K.

Campbell Co. Historical Society. *Campbell County, Kentucky, 200 Years, 1794–1994.* Alexandria, Ky.: Campbell Co. Historical Society, 1994.

"Church Building," *KP,* May 5, 2004, 2K.

Main, Frank. "39 Tombstones and a Lot of Questions," *KP,* April 29, 1995, 1K.

Elizabeth Comer Williams

FIRST BAPTIST CHURCH, BELLEVUE. This church was organized on April 12, 1904, with the support of the Bellevue Sunday School Mission, which was established by the Campbell Co. Baptist Association with the intention of incorporating a Baptist church in Bellevue; the neighboring Baptist churches of Dayton and Newport offered their support and sponsorship. The first service, attended by 34 charter members, was held at Ideal Hall on Bellevue's Fairfield Ave. T. J. Johnson served as the church's first pastor. In August 1904 the church purchased a building lot on the corner of Washington and Prospect Sts., and the church's first sanctuary was dedicated on November 24, 1907. Church membership increased, and on November 26, 1922, the church dedicated an addition that provided Sunday school classrooms, an auditorium seating 600, and a gymnasium complete with a large spectator balcony. In 1931 the Covington **YMCA** sponsored an amateur basketball church league, in which the First Baptist Church of Bellevue won first place in its division of competition. As the ministry and the congregation expanded, there was a need for a larger and more modern structure. A new church was erected on the original site, and the congregation moved into its second sanctuary in 1973. In 2003 a steeple was donated to the church by the Hebron Baptist Church. The First Baptist Church at Bellevue celebrated its 100th anniversary in 2004.

"Church League Opens; 28 Teams in Cage Play," *KP*, November 29, 1931, 9.

Good, Cecil, comp. *First Baptist Church of Bellevue: One Hundred Years of Service*. Bellevue, Ky.: Bellevue First Baptist Church, 2004.

"New Addition to Bellevue Church Will Be Dedicated," *KTS*, November 24, 1922, 41.

Robin Caraway

FIRST BAPTIST CHURCH, COLD SPRING. The First Baptist Church of Cold Spring has been known also as the Mouth of the Licking Baptist Church, the Licking Church, and the Old Licking Church. It was organized in October 1794 by eight Northern Kentucky members of the Columbia Baptist Church at Fort Columbia in what is now eastern Cincinnati, near the mouth of the Little Miami River. They had withdrawn with the blessing of the Columbia Baptist Church. This church in Ohio, organized in 1790, was where the early Baptists of Northern Kentucky worshipped. The new church was called at first the Mouth of the Licking Baptist Church and began in the home of William DeCoursey, west of the Licking River in present-day Kenton Co. His house was about six miles from the Ohio River. For six years the church met at the homes of its members. A movement was then started to secure land and a meetinghouse east of the Licking River. The church became a member of the Elkorn Association (Baptist) in 1795 or 1796. An early preacher-statesman who preached there on several occasions was James Garrard, who was elected the second governor of Kentucky in 1796.

Around 1800 the church erected a log building near Leitch's Station (see **David Leitch**), on the east side of the Licking River, and with that move became known as the Licking Church. In 1805 the church secured property and moved to its location on Alexandria Pk. (**U.S. 27**) in Cold Spring. In 1820 the name was changed to Old Licking Church. On May 1, 1841, a committee was named to secure the services of Rev. **James Monroe Jolly**, who erected a new building, since replaced. In 1910, with 71 members, the church celebrated its centennial, which had been overlooked for 16 years.

The name of the church was changed again, to the First Baptist Church of Cold Spring, in the 1940s. In 1944 the church celebrated its sesqui centennial, and on November 6, 1949, the cornerstone of a new building was laid. Construction of a new auditorium began on September 26, 1949, with much of the work being done by the members of the church under the leadership of Charles Graziani, Charles Howe, and Henry Reder. The first service in the new building was held on June 3, 1951, and the dedication service on July 15. A new education building was erected and dedicated on November 1, 1959. In May 1989 a long-range planning committee was formed to seek land on which to build a new church. A location was found just to the south, at the corner of Murnan Rd. and U.S. 27 in Cold Spring, and was purchased for $275,000. The church continued to grow in subsequent years. In the early part of 2004, however, about 230 people left the church to form the Christ Baptist Church.

"After Split, New Church Making It on Its Own," *KE*, June 12, 2005, B1.

"Christ Baptist Members Buying Rolling Hills Site," *KE*, June 20, 2004, C4.

"History of First Baptist Church of Cold Spring," *News of Northern Kentucky Association*, May 27, 1976.

Donald E. Grosenbach

FIRST BAPTIST CHURCH, COVINGTON. A committee from six area Baptist churches met on March 10, 1838, to discuss plans to establish the First Baptist Church of Covington. The meeting was held in a schoolhouse at the corner of Fourth and Scott Sts. Exactly where the church held its first services is not known, but it is believed that some of the meetings were conducted at a pork packing plant on Greenup St., north of Second St. The church's first building was constructed in 1842 and was described as a modest, one-room structure. In 1855 that building was enlarged and remodeled to better serve the congregation. During the **Civil War**, the congregation of the First Baptist Church of Covington was divided in their loyalties, as were many other area congregations, but the Covington church managed to survive and prosper.

By 1870 the congregation had grown so much that a new building was needed. The old church building was demolished, and a new, larger one was built on the original site, along W. Fourth. The architects were from the Cincinnati-based firm of

First Baptist Church, W. Fourth St., Covington, ca. 1915.

Walter and Stewart. During the two years of construction, the church held services at the Franklin Library Hall in downtown Covington. On December 13, 1873, the church's pastor, W. H. Felix, dedicated the new building. In 1883 the church announced that all debt had been retired.

The congregation of the First Baptist Church of Covington was instrumental in starting several new churches in Covington, including the Southside Baptist Church and the Madison Avenue Baptist Church. During **World War I**, the pastor of the First Baptist Church of Covington, Llewellyn L. Henson, helped to organize a $6.5 million drive among Baptists statewide for foreign missions. While Henson was pastor, a building next to the church was bought for educational purposes and the church's membership grew from 621 to 841.

The congregation at the First Baptist Church of Covington encountered problems during the 1930s as a result of the **Great Depression** and the **flood of 1937**, but they managed to suffer through those trials. In 1957 the church had a new 40-room addition built onto its educational complex, and church membership peaked at around 1,200. However, incursion into the area by business and industry and flight to the suburbs by many members of the church's congregation during the 1950s and 1960s took their toll. The church, once filled to capacity, now suffers the plight of many other inner-city churches and has few worshippers. Over the long history of the church, many pastors have served, but because church records were lost during the 1937 flood, a complete list is not available.

"The City—Free of Debt," *DC*, July 2, 1883, 2.

"Congregation Will Erect New Building," *CJ*, October 29, 1870, 3.

"Congregation Will Occupy Franklin Library Hall," *CJ*, December 9, 1871, 3.

"First Baptist Church, Covington," vertical file, Kenton Co. Public Library, Covington, Ky.
Reis, Jim. "Church Pioneered Other Baptist Missions." In *Pieces of the Past,* by Jim Reis, vol. 2. Covington: Kentucky Post, 1991.
Tenkotte, Paul A. *A Heritage of Art and Faith: Downtown Covington Churches.* Covington, Ky.: Kenton Co. Historical Society, 1986.
"To Organize New Church," *KP,* September 28, 1907, 2.

FIRST BAPTIST CHURCH, COVINGTON [AFRICAN AMERICAN]. In August 1864 Rev. George W. Dupree, along with 22 charter members, organized the First Baptist Church of Covington, which was first known as the Bremen St. Baptist Church. It is the oldest African American congregation in Northern Kentucky. The church's first building was located on Bremen St. and **Jacob Price** was its first pastor. From its earliest days, the church has been involved in community activities, including education and civil rights. Under the leadership of Price, the Baptist church hosted a number of rallies and organizational meetings to prepare the way for local African American private schools. In April 1866 the first private school opened at the church, directed by the Freedmen's Aid Commission and the Freedmen's Bureau. In late 1866 the Ninth St. Methodist Episcopal Church was formed out of the Bremen St. Baptist Church.

In 1869 the church on Bremen St. moved to Third St. and changed its name to Third St. Baptist Church; the school remained on Bremen St. It was after this move that Jacob Price and a small group of parishioners left the congregation following a disagreement with other members. In 1870 the Third St. Baptist Church called **William Blackburn** as pastor. When citizens of Covington were asked to select delegates to attend the first statewide African American political convention in Frankfort, the delegate-selection meeting was held at the Third St. Baptist Church. Through the ensuing years, the church grew and became more involved in the struggles of the African American community.

In 1874 the Third St. Baptist Church moved from Third to Robbins St. and erected a building at the new location; the congregation moved again in 1877 to a site on W. 13th St., where another church building was built. At that time, it changed its name to the First Colored Baptist Church of Covington. Placed in the cornerstone, laid on May 20, 1877, were copies of the Bible, several religious periodicals, Covington's 1877 city directory, a list of prominent city officials, and copies of that day's newspapers: the *Ticket,* the *Enquirer,* the *Volkesblatt,* the *Volksfreund,* and the *Commercial Gazette.* After the move to 13th St., Price and his splinter group returned, and Price succeeded in uniting the congregations briefly. A second separation resulted in establishment of the Ninth St. Baptist Church by departing members.

A number of pastors followed Blackburn at the First Baptist Church. In 1911 Rev. F. C. Locust became pastor. On July 7, 1915, a tornado destroyed the church building. Then in 1916, the church purchased a site on E. Ninth St. and construction began. One of the guest speakers at the new church dedication, April 7, 1917, was Mrs. **L. B. Fouse** of Lexington. The new structure included beautiful stained-glass windows, financed by some of the oldest African American families of Covington and by the auxiliaries of the church. On August 30, 1941, Rev. Locust and First Baptist Church celebrated his 30th and the church's 77th anniversary. In 1947, when Locust was suffering from a serious illness, William P. Halbert was called to serve as his assistant. Halbert officially became pastor in July 1948, after Locust's death, and the congregation prospered under his leadership. He organized new auxiliaries and led a progressive program of development and advancement, encouraging community and civic involvement. The L. B. Fouse Civic League's leadership drew much of its membership from the First Baptist Church. Halbert retired in 1971, and A. B. Moore was called to serve as pastor in 1972. Moore served two years and resigned; he later founded Crucifixion Baptist Church on E. 10th St. On October 26, 1975, Willie R. Barbour became pastor of the First Baptist Church and served until 2001. On June 22, 2003, the First Baptist Church appointed Adam P. Crews Sr. as its new full-time minister.

"Colored Baptists to Dedicate Church," *KP,* April 7, 1917, 1.
Covington Ticket, May 19, 1877, 1; May 21, 1877, 3.
"New Church to Be Erected," *KP,* January 9, 1915, 1.
Newport Local, May 22, 1877, 2.
125th Anniversary Booklet. Covington, Ky.: First Baptist Church, 1989.
Reis, Jim. "Black Churches Offered Stability in Troubled Times," *KP,* January 20, 1997, 4K.
——. "Black Past Often Unsung," *KP,* February 5, 1996, 4K.
"Two Anniversaries for Negro Baptist Church," *KP,* August 30, 1941, 1.

Theodore H. H. Harris

FIRST BAPTIST CHURCH, DAYTON. This church began in Jamestown in May 1850, before the communities of Jamestown and Brooklyn merged in 1867 to form Dayton. Sixteen members assembled in the Jamestown's old district schoolhouse to establish the First Baptist Church. Among them were Ann Bennett, William Bennett, Margaret Hatfield, Mrs. Jefferson McArthur, Rev. James Vickers, Margaret Vickers, Sarah Vickers, Thomas S. Vickers, Isaac N. Walker, James H. Walker, and John O. Walker. The church chose Rev. Asa Drury as its first pastor and established its first meetinghouse at what is now Fifth and Main Sts. in Dayton. This first building served the church for many years, thanks to additions and modifications, but eventually it became clear that the growing church needed a larger building.

The congregation erected a beautiful new church at the corner of Fifth St. and Dayton Ave., on land valued at $1,100 that Henry Walker donated in 1895. Lula Mason, F. M. Spillman, William Tieman, and Henry Walker made donations for beautiful stained-glass windows in memory of beloved deceased citizens. O. F. Barrett gave a pipe organ in memory of his parents. The total cost for the new church was $25,000. At the time the church had a membership of 340, a Sunday school, and a young people's society.

When the United States entered World War I in 1917, Rev. E. H. Mariner, a native of Newport who was the church's pastor, was given a leave of absence to serve as an army chaplain . The church hosted a flag-raising ceremony in 1918 in honor of its serviceman. A diamond jubilee celebration was held at the church in 1925. Later, a tower music system was installed as a memorial to the young men and women who served in **World War II**. In 1995 the First Baptist Church had a centennial celebration, remembering the many years that had been spent in the church's beautiful building. The celebration included several special events, such as concerts, guest speakers, information booths, and the ordination of a former member of the congregation.

Then came the calamitous morning of January 16, 2004, when roofers using a blow torch to work on the education section of the church building ignited something flammable under the roof's surface. Firefighters from five area fire departments responded, but the fire spread to the entire inside of the church, popping out stained-glass windows and destroying the antique pump organ along with much of the church building. Fortunately, the educational wing and the gym were protected by firewalls, but the offices sustained smoke and water damage.

The shock of this sudden loss was somewhat offset by the immediate supportive response of the community. Church services were initially held in several places, including the **YMCA** and other churches, but the membership wanted to return home and use the two-thirds of their complex that was not damaged. Worship services were held in the gym, using folding chairs instead of pews. Insurance coverage paid for most of the $1.9 million loss and made it possible for the church to rebuild on the same site, incorporating improvements into the new building such as handicap access, projection screens, and better heating and air conditioning. The tower, several stained glass windows, and some of the stones from the former church were saved and used prominently in the new structure. The 25-by-15-foot stained glass window in the original church was repaired and included in the new sanctuary. On April 17, 2006, the First Baptist Church of Dayton reopened with a special sunrise service on Easter Sunday.

"Burned Church Restored on a Strong Foundation," *KE,* May 1, 2006, B1.
"Celebrating 150 Years," *KP,* April 25, 2000, 8K.
"What Becomes of Old Churches," *KP,* August 27, 1913, 4.

Daryl Polley

FIRST BAPTIST CHURCH, FORT THOMAS. In August 1915, 52 people met in the Fort Thomas City Building to organize the First Baptist Church of Fort Thomas. Shortly thereafter, 77 members of the **First Baptist Church** of Newport joined the congregation. The church hired as its first pastor Rev. Frank G. McFarlan and affiliated itself with the Campbell Co. Baptist Association. For the next six years, the church held services in the Central Public School building. The City of Fort Thomas also used part of the school as its municipal building.

The congregation purchased a lot in 1924, and another in 1927, where they planned to build their first sanctuary. In 1929, during the pastorate of Rev. Frederick Ellsworth Wolf, a Gothic Style edifice was constructed of pure limestone at 600 N. Fort Thomas Ave. **Weber Brothers Architects** designed and built the facility, which included a sanctuary, Sunday school rooms, a social hall, a kitchen, a pastor's study, a nursery, and a choir room.

The First Baptist Church of Fort Thomas held its 25th anniversary service on August 11, 1940; the pastor, Rev. Jesse M. Rogers, preached a sermon entitled "The Romance of Twenty-five Years."

The longest-serving pastor of the fellowship was Rev. George Stephenson Munro, who came to the United States from New Zealand in 1948. He attended the Southern Baptist Theological Seminary in Louisville and received his BA from Georgetown College (Ky.) in 1953. He later earned his MA from the University of Kentucky in Lexington. Munroe served as pastor of First Baptist from 1955 until 1984.

The First Baptist Church of Fort Thomas now has about 400 members, and the pastor is Rev. Joseph D. Boone, who has been there since 2000.

"Baptists Plan New Church," *KP,* September 24, 1929, 5.
"Baptists to Start New Church in Ft. Thomas," *KP,* August 10, 1915, 1.
"Cornerstone of Ft. Thomas Church to Be Laid Sunday," *KTS,* October 12, 1921, 25.
"First Baptist Church of Ft. Thomas," *KP,* May 27, 2004, 4K.
"Ft. Thomas Baptists Plan New Building," *KP,* July 18, 1930, 1.

FIRST BAPTIST CHURCH, LUDLOW. This church is one of the oldest continuously operating churches in Northern Kentucky. Evidently, it was begun in 1847, as a mission of the Second Baptist Church, Covington. That would place its origin at 15 years before the incorporation of the City of Ludlow and just 7 years after Kenton Co. was formed from Campbell Co. The group held its first services in a public school building in Ludlow on Ash St., just east of Locust St. Sponsored by Covington's Second Baptist Church, the new group officially became the First Baptist Church of Ludlow on December 11, 1849.

William Hay, who later served as a Ludlow city councilman, gave the church a lot at the corner of Carneal and Hay Sts., where a small meetinghouse was built. One individual, C. W. Scott, paid the entire cost of construction. The new church group affiliated itself with the North Bend Baptist Association but withdrew in 1870, when a resolution was passed forbidding women or minorities from serving as delegates to their meetings. The church then joined the Miami Baptist Association of Ohio. In March 1875, to emphasize further its commitment to minority rights, the First Baptist Church of Ludlow brought in a black minister, Rev. Daniel H. Davies, to conduct special services.

Growth of the congregation was slow in the early years; however, the pace picked up in 1875, when Rev. Samuel H. Burgess became pastor. Burgess suggested that a new, larger facility be built farther away from the Ohio River, in an area where most of the city's growth was occurring. The new edifice was constructed at Kenner and Linden Sts. and was dedicated on October 25, 1891. The new church building caused renewed interest within the congregation, and attendance soon reached 145. Because of sacrificial giving by dedicated members, all church debt was retired by 1906. A parsonage was purchased in town in 1920, on Oak St., between Adela and Helen Sts.

In 1924 the First Baptist Church of Ludlow participated in an ecumenical service at the Ludlow Presbyterian Church in honor of seven area soldiers who had been killed during **World War I**. Many other Protestant and Catholic churches in the area also joined in that memorial service.

By 1926 the First Baptist Church of Ludlow had grown to 471 members, creating the need for a larger facility. A two-story addition was built at a cost of $27,000 and was dedicated on April 1, 1928. By the time of the church's centennial service on December 17, 1949, membership had increased to 577. During the next several years, additional land was purchased to allow for future expansion. A new larger facility was constructed in 1964, at a cost of $300,000. The pastor at that time was James E. Howell, who served the congregation from about 1955 until his death in 1976. During his pastorate, church membership reached 1,000.

A new multipurpose building, containing classrooms, offices, a library, and a fellowship hall, was built in 1988, at a cost of $379,859. The larger membership required that more parking spaces also be provided. Several buildings across the street from the church were purchased and razed for that purpose. By 2000, church membership had climbed to 1,100, and the pastor was Rev. James P. Daniels. In 2007 Rev. Paul Anglin Jr. became pastor. The First Baptist Church of Ludlow is now affiliated with the Northern Kentucky Baptist Association.

Reis, Jim. "Congregation Plans Celebration of 150th Birthday," *KP,* December 6, 1999, 4K.
———. "First Baptist of Ludlow Reflects Proudly on Its Past," *KP,* December 6, 1999, 4K.

FIRST BAPTIST CHURCH, MAYSVILLE. The present-day First Baptist Church of Maysville began in 1838 through the work of Thomas J. Fisher and his revivals. Rev. Gilbert Mason was the new church's first pastor. The next year, Thomas Y. Payne gave the church a bell from the Verdin Bell Company in Cincinnati. During this period the former slave **Elisha W. Green**, remembered as a person who loved to sing, was a janitor in the church. Green later formed the **Bethel Baptist Church** in Maysville, even before his ordination in 1847. In 1858 several men from the First Baptist Church of Maysville collected $850 to purchase the freedom of Rev. Green's wife and their three children so that the family could live together. The church started a Sunday school in 1840. In 1875 Dr. J. M. Frost Jr., of the church, helped organize the Baptist Sunday School Board of the Southern Baptist Convention and served that organization as its first executive secretary. In 1886 the Gothic-style structure of the First Baptist Church was built on Market St. using the old cornerstone. Then in 1902 Mary Caroline Cox donated money for the purchase of a pipe organ for the church.

The First Baptist Church of Maysville celebrated its centennial in 1938 under the leadership of Dr. A. D. Odom. Because large crowds were attending, the church built a full basement under the building to accommodate Sunday School classes and fellowship meetings. In 1973 this church hired its youngest pastor, Rev. Jim England, who helped find a home for the Day Care Center for Retarded Children, sponsored by **Comprehend Inc**.

Calvert, Jean, and John Klee. *Maysville, Kentucky: From Past to Present in Pictures.* Maysville, Ky.: Mason Co. Museum, 1983.
Cathcart, William. *The Baptist Encyclopaedia: A Dictionary.* Philadelphia: Everts, 1883.
Hughes, Gary K. "150 Years of Faith and Witness," Church Bulletin, May 29, 1988, First Baptist Church, Maysville, Ky.
Vertical files, Kentucky Gateway Museum, Maysville, Ky.

Alex Hyrcza

FIRST BAPTIST CHURCH, NEWPORT. A group of Baptists in Newport wanted a place to worship, and on August 8, 1812, the First Baptist Church of Newport was formed by seven charter members. One month later, on September 12, 1812, the church was formally received into the North Bend Baptist Association. Since this church group did not have a regular pastor for about five years, the members met in the homes of its members. In 1828 the church changed its name to the Covington Baptist Church, because most of its members lived in Covington. By 1840 the church was once again reorganized and was renamed First Baptist Church of Newport.

From February 1840 until 1843, the First Baptist Church of Newport held church services at the Newport Court House, at the Newport Seminary, and at various city school buildings. In 1844, **James Taylor Jr.** transferred property on the south side of Bellevue St. (Fourth St.) between E. Row St. (Washington Ave.) and Saratoga St. to the church trustees, for the sum of $1.00. Although the church was strapped for construction funds, the members donated services to finish the project, and the first church building was completed sometime in the late 1840s.

In 1881 the congregation purchased a frame building at Ringold (now Eighth) and York Sts.

This building was previously occupied by the town's Congregational Church. Over a period of time, Newport's First Baptist Church organized various missions, including one in town known as the Walnut Street Mission at Ninth and Patterson Sts. An 1889 report of the North Bend Baptist Association indicated that the First Baptist Church of Newport was operating two mission Sunday schools as well as one in the main church building.

The present church building at Eighth and York Sts. was dedicated on Sunday, February 14, 1892. The architects were S. W. Rogers and Son, and the auditorium seated nearly 700. In 1902 the building's auditorium was enlarged, giving additional space to the front of the church. Another local off-site mission effort, called the West Side Mission, was organized in 1914. Initially, this mission was located at 327 W. Sixth St. Later, it moved to Eighth and Brighton Sts. and became Newport's Brighton St. Baptist Church.

On August 15, 1916, the First Baptist Church of Fort Thomas was organized, with 77 members from Newport taking their membership transfer letters to unite with the newly formed church. In spring 1924, plans were drawn up by the First Baptist Church of Newport to add an additional Sunday school building, located on York St., adjacent to and on the south side of the current church building. In 1933 the church established a work program (called the Good Will Center) for the unemployed in Newport at 519 Isabella St.

In 1940 about 41 members left the First Baptist Church of Newport to form the Trinity Baptist Church of Newport. On June 29, 1958, the cornerstone was laid at the First Baptist Church of Newport for a new three-story educational building, to house Sunday school rooms, the church office, and a gymnasium. A new educational building was constructed on Eighth St., adjacent and to the rear of the church, and was dedicated on April 19, 1959. During the 1960s, members of the church became active in the Committee of 500 to clean up **gambling** and crime in Newport. In 1987 the congregation held a special celebration commemorating the church's 175th anniversary.

"First Baptist. Dedication of the New Church Tomorrow," *KJ*, February 13, 1892, 1.

History of the First Baptist Church, Eighth and York Streets, Newport, Kentucky. Newport, Ky.: First Baptist Church, 1987.

Stegar, J. W., et. al., comps. *History of the First Baptist Church, Newport, Kentucky, 1812–1962.* Newport, Ky.: First Baptist Church, 1962.

Donald E. Grosenbach

FIRST CHRISTIAN CHURCH, COVINGTON. Educator **James Grimsley Arnold** moved to Covington in 1818 and helped to form the First Christian Church there in 1827. Serving as first elder of the church, he played a major role in its growth and success until his death in 1876. Arnold began First Christian with the assistance and guidance of a friend, James Challen, who was the first minister of the Sycamore Christian Church in Cincinnati. The Christian Church (Disciples of Christ) was a new denomination begun in Paris, Ky., in 1804 by a group of Presbyterian ministers. They signed a document at the Cane Ridge Meeting House in Paris that "called for unity among Christians along non-sectarian lines." It was one of the first denominations to get its start in the United States. In Covington, 15 people met in a one-room house on Second St. In 1833 the congregation was virtually wiped out by a cholera epidemic, and it disbanded. Arnold, a businessman and politician who eventually made his fortune in real estate and tobacco, revived the church in 1840. Members worshipped in his tobacco warehouse, probably on lower Greenup St. Arnold was determined to build a church and, in 1843, donated land on the south side of Third St. He bought building materials and hired construction workers and paid the costs himself—in silver half dollars.

When the congregation outgrew that space, Arnold bought another plot of land, at 14 W. Fifth St., next to his home, for $4,000. Then he loaned the congregation $3,000 to build the church, which was dedicated on March 23, 1867. Five years later the loan had not been completely repaid, and Arnold himself pledged $275 toward the $700 balance. In 1875 a disagreement over the recalling of a minister divided the congregation. The result was the formation of Madison Avenue Christian Church, called the Fourth Street Christian Church at the time. On March 5, 1893, a fire that started in the Fred J. Meyers Company, a manufacturer of iron products on nearby Madison Ave., destroyed the First Christian Church and the buildings surrounding it. The congregation raised the money to rebuild the church, making the new building a little larger than the old one. Designed by the architectural firm of **Dittoe and Wisenall**, the new church building had stained-glass windows from the Artistic Glass Painting Company of Cincinnati and was dedicated on October 14, 1894.

The congregation grew over the years. In the 1940s, First Christian was famous for its Election Day turkey dinners. In the 1950s a major renovation took place. The front of the sanctuary was remodeled, the organ and choir being moved to the rear of the church. New lighting and furnishings were purchased and an 11-room Sunday school was added. The congregation bought the Arnold house next door and used it as an annex. In the 1980s two important events happened to the church: another rift and the advent of an evangelical program. A "number of good folks" left First Christian over a disagreement about the minister. "From these painful experiences of division in the church family, the congregation renewed the desire for unity in the body of Christ and for the ability as Christians to learn how to better accept each other, even when we disagree," a church history claimed. The congregation embarked on a 10-year evangelical program. The purpose was to bring worshippers back to the urban church. In 1985 a capital improvement campaign raised more than $130,000, which was used to install air conditioning and protective covers for the stained-glass windows and to purchase a church bus. An elevator, added in 1990, was large enough to carry a casket from the ground level to the third-floor sanctuary. The pipe organ was renovated and moved once again to the front of the sanctuary. "In the 1990s, the congregation decided to reach out to the community," Patricia Hatfield, the church's pastor, said. First Christian joined the Interfaith Hospitality Network, and now about every eight weeks the church houses families who need temporary shelter. "The program keeps families together," said Kay Peacock, copastor, in 1994. In 2000 the church's pastor inaugurated a Sunday worship service for senior citizens at the nearby Panorama Apartments, and in fall 2001 the congregation started offering free community dinners every Saturday night for those in need.

Biographical Encyclopedia of Kentucky. Cincinnati: J. M. Armstrong, 1878.

DeVroomen, Sacha. "Hearts, Doors Open to Homeless Families," *KP,* December 8, 1994, 14A.

Hatfield, Patricia N., pastor, First Christian Church. Interview by Ann Hicks, June 8, 2005, Covington, Ky.

Nichols, Edythe. "Narration for 'The Church's One Foundation,' for the Musical Celebration and Dedication of the Refurbished Church Organ, Grand Piano, Elevator and Chancel Renovation," October 6, 1991, First Christian Church, Covington, Ky.

Reis, Jim. "Church Arose from Ashes—First Christian Still Covington Landmark," *KP,* August 5, 2002, 4K.

———. "James Arnold Left Bourbon Co. to Find His Fortune in Covington," *KP,* April 16, 2001, 4K.

Stein, Tim. "Reborn First Christian Conquers Inner City Blues," *KP,* April 6, 1991, 7K.

Tenkotte, Paul A. *A Heritage of Art and Faith: Downtown Covington Churches.* Covington, Ky.: Kenton Co. Historical Society, 1986.

Ann Hicks

FIRST CHRISTIAN CHURCH, MAYSVILLE. The First Christian Church in Maysville is one of the earliest churches of the **Disciples of Christ** movement. Occupying a strategic position as a port of entry into Kentucky, Maysville was visited on many occasions by Thomas and **Alexander Campbell**, Scottish immigrants who espoused the ideas of doctrinal reform in the Baptist churches. Thomas Campbell, a schoolmaster and a Presbyterian minister, had come to the United States in 1807 from Scotland seeking a more healthful environment. A graduate of Scotland's University of Glasgow and its divinity school, Campbell was assigned to the Presbytery of Chartiers in Washington, Pa. He soon found himself in disagreement with the beliefs of this religious body. Upon the urging of friends, he wrote the *Declaration and Address,* a document that proved to be the basis for a new religious movement, the Disciples of Christ.

Thomas Campbell's son Alexander, also a graduate of the University of Glasgow, expressed his agreement with the articles of faith articulated in his father's published declaration, and together the two men made a great impact on the lives of people in Maysville and the surrounding areas. The Maysville First Christian Church was the direct result of the influence of Thomas and Alexander Campbell on the local Baptist church.

Alexander Campbell's first visit to Kentucky was in 1823 to participate in a debate on baptism with the Presbyterian minister, Rev. William McCalla of Augusta. The Campbellite Reform Movement was spreading rapidly through the Baptist churches in all parts of the state. It divided the Baptist Church in Maysville, most of whose members in 1828 united with the Reformed Church; the remainder joined the Baptist Church in nearby Washington.

Since the 28 charter members of the new First Christian Church in Maysville constituted a majority, they retained the use of the building, paying an annual rent to the regular Baptists in Washington. But during a meeting held by Elder John O'Kane, the Reformers were forced to leave and find a temporary home in a carpenter's shop in Graves Alley. With a membership of 84 in 1836, they built a church on Third St. in Maysville at a cost of $1,638. The church, built by William B. Mooklar, was constructed of red brick in a simple style. The sanctuary was the only room. Since there was no baptistery, candidates for baptism were immersed in the Ohio River at the foot of Fish (now Wall) St. in Maysville.

The first 48 years after the church's founding were marked by such rapid growth that a new building was built in town on E. Third St. in 1877. The Gothic structure was erected on a lot 60 by 300 feet, running from street to street, at a cost of $24,000. The architect and builder was E. H. Hanna of Dover. One of the features of the new church, the baptistery, was far in advance of those being used by most immersionist churches of the time.

The Maysville Christian Church continued to grow in membership and activities. In 1923 a new 15-room educational plant was completed, built by J. F. Hardymon. Included were a gymnasium with lockers and showers, and a kitchen. The gymnasium was furnished to make it a complete physical department for both children and adults. The Maysville Christian Church was one of the first churches in the state to recognize the need for such facilities. For many years this was the only gymnasium in town, and high school games were played there. In 1951 the basement was excavated to provide additional classroom space. An associate minister was added to the church staff, and an outstanding program for youth was established. In 1964 a three-level addition was constructed for expansion of the Sunday school and offices for the ministers. Membership reached its peak in 1954, when 316 persons were added on a single Sunday. This was the culmination of a membership drive directed by Rev. Bayne Driskill, a guest evangelist.

The Maysville First Christian Church has contributed several ministers to the Disciples of Christ ministry: Marla Wilson Brock, Walter Cady, James Cox, Joseph Frank Jr., Lawrence Hay, and John Shackleford.

Decreases in membership to 474 and an average attendance of 145 have prompted the First Christian Church in Maysville to define its vision for the future. A plan for revitalization is in progress under the guidance of Dr. Richard L. Hamm, former general minister of the Christian Church, Disciples of Christ. The plan calls for 99 members to be divided into groups of three, who will meet for 100 days of prayer and contemplation. The minutes of these meetings will be sent to Hamm, who will develop a plan to be presented to the congregation for approval and implementation. Rev. C. Wayne Barnett, senior minister, looks upon this plan as the most meaningful of his three decades of ministry. Together with Barnett and the associate minister, Rev. Marla Wilson Brock, the church has become a Bible-studying congregation.

Braden, Gayle A., and Coralie J. Runyon. *A History of the Christian Church, Maysville, Kentucky.* Lexington, Ky.: Transylvania, 1948.
"Church Says 'Amen' as Mortgage Burns," *KE*, January 18, 1971, 18.
Mason Co. Deed Book 70, p. 75, Maysville, Ky.
Maysville Bulletin, January 20, 1877.
Maysville Eagle, January 17, 1877.

Coralie Runyon Jones

FIRST NATIONAL BANK AND TRUST COMPANY OF COVINGTON. One of Covington's earliest and largest financial institutions, the First National Bank of Covington was organized in 1864 by prominent Covington residents **John G. Carlisle**, **John Fisk**, **Amos Shinkle**, and others. Shinkle served as its first president, and the bank's first location, officially opened on January 10, 1865, was in the Odd Fellows Hall on the northeast corner of Fifth and Madison Aves. (see **Covington, Downtown**). By 1878 the bank had moved to an Italianate-style building at 515 Madison Ave. After the death of Shinkle in December 1892, the board of directors named Frank P. Helm, formerly of the Farmers and Traders National Bank in Covington, the second president in January 1893. About the same time, First National merged with the Covington City National Bank.

Helm held the position of president of First National until January 1907, when he was succeeded by **E. S. Lee**, who served as president until his death in 1932. Lee oversaw a period of great expansion, including acquisition of the Merchants National Bank of Covington in 1908 and merger with the Farmers and Traders National Bank in Covington in 1910, at which time the First National Bank moved its headquarters to the Farmers and Traders National Bank on the northwest corner of Sixth and Madison Aves. The six-story Beaux Arts–style headquarters, designed by Cincinnati architect Harry Hake in association with architects **Lyman Walker** and George W. Schofield of Covington, had been completed in 1904. Lee also applied to establish a trust department, and following the Federal Reserve Board's approval, the bank's official name was changed to First National

First National Bank and Trust Co., Sixth and Madison Aves., Covington.

Bank and Trust Company of Covington in January 1926.

After the 1932 death of Lee, Ben Bramlage became the bank's fourth president in 1933. In March 1933, during the **Great Depression**, President Franklin D. Roosevelt (1933–1945) declared a "bank holiday" to allow government officials time to examine the solvency of banks nationwide. Federal examiners found First National's situation less than satisfactory, although some directors claimed that the report was politically motivated. The bank was forced to close, but it reorganized and secured sufficient assets to reopen. In September 1933, E. A. Vosmer became the fifth president of the reorganized First National and guided it successfully through the remainder of the Great Depression. The bank's assets more than doubled between 1933 and 1943.

The year 1950 witnessed the naming of a new president for the bank, Harry J. Humpert, under whose guidance the bank announced a merger with the First National Bank of Latonia in August 1961. The assets of the First National Bank and Trust Company of Covington reached nearly $17.3 million by the end of 1961, and deposits were $15.2 million. In 1962 T. Byron Stephens succeeded Humpert as president of the bank and served until 1970. A succession of presidents followed: V. J. Hils, Harold C. Truitt, and Harry K. Lowe (1974–1983). Suburban development in the 1960s and 1970s led to the opening of branch offices, including branches at Latonia Plaza (1964), Expressway Plaza in Fort Mitchell (1967), Crescent Springs (1969), and Elsmere (1975).

With the impending passage of new federal and state banking laws in the 1980s, bank holding companies were formed to acquire the assets of banks. David Barry Briggs of Kentucky Bancorporation Inc., representing a number of investors, including Central Bancorporation (the parent company of Central Trust Company of Cincinnati), purchased First National in 1983; the Federal Reserve Board approved the acquisition in autumn of that year. Kentucky Bancorporation Inc. operated subsidiaries under the name of Kentucky National Bank (KNB), including the First National Bank, which was officially renamed Kentucky National Bank in 1985. In 1990 it moved its headquarters to RiverCenter in Covington, where it leased 37,500 square feet on five floors. In turn, RiverCenter's developer, **Corporex**, purchased the bank's former Sixth and Madison Aves. home offices. The following year, 1991, Cincinnati-based Star Banc Corp. acquired KNB, and the bank became known as Star Bank, N.A., Kentucky. In 1993 it moved its headquarters from RiverCenter to the old **People's-Liberty Bank** on the southeast corner of Sixth and Madison Aves., the longtime home of Peoples-Liberty Bank, which Star (First National Cincinnati Corp.) had acquired in 1987. In 1999 Star Bank changed its name to Firstar, and in 2000 **US Bank** purchased Firstar.

Hall, Gregory A. "Star, KNB Wrapping up Merger," *KP*, July 2, 1991, 1K.

Hartell, Greg. "First National: A New Image for New Home," *KP*, October 30, 1985, 1K.

Kingsbury, Gilbert W. "History of the First National Bank and Trust Co., Covington, Ky., 1864–1975," vertical files, Kenton Co. Public Library, Covington, Ky.

"Our 100th Anniversary," *KP*, December 10, 1963, special section.

Williams, Tom. "Cincinnati Bank Backs Purchase of 1st National," *KP*, May 9, 1983, 1K.

———. "Federal Reserve OKs Purchase of First National," *KP*, November 2, 198, 6K.

———. "Star Bank Set to Move Home Base," *KP*, July 10, 1993, 2K.

Paul A. Tenkotte

FIRST PRESBYTERIAN CHURCH, MAYSVILLE. The First Presbyterian Church at Maysville was organized June 14, 1817, as part of the West Lexington Presbytery of the Presbyterian Church. Rev. Robert Wilson, Elder William Richey of the **Washington Presbyterian Church**, and Robert Robb and John Boyd of the Cabin Creek Ebenezer Church in Mason Co., Kentucky took on the initial work of establishing the church. This action was the result of the great religious revival that took place in the western states in 1800. The first pastor was Dr. John T. Edgar, who was elected March 29, 1820. Records do not show where the earliest congregation met for worship, but the first building was erected in 1835 where the **Washington Opera House** now stands in Maysville. This first church was affectionately called the Old Blue Church, because of its deep-blue paint and its tall spire modeled after the old English churches.

In 1850 the building was destroyed by fire; services were then held in the courthouse, and Sunday school was held in the local Academy of Rand and Richeson. In June 1850, Andrew M. and Harriet January deeded to the church the present property, where services were first held in December of that year. The building was completed in 1852. In 1867 the church split over the **Civil War**, and the two groups worshipped in the building on alternate Sundays.

In the 20th century, the church building was used as a headquarters for the distribution of clothing after the **flood of 1937**. The church was later given a brass chandelier, made in France. The early 1950s saw an expansion that necessitated the development of a four-level educational unit and an additional chapel. In May 1980 the building was completely redecorated. On July 27, 1980, an earthquake caused minor interior damage to the church.

Pickett, Thomas E. "W.W. Richeson: The Kentuckian That 'Taught' Grant," *RKHS* 9, no. 27 (September 1911): 14–22.

Wilson, Mary L., and Florence Wilson. *A History of the First Presbyterian Church*. Maysville, Ky.: Session of the First Presbyterian Church, 1950.

Young, Bennett H. "Division of the Presbyterian Church in Kentucky," Archives, Eastern Kentucky Univ., Richmond, Ky.

Alex Hyrcza

FIRST PRESBYTERIAN CHURCH, NEWPORT. The First Presbyterian Church of Newport is descended from two older Presbyterian churches within the city, the Old School Presbyterian Church and the New School Presbyterian Church. In September 1845 Newport was selected as the site of a Presbyterian Church, and on January 16, 1847, a Presbyterian church, later referred to as the Old School Presbyterian Church, was incorporated. A church building was dedicated on October 6, 1848.

In 1851, 14 Newport citizens organized the New School Presbyterian Church (so named to distinguish it from the Old School Presbyterian Church). Then in April 1852 it adopted the name Second Presbyterian Church. In 1859 that church built on a site at 520 Columbia St. and changed its name to Columbia St. Presbyterian Church.

When in September 1861, a tornado destroyed the Old School Presbyterian Church's building, the elders of that church approached the members of the Columbia St. Presbyterian Church, asking to use their church building for worship. It appears that subsequently the Old School membership became integrated gradually into that of the Columbia St. church. In May 1870, 40 members withdrew from the Columbia St. Presbyterian Church and formed a new church, the Second Presbyterian Church, resurrecting a former name.

On October 3, 1876, the members of the Columbia St. Presbyterian Church and the Second Presbyterian Church agreed to reunite under the name Westminster Presbyterian Church. However, strong differences of opinion between the two churches prevented the merger from occurring. In spring 1878 the Second Presbyterian Church was removed from the rolls of the Presbytery because it became a Congregational Church.

Another name change took place in January 1888, when the Columbia St. Presbyterian Church became the First Presbyterian Church of Newport. In December 1891 this congregation sold its 520 Columbia St. property to an African American congregation, the **Corinthian Baptist Church**, because the First Presbyterian Church was moving across town to East Newport.

In 1893 the members of the surviving First Presbyterian Church laid the cornerstone of their new building at 625 Overton St.; the structure was dedicated in 1894. In 1896 the congregation purchased a massive Köhnken and Grimm pipe organ. In the early 20th century, before Prohibition, the church became involved in efforts to enforce Sunday closing laws against local saloons. The congregation was dissolved on November 12, 1985. For several years the church building stood vacant and neglected, and then the property was sold on March 21, 1990, to David Hosea. The building was converted into housing; the original Köhnken and Grimm pipe organ has been retained. The smokestack at the rear of the building for the old boiler has been taken down, but otherwise the building, with its stained-glass front, appears much as it has for many years, set in a residential neighborhood. Today, there is no Presbyterian church in Newport.

Campbell Co. Historical Society. *Campbell County, Kentucky: 200 Years, 1794–1994*. Alexandria, Ky.: Campbell Co. Historical Society, n.d. [ca. 1995].

Donald E. Grosenbach

FIRST TWELVE MILE BAPTIST CHURCH. In December 1799 a small group of Baptists began holding services at Camp Springs in Campbell Co. They called their congregated body the Four Mile Baptist Church. Early meetings of the congregation were held in the homes of various church members. In 1822 the group built a tiny meetinghouse nearby, along Twelve Mile Creek, and changed their name to the Twelve Mile Baptist Church. In later years, when another Baptist church was formed in the area, the name was changed to the First Twelve Mile Baptist Church. As the congregation grew, a larger church was needed, and one was constructed in 1836 on a hill high above the creek.

Since the congregation of the First Twelve Mile Baptist Church was small and unable to support a full-time pastor, numerous circuit preachers filled the pulpit in the early years. They included Rev. **James Monroe Jolly**, who built and was pastor of the **Flagg Springs Baptist Church**; Moses Vickers; Elam Grizzle; James Spilman; James Vickers; and Nicholas C. Petit, founder of the **Walnut Hills Academy** in Cold Spring. Most of those early preachers were not paid a salary but were given various amenities, such as having their horses fed and shod; the preachers also received an occasional chicken dinner in the home of a church member. Church records indicate that during the late 1800s the church began paying its part-time preachers a salary of $50 per year. One of the longest-serving of those early pastors was Rev. Jesse Beagle, who was there from 1858 to 1870.

Lightning struck the church building on June 5, 1905, and it was completely destroyed by fire. Undeterred, church members rebuilt immediately on the same site. Construction materials for the new church were floated down the Ohio River from New Richmond, Ohio, to Oneonta, Ky., from where they were hauled overland by wagon. The present church building was completed in September 1905. During the Ohio River **flood of 1937**, the church was surrounded by floodwaters, but since the building was on a hill high above the creek, it was untouched.

Over the years many additions have been made to the building, including a Sunday school wing and a church library. A parsonage was built in 1961 and a fellowship hall in 1985. Most recently, a 10-acre tract of land adjacent to the church was purchased to allow for future expansion. In a church cemetery near the creek, many of the early church members and two of the circuit preachers are buried.

In 1949 the First Twelve Mile Baptist Church hired as its first full-time pastor, Rev. Russ Hayne. He was followed by Bill Pack, Bob Brumback, W. D. Hullette, Elmer Cunningham, J. T. Ryan, Keith Blair, Chris Field, and, since January 2003, the present pastor, Cohen Copley.

"First Twelve Mile Baptist Church Boasts a Rich Heritage," *Kentucky Explorer,* October 2003, 37–38.

"History of First Twelve Mile Baptist Church," First Twelve Mile Baptist Church, Camp Springs, Ky.

"Worship, Drama Mark Holy Week," *KP,* March 22, 1997, 15K.

FIRST UNITED METHODIST CHURCH. The roots of the First United Methodist Church of Covington (now Grace Campus of **Immanuel United Methodist Church**) go back to 1786, when Methodist missionaries and circuit riders were appointed to the area in Covington known as **the Point**.

The original congregation of what became the First Methodist Church of Covington started in 1827 with a membership of 10 persons who met in homes and public buildings. As it grew there was a need for a church structure the congregation could call its own. Its first building was constructed at 233–235 Garrard St. in 1832. With 350 members by 1843, the congregation built a new brick church at 530–532 Scott St. In 1846 the Scott St. church became a member of the Methodist Episcopal Church South, which supported slavery. Dissenting antislavery members withdrew to form Wesley Chapel (later called the Greenup Street Station, then the Union Methodist Episcopal Church, and finally, the First Methodist Episcopal Church), which met in a number of different locations until the congregation built an imposing Gothic Revival church on the southwest corner of Fifth and Greenup Sts. Designed by the noted architectural firm of **Walter and Stewart**, it was dedicated on July 14, 1867. Covington businessman **Amos Shinkle** was a large contributor.

At the same time the congregation was building its new building on Greenup at Fifth Sts., members led by Amos Shinkle and **Jonathon David Hearne** started a Sunday school at Powell and Stevens Sts. (now 15th and Garrard Sts.). Later, this Sunday school turned into a mission located at 211–215 Byrd St. The mission was known as the Shinkle Mission, although the city directory of 1869–1870 lists the name as the Powell St. M.E. Church. In 1892 this church was formally dedicated as the Shinkle Methodist Episcopal Church and continued to be known as such until it moved to Independence and became known as Faith Community United Methodist Church.

The first "Father's Day" Service in Covington was commemorated by Rev. George Bunton on June 28, 1914. According to the *Kentucky Post* of May 22, 1914, Bunton was the "originator of 'Father's Day' in Covington." During the evening of July 7, 1915, the Union Methodist Church on Greenup St. and the First Methodist Episcopal Church South on Scott St. were damaged by a **tornado** along with more than 1,000 homes in Covington.

On September 1, 1939, the Union Methodist Episcopal Church and the First (formerly Scott St.) M.E. Church South (located within the same block) merged into one church known as the First Methodist Church. This merger was part of a plan of the Kentucky Conference of the Methodist Church to seek mergers of various congregations. The Scott St. Methodist Church South, which from 1928 had been known as the First Methodist Episcopal Church South, was demolished in about 1970 for the construction of the **Kenton Co. Public Library**.

On January 19, 1947, the First Methodist Church suffered a devastating fire that took three hours to control. The fire caused around $100,000 damage, destroying many items going back to the early 1800s. In 1965 the church founded a Day Care Center. In 1968 the First Methodist Church became known as the First United Methodist Church.

Between 1977 and 1985, the First United Methodist Church of Covington and the **Ninth St. United Methodist Church** shared pastors. The Ninth St. United Methodist Church was a predominately African American Methodist Church. Even after 1985, the two churches held joint Vacation Bible Schools, Wednesday Evening Lenten Services, and Thanksgiving and Christmas Services. In respect to the African American membership in the church over the years, the membership roster of 1835 included 15 black members. Cooperation between these two churches goes back to when Amos Shinkle purchased the building for the congregation, which originally housed the Ninth St. United Methodist Church.

In March 1986, a microburst toppled the spire of the First Methodist Church of Covington and caused more than $124,000 damage. Architect **George Roth** assisted the congregation in repairs, including the reconstruction of the spire.

The membership of the First Methodist Church of Covington in 1939, after the merger of the First Methodist Church of Covington and the Scott St. Methodist Episcopal Church, totaled 901. It stayed relatively stable until 1960, when the population of Covington and the river cities began to decline as members moved to the suburbs. Membership and attendance declined into the first four years of the 21st century. As a result, in 2004 the church was closed and reorganized into one of the campus ministries of the **Immanuel United Methodist Church** of Lakeside Park. It is now the Grace Campus of that church, conducting contemporary services in order to meet the needs of the changing Covington community.

Several famous and notable persons visited Union M.E. Church, including President U.S. Grant (1869–1877) whose parents lived on Greenup St. across from the church. His parents owned a pew at the church, and the funeral of his father, Jesse Root Grant, was held there in 1873. The head of the Women's Christian Temperance Union, Carrie Nation, came to the church in 1901. Notable individuals who belonged to the church include actress **Una Merkel**, businessman and philanthropist **Amos Shinkle**, and Covingon's first mayor, **Mortimer Murray Benton**. Four pastors of this church became bishops in the Methodist Church: Davis W. Clark, Urban Valentine William Darlington, Hubbard H. Kavanaugh, and S. M. Merrill. Kavanaugh, a native of Clark Co., was pastor at the Scott St. Methodist Episcopal Church South in 1850. In 1854 he was elected bishop in Columbus, Ga. He was known for his two-hour sermons that could move people from laughter to tears. Darlington was a native of Grafenburg and served as pastor of the Scott St. Methodist Episcopal Church South from 1901 to 1904. At the time he was elected bishop in 1918, he was serving as president of Morris Harvey College in Pittsburgh, Pa.

"Closing Not End of Line for Church—New Home to Outreach Programs," *KP,* June 11, 2005, 3K.

Donsback, Edna Tyson. *Our Church through 175 Years*. Covington, Ky.: First United Methodist Church, 2003.

Immanuel United Methodist. www.immanuelumc.org (accessed October 16, 2006).

Tenkotte, Paul A. *A Heritage of Art and Faith: Downtown Covington Churches.* Covington, Ky.: Kenton Co. Historical Society, 1986.

Paul L. Whalen

FIRTH, JESSIE (b. June 5, 1864, Louisville, Ky.; d. October 10, 1950, Covington, Ky.). Civic-minded Jessie Edith Riddell Firth, the first woman to run for public office in Kenton Co., Ky., was also a leader in the **women's suffrage** and temperance movements. She married Charles F. Firth, a railroad freight agent. By 1913 she was elected second vice president of the Kentucky Equal Rights Association; her election was an honor for both Firth and Kenton Co. Other counties had more members, but Kenton Co. was recognized for its "earned effort to arouse the sympathies of the people." Firth served as chairwoman of the association's state convention in 1914. The Kentucky Equal Rights Association created the Covington Protective League in 1919. Firth was in charge of the league's food distribution program and the "barefoot campaign" to help Covington children who were going barefoot in summer. When the Kentucky Equal Rights Association was reorganized and became the League of Women Voters, Firth was secretary of the state organization and president in Kenton Co.

She received the Republican nomination for state representative from the 64th legislative district in 1923. In announcing her candidacy, she said she wanted better schools and roads. Furthermore, she pointed out: "I believe in honesty and economy in public affairs. I pledge, if elected, to render a full day's work for a full day's pay." She lost the election to Democrat John L. Cushing, although it was said that she "ran far ahead of her ticket." In 1930 Firth was elected president of the Covington Women's Christian Temperance Union. A writer and painter, she served as society editor of the *Kentucky Times-Star* for some 18 years. She was a member of the First Methodist Church in Covington (see **First United Methodist Church**). Firth died in 1950 at her home, 911 Scott St. in Covington, and was buried in Highland Cemetery in Fort Mitchell.

"Covington Woman Is Republican Nominee," *KTS*, October 23, 1923, 33.
Kentucky Death Certificate No. 20963, for the year 1950.
Reis, Jim. "A Big Year for Women's Movement," *KP*, August 3, 1992, 4K.
"Seeks Office," *KP*, October 26, 1923, 1.
"Taken by Death," *KP*, October 11, 1950, 6.
"W.C.T.U.: Mrs. Jessie Firth Named Union President," *KP*, November 12, 1930, 1.

Ann Hicks

FISHER, BOBBY (b. May 28, 1952, Cincinnati, Ohio). Bobby Fisher, an internationally famous liturgical musician, is director of music ministries at **St. Agnes Catholic Church** in Fort Wright, where he has worked since July 1995. He is the son of David and Esther May Kahn Fisher. Bobby Fisher graduated from Woodward High School in 1970 and studied classical guitar and music theory at the College Conservatory of Music at the University of Cincinnati. He played banjo, fiddle, guitar, keyboard, and mandolin in bands throughout the region, including, chronologically, Melange, Smyth Brothers, Coyote, and Jill and Bobby. As a studio musician playing on recordings for well-known pastoral musicians such as Ed Gutfreund, David Haas, Marty Haugen, and the St. Louis Jesuits, Fisher became interested in liturgical music as well as Catholicism. He converted from Judaism to Christianity in 1970 and was baptized a Catholic in 1977.

Fisher has recorded for a number of labels, including GIA Publications Inc. and OCP. His CDs include *Catholic Classics, Vol. III; Go Out and Tell; Guitar Prayer; Hymns and Hers for Happy Hearts; If We Dare to Hope; Misa Santa Bárbara; One Breath* (with Ed Gutfreund); *Play before God; Season of Peace*; and *Waiting for the Light.* Fisher is the author of *The Pastoral Guitarist,* and he has a series of instructional videos entitled *The Liturgical Guitarist.* He gives concerts and leads music workshops worldwide. His workshops include annual guitar schools for the National Pastoral Musicians Association; an annual youth liturgy conference entitled "One Bread, One Cup" at St. Meinrad, Ind.; "Music Ministry Alive!" Summer institute for young people and adults in St. Paul, Minn.; and the Knockadoon Folk Liturgy summer camp for youth in East Cork, Ireland. Recently, Fisher has been working on music for film and television, including a PBS special documentary on Christian-Muslim dialogue (to air in 2010). He lives in Cincinnati with his wife Tarri Baker.

"Bobby Fisher." www.giamusic.com/bios/fisher_bobby.cfm (accessed August 10, 2008).
Fisher, Bobby. Telephone interview by Paul A. Tenkotte, Fort Wright, Ky., August 10, 2008.

Paul A. Tenkotte

FISHING. Fishing in Northern Kentucky is always fresh-water fishing, but beyond that, it varies depending on whether it is done in a river or in a lake. River fishing, along the Ohio, Licking, and Kentucky Rivers, is generally conducted deadline, using a sinker with a taut line back to the reel. A good tug on the line, bending the reel, generally means a fish is nibbling or caught on the hook at the bottom of the stream and that it is a good time to set the hook. Bait for fishing in the rivers is often live bait, worms or minnows; however, dough balls, corn flakes, cheese, or beef smelt (the lining of a cow's stomach) may be used instead.

The other main type of fishing is lake fishing, which may occur in pay lakes, in state or public park lakes, or in farm ponds. Depending on weather conditions, clarity of water, and turbulence of the water, bait for lake fishing can be either live or artificial (spinners, rubber worms, spinning lures, and flies). Smaller farm ponds throughout the region yield nice-sized largemouth and smallmouth bass, which are full of fight and are flavorful when cooked.

Fishing is done in the rivers or lakes from boats, from shore, or with trout lines (baited hooks attached to long lines, which are checked occasionally for catches).

Favorite Northern Kentucky fishing spots along the Ohio River are the areas just above and below the **Meldahl Dam** upriver and the **Markland Dam** downriver. The confluence of the Licking and Ohio rivers between Newport and Covington has yielded countless fish over the years, especially to the vagrant populations living nearby. Carp and channel catfish are common catches there. The area between the Newport shore and the first pier of the old **Louisville and Nashville Railroad** Bridge has given up as many as 75 perch, 8 to 10 inches long, in an hour. Whether one wants to eat these fish or not, such fishing certainly is fun. Up the Licking River south of the I-275 bridge to Falmouth, and in the branches of that river beyond Falmouth, live several varieties of game fish not generally found in the Ohio River. However, as the Ohio River has become cleaner in the past 50 years, more exotic varieties of game fish have begun to appear. The river is full of large catfish, and mythical stories of man-sized catfish lurking in lethargy at the bottom of the dams have been told by the Corps of Engineers divers who inspect that part of the river's bottom.

Pay lakes (sometimes called commercial lakes), where one pays a daily rate for permission to fish, usually with a limit on the catch, are common in some parts of Northern Kentucky; elsewhere in the nation, where streams and lakes are plentiful, pay lakes are rare. The pay lake flourished in the 1940s and 1950s. Stocked sometimes as often as weekly, and advertised in the sports pages of newspapers, with specially tagged fish for prizes, these lakes were located near the urban areas, where people might fish all night in hopes of getting the catch of their life. One of the first pay lakes was Belle Acres in Southgate in Campbell Co.; it was also known as Lake Berry for its owner, **Albert Seaton Berry**. In 1928 cottages were built around the shores of the two lakes at Lake Berry. Today the municipal building–community center in Southgate is located where Lake Berry was. Just downstream to the south was Joe's Fishing Lake, notorious for the fights that broke out there among drunken all-night fishermen. It is reported that the lake, though not the business, remains today just behind **Evergreen Cemetery** in Wilder, teeming with fish jumping up out of the water. Around 1950, Belmont Lake was developed at the top of Belmont Hill in Dayton. Belmont was famous for its annual fishing contest, where young contestants lined the shore shoulder to shoulder, hoping to hook into the largest fish. It was so crowded that it was dangerous, with baited hooks threatening the eyes and faces of participants. Igo's Lake (later known as Wilbur's Lake) was along Grand Ave. in Fort Thomas, and the WLW Lake was along Ky. Rt. 10, beyond Flagg Springs. WLW stood for William L. Woodie, not for the radio station. Farther out in Campbell Co., lakes like Tiemier's in Silver Grove (it is still there); Darlington Lakes, off Uhl Rd. in Melbourne; Dietz's Lake, along Nelson Rd.; Neltner's Lake, off Ky. Rt. 8; Claredan Lake, along John's Hill Rd. in Highland Heights (home to that city's municipal building today); and Cedar Wood Lake, in Claryville, were also pay lakes. Private pay lakes included Bartlett's Lake in Sun Valley, south of Alexandria, Ky., and the Bob White Club (still operating today), along Licking Pk. (Ky. Rt. 9).

Kenton Co. had a few pay lakes. Hatchet Lake, at the west end of 16th St. in Covington, where the cut in the hill for I-75 is today, was a popular fishing location for city boys. Its two lakes drained northward into **Willow Run** Creek. Both of the well-known eateries the **Lookout House**, at the top of the **Dixie Highway**, and Retschulte's (see **Barleycorn's Five Mile House, Lakeside Park**), in old South Fort Mitchell, had places to fish. Funke's Lake was along Turfway Rd., about one mile from Dudley Rd., and Doc's Lake was along Richardson Rd. in Erlanger. In southern Kenton Co. was Ehrhardt's Lake, at Nicholson, and Kenton Lakes, reportedly stocked by the government in 1880. It was along the **Three-L Highway**, near Visalia, as was Redlick's Triple-L Lake, near Ryland Heights. Miller's Lake was near Covington also, along the Three-L Highway. Shady Shore Lake was on the edge of Latonia, in Rosedale, near where Banklick Creek flows into the Licking River. Today, it is the Marshall Schildemeyer **VFW** Post No. 6095.

Boone Co. once had Lake Air View, offering both fishing and cabins, off Hopeful Rd. near Florence. Idelwhile Lake was in Richwood, Dixie View Lake was along U.S. 25 south of Florence, Lake Echo was on Maher Rd., and Henderson's Shady Farm was on Moffett Rd.

During 1953–1954, the drought in Northern Kentucky prompted the state to think about building some recreational and water-supply lakes in the region. Thus appeared Williamstown Lake in 1957, built as a recreation and fishing spot and as the reservoir for Grant Co. Plans are afoot today to enlarge the lake and perhaps make it into a state park. Also in Grant Co. are Bullock Pen Lake, near Crittenden, and Boltz Lake, northwest of Dry Ridge. Owen Co. received **Elmer Davis Lake** (the county reservoir) at about the time the private Elk Lake Shores was built. In Pendleton Co. the state created **Kincaid Lake State Park**, once known as Falmouth Lake State Park, around a dam across Kincaid Creek in the early 1960s. In Carroll Co. the **General Butler State Resort Park** offers fishing; and there is fishing in the lake at the **Blue Licks Battlefield State Resort Park** in Robertson Co. In Kenton Co. the relatively new Doe Run Lake, built for flood control, is now the largest lake in the county. In southern Campbell Co. is the A. J. Jolly Lake at the park of the same name, which was opened in the early 1960s as Campbell Co. Park. Persons 16 years of age or older who fish in these public fishing places or in the rivers are required to have Kentucky state fishing licenses.

Fishing was a popular enough sport that the local newspapers had weekly if not daily fishing columns. For many years John E. Murphy and Bob Rankin both wrote informative and interesting articles in Northern Kentucky newspapers. Their pieces were full of local history, and the newspapers often sponsored area-wide fishing contests. Stores such as Rink's Bargain City, Sports of All Sorts, and Wal-Mart today carry extensive lines of fishing equipment, and at one time it seemed that every river city in Northern Kentucky had its own bait shop. Boys gathered night crawlers after heavy rains and sold them to bait stores for 25 cents per dozen; dealers stored them in old soft-drink coolers before reselling them. In recent years the State of Kentucky has experimented with stocking some local lakes with rainbow trout, to the delight of fly fishers; the problem appears to be that the water temperature of area streams and ponds is generally not cool enough for trout to flourish.

Forest, Wally. "Bullock Pen Versatile Lake," *KP*, May 5, 1970, 26.
Murphy, John E. "Astream and Afield," *KP*, May 31, 1940, 13.
Reis, Jim. "Fishing at the Old Pay Lake," *KP*, August 16, 1993, 4K.

Michael R. Sweeney

FISK, CHARLES H. (b. August 31, 1843, Fiskburg, Ky.; d. October 19, 1930, Covington, Ky.). Attorney and **Civil War** veteran Charles Henry Fisk earned his bachelor and law degrees at Miami University, Oxford, Ohio. At the start of the Civil War, he was instrumental in recruiting a company of men, the "Squirrel Hunters." A volunteer group of Union sympathizers, they were recruited to help defend Cincinnati against an anticipated invasion by Confederate general Kirby Smith's forces. Fisk was admitted to the Kentucky bar in 1865 and practiced law in Lexington for a year. He then moved to Covington and joined the law firm of his father, John F. Fisk. Charles later became president of the Kenton Co. Bar Association, was a 33rd degree Mason, and was secretary of the Covington and Cincinnati Bridge Company. He died at his Covington home in 1930 at age 87 and was buried in the Fisk Mausoleum at Highland Cemetery in Fort Mitchell. The day he was buried would have been his 64th wedding anniversary. He was survived by his wife, Margaret, and a son and a daughter.

"Fisk Is Dead," *KP*, October 20, 1930, 1.

FISK, JOHN FLAVEL (b. December 14 or 15, 1815, Genesee Co., N.Y.; d. February 21, 1902, Covington, Ky.). Educator, Democratic politician, and lawyer John Flavel Fisk was educated in the common schools of New York and then at Cary's Academy in Cincinnati. He began his academic life as principal of the Germantown Academy and later served as principal at Mason Academy in Mason Co. He studied law under Frank Hord at Maysville and under **James T. Morehead** and James Pryor in Covington. He married Elizabeth S. Johnson on October 14, 1842; they had seven children. Fisk served on the boards of directors of many organizations, including the Covington and Cincinnati Bridge Company, the First National Bank of Covington (see **First National Bank and Trust Company of Covington**), the **Highland Cemetery**, the Covington Gas Light Company, and the Kenton Insurance Company. He also served as Covington city attorney, president of the Covington school board, and Kenton Co. attorney. He was a Kentucky state senator from 1857 to 1862 and served as Speaker of the Senate. Fisk was also the lieutenant governor from 1862 until 1863. He returned to the Senate from 1863 to 1865. From 1868 until he retired in 1890, he practiced law with his son Charles Henry Fisk. John Flavel Fisk was considered to be one of the most successful and able lawyers in the region and also an outstanding orator. He was buried in Highland Cemetery.

John F. Fisk.

Biographical Encyclopedia of Kentucky. Cincinnati: J. M. Armstrong, 1878.
"Fisk Is Dead," *KP*, February 22, 1902.
Levin, H., ed. *The Lawyers and Lawmakers of Kentucky.* Chicago: Lewis, 1897.

FISKBURG. Fiskburg is an unincorporated community located in southeastern Kenton Co., in the vicinity of Madison Pk. (Ky. Rt. 17) and Fiskburg Rd. (Ky. Rt. 2046). Settled in the early 1800s, Fiskburg became a small but prosperous farming community. By the 1880s, the town contained several farms, a school, a Grange hall, a general store, and a church. With its tobacco warehouse and cigar-making factory, Fiskburg was a center for tobacco farming. The community presumably received its name from the Fisk family, one of the area's larger families. Well-known members of that family include **John F. Fisk** and his son **Charles H. Fisk**; both were prominent attorneys and politicians in Northern Kentucky during the late 19th and early 20th centuries. Fiskburg's most enduring institution is the **Wilmington Baptist Church**, whose cemetery contains the graves of several local area pioneers. Fiskburg has a rural charm typified by its well-preserved farmhouses and open spaces.

An Atlas of Boone, Kenton, and Campbell Counties, Kentucky. Philadelphia: D. J. Lake, 1883.
"Fiskburg," *Newport Local,* September 5, 1878, 2.

Greg Perkins

FITZPATRICK, THOMAS P. (b. May 14, 1894, Cleveland, Ohio; d. June 22, 1962, Covington, Ky.). Thomas P. Fitzpatrick, a professional boxer and a colorful Democratic politician, was the son of a mill hand, Timothy Fitzpatrick, and his wife Margaret Daly. The family moved to Covington, and there, as a young boy, Thomas attended **St. Patrick** Elementary School. He later graduated from the St. Xavier Business College in Cincinnati. Fitzpatrick served in the U.S. Navy for four months at the end of **World War I**. As a young adult, he became a well-known lightweight boxer and later worked as a boxing referee, promoter, and matchmaker. In partnership with "Biddy Bishop," he was personally responsible for bringing many high-profile boxing matches to the old Riverside Arena at Second St. and Madison Ave. in Covington.

Fitzpatrick was elected as a Kentucky state representative in 1933, a position he held for 10 years. He served as Covington mayor from 1944 to 1946 and as Kenton Co. sheriff the following four years. After his term as sheriff ended, he left politics for four years, before again being elected a state representative in 1954. He held that position for the remainder of his life, serving as Speaker of the Kentucky House of Representatives from 1956 until 1958. On the final day of the 1962 session of the state legislature, Fitzpatrick suffered an asthma attack, for which he was hospitalized and from which he died several months later, at St. Elizabeth Hospital in Covington.

At the time of his death, he and his family were living in Covington at 305 W. Sixth St. Funeral services were held at Covington's St. Patrick Catholic Church, and burial was in St. Mary Cemetery, Fort Mitchell. Thomas P. Fitzpatrick was survived by his wife Ida Welsh Fitzpatrick and a daughter, Charlotte Fitzpatrick Richter. During his long and colorful career, he was a member of many clubs, including the Covington Eagles, the Elks, the **Knights of Columbus**, and the Holy Name Society. He was also a prominent figure in St. Patrick's Day celebrations locally.

"Thomas Fitzpatrick Dies at 68," *KP*, June 22, 1962, 1.
"Thomas P. Fitzpatrick," vertical file, Kenton Co. Public Library, Covington, Ky.
Thomas P. Fitzpatrick U.S. Navy World War I record, on file at the Kenton Co. Public Library, Covington, Ky.

S. S. Kresge Company lunch counter, Madison Ave., Covington, 1965.

FIVE-AND-DIME STORES. These stores were also known as 5-and-10 stores, 10-cent stores, and dime stores. For much of the 20th century, most large and medium-sized Northern Kentucky cities had a Woolworth or a Kresge five-and-dime store, and sometimes both, on their main streets. In 1879 Frank Winfield Woolworth opened one of the nation's first successful five-and-dime stores, selling inexpensive items. Soon he started a national chain of outlets that operated as F. W. Woolworth Company. In 1897 Sebastian Spering Kresge entered a partnership with J. G. McCrory in 5-and-10-cent stores; in 1912 he incorporated the S. S. Kresge Company. These two national chains, Woolworth and Kresge, achieved great success, purchasing inexpensive items in large quantities, so that their stores could sell more cheaply than local independent merchants. An early feature of the dime store was the open display of merchandise on tables, so customers could examine the merchandise themselves before purchase. Before this time, storekeepers generally kept merchandise in cases and behind counters, requiring customers to ask for the items they wanted. Another innovation of dime stores was the inclusion of lunch counters, which soon became affordable and popular gathering places, featuring hot dogs, hamburgers, soft drinks, and daily "blue plate" specials. The 5-and-10-cent stores also provided employment opportunities for women, who were typically called salesgirls.

The prosperity of the Woolworth chain was evidenced in 1913, when it opened a corporate headquarters building, then the world's tallest building, in New York City. By 1922 Woolworth operated 1,174 stores in the United States and Canada. Woolworth's main competitor, S. S. Kresge Company, remained a formidable opponent by pioneering in the use of newspaper ads and radio commercials to advertise its business.

The first Woolworth in Covington opened in 1898 at Pike and Washington Sts., eventually moving to 734 Madison. A cousin and former partner of F. W. Woolworth was Seymour H. Knox, who opened his own chain of 5-and-10-cent stores, including two S. H. Knox & Company stores in downtown Covington, the first at 40 Pike St. and the second at 632 Madison Ave. (the latter opened in 1910). In 1911–1912, Knox merged his 112 stores nationwide with Woolworth's 318; thereafter the S. H. Knox store at 632 Madison became an F. W. Woolworth store. In 1927 the Woolworth store at 632–634 Madison Ave. doubled its size, opening a lunch counter and increasing its salesgirl staff to 35.

By far the largest five-and-dime store in Northern Kentucky was the three-story (plus a basement) F. W. Woolworth on the southeast corner of Seventh St. and Madison Ave. in Covington (currently the Madison; see **Covington, Downtown**). F. W. Woolworth Company built this new Art Deco–style, air-conditioned store in 1941, with a grand opening in March 1942. The store featured candy, perfumes, jewelry, toiletries, sundries, stationery, books and magazines, and a 110-foot-long lunch counter on the entry floor. On the lower (basement) floor were toys, pets, housewares, domestics, and clothing for men, women, and children. The kitchen was located on the second floor, with cutting-edge conveniences such as two large refrigerators, an electric dishwasher and drier, an electric potato peeler, three garbage disposals, and a silverware washer and polisher. Offices, employee washrooms, and a salesgirls' hat-check room were also located on the second floor. The third floor contained a stockroom, a horticulture room where plants were prepared and kept at cool temperatures, and "a locker and shower room for Negro porters."

Downtown Newport also had an F. W. Woolworth, located at 728 Monmouth St., which opened in about 1914. In February 1925, the Newport Woolworth store burned; it reopened in September 1927 with 5,000 square feet of retail space, including a lunch counter and soda fountain. The company opened a new store in the **Newport Shopping Center** in 1956, operating there successfully until the early 1990s, again with a lunch counter, where 35-cent hamburgers were the featured hit. Through 1959, F. W. Woolworth operated both stores in Newport, but by 1960, the downtown Newport location had closed.

S. S. Kresge opened its 15th outlet nationally in Newport in 1916. Eventually, Kresge operated two stores simultaneously within the 800 block of Monmouth St. (812 and 822) in Newport: one was called a dime store and the other a dollar store. In 1941 Kresge built a new building at 822 Monmouth St., continuing to operate out of both locations. The Newport Kresge stores were remodeled in 1963. In the 1970s, Kresge closed its store at 812 Monmouth but continued operations of its outlet at 822 Monmouth before closing in about 1983.

Downtown Covington's S. S. Kresge store, at 618–622 Madison Ave. in the ground floor of the YMCA building, opened in about 1916. In 1932, when an adjoining store moved out, Kresge opened larger quarters in the **YMCA** building at 624 Madison. The downtown Covington Kresge's closed on December 31, 1966.

In Maysville, Woolworth operated a store from 1922 to 1956, and the smaller G. C. Murphy chain was there for 60 years, 1924 to 1985. S.H. Kress & Company, a small chain of stores, also was represented in downtown Maysville for a time. The Ben Franklin dime-store chain operated in Brooksville and Carrollton and also in the Latonia Shopping

Center in Covington. The W. T. Grant chain had an outlet in the Expressway Plaza in Fort Mitchell. There were also small privately owned single-store operations such as Boyer's in Silver Grove, Dayton Dime Store, Erlanger 5¢ to $1.00 Store, Fort Mitchell 5¢ to $1.00 Store, Greenup 5¢ to $1.00 Store in Covington, Latonia 5¢ to $1.00 Store, Ludlow 5¢ to $1.00 Store, and Morris Department Store in Erlanger.

By the 1960s, the heyday of the 5-and-10-cent stores was quickly fading. In 1962 S. S. Kresge Co. opened its first Kmart stores, "big box" discount department stores generally located in suburban shopping centers with plenty of free parking and longer hours of operation. The move heralded the growth of suburbia and the steady decline of downtown retail centers and of dime stores. Likewise, Woolworth's opened Woolco discount department stores, although there were none in Northern Kentucky. Covington's S. S. Kresge store closed in December 1966, and its downtown Woolworth outlet in January 1990. Kmart Corporation sold its remaining Kresge stores to McCrory in 1987; the last Woolworth stores in the United States closed in 1997. The first Kmart in Northern Kentucky opened in Edgewood in November 1972; in addition, there are now Kmart stores in Newport, Florence, and Maysville. If there are modern replacements for the classic five-and-dime stores, they are the contemporary Family Dollar, Dollar General, and Dollar Tree store chains.

"Everything but Miracles Worked by Equipment in New Covington Store," *KP*, March 24, 1942, 1.

Kresge, Stanley S. *The S. S. Kresge Story*. Racine, Wis.: Western, 1979.

"New Business," *KP*, May 10, 1951, 3.

"New 5-And-10 Store," *KP*, September 4, 1925, 1.

Pitrone, Jean Maddern. *F. W. Woolworth and the American Five and Dime*. Jefferson, N.C.: McFarland, 2003.

S. S. Kresge Company Records, Bentley Historical Library, Univ. of Michigan, Ann Arbor, Mich.

Vertical File, Library, Kentucky Gateway Museum Center, Maysville, Ky.

Jack Wessling and Paul A. Tenkotte

FLAGG SPRINGS. The area known as Flagg Springs (also called Flagg Spring) is located in southeastern Campbell Co. in an area along the **AA Highway**, Smith Rd., and Ky. Rt. 10 (originally called the Alexandria–Flagg Springs Turnpike). Flagg Springs is shown on the local 1883 Lake atlas as having a couple of stores, a gristmill, a blacksmith shop, the **Beech Grove Academy**, numerous springs, and the **Flagg Springs Baptist Church**. Although never a part of any incorporated town, the Flagg Springs Baptist Church has long been the area's meeting and social centerpiece.

At first the Flagg Springs area was named Kennedy's Ferry, after the early settlers; it became Flagg Springs in 1817, deriving this name from the Kennedy family's farm, named the Flagg Springs Farm. *Flagg* in the farm's name came from the irises growing in abundance on the farm, and *Springs* refers to the many freshwater springs found there.

The church cemetery at Flagg Springs contains the remains of **Thomas Jefferson McGraw**, one of two Campbell Co. residents executed by Union authorities during the **Civil War** for recruiting for the Confederacy. Flagg Springs had a post office, and several important structures also played a part in the area's history. The oldest and most prominent building, other than the Baptist church, was the Beech Grove Academy. Next door was a campground called the Beechgrove Sunday School Union. Still functioning today, it holds outdoor singing and religious meetings on the site of the former seminary. Later, a smaller school was built on the property of the former seminary; it was also called Beechgrove. The Eastern Campbell Co. Fire Department, is located in town.

Just across the road was a facility called Camp Sunshine. Beginning in 1928, this camp was a place for "city" kids to experience (free of charge) the outdoors and country life. It eventually closed, and the Mentor Baptist Church bought the property and built a new church there in 2001. Today a golf course called Flagg Springs is located next to the church. The development of the AA Highway has impacted the area in that many new homes are under construction and new growth is sprouting up around Flagg Springs.

An Atlas of Boone, Kenton, and Campbell Counties, Kentucky. Philadelphia: D. J. Lake, 1883.

Campbell Co. Historical Society. *Campbell County, Kentucky, 200 Years, 1794–1994*. Alexandria, Ky.: Campbell Co. Historical Society, 1994.

Kenneth A. Reis

FLAGG SPRINGS BAPTIST CHURCH. The historic Flagg Springs (also known as Flagg Spring) Baptist Church is located along Ky. Rt. 10 near Smith Road in southern Campbell Co. Tradition suggests that a small log cabin, and later a frame building, preceded the present brick structure. A stone sign mounted on the front of the building is engraved with the date of December 7, 1833, and according to church records, that is when the church was organized, not when the building was constructed. Rev. **James Monroe Jolly** is thought to have built the present structure, although at that time he was age 15 and living across the Ohio River at Point Pleasant, Ohio. James Moses "Monroe" Jolly moved to rural Campbell Co. about 1840, when he built the Campbell Co. Courthouse. If he constructed the church, it was evidently after 1840. Jolly was a circuit preacher who held services once a month at various local churches. Over the years many different ministers have filled the pulpit at Flagg Springs, including Jolly and his son William. The family names of some of the early church members were Dicken, Jolly, Kennedy, Maddox, Stevens, Taylor, and White. Many of those families remain in the area. Church records indicate that about 700 people became members of the church between 1840 and 1890. However, attendance figures and the number of living members at any given time are not known. There is a graveyard at the church, with the older graves on the north side of the building and the newer ones on the south. The land occupied by the church and the graveyard was donated by the estate of Edward Morin and was originally a public burial ground. Between 1829 and 1890, there were about 140 burials. The most noteworthy grave is behind the church, that of executed Confederate soldier Lt. **Thomas Jefferson McGraw**. Regular services continue to be conducted at the church, and in 2008 the congregation celebrated its 175th anniversary.

Records of the Flagg Spring Baptist Church, Kenton Co. Public Library, Covington, Ky.

Turner, Gary R. "Oral History of the Jolly Family," Northern Kentucky Univ. Oral History Interviews, 1976, Northern Kentucky Univ., Highland Heights, Ky.

Wessling, Jack. *Early History of Campbell County, Kentucky*. Alexandria, Ky.: Self-published, 1997.

FLESCH, STEVE (b. May 23, 1967, Cincinnati, Ohio). Steve Flesch, the son of Jerry and Melinda Flesch, has traveled a long road through professional golf's minor leagues and arrived at a lengthy Professional Golf Association (PGA) career and two victories in PGA Tour events. The left-hander led **Covington Catholic High School**, in Park Hills, to the state golf title in 1985, his senior year. He also played golf at the University of Kentucky at Lexington, where he graduated in December 1990 with a BA in business marketing. Flesch turned professional in October 1990, and beginning in January 1991, he played on the Asian Golf Tour for five years. He returned to participate in the Nike Golf Tour in 1996 and 1997 and earned his PGA Tour card by winning the 1997 Nike Golf Tour Championship. In 1998, at age 31, Flesch earned PGA Tour Rookie of the Year honors, the first left-hander to receive that distinction. He finished 35th on the tour's money list that year, totaling five top-10 finishes, including a second and a third. He posted a runner-up finish in a tournament in 1999 and again at an event in 2000, and in 2000 he totaled 13 top-10 finishes—second only to Tiger Woods on the tour—and finished 13th on the money list with $2,025,781. In May 2003, having totaled 38 career top-10 finishes in 174 starts over six years, Flesch finally won a PGA Tour event, outdueling Bob Estes in a one-hole playoff at the HP Golf Classic at New Orleans. Flesch ranked 21st on the money list that year, then 18th in 2004, with a career-best $2,461,787. In May 2004 he added his second PGA title by winning the Bank of America Colonial Golf Tournament in Fort Worth; he beat Chad Campbell by one stroke. As of June 2006, Flesch's career PGA Tour earnings were $11.8 million, ranking him 48th on the all-time money list. He had finished in the top 100 of the money list each of his first eight seasons on the tour. Flesch lives in Union, Ky., and plays out of the **Triple Crown Country Club**. He married his wife, Lisa, in 1995; they have two children, son Griffin and daughter Lily.

Archer, Todd. "Flesch Living out His PGA Fantasy," *CP*, May 14, 1998, 1B.

Schmidt, Neil. "Elusive Trophy Now in Flesch's Grasp," *CE*, May 8, 2003, B1.

———. "Flesch Rewarded after 7 Years of Roughing It," *CE,* August 10, 1998, D6.

Neil Schmidt

FLINGSVILLE. Flingsville in northern Grant Co. was named for George Fling (1854–1932), who became the first postmaster when the post office was established there in 1876. Earlier, the community was known as Newtown, the origin of the name of the Sherman-Newtown Rd. Located in Flingsville in the 1870s were a tobacco warehouse, a veterinarian, two blacksmith shops, several general stores, a physician, and a chicken hatchery. Nearby was the Liberty Baptist Church, whose building served as a school during the week. The post office closed in 1903. Residents now go to Crittenden and elsewhere for goods and services.

Conrad, John B., ed. *History of Grant County.* Williamstown, Ky.: Grant Co. Historical Society, 1992.

John B. Conrad

FLOOD CONTROL. Heavy rains, sometimes in combination with melting snow, have often caused flooding along the Ohio River and its tributaries. Major floods are known to have occurred in 1883, 1884, and 1913 (see **Flood of 1884**; **Floods of 1913**). Record flooding took place in 1936 and 1937 (see **Flood of 1937**), causing devastation in many Northern Kentucky communities and elsewhere. The federal government responded to these 1930s events, enacting flood-control legislation that created a nationwide comprehensive program for flood control, administered by the U.S. Army Corps of Engineers.

Flood-control programs lessen or prevent flood damage by regulating water flow from reservoirs, by local protection projects, or by combinations of the two means. Channel improvements—deepening, widening, or straightening the channel—may suffice to keep small streams from overflowing during flood seasons. Reservoirs located on tributary streams of the Ohio River store waters during times when downstream floods are likely to occur. (The navigation dams on the Ohio do not provide flood control.) Reservoirs constructed for flood control may also be used for other purposes, including municipal and industrial water supply, development of hydroelectric power, navigation, conservation of fish and wildlife, and recreation. The nearest reservoir to the Northern Kentucky counties is Cave Run Lake on the upper Licking River, near Morehead.

Local protection projects, usually levees and floodwalls, are built along the banks of rivers and are located both on the Ohio River and on tributary streams. Levees are wide-based earthen structures used where land is relatively inexpensive; they are usually located in rural areas. A floodwall, a concrete structure, is more practical for urban areas. Both levees and floodwalls are likely to have devices to close openings that allow movement of traffic at times when flooding is not imminent. In the Ohio River comprehensive flood-control program, the reservoirs and local protection projects are built to provide a level of protection three feet higher than the levels reached in the 1937 flood. In the national flood-control program, the local projects are built by the U.S. Army Corps and, when completed, are turned over to the local governments that shared in construction, operation, and maintenance costs.

In Northern Kentucky the following cities have local protection projects built by the Army Corps of Engineers:

—Covington, Kenton Co. The project is located at the confluence of the Licking and Ohio rivers and consists of work along streams, comprising 1.8 miles of earth levee, 1.1 miles of concrete wall, 10 pumping stations, and 8 traffic openings. Construction began in 1948 and was completed in 1955 at a cost of $8.9 million. Damages prevented by the project are estimated in excess of $5 million.

—Dayton, Campbell Co. The project is located along the Ohio River upstream from Newport and consists of 8,170 feet of earthen levee and 2 pumping stations. It was constructed between 1978 and 1986 at a cost of $13 million. Damages prevented by the project are estimated at around $4 million.

—Newport, Campbell Co. The project is located at the confluence of the Licking and Ohio rivers and consists of work along both streams, comprising 1.5 miles of earthen levee, 1,500 feet of concrete wall, 2,500 feet of cellular steel sheet piling wall, and 3 pumping stations. Construction began in 1946 and was completed in 1951 at a cost of $7.8 million. Damages prevented by the project are estimated in excess of $30 million.

—Maysville, Mason Co. This project is located along the Ohio River and consists of 1.2 miles of earthen levee, 1.5 miles of concrete wall, and 5 pumping stations. Construction was completed in 1956 at a cost of $7 million. Damages prevented by the project are estimated at around $22 million.

The Corps of Engineers fights flood problems also by providing detailed technical information on flood hazards to other federal agencies, state and local governments, and private citizens, through its Flood Plain Management Services Program. This information is used in developing zoning regulations, building codes, sanitary codes, and other measures to reduce property loss and to protect the environment by avoiding unwise development in flood-prone areas.

Project Maps and Data Sheets, Louisville District, Corps of Engineers, Louisville, Ky.

Water Resources Development by the U.S. Army Corps of Engineers in Kentucky. Louisville, Ky.: U.S. Army Corps of Engineers, 1995.

Charles E. Parrish

FLOOD OF 1884. Before the **flood of 1937**, the most devastating flood to strike the Northern Kentucky region took place in 1884, when the Ohio River reached 71.1 feet at Cincinnati, 26.1 feet above the flood stage at that time of 45 feet. The worst recorded flood before 1884 was just the year before, when the river rose to 66.3 feet and it was immediately proclaimed that the river could never get that high again. Late December 1883 had brought snow and cold weather such that the snow had not melted easily but had turned to slush. In mid-January of 1884, the Ohio River began to rise slowly, and on February 14, 1884, it crested at its then new record level of 71.1 feet at 1:00 p.m. Upriver in Mason Co., east Maysville and the city of Chester were completely under water; Augusta in Bracken Co. was also completely covered; the Four Mile Creek Bridge near California in Campbell Co. was lifted and carried away; the residents of Boson in Pendleton Co. saw the Licking River rise 12 feet in one day; the cities of Warsaw in Gallatin Co. and Carrollton in Carroll Co. suffered similar fates; Monterey, up the Kentucky River in Owen Co., was swamped. Petersburg in Boone Co., elevated well above the normal pool of the Ohio River, was the only river city in the region not to be seriously harmed. The ferry in Newport halted service to Cincinnati because the current was too swift. School buildings were turned into houses of refuge for the newly homeless. John C. Dueber, the owner of Newport's **Dueber Watch Case Company**, kept his workers busy building temporary shelters. He opened his Washington St. home in Newport to 25 children who needed care. Dueber also succeeded in placing a request for help on a national newswire, and as a result supplies and help started arriving from around the United States. Homes in Dayton in Campbell Co. were swept off their foundations into the fast-flowing river, and Link's rope factory in that city was washed away. By 63 feet, some 3,000 homes in Newport had been evacuated; the **L&N Bridge** in Newport had a temporary causeway built up to it to keep it usable. Roughly one-third of Newport became submerged. Covington, although flooded in its lower spots, did not suffer as much as Newport. Perhaps the most obvious long-term consequence of the flood of 1884 was the U.S. Army's decision to retreat from the **Newport Barracks**, which had endured floods at the confluence of the Licking and the Ohio rivers since 1803. In a large basin area around present-day Ninth St. in Newport, a low spot, pools up to 10 feet deep persisted long after the river receded. The effects of the flood continued to haunt Northern Kentucky river cities.

Reis, Jim. "Flood of 1884 Wreaked Havoc," *KP,* December 18, 1995, 4K.

FLOOD OF 1937. While many "great" floods are remembered in the Ohio River Valley, none rivals the flood of 1937. Over the course of 10 days, the Ohio River swelled to a height never seen before or since. The final figure of 79.99 feet, more than 27 feet above flood stage, is still one for the history books, as are the experiences of those who lived through the greatest natural disaster seen in Northern Kentucky.

Water levels in 1937 had been rising slowly throughout the course of a very wet January as rain and snowmelt combined to swell both the Ohio River and its tributaries. By Friday, January 22, the

The Depery Home, Keturah St., Newport, after the flood of 1937.

river was recorded at 70.4 feet at Cincinnati. People began to talk about the last record-setting flood, which occurred in 1884, but few believed the river would flood at such levels again. A U.S. weather forecaster predicted that the river would soon crest between 71 and 72 feet. It rose to 72.8 feet the next day, a new record, and continued rising at the rate of about three-tenths of a foot each hour. The City of Cincinnati put pumping crews to work in an attempt to keep the flood out of the electrical stations and other utility plants. Already 12,000 to 15,000 residents of Northern Kentucky had been forced to evacuate their homes.

The vital links connecting the communities of Northern Kentucky with Cincinnati were already disappearing. Lunken Airport, then called the Cincinnati Municipal Airport, was closed as the floodwater reached its runways. The flood eventually covered the entire airfield, leaving only the top of the new control tower above water. The approaches to the **Central Bridge** in Newport and Cincinnati were submerged. The Louisville and Nashville Railroad Bridge (**L&N Bridge**) was closed that Friday, leaving only the **Chesapeake and Ohio Railroad Bridge** and the **John A. Roebling Bridge** for transportation of people and supplies. As the Covington approach to the Roebling Bridge began to flood, a new path was constructed, raising the roadbed out of water that was between two and six feet deep. Martial law was considered for Covington, and special permits were needed to cross the Roebling Bridge and enter the city. Thus bridge traffic was limited to the transport of food and medical supplies.

The next day, January 24, is still known as Black Sunday in the tri-state region. The Ohio River had continued to rise and was now at 75 feet. The utility companies were in danger of being shut down by the flooding, and water rationing was imposed. Then the flood broke an electric cable for the streetcar lines, sparking a fire in the Camp Washington industrial district of Cincinnati that raged out of control in the flooded neighborhood. Gasoline from breached fuel tanks at the Standard Oil storage plant floated on the surface of the water, giving the fire a fast route across the area. Other tanks and drums exploded when the fire reached them, and flames shot 50 feet in the air. Thirty-five fire companies converged at the Crosley Radio Corporation in Cincinnati, struggling to save the radio plant and to halt the fire at that point. Off-duty and retired firemen from all over the area and from places as far away as Columbus, Ohio, responded to the call for help. The fire was eventually stopped, but it left behind $1.5 million–$2 million in damage over three miles of Cincinnati.

An emergency holiday was declared, forcing businesses to close their doors. Only vital shops such as grocery stores were allowed to remain open. Most church services were canceled because of the flooding. Western Union was overwhelmed by the telegrams from out-of-state friends and relatives desperate to learn whether their loved ones were safe. The number of telegrams was so high that the office stopped making deliveries. Instead, lists of the recipients were published in local newspapers with a request that the telegrams be picked up at the office. Police were stationed along the perimeters of Covington to stop people who came from the outlying areas to stare at the incredible site.

As the disaster reached epic proportions, President Franklin Roosevelt (1933–1945) declared a state of emergency and ordered government agencies to respond on a "war-time" basis. National Guard troops were sent to augment the local police. The New Jersey Coast Guard arrived with small cutters to row through the flooded streets. Many people were rescued from rooftops and upper-level windows, often being lowered by ropes to waiting boats.

The electric company fought to keep the power on as long as possible despite flooded plants and substations. Workers traveled to the plants by boat, then crossed plank bridges across abandoned coal cars and entered the buildings through upper-level windows. Sandbag walls inside the buildings protected the equipment from the floodwater. Rail lines were flooded out, and workers carried coal to the boilers in wheelbarrows and in sacks on their backs. By Monday the electric company had lost its fight with the rising waters, and the steam turbines that powered the area were shut down. Water-pumping stations had been flooded and forced to shut down. Even in the more rural areas, outside of the flooded inner cities, wells and cisterns were flooded, the water undrinkable. Water rations were running low, and residents of the area walked to springs and wells outside the flood zone to fill kettles of water. In many areas water was brought in on tanker trucks.

St. Elizabeth Hospital in Covington (see **St. Elizabeth Medical Center**) had been built in a supposedly "flood-free" area, but that was of little help in 1937. After fighting rising waters for three days, firemen finally shut down the boilers and furnaces in the hospital's basement and subbasement ahead of the inevitable flooding. Even emergency power was lost during the night as the electric company's plants flooded. Eventually, limited electricity was restored to the hospital, but not enough to supply heat. Blankets were distributed, and hot drinks were continuously supplied from the hospital kitchens. Two city steamrollers were parked outside the building and surrounded by sandbags. The machines piped steam directly into the maternity ward to keep the newborns warm.

By Wednesday, January 27, the first sunny day in two weeks, the flood was beginning to recede, although the Ohio River was not confined to its banks again until February 5. Residents continued with rationed water and no electricity for weeks. Relief arrived from neighboring communities, which had been almost unaffected by the flooding. The City of Hamilton, Ohio, remembering the help Cincinnati had provided in a previous flood, mobilized residents to send clothing, blankets, food, and other supplies south. Truckloads of supplies were sent into Cincinnati, and much of the total was brought across the John Roebling Bridge to Northern Kentucky communities.

Life continued despite the raging waters. Public officials encouraged churches to reopen for services on January 31, in order to boost morale. At this time most people cooked with gas, rather than electricity, and the flooding did not interrupt gas service in most of the area. Gas pipes ran underground, and the gas company had slowly lengthened the valve handles as the water levels rose, eventually regulating the flow of gas from the roof of the flooded plant. Meals could still be prepared and water could be boiled for drinking. Milk was delivered by boat; the sale of liquor was banned during the emergency. In those areas with electricity, residents were encouraged to limit their use to a single light bulb and a radio, in order to stay abreast of further developments. Boat taxi service sprang up to meet the demand. The streetcars had been shut down, because there was no electricity and several garages full of streetcars were under water, but the **Green Line Company** put buses into service in the dry areas of the tristate region. This shift turned out to be the beginning of a continuing trend, with streetcars disappearing completely in 1951. The C&O Railroad suspended all normal service into and out of Cincinnati but operated a special commuter line between Cincinnati and Dayton, Ky. The service continued until February 4, the last day of the flood. Pontoon bridges were built in some areas, and pontoon ferries were used when the supply of bridge segments ran out.

As the water continued to recede, crews (many from the WPA), followed the water line with brooms and shovels, pushing debris and mud into the water to be carried off downstream. Others began to assess the damage. A number of basin-area buildings had collapsed from the pressure of the water. Portions of streets had collapsed. Houses had been swept away, leaving behind nothing but foundations. Numerous boats were lost, many sunk and others swept away completely. The water was 20 feet deep over home plate at Crosley Field in Cincinnati's West End. As waters receded from the L&N Railroad Bridge, planks were laid along the tracks to accommodate automobile traffic.

In the end, 10 states bordering rivers were flooded. Northern Kentucky communities suffered more than $1 million in property damage and 50,000 residents were left homeless. The final flooded area in Kentucky encompassed 55 percent of Newport, 60 percent of Dayton, 40 percent of Bellevue, and 37 percent of Ludlow. Bromley was an island, completely surrounded by water. The flooded area completely covered Silver Grove, Melbourne, Brent, and Rabbit Hash. One local farmer, Frank Rouse, wrote in his diary, "Rabbit Hash washed off of the map." This turned out to be a slight exaggeration. The Rabbit Hash General Store had survived, though it was completely covered by water. Iron rods installed through the entire structure into the ground secured it against such disasters. According to the store proprietors, there is still river mud in the attic crawl space from the flood of 1937.

Campbell Co. Historical Society. *Campbell County, Kentucky, 200 Years, 1794–1994.* Alexandria, Ky.: Campbell Co. Historical Society, 1994.

"Covington Begins Cleanup as Flood Waters Recede," *CE,* January 30, 1937, 14.

"Flood Expected to Exceed 1884 Record," *CTS,* January 22, 1937, 1.

Frank Rouse diaries, Elizabeth Kirtley Collection, M1996-0507, Special Collections and Archives, Northern Kentucky Univ.

Ludlow Celebrates 125 Years: 1864–1989. Ludlow: Northern Kentucky Typesetting, ca. 1989.

"Ohio River Going toward 80 Feet," *CTS,* January 25, 1937, 9.

Rabbit Hash General Store. "History of the Rabbit Hash General Store." www.rabbithash.com (accessed December 26, 2006).

Reis, Jim. "Coping with Flood of '37," *KP,* January 29, 2001, 4K.

10 Wet Days: A Pictorial History of 1937 Greater Cincinnati Flood. Cincinnati: Cincinnati Times-Star, 1937.

Jennifer Gregory

FLOOD OF 1964, LICKING RIVER. In March 1964 Pendleton Co. was hit with one of the worst floods the county had experienced up to that time. Before 1964 the flood of 1948 had set a record depth of 43 feet, exceeding the **flood of 1937**, which rose to 42 feet. Flood stage at the city of Falmouth in Pendleton Co. is 28 feet.

On Wednesday, March 4, 1964, the first of two intense rains fell on the area, bringing a total of 5¼ inches, with about 3 of those falling in a 24-hour period. Some 50 families were forced to move from the flooded sections in Falmouth, and several mobile homes in Butler were moved. The Licking River at Falmouth crested at 37.5 feet the following day, just short of a major flood. Friday brought cold temperatures as the river began its descent. With skies bright and clear, all danger seemed to have passed, but March 9 still lay ahead. The second rain fell in sheets hour after hour. The Licking River, full from the previous week, was standing at 16 feet when the new rise began. By Monday afternoon, March 9, the river had returned to its peak of 37.5 feet and was still rising. The rain continued as families began moving from low-lying areas. No one expected the river to reach the heights of 1937 and 1948, much less surpass them. The receding waters in the upper reaches of the Licking River were still extremely high. This was a bad sign, since that water would be reaching Falmouth sometime Monday evening.

For the first time in the 173 years of the city's existence, water broke over **U.S. 27** and flowed into the west end of town. It was one of the two Licking River branches at Falmouth, the South Licking, that broke all records and covered west Falmouth. What many people reported was two to three feet of rushing water that resembled a wave crashing on an ocean beach. The floodwaters came so fast that property owners were trapped in their homes and places of business. Rowboats, motorboats, and canoes were used to evacuate residents as the rain continued to fall heavily. Confusion set in; people were in their living rooms with furniture beginning to float around them. Men were wading in waist-deep water, frantically moving furniture up to the second floors of houses.

Falmouth firemen helped to move families from distressed homes. The patients from the Falmouth Rest Home were evacuated by laying them on mattresses in boats. With the rain beating in their faces, the aged residents were soaked by the time they reached ambulances waiting to take them to the school shelter.

By 1:00 a.m. Tuesday morning, March 10, the water was breaking in a waterfall over the railroad tracks in town at Shelby St. Basements in the business district were full of water, and 10 inches or so of water stood on the first-floor levels. Owners were pumping water out of their basements into Wednesday night.

With the exception of **civil defense**, police, and fire radios, the town had no telephone service and no outside contact. Disaster areas were set up. The **American Red Cross** established headquarters at the old **Falmouth High School** building, where they served food. Although many people stayed at the **Pendleton Co. Memorial High School**, the Corral Motel also furnished lodging to residents who were displaced.

The town of Butler also suffered heavily during this flood, many families being forced to leave their homes. An emergency was in effect on Monday afternoon because it was feared that the Falmouth Lake Dam on Kincaid Creek (see **Kincaid Lake State Park**) would break.

A total of 9¼ inches of rain fell between late Saturday night, March 7, and Tuesday morning, March 10, adding to the 5¼ inches from the previous week. It was estimated that three-fourths of the city of Falmouth was under water. Officially, the main Licking River crested at a record 47 feet. About 400 homes were flooded, and some 200 automobiles were lost to the waters. Many boats were overturned and swept away. The estimated loss to the city of Falmouth exceeded $2 million.

Belew, Mildred Boden. *The First 200 Years of Pendleton County.* Falmouth, Ky.: M. B. Belew, n.d. [ca. 1994].

"Falmouth Hi Boys Doing Their Part," *Falmouth Outlook,* March 13, 1964, 2.

"Falmouth Recovering from Flood; Loss Estimated More than 2 Million," *Falmouth Outlook,* March 27, 1964, 1.

"Little Flood on Licking River in Pendleton Causes Inconveniences," *Falmouth Outlook,* March 13, 1964, 2.

"March 9th Will Go Down in History: The Worst Ever Encountered Here," *Falmouth Outlook,* March 13, 1964, 1.

"Near Tragedy in Falmouth Park," *Falmouth Outlook,* March 13, 1964, 3.

"The Night of Monday, March 9th Will Be One to Remember, Surely," *Falmouth Outlook,* March 13, 1964, 2.

Melissa J. Wickelhaus

FLOOD OF 1997, LICKING RIVER. Pendleton Co. has seen many floods over the years, but the flood of 1997 brought more devastation to the area than any of its predecessors. On Friday, February 28, 1997, the depth of the Licking River stood barely above four feet as it flowed under the bridge going into Shoemaker Town. However, in just two days the river swelled to 13 times that depth; it devoured the small town, turning many homes into ruins and some into tombs. The rain began Friday night and continued through Sunday. At about 10:30 Saturday morning, March 1, 1997, the National Weather Service issued its first flood warning, predicting that the Licking River would crest at 40.5 feet at 7:00 Sunday evening. Those whose houses had not been touched when the river reached 42 feet during the flood of 1937 or when it reached 47 feet in the flood of 1964 were not alarmed by the warning, so they stayed. As time went on and the rain continued, it became apparent that Falmouth and the adjacent communities were in trouble.

On Saturday evening, firefighters and police began evacuating the 60 patients from Falmouth's nursing homes. Fire trucks drove up and down the streets and, using loudspeakers, warned the rest of the town's 2,700 residents to evacuate. Based on earlier predictions, rescuers believed that they had more than 12 hours to complete the evacuation of Falmouth, but the river rose faster than expected, and as the flood waters began engulfing the town, residents who were still in their homes had to flee. Some escaped with a few of their personal belongings and many with just the clothes on their backs; others were stuck on the roofs of cars and houses, calling for help in the darkness. By midnight Saturday, both of the converging branches of the Licking River had broken over the banks at the fairground west of town. A mass of water rushed at the town with such force that homes were wrenched from their foundations. One by one, sections of town lost electricity as the water rose. Several homes caught on fire. Phone service was lost by 4:00 a.m. on Sunday, March 2. Trying to keep up with rescue efforts, emergency workers were using hand-held radios.

Meanwhile, residents in Butler and other areas were battling the Licking River's flood waters as well. Flash flooding was reported in low-lying areas. In the early hours of Sunday morning, the residents of Butler were evacuated. About 60 homes and businesses in the town were flooded, the water reaching as high as 17 feet inside buildings along Mill St.

When the sun rose, Falmouth was a brown lake dotted with rooftops. Most of the town's residents had fled, though some were still trapped on roofs or in second floors of homes. Emergency shelters were set up quickly in local churches and schools to accommodate those affected. The National Weather Service continued to update its predictions—and continued to underestimate the crest. Sunday morning it predicted a crest of 50 feet by 1:00 a.m. on Monday. At the time of that update, the water was at 40 feet, a level it had reached 13 hours earlier than the first warning had predicted. The Licking River finally crested at 52 feet around 7:00 Sunday evening. About 80 percent of the town of Falmouth was under water.

Police and sheriff departments responded to calls for help throughout the night and the day. Volunteers and donations began arriving from all over the region. The National Guard, the **American Red Cross**, the U.S. Army Corps of Engineers, and the Federal Emergency Management Administration Agency (FEMA) reached the flooded area and offered their assistance.

Many of Falmouth's residents awoke on Monday morning homeless and in shelters. A list of names was created so that people could find family members and friends at the various sites. As the Licking River began to recede, the city's residents began to see what the river had done. Separated from the flood's edge by yellow police tapes, small groups stared at the destruction before them.

The city was without drinking water, gasoline, kerosene, or grocery stores. The town's two drugstores set up temporary mobile units to fill prescriptions. Tetanus shots were provided for volunteers and residents. Before residents were allowed to return to their homes, volunteer teams had to turn off broken natural gas lines. Houses, businesses, and cars had to be checked for bodies. The streets were cleared of logs, brush, and inches of mud. Crews of firefighters went door-to-door to inspect buildings. A house would be marked with a blue *X* if it had been checked. A red plastic ribbon meant nothing was wrong. An *X* in yellow meant the house was unstable. But if a house had a yellow ribbon, that meant it needed a more thorough search. Most were marked with a yellow *X* and would likely have to be demolished.

On Thursday, March 6, residents boarded busses and were driven through town to look at their homes and businesses; what they saw was startling devastation. No one was prepared for the scene that lay before them: broken windows, smashed buildings, ravaged trees, cars underneath houses, and empty foundations. The New Pastime Theater still advertised its scheduled movie, *Scream*. People made their way into broken houses, through mud up to their knees, and began to clean. Power washers, pumps, and generators roared as houses were emptied of their contents. All work ceased at 7:00 p.m.; the residents moved out and the National Guard arrived. The day's piles of rubble were hauled away by dump trucks.

Countywide, about 78,600 acres of land were flooded. Structural damage totaled more than $36.5 million, more than $29 million in Falmouth and $7 million in Butler. Some 700 buildings were flooded and 110 completely destroyed. Thirty-seven businesses in Falmouth did not reopen. Around 1,500 residents were displaced, and the Licking River had claimed five lives.

Gerth, Joseph, and Michael Quinlan. "Forecasters Missed Licking River's Crest at Falmouth," *LCJ*, March 7, 1997, A9.

Prendergast, Jane, and Kathleen Hillenmeyer. "Mother, Daughter Died Together: Memories and Tears for Four Killed in Falmouth," *CE*, March 7, 1997, A1.

"24 Hours of Terror," *KP*, March 22, 1997, 1.

Melissa J. Wickelhaus

FLOODS OF 1907. The winter of 1907 proved to be a hard one for Northern Kentuckians, especially those in Campbell and Kenton counties. Two devastating floods occurred. In the flood of January 1907, it took five days, from January 16 through January 21, for the waters to crest at 65.2 feet. Then during the night of January 21, temperatures plummeted to the low teens, and a fierce snowstorm with very high winds caused additional damage to property and prevented rescuers from reaching people in peril. The waters receded as slowly as they had risen, prolonging the misery of the thousands of people misplaced by the natural catastrophe.

In Campbell Co., the city of Newport suffered the most, for the Licking River to its west also overran its banks; floodwaters from the Ohio River and the Licking River inundated 45 city blocks of Newport, submerging hundreds of homes and businesses and forcing thousands of residents to flee. Dayton and Bellevue were flooded as well, but not as severely as Newport. In Kenton Co., Covington's difficulties were compounded as Banklick and DeCoursey Creeks overran their banks, causing waters to reach as far as Madison Ave. Ludlow and Bromley also had major areas completely swamped. Another consequence of the high waters was that rail service on both sides of the Ohio ceased, cutting off the delivery of freight and coal. The reported loss was about $7.5 million in business; however, very few people lost their lives as a direct result of the flooding waters.

Northern Kentucky was just beginning to recover from the January catastrophe when, as a result of heavy rains in Pennsylvania and southern Ohio, the Ohio River rose out of its banks again in March and reached 62.1 feet. The river rose quickly between March 14 and 18 and receded rapidly. However, owing to the heavy rains and already-saturated lands, there was considerably more damage caused by mudslides and sinking roads. Buildings that survived the January waters succumbed to the March flood because of their weakened state. Again, men were thrown out of work, rail transportation was disrupted, and people were displaced. This time, though, frigid temperatures did not follow the flood.

KP, January 14–February 1, March 13–21, 1907.

Blanche Gaynor

FLOODS OF 1913 Northern Kentucky experienced severe floods in both January and March of 1913, when the Ohio River and its tributaries crested at new heights of 62.2 and 69.9 feet, respectively. In January 1913, an unusually warm month, there was an exceptionally high amount of rainfall throughout Kentucky, 11.89 inches. Every river in the state flooded. In Campbell Co. the Licking River jumped its banks on January 6 and then combined with floodwaters from the nearby Ohio River. Newport was referred to as "the New Venice." Rescuers came from Cleveland and Louisville, and soon breadlines formed. In Kenton Co., Bromley, Covington, and Ludlow, and in Campbell Co., Melbourne, Ross, and Silver Grove all experienced flooding from the Ohio River and its tributaries. In Mason Co. the floodwaters flowed east of the Limestone Creek Bridge in Maysville. The Ohio River overran the levees in Louisville in Jefferson Co. and at Paducah in McCracken Co.; towns in Ohio Co. along the Green River were submerged. On January 13, temperatures plummeted and a wind and snow storm lashed the Northern Kentucky region, making rescues difficult and flattening houses whose foundations had been weakened by the floodwaters. By the time the flood crested on January 14 in Northern Kentucky, hundreds of thousands of dollars in damage had been done, as many as 8,000 residents were homeless, businesses and schools were closed, streetcar and rail service had been discontinued, and coal shipments had been suspended.

Northern Kentucky was just beginning to recover from the January catastrophe when two months later, from March 13 to 27, heavy rainstorms dropped from two to seven inches of rain in 24-hour periods on the region. There were severe winds, squalls, gales, and snowstorms. The

Looking north on Monmouth St. from Third St., Newport, in April 1913.

resulting floodwaters kept building until April 1, when they crested at 69.9 feet, 7.7 feet higher than the record reached in January. In Campbell Co., Newport once again was marooned, with 90 city blocks under water and 12,000 people homeless. In Kenton Co., the city of Bromley was half submerged and Ludlow was described as marooned. Covington was able to send relief help to Newport, Bromley, and Ludlow. In a contemporary account recording business and personal losses from these floods, the South Covington & Cincinnati State Rye Company stated its loss as "Enormous. Can't estimate." The losses in Newport alone amounted to $200,000. The March flooding left people cut off from food and coal supplies; communities were subjected to grave health concerns and looting, as well as dangers caused by wildlife (for example, snakes sought refuge in the same places where people went); and an unknown number of people died from drowning, exposure, or disease.

While the Ohio and Licking Rivers ravaged Northern Kentucky, the Great Miami River devastated much of the Dayton, Ohio, area, killing 454 people and leaving 40,000 homeless. The state of Indiana also suffered a heavy loss of life due to this same period of flooding. The floods of 1913 made the all-time "Top Disasters: Floods and Tsunamis" list with a total of 732 people killed. In the aftermath of these floods, there was a renewed outcry, from President Franklin D. Roosevelt (1933–1945) and many others, for a congressionally funded flood-control program in the region. In response the Flood Control Act of 1936 was finally passed by the U.S. Congress in June 22, 1936, but it came too late to help prevent the devastating **flood of 1937** that occurred in the Ohio River Valley when once again the Ohio River and its tributaries overflowed their banks.

"Bromley Is Nearly Half Submerged," *KP*, January 29, 1913, 6.

Dick, David, and Eulalie C. Dick. *Rivers of Kentucky*. North Middleton, Ky.: Plum Lick, 2001.

"The Flood in Newport," *KP*, January 31, 1913, 2.

"Flood Waters Have Invaded Newport," *KP*, January 11, 1913, 1.

"Ludlow Marooned; Fights the Waters," *KP*, January 29, 1913, 6.

"North Kentucky Suffers Worse Than in 1884 Flood," *KP*, January 31, 1913, 1.

"Sixty Blocks under Water in Newport," *KP*, January 28, 1913, 1.

"With Cincinnati Cut Off by Flood, Key to Vast Territory Is Lost," *KP*, April 2, 1913, 1.

Blanche Gaynor

FLORA. At the time of the European exploration and settlement of Northern Kentucky, the landscape in this region was primarily covered with closed forests, but pockets of open forests, glades, and prairies were also present. Geographically, the area is about evenly divided between the Outer Bluegrass (OBg) and Eden Shale Belt (ESB) subregions of the Bluegrass region (see **Eden Shale Farm**). Parts of the OBg experienced Pleistocene glaciation, especially deposits of outwash, and these influenced topographic, geologic, and edaphic diversity, which in turn caused biological diversity.

Today's highly modified landscape is the result of more than 200 years of land-use changes including clearing of forests for agriculture (crops and livestock raising), urbanization and suburban sprawl, and the building of roads and highways. Remnants of original vegetation, however, provide information about the region's native flora.

Closed forests are found on uplands and lowlands. Upland forest associations include Mixed Mesophytic, similar to those in Eastern Kentucky but without hemlock. These are most prominent in dissected areas of Kansan glacial outwash. The dominant trees are sugar maple (*Acer saccharum*), basswood (*Tilia americana*), beech (*Fagus grandifolia*), white ash (*Fraxinus americana*), yellow poplar (*Liriodendron tulipifera*), and red oak (*Quercus rubra*); locally, yellow buckeye (*Aesculus octandra*) is found. These forests have a rich herbaceous flora reflecting microenvironmental and microclimatic influences.

Beech and beech-maple forests are now rare but formerly occupied the upland flats where loess deposits and Rossmoyne (glacial) soils predominate. **Newport Central Catholic High School** in Newport was constructed atop a hill on a loess deposit in the mid-1950s. Oak-ash-maple forests are found on slopes where glacial deposits have been eroded. Oak-hickory forests are most prominent on the ridges and V-shaped valleys of the ESB. These forests are dominated by white (*Quercus alba*) and red (*Q. rubra*) oaks and by hickories, shagbarks (*Carya ovata*), and pignuts (*C. glabra*). Sugar maple is now the subcanopy dominant.

Two types of forest are found in the lowlands, on the floodplains of the Ohio and Licking rivers and their leading tributaries. Typical floodplain forests are characterized by various combinations of silver maples (*Acer saccharinum*), cottonwoods (*Populus deltoids*), box elders (*A. negundo*), green ashes (*Fraxinus pennsylvanicum*), and willows (*Salix* spp.). Depression forests along the Ohio River are uncommon. Their dominants are pin oak (*Q. palustris*), red maple (*A. rubrum*), green ash, American elm (*Ulmus americana*), and swamp white oak (*Q. bicolor*). The herbs in this association are adapted to hydric conditions.

Open forests include the blue ash–oak savanna–woodland in the vicinity of Washington and Mayslick, Mason Co. These forests were composed of wide-spaced open-grown trees that were found on rich soils and rolling topography. Blue ash (*Fraxinus quadrangulata*), bur oak (*Q. macrocarpa*), and chinquapin oak (*Q. muehlenbergii*) characterized these communities.

Glades are treeless or almost treeless areas where limestone or dolomitic bedrock is at or near the surface. They may be surrounded by trees, usually red cedar (*Juniperus virginiana*). The flora consists mainly of herbaceous plants. Glades are found in the vicinity of the **Blue Licks Battlefield State Resort Park**.

Prairies in Northern Kentucky are exceedingly rare, but a few have been found on exposed glacial outcrops in Boone Co. Grasses including little bluestem (*Schizacrium scoparium*), Indian grass (*Sorgastrum nutans*), and side-oats grama (*Bouteloua curtipendula*) are common associates along with a number of other herbs.

Across the region, flora is rich and diverse, reflecting both habitat diversity and disturbance. Two federally listed plants, Short's goldenrod (*Solidago shortii*) and running buffalo clover (*Trifolium stolonifera*), are known to occur in Northern Kentucky. Other species of special interest include ginseng (*Panax quinquefolia*), synandra (*Synandra hispidula*), goldenseal (*Hydrastis canadensis*), Great Plain's ladies' tresses (*Spiranthes manicamporum*), and side-oats grama.

Throughout much of the area, nonnative plants (exotics) have become established and pose problems to native plants and communities. The two species that appear to be the most difficult to eradicate are Amur honeysuckle (*Lonicera maackii*) and false garlic mustard (*Allairia petiolata*).

Baskin, J. M., and C. C. Baskin. "A Floristic Study of a Cedar Glade in Blue Licks Battlefield State Park, Kentucky." *Castanea* 50, no. 9 (1985): 9–25.

Bryant, W. S. "Oak-Hickory Forest of the Eden Shale Belt: A Preliminary Report," *Transactions of the Kentucky Academy of Science* 42 (1981): 41–45.

———. "Savanna-Woodland in the Outer Bluegrass of Kentucky," *Transactions of the Kentucky Academy of Science* 44 (1983): 45–49.

Bryant, W. S., S. L. Galbraith, and M. E. Held. 2004. "Natural Terrestrial Vegetation of Boone County, Kentucky," *Journal of the Kentucky Academy of Science* 65 (2004): 132–39.

William S. Bryant

FLORENCE. Florence, the largest and most industrialized city in Boone Co., is located in the east-central part of the county, along I-75. It was designated a third-class city in 1958. Proximity to major transportation avenues has been an important force in the development of this city.

Florence was first called Crossroads, because it was situated where the road to Louisville, the Georgetown Rd. (later the **Covington and Lexington Turnpike**), and the road to Burlington, the county seat, all met. In 1805, 11 people from the Germanna Colonies of Madison and Culpepper counties in Virginia settled in the Crossroads area. They organized the **Hopeful Lutheran Church** in January 1806, which was the first Lutheran church west of the Allegheny Mountains. By 1818 the stagecoach line owned and operated by Abner Gaines of Walton (see **Gaines Tavern**) stopped regularly in Florence to change horses. This stagecoach ran from Cincinnati to Lexington three times a week. In 1821 the town changed its name from Crossroads to Maddentown in honor of prominent citizen Thomas Madden, a lawyer from Covington, who operated the town's Inn & Tavern. By 1825 Madden had moved to Missouri, and the town was renamed Connersville for another prominent land owner, Jacob Conner.

In 1828 Connersville applied to the U.S. Post Office Department for a post office. Although the application was approved, it was necessary to change the town's name, since there was already a Connersville in Harrison Co., Ky. The Post Office Department offered two choices for a new name, and 16 of the 25 eligible citizens voted for Florence as the new name of the post office and the town.

When the Kentucky legislature incorporated Florence in 1830, the town had a population of 63 and a physical area of less than five acres. The town trustees were William T. Bainbridge; Pitman Cloudas, who was also the first postmaster; B. A. Collins; Jacob Shotts; and Henry Stuck. In 1842 the Kentucky legislature expanded the town's limits to just over 50 acres.

The largest influence of this growth, just after Florence's incorporation, was to place it on heavily traveled roads. By about 1840 the Covington and Lexington Turnpike was macadamized to Florence, enabling individual farmers to drive their livestock and crops to the Cincinnati markets. Business boomed in Florence to support the increased traffic. Kentucky historian **Lewis Collins** reported that in 1847 Florence had two churches, three doctors, two stores, two inns, two schools, four mechanics' shops, and a population of 200. Also in 1847, a new road to Union opened, today U.S. 42. Within three years, by 1850, the population of Florence rose by 25 percent, to 252.

Through most of the 19th century, Florence prospered and had a constant influx of residents. Among the families that came to live in Florence during this time was the Nelson and Sophia Lloyd family. The Lloyds, who were both teachers from New York, moved to Boone Co. around 1853, and by 1856 they had settled in Florence. Nelson Lloyd opened a school in the lower floor of the Florence Town Hall. Their son **John Uri Lloyd**, who held an affinity for Florence all of his life, had been born April 19, 1849, in New York. He became a world-famous novelist at the turn of the 20th century and was instrumental in the Eclectic Pharmacy movement. Several novels by John Uri Lloyd were based on his childhood in Florence. His most famous book, ***Stringtown on the Pike***, popularized Stringtown as the nickname for Florence. Lloyd also wrote an account of the **Civil War** fighting that occurred near Florence.

On September 17, 1862, an advance guard of a detachment of the Confederate Army that had camped at **Snow's Pond** met with Union men of the 10th Kentucky Cavalry who were in Florence, and a small running skirmish occurred. As the Confederates were retreating south down the road, firing back, a stray bullet killed Larken Vaughn, a citizen of Florence, who was standing on the corner of Main and Girard Sts. Men who were wounded in this incident were taken to the **Florence Christian Church**, which served as a hospital.

An attraction of the Florence area during the 19th century was the county's agricultural fair. The first fair, in 1855, was on the Kenton-Boone county line. No fairs were held during the war, but they resumed afterward and continued until 1881. A larger fair was organized and incorporated in 1896 by a group called the Northern Kentucky Fair Society. They built an amphitheater and permanent livestock stalls on the land of William Carpenter, located on the southeast corner of U.S. 42 and U.S. 25 (**Dixie Highway**). The site was enclosed by Gibbons St. off of U.S. 42 and Smith St., off of the Dixie Highway. These two streets remain connected today by Fair St. in Florence. The Northern Kentucky Agricultural Fair operated at this location until 1932, featuring events that ranged from livestock showings to horseracing. The fair then moved to the Harvest Home fairgrounds in Limaburg and a few years later moved to its current location, the Boone Co. Fairgrounds in Burlington.

In 1877 the **Cincinnati Southern Railroad**, bypassing Florence, established a depot at Greenwood Lake, currently Erlanger. The railway provided a faster way for farmers to move produce and livestock to the markets of Cincinnati and Lexington. For nearly 50 years during this period, the population and businesses of Florence declined. By the 1880 census, the population had decreased to 309, a loss of 63 people. By 1900, Florence had only 258 residents and one of the oldest hotels operating in town, the Southern Hotel, had closed. In 1920 the population had increased only to 268. Although Florence was no longer a booming city, there were important improvements during this time. It acquired electricity in 1917, natural gas lines in 1926, and city water in 1933. In 1931 a three-story brick school, which stands today, was built on Center St. By 1940 the population of Florence had grown to 776.

The 1940s and 1950s were an active time for Florence. The increased availability of the automobile brought more and more people to settle in Florence, thus turning it into a bedroom community. There were major road projects, not the least of which was the construction of an interstate highway, I-75, which cuts right through the middle

Main St., Florence, ca. 1960.

of Florence. The rationale for the location of this road, in discussions as early as 1945, was based on the thought that a better road from Covington to Erlanger would ensure the longevity of the **Cincinnati/Northern Kentucky International Airport**. The airport, which had been used by the military during **World War II**, was opened in 1947 for commercial flights, stimulating more traffic and business in Florence. Construction of I-75 did not finally begin until 1955, because of necessary changes in the road location. However, Florence was quickly revitalizing and becoming a bedroom community. In the 1950s the **Northern Kentucky Industrial Foundation** started the Florence Industrial Park, which has grown to include 57 industries and employ 8,000 people. In addition, annexation during the 1950s increased the physical area of Florence.

After the opening of I-75 in 1963, Florence was well on its way to becoming the major economic force in Boone Co. It had far surpassed its old rivals of Walton and Erlanger as an industrial center in Northern Kentucky. In 1961 **Carroll "Hop" Ewing** was elected mayor of Florence. During his 20 years as mayor, he was instrumental in the growth of Florence. He helped to create the Florence fire and police departments, and he regularly encouraged industries to build in Florence, spurring further economic growth of the city. He was also directly responsible for the one structure in town that is instantly recognizable by outsiders and has been featured in national magazines and newspapers, the "Florence Y'all" water tower. The water tower was completed in 1974 on land that was donated by the developers of the **Florence Mall**, which was under construction. When the tower went up, the name "Florence Mall" was painted on it, but since state highway regulations forbade such advertising, the water tower had to be repainted. Ewing, after playing with the words, came up with the solution: to paint the legs of the M white, matching the background paint, and add an apostrophe. The "Florence Y'all" water tower is now a landmark seen by thousands of I-75 travelers yearly.

The Florence Mall opened in September 1976. With its proximity to I-75 and easy access from the highway, this new commercial mall soon became a fixture for tri-state shoppers. The economic success of the mall encouraged further development along Mall Rd., where seven separate business complexes have since been built. A revitalization project is currently in the works for the Mall Rd. area.

In the 1980s and 1990s, the shopping district of Florence expanded to include new stores and attractions on Houston Rd. Turfway Park, once known as **Latonia Racecourse**, is a thoroughbred racetrack that has been located in Florence since 1959 and had long been surrounded by farmland. But after Jerry Carroll bought it in 1986 and renovated it, a large number of shops and restaurants have been opened around the track, creating the largest shopping district in Florence today.

The 1980s also saw the development of cultural organizations like the Arts Council; the **Florence Community Band**, started by Carl Biehler in 1984; and the Florence Community Chorus, organized in 1989.

Most of the city's offices and the Florence Police Department moved into a new 90,000-square-foot city building on Ewing Blvd. in 1998, having outgrown their previous location on U.S. 42. The new city building holds all the government offices of the City of Florence as well as some state offices. There are also meeting rooms for public events.

The Florence Recreation and Parks Department in 2003 opened a 20,000-square-foot park featuring the new Aquatic Center and a skate park. The Florence Aquatic Center has a swimming pool, a lazy river, and other water activity areas, as well as skateboard ramps for all skill levels. Also in 2003, Florence acquired a Frontier League baseball team, the **Florence Freedom**, whose home is the Champion Window Field, a stadium next to I-75 that seats 4,500. Its lawn area allows for a maximum capacity of 7,000. The field also has a playground. The baseball games, geared toward families, are well attended; the city of Florence has embraced the team.

Although it has grown from the least-populated city in Boone Co. to the largest in population, Florence has retained its warm atmosphere. Moreover, since Boone Co. is the second-fastest-growing county in Kentucky and new industries are establishing bases of operations in Florence, it seems likely that the population of Florence will continue to increase. In 2000 Florence had a population of 23,551.

Conrad, William. *Yesterdays: An Enriching Adventure in Boone County's Past*. Florence, Ky.: Boone Co. Schools, ca. 1981.

——, comp. *41042, a Story about Florence, Kentucky and the Florence Rotary Club*. Florence, Ky.: The Club, 1989.

——, ed. *Boone County: The Top of Kentucky, 1792–1992*. Fort Mitchell, Ky.: Picture This! Books, 1992.

Reis, Jim. "Birth of I-75, the Groundwork for the Region's Primary Route Was Laid in the 1950s," *KP*, August 22, 2005, 4K.

Tanner, Paul. *Florence, Kentucky: The First Century*. Frankfort, Ky.: Paul Tanner, 1993.

U.S. Census Bureau. "American Fact Finder. Data Set. Census 2000 Summary File 1 (SF1) 100-Percent Data. Custom Table." www.census.gov (accessed September 7, 2006).

Yealey, A. M. *History of Boone County Kentucky*. Covington, Ky., 1960.

Laurie Wilcox

FLORENCE BAPTIST CHURCH. The Florence Baptist Church was constituted in 1855 with 11 members, most of them from the Dry Creek Baptist Church in Kenton Co. The cornerstone indicates that the church's first meetinghouse was built that year. Gen. **Leonard Stephens**, who lived at Beech Grove in what is now the Richardson Rd. area, was one of the earliest leaders in the new church. Like most churches of that time, it met only once a month. A *Covington Journal* article in 1858 referred to the congregation as "the little church at the crossroads," since it was situated at the intersection of the **Covington and Lexington Turnpike** (modern U.S. 25) and the road to Union (modern U.S. 42). The church had a small membership when it began, and a few years after the **Civil War** it had only 29 members.

As the 20th century commenced, and railroads became the primary means of travel, traffic from Covington to Lexington bypassed Florence. When stagecoaches no longer came through town on a regular basis, the town suffered. At this time the church met on an irregular basis for several years. The city was cut off from easy access to other areas, and the church did not thrive.

In 1908 the church was reorganized; a new covenant was drawn up, and 30 members signed it. Under the leadership of W. A. M. Wood, the Florence Baptist Church erected a new building of modified Greek Revival design, which was completed in 1930. It was located in front of the original meetinghouse. By 1931, when the Covington-to-Louisville highway (U.S. 42) was completed, the Florence population had increased to 450 and the church's membership rose to 132. In 1931 Rev. R. F. DeMoisey, a native of Walton, was called as pastor. During his 10-year pastorate, the church's membership nearly doubled, from 132 members to 247. Rev. Harold Wainscott served the church as pastor for six and a half years, during the latter part of **World War II** and the years following. From about 1953 to 1958, Pastor Roy A. Johnson ministered at the Florence Baptist Church, and when he retired in 1958, the church had more than 900 members. Rev. Bob Couch was the next pastor. In 1960 the Florence Baptist Church sponsored the Greenview Baptist Mission on Ky. Rt. 18 and called Bob Campbell, who had grown up in the Florence church, as pastor. The Greenview mission church was organized by the Florence Baptist Church in 1963, and Campbell later became an army chaplain.

Rev. Jack Sanford began serving as pastor in 1963, and he led the church through a major building renovation in 1966–1967. The new structure, with a brick and stone exterior, is contemporary in style and has a 100-foot, diamond-shaped spire. Its seating capacity of 1,000 was enough to accommodate the Kentucky Baptist Convention, which met at the church in 1968. Rev. W. Bill Jones pastored the Florence Baptist Church from 1971 to 1980. During his ministry, the church purchased a bus for the first time, and Rev. William Hodge became associate pastor. The Kentucky Baptist Convention again met at the Florence Baptist Church in 1977. Rev. Gary Watkins, who was called as pastor in 1981, served a little over three years. Dr. Timothy Alexander, the current pastor, came in 1985. In that year, the church dedicated its new preschool-office building. By the beginning of 1987, Florence Baptist Church's membership was greater than 1,700. In the late 1980s, the church began a television ministry. During the 1990s, Herbert Booth, MD, a prominent physician in Florence and a member of the church, began medical mission trips to foreign nations. In 1994 the church began HOPE Ministries, a volunteer group to help the needy. The church has ordained eight men and has licensed seven to preach. In late 1999, the deacons recommended that the church purchase 67 acres at the intersection of I-75 and Mount Zion Road. In September 2006, groundbreaking was held for a new $15 million church facility on Mount Zion Rd. With a sanctuary seating 1,300, the new church, designed by Terry Simmons of Lexington, was opened in 2009.

Capek, Michael. *Church at the Crossroads: The Story of Florence Baptist Church, 1855–2005*. Knoxville: Tennessee Valley, 2005.

"Florence Baptist Ready to Grow," *KE*, August 8, 2004, C3.

"Florence Congregation in Existence 85 Years," *KTS*, May 3, 1930, 5.

"New Church for Florence," *KP*, July 19, 1929, 1.

James R. Duvall

FLORENCE CHRISTIAN CHURCH. The Christian Church in Florence in Boone Co., a **Disciples of Christ** congregation, was organized in 1831 and was the first church built in the city. It was one of the original Disciples of Christ branches in Kentucky. The first sanctuary was a log building that burned within a couple of years. The second structure was built of brick, reportedly in 1835, but the land was not transferred until April 1842, when John Stephens sold the property to the trustees of the church (George McDonald, William Nichols, Thomas Sanford, and James Varner). The brick building served the congregation, with occasional remodeling, until 1965, when the "Little White Church," as it was affectionately known, was torn down and replaced in its present location at the corner of U.S. 25 (see **Dixie Highway**) and U.S. 42 in Florence.

In September 1862 the Union Army under Gen. Lew Wallace, which was stationed at Fort Mitchell, was retreating north after fighting in a small engagement in Walton, at **Snow's Pond**, against some of Confederate general Kirby Smith's men. As the Union soldiers retreated, they were firing back down the road, and a stray bullet killed a civilian named Larken Vaughn at the corner of Main and Girard Sts. According to local author **John Uri Lloyd**, the Union soldiers who were wounded in this running skirmish were taken to the Florence Christian Church, which was being used as a hospital.

The church has a long history of community involvement. Its members helped in the recovery efforts of the Ohio River **flood of 1937** by drying linens for the local St. Elizabeth Hospital (see **St. Elizabeth Medical Center**). Emma Schild organized the church's Ladies Auxiliary in the early 1920s. The Missionary Society was organized in 1920 and led by Mrs. Charles Bradford. Rev. H. C. Runyan initiated Sunday school services in the early 1900s.

In 1948 Rev. Herbert L. Reid of Lexington came to minister to the congregation. He proposed and edited a monthly ecumenical newspaper, the *Stringtown Christian*. Although Reid left in 1951, this publication was continued under Rev. R. C. White. In addition to covering events of all the Christian churches in the Florence area and current events, the newspaper had historical articles written by local historian A. M. Yealey.

The Florence Christian Church's commitment to the community took on a tangible form in 1978 when it opened a day care center. In 1981 the church dedicated the Florence Christian Center. This senior living facility was expanded in 1985 and again in 1995. Today in its four buildings it has 215 one-bedroom apartments in which seniors can enjoy retirement life. More recently, the church has sponsored refugees from Bosnia, gathered items for the victims of Hurricane Katrina, and participated in building houses with Habitat for Humanity.

The current pastors of the church are Jerry and Denise Zehr, a husband-and-wife team hired in 1997 who have shared the duties of pastor. Denise is one of the first female pastors to serve a church in Boone Co. They have also embraced new technologies by hosting a Web page and having their services aired on local cable channels.

Florence Christian Church is looking toward the future: it recently purchased 12 acres in Union, where it will build a new satellite church while retaining the one in Florence. The new church is to be named Harmony Place; a nearby house will be used until the sanctuary is completed.

The Florence Christian Church is a liberal Christian church that has a strong respect for and tolerance of differences, which is emphasized by a sign on the front of the church that reads "Come as you are." Unlike many churches in Northern Kentucky, the church is gaining members. Membership increased from 180 in 1997 to 260 in 2006.

Conrad, William. *Yesterdays: An Enriching Adventure in Boone County's Past*. Florence, Ky.: Boone Co. Schools, 1987.

"Different Kind of Church," *KP*, July 21, 2006, A1.

"Filling a Growing Need Churches Are Establishing Homes for Older Citizens," *KP*, March 13, 1995, 1K–2K.

"Florence Church Building," *KTS*, July 24, 1956, 4A.

Schramm, Lillian. *History of the Florence Christian Church, 1831–1981*, 1981. Available at Boone Co. Public Library, Burlington, Ky.

Laurie Wilcox

FLORENCE COMMUNITY BAND. The Florence (Ky.) Community Band, established in 1984, is the only formally organized community band in the Northern Kentucky region. The band was initially organized by Carl Biehler, a band-lover with a passion for music, who formed the group with 13 members and held rehearsals during the first few summers in his backyard. Neighbors would gather to visit with one another and enjoy the lighthearted spirit of these rehearsals. The band is supported and sanctioned by the city of Florence and other generous sponsors. It is a traditional community band made up of amateur and semiprofessional musicians from both Florence and the surrounding communities. A variety of music is performed, including "traditional" band music, show tunes, marches, and big band music. In age, the band's members range from teenagers to senior citizens; and they represent a wide variety of professions, including area music teachers and band directors. The band normally performs with 30 to 40 musicians playing at any given concert, but the band's "membership" roll has about twice that number.

Performances take place in churches, parks, festivals, parades, and other venues. Summer is generally the most active season, with a concert scheduled every two to three weeks. There are occasional concerts in the other seasons, but that is also when the band reads and prepares new music. Initially, the band practiced in the former Florence City Building, when not rehearsing in Biehler's backyard. When the group grew in numbers, rehearsals were moved to the band room of **Boone Co. High School** in Florence. After several years of growth, both by the community band and by high school bands, scheduling of rehearsals in the high school became problematic and the Florence Community Band moved to a succession of empty office spaces in the Florence area. Currently, it rehearses every Monday evening at the Florence Government Building on Ewing Blvd.; rehearsals take place year-round, with occasional breaks over the winter holidays. Over the years, various individuals have conducted the ensemble, beginning with Biehler and Tom Houston. Other conductors of note have been Gary Adams, Dennis Akers, Tonya Bromley, Royce Crabtree, Keith Howard, Constance Sanders, Todd Whitford, Gary Whitis, and Hugh Wickes, the band's current director.

Harden, Crystal. "Band Hits High Notes with Persistent Director," *KP*, May 10, 1989, 1KK.

Roberts, Alice Kennelly. "Community Band Began with One Man's Dream," *KP*, January 25, 1989, 2KK.

Simmons, Tim. "Florence Band Swings to Merry Melody," *KP*, August 29, 1984, 1K.

Perry Bratcher

FLORENCE FREEDOM. A resurgent interest in minor league **baseball** surfaced in Northern Kentucky in 2003, with the arrival of the Florence Freedom. The team is part of the independent Frontier League based in Zanesville, Ohio, and is not associated with major league baseball (MLB). Without the permission of the Cincinnati Reds, no team can be a part of MLB and operate within 25 miles of downtown Cincinnati. The Freedom team plays in Florence, Ky., at the southeast quadrant of I-75 and U.S. 42, only 10 miles from the home field of the Reds.

The Freedom franchise began in Johnstown, Pa. The team was known as the Johnstown Johnnies before moving to Erie, Pa., where it was called the Erie Steal. After the 2002 season, the franchise was sold and moved to Florence. It played its 2003 home games in Hamilton, Ohio, while a new stadium, Champion Windows Field, was under construction in Boone Co. In 2004 the owner of the Freedom was charged with fraud. Creditors lost some $3 million, and eventually the owner was sentenced to five years in prison. In 2005 Northern Kentucky businessman Clint Brown acquired the team, and 2006 was a successful season.

Several former Cincinnati Reds have been managers of the team: Tom Browning; Chris Sabo, who quit before ever coaching a game; and Pete Rose Jr. It is common to find Freedom players signing MLB contracts—which, after all, is the purpose of minor league baseball. The Freedom has brought the closeness and fun of minor league baseball to Northern Kentucky as affordable family summer evening entertainment, playing teams such as the Zanesville Greys, the Evansville Otters, and the Chillicothe Paints.

Florence Freedom. www.florencefreedom.com (accessed January 25, 2007).
Wikipedia. "Florence Freedom." www.en.wikipedia.org (accessed January 25, 2007).
Wilson, Denise. "For the Love of Baseball," *KP*, August 31, 2002, 1K.

FLORENCE HIGH SCHOOL. The Florence High School was established in 1911 because the new high school in Burlington, the county seat of Boone Co., was so far away from Florence. The **Burlington High School** had been started in response to a 1908 state law that required every county in Kentucky to have at least one high school located in the city that was the county seat. A petition filed with the county judge on April 5, 1909, had paved the way for a two-year, graded high school in Florence. To accommodate it, two rooms were added to the Florence Elementary School at U.S. 42 and Hopeful Rd. Upon completing the two-year program at Florence, students could continue their high school education at the Burlington High School or they could pay tuition and attend high school in Erlanger. The first four-year curriculum at Florence High School began in 1913, and the first class graduated in 1915. Florence High School, along with the Burlington, Hebron, and New Haven high schools, was consolidated into the **Boone Co. High School** in Florence in 1954.

Warner, Jennifer S. *Boone County: From Mastodons to the Millennium*. Burlington, Ky.: Boone Co. Bicentennial Book Committee, 1998

Gail Chastang

FLORENCE MALL. Northern Kentucky's largest shopping mall, Florence Mall, contains 3 department stores and 130 specialty shops. A shopping mall was planned for the Florence area as early as 1968; 100 acres of land was optioned in July 1973, ground was broken on December 31, 1973, and the $30 million project was opened and dedicated on September 22, 1976, initially with 85 retail stores. Sears had closed its retail outlet store in downtown Covington just two days before (see **Covington, Downtown**). Homart Development, the real estate arm of Chicago-based Sears, Roebuck and Company, developed the project. Original tenants included Sears, Pogue's, and Shillito's department stores. JCPenney arrived in July 1978. The mall is located west of and adjacent to I-75 (see **Expressways**), between Ky. Rt. 18 on the north and U.S. 42 on the south. Eventually, it contained 130 stores and 1 million square feet under its roof and was the first two-level mall in Kentucky and Greater Cincinnati; it radically changed retail shopping in Northern Kentucky. Downtown Newport (see **Monmouth St. Business District**) and downtown Covington, affected years earlier by the opening of the **Newport Shopping Center** and places like Expressway Plaza in Fort Mitchell, suffered further commercial decline.

The Florence Mall was sold to the Cincinnati-based Western-Southern Life Insurance Company for around $40 million in 1982, with Homart Development continuing as the mall management company; in 1994 the mall underwent a major renovation; and in 2000 the Woolly Mammoth Playland, a children's play area that tells the story of prehistoric Northern Kentucky, was opened on the mall's ground floor. In 2003 Chicago-based General Growth Properties purchased the mall, hoping to turn its new property into more of a lifestyle center. Through the year 2001, sales increased at Florence each year except for one year in the late 1980s. Occupancy of the mall's stores has generally been at 90 percent.

The Florence Mall has spawned all types of other retail development along the adjacent Mall Rd. The mall and the **Cincinnati/Northern Kentucky International Airport** are the two engines that have propelled the tremendous growth of Boone Co. The Florence Mall has come a long way from the days when Florence mayor **C. M. "Hop" Ewing** was dealing with the prematurely painted name of the mall on its million-gallon water tower and shrewdly came up with "Florence Y'all," in order to conform to statutory law not to advertise. But Florence Mall cannot afford to rest on its laurels, since new competitive venues such as **Newport-on-the Levee** and the reinvigorated **Crestview Hills Town Center** in Crestview Hills, both open-air lifestyle centers, keep springing up.

In recent years the Florence Mall area has become the largest retail market area in the state, generating some $5.1 million in state income tax revenue, $114 million in wages, and more than $15 million in state sales tax (from more than $250 million in total sales revenue).

Crowley, Patrick. "Florence Mayor Pushes for Renovations at Mall," *KE*, July 4, 2003, B3.
Driehaus, Bob. "Mall Led Way for Regional Shopping," *KP*, September 22, 2001, 1K.
——. "The Relentless Fight for Shoppers," *KP*, September 24, 2001, 1K.
"Florence Mall—Y'all," *Boone County Recorder*, June 8, 1988, 2.
"Opening Day Fever Hits Penney's," *KP*, July 8, 1978, 10K.
Paeth, Greg. "Keeping Up," *KP*, April 18, 2006, 1A.
——. "Malls Opening Pulled Retailer from Covington," *KP*, September 22, 2001, 9K.
"Plan Florence Mall," *KP*, September 13, 1968, 1K.

FLORENCE SPEEDWAY. The Florence Speedway is a half-mile, high-banked, clay oval automobile racing track located at 12234 U.S. 42, Union, Ky., approximately nine miles west of I-75 (see **Expressways**) in Boone Co. It was built during the 1950s, damaged by a fire in 1984, and rebuilt and reopened the same year. Jerry and Mona King have operated it since 1984. Since then, it has become one of the premier dirt late-model tracks in Kentucky. Hosting such prestigious dirt late-model events as the North/South 100, the Ralph Latham Memorial, and the Spring 50 has established the track as one of the elite racing venues in the dirt late-model world. The track generally operates on Saturdays from March through October with a regular racing program for late models, modifieds, super dirt stocks, and pure stocks.

"King's Florence Speedway." www.florencespeedway.com (accessed June 28, 2006).
"Racing's Dirty Side," *CP*, August 25, 2001, 9B.
Reis, Jim. "When Autos First Raced, World War I Hero Eddie Rickenbacker Won Race at Latonia," *KP*, May 21, 2001, 4K.
"Saturday Night at the Speedway," *KE*, May 11, 1995, B8.

Gail Chastang

FLOUR CREEK CHRISTIAN CHURCH. An independent Christian congregation, Flour Creek Christian Church is one of the oldest churches in Pendleton Co. William Masters, who became a church elder, organized it in September 1826 in the home of Robert Taylor, along with five charter members. This small band of founders soon moved their meetings to a little log schoolhouse with rough benches for seats, about 50 yards from where the present church, constructed in 1894, now stands. The membership first called George Fisher, an elder, to preach. He accepted the position and remained 35 years. In spring 1832 it was decided to build a more spacious building, and the next year Robert Taylor deeded to Charles Yelton and Samuel Cox, deacons of the church, a half-acre lot on which to build the new structure. A hewn log house measuring about 40 by 30 feet was erected near the location of the present church. By 1865 the log church building was too small for the congregation, so it was replaced with a larger building, dedicated in May 1866. Within 50 years, the church's membership had increased to more than 150. But in 1879 more than 20 members applied for and were given appropriate letters for the purpose of starting a Christian Church in Butler. On February 2, 1879, the Butler Christian Church was organized, and the members held services in what was known as the Union Church, above the town hall, until they could build a church building. In 1883 about 40 Flour Creek Christian Church members were given church letters for the purpose of organizing another church, which was to be known as the Pleasant Hill Christian Church, near Mount Auburn. A building for this congregation was dedicated September 2, 1883. Since it had followed the spin-off Christian Church established at Butler, the church at Pleasant Hill became known as the second daughter of Flour Creek Christian Church. In 1893 services were held by the Pleasant Hill Christian Church in a new white frame church. On June 6, 1920, a new brick building was dedicated at Pleasant Hill by the church, and this building continues in use today. In recent years the church there has been involved in nursing-home support and flood relief for the local community.

Belew, Mildred Bowden. *The First 200 Years of Pendleton County.* Falmouth, Ky.: Privately published, 1994.
Driehaus, Bob. "It Restores Your Faith in Human Race," *KP,* March 15, 1997, 5K.
"Religion Briefs," *KP,* February 19, 1994, 6K.

Mildred Belew

FOLSOM. This settlement, located at the confluence of Ten Mile and Eagle Creeks in a scenic valley in the western part of Grant Co., was first called Lawrenceburg after one of the early families in the area. Other early local family names were Delph, Jump, and Sipple. W. H. B. New donated the land for a schoolhouse at Folsom in the early 1830s. John Ford, who had acquired some of the lands surrounding Folsom in 1811, built a stone house that bears his name near Folsom during the 1830s. Ford died in 1840, and the property passed to his son Elijah. In 1856 a slave named Warrick murdered Elijah Ford. Warrick's trial, conviction, and execution followed in rapid order.

In 1857 the Vine Run Baptist Church, named for a nearby hill covered with vines, was organized at Folsom. Early leaders of the new church included Joseph Ambrose, J. M. Arnold, and J. T. Elliston. The Vine Run Baptist Church and the Old Vine Run Cemetery are located about nine miles northwest of Dry Ridge on the Dry Ridge–Warsaw Rd. (Ky. Rt. 467). When it was inventoried in 1985, the cemetery contained 185 identified graves and about 86 unmarked graves. Located on the same road, about six miles from Dry Ridge, is the New Vine Run Cemetery; it was found to contain more than 260 graves in 1987. In 1931 a serious fire at the store in Folsom caused damage valued at $8,000.

Conrad, John B., ed. *History of Grant County.* Williamstown, Ky.: Grant Co. Historical Society, 1992.
"Store Burns—Blame Lighting for $8000 Blaze at Folsom, Ky." *KP,* June 15, 1931, 1.

John B. Conrad

Newport Catholic High School football game at Newport Stadium, E. Ninth St., Newport, ca. 1949.

FOOTBALL. Football has been played in Northern Kentucky since the beginning of the 20th century. The football rivalry between the nearby University of Cincinnati (UC) and Miami University of Ohio dates back to the 1890s, and many Northern Kentuckians attended these schools or at least supported their teams. The old Covington High School, **Newport High School**, and **Highlands High School** were playing football in the second decade of the 1900s, at places such as Wiedemann Field in Newport's **West End** along the Licking River and at the Covington Ball Park along **Willow Run** Creek. Lester Black, a chemistry teacher, coached the Covington High gridiron squad. The first Highlands coach, Thomas K. "T. K." Lewis, was discovered in his team's huddle, dressed in uniform and illegally playing in a game, just before **World War I**. Enforcement of the meager rules of the game was lax back then. Lewis later participated in both world wars and, during the 1960s, taught chemistry at **Newport Central Catholic High School**.

In 1921 there was a short-lived National Football League (NFL) team in Cincinnati, the Cincinnati Celts, which played a total of four games. The first person from Northern Kentucky to score a touchdown in the NFL was Covington High graduate Earl "Yellow" Hauser, as an end for the Celts. Later in 1933–1934, a second attempt was made to establish an NFL team in Cincinnati, the Cincinnati Reds, but it ended after 17 games. Covington native and **Holmes High School** graduate (1925) Stanley M. Stewart was a member of the NFL Reds. Later he was president of his family's **Stewart Iron Works** from 1944 to 1955. The late 1930s witnessed another fleeting effort to bring professional football to Cincinnati, again before the modern era of the televised game. This team was the original Cincinnati Bengals, which had as its first quarterback **Bill Schwarberg**, a Covington native and a former Holmes High School and UC star. The team played at the home of the National League's Cincinnati Reds, Crosley Field in Cincinnati, on a gridiron squeezed tightly onto the baseball field.

Lasting NFL professional football made an appearance in the region in 1968, with the arrival of Paul Brown's modern Cincinnati Bengals, who played their first two seasons at UC's Nippert Stadium. The team was later moved to Riverfront Stadium, and then to the nearby Paul Brown Stadium, both along the Ohio River, within easy walking distance for Northern Kentucky followers. Before the Bengals, the region's fans of professional football followed the Cleveland Browns, whose games were televised during the 1950s and 1960s on Sunday afternoons and were sponsored by Carling's Black Label Beer (with the jingle "Hey Mabel, Black Label"). Some of those early 1950s Cleveland Brown teams had a backup quarterback from Fort Thomas, Ky., via St. Xavier High School in Cincinnati and the University of Notre Dame, **George W. Ratterman**, who became the reform sheriff of Campbell Co. in the early 1960s.

After the arrival of the modern Bengals in Cincinnati, some team members discovered the value of living in Northern Kentucky: Max Montoya; Boomer Eiasion; Ken Anderson; Chris Collingsworth, present Fort Thomas resident, national television football analyst, and Highlands High School supporter; and of late, former Bengal lineman Bruce Kozerski, who has been coaching football at **Holy Cross High School** in Latonia.

In the rural areas where high schools were small in enrollment and 11-man teams were difficult to raise, an 8-man-team league existed in the 1930s. In Kenton Co., the old **Crescent Springs High School** played in that league, as did **Hebron High School** and **Burlington High School** in Boone Co. before they were closed owing to consolidation.

At the college level, football mostly has been played at one of Cincinnati's two universities (UC or Xavier, the latter through 1971) or at the more distant University of Kentucky (UK) in Lexington. **Thomas More College** in Crestview Hills, Ky., began playing college-level football in 1990; Cincinnati's College of Mount St. Joseph had to become coed before establishing a similar program. Both schools have had some success at their level of play, with many graduates of Northern Kentucky high schools appearing on their rosters. Bill Erpenbeck (see **Erpenbeck Scandal**), a local homebuilder, in the late 1990s led an effort to entice **Northern Kentucky University** to begin a Division IIA football program. The university opted to delay football at the time. When there were military personnel stationed at the **Fort Thomas Military Reservation**, the U.S. Army fielded teams that played such opponents as UC and teams sponsored by the Covington **YMCA**. In 1918 UC beat the Fort Thomas Army (as the team was known), 6-0. The former Army team's gridiron at the fort is the playing field for the Highlands High School's soccer program today.

Football in the region has mainly involved high schools teams. Newport coach William "Blue" Foster kicked off the modern era of high school football on October 31, 1931, when Erlanger **Lloyd Memorial High School** traveled to play Newport High School in the region's first game at night. Newport won 60-6 at GOHI Field in the **West End** of the city. Temporary lighting was installed, and there was an agreement with the neighbors (but not with the nearby steel mill) that the lights would be turned off by 8:00 p.m. After that experiment, large crowds began to attend night games instead of the after-school contests previously held, and Friday evenings in the fall throughout Northern Kentucky have meant high school football and the sounds of marching bands ever since. Soon the 8:00 p.m. rule was no longer being enforced. The Works Progress Administration in the 1930s built lighted stadiums in Bellevue, Dayton, and Newport, Ky. In the 1940s and 1950s, Bellevue and Dayton High Schools had several very successful teams; since 1960 Beechwood, Covington Catholic, and Highlands high schools have dominated local gridirons. Except for Louisville's Trinity High School, Highlands has won more state championships (16) than any other team in the state; Beechwood has won 9, and Covington Catholic has 6 such trophies. Erlanger Lloyd has won 2 state championships: first in 1965, under Jack Turner in Class A, and then in 1976, in Class AAA under fabled coach Jim "Red Dog" Dougherty. Newport Central Catholic High School's coach Bob Schneider became the high school football coach with the most winnings in the state, amassing more than 300 victories over his 40-year career; he won his third state championship in 2006. Bellevue High School (see **Bellevue Public Schools**), **Conner High School** (while competing in its first season in 1983), and Dayton High School (see **Dayton Public Schools**) hold past state football championships.

In the 1920s the William Grant High School (see **Lincoln-Grant School**) of Covington fielded football teams. They played at the Covington Ball Park and at 15th St. and Eastern Ave. in Covington's **Eastside**. Race relations being what they were then, Grant High School, when not scheduled at home against another African American school, was forced to travel long distances out of town to play other African American teams. Paul Redden, a former player at Wilberforce College in Ohio, coached Grant's team. Grant's football program was disbanded after the 1932 season, with the opening of its new school building on Greenup St. in Covington. The team had been undefeated in 1929 and 1932, but the emphasis at Grant shifted to basketball because the school lacked a practice football field.

Numerous players from the region have played football at the professional level. Clearly, particularly after the 2005 professional season, the most notable football player to come out of Northern Kentucky is **Boone Co. High School** graduate (1996) **Shaun Alexander**. A running back in high school for coach Owen Hauck, Alexander went on to the University of Alabama, where in his senior year (2000) in a game against Louisiana State University he scored a record four rushing touchdowns. In 2005, while in his sixth year with the NFL's Seattle Seahawks, Alexander led his team to the Super Bowl. That season, he led the NFL in touchdowns and total rushing yards and was named the league's most valuable player, but he continues in pursuit of a Super Bowl ring. Alexander, much like former Bengal Doug Pelfrey, has set up a foundation to help the disadvantaged. In Alexander's case it is to help fatherless young men from Florence, Ky., where he was raised. The athletic field within the stadium at Boone Co. High School is named for him.

Irv Goode, also from Boone Co. High School (1958) and UK (1962), played the line some 13 seasons, mostly with the NFL's St. Louis Cardinals. The stadium at Boone Co. High School is named in his honor. John Shannon, UK (1987), is the third NFL player to come out of Boone Co. (1983). He played two seasons during the late 1980s with the Chicago Bears as a defensive end. Another NFL player is Marty Moore, from Highlands (1989) and UK (1994), who played linebacker for nine seasons, mostly with the New England Patriots; that team selected him as the last player in the 1994 NFL draft, the "anchor man" of the selection. Moore, although small for a linebacker, is quite a story, for most of his coaches told him he would never make it. Jeff Brady, from Newport Central Catholic High School (1987) and a walk-on player at UK (1991), was another linebacker who played five seasons with multiple teams. One time, as a Minnesota Viking, playing against the Bengals on a Sunday afternoon at Riverfront Stadium in Cincinnati, Brady intercepted a pass and ran it back for a touchdown in front of his family, the hometown crowd, and his former Newport Central Catholic coach, Bob Schneider.

Highlands's Chuck Kyle (1965), a linebacker who earned All-American honors at Purdue University (1969), played in the Canadian Football League (CFL). A plaque honoring Kyle's abilities hangs on a wall in his high school. Bob Dougherty, coach Jim "Red Dog" Dougherty's brother and one of the football-playing Dougherty brothers to come out of Bellevue High School (1949), played guard for the NFL's Los Angeles Rams in the early 1960s. Mark Pike, from **Dixie Heights High School** (1982) and Georgia Tech University (1986), was a special teams expert for more than 10 seasons with the NFL's Buffalo Bills. Bob DeMoss, of Dayton High School (1945), went to Purdue (1949) on a basketball scholarship but finished as an All-American football player and played with the second New York City NFL franchise, the Bulldogs/Yanks, in 1949. That team played "second fiddle" in New York City to the long-established New York Giants, and DeMoss, known as "De Mo," played backup quarterback for the Bulldogs/Yanks to Fort Thomas's George Ratterman. Lineman Hershel Turner, of **Campbell Co. High School** (1960) and UK (1964), played two seasons in the early 1960s with the St. Louis Cardinals. Doug Pelfrey came out of **Scott High School** (1989) and UK (1993) and in college specialized as a place-kicker. He was the field goal kicker for the Cincinnati Bengals for seven seasons, 1993–1999. There were seasons when if there had not been a Pelfrey field goal, the team would not have won a game. Today he continues his charitable work, known as Kicks for Kids, within the region.

There have been other pro players from the area. Bob "20 Grand" Davis, out of Dayton High School (1934) and UK (1938), played in the late 1930s with the NFL's New York Giants. Jack Gearding, from Campbell Co. High (1947) and Xavier University (1951), played in the CFL. Art Mergenthal, from Bellevue, Ky., Cincinnati's St. Xavier High (1939), and several colleges, the last being Notre Dame (1945), played guard and linebacker with the NFL's Los Angeles Rams in the late 1940s, before serving as a principal in the Bellevue School system for 30-plus years. Earl W. "Bill" Murray was part of the class of 1944 at Dayton High School and the Purdue class of 1950 and played in the NFL with the Baltimore Colts for a couple of seasons in the early 1950s as an offensive guard. Bob Ravensberg was from Bellevue High School (1943) and Indiana University (1947) and played two seasons in the NFL with the Chicago Bears during the late 1940s as an offensive end and a defensive back. Jerry Reynolds, from Highlands High School (1990) and the University of Nevada at Las Vegas (1994), played the line for the New York Giants for two seasons in the 1990s. Larry Schreiber, who was a running back at Dixie Heights High School (1965) and went to Tennessee Tech (1969), had a couple of good seasons in the NFL with the San Francisco Forty-Niners in the 1970s. And Jared Lorenzen, a former Greater Cincinnati Punt Pass and Kick Contest winner out of Highlands High (1999) and UK (2004), recently has taken a few snaps as the backup quarterback for the New York Giants.

Many football players from the area, too numerous to mention, ended their careers at the collegiate level. Some became prominent community leaders, including these: Bob White, from Holmes (1956) and Ohio State (1960), who was an All-American fullback under coach Woody Hayes in Columbus; the Burt brothers from Highlands, Jim and John (1959 and 1961), who played at Western Kentucky University; the Chalk brothers, from Newport Central Catholic (Mike [1972] played at Hanover in Indiana, and Dave [1977] went on to Cornell University); Bill Topmiller, from Covington Catholic (1971) and Vanderbilt University (1975), who played in the Peach Bowl in 1974; Phil Taliaferro, from Erlanger Lloyd (1955) and Centre College (1959); Jim Claypool, from Beechwood (1956) and Centre College (1960); Jim "Red Dog" Dougherty, from Bellevue High (1949) and UC (1956), who embarked on a long high school coaching career; Irv Etler, from Erlanger Lloyd (1957) and Xavier University (1961), where he played quarterback; Ed Eviston, from Newport Central Catholic (1998) and Georgetown (Ky.) College, who quarterbacked his team to a national small college championship; Charlie Fredericks, from

Newport Central Catholic (1955), who played at Notre Dame (1959) before returning to his high school to begin his coaching career; Leo Knoll, from Newport High (1948) and Xavier University (1952), where he played guard on the 1951 undefeated team; Judge **James Cammack Jr.**, who graduated from Owenton High School (1920) and played football at UK (1924); **Ralph Mussman**, from Newport High (1937), who went to Morehead College (now University), where he was the athletic of the year in 1941; Hank Pogue, who was a high school All-American at Highlands (1967) and played halfback for Indiana University in the 1968 Rose Bowl; Pat Uebel, from Bellevue High (1952) and Army (1956); John "Deep" Wing, from Dayton High (1950) and Army (1954); Alex "Zeke" Zachella, from Newport High (1938), who played quarterback at Navy (1942); and old Covington High's **Earl Wilson** (1906), brother of radio station owner **L. B. Wilson**. Earl Wilson was the Naval Academy's quarterback in the 1909 season, when he broke his neck; he died the following spring. Collegiate football rules were changed as a result of Wilson's tragic injury, suffered while playing against Villanova at Philadelphia.

One of the most successful collegiate players from the region never played a down as a pro. **Ron Beagle**, who lived in Winston Park, Ky., attended Purcell High School in Cincinnati and went on to the U.S. Naval Academy, where he was named the 1954 College Player of the Year as an end in his junior season. He was commissioned a Marine officer upon graduation from Annapolis. A leg injury prevented him from earning a spot with the 1960 Oakland Raiders of the old American Football League (AFL). He appeared on a players' football card that year. In 1956 Winston Park mayor Thomas Hunkle presented him with the keys to his hometown, and Covington mayor Harry Schneider honored him with an official scroll. Covington's mayor had given Beagle the keys to the city in 1955. Beagle is also a member of the College Football Hall of Fame.

Although he did not play football at the pro level, one more person needs to be singled out. Frank Jacobs came out of Highland Heights, Ky., and Newport Central Catholic High School (1987). In 1986, the first year of the award, Jacobs was named Kentucky's Mr. Football. He went on to play two seasons as a tight end at Notre Dame, catching a pass for a touchdown in the 1988 Fiesta Bowl Game for his national championship team. His football future seemed bright at the time, but he settled on playing only baseball and was selected in the seventh round of the 1991 draft by the National League's New York Mets organization as a first baseman. Although he showed great promise as a minor leaguer, he never played in a big league baseball game.

A few coaches have come out of Northern Kentucky. Among those who have coached professional teams, there is **Homer Rice**, a graduate of Highlands (1945) and Centre College (1950), who returned to his high school to lead its team to their first state championship in 1960. He then coached at UK, UC, and Rice University before spending a lackluster year and a half as the leader of the Cincinnati Bengals. Rice, who holds a doctorate, finished his football career at the University of Georgia as its athletic director. **John Merritt**, from Falmouth, Ky., who played at Kentucky State University, coached a combined 31 seasons at Jackson State (Miss.) and Tennessee State University. Merritt has the third-highest number of college football coaching victories (232). Only coaches Paul "Bear" Bryant and Grambling's Eddie Robinson have won more games. Merritt is a member of the College Football Hall of Fame. Bob DeMoss of Dayton, Ky., returned to Purdue to coach the Boilermakers; he was assistant and quarterback coach (1950–1969), head coach (1970–1972), and assistant athletic director (1973–1993). Billy Lyons, a graduate of Erlanger Lloyd (1991) and Marshall University (1995), spent seven seasons in the NFL with the Green Bay Packers and the Minnesota Vikings as a defensive end. Lyons returned to Northern Kentucky as a defensive coach at Thomas More College.

Leroy Hambrick of Newport, who attended William Grant High School in Covington and played football there on Grant's undefeated teams and later at Kentucky State University, went on to become the first African American to officiate in the NFL. He was a principal at a school in Atlanta, Ga., while he worked Sundays in the NFL into the early 1990s.

During the mid-1990s, the gender barrier was broken for football in Northern Kentucky, as a Bellevue girl, Lacey Mile, went out for and made a Pee Wee football team in her town; playing quarterback, she crossed many lines in addition to the first down marker.

Boehmker, Terry. *Northern Kentucky High School Sports Guide*. Self-published, n.d.

Carroll, Bob, Michael Greshman, David Neft, John Thorn, and the Elias Sports Bureau. *Total Football: The Official Encyclopedia of the National Football League*. New York: HarperCollins, 1997.

FORD FAMILY. Robert Carrick Ford Sr. (b. October 12, 1862, Owenton, Ky.; d. June 16, 1941, Owenton, Ky.) was one of the most prominent members of an Owen Co. family known for their public service, banking, and publishing interests. The fourth child of Francis "Frank" Ford (1820–1894) and his wife Sarah Morton Ford of Bourbon Co., Robert was the great-great-grandson of John Ford Jr., a **Revolutionary War** veteran, and Aphia Petty Ford.

Robert "R. C." Ford's parents settled in Owen Co. many years before the **Civil War**. Their first home, which burned during the war, was located on the first cleared land in Owen Co., where today the junction of U.S. 127 and Ky. Rt. 22 is located. In 1870 Frank Ford built the ancestral house that remains today on S. Main St. in Owenton.

R. C. Ford attended Georgetown College in Georgetown from 1882 to 1885. He returned to Owen Co., served two years as a deputy clerk, began reading law with Judge O. B. Hallam, and was admitted to the bar in 1885. Ford, along with his law partner O. V. Riley, bought the *Owen Democrat* newspaper and published it from October 22, 1886, to June 26, 1888. They then sold the paper to **Ed Porter Thompson**, who later compiled the *History of the Orphan Brigade*, an excellent account of Kentuckians who served in the Confederate Army. Ford was a member of the Owenton Baptist Church and was affiliated with the **Independent Order of Odd Fellows**, the Knights of Pythias, and the Benevolent and Protective Order of Elks (see **Civic Associations**).

On November 10, 1892, he married Emma Garrard, a granddaughter of Kentucky governor James Garrard (1796–1804), a Revolutionary War veteran. In 1895 Ford was nominated on the Democratic ticket for the office of Kentucky state treasurer. In 1896 he established and became president of the Manufacturers' Bank at Middlesborough. He was a U.S. marshal, acting mayor of Middlesborough, and a 32nd-degree Mason. In 1904 the Manufacturers' Bank merged into the National Bank, and Ford remained as president. He later served as president of the First National Bank of Pineville and helped organize the Manchester Bank of Clay Co. In addition to his extensive banking affairs, he had business interests in coal and timber.

R. C. Ford's sons included Robert "Bob" Carrick Ford Jr. (b. October 13, 1909; d. October 3, 1998), who served as Owen Co. attorney for 44 years, and James R. Ford (b. October 12, 1913; d. April 9, 2003), an attorney and judge of Owen Co.

Johnson, E. Polk. *A History of Kentucky and Kentuckians*. Vol. 2. Chicago: Lewis, 1912.

Ford Bible Record, Owen Co. Historical Society, Owenton, Ky.

Murphy, Margaret Alice, and Lela Maude Hawkins. *The History of Historic Old Cedar Baptist Church and Community, 1816–2004*. Frankfort, Ky.: Lynn, 2004.

Perrin, William Henry, J. H. Battle, and G. C. Kniffin. *Kentucky: A History of the State*. Louisville, Ky.: F. A. Battey, 1888.

Margaret A. Murphy

FOREST LAWN CEMETERY. Forest Lawn Cemetery in Erlanger was created in the mid-1930s on a property with a colorful history. Originally part of a 1785 land grant to Robert Johnson and John D. Watkins from the Commonwealth of Virginia, this property later fronted on the **Covington and Lexington Turnpike**. The land came to be owned by the Buckner family and then by Caleb Manley, who built the mansion that now houses the Forest Lawn Cemetery's offices. Manley introduced many new trees and plants on the property and developed it as a small plantation. William H. Wilson and Asahel Hathaway subsequently owned the property briefly; they sold it to James P. Garvey, one of the developers of the city of Erlanger. Following Garvey's death, Anna Bedinger, a descendant of one of Erlanger's earliest families, owned the property. Restaurateur Thomas R. Cody purchased it in 1913 and operated a popular restaurant in the mansion while also using the surrounding grounds for various social activities. Cody's business waned with **Pro-**

hibition, and he sold the property to a group of investors, led by Newport funeral director George Stetter, who intended to establish a funeral home, cemetery, and florist business there. Stetter was a partner in the Newport funeral home operation that bought the **James Taylor Mansion** at 335 E. Third St. in Newport in 1919 and operated it as Vonderhaar-Stetter-Betz Funeral Home until the late 1980s.

Although the development of the property in Erlanger from Manley's ownership on had provided attractive elements, much work on the site was required before burials could begin. The old slave buildings were removed, roads were replaced, and new roads and curbs were built. The sale of graves before the time of need began in 1935, and the first burial was of Joseph Guthrie of Bromley, on January 2, 1937.

George Stetter served as president of the Forest Lawn Board of Directors until his death in 1950. His son-in-law, James L. Owen, managed the cemetery from 1935 until his death in 1961, at which time his wife, Thelma Stetter Owen, became the cemetery's manager. When her health failed in 1976, her son James S. Owen became manager. The Stetter and Owens families were assisted in the development of the cemetery grounds by a very capable staff. Bill Workman served as grounds foreman during the early years and was followed by Joseph L. Schaffer Sr. and Joseph L. Schaffer Jr., who worked at the cemetery for many years. June Schaffer also helped to create the beauty of the cemetery. As a result of the Schaffer family's work, the cemetery has become one of the most picturesque locations in Northern Kentucky. The lake and the cypress trees at the entrance of the cemetery, remnants from Manley's ownership of the property, are among the most frequently used settings for wedding photographs in the area. When widening of the **Dixie Highway** threatened to destroy the lake and the trees, Erlanger city officials worked with the cemetery and the Kentucky State Highway Department to preserve the setting.

The Owens family sold Forest Lawn Cemetery in 1998 to SCI Kentucky Funeral Services Inc., and this company has continued the work of making Forest Lawn one of the finest burial grounds in the area. As of 2005, about 12,500 burials and entombments had taken place in Forest Lawn Cemetery. The first mausoleum, which included a chapel, was constructed in 1994. Two additional mausoleums have been built, and more such structures are planned. A lawn crypt section was added in 2002, and in 2006 family estates with rights to an upright memorial were offered for the first time.

Kenton Co. Deed Book, Covington, Ky.

Onkst, Wayne, ed. *From Buffalo Trails to the Twenty-First Century: A Centennial History of Erlanger, Kentucky.* Erlanger, Ky.: Erlanger Historical Society, 1996.

Wayne Onkst

FORKS OF GUNPOWDER BAPTIST CHURCH. In 1812, when Boone Co. was just over a dozen years old as a county, a group of Kentucky Baptists in the Gunpowder Creek area formed the Forks of Gunpowder Baptist Church. The place chosen for their meetinghouse was where the Gunpowder Creek divided, forming a fork; they built on an island located in the fork. Most contemporary church meetinghouses were log structures, but it is believed that this one was a stone building. Although no regular Indian intrusions into this area of the state were occurring then, there remained a fear of that possibility. This location was considered to be a safe place to worship.

In April of the same year, requests were made to the Bullittsburg and Middle Creek (now Belleview) Baptist churches to help constitute the new church. The church's early records are not extant, but Northbend Baptist Association records from September 1812 indicate that the church had 56 members and that Christopher Wilson was the ordained pastor. This was the third church established in the county. In 1840 the congregation, led by their pastor, Lewis Conner, withdrew from the Regular Baptists and aligned with the "Old School" or Primitive Baptists. That group was opposed to missionary work, Bible societies, education for ministers, and other means of evangelism. The Forks of Gunpowder Baptist Church helped establish the Salem Predestinarian Baptist Association and soon became its leading church. In the 1850s a wooden structure was built to replace the old building on the island. The new meetinghouse had two front doors: the one on the left was used by the women, who sat on that side of the church, and the one on the right was for the men, who sat on the other side. During the following years, besides Pastor Conner, John Underhill and Martin L. Aylor. served as pastors. The church disbanded in 1897 because of a steadily declining membership.

John Uri Lloyd, a local novelist, historian, and scientist of the late 19th and early 20th centuries, seemed fascinated by the predestinarianism of the Forks of Gunpowder Baptist Church, and he mentioned the church in several of his books. One of his novels, *Warwick of the Knobs,* focuses on the family of the pastor of the Forks of Gunpowder Baptist Church during the **Civil War**.

In 1902 a new church, Gunpowder Baptist Church, was established as a Regular Baptist church and met in the building that was once used for services of the Forks of Gunpowder Church. It thrived for a time, but in 1939 this group also ceased to exist. The structure, in a poor state of repair, was dismantled in late 2001 and moved to nearby Richwood, where it was reassembled as a residence.

Forks of Gunpowder Baptist Church Church Book, 1865–1897. Available at Northern Kentucky Univ. Archives, Highland Heights, Ky., along with the records of the church organized later.

James R. Duvall

FORREST, EDWIN (b. March 9, 1806, Philadelphia, Pa.; d. December 12, 1872, Philadelphia, Pa.). Edwin Forrest has been called the greatest American Shakespearean actor of the 19th century. He

Edwin Forrest.

was the fifth of the seven children born to a struggling couple from Philadelphia, William and Rebecca Lauman Forrest. Edwin's father died of tuberculosis when Edwin was 13. As a child, Edwin was very sickly, but through a vigorous exercise program, he developed a healthy, muscular body. He had a keen interest in acting and made his first stage debut at Philadelphia's Walnut Theater in 1820. He joined a traveling troupe, Collins and Jones, which held shows in Pittsburgh and other cities throughout the Ohio River Valley. In 1823 his troupe performed in Lebanon, Ohio, and after that show the group disbanded.

Stranded and penniless, the 17-year-old Forrest walked the 40 miles to Newport, Ky., where he knew Rachel Riddle, a friend from the Prune St. Theater in Philadelphia, lived. She allowed him to stay in her home until he could find an acting job. Out of necessity, he wore his stage costume on the street and rehearsed his parts with the Riddles' daughter Sallie. During his stay in Newport, he met another actor, **James Taylor III** (son of **James Taylor Jr.**, founder of Newport). When the younger Taylor was performing at the Newport Barracks, another actor got drunk and was unable to perform, so Taylor asked Forrest to play the part and gave him $5. From that time, Taylor and Forrest were fast friends. They spent many hours together at the Taylor home or sailing on the Ohio River, rehearsing lines and discussing acting. The two remained in contact for the rest of their lives, and Forrest would often visit Northern Kentucky.

After a month in Newport, Forrest left for Lexington, accompanied by the Riddles' daughter Sallie, who aspired to be an actress. In Albany, N.Y., at age 20, Forrest appeared in a supporting role to English actor Edmund Kean. Forrest admired the fiery performance by Kean and endeavored to develop a similar acting style for himself. In Cincinnati in 1823, Forrest played possibly the first ever blackface character in theater, in *Tailor in Distress.* In 1826 he made his New York City appearance, playing Othello at the Bowery Theater. For the next several years, he performed across the United States and Europe. He became immensely popular and received much critical acclaim. At age 30 he married an 18-year-old English girl, Catherine Sinclair. He said at the time that of all the women he had ever met, she was the only one he had ever considered marrying. They had only one child, a son, who died several days after birth in 1838.

During a trip to Cincinnati in 1839, Forrest purchased a large parcel of land from Israel Ludlow in the hills west of Covington, which had a spectacular view of the Ohio River Valley and the cities of Cincinnati, Covington, and Newport. He built an 11-room home there, which he named Forrest Hill. The house stands today at 309 Wright St., now a part of Covington.

At the pinnacle of Edwin Forrest's popularity, he owned, in addition to Forrest Hill, a castle on the Hudson River in New York, a brownstone mansion in Philadelphia, and a 100-acre country estate. Edwin Forrest dearly loved his wife but was not an attentive husband. After performing in the evening, he would often play cards with his friends and fellow actors until dawn. One evening after a performance in Cincinnati, Edwin returned to his hotel room unexpectedly to find his wife in the embrace of another actor, George W. Jamieson. After 12 years of a seemingly happy marriage, Edwin insisted on a separation and then filed for divorce. A very public legal battle ensued, with salacious accounts of the breakup appearing in newspapers across the country. Some have called it the domestic squabble of the 19th century.

After the 1852 divorce, Forrest's demeanor changed markedly. He became very stern, trusting few people, and seemed to lose his zest for life. Because of the divorce, many of his friends and fans abandoned him, but he continued to act. Most of the plays of that period were by European writers, but Forrest longed to perform an American work. Finding none, he ran a newspaper ad, offering $500 for the best new play by an American writer. The winning entry was by John Augustus Stone, called *Metamora.* It was about an Indian chief of the Wampanoag tribe, who worried about the white man forcing the Indian from his land. The performance was so moving and realistic that some Indians in the audience wept and did a chant, in honor of the beloved chief.

In Europe, Forrest met an English actor, named William Macready, who was a close friend of Charles Dickens. Both Macready and Forrest were excellent actors, but intense jealousy soon developed between them. In 1849, when both were appearing in New York City, their fans clashed in what was called the Astor Place Riot, in which at least 22 people lost their lives. In 1871 Edwin Forrest gave his last performance as Cardinal Richelieu at Boston, Mass. He died in Philadelphia, at age 66, and was buried in the St. Paul's Episcopal Churchyard there. During a distinguished career, he amassed a sizable fortune, which he left in a trust fund. He directed that income from the trust be used to set up a home for aged actors in his former home in Philadelphia.

In the 1930s, his former home in Covington was purchased by Harvey Brownfield, a local vaudeville performer and music teacher and the father of Bruce Brownfield, the bandleader. Harvey was probably best known as an accordion player but also played the calliope on Ohio River steamboats.

Alger, William Rounseville. *Life of Edwin Forrest.* New York: Arno Press, 1977.

"At Cards," *KP,* December 25, 1897, 5.

Classic Encyclopedia. "Edwin Forrest." http://63.1911encyclopedia.org (accessed November 5, 2005).

Grayson, Frank Y. "Historic Spots in Greater Cincinnati," *CTS,* November 25, 1932, 7.

——. "Sonorous Strains of Accordions Now Fill Home Where Great Tragedian Declaimed Deathless Lines," *CTS,* September 27, 1932, 16.

Moody, Richard. *The Astor Place Riot.* Bloomington: Indiana Univ. Press, 1958.

——. *Edwin Forrest: First Star of the American Stage.* New York: Alfred A. Knopf, 1960.

Purvis, Thomas L., ed. *Newport, Kentucky: A Bicentennial History.* Newport, Ky.: Otto Zimmerman, 1996.

"W. Covington," *KP,* February 7, 1910, 5.

Jack Wessling

FORT ANCIENT INDIAN SITES. By A.D. 800–900, the bow and arrow may have been introduced into the cultures of the American Indians inhabiting the Ohio River Valley. Other changes in settlement and subsistence soon changed the character of the Late Woodland–period archaeological record. Soon after 1000, the local American Indian inhabitants of Northern Kentucky practiced maize agriculture, used the bow and arrow, and tempered their pottery with shells instead of grit or limestone. Social and political changes may also have accompanied these changes. Archaeologists refer to this time span (A.D.1000 until after 1600) as the Fort Ancient Period. Divided into three segments (Early, Middle, and Late) by many researchers, the Fort Ancient period produced changes in pottery styles and village layouts or plans throughout its 600-plus years. For the Fort Ancient period, archaeologists have documented that there were permanently occupied villages along most of the major streams in Northern Kentucky. The Petersburg Village site in Boone Co. has recently produced brass or copper artifacts that may date from the 15th to the 16th centuries and likely came from trade with French or other European traders.

Northern Kentucky has many villages of the Fort Ancient period, including documented sites in Boone, Bracken, Campbell, and Kenton counties. In southeastern Campbell Co., the Bintz site lies on two terraces overlooking the Ohio River. Investigated by archaeologists during the late 1940s, the site includes two villages and a large burial mound. For many years, researchers from **Northern Kentucky University** have conducted archaeological field studies at the Dunn Village, another Fort Ancient village in Campbell Co.

Terraces along the Ohio River and major streams of Boone and Kenton counties, including Big Bone Creek, Gunpowder Creek, and Mud Lick Creek, also contain Fort Ancient village sites. The modern-day town of Petersburg lies above villages of both the Middle and the Late Fort Ancient periods. Other well-known villages of the period in Boone Co. include the Cleek-McCabe site, partially excavated by the University of Kentucky in the 1930s, and several village sites at **Big Bone Lick** State Park.

Most of the aforementioned sites were large villages that included houses and in some cases stockade walls. The houses were usually built in a circular pattern, with the doors facing in toward the center of the village, where there was a plaza, or open-space area, used for ceremonies and other community activities.

The Northern Kentucky Fort Ancient peoples farmed corn, beans, and squash or pumpkins. They also hunted deer and many smaller mammals, birds, and fish. Their farmlands were the fertile stream valleys surrounding their village site. From the local streams and rivers, they collected large quantities of mussels, which they ate. The mussel shells were used to temper their pottery and to make tools such as hoes. They buried their dead either in mounds nearby or in small cemeteries located within the village itself. Each village contained at least one community building or meeting place. Other buildings in the village included sweat lodges and houses.

"Ancient Burial Site," *KE,* July 24, 2004, C3.

"Building on the Past," *SC,* August 1, 2004, 1.

"Petersburg Dig Reveals Daily Life of Prehistoric People," *SC,* August 1, 2004, 3A.

"Petersburg's Treasury of History—Bone May Be Those of Ancient Indians," *KP,* July 20, 2004, 1K.

Rafferty, Janet Elizabeth. "The Development of the Ft. Ancient Tradition in Northern Kentucky," PhD diss., Univ. of Washington, 1974.

"Twelve Mile," *KSJ,* February 19, 1885, 3.

Jeannine Kreinbrink

FORT MITCHELL. The modern city of Fort Mitchell, in central Kenton Co., three miles south of Covington along **Dixie Highway** (U.S. 25/42; the old **Covington and Lexington Turnpike**), is the result of mergers and several annexations. The first merger occurred in 1967, when the old city of Fort Mitchell joined with the city of South Fort Mitchell; in 1999 the adjacent small city of Crescent Park was merged with Fort Mitchell. Fort Mitchell now encompasses roughly four square miles.

The original Fort Mitchell (old Fort Mitchell) began in the first decade of the 20th century as a **streetcar** suburb, just after the old Lewisburg streetcar line was extended in 1903 to Highland Cemetery; in 1910 the streetcar line reached its final terminus at a loop (turnaround) opposite where modern Orphanage Rd. intersects. The streetcar passed to the rear (to the west) of the then new **Fort Mitchell Country Club**, which opened in 1904. The city was developed along the streets between that club and the **Dixie Highway**. John Menzies and A. G. Simrall served as the earliest trustees of the town, which was incorporated on Valentine's Day in 1910. Soon, builders such as the Northcutt Brothers and Paul L. Bethel were constructing beautiful homes that remain today as part of Fort Mitchell's historic districts. It was

Dixie Highway, Fort Mitchell. Carl Goetz poses in front of stores near the streetcar's "end-of-the-line," in the 1940s.

not long before city water (supplied by the Covington Waterworks via the Dixie Water Company) and natural gas were brought out along the highway, spurring further development. In the late 1920s, the area known as Fort Mitchell Heights was annexed by Fort Mitchell. Fort Mitchell Heights was the location of the **Civil War**–era Fort Mitchel, one of the many Northern Kentucky **Civil War fortifications** built to defend the region and Cincinnati from attack in 1862 by the Confederate general Henry Heth. He reportedly came as close as the southern end of modern Fort Mitchell before turning back. The fort was named for Union general **Ormsby Mitchel**, but a second *l* was added for the name of the city. One of the best-known homes in Fort Mitchell Heights was the home of **Brady Black**, longtime editor of the *Cincinnati Enquirer*; he lived along a rise to the west along the highway, near where the fortification stood. Another newspaperman, **Ollie James**, lived across the highway from Black, in what his readers knew as Bullfrog Holler.

The city of South Fort Mitchell was incorporated in 1927 with a population of 296. The Dixie Tea Room, later the Greyhound Grill, had already been in operation for a few years at the time. It was at the end of the streetcar line in an area in South Fort Mitchell that locals still refer to as the End of the Line. (See **Gourmet Strip**.) Nearby were the **Blessed Sacrament Catholic Church**, which built a combination church and school on the Dixie Highway in 1920, and the **Fort Mitchell Baptist Church**, opened in 1924. In 1935 **Remke Markets** introduced Northern Kentucky to the first self-serve grocery store at Orphanage Rd. and the Dixie Highway. That same year saw the construction of an underpass beneath the Dixie Highway for pedestrians; traffic had grown enough that crossing the road had become dangerous, especially for the students of Blessed Sacrament School. In 1938 a new city building was dedicated, and it has been expanded since. By 1940 the population of South Fort Mitchell was 2,400. The Fort Mitchell area is served by the high-quality Beechwood Independent School District (see **Beechwood Public Schools**), which disassociated itself from the county school system in 1912. The Beechwood School is almost 150 years old.

The 1960s brought rapid change to the area. In 1962 I-75 was completed through the cities. Traffic increased greatly, and the Expressway Plaza Shopping Center was constructed across from Highland Cemetery, next to the interstate. By that time the streetcar suburb had become a highway suburb. A new Holiday Inn Motel was added to that same intersection of I-75 and the Dixie Highway. Office buildings were also erected near the interstate, and the slow but steady growth of the nearby **Cincinnati/Northern Kentucky International Airport** brought many new visitors and residents to the cities.

In 1967 the city of South Fort Mitchell merged with the adjacent city of Fort Mitchell, and the name Fort Mitchell was retained. The police departments, fire departments, administration, and city services of the two cities were combined. At the time, old Fort Mitchell had a population of 500, while South Fort Mitchell had 5,500.

Fort Mitchell is rich in history. It is home to three cemeteries, where many famous Northern Kentuckians are buried: **St. John Cemetery** (1867), **Highland Cemetery** (1869), and **St. Mary Cemetery**. Five historic districts in the city have been placed on the National Register of Historic Places: the Old Fort Mitchell Historic District, the Fort Mitchell Heights Historic District, the Beechwood Historic District, the Highland Cemetery Historic District, and the Kruempelmann Farm Historic District. The 26-acre Kruempelmann property was a working farm for some 170 years before it recently became the site of a 58-home high-end development. On the southwest end of town, the Deters family opened the Rowntowner Motor Inn in November 1970, and it served as the main Northern Kentucky convention center until a new convention center was built in Covington. Today, the Fort Mitchell facility is known as the Drawbridge Inn Convention Center Motel. At one time a microbrewery operated there. This is also the area where the **Columbia Sussex Corporation** had its offices for many years before its recent move to Crestview Hills.

In 2000 Fort Mitchell had a population of 8,089.

"Board Decides on Underpass," *KP*, October 10, 1935, 1.

"Data on Three Kenton County Communities Prepared by Mrs. Udry," *KP*, October 25, 1940, 17.

"Happy at Home," *KP*, July 11, 1983, 1K.

Keeme, Steve. "Office Building Going Up on Columnist's Beloved 'Bullfrog Holler,'" *CE*, January 16, 1982, D1.

Kleber, John E., ed. *The Kentucky Encyclopedia*. Lexington: Univ. Press of Kentucky, 1992.

Reis, Jim. "Beechwood Memory Lane," *KP*, July 15, 1985, 4K.

——. "Ft. Mitchell Merger Memories," *KP*, January 13, 1992, 4K.

——. "Ft. Mitchell: Town of Tombs Becomes a City," *KP*, April 1, 1985, 4K.

U.S. Census Bureau. "American Fact Finder. Data Set. Census 2000 Summary File 1 (SF1) 100-Percent Data. Custom Table." www.census.gov (accessed May 8, 2007).

FORT MITCHELL BAPTIST CHURCH. The Fort Mitchell Baptist Church was formed in the early 1920s after the North Bend Baptist Association (now the Northern Kentucky Baptist Association) of the Kentucky Baptist Convention authorized establishment of a church. A lot costing $5,000 was purchased at the corner of the **Dixie Highway** and Silver Ave., and a "tabernacle," as it was called, was built. The building was dedicated on Sunday, May 25, 1924. This tabernacle and its congregation were considered a mission until October 9, 1924, when the Fort Mitchell Baptist Church was organized. The pastors from that time to the present, along with highlights of the church's growth, are as follows.

Dr. Andrew Smith, 1924–1926; membership 34 in 1924, 78 in 1926. The first baptism was April 12, 1925; the title for the church property was received from the North Bend Association.

G. B. Bush, 1926–1947; membership 266. A new sanctuary and a parsonage were built; the church became debt-free in 1946.

Darrel C. Richardson, 1947–1954; membership 469. A building committee was formed to plan expansion of the auditorium and the basement.

Dr. Samuel Southard, August 1954–July 1955; membership 503; plans drawn for a future educational building.

Dr. Clarence R. Lassetter, 1955–1964; membership 660. An education building was constructed, two properties (one on Silver Ave. and the other on the Dixie Highway) were purchased for future expansion, and the church began conducting two morning services.

Thomas H. Conley, 1964–1966. Additional property was purchased for future expansions.

James E. Taulman, 1967–1976; membership 602. More property was purchased, and the church hired Tom Mallory, a full-time minister of Christian education, and Dan Arterburn, a minister of music and youth. Five vocal choirs and two handbell choirs were now included as parts of the music program. A mortgage-burning ceremony was held in September 1975. The church also celebrated America's bicentennial with various events culminating in a celebration in "1776 style."

Dr. Gilbert Tucker, 1976–1985; membership 799. Ground was broken in April 1978, and a new church sanctuary was completed in 1980. The church parsonage was converted to offices and later razed for additional parking. In 1983 the sanctuary and the choir loft of the "old church" were converted into additional classrooms.

Dr. C. Michael Watts, 1986–1990; played a major role in the creation of the chapel program at the **Cincinnati/Northern Kentucky International Airport**. The Mother's Day Out program was established in this period by church member Debby Jump. The church's education facility was renovated and reoccupied in 1992, and a new minister of music, Dr. Melanie Williams, was hired.

Dr. Harry M. Rowland, 1992–1996; membership 818. The singles ministry was expanded, the church began participation in the Interfaith Hospitality Network program, Charles Houp became minister of education and youth (serving until 1995), and Jenna Lusby became the part-time children's minister. During the interim period after Rowland left the pastorate, Daniel Mackey was appointed as the church's minister of youth.

Dr. French B. Harmon, 1997–2004; membership just over 1,000. The church expanded its outreach ministries in discipleship and missions, offering several music dramas to entertain the church members as well as the general community. This was also a time of expansion for the Mother's Day Out program and a period of reevaluation of the church's overall structure. After the resignation of Williams, the team of Tony and Joy Burdett led the music ministry's program. Following Mackey's departure in 1999, Cohen Copley filled the youth ministry position until 2001. After he left, the church's staff positions were once again reevaluated and several part-time ministerial positions were created.

Dr. R. Joseph Tricquet Jr., 2005–present.

"Baptist Church Marks 80 Years," *KE*, October 22, 2004, C3.

"Church Celebrates 75th Anniversary," *KE*, October 2, 1999, C1.

"Dedication Service," *KP*, May 26, 1924, 1.

Fort Mitchell Baptist Church. *Church History, June 1, 1924 to October 9, 1999.* Fort Mitchell, Ky.: Fort Mitchell Baptist Church, 1999.

Northern Kentucky Baptist Association. *Annual of the Northern Kentucky Baptist Association*. Erlanger: Northern Kentucky Baptist Association, 1992, 1996.

Perry Bratcher

FORT MITCHELL COUNTRY CLUB. At the turn of the 20th century, the so-called fresh-air movement brought urban residents out of the cities and into the countryside. Some went for walks and rides near their homes, others strolled in the newly developed garden cemeteries (see **Highland Cemetery**), and people who could afford to do so formed their own clubs out in the fresh air, the modern country clubs. In 1904 the Fort Mitchell Country Club (FMCC), the oldest still-existing country club in Northern Kentucky, was incorporated as a private, nonprofit corporation with 128 charter members, including Kenton Co. community leaders **J. T. Hatfield** and **Bradford Shinkle.** The club was located west of the Lexington Pk. (**Dixie Highway**), at the end of Fort Mitchell Ave., in the original section of Fort Mitchell. Formerly, this site was the Perkins family homestead, a 74--acre farm. It was leased for the first two years, and then the club purchased the land that it was quickly improving. Situated along the route of the Fort Mitchell **streetcar** line (see **Green Line**), the club had its own streetcar stop at the rear of its property. In those early days, club events were scheduled to end before the midnight departure of the last streetcar back to Covington, where most members lived.

When the FMCC opened in 1904, its nine-hole golf course was ready for use, as was the baseball field. The former Perkins family home was used as the first clubhouse. A large, open-air dancing platform, considered to be one of the finest dance floors in Northern Kentucky, was constructed for dancing under the stars, a popular activity at the time. The golf course has been redesigned a couple of times, but not enough land is available to add another nine holes. Nevertheless, the FMCC course was the site of the Kentucky State Amateur Golf Tournament in 1913, 1917, and 1920 and the Kentucky Open in 1920 and 1928. Bill Deupree was perhaps the best of the many golfers who have called the FMCC their home course.

The club's first swimming pool was built in 1941, a second, larger one in 1961, and another in the 1980s. Over the years, other activities have included basketball, a shooting range, and tennis (early on, and brought back in 1975). The club has endured some difficult times: at least two fires, a period of bankruptcy in the late 1930s, a cyclone in 1948, a robbery in 1976, and a hepatitis scare in 1983. The new clubhouse was opened in 1971, after a 1970 fire.

Having endured for more than a century, the FMCC continues to be the scene of numerous meetings, from the Kiwanis Club (see **Civic Associations**) to political gatherings, proms, and seasonal thematic dances. Events held there have been attended by many important people, including various Kentucky governors and golfing legend Sam Snead.

"Country Club Is Formed," *KP*, March 7, 1904, 1.

"Day Night Golf Games at Fort Mitchell," *KP*, August 27, 1914, 10.

Edmiston, John H. *A Special Place: History of the Fort Mitchell Country Club, 1904–1994.* Fort Mitchell, Ky.: The Club, 1994.

"Ft. Mitchell an Oldie," *KP*, July 1, 1974, 16K.

FORT THOMAS. Originally incorporated as the District of the Highlands on February 27, 1867, with the help of U.S. attorney general **Henry Stanbery**, this sixth-class city stretches along a five-mile ridge above the Ohio River in northeastern Campbell Co., covering 5.7 square miles. It is bounded by the Ohio River and the Kentucky towns of Dayton, Bellevue, Highland Heights, Newport, Southgate, and Woodlawn. The city was part of a half-million-acre land grant awarded to

Fort Thomas Military Reservation.

the Ohio Land Company in 1749 and surveyed by **Christopher Gist** in 1750. Later, this land grant was preempted by the U.S. Congress to award lands to **Revolutionary War** veterans. Patents for service in the war were issued to **William Kennedy**, **David Leitch**, Benjamin Logan, Laurence Muse, John O'Bannon, Samuel and David Perry, and Edmond Taylor.

The first settlers arrived during the early 1800s to "the Highlands," situated on the hills behind Newport. Among them was William Richard Taliaferro, from Virginia. His wife was Alice Berry, whose father had given the couple 150 acres extending north to the Ohio River, near what today is Rossford and N. Fort Thomas Aves. Taliaferro built a log cabin, which in 1830 was converted into a mansion known as Mount Pleasant. The house remains standing at 1810 N. Ft Thomas Ave. Classes were conducted at this home before a school was built close by on Holly Ln. The Highland Methodist Church held its first worship service at Mount Pleasant. At 370 Newman Ave. in Fort Thomas stands another early log cabin, dating to 1850, which has been enlarged and covered with siding.

Other landowners in the area, many of whom also served as trustees of the town, were John Cline, Jacob Hawthorne, George H. Hilton, Thomas Irvin, Elli Kinney (whose castle became **Carmel Manor** nursing home), John Lilley, and Henry Stanbery (1803–1881). Stanbery, who was the U.S. attorney general under President Andrew Johnson (1865–1869), planned the successful strategies used to thwart Johnson's impeachment in 1867. The first census in 1871 showed that the District of the Highlands (Fort Thomas) had a population of 617.

In 1873 the post office closest to the District of the Highlands was located in Dale, where mail services were restricted to residents of that community. Inhabitants of the rest of the Highlands had to go to Newport for their mail. However, as the town known as the District of the Highlands grew in population, the smaller settlement of Guyville to the north, as well as Dale to the south, were annexed to the city. During the construction of the **Fort Thomas Military Reservation** during the 1890s, Col. Melville Cochran (1836–1904) was instrumental in the closing of the Dale post office branch; a new post office opened on the property of L. L. Ross, just to the north of the entrance of the new fort. This became Station A, Newport, and its postmark designation was stamped as Fort Thomas. In-town mail deliveries began in 1896. The citizens of the town voted to change the name of the District of the Highlands to the city of Fort Thomas in an election during 1914, thus acknowledging their city's close ties to the military base. The post office moved to the Midway, the commercial strip across from the entrance to the fort, in 1918, and later to a more central location, a new structure built at 24 S. Fort Thomas Ave., in 1941. A mural inside this post office depicts Gen. George Henry Thomas (1816–1870) and Gen. Phillip Henry Sheridan (1831–1888) standing together at Missionary Ridge, Tenn., during the **Civil War**. The mural also shows soldiers standing in front of the fort's barracks and the historic water tower at the Fort Thomas military reservation.

A boulevard that runs the length of Fort Thomas, originally named Jamestown Pk., went through many name changes before it came to be called N. Fort Thomas Ave. north of Highland Ave., and S. Fort Thomas Ave. south of Highland Ave. Other major through streets in the town are Covert Run Pk. and Memorial Pkwy. connecting to Bellevue (Memorial Pkwy. was the former right-of-way of the **Green Line** streetcar that served the city); Dayton Pk., which connects to Dayton; Highland Ave. and Grandview Ave., connecting to Southgate; River Rd. and Tower Hill Rd., which lead to Ky. Rt. 8 (the **Mary Ingles Highway**) along the eastern boundary, paralleling the Ohio River; and Waterworks Rd. and Grand Ave., which connect to Newport. In 2000 the city of Fort Thomas had a population of 17,184.

"Ft. Thomas—Re Name for New Fourth Class City Soon to Be Created," *KP*, August 19, 1914, 3.
"Happy Birthday for Ft. Thomas," *KTS*, February 27, 1958, 1A.
"Highlands Soon to Be Ft. Thomas," *KP*, October 6, 1914, 1.
Reis, Jim. "Ft. Thomas Besieged by Indians," *KP*, July 20, 1987, 4K.

Betty Maddox Daniels

FORT THOMAS MILITARY RESERVATION. The deactivated military reservation at Fort Thomas is located in the southeastern portion of the city. The fort's grounds, high above the Ohio River, are bounded by S. Fort Thomas Ave. (Ky. Rt. 1120), River Rd. (Ky. Rt. 445), and the **Mary Ingles Highway** (Ky. Rt. 8). This site, 111 acres of former farmlands and orchards atop the hills of the District of the Highlands (now **Fort Thomas**), was chosen as a replacement after the **Newport Barracks**, at the confluence of the Ohio and Licking rivers, was inundated in the **flood of 1884**, as well as that of 1887. The site was promoted as being desirable both because it was out of the floodplain and because an adequate supply of fresh water was available from the nearby Covington Waterworks. The military installation at Fort Thomas was also accessible to Cincinnati, Newport, and Covington by an electric **streetcar** line. It was served by the Grand Avenue Turnpike for wagons and carriages and had a special siding of the **Chesapeake and Ohio Railroad** for moving building materials and supplies as well as for troop transport. The Kentucky legislature ceded the land to the federal government on the last day of February 1887. Dedicated on June 29, 1890, the base was first named Fort Crook. However, Gen. Phillip Henry Sheridan (1831–1888), chief of staff of the U.S. Army, changed its name to Fort Thomas in honor of his comrade in arms, Gen. **George Henry Thomas** (1816–1870), the Union Army commander known as the "the Rock of Chickamauga." Generals Thomas and Sheridan are portrayed in a 1942 mural by artist Lucienne Bloch that is displayed inside the lobby of the Fort Thomas Post Office at 24 S. Fort Thomas Ave.

In the 1890s the U.S. Army decided to move operations from its remote and scattered posts and garrisons and consolidate some of them in population centers that had railheads. The Cincinnati–Northern Kentucky region, which previously had two significant military installations (Fort Washington at Cincinnati and the Newport Barracks), was a logical choice. Citizens on both sides of the river expressed support for having the military in their midst. And an assignment to the post at Fort Thomas was the number-one choice of West Point Military Academy graduates, because it put them in a quiet suburban neighborhood near a large city with cultural and entertainment opportunities. Units from the Philippines were routinely rotated and assigned to service at Fort Thomas.

Col. Melville Augustus Cochran (1836–1904), of the 6th Infantry Regiment (U.S.A.), was the first commandant. As a career officer during the **Civil War**, he had fought for the Union Army and had been held prisoner by the Confederates for 16 months before escaping. He later served at a number of small military posts in the West. He was responsible for the layout of the fort and overseeing its construction. The commandant's home, No. 1 Carriage Loop (Alexander Circle), was the first building to be constructed. Base commanders lived with their families on-site. Henry A. Schriver (1829–1909), a local contractor, used U.S. Army plans for the red brick buildings that he built on the base. For instance, the mess hall was built according to the same plans as the stone mess halls at the Presidio in San Francisco and at Fort Riley, Kans. The tower in the front of the fort was constructed of limestone blocks. Administrative officers and their families had houses on Alexander Circle; field officers and their families lived on Greene St., where the bachelor officers' quarters (B.O.Q) were also located; and noncoms and their families were housed on Pearson St. These houses, the tower, the armory–drill hall–gymnasium, the mess hall, the hospital steward's house, and the stable remain; only the B.O.Q. is gone. Other service buildings, which have been removed, included the headquarters building, the barracks, the commissary, the hospital, the chapel, the guard house, the firehouse, and the band quarters. The grounds were well landscaped to give the appearance of a college campus, thanks to planning by Colonel Cochran. A baseball field, an amphitheater for **boxing** bouts, parade grounds, and a polo field provided for outdoor recreation.

The stone water tower, which has become the symbol for the city of Fort Thomas, stands on the western edge of the military reservation on S. Fort Thomas Ave. between Pearson and Douglas Sts. Built in 1890, under the direction of Henry Schriver and engineer Patrick Rooney, and no longer in use, it conceals a standpipe 100 feet high, with a capacity of 100,000 gallons. Water was pumped from the Covington Waterworks reservoir just across the street (now the **Northern Kentucky Water District**). The water came from the Ohio River below the military reservation's east boundary through a 30-inch main under the reservation and S. Fort Thomas Ave. The truncated base, of regular coarse granite, measures 23.5 square feet at ground level. The untapered shaft of limestone, with its projecting crown, brings the height to over 102 feet. A wrought iron gate in the base once made the inside spiral staircase to the top accessible. The cost of the entire installation was $16,328, and daily water consumption was 15,500 gallons. The bronze plaque on the west side of the tower honors 28 officers and men who lost their lives in the Spanish-American War (1898). It was "erected by the citizens of Cincinnati, Covington, Newport, and the vicinity of Ft. Thomas." The sculptured work was done by artist **Clement Barnhorn**. A smaller plaque on the south side honors Col. **Harry Egbert** (1839–1899). The 6th Infantry, commanded first by Colonel Cochran and then by Colonel Egbert, was the first military force assigned to duty at Fort Thomas. The unit's first military action came after 250 American lives were lost when the USS *Maine* exploded in Havana Harbor, Cuba, on February 15, 1898. The 6th Infantry was sent to Florida to prepare for battle; however, the unit's commander, Colonel Cochran, became ill and was relieved of his command. Colonel Egbert, a 36-year army veteran, took charge and led the men to victory during the battle at San Juan Hill in Cuba. Their stay in Cuba was short, and they soon returned to Fort Thomas by train and streetcar line, bringing their injured in litters. In front of the tower are two cannons on stone platforms diagonally placed and inscribed "Barcelona. 1 de Junio, 1768" and "Barcelona. 2 de Junio, 1789." Trophies from the war in Cuba, they were captured from Spanish admiral Pascual Cervera y Topete during a naval engagement in Havana harbor when American commanders William T. Sampson and Winfield Scott Schley prevented the enemy from leaving the harbor.

During the Spanish-American War, 15 men had been left at Fort Thomas under the command of Lt. Harry Lee, Sgt. Paulin, and Lt. Col. Henry Gadner, a surgeon. Customarily, a skeleton military crew, sometimes only three, would stay behind at the fort when one company was leaving and another arriving. There were frequent rumors that the post might close during peacetime, but companies of the 2nd, 3rd, 4th, 9th, and 10th infantries came at various times and the post stayed open. Situated near a major population center and easily accessible, the Fort Thomas facility became a major site for military recruitment, inductions, and enlistments as men from western West Virginia, Eastern Kentucky, and southern Ohio regularly arrived to join the service.

To provide extra space during World War I, 20 temporary buildings were added. When 1922 began, only recruiting companies and a few medical corpsmen were on the base, but then the 10th Infantry arrived and remained at the post until 1940. This unit was called upon for community service at times of flooding. During the **Great Depression**, the person in command was an ambitious colonel named Edward Croft, who worked to repair the poor appearance of the post. He directed recent West Point graduates to lead young men from the Civil Military Training Corps in digging up stones from unused areas of the grounds. Then the young men were put to work constructing the walls along the south and west boundaries, the stately gates at the entrances, and steps and benches throughout the grounds. Each group working on the walls made its own patterns; some of the walls were built with jagged tops so soldiers could not sit on them. Local homeowners, who were friendly with the officers, generously contributed shrubs, small trees, rose bushes, and other plants to the beautification crews so that the area could be returned to its former excellent appearance. The commanding colonel insisted that whenever the troops left the base, they were to wear their stately full dress uniform, including white cross belts, white gloves, and highly polished shoes.

Soldiers who came to Fort Thomas, for whatever reason—tours of duty, enlistment, recruitment, a posting to the military police barracks, or for Army Reverse duty—always seemed to remember the mess hall after they left. Finished in 1891, at a cost of $20,407, the building has been returned to its original condition through the diligent efforts of the Fort Thomas Heritage League Inc. and was dedicated as a Community Center on September 26, 1992. The main hall is 150 by 50 feet, without central support. There are double doors on the east, south, and west sides and large arched windows, originally topped with lunettes, around the hall. The original red quarry tile floors are intact throughout, even though they were flooded at times to provide winter ice skating when the structure was not in use for other purposes. The pressed-tin ceiling was rusted and has been hidden by new acoustical tiles. Several coats of paint were removed from the interior buttered-brick tile walls, and outside the brick walls have been repointed. The T-shaped rear section once housed the kitchen, a cork-lined meat locker, storage rooms, and an entrance to the basement. Now this area is divided into a caterer's kitchen, a small museum, a meeting room, restrooms, and storage. With new lighting, ceiling fans, and an air-conditioning system, it serves many public purposes throughout the year.

Another of the remaining buildings is the armory–drill hall. It has a double-door entrance on the west side from S. Fort Thomas Ave. and one from the east side on Cochran St. A rectangular building, it contains 19,900 square feet on its two floors. When it was built in 1896, it cost $50,235. There are large windows at ground level on the north and south sides; larger casement windows above admit plenty of light for the second level. Red tile covers much of the floor of the lower level, which once housed bowling alleys, pool and billiard tables, and refreshment rooms. The second floor has no central supports, depending instead on roof trusses constructed by bolting or riveting a series of compression and tension members. Hardwood flooring covers the 90-by-100-foot floor. In inclement weather, troops drilled there with the officers observing from a balcony. At other times the area was used for social events, hops and dances, bridge tournaments, charity luncheons, graduation exercises, and various indoor sports. Citizens from the surrounding cities put on special events during peacetimes. In the aftermath of the **Beverly Hills Supper Club** disaster on May 28, 1977, in Southgate, the huge armory floor became a temporary morgue. The lower floor now houses city recreation department offices and rooms for games, dancing, meetings, and children's activities. The second floor is busy daily with exercise classes, basketball and volleyball games, sports leagues for all ages, and large dances.

Base housing for the troops was in the four brick barracks buildings, two on either side of the mess hall. The three-story central core contained the company office and billiard, reading, and recreation rooms; the two-story wings on either side had verandas facing the parade grounds. These structures no longer remain, but a fifth barracks, constructed in 1935, is now used as a nursing home–domiciliary by the Cincinnati U.S. Veterans Administration Hospital (see **Veterans Administration Medical Center**).

When the post opened, every officer above the rank of 2nd lieutenant was entitled to a horse. Each one could also have a private mount, as did members of the cavalry attached to the infantry. The resident polo team and the cavalry often performed publicly. A stable was erected on the far southern edge of the property on Carmel Manor Dr. (now part of the Brooks-Lawler Army Reserve Center complex). The road was initially called Boone Dr., since it led to a site where **Daniel Boone** once camped overlooking the river. The stable's building of red brick was constructed between 1889 and 1892 and could house 40 horses and mules. The long, narrow building has rather steep roofs and a clerestory along the ridge. Usually, such military structures do not survive. Now it is used for storage in a fenced-off area.

Carriage Dr. (renamed Greene St.) was the main entryway when the post was new. It begins at S. Fort Thomas Ave. and turns left into Cochran St. to continue past the mess hall and then to the Carriage Loop (Alexander Circle), with Ohio River overlooks. On both sides of the entrance are homes that housed field officers (starting at lieutenant colonels) and their families; the B.O.Q. was there also. The first house on the left of Greene St. was at one time assigned to Colonel Egbert. It is a single-family, two-story building in Georgian Revival style. The entrance is a reception room of generous size, which was used by base commanders for their many formal entertaining events. Three rooms on the first floor, three on the second, servants' quarters on the third, and a full basement complete the interior. Fireplaces in six of the rooms are elaborately carved. A wooden porch and an octagonal bay window grace the front facade. The cost was $6,546 for the 3,489 square feet of living area in the house. Next are four duplexes, two on each side of the street. The overall size of each is 51 by 63 feet, and their cost in 1892 was $13,147. Each of these eight units has a wooden porch and lunettes over a large front window and a door. Each dwelling also has a stairway with ornate landing areas, a fireplace in each room, servant quarters on the third floor, and a basement. The last house on the left is a single-family residence with a floor plan the reverse of Colonel Egbert's house. Across the street was the B.O.Q., which once housed nurses serving the hospital on Cochran St. It was reported that, at a party in the B.O.Q., Alice Roosevelt, daughter of President Theodore Roosevelt, smoked a cigarette and "drank whiskey like a man." Both the hospital and the residence have been removed.

Administrative officers (full colonels), who did not rotate from base to base as field officers, were entitled to homes on the Loop. The commandant's home, built in Queen Anne style, stands at the most prominent position on the circle and provides views of both the Ohio and Little Miami rivers and of downtown Cincinnati. It has a foundation of field stone and walls of locally made red brick. The 15-room structure with three baths, two half baths, a basement, and a porch cost $9,803.53 to build. The front is distinguished by a projection that houses the stairway and by a small balcony on the third floor. Other officers' homes on the Loop include four single-occupant residences and three duplexes, constructed in 1888. The single houses originally had frame siding on the second floor, but that has been replaced. The structures' stone foundations, red brick walls, slate roofs (now covered), and corner cylindrical towers with cone-shaped roofs also represent the Queen Anne style. Parquet floors are laid on the first-floor rooms, and the stairway landings are window seats with art glass windows, which have "USA" etched into the design. Each duplex has an entrance hall, three rooms with fireplaces on the first floor, three rooms with fireplaces on the second, three servants' rooms on the third floor, two staircases, transoms above doors for air circulation in the high-ceilinged rooms, abundant closets, a pantry, and a porch. In 1891 two more duplexes were built on Cochran St. While similar in design to the duplexes on the Loop, the newer ones also have overhanging third-floor dormers. A headquarters building once located next to the latter two has been removed. Veteran's Administration personnel have occupied all of these homes in recent times. The oval green space encircled by the drive and the former rose gardens also attracted many visitors to the post's grounds.

Between 1890 and 1894, six modest homes for noncommissioned officers were built on Pearson St. on the north side of the tower. These modest, 999-square-foot homes contain three rooms on the first floor and one or two rooms and a bath on the second floor. Each house was equipped with a coal cooking range and a laundry stove. They have stone foundations, red brick walls, porches (in most cases, closed in now), and stone lintels above the windows, and they cost $2,100 per house to build. Sgt. **Samuel Woodfill** (1883–1951) and his wife, Blossom, lived on Pearson St. after their marriage, which followed his return from France. Woodfill was awarded the Congressional **Medal of Honor**, by U.S. secretary of war Peyton C. March, for his heroic actions in combat in France against German soldiers during World War I.

Almost immediately after the Fort Thomas Military Reservation was occupied, it was found to be too small. The city was expanding around it, so that there was no room for a very necessary rifle range. To address this need, the Cochran Rifle Range was established on 167 acres purchased from William N. Taliaferro along the Licking River in May 1891. Troops marched 14 miles to the site for frequent practice and often spent a month camping there during summers. When some of the military companies were too large to be accommodated at the post, they set up their tents at the range. Today, the Tri City Sportsman Club Inc. is established at what was the military range's site (4219 Rifle Range Rd.). Similarly, there was no suitable space for a cemetery at the post. However, the **Evergreen Cemetery** in Southgate, just a few miles from the post, reserved an area for soldiers, dependents, nurses, and patients from the Veterans Administration Nursing Home.

In November 1940 the War Department announced that the fort's last major infantry unit, the 10th Regiment, would be transferred to Fort Custer in Michigan. The size of the modern army's regiments had simply rendered Fort Thomas too small. In September 1940 the fort became an induction center only. Throughout World War II, it functioned as such, with recruits undergoing physical and aptitude tests, attending basic lectures and drills, and usually, by the fourth day, being sent by bus and train to army camps elsewhere for basic training. At its peak during World War II, the induction center at Fort Thomas processed about 3,000 recruits per week. Besides its regular staff, it housed about 190 Japanese American soldiers, who performed menial duties.

In June 1944 the War Department suspended the induction center at Fort Thomas and transferred inductions to Fort Benjamin Harrison in Indianapolis. On October 1, 1944, the U.S. Army Air Force (AAF) assumed control of the fort and operated an AAF Convalescent Hospital in the new (1938) barracks during 1944–1945, but the hospital was soon closed because it was not near enough to an airfield. After the fort was controlled by the U.S. Army Corps of Engineers for a short period, the War Department declared the fort surplus property. In October 1946 the Veterans Administration assumed control of it and opened a hospital in 1947. In addition, the army post continued to house military equipment, a guard house (closed in 1960), a PX, a reserve unit, and a small number of personnel. The National Guard operated an artillery unit there from 1955 until 1959. In 1961 the U.S. government granted the City of Fort Thomas 43.87 acres of the property for use as a public park. In 1962 the U.S. Army Reserve built its new Brooks-Lawler Reserve Center on 7.19 acres of the grounds, still home to the 478th Engineer Battalion.

Apparently, small numbers of recruits continued to be inducted at Fort Thomas until April 11, 1964. The property of the fort was declared U.S. government surplus and by 1972 the federal government had divided the fort's property into six tracts of land: the Veterans Administration, which had converted its hospital to a nursing home and which used the homes on Alexander Circle for personnel, received two parcels; the Brooks-Lawler Army Reserve Center received one tract; the U.S. Army Corps of Engineers used one area for its Antennae Farm; and the City of Fort Thomas was given two tracts totaling about 37 additional acres for use as Tower Park (included were the old fort's homes on Greene and Pearson Sts., which the City of Fort Thomas thereafter rented to individuals until September 1992, when the city decided to sell the homes at auction as condominiums with covenants protecting the exteriors). On May 15, 1986, an 86-acre area entitled the Fort Thomas Military Reservation District became a National Register Historic District (the mess hall had been placed on the National Register in 1980). In 2007 President George W. Bush signed legislation permitting the Veterans Administration–owned houses on Alexander Circle to be sold to the City of Fort Thomas, which, in turn, will sell the properties at auction with similar covenants.

Bogart, Charles. "The Military Post at Ft. Thomas, Kentucky," ca. 1985, Kenton Co. Public Library, Covington, Ky.

Daniels, Betty Maddox. "Fort Thomas Military Reservation: Description and History," *NKH* 6, no. 2 (Spring–Summer 1999): 1–22.

Deed Books 347, pp. 44–51; 376, pp. 544–52; 405, pp. 566–73; 406, pp. 371–83; and 463, pp. 283–89, Campbell Co. Courthouse, Newport, Ky.

"Ft. Thomas Center Closes June 15," *KP*, May 24, 1944, 1.

"Ft. Thomas Gets VA Tract," *KP*, December 21, 1972, 2K.

"Ft. Thomas Post Passes to Air Force," *KP*, September 30, 1944, 1.

"Ft. Thomas to Buy Hospital Land," *KP*, September 6, 1972, 2K.

Knapp, Paul T. *Fort Thomas, Kentucky: Its History, Its Heritage*. Fort Thomas, Ky.: Fort Thomas Centennial, 1967.

"Spence to Lead Dedication Parade," *KP*, October 3, 1962, 1K.

Stevens, William R., comp. *Fort Thomas Military Reservation, 1888–1964, Fort Thomas, Kentucky*. Alexandria, Ky.: [Campbell Co. Historical Society?], n.d.

Thomas, Bill. *Images of America: Fort Thomas*. Charleston, S.C.: Arcadia, 2006.

"U.S. Deeds Tract to Ft. Thomas," *KP*, November 10, 1972, 8K.

U.S. Department of the Interior, National Park Service. "National Register of Historic Places Inventory–Nomination Form" for "Fort Thomas Military Reservation District," Kenton Co. Public Library, Covington, Ky.

Wadsworth, Randolph L. "The Military Post at Fort Thomas," *BCHS* 25, no. 3 (July 1967): 184–95.

Betty Maddox Daniels

FORT THOMAS PUBLIC SCHOOLS. Formal education in Fort Thomas began with the Mount Pleasant School, a one-story log building in the northern part of the modern-day city of Fort Thomas, an area known at the time as Mount

Pleasant. This log school was built before 1840 by pioneer resident Richard Taliaferro, on his property. If the school still stood today, it would be at the corner of Holly Ln. and N. Fort Thomas Ave. The Mount Vernon School was started later by a Captain Blackford of Carter's Ln. (now Highland Ave.) along that thoroughfare, opposite Newman Ave.; the Union School was constructed in the south end of the city by the Hawthorne family, next to **St. Stephen Cemetery**. Today the Memorial Park is at that site, at the intersection of old Three Mile Rd. and U.S. 27. A fourth school, the Anderson School, was opened at the southwest corner of W. Villa Pl. and S. Fort Thomas Ave.; it was named for the landowner who owned the dairy there. These schools were called "free schools" and were run by local neighborhood residents.

In 1872 a school system, the predecessor to the modern Fort Thomas Independent Schools System, was formed for the District of the Highlands. Smaller schools were combined or closed to serve the needs of students better. In 1885, as a result of a new state law allowing school districts to issue bonds for new construction, the new Central School began along N. Fort Thomas Ave. (its building later served as city hall). A high school program was initiated that year also, the first in Campbell Co. James McGinniss served as principal and later was named superintendent. The high school's first four-year class, consisting of five boys, graduated in 1891. By 1894 two other schools had been erected: the Inverness School, near the Inverness Golf Course, and the Grant Street School, in the south end of town. By 1907 the Central School had been expanded. In 1911 the Grant Street School closed and a replacement one opened where today's **Samuel Woodfill** School stands.

Highlands High School opened in 1915. Its first principal was Anne B. Regenstein, sister of **Elsworth Regenstein**. That first building, later known as the South Wing, burned to the ground in January 1962. The other wing of the building, the North Wing, was added in 1937. In 1916 the old Mount Pleasant School merged with the Central School. In 1923 the Robert D. Johnson Elementary School opened along N. Fort Thomas Ave.; it has been expanded several times since. The construction of the Samuel Woodfill School along Alexandria Pk. soon followed. In 1931 the Ruth Moyer Elementary School was built, allowing the old Central School to become the city building. In 1962, after the high school's fire, a new building and a gymnasium were built on that campus. In April 2000 the system broke ground for an almost $15 million new middle school, next to Highlands High School. The 95,000-square-foot Highlands Middle School, the first separate middle school in the system, was designed to accommodate up to 600 students in grades six, seven, and eight. Of late, the high school building has been undergoing extensive renovation.

Today the Fort Thomas Independent School System has 2,300 students attending five schools: Woodfill on the south end of town; Moyer in central Fort Thomas; Highlands High School and the new Highland Middle School, both on the same campus along N. Fort Thomas Ave.; and farther north along N. Fort Thomas Ave., the Johnson School. Since 2000 the Fort Thomas Board of Education has occupied a central office at 28 N. Fort Thomas Ave. In June 2007 Dr. Larry Stinson finished his 13th year as school superintendent.

Campbell Co. Historical Society. *Campbell County, Kentucky, 200 Years, 1794–1994.* Alexandria, Ky.: Campbell Co. Historical Society, 1994.

History of Ft. Thomas: The Highlands, 1867–1914. Fort Thomas, Ky.: Fort Thomas Optimist Club, n.d. [ca. 1994].

FORT WRIGHT. Perched atop a hill overlooking Covington to the south, the area that became the city of Fort Wright was once a family farm owned by Robert Samuel Kyle. Kyle had helped build Battery Kyle, a fortification erected during the **Civil War** to help defend Cincinnati from Confederate attack (see **Civil War Fortifications**). Kyles Ln. in Fort Wright is named for the Kyle family. Nearby stood a fort named for Union general **Horatio G. Wright**, an Ohio commander who was a key organizer of the Cincinnati defense. In addition to meritorious service during the Civil War, General Wright went on to civilian fame as the engineer who helped complete the Washington Monument in Washington, D.C.

By the late 1930s, Fort Wright was largely an area of farmland, apple orchards, and dairy cow pastures. But then George Kreutzjans arrived from Lorup, Germany, and recognized the area's potential for residential development. Often referred to as the "Father of Fort Wright," Kreutzjans and an early partner, Theodore Drees (of the Drees Company), built the first homes along Kyles Ln. (see **Building, Residential**). Kreutzjans moved into the area in 1937 after 11 of these houses had been sold. The first homes were available for about $7,000 including the lot. Over time, the area sprouted new streets, including Kennedy, Rose, Augusta, and Barbara. Each street name held a meaning for Kreutzjans; Lorup, for instance, was named for his hometown, and Barbara Circle was named for his wife. Kreutzjans made many other important contributions to the community. He spearheaded the incorporation of the city, served for 20 years on the Fort Wright City Council, and became one of the founding members of the Northern Kentucky Home Builders Association.

In 1941 a group of residents banded together to incorporate the City of Fort Wright as a sixth-class city, bordered by South Hills, Lookout Heights, Covington, and South Fort Mitchell. The first mayor of Fort Wright was Irwin Widmeyer, and he was followed by Fred Wolnitzek, Tom Litzler, John McCormack, Joe Nienaber, Don Martin Sr., Cindy Pinto, Paul Hiltz, and Gene Weaver. City meetings were originally held in various residences, including that of George Kreutzjans, and then were moved to the Fort Wright Civic Club, which opened in the late 1930s.

The Fort Wright Civic Club, located on Kennedy Rd., has long been a driving force in the community. In 1946 the club initiated a community festival to raise funds to start a volunteer fire department, which was something most of Fort Wright's neighboring communities lacked. In 1949 a committee from the Fort Wright Civic Club was responsible for funding, recruiting, and equipping the city's first fire department. Nearly 40 men volunteered for service as firemen, with Vern Ashcraft as their first chief. In 1950 the Fort Wright Civic Club purchased its first piece of fire equipment, a 500-gallon-per-minute Howe pumper. A garage was added to the building to house the pumper, and this became the fire department's home for the next 40 years. In 1952 the Fort Wright Life Squad Service received its humble start when two members of the fire department began responding to emergencies in their own family station wagons. In

Construction on Lorup Ave., Fort Wright, 1955.

1954 a panel van was converted for use as an ambulance and was kept in the equipment bay at the Civic Club.

Fort Wright began to provide fire protection to South Hills under contract in about 1953; this ongoing relationship with South Hills, coupled with shared concerns over being annexed by Covington, led Fort Wright to an amicable annexation of South Hills in 1960. It was the first of several mergers, which garnered for Fort Wright the nickname "The City of Cities." Another neighboring city, Lookout Heights, had similar annexation concerns with Covington. In November 1967, a proposal for Lookout Heights to merge with Fort Wright passed by votes of 389 to 150 in Lookout Heights and 532 to 319 in Fort Wright. Another adjoining city, Park Hills, was originally included in these merger talks, but it elected to withdraw before the vote occurred. In 1968 the newly merged cities briefly operated as Fort Wright–Lookout Heights, with two city buildings and two mayors. The next merger occurred in 1978 with the city of Lakeview, which ran along Madison Pk. (Ky. Rt. 17) from the **Mother of God Cemetery** to roughly where Pioneer Park is located today. Like many small cities, Lakeview suffered from budgetary problems, and it elected to merge with Fort Wright. In November 1977 Fort Wright voted 1,216 to 300 in favor, while the approving vote in Lakeview was 56 to 20.

In 1983 a merger with Kenton Vale was considered. Kenton Vale borders Fort Wright on the east, near the old Lakeview area along Madison Pk. The vote in Fort Wright this time was 1,008 to 953 against merger. Talk of other mergers has arisen from time to time during Fort Wright City Council meetings. A major battle was waged with Covington during the early 1980s over undeveloped property that Covington had annexed in Lookout Heights during the 1960s. Once it had been developed, Covington claimed this property and won it in court in 1980. However, a group of citizens living on the properties in question formed Citizens against Forced Annexation and vigorously fought annexation. Using a new state law, Fort Wright reannexed the disputed area and placed the issue on the ballot. In what amounted to a landslide, a record number of these residents voted to leave Covington. Fort Wright was then required to pay $250,000 over seven years to offset debts Covington had incurred in providing city services to these properties. Some of the money owed was raised between 1981 and 1987 from an annual event in Fort Wright known as the World's Largest Garage Sale, a sale sometimes involving as many as 133 homes in the city's Fort Henry subdivision.

In 1988 Fort Wright purchased five acres at the intersection of Highland Pk. and Kyles Ln. for a new city building where all city operations could be centralized. The new 15,000-square-foot building was occupied on November 20, 1990, and the city's offices were moved from the Lookout Heights Civic Club and the Fort Wright Civic Club. Both social clubs continue to remain active in the community.

Today the Kyle Farm is long gone, replaced by the Kyles Ln. overpass on I-75 (see **Expressways**); Fort Wright has become the de facto crossroads of Kenton Co. with I-275 providing access to points east and west and I-75 and the **Dixie Highway** (U.S. 25) to places north and south. The city is a tight-knit community with many second- and third-generation residents. It is largely residential in nature and is a fourth-class city, covering an area of 3.49 square miles and with a population of 5,681 according to the 2000 census. Fort Wright offers many amenities, including the two civic clubs, a community center (the former South Hills Civic Club), three churches, a school, the Bluegrass Swim Club, the Fort Wright Nature Center, several community parks, and the **James A. Ramage Civil War Museum** at Battery Hooper Park. In addition, the city is home to a thriving community of nearly 500 businesses and an active business association. Fort Wright celebrated its 50th anniversary in 1991 at the city building with a parade and fireworks; the event, according to newspaper reports, was attended by several thousand people. The city was designated Northern Kentucky's Most Livable Neighborhood by *Cincinnati Magazine* in 1995.

City of Fort Wright. *City of Fort Wright 50th Anniversary Booklet.* Fort Wright, Ky.: City of Fort Wright, 1991.

"Park Hills, Ft. Wright, Lookout Heights Talk More on Merger," *KE*, March 21, 1967, 19.

"Pride Fills Ft. Wright's Golden Day," *KP*, August 26, 1991, 3K.

Reis, Jim. "The City They All Seem to Want," *KP*, November 11, 1985, 4K.

U.S. Census Bureau. "American Fact Finder. Data Set. Census 2000 Summary File 1 (SF1) 100-Percent Data. Custom Table." www.census.gov (accessed October 4, 2006).

Dave Hatter

FORWARD QUEST INC./VISION 2015. Forward Quest Inc., a nonprofit corporation, was organized in 1996 to implement Quest: A Vision for Northern Kentucky, a regional community agenda for Boone, Campbell, and Kenton counties. Led by cochairs Bill Butler and Rev. Bill Cleves, the Quest vision was created by 14 task forces and included 44 strategic initiatives (projects) related to economic development, education, human services, culture/parks, governance, and regionalism. Working with a small staff, Forward Quest engaged hundreds of volunteers and more than 60 organizational partners to work collaboratively to implement the Quest projects. The organization was committed to improving the region's quality of life and advancing its best long-term interests.

The Quest vision has been responsible, through Forward Quest, for establishing Legacy, a young professionals' group; the **Urban Learning Center**, which provides college-level instruction for low-income adults; the **Duveneck House**, which offers art classes and programs for inner-city youth; and the **Northern Kentucky Fund** of the Greater Cincinnati Foundation. Forward Quest also sponsored the publication of the *Encyclopedia of Northern Kentucky*, a comprehensive historical resource for the region. In addition Forward Quest conducted advanced education and governance studies that helped inform the community and key stakeholders about trends and opportunities. It supported efforts to secure state funding for the Metropolitan Education and Training Center and the **Bank of Kentucky** Arena at **Northern Kentucky University**, as well as the additional operational funding for Northern Kentucky University and the establishment of **Gateway Community and Technical College**.

Beginning in late 2004, Forward Quest led and supported the community visioning process that produced Vision 2015. The founding director of Forward Quest and of Vision 2015 was Michael Hammons. Northern Kentucky's 10-year strategic plan, a community agenda produced by more than 2,000 people from throughout the community. The visioning process was led by cochairs James "Jim" Votruba of Northern Kentucky University and Andrew "A. J." Schaeffer of the Greenbaum, Doll & McDonald law firm. Extensive studies and public-engagement activities were led by six task forces in the strategic areas of economic competitiveness, education excellence, effective governance, livable communities, regional stewardship, and urban renaissance to address the needs of the community. The final report was released to the public in March 2006. In April 2006 Forward Quest dissolved its Board of Directors, turning to the Vision 2015 Regional Stewardship Council for leadership. The Regional Stewardship Council includes more than 50 diverse members from throughout the community. With the change of leadership, the small staff of Forward Quest changed its operating name to Vision 2015.

The 10-year plan includes specific goals to increase educational attainment, homeownership, the number of high-paying jobs, and the number of parks in the region, as well as to encourage new investment in the urban core, more effective governance, greater public engagement, more women and minorities in key leadership positions, and increased civic volunteerism. Vision 2015 maintains the primary purposes of Forward Quest: to enhance the region's quality of life and advance its best long-term interests. It focuses on Boone, Bracken, Campbell, Carroll, Gallatin, Grant, Kenton, Owen, and Pendleton counties. In November 2006 community leaders from Cincinnati embraced Vision 2015, making a commitment to develop a similar community agenda that could later be integrated with the efforts of Vision 2015 to form a Shared Civic Agenda.

The staff of the former Forward Quest Inc. continues to work with community organizations and stakeholder groups to implement Vision 2015. This organization functions in both leadership and supporting roles in identifying priorities; convening, forming, and supporting coalitions of participating partners; providing research and consultants;

generating financial, governmental, and community support; assuring public engagement; establishing and evaluating outcome measures; monitoring and reporting to the community the overall progress in the implementation of the vision; and celebrating success.

Kara Clark

FOSDICK, WILLIAM WHITEMAN (b. January 28, 1825, Cincinnati, Ohio; d. March 8, 1862, Cincinnati, Ohio). William W. Fosdick, a lawyer and a poet, was the son of Thomas R. and Julia Drake Fosdick. His father, a Cincinnati merchant and banker, died August 1, 1829, when William was a child. His mother was a famous actress, and an aunt, **Mrs. Alexander Drake**, was another famous and talented actress. The Drakes were the pioneer theatrical family of the Ohio River Valley. William was raised in Covington and graduated in 1845 from Transylvania College, where he studied law. He practiced in Covington, Cincinnati, and New York City. The front page of the October 26, 1850, *Covington Journal* included an advertisement of his law office on Third St. in Cincinnati. After his time in New York, he returned to Cincinnati and edited the literary journal *Sketch Club*. He was also a poet and a constant punster, and for a few years he was regarded as the poet laureate of Cincinnati. His novel *Malmiztic* was met with both high praise and loud ridicule. It was said of him that if he had not been consumed by playing chess, he might have accomplished more in literature. Fosdick was buried at Spring Grove Cemetery in Cincinnati.

Advertisement, *CJ,* October 26, 1850, 1.
Coyle, William, ed. *Ohio Authors and Their Books: 1796–1950.* Cleveland, Ohio: World, 1962.
Ford, Henry A., and Kate B. Ford. *History of Cincinnati, Ohio.* Cleveland, Ohio: Williams, 1881.
Hill, West T., Jr. *The Theatre in Early Kentucky: 1790–1820.* Lexington: Univ. of Kentucky Press, 1971.
"Mrs. A. Drake," *CJ,* May 16, 1874, 2.

FOSTER. Foster, an Ohio River community, is located in the northeastern tip of Bracken Co., at the mouth of Holt's Creek. Originally known as Foster's Landing, it was named for landowner Israel Foster. On August 19, 1847, Richard Lindsey established the first post office there. On January 30, 1850, Foster was incorporated as a sixth-class city, and the name of the post office was changed to Foster the same year. Early settlers used the river landing to send tobacco, grain, and other goods to markets in Cincinnati and New Orleans. Foster was an important shipping point, and the landing was used in 1853 to receive materials to construct a suspension bridge at Falmouth. In the late 1870s, Israel Foster donated land to build a Northern and a Southern Methodist Church. The Northern Church was soon disbanded, and its members joined the Southern congregation.

The 1884 atlas of Bracken Co. depicts Foster as a fairly large town, in which the following men conducted business: W. W. Erion, George Holmes, Harry Ketchum, J. J. Ketchum, A. Lively, the Markley brothers, and L. B. Plummer. The railroad, built in 1888, promoted additional transportation and shipping. In 1907 Foster received a natural gas line. A Kentucky Historical Highway Marker relates the story of an early American Indian raid at the mouth of Holt's Creek in summer 1793. The raiders crossed the Ohio River, hid their canoes in Holt's Creek, and proceeded across country to Bourbon Co. to steal horses. Simon Kenton, who was in the area at the time, gathered a group of men to ambush the war party upon its return to the river. After concealing themselves for four days, Kenton's men killed six warriors, scattering the others, and retrieved the stolen horses.

Today, what remains of Foster is located between Ky. Rt. 8 (the **Mary Ingles Highway**) and the **AA Highway**. The new pool level of the Ohio River covers remnants of the old boat landing and of the original town. Foster is no longer incorporated, and the AA Highway has removed most of the traffic that used to pass through town along the Mary Ingles Highway.

Bracken Co. Extension Homemakers. *History of Bracken County.* Bicentennial ed. Brooksville, Ky.: Bracken Co. Extension Homemakers, 2002.
Rennick, Robert M. *Kentucky Place Names.* Lexington: Univ. of Kentucky Press, 1984.

John E. Leming Jr.

FOSTER, RANDOLPH SINKS (b. February 22, 1820, Williamsburg, Ohio; d. May 1, 1903, Newton, Mass.). Randolph Foster, a bishop and an author, was the son of a jailer in Clermont Co., Ohio. The family moved to Kentucky, and he attended Augusta College. In 1837 he was admitted to the Ohio Conference of the Methodist Episcopal Church. Over the years, he traveled widely in his preaching and teaching. In 1852 Foster received his BA from Ohio Wesleyan College, and in 1858 the same school awarded him a DD (doctorate in divinity). He served as president of Northwestern University in Chicago (1857–1860) and of Drew Theological Seminary in Princeton, N.J. (1870–1872). In 1872 he was elected a bishop in the Methodist Episcopal Church. He authored more than a dozen books, the most famous being the religious work *Objections to Calvinism as It Is* (1849), which was written while he was the pastor of a famous Methodist church in Cincinnati, Wesley Chapel. In 1876 he moved to Boston, where he spent the rest of his life. He was an often-requested speaker and traveled widely throughout the country. He died in Massachusetts in 1903 and was buried at the Greenwood Cemetery in Brooklyn, N.Y.

"Bishop Foster," *Newton (Mass.) Graphic Supplement,* May 8, 1903.
Coyle, William, ed. *Ohio Authors and Their Books: 1796–1950.* Cleveland, Ohio: World, 1962.
Mohs, Mayo. "Your Town: Augusta, Ky., Battleground of Giants," *KTS,* June 27, 1956, 21–23.
Rankins, Walter H. *Augusta College.* Frankfort, Ky.: Roberts, 1955.
"Recent Death," *Boston Evening Transcript,* May 2, 1903, 2.
"Translation," *Zion's Herald,* May 6, 1903, 550–56.

FOSTER, STEPHEN COLLINS (b. July 4, 1826, Lawrenceville, Pa.; d. January 13, 1864, New York City). Songwriter Stephen Foster was born at White Cottage, his family's homestead along the Allegheny River northeast of Pittsburgh. He was the 10th of 11 children of William Barclay and Eliza Tomlinson Foster. His mother was the half sister of Dr. Joseph S. Tomlinson, president of **Augusta College**, Augusta, Ky., and Dr. John Tomlinson, an Augusta physician. Stephen and his mother are said to have visited them in Augusta at least once, in May 1833. Today a Kentucky Highway marker in Augusta suggests that Foster was influenced by Negro spirituals he heard there. Foster was schooled at home, as was typical on America's frontier. He evidenced much interest in music and received some formal musical training from Henry Klaber, a German immigrant composer who was influential in Pittsburgh's musical circles. By age 18 Foster was writing words and music, creating the first of his many songs.

At age 20 Foster became a bookkeeper in his older brother Dunning's merchant firm in Cincinnati and continued to pen music. He saw river life firsthand and noted the mingling currents in American culture. His genius blossomed. In Cincinnati he began to write songs in earnest while establishing friendships with musicians, minstrels, and publishers. He gave manuscript copies of "Oh! Susanna," "Old Uncle Ned," and other songs to several acquaintances in Cincinnati. Queen City minstrels sang his compositions, increasing the popularity of these songs. "Oh! Susanna" (1847) became the marching song of thousands of Americans joining the California gold rush. In 1849 Foster decided to devote himself full-time to music composition and sent one of his best songs, "Nelly Was a Lady," to a New York City publisher. He negotiated a favorable contract with this firm, Firth, Pond & Company, and maintained a satisfactory business relationship with it for several years.

Foster returned to Pittsburgh, where the years between 1850 and 1855 were his most successful. He entered into an agreement with Edwin P. Christy, leader of the famous Christy Minstrels, whereby Christy agreed to pay Foster a small fee for the privilege of singing Foster songs before they were published; Foster would then be able to affix "As Sung by the Christy Minstrels" on his music's title pages. Foster's business skills were poor, as he sold the rights to "Old Folks at Home" in 1851 to Christy for a paltry $15; when this song was published, it bore the surprising statement, "Composed by E. P. Christy." More than 160 compositions poured from Foster's pen during these years. Many were of only passing interest, but several enduring favorites were created: "Camptown Races" and "Nelly Bly" (1850); "Old Folks at Home" and "Ring, Ring the Banjo" (1851); "Massa's in de Cold Ground" (1852); "My Old Kentucky Home," "Good Night," and "Old Dog Tray" (1853); "Jeanie with the Light Brown Hair" (1854); and "Come Where My Love Lies Dreaming" (1855).

On July 22, 1850, Foster married Jane Denny McDowell, daughter of a Pittsburgh physician. Their daughter and only child, Marion, was born in Pittsburgh on April 18, 1851. The marriage was not always serene. Even though Stephen was basically kind and sympathetic, he also possessed a genius temperament: moody, and careless about money and practicality. About the time Marion was born, he was working on "Swanee River (Old Folks at Home)." Although he had never seen Florida's Suwannee River, he immortalized it around the world with this song. Stephen Foster has thus become the only American composer who has contributed what became two official state songs: "Swanee River" for Florida, and "My Old Kentucky Home" for Kentucky.

By 1856 Foster's compositions had decreased in number and quality, and by 1857 his financial situation was bleak; he developed the habit of selling his compositions to publishers for outright cash, thereby undervaluing most of them. After composing "Old Black Joe" (1860), he moved to New York City in a effort to regain his financial footing. Except for "Beautiful Dreamer" (1863), Foster's compositions written while he was in New York City were of poor quality. He soon found he could not support Jane and Marion, and they both returned to Pittsburgh. In New York City, cut off from sympathetic friends and family, Foster became lonely and despondent. On January 10, 1864, he fell in his room and was taken to Bellevue Hospital, where he died on January 13, at age 37. He was buried at Allegheny Cemetery in Pittsburgh, not far from his birthplace.

Algier, Keith. *Ante-Bellum Augusta: The Life and Times of a Kentucky River Town.* Maysville, Ky.: Standard Quick Print, 2002.

Emerson, Ken. *Doo-Dah! Stephen Foster and the Rise of American Popular Culture.* New York: Simon and Schuster, 1997.

Rankins, Walter H. *Augusta College, Augusta, Kentucky: First Established Methodist College, 1822–1849.* Frankfort, Ky.: Roberts, 1957.

Karl Lietzenmayer

FOSTER'S CHAPEL UNITED METHODIST CHURCH. Established in the late 1840s by Rev. Jedediah Foster, this Robertson Co. Methodist Episcopal North congregation split off from the Mount Zion Church. Originally the membership met in the chapel of the Foster's Chapel Cemetery, hence its name. It is located 2.5 miles northwest of Mount Olivet along Foster Chapel Ln. After the **Civil War**, a new meetinghouse was built nearby. Later a bell tower and vestibule were added, but the latter was removed by 1962. The area around the church is also generally known as Foster's Chapel.

Moore, T. Ross, ed. *Echoes from the Century, 1867–1967.* Mount Olivet, Ky.: Robertson Co. Historical Society, 2000.

4-H CLUBS. 4-H Clubs have been well represented in the rural areas of Northern Kentucky. It was in the late 1890s and early 1900s that 4-H clubs were established to meet the needs of rural young people in the United States. These clubs united youth through "learning by doing." In 1907, under sponsorship of the U.S. Department of Agriculture (USDA), corn clubs began in the South. Several years later, pig clubs were added to the program. At that same time, canning clubs were organized, using materials furnished by the USDA. In 1911 the 4-H Club's four-leaf-clover emblem was designed, and in 1924 the organization acquired its 4-H name and patented the 4-H emblem.

The 4-H programs, with volunteer leadership, taught children in farming communities the responsibilities of raising animals and crops, using new and improved techniques. Young women were taught sewing and cooking. During **World War II**, Northern Kentuckians plowed victory gardens and bought victory bonds. In early 1943, J. A. Caywood, the Kenton Co. school superintendent, supplemented regular high school classes with victory corps, in order to teach students basic military skills. The Boone Co. 4-H Club organized a victory program to promote basic farming skills. Throughout Kentucky, 200,000 students enrolled in the 4-H victory program.

Now sponsored by the Cooperative Extension Service of the University of Kentucky at Lexington, under the auspices of the USDA, 4-H clubs in the state are mostly urban. Local chapters, which elect their own leadership, have monthly meetings, where they learn about citizenship and life skills. There are wide selections of projects that fit the rural as well as the urban 4-H member, and the clubs are reaching out to new audiences with after-school programs. No longer just about livestock and crops, today's 4-H clubs involve members in equine activities, photography, computer technology, and career development. Members also participate in lifestyle programs, nutrition, and cooking; design and sew clothes; gain knowledge about the environment; engage in community service; attend state and national conferences; and can even be part of international exchange programs.

Each Northern Kentucky county has a 4-H Club program. It is often associated with the county's fair, where there is a strong connection to the organization's agricultural roots. Members of 4-H clubs share with the community their projects: livestock clinics and contests, as well as nonanimal activities such as photography, art contests, vegetable and fruit exhibits, needlework, and foods.

Kentucky, one of the first states to offer 4-H programs, has some famous 4-H alumni, including governors (Martha Layne Collins [1983–1987], Wendell Ford [1971–1974], and Paul Patton [1995–2003]), a senator (Mitch McConnell), a Kentucky commissioner of agriculture (Billy Ray Smith), singers/songwriters (Ricky Skaggs and Kevin Richardson), and a Triple Crown–winning jockey (**Steve Cauthen**).

Today, 9 million youngsters nationally of ages 5–19, whether on the farm, in the cities, or in subdivisions, are involved in 4-H programs. A person who is not a 4-H member but wears the 4-H emblem is subject to a $5,000 fine and a six-month jail sentence, under federal law (U.S. Code 707, section 18). This is the same law that protects the seal of the president of the United States.

Cabot, Susan M., and Michael D. Rouse. *Boone County.* Charleston, S.C.: Arcadia, 1998.

Kentucky 4-H. www.ca.uky.edu/agcollege/4h/partnerships/ydpartnership/ (accessed on July 9, 2006).

Warner, Jennifer S. *Boone County: From Mastodons to the Millennium.* Burlington, Ky.: Boone Co. Bicentennial Book Committee, 1998.

Nancy J. Tretter

FOUSE, ELIZABETH B. COOK "LIZZIE" (b. May 14, 1875, Lancaster, Ky.; d. October 22, 1952, Lexington, Ky.). Lizzie Beatrice Burnside Cook, an African American educator, clubwoman, and social activist, was the daughter of William and Mary Burnside Cook. In 1884 she entered the Model Division at the State University in Louisville (formerly named Simmons Bible College) and advanced the following year to the university's Normal Department. She apparently transferred to Eckstein-Norton Institute in Cane Springs, Ky. when that college opened in 1890, and graduated two years later. At age 17, Lizzie began teaching at the Constitution School in Lexington. She married William Henry Fouse in August 1898, and the couple began a 46-year partnership devoted to uplifting African Americans. In 1908 William Fouse was appointed principal of William Grant High School, and when the couple moved to Covington, Lizzie joined the Ladies Union and Ladies Improvement clubs. Thus she started her lifelong association with the Northern Kentucky community and the African American clubwomen's movement. In 1913 the Fouses moved to Lexington, where William was called to head the Russell and later the Paul Lawrence Dunbar schools. Though for the rest of her life she lived in Lexington, where she was equally well respected for her social activism, Lizzie Fouse did not abandon the social causes in which she was involved in Northern Kentucky; she returned often to support them.

The Fouses lived by the motto "lifting as we climb." Lizzie Fouse was part of the network of African American women who organized on the local, state, national, and international levels. The National Association of Colored Women, the Association of Southern Women for the Prevention of Lynching, the Kentucky Commission on Interracial Cooperation, the Kentucky Negro Educational Association, the National Women's Christian Temperance Union, and the **NAACP** were some of the groups that benefited from her leadership. She was a delegate in 1933 to the International Congress of Women held in Chicago and in 1947 to the world convention of the Women's Temperance Union in England. The L. B. Fouse Civic Center in Covington, which became the site of many **civil rights** meetings during the 1960s, was established in her honor in 1953.

William H. Fouse died June 1, 1944, and Lizzie Fouse died October 22, 1952, each while residing at their home, at 219 N. Upper St. in Lexington. Lizzie was buried at the Greenwood Cemetery (Cove Hill Cemetery today) in Lexington. Networks created across the country by many African American women such as Lizzie Fouse laid the foundation for the success of the civil rights movement of the 1960s.

Fouse Family Papers, folders 1–2, Special Collections, M. L. King Library, Univ. of Kentucky, Lexington.
"Heart Attack Proves Fatal to Mrs. Fouse," *Lexington Leader*, October 22, 1952, 1.
Hollingsworth, Randolph. *Lexington: Queen of the Bluegrass*. Charleston, S.C.: Arcadia, 2004.
Kentucky Death Certificate No. 13381, for the year 1944.
Kentucky Death Certificate No. 23024, for the year 1952.
Pettit, Jennifer L. "Consuming, Organizing, and Uplifting: Elizabeth Fouse and the Production of Class Identity," master's thesis, Univ. of Kentucky, 1998.
Smith, Gerald L. *Lexington Kentucky*. Charleston, S.C.: Arcadia, 2002.

Jim Embry

FOWLER, JACOB (b. 1764, either New Jersey or New York; d. October 16, 1849, Covington, Ky.). One of the earliest settlers of Northern Kentucky, Jacob Fowler built a log cabin in the area of Newport in about 1789. In 1782, at age 18, Fowler fought with Gen. **George Rogers Clark** in Clark's successful campaign against the Shawnee Indians. Fowler also participated in the battles known as Harmar's Defeat in 1789 and St. Clair's Defeat in 1791, where he almost died. Later, he fought in Gen. Anthony Wayne's victorious Fallen Timbers Campaign of 1794. Fowler returned to Newport, and in 1796 **James Taylor Jr.** appointed him Campbell Co. deputy sheriff. In 1793 Fowler was given an in-lot in Newport in payment for clearing land. In 1795 he opened Newport's first tavern in his home, and it soon became a well-known gathering place and the site of some early city meetings. He bought from Taylor out-lot no. 1, which consisted of two acres south of Fifth St. between Isabella and Brighton. Fowler was also one of the founders of the **Newport Academy**, a Newport City Council member, and operator of a ferry (see **ferries**) across the Licking River. When two of Taylor's slaves, Moses and Humphrey, ran away, it was Fowler who helped find them. Fowler also assisted Taylor in surveying the turnpike to Alexandria (**U.S. 27**), which continues south toward Lexington. In the "James Taylor Narrative," Taylor talks of hunting buffalo with Jacob Fowler at **Big Bone Lick**.

In 1821–1822, Fowler was a guide of the Fowler-Glenn Expedition that blazed the Old Taos Trail to New Mexico. His journal of the expedition was subsequently published by the American scientist Elliot Coues as *The Journal of Jacob Fowler*. Fowler moved to Covington sometime after 1826, and his place of burial is not known. He married a widow, Esther de Vie Sanders, who was of French descent. Their granddaughter, **Henrietta Cleveland**, became one of the founders of St. Elizabeth Hospital (see **St. Elizabeth Medical Center**).

"Died," *CJ*, October 19, 1849, 2.
Fowler, Jacob. *The Journal of Jacob Fowler: Narrating an Adventure from Arkansas through the Indian Territory, Oklahoma, Kansas, Colorado, and New Mexico, to the Sources of Rio Grande del Norte, 1821–22*. Ed. Elliot Coues. New York: Francis P. Harper, 1898; reprint, Minneapolis: Ross and Haines, 1965.
Jones, Mary Keturah. *History of Campbell County*. Newport, Ky., 1876. Reprint, Fort Thomas, Ky.: Rebecca Bryan Boone Chapter of the Daughters of the American Revolution, 1974.
Purvis, Thomas L., ed. *Newport, Kentucky: A Bicentennial History*. Newport, Ky.: Otto Zimmerman, 1996.
Taylor, James, Jr. "The James Taylor Narrative," 1840, Kenton Co. Public Library; Campbell Co. Historical and Genealogical Society, Alexandria, Ky.
Wessling, Jack. *Early History of Campbell County, Ky*. Alexandria, Ky.: Self-published, 1997.

FRANCISVILLE. The history of Francisville, a town in Boone Co., is intimately related to its Baptist church. In 1819 in Boone Co., 77 members of the **Bullittsburg Baptist Church**, who lived north of that church, decided to build a place of worship closer to their homes. The group was made up of 54 whites and their 23 slaves. A three-acre site was purchased to build a church; members met in private homes while the building was under construction. The new congregation was named the **Sand Run Baptist Church**, evidently after the sandy dirt road running through the area. Both the church and the town of Francisville date their formation to 1819. The church's building cost $2,100, which was paid partly with money and partly with tobacco, the church group's primary source of income. The small one-room brick church building had a balcony, where the slaves sat during services. Rings were attached to trees in the churchyard so that members could tie their horses. The first pastor of Sand Run was Rev. Chichester Matthews, who remained the pastor until his death in 1828. A cemetery was started behind the church, where Matthews and others were buried. Well known Boone Co. clerk Cave Johnson (see **Cave Johnson House**) and his three wives are buried there. Lighting for the church came from several banks of L-shaped candleholders; a different church member was assigned to light these each week. Drinking water was supplied from a local spring, until members of the congregation dug a well in the churchyard. Soon a general store, a hotel, a post office, a school, and a tobacco warehouse sprang up around the church. The town of Francisville flourished for a number of years and then declined as travel became easier in the area, and the community's businesses moved to other towns. Eventually the public buildings were torn down, leaving just the church building and a number of farms. Today the town has no mayor, no police or fire department, and no businesses.

Reis, Jim. "Tiny Unincorporated Communities Abound in Boone," *KP*, December 9, 1985, 4K.
"Sand Run Baptist Church," 175th Anniversary Historical Edition, Sand Run Baptist Church, Francisville, Ky.

FRANKLIN ACADEMY. In 1795 the citizens of Washington, Ky., petitioned the Kentucky legislature to grant a charter for a new school in Mason Co., to be called the Franklin Academy. The request was approved, and the school opened in 1796 on Washington's Duke of York St. Twenty-five prominent locals were chosen as trustees and assigned the task of running the school. One trustee was a local physician, Dr. **Basil Duke**, who married U.S. chief justice John Marshall's daughter, Charlotte. Another was Dr. Duke's mercantile business partner, Judge **John Coburn**, whose wife was Mary Ann Moss, sister of **Keturah Moss Leitch Taylor**. Another trustee was **Revolutionary War** veteran Capt. **Philip Buckner**, who donated the land on which the town of Augusta was founded. Monsieur Mentelle, a French immigrant for whom Mentelle Park in Lexington is named, was an early teacher at the academy. A physician, Dr. **William Goforth**, was both a trustee and a teacher at Franklin Academy. On the very night he arrived in Washington, Dr. Goforth met the daughter of William Wood, one of the founders of Washington, and fell madly in love with her. The couple later married and moved to Cincinnati. During their stay there, 15-year old **Daniel Drake** left his Mayslick home to study medicine in Cincinnati. The Goforths invited Drake to reside with them during his schooling, and he readily agreed to do so. With the mentorship of Dr. Goforth, Daniel Drake became one of the greatest medical authorities in the area.

Franklin Academy hired highly qualified teachers, and the school soon gained a reputation as one of the best educational academies west of the Alleghenies. However, Franklin, like most early schools, was quite primitive, often using handmade textbooks. Penmanship was accomplished with goose quills and homemade ink. The curriculum was centered on the three R's, plus basic information about the United States and its leaders. Many students arose at daybreak and assisted with chores at their family farms before walking several miles to school. The atmosphere at these early schools was very strict, and corporal punishment was an integral part of a student's training. Exactly how long Franklin Academy existed is not known.

Best, Edna Hunter. *The Historic Past of Washington, Mason County, Kentucky*. Cynthiana, Ky.: Hobson Book Press, 1944.
Clark, Thomas D. *A History of Kentucky*. New York: Prentice-Hall, 1937.

FRANZ, FREDERICK WILLIAM (b. September 12, 1892, Covington, Ky.; d. December 22, 1992, Brooklyn, N.Y.). Frederick Franz, who became president of the **Jehovah's Witnesses**, was the son of Edward F. and Ida L. Franz of Covington. He lived at 102 E. 13th St., and his father worked next door at Kreiger's Bakery. He was baptized Lutheran, according to his father's religion, but attended the parochial school of **St. Joseph Catholic Church, Covington**. He always remembered the quality of the Marianist Brothers' instruction there. Later, adding to the religious diversity of his youth, he became a member of the Presbyterian Church. His family moved to Cincinnati, where he was the valedictorian of his high school class at Woodward High School (then in downtown Cincinnati). He studied Latin and Greek at the University of Cincinnati as preparation for becoming a Presbyterian minister. In 1913 he left the university after his junior year (purportedly giving up a Rhodes Scholarship), to be ordained a minister in Chicago as part of the International Bible Students movement, the group that became the Jehovah's Witnesses. As a minister, he sold religious books for the Watch Tower Bible and Tract Society, the official name of the Jehovah's Witnesses. In 1920 he moved to Brooklyn, N.Y., to work for that organization; in 1945 he became a vice president, and in 1977, after the death of Nathan H. Knorr, he was elected the fourth president of the worldwide Jehovah's Witnesses. He believed in the power of the radio and made use of it often. He was broadcasting as early as 1930, locally on station WBBR. In 1958 he spoke to a combined group of more than 250,000 members gathered at both Yankee Stadium and the Polo Grounds in New York City for an international conference of Jehovah's Witnesses. Considered the primary theologian of his church, Franz is generally credited with being a major contributor to *The New World Translation of the Bible* (1961) as well as a 1966 work entitled *Life Everlasting in the Freedom of the Sons of God.* The latter asserted that the seventh period of 1,000 years of human history would begin in autumn 1975.

Franz died from cardiopulmonary arrest at the age of 99. He spent his last days blind and deaf, living at the infirmary in the church's world headquarters in Brooklyn, where his funeral services were held. He was buried in Resurrection Park, Watchtower Farms, Wallkill, N.Y. Much of the recent success of this 5-million-member worldwide religious organization can be attributed to the formative leadership of this native Covingtonian.

"Frederick W. Franz, a Religious Leader, Dies in Office at 99," *NYT,* December 24, 1992, B6.

Kreimer, Peggy. "Church Leader's Roots in N. KY." *KP,* December 25, 1992, 1K.

Life Everlasting in the Freedom of the Sons of God. Brooklyn, N.Y.: Watchtower Bible and Tract Society, 1966.

Michael R. Sweeney

FREEDMEN'S BUREAU. Northern Kentucky benefited from schools and medical services established in the state by the Freedmen's Bureau. In fall 1865, voluntary freedmen's associations in Boston, Cincinnati, Philadelphia, and New York City sent petitions to the 83rd U.S. Congress, claiming that the services and protection needed by hundreds of thousands of former slaves in the South were overtaxing their limited financial resources. They insisted that the federal government take immediate action. Over strong objections by President Andrew Johnson (1865–1869), the U.S. Congress enacted the Bureau of Refugees, Freedmen, and Abandoned Lands under the War Powers Act and a year later overrode Johnson's presidential veto, thereby extending the act. The new bureau was supposed to be funded from confiscated lands and by fees levied on former Confederates.

The bureau's charter stipulated that it was to supervise and manage all abandoned lands and control all matters relating to freedmen and refugees. The Radical Republicans wanted lands owned by Confederate officers and officials to be distributed among former slaves and wrote into the original act a land distribution of 40 acres to freed slaves that became as famous as it was controversial. Chiefly associated with land reform, education, and social services such as orphanages, homes for the aged, medical dispensaries, and federal banks for freedmen, the new bureau was staffed by army chaplains and regular soldiers.

The Kentucky General Assembly's failure to approve the 13th Amendment to the U.S. Constitution and to eliminate the state's slave code, as well as its outright hostility toward the education of former slaves, caught the attention of Maj. Gen. Clinton B. Fisk, then head of the Freedmen's Bureau in Tennessee. In March 1866 Fisk sent a scathing report about the situation in Kentucky to Washington, D.C.

Shortly thereafter, Rev. T. K. Noble was appointed chaplain and chief superintendent for the bureau's schools in Kentucky. Noble assumed the task of educating former slaves; there were 37,000 illiterate children and nearly 250,000 illiterate adults but only 18 schools with seats for 235 children available in all of Kentucky: two of those schools were in Northern Kentucky, one in Covington at the Bremen St. Baptist Church and the other in Newport on Southgate St., near Saratoga St. (see **Freedmen's Bureau Schools**).

Noble chose not to get into divisive jurisdictional battles in Kentucky. He worked closely with the American Missionary Association (AMA) and the Western Freedmen Aid Commission (WFAC) and gave them credit for opening schools and bringing teachers in from outside the state. Both of those organizations joined in his efforts to open the Ely Normal School at Louisville to train African American teachers who lived in Kentucky. The AMA and the WFAC supported schools at Berea, Camp Nelson, and Covington, as well as at Lexington and Louisville. The Baptist Missionary Association, the Methodist Missionary Association, and the Right Reverend B. B. Smith, an Episcopal Bishop, were encouraged to open and staff schools. The Freedmen's Bureau itself funded the establishment of nearly 100 schools across the state. Most were built with finances contributed by their local Freedmen's Bureaus.

From July 1866 to January 13, 1869, Noble continued to send detailed narrative and statistical reports to Rev. J. W. Alvord, his superior in Washington, D.C. Contained in those reports were a litany of more than 100 incidents and outrages in which Freedmen's Bureau schools and churches were burned, teachers harassed, and freedmen assaulted or murdered. Federal troops had to be deployed to protect the schools in many areas of Kentucky, further fueling local hostility to the Freedmen's Bureau.

Originally stressing education, the Freedmen's Bureau in Kentucky soon became enmeshed in a number of critical social services such as opening orphanages to serve abandoned children, establishing homes for the aged, and setting up needed medical service facilities. In Covington the Freedmen's Bureau established a medical dispensary to supply medicines and medical advice to "invalid and indigent refugees and freedmen" who lived in Covington and Newport. The dispensary was under the supervision of Dr. J. J. Temple, and its headquarters was located on Madison Ave in Covington. That facility was clearly needed, as more freedmen refugees continued to arrive in Northern Kentucky from other parts of the state. A Freedmen's Bank was also established in the state and was one of the more successful ones in the country. In the April 1869 report, there were 950 depositors with $100,000 in savings in Kentucky. However, the Freedmen's Bank never opened a branch in Northern Kentucky; its closest branch was in Lexington.

In September 1868 prominent Republican lawyer and politician Benjamin P. Runkle, who had replaced Noble as the Freedmen's Bureau administrator in Kentucky, was ordered to shut down operations in the state. Between October 1868 and January 1869, Runkle closed the regional offices that had been so successful in developing the Freedmen's Bureau's schools and reassigned five of the eight career officers reporting to him. He eliminated the civilian agent and reduced the number of clerks from 19 to 4, and those 4 were assigned strictly to paying bounties owed to freedmen. By April 1869 the Freedmen's Bureau in Kentucky was down to a superintendent of education, one clerk, and three other clerks paying bounties. Runkle's last report to Washington, D.C., claimed that although "murders and outrages continued" to take place against freedmen in Kentucky, his staff was too small to investigate them and report.

Bentley, George R. *The History of the Freedmen's Bureau.* New York: Octagon Books, 1970.

Du Bois, W. E. Burghardt. "The Freedmen's Bureau," *Atlantic Monthly* 87 (1901): 354–65.

Fisk, Gen. Clinton B., to Maj. Gen. Oliver O. Howard. House Executive Document No. 70, 39th Cong., 1st sess., 1865–1866, p. 230.

Harris, Theodore H. H. "Creating Windows of Opportunity: Isaac E. Black and the African American Experience in Kentucky, 1848–1914," *RKHS* 98, no. 2 (Spring 2000): 155–77.

Webb, Ross A. "Benjamin P. Runkle and the Freedmen's Bureau in Kentucky, 1866–1870." In *The Freedmen's Bureau and Black Freedom,* ed. Donald G. Nieman. New York: Garland, 1994.

———. "The Past Is Never Dead, It's Not Even Past." In Nieman, *Freedmen's Bureau and Black Freedom.*

Diane Perrine Coon

FREEDMEN'S BUREAU SCHOOLS. Before the **Civil War**, free people of color residing in Kentucky could with great difficulty obtain basic reading and writing skills through subscription schools sponsored by their churches or by attending schools in states north of the Ohio River. In some urban areas of Kentucky, church pastors taught in the subscription schools; in rural areas, however, such educational opportunities rarely existed.

Slaves had even more difficulty learning how to read and write. Very few slave owners in Kentucky permitted their slaves to learn to read the Bible; this practice was frowned upon both by social custom and by various local ordinances. In Bracken Co. during the mid-1830s, a slave owner named Jack Tabb taught his slaves to read and "figger" because it suited Tabb's interests to do so. Tabb's actions were quite unusual. Most slave owners feared that slaves, if taught to write, would forge "permission to move" slips and escape to the North. Such fears were particularly acute for persons holding slaves in the river counties of Northern Kentucky. Eventually, one of Tabb's slaves, Arnold Gragston, did just that, leaving Kentucky with his entire family for Canada.

At the end of the Civil War, there were nearly 4 million illiterate freedmen in the nation, and almost 250,000 of them lived in Kentucky. In the massive confusion following the war's end, federal and state governments focused on reestablishing political and economic stability rather than on educating the free blacks and former slaves who lacked a basic education. Rebuilding the railroads and transportation systems were among the war-scarred nation's first priorities. The Radical Republicans in the U.S. Congress sought legislation that would redistribute land from Confederate officials and military leaders to former slaves and provide welfare assistance and jobs for freedmen. Over strong objections and a veto by President Andrew Johnson (1865–1869), Congress enacted legislation in mid-1865 establishing the Bureau of Refugees, Freedmen, and Abandoned Lands (see **Freedmen's Bureau**). Part of its mission was to create a system of education for former slaves.

Initially, Kentucky was not covered under this legislation. However, the Kentucky General Assembly's failure to ratify the 13th Amendment, to eliminate the slave codes, and to provide for the education of former slaves caught the attention of Maj. Gen. Clinton B. Fisk, the Freedmen's Bureau administrator in Tennessee. Fisk's January 1866 report to Washington, D.C., detailing Kentucky's intransigence, led to the establishment of a Freedmen's Bureau in Kentucky, an action seen by Kentucky lawmakers as treating their state as conquered territory.

Northern abolitionists, working chiefly through the American Missionary Association (AMA) and the Western Freedmen Aid Commission (WFAC), poured money as well as preachers and teachers into the South from 1865 to 1867. In Kentucky, these benevolent societies established schools at Covington and then eventually across the rest of the state.

Appointed as chaplain and chief superintendent of Freedmen's Bureau Schools, Rev. T. K. Noble (working under Maj. Gen. Jeff C. Davis, the Freedmen's Bureau's assistant commissioner for Kentucky) began the arduous task of supervising the education of 250,000 former slaves; Noble's priority throughout his tenure as superintendent was to educate the 37,000 freed school-aged children in Kentucky. In December 1865 Kentucky had only 18 schools educating African Americans: 9 subscription schools and 9 schools funded through the AMA and the WFAC.

The federal government funded the Freedmen's Bureau's staff salaries, some limited construction funds for schools, part of the teachers' transportation costs, and a small portion of the teachers' salaries at the Freedmen's Bureau schools. The bulk of funding for these schools in Kentucky was supposed to come from taxes paid by freedmen. Since few African Americans owned property in 1866, the taxes collected were minuscule. For several years, the Kentucky General Assembly insisted that freedmen paupers should receive the bulk of taxes paid by freedmen, leaving very little money for the schools operated by the Freedmen's Bureau. As a result, the Freedmen's Bureau schools were financed only partly by a shoestring budget from the federal government. Religious and abolitionist sources financed some Freedmen's Bureau schools, many of the teacher salaries, and even some teacher training. Tuition fees from freedmen themselves defrayed costs of buildings and paid some of the teachers' salaries. Freedmen, especially in the rural areas, had little access to cash, and therefore most contributions were in kind: freedmen donated their labor in constructing the schools and used their church buildings as schools. Had it not been for the financial resources from AMA, WFAC, and the Baptist, Episcopal, and Methodist missionary associations, the educational effort at the Freedman's Bureau schools would have failed quickly.

Noble established three regional districts in Kentucky—Louisville, Lexington, and Paducah—and began appointing district superintendents, whose task it was to educate black citizens. The Freedmen's Bureau's first statistical report on progress at these schools, by Jesse Duns, was submitted to Washington, D.C., in June 1866; only slight gains had been realized in the first six months, and these were mainly in the urban areas. There were 18 schools in Louisville and Lexington and 7 in the rest of the state, serving 80 adults and 2,800 children. Most of these schools operated only three months each year. Moreover, it was reported that operational budgets at the schools were extremely small.

The task in Kentucky was so monumental that Noble decided to allow the abolitionists to concentrate on developing freedmen's schools in the state while he focused on developing community-based initiatives and support for educating freedmen. Accordingly, Noble encouraged the AMA, a longtime supporter of Berea College; the WFAC, an early supporter of efforts in Covington; and the Baptist, Episcopal, and Methodist missionary societies to continue working on developing the freedmen's schools statewide. By design, the Freedmen's Bureau thereafter focused its limited resources on sharing some expenses of freedmen's churches in order to open their buildings for day and night subscription schools, paying for teacher transportation, and funding school buildings where necessary.

One critical shortage, the lack of qualified teachers, was solved initially by using abolitionist agencies to recruit young black and white teachers from the North, many from Oberlin College in Ohio and from New England and New York. Kentuckians disliked the idea of former slaves learning to read and write and despised these abolitionist teachers from the North. Noble's monthly reports detail examples of the teachers' being harassed and terrorized by local citizens. Noble placed a high priority on establishing African American teacher training and certification at two locations, and with the aid of the AMA and the WFAC, the new Ely Normal School in Louisville was launched with 40 teacher-certification candidates by December 1868; the same resources funded Berea College in Berea, which had space for 150 students, half of them white.

The second critical shortage was the lack of buildings that could be used as schools for the freedmen's children. Most of the earliest schools were housed in African American churches or in buildings described as shacks. Noble lobbied hard to use the meager Freedmen's Bureau funds to build new school buildings. Among the earliest schoolhouses built in Northern Kentucky were a 30-by-60-foot wooden structure at Washington in Mason Co., completed in April 1867; and an 18-by-30-foot schoolhouse costing $200 at Warsaw in Gallatin Co., completed in mid-1868.

In the schoolhouse-construction program, either the Freedmen's Bureau or the local freedmen trustees acquired titles to the land. Under contract with local freedmen trustees, the Freedmen's Bureau supplied the lumber, the nails, and other materials, while local freedmen provided free labor. The Freedmen's Bureau schools were simple structures, no more than rectangular boxes, but at a time when there were few rural common schools for whites, these schoolhouses were treasured by freedmen and despised by many whites. They were often the target of reprisals by night riders, some of whom belonged to the Ku Klux Klan.

In October 1868, according to a report on fall classes, the Freedmen's Bureau maintained 135 day schools, 1 night school, 6 white teachers, and 144 black teachers, with 6,022 students enrolled. However, there were "outrages"; for example, a church schoolhouse operated by the Freedmen's Bureau in Germantown in Mason Co. was burned down by arsonists. By 1869 Ben Runkle, Noble's replacement as superintendent in Kentucky, reported substantial gains, with a total of 248 schools operating. Thirteen schools had been newly constructed with Freedmen's Bureau funds.

In Northern Kentucky, the Freedmen's Bureau activity was uneven. Augusta, Covington, Maysville, and Washington were quick to embrace the education of freedmen. But in the river counties of Boone and Carroll, and inland in the heavily Confederate strongholds of Grant and Owen counties, there was little interest and often violent hostility. In 1870 in Boone Co., for example, there was only one freedmen's school operating at Caledonia, now Petersburg.

In some Kentucky counties, great losses of the slave population immediately before and during the Civil War combined with antipathy to create a general indifference toward educating former slaves. Across the Ohio River at Madison, Ind., the Freedmen's Bureau funded a school in fall 1868 so that freedmen's children from Carroll and Trimble counties in Kentucky could be educated. Hundreds of former slaves from these and other Kentucky counties fled into Indiana and Ohio. The small A.M.E. church school at Hanover, Ind., funded in part by the Freedmen's Bureau, taught 75 students, while another 70 per year were being taught in Madison's black churches. At the same time, the large movement of former slaves out of Northern Kentucky into Cincinnati was being prompted as much by the promise of access to education as by the promise of wage jobs. Boone and Kenton counties in Northern Kentucky experienced 60 percent reductions in their African American populations between 1850 and 1870.

Kentucky's state funding of black schooling remained a chronic problem throughout the five years, 1865–1869, that the Freedmen's Bureau schools were operating in the state. And during the 1870s, once Confederate supporters had taken control of the Kentucky political structure, funding for the freedmen's schools essentially ceased. Ultimately, Northern abolitionists had no sustaining interest in further occupying the South. In January 1869 the Freedmen's Bureau was ordered closed, and by April 1869 its schools in Kentucky were forsaken and still unfunded.

Many of the black churches continued educating former slaves in subscription programs in spite of the lack of cash and blatant hostility toward their activities among whites. Clearly, the Freedmen's Bureau had made a start in the task of educating former slaves. More than 10,750 black children, or about one-third of the total, had received at least three months of schooling. Additionally, more than 100 buildings usable as schools had been designated for freedmen; and a small but eager cadre of newly trained black teachers had graduated from Berea College and the Ely Normal School in Louisville.

One of the most important accomplishments of the Freedmen's Bureau was helping, along with the AMA and the WFAC, to form a statewide convention of black educators. The first meeting, in 1867 in Lexington, petitioned the Kentucky General Assembly for support for black schools; the second meeting, in Louisville, was a three-day conference that featured distinguished national and state speakers. Attended by Covington African American leaders **Jacob Price** and **Isaac Black**, the conference's resolutions petitioned the Kentucky General Assembly to add the African American population to the common school system. The resolutions noted that the Freedmen's Bureau was leaving the state and that it was therefore even more critical for the state to take responsibility.

Cities that had charters from the state legislature, such as Covington and Newport, were able to take advantage of their mayor's or city council's authority to fund their black schools through taxes and then sinking funds, with much drawn from the white school system. However, it was 1874 before the state legislature acted to include African American children in the common school system.

In April 1875 the first of the checks funding segregated black common schools in Kentucky were sent from the state government in Frankfort to Campbell, Carroll, Kenton, and Pendleton counties. The Freedmen's Bureau had established 18 schools in Northern Kentucky with space for 443 students. By 1900, under the common school program, there were 54 schools in Northern Kentucky dedicated to educating 3,959 black students, the descendants of former slaves.

Bentley, George R. *The History of the Freedmen's Bureau.* New York: Octagon Books, 1970.

Marrs, Elijah Preston. "Autobiography of Elijah P. Marrs." In "Documenting the American South at Univ. of North Carolina. Ledger, Superintendent of Schools of Kentucky (Colored), 1875–1885," Kentucky Department for Libraries and Archives, Frankfort, Ky.

Reports to Superintendent of Public Instruction, January 3, 1839–January 3, 1849, Kentucky Department for Libraries and Archives, Frankfort, Ky.

Turley-Adams, Alicestyne. *Rosenwald Schools in Kentucky.* Frankfort, Ky.: Kentucky Heritage Council and African American Heritage Commission, 1997.

Webb, Ross A. "Benjamin P. Runkle and the Freedmen's Bureau in Kentucky, 1866–1870." In *The Freedmen's Bureau and Black Freedom,* ed. Donald G. Nieman. New York: Garland, 1994.

———. "The Past Is Never Dead, It's Not Even Past." In Nieman, *Freedmen's Bureau and Black Freedom.*

Wilson, George D. *A Century of Negro Education in Louisville, Kentucky.* Louisville, Ky.: Univ. of Louisville, 1986. From original Works Progress Administration and Louisville Municipal College documents, ca. 1935.

Diane Perrine Coon

FRENCH, HEATHER (b. December 29, 1974, Fort Thomas, Ky.). The Ohio River cities of Augusta, Maysville, and Louisville, are all homes to this determined, hard-working woman, who was the first Miss Kentucky to become Miss America. Born in Campbell Co., Heather French Henry is the daughter of Diane, a seamstress and child care giver, and Ronni French, a disabled Vietnam veteran. She and her three siblings lived for nine years in Augusta before the family moved to Maysville. She graduated from **Mason Co. High School**, earned a BA and an MA from the University of Cincinnati, and then worked as a fashion designer and an illustration instructor.

By the age of five, Heather dreamed of becoming Miss America, and her dream came true when she was crowned Miss America 2000. The 5-foot, 6-inch brown-eyed brunette then traveled 300,000 miles speaking on behalf of homeless veterans. Her work influenced the Homeless Veterans Assistance Act of 2001.

On October 27, 2000, she married Kentucky lieutenant governor Steve Henry in a ceremony that *People* magazine said was reminiscent of a page from *The Great Gatsby,* "with more pomp and ceremony than Louisville ever knew before." They have two daughters, Harper Renee and Taylor Augusta.

A tireless worker, Heather Henry cohosted Louisville's *Fox in the Morning,* wrote five children's books, and is executive director of the Heather French Foundation for Veterans Inc. In honor of Heather's friend singer **Rosemary Clooney**, she and Steve opened their home in Augusta as the Rosemary Clooney House museum. She often returns there and to Maysville for benefits attributing her success to roots in those river communities. For her work, she has won the respect of many, including President William Clinton, who hosted her at the White House in Washington, D.C.

"Hatchett and Henry," *LCJ,* November 19, 2000.

Henry file, Kentucky Gateway Museum, Maysville, Ky.

"No One's Teasing Miss America Now," *CE,* September 20, 1999, 1A.

John E. Kleber

FRENCH AND INDIAN WAR. The French and Indian War (1754–1763) between Great Britain and France began in conflict between the two nations over control of Northern Kentucky and the entire Ohio River Valley. The war and its aftermath delayed settlement in Kentucky but whetted the appetite of settlers and travelers who heard about the reports of **Christopher Gist** and other explorers. The word was that Kentucky was an enchanted place with bountiful game and salt, where the land was so fertile that giant prehistoric bones could be collected at **Big Bone Lick**, the most curious attraction in the West at the time.

Great Britain's victory determined that the language, culture, and political tradition in Northern Kentucky would be English, but for the first four years of the war, France had the upper hand militarily and it appeared that future settlers in Northern Kentucky might have to learn French. When the war began with Colonial Virginia major George Washington's surrender of Fort Necessity to a superior force in 1754, the French and their American Indian allies took control of the Ohio Valley from Fort Duquesne (now Pittsburgh, Pa.) to the mouth of the Ohio River in what was at the time the Illinois country. French commanders encouraged Shawnee and Delaware warriors from Ohio to conduct long-distance raids on English settlements on the Virginia and Pennsylvania frontier, and using guerrilla-war tactics of speed, surprise, and hit-and-run, the Indian war parties

FREEDMEN'S SCHOOLS IN NORTHERN KENTUCKY, JULY 1867–FEBRUARY 1869

Date and County	*Town*	*Sponsor*	*Teachers*[a]	*Students*
July 1867				[b]
Mason	Washington	Freedmen's Bureau		
April 1868				
Mason	Maysville	Freedmen's Bureau	Amanda Perkins	
Mason	Maysville	Freedmen's Bureau	Avene Casey	
Mason	Maysville	Freedmen's Bureau	Mary E. Wilson	
Mason	Washington	Freedmen's Bureau	Elizabeth Wilkerson	
Bracken	Augusta	Freedmen's Bureau	C. M. White	
Pendleton	Brandywine	Freedmen's Bureau	Mary Southgate	
Pendleton	Falmouth	Freedmen's Bureau	Ellen Kinny	
Kenton	Covington	Freedmen's Bureau	E. C. Wilmot	
Kenton	Covington	Freedmen's Bureau	Ellen N. Leavitt	
Kenton	Covington	Freedmen's Bureau	Richard Singer	
December 1868				
Bracken	Augusta	Church and school	Jeptha Griffin (B)	13 M, 15 F
Campbell	Newport	Alex Howard	Alex Howard (B)	26 M, 16 F
Campbell	Newport	Mary Williams	Mary Williams (B)	12 M, 13 F
Campbell	Newport	Henry Graham	Julia Warner (B)	8 M, 9 F
Kenton	Covington	Church	E. E. Willis (B), Eliza Skillman (W)	44 M, 45 F
Mason	Maysville	Church	Amanda Perkins (B), Green Casey (B) [c]	39 M, 47 F
Mason	Washington	School	Marcia Dunlap (B)	20 M, 21 F
Pendleton	Falmouth	Church	Ellen M. H. Southgate (B)	10 M, 6 F
January 1869				
Gallatin	Warsaw	Freedmen's Bureau		[d]
Bracken	Germantown	Freedmen's Bureau		[e]
February 1869				
Boone	Caledonia	School	Joshua Kendall (B)	18 M, 18 F
Bracken	Augusta	Church		12 M, 15 F
Pendleton	Falmouth	Church	Ellen M. Southgate	9 M, 4 F
Campbell	Newport	Henry Graham School	Mary Warmus (W)	12 M, 13 F
Campbell	Newport			
Kenton	Covington	Church	E. C. Wilmot (W) Eliza Skillman (B)	56 M, 48 F
Kenton	Covington	Church	E. C. Wilmot (W) (night)	17 M, 12 F
Kenton	Union Hall	School	William A. Patterson (B)	20 M, 15 F
Mason	Maysville	Church	Amanda Perkins (B), Green Carey (B), Mary Nelson (B)	50 M, 52 F
Mason	Mayslick	School	Emma Gardner (B)	25 M, 27 F
Mason	Washington	Church	Narcissa Dunlap (B)	20 M, 20 F
Pendleton	Brandywine	School	Mary Southgate (B)	6 M, 6 F

Notes: [a]B = black; W = white.

[b]Wood building 30 × 60 ft.

[c]A third teacher's name is illegible in the records.

[d]Building 18 × 30 ft.; cost, $200.

[e]The Freedmen's church and school burned.

devastated the backcountry. The colonial militia was no match for the raiders, and many settlers fled back east in panic.

The **American Indians** intentionally terrorized the settlers with fear of capture. In July 1755, a Shawnee raiding party kidnapped **Mary Draper Ingles**, her two young sons, and her sister-in-law from their home at Draper's Meadow (Blacksburg, Va.) The raiders took them down the Kanawha River and the Ohio River to the largest Shawnee village in the Ohio Territory, lower Shawnee Town at the mouth of the Scioto River. Adopted as his daughter by the chief of the tribe and therefore given a degree of freedom, Ingles was taken on a salt-making expedition to Big Bone Lick in present-day Boone Co., Ky., and this probably made her the first woman of European descent to enter Kentucky. In September 1755, while at Big Bone Lick, Ingles escaped and returned home to Virginia, less than six months after her capture. She reported the location and number of the Shawnees living at lower Shawnee Town, thereby contributing to Virginia lieutenant governor Robert Dinwiddie's decision to order a militia raid, the only military expedition into Kentucky during the war.

Major Andrew Lewis led about 340 men, including several Cherokee warriors, from southwestern Virginia into Kentucky, intending to move down the Big Sandy River to the Ohio River and attack lower Shawnee Town. The raid began on February 19, 1756, but in the bitterly cold weather, and with their supplies gone, the Virginians became demoralized and Lewis had to turn back.

The retreat of Lewis and the Virginia militia was the culmination of two and a half years (1754–1756) of military misfortunes for the British and the colonials. Their worst defeat coincided with Mary Ingles's capture: on July 9, 1755, British general Edward Braddock suffered a major defeat while marching with a force of 1,400 British regulars and 450 colonials to Fort Duquesne. Surrounded by a smaller force of 900 French and Indians, Braddock and his troops suffered heavy casualties at the Battle of the Wilderness. The excellent road Braddock's troops built on their march toward Fort Duquesne (Braddock's War Road), almost 20 years later became the major pathway from Cumberland, Md., that settlers coming to Kentucky used to embark on flatboats at Pittsburgh. Washington's surrender at Fort Necessity, Braddock's defeat, and Lewis's fiasco had by 1756 opened the frontier for Indians to raid the backcountry at will.

The tide of war changed when William Pitt became secretary of state and head of the king's ministry in England. He placed priority on the war in America and strengthened the war effort by supplying funds to encourage the militia and by committing more British regulars to the fight. In 1758 British general John Forbes captured Fort Duquesne, renaming it Pittsburgh, and the next year British forces defeated the French in Canada. Would-be Kentucky settlers thought the 1763 Peace of Paris, in which France ceded most of its claims in North America to Britain, should open lands west of the Appalachian Mountains for settlement, but British officials realized that while the

French were defeated, the Indians were not. Therefore, the Proclamation of 1763 prohibited settlement west of the mountains, and for about 10 years, Kentucky remained a hunting preserve for Indians and long hunters. Finally, at the time of the outbreak of the **Revolutionary War**, settlers began accomplishing their dream, which had been enhanced by reports from the French and Indian War, of settling Kentucky.

Chinn, George M. *Kentucky: Settlement and Statehood, 1750–1800.* Frankfort: Kentucky Historical Society, 1975.

Rice, Otis K. *Frontier Kentucky.* Lexington: Univ. Press of Kentucky, 1993.

James A. Ramage

FRIENDS OF BIG BONE. The Friends of Big Bone (FOBB) is a nonprofit citizen support organization whose purpose is to promote, preserve, research, and memorialize the history and prehistory of Big Bone Lick and its vicinity in Boone Co. It encourages and promotes research and study in archaeology, paleontology, geology, and other related sciences. The main focus of the group is education, both private and public. Big Bone Lick is of prime importance in the development of American vertebrate paleontology, a science founded by Thomas Jefferson, third president of the United States (1801–1809).

Earlier attempts to establish an awareness-oriented citizen support group occurred in the 1930s, the 1950s, the 1970s, and the 1990s. The first began on June 10, 1935, with the formation of the Big Bone Lick Association by a group of distinguished Kentuckians. Three of these men are known for their literary contributions in Boone Co. Willard Rouse Jillson authored *Big Bone Lick* (1936), which remains the authoritative work on the area. He was the Kentucky state geologist for many years and a prolific writer about Kentucky history. W. D. Funkhouser coauthored *Ancient Life in Kentucky* (1928) with William S. Webb, the father of Kentucky archaeology. Funkhouser was a professor of zoology at the University of Kentucky (UK) in Lexington, and Webb was a professor of physics. Together, the two men founded the department of anthropology and archaeology at UK. During the Works Progress Administration era of the 1930s, they did intensive archaeological work and research in Boone Co. The third founding organizer, **John Uri Lloyd**, is a household name in Boone Co. His series of *Stringtown on the Pike* novels, all set in Boone Co., made him one of the most famous historical novel writers of the 20th-century Midwest. His professional claim to fame, however, was chemistry and his work in the research and development of pharmaceuticals. Specializing in eclectic medicine and pharmacology, he was a founder of Lloyd Brothers Pharmaceuticals and of the Lloyd Library in Cincinnati. Although the Big Bone Lick Association was planned to run 99 years, Jillson's book was its only accomplishment.

In the early 1950s, a renewed interest in Big Bone Lick was fostered by the members of the newly formed Boone Co. Historical Society, and ultimately the Big Bone Lick Historical Association was formed to promote the establishment of the **Big Bone Lick** State Park. After many years of tireless effort in promotion, education, and fundraising, the determined members of the association, through the leadership of Bruce Ferguson, president, and William Fitzgerald, secretary, purchased 16 2⁄3 acres in December 1959 and presented the land to the Commonwealth for use as a state park. In December 1960 the Kentucky Department of Parks announced plans to develop picnic areas and a shelter house. Thus Big Bone Lick State Park, the newest of the four state parks within the Northern Kentucky region, was born.

The FOBB was incorporated on July 8, 1999. At an organizational meeting on February 22, 2000, attended by a group of interested citizens, it was decided to proceed with the concept of the FOBB and its mission. This organization was granted IRS 501(C) 3 nonprofit status in January 2002. The group's purpose is to work with and alongside the Kentucky Department of Parks in furthering the academic and scientific importance of Big Bone Lick and in ensuring its proper interpretation and utilization as one of Kentucky's premier historical and prehistoric theme parks. Activities of the FOBB include scientific research, historical and prehistoric research, presentation of papers, sponsoring guest lecturers, fundraising for a state-of-the-art museum and research center, archaeological and paleontological projects, assisting in the planning and implementing of interpretive displays, educating and training museum docents, promoting the designation of national and international heritage site status for the park, and establishing and maintaining a comprehensive research library.

Thus far, the FOBB has made significant headway in promoting awareness of and education about Big Bone Lick. With assistance, in the form of a grant, from the Boone Co. Fiscal Court, the FOBB has initiated and nearly completed a comprehensive bibliography and database of written and recorded references pertaining to Big Bone Lick. This will continue to be an ongoing project. The FOBB also played a significant role in the Bicentennial Commemoration of the Eastern Legacy of the Lewis and Clark Expedition, highlighting the importance of Big Bone Lick to the scientists, philosophers, and explorers of the day. Because of the dedicated work of the FOBB, Big Bone Lick has been designated one of only four official Eastern Legacy sites on the Lewis and Clark trail east of the Mississippi and Missouri rivers. The FOBB partnered with the Ohio River Chapter of the Lewis and Clark Heritage Trail Foundation Inc. (see **Lewis and Clark in Northern Kentucky**) to purchase and install a commemorative Kentucky Historic Highway marker at Big Bone Lick in conjunction with the Kentucky Department of Transportation.

Numerous fundraising activities and programs have enabled the FOBB to develop its three traveling educational units for use by teachers and schools. These units include lesson plans, written materials, artifacts, and show-and-tell items about Big Bone Lick and the Lewis and Clark expedition. Additional educational projects and plans will be the focus of the FOBB for the future, along with fundraising activities to support and sustain these endeavors.

Don Clare

FRITZ MINERAL WATER COMPANY. In 1873 Felix Fritz started the Fritz Mineral Water Company at the corner of Pike and Craig Sts. in Covington. By 1880–1881 the Covington directory listed Felix Fritz as a manufacturer of mineral water, and his business address was 136 Pike St.; in 1895 Felix Fritz and Son were operating the business at 171 W. Robbins St. in Covington. The Fritzes' company sold champagne cider, ginger ale, seltzers, and vinegar. By 1906 the firm was known as Louis Fritz and Company Inc., and its officers were Louis Fritz, president; Al Welling, secretary and treasurer; and C. H. Feuss Sr., vice president. By 1914–1915 the firm had moved to 254 Pike St. in Covington, where it manufactured a soft drink called American Favorite and also bottled Lithia, cream soda, Dewey, ginger ale mineral and soda water, sarsaparilla, Selzer, and Vichy. Just after the end of **World War I**, in 1918, the company was operating at 340–342 Pike St. In 1923–1924 Fred T. Dotchengall was president, Al Welling was vice president, and Arthur G. Muth was secretary-treasurer. At that time the company sold bottles of Gateway brand soft drinks; Lithia, a white cooler mineral water used as a diuretic seltzer; and Vichy, a sparkling mineral water. In 1931 the firm was the Louis Fritz Mineral and Soda Water Company, "manufacturers of carbonated beverages, Lithia, seltzer, and Vichy." Ten years later the company was producing "13 flavors" of bottled soft drinks and mineral waters: club soda, cream soda, ginger ale, grape, grapefruit, lemon-lime, lime rickey, lithiated lemon, orange, root beer, sarsaparilla, Vichy, and white. The company's president, Fred T. Dotchengall, retired in 1952, and Ben Castleman and William B. Southgate acquired the company. Before the business was closed in 1957, it had been sold again to G. Vincent Seiler and his son John V. Seiler. At that time its modern plant had the capacity to produce 1,000 cases of bottled products each day; the closing ended 81 consecutive years of business operations in Covington for the popular soft drink and mineral water company.

"Fritz Firm Quits after 81 Years," *KTS,* February 21, 1957, 1A.

Murphy, John E. "Fritz Firm Organized When Soft Drinks Were Dubbed 'Pop': 68 Anniversary Being Celebrated by Local Company," *KP,* April 18, 1941, 19.

Reis, Jim. "Records and Memories of Bottling Company Pour a Sip of Local History," *KP,* October 14, 1991, 4K.

———. "Soft Drink Firms Survived Prohibition: Carbonated Drinks Became Alternative to 'Hard Liquors,'" *KP,* October 9, 1989, 4K.

John Boh

FULLER BROTHERS. Alexander Fuller (b. September 1824, Stamping Ground, Scott Co., Ky.;

d. July 8, 1898, Worthville, Carroll Co., Ky.) and his brother Duncan Fuller (b. February 23, 1823, Kentucky; d. August 14, 1865, Gallatin Co, Ky.), were active in the **Underground Railroad**. They lived in Gallatin Co. in the 1840s and 1850s and later moved to Carroll Co. in the Sanders Precinct near Worthville. The Fuller brothers were Unionists; Duncan served with Union Company B, 7th Kentucky Cavalry, was captured at Dalton, Ga., in 1864, and was a prisoner of war until mustered out at Edgefield, Tenn., on July 4, 1865.

Significantly, Duncan and Alexander Fuller were closely related to members of the New Liberty Baptist Church near Quercus Grove, Ind., a known station on the Underground Railroad routes leading from Patriot, Markland, Florence, Vevay, and Lamb, Ind. Rev. **Alexander Sebastian**, the founding preacher of that church, spent time in the Warsaw, Gallatin Co., area.

According to family historians, Alexander and Duncan Fuller voted Republican in the heavily Democratic precinct of Worthville-Sanders. This was a strongly Confederate-leaning portion of Carroll Co., and voting Republican was not only dangerous but foolhardy during the 1860–1880 period. Only the most dedicated Unionists would brave the nearby Ku Klux Klan activities along the Kentucky River and in Owen Co.

Ephraim Fuller, the father of Alexander and Duncan, had settled at Stamping Ground, Scott Co., Ky., before 1830. Ephraim and both sons gravitated to Warsaw, Gallatin Co., in the 1840s, and the two brothers married sisters: Alexander married Amanda Melvina Knox on October 12, 1845, at Warsaw, and Duncan married Angelina Knox on August 14, 1846, also at Warsaw. They were daughters of Robert Knox and Mildred Ann Bohanan, who moved to Warsaw from Franklin Co., Ky., during the early 1840s and were probably associated with the short-lived Presbyterian Church at Warsaw (1837–1867).

Two daughters of Ephraim Fuller, Sarah Ann and Mercy Fuller, married brothers, Enos and David Ellis, respectively, settled in Switzerland Co., Ind., and were associated with the Separate Baptist Church at East Enterprise that merged with the Freewill Baptist Church nearby, forming the New Liberty Baptist Church near Quercus Grove, Switzerland Co. Members of this congregation formed a significant Underground Railroad station, providing safe houses and conductors from Patriot, Markland, Vevay, and Lamb.

The Underground Railroad was active from 1840 to 1861 along the Ohio River between Gallatin Co., Ky., and Switzerland Co., Ind. There were at least five crossing points where runaway slaves from Gallatin and eastern Carroll counties were aided, or at least sighted, by Underground Railroad activists on the Indiana side of the Ohio River: from Sugar Creek, Ky., to Patriot and Florence, Ind.; from Warsaw, Ky., to Markland, Ind.; from Warsaw or Ghent, Ky., to Vevay, Ind.; from Carrollton, Ky., to Lamb, Ind.; and from Prestonville, Ky., to Brooksburg, Ind.

Precisely what role Alexander and Duncan Fuller played in these operations is not clear, but the two represent a substantial number of white yeomen who, together with numerous free people of color, enabled runaway slaves to reach places of safety in southern Indiana.

Coon, Diane Perrine. "Southeastern Indiana's Underground Railroad Routes and Operations," 1999, U.S. Park Service and Indiana DNR, unpublished technical report, Indiana Dept. of Historic Preservation and Archaeology, Indianapolis, Ind.

Duvall, Jeffery, to Diane Perrine Coon, June–July 2006, e-mail correspondence regarding family history and genealogy.

Diane Perrine Coon

FUNERAL HOMES. Generally, funeral homes in Northern Kentucky remain private, rather than corporate, enterprises. Before the **Civil War**, bodies were often preserved for viewing either by placing them on ice or by use of formaldehyde to delay decomposition. Then various events and changing institutions within U.S. life, starting about the time of the Civil War, called for changes in those traditions. The families of soldiers killed on distant battlefields wanted the remains of their sons brought home. Rigor mortis and the general degradation of the corpse, in particular of the face, refused to wait weeks for the funeral of the unprepared body. Thus embalming, a process of preservation that had been toyed with previously, quickly became both necessary and popular. For example, after President Abraham Lincoln (1861–1865) died, embalming was performed on his body; it was carefully prepared for the 20-day railroad tour to Springfield, Ill., with stops in multiple cities. Even when long-distance shipment of the body was not necessary, embalming was appreciated because, when accomplished as soon as possible after death, it helped to preserve a lifelike appearance for viewing. Because the preparation, packing, and shipping of human remains required a modicum of training beyond the skill level of concerned family members or battlefield body collectors, funeral directing developed as a profession.

As the country became more urban, it was no longer fashionable or legal, in most places, to use family property as burial grounds. Burials began to be grouped together in public and private cemeteries (see also **Cemeteries, Rural**), generally away from dwellings or businesses. In larger urban areas, cemeteries, often the most botanical spot in town, were great settings for Sunday family picnics. Concurrently with the appearance of general hospitals (and **nursing homes**), deaths at home became less common. Both the place of death and the place of final visitation were being moved. There arose a need, as the nation began the practice of hiding death—whether intended or not—to hire a disinterested party to handle the burial. The logical person to turn to was the businessman down the street with a livery station, who already had the horse and wagon teams and, after 1920, a hearse, or the furniture dealer who sold wooden coffins. Some of those tradesmen became experts in embalming and extended their line of services. And since families no longer wanted the corpse returned to their living space, the funeral home, a short-term rentable hall for final visitations, with all the amenities of the modern practice of death, was conceived. Families in the midst of grief were willing to pay to bid their loved one a last elaborate adieu; the proliferation of life insurance certainly helped to cushion the cost. In the 20th century, both world wars had an effect on the business of funerals similar to that of the Civil War: survivors expected their loved ones who died abroad to be returned for a funeral. Hence, the funeral business, carrying out tasks that families neither could nor would do, has become a multi-billion-dollar industry.

In Kenton Co., around Covington, there have been several funeral home operators over the years. As early as 1839, Abraham Rose, who was born in Baltimore, Md., was listed in the city directory as a mortician. He made the natural transition from cabinetmaking to coffin making. After the business had passed through several generations with sons and partners, the present Allison and Rose Funeral Home was formed in 1925. Others who became established in the local funeral business were named Linnemann, Menninger, Middendorf, Rich, and Swindler; many of these worked at one time for Allison. John Allison, who began working for the Weaver Funeral Home along Pike St. in Covington during the 1890s, lived in nearby Ludlow and was in business later with partners John C. B. Yates and Gus Menninger, as Allison, Yates, and Menninger; afterward he became associated with Rose along Pike St. In 1932 Allison and Rose moved to a historic home in Covington at Robbins St. and Madison Ave., and it has opened a second facility in recent years along Ky. Rt. 16 in Taylor Mill. Other funeral operators in the county have included Chambers and Grubbs in Independence; Connley Brothers in Latonia; Donnelly Brothers in Covington at 12th St. and Madison Ave., serving the Irish community; Don Catchen and Son on W. 19th St. in Covington and also in Elsmere; Hugenberg and Glindmeyer on Sixth St., today a Linnemann home; Jones & Simpson, traditionally serving African Americans in Covington's eastside (see **Charles E. Jones**; for Covington's earliest African American funeral director, see **Wallace A. Gaines**); Middendorf-Bullock on Covington's Main St., on Elm St. in Ludlow, and on Dixie Highway in Erlanger; Middendorf in Fort Wright; Ronald B. Jones on Elm St. in Ludlow; and Swindler and Currin in Latonia and in Independence. The Linnemanns have funeral homes in Covington, Erlanger, and Burlington today. During the early 1920s, Henry Linnemann drove the first ambulance in Kenton Co.; it was a sideline service utilizing the downtime of the funeral business. The Linnemanns have operated a funeral home in Erlanger for more than 50 years.

In Campbell Co., funeral directors have been in Newport for a long time. The Bunning livery business evolved into the Bunning and Costigan Funeral Home. The Charles E. Smith Funeral Home was in the former George Wiedemann home at Fifth St. and Park Ave. for several years; and the Vonderhaar and Stetter Funeral Home was anchored from 1919 into the 1980s at the former **James Taylor Mansion** on E. Third St. Muehlenkamp, Costigan, and Roll began using the **Peter O'Shaughnessy** home at 835 York St. after O'Shaughnessy's death in the late 1920s, and the home remains a Muehlenkamp-Erschell venture; across the street is the Fares J. Radel funeral home. The Betz Funeral Home operated along E. Sixth St., and Pye and Erschell at Seventh and York Sts.; Frank Pye retired from the funeral business in 1892, and Fred Erschell moved to E. Sixth St. in Newport before relocating his business to Fort Thomas. Erschell's son, also named Fred, continued in the business in Fort Thomas, while also serving as mayor. A. C. Dobbling & Son have funeral homes in Bellevue, Fort Thomas, and Alexandria. In Dayton, from the early 1930s through the late 1940s, there was the Tharp and Stith Funeral Home along Sixth Ave., later a Muehlenkamp operation; Muehlenkamp-Erschell also has an operation in Fort Thomas. In recent years, the family operating the Radel Home (Faris J. Radel) opened a new facility in Highland Heights on the site of a former A&W Root Beer stand, but it moved shortly to another new location farther south along **U.S. 27**, across from **St. Joseph Catholic Church** in Cold Spring. The short life of that venture in Highland Heights shows how difficult it is to open a new location that makes money, even for operators as well established and well known as the Radels. In the southern part of the county, there are Fares J. Radel in Alexandria, the Alexandria Funeral Home Inc. (Middendorf-Bullock, Muehlenkamp-Ershcell) in Alexandria, Peoples Funeral Home on U.S. 27 in Alexandria, and the Cooper Funeral Home on U.S. 27 in Claryville. For many years, as long as the New Richmond **ferry** was in operation, the T. P. White Funeral Home of New Richmond, Ohio, handled much of southeastern Campbell Co.'s funeral business. It was much easier to cross into Ohio than make the trek to Newport.

In Boone Co. there are five funeral establishments. Chambers & Grubbs operates along **Dixie Highway** in Florence and also on Main St. in Walton, the Stith Funeral Home (a descendant of the Tharp and Stith funeral home earlier in Dayton) in Florence and Hebron, the Linnemann in Burlington, and the Hamilton-Stanley Funeral Home in Verona; there is a branch of the Middendorf-Bullock chain in Hebron.

Bracken Co. has four funeral homes: in Augusta, the Metcalfe & Hennessey Funeral Home on E. Fourth St. and the Moore and Parker Funeral Home on Elizabeth St; in Brooksville, a branch of the Moore and Parker Funeral Home, along Hackett Ridge Rd.; and in the eastern part of the county, a Palmer Funeral Home on Ky. Rt. 10 on the Bracken side of the city of Germantown.

Carroll Co. has two homes at Carrollton: the Graham-Dunn Funeral Home on S. Fifth St. and the Tandy-Eckler-Riley Funeral Home on Highland Ave.

Gallatin Co. has one facility, the Carlton-Lowder Funeral Home on Main St. in Warsaw.

Grant Co. has four funeral homes: the **Elliston-Stanley Funeral Home** on N. Main St. in Williamstown and on S. Main St. in Crittenden, the Eckler-Hudson-McDaniel Home in Dry Ridge, and the Rogers Funeral Home in Corinth.

Mason Co. has two funeral homes in Maysville, Brell & Son and Knox and Brothers, both on E. Second St.; and one in Mayslick, Palmer Funeral Home. In that same city, an African American funeral home opened in August 1929. Lexington native Shirley Arnold began operating a "colored undertaking establishment" in Maysville on E. Fourth St. in that year. How long Arnold remained in business is not known. In 1974, a long-standing funeral business tradition in Maysville ended with the closing of the Porter Funeral Home, which had operated for the previous 105 years. Owner Ashby F. Porter was the dean of funeral home directors and owners in the area. With the closing of the Porter Home, its ambulance service also ceased.

Owen Co. has two branches of the McDonald & New Funeral Home, both in Owenton, one along Main St., and another along W. Seminary St. For many years, at New Liberty in the northern part of the county, R. G. Know did the undertaking work. Know was a graduate of the nationally recognized Clark's Embalming School in Cincinnati and was the leader of the profession in Owen county. He also did wallpapering and painting and sold buggies and whips on the side to fill in the slow times of his funeral business.

Pendleton Co. has three funeral homes. Two are in Falmouth, the Peoples Funeral Home and the Woodhead Funeral Home, both on Shelby St. The Woodhead family's firm is one of the state's Centennial businesses. It also does business in Harrison Co., at Berry, having bought the former Roger P. Blair Home during the early 1940s. The other home in Pendleton Co. is Peoples Funeral Home on Main St. in Butler.

Robertson Co. has two homes, both in Mount Olivet: Kain & Kabler on N. Walnut St. and the Robertson County Funeral Home on U.S. 62.

For several years during the 1990s, Covington was home to one of the modern leaders in consolidation of the funeral industry. The RiverCenter building housed the Loewen Group, a conglomerate based in Vancouver, British Columbia, Canada, that aggressively purchased funeral homes, cemeteries, and crematoria and sold burial insurance and prearrangement plans. Covington was Loewen's U.S. headquarters until corporate financing forced a consolidation of the company itself. After its financial difficulties, the restraint of trade investigations by the Federal Trade Commission, and some massive lawsuits, Loewen no longer has offices in Covington. In April 1999, the company reported that it employed some 16,000 workers in 1,097 funeral homes and at more than 426 cemeteries in the United States, Canada, and the United Kingdom, with revenues of $1.1 billion. At the consumer level, Loewen did not mesh well locally.

There is one operating crematory in Northern Kentucky, the Northern Kentucky Mortuary Service at Richwood in Boone Co. The same company also operates Heavenly Paws, a pet burial and cremation enterprise. Whereas nationally 26 percent of all human bodies are cremated, in Kentucky only 8 percent are cremated.

"The City," *KJ*, September 29, 1892, 8.

"Colored Funeral Home Opens Here," August 20, 1929, Funeral Home Vertical File, Mason Co. Museum, Maysville, Ky.

"Henry Linnemann, Funeral Director," *KP*, August 4, 1969, 8K.

Kingsbury, Gilbert W. *Allison & Rose Funeral Home, Inc.* Covington, Ky.: Allison and Rose, 1977.

Laderman, Gary. *Rest in Peace.* New York: Oxford Univ. Press, 2003.

"Maysville Funeral Home, City Landmark, to Close," *CE*, March 13, 1974, 11.

Mitford, Jessica. *The American Way of Death.* New York: Simon and Schuster, 1963.

"Public Inspection of Our New Funeral Home," *KP*, May 18, 1935, 2.

Michael R. Sweeney

FURNITURE AND HOME FURNISHINGS. The thriving furniture industry that flourished in 19th-century Cincinnati spilled over into Northern Kentucky. As the city's suburbs expanded into Kentucky, providers of household furnishings and equipment arose, as did manufacturers of some items. In Cincinnati, the firm of Mitchell and Rammelsberg (1847–1939) became nationally known for the furniture it supplied to the growing West and South. Internationally recognized as the world's largest furniture factory, it employed about 1,500 workers along Cincinnati's Second St. In Northern Kentucky, several retailers opened businesses along Monmouth St. in Newport and Madison Ave. in Covington. Household furniture was also manufactured in those cities, but to a lesser extent than in Cincinnati. The general area was ideal for the making and shipping of furniture: it was near the hardwood forests of the Midwest and was both a river port and a rail center.

Louis Marx & Bros. Furniture, Monmouth St., Newport, ca. 1923.

The talented, trained German craftsmen among the population contributed greatly to supplying the needed manpower.

In Campbell Co., the center of the furniture business was traditionally Newport. City directories suggest that in the antebellum years, there were cabinetmakers or carpenters on seemingly every corner. The Klosterman family was building furniture by the 1880s, as was Newport Industries, which specialized in chairs. Shortly, retail stores appeared. Philip Dine, a former tailor, and his partner Ferdinand Fulner sold carpet, furniture, and stoves roughly between 1880 and 1910 at 518 and 529 York St. In 1910, Dine's nephew Reuben Dine and Joseph Schabell incorporated and at 913 Monmouth St. began the Dine-Schabell Furniture Company, known in later years simply as Dine's. Through fires, burglaries, renovations, and the changing face of Newport, the business operated there until the mid-1980s. Just to the north and across the street was the Louis Marx & Bros. Company, which opened in Newport in 1888 at 842 Monmouth St. Founder Louis Marx died in 1924, but the organization remained in the family until it closed in 1987. Louis Marx built a large multilevel warehouse fronting on E. Ninth St. and connected it to the rear of the main store on Monmouth (see **Monmouth St. Architecture**). The Marx company survived fires, thievery, and a changing market. A third company that tried the Newport market for a short time in the 1930s was the William H. Tillman Company, located at Seventh and Monmouth. Dine's, the Marx company, and Tillman also had stores in Covington, and the latter even ventured into Cincinnati for a short time.

Other operators of furniture ventures in Newport included Camin's at 638 Monmouth, which began as a linoleum and carpet store on York St. in the 1930s and evolved into offering a full range of household goods; Camin's had a warehouse at 1101 Monmouth St., next to the train station. The store began selling furniture in 1954 and continued until the 1980s. From the late 1940s until the mid-1980s, the Hall Swenson Company was located at 728 Monmouth St.; it sold some furniture but mainly provided interior decorating services to an elite crowd of Greater Cincinnatians. The existence of several furniture retailers further created a market for interior and design planning. Newport was home to smaller furniture retailers as well: Finkleman's in the West End at W. 10th and Brighton Sts. and the Bromall family's Kentucky Sales and Service Company at E. 10th and Saratoga Sts., still operating today at that corner since 1920.

Eventually, stoves were added to furniture stores. First came the gas stove, with the introduction of readily available iron and steel. In the beginning stoves were fueled with wood, then with coal oil, and finally with natural gas piped into the home through a line from the street. Dine's in particular sold a vast number of stoves, especially the Red Star Oil brand. The modern stove eliminated the need for summer kitchens and made cooking inside an open hearth unnecessary, allowing for new types of preparation methods (frying, broiling, and baking). The 54 employees of Pomeroy, Peckover, and Company made an average of 30 stoves daily at their factory in Newport in 1876. By 1880 the firm of Moore, Harkness, and Bayless was manufacturing stoves at its plant on Front St. in Newport, east of Washington Ave. A gas stove retail store opened in May 1887 at 707 Monmouth St. The Favorite Stove and Range Company was making stoves in April 1888, the Stubben Manufacturing Company of Newport in 1892. Smaller manufacturers built items that contributed to the overall furnishing of residential homes. In the mid-20th century, the largest employer in nearby Bellevue was **Grote Manufacturing**, a maker of medicine cabinets for home bathroom use.

Electrical appliances, following the introduction of the radio in the 1920s (Crosley, Philco, and Zenith brands), became another wave of product-line expansion. Furniture merchants quickly added radios and, later, televisions to their inventories, and some even sold washers and dryers.

In Kenton Co., the furniture industry began in Covington. Louis Marx renovated the former Latonia Hotel in the 300 block of Madison Ave. and opened for business in 1895. In 1898 he moved to 520 Madison Ave., and the Marx store operated there until 1987. The Covington and Newport stores offered the same product lines, and together they won numerous retailing awards over the course of the company's history. The stores were well known for their unique promotions, and they were major purchasers of advertising space in the ***Kentucky Post***. Dine's Covington store, located at 530 Madison Ave., had closed by 1962. It withstood a fire in March 1923, as did its warehouse at Second St. and Madison Ave. in October 1927. The third firm to operate in both cities was Tillman's, which occupied various buildings, beginning in 1927: 812 Madison Ave., 536 Madison Ave., and for the last 51 years, the northeast corner of Eighth St. and Madison Ave. Tillman's gradually added lines as they became available, closing its doors in 1991 after almost 65 years, a victim of competition from Boone Co.'s **Florence Mall**. Ball Furniture leased Tillman's space from 1992 until 1998. Today, the building is home to a wedding reception hall (see **Covington, Downtown**).

Other Covington furniture merchants included the Bellonby Furniture Company in the building formerly occupied by the **Walsh Distillery** at Front and Scott Sts. It opened in time for the **Great Depression** in 1927 and was not in business long. Modern Furniture, founded by Sam Greenberg in 1915, operated at 513 Madison Ave., once the Salvation Army building, and later built a new store at that site. Son Adrian Greenberg closed the venture in 1987. The A. J. Ostrow Furniture and Appliance Store began small in 1926, selling electronics at 711 Madison Ave., and added appliances and furniture later in another building. At one time, Ostrow's even sold automobile tires.

Charles Bogenschutz was building stoves in Covington at 523 Madison Ave. in 1880. In 1903, that firm was sold to **Ignatius Droege** and made a part of his foundry. The Ohio Scroll and Lumber Company was in Covington for 67 years at the corner of Russell and Stewart Sts. It was owned by the Fuess family of Fort Mitchell. Although mainly known for plaques and other wood decorative products, it made tables, chairs, cabinets, lamps, and other household items. By December 1962, the firm had moved to Cincinnati as a result of the construction of the **Internal Revenue Service Center** in downtown Covington; one of Ohio Scroll's last employees was Charles D. "Carmi" Meyers of Fort Mitchell, who went out on his own and built hundreds of custom cabinets and bars for local residences and such places as the **Beverly Hills Supper Club** and desks or credenzas for the **Kenton Co. Public Library**. He worked out of his shop in Covington for the last three decades of the 20th century.

Other parts of the Northern Kentucky region also participated in the furniture industry. To the southwest along the Ohio River, there were the **Warsaw Furniture Factory** of Warsaw in Gallatin Co. and the **Carrollton Furniture Manufacturing Company** of Carrollton in Carroll Co. The Warsaw operation was owned by the family of **Carl R. Bogardus**, a longtime medical practitioner and historian of that area. Employing almost 200 at its peak, it was established in the early years of the 20th century and specialized in dining room sets and chairs. The Warsaw business left Bogardus ownership in 1969, and the factory was torn down in 1995. The Carrollton Furniture Manufacturing Company began in 1884, operating from two large five-story brick buildings connected by causeways. The company was well known for its high-class bedroom suites and won awards around the nation at furniture shows. Another recognized individual furniture maker for that part of the region was Owenton's William Jones, who died in 1985.

In Mason Co. there have been several individual furniture makers and retailers over the years. Early cabinetmakers include Gerrard Calvert; the mysterious Peter Tuttle, whose "Mason County trunks" have become collector items; and Joseph Wallingford, an apprentice to Archibald Calvert. These cabinetmakers were deceased by 1860. John Foxworthy is a well-respected recent furniture retailer of Maysville. Recent individual furniture craftsmen around Maysville include Joseph Brannen, Johnnie Disher, and Raymond Hester. Maysville furniture retailers over the years have included the names John Brisbois, whose five-story "white palace" began selling furniture in 1908 at 402 W. Second St.; J. H. Brown; Harry Foxworthy; C. L. Mains; Joseph F. Martin; Mattingly; C. H. McEuen; and McIlvain, Humphreys, and Bramel (also undertakers).

In recent years, furniture has also been sold by the long-running Krause Awning Company, which carried trendy outdoor furniture at the northeast corner of Fourth and Monmouth in Newport for 60 years, ending in the 1990s; other Covington merchants have included Mertack's, which went out of business in 1998, only to be replaced by Adobe in the same building on the northeast corner of Fifth and Scott Sts. in 2003; and the now-closed Brock's Furniture at 19th St. and Madison Ave.

In the late 20th century, the Schottenstein family of Columbus, Ohio, opened one of their "big box" furniture stores in Latonia, followed by a second location in Florence. A similar venture is the Furniture Fair chain. Begun in 1963 by Robert Daniels in Erlanger at 3932 Dixie Highway, the firm has eight stores today: the original store is now an outlet facility, and there are operating Furniture Fairs in Florence and Cold Spring, in addition to Cincinnati suburbs. One of the remaining furniture factories to operate in the area was the Duchess Furniture Company of Florence, which closed in May 1976, with 300 workers losing their jobs.

"Furniture File," vertical files, Kentucky Gateway Museum Center, Maysville, Ky.

International Publishing Company. ***Leading Manufacturers and Merchants of Cincinnati and Environs.*** New York: International, 1886.

"Marx, Stores to Celebrate Golden Jubilee," *KP*, March 10, 1938, 4.

"Reuben Dine," *KP*, September 27, 1927, 1.

Sikes, Jane E. ***The Furniture Makers of Cincinnati, 1790 to 1849.*** Self-published, 1976.

Michael R. Sweeney

GAINES, JOHN P., MAJOR (b. September 22, 1795, Augusta Co., Va.; d. December 9, 1857, Quartsburg, Ore.). John Pollard Gaines, a U.S. military officer and governor of the Oregon Territory, was the son of Abner and Elizabeth Matthews Gaines, who moved from Virginia to Boone Co. in 1800. He was educated in local schools. When the War of 1812 erupted, he enlisted as a private in a regiment of the Kentucky Volunteers. Afterward, he speculated in land locally. He married Elizabeth Kinkead of Versailles, Ky., in 1819.

Gaines entered Boone Co. politics in 1825 and was elected to the first of his several terms in the Kentucky legislature. During the **Mexican War**, he enlisted in a Kentucky cavalry brigade, where he held the rank of major. In January 1847 Gaines and 80 of his fellow soldiers were captured at Incarnacion, Mexico, and held prisoner in Mexico City until August of that year. While a prisoner, Gaines was elected to the 30th U.S. Congress as a **Whig** candidate from Kentucky's 10th District, a position he held for two years. When he ran for reelection, he lost to the Democratic candidate, Joseph Lane.

Gaines was an ardent supporter of Zachary Taylor during the 1848 presidential election campaign, and subsequently the party rewarded his loyalty by appointing him governor of the Oregon Territory in 1849. He and his family traveled by ship around Cape Horn on a nine-month voyage to his new assignment. The trip was a disaster for the family, because two of his daughters, Harriet and Florella, died of yellow fever during a stop in Brazil. Shortly after the family arrived in the Oregon Territory, Gaines's wife, Elizabeth, was killed in a fall from a horse, and one of his sons died soon afterward. To protect his remaining children, he sent them back to live with relatives in the East. Gaines's tenure as a Whig governor was marked by fierce partisanship on the part of the territorial legislature, controlled by the Democrats. One of the major controversies he faced in Oregon was whether the state capitol should be located in Oregon City or in Salem. When Gaines's four-year term ended, he did not seek reelection. After leaving office, he remained in Oregon, where he remarried and settled on a farm at Quartsburg, near Salem. He lived there until his death from typhoid fever in 1857, at age 62. Gaines was buried in the Old Pioneer Cemetery at Salem, Ore.

Biographical Encyclopedia of Kentucky. Cincinnati: J. M. Armstrong, 1878.

Pioneer Cemetery Records, Pioneer Cemetery, Salem, Ore.

The Political Graveyard. "Gaines, John Pollard." www.politicalgraveyard.com (accessed December 28, 2006).

Reis, Jim "A Killer Named Cholera Stalked Victims Rich, Poor," *KP*, October 4, 1999, 4K.

GAINES, WALLACE ARKANSAS (b. April 15, 1865, Dayton, Ohio; d. August 1940, Evansville, Ind.). African American businessman and civic leader Wallace Gaines came to Covington with his parents about 1875. He began working for his uncle in Ottoway Burton's barbershop, at 706 Washington St., shining shoes; he continued as a bootblack until he found other employment in the handling of furniture and feathers.

By 1880, Gaines was serving as president of the "colored" Garfield First Voters Club, which supported James Garfield of Ohio for president (1881). He rose quickly within the **Republican Party** and received an appointment in 1881 as a storekeeper in the Federal Revenue collection department. During the administration of President Benjamin Harrison (1889–1893), he was appointed a U.S. gauger; the duties of a gauger included inspecting scales and other measuring devices used to determine the official weight of grains and other supplies. When the Republican Party was out of power, Gaines became a hauling contractor, handling grain and whiskey for distilleries. During this period he joined the United Brothers of Friendship, which by the late 1890s had become the largest African American civic association in the country. Gaines rose through that organization's ranks and by 1897 was the Grand Supreme Master. It placed him at the head of an estimated 300,000 African American voters nationwide. With such backing and political connections, Gaines was mentioned as a candidate for the post of U.S. Registrar of the Treasury. He traveled to Washington, D.C., to lobby for the job but did not receive it; instead he returned home to resume his job as a federal gauger, which he kept only briefly. In May 1898 he was appointed a federal court bailiff but resigned the same day, after it was determined that the job would interfere with his support of the renomination of his personal friend Walter Evans, a Republican congressman.

In 1904, while doing his job as a special revenue agent for the U.S. Treasury Department, Gaines discovered that the wholesale whiskey house of Crigler & Crigler, located on Pike St. in Covington, was moving untaxed whiskey barrels. His report to the tax collector and revenue agent led to action in the U.S. District Court.

Gaines was a founding member, president, and director of the Progressive Building and Loan Association, which was created for the African American community of Covington. The association, which operated from 1906 to 1910, was located at the corner of Seventh and Scott Sts. adjacent to the W. A. Gaines funeral home.

For a number of years Gaines owned the W. A. Gaines Funeral Home at 633 Scott St. He was the first African American funeral director in Covington. In 1908 he started a funeral home in Evansville, Ind. In 1912 he expanded his funeral home businesses to include Henderson, Ky., then in 1913 sold his Covington business to Charles E. Jones. In July 1913, Gaines married Tillie Young, a teacher at Lincoln Grant School and a former treasurer of the Progressive Building and Loan Association, and the couple moved to Evansville, Ind. He died in Evansville and was buried in Highland Cemetery, Fort Mitchell. At the time of his death, he was a 33rd Degree Mason.

"Building Association Will Be Organized," *KP*, May 31, 1906, 2.

"The Colored Garfield First Voters' Club," *DC*, October 25, 1880, 1.

"Colored Man, Who Is Said to be Booked for High Position," *KP*, July 24, 1897, 8.

Reis, Jim. "Blacks at Turn of Century Persevered to Improve Lives," *KP*, January 17, 2000, 4K.

———. "Wallace Gaines Achieved Success in a Difficult Era for African-Americans," *KP*, February 2, 2004, 4K.

———. "When History Is Overlooked," *KP*, February 8, 1999, 4K.

Theodore H. H. Harris

GAINES TAVERN. The Gaines Tavern in Walton in Boone Co. has been used as a stagecoach stop, a tavern, and an antique shop. On early-19th-century maps of Kentucky (such as H. S. Tanner's 1839 *A New Map of Kentucky*) it is referred to as Gaines Crossing, where the road from Covington divided into a route to Lexington (see **Covington and Lexington Turnpike**) and a road to Warsaw.

Abner Gaines, born October 8, 1766, in Orange Co., Va., was the first member of his family to arrive in Kentucky. He married Elizabeth Matthews on December 8, 1792, in Virginia. The exact date when the Gaines family arrived in the state is unknown, but the 1800 census shows Abner living in Woodford Co., Ky. He first appears in the Boone Co. records in 1804.

Estimates for the year the present building was constructed range from the 1790s to 1814. Gaines received clear title to the property in December 1813. As early as 1795 but at least by 1803, Archibald Reid was operating a tavern on the property. Archaeological evidence suggests that an earlier building existed just south of the existing brick structure and may have stood until the 1890s. Gaines appears to have taken over the tavern in 1808, when he was approved for a tavern license. The license allowed him "to keep a tavern at his dwelling house in the county of Boone . . . and provide in his said tavern good wholesome cleanly lodging and diet for travellers and stablage provender or pasturage for horses." According to the license, Gaines was not to "suffer or permit any unlawful gaming in his house nor suffer any person to tipple or drink more than is necessary or at any time suffer any disorderly or scandalous behavior to be practised in his house." The tavern license was renewed by Gaines every year or two through December 1818. The list of rumored guests at the tavern includes Henry Clay, Vice President Richard Mentor Johnson, and Gen. Marquis de Lafayette. Although Gaines was running a tavern in 1808, it appears that he did not own the property until 1809. He lived at his home in Walton until his death on October 30, 1839. Gaines willed the tavern to his unmarried daughter Mildred. After Mildred married Anthony Davies, the couple sold the land to Mildred's brother Archibald in 1850. In 1869 Archibald sold it to Harvey Hicks.

The road to Lexington had existed for many years before Abner Gaines opened his stagecoach line on May 6, 1818. An advertisement in the May 16, 1818, *Western Monitor* in Lexington states that the cost of passage from Cincinnati to Lexington on Gaines's stagecoach was 10 cents per mile, which included 14 pounds of baggage. For 100 pounds or more of baggage, one paid the same rate as for a person. Several of Gaines's sons served as postmasters for the Walton area and used the stagecoach line as a postal connection to Lexington. During winters, the stagecoach line was often closed owing to bad road conditions.

There are several documented stories of suicides occurring at the tavern. The *Cincinnati Daily Enquirer* on April 18, 1867, reported that Maj. John A. Goodson had shot himself at Glen's (Gaines's) Tavern one mile north of Walton. Goodson had been a state representative and served as mayor of Covington from 1860 through 1864. The next day, the newspaper reported that Goodson's funeral would be held at J. G. Carlisle's house in Covington. **John G. Carlisle** was Goodson's son-in-law.

Robert F. and Attila Cleek bought the tavern property in 1873. On September 3, 1883, another suicide occurred. Covington's *Daily Commonwealth* reported that Hugh Ingram had hanged himself on the tavern's property from the beam of a bridge that crossed the **Cincinnati Southern Railroad**. The suicide of Ingram was blamed on a mad dog that had bitten him several years before. The bridge was torn down several years ago, but its stone supports remain on each side of the tracks.

Yet another bizarre incident took place in May 1892 when Cleek's sister-in-law Lizzie Rice was visiting. The *Boone County Recorder* related that while Rice was in the orchard, she poured coal oil on herself and then set fire to it.

John Gault operated the Haunted House Antique Shop in the former tavern for most of the 20th century. In 1989 Alan and Stephanie Gjerde purchased the house and began an extensive restoration of the property. In 2006 the city of Walton received a $300,000 federal grant to purchase the home, continue restoration, and convert it into a transportation museum.

Becher, Matt, to Paul A. Tenkotte, e-mail, July 11, 2008.
Boone County Recorder, May 11, 1892, 2.
Coleman, J. Winston, Jr. *Stage-Coach Days in the Bluegrass.* Louisville, Ky.: Standard, 1933.
"Died," *CDE,* April 19, 1867, 2.
"Suicide of Ex-Mayor Goodson," *CDE,* April 18, 1867, 1.
"Suicide of Hugh Ingram," *DC,* September 3, 1883, 1.
Worrel, Stephen W., and Anne W. Fitzgerald. *Boone County Kentucky Court Orders, 1799–1815.* Falls Church, Va.: S. W. Worrel, 1994.

Elizabeth Comer Williams

GAINESVILLE. See **Idlewild**.

GAITHER, THOMAS (b. 1943, Cincinnati, Ohio). Tom Gaither is best known for his keen understanding of the character of Northern Kentucky, as expressed in his paintings and writings. He is the son of Rudy C. and Bertie M. Gaither and the brother of wildlife artist Bill Gaither. Tom Gaither grew up in Ludlow and currently resides with his wife Gee in Fort Mitchell. His first job in art was as a traveling salesman, selling fine art prints to galleries. He later became a manager at Echo Publications in Amelia, Ohio. Having gained experience in the world of published art, in 1970 he began preparing pen-and-ink illustrations for the ***Kentucky Post***. His friendship with artists **Tom Bluemlein**, Don Dennis, and **Jack Meanwell** influenced him to take up watercolor painting. Then in 1974 he opened a frame and print shop in Ludlow, selling only his own works at first. Because he was familiar with the print business, he made prints of his most popular subjects, and he found that scenes of Northern Kentucky and the Cincinnati area were the most often ordered. In 1990 Gaither was asked to be a contributing writer for the *Kenton Co. Recorder.* His weekly column included stories and recollections from Northern Kentuckians, in addition to his own musings about happenings in his hometown. Many of his sketches of buildings and locations around Northern Kentucky have been reproduced in the *Kentucky Post,* the *Kenton Co. Recorder,* and other publications. Many private collections in the region include his work; his commissioned works may be found at Bowling Green State University in Ohio, Miami University of Ohio, and Auburn University in Alabama. The paintings and prints he contributed to the Tall Stacks celebrations in Cincinnati have a wide distribution.

"Frame Maker Also Can Fill Them," *KE,* April 30, 2006, B5.
Gaither, Thomas. Interview by Rebecca Bilbo, fall 2006, Fort Mitchell, Ky.
"Print Sale to Benefit Museum," *KP,* September 18, 1985, 8K.
"Renaissance '78 Will Bring Arts to Plaza," *Colonel Covington's Chronicles,* April 1, 1978, 8.

Rebecca Bilbo

GALLATIN, ALBERT (b. January 29, 1761, Geneva, Switzerland; d. August 12, 1849, Astoria, N.Y.). Albert Gallatin, the namesake of Gallatin Co., was the son of Jean and Sophia Gallatin, who were members of a noble family but not wealthy; both died before Albert was nine years old. He arrived in America in 1780, settling in Boston, Mass. Gallatin Co. was named after him in 1799. Gallatin was U.S. secretary of the treasury from 1801 to 1814 under Presidents Thomas Jefferson (1801–1809) and James Madison (1809–1817) and a lead negotiator on the Treaty of Ghent which ended the War of 1812. Gallatin was noted primarily for his steadfast defense of the Constitution's allocation of powers and duties among the legislative, executive, and judicial branches of government. He also antagonized and questioned Federalist politicians regarding their monetary policies: Gallatin believed that the Federalists did not give the young nation's debt sufficient consideration. Gallatin died in 1849 at age 88 and was interred in a vault at the Trinity Churchyard in New York City.

Kuppenheimer, L. B. *Albert Gallatin's Vision of Democratic Stability: An Interpretive Profile.* Westport, Conn.: Praeger, 1996.
United States Department of the Treasury. www.ustreas.gov/education.

Bernie Spencer

GALLATIN ACADEMY (Carroll Co. Academy). One of the earliest schools in Kentucky, the Gallatin Academy was chartered in 1813 by an act of the Kentucky legislature. A state law passed in 1798 allowed for seminaries to be established, funded in large part by donations or sale of public lands. In 1813, while serving a second term as the Kentucky governor, Isaac Shelby (1792–1796 and 1812–1816) signed the charter creating Gallatin Academy. The land donated to support the new academy in Gallatin Co. was a 6,000-acre tract located near Hopkinsville in Christian Co., part of the Cumberland River land tract.

The name *seminary* or *academy* did not refer to a theological seminary; nor were such institutions free schools, but rather private schools offering elementary and secondary education. A board of trustees, often tied to a religious group, oversaw a seminary or an academy and hired teachers, charging students tuition to cover expenses.

The first trustees of Gallatin Academy were John Barner, Garland Bullock, Robert Plummer, Carter Tarrant, and William Winslow. Meeting for the first time on May 13, 1813, the trustees selected Port William, today Carrollton in Carroll Co., as the permanent site for the Gallatin Academy. Although it was originally in Gallatin Co., Gallatin Academy became a part of Carroll Co. with the formation of that county in 1838. The school was on land that Benjamin Craig had donated, designated in the original plat of Port William as the "old public ground." The trustees were advocates of quality education. Carter Tarrant was well educated, a leading, though controversial, Baptist and a major antislavery spokesman. Robert Plummer was Port William's first postmaster, and William Winslow, from Spottsylvania, Va., was the father of Dr. Henry Winslow, a graduate of the School of Medicine in Philadelphia.

These early academies functioned as the private schools in Virginia and Maryland did, teaching composition and writing, English literature, Latin and Greek classics, mathematics, physical geography, and rhetoric. The leading families in Carroll, Gallatin, and northern Trimble counties supported the local academy for some years.

It appears that the Gallatin Academy evolved into the Carroll Co. Academy. In 1859 the trustees of the Gallatin Academy included many of Carrollton's town fathers: George W. Boorom, William Cox, Henry Crittenden, William H. Harrison, Richard W. Masterson, and John W. Root. On September 10, 1859, the trustees of Gallatin Academy transferred four to five acres, designated as the Old Public Ground on the Port William plat, to the shareholders of what became the Carroll Co. Academy. This property was the site of the Carroll

Co. Academy, then the **Carrollton High School**, and currently the Carrollton Middle School.

In 1860 incorporation papers by 45 stockholders of the Carroll Co. Academy were filed at Carrollton; the curriculum and selection of teachers were modeled on the best classical education of the times. The Carroll Co. Academy was operating at the time of the 1892 annual report to the Kentucky superintendent of instruction, but it had closed by the time the 1899 report was submitted.

Bevarly, R. W. "History of Education in Carroll County," Master's thesis, Univ. of Kentucky, 1936.
Campbell, Justine Tandy. "History of the Carroll County Schools," 1976, Carroll Co. Public Library, Carrollton, Ky.
Carroll Co. Deed Book, book 7, pp. 251, 258, Carrollton, Ky.
Carrollton Democrat, June 12, 1868.
Hamlett, Barksdale. *History of Education in Kentucky*. Frankfort: Kentucky Department of Education, 1914.
Parker, Anna V. "A Short History of Carroll County," 1958, Carroll Co. Public Library, Carrollton, Ky.
Peters, H. W. *A Study of Local School Units in Kentucky*. Frankfort, Ky.: Superintendent of Public Instruction, 1937.
Tarrants, Charles. "Carter Tarrant (1765–1816): Baptist and Emancipationist," *RKHS* 88, no. 2 (Spring 1990): 121–48.

Diane Perrine Coon

Gallatin Co. Courthouse, Warsaw, built in 1837; the addition dates from 1868.

GALLATIN CO. Located on the western side of the Northern Kentucky region along the Ohio River, Gallatin Co., established in 1798, was the 31st of the Kentucky counties in order of formation. The county was named for **Albert Gallatin**, an early U.S. secretary of the treasury. Several of the county's earliest settlers were enlisted soldiers during the Revolutionary War and arrived with land grants issued for their military services. Gallatin Co. covers an area of roughly 99 square miles, mostly wide and fertile floodplains, and the county's economy is mainly agricultural. Gallatin Co. is bounded by the counties of Boone, Carroll, Grant, and Owen. Warsaw, the county seat, was once an important center of river trade; abundant deposits of natural materials such as sand and gravel are surface-mined there, and tobacco and corn were once cash crops. Small industry such as furniture manufacturing (see **Warsaw Furniture Factory**) was also once part of the local economy.

A portion of Gallatin Co. was taken to form Carroll Co. in 1838, the year Warsaw became the county seat. The **Civil War** was a difficult time for the county. It was highly Confederate in sympathies, and many Southern recruits came out of Gallatin Co. Several minor skirmishes took place within the county. One of the worst steamboat disasters in U.S. history occurred on the Ohio River near Warsaw on December 4, 1868, when the ***America*** and the ***United States*** collided, killing 74 people. In the early 20th century, river trade gave way to travel via highways and interstates, such as U.S. 42, U.S. 127, and I-71. The Ohio River navigation lock and dam at Markland, Ind. (see **Markland Dam**), was completed in 1964; a hydroelectric power plant (see **Power Plants**) was added there in 1967; and a vehicular bridge across the top of the dam came in 1978. In the late 1990s, the **Kentucky Speedway** began operations near Sparta, changing the face of the county, as have the gambling casinos opened close by in Indiana.

In the 1820s abolitionist **Alexander Sebastian** proclaimed his antislave stance throughout the county; Gallatin Co. was the home of Dr. **Lucy Ann Dupuy Montz**, Kentucky's first woman dentist, in the late 19th and early 20th centuries; country music star **Skeeter Davis** was born in Gallatin Co. at Glencoe in 1931; **Alvin Kidwell**, a local nurseryman, served in the Kentucky State Senate from 1941 to 1967; and Dr. **Carl Bogardus**, a medical doctor and a respected local historian who was a native of the county, helped to chronicle much of the area's history until his death in 1992.

Education in the county greatly improved with the opening of the new **Gallatin Co. High School** in 1993 and again in recent years with the additions made to the **Gallatin Co. Free Public Library** at Warsaw.

Incorporated towns within the county are Glencoe, Sparta, and Warsaw. In 1990 the county's population was 5,393, and in 2000 it was 7,870; Warsaw had 1,811 residents at the time. Positioned between the major markets of Louisville and Northern Kentucky, Gallatin Co. today faces pressure from both of those highly populated areas as they expand and develop, spreading into the county.

Bogardus, Carl R., Sr. *The Story of Gallatin County*. Ed. James C. Claypool. Cincinnati: John S. Swift, 2003.
Kleber, John E., ed. *The Kentucky Encyclopedia*. Lexington: Univ. Press of Kentucky, 1992.
U.S. Census Bureau. "American Fact Finder. Data Set. Census 2000 Summary File 1 (SF1) 100-Percent Data. Custom Table." www.census.gov (accessed March 8, 2007).

GALLATIN CO. FREE PUBLIC LIBRARY. During the late 1970s, the dream of a library in Gallatin Co. became a reality through the work of the original Library Board chairman, Charles G. Warnick, and library committee members Mary Evelyn Beverly, William Coates, Doris Combs, Barbara Liggett, and Richard Rider. Appointed by Judge Executive Clarence Davis and the Gallatin Co. Fiscal Court, this committee acquired financial help from the state: a $60,000 library demonstration grant from the Kentucky Department for Libraries and Archives (KDLA), which was used, along with help from the Gallatin Co. Fiscal Court, to support the library for more than two years. The small population of the county (5,367) would have to approve a property tax in order to continue library services once the grant moneys were expended. But the future struggle of getting this tax passed did not dim the enthusiasm of library supporters; dreams and plans were formulated, and a site for the library was selected.

Keith Collins, a graduate of Northern Kentucky University (NKU) and a resident of Glencoe, well known for his civic activities, was employed in June 1978 as the first library director. Brenda Hawkins of Warsaw became the first library assistant. Establishment of the library for Gallatin Co. was under the direction of Philip Carrico, director of the Northern Kentucky Library Development District. Carrico's expert advice and leadership helped Gallatin Co. open its first library in a remodeled laundromat on W. Pearl St. in Warsaw, in September 1978.

Shelves were built by the agriculture class at the local high school and were filled with books, some

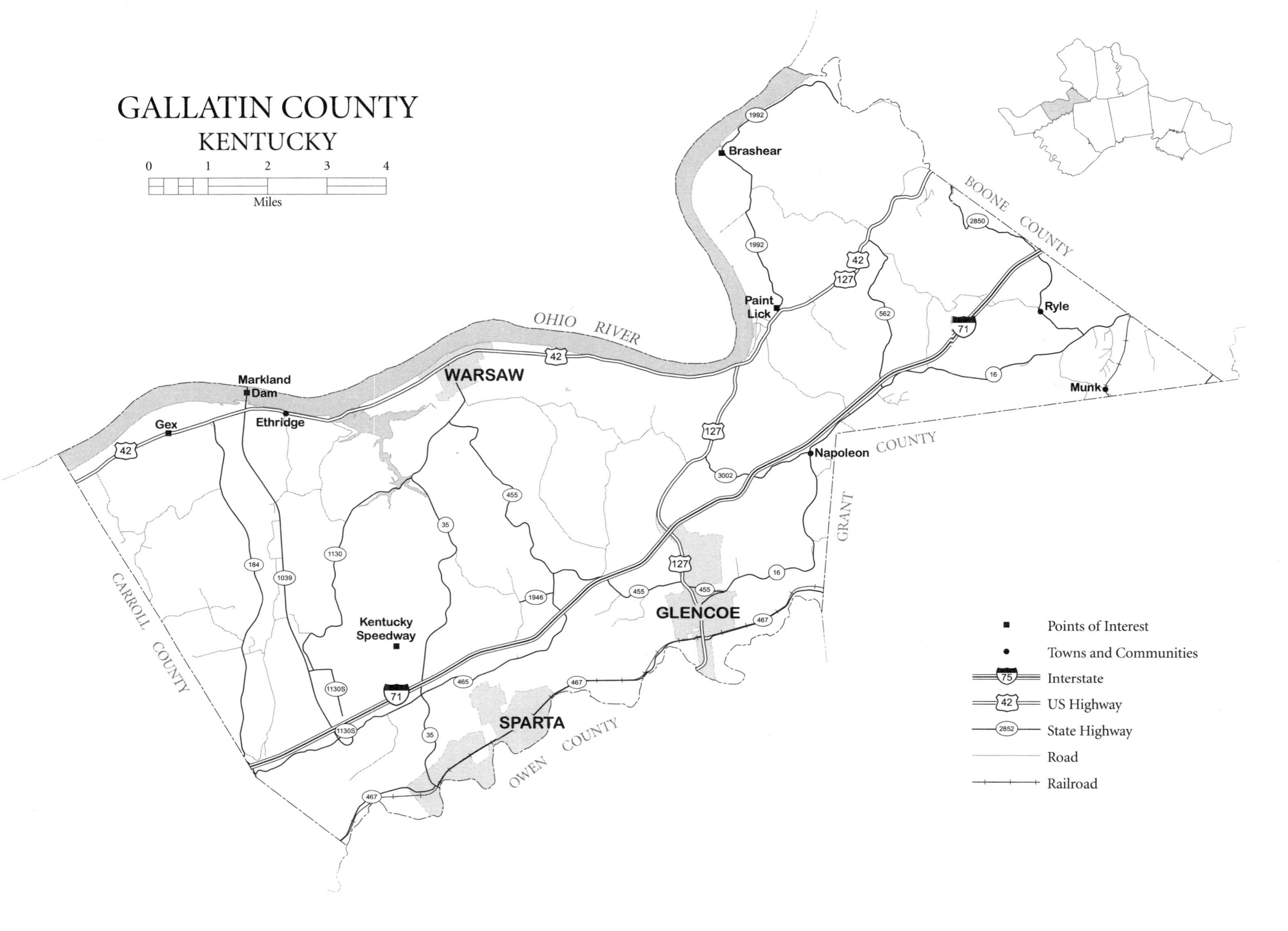
GALLATIN COUNTY
KENTUCKY
0
1
2
3
4
Miles
OHIO RIVER
BOONE COUNTY
GRANT COUNTY
OWEN COUNTY
CARROLL COUNTY
WARSAW
GLENCOE
SPARTA
Brashear
Paint Lick
Ryle
Munk
Napoleon
Markland Dam
Ethridge
Gex
Kentucky Speedway
1992
2850
42
127
562
71
16
3002
455
1946
35
1130
1039
184
1130S
465
467
Points of Interest
Towns and Communities
75
Interstate
US Highway
2852
State Highway
Road
Railroad

donated by other libraries in Kentucky. Curtains made from bedsheets graced the two large windows; volunteers worked diligently to make this first library charming and inviting to the public. Books were hand-stamped for checkout, and office space was one long table equipped with a used manual typewriter. In December 1978 Janet Jackson, a graduate of Ball State University at Muncie, Ind., succeeded Collins as library director. Jackson and her family had moved to Glencoe after her husband, Steve, accepted a teaching position at the Gallatin Co. High School.

The future of the first library was uncertain and depended totally on whether the voters of Gallatin Co. passed the proposed property tax to support the library. In November 1980 the property tax passed by 65 votes, making the library a permanent fixture in the county.

The need for a library building larger than the remodeled laundromat was soon evident, and plans for building a new library were finalized in 1982. The cost of the new construction was supported in part by a matching grant of $250,250 from the KDLA; the remaining costs were covered by a bank loan. The new library, at the corner of 209 W. Market St., directly in front of the existing library, was of Federal design, with white pillars at the entrance, a clock tower, a colonial garden, a brass weathervane, and brick sidewalks. This new structure provided 5,000 square feet of space, four times that of the former quarters. Architect Robert Ehmet Hayes was hired for the project; his blueprints included provisions for an expansion, in case it was ever needed. The new library facility opened its doors in 1984 and has become a model for other libraries built in the smaller counties of Kentucky. The original library building now houses Senior Citizens of Northern Kentucky Inc., but it is still known as the "old library." Brenda Hawkins, employed by the Gallatin Co. Free Public Library since its inception in 1978, became the library's director in September 1986. In July 1991 the library's Kentucky Room was formally dedicated to the memory of the late Charles G. Warnick. More than 200 guests attended the dedication, demonstrating that the community had suffered a profound loss with Charles Warnick's death.

In June 2000 a new library addition of 1,800 square feet was dedicated to the youth of Gallatin Co., to provide modern technology for them, to meet the diverse educational needs of today, and to enhance youthful imagination. The addition was financed by generous donations from businesses and private citizens and by a new grant from KDLA. A plaque recognizing these donors and listing board members hangs in the Children's Room.

The library has served as an example for libraries in other small counties in Kentucky in regard to technology as well as structure, receiving one of the first Empower Kentucky grants for Internet service. The Gallatin Co. Free Public Library has been featured in articles in two issues of *Kentucky Living* magazine.

Although the library is automated with the latest technology and offers a collection of more than 28,000 books, it retains its country charm. An always popular display of Denny French's model trains has been a Christmas staple at the library for 26 years. And hot coffee is provided free to patrons daily, along with warm conversations and friendly directions from members of the library's staff. Library director Brenda Hawkins retired April 1, 2005, after 27 years of service, and Shirley French, a graduate of NKU, became the fourth library director. The Gallatin Co. Free Public Library is a permanent reminder of the generosity and forward-thinking nature of Gallatin Co.'s citizens.

"Gallatin Library Approved," *KP*, August 19, 1977, 11K.
"Gallatin Library Gets $60,000," *KP*, June 20, 1978, 5K.

Brenda Hawkins

GALLATIN CO. HIGH SCHOOL. The Gallatin Co. High School, located on U.S. 42 in Warsaw, the county seat, is the only secondary education institution in Gallatin Co. It opened in 1936 as the consolidated public county high school, accepting students from the former Warsaw High School, Sparta High School, and Glencoe High School. The original building was that of the Warsaw High School, which had been built in 1913. The Works Progress Administration (WPA) constructed a new building in 1937, adjacent to the older 1913 structure, which then became an elementary school. In the school year 1959–1960, a new addition opened, and the elementary and high schools shared some rooms and a cafeteria. Damaged in a 1959 explosion of the Warsaw Pepsi-Cola plant, the 1913 building was demolished several years later when a new addition was constructed in the growing educational complex; further expansions occurred during the 1970s. In 1995 a new high school campus was opened, and the old building was turned into a middle school. When a new upper elementary-middle school was completed in 2008, the old WPA building with its 1959–1960 and subsequent additions was demolished.

The school is under the daily supervision of a resident principal and the school's site-based council. The school system's overall operation is directed by a four-member county board of education, whose members are elected from their respective districts for four-year terms, and a county school superintendent hired by the county's school board. The Gallatin Co. High School is a member of the Kentucky High School Athletic Association, and its sports teams, called the Wildcats, compete under the colors of blue and white. The athletic program offers a variety of interscholastic sports for men and women, including basketball, baseball, football, golf, tennis, cross-country track, volleyball, and softball. In accordance with its relatively small student population, the school is a Class A school for athletic purposes. In addition to its core curriculum, Gallatin Co. High School offers courses in art, music, band, shop, and foreign languages, and students can participate in a variety of extracurricular activities, including the school's interscholastic academic team. Full racial integration of the school system was achieved in 1964 without notable incident. In 2008 the high school had 409 students enrolled.

Bogardus, Carl R., Sr. *The Story of Gallatin County.* Ed. James C. Claypool. Cincinnati: John S. Swift, 2003.

Steve Huddleston

GALLATIN CO. NEWS. The first issue of the *Gallatin Co. (Ky.) News* made its appearance on September 1, 1926; it was edited by Edgar Lamkin and printed at the *Boone Co. Recorder*'s plant in Burlington. The publisher of Gallatin Co.'s new newspaper was R. E. Berkshire. Unfortunately, bound volumes of early editions of the newspaper did not survive; however, from January 1, 1935, on, bound copies of each year's **newspapers** are filed at the office of the *Gallatin Co. News* in Warsaw.

In 1934 Warren P. and Bess Boulton purchased the *Gallatin Co. News.* Printing equipment was acquired, and the newspaper began to be printed at Warsaw. In 1937 Mark Meadows purchased the newspaper from the Boultons and continued printing it in Warsaw. In 1941 he also purchased the *Walton (Ky.) Advertiser.* The *Gallatin Co. News* was next sold to Charles E. Adams, a native of Morehead who came to Warsaw with his wife Frances and his stepson Phil Bradley, who was from Shelbyville, Ky. While working at Morehead, Adams had been employed by that town's newspaper, the *Sentinel-News.* He was an experienced printer, able to operate the complicated Linotype machine of the day, and proved to be an excellent writer-editor. He issued the first number of his paper on August 7, 1941.

Weathering the dark days of **World War II**, with its paper shortages and slow advertising growth, Adams continued printing the *Gallatin Co. News* without interruption. He built a fine new brick building on the courthouse square in Warsaw to house the newspaper's business office and printing facility. An indication that he was active in journalism outside his own venture was that he was elected president of the Kentucky Press Association in 1956. Adams's stepson Phil Bradley joined the *Gallatin Co. News,* serving as editor. But after Bradley's untimely death in 1974, Adams sold the newspaper. Charles and Denny Warnick purchased it on February 1, 1975.

Reflecting the many changes that have occurred with the modernization of newspaper production, the paper is now printed at the Landmark Press in Shelbyville, Ky. The days of hot metal, the flat-bed press, and the Linotype are gone from the newspaper business. Computers are used to write stories and to compose pages, which can be sent electronically to the printing plant. Subscribers' mailing labels for the *Gallatin Co. News* are also computer-generated.

However, the editorial offices of the newspaper, located in a restored 1860 house one block from the Gallatin Co. Courthouse, remain the same. At the death of Charles Warnick in 1984, Denny Warnick became the paper's publisher. The couple's older son, Kelley Warnick, is editor. He is also the newspaper's award-winning photographer and a longtime Kentucky Press Association board member. Younger son Clay Warnick is the newspaper's associate editor and advertising director. Terry Combs-Caldwell is production head and is assisted by Bobbie Hendrix.

Bogardus, Carl R., Sr. *The Story of Gallatin County.* Ed. James C. Claypool. Cincinnati: John S. Swift, 2003.
Cutshaw, Paul, former hot-type printer of the *Gallatin Co. News.* Interview by Denny Kelley-Warnick, March 30, 2006, Warsaw, Ky.
Gallatin Co. News, various back issues.
Gray, Gypsy M. *History of Gallatin County, Kentucky.* Covington, Ky.: Self-published, 1968.

Denny Kelley-Warnick

GALLATIN CO. PLANT NURSERIES. Along each of the three highways leading to Warsaw, the county seat of Gallatin Co., there is a plant nursery. These businesses represent an industry that thrived throughout the 20th century, causing Gallatin Co. to be nicknamed "the nursery county."

The father of these wholesale plant nurseries was John F. Donaldson, a native of England, who began his first nursery on rented land in Warsaw. Later he bought 70 acres in Sparta, along the **Louisville and Nashville Railroad** tracks, over which his plants were shipped to the Midwest and the South. He was well known throughout those regions and hailed as a pioneer whose techniques and supply of offshoot plants gave birth to many others. People who worked for and learned from him began by leasing, then buying land around Warsaw.

William Hill began planting offshoots he had obtained from Donaldson on the eastern and southern edges of Warsaw. He built a greenhouse to grow plants for sale and then established Hill's Nursery, encompassing more than 125 acres along U.S. 42 to the east of Donaldson's Nursery. There he grew bare root stock, from shrubs to trees, until he died in 1963. His son-in-law Harry Roberts continued the operation until 1990.

Chester "Shug" O'Connor went from water boy to foreman at Donaldson's Nursery, learned landscaping while stationed at Norfolk, Va., during **World War II**, and returned to Warsaw to operate a greenhouse. Because his knowledge of grafting and propagating were in high demand, he leased, then later bought, tracts of land in several locations in the county, expanding to more than 167 acres in nursery stock. He owned and operated his business as Arrowwood Nurseries for 35 years, and his son, Terry continued the business for 15 years as O'Connor Nursery.

Raising nursery stock was a year-round occupation. The busy seasons were spring and fall, when the plants were dug from the ground, either bare-rooted or swathed in burlap for transplanting. The plants were hand dug by a mostly local workforce that was expanded during the busy seasons. In winter, since few used a mechanical spade, they could dig only as long as the crust of frosted earth was no deeper than four inches. When winter conditions prevented outdoor work, plants were grafted in clay pots by a smaller, skilled group of workers, so that they would be ready for sale in the spring. It was during this dormant season that owners could research new methods and new plant varieties and prepare pocket-sized price lists. Summers were spent mowing and weeding to control rampant growth.

More nurseries opened west of Warsaw as Harry Hopperton, who had for years bought trees from O'Connor for his garden center in Illinois, purchased a farm on the west edge of town in 1957, converting former corn and tobacco fields to plant stock. When Hopperton retired, he leased his operation to Rick Flynn, who continued the business until 2005.

In 1961, Eddie Mylor transformed 150 acres of his family farm to a balled and burlapped stock of tree liners, which were small plants field grown in rows. Mules, as well as tractors, were used to plow and drag the largest plants from their holes. Former farmhands loaded plants onto flatbed trucks for transport as far away as New York and Wisconsin. Seasonally hired teenagers would accompany the loads to provide labor.

The building of the local interstate highways helped the industry in two ways: the highways provided a faster route to other nurseries and garden centers, which were existing markets; and the roads enhanced the nursery market, since nursery products were needed to landscape and beautify the federal highways.

The American Nurserymen's Association, in which some owners were active, helped promote these mostly family-run businesses. In 1966 R. Waldron Haymond bought Donaldson's original Sparta land, named Willadean Nursery, which had been operated for more than 40 years by Kentucky state senator **Alvin Kidwell**. Haymond renamed it Willadean-Donaldson Nursery, and he, a licensed landscape architect, designed the grounds of many private homes and public projects, such as the **Cincinnati/Northern Kentucky International Airport**.

Plants from Gallatin Co. nurseries were used to landscape a variety of sites, from Bernheim Forest south of Louisville to Kings Island in Mason, Ohio. The industry was affected by events such as the **blizzard** of 1978, which necessitated a long recovery period, and by market trends that included the sale of imported nursery stock by big-box retailers.

In 1991 another family farm was transformed into a plant nursery when Zack Bledsoe started Cloverfarm Nursery with container-grown stock in over-winter-protection poly houses, actually large cold frames. These 14-by-96-foot structures shelter the plants from winter dry-out, before their tops are removed in the spring. The plants, both deciduous and evergreen, ground covers to shade trees, are propagated in a nonsoil medium and are spaced throughout the poly house in order to grow into a pleasing shape. Cloverfarm Nursery supplies Gallatin Co.'s first garden center, Country Blooms, operated by Bledsoe's wife, Janet. In 1992, Jeff Wallace started Rolling Ridge Nursery on his family farm in western Gallatin Co., growing container trees. His operation today includes balled and burlapped trees on five acres of land. Such operations supply a new demand for diverse landscaping plants that container nurseries make possible.

"Former Senator Alvin Kidwell Dies at Age 80," *Gallatin County News*, April 18, 1974, 1.
"Local Nurseryman, J.F. Donaldson Passes Sunday," *Gallatin County News*, March 30, 1950, 1

Jacquelene P. Mylor

GALLATIN CO. PUBLIC SCHOOLS. Education has had high priority for Gallatin Co. residents from the very beginning of the county in 1798. Many log schools existed in the county in early days, such as the Gridley School at Ethridge, the Gullion School between Sparta and Glencoe, and the Orr School in the Drury community. These schoolhouses were one-room structures with split-log seats and served students of all ages. There were a number of private schools and academies before the establishment of the public school system.

Gallatin Co. established a public school in Warsaw in 1885; it built a new building in 1888 and closed in 1913. The city of Warsaw established its own school system in 1904; in 1913 it created **Warsaw High School**.

During the early 1900s, there were still several one-room schools in Gallatin Co. Some of these were the Carlisle School located on Montgomery Rd., the Clay Lick School just outside Glencoe, and others named Concord, Cow Branch, Drury Chapel, Eagle Tunnel, Ethridge, Gex, Hamilton, Hixon's, Hogan, Hoggins, Hughes, Jackson, Lick Creek, Lowe, Montgomery, Napoleon, Oakland, Paint Lick, Sleet, South Fork, Steeles Creek, Stone Lick, Sugar Creek, Ten Mile, Union, and Walnut Valley. In addition, African American schools existed at Warsaw and Park Ridge.

Sparta established its school district during the early 1870s on land donated by A. D. Mason that was partly in Gallatin Co. and partly in Owen Co. This facility was in use as late as 1936–1937 and was known as the Old Red Brick School.

A school established by Glencoe in 1871 held classes in the Christian Church until 1872, when the townspeople, with the help of the Masonic Lodge in town (see **Masons**), built a two-story frame building for the school. In 1910 this school became a grade school, and a new building was built for it in 1914. During the 1936–1937 school year, when the schools in the county were consolidated, this school became the Glencoe Elementary School. The building burned in 1956 and a new building was built in 1957. This school operated until the 1970s; when it closed, all of its classes moved to Warsaw.

The 1935–1936 consolidation of Gallatin Co. schools resulted in the closing of the one-room schools in the county as well as Sparta's school. The two initial county schools were **Gallatin Co. High School** (formerly Warsaw High School) and the Glencoe Elementary School. Today, the Gallatin Co. School District operates four schools: a lower elementary, an upper elementary, a middle school, and Gallatin Co. High School, all located in Warsaw.

Bogardus, Carl R., Sr. *The Story of Gallatin County.* Ed. James C. Claypool. Cincinnati: John S. Swift, 2003.

Gallatin Co. School District. www.gallatin.k12.ky.us/ (accessed June 9, 2008).

Darrell Maines

GALLOWAY, DONALD P. "DON" (b. July 27, 1937, Mason Co., Ky.; d. January 8, 2009, Reno, Nev.). Don Galloway, an actor, a producer, and a director, is the son of Paul Smith and Callie "Malee" Poe Galloway. He grew up just outside Brooksville, graduating from Bracken Co. High School in 1955. Galloway graduated from the University of Kentucky in Lexington in 1959 and then went to New York City to study acting. From 1963 to 1964, he played Mitchell Harris, a character in the ABC television network's drama *Arrest and Trial,* the series that inspired the popular NBC program *Law & Order.* Galloway is retired from a television and movie career that totaled about 60 credits as an actor, a director, or a producer. He is best known for his supporting role as Detective Sgt. Ed Brown alongside lead actor Raymond Burr in the popular NBC television program *Ironsides,* 1967–1975. Galloway resided in Valencia, Calif., with his wife, a former actress, until his death in 2009. They had two daughters. Galloway was cremated.

Bracken Co. Extension Homemakers. *History of Bracken County.* Bicentennial ed. Brooksville, Ky.: Bracken Co. Extension Homemakers, 2002.
"Malee Poe Galloway," *KP,* December 27, 1991, 6A.
McNeil, Alex. *Total Television.* New York: Penguin Books, 1996.
Reis, Jim. "Joy, Sorrow Marked Holidays Past," *KP,* December 21, 1991, 4K.

James C. Claypool

GALVIN, MAURICE L. (b. July 10, 1872, Covington, Ky.; d. August 25, 1940, Cincinnati, Ohio). Attorney Maurice Lee Galvin Jr. worked compulsively, took few vacations, and became one of the most powerful Kentucky Republican "political bosses" and powerbrokers of the 20th century. "His word was his bond and his iron was in his hand," said two-term Kentucky governor Albert B. "Happy" Chandler (1935–1939, 1955–1959) in a letter to Galvin's family. "Even vacations he took when we were young were shortened so he could get back to work," commented his daughter Grace Galvin Nelson, of Covington.

Maurice Galvin Jr. was one of 10 children born to Covington blacksmith Maurice Galvin Sr. and Ellen Cronin Galvin. The Galvin family lived near Fourth and Garrard Sts., and Maurice attended Covington public schools. He graduated from the Covington High School and from Xavier University in Cincinnati. After earning a law degree from the Cincinnati Law School in 1893, he went into practice with his brother John, who later became mayor of Cincinnati. Galvin was the brother-in-law of **Earl Wilson**, the Kenton Co. native who died in 1910 as a result of injury while playing football for the U.S. Naval Academy in Annapolis, and also of radio station owner **L. B. Wilson**, one of Greater Cincinnati's broadcasting pioneers.

Galvin was involved in the management of **Latonia Racecourse**, which operated on the grounds where the Latonia Shopping Center currently stands. In 1939, when the racing industry fell on hard times, Galvin guided the sale of the racing property in Latonia to Standard Oil. He became secretary-treasurer of the Kentucky Jockey Club, an organization headed by Col. Matt Wynn, the man who built Churchill Downs and the Kentucky Derby in Louisville into internationally famous institutions.

Maurice Galvin, July 1921.

Galvin served Kentucky governors from about 1900 through the end of Happy Chandler's first term in 1939. Friends said Galvin worked for the man he thought could do more for Kentucky, whether Democrat or Republican. In 1907 the U.S. Senate approved his appointment as internal revenue collector for the congressional district then centered in Covington, and he took office in February 1908. Several years later, Happy Chandler, in a letter to Galvin, complimented this Northern Kentuckian as "one of my longest and strongest supporters."

A director and cofounder of radio station **WCKY**, Galvin also was attorney for the **Stewart Iron Works**; the Union Light, Heat, and Power Company; the Greene Line Steamers; and the **Chesapeake and Ohio Railroad**. He was director and attorney for the Deering Publishing Company and attorney for the ***Kentucky Post*** when it was an independent newspaper. His law partner for many years was **Frank M. Tracy**.

Galvin died in 1940 of a cerebral hemorrhage; he was age 68. A tribute on WCKY radio quoted *Kentucky Post* editor Carl Saunders: "Mr. Galvin was honest and sincere, modest, and unostentatious. He never forgot his friends." Maurice Galvin was buried at St. Mary Cemetery in Fort Mitchell.

"Death Ends Colorful Career of Leader M.L. Galvin at 68," *KP,* August 26, 1940, 1.
Ohio Death Certificate No. 50253, for the year 1940.
"Program in Tribute to Memory of Maurice L. Galvin," WCKY radio, script from broadcast, Tuesday, August 27, 1940.
Reis, Jim. "Past VIP's: Diverse Group of Politicians, Military Men, and Scientists Made a Difference," *KP,* October 20, 1986, 4K.

Roger Auge II

GAMBLING. Gambling and associated vice industries played an important part in Northern Kentucky's economy from the first decade of the 1800s until the early 1960s. It was during this period that Northern Kentucky gained a national reputation as being a center for vice, especially gambling. In addition, the gambling and entertainment innovations instituted at the **Beverly Hills Supper Club**, one of the region's gambling-entertainment centers, represented an important turning point in the history of casino gambling.

For years in Cincinnati it was commonly said that "things were a bit looser on the other side of the river." Simply put, in the smaller municipalities on the Kentucky side of the Ohio River, it was easier for vice interests to buy off local city officials, thus avoiding the constant threat that laws against vice and gambling in these cities would be enforced. The reputation of Newport for being weak in enforcement of vice and gambling laws began with the arrival of the **Newport Barracks** in 1809 when troopers stationed there began visiting adjacent houses of ill repute.

Until the 1960s, people profiting from the illegal vice activities in Northern Kentucky had been able to weather the reforming impulses of the region's rising middle class. Since vice interests represented a large portion of the economy in Northern Kentucky, many local citizens were hesitant to help clean up the affected cities. The region's proximity to Cincinnati and its distance from state government and state law enforcement officials in Frankfort also helped to promote and perpetuate a sense of regional autonomy that allowed illegal activities to continue to grow and prosper. The situation was magnified during **Prohibition**, when bootlegging allowed criminals who previously might have been small-time outlaws to reap enormous profits through the production, transportation, and distribution of illegal alcohol. Many of America's greatest fortunes, criminal and otherwise, were made during Prohibition. It was the hotbed from which most of the country's major organized crime figures emerged. After the federal government made the manufacture and distribution of alcoholic products legal again in 1933, these nouveau riche bootleggers had to look for other investments. Cincinnatian Peter Schmidt, who fell into this category, was about to make his mark.

Soon Schmidt began to act on a vision that, though not necessarily unique, turned out to be one of the models for the modern-day casino. He had in mind a gambling hall that offered a variety of services, including fine dining and a full bar, in addition to gambling. The idea was to offer to the masses the same gambling amenities usually afforded only to the rich in private clubs. To achieve his dream, Schmidt built the **Beverly Hills Supper Club** in Southgate. Its success prompted envy from the region's largest criminal organization, the **Cleveland Syndicate** (a.k.a. the Mayfield Road Gang). In the late 1930s, the crime syndicate attempted to buy Schmidt out on numerous occasions. Stubborn, Schmidt refused, and the Cleveland Syndicate, through local agents, blew up the Beverly Hills Supper Club in 1937. Schmidt rebuilt the club but eventually, in 1940, agreed to give up his piece of the local gambling turf, and the syndicate from Cleveland arrived.

Although it is easy to view the Cleveland Syndicate as a ruthless criminal organization, much like the Corleone family in *The Godfather,* it is best understood as well-financed businessmen, whose business was largely illegal gambling. This is not to discount their capacity to resort to violence. Their local enforcer was **Red Masterson**, who oversaw the Cleveland Syndicate's local operations. Like most enforcers, he usually dealt with problems through persuasion and cash payments but sometimes used violent means.

With the coming of organized crime in the early 1940s, Northern Kentucky's gambling industry took on the structure that it retained until most of the casinos in the region were shut down in the early 1960s. It was essentially a two-tiered affair, in which larger, better-financed and sometimes glitzy "carpet joints" competed with more rough-and-tumble "bust-out joints." Most of the carpet joints were run by the mobsters and local henchmen associated with the Mayfield Road Gang, but Peter Schmidt's Playtorium and Glenn Rendezvous were also included. They made their money the same way today's casinos in Las Vegas and in Atlantic City, N.J., do—the odds were with the house, which meant that as long as people lost more than they won, profits were made. The take could be enormous, but achieving it required patience and startup capital. To draw in players, the carpet joints were well appointed (hence the name) and usually had nice restaurants and showrooms attached. The Playtorium had a bowling alley, and the Beverly Hills Supper Club booked national entertainment acts.

The bust-out joints operated on a different business model. Smaller, with less capital, most of them were located in downtown Newport. They were often just bars with some gambling in the back. These joints generally played on the naïveté of tourists and other out-of-towners, rigging the games so customers always lost or drugging customers to steal their winnings. Thus, individuals who entered and gambled could not get "out" until they were "busted." Since the cops were on the payroll, these suckers had no recompense, and they would often be blackmailed into keeping quiet by means of pictures that had been taken showing them in a compromising position with a showgirl or prostitute.

The most famous episode in Newport's history was a classic example of bust-out-joint trickery. The reform candidate for Campbell Co. sheriff, **George W. Ratterman**, was hoping to play upon his celebrity as a former professional football player to gain election. Thus, when Peter Tito Carinci, another former football player and the manager of the Glenn Hotel–Tropicana Club, told Ratterman he wanted to get out of the gambling business and could provide important information about corruption in Newport, Ratterman agreed to meet with him. What Ratterman did not know was that he was being set up by Carinci, who was acting on orders from his mobster associates to frame Ratterman. Carinci drugged Ratterman and another man, who had come along with Ratterman to observe, before dinner in Cincinnati and then took them both back to the Glenn Hotel in Newport. Carinci's attempt to have Ratterman photographed with semiclad showgirl-prostitute April Flowers (Juanita Hodges) backfired (the photographer never arrived), but Ratterman was still arrested for soliciting **prostitution** by corrupt Newport police officers who had been paid off and were part of the frame.

The charges against Ratterman quickly proved to be a farce, and the episode destroyed whatever credibility the gambling interests retained in Northern Kentucky. But the incident reveals a lot about the styles of the carpet joints versus the bust-out joints. Once the heat was on in Northern Kentucky, the Cleveland Syndicate's operations shut down, or else the restaurants stayed open and the casino operations closed. But the small-time operators like Carinci had a lot more to lose, and so they attempted to frame Ratterman, using the same techniques that had succeeded in framing thousands of out-of-towners for years. The Cleveland Syndicate preferred to try to buy Ratterman off, but he rebuffed them every time.

Casinos were Northern Kentucky's primary form of gambling during the 1940s and 1950s. Many of them contained the table games—blackjack, craps, and roulette—that today's avid gambler would find familiar. Slot machines were popular, but most serious gamblers stuck to the tables. Slots were more of a diversion than serious gambling, and most of these "one-arm bandits" were found in small bars and cafés in Newport.

Another type of gambling was layoff betting, and much of the money that went through Newport was in this form. As the national center for the horse-racing industry, Kentucky is one of the few states where gambling on horse racing has been never been outlawed. Thus, much of the infrastructure for betting on horses was in place in Kentucky, especially in Newport. Small-time bookies could be found throughout the county. Using the various wire services, the bookies could get up-to-date information on horse races being run anywhere in the country. Most of these handbooks, as they were called, were essentially illegal versions of today's off-track betting houses. Patrons would put money on horse races and, increasingly after World War II, would bet on sports such as football and basketball.

Bookmakers adjusted the betting lines on a contest in order to attract an even amount of betting for each participant. Thus, in order to attract betting for an underdog, a bookmaker offered better odds. Bookmakers wanted an even amount of money on each side because they made their profits from the vigorish, or commission charged to the losing bettor (10%). But sometimes, no matter what the line, there might be uneven betting. So the bookmaker called in a "lay-off" bet to another, usually larger, gambling operation to cover his risk. Many of these lay-off operations were in Northern Kentucky. Often no more than a phone bank, the lay-off house was a key part of the region's gambling business.

Gambling was the core of Northern Kentucky's illicit economy. It is what brought the locals as well as out-of-towners to Newport, the "Sin City on the Ohio River." But there were plenty of secondary businesses that fed off gambling and Newport's economy of crime. The most prominent of these was prostitution. Newport was notorious for its various brothels, which were divided between day and night houses. Day houses serviced customers from the morning until the early evening; evening houses were open until the sun rose the next day. A house would have a light (usually red) turned on if it was open for business. Prostitution, despite its notoriety, is one of the least understood aspects of the region's larger gambling economy.

Other businesses that benefited from gambling included the numerous food, beverage, and linen purveyors that served the restaurants and casinos, as well as the hundreds of people who worked as bartenders, cabdrivers, dealers, and waitresses. All of these people had businesses and jobs that were dependent on the gambling industry, a fact that explains the lack of support reform efforts received in the municipal areas of Newport and Covington.

The least discussed aspect of Newport's gambling business is the economy of corruption, which was one of its most lucrative aspects. In addition to providing jobs for service employees, gambling also provided generous payouts to law enforcement officials in the form of regular payoffs and bribes. The amount of money that was circulated into the economy in this manner should not be overlooked. Officials from the lowest beat cop all the way up to the county judge and solicitor received weekly and monthly payoffs to persuade them to allow casinos and brothels to run without interference. These payments not only provided a powerful roadblock to reform but also were a key part of the gambling economy. Much of the profits from syndicate-run casinos left town, lining the pockets of Moe Dalitz and others, who then invested them in their Las Vegas ventures. But the bribes and payoffs stayed in the region, supplementing the incomes of low-paid civil servants.

Gambling was a large part of the Northern Kentucky economy until the Committee of 500's successful cleanup campaign of 1961. But this cleanup committee's success portended the future of the casino industry in the United States. Committee of 500 members such as Ratterman admitted that they were not really opposed to gambling on moral grounds. They just saw the rampant corruption associated with illegal gambling as a barrier to the region's long-term economic growth. This was part of the gradual change in American attitudes toward casino gambling after **World War II**. Despite the success of cleanup efforts in

Newport and other regional gambling centers, Americans came to believe that casino gambling should be legalized, as long as it was run in a fair and legitimate manner. First in Las Vegas and later in Atlantic City, and now across the country on American Indian reservations and on riverboats, Americans have embraced casino gambling as an acceptable pastime.

Gioielli, Robert. "Suburbs v. Slot Machines: The Committee of 500 and the Battle over Gambling in Northern Kentucky," *Ohio Valley History* 5, no. 2 (Summer 2005): 61–84.

Williams, Michael L. "Sin City Kentucky: Newport, Kentucky's Vice Heritage, and Its Legal Extinction, 1920–1991," master's thesis, University of Louisville, 2008.

Robert Gioielli

GANO, JOHN STITES, MAJOR GENERAL (b. July 14, 1766, New York City; d. January 1, 1822, Covington, Ky.). An early settler instrumental in the founding of Covington, John Stites Gano was the son of John Gano, pastor of the First Baptist Church in New York City, and Sarah Stites Gano. John Stites Gano was given the same name as the oldest child in the family, who had died in 1765 at the age of 11. In 1788 the family, along with other relatives, settled at Columbia, then part of the Northwest Territory. (Columbia was on the east side of modern-day Cincinnati, near where the Lunken Airport is now.) In 1790 Stephen, another son of the family, who was a physician and a Baptist minister, helped a group of settlers establish the Columbia Baptist Church, which was the first church of any kind in the Northwest Territory. John Stites Gano married Mary Goforth of New York and they had seven children, two of whom died at a young age. Gano was appointed justice of the peace in Hamilton Co., Ohio. He was in the Ohio Militia for many years and fought on the frontier against Indians under the command of Gen. Arthur St. Clair, the territorial governor of Ohio. Gano attained the rank of major general. For a time, he was the commander of Fort Hamilton and Fort Washington in the Ohio Territory; the latter fort was on the banks of the Ohio River in Cincinnati. He also fought in the **War of 1812**.

In 1814, along with his brother Richard and **Thomas D. Carneal**, Gano purchased from **Thomas Kennedy** 200 acres at **the Point** in Kentucky, where the Licking River enters the Ohio River. At the time, there were only farms and farmlands west of the Licking River in Kentucky. On February 8, 1815, the Kentucky legislature passed "An Act establishing the town of Covington, at the mouth of the Licking," thereby approving 150 acres of the 200 acres purchased by the Gano brothers and Carneal as constituting the Covington Company; later this land, which was then a part of Campbell Co., became the basis for the city of Covington. The *Western Spy*, a newspaper in Cincinnati, described the property: "This commanding & beautiful situation is generally known throughout the Western country. . . . This situation presents a prospect equal if not superior to any on the Ohio River." The first lots were sold in March 1815. Later that year, Thomas Carneal sold his part of the property to the Gano brothers. Richard, John's brother, died in October 1815 at age 41, and John S. Gano became the company's sole proprietor.

In early 1816 Gano and Carneal received licenses to operate ferries across the Ohio and the Licking rivers. By 1817 Gano began listing lots for sale in Covington. He served as clerk of the Common Pleas Court and the Supreme Court of Hamilton Co., Ohio, until he moved to a nine-and-one-half-acre Covington estate in 1818. Gano died on January 1, 1822. Originally buried at the First Baptist Grounds on Court St. in Cincinnati, his remains were transferred in 1866 to Spring Grove Cemetery, also in Cincinnati.

Cist, Charles. *The Cincinnati Miscellany; or, Antiquities of the West.* 2 vols. Cincinnati, 1846.

Smith, Allen Webb. *Beginning at "the Point": A Documented History of Northern Kentucky and Environs, the Town of Covington in Particular, 1751–1834.* Park Hills, Ky.: Self-published, 1977.

Spring Grove Cemetery Records, Cincinnati.

James R. Duvall

GANO-SOUTHGATE HOUSE. Located in Covington at 405 E. Second St., this historic mansion is officially named the Gano-Southgate House, but it has been mistakenly called the Carneal House for many years (see **Licking-Riverside, Riverside Drive, and Ohio Riverside National Historic Districts**). In 1820 Aaron Gano, son of **John Stites Gano**, one of the founders of Covington, purchased the land on which the house rests, originally lot number 69. Thomas Carneal may have designed and built this house sometime between 1820 and 1822 for Aaron Gano. The design is basically Federal (Adamesque), with obvious influences by the renowned Italian architect Andrea Palladio. The two-story recessed portico features slender columns, surmounted by Ionic capitals on the first floor and Corinthian capitals on the second floor. The recessed windows have arched lintels and Georgian tracery. The bricks are a rich rose.

In 1825 **William Wright Southgate**, who later served as a Kentucky state representative and as Covington mayor, acquired the mansion. He was the son of **Richard Southgate**, a Campbell Co. lawyer and businessman and one of the wealthiest men in Kentucky. In 1835 William Wright Southgate built an addition in Greek Revival style onto the back of the mansion. Over the years, the interior of the house was extensively remodeled, and the building was used for a time as an apartment house. It has beautiful woodwork and impressive fireplace mantels. Most of the interior hardware is silver plated, and there are also several silver-plated metallic stars, which are said to be Masonic emblems. Lately, efforts have been made to determine the original wall locations and woodwork style, so that a total restoration can eventually be made.

An arched tunnel leading to the Licking River was initially built as a service entrance through which supplies could be quietly brought into the house from the riverbank. Some believe that the tunnel and the house were used as part of the Underground Railroad escape network (see **Underground Railroad, Campbell and Kenton Counties**). It is said that many notables have been guests in the Gano-Southgate house, including Henry Clay, Andrew Jackson, and Daniel Webster.

Bricking, Chuck. *Covington's Heritage: A Compilation of the City's Historical Houses and a Short Biography of the Inhabitants.* Covington, Ky.: Privately published, 1980.

Langsam, Walter E. *Great Houses of the Queen City.* Cincinnati: Cincinnati Historical Society, 1997.

Jack Wessling

GARDEN OF HOPE. On three-fourths of an acre of land atop a peaceful hill overlooking I-75 to the west and Covington to the east, lies the Garden of Hope. In the garden is a statue of Jesus Christ, a 25-foot wooden cross, a re-creation of a carpenter's shop, and a rock from the Jordan River, where Jesus was baptized. In the garden's Chapel of Dreams is a piece of marble from the mountain where Jesus delivered his Sermon on the Mount. But the garden's main attraction is an ivy-covered re-creation of the tomb in Jerusalem where it is believed Jesus was buried. Morris Coers, pastor of the Immanuel Baptist Church at 20th and Greenup Sts. in Covington, built the garden in 1958. At the time, it was said to be the only replica of the tomb in the United States. Solomon Mattar, the warden of the Jerusalem tomb, sent the exact measurements to Coers, and Mattar's son Samuel helped build the replica of the tomb. Indeed, visitors who have previously been to Jerusalem have agreed that the tomb strongly resembles the original one. In its early years, the Garden of Hope was always open, and on a typical Sunday, 2,000 people would visit. By 1960 attendance had risen to 150,000 annually. When erosion threatened the hillside, a man wearing bib overalls "came out of nowhere and told Coers what to do," according to legend. No one knew the man or where he had come from, but his advice, to build a retaining wall, solved the problem. In 2000 the Garden of Hope of Immanuel was incorporated. The garden remains a popular spot for weddings and Easter services.

DeVroomen, Sacha. "Obscure Garden, Replica Tomb Inspire Kindness of Strangers," *KP*, April 10, 1992, 1K.

Eigelbach, Kevin. "Hope for the Garden," *KP*, April 10, 2004, 1K.

Hicks, Jack. "Garden of Hope Brings Spirit of Easter Sunday into Visitors," *KP*, April 5, 1999, 1K.

Reis, Jim. "The Garden of Hope: Elusive Dream," *KP*, January 11, 1993, 4K.

Ann Hicks

GARDNERSVILLE. Gardnersville, a small village in northwestern Pendleton Co., is located on Ky. Rt. 491, the Knoxville-Gardnersville Rd. Gardnersville was a booming village in the late 1800s and early 1900s. At its stores, customers could purchase anything from fiddle strings to a buggy or a jolt wagon. There were also a millinery shop, a sewing machine dealer, a post office, two barbershops, and a community hall where the Odd Fellows and the Junior Lodge met. Three blacksmith shops, which later gave way to the largest farm machinery dealership in Pendleton Co., were also operating in Gardnersville. In the late 1800s the town had a saloon where customers could bring their own bottles and have them filled with whiskey directly from the house barrel. The buggy shop manufactured and sold buggies and also did repairs. In the early 1900s, this shop became an automobile garage and upholstering shop where Model T Fords were fitted with new tops, curtains, and glass windows.

Gardnersville once had two doctors, an undertaker, a cemetery, two church houses, and three **tobacco** warehouses. The largest of the warehouses was a two-story building, built during the period when the nightriders roved through Pendleton Co. burning tobacco.

In 1911 the old Simpson School on Center Ridge Rd. was replaced by a new school building, which eventually included a two-year high school program. This school was replaced by the Portland School, built in the mid-1930s, which burned in the 1960s. Several wool buyers were located in Gardnersville, as were two automobile garages and, at various times, four gasoline dealers.

Modern times have changed the little village. At present there are two churches, a cemetery, one store, and a farm machinery dealership.

Belew, Mildred Boden. *The First 200 Years of Pendleton County.* Falmouth, Ky.: M. B. Belew, n.d. [ca. 1994].

GARNER, JOHN "MACK" (b. December 23, 1898, Centerville, Iowa; d. Oct. 28, 1936, Covington, Ky.). Jockey Mack Garner, a 1969 inductee into the Racing Hall of Fame, was the son of T. F. "Dode" and Sarah Clements Garner. Mack's great-grandfather, grandfather, father, and five brothers were also jockeys. In 1915, at age 17 (not 15, as is often mistakenly asserted), Garner led the nation's jockeys in wins, by achieving 151 wins, and in money won. He also was top money winner in 1929, winning $314,975, a record at the time. Garner won the 1929 Belmont Stakes aboard Blue Larkspur, the Belmont again in 1933 aboard Hurry Off, and the Kentucky Derby in 1934 riding Cavalcade. A regular rider at Covington's old **Latonia Racecourse**, Garner's greatest triumph there occurred in November 1923 when he guided **Carl Wiedemann**'s horse In Memoriam to victory over that year's Derby champion, Zev. Garner married Willis M. Leslie of Covington in 1920, and the couple eventually moved into a home in Covington that belonged to his father-in-law. On October 28, 1936, after riding four races (one of which he won) at River Downs in Cincinnati, Garner had two heart attacks at his home. He died during a third attack at Covington's St. Elizabeth Hospital (see **St. Elizabeth Medical Center**) and was buried in Covington's Linden Grove Cemetery. He was survived by his wife and four children. In a 21-year career, Garner rode 1,346 winners and 2,358 other mounts that finished in the money.

Claypool, James C. *The Tradition Continues: The Story of Old Latonia, Latonia, and Turfway Racecourses.* Fort Mitchell, Ky.: T. I. Hayes, 1997.

"Veteran Saddle Artist Dies of Heart Attack," *CP*, October 29, 1936, 20.

James C. Claypool

GARNER, MARGARET (b. 1833, Boone Co., Ky.; d. 1858, Mississippi). Margaret Garner and her children were slaves owned by the Gaines family on Maplewood Farm near Richwood, Boone Co. Her husband, Robert, and his parents were owned by the Marshall family on an adjoining farm. On the cold, wintry night of January 28, 1856, with the temperature hovering around 10 degrees Fahrenheit, the Garner family (as well as 9 other Northern Kentucky slaves, a total of 17) escaped on a large sled, which they abandoned along Pike Street in Covington, and crossed the frozen Ohio River on foot into Cincinnati. The Garners fled to the Mill Creek home of Elijah Kite, a former slave and a cousin of Margaret's. The 9 other fugitive slaves were successful in their escape to Canada via the **Underground Railroad**. The slave owners and a posse soon found the Garners at the Kite home. Rather than allow her two-and-a-half-year-old daughter Mary to be returned to slavery, Margaret killed her with a butcher knife and attempted to kill the other children. The Garners were overpowered and taken into custody.

The Garners stood trial as fugitive slaves in a Cincinnati federal courtroom. The trial provoked near-riots on the streets of Cincinnati and captured national attention. The fugitive Slave Law was upheld and the Garners were returned to their owners. Governor Salmon P. Chase of Ohio sent a requisition to Governor Charles Morehead (1855–1859) of Kentucky for the return of Margaret to Ohio to stand trial for murder, but it arrived after the Garners had been sent down the river to other Gaines brothers. No requisition was ever sent to any other Southern state. The Garners were forgotten and peace was restored to the streets of Cincinnati.

For **abolitionists**, the Garner case illuminated all that was wrong with slavery. It was also a states' jurisdiction issue. The case juxtaposed federal law (the Fugitive Slave Law of 1850) and states' rights (Ohio law for murder). Federal law took precedence over state law. Chase, the Ohio governor and an abolitionist, was personally torn because he was entrusted with enforcement of federal law and had to return the Garners to Kentucky.

This incident was one of several during the 1850s that, along with Harriet Beecher Stowe's 1852 publication of *Uncle Tom's Cabin,* popularized the plight of African American slaves. For Margaret the death of her children was preferable to slavery. Although the Garners failed in their quest for freedom, it was Northern Kentucky's best-known slave escape. Hundreds of abolitionists could not do as much for the antislavery cause as the Garners did, fanning the flames that eventually erupted into the **Civil War**.

Toni Morrison was awarded the 1993 Nobel Prize in literature for *Beloved,* a novel based on this event, and the Cincinnati Opera Company was commissioned to produce *Margaret Garner: A New American Opera,* which debuted in three cities in 2005.

"Boone Farm Confirmed as Slave Home," *KE,* October 9, 1958, B3.

Brunings, Ruth Wade Cox. "Slavery and the Tragic Story of Two Families—Gaines and Garner," *NKH* 12, no. 1 (Fall–Winter 2004): 37–45.

"Escape of Slaves," *CJ,* February 2, 1856, 2.

Margaret Garner. "*Margaret Garner: A New American Opera.*" www.margaretgarner.org (accessed September 20, 2006).

Morrison, Toni. *Beloved.* New York: Knopf, 1987.

"New Opera Will Tell Ky. Slave's Tragic Story," *KP,* February 20, 2003, 14A.

Weisenburger, Steven. *Modern Medea: A Family Story of Slavery and Child Murder from the Old South.* New York: Hill and Wang, 1995.

Yanuck, Julius. "The Garner Fugitive Slave Case," *Mississippi Valley Historical Review* 40, no. 1 (June 1953): 47–61.

GASDORF MUSIC PUBLISHING COMPANY. This Newport-based firm was owned by Alfred Gasdorf, who was born October 30, 1883, in Newport to Conrad and Elizabeth Machinot Gasdorf. By the first decade of the 20th century, Alfred Gasdorf was composing and publishing **ragtime** music for the company. He became one of several Northern Kentuckians involved with ragtime music, which flourished from 1897 to 1920. Alfred's father and brothers also played and performed music locally, when they were not working in their whitewash business. Alfred performed on the stately *Island Queen* steamboat, which sailed out of Cincinnati to Coney Island Amusement Park, and he was known to manipulate its famous calliope. He also played in theater orchestras in Cincinnati and other cities. His ragtime compositions include "Sic' 'Em Prinz: March & Two-Step" (1905), "Coney Island Tickle" (1906), "Mississippi Rag" (1913), and "The Queen of Coney Island: March and Two Step" (1904). By 1910 Gasdorf was living in Denver, Colo.; in about 1918 he began touring the United States with a concert group. In 1920 he had a San Francisco address, but later he settled in Los Angeles, where he died on December 6, 1957. The family's musical tradition continued well into the 1950s, when Newport's Merle Gasdorf, apparently a relative of Alfred, as a young boy played the drums on the old *Ted Mack Amateur Hour* television show around 1955.

There were at least three other notable contributors to the ragtime era who resided in Northern Kentucky. In 1905 Louis H. Mentel, who lived in Covington, wrote and published "A Daisy Girl," one of the 10 rags he composed; in 1910 Covington's William M. Hickman wrote "Diplomat Rag"; and the most famous of this region's songwriters, **Haven Gillespie**, crossed over to collaborate with Lloyd Kidwell and Louis R. Strong in "Kyra: An Oriental One-Step," in 1918. Northern Kentucky, Cincinnati, St. Louis, and Indianapolis were centers of ragtime, as this musical art form (one of the few meldings of German American and African American cultures) was performed on the vessels that traveled up and down the Ohio River and in so many of the communities on or near the river's banks.

Hasse, John Edward. *Cincinnati Ragtime: A List of Composers and Their Works.* Cincinnati: John Edward Hasse, 1983.

"Musician Dies on West Coast: Albert Gasdorf," *CE*, December 8, 1957, 95.

RootsWeb.com. "California Death Index." www.rootsweb.com (accessed December 27, 2005).

Michael R. Sweeney

GAS LIGHTING AND GASWORKS. The City Council of Covington on October 28, 1852, approved a contract with James Southgate and his associates to supply the city with gas. It was a 50-year franchise allowing the city to purchase gas at half price for public streetlamps. The gas was generated by the burning of coal (coke). Besides allowing the city government to set the gas rates for users, the city held the right to purchase the Covington Gas Light Company on or after January 1, 1869, or at five-year intervals thereafter. **Amos Shinkle** became the president of that company. Its gasworks, completed by early 1854, was located along the Licking River, at the east end of Saratoga St., and soon five miles of main lines ran beneath Covington streets.

On June 11, 1857, an arrangement was made with the City of Newport for the Covington works to send gas to that Campbell Co. city via lines across the **Newport and Covington Suspension Bridge**. In October 1864, Newport had public gas streetlights and 2.5 miles of mains. In November 1868, the citizens of Covington voted to purchase the Covington Gas Light Company, but the City Council balked at paying the estimated price of $500,000. By 1880 Newport had 227 gas streetlights, and gas was being supplied by the Cincinnati Gas and Electric Company via a 25-year contract. Later, a small gasworks operated in Newport for a short time as part of the **Dueber Watch Case Company**.

In 1872 the Kentucky legislature chartered the Newport Light and Fuel Company. Future Bellevue mayor Gus Harms became an officer of that concern. Another company, the Newport and Bellevue Gas, Light, and Coke Company, was formed about the same time with the intention of building a plant to manufacture gas from coal for customers in Newport, Bellevue, and Dayton, Ky.

In Maysville, the first gas charter was granted in 1854 to the Maysville Gas Company to install gaslights in that city. That act was amended in 1865 for Solomon Salomon and associates to do the same while building a $32,000 gasworks. In 1886 the charter was revised to allow that company to furnish electric lights and power along with gas within Maysville. That same year, the Citizens Gas Light Company was incorporated to erect a local gasworks and to furnish gas and gaslights to both Maysville and the adjacent city of Chester. In 1903 electric lights were installed in the city of Maysville, but coal gas continued to be available.

Eventually, street lighting became electric with few exceptions, and gas from coal was replaced by natural gas piped into the area from the gas fields in West Virginia and Pennsylvania. Soon, natural gas transmission lines owned by the Columbia Gas Transmission Company, and later Williams Brothers, were crisscrossing Northern Kentucky, and gasworks were no longer needed.

Maysville Centennial Exposition Commission. *As We Look Back: Maysville, 1833–1933.* Maysville, Ky.: Daily Independent, 1933.

Reis, Jim. "Former Bellevue Mayor Found Riches in Mexico," *KP*, July 31, 2000, 4K.

Tenkotte, Paul A. "Rival Cities to Suburbs: Covington and Newport, Kentucky, 1790–1890," PhD diss., Univ. of Cincinnati, 1989.

GASTRIGHT, HANK (b. March 29, 1865, Covington, Ky.; d. October 9, 1937, Dayton, Ky.). Hank Gastright, a professional baseball player, was born Heinrich Carl Gastreich. He was the son of Fredrick and Catherine Borgman Gastreich, immigrants from Sauerland in Northern Westphalia, Germany, who arrived in the eastern United States in 1846. They moved west to Covington, Ky., to join a colony of neighbors who had followed their parish priest there. The entire family had anglicized their name to either Gastrich or Gastright by 1918.

Baseball was quite popular in Covington and Newport before the **Civil War** (see **Kenton Base Ball Association**). In this atmosphere, Hank Gastright was encouraged to develop his baseball skills. He was a six-foot-two-inch, 190-pound pitcher, who both batted and threw right-handed. His first year as a professional was with the Toledo Mudhens in 1888. The Mudhens were in the International Association and were a feeder team for the Columbus (Ohio) Colts (American Association). Gastright's statistics with the Mudhens are unknown, but he was promoted to the major league Colts in 1889.

He made his first major league debut for the Colts on April 19, 1889. He pitched in 32 games that season, compiling a record of 10 wins and 16 losses with an earned run average (ERA) of 4.57. He ranked high in strikeouts, complete games, and wild pitches. His 1890 season with the Colts was outstanding in every way. He appeared in 48 games, winning 30 and losing only 3. His ERA was 2.94, and he struck out 199 batters in 401 innings. In the 1891 season with the Colts, he completed only 28 of the 35 games he started, but his ERA rose to 3.78 with a record of 12 wins and 19 losses.

Gastright was traded to the Washington Senators (National League) for the 1892 season. He appeared in 79 innings in 11 games with the Senators and achieved a record of 3 wins and 3 losses with an ERA of 5.08. A move to the Pittsburgh Pirates in 1893 brought 59 innings pitched with 3 wins and 1 loss, but in midyear he was traded to the Boston Beaneaters (N.L.), where he pitched in 19 games and won 12 and lost 4, the best percentage in the National League. Gastright's combined pitching record for the 1893 season was quite good, and the Boston team finished in first place.

During his last three years, 1894–1896, Gastright played for the Brooklyn Bridegrooms and then played briefly for the Cincinnati Reds. He played in 16 games for the Bridegrooms for a total of 93 innings, his ERA soaring to 6.39. He sat out the 1895 season. For the Reds on June 5, 1896, he appeared in 6 innings in a single game. He gave up 6 runs but did not figure in the decision. For his major league career, he won 72 games and lost 63. In retirement he was honored as a local hero for decades. He worked as a Newport policeman. Gastright was a resident of the Campbell Co. Infirmary in Cold Spring when he died at Speers Hospital in Dayton in 1937. He was buried at St. Joseph Cemetery in Johns Hill.

Ellard, Harry. *Baseball in Cincinnati.* Reprint, Cincinnati: Ohio Book Store, 1987.

James, Bill, John Dewan, Neil Munro, and Don Zminda, eds. *Bill James Presents STATS All-Time Major League Handbook.* Skokie, Ill.: STATS, 1998.

Kentucky Death Certificate No. 27530, for the year 1937.

Joseph F. Gastright

GATEWAY COMMUNITY AND TECHNICAL COLLEGE. Opened in 1998 as Northern Kentucky Community and Technical College District and renamed Gateway Community and Technical College in 2002, this educational institution operates multiple campuses. The main campus, at 500 Technology Way in Boone Co., was dedicated in December 2005. This 30,000-square-foot concrete and glass facility features four two-story laboratories designed to accommodate large industrial equipment, associated observation areas, a computer-aided drafting lab, a library, classrooms, and offices. Other campuses are located at Covington–Park Hills (the former Northern Kentucky State Vocational and Technical School) and at Edgewood (the former Northern Kentucky Health Occupations Center). Gateway offers a variety of programs and degrees, including Associate of Art and Associate of Science degrees, a nursing program, and a computer-aided design program.

In 1940 the Kenton Co. Board of Education began a vocational program at the Park Hills School that included courses in sales and technical fields. By 1941 the school was relocated to the old Federal Building and Post Office, located at Scott and Third Sts. in Covington. Three years later, in 1944, the state board of education assumed control of the Kenton Co. Vocational School, which then became known as Northern Kentucky State Vocational School and operated under that name until the late 1990s. In 1997 the Kentucky General Assembly passed the Kentucky Postsecondary Education Improvement Act, which included the establishment of the Kentucky Community and Technical College System (KCTCS). This law created a system of 16 districts throughout the state that operate together to better serve their communities.

The newly created Northern Kentucky Community and Technical College District (NKCTCD) combined three independent existing campuses in Northern Kentucky, which were operated by the Kentucky Department of Education, into one college with multiple campuses. These were the Northern Kentucky State Vocational and Technical School, which became known as the Covington campus; the Northern Kentucky Health Occupations Center, which became known as the Edgewood campus; and the Northern Campbell Vocational Technical School, which became known as the Highland Heights campus. Michael McCall, the president of KCTCS, announced in September 2001 that the main campus of the yet-unnamed community college would be on 41 acres of newly acquired land in Boone Co., just off the Mount Zion exit of I-75–I-71.

In November 2001, Dr. G. Edward Hughes was named the founding president and chief executive officer of the NKCTCD. Since 1985, Hughes had been president of the Hazard Community College in Hazard and had helped that school become a multicampus district serving about 3,800 students.

In March 2003 the Toebben Companies announced a donation of $650,000 worth of land and improvements to the Mount Zion project. This included the main drive into the new campus, Technology Way, plus all of the water, sewer, gas, and electric line hookups the campus would require. This gift was accompanied by a $500,000 grant from the Kentucky Transportation Cabinet, used to pave the road. The groundbreaking for the new building was held on June 11, 2003.

In 2004 Gateway began a nursing program, in support of which the **St. Elizabeth Medical Center**, located near the Edgewood campus, offered $1.25 million over five years. Classes for this degree started in fall 2004 with 40 students. In July 2004 the Health Resources and Services Administration, a division of the U.S. Department of Health and Human Services, granted the program $739,589 to recruit and train minority nursing students.

In September 2004 the U.S. Department of Education awarded $1.6 million in a five-year "strengthening institutions grant" to improve programs and provide training for professors.

Gateway Community and Technical College was ranked as the seventh-fastest-growing public two-year college in the nation between 2004 and 2005. Gateway's vision for the future includes offering new degrees for the community. The college has articulation agreements with area institutions such as **Northern Kentucky University** and **Thomas More College**, enabling its graduates to pursue four-year degrees at the university level. Gateway earned accreditation by the Commission on Colleges of the Southern Association of Colleges and Schools in 2008.

"Evening Classes in Vocational Education to Be Started in Kenton," *KP*, February 7, 1940, 1.

"Feds Provide $1.6 M Grant," *KP*, September 1, 2004, 2K.

Gateway Community and Technical College. www.gateway.kctcs.edu (accessed June 16, 2005).

"State Votes to Take Over Kenton Vocational School," *KP*, December 16, 1944, 1.

"24-Hour Schedule Is Inaugurated at Vocational School in Covington: Students Urged to Register," *KP*, April 29, 1941, 1.

Elizabeth Comer Williams

GATEWAY REHABILITATION HOSPITAL. This hospital, located on Merchants St. in Florence, Ky., received its first patient in December 2000. The 40-bed, two-story, 66,000-square-foot facility cost nearly $10 million. It is licensed by the State of Kentucky as a Specialty–Acute Care Hospital. The physical plant was originally designed with the potential to easily add a third floor, should more rehabilitation beds later be needed. Physical therapy, speech therapy, and occupational therapy are offered at Gateway, along with aquatic therapy. Stroke, spinal-cord injury, amputation, trauma, and hip fracture are just a few of the many conditions treated. In its short history, Gateway has become a welcome addition to the region's health care continuum, helping to contain spiraling health care costs as it serves a specific clientele. According to Gateway's brochure, its goal is to be "a hospital that doesn't feel like a hospital."

Burcham, James A., CEO and administrator of Gateway Rehabilitation Hospital. Personal communication, November 2004.

GAUNT, WHEELING (b. 1812–1815, Carrollton, Ky.; d. May 10, 1894, Yellow Springs, Ohio). Wheeling Gaunt, described as a mulatto, was born into abject poverty as a slave, but over his lifetime he amassed a large fortune and gave most of it away in philanthropic projects. To this day, the poor families of Yellow Springs, Ohio, receive a Christmas gift of 25 pounds of flour and 10 pounds of sugar from the foundation Gaunt established. The funds for these donations came from a gift to the community of nine acres (now Gaunt Park) that the former slave owned next to Antioch College. And in 1884 Wheeling Gaunt gave a $5,000 financial contribution to enable Wilberforce College (today Wilberforce University) at Wilberforce, Ohio, to become one of the leading traditional black colleges in the United States. Gaunt was a friend and benefactor of Daniel A. Payne, the presiding bishop and an evangelist for the African Methodist Episcopal (A.M.E.) Church and the first president of Wilberforce College.

Wheeling Gaunt's slave owner during the 1840s was John R. Gaunt, an attorney at Carrollton. Wheeling's father was a white man, a leading merchant, who sold Wheeling's mother to a slave trader when Wheeling was very young. In later years, Wheeling claimed that he inherited his knowledge of how to make and save money from that first slave owner–father. Wheeling married his first wife, Amanda, also a mulatto slave, in 1838 in a typical slave wedding.

John R. Gaunt permitted Wheeling to earn his freedom, as a few other Carroll Co. slave owners did for their slaves. The money for Wheeling Gaunt's emancipation was earned by picking apples and shining shoes over and above his regular chores. When John Gaunt died in 1841, his inventory of properties listed "One Negro Man, Wheeling," worth $600. Wheeling and another slave, Louisa, were willed to John's wife Nancy and their children. The emancipation bond of $500, dated May 5, 1845, at the Carroll Co. Courthouse, between Nancy, Alfred R. and John E. Gaunt; William Root; and George Hinkley, witnessed by several justices of the peace of Carroll Co., stated that on that day they emancipated their slave, Wheeling.

Two years later, Wheeling Gaunt, a free person of color, purchased a house and two lots in Carrollton. He then purchased for $200 Nick, a slave owned by M. D. Smith; the contract stated that Nick was to be free on reaching the age of 21. Speculation is that this boy, born in 1841, was Wheeling's son. In 1849 Wheeling purchased in-lots 138 and 139 at the corner of Fourth and High Sts. in Carrollton.

Wheeling purchased Amanda, his wife, for $500 and then emancipated her sometime before the 1850 federal census, which listed the family together as free people of color living in Carrollton. Wheeling Gaunt, then 35, had $1,000 of real estate and was listed as a farmer. His wife, Amanda, was age 29, and Nicholas Gaunt was 9 years old. In 1858 and 1859, Wheeling purchased in-lots 189 at Fifth and Sycamore Sts.; 287 on Seventh St.; 135 at Fourth and Main Sts., a large lot along the Ohio River; and 136 on the southeast corner of Fourth and Main Sts. in Carrollton.

Ten years later, Wheeling Gaunt, age 45, remained in Carrollton, and his occupation was listed as teamster. He had $1,500 in real estate and $3,000 in personal property. His wife was 38 years old, and their son Nicholas was no longer living with them. In 1860 Wheeling cashed out his Carrollton properties for $2,800 and headed for Yellow Springs, Ohio. Greene Co. historians in Ohio speculate that he may have heard about Moncure Conway's emancipated slave colony at Yellow Springs, founded in 1862, or he may have followed Bishop Daniel A. Payne to Wilberforce College. There may be an even better link from Kentucky. The most famous **Underground Railroad** conductor between Louisville and Cincinnati, **Elijah Anderson**, would have known Wheeling Gaunt very well, since it was Anderson who established the Carrollton and Kentucky River route for escaping slaves. Anderson often took groups of runaway slaves up from Kentucky through northwestern Ohio to Sandusky, and he would have known about the abolitionists, black and white, at Yellow Springs.

Although the 1870 census of Greene Co., Ohio, listed Wheeling Gaunt, worth $4,000 in real estate and $6,000 personal property, as just a day laborer, he proved to be an excellent real estate speculator, buying and selling town lots near Antioch College between 1864 and 1890. For his residence, Gaunt built a substantial two-story Greek Revival building near the corner of N. Walnut and Dayton Sts. and four small cottages he called "Gaunt cottages." In 1887, the first year of racial integration at Yellow Springs, Gaunt ran for the city school board.

Although Gaunt never received any formal education, he was very interested in Bishop Daniel A. Payne's concepts of education for black citizens. Gaunt's gifts to Wilberforce College began with his donation of a sizable brick house and property that Gaunt owned at 131 N. Walnut St., on the north side of Yellow Springs. It was, at the time, valued at $1,650. Then in 1884 he gave $5,000 in endowment funds to support Wilberforce College and the Payne Theological Seminary at Wilberforce.

The Gaunt holdings on the south side of Yellow Springs, originally nine acres, became a gift to the community of Yellow Springs and the financial source for the Christmas gifts to the poor. Named in his honor, Gaunt Park now contains Gaunt Pool, baseball fields, and a sledding hill. Wheeling Gaunt was also a major contributor to his church, the Central Chapel, an A.M.E. church at the corner of High and Davis Sts. in Yellow Springs. He donated a bell, the vestibule, and the belfry.

When his wife Amanda died in 1889, Wheeling erected a large, ornate marble tombstone in the Glen Forest Cemetery at Yellow Springs. He married a second time, to Mrs. Elizabeth Nichols of Xenia, Ohio, on July 2, 1890. Elizabeth received a bequest of $7,000 when Wheeling died of Bright's Disease in 1894, and she was asked to care for Wheeling's sister, Louise Chandler, during her lifetime. The remainder of his property Gaunt willed to Wilberforce College and the Payne Theological Seminary. The Yellow Springs *Weekly Citizen* asserted that Wheeling Gaunt was the "richest colored man in Ohio" and stated that he was "known to every distinguished man of his race, from Fred Douglass to Bishop Payne." On May 18, 1894, both blacks and whites from Wilberforce, Springfield, Xenia, and Yellow Springs, Ohio, packed the church and lined the funeral procession for Wheeling Gaunt, the former Carroll Co., Ky., slave. He was buried next to his first wife, Amanda, in the Glen Forest Cemetery.

In addition to more than 15 Virginia black families whom Moncure Conway led to Yellow Springs in 1862, a number of families from Northern Kentucky resettled at Yellow Springs. The 1870 U.S. Census lists the following resettled Kentucky families as residents of Yellow Springs: Tolbert Baker, Alfred Benning, Andrew Benning, Francis Botts, John Cloak, Jackson Coffee, Henry Ford, Mack Ford, Peter Ford, Alfred Henry, Benjamin Grimes, Allen Jones, Eliza Lee, Charles Morgan, Anderson Ramsey, Vincent Smith, William Talber, Charles Webster, Charles Willis, and Harrison Wilson.

Claiborne, Karen. "Emancipated Gaunt Slave Prospered as a Free Man," *Carrollton News Democrat*, February 2, 2004, 4.
Deal, Steve. "Wheeling Gaunt: Our Remarkable Patron: What We Know. What We Think." www.yshistory.org/Gaunt.pdf (accessed July 25, 2006).
Emancipation Papers, Carroll Co. Courthouse, May 5, 1845, Carrollton, Ky.
Freedom from Religion Foundation. "Moncure Conway House Designated Underground Railroad Network to Freedom Sites." www.ffrf.org (accessed July 25, 2006).

Karen Claiborne and Diane Perrine Coon

GAYLE, JUNE WARD (b. February 22, 1865, New Liberty, Ky.; d. August 5, 1942, Owenton, Ky.). June W. Gayle, a legislator, was born in Owen Co. to James and Sallie Green Gayle. He was educated in New Liberty schools, including **Concord College**, and also attended Georgetown College, Georgetown, Ky., for a short time. By age 16 he had become an Owen Co. deputy sheriff, and between 1892 and 1896 he served as the county's high sheriff. A Democrat, Gayle was a member of the state Democratic central committee. When his good friend **James W. Cammack Sr.**, who later served as a judge, was married in Lexington in 1898, Gayle was an attendant. He was an unsuccessful candidate for state auditor in 1899. As a result of the death of **Evan Settle**, he was elected as a Democrat to the 56th U.S. Congress and served a little over one year, from January 15, 1900, to March 3, 1901, before returning to his previous business interests, banking and tobacco. He died in 1942 and was buried at the New Liberty Cemetery.

Biographical Cyclopedia of the Commonwealth of Kentucky. Chicago: John M. Gresham, 1896.
Biographical Directory of the United States Congress. "June Ward Gayle." http://bioguide.congress.gov (accessed June 20, 2007).
Kentucky Death Certificate No. 19042, for the year 1942.

GAYS AND GAY RIGHTS. Before the 1960s, the gay and lesbian community was largely invisible. Legal and societal pressures kept most homosexuals out of the mainstream and out of the press. Kentucky laws against sodomy were used to criminalize and isolate homosexual behavior. Municipal laws against cross-dressing, sometimes referred to as "Halloween ordinances," as in Covington, forbade dressing "with intent to counterfeit the opposite sex." In June 1978 this law was tested before Kenton Co. District Court judge Joseph Condit when four African American men were arrested for cross-dressing and their attorney argued that the law forbidding it was unconstitutional. Condit upheld the ordinance's constitutionality but dismissed the case on a technicality, namely that the court could not determine the sex of the accused individuals with certainty except by a medical examination. The ordinance was rescinded in 1990 when Condit was Covington city attorney.

Cross-dressing and female impersonation had long been a part of the gay subculture. Locally, the first documented reference to the topic involved a man named Peaches, who performed as a "female illusionist" from 1947 until 1949 at the Varga Club at Sixth and York Streets in Newport. Gays and lesbians could gather as a community in places like bars, health clubs, and public parks; evidence of their doing so is derived from police reports. From about 1966 until 1974, the Downstairs Club on Madison Pk. in Kenton Co. was recognized as a gay bar by homosexuals and heterosexuals alike. In November 1968, a health club at 219 E. Second St. in Covington, in the old Gateway Motel, was raided for sodomy. In 1971 the Newport City Commission characterized the Riviera Club at Second and York Sts. in Newport as a gay bar. Within a week, the club was raided for liquor violations. Numerous other gay bars existed throughout the Northern Kentucky region.

A slow change in legal and societal perceptions began to take place by the 1980s. In 1968 a series of articles appeared in the *Cincinnati Enquirer* dealing negatively with gays and lesbians and noting that a Mattachine Society based in Cincinnati was working for civil rights for homosexuals. Part of the national and local change in attitudes derived from the 1969 Stonewall Riots in New York City. During the early and mid-1970s in Cincinnati, a gay church was organized and a pride festival began. By May 1984, Bertram A. Workum, a reporter for the *Kentucky Post*, outed himself as a gay male in an article written for that newspaper. The public announcement of his sexuality was in response to an article by fellow reporter David Wecker, who warned parents and their children not to wear red, the identifying color for gays, at a gay and lesbian day held at the Kings Island Amusement Park in suburban Cincinnati. In July 1986 Sandy Cohen, a well-respected Covington businessman and former two-term city commissioner, mysteriously disappeared. He had not publicly been known to be gay, but Cohen's sexuality was revealed during the days after his disappearance. His badly beaten body was found in Cincinnati days later, and two 22-year-old male hustlers were found guilty of his murder. In 1989 Storer Cable of Northern Kentucky aired a series of programs on gays. In 1994 a **Northern Kentucky University** student group called the Alliance of Gays, Lesbians, Bisexuals, and Friends held a "coming out" event, in conjunction with National Coming Out Day, giving gays and lesbians the opportunity to announce their sexuality. In 2002 Northern Kentucky University's Common Ground Gay-Straight Alliance held a national day of silence to underscore the silence caused by harassment and discrimination.

In January 1999 Kentucky representative Kathy Stein of Lexington first proposed adding sexual orientation to the mandate of Kentucky's Human Rights Commission. The proposal has not yet been enacted. In July 1999 a survey of Northern Kentucky political leaders showed no inclination to favor such an ordinance. In 2000 the Cincinnati chapter of PFLAG (Parents and Friends of Lesbians and Gays) moved its annual banquet to Covington to protest Cincinnati's adoption of antigay language in the city charter. In October 2001 the 11th Annual National Out and Equal Workplace Summit was held in Erlanger, also to protest Cincinnati's discriminatory legislation. In May 2001 the Northern Kentucky Fairness Alliance (NKFA) Chapter of the Kentucky Fairness Alliance was officially formed. The Fairness Alliance objectives are to educate the public about the GLBT (gay, lesbian, bisexual, and transgendered) community. It also works with local and state government to promote legislation supportive of gay rights and to stop discriminatory legislation. In 2002 NKFA featured a talk by Kentucky state senator Ernesto Scorsone of Lexington, who later "came out" as a gay man. On April 30, 2003, the City of Covington, with broad support throughout the community, unanimously passed an expanded Human Rights Ordinance that added protection for sexual orientation and gender identity. Later that year, NKFA celebrated with a fundraiser featuring speaker Judy Shepard, mother of the nationally known slain gay Matthew Shepard. At the same time, Northern Kentucky University studied the possibility of introducing same-sex-partner health benefits for its employees. In December 2003, Greater Cincinnati Community Shares honored Marian

Weage of Fort Thomas with the McCrackin Peace and Justice Award for her advocacy on behalf of homosexuals.

In 1985 the city of Florence, concerned about homosexual activity taking place at the Florence Mall restrooms and I-75 rest areas, toughened its law against sodomy. In November a man challenged the ordinance and was convicted in February 1988. In November 1988 three men were charged with sodomy in Carroll Co. In 1992 the Kentucky Supreme Court ruled that the Kentucky state sodomy law was unconstitutional.

In 2003 Kentucky governor Paul Patton (1995–2003) signed an executive decree providing for protection of executive department employees based upon sexual orientation. In April 2006 Kentucky governor Ernie Fletcher (2004–2008) repealed this order. In 2004 the Kentucky General Assembly proposed a constitutional amendment banning same-sex marriage, which passed in the November election. The amendment followed both state and national Defense of Marriage acts.

Throughout the 1980s and 1990s, the AIDS (Acquired Immune Deficiency Syndrome) crisis was gaining recognition. The earliest newspaper-recorded AIDS death of a Northern Kentuckian was June 1983. From 1985 on, the local newspapers covered the AIDS crisis with growing concern and diligence. In May 1987 Northern Kentuckian **Gary Bauer** expressed the views of some conservatives who espoused abstinence versus condom use (see **Birth Control**) as a check on AIDS and blamed the spread of AIDS on the erosion of moral values. Church leaders did not necessarily agree. For example, William Hughes, bishop of the Roman Catholic Diocese of Covington, was part of a panel of the United States Catholic Conference that sought tolerance for educational programs that described how condoms may prevent the spread of AIDS. Throughout his episcopacy, Hughes continued to seek tolerance for gays and lesbians. He officiated at a mass at a gay symposium in 1992 in Chicago and established an Inclusive Church Commission in the diocese to study and recommend proposals for gays, lesbians, and the handicapped. In 1988 the first Northern Kentucky group to help persons who lost family and friends to AIDS was founded. This organization was followed by others, such as AIDS Volunteers Serving Together (1991), the predecessor of the current AIDS Volunteers of Northern Kentucky. By the 1990s, despite increasing awareness that AIDS affected the homosexual and heterosexual communities alike, a constitutional amendment was proposed in December 1993 in the Kentucky General Assembly against anal sex (sodomy) so as to prevent the spread of AIDS. It subsequently failed. The first acknowledged Northern Kentucky contribution to the national AIDS Memorial Quilt was in November 1992 by Larry Barr.

One of the nationally known activists on behalf of U.S. congressional funding for AIDS research was **Bill Kraus**. Born in Fort Mitchell in 1947, Kraus attended Blessed Sacrament School. When he was 13 years old, his family moved to Cincinnati, where he attended St. Xavier High School. Graduating from Ohio State University with a BA and an MA in history, he moved to San Francisco, enrolled in a doctoral program at the University of California—Berkeley, and became a gay rights activist, serving as campaign manager for Harvey Milk, a San Francisco city supervisor who was assassinated. In the early 1980s, Kraus became a staff member for U.S. representative Phillip Burton of California. Author Randy Shilts, in his best-selling book *And the Band Played On* (1987), detailed Kraus's work on behalf of people suffering from AIDS. The book appeared one year after Kraus's own death from AIDS in 1986, at age 38. In 1993 the book was made into an HBO movie, and actor Ian McKellen played the role of Kraus. In 2008 Northern Kentucky University expanded employee health care benefits to include coverage for domestic partners.

Biesk, Joe. "Kentucky Overwhelmingly Says Yes to No-Gay-Marriage," *KE*, November 3, 2004, A11.

"Bishops Soften Stance: Condoms Accepted in AIDS Education," *KP*, December 11, 1987, 1K.

Bliss, Betsy. "'Homos' Fighting Legal Bias," *CE*, November 11, 1968, 1.

Fogarty, Bob. "Four Win Dismissal of Dress Code Charges," *KE*, June 21, 1978, A2.

Houck, Jeanne. "Florence Toughens Gay Law," *KP*, September 6, 1985, 1K.

Kreimer, Peggy. "New Group Sustains Families through Loss to AIDS," *KP*, November 8, 1988, 1K.

Long, Paul A. "Bishop Said Mass at Gay Symposium: Bishop Hughes Criticized," *KP*, June 16, 1992, 1K.

Rutledge, Mike. "Gay Rights Law OK'd," *KP*, April 30, 2003, 1K.

"Sodomy Law Illegal: Justices Uphold Right of Privacy," *KP*, September 25, 1992, 1K.

Speers, William J. "Living the Gay Life," *CE*, November 4, 1971, Magazine section, 30.

Wecker, David. "Drawing the Line at Kings Island," *KP*, May 4, 1984, 1K.

Whitehead, Shelly. "Hero to Thousands, Unknown at Home: Ft. Mitchell Native Joined AIDS Fight Early," *KP*, September 10, 1993, 1K.

Workum, Bertram A. "Cohen Found Brutally Murdered," *KP*, July 11, 1986, 1K.

Charles King

GEASLEN, CHESTER F. (b. February 21, 1896, Cincinnati, Ohio; d. January 6, 1986, Villa Hills, Ky.). Chester F. Geaslen, athlete, railroad engineer, reporter, and historian, was the oldest of the three children born to Joseph and Clara Geaslen. When Chester was six, the Geaslens moved to 1614 Banklick St. in Covington, to be closer to his father's employer, the **Stewart Iron Works**, which had just relocated to 17th and Madison. In 1917 Chester Geaslen, along with some friends, joined the U.S. Marine Corps. They were sent to Parris Island, S.C., for basic training, then to France to fight in **World War I**. In 1918 Geaslen was wounded in the hand during combat at Verdun, France. When the war was over, he returned to Covington and tried several occupations. A fine athlete, he enrolled at Xavier University in Cincinnati, simply for the chance to play on the school football team. He also tried professional baseball and pitched batting practice for the Cincinnati Reds. When his career with the Reds did not advance, Geaslen signed to play center field in the Blue Grass League for the Paris, Ky., team. Baseball was not very lucrative, so in 1922 Geaslen applied, successfully, for a position with the **Louisville and Nashville Railroad** (L&N). During the **Great Depression**, Geaslen was laid off by the railroad. He then went to work for the ***Kentucky Post*** in Central Kentucky, managing circulation. To help boost the paper's circulation, he carried a notebook and a camera and wrote human-interest stories about people he met along his route. His tactic paid off, with locals subscribing to see whom he had included in his column. When **World War II** began, Geaslen was called back by the L&N Railroad. Although he engineered by day, the writing bug had bitten. He contributed a weekly column, *Strolling along Memory Lane,* for the *Kentucky Post* and wrote historical articles for the ***Kentucky Times-Star*** and the *Cincinnati Enquirer.* Following his retirement from the railroad in 1966 at age 70, he continued to write and to carry out research on Northern Kentucky history. He was the author of three books, which were compilations of his columns. They were titled *Strolling along Memory Lane,* volumes 1, 2, and 3. He also wrote a book called *Our Moment of Glory in the Civil War,* which was reprinted in 2007. Geaslen married Lucille Huber in 1928, and they had four children, Sue, John, Margaret, and Kathy. He died at the Madonna Manor Nursing Home in 1986 and was buried at St. Mary's Cemetery in Fort Mitchell.

"Chester Geaslen, 89, Local Historian, Writer," *KP*, January 7, 1986, 3B.

Geaslen, Chester F. *Strolling along Memory Lane.* 3 vols. Newport, Ky.: Otto, 1971–1974.

Deborah Kohl Kremer

GENERAL BUTLER STATE RESORT PARK. The General Butler State Resort Park in Carroll Co. was formally presented to the Kentucky State Park Commission at the park dedication ceremony on August 12, 1931, as Butler Memorial State Park. The park was named for the illustrious Butler family, known for their military and political contributions from Colonial times through the **Civil War**. Oscar W. Geier of Carrollton, who sponsored the local citizen movement along with the Carrollton Tobacco Board, presented the deed of the old Butler Homestead, known today as the **Butler-Turpin State Historic House**, along with 300 acres, to create the park.

The acreage had been acquired with the help of the Tobacco Board. Since Carrollton was a tobacco market, the Tobacco Board of Trade had formed a plan whereby a small amount of tobacco was contributed by each member of this organization for some years, then sold. In a few years, a sum amounting to $22,000 had accumulated to be used for community benefit. These funds purchased the initial land for the Butler Memorial State Park. The site was developed by the state and federal governments through the Civilian Conservation Corps (CCC), the National Youth Administration, and the Works Progress Administration (WPA). The workers who built the park had little more than a view to begin with; however, the hand-cut stone walls, pavilions, and an overlook that they fashioned still remain as testimonies to their expert stonemasonry.

The National Park Service contributed $155,408 through December 1935 to the building of Butler Memorial State Park. Improvements made with these funds included a bathhouse, shelter houses, a lookout tower, a parking area, a water system, trails, bridges, picnic grounds, trail-side seats, public camp grounds, a custodian lodge, an incinerator, service buildings, latrines, landscaping, guardrails, drinking fountains, picnic tables, camp stoves, park roads, and a lake about one mile long. Through 1941 the federal government continued to fund improvements, including a boathouse, a diving tower, and a service building. With the beginning of **World War II**, further development was delayed.

The next major development occurred during the period 1948 through 1955. Approximately a half million dollars were applied to new construction and renovation. Land acquisitions increased the size of the park to around 800 acres, 10 new cottages were added, the old cottages built by the CCC were renovated, the trading post was renovated and expanded, the bathhouse was rebuilt and the bathing beach was enlarged, the Butler Home was restored and furnished, a complete new group camp was constructed, the picnic facilities were expanded, a new service building was built, a new riding stable and trails were completed, and a new recreation area was developed. Final plans were completed and a contract was let during the latter part of 1955 for a new lodge, but construction was stopped at the foundation stage and the present lodge was not built until the early 1960s.

From 1960 through 1968, approximately $1.7 million was applied to additional development. The largest new facility was the present lodge, completed and placed in operation on October 31, 1962. The setting and architectural character of this lodge make it one of the most spectacular in the Kentucky park system. The lodge was designed by Braun and Ryan, architects and engineers of Louisville. The initial construction included 24 rooms, and 8 additional rooms were financed from a $43 million revenue bond issue in 1965, to bring the total to 32 rooms. Other major developments have included a new nine-hole golf course located near the lodge, a new miniature golf course in the day-use area, a new expanded camping area, renovation or reconstruction of every building in the park, a complete new water and sewerage system, and new roads and parking.

The park retains many of the original elements from the early years. The beautiful stonemasonry construction can still be seen laced throughout the landscape. The manmade lake built more than 75 years ago now looks like a natural lake. It is difficult to believe that the preserved woodland areas, akin to the landscape in Kentucky at the early, unsettled stage, were once barren farmland. The homestead, known today as the Butler-Turpin State Historic House, stands as stately as it did when first built in 1859. The Butler family cemetery is restored and protected. The original log house of the Butler family who settled at the mouth of the Kentucky River in 1796 is now a place where students of archaeology can explore the past.

Brooks, James W. "American History by Motor," *Washington (D.C.) Sunday Star*, January 18, 1931.

"Butler Memorial State Park," *Kentucky Progress* 3, no. 12 (August 1931).

Evelyn Welch

GENE SNYDER AIRPORT. The Gene Snyder Airport, located off Ky. Rt. 22 West, at 400 Gene Snyder Airport Dr., just four miles northwest of Falmouth, was built on the former farm of Henry Auchter and portions of surrounding farms. It was the fifth airport established in Pendleton Co. The first known airport was a grass strip located on the county's old poor farm, on the Licking River bottoms of Hayes Station Rd., just north of Falmouth. The second known airport was also a grass strip, located on the site of the current Pendleton Co. Athletic Park on **U.S. 27** North in Falmouth. The next one was a grass strip at Shannings, just south of Falmouth, during the 1950s. The last grass airstrip to serve Pendleton Co. was located along the Licking River bottoms on Licking Valley Rd., in the vicinity of **Kincaid Lake State Park**, and included five hangars.

The paved Gene Snyder Airport, after being approved by the Federal Aviation Administration (FAA) and the Kentucky Aeronautical Association, was dedicated on August 11, 1984. The founding members of the airport board were Robert Bay, Hildreth Kidd, Dr. Robert McKinney, Lloyd Spaulding, and Paul Tuemler. The first board's attorney was Robert Bathalter. U.S. congressman Gene Snyder of Kentucky and U.S. secretary of transportation Elizabeth Dole were instrumental in obtaining the new airport for Pendleton Co.

The Gene Snyder Airport, whose FAA identifier is K62, sits at an estimated elevation of 898 feet above mean sea level. There is no control tower at the airport. The airframe and power-plant services are classified as major. However, there is no bottled or bulk oxygen available. The 4,000-by-75-foot asphalt northeast-southwest runway is considered to be in good condition. It has a single-wheel weight-bearing capacity of 12,500 pounds, with medium-intensity edge lights on the runway.

Unlike many public landing facilities of its size, the airport offers pilots the ability to refuel on an around-the-clock basis, using a credit card system. Pilots also have access to an outside telephone line and a small terminal. The airport has four small and two large paved hangars, in addition to tie-downs. There are typically five planes in one of the large hangars and as many as nine in the other. The airport is used quite often for refueling and emergency landings.

In April 2006, there were 23 airplanes based at the field, including 22 single-engine aircraft. At that time, the Gene Snyder Airport was averaging 96 aircraft operations per week. There is currently a waiting list to use the airport's hangars. The volunteer airport board is working with the FAA and the Kentucky Aeronautical Association to expand the operation to include taxiways and additional hangars.

AirNov.com. "K62 Gene Snyder Airport, Falmouth, Kentucky, USA." www.airnav.com/airport/K62 (accessed June 5, 2006).

Lovelace, Donnie. Interview by Aprile Conrad Redden, September 29, 2006, Falmouth, Ky.

Michael D. Redden and
Aprile Conrad Redden

GEOGRAPHY. See **Dry Ridge Trace**; **Geology**; **Glaciers**; **Licking River**; **Ohio River**; **Weather and Climate**.

GEOLOGY. Northern Kentucky stretches for more than 110 miles (176 km) along the Ohio River from Mason Co. in the east to Carroll Co. in the west. The northern boundary of seven counties within this area (Boone, Bracken, Campbell, Carroll, Gallatin, Kenton, and Mason) is the Ohio River. The Licking River divides Campbell and Kenton counties, flows through Pendleton Co., and forms the southwestern boundary of Robertson Co. The Kentucky River bisects Carroll Co. and forms the western boundary of Owen Co. Grant Co.'s Dry Ridge is a dividing point between tributaries flowing into the Kentucky River to the west and into the Licking River to the east.

The physiographic regions of Kentucky are defined by the surface topography. Northern Kentucky sits in the northern part of the Interior Low Plateaus Region, in the Outer Bluegrass subsection. This unglaciated area of gently dipping Paleozoic-age sedimentary rocks has relatively moderate topographic relief. The modern surface topography resulted from the entrenchment of the drainage systems that occurred before, during, and after the Pleistocene glacial advances.

The Outer Bluegrass subsection is more highly dissected than the rolling Central Bluegrass. The Northern Kentucky region is characterized by deeper valleys than the other subsections, both because of the nearness of the entrenched valley of the Ohio River and because the bedrock in this area is mostly composed of interbedded Ordovician limestone and shale. These rocks are more easily eroded than other sedimentary formations.

The surface topography is influenced by the kinds of rock that lie underneath. Although sandstone and shale occur throughout the region, much of the area is underlain by limestone. Karst topography, defined by limestone formations that are easily eroded to form sinkholes and underground streams, is well developed where these formations are near the surface.

The Outer Bluegrass overlays the Cincinnati Arch, a positive geologic feature composed of a thick sequence of Paleozoic-era sedimentary rocks. These layers date to between 570 and 285 million years ago, although the oldest rocks exposed on the surface in Kentucky belong to the Ordovician period (505–438 million years ago).

The Precambrian rocks are ancient sedimentary layers that cover much of the Midwest. They are part of the deeply buried Laurentia craton (the large nucleus of the continent) and are buried at least several thousand feet deep. The Laurentia craton is part of the larger North American Plate. How these deeply buried layers were formed is not known. The passive behavior of the Laurentia craton is characterized by subdued subsidence and gentle uplift. These stable layers are called basement features. This long, inactive basement underlies the Paleozoic sedimentary layers.

The Paleozoic era includes seven geological periods dating from 570 to 285 million years ago. These successive layers of sedimentary rock formed in alternating shallow saline seas, swamps, and dry land. Weathering and erosion marked the dry periods, often allowing for little or no soil formation during those periods. Even the rock layers were eroded away. Fossils are found in many of these layers.

The oldest rocks exposed on the surface in Northern Kentucky belong to the Ordovician period (505–438 million years ago), except in eastern Mason Co., where the more recent Silurian-period rocks are the oldest. Ordovician sedimentary formations were deposited in alternating shallow and deeper salt-water seas. Limestone is the predominant resulting bedrock. Shale is also found layered with the limestone, and dolomite forms a deeper subsurface layer from this period. The most common fossils from this period are bryozoans (fossil coral). Other common fossils include brachiopods, cephalopods, trilobites, horn coral, snails, clams, echinoderms, and graptolites.

Limestone is derived from the hard parts of ancient sea life and formed generally in clear water. Shale is formed from silts and clay and often includes calcareous shell and skeletal fragments of sea creatures. Deposits of sediments and the remains of sea animals and plants settled to the sea floor in horizontal layers. Compression over time pressed out any trapped water. The remaining material was cemented together, and the result is modern bedrock of varying types.

At the end of the Ordovician period, the area was again dry land and subject to erosion. The sea soon returned and through the Silurian period varied from shallow to deep water. In eastern Mason Co., dolomite and dolomitic limestone is interbedded with clay shales. In this period, coral reefs were very common. The most common fossils include brachiopods, cephalopods, echinoderms, and clams.

The Ordovician-Silurian transition also saw the gradual uplift that formed the Cincinnati Arch. Buried interior basins of North America are separated by broad uplifted arches such as the Cincinnati Arch. To the east and west, the bedrock dips into the Appalachian Basin on the east and the Illinois Basin on the west.

Erosion and weathering removed all traces of the later Paleozoic periods from the Northern Kentucky region, except in eastern Mason Co., as noted. Ordovician-period rock is present in eastern Mason Co., but the Silurian bedrock, which has not eroded, overlays it. Rocks and fossils from later periods, such as the Devonian, the Mississippian, and the Pennsylvanian, are found elsewhere in Kentucky, but not in this region.

Around the end of the Permian period, a major mountain-building event called the Alleghenian Orogeny occurred. The combined continents of Europe and Africa collided with North America. This event lifted up the Appalachian Mountains and caused further uplift to the Cincinnati Arch. As a result, during the Mesozoic era and for much of the Tertiary period of the Cenozoic era, Kentucky was above sea level and experienced a nondepositional environment. Northern Kentucky was exposed to an erosional, weathering environment through the remainder of the prehistoric time periods up to beginning of the Quaternary period. The uplifted surface was initially a flat plain known as the Lexington peneplain.

This environment prohibited the formation of thick bedrock layers. As a result, no dinosaur bones have been recovered from Northern Kentucky. With no physical record, it is not known whether they roamed Northern Kentucky, but a few remnant fossils have been recovered in the Jackson Purchase in southwestern Kentucky.

This nondepositional environment characterized Northern Kentucky until the Quaternary period of the Cenozoic era. The Quaternary is best known as the Ice Age. During the period from 1.8 million years ago to about 12,000 years ago, **glaciers** advanced into the United States from Canada and retreated. The glaciers had a profound effect on the creation of the local modern drainage system, including the Ohio River, soil formation, and the deposition of glacial outwash along the major river valleys. The Licking River is one of the few local preglacial rivers that still flows close to its old course. The present channels of the Ohio River and other local streams are a direct result of the successive advances and retreats of glaciers in the local region. The glaciers left deposits of loess (windblown) soil and sand, and glacial outwash along the Ohio River. In contrast, the major soil deposits along the Kentucky River and Eagle Creek are from slack water clay and silty alluvium caused by localized flooding, not from glacial deposition.

The modern topography of Northern Kentucky is the result of a combination of factors, then. The underlying bedrock formed as horizontal sedimentary layers in a succession of salt-water seas. These horizontal layers were uplifted to form the Cincinnati Arch. Succeeding geologic periods saw the erosion of surface layers, leaving the Ordovician bedrock layers at the top of the Cincinnati Arch. Glacial advances and retreats during the Quaternary period left varying depths of windblown soil (loess) and glacial outwash, including sand and gravels along the major river valleys. Modern soil formed both from glacial deposits and from weathering of the limestone and shale bedrock. The environment had shifted to a more depositional one during the Pleistocene Ice Age. However, the erosional environment also continues with the downcutting of stream valleys, creating stream channels, ravines, and other dissected features in the old Lexington peneplain.

Davis, Richard A. *Cincinnati Fossils: An Elementary Guide to the Ordovician Rocks and Fossils of the Cincinnati, Ohio, Region.* Cincinnati: Cincinnati Museum of Natural History, 1992.

Kentucky Geological Survey. "Geologic Map of Kentucky." www.uky.edu/KGS/geoky/geologymap.htm (accessed July 25, 2006).

Kleber, John E., ed. *The Kentucky Encyclopedia.* Lexington: Univ. Press of Kentucky, 1992.

KENTUCKY GEOLOGIC PERIODS

Era/Period	*Age (Millions of Years Ago)*	*Occurrence*
Precambrian Paleozoic Era	Before 544 million	Buried deeply, no surface exposure
Cambrian period	570–505	Buried deeply, no surface exposure
Ordovician period	505–438	Central to Northern Kentucky, crest of Cincinnati Arch
Silurian period	438–408	Around edges of Arch, eastern Mason Co.
Devonian period	408–360	Around edges of Arch, not in Northern Kentucky
Mississippian period	360–325	Eastern, South Central, and Western Kentuck
Pennsylvanian period	325–280	Eastern and Western Kentucky coal fields
Permian period	280–248	
Mesozoic Era		Not found in Kentucky, except possibly in Jackson Purchase
Triassic period	248–208	
Jurassic period	208–146	
Cretaceous period	146–65	Jackson Purchase
Cenozoic Era		
Tertiary period	65–1.8	Jackson Purchase
Quaternary period	1.8–present	
Pleistocene epoch	1.8 million–12,000 yrs. before present	Along Ohio River margins in Northern Kentucky, glacial advances; formation of modern river systems
Holocene epoch	12,000 to present	Present-day topography of state

Potter, Paul Edwin. *Exploring the Geology of the Cincinnati/Northern Kentucky Region*. Special Publication 22, Series 11. Lexington: Kentucky Geologic Survey, Univ. of Kentucky, 1996.

Jeannine Kreinbrink

GERMAN AMERICANS. German Americans were one of the major immigrant groups to settle in Northern Kentucky. By 1790 Kentucky's population was 14% German, and by 1990 the population of German descent had reached 22%. The first German settlers came from the Carolinas, Virginia, and Pennsylvania and had immigrated to America before the **Revolutionary War**. Their main route was via the Cumberland Gap into southern Kentucky, and their settlement area of choice was the Bluegrass region. In the 19th century, Germans entered the state directly from Europe, with the Ohio River being the major travel route to Kentucky. By the 1850s, Cincinnati had developed into one of the three major urban centers of the German immigration, along with St. Louis, Mo., and Milwaukee, Wis., thereby making the Greater Cincinnati area, including Northern Kentucky, one corner of the so-called German Triangle. German immigration to and settlement in the region reflected similar patterns and origins.

The first Germans in Boone Co. arrived in 1785. They were the family of Johannes Tanner, who established Tanner's Station, a trading post that eventually developed into the city of Florence; north of the Ohio River, the first Germans did not arrive until 1788–1789. Tanner was a German Baptist preacher from Pennsylvania, whose congregation had moved with him to the German settlement of Germanna, Va. News of Tanner's Station spread back to Germanna, as well as to Pennsylvania, causing more Germans to migrate to Northern Kentucky. For example, in 1805, 14 families arrived from a settlement on the Rapidan River in Virginia in Conestoga wagons, a frontier vehicle devised by the Pennsylvania Germans. The group formed the **Hopeful Lutheran Church** in 1806, the oldest Protestant church west of the Allegheny Mountains. In 1813 they called Pastor Wilhelm Carpenter (Zimmermann) from the Hebron Church in Madison Co., Va., and the congregation grew, attracting more Germans to the area. Carpenter, who had served in the Virginia division of Gen. Peter Muehlenberg during the Revolutionary War, established a church school. As a result of the growing congregation, the town of Florence was founded, but it was not incorporated until 1830. By 1880 its population had risen to around 600, and the town included six churches, several schools, and a brewery.

Campbell Co., organized in 1794, had several Germans among property owners in the city of Newport. Germans were engaged in a variety of occupations; for example, the first tavern was established by a German (1795). They also built roads and introduced the first brewery and the first vineyards in the hills of Campbell Co., and German mechanics helped construct the paddle wheeelers on the Licking River. German women introduced weaving as well.

The first Germans in Kenton Co. were George Jaeger and Johannes Strader (Straeter), who explored the Licking River with **Simon Kenton** in 1771. In 1774 several Germans from Virginia, including Jacob Harrod, Abraham Hite (Heit), and Jacob and Johann Sodowsky, came down the Ohio River and camped at the mouth of the Licking River; both of the Sodowsky brothers lived for a time in Campbell Co. and later moved elsewhere. German settlers began to arrive in the 1790s, especially from Pennsylvania; one of them was Edmund Rittenhaus, a relative of the well-known astronomer and scientist David Rittenhouse. In 1815 the city of Covington was formed and named in honor of Gen. Leonard Covington, whose father had immigrated to Maryland from the Alsace region and whose name originally was written as Korfingthan or Kurfingthan.

After the conclusion of the Napoleonic era by means of the Congress of Vienna in 1815, German immigration greatly increased, especially after the revolutions of 1832–1833 and 1848 in Europe; during this period Germans immigrated for political as well as economic reasons. Many were attracted by the existing German element of the region and by the glowing reports of the area by the German Moravian missionary Johann Heckewelder in 1797 and by travel authors such as Charles Sealsfield and Gottfried Duden, who wrote in the 1820s. These works commented on the beautiful river valley, the rich and cheap farmland, the political and religious freedoms, and the presence of Germans in the area, all factors that attracted immigrants. The emerging German-language press of Cincinnati, beginning especially with the *Volksblatt* in the 1830s, as well as that of Louisville, also helped to publicize the area.

In ensuing years, Florence, Newport, and Covington developed as the major German American urban centers of Northern Kentucky. German congregations especially began to emerge in the 1840s. In 1841 the German Catholics formed their congregation in Covington with Rev. Ferdinand Kühr, considered the German patriarch of Covington. Their church, the Mutter Gottes Kirche, or **Mother of God Catholic Church**, stands today as one of the most majestic church edifices of Northern Kentucky. Other congregations followed in Covington, such as the German Protestant Evangelical Church (1847). Churches also established schools and various charitable institutions and sponsored German-style social events and picnics. For many Germans, life revolved around their particular congregation, which became the center of their religious, educational, social, and cultural life.

German secular societies also developed, such as the Covington Turngemeinde (1855), begun by the Turner Movement. The first such society had been formed in Cincinnati in 1848 by refugees of the 1848 revolution, including Friedrich Hecker, leader of the revolution in Baden, Germany. The word Turner came from the German word *turnen,* which means to turn, move, and exercise; the Turners believed in keeping physically fit. However, they were more than a gymnastic group, because they also believed in a "sound mind in a sound body," keeping intellectually fit as well. Their interests therefore were not only social but also cultural and political.

The influx of German immigrants transformed the region socially, culturally, religiously, and politically and was not without conflict in the 1850s, when German Americans met with nativist opposition in the form of the **Know-Nothing** movement. There was a cultural clash between the predominantly Anglo nativists and the recently arrived immigrants, which was best symbolized by the two groups' differing ideas about Sunday. On the one hand was the notion of the Puritan Sunday and on the other the Continental Sunday. The former held that no business or social activities should take place on Sunday, whereas the latter held that Sunday afternoons were the time for social activities, such as festivals and picnics, and that businesses, such as beer gardens, restaurants, and cafés, should be open. A number of encounters occurred in which the nativists took action against German American activities. For example, in 1856 the Covington Turners were attacked by a nativist mob during a parade held in conjunction with a German-style picnic.

Nativist hostilities subsided with the growing sectional crisis that led to the **Civil War**; German Americans supported the new immigrant-friendly **Republican Party**. Although Kentucky was neutral at the outbreak of the war, Germans from Northern Kentucky joined the ranks of the 9th Ohio Volunteer Infantry Regiment formed by the Cincinnati Turners, the 32nd Indiana Volunteer Infantry Regiment formed by Germans in southeastern Indiana, and other German units formed later in Louisville. Pride in German American achievements, especially having to do with service in the Union Army in the Civil War, led to the formation of the German Pioneer Society of Cincinnati in 1869 and then to the German Pioneer Society of Covington in 1877; another branch formed later in Newport. Information on these groups can be found in the historical journal *Der Deutsche Pionier,* edited by Heinrich A. Rattermann, and in the records of the German Pioneer Society of Covington at the **Kenton Co. Public Library** in Covington.

The growth and development of German American societies nationally led to the founding of the National German American Alliance in Philadelphia in 1901. It was made up of statewide alliances of umbrella organizations of German American societies formed at the city level. Both Newport and Covington had branches of the German-American Alliance; the Covington branch included 27 organizations, such as the Turners and the German Pioneer Society. These and other branches across the state affiliated together as the German-American State Alliance of Kentucky, with headquarters in Covington. Its president was Alfred Reinhardt of Newport, and its secretary, the driving force of the organization, was Alban Wolff, head of the Wolff Printing Company of Covington, located at 404 Scott St.

The German-American State Alliance took an active role in political affairs, strongly opposing **Prohibition** and supporting German bilingual education in the public schools, as well as physical education based on Turner principles. It and its local branches also sponsored the annual celebration of German Day, which marked the founding of the first permanent German settlement in America at Philadelphia on October 6, 1683. For example, in conjunction with the German-American Bicentennial of German Day in 1883, the Newport Turners celebrated their 23rd gymnastic and songfest event at Turner Hall in Newport, and the Covington German Pioneer Society organized a parade. A church service was held at the Salem Methodist Episcopal Church in Newport (see **Salem United Methodist Church**) that also commemorated the birth of the German Protestant reformer Martin Luther. A cross-section of religious and secular institutions and organizations thus joined together in celebrating the German heritage of the nation, as well as of Northern Kentucky. German Americans aimed at blending and uniting their German and American identities as German American. For example, in 1898 Newport's German Day parade included the singing not only of German songs, but also of "My Old Kentucky Home."

In 1909 the German-American State Alliance held its convention at Turner Hall in Covington, and in 1911 the convention was held at various locations in Northern Kentucky. More than 11,000 attended the German Day celebration at the **Lagoon Amusement Park** in Ludlow, and guests included Kentucky governor **Augustus E. Willson** (1907–1911) and Dr. O. Mezger, the German consul for the region. The last major German Day before **World War I** was held in 1916 and included a mass rally at the Carnegie Library Auditorium in Covington. On that occasion strong opposition to American involvement in the war in Europe was expressed.

The entrance of America into World War I resulted nationally in the so-called **anti-German hysteria**, which also found expression in Northern Kentucky. German instruction ceased in area schools, public and parochial. In 1918 the Covington Turngemeinde officially changed its name to the Covington Turners Society, and streets, organizations, and institutions followed suit by translating or Americanizing their names. Some families also changed their names: Braun to Brown, Baumann to Bowman, for example. German churches dropped German-language services, and the German-American State Alliance of Kentucky dissolved, along with its local branches. A pacifist minister was even tied and whipped "in the name of the women and children of Belgium." World War I was followed by the hard times of Prohibition, which struck a direct blow not only at the major industry of brewing but also at German American social life, where beer was a basic ingredient. **World War II** brought another war against the ancestral homeland of Northern Kentucky German Americans, but fortunately without the local excesses of the previous world war.

The post–World War II era ushered in the ethnic heritage and "roots" revival of the 1970s and beyond. In 1976 the **Northern Kentucky Convention and Visitors Bureau** obtained state funding for the creation of **Main Strasse** Village, a German-style village in Covington, which has become a major tourist attraction and the site of annual festivals, such as Maifest and Oktoberfest. In 1989 the German-American Citizens League of Greater Cincinnati sponsored the celebration of German-American Day on October 6 and held the celebration at the **Cathedral Basilica of the Assumption** in Covington with a program of Mozart and other German composers. The program noted that its purpose was "to provide the opportunity to not only celebrate the German heritage but to also explore the many contributions and influences German Americans have made locally and nationally."

German American influences on the region can be found in every possible field, as could be expected, given the percentage of the population that is of German descent. According to the census for Northern Kentucky counties, approximately 45 percent claim some German ancestry, making Northern Kentuckians of German descent the largest ethnic element of the region. The business, industrial, social, cultural, religious, and political life of Northern Kentucky reflects this percentage of the population. Symbolic of culinary influence is, of course, the ever-popular German sausage, **goetta**, which also reflects the geographic origin within Germany of the Germans who immigrated to the area. Census records for Northern Kentucky reveal that more than three-fourths of the German immigration derived from northern Germany, especially northwestern Germany, and the same is true of the German immigration north of the Ohio River. This knowledge provides a key to understanding the German heritage of the region.

German heritage no doubt attracted the Hofbräuhaus to locate its first American outlet at Newport, which now also sponsors Oktoberfest, as does Covington. German influences dot the landscape across Northern Kentucky, from church steeples and city streets to the **John A. Roebling Bridge**, a central landmark. The image of Northern Kentucky has been greatly and definitely influenced by the region's German heritage.

Rattermann, Heinrich A. *Kentucky's German Pioneers: H. A. Rattermann's History.* Trans. and ed. Don Heinrich Tolzmann. Bowie, Md.: Heritage Books, 2001.

Tolzmann, Don Heinrich. *Covington's German Heritage.* Bowie, Md.: Heritage Books, 1998.

——. *German Heritage Guide to the Greater Cincinnati Area.* Milford, Ohio: Little Miami, 2003.

Don Heinrich Tolzmann

GERMANTOWN. Pennsylvania Dutch people originally settled Germantown in about 1788. Initially, the town was located about three-fourths of a mile west of present-day Germantown. The original settlement was a log fort located where Asbury Rd. meets Ky. Rt. 10 and was called Buchanan Station. At one time, there were about 600 inhabitants living at Buchanan Station. Maysville was then only a landing, Augusta had not yet been thought of, and Cincinnati was an unbroken wilderness. Because the location of Buchanan Station was rather remote and because the settlement was some distance from a navigable stream and too hilly for road building, not much growth occurred. This part of Mason Co. had no rock roads, and the nearest town to the settlers' station was Washington, Ky., which was laid out in 1785. All of Mason Co. had fewer than 3,000 people. In 1794, on the nearby high plateau, approximately five miles north of the confluence of Pummell Creek and the North Licking River, and nine miles west of Washington, Whitfield Craig and associates laid out a town of approximately 4,000 square feet. It consisted of Main St., 2,145 feet long; Broadway, 1,089 feet long; Water St., 990 feet long; Frankfort St., 2,705 feet long; and about three and one-half miles of alleys. The Kentucky legislature granted the town a charter and incorporated it as Germantown.

The city was given authority to elect a city council, to enact ordinances for self-government, to regulate the types of business conducted within the city limits, and to enforce the ordinances by fine or imprisonment, providing that no city ordinance conflicted with state or national law. This same form of city-council government continues in Germantown today. Modern-day Germantown has a park with a walking track, a new building housing city offices and the fire department, new town streetlights, and a main sewage system. In 1797 Bracken Co. was formed out of parts of Mason and Campbell counties, and Germantown was divided, with one part in Mason Co. and the other in Bracken Co. Thus the town acquired the nickname of "the best little town in two counties."

The central industry in Germantown was the tannery, consisting of several large vats, which was located on Tanyard Hill. A man named Currans was sent as a young man to Germantown to learn the tanning trade. While working as a tanner, he rescued a 13-year-old girl who fell into one of the vats, and soon afterward he married her. Currans eventually built the first store in Germantown and also operated the Pepper House. Jesse Grant, the father of U.S. president Ulysses S. Grant, learned the tanning trade at the tannery in Germantown. After he finished this training, he went to Point Pleasant, Ohio; there he married Hannah Simpson, and their son, Ulysses, was born there.

The Germantown Fair, which locals refer to as "The Old Reliable," originated at a meeting held in Germantown on July 29, 1854. The first fair was held on Thursday and Friday, October 5 and 6, 1854, in local woodlands. The grounds were enclosed by a post-and-rail fence. Admission was 10 cents, and everyone who came to the fair was given a piece of blue ribbon, which was tied securely to a buttonhole. The first permanent fairgrounds building was built a year later and improved in 1920. In 1967 the fair was moved to its present location. "The Old Reliable" is still going strong and annually draws large crowds during the first full week in August. It has been held each year since 1854, except for the years 1942 and 1943, when the fair was suspended because of **World War II.**

During the **Civil War**, the Union Army camped at the town's fairgrounds. They raided Germantown and took horses and slaves. Local slave owners built slave pits, six feet by six feet, under the floors of their homes to hide their slaves. Two such pits were found in the home of Ruby Ashcraft during recent renovation. The Union soldiers also searched for Southern sympathizers. One of these was Dr. E. C. Dimmitt, who, having discovered that the federal troops were searching for him, took refuge outside of town in the old Humlong Cemetery on Ky. Rt. 10. The Union soldiers passed him by and he went undiscovered.

The early settlers of Germantown were very interested in education, and schools were established as early as 1827. They were held in any place that was available and met for only a few months at a time. The Germantown Hall, one of the oldest buildings in Germantown, began as a school building; school was held on the second floor until 1878, when the school trustees purchased a lot in town for a new building. In April 1879 this new two-story, four-room structure was completed. It was regarded as being a first-class schoolhouse and the best public school in Mason, Bracken, or the adjoining counties. After the school moved to the new building, Germantown Hall was used to house a post office, a lodge, and a jail, which was added to the back of the building in October 1871, at a cost of $280.

The Germantown school that moved to the new site in 1879 became a graded school in 1909 and a high school in 1911; a new four-room brick building was built for it in 1930. The school became a part of the Bracken Co. School System in 1936, and the class of 1939 was the last class to graduate from Germantown High School. The county high schools were consolidated in 1940. The ninth grade was transferred to the Bracken Co. High School (see **Bracken Co. Public Schools**) in 1956, and the Germantown School building was closed in 1987, when the county elementary schools were consolidated. Wayne McGee was the last principal of the Germantown Elementary School. The building is currently owned by Woodmen of the World Insurance Inc.

Early businesses in Germantown included a factory for the making of grey jeans and men's clothing, the Morris Browning Drug Store, the T. T. Hill and Son Grocery, and the Pepper Funeral Home. S. C. Pincard, one of Germantown's early storekeepers, sold everything a person might need, ranging from groceries to furniture and from horses and buggies for hire to coffins costing $1.50–$8.00. It was said that tobacco was received in Germantown in good order, which meant that it was delivered in the summer following the year in which it was grown. There were warehouses in town on Frankfort St. and Bracken Alley, and both structures remain. The Germantown Milling Company was founded in 1910, destroyed by fire on June 25, 1915, and then rebuilt. The company purchased the Sardis Mill in town so it could remain in business while the burned mill was being rebuilt. The Germantown Milling Company was the only mill in Bracken Co. making flour. The Bank of Germantown and the Farmers and Traders Bank were both operating in town in 1910; they merged in 1930 to form the Bank of Germantown. Dr. Joe Browning owned the first automobile in Germantown, and during the 1920s electric lights replaced gasoline lights. The city bought its first fire engine and established a fire department in 1928. It purchased a new firefighting apparatus with a 500-gallons-per-minute pump capacity in 1948.

In 1958 Germantown expanded its city limits for the first time, extending Frankfort St. out Bridgeville Rd. for three-tenths of a mile. In 1960 the town again extended its city limits out Salem-Lowell Rd. 2,200 feet.

Although Germantown is geographically divided between two counties, the residents of Germantown demonstrate loyalty to one another. They frequently band together and sponsor suppers and other such activities to raise money for new playground equipment; they support the fire department's car shows and dances, as well as other fundraisers. Each year in September, the Germantown Festival brings townspeople together. The churches, the fire department, and local homemakers join to run the food booths, make ice cream, bake cakes, work the contests, conduct the festival's dance, and hold baby shows. All funds received are divided equally among the participating organizations.

Bracken Co. Extension Homemakers. *History of Bracken County.* Bicentennial ed. Brooksville, Ky., 2002.

Bracken Homemakers History Committee. *Recollections: Yesterday, Today for Tomorrow.* Brooksville, Ky.: Poage, 1969.

Calvert, Jean, and John Klee. *The Towns of Mason County: Their Past in Pictures.* Maysville, Ky.: Maysville and Mason Co. Library Historical and Scientific Association, 1986.

Rennick, Robert M. *Kentucky Place Names.* Lexington: Univ. of Kentucky Press, 1984.

Mary Lou Simons

GERMANTOWN CHRISTIAN CHURCH. The beginning of the Germantown Christian Church in Mason Co. was tied to the death of a young soldier in 1826. Maj. John D. Morford, a veteran of the **War of 1812**, buried his son on the south side of Germantown that year. Recognizing the need for upkeep of the grave site, Morford donated a plot of ground around the grave for a church to be built. This church began as a Baptist Church and later became a Christian Church. The lovely brick building that remains includes a large auditorium and the original balcony where slaves could be seated. The first service was held in this structure in 1857. The building was enlarged with Sunday school rooms and a basement in 1924. On a Sunday evening in February 1975, the building was almost destroyed by fire set by a serial arsonist. However, it was immaculately restored and reopened in 1976.

Bracken Co. Extension Homemakers. *History of Bracken County.* Bicentennial ed. Brooksville, Ky.: Bracken Co. Extension Homemakers, 2002.

Caroline R. Miller

GEX. The Gallatin Co. community of Gex (pronounced *jay*) began during the 19th century as a boat landing on the Ohio River west of Stephens Creek and east of Agniels Branch. The town was named for the Antoine Gex family, who were among the Swiss immigrants who settled across the Ohio River in nearby Vevay, Ind. A son of that family, John Anthony Gex (1819–1907), his wife Cyrene, and five children ranging in age from 14 to 27 were listed as residents of Gex in the 1850 Kentucky census. The settlement of the area continued as other immigrants moving in began to farm the area's rich river bottomland, pasture livestock on the valley hills, and build clapboard or brick houses near the road that ran between Warsaw and Ghent.

A post office was established on March 19, 1898, when Thomas Mylor Jr., who in 1854 had emigrated from County Wexford, Ireland, was named postmaster. The post office was located in Mylor's general store, and his daughter Maggie served as the assistant postmaster. It remained there until August 15, 1907, when the mail was rerouted to Sanders. The area called Gex remained a farming community and was later assigned a Ghent postal address as part of Rural Free Delivery. A one-room grade school at Gex served the community's children until schools in the county were consolidated. The general store was closed and the building sold in 1932, just after the road running through Gex was repaved and became part of U.S. 42. The end of the 20th century saw industry enter the community of Gex: Gallatin Steel built its plant on the south side of the highway outside of town. A firm known as Steel Technologies also located nearby, and three other manufacturing businesses now occupy what was formerly farmland. A restaurant is the only commercial building in town. Although a few of the original houses remain, most of the homes in Gex are newer structures. An exception is the 1865 Gex house, purchased by Gallatin Steel and preserved along with the house's original outbuildings that overlook the Ohio River.

An Atlas of Carroll and Gallatin Counties, Kentucky. Philadelphia: D. J. Lake, 1883.

Bogardus, Carl R., Sr. *The Story of Gallatin County.* Ed. James C. Claypool. Cincinnati: John S. Swift, 2003.

Jacquelene P. Mylor

GEX LANDING INCIDENT. Resentment against the U.S. Colored Troops (USCT) established by President Abraham Lincoln in spring 1863 dominated Kentucky politics into 1864, and it festered particularly in the north central counties where Confederate sympathies were most pronounced. The Union forces were thinly stretched across Kentucky. Confederate colonel George Jesse had been ordered to collect the scattered remnants of Gen. John Hunt Morgan's Cavalry after Morgan's forces were routed in June 1864 at Cynthiana, Ky. Jesse stationed himself in familiar territory at New Castle in Henry Co. As his now relatively independent forces strengthened, Jesse harassed supply lines and targeted Union supporters throughout the area.

Into this hostile territory in August 1864, recently promoted Lt. Frederick D. Seward led a detachment of Company C of the 117th USCT, mustered at Covington in July 1864. This squad of untrained infantry was sent to protect recruits obtained for the 5th U.S. Colored Cavalry (USCC) among slaves and free people of color in Carroll, Gallatin, Grant, and Owen counties. The officers of USCT and USCC units were white. Indiana native Frederick Seward had completed two years of service with Company E, 9th Minnesota Regiment, before his promotion to lieutenant. About August 22, the USCT squad arrested James Southard, a leading Confederate sympathizer and ferryman at Ghent, Gallatin Co. Southard owned land along the Ohio River that formed the Ghent landing. His brother notified Colonel Jesse, who was in Henry Co., that James Southard had been taken by USCT troops.

Jesse's cavalry caught up with the USCT squad at the plantation of Lucien C. Gex, just outside Ghent, on August 29, 1864. According to eyewitness Virginia Craig, that night the USCT unit had been separated into two groups of six each; one group was fed dinner at the farm of her father, and the other group was fed at an unspecified nearby farm. Jesse's men surprised and captured the USCT soldiers, and in their first engagement with the enemy, the Union troops were scattered across the farms of Albert and John A. Craig. The CSA troops rescued Southard at John A. Craig's farm. There were casualties among the USCT troops, but the exact number of them is unknown. Over the next day or so, several different accounts of the incident were recorded, and thus the tale of the Gex Landing Massacre was established.

On August 30, 1864, Union lieutenant colonel Thomas B. Fairleigh, at Louisville, requested aide from J. Bates Dickson, assistant adjutant at Lexington: "Last evening [Confederate colonel] Jesse with 150 men captured a squad of eight or ten colored troops at Ghent and murdered them. Other squads are in the country where he is hunting. Can't you send some men there?"

Virginia Craig, daughter of Albert Craig, recorded in her diary of August 30, 1864, that six of the USCT soldiers were fed at her house and were surprised and captured by rebel soldiers who had searched the house. She said that Southard was being held at her cousin John's house and was rescued. According to her diary, one USCT soldier had been killed and subsequently buried on Albert Craig's lower farm, two wounded USCT soldiers had been put on the packet steamer *Rowena* bound for Cincinnati, and the rest were captured, including a white recruiter.

A Cincinnati newspaper, the *Commercial Dispatch,* carried the story within the week, claiming that one of the two wounded USCT soldiers had died in transit on the *Rowena.* This story further claimed that there had been 60 USCT and 100 CSA involved in the incident at Ghent.

A highly partisan version of the "massacre" was carried in the August 31, 1864, issue of the *Louisville Daily Journal,* generally a pro-Union newspaper. There it was stated that Jesse's troops had massacred unarmed Negro troops, "shooting them like wild beasts." The next day the *Louisville Daily Journal* reported that Jesse's troops had destroyed Lock No. 1 on the Kentucky River and had "proclaimed vengeance against all Negro soldiers and recruits. It will be [Jesse's] policy to murder all that may fall into his hands. His recent massacre of the blacks at Ghent shows that his words [are] not simple idle bombast."

Two days later, the newspaper corrected its earlier story: "Jesse did not murder negroes at Ghent—none killed except in attack. His men urged him to murder entire party but he refused the barbarous act." Then on September 5, the newspaper reported that "seven of the colored soldiers reached Owenton [Ky.] from Port Royal [Ky.] on Wednesday last where released . . . one a Sgt., two wounded, fifteen captured, eight remained with rebels voluntarily . . . no bad treatment by Jesse."

As if the story were not confused enough by the presence of two different black units at the skirmish, in November 1864 elements of the 5th U.S. Colored Cavalry were assigned to patrol duty at Ghent and Warsaw. Local citizens apparently made no distinction between the USCT and USCC units.

In December 1864, the 117th USCT, stationed at Camp Nelson in Jessamine Co., was folded into the 25th Union Brigade, and white regiments in the brigade were transferred. The 117th regiment under the 25th Corps saw action at Richmond and Appomattox in Virginia and in the final Texas campaign. Compared to these other battles, the Gex landing skirmish was insignificant. The official regimental records of the 5th USCC state that at the Ghent skirmish one soldier was killed, six were captured but later escaped, and five returned to their unit.

The story was embellished further during the early 1900s when A. L. Gex, the son of Lucien Gex, found three graves churned up by a cyclone (tornado) and reported seeing "foot bones in perfectly preserved shoes."

The wide discrepancies concerning the numbers involved in the Ghent incident can be attributed to wartime hysteria and to newspaper reporting that was dependent on local sources for its news coverage. The presence of both cavalry and infantry units among the black troops and recent recruits of slaves from the region added to confusion about the number of deaths and about those who were released or remained with the Confederates.

From the family letters exchanged during the **Civil War**, it appears that the Gex and Craig families originally supported Kentucky's neutrality but were bitterly opposed to the formation of USCT units and the military draft. By 1865 these families had affiliated themselves totally with the Conservative Democrats, a political faction that tipped the balance in the Kentucky legislature toward a pro-Southern position following the Civil War.

Abbett, H. J., Warsaw, to A. G. Craig, July 18, 1865. Craig Papers, King Library, Univ. of Kentucky, Lexington.

Carroll Co. Deed Book 2: 157, 196; 17: 119; 20: 2, Carrollton, Ky.

Cincinnati newspaper clippings, September 1864, made by Lucien Gex. Craig Papers.

Craig, Virginia. Diary excerpt, King Library, Univ. of Kentucky.

Gex, A. L., son of Lucien Gex, embellished narrative, ca. 1900. Craig Papers.

Harrison, Lowell H., and James C. Klotter. *A New History of Kentucky.* Lexington: Univ. Press of Kentucky, 1997.

Louisville Daily Journal, August 31, September 1, 3, 5, 1864.

Prichard, James. "Colonel Jesse," typed manuscript, privately held by James Prichard, Kentucky Libraries and Archives, Frankfort, Ky.

Diane Perrine Coon

GHENT. The town of Ghent in Carroll Co., a thriving Ohio River port throughout the 1800s, began with **Benjamin Craig**'s 1794 settlement of McCoull's Bottom, a 1,000-acre tract purchased from Ann McCoull, widow of Neil McCoull of Fredericksburg, Va. The property had originally been granted to the heirs of Ann's brother, Theodosius McDonald, who died in the **French and Indian War**. The McCool's Creek settlement provided overland access to the Ohio River for several surrounding counties. A ferry soon linked it to Vevay, Ind., which was settled by Swiss immigrants as early as 1802.

In 1810 John and Samuel Sanders purchased from Benjamin Craig, who was their uncle, a 300-acre tract, upon which Samuel Sanders laid out a town of eight streets and 108 lots in 1816. It was called Ghent, and the legend persists that Henry Clay, a signer of the Treaty of Ghent, which ended the War of 1812, suggested the name.

Benjamin Craig sold 200 acres east of the Sanders's tract to his brother, noted Indian fighter Jeremiah Craig. This acreage stretched from Jerry Craig's Creek (now Black Rock) to Ferry St. in Ghent, marking where Jeremiah Craig operated the ferry for his nephew Samuel Sanders. Sanders's Tavern was a popular stopping place in the early 1800s, as was the America House, a nearby hotel. Much of Jeremiah Craig's tract was acquired by Rev. **John Scott** and continues to be owned by Scott descendants today. Scott-Land Gardens, a roadhouse with tourist cabins, operated there during the early 1900s.

In 1814 the "mother church" for the area's Baptist churches relocated to the settlement and built a new brick sanctuary along Ferry St. in 1843, on land donated by John Scott. It is now known as the **Ghent Baptist Church**. "Reformers" split off to form the Ghent Christian Church in 1836, and the two congregations hosted Baptist evangelist T. J. Fisher and Disciples of Christ publisher Ben Franklin in a religious debate at the Baptist Church in 1857. The debate was transcribed and published as a book.

In 1843 Samuel Sanders's nephew **George N. Sanders** organized a political meeting at Ghent, calling upon prospective presidential candidates to declare their position on the annexation of Texas. The response of little-known speaker James K. Polk launched his successful candidacy and led to the **Mexican War**. It also marked the beginning of George Sanders's controversial political career, which ended in exile because Sanders was a suspect in the assassination of Abraham Lincoln.

Ghent's most notable **Civil War** incident occurred in 1864, when a regiment of African American soldiers arrested a man at Ghent and were subsequently ambushed near Gex's Landing in Kentucky at the Gallatin Co. line (see **African Americans in the Civil War**; **Gex Landing Incident**). After the Civil War, African American members split off from the Baptist Church to form the **Ghent Second Baptist Church**, which still meets occasionally under longtime minister Rev. John Sharpe. Little is known of an African Methodist church in Ghent that is mentioned in old deeds. An African American hamlet outside of town may have given Black Rock Rd. its name.

Numerous fraternal organizations thrived in Ghent from before the Civil War through the early 1900s. Surviving Ghent newspapers mention meetings of the Masonic Order, the Independent Order of Odd Fellows, the Knights of Pythias, the Order of Red Men, and others. The Masons and the Odd Fellows built tall brick "temples" downtown. In 1856 the Ghent Cemetery began as a group of adjacent cemeteries, one section operated by the Masons, another by the Odd Fellows, and a later third section operated by the Scott brothers, local undertakers. The Colored Odd Fellows added a fourth section for the black community; when the lodge disappeared, that part of the cemetery fell into neglect and was replaced by an African American cemetery southwest of town.

There were also women's clubs and missionary and literary societies. The Caby M. Froman Club is the oldest active club in the Kentucky Federation of Women's Clubs, and its offspring the Ghent Women's Club still meets. The once-influential Daughters of the Confederacy is gone.

The three-story brick **Ghent College** was constructed on the west side of town in 1867. After 20 years the college closed and the building was used for Ghent High School.

It would be difficult to pinpoint when Ghent reached its peak before its inevitable decline. Perhaps it was in 1899, when Ghent's newspaper, the *Ghent Times,* began a run that lasted several years. Roads and shipping improved, and commerce was bypassing Ghent even before the **Great Depression** came, ending the steamboat culture. Well situated on high ground, Ghent was largely untouched by the **flood of 1937**—but not unaffected, as the already Depression-weakened Ghent Deposit Bank failed after 50 years in business.

In 1932 Ghent's best-known native, **James Tandy Ellis**, returned to Ghent in semiretirement. He was a popular Chautauqua entertainer, poet, and humorist, and in his widely published newspaper columns he often made reference to characters identified with his hometown. Late in life, he wrote a column lamenting Ghent's condition. "Today we linger in the cobwebs," he said. "Our high school gone; our bank gone; our drug store gone, our lumber and coal yard gone. We had a canning factory once, but that evaporated. . . . the town has no scales. We haven't any hotel, and the tourists lam through town at 70 miles an hour." Ellis further regretted that Ghent no longer had its flour mill or its bakery, that Scott's Restaurant on the east side of town had burned, and that the tavern west of town had closed. The town suffered another indignity soon afterward, when the old college building burned in 1940.

In the 1960s industry started to encroach on the town. Ghent prevented construction of a noxious plastics plant to its west, but the Walton Craig house was nonetheless demolished. Kentucky Utilities tore down several antebellum homes in 1973 to build a generating plant a mile east of town. Smokestacks dominate the eastern skyline now, and electrical towers and transmission lines mar the high hills overlooking Ghent.

The automobile traffic from Cincinnati to Louisville along U.S. 42 bypassed Ghent completely once I-71 was completed in 1969; today commuters from Ghent can reach Cincinnati, Louisville, or Frankfort in an hour's drive. In 1977 the *Martha A. Graham,* the last double-wheeled ferry operating on the Ohio River, ceased operation when **Markland Dam** was bridged, ending Ghent's 175 years of shared history with Vevay, Ind. When the elementary school closed in 1972, Ghent lost another measure of local identity. On the site of the old college, the building remains, poorly utilized when not completely vacant.

Longtime town mayor Johnny Davis had few successes in preventing Ghent's decline, which paralleled the decline of tobacco farming, but he did help save Ghent's post office from closure; and before his death in 1992, he secured a sewer system for Ghent, to be shared by the North American Stainless plant being built west of town. The steel plant later expanded greatly and more plants followed, and with expansions of Kentucky Utilities, Dow Corning, and the nearby Belterra casino complex in Vevay, Ghent is surrounded by development without necessarily benefiting from it. The commonwealth of Kentucky is exploring several invasive options to deal with increased plant traffic through town.

Among the Ghent population, formerly consumers of both Cincinnati and Louisville media, the Cincinnati papers now have few subscribers. The sole cable provider picks up local broadcasts only from Louisville, and Ghent has lost much of the affinity it once shared with the Cincinnati and Northern Kentucky area.

Despite all it has lost, many vestiges of Ghent's past remain. The Sibley house on Ferry St. may date from Jeremiah Craig's tenure; the 1833 Theodorick Fisher house and the James Tandy Ellis house (ca. 1861) are now bed-and-breakfasts. The business block on Main Cross is largely empty. A fire in 1915 destroyed several storefronts and weakened the Odd Fellows building; it collapsed suddenly months later and was rebuilt. An arsonist struck the 123-year-old Masonic Building in 1988, and its burned-out shell dominated the downtown for 15 years before being razed.

The Ghent Baptist Church continues to meet in its 1843 sanctuary. The Christian Church closed in 1989, and its 1871 building has been rehabilitated for city offices and a proposed museum. An earlier Christian Church building (ca. 1836) is now a private residence.

Entwined with a sycamore tree in the yard of James Bledsoe Tandy's 1842 house on Main Cross are the remains of what some have deemed the largest grape vine in Kentucky. Across the street, the 1889 Methodist Church is in poor condition; the congregation stopped meeting during the early 1960s. Its previous church building, built in 1859, became the Ghent Deposit Bank and is now the town's post office, operated by Retta Craig Lykins, a descendant of Benjamin Craig. An earlier Methodist Church building on Union St. became the telephone exchange and today is a private residence. Near the post office are the Charlene McPherson and Evelyn Sanders homes, both former hotels.

Many of Ghent's small frame houses are also quite old. Some have become dilapidated, and concerns over their condemnation played a role in the 2006 election of William Mumphrey, Ghent's first African American mayor.

Noteworthy "Ghentiles" not previously mentioned include Russell Dufour, an entertainer and music teacher who wrote articles on local history in the 1950s and 1960s; **Nancy Diuguid**, who became a respected theater director in England and South Africa; **Pam Browning**, a pioneering Kentucky women's basketball player; Princie Brown, an African American businesswoman; Price Chamberlain, a Cleveland arts figure; Verney Sanders, a Louisville sportswriter; legendary steamboat captain C. J. Dufour; Cliff Snell, a notorious barbecue entrepreneur; Dr. J. Sam Brown, a small-town doctor with a statewide reputation; and the brothers James, Luke, and **Attilla Cox**, prominent businessmen. In 2000 Ghent had a total population of 371.

"Ghent Baptist Church to Celebrate 175th," *KP,* August 2, 1975, 1K.

"Town of Ghent in Carroll County, Ky. Dates Back to Year 1812," *KP,* December 18, 1936, 26.

U.S. Census Bureau. "American Fact Finder. Data Set: Census 2000 Summary File 1 (SF1) 100-Percent Data, Custom Table." www.census.gov (accessed April 24, 2006).

Bill Davis

GHENT BAPTIST CHURCH. The Ghent Baptist Church, originally known as the Baptist Church at Port William, was organized on April 5, 1800, as an outcome of a revival held in Port William (now Carrollton) in Carroll Co. Many of its members had been members of the Traveling Church, a church group that migrated from Virginia, fleeing persecution. The new Baptist church of 10 members, constituted at Port William, met at first in homes. Its first building was a log structure at the mouth of McCool's Creek. In 1814 a brick building was erected near McCool's Settlement (now Ghent), and the church was called McCool's Bottom Baptist Church. In 1843 the church built a new and larger building and became known as the Ghent Baptist Church. Donations for the construction consisted of money and farm products, including several barrels of whiskey. This building remains and serves as the present sanctuary of the church.

During its history, the Ghent Baptist Church has assisted in the constituting of 14 Baptist churches. In Kentucky the churches were White's Run Baptist Church (1810), Craigs Creek Baptist Church (1816), Four Mile Baptist Church (1820), Sharon Baptist Church (1825), Carrollton First Baptist Church (1849), Dallasburg Baptist Church (1851), Jordan Baptist Church (1867), Ghent Second Baptist Church (1871), Ohio Valley Baptist Church (1976), and Prestonville Baptist Church (1990). In Indiana the new churches were Indian Creek Baptist Church (1810), Bryants Creek Baptist Church (1815), Log Lick Baptist Church (1818), and Long Run Baptist Church (1818). The churches at Craigs Creek, Log Lick, Four Mile, Sharon, Ohio Valley, and Prestonville no longer exist.

In August 1871 the blacks in the congregation expressed a desire to form a church of their own, and the church issued letters of dismission to any who requested them for that purpose. As a result the Second Baptist Church of Ghent was formed.

When the present church building was built in 1843, space was provided for a cemetery. By 1880, however, the cemetery was full, and by 1911 the cemetery became so neglected that relatives were asked to move the remains of their loved ones to other cemeteries. The graves were removed and the area planted in grass and trees.

In 1900 the Ghent Baptist Church and 11 other churches formed the White's Run Baptist Association. Improvements to the Ghent Baptist Church property in subsequent years included stained-glass windows, electric lights, a new steeple, and new pews. A parsonage was built in 1914, a Sunday school annex was add in 1923, and a new education building was erected in 1969. In April 2000, the church celebrated 200 years of ministry. On several Sundays during the time of celebration, former pastors returned to preach. Ghent Baptist Church has had a total of 52 different pastors during its many years of ministry to the community.

Minutes of the Ghent Baptist Church, 1880 to the present, Ghent Baptist Church, Ghent, Ky.

Ken Massey

GHENT COLLEGE (HIGH SCHOOL). Ghent College in Carroll Co. was founded in 1867, when local citizens, led by James Frank, formed a corporation creating a private nonsectarian college for white students at Ghent. A three-story brick college was built on the western edge of town the following year, at a cost of $31,700. The U.S. Mail steamboat line donated a bell for the new building, which had four classrooms on the ground floor, residences for students and the president on the upper floors, and a dumbwaiter that carried meals from the basement kitchen to a second-floor dining room. It was a coeducational institution with three departments: primary, academic, and collegiate, the latter offering degrees in both classical and scientific courses of study.

The college's first president was Ebenezer N. Elliot, the editor of the collection *Cotton Is King, and Pro-Slavery Arguments* (1860) and a past president of some small colleges in Mississippi. Elliot left to become principal of the Carroll Seminary in Carrollton and was replaced by James Shannon Blackwell, a linguist and philologist who later taught at the University of Missouri at Columbia. H. E. Holton became president in 1870.

John A. Reubelt, a distinguished German-born linguist and author who had recently been expelled from Indiana University at Bloomington and from the Methodist Church in a doctrinal dispute, replaced Holton in 1871. Reubelt resigned in 1875, and the presidency was filled for five years by William J. Barbee, a Mississippi teacher and the author of *Physical and Moral Aspects of Geology.* A native of Kentucky, Barbee had obtained a medical degree before becoming a Disciples of Christ minister.

Reubelt's and Barbee's terms were the high-water mark for the college. It declined later, during G. C. Crowe's five-year tenure as president that began in 1880. In 1883 a local newspaper made an oblique reference to "discouraging circumstances" at the college. Author **James Tandy Ellis**, who had attended the school, attributed its decline to "religious bigotry," which troubled the college even though it had been founded on nonsectarian principles. The trustees invited the commonwealth of Kentucky to acquire the property for an agricultural and mechanical college; failing that, the college was closed in 1887, and its last president, John Thomas Walker, returned to teaching in Owen Co.

During its 20-year history the collegiate department granted 17 BAs and 14 MAD (maid of arts) degrees.

The college building was sold to the Ghent Independent School District, which reopened it as a grade school and the Ghent High School in 1889, graduating five students in 1893. This high school remained for decades a small, underfunded school that seldom employed more than five teachers or graduated more than seven high school students in any given year. Ghent Independent School District merged into the Carroll Co. educational district in 1936, and the Ghent High School was closed; its students were sent to Carrollton High School in Carrollton. Elementary classes continued in the old college building until a fire destroyed the landmark on New Year's Day 1940. On the old college grounds the Works Progress Administration constructed an elementary school building that served Ghent students from 1945 until its closing in 1972. The property today is in private hands.

Bevarly, R. W. "History of Education in Carroll County," MA thesis, Univ. of Kentucky, 1936.
Gentry, Mary Ann. *A History of Carroll County, Kentucky.* M. A. Gentry, 1984.
——, comp. *Memorable Events: 1890—1990.* Carrollton, Ky.: MPS Publishers, 1990.

Bill Davis

GHENT SECOND BAPTIST CHURCH. The Ghent Second Baptist Church is an African American congregation meeting at 405 Liberty St. in Ghent in Carroll Co. It was established by black members of the Ghent Baptist Church and of some other churches. Records are not extant as to the charter, the founders, the first pastor, and the officers of the church. In 1873 Nellie Slaughters came to teach in the public schools and is credited with having organized the church's first Sunday school, and she was its first superintendent. It is believed that this school gave birth to the church and that the congregation worshipped in a livery stable on the east side of town. In 1879 a local white citizen by the name of Turner gave money to purchase, for $85, the front half of lot 93 (now 405 Liberty St.), on which a church building was erected. In the same year, Simeon Dillard, a trustee of the church, bought lot 88 (now 404 Union St.), located behind the church, which later was sold to the Colored Baptist Church and became the site of the church parsonage. On March 18, 1924, the church purchased the Richard Brightwell family cemetery, located at the southeast end of Carroll St., for $300. Additional property was purchased in 1995 and 2003, and as a result the church owns all the land between 405 Liberty and 404 Union Sts. During the 1970s and 1980s, men from the church along with men from the Carrollton Second Baptist, the Warsaw Second Baptist, and the Park Ridge Baptist churches in Gallatin Co. formed the Tri-County Chorus. This group often sang at church and community events throughout the area. The year 2002 witnessed the formation of a mass choir, directed by Raymond Brightwell. Anna Anderson and Richard Brooks were the organists of the group.

Ghent (First) Baptist Church Minutes, Ghent Baptist Church, Ghent, Ky.
Hampton, G. A., ed. "Historical Sketch of the Ghent Second Baptist Church," 2002, Second Baptist Church, Ghent, Ky.

Ken Massey

GIBBS, CLINTON (b. August 8, 1891, Petersburg, Ky.; d. May 1, 1979, Cincinnati, Ohio). Organist Clinton Gibbs was the son of Frances Gibbs. By 1900 the Gibbs family was living along Wayne St. in the Walnut Hills neighborhood of Cincinnati. In 1926 Clinton Gibbs became the organist for the African American First Baptist Church in Walnut Hills, located just to the east and behind the former Lane Seminary complex along Gilbert Ave. Gibbs had studied music theory at Holderbach College with Prower Symon, once an instructor at the Cincinnati College Conservatory of Music. Gibbs also served at Carmel Presbyterian and the St. Andrew's Episcopal churches in Cincinnati. He was the director of the Queen City Glee Club and was on the faculty of the local Lillian Aldrich Settlement School of Music. He became the vice president of the Cincinnati branch of the National Association of Negro Musicians and was a member of the Masonic Order (see **Masons**). He was affectionately called "the Professor."

Gibbs, who never married, died at his home at 2819 Preston St. in Walnut Hills in 1970, and after services at his beloved First Baptist Church, he was buried at the United American Cemetery in the nearby Evanston neighborhood of Cincinnati.

"Clinton Gibbs," *CE*, May 5, 1970, 18.
"Clinton Gibbs Services Tomorrow," *CP*, May 6, 1970, 50.

Warner, Jennifer S. *Boone County: From Mastodons to the Millennium*. Burlington, Ky.: Boone Co. Bicentennial Book Committee, 1998.

GIBSON GREETING CARDS INC. The oldest greeting card company in the United States until it ceased operating in 2000, Gibson Greeting Cards Inc. operated in the Cincinnati–Northern Kentucky region. The firm was founded as Gibson & Company, Lithographers, in 1850 by four brothers, Stephen, Robert, George, and Samuel Gibson, with the help of their father, George Gibson. The elder George Gibson had operated a lithograph business in Scotland before immigrating with his family to St. Louis, Mo. Another brother, John, established a New York City–based lithography business that merged, off and on, with Gibson & Company, Lithographers. That firm, C. R. Gibson, currently of Nashville, Tenn., continues as a stationery company specializing in family albums.

In its early years, Gibson & Company, Lithographers, located in Cincinnati, produced **Civil War** prints and patriotic and reward cards and sold them in Cincinnati–Northern Kentucky shops. The company later became a jobber handling products such as imported Christmas cards from Germany. As the company found these greeting cards popular, it decided to develop its own mass-produced greeting cards for Christmas and later for Valentine's Day and Easter. In 1883 Robert Gibson, the firm's business manager, purchased his three brothers' interests in the company and was the sole proprietor until his death in 1895. Afterward the company was incorporated as the Gibson Art Company, and its shares were divided among Robert Gibson's surviving children (Charles, Arabella, William, and Edwin). The Gibson Art Company became one of the nation's progressive card publishers, using new industrial processes and printing techniques. The greeting card business prospered during **World War I**, as American servicemen were overseas. It was at this time that the Gibson company developed a new form of greeting card called the "French-fold" card—one sheet of paper folded in half—which became the industry standard.

During the **Great Depression** in late 1931, J. R. Gibson, then the head of the Gibson Art Company, hired Helen Steiner Rice, the wife of an unemployed Dayton, Ohio, banker who had lost his wealth in the 1929 stock market crash. Rice suggested that the Gibson company expand public awareness of the annual Christmas seals, which at the time were sold exclusively in the nation's department stores. While many people during the Depression had to forgo buying gifts, they could afford a Christmas seal or a greeting card. Rice underwent training in the greeting card business at Cincinnati and Pittsburgh, Pa. A successful employee with her experience in poetry, marketing, and public relations, she was later appointed as the Gibson company's greeting card editor. She made use of her personally experienced celebrations, tragedies, and illnesses to help her understand the emotional needs of the purchasers and the recipients of the company's cards. One of her own tragedies was that her husband died 10 months after she started working with the Gibson Art Company.

The Gibson Art Company was among the region's businesses affected by the **flood of 1937**. The company encouraged its employees to become involved with the region's flood relief efforts, and Rice participated by preparing news releases on the flooding and related health concerns. During **World War II**, a newsletter called *Gibsonews*, edited by Rice, was mailed to every Gibson company employee stationed in the U.S. armed forces worldwide. In 1950 the Gibson Art Company celebrated its 100th birthday, and Rice wrote the special celebratory verses for tours, invitations, and cards of appreciation. By 1957 the company was among the five largest greeting card companies in the United States. At that time it moved to a larger site at Amberley Village, 10 miles north of Cincinnati. After nearly 40 years, Rice retired in 1971 from Gibson Greeting Cards Inc. (the company had changed to this name in 1960). Because she was respected and well-liked by many people in the Gibson company, they kept in touch with her, including executives Bill Dresman, Fred Wagner, and Jack Wiedemer. As a consultant to the Gibson company following her retirement, Rice had an office and a secretary provided by the firm until her death on April 23, 1981, at age 80.

The popularity of Helen Steiner Rice's poems and books was welcomed by the management of the Gibson company. The firm's executives quickly recognized the potential financial rewards of Rice's poetry and books, especially after the broadcast reading of her poem "The Praying Hands" on the *Lawrence Welk Show* in 1961. This poem turned out to be "the hottest thing on the line" and "a money maker," according to a Gibson company memo. The company then marketed Rice's inspirational poems as a new venture in the form of booklets, stationery, plaques, and wall hangings in stores nationwide. By 1963 Gibson Greetings Cards Inc. reported sales of more than $26 million, with net earnings of $1.8 million. A Gibson company general sales manager, Bruce Forster, wrote to the company's dealers in September 1964, stating, "Never before in the 114-year history of Gibson Greeting Cards has any merchandise received the 'tremendous' acclaim accorded Helen Steiner Rice's Inspirational Books." A Gibson company managing art director from 1959 to 1979, John T. Gimpel, reviewed Rice's poems and approved their artwork on the company's cards. Following a national broadcast of Rice's Christmas poetry on the *Lawrence Welk Show* in 1966, Gibson Greeting Cards Inc. published a collection of her poems, *For Your Christmas*.

The firm was acquired by C.I.T. Financial Corporation in 1964, and the Gibson Greeting Cards Inc. name was retained. C.I.T. Financial also purchased Cleo Wrap Corporation in Memphis, Tenn., which supplemented the Gibson company's greeting card line. In 1975 Gibson Greeting Cards Inc., celebrating 125 years as a company, published *Gibson 1850–1975: Our 125th Anniversary*. In 1980 C.I.T. Financial was acquired by RCA. Two years later (1982), Gibson Greeting Cards Inc. was purchased by a group of Gibson company executives and the Wesray Corporation. In 1983 the Gibson company was renamed Gibson Greetings Inc. and became a publicly owned company on the NASDAQ stock exchange. Gibson Greetings Inc. was now the third-largest greeting card company, behind Hallmark Cards Inc. and the American Greetings Corporation. With its commitment to conservation, Gibson Greetings Inc. was the first stationery company to earn an endorsement from Renew America, a nonprofit environmental organization. The firm expanded into international markets in the early 1990s, with the names Gibson Greetings International Ltd. and Gibson de Mexico, S.A. de C.V.

In the mid-1990s Gibson Greetings Inc. had 4,600 employees and sales of $546.2 million. Through its Store-Within-A-Store program, the company sold its products in more than 50,000 outlets worldwide by 1993. The headquarters remained at Amberley Village until the late 1990s, when a new corporate headquarters was established in Covington, Ky. Gibson signed a 10-year lease in 1998 for corporate-retail space on the Ohio River at Covington's RiverCenter (see **Covington, Downtown**). The company began moving its headquarters to Covington the next year and set up a distribution plant in the Pioneer Valley Industrial Park area of South Covington. Gibson Greetings Inc. continued with its traditional greeting cards for seasons, holidays, birthdays, and inspirations and developed alternative cards such as "A Good Laugh" and "With Thoughts of You." The company was the leader for multicultural products for African American, Chinese, Jewish, and Hispanic communities; it produced "The Family Collection" on African American family life. Gibson Greetings Inc. expanded its Christian market by developing another line, "Messages of Faith, Hope, and Love." Obtaining licenses from specific companies, the Gibson company also sold products that featured characters from the Walt Disney Company and Sesame Street.

Gibson Greetings Inc. suffered financial losses in 1994 and 1995. Wal-Mart stopped selling cards made by the Gibson greeting card company. In 1996 the American Greetings Corporation, based at Cleveland, Ohio, offered to purchase Gibson Greetings Inc. for $292 million, and the offer was rejected. The Gibson company reduced costs in its divisions, eliminated jobs, outsourced artists and art printing, and participated in the Egreetings network. But the company could not compete with the electronic and other marketing successes of Hallmark and American Greetings. Gibson Greetings Inc. lost vital accounts with the Cincinnati-based Kroger Co., a nationwide grocery retailer. In 1999, when sales of the Gibson company's product line were down 42 percent in the second quarter, the American Greetings Corporation again offered to purchase Gibson Greetings Inc., this time for around $162.3 million. The final purchase price was $175 million, according to an agreement completed in March 2000.

In early 2000 the Gibson Gold Collection, commemorating 150 years of the Gibson company's operation, was produced by Bullseye Productions, a unit of Gibson Greetings Inc. The Gibson company's general manager for Bullseye, George White, oversaw this project, for which 48 reproductions of vintage greeting cards from the Gibson company's archives were selected. Later in 2000, American Greetings closed the Gibson company's corporate offices at Amberley Village and at Covington, as well as the distribution plant in South Covington. Greeting cards produced by the Gibson company are kept in the American Greetings Corporation's archives.

"American Greetings Corp. to Acquire Gibson Greetings, Inc. for 0.40 Times Revenue," *Weekly Corporate Growth Report*, November 15, 1999, 10470.

"Business Brief: Gibson Greetings, Inc. Headquarters to be Moved to Kentucky by Next Year," *Wall Street Journal*, Aug. 14, 1998, 1.

C. R. Gibson. www.crgibson.com (accessed April 4, 2006).

Driehaus, Bob. "Beginning of End for Gibson Greeting: Office Jobs Cut; Ky. Plant Remains," *CP*, March 10, 2000, 10C.

Gibson Greeting Cards Inc. *Gibson 1850–1975: Our 125th Anniversary*. Cincinnati: Gibson Greeting Cards, 1975.

"Gibson Jobs Leave," *CP*, June 3, 2000, 9A.

Luken, Charles, and Mark Brown. *Gibson Greetings, Inc.* Memphis, Tenn.: Towery, 1996.

Murray, Matt. "Gibson Rejects $292 Million Bid from Big Rival," *Wall Street Journal,* March 6, 1996, A3.

Margaret Prentice Hecker

GIBSON WINE COMPANY. The Gibson Wine Company operated in Covington from 1934 until 1971. When Robert H. Gibson and Louis W. Schultz founded the company in 1933, **Prohibition** was in force, but rabbis could produce sacramental wines legally. By 1941 William A. Schneider was also a partner in the firm. In 1944 the Gibson Wine Company moved its headquarters to Elk Grove, Calif., near Sacramento, but a small operation remained in Covington at 235 Scott St. Although the firm had moved west, the Cincinnati area remained its top market, and a branch office remained in Cincinnati at 218 W. McMicken Ave., in the Over-the-Rhine neighborhood. In late 1961 the company had plants in both Cincinnati and Covington, employing roughly 150 workers. That year, the firm was acquired by Sanger Winery Associates of Sanger, Calif., and became a part of a wine cooperative owned collectively by 150 California grape growers. The Sanger cooperative's motivation was to ensure the distribution of its product through the Gibson Wine Company's network of outlets. Before the sale, Gibson Wine Company had purchased all of the grapes produced by the Sanger wine cooperative during the previous 10 years. Later, the Gibson Wine Company operated out of 20 W. 18th St. in Covington, in 1962 under vice president Schneider and in 1970, at the same address, under president Schulze. Its Covington plant, a bottling-finishing and warehouse facility, distributed wines throughout Ohio, Kentucky, Indiana, and West Virginia. Gibson Wine Company made fruit wines, rather than table wines. The company was one of the first U.S. wine producers to attempt to quench the thirst of Americans, challenging things cold and sweet such as Coca-Cola. In the late 1950s, "pop" wines such as those produced by the Gibson Wine Company began to be served much as soft drinks were among young people. The emerging popularity of Riunite wines during the 1950s is perhaps the best example of this trend.

Gibson's wines were aimed for the middle-line, price-conscious consumer and the everyday drinker who keeps a jug of wine in the refrigerator for sipping. The company's products were sold mainly in supermarkets, where they competed with inexpensive wines produced by Gallo and Almaden. The Gibson Wine Company also produced several private labels, for supermarkets and liquor stores. In 1981 it had estimated annual sales of $20 million and 9 million gallons of product in storage, making it the nation's 18th-largest winery.

The Gibson Wine Company's Covington operation was not without labor problems. In 1941 the company pled guilty to violating the Kentucky statute regulating the number of hours women were allowed to work. In 1956 there was a vote to determine whether the employees of the plant in Covington wished to be represented by the International Union, Allied Industrial Workers of America, AFL-CIO.

Fields, Gregg. "Gibson Thinks Fruit Wines Are Ripe," *CE*, October 16, 1981, C9.

"Firm Officials Fined on Hours Act Charges," *KP*, June 24, 1941, 1.

"Gibson Wine Acquired by Association," *CP*, November 3, 1961, 4.

"Sanger Acquired Gibson Wine Co.," *CE*, November 3, 1961, 1.

"Union Ballot at Gibson Wine," *KTS*, October 10, 1956. 6A.

GILLESPIE, HAVEN (b. February 6, 1888, Covington, Ky.; d. March 14, 1975, Las Vegas, Nev.). "You better watch out, you better not cry, better not pout, I'm telling you why: Santa Claus is comin' to town." This is the oft-sung lyrical advice that songwriter Haven Gillespie gives children in his classic song "Santa Claus Is Comin' to Town," one of the 10 most popular Christmas songs of all time.

James Haven Gillespie was the sixth of nine children born to William "Will" and Anna Riley Gillespie. The family was poor and lived in the basement of a house on Third St. and Madison Ave. in Covington. Haven's father was a painter and musician with a penchant for the whiskey bottle and a good ear for music, who had once studied for the priesthood. Haven's mother worked as a servant. Later in life, Haven said his most vivid memory of childhood was seeing his father's empty whiskey bottles spread all over the house. The young Haven dropped out of Covington's Third District School in the fourth grade after a composition he wrote won second rather than first prize. He later explained that he had dropped out of school because "he felt he was lacking." In 1902, at age 14, Haven moved to Chicago to live with relatives and found a job as a "printer's devil," which entailed cleaning printing presses and running errands. At the time Chicago was the second-largest

Haven Gillespie, ca. 1949.

city in the United States, and Haven reveled in the city's whirlwind of activity and quick-paced life. As his work as a printer's devil progressed, he focused on words and their arrangement, developing an understanding of the English language that served him well later as a lyricist. Gillespie remained, throughout his life, first of all a printer and secondly a songsmith. As he put it, "I have ink in my blood." By 1907, having become a qualified compositor and printing journeyman, Gillespie returned to Covington and joined the International Typographic Union; he continued as a union member for 67 years. His timing was poor in 1907, however, since that year a strike in the printing trades left him out of work. By 1909 the strike had ended, Haven had returned to his job in the printing industry in Chicago, and he had married his childhood sweetheart from Kentucky, Corene Parker. The couple began married life with a grand total of $16 between them. Gillespie initially could not read or write music, and all his early composing attempts failed. By 1911, therefore, he and his now pregnant wife had returned to Covington. The same year, he took a newspaper printing job with the *Cincinnati Times Star.* Louis Mentel, a **ragtime** musician and president of the Associated Music Company in Cincinnati, helped launch Gillespie's career as a songwriter by publishing eight songs, none of which met with success.

Not until 1917, with the publication of his 46th song, "The Harbor of Love," did the young songwriter make a mark in the music industry. Becoming one of the many passing sentimental hits during wartime, this song reached number three on the music charts and initially earned Gillespie $12,000 in royalties. It was the first big break for Gillespie, who was by then working at the *New York Times*, living in New York City, and trying to become a songwriter in the city's famed Tin Pan Alley. An outbreak of polio that year in the city worried Gillespie's wife so much that the couple returned with their seven-year-old son, Lamont, to Chicago. Gillespie went back to his work in the printing trade, though he was by this time an experienced songsmith with an expanding list of contacts in the music industry. He had collaborated in composing several songs for the vaudeville stage and also had published songs with the Remick Publishing Company, a leading national music publisher. His next big break in the music industry came in 1921, when he met Egbert Van Alstyne, a brilliant composer, pianist, and song plugger 10 years Gillespie's senior, who had worked at the Remick Publishing Company, had written three hit songs, and was then living in Chicago. From Van Alstyne, with whom Gillespie soon paired in songwriting, Gillespie learned the requisite technical skills of lyrical composition. During the 1920s, in collaboration with Van Alstyne and others, he wrote 88 songs, including, in 1923, the lyrics for "You're in Kentucky Sure as You're Born," a brief hit that was for Kentuckian Gillespie a particular delight. By then he was writing with composers, band leaders, and vaudevillians nationwide, and his lyrical compositions, most of which were written in a matter of minutes, were becoming Tin Pan Alley staples. He wrote his favorite song of all time, "Drifting and Dreaming," in 1925 and his first classic, "Breezin' Along with the Breeze" in 1926.

Homesick, the Gillespies returned to Covington in 1929. Haven worked enough in the printing trades during the hard times of the 1930s to maintain his union card, but his main work was as a songwriter. He soon made two important friends, Covington radio owner **L. B. Wilson**, who liked Gillespie and helped promote his songs, and New York native Freddie Coots, who became his songwriting collaborator and longtime friend. Having picked up his father's fondness for whiskey, Gillespie thrived in Covington, especially after the repeal of **Prohibition** in 1933. Dividing his time between work as a printer and trips to Chicago and New York City to promote his songs, he was frequently, when home, seen at the Covington tavern of an old friend, ex-vaudevillian Kern Aylward. Aylward had opened a saloon in 1934 at 530 Scott St., in the heart of Covington's Irish neighborhood, and Gillespie was a regular customer who joined Aylward and others in singing and general merriment. Gillespie loved telling stories and drinking with his friends at Aylward's Saloon and later, during the 1950s, could be found doing the same at Arcaro's Tavern, a bar in Erlanger operated by the father of famed jockey **Eddie Arcaro**. The year 1934 was magical for the new songwriting team of Coots (music) and Gillespie (lyrics). That year they wrote their Christmas classic, "Santa Claus Is Comin' to Town," an immediate hit that charted a second time in 1947 when Bing Crosby and the Andrews Sisters recorded it. Another Coots-Gillespie national hit, "You Go to My Head," was made popular in 1938 by the Glen Gray Orchestra, with vocalist Kenny Sargent. A popular torch song with sophisticated lyrics, it was recorded by top singers such as Billie Holliday, Lena Horne, Peggy Lee, and, a generation later, Linda Ronstadt backed by the Nelson Riddle Orchestra. Between 1939 and 1947, Gillespie published just 14 songs, with only one, "The Old Master Painter" (1945), later (in 1950) becoming a charted success. Gillespie's alcoholism was beginning to affect his work. However, he had an idea that temporarily stayed the decline. In 1949 he published "That Lucky Old Sun," a megahit that Gillespie had first thought about writing several years earlier. He was inspired by sitting in his backyard along Montgomery St. in Covington, watching the sun pass over the twin spires of **Mother of God Catholic Church**. There followed, during the next three decades, a long list of songs written by Gillespie, only one of which, "God's Country," sung by Frank Sinatra, charted. Haven Gillespie published his last song, "I Love to Dream," in 1972. A recovering alcoholic, he was living at the time in Las Vegas.

In a songwriting career spanning six decades, 1911–1972, more than 300 of Gillespie's songs were published, he collaborated with more than 100 other songwriters, and he wrote songs for eight musical revues and variety shows. Forty-four different music publishers printed Gillespie's works; 20 songs that he wrote charted, including 3 that were number one ("Breezin' Along with the Breeze" [1926], "Honey" [1929], and "That Lucky Old Sun" [1949]); and his songs were heard in 17 movies. Haven Gillespie, one of the world's most prolific songwriters, died of cancer in 1975. He was cremated and his remains were buried in Bunker's Memory Gardens in Las Vegas, next to his wife, Corene.

First, William E., and Pasco E. First. *Drifting and Dreaming: The Story of Songwriter Haven Gillespie.* St. Petersburg, Fla.: Seaside Publishers, 1988.

Reis, Jim. "Songwriter Gillespie Brought Santa to Town," *KP*, February 16, 2004, 4K.

Steitzer, Stephanie. "Santa Song No Hit with Writer," *KP*, December 22, 2003, 1K.

James C. Claypool

GIRL SCOUTS. Girl Scouting, which came to Northern Kentucky only a few years after the organization began in the United States, helps cultivate values, social conscience, and self-esteem in young girls, while teaching them critical life skills that will enable them to succeed as adults. Through Girl Scouts, girls discover the fun, friendship, and power of girls together. The organization serves all girls of ages 5 to 17 through various levels: Daisy, Brownie, Junior, Cadette, and Senior. The U.S. branch of the Girl Scouts was founded by Juliette Gordon Low in 1912 in Savannah, Ga.

By 1918 there were several Girl Scout troops in the tri-state area. Because so many Northern Kentucky girls were interested in the program, volunteer leaders soon formed a Girl Scout council in Northern Kentucky, separate from the Cincinnati council. At the time, Girl Scouts participated in numerous events such as first aid, bed-making, and signaling. As the number of Girl Scout troops in Northern Kentucky grew, four more councils were chartered. In 1950 Kentucky Girl Scout leaders combined the five smaller councils into one large council to serve the entire Northern Kentucky region. With this merger, the Licking Valley Girl Scout Council received its charter in 1951 and set up an office in Newport. The headquarters were relocated to Covington in 1973 and to Erlanger in October 1986. In order to comply with standards set by the national organization, the council changed its legal name to Girl Scout Council of Licking Valley Inc. in April 2000. The council served 12 counties: Boone, Bracken, Campbell, Carroll, Fleming, Gallatin, Grant, Kenton, Mason, Owen, Pendleton, and Robertson.

In 1955 the Girl Scout Council of Licking Valley received from the Campbell family a generous donation of 211 acres in Fleming Co. for use as a camp. This property, which became known as the Campbell Mountain Girl Scout Camp, opened to the first group of girls in 1959. It eventually included two camping units, each containing platform tents, restrooms, a shower house, a unit house–bunkhouse, and a cabin for staff housing. Camp facilities also include a dining hall, a swimming pool, a health center, a camp office, a trading post, and a craft center. In 2007 the property was sold and the facility was closed.

In 2001 the cities of Newport and Covington chose to honor the thousands of past and present Girl Scouts of Northern Kentucky by naming a new bridge the Licking Valley Girl Scout Bridge. The bridge, a replacement for the former Short-Way Bridge, connects Newport and Covington.

Community service is at the heart of the Girl Scout program. Girl Scouts stresses social responsibility and the importance of helping others. Licking Valley Girl Scouts conduct a variety of service projects, from collecting used books for libraries or baby clothes for women's shelters, to cleaning up local waterways, participating in civic events, and sending personal supplies and Girl Scout Cookies to military personnel stationed overseas.

In 2006 the Licking Valley Council became part of the Girl Scouts–Wilderness Road Council, which still maintains a local office in Erlanger. Because of the merger, one of the Northern Kentucky counties—Carroll Co.—was transferred to the Kentuckiana Girl Scouts Council.

"Council of Girl Scouts Is Started," *KTS*, March 1, 1918, 10.

"Goodies Being Readied for GI," *KP*, February 14, 2003, 1K.

"Our Scouts—Activities of Northern KY Scouts Individuals Listed," *KP*, January 12, 1918, 2.

Elizabeth Comer Williams

GIRTY, SIMON (b. 1741, Chambers Mill [now Dauphin], Pa.; d. 1818, Mauldin, Canada). Simon Girty, who later fought with the British in the **Revolutionary War**, spent his early childhood at Sherman's Creek, in the northwestern part of Pennsylvania. While he was a teenager, his family moved into Fort Granville, in modern central Pennsylvania, because of Indian attacks near their home. In 1755 the fort was overrun by a group of French soldiers and their Indian allies. Simon's stepfather was burned at the stake and his mother and her four children, including Simon, were taken captive. Simon soon learned the Seneca language, was adopted into the Seneca Tribe, and was given the Indian name of Katepacomen. As part of a peace treaty signed in 1758, the Indians agreed to release Simon and all other captives. He reluctantly returned to the European settlements and took up residence near Fort Pitt (Pittsburgh, Pa.). Girty served as a scout and interpreter for various traders and later for the British Army, during Lord Dunmore's War (1774). About that time, he met and became a close friend of Simon Kenton. The two men made a pact, promising to be blood brothers for life. That act later saved Kenton's life when he was captured and sentenced to death by the Indians. In 1778 Girty joined with the British and the Indians to fight in the Revolutionary War. He was a leader during the British-led Indian sieges of Fort Boonesborough and Bryants Station in Kentucky and also at the British victory in the Battle of **Blue Licks** (August 19, 1782) in present-day Robertson Co. He led the British and the Indians in 1779 in the Battle of Dayton, Ky. (see **Rogers' Defeat**), where 60 Kentucky militia soldiers, under Col. David Rogers (see **Rogers' Defeat**) and Col. **Robert Benham**, were ambushed and savagely attacked. Girty played an active role in an Indian victory in 1791 over American frontier military forces (St. Clair's Defeat), as well as in Indian defeat of the Americans at the Battle of Fallen Timbers in 1794. He also assisted the British in the **War of 1812** and participated in the British defeat at the Battle of the Thames in 1813. After the end of hostilities, Girty retired to a farm in Malden, Canada. There he married and raised a family. He attempted to become a good citizen; however, his bad reputation preceded him, and his neighbors would have little to do with a person they considered to be both a murderer and a savage. Simon Girty died at Malden in 1818, at either 76 or 77 years of age.

Ohio History Central. "Simon Girty." Ohio Historical Society. www.ohiohistorycentral.org.

Reis, Jim. "Men Who Fought on the Other Side," *KP*, May 23, 1988, 4K.

RootsWeb.com. "Simon Girty." www.rootsweb.com.

GIST, CHRISTOPHER (b. ca. 1705, Baltimore Co., Md.; d. 1759, Cherokee country [Virginia, South Carolina, or Georgia]). Explorer Christopher Gist was the son of Richard and Zipporah Gist. He grew up in Baltimore. His father, a surveyor, had laid out the city of Baltimore. By 1729 Christopher Gist had married Massachusetts-born Sarah Howard, and he appears to have worked as a surveyor before becoming a fur trader. By 1750 his family was living in the Yadkin River Valley of western North Carolina, not far from the home of another future Kentucky explorer, **Daniel Boone**. The newly founded Ohio Company of Virginia hired Gist to explore its 500,000-acre land grant west of the Allegheny Mountains in preparation for eventual settlement. When he crossed the Ohio River into Kenton Co. during his trip west in 1751, he became one of the first documented white men ever to set foot in Kentucky. His party camped at the confluence of the Licking and Ohio rivers, and he stopped at **Big Bone Lick** in Boone Co. for salt. He then returned to Virginia and reported on the scenic beauty of Northern Kentucky. Gist made two more trips to Kentucky; on one of the occasions, he served as a guide for Maj. George Washington shortly before the **French and Indian War** began. On July 25, 1759, Gist and 62 Catawba Indians left Williamsburg, Va., en route to Winchester, Va. He was attempting to enlist the help of the Indians against the French, but he died of smallpox on this journey. His burial place is unknown. A Northern Kentucky historical society is named in his honor.

Hicks, Irle R. "Christopher Gist, First Ky. Visitor, Also First Reporter," *KP*, February 13, 1964, 4K.

Kleber, John E., ed. *The Kentucky Encyclopedia*. Lexington: Univ. Press of Kentucky, 1992.

Read, Fred. "Gist Served as a Guide for Washington," *KTS*, February 22, 1957, 3A.

GLACIERS. Glaciers profoundly affected the topography of Northern Kentucky. A glacier is a "river" of ice. When the rate of snowfall exceeds the rate of snow melt, the resulting buildup compresses from its own weight. This compression is called firnification, and the compressed snow is known as firn. Over time, the firn compresses further into ice and a glacier is born. Once a large mass of ice reaches more than one square kilometer in size, it is officially designated a glacier. Gradually the glacier's increasing size and mass causes it to begin to move slowly, either downhill or outward from its center.

Glaciers are found in two main forms, alpine and continental. Alpine glaciers originate high in mountainous terrain and are associated with steep mountain valleys. Flowing down the valleys, they impact the terrain but generally stay confined within the original valley walls. Continental glaciers, also known as ice sheets, are very large in scale and may cover an entire continent. A glacier is considered a continental glacier when it grows to more than 50,000 square kilometers (19,305 square miles) in size. At the present time, continental ice sheets are found in Antarctica and Greenland.

A glacial system has three main components: (1) the ice and the sediments contained within the glacier itself, (2) the landscape over which it flows, and (3) any deposits left behind by its advance or retreat. All three components are dependent on one another. As the glacier or ice sheet moves across the landscape, it accumulates sediments, such as rocks, gravel, sand, and other debris. The sediments become embedded in the ice and are carried along with the glacier. As it moves, it leaves some debris behind. Low areas may be filled in, or higher areas may be scoured off and deposited some distance away. These deposits have many names, including kame, esker, moraine, or outwash deposits. Each defines a particular type of collected sediment. As glaciers begin to melt and retreat, large volumes of material are often left behind as outwash deposits in river and stream valleys. Large deposits of sand and gravel found along the Ohio River in Northern Kentucky were left by glaciers. Windblown sediments often accumulate south of the glacier's furthest advance. Called loess, these fine, silty sediments contribute to modern soil development.

The Ice Age is a common name for the geologic period known as the Pleistocene, which is in turn part of the Quaternary period. From 1.8 million years ago to about 12,000 years ago, a series of glaciers advanced from Canada into the United States and later retreated. The glaciers had a profound effect on the creation of the local modern drainage system, including the Ohio River, soil formation, and the deposition of glacial outwash along the major river valleys. The Licking River is one of the few local preglacial rivers that still flows close to its old course. The present channels of the Ohio River and other local streams are a direct result of the successive advances and retreats of glaciers in Northern Kentucky. The glaciers left deposits of loess, eolian (windblown) sand, and outwash along the major stream channels in their path. Modern soil formed both from glacial deposits and from weathering of the limestone and shale bedrock. In contrast, the major soil deposits along the Kentucky River and Eagle Creek derive from slackwater clay and silty alluvium caused by localized flooding, not from glacial deposition.

During the Pleistocene, four major ice sheets directly or indirectly impacted Northern Kentucky. The two oldest, the Nebraskan and the Kansan, often referred to as pre-Illinoian, both occurred before 300,000 years ago. Because of the actions of the two more recent glaciations, the Illinoian and the Wisconsinan, deposits from the earlier glaciers are rare. In Northern Kentucky, deposits from the earlier ice sheets may include thin layers of eroded stony and clayey till. When found, such deposits occur in in-filled shallow preglacial stream valleys.

The time period between the pre-Illinoian glaciations and the Illinoian is known as the Yarmouth interglacial. During this period (approximately 425,000–200,000 years ago), the old Licking River, the old Kentucky River, and the old Eagle Creek continued to develop and became entrenched.

The Illinoian glaciation occurred between approximately 200,000 and 132,000 years ago. Little evidence of this period is found in Northern Kentucky. One well-known geologic feature, however, known as **Split Rock** in Boone Co., may date to the Illinoian period. Split Rock, at the confluence of Woolper Creek and the Ohio River, is a collection of conglomerate rock deposited by a glacier. The only other documented deposit in Northern Kentucky is a narrow band of sediment that stretches from Silver Grove in Campbell Co. into Bracken Co.

After the Illinoian ice sheet retreated, by about 132,000 years ago, the next interglacial period, lasting until about 70,000 years ago, was known as the Sangamon Paleosol. Mature soils developed in Northern Kentucky during this period from weathering bedrock and older glacial till.

The last glacial advance that affected Northern Kentucky, albeit indirectly, was the Wisconsinan (also called Wisconsin), which occurred between 70,000 and at least 10,000 years ago. Divided into three individual glacial advances and retreats, this final stage reached its maximum extent about 20,000 years ago and had retreated by about 10,000 years ago. The glacial ice did not reach directly into Northern Kentucky, but it did influence stream drainages by depositing sand and gravel in the Ohio River channel, and loess reached the northern tier of hills in Boone, Kenton, and Campbell counties. In the northern parts of the counties, soil types such as Nicholson also formed partly from loess, windblown soils deposited during the Pleistocene glacial advances. Some soils along the ridgetops were formed partially from glacial till and have a thin loess cap.

One of the most famous Northern Kentucky geologic features, **Big Bone Lick** in Boone Co., was formed partly as a result of indirect glacial impacts. The geology and the soils at Big Bone Lick that created its unique landform characteristics are the indirect results of the Pleistocene glacial advances. The drainage features that developed throughout the Big Bone area initially were part of the Teays River system, which was the major, northward-flowing preglacial river of the area. Several periods of glacial advancement and retreat, however, forced the abandonment of the Teays River system, and the modern Ohio River system of today developed as a result. During the most recent glacial retreat (the Wisconsin), the floods of meltwater carried by the Ohio River (to the north of Big Bone Lick) deposited in the major valley vast quantities of sand and gravel, which built up and trapped the waters of the northward-flowing Big Bone Creek, forming temporary lakes. During these periods the lacustrine silty clays and clayey silts ("blue clay") that provided the soils in which the Pleistocene mammals became entrapped were deposited in these lakes. The combination of mineral springs and clay beds contributed to the formation of the Pleistocene animal fossil beds for which Big Bone Lick is famous.

Hedeen, Stanley. *Big Bone Lick: The Cradle of American Paleontology.* Lexington: Univ. Press of Kentucky, 2008.

——. *Natural History of the Cincinnati Region.* Cincinnati: Cincinnati Museum Center, 2006.

Kentucky Geological Survey. www.uky.edu/kgs (accessed October 6, 2006).

McDowell, Robert C., and Wayne L. Newell. "Contributions to the Geology of Kentucky: Quaternary System." http://pubs.usgs.gov/prof/p1151h/quat.html (accessed October 6, 2006).

Potter, Paul Edwin. *Exploring the Geology of the Cincinnati/Northern Kentucky Region.* Kentucky Geological Survey, Special Publication 22, Series 11. Lexington: Univ. of Kentucky, 1996.

Teller, James T. "Preglacial (Teays) and Early Glacial Drainage in the Cincinnati Area, Ohio, Kentucky, and Indiana," *Geological Society of America Bulletin* 84, no. 11 (1973): 3677–88.

Jeannine Kreinbrink

GLENCOE. Glencoe is situated along the northern bank of Eagle Creek, which forms the southern boundary of Gallatin Co. In the 1780s, **Daniel Boone** surveyed a trace road through this part of Northern Kentucky; his road has become Ky. Rts.16 and 467 and the Boone Rd. Glencoe is the third-oldest incorporated town in the county, although there is some debate as to when the community was originally founded and about the origin of its name. The name is said to derive either from Glen Coe, Scotland, where the Campbells massacred the McDonalds in February 1692, or from "glen of crows," a reference to the large flocks of crows in the area. A third possibility is that the town was named for a famous racing stud, Glencoe, which was active in Kentucky until the early 1850s.

The original land grant in the area was made around 1795 to Col. Robert Johnson, who built and operated a gristmill on a natural millrace just north of the town before 1800. Johnson later sold a substantial portion of his land holdings, including the mill, to John Castleman. The Castleman family operated the mill into the early 20th century. Glencoe is adjacent to an important intersection of two of the earliest roads that passed through the county—Boone's Trace and Steele's Rd (U.S. 127).

The first post office was established in March 1848, and the town was incorporated in February 1876. Some accounts argue that the town was founded later, with the construction of the **Louisville, Cincinnati, and Lexington Railroad**, between 1867 and 1869. In 1869 M. J. Williams laid out land on the west side of Steele's Rd. in lots, creating the core of the settlement. That same year, Dr. O. B. Yager, a Confederate physician and a friend of Frank and Jesse James, settled there, where he practiced until his death in 1934. During the 1870s, two churches, a school, and a Masonic lodge (see **Masons**) were established. Businesses included a hotel, two general-merchandise stores, a drug store, a shoe and saddle maker's shop, an undertaker's establishment, and a blacksmith business owned by James Ruddle, the inventor of the Ruddle hoe. By the early 20th century, there was also a movie house, an egg hatchery, a tomato cannery, a tobacco warehouse, a coal yard, and a lumberyard. The **Great Depression** of the 1930s and **World War II** had a devastating impact on Glencoe; from the 1950s, with the decline of the railroad, the town declined also, losing most of its commercial businesses, in addition to population.

Notable residents have included Yager and Ruddle, as well as Pascal H. Duncan, a member of the Kentucky legislature in the 1870s; Franklin R. Shirley, a professor of drama, debate, and communications at Wake Forest University in Winston-Salem, N.C.; Henry Beach Jr., president of Georgetown College, Georgetown, Ky.; and Mary Frances Penick, better known as country singer **Skeeter Davis**. In 2000 Glencoe had a population of 251.

Bogardus, Carl R., Sr. *The Story of Gallatin County.* Ed. James C. Claypool. Cincinnati: John S. Swift, 2003.

Gray, Gypsy M. *History of Gallatin County, Kentucky.* Covington, Ky.: Self-published, 1968.

Perrin, William Henry, J. H. Battle, and G. C. Kniffin. *Kentucky: A History of the State.* Louisville, Ky.: F. A. Battey, 1888.

U.S. Census Bureau. "American Fact Finder. Data Set. Census 2000 Summary File 1 (SF1) 100-Percent Data. Custom Table." www.census.gov (accessed July 15, 2006).

Welcome to Gallatin County. www.gallatincountyky.com (accessed June 29, 2006).

Sabrina Alcorn Baron

GLENCOE BAPTIST CHURCH. In April 1877, **Lewis H. Salin**, a converted Jew and a Baptist preacher, began a religious meeting lasting several days in Glencoe in Gallatin Co., first in a barroom and then in a blacksmith shop. On January 11, 1878, a council was called by a company of men and women to establish an independent church at Glencoe. Messengers from the **Ten Mile Baptist Church**, the Poplar Grove Baptist Church, the Oakland Baptist Church, and the Pleasant Home Baptist Church, upon hearing the covenant and the articles of faith read, agreed unanimously to include them in the constitution of the new church. Salin was elected the Glencoe Baptist Church's first pastor.

The first church building was built in 1878, at a cost of $656. In July 1898 a new church building, 35 by 55 feet in size and costing $1,550, was dedicated on the site of the present church. In 1921 the church was remodeled at a cost of $6,306. In 1952 a concrete-block educational-recreational building was built. In June 1969 the property of Mae Duvall was purchased and the five-room house on the lot was converted into the Sunday school building for the church. In 1975 a new educational building was added at a cost of $69,860.

The Glencoe Baptist Church joined the Ten Mile Baptist Association in 1878 and has participated in the Southern Baptist Convention's Cooperative Program for many years. It has used Southern Baptist materials and programs and has supported numerous Southern Baptist mission endeavors. Glencoe Baptist Church has been listed in the top 100 churches in per capita gifts to the Kentucky Baptist Convention for several years. In fiscal year 2004, the church ranked 30th, with a per capita gift of $157.

No church meetings were held from September 1918 through January 1919, because health authorities canceled meetings in response to the outbreak of the Spanish influenza. The church was closed again in March 1919, when there was a smallpox outbreak.

In July 1936, Mr. and Mrs. J. L. Hendrix willed their home to the Glencoe Baptist Church for use as a parsonage. A new, brick parsonage was built on the site in 1963, at a cost of $12,700. Lucille Courtney was elected church clerk in 1959. The first woman to hold an elected office in the Glencoe Baptist Church, she served for 13 years. No church members served in the military in **World War I**. But in **World War II**, seven members of the church served: Raymond "Bud" Beverly, 8th Air Corps; M. E. "Dude" Boots, navy; Russell Eugene Clark, army, as a member of the invasion force at Normandy in 1944; Allen Eugene Hamilton, army (awarded a Purple Heart for wounds received in Italy); Oran "Mac" McKinney, marines, South Pacific; J. D. Poland, army; and Rev. Everett Rountree, army. While Rountree was stationed at Paris, France, he was secretary to Gen. Dwight D. Eisenhower.

Two pastors have had long tenures: Roundtree, 1966–1981, and Rev. Hardin Lowe, 1989–2005. The Glencoe Baptist Church remains a thriving part of the community.

Bogardus, Carl R., Sr. *The Story of Gallatin County.* Ed. James C. Claypool. Cincinnati: John S. Swift, 2003.

McKinney, Maureen, and Everett Roundtree. "A History of the Glencoe Baptist Church," 1978, Glencoe Baptist Church, Glencoe, Ky.

Hardin Lowe

GLENN, DUDLEY A. (b. October 2, 1847, Boone Co., Ky.; d. October 11, 1911, Latonia, Ky.). Dudley A. Glenn, a lawyer, was the son of Jerimiah "Jerry" and Louisa Yelton Glenn. His father was a farmer and livestock dealer and, at one time, was the innkeeper at the **Gaines Tavern**, Walton. He attended public school, graduated from Transylvania University in Lexington, and studied law at the Lebanon Law School in Tennessee. In 1870 Glenn was admitted to the bar; he moved to Covington in 1872.

Glenn was elected to the Kentucky legislature for one term (1877–1878), representing Covington, and was a member of the Constitutional Convention of 1890. In 1897 he was elected commonwealth attorney. He was instrumental in the formation of the town of Latonia (now part of Covington) in 1894 and served on its first town council as a trustee. Glenn was a member of several fraternal organizations.

He married Lucy Mason, the daughter of George and Mary Mason. The Mason estate became the Dinmore Park section of Latonia, and the Glenns settled there. After their first home burned, they lived at 3612 Glenn Ave. They were devout Episcopalians, and some of the organizational meetings for the establishment of St. Stephen's Episcopal Church took place in their parlor. Lucy Glenn was the organist for the small parish for many years.

In 1910 Dudley Glenn suffered a stroke at Covington City Hall and was left partially paralyzed, so he traveled to Florida to recuperate. After returning to Latonia, he died in 1911 at his home and was buried in Highland Cemetery, Fort Mitchell. His wife and all seven of their children survived him.

"Dudley A. Glenn Passes Away at Home in Latonia," *KP*, October 11, 1911, 3.

Kentucky Death Certificate No. 26252, for the year 1911.

"Miss Olive Glenn," *KP*, June 7, 1971, 4K.

Karl Lietzenmayer

GLORIA DEI LUTHERAN CHURCH. Although it can trace its origins back to 1916, Gloria Dei Lutheran Church, in Crestview Hills, was actually established in 1982 with the merger of the Zion Evangelical Lutheran Church and the Faith Evangelical Lutheran Church.

Zion Evangelical Lutheran Church (originally First English Lutheran Church) was founded in 1916 to serve the growing number of Lutherans, many of German heritage, in Covington. In 1917 the church received its first resident pastor, Rev. Henry W. Little. After worshipping in a remodeled house on Madison Ave. in Covington, in 1934 the congregation voted to move to Park Hills; they changed the church's name to Zion Evangelical Lutheran Church and broke ground for a new building at the corner of Amsterdam and Hamilton Rds. on June 9, 1937. The financial constraints of the **Great Depression** forced the church to rein in its building plans, so initially only the finished basement was completed. On February 27, 1938, the church held its first service, dedicating the completed portion of the building. The church continued to add onto its building over the next two decades and finally completed the structure in 1955. The acquisition of a nearby existing building in 1963 allowed the Zion Evangelical Lutheran Church to expand again by adding an education center and office space in Park Hills.

The other church involved in the formation of Gloria Dei Lutheran Church was Faith Evangelical Lutheran Church of Erlanger. This church began as a small group worshipping in the homes of members, with the assistance of Rev. Lorin L. Spenny, the pastor at Zion Evangelical Lutheran Church in Park Hills, and Rev. J. Paul Rimmer, the pastor at Hopeful Lutheran Church, near Florence, Ky. In 1946 the group grew large enough to need different accommodations, worshipping at several different locations. In 1947 the congregation purchased property at 3804 Dixie Highway in Erlanger and worshipped first in the existing two-story house on the property, which at that time was used both as a chapel for worship services and as the home of the church's pastor. Due to the small size of the congregation, finances were extremely limited. Though a parsonage was erected at 49 Price Ave. in Erlanger in 1953, the congregation did not begin building the main sanctuary until 1961. The old chapel was demolished and the new building was erected on the site and opened in 1962.

In the early 1980s, both churches remained small. After Faith Evangelical Lutheran Church lost its pastor, one of the pastors helping out was the new minister in Park Hills. Zion Evangelical Lutheran Church was in somewhat better circumstances, having a new full-time pastor, but its congregation remained small. Both congregations were struggling financially. As the two churches were located so close to each other and were, to a limited extent, being served by the same minister, they began to consider merging. The merger became official on October 3, 1982, and an interim church council was selected. The first service of the new Gloria Dei Lutheran Church was held in Zion Evangelical Lutheran Church's building on January 15, 1983.

Eventually it was decided that the church needed to move into a different building to provide the merged congregations a fresh start as a unified body. The Faith Evangelical Lutheran Church's building was sold to Dixie Nautilus & Fitness, the Zion Evangelical Lutheran Church's building was sold to the Faith Christian Center, and Gloria Dei purchased land in Crestview Hills, halfway between the merged churches' former locations, for a new church site. In the meantime, the new church rented a storefront in the Heritage International Shopping Center in Erlanger. With the resources of both churches now available, the congregation began to grow.

Ground was broken for the current church building on May 12, 1985, but all did not go smoothly. Halfway through construction, the contractor went bankrupt. The bonding agency soon afterward went bankrupt too. In anticipation of the move, the merged church's rental contract at the shopping center had not been renewed, so the young church was forced to relocate yet again, this time to nearby **Dixie Heights High School** in Edgewood. The congregation of Gloria Dei Lutheran Church struggled together through these difficult times and continued to grow. After a generous loan from a Lutheran church in Indiana, construction finally resumed, and the completed building was dedicated on October 26, 1986. An education wing was added early in 1989, allowing the church to move forward on a new project, a preschool. Under the leadership of the pastor, Rev. Vicki Garber, the Gloria Dei Lutheran Church launched a fund drive and broke ground for an $850,000 addition in 2008, completed in January 2009.

Carmack, Anita, church organist. Interview by Jennifer Gregory, July 25, 2006, Crestview Hills, Ky.

"Church to Offer Classes: Preschool Opens in September," *KP*, July 25, 1989, 2K.

"Gloria Dei Historical Timeline," Gloria Dei Lutheran Church, Crestview Hills, Ky.

Waltman, Henry G., ed. *History of the Indiana-Kentucky Synod of the Lutheran Church in America.* Indianapolis, Ind.: Central, 1971.

Jennifer Gregory

GOEBEL, WILLIAM (b. January 4, 1856, Sullivan Co., Pa.; d. February 3, 1900, Frankfort, Ky.). William Goebel is the most recent governor of Kentucky (1900) who was a resident of Northern Kentucky. He is also the only governor in U.S. history who died in office as a result of an assassination.

William Justus Goebel, the oldest child of German-born immigrants William (Wilhelm) and Augusta Goebel, spoke only German in his early years. His father served in the Union Army during the **Civil War** and then moved to Covington, where he held a variety of jobs and was a member of numerous organizations. Although the younger Goebel later emphasized his family's poverty, an area newspaper described the elder William Goebel, at his death in 1877, as "one of the most prominent and highly respected German citizens." Three years later, Goebel's mother died and he, in his early 20s, became the guardian of two younger siblings.

Ambitious, hard-working, highly intelligent, and strong willed, Goebel had sold newspapers and worked as an apprentice at Duhme's Jewelry Store in Cincinnati while he pursued his education. He attended Kenyon College's Grammar School at Gambier, Ohio, and in 1877 graduated from the University of Cincinnati Law School. His abilities had attracted the attention of the two most powerful political figures in Covington, and he eventually served as a law partner of **John White Stevenson**, U.S. senator and former Kentucky governor (1867–1871), and Covington native **John G. Carlisle**, Speaker of the U.S. House and secretary of the treasury. Goebel soon became a wealthy attorney, specializing in cases against corporations and railroads. He also served as a director of Covington's Citizens National Bank.

Despite his success, Goebel lived simply. He resided in boarding houses and apartments on Sixth and Seventh Streets, near his office at 11 **Boone Block** on Scott St. in Covington. He read studiously, had few friends, and apparently had almost no female attachments. He never married. Instead, Goebel focused almost solely on his work and on his new interest of politics. When the Democratic Club organized in 1880, members elected Goebel as the first secretary; within four years he sat on the local Democratic Executive Committee. Backed by powerful friends, the 31-year-old Goebel decided to run in 1887 to fill a vacant seat in the Kentucky Senate. Republicans supported the Union Labor Party candidate in the election, and that political combination almost defeated Goebel, but he won by 56 votes.

Goebel differed in several ways from typical Kentucky politicians of his era. At a time when well-to-do ex-Confederates or Confederate sympathizers dominated his Democratic Party, his nonaristocratic family had supported the Union. Moreover, his German background varied from the more typical English or Scotch-Irish origins of state leaders in Kentucky. And his approach to power was out of the ordinary. In the absence of good speaking skills or a pleasing public personality, he operated behind the scenes, making deals, working out coalitions, scorning established ways. As a result he became known as a machine politician, "Boss Bill," "the Kenton King." Such tactics also made him seem atypical. In addition, he led a younger group of voters who challenged an establishment he portrayed as venal and corporate-controlled. Goebel supported black rights and women's rights; he advocated strict controls on the powerful **Louisville and Nashville Railroad** (L&N) and its lobby; he pushed for an end to the corrupt lottery; he initiated laws aiding laborers; he advanced restrictions on convict labor; he reduced or ended road and bridge tolls. He was an unusual figure in the politics of the commonwealth of Kentucky. In something of a contradiction, Goebel used the methods of the political boss to achieve his urban progressive goals. Some people opposed both the means and the ends. Others saw him as a long-overdue reformer.

In his hometown of Covington, his stands and tactics also angered important leaders, such as **Theodore Hallam** and **Harvey Myers Jr**. Another opponent was John Sandford (also spelled Sanford), who countered Goebel on several fronts. "Boss Bill" purchased the *Covington Ledger* to present his views, and soon it referred to Sandford as "Gon_h_ea John." On April 11, 1895, the two men accidentally met in front of a bank and shots rang out. Goebel had a bullet hole in his coat, and Sandford had one in his head. Goebel's opponent soon died. A judge determined that "reasonable doubt" existed over which man had drawn his pistol first, so Goebel went free. Later a grand jury failed to indict Goebel. But now his growing list of enemies saw him not only as a political boss, a demagogue, and an upstart, but also as a murderer.

The Sandford shooting seemed to have little effect on Goebel's continuing rise to power, however. In 1889 he had won reelection to the state senate without opposition. After that, he had served on the convention that drafted the Kentucky's current constitution. In 1893 he had successfully defeated Hallam in the primary and had kept the seat by a three-to-one margin. Then in 1897—two years after the Sandford affair—Goebel overcame primary opponent John C. Droege (a bank director at Sandford's old bank) and subsequently defeated Republican Charles E. Clark in the general election by a 5,553–4,696 count. First named Kentucky Senate president pro tem in 1894, Goebel continued to hold that post through 1900. With his political base secure, Goebel now turned his eyes to the governorship.

In 1898 Goebel introduced, and the Kentucky legislature passed, a controversial bill to change the system of regulating elections. Numerous members of his own party opposed what became known as the Goebel Election Law, while some Republicans viewed it as a dangerous attempt to ensure the "Kenton Czar's" eventual election. In the midst of that unrest, the Democratic convention met at the Music Hall in Louisville in June 1899 to select a gubernatorial nominee from among P. Wat Hardin, the leader; William J. Stone, who commanded the second-largest number of delegates; and Goebel, who trailed the field going into the convention. But Stone and Goebel joined forces to get rulings unfavorable to Hardin's cause, and then Goebel outmaneuvered Stone and narrowly received the nomination on the 26th ballot. Disgruntled Kentucky Democrats formed a third party and nominated ex-governor John Young Brown (1891–1895). Thus, a divided party faced Republican nominee William S. Taylor. Observers predicted a very close race, with every vote important.

Though faced with opposition from his former law partner Carlisle and other key party leaders, Goebel continued speaking out against trusts and concentrated wealth, saying the question was "whether the Louisville and Nashville Railroad Company is the servant or the master of the people of this Commonwealth." The L&N then poured huge sums of money into opposing the nominee. Goebel responded, "I ask no quarter and I fear no foe."

Election Day passed rather quietly, but results showed that Goebel and Taylor were locked in a very close race. The election commission met and, to the surprise of almost everyone, voted 2–1 against Goebel's claims. It certified Taylor the victor with 193,714 votes to Goebel's 191,331 and Brown's 12,140. The third-party ballots had cost Goebel dearly. Three days later, Kentucky's second straight Republican governor was inaugurated.

But the contest had not ended. The legislature was the final judge of the governor's race, and the legislature had a Democratic majority. Goebel's allies filed a "Notice of Contest," arguing that illegal ballots had been used and that those votes should be voided, which would make Goebel the rightful governor. As a 10–1 Democratic joint legislative committee heard evidence, observers expected it to rule soon in Goebel's favor. A few years earlier, similar actions had voided a Tennessee governor's race, and Kentucky Republicans feared the same result. They called in armed allies from Eastern Kentucky—"the Mountain Army"—to put pressure on the legislature, and that action only added to an already volatile mix.

On January 30, 1900, as the contest continued, Senator Goebel walked to the state capitol to preside over the senate. Just a few steps from the building, he was shot. As he battled for life, the legislative committee recommended that he be named governor. Meanwhile, the Republican chief executive declared that a state of insurrection existed, adjourned the legislature to meet in the mountains, and called out a militia force that surrounded the capitol grounds. Democratic legislators termed those actions illegal, met secretly in a hotel room, adopted the committee report, and named Goebel as governor. On January 31, 1900, Goebel was sworn in, and in his only official action he ordered the Taylor troops removed and directed the legislature to reassemble in Frankfort. Some questions about the legality of the actions prompted a second swearing in the next day. At the same time, Goebel's lieutenant governor signed an order replacing the Republican adjutant general with one sympathetic to Democrats. The new appointee called out a militia force friendly to his party. Since Taylor and the Republicans refused to recognize the validity of those actions, two governors, two separate legislative assemblies, and two separate armies—facing each other across a street—vied for power. Civil war seemed possible.

Meanwhile, Goebel's strength ebbed. The rifle bullet had shattered ribs, punctured a lung, and gone through his body. Goebel died at 6:44 p.m. on February 3, 1900, at the age of 44. His officially reported last words were, "Tell my friends to be brave, fearless, and loyal to the great common people." Goebel had been governor for three days and had lived for little over 100 hours following the assassination. He was not governor when he was shot; whether he was governor when he died would now be decided by the judicial system.

State courts found in favor of Goebel. In May 1900 the U.S. Supreme Court (in contrast to its action in the 2000 presidential race decision) ruled that it was a state matter and that the decision of the majority of the legislature should stand. Taylor fled the state, since he was under indictment as an accessory before the fact. Republicans charged that the Democrats had stolen the election; Democrats countered that Republicans had killed their governor. Kentucky's already strong party feelings intensified.

In the end, jurors indicted 16 people in connection with the murder of Goebel. Five went to trial and three were convicted. According to the prosecution's case, Caleb Powers, the secretary of state, had planned the assassination, Henry Youtsey of Cold Spring, a stenographer in the auditor's office, had handed the gun to the assassin and pointed out Goebel, and Jim Howard, a Clay Co. feudist, had pulled the trigger. However, packed juries, partisan judges, and perjured testimony leave the scenario somewhat open to question. Of those known to have been involved, the unstable Youtsey seems a more likely candidate as the assassin. Yet the assassin could also be someone who remains virtually unknown to history. In the end, the Republican-dominated high court in the state invalidated several of the convictions. Seven trials occurred over seven years, and eventually all three convicted men received pardons.

After his death, Goebel lay in state at Odd Fellows Hall (**Independent Order of Odd Fellows**) at Fifth St. and Madison Ave. in Covington and then was buried in Frankfort Cemetery. A statue was later erected over his grave and another was placed in front of the new capitol. A half century later, the statue was moved from the new capitol to the Old Capitol yard, near the scene of the shooting. That monument, which portrays a serene Goebel, contrasts with the controversial nature of his life. To his supporters, he was a martyr to the cause of reform. To his enemies, he stood as a boss who sought power by any means. Whatever the case, Goebel's death and the trials that followed cast a long, dark shadow over Kentucky life.

Hughes, R. E., E. W. Schaefer, and E. L. Williams. *That Kentucky Campaign.* Cincinnati: Robert Clarke, 1900.

Klotter, James C. *William Goebel: The Politics of Wrath.* Lexington: Univ. of Kentucky Press, 1977.

James C. Klotter

GOETTA. The word *goetta,* for a German dish that came with immigrants to Northern Kentucky, is derived from the Low German *Götta,* or High German *Grütze,* which is related to the English word *groats.* The Low German *Göttwurst* (*Grützwurst* in High German) refers to a sausage consisting of pork, beef, oatmeal (pinhead or steel cut), and spices. The recipe and the term were brought by German immigrants from northwestern Germany, especially Hanover, Oldenburg, and Westphalia, to Northern Kentucky and to nearby German American communities in the Ohio-Kentucky-Indiana region. The term *goetta* is a direct German loan into American English as spoken in the area. Moreover, it reflects a specific regional origin in northwestern Germany and the process of chain migration to the Ohio River Valley.

Variations of goetta are produced in other regions of Germany but are known by other terms, especially by the High German *Grützwurst.* An example of *Grützwurst* in America is Pennsylvania German scrapple, which contains similar ingredients but uses cornmeal rather than oatmeal. Goetta is usually made into loaves, but it is also available in sausage links. Some cooks prepare goetta by breaking it up and frying it as ground meat. Family recipes and preparation reflect local preference and tradition. Originally, goetta, like scrapple, was prepared as a loose porridge that was scooped up with bread from a bowl, a practice consistent with goetta's probable medieval origin as a farmhouse food item. By the 19th century, however, goetta in northwestern Germany had a firmer, loaf-like texture, and that preparation method was brought to the Northern Kentucky area.

Traditionally eaten as a breakfast food, goetta is now served at all mealtimes and also as a snack food. The recent innovations such as goetta links and goetta pizza demonstrate goetta's popularity in the region. Goetta is also featured at local restaurants, church events, and German-American functions. And Goettafest is now celebrated during the summer in Covington and Newport.

A basic dietary item in the region, goetta serves as a cultural marker revealing the influence of German immigration. It is produced by several companies and various regional meat markets, the main company today being Glier's Meats of Covington. Glier's produces more than 1 million pounds annually at its Goetta Place address, the largest goetta plant in the United States. Others include Finke's Market in Fort Wright, which makes 50,000 pounds each year, both traditional and hot and spicy flavors, and the Hoffman Sausage Company in Cincinnati. At one time most of the local butcher shops in the region made their own goetta for retail sale. When Finke's operated its 824 Main St. location in Covington, it sold goetta to the nearby Irish, calling it "Irish mush." The family has been making and selling the product ever since George Finke opened his shop in 1876.

Here is a typical recipe for goetta:

8 cups water

2 teaspoons salt

1 pinch pepper

2½ cups oatmeal (pinhead or steel cut). Dorsel's Pinhead Oatmeal is preferred

1 pound ground pork and 1 pound ground beef

1 large onion, sliced (optional)

1 to 4 bay leaves (optional)

(2 teaspoons savory may be used instead of the onion and bay leaves)

Boil the water in a large pot with a lid; add the salt, pepper, and oatmeal. Cover and cook for two hours, stirring the mixture often.

Add the meat, onion, and bay leaves (or savory), and mix well. Cook for another hour with continual stirring. Remove the bay leaf (if used) and pour the mixture into bread pans. Refrigerate overnight.

To serve, goetta can be sliced and fried until it is crispy, or just heated; or it can be crumbled and fried. It may be used as a breakfast food with eggs, pancakes, and so forth or served on bread or rolls to make a sandwich. Anyone who does not want to prepare goetta from scratch can readily find it in regional meat markets and grocery stores or at Findlay Market in Cincinnati's Over-the-Rhine neighborhood.

"Gaga over Goetta—Business Produces about a Million Pounds Annually," *KP,* February 22, 2003, 6K.

Oehler, Martha Finke. "Goetta Making in Covington." Unpublished paper, goetta vertical file, Kenton Co. Public Library, Covington, Ky.

Paeth, Greg. "Gotta Get It to Get a Goetta," *KP,* November 15, 1992, 3K.

"Talk about Goetta, You 'Getta' Finke," *KP,* February 25, 1957, 1.

Tolzmann, Don Heinrich. *German Heritage Guide to the Greater Cincinnati Area.* Milford, Ohio: Little Miami, 2003.

Don Heinrich Tolzmann

GOFORTH, WILLIAM (b. December 25, 1767, New York City; d. May 12, 1817, Cincinnati, Ohio). Physician William Goforth was the son of William Goforth and Catherine Meeks. He studied medicine under Dr. Charles McKnight and the surgeon-anatomist Dr. Joseph Young. Like numerous other medical students and physicians, he left New York City in 1788 amid turmoil and riots fueled by controversy over the use of human cadavers in the study of anatomy. Goforth's westward travels led him first to Maysville and then to Washington, Ky., where he settled in 1788 and practiced medicine for more than a decade. In 1799 he moved to Ohio, eventually settling in Cincinnati, and again established a large medical practice. He was one of the earliest physicians to introduce vaccination to residents of the Greater Cincinnati area.

During his initial journey to Kentucky, Goforth became acquainted with the Drake family and many years later honored a request by Isaac Drake that he someday teach medicine to Drake's then three-year-old son Daniel. Goforth is today highly recognized for this role as preceptor to his apprentice Dr. **Daniel Drake**, another legendary early Cincinnati physician.

Possessing a wide spectrum of interests in the natural sciences, Goforth was also intrigued with paleontology. He was instrumental in leading an 1803 archaeological dig for mastodon and mammoth fossils at **Big Bone Lick** in Boone Co., an event visited that year by Meriwether Lewis of the Lewis and Clark Expedition (1803–1806).

Goforth relocated to Louisiana in 1807. There he became involved in political affairs and served as surgeon to a regiment of the Louisiana militia. He returned to Cincinnati in 1816 and died of hepatitis on May 12, 1817. He was buried at Columbia Grounds in Cincinnati, but his remains were moved to Spring Grove Cemetery in Cincinnati in 1854.

Johnson, Allen, and Dumas Malone. *Dictionary of American Biography.* Vol. 4. New York: Charles Scribner's, 1959.

Juettner, Otto. *Daniel Drake and His Followers: Historical and Biographical Sketches.* Cincinnati: Harvey, 1909.

The National Cyclopedia of American Biography. Vol. 23. New York: James T. White, 1933.

Obituary. *Liberty Hall and Cincinnati Gazette,* June 2, 1817, 2.

Judy L. Neff

GOLDBERG, MAX H. (b. April 5, 1913, Falmouth, Ky.; d. December 18, 2007, Morehead, Ky.).

Max Goldberg, 1978.

Few people have lived a more exciting and fulfilling life than Max Goldberg, the former mayor of Falmouth. He was a racecar driver and a **World War II** bomber pilot and owned businesses including a motel, a restaurant, and several movie theaters. Goldberg attended the local public school and graduated from Falmouth High School. His parents, Solomon (Sol) and Jennie Yanfaki Goldberg, emigrated from Russia around 1900 and operated a clothing store in Falmouth. Max was trained extensively in electricity, aeronautics, and engine mechanics. During the 1920s and 1930s, he began building and racing automobiles at the Falmouth Fairgrounds. As his racing career progressed, he competed at tracks throughout the Northern Kentucky region and as far north as Dayton, Ohio. In the late 1930s, Max took a job with the Wright Aeronautical Corporation in Dayton, where he repaired airplane engines. His employer sent him to England to work as an airplane mechanic.

Max was in England at the outbreak of World War II and while there joined the British Royal Air Force (RAF). He trained to become a pilot of multi-engine propeller-driven aircraft. Shortly after the United States entered the war in 1941, Max left the RAF and became a pilot with the U.S. Army Air Corps. During the war he flew 43 bombing missions over Germany and France. Numerous times his planes were hit by enemy gunfire, so that he had to return them to base, often with only one or two of their four engines running. Twice a plane he was piloting was shot down; one time he parachuted to safety, and the other time he was severely injured in the crash. At war's end, Max went to Knoxville, Tenn., where he operated several drive-in theaters. He later moved to Mason Co., Ky., where he bought the well-known **Washington Opera House**. There, his customers were entertained with live stage performances and motion pictures.

In the 1950s he returned to Falmouth and bought the Past-Time Movie Theatre, which he operated for many years. He became a friend of broadcasting pioneer **L. B. Wilson**, who owned movie theaters and radio stations in Northern Kentucky and Cincinnati. Max entered politics in 1965, was elected mayor of Falmouth as a Democrat, and held that office for 33 years. He was very proud of the way he directed city finances: he never raised real estate tax rates, never installed parking meters, had no city payroll tax, and never required residents to buy automobile stickers. He attempted to pay cash for all public projects, rather than have the city incur debt. His one regret was that he was not able to persuade the Commonwealth of Kentucky to build a Licking River dam at Falmouth, which he felt would help alleviate flood damage and provide recreational jobs. He loved Falmouth and even in his nineties could regularly be seen around town, shaking hands with fellow citizens, chatting with old friends. Max acquired a reputation of romancing ladies from around the world, but he never married. Goldberg died in 2007 and was buried in Riverside Cemetery in Falmouth.

"Falmouth Mayor Makes Few Waves in 30 Years," *KP*, February 24, 1997, B1B.

"Falmouth Says Goodbye to Mayor Max," *KP*, December 11, 1989, 1K–2K.

Goldberg, Max. Interview by Jack Wessling, August 12, 2005, Falmouth, Ky.

Jack Wessling

GOLD VALLEY. Gold Valley, in western Grant Co. not far from the Owen Co. border, was so named because it was mistakenly thought that gold had been discovered there. The first record of community action at Gold Valley was a gift of one-fourth acre of land by Richard Osbourne and his wife in 1856 on which to construct a school and a church meetinghouse. Local schools are now long gone. The church was reorganized as the **Concord Baptist Church** in a new building in 1884. The current building was built in 1922. Concord Baptist Church remains at the center of community life in Gold Valley.

Mount Pisgah United Methodist Church, organized in the late 1800s, is also on Gold Valley Rd. This church's first building burned in 1910. The second building burned in 1962 and was replaced by the current structure. One of the most scenic views in Grant Co. can be seen from the front yard of the Methodist church. It sits 200 feet above one of the larger of the Eagle Creek horseshoe bends and its extensive fertile valley.

Conrad, John B., ed. *History of Grant County*. Williamstown, Ky.: Grant Co. Historical Society, 1992

John B. Conrad

GOLF. Golf began to make its mark as a popular sport in Northern Kentucky during the 1920s as golf courses were established at **Fort Mitchell Country Club** in Fort Mitchell, **Summit Hills Golf and Country Club** in Crestview Hills, Devou Golf Club in Park Hills, and **Twin Oaks Golf Course** in Latonia. In 1940 these four entities formed the Northern Kentucky Golf Association (NKGA) to promote amateur golf and conduct local tournaments. The NKGA, now with golf courses and country clubs from several Northern Kentucky counties listed as members, contributes to the Northern Kentucky Invitational Golf Tournament Scholarship Fund to support the men's and women's intercollegiate golf teams at **Northern Kentucky University** in Highland Heights. The golf association now has established a foundation to extend its contributions to other worthy golf endeavors. The NKGA conducts seven amateur tournaments each summer, with entrants numbering about 1,000. The organization estimates that each year more than 700,000 golfers play rounds on member courses. The NKGA established a Hall of Fame in 2001 to honor Northern Kentucky golfing pioneers, saluting golfers who have "complied with the highest standards of in tegrity, sportsmanship and good conduct in connection with golf."

For more than 60 years, thousands of other young men and women have developed their interest and honed their golf skills by competing in the NKGA Amateur and Junior Amateur tournaments and have gone on to compete successfully in state and national tournaments. In recent years, two Northern Kentuckians have played on the PGA Tour: **Ralph Landrum** and **Steve Flesch**.

Members of NKGA Hall of Fame

William Deupree Jr., a former Northern Kentucky (1952) and Kentucky state amateur (1950) champion and nine-time Fort Mitchell Club Champion who also won two Cincinnati Metropolitan amateur titles (1954, 1959).

Herb Fitzer, who won the Kentucky State High School Championship at Summit Hills in 1937 and has been head professional at both A. J. Jolly Golf Course in Campbell Co. and the Fort Mitchell Country Club.

Robert Gray, a three-time Northern Kentucky Champion (1965, 1966, 1974), Senior Amateur Champion (1982), and Northern Kentucky Player of the Year (1982).

Angie Grubbs, who won the Women's Northern Kentucky Amateur Championship five times between 1959 and 1970.

Gary Herfel, a past champion of the Northern Kentucky Tournament (1983), a two-time winner of the Mid-Amateur (1986, 1999), a four-time winner of the Senior Amateur (1996, 1997, 1999, and 2002), and a Carran Memorial winner (1999). Herfel also has won the Northern Kentucky Invitational Tournaments seven times, has been named Player of the Year three times, and was chosen Senior Player of the Year six times, most recently in 2004, when he won both the Kentucky State Senior Amateur and Open titles. He is the only player to have won all five of the men's NKGA championships in a span of 19 years. Herfel founded the Northern Kentucky Invitational, was president of the NKGA from 1998 to 2003, and has been club champion at Highland Country Club 10 times.

Bud Humphreys, a first-year inductee, who won the Northern Kentucky Amateur Championship in

1960 and 1961, who is a nine-time Fort Mitchell Club Champion, and who won the Kentucky State Senior Amateur in 1989.

Dennis Hurley, who was a member of **Covington Catholic High School**'s State Championship Golf Team in 1969 and winner of the Kentucky Junior Championship in 1971.

Margaret Jones, a part of the first group of inductees, who is a two-time winner of the Northern Kentucky Women's Championship, won the Kentucky State Women's Championship four times between 1962 and 1971, and was a three-time champion of the Cincinnati Metropolitan Women's Tournament.

Spencer Kerkow, who was inducted into the Hall of Fame in 2004, won the Northern Kentucky Amateur and the Central Kentucky Amateur Championships, and was a five-time club champion at Fort Mitchell Country Club before his death at age 26. The Amateur Championship was played in his honor and referred to as "The Kerkow" for a number of years.

Robert Leach, a founding honoree, who won the Northern Kentucky Senior Amateur in 1995 and was the first recipient of the NKGA Distinguished Service Award for his work in promoting local golf. He and Bob Schultz won the two-man Senior Championship in 2003 and 2004.

Harry McAttee, another of the first-year inductees, who was head professional at the Highland Country Club for 36 years, was active in fundraising in the community, and loved to teach golf to old and young alike. The Harry McAttee Memorial Tournament is played each year to benefit the **St. Luke Hospital** Foundation.

John Meyers, a first-year inductee and an original founder of the NKGA, who won the Northern Kentucky Amateur five times between 1946 and 1959, captured a Cincinnati Metropolitan title in 1951, and was a 13-time club champion at Summit Hills.

Robert Schultz, a first-year inductee, who holds four Northern Kentucky Amateur Championships (1956, 1964, 1967, and 1978) and five Carran Memorial Titles, was Senior Amateur in 2001 and 2003, was named Senior Player of the Year in those years, won the Cincinnati Legends of Golf title three times, is a seven-time Summit Hills Country Club titleholder, and was the NKGA president from 2004 to 2006. A member of the **Thomas More College** Hall of Fame, he formerly coached the golf team there.

Ralph "Pete" Stuntebeck, a first-year inductee, who began his golfing life as a caddie at Fort Mitchell Country Club; was the youngest golf professional in the United States, as club pro at Fort Mitchell at the age of 18; regained amateur status in 1937 and won numerous amateur titles including three Northern Kentucky titles and one Cincinnati Metropolitan; turned professional again in 1951 and was the head professional at Twin Oaks Golf Course for 26 years; and won both the Greater Cincinnati Stroke Play and Kentucky State Senior Open championships in 1955.

"Deupree Keeps on Winning," *CP*, May 15, 1998, 1B.

Northern Kentucky Golf Association. www.nkga.com (accessed on December 27, 2006).

Dennis W. Van Houten

GOOCH, DANIEL L. (b. October 28, 1853, Calhoun, Ky.; d. April 12, 1913, Covington, Ky.). Businessman and politician Daniel Linn Gooch (known as Linn) was born near Owensboro, where he was educated in a private school. At age 17 he entered the business world, by starting a company for the manufacture of medical supplies. The business was very successful, and after several years, Linn moved to Covington, hoping to find an even larger market for his products. There he started the Cincinnati Drug and Chemical Company. Linn married Virginia Stout, and the couple had two daughters. The Gooch family lived at 520 Greenup St. As his wealth grew, Linn purchased a summer home, which he called Gooch Island, on the St. Clair River in the Virginia mountains. He entered politics in 1900 and was elected to the U.S. House of Representatives, as a Democrat, serving from March 4, 1901 through March 3, 1905. Linn lived a sedate existence during his retirement years, in the Arthur Apartments, at 545 Greenup St. In 1907 Gooch donated a 127-volume set of books, *The War of the Rebellion*, to the Covington Library (see **Kenton Co. Public Library**). He died in his Covington apartment at age 59 and was buried in the Woodlawn Cemetery in Dayton, Ohio.

Biographical Directory of the United States Congress. "Gooch, Daniel Linn." www.bioguide.congress.gov (accessed November 22, 2005).

"Linn Gooch Dies at Home in Covington," *KP*, April 14, 1913, 2.

GOOD SHEPHERD LUTHERAN CHURCH. Established in 1995 as a grassroots church with a handful of families, Good Shepherd Lutheran Church (a member of the Lutheran Church Missouri Synod) now has about 350 members. The congregation dedicated a new building at 9066 Gunpowder Rd. in Florence, Ky., in 1998, and a Family Life and Education Center was scheduled for completion in spring 2008.

"Good Shepherd Lutheran Bible School to Start," *KE*, July 20, 2006, 4C.

Good Shepherd Lutheran Church. www.gslutheran.org/index.htm (accessed October 9, 2006).

"Good Shepherd to Dedicate Sanctuary," *KP*, November 7, 1998, 6K.

Melinda G. Motley

GOODWILL INDUSTRIES. Since 1916 Ohio Valley Goodwill Industries, which includes several Northern Kentucky counties in its service area, has been providing services for individuals with disabilities and other barriers to employment. The organization moved to its present facility in the village of Woodlawn, Ohio, in 1957 and in 2004 celebrated a grand reopening that marked a complete renovation of its 13-acre campus at 10600 Springfield Pk. Over the years, many new programs and services have been added.

The Goodwill story is a simple but important one. Working in partnership with the community, Goodwill sells donated items in retail stores, and the funds received support programs and services, such as the employment and training programs. At the core of Goodwill's mission is its commitment to assist people with disabilities and provide services that encourage self-sufficiency.

Goodwill's rehabilitation employment and training division offers a multitude of programs and services for individuals with disabilities and other barriers to employment. Services for individuals include work evaluation, occupational skills training, work adjustment training, placement services, job coaching support, and assistive technology. In 2005 Ohio Valley Goodwill provided service to 2,609 individuals who were searching for vocational independence; 735 men and women were placed into competitive community employment.

Goodwill's work evaluation program assesses the individual's need for additional rehabilitation services such as skills training, placement assistance, job coaching, and assistive technology services. To help people develop needed vocational skills, Goodwill offers occupational skills training in four areas: office procedures and computer technology, janitorial services, food service, and grounds keeping and light janitorial.

The job placement department provides services in the areas of job development, vocational exploration, market surveys, job-seeking skills training, and job retention. After individuals obtain employment, the job coaching department provides support including on-site job training, off-site services, training in appropriate work behavior, self-advocacy skill training, travel training, personal adjustment, and long-term follow-up services.

Goodwill's work adjustment training program offers an individualized program that reflects individual goals, wishes, and desires. The program serves individuals sponsored by county boards of mental retardation and developmental disabilities. In addition, Goodwill provides service for transition students from various local school districts who are making the move from school to work.

In 2004 Goodwill introduced its newest program option, CARE (the Center for Advocacy, Recreation and Education). The CARE is a service that diversifies Goodwill's program offerings to individuals with developmental disabilities, particularly those with personal care support needs.

Goodwill also offers assistive-technology support for individuals either at home or in a work setting. The department helps to provide services in a variety of areas including ergonomics, computer access, home accessibility, job-site accessibility, job accommodations, and seating and wheeled mobility.

In Kenton Co., Goodwill has operated stores in Covington since at least the 1950s, in two locations along Pike St. and, for the years 1990–2003, at 25 W. Seventh St. The organization developed and owns the Goodwill Village Apartments for the handicapped along Banklick St. in Covington and has a store along Taylor Mill Rd. in Independence. In Boone Co., Goodwill has a facility along Tanner's Ln. In Campbell Co., after being located for years at Fifth and York Sts. in Newport, the organization now has a store along Donnermeyer Dr. in Bellevue. In Mason Co., Goodwill operates a store at 505 Market Place Drive in Maysville.

"Covington to Have New Goodwill Shops," *KTS*, April 1, 1955, 1A.

"Goodwill Expands," *KTS*, July 20, 1956, 4A.

"Goodwill Relocating Its Covington Store," *KE*, March 28, 2003, B2.

"Goodwill Strengthening N. Kentucky Presence: Tanners Lane Store 12,000 Square Feet," *KP*, March 27, 1993, 11K.

"Invalid Needs 'Job Therapy,'" *KP*, November 19, 1969, 1K.

Ohio Valley Goodwill Industries. www.cincinnatigoodwill.org (accessed October 14, 2006).

"Record Turnout Greet Goodwill Store's Opening in New Location," vertical file, Kentucky Gateway Museum, Maysville, Ky.

George Palmer

GOURMET STRIP. This was the name given to a string of restaurants, nightclubs, and taverns stretching along the **Dixie Highway** (U.S. 25/42), from Covington to Florence, Ky. The Gourmet Strip was a popular destination for Cincinnatians, Northern Kentuckians, and travelers, particularly from the 1930s through the 1970s. Dining varied from fine cuisine to tavern food to the new fast-food **drive-ins** of the 1940s and 1950s. A number of entertainment spots featured illegal **gambling**, such as bookmaking, slot machines, and gaming tables. The end of gambling in Kenton Co. in the 1950s, the opening of I-75 in 1963—diverting interstate travelers—and various fires brought an end to the Gourmet Strip, and only a few buildings remain. Some of the prominent restaurants included these, listed by city.

Park Hills

Hahn Hotel, 1424 Dixie Hwy., a 19th-century inn and tavern where drovers of livestock stopped (see **Meatpacking**).

Marshall's, 1450 Dixie Hwy., which featured a dining room, a cocktail lounge, and party rooms.

Colonial Bake Shop, 1470 Dixie Hwy., open 24 hours daily, offering coffee and baked goods to travelers.

Lamplighters Club of Nick Behle, 1491 Dixie Hwy., a late-night gathering spot principally for musicians and workers from the restaurants and clubs along the strip.

White Horse Tavern, 1501 Dixie Hwy., opened in 1936 and operated by Ben S. Castleman; destroyed by fire on January 26, 1972. Castleman reopened the restaurant across the street in the old Golden Goose, closing it in September 1972. In 1977 he and other investors opened a new White Horse at 3041 Dixie Hwy. in Edgewood, but it closed in 1978.

Gus Sanzere's Golden Goose, 1504 Dixie Hwy., originally known for its Italian food and now the home of the Szechuan Gardens.

Chappie's Tavern, 1560 Dixie Hwy., later renamed Tom and Jerry's and now demolished.

Town and Country Restaurant, 1622 Dixie Hwy., opened in 1936 as the Blue Star Tavern, operated by the Wooten family; now the home of Chuck McHale's The Gardens of Park Hills.

Old Mill Grill, on the northeast corner of Dixie Hwy. and St. James Ave., built for the tourist trade about 1930 or before, with distinctive roadside architecture featuring an operating windmill. Gasoline pumps stood outside, and there was also a restaurant offering chicken and steak dinners.

Fort Wright (including old Lookout Heights)

Jerry's Restaurant, 1663 Dixie Hwy., featuring J-boy hamburgers. It was one of the early drive-in restaurants along the strip. Later it became Clyde's Steak House, and then Cassidy's; the building was demolished in 2006.

Lookout House, 1721 Dixie Hwy., a posh nightclub featuring Hollywood entertainers that was destroyed by fire on August 14, 1973.

Oelsner's Colonial Tavern, 1730 Dixie Hwy., opened in March 1937 and operated by three brothers, Russell, Richard, and Charles Oelsner. It was a favorite gathering place for Cincinnati Reds baseball players during the 1930s and 1940s. The tavern was demolished and a Skyline Chili stands on the site.

Oelsner's Colonial Tavern, Lookout Heights.

Lookout House Supper Club.

Kanebrake Restaurant, 1830 Dixie Hwy., later the Hillcrest Tavern, featuring chicken dinners. The restaurant was demolished and a dry cleaner now occupies the site.

Schilling's Drive-In Restaurant, 1939 Dixie Hwy., demolished and replaced in 1962 by the Hofbrau Haus Restaurant, now called Shimmer's Tavern.

Fort Mitchell

Hearthstone, 2053 Dixie Hwy., currently Indigo's.

Robertson's, 2216 Dixie Hwy., founded by Cliff Robertson in 1959 and closed in 1972.

Frisch's Restaurant, 2498 Dixie Hwy., featuring Big Boy hamburgers, one of the early drive-in restaurants along the strip.

Greyhound Tavern, 2500 Dixie Hwy., opened as the Dixie Tea Room in 1921.

Stevie's Clubhouse, 2501 Dixie Hwy., opened by Joe Stevie in 1901 and later renamed Zimmer's Clubhouse and then Kentucky Tavern. It was demolished in 1957 for a **Remke Market**.

Saddle Club, 2587 Dixie Hwy.

Lakeside Park

Barleycorn's Five Mile House, 2542 Dixie Hwy., an eatery that dated from the 19th century and was later renamed Retschulte's. The current name is Barleycorn's Five Mile House.

Erlanger

McDonald's, 3096 Dixie Hwy., the first of this chain in Northern Kentucky.

Roundup Club, 3100 Dixie Hwy., a nightclub with an eclectic Wild West exterior facade that opened in 1950, closed in 1982, and was demolished.

Cabana, 3126 Dixie Hwy., destroyed by fire on July 13, 1971. The restaurant was rebuilt, operated for a time, and is now the home of shops and offices.

Colonial Cottage, 3146 Dixie Hwy., now at 3140, opened in 1933.

Tom Cody's Farm, 3227 Dixie Hwy., now **Forest Lawn Cemetery**.

Seven Mile House, 3236 Dixie Hwy., just north of the **Cincinnati Southern Railroad** underpass on the west side of the road, later renamed the Rightway Café.

Dixie Club Café, 3424 Dixie Hwy.

Arcaro's (see **Eddie Arcaro**), 3510 Dixie Hwy., previously **Joe Anderson**'s Restaurant.

Dixie Chili, 3702 Dixie Hwy.

Frisch's, 4016 Dixie Hwy.

Elsmere

Swan, 4311 Dixie Hwy., now the home of Swan Florist.

Kenton Terrace, music and dancing, just south of the Swan.

Doc's Place, on Dixie between Park and Eastern Aves.

Florence

Caintuckee Grill, a short-order eatery located on the northeast corner where U.S. 25 and U.S. 42 divide, opened about 1949 by the Cain family. Hilda Ramler purchased the business in 1954, and it closed in 1984.

"Deals Closed for Business Places Here: Roadhouse Building to Be Erected Near Covington, Contractors Reveal," *KP*, July 24, 1936, 5.

"Fire Rips through Restaurant," *CE* (Ky. ed.), July 14, 1971, 13.

Hicks, Jack. "Boone County Movers and Shakers Losing an Old Haunt," *KE*, June 19, 1984, B1.

——. "Breakfast Lovers Losing Landmark on Dixie Hwy." *CE* (Ky. ed.), September 29, 1972, A1.

"History of Famous Old Northern Kentucky Resorts Recalled as Good Beer Comes Back," *KP*, April 6, 1933, 3.

"'Hofbrau Haus' Opened at Motel," *KP*, July 24, 1962, 1K.

Jacobs, Gabriella. "Nightspot Heads for Last Roundup," *KP*, June 25, 1982, 1K.

Johnson, Omer. "Dixie 'Strip' Fades Away into History," *KP*, June 17, 1982, 4K.

"Marshall's Formal Opening Announced," *KP*, February 19, 1955, 1.

"Prosecutor Leads Own Raids of Cabana, Arcaro's, and the Swan," *CE* (Ky. ed.), October 17, 1949, 1.

Reis, Jim. "Dixie 'Gourmet Strip' Outshone Cincinnati with Food, Gambling," *KP*, January 10, 1983, 4K.

"Six Beautiful Dixie Cities Visited by Kentucky Times-Star," *KTS*, June 25, 1957, 5A.

Paul A. Tenkotte

GRACE UNITED CHURCH OF CHRIST. German Protestants living in the **West Side** of Covington established the Grace Evangelical Reformed Church in 1862. On April 18, 1862, 18 individuals met at the home of Heinrich Wilhelm Schleutker at the corner of Pike and Craig Sts. in Covington to organize the congregation. Soon afterward, a lot was purchased in town at the corner of Lockwood and Willard Sts. as a site for the new church. While the church was under construction, the congregation met in a neighboring schoolhouse or in the local fire station. The cornerstone of the new Gothic Revival church was set into place on June 13, 1862, and the structure was dedicated formally on April 6 of the following year. The two-story building included classrooms and meeting space on the first floor and a large worship space on the second floor. Many of the members of the congregation were recent immigrants from the German state of Prussia. The members of Grace Church strongly desired to maintain their German language and traditions, so worship was conducted in German for many years. The congregation established a school, restricted to children of German parents, at the same time as the founding of the church. Tuition of 25 cents per month was charged.

As the German population of Covington increased, so did the membership of Grace Church; by 1868 it had reached 300. Among the early leaders of the congregation was John Schleutker, a German baker renowned locally for his pumpernickel bread. His association with the church was so strong that many Covingtonians referred to the congregation as "the pumpernickel church." Schleutker's son John served as the church organist for more than 50 years.

During the last decades of the 19th century, the congregation continued to expand. In 1889 a new three-story parsonage was erected as an addition to the rear of the church building. In 1894 a daughter congregation, named the Immanuel German Reformed Church, was established in the nearby city of Bromley. A frame church was constructed for the new congregation at the corner of Boone and Harris Sts. in Bromley.

A large-scale renovation of this church building occurred in 1896. At that time, a new Gothic Revival facade was added. The new facade included two entranceways, a large central Gothic window, and a bell tower . At the same time, new art-glass windows were installed in the sanctuary.

The use of the German language in worship slowly declined in the **World War I** period as fewer immigrants settled in Covington. In 1904 Sunday school teachers were given permission to use English classroom materials. At about the same time, the church board agreed to have brief English-language services between the Sunday school classes and the main German Sunday service. In 1913 the congregation voted 80-2 to conduct English and German services on alternate Sundays. The use of the German language was ended entirely when the United States became involved in World War I, and the name of the congregation was officially changed to the Grace Reformed Church.

The Grace Reformed Church remained stable in size during the interwar years. Membership stood at about 300 during this period. During the 1940s and 1950s, however, membership dropped. Many residents of Covington were leaving the city for the suburbs, and as a result, Covington's West End was changing. Once home to thousands of immigrants and their children, the West End was losing population. Most of the newcomers, furthermore, were arrivals from the **Appalachian** region of Kentucky, people whose heritage was British. Despite these struggles, the Grace Reformed Church continued to carry out its mission. In 1957 the congregation officially became a member of the United Church of Christ.

During the 1960s, the church board seriously considered leaving Covington for the suburbs. A number of other Protestant congregations had already made such a move. The congregation voted to remain in the city, however. By 1975 membership had decreased to 103. Seven years later, only 73 active members were on the parish rolls. In 1995, when only 20 active members, many of them elderly, were attending services, the decision was made to close the church. The last services were held on October 29, 1995, and the church building was eventually sold to another denomination. The Grace United Church of Christ, under names changing with the times, had continued for more than 130 years.

Hicks, Jack. "Members Bid Church Goodbye," *KP*, October 30, 1995, 1K.

Seventy-Fifth Anniversary of Grace Reformed Church, Covington, Kentucky, 1862–1937. Covington, Ky.: Grace Reformed Church, 1937.

"Still a Good Neighbor," *KP*, October 28, 1995, 9K.

Vercouteren, Karl J. *The German Churches of Covington.* Covington, Ky.: Self-published, 1977.

David E. Schroeder

GRACE UNITED METHODIST CHURCH. In the mid-1850s, a group of worshippers who had relocated to Northern Kentucky from Cincinnati began meeting as "The Society" in the Bagby home at Eighth and Monmouth Sts. in Newport, led by a missionary named Conrey. Worship meetings continued into spring 1858, when the society united with a Bellevue group and formed a circuit. The Newport link held services in Newport's German Methodist Church, located along Seventh St., until 1861. As membership grew, a larger facility became necessary, and property in Newport on Eighth St. was purchased for $1,250; in 1861 a frame building was erected. After the **Civil War** and growing financial hardships forced the society to sell the church property, the group met on the second floor of Hayman's Hall at Fifth and Monmouth Sts.

In 1863 the area's Methodist circuit was divided and Newport became an independent charge. In May 1866 the Grace Methodist Church paid $4,290 for a lot in Newport along Jefferson St. (now Sixth St.) between Monmouth and Saratoga Sts. Henry Tinsley drew construction plans for a church building, F. A. Stine provided the lumber for the building, J. K Stone supervised the carpentry, and William McGill ground the ornamental figures in the window glass. The finished structure was dedicated as the Grace Methodist Episcopal Church on Sunday, December 2, 1866. Newspaper accounts reported that the Newport church was "one of the most beautiful structures in the city." The building was later enhanced by the addition of a pipe organ; 10 stained-glass windows, many of them donated by the Root family of Newport; and chimes.

From 1880 to 1882, a Rev. Watson served the congregation; under his direction the missionary outreach programs grew and the Women's Foreign Missionary Society began. In 1903 the Women's Home Missionary Society was initiated. In the early 1900s, a parishioner died and willed to the church his home at 18 W. Eighth St. in Newport. That house was then used as a parsonage. On July 7, 1915, a tornado destroyed the church's steeple, which was not replaced. The church celebrated its Golden Jubilee on May 26, 1918.

From 1922 to 1936, the pastor was Rev. W. F. Gregory, who was an active participant in a group working within Campbell Co. to clean up vice activities. In that connection, he testified before the grand jury with other Newport ministers. In 1924 Gregory's home was damaged when an explosion of a carbide and potash mixture was set off by his basement door. A note was left warning him to quit the grand jury investigations.

In 1941 the congregation had 314 members. After **World War II**, Newport's citizens began moving to the suburbs, and as a result, Grace Methodist Church's list of inactive members became the largest in the region's Methodist district. The church celebrated its 90th anniversary in November 1956, as membership continued declining.

In 1975 Rev. Don Drewry reported that the church was set to celebrate its celebrate its 110th birthday. The congregation was presented with a Kentucky Landmark certificate for its historic building, and the church, located in Newport's Monmouth St. Historical District, is listed on the survey of historic sites in the state. In June 2001 the Grace United Methodist Church merged with the Southgate Methodist Church and the Calvary Tower United Methodist in Bellevue to form New Hope United Methodist Church in Southgate. The old Grace United Methodist Church building is currently vacant and for sale.

"Blast Damages Pastor's Home," *KP*, June 18, 1924, 1.
"Dedication," *CE*, November 2, 1866, 2.
"Homecoming Dinner Set to Celebrate 90th Anniversary," *KTS*, November 23, 1956, 9A.
"Memorial Windows," *KP*, May 16, 1905, 5.
Reis, Jim. "Flames Char the Past," *KP*, May 20, 1996, 4K.
"The Reopening of Grace Church," *KP*, May 10, 1906, 5.
Reynolds, Howard. *The History of Grace Methodist Church Newport, Kentucky*. Newport, Ky.: Grace Methodist Church, 1966.
Tortora, Andrea. "Church Tries to Save Itself," *CE*, April 22, 1996, A5B.

Jeanne Greiser

GRANDVIEW GARDENS. From 1933 through the early 1970s, the Santini and Peluso families owned and operated Grandview Gardens at the top of Widrig St. on a knob off Grandview Ave. in Clifton, which was later annexed by Newport (see **Italian Americans**). This Italian restaurant was home to summer fireworks (1940s), dances, **boxing** events (Elgin Harris versus Bobby Leen, 1941), political party conventions (National States' Rights Party, 1970), fish fries (1950s), Santa Claus visits (1940), and gambling. Former Kentucky governor A. B. "Happy" Chandler (1935–1939; 1955–1959) dined there. Pasquale Santini owned and operated the Grandview Gardens until 1967, when he sold the business to Johnny "TV" Peluso, who renamed it New Grandview Gardens. Peluso once proposed building a cable-car ride across the Ohio River to Mount Adams, an entertainment district on the east side of downtown Cincinnati. Another time, Newport Mayor Peluso became embroiled with city commissioners over city crews' blacktopping the road up to the gardens. In 1980 Specialty Restaurants of California took an option on the property in anticipation of making it into an entertainment complex, but neighbors successfully opposed the plans. For awhile the Landmark Baptist Church of Newport used the site on Sundays; in 1988 developers gained zoning approval for a 56-unit housing project, which is known as the Grandview Condominiums today.

"Harris and Leen Are in Main Event," *KP*, February 28, 1941, 14.
"Restaurateur Pasquale Santini," *KP*, October 14, 1982, 3B.
"S. Newport Tots Will See Santa," *KP*, December 20, 1940, 24.
"To State Fireworks Display at Gardens," *KP*, May 29, 1940, 4.

Michael R. Sweeney

GRANT, JESSE ROOT (b. January 23, 1794, near Greensburg, Pa.; d. June 29, 1873, Covington, Ky.). Jesse Root Grant, a successful businessman and the father of U.S. president Ulysses S. Grant (1869–1877), was one of six children. His mother, Rachel Kelly Grant, died when he was 11 years old, and his father, Noah Grant, a shoemaker, was unable to care for all his children. So Jesse migrated to Ohio, and later to Maysville, where he learned the tanning trade from his half brother Peter Grant.

At age 26 Jesse Grant became a partner in a tannery in the river village of Point Pleasant, Ohio. At age 27 he married Hannah Simpson, and the following year (April 27, 1822) his oldest son, Ulysses, was born. Jesse Grant prospered in business, and the family moved to Georgetown, Ohio, where he served a term as mayor. He sent Ulysses to school in Maysville. Without consulting his son, he made arrangements for Ulysses to receive an appointment to the U.S. Military Academy at West Point, where he graduated in 1843. Jesse knew that Ulysses was not a businessman, and besides, he had two other sons who could help him with his business. Jesse Grant accumulated a fortune of more than $100,000.

Jesse Root Grant House, Greenup St., Covington.

For a time Grant and his wife lived in Galena, Ill., where he owned a successful leather goods business. When they moved to Covington in 1855, Grant continued to operate the business from Covington as Ulysses worked in Galena before the **Civil War**. From 1859 to 1873, Jesse Grant lived in the home now known as the Grant House at 520 Greenup St. in Covington. He became semiretired when he moved from Galena to Covington. The family were active Methodists, worshipping at the First Methodist Church at Fifth and Greenup Sts, just across the street from their home. During the Civil War, Gen. Ulysses Grant's wife and children spent extended periods of time at the Jesse Grant home on Greenup St. From 1866 to 1872, Jesse Grant was the postmaster of Covington, appointed by President Andrew Johnson (1865–1869) as a favor to Grant's son Ulysses.

After Ulysses became the 18th president of the United States (1869–1877), Jesse, unlike his wife, loved sharing in the limelight. He made many trips to Washington to stay at the White House. It is said that Hannah did not visit her son in the White House, partly because of shyness and partly because she was a "died-in-the-wool" Democrat.

Jesse Grant died in Covington in 1873 after a long illness. His funeral was held at the First Methodist Church at Fifth and Greenup Sts., and he was buried in Spring Grove Cemetery in Cincinnati, with his famous son in attendance. Today, a Kentucky Highway Marker in front of their church in Covington notes the former presence of the Grants in the neighborhood.

"June 23rd Mr. Grant Celebrated 50th Anniversary," *CJ*, June 24, 1871, 2.
Reis, Jim. "Grant's Father Also Died in 1873," *KP*, July 20, 1998, 4K.
——. "Grants Worshipped at Covington Church," *KP*, November 15, 1999, 4K.
——. "Ulysses S. Grant Linked to Covington," *KP*, February 25, 1991, 4K.
Spring Grove Cemetery Records, Cincinnati, Ohio.

Paul L. Whalen

GRANT, WILLIAM L. (b. April 1, 1820, Lancaster, Ky.; d. May 5, 1882, Covington, Ky.). William Letcher Grant, a lawyer, a businessman, and a politician, was the son of Moses V. and America Letcher Grant. He was a student at the Lancaster Seminary in Lancaster in his early teens when his family moved to Covington. He attended Cincinnati College and later studied law with the Covington firm of Stevenson and Phelps. One of the partners, **John White Stevenson**, became a Kentucky governor (1867–1871) and a U.S. senator (1871–1877). On September 10, 1845, Grant married Laura Southgate, who was the daughter of **William Wright Southgate**, a former Northern Kentucky congressman. Grant served as a Covington city clerk, a councilman, and a Kenton Co. state representative.

A Democrat for most of his life, Grant backed the Union cause during the **Civil War**. In the early 1870s, he was elected to the Covington City Council. He resigned his council seat in November 1874 to become a candidate for state representative. Realizing that he needed the support of the African American community, he met with African American community leaders **Isaac Black**, a Mr. Dixon, George Durgan, and Rev. **Jacob Price**. Grant proposed that if the African American voters supported him for the legislature, and if he was elected, he would amend the City Charter of Covington to provide for an African American public school. He proved to be a man of his word. Grant won election to the state legislature and pushed for the amendment. He deeded over his own land for the school, which was first named Seventh St. School and later William Grant High School. On October 5, 1880, the Seventh St. School opened with an enrollment of 200 students. Grant died on May 5, 1882, and was buried in Linden Grove Cemetery in Covington.

With the annexation of Latonia by Covington in 1908, the Lincoln School in Latonia, another African American elementary school, was combined with the Seventh St. School to form the Lincoln-Grant Elementary School and the William Grant High School. In 1932, when a new school building was completed on Greenup St., all the grades were consolidated into one building. A Kentucky Historical Society Highway Marker, detailing the histories of Covington's African American schools, was placed in front of the building of the former Lincoln-Grant School on August 2, 1997.

"Col. Wm. L. Grant," *DC*, May 3, 1882, 2.
"Death of Wm. L. Grant," *DC*, May 6, 1882, 2.
"Funeral of Col. W. L. Grant," *DC*, May 8, 1882, 2.
"Special Election," *CJ*, November 14, 1874, 3.
"William Grant Helped Launch a Beginning in Education on the Path toward Equality," *KP*, July 8, 1991, 4 K.
"William L. Grant," *CJ*, July 31, 1875, 3.
"William L. Grant," *Covington Ticket*, July 17, 1875, 1.

Theodore H. H. Harris

GRANT CO. Established on April 1, 1820, by an act of the Kentucky legislature, Grant Co. consists of 259 square miles that were taken from the western half of Pendleton Co. Grant Co. is located in the Outer Bluegrass region, where the land is mostly rolling plains with some hilly areas. It is bordered on the north by Gallatin, Boone, and Kenton counties, to the east by Pendleton Co., to the south by Harrison and Scott counties, and to the southwest by Owen Co.

It is believed that the county was named for one or more of the three sons of William and Rebecca Boone Grant, nephews of **Daniel Boone**: Col. John Grant (1754–1826), who developed saltworks on the Licking River; Samuel Grant (1762–1789), who was killed pursuing Indians in Indiana; and Gen. Squire Grant (1764–1833), who became a developer of adjoining Boone Co.

One of the last Indian massacres in Kentucky took place in Grant Co. at the Andrew Brann cabin on Bullock Pen Creek west of Crittenden. It most likely occurred in 1807 rather than "around 1805," as indicated on a historical marker. Brann and some of his children were killed. The mother was scalped, but she and six children survived and resettled in Harrison Co.

In 1827 a small section of land was transferred from Harrison Co. to Grant Co., moving the county boundary line southward from Crooked Creek to the dividing ridge between the Crooked Creek and Raven Creek watersheds. In 1852 a small portion of Kenton Co. adjoining the Crittenden area was transferred to Grant Co. In 1876 the Kentucky legislature transferred an extensive area of Owen Co. into Grant Co. This area became the Corinth and Keefer voting precincts.

During the **Civil War**, more than 500 Grant Co. men, draftees and volunteers, served in military service for the Union, and about as many volunteers served for the South. A number of skirmishes took place in the county, including a Confederate raid in 1864 on Williamstown, in which U.S. moneys and muskets were seized (see **Williamstown Raid**). Also in 1864, three native Grant Co. Confederates, federal prisoners of war, were returned home and executed in reprisal for the killing of the local U.S. marshal and other Northern sympathizers.

Much of the development of Grant Co. took place along the Dry Ridge Trace, the crest of the great dividing ridge that separates the waters of the Licking River on the east from the tributaries of the Kentucky River on the west. The **Norfolk Southern Railway** and U.S. 25 (**Dixie Highway**) follow the crest, where there were no streams to cross or bridges to build. I-75 parallels the dry ridge crest and has interchanges leading into Crittenden, Dry Ridge, Williamstown (the county seat), and Corinth, the incorporated towns in the county. Traveler and tourist facilities are readily available in all four towns. Jonesville, on the western side of the county near Owen Co., was once incorporated but surrendered its charter of incorporation some years ago. There are 28 identifiable communities in Grant Co.

Agriculture has been important historically to the county's economy. Tobacco now has only a limited commercial market, but other crops and livestock production continue to play significant roles in the economy. Major employers include Wolf Steel at Crittenden; the Dana Corporation, Grant County Foods, and Powell Structures at Dry Ridge; and Gusher Pump, Performance Pipe, and Sun Manufacturing at Williamstown.

A major need was met when the Grant Co. Hospital opened its doors in 1964, providing both inpatient and outpatient services. By the mid-1980s, however, some specialist physicians stopped serving at the hospital because of the extremely high malpractice insurance premiums they were being charged. Their departure caused staffing and financial difficulties for the hospital. Corrective steps included the construction of a wing to the hospital that included multiple examination and treatment rooms with added medical facilities. A fully lit helicopter pad was built so that patients could be transported rapidly to other facilities in emergencies. In 1990 a contract was entered into with **St. Elizabeth Medical Center** in Kenton Co. to provide specialized and auxiliary services, an arrangement that continues today.

Northern Kentucky University, whose main campus is located in Highland Heights, has

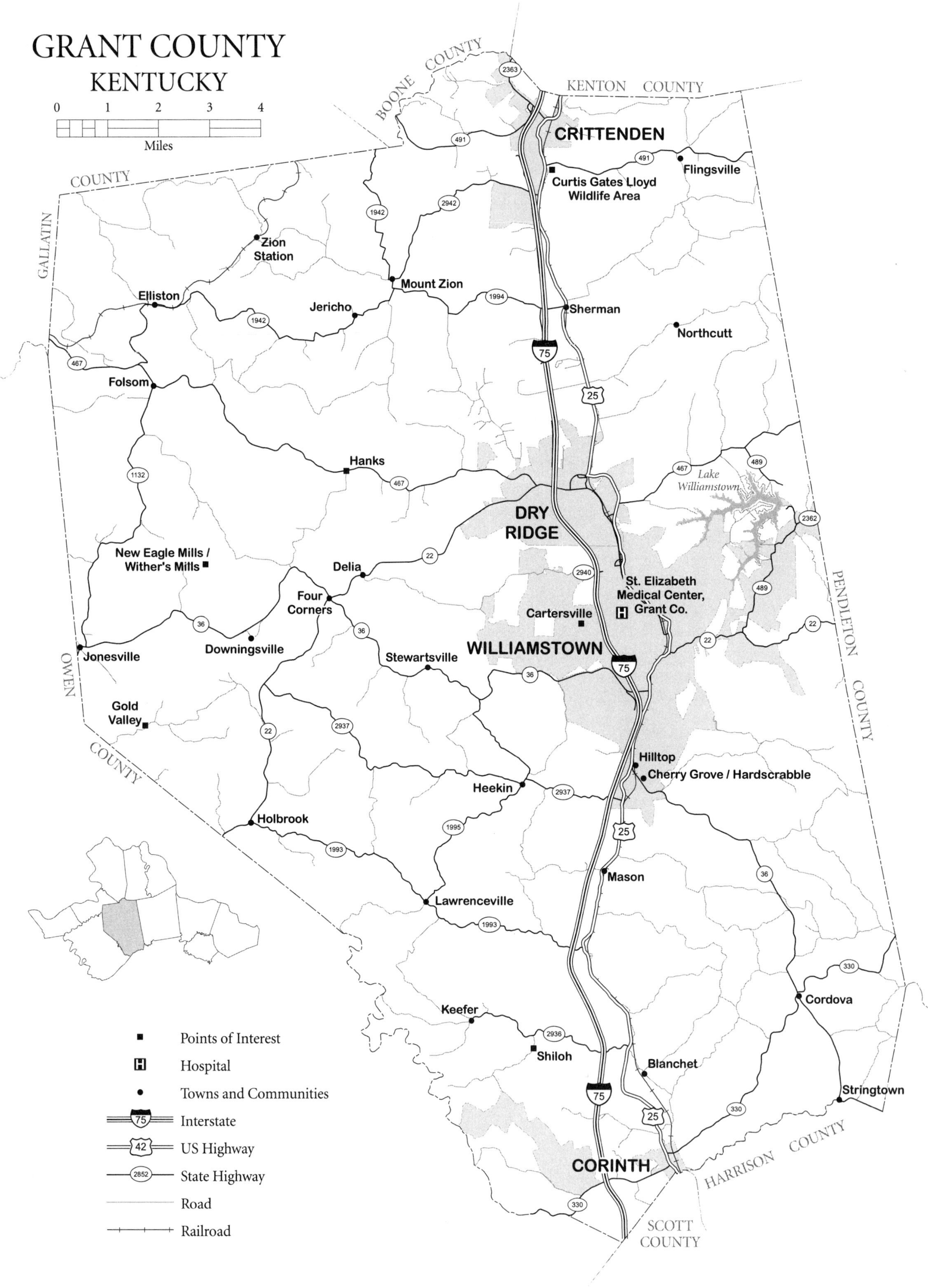
GRANT COUNTY
KENTUCKY
0 1 2 3 4
Miles
BOONE COUNTY
KENTON COUNTY
GALLATIN COUNTY
OWEN COUNTY
PENDLETON COUNTY
HARRISON COUNTY
SCOTT COUNTY
CRITTENDEN
Flingsville
Curtis Gates Lloyd
Wildlife Area
Zion
Station
Mount Zion
Elliston
Jericho
Sherman
Northcutt
Folsom
Hanks
Lake
Williamstown
DRY
RIDGE
New Eagle Mills /
Wither's Mills
Delia
Four
Corners
St. Elizabeth
Medical Center,
Grant Co.
Cartersville
WILLIAMSTOWN
Jonesville
Downingsville
Stewartsville
Gold
Valley
Hilltop
Cherry Grove / Hardscrabble
Heekin
Holbrook
Mason
Lawrenceville
Cordova
Keefer
Shiloh
Blanchet
Stringtown
CORINTH
Points of Interest
Hospital
Towns and Communities
Interstate
US Highway
State Highway
Road
Railroad

opened the Grant Co. Educational Center, making higher education more convenient for Grant Co. residents. The former Williamstown City Building has been remodeled to provide four classrooms, a conference room, technology laboratories, and offices. Twenty-four courses are offered each spring and fall semester. Currently, about 400 students are enrolled, and 180 of these are taking more than one class at a time. An associate degree in liberal studies may be earned upon completion of 64 credit hours.

The population growth of the county is due to its location halfway between Covington on the north and Lexington on the south. Many residents commute to work in these areas. The county had a population of 9,999 in 1970, 13,308 in 1980, 15,737 in 1990, and 22,384 in 2000.

Conrad, John B., ed. *History of Grant County.* Williamstown, Ky.: Grant Co. Historical Society, 1992.
Kleber, John E., ed. *The Kentucky Encyclopedia.* Lexington: Univ. Press of Kentucky, 1992.

John B. Conrad

GRANT CO. ANIMAL SHELTER. In 1988 the citizens of Grant Co. decided that the homeless dogs in the county's care deserved better treatment. The February 9, 1988, *Grant County News* reported that these animals existed, and often died, in horrific conditions—enclosed in one unsanitary pen without enough food or water. On August 23, 1991, Grant Co. dedicated its first shelter for cast-off pets. However, the shelter's five indoor and three outdoor pens quickly became inadequate. Scott Caudill, the dog warden in 1998, told the *Grant County News* that it was too small, forcing him to euthanize dogs quickly to open space for other animals. In 1997, 96 percent of the dogs entering the shelter were destroyed. Again citizens and the fiscal court responded. With help from state funds and from prisoners performing work-release jobs, the county built a larger, modern shelter in two phases. On May 31, 2003, the county dedicated the second wing of the new facility, which accepts both dogs and cats. The facility is located at 204 Barnes Rd. in Williamstown. Also in 2003, the fiscal court created Grant Co. Friends of the Shelter, a group focused on improving shelter animals' conditions and fate. Even with these improvements, many discarded Grant Co. pets die. During the first seven months of 2004, the county euthanized 195 animals.

Clayton, Laetitia. "Shelter Dogs Dying for Lack of Homes," *Grant County News*, October 29, 1998, 1.
"County Animal Control Center Opens for Business," *Grant County News*, August 24, 1991, 1.
"Dog Warden Loses Job over Allegations," *Grant County News*, February 9, 1988, 1.

Brenda L. Wilson

GRANT CO. DEPOSIT BANK. The Grant Co. Deposit Bank opened for business on March 2, 1882, at 106 N. Main St., Williamstown, where its main office remains today. Seven men served on the original board of directors, and by 1886 the bank's capital had grown to $80,000; today the bank has 10 directors and its capital and surplus are worth $4.44 million. The first dividends were paid to stockholders on January 3, 1885, and dividends have continued to be paid annually without interruption. The bank has been honored as one of Kentucky's Centennial Businesses. The Grant Co. Deposit Bank began with six stockholders and has increased to more than 100 shareholders today; some of the stock is still held by descendants of the first stockholders. On August 9, 1984, a bank holding company known as Grant Co. Bancorp Inc. was organized. The Grant Co. Deposit Bank, in an effort to improve its service to the citizens of Grant Co. and its stockholders, has opened branches at five locations. 1100 N. Main St., Williamstown, in 1983; Ky. Rt. 330, Corinth, in 1987; 225 Violet Rd., Crittenden, in 1991; 14830 Jonesville Rd., Jonesville, in 1995; and 26 Taft Hwy., Dry Ridge, in 2001. ATMs are available at all of these branches and off-site at I-75 and Ky. Rt. 36 in Williamstown and at 33 Broadway in Dry Ridge. The bank also offers Internet banking to its customers.

Grant County Deposit Bank. www.gcdb.net (accessed April 25, 2006).
"Northern Kentucky's Well-Seasoned Firms," *KP*, July 31, 2001, 3K.
Williams, Tom. "Bank Sale Means Jonesville Keeps Community Bank," *KP*, June 6, 1995, 8K.

D. W. Dills

GRANT CO. HIGH SCHOOL. A consolidated school that opened in 1954, Grant Co. High School replaced **Corinth High School**, **Crittenden High School**, **Dry Ridge High School**, and **Mason High School**. The county's other secondary school, Williamstown High School, part of the **Williamstown Independent Schools**, remains in operation. Originally located in south Dry Ridge, Grant Co. High School moved in 1998 to a new multimillion-dollar facility at 715 Warsaw Rd. in Dry Ridge. It is centrally located for all county residents and is the hub of school and community activities. Over 40 percent of its student body is classified as "academic achievers," defined as those students who achieve at high levels, attend school regularly, and exhibit exemplary behavior. The high school features modern art studios and science labs. In 1998 Grant Co. High School's marching band won a second-class AA state band championship; it won the state championship in 1995. Roger Bingham, a teacher at the high school, gained national recognition as a participant on the popular network television program *Survivor*, where he was nicknamed "Kentucky Joe" and was frequently asked to make public appearances. In 2008 Grant Co. High School enrolled more than 1,000 students.

Conrad, John B., ed. *History of Grant County.* Williamstown, Ky.: Grant Co. Historical Society, 1992.

James C. Claypool and Paul A. Tenkotte

GRANT CO. HOSPITAL. See **St. Elizabeth Medical Center**.

GRANT CO. NEWS. Robert Lee Westover established the weekly newspaper the *Grant Co. News* at Dry Ridge in 1906. In 1909 the *Grant Co. News* acquired the office and plant of the *Williamstown Courier* and relocated to Williamstown. The *Grant Co. News* was successfully managed and operated by Westover until his death in 1947, at which time Edythe Harrell, who had worked for the paper for 16 years, acquired the newspaper. She sold the paper and the printing plant in 1966 to Clayton Roland, who operated it until his death. The paper was sold in 1975 to the Scripps Howard newspaper chain (see **Newspapers**); Susan Arena became its publisher and W. J. Stanchina its editor.

Landmark Community Papers acquired the *Grant Co. News* in 1988 and installed Ken Stone as publisher. He has maintained and operated the paper since that time. Jamie Baker-Nantz serves as editor and oversees a staff of 12 employees.

Harrell, Edythe G. "History of Newspapers and Journalism in Grant County." In *Grant County Sesqui-Centennial.* Williamstown, Ky.: Publications Committee, 1970.

John B. Conrad

GRANT CO. PARK. The Grant Co. Park is located on U.S. 25 in the south end of Crittenden. It once was part of the Lloyd Wildlife Center (see **Curtis Gates Lloyd Wildlife Area**), where **Curtis Gates Lloyd** had a log cabin and where he built the Lloyd Welfare House, a center established to be used for nonprofit meetings by residents of the county. After Lloyd's death in 1926, the land was deeded to the Kentucky Department of Fish and Wildlife. On March 18, 1969, the Grant Co. Fiscal Court signed a lease with the Department of Fish and Wildlife for the use of the land as a county park. The terms of the lease specified a payment of $1.00 per year. The county cleared some of the dead trees and built restrooms on the property. Other buildings were built as well, and the county fair was moved to the park. On Oct. 7, 1999, the Department of Fish and Wildlife transferred the 55 acres to the Grant Co. Fiscal Court. Subsequently, the county has cleared scrub trees and planted replacement trees. The park now has basketball, baseball, and soccer fields, a horseshoe-pitching area, and a playground for children. The county fair grounds in the park include a cattle barn, a horse ring, a tractor-pull track, and two other buildings for exhibits. Several thousand people come to the park for the fair during one week in the summer. Parties, reunions, and weddings, as well as the District Track Meet, Senior Day, CETA's Art Show, and other events are held in the park. Many people enjoy simply walking in the park each day. The park has a well-kept, rolling landscape and is a great asset to Grant Co.

Grant Co. Lease Book 110, p. 26.
Quit Claim Deed to Grant Co., Deed Book 254, pp. 621–30.

Edna Marie Cummins

GRANT CO. PUBLIC LIBRARY. Tax-supported library service became available to Grant

Co. residents in 1954 when the county's first public library opened in the basement of the courthouse in Williamstown. The **Williamstown Women's Club** and the Grant Co. Younger Woman's Club petitioned the Fiscal Court for space and funds. For decades thereafter, club members volunteered thousands of hours and continued to carry out fundraising efforts to support library efforts.

In 1967 the library moved next door to the Old County Records Building, after the state threatened to withdraw state funds and terminate bookmobile services unless the county increased its investment in library services. In 1976 the county Fiscal Court accepted a petition from residents to create a library taxing district. A two-story building addition was completed in 1978. The library remained at its downtown Williamstown location for more than 35 years, then moved to a new building at 201 Barnes Rd, one-half mile east of I-75 at exit 156.

The new facility is located on a site of more than four acres. The 12,500-square-foot library, built at a cost of nearly $2.2 million, was dedicated on April 27, 2003. The Children's Garden, created with donated labor and funds, and attractive landscaping frame the structure's red-brick exterior. The dramatic interior features exposed trusses, 27-foot ceilings, window walls, and an octagonal reading room. The open floor plan is an ideal environment for the library's collection and services. On the west side of the public service area, children have access to a collection of 14,000 books, educational games, and toys. The building's east side, the adult area, houses a print collection of 21,000 books and magazine and newspaper subscriptions, along with 2,000 media titles that include music and books on CDs, books on tape, and movies in DVD and VHS formats. A teen area was created in 2004. The Kentucky Room is home to reference materials about the county and the state, genealogical information, local and family history files, census records, and the Grant Co. newspapers on microfilm. The Community Room has a fully equipped kitchen and is the site of educational, informational, and cultural programs as well as events for adults and children, including weekly toddler and preschool story hours.

The building was designed with space for 65,000 titles, and at least 15 percent of the library's operating budget is dedicated to collection development. The library's catalog and circulation functions are computerized. The catalog, the calendar, and a variety of online reference sources are available via the library's Web site. Library cardholders may also access their accounts online. Wireless access to the Internet and 15 public-use computers are very popular with patrons.

From a collection of 1,400 books and a part-time and volunteer staff in 1954, the library has grown to 35,000 print and media titles and a staff of nine. Thus the library can fulfill its mission of enhancing the quality of life for Grant Co. residents by serving their informational, leisure, and lifelong learning needs.

Grant Co. Fiscal Court Orders, 16:36, 37, 38.
"Joint Club Meetings," *Grant Co. News,* March 20, 1953, 4.
"Library Plans Move to Square," *Grant Co. News,* April 27, 1967, 1.
Paschke, Margaret. "Club Makes Library Come Alive," *KP,* February 14, 1968, 15K.
Russell, Burl. "Underground 'Book Nook' Emerges into Light of Day: Grant Co. Library on the Move," *KP,* June 28, 1967, 19K.
Williamstown Woman's Club. "Minutes Book, 1942–1958," pp. 299–300, March 12, 1953, Grant Co. Public Library.

Ann Stanchina

GRANT CO. PUBLIC SCHOOLS. When Grant Co. was created by the Kentucky legislature in 1820, two buildings in the county, both crude log structures, were being used for public school purposes. One was located on Fork Lick Creek, at or near where the creek is crossed by present-day Ky. Rt. 36. The first teacher at that school is said to have been James Williams. The other school was located at or near the site of **Campbell's Blockhouse**, east of U.S. 25 (**Dixie Highway**) and just south of the corporation line separating Williamstown and Dry Ridge. The first teacher there was William Littell. Both schools were maintained financially by the tuition that was charged. A surviving record states that Littell charged $1.50 per student per school quarter, "one half to be paid in money and the rest in coonskins."

Kentucky state laws, enacted at various times, made provision for additional schools to be built as the population increased and partially funded by taxes, reducing the tuition paid by the parents. In 1838 Kentucky established a system of common schools, whereby Grant Co., like the other counties, was divided into a number of school districts. Each school was operated by a board of three trustees elected by the male property owners in the district. With the approach of the **Civil War**, the activation of once dormant districts ceased. During the war, many active school districts occasionally were closed for a time. After the war, the schools that had suspended operations reopened. Burl N. Carter, an educator and a lawyer, was elected Grant Co. commissioner of schools. He was successful in restoring the existing districts and establishing new ones, so that by 1870 there were 55 one-room schools functioning in the county, each offering grades one through eight. An interest in education beyond eighth grade led to the establishment of academies in Corinth, Crittenden, and Williamstown.

In 1875 state law required the establishment of "colored" school districts for black children residing in the county. Accordingly, District A was organized at Williamstown, District B at Crittenden, and District C at Corinth. The boundaries of Districts D and E, at Dry Ridge and near Jonesville, were frequently revised because of the large area covered.

During the late 1800s and early 1900s, county school boards were developed and replaced the three-trustee system of managing individual schools. However, not all schools in Grant Co. were managed by the new board. The 1921 minutes of the Grant Co. Board of Education recognize the totally independent status of the Williamstown Graded Free School Board and the Corinth Graded Common School Board, both free of any control by the county board. In 1924 the Corinth board joined the county system in order to finance a new school building that was needed.

The first high school in the county was operating in the Williamstown District by 1891. The Williamstown schools were also the first "free" schools, wholly paid for by taxes (requiring no tuition charges). Other high schools in the county included **Crittenden High School**, which graduated its first class of one in 1911; **Dry Ridge High School**, which graduated its first class of four in 1912; **Corinth High School**, which graduated its first class of three in 1918; and **Mason High School**, which graduated its first class of one in 1921.

Grant Co. High School was opened in 1954 in Dry Ridge to replace the four county high schools. The old high schools graduated their last classes in 1953. Also constructed was a countywide middle school adjacent to the high school. Students in the seventh and eighth grades of the middle school were bussed from all over the county along with high school students. Elementary students in grades one through six continued attending classes at their old school buildings for a time. A new Crittenden–Mount Zion Elementary School was built in 1973 for students in that area. After the old school building in Dry Ridge burned in 1973, a new Dry Ridge Elementary School was built next to the Grant Co. Middle School. A new Mason-Corinth Elementary School was built in 1991 on U.S. 25 between Mason and Corinth.

A large increase in population throughout the county made the county high school in south Dry Ridge inadequate, so a new, larger one was built on the Warsaw Rd. on the west side of Dry Ridge and dedicated in 1998. The county middle school in south Dry Ridge, which was also overcrowded, expanded into the adjacent high school property.

Conrad, John B., ed. *History of Grant County.* Williamstown, Ky.: Grant Co. Historical Society, 1992.

John B. Conrad

GRANT FAMILY. Many Kentuckians with the surname of Grant, including numerous Northern Kentucky persons, can trace their lineage to William and Margery Verner Grant, who came to America in 1725 from the highlands of Scotland, landing at the port of Philadelphia. The first record of the family in America is of a son William II in February 1726. The family moved with a group of relatives and friends to the Yadkin Valley in Rowan Co., N.C. in 1749. Margery, on horseback, with a newborn child, and a female slave drowned while attempting to cross the Yadkin River. In the Yadkin Valley, the Grants lived near the Boones and the Bryans. William II married Elizabeth Boone, daughter of Squire and Sarah Morgan Boone and a sister of the famous pioneer Daniel Boone. They had 11 children, all born in North Carolina. In

1777 the family came to Kentucky and settled with Daniel Boone at Boonesborough. William II sent his son Squire back to North Carolina to finish his schooling and to train as a surveyor. Eventually, Squire was made deputy surveyor for land grants being given by the State of Virginia to North Carolina veterans of the **Revolutionary War**. He surveyed numerous tracts of land in North Carolina, Tennessee, and Kentucky. For his military service, Squire was given a 1,400-acre tract on Elkhorn Creek, near Lexington. While on a salt-making trip to Blue Licks in 1778, Daniel Boone was captured by a band of Shawnee Indians. The Grants, believing Daniel to be dead, went back to North Carolina. They returned to Kentucky in 1780. William II soon became quite discouraged with his new life and in 1783 decided to go once again to North Carolina. In preparation for the trip, he traded 400 acres of his land for an Indian pony, but the next day the pony and all his horses were stolen, making the trip impossible. Reluctantly, he remained in Kentucky for the rest of his life. William II died in 1804; his wife, Elizabeth, died in 1814. Both were buried on land that they owned about 10 miles east of Lexington.

Three of William II's sons, Samuel, John, and Squire Grant, played significant roles in the early history of Northern Kentucky. Samuel, for whom Grant Co. was named, married Lydia Craig, daughter of Capt. Elijah Craig, and they had two children. Indians killed Samuel while he was on active duty with Col. Robert Johnson. John started a salt-making operation at present-day **Grants Lick**, ran several gristmills, operated a ferry across the Licking River to Wilmington, Ky., and served for one term in the Kentucky House of Representatives. John died in Missouri at age 72. Squire lived at Wilmington, on the west side of the Licking, opposite Grants Lick. In 1804 he became a brigadier general of the 4th Brigade of Kentucky Militia. Squire was one of the few soldiers to escape unharmed at the **Battle of Blue Licks** in 1782. He also fought in the Battle of the Thames at Chatham, Ontario, on October 18, 1813, in which the great Shawnee Indian chief Tecumseh was killed. Squire served as sheriff of Campbell Co. in 1810 and also operated a general store and tavern near his brother's saltworks at Grants Lick. He served as a state senator from 1801 to 1806. Squire married three times, fathering 13 children. In 1832 Squire Grant traveled on horseback to Calloway Co., Mo., to visit his son Israel; during his return, he visited his stepdaughter Mrs. Blythe in Indianapolis, Ind. He died on October 6, 1833, at his home in Errondale (later known as Grants Bend), on the Licking River, during a cholera epidemic. During the last 13 years of his life, Squire acquired 40,000 acres in Campbell and Kenton counties but lost all except about 1,000 acres as a result of lawsuits over faulty deeds, overlapping claims, and poorly filed paperwork. In his will he left the remaining land to his children.

Grant Family Files, Kenton Co. Public Library, Covington, Ky.

Jack Wessling

GRANT MANOR HEALTH CARE CENTER. In 1984 a group of Northern Kentucky businessmen recognized a need to establish a long-term health care facility in Grant Co. to provide private, Medicaid- and Medicare-qualified skilled care for area residents. Following several meetings, five men, Dr. R. Michael Goodman, Arthur Moore, W. Michael Stanley, and William C. Wilson, all of Williamstown, and Bernie Poe of Owenton, formed Grant Manor Health Care Center Inc., for the purpose of securing a certificate of need from the Commonwealth of Kentucky to construct and operate a long-term health care facility. After more than two years, their efforts were successful; the certificate of need was granted and Grant Co.'s first modern, completely dual-certified long-term health care facility became a reality. A one-floor brick-veneer building was soon constructed along Barnes Rd. in Williamstown, adjacent to the Grant Co. Hospital, and opened to the public in November 1987. The facility, located on a 10-acre tract of land purchased from the Grant Co. Fiscal Court, was initially certified for 60 beds.

Just before the health care center opened, the corporation was sold to SeniorCare of Louisville, a corporation with much experience in providing long-term health care through its operation of five other similar facilities in Kentucky. The first administrator was Julia Poe, who served for about 18 months. She was succeeded by Glenda Walton and then by the current administrator, Bettye Tackett, who has served since November of 1989.

In 1995 an addition to the facility provided space for 35 more beds, bringing the total number of certified beds to 95. All of the SeniorCare facilities in Kentucky were sold in July 2006 to Harborside Rehabilitation and Nursing Centers of Boston, Mass., which operates Grant Manor as one of its 62 health care facilities, located in 10 states.

Conrad, John B., ed. *History of Grant County.* Williamstown, Ky.: Grant Co. Historical Society, 1992.
"Facility of Year," *KP*, October 15, 1998, 2K.
"Grant Manor Near Completion," *Dixie News*, October 26, 1995, 18.

William Michael Stanley

GRANTS LICK. The salt beds that were deposited 450 million years ago, when Northern Kentucky was covered by the Ordovician Sea, gave rise to many place names in the region. In 1793 Samuel Bryan discovered salt in southern Campbell Co. along Phillips Creek, where he had purchased property. A newspaper article in 1890 mentioned that the spot had always been known as the deer lick because of the number of animals that went there to lick salt. John Grant (see **Grant Family**) drilled a well in the area, and then he and several others formed the Grant and Company Salt Works that gave Grants Lick its name. The need for salt was critical for settlers, and the production and distribution of it led to the early roads and development of southern Campbell Co.

The production of salt was a large undertaking. Once salt water was drawn from the well, it was put into a large kettle and boiled until the water evaporated, leaving only salt. It took approximately 250 to 900 gallons of salt water to distill a bushel of salt. An early report stated that Grant's well was one of the best in the state. There, only 130 gallons of salt water were required, usually, to produce a bushel of salt.

Many hands were needed to cut wood for fires and to tend kettles. These laborers required food, drink, and lodging. So did the buyers and haulers who came to obtain salt for their communities. The horses and oxen doing the hauling needed feed, stabling, and perhaps blacksmith services. So a settlement arose around the lick to meet the demands of men and animals.

Soon after Campbell Co. was created in 1794, road-building began in earnest in the area. Most of the early roads were in the southern end of the county and led to the salt lick. One of the first was from the lick to Wilmington on the Licking River. In 1797 Grant requested a road from the well to Newport, some 20 miles to the north, and to the forks of Harris Creek in Pendleton Co. Again in 1799, Grant asked to have a road constructed locally from Reed's Tavern along the **Dry Ridge** to his saltworks. An 1803 petition was for a road from the Ohio River west across Campbell Co. to Roberts' Ferry (now the Plum Creek area) on the Licking River.

The second post office in the county was established at Grants Lick in 1800. In 1805 Grant petitioned the Campbell Co. court for a tavern license. A store had been in existence there before 1804. A blacksmith shop operated at the site from early times until the 1940s.

In the mid-1820s, the salt water began to become scarce. The competition from other salt makers in Ohio and Virginia began to take its toll on the Grants Lick salt well and, later, on the settlement. A newspaper article in the *Newport Local* in 1878 mentioned that Grants Lick was beginning to rebuild. It had a post office again, three stores, two blacksmith shops, a steam saw and grist mill, two taverns, a large Baptist church, and a district schoolhouse. The Grants Lick area remained rural until recent times, when the widening of **U.S. 27** has been bringing new population and development to the southern end of Campbell Co. Today, the area has two churches, an elementary school, a store, a tavern, and a funeral home. It is also home to the Oakland Cemetery, where **Mary Boone Bryan**, sister of **Daniel Boone**, was buried.

"Correspondence," *Newport Local*, December 5, 1878, 1.
"Dedication Marks Finds at Salt Works," *KE*, April 21, 1979, A3.
"Grants Lick," *KSJ*, April 15, 1890, 2.
Kleber, John E., ed. *The Kentucky Encyclopedia.* Lexington: Univ. Press of Kentucky, 1992.
Vertical files, Campbell Co. Historical and Genealogical Society, Alexandria, Ky.

Martha Pelfrey

GRASS HILLS. Grass Hills was the homestead of **Lewis Sanders** (1781–1861), one of Kentucky's first agricultural experts (see **Agriculture**). Famous as an antebellum experimental farm, Grass

Hills was home to Sanders and his descendants until 1883. It was also the site of many political meetings during the 1830s and 1840s, especially during the buildup leading to the **Mexican War**.

This unusually constructed home was built on 750 acres that Ann Nicholas Sanders, the first wife of Lewis Sanders, inherited from her father, George Nicholas, a politically powerful Lexington attorney. Lewis Sanders began construction on the foundations and barns in 1819. The main house, which dates to 1823, was built chiefly by slave labor of notched logs, shingles, and rafters hewn and shaped by hand on-site. According to biographer **Anna V. Parker**, there was no sawmill available. A stickler for detail, Sanders had his men age the cut flooring in the farm pond for two years to season it before they used the boards as planks.

The main floor of Grass Hills has two large front rooms about 20 feet square connected by a 15-foot-wide main corridor. At the far end of the hall is a dining room with a large kitchen adjacent to the right side. On the left are two small bedrooms. Another three bedrooms, used for guests, are behind the right chimney corner, and a narrow, winding staircase leads around the chimney to an upstairs bedroom. A large veranda fronts the hall, and a small porch at the back is accessed by a door out of the dining room. The two front rooms have large wood fireplaces. All of the rooms are plastered except for Lewis Sanders's own room on the left, which has exposed rafters and chinked logs. There are traces of early Georgian moldings, and some of the staircases are typical of early log construction. In the hall and right (east) large room, Greek Revival elements were added in the 1830s or 1840s, at a time when Sanders hosted many political events at Grass Hills. The basement includes a wine cellar, and when two families occupied the house, Lewis Sanders's kitchen was located there as well. Upstairs are two large rooms, each with a separate stairway, and a wide hall between them.

Grass Hills included the rambling main house, the barns, several outbuildings, a large pond, a 25-acre orchard, a racetrack just beyond the front-yard fence, and fields of experimental grasses, grains, hemp, and other crops. In addition to thoroughbred racing horses, Sanders imported strains of Merino sheep and shorthorn cattle. He became an expert and a judge of Kentucky's hemp and wool production. His longtime friendship with the Dufour family of Switzerland Co., Ind., gave him an interest in vineyards and wine production as well.

There is a Kentucky State Historical Marker at Grass Hills, and on August 22, 1975, the house was listed on the National Register of Historical Places. About 91 acres were taken from the Grass Hills estate when I-71 (see **Expressways**) was constructed through Carroll Co.

Parker, Anna V. *The Sanders Family of Grass Hills.* Madison, Ind.: Coleman, 1966.

Diane Perrine Coon

GRASSY CREEK CHRISTIAN CHURCH. This church, located in northwestern Pendleton Co., was organized in 1838 with 13 charter members. The first church building was constructed of logs and was located along the South Fork of Grassy Creek, but the church building was later moved to a parcel of land donated by Richard Mullins, who had moved to the area from Virginia. In 1851 the original log church was replaced with a frame structure. In 1895 the interior of the building was remodeled so that it had an arched ceiling and a new platform with windows at the rear. The **flood of 1937** damaged the interior of the church, requiring extensive repairs, and the building was also raised up on a three-foot foundation. Nevertheless, several subsequent floods did damage to the church over time. The building was raised again in the 1940s and a basement was added. In 1963 a building fund was started with the idea of moving the church to higher ground. In March 1964, one of the worst floods filled the church with water about four and a half feet deep in the auditorium. Then, on January 31, 1965, shortly after the morning service, a fire broke out in the ceiling of the building and the entire structure burned to the ground.

The congregation rebuilt on higher ground, next to the old Richard Mullins homestead, on land willed to the church by Theodore Blackburn. On June 27, 1965, a groundbreaking service was held and construction began. In spring 1974, the church began work on a new parsonage, where the Richard Mullins homestead once stood.

Belew, Mildred Boden. *The First 200 Years of Pendleton County.* Falmouth, Ky.: M. B. Belew, n.d. [ca. 1994].

"Roads Damaged; One Bridge Washed Out by Sunday's Storm," *KP*, June 27, 1928, 1.

"Rural Store Fills Niche for Village," *KP*, May 19, 1993, 9A.

"Society—Grassy Creek," *KP*, May 7, 1931, 6.

Mildred Belew

GRATZ. Located on the western edge of Owen Co., the community of Gratz sits on the eastern shore of the Kentucky River, six miles west of Owenton along Ky. Rt. 22 and 28 miles upriver from Carrollton. A bridge at Gratz carries Ky. Rt. 22 across the river into Henry Co. It is believed that the city was named for Benjamin Gratz Brown, the grandson of Kentucky's first U.S. senator, John Mason Brown, whose family owned most of the land in the area. A post office was established in 1844 as Clay Lick, from the name of the local creek that empties into the river, but in 1851 the post office was renamed Gratz. There was a resort hotel on Clay Lick Creek, which catered to travelers and their desire for sulfur water, and a saloon was located nearby. The town was surveyed in 1847 and incorporated as a sixth-class city in 1881. The city's three landings were once congested, with wagons busily off-loading coal, hardware, and general merchandise for inland Owen Co. The population of Gratz reached its peak of 300 residents around the year 1900; at that time the town had four churches, two schools (one for whites and one for African Americans), two hotels, a bank, three medical doctors, two drugstores, a dentist, an opera house, a band, and a baseball team. **Showboats** such as Billy Bryant's visited Gratz annually. During the last quarter of the 19th century, **Cedar Grove College** operated in Gratz, and a student there for a short time was Judge **James W. Cammack Sr.** A **lead** mine flourished nearby in the early part of the 20th century. About that same time, there was a ninth-grade school at Gratz. The building it used is today's community center. In recent years, Ky. Rt. 35, which runs along the Kentucky River through Gratz, has been improved and widened as part of a general upgrade to facilitate access to the new **Kentucky Speedway** at Sparta. In the year 2000, the Gratz population was 89.

An Atlas of Owen County, Kentucky. Philadelphia: Lake, 1883.

Dias, Monica. "Town Bristles at Flow of Trucks to Speedway," *KP*, April 25, 2000, 1K.

Houchens, Mariam Sidebottom. *History of Owen County: "Sweet Owen."* Louisville, Ky.: Standard, 1976.

Rennick, Robert M. *Kentucky Place Names.* Lexington: Univ. of Kentucky Press, 1984.

U.S. Census Bureau. "American Fact Finder. Data Set. Census 2000 Summary File 1 (SF1) 100-Percent Data. Custom Table." www.census.gov (accessed February 21, 2005).

Doris Riley

GRAVES, BARTLETT (b. November 22, 1766, Louisa Co., Va.; d. January 6, 1858, Erlanger, Ky.). Bartlett Graves, an early landowner and politician, was the son of Thomas and Isabel Bartlett Graves. He came to Bryants Station in Central Kentucky in 1785 and in the 1790s moved to Newport. There he became a representative to the state legislature and accumulated substantial amounts of property. He moved to modern-day Erlanger shortly after 1800. About 1806, he was widowed for a second time; he later married Elizabeth Leathers, the daughter of **John Leathers**, who owned much land in the area. In 1813 Graves purchased 500 acres, on which much of the city of Erlanger now stands, for $1,375. In 1819 he completed a large colonial home built of bricks made by slaves on the site. He named his home Walnut Grove and established a plantation on the property, where he lived for the rest of his life. Graves remained active in public affairs. He served as sheriff of Campbell Co.; was instrumental in the building of the **Covington and Lexington Turnpike**, which ran near his property in Erlanger; and was also involved in the creation of Kenton Co. from Campbell Co. in 1840. He raised a family of 13 children. Walnut Grove was sold to the Bedinger family after Graves died, and when the property was subdivided, the streets were named Bartlett and Graves in honor of this early settler. Graves died in 1858 and was buried at the Florence Cemetery in Boone Co.

Onkst, Wayne, ed. *From Buffalo Trails to the Twenty-First Century: A Centennial History of Erlanger, Kentucky.* Erlanger, Ky.: Erlanger Historical Society, 1996.

Reis, Jim. "Erlanger Pioneer and Land Owner Bartlett Graves Played an Active Role in the Life of His Community," *KP*, May 17, 1993, 4K.

Wayne Onkst

GRAY, RALPH (b. ca. 1802, England; d. November 30, 1863, Covington, Ky.). In 1848 Ralph Gray, in partnership with **Robert Hemingray**, founded the Gray & Hemingray Glass Works, the predecessor to the **Hemingray Glass Company**. Together they became pioneer industrialists in Covington and were quickly recognized nationwide as leaders in glassware manufacturing.

Ralph Gray came to the United States and settled in Birmingham, an industrial suburb of Pittsburgh, in the early 1840s, with at least two brothers, James and Anthony. Ralph gained employment as a glassblower and mechanic in one of the numerous glassworks located along the south side of the Monongahela River. Following the Great Fire of 1845, which destroyed most of the industrial and commercial district of Pittsburgh, he joined Robert Hemingray in a move down the Ohio River to Covington. Their intent was to establish a glassworks at Covington, taking advantage of a market in great need of domestic and commercial glass products of all descriptions. However, no suitable site was immediately available; they had to lease a small lot just across the river in Cincinnati, where they constructed a furnace and began making glass in late 1848. By 1852 they had moved their factory to Second St. and Madison Ave. in Covington.

Ralph Gray married Ann Frier in Pittsburgh. Although they had no biological children, they raised five children of deceased brothers and sisters. The Gray family resided at 45 W. Fourth St. in Covington.

One of the principal products of the Gray & Hemingray Glass Works was fruit jars. Gray and Hemingray received a patent in 1863 for an improved closure for fruit jars. Those Gray & Hemingray jars were popular with homemakers throughout the Ohio River Valley for many years. During the 1880s the glassworks employed about 500 men and boys at peaks of production.

Ralph Gray died in 1863, at the height of the Civil War. In his will he stipulated that his one-half undivided interest in the glassworks should be sold and the proceeds invested to provide for the comfort of his widow. This requirement caused consternation for Hemingray, who was executor of the will. Not only had he lost his partner and friend, but also he was burdened with the task of securing the future of the glassworks during greatly disturbing times. Robert Hemingray, with the assistance of his brothers Joseph C. and Samuel J.; his brother-in-law, Richard Evans; and a close friend, James L. Foley, was able to buy Gray's interest and ensure the continuation of the glassworks as a family concern.

Ralph Gray's younger brother, Anthony Gray, married Robert Hemingray's sister-in-law, Susan Carroll, in Pittsburgh. In 1848 Anthony came to Cincinnati to work as a glassblower. Although he never became a partner in the company, Anthony remained as a glassblower until 1862, when ill health forced his retirement. Anthony died April 27, 1865, and Susan died in 1868. The five children of Anthony and Susan Gray, two boys and three girls, were taken into the Robert Hemingray home. The glassworks employed the eldest son, John C. Gray, who eventually become plant manager.

Originally buried at Linden Grove Cemetery in Covington, Ralph Gray was reburied at Spring Grove Cemetery in Cincinnati. His widow, Ann, died in 1901 and was buried beside him.

City Directories, Cincinnati, Ohio, Covington, Ky., and Pittsburgh, Pa.

"Death Notice," *CDE,* December 1, 1863, 2.

Hyve, H. G. (Bea). *The Hemingray Glass Co.: A Most Colorful History.* San Diego: Clarice Gordon, n.d. [ca. 1998].

Probate and Deed Records, from Hamilton Co., Ohio (Cincinnati), Kenton Co., Ky. (Covington and Independence), and Allegheny Co., Pa. (Pittsburgh).

Spring Grove Cemetery records, Spring Grove Cemetery, Cincinnati, Ohio.

Glenn Drummond

GRAYSON, TREY (b. April 18, 1972, Fort Thomas, Ky.). Charles Merwin Grayson III (Trey) is the son of Charles Merwin Jr. and Susan Rhodes Grayson. Trey Grayson's father has been one of the most respected bankers in the Northern Kentucky community for more than 40 years. Trey Grayson was educated in the Kenton Co. schools. He attended **Dixie Heights High School** in Edgewood, where he participated in the Kentucky Governor's Cup and other academic competitions. Because of his achievements there, he was named a member of the Hall of Fame of the Kentucky Association for Academic Competition. In 1989 Grayson was named a Governor's Scholar, and the next year he graduated as valedictorian of his high school class. He earned his BA in government from Harvard University in Cambridge, Mass., where he graduated with honors in 1994 , and his MBA from the University of Kentucky at Lexington (UK) in 1998. He received one of the first two Bert Combs scholarships to the UK College of Law. After graduation, Grayson worked as an attorney, focusing on estate planning and corporate law. He married the former Nancy Humphrey of Lexington on January 8, 2000, and they make their home today in Boone Co. with their two daughters, Alex and Kate.

In his first run for political office, Grayson was elected to the office of Kentucky secretary of state in November 2003; he was then reelected in November 2007. During his first three years in office, he modernized the office of the secretary of state by bringing more services online, enhanced Kentucky's election laws through several legislative packages, and revived the civic mission of schools in Kentucky by leading the effort to restore civics education to the classroom.

Grayson is recognized as one of the top young political leaders in the United States. In 2004 the Council of State Governments selected him to participate in the prestigious Toll Fellowship Program, and the United Leaders recognized him as a "Rising Star" in the Republican Party. In 2005 he was selected as part of the inaugural class of the Aspen-Rodel Fellowships in Public Leadership, which recognizes the nation's "emerging leaders." Also in 2005, Grayson was named Outstanding Young Kentuckian by the Kentucky Jaycees. He is currently serving in a variety of leadership capacities, most notably as chairman of the Republican Association of Secretaries of State and as chairman of the elections committee of the National Association of Secretaries of State (NASS). As a former vice chairman of the NASS committee on voter participation, Grayson also serves on the association's committee on business services and the subcommittee on presidential primaries. In 2008 Grayson was elected president of NASS.

Dixie Heights High School Annual. Edgewood, Ky.: Dixie Heights High School, 1990.

Kentucky Secretary of State. "Biography." www.sos.ky.gov (accessed July 10, 2006).

"Official to Speak to United Way," *KP,* May 24, 2006, A2.

David Sorrell

GRAZIANI, BENJAMIN F. (b. November 16, 1858, Newport, Ky.; d. January 13, 1929, Covington, Ky.). Lawyer and legislator Benjamin F. Graziani was the youngest of nine children born to Charles and Emma Sanham Graziani. He lived with his family on a farm near Cold Spring. One of his grandfathers was the Italian count of Oneglia. Benjamin's father, a political exile and an artist who had immigrated to the United States in 1845, was killed on August 6, 1866, by a boiler explosion aboard the steamboat *General Lytle.* Benjamin's early education was in the Campbell Co. public schools. During his early teens, he worked as a salesman for the John Shillito Company in Cincinnati. Graziani entered the Cincinnati Law School in 1882 and received his degree two years later. He was admitted to both the Kenton Co. and the American Bar associations and practiced law in Covington, where he became a highly successful criminal attorney. Graziani handled many of the high-profile cases in Northern Kentucky. In 1890 he was elected to the Covington School Board, which he served as president. He married Eliza York in 1892, and they had five children. Graziani served two terms in the Kentucky legislature as a Democrat. When **James P. Tarvin** was elected Kenton Co. circuit court judge in 1902, he appointed Graziani as Campbell Co. master commissioner. Graziani was an active member of the Scott Street Methodist Episcopal Church in Covington. In 1929 he died at his home at 326 E. Second St., in Covington and was buried in Evergreen Cemetery.

"Death Claims Graziani," *KP,* January 15, 1929, 1.

Perrin, W. H., J. H. Battle, and G. C. Kniffin. *Kentucky: A History of the State.* 7th ed. Louisville, Ky.: F. A. Battey, 1887.

"The 'Squire,'" *KP,* August 22, 1893, 1.

USGenWeb Archives. "Campbell County Biographies." www.rootsweb.com/~usgenweb/newsearch.htm (accessed June 1, 2005).

GREAT DEPRESSION. Of the six economic depressions in U.S. history, the Great Depression (1929–1941), as suggested by its name, is generally regarded as the worst one endured by this nation.

Black Tuesday (October 29, 1929) is often considered the Depression's beginning, but there were earlier portents of the collapse of the stock market and economy. In Covington, the real estate boom had begun falling a few months before. By the time the Great Depression had supposedly ended in late 1941, both the nation and Northern Kentucky had changed. It took entrance into a long-lasting external world conflict, **World War II**, to revive the nation's economy and remove its people from the doldrums of unemployment and general strife. Most importantly, with America's entry into the war in 1941, people no longer believed that they were living during a depression, perhaps the most telltale sign of any recovery.

The federal government's response to the joblessness and hunger of the Great Depression was to create countless programs (known best by their acronyms) to feed, shelter, and provide jobs for the people most affected. Some of those programs continue today. The SEC (Securities and Exchange Commission) was started as a watchdog organization to prevent any future catastrophic economic collapse. Social Security was a relief program aimed at the middle class. Several programs by their very nature were more noticeable within Northern Kentucky.

The most visible of the federal programs in Northern Kentucky was the WPA (Works Progress Administration), which was established in 1935 as part of President Roosevelt's New Deal. Its name changed to Works Projects Administration in 1939. It was the largest and most comprehensive of all the new governmental agencies. In the late 1930s and early 1940s, the WPA funded the building of high school football stadiums in both Dayton and Bellevue, Ky. In 1936 construction began on two new Kenton Co. high schools built by the WPA, **Simon Kenton High School** and **Dixie Heights High School**. During the Ohio River **flood of 1937**, the WPA assisted the **American Red Cross** and the **American Legion** in their flood relief efforts in Campbell Co. At one point, a WPA rescue team found 80 patients, 15 nurses, and others marooned on the first floor of Speers Hospital in Dayton, Ky. (see **Speers Memorial Hospital**). Similar flood-related activities were conducted in Boone, Bracken, and Mason counties. The WPA helped to build the 200-foot sand and gravel extension to the **John A. Roebling Bridge** in Covington to keep the bridge open during the flood. As of February 20, 1937, within the WPA's District 3 (mainly Northern Kentucky), 176 projects were in operation, employing 5,010. Local projects at that time included new sewers in Newport, street improvement in Covington, and renovations at the **Fort Thomas Military Reservation**. In 1937 South Fort Mitchell (later merged into Fort Mitchell) received money for a fire department building, Butler for a waterworks, and Williamstown for work on its courthouse and electric distribution system. In Maysville, the new Limestone Creek Bridge opened for traffic that year thanks to the efforts of the WPA. In 1938 Covington received money for its city infirmary, its waterworks, and its filtration plant. By 1939, as economic conditions improved, WPA workers were being released from the program. Early in 1941 the WPA was responsible for construction within Covington's **Devou Park**, in particular the band shell (see **Devou Park Band Shell**). The agency provided some $45,000 for the construction of a new school in Elsmere and at the same time granted $53,000 for improvements to the roads and streets within the Fort Thomas Military Reservation. The WPA participated in local planning efforts in Boone Co. and funded cultural projects. The agency kept historians working with the writing of historical tour books for both Cincinnati (including the suburbs in Northern Kentucky) and the entire state of Kentucky.

Although no bank failed during the Great Depression in Campbell Co., at least two failed in Kenton Co., one in Latonia and one in Ludlow; and the **First National Bank of Covington** was closed for a few months to regroup its financial structure. In an attempt to preclude any more bank failures, the WPA began a series of monthly reports on each bank, savings and loan, and insurance company offering home loans in the region.

The Civilian Conservation Corps (CCC) was another program that put young men to work during the Great Depression, mainly constructing public structures along highways. The CCC built camps in which the workers lived in tents. Northern Kentuckians who were part of the CCC were required to leave the region and work in places such as Camp Robinson in Eastern Kentucky's Breathitt Co. Jack Kaiser, a 1933 graduate of **Newport High School**, delayed college and went to Camp Robinson that year along with 68 other Northern Kentucky men. They built about eight bridges in the forests of Breathitt Co. As late as 1982, Kaiser was still involved with an organization of former CCC men who were trying to persuade the U.S. Congress to reinstitute the program. Kaiser retired from teaching at **Highland High School** in Fort Thomas, where he directed the school band.

Other similar programs operated in Northern Kentucky. The National Reemployment Service (NRS) placed some 230 workers in employment in 1936, some with private firms. The Civil Works Administration (CWA) funded several street projects in Covington in 1934.

After several of President Roosevelt's relief proposals were ruled unconstitutional by the U.S. Supreme Court, Roosevelt, believing that a friendly court mainly appointed by him would reverse these decisions, made a failed attempt in 1937 to increase the number of Supreme Court justices from 9 to 15; by mid-1938, new programs of the New Deal had ceased. Roosevelt declared, upon signing the Wage and Hours Act of 1938, that the last major act of the New Deal had been taken. Thus, the Great Depression outlasted the New Deal in that respect.

The highest-ranking administrator within the New Deal programs from Northern Kentucky was **Allen Cammack**, a scion of the famous legal family of Owen Co. Cammack was in charge of the National Youth Administration (NYA) Industrial Work Shop Training program for Kentucky from 1936 through 1942.

The Great Depression in Northern Kentucky should not be thought of with the destitute images projected in John Steinbeck's *The Grapes of Wrath*. Northern Kentucky did not have the physical or economic climate of the western American dustbowl. Northern Kentucky, with its more diverse economy, experienced less unemployment than those areas. Life was tough, but Northern Kentuckians survived. Edna Phirman of Dayton, Ky., for example, worked in the shoe factories of Cincinnati and ate beans, rice, and **goetta**, swearing that she would never serve the latter two if she ever got out of the Great Depression. Her son never tasted those items until his own maturity a few decades later.

"Bank in Latonia Shuts Its Doors," *KP*, January 14, 1932, 1.

"554 on WPA Here to Go, Court Told," *KP*, July 27, 1939, 1.

McElvaine, Robert. *The Great Depression*. New York: Times Books, 1984.

National Archives. *Preliminary Inventories Number 125: Records of the Public Works Administration*. L. Evans Walker, comp. Washington, D.C.: National Archives, 1960.

"New County School Work Starts Soon," *KP*, February 25, 1936, 11.

"$100,000 Allotted on 2 Local Projects," February 20, 1941, 1.

Reis, Jim. "CCC Taught Young Men about Living," *KP*, September 27, 1982, 4K.

———. "Depression Years Recalled," *KP*, May 24, 1982, 4K.

"Report on Bank," *KP*, March 11, 1933, 1.

Works Progress Administration. *Guide to Civilian Organizations, Kenton County, Kentucky*. Louisville, Ky.: Works Progress Administration, 1942.

GREEN, ELISHA (b. ca. 1818, Bourbon Co., Ky.; d. November 1, 1893, Maysville, Ky.). Elisha W. Green, founder and pastor of African American Baptist churches in Maysville, Flemingsburg, and Paris, Ky., and one of the foremost African American leaders in post–**Civil War** Kentucky, was born into slavery. His short autobiography printed in 1888 indicates in its subtitle what Green himself saw as his accomplishments—"one of the founders of the Kentucky Normal and Theological Institute—now the State University at Louisville, Ky.; Eleven Years Moderator of the Mount Zion Baptist Association; five years moderator of the Consolidated Baptist Educational Association and over thirty years pastor of the Colored Baptist churches of Maysville and Paris." Those achievements and more were earned in the context of slavery and racism, conditions that Green faced with dignity and courage.

As a youth in Bourbon Co., he barely escaped a group of patrollers who broke up a religious service of slaves with whips. Around age 10, Green was moved to Mayslick in Mason Co. On many occasions through the years he had contact with "negro traders" and remembered particularly a group of 50 slaves who came through the community during his youth. Observing them brought him, and at least one white witness, to tears and led him to write, "The stain of slavery and its degrading impressions will long linger in the minds of generations yet unborn."

Green went through a succession of owners and was put up for auction on the square at Washington, Ky. In the early 1830s, he was converted while plowing a field and baptized six months later in the north fork of the Licking River. In 1835 Green married Susan Young, who was also a slave. In 1838 he moved to Maysville, 12 miles away, and often had to walk that distance to visit his wife, being questioned along the way by skeptical whites as to why he was alone.

Green became a sexton for the white **First Baptist Church** in Maysville and was allowed to attend services. The leaders of that church recognized his devout nature and his singing ability. He was permitted to have services for the African American community in 1844. On May 10, 1845, the Baptist Church licensed Rev. Green to preach, and he organized the **Bethel Baptist Church** in Maysville that year. He founded the Mount Zion Baptist Church in Flemingsburg in 1853 and the First Baptist Church in Paris for African Americans in 1855.

Although Green had contact with operators of the **Underground Railroad** and had many opportunities to escape while he was traveling in Ohio to perform religious services, he did not. After buying his freedom, he was able to purchase freedom for his wife and three of his children in 1858. He and his wife saw the removal of their son John in Maysville and watched him being sold in Paris. They never had contact with him again.

After the Civil War, Green was elected vice president of the Kentucky Negro Republican Party at its convention in Lexington in 1867. In 1875 he and his congregation built a brick structure for the Bethel Baptist Church in Maysville that served the congregation for a century. He continued to pastor his churches, worked for the education of the freedman, and lobbied against discriminatory laws such as those that prevented blacks from testifying against whites in judicial proceedings.

During the period of emancipation, many freed slaves left their former masters or were ejected from their former homes. In Paris a group of such freedmen were housed in a stable for 10 dollars a month. Its chimney was a hole in the roof. Because Green believed it was "as much my duty to look out after the interests of my people as to preach the gospel," he persuaded his Paris congregation to buy houses in a development from Samuel Clay. The lots measured 60 by 75 feet, and on each was built a cottage with a door and a chimney. This led to a community of home-owning African Americans.

On June 8, 1883, while riding the **Maysville and Lexington Railroad** from Paris to Maysville, Green was attacked by two white professors of the Female Millersburg Institute in Kentucky for refusing to give up his seat. Green brought charges against Professors Gould and Bristow in Paris and was awarded damages in the amount of $24. In the controversy that followed, many newspapers in Kentucky commented on the case, favoring Green. The *Maysville Bulletin* called Green a man respected by his own race and "by the white population of Maysville."

Rev. Green baptized some 6,000 individuals, many in the Ohio River. He died at his home in 1893. His funeral was a community event and the church overflowed with mourners. Green was buried in the Maysville Cemetery, which was segregated at the time.

Green, Elisha. *Life of the Rev. Elisha W. Green*. 1888. http://docsouth.unc.edu/neh/greenew/greenew.html (accessed April 2, 2006). Part of the Documenting the American South series.

Kentucky Gateway Museum files, Maysville, Ky.

George Vaughn and John Klee

GREEN DERBY RESTAURANT. The Green Derby Restaurant has long been a fixture at the northwest corner of Ninth and York Sts. in Newport. Its history is tied to the importance of family and friends, which are as essential to a visit there as any ingredient in the food.

Helen Azbill Haller Cummins (1912–1986) started the Green Derby Restaurant in 1947 with her husband. In 1912 the Azbill family had a farm in Clover Bottom (Jackson Co.). Helen's father, William Azbill, was a dentist from Sweden. He had married Mollie McCann, an Appalachian woman of Irish and Cherokee ancestry. In the 1920s many families in that part of Kentucky, including Helen's oldest sister Lula, found opportunities for employment scarce and headed north to the more populated cities of the state. Before long the rest of the family followed Lula north.

Helen married Jacob Haller, a German immigrant employed in Newport at the Interlake Steel Plant (see **Newport Steel**). The **Great Depression** took his job, and the story is that he became an entrepreneur in the "bathtub gin" business (bootlegging). Helen and Jake had four children, John (Jack), Glen, Ron, and Mollie. When her marriage ended, Helen turned to waitressing to support her family. A large picture hangs in the Green Derby Restaurant today showing Helen and her sister Lula at Arnold's Restaurant on Eighth St. in Cincinnati during **World War II**.

Helen married Wilber Cummins, who was an experienced restaurant cook. After the war, they decided to buy the bar on the corner of Ninth and York Sts. and start their own business. Helen named the restaurant the Green Derby because the Brown Derby was a famous restaurant on the West Coast at the time. *Green* in the name was a nod to her Irish ancestry. The place had a red tile floor, high pressed-tin ceilings, dark paneling, a jukebox, and a bar that stretched all the way from the front door to the tiny kitchen. And of course there was a "bookie" (a bookmaker) who sat in the corner booth. Wilber oversaw the business, while Helen, her mother, and two sisters cooked and served food to the bar patrons. Not much is known about the previous history of the building itself, except that it dates from the mid-1800s and that during the Ohio River **flood of 1937**, the water rose to the second floor.

As the Green Derby began to prosper, Helen and Wilber would drive south on **U.S. 27** to vacation in Florida. They made a point of stopping along the way to sample regional foods and specialties. A family story tells of the time they tried a side dish similar to hush puppies but made with mashed potatoes. Helen knew she had found something and marched back to the kitchen. She charmed the astonished cook out of the recipe, made a few changes of her own, and the Green Derby Restaurant's popular Potato Puffs were born. The Derby Salad is also one of her unique adaptations, of hot slaw and wilted lettuce.

All four of Helen's children have been actively involved with the restaurant at one time or another, although Glen and John made their careers in other businesses. In 1989, after retiring from a corporate position with Kmart, John (Jack) moved back to the region. Helen had died and Ron and Mollie wanted help with the business end of the restaurant. So Jack started a new career, and Ron and Mollie had a new partner. Glen, meanwhile, was always there behind the scenes.

There have been many expansions of the restaurant, including the addition of a bar/lounge and a large nonsmoking dining room. The Green Derby Restaurant rose to become the area's "Fish King," lauded by the *Cincinnati Enquirer* many times as having the "Best Fish Sandwich in Town."

The Green Derby Restaurant has witnessed many of Newport's eras and changes. During the 1960s the Jai Alai Club, a notorious local strip club and gambling joint, was located across Ninth St. from the Green Derby. The bus boys would fight over who got to deliver carryout orders to the club. Helen would periodically come out of the kitchen and patrol the seating areas to make sure the girls who worked at the club were not sewing sequins on their outfits in the Green Derby Restaurant during lunch. All were welcome, but the "family atmosphere" was of utmost importance. All had to be comfortable, too.

Through the years, the Green Derby Restaurant has become a favorite in the region. The soups and pies are homemade, and the large menu includes hard-to-find items like beef and chicken liver and country ham with true redeye gravy. Cincinnati Reds and Bengals players, judges and lawyers, politicians and celebrities—all make regular visits for "comfort food." So do many people who have moved out of town, considering a meal at the Green Derby Restaurant a "must" during their return trips.

The Green Derby Restaurant's significance is not that it has been in business for so many years, or that the fourth generation of the family is now working there. The restaurant's lasting impression is as one of the few places remaining where customers frequently stop at three or four tables to visit with other diners before sitting down at their own table. A visit to the Green Derby Restaurant, customers seem to feel, is as much a social event as an eating experience. The restaurant is regarded as a truly unique Northern Kentucky business and appears to live up to its motto, "Good Food, Good Friends, Good Times."

"A Good Fit for Regulars," *CE*, January 5, 2006, E1.
"The Green Derby: 50 Years of Family," *KP*, July 24, 1991, Timeout sec., 16.
"Still the Champion of Fish Sandwiches," *CE*, March 10, 2000, R8–R9.

Lori Haller

GREENE, MARY BECKER (b. June 20, 1868, near Marietta, Ohio; d. April 22, 1949, aboard the *Delta Queen* steamboat on the Ohio River). Pioneer female river pilot Mary Becker Greene was one of eight children born to Peter and Rhoda Becker. Her father was the postmaster at Hill's Post Office in Marietta, Ohio, and the proprietor of a prosperous country store. She attended school in Marietta, where she met her future husband, Captain Gordon Christopher Greene. After their marriage in 1890, she began her life on the river. In 1896 Mary Greene became one of the few women issued a captain's pilot license. After having served five years as a striker on her husband's boat, the *H.K. Bedford,* Greene felt she was entitled to the license; it also allowed her to stay close to her husband. By the time her first son, Henry Wilkins Greene, was born in 1898, her pilot license had been elevated to a master's pilot license. She continued to serve as a pilot on the river. She had two other sons, Christopher Becker, born in 1901, and Thomas Rea, who was born aboard the *Greenland* on February 3, 1904. The *Greenland,* the boat Greene piloted, made a specialty of taking women and children on excursion trips and by 1907 had carried nearly 100,000 passengers. For a short time, Greene thought about leaving the river after the death in 1907 of her first son. She even told reporters that she would never go back to river life. Yet, Greene stayed on the river and continued to pilot the *Greenland.* She later moved to the *Gordon C. Greene,* where she lived onboard for many years. After her husband's death in 1927, Greene continued to carry on the business of the Greene Line Steamers, with help from her two sons Christopher and Thomas. In 1944 her son Christopher, Captain Chris Greene, collapsed and died of a heart attack, leaving Mary and her son Thomas to run the company. Captain Tom Greene bought the *Delta Queen* steamboat in 1948 and moved his mother to her own rooms onboard before the vessel's inaugural passenger cruise on June 30, 1948. Less than a year later, she died aboard the *Delta Queen,* following a voyage to New Orleans, and was buried beside her husband in the Newport, Ohio, Cemetery. Today a bronze statue of Mary B. Greene stands on the Northern Kentucky river walk near Riverside Dr. in Covington, honoring her contributions to river life.

Greene, Letha C. *Long Live the Delta Queen.* Toronto: Saunders, 1973.
"Life Voyage Ends for Mary Greene: Famed Pilot Dies aboard Delta Queen," *CP*, April 23, 1949, 7.
Simcox, Betty Blake. *Greene Line Steamers, Inc. Celebrates Its 75th Anniversary.* Cincinnati: Green Line Steamers, 1965.
"Vikings of the River: Adventure Rewards Mary Greene's Long Time Devotion to Ohio," *CP*, September 14, 1933, 13.
"Woman Captain Leaves River Boat for Her Boy," *CP*, August 14, 1907, 10.
"A Woman Pilot: Mrs. Greene Tells of Her Experience on the River," *Wheeling (W.Va.) Daily Intelligencer,* February 3, 1896, 2.

Sienna Spooner

GREEN LINE COMPANY. The Green Line Company, officially the Cincinnati, Newport, and Covington Railway Company (CN&C), began as an amalgam of four earlier horsecar transportation companies operating from the cities of Bellevue, Covington, Dayton, and Newport in Kentucky to Cincinnati. The first horsecar transport line commenced operation on Covington's Madison Ave. in 1867. Formed in 1887 as the South Covington and Cincinnati Street Railway Company (SC&C), the Green Line Company was initially owned by a group of local investors headed by George F. Abbot (see also **Streetcars**). It came to be called the Green Line because its cars were painted green, to distinguish them from the orange cars of the much larger Cincinnati Street Railway Company that was operating in downtown Cincinnati.

The Green Line began converting its newly purchased horsecar transportation lines to electric streetcar service in 1890. Between 1890 and 1892, the company built new electric streetcar lines to Fort Thomas and the then independent suburban towns of Central Covington, West Covington, Latonia, and Rosedale. Small car-storage facilities in Covington and Dayton (Ky.) were replaced by a new car barn at 20th St. and Madison Ave. in Covington.

The rapid conversion to electric streetcars and the building of new lines put a severe financial strain on the SC&C. As a result the Green Line was purchased, in 1892, by a group of investors from Cleveland and renamed the Cincinnati, Newport, and Covington Railway Company. With an influx of new capital, the CN&C built a new electric streetcar line to suburban Southgate in Campbell Co. and to Ludlow in Kenton Co. In conjunction with the 1895 completion of the Ludlow line, the company developed an amusement park on the Ludlow-Bromley border that it named the **Lagoon**.

In 1896 the Green Line Company was sold to a group of local investors headed by future U.S. senator **Richard P. Ernst**. In 1899 a large brick-and-stone streetcar storage facility (90 by 370 feet), along with electrical, woodworking, and painting buildings, was opened in Newport along the Licking River, bordered by 11th, Brighton, and Lowell Sts. Also developed on Lowell St. was a large electric generating plant to supply power for the Green Line's growing streetcar fleet. Surplus electric power was sold to nearby businesses and homes in Newport and Covington.

Soon the business of supplying electric power overshadowed the Green Line's significant transit business, and a separate subsidiary, the Union Light, Heat and Power Company (ULH&P), was formed. The Green Line and ULH&P were sold to the North American Company, a power conglomerate, in 1902; that entity, in turn, sold them to the Columbia Gas and Electric Company (CG&E) in 1907. **James C. Ernst**, installed as general manager of the Green Line Company in 1896, was apparently a very able executive, since both the North American Company and CG&E retained his services. Ernst remained at the helm of the Green Line Company until ill health forced his retirement in 1914.

A new office building was built for the Green Line at Third and Court Sts. in Covington in 1903, the same year a new electric streetcar line through Park Hills to the **St. John**, **St. Mary**, and **Highland cemeteries** was opened. A new line was also opened to South Bellevue in 1904. The Green Line extended the cemeteries line out the **Dixie Highway** as far as Fort Mitchell's Orphanage Rd. in 1910. With the opening of the Fort Mitchell electric streetcar line, the CN&C reached its zenith, operating about 200 streetcars over some 58 route miles of track in Campbell and Kenton counties. The Green Line's streetcars carried, in 1910, more than 15 million passengers.

In fall 1921 the Green Line streetcars began using the **Dixie Terminal** at Fourth and Walnut Sts. as its downtown Cincinnati terminal. Streetcars from Covington used the **John A. Roebling Bridge** and a newly constructed ramp to reach the Dixie Terminal's upper level and thus entirely avoided traveling Cincinnati's downtown streets. Cars from Newport used Third St. in Cincinnati to reach the terminal's lower level. By 1929 the CN&C employed more than 500 persons and was one of Northern Kentucky's largest employers.

With the advent of paved roads and the maturing of internal-combustion-engine technology, the Green Line faced stiff competition from both private automobiles and numerous upstart bus companies by 1930. Hamstrung also by franchise requirements to charge only a five-cent fare, the Green Line began during the 1930s to replace electric streetcars and their maintenance-intensive tracks with trolleybuses and motor buses. Although trolleybuses needed overhead wires to utilize electricity for power, they ran on regular paved urban streets. Between 1937 and 1939, three major Kenton Co. electric streetcar lines, to Rosedale, Latonia, and Ludlow, were converted to trolleybuses.

Weakened financially by the **flood of 1937**, six competing motor-bus companies were purchased by the Green Line Company. The company also purchased two suburban bus businesses before **World War II**. Acquired in 1940 were the Black Diamond Company, which linked Cincinnati with eastern Newport, Fort Thomas, and Ross; and the **Dixie Traction Company**, connecting Cincinnati with Fort Thomas, Cold Spring, and Alexandria and, west of the Licking River, a whole host of communities along the Dixie Highway from Covington to Florence, Ky.

World War II brought a rationing of tires and gasoline and forced many workers to resort to public transit. The Green Line saw its ridership more than double during the war years, enabling the company to earn a profit for the first time in more than a decade. Because motor-bus production was curtailed during the war, plans to convert the company's one remaining Campbell Co. streetcar line (No. 11–Fort Thomas) and its four remaining Kenton Co. streetcar lines (No. 1–Fort Mitchell, No. 4–Main, No. 5–Holman, and No. 8–Eastern) to motor buses were put on hold.

In 1944 the Columbia Gas and Electric Company sold the Green Line to Allen and Company, a New York City investment house. The sale was prompted by federal legislation mandating that utility companies controlling transit operations must elect to keep either their energy production or their transit operations, but not both. Since the Columbia Gas and Electric Co.'s utility holding in Northern Kentucky, the Union Light, Heat and Power Co., was considerably more profitable than the Green Line Company, the sale of the latter was inevitable.

The peak year for the Green Line was 1946 in terms of ridership: it carried a record 41 million passengers. That year was also significant in that Green Line's general manager, Phillip G. Vondersmith, and its assistant general manager, **David Ringo**, entered into an exclusive contract with the board of the new Greater Cincinnati Airport (later **Cincinnati/Northern Kentucky International Airport**) to provide scheduled bus service between the yet-to-be-opened airport in Boone Co. and downtown Cincinnati. In addition, the Green Line was given exclusive rights to the airport's taxi-for-hire business. The Green Line Company's scheduled service to downtown Cincinnati (later expanded to serve a number of Cincinnati suburbs as well as Hamilton, Ohio) was marketed under the Airporter trade name. Its taxi-for-hire franchise was operated under the Red Top banner. Both services continued under the Green Line until 1973.

With World War II at an end, the Green Line began converting its remaining electric streetcar lines to bus service in 1946. The last electric streetcar line in Campbell Co., the No. 11–Fort Thomas route, was converted to motor-bus operation in 1947. The last streetcar line in Kenton Co., the No. 1–Fort Mitchell line, was changed over to a bus operation on July 2, 1950, thus ending 83 years of either horsecar or electric streetcar service in Northern Kentucky.

By 1954 the Green Line's ridership had been cut in half to 21 million passengers, in just eight years. Statistics compiled by the Covington–Kenton Co. Chamber of Commerce (today's **Northern Kentucky Chamber of Commerce**) revealed that automobile traffic on the **Chesapeake and Ohio Railroad Bridge** and the John A. Roebling Bridge had jumped from 18,000 vehicles a day before World War II to 41,000 vehicles a day in 1953. Therefore the Green Line found it necessary, for the fourth time since the end of World War II, to raise its basic fare, this time to 15 cents. As an economic move, the company sold its Covington car barn at 20th St. and Madison Ave. and its Covington office building at Third and Court Sts. The old electric streetcar machine shop behind the Newport car barn was converted to house the additional buses moved from Covington, and office facilities were relocated to the former Newport powerhouse at 11th and Lowell Sts.

As a result of these moves, along with limited pruning of some early-morning, late-night, and Sunday services, the company remained a profitable enterprise through the remainder of the decade. With the last streetcars gone, the Green Line updated its corporate name in 1956 to the Cincinnati, Newport, and Covington Transportation Company. Its formerly independent subsidiary the Dixie Traction Company was merged into the Green Line Company. In March 1958 the curtain came down on the Green Line's last electric trolleybus operation as the No. 3–Ludlow and No. 6–Rosedale routes were converted to motor-bus service. Expressway construction in downtown Cincinnati was cited as the prime reason for substituting the more flexible diesel buses for the trolleybuses and their fixed-wire power system.

At the end of 1959, the CN&C was still serving 32 cities, towns, and unincorporated communities in Boone, Campbell, and Kenton counties. On the 130 diesel transit buses, 12 fancy Airporter coaches, and 16 Red Top taxi cabs that it owned, it carried some 14 million people.

By the mid-1960s, the CN&C was engulfed in a sea of red ink. In 1964 the Green Line's ridership fell to a record low 10 million, with operating expenses again outstripping revenue. A vicious cycle ensued, wherein, as the Green Line's vehicles carried fewer passengers, it needed additional revenue through fare increases that resulted in more passenger desertions. In 1965 the basic interstate fare was increased to 25 cents. Further weekend service was eliminated on some routes: No. 4 Main–Park Hills–South Hills, No. 13 South Bellevue, No. 18/21 Newport East–North Fort Thomas, No. 19 Newport West, No. 20 Newport South, and No. 23 Bonnie Leslie. Most other routes saw greatly reduced service after 7:00 p.m. on weekdays and all hours on weekends.

By 1960 it had become clear to many transit managers and other observers that privately owned companies, such as the Green Line, had no long-term future. Although transit companies were the safety net transporting people to work and school if they were financially or physically unable to drive, the companies were not true public utilities because they had no public subsidy to fall back on if revenues did not keep pace with operating costs. The ongoing mania for building new expressways and feeder roads encouraged people to forsake public transportation in favor of the automobile. Gridlock, smog alerts, and rising gasoline prices were not yet established factors across the United States.

As part of his Great Society program, President Lyndon B. Johnson (1963–1969) signed the Urban Mass Transportation Act into law on July 9, 1964. This legislation provided a firm base for the granting of transit subsidies. However, such subsidies were conditioned upon local governments forming transit authorities and upon citizens voting to approve funds for a private-system takeover. In June 1971, by action of the fiscal courts in Boone, Campbell, and Kenton counties, the **Transit Authority of Northern Kentucky** (TANK) was created.

Deferred maintenance had reduced the Green Line's available transit fleet. It was made perfectly clear by the Green Line's owners that the company was not going to throw good money after bad for new equipment, or even improve fleet maintenance, in order to keep public transit alive in Northern Kentucky. In March 1972 the Green Line Company announced that it would terminate all public transit service as of November 4, 1972, ending almost a decade of unprofitable operations.

In June 1972 a bond issue for funding the proposed TANK service was authorized by all three county governments for placement on the November ballot. In October the Cincinnati, Newport, and Covington Transportation Company forfeited its state operating license.

At midnight on Saturday, November 4, 1972, the last Green Line Company transit bus rolled into the Newport garage. There was no ceremony to mark the venerable transportation company's demise. The employees going off duty simply locked the doors and went home, ending more than 105 years of transit service by the CN&C and predecessor companies for Northern Kentucky.

Lehmann, Terry W., and Earl W. Clark. *The Green Line*. Chicago: Central Electric Railfans' Association, 2000.

Terry W. Lehmann

GREENWAY, ISABELLA SELMES (b. March 22, 1886, near Petersburg, Ky.; d. December 18, 1953, Tucson, Ariz.). Isabella Selmes, who became a member of the U.S. Congress, was born at the **Dinsmore Homestead** to Tilden R. and Martha Flandrau Macomb Selmes. Following her father's early death, she moved to Wisconsin and then to New York, where she met her first husband, Robert H. Monro Ferguson. They were married in 1905. After Ferguson became ill, the couple relocated with their two young children to New Mexico. It was there that Isabella fell in love with politics, serving as the chairwoman of the Women's Land Army of New Mexico in 1918. A year after Ferguson's death in 1922, she moved to Arizona and married copper baron John C. "Jack" Greenway in November 1923. She served as that state's Democratic national committeewoman after Greenway died in 1926; to the surprise of the Democratic Party, Isabella worked eight-hour days in that position. Following U.S. Representative Lewis W. Douglas's resignation in 1933, she was appointed to fill out his term, and then she was reelected as a representative in the 74th Congress. She was Arizona's first woman representative in Congress. Greenway spent her congressional time tirelessly advocating what she called the "Liberty of Living," which was undoubtedly influenced by the politics of her close friends Franklin and Eleanor Roosevelt. Greenway's plan focused on helping homeowners, the elderly, and persons in economic distress with the intent of improving the quality of life for Depression-era Americans. Greenway also recognized a need for reorganization of the tax system to protect these citizens. She called for fewer taxes on inexpensive homes and land and higher taxes on incomes, inheritances, profits, and financial transactions. She was not a candidate for renomination after her elected term, so she returned to Arizona to run her two cattle ranches and a hotel, the Arizona Inn in Tucson. She was also involved in the ownership of Gilpin Airlines, a small western regional operation. Greenway was married again in 1939 to Harry Orland King and split her time between New York and her beloved Arizona. Isabella Greenway died in 1953 and was buried at the Dinsmore Homestead in Boone Co.

Aikman, Duncan. "Mrs. Greenway Charts Her Own Course," *NYT*, April 21, 1935, SM 9.

Biographical Directory of the United States Congress. "Greenway, Isabella Selmes." http://bioguide.congress.gov.

Miller, Kristie. *Isabella Greenway: An Enterprising Woman*. Tucson: Univ. of Arizona Press, 2004.

"Mrs. J. C. Greenway Wed to H. O. King," *NYT*, April 24, 1939, 15.

Who Was Who in America. Vol. 3. Chicago: A. N. Marquis, 1960.

Amanda C. Kerley

GREENWOOD. Greenwood is located in Pendleton Co. at the junction of the road from Butler, Ky. Rt. 609, and the road from Falmouth and Grassy Creek, Ky. Rt. 17. The town received its name because of the many trees in the vicinity. During the early 1800s, Greenwood was a prosperous small town with many homes, a blacksmith shop, a school, a general store, a tollgate, and a distillery. When the Redbrush School, located only a short distance away, closed because it had too few students, its remaining students attended the school in Greenwood.

Several families near Greenwood raised a variety of sorghum. In the fall the cane was cut, stripped of its leaves, and ground to make juice. The juice was then cooked for about two hours over a fire to make sorghum molasses. This annual activity joined many families in an activity that heightened their sense of community. Once the molasses was ready, the families would get together and have a candy party for the children. The community project died out after the school at Greenwood was closed in 1931 because of consolidation.

The general store, located on the corner of the Butler Rd., was where the families of the area obtained their supplies of food and other items. The farmers used the second floor of the store as a meeting place. After the general store burned in 1893, people had to go to Butler or elsewhere to shop. Farmers took their horses to the blacksmith shop, which was located across from the general store. Families attended church in Mount Moriah, about three miles away, but every Sunday afternoon, Sunday school was held in the schoolhouse at Greenwood. About a half mile from the school was one of Kentucky's largest whiskey distilleries, which, during the early 1800s, was owned and operated by O. W. Cowles. After the whiskey was made, it was placed in locally made wooden barrels and stored in a warehouse to be aged. Eventually, the whiskey was taken to the saloon (or "the Jigger house") on the hill behind the schoolhouse. There it was sold in pints, quarts, or by the glass. Later, the local population voted the distillery out of business, closing down the operation. At Greenwood's tollgate, on the road to Butler, people paid two or three cents per mile to travel on the road. Now the tollgate, the store, the blacksmith shop, the distillery, and the school are gone. Like most of the other small villages in Pendleton Co., Greenwood now has a few houses and nothing else.

Belew, Mildred Boden. *The First 200 Years of Pendleton County*. Falmouth, Ky.: M. B. Belew, n.d. [ca. 1994].

Mildred Belew

GREYHOUND TAVERN. The Greyhound Tavern, originally named the Dixie Tea Room, was opened in 1921 by John Hauer and at first operated as an ice cream parlor, selling candies, ice cream products, soft drinks, cigarettes, and cigars. The tea room was in South Fort Mitchell, near the end of a **streetcar** line. In the 1930s the business was sold to Al Frisch, who named it the Greyhound Grill after his brother Benny, who was a greyhound trainer. Frisch's family operated the business, and in addition to homemade ice cream, the Greyhound Tavern became famous for the whole Jack Salmon fish and fried chicken on its menu. The dinners cost 50 cents. Over the years, the ice cream parlor was eliminated, and as the building was expanded, the menu was expanded also, to include homemade soups, onion rings, hamburgers, and double-decker sandwiches.

The tavern has grown into a favorite dining and social spot for local customers and travelers along what has become a very busy section of **Dixie Highway** (U.S. 25) (see **Gourmet Strip**). Although all of the tavern's traditional food favorites are still available, the menu now also includes steaks, chops, seafood, and specialties offered by a friendly staff. The tavern's original two rooms are still intact and are named the Tavern Room and the Hunt Room. Both have pine paneling; the Hunt Room is decorated with a few paintings of greyhounds, while the Tavern Room houses the bar. At the parking lot entrance, the walls are decorated with photos of **Green Line** trolleys at or near the end of the line in South Fort Mitchell, and an original photo of the Dixie Tea room is the centerpiece below what appears to be the original wooden signboard. In 1987 the Greyhound Tavern hosted a dinner meeting of local politicians that featured a visit by former U.S. vice president Dan Quayle.

Bida, Craig. "Greyhound Tavern Keeps Drawing Crowds in Fort Mitchell," *Cincinnati City Beat*, April 2, 2006.

"Fried Chicken: A Pecking Order," *CE*, July 4, 2003, Weekend section, 19.

"Take a Nostalgic Journey Back to Dixie Highway's 'Gorumet Strip,'" *KP*, March 27, 1997, Weekend section, 17.

Warner, Tess. "Greyhound Tavern—Historic Spot Serves Up Southern Style Cuisine," *CIN Weekly*, December 7, 2005.

John E. Leming Jr.

GRIFFIN INDUSTRIES. Griffin Industries, a multimillion-dollar business with 30 locations in 14 states, got its start when John Lawrence Griffin moved to Falmouth, bought a 1935 Ford truck, and in 1943 began a trade few others wanted to touch. He drove a truck that picked up dead farm animals, which he then sold to rendering plants in Ohio. The Griffin rendering firm, which recycles animal waste products, continues to grow.

When Griffin began in 1943, he had a young wife, Rosellen Van Nest Griffin, an infant son, one truck, and a strong will to work. As the business grew, so did his family, eventually totaling 12 children. In June 1947, Griffin purchased 40 acres, two miles from Ky. Rt. 17 in Pendleton Co., on what is now known as Bryant Griffin Rd. There he built a processing plant. The Griffin family worked hard to build the company into what it is today. At times it was very difficult, but with Griffin's dedication and strong work ethic, which he passed on to his children and grandchildren, the company thrived. It began as Falmouth Fertilizer and later went by the name Griffin Fertilizer Company before arriving at its current name, Griffin Industries. Five sons and one son-in-law operate the company today. Several of the grandchildren also work for the firm.

John Griffin was an avid sports fan. In his earlier years, he sponsored and coached a baseball team on which several of his sons played. During his children's elementary years at **St. Francis Xavier** School, he started the school's basketball program and coached its team. For many seasons, he was a scorekeeper for the basketball team at Pendleton Co. High School (see **Pendleton Co. Public Schools**). In 1989 Griffin was inducted into the 10th Region Basketball Hall of Fame. He was also made an honorary coach at **Northern Kentucky University**. He died April 9, 1995, at age 72, after a long bout of strokes and heart attacks, and was buried at St. Stephen Cemetery in Fort Thomas, next to his wife, who died in 1985.

Dennis Griffin became president of the company in 1970. In 1973 the corporate headquarters moved to Cold Spring in Campbell Co. Today, Griffin Industries remains essentially a rendering business; it has grown and adapted, while other companies in the same business have folded. With nearly 900 employees, Griffin Industries operates a fleet of 400 vehicles and 700 truck-trailers, a ship that plies Caribbean ports in international trade, and a list of 1,000 customers that includes major cosmetics companies, clothing producers, and pharmaceutical firms.

Over the years, Griffin Industries has provided many residents of Pendleton Co. with jobs. The company has also supported a number of local civic projects. Pendleton Co. High School, for instance, has one of the finest fitness centers in the state, the John L. Griffin Fitness Center, thanks to construction funds provided by the Griffin family.

In 1993 the company also built the Griffin Concert Centre at the Pendleton Co. Fairgrounds.

"Opinion: John Griffin—Model Employer, Citizen," *KP*, April 13, 1995, 4K.
"Pioneer Recycler Dies—Griffin Industries Founder Was 72," *KP*, April 10, 1995, 1K.

Mildred Belew

GRISTMILLS. Shortly after pioneers arrived in Kentucky, some of them built primitive gristmills to grind corn into meal and wheat into flour. Gristmill sites were selected along streams with adequate water flow. As counties were developed, it became necessary to secure permission from the county court system, since millponds had the potential for flooding the properties of adjacent landowners. Also, the Kentucky legislature passed laws that regulated milldams, especially those on larger streams, because boat traffic and the movement of fish were considerations.

As time passed, more substantial gristmills were constructed. Many mills were spectacular three- or four-story structures, while others were quite simple buildings. Some of the early mills were constructed from logs; others were of frame, brick, or stone construction. Dams built of logs or stone provided the water supply to power these mills. A millrace or flume (an elevated wooden trough) was constructed to convey the water from the dam to the mill. The mill might be placed immediately below the dam, or it might be built far enough away to require long races or flumes for the water to travel through. The water was converted into power by means of water wheels (overshot, undershot, or breast wheels) or turbines that turned a main shaft. A series of gears, smaller shafts, and belts were used to supply power to various pieces of equipment in the mill.

Of critical importance were the millstones that ground the grain. Small mills had only one pair of stones, while larger ones sometimes had several pairs. Conglomerate millstones from Kentucky or Pennsylvania were often used for grinding corn, but flint millstones from Ohio or Kentucky were also used. For the grinding of wheat, millers preferred imported French burr millstones. Simple grain elevators were installed in some mills to move the grain from floor to floor, and bolters were used to sift flour. By the late 19th century, millstones began to be replaced with steel rollers (known as roller mills). This innovation allowed millers to produce more barrels of flour and meal per day.

Steam engines permitted the construction of mills in small communities far from streams and in urban contexts. By the early 20th century, the water-powered gristmills had nearly disappeared, replaced by larger urban mills that produced enough flour for regional markets. Today, only a few of the original structures have survived; the others lie in ruin or have been obliterated by modern development.

Northern Kentucky once had numerous gristmills, and communities often developed around these mills. The most important mills, historically or in terms of size, are listed in the following paragraphs.

Boone Co.

Petersburg, an important manufacturing center in the 19th century, included the mills of the Petersburg Milling Company in 1891; Ben Belden in 1896; Ferris, Brooks & Company also in 1896, and F. M. Morgan in 1906. In Walton, several mills once ground grain: the Rouse Brothers from 1879 to 1906, Abram Stansifer in 1880, M. & R. Rouse in 1896, the Walton Feed Mills from 1927 to 1929, and the Leonard Cook Company in 1929. The Rouse Brothers flour mill at Walton was a two-story frame structure with horizontal siding. Also in Boone Co., A. S. Crisler operated a water-powered gristmill near Limaburg on Gunpowder Creek; his father, Gabriel Crisler, operated a mill on Long Branch above the forks. Archaeologist Jeannine Kreinbrink has documented the Crisler-Gulley Mill. According to her, Lewis Crisler established the mill between 1817 and 1828 and sold it to Alfred and Joseph Chambers in 1834. The Crisler-Gulley Mill went through a series of owners before Robert Gulley acquired the property in 1918.

Bracken Co.

A steam merchant mill operated in Augusta during 1847. Other mills in Augusta included Darry & Brothers in 1859, J. Cook & Son in 1870, P. S. Blades in 1876, J. R. Powers & Co. in 1876, Stroube & Taylor during 1879 and 1880, B. P. Blades in 1881, N. J. Stroube from 1881 to 1896, William Teagarden from 1883 to 1887, Hanson & Brevard in 1891, Frank Hanson in 1896, G. W. Moneyhon Company in 1896, W. T. Teagarden in 1896, and the Augusta Milling Company in 1906. The Germantown Milling Company operated mills at Germantown in 1929.

Campbell Co.

As early as 1802, **James Taylor Jr.** had built a gristmill on the Licking River. John Gubser operated a mill in the 19th century in the community of Gubser (see **Gubser's Mill**). His mill was a two-story frame structure that was later acquired by the Rittinger family.

Many gristmills operated at various times in Newport, a number of them located along Monmouth St. They included the Newport Roller Flour Mills at 1104 Monmouth St. in 1894, the Newport Flour Mills at 1106 Monmouth St. in Newport from 1895 to 1897; the Wehenpohl Milling Company at 1106 Monmouth St. in 1897, and the Newport Milling Company at 1106 Monmouth St. and later at 1110 Monmouth St. from 1898 to 1903.

Carroll Co.

The great concentration of gristmills in Carroll Co. was in Carrollton. These included Cameron & Company in the early 20th century and the Hanlins Flour Mill, a two-story brick structure at the southwest corner of Sixth and Sycamore Sts.

Gallatin Co.

Several mills operated in Warsaw: J. H. McDaniel in 1859; Perry & Gibson from 1879 to 1883; James A. Howard from 1880 to 1890; and George T. Thompson from 1887 to 1896. Only the Thompson Flour Mill structure, a two-story brick building in Warsaw, has survived.

Grant Co.

The community of New Eagles Mills had mills owned by John A. Collins from 1876 to 1883, Frank Beard in 1881, James F. Salyers in 1883, and J. P. Pettit & Son in 1891. In Williamstown, mill owners included D. L. Cunningham from 1873 to 1896, O. S. Daugherty in 1880, D. D. Cunningham in 1881, Frank Carder from 1881 to 1883, J. H. Brumbach & Son in 1890, Carter & Vallandingham in 1891, D. C. Points & Company in 1896, Rednour & Company in 1896, and D. S. Cunningham in 1906. At Wilson's Mills, Wilson & Beck ran a mill in 1880.

Kenton Co.

At Banklick, James Bird operated a mill from 1879 to 1881, and Michael Morris ran a mill at Erlanger in 1896. Many mills have operated in Covington, including D. & G. Cree at 703 Madison Ave. from 1869 to 1874, D. Cree & Company during 1872 and 1873, Deglow & Bausch at 411 Pike St. from 1872 to 1880, Graves & Cree in 1876, Graves & Bramlage at Pike St. and Russell Ave. from 1878 to 1881, Deglow & Bramlage from 1881 to 1883, J. H. Fedders & Sons from as early as 1883; Covington City Mills at 708 Washington St. from 1894 to 1901; and the mill of Henry Heile & Company located at 517 Pike St. in the late 19th century.

Mason Co.

A primitive horse-powered gristmill was built at Limestone (Maysville) in 1785. Pioneer **Simon Kenton** operated a mill located below the forks of Lawrence Creek. Maysville newspapers contain advertisements for some of the late-18th- and early-19th-century mills in the area. An advertisement in the July 17, 1799, edition of the *Mirror* in Maysville mentioned the desire to purchase a few hundred bushels of wheat to be delivered to Orr's Mill on Lawrence's Creek. In the September 15, 1824, and August 28, 1829, issues of the *Maysville Eagle*, N & N Hixson advised the public that they were paying 40 cents (in 1824) and 50 cents (in 1829) per bushel for wheat at their steam mill in Maysville. The February 7, 1833, edition of the paper advertised the sale of Hixson's Frame Steam Mill in Maysville.

Owen Co.

Three individuals operated mills in Lusby's Mill, including Jacob Anspaw in 1876, D. R. Kinman from 1881 to 1883, and W. R. Kinman from 1887 to 1891. In Owenton, mills were run by M. A. Redman in 1870; the Roland Brothers from 1876 to 1883; Owenton Mills in 1883; H. F. Swope in 1890; and W. E. Arnold, Duke & Son, and C. W. Kenney in 1906. Poplar Grove was home to the following mills: R. N. Hatters in 1876, J. J. G. Brock in 1879, Crouch & Brock in 1883, and Hamilton & Applegate in 1883.

Pendleton Co.

Among the gristmills in the county seat of Falmouth were these: G. P. Gaulding in 1865; J. Woodhead in 1873; A. J. McNeis in 1880; J. E. Thompson in 1880; A. J. McNees in 1881; W. B. Woodhead from 1881 to 1883; J. W. Ashbrook in 1883; B. Bishop in 1883; King, Hamilton & Johnson in 1883; G. W. Galloway during 1883 and 1884; Champion Roller Mills (Applegate & Hamilton) in 1884; Bidge in 1887; Pendleton Flour Mills in 1887; Mary E. Hamilton in 1890; Falmouth Milling Company in 1891; R. B. McDonald in 1891; George Myers in 1891; Farmers' Co-operative Milling Company in 1896; J. W. Galloway in 1896; R. R. Wilson in 1896; Champion Mills in 1906; and Ideal Mills in 1906.

Robertson Co.

The county seat of Mount Olivet had several mills, including J. H. Sabin in 1881, Morrison & Son in 1887, F. P. Bland from 1887 to 1891, Morrison Brothers in 1890, the Robertson County Milling Company in 1890, Morrison & Sons in 1891, Morrison & Sparks in 1891, and Morrison & Company in 1896.

Cawker, E. Harrison. *Cawker's American Flour Mill and Elevator Directory for 1890–1891.* Milwaukee, Wis.: Riverside, 1891.

———. *Directory of the Flour Mill Owners and Millwrights of the United States of America and Canada, 1880.* Milwaukee, Wis.: Grand Opera House, 1880.

Clift, G. Glenn. *History of Maysville and Mason County.* Lexington, Ky.: Transylvania, 1936.

Hawes, George W. *George Hawes' Kentucky State Gazetteer and Business Directory for 1859 and 1860.* Louisville, Ky.: George W. Hawes, 1859.

Hockensmith, Charles D, Kenneth C. Carstens, Charles Stout, and Sara J. Rivers. *Current Archaeological Research in Kentucky.* Vol. 5. Frankfort: Kentucky Heritage Council, 1998.

Hodgman, George H. *Hodgman and Company's Kentucky State Gazetteer, Shippers' Guide, and Business Directory, for 1865 and 1866.* Louisville, Ky.: Hodgman, 1865.

———. *Kentucky State Directory, Travelers and Shippers' Guide, for 1870–1871.* Louisville, Ky.: John P. Morton, 1871.

O'Malley, Nancy. *A New Village Called Washington.* Maysville, Ky.: McClanahan, 1987.

Seiller, Edward F. *Kentucky Natural Resources, Industrial Statistics, Industrial Directory Descriptions by Counties.* Bureau of Agriculture, Labor and Statistics, Bulletin 34. Frankfort, Ky.: State Journal, 1929.

Tenkotte, Paul A. "Rival Cities to Suburbs: Covington and Newport, Kentucky, 1790–1890," PhD diss., Univ. of Cincinnati, 1989.

Young and Company. *Business Professional Directory of the Cities and Towns of Kentucky.* Atlanta, Ga.: Young, 1906.

Charles D. Hockensmith

GROTE MANUFACTURING COMPANY. In 1926 William D. Grote, a pharmacy graduate of the University of Cincinnati, purchased the National Color Type Company, 421 Grandview Ave., Bellevue, which manufactured reflective street signs. In 1930 construction began on a physical plant that eventually was three stories high and contained more than 140,000 square feet. Before buying the company, Grote had owned and operated two chemical companies (the American Chemical Company and the Missouri Chemical Company) and an oxygen company. With the acquisition of National Color Type, he began to make items for the automotive industry, including spotlights and reflectors. As sales increased, Grote was able to sell his chemical and oxygen interests and concentrate more on automotive sales. During the Great Depression, when auto-part sales were not sufficient to sustain the company, he shifted production to the manufacture of street signs. During **World War II**, Grote converted his plant and equipment to the making of blackout lights, devices that cut underwater cable, and other war-related products. After World War II, to capitalize on the dramatic increase in new home construction, Grote converted his wartime equipment to the manufacture of bathroom medicine cabinets and metal mirrors; he also resumed the production of parts for cars and trucks, primarily reflectors and lights. During the 1950s, the Bellevue plant, surrounded by residential housing, lacked room for expansion. Grote had another facility in Seymour, Ind., and the decision was made to build a new plant in Madison, Ind. All production was relocated to the new plant in 1960. The company continues to be known as Grote Industries. Headquartered in Madison, the firm has plants in both Mexico and Canada, where lights, reflectors, mirrors, and electronics, primarily for trucks, off-road vehicles, and cars are made. After Grote Industries moved away from Bellevue, its building was sold to Kent Manufacturing, which continued to build medicine cabinets. The building was later sold to the Henry Hosea Company, an office-furniture firm. At its height in Bellevue, the Grote Manufacturing Company employed 300 to 400 people and for some time was the largest employer in the town. The company was the first in the United States to use plastic injection molding (in the 1920s), it introduced the first repairable long-life lamps for trucks (in 1977), and it brought LED lighting to trucking (in 1990). Today, Grote Industries has 1,200 employees and revenues of $114 million. It is led by the founder's grandson William "Bill" Grote and is still privately held by a family that has been in business for 100 years.

Grote. www.grote.com/ (accessed June 1, 2005).

Peter Grote

GROVER, ASA PORTER (b. February 18, 1819, Ontario Co., N.Y.; d. July 20, 1887, Georgetown, Ky.). Born in upstate New York, legislator Asa Porter Grover was educated in the schools of that area. He moved to Kentucky in 1837 to attended Centre College, from which he graduated. Grover then taught school in Woodford and Franklin counties. Like many other teachers of his day, he took up the study of law, and he was admitted to the bar in 1843. He opened his law office in Owenton in Owen Co. and practiced there until 1881. Entering politics, Grover became a member of the Kentucky state Senate (1857–1865) representing Owen Co.; he was the only Democrat to serve in the Kentucky Senate during the **Civil War**. He attended the Democratic state convention in 1863, and he was elected to the 40th U.S. Congress (1867–1869). He was well respected in Owen Co. Grover moved his law practice to Georgetown in Scott Co. in 1881 and founded the First National Bank of Georgetown, which opened in May 1883. Grover died in 1887 and was buried at the Georgetown Cemetery.

Apple, Lindsey, Frederick A. Johnston, and Ann Bolton Bevins. *Scott County Kentucky: A History.* Georgetown, Ky.: Scott Co. Historical Society, 1993.

Biographical Directory of the United States Congress. "Asa Porter Grover." www.bioguide.congress.gov (accessed June 20, 2007).

GUBSER'S MILL / TWELVE MILE. The community of Gubser's Mill, or Twelve Mile, located in rural south central Campbell Co., has long been associated with its sawmill and gristmill. John Gubser arrived from Switzerland after the area had been settled in the 1860s by English-speaking immigrants. He bought an established sawmill in 1865, and from then on, the name Gubser's Mill has been applied to the village. The other name, Twelve Mile, is a reference to Twelve Mile Creek, which has its source there and flows to the Ohio River. The local 1883 Lake atlas shows a mill, Seiter's Blacksmith Shop, a wagon shop, a post office, and a café. The mill burned twice and was rebuilt but eventually fell into disrepair. It was torn down in 1983. The mill and the adjacent shops were the hub of the community. The mill's steam whistle used to blow each noon to signal local farmers that it was time to stop for lunch.

Besides the mill and its surrounding buildings, the other important element of the community was the St. Peter and Paul Catholic Church. Established in 1853, the church was the religious center for the German Catholics who had settled in the area in the late 1840s. The church began in a log cabin; later a brick church was built, which had to be torn down due to structural flaws. Today, the parish has its present church building, a school, and a cemetery. In order to raise money for its school, the parish sponsors two summer picnics that bring together the entire community. The picnic grounds, called Hickory Grove, have been in operation for more than 100 years. Although public one-room schoolhouses existed in Gubser's Mill/Twelve Mile—some of them named Hickory Grove, Sugar Grove, Kohler, and Old Gubser Mill—the vast majority of children attended the Catholic elementary school associated with the church.

Today, the AA Highway allows the residents of this community to travel to workplaces elsewhere while living in the farming community. It is expected that more new homes will be built in the area by people desiring this lifestyle as the county solves sanitary sewer issues around Gubser's Mill.

An Atlas of Boone, Kenton, and Campbell Counties, Kentucky. Philadelphia: D. J. Lake, 1883.
Campbell Co. Historical Society. *Campbell County, Kentucky, 200 Years, 1794–1994*. Alexandria, Ky.: Campbell Co. Historical Society, 1994.
"Only One in County," *KP*, August 2, 1975, 6K.
"Twelve Mile Baptist Church Observes 135th Year," *KP*, September 24, 1934, 2.

Kenneth A. Reis

GUM LICK BAPTIST CHURCH. The Gum Lick Baptist Church was constituted in December 1882, with 21 charter members. G. B. and Josephine Dance deeded to the church's trustees the lot in southwestern Pendleton Co. on which the church and the cemetery were situated. The first pastor was J. W. Clark, and the first list of deacons appeared in 1895. Church business meetings in the early years began on Saturday evenings and were sometimes resumed after Sunday morning services. Committees were assigned for each job to be done at the church. The church had very strict rules in those years: if members showed bad conduct, they were brought before the church to confess their wrongs, and only then were they allowed back into the fellowship. Failure to confess led to exclusion from membership.

Early baptisms took place in farm ponds and streams. People traveled to church by foot, on horseback, or by horse and buggy. The church was heated at first by a wood stove and later by coal. Kerosene lamps hanging from the ceiling provided lighting. Later, carbide lights were used. Electricity first came in 1948.

In May 1982, lightning struck the church steeple, damaging it severely and also damaging part of the roof. Frankie Jones and other church members erected a new steeple. The church bell, which was repaired, has now been rung in the community for more than 100 years.

Belew, Mildred Boden. *The First 200 Years of Pendleton County*. Falmouth, Ky.: M. B. Belew, n.d. [ca. 1994].
"Eye Catcher of the Week," *KP*, November 15, 1989, 4K.

Mildred Belew

GUNPOWDER (SUGARTIT). The village of Gunpowder in Boone Co., located along Gunpowder Creek at the intersection of Pleasant Valley Rd. and the Florence Union Turnpike (U.S. 42), was also known as Sugartit. In the early 1900s it was home to a blacksmith shop, a general store, a post office, and a sawmill. The **Hopeful Lutheran Church** and the Gunpowder Baptist Church were nearby. The Pleasant Ridge School stood on a nearby hill, just to the east of Gunpowder.

There are several theories regarding how the village received the name Sugartit. (A sugartit was a pacifier for babies, made by tying a piece of sugar into a square of muslin.) In a letter to his grandchildren, Shelly Aylor, the last owner of the town's general store, tells this story: His father, L. P. Aylor, and his uncle John Surface were farmers who lived in the Gunpowder neighborhood. During the winter, when farm chores were not very demanding, the two men would walk to the general store to pick up their mail and exchange news, or in Shelly Aylor's words, to "loaf." Often they would arrive home late for dinner. Their wives, exasperated, said the reason the men were late was that they had to have a sugartit at the store.

Cabot, Susan M., and Michael Rouse. *Boone County*. Charleston, S.C.: Arcadia, 1998.

Michael D. Rouse

GYPSIES. Many of the Gypsies who have come to Northern Kentucky, for short or long periods, have acted in accord with the Gypsy stereotype. Sometimes referred to as a nation within a nation, Gypsies as a group seek no permanent home, preferring to wander about continuously. They call themselves the Roma and live by a strict religious and legal code known as Romany. Their mother tongue is Romany and is derived from Sanskrit, revealing their Indian origins, but *Gypsy* is derived from *Egyptian*. Gypsies are often confused with, or grouped with, Hungarians, Romanians, or Serbs, since they immigrated to the United States just behind those groups in the 1880s. Gypsies are mostly associated with the dark-clothed, high-cheekboned people, speaking with an accent, who stroll into town for a few days; often they depart on their own, just before being asked to leave. In the old days, they arrived via caravans of horses and wagons; today they come in expensive cars and trucks. While in town they perform sundry casual jobs for cash payments: as tinkers, they repair things, from pots and pans to roof gutters; as contractors, they seal driveways with a black concoction that frequently washes away during the next hard rain. Gypsy women, made famous by song and by their specialty trades—palm-reading and fortune-telling—generally stay in camp on the outskirts of town. Their men can sometimes be found siphoning fuel out of the underground storage tanks of closed gasoline stations. Of course, not all Gypsies fit this stereotypical image, and some became respectable members of the community.

One Gypsy family in Newport was the Boswell family, a well-known member of which was Madam Sheba, Irene G. Boswell (Mrs. Frederick C. Boswell), who resided for a long time at 11 E. Third St. Just around the corner was Madam Lena (Mamie Rose Lovell), who lived at 309 York St. Both were "palmists" (according to their signs) whose fortune-telling parlors were positioned just off the end of the old **Central Bridge**. Their scam was part of the notorious business scene in Newport during the 1950s. In their parlors, at all hours of the day and night, customers could pay to have their palms read and learn what the length of their "love line" portended. For a larger fee, and with prior arrangements, a group could schedule a séance at the palm-reader's parlor. However, both Madam Sheba and Madam Lena had to be given enough advance notice to hide assistants in the walls and basement, providing the necessary voices from beyond. The candles, the thick dark drapes, their large earrings, and the large tables were all part of the scene. They seemed to have known many of the customers' deceased relatives but seldom any living ones. Meanwhile, the palm-readers' husbands would be busy hauling things in their trucks, blacktopping, painting driveways, or "honey-dipping," a term for the service of sucking the muck out of septic systems. The modern sanitation district has taken the long, thick, black hose from the hands of people like Bosmac. A member of the Boswell clan, he was Campbell Co.'s longtime honey-dipper; he operated out of his Dayton, Ky., business location well into the 1980s, referring to himself as "a privately employed sanitation worker." Later, there were other Gypsy palmists in Campbell Co.: for example, Sister Mohawk in Dayton and a group of palm readers working out of Cold Spring. In 1978, when Madam Lena died, her funeral in Newport at the Vonderhaar-Stetter-Betz Funeral Home on E. Third St. was one of the largest in that city's history. It was attended by mourners from across the nation. Madam Lena, the so-called "mayor of York St.," was carried in grand splendor by a white, horse-drawn hearse to nearby Evergreen Cemetery in Southgate.

In Fort Thomas, in March 1977, 20 to 25 Gypsies appeared at the IGA Highlander food store, distracting employees with requests for help. Almost as quickly as they arrived, they were gone, as was a large amount of cash from the safe in the store's office. They were last seen headed south on **U.S. 27**. Later that year, Gypsies in Campbell Co. posed as city building inspectors, asking homeowners for identification and demanding cash for their services.

Across the Licking River in Kenton Co., attorney Bill Hagedorn became the negotiator of choice for the Gypsies. He was invited to their parties and gatherings, often large galas held in hotels in Cincinnati; the tab for these Gypsy galas was seldom paid. When in the region, the migratory Gypsies often camped on the outskirts of town, where no permit was required. Madison Pike (Ky. Rt. 17), south of Covington, was one such place. If trouble broke out, Hagedorn was summoned. In February 1977 it was Hagedorn who saved Sister Mohawk from jail after she bilked a widow in Fort Mitchell out of more than $11,000.

In adjoining Boone Co., in May 1974, about 10 Gypsies, described as wearing old clothes and "looking like tramps," entered a convenience store in Florence, and one of the women proceeded to discuss a coupon for a wrinkle cream with the checkout lady and eventually the manager. When the Gypsies left after 15 minutes, the manager discovered that almost $4,000 was missing from that day's bank deposit. The group had driven off in two late-model Cadillacs with red and white license plates.

The migratory Gypsies habitually arrive in Northern Kentucky during the early spring, having worked their way back north from wintering in the Deep South. Perhaps the Williamson family is the best known group of these. During each annual visit, the Williamsons schedule a morning at Spring Grove Cemetery in Cincinnati, formally burying their members who died during the previous year.

Bodies are sent in advance to the vault at the cemetery to await the mass burial ceremony.

Rightly or wrongly, performers in **circuses** are frequently thought to be Gypsies. The image of the Gypsy has entered into the language of child-rearing, much to the chagrin of modern child psychologists. Mothers in the region have often exhorted their children, "If you don't behave right, we're going to give you to the Gypsies."

DeCamp, Graydon. "Those Unbelievable Gypsies." *CE Magazine,* March 14, 1982, 18–23.

Grossman, James R., Ann Durkin Keating, and Janice L. Reiff, eds. *The Encyclopedia of Chicago.* Chicago: Univ. of Chicago Press, 2004.

Hicks, Jack. "NKU Official, Student of Gypsies, Tells of Myths," *KE,* April 6, 1979, A1.

Loftus, Tom. "'Gypsies' Bilk Pair of $137," *KP,* September 6. 1977, 7.

———. "Mourners Flock to Madam(e) Lena's Funeral," *KP,* June 15, 1978, 5.

Remlinger, Connie. "'Gypsies' Swipe $3,887," *KP,* May 7, 1974, 9K.

Workum, Bert. "Gypsy Bands Raiding Homes," *KP,* August 31, 1977, 17.

———. "Widow Gave Gypsy $11,250," *KP,* February 18, 1977, 1.

Michael R. Sweeney

HAILE, RALPH (b. May 18, 1922, Cincinnati, Ohio; d. August 4, 2006, Cincinnati, Ohio). Ralph V. Haile, a well-respected and long-time Covington banker, was the son of Ralph B. and Mary Neal Donoho Haile. He grew up in the Hyde Park neighborhood of Cincinnati and graduated from Walnut Hills High School and, in 1946, from the University of Cincinnati School of Engineering. During **World War II**, he piloted P-51 Mustang fighters in the European theater for the U.S. Army Air Force. After the war he attended the University of Wisconsin's School of Banking in Madison.

Haile served as chief executive of the Peoples Liberty and Trust Company in Covington for 19 years. He was a strong Covington and Northern Kentucky supporter. Famous for the bow ties he wore and the Camaro convertible he drove, Haile was a history lesson in person; he could be counted on to know what had happened and often what was about to happen. Although he lived on the east side of Cincinnati, he generously supported Northern Kentucky. For example, he and his wife donated $2 million to **St. Elizabeth Medical Center** for an addition to its hospice unit. Haile was involved in the Covington Community Center (see **Center for Great Neighborhoods of Covington**), the Covington Business Council, urban renewal, and the development of the Old Town Plaza and the Riverside Condominiums. He contributed to the **Behringer-Crawford Museum**, **Thomas More College**, and the University of Cincinnati Foundation. Haile died in 2006 in Cincinnati and was buried in the Haile lot at Spring Grove Cemetery there. His wife, Carol Ann Homan Haile, died in 2004. The plaza by the U.S. Bank along Madison Ave. in Covington has been named the Ralph Haile Square, in honor of him.

"Banker Laid Foundation for City Rebirth," *KP*, May 24, 1989, 1K.
"A Banker with a Heart of Gold," *KP*, August 5, 2006, 1A.
"Dedication for a Visionary," *KE*, September 1, 2006, B1.
Spring Grove Cemetery Records, Cincinnati, Ohio.
"$2 Million Gift Helps Hospital Add Four Rooms to Hospice," *KP*, December 6, 2006, A2.

HALFWAY HOUSE. The Halfway House was a restaurant, gas station, and motor lodge just south of Williamstown in Grant Co. The site was located at the corner of the **Dixie Highway** (U.S. 25) and Sunset, approximately halfway between Covington, and Lexington. Built in 1928 by John Gilforos, the Halfway House opened on Independence Day in 1929.

The heyday of the Halfway House was the 1950s and early 1960s, when tourist and local traffic made the Dixie Highway one of the most heavily traveled roads in the nation. The Halfway House cabins were routinely filled and the restaurant was kept busy; busloads of passengers stopped by at all hours to enjoy the food, especially the widely known fried chicken.

The completion of I-75 (see **Expressways**) through the area spelled the beginning of the end for the Halfway House. Travelers on the interstate found that restaurants, filling stations, and lodging closer to the interstate highway's exits were the convenient places to stop. The Halfway House faded into memory, replaced by a sporting-goods store called F&R General Sales. The building was destroyed by a spectacular fire on the evening of November 18, 1976. It was rebuilt as a Red Carpet Inn and restaurant.

"Fire Destroys Old Halfway House," *Grant County News*, November 25, 1976, 1.
Northern Kentucky Views. "Halfway House." www.nkyviews.com (accessed August 3, 2006).

Chris Meiman

HALLAM. The community of Hallam in central Owen Co. is on the northwest side of **Elk Lake Shores**, where Ky. Rts. 227 and 330 intersect. It is within East Owenton Precinct, and the 1883 Lake atlas suggests that once there was a school at Hallam. The Beech Grove Baptist Church is just north of town along Ky. Rt. 227. Hallam is the boyhood home of Rear Adm. **Arnold Elllsworth True**, a naval officer who earned many navy medals for his ship and fleet command in the Pacific during **World War II**.

An Atlas of Owen County, Kentucky. Philadelphia: Lake, 1883.
Houchens, Mariam Sidebottom. *History of Owen County: "Sweet Owen."* Louisville, Ky.: Standard, 1976.

HALLAM, THEODORE FRELINGHUYSEN (b. March 10, 1844, Owenton, Ky.; d. May 3, 1905, Covington, Ky.). Theodore Hallam was a descendant of the 15th-century English bishop of Salisbury, Robert Hallam. Theodore's father, James R. Hallam, an attorney, served for a short time as a circuit court judge. The family moved from Owenton to Williamstown, and then to Newport when Theodore was quite young. He served with the Confederate Army in 1861, fighting at the battles of Shiloh and Hampton Roads. Near the end of the war, he held the rank of captain and was assigned to Jefferson Davis, president of the Confederate States. After leaving the army, Hallam was employed as a correspondent with the *Cincinnati Enquirer.* In that position he toured famous **Civil War** battlefields, writing articles under the pseudonym Asperate. Afterward he studied law, became an attorney, and formed the firm of Hallam and Terrill, with offices in Covington and Cincinnati. On May 3, 1875, he married Bettie Stevenson Timberlake. Her father's family, the Timberlakes, and her mother's, the Stevensons, owned most of the land where the cities of Erlanger and Elsmere are today. The Timberlake home still stands along Stevenson Rd. In 1875 Hallam entered politics and was elected to the state House of Representatives, representing the First District of Covington. Later he was elected state senator. He rose to the position of Speaker in both bodies. Hallam was a staunch Democrat (see **Democratic Party**), but in the 1899 governor's campaign, he refused to back fellow Northern Kentuckian William Goebel, siding instead with the Independent, John Y. Brown. Hallam died in 1905 at age 61, at his home, 1034 Scott St. in Covington. He was buried in the Highland Cemetery in Fort Mitchell.

"In Memoriam," *CC*, May 12, 1905, 4.
"Lawyer Suspended," *KP*, December 31, 1900, 1.
"Sketch of Theodore Hallam," *KP*, August 10, 1892, 1.
"Tarvin Sends Lawyer to Jail," *KP*, January 14, 1901, 1.

HALL FAMILY (COVINGTON). John Wortham Hall Sr. was born January 19, 1802 in Orange Co., N.C. He studied theology with Dr. Gideon Blackburn, a Presbyterian missionary to the Indian

Halfway House Restaurant, Williamstown.

tribes of the South, and was licensed to preach in western Tennessee in October 1824. He married Catherine Presley Thornton. After several assignments as a pastor in Tennessee, Ohio, and Huntsville, Ala., during the 1830s and 1840s, he earned a doctorate in divinity from Miami University in 1848 and then became the fifth president of Miami University of Ohio, serving in that role from 1854 to 1866. Hall is often referred to as Miami's Civil War president, for he dealt with the mixed loyalties existing on campus at the time. In 1868 he was elected superintendent of the Covington schools at an annual salary of $2,500. He brought a new structure and new ideas to the city's schools. While he was superintendent, he hired his son John Wortham Hall Jr. as the high school principal. The senior Hall's tenure as superintendent ended in 1878. He continued to preach as a Presbyterian minister until his death. The Hall family lived at 26 E. Fourth St. for many years before moving to 417 Russell St., where John Sr. died on January 4, 1886, at age 83. He was buried at Linden Grove Cemetery in Covington. One month later his wife Catherine was buried next to him.

John Wortham Hall Jr., born in 1830 in Tennessee, was trained as a geologist. However, education was his real interest, and he became a high school principal in Dayton, Ohio. He moved to Covington in 1868 and served as principal of the Covington High School, which eventually was located on the northeast corner of 12th and Russell Sts. He was employed by the Covington schools for more than 30 years, including 4 years, 1889 to 1893, as the superintendent of Covington schools. In 1901, with his health failing, he moved to Denver to be with his son Harry, who died shortly after his father's arrival. John W. Hall Jr. died November 6, 1907 in Colorado, at the home of his daughter-in-law, Harry's widow. He was buried at the Denver Cemetery. Mourners came from as far away as Dayton, Ohio, and Covington for his funeral. In 1928 the Covington School Board, in appreciation of John Wortham Hall Jr.'s long service, changed the name of the Fourth District Junior High School to the John W. Hall Junior High School.

Mary Thornton Hall was born about 1845 at Murfreesboro, Tenn., the daughter of John W. and Catherine Presley Thornton Hall and the sister of John W. Hall Jr., and was educated early in life at the Nashville Academy, excelling in music. In 1870 she was living with her parents in Covington. She graduated from Miami University of Ohio and became a popular newspaper columnist in the Greater Cincinnati area. Hall worked for the *Covington Daily Commonwealth* and the *Cincinnati Enquirer* (the latter for 30 years) as a society columnist. She often wrote about herself in the third person as a writer, singer, social leader, or philanthropist. Mary was active in charitable work. A strong soprano singer, she often sang and played the organ at **Trinity Episcopal Church**. She died July 15, 1916, at her flat in the Woodford Apartments in Covington, affectionately remembered as "the woman who never said or wrote an unkind word about anyone." She was buried at Linden Grove Cemetery after a funeral at Trinity Episcopal Church.

Kentucky Death Certificate No. 18531, for the year 1916.
Linden Grove Cemetery Records, Covington, Ky., available at www.kenton.lib.ky.us.
MacCracken, Henry Mitchell. "The Administration of President John W. Hall, D.D., LL.D.," archives of Miami Univ., Oxford, Ohio.
Mills, Howard H. "A History of Education of Covington, Kentucky," master's thesis, Univ. of Kentucky, 1929.
"Miss Mary T. Hall, 'Kindest Woman in Kentucky,' Is Dead," *KTS*, July 15, 1916, 10.
Nordheim, Betty Lee. *Echoes of the Past: A History of the Covington Public School System.* Covington, Ky.: Covington Independent Public Schools, 2002.

HAMILTON. The village of Hamilton was located at Ohio River Mile 466 in far western Boone Co. Although it had been the landing point for many excursions to Big Bone Springs (see **Big Bone Lick**) for some time, it was first incorporated as the town of Landing by the Kentucky legislature on February 28, 1835. The town's name was changed to Hamilton in 1846 to honor Joel Hamilton, one of the community's founders.

The town prospered during the 19th century owing to its proximity to Big Bone Spring. In 1883 the community had two tobacco warehouses, a mill, a school, and two doctors. Dr. John E. Stevenson of Covington operated the Valley Hotel, also known as the Big Bone Hotel. The waters of Big Bone Spring were advertised to have healing powers, and people came from great distances to stay in the hotel and gain access to the springwater.

During the early 20th century, Hamilton thrived as a port for packet boats on the Ohio River. However, as a result of the decrease in river travel, the improvement of roads, and the burning of the Hamilton High School in June 1953, Hamilton eventually ceased to be a town.

An Atlas of Boone, Kenton, and Campbell Counties, Kentucky. Philadelphia: D. J. Lake, 1883.
Boone Co. Deed Book L, 436.
"Recreations," *DC*, June 6, 1882 4.
Warner, Jennifer S. *Boone County: From Mastodons to the Millennium.* Burlington, Ky.: Boone Co. Bicentennial Book Committee, 1998.

Laurie Wilcox

HAMMON, JOHN (b. January 29, 1760, Goochland Co., Va.; d. 1868, Owen Co.). John Hammon, a soldier and an Indian fighter, was the son of James and Mary Hargiss Hammon. While living in Wilkes Co., N.C., at age 16, he became a **Revolutionary War** soldier and fought at the Battle of King's Mountain (N.C.). Later, he participated in the siege of Bryants Station in 1782 near Lexington, and he accompanied Benjamin Logan on his forays into Ohio Indian Territory. Hammon was living at Mountain Island in what later became Owen Co. by 1806, and in 1822 he and some of his sons were building wooden superstructures in Cincinnati for Ohio River steamboats. He retired to Owen Co. Hammon, a Baptist, was married twice, and when he died in 1868 at age 108, he had fathered 22 children. He was buried in the cemetery of the Mussel Shoals Baptist Church in Owen Co. Hammon was an ancestor of Stratton Owen Hammon, the peripatetic Louisville architect, author, and genealogist.

Hammon, Stratton Owen. *The Saga of John Hammon, Revolutionary War Hero and Owen County Kentucky Pioneer.* Louisville, Ky.: Pilgrim Press, 1979.

HANKS. The Grant Co. community of Hanks was located about four miles from Dry Ridge on the Dry Ridge–Warsaw Rd. (Ky. Rt. 467). The residents at Hanks included C. L. Alexander, operator of a general store in 1890; Jimshack Webster, who lived and farmed across the road; and Ezra Webster, who lived on an adjoining farm. A post office was established there in 1898, with C. L. Alexander as postmaster. There was difficulty in finding an acceptable name for this small village, a name not already in use in the state. But finally Hanks became the approved name. The post office was closed in 1906. In 1921 the general store burned down and was not rebuilt.

Conrad, John B., ed. *History of Grant County.* Williamstown, Ky.: Grant Co. Historical Society, 1992.

John B. Conrad

HANNAFORD, SAMUEL, AND SONS (Samuel Hannaford, b. April 10, 1835, Widdecome Parish, Devonshire, England; d. January 7, 1911, Cincinnati, Ohio; Harvey Eldridge Hannaford, b. October 15, 1857, College Hill, Ohio; d. May 23, 1923, Cincinnati, Ohio; Charles E. Hannaford, b. April 7, 1860, Cincinnati, Ohio; d. July 18, 1936, Cincinnati, Ohio). In 1844 nine-year-old Samuel Hannaford, founder of the prominent Cincinnati-based architectural firm Samuel Hannaford and Sons, immigrated to the United States from England with his parents, Roger and Mary Northcott Hannaford; the family eventually settled on a farm in the small village of Cheviot in western Hamilton Co., Ohio, near Cincinnati. Samuel received his early education in Cincinnati public schools, attended Farmer's College, College Hill, Ohio, in 1853, and in the following year began a period of study and collaborative employment as a draftsman with the architect John R. Hamilton. By 1857, the 22-year-old Hannaford had decided to form his own architectural firm, though he also participated in successful partnerships with two local architects: he practiced with Edwin Anderson from 1858 to 1870 and with Edwin Proctor from 1874 to 1876. Hannaford was married three times and had 11 children. By 1886 Hannaford's two eldest sons, Harvey Eldridge and Charles Edward, had completed their architectural training; they joined their father's business, forming Samuel Hannaford and Sons, a firm responsible for the design of structures throughout Greater Cincinnati and Northern Kentucky. After Samuel Hannaford's death in 1911 and burial at Spring Grove Cemetery in Cincinnati, successive generations operated the firm under the family name until 1964.

Hannaford-designed structures covered a broad range of styles that included, among others, Renaissance Revival, Queen Anne, Victorian, Eclectic, Romanesque, and Beaux Arts. The company designed hospitals, factories, churches, schools, courthouses, waterworks buildings, hotels, and family homes. One of the most notable contributions of the Hannafords to architecture in Campbell Co. is Newport's Beaux Arts–style **Our Lady of Providence Academy**, formerly known as the Academy Notre Dame of Providence. The site at Sixth and Linden Sts. was purchased in 1902 by the **Sisters of Divine Providence** as the new home for their academy and dedicated in 1903 by Bishop **Camillus P. Maes**. The Diocese of Covington (see **Roman Catholics**) sold the building in 1983. Subsequent interior alterations converted the grand old building into apartments and extended-stay suites, and it has recently become a 40-unit upscale condominium complex that bears the name of its celebrated architect. Other Hannaford-designed structures in Newport include the **Salem United Methodist Church** and parsonage at 810 York St. and two stately mansions constructed for members of local beer baron **George Wiedemann**'s family. The George Wiedemann Jr. mansion, located at 401 Park Ave. in Newport's East Row Historic District, was constructed in 1899 for the younger son of the brewery founder. The second structure, an imposing Victorian edifice, was known as the Wiedemann Estate or Mansion. Located at 1102 Park Ave. and constructed in 1895 on a tract in the **Cote Brilliante** neighborhood, this stately dwelling served as the longtime residence of George Wiedemann's son Charles. Samuel Hannaford and Sons also designed several other Campbell Co. structures, including the **St. Bernard Catholic Church** in Dayton and the Newman Samuel residence and the **Altamont Hotel**, both in Fort Thomas. In 1880 Hannaford designed a Classical Revival structure for the Grant Co. clerk's office in Williamstown at 107 N. Main St.

In Kenton Co., Hannaford and Sons designed both incarnations of the Covington Protestant Children's Home; the first structure, located at the southwest corner of 14th St. and Madison Ave., was begun in 1881 and housed 50 orphans; a site in **Devou Park** was later chosen as the location for a larger facility, constructed in the Colonial Revival style, that became known as the **Children's Home of Northern Kentucky** in 1990. Hannaford's firm was also selected by **St. Benedict Catholic Church**, which had outgrown its original church-school combination, to design a church building. Located on E. 17th St. in Covington, the new church was dedicated in December 1908 by Bishop Maes. The firm served as architects for the St. Elizabeth Hospital at 21st and Eastern Aves. in Covington, completed in 1914 (see **St. Elizabeth Medical Center**). After a **tornado** in 1915 destroyed **St. Joseph Catholic Church**'s spire in Covington, Hannaford and Sons was chosen to design a new tower surmounted by a cupola. A Hannaford-designed cupola of 1898 replaced the original dome of the Boone Co. Courthouse in Burlington.

In the 1920s Covington demolished the former **Amos Shinkle** Mansion at 323 E. Second St. It had served as the first home of the **Booth Memorial Hospital**, established by the **Salvation Army** in 1914. Hannaford and Sons was selected to design a more modern facility, which served the people of Covington until 1979, when the hospital relocated to Florence, Ky.; the structure, now known as Governor's Point, houses 49 condominium units. Within Covington's Emery-Price Historic District, the Hannafords designed the Queen Anne–style Emery Row Building in the 800 block (810–828) of Scott St. In 1906 construction was completed on the Hannaford-designed **Mother of God Church** School building. Nearly a decade later, the Covington parish commissioned the Hannaford firm to design a replacement for the arched pediment, which had linked the Mother of God Catholic Church's two distinctive bell towers, because the original had been destroyed when a tornado struck the area on July 7, 1915. Samuel Hannaford and Sons was also responsible for the design of many other Covington buildings, including the German Mutual Fire Insurance Company, the Bell Telephone Company building, and the residence of Rev. Adolph Rupprecht. In Mason Co., the firm designed the **Hayswood Hospital** in Maysville during the early 1920s.

In addition to designing, over the course of about a century, some of Northern Kentucky's most opulent structures, Samuel Hannaford and Sons also served as a training ground for many local architects and engineers, including Louis E. Dittoe (see **Dittoe and Wisenall**), **Lyman R. Walker**, and **Louis Gustave Bouscaren**.

Leonard, Lewis Alexander, ed. *Greater Cincinnati and Its People: A History*. Vol. 4. New York: Lewis Historical, 1927.

Schroeder, David E. "Community History–Covington." Kenton Co. Public Library, Genealogy and Kentucky History. Kentonlibrary.com. www.kentonlibrary (accessed June 4, 2006).

Tenkotte, Paul A. *A Heritage of Art and Faith: Downtown Covington Churches*. Covington, Ky.: Kenton Co. Historical Society, 1986.

Tenkotte, Paul A., David E. Schroeder, and Thomas S. Ward. *To Be Catholic and American in Northern, Central, and Appalachian Kentucky: The Diocese of Covington, 1853–2003*. Forthcoming.

Janice Mueller

HARDEMAN, FLORENCE (b. October 1886, Covington, Ky.; d. after April 1938). Concert violinist Florence E. Hardeman was the daughter of Capt. Thomas W. Hardeman, a Covington postmaster, and was a 1902 graduate of **La Salette Academy** in Covington. The family lived at 316 Garrard St. in Covington. Florence Hardeman made her debut as a violin soloist with the Cincinnati Symphony Orchestra while in her teens, and she earned her graduate degree in music from the Cincinnati College of Music. In 1909 John Philip Sousa engaged her as a violin soloist for his orchestra, and she toured the United States for several years, performing at places like Cincinnati's Music Hall and San Francisco's Civic Auditorium. After touring with Sousa, Hardeman traveled to Berlin, Germany, in 1912 to study under violinist Leopold Auer. She returned to the United States in 1914, before **World War I** erupted, relocated to New York City, and studied with violinist Arrigo Serato. In 1916 she was given a 300-year-old, $10,000 Amati violin that had previously been owned by Ole Bull. The following year she toured the United States with actress Sarah Bernhardt. Florence Hardeman married Frank Hardeman (no relation) of Detroit, Mich., in December 1918, separated from him after eight months in 1919, and was granted a divorce by 1921. As late as April 1938, she was playing at the Plaza Hotel in New York City.

"Florence Hardeman to Study in Berlin," *KP*, June 8, 1912, 2.

"Former Sousa Soloist Given Divorce Decree," *KTS*, July 12, 1921, 25.

"Miss Hardeman to Play with $10,000 Violin," *KP*, March 20, 1917, 3.

"Miss Hardeman to Tour with Sarah Bernhardt," *KP*, July 21, 1917, 1.

Jenny Plemen

HARDIN, THOMAS JEFFERSON, AND WILLIAM DAVID HARDIN (Thomas Jefferson Hardin, b. October 19, 1834, Owen Co., Ky.; d. July 11, 1906, Monterey, Ky.; William David Hardin, b. November 6, 1842, Owen Co., Ky.; d. 1909, Monterey, Ky.). Brothers Thomas Jefferson Hardin, a lawyer, and William David Hardin, a merchant, were both active in the early life of the city of Monterey in Owen Co. Their parents were Thomas Hardin and Rachel Allen. The brothers grew up in Owen Co. on the Hardin Plantation, referred to as "Hardin's Landing" during the heyday of Kentucky River boat traffic and during the **Civil War**. Their ancestors, the Ashbys and the Hardins, were owners of the Hardin Plantation long before Owen Co. was formed in 1819.

Thomas Hardin Jr. assisted in establishing the city government of Monterey, which was formerly known as Williamsburg, Ky. He was engaged in the mercantile business there from 1859 to 1876, was a police judge from 1874 to 1878, and studied to be an attorney. At age 28 Thomas served with distinction as captain of the 9th Kentucky Cavalry during the Civil War, in the Union Army. On February 4, 1864, he married Florence E. Seston. In 1867 he became a charter member of **Monterey Baptist Church**; later, however, he transferred to the Christian Church with his wife and daughter. Thomas was a leading force in getting the town of Monterey enlarged by Kentucky statute in 1874 and again in 1881. He is given credit for organizing the Monterey city government and for writing the acts that established it, which were presented on the first Monday of August 1874. In 1876 Thomas was admitted to the bar at Owenton, where he served 34 years. In 1888 he became the first president of the First State Bank of Monterey. He was twice nominated as the Republican candidate for the U.S. Congress: in 1892 against W. C. P. Breckinridge and in 1898 against **Evan E. Settle**, and he was once a candidate for lieutenant governor of Kentucky.

William David Hardin in 1867 was a charter member of Monterey Baptist Church and served for many years as church clerk. He married Minnie Vories on November 22, 1893, and the couple had five children. A lifetime merchant in Monterey, he began in business in 1872 as a member of the firm Hardin and Calvert. Later he bought Calvert's half of the business and became sole owner. In 1885 William, along with J. M. Abraham and George Lawrence, purchased the steamboat *Falls City II*, which ran from Louisville to Valley View in Fayette Co. from 1898 to 1908. The *Falls City II* was an asset to commerce shipped through the warehouses of Monterey and other landing sites along its way. The Kentucky River profoundly influenced the growth of Monterey as a commercial center. The three partners sold the steamboat in 1908. In 1907 the **tobacco** business was booming in the organized burley district around Monterey. On January 10, 1907, William Hardin and capitalist Lee H. McGraw formed the Monterey Realty and Warehouse to handle and finance the Equity Tobacco Company, which operated as late as 1925. In 1909 William was elected to the Monterey town council.

The Hardin family members are buried at the Monterey Cemetery in Owen Co.

Coleman, Winston J. *Steamboats on the Kentucky River*. Lexington, Ky.: Winburn Press, 1960.

Johnson, Leland R., and Charles E. Parrish. *Kentucky River Development: The Commonwealth's Waterway*. Louisville, Ky.: U.S. Army Corps of Engineers, 1999.

Murphy, Margaret A. *History of the Monterey Baptist Church and Community*. Frankfort, Ky.: Roberts, 1976.

Margaret A. Murphy

HARDING, DUNCAN (b. January 12, 1812, Kentontown, Ky.; d. September 5, 1887, Kentontown, Ky.). Duncan Harding, a Robertson Co. judge and landowner, was born into a family who had arrived in Kentucky before it attained statehood in 1792. Their Virginia land grant of 1,000 acres was situated in the future Robertson Co. Harding became one of the most powerful influences in the formation of Robertson Co., along with **Osmer Sage Deming** and James Ogdon. A Democrat, Harding had served two terms as a state representative from Harrison Co., of which his hometown, Kentontown, was then a part. He also served as postmaster at Kentontown and ran a dry goods store there during the 1840s. His party affiliation served him well in his push to establish a new county, and he hoped that his hometown would become the new county's seat of government. He owned considerable land in and around Kentontown and stood to gain financially if the town became the county seat. It did not, however. The more centrally located Mount Olivet became the seat of the newly formed county by a small majority vote. Nevertheless, Harding became the new county's first judge in 1867 and was among the first attorneys to be accepted to practice law in Robertson Co. Harding also donated the land on which the old Kentontown Christian Church and cemetery were established; he died in 1887 and was buried in the Kentontown Cemetery, next to his wife, Elizabeth Whitehead Harding.

Gifford, Anjanette. "The Formation of Robertson County," *NKH* 8, no. 2 (Spring–Summer 2001): 65–72.

Nagle, Eric C., and Larry L. Ford. *Monument Inscriptions of Robertson County, Kentucky*. Dayton, Ohio: Ford and Nagle, 1995.

Karl Lietzenmayer

HARGRAVES, WILLIAM FREDERICK "BILLY," COLONEL (b. August 18, 1932, Cincinnati, Ohio). William Frederick Hargraves II, an Air Force colonel who was raised in Covington, is the son of William and Annie Leona Thomas Hargraves. Both of Hargraves's parents were educators at Covington's **Lincoln-Grant School**. Hargraves was the first African American from Covington to become both a U.S. Air Force pilot and a Rhodes scholar candidate. He attended Lincoln-Grant grade school, graduated from William Grant High School, and graduated with honors from Miami University of Ohio with a BS in education. While attending Miami University, he was a member of the Air Force ROTC and was commissioned a second lieutenant upon graduation. He entered the U.S. Air Force in 1955 after receiving his MA in physics. Later that year, Hargraves entered the U.S. Air Force pilot training program. In 1956 he earned his silver wings while at Goodfellow Air Force Base, San Angelo, Tex. While in Texas, Hargraves married Maurine Collins of San Angelo on July 5, 1957.

During his varied career in the Air Force, Hargraves served as commander of the 20th Military Airlift Squadron, as an air liaison officer research scientist at the Air Force's Weapons Research Center, as an instructor pilot with the 22nd Military Airlift Command, and as an air liaison officer with the 1st ARVN (Army of the Republic of Vietnam) Division. He returned to Miami University to serve as an assistant professor of aerospace science with the Air Force ROTC program from 1971 through 1974. From 1978 into 1982, he was chief of flight deck development in the Research and Development section at Wright Patterson Air Force Base, Dayton, Ohio; he then became deputy division chief at the Pentagon. He retired from the Air Force in 1982 after 30 years of distinguished service. Colonel Hargraves has received numerous military medals and commendations, including the Distinguished Flying Cross, the Air Medal, an Air Force Commendation Medal with two oak leaf clusters, the Vietnam Service Medal with five bronze stars, and the National Defense Service Medal.

William Hargraves, 1967.

After Hargraves retired from the Air Force, he became an assistant professor and assistant dean of arts and sciences at Central State University, Wilberforce, Ohio. In 1992 he was named to the Black Hall of Fame in Covington. While at Central State University, Hargraves received two awards from the students: in 1997 the Teacher of the Year Award and in 2001–2002 and 2002–2003 the Most Inspirational Teaching Award. Colonel Hargraves resides in Oxford, Ohio, with his wife.

"Center's Events Salute Black History," *KP*, February 22, 1992, 11K.

"Major William Hargraves Earns Air Force Honors," *Oxford Press*, November 11, 1971, 3.

"Military Notes," *KTS*, August 15, 1956, 6A.

"Praise God. Viet Hero Returns," *KP*, February 17, 1971, 2K.

"Silver Wings," *KTS*, August 22, 1956, 6A.

"Tests of Character," *Dayton Daily News*, June 8, 1997, E1.

Theodore H. H. Harris

HARMEYER PAINT COMPANY. One of the many Europeans who came to the United States for business opportunities in the 1850s was John James Joseph Harmeyer (b. 1820) of Hanover, Germany. He and his wife, Mary, settled in Covington, where their son Henry H. Harmeyer (1860–1911) was born. Henry married a woman named Catherine, and their first son, Frederick Joseph "Fred" Harmeyer was born in 1893. The family resided at 402 W. Eighth St. in Covington while Henry commuted to Newport. In 1896 Henry Harmeyer purchased a double storefront at 617–619 Monmouth St. in Newport. The *Newport City Directory* for that year says that he was a clerk. He operated a modest paint and wallpaper store at that location. Additional children were born to the Harmeyers, and eventually they purchased the former **Barney Kroger** home at 624 Monroe St. in Newport. That old brownstone remains standing.

On December 29, 1911, Henry died of consumption at age 51, leaving the Harmeyer Paint Company to Fred, his eldest son. Fred was 17 when he took control of the business and the family of nine children. During **World War I**, he served with the American Expeditionary Force in France, and John Hoover, Harmeyer's good friend, operated the business until Fred Harmeyer returned.

As time passed, the Newport store became too small for the manufacture of paint. Searching for ways to expand the business, Harmeyer met and became a lifelong friend of Ferdinand Derrick. Derrick was in a partnership with Fred Perry at the Perry and Derrick Paint Company. In 1913 Perry and Derrick invested $1,200 each to acquire the John Pfaff Varnish Company at Central and Livingston in Cincinnati. In 1919 Derrick bought out Perry and joined with Fred Harmeyer of the Henry Harmeyer Paint Company. In 1926 they moved the manufacturing operations to Lindsey St., next to the **Chesapeake and Ohio Railroad** in Dayton, Ky. They made paint at this location until September 2, 1957, when the factory suffered the worst fire in Dayton's history.

After this setback, the Perry and Derrick Paint Company moved across the river to Norwood, Ohio, into the former Continental Can Company complex on Highland Ave. A decision to streamline the business in the early 1960s resulted in the corporate absorption of the Harmeyer firm into Perry and Derrick. At its zenith in the 1950s and 1960s, there were 16 Henry Harmeyer paint stores; among them were two stores in Covington and one each in Newport, Lexington, and Winchester, Ky.; Cincinnati, Dayton, and Springfield, Ohio; and Huntington, W.Va. There were many Perry and Derrick–affiliated outlets regionally across four states (Kentucky, Ohio, Indiana, and West Virginia). In various annual contracts, roadways in both Ohio and Kentucky were painted with Perry and Derrick products. The original Monmouth St. store, the beginning of it all, sold its last can of paint on November 30, 1999. The Harmeyer Paint Company was one of the largest chains of corporate enterprise to emerge from the Northern Kentucky region. A Harmeyer Paint Store exists in Newport at 502 E. 10th St., operated by a great-grandson of the founder.

"Eight Dayton Homes Damaged as Fire Destroys Warehouse," *KTS*, September 3, 1957, 1–2A.

Glover, Robert Alan. "Changing Colors—Paint Store Moves Back to Roots in Newport," *CP*, May 28, 2002, 6C.

"Mrs. Harmeyer Dead," *KTS*, August 28, 1915, 3.

Fred C. Harmeyer

HARRIET BEECHER STOWE SLAVERY TO FREEDOM MUSEUM. This brick museum townhouse in Washington, Mason Co., dates from 1807. In 1833 it was owned by **Marshall Key**, a nephew of Chief Justice John Marshall and a brother of Col. Thomas Marshall, who served as a staff officer under Gen. George Washington. That year, Key's daughter became a pupil of Harriet Beecher Stowe (1811–1896), author of *Uncle Tom's Cabin* (1852). After a visit to the house, Stowe received the inspiration for the book's characters Uncle Tom and Topsy. The real-life name of the person who inspired Topsy was Jane, and she later married Isham Anderson. Behind the museum is a small brick structure, known as the Indian Fort, which was used by settlers to ward off **American Indians** who sometimes crossed the Ohio River at nearby Maysville. Included in this museum are the original mantels; woodworking; floor; doors; slavery artifacts, including slave leg irons; period furnishings; and Civil War artifacts. The museum is included on **Underground Railroad** tours.

Admiraal, Karin. "Festival Great Way to Learn History," *KP*, September 17, 2005, 6K.

Harriet Beecher Stowe Museum, Washington, Ky.

Safe Passage. www.safepassageohio.org (accessed June 10, 2006).

Vaughn, Melinda Myers. "A Stop on Freedom Road," *KP*, September 17, 1997, 1KK.

Washingtonkentucky.com. "Washington, Ky." http://washingtonkentucky.com (accessed June 10, 2006).

Kareem A. Simpson

HARRISBURGH ACADEMY/OWEN COLLEGE. These Owen Co. schools were the creations of **Edwin Porter Thompson**, famed Kentucky **Civil War** author and educator, at the end of the 1860s. First came the coeducational Harrisburgh Academy (spelled with an *h* on the end), located at Long Ridge (or Harrisburg), just north of Owenton along the road that is U.S. 127 today. The school was established in 1869. Thompson hired such an esteemed faculty that students came from Owen Co. and elsewhere. The Harrisburgh Academy students made their own boarding arrangements in the neighborhood.

In 1876 the Kentucky legislature chartered Owen College; it essentially amounted to a name change for the Harrisburgh Academy. Owen College had three departments: preparatory, collegiate, and business. Military drill was required of male students. Owen College flourished until the late 1880s. Its last remaining buildings were demolished in the late 1920s.

Houchens, Mariam Sidebottom. *History of Owen County: "Sweet Owen."* Louisville, Ky.: Standard, 1976.

HARRIS CREEK BAPTIST CHURCH. The Harris Creek Baptist Church at Boston Station in northern Pendleton Co. was organized on October 21, 1843. The minutes of the church survive and contain valuable information about the history of the church and of the immediate area. This church operated for some 41 years, disbanding in July 1884. The Butler Union Baptist Church was organized in November 1884 and was a continuation of the Harris Creek Baptist Church.

The Harris Creek Baptist Church began and held services in an old hewed-log schoolhouse that stood along Harris Creek. J. C. Kirby owns that farm today. The school building, dating from 1812 or 1815, was 20 by 30 feet in size, with a large stone fireplace at one end. The Harris Creek Baptist Church minutes dated October 21, 1843, list the persons who formed the new church: colored Jane, Jaily Ducker, Sarah Stewart, Elizabeth Wright, Martha Wright, Matthew Wright, and William Wright. The preacher on that occasion was Brother Morin. The membership of the church consisted of the families of some of the pioneers of that section of Pendleton Co. Many services were held during its 41 years of existence, and for a rural church, it had a large membership.

Soon after organization, the church joined the Union Baptist Association, and it remained an affiliate until disbanding. The congregation worshipped in the old log schoolhouse until 1858 or so; a new schoolhouse was built then, near the center of the county's school district. The new school was located near Boston Station on the Lloyd Kirby farm, a part of the old Ducker farm. The Harris Creek Baptist Church and a group of Methodists shared the new school building on Sundays, holding services on alternating weeks. Some of the names on these church rolls were Barton, Beckett, Bonar, Bradford, Burlew, Byland, Ducker, Ellis, Hendricks, Kirby, Marshall, Mullins, Shoemaker, Williams, and Wright.

In 1884 the Baptists disbanded at Boston and 18 members transferred to the Baptist church at Butler. The Boston school building was left to the Methodists, who continued to use it as a place for itinerant Methodist ministers to preach. The Methodist ministers on this area's preaching circuit served at least three churches and held meetings at Boston on one or two Sundays each month. The little church at Boston was often filled to an overflow capacity of some 40 to 50 worshippers.

Belew, Mildred Boden. *The First 200 Years of Pendleton County.* Falmouth, Ky.: M. B. Belew, n.d. [ca. 1994].

Mildred Belew

HARRISON, HENRY THOMAS "HARRY" (b. April 23, 1831, near Nashville, Tenn.; d. October 28, 1923, Covington, Ky.). This **Civil War** spy is depicted in Ted Turner's epic movie classic *Gettysburg* (1993), an adaptation of Michael Shaara's *The Killer Angels* (1974), which opens with a lone man on horseback riding across the rolling hills of southeastern Pennsylvania. Moving behind the Union Army's lines, the rider is working his way back to Confederate general James Longstreet's encampment. Recently, that character has come alive in Northern Kentucky's history. Confederate spy and later Northern Kentucky resident Henry T. Harrison was that rider, and the information delivered by Harrison to Longstreet made the Battle of Gettysburg not an easy rout of the Southern troops but three of the bloodiest days of fighting during the Civil War.

Harrison first served with Company One of the 12th Mississippi Infantry. By early 1863 he was a plainclothes scout (spy) in the North for Longstreet. Harrison's report on June 28, 1863, led Longstreet to send the messenger spy to General Robert E. Lee. Subsequently, Lee ordered his dispersed troops to converge on Gettysburg, precluding any quick and easy Union victory there.

After Gettysburg, Harrison married a Virginia lady, Laura Broders, in Washington, D.C., on September 28, 1863, while continuing his work as a spy for the South. He quickly proved not to be much of a family man, although the couple had two children. By 1866 Harrison was in Helena, Mont., prospecting for gold, drinking, and gambling. His family remained in Virginia, never to be seen again by Harrison, whose whereabouts from 1867 through 1892 are unknown. His life seemed to be one of espionage and deception. In 1900 Harrison made an unsuccessful attempt to visit Laura and the family.

From 1893 into 1912, Harrison lived in Cincinnati, at first, reportedly, working as an engineer and later as a detective, from 1901 through 1911. In 1912 he applied for and received a Confederate pension from the State of Kentucky, listing his residence as 35 E. Fourth St. in Covington. Later he lived at 307 Scott St. and, for a time, was a resident of the Kenton Co. Infirmary. At age 87, on February 9, 1920, he married a second time to Lucretia Allison in Covington; she was 61 and caring for him in his old age.

In 1923 Henry T. Harrison died of a stroke and was buried at Highland Cemetery in Fort Mitchell. Lucretia Harrison continued to receive his pension until her death in 1936. Harrison's grave remained unmarked and his death unknown to his first family until a great-grandson, with the help of local historians in Northern Kentucky, found him. On May 18, 2003, a formal dedication of his newly marked grave honored the forgotten Civil War spy whose actions changed the course of one of the war's major battles. Although the North under General George Meade claimed victory, Gettysburg is often called "the high water mark of the Confederacy."

"Apoplexy Kills Vet," *KP,* October 29, 1923, 1.
Becker, Bernie. "Civil War Spy Discovered in Covington," *NKH* 10, no. 2 (Spring–Summer 2003): 44–47.
——. "A Man Called Harrison," *America's Civil War,* November 2004, 46–52.
Grayson, Frank Y. "Historic Spots in Greater Cincinnati," *CTS,* June 15, 1933, 11.
Kentucky Death Certificate No. 26219, for the year 1923.
Longstreet, James. *From Manassas to Appomattox.* Philadelphia: J. B. Lippincott, 1895.
"Newport, Dayton, and Covington Residents Are Given Pensions," *KTS,* September 20, 1913, 3.
Shaara, Michael. *The Killer Angels.* New York: McKay, 1974.

Sharon Jobert

Henry T. Harrison.

HARROD, JOHN (b. February 8, 1946, Shelbyville, Ky.). John Harrod is one of the chief contemporary performers and scholars of Kentucky-style fiddle playing. He is the son of Rufus C. and Nancy Van Arsdale Harrod. After graduating from the Shelbyville (Ky.) High School in 1963, he received a BA in English and political science from Centre College in Danville, Ky., in 1967. He went to Pembrooke College of Oxford University in England as a Rhodes Scholar and earned an MA in English language and literature.

With Mark Wilson, Harrod produced the recording *Traditional Fiddle Music of Kentucky* (1997) for Rounder Records in two compact discs: one volume covers the northeastern portion of the state near the Ohio River, and the other covers a region that can be defined as the Kentucky River watershed from the eastern edge of the Cumberland Plateau through the Bluegrass region to the Ohio River. The liner text makes the distinction between ethnomusicologists and those who actively study and play traditional "old time" folk music. By this tradition, music is taught aurally, without notation or conductor. The resulting individuality in versions rendered by players in different regions is one of the main features of Harrod's recordings, in "lessons" from players, and in his own experience in playing the fiddle. Harrod has played with bands such as the Progress Red Hot String Band, the **Bill Livers** String Ensemble, the Grey Eagle Band, and the Kentucky Wild Horse Band.

Most recently, he presented a paper titled "A Keen Cut with the Bow: The Art of Kentucky Fiddling in Berea, Ky." at Berea College's Thirty-first Celebration of Traditional Music in October 2005. He received the Folk Heritage Award on February 18, 2005, in Frankfort. From 1998 to 2006, Harrod taught history at the Frankfort High School. Today he lives with his wife, the former Tona Barkley, and their two children in Owen Co. and is working on various projects.

Harrod, John. Personal communication, October 2006.
Harrod, John, and Mark Wilson, producers. *Traditional Fiddle Music of Kentucky.* Vol. 2, *Along the Kentucky River,* liner text, unsigned. Cambridge, Mass.: Rounder Records 0377, 1997.
Wolfe, Charles K. *Kentucky Country: Folk and Country Music of Kentucky.* Lexington: Univ. Press of Kentucky, 1982.

Rebecca Schaffer Wells

HARSHA, WILLIAM H., BRIDGE. See **William H. Harsha Bridge**.

HARVARD PIANO COMPANY. In 1859 the John Church Company of Chicago and New York City began selling pianos and sheet music in a store located at Fourth and Elm Sts. in Cincinnati. Frank A. Lee began working for the company in 1883. The following year, the company opened the Harvard Piano Company factory at Fifth and Clay Sts. in Dayton, Ky. In 1894 Lee became president of the piano company, which manufactured upright, grand, and player pianos, described as being distinctively styled, well constructed, and among the most popular and salable pianos on the market. The business was so successful that its plant was soon expanded to cover the entire city block on the east side of Clay St. between Fourth and Fifth Sts. The Harvard Piano Company also opened a small branch factory in the former First Baptist Church building, nearby at Fifth and Main Sts in Dayton. During the economic recession of 1907–1908, sales declined significantly and the company suspended operations for several months. However, when market conditions improved, it resumed full production. At the height of its success, the firm had about 400 employees. During **World War I**, the company also manufactured airplane bodies for the U.S. Army. The Harvard Piano Company and the **Wadsworth Watch Case Company**, also on Clay St., were Dayton's largest employers. In later years, Frank A. Lee left the company and moved to Santa Barbara, Calif. Based on piano serial production numbers, the Harvard Piano Company manufactured about 30,000 pianos from 1885 until the business was discontinued in 1925. For many years after it closed, there was a bowling alley in the piano company's former building.

"Newport Shop to Build Air Ships, Report," *KP*, August 18, 1917, 1.
"Piano Plant to Resume Operations," *KP*, February 4, 1908, 5.
Piano World. "Piano Forums." www.pianoworld.com (accessed December 21, 2005).
Renfrow Piano Tuning Home Page. "Cincinnati Piano History." www.pianocincinnati.com (accessed December 21, 2005).
"What Becomes of the Old Churches?" *KP*, August 27, 1913, 4.

HATFIELD, J. T. (b. February 25, 1865, Lincoln, Ill.; d. July 19, 1938, Cape May, Mass.). James Tobias Hatfield, a coal merchant and a philanthropist, was the son of Henry C. and Amelia Hatfield, who moved with their family to Covington when James was a teenager. In 1882 James opened a small coal yard there on 15th St. and from that location delivered kindling wood and coal to homes in his neighborhood, using a small wagon he pulled by hand. As his business grew, he purchased a mule and a cart for making deliveries. Five years later he purchased the Bond Brothers Coal Company and renamed it the J. T. Hatfield Coal Company. Continued business growth led him to branch out into other aspects of the coal business in subsequent years. He operated a coal mine near Reed, W.Va., and bought steamboats and barges to transport the coal to Cincinnati. As he became more successful, he was asked to become a director of many local companies. He was also named president of the Atlas Coal Company, the Great Kanawha Improvement Association, and, in Kentucky, the Pomeroy Dock in Carrollton. About 1920 the Hatfield Coal Company merged with six other coal companies, and Hatfield was made vice president of the newly formed Hatfield-Reliance Coal Company. When the company's president, Julius Fleischmann, died in 1925, Hatfield became president.

Hatfield became involved in many philanthropic causes and often gave free coal to poor families. He was a member of several clubs, including the Covington Industrial Club, the **Fort Mitchell Country Club**, and, in Ohio, the Queen City Club and the Cincinnati Club. He was the founder of the Covington **Boy Scouts** and served as the first council president of that organization. In 1891 Hatfield married Ellen Daisy Methven, and they had eight children. After suffering a stroke in 1933, Hatfield reduced his workload by resigning from many of the positions he held. He died at age 73 at his summer home on Cape May, Mass. Over the years, he and his family lived at several Covington locations. At the time of his death, his home was at 400 Wallace Ave. in Wallace Woods. His wife, Ellen, five daughters, and three sons survived him. He was buried at Highland Cemetery, Fort Mitchell. In 1977 Hatfield's daughters, Louise and Virginia, had a large stained-glass window installed in the Covington **Trinity Episcopal Church** in memory of their father.

"Coal Man Succumbs in East," *CE*, July 21, 1938, 2.
"Eight Northern Kentuckians in 1928 Edition of Who's Who," *KP*, April 4, 1928, 1.
"Hatfield Is Recipient of Fine Testimonial," *KP*, October 16, 1919, 1.
"Patriots Will Dine," *KP*, October 10, 1919, 1.
Steamboats.org. "Sternwheeler Towboat J. T. Hatfield." www.steamboats.org.

Jack Wessling

HATHAWAY, HENRY, JR. (b. March 14, 1804, Belfast, Maine; d. July 28, 1877, Eaton, Ohio). Henry Hathaway Jr., a humanitarian and a reputed abolitionist, was the son of Henry and Abigail Chase Hathaway. His father, born in Massachusetts, became an early and prosperous settler of Cincinnati and left an estate of $2 million when he died in 1852. Henry Jr. married Jane Hubbell, a native of Clark Co., Ohio, in March 1827. For a short time, he operated a store and pork-packing facility in West Alexandria in Preble Co., Ohio, where his son Hannibal Chase was born in 1831. That business failed, and by the late 1830s, Henry Jr. and his family moved to Texas and remained there about five years; their daughter Eliza Jane was born in Texas in 1838. By 1843 Henry Jr. had moved back to Cincinnati, and resided on W. 5th St. in Hathaway's Subdivision in Cincinnati's West End; by 1849 he operated a store on that street. In the same year, he purchased slightly more than six acres of land at 1210 Highway Ave., in what is now **West Covington**, for $14,250. This was a high price for the times and generally confirms the belief that the property already contained a stately home. Situated on a hill overlooking the Ohio River, Hathaway Hall, as it came to be known, featured a spectacular view of the river valley and of the West End of Cincinnati. According to oral tradition, Hathaway used his home as a stop along the **Underground Railroad**. He presumably concealed slaves in a small cellar room, which was entered through a trap door from one of the parlors and was connected to a service tunnel that once led from the house to the river.

The probability of Hathaway's abolitionism is strengthened by a number of facts. First, he was a client and friend of Salmon P. Chase, a noted abolitionist lawyer of Cincinnati and later a member of President Abraham Lincoln's administration (whether Hathaway's mother, Abigail Chase, was related to Salmon P. Chase is unknown at this time). Second, Hathaway's family, as evidenced in legal documents such as wills, were trusted friends of noted Cincinnati abolitionists Samuel Lewis and Nicholas Longworth. Third, Hathaway had familial and property ties to Preble Co., Ohio, a hotbed of the abolitionist movement. Fourth, other family members owned land in areas well known for their abolitionist activity. For instance, his son Hannibal Chase owned 72 acres in Crosby Township of Hamilton Co., west of Cincinnati and along the Underground Railroad routes into Indiana. Finally, Hathaway demonstrated a lifelong commitment to the poor and disenfranchised. He originally belonged to the Enon Baptist Church on Sycamore St. in Cincinnati, which later became a Disciples of Christ congregation. By 1859, he was an elder of a mission church of the Disciples of Christ on the west side of Freeman Ave. in Cincinnati's poor West End neighborhood. The church was within walking distance of Hathaway's home in West Covington, via the Fifth St. Ferry. That ferryboat crossed the Ohio River near Hathaway Hall into Cincinnati's West End, terminating close to yet another "Hathaway's subdivision" with a street named Hannibal (presumably after Henry's son).

In September 1855, Henry and his wife conveyed Hathaway Hall and its six-plus acres to their son Hannibal Chase; however, they continued to reside there for many years. In 1871 Jane Hathaway died at the home, and four years later, in 1875, Hathaway Hall and its acreage were advertised for rent. Henry Hathaway died in 1877 at his residence in Eaton in Preble Co., Ohio. An obituary in the *Christian Standard* stated that "for the last thirty years and more he devoted his time to the preaching of the word among the poor." He was buried in the Wesleyan Cemetery in the Cumminsville neighborhood of Cincinnati.

Hathaway Hall in West Covington was sold in 1952 to Joe Spratt, a local manual arts teacher at **Ludlow High School**, who attempted to restore the house to its original beauty. He found the task overwhelming and eventually sold the property to Arnold Ingram, a real estate developer. Ingram had the house torn down in 1969 and, in its place, built a high-rise senior citizens apartment building, which he named Hathaway Court.

Deed Book 14, pp. 196–97, Kenton Co. Courthouse, Independence, Ky.
"Hathaway Hall Coming Down," *KP*, March 12, 1969, 6K.
History of Preble County, Ohio, with Illustrations and Biographical Sketches. Cleveland, Ohio: H. Z. Williams and Bro., 1881.
Kenton Co. Public Library. "Hathaway Senior Citizens Apartments." www.kenton.lib.ky.us/genealogy/history/covington/article.cfm?ID=218.
Niven, John, ed. *The Salmon P. Chase Papers*. Vol. 1, *Journals, 1829–1872*. Kent, Ohio: Kent State Univ. Press, 1993.
Salmon P. Chase Papers, Library of Congress, Washington, D.C.
Siebert, Wilbur Henry. *The Mysteries of Ohio's Underground Railroads*. Columbus, Ohio: Long's College Book Company, 1951.
"This Old House," *CE*, November 12, 1961, 4F.
Versailles, Elizabeth Starr, ed. *Hathaways of America*. Northampton, Mass.: Gazette, 1970.
"West Covington," *Ludlow Reporter*, April 17, 1875, 2.

Paul A. Tenkotte and Jack Wessling

HAWES, HARRY BARTOW (b. November 15, 1869, Covington, Ky.; d. July 31, 1947, Washington, D.C.). Harry B. Hawes, a U.S. senator, was the son of **Smith Nicholas Hawes** and nephew of Confederate brigadier general **James Morrison Hawes**. Harry Hawes's mother was the former Susan Elizabeth Simrall, daughter of well-known Covington attorney **Charles Simrall**. Harry Hawes moved to St. Louis, Mo., in 1887. He graduated from

Washington University Law School in St. Louis and was admitted to the Missouri bar in 1896. He entered politics in 1916 and was elected to the Missouri House of Representatives. During **World War I**, Hawes served with U.S. Army intelligence and later at the U.S. Embassy in Madrid, Spain. Elected as a Democrat to the U.S. House of Representatives in 1921, he served until 1926, when he resigned his House seat to fill a vacancy in the U.S. Senate created by the death of Selden P. Spencer. On the same day, he was also elected to a full Senate term commencing March 4, 1927. After resigning the Senate in 1933, he devoted his time to wildlife conservation and the practice of law until his death at age 77. His body was cremated and his ashes were scattered along the Current River in Missouri. He was one of several individuals born in Northern Kentucky who rose to high positions in the nation's political circles; Hawes once was considered for the vice presidency.

Biographical Directory of the United States Congress, 1774–1989. Washington, D.C.: Government Printing Office, 1985.

"Harry Hawes, Former Covington Resident, May Be Nominated for Vice President," *KP,* February 21, 1928, 1.

The Political Graveyard. "Hawes, Harry Bartow." www.politicalgraveyard.com (accessed April 3, 2007).

Tenkotte, Paul A. "Rival Cities to Suburbs: Covington and Newport, Kentucky, 1790–1890," PhD diss., Univ. of Cincinnati, 1989.

HAWES, JAMES MORRISON, BRIGADIER GENERAL (b. January 7, 1824, Lexington, Ky.; d. November 22, 1889, Covington, Ky.). James Morrison Hawes, a Confederate brigadier general, was one of six children born to Richard and Hattie Morrison Nicholas Hawes. His father was a prominent attorney who served three terms in the Kentucky legislature and two terms in the U.S. House of Representatives and was also provincial Confederate governor of Kentucky during the **Civil War**.

James Morrison Hawes grew up in Paris, Ky., where in 1841 he received an appointment to the U.S. Military Academy at West Point, N.Y. Four years later, he graduated 29th in his class and was commissioned a second lieutenant. After leaving school, he fought in the **Mexican War**, taking part in the sieges of Vera Cruz and San Juan de los Llanos. He was cited for bravery and gallantry at San Juan de los Llanos and was rewarded by promotion to first lieutenant. In 1848 he returned to West Point to teach infantry tactics and mathematics. Two years later he was sent to Saumur, France, to study advanced military tactics. He returned to the United States in 1852 and was stationed in Texas, where he served in the Utah military expedition of 1857–1858.

On February 3, 1857, he married Marie Jane Southgate, the great-great-granddaughter of **Richard Southgate** and the great-granddaughter of **William Wright Southgate**, a well-known Covington attorney and politician. James and Maria Hawes became the parents of 10 children.

At the outbreak of the Civil War, Hawes resigned from the U.S. Army and joined the Confederate Army as a captain. In less than a year, largely on the sponsorship of Gen. **Albert Sidney Johnston**, Hawes received several promotions and was made a brigadier general on March 5, 1862. He later saw service in Arkansas, Texas, and Louisiana and was severely wounded at the Battle of Shiloh.

At the end of the war, Hawes and his family moved back to Northern Kentucky and lived at 71 E. 15th St. in Covington. James's brother **Smith Nicholas Hawes** also lived in Covington. Shortly after returning, James Hawes entered into a partnership with Herman Wente to operate the Hawes and Wente Hardware store in Covington at 3 Pike St. Hawes and his family found life quite difficult in Covington, mostly owing to discrimination against anyone who had served in the military for the South. Some former Union sympathizers hated Hawes so intensely that they set fire to his store three times.

Hawes spent much of the latter part of his life decorating and maintaining the graves of Confederate soldiers buried in **Linden Grove Cemetery**. He was reported to have personally paid to have seven soldiers' graves moved from a cemetery on the **Dixie Highway** (U.S. 25) to Linden Grove Cemetery. Hawes died in his Covington home at age 65 and was buried in Highland Cemetery, Fort Mitchell. A local well-known descendant of James was *Cincinnati Post* radio and television writer **Mary Wood**, and he was an uncle of U.S. senator **Harry Bartow Hawes** of Missouri.

Kleber, John E., ed. *The Kentucky Encyclopedia.* Lexington: Univ. Press of Kentucky, 1992.

Reis, Jim. "Confederate General Called Covington Home," *KP,* April 29, 2002, 4K.

———. "Fame Came to Both Hawes Brothers," *KP,* May 11, 1987, 4K.

TSHA Online. "Hawes, James Morrison." www.tsha.utexas.edu (accessed October 30, 2006).

HAWES, SMITH NICHOLAS (b. ca. 1843, Paris, Ky.; d. April 9, 1890, St. Louis, Mo.). Smith Hawes, a political boss of Kenton Co. and a corrupt politician, was one of the six children of Richard and Hattie Morrison Nicholas Hawes. Richard Hawes was a Bourbon Co. judge, who also served three terms in the Kentucky legislature and two terms in the U.S. House of Representatives and was the second and last provincial Confederate governor of Kentucky. One of Smith Hawes's brothers was Confederate brigadier general **James Morrison Hawes**. Smith Hawes married Susan Elizabeth Simrall in November 1868, and the couple had two children, **Harry Bartow Hawes** and Richard Simrall Hawes. The family's home was on Russell St. between 10th and 11th Sts. in Covington. Their son Harry Bartow Hawes became a lawyer and then served in the Missouri House of Representatives for four years and in the U.S. Senate for a term of four years.

As the political boss of the Democratic party in Kenton Co., Smith Hawes controlled local patronage and at one time himself simultaneously held five political offices in the county. In 1876, at the pinnacle of his success, Hawes vanished. After examining their books, Covington city officials announced that thousands of dollars were missing from the city's treasury. Several investigating committees discovered an appalling level of corruption in that city's government. In January 1877, Covington city marshal P. J. Bolan arrested Hawes in London, Ontario, Canada. Three prominent Covington attorneys, **John G. Carlisle**, **Theodore Hallam**, and Smith's brother-in-law **Charles Simrall**, traveled to Canada to advise and defend the suspect in an extradition hearing. Hawes was returned to Covington on February 27, 1877. His trial was held in June 1877, but due to technicalities regarding his extradition, Hawes was discharged and returned to Canada. In 1880 his fellow Democrat Kentucky governor Luke Blackburn (1879–1883), an ex-Confederate, granted him a pardon. Hawes and his family returned to the United States, but they settled in St. Louis, Mo., not Covington. Hawes died in St. Louis at age 47, and his body was returned to Northern Kentucky for burial in Covington at Linden Grove Cemetery. Longtime *Cincinnati Post* newspaper columnist **Mary Wood** was a descendant of the Hawes family.

Linden Grove Cemetery Burial Records, Covington, Ky.

"Mrs. Hawes Dead," *KP,* September 10, 1900, 5.

Reis, Jim. "Fame Came to Both Hawes Brothers," *KP,* May 11, 1987, 4K.

Tenkotte, Paul A. "Rival Cities to Suburbs: Covington and Newport, Kentucky, 1790–1890," PhD diss., Univ. of Cincinnati, 1989.

HAYES STATION. Hayes Station, a mid-nineteenth-century station in northern Pendleton Co. along the **Covington and Lexington Railroad**, was originally called Livingood (it was also called Levingood, after an early settler). In 1866 a post office opened there. In 1906, when the post office was moved a half mile north, it was renamed Hayes Station, for Timothy Hayes, a millionaire Cincinnati distiller and the inventor of an improved distiller's yeast. Hayes bought bottomland between the Covington and Lexington Railroad and the South Licking River and built the largest distillery in Pendleton Co.'s history.

Belew, Mildred Boden. *The First 200 Years of Pendleton County.* Falmouth, Ky.: M. B. Belew, n.d. [ca. 1994].

Eighth Annual Report to the Stockholders of the Covington and Lexington Rail Road. November 2, 1857. Cincinnati: Daily Commercial Steam Job Press, 1858.

Rennick, Robert M. *The Post Offices of Northern Kentucky.* Lake Grove, Ore.: Depot, 2004.

Mildred Belew

HAYSWOOD HOSPITAL. In 1907 Maysville resident Mary V. Wilson bought the W. Fourth St., Maysville, property of the former Hayswood Seminary, a private school for girls, and gave it to the city for use as a hospital. As long as Wilson lived there, it was called the Wilson Hospital, but in 1908, after she moved, it became the Hayswood Hospital. A new **Samuel Hannaford**–designed hospital building was constructed in 1925. Its market area included parts of southern Ohio, particularly after the **Simon Kenton Memorial Bridge** at Maysville opened in late 1931. Many babies were born in the hospital over the years, and it earned care awards presented by national accreditation groups. After Pearl Harbor the U.S. Navy used part of the hospital for the rehabilitation of mentally harmed survivors of that attack.

The changing world of modern health care caught up with many small city hospitals, and Hayswood was no exception. For reasons of mere survival, it relinquished its nonprofit status in 1981, as it was sold to the Nashville-based Hospital Corporation of America (HCA). The time had come for a new facility, which the well-capitalized new owner could provide. In the early 1980s, an earthquake centered near Maysville damaged the hospital structurally. Around the same time, its name was changed to the Maysville Hospital, and in 1983 HCA moved the business to a new facility along the **AA Highway** (Ky. Rt. 9) just west of the intersection with U.S. 68, south of town. The Hayswood Hospital closed on February 9, 1983. Reflecting the broader market area it seeks, the 101-bed successor to Hayswood was named the **Meadowview Regional Medical Center**. Meanwhile, the building that had housed the Hayswood Hospital was purchased by Covington developer Esther Johnson in 1994. She had plans to convert it to apartments. Previously senior housing organizations had considered it for a nursing home or retirement apartments, or both. None of the plans have been put into action yet.

Calvert, Jean, and John Klee. *Maysville, Kentucky: From Past to Present in Pictures.* Maysville, Ky.: Maysville and Mason Co. Library Historical and Scientific Association, 1983.

"5 Local Hospitals Win Accreditation," *KTS,* March 10, 1958, 2A.

"Hayswood Hospital to Close Wednesday," *KE,* February 6, 1983, B2.

"New Hospital Opens Feb. 9," *CP,* January 21, 1983, 1C.

HAZEN, EVELYN M. (b. November 8, 1899, Knoxville, Tenn.; d. June 16, 1987, Knoxville, Tenn.). Evelyn Montgomery Hazen, the daughter of Alice Evelyn Mabry and Rush Strong Hazen, gained notoriety for a 1934 suit in Kenton Co. against her former fiancé. A member of Knoxville, Tenn. society, Hazen was descended from prominent and wealthy entrepreneurs. Her father owned a successful wholesale business, served as a bank chairman, and was a member of Knoxville's city council. Her great-grandfather Joseph Alexander Mabry was a prosperous landowner, publisher, and railroad president. He and his son Joseph Mabry Jr. were killed in a shootout on Knoxville's Gay St. in a dispute over a business deal. The incident was memorialized in Mark Twain's *Life on the Mississippi.*

Hazen was reared in her family's antebellum mansion. Sheltered and protected, she attended a private grammar school for young girls. When the school closed, Hazen, at the age of 14, enrolled at the University of Tennessee in Knoxville. Her intelligence, beauty, and youth attracted the attention of Ralph Scharringhaus, the son of prosperous Knoxville businessman Edward Scharringhaus. They became engaged and were planning their future together when the United States entered **World War I**. Scharringhaus joined the armed forces and was sent to a military training camp. While he was off duty for a weekend in 1917, he persuaded Hazen to consummate their love physically.

After Scharringhaus returned from the military, he continued to demand physical relations with Hazen, while putting off their wedding. In 1932 he finally broke their 15-year-long engagement and fled to relatives in Erlanger, Ky., hoping to prevent Hazen from retaliating against him. His plan failed. She tracked him down and filed her landmark lawsuit accusing him of breach of promise to marry, aggravated by seduction.

The case went to trial in February 1934 and generated news coverage throughout the country. After three weeks of emotional testimony, the jury of 12 men awarded Hazen $80,000—a huge fortune in the middle of the **Great Depression**. Hazen's suit set the standard for breach-of-promise-to-marry suits in 20th-century America. As the century drew to a close, several states eliminated breach of promise to marry as a cause of action. The Kentucky Supreme Court struck it down in 1997, ruling that it had become antiquated and unnecessary.

Hazen's legal triumph was a hollow victory. She apparently never received the money, and she never married. After her death, her family's mansion in Knoxville, Tenn., was turned into the Mabry-Hazen House Museum in accord with her last wishes. The Italianate home is listed on the National Register of Historic Places. Hazen was buried in the Old Gray Cemetery in Knoxville, Tenn.

Ryan, Jane Van. *The Seduction of Miss Evelyn Hazen.* Glen Echo, Md.: Glen Echo, 2006.

"Teacher Wins $80,000 Love Verdict," *KP,* February 24, 1934, 1.

Jane Van Ryan

HEALTHPOINT FAMILY CARE. HealthPoint Family Care of Northern Kentucky is a private, nonprofit primary health care organization that provides medical and dental services to all patients but especially to those who lack health insurance or sufficient income to pay for care. HealthPoint was established in 1971 in Covington as a volunteer effort. The organization was then known as the Covington Family Health Care Center. Robert Longshore, MD, was the first medical director, and Howard Hall, DDS, was the first dental director. The Covington Family Health Care Center was incorporated in 1972. In 1978 the Covington Family Health Care Center won its first federal grant from the Bureau of Primary Health Care, a unit of the U.S. Department of Health and Human Services. This funding, which continues today, enables the organization to provide health care services to patients with no ability to pay.

In 1988 the organization changed its name to Northern Kentucky Family Health Centers Inc. and opened a second health care center in Newport. The next year, a walk-in clinic was established in Covington to provide medical care to homeless patients. In 1990 Northern Kentucky Family Health acquired its largest facility, a three-story building at 1132 Greenup St. in Covington, which it purchased for $1 from the City of Covington. That center continues to operate. Later, other centers were opened in Dayton, Ky., in the City Heights neighborhood of Covington, and at 1100 Pike St. in Covington.

Northern Kentucky Family Health expanded into rural Bracken Co. in 1999. Reflecting the expanded service area, the organization changed its name to HealthPoint Family Care in 2002. That year was a major building period for HealthPoint, as a new health care center was constructed in Bracken Co. at the intersection of the **AA Highway** (Ky. Rt. 9) and Ky. Rt. 19, and the organization's leased space in the Bellevue Medical Arts Building was remodeled. HealthPoint then consolidated outdated facilities in Newport and Dayton into the new Bellevue center.

As of 2006, HealthPoint Family Care operated three health care centers and the Pike Street Clinic for the Homeless in Covington, one center in Bellevue, one in Bracken Co., and one in Robertson Co. A medical staff of 33 physicians, dentists, nurse practitioners, and physician assistants provide care for 28,000 patients. HealthPoint's chief executive officer, Christopher M. Goddard, joined the organization in 1999. Medical director Elmer Martin, MD, has been with HealthPoint since 2004. HealthPoint Family Care's mission is "to be the best provider of health services in Northern Kentucky through compassion, innovation, and excellence for all patients and the communities where they live."

Of HealthPoint's 28,000 patients, Medicaid, the government insurance program for low-income people, covers 37 percent. Some 28 percent of patients have no health insurance and are charged fees on a sliding scale based on income and family size. Another 26 percent have private insurance, and 9 percent have insurance through Medicare. HealthPoint's major sources of funding are reimbursement from Medicaid, Medicare, and private insurance companies for patient services. A $1.4 million federal grant from the Bureau of Primary Health Care helps pay for services to low-income, uninsured patients. HealthPoint also raises money for special programs and capital needs through appeals for foundation grants, contributions from corporations and individuals, and other fundraising activities.

"Care Center Updates, Merge," *KE,* July 28, 2002, B1–B1B.

"Health Agency to Build $1 Million Care Center (between Brooksville and Augusta)," *KE,* February 22, 2002, B2.

"Healthpoint Expands Covington Services," *KP,* August 20, 2005, 5K.

Laurel Humes

HEARNE, JONATHAN (b. 1829, Harrison Co., Ky.; d. June 15, 1905, Covington, Ky.). Banker Jonathan David Hearne was the son of Cannon and Sallie Hearne. Orphaned early in life, he grew up to be a successful businessman in Central Kentucky. At the outbreak of the **Civil War**, he was living in

Paris, Ky. Pledging his loyalty and support to the Union cause, Hearne relocated to Covington, where the majority of the residents were Union supporters. He became a shoe jobber in Covington and later a shoe manufacturer. In 1870 Hearne and his partners operated a shoe business in Cincinnati, at 65 W. Pearl St., near the waterfront. In 1866 **Amos Shinkle**, Jonathan Hearne, and some others purchased the H. J. Groesbeck property in Covington for a land development called Park Place. The next year, Hearne personally purchased a portion of this land and built the stately Hearne House, which was completed in 1874 and still stands.

After the Civil War, Hearne's career paralleled that of other wealthy businessmen and bankers of the era. Following passage of the national banking act of 1864, Hearne became involved with more than one of the new "national" banks established in Covington and Cincinnati. In league with Shinkle, Covington's most prominent banker, Hearne tried to upgrade the Covington Branch of the Farmers Bank of Kentucky, where Hearne was president, into the "national system." Failing to accomplish that, in 1871 he organized the City National Bank of Covington and became its president. He also was president of the Cincinnati and Newport Iron and Pipe Company. Then in 1882 Hearne became president of Third National Bank in Cincinnati, while also continuing as a director at City National Bank of Covington.

In 1852 Hearne married Emily Duke Meyers, who was from Garrard Co., Ky. Hearne and his wife belonged to the Union Methodist Church, where he served as president of the board of trustees. In 1872 Hearne was elected to the Covington city council. He also helped organize the YMCA, was president of an organization for the "suppression of vice," and was the first president of the Covington Park Association. He ended his career in banking in 1904 because of poor health. At the time, his worth was estimated to be at least $500,000. Among the recipients of bequests from his will were the Methodist Church, the Covington Protestant Children's Home (see **Children's Home of Northern Kentucky**), the Home for Indigent Women (see **Covington Ladies Home**), and the **YMCA**. He was buried in Highland Cemetery in Fort Mitchell.

Around 1980 a proposed new Licking River bridge and traffic corridor threatened the Hearne House (located in Covington at the end of E. Fifth St.), but thanks to a neighborhood effort, it remains. Now on the National Register of Historic Places, the Hearne House retains its singular prominence.

Bricking, Chuck. *Covington's Heritage: A Compilation of the City's Historical Houses and a Short Biography of the Inhabitants.* Covington, Ky.: Privately published, 1980.

City of Covington Death Certificate No. 486, for the year 1905.

"Death Ends Career of John D. Hearne," *KP*, June 15, 1905, 1.

Greve, Charles Theodore. *Centennial History of Cincinnati and Representative Citizens.* 2 vols. Chicago: Biographical Publishing, 1904.

"J. D. Hearne as a History Maker," *KP*, June 15, 1905, 1.

Kenton Co. Deed Book 15, April 1, 1867, pp. 12, 13, 14; Deed Book 18, May 15, 1868, pp. 40–51; Will Book 9, November, 3, 1904, pp. 527–37, Kenton Co. Courthouse, Covington, Ky.

"Large Real Estate Transaction—Sale of the Groesbeck Property," *CDE*, June 20, 1866, 2.

John Boh

HEBRON. The village of Hebron, located in the southernmost part of the Bullittsville Magisterial District, which constitutes the northernmost part of Boone Co., calls itself the "Top of Kentucky," a phrase coined by Boone Co. historian William Conrad. The town is centered at the junction of Ky. Rts. 20 and 237. Hebron received its name from the **Hebron Lutheran Church**, which was established in this area in 1854 as an offshoot of the **Hopeful Lutheran Church** of Florence, Ky. On February 23, 1858, the U.S. Post Office recognized Hebron as the official name of the town when it granted the town its first post office. There was never any doubt that the community would assume the name of its church as the name for the town.

A community based on yeoman agriculture, Hebron soon became recognized as one of the fastest-growing and most prolific crop-producing portions of Boone Co. An array of businesses, mercantile establishments, tradesmen, and providers of goods and services naturally followed, and a lineal neighborhood took form along the Petersburg Rd., now known as Ky. Rt. 20. Long-established family names from the original German immigrants remain today in the Hebron area. They include Clore, Connor, Crigler, Crisler, Rouse, and Tanner. The German family name Zimmermann was anglicized to Carpenter. Then followed the Dolwicks, the Hempflings, and the McGlassons—all common names in the Hebron environs and still connected to agricultural pursuits in one way or another.

The 1940s introduced a new, identity-altering use for the flat farmland in the area. Boone Co. became home to the Cincinnati airport, winning out over an area in Blue Ash, Ohio, and the Lunken Airport in Cincinnati. The airport was later expanded to become the Greater Cincinnati Airport and then the **Cincinnati/ Northern Kentucky International Airport**. The growth and development that followed at the airport itself and in the surrounding area, in the form of business and residential expansion, soon absorbed most of Hebron's prime crop-producing farmland and eventually much of the town itself. What the airport did not take, the construction of I-75 and I-275, along with the widening and rebuilding of the local North Bend Rd., did. Further airport runway expansions in the 1990s and in the 2000s have claimed even more of what was once the community of Hebron. The main businesses and services are now along the North Bend Rd., both north and south of the expressway interchanges. Hebron is no longer incorporated as a town.

Boone Co. Historic Preservation Review Board. *Historic Structures of Boone County, Kentucky.* Ann Arbor, Mich.: Cushing-Malloy, 2002.

Rennick, Robert M. *Kentucky Place Names.* Lexington: Univ. Press of Kentucky, 1984.

Warner, Jennifer S. *Boone County: From Mastodons to the Millennium.* Burlington, Ky.: Boone Co. Bicentennial Book Committee, 1998.

Don Clare

HEBRON HIGH SCHOOL. The Hebron Consolidated School, which included the high school, was near the intersection of North Bend and Elijah Creek Rds. in Boone Co. It opened in 1923 and closed in 1954. The high school had fine basketball teams, known as the Cardinals. The school produced John Crigler, who was a starter on the 1958 NCAA championship basketball team at the University of Kentucky (UK). By guarding Elgin Baylor, an All-American at Seattle University and later a great professional player, Crigler enabled the UK team to advance. High school athletes also played six-man football; Irv Goode, who played some 13 years with the St. Louis Cardinals in professional football, came out of a six-man programs The building was sold and a few years later was destroyed by fire.

Boone Co. judge **Carrol L. Cropper** named Glenrose Williams, a Hebron High graduate of the late 1930s, the county's first woman sheriff in 1945; she succeeded her father, J. T. "Jake" Williams, upon his death. Secondary education returned to the Hebron area in 1970 with the opening of the Conner High School.

Meiman, Karen. "Friends for Life—Class of '30 Meets," *KP*, May 23, 2000, 8K.

Warner, Jennifer S. *Boone County: From Mastodons to the Millennium.* Burlington, Ky.: Boone Co. Bicentennial Book Committee, 1998.

Gail Chastang

HEBRON LUTHERAN CHURCH. Wars occurring in Europe more than 300 years ago led indirectly to the establishment of this church. When French armies invaded the Alsace region of southwestern Germany in 1674, many citizens fled from their German homeland and came to the New World. After a brief stay in Pennsylvania, some of them moved to the area around the Rappahannock River in Virginia, where they established a community called Germanna and a church, the Hopeful Lutheran Church, which is the oldest continuously used Lutheran church in the United States. They chose the name because they hoped to have a happy and prosperous life in their adopted country. In 1727, under the leadership of Rev. John Casper Stover Sr., a second church, called Hebron Lutheran Church, was begun a short distance from Germanna.

Rev. William Carpenter and some of the members from Hopeful Church in Virginia moved to Northern Kentucky in 1805. Those hardy settlers formed the **Hopeful Lutheran Church** in Boone Co., in modern Florence, on January 6, 1806. In 1854, 16 members from Hopeful Lutheran Church, whose parents and grandparents had previously belonged to the Hebron Lutheran Church in Virginia, met in the home of John J. Crigler, to form a

Boone Co. church named after the Hebron Lutheran Church in Virginia. Hopeful Lutheran and Hebron Lutheran started a joint parish, with one pastor, Rev. David Harbaugh, serving both congregations. He lived in a parsonage midway between the two churches. On July 15, 1854, the cornerstone was laid for the newly christened Hebron Lutheran Church. Its modern address is 3140 Limaburg Rd., just east of today's Connor High School in Boone Co. Trees on the church property were felled for use in construction of the new building, and the bricks were handmade on-site. The building was completed and dedicated on December 3, 1854. The Hebron Lutheran Church of Virginia sent $500 to help pay for construction of its Boone Co. namesake. In 1856 the Ebenezer Lutheran Church was founded in Boone Co. and accepted as a member of the parish. That church continued holding services until 1892, when it merged with the Hopeful Lutheran Church. The Hebron Lutheran Church celebrated its 100th anniversary in 1954. The City of Hebron took its name from the Hebron Lutheran Church.

Several additional acres of land adjoining the Hebron Lutheran Church property were purchased in 1968, and a new, modern edifice was built. A $1 million wing was added in 1991, which contains a social hall seating 450 and educational space. Hebron Lutheran Church, with about 350 active members, continues to be a vibrant, growing church, with a wide range of programs. It is currently a member of the Indiana-Kentucky Synod.

"Celebration Is Set for Boone Church, Founded in 1806," *KE*, June 6, 1956, 1.

"Church Chat," *KP*, March 11, 1967, 1.

Lentz, H. Max. *A History of Lutheran Churches in Boone County, Ky.* York, Pa.: P. Anstadt, 1902.

Waltmann, Henry G. *History of the Indiana-Kentucky Synod of the Lutheran Church in America.* Indianapolis: Central, 1971.

HEEKIN. Heekin is in Grant Co., south of Williamstown on U.S. 25 and west on Ky. Rt. 2937. Named for the Heekin Spice Company of Cincinnati, the neighborhood now consists of a smattering of houses and two churches. The thriving Mount Olivet Church of Christ is engaged in a building program. Nearby is the Grassy Run Baptist Church and its adjacent cemetery. Eagle Creek, Rattlesnake Creek, Clark's Creek, and Grassy Run furnished water needed by the early settlers. The creek beds sometimes served as roads in those days, but landowners were soon made responsible for surveying and maintaining roads in their neighborhoods. The grade schools, which were established about three miles apart, within walking distance for students, included the Independence School, on nearby Chipman Ridge Rd., and the Heekin School. The Heekin School was later consolidated with the Mason School. The Mason School closed its high school in 1953 so its students could enter **Grant Co. High School**. The present Mason-Corinth Elementary School opened in 1991.

Conrad, John B., ed. *History of Grant County, Kentucky.* Williamstown, Ky.: Grant Co. Historical Society, 1992.

Pease, Janet, comp. *Abstracted County Court Records.* Vols. 1 and 2. Williamstown, Ky.: Grant Co. Historical Society, 1985.

Mary Louis Evans

HEHL, LAMBERT, JR. (b. July 22, 1924, Newport, Ky.). Lambert Lawrence Hehl, a judge and a legislator, is the son of **Lambert Lawrence Hehl Sr.** and Martha Daly Hehl. He received his early education at **St. Vincent de Paul** Elementary School in South Newport and went on to graduate from **Newport High School**. In 1943 Lambert Hehl Jr. volunteered for the U.S. Marines; he served as a legal clerk in the Pacific Theater and had achieved the rank of sergeant by the time he left military service in 1946. On May 25 of that same year, he married Helyn Mae Bathiany, and the couple had two daughters. During the early years of his marriage, Hehl worked by day to support his family and attended evening classes at **Chase College of Law**. After receiving his law degree in 1952, he maintained a solo law practice until 1956, when he became an associate, and later a partner, in the Newport firm of Benton, Benton, Luedeke, Rhoads, and Hehl. In 1962 Hehl began a successful law partnership with Norbert Bischoff, which lasted until 1982.

Throughout the 1950s and 1960s, in addition to his burgeoning law practice, Hehl served as president of the Campbell Co. Junior Chamber of Commerce (see **Northern Kentucky Chamber of Commerce**) and as state vice president of the Kentucky Jaycees, and he maintained memberships in the James Wallace Costigan Post No. 11, the American Legion Lawler-Hanlon Post No. 5822, the Veterans of Foreign Wars, and many other civic organizations. From 1953 to 1956, he served as deputy Campbell Co. tax commissioner under his father, who was serving his fourth term as county tax commissioner. On December 2, 1957, Judge **Fred Warren** named Hehl Jr. county judge pro tem so that he could swear his father into office for a fifth term as county tax commissioner.

Lambert Hehl Jr.'s election in 1959 as a Kentucky state senator marked the beginning of his wide-ranging career as an elected official. From 1960 until the end of his term in 1963, he also served as chair of the senate judiciary committee. From 1969 to 1980, he was a member of the central executive committee of the Kentucky Democratic Party and also officiated as a special hearing officer.

His long career in county government began with two terms (1963–1973) as county commissioner with Judge **Andrew J. Jolly**. In 1974 Hehl succeeded Jolly as Fiscal Court judge; he served in this capacity until 1982, although during the last five years of his county judgeship, the position's title was county judge-executive. Kentucky governor John Y. Brown Jr. (1979–1983) appointed Hehl to an interim term as county circuit judge in 1983. The following year, Governor Martha Layne Collins (1983–1987) appointed him as Campbell Co. district judge, a post to which he was twice elected, continuing in this position until 1990. That same year, the chief justice of the Kentucky Supreme Court, **Robert Stephens**, announced Hehl's appointment as chief regional judge of the Sixth Appellate Court District; he served in this capacity until his retirement in 1990.

Throughout Hehl's lengthy tenure in public office, his exhaustive efforts on behalf of his Campbell Co. constituency helped to lay the groundwork for Northern Kentucky's ongoing residential and industrial revitalization. His proactive legislative style and aggressive pursuit of state and federal funds for Northern Kentucky fostered the establishment of intrastate highways and bridges and sparked other projects that have since opened the area to expansive development. His 20-year stint on the Campbell Co. Fiscal Court saw the completion of I-275 through Campbell Co. and across the Ohio River, the construction of I-471, and the construction of the **AA Highway** in Campbell Co. and beyond. Such essential connector routes also fostered the birth of **Northern Kentucky University** at Highland Heights in the late 1960s and the school's growth in the 1970s.

The Commonwealth of Kentucky honored the significant contributions of both Hehl and former Kentucky governor Bert Combs (1959–1963) with the December 19, 1979, dedication of the Combs-Hehl Bridge; its heavily traveled double span carries six lanes of I-275 across the Ohio River at Brent. Hehl is also the recipient of the National Jaycees' Distinguished and Unselfish Service Award and the National Veterans of Foreign Wars' Life Saving Award. Hehl's peers on various professional and government organizations, such as the Chase Law School Alumni, the Campbell Co. Bar Association, the Kentucky Association of County Judge-Executives, the Northern Kentucky Transportation Committee, and the **Northern Kentucky Area Planning Commission**, have selected him as their president.

Since his 1990 retirement, Hehl has remained a driving force of community involvement within Northern Kentucky. He has been active in various civic and fraternal organizations and has honored his hometown roots by serving as president of Newport's Clem and Ann Buenger **Boys & Girls Club** and the Newport High School Alumni Association. In April 1994 Hehl was named chairperson of Newport's Bicentennial Commission, a duty he executed with faithful precision. Hehl's wife of 58 years, Helyn, died in October 2004. He currently resides in Fort Thomas with his present wife, Pat Zint Hehl.

Beasley, David. "Hehl Rode New Highways to Success as County Official," *KP*, October 17, 1982, B2.

———. "Lambert Hehl Helped Bridge NKY and Ohio," *SC*, January 30, 2005, 4B.

Hehl, Lambert. Interview by Jan Mueller, April 28, 2006, Fort Thomas, Ky.

Long, Paul A. "Judge Hehl Will Retire at Year's End—Public Career Began in 1953," *KP*, November 1, 1990, 1K–2K.

Purvis, Thomas L., ed. *Newport, Kentucky: A Bicentennial History.* Newport, Ky.: Otto Zimmerman, 1996.

Janice Mueller

HEHL, LAMBERT, SR. (b. August 4, 1895, Newport, Ky.; d. December 26, 1970, Fort Thomas, Ky.). Lambert Hehl Sr., a respected civic leader, a

World War I veteran, and a longtime Campbell Co. tax commissioner, was the son of Frank and Mary Wilderley Hehl. He grew up in Newport, where he received his early education. In 1917 Hehl was employed as a ticket agent at the Chesapeake and Ohio Railroad depot when the U.S. declaration of war on Germany and the subsequent passage of the Selective Services Act prompted a nationwide conscription effort. Hehl enlisted with the U.S. Marines; by November of the same year, he was undergoing training at Quantico, Va., and awaiting deployment to France. On April 5, 1918, while advancing with his unit, the 6th Marine Brigade, in France's Toulon Sector, Private Hehl was struck in the leg with shrapnel, becoming Campbell Co.'s earliest casualty wounded in action in France during World War I. Another Newport resident from Hehl's company, James Wallace Costigan, died July 31, 1918, from wounds received the month before at Belleau Wood; Costigan was Newport's first World War I casualty. The James Wallace Costigan **American Legion** Post in Newport memorialized Costigan. Hehl later served as that post's commander and for 30 years was its service officer. His interest in veteran affairs was further demonstrated by his longtime assistance to widows and other dependents, securing lawfully allowed benefits due to them.

On June 16, 1920, Hehl married Martha Daly; they had a son and a daughter, **Lambert Hehl Jr.** and Virginia. Although the family experienced its share of tough times during the Great Depression, in 1935 Hehl was appointed assistant county road engineer, a post he held until 1941. The devastating Ohio River **flood of 1937** hit Northern Kentucky during his tenure. Hehl contributed his civic talents to the community by serving as county chair for the local **Red Cross** Disaster Committee. His position as public service officer for the James Wallace Costigan American Legion Post allowed him to utilize the facility's hall as the area's earliest shelter and soup kitchen. By January 21, when the rising waters covered 68 blocks and were continuing to displace more Newport residents, Hehl's emergency shelter was serving two meals a day to almost 200 families.

After the U.S. Congress declared war on Japan and its allies on December 8, 1941, Newport's citizens, fraught by paranoia and fear of saboteurs in the wake of Pearl Harbor, mounted an active defense of the city's businesses and infrastructure. Their coordinated efforts included the establishment of the Municipal Council of Defense, of which Hehl was a member. The defense council organized multiple emergency response teams, including air raid wardens, medical personnel, and rescue squads.

That same year, Hehl had decided to run for public office. He took the tax commissioners' exam and, despite his limited formal education, passed it. This accomplishment was always a source of pride for Hehl, who had undertaken extensive self-education after returning from active duty during World War I. He ran on the Democratic ticket as a candidate for Campbell Co. tax commissioner in 1941 and was elected, beginning the first of six consecutive terms in 1942. For the next 24 years, until his retirement in 1965, Hehl served in this capacity; during his long tenure, the tax commission office's reputation for efficiency was recognized on a nearly annual basis by the state.

In 1953 Lambert Hehl Jr. had been appointed deputy county tax commissioner under his father. After Lambert Hehl Sr. had won his fifth bid for the office of Campbell Co. tax commissioner in 1957, the younger Hehl was offered the opportunity to pay a touching tribute to his father. Judge **Fred Warren** named Lambert Hehl Jr. county judge pro tem, thus allowing the father to be sworn into office by his son.

In addition to his responsibilities as a public official, Hehl Sr.'s political activity included serving as the executive secretary of the Campbell Co. Democratic Committee for almost two decades. Known as a powerful public speaker, he supported his close personal friend U.S. congressman **Brent Spence** by campaigning for him throughout his 32 years in office. On April 27, 1970, Hehl was chosen as the recipient of the second annual Brent Spence Memorial Award, bestowed upon him by members of the Campbell Co. Democratic Committee. Lambert Hehl Jr., by then a seasoned public official in his own right, honored his father with a touching eulogy before introducing him to accept the award. Just a few months later, on December 26, 1970, Lambert Hehl Sr. collapsed at his home at 81 Southview Ave. in Fort Thomas and died. He was buried at St. Stephen Cemetery in Fort Thomas.

Hehl, Lambert, Jr. Interview by Jan Mueller, April 28, 2006, Fort Thomas, Ky.
"Lambert Hehl Dies at 75," *KP*, December 28, 1970, 1K–2K.
Murphy, John. "Tears of Joy Honor Hehl Sr." *KP*, April 28, 1970, 1K.
Purvis, Thomas L., ed. *Newport, Kentucky: A Bicentennial History.* Newport, Ky.: Otto Zimmerman, 1996.

Janice Mueller

HELENA. Helena is located in the southeastern part of Mason Co. near the Fleming Co. line. It was incorporated on March 8, 1854, and for a period during the 1880s was annually electing a police judge and a town marshal. The town was located near the Helena Station on the **Maysville and Lexington Railroad** line that runs between Maysville and Lexington (see **Louisville and Nashville Railroad; TransKentucky Transportation Railroad**). In 1856 the Richland Academy was opened in Helena community as a girls' school. It later became part of the county system and enrolled more than 100 students at the end of the 19th century. The community of Helena had a Masonic Lodge (see **Masons**), a post office, and churches, in addition to the school. The Helena Methodist Church has a long history, and the church's current building dates from 1914. In recent years, a number of Amish people have moved into the general area, and an Amish school now operates across from the railroad tracks in Helena.

Calvert, Jean, and John Klee. *The Towns of Mason County: Their Past in Pictures.* Maysville, Ky.: Maysville and Mason Co. Library Historical and Scientific Association, 1986.
Clift, G. Glenn. *History of Maysville and Mason County.* Lexington, Ky.: Transylvania, 1936.

John Klee

HELLEBUSCH, BERNARD H. F. (b. April 23, 1825, Oldenburg, Germany; d. June 12, 1885, Covington, Ky.). Bernard Hellebusch, an organist and hymnal publisher, came from a musical family. Having immigrated to the United States in search of opportunity, he arrived in Covington by flatboat in January 1844; some of his siblings followed. Hellebusch began to teach school at the German-speaking **Mother of God Catholic Church** in Covington, using the melodeon (a small pump organ) that he had brought with him. Although most of his career centered on the Mother of God Church, he also taught at Holy Trinity Church (Heiligen Dreiheit Kirche) in Cincinnati's West End.

Hellebusch became both a teacher and the principal at Mother of God School, in addition to giving private music lessons. A student of the Enlightenment, Hellebusch promoted the German *Singmesse* tradition, which emphasized the folk song rather than a classical Latin approach to church music. He wrote seven sets of *Singmesse* hymns, 34 in all. *The Catholic Youth's Hymn Book* (1871) was the first to provide English translations of them.

Perhaps Hellebusch's greatest contribution was the German-language hymnal he first published in 1858, *Gesang und Gebetbuch,* through which he introduced for the first time to the U.S. church such hymns as "Holy God" ("Grosser Gott") and "O Sacred Head Surrounded" ("O Haupt Voll Blut und Wunden"), along with many others. This hymnal was used throughout German-Catholic communities, and Hellebusch's modest church salary was enhanced by the royalties from its sales.

During his last years at Mother of God, the present church building was erected. Hellebusch persuaded the pastor, Father Teutenberg, and the parish to install a new organ. No doubt his campaign had the support of his brother Clemens Hellebusch, who was a wealthy jeweler and a parish trustee. The Koehnken organ installation was overseen by Bernard Hellebusch in 1876.

Toward the end of Hellebusch's career, his type of music was falling out of favor in the church, in preference for what was known as the Caecilian Movement. Upon the arrival of Mother of God's new pastor, Rev. William Tappert, and his musician-brother Rev. Henry Tappert, Caecilian music was embraced by the church, and Hellebusch departed to finish out his career at the neighboring **St. Aloysius Catholic Church**, also in Covington.

The Hellebusch family lived at the southeast corner of Fifth and Russell Sts., Covington, when he died in 1885. His first wife, Marian Putthoff, had died in 1860. His second wife, Margaret Merle, bore him 11 children, the youngest of whom was age six at the time of Hellebusch's death. Hellebusch's musical contributions have been largely forgotten, and only archival copies of his very successful hymnal remain. He was buried at Mother of God Cemetery, Covington.

Hellebusch, Juliana Mattei. "B. H. F. 'Teacher' Hellebusch (1825–1885)," *NKH* 1, no. 2 (Spring–Summer 1994): 13–23.

Karl Lietzenmayer

HELM, CHARLES JOHN, SR. (b. June 21, 1817, Hornellsville, N.Y.; d. February 1868, Toronto, Canada). Charles John Helm Sr., who became a lawyer, a military officer, the U.S. consul general, and a Confederate agent to Havana, Cuba, was the first of six children of Francis T. and Sallie B. McKinney Helm. In 1817, his birth year, his family moved to Newport, where in 1834 Francis Helm, a veteran of the **War of 1812**, became Newport's first mayor. Educated in Newport, Charles was tutored in law by **John W. Tibbatts**, a noted attorney, congressman, and infantry colonel, and a son-in-law of Gen. **James Taylor Jr.**, founder of Newport. Upon admission to the bar in 1842, Helm practiced law in Tibbatts's firm until Tibbatts, on April 9, 1847, organized the 16th U.S. Infantry Regiment (which included 4 of the 10 companies from Kentucky), which had been reactivated on February 11 for the **Mexican War**. Helm was appointed a 1st lieutenant and later reached the rank of brevet major. The regiment was disbanded on August 16, 1848, and Helm returned to his law practice in Newport.

Helm was elected to the Kentucky House of Representatives for one term in 1851. President Franklin Pierce named him U.S. commercial agent to St. Thomas, Virgin Islands, in 1853. In 1854 Helm married Louise A. Whistler in Newport. They had five children. Back in St. Thomas, Helm successfully negotiated to have the Danish government revoke certain imposts that had hampered U.S. merchant shipping. In 1858 President James Buchanan appointed Helm as the country's consul general to Cuba. That strategic Spanish shipping hub became very important when the **Civil War** commenced in 1861. Rumors spread that Helm might defect to the Confederacy, whereupon U.S. secretary of state William Seward made several attempts to retain Helm in his position in Havana, even to the extent of sending him a silk flag, according to some accounts. Nevertheless, Helm resigned as consul general and returned to the United States, evading all attempts to have him arrested for his allegiance to the South. Confederate president Jefferson Davis sent Helm back to Cuba in July 1861 as a special agent for the Confederacy; his circuitous journey took him through Canada and England to Havana. Helm worked to ensure Cuba's neutrality during the Civil War, while simultaneously acting as the monitor of Confederate blockade-running activities. After the war, fearful of arrest for treason, Helm moved his family to Toronto, Canada, where an enclave of former Confederate politicians and senior military officers lived. He was in the welcoming party for the visiting Jefferson Davis at Niagara-on-the-Lake, Ontario, Canada, after Davis was released from federal prison in 1867. The exiled Helm died in Toronto in 1868. His wife, Louise, and their three surviving children, Charles John Helm Jr., born in St. Thomas; Louise, born in Havana; and William W., born in Canada, returned to Newport, where Charles Jr. and William practiced law, the former becoming circuit judge.

Charles Helm.

Collins, Richard H. *History of Kentucky.* Vol. 1. Covington, Ky.: Collins, 1882.

Perrin, William Henry, J. H. Battle, and G. C. Kniffin. *Kentucky: A History of the State.* Louisville, Ky.: F. A. Battey, 1888.

Reis, Jim. *Pieces of the Past.* Vol. 2. Covington: Kentucky Post, 1991.

Roberts, William Hugh. *Mexican War Veterans: A Roster of the Regular and Volunteer Regiments in the War with Mexico, 1846–1848.* Washington, D.C.: A. S. Witherbee, 1887.

Robert Michael Venable

HEMINGRAY, ROBERT (b. June 22, 1820, near Johnstown, Pa.; d. December 27, 1898, Covington, Ky.). Robert Hemingray joined **Ralph Gray** to found the Gray & Hemingray Glass Works in 1848. They were pioneer industrialists in the Northern Kentucky region, providing a product eagerly welcomed by a market hungry for a local source of quality glassware. Gray died in 1863, and in 1870 the glass works was incorporated as the **Hemingray Glass Company**. The company became recognized worldwide as a leader in the production of domestic and industrial glassware.

Robert's parents, William and Ann Hemingray, arrived in the United States about 1818 from England and settled on the Conemaugh River, near Johnstown, in western Pennsylvania. William found work making salt from the saline springs that abounded in the area. Robert Hemingray was born in a salt-camp cabin in 1820. William Hemingray moved his family to Pittsburgh in 1825 and opened a small general store. Unfortunately, William drowned November 22, 1832, and Ann died August 29, 1834, leaving Robert Hemingray orphaned at age 14.

Despite trying circumstances, Hemingray managed to obtain a sound education, completing a college course prior to marriage and embarking on his life's work. He was employed by the Phillips Glass Works, located in "Pipetown," an industrial Pittsburgh suburb located east of the city along the Monongahela River. Because of his education, Hemingray was engaged in the business aspects of the company rather than the actual manufacturing of glass. The "Great Fire of 1845" destroyed essentially all of industrial Pittsburgh and most of its residential neighborhoods. The Phillips Glass Works was consumed by the fire as was, most likely, the residence of the young Hemingray family. Conditions in Pittsburgh became grim as thousands were put out of work and many people were left homeless.

Soon after the fire, Hemingray joined forces with Ralph Gray, a glassblower living in Birmingham, Pa., an industrial community across the Monongahela River from Pittsburgh. Together they descended the Ohio River to Covington with hopes of starting their own glass works. The two were unsuccessful in immediately acquiring a suitable site in Covington and were forced to lease a small lot in Cincinnati. They quickly constructed a furnace for making glass, obtained the necessary raw materials, and procured molds; they began producing glassware in late 1848. In 1852 they purchased a small lot near the intersection of Second St. and Madison Ave. in Covington and moved the production of glassware to Covington while maintaining the sales room in Cincinnati until 1881, when it also was relocated to Covington.

Hemingray was progressive as well as innovative in the art of glass manufacturing. Once he and Gray had overcome the obstacles confronting them in their start-up of the glass works, he was able to focus on improvements in operational efficiency and product quality. He received patents for improvements in machinery and product design from 1860 to 1887 and encouraged his partners and employees to seek enhancements that resulted in additional patents assigned to the glass works.

Robert married Mary E. Carroll June 6, 1842, in Pittsburgh, and the couple had eight children.

Gray's younger brother Anthony married Susan Carroll, a sister of Hemingray's wife. Anthony died April 27, 1865, and Susan died two years later. Robert and Mary Hemingray took the five Gray children into their home to be raised to adulthood. The oldest son, John C. Gray, became superintendent of the Hemingray Glass Company in 1897 and was elevated to the position of general manager upon the death of Hemingray.

Hemingray was not politically active. While he voted with the **Whig Party**, he did not seek public office, nor is there any indication that he played a role in politics behind the scenes. Northern Kentucky had strong pro-Union feelings before and during the **Civil War**. When the area was threatened by an attacking Confederate force in September 1862, Hemingray joined **Amos Shinkle**'s Covington militia company as a sergeant. Hemingray's leadership capabilities were sorely tested during the war years, especially after the death of his partner, Ralph Gray; however, Hemingray managed to hold the company together.

Robert Hemingray died at his home at 219 Garrard St. in Covington in late 1898; Mary died in 1901. They were buried in the Hemingray lot at Highland Cemetery in Fort Mitchell.

Covington Health Department Death Certificate No. 759, for the year 1898.
Drummond, Glenn. *A Genealogical Study of the Ancestral Line of Robert "Robin" Hemingray, Conway Taylor Hemingray, Susan Ashley Hemingray for the Purpose of Identifying Their Connection to a Revolutionary Patriot.* Notasulga, Ala.: Glen Drummond, 2003.
Highland Cemetery Records, Fort Mitchell, Ky.
Hyve, H. G. (Bea). *The Hemingray Glass Co.: A Most Colorful History.* San Diego: Clarice Gordon, n.d. [ca. 1998].
"Pioneer Dead—Founder of Company Robert Hemingray Died," *KP,* December 27, 1898, 1.
Probate, Marriage, and Deed Records, Hamilton Co., Ohio (Cincinnati), Kenton Co., Ky. (Covington and Independence), and Allegheny Co., Pa. (Pittsburgh).

Glenn Drummond

HEMINGRAY GLASS COMPANY. The Hemingray Glass Company, once located in Covington, was founded by a partnership of **Ralph Gray** and **Robert Hemingray** in 1848. From a very modest beginning on a small leased lot in Cincinnati, the company grew to become one of the nation's largest manufacturers of domestic and industrial glassware. The factory was moved from Cincinnati to Covington in 1852, then to Muncie, Ind., in 1888; the company's business offices continued to function in Covington until 1919. The Owens-Illinois Glass Company bought the assets of the Hemingray Glass Company in 1933 and closed the firm's operations in 1972.

Gray and Hemingray came to Covington from Pittsburgh. Both had been associated with glass-manufacturing interests in Pittsburgh before the "Great Fire of 1845," which destroyed most of that city. Their initial goal was to build a glass factory in Covington, but because they found no suitable site, they located in Cincinnati, where a glass furnace was constructed fronting on Mayor's Alley (Hammond St.). They began to produce glass products in 1848. Four years later they secured a desired property in Covington, near the northwest corner of the intersection of Second St. and Madison Ave. The factory was moved to Covington as soon as production facilities were completed; however, the warehouse and the sales room remained in Cincinnati until 1881.

The cities of Cincinnati, Covington, and Newport were thriving and growing rapidly. As Cincinnati was the center of commerce for the Ohio River Valley, there was a large demand for domestic and commercial glassware. The nearest sources of these products were the glass houses of Wheeling, W.Va., and Pittsburgh, but the Pittsburgh fire had created an uncertain void in the availability of glassware that the Gray & Hemingray Glass Works (as the firm was first known) quickly filled. Products varied, but the greatest demand was for apothecary glassware, bottles of various forms, fruit jars, oil lamps, and tableware. These products remained the staple of the company throughout its first two decades.

Hard work, a quality product, a rapidly expanding market, and limited competition enabled the Gray & Hemingray Glass Works to flourish during the 1850s. Even when war clouds formed early in the 1860s and the national economy became shaky, the glass works continued to prosper and grow.

The death of Gray in 1863, resulted in great consternation for Hemingray. Gray's will stipulated that, because of the great uncertainty prevailing at the time, his undivided half interest in the glass works be sold and the proceeds invested for the support of his widow. Not only did Hemingray lose a close friend and business partner, but the thought of bringing into the firm an interest outside of the family was particularly unsettling. He was able to marshal a small group of family members and close friends who acquired Gray's half interest, enabling the company to survive. The half interest was equally divided among Joseph C. Hemingray, Samuel J. Hemingray, Richard Evans, and James L. Foley. Joseph C. and Samuel J. were brothers of Robert Hemingray; Richard Evans, Robert's brother-in-law, and James L. Foley were close friends and associates. The subsequent death in 1866 of Samuel J. Hemingray created another episode of uncertainty, because Samuel's widow immediately sold her inherited one-eighth interest to an outsider with no experience in glass production. This dilemma was quickly resolved through the purchase of that interest by Evans and Foley.

Incorporated in the state of Kentucky in 1870, the company continued to grow. Additional land was acquired and new buildings constructed to enable the company to satisfy the expanding market. Fruit jars, oil lamps, and telegraph insulators came to be the primary products. The Hemingray Glass Company eventually became the world's largest producer of glass insulators for telegraph, telephone, and electric power distribution.

The Covington business site offered a number of advantages at the outset, such as easy access to the Ohio River for the shipment of finished products and receipt of raw materials. A block away from the Covington plant was the **Walsh Distillery**, a major user of glass bottles beginning in 1873. However, floods, droughts, ice, and other weather conditions sometimes overwhelmed these advantages. The company suffered severe losses during the floods of 1883 and 1884, which forced work to cease for extended periods. In addition, the **flood of 1884** caused structural damage to the Hemingray Glass Company's buildings. The variable flow rates of the river resulted in frequent periods when low flow prevented the essential delivery of coal, sand, and other necessary raw materials to the plant. Ice jams or running ice on the river would also bring traffic to a standstill (see **Ohio River Navigation**). One of the company's buildings was severely damaged by a tornado that passed along the river in 1860.

Natural gas was the fuel of choice for rival glass manufacturers located in the upper Ohio River Valley by the 1880s, so Robert Hemingray attempted to locate a source of natural gas. He drilled test wells on company-owned property, beginning in 1884. The first well yielded sufficient natural gas to heat the boilers but not nearly enough to fire the furnaces, and further exploration proved fruitless.

In 1887 the company was approached by representatives of the Manufacturers Guarantee Fund Association of Muncie, Ind., with an offer of free property and natural gas in exchange for agreeing to relocate the factory to that city. The offer, coming on the heels of devastating floods and record low water levels in the Ohio River, was attractive enough that company officials chose to accept it. The company began to move production facilities to Muncie in 1888.

Although Robert Hemingray continued to be the president, factory operations in Muncie were under the direction of Ralph G. Hemingray, Robert's oldest son. Daniel C. Hemingray, the youngest son, secretary-treasurer, was responsible for the operation of the business offices, which remained in Covington. Robert C. Hemingray, the second son, was factory superintendent until health problems forced his retirement.

The natural gas reserves had been touted as "inexhaustible." No one knew that the "Indiana Natural Gas Belt" would be depleted within a very few years. An attempt was made in 1900 to reopen the Covington factory on a limited basis, but it was decided to terminate the attempt after operating for one year because of high maintenance costs. In the meantime, efforts were under way to purchase property for a new Covington factory near the intersection of Seventh and Russell Sts. The site was above flood stage, as well as lying adjacent to the Chesapeake and Ohio Railway. Unfortunately, the property owners insisted on a higher price for the land than the company was willing to pay, and negotiations broke down. All thoughts of returning to Covington were abandoned. The final decision was to construct "producer gas" furnaces in Muncie and retain the factory there.

After Ralph Hemingray died, May 11, 1920, the company came under the control of Phillip McAbee, husband of Ralph Hemingray's daughter Carol. McAbee had little glass-manufacturing experience, and the loss of markets during the onset of the **Great Depression** in the 1930s took a toll on the Hemingray Glass Company along with other glass manufacturers. McAbee soon found the firm in debt with no foreseeable opportunity to recover; consequently, he chose to put his glass-making company on the market, and the Owens-Illinois Glass Company bought it.

Hamilton Co. (Cincinnati) and Kenton Co. (Independence and Covington) Deed Records.
Hyve, H. G. (Bea). *The Hemingray Glass Co.: A Most Colorful History.* San Diego: Clarice Gordon, n.d. [ca. 1998].
Pittsburgh, Cincinnati, and Covington city directories and newspapers.

Glenn Drummond

HEMINGRAY GLASS COMPANY ARCHAEOLOGY. A 1986 archaeological project explored the Covington site occupied by the **Hemingray Glass Company** from 1852 until

1888. The property, acquired in at least seven transactions from 1852 to 1880, took in nearly the entire block north of Second St. and west of Madison Ave., as well as portions of the block to the south.

Considerable effort was made in the 1986 archaeological excavations at the Hemingray Glass Company's work site to expose the remnants of the factory complex (see **Covington Urban Archaeology**). Originally, the company's building complex contained a batch house; a bottle-blowing house; company offices; clay, molding, and sandblasting areas; a decorating room; ovens; packing rooms; and steam heated lehrs (ovens through which glassware travels on a belt). The various parts of the complex ranged from one to four stories tall. In total, 315.1 linear meters (1,034 feet) of limestone foundation walls were exposed across the large area. Excavated features included the bases of the glassblowing ovens, a decorating oven, a large cistern, a lehr, and a series of unidentified ovens. In addition, a large excavation unit was placed within massive waste deposits near the north end of the complex. This pit extended to nearly 5 meters (16.4 feet) below the present surface; however, the base of the deposits was not encountered. More than 221.77 kilograms (489 pounds) of glass waste were processed at the screens.

When the Hemingray Glass Company was active in Covington, Ohio River commerce provided coal for the company's glass furnaces, but historical documents indicate that sand was purchased from Missouri and lead from Illinois. Ralph Gray and Robert Hemingray, the founders and owners, produced apothecary glassware, chemical apparatus, decanters, fruit jars, lamp glasses, lightning rods, packing bottles, perfumery glass, pickling bottles, telegraph insulators, and tumblers. The Hemingray Glass Company is well documented in the 1870 U.S. Census Manufacturing Schedule. According to that source, the firm made a capital investment of $250,000 and had 209 employees, 67 of them, or nearly one-third, children. Owing to the extreme heat of summer, the glassworkers were furloughed during July and August. Production materials were valued at $87,350, wages of $88,631 were paid, and sales amounted to $192,000. Flintware, fruitware, greenware, and lantern ware were the company's products listed. Hemingray Glass received 11 U.S. patents for advances in glass manufacturing during its stay in Covington: 4 for improvements in the manufacture of canning jars, 4 for advances in glass telegraph insulators, and 3 for manufacturing techniques. Robert Hemingray's 1871 patent for a threaded glass insulator heralded a shift of focus to mass production of first telegraph and then telephone and electric insulators, which were the firm's mainstay product for the next six decades, well past the company's move away from Kentucky.

Drummond, Glenn. *Hemingray Glass Company, Covington, Kentucky: A Chronological Listing of Pertinent Real Estate Actions, 1815–1899.* Notasulga, Ala.: Glenn Drummond, 1994.

Genheimer, Robert A. "Archaeological Testing, Evaluation, and Final Mitigation Excavations at Covington's Riverfront Redevelopment Phase 2 Site, Kenton County, Kentucky." Prepared by R. G. Archaeological Services, Covington. Submitted to the city of Covington, 1987.

Robert A. Genheimer

HENDERSON, CHARLES L. (b. September 1893, Paris, Ky.; d. December 27, 1918, France). Henderson, the son of Harriet Lee, was the first African American from Covington to be killed in action while serving in France during World War I. On April 1, 1918, Henderson was among the first African Americans to depart Covington for Camp Zachary Taylor in Louisville. He was with the 325th Field Signal Battalion, 92nd Infantry Division. These African Americans, drafted into the U.S. Army by the Covington Selective Service Board, were given a grand send-off by the community, family, and friends, as demonstrated by the brass band that accompanied them to their train. When Henderson died, the military authorities had a difficult time locating his nearest relative, even though his mother, his brother, and a nephew were living in Covington. Henderson was buried at the Oise-Aisne American Cemetery, Fère-en-Tardenois, France.

On September 1, 1919, World War I veterans in Covington decided to honor their fallen comrades by organizing an American Legion post. Henderson was honored by the naming of the Charles L. Henderson American Legion Post No. 166. **William H. Martin Jr.**, a veteran of World War I, was selected as its first commander. In May 1932 Charles H. Bishop became the new commander at an installation held at the Knights of Pythias Hall. In July of that year, a minstrel show was presented under the sponsorship of Post No. 166 at its post home, Prospect and Wheeler Sts. In December 1941 Post No. 166 was reactivated just before Pearl Harbor. The Charles L. Henderson American Legion Post No. 166 remains an active part of the community.

"Legion to Install," *KP*, May 6, 1932, 7.

"Officers Installed," *KP*, May 10, 1932, 2.

"Plan Minstrel Show," *KP*, July 19, 1932, 1.

Reis, Jim. "All Quiet on the Home Front Then Came Pearl Harbor," *KP*, December 7, 1998, 4K.

"Seeking Kin of Dead Soldier," *KTS*, November 4, 1919, 28.

"Selects Start Soldier Life," *KP*, April 1, 1918, 1.

"Soldier's Kin Sought," *KP*, November 4, 1919, 1.

"To Form Negro Post," *KP*, September 1, 1919, 2.

"To Give Minstrel Show," *KP*, July 24, 1932, 8.

Theodore H. H. Harris

HENDERSON-ROUSE TAVERN. Located on the **Dry Ridge Trace** (now U.S. 25, the **Dixie Highway**), on the south side of Crittenden, this six-room log tavern is said to have been built in 1815 by Joseph Meyers. The first proprietor was county magistrate James Theobald, who operated the tavern until 1822. The tavern was large for its day, with three rooms on the first floor and three on the second floor. Each room was about 20 feet square. The south room on the first floor was the barroom. Heated by a large fireplace when necessary, it contained a writing desk, tables, chairs, and a bar along one wall. This room also served as the magistrate's courtroom, where misdemeanor cases were tried, boundary disputes over land claims were settled, and administrators for estate settlements were appointed. The north room on the first floor was the tavern's dining room. The ringing of the first bell at mealtime was the signal for ladies and children to be seated. Men were seated on the sounding of the second bell. A doorway in the west wall led to a detached brick kitchen, where meals were prepared and carried by slave children into the dining room.

Rev. Thomas Henderson of Scott Co. acquired the 340 acres of land that included the tavern in 1822. He served as the tavern owner and operator, a farmer, a schoolmaster, and a Baptist minister until his death in 1846. His family continued to operate the tavern afterward. During the **Civil War**, the property and the tavern suffered considerable damage when the area was occupied by the 18th Michigan Regiment of the U.S. Army. With other changes brought about by time, the tavern became a private residence.

Conrad, John B., ed. *History of Grant County.* Williamstown, Ky.: Grant Co. Historical Society, 1992.

John B. Conrad

HENRY, JOSEPHINE W. (b. February 22, 1843, Newport, Ky.; d. January 8, 1928, Versailles, Ky.). Josephine Williamson Henry, a writer, teacher, and women's rights activist, was the daughter of Captain Euclid and Mary Kirby Williamson and the niece of Captain **John A. Williamson**, steamboat line owner and developer of the **Central Bridge** across the Ohio River at Newport. When Josephine was age 15, she and her family moved to Versailles, in Woodford Co., where she lived for the remainder of her life. She became an accomplished musician and gave piano lessons in her home. She also taught for several years at the Versailles Academy for Ladies. She married Confederate Army veteran Capt. William Henry, and they had a son, Frederick V. Henry, born in 1868. Captain Henry was also a teacher; he started the Henry Academy for Boys in Versailles. Josephine joined the Kentucky Equal Rights Association and espoused many of their ideas. In 1888 she began to campaign for voting rights for women and the following year attacked repressive Kentucky laws dealing with women's property rights. In 1890 Josephine Henry became the first woman in Kentucky to run for an elected state office; she was defeated in her effort to become clerk of the Kentucky Court of Appeals.

Henry's son, Frederick, began publishing a newspaper, which he called the *Versailles Clarion*. In 1891, while in Chicago researching a story for his newspaper, he was killed during a train derailment. It is believed that her son's death caused Henry to become an ardent agnostic. She developed a great disdain for biblical teachings and for Christianity in general. Henry was physically small; she looked more like a schoolmarm than the dynamic speaker and fiery suffragette she later became. She detested many things about the marriage ceremony, especially that the bride had to give up her surname and promise to obey her husband and that the bride was given away like chattel by her father. Henry also wanted women to stop using *Miss* or *Mrs.* before their name, since most men used no similar designation. She proposed that male children carry their mother's surname and female children use their father's. In her view marriage and divorce were the world's biggest problems, and marriage was the worse of the two. She claimed that by Kentucky law it was almost a crime to be a married woman.

Henry wrote two books, *Marriage and Divorce* and *Women and the Bible.* Because of her extreme views concerning religion and marriage, many in the women's rights movement opposed her, and she was later expelled from the Kentucky Equal Rights Association as an undesirable member. However, in 1920 the National American Woman Suffrage Association presented to Josephine Henry its Pioneer Distinguished Service award for her lifetime of dedication to women's issues. Henry suffered a stroke in December 1927 and died about a month later, at age 84. She was buried in a nondescript grave in the Versailles Cemetery, where a simple marker was erected, bearing only her name. Now nearly a century after her death, the fiery suffragette is all but forgotten, even in her home state. However, aided by the tenacity of her convictions, many of the causes she espoused have come to fruition.

"Josephine W. Henry," *LCJ,* August 20, 1995, sec. D, p. 1.

Orr, John. "Josephine W. Henry—A Pioneer for Women's Rights." *Connections Magazine,* March 1997, 6.

"Pioneer Woman Is Dead," *LCJ,* January 9, 1928.

HERITAGE ACADEMY. This Christian school for students in grades K–12 was founded in the early 1980s by Rev. Cleddie Keith, the pastor of Heritage Fellowship (Assembly of God) in Florence, Ky. The primary purpose of Heritage Academy, a Christ-centered alternative to secular education, is to train students in the knowledge of God and the Christian way of life and to give students an excellent education. The teachers at Heritage Academy aspire to foster the development of the whole child: one who is spiritually alert, morally sound, and emotionally and intellectually mature.

The first administrator of the school was Malcolm Pugh. Students come from all over the tristate area. Classes at the school are small, with an elementary student-teacher ratio of 18:1 and a high school ratio of 22:1. In 2005 the school's enrollment was 265; in 2006 Heritage Academy graduated 18 high school seniors.

Gutierrez, Karen. "Grad's Odyssey Gets Last Twist," *KE,* May 22, 2006, 1A.

Gail Chastang

HERNDON, ELIJAH (b. November 27, 1774, Goochland Co., Va.; d. July 26, 1849, Carthage, Ky.). Early settler and Indian-fighter Elijah Herndon was a descendant of European kings and colonial governors. His forebears had come to this country by the early 17th century. He was the son of slave-owning Virginians Lewis and Frances Thompson Herndon. Elijah Herndon arrived in Campbell Co. before 1800, and on August 30, 1813, he joined the 4th Regiment of the Kentucky Militia, whose captain was Squire Grant (see **Grant Family**) and whose commander was Gen. William Henry Harrison, the future president. Herndon and his company participated in the Battle of the Thames at Chatham, Ontario, where Shawnee Indian Chief Tecumseh was killed. Herndon was married three times and fathered 12 children. He and his wife Catherine donated the land on which the Mount Gilead Methodist Church at Carthage in Campbell Co. was built. Mary Gregg Herndon, a daughter, married William Evermont Bryan on October 21, 1845. Another daughter, Elizabeth, married Simeon Dicken; their son **Absolom Columbus Dicken** wrote a **Civil War** diary about his days as a Confederate. On April 18, 1806, Elijah Herndon bought 130 acres of land in Campbell Co. on Washington Trace for $260 from Benjamin Beall and had it surveyed by **William Kennedy**. There, in 1818, he built a house from bricks that had been used as a ship's ballast. The house still stands. According to Elijah's great-grandson Robert Herndon, who died in 1973, the noted author Harriet Beecher Stowe had visited in the Herndon home and referred to it in *Uncle Tom's Cabin.* Elijah Herndon died in 1849 and was buried in the Mount Gilead Methodist Church Cemetery.

Campbell County Kentucky History and Genealogy. Falmouth, Ky.: Falmouth Outlook, 1978.

Wessling, Jack. *Early History of Campbell County Kentucky.* Alexandria, Ky.: Privately published, 1997.

Jack Wessling

HERSHFIELD, OLIVE S. VAIL (b. October 11, 1903, Bellevue, Ky.; d. June 14, 1951, Cincinnati, Ohio.). Olive Vail Hershfield, a well-known performer and dance instructor, was the daughter of Willard and Eliza Mae Hale Vail. Her father worked as a commission merchant and real estate agent. The family moved to 307 Berry Ave. in Bellevue when Olive was four years old. Early in life, she developed a keen interest in dancing and began teaching dancing when she was just 11. She graduated from Bellevue High School and later the Schuster-Martin School of Dramatics in Cincinnati and then operated a dance studio in Bellevue for about 10 years, where she had 250 pupils. Later she studied under some of the top dance masters in New York City; Paris, France; and Berlin, Germany. In 1931 she went to Hollywood, where she appeared in the movie *The Spirit of Notre Dame.* Olive later danced with the Ziegfield Follies and with George White's' Scandals and also toured with an RKO dance troupe. During her stellar career, she performed in 10 countries and mastered numerous native dances. She married Larry Hershfield, and the couple was childless. She retired from dancing in 1941 to take a position with the U.S. Post Office Department, in Washington, D.C. She was diagnosed with a heart problem in September 1950, at age 47, and died of the malady about nine months later at Good Samaritan Hospital, Cincinnati. She was buried at the Mount Zion Cemetery in New Richmond, Ohio.

Ohio Death Certificate No. 37811, for the year 1951.

"Olive Vail Hershfield Dies, Prominent Dance Teacher," *CE,* June 16, 1951, 12.

"Widely Known Dance Instructor Succumbs," *KP,* June 15, 1951, 1.

HESLER. Hesler is a town in Owen Co., located near the intersection of Ky. Rts. 845 and 227. It was founded in 1820 by Daniel McCarthy Payne of Lexington, who purchased its site from Jacob Hesler. Hesler, an early settler, was instrumental in Owen Co.'s formation in 1819. Payne's plat of the town featured a square at the center, on which was planned a courthouse and a jail. Hesler's residence (used as a courtroom for some time) was also on the square, which, in turn, was surrounded by 194 lots, each having a frontage of 66 feet and a depth of 198 feet. Payne had visions of a growing town and very likely of selling off the lots for a profit.

In 1821 part of Gallatin Co., below New Liberty and Bromley, was added to Owen Co., making Hesler no longer the geographic center of the county. Therefore, on January 15, 1822, the court ordered that the county seat be removed to lands owned by William B. Forsee, James Gess, and Andrew Parker, where the city of Owenton is located today.

During the mid-1920s, Hesler was referred to as one of the most flourishing places in the county. It had four stores, two garages, two blacksmith shops, two cream stations, a barbershop, a bank, a church, an elementary school, and a number of progressive-minded citizens. In 1996 city water came to Hesler when additional mains were built by the Tri-Village Water District through the area, along with a 150,000 gallon water storage tank.

Houchens, Mariam Sidebottom. *History of Owen County: "Sweet Owen."* Louisville, Ky.: Standard, 1976.

Johnson, Omer. "Expansion Quenches Owen's Thirst for Water," *KP,* February 14, 1996, 8A.

Vertical files, Owen Co. Public Library, Owenton, Ky.

Doris Riley

HEVING BROTHERS (John Aloysius Heving, b. April 29, 1896, Covington, Ky.; d. December 24, 1968, Salisbury, N.C.; Joseph William Heving, b. September 2, 1900, Covington, Ky.; d. April 11, 1970, Covington, Ky.). The Heving brothers, John and Joe, professional baseball players, were the two youngest sons of a German immigrant family of six boys and two girls. Their parents were Frank and Louise Busse Heving. They became involved in the trades of their father and other close relatives, which were brick making (see **Brickyards**) and carpentry. In their youth the brothers relished informal games on the local baseball sandlots, little realizing the place baseball was going to occupy in their lives.

The older brother, John, played locally with the **Holy Cross** Standards and the Covington Chesters as a catcher. He left in 1920 at the age of 24 for Battle Creek, Mich., to play for a minor league team in

Ontario, Canada. It was there that he met and married Ruth Matthews; the couple had one daughter, June. Other minor league cities where John Heving played included Tulsa, Okla.; Mobile, Ala.; and Toledo, Ohio. He was called up to the major league to play for the St. Louis Browns in 1920, played with the American League's Boston Red Sox between 1924 and 1930, and finished his career with the league's Philadelphia Athletics in 1932. A highlight in his career was playing in the 1931 World Series against the National League's St. Louis Cardinals. After completing his playing career, John became a minor league manager. He retired from professional baseball in 1950. Heving died in 1968 at the age of 72 in N.C. and was buried at the Rowan Memorial Park Cemetery in Salisbury, N.C.

John was influential in persuading his younger brother Joe to give up his job as a carpenter and join a minor league team in Bartlesville, Okla., as an outfielder. Joe also played for teams in Topeka, Kans.; Portsmouth, Va.; Asheville, N.C.; and Memphis, Tenn. The National League's New York Giants called him up to the majors in 1930. They added him to their roster as an outfielder, but he was later switched to a relief pitcher. He pitched throughout the rest of his career. His first major league pitching victory came close to his hometown when he beat the Cincinnati Reds at Crosley Field in Ohio on May 3, 1930. In his baseball career he played with the New York Giants, the American League's Chicago White Sox, the Cleveland Indians, the Boston Red Sox, and the National League's Boston Braves, finishing his career with the last team in 1945. He was jokingly referred to as the only grandfather playing major league ball in 1942. During his early career, he married Emily Bubbenhoffer, and they had one daughter, Evelyn. Later, he married Nancy Abner Carlson, who had two children, Jimmy and Vendela, by former marriages. Together, Joe and Nancy Heving had one daughter, Joelene, and one son, Joe Jr. Joe Heving loved to share stories of his baseball-playing years with family and friends. "One mild regret in my life," he once said, "was the fact that I never pitched for the Covington Blues," Covington's short-lived 1913 entry in the startup Federal League (see Covington Blue Sox). After retirement from professional baseball, Joe continued to play with teams in Northern Kentucky and at times was honored by the Cincinnati Reds at their annual "Old Timers" games. Joe died in 1970 in Covington and was buried at St. Mary Cemetery in Fort Mitchell.

In 2004 the city of Covington honored John and Joe Heving and their baseball careers by placing a Kentucky State Historical Marker in the city and conducting a ceremony attended by officials and local relatives. The marker was fittingly placed near a park where in times past there was a sandlot for enjoying the game of baseball.

"Athletics Drop Heving," *NYT,* June 22, 1933, S7.
James, Bill, et al., eds. *Stats All-Time Major League Handbook.* Skokie, Ill.: Stats, 1998.
"Joe Heving, 65, Giant Pitcher," *NYT,* April 13, 1970, 41.
Rutledge, Mike. "Covington Brothers Played in Big League," *KP,* May 4, 2004, 3K.

Joe Heving Jr.

HIGHFIELD. Highfield is a home located in Owenton in Owen Co., at the corner of N. Adams and E. Blanton Sts., across from the First Baptist Church. The original tract of land included the entire eastern section of Owenton and was purchased by Robert Parker in 1785 from the State of Virginia. In about 1839, Willis Roberts purchased this land and constructed the home now on the site in about 1840. The home was owned and occupied for 101 years by members of the Roberts family. During the 1850s, John C. Breckinridge, campaigning for Congress, spoke from the porch at Highfield (see **Sweet Owen**).

The lumber used in the original house, which had six rooms and two halls, was cut from trees growing on the grounds. The window and door facings, along with the frames and doors, were made by hand. The original singles were hand-hewn. The hand-carved stairway rail and spokes (baluster) are made of cherry. The risers, treads, and floors are ash. The present two-story log cabin at the rear of the home replaced former slave quarters and was once used as a summer kitchen.

Houchens, Mariam Sidebottom. *History of Owen County: "Sweet Owen."* Louisville, Ky.: Standard, 1976.
Vertical files, Owen Co. Public Library, Owenton, Ky.

Doris Riley

HIGHLAND AVE. BAPTIST TABERNACLE. This church owes its existence to the dedicated efforts of Miss Maggie Kuhnhein. In July 1914, the **First Baptist Church** of Newport sent her to start mission work among poor mothers and their families in the **West End** of Newport. The women began worshipping together in a house at 327 W. Sixth St., Newport. As the group grew, they moved services to a larger house at Seventh and Brighton Sts. and began calling themselves the Brighton Street Baptist Church. The congregation soon outgrew that building, leading some men connected with the church to build a crude wooden structure, with sawdust floors, nearby at Eighth and Brighton Sts. The first service was held in the new building on Sunday morning November 23, 1919, with Rev. Harry Drake delivering the sermon. Within a short time, crowds of 300 to 400 worshippers were attending. From the beginning, the church endeavored to hire well-educated, highly qualified men to lead the congregation. In 1920 they employed their first full-time pastor, Rev. O. J. Steger, who in 1952 became pastor of the First Baptist Church of Newport. They hired as his assistant D. B. Eastep, who later served for 35 years as pastor of **Calvary Baptist Church** in Latonia.

In the early 1930s, the Brighton Street Baptist Church changed its name to the Newport Baptist Tabernacle. In 1939 the congregation hired a dedicated young pastor, Rev. Harmon Eggleston, who remained pastor for the next 42 years. During his tenure, he discontinued the practice of passing offering plates, preferring to have donation boxes placed at the doors of the church. During the 1940s, Eggleston had a regular local radio program on station WCPO and later on station WKKY. During the late 1940s, the church began looking for a building that was located outside the Newport flood district. They purchased the old First Church of the Nazarene building in Newport at Seventh and Putnam Sts. in 1950 (see **Nazarenes**). The Newport Baptist Tabernacle purchased a parsonage in town at 46 15th St. in 1954.

After **World War II**, most inner-city churches began losing members, as many people moved to the suburbs. It soon became apparent that if the Newport Baptist Tabernacle was to survive, it would need to find a new site outside the city, where a modern facility with ample parking could be built. In 1973 the church contracted with the Roman Catholic order of the Sisters of Good Shepherd to purchase several acres of adjacent land along Highland Ave. in Fort Thomas. The old church building in Newport was sold and a new, modern, 525-seat sanctuary was built on the Fort Thomas property. The church was pleasantly surprised when about a dozen of the Sisters of Good Shepherd, their next door neighbors at **Our Lady of the Highlands**, attended the Baptist church's dedication service on April 11, 1976. After the move, the church's name was changed to the Highland Ave. Baptist Tabernacle. The financial burden of building the new church seemed insurmountable to the small congregation; however, through the sacrificial giving of dedicated members, all church debt was retired by 1992.

Pastor Harmon Eggleston retired as pastor in April 1981 and subsequently took a position as pastor to the senior members of Calvary Baptist Church in Latonia. Rev. Floyd Arnold served as interim pastor at the Highland Ave. Baptist Tabernacle until Rev. Jack Holmes Jr. was hired as senior pastor in July 1981. Rev. Holmes served until 1984, when a retired Ohio schoolteacher, Rev. Ray Shepherd, became pastor. Shepherd resigned in 1993, and Rev. John Harrison Jr. served as pastor until 2000. The present pastor is Rev. David Simpson, who has been there since 2001. The current membership of Highland Ave. Baptist Tabernacle is about 250.

History of The First Baptist Church, Eighth and York Streets, Newport, Kentucky. Newport, Ky.: First Baptist Church, 1987.
Turner, Robert. "History of the Highland Avenue Baptist Tabernacle, 1911–2006," Highland Avenue Baptist Tabernacle, Fort Thomas, Ky.

Jack Wessling

HIGHLAND AVE. WESLEYAN CHURCH. Covington's Highland Ave. Wesleyan Church is one of the oldest of the congregations in Northern Kentucky that developed into the Pilgrim Holiness Church. The "Pilgrims" were one of the parent bodies of the Wesleyan Church of today. The roots of the Highland Ave. Wesleyan Church go back to 1893, when Rev. Richmond Reed, Rev. L. Shumate, and Rev. John Kennett opened a mission in Covington that became known as the Lifeboat Mission. The mission cooperated with the evangelistic work of the God's Bible School's Salvation Boat of Cincinnati. A permanent location for the mission was purchased by God's Bible School in 1917 at the corner of Pike and Banklick Sts. in Covington, where as many as six services were conducted each week. Often they were preceded by open-air street meetings, accompanied by singing and brass bands.

On May 15, 1918, under the direction of Rev. Lawrence Wade, the ministry became a part of the International Apostolic Holiness Church. The congregation purchased the property it was using from God's Bible School on September 15, 1920. In 1922, following the merger of the denomination, the church's official name became the Pilgrim Holiness Church of Covington. Yet, for many years thereafter it was known as the Pike Street Mission. During Wade's tenure, the Kentucky District conference was held at the Pilgrim Holiness Church.

Rev. C. L. Wireman became pastor in 1923, and then Rev. A. A. Price in 1925. During Price's tenure, the frame building at Pike and Banklick was replaced with a fine brick structure. In 1927 Rev. Plennie Williams and his wife served as copastors, and a year later, they were followed by Rev. Thomas Bishop. The former Kentucky District superintendent Rev. J. T. Johnson was pastor from 1929 to 1933. The second floor of the facility was finished as a parsonage during his term. In 1934 Rev. E. E. Leadingham was called as pastor, but he remained only a short time because he was elected to serve as Kentucky District superintendent. Leadingham was succeeded by Rev. Maurice Finger. In 1939, during the tenure of the next minister, Rev. F. M. Singleton, the church paid its building debt in full. Also under Singleton, a house and lot for a parsonage were acquired on the corner of Homesdale Ct. and Madison Ave. in Covington. In 1949 Rev. Ralph Tromble assumed the pastorate. When Tromble was appointed district superintendent in 1954, his term was completed by Dr. J. R. Mitchell, then dean of theology at God's Bible School.

In February 1955, Rev. E. R. Mitchell began his 14-year pastorate. In December 1955 the congregation purchased property for the construction of a new worship structure at 729 Highland Ave. in Covington. With that purchase came an adjacent lot on W. 19th St. that included a splendid old home, which served and continues to serve as a parsonage. Groundbreaking Day at the new site, with Rev. R. A. Beltz as the guest speaker, was September 16, 1956. On November 24, 1957, the church cornerstone was laid, and in spring 1958 the first services were held on Highland Ave. in the church basement. The new church was dedicated on May 11, 1958, with Rev. William Neff, general superintendent as guest speaker.

In 1968 the Pilgrim Holiness Church merged with the Methodist Church of America, creating the denomination of the Wesleyan Church in the holiness tradition. Consequently, the church became known as the Covington Highland Avenue Wesleyan Church on June 26 of that year, and Rev. Mitchell moved to a new ministry. In 1969 Rev. Hansel D. Wright served as the interim pastor. The year 1970 brought the arrival of Rev. Larry Freels, who directed an energetic outreach. Four buses were transporting individuals to Sunday services, and the church opened its doors to the **Week Day School of Religion**, which was attended by 165 children per week at one time. Freels remained pastor for 12 years. From 1982 to 1986, the pastor was Rev. Daniel Eckart, a gifted writer who authored several denominational articles while in Covington. During the 1980s the bus service was halted in response to economic and other pressures. Rev. Roger Atwood, who followed Eckart, ministered for a short time and was followed by Rev. Donald Lane, who was the minister from 1987 to 1991. The Latonia Wesleyan Church, whose attendance had declined greatly, merged on June 30, 1990, with the Highland Ave. church, and the facilities in Covington were improved. In 1991 Wright again served as interim pastor prior to the arrival of Rev. Kevin Barnsdale in January 1992. Many heating and cooling improvements at the church and the parsonage were made under Barnsdale. In 1993 the church celebrated its centennial anniversary. On November 10, 2002, Rev. F. Keith Biddle became pastor.

"Covington Church Celebrated 100-Year Journey," *KP*, September 18, 1993, 9K.

F. Keith Biddle

HIGHLAND CEMETERY. Located at the intersection of the **Dixie Highway** (U.S. 25) and I-75 in Fort Mitchell, Highland Cemetery has the second-largest acreage of all cemeteries in Kentucky and the largest in Northern Kentucky. Locally, only **Evergreen Cemetery** in Southgate has more burials. Highland Cemetery was dedicated in 1869, just as the burial lands at the old Craig Street Burial Grounds and at the **Linden Grove Cemetery**, both in Covington, were approaching their capacities. Adolph Strauch, a Prussian immigrant and a landscape gardener of the Spring Grove Cemetery in Cincinnati, came to Fort Mitchell to help lay out the new cemetery; George A. Yates was hired as the site's surveyor. Highland Cemetery's first burial was Mary Ann Blythe, on June 12, 1869. Her body was re-interred from Linden Grove Cemetery. During the late 1870s, some 1,700 graves were moved from the Craig Street Burial Grounds to the new suburban Highland Cemetery. Located along the old **Covington and Lexington Turnpike** three miles south of Covington, the Highland Cemetery was originally farmland owned by the Hagerty and Sandford families, consisting of three parcels, a total of 114 acres. The developers of Highland Cemetery paid $27,205 for these properties. The approximately 2,000 people who attended the grand dedication were offered the opportunity to purchase subscription books as down payments on graves. This offer was a means to start cash flowing into the business.

Many prominent Northern Kentuckians have been laid to rest at Highland Cemetery. Some of the better-known families buried there are the Bruces, the Ernsts, the Fisks, the Hemingrays, the Shinkles, the Stewarts, and the Wares; individuals interred at Highland Cemetery include actress **Una Merkel**, Confederate general **James Morrison Hawes**, **Medal of Honor** winner Cavalry M. Young, Confederate spy **Henry Thomas Harrison**, artist **Dixie Selden**, and Jerome Respess, owner of the 1909 Kentucky Derby winner, Wintergreen. The grounds of the cemetery offer a continuously evolving and a veritable history lesson on Northern Kentucky and its citizens. The most impressive monument there belongs to Covington banker **J. D. Shutt**, who is entombed alone within a massive mausoleum; on its top is a life-size bronze likeness of Shutt. A number of eccentric activities have taken place at the cemetery over the years. In 1909, for example, 11 days after the death of **Bradford Shinkle** (a brother of Vincent Shinkle, one of the cemetery's founders), a guard was instructed to open his casket hourly in the holding vault, because Bradford Shinkle had feared being buried alive.

As of April 19, 2006, there were 44,912 interments spread across Highland Cemetery's 251 acres. In recent years, the cemetery owners have acquired the more-than-100-acre Independence Cemetery in southern Kenton Co.; and in 1995 about five acres of the Fort Mitchell cemetery were committed for use as the Highland Pet Cemetery, where an array of pets now rest. Cliff, a beloved Covington canine officer who lived during the 1990s, was buried in the Highland Pet Cemetery in a formal police ceremony in early August 1998. Today, nature lovers and other visitors are drawn to the Highland Cemetery's miles of walking trails that traverse the property's rolling hills, along with many species of plants and wildlife.

"Area History Buried in Ft. Mitchell's Highland Cemetery," *KE*, January 5, 1975, 6.

"Feared Burial Alive: Casket Is Guarded," *KP*, June 10, 1909, 2.

Highland Cemetery. www.highlandcemetery.com (accessed on April 19, 2006).

Linden, Blanche M. G. "Adolph Strauch's Landscape Plan," *QCH* 53. no. 1 (Spring–Summer 1995): 30–45.

Reis, Jim. "Highland Envisioned as Place of Solitude, Beauty for Burial," *KP*, June 25, 2001, 4K.

Sharon Jobert

HIGHLAND COUNTRY CLUB. The Highland Country Club was a continuation of the Inverness Country Club, the first golf club in Northern Kentucky and the second one in metropolitan Cincinnati. It was developed in 1896 by **Samuel Bigstaff** (1845–1912) and his business partners. Located in the District of the Highlands (Fort Thomas), the nearly 25-acre site lay along a former streetcar line (Memorial Pkwy.). The connection to the streetcar line was important because it allowed easy access to and from Covington, Newport, and Cincinnati. The majority of the club's 400 members lived in Covington. The property was bounded by the Newport Waterworks, Southgate Ave., and Mount Pleasant Rd. (N. Fort Thomas Ave.), and one of the nine holes lay across the streetcar tracks, requiring a player to cross the tracks to the fairway located on the waterworks grounds. Wishing to enlarge the course, members unsuccessfully sought to acquire adjacent property. Furthermore, the club had only leased its grounds, and members found that the lease could not be renewed. After the clubhouse was destroyed by a fire, the Inverness

Club closed in 1909. Houses on four new streets, Dixie Pl. and Hartweg, Rosemont, and Strathmore Aves., were built at the club's former location. Club members wanted to utilize the undeveloped hillsides in the southern part of Fort Thomas, and they looked for a new location within walking distance of the streetcar line, which ended close to the intersection of S. Fort Thomas Ave. and Alexandria Pk. (**U.S. 27**).

While some Covington members joined the new **Fort Mitchell Country Club**, a determined group of former Inverness members bought three parcels of land on the west side of Alexandria Pk. for $9,750. These properties, which were located near the streetcar line and close by the intersection of S. Fort Thomas Ave. and Alexandria Pk. (U.S. 27), had been an orchard of apple, cherry, and peach trees, most of which were removed from the new links. Created with $200,000 in capital and with 78 members, the Highland Country Club, with only tennis courts and nine golf holes, opened on Labor Day in 1915. A large crowd gathered and viewed the plans for the proposed clubhouse. The course was completed and ready for play on April 15, 1916, and the wooden clubhouse, with two floors and a basement, was completed in July. It contained a dining room, a ballroom, and a kitchen on the first floor, an office on the second floor, and locker rooms and three bowling lanes with hand-set pins in the basement. The clubhouse was the scene of many social activities in the city and the county, including organized dances, wedding receptions, high school formal events, dinners, and fundraisers.

On the hilly nine-hole golf course, golf professionals gave lessons and managed the course, and some of the early pros even made hickory-shafted golf clubs for members. Since the Inverness club had been instrumental in the formation of the Greater Cincinnati Golf Association, and since the Highland Country Club was an outgrowth of the former club, many of Highland's golfers participated in the association's tournaments over the years. One of the tournament golfers from the Highland Country Club was Johnnie Fischer, who won the 1932 NCAA Collegiate Golf Championship. Fischer found himself stymied on the 18th green in the 1936 U.S. Amateur Tournament in his match with Scotsman Jack McLean. In a spectacular play, Fischer hit his golf ball over his opponent's golf ball to tie the hole and went on to win the match in extra-hole play.

Membership at Highland Country Club was limited to men until the 1950s, when golf became more popular with women; then they became members also. A fire in the kitchen destroyed the clubhouse in 1968, but no lives were lost. As reconstruction began on the original foundation, golfing activities continued. The new clubhouse, whose main dining room and bar area looked out toward the rolling course and its background hills, was opened in 1969. A large swimming pool and tennis courts built adjacent to the clubhouse provide varied activities for member families and their guests.

Since 1924, club members had discussed adding a second nine holes for golf on property to the north across Blossom Ln. After one false start, members finally raised enough money to buy additional land and enlarged the course to 18 holes in 1983. Even though residential sites and I-471, a busy interstate highway, surround its grounds, Highland Country Club received recognition as an Audubon wildlife sanctuary in 1999. Early-morning viewers catch frequent glimpses of deer, foxes, and wild turkeys. At all hours, rabbits, squirrels, and raccoons attempt to share the course with the players. Songbirds are abundant, and owls and falcons have been spotted too.

When the Fort Thomas Military Reservation was active, its officers were given golfing privileges at the club's course, a perquisite that may have contributed to the local post's excellent reputation among officers. For many years, it was said, the Fort Thomas post assignment was first choice for West Point Academy graduates.

Reis, Jim "A Mover and Shaker Little Remembered Today." In *Pieces of the Past,* by Jim Reis, 2: 61. Covington, Ky.: Kentucky Post, 1991.

Skyzinski, Rich, "The U.S. Amateur Turns 100," *Golf Journal*, August 2000.

Betty Maddox Daniels

HIGHLAND HEIGHTS. Formerly, the combined area of present-day Fort Thomas and Highland Heights was known as "The Highlands." When **Henry Stanbery** incorporated the District of the Highlands (today Fort Thomas) in 1867, he did not include the portion now known as Highland Heights, which was referred to in deeds at that time as the Highland Baby Farms. In 1917 the Highlands Real Estate and Investment Company built a model home at the corner of Renshaw Rd. and Main Ave. A streetcar line (see **streetcars**) was extended from S. Fort Thomas Ave. to the area, in an attempt to encourage development, but little occurred. Residents proposed incorporation in 1927 and asked that the city be known as Highland Heights. When incorporated, the new city had exactly 125 residents, the minimum required by law. The first city building was located on Renshaw Rd., but a $1.25 million facility was built in 1980 on Johns Hill Rd. on the ground once occupied by the Claradan Fishing Lake (see **fishing**). Over the years, several attempts have been made to merge Highland Heights with the Campbell Co. communities of Cold Spring and Crestview, but to no avail. Development in the area was sluggish until Northern Kentucky State College (now **Northern Kentucky University**) arrived in 1972. Construction of I-471 and I-275 (see **Expressways**) has also contributed to the city's growth. Many businesses have come to the city, and several housing developments have been built. Today, Highland Heights is a flourishing small city, easily reached from almost anywhere in the tri-state area. In 1990 the city had a population of 4,223; by 2000 it had grown to 6,554. In 2008 Highland Heights annexed the campus of **Northern Kentucky University**.

Campbell Co. Historical Society. *Campbell County, Kentucky: 200 Years, 1794–1994.* Alexandria, Ky.: Campbell Co. Historical Society, 1994.

U.S. Census Bureau, "American Fact Finder. Data Set. Census 2000 Summary File 1 (SF1) 100-Percent Data. Custom Table." www.census.gov.

HIGHLAND UNITED METHODIST CHURCH. Founded in 1830, the Highland United Methodist Church, located between Memorial Pkwy. and N. Fort Thomas Ave. across from **Highlands High School**, is the oldest church in Fort Thomas.

The congregation originally met at Mount Pleasant, the home of William and Alice Taliaferro at now 1819 N. Fort Thomas Ave., in what was originally known as the District of the Highlands (Fort Thomas). The gathering of worshippers at the Taliaferro house was considered a Methodist church. In 1832 a one-room log structure was built on land donated by the Taliaferro family, on the edge of their property and now at the intersection of Holly Ln. and N. Fort Thomas Ave. This building served as the Mount Pleasant Methodist Church and School and often was used as the community's meeting place; for a brief period, the building was also shared with a Baptist church.

In the early years, the ministers of the church were the Methodist circuit riders, who arrived on horseback. In 1852 the cabin was replaced with a frame church building in town at what is now E. Southgate St. and N. Fort Thomas Ave. At that time, the church also was referred to as the Mount Pleasant Church. It housed one of Fort Thomas's early public schools, which attracted students from Newport as well as from homes and communities located nearby on the banks of the Licking River.

With the building of the **Fort Thomas Military Reservation** during the 1890s in the south end of town, the social center of the area shifted. At the same time, **Samuel Bigstaff**, a land developer and streetcar promoter, was building homes in Fort Thomas in the vicinity of what is now N. Fort Thomas Ave. and Memorial Pkwy. In 1899 Bigstaff decided it would be advantageous to have a church in his development, so he donated two lots to the Mount Pleasant Church's congregation, moving its location closer to the center of town.

Plans for the new church building called for a 60-by-94-foot stone Gothic structure. After $6,000 of the $16,000 needed to erect the church building had been collected, the women of the church raised most of the remaining funds to cover construction costs through dinners and ice cream socials. The dedication of the new church, now named Highland Methodist Episcopal Church, took place on July 29, 1900. Concert soprano soloist **Mary Hissem DeMoss**, a California, Ky., native who performed in New York City's Carnegie Hall, sang for those attending.

Owing to an increase in the size of the congregation and the church's growing educational needs, the Highland Methodist Church built an educational building during 1923 and 1924; the two-story expansion contains not only classrooms but a community room, used by groups including scouts (see **Boy Scouts**; **Girl Scouts**) and by **Highlands High School** for its sports banquets. During the **flood of 1937**, many displaced residents were housed at Highlands High School and ate meals at the Highland Methodist Church.

The church began to be known for its music during the 1920s, with the leadership of organist Daniel Humphrey Davies, a native of Wales. He was renowned not only in Fort Thomas but also throughout the Greater Cincinnati area. This tradition continues today with organist Carl Relyea, a graduate of New York City's prestigious Julliard School of Music.

During **World War II**, 148 members of the Highland United Methodist Church served in the military, and 5 of them died in the war. During that war, the **American Red Cross** operated a surgical dressing unit at the church from 1942 through 1945, making dressings and bandages that were packed at the church and sent to U.S. military units serving throughout the world.

In 1954 the present organ was installed; its magnificent pipes are located in the front of the sanctuary. In 1967 the church started a preschool program that was the forerunner of the Bluebird Early Learning Center and now is known as the Bluebird Christian Preschool. In September of that same year, the church's tower was damaged by a fire.

During 1985 the church underwent a major renovation that included the installation of air conditioning. The years of 1998 through 2006 have been a time of expansion and change for the Highland United Methodist Church. Dr. Lowell Ford became its first associate pastor. During this period, the church gave up one of its lots along N. Fort Thomas Ave. in order to build a parking lot that is currently shared with the Fort Thomas School District. During 2004 and 2005, the church purchased a house on N. Fort Thomas Ave. known as the Tudor house for church offices and meeting rooms.

The front entrance to the church was changed with the closing of the Avenue of Champions, originally connecting Memorial Pkwy. with N. Fort Thomas Ave. The church is now connected directly with a new plaza that is used as a gathering place after church and for an occasional outdoor wedding.

"Church Damage Is Undetermined," *KP*, September 4, 1963, 1.

"Highland Methodist Church Tower Burns," *KP*, September 3, 1963, 1.

"New Sunday School for Highlands," *KP*, April 17, 1924, 1.

Reis, Jim. "A Beacon for Mortality—Methodist Church Stood on Firm Ground in Early Fort Thomas," *KP*, November 9, 1998, 4K.

Paul L. Whalen

HIGHLANDS HIGH SCHOOL. Highlands High School, located in Fort Thomas, is the high school for the Fort Thomas Independent School District. The school began in 1886, when Professor James McGinness established a three-year high school course in the Fort Thomas City Building. The first four-year graduating class of the school, which came to be named Highlands High School, took place with four students in 1891. The high school received accreditation from the state in 1912 and from the Southern Association for colleges and schools in 1914. In 1915 the high school moved into a new building at its current location on Memorial Pkwy. in Fort Thomas. There were 93 students by then, and the school's first football team took the field that fall. A library was added in 1932, and in 1935 a Highlands High School student named Jean Megerle was crowned Miss Kentucky. A north building was added to the school in 1937, and the current gymnasium opened in 1955. Extensive renovation was completed in 2007.

Highlands High School is considered one of the best public high schools in Kentucky for academic and athletic achievement. The student enrollment is 800, and there are 48 teaching staff members. The school offers 16 Advanced Placement courses. The school was recognized by the Kentucky Department of Education as a Pacesetter School for superior performance on CATS testing and is a permanent member of the College Board and Council for Academic Success. *Newsweek* magazine ranked Highlands High School as one of "the 1,000 Best High Schools in America" in 2005 and 2006.

In 2005 Highlands High School's graduating class led Northern Kentucky with eight National Merit Finalists and four Commended Students. In 2006 there were four National Merit Finalists and four Commended Students. The We the People team, an elective senior government course, won the state championship and advanced to national competition in 2003, 2005, and 2006.

Highlands has won 17 state football championships and captured state cross-country championships in 2002, 2003, and 2004; state soccer championships in 2005 and 2006; and a women's track-and-field championship in 2008. Sports that students may participate in include archery, baseball, basketball, bowling, cheerleading, cross country, fast-pitch softball, football, golf, swimming and diving, tennis, track and field, and volleyball.

School organizations include Academic Team; Blueprints Literary Anthology; Chamber Choir; Chess Club; Concert Band and Color Guard; Family, Career & Community Leaders of America; French Club; Future Business Leaders of America; Future Teachers Team; German Club; Highlandaries; Jazz Band; Key Club; Marching Band; Mock Trial; National Art Honor Society; National English Honor Society; National Honor Society; National Spanish Honor Society; Poetry Slam; Robotics Team; Science Club; Spanish Club; Speech, Drama, and Debate Teams; Student Council; Treble Choir; and We the People Team.

"First Annual Commencement of the Highland High School," *KSJ*, June 18, 1891, 5.

"New Highlands High School Is Growing," *KP*, June 26, 1914, 2.

"Rapid Growth of School Is Seen," *KP*, April 25, 1930, 1.

Bill Thomas

HILL, THEODORE MCDONALD (b. 1846, Alexandria, Ky.; d. May 4, 1900, Alexandria, Ky.). Ted Hill was the son of William and Elizabeth Nation Hill. His mother died at age 24. He quit school at 15 and joined the Kentucky 5th Infantry of the Confederate Army. He later served under Colonel Henry L. Giltner and also under Gen. Robert E. Lee. After the war, he returned to Alexandria, where he studied law under the renowned lawyer **Richard Tarvin Baker** and was admitted to the bar in 1871. Hill married Mary Isaphine White on January 1, 1868, and the couple had five children. Hill was elected Alexandria police judge in 1872 and served until 1877. He was elected to the Kentucky House of Representatives and served 1877–1881. Afterward, he resumed his law practice in Newport. Upon the death of Campbell Co. judge T. P. Makibben in April 1888, Hill was appointed to succeed him. He served in that position until 1898. Hill became ill at his Alexandria home in spring 1900 and died. Both he and his wife are buried in the Alexandria Cemetery.

Biographical Cyclopedia of the Commonwealth of Kentucky. Chicago: John M. Gresham, 1896.

Levin, H., ed. *The Lawyers and Lawmakers of Kentucky*. Chicago: Lewis, 1897.

Reis, Jim. "A Man of Convictions; Hill Rose to Top in Local Politics," *KP*, September 22, 2003, 5K.

HILLCREST CEMETERY. Hillcrest Cemetery, a public perpetual-care cemetery, is located two miles north of Dry Ridge on the west side of U.S. 25 (**Dixie Highway**). It was opened in 1926, when J. H. Colcord, along with Louis Lucas, Robert M. Lucas, and John L. Vest, incorporated the Dry Ridge Burial Park Association after acquiring 13.71 acres from Colcord Some. Burial lots were sold, but at the onset of the **Great Depression**, the burial association was placed in receivership. In 1932 the property was sold to the Dry Ridge Cemetery Company, incorporated by J. H. Colcord, Mabel Eckler, and Harry J. Eckler, a Dry Ridge funeral director. In 1979 the cemetery's corporate provisions were restated in accordance with Kentucky law to include James Hudson as an incorporator. This well-operated, well-kept cemetery, with hundreds of graves, has burial space for the foreseeable needs of the community.

Conrad, John B., ed. *History of Grant County*. Williamstown, Ky.: Grant Co. Historical Society, 1992.

John B. Conrad

HILLS OF KENTUCKY DULCIMERS. Founded in 1992 by ten local amateur musicians, Hills of Kentucky Dulcimers (HOKD) is a nonprofit organization that seeks to promote Kentucky's state instrument, the mountain dulcimer, and its rich Appalachian heritage throughout the Northern Kentucky and Cincinnati region. HOKD defines its primary mission as "entertaining and educating our neighbors and communities with the beautiful music made by mountain dulcimers and traditional mountain instruments." Members of this family-oriented club work to maintain a powerful local influence regarding Appalachian pride. They encourage people of all ages to learn about the dulcimer and its history, and they present music performances in various public venues, including festivals, hospitals, libraries, nursing homes, and schools. Programs frequently include information about particular songs, customs, and contributions related to Appalachians.

To generate excitement about Appalachian music and culture, especially within young people, HOKD members emphasize exploration and participation. Donations received for performances support general operations and further the club's goal to help people gain hands-on experience with mountain dulcimers. During programs, children are encouraged to learn to play traditional songs such as "Old Joe Clark," "Boil Dem Cabbage Down," "She'll Be Coming Round the Mountain," and "Skip to My Lou." In 2004 HOKD donated 24 cardboard dulcimers to A. D. Owens Elementary School in Newport for use in fourth- and fifth-grade music classes. In 2005 the organization gave funds to Campbell Ridge Elementary School in Campbell Co. to increase the number of dulcimers available to students. Members also shipped three dulcimers to South America to assist a music teacher who helped her students learn music theory and how to play the instrument.

HOKD collaborates regularly with other local institutions to provide creative Appalachian outreach experiences for people in Northern Kentucky. In October 2002 HOKD joined with the Cincinnati Dulcimer Society and **Thomas More College** to sponsor a free public program that featured Jean Ritchie and the Appalachian music tradition. Each spring, HOKD supports the **Northern Kentucky University** event Dreamfest by teaching dulcimer playing to gifted students from area schools. This experience has inspired many of the schools to start dulcimer clubs and classes. HOKD members also offer free dulcimer classes to new members and hold a monthly gospel jam session at a local nursing home. The group's emphasis on music fellowship and family fun has added atmosphere to public entertainment venues such as Paramount's Kings Island, Old Coney's Appalachian Festival, and Tall Stacks.

HOKD has produced one CD, *Hills of Kentucky Dulcimers*, recorded in 2002 by Stephen Seifert, a nationally known dulcimer player who grew up in Northern Kentucky. This musical collection features members playing autoharps, mountain dulcimers, guitars, harmonicas, mandolins, and the washtub bass.

HOKD membership has grown rapidly since the club was formed more than a decade ago. The Cincinnati Dulcimer Society (CDS), which began in 1979, was the only dulcimer society in the area at that time. As interest expanded, members of that organization joined with others to create HOKD. HOKD now has more than 150 members. Whenever members of CDS and HOKD gather to perform, they laughingly call themselves "Both Sides of the River."

Hills of Kentucky Dulcimers. www.hokdulcimer.com (accessed April 4, 2006).

Sherry Stanforth

HINDE, THOMAS (b. July 10, 1737, Oxfordshire, England; d. September 28, 1828, Newport, Ky.). Physician Thomas Hinde received his early education in rural England and studied medicine and surgery at St. Thomas Hospital in London. By age 20 he had become so proficient that he was granted a license to practice from the prestigious Royal Academy of Surgeons. He became a surgeon's mate in the Royal Navy and was sent to America in 1757. There he served with Gen. James Wolfe at the battle for Quebec during the **French and Indian War**. The general was severely wounded, and Hinde valiantly tried to save his life but was unsuccessful. The famous artist Benjamin West's *Death of General Wolfe* (1771) features Hinde as the attending surgeon, holding Wolfe in his arms. Hinde resigned his navy commission and took over the practice of a retiring physician in Essex Co., Va., then later moved to King and Queen Co., Va. In 1767 he married Mary Todd Hubbard, with whom he had eight children. His next move was to Hanover, Va., where he became a close friend of Governor Lord Dunmore and of Patrick Henry, the celebrated orator and statesman. His new friends soon persuaded him to switch his allegiance to the oppressed colonies. During the **Revolutionary War**, Hinde used his personal fortune to make sure that all colonial troops were properly inoculated.

When the war ended, he left Virginia for Newport, Ky., where he spent the remainder of his life. He became the most beloved physician in the area; he was willing to treat illnesses thought hopeless by other physicians. Adept at diagnosing and treating maladies, he was truthful in talking to patients about their conditions. Hinde was an avowed atheist and would often ridicule people who spoke of religion. When his wife became interested in Christianity, he was so exasperated that he placed a blister patch on her neck in an attempt to determine if she had gone insane. When he removed the patch, he claimed to have been miraculously saved by God and made into a zealous Christian. From that day forward, he always insisted on having prayer with his patients before treating them. It was also said that he lost all desire for money and worldly goods. He gave medical treatment to everyone regardless of the person's ability to pay, and he made no attempt to collect unpaid bills. For the next 40 years, his family regularly attended church. Hinde was married for 61 years, and he always told his wife that he wanted them to depart this life together. When near death, he took hold of his wife's wrist and checked her pulse to see if she was ready to go. Reluctantly, he told her that she was in fine condition and that he would have to leave without her. He died in 1828, but his burial location is unknown.

Hartman, Margaret Strebel, and W. Rus Stevens. *Campbell County Kentucky History and Genealogy.* Campbell Co., Ky.: W. R. Stevens, 1984.

Purvis, Thomas L., ed. *Newport, Kentucky: A Bicentennial History.* Newport, Ky.: Otto Zimmerman, 1996.

Reynolds, Charles W. "The Medical Fraternity," *Papers of the Christopher Gist Historical Society* 2 (1950–1951): 1–51.

Wessling, Jack. *Early History of Campbell County Kentucky.* Alexandria, Ky.: Privately published, 1997.

Jack Wessling

HISER, BERNIECE TERRY (b. April 6, 1908, Cowcreek, Ky.; d. January 5, 1995, Williamstown, Ky.). Author and folklorist Berniece Iona Terry Hiser was born along the Beech Fork of the Kentucky River in Owsley Co. to Wilson Edgar and Ruse Wilder Terry. When her father died, he was the last surviving Kentucky veteran of the Spanish-American War (see **National Guard, Spanish-American War**). Berniece grew up in a rural part of Owsley Co., southeast of the county seat of Booneville. She attended Pine Mountain Settlement School through the 10th grade, then left that school at age 16 to attend Berea College in Berea, Ky., where in 1940 she earned a BA in English. She earned an MA in secondary education and library science from the University of Kentucky. An avid folklorist, she continued her studies, which included advanced work in the field of folklore, under William Hugh Jansen, a professor of English at the university. She married Ora M. Hiser, and the couple had two daughters.

Hiser's first book, ***Quare Do's in Appalachia: East Kentucky Legends and Memorats,*** based on "stories of supposedly real happenings (do's), given me by word of mouth by members of my family and in a few cases by friends of Eastern Kentucky," was published in 1978 when Hiser was age 70. Another book, ***The Adventure of Charlie and His Wheat-Straw Hat,*** published eight years later, was a children's book set in Kentucky during the **Civil War**; it earned several children's literature awards for the author. Hiser taught a variety of subjects at various grade levels in Kentucky and Indiana before retiring in 1974. She was also a school librarian. She authored some 50 manuscripts, which included poems, folklore collections, and romances. Hiser, who referred to herself as an "Appalachian-at-large," was well versed in folk remedies (she maintained a card file of herbal, faith, and other treatments), folksinging, dulcimer picking, and mountain crafts, including weaving.

Hiser and her husband lived for many years, following retirement, in Walton, Boone Co., Ky. At the time of her death at age 86, on January 7, 1995, Berniece Hiser was living at the Grant Manor Nursing Home in Williamstown. She was buried in Pleasant View Cemetery, Grant Co., Ky.

Halfman, Janet. "Heard Any Good 'Quare Do's' Lately?" *CE,* September 3, 1978, 8.

Hiser, Berniece T. ***The Adventure of Charlie and His Wheat-Straw Hat: A Memorat.*** New York: Dodd, Mead, 1986.

——. ***Quare Do's in Appalachia: East Kentucky Legends and Memorats.*** Pikeville, Ky.: Pikeville College Press, 1978.

"Kentucky Deaths," *KP,* January 7, 1995, 9A.

Wikipedia. "Berniece T. Hiser." http://en.wikipedia.org/wiki/Berniece_T._Hiser (accessed February 16, 2007).

——. Wilson Edgar Terry. http://en.wikipedia.org/wiki/Wilson_Edgar_Terry.

Kathryn Witt

HISTORICAL SOCIETIES. Most Northern Kentucky counties have formed nonprofit associations, some more active than others, with the goal of preserving their county's history and genealogy.

Many of the historical societies publish a newsletter or some similar publication for their members. In order to preserve the records of their respective counties and cities, such societies may take on projects such as surveys of cemeteries, especially small, private burial grounds. A historical society is likely to be involved heavily in genealogy and willing to respond to queries concerning family history, either gratis or for a modest research fee. Sometimes such organizations fade and are reconstituted later. This was the case in Boone Co., where the present historical society is the third one formed over the years; the same has happened in both Campbell and Kenton counties. In some counties in Northern Kentucky, the functions of genealogy, history, and museum development are combined in one group, as in Campbell Co.; in others, such as Mason Co., they remain separate.

Few if any of these organizations existed before **World War II**. However, the efforts of certain dedicated individuals, such as O. J. Wiggins, resulted in the publication of several worthwhile articles on local history during the 1880s in the Covington *Daily Commonwealth* newspaper. One of the most noteworthy groups organized to record and preserve the history of the Northern Kentucky region was the **Christopher Gist Historical Society**. Organized soon after World War II, its modus operandi was the production of research presented in the form of unpublished oral papers delivered before its membership. Covington attorney **Stephens Blakely** was a founder of the group, as was **Charles B. Truesdell**, and for many years it owned and met at the historic Carroll House, at 216 E. Fourth St. in Covington. This society has left a legacy in the form of several volumes of papers, copies of which are held by the **Kenton Co. Public Library**, the archives of **Northern Kentucky University** (NKU), and the office of the Kenton Co. Historical Society. The society no longer produces research. Its present function is to award small scholarship grants and to hold meetings that feature speakers.

In the 1960s, **Chester Geaslen**, who ultimately published several volumes of the region's history on his own initiative, helped awaken interest in local historical research. His volumes remain in print and are valuable resources. Margaret Strebel Hartman did similar work for Campbell Co. In the 1970s, a group calling itself the Northern Kentucky Historical Society operated in the area, often meeting at restaurants with guest speakers. Its members were known to travel to various historical sites throughout the state. For several decades, ***Kentucky Post*** reporter Jim Reis wrote a weekly column *Pieces of the Past,* relating to the entire Northern Kentucky region. In the course of his career at the *Kentucky Post,* Reis produced more than 1,000 weekly articles. He is also a major player in the long-term success of the Campbell Co. Historical and Genealogical Society, perennially the best-attended historical group in the state. A selected compilation of Reis's work has been published in three volumes by his newspaper.

The Kenton Co. Historical Society was founded in 1977. It has produced a newsletter throughout its existence. Since 1993 it has also published a regional full-size magazine biannually called *Northern Kentucky Heritage.*

In 1978 the Kentucky Historical Society (KHS) wanted to improve outreach and strengthen local heritage organizations statewide, so it began publishing the *Circuit Rider,* through which local groups were surveyed regarding services that might benefit them. The Historical Confederation of Kentucky (HCK) was then formed. The HCK staff offers programs, supplies resources, and organizes seminars to train local historians and curators. This organization has assisted most of the historical societies in Northern Kentucky in one way or another, but especially it has helped the Campbell Co. and Kenton Co. societies in the production of an annual History Day event, usually held in late February. Since 1993 History Day has been scheduled on a Saturday at the campus of NKU in Highland Heights. Attendance of more than 250 participants at lectures, workshops, and exhibits of local history books and items of interest is the norm at History Day.

Historical societies also exist in Bracken Co. (Bracken Co. Historical Society), Carroll Co. (Port William Historical Society), Gallatin Co. (Gallatin Co. Historical Society), Grant Co. (Grant Co. Historical Society), Mason Co. (**Kentucky Gateway Museum Center**; Mason Co. Genealogical Society), Owen Co. (Owen Co. Historical Society), Pendleton Co. (Pendleton Co. Historical Society), and Robertson Co. (Robertson Co. Historical Society).

"Ft. Mitchell Tries to Hang onto History," *KE*, August 18, 2002, B1.

"Historical Society Formed," *Northern Kentucky Observer*, April 7, 1977, 5.

"Historical Society to Be Organized," *KP*, December 11, 1913, 7.

Roberts, Alice Kennelly. "Erlanger Historical Society Celebrates Depot Heritage," *KP*, September 13, 1995, 2KK.

Karl Lietzenmayer

HISTORIC PRESERVATION. Preservationists often say ruefully that no one appreciates old buildings until they are endangered. This was true in the 1950s and 1960s, when it almost seemed as if the United States was at war with itself. Federally funded urban-renewal projects leveled old neighborhoods in the name of progress. **Expressways** ripped through central cities. A pervasive "new is better" mentality toppled countless historic buildings. While Northern Kentucky was spared much wholesale destruction, Covington's old city hall and courthouse, Newport's **Mount St. Martin** mansion, and other landmarks fell to the bulldozers.

In the 1960s, preservationists decided to try to put the brakes on the bulldozers by strengthening the federal government's role in, and commitment to, preserving the nation's architectural heritage. In 1966 the U.S. Congress passed two laws that helped move preservation into the mainstream: the National Historic Preservation Act and the closely related Section 4f of the Department of Transportation Act.

During the same era, middle- and upper-class citizens began to rediscover urban life. In Northern Kentucky, people developed a new appreciation for the fanciful or stately buildings overlooked by earlier generations, as well as rundown but livable old neighborhoods. Affordable and close to downtown Cincinnati, they offered an adventurous alternative to suburban living. Over the next four decades, hundreds of historic residential and commercial buildings across the region were renovated and restored.

The boisterous 1960s also nurtured civic activism, and an energized citizenry fought for its neighborhoods. Residents of Covington's **Licking-Riverside**, then in the early stages of revitalization, successfully resisted redevelopment of their community as high-rise luxury housing and parkland. In 1971 residents nominated Riverside Dr. to the National Register of Historic Places as Northern Kentucky's first historic district. While the designation exerted little control over local planning decisions, it provided valuable recognition of the neighborhood's importance.

Five blocks south, another crisis soon appeared. At Fifth and Garrard Sts., where cars turned left to travel over the Veterans Memorial Bridge to Newport, stood the Jonathan Hearne House, the high-style Italianate residence of a prominent 19th-century Covingtonian. When the Commonwealth of Kentucky proposed building a new bridge where the house stood, it touched off a furor. The bridge project was canceled in the late 1970s, primarily because it was not needed. To disgruntled bridge backers, however, the preserved Hearne home was "the house that stopped the bridge." In the center of Covington, members of **Mother of God Catholic Church** banded together to reclaim their historic neighborhood, which became the **Mutter Gottes National Historic District**.

In Newport, residents of the newly formed **Mansion Hill** Neighborhood Association successfully fought freeway ramps that would have split the neighborhood in two. A court battle over a "compromise" off-ramp ended in an out-of-court settlement.

During the late 1970s, suburban-type shopping centers were still seen as a cure for ailing downtowns. Shopping plazas were proposed for both downtown Covington and **East Newport**. In both cases, strong local opposition brought the plans to a halt.

Often the first step in preservation of buildings was to identify and categorize them. Beginning in the late 1970s, the Kentucky Heritage Council (KHC), the state historic preservation office, funded surveys of historic architecture in many communities. Thousands of buildings were eventually photographed and recorded by the Kentucky Historic Resources Inventory, which was used as a planning tool by local and state governments. KHC also provided matching grants to prepare nominations to the National Register of Historic Places. Over the next three decades, a total of 31 National Register historic districts were created in Northern Kentucky: in Bellevue, Burlington, Camp

Springs, Covington, Erlanger, Fort Mitchell, Lakeside Park, Ludlow, Newport, Rabbit Hash, and Walton.

Early preservation efforts were often led by volunteers and dedicated amateurs. As preservation gained credibility and acceptance, the field became increasingly professionalized. Preservation also began to be a function of local government, like city planning and economic development. Beginning in the mid-1980s, Bellevue, Boone Co., Covington, Ludlow, and Newport joined KHC's Certified Local Government (CLG) program, which provided funds to local communities to set up their own preservation programs. Most CLGs enacted preservation ordinances providing for the designation of local landmarks and historic districts, where high standards for exterior renovation and new construction applied. Among many other duties, preservation commissions enforced these guidelines, educated owners about proper restoration techniques, and honored preservation successes with awards.

Despite good intentions and growing support, inconsistent decisions, work done without permits, lack of enforcement, and political pressure remained problems for local preservation commissions. Across Northern Kentucky, support for local preservation programs, and urban planning in general, fluctuated with shifting political winds. In Covington, for example, the preservation officer position was abolished in 2005 and then reinstated months later.

As a largely rural but rapidly growing county, Boone Co. followed a somewhat different course from its more urbanized neighbors. In 1986 it established a countywide preservation program, the second of its kind in the state. The Boone Co. Historic Preservation Review Board's multifaceted programs included a preservation plan, a historic-cemetery mapping project, and heritage education programs, including the innovative Heritage Tourism Map. In 2002 the board published a book, *Historic Structures of Boone County, Kentucky.*

Beginning in the 1970s, federal and state initiatives were enacted to aid preservation and further urban development. In 1976 the U.S. Congress enacted a tax credit for rehabilitation of income-producing historic buildings, and Kentucky soon became a leader in its use. Among other local projects, the credit helped fund the reconstruction of Covington's **Independent Order of Odd Fellows** Hall, which was gutted by fire in 2002.

In 1979 KHC started the Kentucky Main Street program, which promoted the revitalization of historic downtowns. The closely related Renaissance on Main program, launched in the 1990s, directed grants for downtown revitalization across the state. Eventually Bellevue, Covington, Dayton, Elsmere, Erlanger, Fort Thomas, Ludlow, and Newport became Renaissance communities.

During the 1980s, federal Urban Redevelopment Action Grants were awarded for two controversial development projects in Northern Kentucky. One was a condominium development, markedly different in size and scale from the historic homes around it, that was built at the western end of Covington's Riverside Dr. The other was a proposed redevelopment of the former Wiedemann Brewery in Newport as a mixed-use commercial complex incorporating some of the original buildings. This project was never built, and the brewery was eventually demolished.

Beginning in 1993, federal Transportation Enhancement (TE) grants were used across the country for a variety of civic improvement projects along major transportation routes. In 1996 the City of Walton secured a TE grant to purchase and begin the restoration of the Colonel Abner Gaines House, which dates from about 1814, as the **Gaines Tavern** History Center.

The 1990s also saw renewed attempts at the kind of large-scale urban-renewal efforts that had disrupted cities decades before. In 1996 a privately led regional planning effort called **Forward Quest** called for redevelopment of part of Covington's Emery-Price Historic District, a historically African American Eastside neighborhood, as a marina. Public outcry, however, stopped the project. In Newport, a downtown block was cleared for a proposed Millennium Freedom Tower, which was never built. Lost was the 1927 Newport Finance Building (Campbell Towers), for years the tallest building in Northern Kentucky, which was originally planned for renovation by the same developer.

As urban land became increasingly scarce and valuable, older neighborhoods and commercial districts were threatened by "teardowns." In the late 1990s, an entertainment and shopping complex called **Newport-on-the-Levee** reshaped Newport's riverfront. Lost to the cause was the National Register–listed Posey Flats (1890), the city's oldest apartment house. The eastern half of Newport's **Cote Brilliante** neighborhood was destroyed in 2004 for a shopping center, under construction in 2008. The surviving half of the community, however, became Newport's fifth historic district in 2005. Preservationists feared that such conflicts would intensify and multiply in coming years as development pressures increased.

In Boone Co., the county's rapid rate of land speculation and development made preservation of historic cultural resources a challenge. Old buildings and family cemeteries were particularly at risk. As of 2006, at least 10 percent of the county's Kentucky Historic Resources survey sites had been demolished after being recorded.

Road projects continued to threaten historic resources in town and country alike and push sprawl into the rural hinterland. Following years of controversy, the long-planned widening of Covington's 12th St., which will remove more than 100 buildings between I-75 and Scott St., was begun in 2008.

Allen, Randy. "Developer Seeks OK for Covington Center," *KE*, April 25, 1980, A1.

———. "Town Center Weathers Another Vocal Assault," *KE* April 23, 1980, A1.

Conley, Joe. "Pleas May Save Old Hearne House," *KP*, July 12, 1973, 1.

Driehaus, Bob. "City, Tower's Planners Soothe Neighbors' Fears," *KP*, January 14, 1998, 3K.

Kreimer, Peggy. "Old Tower Must Fall for New—Building to Be Razed for Monument Work," *KP*, January 14, 1998, 1K.

———. "Quest Marina Touches Nerve—Most of Quest Plan Well-Received," *KP*, February 27, 1997, 1K.

Lietzenmayer, Karl. "Riverside Assailed: The Turning-Point of a City," *NKH* 9, no. 1 (Fall–Winter 2001), 10–18.

Morse, Susan. "Neighborhood Spirit Shapes a City," *Historic Preservation* 40, no. 4 (July–August 1988): 24.

Remlinger, Connie. "Mansion Hill, Newport, State to Try for Ramp Compromise," *KP*, October 24, 1985, 14K.

Schoolmeester, Ron. "Rousing Riverside Dwellers Rally to Beat Resolution for Renewal," *KE*, November 22, 1968, 14.

Schroeder, Cindy. "Newport Strikes Deal for Posey Flats," *KE*, November 11, 1997, B1.

Tortora, Andrea. "Marina Proposal Becomes Hot Issue—Covington Commissioners Oppose Plan," *KE*, October 8, 1996, B1A.

Margaret Warminski

HITEMAN, CHARLOTTE B. (b. December 1, 1929, Newport, Ky.). Actress and model Charlotte Hiteman was the daughter of Thurman and Anne Fletcher Hiteman. The family lived at Ninth and Maple Streets in Newport, and Charlotte attended **Newport High School**. By age 15 she had already competed in beauty contests at places such as **Tacoma Park** and Coney Island. In August 1936, before she turned 16, the five-foot-three hazel-eyed blond of 108 pounds won the title of Miss Kentucky. The pageant that year took place at Newport's Hippodrome Theater (see **Movie Theaters**). In the next month, she was on the runway in Atlantic City, N.J., vying for Miss America and claiming to be 18 years old. Although she did not win the national competition, she went on to a career on the stage and as a model. She appeared on the *George White Show* in New York City, which was similar to the Ziegfeld Follies, and with the N.T.G. Revues. Upon her return to Northern Kentucky, she has had an extensive career modeling for the likes of Shillitos and Kroger. Today, Charlotte lives in Southgate and in Florida. She continues to make an occasional guest appearance as the commonwealth's oldest Miss Kentucky.

Hicks, Jack. "Memories Never Fade for Pageant Winners," *KP*, October 9, 1996, 1K.

"Northern Kentucky Girls Will Vie for Beauty Title," *KP*, August 8, 1940, 1.

Reis, Jim. "Oldest Living Miss Kentucky Won in '36," *KP*, October 16, 2000, 4K.

HOAGLAND FAMILY. Members of the Hoagland family were among the early settlers of Hunter's Bottom in Carroll Co. Cornelius Hoagland was the fourth generation of a Dutch immigrant family who in 1657 came from Harlaam, Holland, to New Amsterdam (New York City). Cornelius was born in 1750 on a farm along the Millstone River in Windsor, Middlesex Co., N.J. He was the fourth son of Martinus and Phoebe Van Okie Hoagland. In 1776 four of the Hoagland brothers, John, Martin, Cornelius, and Abraham, volunteered for service in the New Jersey militia. Martin became a captain, and their uncle Okey Hoagland became a major.

In early 1777, Capt. Cornelius Hoagland organized New Jersey's only mounted horse troop at Middlebrook. His unit, along with four mounted horse troops from Connecticut and one from Massachusetts, became the elite Second Light Dragoons Regiment, under the command of Elisha Sheldon. The Dragoons excelled at reconnaissance, and at Gen. George Washington's insistence, they cross-trained with sabers and with rifles as mounted infantry. Operating most frequently in small groups, the Second Light Dragoons staged numerous harassment raids and supply ambushes throughout New Jersey, Connecticut, and upstate New York. Frequently, the Dragoons acted as bodyguards for General Washington or covered retreats of the army, and at Valley Forge, Pa., they patrolled the perimeter. The Second Light Dragoons were the last unit dismissed from service by General Washington at West Point, N.Y., on November 20, 1783.

Capt. Cornelius Hoagland was stationed at Morristown, N.J., in the winter and early spring of 1776–1777. On May 15, 1777, he married Mary Tuttle, daughter of Capt. Moses Tuttle of Mount Pleasant, northwest of Whippany, N.J. Tuttle was the owner of a famous iron mine that produced cannon and shot for the colonies' war effort. The Tuttle family had arrived in Boston in 1635, about the same time the Hoaglands came to New Amsterdam, and were prominent members of society in Connecticut. The original Yale University buildings were erected on William Tuttle's land near the New Haven, Conn., green. Mary Tuttle was related through her mother to the large Ford family; her uncle Jacob Ford's home in Morristown served as Gen. George Washington's headquarters in the winter of 1779–1780, and Mary attended dances and social events there.

Immediately following the war, Cornelius joined his father-in-law in running the iron business. Together, they expanded the enterprise, which included the original mine, forges, and mills. Cornelius and his brother-in-law Charles Hoff, on March 15, 1781, entered land surveys for 1,000 acres each along the Ohio River in what became Hunter's Bottom. A series of financial panics in the middle and late 1780s nearly bankrupted the Tuttle iron business and prevented Hoagland from making use of the Kentucky lands until 1797.

Between 1778 and 1798, the first nine children of Cornelius and Mary Hoagland were born in Windsor, Middlesex Co. In 1793 Cornelius Hoagland paid taxes in Pequannok, Morris Co., N.J. Apparently Hoagland was working through his debts, because he served as a carpenter for the Peter Ogden estate in Morristown; Ogden, a relative of the Tuttles, participated in approving the U.S. Constitution.

The lure of open lands in the West continued to attract Cornelius Hoagland and his family. He and his eldest son, Moses, came to Kentucky in 1797, entered the survey in the Kentucky land records, and cleared their land. Indian mounds were located on the property. They then returned to New Jersey, and Cornelius sold his property there. In 1801 Cornelius brought the entire family, including Mary, eight children, and his sister Anna, to Hunter's Bottom. His older brother Martin Hoagland settled in Lexington that same year. Cornelius and his sons built a low, one-story, rambling house, where **George Rogers Clark** is said to have stayed overnight later. Cornelia and Emily Hoagland were born in 1800 and 1803, respectively.

In 1801, upon the recommendation of Presley Gray, lieutenant colonel of the 51st Regiment, Kentucky governor James Garrard (1796–1804) appointed Cornelius Hoagland a major in the regiment; Hoagland resigned that commission late in 1802. He replaced Presley Gray as assistant judge of the local circuit court on February 25, 1805. The Kentucky circuit of the court's chief justice, Cary L. Clarke, included Boone, Campbell, Gallatin, Harrison, Pendleton, and Scott counties.

While returning from a court session in Port William in July 1806, Hoagland stopped to view work being done to clear land, was struck by a burning tree limb, and died at 56, leaving Mary to raise 11 children in the wilderness. Cultured and educated, Mary Tuttle Hoagland is said to have educated several of the neighborhood children in addition to her own. Her stories of the events she witnessed firsthand during the **Revolutionary War**, and especially stories of George Washington, were part of the lore and legend of Hunter's Bottom. A land partition in 1806 divided the Hoagland farm into 12 equal parts, each child and the widow receiving about 100 acres. Mary died in February 1836 and was buried at Hunter's Bottom.

The Hoagland family's eldest son, Moses Tuttle Hoagland, followed in his father's footsteps, serving in the Kentucky Militia's 2nd Regiment Mounted Volunteers during the **War of 1812**. The family history claimed that Moses served on the staff of Gen. Andrew Jackson and was given a battlefield command as a major at the Battle of New Orleans in January 1815, but there is no validating muster list. He married Sarah Paine (Payne) of Lexington and lived at Hunter's Bottom. Okey Hoagland, an attorney who speculated in land both in Indiana and in Kentucky, bought portions of the Hoagland family's lands from his sister, Delia Morris, and his brother, Martin, who moved west. Okey, who became lame and later blind, constructed what was later known as the Hampton House, a square-set house with a center corridor, from architectural plans he acquired while in New Jersey. Two daughters of the Hoagland family, Mary Caroline and Emily, married sons of John Conway, another early Hunter's Bottom settler, and descendants of the Conway family members continue to live at Hunter's Bottom on farms. Jane Hoagland married William White, and he built them a home at Hunter's Bottom that stood for over 150 years.

Carpenter, Daniel Hoagland. *History and Genealogy of the Hoagland Family in America from Their First Settlement at New Amsterdam, 1638–1891. From Data Furnished Mainly by Daniel Hoogland Carpenter.* New York: J. Polhemus, 1891. Held by the New York Historical Society, New York City.

Hampton, Ella., "Early Settlers in Hunters Bottom," 1965, Carroll Co. Public Library.

Memoirs of the Lower Ohio Valley. Vol. 1. Madison, Wis.: Federal, 1905. Held by the Filson Historical Society, Louisville, Ky.

U.S. Treasury Warrants 2014, 2015 for 1,000 acres on the Ohio River, Ky. Survey No. 2341, filed November 3, 1797, Secretary of State's Office, Frankfort, Ky.

Diane Perrine Coon

HODGE, GEORGE BAIRD, GENERAL (b. April 8, 1828, Fleming Co., Ky.; d. August 1, 1892, Longwood, Fla.). Gen. George Baird Hodge, a Confederate soldier, a lawyer, and a politician, was the son of William Hodge and the former Sarah Baird. He received his early education at the Maysville Seminary (see **Maysville Academy**). After graduation, he entered the Naval Academy at Annapolis, Md., where he received his bachelor's degree in 1845. He served as a lieutenant in the navy for nearly six years, seeing service at the siege of Vera Cruz during the **Mexican War**. He studied law and began his legal practice in Newport. Shortly thereafter, he married Keturah Tibbatts, daughter of lawyer **John Wooleston Tibbatts** and granddaughter of **James Taylor Jr.**, founder of Newport. He ran as a Whig candidate for the U.S. Senate in 1853 (see **Whig Party**) but was defeated by **Richard H. Stanton**. In 1859 he was elected to the state legislature as a Democrat (see **Democratic Party**). In 1861 he left Kentucky to join the Confederate Army; he served under fellow Kentuckian Gen. Simon Bolivar Buckner. Later that same year, he was elected to represent Kentucky's Eighth District in the Confederate Provisional Government. While holding that office, he continued to serve in the Confederate Army. He recruited a company of men from Campbell Co. and led it south, where it became part of Kentucky's "Orphan Brigade." He received several promotions for gallantry and meritorious conduct and was eventually made brigadier general. After the **Civil War**, he returned to Newport and resumed his practice of law. In 1873 he was elected a state senator. When his term ended, in 1877, he left politics and moved to Longwood, Fla. He died and was first buried in Florida. Three children, Judge **John T. Hodge**, Ann Taylor Hodge, and Mrs. Samuel C. Bailey, survived him. He had always told his son that he wanted to be buried in Kentucky; thus, on January 1, 1903, John T. Hodge had his father's remains reburied at Evergreen Cemetery in Southgate.

The Biographical Encyclopedia of Kentucky. Cincinnati: J. M. Armstrong, 1878.

"General Hodge Dead," *KSJ*, August 9, 1892.

"General Hodge Remains Brought to Newport," *KP*, January 1, 1903.

Purvis, Thomas L., ed. *Newport, Kentucky: A Bicentennial History.* Newport, Ky.: Zimmerman, 1996.

HODGE, JOHN T. (b. March 28, 1863, Florence, Ky.; d. February 10, 1934, Newport, Ky.). Judge John T. Hodge's father was Confederate general **George Baird Hodge**. His mother was Keturah Tibbatts Hodge, a daughter of **John Wooleston Tibbatts** and a granddaughter of Gen. **James**

Taylor Jr., founder of Newport. John's early education was in Newport public schools. He entered the Cincinnati Law School and in 1887 graduated third in a class of 118. After leaving school, he apprenticed under lawyer W. H. McCoy in Cincinnati. In 1890 Hodge opened a law office in Newport. He married Virginia Lee Lovell on April 4, 1891. Appointed Campbell Co. master commissioner in 1893, Hodge soon became a prominent figure in local Democratic politics and over the years held many influential positions in the party. In 1897 he was elected to a six-year term as Circuit Court judge. Judge Hodge was a lifelong resident of Newport, where he and his wife were members of **St. Paul's Episcopal Church**. He also served as exalted ruler of the Newport Elks Club. Hodge and his wife Virginia Lovell divorced in 1905, and he married Grace Stewart in September 1906. Hodge suffered a paralyzing stroke in 1931, forcing him to give up his legal practice. In 1934 he died of pneumonia at age 70 at his home at Park Ave. and Nelson Pl. in Newport. He was buried in the Evergreen Cemetery in Southgate.

Biographical Cyclopedia of the Commonwealth of Kentucky. Chicago: John M. Gresham, 1896.

"Former Judge Expires at Newport," *CE*, February 11, 1934, 2.

HOEFKER, JOHN HERMAN, MAJOR (b. May 24, 1919, Covington, Ky.; d. July 18, 1990, Covington, Ky.). Reconnaissance pilot and fighter ace John Hoefker was the son of Harry Herman and Alma Studer Hoefker. He grew up in Fort Mitchell but was sent across the Ohio River to attend high school at St. Xavier in Cincinnati. While at St. Xavier, he played football and graduated with the class of 1937. Following graduation, he worked in his father's grocery store, located at 1634 Holman Ave. in Covington. In August 1941 Hoefker left a manager position at his father's store to join the U.S. Army Air Corps as an aviation cadet and was sent to King City, Calif., for flight training. Following primary and advanced flight training, Hoefker received his pilot wings and the rank of second lieutenant on March 16, 1942. Soon he received orders assigning him to the 153rd Observation Squadron, 67th Observation Group, at Esler Field, La.

Hoefker arrived as the unit was receiving more modern aircraft, including the P-43 Lancer and the P-51A Mustang. The unit spent time familiarizing themselves with the aircraft and developing new techniques and tactics for flying combat reconnaissance missions, and in September 1942 they were declared combat ready. By October 1942 the men of the 67th Reconnaissance Group were shipped to England without their aircraft and assigned to the 8th Air Force. They set up their base in Membury, England, and were assigned a photo-reconnaissance version of the Royal Air Force Spitfire fighter; they began training to familiarize themselves with the European combat theater. By April 1943 Hoefker was reassigned to the 107th Reconnaissance Squadron, and like other members of his unit, he was required to serve temporary duty with a Royal Air Force squadron. He was assigned to the 165th Squadron based at Kenley. While assigned to this unit, Hoefker flew 11 combat missions, including convoy patrols, bomber escort, and fighter sweeps over mainland Europe.

In November 1943 the 67th Reconnaissance Group was reassigned to the 9th Air Force and to Middle Wallop, England. They were reequipped with new F-6D Mustangs, the latest photoreconnaissance version of the P-51 Mustang, which carried lighter armor to increase speed, as well as cameras to photograph enemy targets. On December 20, 1943, lieutenants John Hoefker and Frank Dillon of the 107th Recon Squadron flew the first tactical reconnaissance mission flown by the U.S. Army Air Force over northern Europe. The unit's primary job was to photograph potential targets for bombing missions, but they were also to assess bomb damage of targets after a raid and provide information about enemy troop movements in France. By early 1944 Hoefker was reassigned as a flight leader of the newly formed 15th Tactical Reconnaissance Squadron and was promoted to the rank of captain. From March 1944 through the early part of June, the primary mission of the unit was to document enemy shore installations and troop movements in the Normandy area of northern France. On the morning of June 6, 1944 (D-Day), Hoefker and his men were assigned to fly inland to report German troop movements toward the invasion beaches. During their D-Day missions, men of Hoefker's unit shot down three German aircraft, and on June 7, 1944, Hoefker scored his first victory over a Messerschmitt Me-109 while flying a two-plane reconnaissance flight over Le Mans, France. These were the first of 8.5 victories officially credited to Hoefker. He also had two unconfirmed victories to his credit.

Hoefker's most notable actions occurred during the German Ardennes Offensive of December 1944. The Germans attempted to attack with infantry and tank units through a weak spot in the American lines in the Ardennes Forest on the Belgium border. Using a long period of bad weather that virtually grounded all Allied aircraft, the Germans hoped to split the Allied forces in two and take the port of Antwerp, Belgium. Hoefker and his men flew low-level reconnaissance missions over the Ardennes under difficult conditions in an attempt to locate advancing enemy forces. On December 17, 1944, he and his wingman took off on a flight over the Ardennes in poor conditions. Early in the mission they became separated, and Hoefker continued on the mission alone. Over the Ardennes, he flew low-level, recorded some of the enemy's positions, and was fired upon by German gun positions. On several occasions he engaged enemy fighters in low-level combat, shooting down three German fighters. Toward the end of the mission, he found his wingman, and together they attacked an enemy bomber flying low-level toward American positions. For this mission, Hoefker was awarded the Silver Star. During the period of December 23 to December 31, 1944, Hoefker flew four reconnaissance missions over a heavily defended section of the Ardennes Forest to gain additional information for ground commanders on German positions. Twice during this period, he was shot down by enemy ground fire, and both times he managed to evade capture and return through enemy lines to his unit, once after being wounded. For his devotion to duty during this period, Hoefker was awarded the Distinguished Flying Cross. He continued flying combat missions through May 1945 and then returned to the United States in June 1945 to fly demonstration flights for the Army Air Corps at air shows. By the end of the war, Hoefker had been promoted to the rank of major and had been awarded the Silver Star, 2 Distinguished Flying Crosses, 31 Air Medals, and 2 Purple Hearts. He also was the second-highest scoring ace of his unit and the third-highest scoring reconnaissance ace of the war—an amazing feat since reconnaissance pilots engaged in combat only as a last resort; their primary mission was to gather intelligence and get it back at all costs.

In 1946 Hoefker was assigned to Langley, Va., where he served as a flight leader for the 161st Reconnaissance Squadron flying RF-80 jet aircraft. He served with this unit until his discharge in January 1947. Shortly after his discharge, Hoefker bought a store in Ludlow, Ky., which he operated until 1948. In November of 1947, he married Jean Lubbe of Covington, and they eventually had three children, Jill, Jack, and Jim. In 1948 Hoefker took over his father's Covington store and operated it for 34 years, retiring in 1982. He died of a stroke on July 18, 1990, and was buried in Floral Hills Cemetery in Taylor Mill.

Hoefker, Jill. Interview by Robert Snow, April 19, 2007, Fort Thomas, Ky.

Ivie, Torn. "Fighter Aces of Europe," *Air Classics Magazine*, Winter 1985, 59.

———. "Recon's Finest Hour," *Air Classics Magazine*, April 1992, 32.

Olynyk, Frank. *Stars and Bars: A Tribute to the American Fighter Ace, 1920–1973.* London: Grubb Street, 1995.

Personal papers of Major John Hoefker, in the possession of Jill Hoefker, accessed April 19, 2007.

Robert B. Snow

HOGAN, HENRY LEE, MAJOR GENERAL (b. 1920, Cincinnati; d. April 13, 1986, Melbourne, Fla.). **World War II** general Henry Lee Hogan, after spending his preteen years in the Philippines, graduated from **Highlands High School** in Fort Thomas (1938). He was the son of Lt. Col. Henry Leon and Nell Emily Bolan Hogan, and the family lived at 72 Mayfield Ave. in Fort Thomas. His father was a dentist who practiced in Covington. Hogan graduated from the U.S. Military Academy at West Point (1943), where he was a track star, and became an Army Air Corps pilot flying B-17 Fortresses out of Foggia, Italy. He flew 51 combat missions over Germany in his bomber christened "Lil Abner," sometimes landing at Russian air bases on their western front as part of shuttle bombing runs. After World War II he became the flight instructor and military secretary for Gen. Maxwell Taylor. In the late 1950s, Hogan was involved in the early planning of the U.S. Air Force Academy at Colorado Springs, and he held several command positions within SAC (the Strategic Air Command) and Pentagon assignments of importance before retiring on December 1, 1972. He received many military awards, including the Distinguished Flying Cross, and eventually logged 6,000 hours flying time. Hogan died at the Holmes Regional Medical Center in Florida, and his funeral took place at Patrick Air Force Base, Fla.

"Friendliness of Russians Stressed," *KE*, December 2, 1944, 1.

"H. Lee Hogan Helped Found Air Force Academy in Denver," *KE*, April 15, 1996, A10.

HOLBROOK. Holbrook, in southwestern Grant Co. near the Owen Co. border, is located in the beautiful Eagle Creek valley along Ky. Rt. 22. It is believed that the community was named for Isaac Holbrook, a large landowner. The name was confirmed when a post office was established there in 1876. By 1850 the White Chapel Episcopal Church South was established on land donated by Uriah and Deborah Bickers. The church's first building was destroyed by fire and was replaced by the present structure on land donated by Nelson P. Poe. In 1940 the Uriah Bickers Memorial Association acquired a site adjoining the church property for use as a meeting place for the descendants of the Bickers family, who settled there in 1826. Bethany Baptist Church was organized in 1880. Its building was replaced in 1922 and used for 42 years until it burned. A new modern church building was completed in 1965. In the early 1900s, Holbrook had two general stores. There was also a blacksmith shop, a buggy shop, and a steam-powered mill for grinding wheat and corn into flour and meal. Doctors A. L. Abbott and Allie Agee practiced medicine in the town at that time.

Conrad, John B., ed. *History of Grant County.* Williamstown, Ky.: Grant Co. Historical Society, 1992.

John B. Conrad

HOLLADAY, BEN (b. October 1819, New Liberty, Ky.; d. July 8, 1887, Portland, Ore.). Ben Holladay, a noted owner of stagecoach lines, was one of the seven children of William and Margaret Hughes Holladay. Like many other residents of Owen Co., the family moved westward to Missouri, and by 1837 they were living at Weston, just across the Missouri River from Fort Leavenworth, Kans. Ben's father had driven wagon trains through the Cumberland Cap into Kentucky, and Ben quickly learned that business. In 1840 he married Ann Notley Calvert of Weston.

During the **Mexican War**, Ben Holladay held a contract to supply Gen. Stephen Kearny's Army of the West with provisions, delivered by wagons. By 1852 Holladay moved to California, where he became known as the Stagecoach King. He started, purchased, and consolidated several stage lines running passengers, freight, and the lucrative U.S. mail across the western plains, operating as the Holladay Overland Mail & Express Company. He collected annual fees of more than $650,000 from the postal service for his mail routes, and he eventually owned the famous but short-lived Pony Express in its waning days. Operating more than 3,000 miles of stage routes, he became one of the largest individual employers in the country. He had lavish homes scattered around the United States, in which he often entertained business associates. He befriended Mormon leader Brigham Young, and he greatly improved mail delivery to Denver.

In the mid-1860s, fed up with Indian attacks on his coaches and recognizing the coming impact of the railroad, he sold his stage holdings to Wells Fargo for $1.5 million and entered the steamboat navigation business along the West Coast. That venture was known as the Northern Pacific Transportation Company. Holladay also attempted to build a railroad from California to Portland, Ore., where he owned some of the first street railroads. The Panic of 1873 bankrupted him and his Oregon railroad plans. Holladay died at age 68 in Portland and was buried at the Mount Calvary Cemetery on the west side of that city. Race horses, cigars, and an eastside neighborhood of Portland have been named for Holladay, a transplanted Owen Countian whom some have called the father of modern transportation. Ben Holladay probably made and lost more money than any other person from the Northern Kentucky region.

Frederick, J. V. *Ben Holladay: The Stagecoach King.* Lincoln: Univ. of Nebraska Press, 1989.

Utah History to Go. www.historytogo.utah.gov (accessed June 20, 2007).

Michael R. Sweeney

HOLMES, DANIEL HENRY, JR. (b. July 16, 1851, New York, N.Y.; d. December 15, 1908, Hot Springs, Va.). The poet Daniel Henry Holmes Jr., the third of four children of **Daniel Holmes** and Eliza Kennison Holmes, was raised to take over the family's dry goods business, but he did so for only a very short period. He was sent at age 16 to Manchester, England, to learn the commercial arts, which he disliked intensely. He detested office work and as soon as he could, he moved to Covington and entered law school. His interest in law practice, however, was described as "desultory"; when his law partner died in an accident, he took it as a sign that he should turn to his real interests, writing poetry and music. Holmes subsequently spent four years in Paris, France, at the Lycée Bonaparte. In 1883 he married Rachel Gaff, the daughter of a Cincinnati distiller. The following year he published his first book of poetry, *Under a Fool's Cap: Songs,* and toured Europe with his wife. In 1891, after giving up his law practice, he returned to Europe, where he studied Greek, Latin, Italian, counterpoint, and harmony.

John Wilson Townsend observed that "after Theodore O'Hara and Madison Cawein, Daniel Henry Holmes was Kentucky's finest lyric poet." Holmes's second book of verse, *A Pedlar's Pack,* was published in New York City in 1906. The poems contained in it had been largely written in Dresden, Germany. His final work, *Hempen Homespun Songs,* was published in Cincinnati, also in 1906. He died in Virginia in 1908, and after services at his inherited estate, Holmesdale, in Covington, he was buried in his wife's family plot at Spring Grove Cemetery in Cincinnati.

"Dan Holmes Dies While in Virginia," *KP*, September 15, 1908, 3.

"Dan Holmes' Funeral," *KP*, December 16, 1908, 3.

Gastright, Joseph F. *Gentlemen Farmers to City Folks: A Study of Wallace Woods, Covington, Kentucky.* Cincinnati: Cincinnati Historical Society, 1980.

Holmes, Daniel H. *A Pedlar's Pack.* New York: E. D. North, 1906.

Mosher, Thomas B. Forward to *Under a Fools Cap: Songs.* 3rd ed. Thomas P. Mosher, 1914.

Spring Grove Cemetery Records, Cincinnati.

Townsend, John Wilson. *Kentucky in American Letters, 1784–1912.* Cedar Rapids, Iowa: Torch Press, 1913.

Joseph F. Gastright

HOLMES, DANIEL HENRY, SR. (b. April 28, 1816, Point Pleasant, Ohio; d. July 3, 1898, New York, N.Y.). Daniel Holmes was orphaned at an early age and was raised by his older brother Sam Holmes in the village of Columbia, east of Cincinnati. Eugene Levassor, who lived nearby, hired Daniel Holmes as his valet. Levassor also taught him to speak French and to play the flute. Holmes went to New York City and worked for the Lord and Taylor Department Store (see **Department Stores**). When Lord and Taylor opened a store in New Orleans, La., the young Holmes became its manager. The store was only a modest success, but Holmes bought the store from his employers and reopened it as the Daniel Holmes Store, which became very successful. He purchased all of his merchandise in Europe, where he was known as the "King of New Orleans." By the 1960s, the Holmes Department Store chain operated 18 department stores in three states. It was among the largest independent department store chains in the nation.

In 1847 Daniel Holmes married Eliza Kennison in New Orleans, and the couple had four children; among them was **Daniel Henry Holmes Jr.**, who became a noted Kentucky poet. In the spring of each year, Holmes traveled up the rivers to Cincinnati, where he dropped off his family to visit friends in Covington, Ky., while he continued on to Europe to shop for fashionable dry goods and luxuries. In the 1850s, Holmes began to buy property next to the home of his old mentor Eugene Levassor in Covington. During the **Civil War**, he moved his family to Covington and ran the business from there. After the war, Holmes spent $200,000 on a large High Victorian Gothic house, which he named Holmesdale, just south of Covington. He had a Boston firm design a landscape plan with hundreds of trees, a pond, and a pasture. For many years, the groundskeeper kept a herd of cows and sold milk to neighbors. After his wife died in 1884, Daniel Holmes spent less time in Northern Kentucky. He sold the northern half of his land to developers, who opened the Holmesdale subdivision. His will left the mansion and property to his son Daniel Jr. and divided his money among the other children. He died in 1898 at his New York City apartment. His body was brought to Covington for services at Holmesdale, then was buried in a family crypt in Metarie, La., a suburb of New Orleans. His home and part of his property became **Holmes High School** in 1919.

"Dan Henry Holmes Reigned as Retail King," *KP*, January 5, 2004, 5K.
Gastright, Joseph F. *Gentlemen Farmers to City Folks: A Study of Wallace Woods, Covington, Kentucky.* Cincinnati: Cincinnati Historical Society, 1980.
"Holmes Dead," *KP*, July 4, 1898, 1.
Nordheim, Betty. "Daniel Henry Holmes, 1816–1898," *NKH* 8, no. 2 (Spring–Summer 1996): 28–38.
"School Born of a Castle—Covington's Richest Man Was Also 'King of New Orleans,'" *KP*, October 17, 2005, 4K.

Joseph F. Gastright

HOLMES HIGH SCHOOL. Holmes High School, located along Madison Ave. in Covington, is a unique and historic school marked by classic architecture. When founded (long before it was known as Holmes), it was the commonwealth of Kentucky's first public high school as well as the first coeducational public high school in the state. More than 150 years later, Holmes High School continues to provide high-quality secondary education. Its graduates continue to matriculate at some of the finest universities. Thousands of Holmes alumni have distinguished themselves in their professions and in service to country and to community.

Holmes High School, part of **Covington Independent Schools**, offers classes for students in grades 9 through 12. In 2005 the high school had 86 full-time classroom teachers and 1,057 students; the student-teacher ratio was 12:1, ranking Holmes among the top schools of its category in the state. Covington Independent Schools allocates about $4,760 per pupil for instructional expenses.

Holmes, founded as Central High School in 1853, is the oldest operating public high school in Kentucky. The original school began with 20 students and was located in classrooms of the old Fourth District School at 11th and Scott Sts. in Covington. In 1872 it moved into a new 12-room building at 12th and Russell Sts. and was renamed the Covington High School. In 1919 the school moved to the former Holmes mansion, built by **Daniel Henry Holmes Sr.**, who owned retail stores in Covington and in New Orleans. Holmes built the home of his dreams in 1866. Known as Holmesdale castle, it was a three-story, English Gothic structure with 32 rooms, patterned after a castle in Siena, Italy. Two large pillars guarded the entrance to the estate. Flowers, shrubbery, and large trees brought in from many parts of the world flanked the long driveway and concealed the home. Only the tower, which rose well above these, could be seen from the road. At one point along the drive, Holmes had a sign: "North, South, East, or West—Home is Best." Below and to the east of the main house were a carriage house and stables—these buildings and the arcade leading from today's Junior High Building to the Administration Building are the only parts of the castle still standing. Today the carriage house and the stables have been converted into a residence for the school's custodian and his wife. Holmesdale featured a small lake with an island in the center; the high school football stadium is now located where the lake and the island were. There were four cisterns placed around the building so that water would be available in case of fire.

In 1915 Holmes's heirs sold the palatial home to the Covington Board of Education for $50,000. The following year construction began on a new school building, which was completed in January 1919; at that time the students moved from the old high school building at 12th and Russell Sts. The cafeteria, the band room, and the bookstore were in the Holmes mansion. Gradually, because of its new location, the Covington High School became known as Holmes High School. In 1927 a new building for junior high students, designed by the **Weber Brothers**, was completed. Ten years later, in 1936, the Covington Board of Education decided to demolish the "castle" to make space for a new administration building. Students were given a chance to bid a last farewell to their beloved castle on a cold, windy Wednesday before the 1936 Thanksgiving holiday. Thirty years later, in 1966, a new science building and the David M. Evans Fieldhouse were completed. In 1980 the Virginia Chapman Academic and Vocational School was built on the campus; it merged with the high school in 2000. In 2009 the school's boys' basketball team won its first state championship.

"New Junior High School May Open This Week," *KP*, September 11, 1927, 6.
Nordheim, Betty Lee. *Echoes of the Past: A History of the Covington Public School System.* Covington, Ky.: Covington Independent Public Schools, 2002.

Suzanne C. Wendt

HOLY CROSS CATHOLIC CHURCH. The **Latonia** section of Covington (known as Milldale in the 19th century) was included within the boundaries of **St. Augustine** Parish (established in 1870) until 1890. Catholics from this southern reach of Covington found it difficult to travel to St. Augustine Catholic Church for Sunday mass. At first, the bishop of Covington, **Camillus Paul Maes**, did not agree with requests for a separate church in Latonia because the St. Augustine Church was facing financial difficulties. But with concern that the mostly German Catholic population of Latonia might lose their faith without a more constant presence of the Church in their midst, the St. Augustine Church's pastor, Rev. Paul T. Abeln, agreed to the request of Latonia's Catholics that a church should be built in their village. Bishop Maes finally gave his consent to proceed and put Abeln in charge of the project. Under Abeln's direction, property in Latonia was purchased on Longworth St. (now Church St.) and the cornerstone was laid on August 24, 1890. The brick structure was near enough to completion for the first mass to be celebrated there on Christmas Day by the first resident pastor, Rev. Bernard A. Baumeister. On the Feast of the Finding of the Holy Cross (May 3) in the following year, Maes officially dedicated the new church, named Holy Cross Catholic Church in honor of that feast day.

After Milldale was incorporated as the city of Latonia in 1896, the parish's population grew rapidly. The size of the church and the parish school, staffed by the **Sisters of St. Benedict**, soon proved inadequate. The congregation, led by Rev. John B. Reiter, who had begun his 34-year pastorate in 1898, decided to build a new church, rather than add to the old one, even though many parishioners were newcomers who had debt on the new homes they had recently purchased. The result was a large stone church across the street from the original building, designed by architect Anthony Kunz Jr. In elaborate ceremonies, Maes dedicated the new Holy Cross Catholic Church on November 29, 1908. Also participating were civic leaders and non-Catholic residents, who recognized that the presence of a Catholic church was a boon to the ongoing development of Latonia. The old church was then used temporarily as the school.

With the assistance of a very generous anonymous donor, the heavily indebted parish was able to go forward in 1914 with plans to erect a new school. The Holy Cross Catholic Church managed to build a parish high school in 1930, also with the Benedictine Sisters in charge. After the death of Reiter in 1932, the new pastor, Rev. Louis Fey, emphasized education and worked diligently to update the facilities of **Holy Cross High School**, improving its science and music departments and its library. The high school continues today, although in 1986 it became Holy Cross District High School, serving students from several area parishes, rather than the students of Holy Cross Parish alone. The parish endured a dispute over a controversial renovation plan in the mid-1980s during the pastorate of Rev. Joseph Brink. His successor, Msgr. Elmer Grosser, oversaw a more modest painting and repair of the church in time for the centenary of the parish in 1990.

Feldman, Jim, and Bev Lonneman. *Holy Cross Centennial Book.* Covington, Ky.: Holy Cross Catholic Church, 1990.
Nieberding, Robert H. "History of Holy Cross Parish, Covington, Kentucky," master's thesis, St. Paul Seminary, St. Paul, Minn., 1956.
Ryan, Paul E. *History of the Diocese of Covington, Kentucky.* Covington, Ky.: Diocese of Covington, 1954.
Tenkotte, Paul A., David E. Schroeder, and Thomas S. Ward. *To Be Catholic and American in Northern, Central, and Appalachian Kentucky: The Diocese of Covington, 1853–2003.* Forthcoming.

Thomas S. Ward

HOLY CROSS HIGH SCHOOL. In 1891 a grade school was established at Holy Cross Catholic Church in Milldale (now Latonia) and the **Sisters of St. Benedict** were retained as the teachers at the parish. After a major boom in housing began, a modern 12-room building was completed in 1915 at a cost of $36,000. Sister Lioba, O.S.B., started to accept a few advanced students into a high school program at the grade school. The first high school diploma went to Helen Pernice in 1921. Commercial and pre–liberal arts diplomas were issued in the 1920s.

In 1930, in spite of the **Great Depression**, parishioners built the present high school structure on the site of the original parish church; it was a $40,000 building, complete with a cafeteria, a gymnasium, a library, and 13 classrooms. The commercial department was incorporated into the four-year program. The average class size was between 30 and 40, and the Benedictine nuns ran both schools. The secondary education became known as the Holy Cross High School (HCHS).

The post–**World War II** baby boom swelled enrollment at both schools to capacity. In 1961 Pastor Thomas B. Finn constructed a new building, now named in his honor, with science and language labs, a recreation hall, and a new gymnasium, at the corner of 36th and Church Sts. The gym was provided just in time for legendary basketball coach George Schneider to guide the Holy Cross Indians, the high school's basketball team, to the Kentucky state finals in 1965. One of the all-time-great basketball players to come out of Northern Kentucky, Dave Hickey, was a member of that team.

In 1969 Bob Mark became HCHS's first lay principal. Peak enrollment was 400 between 1968 and 1972, reflecting the baby boom. After 1972 the enrollment saw a steady decline. By 1980 Holy Cross was becoming an inner-city parish. Most of the Benedictines were gone, tuition was steadily rising, and the flight to the suburbs had taken its toll on enrollment; graduating classes were down to about 25 students. The parish could no longer afford to keep the high school on its own. By 1985, when the enrollment was less than 200, Bishop William Hughes of the diocese changed it from a parish high school to a district high school of the Diocese of Covington (see **Roman Catholics**). In 1986 Bill Goller, a longtime teacher at the school, became its principal and guided it until 2001.

In 1988 a grassroots group of alumni formed an association to improve the situation at the high school. Annual appeals, a weekly bingo, and a fall festival were instituted. Today, as a result of these efforts, HCHS boasts an enrollment of more than 400. A wrestling and a football program were started, and a new practice field was added, largely financed by Covington philanthropist Oakley Farris. More than 40 memorial scholarships, some of them endowed, are awarded each year.

Feldman, James, and Beverly Lonneman. *Holy Cross Church, 1890–1990.* Covington, Ky.: Self-published, 1990.

Holy Cross Parish, 1891–1916. Covington, Ky.: Wallenborg Stationery, 1916. Silver Jubilee Souvenir.

Thou Shalt Sanctify the Fiftieth Year. Covington, Ky.: Vesper, 1941.

Jim Feldman and Bill Goller

HOLY SPIRIT CATHOLIC CHURCH. The Holy Spirit Catholic Church in Newport resulted from a decreasing Catholic urban population and the dwindling number of priests in the Diocese of Covington (see **Roman Catholics**). The city of Newport, on the Ohio River, attracted many Catholic immigrants of Irish, German, and Italian extraction in the 19th and early 20th centuries. But in the mid-20th century, many Catholics moved to the suburbs. A large number of people from Appalachia, mostly Protestants, moved into Newport in place of the departed Catholics. Thus, the city that boasted five Catholic churches found it difficult to sustain so many individual Catholic parishes and their schools. The bishops of the Diocese of Covington had to face the reality of changing demographics. In 1969 Bishop Richard H. Ackerman mandated that **Immaculate Conception Catholic Church** (established in 1856) close. The other four churches survived until the late 1990s. It was these four—**Corpus Christi Catholic Church** (established in 1845), St. Stephen Catholic Church (established in 1855) (see **Holy Spirit Catholic Church**), **St. Francis de Sales Catholic Church** (established in 1912), and **St. Vincent de Paul Catholic Church** (established in 1916)—that made up the new parish.

By the mid-1990s, as the pastors of the four separate parishes reached retirement age, Bishop Robert W. Muench decided that he could no longer provide a resident priest for each parish. He decreed in 1997 that the four parishes be suppressed and that a new church, Holy Spirit Catholic Church, be established, with each of the former parishes to serve as missions related to it. The merged school system of the four parishes had already been designated by the name Holy Spirit in 1984. Rev. Richard Bolte was appointed pastor and Rev. Donald Enzweiler parochial vicar of the new church. In 2001 Muench ordered all of the former churches except St. Stephen be closed and put to other uses. St. Stephen Church, renamed Holy Spirit Catholic Church, then became the sole location of worship for Holy Spirit Parish, with Bolte as the pastor. Although parishioners of the former parishes were disappointed to lose their churches, most of them worked together through the difficult transition to make the new parish the home of one Catholic community for Newport.

Decree of Bishop Robert W. Muench, August 28, 2001, Diocese of Covington Archives, Erlanger, Ky.

Decree of Bishop Robert W. Muench, *Messenger,* April 25, 1997, 1.

"Jubilee Cross Visits Holy Spirit Parish," *Messenger,* November 3, 2000, 6–7.

"Newport to Become One Parish, Four Missions," *Messenger,* April 25, 1997, 1.

Ryan, Paul E. *History of the Diocese of Covington, Kentucky.* Covington, Ky.: Diocese of Covington, 1954.

Tenkotte, Paul A., David E. Schroeder, and Thomas S. Ward. *To Be Catholic and American in Northern, Central, and Appalachian Kentucky: The Diocese of Covington, 1853–2003.* Forthcoming.

Thomas S. Ward

HOME BUILDERS ASSOCIATION OF NORTHERN KENTUCKY. It was during the home-building boom that followed **World War II** (1941–1945) that home builders in America formally organized to meet the demands being thrust upon them. In Northern Kentucky, home builders found that multiple local governments issued conflicting regulations administered by people poorly informed about complexities of the industry. Further frustrating entrepreneurs in the home-building business, state officials in Frankfort imposed additional requirements that applied to the commonwealth's metropolitan areas in particular. This was the setting in which the Home Builders Association of Northern Kentucky (HBANK) was founded by sixteen residential contractors in 1955. Builders, remodelers, suppliers, and subcontractors came together in order to interact as a body with government; their purpose was to provide leadership in shaping regulations and legislation, setting standards of construction and consumer relations, educating consumers and their own members, fostering a good public image, and contributing to the community through charitable endeavors.

As early as 1956, bills were introduced in the Kentucky legislature by local attorney **Morris Weintraub** proposing countywide planning and zoning, while eliminating local official jurisdiction over the process. At the time, these bills failed, but planning and zoning legislation did become a major concern of the community and the industry in subsequent years. Interaction with the **Northern Kentucky Area Planning Commission** (NKAPC), created by the Kentucky legislature in 1961, and other planning units consumed significant amounts of time for both builders and city officials as communities in Northern Kentucky continued to experience growing pains.

Beginning in 1956, the HBANK called for consolidating and streamlining governmental operations and supported the planning process, even though many local governments resisted. Wary of those supporting this new process, local governmental officials succeeded in maintaining the status quo—creating considerable controversies especially in the river cities of Boone, Campbell, and Kenton counties. Builders called for consolidation of services, citing the complexity of 44 cities and three counties, each with different building codes and zoning and subdivision regulations. Builders advocated the pooling of services in certain areas rather than eliminating boundaries.

The HBANK sponsored successful legislation that made the NKAPC advisory to cities and local planning commissions, thus eliminating duplicate hearings on planning and zoning issues. Other developmental issues of interest to the HBANK included preservation of hillsides, agricultural lands, and property rights; the Northern Kentucky Property Rights Association was formed in response to the latter concern. The HBANK introduced new concepts in residential planning, including Open Space Communities, Cluster Development, and Planned Unit Development (PUD). PUD, which involves integrating multiple uses in a development, was adopted in Kenton Co. and later used as a model ordinance for adoption nationwide. It was applied in the subdivisions of Beech Grove, in the Prospect Point development that became part of Villa Hills, and later in Boone Co. at the Oakbrook subdivision.

In 1958 the HBANK supported the adoption of a uniform building code in the Northern Kentucky counties of Boone, Campbell, and Kenton that was designed to upgrade the quality of building. A 1963 survey revealed that most of the communities in these three counties had no building code in effect, and while a few others had codes expressed in several typed pages, some of these were still based on code formulations dating from 1895. Code enforcement was sporadic at best and in many cases nonexistent. The HBANK proposed and secured adoption of the National Building Code as the uniform code in the three counties of Boone, Campbell, and Kenton.

In 1976 the HBANK prepared legislation to establish a state department of buildings, housing, and construction, but the Kentucky General Assembly did not approve the legislation until 1978, after the tragic **Beverly Hills Supper Club** fire in 1977. The new department then approved a uniform building code for adoption at the local level and developed a mechanism for enforcement. Northern Kentucky cities and counties, at the builders' urging, adopted the statewide building code, which was placed in effect in August 1981. The One- and Two-Family Dwelling Code and the Building Officials of America Code became the statewide building code adopted at the builders' urging by Boone, Campbell, and Kenton counties and their cities. Also endorsed was centralized building inspection in Northern Kentucky, but this was not directly related to the planning process. Builders throughout the state successfully challenged the state plumbing code in a dramatic confrontation with suppliers and labor. Legislation was adopted in 1966 that opened the way for use of updated materials, notably plastic pipe, in one of the HBANK's most significant and successful endeavors. But bureaucratic delays made the industry and consumers wait five years before the new technology could be implemented.

Because construction standards, a mechanism for handling consumer complaints, and stringent requirements for builders and remodelers were needed in order to maintain good consumer relations and enhance the industry image, in 1990 the HBANK adopted the Registered Builder/Remodeler Program. It requires builders and remodelers to meet a strict set of qualifications, including business ethics, customer references, peer review, and financial integrity. The program includes professional contracts incorporating workers' compensation and liability insurance, a one-year limited warranty, and a complaint-handling procedure that has proved to be of great value to builders-remodelers as well as new owners. A builder's or remodeler's failure to meet these standards is cause for censure.

The expansion of building in the 1960s created an increased demand for tradespeople, so it was necessary to train new people to fill the jobs. The HBANK in 1967 began its Apprenticeship Program, which has been expanded from carpentry to include electricity and HVAC (heating, ventilation, and air conditioning). It is offered in both English and Spanish.

The HBANK sponsors several consumer events each year to show new homes and products: The Northern Kentucky Cavalcade of Homes, begun in 1963, is an annual spring showcase of new homes of various price ranges in locations scattered throughout Northern Kentucky. Homefest has displayed new homes in one location each year since 1974. Citifest is an annual showing of upscale homes in older cities, particularly in Newport, that started in 2002. The Home Products Expo, begun in 1974, is an annual exhibit of products and services for new and remodeled homes. Previously held at either the Drawbridge Inn in Fort Mitchell or the Crestview Mall in Crestview Hills, it now occurs at the **Northern Kentucky Convention Center** in Covington. The home builders' association's television show, *My New Kentucky Home,* first broadcast in 2000, regularly appears on Insight Communications (ICN 6) in Northern Kentucky. It features interviews with builders, remodelers, and suppliers and commentary on home products and services.

A strong demand for apartments was evident in Northern Kentucky by the end of the 1960s. In response, builders sought information on apartment construction, sound control, financing, and management through the Northern Kentucky Apartment Council, established as an arm of the HBANK. Its purpose was to provide a forum for education and information and to inform the public and local governments of the need for this type of housing. Apartment construction has continued to flourish over the years. In 1988 the council merged with the Greater Cincinnati Apartment Association.

In 2006 the HBANK moved to new headquarters on Circleport Dr. in Erlanger, where it has administrative offices, training facilities, and classrooms, as well as an events center that can accommodate more than 200 people.

Home Builders Association of Northern Kentucky. *Industry Standard.* Fort Mitchell: Home Builders Association of Northern Kentucky, 2001.

Wiedeman, Donald M. *Milestones and Memories: The Heartbeat of Housing in Northern Kentucky.* Fort Mitchell: Home Builders Association of Northern Kentucky, 2001.

Donald M. Wiedeman

HOMELAND SECURITY AND 9/11. On September 11, 2001, America found itself at war with neither a country nor an alliance of countries but with a multinational ideology, often divorced from the ruling government of any nation, which proclaimed that the United States was a great evil, to be destroyed by any and all means available. The attacks on the United States and its interests overseas had started years earlier: the USS *Cole,* the U.S. embassies in Africa, and individual U.S. citizens. But those events had not been given credence by the U.S. government as a coordinated attack against the nation and its citizens by those adhering to a violent Islamic ideology.

On September 11, 2001, four airliners were hijacked in the United States and used as flying bombs. Three of them hit their intended targets. Two airplanes hit the World Trade Center in New York City, and another crashed into the Pentagon, in Arlington, Va. The fourth aircraft failed to hit its target when passengers fought back and caused it to crash into a remote farm field in Pennsylvania. **Brian Williams**, a native of Northern Kentucky, died in the attack on the World Trade Center.

The immediate result of these aerial attacks was a shutdown of air transportation within U.S. airspace for two days as the federal government made sure no other aircraft hijack plan was in place and updated the nation's air-transportation security procedures. During the days immediately following the attack, citizens within Northern Kentucky, as elsewhere, took part in church memorial services and vigils remembering those who had been killed. State and county governments opened their emergency operation centers, and law enforcement officers throughout Kentucky were placed on overtime, patrolling areas considered as targets (see **Civil Defense**).

As a result of the attacks, known now as "9/11" because they occurred on September 11, the lifestyles of U.S. citizens changed. The federal government created the Department of Homeland Security, which established an advisory security system. Using the color codes of green, blue, yellow, orange, and red to represent ascending threat levels, Homeland Security warns citizens regarding the likelihood of terrorist attacks.

Among the major impacts 9/11 had on everyday life in Northern Kentucky was that friends and family members could no longer greet or say goodbye to one another at the **Cincinnati/Northern Kentucky International Airport** passenger gates. Airports throughout the nation suddenly increased these and other security procedures. Citizens who enjoyed watching and taking pictures of aircraft, trains, and towboats now had to consider the risk that such activities might make them suspect as terrorists. Government offices became inconvenient to visit because of newly established security policies. Background security checks on individuals became more common, as did the thorough uncovering of false claims regarding a person's education level, employment, military service, and outstanding warrants. New restrictive regulations were implemented by the federal government controlling the movement of cargo by barge, aircraft, train, ship, and truck, while industries were required by various levels of government to upgrade security at their facilities. The open military base, one permitting free admittance without checking, became a thing of the past. All of these changes came at a cost passed on to U.S. citizens through higher prices for goods and curtailed governmental social services. Through July 1, 2004, some $85 million had been spent in Kentucky by the federal Department of Homeland Security, and this figure did not include funds spent by other federal agencies to increase Kentucky's ability to detect, deter, respond to, and recover from a terrorist attack.

"Federal Money Covers Wide Range of Local Safety Needs," *KP,* May 23, 2005, K1.

"Ham Radio to the Rescue," *KP,* June 25, 2005, A12.

"Terrorism 101," *KP,* January 24, 2005, K1.

Charles H. Bogart

HOMELESSNESS AND HOMELESS SHELTERS. Like many other urban areas, Northern Kentucky has a homeless population. The Department of Housing and Urban Development (HUD) defines a homeless person as an individual who lacks a fixed, regular, and adequate nighttime residence, or one who has a primary nighttime residence that is a supervised publicly or privately operated shelter designed to provide temporary living accommodations (including welfare hotels, congregate shelters, and transitional housing for the mentally ill); an institution that provides a temporary residence for individuals intended to be institutionalized; or a public or private place not designed for, or ordinarily used as, a regular sleeping accommodation for human beings. HUD's definition does not include persons who are doubled up with family or friends, living in overcrowded conditions or in substandard housing. Neither does it take into consideration the cost burdens borne by the many low-income households that pay 60 percent or more of their income to live in housing that is inadequate for their needs. HUD says, in other contexts, that housing is affordable to a household when the cost of rent and utilities does not exceed 30 percent of the household's adjusted income.

In an attempt to understand homelessness better, the state's housing finance agency, Kentucky Housing Corporation (KHC), conducted homelessness surveys in 1993 and again in 2001. These studies found that economic instability (resulting from job loss, low wages, divorce, lack of job skills or training, inability to gain access to public assistance, loss of such assistance, and other factors) is a leading cause of homelessness. Additional causes are domestic violence, mental illness, substance abuse, illness, and family rejection.

The KHC surveys found significant differences between the homeless population in the urban areas of Covington and Northern Kentucky, Lexington and Fayette Co., and Louisville, on one hand, and the rural areas of the rest of the state, on the other hand. In the urban areas, the majority of homeless individuals were men; in the rural areas more women than men were homeless. In addition, the homeless people in urban areas are more likely to be unsheltered (living on the streets) than are those in rural areas. In all areas, a significant number of homeless individuals are children.

It is extremely difficult to determine the number of homeless persons, especially those who are unsheltered. A count in January 2005 found a total of 305 homeless persons in Northern Kentucky on one night. The number would likely have been considerably higher had the count been made during the summer months, when the unsheltered homeless are more visible. A 2001 report by Applied Information Resources, funded by the Health Foundation of Greater Cincinnati, estimated that 25,488 individuals had experienced episodes of homelessness in the Greater Cincinnati–Northern Kentucky area in the previous year.

There are many local social service agencies that try to help the homeless find housing and attempt to address the root causes of homelessness in Northern Kentucky. Most of the agencies are members of and participants in the Northern Kentucky Housing and Homeless Coalition. Together, they coordinate efforts to provide affordable housing and supportive services to the homeless. In December 2005, HUD awarded these agencies more than $1.6 million to provide homeless individuals housing, rental assistance, and supportive social services such as case management, mental and physical health care, job training, education, budget management, domestic violence counseling, life-skills training, and substance abuse treatment.

Despite this funding, it has long been recognized that there is a critical shortage of emergency shelter beds available in Northern Kentucky, especially for men. Efforts to correct this problem have been ongoing for more than 10 years. During the late 1990s, the concept of a one-stop day center, social service facility, health care clinic, and shelter evolved and came to be known as the Life Learning Center. The center was to be established in Covington, where the majority of homeless persons are located and where the existing agencies that provide the services have their offices. Despite funding commitments and available sites, the City of Covington twice rejected the project, once by preempting the intended site, using eminent domain laws, and on a second occasion by denying the required zoning change. The projected Life Learning Center in Covington remains a viable concept to address the most critical needs of the homeless but has yet to find the necessary political support.

Several emergency and transitional shelters for the homeless operate in Northern Kentucky, although the number of persons in need far exceeds the number of available beds. **Welcome House of Northern Kentucky**, a typical shelter serving women and children, has turned away more than 2,000 people in need of shelter in a year owing to the lack of available beds or because of household makeup. Efforts to increase the number of shelter beds available routinely face stiff opposition in Northern Kentucky.

Emergency and Transitional Shelters Operating in Northern Kentucky

Boone Co.

Women's Crisis Center, Outreach Office, 11 Shelby St., Florence, for victims of domestic violence, 23 beds.

Campbell Co.

Brighton Center Independent Living Services, Seventh and Park Aves., Newport, a youth transitional living program for ages 16 through 21.

Henry **Hosea House**, 901 York St., Newport, 3 units for transitional shelter.

Interfaith Hospitality Network, 336 W. Ninth St., Newport, for families and children, up to 30 beds.

Salvation Army, 340 W. 10th St., Newport, transitional housing, 2 units.

Transitions Droege House, 925 Fifth Ave., Dayton, a detox center for adult men and women, 9 beds; transitional housing for chemically dependent men, 10 beds.

Veteran's Administration Domiciliary, 1000 S. Fort Thomas Ave., Fort Thomas, for homeless veterans, 10 beds (see **Veterans Administration Medical Center**).

Kenton Co.

Homeward Bound, 13–15 20th St., Covington, for youth, 16 beds.

Madonna House, Fort Mitchell, for single women over 18 in the last trimester of pregnancy.

NorthKey Transitional Apartment Program, 722 Scott Blvd., Covington, for mentally ill adults, supervised living.

Transitions, 1629 Madison Ave., Covington, for chemically dependent women and their children, 15 units.

Welcome House, 205 Pike St., Covington, for women and children, 25 rooms.

Women's Crisis Center, 835 Madison Ave., Covington, for victims of domestic violence.

"Giving Hope a Home," *KP*, January 13, 2003, 1K–3K.

The Health Foundation of Greater Cincinnati. www.healthfoundation.org (accessed January 6, 2006).

"Homeless Shelter Loses Land to City," *KE*, January 24, 2001, B1.

Homes & Communities. www.hud.gov (accessed January 6, 2005).

Barry Grossheim

HOMING PIGEONS. During the first half of the 20th century, homing pigeons were raised in Northern Kentucky, participated in races, and performed their duties as communicators.

Earlier, before the invention of the telegraph, the homing (carrier) pigeon constituted the "overnight express." For instance, when President Andrew Jackson died in Nashville on June 8, 1845, the residents of Washington, D.C., learned of his death one and one-half days later via the homing pigeon network. Generally owned by the stagecoach industry and located in major cities such as New Orleans, Nashville, Lexington, Cincinnati, and Pittsburgh, these birds contributed significantly to keeping the nation informed. Lexington was a major relay point for the pigeons. Individual birds were confined in cages on the roof of the stagecoach station. Each cage was marked with the bird's city of destination. Well fed and well attended, the pigeons were ready to fly at a minute's notice for a premium fee. A note was inserted into a small pouch attached to a bird's leg, and the bird was released. Within three hours the Cincinnati bird would arrive, with the note aboard. Travel times varied with the distance and with winds aloft, but often birds attained a speed of 50 miles per hour and could fly 600 miles to their destination. The only threat was posed by an occasional eagle or hawk en route. Once the pigeon arrived, it would be fed and rested, then placed in a cage for its return stagecoach ride. Some birds had the ability (the instinct) to fly return routes, and those were highly valued. The Lexington-Cincinnati route was discontinued in 1851 with the stringing of the first telegraph lines from Lexington, through Grant and Kenton counties, to Cincinnati.

Homing pigeons were used in the **Civil War**, **World War I**, and **World War II**. Bud Deglow, a Covington resident, for instance, offered the use of his pigeons during World War II. From around 1910 through the 1950s, there were several individuals in the region who raised, trained, raced, and even wagered on their birds. Covington and Bellevue had pigeon racing clubs. There were local races, such as the popular 45-mile Sunday morning run from Dillsboro, Ind., to Bellevue, Ky. Typically, a club member transported the competing birds to Dillsboro and released them at a set time. Meanwhile, back in Bellevue, a clock was mounted on the back wall of each bird's roost, and when the bird landed on its perch, a camera was triggered, recording the bird's arrival time. One bird from the J. H. & S. Loft at 228 Prospect Street, Bellevue, was entered in the 1954 Mountain Empire Futurity, a 320-mile western endurance trip. Of the 450 birds that were entered from 31 states, only 7 completed the run. The J. H. & S. bird won second-prize money. This Bellevue aviary held government contracts for the breeding, raising, and training of birds for national emergencies. Homing pigeons were also used in local celebrations. On May 9, 1913, the opening day of the **Covington Blue Sox** team in the new Federal Baseball League, homing pigeons were released to each of the other cities in the league, announcing that Covington now had major league baseball.

"Bellevue Bird One of Seven to Finish Big Race," *KP*, October 15, 1954, 10.

"Bud Deglow Had Appreciation for Fully Living His Life," *KP*, November 10, 2001, 12A.

Coleman, J. Winston. *Stage-Coach Days in the Bluegrass*. Louisville, Ky.: Standard Press, 1936.

Michael R. Sweeney

HOPEFUL HEIGHTS. The community of Hopeful Heights in Boone Co. grew up around the **Hopeful Lutheran Church**, from which the town's main thoroughfare, Hopeful Church Rd., also received its name. The church's adjacent cemetery contains the graves of many important Boone Countians. For many years, the area was a sleepy neighborhood of farms, but when I-75 was built, it brought the development of the nearby **Florence Mall**. Thereafter, Hopeful Heights began participating in the amazing population growth that has been so much a part of Boone Co.'s recent history. In November 1960, there was a movement by the City of Florence to annex Hopeful Heights, but 22 Hopeful Heights residents filed suit to stop the action in December. In April 1961, Hopeful Heights incorporated as a protective move. With a population of only 550, and in view of the continuing debate regarding the provision of much-needed city services, especially sewers, the sixth-class City of Hopeful Heights faced a severe financial crisis. In 1969 a majority of the city's residents signed a petition requesting the dissolution of their town; in January 1970, the Appeals Court dismissed a suit attempting to block the dissolution, and the city came to an official end. By 1982 about half of Hopeful Heights had been made part of Florence, and by 2000 the entire area had been annexed by Florence.

Becker, Lee B. "Hopeful Heights Off to New Disagreement," *KE*, August 23, 1969, 21.

"Hopeful Heights Is Dissolved," *KP*, January 29, 1970, 1K.

"Hopeful Hts. Had Lost All Hope," *KE*, December 26, 1982, C7.

Reis, Jim. "Annexation Battles Stirred Hopeful Heights," *KP*, July 15, 1996, 4K.

HOPEFUL LUTHERAN CHURCH. Hopeful Lutheran Church, located just outside of Florence in Boone Co., is the oldest Lutheran church west of the Allegheny Mountains. The founding families were members of the Hebron Lutheran Church in Madison Co., Va., and descendants of German colonists who had immigrated to North America during the early 1700s. (See **German Americans**.) The first families coming from Virginia to Kentucky arrived in Boone Co. in November 1805. The members of the group were Elizabeth Hoffman, John and Millie House, George and Elizabeth Rouse, John and Nancy Rouse, Ephraim and Susannah Tanner, and Frederick and Rose Zimmerman. Each family soon built a cabin, with the exception of George Rouse, who pitched his tent not far from where the present Hopeful Lutheran Church now stands.

The first religious services were held at the homestead of George Rouse. Worship services were conducted in German and included hymn singing, prayers, and sermons read by Ephraim Tanner. These settlers' former pastor in Virginia, Rev. William Carpenter, sent a constitution and urged them to form a congregation. They did so on January 6, 1806, and the following men signed that constitution: Daniel Beemon, John Beemon, John House, George Rouse, Jacob Rouse, John Rouse, Michael Rouse, Ephraim Tanner, Simeon Tanner, and Frederick Zimmerman. All signers were from the Hebron Church in Virginia; five had arrived with the original group in November, and the remaining five arrived soon thereafter.

George Rouse donated an acre of ground on which to build the church, and in 1807 a log church was constructed. In his 1854 history of the church, Rev. David Harbaugh described the building: "It was a cabin church in reality, built of unhewn logs. The roof and door were made of clapboards; the floor with puncheons, and the seats were made of saplings. An opening was made at each end by sawing out some logs for windows. These were always open, that is, without sash or lights. They had neither stove nor fireplace in it, yet they met for worship during the winter."

From the beginning, the congregation of the Hopeful Lutheran Church strove to have an ordained minister come at least once a year to administer the sacraments. Rev. William Carpenter came from Virginia at least twice for that purpose. In 1813 he moved to Boone Co. and became the first pastor of the congregation. He served the parish longer than any of his successors, ministering until his death in 1833. Both a new constitution and a new church building were added during Carpenter's pastorate. The new church building was a 25-by-25-foot log church, with an end gallery and a raised pulpit. Before his death, Carpenter wrote to Rev. Jacob Crigler, urging him to take charge of the Hopeful church's parish. Crigler did so in 1834. Pastor Crigler was heartily in favor of the use of English in the liturgy. In the final years of Carpenter's ministry, services had alternated between German and English, but under Crigler, English became the language used exclusively in worship. In 1837 a 35-by-50-foot brick church was built from bricks made from a site near the church. Much of the work was donated, so the final treasurer's report listed only $1,587 in expenses.

In 1854 the Hebron Evangelical Lutheran Church was formed near what became Hebron. The Hopeful and Hebron Lutheran churches formed a joint parish, which lasted until 1947, and a parsonage was built halfway between the two on a lot near Limaburg.

Rev. W. C. Harter began his work at Hopeful Lutheran Church in early 1864 with great promise, but he died after a brief illness on July 31 of that year. After a short vacancy, Rev. Thomas Drake was called to become the church's pastor in 1865. During the **Civil War**, Drake had served as a provost marshal in Fairfield Co., Ohio. The predominant political mood of the congregation was highly in favor of the South, and since some of the people in the county had been arrested or imprisoned by a provost marshal during the war, Pastor Drake was not well received. Although he remained at Hopeful Lutheran Church for two years, he accomplished little because of the bitter feelings regarding his service during the war.

Rev. A. G. Emmerson began his service at Hopeful Lutheran Church in 1867 and was able to bring healing and growth to the church during his two-year ministry. Rev. W. C. Barnett became pastor in 1871 and led the church for the next 10 years. From 1881 to 1883, Rev. A. J. Douglas was pastor of the parish. His son, Lloyd C. Douglas, was an author who wrote such books as *The Robe* and *Dr. Hudson's Secret Journal*. Except for the pastorate of Rev. H. Max Lentz (1890–1900), the period from 1881 to 1916 was one of the shortest terms of service for pastors at Hopeful Lutheran Church. In 1917, during the pastorate of the Rev. George A. Royer, the present brick church building was erected at a cost of more than $12,000.

At the end of Rev. J. Paul Rimmer's pastorate, the Hopeful-Hebron joint parish was dissolved; each church became independent. A brick parsonage was built beside the Hopeful Lutheran Church in 1949, during the pastorate of Rev. Herman V. J. Andres. An educational wing was added, and in 1956 the church celebrated its 150th anniversary. Rev. Robert C. Richter became pastor in 1963 and served the parish until his retirement in 1980. Rev. John H. Pollock followed him in 1981. In 1991 extensive remodeling was begun and a new social hall was added to the church. This work on the church was dedicated in November 1992. In April 1996 Rev. Blair Fields was called to become the church's pastor. In 2005 the church broke ground for a new sanctuary, and in 2006 the congregation celebrated its 200th anniversary. Fields remains the church's pastor.

Church records and archives of Hopeful Lutheran Church, Boone Co., Ky.

Harbaugh, David. *A History of the Evangelical Lutheran Congregation of Hopeful Church, Boone County, Kentucky.* Cincinnati: S. V. Crossman, 1854.

Lentz, H. Max. *History of Lutheran Churches in Boone County, Kentucky.* York, Pa.: P. Anstadt, 1902.

Michael D. Rouse

HORD, REBEKAH HECHINGER (b. January 25, 1899, Maysville, Ky.; d. July 7, 1977, Maysville, Ky.). Rebekah Hechinger Hord, the daughter of Ferdinand and Hattie Oridge Hechinger, became the first woman mayor of a city in Kentucky. She graduated from **Maysville High School** in 1916 and married Dr. Winn E. Hord on April 26, 1920. She was a Democrat and, during the late 1940s, was the first woman to serve as a Maysville city commissioner. She was elected without opposition as mayor in November 1951, after having served as mayor pro tem following the resignation of James M. Collins, the previous mayor. To run for the seat, Hord had defeated former mayor Rex Parker in the Democratic primary. Her subsequent election made her not only the first woman mayor of Maysville but also the first woman ever to hold the position of mayor of a city in Kentucky. She was reelected in 1957 and served through May 1961. As mayor, she was instrumental in securing federal aid to build the town's vital floodwall (see **Flood Control**). After completing her terms as mayor, Hord ran unsuccessfully for the Kentucky legislature in 1960. Her involvement in the Democratic Party extended to the national level when she served as a delegate to Democratic national conventions in 1939 and 1960. Her daughter, **Harriet Cartmell**, was elected mayor of Maysville in 1986. Hord's varied interests led her to participate in many civic and professional organizations, such as the Kentucky Municipal League, the **American Red Cross**, the League of Women Voters, the Humane Society, and the **Nomads** women's club. She died, apparently of a heart attack, in 1977 and was buried in the Maysville and Mason Co. Cemetery.

Calvert, Jean, and John Klee. *Maysville, Kentucky: From Past to Present in Pictures.* Maysville: Mason Co. Museum, 1983.

"Former Maysville Mayor Hord Discovered Dead in Mansion," *CE,* July 11, 1977, 1.

"Mayor Hord Wins Re-Election," *KTS,* November 7, 1957, 1.

"Mrs. Rebekah Hord Is Elected First Woman Mayor of Maysville," *KP,* August 6, 1951, 1.

"Office Oath Taken by City Commission: Mayor Begins Term," *KE,* January 8, 1952, 1.

Thomas S. Ward

HORNER, CHARLES D. (b. August 1859, Tennessee; date and place of death unknown). Charles Horner was the principal of Newport's African American **Southgate St. School** from 1897 to 1904. He married Rebecca Day Minnes, and the couple had six children, including **Charles E. Horner**, who became a medical doctor in Newport. The family resided in the Cincinnati neighborhood of Cumminsville until Charles D. Horner became principal of the Southgate St. School in 1897. Horner was active in the Newport community; for example, in June 1899 he was elected an officer of the Colored Four Hundred Society of Newport. The Horners resided at 152 Van Voast Ave. in Bellevue in 1900, later moving to 404 W. Fourth St. in Newport. In August 1902 Horner helped organize and was a speaker at the Kentucky State Colored Chautauqua, which was held at Electric Gardens at 11th and Brighton Sts. in Newport.

While principal of Southgate, Horner requested that the high school's program be expanded from three to four years, to match the program of Newport High School. His proposal was accepted and implemented, and the Southgate St. High School continued to offer its African American student body four years of high school until the school was closed in 1921. In June 1905, Horner was asked by the Newport Board of Education to resign as principal and was given until the July board meeting to reply to their demand. The board minutes do not indicate the reason for the board's request. He resigned before the July board meeting, and from that time on no further information about Horner is available.

"Horner Must Go," *KP,* June 22, 1905, 5.

"Newport," *CE,* July 18, 1899, 3.

Newport Board of Education. *Fifty-Third Annual Report of the Public Schools of Newport.* Newport, Ky.: Campbell Co. Printing, 1901.

"Newport News," *KTS,* August 15, 1902, 3.

Reis, Jim. "Educator's Son Worked Hard to Be Called 'Doctor'," *KP,* February 4, 2004, 4K.

Theodore H. H. Harris

HORNER, CHARLES E. (b. August 1, 1882, Cincinnati, Ohio; d. October 11, 1948, Cincinnati, Ohio). Charles E. Horner, the son of **Charles D. Horner** and Rebecca Day Minnes Horner, became the first African American medical doctor in Newport. He attended public schools up to the eighth grade, leaving school at age 15. At age 16, he went to work in a restaurant as a cook and a pantryman. In 1899, at age 17, Horner moved from Ohio to Newport and began working as a janitor at the **Southgate St. School**, where his father was the principal; he also waited tables at evening parties. He later held janitorial jobs at two churches and worked as a window washer, a porter in stores, and a waiter at nighttime poker parties.

In 1903, with $300 in his bank account, Horner entered the Eclectic Medical College in Cincinnati, attending classes during the day and working as a waiter at night. He graduated with a degree in medicine from the college in 1907. In 1908 he worked as a Pullman porter stationed in Chicago, traveling throughout the United States, Canada, and parts of Mexico. In 1910 he took the Kentucky State Medical Board examination and passed with an average score of 79. In May 1911 Horner married Emma Walker. He began his medical practice in Newport, where he lived, and treated mostly white patients.

In February 1918 Horner almost lost his life while trying to visit sick patients in a flooded area of Newport. He was in the floodwaters in a flatboat with a man named George Wooding, when the vessel collapsed at Fourth and Isabella Sts. Wooding drowned, but Horner was rescued and recovered.

Horner was active in St. Andrew's Episcopal Church in Cincinnati. He was a 32nd Degree Mason. In the 1930s, Horner was married a second time, to Katharine Berry. In 1943 he retired from medical practice and moved to a farm he owned in Williamsburg, Ohio. He died in 1948, and his remains were cremated at the Cincinnati Crematory.

Dabney, W. P. *Cincinnati's Colored Citizens.* Cincinnati: Dabney, 1926.

"Death Notices," *KE,* October 13, 1938, 32.

"Dr. Charles E. Horner," *KTS,* October 13, 1948, 4.

"Man Drowned When Flatboat Capsized on Flooded Street," *KTS,* February 12, 1918, 11.

"Newport Physician to Face Grand Jury," *KP,* August 8, 1940, 1.

Reis, Jim. "Educator's Son Worked Hard to Be Called 'Doctor'," *KP,* February 4, 2002, 4K.

Theodore H. H. Harris

HORSE RACING. Competitive licensed horse racing in Northern Kentucky has primarily involved thoroughbreds. All thoroughbred horses have unbroken bloodlines drawn from three Arabian stallions (the Byerley Turk, the Darley Arabian, and the Godolphin Barb) and approximately 40 English mares. As pioneers began settling Kentucky during the second half of the 18th century, they discovered that the nutrients in the area's limestone- and mineral-based waters and grasses strengthened horses and made this the perfect place to breed and raise thoroughbreds. Challenge match races and the laying out of private racetracks on farmlands were common during the settlement period and in the years immediately following Kentucky statehood in 1792. One early settler, William Whitley of Lincoln Co., helped to establish the model for competitive thoroughbred racing in America. Whitley, who had fought the British in the Carolinas during the **Revolutionary War**, had a deep personal aversion to anything associated with England, including its long-established horse-racing traditions. Consequently, when he laid out his private racecourse, Sportsman Hill, he decided that racing on it would be conducted counterclockwise and on dirt (not clockwise and on grass, as in England). Both of these changes were soon adopted nationwide as being the "American way" to race thoroughbreds.

The Lexington Association Track, which was built in 1828, was the first racetrack in Kentucky to conduct thoroughbred racing by a set of written rules and to have a formal governing board. The next significant racecourse to open in Kentucky was the Louisville Jockey Club Track (later known as Churchill Downs). It was opened by Col. Matt J. Winn and a group of investors on May 17, 1875, the same day the new track in Louisville ran the first Kentucky Derby. This presence of thoroughbred racecourses in Lexington and Louisville helped convince a group of horsemen and local officials from Central and Northern Kentucky that they too should open a thoroughbred racetrack. Seven men, track president and race judge T. J. Megibben; racing secretary Maj. Elias D. Lawrence; horseman

Col. **Robert W. Nelson**; attorney and Covington councilman Frank P. Helm; judges **George G. Perkins** and **Walter W. Cleary**; and John Taylor, the son of Gen. **James Taylor Jr.**, joined together to form the Latonia Agricultural and Stock Association, which obtained a state charter to race thoroughbred horses in 1882. Having purchased 109 acres in the Milldale District near Covington from Gen. James Taylor, the track's new officers proceeded to build their racetrack, named Latonia (see **Latonia Racecourse**) after the nearby **Latonia Springs**, once a popular summer resort.

On June 9, 1883, Latonia's opening day, the racetrack drew a crowd estimated to number 10,000. Oddly, the featured race that day, the Hindoo Stakes, saw horses named Leonatus, Drake Carter, and Ragland finish first, second, and third, respectively, thus duplicating the exact finish they had achieved a few weeks earlier in the Kentucky Derby at Louisville. The facts that three Derby horses raced in Latonia's opening feature and that the jockey aboard Leonatus was Isaac Murphy, the jockey with the all-time leading win percentage in stakes in American racing history, were strong indications that Latonia was starting out on the right foot.

The Hindoo Stakes, which became the Latonia Derby in 1888, remained Latonia's top race; often in the years that followed, the purse provided to the winner of the Latonia Derby was larger than either the Kentucky Derby's purse or any of the stakes' purses offered at the Lexington Association Track. Racehorse owners were soon rotating their stock from the track in Lexington to the one in Louisville and ending at Latonia, a racing sequence soon christened Kentucky's 3-L Race Circuit. The success of Latonia and the new 3-L Race Circuit (see **Three-L Highway**) spawned three lower-level area copycat tracks, one in Oakley, a northeast suburb of Cincinnati, and two in Northern Kentucky. The first, the Gentlemen's Full Racing Park in Oakley, opened in 1889 and closed in 1904. In April 1896 the Queen City Race Track (1896–1905) opened just south of Newport, along the Licking River. It offered smaller purses and catered to cheaper horses. Even so, one of the nation's top riders, Jimmy Winkfield, who was living in Cincinnati, rode at both the Oakley and the Newport tracks. The third of these tracks, The Rosedale Electric Light Jockey Club (Rosedale, Ky., now part of Covington), which also opened in 1896, found fame by becoming one of America's earliest lighted evening racecourses, but bankruptcy was declared in 1897 and it never reopened.

Latonia's rapid rise to be counted among the top tracks in Kentucky helped to keep its quality of racing at a high level until 1929, the year the **Great Depression** began. Racing at Latonia drew some of the nation's best horses, many noted trainers, the best jockeys, and some of the most famous owners in America. In a period from 1915 to 1928, Latonia led all North American tracks in total purse moneys awarded. Horses racing at Latonia set several speed records, and the prestigious stake races the track added, such as the Clipsetta Stakes and the Latonia Oaks for distaffs, and the open-company Latonia Cup and Fall Championship, garnered nationwide interest, drew prestigious fields, and attracted large crowds. Racing at Latonia peaked in the mid-1920s. Two races held there, Latonia's 1923 Fall Championship and the third leg of the 1924 American International challenge race, were such important events that they are included in all major thoroughbred horseracing histories covering this period.

The ownership at Latonia changed several times over the years, alternating between local and out-of-town owners. The final change occurred in 1919, when a race syndicate headed by Matt J. Winn, called the Kentucky Jockey Club, bought all the thoroughbred tracks in Kentucky. This change in ownership had an immediate impact on the Latonia Derby, which was diminished in importance as Winn concentrated on making the Latonia Derby's rival, the Kentucky Derby, America's most famous race. The 1930s were difficult years at Latonia. Purses were substantially reduced, the top stables no longer raced there, and the track struggled just to survive. Latonia closed suddenly in 1939 after its properties were sold to the Sohio Refining Company (Standard Oil of Ohio).

Thoroughbred racing did not resume in Northern Kentucky until 1957, and at that, it came in a backdoor manner. A five-eighths-mile harness track had been opened during the 1950s in Florence in Boone Co., and in 1957 the Northern Kentucky Turf Association (the parent organization of Kentucky Raceways) obtained a license to conduct a thoroughbred meet. Kentucky Raceways conducted one meet in 1957 (September 7–October 5) and then closed. Meanwhile, plans were in the works to open a second Latonia track, also to be located in Florence. The key founding figure of what was called the Latonia Jockey Club Inc. was Matt Winn Williamson, the grandson of Matt J. Winn. New Latonia (the original track became known as Old Latonia) opened on August 27, 1959, and drew a crowd totaling 10,000. The jubilation associated with the track's successful opening, and its owner's high hopes, did not last long. Undercapitalized, the track fell into receivership in November 1959, emerged barely hanging on, and throughout the 1960s, 1970s, and mid-1980s conducted racing acknowledged as being clearly below the levels established by the earlier Latonia track. In 1965 Corwin Nixon's Ohio-based harness organization agreed to help pay for lighting at Latonia, and from 1965 until the mid-1980s the Latonia Trots held meets at the track.

Briefly, during the 1970s, quarter-horse racing was conducted at Latonia. The track's personable general manager, John Battaglia (1971–1977), whose son Mike remains the track announcer, had helped launch quarter-horse racing, one of the many attempts during Battaglia's tenure as general manager to utilize Latonia's facilities fully and draw more customers to the track. The track's thoroughbred meets in this era produced three memorable firsts. Latonia was the first track to conduct night racing in Kentucky (March 29, 1969) and the first track in Kentucky to offer Sunday racing (December 7, 1980). Then on March 22, 1974, it became the 12th track nationwide, and the lone one in Kentucky, to produce a triple dead heat for a win. Latonia was bought in 1967 by Emprise, which ran Sportservice, the concessionaire that later morphed into the Delaware North Corporation. Nineteen years later, on April 9, 1986, Latonia was sold to the partnership of businessmen Jerry Carroll and James Thornton and renamed **Turfway Park**.

Turfway Park's first meet was held in the fall of 1986. In August 1987 Carroll and Thornton dissolved their partnership after Carroll outbid Thornton for control of the track. While Carroll was running Turfway Park (1986–1999), the track gained attention for the innovations it introduced and its improved quality of racing. Carroll transformed the Spiral Stakes, a contest that began as a $10,000 ungraded stake, into what eventually became a Grade II $600,000 event, the Jim Beam Stakes, a race that produced three Preakness winners (Summer Squall, 1990; Hansel, 1991; and Prairie Bayou, 1993), a Belmont winner (Hansel, 1991), a Kentucky Derby winner (Lil E. Tee, 1992), and three Eclipse Champion Horse Award winners (Summer Squall, 1990; Prairie Bayou, 1993; and filly-champ Serena's Song, 1995).

Carroll spent millions improving the track's racing surface and physical plant. On July 22, 1994, he opened the Race Book, a state-of-the-art simulcasting betting facility soon copied nationwide. Attendance and track revenues peaked in the late 1990s and, true to form, Carroll, the speculator in properties, sold out and moved on to a new enterprise—building a motor sport facility called the **Kentucky Speedway**. On January 15, 1999, it was announced that a partnership consisting of the Keeneland Association; Dreamport, a division of GTECH Corporation; and Harrah's Entertainment had purchased Turfway Park. Each new owner had a specific reason for joining this partnership. Both GTECH Corporation and Harrah's Entertainment were positioning themselves to profit, should video gambling devices be allowed at racetracks in Kentucky, and Keeneland was attempting to block Churchill Downs, which had purchased Ellis Park in Kentucky, from dominating the Kentucky racing circuit and its dates. In 2006 the GTECH Corporation sold out to the other two partners. Turfway Park holds annual Spring, Fall, and Holiday meets and in 2005 became the first North American track to race on Polytrack, a synthetic surface that allows all-weather racing. The track has just completed a multimillion-dollar expansion of the paddock and saddling area, the gift shop, and its food-distribution sites. It has also launched an aggressive campaign to attract new fans to the track by offering discounted food and drink, providing live music entertainment, and hosting special community parties and gatherings. Old Latonia and New Latonia are gone, but their legacy is preserved and lives on at the horse-racing facility that today is named Turfway Park.

Claypool, James C. *The Tradition Continues: The Story of Old Latonia, Latonia, and Turfway Racecourses.* Fort Mitchell, Ky.: T. I. Hayes, 1997.

The Media and Information Guide. Florence, Ky.: Turfway Racecourse, 2000, 2002, 2004, 2006, and 2007

James C. Claypool

HORSESHOE GARDENS. The Horseshoe Gardens was an entertainment resort located along the Ohio River at the foot of Ward St. in Bellevue, Ky. Formerly known as the Riviera Beach and Dance Hall, and before that as the Queen City Beach, it was one of the various Campbell Co. beachfronts on that stretch of the river that helped the City of Cincinnati bring the national Grand Army of the Republic (GAR) convention to the region in 1898. Families of **Civil War** veterans rode streetcars to Bellevue and Dayton, Ky., to frolic on the naturally sandy beaches of the bend in the Ohio River, as the former soldiers reminisced at their convention in Cincinnati.

After the Queen City Beach was sold in 1916, the new owners renovated it, building a lavish dance hall to entice customers on a year-round basis. It advertised a new maple floor that could accommodate 1,000 dancers. A radio bandstand system amplified the music throughout the hall. In 1928 Bellevue native Ed Rohrer purchased the business, by then called the Riviera Beach and Dance Hall, and changed its name to the Horseshoe Gardens. It sported a tropical-island theme and featured the most popular local and regional bands. A newspaper account at the time described it as "brilliance on the Ky. Shore of the Ohio River."

The dance pavilion offered performances by the **Justin Huber** Orchestra, Michael Hauer's Orchestra, the Royal Kentuckians, the Nightingale Orchestra, Bob Ranier, Earl Arnold, Fats Waller, bluegrass singer Harry Willsy, the "Ky. Songbird" Norbert Rechtin, the Mills Brothers, Murray Horton and his band from WLW radio, and the like.

The Horseshoe Gardens also had a large veranda and an outdoor dining area called the Starlight Terrace. Another attraction was the Crystal Floating Palace, a party area anchored to the dance pavilion that featured bright lights in the shape of a giant horseshoe. Customers could get a speedboat ride from the dock for 35 cents. Many special events were held at the Horseshoe Gardens, such as ballroom-dancing contests, concerts, a Bavarian villa, bathing-beauty contests, dinner dances, holiday dances, and Mardi Gras balls. Miss United States for 1932, Ludlow's **Anne Lee Patterson**, led a parade of bathing-beauty winners at the resort one Sunday evening in April of that year.

The Horseshoe Gardens remained a popular entertainment mecca until 1933. The **Great Depression** facilitated its demise, and the **flood of 1937** destroyed any hopes of reviving the business.

In 1955 a group of people who had regularly frequented the establishment formed the Horseshoe Gardens Alumni Association. They renewed friendships and cherished memories at an annual dance and dinner party. Reunions are no longer held, but the sentimental memory of the Horseshoe Gardens lingers on. The site is now the Bellevue Beach Park, which continues to be an important gathering place for community events and open-air summer concerts.

"Miss United States in Style Parade," *KP*, April 17, 1932, 8.

Reis, Jim. "Beach Became Horseshoe Gardens," *KP*, June 12, 2000, 4K.

———. "Cherished Dreams Linger in Memories of Youthful Years," *KP*, May 22, 1995, 4K.

———. "One Peach of a Beach," *KP*, June 12, 2000, 4K.

Robin Caraway

HORSFALL, WILLIAM H. (b. March 3, 1847, Alexandria, Ky.; d. October 22, 1922, Newport, Ky.). U.S. Congressional **Medal of Honor** recipient William H. Horsfall was the second of six children of English-born Jonathan Horsfall and his wife Elizabeth, residents of Alexandria, Ky. By 1860 the family had moved to Newport, where William resided during his adult life. At age 14, he boarded the steamer *Annie Laurie*, which was heading for the Kanawha River in what was then Virginia. The young boy, who was small for his age at just four feet and three inches in height, arrived in Charleston, Va. (today W.Va.), and enlisted on January 1, 1862, in the Union Army's Company G, 1st Kentucky U.S. Infantry, as a drummer. His uniforms and shoes were always too big for him, and he usually walked barefoot, causing blisters and infection throughout his term of service in the military. He also suffered from knee calluses from carrying the cumbersome snare drum. In combat situations, Horsfall used a sharpshooter's 20-pound rifle with a telescope for long-range sighting. He fought in the Battle of Shiloh at Pittsburg Landing, Tenn., and at the battle of Stone River, near Murfreesboro, Tenn. On May 21, 1862, during the siege of Corinth, Miss., Capt. James T. Williamson was shot in the hip and lay helpless between the lines of fire as his unit retreated. Horsfall rested his rifle against a tree, stooped low, and ran to Williamson. The boy slowly dragged the heavier captain by the wrists, as bullets dug into the earth all around him. Finally they reached safety behind the reestablished skirmish line. Gen. William Rosecrans, commander of the Union division fighting there, complimented Horsfall for his bravery. Horsfall was captured on September 10, 1893, at Graysville, Ga., and was held prisoner at Andersonville Prison, Andersonville, Ga., until August 19, 1864. Then on March 1, 1865, he reenlisted in the Union Army in Company K, 4th Regiment, of the U.S. Veteran Volunteers, in Cincinnati. During this term of service, Horsfall contracted a severe cold from exposure to the elements and sleeping on the ground. His untreated illness became progressively worse, though he stayed with his regiment until being discharged on March 1, 1866. For most of his adult life, Horsfall was a semi-invalid suffering from rheumatism and pain in his lungs, back, and limbs, as well as from heart disease. After the war he worked as a notary public; he also authored war poems, wrote music, and sang. Horsfall married Loretta Davis in 1871 and became the father of six children. He was the commander of the William Nelson Post of the Grand Army of the Republic in Newport. President Grover Cleveland (1893–1897) awarded Horsfall the U.S. Congressional Medal of Honor on August 9, 1895, for "most distinguished gallantry in action at Corinth, Miss., May 21, 1862." Horsfall died in 1922 in his home at 218 W. Third St., Newport, at age 75. He was buried in Evergreen Cemetery at Southgate in a GAR plot, where a Kentucky Historical Marker memorializes his bravery and courage.

Civil War Soldiers & Sailors System. "William Horsfall." www.itd.nps.gov/cwss/ (accessed September 26, 2006).

Fiore, C. A. *Young Heroes of the Civil War*. Unionville, N.Y.: Royal Works Press, 1932.

Macon Co., Georgia. Andersonville National Cemetery and Historic Site. www.maconcountyga.org (accessed September 26, 2006).

"War Veteran Dies," *KP*, October 23, 1922, 3.

Garry A. Casson

HOSEA HOUSE. The Henry Hosea House, located at 901 York St., Newport, was renovated and donated by David and Marcia Hosea in 1992 to the Interchurch Organization as a memorial to David Hosea's father and grandfather. The facility, a former VFW hall, now serves as a soup kitchen run by the Interchurch Organization, commonly known as ECHO, a nonprofit agency started by Sister Mary Dorgan, C.D.P., and other ministers and community members from Campbell Co. to help the poor and the homeless (see **Homelessness and Homeless Shelters**). ECHO officially began on April 19, 1991, serving about 30 meals a day at the fellowship hall of the First Church of the Nazarene, located at 830 York St. in Newport; since the move to the Henry Hosea House in 1992, ECHO serves an average of 150 meals each evening. In June 1997 ECHO expanded its meal service to include weekends and to offer other direct services, including a referral service that connects guests with other social agencies. The foot clinic offers on-site care by trained nurses and doctors and provides new shoes and socks for clients.

ECHO also provides blankets, fans, personal-care items, school supplies, and Thanksgiving food baskets. The Adopt a Family for Christmas program recruits businesses, churches, community groups, and families to purchase gifts and food for families that otherwise would not have a holiday. During the winter ECHO operates a program called HUGS, an acronym for Hats, Underwear, Gloves, and Socks. ECHO has four staff members but utilizes more than 400 volunteers at Hosea House throughout the year. The organization depends on the generosity of many agencies, individuals, organizations, and the community.

"Her Kitchen Feeds Their Bodies; She Warms Their Spirits," *KP*, April 14, 1993, 1–2KK.

"Soup Kitchen Adds on Day—Hosea House Expands to Meet Need," *KE*, January 15, 1995, B3.

Gabrielle Summe

HOSPITALS. The first hospital that operated in Northern Kentucky was the medical facility at the **Newport Barracks**, at the confluence of the Licking and Ohio rivers in Newport. Two prominent physicians practiced there, **Nathaniel Burger Shaler** and Gen. **Charles Stuart Tripler**. The widely respected Shaler tended to the ill, both military and civilian, from the height of the cholera epidemic in 1832 almost until his death in 1882. Tripler, a career military officer, was at Newport for a few years during the late 1850s, when he wrote the long-used military medical classic *Manual of the Medical Officer of the Army of the United States*. Tripler also improved upon the U.S. Army's field ambulances by adding a fourth wheel. He participated in local civilian medical societies, especially in Cincinnati. The major U.S. Army medical facility in Honolulu today is named in his honor.

In the early 1850s, two medical practitioners, one named Dr. Holt and his partner, a Dr. Delaney, opened what they called an infirmary in Covington for the treatment of disease, mainly of the eyes and ears. The first civilian general hospital in Northern Kentucky was St. Elizabeth Hospital in Covington, founded in 1861 (see **St. Elizabeth Medical Center**). Operated by the Sisters of the Poor of St. Francis, a Catholic order of nuns, the hospital cared for soldiers from either side of the conflict who were injured in the **Civil War**. As the St. Elizabeth Medical Center, it continues and prospers today, both in Covington and from its modern medical campus in Edgewood. During the Civil War, there were several military hospitals in Covington and at least one in Newport (see **Civil War Hospitals**). They existed temporarily during the conflict as needs required. Another early hospital in Campbell Co. was in the Federal-style home at 185 Ridgeway Ave. in Fort Thomas; it operated just after the war for a short time.

In Campbell Co. in the 1890s, Dr. J. L. Pythian had bedrooms at his office at 810 Washington Ave. in Newport. This was where the autopsy on the headless body of **Pearl Bryan** took place in 1896. From 1895 to 1897, Dr. J. Oliver Jenkins had a similar facility, known as the Jenkins Hospital, at Seventh and Isabella Sts. in the **West End** of Newport. Each structure stands today. Both offered 24-hour care in a hospital-like setting and catered primarily to a clientele who could afford to pay for it. These two facilities, known as transition hospitals, accepted emergency cases, but contagious patients were not admitted. The next hospital in the region was **Speers Memorial Hospital** in Dayton, the first major hospital in Campbell Co. It opened in 1897 and closed in 1973.

In 1908 the **Hayswood Hospital** opened in Maysville. A gift of Mary V. Wilson, it operated until 1983, when it was replaced by the modern for-profit **Meadowview Regional Medical Center**, up on the hill south of downtown Maysville along the **AA Highway**. Meadowview is the largest of the hospitals out in the region away from the Kenton-Campbell urban area. It has 101 beds today and serves seven counties in Kentucky and Ohio.

In 1914 the **Booth Memorial Hospital** opened along E. Second St. in Covington. It served the Covington community until 1979, when competitive forces moved it to Florence in Boone Co. The Booth facility in Covington, which began as a **Salvation Army** home for girls, soon converted into the first general hospital for the Salvation Army in the United States. In 1989, after the hospital moved to Florence, it was sold to the **St. Luke Hospital**, and it operates as St. Luke Hospital West today.

In the period between 1916 and 1919, a proposed hospital for 20th St. and Madison Ave. in Covington was much talked about, but it never got off the ground. In the 1920s, a doctor operated a so-called hospital in a large home in Erlanger, along the **Dixie Highway**, that only lasted a few years; and in Covington, along W. Third St., an African American medical practitioner, Dr. Dunham, ran a storefront hospital. Denied practice privileges at Booth and St. Elizabeth hospitals, he was forced to place his patients somewhere else. From 1921 to 1926, the U.S. Public Health Service ran a convalescent hospital for veterans of **World War I**; the facility was spread over several buildings in Fort Thomas, including three former hotels, the **Altamont**, the **Avenel**, and the **Shelby Arms**. A medical facility that never materialized was the Effie Slaughter Memorial Hospital, planned as a Covington hospital for African American patients. Although fundraising drives were carried out during 1928, further plans for the facility never were completed. In the early 1940s, a local doctor proposed a 10-bed hospital for Fort Thomas near the intersection of Mayo and N. Fort Thomas Ave., but it never developed.

At the end of **World War II**, the U.S. Army Air Force ran a convalescent hospital, one of seven nationally, for almost two years (1945–1946) at the **Fort Thomas Military Reservation**. Injured flight crew members were rehabilitated there. Afterward, the hospital became the first U.S. Veterans Administration (VA) Hospital for the Cincinnati region (see **Veterans Administration Medical Center**). The present VA hospital on Vine St. in Cincinnati opened in 1952, and by 1957 the general-hospital aspect of the VA operation in Fort Thomas had been phased out and moved to Cincinnati; a VA nursing home operates at that site in Fort Thomas today. U.S. congressman **Brent Spence**, the district's representative, tried to retain and expand the VA hospital in Fort Thomas. In the late 1940s, there were plans, which never came to fruition, for as many as 750 VA hospital beds for Fort Thomas.

In 1954 the St. Luke Hospital opened as a public-owned entity along Grand Ave. on the Newport–Fort Thomas boundary in Fort Thomas. The St. Luke Hospital has since expanded into Florence, by buying the Booth Hospital there, and into Falmouth, in a building once known as the Pendleton Co. Hospital, where the St. Luke Hospital runs its alcoholic detoxification unit. In recent years, this hospital has been a member of the Health Alliance of Greater Cincinnati. After Booth Hospital moved from the riverfront neighborhood of Covington to Turfway Rd. in Florence, the Salvation Army sold the business and property to the St. Luke Hospital in 1989. Today, that facility, operating as St. Luke Hospital West, is expanding. Most recently, St. Luke has sought to divest itself of its membership in the Health Alliance, as has Cincinnati's Christ Hospital; both claim that they are not receiving a fair share of the resources. There also have been discussions of a merger between the St. Luke Hospital and the St. Elizabeth hospital groups.

Other Northern Kentucky hospitals include the Grant Co. Hospital, now the **St. Elizabeth Medical Center**, Grant Co. It was founded in 1960 as a 30-bed facility under the direction of leaders such as Dr. **Fred Scroggin**. In Owen Co., there is the 24-bed **New Horizons Medical Center**, which has served Owenton and Owen Co. since 1951 under several different names and managers; and in Carrollton there is the **Carroll Co. Memorial Hospital**, founded in 1954 with 54 beds, which also has had several operators and owners over the years.

In the early days of nursing education, nurses usually attended nursing school at the hospital where they worked. That was how hospitals developed their nursing staffs. The William Booth and St. Elizabeth hospitals in Covington each had a nursing school, as did Speers Hospital in Dayton. When nursing degree programs developed, it became easier for local colleges such as the **Gateway Community and Technical College**, **Northern Kentucky University**, and **Thomas More College** to handle nurses' education. All three schools work closely with existing hospitals in that effort today.

The development of private medical insurance in the 1940s and Medicare and Medicaid in the 1960s, combined with the spiraling cost of modern medical care, have prompted the emergence of cost-saving specialty hospitals in Northern Kentucky. Such facilities do not require all the equipment and space of a general hospital and therefore are able to charge lower rates. Today, on the campus of the St. Elizabeth Medical Center in Edgewood, is the HealthSouth Rehabilitation Hospital, formerly the Rehabilitation Hospital of Northern Kentucky. Not far away in Florence is the Cardinal Hill Rehabilitation Hospital, a division of the Lexington-based Cardinal Hill Hospital. Near the Cardinal facility is the **Gateway Rehabilitation Hospital**.

Donnelly, Joseph. *Newport Barracks—Kentucky's Forgotten Military Installation*. Covington, Ky.: Kenton Co. Historical Society, 1999.

Poweleit, Alvin C., and James A. Schroer, eds. *A Medical History of Campbell and Kenton Counties*. Cincinnati: Campbell-Kenton Medical Society, 1970.

———. *Medical History of Northern Kentucky*. Cincinnati: Campbell-Kenton Medical Society, 1990.

Michael R. Sweeney

HOUSE, GERRY (b. March 28, 1948, Covington, Ky.). Gerald L. House, a radio personality and songwriter, is the son of Homer and Lucille Jacobs House. He grew up in Independence and graduated from **Simon Kenton High School** (1966) and from Eastern Kentucky University at Richmond.

Nicknamed "Mr. Controversy Pants," House is the king of FM radio in the Nashville listening market. He earns top ratings as he broadcasts over 98 WSIX and has been honored with numerous awards from the Country Music Association, the Academy of Country Music, and *Billboard.* His show, which includes various broadcasting sidekicks, is full of skits, comedy routines, and talk. His late mother was a frequent contributor to the on-air action and frivolity via telephone from her home in Independence. House previously worked in Los Angeles; Ithaca, N.Y.; and Jacksonville, Fla. Those stints were during his rock music years.

As a songwriter, he has penned hit songs for the likes of George Strait (*The Big One*), Reba McEntire (*Little Rock*), and his neighbor LeAnn Rimes (*On the Side of Angels*); Randy Travis and the Oak Ridge Boys have recorded other House pieces.

As a comedian, he has cut two albums, *The Cheater's Telethon* and *Bull,* both released internationally. While in Los Angeles, House wrote for the *Roseanne* television show. He has hosted nationally syndicated radio shows, including *Countryline USA, America's Number Ones,* and *The Saturday Night House Party.*

As one of the nation's top country disk jockeys, House continues to command the morning drive radio hours on weekdays with his *House Foundation* broadcast over the Big Six (98 WSIX). He married Allyson Faulkner (also from Northern Kentucky) in 1974. Gerry and Allyson House have one daughter, Autumn, and reside in the Music City of Nashville.

The Big 98. "Gerry House." www.wsix.com (accessed September 17, 2006).

Hicks, Jack. "Maw-Maw and Her Son Chat on the Air," *KP,* June 22, 1992, 1K.

Kingsbury, Paul, ed. *The Encyclopedia of Country Music.* New York: Oxford Univ. Press, 1998.

Wikipedia. "Gerry House." http://en.wikipedia.org (accessed September 17, 2006).

HOUSTON, STANWOOD & GAMBLE COMPANY. The sales office of the Houston, Stanwood & Gamble Company (HSG), which made steam engines, was in Cincinnati, and "Cincinnati, O" was cast into the steam chest covers of many HSG engines, but the firm's factory was actually in Covington. The company was situated on the property once occupied by the **Covington Locomotive and Manufacturing Works**, between Second and Third Sts. along Philadelphia St. Beginning in 1891 and continuing through the mid-1920s, HSG manufactured more than 17,000 steam engines. Testifying to their excellence is the fact that most were still running by 1927. If the number of engines in preservation are a measurement of production, HSG was a major manufacturer. Extant engines are found throughout the South, where the company sold many engines. Ranging from an 8-by-12-inch single-cylinder engine to a massive 16-by-24-inch double-cylinder model, the engines were applied to an array of tasks, not the least among them the powering of sawmills.

Partners Charles R. Houston, James B. Stanwood, and James N. Gamble formed their company in 1891. Only the previous year, the Cincinnati firm of Procter & Gamble had incorporated as the Procter & Gamble Company, with James N. Gamble serving as the company's first vice president. He was the son of James Gamble, the founder of Procter & Gamble, who died in the same year that Stanwood, Gamble, and Houston launched their steam-engine manufacturing company. In 1897 the Covington business incorporated and became the Houston, Stanwood & Gamble Company Inc. Both Houston and Stanwood brought to the firm considerable experience gained during their employment at the Lane & Bodley Company, located directly across the Ohio River in Cincinnati. Lane & Bodley manufactured agricultural traction engines and factory engines. Initially, HSG's main building, made of stone, had been used as a railroad car shop by the Southern Railway. In all likelihood, the stone building had been part of the Covington Locomotive works.

In 1904 the acquisition of the Western Foundry Company gave HSG the ability to manufacture its own gray-iron castings. In 1905 Houston proposed the building of playground equipment for children at Covington's Third District School to serve the neighborhoods where most of HSG's employees resided.

In November 1909, a rail line from the **Louisville and Nashville Railroad** (L&N) to the Houston, Stanwood & Gamble plant was proposed. Eventually, the L&N ran a spur from a southern point where the rails and the streets were on approximately the same level to the northern point, where the company's buildings stood on a level lower than the main line.

When **World War I** erupted, HSG made production changes to aid in the war effort. Early on, the factory converted to the production of engine lathes. In 1915 the Cincinnati Iron and Steel Company paid $200,000 for 200 lathes to use in the manufacture of mortar shells. At the time, HSG employed 250 workers around the clock. Even though the United States did not declare war against Germany until 1917, American merchant ships were transporting loads of American-built matériel to the Allies.

After the war, in 1920, the Covington engine company's Stanwood Smokeless Boiler, boasting a patented downdraft, was marketed and became an immediate success. Architects across the United States regarded the company's new product as the cleanest and most economic boiler being made. Branch HSG sales offices were opened in many U.S. cities, and the firm also engaged in a lively overseas trade.

HSG also built throttle-governing engines and automatic-cut-off engines. The latter featured governors that worked by inertia. Installed in the flywheel, the governors closely regulated engine speed, a refinement necessary in generating electricity. Southern sawmills relied upon the throttling engines. Most of the existing HSG engines are of the side-crank variety, but the company also produced center-crank models. The majority of the company's extant engines have balanced valves, but the firm advertised engines with standard slide valves.

From 1906 to 1927, about 10,000 boilers were manufactured at the Covington factory. In December 1924 the Stanwood Corporation replaced the Houston, Stanwood & Gamble Company Inc. By 1927 the Stanwood Corporation was producing Stanwood Smokeless Boilers, horizontal-return tubular boilers, locomotive firebox boilers, feed water heaters, steel smokestacks, tanks, and steam engines. Around 140 workers were employed. During the first half of the 1940s, the Stanwood Corporation ceased production.

"Enlarging Its Plant," *KP,* December 13, 1905, 8.

"Expensive Improvements," *CE,* November 17, 1909, 10.

"His Answer Filed," *CE,* May 27, 1899, 2.

"Local Plant Gets $200,000 War Order," *KP,* November 27, 1915, 1.

"New Machine Shop," *KP,* December 8, 1914, 4.

"Stanwood Boilers, Made in Covington, Have Proved Superior," *KP,* April 24, 1927, 14.

"Western Foundry Absorbed," *KP,* July 7, 1904, 1.

"Willow Run Road," *KE,* October 7, 1909, 13.

Robert T. Rhode

HOWARD, BENJAMIN FRANKLIN (b. April 1860, Kentucky; d. May 4, 1918, Covington, Ky.). Benjamin Franklin Howard, who established Elks lodges (see **Civic Associations**) for African Americans, was raised in Covington. After he obtained a copy of the Elks initiation ritual—the organization was then all white—Howard rewrote the ritual for use by African Americans and copyrighted it. Because it was denied a charter in Kentucky, the first African American Elks Lodge (Improved Benevolent and Protective Order of Elks of the World) was incorporated in Cincinnati. However, before the lodge was established in Cincinnati, Covington was home to its headquarters. Later, other African American lodges were created under Howard's leadership throughout the United States, laying the foundation for the establishment of an Elks grand lodge. In June 1899 the first Grand Lodge for the African American Elks was assembled in Cincinnati, and Howard was elected the Grand Exalted Ruler. A constitution for the new Grand Lodge was drawn up and approved. Howard served as the lodge's Grand Exalted Ruler until July 28, 1910.

In 1916 the State of Kentucky finally permitted B. F. Howard to incorporate a lodge, called Ira Lodge No. 37, in Covington. Its first Exalted Ruler was Howard. After he failed to become the new Grand Exalted Ruler of the Southern Grand lodge, however, Howard left the organization but continued his fraternal involvement by joining a new organization in Cincinnati, the Fraternal Mutual Benevolent Association. Howard, the founding father of the first African American Elks lodge in the United States, lived in Covington until his death in 1918 and was buried in Covington's Linden Grove Cemetery.

"Black Elks Founder Honored with Marker," *KP,* November 27, 1995, 2K.

"Covington Officials Rededicate City Park," *CE,* August 30, 1998, C1B.

Day, Michele. "Lodged in History, Elks to Host National Ceremony Here for Black Leader Ben Howard," *KP,* October 16, 1987, 7K.

Fisher, John C. K. "Elks in Covington Honor Black Chapter's Founder," *KP,* October 19, 1987, 14K.

Harris, Theodore H. H. "The History of Afro-American Elkdom and Benjamin Franklin (B. F.) Howard in Covington, Kentucky, 1889–1918," *NKH* 1, no. 2 (Spring–Summer 1994): 43–44.
"Park Honors Elks Group Founder," *CE*, December 2, 1995, C3.

Theodore H. H. Harris

HOWARD, FRANCIS W. (b. June 21, 1867, Columbus, Ohio; d. January 18, 1944, Covington, Ky.). The fifth bishop of the Diocese of Covington (see **Roman Catholics**), Francis W. Howard, was the son of Francis Howard, a grocery store operator, and Catherine Sullivan Howard. Francis W. Howard was educated in the Catholic schools of Columbus, Ohio. He studied for the priesthood at Mount St. Mary Seminary in Cincinnati and was ordained by Bishop John Watterson for the Diocese of Columbus on June 16, 1891, at St. Joseph Cathedral in that city. In 1898 Howard received permission to attend graduate school at Columbia University in New York City.

Howard spent many years as a parish priest in the Diocese of Columbus. He was stationed at Jackson, Ohio, and St. Joseph Cathedral in Columbus. For a time, he also served as chaplain of St. Francis Hospital and St. Anthony Hospital in Columbus. He was the organizing pastor of Holy Rosary Parish in Columbus. He supervised the construction of a permanent Holy Rosary Church in 1915 and established a parish elementary and high school. In 1901 Howard organized the first Columbus Diocesan School Board. In the following year, he participated in the establishment of the National Catholic Education Association (NCEA). For the next 42 years, he held offices in the NCEA: he was secretary general from 1903 to 1928, president from 1928 to 1936, and a member of the Advisory Board until his death in 1944.

In 1923 he received word from the Vatican that he had been appointed the fifth bishop of Covington, and he was consecrated a bishop on July 15, 1923, at St. Mary Cathedral in Covington, by Archbishop Henry Moeller of Cincinnati. Howard led the Diocese of Covington through the years of the **Great Depression**, the anti-Catholic bigotry of the Ku Klux Klan (the 1920s), the devastating **flood of 1937**, **World War II**, and the initial development of the suburbs in Northern Kentucky. He greatly expanded the activities of Catholic social services in the diocese and accelerated the growth of the church in the mountain counties served by the diocese. During his tenure as bishop, he established new parishes in Fort Thomas (**St. Catherine of Sienna**), Fort Wright, Hazard, Paintsville, and Southgate. Howard also appointed the first resident pastors at St. Leo Parish in Versailles, Ky., and St. Stephen Parish in Himlerville (Beauty). In 1943 he began organizing the **Our Savior** parish and school in Covington for the **African American** community of Northern Kentucky.

Education was one of Howard's primary concerns. He worked enthusiastically to improve and expand the Catholic school system, overseeing the establishment of several central high schools in the diocese: **Covington Catholic High School**, **Covington Latin School**, Lexington Latin School, and **Newport Central Catholic High School**. In addition, Howard transformed Villa Madonna College (see **Thomas More College**), established in 1921 by the **Sisters of St. Benedict** of Covington, into a diocesan institution under the direction of the three major religious orders of women in Northern Kentucky.

Howard's philosophy of education was at odds with the general thinking of the day. He strongly believed that parents were the primary teachers of their children and that secular authorities should not interfere with this basic right. Consolidation of small rural schools, standardization in education, the expansion of curriculum outside the classical disciplines, and secularization were all rejected by Howard. His education motto summed up his thoughts on curriculum: "teach few things, but teach them well." He also rejected the idea of state funding for Catholic schools, believing that any such aid would come with strings attached and would thus compromise the educational standards of the parish schools.

Howard died in 1944 in Covington. Following a funeral mass at St. Mary Cathedral, he was laid to rest at St. Mary Cemetery in Fort Mitchell.

Messenger, special memorial ed., 1944, 15–18.
Tenkotte, Paul A., David E. Schroeder, and Thomas S. Ward. *To Be Catholic and American in Northern, Central, and Appalachian Kentucky: The Diocese of Covington, 1853–2003.* Forthcoming.

David E. Schroeder

HOWARD, ULIE (b. June 22, 1874, Ghent, Ky.; d. October 17, 1947, Fort Mitchell, Ky.). Lawyer and politician Ulie J. Howard was born in Carroll Co., the son of John and Mary Scott Howard. His early education was in the local public schools. He graduated from **Ghent College** in Ghent and apprenticed law in the Carrollton office of Judge Joseph A. Donaldson. In 1894 Howard began law school at Centre College, in Danville, Ky. He passed the Kentucky bar exam in 1895 and set up practice in Covington. In 1901 he formed a partnership with **Harvey J. Myers Jr.**, to create the law firm of Myers and Howard, which soon became one of the most prominent in Northern Kentucky.

Howard married Carrie Brent Alexander on April 21, 1897, and they had only one child, Charlton Alexander Howard, who was born on December 23, 1900. The family lived at 312 E. Second St., in Covington. Ulie's wife, Carrie, died on November 9, 1917. Ulie married a widow, Aileen Brown Southgate, in 1918, and they made their home in Fort Mitchell. When Harvey Myers Jr. died on July 1, 1933, Ulie created a new partnership with his son, Charlton Alexander "Alex" Howard. They opened an office in the **Coppin's Department Store** building in Covington at the corner of Seventh St. and Madison Ave. In 1927 Ulie Howard was elected Kenton Co. commonwealth attorney. His son became a Kentucky state senator but died young in 1947. Later that same year, Ulie J. Howard died of a cerebral hemorrhage at his Fort Mitchell home. Both he and his son were buried in Highland Cemetery in Fort Mitchell.

Johnson, E. Polk. *A History of Kentucky and Kentuckians.* New York: Lewis, 1912.
Rootsweb. "Ulie J. Howard." www.rootsweb.com (accessed December 31, 2005).

HUBBARD, ANNA WONDER (b. September 7, 1902, Grand Rapids, Mich.; d. May 3, 1986, Payne Hollow, Trimble Co., Ky.). Anna Hubbard and her husband, **Harlan Hubbard**, an artist and writer, were married for 43 years and lived a deliberately simple, self-sufficient life.

Anna was born in Michigan, the daughter of John and Nellie Ross Eikenhout. She graduated with honors from Ohio State University in Columbus and taught French and German at Hope College in Holland, Mich., for two years before moving to Cincinnati to take a position as a fine arts librarian at the Cincinnati Public Library. She met Harlan Hubbard there.

Anna Hubbard was a skilled pianist and cellist and an avid reader in three foreign languages. She was also reserved and quiet like her husband. The Hubbards were married in 1943 and lived for a short time in a tiny studio behind Harlan's mother's home in Fort Thomas. In 1944 they moved to Brent, along the Ohio River in Campbell Co., and lived in a tent on the riverbank while Harlan Hubbard built a shantyboat. They lived for two years in the shantyboat before traveling in it downriver to Louisiana. Their journey took five years to complete.

After their return to Fort Thomas, the Hubbards moved to Payne Hollow, a remote, wooded valley by the Ohio River in Trimble Co., Ky., nine miles downriver from Madison, Ind. It was a place they had fallen in love with on their shantyboat trip. They built their own rustic home and boat and grew their own food, canning fruits and vegetables for the winter months. In the evenings the Hubbards wrote in their journals, read to each other by candlelight, or played music together. Anna Hubbard was a gracious hostess to visitors at Payne Hollow. She died at age 84 in 1986, and her ashes were buried along the path leading to her home at Payne Hollow.

"Anna Hubbard, Woman of Quiet Strength, Dies," *KP,* May 6, 1986, 1K–2K.
Cunningham, Mia. *Anna Hubbard: Out of the Shadows.* Lexington: Univ. Press of Kentucky, 2001.
Hubbard, Harlan. *Payne Hollow: Life on the Fringe of Society.* Frankfort, Ky.: Gnomon Press, 1974.
———. *Payne Hollow Journal.* Lexington: Univ. Press of Kentucky, 1996.

Bill Thomas

HUBBARD, HARLAN (b. January 4, 1900, Bellevue, Ky.; d. January 16, 1988, Madison, Ind.). Harlan Hubbard was a writer, an accomplished musician, and an artist who produced many paintings of the Northern Kentucky countryside and of riverboats and shantyboats on the Ohio River. He is often referred to as the Henry David Thoreau of Kentucky. Hubbard wrote a number of autobiographical books, including *Shantyboat* and *Payne Hollow.*

Hubbard was born in a house on Grandview Ave. in Bellevue, Campbell Co., the son of Frank G. and Rose Swingle Hubbard. His father died when Harlan was seven years old, and a short time later, he and his mother moved to an apartment in New York City, to be closer to Hubbard's two older brothers. Hubbard finished high school in New York and turned down a scholarship offer from Cornell University. Instead, he attended the National Academy of Design in New York for two years. A visit to the Metropolitan Museum of Art was the turning point in his life. After viewing paintings of the great postimpressionist artists, he wrote, "I grasped the meaning of Cezanne, Gauguin, and Van Gogh, and was never the same afterwards." Hubbard returned to his brother's art studio after his visit to the museum and completed his first oil painting. This was the moment he decided to be an artist.

In 1921 Hubbard and his mother returned to Northern Kentucky. His mother rented an apartment in Fort Thomas, and Hubbard went to work doing odd jobs for builders in the community. Rose Hubbard found a job working for a newspaper in Cincinnati, and soon she and her son purchased a lot on Highland Ave. in Fort Thomas. Harlan Hubbard designed and built their home himself. It was patterned after an old farmhouse he had seen while walking in the country. The Hubbards' home is located near Ruth Moyer School.

About the year 1929, Hubbard began to visit the little town of Brent, Ky., on the Ohio River. He stored his canoe there and eventually constructed a crude art studio near the river. He painted many river scenes while he was in Brent. Between 1936 and 1937, he moved his Fort Thomas studio to a hill overlooking the Ohio River and painted more than 100 landscapes of Campbell Co. A year or two later, Hubbard built another studio behind his mother's home in Fort Thomas and began to paint there. His brick studio now sits on the edge of the Highland Hills Park.

Hubbard's personality was well suited for the often solitary nature of landscape painting. His landscapes depict a sense of stability and permanence in nature, both of which are abiding themes throughout his work.

Hubbard married Anna Eikenhout (see **Anna Hubbard**), a Cincinnati librarian, in 1943, a few months before his mother died. The couple went on hiking trips in New England and Michigan and afterward lived in the studio behind the family home in Fort Thomas. During winter 1944 they moved to Brent and lived in a tent along the bank of the Ohio River while Hubbard constructed a shantyboat. The Hubbards lived on the river in Brent for the next two years in their 10-by-16-foot shantyboat. Hubbard rented out his Fort Thomas home in order to have a source of income.

The Hubbards spent the next five years traveling down the Ohio and the Mississippi rivers to the bayou country of Louisiana in their shantyboat. Before returning home, they sold their shantyboat, bought an old car, and took a 10-month tour of the western United States. Hubbard wrote the book *Shantyboat* during this trip. The couple returned to Fort Thomas in 1952 and lived in Hubbard's studio for a short time before deciding that the city was losing some of its small-town appeal—that is, it was becoming too civilized. The Hubbards decided to pack their car and trailer and move to Payne Hollow on the Ohio River in Trimble Co., Ky. They had spent a summer at Payne Hollow on the first leg of their journey by shantyboat to Louisiana. Payne Hollow was so isolated that it could not be reached by car. The Hubbards had to walk down a half-mile path from a farm on the top of the hill to reach their new home. Visitors either walked the same path or arrived by boat. The Hubbards purchased seven acres in Payne Hollow and lived there for the remainder of their lives.

Hubbard built a small home on a hillside above the river. The dominant feature of the house was the large window overlooking the river. The walls, ceilings, and doors were all wood. The main room served as a living room, a kitchen, a dining room, and a bedroom. Hubbard also dug a cistern, made a johnboat, and planted a vegetable garden near the river. He built a studio and workshop on the steep hill next to the house, and there he created paintings and fashioned woodcuts. He also constructed a goat house next to the vegetable garden and a tiny guesthouse on a hill on the other side of a creek.

The Hubbards grew their own food, made their own furniture (except for a grand piano that Anna played each evening), and lived without electricity or running water. Hubbard did most of the heavy work and would take time each day to write in his journal and paint. In the evenings, the Hubbards would read to each other or play music together. Hubbard played the violin and viola.

Although he was an introvert and a difficult person to get to know, Harlan Hubbard was a deep thinker who revealed himself in his writing and paintings. He was a gifted writer with a philosopher's mind. Hubbard's accomplishments as a landscape painter continue, even today, to build his stature in the world of art. His art depicted his life and the world around him; he painted the small towns, hills, valleys, and rivers he loved. It has taken many years for Hubbard's artwork to be appreciated. His entries for the annual exhibit at the Cincinnati Art Museum were rejected nine years in a row, and his paintings from the period 1920–1940 were stored at his studio on Highland Ave. in Fort Thomas for almost 30 years. Today, his paintings are on exhibit at the Behringer-Crawford Museum in Covington and at Hanover College in Madison, Ind.

Anna Hubbard died in 1986, and Harlan Hubbard died of cancer two years later at age 88. He died in the living room of Dr. Robert Canida's home in Madison, Ind., and his ashes were buried along the pathway leading to the Payne Hollow home. There is a stone marker on the rock at the gravesite, carved by Mike Skop, a retired art professor at **Northern Kentucky University**. The carving shows a simple heart with the names Anna and Harlan inscribed inside it.

Berry, Wendell. *Harlan Hubbard: Life and Work.* Lexington: Univ. Press of Kentucky, 1990.

Gateley, Joe, and Faye Gately. Interview by Bill Thomas, October 13, 1999, Fort Thomas, Ky.

Hubbard, Harlan. *Payne Hollow: Life on the Fringe of Society.* Frankfort, Ky.: Gnomon Press, 1974.

———. *Payne Hollow Journal.* Lexington: Univ. Press of Kentucky, 1996.

Skop, Mike, and Kathy Skop. Interview by Bill Thomas, October 22, 1999, Fort Thomas, Ky.

Bill Thomas

HUBER, JUSTIN (b. November 23, 1892, Covington, Ky.; d. September 8, 1969, Grayson, Ky.). Orchestra conductor and composer Edward Justin Huber was the son of Henry and Elizabeth Jane Davis Huber. His father was a barber, and the family lived in Covington. Having a good ear for music, Justin had mastered playing the drums by age four. He was regarded as a child prodigy in music. As a youth he appeared in local vaudeville acts, performing the cakewalk at such places as the Ludlow Lagoon (see **Lagoon Amusement Park**) and the Covington Opera House. In high school he was a member of various musical groups and played the calliope on Ohio River steamboats during the summer. There were very few instruments he could not play.

Huber married a cousin from Ohio, Josephine Eckenroth, on March 15, 1911, in Covington. Soon afterward he published a "catchy" Indian ragtime piece entitled "Fire Water." His employment was as a secretary for a railroad and at the Covington post office. In 1919 he was a pianist for a local jazz orchestra—admirers referred to his "wicked fingers." In the early 1920s, Huber and his family moved to the Hyde Park area of Cincinnati, where he formed an orchestra. First appearing in 1922, his orchestra played in many places, including Chester Park in Cincinnati; **Horseshoe Gardens** in Bellevue; Buckeye Lake, east of Columbus, Ohio; the Ritz Hotel in New York City; the opening of the Florentine Room at the Gibson Hotel in Cincinnati; and various dance palaces throughout Pennsylvania. In addition, orchestra performances were broadcast over WLW radio in Cincinnati. Generally, the orchestra consisted of 10 to 12 members and it played for both round and square dancing. It performed at many corporate functions as after-dinner entertainment. By 1938 the grueling demands of his travels had caught up with Huber. He disbanded his orchestra and went into the coal business, investing in coal mines.

Over the years Huber's musical groups went by various names, depending on the occasion and the type of music requested—symphony or jazz. Mainly, they were known as Justin Huber's Orchestra (early 1920s), the Kentucky Colonels' Orchestra (late 1920s), Huber's Orchestra (1930s), Justin Huber's 10 Piece Orchestra (1930s), Justin Huber and His Original 11 Piece Recording Orchestra (1930s), and, in New York City, Justin Huber and His Cincinnati Society Orchestra (mid 1930s).

Throughout his life Huber also composed music, some of which was published, but none of his music sold in any significant volume. His wife, Josephine, died in 1955, and afterward Huber set up a recording studio in Blue Ash, Ohio. Following a short unsuccessful second marriage, he closed the studio and moved to Charleston, W.Va., to sell pianos at a music store. He spent the last years of his life in Grayson as the music director for radio station WGOH-A.M. Several times each broadcast day, Huber presented live five-minute piano interludes. In Grayson he married for a third time in 1961. A lifelong smoker, Huber died of emphysema at age 77 in 1969 and was buried at Highland Cemetery in Fort Mitchell, next to his parents.

Edward Justin Huber Microfilm Collection, Kenton Co. Public Library, Covington, Ky. A two-microfilm set.
"Justin Huber," *CE*, September 9, 1969, 33.
"Kentucky Jazz Artist," *KP*, November 6, 1919, 1.
Kline, Elinor J. "Edward Justin Huber (1892–1969)," microfilm, Kenton Co. Public Library, Covington, Ky.
"Young Covington Composer," *KP*, December 16, 1911, 3.

HUMPHREY, WILLIAM (b. December 24, 1879, Mason Co., Ky.; d. September 20, 1958, Maysville, Ky.). William Humphrey, a well-known African American teacher, was the son of George and Annetta Berry Humphrey. Professor Humphrey, as he became known, began his academic career at age 13 while working as a school janitor at the colored school in Maysville. He finished 10 grades of school there in 6 years. He then attended Berea College in Berea for five years, working as a headwaiter at the same time. At Berea College, he completed his last two years of high school and three years of college, earning his BA in 1904. A year of graduate study at Harvard University in Cambridge, Mass., followed, but health problems made it necessary for him to return to Maysville for a period of rest. He later earned an MA from Ohio State University in Columbus and a BS at Tuskegee Institute in Tuskegee, Ala.

At this time, Humphrey was asked to work with African Americans in Mason Co., and he helped to rebuild the county's colored school at Mayslick, which had burned. His teaching career began there. The following year, he took a teaching position at the old colored school in Maysville, where he served as principal from 1907 to 1930. In 1930 the **John G. Fee Industrial High School** was built on E. Fourth St. in Maysville, and Humphrey served as its principal for a total of 42 years. Under his direction it became a four-year high school for African Americans. Through his influence, the integration that took place in the late 1950s within the Maysville schools was accomplished more smoothly, even though he had retired in 1949.

In 1930 Humphrey was chosen as president of the Kentucky Negro Education Association. Over the years, he served as a deacon and in every official lay position in Maysville's **Bethel Baptist Church**. From March 1950, when the Maysville Municipal Housing Commission was established to oversee the city's 100-unit low-cost housing program, until his death, Humphrey was part of the four-member governing body of the commission. In 1951 he became a director in the Mason Co. Fund, the forerunner of the United Appeal agency in the county.

Humphrey's wife, whom he married June 16, 1920, was Allie Young, from Bath Co., Ky. They had two sons and also raised a foster daughter and three nephews. Humphrey died in Maysville at his home at 614 E. Third St. in 1958 and was buried in the Washington Baptist Cemetery in Washington, Ky.

Calvert, Jean, and John Klee. *Maysville, Kentucky: From Past to Present in Pictures.* Maysville, Ky.: Mason Co. Museum, 1983.
"Long Useful Life of City's Leading Colored Citizen Ends," *Maysville Public Ledger,* September 22, 1958, 1.
Stout, Louis. *Shadows of the Past.* Lexington, Ky.: Host Communications, 2006.
"W. H. Humphrey Former Head at Fee, Dies," *Maysville Daily Independent,* September 22, 1958, 1.
"William Humphrey an Honor to His Native City, Maysville, and Kentucky," *Maysville Public Daily Ledger,* June 15, 1904, 2.

Mary Ellen Lucas

HUNT, FRANK WILLIAMS, CAPTAIN (b. December 16, 1861, Newport, Ky.; d. November 26, 1906, Goldfield, Nev.). Frank Williams Hunt, who became governor of Idaho, was the son of Thomas Benjamin Hunt, a captain in the Union Army during the Civil War, and Eugenia A. Montmolin Hunt. Frank Hunt attended Newport schools. It was not academics, though, but adventure that interested Hunt; he was a pioneer in the tradition of **Simon Kenton** and **Daniel Boone**. In 1888 Hunt headed west in search of both adventure and business opportunities. He settled in Idaho, where he invested in the mining industry.

Idaho territory in 1888 included not only what is today Idaho but also today's states of Montana and Wyoming. The Idaho Territory, formed during the gold rush, was governed by an appointee of the U.S. president. In 1889 the territorial political leaders met in Boise and drafted a state constitution, which was adopted by territorial leaders on August 6, 1889, and approved by voters in the territory. On July 3, 1890, Idaho became the 43rd state in the union.

Whether or not Hunt was among the 68 leaders who drew up the constitution, he was soon involved in Idaho state politics. In 1893 he was elected to the Idaho state senate. On November 10, 1896, he married Ruth Maynard, the daughter of John W. Maynard of Boise. When the Spanish-American War (see **National Guard, Spanish-American War**) began in 1898, Hunt joined the army with the rank of 1st lieutenant in the 1st Idaho Volunteers. His unit, which shipped to the Philippines, took part in the capture of Manila on August 13, 1898. After the Spanish surrender, Hunt stayed in the Philippines to battle rebels who were angry that the United States had not granted them independence. Hunt ended his military service as a captain and returned to Idaho to resume politics and mining.

In 1900 Hunt ran as a Democratic candidate for governor in the state, which was heavily Republican, and won with 50.8 percent of the votes. He was sworn in as Idaho's fifth governor on January 7, 1901. The term was for two years. It was during his administration that the Academy of Idaho at Pocatello, the forerunner of Idaho State University, was established. As governor, Hunt sought to attract business from the east to Idaho in order to gain more jobs for the people. He also supported the 8-hour workday when 10 hours was a common working shift. Two years later, he sought reelection but was defeated by Republican John T. Morrison.

After his defeat, Hunt settled in Emmett, Idaho, and continued in the mining business. He later was named vice president of the Dewey Combination Lease Company, which operated mines in Goldfield, Nev. He also continued his involvement in Idaho statewide politics. In 1904 he was a state delegate to the national Democratic convention. Hunt died from pneumonia in 1906 at age 44 and was buried at the Masonic Cemetery in Boise, Idaho.

Purvis, Thomas L., ed. *Newport, Kentucky: A Bicentennial History.* Newport, Ky.: Otto Zimmerman, 1996.
Reis, Jim. "Fame Found Out West—Newport Native Served as Fifth Governor of Idaho," *KP*, December 1, 2003, 5K.

Jim Reis

HUNT, ROBERT WOOLSTON (b. December 9, 1838, Fallsington, Bucks Co., Pa.; d. July 11, 1923, Chicago, Ill.). Metallurgist Robert W. Hunt received his early education in the schools of Covington and went on to study analytical chemistry in Philadelphia. In 1860 he established the first analytical laboratory associated with a steelworks in the United States. During the **Civil War**, he was the commandant of Camp Curtin in Harrisburg, Pa., with the rank of captain in the Union Army. It was the largest training camp of the war; almost 300,000 Union troops passed through it. After the war, Hunt assisted George Fritz in building the first Bessemer steelworks for the Cambria Iron Company at Johnstown, Pa. Hunt went on to develop Bessemer mills in Michigan and in Troy, N.Y., where he became associated with the nation's oldest engineering school, Rensselaer Polytechnic Institute. He became a member of that school's board of trustees in 1886, and in 1888 he started the Robert W. Hunt Company to apply demanding standards of inspection and testing throughout the steel and iron industry; the company he founded continues today, based in Pittsburgh. Hunt received several engineering awards, including the John Fritz Medal in 1912 and the Washington Award in 1923. He contributed greatly to the literature of his field of research. A personal friend of Andrew Carnegie, Hunt was the first person in modern history to be awarded an honorary degree by Rensselaer Polytechnic Institute. His estate endowed the Hunt Professorship in Metallurgical Engineering at the school. Hunt died at his home in Chicago in 1923 and was buried at the Oakwood Cemetery in Troy, N.Y.

"Captain Robert W. Hunt," *NYT*, July 12, 1923, 17.
Illinois Death Certificate No. 6019591, for the year 1923.
Oakwood Cemetery Records, Troy, N.Y.

Rensselaer. "Robert Woolston Hunt," in the Rensselaer Polytechnic Institute Hall of Fame. www.rpi.edu (accessed October 28, 2006).

Wilson, James Grant, and John Fiske, eds. *Appleton's Cyclopedia of American Biography*. New York: D. Appleton, 1894.

HUNTER, JACOB (b. ca. 1760, Rowan Co, N.C.; d. March 1856, Owen Co., Ky.). Jacob Hunter was an early pioneer and explorer of the area that became Owen Co., and that is where he settled. In 1780 he was one of the first to file for land in the Owen Co. area, according to Virginia Land Office records. He was a private in the **Revolutionary War**, in the Virginia lines, and in 1833 he received a pension for his service. Hunter was married three times. He died in 1856 in Owen Co. He was originally buried at the Hunter Cemetery on Big Twin, but his remains were moved to the Owenton International Order of Odd Fellows Cemetery in 1983.

Houchens, Mariam Sidebottom. *History of Owen County: "Sweet Owen."* Louisville, Ky.: Standard, 1976.

HUNTER'S BOTTOM. This 10-mile stretch of Carroll Co. bottomland from Locust Creek to Canip Creek was named for Joshua Hunter, who put his rough cabin here and claimed a preemption from Fincastle Co., Va. A long portage trail angling south-southeast from Tippecanoe in northwestern Indiana crossed the Ohio River near Madison, Ind.; this trail led through Hunter's Bottom. There, the first surveyors and settlers found much evidence of American Indian seasonal residence on the banks of the Ohio. The Potawatomi may have been only the latest tribe to inhabit this fertile land; some of the artifacts—arrowheads, ax fragments, bones, shards—trace back to the Adena and Mississippian era several hundred years before any white man arrived. French explorers and traders had also passed through the area. Among the earliest surveys entered in the Hunter's Bottom area were several Fincastle and Kentucky Co. entries: 3,500 acres by John May, 800 acres by Thomas Brown, and 1,700 acres by John Saunders. None of these became permanent settlers.

In 1797 Cornelius Hoagland (see **Hoagland Family**) and his brother-in-law Charles Hoff, both Revolutionary War officers from old-line Dutch families of New Amsterdam (New York City) and New Jersey, entered surveys for 1,000 acres each and cleared some land. But it was not until 1801 that Hoagland brought his family down the Ohio River to settle in the upper stretch of Hunter's Bottom. The Hoagland children and descendants dominated society in the eastern end of Hunter's Bottom until well into the 20th century.

John Conway and his wife Mary Elizabeth Hopwood came to Hunter's Bottom in 1803 from Fauquier Co., Va. They settled on 300 acres at the Canip Creek end of Hunter's Bottom and raised seven children. John Conway, one of the children, married Emily Hoagland, and his brother Peter Conway married Mary Caroline Hoagland Kent, thus cementing family ties between the two ends of Hunter's Bottom. Peter and Mary Caroline Conway settled near the mouth of Locust Creek, and their son George built a large farmhouse that stands today just to the west, owned by Rudy Conway, a descendant.

In 1803 Samuel Fearn (see **Fearn Family**) moved his extensive family from Bourbon Co. to Hunter's Bottom. The Fearns purchased 1,000 acres straddling what became the border between Carroll and Trimble counties at Spillman Rd. By 1850 the Fearn family had built a large gristmill at Milton, dabbled in real estate on both sides of the Ohio River, and constructed large brick houses. After the **Civil War**, the next generation of Fearns operated a packet steamship business, with the *Maggie Harper* serving Louisville, Madison, Carrollton, and the Kentucky River. The Fearns also were founders of the Hunter's Bottom Turnpike Company. The original road through Hunter's Bottom ran on the bank of the Ohio River and was annually flooded, making transport difficult. So the residents moved the road several hundred feet south to the position of Ky. Rt. 36, paying the expenses through subscriptions to the Turnpike Company. The Fearns eventually built more large brick homes. Five gracious homes in Hunter's Bottom were attributed to the Fearn family, including Fearn Hill, on the National Register, the Sam Fearn place, and Richwood, which served as an upscale riding camp and is now a bread and breakfast.

Up on the hillside above Hunter's Bottom, the Taylor family dated from the earliest settlement period. Several branches of this family remain in the area. Cornelius Deweese, Francis Giltner, and William White appeared at Hunter's Bottom in the 1820s. They settled in the middle section of the bottoms on old Hoagland lands. William White married into the Hoagland family. The Deweese place was remarkable for its three-story brick facade, its iron grille upper porch, and its large, formal pear and apple orchards. Cornelius Deweese, although not a Methodist, donated a lot on the northwest corner of his farm where the Hopewell Methodist Church was built.

Several German immigrants arrived at Hunter's Bottom in the 1840s. The Johann Obertödler family was already in residence in 1848, when the Friedrich Detmer family moved from Rising Sun, Ind. A German-speaking Reform congregation was established and met at the Hopewell Methodist Church until 1895; in that year the Methodists moved to Locust. The following year, the families of Friedrich Detmer, Heinrich Hotfil, Johann Obertödler (Obertate), Fred Thiemann, Frank Thiemann, and Karl Walkenhorst formed a German Evangelical Protestant congregation and built a church next to the Hopewell School.

Residing among the landowners at Hunter's Bottom before the Civil War were a number of slaves, at the most 8 to 10 slaves on a large plantation. Relations between slave owners and their slaves varied widely. Two cases—**Adam Crosswhite** and **Richard Daly**—became part of the larger American history.

Hunter's Bottom School, the earliest permanent school built in Carroll Co., was constructed in 1846 as a one-room log structure on one-quarter acre of land donated by William White. When the common school system was organized in 1867, Hunter's Bottom School was designated as School District No. 12. Most of the early teachers at Hunter's Bottom were male. The Hunter's Bottom school district was consolidated when a two-story brick structure was built at Locust in 1910; the children were then bused from the river bottoms to Locust. After the 1963 consolidation of the western area into the combined Carrollton and Carroll Co. school system, both Hunter's Bottom and Locust children were bused into town.

Even though steamboats still ran along the Ohio and would stop at private and public landings as late as the 1930s to take people to Louisville, railroads had made such economic impact that the great days of steamboats were finished. By 1900 many of the old settler families began moving out of Hunter's Bottom, to be replaced by new people.

Carrollton Democrat, May 8, 1884.

Family Bible of Emma McClaran Fearn, in possession of Larry Douglas Smith of Louisville, Ky.

Gentry, Mary Ann. *A History of Carroll County*. Madison, Ind.: Coleman, 1984.

Hammon, Neal O. *Early Kentucky Land Records, 1773–1780*. Louisville, Ky.: Filson Club, 1992.

Smith, Larry Douglas. "The Fearns of Hunters Bottom, Kentucky," Kentucky Historical Society, Frankfort, Ky.

Diane Perrine Coon

HUNTINGTON BANK. P. W. Huntington began working as a messenger for a Columbus, Ohio, bank in 1853, at age 17. He stayed with the bank for 13 years and then in 1866 opened his own bank, named P. W. Huntington and Company; however, in 1905 he incorporated it as the Huntington National Bank of Columbus.

In 1966 Huntington Bank created its International Banking Division, and in 1972 it became the first bank in the United States to offer 24-hour banking. Huntington Bank is currently one of the nation's 40 largest multibank holding companies. It has more than 8,000 employees at 350 offices in eight states, most of them in Indiana, Kentucky, Michigan, Ohio, and West Virginia. With the advent of interstate banking in the 1980s, Huntington Bank moved into the Northern Kentucky market, acquiring Commonwealth Trust Bank Corp., parent of the old Covington Trust Company, in 1986. Covington Trust had its headquarters for many years at the northeast corner of Sixth St. and Madison Ave. in Covington.

Huntington Bank currently operates 49 banking offices with about 800 employees in Cincinnati and Northern Kentucky. Eleven of the bank's offices are located in the two counties of Boone and Kenton. The bank is an avid supporter of many local charities.

Huntington. "Huntington Customer Services: Community Affairs." http:www.huntington.com (accessed April 11, 2007).

HURRELL, GEORGE EDWARD (b. June 1, 1904, Covington, Ky., d. May 17, 1992, Los Angeles, Calif.). George Hurrell, the photographer who set the standard for the glamorized publicity stills in Hollywood, was the son of Edward Eugene and Anna M. Hurrell. His father was a shoemaker; his mother was born in Baden-Baden, Germany. While some sources list Cincinnati as George Hurrell's birthplace, Hurrell himself clearly states in correspondence that he was born in Covington, Ky. He was raised in Cincinnati until age five, when the family moved to Chicago.

At about age eight, Hurrell became interested in painting and drawing. He learned to use a camera to photograph and study his own paintings. When he was 16, in 1920, he attended the Art Institute of Chicago on a scholarship, but he soon found that working as a photographer provided a needed income. In 1925 Hurrell moved to Laguna Beach, Calif., and was commissioned to photograph painters and their paintings. He had more success, however, photographing the society crowd. He moved to Los Angeles in 1927 and worked briefly with the famous photographer Edward Steichen, who influenced him to pursue celebrity portraiture.

Named the "Grand Seignior of the Hollywood Portrait," Hurrell produced images of the Golden Age in the 1930s and early 1940s. His most famous ones pictured Humphrey Bogart, James Cagney, Joan Crawford, Betty Davis, Clark Gable, Greta Garbo, Jean Harlow, Rita Hayworth, Katherine Hepburn, Ramon Navarro, Tyrone Power, Jane Russell, Norma Shearer, and Mae West. His art background as a painter enhanced his instinctive awareness of how to utilize exposure, composition, and contrast in his photographs to present his subjects best, thereby gaining their complete confidence. The unmistakable Hurrell look was achieved by his control of a movable boom light, combined with key lighting at high angles, to create lush and dramatic images that were sensual yet spiritual.

Hurrell's classic glamour Hollywood portraits were discovered by a later generation when they were exhibited at New York's Museum of Modern Art in 1965. Soon, exhibitions in other major museums throughout the world created an ongoing revival of interest in his early works. Numerous art books were published of his glamorized images, placing him in the spotlight for a second career, during which he photographed celebrities such as Warren Beatty, Natalie Cole, Liza Minnelli, Paul Newman, Robert Redford, Sharon Stone, and John Travolta.

After 60 years as the most legendary glamour-portrait photographer of the stars, George Hurrell died of cancer at age 87 in 1992. His portraits of Hollywood luminaries created the idealized images of movie icons from the Golden Age that are highly valued and avidly collected today. A documentary film entitled *Legends in Light: The Photography of George Hurrell* (directed by Carl Colby) premiered on the TNT cable television network in 1995.

"George Hurrell," vertical files, Kenton Co. Public Library, Covington, Ky.

Keating, Michael E. "Looking at Stars for Your Close-ups," *CE*, January 27, 2007, 1E.

Vieira, Mark A., and George Hurrell. *Hurrell's Hollywood Portraits: The Chapman Collection.* New York: Harry N. Abrams, 1997.

John Schlipp

HUTCHERSON, JOSH (b. October 12, 1992, Union, Ky.). Joshua Ryan Hutcherson, one of the nation's up-and-coming child actors, is steadily obtaining larger movie roles. The son of Chris and Christina Michelle Fightmaster Hutcherson, Josh grew up with his younger brother, Connor, in Northern Kentucky. Josh's interest in acting prompted him to sign a management contract with the Heyman Talent Agency in Cincinnati. Afterward, he traveled to Los Angeles, accompanied by his mother, to pursue an acting career.

The young actor has made guest appearances in a variety of television shows: *Jimmy Kimmel Live, Justice League, Line of Fire, The Division,* and *ER*. His movie career includes *Miracle Dogs* (2003), *American Splendor* (2003), *Motorcross Kids* (2004), *The Polar Express* (2004), *Zathura: A Space Adventure* (2006), *RV* (2006), *Bridge to Terabithia* (2007), *Firehouse Dog* (2007), *Winged Creatures* (2008), *Journey to the Center of the Earth 3-D* (2008), and *Cirque Du Freak* (scheduled for release in 2009). Hutcherson has won two Young Artist Awards: in 2004 for "Leading Young Actor in a TV Movie, Miniseries or Special" for his role in *Wilder Days* (TNT) and in 2008 for "Leading Young Actor in a Feature Film," for his role in *Bridge to Terabithia* (Buena Vista Pictures).

Hutcherson, Josh. E-mail to Mary Texter, November 22, 2005.

The Internet Movie Database. www.imdb.com (accessed December 12, 2005).

Mary Texter

HUTCHINSON, CONRAD, JR., "HUTCH," WARRANT OFFICER (b. October 25, 1919, Bloomsburg, Pa.; d. March 5, 1996, Grambling, La.). Conrad Hutchinson, an innovator in music for marching bands, was the son of Conrad and Helen Hutchinson. He earned his BA in music education from Tuskegee Institute in Macon Co., Ala. During **World War II** he served in the U.S. Army's Command Headquarters Band in Calcutta, India, and achieved the rank of warrant officer, junior grade. Hutchinson was awarded the Good Conduct Medal as well as the China, Burma, India Theater Medal, with five battle stars. In 1945 he became music director for the Lincoln-Grant Schools in Covington.

It was while Hutchinson was at the Lincoln-Grant Schools that he initiated marching to contemporary music; the result was the distinctive step style of marching that is commonly performed by many African American marching bands today. Hutchinson would march the high school band around the schoolyard in this style, never missing any of the musical notes. Ever the creative mentor, Hutchinson developed a lasting relationship between his students and their music. He also developed popular school dance and jazz bands, and a number of his students went on to play professionally in clubs in and around Cincinnati. While living in Covington, Hutchinson resided on W. 10th Street, on E. Bush St. and on Russell St.

When Hutchinson was not conducting the school bands, he worked for Cincinnati radio stations WSAI and WLW as staff organist, conducted theater bands and orchestras, and played the organ at churches. He was the staff arranger for Cincinnati's famed King Records and worked with the Big Three Music–Warner Brothers Publishers. He engaged in graduate study at the University of Cincinnati; Case Western Reserve University in Cleveland, Ohio; the New England Conservatory of Music; and Vandercook College of Music in Chicago, where he earned an MA in music education.

In 1952 Hutchinson left Covington and Lincoln-Grant Schools for a job at the Grambling State University in Louisiana, where he served as music director for more than 40 years, receiving numerous awards. In 1996 he died in Grambling, La., and was buried there.

"Celebration of Life, Conrad Hutchinson, Jr., March 9, 1996," Special Collections, A. C. Lewis Memorial Library, Grambling State Univ.

Grantonian, 1950, William Grant High School Year Book, in Theodore H. H. Harris's collection.

Theodore H. H. Harris

HYGEIA. William Bullock, an English naturalist and the owner of the Egyptian Hall Museum in London, England, visited Cincinnati in 1827 on his travels through Mexico and North America. Enchanted by the approximately 1,000-acre Elmwood estate of Northern Kentucky businessman **Thomas D. Carneal** (present-day Ludlow), Bullock purchased it in 1828 and began to make plans for developing a speculative town on the property, to be called Hygeia after the Greek goddess of health. Bullock enumerated the virtues of the locale, which included the beauty and healthfulness of the site, the freedoms and low taxes of the United States, the friendliness of Cincinnati, the fact that it was a thriving city, and the high quality and low cost of goods and provisions. He said, "Every hour I spent in this place . . . served to convince me, that, for the industrious peasant, artisan, manufacturer, or other person, with a small income, arising from capital, no situation I had seen embraced so many advantages as a place of residence." About the Elmwood estate, he wrote, "a finer site for building a small town of retirement, in the vicinity of a populous manufacturing city, could scarcely exist." Bullock anticipated that his proposed town would appeal not only to Americans but also to his acquaintances with limited incomes in Great Britain, where, he claimed, living expenses were three times those of the Cincinnati area. He intended Hygeia to be not merely a speculative town but one of the earliest planned suburban communities in the United States; though never executed, it remains a fascinating episode in American town-planning history.

Speculative towns were commonplace in the 19th-century U.S. West. Carneal had helped to lay out Covington in 1815, and it seems likely that he may himself have considered a town on the Elmwood site and encouraged Bullock in the idea. However, most American speculative towns had nondescript, gridiron plans and lacked the sophisticated layout and architectural character of Hygeia. Bullock recorded his design process: "I made a little model of the land, and determined to have it laid out to the best possible advantage with professional assistance, on my [return] to England." He had expertise to make both plaster and wax molds and evidently created his own topographical model of the site. Once back in London, for "professional assistance," he hired English Regency architect John Buonarotti Papworth (1775–1847) to design the town and its buildings. Bullock had previously retained Papworth, in 1819, to create a new gallery for the Egyptian Hall.

Papworth was a versatile and prolific architect who designed everything from landscapes to furniture and had a large practice in country houses and in urban commercial buildings with iron and glass fronts. He designed a palace for King Wilhelm I of Württemberg in Germany (which was not built) and thereafter made the most of the royal connection. Working-class housing interested him, and he published numerous designs for small villas and cottages. His architecture was eclectic and predicted the multiple styles of the 19th century. He laid out several streets in London and planned additions to nearby Dulwich and to Cheltenham in Gloucestershire. However, Hygeia was his most extensive and complete town-planning scheme.

A striking aspect of the Hygeia plan is its figural elegance. Its multiple geometries make it an arresting image on the page. This feature served Bullock well as he published the plan in his *Sketch of a Journey through the Western States of America*, intended as a description of his travels, a prospectus for his new town, and a laudatory account of Cincinnati. The abstract graphic qualities of the plan have continued to attract interest, and it has been frequently republished in books and articles on urban planning history. Some critics have faulted it for its functional deficiencies, for a lack of synthesis among its complex geometries, and for a "meaningless" use of diagonal streets that "lead nowhere," but such criticisms tend in part to misunderstand the plan, the first purpose of which was to provide a striking visual image to attract the notice of potential investors and residents.

Hygeia would have filled the 1,000 or so acres of Bullock's site, stretching more than two miles from east to west along a curve in the Ohio River, opposite and slightly west, downriver, from Cincinnati, covering much of the central area of current-day Ludlow. The town's northern boundary was the river, while on the south it climbed into the hills of what is now Covington's **Devou Park**. The centerpiece of the plan is a large circle-in-a-square of streets and drives; within the circle is another square, bisected by cross streets, forming four smaller squares composed of rows of townhouses looking outward onto naturalistic gardens containing freestanding villas and ornamental ponds. Four churches, facing north and south, interrupt the uniform ranges of townhouses and create architectural focal points. At the center is a minute, circular "fountain place." From the corners of the smaller squares, four diagonal streets radiate outward. Above the circular centerpiece, uphill to the south, three public buildings occupy the central axis of the plan: a town hall flanked by a museum and a library. Below the centerpiece, on the riverbank to the north, are flower and vegetable gardens, divided into small communal plots for the town residents. The western portion of the plan contains two squares of terraced townhouses facing inward onto central gardens; their perimeters are screened by ranges of outward-facing, semidetached villas (freestanding double houses or duplexes). Farther west are more dispersed streets of semidetached and freestanding villas.

The eastern portion of the plan (nearest Cincinnati), contains orthogonal ranges of semidetached villas; beyond these are communal stables and a market square, bordered by rows of shops, probably with shopkeepers' residences above. Farther east, on a small branch, is a brewery (the town's only manufacturing establishment), with long rows of workers' housing beyond. Near the riverfront are an inn, a public bath, and "Mr. Bullock's House" (the still-existing **Elmwood Hall**), its river view awkwardly blocked by a proposed row of semidetached villas. On a promontory to the southeast is a picturesquely planned cemetery with naturalistic walks and a central chapel like a small classical temple, all of which, as the caption states, are "like Père la Chaise [cemetery] at Paris" (laid out ca. 1803, by architect A. T. Brongniart). Had it been executed, this would have been the first such picturesque cemetery in America. The Hygeia plan has been credited as among the earliest of "garden cities." Indeed, Papworth called it a "Rural Town," and it contains large percentages of green space. Despite Bullock's speculative intentions, the plan exhibits some of the idealizing tendencies of Enlightenment utopias of the period, in this case not an ideally ordered industrial city (such as Robert Dale Owen's New Harmony, Ind., ca. 1825), but a beautiful, "gardenesque" alternative to the chaos and unhealthful conditions of emerging industrial cities.

Hygeia exhibits a further Enlightenment idea: an encyclopedic array of different planning, housing, and architectural typologies. It sums up several decades of British town-planning strategies (orthogonal, radial, and naturalistic, with squares, circuses, and picturesque gardens) and echoes various 18th- and early-19th-century extensions to existing cities, such as Bath, England; Edinburgh New Town, Scotland; and Regent St. and Regent's Park in London, the latter near Bullock's museum in Piccadilly. As was done for Regent St. and Regent's Park—also a speculative planning scheme—Bullock probably meant to build Hygeia in stages, the sales of each portion paying for the development of the next. Unlike the British town plans, however, which usually aimed at middle- and upper-class occupants, Hygeia exhibited a degree of social idealism by providing healthful cottages and small row houses for workers and artisans along with middle-class villas and residential squares. It included around 800 to 1,000 residential units, perhaps meant to accommodate 2,000 or more occupants. (By comparison, Cincinnati in 1827 had a population of about 20,000). As with similar English planned communities, Bullock and Papworth would have controlled the design of Hygeia's public buildings and houses. Papworth provided drawings for a variety of buildings in multiple styles, including Greek, Gothic, Italianate, Roman, and a simplified neoclassicism.

Despite its conceptual elegance, Hygeia failed. First, it was remote and lacked convenient transportation to Cincinnati. Boats and ferries formed the only direct connection to Hygeia. Bridges, roads, and railways to the site were still several decades in the future. Second, there was a lack of jobs: other than shops and the brewery, the absence of factories meant that workers would have no way to make a living. Hygeia was not planned as a wholly self-supporting community and thus posited a "suburban" dependence upon Cincinnati at a time significantly before the larger city developed real suburbs (the Hygeia plan preceded the development of the Cincinnati suburbs of Clifton and Glendale by a quarter century and Mariemont and Greenhills—which it conceptually resembled—by a full century). Hygeia failed to attract either local residents or British emigrants; had it been adjacent to London rather than Cincinnati, it might have succeeded. Finally, Bullock failed to foresee that sites downstream from developing industrial cities like Cincinnati would eventually themselves become industrial communities, while cleaner, upstream sites would become more desirable residential suburbs.

Perhaps needing capital, Bullock sold 710 acres of the estate to Israel Ludlow Jr. in 1831. Shortly thereafter, his friend Frances Trollope, an author who had lived in Cincinnati and visited Bullock at Elmwood Hall, published her famous book *The Domestic Manners of the Americans*, in which she lampooned Americans generally and Cincinnatians specifically, for their lack of culture. Her book perhaps sank Bullock's last hopes of attracting residents from Britain. Conceding defeat, he sold his remaining acreage in 1836, mostly to Israel Ludlow, and eventually returned to England.

From the 1830s on, the Ludlow family and their relatives the **Kenner family** slowly developed the town of Ludlow on the site. It has a simple grid of streets, with nothing of the complex character of Hygeia. In the 1870s, the completion of the **Cincinnati Southern Railroad** and the arrival of its shops and associated industries in Ludlow and the construction of a railway and pedestrian bridge across the Ohio River to Cincinnati solved at once the jobs and transportation problems of the little community, and it became something of a railway boom town, with an eventual population of 6,000. Ironically, several of the Hygeia housing types, such as freestanding houses and cottages, semidetached or double houses, and row houses, all in multiple architectural styles, did appear in Ludlow a half century and more after Bullock and Papworth's similar designs. The later 20th-century decline of the railroad and the gradual disappearance of industry from Ludlow has left it again a residential bedroom community in a quiet river setting, with small and medium-sized houses in a variety of styles, similar to Bullock's original vision (but lacking Papworth's avant-garde planning). Perhaps with preservation of its historic buildings and careful development of its riverfront, Ludlow can yet recapture some of the bucolic character promised by Hygeia.

The great virtue of Hygeia was its striking plan and architectural character. It was one of the earliest and most sophisticated suburbs proposed for America or, for that matter, Europe. Although its plan had little effect on the later development of Ludlow, perhaps the memory of Hygeia unconsciously raised the level of planning in neighboring Cincinnati, with its eventual picturesque cemeteries, garden suburbs, and other urban amenities.

Bullock, William. *Sketch of a Journey through the Western States of North America.* London, 1827. Reprinted in *Early Western Travels,* by Ruben G. Twaites. Cleveland, Ohio: Arthur H. Clark, 1905.

Choay, Francoise. *The Modern City.* New York: George Braziller, 1969.

Costeloe, Michael P. *William Bullock, Connoisseur and Virtuoso of the Egyptian Hall: Piccadilly to Mexico (1773–1849).* Bristol, UK: Univ. of Bristol, 2008.

———. "William Bullock and the Mexican Connection," *Mexican Studies/Estudios Mexicanos* 22 (Summer 2006): 275–309.

McHarcy, George. *Catalogue of the Drawings Collection of the Royal Institute of British Architects: Office of J. B. Papworth.* London: Riba and Gregg International, 1977.

Reps, John W. *The Making of Urban America: A History of City Planning in the United States.* Princeton, N.J.: Princeton Univ. Press, 1965.

Tenkotte, Paul A. "Rival Cities to Suburbs: Covington and Newport, Kentucky, 1790–1890," PhD diss., Univ. of Cincinnati, 1989.

Patrick Snadon

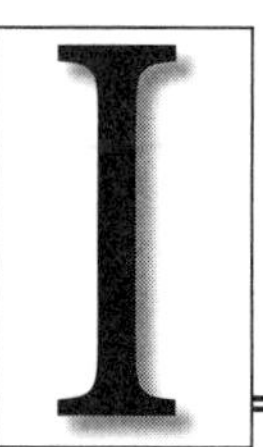

ICEHOUSES. A number of Northern Kentucky icehouses made and sold ice in the 19th and 20th centuries. Before electric refrigeration became widely available, ice played an important role in daily life. Loaded into iceboxes, it was used to preserve food. An icebox was a wooden box that had some resemblance to a present-day refrigerator; it could be as large as a refrigerator or even larger and was well insulated so that the 50-to-75-pound block of ice in a compartment at the top would keep the contents cold. As the ice melted, the water dripped into a pan at the bottom of the icebox. The pan had to be checked and emptied regularly in order to avoid an overflow.

In the early 1900s, well before World War I, the ice for iceboxes came from frozen lakes. During cold weather crews with horses pulling large saws would cut blocks of ice from the lakes. That ice was kept until needed in large storage buildings with thick walls insulated with sawdust.

As electricity became more readily available, ice was manufactured by icehouses, in 300-pound blocks, and kept in storage rooms. The manufacturing portion of the icehouse had large rooms whose floors were a grid of wooden blocks set on a steel frame. Under each wooden block was an ice can that was about 22 inches long, 12 inches wide, and four feet tall. The ice cans were filled with water and set in a brine solution. Large compressors circulated ammonia through a network of pipes that ran throughout the brine solution, chilling the brine enough to freeze the water in the cans. The compressors were cooled with water by the following process. Water was pumped to the top of a cooling tower on top of the ice-manufacturing building. The cooling tower could be as tall as a two-story building. The hot water splashed down through a series of panels that cooled it before it was returned to cool the compressors again. To keep the ice clear, air was blown through the water as it froze. After the block was about 90 percent frozen, the water and impurities were suctioned out and clean water was put in the resulting cavity and allowed to freeze solid. This process was called coring the ice. Each of the wooden blocks had a metal loop in the center, by which workers could lift the lid with a hook and check on the progress of the ice block underneath. Because few households needed such a large block of ice, the ice was cut by a scoring machine with saw blades into sections that could be broken into 25-to-50-pound blocks. The "snow" produced as a by-product of cutting ice was a treat for children during the hot summer months. The smaller blocks could also go into a crusher to produce crushed ice. The storage rooms where the ice was kept were well insulated and could have thick, hollow walls made of cork and filled with sawdust. A large storage room might be several stories high and hold hundreds of 300-pound blocks.

For home use, the iceman delivered these smaller blocks of ice weighing 25 to 50 pounds each. Early on, the iceman used a horse-drawn wagon. He would carry the ice into the customer's house using a set of ice tongs shaped like a figure 8 with a handle at the top and two sharp points on the bottom; the tongs could open and then close on the ice, gripping it securely. When the iceman had to transport a large block of ice, he would grip the block with the tongs and put it on his back to carry it. Trucks were later used to deliver ice, but the work of the iceman did not change. He still used the tongs and his back to transport the ice.

One company that provided both coal and ice during the 1900s was the Latonia Ice & Fuel Company in Latonia. Two brothers, Joe and Phil Mueller, began the company around 1902, and articles of incorporation were filed on September 1, 1908. At first the Muellers cut their ice from a spring-fed lake that was located where the present **Transit Authority of Northern Kentucky** bus barn is on Madison Pike in Latonia. They later built an ice-manufacturing plant on Eugenia Ave. in Latonia, adjacent to the **Louisville and Nashville Railroad** tracks that ran down to Latonia Ave.; there they sold both ice and coal. When the plant was running at full capacity, it could produce almost 100 blocks of ice, 300 pounds each, in 24 hours. After Joe's death in 1938, Phil continued the business. Latonia Ice & Fuel provided ice not only to individual homes and businesses but also for Fruit Growers Express railcars full of produce being shipped to market. By means of a winch, the railcars were positioned on the tracks that ran alongside the large storage room. Inside the storage room, an elevator brought the 300-pound blocks of ice up to the level of the top of the railcars, so that the ice could be moved onto platforms and loaded into the railcars from the top. Each railcar held approximately 160 to 180 of the 300-pound blocks. In the mid-1950s, refrigerated railcars were perfected and their use was phased in gradually over the next six or seven years, eliminating the need for iced railcars.

Phil Mueller died in 1954, and his family continued to operate the business. After the downturn in the demand for ice and coal, Latonia Ice & Fuel turned to selling and servicing Gravely tractors and Toro lawn equipment. The Latonia Ice & Fuel Company complex took up an entire city block, and in the early 1960s the property where the ice-manufacturing plant and the coal yard was located was sold to the Green Trucking Company. The Gravely-Toro business continued to operate across the street from the former icehouse in the building that had been the truck garage. In August 1966 a fire destroyed most of the former icehouse building. Finally, after 60 years, the Latonia Ice & Fuel Company closed in 1968 and the remainder of the property was sold. Part of the original icehouse still stands and is used by the Covington Independent School District as a maintenance garage for school buses. The National Billiard Company now occupies the former truck garage.

Dusing Brothers Ice (now Dusing Brothers Ice Manufacturing Inc.), along U.S. 25, the **Dixie Highway** in Elsmere, was begun in 1928 by brothers Ben and Frank Dusing, and the operation remains in the same location today. They home-delivered ice and supplied ice to trucks that traveled along the Dixie Highway carrying perishable food items. They iced the trucks by blowing crushed ice into them. Dusing Brothers still manufactures ice, but they also operate mechanical ice-making machines that need only to be turned on to produce ice quickly and with less manpower. However, these machines, prone to mechanical breakdown, are far less reliable than the old methods. During the 1950s and 1960s, in times of peak demand for Latonia Ice & Fuel, trucks would make trips from Latonia to the Dusing Brothers icehouse for 300-pound blocks of ice in order to have enough ice for the Fruit Growers Express railroad cars.

The Penn family of Newport ran a similar icehouse along the **Chesapeake and Ohio Railroad** on that city's east side, at E. Ninth St. and Linden Ave. Called the City Ice and Fuel Company, it ceased operations in 1959, and the building began to be used by the Pharo Trucking Company in August 1966.

Ice Wagon.

Centennial Committee, *City of Elsmere Centennial Celebration, 1896–1996.* Elsmere, Ky.: Centennial Committee, 1996.
"Latonia Ice & Fuel (Articles of Incorporation Filed)," *KP*, August 26, 1908, 2.
"Phil Mueller Rites Set for Thursday," *KP*, June 1, 1954, 1.
Russell, Burl. "Fire Destroys Plant as Owner Awaits Surgery," *KP*, August 27, 1966, 1.

Mary Jo Hardcorn

IDLEWILD. Idlewild is located just off I-275 at Ky. Rts. 20 (the old Burlington-Petersburg Turnpike) and 338 (Idlewild Rd.) in northwestern Boone Co. The name of the community started as Gainesville, since much of the land was owned by the county's influential Gaines family. When a post office was established in the community in 1886, the name was Utzinger; then in 1900 the current name, Idlewild, was adopted.

In the late 1800s, the town had a general store, three blacksmith shops, and several businesses. There was a carriage shop, operated by Fred Pfalzgraf, a charter member of the Wells Fargo stage route, which delivered mail from Petersburg to Bromley. Along the delivery route, delivery persons would switch horses in Idlewild, Hebron, and Constance, on the way to Bromley.

During the early 1900s, a public school for black children was located near Idlewild; one of several in the county, it served 10 pupils and provided the students with bus service. There was also a school for whites, a one-room brick building that was later consolidated with that at Hebron. That former school building still stands as a private residence.

During the 1940s, Scothorn Motors and the Scothorn General Store made up Idelwild's business district. The car dealership's building is currently a body shop, but the appliance building is vacant and the old general store is just a shell.

Boone Co. Historic Preservation Review Board. *Historic Structures of Boone County, Kentucky.* Burlington, Ky.: Boone Co. Historic Preservation Review Board, 2002.
Reis, Jim. "Tiny Unincorporated Towns Abound in Boone," *KP*, December 9, 1985, 4K.

Nancy J. Tretter

IMMACULATA ACADEMY. Immaculata Academy opened in Newport on W. Fifth St. in 1857. It was a coeducational Catholic school run by the Sisters of Charity of Nazareth, who also operated **La Salette Academy** in Covington. It the early years, the sisters lived in Covington and traveled to Newport, daily crossing the Licking River by rowboat. With benefactors such as Michael V. Daly and his wife, the parents of Mrs. **Peter O'Shaughnessy**, Immaculata Academy grew and flourished. In 1883 enrollment was 130; in 1919 it was 210. But because a new physical plant was needed, and because there was a desire in Campbell Co. to consolidate Catholic secondary education in separate boys' and girls' high schools, Immaculata Academy closed its doors in August 1932, after operating for 75 years. Many of its students transferred to La Salette Academy. In September 1934, a new high school for boys, **Newport (Central) Catholic High School**, occupied the former Immaculata Academy space.

"1932 Class Will Be Last at Immaculata," *KP*, May 30, 1932, 1.

IMMACULATE CONCEPTION CATHOLIC CHURCH, NEWPORT. The Immaculate Conception Catholic Church was established in Newport in 1855, to provide services for English-speaking Catholics in the city. **Corpus Christi Catholic Church**, the first Catholic congregation in Newport, had been operating since 1845, primarily serving the German-speaking residents of Newport. In March 1855 a lot was purchased along Madison St. (present-day Fifth St.) for the construction of the Immaculate Conception Church building. Bishop George Carrell laid its cornerstone on April 15, 1855, and the structure was dedicated on December 23, 1855.

The first pastor was John Force, who served until 1857, when Patrick Guilfoyle (1817–1892), a native of Kilkenny, Ireland, was appointed pastor. Under Guilfoyle's guidance, Immaculate Conception parish flourished. In 1857 the parishioners financed the construction of a one-story brick school building for boys. That same year, the Sisters of Charity of Nazareth (Ky.) arrived in Newport and opened a school for girls on York St. The sisters also established a private school near the church, which they named **Immaculata Academy**. A three-story academy building was constructed in 1864 under the direction of Mary David Wagner S.C.N. Over time, Immaculata Academy evolved into a grade 1–12 school enrolling both male and female students.

In the years following the **Civil War**, population growth in Newport necessitated the construction of a new church for the Immaculate Conception congregation. The cornerstone of this church, designed by the Piket architectural firm (see **Louis Piket**) was laid in 1869, and the new Gothic Revival church building was dedicated in 1873. Before the facade of the new building was completed, however, the parish suffered a complete financial failure. For many years, Guilfoyle, who believed that all Catholic families should own a home, had purchased lots in Newport, built houses, and sold or rented them to his parishioners. His activities resulted in the construction of perhaps 500 homes in the city. When a massive economic depression during the 1870s brought the construction of homes to a halt, the parish did not have enough funds to pay the debt that Guilfoyle had incurred. Only large donations from two parishioners, **Peter O'Shaughnessy** and James Walsh, saved the parish's property from being lost (see **Walsh Distillery**; **Newport Home Ownership**).

In July 1877 Bishop Augustus M. Toebbe sent James Bent to Immaculate Conception as pastor. In that same year, the facade of the new church was finally completed. In June 1878 James McNerney became pastor. He oversaw the construction of a brick, three-story school building in 1893. He also arranged for the Sisters of Charity of Nazareth to take over the education of the boys, who up to this time had been taught by lay teachers. About this same time, the parish's elementary school was declared a free school; that is, no tuition was charged. A new rectory was completed in 1897 adjacent to the church.

During the pastorate of James L. Gorey (1915–1927), new Gothic marble high and side altars were placed in the church. The old wooden altars were donated to the **St. Paul Catholic Church** in Florence, Ky. Other improvements included a new pulpit and confessionals and the frescoing of the interior.

The 1930s proved a challenging decade for the people of Immaculate Conception Parish. The Sisters of Charity of Nazareth announced the closing of Immaculata Academy in 1932. The academy's buildings had suffered greatly over the years from persistent flooding and were no longer suitable for school purposes, but the expense of rehabilitating them or building new facilities was considered too high. During its last year of operation, the academy enrolled 180 pupils. The defining event in parish life during the 1930s, however, was the **flood of 1937**. Water reached a height of 11 feet inside the church, completely destroying the floors, the pews, and many other furnishings. Floodwaters also did considerable damage to the parish school and the rectory. The lower **West End** of Newport suffered greatly because of the flood. Many residents sold their homes and moved to higher ground in the city or to one of the new suburban communities of Campbell Co.

Newport's lower West End was becoming increasingly non-Catholic. Urban renewal projects in the city had led to the destruction of many single-family homes. By 1964, 20 blocks of downtown Newport had been cleared. Membership at Immaculate Conception Church began to decline significantly. Located on low ground near the Ohio and Licking rivers, Immaculate Conception parish buildings suffered repeated flooding over the years. In 1967 the Kentucky state fire marshal declared the school building unsafe, and the parish elementary school closed the following year. Immaculate Conception Church itself was officially closed on July 31, 1969. The historic church, school, and rectory were demolished to make way for the construction of a Shell gasoline service station; the lot, at the southeast corner of Fifth and Central Sts., is currently vacant.

"Academy to Close after 75 Years," *KP*, May 30, 1932, 1.
Golden Jubilee of the Rev. James McNerney Rector of the Church of the Immaculate Conception, Newport, Ky. Newport, Ky.: Immaculate Conception parish, 1915.
McGill, Anna Blanche. *The Sisters of Charity of Nazareth, Kentucky.* New York: Encyclopedia Press, 1917.
Tenkotte, Paul A., David E. Schroeder, and Thomas S. Ward. *To Be Catholic and American in Northern, Central, and Appalachian Kentucky: The Diocese of Covington, 1853–2003.* Forthcoming.

David E. Schroeder

IMMACULATE CONCEPTION CATHOLIC CHURCH, STEPSTONE. German Catholics initiated the small **St. Joseph Catholic Church** at Four Mile Creek in Campbell Co. in 1846. Soon after establishing it as a parish in 1855, Bishop George A. Carrell appointed Rev. Lawrence Spitzelberger as the second pastor. In 1858 Spitzelberger began attending to the needs of another group of eight German Catholic families at Stepstone Creek in northeastern Pendleton Co., near a landing that made the spot accessible by boat. Under Spitzelberger's guidance, the small German community built a little church in 1861 and named it Immaculate Conception Catholic Church. It served as a mission of St. Joseph Catholic Church until it was transferred to the care of Saints Peter and Paul Catholic Church in Twelve Mile (now California). The small wooden church remains as a mission of Saints Peter and Paul Catholic Church. Although the church building has never had heat or electricity, it is still used for Mass twice a year.

Reder, Diane. "Jubilee Cross Visits Sts. Peter and Paul," *Messenger*, February 4, 2000, 6.

Ryan, Paul E. *History of the Diocese of Covington, Kentucky*. Covington, Ky.: Diocese of Covington, 1954.

Tenkotte, Paul A., David E. Schroeder, and Thomas S. Ward. *To Be Catholic and American in Northern, Central, and Appalachian Kentucky: The Diocese of Covington, 1853–2003*. Forthcoming.

Thomas S. Ward

IMMACULATE HEART OF MARY CATHOLIC CHURCH. The new Immaculate Heart of Mary Church building, dedicated in 1993, is located off Ky. Rt. 18, near the geographical center of Boone Co. It was once a church with a small congregation that met in a sanctuary on Limaburg Rd. near Hebron and served a much more rural community, but today the church building and its membership are in the suburbs. The first church had a membership of some 70 families. In 2002 the Immaculate Heart of Mary parish counted 1,546 households.

Originally, Bishop **William T. Mulloy** on October 1, 1954, named Immaculate Heart of Mary a mission of St. Boniface Catholic Church in Ludlow (see **Saints Boniface and James Catholic Church**); then in October 1955 it became a mission of a new parish called **Mary Queen of Heaven** under Rev. Paul Ciangetti. In 1954 the Diocese of Covington (see **Roman Catholics**) counted 60 Catholic families in the Hebron area. John Weghorn, a member of **St. Paul Catholic Church**, Florence, Ky., donated 15 acres for the building of a church. Arrangements were made to celebrate Sunday Mass with the Passionist nuns on Donaldson Hwy. in adjoining Erlanger. To alleviate overcrowding at the Passionist chapel in Erlanger, the Immaculate Heart of Mary congregation reserved space in a former restaurant to celebrate weekly Mass. But because of an apparent act of religious bigotry, they relocated to the basement of a private home. With the future of the local parish still in doubt, a petition with 66 signatures from the congregation at Hebron reiterated the need for a church and a nearby school for the safety of Catholic students. Finally, Bishop Mulloy approved having Father Ciangetti entertain construction proposals.

In August 1956 the ground was broken for the new sanctuary building, and on Sunday, August 11, 1957, the bishop blessed the newly completed church. A year later, members requested parish status and a school from the bishop. In 1960 Richard Ackerman, the Covington Diocese's new bishop, established the parish of Immaculate Heart of Mary, assigning Father Otto Hering as pastor.

In January 1961 Father Hering announced that Immaculate Heart of Mary parish would build its own elementary school with five classrooms and "temporary" quarters for five teaching sisters. The school building opened in January 1962 with about 75 students. In 1970 the parish consisted of 138 families, 76 students in the school, 85 in public elementary school, and 2 religious and 2 lay teachers, with 4 classrooms in use. During the late 1970s, Bishop Ackerman approved spending $102,500 for a convent and a rectory and for remodeling to provide another classroom, a principal's office, a lounge, and storage space.

By 1981, 800 parishioners per week attended the one Saturday and four Sunday masses. Accordingly, the diocese approved adding a 135-seat wing to the church, extending from the right side of the sanctuary.

As early as 1967, Father Herring had complained that the nearby airport's "new landing and take-off patterns are bringing the planes within a hundred yards or less of our church buildings." On October 21, 1991, the **Cincinnati/Northern Kentucky International Airport** Board voted to purchase all of the Immaculate Heart of Mary parish properties for $1.65 million plus another $20,000 for moving expenses. The parish's new Steering Committee negotiated with the airport, developed a wish list, selected a site for relocation, and hired an architect. The new site chosen was on 15 acres of farmland near Burlington. In November the parish began fundraising.

With a cost estimate of $2,950,000 and $820,000 in pledges, ground was broken for the parish's new facilities on March 22, 1992. On August 29, 1993, Bishop William A. Hughes, Pastor Louis Holtz, Deacon Arthur Jansson, and former pastors John Kroger and Paul Ciangetti dedicated the new building, which had cost more than 4 million dollars.

In 1997 the parish council was considering building a new church and converting the present church into school facilities, an endeavor that would have cost several millions of dollars. However, the projected large indebtedness for these projects swayed the parish instead to build eight additional classrooms at a cost of less than a million dollars. The new classrooms provided the school with two classrooms for each grade. Today, Immaculate Heart of Mary parish is one of the largest in the Diocese of Covington, as is its elementary school.

"Hebron Parish Sold to Airport Board," *Messenger*, October 27, 1991, 1.

"Immaculate Heart of Mary Multi-Purpose Building Dedication," *Messenger*, August 27, 1993, 2A.

"Immaculate Heart of Mary Parish 50th Anniversary," *Messenger*, supplement, December 16, 2005.

"Immaculate Heart of Mary to Build in Burlington," *Messenger*, December 8, 1991, 1.

John Boh

IMMANUEL UNITED CHURCH OF CHRIST. During the late 1880s, a group of Reformed Church people settled in the small Kenton Co. town of Mullinsville. In 1890 the name of the community was changed to Bromley, and it was incorporated as a sixth-class city. Several years later, two religious groups, the Reformed and the Campbellites, began holding German-language services in the same meeting hall, one on Sunday mornings and the other on Sunday afternoons. On March 11, 1894, 30 members of the Reformed group held a meeting at which they formally organized the German Reformed Church of Bromley, Ky. Shortly thereafter, they purchased lot 95, at the northeast corner of Boone and Harris Sts., and began building their first sanctuary. The cornerstone was laid on July 15, 1894, and the structure was completed in September of that year. Many of the members were farmers, who came to church by horse and wagon, so a barn was built at the rear of the property to house the animals during services. Because of the **anti-German hysteria** that arose during **World War I**, the church name was changed in 1918 to the Immanuel Reformed Church of Bromley. Religious services began to be conducted in English rather than German. In 1920 a 20-member choir was formed, directed, until 1932, by the pastor, Rev. William E. Miller. In 1922 the barn was torn down and replaced by an educational building that provided Sunday school classrooms. In June of the same year, the church purchased two lots adjacent to the church property, and the present sanctuary was later built on them. The Ladies' Aid Society played a major role in raising the funds needed for construction. In 1934 Immanuel and most other Reformed churches merged with the Evangelical Church and the organization's name was changed again, this time to the Immanuel Evangelical and Reformed Church.

During the Ohio River **flood of 1937**, the congregation removed the pews from the church, and many of the members stored their belongings there until the floodwaters receded. The local drugstore also moved into the church lecture room, from which it dispensed medicine to area residents.

On February 17, 1957, Immanuel hired Rev. Raymond Kuhlenschmidt as its first full-time pastor. A parsonage was also purchased for his use, on Amsterdam Rd. in Park Hills. Later that year, the Evangelical and Reformed Church and the Christian Church merged, necessitating yet another name change, this time to the Immanuel United Church of Christ. The old sanctuary was torn down in 1959 and replaced by the present modern building. A bell tower was added in 1967, in which members installed the bell from their old church. An educational wing, with a pastor's study, a nursery, a choir room, Sunday School classrooms, lavatories, and a kitchenette, was built in 1983. Through the generosity of dedicated members, the church was debt-free when a dedication ceremony was held in June 1984.

"Immanuel United Church of Christ," *Ludlow News Enterprise,* May 10, 1989, 3.
Immanuel United Church of Christ. *100 Years of Service, 1894–1994.* Anniversary booklet. Bromley, Ky.: Immanuel United Church of Christ, 1994.
"Immanuel United Church of Christ Photos," *KP,* December 10, 1959, 14K.

IMMANUEL UNITED METHODIST CHURCH. This church came about as one of the results of the German revolutions of the 1840s, when large numbers of Germans fled their homeland and came to the United States. A large number of these immigrants were drawn to the Ohio Valley because it reminded them of the Rhine River Valley in Germany. Many chose to settle in Newport and Covington. In 1848 a small group of German Protestants began holding church services in the home of Frederick Dohrmann, at 100 Robbins St. in Covington. Though not originally affiliated with any larger church organization, these worshippers were known as the German Methodist Episcopal Church. Services were conducted in German. The church's first full-time pastor was Dr. Christian Vogel, who assumed the position in 1849. As the congregation grew, the church purchased a frame house at 717–719 Craig St. in which to hold services. A Sunday school was organized in 1853, by which time church membership had grown to 160. Within a few years, a larger building was needed, so in 1866 a lot was purchased on the southeast corner of 10th and Russell. The cornerstone of the new church was laid in 1869, and the first floor was dedicated in 1870. The upper sanctuary was dedicated on February 20, 1876. The edifice, designed by architect F. Armstrong, was described as being one of the finest church buildings in the city. It also contained one of the region's best pipe organs, which facilitated the creation of a music program, including a choir.

Immanuel Methodist Church, 10th and Russell Sts., Covington.

In 1886 a house at 79 W. 10th St., adjacent to the church building, was purchased to be used as a parsonage. In 1889 the congregation joined the Epworth League of Methodist Churches. About 1916 an addition was added to the church, but that was soon outgrown, and the parsonage became the Sunday school building. Because of anti-German sentiments during the **World War I**, the church's name was changed to the Immanuel Methodist Episcopal Church and German-language services were gradually discontinued. In 1929 a site was purchased at Madison and Robbins, with the intention of building a new 600-seat facility. However, before construction began, church leaders rethought their decision. Attendance had begun to fall as older members died and many younger ones began a flight to the suburbs. It was decided that a location outside the city would best serve the needs of the congregation. Many sites were considered, and eventually an 11-acre one at the corner of **Dixie Highway** and Arcadia Ln. in Lakeside Park, the gift of Mr. and Mrs. Henry W. Zimmerman, was obtained in the late 1940s. A new building, which took several years to complete, was started in 1949; the congregation officially moved from Covington to Lakeside Park in September 1950, worshipping in the basement of the unfinished building. The cornerstone of the new sanctuary was laid in June 1955, and the sanctuary opened in May 1956. An educational annex was constructed in 1964, a new Wicks organ was installed in 1973, and a $3.2 million Wesley Hall addition was dedicated in 1998. The church continues to be a healthy and vibrant organization, drawing its members from many Northern Kentucky communities. It hosts a number of community groups, including the Boy Scouts, the Girl Scouts, a basketball league, and self-help groups. Now named Immanuel United Methodist Church, it is one of the largest Protestant churches in Northern Kentucky. In 2005 the church took over the responsibility of operating the closed **First United Methodist Church** in Covington, converting it into its Grace satellite campus. In the same year, the church merged with New Hope United Methodist Church in Southgate and continued to operate the New Hope campus at 22 William Blatt Ave. In addition, Immanuel conducts a large outreach program for **Latinos**.

Immanuel United Methodist Church. www.immanuelumc.org/history.htm (accessed December 19, 2007).
Linn, Molly. "Closing Not End of Church," *KP,* June 11, 2005, 3K.
Reis, Jim. "Heritage Celebrated. Immanuel Marks 150th Milestone," *KP,* September 13, 1999, 4K.

INDEPENDENCE. Independence, one of two county seats in Kenton Co., ranks among Northern Kentucky's largest and fastest-growing cities. Primarily a residential city, Independence covers about 23 square miles and stretches across the middle third of Kenton Co. between the Boone and Campbell county borders. Through annexation and real estate development, the population of Independence grew almost 10-fold from 1970 to 2000. With its suburban present and rural past, Independence touches on two major themes in Northern Kentucky history: the interplay between rural and urban interests and the post–**World War II** population shift from the region's river cities toward the interior of the state.

Unlike most Northern Kentucky cities, the origins of Independence were political, not commercial. The Kentucky statute that created Kenton Co. in 1840 required a central location for the county seat. John McCollum donated land at the present-day intersection of Madison Pike (Ky. Rt. 17) and McCullum Rd. for the Kenton Co. Courthouse. A Greek Revival–style courthouse was erected on the site. Incorporated in 1842, the small community surrounding the new courthouse named itself Independence to commemorate the independence of Kenton Co. from Campbell Co.

Residents of Covington, the new county's center of population, long bemoaned the inconvenience of traveling to Independence to transact legal business. Several times from Kenton Co.'s birth through the early 1900s, Covington business and political leaders attempted to move the county seat to Covington. An 1848 *Covington Journal* editorial pleaded Covington's case: "It seems a very plain matter. Independence is now the Seat of Justice for the county. This is a village of half a dozen houses, twelve miles in the interior, without business, or indeed, anything else, to draw people there. On the other hand, Covington has now a population of ten thousand, which is rapidly increasing; and here, from the nature of things, nearly all of the Court business originates; here the parties, witnesses and counsel reside. In addition to this, the people of all parts of the county come to this place . . . to trade, or attend to other business, and hence it would not be a matter of inconvenience for them to attend the courts here."

The Kenton county seat controversy lingered for decades. By 1860 a dual-county-seat system had developed that split the county in two, with Covington and Independence as the county seats for its northern and southern portions, respectively. The Kentucky legislature, on occasion, considered moving the Kenton county seat. In 1867 and again in 1905, Kenton Co. voters decided to keep Independence as a county seat. Victorious Democrats interpreted the 1905 decision as repudiation by virtuous rural voters of the corrupt Republican Party machine that ran Covington.

During its first 100 years, Independence changed little from the quiet village described by the *Covington Journal*. Independence was a farming community, with businesses such as hotels and law offices to support courthouse traffic. A few county officials, for example Judge Lafayette Shaw, had summer residences or farms in Independence, but they also maintained homes in Covington.

Commerce stagnated in 19th-century Independence, in part because it lacked mass transit. The **Louisville, Cincinnati, and Lexington Railroad**, built through the Banklick Creek valley in 1869, had an Independence depot, but more than a mile of hilly terrain separated it from the city. A stagecoach line also operated between Covington and Independence, but a one-way trip took more than two hours. Small wonder that proponents for Covington as the Kenton county seat contended that it was easier for most people in rural areas to get to Covington than to Independence because more railroads and turnpikes led to Covington.

Despite its relative isolation, Independence teemed with activity when it hosted county court days and other political meetings. These events drew local farmers to town to socialize and sell their products. The political party conventions held in Independence were annual highlights. Many of Northern Kentucky's leading 19th-century politicians, including **John G. Carlisle**, **John White Stevenson**, and **James W. Bryan**, received their nominations for higher office in Independence.

But not all interruptions to the city's tranquility were welcome. During the **Civil War**, at the height of the frenzy stirred by a Confederate advance on Northern Kentucky and Cincinnati, a Confederate force numbering about 1,500 briefly occupied the town in September 1862 and helped themselves to food and other supplies. A few years later, armed Confederate sympathizers harassed the pro-Union men in Independence and wreaked general havoc.

The apex of Independence's quiet country village life probably came in October 1912 with the dedication there of a new Kenton Co. Courthouse. A large crowd attended the ceremonies for the new courthouse, a Beaux Arts structure that cost $35,000 to build. The festivities included speeches from civic leaders, music, and simmering pots of burgoo–a staple of Kentucky political celebrations. Once common, gatherings like this had all but ceased in Independence when party nominating conventions yielded to primary elections during the 1890s.

Although the city was diminishing in political importance, the rise of the automobile kept Independence integrated with the rest of Northern Kentucky. For instance, increased car ownership in the 1920s and improved rural roads enabled Independence's baseball teams to play in Northern Kentucky leagues that had entries scattered throughout the region. School consolidation, made possible by school buses, also brought people to Independence. Even so, as late as the 1950s Independence remained underdeveloped. The city's population hovered at about 300 residents.

During the 1960s Independence began transforming from a quiet country town to a booming residential city. Annexations, starting with the area surrounding the Cherokee Shopping Plaza on Taylor Mill Rd. (Ky. Rt. 16), spurred the city's expansion. By the early 1970s, Independence had grown to five square miles with a population of nearly 2,000. Additional annexations during the 1970s increased the city's area to 12 square miles and quadrupled its population by the end of the decade. Independence added still more territory in the early 1980s by its merger with the City of Ridgeview Heights and by other annexations to the west. Most annexations arose from the lobbying efforts of residents of unincorporated areas who wished to join Independence rather than risk absorption into the expanding Covington with its higher tax rates. In other situations, as in Ridgeview Heights, residents favored annexation because Independence could offer services at a much lower cost.

Rapid growth in Independence also transformed its city government. As late as 1960, Independence offered minimal services to its inhabitants. The city government occupied offices in the Kenton Co. Courthouse. Its police force consisted of only a marshal and a part-time patrol officer. Residents had to use cisterns for their water and had no sewers for waste treatment. This lack of services thwarted annexation attempts by Independence during the 1950s. Because of the city's growth in the 1970s, Independence purchased a building to house city offices, expanded the police department to two full-time officers and six part-timers, built two firehouses for the city's 80-member volunteer fire department, and began the construction of sewage and water systems. Annexations brought a fivefold increase in tax revenue without increasing the tax rate. The revenue windfall and disciplined spending–sometimes to the consternation of those impatient for improvements in city services—kept Independence operating at a surplus while permitting gradual infrastructure upgrading.

Independence continued to grow throughout the 1980s and 1990s. Housing developments started to replace the family farms that surrounded downtown Independence. Annexation was the price new subdivisions had to pay if they wanted to tap into Independence's sewer and water lines. The population of Independence almost doubled between 1980 and 2000.

Independence's most impressive growth may still be on the horizon. A housing boom brought by low interest rates has helped make Independence the fastest-growing city in Northern Kentucky, with an estimated 27 percent population increase between 2000 and 2005. The widening of Madison Pike (Ky. Rt. 17), Turkeyfoot Rd. (Ky. Rt. 1303), Ky. Rt. 536, and Taylor Mill Rd. (Ky. Rt. 16) will improve the city's already enviable access to Northern Kentucky interstate highways and should attract even more development. With new and renovated schools, a new library, abundant parks, and Kenton Co.'s largest public golf course all within its city limits, Independence offers many attractions for families. In addition, a major retail area is emerging at the intersection of Madison Pike and Harris Pike with expectations of more such areas to come. Already Northern Kentucky's largest city in terms of land mass, Independence has the potential to become the region's most populous city. Projections indicate that Independence's population could grow to between 40,000 and 60,000. The population of Independence was 1,715 in 1970; 7,998 in 1980; 10,444 in 1990; and 14,982 in 2000.

"Independence Has Changed Very Little," *KE,* July 4, 1958, 1.
"19,065 . . . and Counting—Independence's Day," *KP,* July 1, 2006, 1A.
U.S. Census Bureau. "American Fact Finder. Data Set. Census 2000 Summary File 1 (SF1) 100-Percent Data. Custom Table," www.census.gov (accessed July 31, 2006).
"Who Runs Independence?" *KE,* September 10, 1979, 2A.

Greg Perkins

INDEPENDENCE HIGH SCHOOL. Established in February 1910, Independence High School was the first county public high school in Kenton Co. The sweeping 1908 Sullivan Law, which revamped Kentucky's public school system, included a requirement that each county have at least one public high school. To comply with the legislation, the Kenton Co. School Board took over a small two-room private high school in Independence that was conducted by Charles V. Lucy. Plans immediately commenced to erect a new county-administered high school at Independence, the county seat. Completed in 1912 at a cost of $10,000, the two-story brick Independence High School housed both elementary and high school students in its eight rooms. Later additions to the school included an auditorium and expanded classroom space. Independence High School closed in 1938 with the opening of the nearby **Simon Kenton High School**; however, its facility continued to be used as an elementary school until 1954. The former Independence High School building, located at 5209 Madison Pike, remains an enduring landmark in Independence and continues to serve the community with its mix of residential, office, and retail space.

Caywood, James A. "A Brief Sketch of the Development of the Kenton County School System," January 14, 1958, Kenton Co. Schools, Fort Wright, Ky.
Kleber, John E., ed. *The Kentucky Encyclopedia.* Lexington: Univ. Press of Kentucky, 1992.

Greg Perkins

Odd Fellows Ringgold Lodge, Market St., Maysville.

INDEPENDENT ORDER OF ODD FELLOWS. The Independent Order of Odd Fellows (I.O.O.F.) in the past had a strong presence in Northern Kentucky, where it sponsored many charitable enterprises. The I.O.O.F. has its roots in 18th-century Great Britain; in North America it was chartered in 1819. Although it was originally a fraternal organization, with a ladies auxiliary called the Daughters of Rebekah, today both men and women can be members of the I.O.O.F. Like the **Masons** of the 18th-century Enlightenment, the I.O.O.F. lodges practiced religious tolerance, requiring only that their members believe in a supreme being. Also similar to the Masons, the I.O.O.F. featured several levels, each composed of degrees. The first level, or Lodge, had three degrees (friendship, love, and truth); the second level was Encampment, with the three degrees of Patriarch, Golden Rule, and Royal Purple; and the third level, the Patriarchs Militant, or Canton, had one degree, the Chevalier. Known as the "The Three-Link Fraternity"—for its tri-linked chain logo with the letters *F, L,* and *T* (for friendship, love, and truth)—the Odd Fellows were considered "odd" in their early days because of their practice of giving charity without expecting anything in return. The I.O.O.F. provided sickness, death, and other benefits for its dues-paying members and contributed to widows and orphans, the **Booth Memorial Hospital**, and many other worthy causes.

Many Odd Fellows lodges operated in Northern Kentucky, in the communities of Atwood, Augusta, Bellevue, Big Bone, Butler, Carrollton, Corinth, Covington (multiple lodges), Dayton, Florence, Foster, Gardnersville, Ghent, Glencoe, Grants Lick, Hebron, Independence, Johnsville, Jonesville, Knoxville, Latonia, Ludlow, Maysville, Mount Zion, Napoleon, New Liberty, Newport (multiple lodges), Owenton, Petersburg, Warsaw, and Williamstown. In addition, there are I.O.O.F. cemeteries in Burlington, Carrollton, Corinth, and Jonesville and three in Owen Co. In the 19th century, the I.O.O.F. owned a picnic grove called the Odd Fellows Grove situated on Waterworks Rd. in Campbell Co.; in 1905, the land was sold to the Woodlawn Land Company, which became part of the later city of Woodlawn. At least four lodges in Northern Kentucky were founded for **African Americans**: the Crispus Attucks Lodge in Covington, the Maysville Star Lodge, the Dunbar Lodge in Newport, and a lodge in New Liberty. The hall where the Crispus Attucks lodge met is still standing in Covington, on the southwest corner of two intersecting alleys in the block bounded by Fourth, Fifth, and Scott Sts. and Madison Ave. Rebekah lodges for women operated in Augusta, Bellevue, Carrollton, Covington, Jonesville, Newport (multiple lodges), and Owenton. Lodges are still operating in Carrollton, Jonesville, Maysville, and Owenton.

Some of the I.O.O.F. lodges built elaborate halls, usually renting the first floor to retail establishments and themselves occupying one or more floors above. The most noteworthy buildings included the Odd Fellows Hall on the northeast corner of Fifth St. and Madison Ave. in Covington; the Browinski Lodge, on the corner of Third and Main Sts., and the later I.O.O.F. Hall on Seminary St., both in Carrollton; the Odd Fellows' Hall (built 1889; demolished 1971) on the northeast corner of Elm and Butler Sts. in Ludlow; two buildings in Maysville; the Odd Fellows Hall on Seminary St. in Owenton; and the three-story I.O.O.F. building at 115 N. Main St. in Williamstown (built 1911). Maysville's DeKalb Lodge No. 12 and Ringgold No. 27 built a three-story hall on the south side of Second St. between Market and Sutton Sts. in 1877–1878; the third floor featured a library and lodge rooms. In 1915 the Ringgold Lodge dedicated a new three-story hall on Market St. (still standing). Designed by the noted architectural firm of **Weber Brothers**, it features a terra cotta front. The three-story Odd Fellow's Building in Covington, dating from 1856, featured a unique second-floor ballroom-auditorium seating 800, unobstructed by columns and suspended by metal rods hanging from above. The third floor contained lodge rooms. The auditorium was used for many civic events, and in 1900 the body of assassinated Governor **William Goebel** (1900) lay in state there. The Odd Fellows sold the building in 1923, and in the 1940s and 1950s the auditorium was used as a roller rink. In 1930 the Washington I.O.O.F. lodge of Covington built a new three-story headquarters at 808–810 Scott St. In 2001 Tony Milburn and Damian and Kelly Sells purchased the old 1856 Odd Fellows Hall at Fifth and Madison, with plans to restore it to its original splendor. A massive fire on May 21, 2002, however, destroyed the inner shell of the building. The owners saved the historic outer walls and built a new five-story office structure inside.

"Building Ready: Odd Fellows Dedicate New $65,000 Structure," *KP,* October 25, 1930, 1.
Conrad, John B., ed. *History of Grant County.* Williamstown, Ky.: Grant Co. Historical Society, 1992.

Emery, George Neil. *A Young Man's Benefit: The Independent Order of Odd Fellows and Sickness Insurance in the United States and Canada, 1860–1929.* Montreal: McGill-Queen's Univ. Press, 1999.
"Fire Ravages Historic Hall," *KP*, May 21, 2002, 1K.
Independent Order of Odd Fellows. http://dev.ioof.org/aboutus.html (accessed August 16, 2008).
Kentucky Gateway Museum, Maysville, Ky. Vertical files.
"Odd Fellows Hall Sold," *KP*, March 5, 1923, 1.
Proceedings of the Grand Lodge of Kentucky of the Independent Order of Odd Fellows: Held at Lexington, Kentucky, October 14 and 15, 1941. Frankfort, Ky.: Roberts, 1941.
The Spirit of a Greater Maysville and Mason County. Maysville, Ky.: Daily Independent, 1930.
Warminski, Margo. *Historic Structures of Boone County.* Burlington, Ky.: Boone Co. Historic Preservation Board, 2002.
"Will Be Dedicated in May," *KTS*, February 16, 1915, 14.

Paul A. Tenkotte

INGLES, MARY (b. 1732, Philadelphia, Pa.; d. 1815, Montgomery Co., Va.). Mary Draper Ingles was the daughter of Irish immigrants George and Elenor Hardin Draper. The Draper family moved to the western frontier, near what is today Blacksburg, Va., in 1748. There, they helped to create a pioneer settlement that was known as Draper's Meadow.

In 1750 Mary Draper married William Ingles and later gave birth to two sons. On July 8, 1755, a band of Shawnee Indian warriors (see **American Indians**) raided the settlement, scalping and killing several settlers, including Mary's mother. The Shawnees took Mary along with her children, her sister-in-law, and a neighbor as hostages. The captives were forced to trek through uncharted territory and reportedly were the first white people to traverse this terrain. Eventually, they arrived at a Shawnee village located in the Ohio Territory on the banks of the Scioto and Ohio Rivers. Mary was separated from her sons there. While in captivity, Mary was taken to **Big Bone Lick** in modern Boone Co., Ky., to help the Indians make salt. She became the first white person to make salt west of Kanawha River and the first white woman to enter territory now included in Indiana, Kentucky, and Ohio.

Mary's opportunity to flee came about when the Shawnees gave her permission to forage the woods for nuts and wild grapes. During one of these gathering expeditions, Mary and another captive escaped from the Indians and made their way through the wilderness on foot, enduring incredible hardships along the way. They used the Ohio, Kanawha, and New rivers to guide them throughout their journey. After traveling more than 800 miles, they finally arrived in Virginia, and Mary was reunited with her husband, whose efforts to find her had been unsuccessful. William and Mary Ingles had four more children and settled in Montgomery Co., Va., where they operated a ferry across the New River. William died in 1782. Mary continued to live in the log house that her husband had built until her death in 1815. She was buried at the Ingles Homestead in Radford, Va. Mary's ordeal has inspired numerous books, movies, and living-history programs, and many historical monuments pay homage to this courageous woman; the **Mary Ingles Highway** in Northern Kentucky is named in her honor.

Furbee, Mary Rodd. *Outrageous Women of Colonial America.* New York: Wiley, ca. 2001.
——. *Shawnee Captive: The Story of Mary Draper Ingles.* Greensboro, N.C.: Morgan Reynolds, ca. 2001.
Hale, John Peter. *History of the Great Kanawha Valley.* Madison, Wis.: Brant, Fuller, 1891.
——. *Trans-Allegheny Pioneers: Historical Sketches of the First White Settlements West of the Alleghenies, 1748 and After, Wonderful Experiences of Hardships and Heroism of Those Who First Braved the Dangers of the Inhospitable Wilderness, and the Savage Tribes That Then Inhabited It.* 1886. Reprint, Charleston, W.Va.: Kanawha Valley, 1931.
Ingles, John. *Escape from Indian Captivity: The Story of Mary Draper Ingles and Son Thomas Ingles, as told by John Ingles, Sr.* Ed. Roberta Ingles Steele and Andrew Lewis Ingles. Radford, Va., 1969.

Robin Caraway

INTERNAL REVENUE SERVICE CENTER. The federal Internal Revenue Service (IRS) has had a physical presence in Covington since at least 1907, when President Theodore Roosevelt (1901–1909) appointed attorney **Maurice L. Galvin** as the local revenue collector. Former Covington mayor Ron Turner (1987) has often remarked that the city's employment turnaround started with the arrival of the modern IRS Center in the 1960s. Located in a multiblock area just to the west of Madison Ave. and north of Fourth St., its first one-level building, with an interior courtyard, was designed by local architect **Carl Bankemper**. The Dugan and Meyers Construction Company of Cincinnati began work in late 1965, and the new $4.5 million IRS Center opened for its first group of 300 employees on May 12, 1967, with plans to employ 3,300 by the end of that year. The formal dedication of the building took place in August 1967. The purpose of the center was to service some 12 million taxpayers, and it soon became one of the 10 IRS databanks across the nation. Within two months after opening, IRS officials were already talking about further expansion in Covington. The operation soon became one of the major employers in Northern Kentucky.

The IRS Center, beginning on a 14.5-acre site, solved a large urban-renewal problem for the City of Covington, while bringing more people into town and increased payroll taxes into the city's coffers, at a time when both were sorely needed. The building contained a cafeteria and three canteen areas, with stonework throughout. In 1989 the IRS added a daycare facility for the children of its employees. In 1990 planning began for the new Gateway Center Building, across Madison Ave. to the east, into which the IRS expanded in 1993. In 2000 the focus of the center changed as it moved to working with small-business taxpayers.

Hopkins, Karen. "Beauty Complements Comfort in IRS Center," *KP*, May 10, 1967, 8K.
"IRS Here Has 20th Birthday," *KP*, August 19, 1987, 6K.
Paeth, Greg. "IRS Asks City to Expand," *KP*, October 3, 1974, 1K.
"Tops in Jobs," *KP*, October 1, 1983, 1K.
Wagner, Arlo T. "Plan 2 Acre Expansion of IRS Center by 1975," *KP*, May 16, 1967, 1K.

INTERSTATE HIGHWAYS. See **Expressways**.

INTERURBANS. Several interurban lines were planned but never built in Northern Kentucky. Nationally, interurban railroad transportation during the first two decades of the 20th century, promoted as a means to move people and goods quickly between cities, was a financial disaster. Interurban railroads were touted as a replacement for the steam railroad. They used electricity drawn from overhead wires to power clean-running, smokeless motors. Interurban cars were the size of steam railroad cars but looked like urban **streetcars**.

Interurban lines were usually built parallel to existing steam operations and often over the public right-of-way. Owing to their frequent, often hourly, service, they stripped steam railroads of much of their passenger business where they competed side by side. Interurbans also claimed a portion of the less-than-carload package business, just as modern overnight air freight companies have done today. By 1916 more than 15,500 miles of interurban line were in service across the nation.

The interurban system's downfall was the development of all-weather highways. Most interurbans ran adjacent to or on existing roads and used local streets to penetrate into the downtowns of cities. This competition between the interurban car and the private truck or automobile was settled in favor of the trucks and automobiles.

Cincinnati, at one time, boasted eight interurban lines; in Kentucky six interurban lines were built statewide, but all had stopped running by 1939; none operated in Northern Kentucky. Although the Northern Kentucky Area saw no interurban lines built, some were proposed. The basic goal of these plans was to tie Northern Kentucky to Louisville and Lexington. Two of the proposals were to extend the Louisville and Indianapolis (L&I) from LaGrange to Covington and to extend the Kentucky Traction Terminal Company (KT&T) from Paris to Covington and Newport.

Between 1910 and 1920, separate charters were granted by the Kentucky legislature to four companies to build interurban lines within Northern Kentucky. The Cincinnati, Louisville, Lexington & Maysville Traction Company was proposed to link Cincinnati, Louisville, Lexington, and Maysville together with interurban track. However, despite some initial news media releases, the company never undertook to build anything. It appears that the company was set up as speculation to sell its franchises to investors who might themselves build an interurban line.

The Newport & Alexandria Electric Traction Company (N&AET) proposed running lines between Newport and Alexandria and, once this route was completed, to continue to Falmouth. News releases speculated that the KT&T would build north to Cynthiana from Paris and that either the KT&T or the N&AET would then close the gap between Falmouth and Cynthiana. A preliminary survey of the route was undertaken by the N&AET, and 1.3 miles of single track was built in 1916 from the end of the **Green Line** streetcar line in S. Fort Thomas southward along Alexandria Pk. and Main St. in Highland Heights. This rump line, subsidized by the Highland Heights Land Company, was operated by the Green Line until 1924. It was far more a streetcar operation than an interurban one.

The Covington & Big Bone Company (C&BB) proposed to connect Covington and Big Bone Lick. The promoters envisioned developing a spa and an amusement park at Big Bone Lick that would attract amusement seekers and give rise to suburban housing developments. The C&BB may be best described as a real estate speculation proposal. Pacific Electric, located in Los Angeles, was a prototype for this type of real estate venture. It involved building a rail line into the country that would allow easy access to the city of origin and then developing residential areas along its path. Outside of some promotional meetings, no start was made on building the C&BB line.

The promoters of the Ohio Valley Traction Company (OVT) proposed to tie Covington with Carrollton, Ky., and Madison, Ind. The route would use a ferry to cross the Ohio River at Madison until a bridge could be built. The promoters also held out the carrot that the L&I would extend its line eastward from LaGrange to meet up with the OVT. This line never progressed beyond plans on paper.

Bogart, Charles H. "A Survey of Kentucky's Traction Interlude." *National Railway Bulletin* 67, no. 2 (2002): 18–27.

Due, John F., and George W. Hilton. *The Electric Interurban Railways in America*. Stanford, Calif.: Stanford Univ. Press, 1960.

Middleton, William D. *The Interurban Era*. Milwaukee, Wis.: Kalmbach Books, 1961.

Charles H. Bogart

IRISH AMERICANS. The Irish were one of the largest groups to settle in Northern Kentucky. They did so in two distinct waves: the first consisted of Scots-Irish people, who were principally Protestant, and the second of Irish Catholics. The Scots-Irish originally hailed from the lowlands of Scotland, and following the systematic conquest of Ireland by Queen Elizabeth I of England (ruled 1558–1603), they settled in Ulster, the northern province of Ireland. Rising rents, drought, and English prejudice against their Presbyterian roots (see **Presbyterians**) were an impetus for hundreds of thousands of Scots-Irish to immigrate to the colonies in North America before the **Revolutionary War** and to the United States afterward. Settling in Pennsylvania and the southern mountains (see **Appalachians**), many made their way to Northern Kentucky in the late 18th and early 19th centuries, for example, **Thomas Kennedy**, whose father was a Presbyterian from Ulster.

The second and largest wave of Irish immigration, mainly **Roman Catholics**, was propelled by a number of causes. The Penal Laws against Catholics in Ireland, the failure of revolts against the British, the enclosure of farmland for herding, the displacement of cottage industries by cheaper British manufacturing, the Great Famine (1845–1850), and subsequent potato failures in the 1870s and 1880s all contributed to the "push factors" motivating millions to leave. "Pull factors" in the United States included economic opportunity, democracy, and religious freedom. Irish immigration to the United States and other places worldwide, as well as other political and economic conditions in Ireland, so impacted the population of Ireland that it literally was halved, from 8.5 million in 1841 to 4.25 million in 1926.

The Great Famine attracted attention throughout the world. According to the *Licking Valley Register*, the citizens of Covington collected $161 in August 1847 for the "destitute of Ireland." More importantly, Covington, Newport, Maysville, and other locations within Northern Kentucky provided employment opportunities for Irish immigrants. As early as 1839, the Covington *Western Globe* reported that Irish workers, whom it called the "'salt of the earth' for public works," were employed among the construction crews of the **Covington and Lexington Turnpike** and later on the **Covington and Lexington Railroad**. But jobs for men in construction were not the only employment opportunities. Sometimes this Irish immigration assumed a form unlike that of other earlier and later immigrant groups, in that a mother or eldest daughter often was sent to the United States first. She would obtain employment, usually as a domestic servant, would save money, and then would send for the next oldest daughter, and then the next, until later the husband and the sons joined the family in America. This was the case with an Irish mother of seven children who, the *Covington Journal* narrated in 1851, immigrated to Covington, became a laundress, saved money, and sent for her eldest and second daughters; finally she sent for her husband, three sons, and two youngest daughters.

The Irish of the Great Famine and afterward were, as a rule, devoutly religious. St. Mary Catholic Church in Covington (founded 1833 and renamed the **Cathedral Basilica of the Assumption**) served their needs, as did the English-speaking congregations of **Immaculate Conception Catholic Church** in Newport (established 1855), **St. Patrick Catholic Church** in Covington (organized 1872), St. Anthony Catholic Church in Bellevue (founded 1889), and St. James Catholic Church in Ludlow (founded 1886) (see **Saints Boniface and James Catholic Church**). The Sisters of Charity of Nazareth, Ky., an English-speaking sisterhood, taught many of the Irish children in Northern Kentucky and also established two schools of their own, **La Salette Academy** in Covington and **Immaculata Academy** in Newport. Irish American priests, such as Rev. Patrick Guilfoyle (1817–1892) of Immaculate Conception Church and Rev. **Thomas McGrady** of St. Anthony, were well beloved by their congregations. Guilfoyle believed that every family should be able to own a home, so he invested church funds in building about 500 affordably priced houses in Newport. Unfortunately, because of an economic downturn in the 1870s, his dream was ended.

In addition to their religious institutions, the Irish established a number of fraternal and political organizations. These included the Ancient Order of Hibernians, which had chapters in Covington and Newport in the late 19th and early 20th centuries; the National Land League (Parnell Branch, No. 1, Newport); and the Fenians (the Irish Republican Brotherhood) of the second half of the 19th century. An estimated 150 Fenians from Covington and Newport joined the 1866 failed invasion of British Canada. The Friends of Irish Freedom, whose members purchased Republic of Ireland Bonds, founded Covington, Newport, and Ludlow branches in 1920.

Irish culture gained American admirers throughout the latter half of the 19th century. One of the most famous Irish visitors to the area was Rev. Theobald Mathew (1790–1856), the "Irish Apostle of Temperance." Mathew toured the United States from 1849 to 1851 and administered a "total abstinence pledge" to 600,000 American Catholics and Protestants; he spoke in Covington on June 29, 1851. The celebration of St. Patrick's Day (March 17) increased in popularity in late-19th-century Cincinnati and Northern Kentucky. For example, in March 1877, there were two metropolitan-based processions, one on Saturday that wound its way through Cincinnati and then across the bridge to Newport and its streets before returning to Cincinnati (see **L&N Bridge**). A Sunday procession also began in Cincinnati, but it traveled over the **John A. Roebling Bridge** to Covington, through the streets of Covington, and back to Cincinnati. The festivities continued throughout the week in Cincinnati, with a musical program at Hibernia Hall featuring Northern Kentucky violinist **Joseph Tosso**, of Mexican heritage, playing a medley of Irish tunes entitled "Souvenirs of Erin."

The fertile economic soil of Northern Kentucky provided many opportunities for Irish immigrants and their descendants to achieve prominence in business, political, religious, and cultural circles. Examples include industrialists and philanthropists **Peter O'Shaughnessy** (1843–1926) and James Walsh (1818–1890) and his son Nicholas Walsh (1855–1915) (see **Walsh Distillery**), judges **Walter Cleary** (1854–1916) and **Michael Shine** (1850–1930), politicians **Thomas Donnelly** (1870–1955) and **August "Gus" Sheehan** (1917–2000), author **Mary McNamara** (1865–1938), songwriter **Haven Gillespie** (1888–1975), singers **Rosemary Clooney** (1928–2002) and **Betty Clooney** (1931–1976), television personality and author **Nick Clooney** (1934–), actor **George Clooney** (1961–), and philanthropist **Helen Theissen** (1906–2005).

Currently, Northern Kentucky has an active Irish American organization entitled the Fenians of Northern Kentucky Inc., whose objectives are "to foster the ideals and perpetuate the history and traditions of the Irish People" and "to promote Irish culture through the following—music, dance, literature, food, language, genealogy, theater, sports, foreign exchange programs, [and] architecture." Since 1997, in conjunction with **Thomas More College**, the Fenians of Northern Kentucky have sponsored an annual lecture series, *Tapestry of Irish History and Culture*. In addition, Thomas More College has had an active "sister-school" relationship with Mary Immaculate College in Limerick, Ireland, since 1998.

Cullen, Kevin. "Irish Tradition Not Forgotten in German Main Strasse," *KE*, March 13, 1983, B1.

"For the Register," *LVR*, August 13, 1847, 3.

Harris, Gen Ann. "Walsh Family Returns Home to the Cathedral." *Cathedral Chimes*, Autumn 1997, 1.

"An Interesting Incident," *CJ*, April 5, 1851, 2.

Miller, Kerby, and Paul Wagner. *Out of Ireland: The Story of Irish Emigration to America*. Washington, D.C.: Elliott and Clark, 1994.

"Notice," *Western Globe*, September 20, 1839, 2.

Reis, Jim. "The Fenian Movement: Local Irish-Americans Recruited for Ill-Fated Invasion of Canada," *KP*, March 15, 2004, 4K.

Sweeney, Michael R. "The O'Shaughnessy and Walsh Families." *Cathedral Chimes*, Winter 2005, 1–2.

Tenkotte, Paul A. "Thomas More College International Studies: Historical Overview, 1990–1998," 1998, Thomas More College, Crestview Hills, Ky.

Tenkotte, Paul A., David E. Schroeder, and Thomas S. Ward. *To Be Catholic and American in Northern, Central, and Appalachian Kentucky: The Diocese of Covington, 1853–2003*. Forthcoming.

Webb, James. *Born Fighting: How the Scots-Irish Shaped America*. New York: Broadway Books, 2004.

Paul A. Tenkotte

IRON AND STEEL MANUFACTURING. Northern Kentucky's industrial history parallels the national experience. Once, Kentucky had a substantial localized charcoal-fueled iron industry. Later, larger-scale coal-smelting "puddling furnaces" produced iron for bridges and rails. After 1860, the Bessemer air blast furnace process provided steel for widespread structural uses. Rivers carried coal from Pennsylvania, including "bituminous coking coal." During the manufacturing era, Covington and Newport ranked second and third to Louisville in production of iron and steel in the state. Besides large iron and steel mills, some local foundries specialized in items such as wire nails and "grey iron castings." Others produced finished items such as wagons, buggies, locomotives, and steam engines. Impressive large steel plants in Owensboro, Ashland, and Newport and smaller casting and forging shops continue to produce iron and steel products.

The number of market products made from iron and steel grew rapidly to meet demands for architectural materials, consumer goods, and railroad construction. In 1831 John McNickel acquired lots in Covington between Madison Ave. and Scott St. at the Ohio River, where he planned to build a factory to roll and split iron and manufacture nails. The 1839–1849 Covington city directories indicated that the rolling mill had cost $75,000. Employing 120, it was manufacturing about 1,800 tons of iron and nails yearly. In 1844 this firm, called the Covington Rolling Mill and Nail Factory, employed around 100 workers, manufacturing 10 tons of iron into sheet, nails, and bar iron of all sizes daily. On average, the factory consumed 600 bushels of stone coal and 800 of charcoal daily. An 1851 Covington map shows that the Covington factory had expanded to **Willow Run** Creek and north to 15th St. In 1860 the rolling mill had become the McNickle Rail Iron Works, owned by Martin, Stephens, and Williams. On September 23, 1865, fire destroyed much of the mill, but only 27 days later, it was back to work producing 45 tons of railroad iron per day. The *Covington Journal* in 1869 reported that Covington-made rails were being laid between Miamisburg and Carlisle, Ohio. The mill in Covington, which employed 160 workers, was producing rolled iron, bar iron, sheet iron, boiler plate, firebed iron, railroad chairs, iron rivets, ironware, and fabricated galvanized tubing, totaling $350,000 in value. Its offices were on W. Second St. in Cincinnati, and its plant was near the **John A. Roebling Bridge**. In 1871 the company sold 550 tons of iron rails at $80 per ton to the **Maysville and Lexington Railroad**. An illustrated advertisement in 1875 showed the Covington Rail Mill (a new name), with James G. and Robert Kyle as proprietors, as a three-story brick structure with factory barns and belching smokestacks. Sitting on about 4 acres and employing around 130 workers, the firm could produce, according to the ad, about 300 tons of rails per week. Just five years later, in 1880, the Covington Rail Mill was closed and offered for sale.

George W. Ball (ca. 1809–1873), John McNickle's brother-in-law, had come from Pennsylvania. Ball helped to build McNickle's iron business. However, in 1854 G. W. Ball, employing 60 workers, operated the Covington Foundry between Third and Fourth and Johnson and Main Sts. and was considering a large expansion in order to meet the demand for stoves. The mill Ball ran in 1856 was called G. W. Ball and Company, as was a plant he had that manufactured stoves and hollowware. In 1861 the mill was still called George W. Ball and Company, but the other business was named the Kentucky Stove Works.

In conjunction with the **Covington and Lexington Railroad**, one of the railroad's developers, Alexander L. Greer, and some of his partners built at Third and Philadelphia Sts. the **Covington Locomotive and Manufacturing Works**, a complex of factory buildings extending to the Ohio River. Included were a main foundry building, 100 feet square and 40 feet high; the machine shop, four stories high, measuring 160 by 45 feet; an assembly shop, 80 feet square; a blacksmith shop, 250 by 45 feet; and a boiler shop measuring 200 by 60 feet, plus brass and tin founding shops and a large yard. The company commenced making railroad locomotives in 1854, but out-of-state railroads canceled their orders, possibly because of the financial panic of 1854 and resulting delays. Nevertheless, during 1854 and early 1855, the Covington Locomotive and Manufacturing Works delivered to the Covington and Lexington Railroad four locomotives, named by the railroad the *Covington*, the *Cynthiana*, the *Paris*, and the *Lexington*. Under new ownership, the factory, now called the Kentucky Locomotive and Machine Works, built two more locomotives, the *M. M. Benton* and the *Sam J. Walker*. However, the panic of 1857 probably hastened the final closing of this locomotive manufacturing firm in Covington.

In 1850 Newport produced 900 tons of iron products; in 1860, 1,550 tons. At the time, Newport had two rolling mills, one operated by Daniel Wolff and the other by men named Swift and Evans. In the next 10 years, the Newport iron industry expanded tremendously, producing 39,500 tons in 1870, with the rolling mill operated by Swift and Evans emerging as the leader. By then Newport was out-producing Louisville, and nationwide only seven states surpassed Kentucky in iron production. But despite constantly favorable reports and having 24 coke ovens, a big crane, and a railroad connection on the rolling mill's eight-acre site, what had become the Swift Iron and Steel Works had to be sold in 1887. In 1891 Joseph and A. L. Andrews started the Globe Iron Roofing and Corrugating Company in Newport. They also purchased the Newport Rolling Mill (successor to the Swift Iron and Steel Works) to provide steel sheets for galvanizing and corrugating. Surviving various economic crises over the years, the Andrews brothers were able to expand Newport's steel industry, tie it into several steel-related businesses they owned, and thus help to make Newport into a major steel-manufacturing center. In 1923 the Newport city directory listed companies run by the Andrews family near the Licking River: the Newport Rolling Mill, the Globe Iron Roofing and Corrugating Company, the Newport Foundry Company, the Newport Culvert Company, and the **Andrews Steel Mill**, one of "the largest steel mills in the south." Descendants of the Andrews brothers finally sold their interests in 1943, having survived the hard times of the 1930s and, during the 1920s, a violent labor strike involving 1,000 workers. After the sale, the Newport Rolling Mill became Interlake Steel and continued to operate on the outskirts of Newport along the Licking River in Wilder. Later, following an extraordinary effort that secured public and private funding during the 1970s, the company, now a part of the NS Group, was reorganized as **Newport Steel** and remains in operation today.

The 1851 city map of Covington also showed, in addition to the Covington Rolling Mill and Nail Factory, a second iron mill in Covington, the Licking Iron Works. In 1850–1851 Phillip S. Bush, a retired cashier for the Covington branch of the **Northern Bank of Kentucky**, and his son John S. Bush opened the Licking Rolling Mill between 11th and 12th Sts., along the Licking River. The Licking Rolling Mill consumed annually 175,000 bushels of coal, 3,000 tons of pig iron, and 1,000 tons of other raw metals in order to produce iron bars, iron sheets, other materials, and hardware. Between 1851 and 1861, city directories listed the

Licking Iron Works and another firm, known as Thomas Phillips and Son, as being ironworks operators. In 1859 a Cincinnati digest reported that the Licking Rolling Mill was one of 10 rolling mills for the Cincinnati market, although located outside of the city. The digest also noted that the Phillips and Son mill in Covington employed 275, operating all days except Sundays and consuming annually 500,000 bushels of coal. It produced 3,000 tons of "small round and square and hoop iron," 2,000 tons of "large round and square, railroad chair iron," 2,000 tons of "fire bed and sheet iron," 1,000 tons of "boiler iron, heads," and 8,000 tons of "iron of all descriptions," averaging $87.50 per ton, with an aggregate value of $700,000. Furthermore, the digest article observed, "The sheet iron made here is annealed on the surface, which renders it apparently equal to the Russia sheets." This plant was located on six and one-half acres.

In the antebellum United States, German immigrants brought old-world industry to Covington. At age 20, **Ignatius Droege** left Germany, where his father owned an iron mill situated on the Ruhr River. After his arrival in Covington in 1849, the Bush and Jordan Licking Rolling Mill hired Droege as a blacksmith. Later in 1861, when a foundry was established in connection with the rolling mill, the new partnership of Phillips and Jordan put Droege in charge. Soon the mill was fabricating iron chains used by Union military forces in the Civil War for naval blockades.

In 1843 Charles Bogenshutz arrived in New Orleans; he moved to Cincinnati in 1856 and soon established a hardware store in Covington on Pike St. between Washington St. and Madison Ave. By 1868 Droege had joined Bogenshutz in a business partnership called the Kentucky Iron Foundry and Machine Shop, which produced well-known brands of heating and cooking stoves popular in the "south and southwest." In 1869 Droege agreed to make iron columns for the new **Mother of God Catholic Church** building. At his E. 16th St. plant in Covington, he cast the columns, almost 50 feet long, in a "horizontal flask form" in sand molds stiffened with a molasses-based formula. He also engineered the delivery of the columns and their erection at the site of the new church. Droege became a full partner with Bogenshutz in 1873. Ignatius Droege and Company, in Covington at 16th St. near the Licking River, claimed to be able to make "anything that could be cast in iron."

That same year, a financial panic saw the Licking Rolling Mill go into receivership. In 1877 Droege borrowed money and purchased a half interest in the financially troubled mill. Henry Worthington purchased the other half, to form the Worthington and Droege Iron and Steel Manufacturing Company. After a decade in the stove business, Droege sold his share back to Bogenshutz. Years later, after some employee "fraud and malfeasance" during the brief presidency of Bogenshutz's son Lawrence, the Charles Bogenshutz Foundry closed in 1903. Afterward, John Casper Droege purchased the business for $10,500.

In 1881 and 1882, the iron and steel workers struck unsuccessfully, trying for a wage increase to $33 per week. In 1897 Ignatius Droege retired at age 69, a wealthy man. In 1905 a big fire, thought by some to have been arson, did almost $100,000 damage to the business. Substantial insurance payments helped overcome the losses. In 1906 a fire hit the Kentucky Iron Roofing and Corrugating Company at 12th and Wheeler Sts., a business partnership formed by John Casper Droege and John H. Mersmann in 1902. In 1906 reorganization placed the Licking Rolling Mill, the I. Droege and Sons Foundry, and the I. Droege and Sons Coal Company under one entity, the I. Droege Iron Foundry and Coal Company, with capital valued at $1 million. Company production reached 25,000 tons of bar iron annually, with sales of $500,000 mostly to industry in the "south and southwest," and a monthly payroll of $3,500, for 350 workers "on average."

In February 1908 another fire caused some $200,000 in damage, and among the items damaged was a much-valued special "steam hammer" that pounded metal into sheets. Insurance covered little more than 10 percent of the loss. Droege's sons had also made heavy California gold investments and engaged in other misadventures, squandering capital and goodwill from other stockholders. After litigation, the disgruntled stockholders achieved a reorganization that temporarily relieved the Droeges of control of the company. However, in June 1908 a federal court in Covington gave it back. The Droeges raised $50,000 and reincorporated as the Licking Rolling Mill. Seeking reemployment at the mill for workers living in Covington, the city voted to give the Licking Rolling Mill a five-year municipal tax exemption. In September 1908 the mill reopened, calling some 300 workers back to work in the midst of a national depression. Ominously, three weeks later the water level in the Licking River dropped so low that production stopped; workers had to lengthen the water supply pipes. In 1911, after the Licking Rolling Mill had declared bankruptcy, a U.S. District Court appointed trustees to handle the company's business affairs. In 1912 the court approved the sale of the property, the machinery, the tools and appliances, a platform scale in the street, and all the scrap iron on hand for $25,500.

On March 22, 1873, the *Covington Journal* reported that John Mitchell, James Tranter, and associates had purchased the former Covington hemp-bagging mill property between Philadelphia St. and Willow Run Creek, extending to the Ohio River. There they operated one of the biggest rolling mills "in the west" as the Ohio Valley Steel and Iron Works; they had a warehouse on W. Second St. in Cincinnati. Walter J. Mitchell was president and Charles Tranter was vice president. In the 1880s about 300 Amalgamated Association of Iron and Steel Workers walked off the job at the factory. In 1898 the firm's management complained that taxes and water rates were too high and city services too slow. The city had denied a right-of-way for a railroad connection. Around 1900 the mill was sold to Republic Iron and Steel, in a trust headquartered at Vandergrift, Pa., that later was relocated to Chicago. Republic Iron and Steel soon laid off or relocated several of its workers in Covington. According to the company, these relocations were necessary "because of high costs and inadequate facilities" in Covington. In 1907, with many of its Covington employees already relocated to Sheffield, Ala., Republic Iron and Steel sold its Covington properties and left town.

Walking on Pike St., on Madison Ave., and on the residential sidewalks of Covington, pedestrians still can read emblems on fencing and iron storefronts that were manufactured by the Covington Iron Works, by Fred J. Meyers, or by the **Stewart Iron Works**. Started in 1856 by John Mieth, the Fred. J. Meyers Wire Works had a store in Covington on E. 12th St. and a factory on E. 10th St. in 1876. By 1886 the company manufactured architectural ironwork, iron storefronts, stairs, and shutters at 419–423 Madison Ave. in two brick buildings. One of the buildings had six stories and measured 47 by 150 feet; the other had two stories and was 23 by 190 feet. In 1893 a fire that did $450,000 in damage, called the largest in Covington's history, gutted the Fred J. Meyers Company, a nearby church, and some of the neighboring businesses. Less than half of the damage, $210,000, was to the Fred J. Meyers Company, but the firm chose not to rebuild.

In 1894 the Covington city directory listed the Covington Architectural Iron Works, John H. Lutter, proprietor, on the east side of Court St. between Fourth and Fifth Sts. In 1900 Lutter and George F. Roth were proprietors at the northeast corner of Ninth and Washington Sts. The 1904–1905 city directory also listed the company under "Jail Works." In the decade 1908–1918, Roth was the proprietor and the firm provided structural and ornamental iron and steel, sidewalk lights, cellar doors, gratings, iron and wire fencing, and grillwork. This was an important local company for several decades, but by 1929 it had closed.

Newport still is home to the Buecker Company, started in 1858 as the Buecker Machinery and Iron works (see **Buecker Iron Works**) by German immigrant Ernst Buecker Sr. The company fabricated iron fencing for many residences in various cities nationwide. It is still located at 29 W. Sixth St. The firm's recent owners, David Buecker and Linda Velton, are fifth-generation members of the family. The Buecker Company still attaches its signature label to a wide variety of custom-made metal consumer and commercial orders. This company is one of Kentucky's Centennial Businesses.

By 1876 another German immigrant, Father Joseph Goebbels, a local Catholic priest, had helped organize the American Wire and Screw Nail Company, "the first of its kind," and he served briefly as its president. Using techniques learned in Germany, the firm made "modern nails." Father Goebbels's activities occasionally are cited as a unique story because while heading this business he was a practicing priest who had his residence at Covington's **St. Augustine Catholic Church**. By 1881 J. L. Stephens was the company's president and treasurer. In 1890 L. H. Gedge was president of the newly named American Wire Nail Company, and the firm was manufacturing "standard wire nails" at its factory on the east side of Washington St. in Covington between 15th and 16th Sts.; F. C. Gedge was first vice president and B. H. Gedge was secretary. By 1894, however, the firm was no longer in business.

By 1892 in Covington, the **Houston, Stanwood & Gamble Company** was manufacturing steam engines and boilers, selling engines to power mills in the South and in the Caribbean, and selling boilers domestically to heat large buildings and laundries. In 1905 the *Kentucky Post* reported that the Houston, Stanwood & Gamble Company was building for its boilermaking department "the largest floor space in the city" at a site in Covington just east of Philadelphia St. In 1910 the company quickly fired 20 men when they chose to strike for a two-and-a-half-cent raise. In 1916 the firm's machinists walked out for a reduction of hours. The company soon offered a reduction from 60 to 52 hours. In 1909 Charles Houston, the company's president, proposed the laying of railroad tracks along Willow Run Creek. Ten years later, there was talk of dredging a harbor at the end of Willow Run. During **World War I**, the Houston, Stanwood & Gamble Company received a $200,000 war order for 200 lathes under a subcontract with the Cincinnati Iron and Steel Company. But electrification, poor management, and the Ohio River **flood of 1937** led to the Covington company's end. The Houston, Stanwood & Gamble Company had cast steam engine blocks, fireboxes, and large flywheels and fashioned boiler tanks.

During the late 1800s and early 1900s, lesser-known companies operating in Covington included the Excelsior Foundry Facing Mills, located on Third St. at the **Chesapeake and Ohio Railroad** (C&O) tracks; the Dean Waterman Company, at 70 W. Ninth St.; the Insurance Foundry, south of 15th St. and west of Madison Ave.; Frank F. Decker, at 125 W. 13th St.; and the Western Foundry Company, at Third and Philadelphia Sts. From the early 1900s, the Moeschel Edwards Corrugating Company manufactured iron and steel roofing, sidings and ceilings, eaves troughs, conductor pipe, and metal shingles; later it made fireproof rolling steel doors and industrial overhead doors, first on W. Ninth St., then at 812 Russell St. This company closed its Covington plant in the 1980s, but the firm's name has been listed in other locations, including Newport. In 1913 C. B. Edwards was this company's president; in 1960 Paul C. Edwards was president and C. B. Edwards was vice president and secretary.

After his father, Lewis Michaels, had started the Michaels Art Bronze Company, Frank L. Michaels relocated the company in 1913 from Cincinnati to Second and Scott Sts. in Covington. In 1954 the company was again relocated, this time to a facility at Kenton Lands Rd. in Erlanger. In 1958 Frank Michaels was chief executive officer and Lawrence Michaels was president. The company did contract work on a University of Louisville building, a Square-D plant in Lexington, and the Prudential Insurance building in Chicago, where it supplied stainless steel column coverings and framework for an observation tower. In the 1950s the Michaels Art and Bronze Company had a local crew of 157 make the gleaming stainless steel curtain walls for the Inland Steel Corporation's skyscraper in Chicago, giving the company, and the structural and cosmetic qualities of its work, national exposure to architectural professionals. In 1958 the Michaels Art and Bronze Company bid to install "wrap-around porcelain" on the then new Kroger Building in Cincinnati. In 1991 the Michaels Art and Bronze Company was purchased by the Crescent Designed Metals Company, "a pioneer in architectural metal work," which was founded in Kentucky in 1870 but now operates in Philadelphia as Crescent Designed Metals–Michaels Art Bronze.

George H. Klaene immigrated to the United States in 1866 with his widowed mother and his family. He helped organize the Star Foundry in Covington and was its president in 1890. Klaene attended **St. Joseph Catholic** parochial school and joined the "molders trade." The firm Klaene founded began as a "jobbing foundry." It specialized in stoves and ranges, employed 40 workers, and sold to markets in Ohio, Indiana, and Kentucky. Star Foundry, located at Third, Main, and Second Sts. and the C&O Railroad, also manufactured "Steel Ranges, Cast Ranges, Stoves, Gas Ranges, Oak Heaters, Hot Blast Heaters, Air Tight Heaters, Franklin Heaters, Cannon Stoves, and Laundry Stoves." In 1938 William H. Hoppenjans was president of Star Foundry; in 1956 the company's president was Robert B. Hoppenjans.

In 1880 Martin and Reynolds operated the Kenton Iron Foundry and Railing Works in Covington on Main St. between Second and Third Sts. In 1890 the William H. Martin and James J. Reynolds Foundry cast grate bars and stove linings. In 1890 Harry H. Martin was secretary-treasurer and general manager; he was a third-generation member of the Martin family. The company sold iron castings throughout the Ohio River Valley. In 1890 Martin reorganized the business as the Germania Supply and Foundry, and in 1914 it was operating in Covington at Second St. and Western Ave. By 1923 the company had been renamed the Martin Foundry; it cast grey iron and other related items, such as steel sewer lids.

By 1932 the Klaene family operated another foundry in Covington at 1530 Russell St. In 1940 it was the Klaene and Kruckmeyer Foundry, in business at 14th and Chesapeake Sts. In 1946 fire destroyed a main foundry building under construction at 1320 Russell St. In 1948, at 1545 Russell St., what was now known as the Klaene Foundry manufactured "grey iron castings," and the Precision Casting Company at the same address produced "aluminum alloy metal."

In 1955 a Molders and Foundry Workers Union strike hit the Martin, the Star, and the Klaene foundries. The city of Covington purchased the Martin Foundry's properties for urban renewal in the mid-1960s. Star Foundry soon ceased operations. In 1975 a $1 million fire "completely destroyed the family-owned Klaene Foundry" at 16th and Russell Sts. in Covington. But the Stewart Iron Works, probably Covington's best-known company, and others still continue to fabricate metal products.

Edmondson, Joyce, Barbara Droege, and James R. Deters. "Immigrant Industrialists: Droege and Bogenschutz." *NKH* 8, no. 1 (Fall–Winter 2005): 2–23.

Lietzenmayer, Karl J. "Stewart Iron Works: A Kentucky Centenary Company," *NKH* 5, no. 1 (Autumn–Winter 1997): 1–14.

Purvis, Thomas L., ed. *Newport, Kentucky: A Bicentennial History*. Newport, Ky.: Otto Zimmerman, 1996.

Reis, Jim. "Church Arose from Ashes," *KP*, August 5, 2002, 4K.

———. "Heritage Shaped along the Licking," *KP*, November 12, 1990, 4K.

White, John H. *Cincinnati Locomotive Builders, 1845–1868*. 3rd ed. Cincinnati: Cincinnati Museum Center at Union Terminal, 2004.

John Boh

I-71, I-75, I-275, I-471. See **Expressways**.

ITALIAN AMERICANS. It has been well over 100 years since more than 4.5 million Italians immigrated to the United States, representing the last of the mass migrations from Europe. Ultimately, the Italian immigrants totaled about 10 percent of the overall U.S. population. That percentage excludes the Italians known as "birds of passage," who came to the United States just so that they could work, send money back home, and then ultimately return to Italy. In Northern Kentucky, the Italians trickled in around the mid-19th century; the mass migration to the region began around 1887 and continued through 1924. According to the most common figures, 4.1 percent of Newport's foreign-born residents were of Italian descent, and they represented 2 percent of the city's overall population. These figures may be unreliable because most of the Italian population resided in the city of Clifton, which was not annexed by Newport until November 26, 1935. Census data and naturalization records were also flawed in that many of the immigrants did not follow the federal guidelines for applying for citizenship and often mistrusted the government's desire to record their whereabouts.

By comparison, the immigration to the Cincinnati area began earlier in the 1800s with a group of Genoese merchants who crossed the Atlantic, passed through the Gulf of Mexico, and arrived in New Orleans. They made their way up the Mississippi River and settled on the banks of the Ohio River in downtown Cincinnati. The early success of these northern Italian immigrants led the way for more to follow. The Italian population gradually built to more than 4,000 living in the downtown area of Cincinnati as early as 1892. The Italians who settled in the Northern Kentucky region were, for the most part, from the southern regions of Abruzzi, Calabria, Campania, Molise, and Sicily, Italy. They came to start a new life away from the devastation brought about in Italy by earthquakes, poverty, and diseases such as malaria that ran rampant throughout the country. Most of these new immigrants, who arrived before 1892, were processed through Castle Garden, New York City, and later through Ellis Island, N.Y., which opened in 1892.

Many Italians worked their way to the Northern Kentucky area by way of Ohio, Pennsylvania, Virginia, and West Virginia. Jobs were plentiful in the steel mills and the coal mines of these neighboring states. Italian immigrants were encouraged to come to the region by employment brokers from the United States, who would visit their hometowns in Italy and recruit them. This was done especially for tailors and stonemasons. In those cases, some came directly to Northern Kentucky and settled. Those who owned and operated their own businesses seemed to settle in the urban areas of Newport and Covington, where they lived in a house or an apartment above their store or business. Others, who were interested in farming or who wanted a more residential area, settled in **Cote Brilliante**. The Italian settlement stronghold, however, was Clifton, later known as South Newport.

Family also influenced the migration to the Northern Kentucky area. Some Italians came to buy property of their own. Once established, they would sponsor other family members or neighbors to come. It was also a common practice for Italian parents to prearrange their children's marriages, often as early as at birth; children were promised to wed when they became of age. For these reasons, many of the Italians who settled in the areas of Cote Brilliante, Covington, Newport, and Clifton, which was known as Spaghetti Knob, were related or at least acquainted with one another. Examples of Italian immigrant families coming from the same small towns are the Arcaro (see **Eddie Arcaro**), Armenti, Farro, Forde, Forte, Giancola, and Vacca families, from the town of Castelpetroso; the Greco, Pellillo, and Ialungo families, from the town of Bagnoli del Trigno; and the Ciafardini and Porfirio families, from the town of Trivento. All three of these towns are in the province of Campobasso (now Isernia), in the region of Molise, Italy. It is easy to see how the Italians decided to settle in a concentrated area such as Clifton, a barren, undeveloped area situated on a hill, resembling many of the families' hometowns in Italy.

One of the earliest immigrants to settle in Campbell Co. was Charles Graziani, who was born in 1806 in the town of Oneglia, in northwest Italy near Genoa, immigrated around 1845, and died August 6, 1866, in a steamboat accident aboard the *General Lytle*. He was an accomplished artist, the son of the count of Oneglia. He married Emma Sanham, settled in Cold Spring, and the couple raised nine children. His youngest child, **Benjamin Graziani**, was born in Cold Spring and became an influential criminal attorney, state representative, and leader of Covington's Italian community.

While many Italian neighborhoods around the nation had groupings called Little Italy, Northern Kentucky had Spaghetti Knob, which was actually the city of Clifton, incorporated on February 15, 1888. Although the Germans and the Irish already occupied this city, a small community of Italians began building homes in the area during the early 1900s. It was just the right place for the Italians to plant vegetable gardens, grow grapes to make wine, and raise goats, pigs, and chickens for the dinner table.

At the heart of this Italian Roman Catholic community was the annual celebration of the Feast of the Assumption of the Blessed Virgin Mary, whose feast day is celebrated on August 15. The Italians were accustomed to honoring their patron saints with traditional feasts, street parades, and festivals, customs brought with them from Italy. With their devotion to the Blessed Mother and their flair for pageantry, they began a tradition of celebrating the Feast of the Assumption of the Blessed Virgin Mary by carrying the statue of the Blessed Mother through the streets of Clifton. The feast was first celebrated on August 14 and 15, 1926, and chaired by Eugene "Gene" Giancola. A festival followed at **St. Vincent de Paul Catholic Church**, and by the following year, first-generation Italian American girls, dressed in authentic Italian costumes, served as waitresses for the Italian dinner served in the school. The celebration continued through the following decades, gradually ending in the 1960s.

Giancola was one of the most prominent and respected Italian Americans. The son of Archangelo and Rufina Armenti Giancola, he was born on a ship that arrived in the United States in 1893. Gene Giancola held leadership roles in every facet of life in Clifton. He was the founder and editor of the *Hill Top Herald,* a community newspaper he created during **World War II** to keep the community and area servicemen informed of what was happening at home and abroad. He married Rosina "Rosie" Porfirio in 1916, and they resided at the corner of Ash and Main Sts.

Rev. Herman J. Wetzels, pastor of St. Vincent de Paul Church, organized a group of cadets in Clifton on August 17, 1920. The cadets, who were preparing to become Knights of St. John, were engaged in various charitable works throughout the community. They also formed a band, marched in area parades, and performed concerts for the general public. The Knights of St. John is an international, multiethnic organization that included many local Italians. It held its meetings at St. Stephen Catholic Church, at Ninth and Washington Sts. in Newport (see **Holy Spirit Catholic Church**). Some of the local Italians active in the organization were Joseph Coley; Carl, Eugene, Frank, Julius, and Paschal Giancola; Joseph and Anthony Larvo; Joseph Ledonne; Anthony Paolucci; and Ralph Zappa.

Along with the Italian families who immigrated came the introduction of Italian cuisine to the general public. Family-owned Italian restaurants opened up throughout the region, each with its own specialty. Forde's Restaurant, owned and operated by Michael and Bernadette Testa Forde, was famous for ravioli. Luigi's Restaurant, known for its pizza, was owned and operated by Tony and Helen Zechella. In fact, Tony's father, Louis "Luigi" Zechella, is said to be the person who first introduced pizza into the Northern Kentucky region. Sam Santini operated Santini's Bar and Restaurant, which later became known as Grandview Gardens in South Newport. For more than 50 years, John Michael "Colonel" and Johanna Coletta "Jay" Pompilio operated **Pompilio's Restaurant**, a casual dining landmark in Newport known for its authentic Italian spaghetti dinners. Of these restaurants, only Pompilio's remains open today; it is currently a family-run enterprise headed by Frank C. and Peter F. Mazzei. Farther east, in Maysville, is Caproni's Restaurant, currently owned and operated by Jerry Lundegan. It opened in 1945 and still retains the name of its founding family.

In Italian culture, life is worth celebrating, and the early immigrants availed themselves of every opportunity to celebrate. In addition to church and family events, Columbus Day was observed as early as 1892 in Cincinnati and Northern Kentucky by all nationalities. Full-scale replicas of the ships the *Nina,* the *Pinta*, and the *Santa Maria* passed by on the Ohio River. The festivities included elaborate parades with decorated floats and wagons. Local militia and military troops from the **Fort Thomas Military Reservation** also participated. In later years, Columbus Day in Northern Kentucky was usually celebrated with a banquet. Today the holiday is organized and celebrated by the Cincinnati Chapter of the Order of the Sons of Italy. Italian Day at the Coney Island Amusement Park on Cincinnati's East Side was first established in 1952 and held every year at the Coney Island Pavilion until the park closed in 1971. The Newport Italianfest, a four-day celebration of family, friends, and entertainment, currently maintains the region's Italian heritage. The festival completed its 15th year in 2006.

Casebolt, Pamela Ciafardini, and Philip G. Ciafardini. *Italians of Newport and Northern Kentucky.* Charleston, S.C.: Arcadia, 2007.

"Company of Cadets Formed in Clifton," *KTS,* August 17, 1920, 19.

Reis, Jim. *Pieces of the Past.* Vol. 2. Covington, Ky.: Kentucky Post, 1991.

Pamela Ciafardini Casebolt

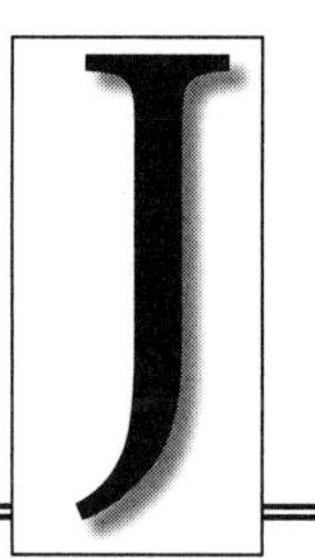

JACKSON, CECIL (b. October 5, 1929, Owen Co., Ky.). Cecil Elmore Jackson Sr. of Dry Ridge in Grant Co., the son of Alvie and Dolly Webster Jackson, worked for the Cincinnati Zoo for more than 50 years, mostly as an animal trainer. He had no idea in 1951, when he went to the zoo to visit his brother, that his career had just begun. From first driving the zoo's passenger train, he gravitated to training horses and ponies and then to training chimpanzees and elephants. Jackson found that he was a natural animal trainer. He has taught chimps to ride bicycles and elephants to stand on two feet. The elephants My-Thai and Ganesh were two of his protégés. He was also present at the birth of many of these animals. Jackson often brought trained zoo animals to parades in the region, to former Cincinnati Reds Baseball Team owner Marge Schott's home, and occasionally even to local marriage ceremonies. Two strokes have partiality disabled Jackson, but his son Cecil Jackson Jr. (b. 1961) has been trained to replace his father, and the animals at the Cincinnati Zoo currently remain under his good handling.

"Pachyderm to Lead Party to the Altar," *KP*, August 9, 1985, 5K.

Roberts, Alice Kennelly. "Zoo Trainer Marks 40 Years with the Elephants," *KP*, January 8, 1992, 2KK.

Whitehead, Shelly. "Half a Century of Zoo Memories: The Elephant Man Remembers," *KP*, April 18, 2000, 1C.

JACKSON, JOHN P. (b. March 7, 1833, Cleveland, Ohio; d. September 25, 1900, San Francisco, Calif.). One-time Newport resident John Putnam Jackson was a Republican Party leader in Kentucky and later an influential journalist in California. Jackson came to Cincinnati as a teenager. After graduating from Cincinnati's Central High School, he studied law in the office of Judge Bellamy Storer, where he began a lifelong friendship with future president Benjamin Harrison (1889–1893). Jackson was admitted to the bar and formed a law partnership with George Hoadly, who later became governor of Ohio. For more than a decade, Jackson lived in Newport with his wife, the former Anna Hooper, with whom he raised nine children. He pioneered team sports in the Ohio River Valley as a member of the Kentucky Town Ball Club (see **Townball**). During the **Civil War**, Jackson supported the Union as a lieutenant colonel in the 23rd Kentucky Infantry Regiment and later served under generals Ulysses S. Grant and Henry Halleck. Jackson's eloquent speeches on behalf of Abraham Lincoln and Ulysses S. Grant during the 1864 and 1868 presidential elections brought him to the forefront of Kentucky Republicans. In 1868 the Republican Party nominated him for governor of Kentucky, but he declined in favor of fellow Campbell Co. attorney **Richard Tarvin Baker**. Jackson also refused the Republican nomination to run for a seat in the U.S. Congress from Kentucky's sixth district.

Jackson's reluctance to seek elected office stemmed in part from his busy legal practice. He went to Europe in 1867 to negotiate bonds for the California Pacific Railroad. He became president of that railroad and moved to San Francisco to supervise its construction. By 1875 Jackson had left his lucrative career in the railroad business and had turned his attention to journalism. As publisher and managing editor, Jackson built the *San Francisco Daily Evening Post* into one of California's leading Republican newspapers. He later became publisher of the *Wasp*, a prominent political satire magazine. In addition to his journalistic pursuits, Jackson was proprietor of the Napa Soda Springs, a popular northern California resort. He finally answered the call of public service when President Benjamin Harrison appointed him assistant secretary of the treasury. At the time of his death in 1900, Jackson was serving as collector for the Port of San Francisco under President William McKinley (1897–1901). Jackson's burial location is unknown.

The Bay of San Francisco: The Metropolis of the Pacific Coast and Its Suburban Cities, a History. Vol. 2. Chicago: Lewis, 1892.

"Jackson," *San Francisco Chronicle*, September 26, 1900, 10. Funeral notice.

"Radical State Convention," *CJ*, February 29, 1868, 2.

West, Richard Samuel. *The San Francisco Wasp: An Illustrated History*. Easthampton, Mass.: Periodyssey Press, 2004.

Greg Perkins

JAMES, NANCY POLMAN (b. August 3, 1953, South Bend, Ind.). Singer and television host Nancy James is the oldest daughter of Louis and Becky Polman's four children. Nancy is a professionally trained vocalist, specializing in the popular standards. She attended the College Conservatory of Music (CCM) at the University of Cincinnati in 1971–1973, where she concentrated on musical theater. Nancy sang professionally at nightclubs, and during that time her agent suggested that she choose a stage name; she selected James, which was her father's middle name. At age 21 she was invited to become a regular cast member and singer in Cincinnati on the live television show *Bob Braun's 50-50 Club*. There, through 1983, she learned the broadcast business, gaining confidence as an on-air personality by interviewing guests and presenting commercials. In 1981 she received a regional Emmy award for On-Air Performer of the Year.

Over the years, James sang with full orchestras and jazz trios at the once famous *Sutmiller's* supper club in Dayton, Ohio, and at *Maggie's Opera House* and the *Playboy Club*, both in Cincinnati. She often participated in *Bob Braun Show* reunions at local venues with other Braun cast members such as Rob Reider, Colleen Sharp, and **Mary Ellen Tanner**, singing favorites from the legendary, locally produced AVCO television programs.

James occasionally leads singing of the national anthem for the Cincinnati Reds baseball home games. She has performed regionally for commercials, narrated industrial films, and hosted trade shows, pageants, benefits, travel tours, and award shows, as well as moderating discussions and debates. She has been a vocalist with the Cincinnati Symphony Orchestra, the **Kentucky Symphony Orchestra**, the Pete Wagner Big Band, and other local orchestras and music groups.

In the late 1990s, Nancy hosted an afternoon show of popular standards, offering informative commentary, on Cincinnati's WSAI radio. In 2005 she returned to television as the host of the local live talk show *Northern Kentucky Magazine* on ICN6, Insight **cable television**.

Nancy is married to Bill Phelan and lives in Western Hills in Cincinnati. She has lived in Cincinnati since her early days attending CCM in 1971. The Phelans have a daughter, Amy, and a son, Billy.

Knippenberg, Jim. "Star Enjoyed ·Helping Others Build Careers," *CE*, January 16, 2001, A4.

Nancy James.net. "Nancy James." www.nancyjames.net (accessed May 3, 2007).

Wood, Mary. "Nancy Giving Up Romance," *CP (TV Plus Magazine)*, April 17, 1976, 2.

John Schlipp

JAMES, OLLIE M. (b. October 16, 1908, Kuttawa, Ky.; d. January 26, 1972, Cincinnati, Ohio). Ollie Murray James, a newspaper columnist and humorist, was born in the small Western Kentucky town of Kuttawa, in Lyon Co. In 1959 Kuttawa had to be moved to higher ground when Barkley Lake was created. Ollie was a nephew of U.S. vice president Alben W. Barkley, for whom the lake and dam are named. The James family moved to Louisville when Ollie was four years old. He was educated in Louisville public schools and at the University of Kentucky in Lexington. After graduating, James took a job as political writer and Washington, D.C., correspondent for the Louisville *Herald Post*. In the mid-1930s, the newspaper filed for bankruptcy, and James became an editorial writer and assistant managing editor for the *Cincinnati Enquirer*. He was promoted to chief editorial writer in 1944. While working for the *Enquirer*, he lived in Kentucky, first in Fort Thomas and later for many years at 1885 **Dixie Highway**, in Lookout Heights (now Fort Wright). The latter home had a swamplike backyard filled with frogs, causing James to refer to his home affectionately as Bullfrog Holler. The house was easily recognized for the many antennae attached to it—he was a ham radio operator as well as a writer.

Ollie James married Elizabeth Hazelrigg, and they had no children. He remained with the *Enquirer* for 35 years and, along with other duties, wrote a daily column called *Innocent Bystander*. His humorous articles made him a local celebrity, and his sayings were widely quoted by an adoring public. He also became a popular after-dinner speaker at social functions. In 1969 Ohio governor James Rhodes presented to James the Governor's

Award, the state's highest honor given for outstanding public service. Owing to ill health, Ollie retired from the newspaper business in July 1971. He died at age 63, in Holmes Hospital, Cincinnati. Funeral services were held at the Allison and Rose Funeral Home in Covington, and he was cremated.

"Everyone Called Him Ollie," *CE*, January 27, 1972, 20.
"Name, Ollie M. James," *CE*, October 9, 1988, suppl., 44.
"Ollie M. James, 63, Columnist," *KE*, January 27, 1972, 24K.
Univ. of Kentucky School of Journalism and Telecommunications. "Ollie M. James." www.uky.edu (accessed March 23, 2006).

Jack Wessling

JAMES A. RAMAGE CIVIL WAR MUSEUM. The James A. Ramage Civil War Museum is located in Fort Wright, at the site of Civil War Battery Hooper. The museum opened on June 30, 2005, and a formal dedication was held on August 20, 2005. The mission of the museum is to inform visitors about the defense of Northern Kentucky and Cincinnati during the Civil War, especially how the community came together to defend the area during the 1862 Confederate invasion, the region's greatest military crisis. Exhibit topics include the history of Fort Wright and the career of Fern Storer, who was food editor for the *Cincinnati Post* from 1951 to 1976.

The museum is housed in the former home of Sheldon and Fern Storer. The couple donated generously to Northern Kentucky University (NKU) in Highland Heights, and when Fern died on May 28, 2002, their home and property were left to the NKU Foundation. At that time, Dr. James A. Ramage, history professor at NKU; Larry Klein, city administrator of the City of Fort Wright; Jeannine Kreinbrink, adjunct archaeology professor at NKU; the Storers' neighbor Kathy Romero; and others formed a committee to save the battery. The NKU Foundation sold the land to the City of Fort Wright in 2003, with the understanding that the battery would be preserved and a park created for students, researchers, and the general public to conduct historical and archaeological research.

Ramage received an NKU University-Community Partnership Grant to work with the City of Fort Wright to involve students and the community in research. Fort Wright mayor Gene Weaver and the City Council named the museum in honor of Ramage's work in the project. Ramage, a native of Paducah, earned a PhD in history from the University of Kentucky in Lexington and began his career at NKU on January 2, 1972. He received the Kentucky Governor's Volunteer Activist Award in 1978 for his work in developing a parks and recreation program for the City of Highland Heights. Ramage has published numerous articles and book reviews in addition to three books: *John Wesley Hunt: Pioneer Merchant, Manufacturer, and Financier* (1974), *Rebel Raider: The Life of General John Hunt Morgan* (1986), and *Gray Ghost: The Life of Col. John Singleton Mosby* (1999). At NKU, Ramage won the Outstanding Professor of the Year Award in 1988 and was awarded the NKU Board of Regents's highest honor, the Regents Professorship, in 1994.

"Battery Hooper Days," *KP*, August 16, 2006, A2.
Cotton, Megan. "Dedication Set for War Museum—Honors Banker Named for Prof," *KP*, August 19, 2005, 2K.
"Fort Wright Dig," *KP*, May 8, 2006, A4.

Andrea Watkins

JAMES TAYLOR MANSION. In about 1814 Gen. **James Taylor Jr.** built his mansion, which still stands at 335 E. Third St. in Newport. The building site was a portion of a 1,500-acre parcel that his father, Col. James Taylor Sr., had purchased from a friend, **George Muse**.

James Taylor Jr. came to Northern Kentucky in spring 1793 to live and to develop his father's land that became Newport; James Taylor Sr. gave his son 500 acres and retained ownership of the remaining 1,000 acres. James Jr. and his slaves built several small log cabins, including one on the site where the mansion later was built. He set aside 180 acres for his personal estate and began the sale of building lots. In about 1817–1819 he replaced his small log cabin with a large masonry house. That building was destroyed in an 1842 fire set by a disgruntled slave. An 1817 letter reveals that the nationally renowned architect Benjamin Henry Latrobe was working with the Taylor family on house plans; further, Latrobe's son, John H. B. Latrobe, asserted in an 1876 biographical essay that he believed his father designed the Taylor estate in Newport called Bellevue (meaning "beautiful view"). In the mid-1840s, following the 1842 fire, the mansion was rebuilt, perhaps using the original foundation, as well as some of the former home's materials. Greek Revival in style, the 1840s Bellevue featured an entrance front of three bays facing north (toward the Ohio River), a one-story portico with Ionic columns, and quoins on the corners of the house.

An unusual feature of the estate was a servant tunnel that led from the mansion's basement northward to the Ohio River. Some have said that it was later used as part of the Underground Railroad. The Ohio River **flood of 1937** destroyed much of the tunnel, and the owners demolished the remainder. When the city of Bellevue later developed adjacent to the mansion, it took its name from the mansion.

The house originally had an unobstructed view of the estate grounds, all the way to the Ohio River. However, over the years, the Taylor family sold off much of their land, and factories and homes were built between the mansion and the river. Because of the diminished view, the front and back of the building were reversed in the 1890s, making the house face Third St. At that time the north portico and both the east and west wings were removed, and the materials were probably used to build a new addition to the north side. A two-story Palladian portico was added to the new front, along with an entry door that featured crystal beveled glass and a window above, displaying the Taylor coat of arms. In the front hall a cantilevered spiral staircase was constructed.

Upon the death of Gen. James Taylor Jr., the house passed to his son Col. **James Taylor III**, then to his grandson John B. Taylor, and finally to John's widow, Betty Washington Taylor. After she died, the estate was unable to pay the real estate taxes, so the property was sold at public auction in 1919. Ben Vonderhaar and George Stetter were the highest bidders, and they began operating the Vonderhaar-Stetter Funeral Home in the mansion. One spectacular funeral that occurred there was for Madam Lena, a Newport palmist. Her body was conveyed from the funeral home to the cemetery in a vintage white carriage, pulled by a team of white horses (see **Gypsies**). In 2003 David Gerner, an attorney-at-law, purchased the Taylor Mansion for law offices. He and his wife Maureen have faithfully restored the mansion to its original elegance, and today it is a signature property in Newport's East Row Historic District.

Fazio, Michael W. and Patrick A. Snadon. *The Domestic Architecture of Benjamin Henry Latrobe*. Baltimore, Md.: Johns Hopkins Univ. Press, 2006.
Reis, Jim. "Four Buildings Preserve a Portion of History That Will Stir Fond Recollections for Many Residents," *KP*, November 9, 1992, 4K.
Tenkotte, Paul A. "Rival Cities to Suburbs: Covington and Newport, Kentucky, 1790–1890," PhD diss., Univ. of Cincinnati, 1989.

JAMES TAYLOR NARRATIVE. James Taylor Jr., **Hubbard Taylor**, Robert Taylor, Richard Taylor, and Gen. **Thomas S. Jesup** each played a part in the writing of this historic narrative consisting of 69 typewritten pages. The first James Taylor came to America from Carlisle, England, in 1682 and settled in King George Co., Va. The Taylor authors, descendants of the original James, tell of their experiences in America. For example, General Jessup provides details about financial assistance given to the U.S. Army by James Taylor Jr. during the **War of 1812**. In addition to details about the lives of Taylor family members, the authors give important genealogical facts about them, tracing their heritage back to its English roots. The document also contains valuable information about U.S. presidents James Madison (1809–1817) and Zachary Taylor (1849–1850).

"The James Taylor Narrative," 1840, Kenton Co. Public Library, Covington, Ky.; Campbell Co. Historical and Genealogical Society, Alexandria, Ky.

JANUARY AND WOOD. The January and Wood Company's cotton mill in Maysville was one of the oldest businesses in Northern Kentucky when it closed sometime after 2006. Cotton grown in the Deep South was shipped to Maysville by steamboat from markets in New Orleans and in Memphis, Tenn. William Shotwell built the cotton mill in Maysville in 1834, and shortly afterward William Goslin bought it. Richard Henry Lee acquired the mill in 1844 and built a four-story building in town on Second St. Lee (a son of Gen. **Henry Lee**) was a surveyor from Virginia who made his home in Washington, Ky. On February 4, 1848, Lee sold the mill to Andrew M. January, Thomas Mannen, Christian Shultz, and William

Stillwell. Henry Cutter purchased Stillwell's share of the mill on January 12, 1849. During 1851 Andrew January and Benjamin W. Wood bought out the other investors and the company assumed the name of January and Wood. Charles Bromley was hired by the January and Wood Company to serve as superintendent and was succeeded eventually by his son Frank Bromley. The January and Wood partnership existed until Andrew January died in 1877. Then January's daughter, Harriet F. January Cochran, and her sister Sarah's son, A. January Grundy, purchased the interests of other January heirs. The surviving founding partner of the company, Benjamin W. Wood, became president after January's death. In August 1896 B. W. Wood sold his half interest in the mill to Harriet Cochran and her five sons. This acquisition brought the cotton mill under complete ownership by January's descendants. Robert Cochran Jr. managed the mill until his retirement in 1926.

Little information is available about the management of the mill between 1926 and 1965. Sometime after 1926, the management shifted from the Cochran family to the Adair family. A Mr. Adair served as company president sometime before 1965. His son William C. Adair, a January descendant, succeeded him in 1965 and served in this capacity until his death in 2001. William C. Adair Jr. assumed leadership of the company after his father died. The 1998 *Kentucky Directory of Manufacturers* listed W. C. Adair as president, but by 2002 Belinda Breslin had become president. The Kentucky secretary of state's online business database listed an annual report for the company as late as June 2006, which showed Brenda A. Breslin as president, vice president, secretary, and director.

The cotton mill experienced a number of improvements and losses over time. The mill's first structure was completed in 1834, and a four-story structure was added on Second St. in 1844. During the 1870s, new equipment, including some acquired from England, was installed. The September 6, 1884, issue of Maysville's *Daily Commonwealth* reported that a fire had destroyed one of the January and Wood Company's cotton mill structures, resulting in a $1,000 uninsured loss. Another fire in May 1915 destroyed the cotton sheds and another building. In early 1916, a three-story addition was added to the mill complex. Two years later in 1918, the dye house was demolished and a brick structure erected in its place. Other changes during 1918 included improvements to the older structures and the installation of electric motors within the mill complex. By 1935, a new addition expanded the facilities. The July 1940 edition of the *Kentucky Post* reported that the company had a new warehouse.

The mill produced the Maysville brand of cordage and carpet warp, and it was sold wholesale, with most of the product going to markets in Cincinnati, St. Louis, and Chicago. The *Centennial Souvenir Book for Maysville* reported that the cotton mill was producing carpet warp, twine, rope, clothesline, batting, and mop yarn wick as well as staging and trout line. The *Kentucky Industrial Directory* for various years provides information on the products of the January and Wood Company. In 1949 it was producing cotton twine, cotton cordage for home weaving, and crocheting yarns. In 1951–1952, the company was making cotton carpet warp, cotton and rayon knitting and crocheting yarns, cotton twine, and small cordage including seine twine and cable cords. By 1955 the company appeared to be focusing on carpet yarn, cordage, and twine. Charles Thompson in his 2003 book *Going on 200* reported that the company only spun and twisted the cotton and had not proceeded to the next stage of weaving or knitting. In the late 1980s, cotton and rayon yarns were manufactured by the January and Wood Company. During 2003 the company was spinning yarns and making twines. The yarns were both pure cotton and a mixture of cotton and polyester. Their products included various types of tying twines and carpet warp that were sold to wholesale distributors. Another family-owned company, the Edgemont Yarn Service, sold January and Wood Company products.

The census of manufacturing for 1870 indicated that the January and Wood cotton mill employed 31 males over 16 years and 25 females over 15 years as well as 70 children and youth. The firm paid $30,000 in annual wages in 1870. During 1922 the company had 150 employees. For 1929 it employed 95 men and 89 women. During 1933, 375 people worked for the company. The *Kentucky Industrial Directory* provides the following employment figures for the second half of the 20th century: 1955–1956, 307; 1957–1958, 350; 1959–1960, 260; 1964, 323; 1969, 250 men and 17 women; 1987, 104 men and 50 women; 1989, 135; 1992, 100; 1994, 100; 1996, 70; 1998, 60; and 2002, 45. The January and Wood Company ceased operations in 2004.

Bodley, Temple. *History of Kentucky: The Blue Grass State.* Vol. 4. Chicago: S. J. Clarke, 1928.
Comer, Mrs. P. W., ed. *As We Look Back: Maysville, 1883–1933.* Centennial Souvenir Book. Maysville, Ky.: Daily Independent, 1933.
Connelley, William Elsey, and E. M. Coulter. *History of Kentucky.* 5 vols. Chicago: American Historical Society, 1922.
Harris Kentucky Manufacturers Directory. Twinsburg, Ohio: Harris Infosource, 1987–2006.
Johnson, E. Polk. *A History of Kentucky and Kentuckians.* Chicago: Lewis, 1912.
Kentucky Industrial Directory. Frankfort, Ky.: Kentucky Department of Economic Development, 1949–1961.
Perrin, William Henry, J. H. Battle, and G. C. Kniffin. *Kentucky: A History of the State.* Louisville, Ky.: F. A. Battey, 1888.
Seiller, Edward F. *Kentucky Natural Resources, Industrial Statistics, Industrial Directory Descriptions by Counties.* Kentucky Bureau of Agriculture, Labor, and Statistics, Bulletin 34. Frankfort, Ky.: State Journal, 1929.
The Spirit of a Greater Maysville and Mason County. Maysville, Ky.: Daily Independent, 1935.
Thompson, Charles. *Going on 200: Century-Old Businesses in Kentucky.* Prospect, Ky.: Harmony House, 2003.

Charles D. Hockensmith

JAYCEES. The U.S. Junior Chamber of Commerce (Jaycees), established in 1920, has been represented in Northern Kentucky by many chapters, which have a long history of developing young leaders. The chapters were founded to give young people between the ages of 18 and 40 the tools to build the bridges of success for themselves in the areas of business development, management skills, individual training, community service, and international connections. Although the Jaycees originally admitted only young men, the organization later expanded to include women, reflecting the growing influence and leadership of women in the nation.

In existence today in Northern Kentucky are the Boone Co. Jaycees, founded in 1957; the Campbell Co. Jaycees, founded in 1934; and the Covington-Kenton Co. Jaycees, founded in 1940. Other places in Northern Kentucky that have or have had Jaycees chapters include Bellevue, Carrollton, Fort Thomas, Grant Co., Ludlow, Maysville, and Taylor Mill.

Clark, John W. *A Legacy of Leadership: The U.S. Junior Chamber of Commerce Celebrates 75 Years.* Commerce, Okla.: U.S. Junior Chamber of Commerce, 1995.
Covington-Kenton County Jaycees. "Chapter History of the Covington-Kenton County Jaycees." www.ckcjaycees.org (accessed August 31, 2006).
"Jaycees Opening to Women; Other Groups Aren't," *KP*, August 4, 1984, 5K.
"Junior Chamber Gets Its Charter," *KP*, March 16, 1940, 3.
NetworkSolutions. "About Jaycees." www.kyjaycees.org (accessed August 31, 2006).
The United States Junior Chamber Jaycees. "USJC History." www.usjaycees.org (accessed August 31, 2006).

Donna M. Bloemer

JAZZ. Jazz is an original American musical art form that began at the start of the 20th century in the southern United States near New Orleans and moved into Northern Kentucky about 20 years later. It is rooted in an amalgamation of African folk music and European musical technique and theory. Jazz utilizes blue notes, syncopation, swing, call and response, strong emotional expression, and improvisation. **Ragtime** and **blues**, as antecedents of jazz, developed unique styles distinctive to the tri-state region. Many scholars imply that jazz could only have developed in the United States, with its rich cultural melting pot. According to legendary jazz singer Tony Bennett, "Jazz is America's greatest contribution to the world—it is our 'classical' music."

Southern migrants and jazz artists passed through Cincinnati and Northern Kentucky via the Ohio River and the railroads in the 1920s. Phonograph recordings, radio broadcasts, movies, dance halls, nightclubs, speakeasies, and jazz bands all developed as part of the post–**World War I** popular culture known as the jazz age. From the 1920s through the 1940s, jazz bands (later known as big bands) were regular attractions in the region at nightspots such as Newport's Columbia St. clubs, the **Lookout House** in Lookout Heights (now Fort Wright), and Cincinnati's Cotton Club.

Artie Mathews, a ragtime pianist and composer, founded the Cosmopolitan School of Music in 1921 in Cincinnati. The first black-owned and operated conservatory in the United States, it inspired regional jazz talent. Mathews's "Pastime Rags" featured rhythmic patterns and methods unique to ragtime, which later influenced jazz piano styles. His most famous composition was "Weary Blues"; it became a major hit of the Tommy Dorsey Orchestra in the 1940s. Famous jazz pianist Jelly Roll Morton made many stops in Cincinnati with the Fate Marable riverboat band. In the 1920s the Vocalstyle Piano Roll Company of Cincinnati issued rolls of Morton's performances.

Cincinnati's WLW radio broadcasts of jazz and big band were popular and, with the station's 500,000-watt reach in the 1930s, drew major musicians to the region, musicians such as renowned pianist Thomas "Fats" Waller, who performed on WLW from 1932 to 1934. His WLW shows included *Fats Waller's Rhythm Club* and *Moon River,* a highly popular late-night poetry program for which he played the organ. Waller performed in person at venues such as the **Horseshoe Gardens** in Bellevue. According to Covington-born jazz legend **Nelson Burton**, Waller also played honky-tonk-style piano in Covington's nightclubs late into the morning after his WLW broadcasts. The Mills Brothers and the Ink Spots, both groups native to the larger region, were also part of WLW radio's roster of local jazz talent in the 1930s. The Mills Brothers played at the Horsehoe Gardens, in particular.

Local venues such as Cincinnati's Cotton Club, at the Sterling Hotel at Sixth and Mound Sts. in that city's west end, hosted nationally famous jazz musicians on tour, such as Bix Beiderbecke, Duke Ellington, and Fletcher Henderson. Nelson Burton also remembers that the bands of Erskine Hawkins and Nobble Sissle visited and performed at Covington clubs during the early jazz years.

While national headliners stopped by, there were many local performing artists. Three of the most notable names residing in Cincinnati were jazz pianist Charles Alexander, who later toured with Louis Armstrong; tenor saxophonist Edgar "Spider" Courance; and Bill Coleman, born in Paris, Ky., who moved to Cincinnati in 1911 and played jazz trumpet with other local stars, such as Edgar Hayes, Clarence Paige, and Zack Whyte. Coleman also made recordings with Fats Waller on numerous occasions. Coleman noted that the prominent black musical culture was originally tied to the needs of social dances at the area clubs. Not until the birth of the big band era in the 1930s did the traditional Cincinnati region as a whole embrace jazz.

Andy Kirk, born in Newport, moved to Denver, Colo., during his youth. Later, in Kansas City, Mo., he became nationally known in the period of the 1920s through the 1940s with the popular Clouds of Joy big band. That band featured the Kansas City Swing style, which utilized southern blues rich with riffs, rhythmic drive, and improvisation.

Territorial bands were popular during the 1920s through 1945. For example, **Justin Huber**, born in Covington, formed a jazz dance orchestra in the 1920s that played at locations all around the tri-state region, including the Horseshoe Gardens in Bellevue. Huber's orchestra also played for WLW radio remote broadcasts from local venues.

George Russell, born in Cincinnati's Walnut Hills, was an important figure of the jazz scene. He published the scholarly book *Lydian Chromatic Concept of Tonal Organization for Improvisation,* considered by many as the definitive theory for jazz musicians. It elaborated on techniques performed by jazz legends such as Miles Davis. Russell built the jazz program at the New England Conservatory of Music in Boston. He grew up in Walnut Hills next to Cincinnati-born arranger and saxophonist Jimmy Mundy, who worked for Count Basie, Benny Goodman, and Artie Shaw. Russell has acknowledged that the diverse jazz talent of the region influenced him to become a composer.

Nelson Burton played in many jazz bands in the region. He was a house musician for Cincinnati's Cotton Club in the 1940s and 1950s and studio musician at Cincinnati's legendary King Records. He told his story in *Nelson Burton: My Life in Jazz,* a memoir of his jazz experiences. Although King Records recorded many **country music** and rhythm and blues artists, it also preserved the works of many jazz performers of the 1950s. Burton worked at King backing famous artists such as Wynonie Harris, Lonnie Johnson, and Maybelle Smith.

Covington-born trumpeter **Christopher Wallace Perkins** was nicknamed "Granddaddy of the Cotton Club" by Burton. From the mid-1930s on, Perkins backed internationally famous entertainers such as Josephine Baker, Nat King Cole, and Tony Bennett. After the local Cotton Club closed, he performed with the Frank Payne Quartet.

Among the later recognized jazz artists, **Rosemary Clooney**, born in Maysville, has become the most widely known from Northern Kentucky. Although jazz singing was not her initial claim to fame, it became associated with Clooney during her career renaissance beginning in the late 1970s, and she provided a lasting legacy on a series of jazz-inspired recordings by Concord Records. Clooney's sultry alto sound had been showcased more than 20 years earlier on her Columbia long-play album *Blue Rose* (1956), a collaboration with Duke Ellington's Orchestra (and Billy Strayhorn's arrangements). It is considered by many music critics to be one of the finest examples of classic jazz singing ever recorded.

Newport's **WNOP**-AM radio station not only played jazz; it was known as the "Jazz Ark," because it broadcasted from a floating barge on the Ohio River. Oscar Treadwell (real name, Art Pedersen), was a WNOP radio personality between 1965 and 1973. Locally known as the "Godfather of Jazz" because of his vast knowledge of jazz music and artists, he continued to educate generations of tri-state-area radio listeners, playing jazz on other Cincinnati public radio stations such as WGUC-FM and WVXU-FM.

The nationally recognized Ohio Valley Jazz Festival was launched in the early 1960s at the Carthage Fairgrounds and later was held at Crosley Field in Cincinnati. In the 1970s the festival was renamed the Kool Jazz Festival and moved to Riverfront Stadium, across the Ohio River from Covington and Newport. Since the late 1980s, the festival has had many name changes and sponsors, has featured more rhythm and blues and hip-hop music, and is currently presented at the Paul Brown Stadium along the Ohio River.

During the 1990s and after, only a few clubs specializing in jazz remained in the region, including downtown Cincinnati's Blue Wisp (founded and operated by Covington native Marjean Wisby) and Chez Nora and Dee Felice, both in Covington's **Main Strasse**. Covington residents **Mary Ellen Tanner** and **John Von Ohlen** perform at jazz clubs in the region. Patsy Meyer, a graduate of Holmes High School and a smooth jazz vocalist and percussionist, has been nominated for three national Emmy awards. Meyer has also recorded jazz albums.

While jazz music is no longer mainstream, FM radio station WMKV in Cincinnati continues to play jazz and big band as its primary musical format. **Northern Kentucky University** in Highland Heights includes a scholarly degree concentration in jazz studies and presents community programs such as jazz and R&B combo performances on a regular basis. NKU also offers a summer jazz camp for children and youth specializing in jazz combo techniques and improvisation.

Burton, Nelson. *Nelson Burton: My Life in Jazz.* Cincinnati: Clifton Hills Press, 2000.

Floyd, Samuel A., Jr., ed. *International Dictionary of Black Composers.* Chicago: Fitzroy Dearborn, 1999.

Gelfand, Janelle. "Cotton Club Led City Jazz Spots," *CE,* February 26, 2006, 5D.

———. "A Faded Jazz Scene," *CE,* February 26, 2006, 1D.

Hasse, John Edward, ed. *Jazz: The First Century.* New York: Harper Collins, 2000.

Hitchcock, H. Wiley, and Stanley Sadie, eds. *The New Grove Dictionary of American Music.* New York: Macmillan, 1986.

Kenney, William Howland. *Jazz on the River.* Chicago: Univ. of Chicago Press, 2005.

Kernfeld, Barry, ed. *The New Grove Dictionary of Jazz.* New York: Macmillan, 2002.

Sadie, Stanley, ed. *The New Grove Dictionary of Music and Musicians.* New York: Macmillan, 2001.

Southern, Eileen, ed. *Biographical Dictionary of Afro-American and African Musicians.* Westport, Conn.: Greenwood Press, 1982.

Yanow, Scott. *Jazz: A Regional Exploration.* Westport, Conn.: Greenwood Press, 2005.

John Schlipp

JEFFERSON COMMUNITY AND TECHNICAL COLLEGE, CARROLLTON CAMPUS.

In 1990 Jefferson Community College in Louisville opened a branch campus in a shopping center in Carrollton (JCTC, Carrollton). Later, with help from an $800,000 grant from the Carrollton College Education Foundation, a three-story building was purchased in Carrollton at Fourth and Main Sts. For some time professionals and civic leaders in Carroll Co. had recognized that an advanced education facility emphasizing practical vocational skills and general education was vital to continue to attract business and industry to the region and to provide good jobs and retain young people in the workforce. It was with the support of these leaders that the campus was developed.

Jefferson Community College, which became Jefferson Community and Technical College in 2005 following consolidation with Jefferson Technical College, had campuses in downtown Louisville and in southwestern Jefferson Co. before it expanded to Carrollton. The college opened a fourth campus in Shelby Co. in 2002 and now has a Jefferson Technical Campus, also located in downtown Louisville.

The JCTC, Carrollton, campus initially offered two-year associate degrees, diploma and certificate programs such as practical nursing, industrial engineering, and business administration, and general education courses that transferred into four-year baccalaureate programs. The student body started out small in numbers and built to about 250–300 students within a couple of years. In 2001 new programs were offered in electrical, maintenance, and industrial chemical technology, all programs helpful to the nearby local chemical and plastics corporations.

Through the years, the campus expanded its course offerings and widened its geographical range. Through a reciprocity agreement, JCTC, Carrollton, serves Dearborn, Franklin, Jefferson, Ohio, Ripley, and Switzerland counties in Indiana as well as Gallatin, Henry, Owen, and Trimble counties in Kentucky. Continuing adult education eventually became a major offering and now surpasses the regular college programs of JCTC, Carrollton. In 2005 the college enrolled more than 600 students in general education and technical studies; adult education served 800 students.

The teaching staff is highly qualified. Instructors in most areas must hold at least a MA degree. Instructors in certain technical concentrations, moreover, have many years of hands-on experience. JCTC, Carrollton, works closely with area business and industry to ensure that programs being offered meet the businesses' training needs. The college has agreements with four-year colleges and universities throughout Kentucky for seamless transfer of credits. Also JCTC, Carrollton, has emphasized dual-credit courses, which allow high school students to earn both high school and college credit simultaneously. Working with **Carroll Co. High School**'s administration, JCTC, Carrollton, developed a system whereby high school students with a 3.0 grade point average or above and with a recommendation from officials of the high school, can elect to take certain college courses.

The enormous growth in students attending the JCTC at Carrollton has led to parking and space problems. Classrooms on the first floor had to be subdivided. Campus director Susan Carlisle also said that there was no space for a campus bookstore or student life activities. That growth prompted the college in 2006 to ask the Kentucky legislature for funding for a new, much-expanded campus. This effort drew support from more than 500 local area civic and business leaders. In April 2006 the Kentucky General Assembly appropriated $12 million for a new community and technical college campus at Carrollton. While the location remains undecided, serious discussions have been held among the college's administrators, Carroll Co. officials, and **Camp KYSOC**, the camp for disabled children run by the Kentucky Easter Seals Society and Cardinal Hill Healthcare and Rehabilitation Services. This camp on 124 acres adjacent to **General Butler State Resort Park**, advantageously located on U.S. 227 between I-71 and U.S. 42, is currently the leading choice as the site for the school's new campus. Overall, the Jefferson Community and Technical College's total student enrollment, for its five campuses, dual-credit, and online programs reached a record high of 14,240 in 2006.

Diane Perrine Coon

JEHOVAH'S WITNESSES (INTERNATIONAL BIBLE SOCIETY). Today there are eight Jehovah's Witnesses churches (Kingdom Halls) in Northern Kentucky: in Butler (Pendleton Co.), Florence, Owenton, Williamstown, Fort Mitchell, Taylor Mill, Fort Thomas, and Maysville. Because members of the group believe that the end of the world is near, they are referred to theologically as "end timers." They are also known for their door-to-door evangelism. The religion comes from the teachings of the Millerites of the 1840s. William Miller taught that on October 22, 1844, Christ would return to the earth. In Cincinnati, for instance, in preparation for Christ's arrival, Miller's followers sold or gave away their property and went up to the higher elevations of Mount Auburn and Clifton to meet the Lord. Twenty years later, Charles Taze Russell, the first president of the Jehovah's Witnesses, who is generally considered the founder of the International Bible Society, revised the date. Russell later proclaimed 1914 as the year ushering in Armageddon and the beginnings of Christ's "thousand year rule on earth." He believed that the "end time" had begun in 1799 and that Christ had returned to the earth in 1874. After 1914 passed and Russell died in 1916, he was replaced by Joseph "Judge" Rutherford. Rutherford revised Russell's date to 1918, and although **World War I** was brutal, it was not what he predicted, and the date was recast again to 1955. The Watch Tower group built a house in San Diego, called Beth Sarim (House of Princes) to shelter the coming "princes on earth"—King David, Samson, and Joseph. Rutherford was the father of the publishing arm of the organization, and under him the name Jehovah's Witnesses was accepted in 1931. The third president was Nathan H. Knorr, who assumed office in 1942 and oversaw the completion of *The New World Translation of the Bible.* In 1977 Northern Kentucky native **Frederick W. Franz** became president. Franz's 1966 book *Life Everlasting in the Freedom of the Sons of God* prompted many members to sell their homes and property in anticipation of the 1975 event he predicted. Amid the subsequent disillusionment, an intense "purging of apostates" inside the organization's Brooklyn's headquarters transpired. Franz survived the turmoil, and the membership of the Jehovah's Witnesses continues to grow. The organization's monthly magazine, *The Watchtower,* has a circulation of almost 14 million. The church is prospering in Latin America, Africa, and eastern Europe. Over the years, it has held several national and international conferences near the Northern Kentucky region, in both Cincinnati and Louisville.

"Frederick W. Franz, a Religious Leader, Dies in Office at 99," *NYT,* December 24, 1992, B6.

Kreimer, Peggy. "Church Leader's Roots in N. KY.," *KP,* December 25, 1992, 1K.

JENKINS, JOSEPH CARTER "J. C." (b. 1818, Orange Co., Va.; d. Boone Co., Ky., 1889). Joseph Carter Jenkins, a noted farmer, was the son of William and Nancy Carter Jenkins. The Jenkins family was descended from Welsh royalty; the Carters were of English descent and among the first immigrants to the colony of Virginia. In 1833 Joseph moved with his family to Boone Co. Ky., and in 1841 he married Elizabeth Berkshire, daughter of William Berkshire.

J. C. Jenkins was renowned as a farmer and grower of champion livestock. Along with William Snyder, owner of the **Petersburg Distillery** in Petersburg, he raised hogs for nearly 30 years. Leftover mash from the distillery became feed for the hogs. Jenkins later became widely known as a breeder of Jersey cattle, Cotswold sheep, and Chester hogs. At one time he owned 1,200 acres south and west of Petersburg. In 1860 he built a spectacular residence on the hilltop overlooking Petersburg. Known as Prospect Farm, the J. C. Jenkins house is Boone Co.'s only representative of the Italian Villa architectural style and has been described as "an artful composition of Italianate, Gothic, Greek Revival and Moorish elements." Prospect Farm was listed on the National Register of Historic Places in 1989.

In addition to farming, Jenkins was one of the owners of the Petersburg Distillery, acquiring half interest in the concern in 1861. Together with minority partners William Appleton and James Gaff, Jenkins operated the distillery through the **Civil War** before selling his part in the business to Freiburg & Workum in 1869. Jenkins died in Boone Co. in 1889 and was buried in the family lot at the Petersburg Cemetery.

Becher, Matthew E. "The Distillery at Petersburg, Kentucky, Part 2: A Kentucky Giant." *NKH* 10, no. 1 (Winter 2003): 35–47.

Boone Co. Historic Preservation Review Board. *Historic Structures of Boone County, Kentucky.* Burlington, Ky.: Boone Co. Historic Preservation Review Board, 2002.

Perrin, W. H., J. H. Battle, and G. C. Kniffin. "Boone County." In *Kentucky: A History of the State.* 7th ed. Louisville, Ky.: F. A. Battey, 1887.

Warner, Jennifer S. *Boone County: From Mastodons to the Millennium.* Burlington, Ky.: Boone Co. Bicentennial Book Committee, 1998.

Matthew E. Becher

JESSUP, MYRTLE STICKRATH (b. February 6, 1896, Ludlow, Ky.; d. April 29, 1990, Xenia, Ohio).

The daughter of David C. and Emma Stickrath of Ludlow, poet Myrtle Isabella Stickrath was born in Ludlow and lived there just a few years before she and her family moved to Dayton, Ohio. Her father was a bartender. Myrtle worked in a bookbindery and in factories around Dayton until 1941 or so, when she married Richard C. Jessup. Although she continued to work full-time, even the day after her wedding, Myrtle still found time to write poems. She enjoyed reciting her compositions at various local clubs and organizations. In 1981 she published *Gems of Truth,* a short book of her poems that tells the story of a woman who loved life, regardless of what it brought—laughter, tears, family problems, or joys. Myrtle Jessup died at age 94 in 1990 in a Greene Co., Ohio, nursing home and was buried in the Memorial Park Cemetery in Dayton, Ohio. Her husband preceded her in death. She was one of numerous minor poets who were born or raised in Northern Kentucky at the turn of the 20th century.

Dayton, Ohio, City Directories, 1900–1990.
"Jessup, Myrtle," *Dayton (Ohio) Daily News,* May 2, 1990, D2.
Jessup, Myrtle Strickrath. *Gems of Truth.* Smithtown, N.Y.: Exposition Press, 1981.
Ohio Death Certificate No. 036094, for the year 1990.

JESUP, THOMAS SIDNEY, MAJOR GENERAL (b. December 16, 1788, Berkeley Co., Va. [today W.Va.]; d. June 10, 1860, Washington, D.C.). Thomas Jesup (also spelled Jessup), of Scotch-Irish descent, was the son of a distinguished **Revolutionary War** officer. His family settled on a farm in Mason Co., Ky., near Washington in the early years of the 1800s. As a youth, Jesup was a voracious reader, always trying to better himself. He worked hard as a clerk in a Maysville store for a few years, exhibiting talents in an area in which he later excelled. In May 1808 he entered the U.S. Army as a 2nd lieutenant. By 1818 he was the quartermaster general, with the rank of brigadier general. His military career spanned from the **War of 1812** almost to the **Civil War**. He fought the British in the War of 1812 and the Seminole Indians under Chief Osceola in Florida, and he was in charge of supplies during the **Mexican War**. He was wounded twice in his military career: at the battle of Niagara during the War of 1812, and during the Seminole War. He was a friend of Henry Clay and was well respected and popular in Washington, D.C. Jesup served as quartermaster general for 42 years and is recognized as the father of the modern Quartermaster Corps. Within the corps, he instituted an improved system of property accountability and experimented with new forms of transportation—canal boats in the East, camel caravans in the desert Southwest, and railroads. He developed the first set of quartermaster regulations, procedures, and forms, while instilling professionalism and ethical standards within the corps. In 1860, while still on active duty at age 71 in Washington, D.C., he became paralyzed on June 8, died on June 10, and was buried at the Congressional Cemetery on June 13. Attending his Episcopalian funeral were President James Buchanan (1857–1861), John J. Crittenden, **John White Stevenson**, Cave Johnson, and Gen. Winfield Scott. The War Department closed for the day to allow its staff to attend the funeral. On April 1, 1862, Jesup's remains were removed to the Oak Hill Cemetery in the Georgetown section of the nation's capital. Military historians have called Maj. Gen. Thomas Sidney Jesup the most colorful and remarkable character ever to hold the position of quartermaster general.

Brigadier General Thomas S. Jesup. www.qmfound.com/BG_Thomas_Jesup.htm (accessed January 8, 2008).
Collins, Richard H. *History of Kentucky.* Vol.2. Covington, Ky.: Collins, 1882.

JEWELL, SUE HAMILTON (b. April 6, 1878, Uniontown, Ky.; d. July 1964, Silver Spring, Md.). Author Susan Steele Hamilton was the fourth of 12 children born to James C. and Ella Hamilton. Educated at Potter College, a finishing school for young ladies in Bowling Green, Ky., Jewell recalled her life in the "horse and buggy days of the gay nineties" in a book entitled *The Sun Shines Bright.* This book "contains family history, biography, autobiography, traditions, mixed metaphors, and just happenings."

On April 28, 1897, Sue Steele Hamilton married Edward Walter Jewell of Louisville. (In 1947, at her golden wedding anniversary, she posed for a photo in her bridal gown, and the photo was reproduced in her book.) After their marriage, the couple lived in Vincennes, Ind., and then near Covington, before settling in Troy, Ohio, in 1900. Sue Jewell became a member of Eastern Star and the Troy Music Club, which she organized in about 1917.

She traveled extensively in England, Scotland, and other parts of Europe and in Canada, Mexico, and the Philippines. Travel letters that she wrote based on her experiences were published in newspapers of the Midwest. A prolific collector, she amassed collections of art objects, china, silver, and dolls. Her doll collection was built particularly from her world travels and included dolls from 23 countries. The collection was described in an article in the 1950 edition of the *American Journal of Antiques.* After a brief illness, Sue Jewell died in 1964 at age 86 at Holy Cross Hospital in Silver Spring, Md., and was buried at the Riverside Cemetery, Troy, Ohio.

Jewell, Sue Hamilton. *The Sun Shines Bright.* New York: Pageant Press, 1952.
"Susan Jewell," *Troy (Ohio) Daily News,* July 13, 1964, 12.

Kathryn Witt

JEWS. There has not been a strong Jewish presence in most of the heavily rural counties of Northern Kentucky, since Jews in America have always resided primarily in urban centers. The cities of Covington and Newport, however, did become home to small Jewish enclaves with organized Jewish institutions around the beginning of the 20th century.

As early as the middle of the 19th century, a few Jews made their homes in Northern Kentucky. For example, a German-born Jewish peddler named Felix Moses (1827–1886) settled in Florence, Boone Co., in the 1850s and became a well-known personality there. During the **Civil War** he served in the Confederate Army, first with General Buckner's Guards and then, after a period of captivity in a Union prison, with Morgan's Raiders (see **John Hunt Morgan**). When Morgan's Raiders briefly held the city of Frankfort, Moses was the man who hoisted the Confederate flag over the capitol building. The story of "Old Mose," as he was called, is told in great detail in **John Uri Lloyd**'s book *Felix Moses, the Beloved Jew of Stringtown on the Pike* (1930). When the first systematic census of Jews in the United States was conducted in the late 1870s, 20 Jews were identified in Northern Kentucky: 18 at Maysville in Mason Co. and 2 at Augusta in Bracken Co. Like most Jews in America at the time, these were almost certainly individuals of central European background, and they probably had come to the river towns of Maysville and Augusta to engage in trade.

In Owen Co. the name of the small town of Gratz on the Kentucky River is connected with the Gratz family of Philadelphia, one of the most prominent Jewish kin groups of colonial America. This family was represented in Kentucky by Benjamin Gratz, who came to Lexington in 1819, the first Jew to settle there. Bernard Postal and Lionel Koppman's *A Jewish Tourist's Guide to the U.S.* (1954) asserts that the town of Gratz was established as a mercantile shipping point by the Gratzes of Philadelphia themselves. More likely, however, is the contention that when the town of Gratz was laid out in 1847 by the heirs of John Brown, Kentucky's first U.S. senator, it was named for his grandson Benjamin Gratz Brown (1826–1885), who had been named in honor of his mother's uncle through marriage, Benjamin Gratz of Lexington, in whose house he was born. It seems that the town of Gratz never had Jewish residents.

The years just before and after 1900 witnessed a massive migration of east European Jews to America, as they fled persecution and economic hardship in places such as Poland and Russia. The Jewish population of the United States rose from about 250,000 in 1880 to more than 4 million by the 1920s. It was during this period that Jews first arrived in substantial numbers in Northern Kentucky, many coming by way of Cincinnati, which had been an important center of Jewish life since early in the 19th century. The Jews who came to Northern Kentucky settled mainly in Newport and Covington and created organized Jewish communities with **synagogues** in those two cities.

The United Hebrew Congregation of Newport established a synagogue in 1897, which moved into a former church building at 117 E. Fifth St. in 1905. In later years one or more alternative prayer groups were established in Newport, but none of these survived for long; the United Hebrew Congregation remained the central institution of Newport Jewry. Because the culture of most east European Jews was heavily influenced by traditional religious norms, the United Hebrew Congregation was Orthodox, even if not all its members adhered to Orthodox practices such as strictly observing the Jewish dietary laws and refraining from work on the Sabbath.

In Covington the Temple of Israel was founded in 1906. Also Orthodox, this congregation built a synagogue on Seventh St. near Greenup in 1915 and remained in that facility until 1937, when the federal government took over the land where the synagogue stood for the construction of a new post office and courthouse. In 1939 the Temple of Israel congregation moved into its second building, a newly constructed synagogue at 1040 Scott St.

The Jews of Covington and Newport, like most Jews of east European background in early-20th-century America, possessed a strong ethnic and cultural identity. Thus their cohesiveness as a community was based on much more than synagogue affiliation. They tended to live near one another, and they supported communal institutions besides congregations. In Newport the Jewish community had organized a Free Hebrew School with 129 supporting members as early as 1907. The school, whose classes met initially in a building on Patterson St., offered educational programs for both children and adults, including English language classes in the evening for Jewish immigrants, most of whom spoke Yiddish. By 1907 Newport's Jews also were supporting a branch of the socialist Zionist society Poale Zion. Many east European Jewish immigrants brought with them to America a certain sympathy for socialism and a strong commitment to the goal of establishing a Jewish homeland in Palestine.

Another institution supported by Newport's Jews during the same period was the Jewish Protective League, created in 1906 with Isaac Hauer, owner of a tailor shop, as its president. Boasting some 200 members, the League was formed to demand better police protection from "hoodlums" preying on Newport's Jews. In 1906 at least two individuals were convicted of attacks motivated by anti-Semitism, although several members of the Jewish Protective League petitioned to have one of them pardoned after he wrote a letter of apology for his actions.

The Jewish Protective League seems to have been disbanded after some success in securing additional attention from the Newport city government, but Newport's Jewish community remained well organized. During the second decade of the 20th century, Newport Jews were supporting a charitable society called the Hebrew Emergency Association, incorporated in 1913; a mutual benefit society called Hebrew Mutual Aid; and the Hebrew Young Men's Association (or Young Men's Hebrew Association), a club that had its own rooms at Fifth and York Sts., at least for a time. An active Zionist society was still maintained in town as well, and during **World War I** the Jews of Newport organized an effort to raise money for Jewish victims of the hostilities in Europe. The Jewish population of Newport was reported to be 600 in 1927; that of Covington, 500.

Like the heads of Jewish households in smaller cities and towns all over the country, those in Newport and Covington made their living primarily in mercantile activities or in skilled trades such as tailoring or shoemaking, with only a few holding factory jobs or involved in professions. Of the 12 men who were officers of the Temple of Israel or members of that congregation's executive committee in 1915, for example, 5 owned clothing stores, 1 was a dry-goods merchant, and 1 had a shoe store. Also among the 12 were a furniture store owner, a restaurateur, a junk dealer, and a "collector" who later owned a store selling second-hand goods. The only professional in the group was the insurance agent Maurice Chase. Similarly, city directories reveal the occupations practiced in the late 1920s by 47 of the 61 men whose names appear on a memorial tablet from the United Hebrew Congregation's synagogue in Newport. Of these 47 men, about 60 percent were in business for themselves, and nearly all the rest were skilled tradesmen. Stores owned by Newport Jews in the late 1920s included Morris Cohn's Newport Furniture Company, the Spector Furniture House, Jacob Jurin's Monmouth Jewelry Company, and the Rosen Auto Supply Company (all on Monmouth St.); others were the K and K Drug Company on Washington Ave., the Rodner Cap Company on York St., and at least six groceries.

The 1920s seem to have been the peak period for Northern Kentucky Jewry, for by the 1930s there were signs of a population decline. The violence that accompanied a steelworkers' strike in the 1920s in Newport's **West End**, where most of the city's Jews lived, may have frightened some of them; and the great **flood of 1937**, which ravaged low-lying communities all along the Ohio River may also have motivated some Jews to leave. By the 1930s it was evident that few new Jewish families were moving into the area and that a fair number of Newport and Covington Jews were relocating to Cincinnati to find a wider range of Jewish social, cultural, and religious activities for themselves and greater educational opportunities for their children. Automobile ownership made it possible even for those Jews who kept their businesses in Northern Kentucky to make their homes in the suburbs of Cincinnati. In 1937 the Jewish population of Newport was down to 475 and that of Covington down to 350. Elsewhere in Campbell Co., there were 15 Jews living in Bellevue, 15 in Dayton, 20 in South Newport, and 25 in Fort Thomas. A few Jews were scattered in other Northern Kentucky towns in 1937, as well: 12 in Falmouth, 13 in Owenton, and 28 in Maysville, for example.

World War II was a difficult time for Northern Kentucky's Jews; they experienced the trauma of the period both as Americans engaged in the war effort and as Jews following events in Nazi-dominated Europe. After the war the population decline evident in the 1930s continued as Northern Kentucky Jewish families' children who had gone off to military service or to college generally chose not to return to their hometowns. Because Jews left Newport and Covington and no significant number of new Jewish families moved into the area, the Jewish community's congregations went into decline and its other institutions were disbanded. The Temple of Israel in Covington ceased functioning completely around 1960, and its synagogue building was sold to the Church of God in 1973. The United Hebrew Congregation closed down permanently around 1966, and its building was sold to the Apostolic Temple of Newport in 1969.

The last president of the United Hebrew Congregation was the Newport-born attorney **Morris Weintraub** (1909–1996), who was perhaps the most prominent individual to emerge from the Northern Kentucky Jewish community. Not only was Weintraub active in Jewish affairs, first in Kentucky and later in Cincinnati, but he was also an important Democratic political figure representing Campbell Co. He served in the Kentucky Senate from 1940 to 1942 and in the Kentucky House of Representatives from 1946 to 1958, rising to the position of Speaker of the House during the administration of Governor A. B. "Happy" Chandler in the mid-1950s. Another famous Jewish son of the region was **Ben Lucien Burman** (1895–1984), author of 22 novels and many articles. Burman was born to Russian Jewish immigrant parents in Covington and lived on E. Eighth St., not far from the synagogue, before leaving town and moving eventually to New York City.

Although organized Jewish life in Newport and Covington had lasted for only six or seven decades, a small number of Jews continued to reside in Northern Kentucky. For a few years in the late 1960s and early 1970s, a group of Jewish professionals transplanted to the area tried to reestablish the Temple of Israel congregation and even investigated rehabilitating its building. In the mid-1980s, yet another small group attempted to organize communal activities under the auspices of an organization calling itself the Jewish Community of Northern Kentucky. Both of these efforts were short-lived, however, and since the final years of the 20th century, Northern Kentucky Jews seeking religious and cultural connections have looked to Cincinnati. Nevertheless, those Jewish families whose roots were in Newport and Covington continued to maintain a connection with each other and with their past, even holding a reunion in Cincinnati as recently as 1994.

Lapides, Leslie. "Judaism Then and Now," *KP*, March 19, 1983, 1K.

Lassetter, Leslie A. "Covington's Schule, the Temple of Israel," 1976, Kenton Co. Public Library, Covington, Ky.

Lloyd, John Uri. *Felix Moses, the Beloved Jew of Stringtown on the Pike*. Cincinnati: Caxton Press, 1930.

Postal, Bernard, and Lionel Koppman, *A Jewish Tourist's Guide to the U.S.* Philadelphia, Pa.: Jewish Publication Society of America, 1954.

Reis, James. "Remnant of Jewish Community Remains," *KP*, August 17, 1987, 4K.

Weissbach, Lee Shai. *The Synagogues of Kentucky: Architecture and History*. Lexington: Univ. Press of Kentucky, 1995.

Lee Shai Weissbach

JOHN A. ROEBLING BRIDGE. On June 27, 1983, the Kentucky Transportation Cabinet (KYTC) designated this historic bridge the John A. Roebling Bridge. Over the years, the span over the

John A. Roebling Bridge, Covington approach, ca. 1920.

Ohio River connecting Cincinnati to Covington had been known by several names—most commonly "the Suspension Bridge"—before it was named for the engineer who designed and built it. John Roebling himself called it "the Ohio Bridge," but for many years it was referred to simply as "the Covington and Cincinnati Bridge."

Discussion of a bridge at Cincinnati over the Ohio River had occurred at least as early as 1815, and the Kentucky legislature granted a charter to build one in 1829. There was apparently little follow-up at this point. Impetus for a bridge was renewed in 1839 when a group from Lexington met to discuss improved commercial ties between Lexington and Cincinnati. Additional meetings in Covington and Cincinnati were held, and eventually the decision was made to push for the completion of the Covington and Lexington Turnpike as the top priority.

A new charter for a bridge at Covington was issued by the Kentucky legislature in 1846. However, heeding opposition from steamboat interests, ferryboat operators, and others, the Ohio legislature took until 1849 to issue a similar charter, and several imposing restrictions were added by the Ohio lawmakers. The bridge must not be built in line with any existing Cincinnati street (Covington's north-south streets had been laid out to align with those in Cincinnati), and the bridge must be at least 1,400 feet long, with a midspan clearance of 112 feet. An amendment in 1856 shortened the length requirement to 1,000 feet but increased the required clearance to 122 feet. It was anticipated that a bridge might enable escaping slaves to cross the river more readily, so provisions were included in both charters addressing that concern.

Little progress was made by the Covington and Cincinnati Bridge Company, which held the two state building charters, until a new president and board of directors took office in 1856. Among the directors was Covington resident **Amos Shinkle**, who reportedly energized the company. In August 1856 John Roebling, an experienced bridge designer and builder from Pennsylvania, was hired as chief engineer for the bridge project. Both Roebling and Charles Ellet had submitted proposals during the mid-1840s to build a bridge across the Ohio River at Covington. Ellet later built the suspension bridge that opened at Wheeling, W.Va., in 1849 to carry the National Rd. across the Ohio River. Roebling was chosen to build the bridge connecting Cincinnati and Covington.

Construction on the bridge Roebling designed began in September 1856 with excavation for the towers. However, the national economic panic of 1857 made it difficult to obtain funds, and work stopped in late 1858, with the tower on the Ohio side at 45 feet in height and the tower on the Kentucky side at 75 feet.

Work on the bridge did not resume until the middle of the **Civil War**. The September 1862 Confederate Army's thrust into Kentucky and the ensuing threat to Cincinnati had helped to reinforce the need for the bridge. A **pontoon bridge** using coal barges had been hastily assembled just upstream of the unfinished bridge towers to move Union forces and supplies to the prepared fortifications in the hills above Covington and Newport. Confederate cavalry patrols probed the area, but the main body of the associated troops remained in Central Kentucky.

With political support now on both sides of the river, the legislatures of Ohio and Kentucky were persuaded to reduce the bridge height requirement to a minimum of 100 feet above the low-water mark. John Roebling then returned to Covington, and construction of the towers resumed in May 1863. Work was also started on the anchorages that same year.

The towers were completed in 1865. Col. **Washington Roebling** had been discharged from the Union Army and was named as assistant chief engineer for the bridge project. John Roebling was at this time involved in planning for the Brooklyn Bridge in New York City and had turned over direct supervision of the work here to his son. The younger Roebling utilized his father's perfected method of spinning the cables in place, and the procedure, begun in November 1865, was completed in June 1866. Installation of the suspenders, the floor beams, the trusses, and the diagonal stays then followed at a relatively rapid pace.

The new bridge was opened for pedestrians on Saturday, December 1, 1866, and according to reports 166,000 people crossed the bridge that weekend. Although the bridge was not totally completed, the company decided to open the span to vehicular traffic on New Year's Day 1867. Freezing conditions that had prevented the local ferries from operating on a regular schedule prompted the decision. A procession of carriages, led by the company's officers and the bridge engineers, formalized the opening. After crossing from Covington, the procession was met on the Cincinnati side by a contingent representing Ohio, and afterward the entire group crossed back to Kentucky At least 45,000 persons were reported to have crossed the bridge that day.

The bridge the Roeblings had completed in 1867 featured the world's longest span, at 1,057 feet between the midpoints of the towers. The stone towers each rested on timber grillage, 75 feet by 110 feet, made up of various native woods. The towers, made of sandstone from the Buena Vista Quarries upriver in Ohio and limestone from quarries in Ohio and Indiana, each weighed more than 30,000 tons. The original anchor houses on each shore covered 11-ton anchor plates connected to the cables by chains of eyebars.

The original cables were made of wrought iron (imported from England because the material was unavailable in the United States during the war). Each cable contained 5,180 wires laid side by side (not twisted); the cables were constructed on-site by a device perfected by Roebling that strung the wires as it traveled back and forth between the anchors. The cable wires were 9-gauge, wrapped tightly with 10-gauge wire, and the diameter of the two original cables was 12 1/3 inches. The cables rested in iron saddles on top of each tower. Roebling constructed brick turrets to protect the saddles and topped them with decorative Greek crosses.

The original floor system and iron trusses hung from suspender cables attached to the main cables. The original flooring was wood. Seventy-six diagonal stay cables radiated from the tops of the towers to help stabilize the suspended spans. These diagonal stays were an innovation by Roebling that added stiffness to his structures. They foreshadowed today's modern cable-stayed bridges, such as the **William H. Harsha Bridge** at Maysville.

The floor of Roebling's bridge was 20 feet wide with 7-foot walkways on either side, for a total width of 34 feet. Narrower walkways went through the 75-foot-high arches, although pedestrians could also walk around the towers. The total cost of the bridge was approximately $1.8 million, well above early estimates owing to inflation fueled by the Civil War. Roebling regretted that the Ohio charter forbade building the bridge in line with the existing streets. He noted that without this prohibition an avenue could have been built that would have been grander than any such boulevard on either side of the Atlantic Ocean.

John Roebling died of injuries he received in Brooklyn, N.Y., and Washington Roebling built the bridge over the East River there that his father had envisioned, completing it in 1883. The Brooklyn Bridge then became the world's longest, with a center span of 1,595 feet. The Cincinnati bridge was a financial success for the bridge company headed by Amos Shinkle, who had become its president in 1866. Because Covington was the northern terminus of the **Kentucky Central Railroad**, the span was used to transport cargo that had arrived by rail to and from Cincinnati by wagon. The river crossing led to an economic boom in Covington and Newport. Horsecars began using the bridge in 1867, and electric streetcars began crossing in 1891. This transit system gradually expanded to serve the basin-area cities of Northern Kentucky.

By the early 1890s, an inspection revealed some weakening of the cable at the span's anchorages due to moisture problems. Local bridge engineer **Gustave Bouscaren** devised reinforcing collars with friction clamps to restore the cable strength. These devices can be seen today at each of the four original anchorages. They clamp onto the cables outside of the anchorage and, on the inside, connect to the same pins that join the strands of cable to the anchor chains.

Despite this successful and vital repair, the weight of the electric streetcars being used during the 1890s raised concerns about the structure's future. The bridge company retained Bouscaren and five other prominent civil engineers to make independent recommendations after inspecting the condition of the bridge. Only the German-born Wilhelm Hildenbrand, who had extensive engineering experience with suspension bridges, suggested retaining the basic structure. He had been employed by John Roebling as a draftsman to prepare plan sheets and promotional illustrations for the Brooklyn Bridge, and he had become one of Washington Roebling's principal assistants in the construction of that bridge. Hildenbrand consulted closely with Washington Roebling in the reconstruction of the Covington-Cincinnati Bridge in 1895–1899. The work was accomplished while maintaining the flow of traffic.

The reconstruction included adding two steel cables and four anchorages. These 10.5-inch cables were designed to support only the central span of the bridge. They are made of 6-guage wire wrapped with 10-guage galvanized wire. The John A. Roebling and Sons Company of Trenton, N.J., produced the wire for the cables. It was necessary to remove Roebling's original turrets to place additional saddles to carry the cables over the towers. The turrets were replaced with dome structures. Hildenbrand's work changed the appearance of the bridge mainly because of the massive steel trusses he added to replace the shallower iron trusses, which had given a much more delicate profile to the bridge. He strengthened the floor with deeper beams and widened the road from 20 to 30 feet. As a result, pedestrians crossing the bridge now had to walk around the towers.

Approximately 1,200 streetcar crossings were made over the bridge each weekday in 1899, and the early part of the 20th century saw tremendous growth in the numbers of automobiles and trucks that were crossing. Highways U.S. 25 and U.S. 42 were routed over the Suspension Bridge. It was the primary roadway span connecting Covington and Cincinnati until the old C&O Bridge was converted to highway use in 1929.

During the record **flood of 1937**, the bridge was the only crossing open on the Ohio River between Steubenville, Ohio, and Cairo, Ill., a distance of more than 800 miles. It was necessary, however, to construct a ramp of sandbags, gravel, and timber connecting the bridge's Covington approach to a point on Greenup St. The crossing provided a critical connection to move food, fuel, medical supplies, and emergency equipment.

The Commonwealth of Kentucky purchased the Covington and Cincinnati Bridge from the company in 1953 for $4.23 million. Kentucky also acquired buildings on each side of the river. The Kentucky Highway Department district office then moved from the **John R. Coppin** Building in Covington to the bridge company's former headquarters on Second St.

Shortly after purchasing the bridge, Kentucky replaced the timber floor with a stronger, yet lighter, open-grid steel floor. Other improvements included reconstruction of the bridge's Ohio approach and the bus ramps to **Dixie Terminal**, the transit portal that accessed the bridge from Cincinnati. The bridge continued to be operated as a toll facility until November 1963. Tollbooths had been located at the ends of the anchor houses with various configurations over the years. In 1930 the portion of the bridge's Ohio approach just south of Third St. in Cincinnati had been widened to a four-lane toll plaza.

Tolls in 1867 were 3 cents for pedestrians, 2 cents for each hog, 10 cents for a horse and carriage, and 5 cents for each additional horse. Rates for autos first appeared in 1901. Toll schedules published in 1935 and in 1953 both show the rate as 1 cent for pedestrians, 5 cents for motorcycles, and 10 cents for autos, as well as 10 cents for "one-horse vehicles."

An observance billed as the Centennial Celebration of the Great Suspension Bridge was held on October 15, 1966. It included a parade across the bridge and ceremonies at Court House Square in Covington. The state governors of Ohio and Kentucky made brief remarks, and the major address was by Charles S. Adams. Marian Spelman sang the national anthem.

The Roebling Bridge was designated a National Historic Landmark in 1975 and a National Historic Civil Engineering Landmark in 1982. The Covington-Cincinnati Suspension Bridge Committee, a local citizens group, began flying flags atop the towers in 1976 to commemorate the U.S. bicentennial. That committee is also responsible for the cable lighting system that was installed on the bridge in 1984 and named in memory of Julia Langsam, a former president of the group and an enthusiastic supporter of the lighting project.

The Roebling Bridge was painted blue at the time of the national bicentennial. The previous color had been green—not unlike the hue of the patina found on many historic fountains, steeples, and other works of art and architecture.

After an in-depth inspection and analysis of the bridge in 1987, the Kentucky Transportation Cabinet (KYTC) pursued a program of repairs and restoration in the early 1990s that cost more than $10 million. The work included replacement of suspender cables; masonry stone, concrete, and steel repairs; restoration of the anchorages, including new metal roofs; reconstruction of the Ohio approach; deck repairs; replacement of the saddle houses with turrets resembling the originals; and dramatic lighting. New ball-and-cross finials were set in place by helicopter on March 7, 1992.

Except for street widening, the approach in Covington had remained basically the same until the KYTC constructed what is termed the "yoke" project. Completed in 1992, it crosses over Second St. in Covington and connects Greenup and Scott Sts. directly to the bridge. On the Cincinnati side, the original approach had been a steep slope from Front St. It was extended to Second St. in 1897 and to Third St. in 1918. Beginning in 1921, ramps carried streetcars and later buses to the Dixie Terminal complex that fronted on the south side of Fourth St. in Cincinnati. These ramps were reconstructed several times and finally removed in the late 1990s. The entire approach in Cincinnati was reconfigured during the late 1960s with the construction of I-71 (see **Expressways**). The Ohio approach was modified again in 1999 when the Fort Washington Way segment of I-71 was totally rebuilt. The bridge now connects in Ohio to **Theodore M. Berry** Way.

In 2006 the bridge carried approximately 9,100 vehicles per day, including 700 **Transit Authority of Northern Kentucky** buses. A repair project was completed in spring 2007 before a long-overdue repainting.

Today, with renewed interest in the riverfronts, the John A. Roebling Bridge has become the symbol of the tri-state area. Its silhouette frequently depicted by artists and photographers, the historic bridge also routinely serves as the background for several local television newscasts.

Files of the Kentucky Transportation Cabinet, District Six, Covington, Ky.

Gastright, Joseph F. "Wilhelm Hildenbrand and the 1895 Reconstruction of the Roebling Suspension Bridge." In *Fifth Historic Bridges Conference*. Columbus, Ohio: Burgess and Niple, 1997.

Lehmann, Terry W., and Earl W. Clark. *The Green Line*. Chicago: Central Electric Railfan's Association, 2000.

"Report of John A. Roebling, Civil Engineer, to the President and Board of Directors of the Covington and Cincinnati Bridge Company, April 1, 1867." In *Reports on the Ohio Bridge at Cincinnati*. Trenton, N.J.: Murphy and Bechtel, 1867.

Stern, Joseph S., Jr. "The Suspension Bridge: They Said It Couldn't Be Built." *BCHS* 23, no. 4 (October 1965): 211–28.

Stevens, Harry. *The Ohio Bridge.* Cincinnati: Ruter Press, 1939.
Tenkotte, Paul A. "Rival Cities to Suburbs: Covington and Newport, Kentucky, 1790–1890," PhD diss., Univ. of Cincinnati, 1989.
Worthington, William F., Jr. "John A. Roebling and the Cincinnati Bridge." In *Fifth Historic Bridges Conference.* Columbus, Ohio: Burgess and Niple, 1997.

Ralph Wolff

JOHN G. FEE INDUSTRIAL HIGH SCHOOL. In 1928 the voters of Maysville approved a bond issue to finance the creation of a black high school, named for **John Gregg Fee**, the famed abolitionist and founder of Berea College, who was born in nearby Bracken Co. Fee had once been a minister in Mason Co. Located on the south side of E. Fourth St., east of the city limits at that time, John G. Fee Industrial High School became noted for its quality academic and vocational training; many of its graduates went on to Kentucky State College (now University) at Frankfort. The school offered both high school and elementary school grades, and its students were drawn from the city and the county. It also had an excellent record in athletics. The 1933 and 1934 girls' basketball teams, coached by Miss E. M. Clement, were state champions; in 1952 the boys' basketball team, under coach John Fields, was the state runner-up, losing to Louisville Central in the finals. Professor **William H. Humphrey** (1880–1958), the first principal of John G. Fee Industrial High School (1929–1949), is remembered as the administrator who oversaw the institution's many achievements; the second and last principal was O. W. Whyte (1949–1957).

The integration of both the Maysville and the Mason Co. school systems began in 1956. That September, the Mason Co. system withdrew 78 students from John G. Fee Industrial, both at the high school and the elementary levels, and enrolled them in previously all-white county schools; the Maysville city schools closed the 10th through 12th grades at the black school and enrolled 23 African American students at Maysville High. John G. Fee Industrial High School continued a few more years until the process of integration was completed in Mason Co. The school building was then leveled for construction of a parking lot.

Calvert, Jean, and John Klee. *Maysville, Kentucky: From Past to Present in Pictures.* Maysville, Ky.: Mason Co. Museum, 1983.
Caron's Maysville City Directory, 1934.
"Integration in Mason," *KTS*, February 16, 1956, 12A.
"Maysville Schools to Integrate," *KTS*, September 3, 1956, 4A.

JOHN H. MOORE HOUSE. The John H. Moore House, located at 9733 River Rd. in Hebron, is one of the most historically significant Greek Revival structures in Boone Co. The house is on the National Historic register and commands a view of Ohio, Indiana, and Kentucky. Capt. John H. Moore built the brick portion of the house in the 1830s. The one-foot-thick walls were built of bricks handmade on the property. In the early days, the house had a wood-shingled roof. The original part of the house was a two-story single-pen hand-hewn log cabin, built between 1789 and 1805, during the time when American Indians were present. William and Nancy Kirtley, the previous owners, probably built the cabin. Nancy Johnson Kirtley was the daughter of the first Boone Co. clerk, Col. Cave Johnson, a previous owner of the land. Moore had many famous relatives, including President William Henry Harrison (1841), who lived across the Ohio River in Ohio, and **Zebulon Pike**, the discoverer of Pike's Peak.

Moore (1799–1885), one of the first native-born farmers in Boone Co., He inherited the farm from his grandparents, William and Peggy Bates and eventually accumulated more than 1,000 acres. He raised cattle, horses, chickens, tobacco, fruit trees, grapes, hay, and vegetables. The family was fairly self-sufficient. The property includes numerous ponds and cisterns, a few springs, and several creeks. On the farm were a buggy-and-harness shop, a water-driven grain mill, an icehouse for cooling food and drinks, and a smokehouse for curing meat.

Dan Moore

JOHNS HILL. Johns Hill, a Campbell Co. community originally located along Ky. Rt. 9 and Johns Hill Rd., was aptly named for the very steep hill that dominates the area. Ky. Rt. 9, the Licking Pk., has been dramatically altered due to land slippages and was relocated westward toward the Licking River during the 1980s and 1990s. Johns Hill Rd. still climbs up the hill, as it has always done, but it is no longer part of Ky. Rt. 9.

The local 1883 Lake atlas shows the Johns Hill community as consisting of a cemetery, a school (Johns Hill Elementary Log School), the Johns Hill house (a tavern), two blacksmith shops, and **St. John the Baptist Catholic Church** and its school. The church began in 1847 on top of the hill in a log building. This structure burned. Leaving its early cemetery behind, the church community built a new stone church at the bottom of the hill along old Licking Pk. in 1858. A school was part of the church property into the 1960s. Another cemetery, known as St. Joseph Cemetery, is next to the current church building. It began as a Catholic cemetery for deceased members of Newport's Catholic churches.

Today, most of the Johns Hill community is located on the very top of the hill. Subdivisions and condominiums are now settled on the hills of the area, even in the area of Battery Wiggins and Battery Holt, two of the **Civil War fortifications** built during the 1860s. To the south and up the hill, I-275 cuts under Johns Hill Road, and the growing **Northern Kentucky University** campus is farther to the south. Johns Hill has developed into a bedroom community, now part of Wilder.

An Atlas of Boone, Kenton, and Campbell Counties, Kentucky. Philadelphia: D. J. Lake, 1883.
Campbell Co. Historical Society. *Campbell County, Kentucky, 200 Years, 1794–1994.* Alexandria, Ky.: Campbell Co. Historical Society, 1994.
Ryan, Paul E. *History of the Diocese of Covington, Kentucky.* Covington, Ky.: Diocese of Covington, 1954.

Kenneth A. Reis

JOHNSON, CAVE, HOUSE. See **Cave Johnson House**.

JOHNSON, DONALD "GROUNDHOG" (b. July 31, 1926, Covington, Ky.). Five-foot-six, right-hand-hitting Don "Groundhog" Johnson, the first African American from Covington to try out for the Cincinnati Reds baseball team, was the son of Howard Johnson and Margaret Battle. Johnson attended **Lincoln-Grant School** in Covington, which did not have a baseball team. He learned baseball by playing with the older kids in the neighborhood.

In 1947 Johnson was a member of a Covington baseball club named the Twenty Counts, which played most of its home games at the old Covington Ballpark along Ninth St. in the Willow Run section of town. Later that year, he tried out for the Cincinnati Reds. Ralph "Buzz" Boyle, the head scout for the Reds organization, had found Johnson. After signing a contract, Johnson was assigned to Ogden, Utah, a Class C Reds farm team, but because of an altercation that occurred before he even got off the train, he returned to Covington and was released by the major league club. In 1948 Johnson began a five-year stint in the Negro Baseball League (NBL). He was in the last group of players before the league folded during the 1950s. Johnson played the infield in both the National and American divisions of the NBL for the Philadelphia Stars and the Chicago American Giants, finishing his career with a respectable lifetime batting average of .335. Afterward, he played semipro ball with the Cincinnati Tigers.

Upon his return to the area, Johnson was employed by Shillito's Department Store in Cincinnati. After his retirement from Shillito's, he was again active in baseball, this time coaching at the Finneytown (Ohio) High School. During the 1980s, Johnson coached at Hughes High School in Cincinnati, when former Covington Lincoln-Grant basketball coach James Brock was that school's athletic director. In 1996 Johnson was inducted into the Negro League Hall of Fame. Today, he works at the Evanston Community Center and coaches baseball at Walnut Hills High School in Cincinnati. Covington mayor Butch Callery renamed the old Randolph field at Ninth and Prospect Sts. in Johnson's honor on August 6, 2005. Johnson currently lives in the Northside area of Cincinnati.

Glover, Robert Alan. "Play Ball! Negro Leagues' Players in the Spotlight on Opening Day," *KP*, March 29, 2003, 6K.
Kenton Co. Public Library. *Images of America: Covington.* Charleston, S.C.: Arcadia, 2003.
Little, Aiesha D. "Cincinnati Kid: Donald Johnson." *Cincinnati Magazine*, April 2005, 70–71.
Lyle, Troy. "'Groundhog' Johnson Honored; Ballfield Named for Black Player," *KP*, July 23, 2005, 3K.

Theodore H. H. Harris

JOHNSON, GERALD WALTER, LIEUTENANT GENERAL (b. July 10, 1919, Owen Co., Ky.; d. September 9, 2002, St. Petersburg, Fla.). Military pilot Gerald Johnson, the son of James B. and Attie Reeves Johnson, grew up on a farm near the small community of Pleasant Home in Owen Co., Ky. Johnson attended the local county schools and graduated from Owenton High School in 1937, then studied at the Bryant and Stratton Business School in Louisville. He worked in various jobs, but his great desire was to become a pilot. In 1939 he entered Eastern Kentucky State Teachers College in Richmond and enrolled in the college's ROTC program. After he had completed two years of college, Johnson's dream to become a pilot was about to come true. In 1941 he entered active military duty as an aviation cadet at Randolph Field, San Antonio, and in April 1942 graduated from flight school with a commission as 2nd lieutenant in the U.S. Army Air Corps.

During **World War II** Johnson was a member of the Eighth Air Force, serving in the 56th Fighter Group. Flying P-47 aircraft, he was the first ace (pilot achieving five combat kills) in the 56th Fighter Group and the second ace in the war's European Theater of Operation. During 15 months of combat duty, Johnson flew 88 missions and was credited with 18 victories (aircraft shot down), 1 probable (unconfirmed) and 4 1/2 (one-half means that his and another plane damaged it) enemy aircraft damaged in combat. On November 29, 1943, Johnson was temporarily assigned by Brig. Gen. **Jesse Auton** to command the 360th Fighter Squadron of the 356th Fighter Group, which was just entering combat and needed an experienced combat pilot. He returned to the 56th in early February 1944, taking command of the 63rd Squadron. On March 27, 1944, Johnson led his squadron on a strafing run of an armed German supply train heading for northern France. On the third pass, his plane was hit by anti-aircraft fire from the train and he crashed in a nearby field. Escaping with minor injuries, he set his plane on fire and ran toward the woods. As he reached the woods, the fire reached the cockpit, setting off the aircraft's guns. Johnson hit the ground as the last of his plane's ammunition passed just above his head. Shortly after this close call, he was captured and sent to Frankfurt, Germany, for interrogation. Being uncooperative, he was held in solitary confinement for 24 days before being sent to a prison camp. He was a prisoner of war for 13 months at Stalag Luft 1 in Barth, Germany. On May 12, 1945, Russian forces liberated this prison camp; then, within three weeks of his liberation, he was turned over to American forces and flown to England aboard a B-17 bomber.

Remaining in the military, Johnson commanded an F-84 fighter wing during the Korean War. In 1953 he led a flight of 20 F-84G fighters nonstop from Albany, Ga., to Lakehurst, England; en route, each aircraft underwent three air-refuelings from KC-97 refueling air tankers.

Johnson was the first commander of the 4,080th Reconnaissance Wing, a combat unit equipped with U-2 and RB-57 aircraft. Following several staff assignments, he left fighter aircraft and transitioned to bombers; he commanded the 305th Bomb wing and flew the B-58 Hustler bombers for three years. During the **Vietnam War**, he was deputy chief of staff for operations at the SAC headquarters in Omaha, Neb. In 1973 Johnson became the inspector general of the U.S. Air Force in Washington, D.C. Prior to this appointment, he was commander of the Eighth Air Force SAC, with headquarters at Andersen Air Force Base in Guam.

Johnson's military decorations and awards include the Distinguished Service Cross, the Distinguished Service Medal with one oak leaf cluster, the Legion of Merit with two oak leaf clusters, the Distinguished Flying Cross with four oak leaf clusters, a Bronze Star Medal, the Air Medal with three oak leaf clusters, an Air Force Commendation Medal, the Army Commendation Medal, and the French Croix de Guerre. In uniform, Johnson wore command pilot wings and the Senior Missileman Badge.

Lieutenant General Johnson retired September 1, 1974, after 33 years of service to his country. He was one of Owen Co.'s two highest-ranking officers, the other being Vice Adm. **Willis A. "Hose" Lee**. Johnson died in 2002 in Florida and was buried at Arlington National Cemetery.

Air Force Link. "Lieutenant General Gerald W. Johnson." U.S. Air Force. www.af.mil/bios/bio.asp?bioID=5958 (accessed November 5, 2006).

Houchens, Mariam Sidebottom. *History of Owen County: "Sweet Owen."* Louisville, Ky.: Standard, 1976.

Johnson, Gerald W. *Called to Command: A WWII Fighter Ace's Adventurous Journey.* Paducah, Ky.: Turner, 1997.

Johnson, Lt. Gen. Gerald, to 1st Lt. Robert Snow, March 5, 1995. Personal handwritten account of service, Robert Snow's private collection.

"Lt. Gen. Gerald Johnson, 83, Native of Owenton," *KP,* October 22, 2002, A6.

Olynyk, Frank. *Stars and Bars: A Tribute to the American Fighter Ace, 1920–1973.* London: Grub Street, 1995.

Vertical files, Owen Co. Public Library, Owenton, Ky.

Wecker, David. "Her Uncle Was a Real Hero," *KP,* October 3, 2002, 1B.

Doris Riley

JOHNSON, LEBUS C. (b. 1910, Greenup, Owen Co., Ky.; d. May 1947, San Antonio, Tex.). Lebus Cooper Johnson, army officer and inventor, graduated from Owenton High School in 1929 and received a BS in metallurgical engineering from the University of Kentucky in 1938. Having joined the U.S. Army in 1942 during **World War II**, he became an officer in an ordnance unit overseas by the end of that year. Eventually, Johnson was in charge of all Allied ammunition in Europe, and after the war it was his responsibility to deal with the disposal of huge stores of unused ammunition from both sides of the conflict. He halted the plan to throw the ammunition into the sea and instead devised machines and methods to convert the remaining munitions into fertilizer and plastics. He reportedly saved the Allies some $300 million; for those efforts, Johnson was highly decorated by several nations. After some 50 months abroad, he returned to the United States in December 1946 and reported to Fort Sam Houston in San Antonio, Tex., where he soon became ill. Johnson died from an acute heart condition in early May 1947 at Brooks Army Hospital and was buried at the **International Order of Odd Fellows** Cemetery in Owenton, Ky., following one of the largest funerals Owen Co. had ever seen.

Bourne, C. H. "Lebus Johnson Dies in Service," *Owenton News-Herald,* May 8, 1947.

Houchens, Mariam Sidebottom. *History of Owen County: "Sweet Owen."* Louisville, Ky.: Standard, 1976.

JOHNSON, WILLIAM C. (b. June 6, 1917, Centerville, Bourbon Co., Ky.; d. May 20, 1999, Warsaw, Ky.). William C. Johnson, the first African American elected to serve on the City Council of Walton in Boone Co., was the son of John Will and Lucy Campbell Johnson. He spent his youth on a horse farm before moving to Lexington, where he attended public schools and graduated from Dunbar High School in 1938. After moving to Northern Kentucky, Johnson worked for the Shillito's Department Store in Cincinnati during the week; on Sundays, for 16 years he served as pastor of the First Baptist Church in Ripley, Ohio. Later he served as interim pastor of several churches, including the First Baptist Church in Burlington, Ky., and the **Zion Baptist Church** in Walton.

Elected to the Walton City Council in 1978, Johnson served for six years. During this period, he was the only African American officeholder in Boone Co. When he resigned for health reasons on August 6, 1985, his distant cousin Johnnie Ann Johnson replaced him. William Johnson died in 1999 at the Gallatin Co. Health Care Center and was buried at the Walton Cemetery.

"Distant Cousin Appointed to Council Man's Vacant Seat," *KP,* August 20, 1985, 5K.

"Only Black Councilman Resigns Walton Seat," *KP,* August 6, 1985, 5K.

"Rev. William C. Johnson Former Walton Councilman," *CP,* May 22, 1999, 13A.

Theodore H. H. Harris

JOHNSON CREEK COVERED BRIDGE. This historic covered bridge is five miles north of the **Blue Licks Battlefield State Resort Park**, near Burika in the southeastern corner of Robertson Co. It originally carried Ky. Rt. 1029 across Johnson Creek, coinciding with a former buffalo trace. The bridge, which can be reached via Ky. Rt. 1029 from U.S. 68, is one of 13 covered bridges surviving in Kentucky (at one time there were more than 400). Jacob N. Bower, a prolific covered-bridge builder, built it in about 1874. Made of poplar wood, the Johnson Creek Covered Bridge is more than 100 feet long and has Smith-type trusses. In 1910 it burned, and in 1914 Bower's son Louis Bower Jr. rebuilt it, adding iron rods and wooden arches. It was closed to traffic in 1966. In 1968 the bridge caught fire again, but the fire was extinguished in time to avoid extensive damage. In 1986 a new roof was added; today, the bridge needs full restoration. The structure was placed on the National Register of

Historic Places in 1976, and there is a Kentucky Highway Marker at the site. Many visitors to Robertson Co. and the Blue Licks Battlefield State Park stop at the Johnson Creek Covered Bridge. For generations, the bridge has also been popular with young lovers.

Laughlin, Robert W. M., and Melissa C. Jurgensen. *Images of America: Kentucky's Covered Bridges.* Charleston, S.C.: Arcadia, 2007.

Powell, Robert A. *Kentucky's Covered Bridges.* Danville, Ky.: Silverhawke, 2001.

JOHNSTON, ALBERT SIDNEY, GENERAL (b. February 2, 1803, Washington, Ky.; d. April 6, 1862, Shiloh, Tenn.). Albert Sidney Johnston, who fought in four wars, was the youngest son of Dr. John and Abigail Harris Johnston. His early education was in local schools, and he then attended Transylvania University in Lexington. After graduating, he was appointed to the U.S. Military Academy at West Point, N.Y., where he graduated in 1926, eighth in his class. He married Henrietta Preston of Louisville in 1829, and they had three children. Albert Johnston was assigned to military posts in New York and Missouri before serving in the Black Hawk War in 1832 as adjutant to the commanding general. Johnston resigned from the U.S. Army in 1834 and returned to Kentucky to care for his dying invalid wife. After her death on August 12, 1835, Johnston moved to Texas, where he took up farming. During the Texas War of Independence from Mexico in the 1830s, he enlisted in the Texas Army and by January 1837 had become the senior general of the Army of Texas.

On February 7, 1837, Johnston fought a duel with Brig. Gen. Felix Houston of the Texas Army, in which Johnston was seriously wounded; as a result, he lost his commission. On December 22, 1838, Mirabeau Lamar, president of the Texas Republic, appointed Johnston as his secretary of war. In February 1840, Johnston resigned from that position and returned home to Washington, Ky. He married Eliza Griffin of Louisville in 1843, and the newlyweds moved to a large Texas plantation, which Johnston named China Grove.

He rejoined the U.S. Army during the **Mexican War**, where he served gallantly as a staff officer under fellow Kentuckian Gen. Zachary Taylor. He participated in the Battle of Monterrey in September 1846. After the war concluded in 1848, Johnston resigned his commission in the U.S. Army and returned to his Texas plantation. Before long he reentered the U.S. Army, and in December 1849 President Zachary Taylor (1849–1850) appointed him, with the rank of major, an army paymaster; he held the position for five years.

During the **Civil War**, Confederate president Jefferson Davis appointed Johnston to be a general in the Confederate Army and made him commander of the Confederate Army's western theater of operations. On April 6, 1862, Johnston led his forces in a surprise attack against Gen. Ulysses S. Grant's forces at Shiloh Methodist Church near Pittsburg Landing on the Tennessee River in Tennessee. During the battle Johnston was hit in the leg by friendly fire and eventually bled to death from the wound. He was buried in New Orleans but was later re-interred in the Texas State Cemetery in Austin, Tex. In honor of Gen. Albert Sidney Johnston, the Texas Historical Commission erected a historical marker near what was once the entrance to his China Grove plantation.

Johnston, William Preston. *The Life of Gen. Albert Sidney Johnston.* New York: D. Appleton, 1878.

Roland, Charles P. *Albert Sidney Johnston: Soldier of Three Republics,* Austin: Univ. of Texas Press, 1964.

Shotgun's Home of the American Civil War. "Albert Sidney Johnston." www.civilwarhome.com (accessed March 17, 2006).

JOHNSVILLE. Fairview, or Johnsville, as it is now known, is a ridgetop hamlet that has been dissected by Ky. Rt. 9 and the **AA Highway**; the town's citizens have to cross the major highway to visit a neighbor. The first structure built in the town appears to have been the Arnold house, built near 1800; later it became known as the William Pepper home. Pepper had been a teacher before settling in the town, and before long he constructed a log schoolhouse on his farm and became the school's first teacher. There was another small school erected in 1865, which served until 1890. At that time the Fairview School was opened as a graded school, with J. T. Watson as its first principal. Other early settlers were the Cooper, Haley, Hiles, Houston, Jordan, Pearl, and Taylor families. About 1872 the post office was started and the town was called Fairview, but soon the name changed to Johnsville, in honor of John Jackson and John Riley, who served as postmasters; the village of Johnsville was incorporated in 1883.

A favorite source of entertainment was the cornet band of local men that was organized in Johnsville in 1880 and led by Captain Smith of the nearby Boude's Ferry. The Fairview I.O.O.F. Lodge No. 276 was another organization of local men, instituted in 1881. One of the businesses that operated in Johnsville was John Hiles's Body Shop, opened during the 1920s. Hiles not only was a blacksmith but also built school buses for the Hiles Centralized School, truck bodies, and horse vans. The Pioneer Cemetery at Johnsville, which contains the grave sites of the early settlers, has been restored. It provides a picturesque view of the village and surrounding hills and valleys.

W. A. Free. "History of Johnsville," *Bracken County News*, March 22, 1934, 4.

Caroline R. Miller

JOLLY, A. J., JR. (b. March 1, 1924, Mentor, Ky.; d. January 12, 1989, Houston, Tex.). A. J. Jolly Jr., a lawyer who served as a judge, was a son of two school administrators: his father, A. J. Jolly Sr., was superintendent of Campbell Co. Schools, and his mother, Caroline, was an elementary school principal. His father died of typhoid fever at age 43, leaving his mother to raise three boys alone. A. J. Jr. attended the **A. J. Jolly Elementary and High School** at California, Ky., which had been named for his father. After graduating from high school there, he entered Miami University of Ohio, where he studied for one year. In 1942 he left school to join the Army Air Force. As a turret gunner on a B-17 bomber, Jolly participated in 35 missions and was awarded several air medals for bravery. He returned home a year and a half later and enrolled at Xavier University, where he earned his bachelor's degree. He received his law degree in 1949 from the University of Cincinnati Law School. A. J. Jolly Jr. married Verna Tarvin, and the couple had five daughters. His political career began in 1949, when he was elected to the first of four terms as Campbell Co. judge (the post now called judge executive). While in that office, he was responsible for the creation of Lakeside Place Nursing Home, Youth Haven Home for Children, and the Campbell Co. Park (now A. J. Jolly Park) south of Alexandria. The park, which carries the name of his father, A. J. Jolly Sr., is situated on about 1,000 acres and has a 250-acre lake, bike trails, picnic areas, baseball and soccer fields, and an 18-hole golf course. Verna Jolly died of cancer on September 17, 1981, and A. J. Jr. died eight years later at the age of 64, after undergoing heart bypass surgery, at St. Luke Hospital in Houston. Both are buried in the Grandview Cemetery at Mentor.

Reis, Jim, "State Legislator Jolly Honored after His Death," *KP*, August 26, 1996, 4K.

Wecker, David. "Andy Jolly." *KP,* July 7, 1982, 1.

JOLLY, JAMES MONROE (b. December 13, 1817, Sallisboro, Lewis Co., Ky.; d. September 25, 1900, Mentor, Ky.). James M. Jolly, both a clergyman and a builder, was the son of John and Martha Mackey Jolly. At times he was referred to as Rev. James Moses Jolly, but his tombstone seems to show his name as Rev. James Monroe Jolly. The first seven of the Jolly children were born in Lewis Co., and then the family moved to Jamestown (known today as Dayton) in Campbell Co., where the last two were born. The family relocated to Point Pleasant, Ohio, in 1827; there James served for three years as an apprentice to William Shaw, learning the bricklaying and plastering trades. Returning to Campbell Co. in 1840, the Jollys settled on a farm near Twelve Mile Rd. On October 11, 1841, James Jolly married America Vickers, daughter of Rev. James Vickers, pastor of the Mouth of Licking Baptist Church (see **First Baptist Church, Cold Spring**). The couple had four children, all sons. Jolly was ordained as a Baptist preacher by his father-in-law in 1842 and became a circuit preacher, holding services once a month in various local churches. In 1843 Jolly and his family moved to Newport, where he preached and worked in construction; then in April 1849 he became the pastor of the **Flagg Springs Baptist Church**. To be closer to the church, the family moved to a farm on Schababerle Rd., about a mile and a half west of the church. Jolly sold his farm at Flagg Springs in 1887 and moved into a new house that he had built in Mentor. Some of the buildings he reportedly constructed are the Campbell Co. Courthouse at Alexandria, the California Christian Church, the

Wesley Chapel Methodist Church, the St. Peter & Paul Church at Gubser Mill, the Flagg Springs Baptist Church, the **Walnut Hills Academy**, the **Beech Grove Academy**, and numerous private homes. After 58 years of marriage, America Vickers Jolly died on March 23, 1900, and James Jolly died in September of the same year. Both were buried in the Grandview Cemetery, along Smith Rd. in Mentor.

Turner, Gary R. "Oral History of the Jolly Family," Northern Kentucky Univ. Oral History Interviews, 1976, Archives, Northern Kentucky Univ., Highland Heights, Ky.

Wessling, Jack. *Early History of Campbell County Kentucky.* Alexandria: Privately published, 1997.

Jack Wessling

JONES, CHARLES EDWARD (b. August 25, 1880, Covington, Ky.; d. March 21, 1947, Covington, Ky.). Charles Edward Jones was the son of Edward L. and Amanda Jones. As a youth, Jones lived at 724 1/2 Sanford St. in Covington. In 1908 he was working for the Wallace A. Gaines Funeral Home as an embalmer; then in 1913 Jones purchased the business from Wallace Gaines and renamed it the C. E. Jones Funeral Home. He moved the enterprise from 633 Scott St., in the heart of the African American business district, to 29 E. Seventh St., adjacent to the original William Grant High School.

Jones was treasurer of the **Ninth St. Methodist Episcopal Church** and president of the local chapter of the National Association for the Advancement of Colored People (**NAACP**). He was a 33rd Degree Mason and a member of the Kenton Masonic Lodge No. 16, the treasurer of the Prince Hall Grand Lodge of Kentucky, and a director in the National Funeral Directors Association. He promoted African American education as member of the community committee designated by the Covington Board of Education to review the plans for the new Lincoln-Grant Schools. The high school later honored him for his efforts by naming its auditorium after him. Jones was involved in many community and fraternal activities. As a member of the African American Businessmen's Association, he helped sponsor an annual summer picnic in the country for the African American community.

In 1920 the C. E. Jones Funeral Home relocated from 29 E. Seventh St. back to 633–635 Scott St., the original location of the Wallace A. Gaines business. From the 1920s until Jones's death, this was the unofficial meeting place of the African American Businessmen's Association. Being **Horace Sudduth**'s brother-in-law (Jones's sister Melvina had married Sudduth) helped Jones to encourage other African Americans to enter into business. Jones died in 1947 and was buried in Covington's Linden Grove Cemetery. After his death, his widow, Anna Mae Watkins Jones, a former schoolteacher at the Lincoln-Grant School, operated the funeral home business until 1961.

Harris, Ted. "Reader Recollection," *KP*, March 2, 1992, 4K.

Reis, Jim. "Funeral Directors Assumed Civic Roles," *KP*, February 2, 1987, 4K.

"School Board Given Bids by Architects," *KP*, January 24, 1931, 1–2.

Theodore H. H. Harris

JONES, FREDERICK MCKINLEY (b. May 17, 1893, Cincinnati, Ohio; d. February 21, 1961, Minneapolis, Minn.). Frederick M. Jones, an inventor, was the son of an Irishman, John Jones, and an African American mother. Jones lived in rooming houses in Cincinnati with his father, who later placed him in the care of Rev. William B. Ryan, a Roman Catholic priest. Father Ryan was the pastor at St. Ann Church in West Covington from 1909 to 1917.

Father Ryan provided Jones with an upbringing that was more typical for an Irish or German Catholic child than for an African American child. It was Father Ryan's view that a child's skin color did not matter. Hence, with Father Ryan's help and guidance, Jones learned to read and write and developed the mathematical and reading skills necessary for a strong foundation in mechanics and science. He became an inventor, an engineer, and a "mechanical whiz" who had special talents in dealing with machinery.

One of Jones's most significant contributions in the early part of his career was the design of a system that enabled refrigerated trucks and trains to keep fresh produce and meats from spoiling as they were transported across the country. Jones also contributed importantly to the nation's efforts during both world wars. During **World War I**, he initially served in France with the U.S. Army's 809th Pioneer Infantry Regiment. Because of his mechanical skills, he became an army electrician and helped to wire several of the army's military installations in France, where he also taught practical electricity in the army's technical schools. During **World War II**, while employed at the United States Thermo King Control Company, Jones designed refrigerators used by the U.S. Army Air Force, the Marine Corps, and the Quartermaster Corps. Machines that Jones designed were also used to cool the cockpits and engines of various aircraft. He also invented a refrigeration unit that allowed blood plasma to be moved throughout the war's Pacific theater.

In the 1930s, when motion pictures were making the transition from silent films to sound films, Jones developed and patented both an electronic-sound-track system and a ticket dispenser for movie theaters. He sold his sound-system patents to Radio Corporation of America (RCA). However, Jones's main focus was the design of mechanical refrigeration in overland trucks and trains and in the air-conditioning of automobiles. Jones is credited with helping to design the refrigeration and air-conditioning units that were marketed by his employer, the United States Thermo King Control Company in Minneapolis. Jones held dozens of patents for his designs and inventions; the ones pertaining to refrigeration and air conditioning were the property of the United States Thermo King Control Company. He was a member of the American Society of Refrigerating Engineers.

Jones died in Minneapolis in 1961, at age 67. He was buried at Fort Snelling National Cemetery in Minneapolis.

Congregation of the Sisters of Divine Providence, St. Anne Convent, Melbourne, Ky., to Theodore H. H. Harris, April 29, 2004.

Frederick McKinley Jones birth record, Archives and Rare Books Department, Univ. of Cincinnati.

Frederick McKinley Jones Military Service Records, Minnesota Historical Society, St. Paul, Minn.

Ott, Virginia, and Gloria Swanson. *Man with a Million Ideas: Fred Jones, Genius/Inventor.* Minneapolis: Lerner, 1977.

Frederick McKinley Jones, ca. 1950.

Saint Ann Church, West Covington. *Kentucky Centennial: The Celebration of Our Centennial,* Sunday, November 20, 1960.
Saint Walburg Monastery, Villa Hills, Ky., to Theodore H. H. Harris, May 15, 2004.
Spencer, Steven M. "Born Handy." *Saturday Evening Post,* May 7, 1949, 22–31.

Theodore H. H. Harris

JONES, THOMAS LAURENS (b. January 21, 1819, White Oak, Rutherford Co., N.C.; d. July 20, 1887, Newport, Ky.). Lawyer and politician Thomas Laurens Jones, the son of George and Elizabeth Mills Jones, grew up in Spartanburg, S.C. He earned his bachelor's degree from the College of New Jersey (later Princeton University) in 1840 and his law degree from Harvard University in 1843. He spent the next two years expanding his horizons, traveling throughout Europe. Jones was admitted to the South Carolina bar in 1846 and practiced law in New York City in 1847. In 1848 he married Mary Keturah Taylor, the granddaughter of Gen. **James Taylor Jr.**, founder of Newport. They spent an extended honeymoon in Europe. In Italy they saw a beautiful house, which greatly impressed them. Upon returning, Mary told her father, **James Taylor III**, about it, and he decided to replicate it for them. The mansion, which was called the Jones Castle and, in recent times, Mount St. Martin's (see **Mount St. Martin**), had 17 rooms and was built on a high hill in South Newport. In 1853–1855, Jones served as a member of the Kentucky House of Representatives. In July 1862, during the **Civil War**, Jones was arrested as a Confederate sympathizer and jailed at the **Newport Barracks**. He was transferred to Camp Chase in Columbus, Ohio, and was told he would remain in custody until he swore allegiance to the Union. He finally did and then returned to Newport. He was elected as a Democrat to the U.S. House of Representatives, where he served 1867–1871 and 1875–1879 (see **Democratic Party**). He ran for governor in 1883 and was narrowly defeated by J. Proctor Knott (1883–1887), the result of what his supporters claimed was a fraudulent count. He intended to run for governor in 1887, but failing health caused his withdrawal. He died that year and was buried in the Evergreen Cemetery in Southgate.

Levin, H., ed. *The Lawyers and Lawmakers of Kentucky.* Chicago: Lewis, 1897.
"Our Honorable Thomas L. Jones Dead," *KSJ,* July 21, 1887, 4.
Perrin, William Henry, J. H. Battle, and G. C. Kniffin. *Kentucky: A History of the State.* Louisville, Ky.: F. A. Battey, 1888.

Jack Wessling

JONESVILLE (GRANT CO.). Jonesville, on the western edge of Grant Co., was so named in the 1880s for the seven unrelated Jones families who owned farms in the vicinity. Earlier names for the community were Nonesuch and Macedonia. The Macedonia Baptist Church began there in 1843, with charter members Margarita and Amanda Hambrick, Jonathan and Julia Johnson, Robert Patterson, William Smith, Lydia Stone, and Wesley and Nancy Wharton. The Macedonia post office was established in 1858 and closed in 1866.

Although a school is known to have existed in the community before the **Civil War**, the earliest public school records now available are from 1885 and list C. H. Beatty, R. McKinsie, and D. L. Stewart as town school trustees at that time. In 1894 trustees A. H. Calendar, Jefferson Davis Renaker, and Thomas V. Toon purchased the Masonic Hall on the Elliston Station Rd. for use as a schoolhouse. After the hall burned in 1931, a two-room frame school was constructed. It was replaced by a brick schoolhouse that was in use until 1966. When the county school system was consolidated, the Jonesville school children were bused to new locations.

The Jonesville Deposit Bank dates to 1893. In 1934 it was recapitalized and the articles of incorporation amended in accordance with the requirements of the Federal Reconstruction Finance Corporation. In 1940 the bank was reincorporated as the Citizens Bank, with its main office at Dry Ridge under the management of B. C. Cotton; the bank's Jonesville office was managed by Carla Mullikin. Currently, it operates as a branch office of **Grant Co. Deposit Bank**.

Jonesville was incorporated from the 1880s until the early 1920s. Being some distance from the Grant Co. sheriff s office and the jail, located at Williamstown, Jonesville maintained its own police force and jail to help keep the peace. As communications and roads improved, the need for a separate police force and jail lessened, and in 1919 the Jonesville jail property was sold to James Caldwell by the town's Board of Trustees, J. M. Beverly, G. W. Caldwell, M. D. Hamilton, A. T. Stewart, and J. W. Stewart. In 1927 a post office was established, with Otis Wilson as postmaster. He was succeeded in 1937 by Margaret Thornton Conrad, who served from 1937 until 1972, when Kathryn Satterwhite became supervisor of the post office.

In 1910 Uriah Bickers donated ground for a new Methodist Episcopal Church South. The church first obtained a parsonage in 1924; then in 1937 a new parsonage was built on a lot near the church.

Today, with two churches, a general store, a bank, and a post office, Jonesville is a successful trading center in a prosperous farming community. In 1998 one of those churches, the Mount Pisgah Methodist Church, experienced a fire. Just to the west of town is another community also named Jonesville, in Owen Co.

Conrad, John B., ed. *History of Grant County.* Williamstown, Ky.: Grant Co. Historical Society, 1992.
Rennick, Robert M. *Kentucky Place Names.* Lexington: Univ. Press of Kentucky, 1984.
"3 Church Fires Raise Suspicions—No Suspects in Grant Co. Blaze," *KE,* November 3, 1998, B1.
"Town Lacks Business, but Not Pride in Unity," *KP,* February 5, 1986, 8K.

John B. Conrad

JONESVILLE (OWEN CO.). Jonesville is one of two hamlets in Owen Co. that straddle the county line: Sparta, in northern Owen Co., is partially in Gallatin Co.; and Jonesville, on the eastern edge, is partially in Grant Co. At one time, Jonesville was called Nonesuch, but since Woodford Co. also had a town named Nonsuch, when seven families named Jones moved into the Nonsuch in Owen Co., its name was changed to Jonesville. The village is located on Ky. Rt. 36, seven miles northeast of Owenton and 10 miles west of Williamstown. The Jonesville post office was established in 1877. Over the years, there have been hotels, blacksmiths, tobacco warehouses, a jail, an undertaker, and barbershops in town. Several doctors have practiced there. In 1911 construction began on a railroad from Dry Ridge in Grant Co. to Owenton via Jonesville, but it was never finished; thus Owen Co. is one of only two Kentucky counties that never had an active railway line. There have been two major fires in Jonesville, and today it has its own volunteer fire department. The Methodists and the Baptists have churches in town.

Houchens, Mariam Sidebottom. *History of Owen County: "Sweet Owen."* Louisville, Ky.: Standard, 1976.
Rennick, Robert M. *Kentucky Place Names.* Lexington: Univ. Press of Kentucky, 1984.

JORDAN BAPTIST CHURCH. The Jordan Baptist Church, located along Ky. Rt. 467 in Carroll Co., was founded on Christmas Day 1867. It started with 25 members, 18 of whom came from the **White's Run Baptist Church** in Dallasburg and the rest from the **Ghent Baptist Church**. Elder Williams Johnson, who became the Jordan Baptist Church's first pastor, preached the dedicatory message, and a man named Baker, from the Wheatley church, assisted. On that same day, a church covenant was adopted. By 1870 a building committee had been organized, and the decision was made to build a 36-by-56-foot meetinghouse. In 1897 the first songbooks were purchased. In 1900 the Jordan Baptist Church, along with other churches, withdrew from the Concord Baptist Association to form the White's Run Baptist Association.

The first Vacation Bible School was held in 1937, and also that year the church gave the State of Kentucky a right-of-way through the churchyard. The church was wired for electricity in 1940. In 1955 the church purchased lumber for a new building. In 1971 aluminum siding was installed, and in 1972 stained-glass panes were installed in the side windows in the sanctuary.

In 1983 the church called a woman, Dr. Molly Marshall Green, to be the pastor; she was the first woman minister in the history of the church or in the White's Run Baptist Association. Another woman minister, Loretta Reynolds, replaced Green in 1985. In 1988 a new roof was put on the sanctuary, and in 1989 inside restrooms were installed. On December 5, 1993, the church celebrated its 125th anniversary. New front doors were installed, and the church was made handicap accessible by adding a ramp to the front door entrance and to the educational building.

Jordan Baptist Church Minutes, Jordan Baptist Church, Carroll Co., Ky.

Ken Massey

JUSTICE, DAVID (b. April 14, 1966, Cincinnati, Ohio). Professional baseball player David Christopher Justice was only four years old when his father, Robert Justice, abandoned the family. David's mother, Nettie Justice, took a job as a housekeeper in order to support her son. Growing up in the North Avondale section of Cincinnati, David spent his time playing sports with the other boys in his neighborhood. Football, basketball, and baseball were his life, and he had dreams of someday playing in the NBA (National Basketball Association). At age 12, Justice began attending the **Covington Latin School** in Northern Kentucky. He was a prime candidate for the school, which requires students to skip at least one grade. Skipping grades was no problem for Justice, because he excelled in academics as well as in athletics, particularly basketball. As a senior, he averaged 25.9 points per game and made the Catholic All-American high school basketball team. Justice graduated from Covington Latin School in 1982, two years early (he had skipped the seventh and eighth grades). He attended college at **Thomas More College**, in Crestview Hills, on a basketball scholarship. During his years at Thomas More, his athletic ability was showcased not only in basketball but also in baseball; the college's legendary coach, **Jim Connor**, mentored him in both sports. When Justice was age 18, he was a junior in college and a favorite prospect of many baseball scouts.

His professional baseball career began in 1985, when he was drafted in the fourth round by the Atlanta Braves. While in the minor leagues, he worked odd jobs during the off-season. He drove a shuttle bus at the **Cincinnati/Northern Kentucky International Airport** and worked as an orderly at University Hospital in Cincinnati. In 1990 he played his first full season in the major leagues and received the National League Rookie of the Year award while playing with the Braves.

On January 1, 1993, Justice made headlines off the field by marrying actress Halle Berry. Their marriage was brief, ending in divorce after three years. In 1994 he was voted one of *People Magazine*'s 50 Most Beautiful People.

During his 14-season major league career, Justice played for the Braves in the National League and in the American League for the Cleveland Indians, the New York Yankees, and the Oakland Athletics. During that time he reached the World Series 6 times and made the baseball playoffs 10 times. Justice was a three-time all-star, who won World Series titles with the Braves in 1995 and the Yankees in 2000. He also holds the major league record for the most post-season games played. His career batting average was .279.

Baseball Almanac. www.baseball-almanac.com (accessed June 30, 2006).
"Baseball Notebook," *Toronto Star*, February 7, 2003.
Bradley, John Ed. "Justice Prevails." *Sports Illustrated*, June 6, 1994, 66.
Croyle, William. "Latin School a Head Start," *CE*, February 10, 2006, 1B.
Johnson, Chuck. "Postseason Justice," *USA Today*, October 1, 2002, 1.
Peterson, Bill. "Coming Home: Once Again, Justice Returns with a Winner," *CP*, June 6, 1998, 3B.

Susan Patterson

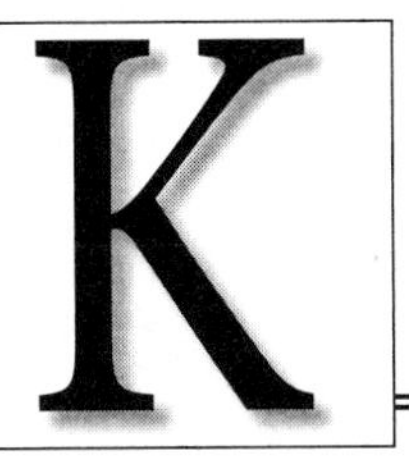

KARSNER, CASPER (b. ca. 1750, place of birth unknown; d. ca. 1798, Kentucky). In 1779 pioneer Casper Karsner (Carsner) was a soldier in the militia of Capt. Benjamin Logan's Company at Logan's Station, near the settlement of St. Asaph's, in modern Lincoln Co., Ky. In June 1780, when he resided at Ruddell's (Hinkston's) Station, which was built by Isaac Ruddell, in modern-day Harrison Co., this station was taken and destroyed by American Indian warriors under the command of British captain Henry Byrd. The people living at Ruddell's Station who were not killed in the attack were captured and held by the British and the Indians. Karsner was held by the British until they sent him to Fort Ticonderoga, N.Y., in 1783, where he was released. Lexington, Ky., trustee records dated May 11, 1785, show that signed deeds for in-lots were issued to Percival Butler, Casper Karsner, and others. On May 20, 1785, Karsner's land grant was given Virginia governor Patrick Henry's seal. On December 10, 1785, Karsner was paid 314 pounds, 15 shillings, and 4 pence for militia service as back pay, four years after the **Revolutionary War** ended. He was 35 at the time and unmarried. In 1786 Karsner married Eveles "Eva" Lail, who had also been captured at Ruddell's Station and had been forced to run the gauntlet to escape the Indians. Four children were born to this couple. In 1789 Casper Karsner was on the Board of Trustees of Transylvania Seminary (1785–1799), the precursor of Transylvania University. Karsner's descendants retained intact the family's original land patents in what is now Owen Co.

On February 11, 1789, Casper and Eva's first son, John Karsner, was born. John Karsner fought and was wounded in the **War of 1812**. He married Sallie Patterson of Jessamine Co. on December 20, 1814, in nearby Fayette Co., and Sallie and John had two children; Sallie died sometime during 1828. John married his second wife, Mary Eaton, on January 8, 1829, and John and Mary became the parents of four children. In 1846 John and his family settled in Owen Co. about three miles from Monterey. John and Mary were buried in the Karsner family's graveyard, just below the Old Cedar Baptist Church on **U.S. 127** near Monterey, where several other members of the Karsner family are also buried. Casper Karsner, however, was buried in Jessamine Co.

Collins, Richard H. *History of Kentucky*. Vol. 1. Covington, Ky.: Collins, 1882.

Murphy, Margaret A. Karsner. *The Karsners of Kentucky: History and Family Album*. Frankfort, Ky., Tingle's, 1981.

Perrin, W. H., ed. *History of Bourbon, Scott, Harrison, and Nicholas Counties, Kentucky*. Chicago: O. L Baskin, 1882.

Perrin, W. H., J. H. Battle, and G. C. Kniffin. *Kentucky: A History of the State*. Louisville, Ky.: F. A. Battery, 1887.

Margaret A. Murphy

KARSNER, HARRY CLARK (b. October 29, 1914, Owen Co., Ky.; d. December 21, 1971, Lexington, Ky.). Owen Co. native Harry Clark Karsner, an aviator and a state official, was the eldest child of Johnathan Albert and Lela Brammell Karsner of Monterey. After graduating from the Monterey High School, he pursued training in aviation. He married Sarah Jane Gill on February 13, 1937, and they became the parents of three children. Karsner received his commercial pilot's license in October 1938. During **World War II**, he was a flight instructor at Ryan's School of Aeronautics in San Diego, Calif., and was appointed a flight commander on August 25, 1942.

After the war, he returned to the Old Cedar community near Monterey, constructed a four-plane hangar on a field near **U.S. 127** called Karsner Field, and began teaching military veterans to fly. The hangar is well known for the neon sign that states, "Christ Is the Answer." Influenced by evangelist Louis W. Arnold, Karsner equipped a plane with a public address system. His wife, Sarah Jane, recorded gospel songs, and Arnold recorded a brief sermon. Each afternoon, Karsner flew the "Gospel Plane" within a 100-mile radius of Frankfort, delivering the message to all those within earshot.

In 1958 Karsner was elected a director of the Burley Tobacco Growers Cooperative Association of Kentucky. In 1959 he became commissioner of aeronautics under Kentucky governor A. B. Chandler (1935–1939 and 1955–1959). Karsner was also a farmer and a landowner in Owen Co. He was chairman of the Owen Co. Board of Education, a magistrate in Owen Co., and a director of First Farmers Bank in Owenton. At Old Cedar Baptist Church, he was chairman of the board of deacons and taught the men's Sunday school class. He died in 1971 and was buried at the Monterey Cemetery.

Murphy, Margaret Alice, and Lela Maude Hawkins. *The History of Historic Old Cedar Baptist Church and Community, 1816–2004*. Frankfort, Ky.: Lynn, 2004.

Trout, Allan M. "Prepare for World's End, Voice from Sky Advises," *LCJ*, October 18, 1949, 5.

Margaret A. Murphy

KEEFER. Keefer is a community in southwest Grant Co. along Ky. Rt. 2936 (Keefer Rd.). Keefer (at one time spelled Kiefer) is believed to have been settled before the county was organized in 1820. Early in its history, the community was also called Priceburg, after John Price, who started the first store there. Other early settlers were Jacob Musselman, a surveyor named Payne, and Francis Simon.

In the 1980s, archaeologists from the University of Kentucky conducted a dig in the area and uncovered numerous arrowheads, broken pottery, and a rock-lined cooking pit estimated to be at least 1,000 years old and thought to have been used by American Indians. There was also a salt spring, where hunters came for water that they boiled down for salt.

The Antioch Church of Christ was founded in Keefer around 1838. It was moved in 1872 to a plot of land donated by J. H. Musselman. The current church building, whose cemetery contains stones dating from 1873, was dedicated in 1957. Tom Marksberry operated a general store across from the church until 1905. Among the businesses in Keefer were blacksmith shops, grocery stores, a gristmill, and huckster routes. Around 1884 a school was established, and the post office followed in 1885. Today the businesses are gone, but the church and several homes remain.

Belew, Mildred J., and Otha Steger. "Never on the Busy Highway—That's Keefer." In *The Grant County Sesqui-Centennial Bulletin, 1820–1970*. Williamstown, Ky.: Grant Co. Sesquicentennial Publications Committee, 1970.

Chandler, Virgil, Sr. *Cemeteries*. Vol. 3. Williamstown, Ky.: Grant Co. Historical Society, 1988.

Conrad, John B., ed. *History of Grant County*. Williamstown, Ky.: Grant Co. Historical Society, 1992.

Barbara Loomis Brown

KEFAUVER COMMITTEE. During the early 1950s, most Americans were introduced to the criminal "conspiracy" of organized crime through the U.S. Senate's hearings of the Special Committee to Investigate Crime in Interstate Commerce. Headed by Senator Estes Kefauver (D, Tennessee), it was more commonly known as the Kefauver Committee, and it had a significant effect on Northern Kentucky. From 1950 to 1952, the Kefauver Committee met intermittently around the nation to investigate and expose the supposed conspiracy of a national crime syndicate. Since the rise of mobster Al Capone and other bootleggers as national figures during the 1920s, the public had always suspected that criminals worked in concert. After **World War II**, this idea gained more currency.

As an attempt to stop any sort of criminal conspiracy, the Kefauver hearings were completely unsuccessful. Their ultimate significance was in providing one of the first major telecasts of a U.S. congressional committee, pioneering the sort of political theater that became famous in 1953 with the attempts by Senator Joseph McCarthy (R, Wisconsin) to root out Communists and continued through to the Watergate hearings of the 1970s and the Iran-Contra hearings of the 1980s. Persons living in Northern Kentucky appeared before the Kefauver Committee; for example, in late March 1951, Jimmy Brink, most closely associated with the **Lookout House**, sat before the committee in Washington, D.C., accompanied by his attorney, **Sawyer A. Smith**.

Millions of Americans sat riveted to their televisions as Kefauver and other committee members interviewed hundreds of criminal figures, attempting to reveal the existence of a shadow government that controlled the nation's criminal enterprises. The Kefauver hearings were arguably the first example of television watching as a mass experience, as people crowded into neighbors' homes, bars, and restaurants to watch. Although no actual law-enforcement action arose from the hearings, Kefauver parlayed the exposure into a failed 1952 presidential run.

The Kefauver Committee hearings were key events in the successful cleanup of Northern Kentucky, even though they preceded it by almost a decade. Northern Kentucky had gained a reputation as the region's haven for gambling and vice. But the committee's hearings in Cleveland in the late winter of 1951 demonstrated how Northern Kentucky was broadly connected to a national criminal network. Connections between the **Cleveland Syndicate** (the Mayfield Road Gang) and gambling in Northern Kentucky were fully revealed, especially how the syndicate had bought up casinos like the Lookout House and the **Beverly Hills Supper Club** after its operations in Cleveland were shut down in the 1940s. Testifying before the committee, Northern Kentucky law enforcement officials professed ignorance of the gambling operations taking place right in their own backyard. The Beverly Hills Supper Club and other casinos closed their doors during the hearings but announced that they would reopen as soon as the committee disbanded.

After the hearings, activities in Newport and Covington were seen as more insidious and dangerous than before. Organized crime was here in Greater Cincinnati and could not be simply relegated to distant ethnic enclaves like Chicago and New York City. The Kefauver hearings sparked the first in a series of reform groups that culminated with the successful work of the Committee of 500 in 1961 (see **Newport Reform Groups**).

Bell, Jack, and John Chadwick. "Local Night Spots Figure in Probe: Two Face Contempt Charges; Mum on Beverly Hills, Lookout House," *KTS*, March 29, 1951, 1.

Robert Gioielli

KEHOE, JAMES A., BRIGADIER GENERAL (b. November 11, 1896, Maysville, Ky.; d. November 29, 1983, Maysville, Ky.). James Arthur Kehoe, an adjutant general for two Kentucky governors and a businessman, was the son of James N. and Hannah M. Kane Kehoe. He attended public school in Maysville and in 1914 was appointed to the U.S. Military Academy at West Point, N.Y. Upon graduation in 1918, he was commissioned a 2nd lieutenant. During **World War I**, he served in China and Siberia and was soon promoted to 1st lieutenant. When Kehoe returned to civilian life in 1920, he became a vice president of the Home Warehouse Company in Maysville. A year later he was appointed secretary-treasurer of the Eastern District Warehouse Corporation, where he served until 1924 (see **Maysville Tobacco Warehouses**). He also was named the president of the **Bank of Maysville** in 1921. Kehoe was appointed Kentucky adjutant general for governors Flem Sampson (1927–1931) and Ruby Laffoon (1931–1935). In 1925 Kehoe married Alice Williams of Frankfort, Ky.; they had two children. He reentered the army during **World War II** and saw service in India and Burma. At the end of the war, Kehoe retired from the army as a brigadier general. His wife, Alice, died shortly after he returned home in 1945. In retirement he built a frame ranch home in Maysville, overlooking the Ohio River, where he lived for the remainder of his life. In 1983 Kehoe was ill for a short time before his death at age 87. He was buried in Maysville Cemetery.

"Brig. Gen. James Kehoe, 87, Helped Build the Burma Road," *KP*, November 30, 1983, 1B.

KEHOE, JAMES N. (b. July 15, 1862, Maysville, Ky.; d. June 16, 1945, Cincinnati, Ohio). Banker, lawyer, and politician James Nicholas Kehoe was the son of James and Nora Conroy Kehoe. He was educated in both public and private schools around Maysville. He took a job with a printing company, and at age 22 became owner of the firm. He later studied law in Louisville under the well-known lawyers Hargis and Easton and was admitted to the Kentucky bar on November 1, 1888. Kehoe set up his practice in Maysville, where he served as city attorney for two terms and as master commissioner of the chancery of the Mason Co. Circuit Court from 1893 to 1900. He also served on the Kentucky Court of Appeals in 1889. He held several leadership roles in the **Democratic Party** and was elected to the U.S. House of Representatives, where he served four years, 1901–1905. He was defeated for reelection in 1904.

Kehoe married Hannah M. Kane of Maysville on September 24, 1892, and they had five children. His wife Hannah died on October 28, 1910, and he married his second wife, Frances Reed Calvert, on April 20, 1918. His son **James A. Kehoe** served in the U.S. Army during **World War I** and **World War II** and attained the rank of brigadier general.

James N. Kehoe served as one of the engineers during construction of the **Simon Kenton Memorial Bridge** during the early 1930s. He was also president of the 1st Standard Bank & Trust Company (see **Bank of Maysville**) and president of the Kentucky Bankers Association. He died at age 82 and was buried in the Maysville Cemetery. In 1940 a new bridge in Maysville was named the Kehoe Viaduct in his honor.

Biographical Directory of the United States Congress. "Kehoe, James Nicholas (1862–1945)." http://bioguide.congress.gov (accessed August 29, 2006).

Levin, H., ed. *The Lawyers and Lawmakers of Kentucky*. Chicago: Lewis, 1897.

"Maysville Viaduct Dedication Is Set," *KP*, October 18, 1940, 6.

Southard, Mary Young, and Ernest C. Miller, eds. *Who's Who in Kentucky: A Biographical Assembly of Notable Kentuckians*. Louisville: Standard, 1936.

The Spirit of Greater Maysville and Mason County. Maysville, Ky.: Daily Independent, 1930.

KELLEY-KOETT COMPANY. Organizer and promoter J. Robert Kelley (1871–1931), aided by a German-born craftsman, Albert Koett (1863–1951), developed the Kelley-Koett Company into a prominent manufacturer and distributor of X-ray equipment and accessories. About 1903, eight years after Wilhelm Roentgen announced his discovery of X-rays, Kelley and Koett met in Koett's backyard shop on Bakewell St. in Covington. Together, these men developed an innovative X-ray model unit that produced a 12-inch spark, and afterward they founded a company to produce X-ray equipment. Their invention was introduced at a meeting of the American Roentgen Ray Society in Niagara Falls, N.Y., and was praised in the first issue of the *American Quarterly of Roentgenology* (October 1906). The National Museum of American History (one of the Smithsonian Institution museums) has displayed Kelley and Koett's prototype under the German title "Grosse Flamme."

Incorporated in 1905, the Kelley-Koett Company moved in 1911 into its permanent new factory and office building on the north side of W. Fourth St., between Russell and Johnston Sts. in Covington, and began marketing the latest X-ray diagnostic and therapy procedures and equipment. From about 12 employees in 1905, the company grew to employ 675 in 1944, not counting office workers and the sales force. Kelley said he foresaw a day when Covington might be called X-ray City. The company donated $1,000 worth of X-ray equipment for the new St. Elizabeth Hospital building (see **St. Elizabeth Medical Center**). According to the ***Kentucky Post***, the Mayo Clinic purchased X-ray equipment only from this company, and in 1916 Kelley hosted a dinner for Dr. R. D. Carman of the Mayo Clinic at the Covington Industrial Club. In 1917 a group of medical and army officials joined with the company's technicians to develop a mobile X-ray table unit for use in treating military casualties. Dr. William David Coolidge, from the General Electric laboratory, developed a compatible portable generator and a compact air-cooled tube to be used in coordination with the Kelley-Koett mobile X-ray unit.

Kelley-Koett developed special relationships with hospitals, clinics, and doctors' offices. For the Mayo clinic, it tested new ideas, solved problems, and sold its instruments at cost, in return for deriving profits from the innovations developed at the clinic by the use of Kelley-Koett products. In 1928 Kelley-Koett recorded $2.5 million in sales; but in 1929 the General Electric Company was number one in the field of X-ray equipment. General Electric held a patent that forced competitors during the 1930s to purchase its "universal Coolidge tube." Meanwhile, the Kelley-Koett Company, continuing to compete, had developed a laminator sensitive to body size and a scanograph that compensated for the naturally distorted focus of X-rays. The company was known for both its quality products and its innovations, including an improved rheostat, a constant-potential transformer, a model surge-protection device, and a long list of others. One of the secrets of the local company's success was cofounder Kelley's ability to make family-like arrangements with independent dealers, many of whom were former employees of the company or suppliers of its accessories. In 1925 the company claimed to have domestic agents and service branches in 37 major cities.

Major troubles came to the company when Kelley died (probably of cancer from X-ray exposure) soon after the stock market crash in 1929. Koett, the company's other cofounder, was at this time approaching age 70. Covington native and long-time company employee George Edward Geise (1889–1958) became the interim president. Another Covington native, Wilbur Stanley Werner (1895–1937), took over and served as president for just three years before dying at age 43. As the company foundered, bank officials on the board of directors took control of the company and also became its financial caretakers. In 1938 one of these men, Donald A. Eddy of the First National Bank of Covington, succeeded Werner as the company's president. After surviving the **Great Depression**, as well as the **flood of 1937**, Kelley-Koett found itself in the hands of officers detached from the company's core culture.

The company still had one great opportunity to turn around and prosper during the 1930s. At the time, cancer rates had been increasing and hospitals worldwide looked for answers. Attempting to capture this market, the Kelley-Koett Company, a deep-therapy innovator, now sold a 250,000-volt unit to the Rockefeller Foundation for a medical center in China. Other orders followed. Werner supervised custom installation of additional units in the Los Angeles Clinic in California, the Harper Hospital in Detroit, Mich., and the Lincoln Hospital in Lincoln, Neb. At Harper Hospital, the installation, which cost the hospital $50,000, included padding the surrounding walls with 26 tons of lead. At the time of his death in 1937, Werner was installing a 1.2-million-volt deep-therapy behemoth costing $76,000 at the Miller Hospital in St. Paul, Minn. In 1938 the **Booth Memorial Hospital** of Covington acquired a 200,000-volt Kelley-Koett deep-therapy unit. In 1939, thanks in large part to the popularity of its deep-therapy units, the Kelley-Koett Company was recovering financially and 15 percent of its sales were overseas.

In 1941 Phillip Meyers, a prominent Cincinnati businessman, purchased the Kelley-Koett Company and appointed an MIT graduate engineer, Adolf Feibel, as president. In the pioneer years for use of X-ray equipment leading up to and through **World War II**, the Kelley-Koett Company's X-ray equipment was a standard-setter and enjoyed prominence. From January through September 1941, the company sold 18 different items to the government for $650,000. During **World War II**, the company sold adaptive industrial X-ray units that were used for testing the integrity of cast-metal airplane propellers and for detecting and helping to disable underwater mines. However, the aggressive Picker X-ray Corporation won a contract for supplying the bulk of the military's X-ray tables, and Picker's competitors, including the Kelley Koett Company, were left to sell accessories.

The war effort still required Kelley-Koett to expand production, to rent off-site warehouse space, to add a second shift, and to hire women. The company also loaned engineers and factory staff to the military for special assignments and product development. Even without the orders that had been lost to the Picker X-Ray Corporation, production on a grand scale at the Kelley-Koett Company required many workers. Complex X-ray apparatus there was always assembled by hand. In 1943 the army awarded the Covington company's officials "E" awards for excellence. After World War II, the Kelley-Koett Company, through a UN relief agency, sold X-ray equipment for the medical treatment of civilian war casualties in the Soviet Union.

In the late 1940s, Kelley-Koett still had its business arrangement with the Mayo Clinic and enjoyed good relations with many loyal customers. But the new managers liked to emphasize sales productivity, and many shortsighted marketing initiatives were tried. They included a cheaper X-ray line, consumer products such as electric blankets, and a cold war radiation-measuring device, manufactured at a company facility in Cincinnati for the Atomic Energy Commission's civilian defense centers. Customers began to sense the company's instability. Nevertheless, at the end, the company professionals in the old factory in Covington still produced a quality line of products, including a new, sleek, 1950s Fleetwood X-ray table. In 1951 Tracerlab of Boston, Mass., purchased the Kelley-Koett Company. After Tracerlab, and then another owner, a French company purchased the business. In 1964 the Covington factory was demolished for urban renewal, but the Kelley-Koett Company's trademark survived into the early 1970s. Several patents are still held by the Kelley-Koett Company and the engineers who worked there.

Boh, John. "An International Edge, the Kelley-Koett Company, 1903–1956." *NKH* 3, no. 2 (Spring–Summer 1996): 39–51.

"Covington Has Reason to Be Called 'X-Ray City,'" *KP*, March 27, 1927, 10.

"A Great Man Passes," *KP*, April 25, 1931, 4.

"New Company Incorporated," *KP*, June 13, 1905, 2.

Reis, Jim. "X-Ray Business Put Covington on Map," *KP*, August 6, 1984, 10K.

John Boh

KELLY, ADAM DAVID (b. July 19, 1860, Carthage, N.C.; d. February 26, 1934, Covington, Ky.). Physician Adam Kelly attended public schools in North Carolina and then entered Bennett College in Greensboro, N.C., receiving his AB in 1892. He married Mary Wendell in Nashville, Tenn., and in 1896 graduated from Nashville's Meharry Medical School. That same year, he moved to Covington, Ky., and established his practice of general medicine and surgery. Kelly became the second African American medical doctor in the city. He was well known throughout Kenton Co. In May 1912, Kelly was an organizer of the State Medical Society of Colored Physicians, Surgeons, Dentists, and Pharmacists, who had gathered in Covington. Kelly also presented a paper, "Progress of Medicine since the Civil War," at that meeting.

On July 23, 1919, tragedy struck Kelly and his family. An intruder shot Kelly and his son in their home at 514 Scott St. while they were sleeping. Kelly's four-year-old son, Garland, died while on the operating table at St. Elizabeth Hospital (see **St. Elizabeth Medical Center**). Dr. Kelly recovered from his wound and continued his medical practice. No one was ever charged with the shooting.

Kelly was a trustee of the Ninth St. Methodist Church and an active member of the local Republican Party. He was also involved with various fraternal organizations: Freemasons, the Eastern Star, the Knights of Pythias, and Odd Fellows. He died at age 73 and was buried at Linden Grove Cemetery in Covington.

"Colored Medical Men Meeting in Covington," *KP*, May 10, 1912, 11.

Dabney, W. P. *Cincinnati's Colored Citizens*. Cincinnati: Dabney, 1926.

"Death," *KTS*, March 1, 1934, 2.

"Investigation into Slaying of Physician's Son," *KTS*, July 24, 1919, 24.

"Negro Doctor and Son Shot by Intruder," *KP*, July 23, 1919, 1.

"Physician and Son Were Shot as They Slept," *KTS*, July 23, 1919, 18.

Theodore H. H. Harris

KELLY, MARY ANN (b. September 15, 1925, Los Angeles, Calif.; d. June 20, 2001, Edgewood, Ky.). Mary Ann Kelly, a television writer and advertiser and an author, was the daughter of John Joseph and Mary "Mayme" Farrell Kelly of Ludlow, Ky. She graduated from the College of Mount St. Joseph in Cincinnati and did graduate work at Marquette University in Milwaukee, Wis., and at Xavier University in Cincinnati. Kelly authored three books, traveled the world, and was already employed as a television program writer at WLW in Cincinnati when the television station went on the air in 1948. She wrote screenplays, conducted advertising campaigns for the Ralph H. Jones Company (Crosley Broadcasting's advertising firm in Cincinnati), and never failed to have a perspective on an issue or an outrageous tale to contribute. Kelly's books summarize her style; *The Trouble Is Not in Your Set* is almost an autobiography of her 40 years in journalism. While at WLW television, she worked with Rod Serling, later the writer of television's *The Twilight Zone*, and with Earl Hamner, the creator of the television series *The Waltons*.

Kelly was a pioneer woman in the written media, in advertising, and in the broadcast world in the region. In her spare time, Kelly wrote songs and was a professional toy creator (see **Toys**). She was a member of the **Mother of God Catholic Church** in Covington. Kelly never married. After her death from heart trouble in 2001 at **St. Elizabeth Medical Center** South, her body was donated for medical research.

Billman, Rebecca. "Mary Ann Kelly," *CE*, July 3, 2001, 4B.

"Her Book Tunes in Early Days on Air of Cincinnati TV," *KP*, December 15, 1990, 1K.

Kelly, Mary Ann. *My Old Kentucky Home, Good-Night*. Long Island, N.Y.: Exposition Press, 1979.

——. *"Rex" and the Single Girl*. New York: Exposition Press, 1978.

——. *The Trouble Is Not in Your Set*. Cincinnati: C. J. Krehbiel, 1990.

"Mary Ann Kelly, Author and World Traveler," *KP*, June 23, 2001, 13A.
"Mary Ann Kelly Wrote Early Television Scripts—Book Looks at City's Broadcasting," *KE*, July 3, 2001, B4.

Michael R. Sweeney

KENNEDY, THOMAS (b. 1741, Chester Co., Pa.; d. August 1821, Covington, Ky.). Covington pioneer Thomas Kennedy was the immigrant son of Scots-Irish Presbyterians from Northern Ireland. In 1767 he married a widow from Philadelphia, Dinah Davis Piersel. In 1789 Francis Kennedy, Thomas Kennedy's brother, arrived in Cincinnati and established a ferry across the river to present-day Covington. Thomas Kennedy followed his brother, and he either rented or made plans to purchase 200 acres at the confluence of the Ohio and Licking rivers from James Welch; he eventually purchased the land in 1801. In the interim, Thomas Kennedy operated the Kentucky side of his brother's ferry and in 1791 obtained a ferry license for himself from Woodford Co., Virginia; in the same year he began construction of a stone house that stood in the rear of what is today Covington's George Rogers Clark Park. In 1814 Thomas Kennedy sold his property to investors in the Covington Company, a group that, in 1815, established the town of Covington. In 1816 the Kennedy family moved to their new home at the northwest corner of Sixth and Greenup Sts. at Covington's southern edge. Both Thomas and Dinah died in 1821 and were buried in the city's pioneer Craig St. burying grounds, located beyond the original town limits at present-day Sixth and Craig Sts.; the couple's remains were later moved to Covington's Linden Grove Cemetery. Considered by some the oldest house in Covington except for the Kennedys' stone homestead, Thomas and Dinah's last residence, at Sixth and Greenup Sts., was razed in 1904. Their stone house was razed in 1909.

"Obituary of Thomas Kennedy," *Lexington Kentucky Register*, August 20, 1821.
Smith, Allen Webb. *Beginning at "the Point," a Documented History of Northern Kentucky and Environs, the Town of Covington in Particular, 1751–1834.* Park Hills, Ky.: Self-published, 1977.
Tenkotte, Paul A. "Rival Cities to Suburbs: Covington and Newport, Kentucky, 1790–1890." Ph.D. diss., Univ. of Cincinnati, 1989.

John Boh

KENNEDY, WILLIAM (b. 1728, Cummock, Ayershire, Scotland; d. May 16, 1799, Mentor, Ky.). William Kennedy was a **Revolutionary War** veteran and surveyor born at Cassiles, his family's estate in Scotland, where he married his first wife. On May 31, 1760, his son James was born to that union. It is believed that his wife died about this time, because in 1765 William arrived in Colonial America alone. He settled in Virginia, where he served with the militia during the Revolutionary War. After the war, he became a surveyor. On September 8, 1778, he married his second wife, Mary C. Lindsey, and they had one child. Kennedy and his family came to Campbell Co., Kentucky, in 1789, and his son James came from Scotland to join them. William and James built a log cabin at Flagg Springs, which they used as a base of operations in surveying most of northern and eastern Campbell Co. At the time, land surveying was a very lucrative occupation, since surveyors typically received one-third of the land surveyed for their services. The Kennedy family soon became one of the largest landowners in the county. William died at Mentor, and it is believed that he is buried nearby in a small family graveyard along Smith Rd.

Wessling, Jack. *Early History of Campbell County Kentucky.* Alexandria, Ky.: Privately published, 1997.

Jack Wessling

KENNER FAMILY. William Kenner, the father of two prominent Northern Kentucky landowners, and his brother-in-law Philip Minor were the earliest known owners of the land in Louisiana that became the Kenner Plantation. The partners made their fortune in the mercantile business and by producing sugar cane. William and Mary Minor Kenner had four sons, Minor (1808–1862), William Butler (1810–1853), George R. (1812–1852), and Duncan F. (1813–1887). When William Kenner died in 1830, his share of the plantation went to his sons Duncan F. and George R. Kenner. In 1839 Duncan Kenner married Nanine Bringier, daughter of a prominent Creole family. As a wedding present to his wife, Kenner had a mansion built in Louisiana, which he named Ashland, after Henry Clay's estate in Lexington, Ky. The brothers William Butler and George Kenner married sisters, Ruhamah and Charlotte Riske, of Cincinnati.

In 1844 George Kenner (died 1852) bought 246 acres that included **Elmwood Hall** in Ludlow, Ky. He bought the property from his brother-in-law Israel Ludlow, to be used as a summer retreat from the Louisiana heat and diseases. The next year he sold nine acres of the land to his brother William, who probably built Somerset Hall nearby, also as a summer residence. In 1852 William Kenner sold Somerset Hall to Thomas Kevan. In 1854 Kevan sold the house to balloonist **Richard Clayton**, who later sold it to the Jenkins family. The **A. B. Closson** family of Cincinnati were the next purchasers, residing there from 1875 until 1925. In 1926 the Unity Lodge of the Free and Accepted Masons purchased Somerset Hall. The house became a private residence once again in 1997, when Stephen and Paula Chapman bought it and restored it to its original splendor.

"How the City of Ludlow Just Missed Being Called Hygeia," *KP*, September 6, 1925, 8.
"Ludlow," *KP*, February 22, 1995, 1KK–2KK.
Marsh, Betsa. "A Legend in Ludlow." *Cincinnati Magazine*, January 2003, 93–96.
"Summer Home, Closson House, now Masonic Lodge," *Ludlow News Enterprise*, January 25, 1973, 1.

KENNETT TAVERN. The old Kennett Tavern is at the intersection of Shelby and Main Sts. in Falmouth, on the main east-west corridor linking the town with the old Buffalo Trace area to the north and with Williamstown to the west (see **Buffalo Traces**). This route was not only a source of stagecoach and wagon travel but also a connection with river commerce at the ports of Maysville in Mason Co. and Foster in Bracken Co. An early stagecoach stop, the Kennett Tavern also housed Union soldiers during the **Civil War**. After 1854 passenger service on the **Kentucky Central Railroad** replaced stagecoach travel as the principal means of transportation in the region. People using the **Falmouth Railway Depot**, a few blocks away, could dine and stay overnight at the Kennett Tavern and later at the Phoenix Hotel and the 3L Building. The Kennett Tavern consists actually of two connected Greek Revival style buildings, built around 1811. The old brick masonry on the building was most likely quarried from nearby clay pits. The lots on which the tavern stands, numbers 34 and 35, are where the first meeting was held to conduct the

Kennett Tavern.

business of the newly founded Pendleton Co. in 1799. In 1814 Tyree Oldham willed this property to his daughter, who married William C. Kennett. Kennett established a tavern in the building. Both the downstairs (the tavern) and the upstairs (hotel rooms and apartments) continued in use into the 1880s. The tavern later gave way to a restaurant, an ice cream parlor, a barbershop, and various other retail businesses. Many of the windows and doorways fronting on Main St. were altered over the years but have been restored to their original configuration. Clark and Zelma Houchen, the last owners of the Kennett Tavern before it was sold to the city for restoration, purchased the building in the 1940s. It is one of 39 buildings on the National Register of Historic Places within the central Falmouth Historic District and is also the oldest commercial building within Falmouth. In 1995 Falmouth received a monetary grant to restore the old tavern. The city clerk now occupies the first floor of the building, while the upper floor remains under restoration.

Falmouth Outlook, February 14, 1995, 6.

Mildred Belew

KENTON, SIMON (b. April 3, 1755, Fauquier Co., Va.; d. April 29, 1836, New Jerusalem, Ohio). Simon Kenton, the namesake of Kenton Co. and **Simon Kenton High School** in Independence, who first came to Northern Kentucky in 1772, is credited with exploring, scouting, and settling much of Ohio and Northern Kentucky, including the Ohio and Licking River valleys and present-day Maysville. He was the seventh of Mark and Mary Miller Kenton's nine children. A contemporary and friend of **Daniel Boone** and **George Rogers Clark**, Kenton fled Fauquier Co., Va., to the frontier in 1771, thinking that while in a jealous rage he had killed a teenage rival. Kenton used the assumed name Simon Butler until 1782, when he learned that the victim of his rage was alive and well. Kenton returned to Virginia and brought much of his family to Kenton Station in Mason Co. He personally welcomed thousands of pioneer families to the area.

Kenton's introduction to the frontier began at Fort Pitt (Pittsburgh, Pa.), where he first heard stories of the dense cane fields south of the Ohio River and where he first became acquainted with **Simon Girty**, a scout and translator known as "the white savage," and with Clark. From Fort Pitt, Kenton and various companions drifted down the uncharted Ohio River more than 500 miles. For two years Kenton traveled up and down the river exploring streams and rivers, until he found the area he was seeking, near present-day Maysville.

During these expeditions he became adept at finding and interpreting the signs indicating that American Indian hunting parties were in the area. He was eager to assist the trappers and traders who occasionally drifted by, and he earned a reputation as an outstanding wilderness scout. Kenton learned the land from often being on the run, beginning with an Indian attack in the winter of 1773 as he and two companions were drying their wet clothes around a campfire. One man was killed, but Simon and the other man escaped. Nearly naked, Kenton wandered the Kentucky wilderness barefoot for a week before finding some lone hunters along the banks of the Ohio River.

In 1774 the six-foot-one-inch Kenton served as a scout, along with Simon Girty, in **Lord Dunmore's War**, an attempt by the governor of the royal Virginia colony to quell Indian threats on the frontier. Kenton crisscrossed the Ohio territory as a courier between Dunmore's troops and backwoods volunteers. During these forays, Kenton continued to learn the land and developed a skill for which he became famous—shooting, reloading his flintlock, and shooting again with marked accuracy while running at full speed. This ability saved Daniel Boone's life when Kenton shot a Shawnee warrior who was about to tomahawk Boone as the pair dashed toward the gate of the Boonesborough settlement in Central Kentucky, while the fort was under siege in April 1777.

In 1778, during a raid on the Shawnee village near Chillicothe, Ohio, Kenton was captured. He was tied, hands bound, behind an unbroken colt that was then sent galloping through the woods and underbrush. Over the next several weeks, the celebrity scout, a prized captive, was paraded before the Shawnee nation—including the 10-year-old Indian boy Tecumseh—and forced to run the quarter-mile gauntlet five times. During Kenton's last ordeal, his skull was fractured and he was unconscious for two days. The Shawnee called him "Cutta-ho-tha," which he later learned meant "condemned man"; the tribe planned to burn him at the stake. As he poised to run his sixth gauntlet, Kenton leaped over his tormentors in one of his celebrated feats of strength, speed, and agility and ran into the nearby woods but was quickly recaptured. Hours before Kenton was to be killed, Girty, who was working for the British and their Shawnee allies, arrived with a returning war party. He recognized Kenton and made an argument to save his life. In Kenton, the Shawnees saw qualities they admired: skill, cunning, strength, and courage, and for three weeks, Kenton roamed free with Girty and memorized the lay of the land. This proved only to be a stay of execution; Kenton was again bound, tortured, and condemned to die. The execution was to take place at the British trading post at Upper Sandusky in the Ohio Territory. During the march to Sandusky, Kenton's arm and collarbone were broken.

British captain Peter Drouillard persuaded the Shawnees to surrender Kenton so that he could be taken to the British fort at Detroit, Mich., for interrogation. Kenton formulated an escape plan and stealthily amassed provisions for the long and hazardous journey back to Kentucky. Rather than flee directly south, as might be expected, he slipped west to the Wabash River in the Indiana Territory and blazed through 400 miles of untracked forest and prairie in 30 days. In 1779, months after his escape, the British and the Indians began an assault on the Kentucky settlements to squash the **Revolutionary War** and end the European invasion of the Indians' hunting grounds. In response, Clark assembled the Kentucky militia to rout the Indians at their towns along the Little Miami River in Ohio, as well as to harass British forts. With Kenton scouting, Clark led 172 volunteers from Fort Kaskaskia in the Illinois Territory 210 miles eastward in 17 days to capture Vincennes in the Indiana Territory.

Kenton was "tall and well proportioned," according to a 1782 description by Joel Collins, who saw him march through Lexington after the **Battle of Blue Licks** in Kentucky, August 19, 1782. At this time, Kenton had the rank of captain. Kenton married Martha Dowden in 1787; after she died, expecting the couple's fifth child, in a house fire in 1796, he married Elizabeth Jarboe in 1797. In all, Kenton fathered nine children. From 1792 to 1794 Kenton fought along with "Mad" Anthony Wayne in Ohio in the Indian Wars.

In April 1792, the middle-aged Kenton first fought Tecumseh, an up-and-coming Shawnee leader. When Tecumseh and 100 Shawnee warriors stole horses from the Kentucky settlements, Kenton and his smaller force tried but failed to stop them. A year later, Kenton led a retaliatory charge against a Shawnee hunting camp in Ohio but failed to catch Tecumseh off guard. While Kenton and his troops plundered the camp, Tecumseh and his warriors rounded up the settler's horses, leaving the Kentuckians without transportation.

By 1795, Wayne had soundly defeated a coalition of 1,500 Indians at the Battle of Fallen Timbers. A new treaty was to be signed at Greenville, Ohio, and each of the affected tribes was to be represented by the principal chief, who had the authority to speak for his people. Kenton was at hand to witness the opening of negotiations, which essentially reaffirmed the area land boundaries established 10 years before. This time around, surveyors wasted no time plotting out new towns where the Indian villages had stood.

In 1799 Kenton moved from Kentucky to Ohio, which was still a territory. In March 1806, while riding with a friend near Urbana, Ohio, he stumbled upon an Indian encampment where Tecumseh was holding a war council. Kenton sounded a general alarm among his neighbors and alerted Ohio governor Edward Tiffin. When Tecumseh was confronted, first by Kenton and a delegation from Springfield, Ohio, then a few days later in a letter from Tiffin, and once again at a banquet in the new state capital of Chillicothe, where the Shawnee chief was an honored guest, Tecumseh assured the Ohioans that his intentions were peaceful. However, Kenton's instincts to the contrary were correct; Tecumseh was biding his time until his preparations were complete for executing his master war plan. He had been building a coalition of Indians from Ohio, as well as from Indiana and Illinois, and he began hostilities with random attacks in the spring of 1812, supported, in part, by the British. In June the U.S. Congress declared war on Great Britain (see **War of 1812**).

A rumor that Kenton's son Simon Kenton Jr., who was serving under Gen. William Henry Harrison, had been captured by Indians, led Kenton, then age 58, to join Gen. Isaac Shelby's forces on their march from Kentucky to Canada. Their purpose was to engage the British general Henry Proctor and his Indian allies. Harrison cornered Proctor on the Thames River in southwestern Ontario, Canada, east of Detroit. The battle was over quickly and Tecumseh was killed while leading the charge. Tecumseh's death, which collapsed the Indian resistance in Ohio, ended Kenton's fighting days. Simon Kenton Jr. returned from the war unharmed. Unable to read or write, Kenton struggled to manage his finances and spent much of his later life in poverty. During an 1820 visit to Kentucky, he was imprisoned for more than a year for his debts. He died in 1836 at New Jerusalem, Ohio. In 1863 he was re-interred at the Urbana Cemetery in Urbana, Ohio.

Clark, Thomas D. *Simon Kenton: Kentucky Scout.* Ashland, Ky.: Jesse Stuart Foundation, 1998.

Crain, Ray. *Simon Kenton: The Great Frontiersman.* Urbana, Ohio: Main Graphics, 1992.

Eckert, Allan W. *The Frontiersmen: A Narrative.* Boston: Little, Brown, 1967.

Edmunds, R. David, "The Thin Red Line: Tecumseh, The Prophet and Shawnee Resistance." *Timeline Magazine* 4, no. 6 (December 1987–January 1988): 2–19.

Kenton, Edna. *Simon Kenton: His Life and Period.* Garden City, N.Y.: Country Life Press, 1930.

Klink, Carl F. *Tecumseh: Fact and Fiction in Early Records.* Englewood Cliffs, N.J.: Prentice Hall, 1961.

Simmons, David A. "Simon Kenton." *Timeline Magazine* 5, no. 2 (April–May 1988): 56–61.

Stephen M. Vest

KENTON, WILLIAM G. (b. August 28, 1941, Maysville, Ky.; d. November 5, 1981, Lexington, Ky.). Legislator William Gordon Kenton was the son of William Gordon Kenton Sr. and Martha Roden Kenton. It was reported that he founded the Mason Co. chapter of the Kentucky Young Democrats at age 14. An early mentor of his was Albert B. "Happy" Chandler, whom he met when Chandler visited Maysville High School in 1955, during Kenton's freshman year. After Chandler (1935–1939 and 1955–1959) was elected governor of Kentucky for his second term that same year, he invited Kenton to a ceremony in Frankfort. The school officials made it known that Kenton could attend but would be charged with an unexcused absence for the day, so Chandler moved the ceremony to Maysville. Kenton left his studies at the University of Virginia in Charlottesville, Va., to work in Chandler's campaign for a third term as governor in 1963; Chandler lost, and Kenton earned his undergraduate degree that year at the University of Kentucky at Lexington (UK). He graduated from the UK Law School in 1966 and began to practice with a firm in downtown Lexington.

As an attorney, he represented the cast of a production in Lexington of *Oh! Calcutta*, a Broadway musical with sexual themes. Kenton won acquittals for his clients, who had been charged with obscenity. He said at the time, "It's not a question of whether it's appealing. My responsibility is to represent clients and protect their rights."

He was elected to the Kentucky House of Representatives from the 53rd district in Fayette Co., serving 1970–1971, and from the 75th District in Fayette Co. for five consecutive terms (1972–1981), serving as House Speaker from 1976 until 1981. He was the youngest Speaker in the history of Kentucky and, at that time, the youngest in the nation. Kenton's grandfather W. T. Kenton was also a member of the Kentucky House of Representatives and served for several terms, and his great-grandfather Eldrige Kenton served in both the Kentucky House of Representatives and the Kentucky Senate in the 1880s.

As House Speaker, Kenton was the principal advocate of his era for greater legislative independence and legislative responsibility. His efforts led to the televising of legislative sessions statewide on Kentucky Educational Television. He believed this was the most important reform in the Kentucky House in his time. He helped to make meetings of legislative committees, where witnesses are heard and key decisions made, open to the press and the public.

During his years as House Speaker, Kenton also championed meaningful legislative oversight of the executive branch, a departure from the custom and practice then prevailing. A series of revelations concerning no-bid personal-service contracts led to the formation of the Program Review and Investigation Committee of the House of Representatives, a committee that continues to operate. And Kenton initiated and led to enactment an amendment to the Kentucky Constitution to permit the legislature to override a governor's veto.

Even given his ambition for legislative independence, Kenton worked well as House Speaker with three different administrations to produce large increases in funding for education at every level. He also sponsored and led to passage the Homestead Exemption, a tax discount for older homeowners that remains law. Kenton campaigned for reelection on his support for the repeal of the sales tax on food, prescription medicine, and utility bills and for the passing of House Bill 44, which remains a significant restraint on increases in local property taxes.

Kenton sponsored legislation to create the Kentucky Cancer Commission and was named its first chairman. He was the principal advocate for the establishment of the Kentucky Horse Park, the tourist attraction located on Ironworks Pk. in Fayette Co. After a brief tussle between Kenton and Governor John Y. Brown Jr. (1979–1983), which Kenton won, the Kentucky Horse Park board was made independent of the Kentucky Parks Department.

Without apology, Kenton espoused state government as an agent for social, educational, and economic opportunity for everyday Kentuckians. He thought politics an eminently respectable profession. A master parliamentarian, he is said to have run a "tight ship" as House Speaker. He was a prominent representative of Kentucky in national and regional legislative associations. With his broad body, his resonant, deep bass voice, his ingratiating manner, and his pristine reputation, Kenton became the appealing public face of the state legislature and dominated the Kentucky House of Representatives during three legislative sessions. He brought order to what had been an often-unruly legislative body. In so doing, he shattered several House Speaker's gavels and met all jokes about it with good humor. He became known affectionately as "Boom-Boom."

From an early age Kenton had wanted to become governor someday, and he made no effort to hide this ambition. He had begun to appear on lists of potential candidates in an upcoming governor's race when he was stricken in early November 1981 with a pulmonary embolism that quickly led to heart and kidney failure. He died at the University of Kentucky teaching hospital named for Chandler, his mentor. As he struggled for life and while details of his illness were front-page news for several days across Kentucky, he was reelected to the Kentucky House of Representatives by his constituents in Lexington's 75th legislative district. Kenton was 40 years old when he died, leaving his wife and two small children; he was buried at Maysville Cemetery. His widow, Carolyn Kenton, was elected to succeed him as state representative in 1982. In a memorial service in the chamber of the Kentucky House of Representatives when the legislature reconvened in 1982, Governor Brown said, "No one person in our lifetime has had such an impact on this body." A Kentucky Historical Highway Marker at Second and Limestone Sts. in Maysville, in front of the old Maysville High School, honors Kenton.

"Assembly Pauses to Honor Kenton," *Lexington Herald*, January 6, 1982, A5.

"The Lost Leader," *Lexington Herald*, November 6, 1981, A14.

Jim Dady

KENTON BAPTIST CHURCH. The Kenton Baptist Church was organized on November 7, 1937, at a meeting of the founders and local Baptist ministers at Kenton Station in southern Kenton Co. The original membership consisted of people from the nearby churches of **Calvary Baptist**, Hickory Grove Baptist, **Latonia Baptist**, Oak Island Baptist, and Baptist churches in Elsmere, Independence, and Morning View, as well as three candidates for baptism. The first pastor, Harold Lee Davis Jr., was called to serve the following week. By September 1939, the church's membership had grown to 57 and the congregation had applied for admittance to the North Bend Association of Baptists (now Northern Kentucky Baptist Association). Weekly services, held in the Kenton Station Rd. church building, began in 1945 after eight years of biweekly worship. In 1952 the church purchased 1.8 acres on Ky. Rt. 177 (Decoursey Pk.) and broke ground for the current facility on April 11, 1965; only the basement was built at that time. On November 14, 1965, after the final Sunday School at the old building, the members marched up Decoursey Pk. to the new church for the first worship service there. Construction on the sanctuary began in July 1970 and was completed in November of that year. Current services continue to be held in this building. The church has from the earliest days been a supporter of missions and various community projects.

"Kenton Baptist Church History," 1987, Kenton Baptist Church, Kenton Station, Ky.
Kenton Baptist Church Minutes, November 7, 1937, Kenton Baptist Church, Kenton Station Ky.

Andrea Watkins

KENTON BASE BALL ASSOCIATION. The Kenton Base Ball Association was a professional baseball team organized in 1883 and based in Covington. The formation of this team, nicknamed the Kentons, signaled a return of professional baseball to Northern Kentucky after a six-year absence. Though unaffiliated with any league, the Kentons were members of the American Alliance, which was a loose collection of teams linked to the American Association, an early rival of the National League that included the Cincinnati Reds among its members. The American Alliance sought to protect owners and suppress player movement by prohibiting member teams from signing players who broke contracts with other Alliance clubs. The Kentons were owned by a group of Covington civic and business leaders, most notably hatter A. L. Brown, building contractor Charles McDonald, and real estate developer and long-time Covington city assessor John Whitney.

The Kentons, sporting white uniforms with maroon caps and red stockings, played at the Kenton Park in Covington. Located at Washington and 17th Sts., near the **Kentucky Central Railroad** tracks, Kenton Park had a covered wooden grandstand with a seating capacity of approximately 3,500. Some adventurous fans avoided the 25-cent admission price by climbing atop freight cars to view the games.

Compared to the Star Base Ball Club of Covington and the Ludlow Base Ball Club that had operated a decade earlier (see **Baseball, Early Professional**), the Kentons were probably a notch or two lower in the professional baseball pecking order. The Kentons, like the Stars and the Ludlows, played professional and amateur teams throughout the Midwest; however, the Kentons played far fewer games against major league teams. While the Stars and the Ludlows sometimes defeated their more established opponents, the Kentons lost all three games they played against major league teams—two of these contests were with the Cincinnati Reds, and one was with the National League Detroit Wolverines. The Kentons' lineup featured several former and future major leaguers, including locals Ed Kennedy of Bellevue, Reddy Mack of Newport, and William "Mox" McQuery and John Shoupe from Covington (see **Baseball**).

Moses Fleetwood Walker, a catcher for the Toledo Blue Stockings, was probably the most famous baseball player to play at Kenton Park. Walker is widely considered the last African American to play major league baseball before Jackie Robinson. The Covington *Daily Commonwealth* urged fans to attend the Kentons-Toledo game to see the "great colored catcher."

Changes to the Cincinnati baseball market since the mid-1870s made profitability elusive for the Kentons. Cincinnati had no professional baseball team when the two earlier teams, the Covington Stars and the Ludlows, entered the professional baseball arena in 1875. The Kenton Base Ball Association, however, found itself competing with a thriving Cincinnati Reds club, the defending 1882 American Association champions. For about the same ticket price, the nearby Cincinnati Reds provided fans better-quality baseball entertainment than the Kentons could. Like most early professional baseball teams, the Kentons were underfinanced. Though successful on the field—the team won over 60 percent of its games—the Kentons sank into debt. Even the scheduling of several popular Sunday home games could not put the team in the black. Faced with liens against its assets, the Kentons baseball team folded during the 1884 season.

"The City," *DC,* March 27, 1883, 2; April 21, 1883, 2.
"Covington," *Cincinnati Commercial Gazette,* October 22, 1883, 7.
Hopkins, G. M. *City Atlas of Covington, Kentucky.* Philadelphia: G. M. Hopkins, 1877.
"Incorporation Notice, Kenton Base Ball Association, of Covington, Ky.," *DC,* March 30, 1883, 3.
"The Kenton Base Ball Club," *DC,* January 22, 1883, 2.
"Local News," *DC,* April 10, 1884, 4.

Greg Perkins

KENTON CO. Situated along the Ohio River, Kenton Co. is bordered by Boone Co. on the west, Campbell Co. on the east, and Grant and Pendleton counties on the south. It encompasses 162 square miles. Bridges connect the county to Cincinnati across the Ohio River and to Newport and Campbell Co. across the Licking River. The Kentucky legislature created Kenton Co. in 1840 out of Campbell Co., with the Licking River, the Ohio River, and Dry Creek as the new county's natural boundaries. The town of Independence, at Kenton Co.'s geographic center, was established as a rural county seat. In the 1850s a second courthouse was established in rapidly growing Covington, the site of most of the new county's court proceedings. The population of Kenton Co. was 7,816 in 1840, 17,038 in 1850, more than 129,000 in 1970, 137,000 in 1980, and 142,000 in 1990. After the Civil War, African Americans moved from the South to the North in steady numbers. Before widespread integration began in the United States during the 1960s, many African Americans had settled north of the Ohio River. Nevertheless, **Eastside Covington** and Elsmere had and continue to have substantial black populations.

Many notable people have been associated with Kenton Co. **Thomas Sandford** (1762–1808) represented Northern Kentucky in 1799 at the second Kentucky Constitutional Convention, in the Kentucky legislature, and in the U.S. Congress from 1803 to 1807. Born in New York City, **Richard Southgate** (1774–1857) was the patriarch of a prominent Northern Kentucky family; he was also a lawyer and a landholder in both Kenton and Campbell counties. **Thomas D. Carneal** (1786–1860), a cofounder of the city of Covington and a land developer in Kenton Co., acquired 968 acres and built Elmwood Hall, still standing in present-day Ludlow. **John W. Stevenson** (1812–1886), a Virginia native and a Covington attorney, became a Kentucky governor (1867–1871) and a U.S. senator. **John G. Carlisle** (1835–1910), a Democrat who had displayed Southern sympathies, became the Speaker of the U.S. House of Representatives, a U.S. Senator, and the U.S. Secretary of the Treasury. Covington attorney **William Goebel** (1856–1900) emerged during the late 1880s as the leader of the Progressive wing of the Democratic Party. After a contentious election for Kentucky governor, Goebel was declared elected in January 1900, was shot, was sworn into office, and died soon thereafter, the only sitting governor in the United States ever to be assassinated. Dr. **Louise Southgate** (1857–1941) was an early female physician and activist. **Richard P. Ernst** (1858–1934), from a banking family in Kenton Co., helped to finance the establishment of the **YMCA** in Covington and later, from 1921 to 1927, was a Republican U.S. senator. Kenton Co. resident **Brent Spence** (1874–1967), from pioneer family stock in Campbell Co., was an influential New Deal congressman from 1931 to 1963; it was Spence who secured for Covington its public housing, its floodwalls, and funding for urban renewal; he is also credited with having Covington chosen as the site of an **Internal Revenue Service Center**.

Historic landmarks abound in Kenton Co. One of the foremost is the **Point**, at the juncture of the Licking and Ohio rivers, a site visited in 1751 by one of Kentucky's first explorers, **Christopher Gist**. **Mary Ingles** is also known to have passed by the Point during her legendary escape from Indians in 1756. On another occasion, in 1771, **Simon Kenton** (1755–1836) and two companions visited the Point. In 1779 the Kentucky militia departed from the Point to engage in war against the Indians living north of the Ohio River; and in 1780 some 1,000 men under **George Rogers Clark** gathered for another Indian campaign north of the Ohio River. A decade later, in 1793, Leonard Covington (1766–1813), for whom Kenton Co.'s largest city was named, drilled militia at the Point under U.S. general Mad Anthony Wayne; and later Kennedy's Ferry, operating from the Point in Covington, served Fort Washington, across the river in Ohio, during the **War of 1812**. In 1832 Simon Kenton, then residing at Urbana, Ohio, because of illness, cut short his return trip to the Point for a promised reunion of veteran militia.

Banklick Creek, which runs along the **3-L Highway** (Ky. Rt. 17), was also an important landmark and one of the parts of Campbell Co. used to form Kenton Co. **James Taylor** (1769–1848), who helped found Newport during the 1790s, when Kenton Co. was still part of Campbell Co., acquired a farm and operated a mill on Banklick Creek. His contemporary, **Revolutionary War** veteran William DeCoursey (1756–1841), for whom Decoursey Pk. (Ky. Rt. 16) in Kenton Co. is named, later also settled at the Licking River near Banklick Creek, where he obtained authorization to operate a ferry.

Of the roads in Kenton Co., a lane at the property of Robert Kyle, who lived near present-day

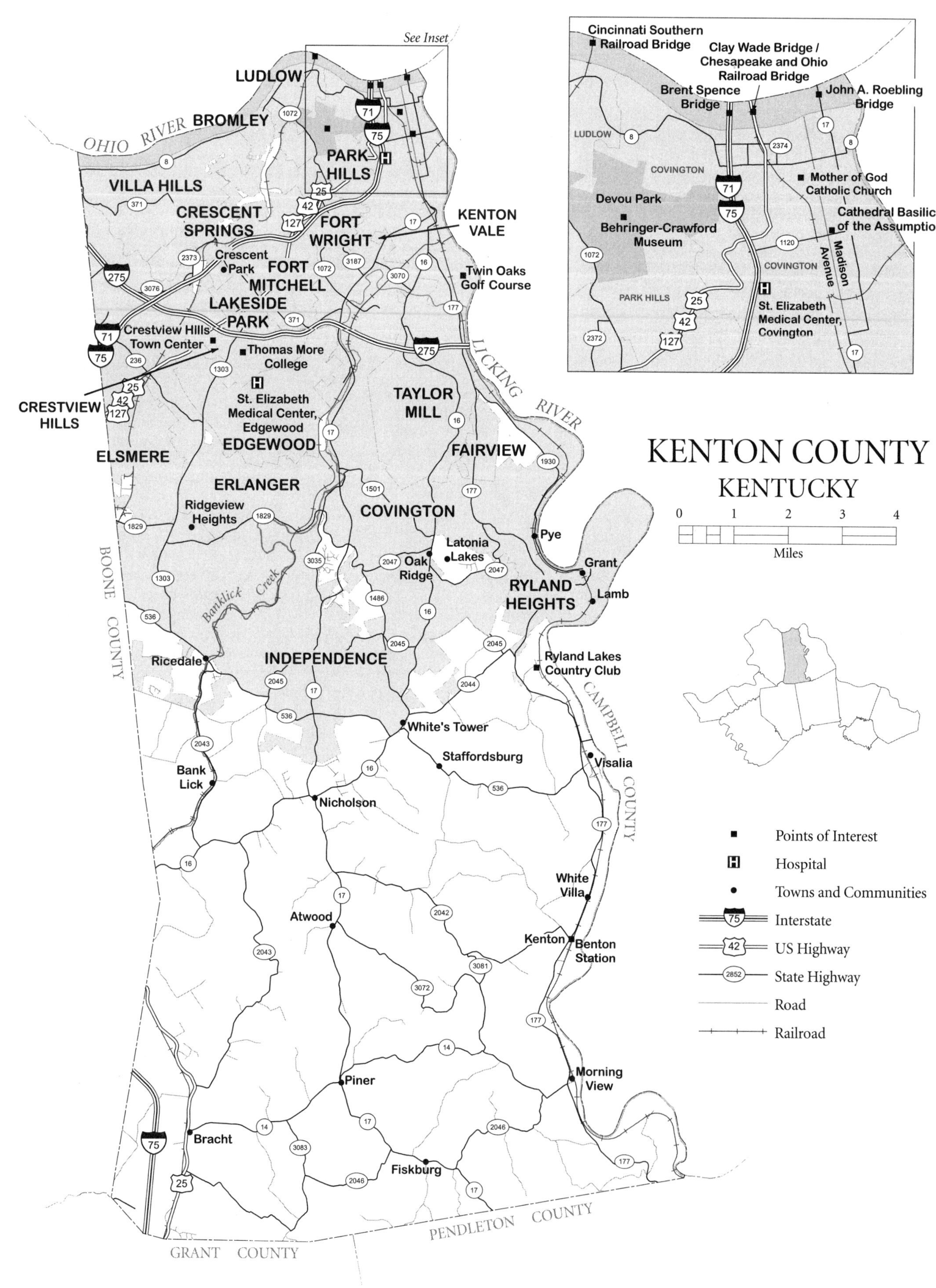

KENTON COUNTY
KENTUCKY
0 1 2 3 4
Miles
Points of Interest
Hospital
Towns and Communities
Interstate
US Highway
State Highway
Road
Railroad
See Inset
Cincinnati Southern Railroad Bridge
Clay Wade Bridge / Chesapeake and Ohio Railroad Bridge
Brent Spence Bridge
John A. Roebling Bridge
LUDLOW
COVINGTON
Devou Park
Behringer-Crawford Museum
Mother of God Catholic Church
Cathedral Basilica of the Assumption
Madison Avenue
PARK HILLS
St. Elizabeth Medical Center, Covington
OHIO RIVER
BROMLEY
VILLA HILLS
CRESCENT SPRINGS
FORT WRIGHT
KENTON VALE
Crescent Park
FORT MITCHELL
LAKESIDE PARK
Twin Oaks Golf Course
Crestview Hills Town Center
Thomas More College
CRESTVIEW HILLS
St. Elizabeth Medical Center, Edgewood
EDGEWOOD
TAYLOR MILL
LICKING RIVER
ELSMERE
FAIRVIEW
ERLANGER
Ridgeview Heights
COVINGTON
Pye
Latonia Lakes
Oak Ridge
Grant
RYLAND HEIGHTS
Lamb
Banklick Creek
BOONE COUNTY
Ricedale
INDEPENDENCE
Ryland Lakes Country Club
CAMPBELL COUNTY
White's Tower
Staffordsburg
Visalia
Bank Lick
Nicholson
White Villa
Atwood
Kenton
Benton Station
Morning View
Piner
Bracht
Fiskburg
GRANT COUNTY
PENDLETON COUNTY

Pike St. and Madison Ave. in Covington, was earlier a **buffalo trace**. In 1793 the Kentucky legislature ordered the marking of a road from Frankfort to Cincinnati. Later, Campbell Co. justices of the peace ordered a road from DeCoursey's Ferry to the Georgetown Rd. Abner Gaines established a stagecoach line between Covington and Georgetown and later built the **Gaines Tavern** (still standing) in present-day Walton. In 1839 the Kentucky legislature chartered the **Banklick Turnpike Company** in Kenton Co. to modernize and macadamize the surface, and then rechartered it in 1845, after a financial panic.

From the mid-1820s, the Banklick Rd. was surpassed in local volume by a road to Lexington that led through eastern Boone Co. In 1834 the Kentucky legislature chartered the **Covington and Lexington Turnpike** Company (bypassing the Banklick Rd.), and the final macadamizing of this turnpike to Lexington in the early 1850s accelerated Covington's development, as did the opening of the **Covington and Lexington Railroad** in 1854 and the **John A. Roebling Bridge** in 1867–1868. For many years, Northern Kentucky truck farmers favored sending their produce to Cincinnati markets. Similarly, in some years producers throughout Kentucky provided half the number of hogs slaughtered in Cincinnati. Businesses with ties to Cincinnati often located in Northern Kentucky as Covington grew and became a bedroom suburb of Cincinnati. Covington's population was 743 in 1830, more than 2,000 in 1840, 9,000 in 1850, and greater than 16,000 in 1860.

In 1862 Confederate soldiers advanced into Boone Co. toward the line of military fortifications constructed in Kenton Co. from Ludlow into Campbell Co. Besides discouraging the invaders, these forts and fortifications (see **Civil War Fortifications**) permanently marked the landscape in both counties as places in **Civil War** history. Union general U. S. Grant's parents resided in Covington, and although consensus favored the Union, pro-Southern sentiments in Covington and other parts of Northern Kentucky were also strong. Thereafter, Covington and most of Kenton Co. joined Kentucky in becoming bastions of strength for the Democratic Party, which had joined with emerging Progressive elements to dominate the county's politics. However, in 2006, for the first time, the number of Republicans registered to vote in Kenton Co. exceeded the number of Democrats.

Throughout the 19th century, Kenton Co. was a focal point for German and Irish settlement (see **German Americans**; **Irish Americans**). After the Civil War, the county African American population steadily grew, as freed black slaves left rural areas for cities such as Covington (see **African Americans**). The institutions that these ethnic groups established made the county a cosmopolitan center for its day. By 1850, ten years after its creation, Kenton Co. was the second-most-populous county in Kentucky, with 16,117 people, and Covington was the second-largest city in Kentucky, with a population of 9,408, trailing only Louisville. Kenton Co. was a major industrial center throughout the 19th and 20th centuries, known for brewing (see **Brewing Industry**; **Bavarian Brewing Company**), **brickyards**, bronze and brass products (see **Michaels Art Bronze Company**), **candy and ice cream** manufacturing, **dairies**, distilling (see **Distilleries**; **Walsh Distillery**; **New England Distillery**), glassmaking (see **Hemingray Glass Company**), **icehouses**, **iron and steel manufacturing** (see **Stewart Iron Works**), locomotives (see **Covington Locomotive and Manufacturing Works**; **Houston, Stanwood & Gamble Company**), lumber, machine tools, **meatpacking** (see **Goetta**), packaging equipment (see **R.A. Jones & Company Inc.**), paper bags (see **Duro Bag Manufacturing Company**), safes and locks, textiles and cordage, **tobacco** products, **toys**, trucks, wine production (see **Gibson Wine Company**; **Monte Casino**), and X-ray equipment (see **Kelley-Koett Company**).

In 1869 the **Louisville, Cincinnati, and Lexington Railroad** (LC&L) reached Covington. In 1883 the Latonia Agricultural Association established the **Latonia Racecourse** adjacent to the LC&L, whose passenger trains conveyed patrons to the famous racetrack. Electric streetcar service was extended to the racetrack in 1893. Racing top thoroughbreds and offering substantial purses, the Latonia Racecourse achieved a status similar to that of Keeneland Race Course in Lexington and Churchill Downs in Louisville. It closed in 1939. In 1877 passenger and freight service began in Kenton Co. on the **Cincinnati Southern Railroad**'s new tracks out of Ludlow. Later, the railroad corporation leasing the tracks established express service between Richwood Station and Cincinnati. With offers of free or discounted commuter service, the railroad enticed homebuyers to populate new subdivision developments in Erlanger and Crescent Springs. West from Covington, along the Ohio River, the Dry Creek Turnpike connected to the **Anderson Ferry** in Boone Co.

In 1912 Kentucky established a state highway commission. At that time, Kenton Co. purchased toll roads and eliminated tollbooths in the county. As a part of the new interstate **Dixie Highway** (U.S. 25), the Covington and Lexington Turnpike in Kenton Co. was widened to 18 feet and modernized to two lanes of concrete. In 1921 contractors completed paving from Covington into Florence. Thereafter gas stations, a **gourmet strip** of restaurants, and other businesses thrived along the new Dixie Highway. Today, traveling on the Dixie Highway south from Covington in Kenton Co., one passes through Park Hills, Fort Wright, Fort Mitchell, Lakeside Park, Crestview Hills, Edgewood, Erlanger, and Elsmere, before entering Boone Co. The old Dry Creek Baptist Church in Kenton Co. still stands as a residence at the juncture of Dixie Highway and Buttermilk Pk. in Fort Mitchell, and the old Five Mile House (see **Barleycorn's Five Mile House**) opposite Turkeyfoot Rd. in Lakeside Park has become a permanent restaurant. I-75, which runs through Kenton Co., was opened in 1962–1963, and in the 1970s the entire I-275 Circle Freeway was completed through Kenton Co. These **expressways** led to a rapid suburbanization. Villa Hills, a postwar suburb incorporated in 1962, was typical of the population changes occurring in Kenton Co. as citizens fled Covington for the suburbs. Numbering a only few hundred residents when first incorporated, Villa Hills by 1990 had a population of 7,739. Likewise, **Delta Air Lines**, with its hub at the **Cincinnati/Northern Kentucky International Airport** in Boone Co., became a major employer drawing many new suburban residents when it built a $46 million terminal in 1987.

In Kenton Co., as in all of the counties of Northern Kentucky historically, tobacco has been an important economic component. In 1845, 22 Covington tobacco businesses manufactured $300,000–$400,000 in products annually. And by 1880 Covington's tobacco companies were producing 2.5 million pounds of plug and fine chewing tobacco. The development of **white burley tobacco** after 1860 led to an increase in the tobacco trade through Cincinnati and Northern Kentucky as more farmers in Northern Kentucky and the Central Bluegrass region of Kentucky began growing this variety. County extension services throughout Kentucky taught boys farming and related skills. Then in 1926, Marie Binder Rich, one of three graduates in 1916 of the Independence High School, helped start an educational extension service for girls by funding home economics training at Kenton Co.'s Piner School.

Truck farming has also been important in Kenton Co. Still operating south of Covington near Erlanger in Kenton Co. is the **Tewes poultry** farm, visible from I-75. The Kruempelmann truck farm on the Dixie Highway in Fort Mitchell operated from about 1865 until 1995. Besides delivering produce to the Pearl St. Produce Market in Cincinnati, Henry Kruempelmann, the farm's owner, supplied the large Castellini produce operation in Cincinnati with fresh farm goods.

In 1929 **L. B. Wilson**, who owned the Liberty Bank and several downtown theaters in Covington, started **WCKY** radio station, just as Covington's population was peaking. But after **World War II**, Covington experienced a population decline. The town's population was almost 30,000 in 1880, almost 43,000 in 1900, 65,000 in 1930, 60,000 in 1960, and 52,500 in 1970. At the time, a Northern Kentucky industrial park, drawing industry away from the cities to the suburbs, had opened in Boone Co. In 1976 the **Florence Mall** in Boone Co. opened with Sears and JCPenney as tenants, both stores having once been successful enterprises in downtown Covington (see **Covington, Downtown**). Locally owned Covington stores, including **Eilerman & Sons, Men's Clothiers** and **John R. Coppin**, went out of business. The new **Northern Kentucky Convention Center** opened in downtown Covington in 1998, and a year later, a new federal courthouse opened nearby on W. Fifth St. The county, after opening a new high-rise building in Covington that houses its offices and the jail, in 1999 also opened its new courthouse in Covington on Madison Ave., near RiverCenter.

Established in 1921 by the Benedictine Sisters of Covington, Villa Madonna College relocated to

Crestview Hills in 1968, and in a dedication ceremony featuring a visit and speech by President Lyndon B. Johnson (1963–1969) became **Thomas More College**. Covington is home to a number of cultural institutions, including the **Baker-Hunt Foundation**, the **Behringer-Crawford Museum**, and the **Carnegie Visual and Performing Arts Center.**

Of the several catastrophes that have occurred in Kenton Co., the Ohio River **flood of 1937**, which inflicted great damage on all the county's river communities, remains the most memorable.

Currently, major employers include **Fidelity Investments** (Covington), the Internal Revenue Service Center (Covington), and the **St. Elizabeth Medical Center** (Edgewood and Covington). In 2002 shipments from Kenton Co.'s manufacturers totaled $1.2 billion, and the county's wholesale trade was nearly $2 billion. In 2000 Kenton Co.'s population, at 151,464, was the third-highest among Kentucky counties.

Crowley, Patrick. "Study: Airport Driving Growth," *KE*, B1–B2.

Gastright, Joseph F. *Gentlemen Farmers to City Folks: A Study of Wallace Woods, Covington, Kentucky.* Cincinnati: Cincinnati Historical Society, 1980.

"Louisville, Cincinnati, and Lexington Railway Time Card," *DC*, September 15, 1879, 3.

Reis, Jim. "Down with the Toll Gates!" *KP*, July 13, 1998, 4K.

——. "Drought of '53–54 Showed Need for New Lakes in Region," *KP*, September 29, 1997, 4K.

——. "Independence' Birth No Accident," *KP*, February 24, 1992, 4K.

——. "Independence Firemen Note 50 years," *KP*, September 14, 1987, 4K.

——. "Old Roads Still Major Thoroughfares," *KP*, July 7, 1986, 4K.

——. "Paving Dixie Highway Quite a Feat Back in 1916," *KP*, January 6, 1997, 4K.

Schroeder, Cindy. "1998 Saw Boom in Construction for Independence," *KE*, January 7, 1999, B3.

Smith, Allen Webb. *Beginning at "the Point," a Documented History of Northern Kentucky and Environs, the Town of Covington in Particular, 1751–1834.* Park Hills, Ky., Self-published, 1977.

Tenkotte, Paul A. "Rival Cities to Suburbs: Covington and Newport, Kentucky, 1790–1890," PhD diss., Univ. of Cincinnati, 1989.

John Boh

KENTON CO. PUBLIC LIBRARY. The Kenton Co. Public Library was created in 1967, when county voters signed petitions establishing the county library district, to be funded by a tax on property owners. The Covington Public Library, the Erlanger-Elsmere Library, and the Kenton Co. Bookmobile were merged to create the county library system.

The Covington Public Library, opened in 1901, provided services free to city residents, since the library was funded with city funds. Located in a Carnegie building at Robbins and Scott Sts. in Covington beginning in 1902, the library periodically made arrangements to provide services to county residents outside the city, but the lack of funding for basic services prevented establishing permanent arrangements for serving county residents.

The Erlanger-Elsmere Library, established by the Erlanger Woman's Club in 1911, provided services for suburban residents. The members of the Erlanger Woman's Club served as a volunteer staff, raised funds for expenses, and received materials for the collection. Limited funding was received from the cities of Erlanger and Elsmere. The library occupied several buildings in Erlanger and Elsmere until 1958, when a house was purchased on Bartlett Ave. in Erlanger. From 1928 until 1942, the Erlanger-Elsmere Library was operated by the Covington Public Library. Lack of funding from the cities of Erlanger and Elsmere resulted in a return of management to the Erlanger Woman's Club until the county library system was established.

In 1953 the Kenton Co. Fiscal Court obtained funding for a bookmobile to serve rural residents of the county. The bookmobile contained more than 3,000 books and made stops throughout the county at schools, firehouses, and other community locations. By 1964 more than 150,000 books had been circulated by the bookmobile. That same year, a small library was established in the Crescent Springs Presbyterian Church.

For each of these libraries and the bookmobile, inadequate funding stood in the way of providing quality services. Consultants reported that the Covington Public Library was operating far below the standards set by the American Library Association, while the Erlanger-Elsmere Library and the bookmobile had no professional staff and limited resources for the purchase of new materials. In April 1967, a committee of Kenton Co. residents began a campaign to form a countywide library district with sufficient reliable funding. A county system would be eligible for state and federal aid. Thousands of free books, records, and films from the Kentucky Department of Libraries would be available to a county system. The new public library system would also allow for the construction of a new $1.1 million main library, expansion of the Erlanger-Elsmere Library, and the addition of another bookmobile. The library would be free to everyone in Kenton Co.

Clyde Middleton and Laurence Grause were cochairmen of a committee that asked for 1,000 volunteers to obtain signatures from county residents for the petition drive, scheduled during the week of April 23–30, 1967. Businesses placed messages about the campaign on their outdoor signs, and volunteers went from door to door asking for signatures. The petition needed 14,865 signatures, or 51 percent of the number of voters casting ballots in the previous general election. The campaign was successful, obtaining more than 16,000 signatures, so the Kenton Co. Fiscal Court accepted the petition and issued an order that the library tax appear on the county's October tax bills.

By October 1967, Covington city commissioners had approved the agreement to transfer the Covington Library operation to the new Kenton Co. Library District. Kenton Co. judge James Dressman appointed a new library board, made up of Mrs. Harry Carl, Mrs. Ruth Eubank, Joseph Gausepohl, Laurence Grause, and George Weidner. By January 1968, Mary Ann Mongan had been appointed the head librarian and the Kenton Co. Public Library had assumed control of the Covington Public Library, the Erlanger-Elsmere Library, and the Kenton Co. Bookmobile. A new $21,000 bookmobile was also purchased and transferred to the country's library system by the state.

One of the first duties of the new board was to select a site for a new library to replace the outdated Carnegie library building in Covington. The City of Covington and the library board agreed on a site in town at the corner of Fifth and Scott Sts. The site was declared an urban renewal project and the city subsequently condemned the property to enable acquisition. Robert Ehmet Hayes was chosen as the architect for the new library building. In December 1971 the official groundbreaking ceremony took place, and construction of a new Kenton Co. library was under way. On Monday, January 21, 1974, at 502 Scott St., it opened its doors. The new $1.4 million library won the prestigious Honors Award of the Kentucky Society of Architects for its designer, Robert Ehmet Hayes and Associates.

The library board now sought a site for a new Erlanger branch library to replace the two-story converted house on Bartlett Ave. In 1976 a site at the corner of **Dixie Highway** (U.S. 25) and Montgomery St. was chosen because it had the greatest volume of traffic and offered good visibility. The new Erlanger branch library, a $1 million, 15,800-square-foot building at 3130 Dixie Highway, with five times the capacity of the former branch, was completed and opened to the public in September 1978.

Joining the Kenton Co. Library staff in 1974 was Covington native Michael Averdick, who served on the library's staff for the next 23 years. As associate director, he was responsible for beginning the local history and genealogy collection that preserved many Northern Kentucky records and was later acclaimed as the region's most outstanding collection.

With the expansion of the library system, operating moneys became an issue during the late 1970s and 1980s because library funding was limited by the Kentucky legislature and double-digit inflation presented additional challenges. Cutbacks in library services were required: one bookmobile was eliminated, library hours were reduced, and spending for books and materials was decreased. Additional financial and material support was received, however, from the Friends of the Kenton Co. Public Library, an organization that was formed in 1979 under the leadership of Kathy Baker and Ruth Eubank, who had worked on the petition drive that created the library. The organization collected donated books and held book sales to support library programs.

Circulation of materials by the library system increased substantially during the 1970s, going from 290,150 in 1969–1970 to 667,412 in 1979–1980. As the suburban population grew and the population in Covington decreased, usage shifted toward the Erlanger branch library. Also, as population in the county moved southward, the bookmobile schedule was adjusted to allow more stops in southern Kenton Co. In the mid-1980s, the county library board asked library staff to complete a feasibility study for constructing a branch library in the southern half of the county. However, since funding was not available to construct a new library branch building at that time, the idea was put on hold.

The library staff also focused on services for persons who were unable to visit the library because of disabilities. Free delivery of library materials was provided for homebound individuals. In 1980 the Northern Kentucky branch of the Kentucky Talking Book Library was established at the main library in Covington to serve an eight-county Northern Kentucky region, offering books recorded on audiocassettes for visually impaired users and those who could not physically hold a book.

Technology became a more important part of the county library's service during the late 1980s. By 1990 the library was ready for automation of all circulation and cataloging records. The library system was closed from August 6 through August 18, 1990, so that scannable barcodes could be added to library items. The process of circulating materials and checking the library's catalog of materials was revolutionized. New formats of materials were also added to the library's collections as technology advanced. Videos were first made part of the library's collection in 1986. As compact discs and CD-ROMs became available, they were also offered to the public.

Once automation of the library's records was completed, attention focused on services for the growing central and southern portions of Kenton Co. In November 1992, the board purchased property at 8477 Taylor Mill Rd. in Independence for a branch, and construction of this long-awaited facility began in 1994. With the opening of the branch library at Independence, the bookmobile, which had served so many rural residents, was discontinued.

At the grand opening of the Independence branch of the Kenton Co. Library, on May 21, 1995, more than 600 residents came to celebrate the new facility. The state librarian of Kentucky, Jim Nelson, speaking at the opening ceremony, remarked that he had never seen such an outpouring of community support at a library opening. During the first full month of operation, the library's branch in Independence checked out more than 18,000 items.

In the mid-1990s, the library board of trustees instituted its first long-range planning process for the library. Directed by board vice-president Richard Gibeau, the process resulted in an ambitious program of improvements adopted by the board in 1997. The improvements focused on areas such as technology and the expansion of facilities, the establishment of a public-relations program, the addition of a human resources department, and the creation of a foundation to provide additional financial support. The plan ushered in a new wave of technology, which played a major role in the growth of library services. Using a grant from the Gates Foundation, the library purchased dozens of computers, and Internet access was offered for the first time. Internet access brought many new users to the library, along with challenges in managing the new resource and providing the funding necessary for its maintenance.

As these improvements were under way, Mary Ann Mongan retired as director of the county library system in 1999, after 41 years of service. In recognition of her devoted service, the board of trustees named the main library in Covington in her honor. The library's associate director, Wayne Onkst, was named her successor as library director.

The building program initiated by the library board during the late 1990s proceeded with the renovation of the main library in Covington in 1998. Replacement of the now outdated Erlanger branch, which had become the busiest public library location in Kentucky, was completed in 2002, with the opening of the branch library building at 401 Kenton Lands Rd. in Erlanger. Construction of a new $8.9 million branch library in Independence, named in honor of William E. Durr, was begun in August 2006 and opened in January 2007. Plans to expand the Mary Ann Mongan Library in Covington are under way.

"Durr Library 'For the People'—New $8 Million Branch Opens," *KP*, January 29, 2007, A1.

"Goodby, Andrew Carnegie," *KP*, August 5, 1969, 6K.

"Here's How New Kenton County Library Will Look," *KP*, July 15, 1970, 13K.

"Library's Hawking Out Dixie Branch Site," *KP*, July 10, 1975, 2K.

Local history file on the Kenton Co. Public Library, Kenton Co. Public Library, Covington, Ky.

Minutes of the Board of Trustees of the Kenton Co. Public Library, Kenton Co. Public Library, Covington, Ky.

Wayne Onkst

KENTON CO. SCHOOL DISTRICT. One year after its formation in 1840, Kenton Co. appointed its first common school commissioners, Robert M. Carlisle, John B. Casey, and Foster Fleming. The first public school outside of the city of Covington was likely at Sanfordtown; it was opened in 1843 with an enrollment of 37 students. In December of that year, the entire county outside of Covington was divided into 23 common school districts; by 1844 four schools enrolled 209 pupils. By 1875 the county had 54 school districts. Although many of the schools were one-room schools, others were graded schools. Most buildings were frame; only a few were brick. By 1889 the last log school was sold. School terms averaged only a few months.

By act of the Kentucky General Assembly in 1884, the state provided for elected county superintendents of schools. In Kenton Co., H. P. Stephens was the first person elected to this post. His written assessment of the county schools in 1887 was honest but depressing, citing poor instructor salaries, ill-prepared teachers, rickety schools, and little parental support, especially among the upper class, who preferred to send their children to private academies. It took Kentucky's "Education Legislature" of 1908 to enact reforms that helped to reverse the negative trends in public education. In that year, the General Assembly created county boards of education, giving them actual authority to operate schools. The legislature also demanded that each county establish a high school by the year 1910. Soon after, the Kenton Co. Board of Education established four high schools: **Crescent Springs High School**, **Independence High School**, **Piner High School**, and Winston Hill High School (1916–1921). During the 1920s, the district pursued consolidation of many of its smaller schools.

By 1934–1935, the county, with the assistance of the state department of education, undertook a study to improve the quantity and quality of the programs it offered. As a result, the last two remaining one-room schools were closed, and two new consolidated high schools were opened: Piner and Independence High Schools were replaced by the new **Simon Kenton High School** (1937), and Crescent Springs High School was replaced by the new **Dixie Heights High School**. Also in 1935, the county board set school terms for both elementary and high schools at nine months. This was the first major change in term length since the early 20th century, when the county had enacted seven months of instruction for elementary schools and nine months for high schools.

After **World War II**, the dramatic rise in births that came to be known as the baby boom prompted the county board of education to undertake a study in 1945 to determine the system's future needs. New schools were built, including Bromley Elementary (1950), Kenton Elementary in Independence (1951), and Taylor Mill Elementary (1954). By 1954 the county's school enrollment had doubled in 10 years and led to the decision to build James A. Caywood Elementary (1956) in Edgewood and to construct additions to the two high schools. In fall 1988 the district reorganized its schools from the K–6, 7–8, 9–12 plan to an updated K–5, 6–8, 9–12 model. The 1960s witnessed the opening of additional schools to accommodate the baby boom: Ryland Elementary School (1960), Twenhofel Middle School (1961), Turkey Foot Middle School (1962), White's Tower Elementary School (1964), and Beechgrove Elementary School (1968). In the 1970s through the 1990s, the following schools were opened: R. C. Hinsdale Elementary School (1972), **Scott High School** (1978), Visalia Elementary School (1982), Woodland Middle School (1988), Fort Wright Elementary School (1992, replacing Park Hills Elementary School, which had opened in 1929), River Ridge Elementary School (1992), and Summit View Elementary and Middle Schools (1998). Two new high-performance school buildings opened in 2005 and 2006, James A. Caywood Elementary and Twenhofel Middle School. A new Turkey Foot Middle School, also a high-performance school, is under construction and will open in the fall of 2010.

Today, Kenton Co. Schools provide services to more than 13,200 students in preschool through 12th grade. Students engage in learning activities that focus on high academic standards, connect to real-world experiences, and support the learning community within each school. One of the primary goals is that each graduate will demonstrate the skills and competencies needed to compete successfully in the global market. To that end, a Career Transitions program was implemented, thereby providing a preschool-through-12th-grade initiative to promote discussion between schools and families about career pathways and the importance of thorough coursework for students. The high schools are organized into transitional freshman academies and smaller learning communities, with career-focused schools of study for the sophomore through senior years.

Technology literacy is integrated into all aspects of curriculum in the Kenton Co. School District. Students use computers as tools for learning and communicating in all classrooms, the library, and computer labs; wireless laptops are available on a regular basis. A technology coordinator and technology resource teachers in each building provide daily assistance to teachers and staff in integrating technology literacy into instruction. In addition, a team of district technology specialists provide technical and instructional support to all schools.

The district has won many awards, including prestigious recognition as a "What Parents Want" selection by SchoolMatch, an independent, nationwide service that helps families find schools that match the needs of their children. This award ranks the system as one of the best school districts in the United States. In 2005 Kenton Co. also received District Accreditation by the Southern Association of Colleges and the Council on Accreditation and School Improvement.

Caywood, J. A. "History and Development of Kenton County Schools," 1958, Kenton Co. Board of Education, Fort Wright, Ky.

The Kenton Co. School District. www.kenton.kyschools.us (accessed December 4, 2006).

Teresa Wilkins

KENTON HILLS. The Kenton Co. community of Kenton Hills, surrounded by the city of Covington and next to **Devou Park**, was incorporated as a sixth-class city in November 1962. The City of Covington had already in January 1958 begun a plan to absorb the community. After a long legal process, Kenton Hills finally was annexed in September 1965, adding 225 new residents and 71 acres of land to Covington. The action had been opposed by two groups, the Kenton Hills Civic Association, led by John Hunnicutt, president of the **Stewart Iron Works**, and homeowners, represented by well-known Covington attorney Andrew W. Clark.

Kenton Hills, perched high above I-75, with a commanding view to the north and east of the Ohio River Valley, is purely residential. Of the four original estates that made up Kenton Hills, one was owned by famed 19th-century actor **Edwin Forrest**. A legend connected with the area is that Kenton Co.'s namesake, **Simon Kenton**, in 1791 pursued the famous Indian chief Wapinotok, killed him, and buried him somewhere in modern-day Kenton Hills. Indian mounds, in fact, were found in the vicinity and excavated. The first homes in Kenton Hills were developed in the mid-1920s by J. J. Weaver; the area was promoted as a haven of clean-air living, located within easy walking distance of Devou Park, with access to all utilities available and with fire protection and water supplied by the City of Covington. Building-lot prices were as low as $1,800, and a model home opened in September 1927. A second wave of construction took place in 1938 as the fears of the **Great Depression** waned. Although part of Covington today, Kenton Hills does not participate in the **Covington Independent Schools**; students from Kenton Hills attend the Kenton Co. Public Schools. Many of Northern Kentucky's business and community leaders, such as longtime ***Kentucky Post*** editor **Vance Trimble** and local athlete and University of Cincinnati coach **Bill Schwarberg**, have had homes in Kenton Hills. A sign of the area's continued appeal is that the Bluff Apartments complex, built in Kenton Hills during the late 1960s, is being renovated for conversion into condominiums.

"'Ideal Home' in Kenton Hills," *KP*, September 4, 1927, 9.

"Indian Chief Killed by Simon Kenton," *KP*, May 22, 1927, 6.

Kenton Circuit Court Case No. 11537, November 7, 1962.

"Kenton Hills Citizens Sue to Prevent Annexation," *KP*, April 14, 1960, 1.

"Kenton Hills Civic Group Has Election," *KP*, January 29, 1941, 1.

KENTON HILLS PORCELAINS INC. Harold Bopp, who started this business, had previously been associated with the Rookwood Pottery of Cincinnati for about 10 years. There he served as director of the color and chemistry departments and later as superintendent of all the company's facilities. As a result of the 1929 stock market crash and the ensuing **Great Depression**, Rookwood Pottery's sales declined so much that the business was no longer profitable. In early 1939 Bopp, discouraged, resigned his position with the Rookwood firm and endeavored to start his own pottery operation. He purchased a one-acre site at 212 **Dixie Highway** (U.S. 25) in Erlanger, Ky., where he set up his factory and showroom. The new company was named the Harold Bopp Manufacturing Company, and production officially began on January 22, 1940. Bopp soon realized that he needed management assistance, so he hired two other Rookwood employees, Arthur Conant and William E. Hentschel.

From the very beginning, the new company was beset with perplexing problems. Bopp lacked the necessary funds to equip and operate the pottery properly, and bank loans were nearly impossible to obtain at the time. Hentschel, his assistant, suggested that Bopp hire David Seyler, whom they had known at Rookwood Pottery and the Cincinnati Art Academy. That proved to be a wise decision, since Seyler had superior business savvy and also had access to the needed capital, through his father, George Seyler. The father agreed to inject into the business an amount of cash equal to Bopp's investment. Thus, on September 21, 1940, Harold Bopp, William Hentschel, David Seyler, George Seyler, and Chester Sterrett signed a partnership agreement that called for the formation of a corporation to be called Kenton Hills Porcelains Inc.

The corporation's first official act was to purchase from a German firm a state-of-the-art gas-fired kiln, which was far superior to the coal-fired one used by Rookwood Pottery. The partners hired a staff of the most talented designers and craftsmen available, capable of producing superior-quality pottery. With its blue-ribbon crew, Kenton Hills Porcelains Inc. soon began production of an impressive line of products. David Seyler traveled the country with samples of the company's wares to establish sales outlets. He was able to sign up numerous high-profile retailers, including Nieman-Marcus in Dallas, Tex.; Marshall Field in Chicago; Gump in San Francisco; and Lord and Taylor and Tiffany in New York City.

During the company's first year of operation, it produced an array of beautiful, high-quality pottery, which sold exceptionally well. The future of Kenton Hills Porcelains Inc. appeared bright; however, **World War II** soon intervened, causing a significant decline in U.S. and European pottery sales. The company became unprofitable, so production was halted and the factory was leased to the government for storage of defense materials. Seyler had always intended to resume operations at the war's end; however, it proved impossible to do so because the kiln was found to be contaminated and unfit for firing pottery. Therefore, the owners sold all the company assets, including the real estate, the inventory, the equipment, and the machinery. The partners moved on to other pursuits.

Bopp and his second wife, Ann, moved to Corning, N.Y., where they took positions with the Corning Glass Company. In their new company, the husband-and-wife team designed the famous blue cornflower logo, which has become so familiar to owners of Corning Ware.

After serving in the U.S. Navy during the war, David Seyler took a position as art director and sculptor at the Belvedere Pottery in Lake Geneva, Wis., but soon became disenchanted with that company and resigned. He worked for a short time as a commercial artist in Chicago and then joined the staff of the University of Nebraska at Lincoln, as an instructor in ceramics, a position he held for the next 30 years. In 1961 he received the ultimate award, when he was named a fellow at the International Institute of Arts and Letters.

Hentschel taught at the Cincinnati Art Academy until 1944, when he retired and began doing oil paintings in his home. His health gradually declined, and he died in 1962.

For a short time, three very gifted artists and craftsmen operated their dream company in Kenton Co.; however, bad timing and world events beyond their control caused their dream to die prematurely. During roughly three years of operation, the corporation produced an estimated 10,000 to 15,000 ceramic works of art. Only about 500 have been identified positively, leaving probably thousands of others undetected in homes around the world.

"Finest Porcelain Pottery in the World Is Aim of Northern Kentucky's New Unique Industry," *KP*, November 8, 1940, 1.

Nicholson, Nick, and Marilyn Nicholson. *Kenton Hills Porcelains, Inc.* Loveland, Ohio: D. A. Nicholson, 1998.

Jack Wessling

KENTONTOWN. Originally chartered in 1795 as Newtown and laid out by John Kenton, brother of the legendary early Kentucky explorer **Simon Kenton**, this Robertson Co. crossroads hamlet at the intersection of modern U.S. 62 and Ky. Rt. 617 is six miles southwest of Mount Olivet. It was later renamed Kentontown in honor of Simon Kenton. A post office existed there as early as 1830; it closed in 1918. The town is one mile north of the Licking River, which at that point is the modern boundary between Robertson and Harrison counties. Kentontown was the home of **Duncan Harding**, the state representative from Harrison Co. who proposed the state legislation establishing Robertson Co. Kentontown, before the creation of Robertson Co. in 1867, was in Harrison Co., awkwardly set north of the Licking River. Harding, who essentially owned the town and the surrounding land, hoped to make Kentontown the seat of his new county, but that honor fell to the more centrally located Mount Olivet. Kentontown was the site of Harding's general store and a Christian Church. The creation of the new county of Robertson made it much easier for Kentontown residents to be represented politically. They could also transact county business in the closer town of Mount Olivet, instead of traveling farther to Cynthiana in Harrison Co., assuming river conditions allowed them to cross the Licking. Today Kentontown remains much as it always has been, a small rural Kentucky hamlet.

Gifford, Anjanette. "The Formation of Robertson County." *NKH* 9, no. 1 (Spring–Summer 2001): 65–74.
Reis, Jim. "A County of Rolling Hills, Winding Roads," *KP*, November 17, 1986, 4K.
Rennick, Robert M. *Kentucky Place Names.* Lexington: Univ. Press of Kentucky, 1984.

KENTON VALE. Kenton Vale is a small city located in north central Kenton Co., sandwiched between Covington and Fort Wright. The city was an unincorporated part of the county until 1949, when residents chose to incorporate to stop planned annexation by the city of Covington. Kenton Vale consists of a small business district on the western side of Madison Pk. and about 30 homes, most of which sit off Kuhrs Ln. The street is named for Ferdinand Kuhr, one of the early priests at **Mother of God Catholic Church** in Covington, who had a home there. Much of the village is nestled in a hillside overlooking the **Mother of God Cemetery**, which lies on the opposite side of Madison Pk. Certainly the most familiar landmark in the city is its oldest business, Jackson Florist, at 3124 Madison Pk.

In the mid-1800s, there was a rock quarry located on Kuhrs Ln. Now a dead-end road, Kuhrs Ln. once continued to the top of the hill and connected with what is now Farrell Dr., near **St. Charles Care Center**. The city has tried twice in recent years to merge with neighboring Fort Wright. In 1981 talks ceased after a conflict over the exact boundary lines of the tiny city. It seems that many residents who thought they lived in Covington actually lived in Kenton Vale. Once the boundary dispute was settled, the merger was placed on the ballot in both cities in 1983. Kenton Vale citizens passed the annexation plan by a vote of 48 to 10. In Fort Wright, however, voters turned down the merger 1,008 to 953. For now, at least, Kenton Vale remains one of the smallest incorporated cities in Kentucky.

"Kenton Vale Dismisses Annex Offer," *KP*, November 19, 1987, 9K.
Reis, Jim. "Tiny Towns," *KP*, November 4, 1986, 4K.
Sesqui-centennial Souvenir Program: 150th Anniversary, 1815–1965, City of Covington, Kentucky. Covington, Ky.: T. and W., 1965.
"Spurned Twice, Tiny City to Continue Merger Effort," *KE*, September 3, 1982, C3.

Robert D. Webster

KENTUCKY CENTRAL RAILROAD. The term *Kentucky Central,* as used for the rail line between Covington and Lexington, was originally an advertising device to promote seamless travel between those two cities. The Kentucky Central consisted of two separate rail lines: the **Covington and Lexington** (C&L), which in 1854 reached Paris from Covington, and the **Maysville and Lexington** (M&L), which linked Paris with Lexington that same year. From the onset, the C&L and its successors were an important means of transporting thousands of cattle stock (mostly hogs) destined for Covington and Cincinnati **meatpacking** operations. Wheat was another profitable item to transport. About that time, the Lexington and Danville (L&D) began service southward from Lexington to Nicholasville. **Civil War**–era documents refer to the entire Covington-to-Nicholasville route as the Central Kentucky Railroad. Promotional material projected Knoxville, Tenn., as its eventual southern terminus. In March 1856 the Kentucky General Assembly permitted the C&L and L&D railroads to use the name Kentucky Central Railroad. In 1858 Robert Bonner Bowler, a director of the Kentucky Central Railroad, persuaded the company to defer debt payment in order to make improvements on the line. A major creditor filed suit, and the railroad was sold at public auction, to Bowler.

During the Civil War, the railroad suffered considerable damage from Confederate forays into Central Kentucky. In 1862, for example, Gen. Kirby Smith's men destroyed most of the line during their reconnoiter from Lexington to the fortifications guarding Covington and Newport. In 1864 Gen. **John Hunt Morgan** and his raiders heavily plundered the line near Cynthiana.

In 1865 the original stockholders filed suit against the heirs of Bowler but lost. In the same year, the C&L and the M&L were sold at a foreclosure sale and bought by the Kentucky Central Association, a holding company, which continued to operate the C&L and the M&L as separate entities. In 1875 the C&L and the M&L were merged as the Kentucky Central Railroad (KC). The M&L at this time consisted of two separate railroads, the line from Lexington to Paris and the road from Paris to Maysville. In 1876 the KC purchased the Paris-to-Maysville road.

In 1881 the KC was sold to Collis P. Huntington for use as the connection route for his **Chesapeake and Ohio Railroad** (C&O) and his Chesapeake, Ohio and Southwestern Railroad (CO&SW). The C&O was building from Huntington, W.Va., to Cincinnati along the Ohio River, and the CO&SW ran from Louisville to Paducah. Connecting service between the C&O and the CO&SW was via the KC and its track rights over the Louisville and Nashville (L&N) between Lexington and Louisville. In 1888 the C&O reached Covington from Ashland. It joined the KC in Covington at KC Junction (16th St. and Madison Ave.) and used the KC tracks northward into Covington for its starting point in building the **Chesapeake and Ohio Railroad Bridge** across the Ohio River into Cincinnati.

Huntington's empire, however, went into receivership, and as part of the reorganization, the L&N in 1891 gained control of the KC. In 1951 the L&N abandoned the Lexington-to-Paris section of the KC. The Covington-to-Paris portion was being operated in 2007 by **CSX** as part of its Cincinnati-Corbin (C-C) division. The L&N sold the Paris-to-Maysville line to the short line **Trans-**

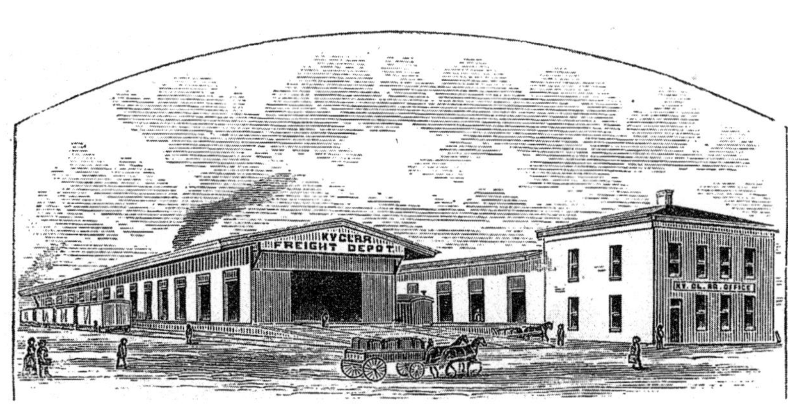

Kentucky Central Railroad Depot, Eighth and Washington Sts., Covington.

Kentucky Transportation Railroad Inc. in 1979.

Herr, Kincaid A. *The Louisville & Nashville Railroad*. Lexington: Univ. Press of Kentucky, 2000.
Tenkotte, Paul A. "Rival Cities to Suburbs: Covington and Newport, Kentucky, 1790–1890," PhD diss., Univ. of Cincinnati, 1989.
Turner, Charles W. *Chessie's Road*. Richmond, Va.: Garrett and Massie, 1956.

Charles H. Bogart

KENTUCKY CONSUMER ADVOCATE NETWORK. The Kentucky Consumer Advocate Network (KYCAN) is a nonprofit organization of mental health consumers that promotes the rights, concerns, and issues of persons with mental illness in Kentucky. It was founded in Nazareth, Ky., in 1988 by a small group of concerned mental health consumers, and the group's main office is in Louisville. KYCAN, a statewide grassroots organization, promotes self-determination, self-advocacy, community integration without discrimination, and freedom of choice on behalf of mental health clients through public education. It exists to empower mental health consumers to have hope, to take personal responsibility, to advocate for needed changes, to educate about mental health issues, and to represent the consumer community before public and governmental bodies. Some of the services available to KYCAN's clients are peer support, voting-rights training and voter registration, a newsletter, seclusion and restraint reduction training, application of the Olmstead Decision (a U.S. Supreme Court decision that requires states to place qualified individuals with mental disabilities in community settings, rather than in institutions, whenever possible), and advanced directives for mental health treatment. There is also a yearly conference with speakers and workshops for mental health consumers.

KYCAN has more than 1,000 members. It has affiliate coordinators in more than 25 counties, including Boone, Campbell, Grant, and Kenton counties in the Northern Kentucky region. All KYCAN programs are free to consumers and their families, as is membership at this time. KYCAN's efforts are supported financially by Kentucky's office of **Protection and Advocacy** and by the Department of Mental Health and Substance Abuse, Community Support Programs, the Substance Abuse and Mental Health Services Administration, and other donations.

KYCAN. "Kentucky Consumer Advocate Network." http://contac.org/kycan/ (accessed March 24, 2006).

Robin Rider Osborne

KENTUCKY CRICKET CLUB. The Kentucky Cricket Club of Newport was formed in 1845 and endured, at least in name, for more than 20 years, until baseball emerged as the region's dominant bat-and-ball game following the **Civil War**. Cricket originated in England during the early 1700s. All-male cricket clubs, complete with bylaws and elected officers, had existed in both England and North America before the **Revolutionary War**.

Cricket first appeared in the Ohio River Valley during the 1840s. The first cricket match played in Kentucky reportedly occurred in 1843 at Louisville. By late 1845, the Cincinnati area had three cricket teams: the Queen City Club, the Great Western Club, and the Kentucky Cricket Club of Newport. English immigrants established these clubs for camaraderie and exercise. One local enthusiast praised cricket as "more beneficial to health than all the drugs and quack medicines this side of the Allegheny Mountains."

Despite such purported virtues, cricket failed to win many adherents outside the English immigrant community. As late as 1860, English natives still made up all or nearly all of the Kentucky Cricket Club's lineup, or "first eleven." Like the German turnvereins and other immigrant institutions, the English cricket clubs demonstrate how European settlers preserved aspects of their culture and, in turn, shaped urban life in the Ohio River Valley.

Although cricket is not widely played in Northern Kentucky today, the Kentucky Cricket Club nevertheless influenced the region's recreation. The club's matches were among the area's earliest spectator events that featured team sports. For an 1860 match against the rival Union Cricket Club of Cincinnati, steamboats departed the **Newport Barracks** every half hour carrying fans to the Kentucky Cricket Club's grounds, located a mile up the Licking River. Moreover, the Ohio River Valley's cricket clubs promoted the growth of other team sports by lending their organizational structures, playing fields, and members to the **townball** and baseball clubs that first appeared in the area during the late 1850s.

"Cricket Match," *CDC*, August 9, 1860, 2.
Kirsch, George B. *The Creation of American Team Sports: Baseball and Cricket, 1838–1872*. Urbana: Univ. of Illinois Press, 1989.
"Sporting Epistle from Cincinnati." *Spirit of the Times* 15, no. 27 (August 29, 1845): 314.

Greg Perkins

KENTUCKY ENQUIRER. The *Kentucky Enquirer* is the Northern Kentucky edition of the *Cincinnati Enquirer,* the daily newspaper with the largest paid circulation in Northern Kentucky. The *Enquirer* also operates a Web site for Northern Kentucky, NKY.com. In the spring of 2008, the *Enquirer*'s Kentucky circulation was approximately 40,000 daily and 52,000 on Sunday, making it the third-largest daily newspaper in the state of Kentucky. The Kentucky edition's front page, local news section, and sports section are either substantially or completely different from the Cincinnati editions of the newspaper. The editorial and business pages also change on some days.

The *Cincinnati Enquirer* issued its first paper on April 10, 1841, focusing that day on the death of the first U.S. president from Cincinnati, William Henry Harrison (1841). From its inception, the paper was a popular resource for news about the arts. Its first editor was John Brough; its circulation at the time was around 1,000. At first called *Daily Cincinnati Enquirer,* the paper later changed its name to *Cincinnati Daily Enquirer,* then to *Cincinnati Enquirer.* Well-known area families have owned the paper during its long tenure: the McLean family for more than 50 years and then later one of Cincinnati's most successful businessmen, Carl Linder. During the **Civil War**, the paper began publishing seven days each week, making it possible to follow the daily happenings of the war in the region. In 1866, when fire destroyed Cincinnati's Pike Opera House, it took the *Enquirer* building next door with it. The publisher quickly recovered from this loss, and through 1991 the paper missed only nine publishing dates. The *Enquirer*'s largest and longest-continuing advertiser, the **Kroger** Company, placed its first ad on March 21, 1897. The *Enquirer* was purchased by the media giant Gannett Corporation in 1978 and became a sister publication of the *Louisville Courier-Journal*.

For many years, extending well into the 20th century, the news of Northern Kentucky, mainly Covington and Newport, was reported on the out-of-town page of the *Cincinnati Enquirer*; the same practice was followed by most other Cincinnati-based newspapers. News items covered included building permits, new construction starts, and the deaths of important individuals, each normally given the space of a short paragraph.

By 1894 the *Enquirer* had an office at 406 Scott St. in Covington, with John M. Vastine as a reporter; in 1900 S. T. Reilly held that job; by 1910 the Covington office had moved to 511 Madison and two reporters were on staff, Charles H. Mohr and Marcella Deutsch; in 1923 Ray A. Cochran gathered the news at 7 W. Sixth. St.; and in 1940 the Covington office was at 35 E. Seventh St. In 1956 the paper's Newport location at 5 E. Sixth St. was consolidated into the Covington location. By 1960 the office had been given the name *Kentucky Enquirer,* with an address of 105 City Building, Covington; in 1970, when Jack Hicks was named Kentucky editor by head editor **Brady Black**, the operation was at 600 Greenup St.; in the 1980s and into the 1990s, the office was at 309 Garrard St.; it moved to 226 Grandview Ave. in Fort Mitchell in the late 1990s. By 2008 about 40 news and advertising people worked in the Fort Mitchell office while staff members for the 10 Community Recorder weekly newspapers worked a floor below. The *Kentucky Enquirer* always has been printed in Cincinnati, first at the plant along Vine St. and recently in Queensgate, and trucked into Northern Kentucky. The *Enquirer* also has two newspaper distribution centers in Northern Kentucky, in Erlanger and Cold Spring.

Over the years, many Northern Kentuckians have worked for the *Enquirer.* Brady Black, Jack Hicks, **Ollie James**, **Robert F. Schulkers**, and **Caroline Williams** are a few who played major roles. Many of the *Enquirer*'s top present-day journalists live and work in Northern Kentucky, including political reporter Patrick Crowley, photographer Michael Keating, and sports columnist John Erardi.

In 1974 *Enquirer* editor Bill Keating announced that coverage of Northern Kentucky would expand because of the importance of four new interstate bridges, the growing airport, the industrial parks, and other areas of growth south of the river. It was then, on Sunday, August 18, 1974, that the Sunday *Kentucky Enquirer* masthead first appeared. The *Kentucky Enquirer* masthead for daily papers has been a fixture since fall 1974. Other overtures of improved coverage and increased staffing to follow the Kentucky market were made later, such as in 1994. That year editor Lawrence Beaupre expanded Kentucky business and sports news. A significant expansion of news and sports coverage began in 2004 with the appointment of a full-time general manager for Kentucky and additional editorial staff. The *Enquirer*'s Kentucky circulation increased significantly in recent years and received an additional boost when the *Kentucky Post* ceased publication on December 31, 2007.

The *Enquirer* also has moved aggressively into the digital world, starting with the launch of Cincinnati.com more than a decade ago. In November 2005 the companion Web site, NKY.com, was launched for the Northern Kentucky audience, combining content from the *Enquirer,* the Community Recorder weeklies, and other information sources. NKY.com was one of the first news Web sites to mesh journalist-produced content with reader-submitted news and photos and was named the best Web site in Kentucky in the Kentucky Press Association's annual contest in both 2006 and 2007. It also offers video, extensive calendar listings, many opportunities for reader interaction, and individual "pages" for the communities of the region with highly localized news, photos, and information. The *Enquirer* has launched products with a Kentucky focus that are specifically designed for mobile phone users as well.

Beaupre, Lawrence K. "Enquirer Expands Kentucky Coverage, Increases Business and Sports News," *KE*, October 2, 1994, A1.

DeCamp, Graydon. *The Grand Old Lady of Vine Street.* Cincinnati: Cincinnati Enquirer, 1991.

"The Enquirer Names New Kentucky Editor," *CE*, January 20, 1970, 6.

Keating, William J. "To Our Northern Kentucky Friends," *CE*, August 18, 1974, 1.

"Kentucky Enquirer Grows to Match Expanding Area," *CE*, July 21, 1974, 6A.

Dennis Hetzel and Michael R. Sweeney

KENTUCKY GATEWAY MUSEUM CENTER. James Wormald, a native of London, England, settled in Maysville with his family as a young man. He engaged in several occupations but eventually became a successful haberdasher and an agent for the Pomeroy Coal Company. In 1876 he donated $2,000 and a lot and house on Sutton St., worth $3,000, for the establishment and endowment of Maysville's first public library and the Mason Co. Historical and Scientific Society (see **Mason Co. Public Library**). Wormald died in 1878, but his legacy has endured. The Commonwealth of Kentucky chartered the new Maysville and Mason Co. Library, Historical, and Scientific Association on March 1, 1878; it is said to be the oldest historical society in continuous existence within the state. The trustees of the association built the current building on Sutton St. to serve as a library in 1881. The adjacent property was purchased early in the 20th century, and the two buildings that were erected served the public through the years. In 1971 the county began public support of the Maysville and Mason Co. Library, and the Historical and Scientific Association spent five years restoring and enlarging the original 1881 building, which opened in 1975 as the Mason Co. Museum with professionally designed exhibits that depict the history of the area. It also contained a genealogical and historical research library.

Plans for an expansion in 2003 led to a change of name to Museum Center, to reflect service to a regional rather than a county area, and in 2006 the official name of the museum was changed again, from Museum Center to Kentucky Gateway Museum Center. The Kentucky Gateway Museum Center continues its mission to acquire, preserve, and display collections for research and educational purposes. The total collection numbers more than 31,000 artifacts, documents, photographs, and works of art. With more than 10,000 documents dating from 1773, the archives have become a nationally recognized repository for regional information. The collection includes letters, land grants, plats, maps, tax rolls, military orders, tavern bonds, and more. There are 18,800 postcards and photographs in a variety of formats, 4,000 research library books, and more than 1,800 artifacts in the collection.

In 2003 Mrs. Louis N. Browning, a native of Maysville, offered her extensive collection of one-twelfth-scale miniatures and an endowment to the museum. This collection, called the Kathleen Savage Browning Miniatures Collection, is one of the three most comprehensive collections of its kind in the United States. The addition of this gift prompted construction to make room for the ever-expanding collections, so the Board of Trustees began a campaign to raise $3.8 million for a new 33,000-square-foot expansion. The Hunt Building that adjoined the 1881 building was razed, and the new addition was completed in 2007. The new facility allows for state-of-the-art preservation of the collection and provides added classrooms, three new galleries, meeting rooms, and staff offices.

Management of the facility is the responsibility of three full-time and seven part-time staff members and a corps of 60 volunteers. A board of 16 area leaders administers the annual budget. Support is provided by a $1.6 million endowment, public and private grants, and donations.

Archives of the Museum Center, Maysville, Ky.

"Death of James Wormald," *Maysville Bulletin,* April 25, 1878, 3.

"James Wormald: A Munificent Donation $5,000 for Establishing and Maintaining a Public Library and Historical Association," *Maysville Republican,* June 3, 1876, 1.

"Maysville Museum Completes Expansion," *KP*, November 24, 2007, 3A.

Lynn David

KENTUCKY POST. For nearly 117 years, the *Kentucky Post* was a part of the fabric of the Northern Kentucky community, recording its everyday events, the milestones in the lives of ordinary citizens, the foibles of its leaders, and the achievements of its local heroes. During those years, editors at the *Kentucky Post* worked to eliminate tolls on the Ohio River and Licking River bridges, won city-manager governments for Covington and Newport, helped save southeastern Kentucky's Cumberland Falls from destruction by a hydroelectric project, promoted efforts to make Boone Co. the site of the **Cincinnati/Northern Kentucky International Airport**, and campaigned to clean up gambling and X-rated entertainment in Northern Kentucky (see **Gambling**; **Newport Second Cleanup**). The *Kentucky Post*'s reporter **Clay Wade Bailey** was so well respected in Frankfort that in 1974, when Kentucky built a new Ohio River bridge linking Covington and Cincinnati, it was named in his honor.

Reporters at the *Kentucky Post* wrote about the Ohio River **floods of 1913** and **1937**, **tornadoes** in 1915 and 1974, airline crashes and fires in 1967 and 1983 (see **Aviation Accidents**; **Fires**), and Northern Kentucky's greatest disaster, the 1977 **Beverly Hills Supper Club** fire. The *Kentucky Post* was so important to the community that during the 1937 flood, newspapers were declared emergency materials and were delivered like food, water, and clothing.

It was because of tenacious crusading by one of the newspaper's editors, **Judy Clabes**, that the Commonwealth of Kentucky began to wake up to its shameless neglect of public education and pushed through the Kentucky Education Reform Act of 1990, a package of reforms that became a national model.

Throughout most of its life, the *Kentucky Post* was the dominant voice in Northern Kentucky, circulating in its peak years nearly 60,000 copies daily. Sometimes an observer, sometimes a common scold, sometimes a booster, the *Kentucky Post* first and foremost always relentlessly chronicled the news. Part of the newspaper's long history of success in Northern Kentucky can be attributed to its accidental alignment with the ideals of the political party that dominated Northern Kentucky for most of the life of the newspaper, the **Democratic Party**. The *Kentucky Post* was grown by newspaper baron Edward W. Scripps, who saw an untapped emerging market in producing a newspaper for the masses. His first newspapers were priced at one penny, well within the budget of a workingman, and they were published in the afternoon, when shift workers were coming home and had time to read a newspaper. Although he prided himself on publishing politically "independent" papers, it was natural that his newspapers tended to be liberal and attuned to the populist interests of his working-class customers. The latter principle found fertile ground in Kentucky, where the Democratic Party had ruled the state since Reconstruction and where, until the decade of the 1990s, the electorate's only real decisions were made in Democratic primaries.

In 1881 Scripps bought the afternoon *Cincinnati Penny Press* from brothers Walter and Alfred

Wellman and soon renamed it the *Cincinnati Post.* As the Cincinnati newspaper flourished, it looked for more readers and found them on the Kentucky shore of the Ohio River. On September 15, 1890, the first issue of the Kentucky edition of the *Cincinnati Post* appeared. Its four pages of news were aimed at the 92,000 residents of Covington, Newport, Bellevue, Dayton, and Ludlow. The new paper had editorial and business offices at 404 Scott St., Covington, and its own staff of 30, but it was printed along with the *Cincinnati Post* in Cincinnati, an arrangement that persisted through 2007.

Telephone and telegraph connections were set up between the Covington and Cincinnati offices, and L. T. Atwood, editor of the *Cincinnati Post,* was placed in charge of the Kentucky newspaper in addition to his duties in Cincinnati. Scripps promised, "The Kentucky Post will tell the truth without fear or favor, irrespective of any political party under all circumstances."

On its first birthday in 1891, the paper in Covington moved to a three-story brick building at Fifth and Scott Sts. Its staff then numbered 40, and it boasted 9,970 paid subscribers. The paper also ceased being called the Kentucky edition of the *Cincinnati Post.* It was renamed the *Kentucky Post* and now had its own editor, William Purnell Campbell. Scripps also ordered that the *Kentucky Post* should be wrapped around the *Cincinnati Post* for circulation in Kentucky. This was a new newspaper concept, publishing two newspapers for the price of one, and still for a penny. This arrangement continued until 2006, when the *Kentucky Post* finally was untethered from its Cincinnati sister. By 2006 the *Kentucky Post* was far the larger of the two papers in circulation, and its price had risen to 50 cents daily and one dollar on Saturday. In the 1880s circulation continued to climb, and in October 1896 the *Kentucky Post* expanded into leased space in Covington at the southwest corner of Fifth St. and Madison Ave. It began printing eight-page papers daily.

One of the new paper's first big stories came with the January 30, 1900, sniper shooting of Covington resident **William Goebel** on the steps of the state capitol in Frankfort. Goebel, who died a few days later, had been declared the winner in a controversial and hotly contested election for Kentucky governor, the closest in Kentucky history. The *Kentucky Post* had covered the campaign closely, and the assassination dominated its pages for days. Circulation was now 12,488. In 1902 the *Kentucky Post* moved into what was its home for the next 100 years. Scripps had purchased a vacant lot in Covington in the middle of the 400 block of Madison Ave., between Fourth and Fifth Sts., and constructed a building on the site where a huge fire had destroyed much of the block. The 30-by-100-foot three-story building was dedicated at an open house on October 31, 1902, that attracted some 2,000 persons. By then every edition of the newspaper contained eight pages of Kentucky news.

In 1904 Harry W. Brown became editor. Then in 1906 Milton J. Bonner took the helm for nine years. Starting in 1915 a series of editors came and went, beginning with Frank Crippen; in 1916 Charles W. Larsh took over. He was followed in 1918 by Albert W. Burhrman, then Edward P. Mills, and in 1919 by Max B. Cook. In 1921 Bruce I. Susong arrived. He was a crusader, and it was during his 10-year tenure that the paper worked to reform government in Covington and Newport and saved the Cumberland Falls from being dammed for a power plant. By 1927 circulation had reached 27,454. On November 30, 1924, Susong started a Sunday edition, which lasted about eight years, until December 18, 1932. Donald E. Weaver was editor during the **Great Depression** years from 1931 to 1936. He ran regular exposés of gambling and uncovered loan sharks who were in league with corrupt justices of the peace. Carl A. Saunders arrived on May 28, 1936, and saw several of his ambitions come to reality, including construction of Greater Cincinnati's main airport in Boone Co. He published an intensely local newspaper, and it was said upon his death in October 1962, "The name of every resident of the area probably appeared in the *Kentucky Post* during his 26 years."

Competition from television, changing lifestyles, and new reader habits were beginning to have an effect on afternoon newspapers as more and more of their customers began to prefer morning papers. The Taft family's local afternoon paper, the *Times-Star,* fell victim to these trends and sold out to the E. W. Scripps Company. On Monday, July 21, 1958, the *Kentucky Post* became the *Kentucky Post and Times-Star,* and the reconstituted newspaper reached its peak of average daily circulation in Kentucky, around 60,000 copies. Eventually, the *Times-Star* name was dropped from the nameplate.

On January 14, 1963, a new editor, **Vance H. Trimble**, arrived from the Scripps-Howard bureau in Washington, D.C., shortly after winning a Pulitzer Prize for national reporting. Trimble brought his aggressive and often irreverent style to the newspaper. A dogged promoter, he at one point ordered a huge reproduction of the *Kentucky Post*'s front page painted on the side of the newspaper's three-story building in Covington, and it was for years a Madison Ave. landmark. Trimble also solidified the newspaper's presence in a 12-county area comprising Bracken, Boone, Campbell, Carroll, Gallatin, Grant, Harrison, Kenton, Mason, Owen, Pendleton, and Robertson counties, branding them "Kentucky Post Country."

The *Kentucky Post*'s now aging building on Madison Ave. had remained largely untouched until 1963, when a $250,000 remodeling created the familiar facade that housed the paper until the structure was sold in 2005 and the newspaper moved its office to RiverCenter II (see **Covington, Downtown**) on the Covington riverfront. The newspaper's old building was extensively remodeled and became the law offices of Morgan, Hazen, Galbreath & Smith.

At the time of its 75th-anniversary celebration in 1965, the *Kentucky Post* had an average daily circulation of about 50,000. Circulation increased and varied between 53,000 and 54,000 through the late 1960s and mid-1970s. Scripps's 1958 purchase of the *Times-Star* only put off the inevitable as profits of afternoon newspapers in metropolitan areas continued to soften. By the mid-1970s, the *Post*'s combined Kentucky and Ohio editions were losing millions of dollars a year, a substantial sum in those days, and in 1977 Scripps negotiated a 30-year arrangement with its local arch rival, the morning *Cincinnati Enquirer,* to take over printing, circulation, and advertising for the *Post*'s Kentucky and Ohio editions, splitting the profits from the joint operation. Scripps continued to operate the newsroom but shed more than 500 employees who did other tasks, mostly in its Cincinnati operations.

Once the *Cincinnati Enquirer* took over circulation, however, the *Kentucky Post* began a long, steady decline, dropping to a circulation of 46,000 through much of the 1980s and to 37,000 by 1995, before leveling off at just fewer than 28,000 by 2000. Trimble retired in 1979, and in December of that year, Paul H. Knue was named editor of the *Kentucky Post.* In August 1983 Knue became editor of the *Cincinnati Post* and was replaced by Judy Clabes, who quickly became noted for her deep commitment to the community.

In 1996 Clabes was named president of the Scripps Howard Foundation, and in a return to the very earliest days of the *Kentucky Post,* Knue became editor of both of the Scripps Cincinnati and Kentucky newspapers. Both the Kentucky and Ohio editions of the *Post* continued to struggle with the growing customer preference for morning newspapers and with the disadvantage of having its marketing and circulation in the hands of its competitor. Although circulation of the *Cincinnati Post* plunged in Ohio, the *Kentucky Post* remained the dominant paper in Northern Kentucky, largely because of the community's continued affection for the *Kentucky Post*'s commitment to the area. Knue retired in 2001, and longtime *Post* news executive Mike Philipps was named editor of the two newspapers; he immediately turned most of the *Post*'s remaining resources toward the booming Northern Kentucky market.

In January 2004 the *Cincinnati Enquirer* announced that it would not continue beyond 2007 its 30-year contract to print and distribute the *Post.* With no incentive to support a possible long-term competitor, the *Cincinnati Enquirer* let the *Kentucky Post*'s circulation slide even further, now limiting deliveries to select areas in Boone, Campbell, and Kenton counties. In July 2007 Scripps announced that the *Cincinnati Post* and the *Kentucky Post* would cease operation, with the last edition of both being December 31, 2007. The announcement left Northern Kentucky without a major daily newspaper that it could call its own for the first time in 117 years. On January 1, 2008, an online electronic version of the *Kentucky Post* began operations as kypost.com, a part of the Scripps media network.

Baldasty, Gerald J. *E. W. Scripps and the Business of Newspapers.* Urbana: Univ. of Illinois Press, 1999.

Duke, Kerry. "The Post to Say Farewell Dec. 31," *KP,* July 17, 2007, 1A.

Stevens, George Edward. "A History of the Cincinnati Post." A thesis submitted to the faculty of the graduate school of the Univ. of Minnesota, 1968.

Trimble, Vance H., ed. *Scripps-Howard Handbook.* Cincinnati: E. W. Scripps, 1981.

Mike Philipps

KENTUCKY RIVER. The Kentucky River forms the western boundary of the Northern Kentucky region. Its waters wash the shores of both Carroll and Owen counties. Before the development of modern modes of transportation, the river was the way people of the Northern Kentucky region met residents of the central and southeastern areas of the state. Carrollton was a destination city where rivermen exchanged goods for transshipment along both the Kentucky and the Ohio rivers. Regional cities such as Worthville, Gratz, and Monterey depended upon the Kentucky River for their economies and communications with the rest of the nation, because for many years overland roads to these places were poor. The Kentucky River has held much the same importance for the western reaches of the Northern Kentucky region as the Ohio River has held for the most northern counties of the region.

The Kentucky River, nearly 255 miles in length, flows from the confluence of the North and South forks at Beattyville on a generally northwesterly course to the Ohio River at Carrollton. The headwaters of the Three Forks of the Kentucky River—the North, the Middle, and the South—rise in the mountains of Eastern Kentucky near Pine Mountain. The river drains an area of nearly 7,000 square miles and drops 226 feet as it flows from Beattyville to Carrollton. In the river basin, the Cincinnati Arch, which crests at Camp Nelson, caused the land to rise during the Pliocene and the Pleistocene epochs (see **Geology**). At one time the Kentucky flowed into the Ohio River far north of present-day Carrollton, but glaciation and constant weathering altered both rivers' courses (see **Glaciers**).

The Kentucky River was vital to both American Indians and European pioneers, and it then became a major transportation route early in state history. Flatboats built on its banks transported tobacco, whiskey, and other agricultural products. Steamboats made their appearance on the river beginning in 1816. Being a relatively narrow and meandering river, the Kentucky in its natural state was subject to periods of flood and low water. There were pools of deep water, impounded by sand and gravel bars or rocky shoals, every few miles throughout the length of the river. As flatboats, keelboats, and steamboats became increasingly important to the state's economy, plans were made for a system of locks and dams to be constructed by the federal government (see **Kentucky River Navigation**). Because no federal funds were forthcoming, the state built five locks between 1836 and 1842, regularizing transportation for less than 100 miles of the river's length. Well-known steamboats such as the *Blue Wing,* the *Argo,* and the *Ocean* used the Kentucky River before the **Civil War**.

When **Railroads** pushed into the region, they superseded much of the river transportation of freight. In 1880 the federal government took over the old system of lock and dams, which were dilapidated and unusable, and began rebuilding numbers 1 through 5. By 1917, 14 locks and dams had been completed from a point four miles above Carrollton to just below Beattyville, creating a channel six feet deep. Already obsolete when completed in 1917, the locks were too narrow and short for the rapid lockages that might have been able to compete with railroads.

At the beginning of the 20th century, such steamboats as the *Falls City II,* the *Royal,* and the *Richard Roe* were the last of their kind to navigate the Kentucky River. As late as the 1920s, gas-powered packet boats such as the *Hanover,* the *White Dove,* and the *Revonah* (Hanover spelled backward) worked the lower river. **Showboats**, such as the *Princess,* brought entertainment to communities during the summertime, until the Great Depression.

Transportation on the Kentucky probably had little overall effect on the cost of internal transportation in the state except for a short while near the end of the 19th century. Nevertheless, for many places along the river from Carrollton to Frankfort, the river offered the most convenient contact with the outside world. Until the construction of highways in the 1930s, small towns such as Lockport, Gratz, and Monterey (see **Monterey Baptist Church**) prospered because of their river links.

Commissions have studied the future of the Kentucky River for decades. The 1990 General Assembly passed a law creating the Kentucky River Authority (KRA), which is empowered to develop comprehensive long-range water-reservoir management and drought-response plans; to maintain locks and dams; to issue administrative regulations for clean water; to develop recreation areas; and to conceive methods of protecting groundwater within the river's basin. In addition, such advocacy groups as Kentuckians for the Commonwealth, Kentucky Riverkeeper, and Kentucky Waterways Alliance participate in the task of monitoring, protecting, and improving the Kentucky River.

One challenge they face is that sewage, salt water from oil and gas wells, runoff from coal mines, and other environmental problems strain the river's ability to regenerate itself. The nonbiodegradable waste floating in the river during spring floods or left hanging in trees along the riverbank is a visible sign of the pollution of the Kentucky River. Sediment constricts the river in many places because of the runoff from mining and agricultural operations and housing developments.

The future of the Kentucky River is uncertain. As the old locks and dams deteriorate, state government and the public at large must make important and costly decisions about replacements. Moreover, as the population of central and Northern Kentucky grows, increasing stress will be placed on the watershed.

Clark, Thomas D. *The Kentucky.* New York: Farrar and Rinehart, 1942.
Coleman, J. Winston. *Steamboats on the Kentucky.* Lexington, Ky.: Winburn, 1960.
Ellis, William E. *The Kentucky River.* Lexington: Univ. Press of Kentucky, 2000.

William E. Ellis

KENTUCKY RIVER NAVIGATION. The Kentucky River, which flows into the Ohio River at Carrollton, is one of the major rivers of Northern Kentucky. The river is formed at the confluence of its North, Middle, and South Forks near Beattyville and flows in a northwesterly direction for 255 miles, reaching the Ohio River at Carrollton. In its course the river drops more than 220 feet in elevation. Because the river channel could be navigated only at high-water stages, and then at peril, boatmen, farmers, and merchants early became interested in improving the river for dependable navigation.

When Kentucky became a state in 1792, the Commonwealth assumed jurisdiction over all the streams within its boundaries. At that time, commerce was moved by flatboats and keelboats. With the advent of the steamboat in 1811, support became strong for developing improved navigation conditions. Shortly after statehood was attained, the state legislature had begun considering improvements, and sections of the river were surveyed over the next several years.

In 1828 the state requested a federal survey of the river to plan a project that could provide a more reliable transportation artery. U.S. Army engineers mapped the river from its mouth upstream to Boonesborough and recommended federal funding for construction of an experimental dam at Frankfort to determine the feasibility of additional improvements. However, no federal assistance was provided. From the 1820s through the early 1830s, the State Board of Internal Improvements approved expenditures allowing for removal of the most treacherous rock and snag obstructions in the channel. In 1835, based on previous surveys and studies, state engineer R. Philip Baker developed plans for a slack-water project to provide a six-foot navigable depth by construction of 17 locks and dams on the Kentucky River, from the mouth to the Three Forks at Beattyville. (Slack water refers to the easily navigable water between one dam and the next dam upstream.)

With authorization from the Board of Internal Improvements, Sylvester Welch, the chief project engineer, directed construction of five locks and dams between 1835 and 1842. These structures established the six-foot depth up to Oregon in Woodford Co., about 95 miles above the mouth of the river. Construction of additional projects was suspended in 1842 because insufficient funds were provided from the state. The five completed projects consisted of rock-filled timber-crib dams and stone masonry locks. Each of the locks was 38 feet wide and 145 feet long, with an average lift of 14 feet. The steamboat *New Argo* was the first to pass through the locks, arriving in Frankfort in February 1840. The project cost just over $1 million. However, it was still 160 miles short of the goal of the Three Forks region and the wish to develop and market the abundant resources of the Eastern Kentucky mountains.

During its early years of operation, the project enabled bustling steamboat commerce. But in the first 25 years of operation, the state collected less than $475,000 in tolls, while expending $315,000 for upkeep and maintenance. The difference of $160,000 was entirely inadequate to extend the system into the mountain region.

During the **Civil War**, care of the system was neglected, and several of the locks received battle-inflicted damage. At the end of the war, the five locks were in bad condition, and the state lacked funds for repairs. Therefore, the state leased the project to the Kentucky River Navigation Company, which agreed to repair the structures and build additional locks and dams up to the mountains. However, that scheme collapsed owing to shortage of funds, and by the 1870s, the five structures had fallen into ruin, becoming more an obstruction to navigation than an aid.

Still, there was the clamor by river men, businesses, and politicians to extend the system upriver to the Three Forks, but adequate funding for repairs and extension of the system was not provided by the state government. The state requested federal aid, and in the Rivers and Harbors Act of 1879, Congress appropriated $100,000 for a survey of the river, directing the U.S. Army Corps of Engineers to undertake the work and stating that the federal government would become the owner of the system. Col. William E. Merrill conducted the survey and study and recommended reconstruction of the five old projects and construction of additional locks and dams to reach the mountain region. Congress adopted this plan, and Kentucky ceded the projects to the United States in March 1880.

The Corps began repairs immediately. Even though it was necessary to completely rebuild several of the old locks and dams, and although floods hampered the work, by 1886 all five of the old structures were reopened. River-borne commerce experienced a resurgence as the locks served steamboats, flatboats, and log rafts. Still the fervor for further expansion of the navigation system simmered. The plan approved by the 1879 act recommended construction of 12 locks and dams to provide navigation to Beattyville. Following failure of an experimental bear-trap dam near Beattyville, the Corps modified the plan to reduce costs by raising the average lift of the new dams from 15 to 18 feet and reducing the number of new projects to 9. Number 6 was completed in 1891, and in subsequent years, in spite of floods and sporadic funding by the Congress, the Corps built all 9 projects, completing number 14 in 1917. Numbers 9 through 14 were constructed of concrete, unlike the old timber-crib dams and quarried-stone locks.

Throughout those years, the driving force was the pervading "boosterism" to complete the system to the mountains for the extraction of timber and coal. Waterborne commerce on the Kentucky River fluctuated greatly in the construction years and following completion of the system. The coming of adequate rail service caused a dramatic decrease in traffic; the navigation system now had to compete with other transportation modes. From 1900 to 1930, commerce in various commodities, and the value thereof, declined precipitously. Movement of coal on the river ceased in the 1960s, and all commercial traffic ended in 2000.

The Kentucky River navigation system simply did not bring about a long-term economic stimulus. In 1986 the Corps of Engineers began leasing the 14 locks and dams to the Commonwealth's Kentucky River Authority. Since then, the Corps has repaired several of the dams in order to maintain an adequate water supply for many Bluegrass communities. The Authority manages the water-supply function and operates the lower four locks specifically for recreational boating in the summer months. Thus, the history of navigation development on the Kentucky River has come full circle. The Commonwealth built the original projects in the early 1800s; the federal government took control in 1880; and since 1986 the Commonwealth has managed the entire system.

Within the Northern Kentucky region, the navigation of the Kentucky River provided important links with the outside world for areas in Carroll and Owen counties. Supplies and goods were delivered to towns that were difficult to reach overland, like Gratz and Monterey in Owen Co. Residents of such areas also had access to entertainment from **showboats**. River commerce made Carrollton the important port that it once was, and it was on the waters of the Kentucky River where central and eastern Kentuckians met Northern Kentuckians, if ever so unintentionally and informally. Modern highways and new forms of communication have replaced, somewhat, the role of the Kentucky River for those parts of the region.

Ellis, William E. *The Kentucky River.* Lexington: Univ. Press of Kentucky, 2000.

Johnson, Leland R. *The Falls City Engineers: A History of the Louisville District Corps of Engineers United States Army.* Louisville, Ky.: Louisville District of the U.S. Army Corps of Engineers, 1974, 1984.

Johnson, Leland R., and Charles Parrish, *Kentucky River Development: The Commonwealth's Waterway.* Louisville, Ky.: Louisville District of the U.S. Army Corps of Engineers, 1999.

Charles E. Parrish

KENTUCKY SPEEDWAY. The nation's newest major spectator sport, NASCAR, came to the Northern Kentucky region with the arrival in Gallatin Co. of Jerry Carroll's Kentucky Speedway. Located along Ky. Rt. 35 just north of I-71 and easily reached from three major markets, Northern Kentucky–Greater Cincinnati, Louisville, and Lexington, this multimillion-dollar venture is changing the nature and the economics of Gallatin Co. The speedway was built on 1,000 acres at a privately funded cost of $152 million and opened in 2000; it seats more than 66,000 and provides parking for more than 30,000 cars and 2,000 recreational vehicles. Having attracted a single-day crowd of 72,312 at a race, the speedway already holds the attendance record for sporting events held in the region. Some 300,000 patrons attended the races in the track's first season, and attendance has grown steadily ever since. The track is a 1.5-mile tri-oval with a state-of-the-art banking design. The racing surface is also one of the best in the nation, often attracting some of NASCAR's top drivers for practice runs. Three types of races are held there: the NASCAR Busch Series (stock cars); the Indy Racing League, using Indianapolis-type open-wheeled cars; and the NASCAR Craftsman Truck Series (race trucks). Of all the major sports, NASCAR is clearly the most family-oriented, and it is marketed to families. Family involvement and family-friendly drivers are a big part of the circuit's appeal. Spectator families love to camp there. Meanwhile, new roads, interstate exits, and sewers have been constructed in Gallatin Co. to accommodate the fans. Hotels, restaurants, and resorts are appearing nearby. Much-needed jobs are coming to both Gallatin and Carroll counties, and a general-aviation airport has been proposed to serve Gallatin, Carroll, and Owen counties. The Kentucky Speedway has begun to host other types of events when not conducting racing: concerts, driving schools, and corporate outings. In 2008, Bruton Smith, chairman and CEO of Speedway Motorsports Inc., purchased Kentucky Speedway, paying $78 million and also assuming $63.3 million in debts. Smith, whose company owns seven other auto racing tracks, stated that he plans to move a NASCAR Sprint Cup Series race to Kentucky Speedway and to boost seating capacity to 115,000. Previous CEO and owner Jerry Carroll has agreed to continue in an advisory capacity.

Kentucky Speedway. "Sprint Cup Race Now Likely," *KE*, May 23, 2008, A1. www.kentuckyspeedway.com.

KENTUCKY SYMPHONY ORCHESTRA. The Kentucky Symphony Orchestra (formerly the Northern Kentucky Symphony) is a professional orchestra with offices in Newport. Founded in 1992 by James Cassidy, its current music director, the orchestra played its first concerts in Highland Heights at the newly opened Greaves Concert Hall on the campus of Northern Kentucky University. Before 1992 a Northern Kentucky Symphony Orchestra existed from 1934 through 1955 as a volunteer community orchestra. This group rehearsed and performed at the Covington YMCA and at the Covington Public Library auditorium (now the **Carnegie Visual and Performing Arts Center**). Its music director at that time was Fritz Bruch. In 1986 a group of local musicians formed the Music Society of Northern Kentucky, based at the Carnegie Center. The organization offered chamber music and ensembles, which were later augmented to form an orchestra, which was under the direction of Jack Kirstein. In 1990, after Kirstein retired, several conductors led the Music Society's orchestra and ensembles, until the orchestra dissolved in 1991.

James Cassidy, having just completed the orchestral conducting program of the University of Cincinnati's College-Conservatory of Music, offered to start an orchestra whose mission would be to make symphonic music attractive, accessible, and affordable to the people of Northern Kentucky and the tri-state area. Central to the mission were innovative and thematic programs that would bring relevant and extramusical ideas to the marketing and presentation of these concerts. The Music Society's dormant corporation was revived, and the corporate name was changed to the Northern Kentucky Symphony Inc. (NKS). Having completed an audition of more than 80 musicians, Cassidy took the new Northern Kentucky Symphony to the Greaves Concert Hall stage on November 21, 1992, with an all-Russian program featuring Russian dancers, familiar show pieces, and a rising local talent, pianist Michael Chertock. The NKS played four programs or performances in its first season, with 14 paid-per-service core members leading each section. The orchestra's 1992–1993 season included its first dinner-concert with a Viennese program at the Oldenberg Brewery and a salute to Richard Rodgers: the orchestra accompanied video clips from the 1960s television documentary *Victory at Sea*. By the orchestra's fourth season, unique programming and collaborations had allowed the NKS to increase its budget tenfold and increase its number of performances and per-service musicians. In 1996 the American Symphony Orchestra League acknowledged that the Northern Kentucky Symphony was "the fastest growing orchestra in America." By 2001 the NKS had collaborated on stage with many local arts groups, including the Cincinnati Opera, the Cincinnati Ballet, the Playhouse in the Park, the Shakespeare Festival, the Ensemble Theatre, the Cincinnati Zoo, the Cincinnati Choral Society, the Cincinnati Observatory, ensembles from Northern Kentucky University and the College Conservatory of Music, and several Kentucky-based visual artists. Featured entities and groups like Hasbro (Trivial Pursuit), NBC's *Saturday Night Live* (*Deep Thoughts by Jack Handy*), the alternative rock group Over the Rhine, the Kentucky National Guard, Blessed Union of Souls, and the University of Kentucky Opera Theatre have also appeared in concert with the NKS. In late August 2001, at a concert in **Devou Park** that drew about 10,000 people from around the region, the NKS shed its local name for a larger regional identity and became the Kentucky Symphony Orchestra (KSO).

Today, the KSO and its music director James Cassidy boast a professional orchestra with a core of 50 quality professionals together with a number of talented charter musicians who helped start the organization. The orchestra offers three series of concerts annually, the Subscription, Education, and Summer Park series. Several KSO subsidiary groups (the Newport Ragtime Band, the Flood Wall Jazz Quintet, the KSO Boogie Band, the KSO Chorale, and the SouthBank Theatre Orchestra) have been formed over the years to afford musicians and audiences alike the opportunity to authentically experience a range of music genres documenting America's relatively young musical heritage. Throughout the course of a year, the KSO and its subsidiary groups perform about 40 concerts for an annual audience of roughly 40,000.

The KSO's innovative approach to programming, together with its commitment to fiscally responsible growth and management, has garnered support from individuals and companies throughout the region who see the KSO as a tangible investment in their community. From concert performances of operas (*Tosca* and *Othello*) and Broadway musicals (*Jesus Christ Superstar* and *Sweeney Todd*), to silent-film accompaniments (*Ben-Hur* and *Phantom of the Opera*), to high-tech theatrical presentations (*Miraculous Mandarin*) and nostalgic re-creations (Spike Jones, Frank Sinatra, and WLW Crosley Square tributes), the KSO offers its audiences the widest possible array of culture and entertainment. Through these performances and additional appearances at special events, grand openings, and civic celebrations, the orchestra continues to enhance the quality of life in Northern Kentucky.

"Kentucky Symphony Orchestra," *CE*, October 13, 2002, E8.

"Making Fine Music South of the River," *CE*, November 9, 1999, C7.

"Northern Kentucky Symphony," *CE*, January 14, 2000, 7.

"Rehearsal Set for Symphony," *KTS*, January 3, 1955, 2A.

James R. Cassidy

KENTUCKY TIMES-STAR. The *Kentucky Times-Star* was, in its day, one of the leading daily newspapers in Northern Kentucky. Like many Northern Kentucky business enterprises, it was a stepchild of a Cincinnati-based organization; and as is often the case with newspapers, it had a tumultuous life cycle. The *Kentucky Times-Star* began its existence on November 2, 1923, when the *Cincinnati Times-Star* launched a separately labeled edition to serve customers in Northern Kentucky. The seeds of the newspaper were planted more than a half century earlier, when the *Cincinnati Times-Star* itself was formed from the consolidation of three competing newspapers. One was the *Cincinnati Times*, founded in 1840 as the *Spirit of the Times*. The *Spirit of the Times* shut down on May 19, 1841, about a month after the launch of the *Cincinnati Enquirer*, but came back a year later as the *Times*, a one-cent afternoon daily. Its publisher was Calvin W. Starbuck, and its first editor was Edwin R. Campbell. Starbuck died a wealthy man in 1870; the value of his estate was estimated to be $750,000—a veritable fortune. The *Times* was appraised at $200,000 upon his death and was sold for two-thirds that amount in 1871 to the publishers of the *Cincinnati Evening Chronicle*, a competitor since 1868. The new owners, including Benjamin Eggleston, Alexander Sands, and Calvin W. Thomas, combined the two publications as the *Times-Chronicle*, but later the name was shortened to the *Cincinnati Times*.

In 1879 Charles Phelps Taft, a lawyer educated at Yale University and a member of the famous Republican Taft family, joined with other investors, H. P. Royden and David Sinton, to buy a controlling interest in the *Cincinnati Times*. It was the beginning of what became a long and legendary association. Taft owned the newspaper until his death on December 31, 1929; control then passed to his nephew, Hulbert Taft, who became editor in chief and president.

One of Charles P. Taft's first acts at the *Cincinnati Times* was to purchase, in 1880, the competing *Cincinnati Star*, another evening paper, which had been in business since 1872. Its price was initially two cents but had jumped to three cents in 1879. The first issue of the new *Cincinnati Times-Star* appeared on June 27, 1880.

The following year brought a development that eventually had a direct bearing on the *Cincinnati Times-Star*. A newspaper entrepreneur named James Scripps bought the *Cincinnati Penny Press*, which had been launched a short time before, from brothers Alfred (Frank) and Walter Wellman. It was a small newspaper, four pages a day, six columns to the page. James's brother Edward Willis Scripps bought control of the paper in 1883 and made it into a feisty workingman's paper that eventually won a toehold in the tough Cincinnati market of 12 newspapers.

In 1890, anxious to capture part of the Northern Kentucky market, Scripps opened a bureau at 404 Scott St. in Covington and hired 30 people to put out a Kentucky edition of the *Post*. It made its first appearance on September 15, 1890.

The *Cincinnati Times-Star* soon followed suit, setting up a Covington bureau a few doors down at 410 Scott St. It later moved to offices in the Moose Lodge at the southwest corner of Fifth St. and Madison Ave. in Covington and opened another Northern Kentucky bureau at 414 York St. in Newport. Joseph Hogan ran the Covington branch at the time, and Thomas Hogan directed the Newport one. That set the stage for what proved to be a lively rivalry between the *Cincinnati Post* and the *Cincinnati Times-Star* and, later, the *Cincinnati Enquirer* for domination of the Northern Kentucky market.

One result was the launch of the *Kentucky Times-Star* as a full-fledged Northern Kentucky newspaper in 1923. Harry Meier was its managing editor, and the *Kentucky Times-Star* declared itself to be the "largest and best" newspaper in the entire state. It was also the only afternoon daily in the region to carry stories from the Associated Press. Published Monday through Saturday, the newspaper sold for two cents. The *Kentucky Times-Star* prospered, and when word came that the Moose Lodge building was about to be sold, the newspaper commissioned one of Cincinnati's leading architectural firms, **Samuel Hannaford and Sons**, to design a proper home for the newspaper enterprise at 421 Scott St. in Covington. It featured hand-carved stone blocks facing the street, heavy bronze doors, and, on the inside, the latest craze in woodworking. "The Kentucky Times-Star" was chiseled into the stone front of the structure. The surest sign the *Kentucky Times-Star* had "arrived" was the fact that it had its own, exclusive telephone number, Covington 4320. "Throngs Visit New Home of Kentucky Times-Star," announced a front-page headline the day the new building opened. The story itself noted, "Many flowers were sent to the offices by citizens who were loud in their praise of the new building, which was declared to be one of the handsomest structures in the city."

For the next 35 years, the *Kentucky Times-Star* fought for control of the Northern Kentucky market with the *Kentucky Post* and, to a lesser extent, the *Cincinnati Enquirer*. In the end it was a losing battle. Because it had long been owned by the Taft family (first Charles Phelps Taft and then his nephew Hubert Taft), the Ohio and Kentucky editions of the *Times-Star* were widely regarded as a conservative, business-oriented Republican voice. But the Kentucky edition of the newspaper was sold in a community that, at the time, was largely blue-collar and heavily Democratic. During the **Great Depression**, the *Kentucky Times-Star*, like the *Cincinnati Enquirer*, struggled to match the popularity in Northern Kentucky of the crusading, blue-collar, Democrat-oriented *Post*. In 1940, although the *Times-Star* outsold the *Post* in Cincinnati, the *Post* was the dominant paper in Northern Kentucky.

By the end of **World War II**, the gap was widening further, and the *Times-Star*, on both sides of the Ohio River, experienced mounting financial pressure. Its executives eventually acknowledged that the *Times-Star* had begun losing money in 1952, with losses exceeding $1 million in the 1957–1958 fiscal year. Although its employees did not know it until after the fact, the *Times-Star* published its last edition on Saturday, July 19, 1958. Its 649 employees in both Cincinnati and Northern Kentucky were notified by telegram and telephone calls that weekend that Scripps Howard, the owner of the *Post*, had purchased the *Times-Star*. Most were told to come to work the following Monday and clean out their desks. That day, July 21, 1958, Northern Kentucky residents were presented with a new evening daily newspaper, the *Kentucky Post and Times-Star*. A story announcing the merger noted that the *Kentucky Times-Star*'s combined circulation at the time had been 22,784, while the *Kentucky Post*'s stood at 42,855. The Northern Kentucky headquarters for the combined publication became the *Kentucky Post* building at 421 Madison Ave. in Covington. The *Post* picked up some *Times-Star* staff members, notably advertising manager George Brady and sports editor Tom Kramer. But most of the other employees of the *Times-Star* were out of work. The *Post* kept the *Times-Star* name for nearly a quarter century, phasing it out of the masthead on the front page and finally dropping it, without fanfare, from the editorial page masthead on May 1, 1982.

"Centennial Edition, 1881–1981," *CP*, October 27, 1981.

Hooper, Osman Castle. *History of Ohio Journalism, 1793–1922*. Columbus, Ohio: Spahr and Glenn, 1933.

Kenny, Herbert A. *Newspaper Row, Journalism in the Pre-Television Era*. Chester, Conn.: Globe Pequot Press, 1987.

"Post Buys Times-Star," *KP*, July 21, 1958, 1.

Reis, Jim. "Newspapers Emerged and Then Merged," *KP*, January 23, 1989, 4K.

"Throngs Visit New Home of Kentucky Times-Star," *KTS*, June 1, 1927, 1.

Trimble, Vance H. *The Astonishing Mr. Scripps: The Turbulent Life of America's Penny Press Lord*. Ames: Iowa State Univ. Press, 1992.

——, ed. *Scripps-Howard Handbook*. 3rd rev. ed. Cincinnati: E. W. Scripps, 1981.

Towles, Donald B. *The Press of Kentucky, 1787–1974*. Frankfort: Kentucky Press Association, 1994.

Robert White

KERLEY, JOHN A. "JACK" (b. December 6, 1951, Newport, Ky.). A former advertising copywriter who has become a suspense-thriller writer, Jack Kerley of Newport published his first novel, *The Hundredth Man*, in June 2004. It made quite a splash in the literary world. The audio and movie rights were sold for more than $1.5 million before the book was even on bookstore shelves. Kerley claims that his stories evolve as he walks along the Ohio River through Covington, Newport, and Bellevue. He carries a small tape recorder to capture ideas as they occur. Kerley is a graduate of Ball State University in Muncie, Ind. He and his wife Elaine have a daughter, Amanda, and a son, John.

"'The Hundredth Man'—Newport Retiree Pens Detective Novel," *KP*, August 13, 2003, 5K.

Kerley, Jack. Interview by Deborah Kohl Kremer, March 2004, Villa Hills, Ky.

Wecker, David. "Ad Man Forsakes Slogans and Sells Detective Novels," *CP*, July 17, 2004, C1.

Deborah Kohl Kremer

KEY, JOHN JAMES, MAJOR (b. 1817, Washington, Ky.; d. October 15, 1886, Washington, D.C.). John James Key, a judge and a **Civil War** major, was the oldest child of **Marshall Key** and Harriet Sellman Key. He worked in the Mason Co. clerk's office with his father and during the 1840s served at least one term as Mason Co. clerk. On December 7, 1842, Key wed Mary S. Reed, and the couple had one child, Joseph R. Key. After Mary died, perhaps during childbirth, John married Hester Ann "Hetty" Rudd on April 18, 1849. Key and his second wife had at least three daughters. In June 1853, Key bought some Perry Co., Ind., real estate, including 102 acres owned by federal judge Elisha Mills Huntington, a brother-in-law of his wife Hetty. Key was elected as a Cannelton, Ind., town trustee and spearheaded a successful effort to make Cannelton the Perry Co. seat. Soon after being admitted to the Indiana bar, he was chosen prosecuting attorney but refused to qualify, to allow his brother-in-law Christopher Rudd Jr. to assume the post. When the Court of Common Pleas was established in 1860 for five Indiana counties, including Perry Co., Key was appointed the first district judge. In November 1861 he resigned to join the Union cause as a colonel in the 60th Indiana Regiment. Later he became a major in the U.S. Army as adjutant to Gen. Henry W. Halleck.

John Key's younger brother, Col. **Thomas Marshall Key**, was Gen. George B. McClellan's aide-de-camp. When a fellow officer asked John Key why General McClellan's forces did not exercise their advantage at the battle of Antietam during September 1862, Key allegedly replied: "That is not in the game. The object is that neither army shall gain much advantage over the other; that both shall be kept in the field until they are exhausted, when we will make a compromise and save slavery." Upon learning of Key's statement, President Abraham Lincoln (1861–1865) summoned him to the White House on September 27, 1862, to interrogate him. Though there was no evidence of disloyalty, Lincoln dismissed Key from the military. Lincoln made it clear that the discharge was an honorable one, but Key begged the president for reinstatement. Ensuing communications from the president to Key are cited by the Gilder-Lehrman Institute of American History as among the most important 600 documents in U.S. history.

Key's setback was made more difficult when he learned that his only son was killed on the battlefield on October 8, 1862, at Perryville, Ky. In early 1863, Key relocated to Terre Haute, Ind., to practice law and sell insurance. For a while, he was a partner with attorney Daniel W. Voorhees, a Democratic congressman and a future U.S. senator from Indiana. In 1876 Key accepted an invitation from U.S. attorney general Alphonso Taft to negotiate cotton claims for the United States in England. In 1878 the family moved to the Georgetown section of the District of Columbia, where Key handled claims against foreign governments. He died in 1886 and was buried at the Holy Rood Cemetery in the Georgetown neighborhood of Washington, D.C.

McCormick, Mike. "Major Statement Got John James Key Booted from Military by Lincoln," *Terre Haute (Ind.) Tribune-Star*, June 16, 2002, D5.

——. *Terre Haute: Queen City of the Wabash*. Charleston, S.C.: Arcadia, 2005.

——. "Unlikely Key Conceives Lincoln's Letter Historic Significance," *Terre Haute (Ind.) Tribune-Star*, June 23, 2002, D5.

Mike McCormick

KEY, MARSHALL "COLONEL" (b. September 8, 1788, Fauquier Co., Va.; d. November 16, 1860, Louisville, Ky.). Marshall Key, a county clerk and a friend of Harriet Beecher Stowe, was the youngest son of James and Judith Keith and the nephew of U.S. Supreme Court chief justice John Marshall. Key relocated to Washington in Mason Co. with his father before 1815 and in 1815 purchased a brick Georgian townhouse, with an elegant curved staircase, that had been erected by Francis Taylor in 1807. On April 18, 1816, Key married Harriet Sellman, daughter of Dr. John and Elizabeth Farrar Sellman of Cincinnati. The couple had six children before Harriet died on July 14, 1832. Key owned a tavern in Washington and was elected Mason Co. clerk. Among his employees were his oldest son, **John James Key**, and Edward Allen Hannegan of Hamilton Co., Ohio. Both men became lawyers. Marshall Key sponsored young Hannegan's education at the law school at Transylvania University in Lexington and helped him establish a law practice in Indiana. Hannegan later became a U.S. congressman and a U.S. senator. After his wife's death, Marshall Key sent his daughter Elizabeth to the Western Female Institute in Cincinnati founded by Catharine Beecher of Hartford, Conn. During the summer of 1833, Colonel Key, as he was called, invited two teachers from his daughter's school, Mary Dutton and Harriet Beecher, to be house guests at the Key home in Washington for a few days. As entertainment, he escorted the young women to witness a slave auction at the Mason Co. Courthouse. According to tradition, it was this experience that inspired Harriet Beecher Stowe to write the controversial best-selling novel *Uncle Tom's Cabin* nearly 20 years later. On June 29, 1857, Key married widow Helen Bullitt Martin and moved to Louisville. He died there in 1860 and was buried at the Bullitt Family Cemetery, near the Oxmoor section of Louisville. The Marshall Key home in Washington is now the **Harriet Beecher Stowe Slavery to Freedom Museum**.

Bullitt Family Cemetery Records, Louisville, Ky.
Calvert, Jean, and John Klee. *Maysville, Kentucky: From Past to Present in Pictures*. Maysville, Ky.: Mason Co. Museum, 1983.
——. *The Towns of Mason County: Their Past in Pictures*. Maysville, Ky.: Maysville and Mason Co. Library Historical and Scientific Association, ca. 1986.

Mike McCormick

KEY, THOMAS MARSHALL, COLONEL (b. August 8, 1819, Washington, Ky.; d. January 15, 1869, Lebanon, Ohio). Thomas Marshall Key, a judge and a **Civil War** colonel, was the second son of **Marshall Key** and Harriet Sellman Key. After attending **Augusta College** in Augusta, Ky., he enrolled at Yale University in New Haven, Conn., and graduated in 1838, before his 19th birthday. While at Yale, he was a member of the exclusive secret society Skull and Bones. Key studied law in Cincinnati under Alphonso Taft, who later became U.S. attorney general under President Ulysses S. Grant (1869–1877); Taft was the father of President William Howard Taft (1909–1913).

When the Commercial Court of Cincinnati was organized in 1848, Key was appointed the first judge and served for five years. In 1858 he wed Elizabeth Boylan and was elected to the Ohio Senate as a Democrat. Following the attack by the Confederates on Fort Sumter, S.C., in 1861, Key was instrumental in securing unanimous legislative support in Ohio for the Union cause, and in April 1861 he was Ohio governor William Dennison's emissary to persuade Kentucky governor Beriah Magoffin (1859–1862) not to aid the Confederates. Named judge advocate and aide-de-camp on the staff of Union general George B. McClellan, Key was given the rank of colonel. While stationed in the nation's capital, he drafted and promoted the passage of a bill abolishing slavery in the District of Columbia. When President Abraham Lincoln (1861–1865) removed General McClellan from command on November 5, 1862, Key returned to Cincinnati, suffering from pulmonary disease believed to have been contracted during the Civil War Antietam campaign. He died of pneumonia in Lebanon, Ohio, in 1869 and was buried at Spring Grove Cemetery in Cincinnati.

Appletons' Cyclopaedia of American Biography. New York: D. Appleton, 1894.
Calvert, Jean, and John Klee. *Maysville, Kentucky: From Past to Present in Pictures*. Maysville, Ky.: Mason Co. Museum, 1983.
Spring Grove Cemetery Records, Cincinnati.

Mike McCormick

KIDWELL, ALVIN (b. November 27, 1893, Trimble Co., Ky.; d. April 12, 1974, Carrollton, Ky.). Trimble Co. native Alvin Kidwell, who became a Kentucky state senator, spent most of his life in Gallatin and Owen counties. He owned the Wiladean Nursery in Sparta for more than 40 years, retiring in 1969, and was a leader in the Kentucky Nurserymen's Association. An army veteran of **World War I** and an American Legion executive committee member, Kidwell often appeared around the region at veterans' groups and Democratic political meetings. He served as a state senator for 26 years (1941–1967) and as president pro tem of the Kentucky Senate during the administrations of governors Lawrence Wetherby (1950–1955) and Earle Combs (1959–1963). His 26th Senate District included Boone, Carroll, Gallatin, Henry, Oldham, Owen, and Trimble counties. He became the dean of the senate, a position that allowed him to vote on all commissions. Because of Kidwell's tenure and seniority in the Senate, and given the rules regarding who is in charge when the governor and the lieutenant governor are not present within the state, Kidwell was the acting governor of Kentucky some 26 times. He died in 1974 at the Carroll Co. Hospital in Carrollton at age 80, survived by his wife Josephine Graham Kidwell. After a Methodist Church ceremony, he was buried in the Warsaw Cemetery.

"Around the Towns," *KTS*, March 1, 1957, 3A.
"Former Senate Dean Dies," *KP*, April 15, 1974, 8.
"Former Senator Alvin Kidwell Dies at Age 80," *Gallatin County News*, April 18, 1974, 1.
Warsaw Cemetery Records. US GenWeb Project. www.rootsweb.com.

KINCAID LAKE STATE PARK. Located four miles northeast of Falmouth in Pendleton Co., along Ky. Rt. 159, the Kincaid Lake State Park was named for the creek that was dammed to create its initial 150-acre lake; the creek, in turn, derives its name from an early pioneer family who lived in the area. For many years, local attorney and prominent historian **Edward E. Barton** often said that the site would make a beautiful state park; he died in 1951, and the park was established in 1958. Kincaid Lake State Park is the result of a unified effort by Boone, Campbell, Kenton, and Pendleton counties. Planning began under Kentucky governor Lawrence A. Wetherby (1950–1955), but it was during the second term (1955–1959) of Kentucky governor A. B. "Happy" Chandler that noticeable progress was made.

Within Pendleton Co., it is generally recognized that George W. Jacobs and Rev. **Charles Lamont Conrad** were the leaders who organized the Kincaid Park Development Association. By July 1958, having acquired some 800 acres of land, the association deeded the property to the state. In August of that year, a contract was awarded to clear trees and brush along Kincaid Creek, and work commenced on a $131,000 earthen dam, 500 feet long and 62 feet high. Built by the Redman Construction Company of Alexandria, the dam was ready within a year, and the state began filling the lake and stocking it with fish, but fishing was not permitted until New Year's Day 1963. Five miles of shoreline were created. Boating, swimming, picnicking, and camping facilities were also constructed.

The administration of Kentucky governor Bert Combs (1959–1963) decided to open the park with the name Falmouth Lake State Park, assuming that the name would be identifiable to travelers; in 1970 the park's name was changed to Kincaid Lake State Park. The dam survived the flood of March 1964 (see **Flood of 1964**), when the water level rose to within six inches of the top of the dam. In 1980 the height of the dam was increased and the spillway was widened, and the lake grew to 183 acres. Over the years, many amenities have been added: a nine-hole golf course, a swimming pool, a 300-seat amphitheater, and a multipurpose building (dedicated September 7, 1980). The park has also been expanded by additional acreage. By 1965 some 100,000 visitors had come to the park; today that number is close to 500,000 annually. The park has become home to the Kentucky Wool Festival and the Kincaid Regional Theater. There is a movement under way to build a lodge at the park, logically the next step. Kincaid Lake State Park has provided some much-needed economic development for Pendleton Co. while delivering more than 900 acres of recreational opportunities to Northern Kentucky. It is one of the four state parks within the region.

A Brief History of the Kincaid Park Develop. Association (Incorporated) and the Final Report of the Treasurer on the Land Purchasing Fund. Falmouth, Ky.: Falmouth Outlook, 1964.
Falmouth Outlook, July 27, 1987.
Johnson, Omer. "Park Offers Variety of Pleasures," *CP*, June 24, 1987, 2B.
Kentucky State Parks. http://parks.ky.gov/.
"Kincaid Dam Is Progressing," *KP*, August 12, 1960, 1.
Reis, Jim. "Kincaid Park Result of Unified Effort," *KP*, July 27, 1987, 4K.

Mildred Belew

KINGSBURY, GILBERT W. "GIL" (b. April 27, 1909, Covington, Ky.; d. August 21, 1995, Lawrenceville, Ga.). Gilbert William Kingsbury's long and varied career as a journalist and a legislator took him from his native Covington, where he herded cows up Main St. as a boy, to New York City and Washington, D.C., and then back to Northern Kentucky. He was the son of William P. and Ruth Naomi Runge Kingsbury. His father worked in the shoe industry, and the family lived at 943 Main St. in Covington. Gil graduated from Holmes High School in 1927 and from the University of Kentucky in Lexington in 1933. He began his journalism career in Covington at the ***Kentucky Post***, where he worked as a reporter and editor before moving to a job with the nearby *Cincinnati Post*. He left newspaper work in 1939 to become an assistant professor at the University of Cincinnati.

Journalism still beckoned, and two years later Kingsbury joined the Crosley Broadcasting Company and moved to New York City to report for radio stations WLW in Cincinnati and WINS in New York City. In 1945 he became WLW's news correspondent in Washington, D.C. Kingsbury continued to work for WLW while serving on the staffs of two U.S. senators from Kentucky, Garrett L. Withers and Earle Clements. Returning to Northern Kentucky in 1951 as the Crosley Broadcasting Company's public relations director, Kingsbury bought a house on Edgewood Dr. in Fort Mitchell. A coworker at WLW said of Kingsbury's work for the radio station, "He did a lot of lobbying work . . . was very articulate and very knowledgeable on all government and legislative matters."

Kingsbury served in the Kentucky House of Representatives from 1958 to 1960. He and his friends, dubbed "the young turks," supported the successful candidacy of Democrat Bert Combs (1959–1963) for governor of Kentucky and criticized incumbent governor A. B. "Happy" Chandler (1935–1939, 1955–1959), who was also a Democrat. In 1962 Governor Combs appointed Kingsbury to the University of Kentucky Board of Trustees. Kingsbury once said his greatest civic accomplishment was working for the Kentucky Better Roads Council. There he helped establish a $100 million bond issue to pay for interstate highways and parks in 1960. Kingsbury died in 1995 at the home of his son in Georgia and was buried in Highland Cemetery in Fort Mitchell.

"Combs Names Kingsbury as UK Trustee," *CE,* June 24, 1962, 6A.

"Gilbert W. Kingsbury, Journalist, Educator," *KP,* August 23, 1995, 16A.

"Gilbert W. Kingsbury Served at UK, Crosley," *CE,* August 25, 1995, 4B.

Hicks, Jack. "Double-Edged Career Gives Kingsbury Twin Perspective," *CE,* August 12, 1981, 1A.

"Kingsbury Appointed as Aid to Senator; Annual Pay $10, 300," *CE,* February 3, 1949, 1.

"Tate Residence Sold to Gilbert Kingsbury," *KP,* June 14, 1951, 10.

Ann Hicks

KIRBY, DURWARD (b. August 24, 1911, Covington, Ky.; d. March 15, 2000, Fort Myers, Fla.). Durward Kirby was a famous television pioneer who played many roles in radio and television over the course of his career. The son of Homer Cleveland Kirby, a train dispatcher, and Alma K. Haglage Kirby, Durward was born at 1815 Greenup St. in Covington. He spent his childhood days there and attended **St. Benedict** School. During his adolescence, his family moved to nearby Fort Thomas, where he attended **St. Thomas** School and later **Highlands High School**. After his sophomore year, he moved with his family (because of his father's railroad career promotion) to Indianapolis, and there he attended Arsenal Technical High School, graduating in 1930.

Kirby started his career in **radio** while he was attending Purdue University, West Lafayette, Ind., as an engineering student. Later, he became a nationally known broadcaster at WLW radio in Cincinnati; there he gained recognition through his reporting about the **flood of 1937**. He also hosted big-band broadcasts for WLW from area nightclubs like the **Lookout House**. The National Broadcasting Company (NBC) took notice of his flood-news reporting and made him an offer he could not refuse, to broadcast for the national radio network from Chicago. During his work on *Club Matinee* radio broadcasts in Chicago, he was associated with Garry Moore for the first time.

After serving in **World War II**, Kirby returned to radio in New York City. His first television broadcast was in 1948. He was best known as the sidekick to Garry Moore on the *Garry Moore Show,* televised in the 1950s and 1960s. Kirby also worked alongside Carol Burnett on the *Garry Moore Show,* the program that helped Burnett achieve stardom. Further, he was the announcer for notable pioneer broadcasts such as the 1953 *Goodyear TV Playhouse*'s production of *Marty,* featuring Rod Steiger.

Kirby cohosted, under Allen Funt, the popular *Candid Camera* television show of the 1960s. Also remembered as a high-profile national broadcast advertisement announcer, he performed in one of the earliest color national television commercials. Kirby continued to play a part in television advertising through the 1970s, earning a Procter and Gamble Award as Outstanding Spokesperson in 1982. He received several other awards for his many broadcast achievements, including induction into the Greater Cincinnati Broadcasting Hall of Fame.

Kirby's popularity was such that he was literally a human giveaway prize for a contest on the *Garry Moore Show* in the 1950s: he spent one weekend as a house guest in the home of a Cleveland, Ohio, winner. Kirby's television fame was spoofed in the 1960s popular *Rocky and Bullwinkle* television cartoon series with a story about the search for the stolen "Kirward Derby," a hat that would make its wearer the smartest man in the world.

Kirby married Mary Paxton in her hometown of Indianapolis in 1941. He had two sons, Randall and Dennis. Durward Kirby authored an autobiography, *My Life . . . Those Wonderful Years!* and *Bits and Pieces of This and That,* as well as a children's book entitled *Dooley Wilson.* Kirby died in 2000 at the Shell Point Village retirement community in Fort Myers, Fla., and was buried at Coburn Cemetery in Sherman, Conn.

"Covington Native Kirby Was Famous TV Sidekick," *KP,* March 17, 2000, 20A.

"Deaths," *Ft. Myers (Fla.) News-Press,* March 16, 2000, 8B.

"Durward Kirby, 88, Sidekick to Television's Garry Moore," *NYT,* March 17, 2000, C19.

Florida Death Certificate No. 35351, for the year 2000.

Kirby, Durward. *My Life . . . Those Wonderful Years!* Charlotte Harbor, Fla.: Tabby House Books, 1992.

John Schlipp

Andy Kirk.

KIRK, ANDY (b. May 28, 1898, Newport, Ky.; d. December 11, 1992, New York City). Andrew Dewey Kirk was the last African American orchestra leader from the big band era who was born in Northern Kentucky. When he was a child, his family moved to Denver, where he studied music under Paul Whiteman's father, Wilberforce. He was a contemporary of nationally known band leaders Duke Ellington, Count Basie, and Jimmy Lunsford. Kirk's Clouds of Joy Orchestra became renowned throughout the nation when, in November 1929, they made their debut recording for the Brunswick label. During Kirk's early years, he maintained his home base in Kansas City, Mo., while he traveled throughout the United States. His band developed a Southeast Jazz style similar to that of Count Basie, also based in Kansas City. After his Clouds of Joy Orchestra broke up in 1948, Kirk continued to tour. During the 1950s he made several stops in the Greater Cincinnati area. On one occasion he added some local talent from Covington to his tour. According to **Nelson Burton**, "Andy Kirk came to Covington and picked up an outstanding left handed drummer named Hoppie and another fellow named Al Sears who lived down in the bottom of Bush Street." Al Sears later left Kirk and went to work with Duke Ellington.

Kirk played occasionally as he began to take up hotel management. During the 1970s, he worked at the Theresa Hotel in Harlem, N.Y. He remained a figure in the New York musical scene through his membership in the city's American Federation of Musicians until he developed Alzheimer's disease. His only child, Andy Kirk Jr., died in 1967. Andy Kirk Sr. died on December 11, 1992, in New York City and was buried there; he had no direct survivors.

Hitchcock, H. Wiley, and Stanley Sadie. *The New Grove Dictionary of American Music.* New York: Macmillan, 1986.

Larkin, Colin. "Andy Kirk." In *Encyclopedia of Popular Music,* vol. 4. 3rd ed. London: Muze, 1998.

Ledin, Lisa, and Simon Anderson. *Nelson Burton: My Life In Jazz.* Cincinnati: Clifton Hills Press, 2000.

Warous, Peter. "Andy Kirk, 94, Big-Band Leader Known for the Kansas City Sound," *NYT,* December 15, 1992, sec. B, 15.

Theodore H. H. Harris

KIWANIS CLUBS. See **Civic Associations**.

KLEIN, ROGER (b. December 8, 1911, Bellevue, Ky.; d. August 11, 2002, Alexandria, Ky.). Roger G. Klein, who coached high school and college tennis in Northern Kentucky for five decades, was the son of Albert F. and Edna Mueller Klein. A 1929 graduate of Bellevue High School (see **Bellevue Public Schools**), Klein went on to earn a BA from the University of Kentucky (UK) in 1933; he was captain of the UK men's tennis team. During the **Great Depression**, Klein strung tennis rackets at an athletic-goods store in Cincinnati and also gave private tennis lessons.

In 1942 Klein returned to Bellevue High School as a teacher and tennis coach. At that time, tennis was not sanctioned as a competitive sport by the Kentucky High School Athletic Association. It was Klein who helped keep the sport alive in Kentucky, organizing state tournaments at Bellevue High School from 1945 to 1951. Bellevue High School's tennis teams compiled a 419-98 record during Klein's 31 years as head coach. His players won 28 regional singles and doubles tennis championships. He retired from Bellevue High School in spring 1974. A few months later, he helped start both the male and female tennis programs at **Northern Kentucky University** (NKU). He had a 114-102 record as the men's tennis coach and a 72-63 record as the women's tennis coach. His men's tennis team won the Great Lakes Valley Conference (GLVC) title in 1986, and that year Klein was named GLVC Coach of the Year.

Klein retired from coaching tennis in 1987. He was inducted into the Northern Kentucky High School Athletic Directors Hall of Fame in 1984 and the NKU Athletic Hall of Fame in 2001. The tennis courts in Bellevue are named in honor of him. He died in 2002 and was buried at Evergreen Cemetery in Southgate.

Boehmker, Terry. "Klein Has Never-Ending Love Affair with Tennis," *KP*, April 11, 1981, 8K.

"Roger Klein, Longtime Tennis Coach at NKU, Bellevue High," *KP*, August 13, 2002, 6K.

"Roger Klein Was Called Mr. Tennis—Coach for Bellevue High," *KE*, August 15, 2002, C6.

Terry Boehmker

KLUEMPER, THEODORE (b. January 30, 1866, Covington, Ky.; d. July 18, 1946, Covington, Ky.). Early childhood responsibilities molded the character of Theodore Kluemper, who served the city of Covington in various ways. He was the son of J. Bernard and Maria Elisabeth Olges Kluemper, both immigrants from Hanover, Germany. In 1872 Bernard Kluemper died, leaving Elisabeth to raise Theodore and his four siblings. At the age of 13, Theodore ended his formal education and, along with his eldest brother, went to work as a cigar maker to support the family. He remained at the Ibold Cigar Company in Cincinnati, for more than 30 years, eventually becoming superintendent, until his political career began unfolding in Covington.

Theodore Kluemper.

Kluemper's long political career, from 1908 to 1940, rode the tide of several changes as Covington experimented with different forms of municipal government. Always a Democrat, he began this second career when he ran for city council, representing the fourth ward, in the election of 1908. He garnered the third-highest number of votes among the 12 elected council members. Reelected three more times, Kluemper served three of his four years on city council as its president, becoming the first in Covington's history to hold this office for three consecutive years. During these four years, both Latonia and West Covington were annexed to the City of Covington. It was a time of great expansion for the city.

In November 1912 the newly elected mayor, George "Pat" Philipps, named Kluemper as his chief of police, which at that time was an administrative appointment and did not require experience in law enforcement. Kluemper assumed these duties when chief Henry Schuler's term expired in May 1913.

The November election of 1913 saw a change in governance as the council's "strong boss" mayor system was replaced by a charter system, which called for an elected mayor and four commissioners. Kluemper was elected the city's first commissioner under the new system and served this term as commissioner of public works. He was reelected a commissioner in 1915 and again in 1917, serving those four years as commissioner of public safety. With this position came the responsibility of directing both the police and fire departments of the city.

During Kluemper's last term as safety commissioner, an incident occurred that turned out to be the highlight of his career. On March 5, 1918, Kluemper was about to enter a board of directors meeting of the Ninth Ward Building Association (see **Savings and Loan Associations**). The annual election of officers in Covington was just getting under way at the association's business office at 12th and Russell Sts., when three men, each aiming a pistol at Kluemper, barged in and demanded money. Kluemper, stalling for time in order to retrieve his firearm from his coat hanging nearby, quipped that the men were "kidding" and told them, "There is no money here." Within seconds, the men re-aimed and fired into the adjoining room, mortally wounding board members John Rehm, 82, and Andrew Nordmeyer, 67. Kluemper, now armed, shot and killed bandit Zeke Moran. The other two fled. Kluemper's ability to identify one of the intruders led to the capture and eventual sentencing and execution of Patrick Kearney and James Lawler. Two days after the shootings, in the midst of accolades, Kluemper returned to work humbly repeating that he "just did what he had to do." The bandage on his cheek revealed his close brush with death as he was shot too; he carried a scar for the rest of his life. As a matter of protocol, a full investigation was held. Theodore Kluemper was not only fully exonerated of any mishandling but was credited with preventing more deaths by his quick thinking. While some witnesses thought Kluemper really believed the bandits were kidding, his statement afterward indicated that he did not: "I saw something in their eyes that wasn't a joke. I knew it was the real thing."

In 1919 Kluemper lost his reelection bid. Using his vast city experience, he reentered the civilian workforce as head of the police department for the Kentucky Jockey Club. He was now in charge of security at various racetracks in Kentucky (including the local **Latonia Racecourse**) and in Illinois.

Again on the ballot in 1923, he was elected city commissioner and served in that capacity until 1929. In November 1929 another change was made as Covington embraced the new city manager system, whose proponents carried the election that year.

Kluemper was still popular, and in 1934 he was appointed city manager by Mayor Joseph Pieper and his four new commissioners. He held this appointment for six years, until Jack Maynard succeeded him in 1940. Thus, the "Old Gray Eagle," as Kluemper had become known, retired at age 73 from Covington politics.

Throughout his years as safety commissioner, Kluemper preached gun control, warned of potential bombings via mail, decried obscene movies, kept local gamblers and saloon keepers in check, and instructed the city to pay "loafers" three dollars a day to shovel snow from the railroad tracks. Although he held many important positions, no title was more respected than that of "Uncle Thee." A lifelong bachelor, Theodore Kluemper accepted the responsibility of head of household and breadwinner for his sister Anna and the several of her nine children who were still at home—the youngest only two years old when Anna's husband, Edward Bergman, died in 1916. Ten years later, Anna died, and Kluemper shouldered the responsibility of seeing the youngest of the children to adulthood.

In his last years, Kluemper made his home with his niece Mary Bergman Eicholz, who honored him with an 80th birthday party. A few months later, on July 18, 1946, he died at St. Elizabeth Hospital in Covington of a ruptured gall bladder. A personal friend, **Brent Spence**, a member of the U.S. House of Representatives, sent condolences from Washington, D.C. Services were held at Mother of God Church in Covington. Kluemper's grave in Mother of God Cemetery in Covington is marked with a simple stone reading "Theodore."

Elsener, Virginia Bergman. Interview by Carol Elsener Rekow, June 2006, Fort Wright, Ky.

Family documents: death card, letter from Brent Spence, and handwritten dates in *Catholic Gems or Treasures of the Church*.

Kentucky Death Certificate No. 15858, for the year 1946.

"Kluemper Elected—President of Council," *CE*, November 27, 1909, 10.

Willis, George Lee. *History of Kentucky Democracy.* Louisville, Ky.: Democratic Historical Society, 1935.

Carol Elsener Rekow

KNAPP, JOHN AUGUSTUS (b. December, 1852, Newport, Ky.; d. March 10, 1938, Los Angeles, Calif.). J. A. Knapp was the only son of John and Margaret Wente Knapp, who also had two daughters. The family resided in Newport. At age 21, after studying at Cincinnati's McMicken School of Design, J. A. Knapp exhibited paintings at the Cincinnati Industrial Exposition (1874) and became a freelance artist. He designed commercial art for United States Printing, Strowbridge Lithography, and Standard Publishing. Knapp married Emily Spring, a Cincinnatian, and in 1880 they had a daughter, Ethel Camilla. The family soon settled in nearby Norwood, Ohio, for many years living on Oak St. there. Their neighbors included the Lloyd brothers, noted pharmacologists **John Uri Lloyd** and **Curtis Gates Lloyd**. A mutual friend was Dr. Jirah Dewey Buck (1838–1916). Buck was an "eclectic" physician (that is, an alternative healer), a Freemason, and a theosophist and later became the president of the Theosophical Society in America. The Knapps joined the society, and J. A. Knapp became a Freemason and studied its esoteric symbolism. When John Uri Lloyd drafted a science fiction novel, *Etidorhpa,* he commissioned Knapp to illustrate it.

Knapp's wife Emily died in 1910. About 12 years later, he married Laura Brickly, an eclectic doctor, and they moved to Culver City, Calif., where Knapp designed posters for Thomas H. Ince (1882–1924), a pioneer in film production. The esoterist Manly P. Hall (1901–1990) sponsored a lecture by Dr. Laura Knapp, in which she spoke on human anatomy from an occult viewpoint. The occasion brought J. A. Knapp into contact with Hall, who was then researching mysticism and planning an encyclopedic survey. Already familiar with the curious graphics in *Etidorhpa,* Hall hired Knapp to illustrate the encyclopedia (now called *The Secret Teachings of All Ages*). Knapp was the illustrator of many of Hall's subsequent publications, including an ambitious Tarot deck of cards (1929). Providing a compendium of doctrines from earlier Tarotists, the cards are eagerly sought by collectors. Knapp's daughter Ethel Knapp Behrman became a poet and published a book of poems, *Doorways,* for which her father designed the cover. J. A. Knapp died in California in 1938 and was cremated.

Decker, Ronald, and Michael Dummett. *A History of the Occult Tarot, 1870–1970.* London: Duckworth, 2002.

"Rites for Father of Cincinnati Poet Held," *CTS,* March 16, 1938, 2.

Ronald Decker

KNAUF, ROBERT (b. August 12, 1924, Covington, Ky.; d. January 15, 2006, Fort Thomas, Ky.). Robert Knauf, a music teacher and performer, was the son of William J. and Annabelle Kuhn Knauf. He grew up in Covington, where he graduated from **Holmes High School**. He earned his BA in music from the University of Cincinnati and his MFA from the University of Kentucky in Lexington and did postgraduate work at Boston University in Massachusetts.

He and his wife Marguerite married in 1948, and the couple had three children. Robert taught music at **Highlands High School** in Fort Thomas for more than 25 years and then took a full-time position at **Northern Kentucky University** (NKU) in Highland Heights, where he had been working as a part-time music instructor. He later became director of NKU's Music Department. At the time of his retirement in 1990, he was serving as the school's vice president for community relations. In 1990 NKU began awarding an annual Robert Knauf Scholarship, in his honor.

Knauf was personable, quick-witted, and a master of repartee. Over the years, he attempted, briefly, to become a professional singer and standup comedian, sang in operettas at the University of Kentucky, and was choral director for the Cincinnati's May Festival and for the city's Choral and Orchestral Music Festival. He was a member of the First Presbyterian Church of Fort Thomas and also belonged to the Newport Elks Club and the Fort Thomas Lions Club. He was an avid sports fan, especially of baseball, golf, horseracing, horseshoes, and tennis.

Knauf died at age 81 in the Highlands of Fort Thomas nursing home in Fort Thomas. Funeral services were held at the Highland United Methodist Church, and he was cremated. His wife of 58 years, Marguerite, survived him.

Knauf, Jim. Telephone interview by Jack Wessling, February 26, 2007.

"Robert Knauf, Music Teacher, Performer," *KP,* January 19, 2006, A8.

KNECHT, ROBERT F. (b. October 27, 1921, Fort Thomas, Ky.; d. February 7, 1944, Anzio Beach, Italy). Robert Knecht, who was killed during service in **World War II**, was the son of Joseph and Lucy Dietrich Knecht. He graduated from Highlands High School in 1937 and enrolled at the Cincinnati College of Pharmacy. During college, he worked at Gottschall's Hy-Pure Pharmacy in Newport. He graduated from the College of Pharmacy in 1941 and worked at Schulker's Pharmacy in Fort Thomas until he was inducted into the U.S. Army in October 1942. Knecht was sent to North Africa, assigned to the 95th Evacuation Field Hospital as a pharmacist. Gen. Mark Clark's 5th Army landed at Anzio on January 22, 1944. The landings went well, but the anticipated breakthrough did not occur. The beach area was quickly jammed with frontline troops, supplies, and hospitals; there were no safe areas. Medical installations were bombed and shelled throughout the landing, and the hospital area came to be known to front-line troops as "Hell's Half Acre." On February 7, 1944, bombs from a German plane fell on the administration and operating tents; 28 hospital personnel and patients died and 64 were wounded. Among those killed was Robert Knecht.

"Athlete Victim of German Bombing of Salerno Hospital," *CE,* March 5, 1944, 18.

"Corporal Robert F. Knecht." *Cincinnati Academy of Pharmacy News* 14, no. 5 (1944): 9.

"Nazi Raid on Hospital in Italy Kills Ft. Thomas Pharmacist," *CE,* March 3, 1944, 13.

Dennis B. Worthen

KNIGHTS OF COLUMBUS. The Knights of Columbus (K of C) remain an active Catholic organization throughout Northern Kentucky. The Knights began in New Haven, Conn., in 1881 when Rev. Michael J. McGivney called a group of his male parishioners to meet in St. Mary Church. They formed an organization to encourage Catholic men in the practice of their faith and foster fraternal ties among them. The new group was chartered by the State of Connecticut in 1882 and soon set up its own insurance company for members and their families. It quickly developed into a nationwide and eventually an international organization. Today, the Knights of Columbus is involved in many activities for the Catholic Church, including prolife work, vocations programs, student loans, and many other social endeavors.

The Knights of Columbus developed a structure based on governing councils, with its Supreme Council and councils on the state and local levels. The Kentucky state council was established in Louisville in September 1903. The oldest local Knights of Columbus council in Kentucky is the Bishop Carrell Council 702 in Covington (named for George A. Carrell, the first bishop of the Diocese of Covington), founded in February 1902. The Bishop Carrell Council's first location was on E. 11th St. near the site of the new St. Mary Cathedral that was being constructed within the same block. A later headquarters for the council was built on Madison Ave. in Covington in 1929. This building later became part of Villa Madonna College (see **Thomas More College**), after the Knights of Columbus sold it to the Diocese of Covington. Today, that building is part of **Senior Services of Northern Kentucky**, located at 1028 Madison Ave.

New councils of the Knights of Columbus sprouted up in Northern Kentucky over the next several decades: the Bishop William T. Mulloy Council in Newport (1908), the Maysville Council in Maysville (1909), the Fr. James Kehoe Council in Ludlow (1914), the Fr. Bealer Council in Erlanger (1954), the Augusta-Brooksville Council in Augusta (1960), the Fr. Louis DeJaco Council in Alexandria (1962), the Msgr. Ahmann Council in Covington (1962), the Bishop Ackerman Council in Hebron (1963), and the Msgr. Borgias Lehr Council in Southgate (1972). The Mulloy Council, which operated for 62 years out of the Southgate House along E. Second St. in Newport, in 1976 moved to a former fishing lake in Cold Spring at Ky. Rts. 8 and 1192, near Brent. The Mulloy group has since moved to Fort Thomas.

Schrode, George E., ed. *Knights of Columbus, Kentucky State Council*. Paducah, Ky.: Turner, 1993.

Thomas S. Ward

KNOW-NOTHING PARTY (AMERICAN POLITICAL PARTY). The Know-Nothing Party, or American Political Party, was born out of the growing anti-immigration and anti-Catholic sentiment that developed in the United States during the 1840s and 1850s. Northern Kentucky, with its substantial immigrant population, experienced Know-Nothing activity in the mid-19th century. Although the Know-Nothing Party became a national political power, peaking in 1856, it was not successful in electing a president and did not last long in the national political arena. The Know-Nothing Party, like the American **Whig Party**, foundered upon the growing sectionalism in U.S. politics over the question of states' rights, in particular, how states' rights related to national expansion and the future of slavery.

The growth of local Know-Nothing Party chapters during the 1850s occurred primarily in cities with relatively large foreign-born populations and was based upon a secret organization called the Order of the Star-Spangled Banner, formed in New York City in 1849. Members of this order were told to reply that they knew nothing when asked about the organization.

Kentucky began to see the emergence of nativism during the late 1840s, yet in Northern Kentucky only Kenton and Campbell counties had foreign-born populations amounting to more than 10 percent of total population, according to the 1850 census. By 1860 Mason Co. joined that list. Nativists organized secret fraternal lodges, or clubs, in most of Kentucky's larger cities before 1854, and these proved useful for political organizing, just as the earlier Whig and Democratic political clubs had been.

Antiforeign sentiment appeared in Kentucky politics as early as 1847, when Stephen F. J. Trabue unsuccessfully ran for the U.S. Congress on a nativist platform in the eighth district, where Whig national leader Henry Clay held the seat. Nativist sentiment was also on display at Kentucky's 1849 Constitutional Convention, where Garrett Davis gave two anti-Catholic speeches and a resolution was made by a "Bluegrass Whig" to limit the voting and office-holding rights of the foreign-born in the state. T. R. Whitney, president of the Know-Nothing Party, was quoted as saying: "Know-Nothingism emerged in Kentucky's local elections of 1854 as an independent anti-party movement that denounced Whigs and Democrats alike." The Know-Nothing Party's first electoral successes came during the summer of 1854, when its candidates were elected in Louisville and Lexington. In November Dr. R. G. Dobyns, the Know-Nothing candidate, became mayor of Maysville, and a clerk of court in Covington aligned with the party. Nativist sentiment and the growing popularity of the Know-Nothings led several formerly Whig newspapers to affiliate with the movement. Local newspapers in Kentucky gave voice to the new party and increased its standing in their communities and throughout the state.

The Covington election of January 1855 illustrates the rapidity with which the Know-Nothings erupted onto the political scene. Because of a budgetary crisis, special city elections were held in Covington; all but two incumbents were returned to office. All of the returning incumbents were Know-Nothings. The election resulted in a complete sweep by the Know-Nothing ticket of 18 contested offices, with incumbent Burshrod W. Foley winning reelection as mayor, C. Butts as sheriff, and **William Ernst** as president of the council. The editor of the Covington *Journal* was pleased with the results, declaring, "if the mysterious order will make it a point in all elections to give us as good a set of officers as they did on Saturday last, there will be very little cause for complaint."

The Covington elections were soon followed, in early March, by Newport's municipal elections. Here Democrats, or "Wild Cats" as they were known locally, managed to retain their majority on the council and won the mayor's race by 34 votes. In May, however, Newport elected two Know-Nothing candidates to the office of justice of the peace.

Successes in local elections in Covington emboldened the Know-Nothings to run candidates at the state level and provided the impetus for incumbents in Northern Kentucky from both the Whig and the Democrat parties to consider adopting the American Political Party's label. Former Whig **Samuel F. Swope**, from Pendleton Co., became the Know-Nothing candidate for U.S. Congress. Former Whigs A. H. Johns and **John W. Menzies** ran as Know-Nothing candidates to represent Kenton Co. in the Kentucky House of Representatives. **Thomas L. Jones**, of Newport, became a Know-Nothing candidate and represented Campbell Co. in the Kentucky House, while Gen. William B. Crupper, a Bracken Co. Democrat, apparently flirted with the Know-Nothing movement but remained a Democrat. The Covington *Journal* reported that in Grant Co. the Know-Nothings had carried all districts except one in the county's recent magisterial elections.

The speed with which the popularity of the Know-Nothings grew was a surprise to Whig political leaders, from whose party the majority of the nativist adherents had come. Yet, it was only after the local elections of 1854 and 1855 that Whig Party leaders realized the extent to which their party was affected. Without strong local party organizations, many Whig leaders concluded that their party was no longer capable of winning statewide elections. Whig leaders began joining the Know-Nothings in 1855, quickly assuming state party leadership positions.

The Know-Nothing ticket won an enormous political victory in the summer of 1855, with Charles S. Morehead (1855–1859), a former Whig, taking the governorship of Kentucky. The Know-Nothing Party also carried both houses in the state legislature, winning 61 out of 100 seats in the House of Representatives and increasing its majority in the Senate from 10 to 14. The party also claimed victories in six of Kentucky's 10 U.S. congressional seats. The Know-Nothing statewide and national successes rested upon the organizational capacity of its local branches and the growing support of the state's formerly pro-Whig newspapers.

In essence, after a short period of spontaneous, dynamic growth in conjunction with the founding of Know-Nothing chapters, particularly in Louisville, Lexington, Covington, and Maysville, the party apparatus, to a great extent, was soon captured by the political remnants of the Whig Party. While the influence of former Whigs helped propel the Know-Nothings to majorities in the two houses of the Kentucky legislature, it also lessened the strength of the anti-immigration and anti-Catholic sentiment espoused by the more radical membership of the party. However, some elements of the Know-Nothing Party continued to engage in antiforeign diatribes, and several violent nativist–led episodes occurred. One such bloody action took place in Louisville in April 1855 and is cited as the most violent election-day riot in Kentucky's history.

Perhaps no Northern Kentuckian is more closely associated with the Know-Nothings than E. B. Bartlett of Covington. A Democrat and a slave owner, Bartlett was active in Covington society and helped to form a local militia unit for the **Mexican War** in 1846. He was elected circuit court clerk in Kenton Co. in 1851. Bartlett probably became associated with the Know-Nothings when the party's national council met in Cincinnati in 1854. By June 1855, he had been elected national president of the Know-Nothings at the party's convention in Philadelphia, Pa. In July 1855, Bartlett and **George B. Hodge** of Newport attended an American Political Party ratification meeting in Louisville, where a speech Bartlett delivered received high praise. The next month, Bartlett was also elected president of the Kentucky Know-Nothings at a quarterly session of the party council in Louisville, while another Covingtonian, A. D. Madeira, was named recording and corresponding secretary.

The Know-Nothings reached their zenith nationally in December 1855, seating 43 members in the U.S. House of Representatives. In 1855 and again in 1856, Bartlett helped fashion the Know-Nothings' national platform, which prioritized the preservation of the Union; however, the party was unable to find a compromise on the issue of slavery that enabled its members to remain politically united. The 1856 presidential elections sounded the Know-Nothings' death knell. The party's presidential candidate, former Whig Millard Fillmore, received 21 percent of the vote and carried only Maryland, and the party's congressional delegation dropped to 12 representatives.

As successful as the party initially appeared to be in the state of Kentucky and on the national stage, almost immediately Know-Nothings began to have internal disputes over the same question that had plagued the Whigs: the future of slavery. Following the failure Fillmore to be elected U.S. president, the national Know-Nothing Party fell apart.

Some Know-Nothings, including Kentucky U.S. congressman Samuel Swope, left the party. Swope did not stand for reelection in 1856 but later sought national office as a Republican. Know-Nothing divisions in Kentucky were based upon whether one had faith in the ability of the national government successfully to solve the dilemma posed by the question of slavery. Increasingly, voters supported the Democrats as the party to preserve the Union.

E. B. Bartlett oversaw the last national council meeting of the Know-Nothing Party in Louisville in June 1857. In the state elections that followed, Know-Nothing candidates won 21 out of 38 state Senate seats and 39 out of 97 House seats but still lost control of the Kentucky legislature. In 1858 Bartlett ran for clerk of the court of appeals in Covington. By 1860 he had left Covington and moved to Memphis, Tenn.

Between 1856 and 1860, Democrats won every Kentucky statewide election; however, the remnants of the Know-Nothing Party held together and changed the party's name to the Opposition. In 1859 the Opposition successfully ran a slate of candidates, winning all statewide offices with the exception of the governorship. The party won a majority in the Kentucky House of Representatives and the Senate and split the state's 10-seat U.S. congressional delegation evenly with the Democrats. In 1860 the Opposition, remnants of the Whigs and the Know-Nothings, and former Democrats who hoped to save the Union, all joined together to form the Constitutional Union Party.

The 1860 presidential election was the last hurrah of what had been known as the Know-Nothings and their spin-off the Constitutional Union Party. In a four-man race for president, U.S. senator John Bell of Tennessee, the Constitutional Union candidate, carried Kentucky but came in last nationally in the race. With the election of Republican Abraham Lincoln (a former Whig) as president (1861–1865) and the secession of several southern states, politics in Kentucky turned to the question of whether the state would remain in the Union.

In early 1861, two new political parties were formed in Kentucky. One, the Union Democracy Party, wanted to remain in the Union; the other, the Southern Rights Party, looked to move the state closer to the South. The Kentucky legislature eventually chose to remain neutral. That summer, the Union Democracy Party overwhelmingly won the elections in Kentucky, and soon afterward Kentucky became closely associated with the Union's cause.

Billington, Ray Allen. *The Protestant Crusade, 1800–1860: A Study of the Origins of American Nativism.* Chicago: Quadrangle Books, 1964.
Brown, Thomas. *Politics and Statesmanship: Essays on the American Whig Party.* New York: Columbia Univ. Press, 1985.
Holt, Michael F. *The Rise and Fall of the American Whig Party: Jacksonian Politics and the Onset of the Civil War.* New York: Oxford Univ. Press, 1999.
Kentucky Weekly News, January 15, 1858.
LVR, June 13, 1846.
Overdyke, W. Darrell. *The Know-Nothing Party in the South.* Baton Rouge: Louisiana State Univ. Press, 1950.
Volz, Harry August, III. "Party, State, and Nation: Kentucky and the Coming of the American Civil War," PhD diss., Univ. of Virginia, 1982.

J. T. Spence

KNOX, FERMON WENDELL (b. August 31, 1923, Dime Box, Tex.; d. October 23, 2001, Erlanger, Ky.). Civil rights leader Fermon Knox was the son of Albert and Carrie Lovings Knox. He was raised in Lee Co., Tex. While at Freeman High School there, he excelled in basketball and football. When he graduated, he received many athletic scholarships for college, but **World War II** began and he was drafted into the U.S. Army. He served in the Philippines for four years and while there contracted malaria. Returning to the states, he was treated at a military hospital in Lexington. When Knox recovered, he was able to attend nearby Kentucky State College (University) in Frankfort on a football scholarship that had been offered to him earlier. Knox became more politically and socially conscious of the world around him during his college years. He, like many other African American soldiers returning from World War II, was no longer willing to accept second-class citizenship after fighting for his country.

After college, he worked for the Monmouth Life Insurance Company, and in 1958 he was transferred to Cincinnati to manage the company's Cincinnati–Northern Kentucky district. He lived in Covington. During the height of the civil rights movement, Knox served as the president of the Northern Kentucky Branch of the **NAACP** and later was the president of its regional division. As he helped to organize and participated in marches, protests, and freedom rides across the United States, he met and worked with such leaders as Rev. **Anthony Deye**, Medgar Evers, Lyman T. Johnson, Mae Street Kidd, Martin Luther King Jr., Fred Shuttlesworth, Roy Wilkins, and his college classmate and friend Whitney M. Young Jr.

Knox was instrumental in lobbying both the Kentucky legislature and the U.S. Congress for passage of the housing desegregation laws and other civil rights laws. He helped to bring about the desegregation of the Covington Public Schools (see **Covington Independent Schools**). He planned the state march on Frankfort in 1965 and served as one of the speakers on that occasion; coordinated efforts in the hiring of African Americans in local businesses; became the first executive director of the Northern Kentucky Community Action Commission; and served as the executive director of the Louisville Community Action Commission. After 31 years in the executive management of nonprofit organizations, Knox retired in 1997 as the chief executive officer of the Emmanuel Community Center in Cincinnati.

Knox was a lifelong member of the Alpha Phi Alpha fraternity. He served as the Kentucky A.M.E. Church Conference lay organization president and historiographer and was an active member of St. James A.M.E. Church in Covington for 43 years. He also served on the boards of many nonprofit organizations. Governor Louie B. Nunn (1967–1971) honored Knox as a Kentucky Colonel. Knox was also nominated to the Kentucky Commission on Human Rights Hall of Fame in 2000 and 2001. He died of a stroke at his home in 2001 and was buried at Forest Lawn Memorial Park in Erlanger.

"Civil Rights Pioneer Dies," *KE*, October 26, 2001, B1.
Knox, Fermon, to Benny Butler, April 1999, Northern Kentucky African American Heritage Task Force Oral History, Archives, Northern Kentucky Univ., Highland Heights, Ky.
KP, June 28, 2001, 4K.
Seguin (Tex.) Gazette Enterprise, January 31, 2001.
"Veteran Rights Crusader Dies," *KP*, October 25, 2001, 1.

Jessica Knox-Perkins

KNOXVILLE. Knoxville is a beautiful little village situated in the west end of Pendleton Co. along the DeMossville-Knoxville turnpike, Ky. Rt. 467, about five miles east of the Grant Co. town of Dry Ridge. In 1889 Knoxville was thriving. It had 30 residents, including Dr. J. T. Scott, a physician-surgeon, and Mrs. L. Stady, who ran the Knoxville House, a hotel and barroom. There were four general stores; a post office; a school; a cemetery; one drug store; Baptist, Christian, and Methodist Episcopal churches; an Odd Fellows Hall; a tobacco warehouse; a blacksmith; a steam grist and saw mill, operated by A. C. Morris; a shoe shop, operated by H. Dahlenburg; and a normal school for teacher training, run by Professor Brough of Williamstown. The town is home to two churches, the Knoxville Baptist Church and the Knoxville Christian Church.

Belew, Mildred Boden. *The First 200 Years of Pendleton County.* Falmouth, Ky.: M. B. Belew, n.d. [ca. 1994].

Mildred Belew

KOREAN WAR (June 25, 1950—July 27, 1953). Like all parts of the nation, Northern Kentucky sent military personnel to fight in the Korean War. At the conclusion of **World War II**, the Korean Peninsula was divided in two. The North was occupied by the armed forces of the Soviet Union, while the South was occupied by the United States. Shortly after both sides withdrew their occupation forces, troop clashes began between the Communist North and the Democratic South. The North wanted to unify the peninsula under Communist rule and by June 1950 had built up its army enough to launch a full-scale invasion of the South on June 25, 1950, aided by the Soviet Union with equipment, pilots, and military advisers. The North took control of much of the South before United Nations forces, primarily made up of U.S. troops, intervened. The first battle fought by American forces occurred on July 5, 1950. The first Northern Kentuckian killed in the war was Campbell Co.'s Pvt. George Schoulthies of the 24th Infantry Division, who was killed after being taken prisoner on July 11, 1950. Between July and November 1950, heavy fighting took place. The North Koreans were beaten back across the 38th Parallel, and almost all of North Korea was occupied. Cpl. Wayne Morgan of Bracken Co. fought in the Defense of Taejon along with combat engineers and was awarded the Bronze Star for this action.

In October 1950, China warned the Allies to stop their advance toward the Chinese border, and in November the Chinese invaded Korea, causing U.N. forces to retreat as far south as Pusan. One of the first major battles between U.S. and Chinese troops was at the Chosin Reservoir in North Korea. Lt. Col. Donald C. Faith, an Indiana native who had attended high school in Fort Thomas, Ky., served at Chosin. He led several counterattacks against advancing Chinese forces in order to free his encircled men. During the action, he was wounded and later died. For his bravery at Chosin, Faith was awarded the Congressional **Medal of Honor**. On March 23, 1951, the 187th Airborne Infantry Regiment made the last combat jump of the war at Munsan-Ni to cut off and destroy a large enemy force north of the 38th Parallel. Bracken Co.'s Pfc. Eugene Estep of the 187th was killed in action there on March 25. By July 1951, the battle lines had stabilized just north of the 38th Parallel. The final two years of the war were spent in a dug-in tug-of-war for hills and valleys along the 38th Parallel as tense peace negotiations were held in Kaesong and Panmunjom. Because of disagreement over a U.N. command proposal for voluntary reparation of prisoners of war, which the Communists staunchly opposed, the war dragged on for almost another year and a half before a cease-fire agreement went into effect on July 27, 1953. The final Northern Kentucky combat casualty of the war was Kenton Co.'s Pfc. Louis W. Baldwin of the 1st Marine Division, who was killed on July 26, 1953. Following the end of hostilities, a demilitarized zone was set up in almost the exact same location as the original dividing line between the North and the South. The DMZ is still being manned by U.S. troops today.

Northern Kentuckians served in every branch of the armed forces. Some volunteered, some were drafted, and some who had been in World War II were recalled to active duty. Of the 868 Kentuckians killed in action, 69 were from the 11 Northern Kentucky counties, as follows: Boone, 3; Bracken, 7; Campbell, 18; Carroll, 2; Gallatin, 1; Grant, 8; Kenton, 23; Mason, 2; Owen, 1; Pendleton, 3; and Robertson, 1. Of these, 1 was Air Force, 55 were Army, 12 were Marine Corps, and 1 was Navy. Although the Kentucky National Guard had units activated during the time of the war, no Northern Kentucky units saw action in Korea; however, some individual Northern Kentuckians serving as replacements in other units, both guard and reserve, saw service in Korea.

The highest-ranking officer to serve from Northern Kentucky was **Jesse Auton**, an Air Force brigadier general from Kenton Co., who served as director of fighter operations for the Strategic Air Command. As a colonel in 1950, Auton flew nine combat missions, including one aboard a Boeing B-29 Superfortress. Northern Kentucky's only Air Force casualty of the war was from Kenton Co., Airman 1st Class Thomas Junior Pettit, who was lost while serving as a gunner on a B-29 of the 28th Bomb Squadron—his aircraft was shot down during a mission on June 10, 1952. The highest-ranking Northern Kentucky soldier killed in action during the war was Grant Co.'s Sgt. 1st Class Thomas P. Pettit of the 25th Infantry Division, who was killed on June 6, 1951.

Kleber, John E., ed. *The Kentucky Encyclopedia*. Lexington: Univ. Press of Kentucky, 1992.

Korean War Project. www.koreanwar.org/index1.html (accessed May 10, 2007).

The National Archives. "U.S. Military Personnel Who Died from Hostile Action (Including Missing and Captured) in the Korean War, 1950–1957." www.archives.gov/research/korean-war/casualty-lists/ky-by-town.html (accessed April 10, 2007).

Reis, Jim. "Memories of Korean War Still Linger," *KP*, July 11, 1988, 4K.

Snow, Robert. "A Veteran Remembered: The Jesse Auton Story." *Northern Kentucky Better Living Magazine*, November 4, 2002, 6.

Veteran-related documents by Caroline R. Miller, Bracken Co. Historical Society, Brooksville, Ky.

Robert B. Snow

KRAUS, BILL (b. June 26, 1947, Cincinnati, Ohio.; d. January 11, 1986, San Francisco, Calif.). William James "Bill" Kraus, a gay activist and politician (see **Gays and Gay Rights**), was the son of Michael S. and Mary E. Schwartz. For his first 14 years, he resided at 12 Idaho Ave. in what was then called S. Fort Mitchell (now Fort Mitchell). He attended **Blessed Sacrament** Parish Grade School through the seventh grade, before his family moved to Colerain Township in northern Cincinnati in 1960, where he completed eighth grade at St. Anne's Parish School and attended St. Xavier High School in Cincinnati, graduating with honors in 1965. While at St. Xavier High School, he was an avid participant in the St. Xavier Forensics Club. In 1965 he began college at Dartmouth College, Portsmouth, N.H., but after one year transferred to Ohio State University (OSU) at Columbus. He earned a BA in 1969 and later an MA in history at OSU. In the late 1960s and early 1970s, while at OSU, Kraus was an activist-organizer for anti-**Vietnam War** protests on campus.

In 1972 he moved to San Francisco and began his career in gay political organization and local Democratic Party politics. He started with on-the-street voter registration for the San Francisco Democratic Party. In 1977 Kraus became the coordinator for Get Out the Vote for Harvey Milk in gay candidate Harvey Milk's third, and finally successful, attempt to win office as a San Francisco city supervisor. Milk, in turn, appointed Kraus as one of his aides on the San Francisco Board of Supervisors and then in 1978 made him co–campaign manager of San Franciscans Against Proposition 6, a proposed anti-gay state initiative authored by state senator John Briggs, which would have banned gay teachers from obtaining California teacher's credentials. In the early weeks of the statewide campaign, the public support for this proposition was strong, but after a series of debates between San Francisco city supervisor Milk and state senator Briggs and a "no on 6" editorial opinion article by California ex-governor Ronald Reagan, public perception of Proposition 6 shifted dramatically, resulting in its defeat by a 2-to-1 margin. Because of Kraus's success in managing the San Franciscans Against Proposition 6, he came to the attention of local Democratic Party leaders. After the assassination of Milk in late November 1978, Kraus became an aide to and campaign manager for Milk's replacement, Harry Britt, in his successful first and second reelection bids following appointment as Milk's replacement.

In 1979 the San Francisco Gay Democratic Club was renamed the Harvey Milk Club in Milk's honor, and Kraus became its president for the next two years. Kraus was also chosen by the California Democratic Party as a Ted Kennedy convention delegate to the 1980 Democratic National Convention in New York City. As a Kennedy delegate in 1980, Kraus was selected as one of the 200 or so convention delegates that made up the Democratic Party Platform Committee. While a member of the Platform Committee, Kraus delivered a powerful gay-rights address before the committee that led to the strengthening of the gay-rights plank in the 1980 Democratic Party Platform.

In 1982 Kraus became cochair of California congressman Phil Burton's successful reelection campaign. Subsequently, Kraus was appointed to Congressman Burton's office as an administrative assistant, where he was successful in organizing the first-ever congressional AIDS epidemic hearings on research funding in 1984 and 1985. Following Congressman Burton's death in 1984, Kraus continued as a congressional aide to Sala Burton, who was appointed to complete her late husband's elected term in the House of Representatives. Kraus continued with his project for AIDS research funding, and Congress approved its first-ever appropriation for AIDS research.

In the early 1980s, as the AIDS epidemic expanded, particularly in San Francisco, Kraus became a forceful and successful advocate for the closure of gay bathhouses, in an effort to stem the spread of the disease. In early October 1984, Kraus was himself diagnosed with AIDS. He followed in the steps of Rock Hudson to the Pasteur Clinic in Paris, France, where there was ongoing experimental treatment for AIDS, and resided there for several months as an outpatient. In fall 1985 he returned to his home in San Francisco, died of AIDS on January 11, 1986, and was cremated.

After Kraus's death, Randy Shilts, a close friend who was a reporter for the *San Francisco Chronicle,* began a project to document the politics and unfolding of the AIDS epidemic. The result was Shilts's bestselling book *And the Band Played On,* which prominently chronicled Kraus's work to try to stem the epidemic in San Francisco and his advocacy for federal funding of AIDS research. The book was subsequently produced as the movie *And the Band Played On,* with Ian McKellan playing the role of Kraus. The Bill Kraus Meadow in Corona Heights Park in San Francisco, affording a spectacular view of the city, was named for him.

"Fighter for Gay Rights Dies of AIDS at 38," *San Francisco Chronicle*, January 13, 1986, 7.

"Hero to Thousands, Unknown at Home: Ft. Mitchell Native Joined AIDS Fight Early," *KP*, September 10, 1993, 1.

Shilts, Randy. *And the Band Played On: Politics, People, and the AIDS Epidemic*. New York: St. Martin's Press, 1987.

———. *The Mayor of Castro Street: The Life and Times of Harvey Milk*. New York: St. Martin's Press, 1982.

Michael Kraus

KROGER, BERNARD H. "BARNEY" (b. January 24, 1860, Cincinnati, Ohio; d. July 21, 1938, Wianno, Cape Cod, Mass.). Barney Kroger, the grocer who began the Kroger grocery chain, was the fifth of 10 children of John Henry and Mary Gertrude Schlebbe Kroger. German immigrant John Kroger first lived in Covington before moving to Cincinnati, where he married Mary Schlebbe on October 31, 1850, at Holy Trinity Catholic Church in the city's West End. John died when Barney was 13, while the family lived on Central Ave. in Cincinnati above the family's dry-goods store. Barney quit school and worked in a drugstore, on a farm, and later as a door-to-door salesman for the Great Northern and Pacific Tea Company. In 1883, with a partner, he opened his first grocery in Cincinnati at 66 Pearl St. A year later, having survived a flood and a delivery-wagon accident, and following the departure of his partner, he opened a second store.

While delivering groceries to customers, which was a common practice at the time, Kroger met the Jansen family of Newport. He married their daughter Mary Emily "Minnie" Jansen on April 28, 1886, at Newport's **Immaculate Conception Catholic Church**. The ceremony was performed by Father James M. McNerney. The couple had seven children. The family lived throughout most of the 1890s in Newport at 624 Monroe Street. On April 22, 1899, having undergone minor surgery at Cincinnati's Jewish Hospital, Mary died from an overdose of an ether anesthetic. She was age 32 at the time.

By 1902, when he incorporated his company as the Kroger Grocery and Baking Company, Kroger was operating some 40 stores, some of them in Northern Kentucky, with total annual revenues of $1.75 million. In the mid-1920s, the Kroger Company acquired, for roughly $800,000, the J. Peter Foltz Grocery and Baking Company, which was a grocery chain of more than 150 units. Covington's Peter Foltz, who lived on Pike St., had stores in Louisville and in Hamilton, Ohio, so Kroger gained a quick entrée into the Louisville market as well as 15 additional stores in Northern Kentucky. In 1928 Barney Kroger sold his interest in the company and retired, having married a second wife, Alice Flynn Maher.

In 1929, after a dramatic growth period of acquiring small urban neighborhood grocery store chains, the Kroger Company reached its peak number of outlets, over 5,500. Within Covington alone, the company operated at least 42 stores between 1928 and 1931; Newport had 18, Bellevue, 6, and Dayton, Ky., 5. Northern Kentucky clearly played an important role in the early formation of the Kroger Company.

In 1938 Barney, Alice, and Barney's doctor took Kroger's personal railroad car to the family's summer home on Cape Cod. Barney, who had been suffering from Parkinson's disease, had a heart attack there and died. His funeral was held at Slantacres, Kroger's palatial home in Columbia Tusculum, on the east side of Cincinnati, and he was buried at the Spring Grove Cemetery in Cincinnati. During his three-hour funeral service on Monday, July 25, 1938, all the Kroger Stores, Albers Super Markets, Atlantic and Pacific Company Stores, and Burke Grocery Stores were ordered closed to show respect to him.

The Kroger Company became a major player in U.S. food retailing. At one time, 10 cents of every U.S. dollar spent on food and groceries was tendered at a Kroger outlet. With the recent acquisition of the Fred Meyers grocery chain of Portland, Ore., the company has become the largest food retailer in the country, surpassing grocery companies such as Safeway and Albertsons. In 2004 Kroger was the second-largest retailer in the United States, with sales of $56.4 billion.

"Body of Kroger Rests in Home; Rites Are Planned," *CTS*, July 23, 1938, 1.

Horstman, Barry M. "Barney Kroger: Hard Work, Marketing Savvy Won Shoppers," *CP*, June 17, 1999, 1C.

Laycock, George. "The Kroger Story." *NKH* 8, no. 1 (Fall–Winter 2000): 47–57.

———. *The Kroger Story: A Century of Innovation*. Cincinnati: Kroger Company, 1983.

Ohio History Central. "Kroger Company." Ohio Historical Society. www.ohiohistorycentral.org.

Spring Grove Cemetery Records, Cincinnati.

Michael R. Sweeney

KUHN, CHARLES H. (b. February 25, 1902, Anderson Twp., Hamilton Co., Ohio; d. August 1, 1989, Middletown, Ohio). City official Charles Henry Kuhn, the third child of Josiah N. and Clara Mudersbach Kuhn, was born on their family farm. At an early age, Charles began to work at planting, harvesting, and tending livestock. He also accompanied his family on peddler routes weekly through the East End of Cincinnati in a horse-drawn wagon. The local school he attended was a one-room brick structure where classes through the eighth grade were taught. After graduating in 1920 from Woodward High School, at 13th and Sycamore Sts. in Cincinnati, he went on to the University of Cincinnati's College of Engineering. There he completed a five-year co-op program, earning a degree in civil engineering in 1925. On August 19, 1925, Kuhn married Florence Mildred Johnson. The couple had two children.

Kuhn began working in the Engineering Department of the City of Fort Thomas, Ky., on December 8, 1925, as an instrument man on a survey team for a salary of $135 a month. He continued working for the city until his retirement on August 1, 1967. Expecting to be employed for only three months in the planning of a sanitary sewer system, Kuhn was soon named assistant engineer for the city. Fort Thomas grew rapidly from a population of 5,000 in 1920 to 10,000 in 1930. New streets were developed and sewer lines added under Kuhn's direction. In 1930 he became city engineer, the equivalent of today's city manager, with increasing responsibilities as Fort Thomas continued to expand.

In addition to his official position, he was influential in creating and serving on numerous boards and commissions from 1937 until 1967: the Playgrounds and Recreation Board, the Planning and Zoning Commission, the Board of Adjustments (Zoning Appeals), the Civil Service Commission, the Committee for Fort Thomas, and the Board of Housing Appeals. For most of these groups he served as secretary. His employment title was eventually changed to city manager-coordinator. During this time the Fort Thomas police force expanded from 4 to 21, the fire department personnel increased from 2 to 15, and the public works division grew from 5 to 29 employees. From 1929 to 1935 the **Great Depression** decreased tax revenues, causing the city of Fort Thomas to cut employee salaries by 10 percent. As both the federal and state governments made new rules, Kuhn's job became more complex. For example, throughout these early depression years, relief laborers were provided at times through Kentucky Emergency Relief, CWA (Civil Works Administration), WPA (Works Progress Administration; later renamed Works Projects Administration), and PWA (Public Works Administration), and it became Kuhn's added responsibility to supervise these programs and the workers provided.

Several other major changes occurred in Fort Thomas while Kuhn was the city manager-coordinator. While he was in charge, the city's parks were expanded to include 210 acres in various locations throughout the city. A new school, the Ruth Moyer Elementary School, was built, and the three other schools in town were expanded. Kuhn worked closely with the elected mayor and six council members throughout these growth years. Kuhn died in 1989 and was buried at Mount Moriah Cemetery, Withamsville, Ohio, east of Cincinnati.

"Charles Kuhn, 87, City Engineer Who Guided Ft. Thomas' Growth," *KP*, August 3, 1989, 10K.

Betty Maddox Daniels

L&N BRIDGE (PURPLE PEOPLE BRIDGE). The **Louisville and Nashville Railroad** Bridge spans the Ohio River, between the **Daniel Carter Beard Bridge** (I-471) upstream to the east and the **Taylor-Southgate Bridge**, downstream to the west, linking the cities of Newport and Cincinnati.

Following the **Civil War**, Cincinnati emerged as a strategic shipment center between the Kentucky and West Virginia coalfields and the industrial heartland of the nation. Recognizing the potential for commercial expansion, business and political leaders in both Ohio and Kentucky organized the Newport and Cincinnati Bridge Company to improve railroad facilities and promote a southern railroad connection. Newport eventually won out over Covington in a bidding war for the proposed bridge, which was to carry the **Louisville, Cincinnati, and Lexington Railroad** (the Short Line) into Cincinnati. Newport's winning proposal included an agreement to grant the railroad the right-of-way to operate trains along the entire length of Saratoga St., an arrangement that, at times over the years, divided the city for hours while a train passed or changed cars. The new bridge's cornerstone was laid at the foot of Saratoga St. on June 3, 1868.

Jacob H. Linville, the nation's foremost railroad bridge engineer, designed the original bridge to carry railroad freight and passengers, with a walkway to accommodate wagons and pedestrians. The Keystone Bridge Company of Pittsburgh, Pa., built the steel superstructure. The Newport approach to the structure consists of a series of small brick arches that were later turned into automobile entrances to the current **Newport-on-the-Levee** parking lot.

When the bridge formally opened on March 20, 1872, it was called the Newport and Cincinnati Railroad and Wagon Bridge. It was the second bridge built to Cincinnati but the first to combine both railway and roadway features; the railroad track was in the center of the bridge, with roadways on both sides. In about 1881, the bridge was widened to accommodate streetcar tracks for horsecars. After the acquisition of the Louisville, Cincinnati, and Lexington Railroad by the **Louisville and Nashville Railroad** (L&N) in the 1880s, the bridge became commonly known as the L&N Bridge.

Although the railroad tracks along Saratoga St. later caused many a traffic jam and a small chorus of citizens' complaints, the acquisition of the railroad represented a major coup for Newport. Railroads were supplanting river commerce as the primary means of moving products and people, so besides adding jobs, the new bridge gave easier access to national and even international markets for the city's manufacturers. Local business leaders used the availability of a railroad depot (at modern-day Fifth and Saratoga Sts.) to promote Newport as a highly attractive place to do business.

The bridge introduced a new phase into the city's economic history: commuter-based suburban expansion. Before the bridge was built, there were only two ways to get from Newport to Cincinnati: via ferry and by going over Newport's Fourth St. Bridge into Covington and then over the **John A. Roebling Bridge**. Once it was completed, the L&N Bridge gave direct access to Cincinnati and its jobs. Employees could conveniently live in Newport and work in Cincinnati. The bridge also attracted many businessmen and families who exploited the new access to Cincinnati. It was then possible to own a business in Cincinnati but live in Newport. By the late 1880s, Newport had become well integrated within the Greater Cincinnati economy as workers and businessmen enjoyed greater access to markets and employment.

The building of the bridge also had an immediate impact on residential development in Newport. Between 1880 and 1900, Newport witnessed a 52 percent increase in the construction of housing, and the city's population swelled 35.4 percent during the same period, with large additions in the eastern part of the city. By 1880 Newport ranked as the 98th-most-populous city in the nation. Because of this population growth in Newport proper, suburban growth also began to occur throughout Campbell Co.

By the 1890s, it had become clear that the existing bridge could no longer accommodate the increased weight of locomotives and railcars, nor that of the heavier electric streetcars. Max Joseph Becker designed a new $700,000 bridge, which was constructed by the Keystone Bridge Company. In September 1896 the channel span of 510 feet was floated on barges to the site and hoisted into place by cables. Approaches on each side of the new bridge were improved; in Newport the rail tracks were elevated over Taylor St. (modern-day Third St.), no longer crossing the streetcar track at grade; they reached ground level just north of modern-day Fourth St. The new L&N Bridge, which included a railroad track on one side and, on the other side, a roadway with two electric streetcar lines and a walkway, opened in May 1897. Streetcars then returned to the L&N Bridge; during the bridge construction, Newport's electric streetcars passed over the **Central Bridge** downriver. In 1904 the Louisville and Nashville Railroad purchased the bridge. The last rail corporation to own it was the **Chessie System**, later known as the **CSX**, until the City of Newport held control of it for a brief period in 2005.

Although an impressive achievement for its time, the bridge had some serious drawbacks. The rail yards on the Cincinnati side could not be expanded because of their location, and the completion of the railroad Union Terminal in western Cincinnati in 1933 put an end to the need for any passenger drop-offs. As automobiles became more of a factor in commuting patterns to and from the suburbs, the bridge's urban location kept it from becoming an important part of automobile traffic patterns between Northern Kentucky and Cincinnati. The Kentucky Department of Highways bought the two-lane vehicular section of the bridge in 1935 and began the unpopular practice of collecting a toll, which lasted until November 11, 1941.

As trucks became the most popular way of transporting products to market, railroads and railroad bridges became less important to the nation's economy. Those bridges that were not torn down, such as the L&N Bridge, began to show the effects of this loss. CSX, when it was utilizing the bridge, refused to paint its side when the Kentucky Department of Highways painted its side blue; the result was an odd two-tone blue-and-rust combination.

The CSX Railroad discontinued its use of the bridge structure in 1984. The tracks on the bridge were removed and the rail approaches at each end were dismantled. The tracks in the city were also removed after railroad traffic ceased; they were replaced in 1987 with a landscaped green space along the middle of Saratoga St.

After the Kentucky Department of Highways determined in 1992 that the bridge was no longer functional to carry modern automobile traffic volumes and weights, proposals were made for its demolition. However, rather than spend the $2 million to demolish the bridge, the City of Newport and the Commonwealth of Kentucky began negotiations to save the structure and turn it into a pedestrian-only bridge, like the Walnut St. Bridge over the Tennessee River at Chattanooga, Tenn. With funding provided by both the City of Newport and the state, this plan became a reality.

The bridge closed to vehicular traffic on October 21, 2001, and reopened as the Newport Southbank Bridge on April 26, 2003. It was then owned and operated by a private nonprofit organization known as the Newport Southbank Bridge Company (see **Southbank Partners**). Much discussion and controversy occurred over what color to paint the bridge. Eventually, purple was chosen because it was deemed to be festive, to age slowly, to fade gracefully, and not to show rust. Thus, the bridge has become known most commonly as the Purple People Bridge. The L&N/Purple People Bridge has been placed on the National Register of Historic Places for its engineering and transportation significance.

"Bridge Formally Open on March 20, 1872," *CJ*, March 23, 1872, 3.

Condit, Carl W. *The Railroad and the City: A Technological and Urbanistic History of Cincinnati.* Columbus: Ohio State Univ. Press, 1977.

Lehmann, Terry W., and Earl W. Clark Jr., *The Green Line: The Cincinnati, Newport and Covington Railway.* Chicago: Central Electric Railfans' Association, 2000.

Purvis, Thomas L., ed. *Newport, Kentucky: A Bicentennial History.* Newport, Ky.: Otto Zimmerman, 1996.

"Span's Ownership Remains with State—Public-Private Transfer Delayed," *KP*, September 16, 2005, 2K.

Tenkotte, Paul A. "Rival Cities to Suburbs: Covington and Newport, Kentucky, 1790–1890," PhD diss., Univ. of Cincinnati, 1989.

Michael Whitehead

LACEY, GENE (b. March 19, 1888, Covington, Ky.; d. July 5, 1965, Covington, Ky.). Businessman Eugene F. Lacey, the son of Samuel and Emma Lacey, was a lifelong resident of Covington. His early education was at **Lincoln-Grant School** in Covington, and he graduated from Woodward High School, on Sycamore St. in downtown Cincinnati. In 1918 he opened his first grocery store, at 508 Scott St. in Covington (currently the site of the Kenton Co. Public Library), while residing at nearby 839 Craig St. In 1919 Lacey married Bessie Merritt of Falmouth, and together they opened a second store in Covington at 205 E. Robbins St., calling it the Gene and Bess Store; the building also served as their home.

Sometime during those years, Gene Lacey found time to attend the University of Cincinnati and the American Institute of Management. He graduated from the Alexander Hamilton Business School, and later the Laceys formed two companies, the Lacey Sausage Company and the Lacey Paper Company. In 1924 Gene and Bess Lacey faced a major challenge to their business when the Great Atlantic & Pacific Tea Company (A&P) and another major grocery chain moved into the neighborhood less than a block away from their small grocery, then located on Greenup St. The Laceys remained competitive not by charging low prices but by the convenience of their store and by employing local people, thus keeping the money spent at their store in the community. In 1926 Lacey closed his store at 508 Scott St.; in 1933 he opened a grocery store at Court and John Sts. in Cincinnati.

Lacey was a 32nd Degree Mason and served on the Southern Jurisdiction of the Supreme Council of Masons, was a member of the Odd Fellow Lodge, and became Exalted Ruler of Ira Lodge No. 37 of the Elks. He was a member of the National Negro Business League, served on the executive committee of the Cincinnati branch of the **NAACP**, and was active in the Ninth St. Methodist Church, serving as treasurer and a trustee for many years. In 1931 Lacey was a speaker for the new Covington City Manager League, which supported the city manager form of government for Covington. There were 300 new members at the time within the Negro Division. Lacey was also a founding member of Covington's **African-American Businessmen's Association**.

A frequent visitor to the Lacey household during the summer months of the 1940s was their nephew, college football coach **John A. Merritt**. Gene Lacey died in 1965 and was buried at Mary E. Smith Cemetery in Elsmere.

Dabney, Wendell P. *Cincinnati's Colored Citizens.* Cincinnati: Dabney, 1926.

"Enroll 300 New Members in Colored Division," *KTS*, July 7, 1931, 2.

"Eugene Lacey, Businessman," *KP*, July 6, 1965, 3K.

Harris, Theodore H. H. "Reader Recollection," *KP*, March 2, 1992, 4K.

Theodore H. H. Harris

LADD, DOROTHY (b. 1902, New Orleans, La.; date and place of death unknown). The Poet Dorothy Ladd was the daughter of Alvin and Bertha Holle Ladd. The family moved to Bellevue when she was age 22 in 1924. Two of Ladd's poems, "Cry in the Night" and "Bread with Jam," appeared in J. T. Cotton Noe's *A Brief Anthology of Kentucky Poetry* (1936). Her work has also been published in the poetry magazine *Letters*. Her father, a printer, died in 1934, and her mother died in 1944. That was the last year Dorothy was found in the local city directories; she was living at 243 Taylor Ave. in Bellevue and was employed as a nurse. Where she lived and what she did after the death of her mother remain to be discovered.

Noe, J. T. Cotton, ed. *A Brief Anthology of Kentucky Poetry: Selections of Poetry Written by Ninety-Three Persons Closely Identified with Kentucky, Most of Them Native Born.* Lexington: Univ. of Kentucky Department of Extension, 1936.

Jenny Plemen

LAFARGE NORTH AMERICA INC. The small Campbell Co. city of Silver Grove was once a bustling railroad town of 1,100 residents. In 1920 the **Chesapeake and Ohio Railroad** built many of the houses in Silver Grove so its employees could be close to their workplace. When the Chesapeake and Ohio Railway closed the 200-acre Stevens rail yard at Silver Grove in 1981, the town suffered greatly. Businesses along the **Mary Ingles Highway** in town lost many of their customers, and homes, now mostly owned by railway workers, became difficult to sell. Over the next 17 years, several companies considered locating on the site of the former rail yard; however, none showed serious interest until a French company, Lafarge, negotiated to buy the property in 1998. The city, county, and state governments offered tax breaks and other incentives to lure the company to the area. The parent company of Lafarge North America Inc. is headquartered in Paris, France, and has been in continuous operation since 1833. It has locations in 75 countries and a worldwide workforce of 77,000. The company is a world leader in the production of construction materials such as cement, asphalt products, and gypsum wallboard. The corporation's North American subsidiary currently operates several facilities in the United States and employs 15,300 people. The Silver Grove plant, which opened in July 2000, was built at a cost of about $100 million and employs 150. The plant produces 900 million square feet of gypsum wallboard each year, for use in the United States and Canada. Strategically located on the Ohio River, the facility has easy access to transportation by water, rail, and highway.

Answers.com. "Lafarge." www.answers.com/lafarge (accessed February 25, 2007).

"Campbell Wooing French Manufacturer," *KE*, December 17, 1998, 2C.

"Lafarge Almost Ready," *KP*, July 21, 2000, 1K.

"Lafarge North America," *KP*, July 27, 2000, 5K.

"Lafarge Plant Revitalizes Silver Grove," *KE*, July 25, 2000, 1B.

"Silver Grove Gets Drywall Plant," *KE*, January 28, 1999, 1K.

LAFFOON, POLK, JR. (b. February 6, 1877, Madisonville, Ky.; d. April 20, 1945, Covington, Ky.). Utility executive and horse-racing enthusiast Polk Laffoon Jr. was the son of Polk Laffoon Sr. and the former Hattie Parker of Madisonville. His father had been a lawyer and a U.S. congressman and had served under Confederate general **John Hunt Morgan** during the **Civil War**. Polk Laffoon Jr. was also a first cousin of Ruby Laffoon, who was a Kentucky governor (1931–1935). Polk Jr. married Emily Woodall in 1914, and they had two children, Polk III and Emily. Polk Jr. was a lifelong horse-racing enthusiast and raised many thoroughbreds on a farm he owned in Kenton Co. on Turkeyfoot Rd. He served as president of the Kentucky Racing Commission and of the Latonia Jockey Club Inc., which operated the (Old) **Latonia Racecourse** in Covington, and was a vice president of the Churchill Downs Racecourse in Louisville. During his long and illustrious career, he also held executive positions with the Peoples Liberty Bank and Trust Company; the Union Light, Heat and Power Company; the Cincinnati Gas and Electric Company in Ohio; and the Cincinnati, Newport and Covington Railway Company (see **Green Line Company**). After a long illness, Polk Laffoon Jr. died at age 68 on his farm, which he called Pokeaway. Funeral services were held at the Trinity Episcopal Church in Covington and he was buried in the Highland Cemetery in Fort Mitchell. His wife Emily and their two children survived him.

"Colorful Figure Passes with Death of Laffoon," *KP*, April 21, 1945, 1.

"Commodore Laffoon Now," *KP*, June 15, 1932, 3.

"Laffoon Estate Is Left to Widow," *KP*, May 5, 1945, 1.

"Laffoon Rites Set Monday at Trinity Church," *KP*, April 21, 1945, 1.

Leonard, Lewis Alexander. *Greater Cincinnati and Its People: A History.* New York: Lewis Historical, 1927.

LAGOON AMUSEMENT PARK. One of the largest and most popular resorts in Northern Kentucky at the beginning of the 20th century was the Lagoon Amusement Park in Ludlow. An 85-acre lake was created for the park by damming Pleasant Run Creek, which empties into the Ohio River nearby; and streetcar lines were extended to the Lagoon entrance at what is today Laurel St. between Park Ave. and Lake St.

The park's grand opening was May 18, 1895. Park patrons paid a fee to enter the park, and additional fees were charged for the major activities. A very important attraction at the Lagoon was its large lake; the clear, fresh water provided for excellent fishing, swimming, and boating. A wide, sandy bathing beach was constructed on the north side of the lake. Another early attraction was the grand clubhouse, a large Victorian structure sporting wide verandas that wrapped around the building. The clubhouse was constructed on high ground, which offered sweeping views of the lake and other parts of the park. Activities at the clubhouse included dancing and fine dining, for which park managers insisted on the best chefs and waiters. The Lagoon dance pavilion, which drew thousands to the park, provided space for hundreds of dancers

Lagoon Amusement Park, as seen from the Cincinnati Southern Railroad Bridge.

and for the large orchestras and bands popular at the time. It boasted the largest dance floor in the United States west of New York City. All of the original buildings at the park were designed by a Ludlow architect, John H. Boll. The first general manager of the park was John Noonan, who held the position from 1895 to 1902. J. J. Weaver was his successor.

Rides available for the first season included a large toboggan sled, a pony track, a miniature gold mine, and a scenic railroad. Of the early rides, one of the most popular was the roller coaster, which was built over the lake and took patrons up and down many times. Riders began on the shore of the lake and were quickly propelled over the water. At the halfway point of the ride, the small cars entered a circular building constructed on piers, where the track spiraled several times inside the building before reemerging into the light for the return trip to the shore. Over the next few decades, many rides were added. In 1896 a chute-the-chutes was constructed on the north shore of the lake. It consisted of small cars that slid down a steep ramp into the lake. Other innovative rides were an Alpine slide, a circular swing, a $10,000 merry-go-round, and a 100-foot Ferris wheel built on one of the lake's many islands. In 1909 the management constructed an elevated automobile ride in the park, featuring full-sized touring cars. The ride carried patrons along a two-mile elevated track, which snaked its way through the woods on the north end of the park.

Various entertainers also drew large crowds; the park's 2,500-seat amphitheatre was available for live productions. A large motion picture theater was also very popular, as were the performances on the park's vaudeville stage. Each weekend there were free vaudeville shows in which local and occasionally visiting performers provided entertainment. Other activities included a large midway with assorted games, refreshment stands, picnic grounds, and several miles of walking trails. By 1905 an Edisonia exhibit was in operation: the large exhibit hall displayed more than 100 recent inventions from across the country.

Current events gave the park managers inspiration for new attractions. In 1898, during the Spanish-American War (see **National Guard, Spanish-American War**), a Cuban village was constructed on one of the lake's islands. Included were an authentic native hut with thatched roof and a small replica farm growing tobacco and sugar cane. A Cuban family (a father, a mother, and five children) fleeing the war was hired to occupy the exhibit. Park visitors were taken to the Cuban village by boat; they could then disembark and tour the exhibit. This early experiment in living history proved very popular.

The victory of the Japanese Navy over Russia in 1905 led to the establishment of a Japanese Fair that same year at the park. This attraction featured a large teahouse built in the traditional Japanese architectural style. A Japanese immigrant operated the exhibit with the assistance of five authentic "geisha girls." The Japanese Fair also offered Japanese music, several Japanese games of chance, and a jujitsu instructor who gave regular demonstrations of his art.

A large wooden motordrome, or motorcycle racetrack, was planned for the grounds in 1912. The quarter-mile oval track was constructed at a 60-degree angle, allowing drivers to reach great speeds. The observation grandstand could seat up to 8,000 spectators, and many more could sit in the infield. The motordrome was officially opened on June 21, 1913, and was an immediate success. Races were held three times each week with an admission charge of 50 cents.

Four events between 1913 and 1920 led to the closing of the park. The costly **floods of 1913** damaged many of the Lagoon's attractions. They were quickly repaired, but at considerable cost. In July 1913 a serious wreck at the motordrome brought notoriety to the Lagoon. A driver named Odin Johnson lost control of his motorcycle on the large wooden track and veered off into a grandstand. The cycle hit a gas lamp, causing burning fuel to spread throughout the stand, and panic set in as the 5,000 spectators tried to flee the fire. Seven people were killed and more than 100 were treated for burns on the day of the accident. Initial newspaper accounts listed the dead as Odin Johnson of Salt Lake City, age 34; Charles Davis of Ludlow, 5; Mrs. Ethel Buchtman of Covington, 20; and Cincinnati residents Henry Andrews, James Carter, Mrs. William Michaels, and William Patterson. Several other spectators died in subsequent days from their burns and other injuries. Injured patrons included residents of Bromley, Covington, and Ludlow, Ky., and Cincinnati and Lima, Ohio. Lawsuits and criminal charges were quickly filed in the local courts. Despite the tragedy, the motordrome was repaired and reopened later in the 1913 season.

Two years later, on July 7, 1915, at the height of the summer season, a large tornado ripped through Ludlow and caused more than $20,000 in damage to the buildings in the park, including the dance hall and the clubhouse. Costly repairs were made and the park was reopened. The final event that spelled doom for the park was **World War I**. For many years, the Lagoon had served the locally brewed Bavarian beer at various locations. But now grain was needed for the war effort; federal officials halted the manufacturing of liquor and beer for the duration of the war. The loss of alcohol sales resulted in a drastic loss in profits, and the Lagoon Amusement Park closed after the 1918 season.

Part of the Lagoon property was developed as a residential neighborhood. Portions of Deverill, Lake, Laurel, Ludford, Park, and Stokesay Sts. were built on the site. Only two buildings from the original park have survived. The clubhouse was converted into an apartment building, and the women's washroom, at the northwest corner of Deverill and Lake Sts., was transformed into a single-family home.

In 1967 the Ludlow Realty Company sold the remaining Lagoon property to Ludlow Development Enterprises Inc. (Carlisle Construction, King Wrecking Company, and other firms) for $28,000. The low-lying areas were later filled and the lake was eliminated.

Centennial Celebration, Ludlow, Kentucky: Commemorating 100 Years of Progress, 1864–1964. Ludlow, Ky.: Ludlow Centennial Committee, 1964.

John Burns Collected Papers, Kenton Co. Public Library, Covington, Ky.

"Ludlow Lagoon Amusement Park," Local History File, Kenton Co. Public Library, Covington, Ky.

David E. Schroeder

LAIDLEY, FREDERICK A. (b. January 28, 1841, Huntington, W.Va.; d. December 14, 1931,

Covington, Ky.). Frederick Alexander Laidley was a prominent businessman in both river and rail transportation and a civic leader in the city of Cincinnati from 1886 until at least 1918. The son of James Madison Laidley, a prominent attorney, and Anna Maria Buhring, he was raised in Charleston, W.Va., and attended public schools there. He started a small store in Charleston and then from 1858 to 1864 manufactured salt in West Virginia on the Kanawha River. In connection with the salt business, he traveled often to Cincinnati. Laidley had become fascinated with steamboats as a boy, and in 1864 he began his career as a river man, getting a job as a clerk on the Ohio River steamer *Annie Laurie*. By 1866 he was captain of that boat. For most of his life, he was best known as a river man and was variously referred to as Captain Laidley or Commodore Laidley (these titles may have been informal, since official licensing of captains and chief mates did not begin until the U.S. Congress established it by legislation in 1871).

Laidley moved to Cincinnati in 1867 as the agent for the Kanawha Salt Company and became a charter member of the Cincinnati Chamber of Commerce. Even though his business was in Cincinnati, he lived in Covington and raised his family there. Laidley engaged in numerous business ventures and partnering associations over the next almost 50 years. From 1873 to 1896, he was in the pork-packing business (see **Meatpacking**); in 1886 he became a prime stockholder of the Louisville & Cincinnati Packet Company, and later (by 1891) served as its general manager and treasurer. With this company, he built and operated two of the finest and fastest boats on the Ohio River, the famed *City of Louisville* and the *City of Cincinnati*. These two steamboats and five others were called the White Collar Line (WCL) or White Packet Line. He was an original stockholder of the Common Carrier Company and president of the Louisville & Evansville Transportation Company. These companies were in the business of transporting freight or passengers, or both, up and down the Ohio River. He was president of the Licking Coal & Towboat Company, which supplied steamboats with coal and provided harbor-towing services, and in 1881 he began shipping meat by rail with the **Cincinnati Southern Railroad** to southern cities such as Chattanooga, Tenn.; Atlanta and Macon, Ga.; Mobile and Montgomery, Ala.; and many others.

In 1866 Laidley married Julia A. Rook from Malden, W.Va., and they had four children. The family lived in what is now known as the **Laidley House**, at 404 E. Second St. in Covington, surrounded by other magnificent homes of the pre–**Civil War** and post–Civil War periods. During the mid-1800s and into the early 1900s, the Laidley home was a center for hospitality known for its glowing lights, grand balls, and lovely parties.

Laidley's lifestyle and his role as a prominent businessman came to an abrupt end after the winter of 1917–1918. During that winter the Ohio and Licking rivers froze in many places, and in 1918 an ice gorge destroyed the *City of Cincinnati*, the *City of Louisville*, and the *Loucinda* (also WCL). Much of Laidley's great wealth was gone. He lived out the rest of his life in his Covington home on Second St. and died after a short illness at age 90 in December 1931. He was buried at Highland Cemetery in Fort Mitchell.

Bricking, Chuck. *Covington's Heritage: A Compilation of the City's Historical Houses and a Short Biography of the Inhabitants*. Covington, Ky.: Privately published, 1980.

Goss, Charles Frederick, ed. *Cincinnati: The Queen City, 1788–1912*. 4 vols. Chicago: S. J. Clarke, 1912.

Kentucky Death Certificate No. 30006, for the year 1931.

"Mourn Laidley—Veteran Riverman Passes in 90th Year," *KP*, December 15, 1931, 1.

Fran Allen

LAIDLEY HOUSE. The Laidley House faces south at the corner of Second and Kennedy Sts. near the Licking and Ohio Rivers in the protected **Licking-Riverside National Historic District** of Covington. The house itself is a Kentucky landmark and is surrounded by historically significant homes.

The Laidley House was built in 1865, at the end of the **Civil War**, in the Second Empire style. A visitor to the imposing and beautiful three-story mansion will first be impressed by its setting on the property and its lovely facade. The home is surrounded by a stone wall topped with an iron fence, and the property is entered through a decorative iron gate. The structure itself is orange red brick with a white Kentucky limestone foundation and massive front steps, and the entrance, corners, and windows are trimmed with limestone. Above the approach to the house is an octagonal cupola sitting on top of the colorful slate-faced mansard roof, like the decorative top of an elaborate wedding cake. After walking up the front steps, one comes to the glass-paneled front door inside an intricately carved, walnut-stained wooden entrance, with folding paneled doors and a black and white, checkerboard-patterned marble floor.

Just inside the front door is a long rectangular entrance hall with an elaborate parquet floor and a winding staircase, which has unusual parquet stair treads. On the right is a poolroom, thought to have been a gentlemen's smoking parlor; on the left is a large living area originally called "the ballroom." The ballroom has a large bay window on the entrance side and wonderful white plaster decorations of morning glories and leaves all around the edges of the 14-foot ceiling. At the end of the entrance hall are two doors: one opens to the dining room, the other to an exterior L-shaped porch with heavy carved pillars and a balustrade, and a view of the Ohio River.

Frederick Alexander Laidley and his family lived in the house from 1880 until 1972. Commodore Laidley, as he was called, owned the White Packet, or White Collar, line of riverboats on the Ohio River. He and his wife, the former Julia Rook, had four children: Frederick Rook, Mary, Marguerite, and Elsie Louise. During the late 1800s and early 1900s, the house was a lively social gathering place. However, the ice gorge of the winter of 1917–1918 crushed five of Commodore Laidley's boats, changing the family's economic status considerably, and social life at the home became a lower priority. The last Laidley occupant was Elsie Louise Laidley More, who died in 1972. Soon afterward, the house was sold at auction to an interim absentee owner who planned to convert it into small apartments. By that time, the house and grounds had been neglected for many years. In 1975 James and Frances Allen purchased the property and restored it to its former glory. They live there today.

Bricking, Chuck. *Covington's Heritage: A Compilation of the City's Historical Houses and a Biography of the Inhabitants*. Covington, Ky.: Privately published, 1980.

Stamm, Michelle. "Riverside Renaissance: Covington's Historic Riverside District from the 18th Century to the Present." *NKH* 1, no. 1 (Autumn–Winter 1993): 1–22.

Fran Allen

LAKESIDE CHRISTIAN CHURCH. This Christian church in Lakeside Park began because in the 1960s men of the Independent Christian Church–Church of Christ felt that a new church was needed in Northern Kentucky. A group of ministers and laymen met in October 1966 to discuss establishing the new church. The New Testament Church Evangelism Committee was formed and incorporated in March 1967, and the Lakeside Park–Crescent Springs area was selected for the church's location. The committee chose Jerry Scarborough to be the minister-evangelist. On September 10, 1967, 73 worshippers attended the church's first Sunday services at the Crescent Springs Elementary School, on Buttermilk Pk. Seventeen adults agreed to form the nucleus of the new church, and at a meeting in December 1967 the name Lakeside Christian Church was chosen. By January 1968 the congregation had grown to 55 members; property was purchased and plans were drawn for the construction of a permanent church, for which ground was broken March 10, 1968. One year later the congregation occupied the new building, at 195 Buttermilk Pk., and on October 1, 1970, Bro. John Russell was chosen as minister-evangelist, since Scarborough had departed to start new churches elsewhere. As the congregation grew, new programs were added and staff members were hired to direct the areas of music, youth, adult involvement, education, and a comprehensive children's program of participation and instruction.

By 1979 continued growth made it necessary to schedule multiple worship services on Sundays, so construction ensued to increase worship service and educational space. The congregation also began to purchase adjacent land along Buttermilk Pk. In 1996 growth again required increasing the meeting space. The building campaign now included a new sanctuary seating about 1,400, as well as renovation of the existing facilities to include a family life–sports complex, meeting rooms for church and community use, and supplementary space for classes and activities.

Lakeside Christian Church endeavors to influence the community by actively participating in charitable needs and by offering beneficial programs—musical productions; men's, women's, and family seminars; and special seasonal drama productions—and also through a comprehensive worldwide mission endeavor: 20 percent of its weekly offerings is used to help people outside the local church body. In 2005 weekly attendance was averaging more than 1,750 in worship services as the church continued to prosper and grow.

"Churches Celebrate Building," *KP,* September 18, 1993, 10K.

"Lakeside Park—Suburban Wrap Up (Expand Lakeside Christian Church)," *KP,* February 12, 1992, 9K.

"Ushers Pass the Construction Hat," *KP,* November 20, 1995, 1K.

Mary Ellen Lucas

LAKESIDE PARK. Lakeside Park is a largely residential fifth-class city in northern Kenton Co. It is surrounded by the cities of Fort Mitchell and Crestview Hills and is bisected by the **Dixie Highway** (U.S. 25). I-275 passes just to the south. Lakeside Park's origins can be traced to a nearly 1,000-acre farm granted to Col. John Leathers, who settled the area in 1785. It was mainly farmland until landowner and Kenton Co. water commissioner Paul Hesser developed the city's first subdivision on 40 acres that he purchased from R. L. and F. D. Crigler. This first neighborhood was placed west of the old **Covington and Lexington Turnpike** (Dixie Highway). The development, along with the formal incorporation of the City of Lakeside Park on May 12, 1930, also championed by Hesser, was specifically arranged to prevent annexation by South Fort Mitchell. Today, Lakeside Park encompasses 530 acres (parts of which were annexed from Kenton Co.) and includes 16 subdivisions, three businesses, a U.S. post office, and four churches. The city has adopted a set of ordinances that promote the city's beauty and limit the number of businesses to three. The three businesses are a restaurant, an automobile window-tinting business, and a branch office of Cincinnati Bell. City ordinances forbid the businesses to expand outside their current boundaries and restrict their sales activity to entities within their categories: food service, automobile service, and communication.

The community is rich with history. The turnpike that runs through town (the Covington and Lexington Turnpike) was a well-traveled route to the South that, during the **Civil War**, was guarded by earthwork forts. **Barleycorn's Five Mile House**, located at Dixie Highway and Hudson Ave., dates from the 1860s. Another historical site is the Dry Creek Baptist Church, a 19th-century brick building on Buttermilk Pk. now serving as a private home.

Lakeside Park includes a formally registered historical area called the Dixie Highway National Historic District. In 2000 the city of Lakeside Park had a population of 2,869, made up mostly of middle- to upper-income residents. Police protection is provided in collaboration with the City of Crestview Hills, while Fort Mitchell supports the fire and life-squad needs of the community.

"Birth of a Police Department," *KP,* June 22, 1998, 4K.

"History of Dry Creek Baptist Church, Kenton County, Kentucky," Lakeside Park Local History Files, Kenton Co. Public Library, Covington, Ky.

Kleber, John E., ed. *The Kentucky Encyclopedia.* Lexington: Univ. Press of Kentucky, 1992.

National Register of Historic Places National Register Form, 1986, Lakeside Park Local History Files, Kenton Co. Public Library, Covington, Ky.

U.S. Census Bureau. "American Fact Finder. Data Set. Census 2000 Summary File 1 (SF1) 100-Percent Data. Custom Table." www.census.gov (accessed June 28, 2006).

Blanche Gaynor

LAKESIDE PRESBYTERIAN CHURCH. In 1961 two churches, the Lakeside Presbyterian Church and the Madison Avenue Presbyterian Church, were merged to create the present-day Lakeside Presbyterian Church in Lakeside Park.

In 1854, 28 members of the First Presbyterian Church in downtown Covington decided to start a new church closer to their homes. They named their new congregation the Second Presbyterian Church, and at first services were held in an old pottery building on Madison Ave., just south of Ninth St., which had also previously been used as a schoolhouse. In 1861 the congregation built their first church building on the north side of Ninth St. just east of Madison. After that structure was destroyed by fire in September 1880, the church's members authorized construction of a new church at 1035 Madison Ave. (today the parking lot of Allison & Rose Funeral Home); the new facility was completed in 1883. The following year, the congregation changed the church name to the Madison Avenue Presbyterian Church. In spring 1886 the new edifice, too, was destroyed by fire, but a replacement was soon built on the same site. In 1916 a house at 1048 Scott St. was purchased to be used as the first parsonage. A new Sunday school section was added to the side of the church in 1922. By 1955 church membership had increased to 420, and that year the Madison Avenue Presbyterian Church celebrated its centennial. About that time, growth had begun to slow in inner-city churches, causing church leaders to consider building new churches in the suburbs. It soon became apparent that financing a new facility would be difficult, given the small size of the congregation. Therefore, in 1960 it was decided to approach the newly formed Lakeside Presbyterian Church about a merger.

The Lakeside Presbyterian Church was organized in 1955, becoming the first new Presbyterian church in Kenton Co. within the past 60 years. From its original 70 charter members, the church grew to 131 members by the end of the first year and to 221 members by 1960. Their initial place of worship was the Dixie Four Star Theater Building in Fort Mitchell (see **Movie Theaters**). On August 4, 1955, the church purchased the stately old George Hill Estate, at 2690 **Dixie Highway** in Lakeside Park. The nine-room house, with a large detached garage, was located on three acres of land. A local artist, **Caroline Williams**, was asked to make a pencil drawing of the house for use in church promotions. Copies of the picture were made available to all church members. The congregation removed several interior walls of the house and made other alterations to make it more suitable for church services. A special offering was taken, which was used to purchase chairs, hymnals, and a Baldwin Orgasonic Organ. In May 1956 the church called Leon Drake to be its first pastor. Shortly after his arrival, he began a church newsletter, the *Lakeside Life*, which soon became a weekly publication. Monthly church suppers were also begun, encouraging fellowship among members. In 1958 the church held its first Vacation Bible School, which was attended by 62 pupils, and purchased a house at 11 Alpine Dr. in Fort Mitchell, for a parsonage. By the end of the church's fifth year, membership had reached 240. Around that time, the Madison Avenue Presbyterian Church approached Lakeside about the merger.

Early in 1961 both churches voted to approve the merger, which was formalized on February 16, 1961. The new church retained the name of Lakeside Presbyterian Church, and 455 members were present at the first combined service. Not all members of the former Madison Avenue Presbyterian Church came to Lakeside. With the increased attendance, it became imperative that a new, larger sanctuary be built. A new church building, constructed on the Dixie Highway property, was dedicated on November 24, 1963. Inspired by having a new building, many members donated money, furnishings, and other items in memory of loved ones. The names of those donors were recorded in a *Book of Remembrance* kept at a place of honor in the church sanctuary. At the dedication of the new building, it was stated that the new church stands as a memorial to those who contributed so generously of their time and money.

"Ground Broken for Lakeside Church," *KP,* March 25, 1963, 1K.

Lakeside Presbyterian Church, 1955–1961. Brochure. Lakeside Park, Ky.: Lakeside Presbyterian Church, 1962.

"Old Covington Landmark Falls," *KP,* March 23, 1963, 1.

"Presbyterian Church Going Up," *KP,* March 25, 1963, 2K.

Tenkotte, Paul A. *A Heritage of Art and Faith: Downtown Covington Churches.* Covington, Ky.: Kenton Co. Historical Society, 1986.

LAMPRECHT, WILHELM (b. October 31, 1838, Altenschoenbach, near Würzburg, Germany; d. 1922, Munich, Germany). The establishment of the **Covington Altar Stock Building Company** in 1862 attracted German-born artists who were skilled in decorating religious edifices, and one of these persons was Wilhelm Lamprecht. There was a great need in the United States for talented painters to add inspirational art to the new churches that had been erected by immigrants during the 19th century. Lamprecht studied at the Munich

Royal Academy of Art in Bavaria between 1859 and 1867. His first teacher was a history painter, who sparked Lamprecht's interest in large-scale historical tableaux. His second was the famous Munich painter Johann von Schraudolph, a specialist in religious art. Von Schraudolph founded a Society of Christian Art, and his pupil Wilhelm Lamprecht became a member and, for a time, president of the Cincinnati Society of Christian Art in Ohio, 20 years later.

In 1867 Lamprecht left Germany for the United States, where during his lengthy career he worked on some 300 churches. That same year, he painted at St. Mary's Abbey Church in Newark, N.J., murals that depict 10 scenes from the life of the Virgin Mary, beginning with her birth and ending with the encounter with her son Jesus after he had risen from the grave. Flanking each scene are paintings of two saints, some of them identifiable as German, for instance St. Cunegund, St. Hermann, and St. Rupert. Lamprecht's murals were painted in oil on dry plaster and placed high in the clerestory. His large canvas painting of St. Benedict greets visitors at the main entrance of the New Jersey church.

Some time after he painted in the Newark church, the artist joined the Covington Altar Building Stock Company. Lamprecht created many exquisite altarpieces and murals throughout North America for the company, which had been established by the Benedictine clergyman Archabbot Boniface Wimmer in 1862 and was managed by the Benedictine lay brother **Cosmas Wolf**.

In 1868 Lamprecht traveled to Canada to decorate the church of St.-Romuald d'Etchemin in Quebec with large murals. Two other German painters accompanied him from Covington, Louis Lang and **Wenceslaus Thien**, to assist. In 2004 this Canadian church was classified as a historic monument by the culture minister of Quebec.

In 1869 Lamprecht worked in Indiana and Pennsylvania. Indiana had attracted a large number of German Catholic settlers, especially in its southern counties. The St. Joseph Church in the hamlet of Millhousen in southeastern Indiana displays today two altarpieces by Lamprecht: *Death of St. Joseph* and *Immaculate Conception.* In Oldenburg, Ind., Lamprecht decorated the chapel of the Immaculate Conception for the Franciscan sisters. The murals are no longer in place, but a canvas by Lamprecht, which he donated to the prioress, still graces the entrance hall of the sisters' house.

The year 1870 brought an important commission for Lamprecht in Vincennes, Ind., to paint three large murals in the Cathedral of St. Francis Xavier, named after the 16th-century Jesuit missionary. The church, built before 1816, was the first Catholic edifice in what became Indiana and was the seat of Bishop Simon Brute, a refugee of the French Revolution. The three Lamprecht paintings are *Crucifixion, Madonna of the Chair,* and *St. Francis Xavier. Madonna of the Chair* is based on the Italian Renaissance prototype *Sacra Conversazione,* which traditionally portrays the Madonna seated on a throne with the Christ child, receiving homage by a group of saints. For the group of saints in his painting, Lamprecht chose the patron saints of the early French bishops of Vincennes: St. Celestine, St. Maurice, St. Simon, and St. Stephen.

Lamprecht returned to Northern Kentucky in 1871 to take part in the interior decoration of Covington's **Mother of God Catholic Church**, where he painted the four Evangelists in the pendentives of the dome. During that same year, he was called to the small town of Quincy in western Illinois on the banks of the Mississippi River. There, for St. Boniface Church, he painted several beautiful murals in the sanctuary: *Christ Handing the Keys to St. Peter, Nativity,* and images of St. Boniface, St. Lawrence, and St. Stephen. Of the small canvases he painted for the church baptistery, only *Blessed Hermann* and *Joseph and the Fourteen Holy Helpers* survive.

In 1876 Lamprecht was in western Pennsylvania, where he painted an altarpiece at St. Mary's Church in a small German settlement called Marienstadt. His painting *The Immaculate Conception* was on display in Philadelphia during the national Centennial Celebration in 1876, where it was widely praised.

Lamprecht's fame spread to Wisconsin, where German settlers had built a large number of churches and monasteries. In Milwaukee two Swiss priests had established the Capuchin Order in 1856. In 1877 Lamprecht decorated their church, dedicated to St. Francis, with a huge mural, *The Triumph of Christianity.* Harking back to his first career as a history painter in Munich, he designed a one-cent stamp for the Trans-Mississippi Exposition in Omaha, Neb., in 1898. It depicts the French explorer Father Jacques Marquette crossing the Mississippi River.

Shortly before his return to Germany in 1901, Lamprecht created a 65-foot-wide painting, *Immaculate Conception,* located in the Immaculate Conception chapel at the Sisters of Charity Mount St. Joseph Motherhouse in Cincinnati. Lamprecht's painting, on a gold-leaf background behind the high altar, is among his most breathtaking works. About the same time, he painted as many as five pieces on the ceiling of old St. Joseph Church at Linn St. and Lincoln Park Dr. (today Ezzard Charles Dr.) in Cincinnati's west end. They represented the Assumption and the four cardinal virtues: prudence, justice, fortitude, and temperance. Some of the paintings survived the transition to the new 1960s church building at the same location. After settling again in Munich, Lamprecht became a much-sought-after portrait painter and died there in 1922, at age 84.

Buerkle, Boniface, O.S.B. *Mary's Legacy, Saint Mary's Church.* St. Mary's, Pa.: McKee Press, 1988.

Humphreys, Henry. "Found in Doomed West End Church," *CTS,* December 12, 1956, 3.

Kuhn, Charles. "Little Known Facts Told by Parish Member: Written and Oral Lore of Old Cathedral," 1933, Vincennes Old Cathedral Archives, Vincennes, Ind.

McPadden, Malachy, O.S.B., ed. *St. Mary's Church, Newark, NJ.* Newark, N.J.: Newark Abbey Press, 2002.

Metz, Jack. "Church Art Salvaged for New Structure," *CTS,* April 17, 1961, 5.

"Wilhelm Lamprecht zum Fest seiner Goldenen Hochzeit, 20. Maerz, 1920," *Allgemeine Abendzeitung,* Munich, March 26, 1920.

Annemarie Springer

LAMY, JOHN (JEAN BAPTISTE) (b. October 11, 1814, Lempdes, Auvergne, France; d. February 13, 1888, Santa Fe, N.Mex.). The subject of Willa Cather's popular fictionalized American novel *Death Comes for the Archbishop* (1927), John Lamy was a Catholic priest of the Archdiocese of Cincinnati, having immigrated in 1839. He was pastor of St. Mary's Church in Covington (later named **Cathedral Basilica of the Assumption**) from 1848 until 1850. Lamy then became the first bishop (1853–1875), and then archbishop (1875–1885) of Santa Fe, N.Mex. He was buried in St. Francis of Assisi Cathedral in Santa Fe.

Horgan, Paul. *Lamy of Santa Fe.* Middletown, Conn.: Wesleyan Univ. Press, 1975.

Ryan, Paul E. *History of the Diocese of Covington, Kentucky.* Covington, Ky.: Diocese of Covington, 1954.

Steele, Thomas J., ed. and trans. *Archbishop Lamy: In His Own Words.* Albuquerque, N.Mex.: LPD Press, 2000.

Tenkotte, Paul A., David E. Schroeder, and Thomas S. Ward. *To Be Catholic and American in Northern, Central, and Appalachian Kentucky: The Diocese of Covington, 1853–2003.* Forthcoming.

Paul A. Tenkotte

LANDRUM, RALPH (b. August 16, 1957, Covington, Ky.). Professional golfer Ralph L. Landrum, who played on the PGA Tour 1983–1985, is the son of Jesse and Betty Landrum. He began playing at **Summit Hills Golf and Country Club**, won numerous junior titles while attending **St. Henry District High School**, and played college golf at the University of Kentucky in Lexington.

Landrum, who currently resides in Burlington, qualified for the 1978 Masters Golf Tournament by reaching the semifinals of the 1977 USGA Amateur Tournament. He played in the Masters Golf Tournament in 1984 as a professional and also competed in six U.S. Open Golf Tournaments; he had seven top 10 finishes on tour. The highlight of his U.S. Open Golf Tournament play was an eighth-place finish in 1983 at Oakmont, Pa. A Class A PGA Member, Landrum operates Landrum Golf Management locally and is the head professional at **Devou Park** Golf Course in Covington. He has always been one of Northern Kentucky's staunchest supporters of junior golf. He and his wife Mary Pat have two children, Kyle and Joe, who also have excelled in amateur golf.

Landrum, Ralph. Interview by Denny Van Houten, June 2005, Covington, Ky.

Dennis W. Van Houten

LANE, WILLIAM LEROY (b. November 27, 1897, New York City; d. December 14, 1968, Fort Worth, Tex.). William Lane, the son of James Robert Lane and Alberteena Martin, became the first African American priest to minister within the

Roman Catholic Diocese of Covington. Lane served at the **Our Savior Catholic Church**, located at 242 E. 10th St. in Covington. In 1917, when the United States entered **World War I**, Lane signed up to become a camp secretary with the Catholic Knights of Columbus organization. After basic training at Camp Zachary Taylor, near Louisville, Ky., he was stationed in France. He was a graduate of Fordham University in New York City and attended St. Mary Seminary in Cleveland, Ohio, and St. Vincent Seminary in Latrobe, Pa. He was ordained in 1933 by Bishop John Swint in Wheeling, W.Va. Before he came to Covington, Lane served in the Diocese of Port of Spain, Trinidad, British West Indies.

Bishop **Francis W. Howard** spearheaded an effort to form an African American church and school as a mission of the **Cathedral Basilica of the Assumption**, and in 1943 the decision was made to do so. At one time, this new parish, named Our Savior Catholic Church, had both a grade and a high school; most of the students were from Covington and Newport. In 1945 the parish priest at Our Savior was Rev. Henry Haacke, assisted by the newly arrived Rev. William LeRoy Lane. At this time and throughout the 1940s, the parish school at Our Savior had 60 students enrolled in grades one through eight. Lane's primary mission was to work with the people of the surrounding neighborhoods and to attract converts to the church. He was of great help to the African American children, as he received clothing in the form of jackets for the boys at the school from the Eilerman Clothing Store (see **Eilerman & Sons, Men's Clothiers**). He sought the assistance of another African American priest from Cincinnati to teach diction in the school. However, Lane was very outspoken on the question of racial prejudices. His efforts had attracted many converts, but it was time for him to move on. Lane left Covington in late 1947.

Afterward, Lane secured temporary assignments in various cities throughout Wisconsin and Minnesota. In 1951 he arrived in the Diocese of Dallas, Tex., after a two-year tour of duty as an assistant priest at the Holy Cross Church in Austin, Tex. Later, he was named assistant pastor of St. Charles Parish in Gainesville, Tex. In 1961 Lane was appointed assistant pastor of Holy Cross Parish in Dallas and became pastor there in 1964. At that time, he was one of only two African Americans among about 300 priests in the Diocese of Dallas. His appointment as pastor of the Holy Cross Parish made Lane the first African American priest to lead a congregation in the Dallas Diocese. Lane's ministry flourished in the racially mixed Holy Cross Parish, which in 1965 consisted of 400 families. He retired as pastor due to failing health in 1967 and served as the associate chaplain of St. Joseph Hospital in Fort Worth, Tex., until his death in 1968. He was buried at Calvary Hill Cemetery in Dallas.

Foley, Albert S. *God's Men of Color.* New York: Arno Press, 1969.
Harris, Ted. "School's Pioneer," *KP,* October 27, 2005, 6K.
The Official Catholic Directory. New York: P. J. Kenedy, 1946–1949.
Reis, Jim. "Our Savior Fills Unique Niche," *KP,* January 17, 1994, 4K.
"Rev. William LeRoy Lane," Archives, Diocese of Dallas, Tex.

Theodore H. H. Harris

LANFERSIEK, WALTER B. (b. February 3, 1873, Cincinnati, Ohio; d. March 1, 1962, Cincinnati, Ohio). Walter B. Lanfersiek, who became a political activist, was the son of William Henry and Elizabeth (Ellerman) Lanfersiek. He graduated from Woodward High School in Cincinnati (1891) and received a Bachelor of Law degree from the University of Cincinnati (1895). Having become enamored with the socialism of Eugene V. Debs, Walter married a kindred spirit, Pearl A. Blanchard, in 1906 in a ceremony performed by noted Cincinnati socialist and future congressman Rev. Herbert Bigelow. After working at various jobs, including that of an actor, Lanfersiek was practicing law in Newport in 1910 and living at 502 Washington Ave (today the Mansion Hill Tavern). He and Pearl crusaded for more city parks, better health care for the poor, and the redistribution of wealth. Lanfersiek ran on the 1910 Socialist ticket for U.S. Congress in the Sixth District of Kentucky; in 1911 he was the unsuccessful Socialist candidate for governor of Kentucky, receiving 8,718 votes. In May 1913 he was elected national executive secretary of the Socialist Party of America and moved to Chicago to fulfill his duties. He held that position until 1916. Over time, Lanfersiek had become a confidant of Debs and a participant in his presidential campaigns. During **World War I**, Lanfersiek became involved in the Socialist Peace movement. In 1917 he changed his name to Walter B. Landell, one of his former stage names, following the practice of assuming an alias that was common with many of his left-leaning contemporaries. He went on to work for the American Red Cross and as a proofreader in several southwestern Ohio cities. He came to believe that communist Russia was the utopia for the future. Lanfersiek died at a nursing home in the Avondale area of Cincinnati, unrecognized locally for what he once had been nationally. He was buried at Evergreen Cemetery, Southgate.

Haines, Randall A. "Walter Lanfersiek: Socialist from Cincinnati," *BCHS* 40, no. 2 (Summer 1982): 124–44.
Papers of Eugene V. Debs, Indiana State Univ. Library, Terre Haute, Ind.
"Socialist and Wife Running for Office Teach Creed to Baby," *KP,* November 4, 1910, 3.

Michael R. Sweeney

LANG'S CAFETERIA. Frank T. Lang (1892–1971), the owner of this Covington restaurant, was the American-born son of German immigrants Theodore and Clara Rauchfuss Lang, who settled in Louisville. As a young adult, Frank traveled to Newport to join his brother Hugo in the baking business. Later he struck out on his own, opening a sandwich shop in 1928 at 623 Madison Ave. in Covington, named simply Lang's. Lang's sandwich shop/Lang's Cafeteria changed and expanded several times over the nearly 40 years at the Madison Ave. location. In the 1930s additional space was acquired and decorated to express a Spanish theme, and the business became Lang's Spanish Tavern. The **flood of 1937** found part of the restaurant under water. Subsequent renovations included a plaque to mark the spot where the floodwaters had reached. At this time there was a cafeteria downstairs; upstairs was a restaurant and sandwich shop. The walls were of decorative stucco and wood paneling, with iron lighting fixtures in a Spanish motif. The cafeteria seated about 90 patrons and was open from 6:00 a.m. until 8:00 p.m. The upstairs stayed open until 1:00 a.m. and was a popular spot for a late-night sandwich and drinks. Beer was the only alcoholic beverage served. On July 4, 1944, a kitchen fire caused the closing of the upstairs. Fortunately, the cafeteria suffered only smoke damage and was able to continue serving customers. The upstairs was not reopened until four years later, because of the lack of adequate insurance and also the scarcity of building materials after **World War II**. The decor upstairs had changed again, by this time, to a more modern theme with indirect lighting and large original oil paintings of Kentucky by George Siegal. Gone were the sandwich and bar areas, and the space was dedicated to table service catering to businessmen and families. The menu also changed from time to time. Frank Lang personally planned all the menus, bought the food, and supervised the cooking. Each morning he drove his large station wagon to "the bottoms" of Cincinnati, where he purchased fresh produce from the warehouses located along the riverfront. Lang was very proud of the quality of his food. The orange juice was fresh squeezed, and pure butter and cream graced the tables. The desserts and rolls were baked fresh daily. By 1967, when the Lang family sold the restaurant to R. B. Cameron and William A. Taylor, it had become Covington's longest-operating restaurant. Two years later, in 1969, the restaurant closed.

Colegrove, Albert M. "A Story of Auld Lang Syne," *KP,* November 20, 1969.
"Lang Restaurant Changing Hands," *KP,* September 4, 1967.

Judy Lang Klosterman

LARRY A. RYLE HIGH SCHOOL. The Larry A. Ryle High School, a public secondary school in Boone Co., is located in the southern part of the county along U.S. 42, in Union. The namesake of the school, Larry A. Ryle, was a superintendent, a school administrator, a teacher, and a bus driver in Boone Co. When it opened in 1992, Ryle High School housed approximately 1,000 students in grades 7 through 12 on what had served as tobacco farmland for several decades. The campus of several hundred acres is also now home to both the Gray Middle School, opened in 1995, and the Mann Elementary School, opened in 2006.

Today, Ryle High School is a comprehensive school with about 1,700 students in grades 9 through 12. The school's goal is to provide the skills for students to excel and to contribute to the leadership, technology, citizenship, and character of the Ryle High School community. The organization of the school is traditional in purpose and design. Teachers work in content area teams, each of which has a common planning and work room, and the classrooms for each content area are located near each other. A variety of professional activities for teachers are offered.

The academic program at Ryle High School includes Advanced Placement courses, recognized by most colleges and universities for credit, in American history, art, biology, calculus, chemistry, computer science, English language, English literature, European history, German language, physics, psychology, and Spanish language. Honors courses in the core academic areas challenge students and prepare them for Advanced Placement courses or other college-level courses. The Career and Technical Education Team offers courses in business, technology, family and consumer science, and agriculture. The Fine Arts Team offers courses in foreign languages (Chinese, French, German, and Spanish), art, choral music, concert band, and marching band.

Ryle High School has distinguished itself for academic success since its founding. *Newsweek* named the school to its listing of the 1,000 best schools in the United States in 2001 and 2006. The school also has met its state-mandated achievement goals in every two-year grading period since 1992. Ryle High School has also been a leader in the awarding of the Commonwealth Diploma for achievement in Advanced Placement classes.

The extracurricular and cocurricular programs at Ryle High School have also been popular and successful. The Future Business Leaders of America (FBLA) have won many regional, state, and national honors: the group has been the largest chapter in the state, and among its members have been a Mr. FBLA, a Miss FBLA, and a national champion. The music program has earned honors and distinguished ratings in both concert band and marching band, and the marching band has reached the state final competition on several occasions. The athletics offered include baseball, basketball, cross-country, fast-pitch softball, football, golf, soccer, track and field, volleyball, and wrestling. Students have been crowned as individual state champions in swimming, track and field, and wrestling. The fast-pitch softball team earned the school's first team state championship in June 2006.

Randall K. Cooper, the founding principal, served Larry A. Ryle High School for 14 years and helped to establish a tradition of excellence. Cooper died in May 2006, and Matthew L. Turner was named as the second principal; he continues in the position.

"Boone to Name School for Larry Ryle," *KP*, September 14, 1990, 5K.

"Cooper Chosen as Principal of Boone's New High School," *KP*, March 31, 1992, 6K.

Larry A. Ryle High School. www.ryle.boone.k12.ky.us.

Larry A. Ryle High School Records, Larry A. Ryle High School, Union, Ky.

Matthew Turner

LA SALETTE ACADEMY. When the Sisters of Charity of Nazareth, Ky., arrived in the city of Covington in 1865, they found a handful of parochial schools operating that were staffed primarily by lay teachers. Bishop George Aloysius Carrell, the first bishop of Covington, had invited the sisters to the city to staff the elementary school of the Cathedral parish (see **Cathedral Basilica of the Assumption**) and to establish a private academy for the young Catholic men and women of the area. The Sisters of Charity found a building for their new academy at the southeast corner of Seventh and Greenup Sts. in Covington. The six rooms and basement of that structure served as both classrooms and convent. Although the building was not large, it was located near the Cathedral Basilica of the Assumption on Eighth St. and near Covington's growing Irish immigrant community. The new school was christened La Salette Academy.

La Salette Academy grew slowly but steadily over the next two decades. The school accepted both male and female pupils. Tuition was charged, but many were unable to pay the full amount. Initially, the academy enrolled only elementary aged students. A formal high school program, for girls only, was created, and the academy's first high school diploma was presented in 1884.

The small size of the original building that housed the academy hampered the development of the school. In 1886 the construction of a new two-story brick academy was begun on the original site, and the building was completed in the following year. The new academy housed both elementary and secondary programs and provided living quarters for the teaching sisters. In 1903 a third floor was added to the building for exclusive use as a convent for the sisters. La Salette Academy earned Kentucky state accreditation in 1923, and in 1930 the academy was granted membership in the Southern Association of Colleges and Secondary Schools.

The sisters began planning for the construction of a new high school building in the 1920s. These plans, however, had to be put aside owing to the **Great Depression**. Land was acquired directly south of the academy's building along Greenup St. for this purpose, and a new two-story Georgian-style brick school with a full basement was eventually constructed. Msgr. Walter A. Freiberg dedicated the new high school building on December 27, 1939.

La Salette Academy continued to flourish during the 1940s and 1950s. With the overturning of Kentucky's Day Law, the school enrolled its first African American student in 1955. From that point on, the academy's minority enrollment continued to grow. A majority of the pupils, however, were drawn from the nearby Catholic elementary schools staffed by the Sisters of Charity of Nazareth. These schools included ones operated by the Cathedral Basilica of the Assumption and **St. Patrick Catholic Church** in Covington, **St. James Catholic Church** in Ludlow, **Immaculate Conception Catholic Church** in Newport, **St. Anthony Catholic Church** in Bellevue, and **St. Catherine of Sienna Catholic Church** in Fort Thomas. All of these schools, with the exception of the St. Catherine school, were located in the older city parishes in Northern Kentucky, the areas most affected by the post–**World War II** migration to the suburbs. This demographic change had a major impact on La Salette Academy.

In 1966 the elementary school program at La Salette was discontinued. The academy's enrollment reached its peak in 1968 at 340. Beginning in that year, a steady decline took place, and by the mid-1970s, the operation of the academy was no longer financially sound. Finally, La Salette Academy conferred its last diplomas in 1977. A private developer eventually acquired the former academy's buildings and transformed them into La Salette Gardens, a residential facility for senior citizens.

Crone, Mary Collette, S.C.N. "La Salette Academy," Archives of the Diocese of Covington, Covington, Ky.

"La Salette Academy to Celebrate Its Seventy-Fifth Anniversary," *KTS*, May 22, 1931, 2.

Ryan, Paul E. *History of the Diocese of Covington, Kentucky*. Covington, Ky.: Diocese of Covington, 1954.

David E. Schroeder

LASSING, JOHN M. (b. 1864, Elm Tree, Boone Co., Ky.; d. October 25, 1936, St. Petersburg, Fla.). John Maurice Lassing, a politician, a lawyer, and a judge, was born in Boone Co., a son of Dr. H. C. and Anna E. Lassing. His early education was in area public schools before he entered Central University (now Eastern Kentucky University) at Richmond, where he graduated in 1886. For the next two years, he taught school and in his spare time apprenticed law under Burlington attorney **Fountain Riddell**. Lassing entered the Cincinnati Law School in 1889 and graduated two years later. He then set up his legal practice in Burlington. Shortly after locating there, he married Mary Lillard Brady, youngest daughter of Robert A. and Susan Brady, and the couple had three sons. For many years, John Lassing was active in state Democratic politics, successfully running the campaigns of Governor James B. McCreary (1875–1879 and 1911–1915) and state senator Thomas S. Paynter. Lassing was elected Boone Co. attorney in 1891, a position he held until 1898, when he was appointed a circuit court judge. He held that post until 1906, when he was appointed an appellate court judge. Lassing bought a home on Nelson Pl. in Newport and moved there in 1908. Because of ill health, Judge Lassing retired from the bench in 1913. He was named president of the Latonia Bank in 1914. Continuing health problems prompted him to begin wintering in Florida. Lassing died in Florida and was buried in the Richwood Presbyterian Church Cemetery in Boone Co.

Boone County Recorder, historical ed., September 4, 1930.

"Lassing's Life Ambition Is Granted," *KP*, June 23, 1906, 2.

"Latonia Bank Reopened," *KP*, June 1, 1914, 3.

Reis, Jim. "Judge Also Headed Boone Baseball League," *KP*, May 6, 2002, 4K.

"Resigns from Bench—John M. Lassing," *KP*, September 15, 1913, 2.

U.S. Gen Web Boone County, Ky. Biographies. www.rootsweb.com.

LATINOS/HISPANICS. Many Latinos/Hispanics, the latest in a long history of immigrants to the region, have recently made Northern Kentucky their home. The term *Latinos,* like *Hispanics,* generally refers to persons of Latin American origin or Spanish descent living in the United States. It is an ethnic, not a racial, category, since Latinos/Hispanics may be of any race or any mixture of races. The U.S. government adopted the category Hispanic for the 1970 census. In current usage, the term *Hispanic* is more common on the East Coast, while *Latino* is more prevalent on the West Coast. Neither term sufficiently describes the rich variety of races and cultures represented by Latin Americans. However, because Latin America and the Caribbean were colonized by the British, the French, and the Dutch, in addition to the Spanish, some scholars prefer the term *Latinos.* It seems more inclusive than *Hispanics,* which implies Spanish linguistic or cultural roots.

Pioneer Kentuckians had a vast, long-standing interest in the politics of the North American colonial empire of Spain. By terms of the Treaty of Paris of 1783, which ended the **Revolutionary War**, Spain regained Florida from Britain (which it had lost at the Treaty of Paris of 1763, ending the **French and Indian War**) and continued to possess New Orleans, as well as the territory of Louisiana west of the Mississippi. Until Spain ceded the expansive Louisiana possessions to France in a secret treaty in 1800, it essentially controlled navigation of the Mississippi River. In 1784 Spain closed the Mississippi River and the port of New Orleans to American citizens, upsetting Kentuckians interested in trade and commerce. In addition, Spain contended that its boundary with the United States lay just south of the Ohio River, while the United States maintained that the border was the 31st parallel. Claiming sovereignty over the Cherokee, Choctaw, and Creek Indians, Spanish authorities promised them an Indian buffer state and armed them, hoping to push settlers in Tennessee and Kentucky east of the Appalachian Mountains. The tense situation was later resolved by the Treaty of San Lorenzo (Pinckney's Treaty) of 1795, whereby both nations recognized the 31st parallel as the boundary between the United States and Spanish Florida and both promised not to incite the American Indians; also, Spain gave the United States a three-year grant of navigation of the Mississippi River and of deposit of goods at the port of New Orleans. In 1803 President Jefferson's administration arranged the Louisiana Purchase. As a result of the Adams-Onís Treaty (1819–1821) between the United States and Spain, the United States gained control over all of Florida. That agreement also fixed the southern boundary of the Louisiana Purchase at the Arkansas, Red, and Sabine rivers, and then westward along the 42nd parallel; this provision essentially waived any claims on the part of the United States to Texas.

In 1821 Mexico declared its independence from Spain. Spain, however, attempted to reconquer Mexico in 1829 and did not formally recognize Mexico until 1836. Also in 1836, Texas declared its independence from Mexico. In 1845 the U.S. Congress admitted Texas as a state, leading to the Mexican-American War of 1846–1848; soldiers from Kentucky and the **Newport Barracks** played a major part in this war (see **Mexican War**). By the Treaty of Guadalupe Hidalgo (1848), Mexico ceded more than half of its territory to the United States for $15 million. The loss of these possessions to the United States left a deep and lasting wound in the minds and hearts of many Mexicans. Continuing U.S. intervention in Latin America throughout the 19th and 20th centuries contributed further to less-than-ideal relations. That Northern Kentuckians maintained an interest in Latin American political affairs is illustrated by newspaper articles of the period and also by the popularity of an 1898 Cuban village exhibit, featuring a real Cuban refugee family, at the **Lagoon Amusement Park** in Ludlow (see also **National Guard, Spanish-American War**).

Throughout most of the 19th and 20th centuries, Northern Kentucky did not attract a large number of Latino immigrants. Rather, **German Americans, Irish Americans, African Americans, Italian Americans**, and **Appalachians** were the major groups to migrate to the region. The number of Hispanics remained negligible until the late 20th century. The musician **Joseph Tosso** (1802–1887), born in Mexico, lived in Kenton Co. as early as 1860, but in the same year, the U.S. Census reported only three other people of Spanish or Latin American birth in Kenton Co.

In the 1980s and after, more Latino immigrants arrived in Northern Kentucky. Some obtained work in the labor-intensive cultivation of tobacco in the region, while others gravitated to service, industrial, skilled trade, and professional positions. The growth of the Latino population in the area generally followed national trends. For instance, in June 2005, the U.S. Census Bureau released a news bulletin stating that the Hispanic population of the United States had passed the 40 million mark. Currently, Hispanics constitute the nation's largest minority. Likewise, in Northern Kentucky, Hispanics are becoming an increasingly important component of the population. The official census figures listed below are merely an indication of the growth in the Latino community; the actual population of Hispanics in the region is much larger than these numbers, owing to a significant undocumented and uncounted population.

In May 2006 the large numbers of undocumented workers in Northern Kentucky made regional and national news. Agents of U.S. Immigration and Customs Enforcement (ICE), part of the U.S. Department of Homeland Security, after a two-year investigation, arrested 76 illegal aliens, largely from Mexico or Guatemala, who were employed for a subcontractor of Fischer Homes of Crestview Hills. Also arrested were four supervisors for Fischer Homes. Michael Chertoff, Homeland Security secretary, stated in an official ICE news release about the Fischer Homes case, "We will continue to bring criminal actions against employers who are consistently harboring illegal aliens." Throughout the following weeks and months, other arrests in the investigation were made, until nearly 100 had been charged. The investigation of Fischer Homes appeared in national news media, including the *New York Times* and *Fortune* magazine.

HISPANIC POPULATION IN NORTHERN KENTUCKY

County	*1990*	*2000*	*2005 (est.)*
Boone	318	1,702	2,622
Bracken	12	39	45
Campbell	319	765	941
Carroll	22	330	408
Gallatin	8	82	187
Grant	36	232	308
Kenton	704	1,669	2,151
Mason	76	160	188
Owen	14	105	123
Pendleton	29	97	125
Robertson	4	21	23
Total	1,542	5,202	7,121

Numerous institutions and programs have been established to serve the needs of Northern Kentucky's growing Latino population, as well as to educate other ethnic groups about Latinos. These include the **Centro de Amistad** (2001); the **Cristo Rey Parish** (2004); **HealthPoint Family Care**'s *Promotores* (Health Promoters Program, 2003); the Hispanic Resource Center (2001); the Latino and Multicultural Center for Regional Development (2005) at **Northern Kentucky University** (NKU); NKU's Latino Student Affairs office (2001); the Latino Police Academy (2003) of the City of Florence; and **Thomas More College**'s many Latin American programs. The college offers a Latin American and Caribbean Studies concentration in its International Studies BA degree program, the Mexico/U.S. Border Studies Program (2000), and the Jamaica Service Learning Program (2001). Thomas More College also keeps in touch with a sister university, Universidad del Sagrado Corazón in San Juan, Puerto Rico. In addition to the Catholic parish of Cristo Rey, Spanish-language religious services are held at Iglesia Cristiana Renacer, Russell St., Covington; the **Immanuel United Methodist Church**, at its old First Methodist Church campus in Covington (see **First United Methodist Church**); the **St. John Catholic Church** in Carrollton; the **St. Patrick Catholic Church, Maysville**; and Unidos en Cristo, at the Madison Ave. Baptist Church, Covington. Northern Kentucky's libraries offer many Spanish materials and programs, **WCVG** in Covington provides Spanish-language radio, and there are television and **cable television** Spanish-language programs. Latino grocery stores, restaurants, and businesses also abound in Northern Kentucky.

Birger, Jon, and Jenny Mero. "Shaking the Foundation." *Fortune*, June 12, 2006, 30.

Collins, Michael. "Fischer Homes Feels Sting of 'Get Tough' Approach," *KP*, June 10, 2006, 1A.

Glover, Robert Alan. "Celebrate Unity: Methodist Church Launches Hispanic Outreach Ministry," *KP*, August 28, 2003, 5K.
Kentucky State Data Center. http://ksdc.louisville.edu (accessed June 19, 2007).
Kreimer, Peggy. "Bienvenidos a Estados Unidos," *KP*, January 10, 2004, 1K.
Long, Paul. "Sentencing Is Delayed in Illegals Case," *KP*, January 4, 2007, 1A.
Long, Paul, and Shelly Whitehead. "Immigrant Raid Hits Homebuilding," *KP*, May 10, 2006, 1A.
Mitchell, Pama. "Living La Vida NKY: Latinos Finding Community Here," *Sunday Challenger*, August 22, 2004, 1B.
Newberry, Jon. "Illegal Workers an Open Secret," *KP*, May 13, 2006, 1A.
Schroeder, Cindy. "Clinicians Fill Need for Hispanics," *KE*, July 26, 2003, B1.
Troutman, Elizabeth. "Morales on a Mission to Help Hispanics," *KP*, July 14, 2005, 4K.
U.S. Immigration and Customs Enforcement. "Fischer Homes Supervisors Charged with Harboring Illegal Aliens in Worksite Enforcement Investigation." www.ice.gov/pi/news/newsreleases/articles/060509washington.htm (accessed June 19, 2007).
Whitehead, Shelly. "Latino Police Effort Wins Annual Award," *KP*, June 12, 2004, 5K.

Paul A. Tenkotte

LATONIA. Latonia in Kenton Co., originally known as Milldale, developed at the intersection of two toll roads, Decoursey Pk. (the **Three-L Highway**) and Taylor's Mill Pk. Decoursey Pk. originally led to a ferry that operated across the Licking River, and Taylor's Mill Pk. led to an early gristmill located on the Banklick Creek. The name Milldale probably was a reference either to James Taylor's early mill or to George Mills, a local entrepreneur who owned a large amount of land and operated an early distillery in the area. Although the community was incorporated in 1894 as South Covington, this name was never used. The name Latonia was borrowed from the famous **Latonia Racecourse** (1883–1939) located in the southern end of the community, now the site of a large shopping center. The name of the racetrack, in turn, originated from a popular 19th-century health springs site located to the south of the city on Madison Pk. (Ky. Rt. 17) at the intersection of Highland Pk.

The historic crossroads of Latonia's business district (known as Ritte's Corner) included banks, groceries, saloons, apartments, drugstores, and hardware stores, which developed along with the racetrack. Walter Ritte ran one of the earliest saloons and groceries, dating from 1890, and lived nearby at the northeast corner of Southern and Church Sts. Ritte's Corner, the five-street crossroads of Decoursey Pk. and Taylor Mill Rds., took its name from Ritte's long-lasting establishment. Johnny's Toys (see **Toys**), perhaps the town's most enduring business, was begun as a small confectionery near Ritte's Corner. In the early and middle 20th century, Nick and Margie Casullo operated Nick's Place, probably Latonia's most popular restaurant of that period. The business continues as Nick's Grove in nearby Independence. Latonia Bakery, now named Bernhard's Bakery, has been a Latonia commercial landmark for more than 80 years.

In the early 1900s, Ritte's Corner boasted a fountain erected in the middle of the crossroads, used primarily to water horses. After the advent of the automobile, the fountain began to be a traffic hazard and was removed after occasionally being struck by motorized vehicles. Fifty years later, the Latonia neighborhood association and the city's VFW raised $60,000 to build a new fountain. A small park was constructed at Ritte's Corner in 2002 to commemorate the 50th anniversary of the conclusion of the **Korean War**. Today, water flows from a fountain facing north at Ritte's Corner. Flowers, benches, and a decorative wrought-iron fence surround the fountain.

Railroad tracks, built in the 1850s, crisscrossed the center of Latonia; the **Kentucky Central** (north-south) and the **Louisville and Nashville** (east-west) were the main railroads involved. These railway lines are now owned by **CSX**. The rail yard just south of Latonia at **DeCoursey Station**, the northernmost point of the Louisville and Nashville main line until the 1930s, was the terminus of coal shipped from southeastern Kentucky. Freight cars were sorted here. The local area's early economy was based on railroad development, and many residents of Latonia worked for the railroads. The DeCoursey Yards were phased out during the early 1980s. Even though little remains of the railroad industry in Latonia, one can still experience the era by visiting the **Railway Museum of Greater Cincinnati** on the western side of Latonia and seeing vintage railroad equipment.

In 1883 Milldale's population was a sparse 700 persons, but with the opening of the racetrack, the community grew rapidly. Local businesses profited exceptionally from the Latonia Racecourse; particularly brisk was the boardinghouse activity in town during the spring and fall meets. Many residents added to their incomes by renting spare rooms to visiting gamblers or people working at the track.

By the turn of the 20th century, the growing community, which began being called Latonia soon after the racetrack opened there in 1883, reached the status of a third-class city, and streetcar service connected Latonia to downtown Covington and Cincinnati. Soon afterward, however, Latonia incurred a large public debt in attempting to install sidewalks and other infrastructure in the city. After lengthy negotiations, Latonia was annexed to the City of Covington in 1909. Covington agreed to assume Latonia's debt, and Latonia became the most politically influential portion of the City of Covington, continuing so for many years. Latonia also accounted for 25 percent of the total population of Covington.

Among Latonia's many churches, some of the largest are the **Calvary Baptist Church**; the **Holy Cross Catholic Church**, with its well-established elementary school and **Holy Cross High School**; the **Latonia Baptist Church**; the Latonia Christian Church; the Runyan Memorial Christian Church; and the Trinity United Methodist Church.

Boeckley Drugs, Conley Brothers, and Swindler & Currin Funeral Homes are examples of long-standing commercial enterprises in Latonia of which several generations of the same families have been owners. Many families in Latonia choose to remain in the community and pass on the homes they have lived in to their children.

"Change the Name—Milldale to Be Known as Latonia," *KP*, September 13, 1899, 1.
Claypool, James C. *The Tradition Continues: The Story of Old Latonia, Latonia, and Turfway Racecourses*. Fort Mitchell, Ky.: T. I. Hayes, 1997.
"Latonia Is Now a Part of Covington," *KP*, November 4, 1908, 1.
"Latonia Will Soon Erect Its Fountain," *KP*, August 11, 1914, 1.

Karl Lietzenmayer

LATONIA BAPTIST CHURCH. The Latonia Baptist Church dates back to 1892, when, under supervision of the Immanuel Baptist Church in Covington, Rev. J. A. Lee began leading the Latonia Mission. Lee's small group first met in the home of O. M. Johnson at the corner of 31st and Rogers Sts. in Milldale (which was annexed to Latonia in 1906). Later, they congregated in other homes, in a hall above Scroggins' Drug Store (later Keller's Hardware Store) on Main St., and in the "old" Methodist Church building. In 1896 a lot was purchased at Main (now Decoursey) and Golden Sts. (or Golding, now 38th St.) in Milldale; a new church building was completed and occupied that same year. On May 14, 1900, an agreement was reached whereby the Latonia Mission congregation would pay $750 and assume the Immanuel Baptist Church's $800 mortgage on the property. A reorganization meeting was held on Sunday, May 20, and on May 27 Rev. C. A. Earl became the reorganized church's pastor. In the fall of 1900, the North Bend Baptist Association granted membership to the congregation as the First Baptist Church of Latonia. The new church in Latonia listed its membership at 39. Although Earl was pastor in 1900 when the church was admitted into the North Bend Baptist Association, W. R. Hutton, a lay preacher and the clerk of Immanuel Baptist Church from 1893 to 1895, led the congregation during 1898–1899 and is regarded as the first pastor of the Latonia Baptist Church.

The present sanctuary, located in Latonia at 38th and Church Sts., was completed in February 1917. A new education building was finished in 1941, and membership grew from 992 to 2,101 between 1941 and 1949. On August 1, 1943, the church began radio broadcasts over the 250-watt WCPO in Cincinnati; on Sunday, August 5, 1945, it aired its first weekly program of *The Glorious Gospel Hour* to 32 states and several foreign countries over Cincinnati's 50,000-watt radio station **WCKY**. In 1954 a new education building was constructed and existing facilities were remodeled to accommodate 1,250 in Sunday school. On September 4, 1959, a kindergarten was opened, and later a preschool program was added; both served to bring generations of children into the church. August 25, 1983, marked the birth of the SUN (Someone Understanding Needs) Group, which provided spiritual development to shut-in individuals, to the **Baptist Convalescent Center** in

Newport, and to Rosedale Manor in Covington. The LBC Television Ministry was launched in February 1984, when the Sunday morning worship service began being taped for broadcasting on the public access channel. Two additional programs were offered as well. This ministry continues to thrive, having received a number of awards.

The church serves as a meeting place for Alcoholics Anonymous, Al-Anon for spouses, and Al-A-Teen for children of alcoholics. Participants have become active members of the church. At least since 1934, the **Boy Scouts** of America have met in the church. The Cub Scouts and the **Girl Scouts** began meeting there in 1970 and 1997, respectively.

In 1998 a minister of family life was appointed, to provide counseling to individuals or groups. In the first two years, about 250 persons, about half of them church members, participated. Women became eligible to serve as deacons when the church bylaws and constitution were revised in 1989. In 1994 the first woman was ordained, and several other women have since become deacons. In 1996 the church purchased the vacant Johnny's Toy Shop property in Latonia in order to provide expanded parking space. In March 1998 a $2.2 million stewardship campaign was initiated with a major church renovation as its objective. On August 17, 2000, Latonia Baptist Church celebrated its 100th anniversary.

Latonia Baptist Church's mission efforts have led to the establishment of other churches locally, including the DeCoursey Baptist Church, the Rosedale Baptist Church, and the Ashland Baptist Church. In 1920, as a result of internal friction at Latonia Baptist Church, a member group established a separate fellowship that five years later was admitted by the North Bend Baptist Association as **Calvary Baptist Church** in Covington Throughout the Latonia Baptist Church's history, it has provided activities such as festivals, picnics, music, parties, and sports for persons of all age groups.

Gibson, Smith H., M. F. Stephens, Frank Hacker, Pauline Hacker, and Emma Batson. *The Spirit of Antioch: A History of Latonia Baptist Church*. Covington, Ky., Latonia Baptist Church, 1969.

"Latonia Baptist Celebrates 75th," *KP*, August 16, 1975, 12K.

Garry A. Casson

LATONIA CHRISTIAN CHURCH. This church owes its existence to a three-week revival series, held by Rev. George A. Miller, at the **First Christian Church** of Covington in early 1898. Miller and 25 charter members met on February 27, 1898, to form the Latonia Christian Church. Their early meetings were held in Bird's Hall at Ritte's Corner in Milldale, which was annexed to Latonia in 1906. Initially, Miller and Rev. P. H. Duncan, pastor of the Ludlow Christian Church, served as dual pastors, preaching on alternate Sundays.

A church member, Elizabeth Whipps, donated a 50-by-50-foot lot in Latonia on Franklin St. (now 36th St.) for a future church building. A subscription drive was held in February 1900, during which sufficient funds were raised to erect a small building. Construction was begun in March 1900, and the church was completed and dedicated on October 7, 1900. The congregation hired as its first full-time pastor Rev. Harlan C. Runyan, who was a graduate of Transylvania College in Lexington. He often told of the first service he held at the church in February 1902, when only 23 members attended and he was paid the entire offering collected, 30 cents. In those early years, the church received financial assistance from the Kentucky Christian Missionary Society. Under Runyan's able leadership, membership doubled by 1907, and an addition was made to the church to accommodate the increased attendance. In January 1911 the church declared its financial independence from the Christian Missionary Society. Owing to the rapid growth of the congregation, a new lot was purchased in Latonia at the corner of 39th and Decoursey Ave. for $5,500 in June 1921, and Cincinnati architect **David Davis** was commissioned to draw plans for a new building. It was erected at a cost of $98,000 and was dedicated on April 8, 1923. At the dedication service, 714 worshippers were in attendance. The church continued its phenomenal growth throughout the tenure of Runyan. Crowds in excess of 1,000 were common at services during the latter years of his ministry. To show their appreciation, his friends and fellow church members sent him and his wife on a tour of the Holy Land in 1926. Church membership had reached about 1,600 by the time Runyan died unexpectedly of heart failure on December 13, 1935.

The grieving congregation hired as their next pastor Rev. Charles D. Carter, who stayed for almost three years. At that time, a serious split occurred in the congregation, with Carter and about 250 members leaving to start a new church in Latonia, which they called the Latonia Church of Christ.

The Latonia Christian Church attendance had dropped to about 350 by the time the congregation hired their next pastor, Rev. Thomas D. Alderson, who stayed for only about a year. On December 3, 1939, the church voted to call as their next pastor Rev. Joseph D. Hill, who served the congregation faithfully for the next 33 years. During his tenure a parsonage was purchased, a new educational wing was built, a church bus began operating, and all debt was retired. When Hill resigned in 1973, he was followed by Rev. Hondel Adams, who stayed for about three years. On April 19, 1977, Rev. Mike Sweeney was hired as pastor, and he has now served the congregation for more than 30 years. The Latonia Christian Church celebrated its 100th anniversary at special services held in April 1998.

Latonia Christian Church, 1898–1948. Anniversary booklet. Latonia, Ky.: Latonia Christian Church, 1948.

"New Latonia Church Formed," *KP*, June 6, 1938, 1.

"New Latonia Church Voted by Dissenters," *KP*, May 23, 1938, 1.

LATONIA LAKES. The small community of Latonia Lakes, incorporated in 1953, was originally developed as a summer resort and weekend getaway destination. It was located on the east side of Taylor Mill Rd., about five miles south of I-275. The cities of Covington, Independence, and Ryland Heights, as well as small pockets of unincorporated Kenton Co., surrounded the tiny community. When the development opened in 1931, more than 900 cottage sites were quickly sold at $77 each. Within a few months, 40 cottages were completed and dozens more were under construction. Many of the homes were built overlooking the four lakes on the property. Residents suddenly enjoyed such attractions as fishing, boating, and swimming. The original clubhouse was renovated in 2004, and several tennis courts were added the following year. At the colony's peak, nearly 300 cottages were situated across the well-maintained property. The construction of new homes diminished during **World War II** as the entire development began a slow, steady decline. Many people who had purchased lots left them vacant. The property that was to become a later phase in the development has remained vacant as well.

Today, only 124 homes remain. The tennis courts are gone, and there is no boating or swimming in the one remaining lake. Several attempts to annex this former resort, by both Covington and Independence, had been rejected. However, suffering from too few tax dollars to cover necessary repairs to the roads and infrastructure, residents of the city voted 32-29 in November 2006 to dissolve the city. It came to an official end in December of the same year and is now part of unincorporated Kenton Co.

Hassert, Dan. "Last Rites for Latonia Lakes Near," *KP*, January 10, 2007, 1A.

Latonia Lakes advertisement. *KP*, May 27, 1932, 4.

"Latonia Lakes Clubhouse," *KP*, May 29, 1932, 2.

"900 Cottage Sites Established at Latonia Lakes," *KP*, June 14, 1931, 9.

Robert D. Webster

LATONIA RACECOURSE. The original Latonia Racecourse (1883–1939), located adjacent to 38th St. and Winston Ave. in what was once Latonia (now Covington), was for several decades one of the leading thoroughbred horse racing facilities in North America. Founded in 1882 by the Latonia Agricultural and Stock Association, Latonia Racecourse's first day of competition, June 9, 1883, drew an estimated 10,000 patrons and featured the Hindoo Stakes, a race that by 1888 was renamed the Latonia Derby. The Latonia racetrack immediately became part of Kentucky's famed "3-L" (Latonia, Lexington, and Louisville) race circuit, and racing there was equal in quality to that at the older facilities, the Association Track in Lexington (1828) and Churchill Downs in Louisville (1875).

Black jockeys were prevalent at southern and midwestern racecourses in the post–Civil War era, and the Latonia track was no exception. Isaac Murphy (1861–1896), acclaimed as the greatest black jockey, and several of his peers dominated Latonia's race stakes, winning with such regularity that they were preferred as riders over their white contemporaries. From the outset, the list of owners, trainers, and horses appearing at Latonia's racing facility was impressive. Top national racing stables were represented, such as the Chicago Stable of

Old Latonia Racecourse, ca. 1920.

Hankins and Johnson, "Lucky" Baldwin's west-coast stable, and many of the most prominent stables from Kentucky. Horses competing at the Latonia track were among the finest racing nationwide and included, between 1883 and 1929, 27 Kentucky Derby winners as well as many winners of prominent national stakes races.

Between 1883 and 1919 the track changed ownership several times; control alternated between locals and owners based in Louisville. In 1919 Latonia was sold to the Kentucky Jockey Club, a newly formed race syndicate led by Matt J. Winn. Winn, the man who had made the Kentucky Derby famous and arguably the most aggressive promoter of horse racing in America, thus entered the Latonia scene. Winn had always viewed the Latonia Derby as a serious rival to his beloved Kentucky Derby (he had been the chief figure at Churchill Downs since 1902), and with good reason, for the Latonia Derby had frequently offered a higher purse to its winner than that offered in Louisville. Winn moved immediately to correct the problem by introducing in 1919 a new featured race at the Latonia track, the $50,000 Fall Championship. This step prepared the way for the Latonia Derby's subsequent decline, because the new race downplayed Latonia's top-stakes race.

The new owners, operating first as the Kentucky Jockey Club and later as the Latonia Jockey Club, had purchased a thriving urban racetrack that throughout the second and third decades of the 20th century consistently led the nation in total purse money awarded. A track noted for its beautiful landscaping and a scenic infield lake, Latonia was often portrayed as one of America's finest race facilities. The "roaring 20s" were Latonia Racecourse's heyday. Legendary Kentucky Derby winners such as Black Gold (1924) and Clyde Van Dusen (1929) raced at the Latonia course, as did Upset, who took the Latonia Derby in 1922, two years after having become the only horse ever to defeat the great horse Man o' War. National and international champions such as Harry Sinclair's Zev (1923) and the French Champion Epinard (1924) also competed. Present at the Latonia track were many of the top riders, including Hall of Fame jockey **Mack Garner**, a Covington resident, as well as the famed Kentucky horseman E. R. Bradley, who for many years was a regular at the track. Exterminator (known to his many faithful fans as "Old Bones") won his maiden victory at the Latonia course in 1917 and while racing there (1917–1922) finished first, second, or third in seven out of eight races. Later inducted into the Racing Hall of Fame, he also placed first, second, or third in 50 of 100 races during his unrivaled eight-year career.

Speed always seemed to rule at Latonia, where the track was lightning fast and new national and world speed records were common. Two events marked the pinnacle of racing at the original Latonia track. First, Latonia's 1923 Fall Championship featured a thrilling battle between two-year-old champion and Kentucky Derby winner Zev and In Memorium, owned by local **Carl Wiedemann**. Zev was beaten, much to the delight of the locals, but weeks later avenged his loss to In Memorium in a still-disputed finish of the match race Winn had arranged for them at Churchill Downs. Second, a star-studded field competed in the third leg of the American International race run at the Latonia track on October 11, 1924. The American International race was won by Mrs. William K. Vanderbilt III's Sarazen, saddled by legendary trainer Max Hirsch, giving the French champion Epinard his third straight defeat and concluding a series meant to match America's best horses against the finest ones from Europe.

The fall of the stock market in October 1929 and the ensuing Great Depression ended "the glory days" at the old Latonia Racecourse. The size of Latonia's race purses dropped, the top jockeys, trainers, and owners departed, and the quality of the horses competing declined dramatically. The 1930s, especially the later part of the decade, were desperate times at the track. An assortment of gimmicks, such as lottery-type betting pools and lower admissions, were introduced in the attempt to survive. When these did not work, post times were set later in the afternoon, to attract fans who had completed their day's work. At best, the Latonia Racecourse was in a holding pattern with no relief in sight. The once-proud track's grounds were being used for political rallies, picnics, auto races, air shows, and even steeplechase racing. Ironically, the Latonia track's fame in racing history for having introduced "the 2 dollar bet" in 1911, for paying a record $1,885.50 win mutual in 1912, and for being where local jockey legend **Eddie Arcaro** got his start in 1931 was already assured, but the track's survival was not. Ultimately, Matt Winn and his partners, straining to sustain both Churchill Downs and the Latonia Racecourse during hard times, were forced to act. On July 29, 1939, the track in Latonia concluded its last meet. A few days later, the property was sold to the Standard Oil Company of Ohio, and demolition of the facilities began immediately.

Fortunately, many of the traditions and legacies of the original Latonia Racecourse have been continued, first at the modern Latonia Racecourse (1959–1986) in Florence, Ky., established and named as a tribute to the old track, and today by Turfway Park, an enterprise begun by Jerry Carroll in 1986 when he bought and renamed the Florence track. Turfway Park, which was sold again in 1999 to a partnership consisting of the Keeneland Association, Harrahs Entertainment, and GTECH Corporation, has also attempted to preserve the original track's legacy by continuing to run several races named for stakes first run at the original Latonia track. Lingering also are treasured recollections of the first Latonia Racecourse's glorious past as locals recall and recount either firsthand or passed-downed memories of the time when the track, affectionately referred to as "Old Latonia," was unquestionably one of the finest racecourses in all of America.

Claypool, James C. *The Tradition Continues: The Story of Old Latonia, Latonia, and Turfway Racecourses.* Fort Mitchell, Ky.: T. I. Hayes, 1997.

"The Minute Book of the Latonia Agricultural and Stock Association," archival collection of the Kenton Co. Library, Covington, Ky.

James C. Claypool

LATONIA SPRINGS. In mid-September 1788, a party of 30 or so settlers was scheduled to leave Lexington to mark out a road to the Mouth of the Licking River. Each settler paid a $1.50 survey fee for a one-half-acre in-lot and a four-acre out-lot in a new town located on the shore opposite the Mouth of the Licking. The deal would become permanent if the settler built a house on the in-lot and if, on the out-lot, two successive one-acre crops were planted.

The buffalo path (see **Buffalo Traces**) traveled by these settlers followed the Banklick Creek valley from near modern Walton toward the Mouth of the Licking. The settlers noted the large buffalo lick located five miles south of the mouth. The salty mineral water flowing from the ground looked like a buffalo lick to this generation, but like a medicinal spa to the next.

By summer 1829, Ralph Letton, proprietor of the Western Museum in Cincinnati, was building a hotel and spa on the buffalo lick, where today Highland Ave. meets Madison Pk. (Ky. Rt. 17; see **Three L Highway**). The hotel was located on the northeastern corner, while the springs were across the road under a lake. It was claimed that the Latonia Springs offered four different types of water: the first was strongly sulfured; the second was a solution of Epsom salts with sulfur and carbonic acid gas; the third was similar but more potable; and the fourth, although slightly saline, afforded a cool and pleasurable drink. The waters cured diseases that were variations on an upset stomach (indigestion, biliousness). **Daniel Drake** was among the visitors to the springs. J. Winston Coleman states that "Kentucky became the social center of the south because of the springs," but also that "trading horses, political opinions, and marriageable daughters [was] the real business at the springs."

The name Latonia probably comes from the ancient Greek goddess Leto, called Latona by the Romans. She was the mother of Apollo and Diana. The springs declined after the **Civil War**, but not before they gave their name to the fairgrounds, the **Latonia Racecourse**, and the small city containing the springs. Around 1900 the mineral waters stopped flowing at Latonia Springs and at hundreds of other locations in Kentucky.

Cist, Charles. *Sketches and Statistics of Cincinnati in 1859.* Cincinnati: Charles Cist, 1859.

Coleman, J. Winston. *The Springs of Kentucky.* Lexington, Ky.: Winburn Press, 1955.

Gastright, Joseph F. "Latonia Springs." *Bulletin of the Kenton County Historical Society,* May 1997, 2–3.

Reis, Jim. "Stories Flow along the Banklick," *KP,* April 22, 1991, 4K.

Joseph F. Gastright

LATTA, ALEXANDER BONNER (b. June 21, 1821, near Chillicothe, Ohio; d. April 28, 1865, Ludlow, Ky.). Alexander Latta, an inventor, was the youngest of six children of John and Rebecca Bonner Latta. Following a few years of elementary education, he worked in various industries, including a cotton factory, woolen mills, shipbuilding, a brass foundry, and a machine shop. At the machine shop, Latta gained important experience and many new skills. In the early 1840s, he moved to Cincinnati and became the superintendent of the Anthony Harkness Shop, one of the largest machine shops in the city. While at this firm, he was primarily responsible for the construction in 1845 of the first railroad locomotive west of the Allegheny Mountains. He also designed an innovative steam locomotive for the Boston and Maine Railroad. In 1846 Latta and his two brothers Edmundson and Findlay established the Buckeye Works on Race St. in Cincinnati.

The major accomplishment of Alexander Latta was designing the first practical steam-powered fire engine in the United States. The engine, which was first publicly tested on January 1, 1853, at the corner of Second St. and Broadway in Cincinnati, proved highly successful and profitable. In time, Latta improved on the design and sold many of his engines to fire departments throughout the United States.

Latta married Elizabeth A. Pawson of Cincinnati on October 21, 1847, and two of their children survived. The Latta family lived in Ludlow, Ky., for many years. Alexander Latta was a prominent citizen of Ludlow and was elected to the first city council in 1864. He was reelected in 1865 but died in 1865, before his term was completed. He was buried at Spring Grove Cemetery in Cincinnati.

The original Latta family home in Ludlow stood on Butler St. near Elm. This was the home Alexander and Elizabeth Latta lived in for many years. Latta's son, G. Taylor Latta, inherited the Ludlow property. In 1900 he had the old family home demolished and began construction of a new residence. This new brick home was designed in the shape of a dodecagon (12 equal sides) and is one of only a few such shaped homes in the United States. G. Taylor Latta was also responsible for subdividing the original Latta property and for constructing the appropriately named Latta Ave., which runs in front of the family home.

Alexander B. Latta Local History File, Kenton Co. Public Library, Covington, Ky.

"Architectural Freak," *KP,* July 6, 1931, 4.

Malone, Dumas, ed. *Dictionary of American Biography.* Vol. 6. New York: Charles Scribner's, 1961.

Spring Grove Cemetery Records, Cincinnati.

David E. Schroeder

LAWRENCEVILLE. Lawrenceville in Grant Co. is located southwest of Williamstown, at the junction of Lusby Mill and Heekin Rds. Streams in the area are the Eagle, Musselmans, and Wicked Willow (Grassy Run) Creeks. According to longtime Lawrenceville resident Christine Mitts, the town at one time had a store, a creamery, a blacksmith, and a Baptist church (organized in 1874). Lawrenceville's economy was rural, and the early local farms were largely self-sufficient. Today, the Lawrenceville Baptist Church has a well-kept building and grounds. Its building, which formerly belonged to the St. Joseph Catholic Church, was moved from Blanchet to be used as the Baptist church.

Early landowners in Lawrenceville were required to furnish labor for surveying and maintaining the roads to the mills, the churches, and the markets. Among the families responsible for the roads were the Chipmans, the Clarks, the Gaughs, the Hickses, the Jumps, the Simpsons, the Sipples, and the Wilsons. Later, toll-road companies, including the Mason and Lawrenceville Company, the Cincinnati Southern & Lawrenceville Company, and the Williamstown and Owen Line, attempted to maintain gravel roadbeds from usage revenues that they collected. Before 1900, the stockholders of these companies deeded their roads to the county.

The Cross Roads (Lawrenceville) School was on the John Mitts farm. The Grant Co. School Census of 1888–1889, District 52, listed G. W. Winters as trustee and H. Z. Alphin as teacher, with 31 children between 6 and 20 years of age enrolled. In the school year ending June 30, 1895, there were 110 pupils. The Lawrenceville School later was consolidated with the Mason School.

The Mount Olivet Church cemetery, on the Heekin-Crossroads Pk., remained when the church moved to Heekin. That cemetery is also called the Scroggins-Fortner graveyard. Another well-known local cemetery, the Musselman Children's Cemetery, is located on the Lawrenceville Rd.

The post office at Lawrenceville was established in 1876 and closed in 1906. Lawrenceville continues to be a close-knit community of good neighbors. Descendants of early settlers who have stayed on their families' land share their pleasant memories with those who return to visit.

Chandler, Virgil, Sr., comp. *Grant County Cemeteries.* Williamstown, Ky.: Grant Co. Historical Society, 1988.

Conrad, John B., ed. *History of Grant County.* Williamstown, Ky.: Grant Co. Historical Society, 1992.

Grant Co. Board of Education Records. Grant Co. Board of Education, Williamstown, Ky.

Pease, Janet, comp. *Kentucky Abstracted County Court Records.* Vol. 9. Williamstown, Ky.: Grant Co. Historical Society, 1992.

Mary Louis Evans

L. B. WILSON RADIO COMPANY. L. B. **Wilson** was born in Covington and spent his early years traveling in a theatrical group. In 1912 he returned to Covington and by 1913 had opened a smoke shop. He eventually became president of the Covington Industrial club, the forerunner of the local Chamber of Commerce (see **Northern Kentucky Chamber of Commerce**). Along with several other local men and Kentucky senator Fred M. Sackett, Wilson applied for a 5,000-watt radio station license that was granted and became **WCKY** radio in Covington. Wilson also started a radio manufacturing company that introduced three models of radios just in time for the opening of the radio station in September 1929. Two of the models were named Kenton and Campbell after the two northernmost counties of Kentucky, and the third was named the Kentuckian. They were displayed at the 1929 Radio Show at Music Hall in Cincinnati. The *Kentucky Post* sponsored a radio show in Covington in October 1929, and the Wilson sets were featured at some of the show's numerous radio display booths. The complete line of Wilson receivers were sold locally by Wilson himself and by the Dixie Sales and Service Company and the Johnson Radio shops. Wilson claimed to be Northern Kentucky's only radio manufacturer, and his company was chosen as the area's exclusive dealer for Howard Radios, which were very well known among radio manufacturers. The three radio models introduced by Wilson were Screen Grid receivers, and Wilson chose Magnavox Dynamic speakers as standard equipment. The Kenton and the Kentuckian were standard radio consoles, while the Campbell was a "highboy" version. All three featured various degrees of elaborate inlays and imported veneers, and the Kentuckian was available in two models with different complexities of cabinet design. All of the cabinets had the initials "LBW" carved into the scrollwork. The Robert Mitchell Company manufactured the radios in Cincinnati. At a time when the radio market was intensely competitive and many of the smaller manufacturers had already gone out of business, apparently Wilson radios did not sell well; it appears that they were manufactured and sold for only one year.

"Famous Set on Market," *KP*, September 15, 1929, supplement.

"Highboy Console Model of Radio Is Being Shown," *CTS*, Special Radio Show ed., September 16, 1929.

"One Station Is Due to Kentucky," *KP*, February 6, 1929, 1.

John E. Leming Jr.

LEADERSHIP NORTHERN KENTUCKY. Founded in 1979 by the **Northern Kentucky Chamber of Commerce**, Leadership Northern Kentucky (LNK) is a highly respected, community-based leadership development program designed to fulfill the community's need for informed and engaged leaders.

The mission of LNK is "to use the community as a classroom to develop leaders to effectively serve the region." This is accomplished through a curriculum delivered as a series of eight daylong training sessions, one overnight retreat, a community project, and a graduation program. The following topics are included in the curriculum:

—arts and literature: covers Northern Kentucky cultural history, the community impact of the arts, and the challenges facing arts organizations;

—health and human services: exposes members to the societal ills faced by many local individuals and families and the governmental and community organizations striving to end these problems;

—justice: teaches about the justice system and its impact on the community through visits to local jails, courts, and police organizations;

—diversity: introduces members to the community's diversity;

—government: includes meetings with public officials and observation of public meetings, including a trip to observe the Kentucky General Assembly;

—education: discusses all aspects of the K-16 educational system, including its many challenges and the opportunities for members to support and contribute;

—economic development: deals with the current economic climate and the importance of economic development on the region's health and well-being; and

—media: introduces members to the print, radio, and television media and explains how media can promote community issues.

Each year, approximately 40 new class members are selected by a panel of judges based on three required reference letters, individual professional accomplishments, community service contributions, and the individual's desire to contribute to the community. A growing alumni network of 800 members also helps to foster participation in community activities such as board memberships and charitable work.

"Business People," *CE*, August 28, 2004, D1.

"Formula for Success," *KP*, December 14, 2004, 4K.

Leadership Northern Kentucky Foundation. www.nkyleadership.com (accessed July 3, 2006).

"Leadership Program Sparks Change," *KP*, February 5, 1990, 3K.

Dave Hatter

LEAD INDUSTRY. Lead was mined along the southwestern fringes of Northern Kentucky, where early settlers found substantial lead deposits in present-day Owen Co. The industry was also active in the adjacent counties of Franklin and Henry. Lead deposits were discovered in the lower Kentucky River valley by 1780. Initially, the lead was utilized for making bullets. Later occupants made shot, white lead, and pipes from the lead. In more modern times, lead has been used in storage batteries, paint, ceramic glazes, gasoline, and alloys.

Lead, or galena as it is properly known, is usually found in association with other minerals such as barite, calcite, and sphalerite, which occur in narrow, nearly vertical veins. Galena occurs in the form of small gray cubes that are frequently embedded in barite, a dense white mineral. Once lead was discovered, miners would prospect the area to determine the direction and length of the vein. Veins exposed near the surface could be exploited by following the lead downward in narrow trenches. To reach deeper deposits, vertical shafts were sunk and hoists were used to raise the ore to the surface. Drift shafts were commonly excavated horizontally off the vertical shaft following the vein. The drift shafts were often placed at 100-foot vertical intervals. After the ore was removed from a mine, the galena had to be cleaned and separated from other minerals occurring with it. Wooden troughs, called jigs, were used in conjunction with a stream of water to wash the ore. A concentrating mill separated the galena from the barite.

Early furnaces for smelting lead ore were simple stone foundations built into the side of a hill. The lead ore and logs were placed in alternating layers. As the wood burned, the galena melted and settled to the bottom, where it was later collected. More complex and efficient furnaces were developed as time passed. The reverberatory or cupola furnaces, with tall chimneys and with separate fireboxes that kept ashes out of the lead, replaced the old log furnaces. Reverberatory furnaces could operate continuously, unlike the primitive log furnaces, which were burned only once per firing.

Lead mining started in Owen Co. about 1812 and continued until around 1940. Four lead veins, named the Barnett, Cantor, Gratz, and Hoosier veins, are known in the county. The Barnett vein, mined to a very limited extent, was narrow and had a 20-foot-deep shaft sunk into it in 1913. The Cantor vein, up to three feet wide, was exploited by the Twin Creek Mining and Smelting Company Inc., incorporated in 1901, which excavated vertical shafts to depths between 80 and 90 feet. Drift shafts were placed horizontally near the bottom of the vertical shafts to follow the veins.

The Gratz lead vein, first mined about 1825, was the one most extensively mined in Owen Co. The Ohio Lead Mining Company of Portsmouth, Ohio, operated the mine at Gratz that exploited this vein. At Gratz a vertical shaft was excavated to a depth of 325 feet. Horizontal shafts up to 1,040 feet long were placed at 100- and 200-foot levels in the shaft. The Twin Creek Mining and Smelting Company also mined the Gratz vein. Geologist Charles Norwood visited this mine in 1875 and noted that the shaft was 76 feet deep and the vein was 22 inches wide at 54 feet below the surface. In the early 20th century, it was found that this vein went as deep as 480 feet below the surface. Occasional swells in the vein were reported to be five to six feet wide. The Hoosier vein was mined by the Lead Mining Corporation of America, which excavated a shaft to 130 feet deep to exploit a lead vein ranging up to 14 inches wide. The mine and the concentrating mill appear to have closed by 1905. The deposits removed from these mines were often sent to be assayed by the Hartsfeld Reduction Works along Thornton St. in Newport. Some small lead veins in southern Campbell Co. were discovered around the time of the Civil War.

The once important lead industry is all but forgotten. The plants and furnaces have long since been dismantled, and most of the mineshafts and trenches have been filled in for safety reasons.

"Important Discoveries in Campbell County," *CDE*, June 7, 1865, 3.

Jillson, Willard R. *Lead Mines of the Lower Kentucky River Valley.* Louisville, Ky.: John P. Morton, 1941.

"Lead—A Valuable Owen County Mine," *KJ*, June 23, 1893, 4.

Norwood, Charles J. *A Reconnaissance Report on the Lead Region of Henry County, with Some Notes on Owen and Franklin Counties.* Frankfort, Ky.: Kentucky Geological Survey, 1877.

Charles D. Hockensmith

LEATHERS, JOHN W. (b. 1809, Kenton Co., Ky.; d. May 17, 1873, Kenton Co., Ky.). Kentucky legislator John W. Leathers was the third child of John W. and Elizabeth Leathers. A farmer by occupation, he lived on Lexington Pk. (**Dixie Highway**) about five miles south of Covington. Leathers spent almost his entire life on his family's farm. In his public life, he was described as a lifelong Democrat (see **Democratic Party**) who was frank and outspoken but always true to his principles. In his private life, he was described as a good husband, father, friend, and neighbor who inspired love, honor, and respect from those around him. Leathers served in the Kentucky Senate (1849–1851) and in the Kentucky House of Representatives (1867–1869). He also was for many years a director of the **Covington and Lexington Turnpike** Company and a strong advocate for improved roads and other public projects. Leathers suffered a stroke on May 12, 1873, and died five days later at age 64. His funeral service was held at his home and was attended by a large crowd. He was laid to rest in the Highland Cemetery in Fort Mitchell.

Collins, Richard H. *History of Kentucky.* Vol. 1. Covington, Ky.: Collins, 1882.

"Death of John W. Leathers," *CJ,* May 24, 1873, 2.

Reis, Jim. "Leathers Family Member Made Mark in State Politics and Real Estate Deals," *KP,* November 4, 1991, 4K.

LEBANON PRESBYTERIAN CHURCH. The second church organized in the area that later became Grant Co. was the Presbyterian Church at Lebanon, which was started in 1796. The Lebanon community, west of Crittenden, was settled by Virginians William Anderson, Nathaniel Bullock, Andrew Kincaid, William Martin, Andrew McCluir (McClure), and their families. Later, Joseph Canady, Thomas Canady, Alexander McClure, Moses McClure, Nathaniel McClure, Alex McPherson, Joseph Meyers, and Robert Stewart joined them. These pioneers petitioned the Synod of Virginia to organize a Presbyterian Church at Lebanon, and it was established by Elder Samuel Rannells in the home of Andrew Kincaid. William Martin and Robert Stewart soon erected a small log building near Bullock Pen Creek, where worship services were conducted. Men and women sat on opposite sides of the church, and the only hymns sung were the Psalms.

An Indian attack against the Andrew Brann family in 1807 or 1808 resulted in a fire that destroyed the log church. With help from his fellow church members, Joseph Meyers constructed a second log church in 1808 on Big Bone Rd., where the Lebanon Cemetery is located. Alexander McClure, Joseph Meyers, and Jonas Stephenson donated the land for the new church.

In 1826 on a nearby hill, a noted former Presbyterian minister named Barton Stone held a series of meetings in which he questioned several points of doctrine held by the Presbyterian church. As a result several members of the church decided to form a separate church adhering to Stone's beliefs, the Crittenden Christian Church. The Lebanon Presbyterian Church lost some additional members in 1842 when they left to form the Crittenden Presbyterian Church. The Lebanon Presbyterian Church continued to be active until the 1950s, but eventually its membership dwindled, and in August 1968 Rev. Ralph Hoffman conducted the Lebanon Presbyterian Church's final service. In 1988 the Presbytery merged the Lebanon and Dry Ridge Presbyterian churches; the surviving members of the Presbyterian church in Lebanon transferred their memberships to the Dry Ridge Presbyterian Church.

Conrad, John B., ed. *History of Grant County.* Williamstown, Ky.: Grant Co. Historical Society, 1992.

John B. Conrad

LEDGER INDEPENDENT **(MAYSVILLE).** Although Maysville's daily newspaper, the *Ledger Independent,* is only 40 years old, its roots can be traced back for more than a century. The *Ledger Independent* was first published on October 1, 1968, following the simultaneous purchase of the city's two daily newspapers, the *Public Ledger* and the *Daily Independent,* by the Gadsden (Ala.) Times Publishing Corporation. The newly chartered Maysville Publishing Corporation, with former *Gadsden Times* business manager James M. Striplin as its president and publisher, continued publication of an afternoon edition of the *Public Ledger* while the company's morning edition carried the masthead of both papers. By early 1969 the Maysville Publishing Corporation was printing one morning edition six days a week under the combined *Ledger Independent* masthead. Both the *Ledger* and the *Independent* had been family-owned and family-operated newspapers.

The *Public Ledger* started publication in 1892 under eight incorporators, including Thomas A. Davis, who soon became sole owner. The paper was bought by Arthur F. Curran in 1909 and later was sold to Clarence Mathews and William D. Cochran in 1915. By 1920 the *Public Ledger* was under the sole ownership of Mathews, remaining in the family until the 1968 sale to Gadsden and the Maysville Publishing Corporation. Mathews served as publisher until his death in 1958. His son, William B. Mathews, became the fourth and last sole owner and publisher. Mary Mathews, the publisher's wife, served as editor of the *Ledger,* and she followed her husband into retirement after the sale.

The *Daily Independent,* first published as the *Mason Independent* in 1907, was founded by James and John L. (Jack) Purdon. In 1911 the paper came under the sole ownership of James Purdon, but by 1913 Purdon had acquired another partner, L. F. Schatzman. Schatzman continued his association with the publication until his death, at which time the newspaper reverted to the sole ownership of the Purdon family.

The *Daily Independent* absorbed its morning rival, the *Daily Bulletin,* in 1936. **Martha Purdon Comer**, who served as editorial consultant to the *Ledger Independent* until her death in 2003, began her career with the family-owned *Daily Independent.* She succeeded her brother, J. Clifford Purdon, as editor in 1935. In 1980 the *Ledger Independent* was sold to Howard Publications Inc., a Delaware corporation with headquarters in Oceanside, Calif.

Howard Publications owned 17 daily newspapers nationwide. Gary Quinn, who came to Maysville with the Striplins in the late 1960s, assumed the position of publisher and retained that position until 1991, when he accepted a similar position with another Howard newspaper, the Freeport (Ill.) *Journal-Standard.* Robert L. Hendrickson, who began his journalism career with the *Ledger Independent* as a reporter in 1978, served as editor of the newspaper before Quinn's departure. At that time he was named publisher, a position he currently holds.

In 2002 Lee Enterprises Inc., based in Davenport, Iowa, purchased the Howard publishing group, including the *Ledger Independent.* At the time of the purchase, Lee Enterprises Inc.'s chairman and chief executive officer, Mary Junck, cited the Howard newspapers' focus on local news, which was also the primary focus for the Lee group. Lee Enterprises owns 38 daily newspapers and has a joint interest in 6 others, along with associated online services. Lee Enterprises also publishes nearly 200 weekly newspapers, shopper guides, and classified and specialty publications.

Located in the heart of a seven-county area of Northern Kentucky and southern Ohio, the *Ledger Independent* has shown tremendous growth in both quality and quantity in the last several years, meeting the expanding needs of the community. One added service is community Web sites serving the newspaper's market. The newspaper has made great strides in technology and newsgathering capabilities, including the addition of computer networks for news, advertising, photo scanning, and layout pagination.

"Looking Back on a Century of Publishing," *Ledger Independent,* September 10, 2004, supplement.

"Martha Comer Led Maysville Paper—Editor, Columnist, Advocate Dies at 96," *CE,* March 7, 2003, B4.

LEDOUX, ALBERT REID (b. November 2, 1852, Newport, Ky.; d. October 25, 1923, Cornwall-on-Hudson, N.Y.). Mining engineer and metallurgist Albert Reid Ledoux was the son of Rev. Louis P. and Katharine Reid Ledoux. Following his graduation from the School of Mines at Columbia University in New York, in 1873, Ledoux studied at universities in Berlin and Heidelberg; he received his doctorate from the University of Göttingen in 1875. Ledoux began his career as a state chemist and a member of the State Board of Health in North Carolina. He received an honorary master's degree from the University of North Carolina in 1880. Ledoux relocated to New York and worked with major corporations as a consulting engineer, a metallurgist, an assayer, and a chemist; he served as an expert in chemistry and engineering cases. Partnered with his brother Augustus and Columbia University professor Pierre de P. Ricketts, Ledoux opened his own research laboratory, Ledoux and Company. Ledoux rose to fame in U.S. industry after solving one of the most pressing issues facing the copper industry in the late 19th century. At the time, nearly all U.S. copper exports had to be weighed and tested in Europe, utilizing antiquated Cornish testing procedures, before European markets would make payment for shipments. This requirement resulted not only in delays but also in loss of the silver found within the copper. Ledoux decided to open his own assay laboratory in his New York–based company to decrease the losses faced by American copper exporters. As Ledoux and Company gained a reputation in the eyes of European importers as a reliable assay firm, other U.S. copper exporters began to use its services, so that they could receive payment for their exports before shipping to Europe. In 1903 Ledoux was the president of the American Institute of Mining Engineers. He was also a member of the Scientific Alliance, the American Chemical Society, the Canadian Mining Institute, and the New York Academy of Sciences, among other scientific and professional organizations in the United States, Great Britain, and Germany. He was also involved as an expert in the New York Electrical Subway Commission, was vice president of the Assurance Company of America, consulted for the American Bureau of Mines, and served as vice president of the Chapultepec Land Company. Two years after the death of his first wife, Anne Van Vorst Powers, in 1918, Ledoux married Alice M. Baird. He was the father of the author and poet Louis Vernon Ledoux. Albert Ledoux died In 1923 at his home in Cornwall-on-Hudson, New York.

"Albert R. Ledoux Dies," *NYT*, October 25, 1923, 19.

Purvis, Thomas L., ed. *Newport, Kentucky: A Bicentennial History.* Newport, Ky.: Otto Zimmerman, 1996.

Who Was Who in America. Vol. 3. Chicago: A. N. Marquis, 1960.

Amanda C. Kerley

LEE, CATHERINE "DIXIE" (b. September 21, 1916, Covington, Tenn.; d. August 5, 2001, Cincinnati, Ohio). Dixie Lee, a political activist and socialite, was born Catherine Boshers, the daughter of John Pershing and Clara Woods Boshers. Her father operated a string of movie houses and her mother was a school teacher. Clara Boshers died in a kerosene explosion in their home when Catherine was five years old. When she was six, the family moved to Clarendon, Ark., where she grew to maturity. She attended Vanderbilt University in Nashville, Tenn., and earned a BA in psychology from Butler University in Indianapolis, Ind. She also earned a MA in French at the University of Cincinnati. In 1939 Catherine enlisted in the U.S. Navy Nursing Corps and served for six years, until after **World War II** ended, achieving the rank of lieutenant commander. During the war Catherine was stationed at the Great Lakes Naval Station in North Chicago, Ill. When she worked as a nurse in Akron, Ohio, her friends started to call her "Dixie Belle," a nickname that Catherine disliked. She succeeded eventually in getting rid of the "Belle" part; however, "Dixie" stayed with her for the rest of her life. While stationed in San Diego, she met Dr. W. Vernon Lee, whom she married in 1946. Lee, a surgeon who came from Brooklyn, N.Y., was also in the U.S. Navy. In the 1950s Dixie Lee taught at the University of Kentucky Northern Community Center (later **Northern Kentucky University**) in Covington.

When Lee began running for office, she wanted to change her name legally to Dixie so that the ballot would show the name by which she was known and recognized. However, attorneys found that Kentucky law did not permit a married woman to change her name. In 1966 Lee was the first woman in Kentucky to make a run for the U.S. Congress; she was a Democrat at the time. Although she lost in the primary to former mayor and Kentucky state senator John Moloney of Covington, she came in second in the Boone Co. portion of the congressional district. The following year, when she failed to obtain her party's nomination, she filed as an independent People's Choice candidate. Lee also ran for the U.S. Senate. She made her final bid for office in a campaign for the Kentucky Senate in 1969.

Lee continued to participate in politics by working for the Democratic Party for many years. In 1992, however, she endorsed Ross Perot, the Independent Party candidate for U.S. president. She liked the direct democracy inherent in Perot's electronic-town-hall campaign. Her local political involvement included a December 1995 challenge to the City of Covington to deal with traffic hazards on Garrard and Greenup Sts.

Dixie Lee loved political galas. In 1976 she attended the inauguration of President Jimmy Carter (1977–1981). In January 1992 she was determined to attend the inauguration of Bill Clinton as president. With the help of an old-time friend from Kentucky, U.S. senator Wendell Ford, chairman of the Inauguration Committee, Lee did attend the inauguration, accompanied by Rick Sacksteder.

She was also a gourmet cook and one of Kentucky's premiere hostesses. She entertained such luminaries as tennis players Jimmy Connors and Vitas Gerulaitis at her Fort Mitchell home, and visitors at her oceanfront villa on the Italian island of Sardinia included the English rock group the Rolling Stones and Prince Karim Aga Khan, a wealthy Muslim leader. In 1977 she wrote an article entitled "How to Throw a Party," in which she maintained that "the most important ingredient for any party is without a doubt the right combination of people." Lee was a unique woman who not only had qualities of leadership but was also was very insightful. ***Kentucky Post*** editor **Vance Trimble** said, "She could look you in the eye and read your mind. She would let you have your foibles and not take you to task about it." Lee was also opinionated, compassionate, and unpredictable.

After her husband died in 1996, Dixie Lee moved to Ball's Row in Covington, where she lived until her death at Cincinnati's Christ Hospital in 2001. Her ashes were buried in Clarendon, Ark. She was survived by her two children, Wellington Lee of Lakeside Park, Ky., and Jeanette Lee of Brooklyn, N.Y. As a *Kentucky Post* editorial commented, "No one will fill Dixie Lee's high heels."

"Dixie Lee," *KP*, August 10, 2001, 4K.

"Dixie Lee, State's Ultimate Socialite, Dies," *KP*, August 8, 2001, 1K.

Lee, Jeanette. Telephone interview by Rick Sacksteder, August 23, 2006.

Lee, Wellington. Telephone interview by Rick Sacksteder, June 10, 2006.

Ohio Death Certificate No. 72440, for the year 2001.

Reis, Jim. "Turmoil, Tragedy Defined Congressional Race of '66," *KP*, May 18, 1998, 4K.

Richard M. Sacksteder

LEE, E. S. (b. May 23, 1862, Danville, Ky.; d. December 8, 1932, Covington, Ky.). Edmund Shackleford Lee, a longtime Covington banker and local park commissioner, was the son of Joshua E. and Elizabeth Waller Lee. He came to Covington in 1884 and took his first banking job with the **Northern Bank of Kentucky**. His first wife was Frances Penn, and on June 22, 1886, he married his second wife, Stella Collins, at the Madison Ave. Presbyterian Church in Covington. In 1899 Lee became treasurer of the Kenton Building Association. He moved to the First National Bank and Trust Co. in Covington in 1900, where he served as cashier. In 1905 he was promoted to president of the bank. In 1909 the bank he headed merged with the Farmers and Traders Bank to form the First National Bank of Covington (see **First National Bank and Trust Company of Covington**), and Lee was named president of the combined bank. He also served as a director of the Federal Reserve Bank in Cincinnati and was chairman of the Liberty Loans campaign in Covington during World War I. Lee sold his home and 40 acres of land in Villa Hills to **Villa Madonna Academy** in 1922. He was also instrumental in gaining the donation of land by the millionaire businessman William P. Devou to the City of Covington for the park bearing Devou's name. As a result, Lee was named park commissioner. E. S. Lee died of a heart attack in his home at 1114 Cleveland Ave., in Park Hills, and was buried at Highland Cemetery in Fort Mitchell. His wife and eight children survived him. One son, D. Collins Lee, is generally regarded as the founder of the City of Park Hills.

"Banker," *KE*, December 9, 1932, 1.

"Covington Banker Found Dead in Bed, Heart Attack Victim," *KTS*, December 8, 1932, 1.

"Covington Park Board Pays Tribute to E. S. Lee," *KP*, December 16, 1932, 1.

"Details of Merger of First National Bank and Farmers & Traders Bank," *KE*, December 28, 1909, 9.

"Heart Attack Proves Fatal to E. S. Lee," *KP*, December 8, 1932, 1.

Kenton Co. Marriage Book 6, p. 181, Kenton Co. Public Library, Covington, Ky.

Kentucky Death Certificate No. 29838, for the year 1932.

Kerr, Charles. *History of Kentucky.* Vol. 5. Chicago: American Historical Society, 1922.

"Normal School to Be Erected," *KTS*, July 17, 1922, 16.

LEE, HENRY, BRIGADIER GENERAL (b. 1757, Virginia; d. October 24, 1845, Washington, Ky.). **Revolutionary War** veteran Henry Lee, an early Kentucky settler and prominent political figure, was born and raised in Virginia. Lee laid claim to 1,400 acres of land in what is currently Mason Co., Ky., by a process known as preemption, whereby he cultivated a crop of corn in 1775 and moved to the area, residing there at least twelve months before the year 1778. During the Revolutionary War, he left Northern Kentucky to serve in the Virginia line of the American army, where he attained the rank of lieutenant colonel. For his seven years of service in the war, he was given a patent for 7,777 2/3 acres of land. In 1785 he returned to the Mason Co. area and established Lee's Station, two miles from present-day Maysville. One year later, he became a trustee of Washington, Ky., and in 1787 he served as trustee of the newly chartered town of Maysville. In 1787 Lee served as a delegate to a convention in Danville, Ky., seeking statehood for Kentucky from Virginia. He was among the petitioners to the Commonwealth of Virginia for the establishment of Mason Co. in 1788. In 1792 he was one of five commissioners who chose Frankfort as the new state capital of Kentucky. Lee served in the

Kentucky Militia and was promoted to brigadier general of its 5th Brigade, which included the 15th, 28th, 29th, and 30th regiments. As compensation for his work as a surveyor for many years, he acquired substantial landholdings in Mason Co.

Henry Lee married 26-year-old Mary Young Fox, the widow of Arthur Fox Sr. and mother of 5 small children, and Henry and Mary Lee had 10 children of their own. As a result of the marriage, Lee gained additional land and became one of the largest landowners in Mason Co. He built a stately home for his family, which he called Clover Hill. As their family grew, the Lees found it necessary to build an addition onto the house. Today, Clover Hill remains and is known as Leewood, but the addition to the home has been removed.

During a storied lifetime, Henry Lee held many influential positions in the region, including county lieutenant, associate Circuit Court judge, city trustee, and president of the Washington branch of the **Bank of Kentucky**. Lee died at age 88; his place of burial is unknown.

Biographical Cyclopedia of the Commonwealth of Kentucky. Chicago: John M. Gresham, 1896.

Brumbaugh, Gaius Marcus. *Revolutionary War Records Virginia*. Reprint. Baltimore, Md: Genealogical Publishing, 1995.

Calvert, Jean, and John Klee. *The Towns of Mason County: Their Past in Pictures*. Maysville, Ky.: Maysville and Mason Co. Library Historical and Scientific Association, 1986.

Clift, G. Glenn. *History of Maysville and Mason County*. Lexington, Ky.: Transylvania, 1936.

LEE, WILLIS AUGUSTUS, JR., VICE ADMIRAL (b. May 11, 1888, Owen Co., Ky.; d. August 25, 1945, Atlantic Ocean, off the coast of Maine). Willis Augustus Lee Jr., a prominent naval officer, was the son of Judge Willis Augustus Lee and Susan Arnold Lee. According to family accounts, he particularly enjoyed outdoor activities and target shooting during his youth. He graduated from Owenton High School in 1904 and promptly received an appointment to the U.S. Naval Academy at Annapolis, Md. At the time barely 16 years old, he was the second-youngest member of the academy's class of 1908. During his years at Annapolis, he was the academy Rifle Team's star member, winning first place in both the rifle and the pistol competitions at the 1907 National Rifle Match.

Lee's shooting abilities led his superiors to steer him toward gunnery and ordnance positions after he graduated, and he started with gunboat service in the Asiatic fleet. Beginning in 1915, Lee put his knowledge and experience of weaponry to use as an inspector of ordnance. He went on to spend most of **World War I** in that position, overseeing quality control in the various munitions factories that were supplying the navy's war effort.

In 1920 Lee was temporarily relieved from naval duty so he could compete with the U.S. Rifle Team at the Olympic Games in Belgium. Individually, he won five gold medals, one silver medal, and one bronze medal. Additional medals were awarded to Lee and Capt. Carl T. Osburn for team shooting events. Lee's marksmanship talents were even more remarkable because a childhood firecracker mishap had almost blinded him, making it necessary for him to wear thick corrective lenses for the rest of his life. Under modern Naval Academy admissions standards, Lee would have been summarily rejected on account of his poor eyesight.

Throughout the 1920s and the 1930s, Lee alternated between sea and shore assignments. As war began to brew in Europe, the navy tapped his experience to educate the next generation of sailors. Lee was posted to the Division of Fleet Training, where he first headed up the gunnery and tactical sections. He soon rose to become assistant director, and ultimately director, of the entire Division of Fleet Training.

After Pearl Harbor, Lee was promoted to rear admiral and became assistant chief of staff to the commander of the U.S. Fleet, a post he held for only six months, before being summoned to the Pacific. Lee is best known for his pivotal role in the campaign for Guadalcanal. In November 1942 he led a task force of American battleships into combat against a much larger Japanese force, sinking a battleship and a destroyer and preventing the Japanese from recapturing a strategic stronghold in the region. As a result of this accomplishment, Lee was placed in charge of all the battleships in the Pacific theater.

The Pearl Harbor attack in December 1941 had decimated the Pacific fleet, and the new battleships that were being built to replenish U.S. forces were faster than their predecessors. They were able to keep pace with the aircraft carriers that had become the preferred mode of naval warfare. Lee's battleships acted as escorts to aircraft carriers, using their guns to defend the carriers while they carried out bombing missions. Despite decades of training and service in the traditional model of battleship warfare, Lee quickly adapted to the new supporting role. At least one military historian of the Pacific theater has credited Admiral Lee with raising carrier defense to an "art form."

Lee spent almost three full years at sea during **World War II** and participated in every single major action in the Pacific except the Battle of Midway. He was promoted to the rank of vice admiral in 1944, in recognition of these achievements. In May 1945 he was sent to the Atlantic to research possible defense strategies against Japanese kamikaze attacks. While on this special mission, off the Maine coast, he died suddenly on August 25, 1945, of a massive heart attack.

Lee was buried in Arlington National Cemetery with full military honors. His numerous awards included the Navy Cross, the Legion of Merit, the Distinguished Service Medal with Gold Star, and the World War II Victory Medal. In 1952 a ship was christened the USS *Willis A. Lee* in his honor. At a final cost of $29.5 million, it was one of the largest destroyers that had ever been launched. The *Willis A. Lee* served with distinction in the Atlantic, the Mediterranean, and the Caribbean until it was scrapped during the 1970s. In 2001 the U.S. Naval Academy's Rifle Team honored Vice Admiral Lee by placing a wreath on his Arlington gravesite on the 56th anniversary of his death.

Houchens, Marian Sidebottom. *History of Owen County: "Sweet Owen."* Louisville, Ky.: Standard, 1976.

James, Edward T., ed. *Dictionary of American Biography*. Supplement 3, 1941–1945. New York: Scribner's, 1973.

Kleber, John E., ed. *The Kentucky Encyclopedia*. Lexington: Univ. Press of Kentucky, 1992.

"Navy Rifle Squad to Honor VADM Willis Augustus Lee, Jr., USN '08." Naval Academy Varsity Athletics. www.navysports.com (accessed September 29, 2006).

Deborah Diersen Crocker

LEE HOUSE. One of the most famous buildings in Maysville is the Lee house, located at Front and Sutton Sts. It was built in three stages, the first about 1798, the second about 1840, and the third about 1850. The oldest section of the house is a Federal-style building on Sutton St. that is thought to have been originally a section of row houses. Two enterprising brothers, Peter and Henry Lee, built the house's second section in the Greek Revival style. They used the buildings as a hotel, to which they gave their family name. Henry Lee was a trustee of the town of Maysville and also president of the local branch of the **Bank of Kentucky**. During the summers, the Lee House was a convenient stop for travelers along the Ohio River and for tourists on their way to Lexington or to the mineral springs at the nearby **Blue Licks**. The Marquis de LaFayette, who had been a general in the **Revolutionary War**, visited Maysville on May 21, 1825, and it was said that he spoke from a balcony at the hotel. What is known is that General LaFayette dined at John T. Langhorne's hotel (then the **Eagle Tavern**, later called the Goddard House, and now demolished) on Front St. near Market St. in Maysville. In later years, when the Lee House was no longer in use as a hotel, it was erroneously named the Lafayette Apartments.

Many prominent people stopped at the Lee House, as attested by its guest register, which is on display at the **Kentucky Gateway Museum Center** in Maysville. Probably the most famous American guest was Kentuckian Henry Clay. He signed the register on May 31, 1852, listing his address as "Ashland" and his destination as "Heaven, I Hope." Over the years, the building has had a long succession of owners, some of whom called it the Lee House, others the Hill House, and still others the Lafayette Apartments. The house is listed on the National Register of Historic Places and is currently being restored.

Calvert, Jean, and John Klee. *Maysville, Kentucky: From Past to Present in Pictures*. Maysville, Ky.: Mason Co. Museum, 1983.

Clift, G. Glenn. *History of Maysville and Mason County*. Lexington, Ky.: Transylvania, 1936.

National Register of Historic Places Inventory—Nomination Form (for the Lee House), Kentucky Gateway Museum Center, vertical files, Maysville, Ky.

LEGAL AID OF THE BLUEGRASS. The Northern Kentucky Legal Aid Society, known today as Legal Aid of the Bluegrass (LAB), is a nonprofit organization that provides quality legal assistance to families and individuals who otherwise cannot afford it. As early as the 1920s, the legal community recognized the importance of legal justice for all. The Northern Kentucky Legal Aid Society formed more than 30 years ago in an effort to address equal justice in eight Northern Kentucky counties. In its infancy, the program included only two Covington locations. The Northern Kentucky Legal Aid Society first merged with Northeast Kentucky Legal Services. Then on January 20, 2002, the organization merged with Central Kentucky Legal Services to form LAB. Today, it serves 33 counties in Kentucky and is staffed by attorneys, management personnel, paralegals, and support staff. It operates five offices, with its main office in Covington; the eligible population served by LAB is about 139,000.

LAB supports client-specific legal services in civil matters, defending the integrity, safety, and well-being of families and individuals. It believes that people have a right to be safe and secure in their own homes and to enjoy economic stability. The health issues of Kentuckians are a priority, and particular attention is paid to the rights of the elderly, children, and all vulnerable individuals in society.

Although justice for all is a constitutional right, there is no law mandating legal representation in civil cases. Thus, funding to provide quality legal services is limited, and LAB cannot respond to the entire demand of the communities. Today there is nearly $4 million in funding sources, yet this cannot meet more than a fraction of the legal needs of low-income clients. Therefore, LAB makes use of case-acceptance guidelines that prioritize the most urgent needs, which are determined by input from clients, social services, legal communities, and the general public. There is a constant struggle to find alternative funding sources. LAB operates an active pro bono program, wherein private attorneys work for the good of the public, rather than for fees. Through this effort, attorneys assist low-income persons at no cost to the client. The organization receives only about 30 percent of its funding from federal sources, so community funding is vital to the life of this organization.

Despite the funding issues, the attorneys and staff are dedicated professionals who want to provide outstanding public service. Although the salaries for the attorneys and the staff are generally low, the workforce consists of highly skilled specialists, usually with many years of experience. Everyone has staggering workloads. Yet, these dedicated individuals enjoy a high rate of successful outcomes for their clients.

The American Bar Association honored LAB with its 2005 Hodson Award for Public Service. This national award honors one government or public-sector law firm annually.

American Bar Association. www.abanet.org (accessed July 27, 2006).

Cullison, Richard. "Two Legal Services Merge Office," *KP*, May 3, 2002, 2K.

"Justice for All," *KP*, January 8, 2003, 4K.

"Legal Aid Need Is Stressed," *KP*, February 14, 1928, 1.

Steven D. Jaeger

LEITCH, DAVID, MAJOR (b. September 11, 1753, Glasgow, Scotland; d. November 9, 1794, Leitch's Station, Ky.). At an early age, David Leitch immigrated to America with his older brother, James, and the two later went into business in Manchester, Va. David served in the army as a major during the **Revolutionary War**. When land grants were being given out to veterans of that war, he, in partnership with others, began speculating in land. Leitch came to own many thousands of acres in Kentucky; his holdings comprised most of the modern-day cities of Alexandria, Cold Spring, and Wilder, as well as much of southern Campbell and Kenton counties. The Commonwealth of Virginia granted him 13,800 acres along the Licking River in 1785; 10 years later, he deeded 4,600 acres of these to **William Kennedy**.

Leitch first came to Kentucky in the 1780s and was a member of the December 1784 convention in Danville that initially sought the separation of Kentucky from Virginia. In 1790 he married Keturah Moss of Bryants Station and around the same time built a blockhouse called Leitch's Station along the Licking River, about five miles upriver from its confluence with the Ohio. The site of Leitch's Station was formerly thought to be in the vicinity of Tippenhauer Rd. in Campbell Co., but later research placed it farther north, closer to present Beacon Dr. and the **AA Highway**. On a hillside east of the blockhouse, Leitch built a one-and-a-half-story log house, with a stone chimney and hewn walls inside and outside; still standing but in bad condition, it is located on the old Licking Pk. In 1794, while surveying a piece of land he was selling, Leitch slept outside all night in a cold rain; afterward he caught a bad cold and likely developed pneumonia. When he returned home, his wife's brother-in-law, Capt. George Gordon, and a surgeon from Fort Washington came to treat him, but Leitch died. On the day before he died, he had signed a will leaving his entire estate to his wife, Keturah Leitch. He was buried in the yard of the Leitch home, but in 1853 Keturah had his remains moved to the Evergreen Cemetery in Southgate. She had an impressive monument erected there, detailing significant events in David's life but incorrectly listing his date of death. In 1795 Keturah Leitch married **James Taylor Jr.**, the founder of Newport, with whom she bore 11 children; only four survived infancy. When Keturah died on January 18, 1866, she was buried next to David Leitch in the Evergreen Cemetery.

Bond, Beverley W., Jr., ed. "Memoirs of Benjamin Van Cleve." *Quarterly Publication of the Historical and Philosophical Society of Ohio* 17 (January–June 1922).

Hartman, Margaret Strebel. "Major David Leitch and Leitch's Station." In *Campbell County, Kentucky History and Genealogy, Falmouth Outlook*, December 15, 1978, supplement.

"The James Taylor Narrative," 1840, Kenton Co. Public Library, Covington, Ky.; Campbell Co. Historical and Genealogical Society, Alexandria, Ky.

Lindsey, Helen Bradley. "Leitch Station in Campbell County, Kentucky." *Papers of the Christopher Gist Historical Society* 1 (1949–1950): 35–42; reprinted as a pamphlet by the author and available in the collections of the Cincinnati Historical Society, Cincinnati.

Reis, Jim. "Birthright: Campbell County Grew from Leitch's Station," *KP*, October 3, 1983, 4K.

Tenkotte, Paul A. "Rival Cities to Suburbs: Covington and Newport, Kentucky, 1790–1890," PhD diss., Univ. of Cincinnati, 1989.

Jack Wessling and Paul A. Tenkotte

LENOXBURG. Lenoxburg, located on the western border of Bracken Co. and the eastern border of Pendleton Co., was named for Samuel B. Lenox, who owned the general store and was the community's postmaster for several years. The town's economy was dominated by the transport of tobacco to larger markets. In 1887 local citizens could purchase brooms from the E. C. Gosney broom factory. Lenoxburg also had a coffin shop, located in the basement of a house in town; that was where the coffins were displayed, and additional stock was stored in a nearby tobacco warehouse. Some residents vividly remember the large tobacco screw press, which remained until the warehouse was destroyed. Another such press was reported to have been in the tobacco warehouse in Foster; it was probably a John P. Parker press, manufactured in nearby Ripley, Ohio. Lenoxburg remains much as it began, a lovely small community with fine farms surrounding it.

Bracken Co. Extension Homemakers. *History of Bracken County*. Bicentennial ed. Brooksville, Ky.: Bracken Co. Extension Homemakers, 2002.

Caroline R. Miller

LEVASSOR, EUGENE (b. ca. 1789, Rouen, France; d. November 6, 1881, Covington, Ky.). Businessman Eugene Levassor was born in France, where his family and Gen. Marquis de Lafayette, one of the heroes of the American Revolution, were close friends. As a youth, Levassor became an accomplished pianist and was a friend of the renowned composer Wolfgang Mozart. Levassor served as a captain in the army of Napoleon Bonaparte. Upon Napoleon's downfall in 1814, Levassor fled in exile to Santo Domingo and then to the United States. He married his wife, Sofia, in 1815, and they had two children, Armand and Clara. Levassor moved to Cincinnati around 1820, where he started a grocery and dry-goods business in 1829 and became quite wealthy. Lafayette visited Cincinnati in 1825 and, while there, gave Eugene Levassor a present of a solid mahogany desk that had recently been given to him by the Philadelphia Chamber of Commerce. The desk became a treasured possession of the Levassor family.

About that time, Daniel Holmes took a job as Levassor's personal valet. Levassor taught his young employee to play the flute and to speak French. While working for Levassor, Holmes became enamored with his mentor's lifestyle and longed to pursue a business career himself. It was said that one day the two men had a heated argument, which caused Holmes to quit his job. He told Levassor that he was going out into the business world but would return someday, after becoming successful. Holmes traveled to New York City and took a job with the dry-goods firm of Lord and

Taylor. When his employer decided to open a new store in New Orleans, Holmes was chosen to be the manager because he spoke fluent French. He later purchased the store from Lord and Taylor. Holmes was very successful and to many was known as the "King of New Orleans."

The mid-19th-century Covington farm estates known as Wallace Woods, Holmesdale, and Levassor Park owe their existence to the three businessmen Levassor, Holmes, and Robert Wallace. Wallace and Levassor ran businesses in Cincinnati, and Holmes had his business interests in New Orleans, but all three loved to retreat to the tranquility of this part of Northern Kentucky.

Levassor purchased several parcels of land totaling 50 acres, close to the property of Robert Wallace. He built his first home there, between Catalpa St. and Holmesdale Ct. Later, he built a new, larger home nearby, which some called the Levassor Castle. He retired from his dry-goods business in 1845. In the mid-1850s, Daniel Holmes returned in triumph, as he had earlier promised Levassor, and purchased much of the land between Wallace and Levassor Aves. Holmes built his home on the site of present-day **Holmes High School** and renewed his friendship with Levassor. Levassor died in 1881 at age 92. At the time of his death, besides his holdings in Covington, he owned 5,000 acres of land in Virginia, nine houses in Cincinnati, and land in the West. He was a devout Catholic, and his memorial service was held at St. Mary Cathedral (**Cathedral Basilica of the Assumption**) in Covington. He was buried at St. Mary Cemetery in Fort Mitchell.

Dressman, Elmer H. "Lafayette's Desk Preserved in Covington Residence," *KP*, May 31, 1925, 1.

"A Drive out the Madison Pike." *Papers of the Christopher Gist Historical Society*, January 26, 1954, 49–56.

Gastright, Joseph F. *Gentleman Farmers to City Folks: A Study of Wallace Woods, Covington, Kentucky.* Cincinnati: Cincinnati Historical Society, 1980.

"Levassor Place Has Interesting History," *KP*, May 15, 1927, 9.

Reis, Jim. "Wallace Woods, Covington's First Suburb Sprang from Wooded Estate," *KP*, December 4, 1995, 4K.

"Sudden Death," *DC*, November 7, 1881, 1.

Jack Wessling

LEWIS, HOMER DICK (b. October 4, 1926, Covington, Ky.). Nuclear scientist Homer Dick Lewis is the son of Homer Dewey and Viola Codey Lewis. He grew up on W. 34th St. in Latonia, where his father was an engineer for the **Chesapeake and Ohio Railroad**. He attended Covington schools and graduated from **Holmes High School** (1944). After a stint in the U.S. Navy, he earned a BS in metallurgical engineering in 1952 from the University of Cincinnati. He also holds graduate degrees from the University of New Mexico. Lewis quickly became a leading nuclear scientist, researching and writing widely in his field of powder metallurgy. He has contributed entries in several books, has presented papers around the world, and holds patents relating to his specialty. He has worked for the Boeing Company and at the Los Alamos Scientific Laboratory in New Mexico. Lewis's work in powder metallurgy has brought about improvements in U.S. security and helped to end the cold war. In his retirement, Lewis lives with his family in Farmington, N.Mex. He remembers his Holmes High School days as being the impetus for his stellar career.

Holmes High School Alumni files, Holmes High School, Covington, Ky.

Who's Who in America, 2004. New Providence, N.J.: Marquis Who's Who, 2003.

Michael R. Sweeney

LEWIS, LYDA (b. September 17, 1948, Maysville, Ky.). Lyda Florence Lewis was the first African American to be named Miss Kentucky; she was the third African American and the first from the South to participate in the Miss America pageant. Lewis wanted others to view her for her talents and accomplishments, without race as a factor. She is the daughter of Edward Holt Lewis and Alice Kirk Johnson Lewis. Lyda Lewis's pioneering firsts in beauty competitions paved the way for other black women in the state and nation. Lewis graduated in 1966 from **Maysville High School**, where she was one of the first African American cheerleaders in the recently integrated schools. She also won awards for her academic work. She attended Morehead State University (MSU) in Morehead and graduated in 1970. She was the MSU homecoming queen in 1967, the first African American so named from any of the Kentucky colleges that were previously open only to whites. Since the MSU queen was selected by a vote of the student body, her selection is a testament to her popularity among her peers; it was also noted in *Jet* magazine. Lewis was the first African American to compete in Kentucky's Mountain Laurel Festival Pageant, where she was named Miss Congeniality. She was crowned Miss Jeffersontown in 1972 and Miss Louisville in 1973, and while competing as Louisville's representative in the state beauty pageant, she became Miss Kentucky in 1973. In 1974 she toured with the Miss America United Service Organizations Far East troupe. Lewis signed with the Ford Agency and worked as a model and an actress in New York City during the 1970s and 1980s.

"Black Is Beautiful for Lyda," *KP*, September 4, 1973, 4K.

Lyda Lewis file, Kentucky Gateway Museum Center, Maysville, Ky.

"Lyda Lovely Loses," *KP*, September 10, 1973, 3K.

"She's First Black Miss Kentucky," *KP*, July 16, 1973, 2K.

John Klee

LEWIS AND CLARK IN NORTHERN KENTUCKY. Before the names of Meriwether Lewis (1774–1809) and William Clark (1770–1838) were linked as explorers of the Louisiana Purchase and the Northwest, they undertook separate missions or adventures in Northern Kentucky. Clark viewed the land from Mason to Carroll counties at age 14 in 1785 when he migrated to Kentucky from Virginia along the "Great Ohio River Highway" with his parents, John and Ann Rogers Clark. The first visit to the region by Lewis occurred between 1797 and 1801, while he was on military duty serving at Fort Pickering (present-day Memphis, Tenn.). His later travels as regimental paymaster, between Pittsburgh and Fort Washington (now Cincinnati), Detroit, and other scattered military units, added to his experience in the region.

Clark was commissioned a lieutenant in the regular infantry on March 7, 1792. His assignment under the command of Gen. James Wilkinson and later Gen. "Mad" Anthony Wayne gave him a first-hand view of Northern Kentucky. In 1793 Clark was sent to the mouth of the Kentucky River, the future site of Port William (modern-day Carrollton), to build a depot for corn and other supplies.

Lewis, a militia veteran of the Whiskey Insurrection of 1794, met Clark in 1794 at Fort Greenville, now Greenville, Ohio, when General Wayne transferred Lewis to Clark's Chosen Rifle Company of the 4th Sub-Legion. Lewis and Clark's service together in Wayne's Legion was short because Clark resigned his commission on July 1, 1796, to assist in settling the tangled financial affairs of his brother Gen. **George Rogers Clark** as well as for personal health reasons. After leaving the army, however, William Clark maintained a correspondence with Lewis, and on March 10, 1801, when Lewis accepted the invitation of the newly elected president, Thomas Jefferson (1801–1809), to be his private secretary, the names of Lewis and Clark were about to become linked forever. On June 19, 1803, Lewis wrote to Clark at Louisville, inviting him to be a co-commander in what was later called the Corps of Northwest Discovery. The letter carried an assurance that the offer was supported by President Jefferson.

As Lewis descended the Ohio River during fall 1803, on his way to meet Clark, he stopped in Limestone (future Maysville), where he met and recruited **John Colter**. Colter, who was one of the "Nine Young Men from Kentucky," became a legend as a mountain man after the expedition. Lewis rested his men and resupplied his boat in Cincinnati, then traveled across country to **Big Bone Lick** in Boone Co. His crew brought the boat to Landing Creek while Lewis dug for mastodon bones for President Jefferson. Lewis was successful with the excavation, but the bones were lost in a boat accident near present-day Memphis, Tenn. Jefferson also asked Lewis and Clark to look for living mastodons in the west during the expedition. The explorers found none, and the president sent William Clark to Big Bone Lick in 1807, following the expedition, for a second effort to secure bones from the site. Jefferson knew the property owner, David Ross, and made arrangements for Clark's dig. Clark arrived at Big Bone Lick on Sunday, September 6, 1807, with his older brother George Rogers Clark and York, William Clark's slave. A crew of eight worked in the mud to recover bones, teeth, and tusks for President Jefferson. They found stone tools and Clovis points as well, but the collateral material was not recognized as significant for almost 200 years. The Clovis point excavated by William Clark in 1807 became part of the collection of Dr. **William Goforth**, who had helped Clark with his dig at Big Bone Lick. Today, those Clovis points are at the Cincinnati Museum of Natural History.

Experience and leadership skills learned by Lewis, Clark, Colter, and York in Northern Kentucky were important to the success of the 1803–1806 Lewis and Clark Expedition. On December 2, 1806, 484 square miles of Mason Co. were spun off to become Lewis Co., the first government jurisdiction named in honor of a coleader of the Lewis and Clark Expedition.

Ambrose, Stephen E. *Undaunted Courage.* New York: Simon and Schuster, 1996.

Clark, William. *Dear Brother: Letters of William Clark to Jonathan Clark.* Edited and with an introduction by James J. Holmberg. New Haven, Conn.: Yale Univ. Press, 2002.

Foley, William E. *Wilderness Journey: The Life of William Clark.* Columbia: Univ. of Missouri Press, 2004.

Jackson, Donald. *Letters of the Lewis and Clark Expedition with Related Documents, 1773–1854.* 2nd ed. Urbana: Univ. of Illinois Press, 1978.

Jillson, Willard Rouse. *Big Bone Lick.* Louisville, Ky.: Standard, 1936.

Jones, Landon Y. *William Clark and the Shaping of the West.* New York: Hill and Wang, 2004.

Kleber, John E., ed. *The Kentucky Encyclopedia.* Lexington: Univ. Press of Kentucky, 1992.

Tankersley, Kenneth. *In Search of Ice Age Americans.* Salt Lake City, Utah: Gibb Smith, 2002.

James L. Mallory

LEWISBURG (COVINGTON). The Lewisburg neighborhood of southwest Covington developed along a branch of **Willow Run** Creek. Today, the National Register of Historic Places defines the Lewisburg historic district as located between I-75 and Covington's boundary with Park Hills and Devou Park. The district extends north to the Ohio River. Lewisburg was annexed by the City of Covington in the 1840s.

After 1842 German Catholics in Lewisburg could attend Mutter Gottes (**Mother of God Catholic Church**), the new German-speaking church located in nearby Covington. In 1848 Lewisburg residents attending Mutter Gottes began lobbying to build a Catholic elementary school nearby. Backers purchased three lots and a fourth one was donated; the school opened in 1848. In 1854, a year after the Diocese of Covington was formed, **St. John Catholic Church** in Covington was built.

Several breweries (see **Brewing Industry**) operated in Lewisburg: the Lexington Brewery, opened by Duhme and Company in 1859 on the north side of Pike between Lewis St. and Western Row; the Lewisburg Brewery, which Charles Lange and Frank Knoll established in 1866 at the northwest corner of Lewis and Baker Sts.; and the **Bavarian Brewing Company**, started by Julius Deglow and Charles Best in 1866 on Pike St. east of Willow Run Creek.

Lewisburg was the home of many **tanneries**, as well as slaughterhouses (see **Meatpacking**). Local historian Chester Geaslen once recalled six slaughterhouses (including those of Conrad Walz, Charlie Hais, and Charlie Kraus and Sons), mostly along Lewis St. Moonshiners operated in a barn not hidden from the neighborhood, and more than one public establishment hosted cock (rooster) fights. At the corner of Lewis and Worth Sts. were Fromandi's Beer Saloon and, next door, Fromandi's Zoo, which had a bear, a wolf, a fox, a weasel, a raccoon, a monkey, a wildcat, an alligator, and two snakes. By 1957 Fromandi's grandson John M. Zembrodt operated Fromandi's, then called the Hillside Café.

Streetcar service began in the Lewisburg district in 1890, and the Lewisburg line also became the first leg in a very scenic route up Montague and Amsterdam Rds. that eventually included a view of lovely Park Hills (see **Streetcars**). This was a streetcar ride on high trestles over Sleepy Hollow Rd. and over the entrance to St. John Cemetery, a run along the Dixie Highway past Highland and St. Mary cemeteries, Blessed Sacrament Church, and residential streets in Fort Mitchell to the turnaround at the end of the line in Fort Mitchell, opposite Orphanage Rd.

Most of the buildings in Lewisburg were built between 1865 and 1900. Lewisburg had a flourishing business district along Pike St. that included a post office, a kindergarten operated by the City of Covington (the teacher for many years was "Miss Daisy"), Vogt's Pharmacy, Dr. King's chiropractic office, Tinglehoff's Bakery, Ed Schmidt's Supermarket, and Zimmer's Hardware (closed in 2008). Grander than most of the homes in Lewisburg are 618 W. 11th St., once the home of H. H. Helman, a grain merchant, and 708 Lewis St., at one time owned by Charles Lang of the Lewisburg Brewery. The architecture of Lewisburg is typical of the other parts of Covington.

Chris Papas, who had opened a candy-manufacturing shop, Lily's Candies, in Covington on Madison Ave. in 1935, later relocated the manufacturing function to 921 Baker St., the former site of the Lewisburg Brewery. When Papas retired in 1951, his son took over Chris A. Papas and Sons, a wholesale candy business on Baker St. in Lewisburg, still known for its Easter candies (see **Candy and Ice Cream**). In 1946 Robert L. Glier ran a butcher shop at 439 Pike St. In the mid-1950s, the shop (now Glier's Meats Inc.) began making **goetta** and soon opened a second plant in Cincinnati. In 1967 the Glier's meat company concentrated its operations at 533 W. 11th St. in Lewisburg in a former dairy bottling plant adjoining the Bavarian brewery's complex. In the 1990s, selling locally and regionally, the Glier's meat company doubled production. In 2002 Glier's Meats Inc. sold 1 million pounds of goetta and Covington renamed a section of 11th St. in Lewisburg Goetta St.

Herb and Thelma's (operated by the Boehmker family) is a neighborhood tavern along Pike St. that displays both old and new beer signs and serves soup, chili, steak hoagies, mettwurst, hot dogs, and especially hamburgers and cheeseburgers, to patrons who might be focusing on television sporting events. The business is located in a building dating to 1859, at the site of the old Lexington Brewery. Like the Standard Club, between Baker St. and the expressway in Lewisburg, Herb and Thelma's has hosted neighborhood "social clubs," card playing, and sports activities. Butler Plumbing and Heating, once located at 957 Western Ave. in Lewisburg, returned there after Knochelmann Plumbing and Heating moved to a larger facility. Dixie Novelty, started 45 years ago by Doug, Derek, and Dan Bosse, the third generation of the Bosse family, is at 934 Baker St. in Lewisburg. Dixie Novelty sells party decorations, ceremonial award items, and supplies for such charitable gaming activities as bingo and Monte Carlo.

The construction of I-75 in the early 1960s impacted Lewisburg significantly (see **Expressways**), displacing many homes, the nearby historic Covington Ball Park (see **Baseball**), and some playgrounds. The Lewisburg Neighborhood Association, which began in 1993, has organized a neighborhood Block Watch in an effort to prevent crime. In early 1997 a convenient and affordable family health center (see **HealthPoint Family Care**) opened in the old Schmidt's Supermarket on Pike St., replacing the old tile storefront with a brick front reminiscent of the 19th-century architecture of the neighborhood. The Veterans of Foreign Wars post at 945 Montague Rd. (see **VFW**) has sponsored the War Memorial across from the post's meeting hall in Lewisburg. The memorial features two field artillery pieces, a large flagpole, and a marker commemorating members of the post who were killed in **World War II**. In 1994 the Lewisburg Neighborhood Association, using federal grant money, transformed an unkempt space across from the VFW into the landscaped Quarry Pointe and War Memorial located near the entrance to Devou Park.

Geaslen, Chester F. *Strolling along Memory Lane.* Newport, Ky.: Otto, 1971–1974.

Schmitz, Raymond A. *St. John's Catholic Church, Covington, Kentucky, 1854–2004.* Covington, Ky.: St. John Catholic Church, 2006.

John Boh

LEWISBURG (MASON CO.). The town of Lewisburg in Mason Co. is approximately halfway between Maysville and Flemingsburg on the main road and six miles south of Maysville along the North Fork of the Licking River and the **Louisville and Nashville Railroad** line. Lewisburg was established on December 17, 1795, by the Kentucky legislature on the land of George Lewis, after whom the community was named. Lewis was a pioneer and a founder of the county. He had reestablished Clark's Station at Lewisburg in 1789 (see **Mason Co. Stations**), was one of the signatories requesting that the Virginia legislature establish the town of Washington in Mason Co., was one of Mason Co.'s representatives to the convention in Danville in 1792 that wrote Kentucky's first constitution, and later served in the Kentucky legislature. Lewisburg quickly became a thriving community. Lewis built a mill and a dam, and then a canal was constructed to direct water to the mill. A woolen mill operated in town in the 1840s, using wool purchased from local farmers. The Lewisburg Baptist Church was established in 1843, across the North Fork on the edge of town; according to tradition, Lewis did not want a church built in the town proper. The congregation of the Lewisburg Baptist Church continues to use the original church building. The town also had a distillery. Residents crossed the Licking River from early in the 19th century until 1930 using a covered bridge located in Lewisburg. Schools in the town included the Lewisburg Academy, the Lewisburg Male and Female Institute, and the Lewisburg High School, which in 1926 consolidated the local one-room schools. That school served the community in some form until 1973, and its gym continues to be used by the community through the Lewisburg Lions Club. The railroad came through town during the 1870s, and the rail station was named Marshall's Station. The post office at Lewisburg was called North Fork. The new Fleming-Mason Airport was opened in recent years just south of Lewisburg.

Calvert, Jean, and John Klee. *The Towns of Mason County: Their Past in Pictures.* Maysville, Ky.: Maysville and Mason Co. Library Historical and Scientific Association, 1986.

Clift, G. Glenn. *History of Maysville and Mason County.* Lexington, Ky.: Transylvania, 1936.

Rennick, Robert M. *Kentucky Place Names.* Lexington: Univ. Press of Kentucky, 1984.

John Klee

LIBRARIES. Libraries in Northern Kentucky first appeared in the urban areas located along the Ohio River: Covington, Maysville, and Newport. The earliest known library was the Covington Social Library, established in 1824. For the next 75 years, numerous libraries operated in Covington for brief periods, usually as subscription services for those who could pay a minimal fee. In 1839 the Kentucky legislature chartered the Maysville Lyceum to operate a library and reading room. The first public library in Northern Kentucky was established in Maysville in 1878 with a bequest from an unknown Englishman along with a gift from Maysville hat and umbrella merchant James Wormald. It opened along Sutton St. and remained in that block for the next 117 years (see **Mason Co. Public Library**). In the 1870s and 1880s, a series of groups including the Odd Fellows established subscription libraries in Newport.

The 1890s brought a dedicated effort by local governments to establish free public libraries in Newport and Covington. Committees of prominent citizens in each city approached Andrew Carnegie for financial assistance for library construction. Carnegie provided funding that resulted in new libraries in Newport in 1902 and Covington in 1904. In the meantime, temporary libraries had begun in Newport in 1899 and in Covington in 1901 (see **Covington Public Library**; **Kenton Co. Public Library**; **Campbell Co. Public Library**; **Newport Public Library**).

Outside the major cities, women's clubs were responsible for establishing many public libraries throughout Northern Kentucky. The Erlanger Woman's Club was organized in 1914 to provide library service in Erlanger and Elsmere that continued until 1967. The Owen Co. Women's Club began library service with a library in Owenton in 1946 (see **Owen Co. Public Library**). The Carrollton Woman's Club opened a library in that city during the late 1940s using **World War II** bonds for funding. Building on this foundation, the Library Commission of Carroll Co. was formed in the late 1940s to receive a state grant for providing countywide service. The **Williamstown Women's Club** and the Grant Co. Younger Women's Club petitioned the Grant Co. Fiscal Court for funding, which made it possible to open the **Grant Co. Public Library** in 1954. The Town and Country Women's Club of Brooksville received a grant from the Kentucky Department for Libraries and Archives (KDLA) in 1983 to create a library in Bracken Co. (see **Bracken Co. Public Library**).

As the region developed, other groups also attempted to establish libraries. Several groups opened libraries in Boone Co. beginning in the 1940s, but none were successful in obtaining the necessary funding. A coalition of organizations in Pendleton Co. received a grant from the state in 1953 to open the county's first library in the Falmouth City Hall (see **Pendleton Co. Public Library**).

Library service in the region improved during the 1950s as a result of a statewide bookmobile program. Kenton, Owen, and Pendleton counties received their first bookmobiles as a result of this program during the early 1950s. In 1952 the **Robertson Co. Public Library** was founded in Mount Olivet.

By the mid-1960s, it was apparent that public library service across Northern Kentucky was inadequate for modern communities. Even the Carnegie libraries in Newport and Covington were chronically underfunded. The Commonwealth of Kentucky became more active in promoting public libraries, and the KDLA assigned Philip N. Carrico to the position of regional librarian for Northern Kentucky to promote the development of public libraries. Carrico immediately began to establish or support public libraries in each county. State law allowed the creation of special taxing districts that became the method of support for libraries. Kenton Co. created such a district in 1967, combining the Covington Public Library, the Erlanger-Elsmere Library, and the Kenton Co. bookmobile. Mason Co. followed suit in 1971, along with Owen and Boone counties in 1973, Carroll Co. in 1975, and Grant Co. in 1976 (see **Carroll Co. Public Library**; **Boone Co. Public Library**).

Gallatin Co. obtained a grant from the KDLA in 1978 for a demonstration library that led to the creation of a county library system in 1980. A petition drive led by Betty Daniels in Campbell Co. resulted in the creation of the Campbell Co. Public Library district in 1978. The Women's Club demonstration library in Bracken Co. was closed in 1987, owing to the lack of continued funding, but a dedicated group of residents persisted through many obstacles to create the Bracken Co. Public Library District in 1991.

As Northern Kentucky continued to grow, so did public library facilities. New libraries were opened in 1973 in Owen Co. (Owenton); in 1974 in Kenton Co. (Covington); in 1976 in Boone Co., Kenton Co. (Erlanger), and Pendleton Co.; in 1981 in Carroll Co.; in 1984 in Campbell Co. (Cold Spring) and Gallatin Co. (Warsaw); in 1989 in Boone Co. (Hebron); in 1994 in Boone Co. (Walton); and in 1995 in Bracken Co. (Brooksville), Campbell Co. (Fort Thomas), Kenton Co. (Independence), and Mason Co. (Maysville). The Pendleton Co. Public Library (Falmouth) was devastated by flooding in 1997 but was restored and reopened with a new collection and new technology.

The new millennium brought a generation of new libraries with expanded services and facilities. Libraries were constructed or expanded in 2000 in Boone Co. (Union) and Gallatin Co. (Warsaw); in 2001 in Owen Co. (Owenton); in 2002 in Kenton Co. (Erlanger); in 2003 in Campbell Co. (Newport), Grant Co. (Williamstown), and Mason Co. (Maysville); in 2004 in Bracken Co. (Brooksville); and in 2007 in Kenton Co. (Independence).

Northern Kentucky libraries were also at the forefront of the technology revolution in the late 1990s. Automated card catalogs were developed throughout the region, beginning in Kenton Co. in 1990. The Internet brought the world of information to Northern Kentucky public libraries, with public access to the Internet beginning in Boone Co. in 1996. With strong funding and heavy usage by the public, libraries in Northern Kentucky are among the strongest in Kentucky.

Mueller, Jan. *Soul of the City: A Centennial History of the Newport Public Library.* Cincinnati: Specialty Litho, 2004.

Wayne Onkst

LICKING RIVER. The Licking River, a tributary of the Ohio River, flows about 320 miles from Magoffin Co. northwest to its confluence with the Ohio River between Covington and Newport, opposite Cincinnati. The watershed of the Licking drains about 3,707 square miles, or about 10 percent of Kentucky. The **Dry Ridge Trace** in Northern Kentucky is the geological division between the watersheds of the Kentucky River, to its west, and the Licking River, to its east. That is, most streams to the east of the Dry Ridge Trace flow into the Licking River, and thence into the Ohio River; creeks to the west of the Dry Ridge generally flow into the Kentucky River, and from there into the Ohio. Of course, some streams on both sides of the Dry Ridge Trace flow directly into the Ohio River.

The Licking River has three main forks in Northern Kentucky: Middle (sometimes referred to as the Main Licking), South, and North (not to be confused with the Upper North Fork of the Licking in Morgan and Rowan counties). The Middle Fork of the Licking River, the longest of the three, originates in the Cumberland Mountains (see **Appalachians**) in Magoffin Co. and flows in a northwesterly direction through Morgan Co., where it joins Cave Run Lake, an 8,270-acre body of water in Daniel Boone National Forest, impounded by the earth and rock-fill dam in Rowan Co. completed by the U.S. Corps of Engineers in 1973. North of the dam, the Middle Fork of the Licking River continues, forming all or part of the boundaries between Rowan and Bath counties, Bath and Fleming counties, Nicholas and Fleming counties, Nicholas and Robertson counties, and Robertson and Harrison counties. Fed by the North Fork of the Licking River, which joins the Middle Fork near the southeastern boundary of Pendleton Co., the Middle Fork continues to Falmouth. At Falmouth the Middle Fork and the South Fork join and continue in one main Licking River, which then travels northward through Pendleton Co. and continues north, serving as the boundary between Kenton Co. on its western banks and Campbell Co. on its eastern banks. The South Fork of the Licking River begins in Bourbon Co., at the juncture of Stoner and Hinkston Creeks, and flows northward through Bourbon and Harrison counties to Pendleton Co., where it joins the Middle Fork at Falmouth. The North Fork has its headwaters in the northeastern section of Fleming Co. and flows northwest, dividing Lewis and Fleming counties, traverses Mason Co., then forms a part of the boundary between Mason and Robertson counties; it proceeds through Bracken Co., constituting a portion of the boundary between Bracken and Robertson counties, and continues through Bracken Co. to the Middle Fork of the Licking near the southeastern line of Pendleton Co.

Geologists refer to three stages of the Licking River: the Old Licking, the Deep Stage Licking, and the modern Licking (see **Geology**). The Old Licking River and the Old Kentucky River, before the Pre-Illinoian Glacier of about a million years ago, flowed north into what is now the state of Ohio, joining near the current city of Hamilton, Ohio (see **Glaciers**). The Pre-Illinoian Glacier blocked the channels of old rivers and streams, forcing the development of the Deep Stage Ohio River and the Deep Stage Licking River. The Deep Stage Licking River was shifted westward from the Old Licking River, essentially forming the valley that it uses today in Northern Kentucky. Then the Deep Stage Licking River proceeded north through the present-day Mill Creek Valley along I-75 (see **Expressways**) in Cincinnati, where it flowed into the Deep Stage Ohio at St. Bernard, Ohio. About 200,000–250,000 years ago, the Illinoian Glacier's ice blocked the Deep Stage Ohio and formed the current Ohio River channel stretching from Lunken Airport on the east side of Cincinnati to Lawrenceburg, Ind. At that time, the modern Licking River began to empty into the modern Ohio River between what later became Covington (the **Point**) and Newport.

American Indians, prehistoric animals, and white settlers all availed themselves of the salt licks along the Licking River, probably giving rise to the river's eventual name. American Indians followed the **buffalo traces**, one of which led from the Point into the interior. The best-known salt licks were **Grants Lick**, the Upper Blue Licks, and the Lower Blue Licks (see **Blue Licks**). The latter was the site of the Battle of the Blue Licks (see **Blue Licks, Battle of**; **Blue Licks Battlefield State Resort Park**).

The Licking River was known to French explorers and traders of North America. Kentucky geologist Willard Rouse Jillson cited a 1744 *Carte de La Louisiane* (map of Louisiana) by Jacques Nicolas Bellin and a 1746 map by Jean Baptiste Bourguignon D'Anville, both of which made reference to salt licks, most likely the Blue Licks. Dr. Thomas Walker of the Loyal Land Company (Virginia) explored Kentucky in 1750 through the Cumberland Gap (which he named) and called the Licking River the Frederick's River. The following year, **Christopher Gist** of the Ohio Company (Virginia) explored the Ohio Valley, crossing the Point in 1751. Early settlers of the area established posts along the Licking River, such as Leitch's Station (see **David Leitch**). In 1802 Campbell Co. officials gave **James Taylor Jr.**, who married Leitch's widow Keturah, permission to build a two-foot-high dam, with a 17-foot-wide gate for the passage of boats, across the Licking River about five miles south of Newport. The mill dam provided power for a saw and grist mill that Taylor constructed (see **Taylor Mill**).

The development of the cities of Covington and Newport at the Licking River's mouth brought urbanization, industrialization, and pollution to the lower reaches of the river. The U.S Army's **Newport Barracks**, built at the mouth of the Licking in 1803–1804, operated until 1894. Like Newport's **West End**, the barracks were subjected to the **flood of 1884** and other flooding. Situated higher, the residential areas of Covington's current **Licking-Riverside, Riverside Drive, and Ohio Riverside National Historic Districts** were less susceptible to flooding. **Iron and Steel manufacturing**, as well as **meatpacking** establishments, lined the Licking River's Covington and Newport shores. **Ferries** operated along the Licking, and the **Newport and Covington Suspension Bridge** connected the two cities in 1853 (a suspension bridge opened upriver in the same year at Falmouth; see **Falmouth Suspension Bridge**); the **Shortway Bridge** opened between Covington and Newport in 1892.

In the 1830s the State of Kentucky proposed the building of 21 locks and dams along the Licking River to enable slack-water navigation to West Liberty, Ky., a distance of 231 miles (see **Licking River Navigation**). Construction was begun on the first five locks, but not yet the dams, in about 1839; completion of these would have enabled navigation to Falmouth, 51 miles from the mouth. State financial problems resulted in the permanent suspension in 1842 of the construction project, a disappointing expenditure of $372,520. Some of the stonework was later sold and used in building the **John A. Roebling Bridge** between Covington and Cincinnati. A rockbar, situated in front of the mouth of the Licking River, further impeded navigation. Beginning in 1887, the U.S. Army Corps of Engineers began underwater blasting of the Licking rockbar and by 1895 had removed 29,862 cubic yards of material. Removal of the rockbar was continued after 1900.

Without locks and dams, the upper reaches of the Licking were navigable only during the rainy seasons of late fall and early spring. At those times, large flatboats carrying coal from the Kentucky mountains could be floated downstream from West Liberty in Morgan Co. Timber from the Cumberland Mountains was tied together as makeshift rafts and also floated downstream to mills in the cities.

The 19th-century locks and dams proposed for the Licking River were designed for navigation purposes only, not for **flood control**. In 1936 the U.S. Congress authorized construction of a dam about nine miles above Falmouth, designed primarily for controlling flooding. The funds for this project were not forthcoming, although efforts to secure them were pursued again and again. In 1980 the Kentucky legislature passed a resolution opposing the use of state funds for the dam, and in 1981 the U.S. Army Corps of Engineers shelved the Falmouth Dam project. U.S Representative **Gene Snyder** made one last-ditch effort to resurrect it, but to no avail. Following the tremendous destruction of the **flood of 1937**, the U.S. Army Corps of Engineers built floodwalls in Covington and Newport to protect those cities from the floodwaters of both the Ohio and the Licking rivers. The catastrophic Licking River floods of 1964 and 1997 (see **Flood of 1964, Licking River**; **Flood of 1997, Licking River**) did extensive damage to the cities of Falmouth and Butler.

The Kentucky Chapter of the Nature Conservancy has designated the Licking River watershed—what it calls the Licking River Buffalo Trace Preserve—as worthy of conservation efforts. Including over 1.8 million acres, the Nature Conservancy's Licking watershed project area contains 100 fish species and more than 50 species of freshwater mussels, 11 of which are endangered. The Kentucky Chapter and its partners in federal, state, and local government, as well as private organizations, seek to educate the public about the dangers of pollutants to the Licking River ecosystem and to work with landowners in protecting lands in the watershed. Another group, entitled the Licking River Region Team, also promotes monitoring and conservation of the watershed. Finally, the **Northern Kentucky Port Authority** exemplifies how reclamation and economic development can be complementary. With the EPA (Environmental Protection Agency), the Port Authority participated in a cleanup of the old Newport Landfill in Wilder, along the Licking River. A clay cap was placed over the landfill site, and other appropriate reclamation and vegetation actions were taken, so that the site is now safe for humans and the environment and can be marketed for development.

Hedeen, Stanley. *Natural History of the Cincinnati Region.* Cincinnati: Cincinnati Museum Center, 2006.

Jillson, Willard Rouse. *A Bibliography of the Licking River Valley in Kentucky.* Frankfort, Ky.: Roberts, 1968.

Kentucky Department of Fish and Wildlife Resources. *Inventory and Classification of Streams in the Licking River Drainage*, by Albert R. Jones. Kentucky Fisheries Bulletin No. 53, 1970, Frankfort, Ky.

Kerr, Charles, ed. *History of Kentucky*. Vol. 1. Chicago: American Historical Society, 1922.

"Licking River," *Maysville Bulletin*, February 9, 1871, 3.

Licking River Region Team. "The Licking River Region in Kentucky: Status and Trends," November 1998. www.watersheds.ky.gov/ (accessed June 17, 2007).

The Nature Conservancy. "Places We Protect." www.nature.org/wherewework/northamerica/states/kentucky/preserves/ (accessed June 17, 2007).

Smith, Allen Webb. *Beginning at "the Point": A Documented History of Northern Kentucky and Environs, the Town of Covington in Particular, 1751–1834*. Park Hills, Ky.: Privately published, 1977.

Tenkotte, Paul A. "Rival Cities to Suburbs: Covington and Newport, Kentucky, 1790–1890," PhD diss., Univ. of Cincinnati, 1989.

U.S. Army Corps of Engineers. "Cave Run Lake." www.lrl.usace.army.mil/crl (accessed June 17, 2007).

Paul A. Tenkotte and Vic Canfield

LICKING RIVER NAVIGATION. The Licking River, one of Kentucky's major waterways, is formed in Magoffin Co., flows 320 miles through numerous additional Kentucky counties, and empties into the Ohio River at Covington and Newport. The origin of the river's name is uncertain, but most likely it is taken from the numerous salt licks found along the river's course in the pioneer period. During the 18th and early 19th centuries, flatboats were used on the Licking River for the movement of agricultural produce. As early as 1788, Virginia state law had established several inspection stations along the Licking River in Kentucky for assurance of "quality control of commodities." After Kentucky gained statehood in 1792, county courts, along with the state legislature, passed various measures to provide for navigation improvements on certain of the waterways of Kentucky, mainly the removal of channel obstructions and the regulation of milldams.

At the request of the Commonwealth of Kentucky, U.S. Army officers conducted the first survey of the Licking River in 1829; later, based on another survey in 1837, federal engineers recommended the construction of 21 locks and dams to overcome a fall of 310 feet from West Liberty to the river's mouth. The State Board of Internal Improvements awarded contracts for the first five projects in 1837, to be built of the typical stone lock chambers, with dams of stone-filled timber cribs. Over the next several years, construction was slow and sporadic, owing to lack of state funds, which were concentrated on improvement projects on the Kentucky River and on the Green River, located in the west-central part of the state. By 1842 all work on the Licking River was suspended, and the five projects begun earlier were left only partially completed. For the next 25 years, political and business leaders in the Licking River valley petitioned the state legislature for resumption of funding support in order to push the project to completion, citing the importance of the improved river to Northern Kentucky. As with the proposals for improvements on the Kentucky River, these leaders sought improvements on the Licking in order to move the farm products and natural resources from the upper valley. By the 1860s, some of the Licking's locks had been dismantled and the stone used for building the piers of the Covington and Cincinnati bridge over the Ohio River (see **John A. Roebling Bridge**).

The U.S. Congress, in 1936, authorized construction of Falmouth Lake by impounding the Licking River about nine miles above the town of Falmouth. The project was placed in the inactive category in 1981, because lack of funding support by the state government, and no construction has ever commenced. In 1984 the U.S. Army Corps of Engineers completed construction of Cave Run Dam, 174 miles above the mouth, for flood control and associated purposes. Cave Run Lake has become a fishing and recreation mecca in the region. Today, the Licking River is made navigable for about seven miles above its mouth by waters impounded by the **Markland Dam** on the Ohio River.

Tenkotte, Paul A. "Rival Cities to Suburbs: Covington and Newport, Kentucky, 1790–1890," PhD diss., Univ. of Cincinnati, 1989.

"Water Resources Development in Kentucky, 1995," U.S. Army Corps of Engineers, Louisville District, Louisville, Ky.

Charles E. Parrish

LICKING-RIVERSIDE, RIVERSIDE DRIVE, AND OHIO RIVERSIDE NATIONAL HISTORIC DISTRICTS. The Licking Riverside, Riverside Drive, and Ohio Riverside National Historic Districts are located in Covington at the confluence of the Ohio River and the Licking River. This area was one of the first established neighborhoods in Kenton Co. and in all of Northern Kentucky and is often referred to as "The Point."

The first person known to explore the area was **Christopher Gist**, an agent of the Ohio Company, and the year was 1751. Key moments in the early life of the Licking Riverside Historic District include the launching of expeditions by John Bowman, and later by **George Rogers Clark**, to fight the Shawnee (1777, 1780, and 1782); the establishment of "The Point" as a base for the military excursions for **Daniel Boone**, **Simon Kenton**, and Benjamin Logan throughout the 1770s and 1780s; and the gathering of 4,000 troops under the command of Kentucky governor Isaac Shelby (1792–1796 and 1812–1816) before he led the troops to victory at the Battle of the Thames (1813).

Significant figures associated with the area and honored by bronze statues along the riverfront are **John James Audubon**, wildlife artist and renowned painter of birds; **Daniel Carter Beard**, founder of the **Boy Scouts**; **James Bradley**, the only ex-slave to participate in the famous Lane Seminary debates on slavery and abolitionism; Captain **Mary B. Greene**, a licensed boat master and river pilot; Simon Kenton, explorer and soldier; Chief **Little Turtle**, the great Miami war chief who fought to protect the Indians' hunting grounds; and **John A. Roebling**, the designer of the **John A. Roebling Bridge** and the Brooklyn Bridge.

Architects, historians, and preservationists have noted that an example of nearly every major architectural style from 1815 to 1920 can be found within the historic districts here.

The George Rogers Clark Park within the district was originally the site of the **Thomas Kennedy** House and Inn (1791). Kennedy and his family traveled by flatboat from Pittsburgh to the mouth of the Licking River, where he purchased and settled the area that became Covington. Kennedy established a ferry operation across the Ohio River.

The oldest surviving structure, the **Gano-Southgate House**, is thought to be the first brick structure in Covington and possibly one of the best examples of a house of its era in the United States. The deed shows that Thomas Kennedy sold it in 1814 to Thomas D. Carneal, Gen. John S. Gano, and Richard M Gano. Local legend holds that the tunnel leading from the house to the Ohio River served as a stop on the **Underground Railroad**; however, it was likely just a service tunnel to load and unload provisions for the large household.

Other significant homes in the district include the Riverside House (ca. 1916), built by **Charles McLaughlin**, architect and artist at Rookwood Pottery in Cincinnati; the **Laidley House** (ca. 1865), owned by Commodore Frederick A. Laidley, president of the Louisville and Cincinnati Packet Company and owner of the Cincinnati, Pomeroy & Charleston Packet Company, nicknamed the White Collar Line; and the Porter-Fallis House (ca. 1852), also known as the Mimosa House, built by merchant Thomas Porter and later owned by banker Daniel Fallis (see **Porter-Fallis-Lovell House**).

Of special note is the Daniel Carter Beard House (ca. 1820), childhood home of **Daniel Carter Beard**. This structure has the additional distinction of being designated a National Historic Landmark, the highest accolade given by the National Park Service. It was also home to **Mexican War** soldier and poet **George W. Cutter** and his wife, actress **Mrs. Alexander Drake**.

There are two outstanding examples of the row-house style in the district—Ball's Row (ca. 1840) on Garrard St., illustrating Greek detail and early row-house construction, and Shinkle Row (ca. 1880) on East Second St., exemplifying the English-style row house known as Renaissance Revival. **Amos Shinkle**, one of the financiers of the Roebling suspension bridge, built Shinkle Row.

Many other architectural building styles are represented, including coach houses, frame houses, Federal, Gothic Revival, Greek Revival, Italianate, Regency-style townhouse, Victorian Gothic, and Chateauesque; it is this rich architectural heritage that brings professors, students, and tourists to the area in large numbers each year.

Though well respected and valued now, the area was in grave danger of being destroyed and replaced by urban renewal projects, especially during the late 1960s. Throughout the 1960s, the City of Covington's financial situation steadily declined, as it lost population in a mass exodus to the suburbs and consequently had few prospects for expansion of its property tax base. This increasingly grim situation forced Covington's leaders to look at ways to improve the economic base of the city. To some, the riverside had the brightest potential for redevelopment, positioned at a prized location on the Ohio River and just across the river from the soon-to-be-built Riverfront Coliseum in Cincinnati, which was completed in 1970.

Coinciding with Covington's economic problems was the emergence of a new city council as a result of the 1967 election. The council included newly elected mayor Claude E. Hensley; newly elected council members Vera Angel, Edward Drahmann, and Ron Turner; and reelected councilman Raymond Wehrmann.

Throughout 1967 both sides established their roles in what proved to be "a contest of wills that raged for nearly two years," as the *Preservation News* described it. The stage was set for a major fight over the fate of the area. Preservation groups began focusing their attention, and several of them banded together to fight the urban renewal projects being discussed. These groups included the Cincinnati Historical Society, the Kentucky Heritage Commission, the **Northern Kentucky Heritage League**, the Miami Purchase Association, and the Riverside Preservation Society. Key leaders from the citizens' groups included Patrick Flannery, Steve McMurtry, Dave Surber, George Thompson, and **Mary Wood**.

In December 1967 the Covington commission voted to lease the riverfront; the Northern Kentucky Heritage League opposed the vote and asked that the leased property be restricted to the western end of Riverside Dr. Some criticized the Northern Kentucky Heritage League, claiming that it was willing to sacrifice one block for urban renewal and that such an action was not justified, even if it might save the rest of the neighborhood.

In October 1968 the contest of wills arrived at its most heated period. On October 31, a public hearing was held in order to discuss declaring a section of the area a city urban renewal project, referred to as a CUR-1. This initial phase focused on a specific section, of which Riverside Dr. and Greenup, Garrard, and Second Sts. marked the perimeter. One set of structures slated for demolition under this plan was Shinkle Row. In all, 20 structures on 11 different pieces of property were to be destroyed. In their place, the commission planned to build a high-rise apartment, hotel, and office complex that would rest on top of a five-story parking garage. Mayor Hensley referred to the plan as his "pet project."

On November 1, 1968, the headlines of the *Kentucky Post* read, "People 'Save' Riverside: City Hall Bows Out on Renewal Project." The proposal had failed. However, the residents of the riverside had little time to enjoy their victory. On November 21 another resolution for an urban renewal project for the district was added to the commission's agenda. Patrick Flannery, a resident of Riverside Dr., an attorney, and one of the leaders of the community group fighting the resolutions, claimed that this was the same resolution that had been proposed and voted down two weeks earlier. The November resolution also failed, by a vote of 3 to 2.

Ray Wehrmann brought up the issue yet again at the December 5 meeting. The resolution had a new look this time, as Wehrmann asked that only a one-block section of Riverside Dr., from Garrard St. to Greenup St., be declared an urban renewal project. Commissioners Vera Angel and Ron Turner protested, asking why this proposal had not been included on the agenda for the December 5 meeting. When the resolution was read, only three residents of the district were in attendance. One of the three left the meeting to rally support from the other citizens, especially since none of them had been aware that a new resolution would be discussed that evening. Residents then began pouring in, many in their house slippers, to protest and to question the legitimacy of the proposed resolution. The meeting ended without passing of the resolution; however, the question remained as to how the citizens might come to an agreement with the city, so that they would not be forced to attend every council meeting in an effort to protect their property.

Between the December 5 and December 12 meetings, another assault on the riverside came, this time from a new source—the Covington-Kenton-Boone Chamber of Commerce (see **Northern Kentucky Chamber of Commerce**). The chamber's proposed plan, which it intended to present to the city, was to redevelop three blocks of the area in a multimillion-dollar venture financed with private funds.

Meanwhile, on December 12, the commission voted again, and now the vote swung in favor of the urban renewalists; Wehrmann's favorable vote was the deciding vote. This was the fourth time within six weeks that the resolution had been considered. Although many preservation groups were there to support the riverside residents, the *Kentucky Post* observed that the Northern Kentucky Heritage League was "conspicuous in its silence." Refusing to concede defeat, the residents of the area created a petition for referendum on the resolution and also one for the recall of Mayor Hensley. They succeeded, gathering 3,300 signatures that they presented at the Covington commission's December 19 meeting.

At the beginning of that meeting, Wehrmann requested that the resolution be read again (for the fifth time) so that he could ask for its repeal, citing a lack of commitment from a developer as his reason. In spite of this reprieve, Patrick Flannery requested that the 3,300 signatures for the petition be filed and recognized in the hope of avoiding future resolutions. Mayor Hensley agreed to file them. Commissioner Turner added a rider to the repeal, stipulating that the issue of urban renewal would not be brought up again during their commission. The rider was accepted.

The citizens finally achieved victory, and this time with such support from the commission that they could feel confident for the time being. Instrumental in the fight was what Flannery referred to as "the Underground Press." A hobby of Dr. George Thompson, a University of Cincinnati professor who was a district resident, this was a printing press operated out of his townhouse in Shinkle Row. It allowed the citizens' group to act quickly, using techniques popular at the time with civil rights groups and antiwar protesters. They could produce flyers, petitions, and signs in response to commission meetings, a helpful aid in gaining the support of fellow area residents.

Another battle ensued during the 1980s, in the form of a dispute with the Bernstein family, owners of **Mike Fink Floating Restaurant**, over the riverbank and the landing. A lawsuit resulted. It went to the Kentucky Supreme Court, which granted a favorable ruling for the residents of the district, further helping to preserve and protect the area that Patrick Flannery refers to as "the commons."

In 1971 the National Register of Historic Places selected the Riverside Drive Historic District for inclusion. Its basic boundaries are from the alley between Greenup and Garrard Sts. east to the Licking River, and from Fourth St. north to Riverside Drive. In 1975 a second district, the Licking Riverside Historic District, was added to the National Register of Historic Places. It generally includes the area south of Fourth St. to Eighth St., west to Scott St., and east to the Licking River. In 1987 the Ohio Riverside Historic District Boundary Extension was approved for sections of Third, Fourth, Court, and Greenup Sts. Throughout the 1970s, 1980s, and 1990s, many of the homes in these districts were restored, and some now serve as bed-and-breakfast commerical operations, while most are still residences.

Today the riverside area continues its distinguished tradition of architectural significance. In 2007 the Ascent at the John Roebling Bridge will be the newest addition to Covington's architectural heritage; it is an 80-condominium tower designed by world-renowned architect Daniel Libeskind. Libeskind, the architect of the new World Trade Center in New York City, was inspired by the cables of the Roebling suspension bridge and by the river itself.

For more than 250 years, the riverside area has been the scene of change and often of turbulent, dramatic events. In the midst of controversy, it has survived because citizens supported their right to exist. Oblivious to the world and events around it, this unique and historic place stands as a sentinel, a witness to its history and evolution.

Flannery, Patrick. Interview by Jennifer Reynolds, December 7, 2005, Covington, Ky.

Lietzenmayer, Karl. "Riverside Assailed: The Turning-point of a City," *NKH* 11 (Fall–Winter 2001): 10–18.

"Local History," vertical file, Kenton Co. Public Library, Covington, Ky.

National Trust for Historic Preservation. *Preservation News* 9, no. 3 (March 1969): 1–2.

"People 'Save' Riverside: City Hall Bows Out on Renewal Project," *KP*, November 1, 1968, 1.

Jennifer Adkins Reynolds

LIMABURG. The community of Limaburg was located in Boone Co., three miles west of Florence and two miles east of Burlington. It ceased to exist in the early 1970s with the widening of Burlington Pk. (Ky. Rt. 18). Limaburg was at the intersection of three county roads: Burlington Pk., North Bend Rd., and the Anderson Ferry Rd. The village had first been known as Needmore and then as Florence Crossroads. In 1884 the residents of Florence Crossroads petitioned for a post office to be established in their community. After some debate, the residents had decided that Lima should be the new name of the village. Postal officials, however, thought that confusion might result from having a Lima, Ky., and a Lima, Ohio, and suggested an alternative name, Limaburg. This suggestion was accepted, and on February 17, 1885, a cancellation stamp with the appropriate designation was granted to the community of Limaburg.

By 1885 Limaburg was well established and growing. At its peak it was home to a mill, a general store, a blacksmith shop, a school, the town's post office, and the Harvest Home fairgrounds. Although it had no church, Limaburg was the site of the Lutheran parsonage. The earliest business in Limaburg was the gristmill built by Jeremiah Beemon in 1849. In 1859 Israel and Robert Rouse joined him in business, and the operation became both a sawmill and a gristmill. More than 100 years later, the last owner of the mill, William Waters, was still using the original grindstones that had been imported to Limaburg from France. The heart of Limaburg was the general store. Operated by the brothers Silas and Jacob Rouse, the store boasted an inventory valued at $3,100 in 1880. The last owner of the store, John "Proc" Brothers, was famous for the quality country hams he sold. At his death in 1957, the store closed.

The Lutheran parsonage in Limaburg was the boyhood home of author Lloyd C. Douglas, among whose works were *The Robe* and *Dr. Hudson's Secret Journal*. The latter book was the basis for a television series of the same name during the 1950s. Limaburg was also home to William C. C. Rouse, who in March of 1879 patented a design for an automatic safety gate for railroads. Today, a few homes and the buildings that housed the school and the blacksmith shop are all that remain of this once thriving community.

CE, Sunday Pictorial Magazine, August 3, 1947.
Warner, Jennifer S. *Boone County: From Mastodons to the Millennium*. Burlington, Ky.: Boone Co. Bicentennial Book Committee, 1998.

Michael D. Rouse

LIME INDUSTRY. Lime was an important commercial product in Northern Kentucky. In addition to many uses in the building trades (it was used in mortar and plaster), lime was spread on agricultural fields, was an ingredient in many commercial products, and was used in various chemical processes. Lime could be produced in any area where suitable deposits of limestone were available. Massive stone kilns, both round and rectangular, were constructed to reduce limestone to powder. The burning of limestone altered its chemical properties by driving off the carbon dioxide. Early kilns were usually built into the side of a hill so that they could be loaded, or "charged," from the top. Layers of broken limestone and wood were alternated in the kiln. A fire was then built in the bottom of the kiln and allowed to burn for several days. Once the kiln had cooled, the lime was removed from an arch at the base. Later kilns were designed with separate fireboxes so that the lime was not contaminated with wood ashes. Fresh lime from the kiln was unstable until it was slaked (mixed with water). When the lime came into contact with water, a chemical reaction occurred that generated heat. However, once the lime had been slaked, it was safe to transport it to markets.

The extent of lime manufacturing during Northern Kentucky's early history is not currently known, since few records have survived. Kenton Co. appears to have been the primary area for production. The 1850 Census of Manufacturing in Kenton Co. listed seven individuals as lime makers. In the 1860 census, only John Kearney and Clements Resenbeck were listed; in 1870 A. D. Easton and Eli T. Rusk were listed; and by 1880 only Clem Resenbeck and Frank Wolking were listed.

In Covington and nearby communities, many individuals and firms sold lime. Among them were Edward Spinks of Covington, who engaged in the enterprise in 1876–1907; T. W. Spinks, 1897–1913; Richard Wolking's Sons, 1878–1879; Wolking Brothers, 1880–1885; Bernard Wolking, 1886–1899; and Ben Wolking, 1892.

In Newport Charles Spinks was a seller of lime during 1878–1892 and was succeeded by Charles Spinks & Son, 1894–1905. Others were Louis D. Emert, 1880–1903; the Newport Lime Kilns, 304 Monmouth St., operated by H. and F. Boehne, 1886–1887; Marion M. Allen, 1886–1907; and M. M. Allen & Bro., 1888–1911. The Spinks family became a major landholder in northern Campbell Co., owning properties such as **Taylor's Bottoms** and the hill on which **Newport Central Catholic High School** was later built.

No lime producers were found for Bracken, Gallatin, Grant, Owen, or Robertson counties. W. H. Chaplin sold lime in Petersburg in Boone Co. during 1876; William L. Smith sold lime in Carrollton in Carroll Co. in 1876–1877; and Sphar & Cooper of Maysville in Mason Co. produced lime during 1887–1888.

The physical remains of the old limekilns have long since disappeared from the region, but the lime industry has been revived in Mason and Pendleton counties. The Black River Mining Company in Pendleton Co. was established along the Ohio River in the 1960s. The company was owned jointly by the Armco Steel Corporation, the Southwestern Portland Cement Company, and Marble Cliff Quarries in 1968. Three large rotary limekilns and a quicklime plant were located at the quarry. In 1979 the company added a hydrated-lime production facility as an adjunct to its plant. By 1986 the Black River Mining Company had been purchased by the Dravo Lime Company. Carmeuse North America, a Belgian company, acquired the Pendleton Co. plant in 1996. The Black River plant produces lime for the steel industry, the paper and pulp industries, chemical plants, and wastewater plants and for gas desulfurization and other uses.

The Dravo Lime Company constructed a lime-processing plant on the Ohio River near Maysville in Mason Co. during 1973. This was one of the largest mines and lime-production facilities in North America. Three large rotary kilns burn the limestone into lime. The lime from the Mason Co. plant is used primarily for scrubbing sulfur dioxide in power plants. Barges on the Ohio River ship much of the lime. The Dravo and Black River plants are still actively producing lime.

Hockensmith, Charles D. "An Overview of Kentucky's Historic Lime Industry." In *Current Archaeological Research in Kentucky*, vol. 7, ed. Charles D. Hockensmith and Kenneth C. Carstens. Frankfort, Ky.: Kentucky Heritage Council, 2004.
U.S. Bureau of the Census. "Manufacturing Census Schedules for Kenton Co., Ky., 1850–1880." Microfilm copies on file at the Kentucky Historical Society Library, Frankfort, Ky.

Charles D. Hockensmith

LIMESTONE AND LIMESTONE CREEK. The community that became Maysville in Mason Co. and the creek that first attracted settlers there were both named for the local sedimentary rock, limestone, which continues to be quarried in the area. Both the rock and lime obtained from it were used for roads, and limestone was the raw material for early buildings and foundations of buildings, as well as for rock fences throughout the vicinity. Lime was also used on fields. Today, lime is used to clean the smokestacks of coal-fired **power plants** in the region and beyond. Local farmers and gardeners have long believed that the lime in the soil was responsible for the high quality of the tobacco and other agricultural products that they grew.

During the 1770s, the creek that emptied into the Ohio River at Maysville attracted numerous explorers. The inlet created by the creek served as a natural landing and also tied into a trace used by American Indians and animals for untold numbers of years. In 1773 Capt. John Hedges named this spot Limestone, a name that was used by some residents and even in court documents, into the 1820s. In 1777 **Simon Kenton** hid gunpowder at Limestone to keep it safe from Indians until he could transport it to Fort Pitt in Pennsylvania.

Several attempts were made to form a permanent settlement at Limestone; Simon Kenton and others built a fort there in April 1780, but it was abandoned because of British and Indian incursions into the region during the final years of the **Revolutionary War**. In 1784 George Lewis and Edward and **John Waller** built a blockhouse on Limestone Creek, and settlement of the area was steady thereafter. Limestone landing became an important stop for settlers as they moved south along the Buffalo Trace (see **Buffalo Traces**), north into what became Ohio, or west down the Ohio River. Most of the early inhabitants of Limestone were from Virginia. They built largely brick homes, along with the needed taverns and businesses. Among the many travelers who stopped in Limestone was, in 1785, U.S. congressman and future president James Monroe. Both **Jacob Boone** and **Daniel Boone** were Limestone tavern owners. Daniel Boone became prosperous in Limestone during the late 1780s and held several slaves. The first gristmill in Kentucky was built at Limestone in 1787 (see **Gristmills**). Also that year, the Virginia legislature established a tobacco-inspection warehouse in the town (see **Maysville Tobacco Warehouses**). Limestone is prominently featured on maps from the 18th century, such as the map of General Collot, a French explorer, printed in 1796. Meriwether Lewis passed through Limestone in the early fall of 1803 and recruited **John Colter** to be part of the famous expedition to explore the Louisiana Territory (see **Lewis and Clark in Northern Kentucky**). The Bank of Limestone was established in 1818. However, by then the name Limestone was going out of common usage; the town of Maysville was established on 100 acres in December 1787 by the Virginia legislature. It was so named because that land was owned by **John May** along with Simon Kenton. Daniel and Jacob Boone, Thomas Brooks, Arthur Fox, **Henry Lee**, and George Mefford were the first trustees.

Limestone Creek marked the area of original settlement, but it later became a deterrent because it stood in the way of development. The creek has been rechanneled several times and now empties into the Ohio River a short distance east of the original inlet. Limestone St. in Maysville now occupies the original site of the creek bed. Bridges over Limestone Creek eventually tied the community together, and the eastern sections of the community were annexed to Maysville. In 1940 the Kehoe Viaduct (see **James N. Kehoe**) brought the roadway away from the potential flooding of the creek and separated the railway from the roadway. This new channeling and earlier changes created several pools of water that still stand in the city. Today, the mouth of Limestone Creek empties through an opening in the Ohio River floodwall at Maysville, which was completed in the 1950s. During high water, floodgates seal Limestone Creek and pumps go into operation to empty Limestone Creek into the swollen Ohio River.

The name Limestone has experienced a renaissance of usage in the past few decades. Many businesses and other entities have incorporated *Limestone* into their name. Limestone Landing was reborn in 1992, with an opening in the floodwall, a park, a dock, and a fishing pier; floodwall murals followed that trace the early history of Limestone and Maysville. Just as the landing attracted settlers in the 1790s, the same spot today attracts visitors and is a favorite for festivals and community activities.

Calvert, Jean, and John Klee. *Maysville, Kentucky: From Past to Present in Pictures.* Maysville, Ky.: Mason Co. Museum, 1983.

Clift, G. Glenn. *History of Maysville and Mason County.* Lexington, Ky.: Transylvania, 1936.

John Klee

LINCOLN-GRANT SCHOOL. Lincoln-Grant was the last in a succession of public African American schools opened in Covington. Until 1932 these schools were commonly known by either their street location or their church affiliation. In that year, after construction of the Lincoln-Grant School building at 844 Greenup St., the elementary school was named Lincoln-Grant School, and the high school, located in the same building, was named William Grant High School. The building that housed both elementary and high school grades was commonly called Lincoln-Grant School.

The names of the schools honored **William L. Grant**, a white businessman and former member of the Covington City Council. When Grant decided to seek the Democratic nomination for Covington's seat in the Kentucky legislature, African American education received a boost. Recognizing the importance of the African American vote and aware of the poor conditions in black schools, he met with a few of the most prominent leaders of the African American community: **Isaac Black**, a Mr. Dixon, George Durgin, and Rev. **Jacob Price**. Grant made a proposition: If African American voters supported him and if he was elected, he would have the city charter of Covington amended to include a new provision to establish an African American public school. Grant received the nomination, and, as promised, the city's revised charter created an African American school that opened one year later, in 1876.

In March 1876, the Kentucky legislature specifically mandated that the Covington Board of Education, "out of funds in their hand, derived by taxation under and by virtue of the City Ordinances of said City, be, and are hereby authorized and empowered to establish and maintain schools for the colored children of the city in such numbers and localities as in their judgement will furnish sufficient educational facilities for the colored children of the city." It stipulated, "Said schools shall be under the same control, rules and regulations as govern other schools of the city."

In response, the Covington Board of Education hired John S. McLeod, former principal at a private school for African Americans, as the first African American principal employed by the Covington board. In September 1876, the school housed in the Methodist church on Madison became known as the Madison Ave. School, with McLeod as principal and Arzelia Ross as the first assistant. By this time, the First Baptist Church had moved from Third St. to Robbins St., and this school became known as the Robbins St. School, with Constantia H. Taylor as teacher. In 1879 McLeod resigned and became a U.S. government gauger.

The Robbins St. School closed in 1880 and was replaced by one on land donated by William L. Grant. First called the Seventh St. School, it opened with 200 pupils, a new principal, Darius L. V. Moffett, and two teachers, Hattie Todd and Clara Grandstaff. In 1883, Samuel R. Singer became the school's new principal and Darius Moffett was one of its teachers. Singer was still principal in 1888 when a new 12-year school opened. It included a high school, which the Board of Education named William Grant High School after the businessman who donated the land.

On June 21, 1889, William Grant High School held its first graduation exercise. The two graduates were Annie E. Price, daughter of prominent minister Jacob Price, and Mary E. Allen. In 1894, commencement was held at the Odd Fellows' Hall (see **Independent Order of Odd Fellows**) in Covington. This graduation attracted a large and enthusiastic audience. Board of Education president **James A. Averdick**'s address was well received, and board superintendent W. C. Warfield spoke also and presented diplomas.

Lincoln-Grant School faculty, 1929.

The 1896 superintendent's annual report to the Board of Education recommended prompt action on the renting of schoolrooms as quickly as possible in the southeastern part of the city. This was done and relieved the crowded conditions at the Seventh St. School. A result was expansion of the elementary school into what was called the Sixth St. Annex. On August 23, 1900, Singer was asked to resign as the principal of William Grant High School and Seventh St. Elementary School, and in September, the board hired Frank L. Williams, a native of Louisville, to replace Singer. Williams, who was actively involved in the community, was one of the founding members of the **Progressive Building and Loan Association**. On June 19, 1908, the high school's 19th annual commencement took place at the public library auditorium. In July, Williams resigned his position at the Seventh St. School and accepted a similar position in St. Louis, Mo. The next principal was William H. Fouse (see **Elizabeth B. Cook "Lizzie" Fouse**), a native of Lexington. In May 1909, the name of the elementary school was changed from Seventh St. School to Lincoln School. A month later, Robert P. Johnson's one-teacher school in Latonia was merged into the Lincoln School. Johnson became a teacher at Lincoln School and his students were picked up and transported there by car. William Fouse resigned as principal in 1913 and was replaced by Robert L. Yancey. In October 1914, a night school, serving African American adults who had missed their opportunity for an education earlier, opened at Lincoln-Grant School. Some Campbell Co. students began attending Lincoln-Grant School after the African American school in Southgate in Campbell Co. closed in 1921. The elementary students there were sent to an African American grade school in Newport, but the high school students were sent to Lincoln-Grant in Covington. The Newport school continued to pay $50 tuition annually per student until the 1955–1956 academic year, when African American students from Campbell Co. finally began attending Newport High School.

In 1925, the Covington Board of Education decided to build a new Lincoln-Grant School. Lincoln-Grant's principal, Robert Yancey, attended a special board meeting to complain that only $100,000 would be spent on his new school, while $425,000 was earmarked for a white school. The board remained unchanged, and Yancey eventually resigned in 1926. He was replaced by a teacher, Henry R. Merry, who continued as principal until retiring in 1955.

In May 1929, during site selection for the new African American school, the Julius Rosenwald Foundation of Chicago, financer for several African American schools in rural Kentucky, became involved. The preferred building site, on Greenup St. between Ninth and Saratoga Sts., had seemed too expensive. However, the foundation said it would help finance the purchase and also buy machine-shop and wood-shop equipment for the school. Several hundred citizens attended a special board meeting called to discuss site selection for the new school. Businessman **Charles E. Jones** presented a resolution from the Utopia Club showing that that organization favored the Ninth and Greenup location; the same view was expressed by the Covington Ministers Alliance and the William Grant Alumni Association, represented by **Horace Sudduth**. The board chose the site unanimously, and the new Lincoln-Grant School, financed in part by the Julius Rosenwald Foundation and costing $250,000, was dedicated on March 31, 1932. At the dedication, principal Henry R. Merry was the speaker of record; former principal Robert L. Yancey extended his greetings as well.

In 1927 Paul Redden came to William Grant High School to teach physical education and to coach football and basketball. His football teams were undefeated and won the African American Kentucky State Football Championship in 1929 and 1932, but football was dropped that year because the school had no football field. Redden continued to coach basketball until he left to become head football coach at Knoxville (Tenn.) College in 1952. He had started a winning tradition in athletics at Lincoln-Grant that was extended into the mid-1960s by coach James Brock.

Teachers at Lincoln-Grant stressed having a well-rounded education and fostered a variety of extracurricular activities. Dr. Clarence Cameron White, the world-renowned African American opera composer and director, visited Lincoln-Grant in November 1938. He conducted several institutes on music. To keep the community involved, a training session was held in the evenings at Ninth St. Baptist Church and at the First Baptist Church. The training period resulted in a memorable public concert featuring students and adults performing African American spirituals.

Throughout the history of Lincoln-Grant School, the Parent-Teachers Association encouraged academic excellence and parental involvement. So too did Lincoln-Grant faculty, whose qualifications were considered grade "A" within the state. Each teacher had at least a bachelor's degree, and most held a master's degree or were continuing their education through graduate study at leading universities. After 1932, the school faculty continued to improve, as did the graduation rates and the numbers of graduates attending college. In the 1950s five high school faculty members held master's degrees or double master's degrees, and one had a PhD. The school always received high marks from the Southern Association of Schools.

The Covington Board of Education took note of the 1954 U.S. Supreme Court decision in *Brown v. Board of Education of Topeka* at their July 1955 meeting. In May 1956, the local branch of the **NAACP** sent a letter to superintendent Glenn O. Swing concerning desegregation of the schools. In 1957 one African American student, Jessie Moore, attended Holmes High School. **Covington Independent Schools** were divided into districts, with the exception of Lincoln-Grant School, and desegregation took place within the districts and on a district-by-district basis. In 1959 African American students living in Peaselburg (a section of Covington) began attending Seventh District School; other African Americans began attending their neighborhood schools in 1961. Some students were moved from Lincoln-Grant to John G. Carlisle School, if they lived in the Russell St. area. The Board of Education never mandated that African American high school students attend Holmes High School until William Grant High School was closed in 1965. Lincoln-Grant School was integrated after it was renamed the Twelfth District School in 1967. In the 1970s, the integration of Covington Independent Schools was finally complete, with the U.S. Department of Health, Education, and Welfare's encouragement, through redistricting and the busing of students.

The 1954 U.S. Supreme Court decision impacted the area of athletics also. William Grant High School, which fielded only a basketball team, was admitted to the Kentucky High School Athletic Association (KHSAA) in December 1956. For the remainder of that school year, the school was permitted to remain in the Kentucky Negro Basketball Conference, which became defunct when other African American teams were admitted to the KHSAA. In March 1957, William Grant High School was eligible for the KHSAA district tournament. In that tournament, their first, the school's team won the 34th District championship and was runner-up to the Ninth Region winner **Dixie Heights High School**. In the eight years from 1957 to 1965, William Grant High School won four regional championships and six district championships; it was runner-up in the district once and in the region twice. The basketball team has the best winning percentage within the region.

After Henry R. Merry retired in 1955, having served 30 years as principal, teacher Charles L. Lett became principal. Lett resigned in 1964 and was replaced by Matthew L. Mastin. It was during Mastin's tenure that Lincoln-Grant School was integrated, placed in the Covington school district system, and renamed Twelfth District School. Mastin left the school in 1973, replaced by James K. Burns. The school closed in 1976 and was later purchased by the Northern Kentucky Community Center. The Lincoln-Grant building became the William H. Martin III Northern Kentucky Community Center. Facing fiscal problems, the community center was closed; it is currently vacant.

"Colored Graduates," *KP*, June 22, 1894, 4.

"Colored Night School Opens," *KP*, October 6, 1914, 1.

Crosby, Leconia Franklin. "A Study of Pupil Marks, William Grant High School, Covington, Kentucky, 1918–1929," Master's thesis, Univ. of Cincinnati, 1929, 4–7.

"Famed Negro Composer Heads Music Institute," *KP*, November 30, 1938, 2.

Hargraves, William F. "Comparative Study of the Educational Effectiveness of the White and Negro Schools of Covington, Kentucky," Master's thesis, Miami Univ., 1935, 1–20.

Harris, Theodore H. H. "Creating Windows of Opportunity: Isaac E. Black and the African American Experience in Kentucky, 1848–1914," *RKHS* 98, no. 2 (Spring 2000): 155–77.

———. "Reader Traces Effort to Build First School for Blacks," *KP*, July 29, 1991, 4K.

Jackson, Jewell Rebecca Smith. "A Proposed Course of Study in Speech in William Grant High School,

Covington, Kentucky," Master's thesis, Univ. of Cincinnati, 1945, 1–25.
Nordheim, Betty Lee. *Echoes of the Past—A History of the Covington Public School System*. Covington, Ky.: Covington Independent Public Schools, 2002.
"To Dedicate New School," *KP*, March 31, 1932, 3.

Theodore H. H. Harris

LINDEN GROVE CEMETERY. Dedicated in 1843 and today consisting of 21 acres, Linden Grove Cemetery in Covington is an invaluable public asset as well as the scenic burial site of pioneers; political, civic, and business leaders; war veterans; and hundreds of other citizens. It began when the board of the **Western Baptist Theological Institute** of Cincinnati, which had purchased some 350 acres south of Covington, established a new public cemetery for the growing city of Covington on part of that acreage.

The earliest known reference to a burying ground in Covington is dated January 11, 1823. It noted existing burials west of the original town at Sixth and Craig Sts. on property purchased by local pioneer **Thomas Kennedy**. Development soon crowded around this cemetery, making it obsolete. In 1872 city planners decided to move the remains buried at this cemetery to **Highland Cemetery** in Fort Mitchell, Linden Grove Cemetery, or other places chosen by the families of the deceased. Before long, however, residential development crowded Linden Grove Cemetery as well.

In 1998 George C. Dreyer published two volumes—a difficult compilation—that reviewed the cemetery's mishandled records and cataloged the burials at Linden Grove Cemetery. According to Dreyer, the cemetery's original name was Cincinnati-Covington Cemetery before it was changed to Linden Grove Cemetery. At least 34 tombstones in the cemetery date from before 1835. On May 1, 1858, the *Covington Journal* listed the numbers of interments at Linden Grove Cemetery from 1845 through March 31, 1858. The total was 2,086, and it included 880 children younger than age six, 112 of whom had died of cholera in the four years beginning in 1849. Nineteen children had died of smallpox in 1849–1850. But Dreyer found only 91 of the numbers mentioned in this article listed in the cemetery's records. Nearly 2,000 records were missing.

Linden Grove Cemetery once extended from about Holman St. to Willow Run Creek, but overseers of the cemetery sold land on its western end for city street development. In 1849 some original trustees of the Western Baptist Theological Institute, Cave Johnson, Samuel Lynd, John Stevens, and Henry Wingate, became overseers of Linden Grove Cemetery. Some of the cemetery's disrupted burial records date back to the dividing of seminary assets and sales of assets to the Baptist Educational Society at Georgetown, Ky., in 1848 and to Northern Baptists at the Fairmont Theological Seminary of Ohio in 1855.

Even before the **Civil War**, lack of upkeep and vandalism became concerns at the Covington cemetery. The Linden Grove Cemetery board in 1860 included prominent leaders: P. S. Bush, **William Ernst**, **John W. Finnell**, W. H. Gedge, and **Amos Shinkle**. Some of them purchased unsold lots to help pay for upkeep at the cemetery. In 1862 the board was requiring admission "tickets" to the cemetery as an attempt to prevent rowdy behavior on Sundays by young men. Over the years, people desecrated grave makers with paint, left trash, and broke into the mausoleums. In 1905 the city council of Covington voted to ban further burials, but this action was later nullified. As a result of newspaper publicity about neglect, citizens in 1928 formed the Linden Grove Memorial Association, which oversaw the paving of a central driveway, grass and plant trimming, the planting of new bushes and trees, and the resetting of grave markers. But desecrations kept occurring. In April 1945 vandals upset almost 30 markers, and in October 1980 around 80 markers. From time to time, individuals and groups volunteered to clean up the cemetery, but such efforts were never long-lasting.

In 1870 about 200 people commemorated a section of Confederate soldier grave sites in Linden Grove Cemetery. Decorating both Union and Confederate soldiers' graves became an annual Memorial Day event that at least once drew a crowd of more than 1,000 and included music and speeches. In 1912 the federal government provided $200,000 for the marking of Confederate prisoner-of-war graves nationwide, including 10 graves at Linden Grove Cemetery. In the 1930s, Spanish-American War veterans began commemorating Civil War soldiers, while also setting a plaque and recognizing deceased veterans of the Spanish-American War. In 1953 an American Legion post brought former vice president Alben W. Barkley to the cemetery for a Memorial Day address. The post also sponsored a commemorative marker for Civil War veterans. Updated plats of the cemetery show a section of Grand Army of the Republic (GAR) Civil War burials. Section 25 was marked for African American burials.

People well known in local history are interred in Linden Grove. The body of **Thomas Kennedy** (1795–1869), owner of the farm where the original town of Covington developed, was moved from the Craig St. burying grounds to Linden Grove. **B. F. Howard**, founder of the African American Elks, lies at Linden Grove Cemetery. So do U.S. congressman and judge **William E. Arthur**, industrialist Alexander Greer, and U.S. congressman **William Wright Southgate**. In 1910 public offices closed and children were excused from school for the interment, attended by hundreds, of Covington-born statesman **John G. Carlisle** and his wife Mary Jane at Linden Grove Cemetery. Besides holding local and state offices, he had been a U.S. Speaker of the House, a U.S senator, and the U.S. Secretary of the Treasury.

In recent years, the Kenton Co. Fiscal Court and the City of Covington began implementing a list of capital improvements at the cemetery: new fencing, cleanup, marker work, improved drainage, landscaping, restoration of the caretaker's house, and relocation of the entrance from Holman St. to the more accessible 13th St. In addition, the city placed signage along roadways announcing the "Historic Linden Grove Cemetery."

Dreyer, George C. *Linden Grove Cemetery*. 2 vols. Covington, Ky.: Kenton Co. Historical Society, 1998.
Reis, Jim. "Monument to Our Past, Covington Cemetery off the Beaten Path but Rich with History," *KP*, May 31, 1999, 4K.

John Boh

LINSTAEDT, HERSCHEL J. (b. 1909, Newport, Ky.; d. December 28, 1966, Cincinnati, Ohio). Herschel J. Linstaedt, a teacher of piano and organ, was the son of Dr. William J. and Freda Aschenback Linstaedt. His father was an optometrist. Herschel grew up in Fort Thomas, graduated from **Highlands High School** (1927), and studied at the Cincinnati College of Music (now the University of Cincinnati's College Conservatory of Music), where his mentors were Leon Conus and the world-renowned Albino Gorno. He went to New York City to study with Conrad van Bos, the famed voice coach and accompanist. Linstaedt became a popular teacher of piano and organ throughout Greater Cincinnati and was often invited to perform with celebrated musical visitors to the area. He taught at his home on W. Southgate Ave. in Fort Thomas, at a private studio on W. Fourth St. in Cincinnati, and at his alma mater, the College of Music. For many years he was the organist at Christ Church in Fort Thomas. At age 57 in 1966, he collapsed during lunch at a College Hill restaurant, apparently from a heart attack, and died at Good Samaritan Hospital in Cincinnati. Linstaedt was buried at Evergreen Cemetery in Southgate. He was a veteran of **World War II**.

"Herschel Linstaedt, 57, Collapses in Restaurant," *CE*, December 29, 1966, 18.
"Music Teacher, Pianist Dies," *CP*, December 29, 1966, 14.
Ohio Death Certificate No. 93888, for the year 1966.

LIONEL FLYING FIELD. The Lionel Flying Field in Edgewood, with its grass runway, was thought to be the future of aviation in Northern Kentucky when it formally opened on Sunday, May 4, 1930, with 1,500 spectators in attendance. The new airfield sat on 11 acres situated on the west side of Dudley Pike, between the present site of President's Park and Turkeyfoot Rd., across the road from the **Summit Hills Golf and Country Club**.

The field's name honored Lionel E. Stephenson, who, with his partners, leased the property for $12,000 per year. The land was owned by J. Stanley Durrell and F. W. Belberbe. Stephenson (1897–1968), a native of Covington, built a nationally recognized career around aviation and aeronautics. Previously, he had worked for the Triangle Parachute Company in Cincinnati as a parachute tester. He frequently competed around the Midwest as a barnstorming parachute jumper. Through the Lionel Flying Service, which Stephenson had established and of which he was president, he trained student pilots and offered charter flights and parachute jumps at the field's airport.

The Lionel Flying Field lasted barely one year. In its short history, it provided entertainment for community celebrations, through stunt shows and aerial parades. More importantly, the airfield was an attraction that lured new residents to Edgewood. An advertising campaign encouraged people to visit the new Edgewood subdivision development when they attended events at the Lionel Flying Field.

During the 1940s, Stephenson worked for the federal government at Wright-Patterson Air Force Base in Fairborn, Ohio. Later Stephenson, who was also an artist, owned and operated several printing companies in Covington for 30 years. He died in 1968. His airfield at one time, along with the Crescent Air Park in Crescent Springs and Boyer Field in Ross, marked the beginnings of general aviation in Northern Kentucky before the opening of the **Cincinnati/Northern Kentucky International Airport** in Boone Co.

"Contract of Leasehold," Kenton Co. Courthouse Records, Covington, Ky.
"Crowd Thrilled: Stunt Fliers Do Their Stuff as New Field Opens," *KP*, May 5, 1930, 2.
"Lionel Stephenson, Artist-Aviator," *KE*, February 10, 1968, 20.
"Seeks Honors at Air Show," *KP*, August 30, 1931, 1.

Steven D. Jaeger

LIONS CLUBS. As members of Lions Clubs International, Northern Kentucky's Lions chapters share in the mission "to serve their communities, meet humanitarian needs, encourage peace and promote international understanding." In 1917 Melvin Jones, a Chicago businessman, convened a group of business clubs interested in supporting unselfish causes. Before this time, many such clubs were primarily interested in the betterment of their own members. The Lions were subsequently organized, and chapters opened quickly nationwide and throughout the world. In 1925 Helen Keller addressed the international convention of the Lions in Cedar Point, Ohio, asking them to adopt work on behalf of the **blind and visually impaired**. They accepted the challenge and have become known for their philanthropy in this area, as well as their programs for the disabled, the **deaf and hearing-impaired**, youth, and the environment. They also sponsor diabetes education and provide international disaster relief. Lions membership numbers 1.3 million men and women in 45,000 clubs, which are located in 202 nations.

The oldest Lions Club in Northern Kentucky is the Maysville one, established in 1929. By the 1940s additional chapters had been organized in Brooksville, Butler, Corinth, Covington, Dayton, Erlanger, Fort Thomas, Newport, Owenton, and Warsaw. From the earliest days, Lions Clubs' benevolence in behalf of eyesight has ranged from sponsoring visual-screening programs for schoolchildren, to buying glasses and paying for cataract surgery for persons unable to do so, to purchasing and training seeing-eye dogs. The Lions Clubs also funded sight-saving classes for the visually impaired at Covington's 10th District School, a program started in February 1955. Fundraising activities have been varied. The Northern Kentucky clubs sponsored an annual Mile-of-Dimes campaign, often with the slogan "Give That Others Might See." This campaign featured "tag days" in downtown areas, where volunteers manning booths accepted donations and gave tags in return. In schools, the clubs distributed cardboard holders with slots for the placement of dimes so that young children could become involved. The Covington Lions Club, and later Ludlow's chapter, sponsored an annual Turtle Derby, and the Erlanger Lions Club began an annual carnival in 1946. In 1954 the Erlanger Lions purchased property on Commonwealth Ave. in Erlanger as the site for their carnival, and they held it there through 1961. In 1958 members of the Erlanger club were instrumental in establishing the Triple "E" Swim Club, the first community swim club in Northern Kentucky. Erlanger Lions Park, on 27 acres on Sunset Ave. in Florence, is the current home of the Lions Club.

Northern Kentucky chapters of Lions Clubs International now operate in the following places, established in the years indicated: Alexandria (1965), Bellevue (1957), Brooksville (1940), Butler (1945), Carrollton (1987), Corinth (1948), Covington–Kenton Co. (1940), Erlanger (1945), Falmouth (1966), Florence (1952), Fort Thomas (1940), Hebron (1956), Independence (1981), Lewisburg–Mill Creek (1966), Mayslick (1959), Maysville (1929), Orangeburg (1988), Owenton (1945), Sardis (1986), Taylor Mill (1961), Warsaw (1946), and Washington (1960). Clubs existed earlier in Bellevue, Dayton, Fort Mitchell, Ludlow, and Newport.

"Covington Lions Club to Receive Its Charter," *KP*, November 15, 1940, 1.
Lions Clubs International. www.lionsclubs.org/EN/index.shtml (accessed September 5, 2008).
"Lions Clubs of Northern Kentucky Launch Annual Mile-of-Dimes Campaign," *KP*, December 5, 1945, 1.
Local history vertical files, Kenton Co. Public Library, Covington, Ky.
Reis, Jim. "Festive Challenges: Lions Overcome Ups and Downs to Continue Their Money-Making Carnival," *KP*, July 16, 1984, 8K.
"Sight-Saving Work Outlined for Lions," *KP*, March 5, 1955, 1.

Paul A. Tenkotte

LIPPERT, LEON (b. March 15, 1863, Sailauf, Germany; d. June 27, 1947, Newport, Ky.). Born Leonard Lippert, this portrait painter was the youngest son of Johann and Anna Maria Bergmann Leonard Lippert. He left his life as a poor shepherd boy in Germany and sailed for the United States in 1880 to pursue a career in fine art. He settled in the Cincinnati area in 1885 and later, for a short time, resided with relatives at John's Hill (modern Wilder) in Campbell Co. He was living in Sedamsville, Ohio, when he met his future wife, Wilhelmina Miller. At that time Lippert worked as a cooper by day and studied evenings at the Art Academy of Cincinnati. He moved to Newport, married in 1890, and resided in Newport the rest of his life.

Possessing a natural talent for drawing faces, Leon Lippert opened his first Cincinnati portrait studio in 1889 and maintained a downtown studio at various addresses for the next 58 years, painting mostly in oils or pastels. His brush styles ranged from academic realism to strong American impressionism. He deviated briefly from his career in 1897–1900, when he partnered with entrepreneur Charles G. Cox to form the Reliable Art Company in Cincinnati at 621 Main St. Success in producing crayon portraits, sold from six wagons and produced with the aid of a staff of 40, brought prosperity to the Lipperts and their children, Elsie, Raymond, and Ralph. Lippert attended the Life Classes of **Frank Duveneck** faithfully for nearly 20 years and was active in the Cincinnati Art Club as a director (1905), vice president (1922), and ultimately an honorary life member (1938). Periodically, he supplemented his income through commercial art for use in advertising, most of which depicted females attired in 1920s-era finery or American Indian costumes. Numerous pupils apprenticed in his art studio.

Lippert's first important painting commission (1904–1908), for the Loyal Legion, was to create portraits of Union Army officers who had Ohio connections. The most famous of these is a portrait of Gen. Ulysses S. Grant, now hanging with others in the series at Lincoln Memorial University in Harrogate, Tenn. Lippert painted portraits of many notable persons on both sides of the Ohio River and from 1915 to 1930 painted members of the prominent Wagner and Thedieck families in Sidney, Ohio. Independently, he painted from photographic sources U.S. presidents George Washington, Abraham Lincoln, Theodore and Franklin D. Roosevelt, and all the Ohio-born presidents. Commissions to portray religious subjects and clerics for the Diocese of Covington (see **Roman Catholics**) were undertaken during the 1930s, culminating in an assignment to paint the entire line of Covington bishops, a task Lippert completed during the last four years of his life. In his final decade of work as a painter, he produced mostly landscapes and flower paintings in addition to some portraits and religious works.

Lippert regularly received mural commissions from churches and commercial establishments. Extant examples of such works in Northern Kentucky include two 9-by-5-foot canvases (1915) that were removed from the **Corpus Christi Catholic Church** in Newport on the closing of that church. The murals were restored and reinstalled at **Holy Spirit** Parish in St. Stephen Church on Washington St. in Newport. In addition, there are three large sanctuary murals at **St. Joseph Catholic Church**, Camp Springs, Ky. (1917), and 36 Gospel narrative scenes in **Sacred Heart Catholic Church** (now Divine Mercy Parish), Bellevue (1924). The St. Stephen Church was Lippert's own parish, where he was married and where his funeral was conducted. There in the church he attended hang colorful Stations of the Cross that he painted on copper for the dedication of the parish's new church in 1938. Earlier Stations of the Cross at Corpus Christi Church and at **St. John the Baptist Catholic Church**, John's Hill, Ky., credited to Lippert, have been lost, as have been murals in the Cincinnati churches

Blessed Sacrament and St. Augustine. Murals for the dome of Longview Hospital in the Bond Hill area of Cincinnati and a wall mural titled *Protection* in the lobby of the Central Savings Bank and Trust Co. at Eighth and Monmouth Sts. in Newport were lost in reconstruction. English hunting scenes on the walls of downtown Cincinnati's Wiggins Tavern were mostly saved, however, as was a mural *Washington's Reception* from the Cricket Tavern, moved by the Elsaesser family to the reception hall called The Farm in their Anderson Ferry Rd. restaurant.

Two Lippert canvases are in the Cincinnati Art Museum: *Young Apprentice* (a portrait of John Kohl), signed and dated 1907, and *Fountain Square 1929.* His notable posthumous portrait of Frank Duveneck is featured with other pieces in the Cathedral Museum in Covington. Lippert died at his Newport home, 658 Nelson Pl., in 1947 and was buried at St. Stephen Cemetery, Fort Thomas.

In 2007 a Lippert painting of Christ, which originally adorned Corpus Christi Church in Newport and was thought to have been destroyed, was found at **St. Cecilia Catholic Church** in Independence. It was restored and now hangs in that church's sanctuary.

Ader, Mary. "Tending Flower Garden and Long Walks Hobbies of Prominent Portrait Painter," *CTS,* September 5, 1932, 3.

Alexander, Mary L. "The Week in Art Circles," *CE,* April 14, 1935, sec. 3, p. 6.

Lippert, Thomas J. *Leon Lippert: Rediscovering the Art and the Man.* Cincinnati: ArtLeaf, 2001.

"A Page of Portraits by the Cincinnati Artist, Leon Lippert," *CC,* January 15, 1922, Gravure sec., 2.

Prichard, Vicki. "A Lippert Original: Valuable Painting Restored, Returned to Church Sanctuary." *KP,* October 16, 2007, 1A.

Thomas J. Lippert

LITERATURE. Northern Kentucky has had an active and prolific literary tradition, beginning in the early 19th century. Numerous newspaper editors and journalists; other nonfiction writers; writers associated with the radio, television and motion-picture industries; poets; and novelists have lived and worked in the region. In addition, several nationally known writers have passed through the area at some time in their lives or have had some connection with the area; examples are Mark Twain, **Harriette Simpson Arnow**, **Walter Tevis**, and **Ed McClanahan** (Tevis and McClanahan both taught at **Northern Kentucky University**). Harriet Beecher Stowe received inspiration for her bestseller *Uncle Tom's Cabin* by visiting the Maysville-area home of Marshall Key in Mason Co. (see **Harriet Beecher Stowe Slavery to Freedom Museum**). Toni Morrison utilized the Northern Kentucky setting and the true story of **Margaret Garner** for her novel *Beloved.* Northern Kentucky, unlike Appalachian Eastern Kentucky, the Central Bluegrass, or the Western Pennyrile, has not produced a distinctively regional literature but a literature eclectic in subject matter, style, and genre. No single subject, like coal mining, farming or horse racing, has dominated the literature of the region. The one distinctive subject of fiction writers of the region has been life along and on the Ohio River.

Journalists

Some of the influential and noteworthy editors, reporters, and writers who have lived and worked in the Northern Kentucky region have achieved national reputations. Among the most prominent was **Clay Wade Bailey**, affiliated with the ***Kentucky Post***, who has been called the "dean of Kentucky journalists." Bailey covered Kentucky state government and was well known to everyone in the state capitol. One of the bridges across the Ohio River from Covington to Cincinnati was named for him. **Judy Clabes**, former editor of the *Kentucky Post* and now CEO of the Scripps Howard Foundation, is a Northern Kentucky citizen with a long list of civic involvements, including being a founding member of **Forward Quest** and a member of the Governor's Task Force on the Economic Status of Women. Other well-known journalists affiliated with the *Kentucky Post* have been **Gilbert W. Kingsbury**, who also reported for radio station WLW and was a news correspondent in Washington, D.C., and **Craig M. Brown**, a columnist for the paper. **Nick Clooney**, a Maysville native and a current resident of Augusta, has been one of the most famous recent columnists for the *Cincinnati Post.* Clooney, of course, is also well known in radio and television. Northern Kentucky resident **Brady F. Black**, a Pulitzer Prize juror, was an editor of the *Cincinnati Enquirer.* **Robert S. Allen**, a journalism partner of Drew Pearson, achieved a national reputation as a political investigative journalist. Allen and Pearson wrote exposés of the Washington scene in the New Deal–era column *Washington Merry-Go-Round.* With Pearson, Allen also coauthored two works about the U.S. Supreme Court, *Nine Old Men* (1936) and *Old Men at the Crossroads* (1937).

Several creative writers and nonfiction writers were also associated with the field of journalism. Perhaps best known as a novelist, **Ben Lucien Burman** was also an editor of the *Cincinnati Times-Star.* **George Elliston**, well known for her poetry and encouragement of poetry writing, began her career as a writer for the ***Kentucky Times-Star*** newspaper, later becoming its society editor. She was also a reporter for the *Cincinnati Times-Star.*

Maysville has had a remarkable number of men and women in the journalism and editing field, beginning with Judge **Lewis Collins**, who became the editor and publisher of the *Maysville Eagle* in 1820, a position he held for more than 20 years. Collins was also the author of the highly acclaimed *Historical Sketches of Kentucky* (1847). His son **Richard Collins** followed after his father as editor of the *Maysville Eagle* and revised and republished his father's famous history. **Henry T. Stanton**, a veteran of the **Civil War**, edited the *Maysville Bulletin* (Stanton was also a poet). **Martha Purdon Comer**, a lifelong resident of Maysville, began her career with the *Daily Independent,* which was edited by her brother J. Clifford Purdon. When the *Daily Independent* merged with the *Ledger* in 1968, Comer became the editor of the Maysville ***Ledger Independent***.

Other famous journalists with Northern Kentucky connections have been **Mary Cabell Richardson**, a reporter for the *Cincinnati Commercial Times,* and another poet, **Forceythe Willson**, who was an editorial writer for the *Louisville Journal.*

Writers of Nonfiction Books

Other nonfiction writers have also contributed to the literary scene in Northern Kentucky. Among those who have achieved prominence is Judge Lewis Collins, mentioned above in connection with the newspaper industry. Collins stands out as an eminent man of letters. In 1847 he published *Historical Sketches of Kentucky,* which was based on the materials of his brother-in-law Henry Perviance Peers, who died before he could finalize his work. *Historical Sketches* was revised and republished in 1874 by Collins's son Richard. Judge Collins's history was considered the most complete history of the state at the time of its publication and is invaluable to modern historians (it is referenced in the *Encyclopedia Britannica* online as a major source of Kentucky history).

Covington's **Daniel Carter Beard**, after whom another one of the bridges spanning the Ohio River between Kentucky and Ohio is named, is best known as the founder of the **Boy Scouts** of America. His reference guide for that organization (and its forerunner the Sons of Daniel Boone) was *The American Boys' Handy Book.* Beard's sisters **Lina and Adelia Beard** wrote *The American Girls' Handy Book.*

Civil War veteran **Alfred Cobb**, author of *Liffy Leman; or, Thirty Years in the Wilderness,* wrote colorful stories about life in 19th-century Owen Co. and Northern Kentucky. One of his most interesting accounts concerns the Ohio River collision of the steamboats ***United States,*** on which Cobb was a passenger, and ***America***. Novelist and motion-picture writer and director **Elizabeth Pickett Chevalier** was, in addition, the author of the nonfiction works *History of Red Cross Nursing* and *The American National Red Cross: Its Origin, Purposes, and Service.* **G. Glenn Clift** wrote *History of Maysville and Mason County* and other historical works. **George Dallas Mosgrove**, author of *Kentucky Cavaliers in Dixie,* and Craig M. Brown, author of the controversial *Caketown USA* about Fort Thomas, were also well-known nonfiction writers of Northern Kentucky.

Several writers are known for their biographical, autobiographical, and personal writings. Regarded as an exemplar of genealogical and family history writing is **Anna Virginia Parker**'s *The Sanders Family of Grass Hills* (1966). **Sue Hamilton Jewell**'s *The Sun Shines Bright* (1952) contains autobiography, history, and biography and recounts traditions of life in the 1890s. Schoolteacher and librarian **Berniece Terry Hiser** of Walton, a graduate of Berea College, is the author of a collection of local traditions and folklore entitled *Quare Do's in Appalachia: East Kentucky Legends and Memorats*, her first book, published when she was age 70. Hiser also published a children's book set in Kentucky during the Civil War, *The Adventure of Charlie and His Wheat-Straw Hat*. Dr. **Darrell Richardson**, a Baptist minister in the area (at one time pastor of the **Fort Mitchell Baptist Church**), was also a prolific writer on many subjects. Among his best-known nonfiction works are *Max Brand: The Man and His Work*, *Counseling in Times of Crisis*, and *A Christian Facing a World of Change*. Like many other literary figures in the area, Richardson was very publicly engaged and held positions in many local church and civic organizations. In the 1950s, for example, he was one of the leaders in the movement to eradicate gambling and the crime syndicates in Northern Kentucky.

Radio, Television, and Movie Writers

Writers for radio, television and motion pictures have included Craig M. Brown, a scriptwriter for television, the aforementioned Elizabeth Pickett Chevalier, a motion-picture writer and director who worked for Fox and Paramount Studios, and **Mary Wood**, a writer for the *Cincinnati Post* who also wrote soap operas for the WLW radio station. Local celebrity Nick Clooney had a long career in radio and television in addition to his newspaper column in the *Cincinnati Post*. **Jean Shepherd** is known for his screenplay *A Christmas Story*, which has become a popular Christmas classic.

Poets

Among the best known of the poets in Northern Kentucky who have achieved local fame is George Elliston, a graduate of the old Covington High School. Elliston was the society editor for the *Kentucky Times-Star* as well as writing poetry and promoting the writing of poetry as the editor of *The Gypsy: A Poetry Magazine*. Her most famous book of poems was *Cargoes: Poems for Poets and Those Who Love Poetry*. Through the George Elliston Poetry Foundation, which she established at the University of Cincinnati, the university sponsors a visiting poet each year and supports the George Elliston Poetry Room. **George Cutter**, a lawyer who came to Covington in 1840 and soon became the captain of a company during the Mexican War, was also a well-known poet during the first half of the 19th century. Among his most famous poems are "Buena Vista" and "The Song of Steam," which extols the rise of steam technology in the 1820s and 1830s. Another poet of the early 19th century was **Mary E. Wilson Betts** of Maysville, whose poem "A Kentuckian Kneels to None but God" became an inspiration to Kentuckians during the Spanish-American War. Other poets in the area include **Frank E. Schoolfield**, called the "poet laureate of Northern Kentucky"; **Daniel Henry Holmes Jr.**, praised as one of Kentucky's "finest lyric poets" by John Wilson Townsend in his *Kentuckians in History and Literature*; newspaper reporter Mary Cabell Richardson, actively involved in the **Daughters of the American Revolution** and in **Trinity Episcopal Church**; Maysville native Henry T. Stanton; Forceythe Willson; **Eleanor Duncan Wood**, whose poem "In Memoriam" is engraved on the side of the Memorial Building at the University of Kentucky; **Julia Dinsmore**, of the prominent Dinsmore family; **William Whiteman Fosdick**, editor of the literary journal the *Sketch Club*; Newport schoolteacher **Margaret Estes**; **Annette Cornell**, who also published a magazine of poetry; **Myrtle Stickrath Jessup**; **Dorothy Ladd**; **Ninona Miller**; **Helen Truesdell**; **Rena Lusby Yancey**; Clement M. Byrne; and **Mary L. Mitchell Cady**. A unique poet and publisher in the area is **Gray Zeitz** of Owen Co., whose Larkspur Press publishes handmade limited-edition chapbooks. Zeitz has published the work of major Kentucky writers, including Wendell Berry, Gurney Norman, Bobbie Ann Mason, Guy Davenport, Richard Taylor, and James Baker Hall.

Writers of Fiction

Fiction writers of Northern Kentucky have been diverse in their subjects and genres, ranging from historical novels, adventure novels, science fiction, and suspense thrillers to children's and young adult fiction, graphic novels, and "chick lit" novels. The subject of life along the Ohio River is exemplified by one of the region's best-known novelists, Ben Lucien Burman. A graduate of **Holmes High School** and a **World War I** veteran, Burman was called "the new Mark Twain" because of his many books about the Ohio and Mississippi Rivers. Among these are his most famous work, *Steamboat Round the Bend* (1933), which was made into a motion picture starring Will Rogers, and his other humorous Catfish Bend stories. As renowned in the area as Burman was **John Uri Lloyd**, best known for his Stringtown books, set in late-19th-century and early-20th-century Florence, Ky., which is the Stringtown of the books' titles. Some of the most famous of them are *Stringtown on the Pike* (1900), *Warwick of the Knobs* (1901), and *Felix Moses: The Beloved Jew of Stringtown* (1930). Lloyd, after whom **Lloyd Memorial High School** was named, was also the author of a fantasy–science fiction novel, *Etidorhpa; or, The End of the Earth* (1895), his first novel, written in the vein of Jules Verne and H. G. Wells.

Journalist and motion-picture director and writer Elizabeth Pickett Chevalier achieved a national readership with her novel *Drivin' Woman*, which covers the 50 years after the Civil War in the life of heroine America Moncure. Popular in his day was **Robert F. Schulkers**, a writer for the *Cincinnati Enquirer* but best known for his young adult series centered around the character of Seckatary Hawkins and the Fair and Square Club with its rules of morality, decency, and honesty.

Novelist and poet **Hollis Summers** was an English teacher at Holmes High School. When he later taught English at the University of Kentucky, Summers and his colleague Robert Hazel were influential in the development of writers Wendell Berry, Bobbie Ann Mason, Gurney Norman, Ed McClanahan, and James Baker Hall. **Ruth Wolff**, a graduate of **Newport High School** and a resident of Newport and later Fort Thomas, was the author of several novels, including *A Crack in the Sidewalk*, a story about hill people from Eastern Kentucky living in Newport in the 1950s. Contemporary writer **Barbara Paul** of Maysville has written 24 novels thus far in the science fiction, mystery, and detective genres. **Jack Kerley** is a suspense-thriller author, while **Sheila Williams** is a writer of popular romance. Northern Kentucky University graduate **David Mack**, writer and illustrator of the Kabuki series of graphic novels, is internationally known.

Noe, J. T. Cotton, ed. *A Brief Anthology of Kentucky Poetry: Selections of Poetry Written by Ninety-Three Persons Closely Identified with Kentucky, Most of Them Native Born*. Lexington: Univ. of Kentucky Department of Extension, 1936.

Townsend, John Wilson. *Kentucky in American Letters, 1784–1912*. Cedar Rapids, Iowa: Torch Press, 1913.

Ward, William S. *A Literary History of Kentucky*. Knoxville: Univ. of Tennessee Press, 1988.

Danny Miller

LITTLETON, ROBERT (b. October 1850, Tennessee; d. July 27, 1909, Newport, Ky.). Robert Littleton spent most of his life in Newport, where he was one of the leading African American figures for more than 35 years. He married Josephine Smith of Covington on September 15, 1884; they raised two daughters and a son. In November 1872, Robert Littleton was involved in the organization of the **Corinthian Baptist Church**, located in Newport on Roberts St. In February 1873, Littleton, Rev. Dennis Lightfoot, **Washington Rippleton**, and a delegation from Newport attended the Colored Education Convention held in Louisville, where attendees were informed of the proposed new state law that would allow for public schools for black children. After the convention, Littleton and the other Newport delegates took the next step by encouraging the Newport Board of Education to include African American children in their plans for new schools. The delegation's efforts resulted in the establishment of the Southgate St. School in Newport.

Littleton, along with his close friend Rippleton, became involved in Republican politics in Campbell Co. during the 1890s. In August 1891, Littleton, Rippleton, and a group of other black Republicans from Campbell Co. formed the first Republican League Club. Littleton was one of five people to serve on its executive committee. In March 1892, when the league elected new officers for the ensuing year, Robert Littleton was chosen as secretary. At this time the league had 80 members. In May 1894 the African American Republican League Club was renamed the Crispus Attucks Club.

In 1882 Littleton was employed by the Cincinnati and Newport Iron and Pipe Company. His family continued to attend the Corinthian Baptist Church and his children went to the Southgate St. School. From 1888 until his death in 1909, Littleton and his family lived at 837 Putnam St. Littleton died at age 59 and was buried in Evergreen Cemetery in Southgate.

Annual Report of Board of Education of Newport, Kentucky. Newport: Newport Printing, 1873.
"Colored Club," *KJ*, May 25, 1894, 6.
"The Colored League," *KJ*, March 4, 1892, 4.
"First in the State," *KJ*, August 13, 1891, 5.
"Newport Briefs," *CE*, August 2, 1909, 3.

Theodore H. H. Harris

LITTLE TURTLE (MISHIKINAKWA) (b. 1747, Miami Nation; d. July 14, 1812, Fort Wayne, Ind.). Mishikinakwa, or Little Turtle, as the early Europeans knew him, was the son of Chief Mishikinakwa, who signed the 1748 Treaty of Lancaster in Pennsylvania (see **American Indians**). That treaty led to the relocation of various Algonquian tribes into the Ohio Territory. Little Turtle, a Miami Indian war chief and political leader himself, became a leader in the Miami tribe during the **Revolutionary War**. He led the resistance of the Algonquian tribes against American settlement within the Old Northwest Territory in the period from 1780 until 1795, conducting offensive and defensive operations north of the Ohio River and dispatching raids south of the river. In 1780 Little Turtle won his battle of note when he led a war party that defeated a French force, operating in support of the American colonists, under the command of Augustin Mottin de La Balme near present-day Fort Wayne.

After the Revolutionary War, Great Britain transferred the Old Northwest Territory to U.S. jurisdiction via the 1783 Treaty of Paris. The U.S. government, as a result, viewed the Old Northwest Territory as ceded land open for settlement. The Algonquian tribes, however, rejected this interpretation of the Treaty of Paris. The result was a low-intensity guerrilla war of the Miamis and their allies against the European settlers. It soon escalated into full warfare.

In response to complaints from settlers within Kentucky, Virginia, and the Old Northwest Territory, the U.S. Congress authorized President George Washington in 1789 to organize an army, consisting of many Kentuckians, including Northern Kentuckians, to pacify the Algonquian tribes. In 1790 Gen. Josiah Harmar led an American army, much of which had been assembled in Covington, north from Fort Washington (Cincinnati) to crush the Miami and other tribes of the Great Miami River basin. After an initial successful attack on the village of Kekionga, Harmar and his troops were led into an ambush orchestrated by the masterful Little Turtle. Harmar lost 183 men in the ambush and was forced to retreat to Fort Washington, abandoning the field to Little Turtle.

The next year, 1791, leading a rebuilt American army, Gen. Arthur St. Clair marched north from Fort Washington to destroy the Indians in present-day central Ohio and Indiana. Little Turtle once again drew the American troops into an ambush and inflicted upon St. Clair's army the worst defeat American soldiers ever sustained in a battle with American Indians. More than 700 officers, men, and camp followers were killed, including many Kentucky soldiers.

In 1794 a newly raised and trained American army, under the direction of Gen. "Mad" Anthony Wayne, set out from Fort Washington to vanquish the Algonquians. Little Turtle, realizing that this time he was up against a competent foe with superior arms, urged the tribes to sue for peace. But Little Turtle's proposal for peace was defeated in council, and Chief Blue Jacket of the Shawnees was appointed war chief of the tribes. Little Turtle's observation of the capability of General Wayne's troops was proved correct, as Blue Jacket lost to Wayne at the Battle of Fallen Timbers on August 20, 1794.

Little Turtle was now called forth to be the Algonquians' principal negotiator with Wayne at a peace conference held near present-day Greenville, Ohio. During the negotiations Little Turtle had entered into the treaty's documentation various claims by the Miamis for land in the Old Northwest Territory. The U.S. government later recognized these claims as valid statements of Miami ownership and provided land-transfer compensation. However, the result of the Treaty of Greenville, signed on August 3, 1795, was that the Algonquians surrendered their claim to land in much of present-day Ohio and Indiana.

After the signing of the Treaty of Greenville, Little Turtle settled with his family near Fort Wayne. He soon lost credit with his tribe, but he was still recognized by the United States as the chief of the Miami tribe. In 1803, 1804, 1805, and 1809, Little Turtle signed treaties with the United States, giving up most of the land claimed by the Miami Indians in the Old Northwest Territory. He placed his name on these treaties as carrying out the will of the Miami Indians, without consulting with the tribal council or receiving its authorization to sign. In 1809 the Miamis publicly rejected Little Turtle as their leader and directed that all further negotiations with the United States concerning Miami lands be through their new chiefs, Owl, Pacanne, and Peshewa. Little Turtle died in 1812, having never lost to an American army. At the end of his life, he was the recipient of a pension from the United States.

The Miamis and the other Algonquian tribes were caught up in the struggle between the Canadians and the Americans for supremacy over the Great Lakes, and Little Turtle's village was burned during the conflict and his family scattered. The power of the Algonquian tribes was forever destroyed at the Battle of Thames in Ontario, Canada, in 1813. The remaining Algonquin tribes were pushed west of the Mississippi River and north into Canada, and the threat of Indian attack was lifted from the Northern Kentucky region. Today, a statue of Little Turtle stands on Riverside Drive in Covington.

Anson, Bert. *The Miami Indians.* Norman: Univ. of Oklahoma Press, 1970.
Carter, Harvey L. *The Life and Times of Little Turtle.* Urbana: Univ. of Illinois Press, 1987.
Dowd, Gregory A. *A Spirited Resistance: The North American Indian Struggle for Unity, 1745–1812.* Baltimore: Johns Hopkins Univ. Press, 1992.

Charles H. Bogart

LIVERS, WILLIAM "BILL" (b. August 3, 1911, near Owenton, Ky.; d. February 7, 1988, Owen Co., Ky.). Musician Bill Livers, the son of Dave and Lula Thurston Livers, was born about three miles south of Owenton on the Monterey Rd. His father was a tenant farmer, and Bill followed in his father's footsteps. Bill grew up in and around the county's Long Ridge community and was well known for his stories as well as for his fiddling. Living as an African American in a mostly white community did not seem to affect Livers in any way. He was always welcomed into a group regardless of its ethnic mix, fitting in perfectly.

Livers's greatest joy was to have friends gather to play "the old songs," have plenty of "good eatin's," and enjoy fellowship. When the word got out that Bill was having a fish fry, people would come from miles around, filling the yard and overflowing into the field nearby. They would bring food, chairs, and blankets, prepared to have an enjoyable time into the early hours of the morning.

The major entertainment for farmers was music; Livers had family and assorted friends who played the fiddle, the guitar, the French harp, the mandolin, the banjo, and the harmonica. During the late 1920s, Livers first taught himself to play the French horn, an instrument for which he had paid a mere 50 cents, one tune at a time. The first horn pieces he learned to play were "Down Yonder" and "Yes Sir, That's My Baby." In 1937 he purchased a 200-year-old fiddle and on it learned to play "My Old Kentucky Home." The ability to play a fiddle allowed him to find employment in the evenings playing for square dances. He had an uncanny ability to pick up melodies easily. He told the story that the first fiddle he played came from a man who played left-handed. Livers was right-handed, but he had to learn to play left-handed because the fiddle was strung that way. Later he got a fiddle strung for a right-handed player, and it took him almost a year to relearn how to play it. But learn he did, and he could play both ways. Livers would ride a horse for miles and play all night, returning home to work in the field at his farm all day. He played at homecomings and square dances and for anyone or any group who asked him. As early as 1928, he was performing a song titled "The Carroll County Blues," but it was in 1942 that he began playing the blues seriously with his rendition of the "St. Louis Blues." He was later featured playing the blues at the Capitol in Washington, D.C., and at the World Fair in Knoxville, Tenn. Numerous articles have been written about Livers and published in *Newsweek, Time, Living Blues,* and other such publications. His work is captured on several record albums; included on them are two of Bill's favorite tunes: "Up and Down Old Eagle Creek," reflecting his Owen Co. heritage, and a popular fiddle tune, "Old Virge."

During Livers's memorial service at Owenton's Second Baptist Church, his importance in the community was described by the person who said, "God bless you Bill for being our friend and making the hard times seem like good times and helping us realize that we have so much [more] to be thankful for than sorry for." Bill Livers was buried at the Maple Cemetery in Owen Co.

Vertical files, Owen Co. Public Library, Owenton, Ky.
Ware, Burnham. "Bill Livers: Tenant Farmer and Rural Musician." *Living Blues* 51 (Summer 1981): 31–33.
"William 'Bill' Livers," *KP*, February 9, 1988, 3B.

Doris Riley

LLOYD, ALICE (b. October 22, 1864, Germantown, Mason Co., Ky.; d. January 21, 1951, Nashville, Tenn.). Alice Lloyd became Maysville's foremost leader for **women's suffrage**, temperance, and women's rights. (She is not connected with Alice Lloyd College in Knott Co., Ky.) Lloyd, the eldest daughter of Evan and Lydia Cheeseman Holton Lloyd, grew up on the family farm, The Pines, in western Mason Co. Prominent land-owners, the Lloyds were early residents of the region. Alice was educated at Miss Park's School in Maysville, Daughter's College at Harrodsburg, Ky., Hamilton College in Lexington, and Ward Belmont in Nashville, Tenn. She became president of the Madison Female Institute in Richmond, Ky., and served from 1890 to 1898. Lloyd was a teacher for most of her life; at various times she was on the faculties of Transylvania and Hamilton colleges in Lexington. But social causes drove her when she was outside the classroom. She was a member of the Women's Christian Temperance Union (WCTU) and the Kentucky Equal Rights Association. She was a speaker at the Democratic platform convention in Louisville in 1919, where she called for a plank supporting the franchise for women. Surprisingly, she was opposed by her good friend Laura Clay. Clay was a proponent of women's suffrage but did not agree with Susan B. Anthony's and Lloyd's support for a federal constitutional amendment legalizing suffrage.

Having been raised on a tobacco farm, Lloyd fought on the side of growers against the large tobacco trusts of the day. She was often found in Frankfort, lobbying on behalf of her causes and frequently lecturing Kentucky governors—particularly Augustus P. Wilson (1907–1911) and A. B. "Happy" Chandler (1935–1939)—about issues.

During the 1928 presidential campaign, Lloyd did not support Democrat Al Smith, because "He was wet," meaning anti-Prohibition. She persuaded the Kentucky state legislature to increase the legal age of marriage from 16 to 18 years. She often appeared in Covington and Newport espousing her causes. In 1928 she spoke at the Immanual Baptist Church in Covington at 20th and Greenup before the WCTU's annual convention. She lived mainly in Maysville, Lexington, and Louisville. In her last few years, she resided with her sister in Nashville, Tenn. Alice Lloyd died in Nashville in 1951. Her funeral was held at the Christian Church in Germantown, and she was buried in the nearby Maple Grove Cemetery.

Calvert, Jean, and John Klee. *Maysville, Kentucky: From Past to Present in Pictures.* Maysville, Ky.: Mason Co. Museum, 1983.
"Miss Lloyd Dies at 86: Long Was Public Figure," *Maysville Ledger Independent,* January 23, 1951, 1–2.
Thomas, Mike. "In Search of the 'Other' Alice Lloyd," *Maysville Ledger Independent,* March 27, 1986, 2.

LLOYD, CURTIS GATES (b. July 17, 1859, Florence, Ky.; d. November 11, 1926, Cincinnati, Ohio). Curtis Gates Lloyd, a mycologist, was the youngest of three sons of Nelson Marvin and Sophia Webster Lloyd. His brothers were **John Uri Lloyd** and **Nelson Ashley Lloyd**. The Lloyd boys spent long hours exploring the woods of Northern Kentucky, developing an interest in natural history, especially botany. Their youthful interest grew into a passion for Curtis, ultimately influencing the direction his life took. He moved to Cincinnati in the late 1870s and, like his brothers, entered pharmacy practice. While working to earn his pharmaceutical certificate, Lloyd continued studying plants. In 1886, with his brothers John Uri and Nelson Ashley, Curtis Lloyd became a partner in Lloyd Brothers Pharmacists. His assignment in the partnership was to specialize in locating and describing plants with potential medicinal properties; however, a turning point came in 1887 when Curtis Lloyd met A. P. Morgan. Morgan, a local mycologist (student of fungi), introduced him to the scientific study of mushrooms, which was developing into a specialized branch of botany. Lloyd's scientific enthusiasm was ever after focused on mushrooms. He was excused from most duties connected with the family business, and he devoted his time and energies almost exclusively to mycology. He never married.

Lloyd maintained offices in Cincinnati; Paris, France; and London and traveled extensively, examining and collecting specimens and studying existing works on mycology. He freely disseminated his own findings in the self-published serials *Mycological Notes* and *Puff Ball Letters.* He also published several monographs, and his writings appeared in the Mycological Series of the *Bulletin of the Lloyd Library and Museum of Botany, Pharmacy, and Materia Medica.* All of his writings were gathered and bound into seven volumes titled *Mycological Writings of C. G. Lloyd.* Through his many contributions, he became a prominent authority in the study of mycology and was regarded by some as a leading architect of the science. Although he was opposed to using personal names in the scientific names of mushrooms, several genera bear his name. With his brothers, Lloyd was also instrumental in development of the Lloyd Library and Museum in Cincinnati. In 1917 he executed the trust that enabled the library to be maintained into the future. He also established **Lloyd's Welfare House** in Crittenden (Grant Co.) for the recreation of the city's various church and school groups. Lloyd's formal education consisted of a few years at schools in Florence, Ky., and in Crittenden (Grant Co.), where his parents taught; however, in June 1926 the University of Cincinnati awarded him an honorary degree of doctor of science. A few months later, Lloyd died of diabetes at Bethesda Hospital in Cincinnati. According to his wishes, his body was cremated and the ashes spread on a property in Crittenden that he had inherited and on which he had established the Lloyd Library Botanical Park and Arboretum, now the Curtis Gates Lloyd Wildlife Area (see **Curtis Gates Lloyd Wildlife Area**). A part of that land is today's **Grant Co. Park**.

Curtis Gates Lloyd Papers, 1859–1926, Collection 11, Lloyd Library and Museum Archives, Cincinnati.
Fitzpatrick, H. M. "Curtis Gates Lloyd." *Mycologia* 19, no. 4 (1927): 153–59.
"Lloyd's Ashes Are Scattered to Four Winds," *KP*, November 12, 1926, 1.
Mayo, Caswell A. "Curtis Gates Lloyd." *Bulletin of the Lloyd Library of Botany, Pharmacy, and Materia Medica* 28 (1928): 16–24.
Simons, Corinne Miller. "Curtis Gates Lloyd, Mycologist, 1859–1926." *National Eclectic Medical Quarterly* 43, no. 1 (1951): 13–16; no. 2 (1951): 11–14.

Maggie Heran

LLOYD, JOHN URI (b. April 19, 1849, W. Bloomfield, N.Y.; d. April 9, 1936, Van Nuys, Calif.). John Uri Lloyd, a pharmacist and an author, was the first of three sons born to Nelson Marvin and Sophia Webster Lloyd; the second was **Nelson Ashley Lloyd**, and the third **Curtis Gates Lloyd**. At age four, Lloyd moved with his family to Burlington, Ky., where both parents worked as teachers, following opportunities for employment around Northern Kentucky. The family moved from Burlington to Petersburg, then Florence, and later Crittenden. The Lloyd sons had very little formal education; however, under the tutelage of their teacher-parents they were well educated and encouraged to learn from their experiences and interests. For John Uri Lloyd, those lay in the local flora and fauna. His parents encouraged his fascination with nature and prodded him to learn through conducting experiments. As an adult, Lloyd said his apprenticeship in pharmacy essentially began at home when, as a young boy, he was guided in chemistry experiments.

In 1863, when Lloyd was age 14, his parents decided to find him a position as a druggist's apprentice. Since formal education for pharmacists was largely a post–**Civil War** development, apprenticeship was the accepted way to enter the trade. After a long search, Lloyd found a position at W. J. M. Gordon & Brother in Cincinnati, where he apprenticed for two years. In order to gain further knowledge and skill, Lloyd apprenticed with George Eger for an additional two years and afterward returned to Gordon's drug shop. During this time Lloyd met some of the most influential physicians and pharmacists in Cincinnati. Dr. John King, a prominent physician of the eclectic branch of sectarian medicine, was especially impressed with young Lloyd and his abilities; Lloyd could not only compound prescriptions but also suggest innovations in the formulas. King arranged for Lloyd to take a position as a chemist in the firm of H. M. Merrell, a pharmacist who specialized in eclectic preparations. Eclecticism was one of many healing philosophies of the 19th century that disagreed with what was then called regular medicine, in which practitioners adhered to a very harsh regimen of purging, bleeding, and blistering. Eclectic practice relied heavily on medicinal plant treatments. Compared to other pharmacists who compounded botanical preparations, eclectic pharmacists sought to use substances that were more

The Lloyd brothers: *left to right,* Curtis Gates, Nelson Ashley, and John Uri, ca. 1880s.

highly concentrated and fresh rather than dried; they also preferred native American plants. Taking the position at Merrell's firm in 1870 placed Lloyd firmly in the eclectic camp.

As a chemist at Merrell's firm, Lloyd continued his pharmaceutical research and learned well the role of an eclectic pharmacist. By 1877 he became a partner with Merrell and T. C. Thorp in the firm Merrell, Thorp, and Lloyd. Lloyd made some attempts to go into business with his younger brothers, also trained pharmacists, but it was not until 1885 that they formed **Lloyd Brothers Pharmacists Inc.** The business was extraordinarily successful and remained in family hands until 1938, when it was sold to the S. B. Pennick Company.

Yet Lloyd was much more than a highly skilled pharmaceutical manufacturer. A largely homeschooled country boy, he became a scholar in his own right. His business interests in manufacturing eclectic preparations motivated him to do serious phytochemical research that resulted in an astonishing number of publications; the first of them was an 1870 contribution to the *Eclectic Medical Journal*. The steady stream of articles that followed, published in medical and pharmaceutical periodicals, led to recognition for Lloyd throughout the pharmaceutical profession. Lloyd's scholarship extended to teaching and professional leadership. He taught chemistry and pharmacy at the Cincinnati Eclectic Medical Institute from 1878 to 1895 and held a similar position at the Cincinnati College of Pharmacy from 1883 to 1887. He was also president of the American Pharmaceutical Association (APhA) in 1887. He received three Ebert Prizes (1882, 1891, and 1916) for outstanding original research in pharmacy and the Remington Medal (pharmacy's highest honor) in 1920 for his lifetime of distinguished service. In addition, he founded the Cincinnati Chapter of the American Chemical Society and was instrumental in establishing a History Section in the APhA.

Lloyd's accomplishments included inventions and discoveries. He held several patents on various apparatuses and compounds. Among the more significant were his "Cold Still Extractor," an improvement on distillation methods; an atropine sulfate used in eye wounds during **World War I**; a "Percolating and Concentrating Apparatus," another enhancement of pharmaceutical equipment; and an improved "Medicine Dropper or Syringe." Perhaps Lloyd's greatest innovation was his work on "mass action" in chemistry, which established him as a pioneer of colloidal chemistry.

Throughout his life Lloyd voraciously collected books. He felt that he needed readily available resources to manufacture the finest eclectic preparations. Lloyd's working library began with a few books he had as an apprentice, and he added medical journals. While he was working at the Merrell drug firm, Lloyd's mentors, Drs. John King and John Scudder, helped him acquire books and journals donated from colleagues throughout the country. By the time Lloyd Brothers Pharmacists was established, Lloyd had amassed a rather impressive collection; it grew even more rapidly with his brothers' assistance. Curtis Gates Lloyd eventually assumed the role of chief acquisitions officer for the growing library, which was augmented in 1893 when King died and the library received his extensive collection. Although John Lloyd did not intend to continue the library venture and assumed that one day it would become part of an academic institution, ultimately he could not part with the library he had worked so hard to build. He moved to ensure its autonomy and future by incorporating it in 1898. Curtis Gates Lloyd further guaranteed its future by establishing a trust fund for the library in 1917. The Lloyd Library in downtown Cincinnati continues to operate from moneys generated by the trust.

Lloyd was the quintessential 19th-century Renaissance man. Chemist, pharmacist, businessman, teacher, inventor, author of influential scientific treatises, and founder of an important research library, Lloyd also wrote eight successful novels. His first, published in 1895, *Etidorhpa; or, The End of the Earth* (*Etidorhpa is* Aphrodite spelled backward), told of a fantastic journey reminiscent of tales by Jules Verne and H. G. Wells. Lloyd's many other novels, such as the *Stringtown* series, vividly recalled the Northern Kentucky of his youth. His best-known novels were *Stringtown on the Pike* (1900), about Florence, Ky.; *Warwick of the Knobs* (1901); *Red Head* (1903); and *Felix Moses: The Beloved Jew of Stringtown* (1930).

In addition, Lloyd was civic-minded and active in community affairs. In 1935 he and others formed the Big Bone Lick Association for the scientific study and preservation of the site in Boone Co. that today is the **Big Bone Lick** State Park. Lloyd served as the association's first president and wrote the forward to its 1936 publication *Big Bone Lick: An Outline of Its History, Geology, and Paleontology.*

Lloyd married Adeline Meader on December 27, 1876, but she died 11 days later of acute peritonitis. In 1880 he married Emma Rouse, daughter of Thomas Rouse; they raised three children: John Thomas, Anna, and Dorothy. Lloyd died in 1936 of pneumonia while visiting his daughter Annie Welbourn in California, and his cremated remains were buried in the Hopeful Lutheran Church Cemetery, in Boone Co., Ky.

"Ashes of John Uri Lloyd to Rest amid Scenes of His Boyhood Days," *KP,* April 11, 1936, 1.

Flannery, Michael A. *John Uri Lloyd: The Great American Eclectic.* Carbondale: Southern Illinois Univ. Press, 1998.

———. "John Uri Lloyd: The Life and Legacy of an Illustrious Heretic." *QCH* 50 (Fall 1992): 3–14.

Heran, Maggie. "Lloyd Brothers' Community Involvement." *Lloydiana* 10, nos. 2, 3 (2006): 5–9.

"John Uri Lloyd Dies; Kentucky Life Recalled," *KP,* April 10, 1936, 19.

John Uri Lloyd Papers, Collection 1, Lloyd Library and Museum, Cincinnati, Ohio.

Kleber, John E., ed. *The Kentucky Encyclopedia.* Lexington: Univ. Press of Kentucky, 1992.

Maggie Heran

LLOYD, NELSON A. (b. November 19, 1851, Lima, N.Y.; d. January 27, 1925, Cincinnati, Ohio). Nelson Ashley Lloyd, a businessman and co-owner of baseball teams, was the second of three sons born to Nelson Marvin and Sophia Webster Lloyd; his older brother was **John Uri Lloyd**, and his younger brother was **Curtis Gates Lloyd**. When he was two years old, Nelson A. Lloyd moved with his parents and older brother to Northern Kentucky, and the brothers grew up on their parents' farm near Florence, Ky. Lloyd followed the advice of his parents and the footsteps of his brother John Uri by apprenticing in W. J. M. Gordon's Pharmacy in Cincinnati. He became a trained pharmacist and, in 1886, a partner in **Lloyd Brothers Pharmacists** when it was established. Nelson spent the greatest part of his life tending to the financial and business affairs of the company, serving as its treasurer.

Nelson A. Lloyd is perhaps best known for his involvement with baseball, particularly the Cincinnati Reds. For many years he and John T. Brush were co-owners of the team. Lloyd also served as the team's secretary and treasurer. During their tenure, Lloyd and Brush introduced the baseball world to the practicality of abandoning wooden stands in favor of concrete ones. After a major fire in the Cincinnati Reds' ballpark, the grandstand was rebuilt with concrete in 1912, it featured pillars and columns carved by hand. Referred to as "The Palace of the Fans" by baseball historians, it was baseball's first concrete grandstand.

After Lloyd and Brush sold the Cincinnati baseball club to Cincinnatians George B. Cox, Julius and Max C. Fleischmann, and August Hermann, the two men purchased a controlling interest in the New York Giants baseball team (National League). Lloyd was involved with that team for many years, serving as its treasurer. Among his many other interests, Lloyd was a well-known collector of art, especially the works of renowned local artist **Henry F. Farny**. He was a trustee of the Cincinnati Children's Home, where his role was far more personal than official. Lloyd was a frequent visitor to the orphanage, often paid bills so that important activities could be maintained, and ensured that all drugs and medicines needed were supplied free of charge from Lloyd Brothers Pharmacists. He was active in civic affairs, once serving on a commission to investigate the natural drainage of Norwood, Ohio. A modern sewage system was built as a result of that study. At one time Lloyd was offered the opportunity to run for mayor of Cincinnati, but he declined. Together with his brothers, he not only ran the pharmacy business but also contributed to the development of the Lloyd Library and Museum in Cincinnati.

Lloyd married Olive Augusta Gardner in Champaign, Ill., in 1877. They had one daughter, Marcia Olive Lloyd, who later became the wife of Judge George E. Mills. Lloyd died in Cincinnati in 1925 after a brief bout with pneumonia and was buried at Spring Grove Cemetery in Cincinnati.

"Ashley Lloyd Died after Brief Illness," *CTS*, January 27, 1925, 1.

"Career of N.A. Lloyd Ended," *CE*, January 28, 1925, 12.

John Uri Lloyd Papers, 1849–1936, Collection 1, box 21, vol. 4, Lloyd Library and Museum Archives, Cincinnati.

Mayo, Caswell A. "Nelson Ashley Lloyd." *Bulletin of the Lloyd Library of Botany, Pharmacy, and Materia Medica* 28 (1928): 24–36.

Reds Ballparks. "Ballparks: 1869–Present." http://cincinnati.reds.mlb.com/NASApp/mlb/cin/history/ballparks.jsp (accessed January 13, 2006).

Simons, Corinne Miller. "Nelson Ashley Lloyd, 1851–1926." *National Eclectic Medical Quarterly* 47, no. 1 (1955): 14–18; no. 2 (1955): 14–15.

Spring Grove Cemetery Records, Cincinnati.

Maggie Heran

LLOYD BROTHERS PHARMACISTS INC. (1885–1938). The journey to the independent, family-owned drug-manufacturing firm of Lloyd Brothers Pharmacists Inc., Cincinnati, could be said to have begun in 1877, when Northern Kentuckian **John Uri Lloyd** became a partner of H. M. Merrell and T. C. Thorp to form Merrell, Thorp, and Lloyd. During that era, large-scale drug firms saturated the market with botanical products and created an increasingly competitive environment. As the partnership endeavored to not merely survive but to thrive in this atmosphere, Lloyd, the youngest partner, was asked to develop new drugs. Lloyd rose to the task by expanding the firm's product line and creating his distinctive Specific Medicines, which were associated with an eclectic therapeutic and diagnostic system. Eclecticism was one of many 19th-century healing philosophies opposed to the harsher regimens of the regular physicians. Lloyd's Specific Medicines were highly concentrated, unofficial tinctures of plant constituents extracted by maceration or percolation. Eclectic pharmacists also preferred using fresh rather than dried botanicals and native American specimens rather than the diverse materials used by other drug manufacturers.

These and other new products developed by Lloyd brought the firm prosperity; however, success bred discord among the partners. Merrell left the partnership in 1881 to start a drug business with his son. Lloyd's younger brother, **Nelson Ashley Lloyd**, also a trained pharmacist, purchased Merrell's share, and the company became known as Thorp and Lloyd Brothers; it consisted of T. C. and Abner (T. C.'s son) Thorp, Nelson Ashley Lloyd, and John Uri Lloyd. By 1884 its catalog contained 80 pages of pharmaceuticals in addition to an assortment of medical supplies and apparatuses—the company declared itself "Physicians' Headquarters for Pure Medicines." Of all its products, Lloyd's Specific Medicines were the most publicized. Inevitably, with the successful formulation and marketing of these products, the Thorps' involvement in the business waned, and late in 1885 the Thorps left the company. Their departure provided an opportunity to bring in the youngest Lloyd brother, **Curtis Gates Lloyd**, also a trained pharmacist, and Lloyd Brothers Pharmacists Inc., owned by three Northern Kentuckians, was born.

Each brother made a unique contribution to the company. Curtis Gates's boyhood interest in botany had grown into a fervent avocation and positioned him to serve as field representative, traveling extensively to explore new medicinal plants and examine foreign supply sources. Ashley was the business manager; he handled all financial aspects of the company. John served as chief researcher and developer of pharmaceutical products and was the undisputed head of Lloyd Brothers. The mainstay of the business continued to be the Specific Medicines, and well into the 20th century, pharmacists dispensed what came to be known as Lloyd's Specifics.

The business prospered and remained in family hands until the deaths of the brothers. Ashley and Curtis died in 1926, and John died in 1936. In 1938 S. B. Penick purchased the firm from the Lloyd estate and continued to manufacture its products largely unchanged from the original Lloyd formulas. Over the next decade or so, ownership passed to several different pharmaceutical manufacturers; however, the Lloyd name was retained on many products. When the German firm Hoechst gained control in 1960, the company moved, and the Lloyd name ceased to be found on its pharmaceutical output.

Flannery, Michael A. *John Uri Lloyd: The Great American Eclectic.* Carbondale: Southern Illinois Univ. Press, 1998.

———. "John Uri Lloyd: The Life and Legacy of an Illustrious Heretic." *QCH* 50 (Fall 1992): 3–14.

John Uri Lloyd Papers, Collection 1, Lloyd Library and Museum, Cincinnati, Ohio.

Lloyd Brothers Pharmacists Inc. Papers, Collection 6, Lloyd Library and Museum, Cincinnati, Ohio.

Maggie Heran

LLOYD MEMORIAL HIGH SCHOOL. The Lloyd Memorial High School in Erlanger was established in 1928, after the Erlanger and Elsmere school systems consolidated. Former U.S. congressman **Arthur B. Rouse** suggested that the new school be named after **John Uri Lloyd**, a well-known local scientist and author of several books, including *Stringtown on the Pike*. It was hoped that Lloyd would donate a large sum of money to the school. The school board voted unanimously to name the new high school Lloyd Memorial High School, and Lloyd did make contributions to the school, but not in the large sums dreamed of by the school founders. He donated several books to the library and established a fund to support the Lloyd Medal, an award given to an outstanding student each academic year.

The new high school was housed in the old Locust Street School in Erlanger while a new building was being constructed. Many former parochial high school students, as well as students from the former Erlanger and Elsmere high schools, enrolled at the new school, creating a student body large enough to field a football team and bolstering the school's competitive position in other sports. For school colors, it was decided to take one color from Elsmere High School's green and gold and one from Erlanger High School's orange and black. Lloyd Memorial High School's colors were black and gold, changed to blue and gold in the 1940s. The first football team was formed during the 1928–1929 school year. Players and parents cleared a locust thicket to make a playing field. Local residents rallied around the school and staged minstrel shows and "womanless weddings" to raise funds to develop an adequate football field. The school's mascot was also chosen during the first football season. According to oral history, a *Cincinnati Post* reporter wrote that the Lloyd football team played "like a juggernaut," and the unique nickname stuck. There are no other high school or college Juggernauts in the United States.

During this first year of the school's existence, the new school building was completed. A plot of about five acres of land near the fairgrounds in

Erlanger was purchased and bonds were sold for school construction. Access was created by building two roads: Bartlett Ave. from the school to the **Dixie Highway** (U.S. 25) and an extension of Cowie Ave. from Graves Ave. to Bartlett Ave. The new school building's auditorium was completed in time for the 22 members of the first graduating class to hold graduation exercises in a school they had never attended. The new school had many modern features, including a cafeteria with a paid staff and a new type of desk with straight chairs and an enlarged armrest for writing.

In the 1930s debates, plays, musicals, operettas, and choral programs were popular at the school. Lloyd High School had football, basketball, and track teams. The school's first yearbook was published in 1936. In the late 1940s, the school board, using money loaned at a low interest rate by six residents, purchased land adjacent to the high school (formerly the Erlanger Fairgrounds). Fundraisers were also held to build a new football field and stadium on the site. The old building was demolished, and a new structure, completed in 1956, is in use today.

During this time of growth, the Erlanger-Elsmere Schools achieved racial integration, and the process went so smoothly that the schools were featured in an article in *Life* magazine. In 1979 the Scheben Gymnasium was built on the grounds between Lloyd Memorial High School and Tichenor Middle School. Dietz Auditorium was added to that facility in 1996.

The Lloyd Memorial High School Alumni Association was formed in 1988. The organization works to connect alumni, preserve school history, and lend support to the school. The Alumni Association awards thousands of dollars in scholarships each year to Lloyd Memorial High School graduates.

Over the years, Lloyd Memorial High School has been successful in academics, sports, band, chorus, and speech and drama. The school's test scores consistently rank in the top 10 percent of the state, and the school is accredited by the Southern Association of Colleges and Schools. The school and district have been awarded the What Parents Want Award for excellence in education. In 2006 Lloyd Memorial High School separated all freshmen and sophomores by gender for core courses, because teachers felt they were better able to meet the needs of the students in separated classes. The move resulted in fewer discipline problems and more focused students. Lloyd Memorial High School was named one of "America's most innovative high schools" by *Newsweek* magazine because of this approach to learning. In fall 2008, a $5.5 million addition was opened, as part of a five-phase $25 million project; it included new spacious hallways, administrative offices, five special education classrooms, five science classrooms, and two science labs.

Onkst, Wayne, ed. *From Buffalo Trails to the Twenty-First Century: A Centennial History of Erlanger, Kentucky.* Erlanger, Ky.: Erlanger Historical Society, 1996.

Deborah Onkst

LLOYD'S WELFARE HOUSE. Located on the grounds of Curtis Gates Lloyd Wildlife Area (see **Curtis Gates Lloyd Wildlife Area**), the Welfare House was built in 1921 and dedicated on Saturday, January 28, 1922. **Curtis Gates Lloyd** built it for the welfare of the Crittenden community of Grant Co.

Lloyd's Welfare House is a frame building consisting of an auditorium and a stage. The auditorium is 30 feet wide and 64 feet long, with two windows in the front and three on each side. Five brass lights were located down each side. It has four-foot wainscoting all around and two fireplaces on its north wall; originally there were four murals on the south wall. The stage is 30 feet wide and almost 10 feet deep. It had panels that could be removed to open the silver screen (which is still there today) for motion picture shows.

The Welfare House could be used for any approved gathering or entertainment as long as it was not used for commercial profit. Any profits made were to go to maintenance of the Welfare House or to the Recreational Area.

The building sat empty for years and was beginning to need repairs, so in 1992 a group of concerned local citizens raised sufficient funds to fix the roof and begin repairs. After several years of bake sales, yard sales, and quilt raffles, the old building began to come alive again. The Grant Co. Fiscal Court matched the money that had been raised, so that the total was enough to add bathrooms and install siding on the exterior. Today it has been deeded over to the Grant Co. Fiscal Court and is used for family reunions, birthday and anniversary parties, graduation parties, and weddings.

Curtis Gates Lloyd Collection, Lloyd Library, series 9, box 22, folders 608–38, Cincinnati.

Edna Marie Cummins

LOCUST. From 1880 to 1940, the hamlet Locust was the commercial, religious, and educational center for the extreme northwestern section of Carroll Co., a hilly district drained by Locust Creek as it cascades north into the Ohio River. Locust is situated west of the Little Kentucky River and southeast of Hunter's Bottom.

The Locust General Store was constructed originally at the Forks of Locust Creek, at the confluence of the East and West Creek Prongs, just downstream of Locust Falls. The store and its adjacent residence were flooded frequently as a result. The store's earliest proprietors included persons named Ginn, Hundley, and Metzler, who occupied the L-shaped section of the store. James G. Mosgrove added an addition to this store section that measured 30 by 32 feet and was 20 feet high; it featured a half story above the first floor. When Mosgrove died in 1882, John M. and W. Harvey Conway purchased the store and expanded its offerings of agricultural equipment, feed, hardware, groceries, and supplies. In 1903 the Conway brothers used skids and horses to move the store and its adjoining house about one-half mile to higher ground at the junction of Locust Rd. and Wrights Ridge Rd. A creamery and an icehouse were added, and customers could then purchase ice cream cones. In the last half of the 20th century, the Locust Store was run by Elmer Dunn, Jim Dowd, and Ralph and Katie Yocum, and then by Cookie and Donna Yocum.

Locust also had both an elementary and a high school, even though the town's total population was never more than 60 people. The Locust School was built in 1895 as a large two-story brick structure. It had four large rooms on the first floor and a gymnasium on the second, with a large encased dome on its roof (see **Locust High School**). When the school at Locust was demolished in 1963, the iron girders from the dome were saved as supports for a bridge that led to a private dwelling along the East Fork of Locust Creek.

The **Great Depression** hit the backcountry in Kentucky very hard. Tobacco provided the farmers' only cash crop, and they used every possible space on the hills and tiny valleys for cultivating tobacco plants and building tobacco barns to house their crops. The tobacco market at Carrollton meant economic success or failure for the hardscrabble farmers living in and around Locust.

The Locust Baptist Church was constructed in 1866 on land owned by S. W. Fallis on Wright's Ridge Rd. along the East Prong of Locust Creek. The trustees at the time were Edward Holmes and S. W. Fallis. Although in poor condition, the small stone church still stands today. It was a member of White's Run Baptist Association for many years.

The Hopewell Methodist Church dates to 1842, when Henry Wise donated land in Hunter's Bottom on the banks of the Ohio River; the trustees were George Harsin, Martin Hoagland, Moses T. Hoagland, Okey Hoagland, and Jefferson V. King. In 1895, because of the frequent flooding of the Ohio River, the Hopewell Methodist Church congregation moved its entire log church by horse-drawn wagons from Hunter's Bottom two and a half miles and 700 feet higher to the West Prong of Locust Creek. Then in 1910 the Methodists built a brick Greek Revival structure on that site, and it is still in use today. Elements of the old log church are still visible: a huge threshold stone, a chimney, and interior planking.

Carrollton Democrat, May 8, 1884.
Gentry, Mary Ann. *A History of Carroll County.* Madison, Ind.: Coleman, 1984.
Hammon, Neal O. *Early Kentucky Land Records, 1773–1780.* Louisville, Ky.: Filson Club, 1992.

Diane Perrine Coon

LOCUST HIGH SCHOOL. When the common school system in Kentucky was instituted during the 1850s, James Crawford taught at the school at Locust in District 19 within Carroll Co. Other common schools in Carroll Co. were started at Hunter's Bottom, Kings Ridge, and Notch Lick. In 1878 school district trustees George Clegg, Owen Driskell, and James G. Mosgrove sold the old log schoolhouse on the East Prong of Locust Creek and built a new school next to the Locust Baptist Church. In 1882 the schoolhouse burned under suspicious circumstances, but the community rebuilt it in time for the fall term. The Ohio River **flood of 1913** greatly damaged the new school, but it was repaired and refurbished. That school was used until 1928, when a large brick school was constructed for the Consolidated Locust School and High School near the Forks of Locust Creek and the center of the community of Locust.

The Locust High School had been established as a two-year school in 1912, and it occupied one room of the original large two-story schoolhouse. Children attending the school came from Hunter's Bottom, Wrights Ridge, Kings Ridge, Locust Rd., and Painter's Hollow. By 1927 J. B. Pullium was teaching 8 pupils at Locust High School, in a school term that ran eight months, and the next year he taught 13. Rev. Graham Good was the high school's teacher in 1929; that year he had 9 students and in 1930 he had 8. Then in 1930 R. J. Wade taught 10 students at the high school. R. Bernhardt Bauer, who had attended Georgetown College in Kentucky, was teaching 14 students at the Locust High School in 1933.

The Locust High School basketball team had to adjust its offense and defense around a pot-bellied stove that sat in the middle of the gym. A skylight provided light to the second-floor gymnasium. The high school closed while Allan McMannis was principal of the Consolidated Locust School in 1938. Students from Ghent, English, and Locust Schools in Carroll Co. were then bused to the **Carrollton High School** (CHS). The first year after its closing, the Locust Consolidated School sent 22 students to CHS.

Bevarly, R. W. "History of Education in Carroll County," Master's thesis, Univ. of Kentucky, 1936.

Campbell, Justine Tandy. "History of the Carroll County Schools," Carrollton, Ky.: Carroll Co. Public Library, 1976.

Carroll Co. Deed Books, 4, pp. 36, 38, 299, Carrollton, Ky.

Carrollton News-Democrat, February 2, 1878; September 15, 1938.

Diane Perrine Coon

LONG RIDGE. This Owen Co. hamlet, located three miles north of Owenton at the intersection of U.S. 127 and Ky. Rt. 36, sits along the long ridge that cuts north-south across the county. Long Ridge is near the former location of **Ed Porter Thompson**'s short-lived **Harrisburgh Academy/Owen College**, in an area Thompson had named Harrisburg during the late 1860s. In 1909 the community's name was changed to Long Ridge owing to the common postal confusion with the Harrisburg community in Mercer Co. Thompson opened the post office at Long Ridge in 1873, and it operated until 1966. Long Ridge was home to the well-known Kentucky blues fiddler **Bill Livers**, whose farm was along Old New Liberty Rd (Ky. Rt. 1978).

Houchens, Mariam Sidebottom. *History of Owen County: "Sweet Owen."* Louisville, Ky.: Standard, 1976.

Rennick, Robert M. *Kentucky Place Names.* Lexington: Univ. Press of Kentucky, 1984.

LOOKOUT HEIGHTS. The city of Lookout Heights was located on the west side of the **Dixie Highway**, overlooking Park Hills and Covington. Much of the early housing development, including the Fort Henry and General Dr. subdivisions and the streets along Park Rd. and the west side of Sleepy Hollow Rd., was done by Nick Kreutzjans, Fred Riedinger, and Joseph Trenkamp. Lookout Heights was incorporated as a sixth-class city in 1937, after a campaign led by a group of residents known as the Dixie Welfare Association, who were troubled by insufficient fire protection.

Although largely residential, Lookout Heights had a diverse set of business and community organizations, among them **St. Agnes Catholic Church** and school, the Dixie Gardens Drive-In Theatre (see **Drive Ins**), Oelsner's Colonial Inn, the Hillcrest Tavern, the Lookout Motel, Lookout Bowl, a goldfish farm, a golf driving range, and the Dixie Bicycle Club, which offered bicycle paths, horseshoe courts, an archery range, and canoeing. The most famous locale was the **Lookout House**, a well-known nightclub along the **Gourmet Strip** of Dixie Highway. Offering casino-style gambling and national entertainers such as Frank Sinatra, it became notorious for its ongoing gambling problems. The Lookout House, after a decades-long run, burned to the ground in 1973. In 1964 the Lookout Heights Civic Club building opened and became a central gathering spot for the community as well as the seat of city government. Former mayors of Lookout Heights include Russell Oelsner (owner of Oelsner's Colonial Inn), J. R. Blumlein, Howard Schambach, and Alfred Beasley.

Annexation was an ongoing topic in Lookout Heights as in neighboring towns, leading to a major battle with Covington in the early 1980s. Covington tried to annex undeveloped land in the Fort Henry subdivision in the 1960s, but the landowners sued to block annexation, and the matter languished in court for over two decades. In 1980 the court ruled in favor of Covington; however, Fort Wright used a new state law that permitted reannexing land and put the issue on the ballot. Residents voted overwhelmingly to leave Covington and return to Fort Wright.

In the interim, seeking better fire protection and wishing to prevent annexation by Covington, Lookout Heights merged with Fort Wright. In November of 1967, Fort Wright voted 532 to 319 in favor of the step, while Lookout Heights voted 389 to 150 for the merger; in 1968 the merger was complete, and the Lookout Heights name was dropped in favor of Fort Wright.

City of Fort Wright 50th Anniversary Booklet. Fort Wright, Ky.: City of Fort Wright, 1991.

"The City They All Seem to Want," *KP,* November 11, 1985, 4K.

"Dixie Bicycle Club Takes Over Plot for Recreation Project," *KP,* March 14, 1941, 18.

"Lookout Heights Has Vigor of Youth," *KE,* June 26, 1958, 1K.

"Park Hills, Ft. Wright, Lookout Heights Talk More on Merger," *KE,* March 21, 1967, 19.

"Town Groups Organize Dixie Municipal League," *KP,* March 20, 1940, 1.

Dave Hatter

LOOKOUT HOUSE. The Lookout House, a thriving nightspot for almost a century in Northern Kentucky, was located in Fort Wright, on the southeast corner of Kyles Lane and the **Dixie Highway**. The restaurant was well known for its gourmet dinners, gambling rooms, and live entertainment shows.

In 1886 Aloise Hampel, a German immigrant, purchased the land on which the restaurant was to be built. The facility initially was a three-story brick structure with a slaughterhouse and an underground passageway that was used as a natural refrigerator for storing cut meat. The building also had a large tower in the front, which attracted visitors wishing to have a spectacular view of Northern Kentucky and Cincinnati. The popularity of this feature led Hampel to name his building the Lookout House. Many locals have speculated, erroneously, that the restaurant was so named because it had been used as a lookout point by Union troops during the Civil War.

Hampel operated a successful restaurant at the Lookout House, and later he added a beer garden and a dance pavilion. During Hampel's ownership the Lookout House was famous for excellent food and accommodations. After his death in 1912, Hempel's children sold the business to Bill Hill for $25,000. Hill already had a national reputation as a saloon owner. Under his management, the Lookout House flourished as a nightclub; however, the business later struggled during the era of **Prohibition**, 1919–1933.

In 1933 the Lookout House was sold to Jimmy Brink, who remodeled the restaurant and added Las Vegas–style gambling and live entertainment. Gambling was illegal in Kentucky, and in the 1930s Brink was charged numerous times but never convicted.

In 1948 Brink was again charged with permitting gambling on the Lookout House premises. Harriett Shelander of Erlanger, along with several other witnesses, appeared in court and testified against Brink. It was also during this time that national investigators led by U.S. senator Estes Kefauver (see **Kefauver Committee**) uncovered a connection between Brink and the Chicago-based Capone crime organization. Two local mobsters, Morris Kleinman and Louis Rothkopf, were regular high-stakes gamblers at the Lookout House. Both men were connected to Jacob "Greasy Thumb" Guzik, who was known to be part of Capone's gang. None of the three men, however, admitted to any involvements that connected themselves or the Lookout House to underworld activities. Before the case against these three men could be tried, Brink was killed in 1952 in a suspicious private plane crash at an airport in Atlanta, Ga. The Kenton Co. Circuit Court ruled that "there was a possibility Brink caused the crash through negligence by turning over the controls of the plane to Charles Drahmann." Both men had been facing prosecution on gambling charges.

Brink's activities in Northern Kentucky at this time would suggest that organized crime was involved at his restaurant. He was nicknamed "Mr. Big," and it was said that "everyone bowed to them

[Jimmy Brink and his wife] . . . and it was political suicide to get on the bad side of the Brinks." A commonly held axiom in Kenton Co., while Jimmy Brink was alive, was that if Brink did not approve of a certain person running for political office, that person was expected to accept this fact and drop out of the race.

After Brink's death the Lookout House was taken over by veteran local restaurant proprietors Bob and Dick Shilling, and illegal gambling continued in a partitioned casino room with slot machines, blackjack tables, roulette, and dice games. The years during which the Shillings owned and operated the Lookout House were characterized by times of either boom or bust. Occasionally, the illegal gambling was shut down during a police raid, but more frequently the shutdown occurred when the Shillings had been tipped off that a raid was imminent. The nightclub, which sat next to a busy drive-in movie facility, the Dixie Gardens, was also regularly vandalized late at night during these years. One particular act, in 1958, caused $3,000 worth of damage.

On August 14, 1973, tragedy struck the Lookout House just months before the scheduled date of a grand reopening. A fire blazed through the rooms of the famous nightclub while it was closed for maintenance. It is remembered as being "one of the most dramatic fires in local history . . . as smoke and flames ate away generations of Northern Kentucky's entertainment history." Hundreds of spectators lined up outside the restaurant to witness its destruction. The fire supposedly started in the kitchen as a simple grease fire that got out of control, and it was especially difficult to subdue because the restaurant had been remodeled several times, preventing access that firefighters needed. The Lookout House has never been rebuilt; instead, the Lookout office complex and a savings bank building now occupy the property.

"Attorney Assailed for Testimony in Lookout House Case," *KTS*, October 15, 1937, A1.
"Brink Case before Kenton Grand Jury," *KTS*, September 20, 1948, A1.
"Brink Plea Overruled," *KTS*, June 8, 1956, 1A.
Dressman, Elmer. "Big Man Is Gone and Scene Changes for Kenton County," *KE*, August 6, 1952, A1.
Hampel, John E. To the Editor, *KP*, January 23, 1987.
Kennedy, John. "Union Troops Marched by More Than a Century Ago," *KP*, August 15, 1973, 1.
KP, August 28, 1912, 2; April 14, 1925, 1A; April 15, 1925, 1A; August 15, 1973, 1A.
"Lookout House Damaged by Vandals," *KTS*, March 1, 1958, A1.
"Trial Dates Set by Kenton Court," *KE*, June 30, 1936, A1.

Craig Schneider

LORD DUNMORE'S WAR. In 1768 the Iroquois Indians signed the Treaty of Fort Stanwix, N.Y., allowing European settlers to enter the land south and east of the Ohio River. By 1774, however, European settlers' demands for the area north of the Ohio River had intensified. Settlers from both Pennsylvania and Virginia were moving into the Ohio River Valley below Pittsburgh, and clashes between the Europeans and the American Indians under Chief Cornstalk began to increase. In response to cries for governmental support from the settlers in and around Pittsburgh, Lord John Murray, Earl of Dunmore (1732–1809), the last royal governor of Virginia, in 1774 called out the Virginia militia. Dunmore was not averse to using the cries of help from the settlers to advance his colony's claims to land beyond the Appalachian Mountains.

The Virginia troops came into the Upper Ohio Valley in two columns during fall 1774. Dunmore led the northern (main) column, and Gen. Andrew Lewis led the smaller, southern column to the Ohio River. Cornstalk led his warriors against Lewis. Cornstalk's plan was to defeat Lewis and then attack the main column, hoping that the news of the defeat would demoralize Dunmore's troops and cause them to retreat. On October 10, 1774, Cornstalk's warriors ambushed Lewis, who was in camp at Point Pleasant, (West) Va. Although the attack was initially successful, Lewis was able to rally his troops and drive the Indians from the field of battle. Casualties were about even between the two forces, but Cornstalk was unable to hold his warriors together to renew battle on the next day.

Unable to mount a military defense against the advance of Lewis and Dunmore, Cornstalk entered into peace talks with Dunmore. Part of the initial agreement was that Dunmore would stop all troop movements during negotiations. However, Dunmore's order to Lewis to stop his advance was met with disgust by Lewis, who continued to advance and destroy abandoned Indian villages. When Dunmore stated that he would use royal troops to protect Cornstalk's village from Lewis's men, open rebellion almost broke out among the militiamen. This act of Dunmore to protect Cornstalk and his people was later cited as a justification for the colonists' rebellion against the Crown.

The result of the peace negotiation between Cornstalk and Dunmore was the Treaty of Camp Charlotte, which opened the Ohio River to navigation and reconfirmed that the Indians were to stay north of the Ohio River. The immediate result of Lord Dunmore's War was to cause the American Indian tribes in the Old Northwest Territory to focus their attention on their eastern border. As the Indians guarded their eastern border during 1775 and 1776, European settlers moved into Kentucky via the Cumberland Gap and established Forts Boonesborough, Harrodsburg, and Logan, eventually helping to populate the lower counties of the Northern Kentucky region.

De Hass, Wills. *History of Early Settlements and Indian Wars of Western Virginia*. Parsons, W.Va.: McClain, 1989.
Withers, Alexander S. *Chronicles of Border Warfare in Western Virginia*. Parsons, W.Va.: McClain, 1975.

Charles H. Bogart

LORING, CLARA B. (b. 1896, Covington, Ky.; date and place of death unknown). Vocalist Clara Loring was the daughter of Frank Loring. By 1914 she was performing operatic concerts at the College of Music in Cincinnati, where she was the youngest singer at the school. She graduated that year and spent the following season in New York City, studying voice and doing concert work. In 1915 she became the first American pupil to be awarded a $5,000 scholarship to the elite International Academy of Opera in Paris, France. That May, she and her mother set sail for Paris. One evening in 1916, Clara was called upon to perform at New York City's Metropolitan Opera after the lead singer became ill. The next morning newspaper reviewers raved about Loring's great potential. Contract offers came flooding in to the beautiful and talented 21-year-old singer from Covington. Afterward, she and her mother spent two winters in Havana, Cuba. In early 1918 Clara was called home because her father, a **Chesapeake and Ohio Railroad** train engineer, had been killed accidentally at the rail yard in Russell. Clara's former neighbors along Greenup St. in Covington were amazed to learn that she was receiving $800 each time she sang.

"Covington Girl Is Awarded Scholarship," *KTS*, May 11, 1915, 10.
"Funeral of Wreck Victim," *KTS*, January 25, 1918, 16.
"Miss Loring to Sing," *KTS*, February 28, 1914, 1.
"Sudden Rise to Fame," *KTS*, November 29, 1916, 2.

LOUISIANA HOTEL. This local landmark in downtown Mount Olivet, the county seat of Robertson Co., was financed by merchant and tobacco buyer James Cumber and originally named the Cumber House. At the time of its construction in 1869, cost estimates ranged from $12,000 to $15,000 for the three-story structure. The original interior, which boasted solid poplar woodwork, was configured to include 23 guest rooms along with a large ballroom on the top floor.

The property changed hands at least eight times before 1930, often under interesting circumstances. During the 19th century, playing the Louisiana Lottery was an extremely popular pastime in Robertson Co. Citizens would pool their money to buy tickets through the mail. A local teacher, S. H. Bettys, won $7,500, a modest portion of that lottery's grand prize, in 1886 and used his winnings to buy and refurbish the hotel. He changed its name to the Louisiana Hotel to honor the source of his newly acquired wealth.

According to local accounts, during its heyday of the late 1800s and early 1900s, the Louisiana Hotel had many visitors, including various governors of Kentucky and, occasionally, a U.S. senator or a U.S. Representative. Unfortunately, however, the facts about the hotel have become somewhat confused in the retelling of stories over the years. For example, many people in the region now believe that the hotel was originally built by someone who moved from Louisiana to Kentucky after winning the Louisiana Lottery's grand prize; this erroneous account has even been published on at least one occasion by a regional Kentucky newspaper.

In 1930 two owners of a Robertson Co. car dealership purchased the hotel and an adjoining lot for the sum of $4,000. They removed interior walls from the hotel and turned the first floor into a Chevrolet showroom. This phase in the building's life was short-lived, however. Just two years later, in 1932, the business partnership dissolved, and one of the partners took the title to the hotel. The Louisiana Hotel then became a private residence.

The once grand Louisiana Hotel still stands on Main St. in downtown Mount Olivet. The first floor houses a floral shop, while the upper level is an apartment. No sign or historical marker commemorates the building's rich and storied past.

Moore, T. Ross, ed. *Echoes from the Century, 1867–1967.* Mount Olivet, Ky.: Robertson Co. Historical Society, 2000.

Pearce, John Ed. "Robertson County." *LCJ Magazine*, January 11, 1981, 6–12.

Robertson County Tribune, April 24; May 1, 15; June 5, 1884. Available on microfilm at W. T. Young Library, Univ. of Kentucky, Lexington, Ky.

Deborah Diersen Crocker

LOUISVILLE, CINCINNATI, AND LEXINGTON RAILROAD. Cincinnati and Northern Kentucky in the 1850s and 1860s found themselves at a disadvantage in serving the growing Southern trading markets. East Coast cities were being linked with the South by railroads running down through the Tidewater region of America. In Kentucky two railroads had been completed from the Ohio River into the heartland of the South. The Illinois Central (IC) extended south from Chicago to Cairo, Ill. At Cairo a railcar ferry transferred IC rolling stock across the river to Columbus, Ky., and to a connection with the Mobile and Ohio, whose track ran to Mobile, Ala. Upstream at Louisville two railroads, providing connections with Detroit and Chicago, terminated on the north shore of the Ohio River: the New Albany and Salem Railroad and the Jeffersonville, Madison, and Indianapolis Railroad (JM&I) in Indiana. Goods were carried by wagons and ferried from railcars that had arrived at Jeffersonville and New Albany to Louisville and loaded onto **Louisville and Nashville** (L&N) equipment headed for Nashville, Tenn., and points further south.

Cincinnati by 1860 had developed two limited rail routes to reach the South. The first was by the 6-foot broad-gauge Ohio and Mississippi Railroad, which intersected with the JM&I at Seymour, Ind., and with the IC at Sandoval, Ill. Since both of these two later railroads were standard gauge (4 feet 8.5 inches), cargo had to be transloaded at these connections. The second route used the **Kentucky Central Railroad** (KC) at Covington to reach Lexington; merchandise then was transferred to the Lexington and Frankfort (Lex&F) and the Louisville and Frankfort (Lou&F) to reach Louisville. The Lex&F and the Lou&F were built to standard gauge, but in 1863 the War Department converted them to 5-foot gauge, the same gauge as the L&N. The roundabout nature of both of these routes added to the cost of shipment to Louisville. The conversion to the 5-foot gauge was a rare event in U.S. railroad history, done for the sake of expediency in the Union war effort.

To stay competitive, what Cincinnati wanted and needed was a more direct rail connection with the South. The solution proposed by some in Cincinnati was to build a railroad along the Kentucky side of the Ohio River to Louisville, connecting with the L&N. When the charter to build this railroad was issued by the Commonwealth of Kentucky, it called for the building of standard-gauge rail between the cities. Goods would have to be transloaded at Louisville, providing jobs in Louisville and adding to the cost of shipment.

The Lou&F and the Lex&F combined their resources to build a connecting rail line between Louisville and Cincinnati. The two railroads in 1869 reorganized themselves as the Louisville, Cincinnati and Lexington Railroad (LC&L). The route the LC&L chose ran somewhat inland from the Ohio River and for most of its distance perpendicular to the natural drainage system, thus requiring the construction of numerous bridges and six tunnels. Because this railroad, upon completion, would shorten the rail distance between Cincinnati and Louisville, it quickly gained the title the Short Line. Regular traffic on it between Louisville and Covington began in June 1869. With the completion of the Newport and Cincinnati Bridge (the **L&N Bridge**) in 1872, the LC&L reached Cincinnati.

The rail line, as built, was 113 miles long. It crossed the Ohio River from Cincinnati by bridge into Newport, where it ran south along Saratoga St. to its own private right-of-way south of 11th St. The road then went down the Licking River Valley to Wilder, where it crossed the Licking River into Latonia. At Latonia the LC&L crossed the KC at grade. From Latonia the railroad ran along Banklick Creek, climbing to the plateau above the river valleys via two high trestles, one at Banklick Creek and one at Independence. Once on top of the hill, the rail line ran south to Walton, before turning west for LaGrange, where it met the Lou&F line. Between Walton and Glencoe, the terrain is rough; it had necessitated numerous cuts and fills and had required construction of the 636-foot Eagle Creek Tunnel in northwest Grant Co. West of the tunnel is the Eagle Creek Valley and the towns of Glencoe and Sparta. Glencoe served as the railhead for Warsaw in Gallatin Co., and Sparta for Owenton in Owen Co. At Worthington the railroad crossed the Kentucky River and began its climb up Mills Creek for LaGrange and Louisville via Campbellsburg. At LaGrange the LC&L ran over the existing Lou&F rails into Louisville. In 1959 the Lou&F's Frankfort Junction at LaGrange was taken up and rail service between Louisville and Frankfort was rerouted through Shelbyville in Shelby Co.

The bridge between Newport and Cincinnati was built by the a subsidiary of the Pennsylvania Railroad (PRR); the PRR sold the bridge to the L&N in 1904. The Little Miami station at Pearl and Butler Sts. in Cincinnati was the northern terminus of the LC&L. For a short period before the bridge to Cincinnati was completed, the northern terminus was the Newport station, located along the east side of Saratoga St. between present-day Fifth and Sixth Sts. Until the combined station of the C&O and the L&N was opened at 11th and Monmouth Sts. (called the NX Cabin) in 1888, the old station served Newport as both a freight and a passenger stop; after the passenger depot moved to the combined station at the Newport diamond, it remained a freight depot for the L&N for many years. Concrete marks can be seen today in the sidewalk where the sidings from the main line once entered the small station yard. In its last days, the Newport city sign could be seen on the freight station, which served local Newport businesses. That property became Art's Rental Equipment in the late 1960s.

The Short Line did not attract the business its promoters believed it was capable of supporting. The problem was the excessive grades and curves on the line, which limited the loads that could be pulled by the steam engines of that era. More than 25 miles of the Short Line have grades greater than 1 percent, and another 20 miles have a grade of between 0.75 and 1 percent. The ruling grade is a 2.72 percent climb as part of a 5-mile overall 1.16 percent climb. The right-of-way has no straight stretch longer than 2 miles, and only two other stretches are straight for more than 1 mile. In one section of the line there are 5.7 miles of curves within 7.4 miles of track. The maximum curve on the line measures 7 degrees 10 minutes. Curves of 3 degrees and more, however, are common, and many occur on a grade. This configuration made for stress on the engines pulling cars over the line. Accepted railroad practice of the day allowed that an engine that could move 1,000 tons on level grade could move only 200 tons on a 0.05 percent grade, a rise of 6 inches in 100 feet. Therefore, watering points were established at Walton and Glencoe, and both coaling and watering facilities were provided at Worthington.

As a result of the lack of business, which only grew worse with the opening of the **Cincinnati Southern** in 1877, the LC&L went into bankruptcy in 1881. The line was then bought by the L&N to keep competitors away. Over the years the L&N straightened a few curves, lowered some grades, and daylighted all but the Eagle Creek Tunnel, but the route still presents a challenge for engineers who attempt it.

In 1875 the Cincinnati Southern crossed the LC&L by a bridge at Walton, and the **Chesapeake and Ohio Railroad** (C&O) in 1888 crossed the LC&L on grade in Newport at NX Cabin (11th and Monmouth Sts.).

In 1980 the Short Line became part of **CSX.** In 1984 CSX embargoed traffic along Saratoga St. in Newport, shifting service into Ohio over the C&O Bridge. CSX donated the L&N Bridge to the City of Newport in 1999, and it is used today as a pedestrian bridge, affectionately called the Purple People Bridge because of its color. The Short Line today terminates in a connection with the former C&O Railway track at NX Cabin in Newport, and both are parts of CSX. In recent years the line has seen a growth in traffic, moving up to 16 trains daily.

The first LC&L Bridge over the Licking River remains between Wilder and Latonia, but it is not in use. Replaced in the 1920s by a bridge able to carry heavier loads, the 1869 bridge serves as a support structure for water lines crossing the Licking River. The LC&L Bridge across the Kentucky River was also replaced in the 1920s.

Appleton's Railway and Steam Navigation Guide. New York: Robbins and Appleton, 1870.
Condit, Carl W. *The Railroad and the City.* Columbus: Ohio State Univ. Press, 1977.
Herr, Kincaid A. *The Louisville & Nashville Railroad.* Lexington: Univ. Press of Kentucky, 2000.
Tenkotte, Paul A. "Rival Cities to Suburbs: Covington and Newport, Kentucky, 1790–1890," PhD diss., Univ. of Cincinnati, 1989.

Charles H. Bogart

LOUISVILLE AND NASHVILLE RAILROAD. The Louisville and Nashville Railroad (L&N) served Northern Kentucky via two rail lines. The first ran west from Northern Kentucky to Louisville, and the other ran south to Winchester. The L&N received a charter in 1850 to build a line between its two namesake cities, and it completed construction of that line in 1860. The L&N was heavily damaged during the **Civil War** but also made a profit as a carrier of supplies to Union troops in Tennessee. After the war, therefore, the L&N was able to expand by acquiring local lines and merging them into its system. The L&N eventually owned track from Chicago to New Orleans and became the predominant railroad in Kentucky.

The L&N first reached Northern Kentucky over the Short Line, which was built between 1869 and 1870 as the **Louisville, Cincinnati, and Lexington Railroad** (LC&L) to provide a connection with the South for merchants in Cincinnati. The LC&L reached Cincinnati in 1872 by crossing the Licking River at Latonia into Wilder and then running down the middle of Newport's Saratoga St. to the Cincinnati and Newport Bridge, now the **L&N Bridge**, over the Ohio River. (Train traffic ended on Saratoga St. in 1984, and the bridge was donated to the City of Newport by **CSX** in 1999.) Once across the Ohio River, the rail line connected with the Pittsburgh, Cincinnati, and St. Louis Railway via the tracks of the Little Miami Railroad, later the Pennsylvania Railroad.

The rail line built by the LC&L was constructed to standard gauge, 4 feet and 8.5 inches. The L&N, whose track extended into the South, was built to a 5-foot gauge. The result was that the LC&L cars could not interchange with the L&N at Louisville; goods moving south had to be transferred to cars of the other railroad. Thus, there was an extra charge for transportation of goods between Cincinnati and southern destinations. When the LC&L went into receivership in 1881, it was bought by the L&N. This purchase allowed Louisville to continue to set the price for goods originating in Cincinnati and destined for a southern state. These actions by Louisville led to the building of the **Cincinnati Southern Railroad**.

The predecessor L&N line due south from Northern Kentucky had been started in 1850 to gain Cincinnati a rail route to Tennessee and Georgia. The road was built by three separate companies: the **Covington and Lexington** (C&L) from Covington to Paris, the **Maysville and Lexington** (M&L) from Paris to Lexington, and the Lexington and Danville (L&D) from Lexington to Nicholasville. This rail line was projected to cross the Kentucky River near Wilmore via High Bridge, a suspension bridge designed by **John Roebling**, and continue to Burnside, Ky., and Chattanooga, Tenn. The outbreak of the Civil War caused this plan to be temporarily shelved. This line operated under the advertising title of **Kentucky Central Railroad**. After the Civil War, the Kentucky Central route was not available for Cincinnati's scheme to build south to Atlanta, Ga., so the Cincinnati Southern was forced to build its own route south.

In 1865 the C&L and the M&L were acquired by the Kentucky Central Association and in 1875 were merged as the Kentucky Central Railroad (KC). The KC languished in the years after the Civil War until, in 1881, it was bought by Collis P. Huntington, who was building westward from Ashland, Ky., to Cincinnati with his **Chesapeake and Ohio Railroad** (C&O). Huntington also owned the Chesapeake, Ohio, and Southwestern (CO&SW), which ran from Louisville to Paducah. To gain access to the CO&SW from the C&O, he bought the KC, which provided access to Lexington. At Lexington he used track rights over the L&N line between Lexington and Louisville to reach the CO&SW. Unfortunately, a recession caused the whole venture to go into receivership. The L&N then stepped in and bought the KC in 1891. The KC at this time consisted of three parts, a road from Paris to Maysville, the line from Covington to Lexington, and track from Paris to Sinks.

The L&N in the 1890s began a program to turn the KC into a major hauler of coal to the northern markets. The southern terminus of the line was shifted from Lexington to Corbin. The line between Cincinnati and Corbin became the CC Division. Then in 1916 the L&N built a new line from Winchester to the coalfields of Perry Co., the Eastern Kentucky Division.

The Paris-to-Maysville rail line remained a branch line with the L&N. Because of steep grades and tight curves, which mandated slow speed, the line never developed through freight service. This line connected with the Chesapeake and Ohio Railway at Maysville and with the Flemingsburg and Northern Railroad at Flemingsburg Junction. In 1979 the L&N sold the line to **Transkentucky Transportation Railroad Inc.**, which developed a market niche of moving Eastern Kentucky coal to the Ohio River coal terminal at Maysville.

In 1902 the Atlantic Coast Line Railroad gained a controlling interest in the L&N. The L&N, however, continued to operate as a separate company. In 1967 the Atlantic Coast Line and the Seaboard Air Line Railway merged to form the Seaboard Coast Line Railroad, a subsidiary of Seaboard Coast Lines Industries. The Seaboard Coast Line began a marketing campaign in which its components, including the L&N, were referred to as the Family Lines. In 1980 Seaboard Coast Line Industries merged with the **Chessie System** Railroad to form the CSX Corporation, which created CSX Transportation operators of CSX's railroad properties. In 1982 the L&N, as part of the Seaboard Coast Line, lost its corporate identity with the forming of the Seaboard System Railroad. The Seaboard System Railroad in turn was folded into CSX in 1986. Repainting of L&N rolling stock with CSX colors, however, had begun as early as 1980.

The heart of the L&N presence in Northern Kentucky, during its last years of existence, was the DeCoursey Hump Yard south of Latonia, which was built in 1918 and rebuilt in 1963. During its operational life, with its two humps, the yard was one of the largest hump freight classification yards in the nation. It was among the first of the hump yards to have retarders installed; the north hump received its set in 1940, and the south hump in 1964. At the hump yard L&N freight trains were broken down and their component cars forwarded to other railroad yards in the Greater Cincinnati area, and cars received from other yards were built into trains for dispatch over the L&N. A shift in movement of goods from boxcars to containers, the use of unit coal and auto trains, and the opening of Queensgate Yard in 1981 at Cincinnati spelled the end of DeCoursey as a hump yard. The yard was used for a time for the storage of bad-order and excess cars by CSX before portions of it were sold off during the 1990s.

The L&N operated a number of named and local passenger trains south from Northern Kentucky until it terminated passenger service in 1971. The named trains included the Pan American, the Humming Bird, and the Azalean to New Orleans, and the Southland and the Flamingo to St. Petersburg, Fla. The L&N's passenger depot in Cincinnati had been served via the bridge between Newport and Cincinnati, but in the early 1930s, with the opening of the Cincinnati Union Terminal, L&N passenger trains began to use the C&O Bridge between Covington and Cincinnati as their gateway into Ohio. This was not the first use of the C&O Bridge, as it had been used to transfer freight cars between the railroad transfer yard in Latonia and the railyards of other railroads in Cincinnati.

"A Fond Farewell," *KP*, August 24, 1984, 4K.
Herr, Kincaid A. *The Louisville & Nashville Railroad.* Lexington: Univ. Press of Kentucky, 2000.
Klein, Maury. *History of the Louisville & Nashville Railroad.* New York: Macmillan, 1972.
Trains Magazine. *The Historical Guide to North American Railroad.* Waukesha, Wis.: Kalmbach Books, 2000.

Charles H. Bogart

LOVELL HOUSE. See **Porter-Fallis-Lovell House.**

LUCAS, KEN (b. August 22, 1933, Kenton Co., Ky.). Kenneth Ray Lucas became a successful businessman and an elected public official. After graduation from the University of Kentucky at Lexington in 1955, he joined the U.S. Air Force and served until 1967. Lucas worked many years as a financial planner in Northern Kentucky. He began his political career as an elected member of the Florence City Council from 1967–1974. He then was elected as a Boone Co. commissioner, serving from 1974 to 1982. In 1970 he earned his MBA degree from Xavier University in Cincinnati. Lucas was judge-executive of Boone Co. for six years (1992–1998). He sat for 23 years on the Board of Regents at **Northern Kentucky University**, and for 13 of those years he was the board's chairman. He also saw service as the president of the **Northern Kentucky Chamber of Commerce**, and over the years he has volunteered as a worker for many other civic organizations and causes.

In 1998 Lucas was elected to succeed Representative **Jim Bunning** as the Kentucky 4th District U.S. congressman. Lucas served three terms in the U.S. House of Representatives and then chose not to seek reelection in 2004. In November 2006 he ran for his former congressional seat, occupied by congressman **Geoff Davis**, and lost. As a congressman, Democrat Lucas was a member of the fiscally conservative Blue Dog Democrats, championing economic development issues, education, and social security. He is married to Mary Kappas, and they have five children.

Biographical Directory of the United States Congress. "Lucas, Ken." http://bioguide.congress.gov (accessed March 6, 2006).

Robert Schrage

LUDLOW. Ludlow is located in northern Kenton Co. on the Ohio River. The city is bordered by Covington to the east, Bromley to the west, and Fort Wright to the south. The first permanent resident in what is today the city of Ludlow was **Thomas D. Carneal**, a member of Kentucky's General Assembly and a wealthy landowner. Carneal acquired 1,200 acres of property and began in 1818 constructing a grand home, which he called **Elmwood Hall**. An early visitor to the estate described it in this way: "I have not, since I left England, seen a house so completely furnished with all the elegancies and refinements of society, nor a more hospitable and abundant board, which is wholly supplied from his own grounds." The home sat on a small rise of ground facing the Ohio River.

Carneal and his family lived in Elmwood Hall until 1827, when it was sold to Englishman **William Bullock**, the owner of London's Piccadilly Circus and Egyptian Hall. Bullock intended to live in Elmwood Hall and establish a model community on the spacious grounds. He acquired the services of architect I. B. Papworth to draw plans for this new community, which he called **Hygeia**, a word of Greek derivation meaning "health." Plans for the community included a central fountain surrounded by four city blocks named Adams, Franklin, Jefferson, and Patterson squares. A circular boulevard was to surround the four squares. The plans also included a theater, churches, a library, a museum, a cemetery, a tavern, and many single-family residences. It was Bullock's intention to entice Englishmen and their families to purchase lots and take up residence in Hygeia; however, he had little success, and the planned community of Hygeia was never built.

In 1831 Bullock sold most of his property to Israel L. Ludlow, a son of one of the founders of Cincinnati. During the ensuing decade, a few individuals purchased portions of the Ludlow estate and built large residences. One of these homes was Somerset Hall, a large Federal style structure built by the **Kenner family** of Louisiana. Casper Ritchie, a Swiss immigrant, constructed a grand home at the northwest corner of Elm and Locust Sts. Matthew Bentley built another early home at the northwest corner of Elm and Butler Sts. In 1846 Israel Ludlow laid out a small town on his property and began selling lots for residential and business uses.

In the years before the **Civil War**, the little village of Ludlow evolved into a quiet country hamlet of small homes surrounded by lush gardens and beautiful orchards. The village was connected to Covington by River Rd. and to Cincinnati by a ferry. River Rd., however, was prone to flooding and was not always properly maintained. The owners of the ferry did not keep a regular schedule. A number of prominent town residents suggested that the area incorporate. They hoped that a local government would be able to regulate the infrequent and expensive ferryboat service to Cincinnati. The Commonwealth of Kentucky officially incorporated the city of Ludlow on February 20, 1864.

The State of Kentucky operated the first public school in the city. Classroom space was acquired on the first floor of the Christian Church at the corner of Elm and Locust Sts. When the city was incorporated in 1864, town officials established a school district under the supervision of city government. Ludlow voters approved a $3,000 bond issue to build a permanent school building (see **Ludlow Independent School District**). That same year, work began on a new school building on Linden St. The brick building contained two classrooms. In 1879 an addition to the building was built to house the growing enrollment. **Ludlow High School** began operation in 1886.

The Ludlow Police Department was established in 1864 with the appointment of the town's first marshal. In 1882 the first town hall was built on Oak St. The building housed the police department, city offices, and the jail. The office of town marshal was changed to chief of police in 1893 with the passage of Kentucky's new constitution. That year, Robert E. Callahan was elected the first Ludlow chief of police. Callahan became a beloved figure in the community and held the position of chief from 1893 until his death in 1936, a period of more than 43 years. The Ludlow Volunteer Fire Department was established in 1884, following a tragic fire that destroyed two businesses and a home. The department was reorganized in 1890. The first firehouse was built on Oak St. near the new city building.

Churches played an important role in the early development of the city. The first congregation established within the city was the Ludlow Christian Church in 1841. Early city government was conducted in the old church building at the southeast corner of Elm and Carneal Sts. Baptist residents living in the area established the **First Baptist Church, Ludlow**, in 1849. Eventually, the congregation built a large church on Linden St. The **Wesley United Methodist Church** was founded in 1853 and constructed a small Gothic Revival edifice on Oak St. In 1872 the German Catholic community in Ludlow established St. Boniface Church and School on Adela Ave. in the city's west end. That congregation also sponsored a school from the time of its founding. An impressive Romanesque Revival church building was dedicated in 1893. In 1887 the city's Irish Catholics founded St. James Parish on Carneal St. A parish school was established in 1893 and a new Gothic Revival church was constructed on Oak St. in 1903–1904 (see **Saints Boniface and James Catholic Church**).

Ludlow changed from a rural area to a working-class suburb during the 1870s, with the arrival of the **Cincinnati Southern Railroad** (also known as the Queen and Crescent Route). Many new residents, especially German and Irish immigrants, were attracted to Ludlow by the abundance of railroad jobs (see **Cincinnati Southern Railroad Yard**). Frequent and dependable railroad service also attracted many other new businesses to the community. The railroad bridge to Cincinnati was completed in 1877. In 1885 the residents of Ludlow passed a bond issue to construct a footpath on the bridge.

The 1890s witnessed much development in the city. In 1893 streetcar service between Covington and Ludlow began over the new Highway Ave. That same year, the Pullman Company constructed a large plant in the city to repair luxury railroad passenger cars. During the height of operations, the Pullman Shops employed 200 area residents. The shops were destroyed by fire on May 20, 1919. In 1894 investors in the South Covington and Cincinnati Street Railway Company opened the **Lagoon Amusement Park** along Pleasant Run Creek, west of the city. The creek was dammed, forming a large lake. Along the shores of the lagoon were built park rides, assorted carnival amusements, and many other attractions. Ludlow became an attractive entertainment destination for many people living both in and outside of the Greater Cincinnati area.

Significant progress was made by the Ludlow Public Schools in the 1890s, as well. In 1895 William and Albert Ludlow donated a lot at the northwest corner of Oak St. and Adela Ave for the construction of a new school building. On June 29, 1895, the cornerstone of the new school was laid, with impressive ceremonies, and the building was dedicated on June 12, 1897. A Cincinnati newspaper declared, "The new building has no equal in the State of Kentucky in point of comfort, beauty, and general utility for educational purposes." In 1915 a second building was constructed to house the growing number of pupils in the district. The Ludlow Board of Education oversaw the construction of a modern high school building at the southwest corner of Elm St. and Adela Ave. in 1932. The new George Washington High School contained classrooms, a large auditorium, and a gymnasium. In 1937 Rigney Stadium was constructed for athletics, using Works Progress Administration (WPA) funds.

Ludlow experienced another building boom in the years following **World War I**. In the eastern end of town, the Morningside Addition was constructed along the south side of Highway Ave. Much of the city's west end was also developed during this era on the former site of the Lagoon

Amusement Park, which had closed in 1918. In 1923 a bond issue provided the funds to build a new combination city hall and firehouse, which was erected on Oak St. after the old firehouse and city hall there were demolished. Ambulance and life-squad services were initiated in the city in 1932. In 1926 William Ludlow donated to the city five acres on the north side of Elm St. for park purposes. The donation was made in memory of his brother, Albert S. Ludlow. A park board was established in 1926, and playground equipment was installed in 1928. The current park shelter house was constructed in 1932.

The **flood of 1937** was the largest natural disaster in the history of Ludlow. By January 22, Ludlow's residents living in low-lying areas began moving their furniture and other belongings to high ground. At this time Hooper, Somerset, and Forest Aves. were under water. Also, water was creeping up the lower portions of Euclid, Butler, and Kenner Sts. The Ludlow Streetcar line was blocked in Covington, and egress through Bromley was impossible. The only reliable way out was through **Devou Park** to the north. The **Green Line Transit Company** began running buses to Ludlow through Devou Park. The river reached a crest of 79.99 feet on January 26. More than 500 families were forced to leave their homes, and more than 43 percent of the city was under water. Residents stored their furniture in the Odd Fellows Hall, St. Boniface School, St. James School, the Masonic Hall, the Wesley Methodist Church, the First Baptist Church, the Knights of Columbus Hall, and the Dixie Metal Tag Company. The **American Red Cross** established a relief center at the First Presbyterian Church. Emergency meals were served at both the Presbyterian Church and St. Boniface Church. Because Ludlow was without running water and gas, residents were forced to cook their food on outdoor fires. Most of the city was also without electricity; only the line that supplied the city hall was operational. Men from the Civilian Conservation Corps (CCC) helped the citizens recover from the flood. These workers were housed at St. James School. The Ludlow Volunteer Fire Department and the Ludlow Police Department worked around the clock to ensure the safety of residents. All flooded homes were sanitized and inspected before residents were permitted to return.

The baby boom following **World War II** filled Ludlow's schools and churches. Several new developments were built at this time, including the 600 blocks of Laurel and Linden Sts. By 1950 the population had reached 6,374. The 1950s also witnessed the development of Ludlow Heights on the south side of Highway Ave. In 1957 the old Ludlow Elementary School was demolished to make way for the current structure, which was dedicated to Mary A. Goetz, a teacher in the Ludlow Schools for 52 years.

The population of Ludlow began to decline during the late 1960s. Many Ludlow residents were drawn to the new suburban cities located south and west of the town. By the early 1980s, the city's population had stabilized at 4,500. More recently, Ludlow has continued to advance with an addition to the firehouse in 1989 and the construction of the Highpoint Senior Citizens Apartments in 1980. Ludlow's reputation as a city of fine homes was strengthened in 2001 with the groundbreaking for the River's Breeze Condominium Complex on Pigeon Point. This development offers spectacular views of downtown Cincinnati. In 2000 the U.S. Census Bureau reported that Ludlow's population was 4,409.

Centennial Celebration, Ludlow, Kentucky: Commemorating 100 Years of Progress 1864–1964. Ludlow, Ky.: Ludlow Centennial Committee, 1964.

Hunnicutt, John M. *History of the City of Ludlow.* Ludlow, Ky.: Ludlow Volunteer Fire Department, 1935.

Tenkotte, Paul A. "Rival Cities to Suburbs: Covington and Newport, Kentucky, 1790–1890," PhD diss., Univ. of Cincinnati, 1989.

David E. Schroeder

LUDLOW HIGH SCHOOL. Ludlow High school was established in 1886, to further the educational goals of the Ludlow Independent School District. Before this date, students from Ludlow who wished to continue their education paid tuition to attend the Covington High School or one of the region's private schools. The high school program in Ludlow began modestly in the district's elementary school building along Linden St. In 1889 the first graduating class received diplomas. These first graduates were Alice Closson, Grace Harwood, Elizabeth Hankins, Margaret Hill, Jessie Howe, Anna Nixon, Robert Rigdon, George Price, and Bertha Vanderbilt. Enrollment at the school grew slowly in the years before **World War I**. Between 1890 and 1893, 30 students received diplomas. No diplomas were awarded in 1894 or 1895.

In 1915 a separate building was constructed to accommodate the growing number of junior high and high school pupils. The architectural firm of Weber, Werner, and Adkins of Cincinnati designed the building. The structure contained five classrooms, a science laboratory, a study hall, a library, a small auditorium, a gymnasium, and a lunchroom. This building quickly became inadequate to serve the educational needs of the district. During the 1920s, more students began attending high school, and the need arose to obtain a larger building. In 1932 a new high school was constructed at the southwest corner of Elm St. and Adela Ave. Architect F. J. Porter designed the structure, and it cost $164,000. The new Collegiate Gothic style building was dedicated formally on April 30, 1932. It contained 16 classrooms, an 800-seat auditorium, and a gymnasium. Each classroom was equipped with a radio. Officially, the name of the school is the George Washington High School. However, throughout its history, the school has been referred to as the Ludlow High School.

The Works Progress Administration (WPA) financed the construction of Rigney Football Stadium on Ludlow's riverfront in 1937. The stadium was dedicated on October 8, 1937. Lights were added to the stadium in 1960, and an electronic scoreboard was installed in 1963. The need for more modern sports facilities resulted in the construction of a new gymnasium at the high school in 1970. The 1,300-seat facility was built on a site near the elementary school on Oak St. In November 1975 the Ludlow High School football team defeated Heath High School (7-6) to win Ludlow High School's first state championship. A second state title was won in 1999 by the Ludlow High School Girls Cross Country team.

Benson, George S. "Looking Ahead," *Ludlow News Enterprise,* April 16, 1970, 1.

"Dedication of School Is Set," *KP,* April 23, 1932, 1.

"Early Ludlow Public Schools," *Kenton County Historical Society Newsletter,* August 1990.

"Local Crowd Follows Team to Western Bowl," *News Enterprise,* December 4, 1975, 1.

Ludlow Centennial Celebration, Inc. *Ludlow Centennial Souvenir Program, 1864–1964.* Newport, Ky.: Acorn-OTTOmatic Printing, 1964.

David E. Schroeder

LUDLOW INDEPENDENT SCHOOL DISTRICT. The Commonwealth of Kentucky operated the first public school in the city of Ludlow. Classes were held on the first floor of the old Christian Church at the corner of Elm and Locust Sts. When Ludlow was incorporated in 1864, town officials established a school district under the supervision of city government. Enrollment at that time was 130. The first school board consisted of Levi Bavis, Fred Gottlieb, and C. W. Harwood.

In 1869 Ludlow voters approved a $3,000 bond issue to construct a school building, which was built on Linden St. and contained two spacious classrooms. In 1879 an addition was erected to accommodate the increasing number of pupils. In 1887 additional classrooms were opened in a nearby cottage that was purchased by the school board. William and Albert Ludlow donated a large parcel of property at the northwest corner of Oak St. and Adela Ave. for a new school building in 1895, and the architectural firm of Fasse and Company was chosen to design the new structure. Plans called for a school measuring 90 by 120 feet with a circular tower at each corner. The cornerstone was set on June 29, 1895, and the facility was dedicated on June 12, 1897, with impressive ceremonies. This building contained 10 classrooms, a room for music instruction, and a lunchroom.

A high school program was begun in Ludlow in 1886. The first high school graduation class, consisting of nine students, received their diplomas in 1889. The school board named the school George Washington High School. As the population of Ludlow increased, so did the need for additional school facilities, especially for the high school. By 1915 the school building at Oak St. and Adela Ave., which housed both the elementary school and the high school, was operating beyond capacity. The citizens of Ludlow approved a bond issue for the construction of a new building to accommodate the high school classes. In 1915 a new high school (currently the junior high school building) was opened near the elementary school. The architectural firm of Weber, Werner, and Adkins of Cincinnati designed the building. The years following **World War I** witnessed a sharp increase in attendance at Ludlow High School. In 1932 the district built a modern high school building at the southwest corner of Elm St. and Adela Ave. Architect F. J. Porter designed the structure, which was constructed at the cost of $164,000.

The current elementary school building opened in 1957. The modern steel-and-glass building was dedicated to the memory of Mary A. Goetz, who taught there for more than 50 years. Born of immigrant parents, Goetz and her two sisters, Christina and Esther, devoted their lives to the education of children. All three sisters taught within the Ludlow school system. In 1998 Ludlow school officials approved an addition to the school building, which was erected in the area between the high school and elementary school buildings facing Adela Ave. The Ludlow Independent School District is known for its dedicated faculty and staff and for its consistently high achievement on national and state standardized tests.

Benson, George S. "Looking Ahead," *Ludlow News Enterprise,* April 16, 1970, 1.

"Contract for School Is Let," *KP,* June 16, 1931, 13.

"Dedication of School Is Set," *KP,* April 23, 1932, 1.

"Early Ludlow Public Schools," *Kenton County Historical Society Newsletter,* August 1990.

"Local Crowd Follows Team to Western Bowl," *News Enterprise,* December 4, 1975, 1.

Ludlow Centennial Celebration, Inc. *Ludlow Centennial Souvenir Program, 1864–1964.* Newport, Ky.: Acorn-OTTOmatic Printing, 1964.

"Ludlow Schools Forming Foundation," *KP,* November 21, 2001, 2K.

"Ludlow Tells Plans for Middle School," *KE,* December 13, 1998, B1B.

"Middle School Going Up," *KP,* June 15, 1999, 2K.

"New Ludlow High School Nearly Ready," *KP,* April 7, 1932, 1.

David E. Schroeder

LUKOWSKY, ROBERT O. (b. August 23, 1927, Covington, Ky.; d. December 5, 1981, Cincinnati, Ohio). Robert O. Lukowsky Jr., an acclaimed judge, legal writer, and teacher of law, was the son of Robert O. and Esther Agnes Cole Lukowsky. His grandparents, Joseph and Rebecca Lukowsky, emigrated from Odessa, Russia. Robert Lukowsky Jr. grew up at 316 Madison Ave. in Covington and attended St. Xavier High School in Cincinnati (class of 1945) and the University of Cincinnati. He graduated from the university's College of Law and was admitted to the Kentucky bar in 1949.

Lukowsky served in the Corps of Engineers of the U.S. Army at the close of **World War II**, was commissioned in the Judge Advocate General's Department of the U.S. Air Force during the **Korean War**, and retired from active service in the Air Force as a lieutenant colonel.

He was appointed and served as judge pro tem and trial commissioner of the Kenton Co. Court from 1952 to 1955. During that time he helped to found the court's Juvenile Session and also served on a three-member committee that drafted rules of practice and procedure for the Kenton Circuit Court. He was appointed a Kenton circuit judge in 1962 by Governor Bert T. Combs; at the time he was the youngest circuit judge in the history of Kentucky. He was reelected circuit judge in 1969. He was elected without opposition in 1974 to the Kentucky Court of Appeals, Kentucky's highest court at the time.

According to a resolution passed by the Kentucky Supreme Court in 1986, Lukowsky "took the lead to push for passage of the Judicial Reform Act, which amended the Kentucky Constitution in the mid-1970s." Known then as the Judicial Article, this set of comprehensive reforms rationalized the organization of hundreds of petit courts across the commonwealth and incorporated them into a unified judicial system. The Judicial Article required that all Kentucky judges be lawyers, it vested all litigants with the right of at least one appeal, and it created the new Kentucky Supreme Court. The enactment of the Judicial Article and its implementation in the succeeding years brought Kentucky into the front rank of states in the cause of progressive court reform.

Lukowsky was appointed by three different governors to the Kentucky Crime Commission. He also served on a committee that revised the Kentucky Rules of Civil Procedure and was a member of a commission that reviewed Kentucky's substantive criminal law, leading to the enactment of the Kentucky Penal Code. He was a member of the first class of the National College of State Trial Judges in 1964 and served on the faculty of the judicial college as a lecturer and seminar leader of the judicial conferences in 18 different states. Lukowsky was an adjunct professor of law at **Chase College of Law** at **Northern Kentucky University** and served as a consultant to the Institute of Court Management on the subject of rural court administration.

Upon enactment and implementation of the Judicial Article, Lukowsky was elevated to the Kentucky Supreme Court in 1978, representing a district that included metropolitan Northern Kentucky and several rural counties nearby. He was the first Northern Kentuckian to serve on the Kentucky Supreme Court.

Lukowsky enjoyed a reputation for prodigious intellectual capacity, he wrote pungent appellate opinions, and his tutelage in law and procedure was venerated by lawyers and judges, who embraced his high standards and mordant wit. He believed that law, vigorously practiced, was fundamental to a just society. He "possessed great literary skill," according to Kentucky Supreme Court chief justice John S. Palmore, who served with him in the inaugural term of the high court. Lukowsky believed that lay people as well as practitioners should understand legal writing. One could never be in doubt about Lukowsky's position on the issues at hand after reading one of his opinions. His appellate opinions were gems of literacy, clarity, and wit. Each is a small legal-literary classic.

Lukowsky thought that the Kentucky legislature had made a muddle of part of the workers' compensation statute in its 1978 session. Nevertheless, he voted with the court majority to uphold the act, damning the legislature with faint praise: "In the last analysis, the palate of the people determines the legislative diet. As President Ulysses S. Grant put it in his Inaugural Address on March 4, 1869, 'I know of no method to secure the repeal of bad or obnoxious laws so effective as their stringent execution.... The constitutional ring is closed. The legislature gave. The legislature has taken away. This court shall respect the function of the legislature.'"

Perhaps his best-known and most controversial opinion was in the case that upheld the legislature's enactment of a law requiring the posting of a copy of the Ten Commandments in every public school classroom in the state. It may have been in deference to what were apparently his own strong religious beliefs that Lukowsky took five double-columned pages to explain his dissent, which included these comments:

> Section 5 of the Kentucky Bill of Rights is unequivocal: "No preference shall ever be given by law . . . to any particular creed. . . ." It is an inescapable conclusion that the Ten Commandments are a religious creed. . . . The same power which could place a copy of the Ten Commandments on the wall of every public elementary and secondary classroom could place a copy of the Communist Manifesto on the same wall. The same state that could require a pledge of allegiance to the "Stars and Stripes" could require a salute to the "Hammer and Sickle." . . . The wall that separates church and state protects as it restricts.

Justice Lukowsky's position was adopted when the U.S. Supreme Court overturned the Ten Commandments decision.

He was considered for a seat on the U.S. Court of Appeals for the Sixth District that sits in Cincinnati but was heard to say that he had been out-maneuvered in the hurly-burly of the nomination process, and the appointment went to another judge.

At the peak of his reputation and influence and seven years into an eight-year term on the Kentucky Supreme Court, Lukowsky was stricken with cancer. He died at Good Samaritan Hospital in Cincinnati in 1981. He was 54 and had been a judge for 29 years. He had resided in Fort Mitchell. "He loved the law. His total life was the law," said his widow Rosemary Domashko Lukowsky upon his passing. "He was one of the most dedicated and courageous men I have ever met," observed Kentucky Supreme Court chief justice **Robert Stephens** at the time of his passing.

Lukowsky was a practicing Catholic who attended Mass on Saturday evenings at the **Cathedral Basilica of the Assumption** in Covington. He was a member of the Ralph W. Fulton Post 6423 of the Veterans of Foreign Wars and the Latonia Post 2032 of the American Legion.

His memory is preserved at Chase Law School with an award given in his name each year to the outstanding professor, as selected by the students. The law library at the Kenton Co. Justice Center bears his name. A portrait of Lukowsky by the artist Maria Simmons of Elizabethtown, Ky., was hung in the capitol at Frankfort on June 11, 1996. At the unveiling, Chief Justice Stephens, himself a Covington native, wrote in remarks placed in the record of the Supreme Court, "No one fought more fiercely to preserve the integrity of our courts than Bob Lukowsky."

"Annexation," *Lexington Herald,* January 23, 1970, 1.
"A Fitting Tribute," *KP,* June 13, 1996, 4K.
Chase Law School Archives, Northern Kentucky Univ., Highland Heights, Ky.
Long, Paul A. "Portrait Honors Jurist's Impact on State," *KP,* June 11, 1996, 5K.
Memorial Resolution of the Kentucky Supreme Court, November 7, 1996.
Neikirk, Mark, and Bill Straub. "The Law Loses a Fine Mind in Lukowsky," *KP,* December 7, 1981, 1K.
"Robert Lukowsky Dies at 54: Kentucky High Court Judge," *NYT,* December 7, 1981, D18.

Jim Dady

LURTON, HORACE HARMON (b. February 26, 1844, Newport, Ky.; d. July 12, 1914, Atlantic City, N.J.). Horace Harmon Lurton, a Confederate soldier, a lawyer, and a U.S. Supreme Court justice, was the son of Dr. Lycurgus L. and Sarah Ann Harmon Lurton. In the 1850s the family left Newport for Clarksville, Tenn. Lurton's early education was by private tutor; he then entered Douglas University in Chicago at age 15. After his second year in college, the **Civil War** began, and he joined the Confederate Army. He intended to enlist in a Kentucky regiment, but, encountering none, he joined the 5th Tennessee Infantry. By age 18 he had been promoted to sergeant major, the highest rank attainable for an enlisted man. Then he joined the 1st Kentucky Infantry CSA. He was captured at Fort Donelson, Tenn., and imprisoned at Camp Chase in Columbus, Ohio. After escaping from the prison, he joined the 7th Kentucky Cavalry CSA. When Morgan's Raiders (see **John Hunt Morgan**) surrendered in July 1863 during their invasion of Ohio, Lurton was imprisoned again. This time he was taken to Camp Johnson's Island, near Sandusky, Ohio. He became seriously ill with what was thought to be tuberculosis, and his mother was able to persuade President Abraham Lincoln (1860–1865) to allow him to come home. After regaining his health, Lurton was admitted to Cumberland Law School, at Lebanon, Tenn. He received his law degree in 1867 and set up practice in Clarksville, Tenn. That same year, he married Mary Frances Owen. Lurton was elected to the Tennessee Supreme Court in 1886, becoming chief justice in 1893. President Grover Cleveland (1885–1889 and 1893–1897) appointed him to the U.S. Sixth District Court of Appeals in 1893. In 1898 he began teaching constitutional law at Vanderbilt University in Nashville, Tenn., and was promoted to dean of the law school in 1905. President William Howard Taft (1909–1913) nominated Lurton as an associate justice of the U.S. Supreme Court in December 1909. His performance with the court was considered outstanding; it was said that he wrote clear, scholarly opinions. Because of failing health, he took a leave of absence in December 1913 and spent the winter in Florida trying to recuperate. He returned the following year, but his health continued to decline and he died at Atlantic City, N.J., of heart disease. He was buried in Greenville Cemetery in Clarksville, Tenn.

"Lurton, a Newport Boy on the Bench," *KJ,* March 31, 1893, 4.
"The New Judge a Campbell County Boy," *KJ,* March 23, 1893, 8.
Purvis, Thomas L., ed. *Newport, Kentucky: A Bicentennial History.* Newport, Ky.: Otto Zimmerman, 1996.
Reis, Jim. "Seven Left Mark on Supreme Court," *KP,* October 3, 1988, 4K.

LUSBY'S MILL. Lusby's Mill in Owen Co. is located six miles east of Owenton along Ky. Rt. 330 and Eagle Creek. In the early years of the county's history, this area was settled by the Cobb family, hence its earliest name, Cobb's Mill. William Jones built a mill there for the Cobbs. Before 1852 John or William Lusby had acquired the mill, and the area came to be called Lusby's Mill. It had a post office from 1852 until 1904 and was incorporated as Lusby's Mill in 1869. The town also had a grade school and the Lusby Central High School; the latter closed in 1934 after the last class graduated. During the **Civil War**, Camp Humphrey, a Confederate recruiting and training center, was just up an adjacent steep hill. There have been several churches in the town, and until 1897 there was a distillery. Lusby's Mill was the home of nostalgic poet Perry Jones, who was raised by Margaret McGibney "Aunt Marge" Hammon (1832–1929). She donated the land for the first school in town. After a bypass road was constructed, business activity declined greatly. No recent population estimates are available.

An Atlas of Owen County, Kentucky. Philadelphia: Lake, 1883.
Houchens, Mariam Sidebottom. *History of Owen County: "Sweet Owen."* Louisville, Ky.: Standard, 1976.
Rennick, Robert M. *Kentucky Place Names.* Lexington: Univ. Press of Kentucky, 1984.

LUSTRON HOMES. Northern Kentucky contains a number of Lustron homes, an interesting architectural development of the mid-20th century. The Lustron Corporation manufactured porcelain-enameled steel prefabricated ranch-style houses during the immediate post–World War II period. With financial support from the federal government, Lustron was the largest manufacturer of factory-made prefabricated housing for a brief time until its collapse in 1951. A shortage of affordable housing for returning veterans created a favorable climate for new approaches to housing construction, and Lustron capitalized on the market demand, using advanced production technologies and timely political connections.

In 1946 Kentucky native Wilson Wyatt, head of the veterans emergency housing program under President Harry S Truman (1945–1953), selected Lustron as an exemplar of new thinking about factory-produced housing. He hoped that large-scale manufacturing would make decent housing available to middle-income families just as mass production had done for automobiles. Although Wyatt soon left the administration, he succeeded in establishing Lustron as a viable enterprise, and the company eventually received $37 million in federal funds.

Lustron had limited success, but the large commitment of taxpayer dollars to the firm made it an easy target for those opposed to federal funding of private firms in peacetime. The automobile analogy proved misguided, as factory-produced and dealer-distributed housing presented far more obstacles. Success required fundamental changes in the financial, legal, and social underpinnings of the housing industry, an industry notoriously resistant to change.

Lusby's Mill.

Lustron produced approximately 2,500 houses from 1949 to 1951 and distributed them through regional dealerships. With the United States embroiled in the Korean War and traditional home builders expanding production, Congress cut Lustron's funding and the company drifted into receivership. In the years following the company's demise, prefabricated housing gained greater market share and customer acceptance. Many of Lustron's technical innovations, especially its steel framing system, have become increasingly common in residential construction.

Northern Kentucky Lustrons can be found in Alexandria (1), Edgewood (2), Fort Wright (1), and Owenton (4). The houses were durable, attractive, and popular with their owners. Twenty-five Lustrons are currently on the National Register of Historic Places, and nearly all the homes produced remain standing.

Knerr, Douglas. *Suburban Steel.* Columbus: Ohio State Univ., 2004.

Douglas Knerr

LUTHERANS. As German immigrants moved into Northern Kentucky in the 19th century, Lutherans were among them, although they were greatly outnumbered by German **Roman Catholics** (see **German Americans**). The Lutheran tradition of Christianity originated with the Reformation during the early 1500s. Martin Luther (1483–1546), a Roman Catholic Augustinian monk, priest, professor, and theologian, is considered the founder of Lutheranism. The first Lutherans to arrive in North America came from Holland as early as 1623 and founded the city of New Amsterdam (New York City). Henry Melchior Muhlenberg (1711–1787) may rightfully be called the patriarch of the Lutheran Church in America. Arriving in Charleston, S.C., after a 14-week voyage in 1741, Muhlenberg was a tireless worker who helped organize churches in the colonies until his death in October 1787. Three of Muhlenberg's sons became ordained Lutheran ministers and were prominent in other fields including botany, the military, and politics. One son, John Peter Gabriel (1746–1807), is the namesake of Muhlenberg Co. in Western Kentucky.

Lutherans moving westward in frontier America during the early 1800s were typically German-speaking farmers. A lack of strong church leadership and the scarcity of pastors made church organization difficult. The freedom-minded Lutherans found slavery repulsive, and furthermore, the terrain and soil were not very conducive to their farming needs and skills. These are some of the reasons why more congregations were not founded in Northern Kentucky.

From 1820 to 1970, Lutheran synods evolved by regions and doctrinal beliefs. While the General Synod of the northern states, including northern Indiana, was generally more liberal, evangelistic, and socially active, the General Council of southern Indiana, Kentucky, and Tennessee was more orthodox, separatist, and silent on public issues. In 1917 a merger of the General Synod, the General Council, and the United Synod in the South created the United Lutheran Church in America. Kentucky had about 3,900 members, and there were almost 1,300 Kentuckians in the Missouri Synod. By the 1920s, most Kentucky mission churches were urban. In 1934 the Kentucky-Tennessee Synod was organized, and although most of its constituency was in Louisville, its first convention was held in Newport. Overcoming the hardships of the **Great Depression** and **World War II**, the synod was held together by placing emphasis on the importance of the individual and in authentic fellowship. Common goals in Christian service were pursued. By 1962, membership had doubled, and in 1963 the reorganized Indiana-Kentucky Synod became operative with a Gospel-centered ministry as its focus.

The Lutheran Church–Missouri Synod began in 1839, with 750 Saxon immigrants who, seeking religious freedom, settled in Missouri. Pastors sent from Germany helped form the German Evangelical Lutheran Synod of Missouri, Ohio, and Other States, and its first convention was held in Chicago in 1847. One hundred years later, in 1947, the name was changed to the Lutheran Church–Missouri Synod. This arm of the Lutheran Church maintains some theological differences with the Evangelical Lutheran Church of America (ELCA) in biblical interpretation, such as holding the ordination of women as contrary to scripture. The ELCA has ordained women ministers since 1970, while European Lutheran churches began ordaining women in the 1920s.

In 1988 three Lutheran church bodies in the United States formed the ELCA—the American Lutheran Church, the Association of Evangelical Lutheran Churches, and the Lutheran Church in America. The ELCA is the largest body of the Lutheran church in the United States today, numbering more than 5.5 million people. The second-largest Lutheran Church group in the nation is the more conservative Lutheran Church–Missouri Synod (LCMS), with more than 2.6 million members. Other organized bodies currently include the Wisconsin Evangelical Lutheran Synod (WELS) and the Association of Free Lutheran Congregations. There are about 82.6 million Lutherans worldwide—primarily in Africa, Asia, Denmark, Finland, Germany, Indonesia, North America, Norway, South America, and Sweden.

On a global level, the organized body of the Lutheran Church helps support the missions of Lutheran Disaster Response (LDR) and Lutheran World Relief (LWR), which are among the world's largest immediate-response efforts to assist in domestic and global emergencies. LDR, a collaborative ministry between the ELCA and the LCMS, provides care to anyone in need domestically through Lutheran Social Service. It has acted in recovery efforts following natural disasters in Florida and along the Gulf Coast after the hurricanes of the early 21st century. LWR supports global ministerial efforts such as recovery from the tsunami that impacted Africa, India, and Indonesia on Christmas Eve 2004. It also advocates fair trade to help developing-world farmers and artisans overcome poverty and to create better communities and environments. These organized, corporate church bodies exemplify joint efforts by all facets of the Lutheran Church to provide assistance in emergency situations with immediate aid in counseling, medical and material assistance, and supplies.

Thrivent Financial for Lutherans is a Fortune 500 company—the result of a 2001 merger between two early-20th-century fraternal benefit companies founded by Lutheran leaders in Minnesota and Wisconsin. The not-for-profit organization provides financial products to members and gives profits back to the larger community through its sponsored programs, such as Thrivent Builds, Habitat for Humanity, and broadcast programs such as Minnesota Public Radio's *Speaking of Faith*—conversations about religion, meaning, ethics, and ideas.

From the establishment of **Hopeful Lutheran Church** in Florence, Ky., in 1806, to the rebuilding of **St. Luke Evangelical Lutheran Church** in Cold Spring in 2008, this faith tradition persists. Reformation is an ongoing, perpetual process as the eight ELCA, four LCMS, and one WELS Northern Kentucky Lutheran congregations minister to the needs of all people with physical, social, and spiritual service.

Existing Lutheran congregations in the early 21st century and their founding dates in Northern Kentucky include the following eight ELCA churches: Hopeful Lutheran Church in Florence (1806), **Hebron Lutheran Church** in Burlington (1854), **St. John Lutheran Church** in Melbourne (1861), **St. Mark Lutheran Church** in Newport (1897), **St. Paul Lutheran Church** in Chatham (1928), **St. Luke Evangelical Lutheran Church** in Cold Spring (1953), **Prince of Peace Lutheran Church** in Bellevue (1978), and **Gloria Dei Lutheran Church** in Crestview Hills (1982). There are also four LCMS churches: **Trinity Lutheran Church** in Maysville (1929), **Bethany Lutheran Church** in Erlanger (1934), **Good Shepherd Lutheran Church** in Florence (1995), and Immanuel Lutheran Church in Dry Ridge; and there is one WELS congregation, Amazing Grace Lutheran Church in Boone Co. The founding dates of the Immanuel and Amazing Grace congregations are unknown.

Evangelical Lutheran Church in America. www.elca.org (accessed October 10, 2006).

The Lutheran Church—Missouri Synod. www.lcms.org (accessed October 10, 2006).

MacCulloch, Diarmaid. *The Reformation: A History.* New York: Penguin Group, 2003.

Muhlenberg, Henry Melchior. *The Journals of Henry Melchior Muhlenberg.* Trans. Theodore G. Tappert and John W. Doberstein. Philadelphia: Evangelical Lutheran Ministerium of Pennsylvania and Adjacent States, 1958.

Nafzger, Samuel. *An Introduction to the Lutheran Church—Missouri Synod.* St. Louis, Mo.: Concordia, 1994.

Waltmann, Henry G., ed. *History of the Indiana-Kentucky Synod.* Indianapolis, Ind.: Central, 1971.

Melinda G. Motley

LYNCHING OF PETER KLEIN. On March 7, 1879, an African American vagrant from Ohio, Peter Klein, spent the evening drinking whiskey in the bars of Cincinnati. Later that night he crossed the Ohio River and continued drinking in the saloons of Newport. He wandered into the District of the Highlands (modern Fort Thomas) drunk and destitute. Returning toward Newport, he approached the farmhouse of Charles Truesdale (Truesdell) along modern-day Waterworks Rd. Klein knocked on the door, which was answered by Truesdale's 24-year-old pregnant wife, Carrie. After Klein concluded that Carrie Truesdale was home alone, he forced his way into the home. He beat her, hitting her in the head and kicking her in the stomach, and dragged her into a closet, where he tied her up and raped her. Klein then proceeded to ransack the home in search of valuables. He left with some change and Carrie Trusedale's gold watch. Trusedale's husband returned several hours later to find his wife unconscious. He ran to the home of his neighbors, the Jollys, who proceeded to "raise the county."

Carrie Truesdale gave a description of Peter Klein, and the manhunt began. The Southgate brothers offered a large reward for the capture of the culprit, as did the local county judge and the governor of Kentucky. On March 16, Peter Klein was found in a saloon on Isabella St. in Newport. He matched the description of the suspect and, more importantly, had Carrie Truesdale's gold watch in his pocket. He was immediately lodged in the Newport jail, and he gave his confession of the crime. Word spread throughout the county that the fugitive had been caught. Officials planned to move Klein to the jail in Covington later that evening for safety reasons, but before they could execute their plan, a large mob stormed the Newport jailhouse. Several hundred citizens armed with shotguns and axes marched through town in a blinding snowstorm to reach Klein. Newport mayor William Harton tried to dissuade the mob from taking Klein. The crowd carried the mayor out of the building and threw him over the fence. The jailer's keys were confiscated and Klein was seized from his cell. The mob, headed by several prominent citizens, marched him into the snowy streets, shouting, "All of you who have mothers, wives, or sisters, come on!" The crowd grew to an estimated 1,500 in number. Klein was forced to return to the scene of his crime and was brought before Carrie Truesdale, who positively identified Klein as her assailant.

The angry army of citizens showed Klein no mercy. They marched him to an oak tree in the nearby Odd Fellows Grove along Waterworks Rd. A noose was thrown around his neck and he was placed in a wagon under the tree. Klein protested, "This is not the law!" "This is Kentucky law!" was the reply. Klein was hanged and the lynch mob riddled his hanging body with bullets. Klein's body was not taken down until the next morning. As news of the lynching gained national attention, many newspapers, including the *New York Times*, ran editorials expressing their sentiments about the lynching. Public opinion was divided: some thought that Klein got what he deserved and that justice was served. Others were embarrassed by the incident and thought it reflected badly on the city and the state. Although some well-known citizens were known to have participated in the lynching, no charges were ever filed. Kentucky governor James McCreary (1875–1879 and 1911–1915) came under attack for not having sent for a military guard, especially since he had been previously warned about the mob's intention. The *Covington Daily Commonwealth* summed up the matter by saying, "So ends one of the most horrible and disgusting events that has taken place in this county."

"Echoes of the Outrage," *DC*, March 12, 1879, 1.
"Hanged without a Trial," *NYT*, March 17, 1879, 1.
"Law vs. Mob Rule," *CDC*, March 18, 1879, 1.
"Snowstorm Recalls Hanging to Pioneers," *KP*, March 17, 1926, 1.
"Taken Out and Done For," *CDC*, March 17, 1879, 1.

Robin Caraway

LYNCHINGS. Although extralegal executions had taken place in Kentucky before the **Civil War** as so-called citizen's committees carried out the sentence of "Judge Lynch," postwar Kentucky suffered an epidemic of lynchings, and some of these took place in Northern Kentucky. Most Kentucky lynchings were racially motivated as white supremacists attempted to maintain control over newly emancipated slaves. Sometimes calling themselves "Negro Regulators," bands of white marauders terrorized free black households and communities for several years after the war. During this time, lynch mobs often justified their actions by arguing that the legal system had failed to serve timely justice to alleged perpetrators of murder, rape, and theft. For example, on June 23, 1876, several dozen masked men forcibly removed a black man named Smith Williams from the Boone Co. jail in Burlington, where he had spent nine months awaiting trial for shooting a white man during an altercation. Once out of town, the mob stripped and hanged Williams, then riddled his body with bullets. Northern Kentucky mobs also seized and executed several white men during this era, but African Americans, though a small minority of the population, were lynched with greater frequency and more overt brutality.

By the late 19th century, racially motivated lynchings often took the form of public spectacle and had at least tacit support from local authorities. On December 9, 1899, Richard Coleman, a young black man from Mason Co. being held in jail at Covington pending trial for the rape and murder of a white woman, was placed on a train bound for Maysville. Before marshals could deliver their prisoner to the local jail, a large group of citizens, led by the victim's husband, demanded that Coleman be handed over to them. His guards complied, and a subsequently convened sham court sentenced the accused to be roasted alive. Hundreds of Mason Co. residents, young and old, male and female, participated in the lynching by adding fuel to the pyre as the victim was tortured and burned to death over a four-hour period. Although the lynching took place in broad daylight, none of the participants bothered to disguise themselves, and none faced charges afterward. Once the fire had died down, what remained of Coleman's corpse was dragged through the historic port city in a macabre parade. Newspapers from Chicago to Cincinnati to New York City reported the ghastly details of Coleman's death, yet national notoriety, even combined with new antilynching laws, did not bring an end to the practice in the commonwealth of Kentucky.

Grant Smith, a black resident of Maysville, was lynched in March 1920. According to an **NAACP** investigation following his death, Smith, who was married, appears to have been guilty of nothing more than an affair with an unmarried white woman. However, he was accused of rape, held in Covington pending trial, and finally sent by rail to Maysville. A group of about 40 men stopped the train and took Smith from it after making public their intent to give him the same treatment Coleman had received. Not enjoying the same level of community support, particularly from local authorities, this lynch mob decided instead to hang their victim unceremoniously from a Bourbon Co. telephone pole. As the 20th century progressed, Kentucky authorities gradually undermined public support for racially motivated lynchings, in part by allowing swift prosecution of black defendants before hostile, all-white juries, a practice that frequently resulted in what historians have called "legal lynchings." See also **Lynching of Peter Klein**.

Lucas, Marion B. *A History of Blacks in Kentucky*. Vol. 1, *From Slavery to Segregation, 1760–1891*. Frankfort: Kentucky Historical Society, 1992.
Waldrep, Christopher. *The Many Faces of Judge Lynch: Extralegal Violence and Punishment in America*. New York: Palgrave MacMillan, 2002.
Wright, George C. *A History of Blacks in Kentucky*. Vol. 2, *In Pursuit of Equality, 1890–1980*. Frankfort: Kentucky Historical Society, 1992.
——. *Racial Violence in Kentucky, 1865–1940: Lynching, Mob Rule, and "Legal Lynchings."* Baton Rouge: Louisiana State Univ. Press, 1990.

J. Michael Rhyne

MACHINE TOOLS. The steamboat traffic on the inland rivers of the United States, starting in 1811, accelerated the movement of farm commodities and the development of towns and cities and eventually inspired a strong machine-tool industry. In 1826 Cincinnati had six iron foundries and two steam-engine builders. By 1850 Cincinnati was the second-largest city west of the Allegheny Mountains, and was also prominent in the output of manufactured goods. By 1817 at least one Cincinnati firm was using "lathes and a boring mill"; by 1851 a Cincinnati company was building its own "planing machines." After the **Civil War**, new enterprises sprang up that specialized in machine tools.

Cincinnati's strong steamboat industry prompted related businesses in Northern Kentucky. In 1852 **A. B. Latta**, a Ludlow inventor who owned the Buckeye Works, introduced in Cincinnati what was described as "the first practical steam fire engine." Late in the 19th century, the **Houston, Stanwood & Gamble Company** began manufacturing steam engines and boilers in Covington. That company sold engines for mills in Central America and for heating and use in commercial laundries in the United States. Electrification was, at the time, rapidly replacing steam, but in 1915 the Houston, Stanwood & Gamble Company received a $200,000 war order for lathes to be used to produce steam engines.

By 1900 Cincinnati's commercial successes in the machine tool industry were spilling into Northern Kentucky. Newport listed in its 1900 city business directory, under the category of machinists, Henry F. Buecker (see **Buecker Iron Works**), Frank Osburg, and William Roettinger and Son. Covington in the same year listed the Anthe Machine Works, the H. J. Averbeck Company, and the Sebastian Lathe Company. The 1926–1927 Covington business directory included the Anthe Machine Works, the Averbeck Machine Company, the Avey Drilling Machine Company, the Precision Truing Machine and Tool Company, the Willard Machine Tool Company, and other shops.

The Avey Drilling Company enjoyed a national reputation, as did other similar companies in Northern Kentucky. The Avey firm started as the Cincinnati Pulley Machine Company and then was moved to Covington in 1910. In 1913, after a devastating fire, the firm chose to stay and build a new plant in Covington on Third St. between Scott St. and Madison Ave. In 1919 the business was renamed the Avey Drilling Machine Company. It prospered during **World War II** and grew to 157 employees by 1956. Its machine tools were sold worldwide to corporations such as Chrysler, Ford, General Motors, International Business Machines, Pratt and Whitney, and Westinghouse. In 1957 the Avey Drilling Machine Company became a division of the Motch and Merryweather Company of Cleveland, Ohio, a firm that claimed to be the largest distributor of machine tools in the world. The Avey Drilling Machine Company made special transfer and indexing machines and drilling, reaming, and tapping tools. In 1965 it built a large addition at its plant in Covington. In 1966 it participated in a federal job training program for the operating of lathes, cutter-grinders, jig borers, milling machines, and radial drills. In 1975 word came that the company might close. After the City of Covington proposed issuing industrial revenue bonds to save jobs, the Cross Company from Fraser, Mich., a large builder of automated tools, purchased the Covington-based firm. In 1976 the Cross Company oversaw a strike at its plant in Covington. In 1981 Cross employed 81 workers and was specializing in metal cutting tools. By 1982 layoffs had reduced the number of employees to 20; the business was closed in 1983 and the plant was demolished in 1985.

Another major toolmaker in Covington suffered the same fate as the Avey Drilling and Machine Company in the decade of the 1980s. The Averbeck Machine Company and the Averbeck residence and shop buildings, plus all the buildings in the block just east of the **John Roebling Bridge**, were demolished in 1988. However, the Precision Truing Tool and Manufacturing Company, General Machinery, still operates at 13 E. 16th St., Covington. Also, at 407 Madison Ave., the fourth generation of the Anthe family now oversees the Anthe Machine Works, which has specialized for years in woodworking tools, cutters, router bits, carving cutters, and cutter-shapers. The tools are customized for the furniture manufacturers that are prominent among the company's 500 customers in the United States and Canada. Many small machine shops and factories also continue to operate today in Northern Kentucky.

Friedberg, Mary. "Toolmaker on Cutting Edge," *KP*, April 23, 1996, 8K.

Reis, Jim. "Avey Symbolized Industrial Base," *KP*, November 14, 1994, 4K.

———. "Street Has Seen River of Change. Second Street Evolves as Center of Commerce," *KP*, June 1, 1992, 4K.

Wing, George A. "The History of the Cincinnati Machine-Tool Industry," PhD diss. Indiana Univ., 1964.

John Boh

MACK, DAVID (b. October 7, 1972, Cincinnati, Ohio). Internationally acclaimed artist, writer, and comic book illustrator David Mack is the son of Wilson Grant and Ida May Mack. His father was an accomplished musician who played several instruments, and his mother taught first grade. While growing up with modest resources, David and his brother Steven entertained themselves by making artworks and toys from recycled school supplies their mother brought home. David graduated from Ludlow High School in 1990 and from **Northern Kentucky University** at Highland Heights in 1995 with a BFA. He is the creator, author, and artist of the Kabuki Graphic Novels, the writer and artist of *Daredevil* from Marvel Comics, and the author and artist of the children's book *The Shy Creatures*. Mack's work has been nominated for six Eisner Awards, five International Eagle Awards, and both the Harvey and Kirby awards in the category of best new talent, and he has received many other national and international awards and nominations as well. Mack's writings, some of which are autobiographical, show influences ranging from the early ancient Greek philosophers to modern-day novelist-philosopher Kurt Vonnegut. Mack's art is equally diverse. He is partial to using metaphors and symbolism in his publications, and the art Mack conveys thereby can range from mature portraiture and delicate line drawing to doodles and Picasso-like futuristic renderings. Consistently, his aim is to provoke thought through his writings and art. Mack has become one of the recognized spokesmen of the new generation of graphic and pop-culture artists, and he has a worldwide following. When not in Japan, where his Kabuki works are revered, or traveling to some other far-away place, he can be found living and working in the modest two-story frame home in Bromley that was once owned by his mother.

Mack, David. Interview by James C. Claypool, February 9, 2007, Bromley, Ky.

Samples, Karen. "Artist Living in Quiet Fame," *KE*, August 2, 1998, C1–C1B.

James C. Claypool

MACK, EDGAR L. (b. August 8, 1930, Pleasureville, Ky.; d. April 21, 1991, Brentwood, Tenn.). **Civil rights** activist and religious leader Edgar Leroy Mack was the son of Edgar W. and Sarah L. Johnson Mack. He attended the Lincoln Institute at Shelbyville, Ky., and in 1953 graduated from Wilberforce College in Ohio. In 1955 he received an MA in divinity from Payne Theological Seminary in Wilberforce, Ohio. Later he received an MA in social work from Ohio State University in Columbus. For most of his adult life, Mack was a leader in the **NAACP** and the African Methodist Episcopal Church (A.M.E.). In 1963 he served as president of the Frankfort NAACP and as the leadership-training director for the Kentucky NAACP youth councils and college chapters. In 1964 he was made pastor at the **St. Paul A.M.E. Church** in Newport and was elected as the executive secretary of the Northern Kentucky NAACP.

Mack was blessed with excellent organizational skills, which he used frequently in civil rights activities throughout the state. He served as cochairman of the Northern Kentucky organizing committee for the March 5, 1964, Freedom March on Frankfort, which featured Martin Luther King Jr. Mack was instrumental in taking 300 people from Northern Kentucky to that important civil rights event. In April 1968, soon after King was killed, Mack planned numerous memorial services around Northern Kentucky and was active in quelling violent responses. In 1973 Mack was named chairman of the United Negro College Fund Advisory Committee in Cincinnati. He moved to Lexington, where he became pastor of the Quinn Chapel

A.M.E. Church and a professor of social work at the University of Kentucky. Mack was named general secretary of the A.M.E. Church in 1980 and moved to the Nashville, Tenn., area. In that position he developed interdenominational relationships that created enduring church partnerships. In 1988 he authored the book *Our Beginning: The African Methodist Episcopal Church.* Mack held his office within the A.M.E. Church until his death in 1991. He was buried at the Lexington Cemetery in Lexington.

African Methodist Episcopal Church. www.ame-church.com (accessed January 17, 2007).

"Funeral Obituary," read at the Quinn Chapel A.M.E. Church, Lexington, Ky., April 27, 1991.

"Mack Head of College Fund Unit," *CP,* May 2, 1973, 29.

Papers of the NAACP. Microform version available at Univ. of Virginia Library, www.lib.virginia.edu (accessed January 14, 2007).

Reis, Jim. "King Marched in Frankfort in 1964," *KP,* January 20, 2003, 4K.

Jim Embry

MACK, LONNIE (b. near Harrison, Ind., 1941). Lonnie Mack became a roadhouse blues-rock legend and rock music's first true guitar hero. His connection with Northern Kentucky is that during the late 1950s and 1960s, he played at many of the local music venues, including Ben Kraft's Guys 'n Dolls Club (today the Cold Spring Roadhouse) along **U.S. 27** in Campbell Co. His 1963 instrumental version of Chuck Berry's "Memphis" placed near the top of the charts. Mack continues to perform and even occasionally returns to play in Northern Kentucky. His style has influenced other musicians, such as Eric Clapton, Keith Richards, and Stevie Ray Vaughan. In recent years there has been a resurgent interest in the career of Lonnie Mack, a performer who got his start in Northern Kentucky.

"King Records Legends Win Lifetime Cammys," *CE,* February 10, 2002, E1.

"Mule Train: He's Been a Rock 'n' Roll Star, a Cult Hero, and an Influence on Some of the World's Greatest." *Cincinnati Magazine,* October 1, 2000, 74.

"20 Years after Hittin Big Time . . . Pickin in the Clubs," *CE,* January 8, 1983, C3.

MACKOY, WILLIAM H. (b. November 20, 1839, Covington, Ky. ; d. September 14, 1923, Covington, Ky.). Noted attorney and Covington city councilman William H. Mackoy was the son of John and Elizabeth G. Hardia Mackoy. William was educated in local schools and in 1865 began his legal education. He married Margaret Chambers Brent of Paris, Ky., in 1868, and they had four children, but only two lived to maturity. Mackoy was a founding member of the Cincinnati, Kenton Co., and Kentucky bar associations. He became a law partner with his son Harry in the Cincinnati firm of Mackoy and Mackoy. William served on the Covington City Council from 1883 to 1889. As a member of its law committee, he drafted the amendment that authorized construction of the Covington Reservoir in the District of the Highlands (now Fort Thomas). William Mackoy retired in 1920 after 55 years as an attorney and moved to Lexington. However, after a short stay there, he returned to Covington to live with his son Harry. William Mackoy died in 1923 and was buried in the Highland Cemetery in Fort Mitchell.

"William H. Mackoy Is Dead," *KP,* September 14, 1923, 1.

MADISON AVE. Named after the fourth Kentucky governor, George Madison, who served in that office barely more than one month in 1817, Madison Ave. in Covington stretches from the Ohio River south to Latonia. Madison Pk., Ky. Rt. 17, continues the roadway to Pendleton Co. City officials once thought that Main St., on the western side of Covington, would live up to its name, but the city's commercial district shifted eastward instead. Residential development toward the Licking River once led some officials to promote Scott Blvd. (today Scott St.) as Covington's main thoroughfare. But the opening of the **Covington and Lexington Railroad** just west of Madison in 1854 relocated the commercial heart of Covington to Sixth, Pike, and Seventh Sts. at Madison Ave. In the late 1850s, the railroad built a roundhouse at 13th St. and Madison Ave.; this, along with other developments, made Madison Ave. Covington's fashionable main thoroughfare.

Selecting sites near Madison Ave. at the Ohio River, entrepreneurs started the Covington Cotton factory (1828), the Covington Rolling Mill, numerous tobacco processing firms, the **Hemingray Glass Company** (relocated from Cincinnati in 1852), and later the **Walsh Distillery** (1872) and an ice manufacturing company. In 1856 **Amos Shinkle** and others dedicated the landmark Odd Fellows Hall (see **Independent Order of Odd Fellows**). St. Elizabeth Hospital (see **St. Elizabeth Medical Center**) once occupied the former **Western Baptist Theological Institute** building on 11th St. near Madison Ave. Beginning about 1903, at 17th St., the famous **Stewart Iron Works** manufactured fences, jail equipment, iron furniture, and even trucks (1913–1928) for nationwide customers. The opening of the **Latonia Racecourse** for thoroughbred horse racing in 1883, and electric streetcar service to it by 1892, further advanced the prominence of Madison Ave.

The intersection of Madison Ave. and Sixth St. once was Northern Kentucky's commercial banking center, and banks still occupy two of the corners. **L. B. Wilson**'s **WCKY**, a pioneer radio station that was later moved to Cincinnati, occupied an upper floor of the **First National Bank** building (see **First National Bank and Trust Company of Covington**). The Covington police station remains on the old streetcar barn site at 20th St. and Madison Ave. The imposing **Holmes High School** (formerly Covington High School) campus stands at 25th St. off Madison Ave.

Madison Ave. intersects with busy east-west traffic arteries; however, many of the well-known and busy stores and businesses that once sat on Madison Ave. have closed. In recent years, the commercial district has been restored and redeveloped as an arts and wedding district (see **Covington, Downtown**).

The Covington Odd Fellows Hall has been rebuilt to remain a distinctive landmark. City Hall now occupies the old **Coppin's Department Store** building. The Madison Theater building (see **Movie Theaters**) has reopened as a performance hall in the 700 block of Madison Ave. Landwehr Hardware still does business in the 800 block of Madison Ave. Since the 1870s, **Motch Jewelers** has served customers at Pike St. and Madison Ave., and that firm owns the landmark Covington antique street clock. In 1987 the Stewart Iron Works resumed manufacturing fences and lawn furniture at its old site, at 17th St. and Madison Ave.

Gastright, Joseph F. *Gentleman Farmers to City Folks: A Study of Wallace Woods, Covington, Kentucky.* Cincinnati: Cincinnati Historical Society, 1980.

Reis, Jim. "Madison Pike Named for Cousin of President," *KP,* November 27, 2000, 4K.

Smith, Allen Webb. *Beginning at "the Point," a Documented History of Northern Kentucky and Environs, the Town of Covington in Particular, 1751–1834.* Park Hills, Ky.: Self-published, 1977.

John Boh

MADISON AVE. BAPTIST CHURCH. Located on the northeast corner of Madison Ave. and Robbins St. in Covington, the Madison Ave. Baptist Church was formed in 1857 by members of the **First Baptist Church, Covington**. Its organizational meeting was held on the property of the former **Western Baptist Theological Institute** (WBTI) in Covington, and its original name was John's Baptist Church. Two ministers assisted the young congregation: Asa Drury, pastor of Dry Creek Baptist Church (see **Lakeside Park**) and a former professor at WBTI, and James A. Kirtley, a member of a family long associated with the **Bullittsburg Baptist Church**. The new church's first pastor was Rev. Samuel Smith, who stayed until November 1859. In 1860–1861, the church fell prey to R. L. Jeffrey, who claimed to be a duly-trained minister from England. When his credentials were proven false, the congregation lost respect and lacked a full-time pastor for about six years. Despite a decline in membership from 57 in 1861 to 36 in 1867, the members persevered, purchased a lot on Russell St. in Covington in November 1866, renamed the congregation the Russell St. Baptist Church, and held services temporarily at the Welch Mission on Lynn St. in Covington. Rethinking their decision, they purchased a lot at Madison Ave. and Robbins St. in June 1869, where they dedicated a new building on January 9, 1870, then becoming the Madison St. Baptist Church. A series of full-time pastors stayed for short periods of time, indicating that the congregation was still young and unable to offer a competitive salary. By 1877 the church had 196 members, but its membership rose and fell as other Baptist churches were formed in the city. In November 1884 the congregation changed its name to reflect the city's renaming of Madison St. to Madison Ave.; the church was now Madison Ave. Baptist Church. In 1911 the congregation decided to demolish their old building at Madison and Robbins and build a new one. The new, and present, church was dedicated on June 15, 1913.

Dr. Henry Dodson Allen served as pastor for nearly two decades, from 1919 until 1938. Under his direction, architect and church member Charles L. Hildreth designed a balcony for the church in 1921, as well as a three-story Sunday school addition to the rear of the church in 1925. In 1924, about 40 members of the congregation were granted letters to organize the **Fort Mitchell Baptist Church**. During the **flood of 1937**, the church cared for 336 refugees. In 1938 Rev. Frank H. Malone became pastor and led the congregation through the latter part of the **Great Depression** and all of **World War II**. The church provided entertainment and gifts for soldiers and collected clothes and funds for European refugees. In 1941 a new pipe organ was installed. In 1947 Rev. Malone left to pastor another church, and Dr. Paul B. Clark served as interim pastor (1947–1948) until the appointment of Rev. P. Ennis Taylor in 1948. Taylor believed that the church was a "sleeping giant," since Covington had attracted many rural migrants during and after World War II (see **Appalachians**). With the assistance of seminary students, he took censuses of the neighborhood and visited its people. The highly mobile population did not produce as many members as he had hoped, but instead, revivals at the church brought in new members. By 1958 the congregation reached its highest membership, 1,165. A new educational building, designed by architect Bill Batson, was dedicated on May 5, 1968. In 1969 the church became the headquarters for a new inner-city ministry, in cooperation with both the state and home mission boards. Rev. Taylor retired in 1972. Suburban development gradually took its toll on membership, which declined to 675 by 1982. In 1997 the church celebrated its 140th anniversary.

"Dedication Set: New Covington Church Addition Costs $21,000," *KP*, October 23, 1925, 1.

Taylor, P. Ennis. ***In the Mainstream of God's Purpose: A History of the Madison Avenue Baptist Church, Covington, Kentucky.*** Covington, Ky.: Madison Ave. Baptist Church, 1977.

Paul A. Tenkotte

MADISON AVE. CHRISTIAN CHURCH. On November 13, 1913, the Madison Ave. Christian Church dedicated its new facility "to the service and worship of Almighty God." The new church was the result of a merger of the Fourth St. Christian Church and the Central Christian Church in Covington. The Fourth St. Christian Church began when approximately 60 members of the Fifth St. Christian Church (currently Covington's First Christian Church) left to organize a new congregation in 1874. After meeting for six months in Cooper's Hall at Sixth St. and Madison Ave. in Covington, the group purchased from the Presbyterian Church a building at 115 E. Fourth St. This was their home until 1913. The Central Christian Church started as a result of a "tent meeting" in the fall of 1909 at 18th and Greenup Sts. The church met first in a private home and later in a building near 18th and Greenup Sts.; in 1910 the Central Christian Church purchased a lot at 18th St. and Scott Blvd. and began raising money for a building.

In the meantime, the Fourth St. Christian Church had been considering the need for a more adequate church building in a better location as the residential area of Covington began to move south from the Ohio River. After plans fell through on a chosen lot in 1911, discussions with the Central Christian Church led to a vote to consolidate the two churches. The Central church sold its lot for $1,980; the Fourth St. church sold its property to the Knights of Pythias for $6,000; and a lot at 1530 Madison Ave. was purchased for $7,500, a gift to the church by Florence Kennedy. Articles of incorporation were filed on April 13, 1912, for "the Madison Avenue Christian Church"; ground was broken for the new building on August 1; and the cornerstone was laid on November 9, 1912, by deputy grand master **Orie S. Ware**. The last services were held at the Fourth St. and the Central churches on July 27, 1913, and the new united congregation met for the first time in its Fellowship Hall on August 10, 1913. Rev. Joseph W. Hagin, who had served as minister of the Fourth St. church since 1904, and under whose leadership the new church was built, was called unanimously to be the first minister. The united congregation totaled about 400 members, the majority originally drawn from the Fourth St. church.

The church building, in the Neoclassical Revival style, was designed by local architects C. C. and E. A. Weber (see **Weber Brothers**). The total cost of the building and its lot was $55,941. The formal dedication of the building took place on November 30, 1913, with Rev. F. M. Rains of Cincinnati as the principal speaker. In addition to the large dome, the four large stained-glass windows are impressive features of the facility. The Hanks Memorial window, of Belgian Tiffany glass and depicting the theme "I am the Resurrection and the Life," and the window "Christ Blessing the Children" were installed in 1913. The Fant-Pearce window, depicting sunrise on Easter morning, was installed in 1930, and the "Come Unto Me" window was added in 1951. Other than the window additions, the sanctuary remained virtually unchanged until 2006, when a large staging area was constructed. The original organ, which had been moved from the Fourth St. church, was replaced in 1926 with the Moller pipe organ that is still in use today. The church building has become a Covington landmark.

The Madison Ave. Christian Church continued to grow and flourish during the 1920s and 1930s. Brother Hagin moved to another church in 1927, and Rev. Kenneth Bowen was called to be the second minister in the same year. Despite a railroad strike in the late 1920s that affected many in the church, and the stock market crash of 1929, an educational wing was added to the rear of the church and was dedicated on April 20, 1930. The sacrifice that many members made to accomplish this construction during the **Great Depression** remains one of the more vivid memories of those years. In 1945 Bowen left to assume the presidency of the College of the Bible (Lexington Theological Seminary), indicating the prestige that had been attained by both the church and its minister.

Rev. Barton A. Johnson became the third minister in 1945, bringing with him his dynamic wife, Vivian. For the next 20 years, they led a vibrant church, an important church in the life of the community. Many community leaders were among the members at that time. Henry Mann became part of the church in the 1940s, served as the chairman of the church board in 1965, and served the community of Lakeside Park as councilman and mayor in the 1970s and 1980s. The Madison Ave. Christian Church probably reached the height of its attendance and membership around 1960. In the subsequent years, as many members moved to the suburbs, attendance began a slow decline. However, the church resisted the temptation to move, hoping to stay and serve the inner city, with varied success.

In 1965 Barton and Vivian Johnson retired. Over the next 25 years, Rev. Lawrence Crane, Rev. Robert Anderson, Dr. Philip Miller, and Rev. Peter Moon served the church. While much smaller, the congregation continued to include quite a few active civic leaders. One of them was Claudia Branham, unofficial church historian and church leader, who served on numerous community boards, such as the **Week Day School of Religion** board. In 1990 Rev. J. Michael Delaney became the eighth minister of Madison Ave. Christian Church. His 11 years of ministry marked a period of transition in the life of the church. Attendance hovered around 100 during those years, but the complexion of the church changed drastically, from the remnants of a once mighty but aging congregation in 1990 to a church with a small core of younger leaders in 2001. A 1997 long-range plan pointed the church in a new direction of evangelism and community service, including the implementation of an inclusion program. In 2002 an architect's report recommended a $1.2 million renovation to the building. Shortly thereafter, the "car parts" building (and former Robert Hall men's clothing store) adjacent to the church on the north was purchased and demolished. A new garden parking area, a new entrance, and Fellowship Hall renovation were completed in 2006, with dedication planned for 2007—the first major physical changes in the church since 1930. These actions reaffirmed the commitment of Madison Ave. Christian Church to stay at its location in Covington and to serve the community. The Monday evening community dinners and the successful inclusion ministry are two examples of that commitment. Rev. Chinna Simon was called in 2004 to be the ninth minister.

Branham, Claudia. "History of the Madison Avenue Christian Church," Madison Avenue Christian Church, Covington, Ky. Printed in the church bulletin of December 13, 1953.

Golden Anniversary Booklet of the Madison Avenue Christian Church. Covington, Ky.: Madison Avenue Christian Church, 1963.

"Madison Avenue Christian," *KP*, January 13, 2005, 4K.

Madison Avenue Christian Church, vertical file, Kenton Co. Public Library, Covington, Ky.
Manker, Donn. "A Journey through Time at Madison Avenue Christian Church, 1913–1999," 1999, Madison Avenue Christian Church, Covington, Ky.

Donn Manker and Linda Maus

MAES, CAMILLUS PAUL (b. March 13, 1846, Courtrai, West Flanders, Belgium; d. May 11, 1915, Covington, Ky.). Camillus Paul Maes, the Catholic bishop of the Diocese of Covington (see **Roman Catholics**) from 1885 until 1915, was the son of John Baptist and Justine Ghyoot Maes. Camillus Maes enrolled at St. Amandus College in 1859, at the age of 13. Two years later, after the death of his father, he took a job as a clerk in a civil engineer's office while also studying with a Courtrai architect. His mother died in June 1862, and he moved to the home of his uncle John Ghyoot. In autumn 1862 Maes resumed his studies at St. Amandus College, graduating in 1863. Interested in the priesthood, he enrolled at a seminary in Roulers for his philosophical (minor seminary) training in autumn 1863 and advanced to his theological studies (major seminary) at Bruges in 1865. In 1867 Bishop Peter P. LeFevre of the Diocese of Detroit, Mich., traveled throughout Europe looking for priests for his growing but understaffed diocese. Maes volunteered, and in the same year he was sent to the American College of Louvain (Belgium) for completion of his studies. In 1868 he was ordained a priest, and in 1869 he immigrated to the United States, reaching Detroit in May. Maes served as a pastor of churches in Mount Clemens and Monroe, Mich. In 1880 he published a scholarly book entitled *The Life of Rev. Nerinckx*, about a pioneer priest of Kentucky. In the same year, Maes was appointed chancellor of the Diocese of Detroit; it was probably at that time when he became familiar with Leon Coquard (1860–1923), the architect of St. Anne's Church in Detroit. In 1884, with the death of Bishop Augustus Maria Toebbe of the Diocese of Covington, the pope appointed Maes as bishop of Covington.

Camillus Paul Maes was officially consecrated bishop of Covington on January 25, 1885, in the old St. Mary's Cathedral on E. Eighth St. in Covington. His episcopacy lasted 30 years, until his death in 1915. During it, Maes oversaw construction of Covington's **Cathedral Basilica of the Assumption**. His abiding interest in architecture dated from his earlier studies. With the generous support of the Walsh family (see **Walsh Distillery**) and **Peter O'Shaughnessy**, Maes broke ground for his new cathedral at 12th and Madison Ave. in 1894 and engaged Leon Coquard as architect. Opened in 1901, but still incomplete, the cathedral awaited finishing touches that were to be made after further donations from the Walsh family. Maes then commissioned architect **David Davis** (1865–1932) to complete the edifice's west facade, which was dedicated in 1910.

Maes also assumed a national prominence in the Catholic Church. He was a strong advocate of Americanism, that is, the movement that hoped to make the Catholic Church more adaptable to American cultural standards. In this regard he stood among an enlightened and educated group of Catholic clergy that included James Cardinal Gibbons, archbishop of Baltimore, Md.; John Ireland, archbishop of St. Paul, Minn.; John Keane, bishop of Richmond, Va.; Kentucky native John L. Spalding, bishop of Peoria, Ill.; and Denis O'Connell. rector of the North American College in Rome, Italy, and later rector of the Catholic University of America in Washington, D.C. With Gibbons, Keane, and others, Maes was one of the pioneers and longtime trustees of the Catholic University of America. He also served as president of the Board of Directors of the American College of Louvain.

Bishop Maes maintained a strong interest in Appalachia (see **Appalachians**), then a part of the Diocese of Covington, creating churches and schools throughout that region. He was also an advocate of education for **African Americans** and established, in 1887, a Catholic school in Lexington for blacks. Maes oversaw the building of many churches and schools throughout the diocese, which then extended over 57 counties, and introduced the **Sisters of Divine Providence** to Kentucky. Bishop Maes was buried at St. Mary Cemetery in Fort Mitchell.

Maes, Camillus P. *The Life of Rev. Charles Nerinckx.* Cincinnati: Robert Clarke, 1880.
Ryan, Paul E. *History of the Diocese of Covington, Kentucky.* Covington, Ky.: Diocese of Covington, 1954.
Sisters of Divine Providence, Newport, Kentucky. *Character Sketches of the Rt. Rev. C. P. Maes, D.D.* Baltimore: John Murphy, 1917.
Tenkotte, Paul A., David E. Schroeder, and Thomas S. Ward. *To Be Catholic and American in Northern, Central, and Appalachian Kentucky: The Diocese of Covington, 1853–2003.* Forthcoming.

Paul A. Tenkotte

MAIN STRASSE GERMAN VILLAGE. Main Strasse, which occupies the center of Covington's old West End or **West Side** neighborhood, is a German-themed tourism district that opened in 1979. It has attracted large crowds and new businesses that constitute an economic boon, but its relationship with residents has not always been serene.

Main Strasse was the first addition to the original town of Covington. It extends roughly west to Willow Run Creek and from the Ohio River south to the former Covington-Lexington Turnpike, now Pike St. The German village project is bounded on the east by elevated **Chesapeake and Ohio Railroad** tracks and on the west by I-75, which was built over the old Willow Run Creek.

The Main Strasse Village is German, but its neighborhood once had an Irish flavor. From 1935 to 1953, Kern Aylward, a former singing and dancing professional, operated a popular Irish saloon at 530 Main St. Aylward was a friend of nationally known songwriter **Haven Gillespie**, a native of Covington and one of Aylward's good customers. Aylward's saloon was for many years the gathering place for the Irish, and many Irish jigs were danced there to Irish songs.

Residents of the neighborhood attended nearby churches, including **St. Patrick Catholic Church** (1872–1967), Main Street Methodist Church, Grace Reformed Church (see **Grace United Church of Christ**), and **St. Aloysius Catholic Church**. In 1985 a fire destroyed St. Aloysius, and the Main Street Methodist Church closed recently.

The organizers of Main Strasse began in the late 1970s planning a village that would feature cuisine, music, dancing, architecture, and various crafts associated with German culture. Originally, the developers planned and implemented the project with an antique-mall motif. It had few restaurant businesses and only limited night life. In 1975 the city designated the Sixth St. and Main St. blocks for renewal and in 1977 received funds for the project from the administration of Kentucky governor Julian Carroll (1974 and 1975–1979). Main Strasse developers then purchased 19 land parcels for a new parking lot between Fifth and Sixth Sts. on Bakewell St. They also financed sewer improvements and had utility wires buried underground on the streets slated to be used for the project. The street improvements have continued in the area. Today smooth, rectangular sidewalk paving blocks mark the intersections on grass medians flanking the trees that line Sixth St.

A grand opening of the $7 million Main Strasse occurred on September 8 and 9, 1979, in conjunction with the German village's first annual Oktoberfest. In May 1980 the Main Strasse Festivals Association inaugurated its annual Maifest. The Goose Girl Fountain at Sixth and Main Sts., inspired by a fairy tale written by the Brothers Grimm and designed by noted sculptor Eleftherios Karkadoulias, was dedicated in October 1980 and became the village's centerpiece . At the same intersection, a Kentucky state historic highway marker commemorates **Margaret Garner** and her family's desperate, failed attempt to escape slavery. In Goebel Park, on the west side of the village, improvements included new shelter houses and the emblematic **Carroll Chimes Bell Tower**, featuring mechanical musical fairytale figures that revolve and a 43-bell carillon for timekeeping.

By 1981 Main Strasse's Oktoberfest attracted 150,000 people, and by 1985 the American Bus Association listed it among the top 100 events in North America. In 1983 a large portion of the area, bounded essentially by the C&O Railroad and by Sixth, Philadelphia, Dalton, Pike, and Robbins Sts., was listed in the National Register of Historic Places as the West Side–Main Strasse Historic District.

The Oktoberfest and the Maifest, as well as a Christmas festival, drew large crowds, so the village had busy shops served by tour buses during the day—but little daytime restaurant activity and hardly any nightlife. As the lack of restaurants and evening entertainment continued, by 1990 the number of tour buses arriving at the village had decreased. New flourishing restaurants and bars were added and have helped to compensate for the slowdown of visitors, but some of these new businesses have increased property blight rather than neighborhood prosperity. For example, one advertisement announced a "pub crawl" visiting some 20 bars and restaurants. Many shop owners and residents in and around the village loudly refused to tolerate the noise, trash, nudity, public urination, and parking problems such events created, even though they were for the sake of enhancing prosperity. Reform efforts for the village soon followed: the Main Strasse Association development committee was formed, and a study by marketing experts at Northern Kentucky University was commissioned. The city and the association improved signage and lighting on Sixth St. City planners then considered a housing rehabilitation program for the area's residents. The new association also asked the city to slow down the rapid proliferation of bars and restaurants in the village through Board of Adjustment rulings and by holding stringent public hearings before allowing any more such businesses to open.

In 1998 a crowd of between 25,000 and 30,000 people came to the village association's third annual Mardi Gras. There were Friday and Saturday night festivities featuring parades, street performers, clowns, jugglers, fortunetellers, contests, Cajun food, and two entertainment tents measuring 20,000 square feet each. In 2000 the Mardi Gras crowd reached 50,000 and produced a lot of negative publicity. The rowdy crowd destroyed residential property and shocked residents with displays of seminudity that they associated with Bourbon Street in New Orleans during that city's Mardi Gras celebration. The outcry gained the attention of city officials, who immediately took corrective action.

To draw more traffic to Main Strasse businesses, in 2005 city officials proposed periodically closing some of the village's streets. Customers would then be able to walk with open containers of alcoholic beverages, free from vehicular traffic. At a public hearing concerning this proposal, 100 opponents showed up to voice their fears that the village was trying to imitate the laxity allowed on New Orleans's Bourbon Street. They further argued that losing parking spaces could be counterproductive, violence and vandalism could get worse, and residential side streets and alleys could be overburdened. Proponents of the plan countered that the drunkenness and parking-problem concerns raised by these critics were exaggerated and could be managed. One city official tried to mediate by saying that the proposal could generate restrained activities like the existing monthly "gallery hops" at the village, during which visitors might enjoy having a glass of beer or wine. However, the implementation of an open-container policy at events in the village has thus far been deferred.

The Convention and Visitors Center service building, once located in the village next to Goebel Park on Philadelphia St., has been relocated to RiverCenter in Covington (see **Covington, Downtown**). As to growth in the village, after extensive remodeling, the historic Park Hotel at Sixth and Philadelphia Sts. has been reopened as a law firm's office. Historic Kentucky State highway markers line Goebel Park to commemorate noteworthy Covington natives and former residents and help draw visitors to the village. The Main Strasse German Village continues to be one of the main gateways to Covington as vehicles pass by or through the village after exiting I-75 at Fifth St. A medieval-theme boutique called Ottoman Imports and other specialty shops complement the popular Dee Felice and Chez Nora's Jazz bar-restaurants in the village. Besides its evening food services and entertainment, Chez Nora's offers a popular lunch and Sunday brunch menu that attracts people of all ages, keeping the restaurant busy day and night. There remains an ebb and flow of businesses and scheduled activities as Covington's Main Strasse German Village continues establishing an identity.

Beasley, Dave. "Festival Helps Put Covington on Map," *KE*, September 8, 1985, B1.

Boh, John H., and Howard W. Boehmker. *Westside Covington*. Cincinnati: Cincinnati Historical Society, 1980.

Cullen, Kevin. "Irish Tradition Not Forgotten in German Main Strasse," *KE*, March 13, 1983, B1.

Franzese, Kim. "Mardi Gras Crowd Swells to 50,000—-Main Strasse Hosted Event," *KE*, March 6, 2000, B1.

Kreimer, Peggy. "Main Strasse: Looking toward the Next Decade," *KP*, September 6, 1997, 1K.

Neikirk, Mark. "'Goose Girl' on Its Way to Covington," *KP*, October 8, 1980, 1K.

Reis, Jim. "From Pipe Dream to City Landmark," *KP*, July 18, 1994, 4K.

——. "Remembering Main Street," *KP*, August 2, 1999, 4K.

Pressley, Darrell S. "Main Strasse's Oktoberfest Has Something for Everyone," *KE*, September 8, 1996, B1A.

Van Benschoten, Amanda. "Cold Beer, Heated Debate, Open Containers Split Main Strasse," *SC*, June 26, 2005, B1.

Wiegand, Rolf. "A Little Bit of Germany Right Here," *KE*, September 9, 1979, 1.

John Boh

MAIN ST. UNITED METHODIST CHURCH. The Main St. United Methodist Church, founded in 1857–1858 as a member church of the Kentucky Conference, was one of the principal congregations serving the **West Side** of Covington). Its first building was of frame construction and stood on Main St.; the first pastor was Rev. S. S. Belville. The Main St. Methodist Episcopal Church, as it was then called, remained in support of the Union during the **Civil War**. By the late 1860s the church's Social Union, which sponsored oyster suppers and other events, flourished, as did its Sunday school. In 1888 the congregation purchased a lot on the northeast corner of Eighth and Main Sts. Construction of a brick church began in April 1888, and it was dedicated on November 4, 1888. Of the total cost of $17,500, **Amos Shinkle**, a member of Union Methodist Episcopal Church (see **First United Methodist Church**) donated $7,500. Women were instrumental in the church, promoting the cause of temperance in the late 1870s and carrying out the work of the congregation's Ladies' Aid Society. In 1892 the church sponsored a three-week revival featuring the traveling evangelist Adelaide Sherman, and 150 people were converted. In 1903 Rev. James Marcus Newton became pastor. He oversaw a three-month canvassing of neighborhood homes, conducted with the help of women from the Elizabeth Gamble Deaconess Home in Cincinnati. As a result, the congregation increased in membership. In 1904 **Jonathan David Hearne**, a member of Union Methodist Episcopal Church, donated a house at 832 Willard St. for a parsonage.

With members moving to the suburbs, the church declined in numbers during the latter half of the 20th century. In the 1950s, the church spire, in need of repair, was removed. In 1968, following the national merger of the Methodist Church and the Evangelical United Brethren Church to form the United Methodist Church, the congregation became known as Main St. United Methodist Church. In 2004 it closed; the building was sold at auction and is now a shop in the **Main Strasse German Village**.

Newton, James Marcus. *A Brief History of the Main Street Methodist Episcopal Church with Incidents of the Kentucky Conference*. Cincinnati: George P. Houston, 1905.

Paul A. Tenkotte

MAJOR, THOMAS SMITH (b. July 13, 1844, Paris, Ky.; d. August 22, 1911, Frankfort, Ky.). Thomas Major was the son of Dr. Frank W. and Ann F. Smith Major. In May 1847 Thomas's 24-year-old mother died, and by 1850 his father had moved to Covington, where the elder Major practiced medicine. It is likely that Thomas and his younger brother George remained in Paris, Ky., with their maternal grandparents until their father remarried in the 1850s. Thomas attended public schools in Covington and also studied for one year at **Mother of God** School, where he learned German. He was a student at Transylvania University in Lexington and in September 1862 enlisted in Lexington as a private in Company C of Col. **John Hunt Morgan**'s 2nd Regiment Kentucky Cavalry (Confederate), known as Morgan's Raiders. During Morgan's Great Ohio Raid of 1863, Major was shot in the arm, captured by Union troops, and eventually sent as a prisoner of war to Camp Douglas in Chicago. He and other prisoners escaped by digging a tunnel, and Major fled to Canada and subsequently to Cincinnati. There he was nursed back to health by two wealthy Catholic converts, Sarah Worthington King Peter and **Henrietta Scott Cleveland**. Near the end of the **Civil War**, Thomas Major escaped over the Rio Grande to Mexico and then set sail for Halifax, Nova Scotia. At war's end, he returned to the United States and studied medicine for awhile. At some point, he converted to Catholicism (see **Roman Catholics**). He decided to become a Catholic priest, the only known member of Morgan's Raiders to do so. Major studied at Mount St. Mary Seminary of the West in Cincinnati and also at St. Joseph College (now Spring Hill) in Mobile, Ala.

Bishop Augustus Toebbe of Covington (bishop 1870–1884) ordained Thomas Major a priest in November 1875. Major served the Catholic Diocese of Covington at St. Edward Church in Cynthiana and at St. Paul Church in Lexington. Thereafter, he served in the dioceses of San Antonio, Tex., and Peoria, Ill., before returning to the Diocese of

Covington in 1892 as pastor of St. Joseph Church in Winchester. He spent his final years, from 1895 until 1911, as pastor of Good Shepherd Church in Frankfort. Major lectured throughout the nation on the topic of his conversion, using the title "From the Army to the Altar." The prototype of author Irvin S. Cobb's *Judge Priest* stories, he was also a friend of Rev. Abram Ryan, the "poet-priest of the Confederacy." Major died in Frankfort, and his funeral mass was held at Good Shepherd Church. He was buried in the Frankfort Cemetery.

Agnes Willson Major Collection, Kentucky Historical Society, Frankfort, Ky.

"Father Major Will Be Laid to Rest Friday," *Frankfort News-Journal*, August 23, 1911, 1.

Tenkotte, Paul A., David E. Schroeder, and Thomas S. Ward. *To Be Catholic and American in Northern, Central, and Appalachian Kentucky: The Diocese of Covington, 1853–2003*. Forthcoming.

Paul A. Tenkotte

MANLEY, CALEB, HOUSE. See **Caleb Manley House**.

MANN, DAVID S. (b. September 25, 1939, Cincinnati, Ohio). David Scott Mann is the son of Henry M. and Faye Mann. His father is a developer and a banker and has served as mayor of Lakeside Park, Ky. David grew up in Park Hills, where he attended **Dixie Heights High School**, graduating in 1957. He received his undergraduate degree from Harvard University at Cambridge, Mass., in 1961 and then served for four years as an officer in the U.S. Navy. Mann completed a law degree at Harvard University in 1968. He became a well-respected tax lawyer in the Greater Cincinnati area; he served on the Cincinnati City Council from 1972 through 1992 and as mayor of Cincinnati from 1980 to 1982 and again in 1991. He was elected to the 103rd U.S. Congress for the years 1993–1995 from the First District of Ohio but failed in his subsequent reelection bid. He is generally described politically as a liberal Democrat. David Mann is an example of a Northern Kentuckian who crossed over the Ohio River to Cincinnati and successfully broke into politics there, just as Erlanger resident **Roxanne Qualls** did later and **Theodore M. Berry** had done before. Mann currently practices law with his son in their Cincinnati law firm, Mann and Mann LLC.

"Kentucky Native Masters Cincinnati Politics," *KP*, November 9, 1981, 2K.

Biographical Directory of the United States Congress. "David Mann." http://bioguide.congress.gov/biosearch/biosearch.asp (accessed June 25, 2007).

MANNING, JOSEPH (b. September 13, 1928, Chicago, Ill.; d. June 19, 2001, Plantation, Fla.). A longtime Pendleton Co. resident, artist Joseph Manning was the fourth of seven sons of Italian immigrants, Joseph Nathan and Lena Gilio Manning. He was raised in Forest Park, Ill., and began three years of evening studies at the Art Institute of Chicago at age 13. After high school he entered a two-year program at the Chicago Academy of Fine Arts; later he studied for a year at the Ray Vogue School of Chicago. Nonetheless, Manning claimed to be a "self taught artist." He spent 18 years in Villa Park, Ill., engaged in a commercial art career. While at the height of his fame as a noted commercial artist, he turned full-time to the fine arts.

At age 38 Manning moved to Knoxville, Ky. He lived on a 72-acre farm that provided the setting for many of his landscape paintings, then in 1979 moved to Plantation, Fla. On the advice of his heart doctor and long-time friend, Erin Vasquez, he spent time in Italy studying the painting techniques of the masters. Manning painted in an ultrarealistic style, using mediums such as watercolors and egg tempera; the latter was a popular medium centuries ago in his Italian ancestral homeland. His work has been exhibited in select and important art shows around the United States, and he has won many first-place prizes and other awards. Manning was awarded signature memberships in prestigious societies of art such as the National Water Color Society and the International Watercolor Society.

His works have appeared in many art publications. The uncanny detail and emotions he put into his paintings, such as *Until Death Do Us Part,* a portrait of his late wife's 26-year battle with cancer, have been described as spirit-tingling by Paul Russell, the director at the Colangelo Gallery in Plantation, Fla. One of Manning's last works, his self-portrait titled *Coping with Cancer,* received the High Winds Award as well as a Society Signature Membership at the American Watercolor Society's 133rd International Exhibition. The accuracy in his paintings was startling. His works have often been exhibited with a magnifying glass provided nearby. Manning sold more than 100 paintings in art shows alone; at one Chicago show, he once sold 21 works in one hour.

Manning was a very colorful but down-to-earth person. He loved to talk, to cook, to farm, and to build things. He joked all the time and never seemed to allow himself to be in a bad mood. He loved life, believing there was always something to learn and experience. With his art, he has left a legacy that few can match. Suffering from cancer, Manning died in 2001 and was cremated.

Florida Death Certificate No. 79518, for the year 2001.

Mildred Belew

MANSION HILL HISTORIC DISTRICT. Newport's Mansion Hill Historic District derives its name from the mansion of Gen. **James Taylor Jr.**, founder of Newport, which stands today along E. Third St. Beginning in the 1860s, **James Taylor III**, son of James Taylor Jr., began to plat this increasingly valuable acreage into a series of subdivisions. Sales accelerated after 1889, when E. Third St. was extended eastward from Washington Ave. and Overton St. was brought north to intersect with Third St. The neighborhood's convenient location, flood-resistant elevation, and, perhaps, the cachet of the nearby Taylor Mansion, drew large numbers of middle- and upper-class buyers.

Mansion Hill's growth coincided with the apogee of Newport's development. From about 1875 to 1920, hundreds of narrow, two- to three-story dwellings, mostly brick, were built in the neighborhood, beginning at its western edge and slowly moving east. Popular housing styles of the late 1800s and early 1900s included the Italianate, the Queen Anne, and the Colonial Revival. After 1910 occasional Craftsman and bungalow-style residences appeared as well. Local builders could choose from a wide variety of local suppliers, including planing mills, brick and stone yards, and even art-tile and stained-glass studios. The result was a visually rich cityscape with considerable variety and individuality.

Mansion Hill became a favorite of wealthy business owners, merchants, and professionals during the late 1800s. Among them were county attorney Johathan S. Ducker (236 E. Fourth St.), Judge **John T. Hodge** (Nelson Pl.), lumber dealer Frank Voss (500 Monroe Ave.), and brewer George Wiedemann (401 Park Ave.) (see **Wiedemann Brewing Company**). **Samuel Bigstaff**, real estate developer and trustee of the Taylor estate, resided at 337 Washington Ave. Businessmen from Cincinnati made their homes there as well, including boiler manufacturer Thomas McIlvaine (301 Overton St.), music dealer **Charles Willis** (525 E. Fourth St.), and grocer Henry Willenborg (306 Overton St.). In the late 1880s, the Taylor family's descendants briefly considered tearing down the family mansion and extending Overton St. north to Second St. Instead, they chose to remodel the house, which originally faced the river, and reorient it toward the new homes being built around it.

In the early 1880s, the **Dueber Watch Case Company** built a factory complex (now partly demolished) at Sixth and Washington Sts. While much larger than surrounding houses, the multistory factory buildings were visually compatible with their neighbors. In 1902 the **Sisters of Divine Providence** founded the Academy Notre Dame of Providence (see **Our Lady of Providence Academy**), a Catholic girls' school, at E. Sixth St. and Linden Ave. The firm of **Samuel Hannaford and Sons** designed the stately Beaux-Arts Classical building.

After the first generation of property owners moved on, Mansion Hill residences began to be converted to multifamily use. This process was joined by the **Great Depression** of the 1930s and the housing shortages of the 1940s. Following **World War II**, many of the older families joined the middle-class suburban migration. Investors purchased the aging buildings and rented them to low-income families, many of whom had poured into Greater Cincinnati during the war years. Maintenance suffered, and the neighborhood began a slow decline.

In 1971 I-471 began to be built through Campbell Co. To make way for the road, the Kentucky Highway Department demolished more than 100 buildings on the eastern border of Mansion Hill, including many of its best-kept dwellings. The Highway Department also made plans for on- and off-ramps along Fourth and Fifth Sts., bisecting the neighborhood. Some residents feared that these ramps would tie into a proposed Covington-

Newport crosstown expressway (never built) linking I-471 with I-75. This new uncertainty about the neighborhood's future led to even more disinvestment.

At the same time, however, a younger generation of homebuyers began to rediscover the inner-city neighborhoods that their parents and grandparents had abandoned. These young people bought rundown but sturdy old houses at bargain prices and began renovating them, in many cases converting them back to single-family use. In 1979 new and old residents joined together to form the Mansion Hill Neighborhood Association. They published a newsletter, held successful house tours to raise funds and awareness, and worked hard for better city policies and services. As a result, the neighborhood, which had been zoned for multifamily use, was "downzoned" to an innovative one-and-two-family urban zone that recognized mixed land uses. In 1980 the neighborhood was listed in the National Register of Historic Places, becoming Northern Kentucky's second historic district.

The galvanizing issue of the neighborhood, however, was I-471. After the Fourth and Fifth St. proposals were finally scrapped, a northbound off-ramp was built at Third St. This roadway emptied traffic into the neighborhood, putting residents at risk of speeding cars and creating an environment more suitable to a commercial strip rather than a residential neighborhood. Because the road was considered to be temporary, no environmental impact statement was prepared. The Mansion Hill District's residents hired engineers to draw buildable alternate plans that would have removed the traffic from the neighborhood, but these were rejected by the state.

In 1983 the Mansion Hill Neighborhood Association took the unprecedented step of suing the Kentucky Highway Department, contending that the traffic coming off the interstate had a negative impact on the neighborhood. Two years later the case was settled out of court. The state agreed to place concrete barriers at E. Third St. and Park Ave. to funnel traffic north along Park Ave. to Ky. Rt. 8. Although most of the neighborhood benefited from a dramatic drop in traffic, not all residents were pleased. Some residents of lower Park Ave. and Second St. were angered about taking the burden of the traffic, and some residents of other neighborhoods resented being forced to travel north on Park Ave.

During the early 1980s, Newport was actively seeking new sources of revenue to fill city coffers. Therefore, they seized on a proposal by National Redevelopment Inc. to build a high-rise office building on a rundown trailer park at the north end of the Mansion Hill Historic District and secured a federal Urban Development Action Grant for the project. The proposal split the neighborhood. Many were angered at losing their river views, which would be blocked by the new structure; by the demolition of historic buildings on lower Washington Ave.; and by the juxtaposition of a tall modern building within a low-scale Victorian neighborhood. Still others saw development of the site as inevitable and did not oppose the project. Since federal funds were used, the project was subject to federal historic preservation review. To help prevent similar threats to Newport's historic neighborhoods in the future, the Kentucky Heritage Council required the City of Newport to enact a historic preservation ordinance to create a higher level of protection for its historic neighborhoods. After several delays, the high-rise Riverfront Place was occupied in 1990.

Luxury apartment living came to the Mansion Hill area in the mid-1980s, when the shuttered Our Lady of Providence Academy was converted to upscale housing using federal historic preservation tax incentives. Likewise, the Martha Saunders Mansion at 337 Washington Ave., built for a Taylor descendant, was converted from a multifamily tenement to condominiums.

In 1989 the adjacent Mansion Hill Historic District and Gateway neighborhoods became part of the locally designated East Row Historic District, which included 1,070 buildings. This historic overlay zone sought to preserve the historic character by regulating exterior alterations, demolition, and new construction. The two neighborhood associations merged in the 1990s to become the East Row Historic Foundation. In 2006 the East Row district was expanded to take in several additional blocks. Property values escalated rapidly as more and more homes were renovated, the neighborhood's revitalization gained national coverage, and homebuyers appreciated the allure of living in a cohesive, well-preserved historic community.

"Economic Sprouts Appear," *KP*, December 31, 1987, 1K.

Key, Stephen. "New I-471 Ramps Plan Tied to Development," *KP*, September 4, 1980, 3K.

"Mansion Hill Group Files Appeal of I-471 Ramp Case," *KP*, September 11, 1985, 5K.

Purvis, Thomas L., ed. *Newport, Kentucky: A Bicentennial History*. Newport, Ky.: Otto Zimmerman, 1996.

Remlinger, Connie. "Mansion Hill, Newport, State to Try for Ramp Compromise," *KP*, October 24, 1985, 14K.

——. "Newport, Mansion Hill Resolving I-471 Ramps Dispute," *KP*, November 5, 1985, 2K.

——. "Newport High-Rise Revived," *KP*, April 12, 1986, 1K.

Stevenson, Larry, and Nick Rechtin. "Mansion Hill Historic District," National Register nomination, 1979. Available at Kentucky Heritage Council, Frankfort, Ky.

Stricharchuk, Gregory. "City That Provided the Sin in Cincinnati Is Being Cleaned Up," *Wall Street Journal*, November 26, 1985, 1.

Workum, Bertram A., and Mark Neikirk. "Mansion Hill Suit Rests on Single Issue," *KP*, November 29, 1984, 1K.

Margaret Warminski

MAPLEWOOD CHILDREN'S HOME. The Maplewood Children's Home in Boone Co., now under the direction of the Children's Home of Northern Kentucky, has a 158-year history of change and service. Established September 14, 1847, when the Boone Co. Court provided 20 acres of land to build a home for the indigent and infirm, the home served as the county's poorhouse until 1969. Upon completion in 1969 of the Woodspoint Nursing Home in Florence, the remaining 13 residents were transferred to the new facility.

Boone Co. judge Bruce Ferguson, recognizing a need for temporary shelter of dependent children and juvenile offenders, moved quickly to take advantage of the home's potential. He named the home Maplewood, after the beautiful maple trees on the grounds. He issued an order opening the home for its new use, and on January 20, 1970, Maplewood received its first juvenile resident. By the end of the month, 10 children were residing at Maplewood. Soon after, several individuals, local churches, and civic organizations launched a campaign to restore and redecorate the old home to make it more cheerful for its new occupants.

In time, there was need for labor and financial support to sustain the operation of Maplewood. A 13-member advisory committee was assembled and instituted a guild to promote Maplewood and raise unrestricted funds. By 1984 the committee concluded that the century-old building had a limited life span. On August 4, 1986, ground was broken for a new building. Finished by October, the new facility housed 12 boys and 12 girls. Soon thereafter, the Commonwealth of Kentucky licensed Maplewood to house 29 children.

From 1986 to 2004, more than 4,000 children in need of acceptance, nurturing, and love passed through the doors of Maplewood; however, by the beginning of 2004, it was apparent that Kentucky's need for temporary shelters had declined, while the need for residential treatment services had increased. In late spring 2004, the Boone Co. Fiscal Court agreed to lease Maplewood to the Children's Home of Northern Kentucky in Kenton Co., a multiservice agency providing care to children and families and accredited by the Council on Accreditation. The Children's Home has a noted residential treatment program for up to 36 abused and neglected boys, ages 7 through 17. It welcomed the opportunity to expand its services into Boone Co. In 2009 the program closed when the county failed to renew its lease. In its place, a Head Start program began.

Children's Home of Northern Kentucky. www.chnk.org.

Warner, Jennifer S. *Boone County: From Mastodons to the Millennium*. Burlington, Ky.: Boone Co. Bicentennial Book Committee, 1998.

Susan Claypool Kettles

MARKLAND DAM. Before the construction of dams in the 20th century, the Ohio River in Northern Kentucky occasionally became as shallow as two or three feet in depth. When that happened, river traffic became impossible, causing shortages of food and other supplies in communities along the river. For many years citizens tried to interest state and federal officials in finding a solution to the problem.

In the early 20th century, a system of 46 locks and dams was built along the Ohio River from Pittsburgh, Pa., to Cairo, Ill. The dams created a minimum pool stage of nine feet. By the 1950s it became apparent that new locks and dams were needed to create an even deeper pool, which would accommodate larger boats. A series of 19 new high-lift dams was proposed to replace the 46 that were in place. One of the new dams was Markland, which was built three and a half miles downriver from Warsaw in Gallatin Co., at a cost of $63.1 million. The name was taken from the nearby city of Markland, Ind., where the Markland family once lived. Construction began in 1956 and was completed in 1963. Markland Dam replaced five of the low-level dams. It is 1,395 feet long and has 12 gates, each 110 feet wide and 42 feet high. There are two locks on the Kentucky side, one 110 by 600 feet and the other 110 by 1,200 feet; the dam's locks are capable of raising or lowering a vessel 35 feet. A hydroelectric power plant operates on the Indiana side. The pool created by the Markland Dam extends 95 miles upstream to Meldahl Dam above Cincinnati, near Foster in Bracken Co. There are three navigable streams that enter the pool, the Big Miami, the Little Miami, and the Licking rivers. A bridge was built over the dam in 1978 to connect U.S. 42 in Kentucky with Rt. 156 in Indiana. Although the new dams have not solved all river problems, such as ice jams and runaway barges, they have greatly improved riverboat traffic and have provided additional recreational opportunities.

"Markland Dam Creates River Boom," *KTS*, January 21, 1957, 4A.

Reis, Jim. "Controlling the Ohio Flow," *KP*, February 24, 2003, 4K.

"River System Varies as Power Source," *KE*, August 12, 2001, 4B.

Jack Wessling

MARKS, JOE E. (b. June 15, 1891, New York City; d. June 14, 1973, New York City). Born on the side streets of New York City, Joe Marks had a show-business career of more than fifty years. His lifestyle was so urban that he was 13 before he ever saw a live cow. This small-in-stature man became a star of vaudeville and appeared on the Broadway stage, in some 20 movies, and in early television as a comedian and a character actor. He also became known as a playwright.

Marks's credits began in the 1920s and continued into the 1970s. On the stage, he played Pappy Yokum in *Li'l Abner* (1957). For television he was Smee in *Peter Pan* (1960). He appeared on the *Colgate Comedy Hour* (1951), and in 1952 he had his own show on WLW-television in Cincinnati playing Mr. Wumpy on *The Play Club*. Afterward, he performed on the *Kraft Television Theatre* (1953–1954) and, in 1963, in a popular TV show, *Car 54, Where Are You?* As late as 1967, he was part of the cast of *Illya Darling* back on Broadway.

For many years Marks called Covington his home. In 1920 he married Mae McCollough, a Scotch-Irish dancer from Frankfort, Ky. The pair traveled the country performing as Joe Marks & Company with Mae Leonard. In 1931 they purchased from D. Collins Lee a 12-room Park Hills home at 843 Arlington Rd. Mae retired in 1935, but they owned that house as late as 1951 and lived in it while visiting relatives in Northern Kentucky. These visits gave them a convenient respite as they traveled across the country. Marks appeared with the likes of Nanette Fabray, Mary Martin, Jean Arthur, and Boris Karloff. He died in 1973 in New York City.

"Actor and Playwright Visits His Home Here," *KP*, September 26, 1940, 3.

"Purchase 12-Room Home Here," *KP*, November 9, 1931, 2.

Taylor, Carol. "Broadway's Pappy Yokum Calls Covington His Home," *CP*, January 11, 1957, 13.

MARSHALL, THOMAS (b. April 2, 1730, Westmoreland Co., Va.; d. June 22, 1802, Mason Co., Ky.). Although not formally educated, Thomas Marshall was an intelligent man who found employment through his childhood friend George Washington as one of Lord Thomas Fairfax's Virginia surveyors and land agents. Throughout his years in Virginia, Marshall served as sheriff, tax collector, magistrate, and representative to the House of Burgesses for Fauquier Co. In 1754 he married Mary Randolph Keith, and they had 15 children. Their oldest son was John Marshall, chief justice of the U.S. Supreme Court. Thomas Marshall was well known for his bravery. As an officer in the 3rd Virginia Regiment during the **Revolutionary War**, he was given credit for halting the advance of British general Charles Cornwallis's troops at the Battle of Brandywine and preventing the capture of General Washington's army. Thomas Jefferson, governor of Virginia, sent Marshall to survey Fayette Co. in the eastern portion of the Kentucky Territory in 1780. He made the 500-mile trip, accompanied by his nephew Humphrey Marshall, in only three weeks. Thomas Marshall then brought his own family to settle in Kentucky in the early 1780s. They arrived at Limestone (present-day Maysville) after coming down the Ohio River on a flatboat. Marshall's position as chief surveyor of Virginia's Fayette Co. allowed him to lay claim to valuable lands, since he could claim half of the lands he surveyed as payment for expenses. Marshall established homes in present-day Mason and Woodford counties. President Washington (1789–1797) appointed Marshall the federal tax collector for Kentucky after ratification of the U.S. Constitution, and Marshall held the post until 1797. Marshall's friendship with Washington continued throughout their lives. At his plantation at Mount Vernon, Va., Washington planted seeds of native Kentucky grass and nuts sent to him by Marshall in the 1780s. Several of these seeds were also sent to the Marquis de Lafayette, a French general and hero of the Revolutionary War in America, for planting at Versailles in France. Marshall died in 1802 and was buried at the Marshall family farm in Washington in Mason Co.

Biographical Cyclopedia of the Commonwealth of Kentucky. Chicago: John M. Gresham, 1896.

Collins, Richard H. *History of Kentucky.* Vol. 1. Covington, Ky.: Collins, 1882.

Jackson, Donald, and Dorothy Towhig, eds. *The Diaries of George Washington, July 1786–December 1789.* Vol. 5. Charlottesville: Univ. Press of Virginia, 1979.

Smith, Jean Edward. *John Marshall: Definer of a Nation.* New York: Henry Holt, 1996.

Andrea Watkins

MARSHALL, THORNTON F. (b. July 4, 1819, Augusta, Ky.; d. March 25, 1901, Augusta, Ky.). Descended from early Bracken Co. settlers and a family involved in the law and public service, Thornton Marshall played a pivotal role in determining Kentucky's position during the **Civil War**. He was the son of Martin and Matilda B. Taliaferro Marshall. After attending **Augusta College** and Centre College, he began to study law with his father in 1830. He established deep roots in Augusta, marrying Ann Eliza Mackie in 1841 and opening his own law practice there in 1842. The following year, he was appointed Bracken Co. attorney, and after a new state constitution was adopted in 1851, he was elected to the same office, serving for a total of 16 years. He ran for state senator on the Democratic ticket in 1851, and his election put him in the Kentucky legislature that decided Kentucky's official stance during the Civil War.

After refusing to honor the request of President Abraham Lincoln (1861–1865) for four regiments of Kentucky troops to fight the Confederates, Governor Beriah Magoffin (1859–1862) called a special session of the legislature in May 1861, hoping for a secession vote. Instead, the legislature proposed that Kentucky remain strictly neural in the conflict. State senator Thornton Marshall is credited with casting the deciding vote. On May 20, 1861, Magoffin officially proclaimed the neutrality of Kentucky.

The house where Marshall lived in the 1840s, on historic Riverside Dr. in Augusta, still stands, though buildings on both sides were among the 30 houses torched in 1862 when the 350-man Morgan's Raiders attacked the city, defended by 100 Home Guards under the command of Col. William Bradford (see **Augusta Civil War Raid**).

Marshall was an elector-at-large for the state in the national election of 1865, when Kentucky, Delaware, and New Jersey cast their Electoral College votes for George B. McClellan for president. Marshall died in his home in Augusta in 1901, at age 82 and was buried next to his wife in the Augusta Hillside Cemetery in Augusta. Marshall was honored as one of the oldest and most prominent retired lawyers in Northern Kentucky. In his will, he left to the City of Augusta a sizable grant to build a waterworks and an electric light plant. The Marshall family had come to Kentucky from Virginia and was related to a number of famous Americans, including John Marshall, chief justice of the U.S. Supreme Court from 1801 to 1835, and Secretary of State George Catlett Marshall, originator of the Marshall Plan for Europe's economic recovery after **World War II**.

"Hon. T. F. Marshall," *Daily Public Ledger*, March 27, 1901, 4.

"Hon. Thornton F. Marshall," *Maysville Bulletin*, March 28, 1901, 3.

Marsh, Betsa. "Augusta B&B Is One Room with a River View," *KE*, March 5, 2006, F1.

Perrin, William Henry, J. H. Battle, and G. C. Kniffin. *Kentucky: A History of the State.* Louisville, Ky.: F. A. Battey, 1888.

"Thornton F. Marshall Dead," *LCJ*, March 26, 1901, A8.

Rebecca Mitchell Turney

MARSHALL, WILLIAM LOUIS, GENERAL (b. June 11, 1846, Washington, Ky.; d. July 2, 1920, Washington, D.C.). Military engineer William L. Marshall, one of the many famous Marshall family members of Mason Co., was the son of Col. Charles A. and Phoebe A. Paxton Marshall. His great-uncle was U.S. Supreme Court justice John Marshall. William Marshall attended Kenyon College grammar school and college in Gambier, Ohio, before the **Civil War** and then spent one year fighting for the Union Army's Kentucky 10th Cavalry. Ill health forced him to resign in 1863, but he recovered and received an appointment to the U.S. Military Academy at West Point, N.Y. In 1868 he was commissioned a 2nd lieutenant in the Army Corps of Engineers.

During his long military career, he discovered the Marshall Pass across the Rocky Mountains and constructed the Ambrose Channel within New York Harbor at New York City. He was involved in several major engineering projects, including the Hennepin Canal in Illinois, part of the Illinois Waterway that connected Chicago to the Mississippi River. He served as chief of engineers from 1908 until 1910, when he retired. He later became a consulting engineer to the U.S. Reclamation Service. He died in an army hospital in the nation's capital and was buried at Arlington National Cemetery in Virginia.

"Fifty Years Ago, July 8, 1920," *Maysville Ledger Independent*, July 8, 1970, 4A.

Malone, Dumas. *Dictionary of American Biography.* Vol. 6. New York: Scribner's, 1933.

MARTIN, DOUGLAS (b. December 8, 1966, Bluffton, Ohio). Doug Martin, who in 1984 ranked as the nation's top youth golfer, is the son of Lynn Martin and his wife, Karen. While at Van Buren (Ohio) High School, from which he graduated in 1985, Martin ranked number one nationally in the Junior Amateurs, for golfers under 18. He became a three-time All-American in golf at the University of Oklahoma at Norman. He finished as national runner-up as a senior in 1989, when he led the Sooners to the NCAA team championship. Martin left school after his senior season, reaching the semifinals of the 1989 U.S. Amateur golf tournament and then representing the United States internationally in the Walker Cup.

He moved to Northern Kentucky in fall 1989, the year he debuted professionally. He spent his first season on the PGA Tour in 1992, won the South Texas Open while playing on the Nike Tour in 1993, and then, in 1994, returned to the PGA Tour for seven more seasons. His best PGA tournament finish was as runner-up in the 1995 Buick Classic, when future world number one golfer Vijah Singh bested him in a five-hole playoff, the longest playoff round on the PGA Tour in six years. Martin's best season was 1997; that year he carded 10 top-10 finishes. In 1997–1998 he served two years on the PGA Tour's Players Advisory Council. He earned $1.7 million during his 11-year professional golfing career. A degenerative back injury forced Martin to retire in spring 2000. In 2001 he began a second career as a teaching pro in Northern Kentucky. Martin has lived in Florence and Edgewood and now resides in Union. He married his wife, Gaylynn, in 1988, and they have two children.

Dorman, Larry. "For Singh, It's Par for the Course until the Very End," *NYT*, May 22, 1995, C5.

Rosaforte, Tim. "Singing a New Tune." *Sports Illustrated*, May 29, 1995, G18.

Neil Schmidt

MARTIN, WILLIAM HENRY, JR. (b. January 19, 1895, Lexington, Ky.; d. February 10, 1952, Dayton, Ohio). Businessman William Henry Martin Jr. was the only child of William Henry and Alice M. Martin, who brought him to Covington at age six. William Jr. attended **Lincoln-Grant School** and graduated from William Grant High School in 1913 and from Miami University in Oxford, Ohio, in 1917. In 1918 he joined the U.S. Army and served during **World War I**. Upon his discharge, Martin went to Lexington, where he worked for a tailor named George Washington. Some time later, Martin moved back to Covington and by 1927 had opened his first dry-cleaning and tailor business at Athey Ave. and Craig St. That same year he married Alice Arnold, a schoolteacher in Lexington. In 1928 he moved his business to 508 Scott St. In 1932 Martin opened a second dry-cleaning business at 1015 Greenup St., near the corner of Clinton Ct. and Scott St. In the late 1930s, Martin closed the Greenup location to concentrate on the business at 508 Scott St., which he moved in 1948 from 508 Scott to 522 Scott.

William Martin (*left*) and Rev. Edgar Mack, 1973.

Martin was a member of the **First Baptist Church** and was actively involved in church affairs, the **American Legion**, the Utopian club, and the **African-American Businessmen's Association**. He was a charter member and the first commander of **Charles L. Henderson** American Legion Post No. 166.

Martin died at Veterans' Hospital, Dayton, Ohio, on February 10, 1952, and was buried in Mary E. Smith Cemetery, Elsmere. His wife kept the business open until 1957. Martin's son William III "Bill" was the longtime executive director of the Northern Kentucky Community Center.

Harris, Ted. "Reader Recollection," *KP*, March 2, 1992, 4K.

"Journey's End," *KE*, February 12, 1952, 23.

Martin, Alice Arnold. Interview by Theodore Harris, January 15, 1992, Covington, Ky.

Martin, William Henry, III. Interview by Theodore Harris, January 14, 1992, Covington, Ky.

Theodore H. H. Harris

MARYDALE. In 1946 the **Roman Catholic** Diocese of Covington purchased the 350-acre Williamsdale property on Donaldson Hwy. in Erlanger. The former horse farm was acquired with the intention of making it a permanent location for a Christian camp. A few years earlier, Rev. **Anthony Deye** had initiated a camping program for underprivileged children. Having a diocesan-owned property would mean that **African American** children would not have to be excluded because of the strictures of segregation enforced locally at public campgrounds. Bishop **William T. Mulloy** changed the name of the property to Marydale and appointed Deye as the first director of the camp.

A large horse barn was cleaned and converted into a lodge with a kitchen. Tents were erected for the first campers in summer 1947. Boys and girls from the various parishes of the diocese spent a week camping under the guidance of diocesan seminarians and female students of Villa Madonna College (now **Thomas More College**) in Covington, who served as counselors. Mulloy and Deye resisted pressure from some parents to schedule separate camping weeks for black and white children. As the popularity of Camp Marydale grew during the next two decades, log cabins were constructed for the campers; over the years, several large lodges were built, including the Timbers and Saga lodges. A swimming pool was built in 1968 to supplement water-related activities at the lake that had been dug as an expansion of the creek flowing through the property. Campers enjoyed riding horses, canoeing, archery, and many other sports. After each camping season, a reunion was held for all of those who had attended camps that summer.

In the early 1950s, a lay retreat group appealed to Mulloy to begin a retreat program on the property. The group chose the name "the Men of Marydale

Retreat League" in 1952, and they took responsibility, with assistance from the **Knights of Columbus**, for raising funds to renovate the horse barn into the first retreat house. When the size of the barn proved inadequate, a hill overlooking the lake was chosen as a site for a new diocesan retreat house. The architectural firm of Betz and Bankemper (see **Carl C. Bankemper**) designed the one-story brick ranch-style structure, which opened at Marydale in 1957. Rev. Carl Tillman, the first director, died that same year of a brain tumor. Rev. Thomas Middendorf succeeded him and served as director through the retreat center's early years. A new south wing with 14 rooms was added to the facility in 1965.

For many years, Marydale remained a rural oasis of natural beauty in the midst of the urban and commercial development all around it. I-71 and I-75 ran along the eastern boundary of the property, and the often-expanded **Cincinnati/Northern Kentucky International Airport** was only a few miles to the west. Pressure for greater access in the expanding commercial areas led to requests by the State of Kentucky to buy a portion of the Marydale property on which to build a connector from Donaldson Hwy. to Houston Rd. in order to help alleviate traffic problems. Bishop William A. Hughes sold just over seven acres for a road. Most of the camping facilities were thus cut off from the retreat house, and as a result the camping program was discontinued in 1988. The diocese hired the PHH Fantus Corporation to form a plan for utilizing the property cut off from the retreat house by the new road. The diocese then entertained proposals from many entities desiring to buy land at Marydale. Some property north of Donaldson Rd. was used to build the new **St. Henry District High School**, which opened in 1998. In 1996 Citicorp (see **Citigroup**) purchased 81.3 acres on the east side of the new Houston Rd., thereby greatly reducing the size of Marydale. In 2006 the Diocese of Covington sold another 226 acres to fund a court-approved settlement of sexual-abuse claims against diocesan clergy. The retreat house was part of the property sold. The diocese plans to renovate the recently closed Catholic Center (formerly the **Seminary of St. Pius X**) as a new center for the retreat program that will utilize the remaining 40 acres.

"Bishop Finalizes Property Deal with State," *Messenger*, February 24, 1991, 3.

"Citicorp Buys 81 Acres of Camp Marydale Property," *Messenger*, June 21, 1996, 1.

Deye, Anthony, "Marydale Memoir," 1954, 13.09, Camp Marydale, Archives of the Covington Diocese, Covington, Ky.

"Diocesan Retreat House Opens: Bishop Explains Marydale Plan," *Messenger*, August 31, 1952, 1A.

"Diocese Sells 226 Acres of Marydale/Catholic Center Property to Fund Class Action Settlement," *Messenger*, March 3, 2006, 3.

Marydale: Center of Christian Renewal, 25th Anniversary Booklet, 1972. Archives of the Diocese of Covington, Erlanger, Ky.

"Marydale Launches Men's Retreat Program: New Building Combines Rural Site, Modern Comforts," *Messenger*, September 15, 1957, 12A.

"No Color Line at Camp," *Messenger*, August 24, 1947, 4.

"Statement Released Concerning Marydale," *Messenger*, July 31, 1988, 3.

Thomas S. Ward

MARY INGLES HIGHWAY. The Mary Ingles (Inglis) Highway, also known as Ky. Rt. 8, was named in honor of the white woman who was reportedly the first to set foot in Kentucky. In 1755 Shawnee Indians captured Mary Draper Ingles and her two sons at Draper's Meadow, Va. (modern Blacksburg, Va.). She was brought to Big Bone Springs (see **Big Bone Lick State Resort Park**) in Boone Co., Ky. Ingles eventually escaped without her children and followed the southern shore of the Ohio River eastward, ultimately returning home in part by the modern-day pathway of the Mary Ingles Highway.

The original intention of this road was to connect Northern Kentucky with Ashland, Ky., and to make Maysville more easily accessible. In 1925 Kentucky state senator **Charles B. Truesdell** of Fort Thomas introduced legislation to designate the proposed route as Ky. Rt. 8. At the same time, Mrs. James G. Johnson of Dayton, Ky., suggested that the highway be named for courageous pioneer Mary Ingles. Thus began the formation of the Mary Ingles Highway Association. On March 13, 1925, a meeting was held at the Eagles Hall in Bellevue to discuss the proposed highway. Governor William J. Fields (1923–1927), Truesdell, and State Representative A. J. Jolly were present, along with city officials from towns that would connect with the planned thoroughfare. It was decided that the road would be built using county, state, and federal funds; but in actuality it was the state that ultimately allocated the funds for the road.

Not much progress occurred during the latter half of the 1920s. After several attempts by Northern Kentucky officials to press for completion of the road, state highway commissioner **J. Lyter Donaldson**, from Carrollton, gave assurance to a frustrated Campbell Co. Fiscal Court that construction would begin in the "current year" (1935). Construction of the 24-foot wide road, wide enough for three cars to travel side by side, was to begin in Dayton and extend through the eastern section of the county. Contracts were let to Francisco Construction of Cincinnati for a 3.5-mile section from California, Ky., to the Pendleton Co. line for the sum of $31,870 and to Pryor and Johnson Construction of Mayfield for the 4.6 miles from Dayton to Brent for $78,000, not including the cost of the underpass beneath the **Chesapeake and Ohio Railroad** tracks at Coal Haven. Until the $250,000 underpass was completed in about 1937, that section of the road could not be used; and the roadbed east of the underpass had to be cleared and cut out of the steep hillside along an old bridle path above the railroad to connect with River Rd., which was part of the old **Twelve-Mile Turnpike**. Later, other sections of construction were proposed and built incrementally. The other bottleneck in construction was the new bridge over Twelve Mile Creek just east of Oneonta. Delays, miscommunications, studies, and more studies, with public meetings following endless other meetings, marked the history of the road. Changing administrations in Frankfort did not help matters. Outside of Campbell Co., few legislators were interested in the project.

In Bracken Co., Brooksville civic leaders such as county attorney Patrick Flannery understood the importance of the proposed highway to his city. He and his group knew that although the road would not pass through Brooksville proper, it would greatly ease the process of bringing goods and services to their town. As recently as 1931, Brooksville had lost the **Brooksville and Ohio Railroad** connection with the **Chesapeake and Ohio Railroad** at Wellsburg. Bracken Co. leaders attended the many intercounty meetings—eventually about 200 of them—that were held regarding the highway. Their association supporting the road was known as the Mary Inglis Trail Boosters.

During **World War II**, the Mary Ingles Highway Association discontinued its activities. After interest in the highway returned, in 1947, a mass meeting was held in Frankfort at the office of the state highway commissioner. More than 500 persons attended, and the Mary Ingles Highway Association was resurrected. The same old prewar off-and-on process continued into the 1950s. As late as 1955, during a highway inspection trip led by **Martha P. Comer**, editor of the *Maysville Independent,* Comer's car, full of media people, became stranded in the mud on Dover Hill west of Maysville and was unable to continue to a scheduled dinner at the Riverdale Hotel in Ross, celebrating the road's "completion." Campbell Co. Judge **Fred M. Warren** warned at that gala that even though the Mary Ingles Highway Association was a nonpolitical organization, "a good share of Republican votes could be captured" if the road was not properly finished as soon as possible.

The road was less complete to the east. The original thought of continuing to Ashland seems to have died early. There was simply not enough political interest in the project east of Maysville for a Campbell Co.–inspired idea. Towns such as Ashland and South Shore in Lewis Co. already had high-quality federally built highways. Even Augusta in Bracken Co. had its easy **Augusta Ferry** connection with U.S. 52.

In many respects, the road never was properly completed. At least three sections have vexed highway department personnel. The part west of Bromley in Kenton Co. hugs an ever-slipping hillside, bubbling up asphalt as quickly as it can be laid; the same is true of the section from Coal Haven east to Brent in Campbell Co., and the portion between Twelve Mile Creek and Ky. Rt. 1996, in eastern Campbell Co. Each of these areas has cost several lives over the years, as cars have literally bounced off the road surface.

The road passes through Boone, Kenton, Campbell, Pendleton, Bracken, and Mason counties. It has always been a favorite route for families taking Sunday afternoon drives. However, its importance as a regional transportation artery has diminished with the opening of the more inland, more direct, and somewhat safer modern **AA Highway**.

"Cry Raised for Work on Inglis Highway; Court Action Is Urged," *KP*, January 27, 1938, 1.
"Heroic Mary Ingles Honored by Women of Kentucky," *KP*, March 25, 1925, 1.
"Highway Is Discussed," *KP*, November 24, 1929, 16.
"Inglis Highway Plans Outlined," *KP*, July 30, 1937, 1.
"Inglis Highway Work Is Begun," *KP*, July 31, 1935, 1.
"Mary Ingles Group Meets," *KTS*, January 5, 1957, 4A.
"Mary Inglis Meeting," *Bracken Chronicle*, July 4, 1935, 3.
"Mary Inglis Road First, Group Hears," *KP*, March 7, 1935, 2.
"State Orders Survey of Incomplete Road," *KTS*, February 17, 1955, 1A.
"Top Officials to Tour Mary Ingles Highway," *KTS*, February 9, 1955, 2A.
"Work on Inglis Highway to Be Started This Year," *KP*, February 6, 1935, 1.

Robin Caraway

MARY QUEEN OF HEAVEN CATHOLIC CHURCH. The Mary Queen of Heaven Church's parish is bounded by the **Cincinnati/Northern Kentucky International Airport**, I-75 (see **Expressways**), and the Boone-Kenton county line. The church is near Marydale, the Passionist convent, and the new **St. Henry District High School**.

The congregation of the parish first worshipped in the chapel of the Passionist nuns and served 73 families in 1955. In 1956–1957 the congregation built a church, a school, and a convent building on former Marydale property. A series of celebrations marked the church's beginning: in September 1957 the first mass was celebrated in the new church; and in October 1957 the church auditorium, four classrooms, the cafeteria, and the convent were blessed by the bishop. In 1961, with 150 families now being served, the parish purchased a nearby residence for a rectory. In January 1964, with 197 families, the bishop approved two more classrooms. The diocese approved the addition of four more classrooms in 1967. During the late 1980s, the parish doubled the size of the school's parking lot; erected a six-foot-tall, brightly illuminated message sign; and built athletic facilities. In 1990 the convent was converted for use in the preschool and kindergarten programs.

The parish began a Community Service outreach in 2002 and in 2004 established a chapter of the St. Vincent de Paul Society. Other ministries include Respect for Life, Family Life, Adult Education, and a Youth Group for high school students.

In 1998 the parish broke ground for a library and a multipurpose gymnasium, dedicated October 10, 1999, in honor of Father John J. McGuire, the parish's second pastor (1986–2000). Soon, work began on another phase of capital improvements. A capital campaign chaired by Jerry Cook achieved pledges of $1.1 million, and Dennis Behle chaired the Building Oversight Committee. Improvements, dedicated on November 14, 2004, by Bishop Roger Foys and Pastor Richard Worth, included a new gathering-place addition, a renovated church interior, Stations of the Cross (acquired from St. Walburg Monastery [see **Sisters of St. Benedict**]), a banner and a wooden statue of Mary in the nave, and other improvements. The Mary Queen of Heaven parish served 622 families in 2002.

"Erlanger Parish Celebrates Jubilee," *Messenger*, September 28, 1980, 2.
"Mary Queen of Heaven," *Messenger*, November, 19, 2004, supplement.
"Mary Queen of Heaven Addition," *Messenger*, April 8, 1990, 7.
"New Buildings Evidence Growth of Mary, Queen of Heaven Parish," *Messenger*, October 20, 1957, 12A.
"Parish Holds Ground-Breaking Ceremonies for New School," *Messenger*, November 25, 1956, 3A.

John Boh

MASON. Mason, in southern Grant Co., situated along U.S. 25 (**Dixie Highway**), was for many years known as Gouge or Gouges, for James Gouge and his brother, who operated a tavern there around the beginning of the 19th century. The community's first post office was named Gouge in 1858. The town's name was changed in 1878 to Mason, for the contractor who completed the construction of the **Cincinnati Southern Railroad** through the area.

The first church organized at Mason was the Lystra Church of Christ, established in 1841. Now it occupies its third church building. The Bethel Methodist Episcopal Church South, the second church in Mason, closed in 1952. The Mason Baptist Church, organized by 1883, remains active.

Three county school districts were merged in 1918 to form the Mason Consolidated School, the first in Grant Co., which offered 12 grades; the first high school class graduated in 1921 (see **Mason High School**).

Bruce's General Store is operated by the third generation of Bruces at the store's original location. The Mason post office is next door, where Jewel Bruce is postmistress.

Conrad, John B., ed. *History of Grant County*. Williamstown, Ky.: Grant Co. Historical Society, 1992.
Rennick, Robert M. *Kentucky Place Names*. Lexington: Univ. of Kentucky Press, 1984.

John B. Conrad

MASON, GEORGE (b. December 11, 1725, Fairfax Co., Va.; d. October 7, 1792, Lorton, Fairfax Co., Va.). George Mason, after whom Mason Co. was named, was born in 1725. He was a Virginia planter and became a jurist and state legislator in his home state. In 1752 he was named treasurer of the Ohio Company, a Virginia land company that sponsored exploration of Kentucky and claimed lands there. He continued to serve in that position until his death in 1792, which effectively ended the land company's claims in Kentucky. Mason was instrumental in gaining the support from Virginia that **George Rogers Clark** needed to defeat the British and their American Indian allies during the **Revolutionary War**; Clark's series of military victories helped consolidate the colonists' hold on the Ohio River Valley.

Mason, one of the key leaders and political thinkers of the American Revolution, also wrote the Virginia Bill of Rights, which clearly influenced Thomas Jefferson's Declaration of Independence as well as the first 10 amendments to the U.S. Constitution. In many cases the same language that Mason penned in the Virginia Bill of Rights can be found in those two later documents.

As a delegate to the Constitutional Convention at Philadelphia, Mason was influential in the deliberations but opposed the final draft of the Constitution, partially because it did not contain a bill of rights. His insistence on the need for a bill of rights ultimately influenced its inclusion as part of the U.S. Constitution in 1791. Mason's place among the founding fathers was negatively affected by his opposition to the final passage of the U.S. Constitution; nevertheless, Virginia honored this early American statesmen in 1788 by assigning his name to one of the nine counties the Virginia legislature established in Kentucky, before Kentucky became a state in 1792. Mason Co. was carved out of Bourbon Co.

George Mason died in Virginia at his plantation at age 66 and was buried at his plantation, Gunston Hall, in Lorton, Fairfax Co., Va. George Mason University, Virginia's largest public institution of higher learning, also bears his name.

Miller, Helen Hill. *George Mason: Gentleman Revolutionary*. Chapel Hill: Univ. of North Carolina Press, 1975.
——. *George Mason of Gunston Hall*. Lorton, Va.: Board of Regents, 1958.

John Klee

MASON CO. Mason Co., established by the Virginia legislature in 1788, was the eighth county formed in what became the Commonwealth of Kentucky. The county was named for **George Mason**, whose Virginia Bill of Rights was an inspiration for the first 10 amendments to the U.S. Constitution. At that time, Mason Co.'s western boundary stretched from the source of the Licking River to its mouth, and its eastern border ran from the Virginia border north along the Big Sandy River to the Ohio River and back to the mouth of the Licking River. Today, the county covers 241 square miles and is bounded by Lewis, Fleming, Bracken, and Robertson counties and the Ohio River. The original county seat, Washington, Ky., was the first town in the United States named for President George Washington (1789–1797). After an intercity struggle, the county seat was moved to Maysville in 1848.

The land that became Mason Co. was part of a seabed millions of years ago, and as a result fossils can be found today in every cut along the county's highways and in the excavations being done by a major local lime operation (see **Geology**). The limestone that formed from the ancient sea provided rich soil, later worked by **American Indians**. Prehistoric foundations and artifacts that have been uncovered reveal a sophisticated community at Fox Field in southern Mason Co. Mounds and other evidence of prehistoric life are common. Prehistoric animals and later bison beat down a trail from the Ohio River to Central

MASON COUNTY
KENTUCKY

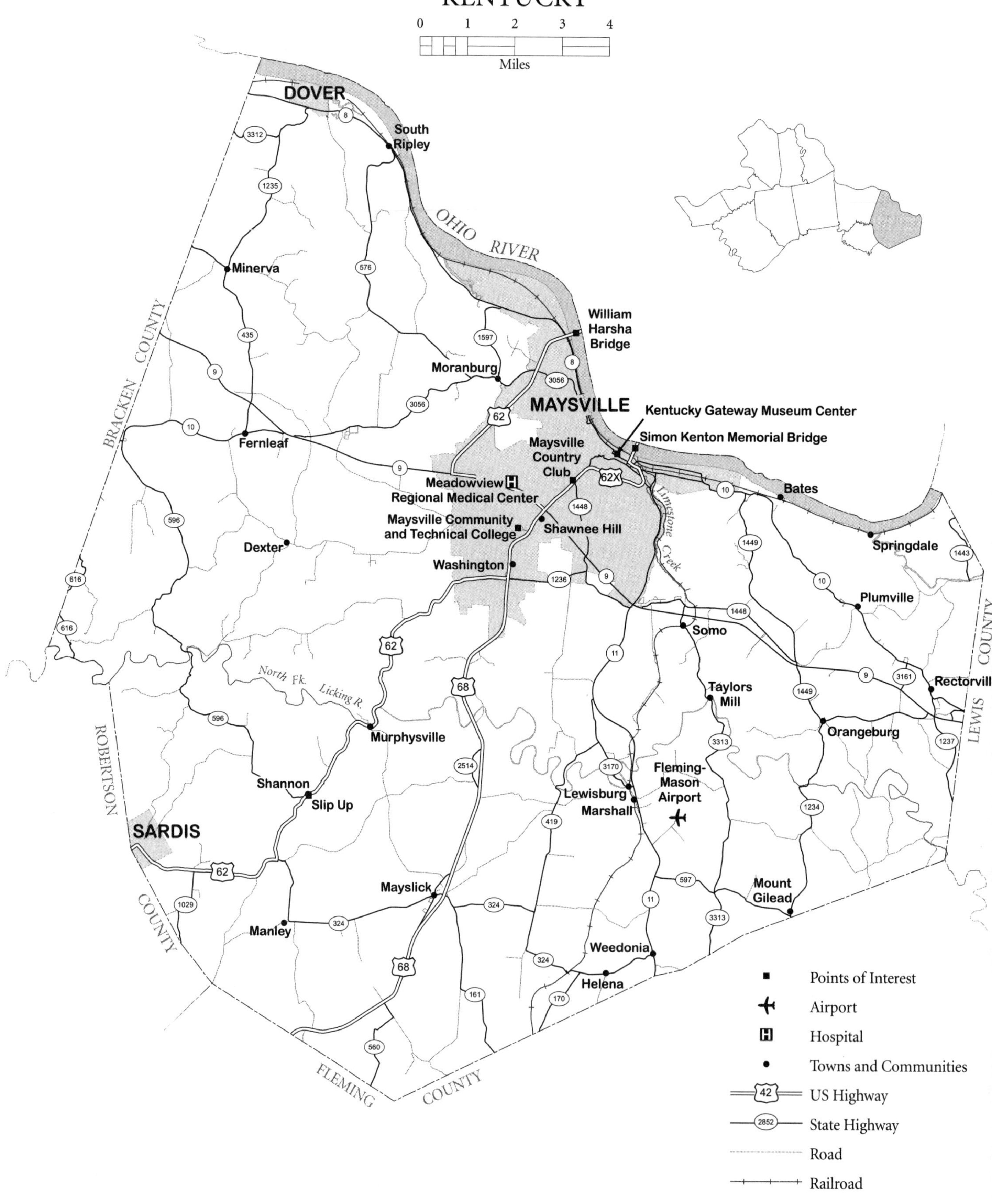

The Mason Co. Courthouse, Maysville, built in 1845, and the First Presbyterian Church, built in 1852. Pictured in ca. 1917.

Kentucky through the salt lick at what is now **Blue Licks**, and it was this road that led the first white settlers to the area (see **Buffalo Traces**). There were no permanent American Indian settlements in Mason Co. contemporary with white settlement. However, in the last half of the eighteenth century, the county was frequently traversed by Indian groups, particularly the Shawnee tribe, and reports of their famed leader Tecumseh in the area are numerous.

One of the first white explorers of the region was Christopher Gist, who came in 1751. In 1755 **Mary Ingles** traveled through the county as she escaped the Shawnees. **Simon Kenton** made repeated visits to the place where Limestone Creek emptied into the Ohio River, and in 1784 he built a station nearby, where he had found rich cane lands. The settlement of Limestone that developed there was a first stop for many people who were on their way to settle in the West, since the Ohio River was the preferred path for that journey after 1780, especially for those headed into Kentucky.

Arthur Fox and William Wood, on 400 acres that they bought from Kenton, developed the town of Washington, and it became the center of commerce, education, law, and politics in early Mason Co. In 1790 Washington was the second-largest town in what became the new state of Kentucky. Lewis Craig, who had led his traveling Baptist church congregation out of persecution in Virginia to Mason Co., built the courthouse in Washington in 1794. In the same period, he built an extant Greek Revival–style brick church building for his congregation in Minerva, in the northern part of the county. The three-mile trail or trace between Limestone and Washington became, in the early 1800s, the first macadamized road in Kentucky. In 1809 future president Zachary Taylor (1849–1850) was a military recruiter in Washington. **Thomas Marshall** moved to Washington in 1788 and served as the first Mason Co. Court clerk. His parents also moved to the community and were buried there. Another son of theirs, John Marshall, chief justice of the U.S. Supreme Court for 30 years, visited when he could. In 1823 **Alexander Campbell**, a founder of the Disciples of Christ, debated a Presbyterian minister, Rev. W. L. McCalla, at the Washington Baptist Church. Harriet Beecher, who visited from Cincinnati with her student Elizabeth Key (see **Marshall Key**), a Washington resident, may have witnessed slave auctions that were held just a few doors down from the Key house on the grounds of the Mason Co. courthouse. In 1803, in a house across an alley from that courthouse, Confederate general **Albert Sidney Johnston** was born. Later Gen. **William "Bull" Nelson** of the Union Army lived in the same house.

About 10 miles south of Washington along the buffalo trace, another settlement, Mayslick, was established in 1787. One inhabitant of Mayslick was **Daniel Drake**, who lived there in his youth and later returned to the town to serve as a physician for a year. Dr. Drake was a founder of what became the University of Cincinnati Hospital and its medical college. His book *Pioneer Life in Kentucky, 1785–1800,* published in 1870 after his death, drew on his experiences as a child in Mayslick.

As the 19th century progressed, Limestone, renamed Maysville, gradually became more prominent than Washington. The conflicts with American Indians in Mason Co. ended, making life in Maysville more attractive than it had been. Maysville was a commercial hub and continued to be a stop for settlers, who now were moving south into Central Kentucky, north on what later became a link (Zane's Trace) to the National Road, and west on the Ohio River to Cincinnati, Louisville, and beyond. Even **Daniel Boone** lived on the riverfront in Maysville in the late 1780s. The advent of steamboats in the 1820s and the resultant economic effects led to increased population and trade, and by 1830 Maysville's population of 2,000 was more than double that of Washington. In 1833 Maysville became an incorporated city, and in 1848 the Kentucky legislature approved moving the county seat there from Washington.

Mason Co.'s importance in the state was often on display in the early 19th century. The Marquis de Lafayette made it a stop on his grand tour of America in 1825. Henry Clay was a frequent visitor as he traveled to and from Washington, D.C. In 1825 and 1827, the community held public dinners for Clay, the latter one drawing 2,500 participants. Zachary Taylor, Daniel Webster, Meriwether Lewis and William Clark, and others made Maysville a stop on their travels. In 1830 Mason Co. was the center of a national debate over the role of the national government in funding improvements within a state: the **Maysville Road Bill**, which called for building an improved road between Maysville and Lexington, Ky., was passed by the U.S. Congress but vetoed by President Andrew Jackson (1829–1837) in 1830. Mason Co. also became a destination for immigrants of Irish and German descent, beginning in the 1840s, and their increasing numbers led to the establishment of three Roman Catholic churches in the county.

Slavery was an important institution in Mason Co.; on the eve of the **Civil War**, the county had more than 4,000 slaves in a total population of 18,000. Slave auctions and slave pens were part of life in the county. There were no Civil War battles in the county, but Confederate raids occurred in Maysville, Sardis, and along the Maysville and Lexington Turnpike. The Union formed a recruiting camp, Camp Nelson, near Maysville. Freedmen faced many difficulties after the war, including the threat of arrest if they were unemployed or vagrant. The African American population declined steadily after the Civil War to a little more than 1,000 at the turn of the 20th century, while the county's total population remained about the same as in 1850.

Maysville, Washington, and Mayslick, as well as Mason Co.'s other small communities, depended on agriculture for their prosperity. In the 19th century the main crops were tobacco and hemp. However, farming was diversified with wheat, corn, garden crops, and livestock, particularly pigs. Well into the 20th century, hog-killing and making sorghum from cane were common events. Communities throughout Mason Co. in the 19th century had their own churches, mills, professionals, schools, and stores. Many had high schools that served through the mid-20th century.

The town of Dover was established on the Ohio River in 1836, and by the 1840s it had one of the largest tobacco markets in the country: 3 million pounds a year were bought there. The Mason Co. City of Germantown, largely settled by Germans, since 1854 has hosted an agricultural fair that draws participants from several counties annually. **Alexander Doniphan**, a Germantown native, moved to Missouri and won important victories in the **Mexican War** as a brigadier general.

Sardis, incorporated in 1850, is in the general area where **Joseph Desha**, governor of Kentucky from 1824 to 1828, had his home and plantation. Sardis was also the location of a raid by Confederate general **John Hunt Morgan**. Minerva, incorporated in 1844, was the site of Lewis Craig's traveling Baptist church. He was buried nearby. Minerva also was the home of Justice **Stanley Reed**, solicitor-general in the administration of President Franklin Roosevelt (1933–1945) and an associate justice of the U.S. Supreme Court from 1938 to 1957. Minerva College served the community from 1856 until 1909 and counted among its graduates Herman Donovan, who became the president of the University of Kentucky at Lexington. In Mayslick the first consolidated grade and high school south of the Ohio River that provided transportation for its students was organized in 1909. Other communities of note in the county are Lewisburg and Orangeburg.

Mason Co.'s growth after the Civil War did not match its early development. Railroads were the new engine of growth in the United States, and Mason Co. did not complete its rail connections to Lexington and Cincinnati until late in the 19th century. Significant floods in the 1880s and 1890s also negatively affected the towns along the river. The county clung to its agrarian, small-town identity while the rest of the nation moved toward urbanization and industrialization. As the 19th century closed, some industry came to the county. The Ohio Valley Pulley Works (see **Browning Manufacturing/Ohio Valley Pulley Works**) began in 1886 and has remained in operation for more than a century in different incarnations. Mule-drawn streetcars began making runs in 1896 in Maysville. The Farmers and Tuckahoe tobacco warehouses were established in 1909 and 1910. These were auction warehouses, the second and third ones in the state, and established Mason Co. as the second-largest loose-leaf tobacco auction market in the world for most of the 20th century. Important names in state and national history continued to be linked to the county. **Charles Young**, born and educated in the Mayslick area, became only the third African American to graduate from West Point Military Academy in New York in 1889. Two Maysville residents, **Augustus Willson** and **William Cox**, served as Kentucky governor and lieutenant governor, respectively, from 1907 until 1911. **Alice Lloyd** of Maysville lobbied the Kentucky legislature on the issues of prohibition, women's suffrage, and protection of tobacco farmers against the tobacco trust.

The 1920s were a time of severe hardship for farmers. For Mason Co. this period initiated a continuing downturn in numbers of farms, tenants, and African American farmers. In the 1930s the tobacco program established following the Agricultural Adjustment Act stabilized prices for that important commodity. Until the 1980s, tobacco was the linchpin of the county's economy, from farming to the various enterprises that served tobacco farmers to the warehouses and tobacco processing. Parker Tobacco Company, which processed tobacco for later sale, was the largest employer in Mason Co. for some years during the 1970s and 1980s. But farming declined in the last two decades of the 20th century with the falling fortunes of tobacco. Remaining farm operations concentrated on beef cattle, dairy, forage crops, and various attempts to diversify.

The **flood of 1937** was devastating for Maysville, Dover, and residents along the Ohio River. River and rail traffic declined in the post–**World War II** period and major roads bypassed the city. In the 1950s, Mason Co. took great pride in native daughter **Rosemary Clooney**, who honored her hometown by premiering the movie *The Stars Are Singing* in Maysville in 1953. The smaller communities lost their schools to consolidation in the 1950s, 1960s, and 1970s, and the decline in farming hastened the towns' decline in population and importance. Meanwhile, as roads were improved and new roads built, Maysville became a regional center for education, employment, medical care, and shopping. The hills that had restricted travel to the river town were finally breached. The change began with the building of the **Maysville Community and Technical College** in 1969 in Washington. Retail establishments followed, and after the **AA Highway** was built in 1983, the hospital (see **Meadowview Regional Medical Center**) and the retail hub of the city moved to the "top of the hill." New industry also located there. Along the Ohio River, where Mason Co.'s second incorporated town, Charlestown, was planned in 1787 but never developed, East Kentucky Power built an electric generating facility in 1977 (see **Power Plants**). That plant has continually expanded and provided stable employment for residents. It also attracted a neighboring business, Inland Container, which uses the steam generated by the power plant to recycle cardboard. The need for coal by that plant and by nearby electric producers helped rejuvenate the rail line from Lexington, which had been abandoned but now transports coal from Eastern Kentucky to Mason Co. River traffic, especially barges and pleasure boats, has increased since the 1970s. The communities throughout the county, which at one point seemed distant from the county seat, are now less than fifteen minutes away from most of the county's entertainment, health care, and retail sites. Maysville expanded its borders greatly, even annexing its old county-seat rival, Washington, in 1990. In the 1980s, Mexicans were brought into the county to work in the tobacco fields. Many stayed, moved their families, and have become permanent residents. Mennonites, who moved into the area after 1995, brought their language and customs, so that German is the primary language of around 300 Mason Co. residents and horses and buggies have become familiar sights on county roads.

Mason Co. celebrates its historical role with numerous festivals, several museums, and several restored buildings in Washington open to the public. Its diversified economy and role as a regional hub have created a county with excellent homes, low unemployment, and a tax base that supports impressive schools, parks, and cultural institutions.

Calvert, Jean, and John Klee. *Maysville, Kentucky: From Past to Present in Pictures.* Maysville: Mason Co. Museum, 1983.

Clift, G. Glenn, *History of Maysville and Mason County.* Lexington, Ky.: Transylvania, 1956.

Collins, Richard H. *History of Kentucky.* Vol. 1. Covington, Ky.: Collins, 1882.

John Klee

MASON CO. COURTHOUSES. Mason Co.'s first courthouse was at Washington, which served as the county seat from 1794 until 1848. An imposing two-story Federal structure built by the pastor Lewis Craig, it was the site of court proceedings, slave auctions, court days, and public meetings concerning religion and slavery. After the move of the county seat to Maysville, it served as a school and the town hall. The structure burned in 1909.

In 1848 the Mason Co. seat moved to Maysville. The courthouse there was a Greek Revival building, constructed in 1845 as the Maysville City Hall. At the time of its construction, plans were already being made to move the county seat from Washington to Maysville. In 1844 a building committee, consisting of Richard Collins, A. M. January, H. McCullough, and F. T. Hord, had been appointed to supervise construction. Ignatius and Stanislaus Mitchell provided and laid the brick for the building, at three dollars per 1,000 bricks. Lenin Purnell and Christopher Russell are believed to have been the carpenters who created the cherry staircases that spiral up three floors. Other woodwork around the doors and windows and in the main courtroom is also original. The old courthouse in Maysville faces Third St. running south to north toward the Ohio River and has four imposing Doric columns. In 1957 the street on the side of the courthouse was renamed **Stanley Reed** Ct. to honor the U.S. Supreme Court justice from Mason Co., and an explanatory plaque was attached to the courthouse. The courtroom in the building looks today the same as over a century ago, with a raised seating area facing the judge's bench and spittoons available for the lawyers and the jury; it is still used on special occasions. The county-judge executive offices are on the first floor of the courthouse.

In 2000 Mason Co. opened a new courthouse on the south side of Third St. It, like the 1845 courthouse, has Doric columns; a cupola and other features are also reminiscent of the Greek Revival style.

Calvert, Jean, and John Klee. *Maysville, Kentucky: From Past to Present in Pictures.* Maysville, Ky.: Mason Co. Museum, 1983.

John Klee

MASON CO. HIGH SCHOOL. Mason Co. High School, the only public high school in Mason Co., opened in fall 1960. It is located at the "top of the hill" on U.S. 68 in the city of Maysville, approximately midway between the Ohio River and Washington, Ky. The 25-acre site for the school, formerly the Chenault farm, was purchased for $27,500. Ground was broken for the new high school in July 1959, and classes began on September 6, 1960.

Mason Co. High School consolidated the high schools at May's Lick, Minerva, and Orangeburg, schools that had been established as other high schools in Mason Co. were closed. In 1936 the Sardis High School was closed, and its students were transferred to the high schools at Washington and May's Lick. In 1942 the Washington High School closed, and its students enrolled at the May's Lick High School. In 1934 the students who had attended the 9th and 10th grades at the Rectorville School were consolidated into the Orangeburg High School. During the 1940s the Lewisburg High School was closed, and its students entered the high schools at May's Lick and Orangeburg. In 1929 African American students enrolled in the 9th and 10th grades at the May's Lick "Negro" School were sent to the segregated **John G. Fee Industrial High School** in Maysville. In 1956 the John G. Fee High School was incorporated into **Maysville High School**, part of the separate Maysville Independent School District. Thirty-five years later, in 1991, Maysville High was consolidated into Mason Co. High School.

The consolidation of the county's three high schools into one school in 1960 provided several new opportunities for the Mason Co. school district: economies of scale could be achieved by operating a single high school, it would allow for expanded offerings, and it would permit replacement of aging facilities. Furthermore, the space freed up in the remaining schools could be used for kindergarten and other programs. The consolidation of the county's high schools also constituted the final step of integration for the schools in the county.

Mason Co. High School began classes in fall 1960 with few extracurricular activities by today's standards. Girls could cheer, but there were no sports programs for them. Although the school's music program did not include a band, it was announced that Coralie Runyon would become the coordinator of music. Her contributions included forming and directing renowned choirs at the school that performed on several overseas tours. Elza Whalen Jr., the first principal, helped the school get off to a successful start. Almost immediately a rivalry, particularly in sports, developed with Maysville High School and to a lesser extent with the schools of the surrounding counties. Blue and white were selected as the Mason Co. High School colors, with Royals as the teams' nickname and a crown as the school's symbol.

Mason Co. High School has established a benchmark of excellence over the years in academics and extracurricular activities. In the 1970s a large gymnasium was built to seat 6,000. It is the largest indoor space in the county and has served as the site for concerts, various celebrations, and athletic competitions for both the school and the community. In 1981, when the Mason Co. High School's boys' basketball team reached the state finals and played a team from another Northern Kentucky school, **Simon Kenton High School**, 17,500 fans were in attendance at Rupp Arena in Lexington. It was one of the largest crowds ever to see a high school basketball game. In 2003 and 2008 the Mason Co. High School's boys' basketball team won the state championship; it was state runner-up in 2004. Opportunities for students have expanded greatly since the high school opened. Beginning in the 1970s, women's sports teams were added, and the school now has a band, academic teams, and a wide variety of special-interest clubs and organizations. Moreover, Mason Co. High School teacher salaries and student test scores are higher than those in neighboring counties.

Several graduates of Mason Co. High School have established distinguished careers around the country. **Heather French** Henry, a 1992 graduate, was crowned Kentucky's first Miss America in 2000, has become a recognized leader in fighting for veterans' rights nationwide, and married the former lieutenant governor of Kentucky, Steve Henry. Chris Lofton, a 2004 graduate, was Kentucky's Mr. Basketball and continued his playing career at the University of Tennessee at Knoxville. Mason Co. High School's enrollment today is approximately 800.

American Association of University Women (Maysville Branch). *From Cabin to College: A History of the Schools of Mason County.* Maysville, Ky.: G. F. McClanahan, 1976.

"In Mason County—$1.4 Million Gym Opens," *KE*, January 14, 1965, 2.

"Mason-Co. Inaugurates Football Program," *KP*, September 21, 1977, 1K.

John Klee

MASON CO. PUBLIC LIBRARY. As early as 1839, a group of local citizens obtained from the Kentucky legislature a charter for the Maysville Lyceum, which was to provide a city library, a public reading room, and a society for literary discussions and debate. This ambitious project was never realized, but in 1870 an unknown Englishman living in the country left a small amount of money for founding a public library. The money was held until 1876, when James Wormald, a local hat and umbrella merchant, donated $2,000 and the Culbertson home on Sutton St. in Maysville to establish a local library. Wormald's other contributions inspired by his generosity were used to create the Maysville and Mason Co. Historical and Scientific Association. The Mason Co. Public Library was then chartered by the Kentucky legislature on March 1, 1878, and its five trustees were chosen by Wormald. It was open by 1879.

The first librarian was William D. Hixon (1828–1908), a former genealogist, historian, newspaper editor, and teacher, who served for 30 years. After his death, Miss Mary Eliza "Mame" Richeson succeeded him, continuing as head librarian until her death in 1935.

In 1910 the library received the final settlement from Wormald's estate, and the trustees purchased the structure next door, which the **Bank of Maysville** had occupied since the early 1830s. In 1952 the Mason Co. Public Library moved into a new building. It was built, behind the original library building, as a memorial to the late John M. Hunt by his wife. The Hunt Building later became the Mason Co. Museum, which was razed in 2005. In June 1971 the Mason Co. Library District was established as a separate taxing district. The library moved once again, to its present location at 218 E. Third St. in Maysville, a facility dedicated on September 10, 1995. A children's wing was added to the library and dedicated on May 4, 2003. A bookmobile provides service to rural areas and schools.

"It's Not about Books," *KP*, June 19, 1990, 4K.

"Location Dispute Kills Library Grant," *KP*, June 9, 1990, 9K.

"New Librarian Named for Mason County," *KE*, April 22, 1980, A4.

Evelyn G. Cropper

MASON CO. PUBLIC SCHOOLS. Public schools in Mason Co. date back to at least July 1835, when the City of Maysville established a free endowed school to serve students between the ages of 6 and 14. This was the start of the system that became the Maysville Independent School District. It developed elementary schools, including the First District School, the Fifth St. School, the Woodleigh School, the Sixth Ward School, and the Center District School. An elementary school and the **John G. Fee Industrial High School** for African American students were also a part of this system. In 1972 the elementary students were consolidated into the expanded Woodleigh School, renamed the Earle Jones Elementary School. The junior high was placed inside the former Fee school. Maysville High School was downtown at the corner of Limestone and Second Sts. in a building built in 1908. The Maysville system was consolidated into the Mason Co. system in 1991.

Public schools in Mason Co. were originally situated in geographic districts that allowed children to walk or use horses to get to school. At first, the district schools were either one- or two-room units. Each local district had its own trustees, who employed the teachers and established the curriculum. Most of Mason Co.'s larger towns had seminaries, academies, or colleges, most of them private. Some of these developed into area schools, including high schools, and were later brought into the county public school system.

Public schools were created in the 1830s in every Kentucky county during the administration of Governor James Clark (1836–1839). Mason Co.'s school system developed at that time and continued to consolidate and take over locally controlled schools well into the early 20th century. A report from the *Maysville Bulletin* in March 1882 gave a count of 46 white school districts and 12 black school districts in Mason Co. There were 5,000 white children and 1,000 black children enrolled, but the total attendance recorded at the schools was less than half that number. Most of the schools had five-month terms, although a few met for only three months. There were 5 log schoolhouses operating in the county in 1882, 20 private schools, and 5 academies or high schools.

Over the next three decades, most of the private schools in Mason Co. closed or were consolidated into the county system, and a system of high schools was established. One of the significant steps forward for the schools in the county was the consolidation of schools and the institution of a tax for schools in May's Lick. As a result, in 1911 the first consolidated school with publicly funded transportation in Kentucky and in the South, May's Lick High School, was established there. The high school remained in operation until 1960. The community of Minerva in Mason Co. had a long tradition of education, of which Minerva College (high school) was a centerpiece. Herman Lee Donovan, a 1905 graduate of Minerva College, became the first student at the Western Kentucky State Normal School (now Western Kentucky University) in Bowling Green, returned to Mason Co. to teach, and then became president of Eastern Kentucky State Normal School (now Eastern Kentucky University) at Richmond and later the fourth president of the University of Kentucky at Lexington. Minerva College became part of the Mason Co. school system in 1909, and the 25 members of the class of 1960 were the last to attend Minerva High School. The other county high school that lasted until the countywide high school consolidation in 1960 was the Orangeburg High School, which had earlier taken in the schools in several surrounding communities including Lewisburg, Plumville, and Rectorville. Lewisburg, Sardis, and Washington had both high schools and grade schools that came to be incorporated into other area schools. Dover, Rectorville, and Moransburg also once had substantial consolidated grade schools that took in the students from smaller district schools in the county.

Miss **Jessie O. Yancey**, the first woman elected to public office in Mason Co., was school superintendent when many of these school changes took place during the early 20th century. She was the force behind consolidation, building, and the transportation plan for the county's public schools in 1912. New schools were built at May's Lick, Washington, Rectorville, and Orangeburg between 1910 and 1922 as part of this arrangement.

Mason Co. High School was made up of students who would have attended the high schools that closed in 1960. The remaining county schools, those for the lower grades, were consolidated during the 1970s, and two new schools, the Straub Elementary School, named for former superintendent Charles Straub, and a middle school for grades six through eight, were built next to the high school. When the Maysville Schools were incorporated into the county system in 1991, the Jones Elementary School was converted to grades four and five. A new intermediate school was completed in 2005 and opened in January 2006, on new property along Clark's Run Rd., approximately two miles from the high school.

Today, there are nearly 3,000 public school students in Mason Co. attending classes in four buildings (Mason Co. High School, Mason Co. Middle School, Mason Co. Intermediate School, and Straub Elementary) on two campuses a short distance apart, which constitute the Mason Co. Public School System.

American Association of University Women (Maysville Branch). *From Cabin to College: A History of the Schools of Mason County.* Maysville, Ky.: G. F. McClanahan, 1976.

Clift, G. Glenn. *History of Maysville and Mason County.* Lexington, Ky.: Transylvania, 1936.

Collection of the Kentucky Gateway Museum, Maysville, Ky.

"Integration in Mason," *KTS*, February 16, 1956, 12A.

John Klee

MASON CO. STATIONS. During the early years of Kentucky settlement, small groups of men, often with their families, clustered their cabins together for mutual protection against the depredations of American Indians who opposed the influx of white settlers. These settlements were referred to as stations and were usually named for one of the founders. Sometimes a blockhouse was erected to serve as a refuge during attack.

One of the earliest and most important stations in Mason Co. was **Simon Kenton**'s Station, established by the famous frontiersman. In 1775, on one of his early visits to Kentucky, Kenton traveled up Limestone Creek with companion Thomas Williams. About three miles from the mouth of the Limestone Creek on the Ohio River, Kenton and Williams found the canebrake they were seeking. There, at a fork in Lawrence Creek near Drennon's Spring, they cleared some land and planted corn. Kenton recognized it as a good place for a station and planned to return there eventually. In 1784 he finally established a small station with a blockhouse, with which he intended to offer security and protection from Indian attacks to the settlers in the area. Two years later, his brother John established another station about two miles away, a mile southwest of the present-day town of Washington. It became known as John Kenton's Station to distinguish it from Simon's. Washington itself originated as Fox's Station; in 1786 it was parceled out in lots for the town by Arthur Fox, who had purchased the site.

Several other stations were built in the Limestone-Washington area starting in 1785. In that year, James McKinley erected a blockhouse on the old **Buffalo Trace** (now U.S. 68) south of Maysville, then known as Limestone. Also in 1785, Gen. Henry Lee established his station two miles southeast of Limestone, and Waring's Station was founded by Col. Thomas Waring a mile and a half southwest of the town. Mefford's Station was established by George Mefford of Maryland in 1787. He and his family sailed down the Ohio River in a flatboat to Limestone, and Mefford then selected a site for his station about two and a half miles south of Limestone. Once the site was chosen, Mefford disassembled his flatboat and used the timbers to construct a home. The cabin was moved to the town of Washington (now part of Maysville) in 1969. George Clark established his station seven miles from Limestone, on the North Fork of the Licking River near present-day Lewisburg. The station was built in 1787 but subsequently abandoned. When George Lewis renewed settlement there in 1789, he renamed the station for himself.

Little information is available about some additional stations. Curtis's Station and Whaley's Station were both built in 1790 in the same vicinity two miles southwest of Limestone. Bailey's Station originated in 1791 between Washington and Limestone. Bosley's Station was founded in 1791 near the main fork of Well's Creek. Byne's Station was also founded on the North Fork, and Daniel Feagan settled his station about 10 miles west of Limestone near Germantown.

Best, Edna Hunter. *Historic Washington Kentucky.* 1st ed., 1944. Reprint, Maysville, Ky.: Limestone Chapter of the DAR, 1971.

Clift, G. Glenn. *History of Maysville and Mason County, Kentucky.* Lexington, Ky.: Transylvania, 1936.

Collins, Richard. *History of Kentucky.* Vols. 1 and 2. Covington, Ky.: Collins, 1882.

Laycock, George, and Ellen Laycock. *The Ohio Valley: Your Guide to America's Heartland.* Garden City, N.Y.: Doubleday, 1983.

Update: Guide to Kentucky Historical Highway Markers. Frankfort, Ky.: Kentucky Historical Society, 1989.

Thomas S. Ward

MASON-DIXON LINE. Songs have been written about it; moving van lines, interstate bus companies, and airlines have been named for it; and many people talk about it, but few people know precisely where the Mason-Dixon Line lies. A portion of it, in fact, constitutes the northern boundary of Northern Kentucky. The line has historical origins in an 18th-century boundary dispute between two families: the Calverts, who administered the Maryland Colony, and the Penns, who oversaw the Colony of Pennsylvania. After litigation from the dispute reached London, England, two British surveyors were hired to draw a boundary line: Charles Mason, a mathematician and an astronomer, and Jeremiah Dixon, a mathematician and a renowned land surveyor. Their work began in 1763, and it took almost four years to survey the disputed boundaries. Once the surveyors had carved out what was to become the State of Delaware from the Delmarva Peninsula, their survey line arrived at a point 15 miles south of Philadelphia and headed west, at roughly 40° north. The line was extended about 244 miles west, to a point 36 miles east of the Ohio River, south of modern Pittsburgh. For its first 60 years or so, the boundary line generally was thought to be a local border; when Maryland and Pennsylvania became states, this line formed the border between them. With the passage of the Missouri Compromise by the U.S. Congress in 1820, the Mason-Dixon line was extended farther and gained a whole new importance. The Compromise pushed it westward to the Ohio River and southwesterly along the Ohio River to where it joins the Mississippi River at Cairo, Ill. From there the line headed due west through Missouri, along latitude 36° 30. According to the Missouri Compromise, all states north of the Mason-Dixon line would be free of slavery, and those south of it were to be slave states. Thus, as it relates to the Northern Kentucky region, the Mason-Dixon line forms the very northern boundary. In terms of dialects within the United States, the Mason-Dixon line also has been dubbed "the line that separates 'y'all' [the Southern term] from 'youse' [its Northern equivalent]."

About.com: Geography. "The Mason-Dixon Line." http://geography.about.com (accessed June 25, 2007).

Danson, Edwin. *Drawing the Line: How Mason and Dixon Surveyed the Most Famous Border in America.* New York: John Wiley, 2001.

Michael R. Sweeney

MASON HIGH SCHOOL. Mason High School was the last to be established of the four local high schools operated by the Grant Co. Board of Education. Officially referred to as Mason Consolidated High School, it was established in 1918 by the merger of three adjoining elementary school districts into one district. All 12 grades were offered by the new school. The school's first principal was Nell Jordan, who served only a brief term, and D. B. Hubbard was the second. The first graduating class in 1921 consisted of one member, Thelma Threlkeld True; the last class, in 1953, had 23 graduates. Thereafter, high school students were bussed to **Grant Co. High School** at Dry Ridge, and students in the seventh and eighth grades were bussed to the adjoining new Grant Co. Middle School. Students in the first six grades continued to attend the Mason Elementary School in the old school building until the 1991 opening of the Mason-Corinth Elementary School, on U.S. 25 between Mason and Corinth.

Conrad, John B., ed. *History of Grant County.* Williamstown, Ky.: Grant Co. Historical Society, 1992.

John B. Conrad

MASONS. Masonic lodges have played influential roles in fellowship and philanthropy throughout Northern Kentucky. The historical roots of freemasonry, as the movement is called, are obscure. Some scholars claim that a number of the rituals and symbols of Masonic lodges date back to the Middle Ages of Europe, to the guilds of stonemasons who traveled "freely" between towns, building medieval cathedrals. Others maintain that some of the traditions hark back to the Knights Templar, a religious order that was originally established to protect Christian travelers to the Holy Land. Modern freemasonry emerged during the height of the Enlightenment in the 18th century and included such founding fathers of the United States as George Washington, Benjamin Franklin, and John Hancock. Known for their religious tolerance, Masons did not require a member to be a Christian—only to espouse belief in a supreme being. Freemasons in Europe generally supported the French Revolution and the unification of Italy, both of which the Roman Catholic Church opposed. Catholic popes condemned freemasonry, discouraging Catholics from becoming members of Masonic lodges; so Catholic men established their own fraternal organizations, including the **Knights of Columbus**.

Free and Accepted Masons (F.&A.M.) are fraternal organizations (historically accepting only men) and have three degrees of initiation, Entered Apprentice, Fellowcraft, and Master Mason. After attaining the rank of Master Mason, a member can proceed to the York Rite, which has further degrees, including those of Royal Arch Mason and Knights Templar, or to the Scottish Rite (Ancient and Accepted Scottish Rite of Freemasonry [A.A.S.R.]), which has 33 degrees.

Like many other fraternal organizations of the 19th and 20th centuries, Masonic lodges provided their members various benefits later supplied by Social Security, unemployment benefits, workmen's compensation, and Medicare. For instance, by the 1870s, the Golden Rule lodge of Covington paid $1.50 per week to hospitalized members who had no one to care for them. Member dues and the proceeds of fund raising events were also used for donations to the Masonic Widows and Orphans' Home in Louisville and the Old Masons' Home in Shelbyville. Many other worthy causes were recipients of the Masons' philanthropy as well, including **Booth Memorial Hospital**, the Covington Protestant Children's Home (see **Children's Home of Northern Kentucky**), and the **YMCA**.

The earliest Masonic lodge in the region was Military Lodge No. 58 (1793–1794) at Fort Washington in what is now Cincinnati. F.&A.M. lodges developed quickly in the region thereafter. In 1820 Temple Lodge No. 64 of Covington was chartered; it met in a building owned by John Casey on the west side of Scott St. between Third and Fourth Sts.; an 1833 fire destroyed the lodge and all of its records. Covington No. 109 was chartered in 1839 and convened in a building owned by **James G. Arnold**, and in 1847 Colonel Clay No. 159 lodge was established in Covington. When A. L. Greer, owner of the **Covington Locomotive and Manufacturing Works**, built the Greer Building in 1849 (on the east side of Scott St. between Fourth and Market Sts.), the Covington No. 109 and Colonel Clay No. 159 Masonic lodges used the third floor of the building; orators at its dedication included two members of No. 109, W. W. Arthur and former governor **James T. Morehead** (1834–1836). In July 1852 the Greer Building was damaged by fire but was repaired (today the 1897 Bradford Building stands on the site). Divisions between proslavery and **antislavery** factions may have played a role in the 1857 charter of the Golden Rule F.&A.M. No. 345 lodge of Covington. Some referred to the Golden Rule as the "Republican lodge," and others derogatively called it the "Yankee lodge." **Amos Shinkle**, a Republican and an antislavery advocate, was one of its prominent members, as was Henry Bostwick, who helped organize the 41st Kentucky Union regiment during the **Civil War** and later served as Grand Master of the Grand Lodge of Kentucky (1874–1875).

In 1866 the Masonic lodges of Covington began meeting in the new three-story Fechter Drug Store Building, on the southwest corner of Fourth and Scott Sts. (still standing), where they remained until fall 1870; the lodges later occupied the Walker Building (1870–1877) and then the Planters Building (1877–1899), both on Madison Ave. In 1899 the Masonic lodges of Covington moved to leased quarters in Bradford Shinkle's building on the northwest corner of Fourth and Scott Sts. Shinkle hired the architectural firm of **Dittoe and Wisenall** to remodel the structure. Described as the "most commodious headquarters of any lodge in the state," the temple—featuring electric lights—had a banquet hall on the second floor and an auditorium, a library, parlors, and smoking rooms on the third; the fourth floor held the armory of the Knights Templar. In 1911 the Covington Masons incorporated a Masonic Temple Association that subsequently purchased the building from Shinkle. The Covington lodges had a combined membership of over 7,000 by 1923. The Masons remained at their Fourth and Scott hall until 1956, when the Scottish Rite completed an impressive temple at 1553 Madison Ave. All of the Covington lodges (including Latonia and Unity in Ludlow) currently meet at the Scottish Rite Temple on Madison Ave., with the exception of the Golden Rule Lodge 345, which has its own hall at 12 Inez Ave. in Covington.

The Ancient and Accepted Scottish Rite (A.A.S.R.) of Freemasonry of the Valley of Covington and the Orient of Kentucky had its beginnings in about 1877. By 1909, however, the group was no longer active, so **Charles H. Fisk** and others reactivated the Covington rite; a class was established in January 1909 and degrees were conferred upon 27 men, including **Orie S. Ware**, an active member of the Masonic Order for 71 years and Grand Master of the Grand Lodge of Kentucky in 1913–1914. In September 1909 the Grand Consistory at Louisville granted the Covington A.A.S.R. a charter. Covington has the only A.A.S.R. temple in Northern Kentucky.

Other cities in Northern Kentucky also had historic Masonic halls, including Brooksville, Dayton, Ludlow, Maysville, and Newport. Brooksville's No. 154, chartered in 1847, still occupies its hall on Frankfort St., which dates from about 1853. Brooksville also produced one of the Grand Masters of the Grand Lodge of Kentucky, James W. Stanton, who served in 1893–1894. Dayton's Henry Barnes Lodge No. 607, chartered in 1879, dedicated a new four-story Masonic Hall on the northwest corner of Sixth Ave. and Vine St. in 1923 (still standing). The Samuel Reed No. 478 Lodge of Ludlow, established in 1869, built a three-story Masonic Hall in 1884, on the northeast corner of Elm and Euclid Sts. (still standing). In 1925, when Ludlow's two Masonic lodges merged to form the Unity Lodge, they purchased the historic **Somerset Hall**. In 1887 Maysville Masons dedicated their hall in the newly constructed four-story Cox Building on the southeast corner of Third and Market Sts. The fourth-floor banquet room could accommodate 300 people. **William H. Cox** and George L. Cox were the owners of the building. The City of Maysville purchased the Cox Building in 2006 with plans to restore it. Newport's Masonic lodges met in a four-story Masonic Hall constructed in 1886 on the northeast corner of Mayo (now Seventh) and York Sts. In 1922 Newport Lodge No. 358 purchased a large residence on the northeast corner of Sixth St. and Park Ave. for its headquarters; in 1964 it built a new hall on the site.

The York Rite of Freemasonry in Kentucky consists of the Royal Arch Masons (R.A.M.), the

Royal and Select Masters (R.&S.M.), and the commanderies of the Knights Templar (K.T.). The R.A.M. have chapters in Carrollton (No. 55), Covington (No. 35), Dayton (Temple Chapter No. 172), Fort Thomas (No. 177), and Maysville (No. 9). The Covington chapter, established in 1848, meets at the Scottish Rite Temple at 1553 Madison Ave. The R.&S.M. have councils in Covington (Kenton No. 13, chartered in 1851), and Dayton (Jeffries No. 33). The K.T. have commanderies in Covington (No. 7, chartered in 1852) and Newport (No. 13).

The Order of the Eastern Star, which enrolls both men and women, established a number of early chapters in Northern Kentucky, including Bradford No. 493 (Independence, 1948); Bristow No. 15 (later No. 31, Erlanger, 1896); Burns No. 31 (Maysville, 1909); Covington-Daylight No. 375 (Covington, 1923); Dora No. 2 (Dayton); Emera No. 392 (Covington, 1924); Fiskburg No. 334 (Fiskburg, 1921); Gertrude No. 19 (Newport); Keturah No. 50 (Latonia, 1905); Lucille (Brooksville); Miriam No. 365 (Bratton); Rosebud No. 39 (Covington, 1905); and Vashti No. 39 (later No. 22, Ludlow). Currently the Order of the Eastern Star has 13 chapters in Northern Kentucky, in Augusta, Brooksville, Carrollton, Covington, Dayton, Falmouth, Florence, Independence, Mount Olivet, Newport, Tollesboro, Warsaw, and Williamstown.

A.A.S.R.: Third Spring Reunion: Institution of the Consistory: Orient of Covington: Valley of Covington. Cincinnati: Sellers, Davis, 1911.

Bracken Co. Extension Homemakers. *History of Bracken County.* Bicentennial ed. Brooksville, Ky.: Bracken Co. Extension Homemakers, 2002.

Grand Lodge of Kentucky: Free & Accepted Masons. www.grandlodgeofkentucky.org/about/about.htm (accessed August 16, 2008).

Guthrie, Charles Snow. *Kentucky Freemasonry, 1788–1978: The Grand Lodge and the Men Who Made It.* Masonic Home, Ky.: Grand Lodge of Kentucky, F.&A.M., 1981.

Knight, William F. *Golden Rule Lodge No. 345. F. & A. M. Centennial, 1857–1957.* Covington, Ky.: T. & W., 1957.

"Masonic New Quarters," *CE,* January 2, 1899, 8.

"New Masonic Temple!" *Maysville Daily Evening Bulletin,* February 23, 1887. Available in the vertical files of Kentucky Gateway Museum, Maysville, Ky.

Pictorial and Industrial Review of Northern Kentucky. Newport, Ky.: Northern Kentucky Review, 1923.

"Square and Compass: Dedication of the Splendid New Masonic Temple," *DC,* October 26, 1877, 1.

Paul A. Tenkotte

MASTERSON, ALBERT "RED" (b. December 22, 1905, Columbus, Ohio; d. December 12, 1972, Cincinnati, Ohio). Albert "Red" Masterson, also known as "The Enforcer," stood six feet tall, weighed more than 200 pounds, and had distinctive red hair. From the 1930s into the 1950s, Masterson worked for the **Cleveland Syndicate**, which controlled organized crime in Newport. He was the son of William W. and Elizabeth "Bettie" Sampson Masterson; William was a bootlegger, and by 1920 the family lived in Newport's **West**

F.&A.M. LODGES IN NORTHERN KENTUCKY

Name	*No.*	*Location*	*Dates*
Boone Co.			
Belleview	544	McVille, Grant P.O.	1874–1945; merged with Burlington in 1945
Boone	100	Petersburg	1837–1854
Boone Union	304	Union	1854–
Burlington	56	Burlington	1819–1841
Burlington	264	Burlington	1853–
Florence	949	Florence	1956–
Good Faith	95	Florence	1835–
Hamilton	354	Big Bone	1858–1889
Hebron	757	Hebron	1904–
North Bend	540	Francisville	1873–1886
Petersburg	579	Petersburg	1876–1893
Petersburg	693	Petersburg	1895–1903
Petersburg	926	Petersburg	1924–
Verona	876	Verona	1914; merged
Walton-Verona	719	Walton	1899–
Bracken Co.			
Augusta	80	Augusta	1826–1848; 1849–
Brooksville	154	Brooksville	1847–
Foster	274	Foster	1854; closed
Germantown	207	Germantown	1850; closed in the 1990s
Milford	476	Milford	1869–1892
Milford	767	Milford	1905; closed
Campbell Co.			
Alexandria	152	Alexandria	1847–
Aspen Grove	397	Grants Lick	1864; closed
Fort Thomas	808	Fort Thomas	1908–
Henry Barnes	607	Dayton	1879–
Licking Valley	135	Newport	1844–1856
Mayo	198	Silver Grove	1850–
Newport	358	Newport	1858–
Robert Burns	163	Newport	1848–
Silver Grove	916	Silver Grove	1922–
Carroll Co.			
Carrollton	134	Carrollton	1844–
English	724	English	1900–1945; merged with Carrollton in 1945
Eureka	867	Sanders	1913–1937
Ghent	344	Ghent	1857; closed
Owen	68	Port William, now Carrollton	1821–1836
Worthville	681	Worthville	1893–1970; merged with Carrollton in 1970
Gallatin Co.			
Glencoe	498	Glencoe	1870–1874; 1877–
Napoleon	216	Napoleon	1851–1930
Sparta	260	Sparta	1853–1942; merged with Tadmor in 1942
Tadmor	108	Warsaw	1839–
Warsaw	94	Warsaw	1831, probably never organized
Grant Co.			
Carter	458	Mason	1867–1903
Corinth	584	Corinth	1887–1947; merged with Grant in 1947

End at 340 Patterson. At an early age Red was involved in crime; he claimed he got his "first square meal in a Newport whorehouse." At age 19, Masterson and David Whitfield were accused of shooting at a man named Edmond Fitters, but the charges were dropped. On December 23, 1925, Masterson took part in a robbery at an Elmwood, Ohio, **gambling** house. For this, he was jailed for the first time.

In the mid-1930s, Masterson began to work for the Cleveland Syndicate, just as it was beginning to push the Chicago mob out of Newport. The murder of pugilist John Rosen was a part of this effort. Masterson was tried for the murder but not convicted. On behalf of the Cleveland Syndicate, Masterson burned buildings, committed murders, and also, for some 20 years, managed the notorious Merchant's Club, located on Fourth St. in downtown Newport. Older Newport residents still recall the fancy red Cadillac he drove through the city's streets.

On August 5, 1946, a shootout between Masterson and Ernest "Buck" Brady helped to call attention to the Newport crime scene. The incident was later cited by the **Kefauver Committee** during U.S. Senate hearings on organized crime as an example of mob violence. It was also a factor in reform candidate **George Ratterman**'s election as Newport's sheriff in 1961. Masterson helped to create and headed the Newport Civic Association (NCA), a group of local businessmen supporting a "clean up, not close up" of Newport gambling. The NCA complicated matters in Newport by enlisting several honest business people on Masterson's side, but the organization dissolved once Ratterman had been elected sheriff and Masterson had been implicated in the criminal attempt, on behalf of the mob, to frame and defeat Ratterman. One of Masterson's most shortsighted observations was his September 1960 statement to *Louisville Courier-Journal* investigative reporter and author Hank Messick that "Newport would never clean up. The town would die."

In 1972, at age 66, Masterson died in a Cincinnati nursing home. He was buried in Evergreen Cemetery.

Edstrom, Ed. "Gambling War Has Put Newport on the Spot," *CJ*, August 8, 1946.

Messick, Hank. *Razzle Dazzle*. Covington, Ky.: For the Love of Books, 1995.

——. *The Silent Syndicate*. New York: Macmillan, 1967.

——. *Syndicate Wife*. Covington, Ky.: For the Love of Books, 1995.

Moncrief, Nancy. "'Red' Masterson, Crime Figure, Dies," *KP*, December 13, 1972, 1.

Ohio Death Certificate No. 09528, 1972.

Reis, Jim. "Former Pugilist Shot to Death in Newport," *KP*, April 21, 1997, 4K.

——. "'Red' Masterson No Stranger to Gun Play," *KP*, February 10, 2003, 4K.

Shearer, Jason G. "Urban Reform in Sin City: The George Ratterman Trial and the Election of 1961 in Northern Kentucky," *RKHS* 98, no. 4 (Autumn 2000): 343–65.

Brad Sayles

Name	*No.*	*Location*	*Dates*
Corinth	611	Corinth	1880–1887; merged with Corinth No. 584 in 1887
Crittenden	150	Crittenden	1846–1874
Crittenden–Dry Ridge	694	Crittenden	1895–
Dry Ridge	849	Dry Ridge	1912–; merged with Crittenden
Grant	85	Williamstown	1827–
John H. Leathers	598	Mount Zion	1887–1888
Stewartsville	519	Stewartsville	1872–1911
Kenton Co.			
Bradford	123	Independence	1842–
Col. Clay	159	Covington	1847–
Covington	109	Covington	1839–1864; 1867–
Golden Rule	345	Covington	1857–
Good Will	936	West Covington	1928–1970; merged with Col. Clay in 1970
Latonia	746	Latonia	1903–
Ludlow	759	Ludlow	1904–1924; merged with Samuel Reed to form Unity
Samuel Reed	478	Ludlow	1869–1925; merged with Ludlow No. 759 in 1925 to form Unity
Temple	64	Covington	1820–1834
Unity	478	Ludlow	1925–
Walton	202	Fiskburg	1850–1883
William O. Ware Lodge of Research	999	Covington	1965–
Wilmington	362	Fiskburg	1859–
Mason Co.			
Fox	386	Dover	1861; closed
Helena	337	Helena	1856–1891
Hiram Bassett	395	Lewisburg	1864–1905
Mason	342	Maysville	1857–1897; merged with Maysville in 1897
Mayslick	74	Mayslick	1822–1830
Maysville	26	Maysville	1814–1830
Maysville; founded as Philips in 1818, name later changed to Confidence and then to Maysville	52	Maysville	1818–
Minerva	116	Minerva	1841–1890
Sardis	196	Sardis	1850–1972
St. Mary's	240	Tollesboro	1852–
Owen Co.			
Bethany	560	Caney Fork Church	1874–1926
Dallasburg	621	Wheatley	1885–
East Owen	411	Lusby's Mill	1866–1901
Jonesville	637	Jonesville	1888; closed
Keystone	470	Gratz	1868; closed
Liberty	126	New Liberty	1843–1866
M. J. Williams	409	New Liberty	1866–1890
New Columbus	546	New Columbus	1874–1930
Owen	128	Owenton	1868–
W. G. Simpson	472	Monterey	1868–

(continued)

Name	No.	Location	Dates
Pendleton Co.			
Bostwick	508	Butler	1871; closed
DeMoss	220	DeMossville, later Butler	1851–
Knoxville	554	Knoxville	1874–1908
Orion	222	Falmouth	1851–
Robertson Co.			
Bratton's Mills	475	Bratton	1868–1937; merged with Mount Olivet
Mount Olivet	291	Mount Olivet	1854–

MASTERSON HOUSE. Presumably built by Richard and Sarah Shore Masterson in fall 1790, this two-story brick home is believed to be one of the earliest brick homes constructed between Louisville and Cincinnati. Others claim that the home dates to about 1803. It sits just east of Carrollton on a bluff overlooking the Ohio River and is visible from the old Louisville Rd. (U.S. 42).

Slaves erected the house with bricks made on-site from native clays burned on the farm. The bricks were laid in Flemish Bond style, with vertical and horizontal grooved mortar and brick foundations. The original openings in both the main story and the basement had brick jack arches. The facade is asymmetrical, with two windows on the left side and one on the right. Originally, there were two rooms on the first floor, one large room plus a smaller room; upstairs was one large room, probably a dormitory bedroom space; and a kitchen was located in the basement. The window frames retain the original wooden pegs. The back door has been bricked over. The house remained in the Masterson family from 1790 to 1850.

Richard Masterson (b. 1782, Fairfax Va.; d. 1806, Port William [Carrollton], Ky.) came to Kentucky about 1784, a date verified when he was registered as a deputy surveyor associated with Thomas Marshall, Fayette Co's. surveyor. Masterson first settled at Masterson's Station, near Lexington. Richard and Sarah Masterson were early converts to Methodism at Lexington through the preaching of Joseph Haw and Benjamin Ogburn, the first Methodist missionaries in Kentucky. In 1788 Richard constructed the first Methodist church building in Kentucky, at Masterson's Station. Bishop **Francis Asbury** and six circuit riders were entertained at the house there, at the first Methodist Conference held west of the Alleghenies.

By mid-1790, Masterson had settled on the Ohio River just east of Port William and had become influential in what was then Gallatin Co. politics. In 1798 the charter to form Gallatin Co. was granted by the Kentucky General Assembly. At the time, there were too few voters to entitle the new county to a seat in the legislature. On December 13, 1794, the trustees of the newly incorporated town of Port William, Jeremiah Craig, Cave Johnson, and Thomas Montague, met at the Masterson House. On May 14, 1799, the first court of Gallatin Co. met there. Justices of the peace included Benjamin Craig, Hugh Gatewood, John Grimes, Martin Hawkins, Gresham Lee, and William Thomas. John Van Pelt was the county's first sheriff, and Percival Butler was appointed clerk of the court. Sarah Masterson is said to have fed the entire assembly. The court met at the Masterson House until 1808, when the first courthouse was erected in Port William, now Carrollton.

From 1790 to 1795, Methodist meetings were held at the Masterson House, and after Rev. Henry Ogburn located nearby, services alternated between the Ogburn home and that of Richard Masterson. Bishop Asbury's journal states that he visited Port William in 1808 and was entertained during his stay by the widow Masterson, who took him to see the burying ground where Richard and several of her children were buried. The first Methodist church building at Carrollton was erected in 1810.

Elf Atochem, a corporation formerly known as M&T Chemical, located south of U.S. 42, deeded the Masterson House and five acres of land to the Port William Historical Society. Through the efforts of Mrs. Rex Guiguid and Kathryn Salyers, the house was listed on the National Register of Historic Places of the National Parks Service in May 1975 and received a Kentucky State Historical Marker from the Kentucky Historical Society. The Port William Historical Society members obtained a substantial grant in 1980 from the U.S. Department of Interior and the Kentucky Heritage Commission, permitting a major restoration of the house. Today, the Masterson House is one of the main heritage tourism sites in Carroll Co.

Adkinson, Ruth. "Masterson House Was Built Near River in 1790," *Carrollton Democrat,* May 26, 1999.

An Atlas of Carroll and Gallatin Counties, Kentucky. Philadelphia: D. J. Lake, 1883.

Bogardus, Carl R., Sr. *The Story of Gallatin County.* Ed. James C. Claypool. Cincinnati: John S. Swift, 2003.

Gentry, Mary Ann. *A History of Carroll County.* Madison, Ind.: Coleman, 1984.

Diane Perrine Coon

MAURER, EDWARD (b. July 24, 1877, Grant, Ky.; d. June 17, 1953, Louisville, Ky.). Steamboat pilot Edward Maurer was the son of Joseph and Rebecca Cook Maurer of Grant (now Belleview Bottoms). He was an apprentice on several steamboats on the Ohio and Mississippi rivers. In 1900 he earned his first-class pilot license and two years later became a master pilot. Traveling 1 million miles without a serious accident, he piloted primarily on the steamers *City of Louisville* and *City of Cincinnati* for 17 years. Four of those years, he and his brother William partnered on the *City of Cincinnati.* Edward Maurer's record-making Louisville-to-Cincinnati sprint on the new *City of Louisville* side-wheeler began at 3:00 p.m. on April 19, 1894. At 12:42 a.m., nine hours and 42 minutes later, the steamboat docked at the foot of Cincinnati's Main St. To celebrate, the numbers 9-42 were painted on the pilothouse sides and a set of deer horns was mounted over the bell roof. The horns were still on the bell roof in January 1918, when the boat was lost in ice at Cincinnati. Maurer married Martha Board in 1915, and they had two children. Appointed a local inspector of hulls for the U.S. Steamboat Inspection Service in 1917 at Pittsburgh, he transferred to Louisville in 1922. In 1934, by presidential appointment, Maurer became the U.S. supervising inspector of the Sixth District. He was the last man in the United States to receive such an appointment. In February 1942, when the Coast Guard took over the marine inspection service, he was made officer in charge of the Louisville District. In 1947, after more than 50 years on the river, Maurer retired, holding the rank of full commander in the U.S. Coast Guard. He was buried in Resthaven Cemetery in Louisville.

Boone County Recorder, illustrated historical ed., September 1930.

"Capt. Edward Maurer," *CP,* June 23, 1953, 17.

Warner, Jennifer S. *Boone County: From Mastodons to the Millennium.* Burlington, Ky.: Boone Co. Bicentennial Book Committee, 1998.

Way, Frederick, Jr., comp. *Way's Packet Directory, 1848–1983.* Athens: Ohio Univ., 1983.

Nancy J. Tretter

MAY, JOHN (b. December 20, 1737 or 1744, Dinwiddie Co., Va.; d. February 1790, Ohio River near Portsmouth, Ohio). John May, the namesake of the city of Maysville and one of the founders of Kentucky, was the son of John May Jr. and Agnes Smith May. In 1769 he became the first clerk of Botetourt Co., Va., after apparently fighting in the **French and Indian War**. The clerkship allowed May to pursue other goals, and in 1770 he was made quartermaster of the militia and was working as an attorney. He was also buying land, and he was so highly respected that in 1773, and again in 1776, he was chosen to be part of committees to examine land claims in Kentucky Co., Va.

In the midst of the **Revolutionary War** in 1778, May became clerk of the General Court of Virginia at the state capital, Williamsburg, Va. His travels were frequent, and in 1779 or 1780, he was in Central Kentucky around Harrodsburg. He was the first teacher at McAfee Station, and thus one of the first of that profession in the state. In 1780 he was involved in the Battle of King's Mountain in North Carolina, a turning point of the war. Back in

Kentucky in 1781, he became the Jefferson Co. clerk and that county's elected representative to the Virginia legislature, one of four delegates from Kentucky. In 1780 he was named by the Virginia legislature as one of the trustees of lands donated by Virginia to form a school, which became Transylvania Seminary. Fellow trustees included **George Rogers Clark**, David Rice, and Isaac Shelby.

While May served as a delegate in Richmond, Va., in 1782, discussions were held about Virginia Supreme Court positions in Kentucky. It was decided that May would be an assistant judge, but he became clerk of the court when it held its first session in Harrodsburg in 1783. May and Virginia attorney general Walker Daniel were given the responsibility of finding a site and having a courthouse built. The resulting log structure was placed in the town that carried the name of Walker Daniel, Danville, Ky. In the mid-1780s, May was again traveling back and forth between Virginia and Kentucky.

Throughout these years, May accumulated property. As a result of his various positions as clerk, his role in settling land disputes, his various partnerships, his explorations, his legal knowledge, and surveying by his brothers, he had claims, by himself and in partnerships, to more than 800,000 acres by 1790. It was on 100 acres of those lands, which he owned in partnership with **Simon Kenton**, that the Virginia legislature on December 11, 1787, established the town of Maysville on the Ohio River. **Daniel Boone** was one of its original trustees. The landing and community had been called Limestone, and that name was still in use by many for several subsequent decades. Mason Co. was formed the following year, and in 1848 Maysville became the county seat, replacing the pioneer town of Washington.

May, however, never lived in the town that bore his name. In February 1790, with his secretary, Charles Johnston, May was on one of his many journeys to Kentucky. His destination was Maysville, to conduct legal work on land claims. Reports of that voyage, May's final, were written by Johnston and other participants. The group purchased a boat at the mouth of the Kanawha River, and May, Johnston, and a merchant named Jacob Skiles, with goods bound for Lexington, Ky. were the passengers. At Point Pleasant (in modern-day West Virginia), they were joined by a man identified as Flinn and sisters by the name of Fleming. A scheme often practiced by Indians was to use white renegades or captives to lure boats close to shore and overtake them. This is what happened to the seasoned pioneer May and his companions. Two white men, at the mouth of the Scioto River near what is modern Portsmouth, Ohio, hailed the May flatboat, pleading to be taken aboard. May was skeptical, but the other travelers were swayed by the wails of the men, who said they had escaped from their Indian captors and that the Indians were close behind. When the boat neared the shore, the Indians attacked. May was killed by a shot to the head, as was one of the women. Flinn was later burned to death, Skiles escaped despite wounds, and eventually the other Fleming woman and Johnston were released. The two white men used as bait claimed they were captives and had agreed to the plan in the hope of being released. What happened to May's body is unknown.

May left a young wife, Ann Langley, and two young children. The legal battles growing out of May's estate involved such prominent lawyers as Henry Clay and John Rowan and dozens of people across several states. The new State of Kentucky adopted laws that essentially denied that May had ever been a legal resident, ignoring his political offices and long periods of time living in Kentucky. His heirs saw little of the estate. Today, John May is largely remembered for the town that bears his name, his other contributions to the states of Virginia and Kentucky forgotten.

Clift, G. Glenn. *History of Maysville and Mason County.* Lexington, Ky.: Transylvania, 1936.

Coke, Ben H. *John May, Jr. of Virginia: His Descendants and Their Land.* Baltimore: Gateway Press, 1975.

Collins, Richard H. *History of Kentucky.* Vol. 1. Covington, Ky.: Collins, 1882.

John Klee

MAYSLICK (or Mays Lick or May's Lick). Mayslick is a small Mason Co. community nine miles southwest of Maysville, which owes its importance to its place on the **Maysville and Lexington Turnpike**, now U.S. 68. For those traveling south on that route, Mayslick was the first community they came to after Washington, Ky. In 1773 William Thompson surveyed the area, and the founder of Lexington, Col. Robert Patterson, explored the area in 1775. It was a group of related families who actually established the settlement in 1787; they included brothers Abraham, Cornelius, and Isaac Drake; David Morris; and John Shotwell, along with their families. They bought 1,400 acres of land through a land agent, Judge Harry Innes. The land had been surveyed and claimed originally by William May, for whom May's Spring and Mayslick were named. William May was the brother of Maysville's namesake, John May, a fact that has caused confusion over the origin of the name. The land was rolling and rich for farming, with a salt lick to provided salt for the pioneers and a large spring for water. Much of the information about early Mayslick comes from Isaac Drake's son **Daniel Drake**, whose letters to his children plus some additional information were turned into a book, *Pioneer Life in Kentucky.* After landing at Limestone and staying for a short time in Washington in a shed built for sheep, the families moved to what became Mayslick. Isaac Drake was married to Elizabeth Shotwell, whose Quaker family strongly disapproved of her marriage to the Baptist Drake. William Wood, the Baptist minister who founded Washington, was instrumental in attracting the families to Mason Co. Pioneer life in Mayslick, as described by Daniel Drake, included log cabins, Indian problems, and the hardscrabble life of farming.

It was Abraham Drake's tavern, where travelers stopped on their way west, that gave the town its early success. David Morris and John Shotwell also had tavern licenses. Early visitors, such as F. A. Michaux in 1793, commented on the lack of development and sophistication in the town. However, in 1810, with 132 residents, it was the third-largest town in the county. The founders were loyal to their religious convictions, establishing a Baptist church, the first in the town, in 1789. On February 1, 1837, Mayslick was incorporated, and Jonas Eddy, E. H. Herndon, John L. Kirk, Asa Runyon, and Samuel Sharp were its trustees. Among Kirk's slaves was **Elisha Green**, who lived in Mayslick from 1828 to 1832 and recounts in his autobiography the hard life of a slave. Green later bought his freedom, established African American churches throughout the area, became a leader in the **Republican Party**, and spoke out for the rights of the freedman.

Slavery was a hot issue in the town. The **Maysville Colonization Society** met in Mayslick in 1823. Slaves accounted for one-third of the town's population of 200 at the time of the **Civil War**. **John Hunt Morgan** made his way through Mayslick on one of his raids, and a pro-Union meeting on October 22, 1864, attended by former governor James Robinson (1862–1863) and Governor Thomas Bramlette (1863–1867), attracted 1,000 persons.

An African American school was established on August 27, 1868, after the Maysville and Lexington Turnpike company conveyed property to Stephen Breckinridge, Henry Jackson, and John Middleton, who were trustees of the Second Baptist Church. The land was to be used for a church and a school. The church stands today on the property, but neighboring property was purchased for a better school. Schools for black students were built there, the last one finished in 1921; it closed in 1960, despite a petition opposing the closure, when all black students in the county were integrated into the county system. The school building remains. Other schools flourished, both small district schools and more substantial private schools. The Baptists had schools from the beginning, such as the one that Daniel Drake attended. James Blaine, later U.S. secretary of state, is believed to have taught at Mayslick, perhaps while he also taught in the 1840s at the Western Military Institute at Blue Licks, just 10 miles southwest on the Maysville and Lexington Turnpike. Hedge College was a late-19th-century private school. In 1909 a public high school opened in Mayslick. In 1910, a Shannon Creek flood washed away a small rural school called Arthuranna. Local citizens then lobbied to consolidate that school and the schools at West Liberty, Mayslick, and Peed, along with part of the Helena Station district. It became the first consolidated school with transportation in Kentucky; horse-drawn buses transported students. A three-story brick school was started in 1909, and a gym was added in 1929. Mayslick High School closed in 1960 and was consolidated into **Mason Co. High School**. It had previously taken in the students from the closed Sardis, Lewisburg, and Washington schools. Before consolidation, the school was the center of the community, which had grown to more than 300 residents in the early 20th century. For example, in 1931, the team of eight Mayslick High School girls won the basketball district tournament and reached the final four in the state championship.

Mayslick had many churches over the years. The role of the **Mayslick Christian Church** at a historic turning point stands out. In the late 1820s, Thomas and **Alexander Campbell** preached in the area, and as a result the Mayslick Christian Church, one of the first Disciples of Christ churches, was established in 1830. The Disciples of Christ, which had grown out of the Cane Ridge movement, became a distinct denomination at about the same time. Walter Scott, another founder of the Disciples of Christ, later was pastor of the church in Mayslick and is buried in the community cemetery. The Mayslick Christian Church, where Scott became the first full-time pastor, was built 1841 by **Lewis Wernwag**, a prolific covered-bridge builder.

The Mayslick Baptist Church suffered a loss of membership when the Campbellites left, but the church nevertheless proceeded to outgrow several structures and today worships in a building enlarged around the 1870 church. Both the Baptist and the Christian churches had black members but eventually sponsored separate churches for African American members. The Second Baptist Church began in 1855 with more than 100 members and has worshipped in the same church building since 1913. The Second Christian Church congregation began worship in their own church in 1889, but the church closed a century later. The Presbyterian Church, which started on Johnson Fork in 1793 and moved to Mayslick in 1850, now has only a few members. Bricks from the original church were used in the 1850 structure and in the 1876 rebuilding after a fire. That church, with some of the 18th-century bricks, stands today.

After the mid-19th-century influx of mostly Catholic immigrants from Ireland and Germany, Rev. John Hickey was appointed in 1864 to serve the needs of them and other Catholics in the area. A church building at Mayslick was purchased from the Methodist Episcopal South Church in 1867 for $600, another church was built in 1886, and the present St. Rose of Lima Church was built in 1928. Still today many of the farming families in the Mayslick area, descendants of the 19th-century immigrants, have Irish or German names.

In the early 20th century, a new bank opened in Mayslick; the Farmer's Bank of Mayslick was chartered in 1902 and remained in some form until the 1990s in the same building. Beside the brick bank building, an impressive **Independent Order of Odd Fellows** Hall was built in 1904 with a second floor large enough to house a skating rink at one time. Both buildings stand today. The community was a hot spot during the tobacco wars, having an active group of **Night Riders** in the first decade of the 20th century.

Large estates and plantations were established in the Mayslick area. It was called the "asparagus bed" of Mason Co., as it was believed to be the site of richest farmland. In the mid-1800s, the Mayslick Importing Company did a thriving business in mule breeding stock. Agricultural fairs were held in the early 1900s, and impressive houses built from the settlement period to the early 1900s dot the area. Examples include a stone house believed to be built by Thomas Metcalfe, who was called Stonehammer at the time but later was elected governor of Kentucky. Another unique example is the William Pepper Fox house, built in 1854, which had an entrance hall that measured 14 by 30 feet. On this estate is Fox Field, a federally protected **Fort Ancient** archaeological site. What is known as the Longnecker house was finished in 1825; its front door shows damage from the buckshot fired by tobacco Night Riders. James Mitchell, president of the First National Bank of Maysville, picked one of the highest spots in the county near Mayslick to build his home, Maplewood, in 1889; it is a Romanesque showplace with stained glass and impressive stonework. In that same year, **Charles Young**, who was born in a log cabin just down the road from Maplewood, became only the third African American to graduate from the U.S. Military Academy at West Point, N.Y., and the first in a generation.

Today, the town square of Mayslick is no longer active with its former hardware store, pool hall, grocery stores, bank, and other businesses. A few businesses remain, along with the churches and a large number of homes, which continue to be built in the area for those who want country living only a short distance away from work. The area has flashes from the past in the significant number of older Amish people who have moved into the Mayslick area in the past decade. They are active members of the community, participating in community events, and their horses and buggies are common sights on the local roads.

Mayslick became the name of the town after it had first been called May's Spring. Mayslick came into common usage in the 20th century, and today both spellings are used, along with Mays Lick and May's Lick.

Calvert, Jean, and John Klee. *The Towns of Mason County: Their Past in Pictures*. Maysville, Ky.: Maysville and Mason Co. Library Historical and Scientific Association, 1986.

Clift, G. Glenn. *History of Maysville and Mason County*. Lexington, Ky.: Transylvania, 1936.

Collins, Richard H. *History of Kentucky*. Vol. 1. Covington, Ky.: Collins, 1882.

David, Lynn, and Liz Comer. "Mayslick: Asparagus Bed of Mason County," *NKH* 12, no. 2 (Spring–Summer 2005): 37–49.

Rennick, Robert M. *Kentucky Place Names*. Lexington: Univ. of Kentucky Press, 1984.

John Klee

MAYSLICK CHRISTIAN CHURCH. The Mayslick Christian Church, located in the center of Mayslick, is tied to three of the founders of the Disciples of Christ movement, **Alexander Campbell**, Thomas Campbell, and Walter Scott. The history of the Mayslick Christian Church can be traced to 1789 and the first church in the community, the Church of Jesus Christ, Regular Order of First Day Baptists. The Mayslick Christian Church developed out of that group about 30 years after Barton Stone, another prominent Disciples of Christ figure, led the 1801 Cane Ridge revival in Bourbon Co., setting off several decades of religious debate in Kentucky. In the 1820s and 1830s, Thomas Campbell and his son Alexander articulated a set of beliefs growing out of Cane Ridge, around which the Disciples of Christ movement was founded.

The Mayslick Christian Church was one of the first Disciples of Christ churches. Visits from the Campbells to the Baptist Church in 1828 and 1829, and debates in the area, led to its formation in 1830. The number of Baptists in the area was reduced by half as members joined the rapidly growing number of Campbellite churches. The congregation of the Mayslick Christian Church first met in a stone schoolhouse. Its church building, which is still used, was constructed in 1841 by **Lewis Wernwag**, a renowned Virginia builder of covered bridges, who also built the house next door that served as the parsonage from 1911 to 1970. The church, similar in style to many of the period, had two entrances, from which members entered facing the congregation. Alexander Campbell, who preached at the church in 1841, afterward stated that he was able to address 1,000 people who were seated on the floor of the church.

Walter Scott became the first full-time minister in April 1850. Scott was another of the Disciples of Christ founders and had preached in many states. He introduced a teaching method on the process of faith based on the five fingers of the hand. The steps in the process were "faith, repentance, baptism, remission of sins, and the gift of the Holy Spirit." Scott left the church but later returned to Mayslick, where he died in 1862 and was buried in the cemetery within sight of the church.

In 1882 the church bought property for an African American congregation, and in 1889 a building was completed for that congregation, named the Second Christian Church. This church closed during the 1990s. In 1891 a major renovation of the 1841 church building uncovered the ceiling support beams of the original church, which displayed the practical and beautiful handiwork of Wernwag. These beams were finished and are now part of the striking interior of the church. On February 4, 1975, an arsonist, who had already burned three other churches in the county, set fire to Mayslick Christian Church. It survived, the damage having involved mostly the Sunday school rooms. Today the church has about 100 members.

Braden, Gayle Anderson, and Coralie Jones Runyon. *A History of the Christian Church, Maysville, Kentucky*. Maysville, Ky.: Maysville Christian Church, 1948.

Calvert, Jean, and John Klee. *The Towns of Mason County: Their Past in Pictures*. Maysville, Ky.: Maysville and Mason Co. Library Historical and Scientific Association, 1986.

Documents and brochures, Mayslick Christian Church, Mayslick, Ky.

John Klee

MAYSVILLE. Maysville, originally called Limestone, is the county seat of Mason Co. It was established at the mouth of Limestone Creek where it empties into the Ohio River, 400 miles downriver from Pittsburgh, Pa., and 60 miles upriver from Cincinnati. Maysville was the original gateway to the nation's West. The Cumberland Gap opened up Kentucky, but people traveling west soon discovered that the Ohio River was a more effective route, and for those settlers Maysville was an early gateway.

European exploration of the region dates to the 1600s. It was Pennsylvanian **Simon Kenton** who was the key to settling Limestone, the nearby town of Washington, and the county. Another explorer of the area was Robert McAfee, who arrived in June 1773. John Hedges gave the site its original name of Limestone earlier in 1773. But it was Kenton, on his fourth visit in 1775, who found Limestone cove and the canebrakes three miles south of Limestone that became part of pioneer legend. Here Kenton built his cabin and began promoting the area. The site of Limestone was locked between the river and hills with insufficient land for farming and vulnerable to Indian attacks. Most settlers moved to the hills above Limestone or migrated farther to the west.

In 1776 numerous exploring parties came to Limestone, and Kenton welcomed them and helped guide them to their destinations. Local tradition holds that he urged only those visitors he found especially promising to stay in the area. Indian attacks kept most settlers away before 1784, the year Kenton returned to Limestone with 60 men. William Bickley, Edward Waller, and **John Waller** of that party built at the mouth of Limestone Creek a blockhouse that was the beginning of Maysville.

Limestone was named a tobacco inspection site in 1787, establishing a relationship of that crop to the town that was especially important over the next two centuries. On December 11, 1787, the Commonwealth of Virginia established the town of Maysville in what was then Bourbon Co., "on the lands of John May and Simon Kenton." The name Maysville was chosen instead of Limestone because John May was considered a founder of the town and owned the land with Kenton. **Daniel Boone** was among the original trustees, whose job it was to lay out the streets and build the town.

The next year, 1788, Mason Co. was established, and nearby Washington was made the county seat. Washington's prominence was short-lived, however. Maysville grew after Mad Anthony Wayne's victory in northern Ohio at Fallen Timbers in 1794 largely eliminated the Indian threat. Another factor in Maysville's favor was its prime location on the river. By 1789, 30 flatboats were landing at the town each day. Although small, Maysville was seen by early travelers "as the most important landing place on the river."

The first paved (macadamized) road in Kentucky was completed on November 7, 1830, between Maysville and Washington. It later extended to Lexington (see **Maysville and Lexington Turnpike**), opening with six covered bridges and 13 tollhouses in 1835. The road had been the subject of national debate as Congress voted $150,000 in 1830 for its construction. During the congressional debate, U.S. senator Richard M. Johnson, a Kentuckian, called the Maysville road the most traveled in the nation other than roads on the East Coast. The road was a pet project of Henry Clay, who wanted to build the nation through internal improvements. However, President Andrew Jackson (1829–1837) vetoed the **Maysville Road Bill** because he considered the road an internal improvement that would benefit only one state.

Between 1810 and 1830 the population of Maysville grew sixfold to more than 2,000; by the end of the **Civil War**, its population was 4,700. In the 1820s steamboats largely replaced the flatboats. Maysville became the region's cultural and economical center, a status illustrated in many ways. In September 1824, Rev. **Alexander Campbell**, a founder of the Disciples of Christ denomination, preached in Maysville. When the great Choctaw chief Mingo Pusksbunnubbe died accidentally in Maysville in October 1824 on his way to the nation's capital, he was given a grand funeral here with full military honors. On May 21, 1825, the French general the Marquis de Lafayette visited, and merchants literally laid down red carpets for this hero of the Revolutionary War. Henry Clay was a frequent visitor as he traveled back and forth to Washington, D.C. In 1827, 2,500 people gathered for a dinner for Clay to show their support after he had been accused of a "corrupt bargain" that gave John Q. Adams the presidency. President Adams (1825–1829) was also given a warm welcome when he visited Maysville on November 4, 1843. When the parents of the future president Ulysses S. Grant (1869–1877) wanted to give their son the best education, they sent him to Maysville in fall 1836 to attend the Maysville Academy.

This prominence led to Maysville's incorporation as a city in 1833, and then in 1848 the Kentucky legislature moved the county seat to Maysville. An impressive Greek Revival building that had been built in 1845 became the county courthouse. As the community grew, so did its businesses, industry, and public institutions. Examples in the 1840s and 1850s included the Maysville Manufacturing Company, new gas and coal companies, ropewalks that made rope from the local hemp, and telegraph lines: one to Nashville, Tenn., and another to the north, passing through a cable laid under the waters of the Ohio River.

Maysville reflected the state and the nation in cultural and social issues in the antebellum period. The cholera epidemic in 1833 took the lives of both the first mayor of Maysville, Charles Wolfe, and Capt. John Langhorne, who had entertained famous individuals and others locally at his Eagle Tavern. There were several other cholera outbreaks during the 1840s and 1850s. Despite some anti-Catholic sentiment in the community, Irish and German immigration led to the establishment of a Catholic parish and the **St. Patrick Catholic Church** in 1847. The bank issue of the 1820s was played out locally, too: one of the controversial state branch banks had been established in the town in 1818, and the politician in the middle of the controversy, Kentucky governor Joseph Desha (1824–1828), was a resident of the county.

Like many Kentucky towns, Maysville's citizens were split on the issue of slavery. On the one hand, a slave who had bought his freedom, **Elisha Green**, established the **Bethel Baptist Church** in 1845 for the African American citizens of the community and continued as the church's pastor for 52 years. On the other hand, in the decades before the Civil War, a slave pen was located near the site of the first blockhouse built in Maysville. In 1838 an Ohio minister, John Mahan, was prosecuted in Maysville for helping slaves escape from Mason Co. Since it could not be established that Mahan had committed any crime in Kentucky, he was found not guilty. His actions were an example of **Underground Railroad** operations in the area. Meetings were held in Maysville in 1845 condemning Cassius Clay's Lexington newspaper the *True American* and those who helped slaves escape. On February 12, 1849, there was a meeting in the city to discuss the gradual emancipation of slaves.

Soon after the start of the Civil War, two Union camps were set up near Maysville, Camp Lee and Camp Kenton. Confederate general **John Hunt Morgan**'s men raided Maysville in 1862, 1863, and 1864. During the 1864 raid, James Conrad tried to cross the Ohio River for help and was killed. A former mayor of Maysville, William Casto, fought Col. Leonidas Metcalfe, a son of Kentucky's governor, in a duel on May 8, 1862, over Civil War issues. Casto had been imprisoned for his Southern sympathies and blamed Metcalfe for his arrest. The participants fought the duel in nearby Bracken Co. to escape Maysville's officials. Casto was killed in the fight (see **Casto-Metcalfe Duel**). When the Emancipation Proclamation was issued in January 1863, by President Abraham Lincoln, one Maysville Union Army officer and prominent citizen, Col. John C. Cochran, resigned his commission in protest.

African Americans have always constituted a significant part of the population in Maysville. They faced special challenges after the Civil War. Freed slaves who could not show evidence of having a job were subject to arrest. Local black minister Elisha Green responded to the tensions by staying in Maysville and fighting for civil rights. He was active in the state Republican Party. In 1883 he took a white man to court for physically abusing him when Green refused to give up his seat on the train while traveling from Maysville to Paris, Ky., to preach. Many talented African Americans left the city, however. **James Mundy**, for example, the son of a former slave, moved to Chicago in the 1920s and became one of the most famous choir directors in the nation. His choirs were invited to perform at the dedication of the Navy Pier and at the closing of the 1933 World Fair in Chicago. The worst manifestation of racism in this period was lynching. The public burning of Richard Coleman in 1899 in the city was so horrendous, with hundreds of participants, that it was condemned in the *New York Times*. By 2005 the percentage of blacks in Maysville was approximately 11.5, or around 1,000, a number that had decreased since 1865.

After the Civil War, the nation was becoming more industrial, but Maysville continued to be largely dependent on its surrounding agricultural base. The stockyards, for example, were located near the center of town well into the 1980s. The community did not attract immigrants, and the population of Mason Co., between 16,000 and 20,000, has been constant since 1870. The city of Maysville has increased in population (8,993 in 2000; 9,179 in 2006), although much of the increase was due to expansion of the city through annexation that has physically doubled the size of the city several times. Even the original county seat, Washington, was annexed in 1990.

Railways connecting Maysville to both Cincinnati and Lexington were completed after the Civil War and were frequently used by locals until the 1950s. The look of Maysville was altered in the 30 years leading up to the 20th century, as downtown businesses with three or four stories, cast-iron ornamentation, and upstairs apartments were constructed. In the second half of the 19th century, the County Clerk's Office, in Gothic Revival style; a jail, in the Second Empire style; a block that is largely Romanesque in character; and several fine examples of Italianate houses were built. Brick streets were laid in town and mule-drawn streetcars began service in 1883. Maysville suffered from significant floods in 1883 and 1884 (see **Flood of 1884**).

In 1901 a visitor to Maysville might have seen Mayor Tom Russell driving the first automobile in the town alongside the streetcars and horses and wagons. In the early 20th century major entertainers, such as John Philip Sousa and Buffalo Bill Cody, came to town, usually performing at the **Washington Opera House** on Second St. **Showboats** were frequent visitors. Local activist **Alice Lloyd** devoted her life to causes such as the fight of tobacco farmers against the trusts, temperance, and women's rights. Mary Wilson in 1908 donated the Hayswood Seminary for use as a hospital (see **Hayswood Hospital**). From 1907 to 1911 the executive branch of the State of Kentucky was in the hands of native Maysvillians Governor **Augustus E. Willson** (1907–1911) and Lieutenant Governor **William H. Cox** (1907–1911).

The Farmers and Tuckahoe tobacco warehouses opened in 1909 and 1910, respectively (see **Maysville Tobacco Warehouses**), reflecting the increasing importance of tobacco to Maysville. These were loose-leaf tobacco auction warehouses, only the second and third of the kind to be established anywhere. Maysville became the second-largest auction market for burley tobacco in the world and remained so until the changes in tobacco marketing that occurred in the 1990s. When the local radio station opened in 1948, founder James M. Finch traded an out-of-state radio station owner a country ham so he could obtain for the new station the call letters WFTM, which stood for "World's Finest Tobacco Market." Dozens of warehouses opened in the community, and a large tobacco-processing plant, Parker Tobacco, was once the community's largest employer.

Sports have been important to the people of Maysville. Beginning soon after pioneer times, racetracks for horses were laid out in the town. Forest Ave. was once named Race St., and Hillcrest Dr. has a circular shape because it once served as a horse track. In 1910 Maysville had a team in the Bluegrass Baseball League that featured Casey Stengel as a player. In 1925 the Maysville High School girls' basketball team won a state championship. A team led by legendary coach Earl Jones won the boys' state basketball championship in 1947. Also in Maysville, Coach John Fields coached the African American **John G. Fee Industrial High School** boys' basketball team to a state runner-up finish in 1952. Both of those schools eventually became part of **Mason Co. High School**, which captured the state basketball crown in 2003 and 2008. The people of Maysville did more than watch others participate in sports and sporting activities. From the 1890s until the 1930s, the Princess Roller Rink was a popular spot for skating and dances. City residents also had access to recreational baseball parks in the community and other community parks, including Beechwood Park, which has been in continual use since it opened in 1884. A number of golf courses opened, and the Country Club was established at its present location in 1925. Houseboat cruises and swimming in the Ohio River were also popular in the early 20th century.

The hard economic times that swept the nation during the 1930s commenced in the 1920s in Maysville, because of the community's agricultural economic base; the great **flood of 1937** exacerbated the hard times. Despite these conditions, in 1932 the city opened the **Simon Kenton Memorial Bridge** (a suspension bridge) across the Ohio River, ending the ferry service in Maysville that dated from the 1790s. A second bridge, the **William H. Harsha Bridge**, built in a cable-stay design, was dedicated in 2000. Maysville built a floodwall in the 1940s. Urban renewal in the 1960s destroyed some of the oldest buildings in the town. It was also during the 1960s that Maysville began to extend westward to the "top of the hill," and annexation followed. Institutions that moved away from the historic district downtown include the hospital and most health care providers, the consolidated school system, and most retail shopping. Industrial parks that opened along the **AA Highway**, constructed during the 1980s, contain many of the factories in the city.

Famous people who had a connection to Maysville and came to national prominence in the last half of the 20th century include **Nick Clooney**, a popular and respected newscaster in the Cincinnati area and other cities. He continues to write columns and books and is involved in community services throughout the region. **Rosemary Clooney** was simultaneously a movie star, a recording artist, and a television performer during the 1950s. She premiered her movie *The Stars Are Singing* on January 28, 1953, at the **Russell Theater** in Maysville. **Heather Renee French** became Miss America in 2000, and today she works for veterans' rights and writes children's books. **William Kenton**, a descendant of the pioneer Simon Kenton, was a rising star in Kentucky politics and was the Speaker of the Kentucky House of Representatives at the time of his death in 1981. **Lyda Lewis** was the first African American to become Miss Kentucky (1973) and afterward traveled with the USO in the Far East. **Stanley Forman Reed** was a justice on the U.S. Supreme Court that handed down the 1954 *Brown v. Board of Education* decision. He served on the Court from 1938 to 1957.

In 1977 East Kentucky Power built an electric generating facility, later annexed by Maysville, that provides stable employment and good wages to its employees in Maysville (see **Power Plants**). The state-of-the-art plant has been expanded several times and also attracted the Inland Container Corporation, which uses steam from the power plant to break down and reconstruct paperboard products. The Emerson Electric Company now operates the former **Browning Manufacturing** plant, which dates from 1886 and remains a large employer. **Maysville Community and Technical College**, now annexed into the city, has expanded its educational offerings significantly since 1995. Maysville is no longer tobacco-dependent, and agriculture has a reduced role in the local economy. Embracing the Ohio River, Maysville has introduced an opening in the floodwall and encouraged greater recreational use of the river. Now a regional hub for education, health care, and retail shopping, the community also publicizes its history and natural features to promote tourism.

Calvert, Jean, and John Klee. *Maysville, Kentucky: From Past to Present in Pictures.* Maysville, Ky.: Mason Co. Museum, 1983.

———. *The Towns of Mason County: Their Past in Pictures.* Maysville, Ky.: Maysville and Mason Co. Library Historical and Scientific Association, 1986.

Clift, G. Glenn. *History of Maysville and Mason County.* Lexington, Ky.: Transylvania, 1936.

Collins, Richard H. *History of Kentucky.* Vol. 1. Covington, Ky.: Collins, 1882.

Friend, Craig Thompson. *Along the Maysville Road: The Early Republic in the Trans-Appalachian West.* Knoxville: Univ. of Tennessee Press, 2005.

John Klee

MAYSVILLE ACADEMY. The Maysville Academy, Maysville, Ky., was also known as the Maysville Seminary. In 1829 a local contractor, Thomas D. Richardson, built the school's red brick building at 109 West Fourth St. in downtown Maysville. Two noted scholars, Jacob W. Rand and William W. Richeson, opened the school in 1830; they also served as instructors. In the beginning, Maysville Academy was an all-boys' school, but later it became coeducational. One of the school's teachers was **John Flavel Fisk**, who became a Kentucky state senator, representing Campbell and Kenton counties. Some well-known people educated at the Maysville Academy include U.S. president Ulysses S. Grant (1869–1877); Walter N. Haldeman, founder and president of Louisville's *Courier-Journal* newspaper; **William H. Wadsworth**, ambassador to Chile; John J. Crittenden, U.S. attorney general; **Thomas H. Nelson**, ambassador to Chile and Mexico; Gen. **William "Bull" Nelson**; **Henry Thomas Stanton**, Kentucky's poet laureate; and historian **Richard H.**

Collins, son of **Lewis Collins**, who authored the classic work *History of Kentucky.* The school's most illustrious student, Ulysses S. Grant, lived with his family in Georgetown, Ohio, as a young child but at age 14 was sent to live with his uncle, Peter Grant, in his uncle's home on Front St. in Maysville. Grant attended Maysville Academy during the school year 1836–1837.

William Richeson bought Jacob Rand's interest in the school in 1860 and continued to operate the Maysville Academy until 1868, when he took a position as principal of the Maysville High School, which had just opened. At that time he closed the Maysville Academy and sold the school's building. Over the years, the structure that had housed the school was used as a single-family and later as a two-family residence. Having deteriorated, the building was condemned in 1983. The City of Maysville took possession of it in early 1997. Several interested parties attempted to secure funding for restoration of the building, but none of these efforts were successful. Later in 1997 part of the front wall collapsed, and authorities decided to raze the structure. During demolition, a secret passageway containing a stash of alcohol was found under the building. Because the bottles had screw-on caps, it was determined that the alcohol was of recent vintage, not from the structure's early history. Some have speculated that the passageway may also have been used as part of the **Underground Railroad**.

"Grant's School to Fall," *KE,* December 22, 1997, C2.
"Historic School to be Razed," *KP,* December 19, 1997, 16A.
Kentucky Historical Society. "Kentucky Historical Marker Database." http://kentucky.gov/kyhs/hmdb/ (accessed January 25, 2007).
Reis, Jim, "Governor Was Torn by War," *KP,* August 18, 2003, 4K.
RootsWeb.com. "Walter H. Haldeman." www.rootsweb.com (accessed February 3, 2006).
"Schoolhouse Mystery," *KP,* December 24, 1997, A6.

MAYSVILLE AND LEXINGTON RAILROAD. At the end of the 18th century, Lexington was the major city west of the Appalachian Mountains. Unfortunately, though, it was not located on a navigable waterway. Goods coming from the east were transported overland to Wheeling, Va. (now W.Va.) and were taken from there by boat down the Ohio River to Limestone (Maysville), where they were reloaded onto wagons for travel over what became the **Maysville and Lexington** Turnpike to Lexington. Overland transportation was expensive and slow. Costs doubled for every 100 miles moved, and because wagons generally traveled at a speed of 12 miles per day, perishables could not be carried any appreciable distance.

By the mid-19th century, Cincinnati and Louisville had become important commercial centers of the West, at the expense of Lexington. In an attempt to regain its place as the leading city of the West, Lexington advanced the canalization of the Licking and Kentucky rivers and the development of railroads. Lexington promoted four railroads, each leading to the Ohio River: the Lexington and Ohio to Louisville, the **Covington and Lexington** (C&L) to Covington, the Lexington and Big Sandy to Catlettsburg, and the Maysville and Lexington (M&L) to Maysville.

The M&L began construction north from Lexington in 1854, meeting the C&L at Paris, where the C&L provided service to Covington beginning in December of that year. In March 1856 the Kentucky General Assembly permitted the C&L and the L&D (Lexington and Danville) railroads to use the name **Kentucky Central Railroad**. In 1858 Robert Bonner Bowler, a director of the Kentucky Central Railroad, persuaded the company to defer debt payment in order to make improvements on the line. A major creditor filed suit, and the railroad was sold at public auction. In 1865 the original stockholders filed suit against the heirs of Bowler but lost. In the same year, the C&L and the M&L were sold at a foreclosure sale and bought by the Kentucky Central Association, a holding company, which continued to operate the C&L and the M&L as separate entities. The revived M&L began laying track from Paris to Maysville that year; in March 1872, the first train from Maysville arrived at Paris. In 1875 the C&L and the M&L were merged as the Kentucky Central Railroad (KC). The M&L at this time consisted of two separate railroads, the line from Lexington to Paris and the road from Paris to Maysville. The KC, in turn, was sold to Collis P. Huntington in 1881 to provide a connecting route between two of his railroads, the **Chesapeake and Ohio Railroad** (C&O) on the east and the Chesapeake, Ohio, and Southwestern on the west. These railroads were part of his grandiose plan to build a seamless coast-to-coast rail system. Shortly after Huntington purchased the KC, his railroad empire went into receivership, and the KC was sold in 1891 to the **Louisville and Nashville Railroad** (L&N).

The L&N had aspirations for the Paris-to-Maysville line and built a large depot in Maysville (now the Maysville Police Department). Traffic, however, did not develop. When the C&O opened its line from Ashland to Lexington in 1895, after purchase of the Elizabethtown, Lexington, and Big Sandy Railroad, through traffic from the east to Lexington was switched to the more direct Ashland-Winchester-Lexington road. The Maysville section became solely dependent upon local traffic and limited to seasonal agricultural products. The building of the **Covington, Flemingsburg, and Pound Gap Railroad** (CF&PG) eastward from Flemingsburg Junction (along the M&L) in 1877 hinted at some future coal business for the M&L, but the CF&PG failed to extend eastward beyond Hillsboro.

In 1908 the L&N acquired the Frankfort and Cincinnati Railroad (F&C), which operated from Frankfort and Georgetown to Paris. The L&N planned to open a Louisville-to-Maysville service via that route, but the Kentucky Railway Commission ordered the L&N to divest itself of the F&C for antimonopoly reasons.

After **World War II**, the M&L was losing money. There was no through-line activity to sustain the line, and local business was switching to trucks. In 1951 its track between Lexington and Paris was abandoned, and in 1979 the L&N sold the Paris-to-Maysville track to **TransKentucky Transportation Railroad Inc.**, a modern short-line operator that uses it to haul Eastern Kentucky coal from its connection with the L&N and CSX's Covington-Corbin division at Paris to an Ohio River barge terminal at Maysville.

"First Railroad Trip to Paris," *Maysville Bulletin,* March 7, 1872, 3.
Herr, Kincaid A. *The Louisville & Nashville Railroad.* Lexington: Univ. of Kentucky Press, 1964.
Tenkotte, Paul A. "Rival Cities to Suburbs: Covington and Newport, Kentucky, 1790–1890," PhD diss., Univ. of Cincinnati, 1989.
Turner, Charles W. *Chessie Road.* Richmond, Va.: Garrett and Massie, 1956.

Charles H. Bogart

MAYSVILLE AND LEXINGTON TURNPIKE. The road between Maysville and Lexington dates to prehistoric times and has been an important transportation link ever since the time when Kentucky's first settlers traveled it. The road has also been at the center of local and national debate. Both prehistoric and historical animals, especially American bison, beat down a path or trace (see **Buffalo Traces**) from the Ohio River at Maysville to the salt springs at Blue Licks and then on to Central Kentucky. A large **Fort Ancient** village near Mayslick once flourished along the route, attesting to the path's early use. The Indian trail was called Alanant-O-Wamiowee, or the **Warrior Trail**, and used by American Indians into the historical period. The path was also used by early Kentucky explorers such as **Daniel Boone** and **Simon Kenton**. In the early pioneer period, the route from Limestone to the Licking River was also called Smith's Wagon Rd.

In the 1790s, Limestone (later Maysville) was the departure point for western settlers. Unless they traveled on down the Ohio River, their usual route in those early years was westward into Central Kentucky. The first stop was Washington, three miles from Limestone. It was a day's journey, because the first part of the trip was up a steep hill, and with livestock, belongings, and family, it was a difficult trip. Communities eventually sprang up along the road to Lexington. After Washington, Mayslick was the first substantial town along the route. Blue Licks was desired for the salt it provided pioneers, but later it developed into a substantial town anchored by a large spa. It attracted visitors from around the country in the mid-19th century. The next community was Ellisville, which was the county seat of Nicholas Co. until 1805. Millersburg came next, and then Paris, the county seat of Bourbon Co. These towns were approximately 10 miles apart along the route, and each eventually had a tollhouse on what became the Maysville and Lexington Turnpike.

The road was seen as key to the development of the western United States. Even before the National Road was built, Ebenezer Zane was concerned about the dependability of the Ohio River route from Wheeling, Va. (today, West Virginia), to

Limestone, and about access from there to the road to Lexington. When Congress in 1796 granted Zane's request to build an overland route, he began building a road (Zane's Trace) from Limestone to what became Zanesville, Ohio. This reduced the distance to Maysville from Wheeling by 100 miles and was not subject to difficult Ohio River conditions and the pirates who troubled travelers. When the National Road reached Wheeling in 1818, Maysville and points west were already connected by Zane's Trace. Some 19th-century cast-iron highway markers remain in Maysville, showing the directions to Zanesville, Lexington, and Nashville, Tenn.

Local residents understood the importance of the Maysville and Lexington Turnpike and continually made improvements. Mail had long traveled along the route, but in 1829, during the Andrew Jackson (1829–1837) administration, the road was made part of a mail system that connected it to the North, to the East Coast via the National Road, and to the South from Lexington all the way to New Orleans. The Maysville and Washington Turnpike Company was formed on January 29, 1829, and by November 1830 the road between those two cities had been paved, based on the principles espoused by John McAdam. The McAdam system, the preferred road system, was adopted throughout England and the United States in the 1800s. The road between Maysville and Washington was the first macadamized road in the West.

The turnpike company became the Maysville, Washington, Paris, and Lexington Turnpike Company and by 1835 had completed the road. It included six covered bridges and 13 tollgate houses. Henry Clay proposed that the national government should support this company by buying stock and thus completing this major internal improvement. The road was an important part of Clay's American System, and it was also a road that Clay traveled often on his journeys between Washington, D.C., and his hometown of Lexington. Congress passed the bill in 1830, because roads and canals were seen as central to the growth of the republic and worthy of national support. President Jackson, Clay's political enemy, used the **Maysville Road Bill** veto to make his point that the federal government should not support projects of a "local character." The message was sent that internal improvements were the responsibilities of the states, and this philosophy prevailed for a generation.

The Maysville and Lexington Turnpike, like most 19th-century roads, was kept in poor repair and was difficult to travel, particularly in winter. However travelers, settlers, teamsters with commercial goods, and slaves made the trek. Coffles of slaves were often seen moving in either direction, generally traveling after having been sold or going to a slave auction. By the 1890s, Kentucky citizens had become weary of paying tolls, and violence against the road system became so widespread it was termed the "tollgate wars." County governments, and later the state government, took over the highway and abolished the tolls. One of the last tollhouses was on the Nicholas Co. line near Millersburg.

Eventually the road was paved and the covered bridges replaced. However, the Maysville-to-Lexington road still essentially followed the original buffalo trace. It was thus a curvy, dangerous highway. Beginning in the 1950s, the state began making major improvements. By the 1970s, the old highway to Blue Licks had been replaced, often taking a slightly different route, bypassing the towns of Washington, Mayslick, and Blue Licks. Now called U.S. 68, the road was straighter with fewer hills. It had wide shoulders and passing lanes.

Two sections remained that had not been upgraded in the 1990s. The road from Paris north to a few miles out of Millersburg and the Paris Pk., between Paris and Lexington, had not been improved greatly. There was, however, a completed bypass around Paris. The Paris Pk. section was debated as opposition organized against improvements that would destroy historic rock fences, trees, and the beautiful vistas of the road. The debate raged from the 1960s until a new road was finished in 2003. That road included wooden guardrails, the protection of rock fences and plants wherever possible, and the building of new rock walls and bridges with rock facades. The four-lane highway also has grass shoulders and new plantings.

The road between Lexington and Maysville remains the link between northeastern and Central Kentucky. With its natural setting, limestone road cuts, horse farms, and attention paid to preservation, it is one of the most picturesque roadways in the country.

Friend, Craig Thompson. *Along the Maysville Road—The Early Republic in the Trans-Appalachian West*. Knoxville: Univ. of Tennessee Press, 2005.

"To Straighten Road," *KP*, February 21, 1931, 3.

John Klee

MAYSVILLE BRICK COMPANY. The Maysville Brick Company was located on the south bank of the Ohio River in Mason Co., about three miles southeast of the courthouse in Maysville. The *Maysville Daily Independent* reported in 1935 that John H. Hall, Sallie S. Hall, A. C. Sphar, and Elizabeth D. Sphar had organized the brick company in July 1894. However, the *Kentucky State Gazetteer and Business Directory for 1879–1880* included a listing for A. C. Sphar and Company, suggesting that the brickyard may have started some years earlier (see **Sphar Brick Company**). A. C. Sphar served as the firm's president, and John Hall was secretary and treasurer until his death in 1902. Initially, the company had $15,000 of capital stock. During the spring of 1912, Sphar sold the company to William H. Hall, son of John H. Hall, and G. J. Thomas, a son-in-law of John H. Hall, with Elizabeth Hall retaining one-half interest in the company. William Hall became president and general manager; Thomas served as secretary and treasurer. G. J. Thomas died in 1917, and another of William Hall's brothers-in-law, Howard Curtis, became secretary and assistant manager. In 1919 the Maysville Brick Company increased its stock capital to $35,000. By 1929 the thriving brickyard employed 40 men. Following the expiration of the original corporation, the company was incorporated again under the same name in 1947. Esther Curtis, Howard Curtis, Elizabeth Wells Hall, and Adella T. Wade owned this second corporation. The company completed its history under the leadership of Howard Curtis and his son Houston Curtis, ceasing operations sometime between 1955 and 1957.

The local Sanborn Insurance maps provide some insights into the Maysville Brick Company. In 1895 the company had four brick clamps, drying racks, a clay pit, and two structures housing the clay-mixing equipment and the engine room. The **Chesapeake and Ohio Railroad** transported the bricks produced by the company. By 1908 changes to the property included a fifth brick kiln, new drying racks, a brick machine, and an 80-horsepower engine. By 1914 a small building and a water tank had been added on the property. Initially, the company used a Henry Martin Wooden Brick machine, which produced about 25,000 bricks per day. By 1907 brick production was increased to 40,000 bricks per day by utilizing new equipment, and in 1917, 45,000 bricks were being made each day. Sometime after 1922, a stiff-mud brick machine was installed at the yard. By 1935 the cherry red bricks produced by the Maysville Brick Company were sold in Kentucky, Ohio, Indiana, Virginia, West Virginia, Tennessee, and North Carolina.

Two published historic photographs of the brickyard and its facilities provide a glimpse of the company during the 1920s and 1930s. The Kentucky Geological Survey first published a view of the brickyard in 1922, showing two of the updraft kilns, railroad cars, and structures next to the Ohio River in the background. The *Daily Independent* published another photograph in 1935 that reveals the addition of an office, a barn, and miscellaneous structures. In 1994 the surviving ruins included a standing kiln, remnants of three other kilns, the brickyard office, a barn, the clay pit, and an old steam shovel. The company produced the Maysville brand of bricks made by the soft-mud method (made in a mold). The last bricks produced at the yard were unmarked three-hole stiff-mud bricks (made from a column of stiff clay that was cut into bricks by wire).

The Maysville Brick Company was a major industry in Mason Co. and played an important role in supplying bricks to the building trades regionally. Although the company closed a half century ago, many of its bricks undoubtedly survive in historic structures that are still standing.

Hockensmith, Charles D., and M. Jay Stottman, "Investigations at the Maysville Brick Company: An Example of Industrial Archaeology in Kentucky," *Ohio Valley Historical Archaeology* 12 (1997): 89–111.

Ries, Heinrich. *The Clay Deposits of Kentucky: An Economic Consideration of the Pottery, Brick, and Tile Clays, Fire Clays, and Shales of Kentucky, with Notes on their Industrial Development*. Series 6, vol. 2. Frankfort, Ky.: Kentucky Geological Survey, 1922.

The Spirit of Greater Maysville and Mason County. Maysville, Ky.: Daily Independent, 1935.

Charles D. Hockensmith

MAYSVILLE COLONIZATION SOCIETY. The Maysville Colonization Society of Mason Co., which was active from at least 1822 to 1827, was associated with the state and national colonization societies. The group first met on December 26, 1822, in the Methodist Meeting House to "form a colonization Society in this place, auxiliary to the American Colonization Society of Washington City for the purpose of colonizing blacks of the United States on the Continent of Africa." Meetings were generally held in church meetinghouses, and Rev. John T. Edgar, one of the organizers, chaired the first meeting. Many prominent citizens were involved in the original group, including George Corwine, Peter Grant (the uncle of future U.S. president Ulysses S. Grant), William Grinstead, and Andrew Wood. Later members included **Lewis Collins**, a newspaper editor and an early Kentucky historian, and A. M. January. The Maysville Colonization Society met again two days after its first meeting and approved a constitution that stated the goal of raising money to pay for "the emigration and colonization of all people of colour who are willing to join the colony." Much of the local society's time was occupied with the administration of the group, although they also informed the public of their goals and raised money for their stated purpose. On February 23, 1824, the Maysville Colonization Society petitioned Henry Clay, a U.S. Senator from Kentucky, to support the congressional incorporation of the American Colonization Society.

In 1825 the group selected members to meet with the Marquis de Lafayette, if he were to stop in Maysville, and ask him to meet with the society. There is no record that such a meeting took place, but Rev. Edgar and Johnston Armstrong, members of the Maysville Colonization Society, were selected to be part of the welcoming committee for the French general. There is no evidence that the local society's efforts were very successful, despite the organization's efforts to have "the managers of the Society see and converse with free blacks in our town and neighborhood and show them the advantages resulting to them by their moving to the colony of Liberia."

Maysville Colonization Society Record Book, 1822–1827, Kentucky Gateway Museum Center, Maysville, Ky.

John Klee

MAYSVILLE COMMUNITY AND TECHNICAL COLLEGE. Part of the Kentucky Community and Technical College System (KCTCS) since 1997, Maysville Community and Technical College (MCTC) was founded in the late 1960s as Maysville Community College and enrolled students for the first time on August 27, 1968. Community colleges were popular innovations during the 1960s, created to meet the needs of the baby-boomer generation and specifically to increase opportunities in higher education. Kentucky was part of this trend in education, and in 1966 the Kentucky legislature named Maysville as a possible site for a community college. That decision, later confirmed by the University of Kentucky (UK), was partially attributable to the political influence of local state representative **Mitchell B. Denham**, who had close ties to Kentucky governor Edward Breathitt (1963–1967). From February through June 1966, more than $200,000 was raised for the new community college, and the Wood family's farm on U.S. 68 in the community of Washington, three miles south of downtown Maysville, was chosen as the specific site of the campus. Ground was broken for the school on November 15, 1967, with Governor Breathitt and UK president John Oswald in attendance. The Maysville Community College opened in 1968, at first holding its classes in church buildings downtown. The first director of the school was Dr. Charles T. Wethington, who was soon promoted to be head of Kentucky's community college system. Dr. James Shires was named the second director of the college in 1971 and held that post until 1996 (his title was changed to president in 1987). The first faculty member selected was Dr. Robert K. Berry; he taught chemistry and agriculture at the college for 30 years.

In the early history of the community college, most students at Maysville and throughout the state's community college system took liberal arts classes with the intention of transferring to colleges offering four-year degrees. The Associate in Applied Science (AAS) programs quickly grew, though; graduates of these two-year programs generally went immediately into the workforce with skills in their chosen field of study. The first AAS programs offered were in agricultural and secretarial studies, and the associate degree in nursing followed in 1972. Other programs were added in subsequent years. The Kentucky Postsecondary Education Improvement Act of 1997 created KCTCS and organized the community and technical colleges in the state into one system. Maysville Community College then began to offer diplomas and certificates in dozens of technical areas, while continuing to grant two-year degrees.

In 1983 a building named for Representative Denham was added to the school's campus. Off-campus classes began to be offered during the 1980s in Vanceburg, Flemingsburg, and other nearby communities. An official off-campus site developed in Cynthiana in 1988, and a permanent building was opened there in 2002. In 1992 a student center was added to the campus in Maysville and named for Mrs. C. C. Calvert, an early proponent of the college, a noted local historian, and the chair of the school's Board of Directors from the college's beginning in 1967 into the 1990s. In 2003 a 45,000-square-foot technical center was added to the Maysville campus. With its four attached buildings, the Maysville facility now totals 145,000 square feet.

In 2004 Rowan Technical College in Morehead and Maysville Community College were merged, and the resulting college officially became Maysville Community and Technical College. MCTC, through an agreement with the Kentucky Department of Corrections, also oversees the educational programs at the Eastern Kentucky Correctional Complex near West Liberty.

The total enrollment of MCTC's multiple campus sites had grown to more than 3,600 by 2007. MCTC was a leader in incorporating technical offerings into its curriculum during the late 1990s and was a pioneer in the use of distance learning. Following Dr. Shires's long tenure as the school's leader, Dr. Hans Kuss served as president from 1998 to 2000, and Dr. Augusta Julian was named president in 2001.

The Maysville college's basic goals since its beginning have been to provide college courses for those wishing to transfer afterward for further studies and for those who want to learn a particular skill to enter the workforce, to provide continuing education for the community, and to train students for jobs in businesses and industry. Partner four-year colleges have offered programs leading to BAs beginning in 2000, largely through classes held on the weekends. MCTC also sponsors and cosponsors events such as health fairs, plays, lectures, pageants, art shows, and musical performances. The faculty and staff of MCTC serve the community as science fair judges, speakers, experts in specific fields, and in many other such service capacities.

Maysville Community and Technical College. www.maycc.kctcs.edu/ (accessed January 5, 2006).

John Klee

MAYSVILLE COUNTRY CLUB. The Maysville Country Club, located on U.S. 68 South in Mason Co., was established in 1925 as a private country club. The club actually began as the Edgefield Club on Maple Leaf Rd. in Mason Co. near the current **AA Highway**. Dues were $50 a year and the Edgefield Club's first president was J. Barbour Russell (see **Russell Theater**). The Edgefield Club had a nine-hole golf course that closed in 1925. Afterward, it was reconstituted and renamed Maysville Country Club. Another nine-hole course was built in 1927 at the Maysville Country Club's current location, and in 1993 nine more holes were added. The club has a swimming pool and tennis courts as well, and its membership typically numbers 200–250. It is now a semiprivate club with restaurant and bar facilities and hosts several banquets and weddings during the year. A major fire in 1959 destroyed much of the country club's kitchen facilities.

Maysville Country Club's annual Chippeways three-day golf invitational tournament is the golfing highlight of each season. Its 70th Chippeways Golf Tournament was in 2005, and the club has been hosting a Junior Chippeways Golf Tournament for more than 40 years. One of its junior golfers, Mark Blakefield, went on to play college golf at the University of Kentucky at Lexington, earning All-South Eastern Conference Second Team honors during his senior year, in 2005.

"Maysville Country Club." www.thegolfcourses.net (accessed June 26, 2006).

Rains, Laura. "Greener Pastures," *Maysville Ledger Independent*, July 15, 2005.

Dennis W. Van Houten

MAYSVILLE HIGH SCHOOL. The Maysville High School, in Maysville, provided for the educational needs of adolescents from the end of the **Civil War** until 1991, when the school was consolidated into **Mason Co. High School**. Before Maysville High School was started, there were private academies in the city, such as the Rand and Richeson School, also called the **Maysville Academy** (for boys), the Maysville Collegiate Institute, and the **St. Francis de Sales Academy** (for girls).

In November 1864 the Maysville High School was established in what was called Neptune Hall at the corner of Market and Fourth Sts. in Maysville, and classes began in 1865 with 29 students; Professor Andrew January Grundy was the school's first principal. The first four diplomas were awarded in 1876. Two years later, the senior class included 10 girls and 10 boys, but only the girls graduated; the boys refused to take their exams. Mollie Blanchard Owens was a member of that class. A new building was built on the same site in 1879. The Maysville school system was further organized in the first decade of the 20th century, when the position of city superintendent was established and a building program planned. A result of the building program was that a large high school was built on the corner of Limestone and Second Sts. and dedicated on May 14, 1908. This was the location of the first building in Limestone (Maysville's earlier name), close to the mouth of Limestone Creek. The 1908 structure served as the Maysville High School until 1991.

A bond issue passed in 1928 resulted in the building of an auditorium and a gym for the Maysville High School and the construction of the **John G. Fee Industrial High School** for African American high school students. Before the gym was built, the basketball court was on the top floor of the school. Maysville High School provided a diverse curriculum that over the years was adjusted to meet changing needs. Extracurricular activities included a variety of sports, music, and academic clubs. The students and the community had a strong interest in basketball, and Maysville's boys' and girls' basketball teams were known throughout the state. In 1926 Coach Flossie Jones led the girls' basketball team to a state championship; boys' basketball teams, coached by Earle D. Jones, won the state championship in 1947 and took second place in the state in 1938 and 1948. Maysville High School's colors were black and gold, and its mascot was the bulldog. When the John G. Fee Industrial High School was integrated into Maysville High School beginning in 1956, teachers as well as students became part of an integrated system. During the first year of integration, the high school's enrollment stood at 578. In 1962 an addition to the school provided art, music, and office facilities. In 1960 Mason Co. High School was opened, consolidating the remaining high schools in the county, except for Maysville High School, which remained separate until 1991. The school districts in Maysville were long established, but housing, business, and industry shifted from the old downtown area to the suburbs "on the hill" over the next decades. This caused both declining enrollment and a reduced tax base for the Maysville City Schools, including the high school. In the 1970s, the John G. Fee Industrial High School had become a junior high, and in 1983 it was closed and the Maysville High School became the Maysville Junior-Senior High School. In 1990 the Maysville Independent and Mason Co. school boards voted to consolidate the schools; the last graduating class of Maysville High School was 1991. The City of Maysville bought the high school building and sold it to Classic Properties of Covington in 1994. That firm converted the building into apartments maintaining the look of the school. The auditorium, the 1962 addition, and the high school's gym continue to be used by the Mason Co. school district.

Lyda Lewis, a Maysville High School graduate of 1966, was the first African American to become Miss Kentucky (1973).

American Association of University Women (Maysville Branch). *From Cabin to College: A History of the Schools of Mason County.* Maysville, Ky.: G. F. McClanahan, 1976.

"Maysville Schools to Integrate," *KTS*, September 3, 1956, 4A.

"Maysville's Surprising Foes," *KP*, October 4, 1974, 10K.

"Old School May House Apartments," *KP*, January 11, 1994, 7K.

Reis, Jim. "Changing Times Bypassed Schools," *KP*, June 15, 1952, 4K.

John Klee

MAYSVILLE HISTORIC BUILDINGS. Many historic private and public buildings, especially dating from the 19th century, remain in Maysville, one of Kentucky's earliest communities. A few structures still survive from earliest times, including the original log houses known as Bickley's Station and the Canebrake. These are mostly in Washington, a town annexed by Maysville in 1990.

On the corner of Market and Second Sts. in downtown Maysville, a log house called the Reverend Martin house dates from 1800. The log structure has been covered with other facing materials, but inside, the original doors are in use and the log infrastructure retains its bark. This is the oldest building standing from early downtown Maysville. A log house and tavern built around 1795, known as the Newdigate-Reed house, sits atop the hill on the Buffalo Trace. The structure, which now belongs to the City of Maysville, served as a tavern and inn for early travelers and later became the home of U.S. Supreme Court justice **Stanley Reed** when he visited his home county.

In the 19th century, the prosperity of Maysville and its citizens was manifested in many of the buildings in use today. Dr. Charles Shackelford, who provided medical care to both Union and Confederate soldiers during the **Civil War**, improved the front section of a 1790s house on Fourth St. in a classical Federal style during the 1820s. The second mayor of Maysville, W. B. Phillips (or Philips), began construction of his home at Third and Market Sts. in 1825, and then, according to legend, ran out of money. The project came to be called "Phillip's Folly." Finally, after a successful gambling trip to New Orleans, Phillips was able to complete the large Greek Revival house in 1831. In the same year, along W. Third St., the renowned educator John Richeson finished his Greek Revival home. **Rosemary Clooney** later lived there, and it is now known as her home; it sits at the head of the street renamed for her in the 1950s. Kentucky historian **Lewis Collins**, the editor of the *Maysville Eagle,* built his impressive Greek Revival home overlooking the Ohio River at Third and Short Sts. in 1834. It was later used as the First District School, then as a funeral home, and again served as a private residence in the 1950s. The brothers Peter and **Henry Lee** enlarged the 1798 hotel at Front and Sutton Sts. in the 1840s. The **Lee House** entertained many important guests, including Henry Clay, who stayed there several times. The A. M. January House, a long structure, as befits its lot, was built in 1838 on Third St. It has been passed down to the eldest female descendant of the family since that time. The house features descending parapets, a common decorative feature in the town. Because of the town's narrow lots, homes in the community also often had long side porches.

The early 1800s saw the building of many row houses in Maysville. On W. Second St. are the row houses built by John Armstrong during the 1820s, believed to be for workers in his various businesses, including the nearby **cotton mill** he owned. One of the homes was deeded to a plasterer, revealing that Armstrong traded one of these houses for plasterwork on the rest. Along Third St. are several sets of row houses built from the 1820s to the 1840s. Near the Lewis Collins house are several of the oldest row homes, simple in their design. Across from the post office are the row houses of Benjamin, James, John, and Lewis Jacobs, called Jacobs' Row. The Jacobses, plow manufacturers, were able to afford these larger row houses, which also have undergone many changes and have had decorative features added over the years. What is called Mechanics Row, built during the 1840s on Third St. near the center of town, has decorative iron fences, porches, and other features said to have been influenced by the architecture of New Orleans. Other extant examples of early row houses can be seen on Limestone St.

The Maysville City Hall was built in 1845 and became the Mason Co. Courthouse in 1848. Built on a narrow lot, it is a classic three-story Greek Revival building with Doric columns two stories tall and a clock tower. It was the center for law, politics, and county administration for a century and a half. Other important meetings were held in this building, even church services such as a 1925 revival sponsored by the **Bethel Baptist Church**. Nearby is the house of silversmith Pleasant Baird, which dates from 1817 and is now the sheriff's office. In 1850 the Maysville Presbyterian Church, next to the courthouse, opened services in the same building used today. The year before, Maysville's Church of the Nativity began services for the Episcopalians in the Tudor Gothic–style church on Third St.

A house on W. Fourth St. at the head of Sutton St. is the location of the **Underground Railroad** Museum. Carriage maker Jonathan Bierbower built it in 1847. The large house, with two-story porches that run across its entire front, was also the home of Col. Frederick Bierbower, who was with the Perry expeditionary group that opened up Japan. Oral history has linked the Bierbower House and Phillip's Folly to the Underground Railroad as safe houses.

The Gothic Revival style was less popular than other styles in Maysville, but the County Clerk's Office, built in 1860, is one example of this style. The iron doors and shutters provide unique styling and safety for the building. Above the doors, also in iron, is a representation of Justice holding scales. The late 19th century saw a boom of building in town, with much variety, and many of the structures are still standing. In 1881 a library building was erected on Sutton St.; a second floor was added later in that decade, and a new facade matching the original architecture was built in 1976. Beginning then, the building, which has round-topped windows extending from floor to ceiling and an open floor plan, housed the Mason Co. Museum, now renamed the **Kentucky Gateway Museum Center**. Around the corner on Third St., a new jail was finished in 1882 in the French Empire style, complete with a Mansard roof and appropriate window treatments. It is currently used for state offices. In 1898 the **Washington Opera House** on W. Second St. was rebuilt in the Renaissance Revival style with an intricate brick design. This theater is the fifth-oldest operating theater in the nation.

Throughout the business district of the town, two-, three-, and four-story buildings, many of them featuring iron treatments around the doors and windows, were constructed during the late 1800s for businesses, warehouses, and living quarters. On Second St., the Zweigart block, which was remodeled in 1884, is an example of the business buildings that lined Front, Market, and Second Sts. The four-story Russell building, constructed in 1892, was the headquarters of a warehouse grocery business and has been a landmark with many uses since. Another four-story brick structure from the same time period stands on Market and Second Sts. A painted sign on the Market St. side of the building advertises the J. Wesley Lee Clothing and Tailoring business, which was housed there around 1900. The Glascock building, whose door opens onto Market and Second Sts., was new at that time and housed the First National Bank. There are dozens of examples of 19th-century business buildings in downtown Maysville, most in a good state of repair.

Fraternal organizations built many of their lodges in this time period, with beautiful results. The most impressive is the Masonic Temple (see **Masons**), built by future Kentucky lieutenant-governor William Cox in 1886 on the southeast corner of Market and Second Sts. It featured a large ballroom where colored light filtered through the round stained-glass window when the Masons held their initiations. The rest of the building was used for apartments and businesses, including, for a time, the post office and Kilgus' Drug, which had a popular soda fountain. On the outside of this Richardsonian Romanesque–style stone building are gargoyles, towers, and the symbols of Masonry around the stained glass. The DeKalb lodge on Third St. also features Masonic symbols in stone, and another lodge building still stands on lower Sutton St. On Market St., in 1915, the Ringgold Lodge was finished with a facade that features Italianate-style windows and a striking use of colors.

Private homes were designed in a variety of styles in the 19th century. In 1848, along the Fleming Rd., John Dobyns built a two-story octagonal house called Glen Alice. A house called Buffalo Trace overlooked Maysville from the top of a hill on the Buffalo Trace Rd. This 16-room Gothic Revival house was finished in 1862. Nearby on the same road is Point au View, an 1860 Italianate house that features a three-story tower in the center and distinctive arched windows. The 1888 Cox-Russell house, a few doors down from the Cox building, is also in the Romanesque style and has a turret decorated with seashells. At 128 W. Third St. is the 1880 Queen Anne–style home of Mayor **Rebekah Hord**, who in the 1950s was Kentucky's first woman mayor. In this house she entertained Justice Stanley Reed and Chief Justice Earl Warren of the U.S. Supreme Court. In 1888 Cox built a set of seven row houses on upper Market St., which alternate features and go by the nicknames of the days of the week. They and several other homes in the vicinity are Queen Anne style with a mix of other influences.

Several churches were built in this period. The 1876 Maysville Christian Church on Third St. was restored in 2006 (see **First Christian Church, Maysville**). The **First Baptist Church** on Market St., built in 1886, was the third and last built on the site. The Scott United Methodist Church on Fourth St. was built by its African American congregation with their own hands in 1884. In 1909 Roman Catholics finished their second church on a site at Second and Limestone Sts. in the Gothic style. It featured large stained-glass windows depicting St. Patrick and St. Boniface, the patrons of the many Irish and German immigrants in the congregation.

Maysville growth slowed at the beginning of the 20th century, and when it resumed at the end of the century, it was focused on the "top of the hill," away from the traditional downtown area. The result was that few of the older buildings were destroyed. Some historic building activity did occur in the first decades of the 20th century. Both the **Louisville and Nashville Railroad** and the **Chesapeake and Ohio Railroad** depots remain, as well as the "new" C&O depot, which opened in 1918. A post office still in use was built in 1905. The loose-leaf tobacco auction system began in the teen years of the century in Maysville, and eventually there were more than 20 tobacco warehouses in the city, some impressive brick buildings. Many of them remain today, although the tobacco floor auction system has nearly disappeared. A large three-story tobacco manufacturing and processing plant that started in 1913 stands empty on Forest Ave. It once housed R. J. Reynolds and later the Parker Tobacco Company. Factories, including Browning's (see **Browning Manufacturing/Ohio Valley Pulley Works**) and Wald's, were expanded throughout the 20th century and are still in business in what is called the east end of Maysville.

In downtown Maysville, the new **Hayswood Hospital** opened on Fourth St. in 1925 and served as the city's hospital until 1983. Montgomery Ward built an impressive Art Deco–style building in 1928 that still displays the symbol of progress in the tiles at the top of the building (see **Department Stores**). The **Russell Theater**, whose tiles, colors, and decorative features make it hard to characterize, was completed in 1929. Its style is Moorish; inside, the lights in the ceiling represented the stars. At age three Rosemary Clooney gave her first on-stage performance at the Russell Theater, and she later premiered her movie *The Stars Are Singing* there in 1953.

Many other historic buildings existed in Maysville and have been lost. When Front St. buildings were destroyed in the 1960s urban renewal period, residents interested in historic preservation mobilized. Most historic buildings have been saved since that time, often with private-public partnerships.

Calvert, Jean, and John Klee. *Maysville, Kentucky: From Past to Present in Pictures*. Maysville, Ky.: Mason Co. Museum, 1983.

John Klee

MAYSVILLE ROAD BILL. The proposed Maysville Road Bill was legislation pushed by Henry Clay and the National Republicans in 1830, stipulating that the federal government would subscribe $150,000 to the Maysville, Washington, Paris, and Lexington Turnpike Company (see **Maysville and Lexington Turnpike**) for the macadamizing of the dirt highway from Washington, Ky., to Lexington. The Maysville-to-Washington section of the road, approximately four miles, had been completed already in 1830. The bill passed the U.S. Senate on May 15, 1830, by a vote of 24 to 18, having previously passed the U.S. House of Representatives by a vote of 102 to 84. Senators Daniel Webster and John Rowan were among the bill's supporters. Other than the congressmen from Kentucky, representatives from the South gave the bill almost no support. President Andrew Jackson (1829–1837) vetoed the bill on May 27, 1830, and efforts to override the veto failed.

The Maysville Rd. was already connected through Ohio to the National Rd. at Zanesville, Ohio. It was the stepping-off point for many settlers who came west down the Ohio River and moved from Maysville along the route into the interior of Kentucky. The Maysville Road Bill was part of Clay's program called the American System, an effort to help the nation prosper from government support of business and internal improvements. For Clay, an improved Maysville Rd. was a bonus since he traveled the route often between Washington, D.C., and his home in Lexington. Support for the road in the areas it would cover in Kentucky was strong. In April more than $30,000 in stock had been sold at Paris, Ky., and more than $30,000 in other communities on the road's path. In the U.S. Congress, many felt that supporting this project would encourage development of similar local-interest projects around the country.

From Jackson's perspective, there were several reasons to veto the measure. Doing so gave him an opportunity to state his position that the federal government should not fund internal improvements that do not clearly benefit all the people. He also simply stated that the bill was unconstitutional; it was his "conviction that Congress does not possess the power, under the Constitution, to pass such a law." For example, the federal government was not empowered by the Constitution to take money from the national treasury and give up jurisdiction by turning it over to the states. Jackson proposed instead that, in the event of a surplus, moneys should be proportionally appropriated to the states. Jackson was also able to use the veto to strike a blow against his political enemy Henry Clay. U.S. secretary of state Martin van Buren largely authored the veto message. Public meetings protesting Jackson's veto were held in Kentucky.

The Maysville Road Bill was the center of a national debate on the power of government and the direction of the federal government. A first-class road between Maysville and Lexington, in Clay's opinion, would benefit the entire country. It would facilitate commerce, trade, and even national defense and thus deserved the support of the national government. Jackson's position was the one that prevailed, however. Because the Maysville Rd. was totally within the confines of a single state, he believed it did not deserve federal support. Also, in his strict-constructionist viewpoint, the Constitution did not allow for such support. This view of the role of the national government dominated national thinking up to the **Civil War**. It left internal improvements in the hands of the states. It also permanently stymied the development of the section of Kentucky that lay along the proposed road's path. No first-class highway between Maysville and Lexington has ever been completed.

Collins, Richard H. *History of Kentucky*. Vol. 1. Covington, Ky.: Collins, 1882.

Friend, Craig Thompson. *Along the Maysville Road: The Early Republic in the Trans-Appalachian West*. Knoxville: Univ. of Tennessee Press, 2005.

Kleber, John E., ed. *The Kentucky Encyclopedia*. Lexington: Univ. Press of Kentucky, 1992.

Library of Congress. *A Century of Lawmaking for a New Nation: U.S. Congressional Documents and Debates, 1774–1875*. Register of Debates, 21st Congress, 1st session. http://memory.loc.gov/ (accessed September 23, 2006).

John Klee

MAYSVILLE TOBACCO WAREHOUSES. Maysville, in Mason Co., is a tobacco town. Despite tobacco's decreasing popularity in recent years, the crop remains a staple among Maysville farmers. Accounts of smoking tobacco date to the 1500s when Amerigo Vespucci recorded its use by American Indians. **White burley tobacco** is the type grown in Mason Co. Once burley was brought to the Maysville area, farmers realized very quickly that it grew well in the fertile, limestone soil of the bluegrass region. By the late 1800s, farmers in Mason, Fleming, and Bracken counties were producing more tobacco than anywhere else in the nation.

Not only is growing tobacco a long-standing tradition in Maysville, but also the warehouses where tobacco is auctioned and sold have a special place in the city's history. With the rapidly increasing production of tobacco in the late 1700s and early 1800s came construction of the first tobacco warehouses in northeastern Kentucky. By order of the Virginia legislature, the Limestone Warehouse was built in Mason Co., in 1787. (Maysville was not yet a city then, and the territory that became Kentucky was a county of Virginia.) The Limestone Warehouse later was called Farmers and then Independent No. 2. Independent No. 2 no longer houses tobacco but is rented out to a manufacturing company.

Through the years, Maysville has ranked second in the world, behind Lexington, as the leading burley tobacco market. Many farmers have traveled from Eastern Kentucky, and some from even greater distances, such as from West Virginia, Indiana, Mississippi, and Kansas, to sell their tobacco at warehouses in Maysville. In 1912 the largest tobacco warehouse in the world, the Home Tobacco Warehouse, was built in Maysville. The 1933 harvest saw tobacco arriving from six different states. By 1974 Maysville had 14 warehouses, where 23.3 million pounds of tobacco were sold. Just nine years later, in 1983, Maysville sold 49 million pounds in 18 different warehouses. During their heyday, tobacco warehouses featured the chanting of auctioneers as buyers traveled down the rows where burley leaves filled the floors.

The sale of tobacco in Maysville has decreased dramatically, from 503 million pounds in 1997 to 95 million in 2001. The switch to contracts with cigarette companies and large quota cuts are mainly to blame for this massive decrease. Also, the negative connotation that smoking has developed over the years has damaged tobacco's reputation, forcing many farmers to rely on alternative crops. Farmers have endeavored to grow different crops with the aid of the Master Tobacco Settlement and with help from extension offices.

Of the 31 tobacco warehouses grouped around Maysville, only 5 were being used for tobacco in 2004. Two of those are running under contracts, and the other three still conduct auctions. Finding new ways to use these rundown, empty warehouses has been a challenge for city officials in Maysville. Many warehouses are rented to manufacturing companies, others are sitting empty, and some are facing demolition. With purchasers buying directly, there is not much need for these facilities.

Alexander, John. "Maysville Ranked Second among Kentucky Markets," *Maysville Ledger Independent*, November 24, 1974.

Coutant, Betty. "Bills Related to Tobacco Moving in Statehouse," *Maysville Ledger Independent*, February 28, 2001.

Fryman, Virgil. "Maysville Leaf Market First," *Maysville Ledger Independent*, October 26, 1960.

"Kentucky Expansion," *Maysville Ledger Independent*, Tobacco ed., November 20, 1986.

Maysville Centennial Exposition Commission. *As We Look Back: Maysville, 1833–1933*. Maysville, Ky.: Daily Independent, 1933.

Peterson, Bill. Interview by Heather Gulley, December 7, 2004, Maysville, Ky.

The Spirit of a Greater Maysville and Mason County. Maysville, Ky.: Daily Independent, 1930.

"Warehouses Built in 1783," *Maysville Ledger Independent*, Tobacco ed., 1974.

Heather Gulley

McARTHUR, JAMES MADISON (b. January 3, 1810, Georgetown, Ky.; d. February 10, 1900, Dayton, Ky.). James McArthur, a legislator, developer, and city official, was the son of Peter and Mary Michie Tomkins McArthur. James's father, a surveyor, was employed to locate land warrants for veterans of the **Revolutionary War**. As payment for his services, he was given part of the land he surveyed, and by this means he acquired vast amounts of real estate. The family moved to Newport in 1815, where James was educated in the best private schools of the day. He then entered Centre College at Danville, Ky., at age 15, but remained there just one year, preferring to pursue a business career. After his father died on July 21, 1828, James took over management of his father's holdings and managed the estate. He married Mary J. Stricker on March 28, 1837, and they had seven children. McArthur began investing in real estate and soon became one of the largest landowners in Campbell Co. He was responsible for much of the early development of Newport, where he built numerous homes and businesses. He was elected a magistrate in 1833, and he served as president of the Newport City Council for 10 years. He entered into a partnership with James Berry and Henry Walker in 1848 to plat and develop the city of Jamestown (now part of Dayton, Ky.). McArthur moved there, where he served as president of the Jamestown City Council for eight years. He was responsible for extending the street railway from Newport to Jamestown, encouraging the development of that area. McArthur also played a key role in the creation of the Newport Safety Fund Bank and served as its president from 1852 to 1856. Because he was so generous in the granting of loans, the bank eventually failed. He was twice elected to the Kentucky House of Representatives, once in 1846 and again in 1873. While serving as a legislator, he sponsored a number of consumer-protection laws, such as the Mechanic's Lien Law, the Cemetery Act, and a law authorizing the taxing of real estate to fund the public school system. James and Mary McArthur had been happily married for 56 years when she died on April 6, 1893. James died in 1900 and was buried in the Evergreen Cemetery in Southgate.

The Biographical Cyclopedia of the Commonwealth of Kentucky. Chicago: John M. Gresham, 1896.
The Biographical Encyclopedia of Kentucky. Cincinnati: J. M. Armstrong, 1878.
Campbell County Kentucky 200 Years: 1794–1994. Alexandria, Ky.: Campbell Co. Historical and Genealogical Society, 1994.

McBRIDE, JAMES (date and place of birth unknown; d. 1791, Fayette Co., Ky.). According to John Bradford, the distinguished editor of the *Kentucky Gazette,* in 1754 James McBride and others came down the Ohio River in canoes and landed at the mouth of the Kentucky River, "where they marked on a tree, the initials of their names and the date of the year." The tree with the carved initials could be seen in Port William (Carrollton) as late as 1784. Thus, McBride became one of the earliest Anglo-Colonial explorers of Kentucky, along with Dr. Thomas Walker in 1750, Christopher Gist in 1750, Capt. James Smith in 1766, and John Finley in 1767–1769.

In April 1779 McBride joined Robert Patterson and several men from the fort at Harrodsburg, Ky., to construct the first permanent settlement at what became the city of Lexington. In January 1780 McBride purchased Outlot H, five acres on Mulberry St. between Second and Short Sts. in the original town plat of Lexington. He also owned land in other parts of Kentucky.

In August 1782 McBride fought at the **Battle of Blue Licks**. He survived and settled on his farm along the South Elkhorn Creek. Apparently, he died in 1791. His estate was entangled in suits and countersuits for the next 10 years; such land-interference claims were prevalent in the settling of Kentucky.

"Battle of Blue Licks," *RKHS* 47, no. 158 (January 1949): 247–49.
Samuel Mackay Wilson Papers, 1871–1946, Special Collections, King Library, Univ. of Kentucky, Lexington, Ky.
Staples, Charles R. *The History of Pioneer Lexington, 1779–1806.* Lexington: Univ. of Kentucky Press, 1939.
Stipp, G. W., comp. *John Bradford's Historical Notes on Kentucky from the Western Miscellany.* 1827. Reprinted by John Wilson Townsend, San Francisco: Grabhorn Press, 1932.

Diane Perrine Coon

McCARTHY, AILEEN (b. September 19, 1886, Covington, Ky.; d. January 25, 1982, Fort Wright, Ky.). Aileen McCarthy, the third daughter of Jeremiah and Cordelia Lambert McCarthy, taught private art lessons from her home on 21st St. in Covington. While public and private schools offered art lessons to students in the Peaselburg area of Covington, it was more prestigious to attend McCarthy's private lessons. McCarthy began drawing as a child and studied under Sister Josina Whitehead at **La Salette Academy**. When she graduated from La Salette in 1905, she continued her education at the Cincinnati Art Academy, where she won scholarships and was tutored by **Frank Duveneck.** She also studied under sculptor **Clement Barnhorn**, artist George Elmer Browne, and landscape artist Emile Gruppe of Gloucester, Mass.

McCarthy taught at La Salette from 1915 to 1923; she opened her own studio in 1927 in her home and continued to teach at 321 W. 21st St. until 1974. Two of her better-known students are Bernard Schmidt, who was a celebrated artist in his own right and served as chair of the art department at **Thomas More College**, and Marlene Von Handorf Steele, a distinguished pastel artist who followed McCarthy's example by attending the Cincinnati Art Academy and teaching at various local schools in addition to giving art lessons from her own home studio on Oliver St. in Cincinnati. McCarthy was best known as a portrait artist; her subjects included her well-regarded teacher Frank Duveneck. She is best remembered, however, as a teacher who helped young artists to see more clearly and thus paint more realistically.

The Covington Deanery Diocesan Council of Catholic Women honored McCarthy in 1975, and she was named a Kentucky Colonel. In 1976 she was awarded a Medallion by La Salette Academy, along with two other prominent citizens: Dr. **J. E. Randolph**, the first African American physician on staff at St. Elizabeth Hospital (see **St. Elizabeth Medical Center**), and **Mary Moser**, who founded the Catholic Social Services (see **Catholic Charities**) in 1948. These recognitions show how treasured she was by the community.

An active member of her community, McCarthy was president of the La Salette Alumnae Association, which was formed in 1931. She presided over teas and organized rummage sales as fundraisers for the school. She was also an active member of the Cincinnati Women's Art Club. When she was no longer able to live on her own, she moved to **St. Charles Care Center**, but she did not stop drawing. She was known at St. Charles for the sketches she drew as long as she could move a pencil to form the images she could barely see. She died at the St. Charles facility in 1982 and was buried at Highland Cemetery, Fort Mitchell.

Aileen McCarthy, ca. 1970.

"Aileen McCarthy, Last Art Student of Frank Duveneck," *KP,* January 25, 1982, 8B.
"Former Pupil of Duveneck," *KTS,* March 18, 1919, 4.
"Society—Covington," *KP,* January 12, 1931, 4; January 16, 1931, 4; April 11, 1931, 4; November 17, 1939, 4.
"Three Receive LaSalette Recognition," *CE,* February 19, 1976, D1.

Katherine Meyer

McCLANAHAN, EDWARD POAGE "ED" (b. 1932, Brooksville, Ky.). Author Ed McClanahan, best known for his novel *The Natural Man* and his writings for *Esquire, Playboy,* and *Rolling Stone* magazines, is the only child of Edward L. and Jessie Poage McClanahan. The family moved to Maysville in 1948, and McClanahan graduated from Maysville High School in 1951. He attended Washington and Lee University, Lexington, Va., for a year before transferring to Miami University in Ohio, where he graduated in 1955. After enrolling in graduate work at Stanford University, Stanford, Calif., McClanahan transferred to the University of Kentucky and earned an MA in English there in 1958. At UK he became associated with other Kentucky-born writers such as Wendell Berry, Gurney Norman, and Kentucky Poet Laureate James Baker Hall—all of whom had received the prestigious Wallace E. Stegner Fellowship in Creative Writing at Stanford University. From 1958 until 1962, when McClanahan moved back to California to accept a Stegner Fellowship, he taught freshman English and creative writing at Oregon State University. Through one of his students, Ken Kesey, McClanahan became acquainted with a group of political radicals in Haight-Ashbury in San Francisco. Included were Kesey's Merry Pranksters, Beat Generation icon Neal Cassady, the Black Panthers, and Jerry Garcia, lead singer of the rock group The Grateful Dead. Many of McClanahan's adventures and misadventures during this period, which has been characterized as the passing of the Beat Generation and the rise of the Flower Children, found their way into his fiction and nonfiction, such as *Famous People I Have Known* (1985), *A Congress of Wonders* (1996), and *My VITA, If You Will: The Uncollected Ed McClanahan* (1998). His long prizewinning meditation about Garcia and the fanatical devotion of his fans, "Grateful Dead I Have Known," is just one example. As a lecturer at Stanford, McClanahan, using the moniker Captain Kentucky, often sported a knee-length red velvet cape, granny glasses, and Peter Pan boots. In 1964 *Esquire* magazine included McClanahan in a list of up-and-coming writers.

After Stanford, McClanahan taught creative writing at the University of Kentucky for a year, and then at the University of Montana from 1973 until 1976. After that he returned to Kentucky, where he makes a living doing farm work in Henry Co. for his old friend Wendell Berry while continuing to work on his books. Also, on occasion, he has taught creative writing as a part-time instructor at Northern Kentucky University. "My career has been a series of fits and starts," McClanahan said. "I am, what you might call, a meticulous writer. I don't just write—I compose." McClanahan's work, though limited in quantity, has been well received. The title story of *A Congress of Wonders* was turned into a prizewinning short film in 1993, and in 1994 McClanahan was the subject of an hour-long documentary on Kentucky Educational Television. "Ed is a stylist—a man intricately aware of how he sounds, meticulously attentive to the nuances of diction, rhythm, syntax," said Berry. "Ed's language is his compass and map."

Of the stories McClanahan has written, a long, reflective profile of Little Enis, "the World's Greatest Left-Handed, Upside-down Guitar Player," which appeared in *Playboy*, is his personal favorite. McClanahan founded, directed, and chaired the Ohio-Kentucky-Indiana Writers' Roundtable, held annually since 1998 at Hanover College in Madison, Ind. In 2002 Larkspur Press in Monterey, Ky., published McClanahan's memoir *Fondelle; or, The Whore with a Heart of Gold.* In 2003 McClanahan served as editor of *Spit in the Ocean #7: All about Kesey,* a tribute issue of the late Kesey's self-published magazine, and he contributed the introduction to *Kesey's Jail Journal,* a volume featuring Kesey's artwork. McClanahan's most recent work, *The Return of the Son of Needmore,* is based on his hometown of Brooksville and includes the revival of his self-based character, Harry Eastep.

McClanahan, who has been married three times, has five children. He and his third wife, Hilda, live in Lexington, which he has called home since 1991.

McClanahan, Ed. Interview by Stephen M. Vest, December 11, 2004, Lexington, Ky.

———. *My VITA, If You Will: The Uncollected Ed McClanahan.* Washington, D.C.: Counterpoint, 1998.

O'Bryan, Danny. "Captain Kentucky," *Kentucky Monthly,* January 2001, 41.

Stephen M. Vest

McCLUNG, JOHN A. (b. September 25, 1804, Washington, Ky.; d. August 6, 1859, Niagara River, N.Y.). A distinguished preacher, lawyer, and writer, Rev. John Alexander McClung was the son of Judge William McClung, a grandson of Col. **Thomas Marshall Jr.**, and a nephew of John Marshall, chief justice of the U.S. Supreme Court. McClung was educated in a private school near Versailles in Woodford Co., Ky., run by his uncle Dr. Louis Marshall. At age 18 he entered the Princeton Theological Seminary in New Jersey, where he studied for two years. In 1825 he married Eliza Johnson, a sister of Judge Josiah Stoddard Johnson and of Gen. **Albert Sidney Johnston**. McClung was licensed to preach in 1828 and for the next two years served as pastor of the Presbyterian Church at Washington, Ky.

McClung left the ministry in 1830 to pursue a career as a writer. His first book, *Camden, a Tale of the South,* was published that year; in 1832 another one, *Sketches of Western Adventure,* was published. He also wrote numerous newspaper articles during those years. He became a friend of noted Kentucky historian Judge **Lewis Collins** and made significant contributions to the first edition of Collins's *History of Kentucky.* McClung was considered one of the best historical writers of his day. However, he often added details from his fertile imagination that were later retold as fact by other writers. Some of the events for which his version deviates from the accepted one include the **Battle of Blue Licks**, the Siege of Bryants Station, and the Battle of Dayton, Ky. (see **Rogers' Defeat**).

McClung began the study of law in 1834 and was admitted to the bar the following year. He began practicing law in Mason Co. in 1835 and soon became one of its most prominent attorneys. In 1838 he was elected to the Kentucky legislature. He returned to the ministry in 1849 and for the next nine years pastored churches in Louisville, Indianapolis, Maysville, Cincinnati, and Augusta, Ga. He was offered the presidency of Hanover College in Madison, Ind., in 1858, but he declined.

McClung was an excellent leader and orator; however, he preferred to spend his leisure time alone, seldom developing close relationships. Because of his hectic schedule, he developed health problems, which were diagnosed as dyspepsia (possibly stomach ulcers). As treatment, he was placed on a strict diet and told to take long walks as exercise; however, his severe pain persisted. Hoping to improve his health, he took a vacation to Niagara Falls, N.Y., in 1859. While swimming in the Niagara River, about three miles above the falls, he drowned. His body went over the falls and was retrieved four days later near the mouth of the Niagara River. Some considered his death an accident, while others speculated that it might have been suicide. His body was brought back to Mason Co. and buried in the Maysville Cemetery.

Biographical Encyclopedia of Kentucky. Cincinnati: J. M. Armstrong, 1878.

Cyclopedia of the Commonwealth of Kentucky. Chicago: John M. Gresham, 1896.

Ward, William S. *A Literary History of Kentucky.* Knoxville: Univ. of Tennessee Press, 1988.

McEVOY, WILLIAM (b. June 28, 1915, Clermont Co., Ohio; d. December 23, 1989, Florence, Ky.). County attorney William Peter McEvoy was the son of John and Jenny Jameson McEvoy. He graduated from **Lloyd Memorial High School** in Erlanger, attended Centre College in Danville, Ky., on a football scholarship, and went to the **Chase College of Law**. In 1940 he married Margaret Kaelin, and they had one child. McEvoy was a 1st sergeant in the U.S. Army during **World War II**. He served as an associate justice of the U.S. Supreme Court by appointment in 1948. McEvoy, the first Catholic to be elected in Boone Co., was the county attorney for 28 years, retiring in 1977. After his first election, he ran unopposed. He was chairman of the Boone Co. Democratic Party for 18 years, a member of the Democratic State Executive Committee for 20 years, and chief counsel for the state Democratic Party more than five years.

A founding member of the **Cincinnati/Northern Kentucky International Airport** Board, McEvoy was also chief counsel for the airport. He served as chairman of the board (20 years) and legal counsel (25 years) for the Florence Deposit Bank, at that time the largest bank in Florence, Ky. He served as president of the Kentucky County Attorneys Association and of the Florence Rotary Club and was a Paul Harris Fellow of the Florence Rotary Club. McEvoy was an original member of the Northern Kentucky Businessmen's Association and a **Northern Kentucky University** Foundation board member, as well as a member of **St. Paul Catholic Church** in Florence.

It was said that organized crime wanted no part of Boone Co. while McEvoy was the county attorney. He was approached many times to run for state office but did not want to leave Boone Co. He loved practicing law; that was his passion. He died in 1989 and was entombed at **St. Mary Cemetery** Mausoleum in Fort Mitchell.

"William P. McEvoy, 74, Attorney, Political Leader," *KP*, December 25, 1989, 9K.

Nancy J. Tretter

McFARLAND, ROBERT WHITE (b. June 16, 1825, Concord Twp., Champaign Co., Ohio; d. October 23, 1910, Oxford, Ohio). A university professor and administrator, he was the son of Robert and Eunice Dorsey McFarland and a descendant of the frontier scout **Simon Kenton**. Robert W. McFarland began his college education at **Augusta College** in Bracken Co. He received his BA (1847) and his MA (1850) from Ohio Wesleyan in Delaware, Ohio. From 1851 through 1856, he taught at Madison College in Antrim, Ohio. From there, he moved on to Miami University, Oxford, Ohio, where he became a professor of mathematics and astronomy. An excellent teacher with a great sense of humor, McFarland demonstrated the stars to his students from a wooden platform built above the roof of his home. On two separate occasions during the **Civil War**, he commanded contingents of Miami University students serving in the 86th Ohio Volunteer Regiment. His unit was given the assignment of transporting Confederate general **John Hunt Morgan** and Morgan's band of marauders to prison at Camp Chase in Columbus, Ohio, and the task was accomplished without one prisoner escaping. In 1873 McFarland received the keys to Miami University's physical plant as the school was being shut down. He then became one of the first professors at the opening of the new agricultural and mechanical school, Ohio State University, in Columbus. In September 1885, with the reopening of Miami University, he returned as its eighth president. He served only three years, resigning because of a conflict with the board of trustees over the need for reforms. He spent his last years working as a consulting engineer. He died at home in Oxford in 1910 and was buried at the Oxford Cemetery. McFarland is one of many prominent academics once associated with Northern Kentucky's Augusta College.

Havighurst, Walter. *The Miami Years: 1809–1984.* New York: G. P. Putnam's, 1984.

Rankins, Walter H. *Augusta College*. Frankfort, Ky.: Roberts, 1955.

McGRADY, THOMAS (b. June 6, 1863, Lexington, Ky.; d. November 27, 1907, San Francisco, Calif.). Rev. Thomas McGrady was a nationally known Socialist author and lecturer (see **Socialist Party**). The son of parents who fled Ireland during the Great Famine, he became a lifelong advocate of the oppressed. In 1887 he was ordained as a Catholic priest in Galveston, Tex. and transferred to the Diocese of Covington (see **Roman Catholics**) in 1891. Bishop **Camillus P. Maes** appointed him pastor of St. Edward Church in Cynthiana and then, in 1895, of St. Anthony Catholic Church in Bellevue. Initially a supporter of the populist position favoring unlimited coinage of silver, McGrady had become a Socialist by 1899. He walked in picket lines to support laborers, lectured nationally, and published several works, including *The Mistakes of Ingersoll* (1898), *The Two Kingdoms* (1899), *Beyond the Black Ocean* (1901), *Socialism and the Labor Problem: A Plea for Social Democracy* (1902), and *The Catholic Church and Socialism* (1913, with Frank Bohn). Bishop Maes, a liberal but not a Socialist, was tolerant of him, but when other bishops and Catholics throughout the nation began to complain about McGrady's Socialist views, which were at odds with Vatican teachings, Maes was forced to respond. He asked McGrady to retract a letter that he had published in *Wilshire's Magazine* in July 1902. Instead, McGrady chose to resign as pastor of St. Anthony's and left the diocese. He remained a priest, continuing to write and lecture elsewhere, and eventually moved to San Francisco and practiced law. He died at St. Mary Hospital, San Francisco, of a heart condition and was buried in the Catholic cemetery in Lexington.

Scibilia, Dominic Pasquale. "Edward McGlynn, Thomas McGrady, and Peter C. Yorke: Prophets of American Social Catholicism," PhD diss., Marquette Univ., 1990.

Tenkotte, Paul A., David E. Schroeder, and Thomas S. Ward. *To Be Catholic and American in Northern, Central, and Appalachian Kentucky: The Diocese of Covington, 1853–2003*. Forthcoming.

Terrar, Toby. "Catholic Socialism: The Reverend Thomas McGrady," *Ecumenist* 21 (November–December 1982): 209–35.

Paul A. Tenkotte

McGRAW, T. J. (b. ca. 1837, Flagg Springs, Ky.; d. May 15, 1863, Johnson's Island, Ohio). Thomas Jefferson "Jeff" McGraw spent his childhood years in southern Campbell Co. He was a friend of **William Francis Corbin**, who lived on **Washington Trace Rd.**, and **Absolom Columbus "Lum" Dicken**, who lived on California Crossroads. He moved with his family to Virginia during his teenage years. On April 17, 1862, McGraw enlisted in the Confederate Army at Moccasin, Va. He asked to be attached to the Kentucky 4th Cavalry, where he would serve with his friends from Campbell Co. McGraw must have been fairly well educated, because he held the rank of captain in the Kentucky Cavalry. Will Corbin was a 1st lieutenant, and Lum Dicken was a private. On February 20, 1863, with the Confederacy in dire need of additional troops, McGraw and his friend Corbin were ordered by Gen. Humphrey Marshall to return to Northern Kentucky and recruit a company of men. While doing so, they were captured by a squad of Union Home Guard troops at the home of Garret Daniel, near Rouse's Mill and the Wesley Chapel Church. The men were taken to Demossville, Ky., then to Cincinnati, and eventually to a military prison on Johnson's Island, near Sandusky, Ohio. There they were tried by a military court and sentenced to death by firing squad. The action appears to have been illegal, since the men were arrested on April 8, 1863, and Union general Ambrose Burnside's order, which they were charged with violating, was not issued until April 13, 1863. Upon hearing the news of the sentences, their families were horrified. Will's sister, Melissa Corbin, traveled to Cincinnati to plead their case before General Burnside, but he refused to change the decision. Undeterred, she traveled to Washington, D.C., in an attempt to persuade President Abraham Lincoln (1861–1865) to spare the men's lives. The president refused to see her, but an aide said that the request would have to be submitted in writing. She then went to the pastor of the church that Lincoln attended in Washington and asked for his assistance. A Rev. Sutherland was sympathetic to her cause and helped her compose a written request for clemency. The next day, the pastor went to the Capitol and met with Lincoln, but the president refused to read the request. Heartbroken, Melissa returned home the next day to await the men's fate. On May 15, 1863, Jeff McGraw and Will Corbin were executed by firing squad at the prison. Several days later, the men's bodies were returned home and were laid out in the Corbin home on Washington Trace. Jeff McGraw was buried in the **Flagg Springs Baptist Church** Cemetery, and Will Corbin was buried on the Corbin family farm. For years later, residents of the area, whether Union or Confederate sympathizers, bristled with anger at the mere mention of the executions.

Demoss, John C. *The Short Story of William Francis Corbin*. Privately published, 1897.

Dicken, Absolom Columbus. "Civil War Diary of Absolom Columbus Dicken, 1862–1865," Kenton Co. Public Library, Covington, Ky.; Campbell Co. Historical Society, Alexandria, Ky. Also available at the National Archives, Washington, D.C.

Wessling, Jack. *Early History of Campbell County Kentucky*, Alexandria, Ky.: Privately published, 1997.

Jack Wessling

McKINNEYSBURG. This small town, whose name is sometimes spelled "McKenneysburg," is located in Pendleton Co., six miles south-southeast of Falmouth. McKinneysburg sits within a bend of the Licking River, almost in Harrison Co., and is one of the most southern cities of Northern Kentucky. The town was named for the many members of the McKinney family who lived in its vicinity. The historic McKinneysburg Bridge across the river at McKinneysburg was constructed in 1862; it survived the **floods of 1937** and 1964, but not the flooding of March 1997, when its center section collapsed into the water. This spot along the Licking River is where in 1994 the federal government removed one of its 18 automatic river-level gauges in Kentucky, for budgetary reasons. Many people contend that the gauge, if it had not been removed, might have alleviated flood conditions farther downstream at Falmouth in 1997. Today, a river gauge has been installed again to that part of the Licking River. The **Pendleton Co. Public School** system once had an elementary school at McKinneysburg, and it was attended by Dr. **Phillip A. Sharp**, the 1993 Nobel Prize laureate in Physiology or Medicine. He was a student there during the late 1940s and early 1950s, and he remembers appreciatively the fine training he received at the school.

Dreihaus, Bob. "Old Bridge Bows to a Flow," *KP*, March 11, 1997, 1K.

"Feds Mum on River Gauge," *KP*, December 22, 1997, 2K.

Rennick, Robert M. *Kentucky Place Names*. Lexington: Univ. of Kentucky Press, 1984.

McLAUGHLIN, CHARLES J. (b. June 6, 1888, Covington, Ky.; d. September 10, 1964, Charlottesville, Va.). Charles Jasper McLaughlin, a multitalented artist and architect, was the son of Edward Ball and Nancy Waller Sandford McLaughlin. His paternal grandfather once owned the **Big Bone** Mineral Springs Resort Hotel, in Boone Co. Born and raised in Covington, McLaughlin studied art under the renowned artist **Frank Duveneck** and later continued his art education at the Sorbonne, Paris, France, and in Belgium, Italy, and Greece. McLaughlin painted portraits, pictures of animals, and scenes of everyday life, using oil on canvas. He worked for the Rookwood Pottery on Mount Adams in Cincinnati from 1913 to 1920, and there he displayed his artwork on Rookwood pottery. McLaughlin married Dorothy Kellogg and they had two children, Nancy and Ralph. In 1916 Charles designed and built the family home at 321 Riverside Dr. in Covington. The house had two apartments on the first floor, and the McLaughlin family lived on the second, with 15-foot ceilings and large windows, affording a spectacular view of the Ohio River. The McLaughlins used their home to entertain many celebrities, including actors, musicians, and opera stars. On July 30, 1922, Dorothy McLaughlin died of suicide, at age 34.

For several years, McLaughlin taught architecture and design at Texas A&M College, College Station, Tex. He was a member of the **Christopher Gist Historical Society**, the Cincinnati Art Club, and the McDowell Society. Later in life, he spent summers in Covington and winters at his art studios in Saldillo, Mexico, and Twenty-Nine Palms, Calif. He died at age 76 while visiting with his daughter, Nancy McLaughlin Dammann, in Charlottesville, Va. He was cremated and his ashes were returned to Cincinnati for burial next to his wife, in Spring Grove Cemetery.

"Charles McLaughlin: Widely-Known Artist," *CE*, September 11, 1964, 38.

"McLaughlin, Noted Artist, Dies at 76," *KP*, September 10, 1964, 1.
Peck, Herbert. *The Book of Rookwood Pottery*. New York: Crown, 1968.
Spring Grove Cemetery Records, Cincinnati.
Stamm, Michelle. "Riverside Renaissance: Covington's Historic Riverside District from the 18th Century to the Present," *NKH* 1, no. 1 (Autumn–Winter 1993): 1–22.

McLEOD, JOHN C. (b. September 27, 1877, Covington, Ky.; d. March 24, 1962, New Rochelle, N.Y.). John C. McLeod, a black veterinarian, was the son of John S. and Anna McLeod. His father was the first principal of **Lincoln-Grant School** in Covington. The family eventually moved to Cincinnati, where McLeod attended public schools and graduated from Hughes High School. He was employed at the Phoenix Grain and Stock Exchange in Cincinnati as an assistant bookkeeper. On October 5, 1901, he married Elvira Cox of Cincinnati, and the couple had a son. John McLeod entered the Cincinnati Veterinary College, where he studied veterinary surgery and earned a DVM. After graduation he was appointed the U.S. Veterinary Inspector in the Bureau of Animal Husbandry and served in the stockyards at Chicago. Before he left for Chicago, McLeod was the only African American veterinarian in Cincinnati.

McLeod was active in the Masonic Lodge; he was a 32nd degree Mason, a Shriner, and a Past Master of the St. John's Lodge in Cincinnati. During the 1930s he moved to New Rochelle, N.Y., where he continued working as a veterinarian with the U.S. Public Health Service. He died in that city in 1962 and was buried at Malden, Mass.

"Births," *KTS*, August 9, 1902, 11.
Dabney, W. P. *Cincinnati's Colored Citizens*. Cincinnati: Dabney, 1926.
"Death Notices," *CP*, March 26, 1962, 4.
"Journey's End," *CE*, March 26, 1962, 37.

Theodore H. H. Harris

McMILLEN, FRANCIS (b. March 25, 1832, Bracken Co., Ky.; d. March 8, 1913, Dayton, Ohio). During the **Civil War**, Bracken Co. native Francis M. McMillen enlisted in the Union Army at South Charleston, Ohio, on August 15, 1862. He rose to the rank of sergeant in the 110th Ohio Infantry and was mustered out with his regiment on June 25, 1865, at Columbus, Ohio. McMillen captured an enemy flag on April 2, 1865, at the Battle of Petersburg, Va.; this deed earned him the Congressional **Medal of Honor**, which he received on May 10, 1865. Only an act of conspicuous gallantry, far above the call of duty and in the presence of an armed enemy, merits this medal, the nation's highest military honor. McMillen placed his life in danger during the Appomattox Campaign, and the act of seizing the flag spoke highly of his heroism. McMillen's career after the war was in carpentry. He died in 1913 at the National Military Home in Dayton, Ohio, at age 80, and was buried in the Washington Cemetery in Washington Court House, Ohio. His wife had preceded him in death. A descendant donated his military medals to the Fayette Co. Museum in Washington Court House. McMillen's name was listed with 55 others from Kentucky on a Medal of Honor memorial in Louisville, dedicated on November 12, 2001.

Bradford, Valerie S. "Civil War Soldier of Bracken County Received Medal of Honor in 1865," *Kentucky Explorer*, February 2006, 19.
Ohio Death Certificate No. 17811, for the year 1913.
Witherspoon, Carol A. "Two Medals of Honor Awarded," Fayette Co. Museum, Washington Court House, Ohio.

Caroline R. Miller

McNAMARA, MARY C. (b. September 2, 1865, Covington, Ky.; d. November 4, 1938, Covington, Ky.). Author Mary Catherine McNamara was the daughter of a Covington tobacco merchant, Patrick J. McNamara, and his wife Catherine. The McNamara family arrived from Ireland in New York City's harbor aboard the *Alexina* on July 6, 1849. They settled in Virginia but by 1860 had moved to Covington. McNamara spent much of her early life in Covington, where the family belonged to St. Mary Cathedral (later named **Cathedral Basilica of the Assumption**). An 1892 city directory lists her as living at 735 Garrard St. in Covington with her mother; McNamara's 1925 will was drawn up in Covington, where she was a resident at that time too.

McNamara wrote her 1930 book, *"Glory" of the Hills*, while staying at the Lynch Hotel in the Appalachian coal town of Lynch, Ky. The novel is set in Kentucky and dedicated to her parents. It was reviewed in the fall of 1930 at the inaugural meeting of the Covington Business and Professional Women's Club, held at the Covington Chamber of Commerce (see **Northern Kentucky Chamber of Commerce**). McNamara also wrote "several other pieces of literature of lesser importance."

In the years just preceding her death, McNamara lived in Asheville, N.C., although she visited Northern Kentucky frequently, often staying at **Mount St. Martin** in Newport. It was during one of her Kentucky visits, in March 1938, that McNamara became ill and was hospitalized at St. Elizabeth Hospital (see **St. Elizabeth Medical Center**) in Covington. She died later that year and was buried at St. Mary Cemetery in Fort Mitchell. She left her estate to the Diocese of Covington (see **Roman Catholics**) as the Miss Mary McNamara Bequest to the Mountain Missions. The bequest was used to construct St. Michael Church in Paintsville, Ky.

Arnim, Margaret. "Society," *KP*, September 18, 1930, 4.
Kenton Co. Will Book, book 23, pp. 469–71.
"Kentucky Author Is Taken by Death," *KTS*, November 5, 1938, 1.
Kentucky Death Certificate No. 27870, for the year 1938.
McNamara, Mary. *"Glory"of the Hills*. Louisville, Ky.: John P. Morton, 1930.
Tenkotte, Paul A., David E. Schroeder, and Thomas S. Ward. *To Be Catholic and American in Northern, Central, and Appalachian Kentucky: The Diocese of Covington, 1853–2003*. Forthcoming.

Kathryn Witt

McVILLE. McVille is a quiet, close-knit community nestled in the valley of the Ohio River in western Boone Co. Rich farmland and historic homes such as the Thomas Sutton Farm touch the boundaries of this town that once centered its livelihood on the river. An ancient American Indian village, south of the present-day town, left behind artifacts that locals once gathered by basketfuls (see **Fort Ancient Indian Sites**). McVille, established by Green McMullen in 1881, was a steamboat town, like its older sister city, Belleview. The local 1883 Lake atlas shows four city blocks in McVille bordered by Scott, Vine, Center, Main, and Front Sts. McMullen, a contractor, paint dealer, and wharfmaster, owned 2 of the 17 town lots.

The need for an improved system of locks and dams brought little McVille to the forefront of Ohio River commerce. The river level would sometimes drop as low as two feet, and river traffic would come to a standstill. At other times, the river was a raging torrent, spilling over its banks to a depth of 71 feet. U.S. Lock and Dam No. 38 opened near McVille in 1926 and became one of a series of navigation dams along the Ohio River system (see **Ohio River Locks and Dams**). In its day, before the construction downstream of the **Markland Dam** near Vevay, Ind., McVille's Dam No. 38 was a critical link in this navigation system. Crops reached their destinations with speed and efficiency when the river level was under control. The river was as essential to commercial shipping as the interstate highways are today.

On October 8, 1962, the scheduled detonation of 5,000 pounds of dynamite ended McVille's era as a vital part in Ohio River commerce. The structures once used for the day-to-day operations of Lock No. 38 became housing for a women's detention center called the Daniel Boone Correctional Center. Today, the former dam's buildings are rented living space.

An Atlas of Boone, Kenton, and Campbell Counties, Kentucky. Philadelphia: D. J. Lake, 1883.
Boone Co. Historic Preservation Review Board. *Historic Structures of Boone County, Kentucky*. Ann Arbor, Mich.: Cushing-Malloy, 2002.
Reis, Jim. "Controlling the Ohio's Flow," *KP*, February 23, 2003, 4K.
———. "Tiny Unincorporated Towns Abound in Boone," *KP*, December 9, 1985, 4K.
———." What's in a Name?" *KP*, June 5, 1995, 4K.

Jannes W. Garbett

MEADOWVIEW REGIONAL MEDICAL CENTER. Located along the John Y. Brown Jr. **AA Highway**, on a ridge south of Maysville in Mason Co., this 101-bed acute-care hospital provides health care in the eastern part of the Northern Kentucky region. As the successor to the **Hayswood Hospital** in Maysville proper, the center serves a seven-county market area: its home county of Mason, Brown and Adams counties across the Ohio River in Ohio, and four additional Kentucky counties, Robertson, Fleming, Lewis, and Bracken. The new $6 million, three-story facility was dedicated on January 23, 1983, and opened as the Meadowview Regional Hospital. It was first owned and managed by the Hospital Corporation of American (HCA); the name was changed to Columbia Hospital Maysville in 1996 as a result of the merger of Columbia Healthcare Corporation with HCA, both major players in the national acute-health-care industry. The facility's name was later changed to the Meadowview Regional Medical Center for public relations reasons and to emphasize its regional market. The center offers most of the standard specialties of a major hospital, since there is no other acute-health-care facility within many miles. The replacement of the not-for-profit Hayswood Hospital by a for-profit health care center has pumped new blood (capital, resources, talent, and experience) into hospital care in this area. For 5 of the past 10 years, the Joint Commission of the Accreditation of Hospitals Organization has ranked the Meadowview Regional Medical Center among the top 100 hospitals in the United States. The Meadowview Regional Medical Center is the largest of the rural hospitals in this part of Kentucky, and for trauma victims who need medical attention within that first critical hour, the center has proven to be literally a lifesaver.

"Maysville Hospital Reverts to Old Name," *KP*, January 24, 1998, 1.
"Maysville's Meadowview Ranks among Top 100 U.S. Hospitals," *KP*, December 7, 1995, 16A.
Meadowview Regional Medical Center. www.meadowviewregional.com (accessed June 25, 2007).

MEANWELL, JACK L. (b. February 6, 1919, Winnipeg, Manitoba, Canada; d. June 7, 2005, Cincinnati, Ohio). The painter John "Jack" Leonard Meanwell was the son of Leonard William and Mary Eleanor Jenkins Meanwell. Jack Meanwell's father, an architect, was born in Rugby, England, and immigrated to the western provinces of Canada. Not finding a demand for architects there, he moved his family eastward to Windsor, Ontario, where he secured a lifelong position at the internationally renowned architectural firm of Albert Kahn in Detroit, Mich. Jack shared his father's artistic talents, as well as his mother's, aunt's, and grandfather's interests in painting. He began his study of art with figure drawing in high school and received further training at Meinzinger's Art School and at the Society of Arts and Crafts, both in Detroit.

The **Great Depression** led Meanwell to learn business art in a technical school. **World War II** followed. After a month in the Essex Scottish Infantry, he joined the Royal Canadian Air Force, where he instructed aircrews in radar for four years. On June 27, 1942, he married Marjory Wallingford, of Fort Mitchell, in Windsor, Canada. He had met Marjory when she visited McGregor Bay, Canada, with her neighbors the Eatons. Meanwell was working on the mail boat in McGregor Bay for his aunt Ethel, who ran the store and the post office there.

In 1945 Meanwell joined Greenhow Art Studios in Windsor, Canada, which handled advertising art for the Chrysler and Ford auto companies. This type of technical work proved stifling for him, so he moved with his wife and their first son to the Cincinnati area in 1947, taking up residence in Northern Kentucky. Jack lived with Marjory's parents in Fort Mitchell. Soon, Meanwell received half of the Wallingford Coffee business from Marjory's father. Eventually, the Meanwells moved to Erlanger. Much later, Jack Meanwell took up residence in Southgate, where he lived until the early 1980s.

In 1972, seeking to devote himself full-time to his painting, Meanwell sold his half interest in the Wallingford Coffee Company. By 1976 he was teaching at the Art Academy of Cincinnati, where he remained for the next 25 years. In addition, beginning in 1979, he taught art at **Northern Kentucky University** at Highland Heights.

Following a divorce, Jack Meanwell married two more times, the last time to Mary Ann Shaffer, and moved to Cincinnati, where he lived the rest of his life. He did, however, operate an art studio for about 25 years at **Elmwood Hall**, in Ludlow.

The Meanwells spent many summers in the rugged wilderness of Canada's McGregor Bay, where Jack found inspiration for his landscapes. His grandparents the Jenkinses were the first non-native people in McGregor Bay, and the McGregor tradition continued with his parents, who also had a summer home there. Eventually, Jack bought his own home and island in the same area and returned year after year.

As Meanwell was becoming one of Cincinnati and Northern Kentucky's most accomplished modern painters, his works were displayed in nearly 100 exhibits at many galleries in Kentucky and Ohio, with an occasional show in New York City, Chicago, Toronto, and Windsor. The first of his local exhibits was in 1969. Meanwell had the privilege of exhibiting in the governors' mansions in both Ohio (1974) and Kentucky (1979). In 1981 he participated in the Cincinnati Art Museum's traveling exhibition, as well as its Invitational. Merida Galleries in Louisville hosted Meanwell in 1977, 1979, and 1982. One of his earliest one-man shows was in 1979 at the Shaw Rimmington Gallery in Toronto. In February 1981 the Gallery at Ohio University, Lancaster, featured an exhibit of his watercolors. In 1983 he was one of fewer than 20 Northern Kentuckians to show artworks in "Kentucky Revisited, 1983" in Frankfort.

Jack Meanwell, 1964.

By 1984 Meanwell's reputation prompted an interview by the *Cincinnati Enquirer* art critic Owen Findsen. The interview focused on Canada's Group of Seven show at the Cincinnati Art Museum, as well as Meanwell's shows at both locations of the Closson galleries in Cincinnati. Findsen said Meanwell's paintings were "charged with color and energy" and had "a freedom that is far beyond the Group of Seven." In 2001 the curator of collections at the Miami (Ohio) University Art Museum, Edna Southard, described the Meanwell works exhibited there as "dramatic landscapes and figures painted with bright bold colors and energetic brushstrokes." She added, "The bright, abstract images are infused with power and originality."

Closson's was the primary gallery that represented the prolific Jack Meanwell throughout much of his career. One of Closson's early Meanwell shows (1979) was described as a "Forceful Art for a Vast Landscape" by art critic Findsen. Closson's held multiple exhibits of Meanwell's work at its downtown Cincinnati store. On February 3, 1996, Closson's opened "25 Years with Jack Meanwell" in downtown Cincinnati; the exhibit was shown at the firm's second gallery in Kenwood on March 28 of the same year.

In February 2001 the Art Academy of Cincinnati held a retirement party for Meanwell. Findsen, by then retired himself, was the master of ceremonies. He presented to Meanwell an honorary doctor of fine arts degree, which Meanwell greatly treasured. On October 31, 2001, the Mary Ran Gallery of Hyde Park (a suburb of Cincinnati) organized and presented a major exhibit of 40 of Meanwell's strongest paintings at Miami University in Oxford, Ohio. A very handsome catalog, the only catalog of his work ever prepared, was developed for this exhibit. In November 2004 the Ran Gallery presented Meanwell's last exhibit while he was alive.

The works of Jack Meanwell have been gathered for numerous corporate and individual collections. In Kentucky, there are collections at the Bardstown Gallery, Bardstown, and at the Commonwealth Hilton in Florence. In Ohio, Meanwell works are included in collections at Cincinnati Bell, American Financial (Cincinnati), Marietta College (Marietta), Western and Southern Life (Cincinnati), and the Cincinnati Art Museum. In Canada, the University of Windsor and the Windsor Art Gallery have collections. And among individual collectors are **Tom Gaither** and Rick Sacksteder. At the 2003 opening of the Cincinnati Wing of the Cincinnati Art Museum, two of Meanwell's paintings were put on permanent display.

Meanwell died on June 7, 2005, in Cincinnati, and was cremated. After his death he was acclaimed throughout the Greater Cincinnati area. Daniel Brown, author of the *Blue Book of Cincinnati,* wrote in the 2006 edition, "Greater Cincinnati lost one of her most popular and gifted painters when Jack Meanwell died in 2005." Cliff Radel reported in the *Cincinnati Enquirer* that "Jack's death left a void in the local art scene. He was one of the giants of Cincinnati's artists."

There have been two one-man shows of Meanwell's work since his death. On May 5, 2006, the Mary Ran Gallery in Hyde Park, Cincinnati, featured an exhibit "pegged as the first anniversary exhibit of Jack's death" and "filled with muscular, thickly painted abstract landscapes, seascapes, and figurative works that were his signature." On December 7, 2006, the second exhibit, "Jack Meanwell, a Cincinnati Treasure," opened at Closson's in Montgomery, Ohio. At the opening, Marie Rigney, the curator of this extensive one-man show, reported to former student and collector Rick Sacksteder that she had pulled together 60 of Meanwell's works on paper and oils on canvas. The subjects of the images were the familiar female figure, landscapes, and florals that were so representative of his abstract expressionist work during the last 25 years of his life.

Bauer, Marilyn. "Weekend Art Warrior: Update." Cincinnati.Com. http://frontier.cincinnati.com/blogs/art/2006/05/weekend-art-warrior-update.asp (accessed December 13, 2006).

Findsen, Owen. "A Forceful Art for a Vast Landscape," *CE*, February 18, 1979, F8.

———. "Local Artist Creates His Own Vision of Mystic North," *CE*, April 1, 1984, D19.

Kreimer, Peggy. "Northern Kentuckians Taking Their Artwork to Frankfort," *KP*, November 25, 1983, 5K.

Lansdell, Sara. "Meanwell at Merida," *LCJ*, October 7, 1979, H16.

Meanwell, Marjory. Telephone interview by Rick Sacksteder, June 14, 2006, Covington, Ky.

Meanwell, Mary Ann. Telephone interview by Rick Sacksteder, June 14, 2006, Cincinnati.

Radel, Cliff. "Painter's Death Leaves Void in Local Art Scene," *CE*, June 13, 2005, 1.

Smith, Gregory A. "Jack Meanwell—Painter, Teacher, and Friend," *Art Academy of Cincinnati News* (Summer 2005): 1.

Richard M. Sacksteder

MEATPACKING. Meatpacking was one of the major industries of Northern Kentucky during the 19th and early 20th centuries. As early as the 1840s, cattle drovers were herding stock, mainly hogs, north into Northern Kentucky and Cincinnati for slaughter, dressing, packing, local consumption, and shipment to distant markets. Cincinnati may have deserved its former nickname of "Porkopolis," but Covington also has had its share of meatpacking. In some years, as much as 30 percent of the livestock packed in Cincinnati came from the Central Kentucky area (Winchester, Cynthiana, and Paris), through Northern Kentucky. Herds were driven northward for as long as a week's time to Covington stockyards. Some of these livestock were processed totally in Northern Kentucky and some were killed in Northern Kentucky and sent immediately to Cincinnati meatpackers. Others were taken alive across the Ohio River on ferries, or sometimes driven over the frozen river (later over the **John A. Roebling Bridge**); the animals were taken through the streets of downtown Cincinnati to slaughterhouses in the Deer Creek valley on the east side and, later, to the Brighton area on the west side.

Milward and Oldershaw, pork packers, Covington.

Before the **Covington and Lexington Railroad** was built, herds of livestock traveled along the **Covington and Lexington Turnpike**, spending the night in pens adjacent to hotels; the animals were watered and fed at such stops. Usually their first Northern Kentucky destination was the Drovers' Inn, where the Fort Mitchell Garage stands today along the **Dixie Highway** in Park Hills. With a little luck, the drive team found buyers from meatpacking operations and struck a deal. Prices received at the Drovers' Inn were published in the newspapers of the day, as were the number and type of livestock arriving in a given day. The Drovers' Inn later became known as the Hawkins House. Housing up to 100 herders, it was also a gathering place for political rallies of all sorts. It closed in 1868. Local historian John Burns has noted that Covington had as many as 19 similar places of rest, and it is possible that the parents of Kentucky governor **William Goebel** (1900) ran such an establishment.

Once a deal was negotiated and the herd was no longer the responsibility of the seller, the drovers were free to spend a night or two "on the town" in Covington, before returning home. Cattle that did not change hands at the Drovers' Inn were herded down the hill to Lewisburg, where Covington's first stockyard was located. Business activity was somewhat seasonal; the peak numbers of hogs arrived beginning about the first of November of each year. Other animals had different peak seasons. It was easier and less expensive for farmers to sell their animals rather than to feed them over the winter. Other factors that influenced the industry were the amounts of grain available for feed purposes and the quantities of rainfall during growing seasons. Drought conditions frequently made it necessary for producers to send their animals to markets to be slaughtered prematurely.

At the slaughterhouses, the animals were killed with a blow to the head or a knife to the throat, cut up into the various sides, hung to dry, dressed, packed in salt from West Virginia's Kanawha River (see **Frederick Laidley**), and shipped to East Coast markets such as New York City and Philadelphia. Some hogs were shipped to England, where consumers preferred to have their pork prepared differently: the pigs' bristles were singed in large, airtight hot rooms before shipment. Most local pigs lost their hair by being dipped in scalding hot water. There were years when 500,000 hogs were slaughtered and processed in Cincinnati while another 100,000 were being processed in Covington. It has been said that Cincinnati fed the Union Army during the **Civil War** with its pork; reportedly, a portion of that pork also found its way illegally to the Southern army. Pork was the preferred meat, for, unlike beef, it could be packed and salted away for years in 31-inch white or burr oak barrels. In addition, some hogs provided as much as 30 pounds of lard, which was used for lubrication, cooking, candle-making, and soap; cattle hides were used for such things as the manufacture of shoes and baseballs.

Once the railroad arrived in Covington, the stockyards moved to a location near the Covington and Lexington's rail line at 22nd St., between modern Donaldson Ave. and the tracks. It became known as the Central Covington Stockyards, and the yards remained, though not in operation at the end, until sold to the Donaldson Lithographing Company of Newport, in 1913. The livestock pens were wedged between the tracks and the old Banklick Rd., making it easy to receive stock either from the trains or via the Banklick Turnpike. As many as four trains per day arrived from Central Kentucky. The days of the weeklong drives were gone by this time, so the animals sent to slaughter arrived faster and generally in better health. Central Kentucky farmers owned the Northern Kentucky stockyards and thus had both a vested interest in the successful operation of the businesses and a place to sell their livestock. Once the railroad was able to cross the Ohio River in Newport over the **L&N Bridge** (1872), in Ludlow across the **Cincinnati Southern Railroad Bridge** (1877), and in Covington via the **Chesapeake and Ohio Railroad Bridge** (1888), most cattle were shipped directly into Ohio; cattle destined for Covington packers were offloaded at the Covington rail yards. When refrigeration became available, the major packers moved on to Chicago.

Over time, several stockyards did business in Covington along the railroad into the city. Many were situated on Russell St., near 16th St., and replaced the Central Covington yards farther south. The newer ones, north of the Kenton Junction railroad intersection, allowed for the easy loading of cattle cars from the east off the Chesapeake and Ohio Railroad after 1888, in addition to the **Louisville and Nashville** (formerly the **Kentucky Central** and the Covington and Lexington) Railroad. Other stockyards in Covington included the Jennings and Wilkerson facility that opened for business in 1875; that same year, the Nagel Slaughter House was operating in Lewisburg, and the Benzinger Slaughter House on Burnet St. in Austinburg burned. Fire was a common problem for meatpacking companies.

The foremost packer in Covington's history operated for only a decade. The firm of Milward and Oldershaw was situated along the banks of the Licking River and flourished during the 1850s. Its specialty was singed pork for the English market. The firm was the largest pork processor in the United States in 1850, with the capacity to prepare as many as 1,000 hogs per day. During the 1849–1850 season, Milward and Oldershaw packed 25,000 hogs. Its plant burned to the ground in 1859. That same year saw Daniel Ruttle begin his meatpacking firm, and in 1862 that company became the Ruttle-Schlickman Company. Its plant was on W. 12th St., and it gained a national reputation for its quality pork products. In 1885 Ruttle's retail operation at Seventh and Madison Ave. burned, and by 1902 both Ruttle and Schlickman were dead. In 1904 the company went bankrupt, and the business was assigned to John Osterholt by the Kenton Co. Fiscal Court. Ruttle's descendants became well-known Covington florists. In 1928 Covington experienced a cattle stampede, when a herd being driven from the Russell St. pens to the C. Rice plant on the east side became unruly and got out of hand at 16th and Madison Ave. Traffic was stopped for an hour before the herd could be regrouped.

At one time, Augusta, Falmouth, and Williamstown had stockyards where the buying, selling, and trading of livestock took place on specified days each month. Maysville still has a small stockyard facility. That city lost two stockyards to fires: in 1940 the old Carlisle Stockyard burned, and in January 1994 its replacement, Maysville Stockyards, burned. In the 19th century, there were slaughterhouses in Finchtown, just south of Newport along the Short Line (**Louisville, Cincinnati, and Lexington Railroad**) to Louisville. Today, **Bobby Mackey's** nightclub on the Wilder Pk. just outside Newport sits on land where a slaughterhouse once operated. Meatpacking now takes place in southern Campbell Co. in Claryville, at the Kahn's plant, owned by the Sara Lee Corporation; Kahn's used to be located along Spring Grove Ave. in Cincinnati, near that city's former stockyards. Smaller Northern Kentucky packers have included C. Rice Packing (Direct Meats), once at Patton St. and Eastern Ave., and another Rice family operation, Bluegrass Meats in Crescent Springs. Long gone are the days when local butcher shops, such as Ebert's Meats in Newport, led live animals into their basements, where the animals were killed and processed on the spot.

"Cattle in Stampede," *KP*, September 18, 1928, 1.
"Council to Close Street for New Plant," *KP*, October 21, 1913, 2.
"New Stockyards," *CE*, April 9, 1899, 3.
"Plant," *KP*, April 4, 1904, 1.
Pork Packers Association of Chicago. *Packing of the West*. Chicago: Pork Packers Association, 1876.
Tenkotte, Paul A. "Rival Cities to Suburbs: Covington and Newport, Kentucky, 1790–1890," PhD diss., Univ. of Cincinnati, 1989.
"Will Wreck Landmark," *KP*, October 26, 1917, 1.

Michael R. Sweeney

MEDAL OF HONOR, CONGRESSIONAL. Through 2008, 56 Medals of Honor have been awarded to Kentuckians, 16 of whom had Northern Kentucky connections.

During the **Revolutionary War**, Gen. George Washington began the practice of awarding medals to soldiers for individual acts of heroism. Those early awards were called Badges of Military Merit. Awards were also made during the **Mexican War** (1846–1847) but were called Certificates of Merit. On July 25, 1863, President Abraham Lincoln signed legislation creating the Medal of Honor. Congress changed the name to the Congressional Medal of Honor in 1918. The purpose of the medal was to honor members of the armed forces who displayed acts of heroism beyond the call of duty. Initially, the medal was given only for heroism in armed conflict, but later it was also awarded for noncombat heroism. Each branch of service designed its own version of the medal. The Congressional Medal of Honor is the only medal issued by the armed services that is worn on a ribbon around the neck. The medal is usually presented in person by the president of the United States. More than 3,400 individuals have received the honor, more than half of them posthumously. Recipients of the award have come from all 50 states. Twenty individuals have been awarded the medal twice. The only woman to receive the Medal of Honor was Dr. Mary Edwards Walker (1832–1919). Some of the famous people honored in this way are Buffalo Bill Cody, Adm. Richard Byrd, Jimmy Doolittle, Eddie Rickenbacker, Douglas MacArthur, Theodore Roosevelt, and Charles Lindberg. Two recipients of the medal have had movies made about the military actions that led to the award: **World War I** hero Alvin C. York (1887–1964) and the most decorated **World War II** veteran, Audie Leon Murphy (1924–1971). A Veteran's Convention is held each year, at which living Medal of Honor recipients are recognized and their exploits recounted.

The first Northern Kentuckian to receive the Medal of Honor was Sgt. John S. Darrough (1841–1920), who was born at Maysville, in Mason Co. He received his medal for saving the life of a captain at Eastport, Miss., on October 10, 1864. Darrough was buried in the Grand Army of the Republic Cemetery, Watseka, Ill. Carroll Co. native Pvt. John Davis (1838–1901) received his medal for capturing the Confederate flag of the Worrill Grays in February 1865 at Cullodon, Ga. He was buried in the Fort Logan National Cemetery in Sheriden, Colo. Sgt. **Francis M. McMillen** (1832–1913), who was born and raised in Bracken Co., received his medal for capturing the Confederate flag at Petersburg, Va., on April 2, 1865. He was buried in the Washington Cemetery at Washington Court House, Ohio. **Civil War** drummer **William H. Horsfall** (1847–1922), was born and raised in Newport. At the age of 14, he was one of the youngest ever to receive the medal. He was credited with rescuing a wounded officer who was trapped between battle lines at Corinth, Miss. He was buried in **Evergreen Cemetery**, Southgate. Pvt. William Steinmetz (1847–1903), also born and raised in Newport, was awarded the medal for gallantry during a charge by his volunteer storming force at Vicksburg, Miss. He was buried in the Wesleyan Cemetery in Cincinnati. Pvt. Charles Wesley Rundle (1842–1924) grew up in Covington. He received his medal for gallantry with the same volunteer storming force. He is buried in the Los Angeles National Cemetery. Sgt. Cavalry M. Young (1840–1909) was awarded his medal for capturing Confederate Gen. William Cabell in Osage, Kans. He was buried in **Highland Cemetery**, Fort Mitchell.

Covington-born Sgt. **Thomas Shaw** (1846–1895) was a member of the African American cavalry regiment known as the Buffalo Soldiers. He won his medal for stubbornly holding his ground, in an extremely exposed position, against a superior force of Indians at Carrizo Canyon, N. Mex., on August, 12, 1881. He was buried at Arlington National Cemetery. Pvt. Thomas Sullivan (1859–1940), also born in Covington, was awarded the medal for gallantry in action against Indians on December 29, 1890, in the Chiricahua Mountains of Arizona. He was buried in the Holy Sepulcher Cemetery in Orange, N.J. German-born Sgt. Louis (Lehman) Hineman (1839–1920) received his medal in August 1875 for gallantry against the Apache Indians during the winter of 1872–1873. He died at his home in Newport and was buried in **St. Stephen Cemetery**, Fort Thomas. Minnesota-born Col. Harry Leroy Hawthorne (1859–1948) was stationed for a time at the **Newport Barracks**, and his parents lived nearby in the city of Newport. As a 2nd lieutenant with a U.S. Army artillery unit, he won his medal for distinguished conduct in battle at Wounded Knee, S.D., during the Indian Wars on October 11, 1892. He was a career officer who later served in **World War I**, where he was awarded a Purple Heart and a Silver Star. He was buried at Arlington National Cemetery.

Seaman Edward W. Boers (1884–1929) was born in Cincinnati but later moved to Bellevue, Ky. He won his medal in peacetime by displaying extraordinary heroism in helping injured sailors after a boiler explosion aboard the U.S.S. *Bennington* on July 21, 1905, in San Diego Harbor. Boers was buried in the Vine Street Hill Cemetery, Cincinnati.

Irish-born Cpl. Thomas M. Doherty (1869–1906) won his medal for rescuing wounded soldiers from the front lines while under heavy fire at Santiago, Cuba, on July 1, 1898. After the war he was stationed at the **Fort Thomas Military Reservation**, where he committed suicide in the restroom of what is known today as the Midway Cafe across the street from the fort. He was buried in Evergreen Cemetery, Southgate.

Samuel Woodfill (1883–1951), who was a 1st lieutenant when he received the medal, was described by Gen. John (Black Jack) Pershing as "the most outstanding soldier of World War I." Woodfill was awarded the Medal of Honor for destroying three machine gun nests near Cunel, France, on October 12, 1918, even though he had just inhaled mustard gas. After the war Woodfill lived in Fort Thomas, where a school is named in his honor. He was buried in Arlington National Cemetery.

Lt. Col. Donald C. Faith Jr. (1918–1950) grew up in Fort Thomas, graduating from **Highlands High School** and from Xavier University in Cincinnati. He was awarded the Congressional Medal of Honor for leading a counterattack on November 27, 1950, against Chinese troops at the Chosin Reservoir in North Korea. Faith was mortally wounded while clearing an enemy roadblock, thereby permitting his battalion to escape encirclement. He was buried in Arlington National Cemetery.

Charles Clinton "Chalky" Fleek (1947–1969) was born and raised at Petersburg in Boone Co. He received the Congressional Medal of Honor for bravery in the Vietnam War. On May 27, 1969, he gave his life by throwing himself on an enemy hand grenade to save his fellow soldiers from harm. He was buried in the Petersburg Cemetery in Petersburg.

About: Women's History. "Mary Edwards Walker." www.womenshistory.about.com (accessed April 25, 2006).

Congressional Medal of Honor Society. www.cmohs.org (accessed April 25, 2006).

"Ft. Thomas Man Awarded Medal," *KTS*, February 6, 1919, 20.

Home of Heroes. "Hometown Heroes of the Bluegrass State." www.homeofheroes.com (accessed April 26, 2006).

Kentucky Medal of Honor Memorial. www.kymoh.com (accessed April 25, 2006).

Reis, Jim. "Memories of the Korean War Still Linger," *KP*, July 11, 1988, 4K.

"20 Years Later a Soldier's Sacrifice Is Not Forgotten," *KP*, May 24, 1989, 1K.

MEDICINAL HERBS. In 1797 Gilbert Imlay, who had been a captain in the U.S. Army, wrote a topographical description of the western territory of the United States, including Kentucky. Historian Michael Flannery later remarked that Imlay's description of the fertility foretold of the many botanical medicines native to Kentucky. Medicinal products before the 20th century were predominantly natural substances. Although some medicines came from distant lands, such as cinchona, the source of quinine, and the poppy, the primary source of opium, many were from indigenous sources. Among the most important medicinal herbs that grew in Northern Kentucky were goldenseal (*Hydrastis canadensis*), black snakeroot (*Cimicifuga racemosa*), mayapple or mandrake (*Podophyllum peltatum*), and ginseng (*Panax quinquefolius*).

Goldenseal was found in open woods where there was a rich layer of leaf mold. The plant was abundant in the wild but quickly disappeared when woods were cut and the land cultivated. Used as a yellow dye by **American Indians**, its medicinal properties were first exploited by the eclectic physicians, who found it effective in the treatment of inflammation of the mucous membranes. Goldenseal was especially valued for its effects in ophthalmologic and gynecologic treatments.

Black snakeroot, widely available in the Ohio River Valley, reportedly was used by early Indians. Professor John King of Cincinnati was probably the first to popularize its use for gynecologic conditions. It later became an important ingredient in Lydia Pinkham's Vegetable Formula.

Mayapple was a common plant in the woods of the Ohio River Valley. The active constituent of the plant in resin form, podophyllin, was a potent cathartic, sometimes called "vegetable calomel." Eclectics used it in place of the mercurial preparations previously favored by many physicians. William S. Merrell of Cincinnati was the first to manufacture the product; it remained a popular ingredient in laxatives for many decades.

Ginseng was also an important plant in the Ohio River Valley. Although it never achieved general acceptance as a medicine in North America, eclectics described its use as a mild tonic and stimulant, noting that some people believed it increased virility. Ginseng was an important commercial product as early as the end of the **Revolutionary War**. **Daniel Boone** was involved in the trade during his time in Kentucky, shipping 15 tons of the plant up the Ohio River in 1787–1788.

Other botanical medicines were also indigenous to the fields and woods of Northern Kentucky, such as echinacea (*Echinacea purpurea*), skullcap (*Scutellaria lateriflora*), and puccoon (*Sanguinaria canadensis*).

Flannery, M. A. "For a Voluptuous Glow of Health and Vigor: Medical Botany in Kentucky, 1792–1910," *Journal of the Kentucky Academy of Science* 60 (1999): 15–30.

Imlay, Gilbert. *A Topographical Description of the Western Territory of North America.* 3rd ed. London: J. Debrett, 1797. Reprint, New York: Augustus M. Kelly, 1969.

Dennis B. Worthen

MEDICINE, HISTORICAL REVIEW. Before the establishment of accessible medical schools, physicians in Northern Kentucky, as elsewhere, were educated through medical apprenticeships. They were referred to as "doctors of physic" and often served wide geographic areas. Because no formal medical facilities were available, patients were usually treated at home. With few diagnostic tools, early medicine was undoubtedly challenging: even simple X-rays were not discovered until 1895, and laboratory tests were similarly lacking. The earliest physicians had little except their own senses and skills to guide their diagnoses. Then, even if a doctor was fortunate enough to reach a correct diagnosis, successful treatment was anything but assured. There was no benefit of prior research, nor any extensive medical experience to refer to. When the causes of diseases were a mystery and treatment options nearly as scarce as diagnostic tools, mortality rates were understandably very high.

Abundant health challenges confronted the early medical community. Diseases prevalent during the early years in Northern Kentucky included the familiar illnesses of cholera, typhoid, and smallpox. However, some other diagnoses of the times are less well known today. One was milk sickness, also known as "the trembles" or "the slows." Later the cause of this sometimes-fatal disease was identified as the white snakeroot plant (*Eupatorium rugosum*). A toxin from this plant would pass into the milk of cows feeding on it and cause disease in unknowing humans who ingested the seemingly wholesome milk. Milk sickness is believed to have claimed the life of Abraham Lincoln's mother, Nancy Hanks Lincoln, when Abraham was nine years old. Dropsy was a widespread cause of illness and death. It denoted swelling, usually caused by what is known today as congestive heart failure or, less frequently, by kidney disease. **Tuberculosis**, called "consumption," took the lives of many. Syphilis was known as "bad blood." "Milk leg" referred to a postpartum blood clot in a leg vein. Rabies was termed "hydrophobia" because of an affected person's aversion to water. "Catarrh" meant an upper respiratory infection, what we now call the common cold. Pregnancy was an especially risky condition during early times, and childbirth was likewise hazardous. Hemorrhage or infection frequently resulted in the death of the mother or the baby or both.

Northern Kentucky did not escape the global pandemic that struck in 1918. Between September 1918 and March 1919, churches, schools, saloons, and theaters closed. Families were told to keep their children at home. In Covington alone some 260 died from the Spanish Flu or "La Grippe." Dr. John Todd, the well-known Health Department director in Newport, managed to survive, though some of his fellow city workers did not. Newspapers reported almost daily the deaths of Northern Kentuckians away in the military, many of them aboard ships at sea. The **Fort Thomas Military Reservation** was quarantined until early November 1918; Halloween ceremonies that year were canceled. Worldwide, the number of people who died from the flu, at least 20 million and perhaps 40 million, exceeded the number killed in **World War I**.

Newspaper advertisements from the early years in Northern Kentucky paralleled those of other cities, offering an abundance of cures for nearly anything that could afflict a person. If a person had an ailment, there were tinctures, balsams, liniments, or bitters to cure it. The lack of proven treatments opened the door to abuse by unethical individuals, referred to as quacks or charlatans. Eventually, the formation of medical organizations helped to abolish quackery within the medical community.

Phrenology was an attempt at diagnostic technique that was popular in the 1800s. This pseudoscience claimed that a person's character traits, mental capacity, and even criminality potential could be discerned by observing the shape the person's skull and examining the bumps on his or her head.

The concept of humoralism formed the basis for many treatments of early ailments. Disease was believed to result from an imbalance of the body's four humors or fluids—specifically blood, phlegm, black bile, and yellow bile. Treatments consequently involved attempts to rebalance those substances by purging with either emetics or laxatives or by performing the ever-popular bleeding or bloodletting. Cupping (drawing blood to the skin with heated glass cups) was also utilized, as were leech treatments. Gradually medical advances such as the acceptance of germ theory, the recognition of contagion as a factor in disease transmission, the use of antiseptics during surgeries, and improvements in nutrition led to better community health and longer lives.

In the 1800s there was a proliferation of medical schools throughout the United States. Many early Northern Kentucky doctors who received the benefit of formal training attended the Medical College of Ohio (later the University of Cincinnati College of Medicine), which graduated its first class in 1821. Also educating physicians in the region were the Eclectic Medical Institute at Worthington, Ohio, which graduated its first class in 1833, and the Woman's Medical College of Cincinnati (later the Laura Memorial Woman's Medical College), which graduated its first class in 1888. Although some pioneer physicians of the Midwest went to eastern medical schools or institutions abroad, not many local physicians did so.

The **Newport Barracks**, a military establishment, played a role in the development of medicine in the Northern Kentucky area by drawing skilled and accomplished physicians to the region. Besides serving the U.S. Army, the Newport Barracks also treated nonmilitary people in surgical emergencies. Dr. John Sellman was the institution's first surgeon. Like many physicians of the time, he did not hold a formal medical degree, but later in his life he received an honorary doctor of medicine degree from the Medical College of Ohio. Other practitioners at the Newport Barracks included Dr. **Nathaniel Shaler** and Gen. **Charles S. Tripler**.

Numerous early physicians influenced the Northern Kentucky community. One pioneer physician who had a direct impact on patient care was Dr. **Joshua Taylor Bradford** of Augusta. He was a **Civil War** surgeon; however, his career is most notable for the revival and refinement of ovariotomy, an operation used to treat "ovarian dropsy" (abdominal swelling caused by ovarian cysts or sometimes ovarian tumors). The procedure had been abandoned, and in fact was condemned, because of high mortality rates. However, Bradford performed a series of such surgeries with a much better survival rate than had been previously experienced, and subsequently many patients began to benefit from this treatment—a direct result of his courageous resumption of the controversial therapy.

Two very early Washington, Ky., physicians included Dr. **William Goforth** and Dr. **Basil Duke**. Although better known for his work in the Cincinnati medical community, Dr. Daniel Drake was from Mason Co., where he spent most of his youth before moving to Cincinnati to apprentice under Dr. William Goforth. He then practiced briefly in Mayslick. Dr. Drake became a prominent medical figure in Cincinnati and in 1819 founded the Medical College of Ohio.

Dr. **Thomas Hinde**, from England, is the first medical doctor known to practice in the Covington and Newport areas; he was practicing medicine in Newport as early as 1799. Earlier, Hinde, an officer in the British Navy during the French and Indian War, had been portrayed and immortalized as the attending naval physician in the famous painting *The Death of General Wolfe*. Dr. Thomas Madden was the first physician of Florence, Ky., in 1818. Dr. C. B. Schoolfield of Dayton, Ky., was the first president of the Northern Kentucky Medical Society. Dr. James Barnsfather, originally of Scotland, practiced in Dayton, Ky., as well as in Cincinnati. Remembered as one of Northern Kentucky's earliest microbiologists, he provided detailed early descriptions of organisms associated with scarlet fever and tuberculosis. There are claims that he discovered these two microbes many years before their official discoveries were credited to other individuals. He reportedly failed to share or publish his findings, perhaps unaware at the time of their great significance. **Dr. Alvin C. Poweleit** of Newport, a survivor of the Bataan Death March in **World War II**, was reputed to be the first physician to earn a combat decoration during the war. He received the silver star for an act of heroism.

Early women physicians of the area included Dr. Dell Edwards, Ludlow's first female doctor. Dr. Anna Wolfram, Bellevue's first woman physician, was practicing in that city by 1892. Dr. Julia Thorpe, who moved to Covington in the late 1870s from New York, where she attended medical school, is recognized as Covington's first female doctor. Dr. **Louise Southgate** received her medical degree in 1893 and also practiced in Covington. She is remembered as an early women's rights activist as well. Dr. **Sarah Siewers** of Newport graduated from the Eclectic College of Medicine in Cincinnati in 1891 and was an early lecturer on alcoholism and tobacco abuse.

The Northern Kentucky area also benefited from the care of early minority physicians. Dr. **Simon J. Watkins**, a physician and dentist who practiced from 1891 until 1946, was Covington's first African American doctor. Dr. **James Randolph** established a practice in 1922 on Greenup St. in Covington and was reported to be the first African American physician on staff at St. Elizabeth Hospital (see **St. Elizabeth Medical Center**) as well as the first African American member of the Campbell-Kenton Medical Society. Two early Campbell Co. African American physicians were Dr. **Charles Horner** and Dr. **Percival Bacchus**.

In the 1800s medical facilities other than doctors' offices began to appear in Northern Kentucky. Altruism was the common foundation for several of them. During the **Civil War**, at least five temporary Northern military rehabilitation hospitals appeared, mostly in Covington. Staffed mainly by women volunteers from the area and housed in rented hotels, they cared for persons injured in the Tennessee and Mississippi campaigns, who were brought to the region via steamboats. As the war wound down, these facilities were consolidated and closed (see **Civil War Hospitals**). Opening in 1897, the **Speers Memorial Hospital** resulted from the benevolence of Elizabeth Speers, a widow and philanthropist who left provisions in her will for the establishment of a hospital in Dayton, Ky. The **Booth Memorial Hospital** opened in 1914 in a building that had been donated to the **Salvation Army**, the former **Amos Shinkle** mansion along E. Second St. in Covington. Three nuns were sent from the Little Sisters of the Poor of St. Francis in Cincinnati to establish a hospital in Covington to care for the poor. From this mission St. Elizabeth Hospital (see **St. Elizabeth Medical Center**) was born in 1861, providing care for anyone in need, including the poor, orphans, and veterans. Campbell Co.'s St. Luke Hospital (see **St. Luke Hospitals Inc.**) opened in 1954, after voters approved a bond to support its establishment. One medical facility that never materialized was the Effie Slaughter Memorial Hospital, planned as a Covington hospital for African American patients. Although fundraising drives were carried out during 1928, further plans for the facility never evolved.

Several other small medical facilities existed in early Northern Kentucky. Founded in the 1890s on Washington Ave. in Newport by Dr. John Pythian, the Emergency Hospital was Campbell Co.'s first nonmilitary hospital. The Jenkins Hospital, operated by Dr. J. Oliver Jenkins, existed for only two years, from 1895 to 1897, at Seventh and Isabella Sts. in Newport. The U.S. Public Health Service Hospital in Fort Thomas was created in 1921 to care for World War I veterans. Also known as Hospital No. 69, this facility encompassed several buildings, including the renowned **Altamont Springs Hotel**. The hospital closed in 1926. Twenty years passed before a second facility for veterans was founded in Northern Kentucky. The Veterans' Hospital (see **Veterans Administration Medical Center**) was opened in 1946 in Fort Thomas, after the short-lived military service branch called the U.S. Army Air Force departed the premises at the end of **World War II**. The Pest House near Kyles Lane in Covington was established to isolate individuals who had smallpox. In 1938 it became the Covington–Kenton Co. Tuberculosis Sanitorium, also dedicated to public health.

In the 1940s poliomyelitis, or polio, appeared in Northern Kentucky along with the rest of the United States, affecting children especially. In 1944, during the first seven months of the year, 412 cases were reported in Kentucky. In 1952 the **YMCA** Camp Ernst in Boone Co. was closed due to the threat of contracting the disease. After Dr. Jonas Salk developed an immunizing injection in 1955 to prevent the spread of polio, more than 27,000 children received vaccinations locally. Festivals, dances, and all sorts of fundraisers were held to collect money for the fight against polio. In 1957 Dr. Albert Sabin improved the vaccine so that it could be administered in an oral sugar-cube dose, and this vaccine also was offered throughout Northern Kentucky. For example, **St. Therese Catholic Church** in Southgate was where many Campbell Co. citizens received their dose of the Sabin cubes.

Great respect and gratitude are due those medical pioneers who daringly stepped onto the unknown road of medicine during its infancy. The sophisticated medical care we enjoy today stands as a tribute to their bravery.

Ellis, John H. *Medicine in Kentucky.* Lexington: Univ. of Kentucky Press, 1977.

McCormack, J. N., ed. *Some of the Medical Pioneers of Kentucky.* Bowling Green: Kentucky State Medical Association, 1917.

Poweleit, Alvin C., and James A. Schroer, eds. *A Medical History of Campbell and Kenton Counties.* Cincinnati: Campbell-Kenton Medical Society, 1970.

———. *Medical History of Northern Kentucky.* Northern Kentucky Medical Society, 1989.

Judy L. Neff

MEEHAN, JAMES (b. October 1834, Ireland; d. February 28, 1908, Covington, Ky.). James Meehan, a master railway mechanic and inventor, came to the United States with his parents in 1840, just before the potato famine that brought so many of their countrymen. The family settled in Covington.

As a young man, Meehan found a job as a machinist at the **Covington and Lexington Railroad**'s repair shop. When the **Civil War** started, he joined the Confederate Navy, and thus began a series of unexpected adventures. He was captured by Union forces but escaped and hid in Florida briefly before fleeing first to Cuba and then Mexico. In Mexico, Meehan became active in railroad construction; during those years Maximilian was emperor of Mexico. After the emperor was executed in June 1867, rebels seized Meehan. They were convinced that the U.S. engineer was a confidant of the late emperor and knew the location of certain treasures. Meehan knew nothing, but his Spanish was not adequate to persuade his captors of his lack of knowledge. He was going to be shot for not revealing the treasure site, but fortunately another U.S. citizen among the Mexican loyalists explained the facts in this matter to the rebel chief. Meehan was set free and made a speedy exit across the Rio Grande River. He returned to Covington and spent the next several years working in a local machine shop.

Late in 1881 Meehan was appointed master mechanic at the Cincinnati, New Orleans, and Texas Pacific Railroad (CNO&TP, the lessee of the **Cincinnati Southern**) shops in Ludlow. When the shops burned a few years later, he designed a new and much enlarged repair facility. While handling this demanding position, he found time for invention. One of his patents, a special type of railcar brake shoe, proved popular and made Meehan a wealthy man. He resigned his position with the CNO&TP in 1893 to devote his full energies to promoting the brake shoe. A large plant was built in Chattanooga, Tenn., to manufacture his invention, the Ross-Condon-Meehan brake shoe, as more railroads adopted it. In 1906 Meehan built a stylish new house in Hyde Park, a fashionable suburb of Cincinnati, and so ended his longtime residency in Covington. He died in 1908 and was survived by his wife, Eleanor, and their five children. His remains were returned to Kentucky for burial in St. Mary Cemetery in Fort Mitchell.

"Inventor Dies at the Age of 74," *CC,* February 29, 1908, 3.

"James Meehan Dead," *KP,* February 28, 1908, 3.

"Meehan Was Sentenced to Death in War," *CP,* March 3, 1908, 2.

White, John H., Jr., *On the Right Track: Some Historic Cincinnati Railroads.* Cincinnati: Cincinnati Railroad Club, 2003.

John H. White

MEIER, JANE SCHEPER (b. March 14, 1951, Covington, Ky.). Mary Jane Scheper Meier, athletic director at **Northern Kentucky University** (NKU), is the daughter of William and Marianne Kennel Scheper. The eldest of eight siblings, Jane had a passion for sports even as a child. In her youth, Meier played softball for the **St. Pius X** Elementary School, in Edgewood, and swam competitively for the Cincinnati Marlins. During her high school years at the all-girl **Villa Madonna Academy**, Meier competed in swimming, tennis, basketball, and volleyball. Thanks to the influence of her physical education teacher–high school coach, Mary Lou Elgrim, Meier knew by her sophomore year that she wanted to become an athletic director. From 1969 through 1973, while completing her BA in physician education and health at the College of Mount St. Joseph in Cincinnati, Meier excelled in volleyball, basketball, and tennis. Her volleyball team competed in the first-ever collegiate volleyball championship sponsored by the Association for Intercollegiate Athletics for Women. After college, Meier spent three years at **Notre Dame Academy**, a girls' school, where she was a physical education–health instructor, a coach for several sports, and the athletic director. At Notre Dame Academy, she initiated basketball, softball, swimming, tennis, and track and field programs. In 1976 she received a graduate assistantship from Eastern Kentucky University (EKU) in Richmond; while pursing her degree there, she served as an assistant volleyball coach. In 1977 Meier completed an MS in physical education, with a sports administration emphasis, at EKU. She spent the next year as head volleyball coach at Northern Michigan University in Marquette, Mich. Meier returned to Northern Kentucky for the 1978–1979 school year as the head volleyball and softball (slow-pitch) coach at NKU. In 1982 NKU's president, Dr. A. D. Albright, asked her to serve as the head women's basketball coach. During her two-year commitment as basketball coach, Meier hired former NKU basketball player Nancy Winstel as her assistant. Meier returned to softball coaching in 1985, while retaining her volleyball coaching position. She also accepted an appointment as cocoordinator of NKU athletic programs. In 1988 following the resignation of the institution's athletic director, Meier served as interim athletic director for three months. Dr. Leon Boothe, then NKU president, subsequently selected Meier as the school's first female athletic director, beginning during the 1988–1989 school year. Her appointment came at a time when there were far fewer female NCAA (National Collegiate Athletic Association) athletic directors than there are today. Meier's resourcefulness and leadership has helped NKU's athletic program to win numerous conference and regional championships. The program had made 48 national tournament appearances by 2005, thereby providing increased visibility and prestige to all of NKU's NCAA Division II athletic programs. Meier has set her sights on continuing to develop the university's athletic facilities and on the possibility of an upgrade of the program to NCAA Division I status.

Northern Kentucky Univ. www.nku.edu.

Paul A. Carl Jr.

MELBOURNE. Frank and Hubbard Helm established the city of Melbourne, Ky., in 1890. The Helms were from Australia, and it is thought that they named the city after the one they had left in that country. Melbourne is on the Ohio River, just to the south of Silver Grove. A civil engineer, John Ellis, laid the town out into lots in 1891. The first city officials were Dr. Jules Pinguely, William Haigis, John Greis, and Frank Springer, trustees, and Joseph Good, marshal and assessor. A post office was established that same year, and Robert A. Carnes was named postmaster. The Helms ran excursion boats along the Ohio River and operated a carriage factory, which was severely damaged by the **flood of 1913**. Several times floods have inundated the city, discouraging new housing, business, and industrial development. Melbourne was incorporated as a sixth-class city in 1912. In 2000, the city had a population of 457. In 1988, the Hollywood film industry injected some unexpected excitement into this sleepy little city when several scenes from the movie *Rain Man* were filmed at St. Anne's Convent, located along Ky. Rt. 8, the main road through Melbourne.

Kleber, John, ed. *The Kentucky Encyclopedia.* Lexington: Univ. Press of Kentucky, 1992.

Reis, Jim. "Buggies, Fairgrounds Put Melbourne on Map," *KP,* December 16, 1996, 4K.

U.S. Census Bureau, "American Fact Finder. Data Set. Census 2000 Summary File 1 (SF1) 100-Percent Data. Custom Table." www.census.gov (accessed November 9, 2007).

MELDAHL DAM. This U.S. Army Corps of Engineers high-lift dam is located 2.5 miles east of Foster, Ky. The official name of the structure is the Captain Anthony Meldahl Locks and Dam; it was named for a renowned Ohio River pilot of the late 1800s and early 1900s. Construction was begun in 1958 and completed in 1962. The locks, located on the Ohio side of the river, consist of a small lock chamber and a large lock chamber; the larger lock chamber was designed to accommodate the biggest tow of barges used on the river. The dam wall contains a series of gates that are lifted from the bottom of the river to control water level in the pool above (behind) the dam. The gates are balanced using counterweights so that they can be controlled by low-horsepower electric motors. Contrary to a popular misconception, the Ohio River dams are not for flood control; rather, they were built for navigational purposes only. When the water level in the river exceeds the height of the pier wall, flood stage for that dam has been reached, and all control of water depth is lost. The upper and lower gates to the lock chambers are opened, the gates in the dam wall are lifted to the top, and the river is declared an open river. During flood stage, the water level is equal above and below the dam. Towboats pass freely through the opened lock chambers.

The City of Augusta holds a license from the U.S. Federal Energy Regulatory Commission for the Meldahl Hydroelectric Project. When completed, the project is expected to use "drop in" generators in some of the gates in the dam wall. These generators will harness the power of the water flowing under the gates to generate electricity.

The lock chambers can be viewed from the public park area adjacent to the dam on the Ohio side of the river. The fishing and sand-beach areas below the dam on the Kentucky side of the river can be accessed from the parking area adjacent to the dam on that side. The fishing area provides a dramatic view of the dam wall and gates, where the force of the water flowing under the gates is evident.

Construction of the dam created a pool of water extending more than 90 miles upstream. The depth of the pool exceeds 40 feet in some areas immediately above the dam. This massive pool of deep water has changed the ecology of the river in the dam area and has also created a microclimate change in the immediate area of the locks and dam. Species of fish and wildlife not indigenous to the area, such as spoonbill catfish, sauger, and freshwater gulls, now populate the dam site. From early spring to late fall, the valley immediately adjacent to the dam is subject to nightly fogs, which, before construction of the dam, were uncommon. Towboats deal with the fog with the convenience of modern radar.

The pool above the dam provides excellent recreational boating and fishing. Numerous boat-launching and marine facilities are located along the pool. The pool has also affected creeks that enter the Ohio River above the dam. Some that were partially dry streambeds now have permanently deep water navigable for some distance upstream from the river and provide excellent fishing for bass, crappie, and other sport fish. Two examples are Snag and Locust creeks in Kentucky.

Johnson, Leland R. *Men, Mountains, and Rivers: An Illustrated History of the Huntington District, U.S. Army Corps of Engineers, 1754–1974.* Washington, D.C.: U.S. Government Printing Office, 1977.

Kentucky Atlas and Gazetteer. Yarmouth, Maine: DeLorme, 1997.

U.S. Army Corps of Engineers, Huntington District. www.lrh.usace.army.mil/contact/ (accessed March 19. 2007).

John A. Lenox

MENTAL HEALTH. See **Comprehend Inc.**; **Kentucky Consumers Advocate Network**; **Mental Health America of Northern Kentucky**; **NorthKey Community Care**.

MENTAL HEALTH AMERICA OF NORTHERN KENTUCKY. This organization grew out of the Mental Health Association of Kentucky, which was initiated in 1951. The modern self-help and advocacy movement of people diagnosed with mental illness began about 30 years ago. But as early as the mid-19th century, former psychiatric patients worked to change laws and public policies concerning the "insane." For example, in 1868 Elizabeth Packard, founder of the Anti-Insane Asylum Society, published a series of books and pamphlets describing her experiences in the Illinois Insane Asylum, to which her husband had had her committed. But in the 19th century, individuals fighting for patients' rights met great opposition. Owing to ignorance and fear, many still believed that mental illness was the result of demonic possession. Thus, such early attempts at activism were largely ignored.

A few decades later, another former psychiatric patient, Clifford W. Beers, founded the National Committee on Mental Hygiene, which eventually became the National Mental Health Association. Beers, a Yale University graduate, sought to improve the plight of individuals receiving public psychiatric care, particularly those committed to state institutions. His book *A Mind That Found Itself* (1908) described his experience with mental illness and the treatment he encountered in mental hospitals. Beers's work was significant because he stimulated public interest in the care and treatment of people with mental illness. He used his connections to involve concerned citizens who had standing in the community. However, there was still enormous opposition to the idea of patients' rights.

The Mental Health Association of Kentucky (MHAKY) was incorporated in 1951 to promote mental health, prevent mental illnesses, and improve the care and treatment of persons with mental illness. Its founding members and early supporters included Dr. Spafford Ackerly, Barry Bingham Sr., Dr. Frank Gaines, Dr. Arthur Kasey, Dr. William Keller, Dr. Harold McPheeters, and Cornelia Serpell. Under the guidance of Ackerly and Bingham, the MHAKY took a survey of state hospitals, and when Kentucky governor Lawrence Wetherby (1950–1955) saw reports of the survey in newspapers, he responded to the urging of the MHAKY and agreed in 1951 to create a separate government agency, the Department of Mental Health, focused on caring for people with mental illness. Continuing its advocacy work, the MHAKY sponsored, funded, and published *Pattern for Change* in 1966, which provided the infrastructure for comprehensive mental health care in every region of the state. In 1972 the *Survey of Mental Health Needs in Kentucky* was made public, and *Blueprint for Mental Health in Kentucky* was published in 1979.

In July 1954 the Northern Kentucky Mental Health Association was incorporated as a nonprofit agency by Mae Emmett, Patricia Kysar, June H. Lukowsky, **Mary Moser**, Rev. John. F. Murphy, Bruce A. Weatherly, and Marie Williams. A clinic was opened in Covington at the **Trinity Episcopal Church**. Rev. Bruce Weatherly was the first duly elected president, and Caty Bottorff Nienaber was the first director. The agency's first office was along Fourth St. in Covington in the Trinity Building. Thus, mental health services began in Northern Kentucky in 1955. In 1956 the association became a Community Chest or United Way member agency. In 1958 it moved to 19 W. 11th St. in Covington; in the 1960s its programs expanded to include training for pastors, which was revived in the 1990s to focus on lay ministries to people with mental illness. Board chairmen in the 1950s were George Higdon, C. Gordon Walker, and Rev. Bruce Weatherly; in the 1960s, Dr. Charles Baron, Charlotte Baron, Rev. John Keller, and Rev. Clarence Lassetter. In 1962 the association, having outgrown its three rooms, moved to 412 Garrard St., also in Covington. In 1965 the association and the clinic separated at the request of the state. The clinic became Comprehensive Care (see **NorthKey Community Care**). The Mental Health/Mental Retardation Regional Boards were formed in January 1966.

In 1970 President Richard Nixon (1969–1974) signed into law the Community Mental Health Centers Act.

Chairmen of the MHAKY in the 1980s included attorney Bob Lotz, who embodies in life and actions what advocacy is all about and strongly advocated in the Kentucky legislature; Bob Lilly, who planned with Lotz and developed the home incarceration bracelet to allow authorities to track offenders. In 1984 the Exodus Jail Ministry program began to help meet needs of persons incarcerated in jails. The Christmas Day Dinner began in 1989 and continues today. In 1998 the Northern Kentucky association moved to 605 Madison Ave. in Covington.

In the 1990s there was an explosion of research, new medications, and technology. The 1990s brought the Supported Living Service and a mentoring program. The Exodus and the Christmas Day Dinner won awards for excellence. To crown the association's 40th year, 1994, the Kenton Co. Fiscal Court granted money that allowed for the purchase of the office building at 605 Madison Ave. in Covington. In the 1990s mental illness made headlines. It is the association's mission to be there and to help fill the gaps in services and build bridges between mental health services. The decade of 2000 is the decade of recovery. Under President George W. Bush (2001–2009), the New Freedom Commission on Mental Health has become a consumer-driven industry instead of provider-driven. The Recovery Network is an independently operated consumer resource center in collaboration with the Mental Health Association. It also offers classes and support groups.

In 2006 the Mental Health Association of Northern Kentucky, one of 340 affiliates of the National Mental Health Association nationwide, followed in the footsteps of its national body in adopting a new name—Mental Health America of Northern Kentucky. In 2005 the organization reached 2,000 people through screenings and education programs, 500 within its Recovery Network, and with 45 volunteers, it visited 500 inmates in confinement.

Kreimer, Peggy. "Mental Health Group Renamed," *KP*, November 20, 2006, 2A.
Mental Health America of Northern Kentucky. www.mhaky.org (accessed December 6, 2006).

Robin Rider Osborne

MENTOR. Mentor is a small town, about one mile square, located along Ky. Rt. 8 (the **Mary Ingles Highway**) and the Ohio River in southeastern Campbell Co. Settled during the mid-1800s, the town was incorporated in 1957. Its history goes back to the days of a large **American Indian** presence, as evidenced by the artifacts from the Adena era found along the riverbank. Originally, this town was called Belmont. When the railroad came through during the late 1880s, the town was assigned a post office, but there already was a town named Belmont in Kentucky, so the name Mentor was chosen as a replacement; the post office at Mentor closed in the 1970s.

The story of Mentor had several major episodes. First were the coming of the **Chesapeake and Ohio Railroad** and the various Ohio River floods, permanently altering life in this small, mostly agricultural area. A brickyard operated here from the 1880s until 1918. The bricks were stamped "Mentor," and many Campbell Co. residents have retained them today as treasures. Mentor bricks were shipped off by rail and used in buildings throughout the region (see **Brickyards**). In the 1960s, when the Black River Mining Company arrived in Carntown, a small community just down the road from Mentor, the company's trucks created dust and made dusty conditions a constant feature in the area (see **Lime Industry**). During the 1970s, the prospect of the Zimmer Nuclear **Power Plant** across the Ohio River in neighboring Ohio brought concerns to the residents of Mentor. After pressure was applied on the power company by concerned citizens living on both sides of the Ohio River, the nuclear aspects of the operation were dropped, and today the Zimmer Power Plant is a coal-fired facility.

The Mentor Baptist Church, the only church in town, for years was the town's meeting place. Recently, the congregation built a new church nearby in Flagg Springs. The grocery store at Mentor, affectionately called the Mentor Mall, and the feed store, Dickens Mill, both longtime fixtures, now are gone. Mentor continues as a quiet town sitting along the river, just as it has been for more than 150 years. Traffic through the town has been greatly reduced with the opening of the **AA Highway**, which bypasses Mentor on the south. In 2000, Mentor had a population of 181.

An Atlas of Boone, Kenton, and Campbell Counties, Kentucky. Philadelphia: D. J. Lake, 1883.
Campbell Co. Historical Society. *Campbell County, Kentucky, 200 Years, 1794–1994.* Alexandria, Ky.: Campbell Co. Historical Society, 1994.
U.S. Census Bureau, "American Fact Finder. Data Set. Census 2000 Summary File 1 (SF1) 100-Percent Data. Custom Table." www.census.gov (accessed June 4, 2008).

Kenneth A. Reis

MENZIES, JOHN WILLIAM (b. April 12, 1819, Bryants Station, Ky.; d. October 3, 1897, Falmouth, Ky.). John Menzies, a lawyer and a legislator, attended local common schools and then entered the University of Virginia at Charlottesville, from which he graduated in 1840. He began the study of law and was admitted to the bar in 1841. That year he moved to Covington to begin his practice. During his career he served as Covington city attorney, city clerk, and city councilman. In 1848 and again in 1855, he was elected to the Kentucky House of Representatives, representing Kenton Co. He also served in the U.S. Congress from 1861 to 1863. When that term ended, he returned to Covington and resumed the practice of law. In 1864 he was a delegate to the Democratic national convention in Chicago, which nominated George B. McClellan for president. In 1867 he moved to Bracken Co., where in 1873 he was elected judge of the 12th District Chancery, at Brooksville. He served in that position until it was abolished in 1892. At that time, he again returned to his law practice in Covington. When he died in Falmouth at age 79, Menzies was said to be one of the oldest practicing attorneys in the state. The Menzies Bottom area in northern Pendleton Co., where Menzies had a farm, is named after him. He was buried in Linden Grove Cemetery, Covington. His wife, a son, and six daughters survived him.

Lanman, Charles. *Biographical Annals of the Civil Government of the United States.* Washington, D.C.: James Anglim, 1876.
Reis, Jim. "They Served as Legislators When War Clouds Billowed," *KP*, January 27, 2003, 4K.

MENZIES STATION. Menzies Station, or Menzies Bottoms as it was once known, is a community in Pendleton Co. It was originally named Irvine Station, after Elisha Irvine and his wife, Sallie Bonar Irvine, and the first school in that area was called the Irvine School. The area was renamed Menzies Station after **John W. Menzies**, who for years served as chancery judge of the circuit court of Kenton, Pendleton, and Harrison counties. He made his home in the community and was buried there in a plot on his family farm. Some other early residents of Menzies Station were Reuben Mullins and his wife, Betsy Love Mullins, and their son, Gabriel Mullins. Menzies Station is just south of Boston Station off **U.S. 27**. There is an elementary school at Menzies Station today.

Belew, Mildred Boden. *The First 200 Years of Pendleton County.* Falmouth, Ky.: M. B. Belew, n.d. [ca. 1994].

Mildred Belew

MERKEL, UNA (b. December 10, 1903, Covington, Ky.; d. January 2, 1986, Los Angeles, Calif.). Known as a wisecracking supporting actress in classic motion pictures and later as a dramatic actress on the stage, Una Merkel was the only daughter of Arno E. Merkel Jr. and Elizabeth Phares Merkel. Through her mother, Una was related to Nancy Hanks Lincoln, Abraham Lincoln's mother. Una attended the First and Sixth District schools in Covington. She also studied elocution under **Patia Power**. Her family moved to Philadelphia when she was a young teenager, and she attended the Girl's Annex there. Later she enrolled in dramatic and dancing classes in New York City.

While she was studying in New York, in 1920, Merkel became a stand-in for Lillian Gish because of Una's resemblance to the silent-screen actress. Merkel appeared in multiple Hollywood films for movie director D. W. Griffith. In one of them, her first feature film credit, she had the leading role in *The Fifth Horseman* (1924). She also performed in stage productions during the 1920s. The highlight of her early stage career was her casting with Helen Hayes in *Coquette* (1927), which ran for nearly two years at the Maxine Elliot Theatre in New York City.

Merkel returned to Hollywood in 1930 when the film industry was in need of photogenic actresses with good voices. Because of her stage experience, she was among the few silent-film personalities to successfully make the transition to sound

Una Merkel.

motion pictures. Her career flourished especially during the 1930s, when she made nearly 60 film appearances. Her perky personality enlivened comedies and musicals and, on occasion, a serious drama or suspense. Impressive highlights of her early sound work in movies included the role of Ann Rutledge in Griffith's first sound production, *Abraham Lincoln* (1930), and a memorable performance in the well-crafted comic thriller *The Bat Whisperers* (1930), both made at United Artists.

During her coveted seven-year contract with Metro-Goldwyn-Mayer (MGM), Merkel was loaned to Warner Bros. productions, appearing as a sarcastic chorus girl beside Ginger Rogers in the cutting-edge musical *42nd Street* (1933). At MGM she played her trademark wisecracking support role for Jean Harlow in *Bombshell* (1933) as well as for Clark Gable in *Saratoga* (1937). However, it is her chirpy image in the MGM musicals that have become favorites of classic film buffs. She appeared in the extravagant *Broadway Melody of 1936* (1935) and *Born to Dance* (1936) with Eleanor Powell, in *The Merry Widow* (1934) with Maurice Chevalier and Jeanette McDonald, and in the later remake of *The Merry Widow* (1952) with Lana Turner and Fernando Lamas.

Merkel's comedic talents were showcased on a radio variety program, the *Texaco Star Theatre,* from 1938 through 1940. Shortly after her studio player contract with MGM ended, she performed in a famous brawl scene with Marlene Dietrich in the classic *Destry Rides Again* (1939) and as W. C. Field's daughter in *The Bank Dick* (1940), both for Universal Studios. She also appeared in a supporting role with Bob Hope and Bing Crosby in *The Road to Zanzibar* (1941) at Paramount Studios.

During **World War II**, Merkel went on a 23,000-mile USO (United Service Organizations) tour in the South Pacific with Gary Cooper. Although her film career slumped through the 1940s, Merkel remained popular as a regular cast member, Leila's cousin Adeline Fairchild, on one of classic radio's most endearing situation comedies, *The Great Gildersleeve.* She briefly returned to Broadway in 1944 to star in *Three's a Family.* After years of more mature supporting parts in comedy and musical films, she landed a serious role in *The Kentuckian* (1955) with Burt Lancaster at United Artists.

Back on Broadway again, she won an Antoinette Perry (Tony) Award for best supporting actress in *The Ponder Heart* (1956). She later received an Academy Award (Oscar) nomination for her performance in Tennessee Williams's film *Summer and Smoke* (1961) at Paramount Studios. Although her Academy Award nomination did not produce more serious roles, she appeared in the family favorites *The Parent Trap* (1961) and *Summer Magic* (1963) for the Walt Disney Studio. Merkel appeared in Cole Porter's television broadcast of the musical *Aladdin* (1958). The following year she returned to Broadway to star in *Take Me Along* (1959), a musical version of Eugene O'Neill's *Ah, Wilderness,* with Jackie Gleason.

From the first of her silent films for D. W. Griffith through her final screen role in MGM's *Spinout* (1966) with Elvis Presley, Merkel appeared in about 100 motion pictures (40 of them at MGM). She married aircraft designer Ronald Burla in 1932; they divorced in 1947, with no children, and she did not remarry. She died in 1986 at age 82 in Los Angeles and was buried near her parents at Highland Cemetery in Fort Mitchell. A Kentucky State Highway Historical Marker along Philadelphia St. at Covington's Goebel Park honors Una Merkel for her achievements.

Commire, Anne, ed. *Women in World History.* Vol. 11. Waterford, Conn.: Yorkin, 2001.

Dunning, John. *On the Air: The Encyclopedia of Old-Time Radio.* New York: Oxford Univ. Press, 1998.

Folkart, Burt A. "Una Merkel, 82, Covington Born," *CE,* January 4, 1986, C4.

Garraty, John, and Mark Carnes, eds. *American National Biography.* Vol. 15. New York: Oxford Univ. Press, 1999.

Harrison, Warder. "Almost Forgotten Today, Movie Star Una Merkel Has Many Kentucky Roots." *Kentucky Explorer,* November 1996, 68–69.

Juran, Robert A. *Old Familiar Faces: The Great Character Actors and Actresses of Hollywood's Golden Era.* Sarasota, Fla.: Movie Memories, 1995.

Parish, James, and Ronald Bowers, eds. *The MGM Stock Company: The Golden Era.* New York: Bonanza, 1972.

Reid, Alexander. "Una Merkel Dies at Age of 82; From Silent Films to a Tony," *NYT,* January 5, 1986, 24.

John Schlipp

MERRITT, JOHN AYERS (b. January 26, 1926, Falmouth, Ky.; d. December 15, 1983, Nashville, Tenn.). "Big John" Merritt, who became a football coach, was the son of Bradley and Grace Merritt. He received his early education in the segregated public school system of Falmouth. During summers, John often visited his aunt and uncle at the Gene and Bess Lacey Grocery Store in Covington, where they discussed various topics. **Gene Lacey** was a member of Covington's **African-American Businessmen's Association**. In later years, these exchanges at his aunt and uncle's store inspired Merritt to become involved with community activities in Nashville. When Merritt reached high school age, he moved to Louisville, where he attended Central High School and played guard on the football team; he graduated in 1943. He served in the U.S. Navy during **World War II** and was discharged in 1946. Thereafter, he enrolled at Kentucky State College in Frankfort, where he again played football, and earned his BS in 1950. In 1952 he received his MA degree from the University of Kentucky in Lexington and immediately was appointed head football coach at the segregated Versailles High School in Woodford Co.

Coach Merritt began his college coaching career in 1953 at Jackson State College in Mississippi as the school's head football coach. He spent 10 highly successful years at Jackson State before accepting the head football coaching position at Tennessee State College in Nashville in 1963. While coaching at Tennessee State, he had 21 consecutive winning seasons. Over the course of his high school and college football coaching career, Merritt achieved more than 30 straight winning seasons. In 1982 Coach Merritt's coaching record totaled 215-64-9, third-best behind Bear Bryant of the University of Alabama and Eddie Robinson at Grambling University. Merritt placed more than 200 players in the National Football League. In 1982 the City of Nashville honored him by renaming its Centennial Blvd., running from 28th to 44th Aves., John Ayers Merritt Blvd. Merritt died in Nashville in 1983, at age 57, and was buried at the Greenwood Cemetery there. In 1994 he was elected to the College Football Players Hall of Fame.

John Merritt.

Climer, David. "One of a Kind Merritt Nears 200th Victory," *Tennessean,* August 1980.

"Coach John Merritt," Special Collections, Brown-Daniel Library, Tennessee State Univ. Memorial Service, Coach "Big" John Ayers Merritt, Tennessee State Univ., December 18, 1983.

Theodore H. H. Harris

METHODISTS. Methodists have been worshipping in Northern Kentucky since before 1790. The Methodist Episcopal Church was organized in the United States in 1784, although there had been Methodists in America for more than two decades at that time. There are more than 23 separate Methodist denominations in the United States, the largest of which is the United Methodist Church. In Northern Kentucky one can find United Methodist churches as well as African Methodist Episcopal churches.

Services were originally held in homes, public buildings, or outdoors until church buildings were built in the early 1800s. During the first 100 years of Kentucky's history, Methodist churches relied heavily upon lay leadership of congregations, since trained Methodist preachers were primarily circuit riders on horseback, who served many churches in a large geographical region. Methodism came to Kentucky under the direction of Bishop **Francis Asbury** and Thomas Coke. Asbury was directly responsible for the founding of at least two churches in Northern Kentucky, including **Asbury United Methodist Church** in Cold Spring.

The Methodist Church is divided into conferences, each one usually presided over by a bishop. Conferences are divided into districts, which are headed by a district superintendent who advises the bishop and supervises the churches in the district. Unlike Baptists and many other Protestant denominations, the United Methodist Church is a connectional church or denomination; local pastors are assigned by the bishop of the conference (the equivalent of a diocese), and church property is owned by the conference rather than the local congregation.

During the first 100 years of Methodism, there were several branches due to cultural, social, and political differences of American settlers who called themselves Methodists. Here, the subject is primarily the church that in 1968 became the United Methodist Church. The predecessors of that denomination included the Methodist Episcopal Church, the Methodist Episcopal Church, South, the Evangelical United Brethren Church, and the German Conference of the Methodist Church.

The national Methodist Episcopal Church also had the Central German Conference. The **Immanuel United Methodist Church** in Covington (now in Lakeside Park) and the **Salem United Methodist Church** in Newport were part of the Central German Conference. Wilhelm (William) Nast, the founder of German Methodism, arrived in Cincinnati in 1835. A year later, he was appointed as a Methodist missionary to the Germans of all Ohio. He spent that year as a circuit rider and in 1837 returned to Cincinnati as a missionary to the city's German population. By summer 1838, Nast organized the first German Methodist society (not church) in Cincinnati. One of Nast's early converts, John Zwahlen, had by 1838 built a congregation in Wheeling, Ohio, that became the first German Methodist Church in the United States and perhaps in the world. These Methodist Episcopal Churches used the German language until **World War I**. In 1939 the churches in the Central German Conference in Newport and Covington became part of the Kentucky Conference of the Methodist Church.

There is evidence that several Methodist families lived on the west bank of the Licking River (Covington and Kenton Co.) and worshipped with Methodists in Newport as early as 1802. By 1804 there was a preaching point for Methodists in the Covington School House on the west corner of Third and Greenup Sts. in Covington. The **First United Methodist Church** claims to be descended from Methodists who met in homes in the Covington area as early as 1796.

The Methodist Church grew during the Second Awakening as a result of revivals and camp meetings of the 19th century. Methodists participated in the Cane Ridge Rival in Bourbon Co. as well as others throughout Kentucky and the West.

Methodists were active in promoting education generally and in the Sunday school movement of the 19th century. Originally established to supplement public education, Sunday schools were for both adults and children to learn the Bible and responsibilities of Christianity and worship. Methodists still today support a strong public school system.

In 1820 the Ohio and Kentucky Conferences cooperated to found **Augusta College** in Augusta, as part of the Methodist emphasis on training ministers and teachers in institutions of higher learning. Peter Cartwright, a famous Methodist preacher and evangelist who gained fame in Illinois and other midwestern states for his brawling style of preaching, was present at the meeting that established Augusta College. In 1846 Cartwright lost a race for the U.S. Congress to Abraham Lincoln. Augusta College began classes in 1822 but was forced to close in 1849 when the Ohio Methodists withdrew their financial support during a dispute over slavery with Kentucky Methodists. Despite its short existence, Augusta College produced some distinguished graduates, including **John G. Fee**, who founded Berea College in Kentucky; Bishop **Randolph Sinks Foster**; and **Alexander W. Doniphan**. Kentucky Wesleyan College in Owensboro is a descendant of Augusta College. Other Methodist colleges in Kentucky include Union in Barbourville and Lindsay Wilson in Columbia.

The slavery question was responsible for major denominational splits. John Wesley, the founder of the Methodist movement, and Methodists in Great Britain were ardent opponents of slavery, and it was partly due to the urging of Methodists that the British Parliament outlawed slavery throughout the British Empire in 1833, 30 years ahead of the United States. In this country, however, the Methodist Church generally avoided speaking about slavery until the General Conference of 1844, the year of the denomination's great national schism over slavery. In May 1845 at Louisville, the southern conferences formed the Methodist Episcopal Church, South, and most Kentucky Methodists joined that southern branch of Methodism. In 1861 the Methodist Episcopal Church, South, in Kentucky had some 41,000 members, whereas the northern Methodists counted only 3,405 members. However, it must be stated that the Methodist Episcopal Church, South, in Kentucky had many loyal Union Army men in its ranks.

An example of the split in Northern Kentucky is seen in the former Scott St. Methodist Episcopal Church in Covington. Due to the issue of slavery, some members, including **Amos Shinkle**, formed the Greenup St. Chapel, which eventually became the Union Methodist Episcopal Church. In 1939, when the Methodist Episcopal Church, South, and the Methodist Episcopal Church merged, the Union Methodist Episcopal Church merged with the First (formerly Scott St.) M E. Church, South.

One of Kentucky's best-known evangelists of the late 19th and early 20th centuries was Dr. Henry C. Morrison, who was born in Bedford in Trimble Co. As a young Methodist preacher, he served the Concord Circuit in Mason Co., as well as churches in Covington and Ft Thomas. In 1890 he became a full-time evangelist.

The issue of clergy rights for women became an issue for Methodists during the 1800s. Women had been leaders in Methodism since 1760, with the leadership of Barbara Heck in New York. The United Brethren Church approved ordination of women in 1889, but the Methodist Episcopal Church, South, did not grant full clergy rights to women until its reunion with the Methodist Episcopal Church in 1939, when the two groups became the Methodist Church. It is estimated, based on present seminary enrollment trends, that by 2025 more than half of the pastors in the United Methodist Church will be women.

During the 20th century, the way Methodists worship became more formal. Ministers as well as choirs began to wear vestments. Candles joined the cross on the Communion tables. The circuit rider on horseback, a symbol of Methodism, became a thing of the past within the first decades of the new century.

In the 1926 Newport Church Census, the membership in Methodist denominations in Newport was as follows: Methodist Episcopal Church, 2 churches, 730 members; Methodist Episcopal Church, South, 1 church, 193 members; African Methodist Church, 1 church, 176 members; and United Brethren in Christ, 1 church, 196 members.

Kentucky has the smallest percentage of Methodists of any of the states in the Southeast Jurisdiction. In 2005, the Kentucky Conference experienced a net growth in membership. In 2006 there were 941 United Methodist congregations in Kentucky, with a combined total of more than 254,503 members. The Web site for the Covington District of the United Methodist Church listed 73 congregations in 2006 in Northern Kentucky.

As a connectional church, Methodists from Northern Kentucky work with Methodists throughout the Kentucky Conference and the world to support missionaries and mission programs as well as relief efforts throughout the world. On some occasions, Northern Kentucky is the mission field, such as when the Licking and Ohio Rivers rose in the **flood of 1997**. At that time, Methodists and others worked from a building at Butler United Methodist Church to serve people in Pendleton, Harrison, and Campbell counties whose homes and businesses had been damaged in the flooding. In 2005–2006, Methodists from Northern Kentucky sent volunteers (for more than a year) through the United Methodist Committee on Relief (UMCOR) to assist in relief efforts from Hurricane Katrina in Mississippi and Louisiana.

Today, the large Methodist churches in Covington and Newport are memories of the past. With the migration of population to the suburbs, most of the larger Methodist congregations are now located in the suburbs of Northern Kentucky, where there is an abundance of parking near suburban homes and room to expand.

Archives and History, First United Methodist Church, Covington, Ky.

Kentucky Conference Archives, Asbury Theological Seminary Library, Wilmore, Ky.

Kinghorn, Kenneth Cain. *The Heritage of American Methodism.* Kentucky Annual Conference ed. Nashville, Tenn.: Abingdon Press, 1999.

Short, Roy H. *Methodism in Kentucky.* Rutland, Vt.: Academy Books, 1979.

Wittke, Carl. *William Nast: Patriarch of German Methodism.* Detroit, Mich.: Wayne State Univ. Press, 1959.

Paul L. Whalen

MEXICAN WAR. The Mexican War significantly impacted Northern Kentucky, through the efforts of the men who fought, the politicians who made use of the war in their careers, and even the average everyday folk who read the newspaper accounts of the soldiers in Mexico and who voted for the politicians.

On May 13, 1846, President James K. Polk (1845–1849) declared that a state of war existed between the United States and Mexico, and Congress ratified the declaration two days later. These actions followed months of increasingly tense confrontations surrounding the U.S. annexation of Texas in December 1845, which made Texas the 28th state in the Union. The annexation sparked a war with Mexico because Mexico continued to claim Texas as its national territory.

Discussions of the possible annexation of Texas had kept the idea of an ensuing war with Mexico in front of the American people for years. For more than two years, newspapers in Northern Kentucky had applauded the idea of annexation and exhorted readers to prepare for anything that might happen when it came about. Throughout that period, frequent mention was made in the local papers of militia or volunteer units that had organized themselves in response to war rumors. As the annexation drew nearer, newspapers across the nation were full of war fever and rumors of battles, keeping the American public in a state of agitation. Northern Kentucky was no different. Weekly, newspapers speculated that war was imminent or had indeed already begun. Enthusiasm swept the region. When the call for volunteers finally came, Northern Kentuckians were ready.

On May 17, 1846, Governor William Owsley (1844–1848) issued a call for volunteer companies to form and present themselves in the three regiments, two infantry and one mounted, that comprised Kentucky's quota of 2,400 men. The volunteers were needed because of the small size of the regular U.S. Army. At that time the federal army consisted of approximately 8,700 officers and men, a number completely inadequate to fight the new war.

Across the commonwealth of Kentucky, more than 13,000 men rallied to the flag. In Covington alone, three companies of infantry organized, as did companies in Newport and Boone Co. However, not all of these companies were accepted into government service. In his desire to support Gen. Zachary Taylor's small army in Texas, Governor Owsley decided to have the first companies report to him in Frankfort. Geography and accessibility gave preference to companies from the bluegrass region and from Northern Kentucky. In the name of expediency, Owsley also accepted an entire militia regiment, the Louisville Legion, into service as the 1st Kentucky Infantry, reducing the number of positions available for the companies forming around the state. Owsley's decisions angered many state citizens, notably those of **Democratic** persuasion, who viewed the governor's actions as benefiting his **Whig** constituents unfairly. In Northern Kentucky, however, the consensus was that Owsley had acted appropriately for the good of the country.

Northern Kentucky companies accepted into the first requisition included two Covington companies in the 2nd Kentucky Infantry and a company from Gallatin Co. in the 1st Kentucky Cavalry. The infantry boated down the Mississippi River to New Orleans and then on to Texas, while the cavalry disembarked in Arkansas and traveled cross-country to northern Mexico. Both regiments joined Zachary Taylor at Monterrey, Mexico.

The Northern Kentucky volunteers typified the volunteers employed by the federal government in this conflict. In camp or garrison they were belligerent, disorganized, slovenly, and unhygienic; in battle they performed effectively, earning the praise of Gen. Zachary Taylor after the battle of Buena Vista.

On February 22 and 23, 1847, General Taylor's small army of fewer than 5,000 men, untested volunteers bolstered by a small contingent of regular army troops, met Gen. Antonio Lopez de Santa Anna's 15,000-man force of raw recruits near the hacienda of Buena Vista in northern Mexico. In a fierce two-day contest, the American forces were badly mauled, suffering 665 casualties. At the end of the battle, they held the field after inflicting approximately 2,100 casualties on the Mexican army. Nineteen Northern Kentuckians lost their lives in this battle. In his reports of the battle, General Taylor singled out the Kentucky regiments for special praise. He wrote "The First and Second Illinois, and the Kentucky regiments, served immediately under my eye, and I bear a willing testimony to their excellent conduct throughout the day. The spirit and gallantry with which the First Illinois and Second Kentucky engaged the enemy in the morning restored confidence to that part of the field, while the list of casualties will show how much these three regiments suffered in sustaining the heavy charge of the enemy in the afternoon."

In August 1847 a second requisition was received for Kentucky volunteers. This time, in response to his critics, Governor Owsley apportioned the 20 companies to be raised among the state's congressional districts. Boone, Fleming, Campbell, and Mason counties all raised infantry regiments, but only the first two were accepted. The regiments of the second requisition, the 3rd and 4th Kentucky Infantry regiments, saw only garrison duty, not battle.

At the same time as this requisition, the U.S. Army was expanded by a number of regiments, including the 16th Infantry. One of the 16th's battalions, four companies, formed at the **Newport Barracks**. Many Northern Kentuckians joined this regiment, which was commanded by **John W. Tibbatts**, a Democratic congressman from Northern Kentucky.

While the combatants struggled on the field of battle and suffered through the onerous duty of occupying a foreign nation, daily life in Northern Kentucky continued very much unchanged; this first U.S. foreign war did not significantly impact the region directly. However, people near the Ohio River viewed a steady stream of boats and barges shipping supplies downriver to the scene of battle. Newport Barracks served as a personnel depot, processing a continuing stream of recruits and reaching a peak of 450 men in September 1847.

One of the few instances of domestic excitement revolved around the federal government's purchase of mules in August 1846. For several days nearly 800 animals, purchased throughout Northern Kentucky at the substantial sum of $75 a head, overran the streets of Covington and Newport.

As the war dragged on with little sign of a Mexican capitulation, opposition to President Polk and the Democratic Party grew. In Northern Kentucky, newspapers attacked one another and their political affiliates, while staunchly defending the soldiers abroad and wishing and praying for their speedy and safe return.

The war also proved notable for the political activity of soldiers themselves, not just left-behind politicians and newspapermen. Maj. **John P. Gaines** of the 1st Kentucky Cavalry, a prominent Boone Co. landowner and politician, ran for election to Kentucky's 10th congressional seat from a Mexican prison, where he was a prisoner of war. Despite his captivity, Major Gaines was elected to the office by a margin of 124 votes. After the war Gaines used his experiences to help him gain appointment as governor of the Oregon Territory.

Capt. **George W. Cutter** of the 2nd Kentucky Infantry, a former Indiana legislator and a Covington lawyer and poet, parlayed his military experience into a post with the U.S. Treasury Department. Major general of volunteers **William Orlando Butler** used his experiences to gain the Democratic nomination for U.S. vice president in 1848.

The war left a legacy in Northern Kentucky that can be seen in places like the town of Monterey, in Owen Co., which is named for the Mexican city seized early by General Taylor's army, and in the fact that both Covington and Newport have neighborhoods named for the battle of Buena Vista. The Carroll Co. park named for William Orlando Butler, **General Butler State Resort Park**, commemorates not his governorship in Oregon, but rather his **War of 1812** experience and his generalship in Mexico.

Federal Writers' Project of the Works Projects Administration for the State of Kentucky. *Military History of Kentucky.* Frankfort, Ky.: State Journal, 1939.

Tim Herrmann

MICHAELS ART BRONZE COMPANY. From 1914 until the early 1990s, the Michaels Art Bronze Company and its successor corporations operated in Covington, Erlanger, and Florence. The business specialized in ornamental bronze, aluminum, and stainless steel casting products. Founded in 1879 in Cincinnati by Lewis Michaels at 182 W. Pearl St., the company moved to 230 Scott St. (formerly a Standard Oil Company building) in Covington in 1914 under Frank L. Michaels with 50 employees, and by 1927 it had a payroll of 150 workers. Both E. C. Kelley and **Maurice Galvin**, Covington businessmen, were officers in the corporation in its early days in Kentucky. During its heyday, Michaels produced parking meters, signs, post office equipment, pinball machine parts, exhibit cases, and even a 560-pound bronze crucifix for Holy Family Church in Dayton, Ohio. In 1937 Michaels supplied the aluminum work for the 40-story First National Bank tower in Oklahoma City, Okla. At the time, it was the largest aluminum work contract ever awarded in the United States. The company prospered during **World War II** with its specialty production, amassing back orders in the amount of $3 million.

In 1955 the Michaels plant and offices moved to Kenton Lands Rd. in Erlanger. During the 1950s, the company had become the nation's largest producer of parking meters (the Mi-Co Meter). In 1958 Chicago's Inland Steel building was encased in a 250-ton sheath of gleaming Michaels stainless steel. For that project, the company won numerous national awards. Locally, Michaels did work on the St. Elizabeth Hospital (see **St. Elizabeth Medical Center**) and **St. Benedict Catholic Church** in Covington, and the **Kroger** building in downtown Cincinnati, and at the University of Cincinnati. In 1965 Frank L. Michaels died of a stroke, having served the company for many years as well as being a Northern Kentucky civic and business leader. In 1991 Michaels Architectural Inc. was located in Florence, doing business in a much reduced state, when it was acquired by Crescent Designed Metals of Philadelphia, Pa., where the operation moved.

"Another New Plant for Covington," *KP*, November 24, 1913, 7.

Carr, Joe. "Death Ends Busy, 94 Year Career of Frank L. Michaels," *KP*, June 21, 1965, 1.

——. "'Made by Michaels'—for 100 Years," *KP*, August 27, 1970, 44K.

"Michaels Art Bronze Plant Gaining Status with Steel," *KP*, April 17, 1958, 1.

MIKE FINK FLOATING RESTAURANT. The Mike Fink Floating Restaurant was built in 1936 by the Dravo Corp., Neville Island, Pittsburgh, Pa., with a length of 171.5 feet, a beam of 34.6 feet, and a hold 7.2 feet deep. This sternwheeler steam towboat was originally christened the *John W. Hubbard*, for a Pittsburgh financier who held an interest in the Campbell Transportation Company of Pittsburgh. Sold to the Ohio River Company in 1947, the vessel was renamed the *Charles Dorrance* in September 1950. The following year it was sold again, this time to Point Towing Company, Kanauga, Ohio, and entered service as a harbor boat until the Todd Marine Service of Cincinnati bought it in June 1959. Captain **John Beatty** purchased the vessel in about 1967 and converted it to a floating restaurant, which he named after the legendary river man Mike Fink. Beatty moved the *Mike Fink* to the Covington riverfront in May 1968 after successfully battling the Kentucky Heritage League (which opposed allowing a commercial entity to encroach upon the city's historic Riverside Dr.) and after winning the approval of Covington's Board of Adjustment by 1 vote (see **Licking-Riverside and Ohio Riverside National Historic Districts**).

During the Beatty family's ownership, hundreds of student tours were conducted aboard the vessel. Besides attracting a regional clientele, the restaurant was frequented by international celebrities including Bob Hope, Perry Como, Raymond Burr, Peter Graves, David Frost, and Mickey Rooney, who became a regular because he swore that the Mike Fink Floating Restaurant served the best bean soup in the world. Under its first two names, the *Mike Fink* had carried the whistle and the roof bell from the *Queen City* steamboat, considered by many to be the classiest packet ever built, and these two items were still aboard when Beatty Inc. purchased the boat. Under the corporate name of International Food Service Corporation, restaurateur **Benjamin Bernstein** (see also **Betty Blake**) purchased the boat on October 1, 1977, and it continues in business today under the ownership of his widow, Shirley Bernstein, and their son, Captain Alan Bernstein (see **BB Riverboats**). In 2008, after suspending restaurant operations for four months, the boat completed a $500,000 restoration and reopened for business.

Huffman, Barbara. *Beatty's Navy: The Life and Times of Capt. John L. and Clare E. Beatty.* Vevay, Ind.: Spancil Hill, 2004.

Way, Frederick, Jr., comp. *Way's Packet Directory, 1848–1994.* Athens: Ohio Univ. Press, 1994.

Barbara Huffman

Frank Milburn.

MILBURN, FRANK S. (b. 1910, Louisville, Ky.; d. February 11, 1984, Burlington, Ky.). Frank Sinton Milburn, called the "Cornfield Edison," was considered to be the inventor's inventor. He dedicated his life to helping others develop their ideas into reality. He was the son of John William and Grace Barrington Sinton Milburn. Frank's family relocated to Fort Mitchell by 1920. His first workshop was in the basement of the family home, where he repaired record players and made models of inventions. Milburn graduated from the Ohio Mechanics Institute in Cincinnati in 1931 and soon began developing inventions under the name Frank S. Milburn Experimental Station. From these early efforts, he received patents for an "apparatus for fertilizing" (U.S. Patent 2,057,785) in 1936 and for a "bottle holder" (U.S. Patent 2,075,217) in 1937.

In 1938 Milburn bought 50 acres in Burlington and built a concrete-block machine shop, an extension of his Milburn Products Company in Osgood, Ind., which manufactured lathes, dies, and other metal items. During **World War II**, the Burlington machine shop subcontracted with the Gruen Watch Company of Cincinnati to make a component of the Norden bombsight. Milburn employed local women as workers in the shop during the war. Throughout his career, he served as a technical consultant to the U.S. military, and it was this work that paid the bills. With the help of his associate Henry Jenisch, who later served as industrial director for the City of Covington, Milburn helped amateur inventors develop working models of their inventions. In 1947 he began ghostwriting a weekly column, *Genius at Work*, in the *Cincinnati Enquirer.* A feature article by him, published in the June 1950 issue of *Popular Mechanics,* generated more than 30,000 letters and 500 visitors to his Burlington machine shop. That year, Milburn began writing a twice-weekly *Cincinnati Post* column called *The Invenoscope,* using his own name. The column showcased real-life success stories and gave practical advice to budding inventors. During the 1950s, more than 600 of the *Invenoscope* columns, together with a short-lived *Inventions for Sale* television show in 1952 and several nationally syndicated feature articles, brought more than 100,000 letters and thousands of would-be inventors to Milburn's shop in the quiet hamlet of Burlington. Frank Milburn was always a champion of the "little guy," and his long-term goal, never realized, was to develop an institute in Burlington where inventors could vacation with their families and concentrate on inventing.

In 1948 Milburn ventured into activism when he organized citizens in Boone Co. to protest against the Consolidated Phone Company's services; as a result, this company was forced by the Kentucky Public Services Commission to upgrade significantly the services it was offering in Boone Co. The talented Milburn was also a particularly adept ham radio operator and photographer. Some of the finest photographs featured in a local-photography book, *Images of America: Burlington,* were taken by Milburn and developed in his

Fort Mitchell darkroom. Milburn died at home in Burlington in 1984 and was cremated. He was survived by his wife, Dr. Carol Swarts Milburn, a cancer specialist.

Becher, Matthew E. "Burlington's Cornfield Edison," *NKH* 13, no. 2 (Spring–Summer 2006): 13–47.
Becher, Matthew E., Michael A. Rouse, Robert Schrage, and Laurie Wilcox. *Images of America: Burlington*. Charleston, S.C.: Arcadia, 2004.
"Bring on Your Inventions!" *Popular Mechanics Magazine*, June 1950, 158.
"Frank Milburn, 73, Helped Develop Nordon Bomb Sight," *KP*, February 13, 1984, 8A.
Laycock, George. "When an Inventor Needs a Friend," *Mechanix Illustrated*, October 1953, 86.

Matthew E. Becher

MILES, JULIET (b. date unknown, Bracken Co., Ky.; d. 1861, Frankfort, Ky.). Juliet Miles began life enslaved on the John Fee Jr. farm near Germantown. She married Add Miles, a slave on a neighboring farm, but continued to care for the Fee children. Fee's son John Gregg Fee purchased Juliet from his father after the elder Fee threatened to sell her "down south." Although Fee emancipated Juliet, she preferred to continue living at Fee's farm in order to be closer to her children. After much persuasion, coupled with Add's ability to purchase his own freedom, the couple and their freed son Henry moved to Felicity, Ohio. However, Juliet's other children and her grandchildren remained in bondage in Bracken and Mason counties, Ky., where their owner, the elder Fee, threatened to sell Juliet's family to a slave trader.

In 1858 Juliet made plans to return to Kentucky, collect her children, and flee with them back across the Ohio River. She retrieved her children first from the Elijah Currens plantation, west of Germantown, before entering Feeland to lead her remaining family to the appointed crossing at Rock Springs, west of Augusta in Bracken Co. Whoever was to provide them with skiffs for the crossing at Chalfont Creek did not show up, and Juliet was met by local patrollers, who seized the fugitive band and escorted them to the Bracken Co. jail. After a few days, the children were released but then were sold to a trader and shipped to New Orleans.

Juliet remained in jail until her trial, where she was found guilty and sentenced to three years in the penitentiary at Frankfort. There she found favor with the penitentiary warden, who recognized Juliet's Christian values. She died at the penitentiary two years later. Her son Henry continued his life in Ohio and joined the Union Army during the **Civil War**. The other children's fates remain unknown.

Bracken Co. Court Records, October 28, 1850; October 4, 1858, Brooksville, Ky.
Fee, John Gregg. *Autobiography of John G. Fee, Berea, Kentucky*. Chicago: National Christian Association, 1891.
Miller, Caroline R. "Juliet Miles and Matilda Fee: Willing Participants in John G. Fee's Anti-Slavery Crusade," Northern Kentucky Univ. Borderlands Conference, 2004, Highland Heights, Ky.

Caroline R. Miller

MILFORD. Milford, one of the early pioneer settlements in Bracken Co., is located near the North Fork of the Licking River. It sits on Ky. Rt. 19 just north of Ky. Rt. 539, some seven miles southwest of Brooksville. Its origins date back to 1831 when the village was founded by John Ogdon, who operated a store. The name came from a water-powered grain mill that was at a ford in the river. The post office began in 1850. Over the years the community has had a bank, several stores, and the Milford Christian Church, first organized in 1853. The town was home to longtime medical practitioner Dr. W. A. Moore. Milford has survived several fires and many floods. A flood-control dam at Falmouth that might have saved Milford from inundation was first proposed in the 1920s and was often discussed thereafter but was never built. In 2000 the U.S. Census Bureau reported fewer than 150 people living in the now unincorporated town of Milford and its immediate environs.

Bracken Co. Homemakers. *Recollections: Yesterday, Today for Tomorrow*. Brooksville, Ky.: Poage, 1969.
Dressman, Elmer. "Sounds Death Knell for Kentucky Towns and Villages," *KP*, April 12, 1925, 13.
Rennick, Robert M. *Kentucky Place Names*. Lexington: Univ. Press of Kentucky, 1984.
U.S. Census Bureau, "American Fact Finder. Data Set. Census 2000 Summary File 1 (SF1) 100-Percent Data. Custom Table." www.census.gov (accessed April 7, 2005, for Blocks 4012, 4021, and 4025, Block Group 4, Census Tract 9503, Bracken Co., Ky.).

MILLENNIUM MONUMENT WORLD PEACE BELL. At the southeast corner of Fourth and York Sts. in Newport, the World Peace Bell hangs poised to ring as it glistens in the daytime sunlight, a monument to hope and fulfillment of a dream that began in 1992. That year, David Hosea, a member of the local planning organization Quest, suggested building a 1,000-foot-plus millennium tower, designed to accommodate a carillon of 83 bells, and a large free-swinging bell housed in a freestanding tower. He took the idea to local businessman Wayne Carlisle, who agreed to finance the project. However, only one-third of the project, the World Peace Bell and its smaller tower, was completed. The bell weighs 66,000 pounds and is 12 feet in diameter and 12 feet high. Its clapper weighs 7,000 pounds, and the yoke in which the bell swings weighs an additional 30,000 pounds. The heavy bell rings with a deep and resonant tone. Made in Nantes, France, and decorated with symbols representing peace, it was shipped to New Orleans in 1999 and then transported to Northern Kentucky via the Mississippi and Ohio rivers by a barge attached to the *Belle of Cincinnati* steamboat. Along the way, it stopped at various sites, where celebrations were held to welcome it and where citizens could write notes about peace in special World Peace Bell ledgers. Inscribed on the bell is this message: "The World Peace Bell is a symbol of freedom and peace, honoring our past, celebrating our present and inspiring our future." At midnight on December 31, 1999, the bell was rung in public for the first time to celebrate the advent of the new millennium and to focus on the hope for peace. The Verdin Bell Company of Cincinnati, which designed it, administers the World Peace Bell and the 54-foot glass and steel tower where it is housed. Thousands of visitors annually come to view it, various organizations use it for peace-themed ceremonies, and the bell is rung each day.

Claypool, James C. "A Bronze Star Is Born: The Story of the World Peace Bell," 1999, unpublished manuscript, author's file.
Flynn, Terry. "Belle and Bell Readied for 3-Week Journey," *CE*, July 4, 1999, C1.

James C. Claypool

MILLER, BARTLETT T. (b. May 15, 1891, Johnsville, Ky.; d. May 1, 1986, Hartford, Conn.). Bartlett T. Miller, the son of Frank and Mattie Yelton Miller, became a vice president of marketing for AT&T in New York City. He and his brother Charles were placed in a Lexington Odd Fellows orphanage after their father's early death and the onset of their mother's terminal illness. While in the orphanage, Bartlett Miller was called to talk with his mother via a new method of communication, the telephone. When he later returned to Northern Kentucky, his first job was with the **Louisville and Nashville Railroad** in Latonia; but while visiting his family in Denver, Colo., on a trip he made using his railroad pass, Miller accepted a new position in the telecommunications field.

By 1915 long-distance telephone services were being slowly extended westward in America. Miller had joined the pioneering group of people trying to put these new telephone systems together. He spent the duration of **World War I** working on line problems for AT&T, solving problems, and perfecting techniques. After a brief assignment assisting the vice chairman of the War Production Board, Miller was transferred to New England, where he became a vice president with AT&T. He was put in charge of developing transmission and reception of microwave lines from New York to Chicago. Soon thereafter, Miller introduced the concept of market research to his corporate bosses and was given the job of redesigning and marketing a revolutionary telephone, the lightweight, attractive 701 Princess telephone, which, as Miller had envisioned, became one of his company's most popular products. When Miller died, he was buried, according to his request, in Johnsville.

The Princess Telephone. http://web.ukonline.co.uk/freshwater/princess.htm.
Terry, Carol. *GP, Grandpa*. Denver, Colo.: Privately published, 1981.

Caroline R. Miller

MILLER, JOSEPH BERNARD (b. May 26, 1902, Owen Co., Ky.; d. August 18, 2002, Lexington, Ky.). Joseph Miller, who became a violin-maker, was one of 11 children born to George Harrison Miller and Anna Bell Dickerson. He was raised on a **tobacco** farm in Gratz in western Owen Co., later lived in Frankfort, and moved to Lexington in 1933. After working as a barber for more than 40 years, Miller retired in 1964 and devoted the remainder of his life to making and repairing violins. He happened into his craft by being asked to repair his brother's broken violin in 1927. He did such an excellent job that he was encouraged to learn the trade and completed making his first violin in 1929. A self-taught violin-maker, he created more than 40 violins in his lifetime, as well as a few violas, mandolins, and guitars. He held a guitar design patent and even designed an upright guitar. It was estimated that about 100 hours of labor were put into each of Miller's violins. Some of them sold for as much as $3,500. His clientele included university students, symphony orchestra musicians, and **bluegrass** and **country** stars, including Roy Acuff. In 1995 Miller was inducted into the Stringed Instruments Maker Hall of Fame in Scott Co. He died of congestive heart failure in Lexington at the age 100 and was buried in the Bluegrass Memorial Gardens in Jessamine Co.

Hewlett, Jennifer. "Famed Violin Maker, Repairer Dies," *Lexington Herald-Leader,* August 20, 2002, B1.
McClelland, Robert L. "Where I Got My Wood," *Devil's Box* 31, no. 2 (1997): 45–47.
Peck, June. "J.B. Miller Made His First Violin in 1929 and Is Still Going Strong," *Kentucky Explorer,* July–August 1999, 23–24.
Warren, Jim. "After 51 Years of Service, J.B. Miller Is Hanging Up His Bow," *Lexington Herald-Leader,* December 31, 1979, A4.
——. "Fit as a Fiddle," *Lexington Herald-Leader,* 1988, D1.

Jenny Plemen

MILLER, NINONA "NONA" (b. November 6, 1916, Newport, Ky.; d. March 20, 2003, Fort Thomas, Ky.). Ninona Luella Miller Kew Scott, the daughter of Rev. William M. and Margaret J. Metcalfe Miller, was 19 years old when she first was recognized for her ability to write poetry. Four short poems by her, "Flight," "I Love You So," "Triad," and "New Moon," were published in J. T. Cotton Noe's *A Brief Anthology of Kentucky Poetry* in 1936. The subjects of the poems were love, religion, and nature.

Ninona Miller graduated from **Newport High School** in 1933. She attended Morehead State University in Kentucky and received a BA from the University of Cincinnati in 1957 and an MA in education from Northern Kentucky University in 1976. In September 1938 Nona married George Willard Kew, a minister, in Newport. She gave birth to a son, William Earl Kew in 1940, and a daughter, Mary Margaret Kew, in 1941. From the early 1940s until the 1970s, she lived along Ohio Ave. in the **Cote Brilliante** neighborhood of Newport. Miller was the treasurer of the Newport and Fort Thomas boards of education from 1948 through the early 1960s. From the late 1960s through the 1970s, she taught English and the Bible as literature at **Campbell Co. High School**. She was also a member of Latonia Christian Church, Dora Chapter Number Two Order of the Eastern Star, Campbell Co. Retired Teachers Association, Northern Kentucky Virginia Asher Bible Council, and the Campbell Co. Historical Society. In 1972 she married Floyd W. Scott, who died in 1982. Ninona died of congestive heart failure in 2003 and was buried in the Alexandria Cemetery in Alexandria.

Campbell Co. Kentucky Marriage Book 164, p. 102.
"Ninona M. Miller, 86, Sunday School Teacher," *KP,* March 22, 2003, A13.
Noe, J. T. Cotton, ed. *A Brief Anthology of Kentucky Poetry: Selections of Poetry Written by Ninety-Three Persons Closely Identified with Kentucky, Most of Them Native Born.* Lexington: Univ. of Kentucky Department of Extension, 1936.

Jenny Plemen

MILLER, WILLIAM O. "BILLY" (b. September 15, 1914, Johnsville, Bracken Co., Ky.; d. February 8, 1986, Lexington, Ky.). William O. Miller, a war crimes investigator and prosecutor, was the son of William E. and Beatrice Lytle Miller. He graduated from Brooksville High School and from the University of Kentucky in Lexington and attended the University of Louisville's Jefferson School of Law in Louisville. After practicing law briefly in Bracken Co., he was selected to be a U.S. Attorney investigating war fraud in Chicago. Subsequently, he was appointed as an investigator at the International Military Tribunal (IMT) in Nuremberg, Germany, and later transferred to the distinctive legal unit of 75 counsels serving in the 7708th War Crimes Group based at Dachau, Germany, in 1946–1947. In 1950 Miller married Leona Mumedy, who was also a member of the 7708th Group and served as a court stenographer.

The cases at Dachau that Miller was assigned to prosecute pertained to the actions of the commandants and guards of the death camps at Buchenwald, Dachau, Flossenburg, Mauthausen, and Mühldorf. Dachau's concentration camp was the paradigm of inhuman treatment, torture, and murder. However, the Mauthausen camp, along with its 60 subcamps, housing 70,000 prisoners, was given the title of a death factory for its operations of the "Vienna Ditch" and the so-called scientific research conducted there, which killed one-third of these facilities' 206,000 detainees.

While Miller was an investigator at Nuremberg, under the newly formed Nuremberg Military Tribunal (NMT), 22 major Nazi directors from seven separate concentration camps were prosecuted. The proceedings of the 7708th Group differed from those of the IMT and the NMT in that persons who were tried in proceedings at Dachau had directly ordered or committed atrocities. The court at Dachau conducted 489 trials, convicted 1,416 criminals, acquitted 256, and sentenced 426 defendants to die.

The cases Miller prosecuted involved a wide variety of crimes, including one case that Leona did the stenographer's work for, involving a commandant of the Dachau Camp named Piorkowski. The conviction in this case set the legal precedent that commanders at the concentration camps were to be held responsible for atrocities they oversaw. Normally, six to eight courtrooms were in daily operation during the trials at Dachau; during these proceedings Leona normally recorded for two hours and transcribed for six. According to military records, Miller prosecuted 35 accused commanders and guards and was the prosecuting attorney responsible for sending 25 war criminals to their deaths.

After the trials at Dachau had ended, Miller returned home and set up a legal practice in Maysville. However, he continued to provide the review courts in Germany with correspondence and legal points as part of the appeal process of the defendants in the last Dachau trial he prosecuted. Miller ran for commonwealth attorney in the 19th Judicial District, and won in August 1951; he was the youngest commonwealth attorney in Kentucky. In 1956 Kentucky governor A. B. Chandler (1935–1939 and 1955–1959) appointed Miller to the Workman's Compensation Board, and he became the board's chairman two years later.

The experiences Miller had during the Dachau war crimes trials continued to vex him. When in 1982 he was asked to testify at a West German trial of a Buchenwald executioner, an SS guard related to one of Miller's cases, Miller did not comply. The trial transcripts and photographs Miller gathered remain as a record of his experiences during the world's first attempt to bring just punishment to persons responsible for the crimes committed during the Holocaust and World War II. Miller died in Lexington in 1986.

Harris, James Russell, and Caroline R. Miller, ed. "Dachau Album: Perspectives from War Crimes Prosecutor William O. Miller and Court Reporter Leona Mumedy Miller, 1946–47," *RKHS* 95, no. 2 (Spring 1997): 135–80.
"Mrs. Rebekah Hord Is Elected First Woman Mayor of Maysville," *KP,* August 6, 1951, 1.
Personal History Statements, William O. Miller and Leona Mumedy, January 15, 1948, National Personal Records Center, St. Louis, Mo.
War Crimes Case Files, National Archives, College Park, Md., Record Group 338, boxes 358–60.

Caroline R. Miller

MILLIKEN, JAMES B. (b. August 8, 1900, Louisville, Ky.; d. August 11, 1988, Frankfort, Ky.). Chief justice James Butler Milliken was the son of Herbert B. Milliken, a **Louisville and Nashville Railroad** engineer, and Sarah Milliken. The family moved to Northern Kentucky, and James graduated from **Bellevue High School** in 1918. He spent three months in the military during **World War I**. He received his undergraduate degree from Centre College in Danville, Ky. (1922), and entered law school at the University of Cincinnati, finishing at Yale University in New Haven, Conn. (1926). Milliken married Janet Pugh of Bellevue, and they resided in Cold Spring. Besides teaching classes at Dayton High School (see **Dayton Public Schools**), Milliken coached basketball. He often joked that he had a better record at the high school than his successor, the legendary UCLA basketball coach **John Wooden**. Milliken served as the city attorney for Southgate and practiced law in Campbell Co., Ky., and in Cincinnati. A Democrat, he was elected to the Kentucky House of Representatives in 1933, and he was the campaign manager in Campbell Co. for A. B. "Happy" Chandler's 1935 successful campaign for governor. Later, Milliken worked in state government under Kentucky governors Chandler (1935–1939 and 1955–1959), Keen Johnson (1939–1943), and Simeon Willis (1943–

1947). Milliken was a member of the Kentucky Court of Appeals (the supreme court for the state) from 1951 to 1975, and he was chief justice of that court three times: 1956–1957, 1963–1964, and 1971–1973. For many years, he was regarded as one of the few persons from Northern Kentucky within the inner governing circle at Frankfort. After retiring from the bench, Milliken taught at the **Chase College of Law** of **Northern Kentucky University** at Highland Heights. He died at the King's Daughters Memorial Hospital in Frankfort, and his cremated remains were buried at Evergreen Cemetery in Southgate.

"Milliken Remembered as Likeable but Principled Judge," *Frankfort (Ky.) State Journal*, August 14, 1988, 6.

MINERVA. Minerva, often called the town of beautiful homes and famous people, is located at the junction of Ky. Rts. 435 and 1235, eight miles northwest of Maysville in Mason Co. The town was named for Minerva Green, an early settler and the first white woman to live there. Preacher and stonemason Rev. Lewis Craig built the first church at Minerva in 1793. The church, which was completely restored in 2005, is one of the oldest buildings in Mason Co. Its grandiose Greek Revival design seems to indicate that early residents hoped to create a town of high-quality buildings. Craig built a number of other structures in Mason Co. as well, including the first school in Minerva and the courthouse at Washington. A post office was established at Minerva in 1812, with James M. Runyon serving as postmaster. Minerva was incorporated on January 31, 1844; however, that town charter was later rescinded. The city's first newspaper, the *Minerva Mirror*, began publishing in the mid-1850s. The 1876 atlas of Mason Co. listed a general store, a Masonic Order lodge (see **Masons**), and a tobacco warehouse in the town.

The most famous person born and raised in Minerva was **Stanley Forman Reed**, who became a Kentucky state senator and later a U.S. Supreme Court justice. His father, Dr. John A. Reed, was a physician in Minerva for many years. On nearby Tuckahoe Ridge there were several large plantation homes, which were described and made famous in a novel entitled *Drivin' Woman*, by **Elizabeth Pickett Chevalier**, who lived on the ridge. Another of Minerva's claims to fame was the town's educational facilities. An 1885 newspaper article said that Minerva had about 200 residents and 5 schools, the largest number of schools per capita in Mason Co. The best known of the schools was Minerva College, a high-quality grade and high school. Monthly tuition was two dollars for the grade school and three dollars for the high school. Class sizes were very small, and the typical graduating class had only five or six members. A Minerva College graduate, Henry L. Donovan, later served as president of the University of Kentucky at Lexington. Another graduate, Cleo Gillis Hester, served for 33 years as registrar of Murray State University at Murray, where a dormitory, Hester Hall, was named in her honor. Minerva College operated from 1855 to 1909 and was then taken over by the Mason Co. School Board. Ironically, although Minerva now has a much larger population than during the 1800s, there are no schools operating in Minerva.

"College Town," *KP*, December 4, 1975, 5K.
EachTown. "City of Minerva, Kentucky." www.eachtown.com (accessed January 22, 2006).
Kentucky Atlas & Gazetteer. "Minerva, Kentucky." www.uky.edu/kentuckyatlas (accessed January 22, 2006).
Lake, Griffing & Stevenson. *An Illustrated Atlas of Mason County, Kentucky.* Philadelphia: Lake, Griffing & Stevenson, 1876.
Rennick, Robert M. *Kentucky Place Names.* Lexington: Univ. Press of Kentucky, 1984.

MINERVA UNITED METHODIST CHURCH. In the northwestern Mason Co. community of Minerva stands the Minerva United Methodist Church, founded in 1836. A stone from the original church building, which burned in the 1890s, says "Wesleyan Chapel, Founded 1836." The church was called Minerva Methodist Episcopal Church South in the mid-19th century. The present church building was built in 1894, and in 1994 the church celebrated its centennial. People with connections to the church came from throughout Kentucky and the Ohio River Valley. People from all walks of life have attended Minerva Methodist Church. Justice **Stanley Foreman Reed**, an associate justice of the U.S. Supreme Court who was born and grew up in Minerva, was a member. Thomas Donavan, who became president of the University of Kentucky, also occasionally attended the church. Although the congregation in the early 21st century is small, the church continues to generously serve the community and individuals by providing a location for civic events, weddings, and funerals.

"Commission Has New Director," *KE*, September 9, 2006, B3.

Paul L. Whalen

MISKELL, CAROLINE "CARRIE" (b. Caroline Scales, September 15, 1873, Covington, Ky.; d. October 2, 1898, New York City). Actress Carrie Scales was the daughter of Christopher Columbus and Mary Menzies Scales. Her father was a tobacco dealer, and her mother was a niece of Kenton Co. judge **John W. Menzies**. Carrie studied at the Cincinnati Art School and performed as an actress at local theaters in and around Covington. Soon, she found her way to New York and the Broadway stage, appearing under the name of Caroline Miskell. She debuted with Augustin Daly's stock company and later worked with Charles Hale Hoyt. In 1894 she married Hoyt, a former *Boston Post* theater critic, who had become one of America's wealthiest playwrights. In 1896 Carrie starred in her husband's production of *A Contented Woman*, one of 18 comical farces that Hoyt wrote and produced between 1893 and 1898. In 1898 Carrie, age 25, died while giving birth to the couple's first child, a son, who also died. The two were buried next to the Episcopalian Church in Charlestown, N.H., near the Hoyts' country estate, with hundreds of friends, co-workers, and well-wishers in attendance.

"Death," *KP*, October 3, 1898, 4.
"Hoyt's Choice—The Famous Playwright Selects a Wife: Will Marry Miss Scales, an Ex-Covingtonian," *KP*, January 25, 1894, 1.
"Mrs. Hoyt Buried," *KP*, October 5, 1898, 1.

MITCHEL, ORMSBY MACKNIGHT, MAJOR GENERAL (b. July 28, 1809, Morganfield, Ky.; d. October 30, 1862, Beauford, S.C.). Ormsby MacKnight Mitchel, an astronomer and a **Civil War** general, was the youngest child of John and Elizabeth MacAlister Mitchel. After the death of his father, the family moved to Lebanon, Ohio, in 1816. There, Mitchel studied Greek, Latin, and arithmetic. In 1825 he entered the U.S. Military Academy at West Point, N.Y., where he graduated in 1829 in the same class as Robert E. Lee. He married Louisa Clark Trask in 1831. Mitchel resigned his commission the next year and moved to Cincinnati, where he was admitted to the bar, became a professor of mathematics and engineering, and was the chief design engineer of the Little Miami Railroad. However, astronomy was his love. He sold 300 shares of stock to citizens, rich and poor, to fund the construction of the first large U.S. observatory. In 1843 John Quincy Adams laid the facility's cornerstone atop Mount Ida (today, Mount Adams) in Cincinnati. It became the U.S. Weather Bureau. In 1860 Mitchel left Cincinnati for the Albany, N.Y., observatory. When the Civil War began, Abraham Lincoln appointed him a brigadier general. He was assigned to fortify Cincinnati. Reassigned to Beaufort, S.C., Mitchel died of yellow fever in 1862 and was buried in Brooklyn, N.Y. Today, his telescope is at the Cincinnati Observatory Center in the Hyde Park section of that city. The city of Fort Mitchell was named for him, and why the town's name is spelled with two l's remains a mystery.

Ormsby Mitchel.

McNutt, Randy. "From the Heavens, Mitchel Watches His City," *CE*, June 15, 2004, G13.
Mitchel, Frederick A. *Ormsby MacKnight Mitchel: Astronomer and General*. Boston: Houghton, Mifflin, 1887.

Ann Hicks

MODEL-EVANS PHARMACY. The Model-Evans Pharmacy was the first pharmacy owned and operated by African Americans in the Northern Kentucky region, and thus far it is the only one. In 1923 Charles W. Anderson was the manager of the Model Drug Store, at 1039 Greenup St. (on the northwest corner of Lynn and Greenup Sts.) in Covington. It was one of the branches owned by the Model Drug Stores Company of Cincinnati, a chain owned and operated by African Americans. In 1926 Mrs. Richie Kyles Smith, a pharmacist, was manager of the chain's Covington store. Smith received her training at Meharry Medical School, Nashville, graduating in 1916. Before coming to Covington, she was employed at Bright's Pharmacy in Louisville for two years.

In 1928 the Covington drug store was sold to Evans Noble, a pharmacist, thus becoming known as Model-Evans Pharmacy. In October 1930 thieves ransacked the building and stole money, cigars, and sundry drug articles. As a result of this break-in, an investigation by the Covington license inspector cited Evans to Police Court and charged him with violation of the city's license law for failure to secure a separate license for the sale of bottled soft drinks. Evidence of his and his store's importance in the African American community is that Evans was selected in March 1932 to represent the African American businessmen at the dedication of the new Lincoln-Grant School in Covington. Evans operated his drug store until late 1932, when it closed. He and his wife, Ethel, lived in Covington at 207 Lynn St. until 1939.

In 1936 the store at 1039 Greenup St. became a shoe repair shop operated by Napoleon Waddell. Later, during the 1940s and 1950s, Raleigh Fender had a restaurant there. Throughout the late 1950s and early 1960s, the Walton family ran a candy and soda fountain shop at this address. And from the late 1960s through 1971, Claude Grubbs had a barbershop in the building. Various other businesses were located there until finally, in the early 2000s, the old Model-Evans Pharmacy building was torn down.

Dabney, Wendell P. *Cincinnati's Colored Citizens*. Cincinnati: Dabney, 1926.
"Docket Is Light," *KP*, October 20, 1930.
"Drug Store Looted," *KP*, October 20, 1930.
"To Dedicate New School," *KP*, March 31, 1932.

Theodore H. H. Harris

MONMOUTH ST. ARCHITECTURE. The architecture of Monmouth St. in Newport reflects the street's history as the main street of Campbell Co. from the mid-1800s to the mid-1900s, as well as a century and a half of architectural fashions. The oldest surviving buildings there are houses built before the **Civil War**, some of which were later converted to commercial use. Earliest of all may be the Federal-era Captain James Curtis Reed House at 336 Monmouth St., which dates from the 1830s.

Most commercial buildings erected in downtown Newport from roughly 1860 to 1910 are two to three stories tall, with ground-floor storefronts and upper-floor apartments. From around 1865 to 1885, the Italianate style was dominant. "Phoenix Halle," a German American social club at 923 Monmouth St., has an austere Italianate design with arched stone hoodmolds and a paired-bracket cornice. Similar details can be found in the structure at 911–913 Monmouth St., which also features a denticulated (toothed) wood cornice with elliptical frieze windows. The building was later expanded to take in a tiny one-story building next door. Good examples of the style on Monmouth St.'s 600 block, all of which have been sympathetically renovated, include buildings at 623, 627, 631 and 635. Oldest of the group is the one at 621, built in transitional Greek Revival–Italianate style in about 1865.

High Victorian eclecticism reigned on Monmouth St. in the 1880s and 1890s. The asymmetrical facade of the 1888 Marx Furniture Store Building at 840 is a showplace of the bricklayer's art, with four different kinds of arches. The Rust Cornice Works at 935, which produced sheet-metal architectural ornamentation, displayed the firm's artistry in a deep concave cornice with Gothic arches and in segmental (flattened) brick arches. The structure at 646 Monmouth St. is a fine example of the Commercial Queen Anne style, popular from 1885 to 1899. It features an arcaded brick corbel table (stepped brickwork), stained-glass transoms, and a mansard-front roof of patterned slate.

The Neoclassical Revival brought a new symmetry and restraint to commercial architecture in the 1900s. The Kentucky Enterprise Savings Building at 800 Monmouth St., clad in pure white limestone and white terra cotta, is encircled by Corinthian pilasters (flat columns). During a 1960s modernization, the storefront was severely altered and the upper stories hidden by metal screening, which has since been removed.

The 20th century also introduced novel materials, including glazed and wire-cut brick, terra cotta, prism glass, and center-pivot windows, and structural systems such as steel beams and reinforced concrete. Virtually unaltered on the exterior since its construction, the Cookie Jar Bakery at 919 Monmouth St. features glossy white brick, metal casement windows, and an original hanging sign. The wire-cut brick facade of the structure at 828 Monmouth St. is relieved by green and white terra cotta and large, center-pivot windows. The "zigzag" storefront, which revealed only part of the window display from any vantage point, was designed to draw passersby into the store. In 1926 Marx Furniture built an L-shaped addition, a four-story, brick-faced concrete warehouse that wrapped around to Ninth St., designed by **Weber Brothers** architects. Color contrast and subtle details, including Gothic arches, brightened an otherwise utilitarian design.

The 1930s brought a machine-age aesthetic to Monmouth St., with "modern" synthetic materials such as opaque glass and streamlined metal trim, and with aerodynamic curves. The stylish storefront of Dixie Clothiers at 809 Monmouth St. features curved glass, Deco lettering, glass block, and a polychrome terrazzo floor. Built in the 1940s, the American National Bank (647 Monmouth St.) and Security Federal Savings (735 Monmouth St.) buildings meld modernism with traditional forms.

Many Monmouth St. storefronts retain original details designed to catch the pedestrian's eye. Examples are the storefronts at 635, a wood storefront; 621, stone piers; 900, amethyst glass transoms; 722–724, stained and beveled glass; 625, faux painting, a tin ceiling, and wood cabinets; and 817, a patterned tile floor.

Although most Monmouth St. buildings were probably created by local contractors, two high-style, architect-designed landmarks anchor the corner at Fourth St. The Newport Mutual Fire Insurance Building, built in 1872, is one of the few surviving commercial works of James W. McLaughlin (1834–1923), one of 19th-century Cincinnati's greatest architects. It is a dignified Renaissance Revival design in brick and sandstone. Diagonally opposite is the Newport Carnegie library (1903), a Beaux-Arts Classical design of dressed limestone dominated by a monumental Roman arch. The competition for its design was secured by Cincinnati architects Werner & Adkins.

Numerous Monmouth St. buildings were poorly altered during the district's nadir in the 1960s and 1970s. Since the 1990s, the designation of Monmouth St. as a National Historic Register site, a facade-improvement program, and a business revival have renewed interest in the street's distinctive architecture, and many buildings are being restored to their original character.

Langsam, Walter E. "Biographical Dictionary of Architects Who Worked in the Greater Cincinnati Area Prior to World War II," 1986, Cincinnati Preservation Association, Cincinnati.
Warminski, Margo. "Monmouth Street Historic District," National Register of Historic Places nomination, 1995, Kentucky Heritage Council, Frankfort, Ky.

Margaret Warminski

MONMOUTH ST. BUSINESS DISTRICT. Monmouth St. in Newport was once one of the major retail shopping districts within the state. Before the city's floodwall was built, Newport's downtown business district stretched from the Ohio River on the north to 11th St. on the south, at the underpass. People came to shop not only from Campbell Co. but from all over the Northern Kentucky region. **U.S. 27** follows Monmouth St. through Newport, and until 1951, when it became one-way northbound, that federal highway ran through the middle of the district for vehicles going either north or south. Located within the town's business district were banks, bars, butcher

Monmouth St., Newport, looking north, ca. 1940.

shops, candy stores, chili parlors, **five-and-dime stores**, grocery stores, hardware stores, jewelers, movie houses, restaurants, shoe stores, and nightclubs. Several of the mafia's nightclubs stayed open 24 hours per day. Special shopping events, such as Fashion Week, were scheduled by the merchants throughout the year, complete with valuable prizes, food, and beauty competitions.

Many shoppers rode buses to Newport. Green Line bus routes ran along Monmouth St., and the crosstown route to Newport brought riders to and from Covington. The Monmouth Street Merchants Association operated its own bus, the Merchants' Bus. Maintained and operated by the Green Line bus company, it was often seen parked on the east side of Monmouth St., at Ninth St., in front of the Crystal Chili Parlor, waiting to begin its scheduled run north on Monmouth St. and east through Bellevue and Dayton, Ky., and back. Originally, it was a free ride. The existence of the bus underscored the importance of downtown Newport as a shopping destination, as well as the support its merchants received from the residents of Bellevue and Dayton. During the 1930s the Monmouth St. merchants provided storefront space for a small bus station near Eighth and Monmouth Sts. The bus operated from 1919 well into the 1970s.

Kresge's Five and Dime Stores (the forerunner of Kmart) had two stores within the 800 block of Monmouth St. on the west side: one was a five and dime store, and the other was a dollar store. The Kresge store's major national competitor, Woolworth's Five and Dime Stores, was located just down the street in the next block. In early 1956, with the opening of the Newport Shopping Center just a little south of the district along U.S. 27, shopping patterns in the region shifted. The new shopping center offered something that the landlocked Monmouth Street Business District could not: free, spacious, and convenient parking. The Kroger grocery store and the Woolworth Five and Dime Store in Newport's downtown business district quickly moved to the shopping center, and the slow decline of the downtown began. In recent years the downtown has experienced a resurgence, partially fed by the construction of a new City Hall there, as well as developments such as **Newport-on-the-Levee**.

"Bus Station Is Fixed," *KP*, June 13, 1930, 1.
"Light Donations Not Expanded for Lights," *KP*, December 4, 1930, 1.
"Newport Sidewalk Days," *KE*, July 30, 1996, B1A.

MONTE CASINO CHAPEL (MONTE CASSINO CHAPEL). Monte Casino Chapel derives its name from the famous Italian abbey (spelled Monte Cassino) founded by St. Benedict, the Roman Catholic founder of the Benedictine order. The Benedictine priests and brothers who came to Covington from Latrobe, Pa., operated a vineyard called Monte Casino in Covington, where this chapel originally stood. Bottles from their wine operation were clearly marked "Monte Cassino," the Italian spelling with which the Benedictines were accustomed. Exactly when and how the localized and improper spelling "Monte Casino" evolved over the years is unknown.

In 1901 several Benedictine monks built the tiny Monte Casino Chapel on the grounds of their Monte Casino Monastery on a hill above the **Peaselburg** neighborhood of Covington. Six monks lived on the property and tended the vineyards growing there. For many years they made wine at the monastery, for sacramental and commercial purposes. One of the monks, Father Otto Kopf, conceived the idea of building a small church at the monastery, to be used by the residents for meditation and prayer. Kopf asked permission from his superiors to construct the building, but his request was denied. The leaders felt that the community was too small and the expense too great to justify such an endeavor. Kopf had already collected much of the needed stone, so he decided to build a small shrine instead. Another monk, Brother Albert Soltis, who had been a stonemason in Germany, agreed to dress the stones for the workers. The monks built the tiny building entirely (even the roof) of natural limestone found on the property. When completed, the miniature church was an architectural marvel, with two stained-glass windows and an impressive 10-foot-tall steeple. The interior was six feet wide and nine feet deep, with an eight-foot ceiling. The church furniture consisted of two prayer benches and a small shrine, on which stood wooden statues of the Virgin Mary and Jesus. The chapel was designed to contain many of the features found in full-size edifices. Over the years, Monte Casino Chapel has gained considerable fame, and much has been written about it; however, that was not what the monks originally intended.

With the passage of **Prohibition**, the vineyards and the monastery were closed, and the monks returned to their provincial house in Latrobe, Pa. With no one to maintain the small church, it soon fell into disrepair. The Diocese of Covington (see **Roman Catholics**) had the building dismantled in 1965 and rebuilt near a lake on the **Thomas More College** campus in Crestview Hills. Moving the 50-ton structure proved to be a daunting task, requiring four months of difficult labor. In the course of the move, Carlisle Construction broke the drag (flatbed trailer) that transported the chapel.

In 1922 Robert Ripley, of *Ripley's Believe It or Not* fame proclaimed Monte Casino Chapel "the smallest church in the world." A retired local volunteer, George Windholtz, obtained permission from the diocese to renovate the building at his own expense in 1992. He tuck-pointed all of the mortar joints, repaired the metalwork, added an exterior concrete bench, and planted two blue spruce trees.

Originally built in an obscure location, Monte Casino Chapel today stands next to a beautiful lake, where it is easily accessible from the Thomas More College campus and surrounding highways. Many local residents regularly visit the lake and the tiny church, to feed the ducks and enjoy the peaceful atmosphere. The diocese does not allow weddings to be held at the chapel; however, many exterior wedding pictures have been taken there. A motion picture was made in 1929 extolling significant points of interest in Kentucky, and the Northern Kentucky sites featured were the Monte Casino Chapel and the **John A. Roebling Bridge**.

"Chapel's Story Largely Untold," *KE*, April 14, 1991, B1.
"He Greets the Lord Daily by Restoring Tiny Chapel," *KP*, July 13, 1992, 1.
"Miniature Chapel Only a Place of Prayer," *KP*, March 9, 1930, 3.
RoadsideAmerica.com. "Tiny Churches." www.roadsideamerica.com (accessed November 8, 2006).

MONTEREY. Monterey in Owen Co. was settled by John and Mary Williams, who arrived in 1795 and between 1805 and 1810 were living in the southern part of today's Owen Co., along the

Kentucky River. Another early area landowner was Stephen French, a surveyor. The pioneer settlement at the site of Monterey was called the Mouth of Cedar, in reference to the location where Cedar Creek empties into the Kentucky River. By 1816 circuit-riding preachers were visiting the Mouth of Cedar Meeting House, the only place of worship in the vicinity. The Williams's youngest son, James, established a trading post at the Mouth of Cedar named Williamsburg. In February 1817 Turner Bramham established the first mail service, and T. B. Calvert was postmaster. In 1819 Owen Co. was formed from Franklin, Gallatin, and Scott counties, and the Williamsburg trading post continued to operate.

In 1821 John Weems, a Scotsman, ran a small store that chiefly sold coffee, **lead**, powder, salt, sugar, tallow candles, and whiskey. The town was officially established by an 1845 statute of the Kentucky legislature. On February 23, 1847, its name was changed from Williamsburg to Monterey to commemorate the **Mexican War** Battle of Monterey. The town has been enlarged by legislative statute three times: in 1847, 1874, and 1881.

Monterey was visited by numerous steamboats and had considerable industry in the 19th and early 20th centuries. Kentucky River traffic and commerce hastened the growth of the town; it flourished as a shipping point once locks and dams were established on the Kentucky River in about 1838–1842. Monterey was a tobacco-marketing center from 1840 through 1910. The Monterey Local of the Burley Tobacco Society was the first to be organized in the region's Burley District. Lee H. McGraw, a local capitalist, and W. D. Hardin formed the Monterey Realty and Warehouse to handle and finance the business that became Monterey's Equity Tobacco Company. In March 1907, the Ware Tobacco Company began to manufacture tobacco in town.

A **Civil War** skirmish occurred at Monterey on June 11, 1862. In 1868 the W. G. Simpson Masonic Lodge 472 was established. In 1885 a disastrous fire destroyed a hotel and a whole block of business structures in town. In 1869 the Union Church was built, where different denominations worshipped on designated Sundays. On the last Sunday in June 1901, a new building for the **Monterey Baptist Church** was dedicated after the congregation had been using the old Union Church for 32 years. In a June 1908 visit to the town, **James Tandy Ellis** wrote a renowned poem, "Among the Hills of Monterey."

Monterey is divided by Cedar Creek, which at one time was spanned by a covered bridge constructed by Paddy Byrns and in use until 1910. A 210-foot iron truss span replaced it, and in 1931 the Works Progress Administration built the current concrete bridge, which remains in use.

The first school building was erected in Monterey about 1880, on a lot adjacent to the Union Church that was leased from the church in September 1878 for 32 years. On June 17, 1901, the trustees of the school at Monterey bought a site for a second school building from Samuel Sanders for $150. The building was available for use beginning with the school year of 1902–1903. On September 10, 1926, students attended their first classes at the newly organized Monterey High School. An addition was built onto the elementary school building to accommodate the high school, which was used through the year 1934. In fall 1935, area high school students began attending the Owenton High School. On December 15, 1938, the Monterey elementary school building burned. A new school building was finished for the fall classes in September 1939, along Owenton Rd., and it served the community for 31 years. In fall 1970 the town's elementary-school students began attending the Owen Co. Elementary School in Owenton.

Monterey experienced challenges in the mid-to-late twentieth century. River commerce and industry declined, the **flood of 1937** completely covered the town, and on April 12, 1952, flames destroyed a portion of the business section, including the post office, on Worth St., just off Ky. Rt. 35. Furthermore, in April 1969, the Monterey Post Office closed, and residents were required to place rural delivery boxes in front of their houses in order to receive mail.

In 1997 the Kentucky Heritage Council listed Monterey's Downtown Historic District on the National Register of Historic Places. The area is bounded on the north by Hillcrest St., on the east by U.S. 127, on the south by High St., and on the west by Taylor St. Agriculture is the major local industry. Most residents of Monterey work in stores, factories, or in state government in Frankfort, and others travel to Florence or Georgetown for employment. There are two Kentucky State Highway Markers in Monterey: one of them chronicles the history of the town, and the other concerns the life of Col. **Henry Sparks**. The U.S. Census Bureau listed the population of Monterey as 167 in 2000.

Houchens, Mariam Sidebottom. *History of Owen County: "Sweet Owen."* Louisville, Ky.: Standard, 1976.

Kentucky State Land Office. Historical Land Records. Frankfort, Ky.

Logsden, Donna G. *Final Survey Summary Report of Monterey, KY.* Hardyville, Ky.: Logsden and Logsden Architects, 1997.

Murphy, Margaret A. *History of the Monterey Baptist Church and Community*, Frankfort, Ky.: Roberts, 1976.

Murphy, Margaret Alice, and Lela Maude Hawkins. *The History of Historic Old Cedar Baptist Church and Community, 1816–2004*. Frankfort, Ky.: Lynn, 2004.

Margaret A. Murphy

MONTEREY BAPTIST CHURCH. Monterey Baptist Church, located at 44 High St. in Monterey, near U.S. 127 in southern Owen Co., was established as a mission of the Baptists' Concord Association in 1867. On October 28, 1867, lot 34 in Monterey was transferred to Daniel S. Clark, James E. Duvall, Michael Jewett, G. S. Sparks, and George W. White, founding fathers of the Union Church, as it came to be known. The Union Church was built between 1869 and 1871. Several denominations worshipped in the Union Church on their designated Sundays, and there was a Sabbath school each Sunday. This grand old church served the area for about 80 years before it burned on November 18, 1953.

Baptists worshipped in the Old Union Church from 1871 to about 1901 as an organized church. Elder John Alfred Head was the first pastor, and there were 46 charter members. At the turn of the century, the current building was constructed about two blocks down the street from the Union Church; it was dedicated on the last Sunday in June 1901. The church overlooks bottoms at the edge of Cedar Creek facing the Kentucky River. The one-story brick building was designed in the Gothic Revival style with an auditorium seating about 250. The first pastor at this location was Thomas C. Ecton.

The Kentucky Heritage Council listed the Monterey Historic District in the National Register of Historic Places on August 19, 1997, and the Monterey Baptist Church property is located within the district. Although the town of Monterey has flooded many times, the church has never been flooded. During the **flood of 1937**, many families found refuge in the building.

In 1950 construction of a 10-room brick addition began. A library was added in 1960 and closed in 1993. Many important files and books of local history were rescued and remain available at the home of Margaret Alice Murphy near Monterey. Also, the church's archives of births, marriages, and deaths are being kept by Murphy. A church parsonage built adjacent to the church was dedicated in 1958. The church museum opened for the first time October 3, 1965. Valuable artifacts, documents, and photographs are housed there, some dating from the **Civil War**. Showcases containing artifacts and histories are dedicated to local servicemen serving in all wars, beginning with the **Revolutionary War**. A 360-page history entitled *History of the Monterey Baptist Church and Community* was released October 10, 1976. Tony Watkins, the current pastor, celebrated his 10th anniversary of service on June 4, 2006. In 2005 the church membership was 375.

Houchens, Mariam Sidebottom. *History of Owen County: "Sweet Owen."* Louisville, Ky.: Standard, 1976.

Murphy, Margaret A. *History of the Monterey Baptist Church and Community*. Frankfort, Ky.: Roberts, 1976.

Margaret A. Murphy

MONTZ, LUCY ANN DUPUY (b. December 30, 1842, Gallatin Co., Ky.; d. March 23, 1922, Madison, Ind.). Lucy Ann Dupuy Montz, the first woman dentist in Kentucky, was a leader in gaining acceptance of Gallatin Co. women into professions traditionally held by men. Her father, John T. Dupuy, a descendant of French Huguenots, came to Gallatin Co. from Virginia and married Lucy's mother, Henrietta Ross, in 1841. When John Dupuy heard of the discovery of gold in California, he left for the West in 1849 and was never heard from again. Lucy was the eldest of three surviving children. Her two brothers served in Union regiments during the **Civil War**. Lucy was 18 when she married Frank P. Montz, a steamboat man, in Louisville. They had a daughter who lived only a short time, and by age 20 Lucy was widowed. Her early education and the years immediately after her husband died are a mystery, but a photograph dated 1877 shows Lucy Montz among a group of teachers at Scott Street School in Covington. In that same year, the Covington School Board recognized her excellent teaching skills by promoting her to teach a higher grade level. She was 34 at the time. While teaching, she attended the Cincinnati College of Dental Surgery and graduated with honors on March 4, 1889. She became a member of the faculty of that school. In 1893 the Kentucky State Board of Dental Examiners issued her a license registered in the Gallatin Co. Clerk's office. Dr. Lucy, as she was called, practiced in the front room of her home, a house that remains standing at 301 W. High St. in Warsaw, overlooking the Ohio River. She had an active practice until 1921, when she retired, sold her real estate and personal items, and moved to Madison, Ind., to live with a niece. Montz died in 1922 in Madison and was buried at the Warsaw Cemetery.

Bogardus, Carl R. "Kentucky's First Woman Dentist," *Kentucky Dental Journal* 36, no. 2 (March–April 1984).

"Death Notice," *KTS*, March 23, 1922, 43.

"Death of Dr. Lucy D. Montz," *Madison (Ind.) Courier*, March 23, 1922, 1.

"Local Personals," *Covington Ticket*, November 17, 1877, 3.

"Taught School for Many Years," *KTS*, March 23, 1922, 43.

Judith Butler Jones

MOORE, JOHN H., HOUSE. See **John H. Moore House**.

MORA, PATRICIA "PAT" (b. January 19, 1942, El Paso, Tex.). Pat Mora, a noted author of children's books, a poet, and an activist, lived for six years (1998–2004) in Edgewood. The daughter of Raúl Antonio and Estela Delgrado Mora, she received her BA and MA in English from Texas Western College (now the University of Texas, El Paso [UTEP]) in 1963 and 1967. She was a teacher in the El Paso Independent School District, a part-time instructor of English both at the El Paso Community College and at UTEP, and an assistant to the vice president of academic affairs and to the president at UTEP. Since 1989 Mora has been a full-time writer. Her many awards include a Kellogg National Fellowship (1986–1989), a National Endowment for the Arts fellowship in creative writing (1994), a Civitella Ranieri Fellowship to write in Umbria, Italy (2003), honorary doctorates from the State University of New York (SUNY) at Buffalo (2006) and North Carolina State University (2008), and honorary membership in the American Library Association (ALA) (2008). Mora was the founder of the family literacy initiative entitled El día de los niños/El día de los libros (Children's Day/Book Day), now a part of the ALA. Her many children's books include *A Birthday Basket for Tia* (1992); *Agua, Agua, Agua* (1994); *Pablo's Tree* (1994); *Confetti: Poems for Children* (1996; named a Notable Book for a Global Society by the International Reading Association); *Tómas and the Library Lady* (1997); *This Big Sky* (1998); *The Rainbow Tulip* (1999); *Doña Flor: A Tall Tale about a Giant Woman with a Great Big Heart* (2005; named an ALA Notable Book and also awarded the Golden Kite Award of the Society of Children's Book Writers & Illustrators); *Yum! Mmmm! Que rico!* (2007; winner of the Américas Award), and a new bilingual series entitled *My Family/Mi Familia*. Mora lives in Santa Fe, New Mexico.

Mora, Pat, to Paul A. Tenkotte, e-mail correspondence, July 18, 2008.

Pat Mora. www.patmora.com/ (accessed August 10, 2008).

Paul A. Tenkotte

MOREHEAD, JAMES T. (b. May 24, 1797, Shepherdsville, Ky.; d. December 28, 1854, Covington, Ky.). James Turner Morehead, a Kentucky governor, was the son of Armistead and Lucy Latham Morehead. When he was about three years old, his family moved to Russellville in Logan Co., where he was educated in local schools; he then attended Transylvania College in Lexington. After graduation he returned to Russellville. He studied law under circuit court judge H. P. Broadnax and John J. Crittenden, was admitted to the bar in 1818, and began the practice of law in Bowling Green. He married Susan A. Roberts in 1823, and they had two children, Robert and Joseph. In 1828 he was elected to the Kentucky legislature from Warren Co. and served until 1831. Elected lieutenant governor of Kentucky in 1832, he held that office until the death of Governor John Breathitt (1832–1834) in 1834, when he succeeded Breathitt. Morehead became the 12th governor of the state, serving from 1834 to 1836, and the first who was native born. After leaving office in 1836, he became the president of the Kentucky State Board of Internal Improvements. The following year, he returned to the practice of law in Frankfort. Morehead was elected to the Kentucky legislature again in 1837, this time from Franklin Co. In 1841 he was appointed to the U.S. Senate, where he served for the next six years (1841–1846). He was a close ally of Henry Clay, leader of the Whig political party. Morehead subsequently set up his law office in Covington, where he died in 1854 at age 57. He was buried at the Frankfort Cemetery.

Collins, Richard H. *History of Kentucky*. Vol. 1. Covington, Ky.: Collins, 1882.

"Death of Honorable James T. Morehead," *CJ*, December 30, 1854, 2.

"Hon. James T. Morehead Leaves Frankfort and Sets Up Residence in Covington," *LVR*, September 9, 1843, 3.

Powell, Robert A. *Kentucky Governors*. Lexington, Ky.: Kentucky Images, ca. 1989.

MORGAN. Morgan in western Pendleton Co. was known in the early days as Fork Lick, after a long creek that enters the Licking River at that point. The settlement was on the west side of the Licking River at the mouth of the creek. There were several stores, a sawmill, a gristmill, a tavern, and a large tannery operated by Thomas L. Garrard and Jonathan Callen. The community had a well-known racetrack, where local breeders raised fine Kentucky thoroughbreds. Morgan was also once called Stowers Station or Stowersville in honor of Richard Stowers, who lived there and was one of the directors of the **Kentucky Central Railroad**, which passed through Morgan. One of the oldest houses in this community was built of stone by John Myers. Fork Lick, a large creek originating in Grant Co., empties into the South Licking River at Morgan. The word *lick* was used to designate a place where salt was available for wild game; several miles up Fork Lick was such a site. In the early days, Tyree Oldham, father of Thomas J. Oldham, leased or purchased the right to bore a well to make salt at the lick. He dug a hole to some depth but later abandoned the project because of a disagreement with a partner. Robert Taylor, from Virginia, purchased the well and a large amount of adjoining land and established a health resort called Gum Lick Springs. It was located near the creek just west of what is now known as the John Denny Rd.

Belew, Mildred. *The First 200 Years of Pendleton County*. Falmouth, Ky.: M. B. Belew, n.d. [ca. 1994].

Mildred Belew

MORGAN, JOHN HUNT. When the Confederate general John Hunt Morgan raided into Kentucky, he gave Northern Kentuckians some of their most suspenseful moments during the **Civil War**. The great alarm was during his First Kentucky Raid in July 1862, when he struck the Bluegrass and appeared to be marching toward Newport and Covington. By then Morgan, world famous, was moving behind Union lines, where resistance was weak and where he seemed almost invincible.

Morgan was born in Huntsville, Ala., and grew up in Lexington, Ky. He was manufacturing uniforms when the war began. On the Green River in Kentucky and around Nashville, Tenn., his success with irregular warfare thrilled the Southern people, and they identified with him as a chivalrous knight, a cavalier from a romantic novel come to life. Southerners called him "Marion of the War," for Francis Marion of the **Revolutionary War**, and he was the model for the Confederate Partisan Ranger Act, authorizing guerrilla warfare behind enemy lines. Morgan never intended to be a folk hero, but he stands today as one of the greatest guerrilla commanders in history. Tactics that he employed are used today by special military forces. He sent scouts in every direction, detached squads to burn railroad bridges, and practiced intelligence preparation of the battlefield by sending companies to threaten strongholds he had no intention of attacking. One of the first to use the telegraph, he confused the enemy with imitative communications deception. George "Lightning" Ellsworth tapped Union telegraph lines and sent messages that lured railroad trains into ambush and made it seem that Morgan's men were threatening when actually they were miles away. The *London Times* heralded Morgan's use of the telegraph as one of the first innovations of the war. Morgan's raids diverted Union forces from the front and caused the Union army to expend a great deal of effort in false alarms. Describing how the raiders traveled light, the *Louisville Journal* noted: "They carry nothing but their arms, which are first class, and their blankets—no haversacks, or any other encumbrance, and live upon the country through which they pass."

The First Kentucky Raid

The First Kentucky Raid gave citizens of Northern Kentucky and Cincinnati their first significant alarm in the war. The raiders marched to Glasgow in south-central Kentucky, and Morgan published a broadside challenging fellow Kentuckians to rise and join his band. "Strike—for your altars and your fires!" he urged, and when Northern Kentuckians read the challenge in Cincinnati newspapers, they imagined that Kentuckians were responding en masse. From Louisville came word from the Union commander in Kentucky, Gen. Jeremiah T. Boyle, that Morgan was attracting large numbers of recruits and that his force was increasing as he moved into the state. Morgan had a brigade of about 850 men, although Boyle estimated that it had increased to 3,000. He wired Cincinnati mayor George Hatch: "Send artillery to Lexington and as many men as possible by special train without delay." In reality, Morgan gained fewer than 300 recruits on the expedition. From July 4 to July 28, 1862, the raid continued: the raiders marched from Glasgow into the Bluegrass, captured Cynthiana, and withdrew in victory, totally eluding the Union pursuit force of 3,000 under Gen. Green Clay Smith. They caused so much confusion and disruption that President Abraham Lincoln (1861–1865) told Gen. Henry Halleck, "They are having a stampede in Kentucky. Please look to it."

"To Arms!" challenged the *Cincinnati Commercial,* calling able-bodied men to join the home guards. A telegram from Frankfort, received in Covington on Friday afternoon, July 11, 1862, broke the news that Morgan was at Glasgow and rapidly moving toward Lexington. The news spread rapidly, and mass meetings were scheduled in Newport and Covington for 8:00 p.m. Saturday. A large crowd gathered for the Covington rally, at the Union Armory at Fourth and Greenup Sts. Speakers read the latest telegrams, and 150 men volunteered to take the train to Lexington to fight Morgan. In Newport, at the meeting in the courthouse, about 70 men stepped forward. The volunteers from both cities departed from the Covington depot of the **Kentucky Central Railroad** the next day.

That Sunday, July 13, 1862, was one of the most exciting days in Covington's history. In response to General Boyle's pleading, detachments of armed Union soldiers and home guards converged on Covington to board trains and get to Lexington as soon as possible. A sense of urgency filled the air as steamboats brought men over the river from Ohio and Indiana; trains arrived and departed every few hours. First came 280 Union soldiers from Camp Dennison, northeast of Cincinnati; they crossed the river about midnight and departed on a special train at 2:15 a.m. During the day, a regiment came from Camp Chase in Columbus, Ohio, and another arrived from Indiana. The Covington volunteers departed about noon, and the men from Newport left in the evening along with 120 heavily armed Cincinnati policemen and other Union units from Ohio.

Then on Monday, July 14, officials realized that if Morgan bypassed Lexington and Frankfort and came to Northern Kentucky, there was no one to defend the area. New home guards were required immediately. "Attention! Attention! Union People of Newport!" proclaimed a Newport broadside. "There will be a meeting of all lovers of the Union, at 8 p.m., this [Monday] evening, at the Court House, to organize a Home Guard, as all the military companies have gone to Lexington. All friends of the country are requested to be present." Men volunteered in Newport, Covington, and Cincinnati, but the tension continued through the week for a total of eight days from the beginning. Race riots broke out on the riverfront in Cincinnati between African American workers and white stevedores, contributing to the tension. Pro-Confederate Northern Kentuckians identified with Morgan, and in Covington several families celebrated the raid by inviting their friends to secession meetings in their homes. The Union provost marshal heard about these gatherings and ordered them halted. Newport mayor R. W. Hawkins proclaimed that Newport required "perfect loyalty of her people."

As the Northern Kentuckians feared, Morgan avoided the forces that Boyle deployed in Lexington and Frankfort and marched northward between the two cities. When the raiders camped at Georgetown on July 16, people imagined that they were advancing toward Covington. The *Cincinnati Gazette* inquired: "Are the fortifications back of Covington and Newport properly manned?" The answer was obviously no, and that night at 11:00 p.m. a mounted courier from Independence raced into Covington with the false rumor that Morgan's entire force was 11 miles south of Independence and therefore only about 30 miles from Covington. The alarm bells rang to call out the home guards, and about 50 guards walked to the armory, where they talked it over and voted to send a rider to Independence to confirm the news before manning the fortifications. Two days later another false report had Morgan steadily moving toward Northern Kentucky. "Another day's hard riding in this direction," declared the *Cincinnati Commercial*, "and there is no adequate force to detain them, and they are at our very doors. We must be fully prepared *this day* for any emergency." The next day was Saturday, July 19, and tension overwhelmed Union authorities in Covington. They declared martial law, posted guards at all roads into town, and warned that anyone on the streets after the 9:00 p.m. curfew would be shot.

Most of the Union men who passed through Covington toward the Bluegrass on July 13 helped defend Lexington and Frankfort and experienced no fighting. But home guards from Newport and Cincinnati and firemen from Cincinnati were among the Union force of 345 that fought the raiders in the first battle of Cynthiana on July 17, 1862. The Federals fought bravely and Morgan was surprised at their determination. When they surrendered, Morgan paroled them and they returned home along with the other volunteers. Morgan and his men turned southeast from Cynthiana and the raid ended, but the emergency left Union defenders better organized and with strengthened home guards. Covington had experienced martial law, and the crisis prepared citizens for the real threat two months later when, during Bragg's invasion of Kentucky, Gen. Henry Heth conducted a demonstration in Northern Kentucky with about 8,000 infantry, artillery, and cavalry.

The Great Raid

The following July, during Morgan's Great Raid, manning the defenses south of Newport and Covington was not an issue because Morgan and his raiders, violating commanding general Braxton Bragg's instructions not to cross the Ohio River, stormed through southeastern Indiana, moved into Ohio, and marched toward Cincinnati's vulnerable right flank. He had a division of 2,400 men and the threat was not as great as it had been from General Heth, but the three cities prepared for an attack. Gen. Ambrose E. Burnside, who was in Cincinnati organizing an army to invade East Tennessee, closed all traffic on the river to prevent Morgan's men from using boats to escape. He and other authorities closed businesses, called out the home guards, and declared martial law in Cincinnati, Covington, and Newport. However, Morgan never intended to attack Cincinnati. He conducted an all-night march around the city to the north on July 13, 1863, but Union cavalry under Gen. Edward Hobson and Gen. Henry Judah overtook him in Meigs Co. In the battle of Buffington Island in the Ohio River, near Pomeroy, Ohio, the Union cavalry captured 700 of his men, including Basil Duke, Morgan's second-in-command, and **Thomas Major**, and killed and wounded more than 100. Morgan withdrew with most of his men and continued the raid for another week.

The Confederate soldiers captured at Buffington Island were loaded onto three steamboats and transported down the Ohio River to Cincinnati. They arrived on the morning of Thursday, July 23, four days after their capture, and the steamboats anchored in the middle of the river between Newport and Cincinnati while preparations were made for guarding the prisoners. Word spread through Newport, Covington, and Cincinnati that the famous raiders had come, and people rushed to the river to see them. They gathered along the landings and on the wharves and stood on rooftops and balconies. It was probably the largest crowd on the river until recent times. As people watched, the prisoners were unloaded and taken through the city to the train station, from which they were transported to prison camps.

On July 26 Morgan and the remainder of his command were captured near West Point, Ohio.

Afterward, Morgan and 67 of his officers captured during the raid were incarcerated in the Ohio State Penitentiary in Columbus. They tunneled for weeks with improvised tools, and on November 27, Morgan and six of his men escaped. Morgan and Capt. Thomas Hines took the night train to Cincinnati. Early the next morning, they jumped off north of Cincinnati, walked to the river, and hired a boy with a skiff to take them to the first stop on the Southern underground railroad, the home of Helen Ludlow (the wife of Israel Ludlow) in Ludlow, Ky. She gave them breakfast and supplied them with horses and $60 in gold. From Ludlow, Morgan and Hines cut across northern Kenton Co., stopping at the Thomas and Cleveland homes before meeting up with Benjamin F. McGlasson at the home of Francis S. Tupman, located along Dry Creek south of the Anderson Ferry. At Tupman's house, they were given fresh horses and led into northern Boone Co., where they followed Zig Zag Rd. down Gunpowder Creek to Pleasant Valley Rd. (Ky. Rt. 237). They went to Dr. John Dulaney's house on Pleasant Valley Rd., and Dulaney led them through Sugartit (see **Gunpowder [Sugartit]**) and then south on the Florence Turnpike (U.S. 42) to the home of Daniel Piatt. The Piatt-Fowler house is one of the best-known stone houses in the county. It still commands a sweeping view of the land along U.S. 42 in Union. From the Piatt house, Morgan and Hines were conducted along Clarkston Ln. and Hathaway Rd. (Ky. Rt. 536) to the home of Henry Corbin on Big Bone Rd. They reached Corbin's house at 10:00 p.m. and rested for the night.

The news of Morgan's trip through Boone Co. spread quickly, and the following morning many members of the Big Bone Baptist Church came to pay their respects. Morgan and Hines accepted fresh horses and visited with the congregation for a time before continuing their journey south along Gum Branch Rd. past the church. Although this road is now closed, the Civil War–era roadbed is clearly visible next to the parking area at the Adair Wildlife Management Area. With Henry Corbin's son Perry as a guide, the men passed **Big Bone Lick** and continued south along Bender Rd. They crossed Mud Lick Creek and followed Big Bone Creek to Big South Fork, making their final Boone Co. stop at the Richardson house on South Fork Church Rd.

Morgan and Hines passed into Gallatin Co. late on Sunday, November 28, less than 40 hours after their daring escape from the penitentiary in Columbus. With the aid of a network of Confederate sympathizers, Morgan and Hines traveled all the way through Kentucky to Tennessee. The Great Raid served to boost Southern morale and delayed Burnside's advance for one month.

The Last Kentucky Raid

Assigned to southwestern Virginia and with 2,000 men, Morgan led the Last Kentucky Raid in June 1864. He captured Lexington on June 10, and on that day a false alarm in Northern Kentucky and Cincinnati reported that the raiders were fifteen miles from Covington and riding hard for the city. Union soldiers and home guards manned the defenses, but the alarm was nothing compared to two years before. Morgan captured Cynthiana and returned south. He was killed on September 4, 1864, in Greeneville, Tenn., and ultimately was buried at the Lexington Cemetery.

CC, July 14, 17, 18, 1862.

CDG, July 16, 1862.

Duke, Basil W. *A History of Morgan's Cavalry*. 1867. Reprint, West Jefferson, Ohio: Genesis, 1997.

Ferguson, Bruce. "The Story of John Hunt Morgan Presented by Bruce Ferguson," presented to the Boone Co. Historical Society, March 21, 2002. Videotape available at the Boone Co. Public Library, Burlington, Ky.

Holland, Cecil F. *Morgan and His Raiders: A Biography of the Confederate General*. New York: Macmillan, 1943.

Horwitz, Lester V. *The Longest Raid of the Civil War: Little-Known Stories of Morgan's Raid into Kentucky, Indiana, and Ohio*. Cincinnati: Farmcourt, 1999.

Houchens, Mariam Sidebottom. *History of Owen County: "Sweet Owen."* Louisville, Ky.: Standard, 1976.

Louisville Journal, October 22, 1862.

Ramage, James A. *Rebel Raider: The Life of General John Hunt Morgan*. Lexington: Univ. Press of Kentucky, 1986; 2nd ed., 1995.

James A. Ramage and Matthew E. Becher

MORGAN ACADEMY. The Morgan Academy in Burlington was a private school established in 1814 by the sale of seminary lands set aside by the government of Kentucky. It opened as Boone Academy and operated under that name from 1814 to 1832, then as Burlington Academy (1833–1841), and finally as Morgan Academy (1842–1897). Instructors Thomas Campbell, Dr. B. W. Chamblin, Willie Gaines, and Lovette Whitehead were among the school's leaders.

By 1842 the new name, Morgan Academy, had been cut in stone and etched in gold leaf on the front of the academy's building. Boone Co. resident Allen Morgan had died without a will or heirs, and Kentucky law said that such estates were to be donated for educational purposes; therefore, Boone Academy inherited Morgan's estate and adopted his name.

A partial honor roll list dated October 29, 1886, named Annie Cowen, Harry Fisk, and Katie Huey as high achievers, having marks in the 90th percentile. Tuition was $1.50 per month for primary students, $2.50 for intermediate students, and $4.00 for those attending high school. Students who boarded at the school were charged an additional $2.50 to $3.50 per week. A few of the Boone Co. leaders of the 19th and 20th centuries who attended Morgan Academy were **J. W. Calvert**, Dr. Otto Crisler, J. W. and **Fountain Riddell**, and Dr. Elijah Ryle.

In the final years of the academy, Professor Henry Newton was both teacher and principal. Newton was said to resemble John Wilkes Booth, was very closed-mouth as to his personal life, and limped on his disabled foot.

Morgan Academy closed its doors in 1897. The school building was demolished many years ago.

Boone County Recorder, August 27, 1878, 3; August 18, 1886, 3.

Conrad, William. *Yesterdays*. A project of the Kentucky 200th Anniversary, Judy Clabes, ed. Fort Mitchell, Ky.: Picture This! Books, 1992.

County history files, Boone Co. Public Library, Burlington, Ky.

Kentucky Death Certificate No. 18053, for the year 1924.

"Old Burlington Cemetery Contains Remains of Many Prominent People," *Boone County Recorder*, July 7, 1955, 7.

Russ, Gina. "Morgan Academy—Burlington's Earliest," *NKH* 16, no. 1 (Fall–Winter 2008): 39–45.

Jannes W. Garbett

MORGAN HIGH SCHOOL. By 1909, Pendleton Co. had three independent high schools, one of which was the Morgan Graded and High School. This institution's first schoolhouse was a multistory brick structure located near the banks of the Licking River. In 1920, Morgan High School's first graduating class consisted of Kate Hand Douglas and Minerva Rigg. Between 1920 and 1928, the 12th grade was not offered at the school; to finish high school, students completed their senior year elsewhere, typically at **Falmouth High School** or **Butler High School**. When Charles S. Brown began serving as principal at Morgan High School, in 1928 or 1929, he reinstated the final year of the high school curriculum. As a result, in spring 1929 diplomas were awarded to four students. During this same year, the school added a gymnasium.

Morgan High School joined the **Pendleton Co. Public Schools** and began using buses for transportation in 1930. In 1939, a new brick building was added for the high school, providing additional classrooms for the lower grades in the original structure. Also in 1939, the school added a lunchroom, a very modern convenience for a rural school at the time. An old church building near the campus was secured in 1947 and converted into a home economics facility.

In 1941 Morgan High School graduated its largest class, totaling 31 students. By the time its last class graduated in 1959, an estimated 600 students claimed the Morgan High School as their alma mater. The school's colors were royal blue and gold, its mascot was the Raiders (a pirate head was the symbol), and the school newspaper was *The Sky Rocket* (printed from 1940 to 1959). The freshman basketball team was known as the Morgan Midgets. The Morgan High School yearbook, *The Morganeer*, was published for the last 10 years the high school operated and included information on all grades, 1 through 12.

Morgan High School ceased to exist at the close of the 1958–1959 school year, and the Pendleton Co. Board of Education consolidated the upper grades from Butler and Morgan high schools into the newly constructed **Pendleton Co. Memorial High School** in fall 1959.

At least 11 principals served Morgan High school. The high school's alumni reside in 18 states and a few live in foreign nations. Seventy-five or more of the high school's graduates served in the armed forces during **World War II**. Included among the more distinguished graduates is **Kenny Price**, who was a popular recording artist and star on the television program *Hee Haw* until he died in 1987. An alumni organization was formed in 1935. After several dormant years, a more active alumni organization was formed in 1951 and continues to meet semiannually.

From fall 1959 until the early 1970s, the high school's building served as one of the county's primary schools, housing grades one through eight. For many years afterward, the building served as a recreation center, including a gym for church league basketball and a roller skating rink. Today, the building is privately owned.

Belew, Mildred Bowen. "History of Pendleton County Schools." www.rootsweb.com/~kypendle/school history.htm (accessed September 30, 2006).
Dennie, Debbie, and Patty Jenkins, comps. *Forks of the Licking, Bicentennial Edition, 1798–1998.* Falmouth, Ky.: Falmouth Outlook, 1998.
Morris, Linda S. Thornton, ed. *The Pendleton Echo, 1960.* Falmouth, Ky.: Pendleton High School, 1960.
Wilson, Lois. Interview by Aprile Conrad Redden, September 20, 2006, Falmouth, Ky.
Wolfe, Ronald Glenn, ed. *The Morganeer, 1958–1959.* Morgan, Ky.: Morgan High School, 1959.

Michael D. Redden and Aprile Conrad Redden

MORNING VIEW. Morning View is an unincorporated community located in the Licking River valley in Kenton Co.'s southeastern corner. Before the **Covington and Lexington Railroad** arrived in 1853, the Licking River and the American Indian trail that followed it served as the main transportation arteries for this area, which had been primarily a farming community. The area comprising Morning View was called Mullins Station for a time after the railroad arrived. The establishment of a post office in 1855 officially changed the community's name to Morning View. Tradition has it that the name Morning View came from a passenger on a morning train who enjoyed the valley's scenery. George H. Mullins, a prominent Morning View resident during the early period, lent his name to the train station. The Mullins family also operated a hotel and saloon, established a local school, and donated land for a train depot. When Mullins's hotel burned down in 1883, the town rallied to support the family by staging a festival to raise funds for reconstruction. By the mid-1870s, Morning View was a bustling railroad stop with a population of about 75. Morning View's farmers shipped grain, hay, livestock, and tobacco.

The railroad provided more than just convenient shipping for Morning View's farm products; it also allowed affluent businessmen to reside in the country and commute to their jobs in Covington and Cincinnati. James Threlkeld was one of the commuters. A native of Flemingsburg, Threlkeld was a prosperous and well-connected Cincinnati merchant who moved to Morning View during the late 1860s. His brother-in law Richard M. Bishop was mayor of Cincinnati during the early 1860s and governor of Ohio during the late 1870s. In 1870 Threlkeld's real estate holdings, which included a 600-acre farm in Morning View, were valued at $21,000. Upon his death in 1877, a correspondent of Covington's *Daily Commonwealth* credited the civic-minded Threlkeld for much of Morning View's prosperity and noted that the town "could not have had so great a loss in any other person."

Two of Morning View's most enduring institutions are churches, **St. Mary of the Assumption Catholic Church** and Morning View United Methodist Church. Located on Decoursey Pk., St. Mary's was built in 1869 to serve the needs of German Catholic railroad workers. The parish also operates a school. The congregation that became the Morning View United Methodist Church first met in the Mullins School. In 1887 the church acquired property and constructed a one-room frame church building. The present church building was dedicated in 1974.

Morning View's rural setting has made it a center for outdoor recreation in Northern Kentucky. During the 1880s, Threlkeld's Grove was a popular site for picnic excursions. For several years, Morning View was a hub of area Boy Scout activity. Camp Hatfield, located near Brady's Lake in Morning View, hosted several scout gatherings during the 1920s. The camp was named for local Boy Scout leader Capt. **J. T. Hatfield**. In 1929 the Northern Kentucky area Boy Scouts established a new campground in Morning View. Named after a Covington grocer who donated land for the site, Camp George W. Hill comprised 40 acres.

Southeastern Kenton Co., including Morning View, retains its rural atmosphere. But, though housing subdivisions and strip malls have yet to encroach upon the area, the major redesigns of Ky. Rts. 17 and 536 in central and southern Kenton Co. portend a level of development in Morning View unseen since the railroad first arrived.

An Atlas of Boone, Kenton, and Campbell Counties, Kentucky. Philadelphia: D. J. Lake, 1883.
"Camp Is Ready," *KP*, June 22, 1929, 1.
"Morning View," *DC*, November 29, 1877, 2.
Morning View United Methodist Church. www.mvumc.faithweb.com (accessed April 8, 2006).

Greg Perkins

MORRIS, BUCKNER STITH (b. August 19, 1800, Augusta, Ky.; d. December 16, 1879, Chicago, Ill.). Buckner Stith Morris was the son of Dickinson and Frances Buckner Morris. His father was the county surveyor in Pendleton Co., and his maternal grandfather laid out the town of Augusta. Buckner was educated at home and worked on a farm as a youth, where he also hunted small game. In 1824 he began to study law and in 1827 opened a law practice in Augusta. He was elected to the Kentucky legislature at age 29 and served two terms. Politically, he was a conservative Whig. In 1832 he married Evilina Barker of Mason Co., and in 1834 he left Kentucky on horseback for Chicago. When he set up his law practice in Chicago, there were only 37 homes in the city. He participated in the incorporation of Chicago in 1837, and on March 6, 1838, as a Whig, he was elected the second mayor of Chicago, defeating the Democrat William Jones. He served two years as mayor, 1838 and 1839. His work as mayor was hindered by the economic effects of the panic of 1837 and a poor real estate market. In 1851 he was elected to a judgeship in the Illinois circuit court. In 1860 he was a candidate for governor of Illinois. During the **Civil War**, because of his Southern leanings, he was generally thought to be a copperhead (a Northern resident with Southern sympathies). In the early days of Chicago, Morris had invested well in real estate, and though not fabulously rich, he lived comfortably throughout his last years. He married three times; his first two wives preceded him in death. Morris was a Roman Catholic. He died in 1879 in Chicago and was buried in the Chicago area's largest cemetery, Rosehill.

Politicalgraveyard.com. "Buckner Stith Morris." www.politcalgraveyard.com (accessed June 25, 2007).
Grossman, James R., Ann Durkin Keating, and Janice L. Reife, eds. *The Encyclopedia of Chicago.* Chicago: Univ. of Chicago Press, 2004.

MOSER, MARY (b. March 17, 1897, Covington, Ky.; d. December 28, 1987, Covington, Ky.). Mary Moser, a social worker, was born Mary Catherine Macke, the daughter of Frank J. and Julia Walsh Macke. She grew up in Covington, attending St. Mary Grade School and **La Salette Academy**. Mary married Ralph E. Moser upon his return from **World War I**, and they had four daughters; Ralph started the first unemployment agency in Northern Kentucky. The family moved to Idaho Ave. in Fort Mitchell. Ralph died prematurely in 1935, leaving Mary to support the family, and she went to work for the Kenton Co. Welfare Department as a social worker when that profession was still in its infancy. In 1948 Mary Moser became one of the founders of Catholic Social Ser-

Mary Moser.

vices in Northern Kentucky (see **Catholic Charities**), the social services delivery arm of the Diocese of Covington (see **Roman Catholics**). She worked tirelessly helping people and families in need, and over the course of her employment arranged for more than 300 children to be placed in adoptive homes. In 1980 Moser was honored for her years of effort by being chosen the national social worker of the year at a convention in Rochester, N.Y. At age 90 she continued to visit "her old people" in nursing homes in the region. Mary Moser died in 1987 at St. Elizabeth Hospital in Covington and was buried at St. Mary Cemetery in Fort Mitchell.

"Dedication Marked Mary C. Macke Moser," *KP*, December 30, 1987, 1.

Ott, James. *A Brief History of the Diocese of Covington*. Strasbourg, France: Editions du Signe, 2002.

Tenkotte, Paul A., Thomas S. Ward, and David E. Schroeder. *To Be Catholic and American in Northern, Central, and Appalachian Kentucky: The Diocese of Covington, 1853–2003*. Forthcoming.

Anne Moser Flannery

MOSGROVE, GEORGE DALLAS (b. August 18, 1844, Lousiville, Ky.; d. February 21, 1907, Carroll Co., Ky.). Writer George Dallas Mosgrove was the son of William and Elizabeth Mosgrove. Where he was educated is not known, but it is obvious from the style of his famous work *Kentucky Cavaliers in Dixie* that he learned how to write well. He enlisted in the 4th Kentucky Cavalry Regiment CSA (Confederate States of America) on September 2, 1862, at New Liberty in Owen Co. and remained a private throughout his time of service. He was assigned as a clerk to the regimental, and later the brigade, headquarters, where he was a copyist and a messenger. He had the opportunity to meet and work with many famous participants in the **Civil War**, such as John C. Breckinridge, **John Hunt Morgan**, Humphrey Marshall, Basil Duke, and Jubal Early. As the events of the war transpired, he had the presence of mind to record them, and it resulted in his book *Kentucky Cavaliers in Dixie* (1895). This work presents short biographies of many of the members of the 4th Kentucky Cavalry Regiment. It is far more than the standard regimental histories that were published after the Civil War. When the war ended, Mosgrove moved to Carroll Co., where he taught in a one-room school at Locust Grove near Carrollton. He wrote many articles for various local and national publications. One morning in 1907, he was found dead along the road from Carrollton to Locust Grove, having apparently died of heart failure. His gravestone at the **International Order of Odd Fellows** Cemetery in Carrollton notes his allegiance to the South. His famous work continues to be reprinted because of its value as a primary historical source.

Mosgrove, George Dallas. *Kentucky Cavaliers in Dixie*. Ed. Bell Irvin Wiley. 1895. Reprint, Wilmington, N.C.: Bradford, 1987.

MOSHER, KATE E. P. (b. July 11, 1836, Warsaw, Ky.; d. April 5, 1926, Covington, Ky.). Kate E. Perry Mosher, a Confederate activist and a wood carver, was the daughter of Thornton and Julia A. Keene Perry. She became deaf at age 20, having contracted meningitis after attending a ball at the **Newport Barracks**. Shortly after her marriage to William Webster Mosher, whose family owned the **Latonia Springs** Hotel in Latonia, she moved to Covington. William Mosher died in 1897.

Kate Mosher was a Southern sympathizer during the **Civil War**. She was known to render aid to Southerners who passed through Covington. She also helped some 50 prisoners escape from the Rock Island Arsenal, a prison in Illinois near the Mississippi River for captured Southern soldiers. She entered the prison allegedly to visit a prisoner and later used information gathered during her visit to effect the Confederate prisoners' escape. After the fighting ended, she assisted homeless persons in Northern Kentucky who were victims of the war.

As a clubwoman, Mosher was a charter member of the **Covington Art Club**. She organized the United Daughters of the Confederacy in Kentucky and started the organization's Henrietta Hunt Morgan chapter in Newport and its Basil Duke chapter in Fort Thomas.

As an artist, she was a student of famed Cincinnati wood carver Benn Pitman. Mosher's carved furniture was exhibited at the Centennial Exposition in Philadelphia in 1876 and at the Columbian Exhibition in Chicago in 1893. A member of **Trinity Episcopal Church** in Covington, she oversaw and contributed to the wood carving done on its altar and in the chapel during the 1890s.

Mosher died in 1926 at the home of a relative on Madison Ave. in Covington and was buried in the Mosher family lot at Spring Grove Cemetery in Cincinnati.

Kentucky Death Certificate No. 10669, for the year 1926.

"Mrs. Kate Mosher Called by Death," *KP*, April 6, 1926, 1.

Roth, George F., Jr. *The Story of Trinity Episcopal Church in Covington*. Covington, Ky.: Trinity Episcopal Church, 1991.

Spring Grove Cemetery Records, Cincinnati.

MOTCH JEWELERS. In 1857 Michael C. Motch, a watchmaker and jeweler from Cincinnati, opened the Motch Jewelry Store in Covington (see **Covington, Downtown**). The store advertised its expertise in watch and jewelry repair as well as the best prices and selection available for clocks, new jewelry, and fancy articles. Motch's watch, jewelry repair, and restoration business thrives today, and complete appraisal services have been added. The enterprise continues to be family owned and operated. It is the oldest jewelry store in the Midwest, having been at its current location, 613 Madison Ave., since 1871. The original display cases are in the store, as is a 10-foot-tall George Jones regulator clock. A street clock from Boston's E. Howard & Company stands on the sidewalk in front of the store and is a Covington landmark. Motch's displays watches, eyeglasses, and letter openers that were samples 100 years ago.

The first store was located at 512 Madison Ave. Success enabled Motch to retain Cincinnati architect James W. McLaughlin to design a new jewelry store building. In September 1871, the business moved across the street into the new structure. Advertisements for the Grand Opening acclaimed the building as a work of art and encouraged citizens to visit just to see the "adornments." Upon his death in 1900, Motch was said to be one of Covington's wealthiest residents.

Covington City Directory, 1869.

"Dropped Dead," *CE*, January 2, 1900, 5.

Kenton Co. Death Records, for the year 1900, Kenton Co. Public Library, Covington, Ky.

"M. C. Motchs New Store Opened," *CJ*, September 23, 1871, 3.

"Motch Jewelers." www.motchjewelers.com/ (accessed August 17, 2007).

Motch Jewelers, ca. 1905.

Nelson, Kristi. "Business Is Good—and Long-Lasting," *KE*, November 8, 1996, B1C.

Jeanne Greiser

MOTHER OF GOD CATHOLIC CHURCH. Established in 1841 for German-speaking Catholics of St. Mary Church (now the **Cathedral Basilica of the Assumption**), the architectural and artistic masterpiece Mother of God Church in Covington holds the distinction of being the "mother parish" of German-speaking Catholic "daughter parishes" throughout Northern Kentucky. In addition, its early brother-pastors **William** (1848–1907) **and Henry** (1855–1929) **Tappert** promoted German American Catholicism in the United States outside of Kentucky. For instance, William Tappert was one of the incorporators of Leo House in New York City (1888), which offered temporary overnight accommodations, the Sacraments, and assistance to German-Catholic immigrants arriving at New York harbor.

The present church edifice, dedicated in 1871, is considered one of the premier examples of Italian Renaissance Revival architecture in America. Designed by the noted Cincinnati architectural firm of **Walter and Stewart**, it was the tallest structure in Covington until the building of skyscrapers in the late 20th century. It is distinguished as a landmark by its 150-foot dome and its twin 200-foot bell towers, long used by steamboat pilots as a guide point in their navigation along the Ohio River. The church's interior is embellished by *a secco* paintings on the ceiling and the sanctuary walls, mainly by the German American artist **Wenceslaus Thien** (1838–1912). Five large murals by the renowned German American artist **Johann Schmitt** (1825–1898) depict the five Joyful Mysteries of the Rosary. Thien's symbolic depictions of the five Sorrowful Mysteries wrap around the apse of the sanctuary, and his finely rendered symbols of the Glorious Mysteries flank the main reredos altar and crucifixion scene. The altars, the communion rail, and the furnishings of the sanctuary are of hand-carved oak. The statues of the altar's crucifixion scene, imported from Germany, are of hand-carved wood covered by gesso (a thin layer of plaster). The outstanding stained-glass windows were, for the most part, executed by the Munich firm of Mayer and Company. The Stations of the Cross were the work of the Swiss artist Paul Deschwanden. The organ, by the Cincinnati firm of Koehnken and Grimm, was built in 1876. In recognition of the outstanding architecture of Mother of God Church, it was added to the National Register of Historic Places in 1973.

Mother of God Catholic Church.

Mother of God's school building, designed by the famous Cincinnati architectural firm of **Samuel Hannaford and Sons** and dedicated in 1906, was perhaps the finest parochial school edifice in the Diocese of Covington. The building included 10 classrooms, a teachers' conference room, an auditorium seating 900 (with a gallery and four boxes), a music recital hall, a gymnasium, club rooms for Catholic men and women of the city, a reading room, a billiard room, a kitchen, and shower and tub rooms. At the time of its dedication, the school enrolled about 565 students. When the Cincinnati Symphony Orchestra visited Covington, it regularly played in the school's acoustically perfect auditorium. By the early 20th century, the school had lost enrollment as families left the downtown area and moved to other neighborhoods of Covington, as well as to outlying suburbs. In absolute numbers, the parish reached its peak about 1915, with 4,000 members.

From about 1950 until the 1970s, Mother of God was an inner-city, downtown congregation facing the twin crises of urban renewal and suburban flight. By 1950 the parish had declined to a membership of 1,400, and its school enrolled a mere 112 students. The decrease in the parish's elementary school enrollment actually proved beneficial to other educational institutions, as parts of the mammoth school building were utilized as an "incubator." **Covington Catholic High School** (for young men) was housed in the building from 1925 until January 1955, and from September 1957 until June 1967, Villa Madonna College (now **Thomas More College**) leased space for its science laboratories. A Braille Classroom of the Society for Visually Handicapped Children (see **Blind and Visually Impaired**) was opened in the school in 1958. Mother of God School closed at the end of the 1961–1962 academic year, and its children attended neighboring **St. Aloysius** School. The closing of Mother of God School enabled Good Counsel School (see **Riverside–Good Counsel School**) to occupy the building from September 1962 until June 1971.

In June 1966 Bishop Richard Ackerman asked Msgr. Edward T. Hickey, chancellor of the diocese, to become pastor. At that time the parish had more than 600 active households. Urban renewal, suburban migration, and an aging urban core quickly took their toll, and by 1969 the parish had declined to about 350 active households (537 parishioners), many of whom were senior citizens, widows, widowers, or single. Only 30 traditional family units with children remained. The parish council hired Community Action Associates of Pittsburgh, Pa., in late 1969 to study the future of the parish. As a result of that study and the members' resiliency, the parish determined to remain open and to replace the church's furnace and leaking roof, carry out other necessary repairs and renovations, demolish the school building for additional parking, and construct a parish hall in the undercroft of the church. Rev. William Mertes (1921–2003) (administrator 1971 and pastor 1971–1981) oversaw construction of the parish hall, which was designed by the architectural firm of Robert Ehmet Hayes and Associates of Fort Mitchell. The nearly $75,000 construction project was completed by Martin Zalla of Building Crafts Inc. of Newport. The demolition of the school followed in 1974, with the construction of a parking lot in its place.

In 1974 Mertes became instrumental in sparking a neighborhood restoration movement, when he and 12 other "urban pioneers" formed the Covington Avenue Property Partnership. This group originally rehabilitated nine homes on Covington Ave. and has since sponsored more restoration projects, as well as construction of new in-fill housing in the neighborhood. The area is now appropriately listed in the National Register of Historic Places as **Mutter Gottes** (German for "Mother of God") **National Historic District**.

In 1981 Rev. Ralph Hartman, formerly director of **Campbell Lodge**, became pastor of Mother of God Church. Hartman's indefatigable labors on behalf of Mother of God saw the parish through three difficult crises. First, on May 16, 1985, lightning struck nearby St. Aloysius Church at W. Seventh and Bakewell Sts., and the resultant fire destroyed the historic building and its famous grotto. The diocese subsequently (January 1, 1986) merged that parish with Mother of God. Second, on March 10, 1986, a "micro blast" of tornadic winds (see **Tornadoes**) struck Covington. As Mother of God Church was undergoing repairs necessitated by the storm, the third crisis occurred. On the evening of September 25, 1986, workmen accidentally set the church dome afire. The fire caused extensive damage to the dome, as well as smoke and water damage to the historic interior. A subsequent $1.5 million restoration, overseen by Hartman and parishioners Victor Canfield and Paul Tenkotte, faithfully recovered the church's former historic appearance. Bruce Goetzman, a well-known restoration architect and professor at the University of Cincinnati, was hired, and Martin Zalla of Building Crafts Inc. of Newport served as general contractor. The lantern of the dome was rebuilt to the exact specifications of the old. Canvas paintings were carefully consolidated, cleaned, and restored. The plaster capitals of damaged columns and pilasters were remolded to exact specifications and covered with gold leaf. The repainted sky scene in the dome was painstakingly matched to surviving plaster pieces. The entire process of restoration was professionally photographed and documented. The Miami Purchase Association for Historic Preservation of Cincinnati recognized the restoration in a 1987 annual awards ceremony. The restoration received national acclaim at the 42nd Annual Conference of the National Trust for Historic Preservation (Cincinnati, 1988) and at the 44th Annual Meeting of the Society of Architectural Historians (Cincinnati, 1991).

In 1991 Rev. Raymond Holtz (1932–2003) became pastor, just as the parish was marking its sesquicentennial. In the following year, the church installed a lift for disabled persons. Then the parish commissioned Goetzman to design a new educational and meeting facility, the St. Aloysius Center, which was dedicated in 1995.

Long recognized for its generous commitment to social concerns, Mother of God Church expanded these efforts during the leadership of many pastors. In 1931 Bishop Francis W. Howard appointed Rev. Edward Klosterman (1884–1961) (pastor 1930–1961) as chairman of the diocese's Charity Association, the predecessor of the **Catholic Charities**. Klosterman's charitable work during the **Great Depression**, the **flood of 1937**, and **World War II** was legendary in Northern Kentucky. He was instrumental in the founding of the Kenton Co. Relief Committee in 1931 and served as its first chairman. He was a member of the board of directors of the Kenton Co. chapter of the **American Red Cross**, a strong supporter and advisory board member of St. Elizabeth Hospital (see **St. Elizabeth Medical Center**), and influential in the founding of both the Kenton Co. **Tuberculosis** Sanatorium and the Carmel Manor Nursing Home (see **Nursing Homes and Retirement Housing**). In 1946 Klosterman was involved in establishing the **Society of St. Vincent de Paul**'s Salvage Bureau, originally located on Greenup St.; it later moved to 241–243 Pike St. The store, managed by Mother of God parishioner Andrew Lonneman, sold used clothing and furniture at reasonable prices to the poor. In the same year, Bishop William Mulloy announced the establishment of a central office of the Bureau of Catholic Charities in the St. Vincent de Paul building. Klosterman continued as director, while the daily operations of the bureau were placed in the capable hands of Mrs. **Mary Moser**. Succeeding Klosterman as director of Catholic Charities was Msgr. John A. Bankemper (1888–1972), appointed to this post by Bishop Mulloy in 1960. In the following year, Bankemper became pastor at Mother of God Church. Mertes was appointed director of the Catholic Social Service Bureau following his term as pastor.

In 1974 Mertes and parish leaders founded the **Parish Kitchen** to feed the poor of the area. The kitchen was housed in a building at the southeast corner of Pike and Russell Sts. In 1976 parishioners expanded the operations to include an emergency food shelter to dispense groceries to the poor. Mertes began an intensive campaign in 1977 seeking grants to establish a home for abused women, later named **Welcome House** and officially opened in 1982. In 1980 the parish purchased and renovated a one-story building at 531 Russell St. Subsequently a not-for-profit corporation, 531 Building Inc., whose purpose was "to encourage sobriety . . . and carry out the ideals and objectives of Alcoholics Anonymous" (see **Substance Abuse Treatment**), leased the building from the parish as a meeting hall.

Mother of God Church has long excelled in the liturgical arts. From the 1840s until the 1870s, **B. H. F. Hellebusch** (1825–1885) was the organist and a teacher at Mother of God. Hellebusch, through multiple editions of his best-selling German American hymnal *Gesang und Gebet Buch*, popularized many German songs in America, including "O Come Little Children," "Holy God, We Praise Thy Name," and "Hail Holy Queen Enthroned Above." From 1895 until 1955, Professor **Edward Strubel** (1875–1964) was organist. Born in Bavaria in 1875, he studied at the musical conservatories in Speyer and Würzburg, Germany, and immigrated to the United States in 1894. As a composer of secular and religious works, he was perhaps best known for his composition "When Evening Shadows Fall." Mother of God's Choral Club, which may have been the first diocesan choir to feature both male and female voices, was founded in 1938. For many years, it was under the direction of Leo J. Grote. In 1941 it began its highly successful Lenten meditation the "Seven Last Words of Christ," by Theodore Dubois. In 1949 it earned the grand prize at a three-state music festival at Indiana University in Bloomington, Ind., qualifying it to sing at the Chicagoland Music Festival at Soldiers' Field. There, it placed third in national competition.

Today Mother of God parish continues its commitment to historic preservation with its National Register church, to fine music with its Choral Club and its Folk Ensemble, and to community service in the inner city. The congregation numbers about 1,900 people, drawn from throughout the Northern Kentucky and Cincinnati metropolitan region.

Ryan, Paul E. *History of the Diocese of Covington, Kentucky*. Covington, Ky.: Diocese of Covington, 1954.

Tenkotte, Paul A., David E. Schroeder, and Thomas S. Ward. *To Be Catholic and American in Northern, Central, and Appalachian Kentucky: The Diocese of Covington, 1853–2003*. Forthcoming.

Paul A. Tenkotte

MOTHER OF GOD CEMETERY. The **Mother of God Catholic Church** in Covington established the current Mother of God Cemetery. The Buena Vista Cemetery (also known as Mother of God Cemetery or as St. Joseph's Cemetery) was the first cemetery for Covington's Catholics. Located on E. 26th St in Covington, the Mother of God Cemetery began interments in 1849. Since the Diocese of Covington (see **Roman Catholics**) was not organized until 1853, Bishop John Purcell of the Archdiocese of Cincinnati signed the deed to purchase the Buena Vista Cemetery property. Organized for the Mother of God Church, the Buena Vista Cemetery soon accepted burials from other Catholic churches The **St. John Cemetery** on the **Dixie Highway** (U.S. 25) in Fort Mitchell did not open until 1867. By the 1880s, the Buena Vista Cemetery had reached its capacity.

On November 2, 1887, parishioners of the Mother of God Church organized the Mother of God Cemetery Association of German Catholics. As their first task, they purchased land near the intersection of Madison Pk. and Latonia Ave. in Latonia and laid out the new cemetery, designed in the rural style. Burials, which began almost immediately, were on lots organized along winding lanes.

After the closure of the Buena Vista Cemetery, many families paid to have their family members' graves moved to the new Mother of God Cemetery. In 1902 the Diocese of Covington organized the transfer of the burials of local priests, including Ferdinand Kuhr, who organized the Mother of God Church in 1841. They were moved into the new cemetery in October of 1902.

The cemetery lies on a gently rolling terrace of the Licking River. Narrow roads wind through the cemetery, creating interesting perspectives and focal points. A beautiful Crucifixion scene sculpted by **Clement Barnhorn** and dedicated on November 1, 1915, provides one focal point in the cemetery; another is the grave of famed Covington artist **Frank Duveneck**. Noted local artist **Johann Schmitt** also rests there.

During the first half of the 20th century, as the Buena Vista Cemetery fell into disrepair, more graves were moved to the new Mother of God Cemetery. A final effort was made in 1960 to move any remaining graves. The Mother of God Church leased the land on E. 26th St. to the City of Covington for use as a boys' club. A few unclaimed grave markers were gathered and placed inside a small fenced area but have since been removed.

The Mother of God Cemetery has remained in private ownership under the direction of a board of trustees. It has become a regional Roman Catholic cemetery. Originally, trustees were chosen from among the German-speaking Catholic parishes in Covington, but now they are selected from across Northern Kentucky. The Diocese of Covington established the Cemetery Office in the 1960s; however, the Mother of God Cemetery remained independent. Today, the cemetery includes both aboveground and inground mausoleum and crematorium facilities and has maintained its peaceful, rustic character.

Cemeteries file, local history files, Kenton Co. Public Library, Covington, Ky.

"New Monument Will Soon Be Erected—Clement Barnhorn Will Design a Crucifixion Monument," *KP*, March 21, 1911, 3.

Reis, Jim. "Cemeteries," *KP*, April 21, 1986, 4K.

"Removing Bones from Old to New Cemetery," *KTS*, October 27, 1902, 3.

"Seeks to Move Body," *KP*, February 6, 1932, 1.

Tenkotte, Paul A., David E. Schroeder, and Thomas S. Ward. *To Be Catholic and American in Northern, Central, and Appalachian Kentucky: The Diocese of Covington, 1853–2003*. Forthcoming.

Jeannine Kreinbrink

MOUND BUILDERS. Many researchers have referred to the creators of above-ground earthworks in the Ohio River Valley as Mound Builders. This is a collective term used in the past for the

builders of all the different burial mounds, ceremonial mounds, and nonburial earthworks found in the region. The above-ground mounds were built by at least four different cultures or traditions. The Adena Culture of American Indians built the earliest mounds and earthworks during the period of roughly 500 B.C.–A.D. 200. These were conical burial mounds, and many of them are found in Boone Co. Other earthworks attributed to the Adena people are circular, nonburial earthworks. None of these have been documented in Northern Kentucky, although some are known from locations in southwest Ohio and Central Kentucky.

The Hopewell tribes, which were centered in central Ohio and extended into southwest Ohio in the Cincinnati area, built many geometric earthworks that were used for ceremonial purposes. Other above-ground features included burial mounds and hilltop enclosures such as **Fort Ancient** in Warren Co., Ohio. Little evidence for the well-known Hopewell ceremonial earthworks exists in Northern Kentucky. Only a few such sites have been documented in all the 11 Northern Kentucky counties, and these include Hopewellian diagnostic artifacts such as bladelets. Only one is a mound that has been characterized as belonging to the Middle Woodland Period (ca. 200 B.C.–A.D. 500); the others are represented by diagnostic artifacts found at open sites such as artifact scatters in agricultural fields.

In the early Late Woodland period (A.D. 500–ca. 700), the American Indians of Northern Kentucky lived in small villages and buried their dead in low mounds that were often covered with limestone. These mounds are found in two types of situations. Some are adjacent to village sites, and other stone-covered mounds are found high on narrow ridgetops, often overlooking permanent streams. Sites such as the Rogers burial site in Boone Co. are typical of this time period. The Rogers site includes two adjacent villages and one burial mound next to one of the villages. Stone mounds have been documented in Boone, Bracken, Mason, and Owen counties in Northern Kentucky. Since these counties are not contiguous with one another, it is likely that stone mounds exist in other counties but have not been reported as being stone-covered mounds owing to lack of excavation. The Rogers burial mound was covered with limestone but had a layer of soil above the stone, obscuring the stone until excavation.

Mound Builders seem to have ceased their activities for several centuries during the latter part of the Late Woodland period (after about A.D. 700). The Fort Ancient Period of the Late Prehistoric saw a resurgence of mound-building for burials. Some Fort Ancient Period villages have burial mounds associated with them. The mounds are rounded earth constructions that are usually found near the edge of a village site. At least one site in Boone Co., near Mudlick Creek, had an associated burial mound. The University of Kentucky at Lexington excavated the site and the mound many years ago.

Lewis, R. Barry. *Kentucky Archaeology.* Lexington: Univ. Press of Kentucky, 1996.

Pollack, David, ed. *The Archaeology of Kentucky: Past Accomplishments and Future Directions.* 2 vols. State Historic Preservation Comprehensive Plan Report No. 1. Frankfort, Ky.: Kentucky Heritage Council, 1990.

Jeannine Kreinbrink

MOUNTAIN ISLAND. Mountain Island, which is unique because it came to be entirely owned by African American families, is a 110-acre island in Eagle Creek in northern Owen Co. That stream flows northwest into the Kentucky River just south of Carrollton, splitting into two channels on the eastern side of Mountain Island. The island is composed of limestone bedrock that resisted the flow of Eagle Creek, which divided instead of carving through the hill. The two channels rejoin on the southwest corner of the island, where Caney Fork Creek merges into Eagle Creek. The island consists of three microtopographic zones: floodplain, steep hill slopes, and a narrow ridgetop.

A road right-of-way reference to Mountain Island as early as 1792 has been found in Scott Co. records; at that time Owen Co. was part of Scott Co. The earliest record of settlers on the island coincides with the founding of the Mountain Island Baptist Church in 1801. By 1832 the church had moved several miles up Eagle Creek and changed its name, first to Rocky Point Baptist Church and then to Pleasant View Baptist Church. The initial church membership rolls include no reference to the Herndons or the Rogerses, the two families that were most influential in Mountain Island's earliest history, but James Herndon was mentioned in the later records of the Mountain Island Baptist Church. The Herndon and Rogers families (Herndon's sister) were apparently not active in the church. Several disputes occurred, after which members with abolitionist tendencies left the rolls. Since both James Herndon and Susannah Herndon Rogers freed their slaves upon their deaths, perhaps they stayed away from the church because most of its membership supported slavery.

James Herndon first appears in Scott Co. records in 1797. In 1802 Herndon was the administrator of Lewis Herndon's will; he and his sister later took control of the property that had been owned by Lewis Herndon. James Herndon owned Mountain Island and some of the surrounding mainland until his death in 1853. He built a mill "on main Eagle Creek on the lower part of the Mountain Island above the mouth of Caney Fork [Creek]" in 1812. His sister Susannah Herndon Rogers owned land on the mainland east of Mountain Island. She died in 1847, and according to the provisions of her will, freed her slaves and gave them land surrounding the island. James Herndon applied to the Owen Co. court in 1850 in an attempt to free his slaves but was told to pay a high bond on each one. He refused and freed 23 persons in his will. He divided his estate among them and gave allotments of property to the adults. The settlement contained 21 parcels, with lots 1–15 on the island and lots 16–21 on the mainland. All of the lots included creek frontage. Herndon took care to ensure that each lot had access to the creek and to either bottomland or ridgetop tillable land. The list of the recipients of this land division survives. Twenty-one of the 23 persons listed received property. Only Joshua Junior and Masiat did not; perhaps they were minors at the time of emancipation. The family names of Vinegar, Carroll, and Smith dominate these lists.

The 1883 atlas for Owen Co. depicts the division of the island but is silent about the African American owners of Mountain Island. The atlas shows no structures on the island or in the immediate surroundings. Apparently, either the surveyors did not approach the African American owners, or those owners did not subscribe to the atlas in order to obtain a listing therein (a common practice when making such maps). Census records from the late 19th century identify several members of the Vinegar and Carroll families.

Mountain Island contains significant archaeological resources related to the black families. In 1998 the **Behringer-Crawford Museum** in Covington conducted an archaeological survey of the island to document the locations of the sites associated with the African American ownership and occupation. The survey found the following archaeological sites that are associated with the families who took ownership after the resolution of Herndon's will in 1860: five house sites, a barn, a limestone wall, scattered historic artifacts, and a mill site on the mainland bank of Eagle Creek.

The Mountain Island community lasted until the early 20th century. The **Great Depression** and local hardship forced inhabitants to look elsewhere for employment. Family members still own the island but do not live there. Perhaps the foremost descendant of the island's families was the successful horse trainer **Theodore Vinegar**.

Bryant, James C. *Mountain Island in Owen County, Kentucky: The Settlers and Their Church.* Owenton, Ky.: Owen Co. Historical Society, 1986.

Jeannine Kreinbrink

MOUNT HERMON BAPTIST CHURCH. The Mount Hermon Baptist Church was founded in July 1909 by Carroll Co. Baptists of the Union Grove Church. The members decided that, instead of constructing a new church building, they would purchase a log church building that the Mount Hermon Methodists owned on King's Ridge Rd. The congregation added to the building a new roof and a new foundation and lowered the log building, which had been on stilts, onto the new foundation. They held their first service there that December. It was not until November 5, 1910, that the Baptists decided to adopt the name Mount Hermon Baptist Church. Before the name change, the church had been known as the Union Grove Baptist Church, a name the members briefly kept after moving to the log church building. That year the church reported having 109 members.

In 1977 the church added four Sunday school rooms and two restrooms. On July 14, 1985, the church observed its 75th anniversary and held a homecoming celebration. Members and friends dressed in turn-of-the-century clothes for the worship service, dinner-on-the-grounds was served, recreational activities were available, and baptisms took place in the creek. From June 6 through 14, 1997, a group of 40 people from the Sulphur Fork Baptist Association Baptist Builders near La Grange came to a site that had been chosen as the location of a new Mount Hermon Baptist Church in Trimble Co., about a mile west of the old building, and erected the framing and roof for the new building. In 1998 the new modern sanctuary and educational building were finished. In 1999 the church paved the parking lot at the new location and sold the building and grounds of its old location in Carroll Co.

Gentry, Mary Ann. *A History of Carroll County.* Madison, Ind.: Coleman, 1984.

Ken Massey

MOUNTJOY HOUSE. The Mountjoy House was the first house in Falmouth, built for Alvin Mountjoy, a **Revolutionary War** veteran, on N. Chapel St. The land where it stands was a grant to John Waller and was sold to Mountjoy for $750. The chimneys in the house were built of locally hand-molded brick. The structure has hand-hewn joists and pegged rafters and was equipped with four fireplaces: one on the second floor, two on the first floor, and one in the full basement. The trustees of Falmouth met at the house of Alvin Mountjoy on June 4, 1799. On that day, the first county court session was held in Pendleton Co., the act creating the county having gone into effect May 10, 1799. In 1837 the Mountjoy House was sold to George Lightfoot, who deeded the property to his daughter, Savannah Holton, in 1848. A lean-to was added at the rear of the house in the late 1800s. It changed hands several times afterward. In 1975 Carrol and Nancy Houchen purchased the house and restored it.

Alvin Mountjoy was born January 17, in either 1745 or 1746, at Overwharton Parish, Stafford Co., Va. He served as a 1st lieutenant in the 3rd Regiment of the Continental Army during the Revolutionary War and resigned in December 1777. On September 2, 1777, in his home county in Virginia, he married Mary "Molly" Edwards. The Mountjoys moved to the area that later became Bourbon Co., Ky., in 1786, where Alvin was closely associated with his brother-in-law, future Kentucky governor James Garrard (1796–1804). He served as the county's justice of the peace and high sheriff. By 1794 Mountjoy had acquired land along the South Fork of the Licking River and also a number of town lots in Falmouth. From that time until his death on November 3, 1827, Alvin's name appeared in many Pendleton Co. official records. It is believed that he and his wife were buried in the "Old Cemetery" on Mountjoy St. in Falmouth. In the 1930s, the tombstones from that graveyard were ground up for use on streets.

"Alvin Mountjoy Log Cabin," *KP*, October 11, 1991, 4K.
Belew, Mildred Boden. *The First 200 Years of Pendleton County.* Falmouth, Ky.: M. B. Belew, n.d. [ca. 1994].

Mildred Belew

MOUNT OLIVET. Mount Olivet, the county seat of Robertson Co., was founded around 1820 and incorporated on December 27, 1851. This fifth-class city was in Nicholas Co. before Robertson Co. was created in 1867. The town was once known as Hell's Half Acre. Mount Olivet is located at the intersection of U.S. 62 and Ky. Rt. 165. It was chosen as the county seat owing to its central location, even though the state representative who promoted the formation of Robertson Co., **Duncan Harding** of Harrison Co., had hoped that his hometown of Kentontown, six miles to the southwest, would be the county seat. The name Mount Olivet was derived from biblical sources.

In 1870 Mount Olivet had a population of 254; in 2000 it had 289 residents. Mount Olivet is where the court house, the jail, most of the churches in the county, the Masonic Hall (see **Masons**), the offices of lawyers and doctors, the drug stores, the hotels, and the grocery stores are located. The **Penn Grove Camp Meeting** grounds are on the edge of town. The Robertson Co. Fiscal Court meets in Mount Olivet. In recent years, a new nursing home, the Robertson Co. Health Care Facility, has opened in town. Mount Olivet is also the home of the one school in the county, the Deming High School (see **Robertson Co. Public Schools**).

The stately hotel known as the **Louisiana Hotel** (initially the Cumber House) opened in Mount Olivet in 1869 and consisted of three stories with 23 rooms. Its large ballroom was the scene of several festive galas over the years, and many famous people were guests there. The name of the hotel goes back to owner S. H. Bettys, who in 1886 reportedly bought the property with winnings from the Louisiana Lottery. At times over the years, the hotel was closed for various reasons, and often the building has been used for apartments. During the 1930s, part of the building was converted for use as a Chevrolet auto dealership.

Moore, T. Ross, ed. *Echoes from the Century, 1867–1967.* Mount Olivet, Ky.: Robertson Co. Historical Society, 2000.
U.S. Census Bureau. "American Fact Finder. Data Set. Census 2000 Summary File 1 (SF1) 100-Percent Data. Custom Table." www.census.gov (accessed June 3, 2006).

Mountjoy House.

MOUNT OLIVET BAPTIST CHURCH. This church, organized at Mount Olivet in Robertson Co. in January 1851, was an offshoot of the former Two Licks Baptist Church. The Mount Olivet Baptist Church's first building was a log structure on the east end of town. A new church building was completed in November 1877, near the old Baptist Burial Grounds in town. The church ran a successful Sunday school in the basement of the Knights of Pythias hall in Mount Olivet for many years. A new church building was dedicated in May 1908; in 1928 a parsonage was built. The Mount Olivet Baptist Church was often called the "proving grounds" for Baptist ministers in the region. In 1953 the church was remodeled, and in 1960 a Sunday school annex was constructed. The church, because of its small membership, has always had trouble finding and retaining a minister.

Moore, T. Ross, ed. *Echoes from the Century, 1867–1967.* Mount Olivet, Ky.: Robertson Co. Historical Society, 2000.

MOUNT OLIVET CHRISTIAN CHURCH. Organized in Robertson Co. at Mount Olivet in October 1860, the Mount Olivet Christian Church first held services in a private residence. The group followed the teachings of Alexander Campbell.

The Christian Church has always been strong in Robertson Co., and many Christian Church ministers have come from area families. Soon, a church building was constructed and the church's congregation grew rapidly. That building was remodeled in 1911, and the church's membership continued to rise. In 1947 the church sustained major damage in a fire, prompting interest in building a new structure. The new building was dedicated 13 years later, in 1960, during the congregation's 100th anniversary. The Mount Olivet Christian Church will soon reach the age of 150 years.

Moore, T. Ross, ed. *Echoes from the Century, 1867–1967.* Mount Olivet, Ky.: Robertson Co. Historical Society, 2000.

MOUNT OLIVET MALE AND FEMALE ACADEMY. Before there was any public secondary education in Robertson Co., the Mount Olivet Male and Female Academy offered education at this level, making it possible for students in the county to prepare for college. It was around 1893 when W. C. Deming joined with Professors R. H. Keys and J. W. Rile in establishing this first secondary school in the county. Classes were conducted on the second and third floors of the county courthouse at Mount Olivet. The academy employed seven teachers, and its reputation was such that it drew students from several adjacent counties. The Mount Olivet Male and Female Academy continued until 1905, when it was replaced by Professor C. E. Colyer's Special School. Colyer was also the editor of the *Robertson County Advance* newspaper, and he constantly published appeals for the county to provide a free public high school. In 1910, with the help of **Kate Zoller**, a free public high school was opened, with about 17 freshman students enrolled; the new school replaced Colyer's school.

Moore, T. Ross, ed. *Echoes from the Century, 1867–1967.* Mount Olivet, Ky.: Robertson Co. Historical Society, 2000.

MOUNT OLIVET METHODIST CHURCHES. Methodists have lived in Robertson Co. since early pioneer days, and initially their spiritual needs were ministered to by circuit riders. By 1836, however, two permanent Methodist Episcopal Churches had been established: one was the Mount Olivet Methodist Episcopal Church in town, and the other was the Mount Zion Methodist Episcopal Church along Pinhook Pk., where the Mount Zion Church is located today.

In 1844 the congregation of the Methodist Episcopal Church in Mount Olivet split over the issue of slavery. Subsequently, the town had two Methodist churches, North and South. The Methodist Episcopal Church South dedicated a new frame building just before the start of the **Civil War**. In 1869 a two-story parsonage was added. In 1890 the church burned, and in 1926 a large oak tree fell on the rebuilt church during a storm. The sanctuary was extensively remodeled and expanded following that incident. The Mount Olivet Methodist Episcopal Church North remained independent of the Methodist Episcopal Church South until May 1939, when the churches were consolidated. The South church's building, due to its size and age, was chosen as the home of the combined Mount Olivet Methodist Church, which continues. Few examples better illustrate the long-term effects of division over the issue of slavery within the world of religion than that experienced by the Methodists who attended church in Mount Olivet.

Moore, T. Ross, ed. *Echoes from the Century, 1867–1967.* Mount Olivet, Ky.: Robertson Co. Historical Society, 2000.

MOUNT ST. MARTIN. An Italian Villa–style mansion, demolished in 1977, that crowned the hillside just east of 13th and Monmouth Sts. in Newport was for more than a century one of the city's most recognizable architectural landmarks. It had long been known as Mount St. Martin, a name assigned by the **Sisters of Divine Providence**, who occupied the structure in 1889. Based in France's Alsace-Lorraine region, this Roman Catholic teaching order of nuns named its newly established U.S. provincial house in honor of the order's founder, the Venerable Jean Martin Moye, a parish priest from the Diocese of Metz in France. For more than 80 years, the "castle," as it was also known, served as a mother house, an academy, a home for working girls, and later as a retirement home for elderly women. Yet, decades before the French order of nuns took up residence there, this stately antebellum mansion and the land on which it stood was an exceedingly generous wedding gift from a loving father to his brilliant and beautiful young daughter.

Mary Keturah Taylor was one of Kentucky's most accomplished and cultivated young women. A scholar and a writer of history and poetry, Mary was also the granddaughter of Newport's founder, Gen. **James Taylor Jr.** On September 12, 1848, she married **Thomas Laurens Jones**, a promising young lawyer from Rutherford Co., N.C., who later achieved distinction as a representative from Campbell Co. in the Kentucky legislature and as a member of the U.S. Congress.

While on their honeymoon in Europe, the newlyweds fell in love with an Italianate-style castle in England; and as the couple's wedding gift, Mary's father, Col. **James Taylor III**, offered to replicate the structure on the site of their choosing from among his substantial landholdings. Mary and her husband selected a rural, densely wooded hillside in the area then known as the Newport Highlands, located at the head of Monmouth St., near the modern-day intersection of **U.S. 27** and Carothers Rd. From this remote but well-chosen promontory, the Joneses were afforded a sweeping view of Newport, Cincinnati, and the Ohio River.

After culling the remembered details of the structure in England from the newlyweds, Cincinnati architect Robert A. Love designed the stately 22-room, three-story gray brick mansion, complete with twin towers. He estimated that the building would cost $3,500 to construct. Many workmen and artisans were needed to complete the massive structure, including James Hall, plasterer; George Pagan, painter and glazier; Charles Stricker, bricklayer; and Thomas Westcott, carpenter. The final construction costs for the Jones Mansion totaled $7,552, though $2,500 of this cost was for one of the structure's most striking architectural features, the cornice, which unified the three-sectioned exterior facade with its repeating pattern of closely spaced, delicately curved brackets. Despite his great wealth, Colonel Taylor balked at the total cost of construction, which had more than doubled after the final bill had been tallied. The wealthy businessman evidenced his displeasure over the inflated figure by refusing to pay Westcott, the carpenter Love had hired, more than the $1,600 that had been originally estimated. The impasse was resolved only after a lawsuit was brought against Taylor for nonpayment.

Construction on the Jones family's impressive mansion had begun in 1851, but their first child was two years old before Thomas and Mary were able to move into their new home in 1853. The completed structure comprised three sections: the two-story central section featured four triple-sectioned windows set in arched, recessed panels and was flanked on either side by two four-story towers with tall, narrow, one-over-one windows. The northwest tower, the taller of the two, was surmounted by a four-sided belvedere and enclosed the building's stunning mahogany spiral staircase; its 70 steps led to a unique, windowless room with a circular, balustraded opening in the ceiling and a side stairwell by which the belvedere and its spectacular, full-circle view of the surrounding area could be accessed. The building's eye-catching exterior was richly complemented by its interior accoutrements, which included marble and tile floors; ornate ceilings festooned with decorative plasterwork such as molded fruits, acanthus, and garlands; several hand-carved fireplaces; and rare red Bohemian glass transoms above the stair hall's main entry doors.

The magnificent mansion provided the perfect backdrop for the lavish gatherings and gala events hosted by the socially prominent couple. Newspaper accounts of the time noted the Jones couple's propensity for entertaining; members of Newport's high society and Kentucky's political elite as well as the Commonwealth's brightest literary luminaries frequented the lofty hilltop home. The home was also the site of joyous family celebrations; on April 17, 1879, Thomas and Mary Jones held a reception for their only daughter, Elizabeth Mills Jones, on the occasion of her marriage to Col. Brent Arnold.

After Thomas Jones's death on July 20, 1887, Mary lost interest in the house in which she and her husband had so happily resided. She eventually moved into a smaller home located at Fifth St. and Park Ave. in Newport, and on September 7, 1889, Mary sold her former home to the Diocese of Covington (see **Roman Catholics**). The year before, Bishop **Camillus Paul Maes** had begun corresponding with Mother Anna, superior general of the Congregation of the Sisters of Divine Providence at the general motherhouse of the St.-Jean-de-Bassel Convent in Mosselle, France. Mother

Anna had written the bishop regarding the order's search for a mission diocese in which to establish a U.S. province. As he had promised in his yearlong correspondence with the superior general, Bishop Maes had found a suitable home for the sisters' Northern Kentucky convent—the former Jones Mansion.

On August 7, 1889, the three sisters who had been selected by Mother Anna to form the nucleus of the community's new colony in the United States set sail from Le Havre, France. Sister Mary Chantal Arth, Sister Mary Lucy Damidio, and Sister Mary Camilla Schaff arrived in Covington on August 23, 1889. Because provisions for their future home in the recently purchased Jones Mansion had not yet been made, the sisters temporarily resided with the Sisters of St. Francis at St. Elizabeth Hospital (see **St. Elizabeth Medical Center**) in Covington.

On October 20, 1889, Bishop Maes blessed the new convent and provincial house; thus, the former Jones Mansion became the Mount St. Martin Convent. That fall, the sisters promptly opened a day school, Mount St. Martin Academy, with an enrollment of three pupils: Emma Fischer, Clementine Hurley, and Clara Nagle. Given the curriculum's European influences, the school soon became known as the French Academy. Over the next decade, as the ranks of the order continued to swell with newly arriving French postulants and growing numbers of American applicants, a clapboard wing and chapel were added to accommodate the convent's flourishing novitiate.

The mansion's original owner, Mary Keturah Jones, died in February 1896. Her funeral, officiated by Bishop Maes, was held at Newport's **Immaculate Conception Catholic Church**, and she was laid to rest among her prestigious forebears in the Taylor family plot of Evergreen Cemetery in Southgate.

By 1901, Mount St. Martin Academy's expanding enrollment made it necessary to move the school to a new facility. That same year, the sisters purchased a site at Sixth and Linden Sts. in East Newport. Forty-six students attended Mount St. Martin Academy during its final school year of 1902–1903; Stella Carius was the lone and final graduate that year. Though Mother Maria Houlné, provincial superior, had pressed the family to postpone the graduation until the new building opened in 1903, they were unwilling to wait. Because Stella's parents were the only guests, the commencement was held in the parlor rather than in the chapel. The simple program included some music, Stella's valedictory address, and the conferment of her diploma. Father L. G. Clermont of St. Ann Catholic Church in West Covington officiated at the ceremony, since Bishop Maes was traveling in Europe.

In 1903 the new facility was completed and christened Academy of Notre Dame of Providence (later **Our Lady of Providence Academy**) at its dedication by Bishop Maes on August 23. Even with the academy's relocation, the congregation was rapidly outgrowing its original Kentucky motherhouse. In 1909 **Peter O'Shaughnessy**, a generous benefactor of the diocese and one of Newport's wealthiest businessmen, served as an undisclosed agent for the sisters, assisting them in their acquisition of a picturesque 77-acre farm along Ky. Rt. 8 in Melbourne. On May 16, 1910, Bishop Maes blessed the satellite community, to be known as St. Anne Convent. For 27 years, the convent had buried its dead in an old cemetery adjoining the Mount St. Martin mansion. By November 1918, in preparation for the motherhouse's relocation to rural Campbell Co., all 31 burials had been removed and re-interred in the new cemetery on the spacious grounds of St. Anne Convent. The Sisters of Divine Providence retained Mount St. Martin as their primary motherhouse until 1919, when the spacious new provincial house and novitiate in Melbourne were completed.

After some needed renovations were completed, the former provincial house was converted into a home for young working women. On January 20, 1919, the Mount St. Martin Young Women's Institute was formally opened, with Sister Providentia serving as superior. Up to 30 young women could be accommodated at the institute. In its later years, the sisters operated the aging Newport landmark as a retirement home for elderly women. By 1974, the order finally voted to close the financially troubled facility. In 1975 the stately old mansion was pressed into service one last time, functioning as temporary home for Vietnamese refugees. The following year, the Sisters of Divine Providence put the building up for sale. The asking price for the home, the outbuildings, and the surrounding acreage was $350,000.

Although concerned citizens had worked tirelessly to get the former Jones Mansion added to the National Register of Historic Places in February 1976, their efforts did not save the historic structure from the wrecking ball. American Diversified Developments Inc., which owned both the **Newport Shopping Center** and the Newport Plaza, saw the vacant mansion and its wooded surroundings as a prime opportunity for property expansion. In October 1976 the Cleveland, Ohio, developer purchased the site, but controversy over traffic congestion and the new center's impact on Newport's blighted downtown shopping district temporarily stalled the deal.

In December 1976 Newport city commissioners finally approved the contested zoning change. On April 22 and 23 of the following year, approximately 3,000 items housed within the mansion, including antiques, glassware, china, jewelry, furnishings, architectural features, and religious items, were sold at public auction. In July 1977, while assisting with the demolition of the Newport landmark, Melvin H. Brown, a 60-year-old semiretired construction worker from Independence, was killed after falling 150 feet from a scaffold. A Kmart store now stands on the partially leveled hillside that was once home to one of Newport's most strikingly aesthetic, historically important, and architecturally significant antebellum landmarks.

Archives of the Congregation of Divine Providence, Melbourne, Ky.

"Mount Saint Martin," Local History files, Campbell Co. Public Library, Newport, Ky.

"Mount Saint Martin," Local History files, Kenton Co. Public Library, Covington, Ky.

"Old Cemetery in Newport Is Abandoned," *KP*, November 15, 1918, 20.

Purvis, Thomas L., ed. *Newport, Kentucky: A Bicentennial History*. Newport, Ky.: Otto Zimmerman, 1996.

Reis, Jim. "Graceful Castle Crowned Newport," *KP*, March 18, 1991, 4K.

Russell, Burl. "Young Women's Home Is a Castle—Mount St. Martin's Was Wedding Gift," *KP*, March 6, 1959, 1.

Ryan, Paul E. *History of the Diocese of Covington, Kentucky*. Covington, Ky.: Diocese of Covington, 1954.

Janice Mueller

MOUNT VERNON BAPTIST CHURCH. See **Truesville**.

MOUNT ZION (GRANT CO.). Today only a crossroads near a Baptist church, during its heyday Mount Zion in northern Grant Co. was a prosperous farming community with a school, two general stores, a filling station and garage, the Mount Zion Baptist Church, and a bank. It had as many as a few hundred inhabitants. Mount Zion was where Ky. Rt. 1942 and Ky. Rt. 2942 intersect today. The Mount Zion Baptist Church was founded in 1827 with 19 members, under the direction of Pastor David Lillard.

The community of Mount Zion was at the center of two of Northern Kentucky's most interesting tales, the first one true and the other probably not. On the morning of April 6, 1931, the Mount Zion Deposit Bank, founded in 1903, was robbed of more than $2,000 by the legendary Charles Arthur "Pretty Boy" Floyd and his partner, Bill "The Killer" Miller. The two entered the bank at 10:00 a.m., asked for change for a $20 bill, and pulled revolvers on the teller, W. Carl Smith. They then ordered Smith to the floor, bound his hands, and covered his mouth with "sticking plaster." Floyd and Miller drove four miles to the farm of Charles M. Flege, near Sherman, and spent the day touring the property pretending to be interested in buying it. According to the *Grant County News*, "Flege fed the party (which included the criminals' girlfriends) and drove them around, showing them his own farm as well as others, showing them real Kentucky hospitality." By nightfall, the search was suspended and the party drove away undetected.

Mount Zion was also the longtime home of Henry Newton, an educator and school administrator who, local legend asserts, was actually John Wilkes Booth, the assassin of President Abraham Lincoln (1861–1865). Newton had a mustache, quoted Shakespeare, and walked with a limp—supposedly from his fall from the balcony at Ford's Theater.

The first house built in Mount Zion was completed in 1790, by John Martin Franks (1751–1817), a fur trader born in the Michigan Territory, and his father, Jacob, a German immigrant. John Franks's grandson, D. A. Franks, started the first general store in the community in 1885; it was owned by

Clyde Franks at the time of the Floyd robbery. John Franks and his wife Elizabeth were charter members of the Mount Zion Baptist Church and donated the land upon which the church stands.

Conrad, John B., ed. *The History of Mt. Zion Baptist Church, Mt. Zion, Kentucky, 1827–2002.* Grant Co., Ky.: Privately published, 2002.

"Did Booth Escape to Kentucky?" *Kentucky Monthly,* July 2004, 28–29.

Grant County News, April 10, 1931, 1; April 24, 1931, 1; May 8, 1931, 1.

Nash, Jay Robert. *Bloodletters and Badmen: A Narrative Encyclopedia of American Criminals from the Pilgrims to the Present.* New York: M. Evans, 1995.

Stephen M. Vest

MOUNT ZION CHURCH SCHISM. Like many Methodist congregations in Kentucky, members belonging to the Mount Zion Church in Bracken Co. depended on the "peculiar institution" of slavery to provide workers as household domestics and as farm laborers. Slavery's economic benefits brought growth and prosperity that allowed the Dora and Bradford families to become principal contributors toward the construction of a permanent Methodist brick chapel in 1837.

When Rev. A. H. Redford arrived in 1843, the Minerva Methodist Preaching Circuit in this region of Kentucky included Dover, Germantown, and Mount Zion. The church at Augusta remained connected to **Augusta College**, the first Methodist college in Kentucky and the third one in the United States. Its president, Joseph S. Tomlinson, and members of the faculty joined with students to lead meetings at Mount Zion where they talked openly about the abolition of slavery.

At the 1844 General Methodist Church Conference in New York, Bishop James O. Andrew's connection to slavery created an acrimonious debate that led to a "Plan of Separation." Augusta College president Tomlinson opposed the plan and later submitted several resolutions against division when the Quarterly Conference met at Mount Zion Methodist Church on February 8, 1844. A majority of the congregation felt the church should respect and follow the region's social and racial customs. They also believed that the issue of slavery would be better resolved through accommodation than by abolition. With the exception of those at Augusta College and a small minority at Mount Zion, all of the churches in the Minerva Circuit elected to become part of the Southern Methodist Church.

Tomlinson did his utmost to keep the Minerva Circuit within the Methodist Episcopal Church (North). He and his supporters sought grand jury action against Redford, the Mount Zion Methodist Church leader, for disturbing the peace; but when the jury learned that Redford had acted under a mandate from the Kentucky Conference of the denomination, the charges were dismissed. Afterward, Tomlinson and Redford engaged in a series of public debates defending their respective viewpoints before a number of local congregations.

Delegates from the Southern states in the Methodist Church met at the Fourth St. Church in Louisville on May 1, 1845. By May 19 the groundwork had been laid for the Methodist Episcopal Church, South. When the Methodist Church's Annual Conference convened at Frankfort on September 1, 1845, the church at Augusta was the only one to adhere to the Northern church's policies laid out at the Ohio Conference on June 1, 1845. The conference in Frankfort withdrew all aid for Augusta College and transferred its support to Transylvania College in Lexington, effectively leading to the demise of Augusta College. On October 24, 1845, William Dora and others met at Mount Zion Methodist Church to elect a Board of Trustees that would follow the church disciplines established by the Methodist Episcopal Church, South. On November 3, 1845, a dissident group of Mount Zion Methodist church members met at the home of Thomas H. Bradford because they believed Dora and the others had forfeited their positions at Mount Zion by their stance in favor of slavery. It made no difference: the proslavery faction had won out in the battle for control of Mount Zion Methodist Church. The minutes of the minority group were not certified and recorded in the Bracken Co. Court until November 1849; by then the issue was moot.

Arnold, W. E. *A History of Methodism in Kentucky.* 2 vols. Louisville, Ky.: Herald Press, 1936.

Court Order Books, C, p. 464; D, pp. 112, 162, Bracken Co. Courthouse, Brooksville, Ky.

Ockerman, Elbert W. "The Separation of Methodism in Kentucky," Master's thesis, Univ. of Kentucky, 1940.

Redford, A. H. *Methodism in Kentucky.* 3 vols. Nashville, Tenn.: Southern Methodist Publishing House, 1870.

"Schismatic Decided Action in Augusta, Ky." *True American,* July 29, 1845, 1. From the *Western Christian Advocate.*

Donald A. Clark

MOUNT ZION METHODIST CHURCH. This church was organized at Mount Zion in Robertson Co. during the 1830s. Around the time of the **Civil War**, a group of people split off from the Mount Zion Methodist Church because of their opposition to slavery. They became the Foster's Chapel Church, under the Methodist Episcopal North conference. The Mount Zion Methodist Church remained associated with the Methodist Episcopal South conference. After the split, and continuing for many years, a minister from nearby Mount Olivet traveled to the Mount Zion Methodist Church to preach on one Sunday each month. In 1901 the church building was either remodeled or rebuilt. In 1927, with the congregation dwindling rapidly, the structure was deeded over to Mount Zion's African American Methodists. The church is used today occasionally, on an integrated basis.

Moore, T. Ross, ed. *Echoes from the Century, 1867–1967.* Mount Olivet, Ky.: Robertson Co. Historical Society, 2000.

MOVIE THEATERS. Sandwiched between the era of live variety shows and the era of television and **drive-in** theaters, stood the local neighborhood movie theater, a fixture in Northern Kentucky as in other regions. Generally located in an urban setting; seating upwards of 1,000 patrons; selling popcorn, soft drinks, and assorted candies; showing cartoons and newsreels along with feature films; and often offering some of the first air-conditioned space in the area, the local movie house reigned from roughly the 1920s through the 1950s. Downtown Cincinnati had at least 10 large, plush movie theaters, which were mainly corporately owned, seated as many as 4,000, had private smoking areas and sometimes even thick red carpet, and were easily reached by Covington and Newport residents. Northern Kentucky had several of these venues, smaller in scope.

In 1905 the Edison Company's film division advertised its moving-pictures slate for November 30. At the Edisonian Annex at 521 Madison Ave., second floor, in Covington, that evening's selection included the silent films *The Great Train Robbery, Peck's Bad Boy,* and other short subjects. Admission was five cents, including seat. As technology improved, the Edison method was soon replaced by other methods. Covington had more theaters than most cities in Northern Kentucky. In 1883 Nowland's Opera House had opened for live variety at Seventh and Washington Sts. in downtown Covington. On that site in 1912, a 700-seat movie house was constructed, known as the Hippodrome Theater. In 1928 movie-theater mogul **L. B. Wilson** acquired it and held a contest to rename it; thus it became the Broadway. The Broadway closed in 1950 and was torn down by 1954; today a parking lot occupies its spot. **Pop Eckler** and his country music group were known to perform at the Broadway. It was common for theaters to have contests and other promotions, just to get people to come through the doors. The Colonial Theater, along Madison Ave. between Fourth and Fifth Sts., was a favorite venue for **Patia Power**, the mother of Hollywood heartthrob actor Tyrone Power, to stage her theatrical productions. The last movie show to operate in Covington was the Madison, at 728 Madison Ave., which opened in 1912 and closed in 1977. It began as the Kozy and changed to the Lyric and then the L. B. Wilson, before becoming the 1,350-seat Madison. Today it is a concert hall, having been rebuilt in 1928 and then again in 1946 as the result of a 1944 fire. It still has the name Wilson in lights at the top of the front of the building. Other Covington movie ventures included the Shirley, 1813 Holman St.; the Family Theater, 633 Main St.; the Strand, 132 Pike St.; and the Liberty, 608 Madison Ave. Finally, at 17th St. and Eastern Ave. stood the De Milo Theater in the 1930s. Famous Covington songwriter **Haven Gillespie**, a self-proclaimed devotee of movie houses, kept a log of the many theaters he visited throughout the nation.

Other movie theaters in Kenton Co. included the several in Ludlow: the Dixie and the Elm, both on Elm St., and the Wilma, the Ludlow, and one at the Ludlow Lagoon (see **Lagoon Amusement Park**). Latonia was home to the Grand and the Delbee (later the Derby), both on Decoursey Ave., and the Kentucky, on W. Southern Ave., which replaced the old Latonia Theater in 1939 but was vacant by 1962. Elsmere had the Village Cinema, 107 **Dixie Highway**, previously named the Gayety. Fort Mitchell was home to the 600-seat Four Star Dixie Theater, which opened in 1940 at 2497 Dixie Highway and closed in the mid-1950s; Columbia Federal Saving & Loan moved into the building and eventually remodeled the structure. Farther south on the Dixie Highway in Walton was the James Theater.

Newport had the Strand, 827 Monmouth St., a parking lot today; the Hippodrome, 711 Monmouth St., another parking lot today; the State, 716 Monmouth St., later to become **Cinema X**; and the Music Hall Theater, 11th and York Sts., which was torn down, and its site became part of the **Trauth Dairy** complex. The Hippodrome was the site of the 1936 Miss Kentucky contest, where Newport native **Charlotte Hiteman** took home the honors. The "Hipp," as it was called, ran into the early 1960s, and *The Three Stooges in Orbit* (1962) continued to be advertised on its marquee for years after its last picture show. Major league baseball player **Bill Sweeney** put on a benefit in which he performed for the victims of the **flood of 1913** at the Music Hall Theater. Even after the arrival of "talkies," movie establishments were used for other purposes.

Other Campbell Co. theaters were in Dayton, such as the Princess, 711 Sixth St., which became Klingenberg's Hardware, and the Dayvue, 115 Sixth St., today a printing company. When the 750-seat Dayvue opened in June 1941, its owners, Jerome and Woodrow Bressler, closed Dayton's Liberty Theater, at 512 Berry St. The Dayvue was out of business by summer 1955, although it tried a brief and unsuccessful comeback in the late 1960s. Bellevue had the Marianne, 607 Fairfield Ave., an Art Deco structure that operated into the 1990s, vacant today, and the Sylvia, 314 Fairfield Ave. Fort Thomas was home to the Hiland, 18 N. Fort Thomas Ave., an office building today, and the Fort, at the top of River Rd. near S. Fort Thomas Ave., across from the **Fort Thomas Military Reservation**. Countless soldiers were entertained there.

In Maysville was the **Russell Theater**, 9 E. Third St., which is being restored today; it was the site of local entertainer **Rosemary Clooney**'s 1953 movie premier of *The Stars Are Singing*, her movie debut. **Max Goldberg**, longtime mayor of Falmouth, showed motion pictures in the **Washington Opera House**, 116 W. Second St. in Maysville, and there was a Pastime Theater in that town also. Goldberg later owned the Pastime Theater in Falmouth, which was closed for a few years, only to reopen recently. Bracken Co. had two movie theaters. The Lyric was in Brooksville, along E. Miami St, and operated from 1925 until 1963. The Odeum, in Augusta, near the Beehive Tavern, operated from the 1930s into the late 1950s. Owenton in Owen Co. had a Pastime Theater, which was damaged by fire in 1955.

Another Northern Kentuckian, besides L. B. Wilson, who owned movie theaters was **Anna Bell Ward**, who began as an actress in Covington. She owned and operated the Phoenix Amusement chain of theaters (35 in number), based in Lexington. She started as the owner-manager of the Pastime Theater at Maysville.

As early as 1910 in Covington, the ministerial association fought to ban certain films that were considered immodest. Around 1915 there were rumors that the Ludlow Lagoon (see **Lagoon Amusement Park**) might be sold to a film production company for use as a set. About the same time in Fort Thomas, there was a proposal to build a film plant, the Highland Film Company. The movie theaters of the 20th century were a far cry from today's modern multiscreen cinemaplexes that are planted in shopping centers and similar settings in suburbia. Gone are the promotions (plate ware, chances to win cars, and so forth) to lure people inside, and organists no longer surface from below the stage playing music such as "The Surry with a Fringe on Top." Only the popcorn remains.

"Edisonian Annex," *KP*, November 30, 1905, 2 (advertisement).

"Elsmere's Gayety Has Long History," *KP*, June 14, 1957, 7.

Gillespie, Haven. "Haven Gillespie's File of Movie Theatres in the 20s, 30s, 40s Found in the Basement of His Former Home on Montgomery St., Covington, Ky.," 1950–1989, Kenton Co. Public Library, Covington, Ky.

Reis, Jim. "Late 1930s Saw Movie Theaters Abound," *KP*, February 26, 1996, 4K.

———. "Movie Houses Still Stand but Silver Screens Silent," *KP*, December 9, 1996, 4K.

Singer, Allen J. *Stepping Out in Cincinnati*. Charlestown, S.C.: Arcadia, 2005.

MOXLEY. Moxley in Owen Co. was situated along the eastern banks of the Kentucky River some 13 miles northwest of Owenton and near Perry Park. The homes and stores are gone, and the **Showboats** that once provided entertainment for the community's residents no longer tie up to the dock, but the name Moxley still identifies the area. The general mercantile store, which housed the post office, made up the business district. The first post office in Moxley was established in 1886 and continued until about 1928. The mail was transported from Eagle Station to Moxley. Typically, a trip to Eagle Station delivered produce, poultry, animal skins, rabbits, and other farm products to the **Louisville and Nashville Railroad** depot for shipment to Louisville or Newport. Returning to Moxley, the freighter brought staples, stock for the store, and huge baskets of fresh bread, stacked in unwrapped loaves, a luxury directly related to Moxley's proximity to the railroad. Riley Dillender carried the local mail and hauled the freight between Eagle Station and Moxley. If Eagle Creek was too high to ford, he would unhitch the mule from the wagon and swim the animal across, returning with only the mail. Dillender, who during the Civil War had been a Union prisoner for several years at the South's notorious prison at Andersonville, Ga., always had interesting war stories to relate.

Perhaps the best-known story about the community concerns the Alexander home, which once stood atop the hill overlooking the river community. Near the intersection of Ky. Rt. 335 and Moxley Rd., about one mile west of the Alexander home, a historical marker tells of a visit of Confederate general **John Hunt Morgan** to the home of J. J. Alexander in 1863. Several Owen Co. men were members of Morgan's group.

Houchens, Mariam Sidebottom. *History of Owen County: "Sweet Owen."* Louisville, Ky.: Standard, 1976.

KYHistorical Society. "Kentucky Historical Marker Database." www.kentucky.gov/kyhs/hmdb (accessed October 15, 2005)

Vertical files, Owen Co. Public Library, Owenton, Ky.

Doris Riley

MULLINS, PAMELA E. (b. January 22, 1953, Covington, Ky.). Pamela Mullins is one of the six children of Robert and Shirley Jennings Mullins. During her early childhood, Mullins's father and mother worked long hours as a factory worker and a day laborer, respectively, in Covington. As she observed their circumstances, she came to believe in the linkage between a quality education and the expansion of one's socioeconomic opportunities. In her early years, Mullins did not desire a life as a social activist or a career in public service. However, her goals changed gradually. Mullins became a student activist at Covington's **Holmes High School**, partly because of her admiration of various national and local leaders of the **civil rights movement** during the late 1960s and early 1970s. She and several of her classmates organized a student demonstration at Holmes that was generated by the school's inability to hire an adequate number of African American teachers, as well as the use of a history curriculum that disregarded the experience of black Americans.

After she graduated from Holmes High School in 1971 and earned a BS degree in marketing from the University of Cincinnati in 1983, Mullins took a more active leadership role in the city of Covington. For example, in 1988 she became the first African American woman elected to the Covington Board of Education, where she served until 1996. During her tenure there, Mullins aimed at improving public education for African American students as well as other underrepresented pupils. When asked about some of her major accomplishments as a member of the school board, Mullins proclaimed, "Although it was a hard fight, I was successful in enhancing the educational experience of African American students in the Covington school system as well as the sponsoring of legislation that focused on such issues as site-based management, diversity, and multicultural [education]."

In 1996 Mullins was elected to the Covington City Commission, the first African American to hold such a position in Northern Kentucky. She left this position in 1998. Among her many achievements in the political arena, Mullins sponsored several neighborhood economic development projects, worked on a regional transportation commission, and helped to create the Covington Human Rights Commission. Through it all, she has worked to improve the lives of all the residents of Covington.

"African-American Day Celebrates Roots," *KP*, April 27, 1990, 2K.
Covington Board of Education Meeting Minutes, Board of Education, Covington, Ky., 1996.
"Covington Elects First Black to School Board," *Suspension Press*, November 1988, 1.
Driehaus, Bob. "Mullins Brings Diversity to Covington Commission," *KP*, November 6, 1996, 1K.
Mullins, Pamela E. "Editorial: A Graduation of Sorts," *KP*, September 27, 1998, 4K.
——. Telephone interviews by Eric R. Jackson, September 15 and October 4, 2006.
Vance, Debra Ann. "Chapman Returns as School Chair," *KP*, January 19, 1991, 3K.
——. "Covington Board Member Pushes for Race-Gender Data," *KP*, September 14, 1991, 3K.
——. "School Board Won't Seek Test-Score Breakdown—Gender, Race Analysis Rejected," *KP*, September 18, 1991, 8K.

Eric R. Jackson

MULLOY, WILLIAM T. (b. November 9, 1892, Ardoch, N.D.; d. June 1, 1959, Covington, Ky.). William Theodore Mulloy, who became a bishop of the Diocese of Covington, was the son of William James and Margaret Ann Doyle Mulloy. After studying at St. Paul Seminary in St. Paul, Minn., Mulloy was ordained a priest for the Diocese of Fargo in North Dakota on July 7, 1916. His boyhood on the farm and his service as a priest in rural parishes made him an advocate for Catholic farmers in their difficulties on the land. He became an early member of the National Catholic Rural Life Conference (NCRLC) and helped formulate its Manifesto on Rural Life. He was the president of NCRLC from 1935 to 1937 and again from 1946 to 1948, the latter term while he was bishop of Covington. Rev. Mulloy also dedicated himself to improving Catholic education in the Diocese of Fargo and was appointed superintendent of diocesan education in 1938. In the same year, he was made pastor of St. Mary Cathedral in Fargo, N.D., and he was made a monsignor in 1941.

Mulloy received word from the Vatican on November 11, 1944, that he had been appointed the bishop of Covington, Ky. He chose "Teach Your Sons" as his episcopal motto. His consecration occurred on January 10, 1945, in St. Mary Cathedral in his home diocese; he was officially installed in his new diocese with an impressive ceremony at the Cathedral Basilica of the Assumption in Covington on January 25, 1945. As bishop of Covington, Mulloy greatly increased the number of Catholic churches and schools in the diocese and established several Catholic hospitals in the mountains of Eastern Kentucky. The new **Covington Catholic High School** and **Newport (Central) Catholic High School** were two of the largest educational facilities that he approved. In 1946 he purchased the Marydale property on Donaldson Rd. in Boone Co. and created there Camp **Marydale**, the Marydale Retreat House, and the **Seminary of St. Pius X** (now the Catholic Center). He was also responsible for a major renovation of the Cathedral Basilica of the Assumption in 1950. It was at this time that the large carved-wood baldachin was erected above the high altar. Mulloy put a high premium on religious vocations, especially the priesthood. His episcopacy saw numerous ordinations at the Cathedral Basilica of the Assumption. Mulloy died in 1959 at St. Elizabeth Hospital and was buried in St. Mary Cemetery in Fort Mitchell.

"Bishop-Elect Leads Busy Life," *Messenger*, December 21, 1944, 12.
"Diocese Goes into Mourning for Death of Bishop Mulloy," *KP*, June 2, 1959, 1–2.
Ryan, Paul E. *History of the Diocese of Covington, Kentucky*. Covington, Ky.: Diocese of Covington, 1954.
"Tributes to Bishop Mulloy from Fargo Diocese: Bishop Mulloy as an Educator," *Messenger*, January 22, 1945, 18.
Tenkotte, Paul A., David E. Schroeder, and Thomas S. Ward. *To Be Catholic and American in Northern, Central, and Appalachian Kentucky: The Diocese of Covington, 1853–2003*. Forthcoming.

Thomas S. Ward

MUNDY, JAMES (b. July 9, 1886, Maysville, Ky.; d. December 25, 1978, Chicago, Ill.). James Ahyln Mundy, the son of a former slave, became one of the premier choir leaders in the United States. He directed choirs, primarily in Chicago, from 1913 to 1978. While Mundy lived in Maysville, he served as organist for the **Bethel Baptist Church** in Maysville, and the church gave him some support as he attended Simmons Normal School in Louisville. Upon the death of his father, Mundy moved to Chicago with his mother. He later commented, "I had heard that up in Chicago a colored man could even work in the post office." Actually employed at a post office in Chicago, Mundy attracted the attention of civil rights leader Ida Wells Barnett, who learned of his musical ability and asked him to form a choir to perform as part of an appearance of W. E. B. Du Bois in Chicago. The day when James Mundy led the choir, January 12, 1913, was the first time an African American group performed in Chicago's Orchestra Hall. Mundy enjoyed creating combined choirs from Chicago's black churches in addition to arranging music and giving private voice and piano lessons. In 1916 he directed his group, named the Mundy Choristers, at the dedication of Chicago's Navy Pier. In 1931 Mundy was chosen to lead the choir at the rededication of Abraham Lincoln's tomb in Springfield, Ill., where President Herbert Hoover (1929–1933) gave the address. When Chicago hosted the World Fair in 1933 and 1934, the Mundy Jubilee Singers provided biweekly entertainment. Mundy took pride that only his group and a police band were invited to reappear at the closing, where 400,000 people witnessed the performances. Beginning in 1935, Mundy directed a Works Progress Administration–funded group of singers that delivered more than 5,000 performances in Chicago area schools over the course of seven years. In 1946 a Mundy-directed choir of 1,000 voices performed at Carnegie Hall in New York City. Mundy directed tens of thousands of singers, and his choirs performed for combined audiences numbering in the hundreds of thousands. He led his last choir, the Olivet Baptist Church Choir, on Thanksgiving Day in 1978. Mundy was still teaching and directing when he died on Christmas Day of 1978.

Grossman, James R., Ann Durkin Keating, and Janice L. Reife. *The Encyclopedia of Chicago*. Chicago: Univ. of Chicago Press, 2004.
Jarrett, Vernon. "James Mundy Still Stirs Yule Spirit," *Chicago Tribune*, December 29, 1974, A6.
"Prof. Mundy, Who Raised Black Voices in Song, Dies," *Chicago Tribune*, December 27, 1978, A11.

George Vaughn and John Klee

MURPHY, RAYMOND L. (b. February 17, 1905, Cincinnati, Ohio; d. November 10, 1969, Fort Thomas, Ky.). Judge Ray Murphy began working at age 13, selling newspapers on the street and running a projector in a local movie theater. He graduated from the Woodward Night High School in Cincinnati and later took evening classes at Xavier University in Cincinnati and at the old Cincinnati **YMCA** Law School. He was admitted to the Kentucky bar in 1928 and then began his law practice. Early in his career, he served as Newport city solicitor and was a state assistant attorney general under Kentucky governor Ruby Laffoon (governor 1931–1935). Over the years Murphy campaigned for several key Democratic candidates, including U.S. vice president Alben Barkley, a native Kentuckian. In 1940 Murphy was appointed a judge by Kentucky governor Keen Johnson (1939–1943) to succeed Roger L. Neff. Murphy was elected to four consecutive six-year terms as a circuit court judge in Campbell Co. before being defeated by **Fred Warren**. Judge Murphy was regarded as a "down-to-earth" jurist; his decisions were seldom overturned by higher courts. His personality and sense of fairness were two of the positive traits that characterized his long tenure as judge in Campbell Co. After his judgeship, he joined **Morris Weintraub** and Ban Sampson in their law firm (Weintraub and Sampson) and remained until his retirement in 1967. Murphy died at St. Luke Hospital two years later and was buried at St. Stephen Cemetery in Fort Thomas. His wife, Alma E. Horne Murphy, and a son, William Murphy, survived him.

"Colorful Campbell Judge Murphy Dies," *KP*, November 11, 1969, 1–2.
Social Security Death Index. www.rootsweb.com.

MURPHYSVILLE. Murphysville is today a small collection of homes nine miles southwest of Maysville, along U.S. 62 where it crosses the North Fork of the Licking River in Mason Co. A prosperous community existed there in the mid-19th century. The town was named either for an early settler, William Murphy, or for the first person who dammed the North Fork and built a mill there. A post office was established in 1830, and in 1867 a large woolen mill with a 120-foot-long dam was established in the town. The pool created by the dam was used by residents for fishing and swimming. The mill, a substantial enterprise, was described in the June 29, 1867, edition of the *Maysville Republican* as "one of the best in the United States." It was highly mechanized. The newspaper article described the process, from sorting the wool to the seven looms that produced the finished plain and plaid cloth. The 1876 Mason Co. atlas indicates that the Murphysville precinct had 786 people. An 1877 newspaper reported that the town had two doctors, the woolen mill, a flour mill, businesses, a lawyer, and "several loafers." The local chapter of the International Organization of Good Templars was noted for its excellence and for its successful effort to have liquor banned "forever" in Murphysville by the Kentucky legislature. The flour mill produced so much flour that a group of nearby houses was nicknamed "the white row" because they often were covered with flour. The town's location on the North Fork made it subject to frequent flooding and was the major reason for its decline. The post office closed in 1906, and the large woolen mill was torn down in 1921. "High water at Murphysville" was local shorthand for flooding that repeatedly closed U.S. 68 until a new bridge and roadway were built in the 1990s.

Calvert, Jean, and John Klee. *The Towns of Mason County: Their Past in Pictures.* Maysville, Ky.: Maysville and Mason Co. Library Historical and Scientific Association, 1986.

Rennick, Robert M. *Kentucky Place Names.* Lexington: Univ. of Kentucky Press, 1984.

John Klee

MURRAY, THOMAS PETER "TOMMY" (b. January 1, 1902, Covington, Ky.; d. January 18, 1963, Cincinnati, Ohio). Jockey Thomas Peter Murray was one of 10 children of Irish immigrants Martin and Margaret Gavin Murray. The family attended **St. Patrick Catholic Church** in Covington.

"Hey Livingston, I need one of your monkeys in the sixth race to show [my horse] Money Maker what the finish line looks like. Let me have Murray." Spoken by horse-owner K. Spence and addressed to fellow horseman J. R. Livingston on July 1, 1919, this request and similar ones were commonly heard mornings in the stables at old **Latonia Racecourse** in Latonia, where the Latonia Shopping Center now sprawls. A few weeks earlier, May 31, 1919, Lillian Shaw, another of Livingston's horses, had been ridden to victory in the fifth race at Churchill Downs in Louisville, by jockey Thomas Peter Murray. That race was the 45th running of the Kentucky Oaks, a race considered the Kentucky Derby for three-year-old fillies.

"Monkey" was what a jockey was sometimes derisively called. In those times, jockeys did not ride as independent agents; instead, they were employees of the owners, who controlled when, where, and how often jockeys worked. Sometimes when an owner needed a rider for one of his mounts, he would pay another owner for the services of one of that person's jockeys.

Murray was one of the smaller jockeys, riding at a weight of 107 pounds and standing not quite five feet tall. In 1919, when he won the Kentucky Oaks and was second leading jockey in the country, his winnings totaled $140,562. That year he had 832 mounts and 157 first-place finishes. Jockey Clifford Robinson beat him out for the national riding title by a mere six wins. There was not an avid horseplayer in the country who did not recognize Tommy Murray's name—he was the jockey sensation of the day. Remarkably, Murray, who begun his racetrack career mucking horse stalls, had become an elite jockey in only two years.

"We're shantyboat Irish," Murray would proudly remind his four children. As a young man, he hung out at the Latonia Racecourse in Covington, where he nurtured his horse-racing interests by observing, asking questions, and meeting people, all the while building his determination to become a jockey. It was certainly not an easy career path for Murray, who later recalled how he worked his way up from the bottom. "When I was broken in by Kay Spence, I walked horses and cleaned out stalls for a year before I got on a horse. Now some of the kids are riding in less than a year's time," he lamented to Louisville newspaper reporter Marvin N. Gay in a 1950 interview. Murray was working at the time as a valet in the Churchill Downs jockey quarters; he was 48. Murray was always a proponent of weight control through exercise. "The only way to really hit riding trim is to jog around the track," he insisted in the interview. But family members recall seeing Murray leave the supper table and go into the bathroom, where he would thrust his finger down his throat in order to regurgitate—still a popular method of weight control among jockeys.

In 1918 at age 16, Murray rode his first race, at Douglas Park in Louisville. His first win was the same year at Latonia on a mount named High Gear. During his career, Murray rode at practically every racetrack in the United States as well as at tracks in Canada and Cuba. He rode such famous horses as Kentucky Derby winner Old Rosebud, Busy Signal, and the notoriously bad-acting horse Flags. His slam-bang stretch duel in the Kentucky Oaks of 1919 at Churchill Downs against legendary jockey Earle Sande is considered a classic. Of his famous ride in the Kentucky Oaks, Tommy reminisced, "I was on Lillian Shaw, the winner, and Earle Sande was on Milkmaid, who ran second. Coming down the stretch, he grabbed my saddle and I took my stick and half beat him to death. We had a ding-dong battle that afternoon." Tommy got his only ride in the Kentucky Derby in 1920 aboard Bersagliere, who broke third but faded after a half mile, placing ninth in a 17-horse field. The last time Murray recorded more than 10 wins as a jockey was in 1929, when he had 134 mounts, with 21 first-place finishes and earnings that totaled $22,840. That year the stock market crashed, as did Tommy's riding career.

After 14 years as a jockey, Murray retired from riding in 1931 at age 30. His riding career abruptly ended, Murray was reduced to near poverty and struggled to support his wife Virginia (Conley) and their two daughters and two sons. He eventually became a trainer, but to maintain a trainer's license he was required to win 10 races annually, something he accomplished only in 1935, with 14 wins and $9,290 in purses, and in 1940, with 10 victories and purses of only $3,120. Murray's story of riches to rags was typical for the times.

On September 22, 1942, Murray joined the U.S. Army as a private and served on active duty until May 10, 1943. Afterward he was assigned to the Enlisted Reserve Corps. When he left the military, Murray returned to the racetrack in various capacities, finishing his career as a jockey's valet. He died at age 61 in 1963 at the Dennison Hotel in Cincinnati, where he had taken a room after having surgery 10 days earlier at the Cincinnati Veterans Administration Hospital. He was buried at St. Mary Cemetery, Fort Mitchell.

Chew, Peter. *The Kentucky Derby—The First 100 Years.* Boston: Houghton Mifflin, 1974.

Gorham, Bob. *Churchill Downs 100th Kentucky Derby—First Centennial.* Louisville, Ky.: Churchill Downs, 1973.

"Jockey Tom Murray Rites Are Tuesday," *KE,* January 20, 1963, 6A.

Leach, Brownie. *The Kentucky Derby Diamond Jubilee, 1875–1949.* Louisville, Ky.: Gibbs-Inman, 1949.

"Tommy Murray," *KP,* January 21, 1963, 4.

James C. Claypool and Don Clare

MUSE, GEORGE, LIEUTENANT COLONEL (b. 1720, England; d. 1790, Nelson Co., Ky.). Lt. Col. George Muse was a Caroline Co., Virginia officer, who served under Col. George Washington during Braddock's campaign in the **French and Indian War**; Muse was properly discharged in 1754. For his services in the war, based upon his rank as lieutenant colonel, Muse was granted 5,333 acres of land. Five of his tracts, or a total of about 2,700 acres, were located in Northern Kentucky; thus Muse was the first American to own the territory that became Covington, Newport, Bellevue, and Dayton, Ky. Muse sold part of this Northern Kentucky land to his friend James Taylor Sr. of Caroline Co., Va. However, as part of the deal, he asked that the eastern 1,000-acre tract (where Dayton now stands) be deeded back to his two daughters Katy and Caroline Muse. James Taylor Sr. had all the tracts surveyed by his son **Hubbard Taylor** and then gave 500 acres to another son, **James Taylor Jr.**, in exchange for managing the Campbell Co. properties. On May 3, 1793, James Jr. moved to Northern Kentucky and had the 1,500-acre tract on the eastern side of the Licking River laid out in lots. He named it Newport, after Christopher Newport, the captain of the first ship bringing English settlers to Jamestown, Va. The Muse daughters later sold their 1,000-acre tract to **Washington Berry**, a brother-in-law of James Taylor Jr. George Muse is said to have taught military tactics to Gen. George Washington during the **Revolutionary War**. Several land transactions between the two men are listed in Washington's will.

"The James Taylor Narrative," 1840, Kenton Co. Public Library; Campbell Co. Historical and Genealogical Society, Alexandria, Ky.

Tenkotte, Paul A. "Rival Cities to Suburbs: Covington and Newport, Kentucky, 1790–1890," PhD diss., Univ. of Cincinnati, 1989.

Wessling, Jack. *Early History of Campbell County Kentucky.* Alexandria, Ky.: Privately published, 1997.

Jack Wessling

MUSIC. The first professional musician known to reside in Northern Kentucky was Mexico-born **Joseph Tosso**, who was of Italian descent. He arrived in Cincinnati in time to play for Gen. Marquis de Lafayette's visit to Northern Kentucky in 1825 and performed regularly at Mrs. Trollope's bazaar, located along E. Fourth St. in the Queen City. The music professor, as Tosso was called, soon moved his family to Covington, and later to Latonia, and played at concerts and important events in both Newport and Covington. He was well trained in classical music and also was a talented fiddle player. He often played his own compositions, including "The Arkansas Traveler," which became a popular fiddle tune. Tosso died in Covington in 1887, having performed locally for more than 60 years. He was a founder of the first school of music in Cincinnati.

Religious music played a large role in Northern Kentucky. Several musicians were associated with **Mother of God Catholic Church** in Covington. **Bernard H. F. Hellebusch** was a teacher and the principal at the Mother of God School beginning around 1850. As a musician, he practiced the German *singmesse* tradition of church music, emphasizing the folk song in contrast to the traditional classical Latin style. He wrote and published some 34 *singmesse* hymns, as well as a popular hymnal entitled *Gesang und Gebetbuch*, before his death in 1885. Henry Tappert (see **William and Henry Tappert**) replaced Hellebusch's *singmesse* style with newer Cecilian reform music, stressing polyphony and chant. He published his compositions in his *St. Cecilia Hymnal.* In 1895 Tappert hired **Edward Strubel** as an organist at the church. Strubel, a virtuoso on the organ and a talented composer, served in that capacity for 55 years. Ecclesiastical music was a much larger part of parish life in the early years of Catholicism in Northern Kentucky, and it was played in all parish churches, not just Mother of God Church in Covington.

Two new types of secular music appeared in America at the turn of the 20th century. **Ragtime** was popular for the first 20 years of the new century, and the **Gasdorf Music Publishing Company** of Newport helped to popularize ragtime, including an occasional piece written by a young composer from Covington, **Haven Gillespie**. The **blues** soon followed, brought up the Ohio River on the riverboats; it prospered in Covington and Newport, as well as in the west side of downtown Cincinnati. Longtime area blues-players such as James "Pigmeat" Jarrett and "H. Bomb" Ferguson performed regularly at Northern Kentucky entertainment venues. Currently, the Mansion Hill Tavern in Newport is a prominent gathering spot for performances of the blues.

Country music arrived with the **Appalachian** migration into the area during the 1920s. Barn dances held in Grant Co. and the **Boone County Jamboree** (later to become both a radio and a television show) provided a venue for this new musical style. Early country music performers from the area included Grant Co.'s singer-composer **Pop Eckler**, the Bird Family from Covington; fiddler **Bill Livers** from Owen Co., and **Blanche Coldiron**, who had family ties to Grant Co. Radio station WLW in Cincinnati and **L. B. Wilson**'s **WCKY** in Covington regularly played country music for their listeners. Today, in Nashville, Tenn., the top-rated country music disc jockey is **Gerry House**, a native of Kenton Co. Later in his career, Pop Eckler performed **bluegrass** music.

The 1920s also saw the beginning of swing-era dancing music. A popular Northern Kentuckian involved in this type of music was Covington's **Justin Huber**, whose bands and orchestras, from the early 1920s through the late 1940s, played at ballrooms regionally. His groups were booked at company gatherings and parties, as well as at the **Horseshoe Gardens** in Bellevue. It was at the Horseshoe Gardens that the famous Mills Brothers got their start. In that same era, Newport native **Tommy Ryan** went from steel-mill worker in his hometown to major national band leader during the 1940s and 1950s. Club musicians playing piano lounge music locally included **Larry Vincent**, who died in 1977, just months before the fire that destroyed the **Beverly Hills Supper Club**, where he often performed. Vincent's good friend Haven Gillespie was the lyricist who produced the most famous song written by a native of Northern Kentucky, the best-selling "Santa Claus Is Comin' to Town." Gillespie, who died in 1975, wrote lyrics to more than 1,000 works in his life, including several that became popular hits.

Also around the turn of the 20th century, several Northern Kentucky women excelled as musical performers. Local voice teachers such as **Patia Power** trained students who made it to the Broadway stage. Vocalist **Clara Loring** from Covington wowed the New York crowds for several years in the second decade of the century. **Mary Hissem DeMoss**, from California, Ky., sang at prestigious Protestant churches in New York City and throughout New England. She taught voice well into the 1950s at her home in New Jersey. **Katherine Hall Poock**, a descendant of a family of Covington educators, spent years singing and teaching voice around Greater Cincinnati. **Elizabeth Parks**, also from Covington, sang for the troops in Europe during **World War I**. In the 1920s, **Eugene Ysaye** wrote music and produced musical concerts for the Cincinnati Symphony Orchestra while living in Fort Thomas. In recent years, **Lee Roy Reams**, a 1960 graduate of Covington's **Holmes High School**, has shared top billing with the greats of the musical theater in New York City, such as *Hello Dolly!* and with road companies throughout the United States, such as the Fantastics.

Along with the Beverly Hills Supper Club, which booked nationally known entertainers, there were other high-caliber musical venues in Northern Kentucky. Kenton Co. had its similarly famous **Lookout House**, where Larry Vincent also performed as well as top-name entertainers such as Dizzy Gillespie, Ted Lewis, Frank Sinatra, and the like. Some of these entertainers even performed for free at the **Devou Park Band Shell** (amphitheater) before thousands of appreciative fans. In Campbell Co., gambling spots such as Glenn Schmidt's, the Latin Quarters, and the Tropicana booked topflight entertainers, some of whom were seen gambling or "bar hopping" after their performances. Maysville's historic **Washington Opera House**, located in that city's downtown area, also hosted shows by several famous performers.

Military band music has long been popular in Northern Kentucky. In the 19th century, the presence of the U.S. Army at the **Newport Barracks** gave the area the Army Band for musical entertainment at important events. The musical Gasdorf family of Newport sponsored the popular Gasdorf Military Band, which performed in the decade beginning 1910, and John Philip Sousa's Naval Band performed before large crowds in Covington in 1918. Later, after the army relocated to the Fort Thomas Military Reservation, the Army Band performed at parades and on Decoration Day at **Evergreen Cemetery** and, during the 1920s, gave free public concerts on the fort's grounds.

Other types of bands that performed or now perform locally include the Newport Jug Band at the turn of the 20th century, today's **Florence Community Band**, and several bands that have had modern rock connections. The area's best-known rock band is **Pure Prairie League**, a musical group that includes several members raised in Northern Kentucky. High schools such as **Beechwood**, **Highlands**, and Covington **Holmes** have won statewide band competitions. Local groups like the McCormick Fiddlers were featured on the ***Boone County Jamboree*** and later regional television's *Midwestern Hayride.* During the first three decades of the 20th century, the **Harvard Piano Company** of Dayton, Ky., manufactured almost 30,000 pianos for use nationwide.

The academic world has also contributed to music in Northern Kentucky. Since it opened in 1970, **Northern Kentucky University** (NKU) has been developing its music department. Internationally renowned Russian immigrant **Sergei Polusmiak** teaches piano there; **Robert Knauf**, the longtime choral director of the Cincinnati Symphony's May Festival, taught choral music and also served as the music department's first chairman; and a number of students and performing groups who have studied music at NKU have performed with distinction nationally and internationally. **Herschel Linstaedt** of Fort Thomas had a distinguished career as a music teacher at the College Conservatory of Music in Cincinnati, and **jazz** musician **Roger Schueler** (see **Dixie Heights High School**) founded and directed a highly successful high school jazz band during the 1960s; several of his students became professional jazz musicians.

The foremost recording artist from Northern Kentucky is Maysville's **Rosemary Clooney**. Her successful musical and movie career spanned more than seven decades. She and her sister **Betty Clooney** performed during their teenage years as the Clooney Sisters until Rosemary struck out on her own after landing a singing part in the 1953 movie *The Stars Are Singing*. Her brother **Nick Clooney**, a former radio and television personality who now writes opinion columns for the *Cincinnati Post* and the ***Kentucky Post***, also recorded songs but produced no hits. Another entertainer, the late **Bob Braun** of Ludlow, also had a highly successful career in regional television and radio, but the songs he recorded never became hits.

Lonnie Mack, remembered for his hit song "Memphis," filled Ben Kraft's Guys 'N Dolls Club in Cold Spring during the 1960s, as did rock and roller Billy Joe Royal singing his biggest hit, "Down in the Boondocks." Later, **Adrian Belew** from Boone Co. gained national acclaim as an electrical guitar player. Country singer **Skeeter Davis**, born Mary Frances Penick in Glencoe, had a country music crossover hit in 1962 entitled "The End of the World"; **Bobby Mackey's** in Wilder remains the longest-running country night spot in Greater Cincinnati; and **Kenny Price**, once dubbed the "Sheriff of Boone County," went from the *Midwestern Hayride* to *Hee Haw* on national television with his robust country style before his death in 1987. Southern Gospel singing has been represented for 30 years by the touring **Ball Family** of Covington; **Nelson Burton** from Covington played jazz backup for many visiting musical groups; African American music is represented by the internationally acclaimed singing group from Covington's **Eastside**, the **Northern Kentucky Brotherhood**, whose appealing harmonies have carried them around the world; ecclesiastical music and pipe organ pieces are well represented by the performances of **Robert Schaffer** and his family at the Roman Catholic **Cathedral Basilica of the Assumption** in Covington; and both **Nancy James** and **Mary Ellen Tanner**, former Cincinnati television vocalists with Northern Kentucky ties, continue to entertain in the area—James with the **Kentucky Symphony Orchestra** and Tanner on Sunday evenings at Chez Nora's in **Main Strasse**.

MUSSMAN, RALPH G. (b. February 3, 1919, Newport, Ky.; d. March 25, 1987, Newport, Ky.). Politician Ralph Mussman was the son of Ralph G. and Josephine Beazley Mussman. For more than 30 years, he had a truly remarkable public life. Ralph grew up on E. Third St. in Newport and graduated in 1936 from Newport High School, where he played football and basketball; in his senior year, he was captain of both of those teams. He also engaged in sports at the college level and in 1941 was voted the most outstanding athlete at Morehead State College in Morehead. In 1984 he was inducted into the Northern Kentucky High School Sports Hall of Fame.

During **World War II** Mussman served as a navigator in the U.S. Army Air Corps and attained the rank of captain. He was stationed in New Guinea in the South Pacific. During the Battle of the Bismarck Sea (March 2–4, 1944), the combat aircraft he was navigating participated in the sinking of one of the four destroyers that the Japanese lost.

He began his career in public service as Newport's first recreation director, for the summer of 1951. Later, he taught history and coached football at **Holmes High School**. For 10 months during 1957 he served as Newport's city manager, a post that he held three times. He was the mayor of Newport from 1960 through 1964. He taught school in Cincinnati for a short time before becoming the principal of the Arnold Elementary School in Newport (1967–1970). At other times during his career, he sold real estate. He became city manager of Newport for the second time in 1976 and served until he was fired and soon rehired in 1980. He then continued as city manager until he retired in 1984. In 1985 he was elected to Newport's city commission.

In his early days of public life, Mussman was accused of being too harsh on Newport's gambling element. He softened somewhat on the gambling issue as time passed, but he never stopped wanting to rid his hometown of vice and corruption and of those who promoted them. In September 1961 he was indicted for not enforcing the state's gambling laws, but a jury found him not guilty. As mayor, he helped to bring the Newport Mall to W. Fourth St. He is often recognized as the person who, during the mid-1980s, initiated the early redevelopment of Newport's riverfront. Mussman worked with the Shilling family to bring to the Newport shore the Islands floating restaurant, the first of a long line of developments—still continuing—along the city's Riverboat Row.

Mussman's first wife died early in their marriage. His second wife, Kathryn L. Poff Mussman, survived him; she died in early May 2005. Ralph Mussman died in 1987 of a heart attack at his long-time home on Monroe St. in Newport. The flags were at half-mast as he was buried at Evergreen Cemetery in Southgate. Athlete, war hero, educator, and politician, Ralph Mussman is still remembered by many as deserving of his nickname "Mr. Newport."

"Athlete, War Hero, Politician—Ralph Mussman," *KP*, February 26, 1987, 1–2.

Michael R. Sweeney

MUTTER GOTTES NATIONAL HISTORIC DISTRICT. The Mutter Gottes (Mother of God) National Historic District in Covington was established in 1980 in a neighborhood in the city's West End. The focal point of the neighborhood is the **Mother of God Catholic Church**, which is itself listed on the National Register of Historic Places. The boundaries of the neighborhood are Kentucky and Covington Aves.; Montgomery St.; portions of W. Fourth, Fifth, and Sixth Sts.; and portions of Craig, Johnson, and Russell Sts.

When Rev. Ferdinand Kuhr established Mother of God Parish in 1841, the parish was the first German Catholic congregation in Northern Kentucky. The parish grew quickly with an influx of German immigrants to the city. In 1870–1871, the congregation built the current Italian Renaissance Revival structure on W. Sixth St. The neighborhood around the Mother of God Church developed along with the parish. Beginning in the 1840s, residents began constructing primarily Italianate-style row houses in the vicinity of the church. These two-story frame-and-brick homes were built close to the street and had small backyards. Family-owned and -operated businesses were also scattered throughout the neighborhood, including grocery stores, taverns, and a pharmacy.

In the years following **World War II**, residents began leaving Covington for the suburbs, and the neighborhood surrounding the Mother of God Church began to deteriorate. In 1962 Mother of God School, which had existed in the neighborhood for 120 years, closed because of low enrollment. In 1972 the beautiful school building on W. Sixth St. was demolished. Parish membership had declined to less than 200 families. The parish experienced a revival, however, under the leadership of Rev. William Mertes, who arrived in the parish in 1969. The parish began a number of outreach efforts in the community, such as the **Parish Kitchen** and the **Welcome House**.

The revival of the Mother of God Church also had an impact on the health of the neighborhood. In 1974 Reverends Ray Holtz, William Mertes, and Paul Wethington and a small group of dedicated laypeople established Covington Avenue Properties Inc., a partnership that purchased 12 dilapidated homes on Covington Ave. for $59,000 with the intention of rehabilitating the properties. Only persons who agreed to restore and live in the homes were permitted to participate. Within several years, Covington Ave. had been transformed. The success of the Covington Ave. project led to the creation of the Russell Row Partnership and the Kentucky-Craig St. Project, which resulted in the restoration of 25 historic structures. The success of all these efforts prompted the neighborhood to apply for National Register Historic District status.

Mutter Gottes Historic District, National Register of Historic Places Inventory-Nomination Form, 1980, U.S. Department of the Interior, Washington, D.C.

Tenkotte, Paul A., David E. Schroeder, and Thomas S. Ward. *To Be Catholic and American in Northern, Central, and Appalachian Kentucky: The Diocese of Covington, 1853–2003*. Forthcoming.

David E. Schroeder

MYERS, HARVEY, JR. (b. December 24, 1859, Covington, Ky.; d. July 1, 1933, Latonia, Ky.). Harvey Myers Jr. was a noted attorney, politician, and sports enthusiast. His father was **Harvey Myers**, and his mother was the former Susan C. Scott. Harvey Jr. was educated in the Covington Public Schools (see **Covington Independent Schools**) and after graduation worked for the Cincinnati *Times* newspaper. In 1879 he married Cara Wells, and they had four children. Harvey studied law under **Theodore F. Hallam** and was admitted to the bar in 1881. He was a partner of Hallam in the firm of Hallam and Myers for thirteen years.

Unlike his father, who was a Republican, Harvey Myers Jr. was a Democrat (see **Democratic Party**). He served in the Kentucky House of Representatives from 1886 to 1890, where he held the office of Speaker. Although all three men were Democrats, by about 1890 Myers and Hallam became vehement opponents of **William Goebel**. For a number of years, Myers was head of the Latonia Jockey Club and a member of the Motor Club. He was responsible for organizing the Twin Oaks Golf and Country Club in 1927. Myers suffered a stroke at his law office in 1931 but continued his regular work. After a half century of law practice, he died of a cerebral hemorrhage at his home on 45th St. in Latonia. His second wife, Anna Belle Menefee, whom he married in 1904, and five children survived him. Burial was in the Highland Cemetery, Fort Mitchell.

Biographical Cyclopedia of The Commonwealth of Kentucky. Chicago: John M. Gresham, 1896.
"Harvey Myers, Jr. Dead," *KP,* July 3, 1933, 1.
Johnson, E. Polk. *History of Kentucky and Kentuckians.* Vol. 2. Chicago: Lewis, 1912.
Levin, H., ed. *The Lawyers and Lawmakers of Kentucky.* Chicago: Lewis, 1897.
Perrin, William H. *Biographical Sketches from Kentucky.* Vol. 7. Louisville, Ky.: F. A. Battey, 1887.
"The Secret Hand Revealed," *KP,* July 9, 1894, 4.

MYERS, HARVEY, SR. (b. February 10, 1828, Chenango Co., N.Y.; d. March 28, 1874, Covington, Ky.). Noted attorney Harvey Myers Sr. was the son of Aaron and Aurelia Bridgman Myers. In about 1852 he moved to Trimble Co., Ky., where he taught school, studied law, and was admitted to the bar. After a few years, he moved to Covington and in 1858 married Susan Clark Withers. His children included **Harvey Myers Jr.**

As a Republican, the senior Myers was a strong supporter of the Union during the Civil War (see **Republican Party**). In 1865 he was elected as a representative to the Kentucky General Assembly from Kenton Co., but he refused the office when he learned that soldiers had been assigned around the county polls, arresting voters and holding them in custody until the day after the election. In 1866 Myers purchased a large brick home at Shelby St. and Riverside Dr. in Covington; the historic home is still standing. In the 1860s he formed a law partnership with Governor **John W. Stevenson** (1867–1871). Myers published a code of practice for Kentucky attorneys, as well as a supplement to the general statutes of Kentucky. In November 1872, he ran for the U.S. House of Representatives in the Sixth Congressional District but lost to incumbent **William E. Arthur**. In the early 1870s Myers and **Oliver Root** were representing Mrs. W. G. Terrell in a divorce case. On March 28, 1874, while working in his office, Myers was approached by Mr. Terrell. An altercation ensued, and Terrell shot and killed Myers. Myers's funeral services were held at **Trinity Episcopal Church** in Covington, and he was buried in Highland Cemetery in Fort Mitchell.

Terrell was found guilty of voluntary manslaughter and sentenced to eight years in prison. In 1877 Terrell's attorneys successfully appealed his case to the Court of Appeals of Kentucky, then Kentucky's highest court, on the basis that procedural errors had been made. These errors included the refusal of the lower court to grant a continuance until Nicholas Corcoran, the only other person in Myers's office that day, could appear as a witness for the defense. The Court of Appeals ruled that Terrell should be retried, and in 1879 he was acquitted.

Biographical Cyclopedia of The Commonwealth of Kentucky. Chicago: John M. Gresham, 1896.
"Deplorable Tragedy: Hon. Harvey Myers Shot and Killed by Col. W. G. Terrell," *CJ,* April 4, 1874, 1.
Johnson, E. Polk. *History of Kentucky and Kentuckians.* Vol. 2. Chicago: Lewis, 1912.
"Sixth Congressional District: Official Statement of the Result," *CJ,* November 16, 1872, 2.

Paul A. Tenkotte

NAACP. The Covington branch of the NAACP (National Association for the Advancement of Colored People) was formed in 1919, when the national office sent Walter White around Kentucky to establish local chapters that would collaborate with other organizations to oppose lynching, mob violence, and Jim Crow laws. During the next 40 years, the organization's Covington branch saw periods of both activity and inactivity.

Founded in 1909, the NAACP has worked primarily to obtain legislative and judicial solutions to civil rights issues. Using courtroom and legislative victories, it has brought about dramatic changes in the educational, legal, and economic conditions of **African Americans**.

Legal counsel provided by the Covington NAACP proved beneficial in numerous cases, helping African Americans avoid unjust jail sentences and the death penalty. In 1930, during a time when the local NAACP was inactive, the Anderson McPerkins case caused it to revive and gain McPerkins's release from prison. In 1934, with the case of Huston Mosler, who was charged with murder, the NAACP was able to persuade the courts to decide on life imprisonment rather than execution. In cases involving John Pete Montjoy (1935) and Harold Van Vension (1938), in which the men were convicted of raping white women, the NAACP, the ACLU (American Civil Liberties Union), and the ILD (International Labor Defense) failed in attempts to alter the death sentences. Both were hanged in front of the Covington city-county building. In late 1938, after two decades of antilynching efforts, the NAACP and other organizations were successful in persuading the Kentucky legislature to outlaw public hangings.

For the next 10 years, the NAACP's Covington branch was again inactive, but it revived in 1948, when the national NAACP received a letter from Louis Brown of Covington, expressing the desire to reorganize the branch. In 1949 Jack Delaney of Covington was elected as a board member to the state conference of the NAACP. Nevertheless, the branch slipped into inactivity again.

The 1954 U.S. Supreme Court decision in *Brown v. Board of Education* signaled the end of "separate but equal" schools and brought about the integration of public schools in Northern Kentucky. This victory by the NAACP national legal defense team inspired the local chapter to reorganize in April 1959. Rechartered as the Covington-Newport branch, it elected Mrs. E. Conley president and Mrs. M. Miles secretary. The group investigated, negotiated, and provided legal advocacy when incidents of abuse, loss of jobs, and other forms of racial discrimination were experienced by African American students, teachers, staff, and faculty during the early years of school integration. Another area of interest to the NAACP was housing discrimination. City urban renewal programs and discrimination by lending institutions had forced many African Americans to leave Covington and Newport and seek housing in Cincinnati or other cities. After considering a lawsuit, the local branch instead worked with officials to dismantle discrimination practices; such cooperation led to open-housing ordinances and commissions.

In July 1960 the NAACP organized community meetings at Covington's Fouse Center (see **Elizabeth B. Cook "Lizzie" Fouse**) to protest a "white only" bathroom sign at **Coppin's** department store that had been there for more than 45 years. These community meetings did not move into direct action until November 1960, when the **Congress of Racial Equality** organized a chapter in Northern Kentucky. While some people were members of both organizations, CORE during the next three years galvanized the local movement and successfully desegregated public accommodations in Northern Kentucky, before the Civil Rights Act of 1964. In addition, CORE and the NAACP worked to eradicate discrimination in employment, housing, and educational access faced by African Americans during that era.

CORE closed its chapter in Northern Kentucky in 1963, and the NAACP, guided by Mrs. E. Conley, president; Rev. **Edgar Mack**, executive secretary; and **Fermon Knox**, reemerged as the primary civil rights organization in the region. It worked closely with the Cincinnati NAACP, the Greater Cincinnati Commission on Religion and Race, the Human Rights Commission, and the Catholic Interracial Council on issues such as education, employment, and housing.

The Northern Kentucky NAACP was an active participant in the Allied Organizations for Civil Rights in Kentucky, which sponsored the Freedom March on Frankfort, held on March 5, 1964. The march was called to show support for a public-accommodations bill being considered by the Kentucky legislature. That demonstration involved more than 10,000 people, with 300 participants from Northern Kentucky.

When Martin Luther King Jr. was assassinated in 1968, the Northern Kentucky NAACP collaborated with numerous local groups to hold memorial services for the purpose of healing the community and quelling any possible violent responses. During the next few years, the NAACP worked on racial injustices in housing, education, politics, and employment. On August 14, 1983, the NAACP organized a march across the **John A. Roebling Bridge** to dramatize the need for African Americans to register and vote. The speakers included Benjamin Hooks, executive director of the NAACP; activist Julian Bond; and Fermon Knox, president of the local and state NAACP.

Often accused of being too moderate or distant from the acute conditions of urban life, the NAACP has most recently been involved in economic development and youth programs, while continuing to be the organization for legal advocacy on civil rights issues.

"Getting Blacks Involved," *KP*, February 3, 1984, 4K.

The Papers of the Congress of Racial Equality, 1941–1967. Frederick, Md.: University Publications of America, 1983. Microform. Available at the Univ. of Kentucky, Lexington; the Univ. of Louisville; and the Univ. of Cincinnati.

Papers of the NAACP. Microform version available at Univ. of Virginia Library, www.lib.virginia.edu (accessed January 14, 2007).

"A Voice on Civil Rights," *KP*, July 6, 2000, 4K.

Wright, George C. *A History of Blacks in Kentucky.* Frankfort, Ky.: Kentucky Historical Society, 1992.

Jim Embry

NAPOLEON. Nestled in eastern Gallatin Co., near Grant Co., along what is now Ky. Rt. 16, is the tiny village of Napoleon. Today it consists of one grocery store and about a dozen private residences.

In 1803 the area was settled by a group of families who came down the Ohio River by flatboats, most likely from Pennsylvania. Initially their community was called Connors, in honor of one of the first settlers, Samuel Connor (1777–1863). Connor married Catherine Spenser, and both were buried in the Ten Mile Cemetery, just behind the present-day **Ten Mile Baptist Church**, approximately one-quarter of a mile to the west of the church.

Myrix J. Williams was appointed the first postmaster of Connors sometime before 1831. He was born July 14, 1811, and was buried in the Williams Cemetery at Glencoe. On January 30, 1841, while Philip Hanna was postmaster, the post office at Connors was renamed Napoleon and the town's name was changed accordingly. The post office at Napoleon was discontinued before 1913.

There were several medical doctors who practiced and lived in Napoleon during the mid-1800s and into the early 1900s. A young doctor named J. W. Shupert began his practice there. Later, he moved with his family and practice to Warsaw, a more populated area. Family names mentioned at Napoleon in those days were Bledsoe, Brashear, Carleton, Lillard, McNeeley, Skirvin, and Turley. During the early 1900s, mail was delivered to Napoleon from Glencoe. John Hall, a federal employee, had the mail route to Napoleon, daily delivering the mail from a horse-drawn wooden wagon.

Between 1844 and 1850, a Presbyterian church, the Napoleon Presbyterian Church, existed in the hamlet. Around 1900 the road servicing Napoleon (Ky. Rt. 16) was nothing but mud, with a scattering of rocks. There were two grocery stores: one owned and operated by Holt Wallace and Andrew McGee and another belonging to Nolan Richardson. These stores were stocked with the usual commonly needed articles, such as 100-pound burlap bags of coffee beans (often the coffee beans were still green and required a quick roasting in the oven before grinding). Stalks of bananas hung from overhead at seasonal times, such as just before Christmas. Every grocery also sold kerosene and wicks for lamps and lanterns.

Walker W. Spaulding owned the blacksmith shop, the hub of activity for the village. In addition to his metal work, Spaulding ground wheat for flour and corn for meal. In the late 1920s, telephones came to Napoleon, for the few who could afford them, but it was not until the late 1930s that rural electrification arrived.

Bogardus, Carl R., Sr., *The Story of Gallatin County.* Ed. James C. Claypool. Cincinnati: John S. Swift, 2003.

"Center of Town," *KP*, November 14, 1975, 4K.

Gray, Gypsy M. *History of Gallatin County, Kentucky.* Covington, Ky.: Privately published, 1968.

Rennick, Robert M. *Kentucky Place Names.* Lexington: Univ. of Kentucky Press, 1984.

Rider, Jack. Interview by Joy Higgins, April 14, 2005.

Joy Higgins

NATIONAL GUARD, POST–WORLD WAR II TO IRAQ WAR. Boone Co. has had a Kentucky National Guard unit since November 1, 1975, when the 118th Maintenance Company was established in Burlington. Exactly one year later, this unit was transferred to Walton, underwent a few reorganizations, and was redesignated the 130th Maintenance Company and Detachment 1, 207th Engineer Company. On March 6, 1999, the present-day Detachment 1, Battery A, 2nd Battalion, 138th Field Artillery, was formed. On October 1, 2002, the 940th Military Police Company became the second unit assigned to meet at Walton. The 2nd Battalion, 138th Field Artillery, served on federal duty from May 5, 2003, until May 4, 2004, providing post security for Fort Campbell's 101st Airborne Division. The 940th Military Police Company was placed on federal duty November 29, 2004, and after some additional training was assigned to service in Iraq.

Campbell Co.'s Battery A, 242nd Field Artillery Battalion, was organized on November 10, 1956, at **Fort Thomas Military Reservation**. In September 1959 federal recognition was withdrawn when the unit fell below its required troop strength. On November 1, 1980, Company B (Medical), 103rd Support Battalion, 149th Armored Brigade, was established, and on November 1, 1985, this unit was transferred to Louisville and redesignated.

The Carroll Co. National Guard unit was organized on October 15, 1949, as Company A, 201st Engineer Battalion. During the Korean War, it served on active duty from May 1, 1951, until April 30, 1953. The unit was stationed at Fort McCoy, Wis. On October 1, 1959, it was redesignated as Battery A, 2nd Battalion, 138th Field Artillery Battalion. On May 13, 1968, the battalion was activated for combat service in Vietnam. It was in Vietnam from October 1968 until October 1969. This artillery battalion is the only Kentucky National Guard unit to serve in Vietnam. The battalion fired over 150,000 rounds at enemy targets. On March 6, 1999, the unit was redesignated Battery A (Less Detachment 1), 2nd Battalion, 138th Field Artillery, with the detachment's drill meetings held in Walton. The 2nd Battalion, 138th Field Artillery, served on federal duty from May 5, 2003, until May 4, 2004, providing post security at Fort Campbell.

Mason Co., the oldest county in Northern Kentucky, has had a military presence since 1788. On October 1, 1985, Company A, 206th Engineer Battalion, of the Kentucky National Guard was activated in Mason Co. On October 1, 2002, the unit became the 301st Chemical Company (Smoke/Decontamination). This new unit was ordered into federal service on November 29, 2004, and was sent to Iraq. While there, they trained the Iraqi police, provided base security and guarded detainees for the U.S. Army. The unit returned home January 9, 2006.

Alfaro, Armando J. *Paper Trail of the Kentucky National Guard.* Utica, Ky.: McDowell, 2003.

Al Alfaro

NATIONAL GUARD, SPANISH-AMERICAN WAR. The men of the commonwealth of Kentucky demonstrated their loyalty to the nation when the "sinking" of the battleship USS *Maine* on February 15, 1898, in Havana Harbor, Cuba, sparked the Spanish-American War. A naval investigation on March 28, 1898, revealed the ship had hit a mine. However, it gave the United States a pretext to try to free Cuba, Puerto Rico, and the Philippines from Spain's control. The United States declared war on Spain on April 25, 1898.

Kentuckians clamored to enlist in the Kentucky State Guard units of the 1st, 2nd, 3rd, and 4th Army Infantry Regiments, plus Troops A and B of the Army's 1st Cavalry. The initial strength mandated by the governor of Kentucky was 104 men per company. It appeared there would not be enough weapons and uniforms to supply that many troops, so he decreased each unit's size to 84 men. When the Presidential Proclamation requesting states to meet their respective federal troop quotas reached Governor William O. Bradley (1895–1899) , the Kentucky State Guard was ready.

Capt. Thomas W. Woodyard, commander of Company G, 2nd Infantry Regiment, Kentucky State Guard, was actively recruiting members from Newport and the surrounding counties in preparation for the unit's activation into federal service. On May 6, 1898, this company moved by rail to the south side of Lexington, Camp Collier at the Tattersall's horse farm. The horse barns were used as living quarters because no tents were available. On May 20, 1898, the regiment was mustered into federal service as Company G, 2nd Kentucky Volunteer Infantry Regiment (U.S.).

On May 25, 1898, Kentucky's federalized 2nd Volunteer Regiment made a 250-mile journey by rail to Camp George H. Thomas, at Chickamauga Park, Ga., arriving the next day. The regiment, along with the New York 9th Infantry and the Arkansas 1st Infantry, comprised the 1st Brigade, 2nd Division, 3rd U. S. Army Corps. During its stay at Camp Thomas, the Kentucky unit engaged in sham battles, routine training, and regimental reviews. The infantry regiment was issued new weapons and uniforms, and the cavalry troops were issued horses and spurs.

The U.S. 2nd Kentucky Volunteer Regiment was eventually sent to Anniston, Ala., for additional training. A peace protocol signed in Washington, D.C., on August 12, 1898, ended all hostilities. Company G, along with other U.S. 2nd Kentucky Volunteer Regiment units, traveled by rail on September 12, 1898, to Lexington, arriving the next day. On September 19 the unit was placed on regimental furlough for 30 days. The regiment reassembled at Lexington on October 18 and performed routine duties until being mustered out of federal service on October 31, 1898. The unit returned home as Company G of the 2nd Infantry Regiment, Kentucky State Guard, on November 1, 1898.

Alfaro, Armando J. *Paper Trail of the Kentucky National Guard.* Utica, Ky.: McDowell, 2003.

Works Progress Administration. *The American Guide Series: Military History of Kentucky.* Frankfort, Ky.: State Journal, 1939. Reprint, Utica, Ky.: McDowell, 2003.

Al Alfaro

NATIONAL GUARD, WORLD WAR II. The organizational charts used by the Kentucky National Guard in **World War II** date to 1860. Records for that year show that Covington had a militia unit named the Covington Light Guard, Maysville had the Mason County Guards, and Carroll Co. had the Butler Guards. During **World War I**, while the National Guard's mobilized troops were on federal active duty, a security force of five other guard units was activated across the state. Covington's Company D, Kentucky State Guard, was organized and frequently activated between August 5, 1917, and March 20, 1921. On March 21, 1921, this unit became a part of the U.S. 38th Division Tank Company. In June 1932 the new division was moved to Harrodsburg, in Mercer Co. Two other military units remained in Covington, and on July 10, 1929, and May 1, 1930, the Headquarters 2nd Squadron and Troop F 123rd Cavalry Regiment, respectively, were designated federal units.

Just before entering federal service, on February 24, 1940, these units were reorganized. Troop F 123rd Cavalry Regiment was converted into Battery C 103rd Coast Artillery Battalion (anti-aircraft), and the HQ and the HQ Company, 2nd Squadron, 123rd Cavalry, was converted into HQ and HQ Company, Battery 106th Coast Artillery Battalion. Both battalions served in the European theater of operations during World War II. Their tours of duty lasted from February 24, 1940, until December 3, 1945.

Troop F of the 123rd Cavalry Regiment left New York on April 30, 1942, and arrived in Northern Ireland on May 15, 1942. The unit was later sent to North Africa, arriving on December 8, 1942, where it was attached to the 34th Coast Artillery Brigade (anti-aircraft). On July 2, 1943, Covington's cavalrymen landed in Sicily and participated in the Sicily Campaign from July 9 to August 27, 1943. On November 13, 1943, the unit was redesignated as the 103rd Automatic Weapons Battalion. From December 1943 until September 1944, the battalion was stationed in England. On November 25, 1944, it was assigned to the 1st U.S. Infantry Division; then, from October 1944 until April 28, 1945, it became part of the 3rd U.S. Infantry Division in Germany. After a short tour of occupational duty in Czechoslovakia, the battalion arrived in Germany on May 6, 1945. The unit departed Marseilles, France, for home on November 20, 1945, aboard the USS *Bardtown Victory.* It arrived in New York on November 30, 1945, and on December 1, 1945, the 103rd AW Battalion was deactivated.

The second Covington unit, the HQ and HQ Company, Battery 106th Coast Artillery Battalion, was activated into federal service on January 6, 1941, at Covington. It trained at Camp Hulen, Tex., from January 15, 1941, until March 31, 1942. The battalion was assigned to the 5th Army Corps in February 1942. It departed New York City and arrived in Northern Ireland on May 15, 1942. On November 7, 1942, it landed in North Africa. The unit participated in the Tunisia Campaign from November 17, 1942, until May 13, 1943. It arrived in Sicily on July 10, 1943, and was attached to the 2nd Army Division, participating in the Sicily Campaign between July 9, 1943, and August 17, 1943. The battalion left Sicily on September 16, 1943, and moved to the Italian peninsula to participate in the Naples-Foggia Campaign. On July 14, 1944, the unit reorganized as an automatic weapons battalion. On August 15, 1944, the newly formed battalion landed in southern France. Upon arrival, the unit was relieved of its North African theater of operations responsibilities, instead becoming part of the European theater of operations. On December 20, 1944, the battalion departed France for Germany. On November 1, 1945, the unit shipped home on the USS *David Shanks,* arriving in New York City on December 2, 1945. The battalion was deactivated on December 3, 1945.

The Maysville National Guard unit, HQ and HQ Company, 2nd Battalion, 149th Infantry, became a federal unit on June 1, 1934. On January 1, 1941, President Franklin D. Roosevelt ordered the entire National Guard (nationwide) into federal service for a year of intensive training, later changed to 18 months because of the military emergency brought about by the outbreak of World War II. Accordingly, on January 17, 1941, all Kentucky National Guard units were activated. The 149th Infantry Regiment unit was assigned to Camp Shelby, Miss., and trained with the 38th Infantry Division (Cyclone). The division consisted of guardsmen from Kentucky, Indiana, and West Virginia. On January 20, 1944, the troop ships carrying the 38th Infantry Division passed through the Panama Canal and landed at Oahu, Hawaii. On Thanksgiving Day 1944, the 38th Infantry Division left New Guinea for Leyte, in the Philippines. The 149th Infantry landed there December 6, 1944. While the unit was at the airport, the Japanese dropped paratroopers on the airfield, and for six days, in a torrential rain, the 149th Infantry fought their enemies before gaining control of the airfield. In January 1945 plans for the attack on Luzon were being formulated; this was where the infamous Bataan Death March had occurred in 1942. The 149th Infantry found itself able to liberate the 38th Tank Company, from Harrodsburg, Ky. (some of which had been members of Covington's Company D), from the Japanese prison camp. The attack on the prison camp started on the morning of January 29. This operation consisted of four separate campaigns over the next five months: Zigzag Pass (January 29–February 14); Bataan and the adjacent islands in Manila Bay (February 11–April 7); the Stotsenburg area (March 7–April 30); and the territory east of Manila (April 30–June 30). At the end of these operations on June 30, the division's statistics were 20,547 Japanese killed and 645 taken prisoner, 37 officers and 527 U.S. personnel dead, and 109 officers and 1,950 U.S. men wounded. The Kentucky 138th Field Artillery Regiment fired 54,375 rounds of ammunition during these battles and was a part of the division given the nickname "The Avengers of Bataan."

By the end of October 1945, the troops from Kentucky who had fought in the Philippines, as well as the liberated prisoners from Kentucky, were on ships destined for Los Angeles. Once back in the United States, the soldiers were transported to Camp Atterbury in Indiana, and within 48 hours most were separated from the service; some of the liberated prisoners remained because they needed additional medical care. The anticipated 12-month call-up to federal military service had turned into a 58-month commitment.

Alfaro, Armando J. *The Paper Trail of the Kentucky National Guard.* Utica, Ky.: McDowell, 2003.

Craft, Joseph R. "Kentucky National Guard History, 1937–1962," War Department Records, Frankfort, Ky.

Al Alfaro

NATIONAL UNDERGROUND RAILROAD MUSEUM, MAYSVILLE. Because of its proximity to the Ohio River, and because it contained one of the largest holding pens for recaptured slaves along the North-South border, Maysville was a hotbed of pro- and antislavery forces during the first half of the 19th century. A movement was begun by many concerned individuals, churches, and organizations to assist slaves attempting to escape to the North. Maysville and nearby Ripley, Ohio, were among the first communities to support **antislavery** societies and to set up **Underground Railroad** stations. The Underground Railroad consisted of a vast network of people who worked together to provide assistance to the fugitives. The operation was risky, and many whites and free persons of color were jailed or fined, or both, for aiding or encouraging the flight of slaves. Secret codes and special railway jargon often were used to protect the participants and to conceal their operations. "Conductors" took fugitives to safe houses, situated about 20 miles apart, where they could get food, clothing, and rest for a short time before moving on to the next station.

Two stations set up in Maysville were Phillip's Folly, at 227 Sutton St., and the Bierbower House, at 38 W. Fourth St. Carriage-makers Frederick and Jonathan Bierbower owned the Bierbower House and were known to hide slaves in their home, which soon became an important stop on the Underground Railroad. The Bierbower House is now the home of the National Underground Railroad Museum of Mayville. The building has been restored to closely resemble the way it may have looked when slaves were hidden there. Many photos, slave artifacts, and memorabilia are on display at the museum.

Crawford, Byron. "Maysville's Own Underground Railroad Museum Tells Story of Slavery," *KE,* September 14, 1998, B1.

PBS. "The Underground Railroad." www.pbs.org (accessed January 23, 2007).

Welcome to . . . Maysville, Kentucky. "The National Underground Railroad Museum." www.cityofmaysville.com (accessed January 23, 2007).

NATIVE AMERICANS. See **American Indians**.

NATIVITY, CHURCH OF THE (EPISCOPAL), MAYSVILLE. The Right Reverend William Meade, the Episcopal bishop of Virginia, considered establishing an Episcopal church in the Maysville area when he visited in 1831. In 1838, when Bishop B. B. Smith, the first ordained bishop of Kentucky, assigned Deacon N. Newlin Cowgill to begin a church in Maysville, progress began in earnest. The original group of Christians attending Episcopal church services met in the council chamber of the Maysville Market House. Deacon Cowgill was successful in raising $1,500 in pledges for a building, but when he was transferred, the building plans were put on hold.

From 1839 to 1847, the congregation met in a private room. By February 1850 services were being held in an unfinished building that later became the church. In 1854 the completed church building was consecrated as part of the Diocese of Lexington. That same year, the church purchased a Louisville-made pipe organ, the first one in Maysville. In the 1860s Father Frank M. Gregg, attempting to forestall a church division, advised his congregation never to discuss Civil War issues on church property; throughout the nation many congregations were dividing over war issues.

About a century later, the church in 1955 gained possession of the Old Opera House bell that was originally used in 1873 to summon firemen in Maysville for an emergency. The bell was dedicated and blessed by the Right Reverend William R. Moody. In 1961, the church made plans for an alcohol rehabilitation center to address the problems of men in the community who were addicted to alcohol. The rehabilitation center, founded by Dr. Robert Blake and others, became St. Luke's Hostel. It was able to help about 110 patients in only two years, closing in July 1965 because of a lack of funding.

Barr, Frances Keller. *Ripe to the Harvest: History of the Episcopal Diocese of Lexington, 1895–1995.* Lexington, Ky.: Diocese of Lexington, 1995.

Moore, T. Ross. *Church of the Nativity: A Historical Sketch.* Maysville, Ky., Privately published, 1977.

"Old Opera House Bell Becomes Church Bell Here," *Daily Independent,* February 8, 1955.

Swinford, Francis Keller, and Rebecca Smith Lee. *Great Elm Tree: Heritage of the Episcopal Diocese of Lexington.* Lexington, Ky.: Faith House Press, 1969.

Alex Hyrcza

NATLEE. Natlee is an Owen Co. community in the southern part of the county near the Scott Co. border. It was named after Nat Lee, who helped build the covered bridge that was once located nearby. Natlee, at the intersection of Ky. Rt. 2018 and the New Columbus Rd., is about two miles west of New Columbus. According to the best information available, there has not been a school at Natlee. The Pleasant View Baptist Church is close by, and the 1883 Lake atlas suggests that there was a winery and distillery at Natlee, along with a tollhouse on the way to New Columbus. Natlee is the birthplace of one of Owen Co.'s most famous military sons, Vice Adm. **Willis Augustus Lee Jr.**

An Atlas of Owen County, Kentucky. Philadelphia: Lake, 1883.

Houchens, Mariam Sidebottom. *History of Owen County: "Sweet Owen."* Louisville: Standard, 1976.

Rennick, Robert M. *Kentucky Place Names.* Lexington: Univ. Press of Kentucky, 1984.

NAZARENES. Probably the oldest Nazarene congregation in Northern Kentucky is the Newport First Church of the Nazarene, founded in 1904 as the Apostolic Holiness Church at the home of Mr. and Mrs. Daniel Blott of Newport. The congregation later acquired the old German United Brethren Church building at 210 W. 7th St. In 1909 it joined the nascent national Church of the Nazarene and by 1910 purchased a lot at 317 W. 6th St. in Newport, building a church and worshipping there until moving back to the W. 7th St. location in 1913. From 1919 until 1922, the members worshipped in a rented hall at 7th and York Sts., and in 1922 they purchased a lot at the southeast corner of W. 7th and Putnam Sts., where they built a frame structure. In 1928 the congregation replaced the frame building with a new brick church, designed and built by church member J. M. Wilson and containing a large auditorium surrounded by 11 classrooms. By 1930 the church had grown to 300 members. The present church at 830 York St. was dedicated on May 28, 1950, and the Educational Annex was constructed in 1965.

Founded in 1935, the Covington First Church of the Nazarene began renting the old Scott Street Methodist Church at 530 Scott St. (now the parking lot of the **Kenton Co. Public Library**) in Covington in 1939 and purchased it in 1944. In 1967 the congregation dedicated a new 300-seat church along the **Dixie Highway** in Park Hills, and further additions were completed in 1985 and 1991.

The Central Church of the Nazarene in Fort Wright began as the First Church of the Nazarene Ludlow in 1939. In May 1941 the congregation broke ground at the southeast corner of Oak and Davies Sts. in Ludlow for a new church; that building is now the headquarters of the **Duro Bag Manufacturing Company**. In 1966, after many of the congregation's members had moved from Ludlow to other suburban communities in Northern Kentucky, the church's pastor, Rev. Arthur O. Little, began construction of a new 26,000-square-foot facility on a four-acre tract of land on Pieck Ln. in Fort Wright, alongside I-75. Little drew the blueprints for the church, which was built entirely by the labor of church members and officially dedicated in April 1972.

The East Side Church of the Nazarene, now at 2505 Eastern Ave. in Covington, was founded in 1940 by Rev. John Knapp, the brother of Rev. Martin Wells Knapp, founder of God's Bible College in Cincinnati. Originally located at Bird and Garrard Sts., the congregation moved to its present site in 1965.

In Northern Kentucky there are a number of Nazarene congregations that belong to the Eastern District of Kentucky, including Augusta, Central Church (Fort Wright), Covington First (Park Hills), Crittenden (Dry Ridge), Dayton, East Side (Covington), Elijah (Hebron), Erlanger First, Florence Community, Immanuel (Highland Heights), Maysville, and Newport First.

The Church of the Nazarene, an international Christian denomination founded in the early 20th century in the United States and headquartered in Kansas City, Mo., has more than 14,000 congregations worldwide. A descendant of the Holiness Movement that arose among some U.S. Methodists in the mid-19th century, the Church of the Nazarene stresses "entire sanctification." To Nazarenes, the process of repentance and acceptance of Jesus Christ by persons of responsible age precedes justification and regeneration, made possible by the Crucifixion of Jesus. Justification and regeneration, in turn, precede "entire sanctification," which frees believers from original sin through the baptism of the Holy Spirit as they strive to grow in "holiness" throughout the remainder of their lives.

"Building Anniversary," *KP,* June 22, 1951, 3.

"Church of the Week," *KP,* October 16, 2003, 5K.

Covington First Church of the Nazarene. www.covingtonfirstnazarene.com/ (accessed December 3, 2006).

"Erlanger Church Work to Begin," *KP,* July 17, 1958, 24.

"First Service: New Church in Newport Will Be Opened Sunday," *KP,* January 23, 1928, 1.

Little, Rev. Arthur O. Interview by Paul A. Tenkotte, December 4, 2006, Fort Wright, Ky.

100 Years. This Is Our Story: First Church of the Nazarene, Newport, Kentucky. Newport, Ky.: First Church of the Nazarene, 2004.

"Plan New Church in Ft. Wright," *KP,* May 20, 1966, 2K.

"Reverend, Church Both Have Big Days Sunday," *KP,* June 19, 1999, 7K.

Tenkotte, Paul A. *A Heritage of Art and Faith: Downtown Covington Churches.* Covington, Ky.: Kenton Co. Historical Society, 1986.

"To Break Ground Sunday for New Ludlow Church," *KP,* May 3, 1941, 1.

"Wesleyan Interpretations of Gospel Taught by Nazarene Church: Congregation Is Housed in New Tabernacle," *KP,* April 8, 1930, 1–2.

Paul A. Tenkotte

NEAVE. Located in southwestern Bracken Co. along Ky. Rt. 22, Neave was once known as Holton's Corner, a tribute to Abner Holton, who had the first general store there during the mid-1800s. The Holtons operated a store at Neave for several decades, and perhaps they were the first to refer to the settlement as a "string town." Many of the homes and barns in this area were destroyed by a tornado on March 12, 1923; another tornado ripped apart the general store in 1927. As in most small towns, there were blacksmith shops and produce storehouses before the modern buildings in town were constructed. Many of these sturdier brick buildings were ruined too, however, in the tornadoes that struck the town during the 1940s and by another that struck in 1968, killing two people and destroying dozens of buildings. Little remains of the once-thriving town of Neave except for a few hardy citizens who farm the nearby fields or commute to work in larger communities elsewhere. There was a school at Neave, but it was closed in 1940 when the county school system was consolidated.

Bracken Co. Extension Homemakers. *History of Bracken County.* Bicentennial ed. Brooksville, Ky.: Bracken Co. Extension Homemakers, 2002.

Caroline R. Miller

NEEDMORE (BRACKEN CO.). The Bracken Co. Needmore, Ky., is located at the intersection of Dutch Ridge and the Augusta-Minerva Rds., just southeast of Augusta. Originally, a tollhouse was located at Needmore. Over the years, several large Victorian-style homes were constructed near the Frolicher windmill, which supplied well water to the area. This water was at times sold in bottles at the house currently owned by the George Kelsch heirs. The winery, at the west end of Needmore, is a massive and impressive structure (see **Viniculture**). The vaulted limestone cellar is 100 feet long, 40 feet wide, and 37 feet high. The entrances have keystone arches and timbers that are 12 inches by 12 inches. This enormous structure is being restored to recapture its former beauty and reestablish its nationally ranked wine production. Perhaps the best account of Needmore can be found in the book *The Natural Man,* by Bracken Co. native **Ed McClanahan**. McClanahan was born in Brooksville and is the author of several books.

Bracken Co. Extension Homemakers. *History of Bracken County.* Bicentennial ed. Brooksville, Ky.: Bracken Co. Extension Homemakers, 2002.

Caroline R. Miller

NEEDMORE (OWEN CO.). The Owen Co. village of Needmore is one of at least five places in the commonwealth of Kentucky sharing that name over the years. It is on the eastern edge of the county, along the Grant Co. boundary, where Ky. Rt. 22 and Fortune Ridge Rd. meet. Needmore is just east of the village of Sweet Owen. According to the best information available, there has not been a school at Needmore. The Mount Hebron Baptist Church is located here.

An Atlas of Owen County, Kentucky. Philadelphia: Lake, 1883.

Houchens, Mariam Sidebottom. *History of Owen County: "Sweet Owen."* Louisville: Standard, 1976.

NELSON, GEORGE EATON (b. January 31, 1899, Covington, Ky.; d. July 8, 1985, Covington,

Ky.). George Nelson, an army colonel and a long-term member of the Kentucky National Guard, was the son of Nathan Ulysses Nelson of Paducah, a traveling candy salesman, and Mammie Eaton Nelson. He attended the Ohio Military Institute in Cincinnati from 1910 to 1914 and the Staunton (Va.) Military Academy in 1914 and graduated from the old Covington High School in 1916. He entered **World War I** in 1917, not long after his 18th birthday. He embarked for England in 1918, near the end of the war, and was discharged in January 1919. Nelson married Grace Galvin, the daughter of **Maurice L. Galvin**, a prominent Republican driving force who was also Kentucky commonwealth attorney from 1903 to 1905, and the Nelsons had two children, a daughter, Grace Galvin Nelson Auge, and a son, Maurice Galvin Nelson.

Between the wars, from 1924 to 1940, Nelson served in the Kentucky National Guard. During that period he organized Horse Cavalry Troop F, which manned barracks and stables in Sanfordtown and also, between the wars, provided a social fabric for Northern Kentucky and Greater Cincinnati. Judges, bookies, company owners, doctors, lawyers, and grocery store owners made up the troop. It even sponsored a polo team. For a short time, when martial law was declared during the Ohio River **flood of 1937**, Nelson served as police chief in Covington and Troop F provided security. Next to swimming in the Licking and Ohio rivers as a boy, commanding Troop F on horseback was Nelson's greatest joy outside his family, he wrote in his autobiography.

Activated for regular duty by the U.S. Army in May 1941, as **World War II** was brewing, Nelson entered the army a second time. He became a lieutenant colonel and served in the Adjutant General's Office of the 100th Division; he held the same office with the 22nd Corps at Camp Campbell, Ky. Nelson sailed for England in November 1944. On the transatlantic ship passage, he caught pneumonia. He returned to the United States in January 1945, retiring from the army as a colonel on January 21, 1945.

George Nelson as a cadet at Ohio Military Institute, ca. 1911–1912.

The Nelson home was at 411 Wallace Ave., Covington, from 1928 to 1994. George and Grace Nelson belonged to the Queen City Club, the Cincinnati Country Club, and the **Fort Mitchell Country Club**, where Nelson served as president in 1966–1967. Nelson managed the Kosmos-Portland Cement Company's regional office, based in Cincinnati, between 1945 and 1964. He worked in public relations and sales for the H. C. Nutting Company from 1965 until his retirement in 1976. In 1983 Nelson was named a Kentucky Colonel, an Ambassador of Goodwill, and an Admiral of Kentucky Waters by Kentucky governor John Y. Brown Jr. (1979–1983). In 1985 Nelson died at St. Elizabeth Hospital North in Covington and was buried in St. Mary Cemetery at Fort Mitchell, next to his wife of 65 years.

"George Nelson, Family Patriarch," *KP*, July 9, 1985, 3D.

Nelson, George E. "Autobiography," typewritten manuscript in the possession of Roger Auge II.

——. "My Service in the U.S. Army, World War II, January 6, 1941, to November 21, 1945," typewritten manuscript in the possession of Roger Auge II.

Roger Auge II

NELSON, ROBERT W. (b. April 3, 1845, Alexandria, Ky.; d. January 9, 1927, Newport, Ky.). Robert William Nelson, a mayor and a state legislator, was the son of John H. Nelson. Robert Nelson was educated in local schools and then studied law under **John G. Carlisle** in Covington. He began his law practice in Alexandria but in 1869 moved it to Newport. At various times, he served as mayor of Newport, Campbell Co. attorney, state representative, and state senator. He played a major role in securing funds to construct the **Central Bridge** from Newport to Cincinnati, the streetcar line (see **Streetcars**) from Newport to Fort Thomas, and the **Latonia Racecourse**. During the **Pearl Bryan** murder trial in 1896, he was one of the prosecuting attorneys and presented the closing arguments, in which he sought the death penalty for the defendants, Scott Jackson and Alonzo Walling. Nelson was also instrumental in organizing the German National Bank in Newport, later known as the American National Bank. His home in Newport was on the corner of Park Ave. and Nelson Pl., where the **St. John United Church of Christ** now stands. Nelson Pl. was named in his honor. He was married twice; his first wife, Maria Sallee, died October 30, 1878, after just 15 months of marriage and shortly after giving birth to a daughter. His second wife, Mary Winston Berry Nelson (married 1893), was a niece of **Albert Seaton Berry** and a granddaughter of James Berry, founder of Jamestown, Ky. (now Dayton). She was also a great-granddaughter of **Washington Berry** and Alice Taylor Berry, sister of **James Taylor Jr.**, founder of Newport. Nelson died at age 81 and was buried in Evergreen Cemetery in Southgate. His wife and two daughters, Judith Nelson and Mary Nelson Jordan, survived him.

"Elected County Judge," *CJ*, August 12, 1854, 2.

Kerr, Charles. *History of Kentucky*. Vol. 4. Chicago: American Historical Society, 1922.

Reis, Jim, "Robert William Nelson," *KP*, January 29, 1996, 4K.

"Robert W. Nelson Dies," *KP*, January 10, 1927, 1.

"Will Probated," *KP*, January 13, 1927, 1.

NELSON, THOMAS HENRY (b. October 20, 1820, Mason Co., Ky.; d. March 14, 1896, Terre Haute, Ind.). Ambassador Thomas H. Nelson was the second child of Dr. Thomas Washington and Frances Doniphan Nelson. He was educated at **Maysville Academy** and became a lawyer. Nelson married Elizabeth Key, daughter of **Marshall Key** and Harriet Sellman Key, on December 11, 1843, and the couple relocated to Rockville, Ind., in early 1844. He made a significant impact on the western Indiana legal community. Already a dynamic public speaker though only 25 years old, Nelson was drafted to represent the **Whig Party** in the 1846 congressional election; however, he withdrew as a candidate in favor of former Indiana congressman Richard W. Thompson. In 1847 Nelson relocated his law practice to Terre Haute, the major city in western Indiana. A chance meeting there with Illinois congressman Abraham Lincoln in 1849 altered his life. Though he later lost the 1860 congressional election to Democrat Daniel W. Voorhees in a campaign marred by the death of two of Nelson's children, Nelson was lauded for mapping out a successful strategy at the Indiana Republican convention.

Soon after the election, Lincoln, the newly elected Republican U.S. president (1861–1865), asked Nelson to serve as the nation's ambassador to Chile. Nelson was residing in Santiago when he learned that his brother, Gen. **William "Bull" Nelson**, had been killed in an argument on September 19, 1862, at Louisville, by fellow Union general Jefferson Columbus Davis, a native of Indiana. While serving in Chile, Ambassador Nelson was declared a Chilean national idol for fearlessly saving the lives of trapped postulates during a catastrophic fire, which consumed the Catholic Church of the Compania in Santiago on December 8, 1863. Despite Nelson's heroism, more than 2,300 people, mostly young women, perished. Nelson also drew praise later for his adroit diplomacy during Spain's bid between 1863 and 1865 to reclaim its Latin American empire. He resigned from his duties in Chile and, on March 12, 1866, returned with his family to Terre Haute.

Nelson later toured the country, giving lectures and advising presidents Andrew Johnson (1865–1869) and Ulysses S. Grant (1869–1877) on Latin American affairs. During this period Nelson maintained residences in both New York City and Washington, D.C. President Grant, concerned about Mexican president Benito Juarez's unstable government, in 1869 persuaded Nelson to become the U.S. ambassador to Mexico. When Elizabeth Nelson died on March 22, 1872, in Maitrata, Mexico, the grieving Thomas Nelson tendered his resignation. However, because President Grant was unable to find a suitable replacement, he did not honor Nelson's request until 1873. Nelson died in

1896 and was buried at Terre Haute's Woodlawn Cemetery.

Bradsby, H. C. *History of Vigo County, Indiana, Illustrated.* Chicago: S. B. Nelson, 1891.

Davis, William Columbus. *The Last Conquistadores: The Spanish Intervention in Peru and Chile, 1863–1866.* Athens: Univ. of Georgia Press, 1950.

Mike McCormick

NELSON, WILLIAM "BULL," MAJOR GENERAL (b. September 27, 1824, Mason Co., Ky.; d. September 29, 1862, Louisville, Ky.). The peculiar death and controversial bearing of this **Civil War** general have caused him to be greatly misunderstood rather than praised for his selfless actions that helped keep Kentucky loyal to the Union. Characterized as an ox of a man, William Nelson stood six feet four, weighed some 300 pounds, and had flashing black eyes that accented his excitable temperament. He was the son of Dr. Thomas W. Nelson and Frances Doniphan. His maternal grandfather, Dr. Anderson Doniphan, influenced Nelson toward his dreaded anger, whereas his paternal grandfather, "Captain" Thomas Nelson (ca. 1770–1841), provided him with invaluable social and political connections. William Nelson attended the **Maysville Academy** and graduated from Norwich Academy (university) in Vermont. In 1840 he was appointed a midshipman in the U.S. Navy. The impressionable 15-year-old Nelson set off and, for the next five years, sailed the South Seas and experienced the hard ways of Navy life.

In fall 1845 Nelson reported to the newly established Naval School (academy) at Annapolis, Md. He graduated as a midshipman in July 1846 and was posted to serve in the **Mexican War**. He saw duty at Naval Battery No. 5 in the siege of Vera Cruz, Mexico, and with the 2nd Artillery Division in a military action known as the Tabasco Expedition. At the conclusion of the war, Nelson was given a sword for his heroism and proficiency as an artillerist.

By February 1848 Nelson had become acting master on the *Scourge.* He was serving in that same capacity when the famed Hungarian revolutionary Louis Kossuth boarded the *Mississippi* at Smyrna, Turkey, on September 1, 1851. The following December Nelson became an escort for Kossuth's famous tour of the United States. Nelson joined U.S. commodore Matthew C. Perry's second voyage to Japan in 1854, becoming a sailing master on September 19, 1854, and a lieutenant on April 18, 1855. He then commanded the store ship *Fredonia* at Valparaiso, Chile, an assignment of civil charity that endeared him to the people of that country. In September 1858 he joined the steam frigate *Niagara* and helped return captured slaves to Monrovia, Liberia. When Nelson became an ordnance officer at the Washington Navy Yard in 1860, Kentucky's allegiance to the Union appeared suspect. In April 1861 he went to Louisville and reported on how the political currents seemed to be running, and his report led to a meeting with President Abraham Lincoln (1861–1865), at which Nelson received permission to distribute federal arms within Kentucky. On May 7 he met with Union leaders at Frankfort and arranged for 5,000 "Lincoln Guns" to be put in the hands of loyal Kentuckians. Soon afterward, the U.S. War Department detached Nelson from the Navy to organize a military campaign into East Tennessee. He recruited Union soldiers throughout July, and on August 6, 1861, those volunteers marched into Camp Dick Robinson in Garrard Co., Ky., under his orders.

Nelson became a brigadier general of volunteers on September 16, 1861, and in the months that followed, he drove the Confederates from the Big Sandy Valley of Eastern Kentucky. He then joined the Army of the Ohio and received command of its 4th Division. Nelson became the first to enter the Confederate stronghold of Nashville, and his extraordinary performance at the battle of Shiloh in Tennessee led to a promotion to major general. The 4th Division led the way into Corinth, Miss., and Nelson soon had the key command for the ill-fated Chattanooga, Tenn., Campaign. The Confederates' Heartland Offensive into Kentucky brought Nelson to Louisville on August 22, 1862. He took command of the newly organized Army of Kentucky at Lexington, and seven days later his field commander committed raw Union recruits against a seasoned Confederate army. Nelson raced to the field, receiving a serious thigh wound when he desperately tried to rally the panicked troops. He managed to elude capture but could not escape the severe criticism connected to this horrendous defeat.

By September 18, 1862, Nelson had recuperated enough to command the forces at Louisville. Days later he gave Brig. Gen. Jefferson Columbus Davis (1828–1879) responsibility for organizing the Home Guard troops. Davis considered the assignment demeaning, and when his view became apparent to Nelson, the fiery Nelson became incensed. On September 29, 1862, Nelson publicly shamed Davis in the main lobby of the Galt House in Louisville. In response, Davis obtained a pistol from a lawyer friend and shot Nelson in the heart. Davis was returned to duty and never received any punishment for this perceived "affair of honor." Out of respect for the victim, however, authorities named the newly formed Camp Nelson in Jessamine Co., Ky., in the slain commander's honor on June 12, 1863. Nelson was buried in the family plot at the Maysville Cemetery. The Camp Nelson National Cemetery, established below Nicholasville in 1868, represents a lasting memorial to the praiseworthy service of Kentucky's "quarterdeck general."

Ellis, Anderson Nelson. "Sketch of William Nelson." In *The Biographical Cyclopedia and Portrait Gallery with an Historical Sketch of the State of Ohio.* 6 vols. Cincinnati: Western Biographical, 1894.

Fry, James B., *Killed by a Brother Soldier.* New York: G. P. Putnam's, 1885.

Stevenson, Daniel. "General Nelson, Kentucky, and Lincoln Guns," *Magazine of American History* 10 (August 1883).

Donald A. Clark

NEW. The Owen Co. community of New is seven miles south of Owenton, along Highway 607 west of Ky. Rt. 227. Sandridge Creek flows through the area, and there was once a post office in town, established in 1895 by William J. New. There is no evidence that there was a school at New, but the 1883 Lake atlas depicts the town as lying within the old Monterey Precinct and shows a tollhouse on the edge of town. At that time there were two churches nearby, the Sandridge Church and the Elk Lick Church.

An Atlas of Owen County, Kentucky. Philadelphia: Lake, 1883.

Houchens, Mariam Sidebottom. *History of Owen County: "Sweet Owen."* Louisville, Ky.: Standard, 1976.

Rennick, Robert M. *Kentucky Place Names.* Lexington: Univ. of Kentucky Press, 1984.

NEW BETHEL BAPTIST CHURCH. New Bethel Baptist Church was founded in March 1840 by 25 people who had separated from the Salem Baptist Church to establish a new church in the Verona area of Boone Co. On June 22, 1840, the founding members, along with delegates from the Ten Mile, Mount Zion, Poplar Grove, and New Salem churches, named the church the Regular Baptist Church of Christ at New Bethel. The founders wrote the Church Covenant, adopted articles of faith, and copied their Rules of Decorum from the Salem Church's book. In July 1840 the church called David Lillard as pastor, and he held services on the third Saturday of each month.

Initially the congregation met at members' homes. When the church quickly outgrew the homes, meetings were held in Zadock Stephenson's barn. On August 2, 1845, Zadock and Delphia Stephenson donated one acre of land to the trustees of New Bethel for construction of the first church building. Today, that building site is on the grounds of New Bethel Cemetery. In March 1880, with only 70 cents in its treasury, the church voted to construct a new building on the donated land. During construction, services were held at the Verona Methodist Church. The new building was completed for $2,036, with members hauling supplies by horse and wagon and donating many hours of labor. After all of the bills were paid, the balance in the church treasury was $2.95.

In July 1926 the trustees purchased the old Verona Methodist Church building in downtown Verona for $1,000. In 1950 the New Bethel congregation voted again to construct a new building, which is still being used by the church. Subsequent additions include a nursery and youth building added in the 1960s, a steeple and chimes added in the 1970s, and a new sanctuary and fellowship hall added in 1980. New Bethel has about 300 members.

Deed Book 66, p. 15, Boone Co. Courthouse, Burlington, Ky.

History of New Bethel Baptist Church. Homecoming program, 1971.

Minutes of the New Bethel Baptist Church. Book 2, 1859–1889. New Bethel Baptist Church, Verona, Ky.

Phillips, Bob. *History of New Bethel Baptist Church.* Dedication program, 1980.

Roy McCubbin Diary. Used with permission of his daughter, Faye Morrisey, Verona, Ky.

Karen L. Leek

NEW COLUMBUS. New Columbus is about three miles west of the point where the Kentucky counties of Grant, Scott, Harrison, and Owen meet in southeastern Owen Co., along Ky. Rt. 607, some 10 and a half miles southeast of Owenton.

The first settler at New Columbus is thought to have been John Guill from Carolina Co., Va., who had fought for three years during the **Revolutionary War** under the command of Colonel Holcomb. Guill arrived in the area in 1780. He built a home on a small stream that emptied into Big Eagle Creek in the area that came to be known as Guill's Branch. Soon Ben Franklin Parr from Scotland, a Mr. Hughes and his wife from Culpepper Co., Va., and Billy Radcliffe joined families named Jones, Lee, Marshall, Prather, True, and Works, who, with some other families, settled in the New Columbus area. Many descendants from these founding families still reside in the vicinity.

About two miles southeast of New Columbus, as the crow flies, is Eagle Creek, where several grist mills were once located, including mills operated by the Mallory, Lee, Hammon, and Lusby families. Lee's Mill was the name given to the area's first post office, established in 1840; however, in 1854 the name was changed and the post office moved to New Columbus. The post office was discontinued in 1864, reestablished in 1868, and permanently discontinued in 1908. Thereafter mail was delivered from Corinth, in Grant Co.

Over the years, New Columbus grew large enough to support, at one time, two general stores, several doctors, a drugstore, a millinery shop, some blacksmiths, an undertaker, and two churches. The Methodist church had its beginning in prayer meetings that were taking place during the early 1800s. After the church moved from one building to another several times, its final site, in 1888, was across the road from the Baptist church.

The community's cemetery was chartered and opened in 1882. Records of the sales of lots and of burials there were destroyed by fire in 1920; however, during the early 1990s a survey team walked through the cemetery and recorded information from all identifiable monuments.

Houchens, Mariam Sidebottom. *History of Owen County: "Sweet Owen."* Louisville, Ky.: Standard, 1976.

"New Columbus," vertical files, Owen Co. Public Library, Owenton, Ky.

Doris Riley

NEW EAGLE MILLS/WITHER'S MILLS. The community once known as New Eagle Mills or Wither's Mill (1810–1920s) was centered on the mill at the mouth of Clark's Creek, where it flows into the Big Eagle Creek, in the west central portion of what is now Grant Co., Ky. The community at and around the mill was of such importance that its road, Wither's Mill Rd., was mentioned in Pendleton or Grant Co. court orders for decades, as neighbors were assigned the duty of maintaining its roadbed. The Wither's Mill Rd. stretched all the way to Williamstown, along Clark's Creek. The mill site was first mentioned in March 1810, when John Weathers or Withers asked for permission to build an "inbutment" for a water grist mill on the east side of Big Eagle Creek, apparently on land that was owned by heirs of Allen Withers.

In 1868 John and Julia Clark Collins from Crittenden, Ky., bought 100 acres on the west side of Big Eagle Creek and built a mill store and dwelling on the property, changing the mill's name to New Eagle Mills. A post office operated there (1870–1905), and according to the 1876 *Kentucky Gazetteer,* New Eagle Mills was "five miles from Elliston Station" and had a blacksmith, a general store, a miller, and a wool carder. In 1890 the Thomas Pettit family bought the mill property. They operated a wool-carding mill (Pettit's Mill) at the end of the Eagle Mill Ford Rd. until the 1920s. Nearby were the Pettit School (1856–1937) and the Wesley Chapel Methodist Church (1855–1945). One of the most scenic views in Grant Co. is from the vantage of Mount Pisgah United Methodist Church. From there one can look down on the beautiful bottomlands of Eagle Creek and the creek's horseshoe bend where water flows toward the old site of New Eagle Mills.

Conrad, John B., ed. *History of Grant County.* Williamstown, Ky.: The Grant Co. Historical Society, 1992.

Hutzelman, Tom. *1858 Atlas of Grant County.* Williamstown, Ky.: Grant Co. News, 1998.

Pendleton Co. Court Order Book, Falmouth, Ky.

NEW ENGLAND DISTILLERY. The Covington-based New England Distillery became one of the largest distillers in Northern Kentucky. It was originally located at 61 Pike St. and later moved to a building that partially remains at 115 Pike St., across the alley (which was once a rail siding) from the parking lot where the **Louisville and Nashville Railroad** had its freight depot. The New England Distillery operated from 1885 until the 1960s. It survived during **Prohibition** by making specially exempted distilled alcohol products for medicinal purposes. In 1926 the officers of the corporation were Herbert Hoffheimer, president; Lester E. Jacobi, vice president; and Maysville resident Henry E. Pogue, secretary and treasurer. In 1935 the enterprise was sold to a giant distilled-spirits conglomerate, the Shenley Distillery Corporation. The Covington division then became one of the world's largest producers of industrial rum for the baking industry, for confectionery additives, and for use in tobacco products. The smell of its production output permeated the surrounding parts of Covington's downtown. The warehouse remains as a large concrete structure with few windows, along the north side of W. Eighth St., just east of the railroad overpass, and is now used for other types of storage.

Covington City Directories, 1927–1937, Kenton Co. Public Library, Covington, Ky.

Geaslen, Chester. "There Ran a Distillery or Two in Covington," *KE,* December 15, 1966, 2.

Reis, Jim. "Distilleries a Vital Part of Northern Kentucy's Past," *KP,* January 6, 1996, 4K.

NEWHALL, JUDSON L. (b. March 26, 1870, Louise, Quebec, Canada; d. July 23, 1952, Park Hills, Ky.). Judson Lincoln Newhall, who became a congressman, and his parents moved from Quebec, Canada, to Covington in 1874. Judson was educated in local public schools and later graduated from Covington's Martin Academy and, in 1898, from the Indiana University Law School at Bloomington, Ind. In 1905 he became music director of the Covington Public Schools (see **Covington Independent Schools**). Newhall married Nellie J. Kinsley on September 1, 1891, in Covington, and they had three children, Elwood, Lucy, and Gail. During **World War I**, Newhall ran a **YMCA** canteen in St. Nazaire, France, for the entertainment of American servicemen. Upon the war's end, he returned to his former position as music director of the Covington Schools. He took several academic courses at the University of Cincinnati from 1926 to 1928. Newhall entered politics in 1928 and was elected as a Republican to the U.S. House of Representatives (1929–1931). At the end of his two-year term, he ran for reelection but was defeated by Fort Thomas Democrat **Brent Spence**. Although Newhall ran for Congress several additional times, he was never again elected to public office. Later in life, he owned and operated a Standard Oil gasoline station in Erlanger. Newhall was a member of the **First Baptist Church** of Covington for more than 70 years; he served there as choir director. He died at age 82 at his home at 1152 Old State Rd., Park Hills. He was buried in Forest Lawn Cemetery in Erlanger. His wife, Nellie, and their three children survived him.

Biographical Directory of the United States Congress. "Newhall, Judson Lincoln (1870–1952)." http://bioguide.congress.gov (accessed December 31, 2005).

"Daughter Born," *KP,* June 2, 1892, 4.

"Honor Newhall," *KP,* February 8, 1930, 1.

Reis, Jim. "Bracken Native Overcame Long Odds," *KP,* November 23, 1998, 4K.

NEW HORIZONS MEDICAL CENTER. There has been a hospital in Owen Co. at Owenton since July 1951. Designed by Louisville architects Thomas J. Nolan and Sons, the original 21-bed Owen Co. War Memorial Hospital was housed in a 45-by-145-foot building. It has been expanded a few times over the years and has had several owners and operators. The New Horizons Medical Center is the present name of the hospital. A 24-bed, 24-hour-a-day, 7-day-per-week operation, it is located on the north side of town along U.S. 127. It is in the center of a triangle of hospitals at Carrollton, Frankfort, and Williamstown, and its mere existence has been life-saving for trauma cases in which a patient needs attention within that critical first hour after injury.

Dr. O. A. Cull arrived in Owenton in 1951 and was still practicing at the hospital in 2005. For 15 years, beginning in 1956, **Herbert Lee "Hub" Smith** was the hospital facility's administrator. The hospital is fully certified and operates with a staff of seven doctors. Most medical problems can be treated there, and trauma cases needing more specialized care can be airlifted via helicopter to major medical centers in Northern Kentucky, Lexington, or Louisville. Over time, this medical center has suffered the same fate as most small rural hospitals in the United States: its inherent diseconomies of scale make the facility's per-unit costs higher than those in larger facilities. In the world of modern private insurance and governmental reimbursement caps, some treatment procedures simply are not adequately reimbursed, resulting in red ink for the hospital. However, for the patient passing through its emergency room door, the New Horizons Medical Center still provides critical service.

New Horizons Medical Center. www.newhorizonsmedicalcenter.com.

Bernie Poe

NEW LIBERTY. Although the exact date of the first house built in New Liberty, Owen Co., Ky., is unknown, the town was large and thriving in 1800, 19 years before the county was created. Located about 10 miles northwest of Owenton on Ky. Rts. 227 and 36, the community continues to be a place of tranquil residential living.

For many years New Liberty was the largest and most prosperous town in the county. It is believed that the first building was a two-story, 10-room log house built by John Gayle and his slaves in 1806. A portion of the structure remains standing and has been converted into a barn. Early commercial goods were shipped to New Liberty via boat on the Ohio River to Ghent and via wagon from Ghent. After the **Louisville and Nashville Railroad** was built, merchandise was shipped to Liberty Station (Sanders) and transported from there by wagon.

The Owen Union Agricultural and Mechanical Association Fairgrounds was the center of much interest and many varied attractions. Organized in 1859, the fairgrounds remained quite active until 1886, except for a period during the **Civil War**; it comprised several buildings, including stables and a large dining room for visitors. Horse racing became popular, and many of the local gentlemen owned horses that proved to be exceedingly fast. During the Civil War, when Union soldiers used the fairgrounds as a camp, a smallpox outbreak resulted in the death of many of them. It is reported that the soldiers used the bell tower of the **New Liberty Baptist Church** for target practice.

One of the earliest schools in New Liberty was a combined school already existing by 1850. **Concord College** was established in town in 1867 for both male and female students. The last building of the college was constructed in 1921. The town's first high school opened in the 1906–1907 school term. When the county's high schools were consolidated in 1951, this building was converted to an elementary school, which closed in 1970 owing to further consolidation.

The town's first bank, incorporated in 1886 as Citizens Bank, remains a vital part of the community. At one time the businesses in town included a tanning yard, a woolen mill, the Gayle House Hotel, the first newspaper in Owen Co. the *Owen News* (1868), a tobacco warehouse, stores, livery stables, an undertaker, churches, and a bank. In 1864 the most important business and residential parts of town were destroyed by fire; another fire in 1904 destroyed much of the rebuilt section of the town.

The first church, established in 1801, was the Baptist Church of the Twins, called that because of its location between two creek branches known as Little Twin and Big Twin. By 1965 it was known as the New Liberty Baptist Church. During the early 1830s, there was a large Christian Church (Campbellites) revival movement in Kentucky, and some members of the Baptist church joined together to become part of the Christian Church denomination. The resulting New Liberty Christian Church is believed to have begun in 1833. There are no records about the first church building, except for the knowledge that bricks from it were used to construct the Second Baptist Church between 1919 and 1921.

Today New Liberty no longer shows its former prosperity. It never totally recovered from its two devastating fires. A bank, a general store, a firehouse, a post office, and three churches remain in the town.

Houchens, Marian Sidebottom. *History of Owen County: "Sweet Owen."* Louisville, Ky.: Standard, 1976.

"New Liberty," vertical files, Owen Co. Public Library, Owenton, Ky.

Doris Riley

NEW LIBERTY BAPTIST CHURCH. This church was originally known as the Baptist Church of the Twins, for the two branches of the Kentucky River, Big Twin and Little Twin creeks, that flow through New Liberty, Ky. The church dates back to 1801, when services were held in the homes of its members. In 1810 a log building was constructed with a balcony for slaves to sit in during worship services. A brick building, erected in 1819, burned in 1836, but the members lost no time in rebuilding; they reused the bricks from the walls of the previous structure. This building, with some modifications, remains the house of worship for the church. The church name was changed in 1842 to the Baptist Church of New Liberty; by 1965 it was known as the New Liberty Baptist Church. Up to that time, a total of 39 pastors had served the church, and it had functioned as the mother church for 10 other Baptist churches. The congregation has supported strong programs in Sunday School, Bible School, and mission ventures in its more-than-200-year history.

"History of the New Liberty Baptist Church," 1951, New Liberty Baptist Church, New Liberty, Ky.

Houchens, Mariam Sidebottom. *History of Owen County: "Sweet Owen."* Louisville, Ky.: Standard, 1976.

NEWMAN, ERICA (b. August 31, 1904, Oberkirch, Germany; d. February 20, 1992, Covington, Ky.). She was known as Erica A. Newman by her acquaintances in Northern Kentucky, where she spent two decades in her later life, after her performing career had ended. Erica's father was Maximillan Herrmann, and all that is known of her mother is that her maiden surname was Ebner. As a dancer, model, singer, and actress, Erica Herrmann was one of the most photographed persons of the 1920s. She arrived in Hollywood in 1933 and appeared in movies with James Cagney, Bette Davis, and Edward G. Robinson. She was in *I've Got Your Number* (1934) with Joan Blondell and Pat O'Brien and in *Strike Me Pink* (1936) with Jimmy Durante. In 1939 Herrmann appeared in *Wife, Husband, and Friend* with Caesar Romero and Loretta Young. She became a good friend of Shirley Temple. Herrmann had two different Hollywood performing names: for her early years at Warner Bros., she used the screen name Rickey Newell; for Fox Studios, at the end of her Hollywood career, she was billed as Alice Armand.

Herrmann appeared on Broadway in Flo Ziegfield's rendition of the musical *Showboat* (1927). In January 1939 she was one of eight studio starlets to make a 12,000-mile airplane promotional tour in connection with Twentieth Century–Fox's release of *Tail Spin*. She retired from entertainment in the mid-1940s and later married New York City policeman Vincent Joseph Newman. She moved to Northern Kentucky in the mid-1970s to be near her son and lived in Florence and then in Covington, in two nursing homes, the St. John Nursing Home and the Garrard Convalescent Center. She remained vibrant, sharp, and interesting until her very last days, recounting stories about her career and sharing items from her scrapbook. She died at St. Elizabeth Hospital in Covington and was cremated.

"Erica Newman," *KP*, February 21, 1992, 6A.

Kentucky Death Certificate No. 4288, for the year 1992.

"Passages," *KP*, January 1, 1993, 1K–2K.

"Screen News Here and in Hollywood," *NYT*, February 7, 1939, 23.

"Time Can't Face a Startlet's Luster," *KP*, May 28, 1990, 1K.

NEW PERCEPTIONS INC. For more than 50 years, the organization now known as New Perceptions Inc. (NPI) has served the special needs of individuals in Boone, Carroll, Gallatin, Grant, Kenton, Owen, and Pendleton counties. NPI has been a leader in promoting the advancement of people who have developmental disabilities and other personal barriers.

NPI was founded by a group of concerned parents in 1952 because no appropriate services for their special-needs children existed. Its origins were in the Riverside School, in the basement of the First Presbyterian Church (now **Community of Faith Presbyterian**) in Covington. A similar school, Good Counsel, opened soon after in two locations: the **Corpus Christi Catholic Church** in Newport and the **St. Aloysius** School in Covington. Both schools were successful, and in order better to serve their clients, they merged in 1960. Then, as public demand grew, **Riverside–Good Counsel** built its own school building in 1972, offering grades K–12 and related programs.

During the next years, Riverside–Good Counsel brought developmental education into the home, so that families could participate in preparing their children for the future. It also opened an activity center that engaged adults in meaningful employment. During the 1970s it was federally mandated that school-age students be transitioned into public school programs by 1976. Riverside–Good Counsel then began to focus on expanding adult employment programs, as well as offering more preschool education to individuals with mental retardation or other developmental disabilities. Riverside–Good Counsel officially changed its name to NPI in 1985.

Infant and toddler clients benefit from a variety of programs, which include physical, occupational, and speech therapy. NPI offers developmental intervention, provided by staff educators specializing in early childhood education. Children and their families are given the foundation they will need to be successful in life.

Adult clients receive the support and learn the skills necessary for employment within the community or in site-based work programs. One example is a local collaborative effort with **St. Elizabeth Medical Center** and the **Kenton Co. School District** for work transition programs providing evaluation, training, and ultimately employment in a medical setting. NPI also runs a community-based supportive employment program, which offers in-depth one-on-one job placement and support in organizations throughout the community.

The site-based employment program, located in Edgewood, offers clients assembly and packaging jobs, as well as other on-site services such as the life skills program, in which clients have the opportunity to transition away from full-time work so that they are able to set and achieve personal, recreational, and social goals.

NPI provides a service throughout the stages of life to hundreds of Northern Kentucky families, supplying them with the confidence and tools to be able to set and reach their goals. The organization believes in the abilities of clients with developmental disabilities to achieve success, and to that end it provides opportunities for education, growth, and employment in a normalized setting in order to facilitate each individual's achievement of his or her maximum potential. Today NPI serves more than 700 children and adults with developmental disabilities. What began as concerned parents wanting the best that life had to offer for their disabled children has become an organization driven by concern for those individuals who at one time were lost within a system that did not understand their special needs.

"Long Wait for Skills Training—Program Helps Disabled Find Jobs," *KP*, July 24, 1997, 2K.

New Perceptions, Inc. www.newperceptions.org (accessed March 14, 2006).

"New Perceptions—Riverside Good Counsel Renamed New Perceptions, Inc." *KP*, January 2, 1985, 8K.

Robin Rider Osborne

NEWPORT. Newport is a second-class city located in Northern Kentucky at the confluence of the Ohio and Licking rivers, directly south of Cincinnati and east (upriver) of Covington. Newport is one of the two county seats in Campbell, Co.; the other is Alexandria. Newport's physical size is 3.5 square miles. Until 1792, Kentucky was a part of the Commonwealth of Virginia. After the **French and Indian War**, a Virginia aristocrat named Col. James Taylor Sr. purchased 2,700 acres from fellow Virginian **George Muse**; it was land awarded to Muse for his services during the Revolutionary War. James Taylor Sr. never visited these lands but sent his sons, Hubbard and James Jr., to survey and settle the area. When Hubbard Taylor arrived in 1785, he discovered pioneer **Jacob Fowler** already settled in the area. Hubbard laid claim to the land that is now Newport (as well as Bellevue and Dayton, Ky.) and in 1791 laid out the first streets of Newport. He named the city after Christopher Newport, captain of the first ship to land at Jamestown, Va., in 1607.

James Taylor Jr. arrived in town in 1792 and quickly became Newport's leading citizen, businessman, and developer. His first major accomplishment was obtaining from the Kentucky legislature a charter establishing the City of Newport on December 14, 1795. Newport thereby became the first incorporated city north of Lexington. The federal census of 1800 listed a population of 106 for Newport. In 1805 Taylor persuaded the U.S. government to locate a military barracks and arsenal in Newport. The presence of the **Newport Barracks** was a significant influence upon the city's early economic and social atmosphere. In its day, the barracks was the most important military post on what was then the western frontier of the United States.

Newport grew between 1831 and 1870. Taylor built his residence in town in 1840. The availability of first river transportation and later railroads and its proximity to markets in states to the north made Newport an attractive location for both manufacturing and retail businesses. Textile factories, which had begun to appear on the banks of the Ohio and Licking rivers, eventually were replaced by iron and steel factories. By 1870 Newport had become the center of iron manufacturing in Kentucky and ranked 22nd in the country in this industry. Even into the 20th century, Newport had the second-highest concentration of heavy industry in Kentucky. These factories have long been closed, with the exception of the **Newport Steel** Company, which remains as a descendant of Newport's **Andrews Steel Mill**, founded in 1891.

Newport Finance Building, also known as Campbell Towers, southeast corner of Fourth and York Sts., Newport. It was built in 1927 and demolished in 1999.

Slavery was not a big factor in the economy of the city of Newport. James Taylor Jr. brought his slaves with him from Virginia, and slaves accounted for 28 percent of the city's population in 1820. However, by 1840 only 4 percent of the city's residents were listed as slaves, and most of them were house servants or factory workers. As elsewhere in Kentucky, Newport had divided loyalties during the **Civil War**. After several civil disturbances between the differing partisans, Newport was placed under martial law for most of the duration of the conflict. The bitterness created by the war remained a dividing factor among Newport's citizens for several generations. By the end of the Civil War, the number of residents in Newport had grown to 15,000.

The construction of several bridges over the Ohio River in 1872 (see **L&N Bridge**) and 1892 (see **Central Bridge**) facilitated both residential and commercial development of the city in the later part of the 19th century. The period of 1870 to 1900 was critical in developing the broadest range of municipal services, urban infrastructure, and public transportation. Modern utilities were also introduced, with the most important being the construction of city water and sewerage systems, begun in 1873. These systems made urban living cleaner and safer and accounted for dramatic increases in Newport's population during this period.

Taylor opened the first facility for the education of the city's youth as the Newport Academy in 1800, and several other private schools operated for the first half of the 19th century. The first public schools in town opened in 1847. By the 1870s, three separate educational systems existed side by side in Newport: public schools for whites, segregated public schools for blacks, and parochial schools for Catholics. The first Catholic schools were begun in 1848 and provided elementary education to approximately 30 percent of the city's school-age children through the end of the century. Newport's public high school opened in 1860. The **Southgate St. School** for black children began operation in 1873 and continued until the entire public school system in Kentucky was integrated in 1956. The institution that evolved into **Newport Central Catholic High School** began educating males in 1929. Females attended **Our Lady of Providence Academy**, located on Sixth St. in town.

From its beginning until 1868, Newport relied on volunteers for firefighting. The first organized volunteer outfit was the Washington Fire Engine and Hose Company, which formed in 1850. A full-time professional paid firefighting service was established in 1868. In the city's formative years, law enforcement was provided by a town marshal who was elected for a two-year term and the deputies of his choosing. The first full-time police force was formed as an emergency measure during the Civil War. The office of police chief was created in 1873, and a more professional police force dates from that period.

All employment with the city suffered from the negative effect of the spoils system of political patronage, which allowed a mayor to replace employees after every election. A change in Kentucky's constitution in 1891 forced mayors to share this appointment power and established a clearer line of authority between the executive and legislative branches. A formal civil service system based on merit was not adopted until 1939.

In 1930 the people of Newport voted into place a city-manager form of government, which assigned the daily operational and financial responsibilities to an appointed public administrator. Sentiment in the city was so evenly split on this issue that it was approved by a margin of only 2 votes.

Although having access to two rivers was crucial to the city's economic and commercial development, it also forced city leaders to deal with the sometimes-severe problems caused by periodic flooding. Between 1859 and 1900, the Ohio River overflowed flood stage 24 separate times. Major **floods** occurred in 1883, **1884**, 1898, and **1913**. Besides causing substantial human and economic suffering, back-to-back floods during the 1880s persuaded the federal government to relocate the army post from Newport to Fort Thomas in the 1890s. The most damaging flood on record occurred in 1937 (see **Flood of 1937**). It covered 25 percent of the city's surface and displaced 40 percent of its residents. This level of destruction spurred the construction of a floodwall in 1947, which continues to protect the basin area of the city.

During the first 50 years of Newport's existence, the makeup of the city's population reflected the ancestry of its founders—mostly people of English heritage. Since most of the early prominent residents of the city were from below the **Mason-Dixon Line**, the culture of the city also had a flavor of the Old South. This began to change after the Civil War when a huge influx of German and Irish immigrants gave the city a more cosmopolitan flavor. By 1880, 46 percent of residents had been born in Europe, 43 percent were of German ancestry, and 14 percent had Irish roots. This pattern continued until the **Great Depression** of the 1930s forced the migration of **Appalachians**, mainly of Scotch-Irish descent, from the mountain regions of Eastern Kentucky.

The arrival of the automobile in the early part of the 20th century eventually spurred the movement of people to the suburbs, and the city's population leveled off at 30,000. Newport began a series of annexations of the neighboring cities: Cote Briliante in 1924, Clifton in 1935, and Ingalls Park in 1936. These annexations doubled the city's land area to its present size.

The period from 1900 to 1930 could be considered the golden age of Newport. Its population of 30,000 made it the third-largest city in Kentucky. By 1910 its retail economy had also become the third-most-robust in the state. Its industrial base was second-largest in Kentucky.

The 1920 passage of the 18th Amendment to the Constitution, banning the sale and consumption of alcoholic beverages, led to the growth of the bootleg liquor industry and the arrival of organized crime syndicates, which exerted considerable influence over the city's economy and politics for the next 40 years. After **Prohibition** was repealed in 1933, the crime syndicate moved its resources into bars and nightclubs that provided entertainment and **gambling**. By the 1950s, Newport had gained a national reputation as the Sin City of the Midwest. The pervasiveness of this reputation has tended to obscure the importance and accomplishments of the other parts of Newport's history, both before and after.

In the decade of the 1950s, a local citizens' effort in Campbell Co. to eliminate the influence of organized crime caught the attention of U.S. attorney general Robert Kennedy. A combined effort of federal and local law enforcement efforts eventually resulted in the closing of the gambling and prostitution houses. These businesses came to be replaced by other adult-oriented businesses, which proliferated during the 1960s and 1970s, continuing Newport's reputation as a regional center for that type of activity.

By 1960 the city was experiencing its share of the general decline in business and residential communities that was adversely affecting many older urban areas in the country. Added to the suburban flight was the demolition of many homes in otherwise stable neighborhoods to make way for the construction of the I-471 expressway. The opening of the **Newport Shopping Center** in South Newport in 1956 further weakened the older central business district. Between 1960 and 1990, Newport's population declined from 30,000 to 18,000. The percentage of persons living below the poverty line increased from 16 percent in 1970 to 26 percent in 1990. The city's economy received two severe blows when its two largest employers closed their businesses: Interlake Steel (later named **Newport Steel**) in 1980 and the **Wiedemann Brewing Company** in 1983. With its oldest neighborhoods declining and its economy on the ropes, Newport reached a low point.

The decade of the 1980s saw resurgence in the city's vitality. A core of young urban pioneers began buying up some of the historic homes on Newport's East Side at the same time that the **Newport Citizens Advisory Council** began holding meetings in all sections of the city to consider ways to improve the quality of life. This rebirth of civic activity eventually led to a more overtly politically active organization called NEWPAC, which began supporting its own candidates for election in local races.

In 1982 a reform-minded city commission began a campaign to clean up the city's neighborhoods and its image in order to attract new businesses and homeowners. The demographic slide seems to have ended as a result, and the population is stabilizing. Newport has moved decisively to rehabilitate its reputation, housing, and economy. A historic district was established in 1982 and has grown into the largest contiguous such district in Kentucky. Tours of the renovated historic homes are annual events. A coordinated effort of city, county, and state officials gradually closed most of the adult businesses. Economic development efforts have led to the development of restaurants and corporate offices along the city's riverfront, culminating in the opening of the **Newport Aquarium** in 2000, the **Newport-on-the-Levee** entertainment complex in 2001, and the Hofbrauhaus Restaurant in 2003. In 2004 the former **L&N Bridge** was converted from vehicular traffic to a pedestrian-only structure. Many outdoor festivals are held in the city's new Festival Park on the banks of the Ohio River. The most spectacular is the gigantic fireworks display on Labor Day Weekend known as Riverfest, attended by huge crowds. In 2000 the city's population was officially stated as 17,048. City officials later challenged the accuracy of that figure and estimated that the correct figure was closer to 22,000.

Donnelly, Joseph. *Newport Barracks—Kentucky's Forgotten Military Installation*. Covington, Ky.: Kenton Co. Historical Society, 1999.

Mueller, Jan. *Soul of the City: A Centennial History of the Newport Public Library*. Highland Heights, Ky.: Self-published, 2004.

Neff, Judy L., and Peggy Wiedemann Harris. *Newport*. Charleston, S.C.: Arcadia, 2004.

"Newport's Old Story: City's Rise Spurred by Army, Dampened by Flood," *KP*, August 12, 1985, 3K.

Purvis, Thomas L., ed. *Newport, Kentucky: A Bicentennial History*. Newport, Ky.: Otto Zimmerman, 1996.

U.S. Census Bureau. "American Fact Finder. Data Set. Census 2000 Summary File 1 (SF1) 100-Percent Data. Custom Table." www.census.gov (accessed July 19, 2006).

Michael Whitehead

NEWPORT ACADEMY. The first public school in Northern Kentucky was the Newport Academy, chartered in 1798 and opened in 1800 in Newport. It was the first academy in the Cincinnati area. The State of Kentucky gave the City of Newport 6,000 acres of land, south of the Green River in Western Kentucky, and empowered the town's government to sell the land to help finance the construction and operation of the school. The Newport Academy was erected on a two-acre site along the north side of Fourth St., between Monmouth and Saratoga Sts., which had been donated by **James Taylor Jr.** The state charter required that a 12-member board of trustees be appointed to run the school. The first trustees included **Washington Berry**, **Thomas D. Carneal**, John Grant (see **Grant Family**), **Thomas Kennedy**, **Thomas Sandford**, **Richard Southgate**, Rev. Robert Stubbs, and James Taylor. Stubbs, an Episcopal minister, was hired as principal and given a house, 15 acres of cleared land, and a salary of 75 British pounds sterling per year. Many of the school's first teachers held other jobs, such as surveying or serving as clergymen. Stubbs resigned after just one year and opened a private boarding school for boys in Campbell Co., near the Two Mile House on Alexandria Pike.

A subscription drive was conducted in 1800 to raise funds for construction of a one-room stone schoolhouse for the Newport Academy; the school building measured 20 by 32 feet. Newport Academy's early curriculum consisted primarily of reading, writing, and arithmetic, coursework for which students were charged tuition of $8 per year. However, some advanced instruction was also given, at a cost of $20 per year, in English grammar, the Latin and Greek languages, geometry, astronomy, logic, and rhetoric. The Newport Academy was technically a public school, even though it charged tuition. It operated successfully until 1850, when it was merged with the **Newport Independent Schools**. The original schoolhouse was used until 1873, and then it was demolished and replaced by a new building to house the Newport High School. The Fourth Street Elementary School now occupies the site of the original Newport Academy.

Cobb, James L. "History of the Public Schools of Newport, Kentucky," MEd thesis, Univ. of Cincinnati, 1939.

"History of Campbell County." Paper prepared and read by Mary Keturah Jones at the Independence Day Celebration, July 4, 1876, Newport, Ky.

Newport Independent Schools. "Our History—A Great Tradition." www.newportwildcats.org (accessed October 17, 2006).

Purvis, Thomas L., ed. *Newport, Kentucky: A Bicentennial History.* Newport, Ky.: Zimmerman, 1996.

Tenkotte, Paul A. "Rival Cities to Suburbs: Covington and Newport, Kentucky, 1790–1890," PhD diss., Univ. of Cincinnati, 1989.

Jack Wessling

NEWPORT AND COVINGTON SUSPENSION BRIDGE. The Kentucky legislature incorporated the Licking Bridge Company on January 27, 1830, with a capitalization of $15,000 on 30,000 shares. Despite the support of leading citizens in Covington and Newport, on both sides of the Licking River, stock sales were insufficient and the corporation failed. In 1844 the bridge issue was raised again, and this time a wire suspension bridge was recommended as ideal for the high banks of the Licking River.

Support for the proposed suspension bridge over the Licking River was much higher on the Campbell Co. side of the river, where the bridge was promoted for its effect on commerce and real estate in Newport. The newspapers reported that 2,000 shares of the bridge company's stock had been sold, but money ran out before the bridge was completed; only a pier on the Newport side stood in testimony to the project. In February–March 1849, the noted bridge engineer Charles Ellet came to Northern Kentucky to revive the project, apparently being given all the privileges of the original charter, on condition that construction of the suspension bridge begin by April 1 and be completed

Newport and Covington Suspension Bridge.

by December 1, 1849. Again, however, the project languished.

In January 1852 the Kentucky General Assembly granted a bridge charter to the Newport and Covington Bridge Company, with the provision that either Newport or Covington, or both cities, could purchase stock in the corporation. By June 1853 a wire suspension bridge to link Newport with Covington was well under way at the end of Fourth St. in Covington, under the supervision of George C. Tarvin. The on-site engineer was John Gray of Pittsburgh, who may have been a protégé of Charles Ellet. At least Gray was using Ellet's bridge-building methods, which included fabricating the bridge cables on the ground rather than spinning the cables in place (bridge-builder John Roebling's practice; see **John Augustus and Washington Augustus Roebling**). Ellet also generally used six to eight cables instead of two, and he did not consider it important to stiffen the floor with a heavy truss, as Roebling did. From 1850 to 1853, Ellet was the chief engineer of the Virginia Central Railroad; in case Gray was associated with Ellet, Ellet's crowded schedule could be the reason John Gray, instead of Ellet himself, had the contract at Newport.

After all the delays, work on the Newport and Covington Suspension Bridge proceeded rapidly. The eight 902-foot-long cables for the bridge were fabricated on the streets of Newport. The wire was pulled around two vertical poles set up in the streets. Six of the eight cables contained 350 wires each, while the other two contained 308 wires each. The anchorages were built on the riverbanks by constructing boxes 15 by 20 feet by some 30 feet high, using one-foot oak pilings. Wrought iron anchor plates, cast to receive anchor chains, were buried at the bottom of the boxes, which were filled with rock to hold the cables. (During the 1870s, the southwestern anchorage of the bridge began to slip, and an additional layer of iron-tipped oak pilings was added to stabilize it.)

The 93-foot-tall towers were built of brick. They were located at about the low-water point on each shore, to assure the widest possible span over open water. At some time, the towers were painted and advertisements were applied on them. (In the 1870s galvanized metal caps were fabricated to cover the lubricated rollers on top of the towers.) The cables were attached to the anchor chains on the east side, and at the other end they were attached to a heavy rope and pulled to the Covington shore, where they were attached to a wagon pulled by six horses. Then, aided by pulleys on the Covington side and rollers on both sides and on steamboats on the Licking River, the cables were pulled into place and attached to the anchor chains in the bridge's west-side anchorages. The suspenders were then attached to the cables, and the floor beams were attached to the other end. On December 28, 1853, superintendent Tarvin and Covington mayor Bushrod Foley rode across the bridge in a buggy to open the bridge.

On January 16, 1854, less than three weeks after the opening, at 5:30 p.m., the toll collector left his small toll booth to watch 15 cattle start across the bridge, when without warning, the roller from the top of the east tower plunged through the booth behind him. The bridge floor flipped to a vertical position, hanging from the southern towers. Eight of the 15 cattle were killed in the fall, and butchers were summoned to the shore to use the beef. Because the stonework had not been damaged, work began immediately on repairs. The damage was estimated at $14,000, and the span was reopened in May at a total estimated cost of $81,000.

As early as the 1860s, the need for strengthening the bridge was apparent. Washington Roebling was finishing up the Covington-Cincinnati Suspension Bridge when he agreed to provide plans and specifications for improving the cable for a fee of $150. He ordered $307 worth of cable from the J. A. Roebling Company, castings from

Miles Greenwood, and iron from D. Wolf. It is likely that he wrapped the four cables into one, since he did something similar a few years later on the Wheeling Bridge. In 1868 the Roeblings supplied another $1,107 worth of wire and service. W. Morton, a civil engineer, was hired in 1872 to develop further plans to strengthen the bridge, and an assistant was hired to help him. Washington Roebling supplied materials and plans for cable stays. Morton was the on-site engineer at a salary of $100 per month. The J. A. Roebling Company was paid $900 for wire and advice. Weight limits were promulgated for the bridge: no more than 12 head of cattle at a time were permitted on the bridge.

In 1875 the bridge board decided to employ an engineer to develop plans and specifications to build a central pier on the bridge and other features to strengthen it. The pier construction was awarded to a local company at a cost of $21,478. The ironwork contract went to John Gray for $3,559, and he agreed to supervise the pier construction for free. The pier was located 404 feet east of Fourth and Garrard Sts. in Covington. B. R. Morton and John Gray carried out the engineering services, and the total cost of the new pier was $39,061. The pier construction firm sued the bridge company for nonpayment. When **Gustave Bouscaren**, the chief engineer for the **Cincinnati Southern Railroad**, was employed to inspect the bridge condition, his verdict about the quality of the work just completed was that it was unsatisfactory. Arrangements were made to advertise for plans and specifications for two new bridges, one a suspension bridge and the other a truss bridge. Morton was authorized to spend almost $4,000 to repair the floor of the bridge scheduled to be replaced. A Colonel Payne of Brooklyn, N.Y., who was Washington Roebling's assistant on the Brooklyn Bridge, was employed to inspect the bridge and comment on Bouscaren's negative report. The suit about the new pier was not settled, and the Covington City Council warned the bridge board to take no action before obtaining the city's permission. Payne's report was far more negative than Bouscaren's, and he advised immediate replacement of the bridge. The bridge board was so negative by now about suspension bridges that they advertised only for a truss bridge. Five companies responded, and the bridge board decided in favor of the sturdiest option, which was provided by the Keystone Bridge Company of Pittsburgh. The consulting engineer was C. R. Stroebel. B. K Morton was hired at $100 per month to oversee the construction. Morton agreed to run a ferry for passengers and vehicles for the period when the bridge was shut down. The old bridge was demolished in the summer of 1886, and the new bridge was opened the same year. In 1934 the 1886 span was demolished, and in 1936 a new bridge dedicated to veterans was opened.

Burns, John E. "A History of Covington, Kentucky through 1865," vol. 3, Kenton Co. Public Library, Covington, Ky.

Coley, Jeannette Cabell. "A Biography of Charles Ellet, Jr." *Smithsonian Associates Civil War Newsletter* 5, no. 5. http://civilwarstudies.org (accessed August 21, 2006).

Reis, Jim. "World War Veterans Memorial Bridge: Providing a Vital Link," *KP*, July 19, 2004, 4K.

Tenkotte, Paul A. "Rival Cities to Suburbs: Covington and Newport, Kentucky, 1790–1890," PhD diss., Univ. of Cincinnati, 1989.

Joseph F. Gastright

NEWPORT AQUARIUM. The Newport Aquarium is located in Newport at **Newport-on-the-Levee**, a commercial center situated along the Ohio River and made up of retail stores, restaurants such as Mitchell's Fish Market, and entertainment facilities including the AMC movie theater. Newport on-the-Levee was designed as a place where people could gather in a social setting. The levee is widely acknowledged as the major force in the recent renaissance of the city of Newport.

One of the levee's biggest attractions is the Newport Aquarium, which was begun by five businessmen in the Greater Cincinnati area, doing business as Aquarium Holdings, who wanted to build something that would express their shared concern for sea life. It took nearly 10 years for the aquarium to come to life, however. Initial plans, as discussed in 1990, called for building the aquarium on the Ohio side of the river, but the owners were persuaded by Newport city officials to change their plans and place the facility in Newport along the Kentucky shoreline. Ground was broken in 1997, and on May 15, 1999, the aquarium opened to the public. Its stated mission was "to captivate, educate, and advocate conservation."

Consistent with its goal of promoting interest in conservation of the world's sea life, the aquarium is populated with fishes, mammals, birds, and other water animals—housed in 1 million gallons of water—that take visitors on a visual tour of the world's oceans, seas, straits, channels, and other waterways. The aquarium has five seamless underwater tunnels made of solid acrylic, see-through floors, two and a half viewing levels, 7,000 marine animals from 600 species, and 66 separate exhibits, to offer visitors a unique and memorable experience. Throughout the building are 17 murals designed and created by Eric Henn, an artist from Franklin, Ohio, and 16 original musical soundtracks play daily throughout the facility.

The aquarium has been a commercial success and continues to grow. In 2004 a permanent exhibit of Asian river otters, lorikeets, and pythons was opened as part of a $4.5 million expansion. Further exhibit development in 2005 took the shape of a "summer of sharks." The new, world-renowned exhibit both displays sharks and provides new ways for visitors to learn facts about them. The Shark Central exhibit allows visitors to touch sharks. In 2008 a new Frog Bog exhibit opened, featuring 20 species of exotic frogs from around the world.

At the waterfront in Camden, N.J., in summer 2005, a corporate sister aquarium of the one in Newport opened.

"Aquarium Symbol of Rebirth," *KP*, November 20, 1997, 1K.

Newport Aquarium. www.newportaquarium.com.

"Prep Work Begins for Aquarium," *KP*, December 24, 1997, 2K.

"Sweet Pea the Shark Is Moving to Newport," *KP*, June 9, 2005, K3.

Michael J. Poehner

NEWPORT BARRACKS. By 1800 it was evident that the city of Cincinnati neither needed nor wanted the military installation located on its riverfront, Fort Washington. The fort occupied increasingly valuable land as the city's downtown grew. Clearly, it was only a matter of time before Fort Washington would be shut down. Meanwhile, just across the Ohio River in Newport, **James Taylor Jr.**, Newport's founder, recognized an opportunity to capitalize on and profit from this situation. Taylor was from an influential family; he was a cousin of future presidents James Madison (1809–1817) and Zachary Taylor (1849–1850) and was the wealthiest landowner in Campbell Co.

James Taylor carried on a lively correspondence with his family, the U.S. Army, and the federal government and in spring 1803 learned that Gen. Charles Scott (governor of Kentucky from 1808 to 1812) had been chosen to seek a suitable location for an arsenal. Scott concluded that the best location was near the mouth of the Licking River, and the U.S. secretary of war authorized him to purchase four to six acres there. The land was expected to accommodate a boat landing within the Licking River and to be at an elevation high enough to protect the arsenal's buildings from the spring freshets, even if it meant locating a mile or so up the river. The story of the Newport Barracks, and indeed of the village of Newport, would have been different if this instruction to build the arsenal upstream on the Licking River had been heeded.

On November 10, 1803, Scott completed negotiations for "a magazine at the mouth of the Licking." Taylor was informed that the most eligible site was on the land he had generously donated, rather than the upriver site first considered, and that he (Taylor) should superintend the construction. The U.S. Treasury issued him money to pay for the materials and labor required to begin construction of the arsenal. He was instructed to erect three buildings, a brick two-story arsenal with a cellar, a barracks, and a circular brick powder magazine. The facility was under construction when Capt. Meriwether Lewis, the coleader of the Lewis and Clark Expedition of 1803–1806, passed on his way to **Big Bone Lick** in nearby Boone Co. to collect specimens for President Thomas Jefferson (1801–1809). Lewis was traveling to meet Capt. William Clark to explore the still undefined lands acquired by the United States in the Louisiana Purchase of 1803. By 1806 a detachment including a sergeant and 12 enlisted men had arrived at the arsenal in Newport, led by an inexperienced Pennsylvanian, Ensign Jacob Albright. Because the barracks were unfinished, Albright had to bed down his men at first in the cellar of the arsenal.

Newport Barracks.

There was no general kitchen; each room in the barracks had a fireplace fitted with a spit and pothook so that the men could cook their rations in their rooms. They slept in wooden, double bunks on ticks stuffed with straw. Poor food, dimly lit quarters, and monotony were consistently the lot of the soldiers stationed at the Newport Barracks. Desertions were frequent even though deserters faced the threat of harsh punishment. Soon Capt. Thornton Posey, the senior U.S. Army officer in Kentucky, was ordered to the Newport Barracks to assume command. Newport was an arsenal and an ordnance depot for its first 15 years, but it was also a recruiting station and remained so until the installation was deactivated.

The Newport Barracks was of great importance during the **War of 1812** as a mustering and supply post, particularly in the gathering of troops on their way to fight the British in Canada. Gen. William Henry Harrison's victory at Moravian Town in Canada in 1813 brought about 600 British and Canadian prisoners to Newport Barracks for internment for the duration of the war. The Newport Barracks remained a small but important installation through the **Civil War** and even, for a time, included a school for military bands. The post was perennially threatened by floods, however, and was viewed as an undesirable posting, since the facility often smelled of mold and was in need of reconstruction after each flood.

The Newport Barracks had lost its usefulness following the **Mexican War**. During the Indian Wars in the West, the post served as a supply depot as well as a recruiting center. Military company posts were, by this time, giving way to larger installations. Moreover, the Newport Barracks' days seemed numbered after the installation was flooded in three consecutive years, 1882, 1883, and 1884 (see **Flood of 1884**). These floods made some of the buildings uninhabitable; the resulting warped floors also made for cold and drafty lodgings.

In 1887 the post surgeons recommended that the barracks be abandoned, and the general-in-chief of the U.S. Army, Philip Sheridan, concurred. The U.S. Congress directed the U.S. secretary of war to purchase a nearby tract of land of about 112 acres located on a hill above the Ohio River in the District of Highlands (Fort Thomas). Suffering through yet another flood in 1889, the Newport Barracks was kept open while the new military installation was being constructed. A drought followed that year, which lowered the level of the Ohio River, adding to the stench and unhealthful conditions. Not until November 1894 were all personnel and equipment transferred from the Newport Barracks to the new military facility located above the Ohio River.

Congressman **Albert S. Berry** labored to have the Newport Barracks retained on the military's active list and then, when that failed, to have the facility presented to the City of Newport. The Newport City Council argued over the value of the gift, and six of its members even opposed accepting it. However, on New Year's Day 1896, the mayor of Newport signed a receipt presented by Col. Melville A. Cochran, commandant of the military's new post nearby, confirming that the former Newport Barracks and their grounds were now city property. Because of the cold weather, no public celebration was planned, and the Newport Barracks unceremoniously receded into history, later serving as a Newport city park for many years.

Donnelly, Joseph. *Newport Barracks—Kentucky's Forgotten Military Installation*. Covington, Ky.: Kenton Co. Historical Society, 1999.

"Newport Barracks Supplied the West during War," *CE*, November 17, 1996, D7.

"Newport's Old Story: City's Rise Spurred by Army, Dampened by Flood," *KP*, August 12, 1985, 3K.

Reis, Jim. "Newport Barracks Both Blessing, Curse," *KP*, November 29, 2004, 4K.

Karl Lietzenmayer

NEWPORT CENTRAL CATHOLIC HIGH SCHOOL. This high school is an amalgam of several other schools. After **World War I** many people came to recognize the need for secondary education, and public and private secondary schools were established nationwide during the 1920s. In the **Cote Brilliante** neighborhood of Newport, the **St. Francis de Sales** parish operated an evening commercial school for students of high school age in 1924. Elsewhere in Newport, both the **Corpus Christi** parish and the St. Stephen parish (see **Holy Spirit Catholic Church**) opened high schools in the 1920s. In 1927 the St. Stephen High School graduated four male students and the Corpus Christi High School graduated 16 students, 8 females and 8 males; in 1930 the St. Stephen High School produced 23 graduates, both males and females. By 1932 the Corpus Christi High School had closed, and the high school operated by St. Stephen parish had evolved into the Campbell Co. Catholic High School for Boys. For the school year 1932–1933, enrollment was 94 students. In 1934, because of overcrowding, the school was moved to the building of the former **Immaculata Academy** on W. Fifth St. near Columbia St. in Newport, and the school's name was changed to Newport Catholic High School. In 1945, faced with the continual growth of its student body, Newport Catholic High School moved to the campus of Corpus Christi Church in Newport, on the corner of Isabella and Ninth Sts. Some students came to Newport Catholic High School from Kenton Co., since **Covington Catholic High School** did not offer football until 1968; Newport Catholic High School itself lost potential students to the highly selective Covington Latin School and to the prestigious St. Xavier High School in Cincinnati.

On December 15, 1954, Newport Catholic High School's basketball team played the first game in its new gymnasium, the largest in Northern Kentucky at the time, and on May 8, 1955, the school's new $857,000 building, on the hill behind Mount St. Martin's in South Newport, was dedicated. Until 1964 the school was administered by the Diocese of Covington (see **Roman Catholics**) and many of the teachers were priests and sisters. The Right Reverend Msgr. John V. Hegenauer was a longtime principal who did much to keep the school solvent. He had an uncanny ability to get donations from local mobsters. Annual tuition at the school in the fall of 1963 was $125 for students coming from one of the 10 supporting parishes. In September 1964 the Christian Brothers, a Catholic order of teaching brothers (today known as the LaSallian Brothers), assumed administration of the school. Brother Julian Mark Sullivan F.S.C. was the first principal during this period. The graduating class of 1965, numbering 198 and made up of baby boomers, was the largest in the school's history. When enrollment peaked at 752 students in 1968, almost all usable space was occupied. In 1982 Newport Catholic High School merged with **Our Lady of Providence Academy** (formerly the Academy of Notre Dame of Providence, also in Newport), becoming the coeducational Newport Central Catholic High School. The 1955 building on the hill was retained for the combined school. Demographic changes in Campbell Co. and financial reasons led to the merger. The 1978 appointment of Carl R. Foster, a 1964 alumnus (and at one time the leading basketball scorer in the school's history), as principal marked the end of the Christian Brothers' administration of the school;

the last Christian Brothers (Brothers Phil Jones and Richard Merkle) departed in 1992. The teaching order, suffering from declining manpower, was no longer able to staff the school. In 2004 enrollment at the school was about 450. In 2008 the school broke ground on a $7.5 million construction and renovation project.

DeBord, Matthew. "Newport Catholic: The Steps on the Way to the Hill," manuscript written for the History Senior Seminar, Thomas More College, Fort Mitchell, Ky., November 2004.

"Ground Is Broken," *KP*, September 4, 1954, 1.

Ryan, Paul E. *History of the Diocese of Covington*. Covington, Ky.: Diocese of Covington, 1954.

Schroeder, David E. "From the Formation of High Schools to a College," *Kenton County Historical Society Bulletin*, January 1997, 2–4.

Michael R. Sweeney

NEWPORT CITIZENS ADVISORY COUNCIL. The Newport Citizens Advisory Council (NCAC) was formed by a resolution of the Newport City Commission on April 26, 1976, to comply with federal regulations involving a Community Block Grant the city received in 1974. The NCAC's initial responsibility was to provide input pertaining to the expenditure of those funds. However, the organization's responsibility was soon expanded to include providing citizen input on all matters of city life. It is in this capacity as a mechanism for civic involvement in Newport that the NCAC has played a major role in helping to change the direction of the city, beginning in the 1970s and continuing to the present. The organization's first meeting was held in September 1976.

Newport was divided into nine geographical neighborhoods, and the interested residents of each neighborhood elected the neighborhood's representative. Three at-large members were appointed by the NCAC Board of Commissioners. Each neighborhood eventually adopted a name of its own choosing: Two Rivers I and II in the northwestern part of the city, **Buena Vista** in the southwestern part, Taylor's Landing in the Central Business District, **Mansion Hill** and Gateway in the eastern sections, **Cote Brilliante** to the southeast, and **Clifton** and Cliffview to the south. The first neighborhood representatives were Herbert Bass, Laura Bradley, Rev. **Anthony Deye**, Tom Ferrara, Robert Freking, Thomas Fromme Sr., Kenneth Mullikan, Anna Murphy, and Rev. Robert Ryan.

Staffing assistance in the initial years was provided by **Brighton Center** and the **Northern Kentucky Area Development District**. At first, each neighborhood was granted $500 per year to promote neighborhood events. Later some neighborhoods began fundraising on their own and were influential in organizing the city's participation in the annual River Fest fireworks display as a way of raising funds for neighborhood groups.

Each neighborhood unit met monthly. The original concept was for the NCAC to be a conduit of information on city business—neighborhood representatives conveying information to their communities from the Newport City Commission and bringing information back to the City Commission. Eventually, the NCAC was granted a permanent seat at Newport City Commission meetings and a regular place on the agenda. This task of acting as a liaison quickly required the NCAC to maintain a delicate balance between maintaining its independence and at times advocating a position that was not favored by some members of the City Commission.

However, as neighborhood meetings continued, some began independently to address problems of concern to them. At first, these activities involved events that would improve residential life without causing much controversy. They included such things as organizing litter cleanups, voter registration, education drives, tree plantings, historic home tours, and leadership training programs. Several neighborhoods also began publishing their own monthly newsletters, and several of these publications continue today. The Mansion Hill Neighborhood was instrumental in advocating for the placement of the entrance and exit ramps for I-471 in a way that would not further damage the historic buildings in the eastern part of the city.

But the NCAC and its member neighborhoods also began to push for more aggressive action on issues that inevitably caused conflict between the organization and certain elected officials. The late 1970s and early 1980s was the time during which the most confrontations erupted. Disagreements arose over issues involving housing-code enforcement, bars in residential neighborhoods, access by citizens to public information, hiring and firing of city employees based on merit and not on political connections, protection of residential zones from encroachment by business interests, and methods of controlling the operation and expansion of adult-entertainment businesses within the city. The NCAC was crucial in providing initial support for the adult-entertainment ordinances the Newport City Commission passed during the 1980s and 1990s that have proved so effective in changing the image of the city and laying the groundwork for the economic development that followed.

In 1980 the NCAC was recognized by the regional field director of HUD (Housing and Urban Development) as one of the best-informed and most active organizations of its kind in Kentucky. In 1979 the NCAC was also featured on a regional television program broadcast on WCET in Cincinnati, called *The People Speak.*

In addition to providing opportunities for civic involvement and action, the NCAC has acted as a training ground for people who were interested in running for political office. Thomas Ferrara, Jan Knepshield, Kenneth Mullikin, and Laura Roberts were all active members of the organization's Advisory Council before being elected to the Newport City Commission. Many of the neighborhood activists who later went on to form the core of the Newport Political Action Committee got their initial exposure to civic involvement and political organizing as members of neighborhood councils and the NCAC.

As the issues in Newport have evolved, the involvement of the NCAC has also changed. While the organization still maintains its seat at the Newport City Commission meetings and continues to sponsor several civic events, its role as a controversial driving force behind civic improvements has waned in recent times. Throughout its history, there has been an ebb and flow of activity, and the neighborhood organizations have always had differing levels of participation and organizing ability. At times, certain neighborhood associations may have even eclipsed the NCAC itself in terms of political influence. But the NCAC remains to function as a source of resident input in Newport and as an example of what can be accomplished in government by residents banding together to improve the quality of life in their communities.

"Advisory Council's Opposition Sets Up Debate on Shelter," *KP*, September 10, 1983, 2K.

"Building Codes Divide Newport City Leaders," *KP*, May 3, 1983, 1K.

"Council Marks Birthday—Newport Group Remains Strong," *KP*, April 1, 1986, 3K.

Michael Whitehead

NEWPORT HIGH SCHOOL. In 1856 Newport had five public common schools and one high school. However, the Newport High School did not come into existence until 1860, when it was chartered by the state. The school's first location was in town on the north side of Fourth St. between Monmouth and Saratoga Sts., where the **Newport Academy** once stood. In those early days, attending high school was a luxury that few could afford; in most families the children became workers after completing the sixth grade. The parents who could afford some form of higher education thought of high school as a sort of "people's college." In the Newport High School's earliest years, its curriculum consisted of such a large number of required courses that it was virtually impossible to meet the graduation requirements in four years. Therefore, the school board decided to reduce the number of subjects required and shorten the length of high school training to three years. Under the old standards, no graduation exercises were held at Newport High School between 1856 and 1874. However, under the new, lowered standards, 519 students graduated between 1874 and 1900.

In 1872 a new home in Newport was built for the high school, on Columbia St. between Eighth and Ninth Sts., where a cemetery was located. Before construction began, the graves were moved to **Evergreen Cemetery** in Southgate. Because the site had once been a graveyard, many superstitious people claimed that the building and grounds were haunted; numerous sightings of ghosts were reported.

In 1880 the population of Newport was 20,433, with 2,972 students enrolled in various schools, but only 108 at Newport High. By 1900 the population of the city had grown to 28,301, with 3,646 students enrolled in schools and 195 of these in Newport High School. Between 1906 and 1908, Newport High School's boys were required to take military training with a unit called the Hammond Rifles. In 1908 the high school's course of study was changed back to four years, and a commercial course of study was added. In 1925 the school board decided to build a new high school and a new building for Arnold Elementary School. When the Arnold Elementary School's building on Central Ave. in Newport was completed, it was used for high school classes while the new high school was under construction at Eighth and Columbia Sts. in town.

By 1925 the city's population had reached 29,420, and 416 students were attending the high school. In 1928 a new gymnasium was added to the high school, and in 1939 a sports stadium was built nearby in **Taylor's Bottoms**. At that time Newport was operating one high school, a junior high, and nine elementary schools. After many years at the Eighth and Columbia Sts. location, Newport High School moved in 1980 to a new, modern building in town at 900 E. Sixth St., next to the elevated I-471.

Over the years, Newport High School has been dedicated to providing quality education to its students. Among the school's graduates who have become leaders in their chosen professions are 2000 Republican presidential primary candidate **Gary Bauer**, Ohio River historian **Virginia Bennett**, famed basketball coach **Jim Connor**, comedian and author **Greg Fields**, civic leaders **Lambert Hehl Sr.** and **Lambert Hehl Jr.**, Miss Kentucky of 1936 **Charlotte Hiteman**, Newport mayor–city manager **Ralph Mussman**, rocket scientist **Eugene Jimmy Palm**, noted physician–historian **Alvin C. Poweleit**, medical doctor and suffragette **Sarah M. Siewers**, Judge **Fred Warren**, noted architects Edward and Christopher Weber (see **Weber Brothers Architects**), Judge **Otto Daniel Wolff Sr.**, noted architect **Otto Daniel Wolff Jr.**, and novelist **Ruth Wolff**.

Newport High School was the runner-up state basketball champion in 1935 and 1954. The school won two state baseball championships during the early 1940s, one with Jim Connor as a player. Over time, the school produced a number of star athletes, including right-handed pitcher Tommy Reis, a major league baseball player; basketball's **John Turner**; Ohio State football All-American Bob White; and army football quarterback Zeke Zachella.

Cobb, James L. "History of the Public Schools of Newport, Kentucky," MEd thesis, Univ. of Cincinnati, 1939.

The Newportian. Newport, Ky.: Newport High School, 1999. 1999 yearbook.

Newport Independent Schools. "Our History." www.newportwildcats.org (accessed October 17, 2006).

Reis, Jim. "Newport Public School Heritage," *KP*, January 29, 1990, 4K.

NEWPORT HOME OWNERSHIP. High rates of home ownership were a feature of Newport's early years as a major Ohio River Valley iron and steel town. With expanding industrial employment in companies such the Swift Iron and Steel Works, Newport in the early 1870s was a prosperous city of more than 15,000 inhabitants (see **Steel and Iron Manufacturing**; **Andrews Steel Mill**; **Newport Steel**). Industrial jobs brought large numbers of immigrants, and the city became distinctively German and Irish (see **German Americans**; **Irish Americans**).

Owning a house rather than renting was possible for a great many families: about 35 percent of male-headed households owned (or were paying for) their own homes, and 54 percent of those who had lived in the city five years or more (for the period 1870–1874) were home owners. A comparable commercial city of similar size at a similar point in its prosperity (Alexandria, Va., just before the Civil War) had home-ownership rates half as high as Newport's. In terms of home ownership, Newport was, comparatively speaking, a "stakeholder community."

Moreover, Newport home ownership was also quite equally spread across economic groups. Even among the least skilled of Newport's residents, nearly 30 percent owned their own homes, compared with 9 percent in Alexandria. Wealth was also more equitably distributed in Newport than in Alexandria. There was, to be sure, a great gap between the wealth of those at the top and those at the bottom, and the poor did not have much, but the gap between rich and poor was smaller in Newport and the poor had more.

Home ownership meant fewer moves, a growing association with place, and a sense of belonging. These advantages are associated with fuller participation in community life, including voting. Perhaps these factors also help explain why in Newport more people, even those employed in unskilled and semiskilled occupations, went to the polls than in Alexandria.

Why was home ownership so widespread in Newport? Three factors stand out. First, **James Taylor Jr.**, the founder of Newport, and his family frequently sold off sections of land platted into small lots, and the City of Newport quickly adjusted the city boundaries to take in these sections. For example, the Buena Vista Addition, named by Taylor for the great Mexican War victory of his cousin Gen. Zachary Taylor, was platted into 750 lots, almost all of which were very small, measuring 30 by 93 feet.

Second, local builders saw an opportunity to build very large numbers of modest houses—one- or one-and-a-half-story structures, wood or brick, with shingle roofs—on these small lots. Henry Schriver established a carpentry firm on Columbia St. between Fifth and Sixth Sts. especially for this type of building, putting up houses of his own design. Thus Newport came to have single-family homes in large numbers. As a result, sometimes there were 17 homes on a single block face, as on the west side of Columbia St. between 10th and 11th Sts.

Workingmen intent on home ownership found the small, locally designed houses on small lots attractive, but there remained the problem of money. The third factor that made home ownership widespread in Newport was that local savings associations served as intermediaries in the purchase of a lot and the building of a home (see **Savings and Loan Associations**). For this purpose there were five building associations in Newport in the early 1870s, each with capital of about a half million dollars. Henry Schriver served as treasurer of one of the two German building associations. Such arrangements were also conducted within churches, especially those associated with the city's large immigrant populations.

Associations within immigrant groups were important, for in the 1870s more than a quarter of all Newport's residents and nearly half of all adults had been born overseas. The largest groups were the Germans (one-third of all adults) and the Irish (one-seventh of all adults). Not surprisingly, land sales were advertised in both English and German.

Facilitating home ownership through informal savings associations was not without its peril, however, as the case of Father Patrick Guilfoyle illustrates. He was born in Kilkenny, Ireland, immigrated to the United States at age 25, studied at St. Thomas Seminary in Bardstown, Ky., and in 1854 was ordained at St. Mary's Catholic Church in Covington. Three years later he became pastor of Newport's newly created **Immaculate Conception Catholic Church**, the city's first English-speaking Catholic congregation, where he undertook to build the church's membership and its infrastructure. Guilfoyle saw an opportunity to accomplish his goals using Newport's economic expansion and land availability; he devised a plan that would increase parishioners' savings, contribute to home ownership for parish members, and turn a profit with which to build the parish's physical plant. Initially, the plan worked well; by some estimates Guilfoyle was involved in the building of more than 500 homes in Newport, and for his parish he built not only a rectory, a convent, and schools but also the beautiful Immaculate Conception Catholic Church on Fifth St. between Central and Columbia Sts. The church was dedicated in 1873, just in time to witness the panic of that year, which set off a profound economic depression. Wages were reduced at the iron mills, Swift's workers went on strike, violence flared, and economic calamity spread. The parish quickly found itself in an impossible economic situation. Guilfoyle resigned in November 1874 and left Newport for Chicago, and many parishioners lost their hard-won homes.

Newport became a workingman's city not by accident or because of great social forces but because of the actions and vision of individuals, such as great landowners like Taylor, self-made entrepreneurs like Schriver, and leaders of community groups like Guilfoyle. But there was always the possibility that gains achieved locally could readily be destroyed by outside forces.

City of Newport, Municipal Poll Books, March 2, 1874, Division of Archives and Records, Frankfort, Kentucky.

City of Newport, Municipal Tax List, 1874, Campbell Co. Tax Lists, Division of Archives and Records, Frankfort, Kentucky.

Purvis, Thomas L., ed. *Newport, Kentucky: A Bicentennial History*. Newport, Ky.: Otto Zimmerman, 1996.

Ryan, Paul E. *History of the Diocese of Covington, Kentucky.* Covington, Ky.: Diocese of Covington, 1954.

Thernstrom, Stephen. *Poverty and Progress: Social Mobility in a Nineteenth Century City.* Cambridge, Mass.: Harvard Univ. Press, 1964.

William's Newport Directory for 1873. Williams, 1873.

Don DeBats

NEWPORT INDEPENDENT SCHOOLS. Newport has a long history of providing quality education for its citizens. The tradition began with the chartering of the **Newport Academy** in 1798, and its opening in 1800. The academy was the first public school in Northern Kentucky and preceded the first similar academy in Cincinnati by 16 years. Before 1839 most schools were privately owned and were usually available only to the elite and wealthy. Many of those early schools were located in private homes.

The first "free school" opened in Newport in 1805. Free schools were usually subsidized by wealthy individuals and were meant to provide rudimentary education to children of the poor. A Professor Blinn, Thomas Lindsey, **Ira Root**, and Charles Thornton started the first free school, and classes were held in rented quarters at Newport's Methodist Episcopal Church. In 1815 a three-story brick schoolhouse was erected in town between Eighth and Ninth Sts. on Columbia St. as a permanent home for the school.

In 1836 a new, larger school was built in Newport on Central Ave. between Fifth and Sixth Sts. and was named the Cabot Free School. Only 25 students enrolled that first year; however, enrollment more than doubled to 54 the second year. In about 1890 the name was changed to the Arnold School, likely for James M. Arnold, president of the Newport Board of Education. In 1847 a state law was passed authorizing the taxing of real estate to fund public education. In Newport a property tax of two cents for every $100 valuation was assessed to support schools. The date of that legislation is now used as the official starting date of the modern Newport independent public school system.

In 1856 Newport was operating five free schools and one high school. The progress of public education suffered during the **Civil War**, when attendance fell, funding suffered, and public interest waned. After the war, interest in education was renewed. Additional schools were built, better textbooks were provided, and the first meaningful effort was made to educate black children.

L. T. Hubbard was named the first superintendent of Newport Public Schools in 1869. Over the years, some of the other superintendents have been A. D. Owens, **Ellsworth Regenstein**, James L. Cobb, and the present one, Michael Brandt.

In the fall of 1875, a night school was opened to accommodate those unable to attend daytime classes. From 1906 to 1908, military training was required of all Newport High School boys in a military unit known as the Hammond Rifles.

By 1900 Newport citizens had a much higher literacy rate than the rest of the state and the nation. In addition to quality schools, a factor that contributed to the literacy rate was the area's many newspapers, which were widely read. In 1904 a new 16-room Newport High School building was built at Eighth and Columbia Sts. and a 4-room school at 10th and Patterson Sts. Weber Brothers Architects designed these two buildings. A new Arnold School was built as an addition to the old one and was opened in September 1926. Another project undertaken that year was construction of the York Street School on 11th St. Two schools became part of the Newport system as a result of annexation: in the 1920s the Cote Brilliante School, a former county school at Park and Grand Aves., joined the Newport Schools, as did the Clifton School when Clifton was annexed by Newport in the 1930s. Both of those schools left the Newport system in September 1960; they were consolidated into the new Mildred Dean School along Grand Ave., adjacent to **St. Luke Hospital**. Arnold School was razed in 1997 and replaced by a Campbell Co. Jail complex.

The Newport Independent School district now operates five schools, with a student population of about 2,200. In 1980 Newport High School moved into a new building in the city at 900 E. Sixth St., next to the I-471 expressway. Energized by the recent renaissance of the city, the high school's staff has embarked on a five-year plan to improve the curriculum and services offered.

Cobb, James L. "History of the Public Schools of Newport, Kentucky," MEd thesis, Univ. of Cincinnati, 1939.

Newport Independent Schools. "Our History." www.newportwildcats.org (accessed October 17, 2006).

Tenkotte, Paul A. "Rival Cities to Suburbs: Covington and Newport, Kentucky, 1790–1890," PhD diss., Univ. of Cincinnati, 1989.

Newport Free School, Fourth St., Newport.

NEWPORT MINERAL WATER COMPANY. This company, located at 18 E. Sixth St. in Newport, produced and distributed soft drinks long before the national consolidation of the industry. The original business was founded in 1886 by Baron H. Woodbury and Dietrich Theodore Buschmiller as the Woodbury and Buschmiller Company; it was sold in 1912 to the Newport Mineral Water Company. The firm manufactured soda water, mineral water, and seltzer water and delivered its products mainly to groceries and drug stores. The drinks were sold in 6.5-ounce emerald or white bottles and 24-ounce light green bottles imprinted with the company name. The bottles have become collector items. The product line was expanded to include other soft drinks, ginger ale, vichy water, litihia water, and similar carbonated and noncarbonated beverages. Soft drink flavors included cream soda, Hawaiian punch, lemon-lime, orange, root beer, and sarsaparilla. The company seldom had more than eight employees. For special events, an extra delivery truck would be loaded and driven to the site of an outing; it would remain until the truck was out of stock. Stiff competition from the national brands began during the early 1950s, and the company tried to compete by introducing two new drinks in 12-ounce bottles, "Mr. Newport" and "Thin," but the company ceased operations in the summer of 1955. In late August of that year, both the company's equipment and its real estate were sold at auction.

"Going Going Gone," *KP*, September 1, 1955, 19.

Reis, Jim. "Records and Memories of Bottling Company Pour a Sip of Local History," *KP*, October 14, 1991, 4K.

NEWPORT-ON-THE-LEVEE. Newport-on-the-Levee, a 350,000-square-foot regional entertainment complex, was the catalyst for the redevelopment of Newport's Ohio River shore. A city-built, 4-level parking garage beneath the development has capacity for 1,800 vehicles. **Newport Aquarium** was the first venue to open, in May 1999. Although the complex had not yet been fully completed, a number of restaurants and shops opened in fall 2001. Major anchors include the aquarium, a two-level Barnes and Noble bookstore, a 20-screen movie theater (see **Movie Theaters**), specialty shops, gourmet and ethnic restaurants (American, Chinese, Irish, Italian, Japanese, Latin American, and Turkish), two amusement game centers, and live performance venues like the Shadowbox Sketch Comedy and Rock-n-Roll Club and the Funny Bone Comedy Club. A hotel is planned for the future. Newport-on-the-Levee is owned by the Price Group of La Jolla, Calif.

Newport-on-the-Levee. www.newportonthelevee.com/ (accessed June 19, 2008).

Rutledge, Mike. "Newport Ties Rebirth to Levee," *KP*, July 19, 2001, 1K.

Wood, Roy. "Newport's New Face," *KP*, April 7, 2001, 1K.

Thomas S. Ward

NEWPORT POLITICAL ACTION COMMITTEE. The beginning of the 1980s was a tumultuous time in Newport politics. A majority with a reputation for wanting to reform city government was elected to Newport's City Commission in 1970 and then voted out of office in 1979. In its place was a new majority that supported various policies of the past, including tolerating the alcohol and sexually oriented businesses that were abundant throughout the city. Public conflicts between the new majority and supporters of restricting these businesses became a frequent topic on local television stations and in the newspapers.

Some citizens were prevented from speaking at city commission meetings, and when they tried, they were shouted down by their elected officials. One particularly vicious verbal attack caught the media's attention. Neighborhood activist Ian Budd was an immigrant from England, where he had been involved in political organizing, and had been promoting civic events in Newport, including the city's initial involvement in the tri-state WEBN fireworks festival. While making a presentation for the 1980 event, Budd was attacked by then Newport commissioner A. J. Tony Warndorf as a "damn Limey" and a "Communist," who had no right to speak at commission meetings. Budd eventually resigned from his post, but the fallout from this attack, which had been aired on local television, had a profound influence on the future direction of Newport politics and government.

The intensity of the political conflict led some citizen leaders to believe that a new force was needed to bring stability, civility, and continuity to Newport government. This desire for a new way led to the formation of the Newport Political Action Committee (NEWPAC) in 1981. Budd was instrumental in forming and directing the early activities of the group. Other influential founding members were Allen Dube, local businessman Peter Garrett, and Owen Kramer. All had had extensive experience in organizing community events sponsored either by their local neighborhood association or by the **Newport Citizens Advisory Council**.

Word of the group's formation attracted like-minded citizens from throughout Newport. Membership was open to all citizens and business owners in the city. Three officers were elected to plan the overall strategies for the organization, subject to approval by the membership. Their purpose was to develop a policy platform for the future of Newport and to endorse and support those candidates for city offices who seemed likely to support that platform.

A questionnaire was developed and sent to each candidate for office, who was given an opportunity to address the group's membership. Not all candidates cooperated, but the meetings themselves were very well attended. Eventually, NEWPAC decided to endorse Laura Bradley, Steve Goetz, Tom Ferrara, and Fred Osburg as candidates for city commissioner. There was no race for mayor that year.

While NEWPAC provided no money to any candidates, its members did use their human resources to organize three different citywide flyer drops before the primary and the general election. In addition, on election day they provided volunteers to stand at the exits of the bridges leading from Cincinnati with signs encouraging citizens to support the reform group's slate of candidates. All four candidates won.

Once the 1981 election was over, NEWPAC members took only a limited role in influencing government policies, leaving that task primarily to the people they had helped elect. Most members continued their involvement with their neighborhood associations and the Newport Advisory Council, which continued to have an impact on the development and execution of new policies for the city. The commissioners adopted much of NEWPAC's platform, including restrictions on adult entertainment and hiring personnel to foster economic development in the city.

Some tension developed between the four commissioners and NEWPAC members, mostly over the board's decision to retain **Ralph Mussman** as city manager, but by 1983 enough progress had been achieved that the same four persons plus candidate Irene Deaton, who had been mayor, were endorsed and elected. According to newspaper accounts of this election, the reelection of four incumbent commissioners was a feat that had not been accomplished since 1941.

By 1985 many NEWPAC members had decided that city government in Newport was on a good course and that a new spirit of political cooperation existed. Deciding that NEWPAC's political services were no longer needed, the group decided to disband. But the group of candidates that NEWPAC had supported provided much of the stability and staff needed to launch the city on its path to restoration, which began in the 1980s and had reached a high level of success by the turn of the century.

"Mayor Won't Seek Group's Endorsement," *KP*, March 17, 1983, 12K.

"New—PAC to Politick," *KP*, January 29, 1983, 2K.

"NEWPAC Has Key Election Role," *KP*, February 14, 1983, 1K.

Michael Whitehead

NEWPORT PUBLIC LIBRARY. The Newport Public Library officially opened on January 16, 1899. By April of that year, the increasing patronage and circulation numbers at the library necessitated the hiring of an assistant librarian. Henrietta Litzendorff was selected to fill the newly created position; she remained a faithful employee of the library for 52 years, eventually becoming the third and longest-tenured head librarian.

The library's board of trustees next set their sights on obtaining a grant from the Andrew Carnegie Foundation to fund the construction of a new facility. In a letter dated October 10, 1899, board member and Episcopal minister W. G. McCready solicited Andrew Carnegie, the Scottish-born philanthropist, for library construction funds. The following month, Rev. McCready was notified that Carnegie had approved a $20,000 grant, which would finance the building with an auditorium. Though exceedingly generous, Carnegie's munificence came with a few stipulations. Grant funds were to be used solely for building construction, and they would be disbursed only after library trustees, city officials, and citizens had secured a suitable site, either through donations or by utilization of public funds. Carnegie also insisted that, since the community owned the building, the city's residents had to agree to an annual maintenance fund pledge equal to at least 10 percent of the total amount he had granted.

Though buoyed by Carnegie's generosity, Newport encountered one of the most frequent problems experienced throughout the country by previous recipients of Carnegie library grants: disputes over the selection and location of a mutually agreed-upon site for the new facility. Because Newport had been the first city in Kentucky to receive a Carnegie library grant, an honor the city did not want to lose, a concerted effort was made to mobilize a subscription drive to fund the purchase of land for a building site. In May 1900, a 77-by-66-foot lot at the southeast corner of Fourth and Monmouth Sts. in Newport was, at last, agreed upon; the site, which had been offered by U.S. congressman and Newport native **Albert S. Berry**, was purchased for $3,350.

Once this lot at 403 Monmouth St. had been secured, the building's design and appearance now had to be decided. The library trustees eventually selected a simple yet classically elegant Italian Renaissance facade designed by Cincinnati architects Werner & Adkins.

As the construction phase drew to a close, and the costs began to exceed original estimates, the trustees again appealed to Andrew Carnegie for an additional funding; a second grant, in the amount of $6,500, was approved. The library board's cash shortfall was further alleviated after Newport's city council passed a resolution allocating $22,650 in funds for library use. The library board's members were at last able to procure the furnishings and accoutrements befitting the library's grand exterior: interior embellishments included an ornate spiral staircase leading to the second-floor auditorium (named Carnegie Hall), a marble-countered circulation desk framed by twin columns, and vaulted ceilings adorned with dentil, egg-and-dart, and reed moldings.

The new Newport Public Library was dedicated on June 25, 1902. At its opening, the library had a collection of 2,202 volumes; by 1905 the library's holdings had increased to 6,588 volumes, of which 191 were in German. Though Newport's citizenry was comprised of many ethnic backgrounds, especially Irish and Italian, according to the 1880 census, those claiming German ancestry formed a large percentage of the city's population. Newport's embrace of its ethnic diversity was further evidenced by the library's early efforts to provide racially integrated service to black patrons.

Despite ongoing budgetary concerns and financial shortfalls, by 1928 the Newport Public Library had become a firmly established municipal institution; that year's annual report noted that 6,527 registered library patrons were provided with access to 17,534 volumes, amounting to a respectable circulation total of 72,908 items. In the aftermath of the October 1929 U.S. stock market crash and the subsequent onset of the **Great Depression**, the Newport Public Library sought to serve its dedicated patron base by participating in the Campbell Co. Association's "make-a-job" program, though its effort to employ citizens in a building renovation project via the federal Works Progress Administration were denied because the library's interior had already been painted within the previous 15 years.

Though the Ohio River **floods of 1913** and **1937** exacted a terrible toll from the city and its residents, the Newport Public Library and its fragile contents survived both events. Later, the library provided a much-needed place to escape the daily tribulations Newport's citizens encountered throughout the Great Depression. In March 1941, the PTA in Bellevue had unsuccessfully attempted to organize a countywide library system. Later that year, a decade before the U.S. Congress passed the Library Services Act to supply funding for the establishment of library services to rural areas, the Newport Public Library sought to extend borrowing privileges to Campbell Co. residents living outside the Newport city limits. Rural residents of Campbell Co. could borrow library materials by paying a one-dollar annual fee and by having their library card application signed by a Newport property owner.

Over the next several decades, Newport experienced a substantial outmigration, which, by the late 1960s, had begun to impact the library's patron base. The formation of the Northern Kentucky Regional Library System in 1968 was followed by renewed efforts to establish a countywide library district, though initially these efforts were met with failure. Furthermore, by 1971, Newport's Public Library, the county's first home of free public library service, was facing a financial dilemma: how to pay for costly renovation and modernization projects with shrinking municipal funds.

In 1976 county officials and residents initiated a well-organized demonstration project to secure funds for a multibranch, countywide library district. Legal concerns and turf issues kept the Newport Public Library from participating in the project. The newly formed Campbell Co. Library Board overcame this difficulty by opening its own Newport branch within a leased mobile home unit located at the **Newport Shopping Center**.

The successful passage of a three-cent library tax levy in 1978 marked the end of the Newport Public Library's long-held and closely guarded autonomy. The new District Library Board purchased the contents of the library, though the city maintained ownership of the building; an arrangement was made whereby the newly established Campbell Co. Public Library System would lease the Newport Public Library's building from the city for one dollar per year. Thus, after 76 long and memorable years, Newport's Carnegie Free Library, as of January 1, 1979, became known as the Newport Branch of the Campbell Co. Public Library.

In May 1982, an ordinance was passed by the Newport City Commission deeding the library building to the Campbell Co. Library Board in return for its trustees' compliance with two conditions: the first required the county's library board to complete at least $100,000 worth of improvements over the next five years; and the second noted that if the library building on Monmouth St. were ever to be sold, all proceeds from the sale would be allocated for the construction of new library within Newport. By 1984 initial improvements had been made, including the purchase and paving of an adjacent lot for additional parking as well as the installation of new stairs and handrails at the library's main Monmouth St. entrance. In early 1987, the county library board approved a major renovation project for the Newport branch; the cost of the aging facility's extensive interior and exterior modernization and remodeling totaled over $260,000 and took two years to complete.

The automation of the Campbell Co. Public Library System's card catalog in 1987 precipitated a technological avalanche that soon overwhelmed the facilities available within Newport's 9,700-square-foot Carnegie building. By November 1997, banks of public-access computers had been installed throughout all the county's library branches, and the system's holdings had rapidly expanded to include compact discs, books on tape, CD-ROMs, and informational and educational movies on videocassettes and later on DVDs. As a result, the Newport branch library's quaint charm no longer camouflaged its sadly outdated condition. As staff and patrons turned out to celebrate the Newport branch library's 100th anniversary in April 1999, its future was in question.

Throughout the remainder of the 1990s and into the new millennium, rumors abounded regarding the possible relocation of the Newport branch library and the potential sale of the Carnegie building at Fourth and Monmouth Sts. In April 2000, the rumors were confirmed when the county library board of trustees took legal action to secure a site for a new library facility to be located at 901 E. Sixth St. in Newport, near the city's border with Bellevue. The rectangular brick structure there had once been an A&P Supermarket and had since become the home of the 471 Antique Mall. By October 2001 the trustees had successfully acquired the location.

Despite the interest of other perspective buyers, the Carnegie library building's long and intimate history with the city of Newport quickly led to earnest negotiations between the Newport Library Board's trustees and city officials on a selling price for the historic structure. Meanwhile, in January 2003, the Morel Construction Company Inc., of Fort Thomas began construction on the $3.8 million, 27,000-square-foot building that would replace the library on Monmouth St. In July of that same year, the Newport City Commission and the Campbell Co. Library's board of trustees agreed upon a $375,000 selling price for the Carnegie building, ending nearly a year and a half of worried conjecture over its future and returning the building's ownership to the city.

On May 1, 2004, current and former library staff members of the Newport Public Library gathered along with past and present Newport residents, faithful library patrons, city officials, and local dignitaries for the closing ceremony of the former Newport Public Library. A half month later, on May 16th, many of the same faces, along with many new ones, celebrated the continuation of Newport's public library service at the grand opening of the new Newport branch library on Sixth St.

In July 2007, local businessman David Hosea purchased the old Carnegie library building and renovated it into the Carnegie Event Center, which includes a tea room, a reception hall, a museum, and a gift shop. The facility opened in 2008.

Mueller, Jan. *Soul of the City: A Centennial History of the Newport Public Library.* Cincinnati: Specialty Litho, 2004.

"Newport Library Relocating," *KE*, April 26, 2004, B1.

"Newport May Buy Old Library Building," *KP*, March 14, 2000, 3K.

Reis, Jim. "Newport Library Turns Page on Second Century," *KP*, April 5, 1999, 4K.

Janice Mueller

NEWPORT REFORM GROUPS. The reform group formed in Northern Kentucky during the early 1960s, known as the Committee of 500, often receives all the credit for the cleanup of Newport's casinos and brothels, but efforts to reform Newport extend back all the way to the 1940s. The success of the Committee of 500 must be seen within the context of the efforts of these other groups, especially the Newport Ministerial Association's Social Awareness Committee (SAC).

The first efforts to clean up Newport were usually blocked by factions within the gambling business. When the police raided an operation, it was most likely because one faction had succeeded in paying off law enforcement officials to shut down a rival. The Newport Civic Association (NCA) was the best known of early ineffective reform organizations. Running under the slogan "Clean Up, Not Close Up," the NCA was co-opted by the **Cleveland Syndicate** in the early 1950s as the NCA was attempting to rid Newport's gambling establishments of some of their seedier side effects, such as prostitution. The NCA was successful only in closing up a few operations temporarily. Real reform did not occur until the end of the decade, with the founding of the of the Newport Ministerial Association's Social Awareness Committee. The SAC is notable because it was the Northern Kentucky region's first truly independent reform group and because it paved the way for the Committee of 500.

The driving force behind the SAC was Christian Siefried, a postman who was one of the lay members of the committee. Under Siefried's leadership, the SAC focused its attention on gambling and vice. Despite the group's tenacity—its members fought continually against gambling for almost four years—its mission and structure ultimately prevented it from accomplishing real reform. Consisting of likeminded souls from numerous Newport Protestant churches, the SAC followed the tenets of Christian social action, which argued that the necessary reforms could be carried out by simply studying a problem and alerting local officials to its existence.

Two years of study helped Siefried and the SAC realize that simply alerting local officials would do no good. Most elected and law enforcement officials were either sympathetic to the gambling interests or directly on the "take." The only way truly to reform Newport was to remove the corrupt officials from office. The SAC attempted to do so, using Kentucky's impeachment system, whereby the governor appointed a committee to investigate the offending officials and then have them removed.

In order to pursue the impeachment process, the SAC needed a lawyer, and this is how the Committee of 500 came into being. Jack Wadsworth, who was in the road-paving and construction equipment business, was spurred on by the recent serious embarrassment that Newport gamblers had caused him. One of his clients, in town for a sales convention, had been "rolled" in one of Newport's seedier casinos. Wadsworth approached Claude Johnson, who sold electrical equipment, about funding the SAC effort to push for ouster proceedings.

Johnson had also been watching the SAC from the sidelines and agreed with Wadsworth that they should approach their fellow businessmen to fund the SAC. Johnson thought they should also form their own group that would be more expressly political in nature. Over the course of the late winter and spring of 1961, the group Wadsworth and Johnson envisioned, the Committee of 500, came into being. Its goals, though similar to those of the SAC in that they wanted to rid Newport of gambling and vice, were more political and secular. Johnson, Wadsworth, and the other area businessmen who formed the core of the Committee of 500 wanted to clean up Newport and Campbell Co. not only for moral reasons, but because they saw how the economy of vice and corruption was hindering Northern Kentucky's economic future.

By the 1950s Northern Kentucky was fully a suburb of Cincinnati. Ninety percent of Northern Kentucky residents commuted across the Ohio River for work; Wadsworth, Johnson, and other prominent citizens wanted to change that situation. But they had seen efforts to recruit new businesses and industry stumble because of the rampant corruption in local politics. Large corporations would not invest in Campbell Co. because they felt that a political apparatus controlled by the gambling interests would be hostile to their needs. Thus, the Committee of 500 focused on cleaning up Newport not for any altruistic reform purpose, but because they wanted to replace the political economy of gambling and corruption with the political economy of the modern corporation and jobs.

In order to accomplish their goal, the Committee of 500 needed to gain control of the political apparatus. Since their political base was in the suburbs of Campbell Co., they focused on running a candidate for county, not municipal, office. They decided on the county sheriff's seat because that office had broad powers to enforce state and federal antigambling statutes. Their candidate was **George W. Ratterman**, a former football star who was a real estate lawyer in a prominent Cincinnati investment firm. Besides possessing charisma and connections, Ratterman was Roman Catholic, a fact that helped the Committee of 500 enlist the assistance of the county's Catholic population.

Despite an ill-fated attempt to frame Ratterman by **Tito Carinci** and his bosses at the Glenn Hotel in Newport, Ratterman won the race for Campbell Co. sheriff in late 1961. Ratterman's strongest support came from outside of Newport, especially from supporters in Fort Thomas, the core of the committee's constituency. Over the course of his four-year term, Ratterman succeeded in running most of Newport's small-time casino operators out of Newport and the rest of Campbell Co. (the larger operations, run by the Cleveland Syndicate, had left town voluntarily once they saw how powerful and serious the reform efforts were). During the 1960s the Committee of 500 elected their candidates to the commonwealth attorney and district judge offices, making sure that the gambling interests could not return to power and that illegal gambling would no longer be the center of the region's economy.

Gioielli, Robert. "Suburbs v. Slot Machines: The Committee of 500 and the Battle over Gambling in Northern Kentucky," *Ohio Valley History* 5, no. 2 (Summer 2005): 61–84.

Shearer, Jason G. "Urban Reform in Sin City: The George Ratterman Trial and the Election of 1961 in Northern Kentucky," *RKHS* 98, no. 4 (Autumn 2000): 343–65.

Williams, Michael L. "Sin City Kentucky: Newport, Kentucky's Vice Heritage, and Its Legal Extinction, 1920–1991," master's thesis, University of Louisville, 2008.

Robert Gioielli

NEWPORT SECOND CLEANUP. Newport's so-called second cleanup occurred during the 1980s, when during about a 10-year period, prosecutors and law enforcement came together to combat the town's "Sin City" label, first imposed during **Prohibition**. Their contributions ultimately redefined Newport's central business core.

In the late 1960s, after organized gambling departed Campbell Co. (see **Cleveland Syndicate**), elections filled Campbell Co. judgeships and the Commonwealth attorney's office with men of integrity. But the late 1960s and 1970s also brought to Newport's central business core a concentration of adult bars featuring nude and seminude dancing, "B-girls," "XXX" adult theater (see **Cinema X**), and the Adult Bookstore, mostly along a five-block stretch of Monmouth St. The "Sin City" stigma remained. For this Newport problem, the solution was reached mostly in courtrooms and hearing chambers, but only after sound law-enforcement investigative efforts and the coming into office of an intense and aggressive Campbell Co. attorney in 1978.

Although a few businesses made feeble attempts at traditional burlesque, most of the 20 or so establishments were poor imitations. In those strip bars, **prostitution** was the real attraction, and alcohol was the medium of exchange; these activities were quite illegal, of course. Cinema X, owned by an out-of-state concern, and local nightlife figure Sammy Wright's Adult Bookstore, both in the 700 block of Monmouth, contained several coin-operated "peep show booths" offering sexually explicit movies. Since the booths were large enough for at least two persons, the Cinema X and Bookstore offered yet another activity for non-Newport patrons, the usual crowds that clogged Monmouth at night. Promoting the long-held myth that adult entertainment was economically good for Newport, the three-member majority of the 1980–1981 Newport City Commission turned a blind eye to the vice that permeated Monmouth St. and a deaf ear to the citizens groups and the ministerial association (see **Newport Reform Groups**) that pleaded for antivice actions. Antivice forces saw hope during 1978 and 1979 when Newport detective Al Garnick's investigative teams began to show results through raids and prosecutions, but the antireform three-member majority did not support those efforts in 1980–1981. The two reform-minded minority members, Mayor Irene Deaton and commissioner Steven Goetz, tried to "stay the course," unaware that someone had, in fact, heard the appeals and was quietly preparing to act forcefully and with a persistence that the vice purveyors could not have expected.

County attorney Paul Twehues began in April 1980 to act aggressively against vice along Monmouth. He was assisted by his associates Bill Schoettelkotte, Justin Verst, and Bill Wehr; the Kentucky State Police; the Campbell Co. Police; and later, when the City Commission majority did not impede them, the Newport Police. Over the next 24 months, the Cinema X was raided and convicted seven times with obscenity violations. The Adult Bookstore was targeted and tried for obscenity violations as well. By early 1982 both establishments, the chief marketers of obscenity and two stark symbols of the "sin" in Newport's "Sin City" nickname, were permanently closed.

Undercover detectives with the Kentucky State Police and, later, with the Newport Police, conducted antiprostitution campaigns inside the bars, and state and local liquor law infractions were investigated; offending license holders were prosecuted. Prostitution convictions, if there were enough of them, permitted sanctions against liquor license holders, which were effected by Newport's liquor administrator, Michael Whitehead (hired in 1982), or by county attorney Twehues through civil lawsuits. Twehues and his assistant Justin Verst brought civil suits against strip bars under a little-known act that allowed a circuit judge to declare a business a "house of prostitution" based upon the number of prostitution convictions, closing the establishment for up to a year. Closures placed the businesses' license and zoning status in jeopardy. Because of these and similar measures by the city and by Twehues's office, the number of undesirable establishments began to shrink as strip bar owners foolishly tried to challenge the resolve of city administrators, police, and prosecutors.

Mayor Deaton and commissioner Goetz's persistence was rewarded in 1982, when the City Commission was populated entirely by reform-minded individuals. The commission promptly enacted Newport's first anti-nude dance ordinance in October of the same year. Drafted by new city attorney Wil Schroder and his staff, and patterned after a U.S. Supreme Court decision from New York (*New York State Liquor Authority v. Dennis Bellanca, dba The Main Event, et al.*, 1981), the ordinance forbade any further nude dancing in Newport establishments having liquor licenses. The ordinance was immediately challenged through the state and federal court systems. The U.S. Supreme Court ultimately upheld the Newport ordinance in the case of *City of Newport, Kentucky v. Nicholas A. Iacobucci, dba Talk of the Town, et al.*, 1987. Newport's ordinance became a model for other cities that wanted similar legislation.

Throughout the 1980s, some adult entertainment businesses survived, but their numbers continued to shrink. Mike Whitehead, the police, and Twehues's office continued the pressure when criminal infractions occurred, but some bars surrendered their liquor licenses to resume nude dancing, thereby avoiding the *Bellanca* decision and the Newport antinudity ordinance, both of which applied only to businesses having liquor licenses. Help came when the U.S. Supreme Court decided the case of *Glen Theatre, Inc. v. Michael Barnes, Prosecuting Attorney of St. Joseph County, Indiana*, 1991. Ironically, the Glen Theatre could trace corporate ownership to the group that had owned Newport's former Cinema X. Holding that a state or local government may prohibit public nudity regardless of whether liquor was involved, concurring justice David Souter reminded cities that adverse "secondary effects" on communities near adult-entertainment businesses were valid considerations when contemplating zoning and other legislation. City attorney Mike Schulkens, a skilled trial lawyer accustomed to exploiting legal opportunities afforded by court decisions, who once had represented adult-entertainment owners, quickly prompted city manager James Parsons and other city leaders to fashion zoning and other laws to take advantage of the *Barnes* case. Newport's dancers' costumes became more conservative, and the number of strip bars, if they could be termed such anymore, numbered only three by the late 1990s. The "Sin City" label became assigned to history.

Newport's current model-community status is attributed to the economic vision of former city leaders such as Laura Long (economic director), mayor Irene Deaton, commissioner Steven Goetz, and Philip G. Ciafardini (finance director and city manager), to name a few, and many dedicated Newport citizens who struggled to maintain their neighborhoods. Today, families stroll unhesitatingly in Newport, day or night, to enjoy a town that has always been there but was for years concealed under the "Sin City" veneer.

City of Newport, Kentucky v. Nicholas A. Iacobucci, dba Talk of the Town, et al., 479 U.S. 92, 107 S.Ct. 383, 93 L. Ed. 2d 334 (1986).

Glen Theatre, Inc. v. Michael Barnes, Prosecuting Attorney of St. Joseph County Indiana, et al., 501 U.S. 560, 111 S.Ct. 2456, 115 L. Ed. 2d 504 (1991).

New York State Liquor Authority v. Dennis Bellanca, dba The Main Event, et al., 452 U.S., 714, 101 S.Ct. 2599, 69 L. Ed. 2d 357 (1981).

Williams, Michael L. "Sin City Kentucky: Newport, Kentucky's Vice Heritage, and Its Legal Extinction, 1920–1991," master's thesis, University of Louisville, 2008.

Mike Williams

NEWPORT SHOPPING CENTER. The first modern outdoor shopping plaza of its type in Northern Kentucky, Newport Shopping Center is located where Carothers Rd. meets Alexandria Pk. (**U.S. 27**) in Newport. It formally opened amid much fanfare on Thursday February 2, 1956, with more than 30 stores, though some stores had already opened, and others came a little later. Pages of advertisements and publicity in local newspapers preceded this gala event. The center was developed by Cleveland-based Sanford Homes Inc. and constructed by the Harrison Construction Company on the property of the Schuerman family's dairy farm. The site had once been considered for the **St. Luke Hospital** (East). The budget for land and construction was $2.5 million, including 1,500 parking spots on 33 acres, but the final cost came in at nearly $3 million, with almost 3,000 parking spots. It was this seemingly endless supply of available parking that differentiated the modern shopping center from previous forms of retail. Extensive site work was required because of the large storm tunnel beneath, which carries the waters of the West Fork of Duck Creek. The exposed shaved hill behind the center indicates the volume of earth-moving that was necessary. That hill had to be scraped level for the pad on which the center rests. Adjacent residents still recall the blasting that was needed to carve out the site. Immediately, the Newport Shopping Center was where thousands shopped. It had a JCPenney department store, Kroger and Albers supermarkets, a Walgreens drugstore, a Western Auto, a Richman Brothers men's clothing store, a Woolworth's **five-and-dime store**, a Martin's women's clothing store, an American National Bank, a Hart Hardware, and a Carter's Drive-In Restaurant. Traffic patterns changed as car after car passed through nearby **Cote Brilliante** from Dayton and Bellevue en route to the center via the newly constructed Carothers Rd. In front of the center was a car wash operated by former Campbell Co. sheriff Al Howe, and many youngsters played their first round of miniature golf at the course there. There were amusement rides at the Kissel Brothers' Playland next to Walgreens, and carnivals, square dancing, and other entertainment productions—including for a time Newport's ItalianFest—used the shopping center's parking lot as a venue. In the 1960s a bowling alley, Walt's Center Lanes, was added next to the Western Auto, and later a separate addition of five stores was placed south of the bowling lanes. In late 1966 the center expanded eastward down Carothers Rd., anchored originally by an Ontario's discount store. Today the major tenants of that lower section are Sears Hardware and **Remke Market**.

Shifting demographics have impacted the center. Gone are many of the shopping center's original tenants, including the JCPenney department store. A Bob Evans Restaurant sits where miniature golf was once played. Walgreens has moved to an outer location at the corner of Carothers and Alexandria Pk., away from the end position in the shopping center that it formerly held. In recent years, the remodeling of storefronts has brought new businesses to the center. In 1991 Morris Wakser, the Cleveland developer who inspired the Newport Shopping Center, died. His family continues to own and manage the center under the name of American Diversified Developments Inc.

KP, week of January 30, 1956. Stories and opening-day announcements.

Reis, Jim. "Newport Center Led the Way," *KP*, August 26, 2002, 4K.

——. "Shopping Center a First," *KP*, September 20, 2004, 8K.

Michael R. Sweeney

Square dancing at Newport Shopping Center in the late 1950s in front of JCPenney.

NEWPORT SILK MANUFACTURING COMPANY. This firm, which made all types of superior handkerchiefs and other quality silken goods, began in October 1844 in Newport, as one of the first operations of its kind in the United States. It was started by William B. Jackson and his partner, a man named Brothers. Before October 1846, Jackson had already obtained and subsequently lost a second partner, John Orme. The silk that was manufactured came from silkworms raised at first in Kentucky and later in Ohio around the Marietta area. The raw material was spun and woven at the Newport plant, which paid four dollars per bushel for high-quality silkworm cocoons. A challenge faced by the business was that the supply of raw material was inadequate to keep up with the demand for the product. Handkerchiefs sold for $1.25 each, and silk products were sold as quickly as they were made. In 1852 **Richard Southgate**, who had become involved in the business, accepted a medal at the New York Crystal Palace Exhibition at New York City "for production and general excellence for silk made from cocoons," on behalf of the company. The business was in operation as late as 1889 and continued into the early 1900s under the name Campbell Co. Silk Culture and Manufacturing Company.

Collins, Richard H. *History of Kentucky.* Vol. 1. Covington, Ky.: Collins, 1882.
"History," *KSJ*, April 13, 1889, 1.
"Silk Factory," *LVR*, April 20, 1844, 3.

NEWPORT STEEL. On April 15, 1981, four persons who had been employed in managerial positions at the recently closed Interlake Steel Plant in Newport formed the Newport Steel Corporation. The company's office is located on W. Ninth St. in Newport, and the plant itself is sprawled over 250 acres in both Newport and Wilder, along the Licking River. Included are two welded-pipe mills, a river-barge facility, machine and fabricating shops, and storage and repair facilities, all served by **CSX** rail sidings. The production buildings occupy about 675,000 square feet, and the current staff, including hourly and salaried employees, exceeds 1,100. Newport Steel Corporation is managed and operated by the parent company NS Group Inc., which also owns Koppel Steel in Ambridge, Pa. In 1990 the NS Group was listed on the New York Stock Exchange. Newport Steel manufactures seamless and welded tubular steel products that are used primarily for oil and natural gas drilling by energy companies when they explore for and produce oil or natural gas, both onshore and offshore. The tubing is used to carry oil and natural gas to the surface. Most customers are located in the United States and Canada.

The modern company sits partially on the same site as the Swift Iron and Steel Works, founded in 1867 by Alexander Swift in the **West End** of Newport. The Swift company employed more than 5,000 people, mostly from that side of town, and was the city's largest employer at the time. Swift Iron and Steel Works, with 32 puddling furnaces, manufactured steel rails and plates. E. L. Harper, a pig-iron merchant and a founder of the local Fidelity National Bank, purchased the company in 1880. After a $10 million wheat deal failed, the bank closed, the Swift plant closed, and Harper was sent to prison. In 1887 the Swift company sold its supplies and materials to Henry A. Shriver, who, with his partner, Adam Wagner, organized the Newport Iron and Steel Company. In 1889 John Trapp, Joseph Weingartner, and **Carl Wiedemann** purchased the company and changed its name to the Newport Rolling Mill. Wiedemann died the following year, and the company was sold again to Col. Joseph and A. L. Andrews in 1890. The Andrewses, who also operated an iron roofing and corrugating operation, the Globe Iron Roofing and Corrugating Company locally, purchased the mill to supply steel sheets for their roofing products. In 1905 the **Andrews Steel Mill** was built in Wilder on the grounds of a former horseracing track, to produce ingots that were rolled into sheet bars for the rolling mill. Mule carts loaded by hand were used to haul pig iron and scrap to the furnaces. During **World War I**, the demand for steel increased, and five more open-hearth furnaces were built. The Andrews Steel Company also owned the Hardy Burlington Coal Mine.

The Andrews Steel Company was sold 12 times between the years 1943 and 1981. Herman Schriver bought it for $5 million in 1943; subsequent owners included, among others, the International Detrola Company, a man named Wolfson, and the Acme Steel Company, which purchased it in 1956. In 1964 the Acme Steel Company merged with Interlake Steel and assumed the Interlake name. During contract negotiations in 1980, Interlake closed the Wilder plant. The plant reopened in 1981 under the name of the Newport Steel Corporation. In

Newport Steel, Wilder.

2006 the Canadian firm of IPSCO Inc. purchased the Newport Steel Corporation for about $1.46 billion.

Paeth, Greg. "Steel Maker to Buy NS Group," *KP*, September 12, 2006, 1A.

Jeanne Greiser

***NEWS ENTERPRISE* (LUDLOW).** The *News Enterprise,* originally called the *Ludlow News,* was a newspaper published in Ludlow for about 54 years, beginning December 11, 1936. The editor of the *Ludlow News* had also created the local *Dixie News.* In 1940 the *Ludlow News* merged with the competing *Dixie Enterprise,* and the name was changed to the *News Enterprise.* During **World War II**, one Ludlow resident, Mary Schrage, became well known for sending weekly issues of the *News Enterprise* to soldiers from the local region who were stationed worldwide.

The longtime editor of the *News Enterprise* was **August "Gus" Sheehan** of West Covington, who served many years as a Kentucky state senator representing Bromley, Covington, Ludlow, and Villa Hills. When first published, the paper covered other areas as far south as Florence, Ky., in addition to Ludlow. However, early on the *News Enterprise* began concentrating on Ludlow and its surrounding area. Sheehan wrote a weekly column called *Editor's Corner.* Local news was covered, and regular features included sections for letters to the editor and births, as well as two regular columns: *Agree or Not,* by S. C. Van Curon, and *Looking Ahead,* by Dr. George S. Benson, president of the National Education Program. The paper, published in a building on Elm St. in downtown Ludlow, found a dependable supply of advertisers for each issue. Sheehan sold the *News Enterprise* in 1988 to Steppingstone Publications, which issued its first edition on June 22, 1988. In 1991 Steppingstone Publications was purchased by the **Recorder Newspapers**, and the *News Enterprise* ceased operation.

"'Legend' Gus Sheehan Dies—Veteran Legislator, Lawyer, and Publisher," *KE*, October 31, 2000, B1B.

"News Enterprise," *Ludlow News Enterprise,* April 25, 1957, 2.

"The Old and the New," *Ludlow News Enterprise,* November 4, 1965, 7.

"Suburban Recorder Papers Bought," *KP,* January 9, 1991, 8K.

Robert Schrage

NEWSPAPERS IN NORTHERN KENTUCKY. In pioneer days, newspapers were the only mass medium. They were read, reread, and passed from hand to hand so often that they fell into tatters. Many were lost to history, but they were essential for a young country to form its republican culture. John Nerone, in *The Culture of the Press in the Early Republic: Cincinnati, 1793–1848,* quoted an editor's boast in the June 23, 1818, *Cincinnati Inquisitor* and *Cincinnati Advertiser:* "The superiority which newspapers seem to possess over other methods of diffusing political or practical knowledge among the people, has occasioned an extraordinary multiplication of them in this country over the last 25 years. From their uncommon cheapness, their pages are made accessible to every individual, however humble and indigent: Thousands of worthy freemen are consequently instructed and benefited by this means, who would otherwise be doomed to a life of perpetual ignorance."

The newspaper business in Northern Kentucky typified that of the entire country—newspapers sprouted, struggled, merged, and often folded. A list of "all newspapers ever published," compiled in 1994 for the Kentucky Press Association by University of Kentucky librarians, listed 166 newspapers in the 11 counties of Northern Kentucky. The list may include duplicates, since some newspapers changed names, and it certainly omits some: for example, absent from the list are at least five German-language newspapers that, according to *Kentucky Post* reporter Jim Reis, were published in Covington and Newport in the 1800s. Today, with the mass media everywhere, readers have turned away from newspapers to watch television, listen to the radio, or surf the Internet, and newspapers are shrinking or failing. Fewer than two dozen newspapers circulated in Northern Kentucky in 2006. The *Sunday Challenger,* a weekly based in Covington, ran only 19 months, publishing its last edition in February 2006.

The first newspaper in Kentucky was the *Kentucke Gazette,* published in Lexington in 1787, before Kentucky was a state. The earliest newspaper in Northern Kentucky and the third in the state, the *Mirror,* began in 1797 in Washington, a city later annexed by Maysville that was important because of its location on the Maysville Rd., a key thoroughfare for pioneers. Images of some ragged 18th-century editions of the *Mirror* are preserved on microfilm at the University of Kentucky, the pages reflecting early Kentucky life. There was slavery: in the *Mirror* of June 28, 1799, a slaveholder offered $6 to anyone who returned "a Negro man named Billy, about five feet eight inches high, twenty-six years of age, of a pleasing countenance." There were also American Indians: "Several reports have been in circulation respecting hostilities on the part of the Indians, which have occasioned some degree of alarm among the frontier settlers," the editor wrote on May 31, 1799.

Like other newspapers of the time, the *Mirror* printed much news copied from other papers, some of it from abroad and some of it weeks old. It did not matter to readers; historians believe that isolated, early settlers in small towns already knew the local news and were eager to learn of happenings elsewhere. What local news there was often took the form of advertisements; in Maysville it was common to see ads offering huge parcels of land for sale. One notice in the *Mirror,* for example, advertised 7,000 acres in Pendleton Co., noting that the owner would take "Negros, horses or produce in payment." It also declared the property's title to be "indisputable," an important point at a time when competing claims for property regularly led to litigation.

The earliest newspapers also filled their pages with verbatim laws, speeches, minutes, and government reports; "official" newspapers were awarded government contracts for this purpose. They often were owned by a lone printer-editor-publisher who reprinted news from steamship captains, other newspapers, and government documents. Reporters did not exist yet. In Cincinnati, newspaper articles by reporters began to appear after about 1815, but by the 1840s, Cincinnati papers routinely employed reporters. South of the Ohio River the same trend likely was seen, and it meant newspapers had begun to take their modern form. Unlike modern papers, however, newspapers of the mid-19th century still printed fiction, poetry, and letters from people using assumed names, and newspapers proudly allied themselves with a political party. Some printed pointed and personal attacks about rivals. In fact, Kentucky editors were not infrequently challenged to duels; many editors in the early days of Kentucky journalism carried arms.

By 1824 the United States had 598 newspapers, and Kentucky had 18. Soon the numbers exploded, as the invention of steam-powered presses in 1830s sped news into print. A hand press could make about 250 newspapers an hour, but a steam press could make more than 1,000. In the late 1840s, newspapers became linked by telegraph, with almost instantaneous transmission of highly condensed news—and much more of it than was previously available. Because telegraphed news was expensive, papers would proudly note in their headlines when news came "By Telegraph."

By the middle of the 19th century, even small towns in Kentucky had three or four newspapers competing for news and advertisements. Some of them had begun printing more than once a week, even daily in some cases. In a speech to historians on August 11, 1887, William Henry Perrin noted that the first daily in Kentucky (and in the entire West), the *Public Advertiser,* edited by Scott Co. native Shadrach Penn, was printed April 4, 1826, in Louisville. Records are scanty, but the first daily in Northern Kentucky may have been the *Covington Daily,* which lasted only 16 days in 1844. Others soon followed. The abolitionist movement's *Register* spawned a controversial daily on March 7, 1850: the *Newport and Covington Daily News.* That paper's office was burned to the ground October 10, 1851, almost killing its feisty editor, **William S. Bailey**, and his family, who lived in the building. Bailey later started another paper, named the *Free South,* but a mob threw its printing press in the Ohio River in 1858.

By the late 1800s, Cincinnati's current dailies, the *Enquirer* and the *Post,* which later grew to dominance, had added Northern Kentucky editions. James E. Scripps bought the Cincinnati *Penny Paper,* and his brother Edward W. Scripps took over the paper and renamed it the *Cincinnati Post* in 1881. He set up an office in Covington to put out the Kentucky edition of the paper on Sep-

NEWSPAPERS IN NORTHERN KENTUCKY

Newspaper	*Owner*
Dailies	
Kentucky Enquirer	Gannett Inc., McLean, Va.
Kentucky Post	E. W. Scripps Inc., Cincinnati
Maysville Ledger Independent	Lee Enterprises Inc., Davenport, Iowa
Weeklies	
Bracken County News	Bay Publishing
Carrollton News-Democrat *Grant County News* *Grant County Express* *Owenton News-Herald*	Landmark Community Newspapers, Shelbyville, Ky.
Falmouth Outlook	Delphos Herald Inc., Delphos, Ohio
Gallatin County News	Denny Warnick
Community Press/Community Recorder Newspapers *Alexandria Recorder* *Boone County Recorder* *Boone Community Recorder* *Campbell Community Recorder* *Campbell County Recorder* *Community Recorder* *Erlanger Recorder* *Florence Recorder* *Fort Thomas Recorder* *Kenton Community Recorder*	Gannett Inc., McLean, Va.

tember 15, 1890. In 1891, what was then named the *Kentucky Post* was delivered to Northern Kentucky homes wrapped around the *Cincinnati Post.* In Northern Kentucky and elsewhere, however, weeklies outnumbered dailies. In 1872 more than 70 of Kentucky's 90 newspapers were weeklies. The Kentucky legislature once considered paying for this kind of paper, a weekly "country paper," for every family, to combat illiteracy in the state.

While Northern Kentucky has a long tradition of community newspapering, it has had little hard-hitting, investigative reporting. In the 1930s and for decades afterward, Newport possessed a "Sin City" reputation for its open gambling and prostitution abetted by organized crime. Stories about the crackdown that forced out the mob were followed doggedly by Hank Messick of the *Louisville Courier Journal* in the 1960s. In an interview by two Northern Kentucky University professors on July 14, 1979, Messick blamed the local press for allowing the situation to continue, saying, "If those Cincinnati papers had done their job, then they would never have had Newport." Later, when the **Beverly Hills Supper Club** in Southgate burned, killing 167, the Pulitzer Prize in 1978 went to the *Courier-Journal* for coverage of both the fire and the lax enforcement of state fire codes. Gary Webb was perhaps Northern Kentucky's best-known investigative reporter in the 1970s and early 1980s, but the stories that earned him fame were written after he left the *Kentucky Post* for the *San Jose Mercury News* in San Jose, Calif.

In the latter part of the 20th century, newspapers began to suffer, as readers abandoned them for other media. "The number of daily newspapers declined an average of one per month in about the last 70 years of the [20th] century," noted the *History of the Mass Media in the United States: An Encyclopedia.* The Internet, the newest mass medium, peeled more readers away from newspapers. New technology caused layoffs: when the computer entered newsrooms in the 1970s, reporters and editors began to take on work formerly done by printers. Corporate owners, emphasizing profit, cut staffing. The *Cincinnati/Kentucky Post*'s 188,000 circulation in 1997 fell to about 42,000 by 2004; it reduced staff four times between 2000 and 2006 and stopped publishing altogether on December 31, 2007. Nevertheless, the *Kentucky Enquirer*'s editor wrote in August 2006 that his newspaper had added 2,000 subscribers in two years. The paper launched www.nky.com in November 2005, where it also published news from the *Post* and from WCPO television.

Prominent reporters and editors made their homes in Northern Kentucky. These included Latonia-born **Robert S. Allen**, who, with Drew Pearson, wrote the Washington, D.C., column *Washington Merry-Go Round;* **Clay Wade Bailey**, the "dean of Kentucky journalists" who covered state government for the *Kentucky Post* and for whom an Ohio River bridge is named; **William R. Burleigh**, a former editor of the *Cincinnati Post* and the ***Kentucky Post*** and chairman of the board of the E. W. Scripps Company, who retired to a Boone Co. farm; **Judy Clabes**, a former editor of the *Kentucky Post* and president and CEO of the Scripps Howard Foundation, and her husband, Gene Clabes, now a journalism professor and formerly a publisher of the Community Recorder Newspapers; **Nick Clooney** of Maysville, a print and television journalist for more than 50 years; **Martha Purdon Comer**, a reporter, columnist, and editor of the *Maysville Daily Independent* and the *Ledger Independent*; **Ollie M. James**, a popular columnist and the chief editorial writer for the *Cincinnati Enquirer*; and **Vance H. Trimble**, a Pulitzer-Prize-winning reporter and a demanding former editor of the *Kentucky Post.*

Best, Edna Hunter. *Historic Washington Kentucky.* 1st ed., 1944. Reprint, Maysville, Ky.: Limestone Chapter of the DAR, 1971.

Blanchard, Margaret A., ed. *History of the Mass Media in the United States: An Encyclopedia.* London: Fitzroy Dearborn, 1998.

CJ, August 7, 1875, 3.

Clark, Thomas D. *A History of Kentucky.* Lexington, Ky.: John Bradford Press, 1960.

———. *The Rural Press and the New South.* Baton Rouge: Louisiana State Univ. Press, 1948.

Evans, Herndon J. *The Newspaper Press in Kentucky.* Lexington: Univ. of Kentucky Press, 1976.

"Gary Webb, 49, Former Reporter for the Post," *KP,* December 13, A10.

Hetzel, Dennis. "A Letter to Our Readers," *KE,* August 27, 2006, 1B.

"Lands for Sale in the State of Kentucky," *Mirror,* May 31, 1799, 3.

Messick, Hank. Interview by Lew Wallace and Frank Steely, July 14, 1979, Archives, Northern Kentucky Univ., Highland Heights, Ky.

Nerone, John. *The Culture of the Press in the Early Republic: Cincinnati, 1793–1848.* New York: Garland, 1989.

Reis, Jim. "Campbell's Largest City Named for British Explorer." In *Pieces of the Past,* by Jim Reis, vol. 1. Covington, Ky.: Kentucky Post, 1988.

———. "A Host of Papers Deliver News to Northern Kentucky." In *Pieces of the Past,* by Jim Reis, vol. 1. Covington, Ky.: Kentucky Post, 1988.

Share, Allen J. *Cities in the Commonwealth: Two Centuries of Urban Life in Kentucky.* Lexington: Univ. of Kentucky Press, 1944.

"Six Dollars Reward," *Mirror,* June 28, 1799, 3.

"Southgate Accused of Fraud," *Yankee Doodle Extra,* June 17, 1840, 4.

Towles, Donald B. *The Press of Kentucky, 1787–1994.* Frankfort: Kentucky Press Association, 1994.

Trimble, Vance H. *The Astonishing Mr. Scripps: The Turbulent Life of America's Penny Press Lord.* Ames: Iowa State Univ. Press, 1992.

Venable, W. H. *Beginnings of Literary Culture in the Ohio Valley: Historical and Biographical Sketches.* 1891. Available at Kentuckiana Digital Library. http://kdl.kyvl.org/.

"Washington, May 31," *Mirror,* May 31, 1799, 3.

Mary Carmen Cupito

NICHOLSON. Regardless of what the "Nicholson City Limit" welcome signs imply, Nicholson, Ky., is not an actual city. It is an unincorporated community located in south-central Kenton Co. at the crossroads of Taylor Mill Rd. (Ky. St. Rt. 16) and Madison Pk. (Ky. St. Rt. 17). According to tradition, Nicholson owes its name to Maysville, Ky., native Dr. **Henry C. Nicholson**, a distinguished inventor and electrician who lived in the vicinity. In 1879 Henry Nicholson lost a patent dispute with Thomas A. Edison over the quadruplex telegraph, an innovation that enabled the sending of multiple simultaneous messages over a single telegraph line. Until the late 1800s, the Nicholson area was called California. The name change to Nicholson likely occurred to avoid confusion with California, Ky., in eastern Campbell Co. Nicholson was a rural farm community well into the 20th century.

Since **World War II**, however, suburbanization has crept into the area. The number of farms in Nicholson has decreased, replaced by a few subdivisions and several modern single-family homes set on large lots. Its relative isolation from Kenton Co.'s expanding cities has protected Nicholson from the annexation boom that has beset central Kenton Co. since the 1960s. Nicholson retains a rural ambiance; however, the pace of change is increasing. The planned reconstruction of Ky. St, Routes 16, 17, and 536 should spur more development in the area.

"Aged Inventor Dead," *KP*, May 1, 1896, 8.

An Atlas of Boone, Kenton and Campbell Counties, Kentucky. Philadelphia: D. J. Lake, 1883.

"Library Sites Considered," *CE*, March 30, 2004, 3C.

"Nicholson vs. Edison—Quadruplex Telegraphing," *Chicago Daily Tribune*, May 5, 1879, 3.

Reis, Jim. "What's In a Name?" *KP*, June 5, 1995, 4K.

Greg Perkins

NICHOLSON, HENRY C. (b. June 18, 1824, Maysville, Ky.; d. May 1, 1896, Nicholson, Ky.). A Civil War surgeon, a local physician, and an inventor, Henry Clay Nicholson, MD, was the son of Thomas and Annah Boon Nicholson and the grandson of **Jacob Boone**. He married Mary Askren, with whom he had eight children, including the prominent Boone Co. builder George Pendleton Nicholson. Although Henry Nicholson was born and died in Kentucky, he spent most of his adult life in Mount Washington, Ohio, on the east side of Cincinnati, where he practiced medicine and spent his spare time working on changes and improvements in electric telegraphy. Frequently described as an eccentric, Nicholson co-invented several types of hermetically sealed fruit and biological specimen jars. His most important invention, however, was the quadruplex telegraph, a major step forward in the field of electric telegraphy. Using the principles of positive and negative electric polarity, Nicholson devised a type of telegraph that could send two messages over a single wire at the same time. Previously only one message could be sent at a time. Almost simultaneously, renowned inventor Thomas Edison was working on a similar device that he had patented, and a long, bitter dispute ensued in the U.S. Patent Office about who had come up with the idea first. Because Nicholson had invented a new telegraphic alphabet (which never came into use) before inventing the quadruplex, with which it was to be used, Nicholson was finally, about 1885, given credit for the invention. Physically, mentally, and financially eroded by the years-long patent dispute with the far more influential Edison, Nicholson was forced to sell his home in Ohio and relocate to Kentucky before the dispute was settled. He died at his home in Nicholson, southern Kenton Co., in 1896 and was buried in the Independence Cemetery in Independence. The town of Nicholson, where he died, reportedly was named for him.

"Aged Inventor Dead," *KP*, May 1, 1896, 8.

The Edison Papers. http://edison.rutgers.edu/ (accessed December 31, 2005).

Nicholson, James B. *Nicholson, Bruner and Getz Family History.* Philadelphia, 1930.

"What's in a Name?" *KP*, June 5, 1995, 4K.

Amber L. Benson

NIGHT RIDERS. The Night Rider movement began in Northern Kentucky around 1904 as a result of a tobacco trust, or monopoly, which paid tobacco farmers less and less for their crops. Because there were virtually no other buyers, "the Trust," led by James B. Duke (later of Duke University and Duke Power fame), reached a point where it was paying farmers less for their crop than their costs to grow it.

As the number of farmers rebelling against the trust increased, they united in forming the American Society of Equity, or ASE. The ASE urged farmers either not to raise tobacco or, if they raised it, not to sell it. There was a small crop in 1907, but in 1908 there was virtually no burley tobacco raised. "Do not raise tobacco, but raise H__l with the tobacco trust," urged the *Carrollton News*, as quoted in the *Falmouth Outlook*. Neighbors were strongly encouraged to join the movement. Rallies in various communities drew large crowds to support the ASE. Augusta had a parade of 5,000 men supporting the cause in 1908. Social pressures to join were enormous, and masked men riding in the night, while not endorsed by the official organization, enforced compliance by vandalism, arson, murder, and other violence. The Night Riders, the lawbreaking element of the organization, were officially disavowed.

Plant beds were scraped, salted, or sown with clover by the Night Riders. Empty graves were dug as threats. Barns and tobacco warehouses were burned in at least Augusta, Brooksville, Carrollton, Covington, Germantown, Maysville, Owenton, Sanders, and Walton. The election of Augustus Willson as governor of Kentucky (1907–1911) and his use of National Guard troops, along with a U.S. Supreme Court decision against Night Rider activities, finally put an end to the Night Riders.

"A.S. of E. Rally at Fair Grounds," *Falmouth Outlook*, July 7, 1907, 1.

Cunningham, Bill. *On Bended Knees: The Night Rider Story.* Nashville, Tenn.: McClanahan, 1983.

"Masked Riders Destroy Trust Tobacco Barn," *KP*, September 27, 1907, 1.

Nall, James O. *The Tobacco Night Riders of Kentucky and Tennessee.* Kuttawa, Ky.: McClanahan, 1991.

"Night Riders Burn Covington Warehouse," *KP*, March 26, 1908, 1.

"Nocturnal Visitors," *Maysville Bulletin*, March 26, 1908, 1.

"No 1908 Crop," *Falmouth Outlook*, April 10, 1908, 4.

Warsaw Independent, May 11, 1907, 3.

Bernie Spencer

NINTH ST. METHODIST EPISCOPAL CHURCH. The Ninth St. Methodist Episcopal (M.E.) Church of Covington, established in the early 1800s, originally met in a small building at Second and Scott Sts. Several church members began to sponsor weekly prayer meetings and worship sessions in hopes of inspiring the local African American community to continue to resist racial segregation and daily discrimination. These objectives were pursued more intensively during the 1870s and early 1880s, when the congregation, under the successive direction of Rev. G. S. Griffin, Rev. James Courtney, and Rev. G. W. Giegler, formed a coherent mission statement and developed an outstanding outreach program that sought to make the facility a shining "light in the community."

During the late 1880s, as the African American population of Covington increased, the church membership also increased greatly. As a result, in 1889, the church moved to 18 E. Ninth St. This property was provided by the Board of Church Extension of the Methodist Church, and funds to construct a new building were obtained through an enormous membership drive campaign and a generous donation by **Amos Shinkle**, a prominent local businessman. The church was designed by noted regional architect James W. McLaughlin.

From the late 1880s to the 1920s, the membership of the Ninth St. M.E. Church continued to grow dramatically because of the vision and activities of several dynamic church leaders during this period, such as Rev. C. E. Ball, Rev. R. F. Broaddus, Rev. W. H. Evans, Rev. John W. Robinson, and Rev. J. H. Ross. These pastors encouraged the church to organize events such as annual revival meetings, weekly family-oriented entertainment programs, and weekend social activities for the youth. Various community leaders and civil rights organizations, galvanizing the local black community over the issues of political oppression and racial violence, also used the facility. For instance, in 1922, a vocal rally and endorsement meeting for the passage of a national "anti-lynching" bill was held at the church.

From the 1930s to the 1980s, the church membership continued its community-based agenda by sponsoring numerous local and church events like the regional Women's Society of Christian Service conference in 1931, a daylong dedication service celebrating acquisition of the church's new pipe organ in 1954, a powerful prayer service led by Bishop Frank Robinson in 1978, and several community activities throughout the 1980s. In

2006 the church closed, the victim of a dwindling congregation.

"Anti-Lynching Bill Indorsed," *KTS*, September 30, 1922, 14.
"The Church Record of the 9th Street Methodist Episcopal Church, 1887–1901," Northern Kentucky African American Heritage Task Force Collection, box 1, folder 13, W. Frank Steely Library, Northern Kentucky Univ.
"The City," *DC*, October 3, 1881, 1; February 14, 1882, 2; July 11, 1883, 4.
"Local News," *DC*, July 9, 1884, 4.
"Ninth Street Methodist Episcopal," vertical files, Kenton Co. Public Library, Covington, Ky.
Reis, Jim. "Four Churches That Made a Difference," *KP*, January 20, 1997, 4K.
——. "Knights of Pythias Born in 1864," *KP*, October 24, 1994, 4K.
——."When History Is Overlooked," *KP*, February 8, 1999, 4K.
"Religious," *DC*, October 29, 1881, 1; February 6, 1882, 2.

Eric R. Jackson

NINTH ST. UNITED METHODIST CHURCH. In the summer of 1894, a nondenominational group of Christians decided to form a church in Newport and began to worship there on W. 10th St., between Isabella and Patterson Sts. On August 20 of the same year, about 60 people chartered a church and began to hold services as the Bethel Church of the United Brethren in Christ. In early 1895 the congregation relocated to a frame building at Ninth and Ann Sts. in Newport, where the worship services were held on the first floor and the pastor lived on the second floor. The congregation was known as Bethel Mission. In November 1901, the church dedicated a new building at the same site and changed its name to the Ninth St. United Brethren Church. In July 1927 the trustees purchased the property to the rear of the church to provide space for a better program of Christian education.

In November 1946, when the Church of the United Brethren in Christ and the Evangelical Church merged to become the Evangelical United Brethren Church, the church in Newport became known as the Ninth St. Evangelical United Brethren Church. In 1968, as a result of the national merger of the Methodist Church with the Evangelical United Brethren Church, the church became part of the United Methodist Church and its name changed to the Ninth St. United Methodist Church. The Ninth St. United Methodist Church had the distinction of being the only former Evangelical United Brethren Church in the Kentucky Conference of the United Methodist Church. By 1970 the church on Ninth St. had closed.

"Church Dedication," *KP*, November 23, 1901, 5.

Donald E. Grosenbach

NOMADS. Nomads, the oldest women's club in Maysville, celebrated its 100th birthday in 1995. The organization continues to pursue the study of literature today, as it has done since its founding, selecting literary works to review that reflect the diverse tastes of its members—travel, drama, classics, biography, best sellers, and pop literature.

The first meeting of Nomads was held in the spring of 1895 at the instigation of Miss Emma Campbell, who had several times been a guest at a literary club in Walnut Hills, a suburb of Cincinnati. With the help of four friends, she established the Maysville organization. They chose the name Nomads not only to honor the Cincinnati group so named but also to remind themselves that they too were wanderers on land and on sea through the pages of literature.

What makes the founding of this organization so significant for Maysville is that it was the first women's club in the region whose focus was not on a church or a school. Nomads thus serves as a reminder of the efforts of 19th-century women to achieve their own identity, to acquire knowledge, and to elevate personal ideals through women's clubs.

Although early records are sketchy, the club's constitution and annual program books provide insight into Nomads history. In the organization's first constitution, membership was limited to 25 women, who would join by invitation only; dues were one dollar per year. Meetings were usually scheduled for evenings or at various times on Sundays. The format of meetings in the early years reveals that topics were studied in depth. A chairman provided a list of questions to be discussed and answered by various members. At present-day luncheon meetings, members review books of their choice.

Membership through the years has included some outstanding women, but of special note are three members from the 1930s: Mrs. Francis Goggin Maltby, a short-story writer whose biography of O. Henry's wife, *The Dimity Sweetheart,* won her special recognition at an O. Henry memorial dinner in New York City; Mrs. **Eleanor Duncan Wood**, whose poem "In Memorium" won the prize in a memorial poem contest in which only Kentucky poets were entered; and **Elizabeth Pickett Chevalier**, a writer whose motion picture screenplay *Red Skin* was much acclaimed, as was her novel about Mason Co., *Drivin' Woman.*

Since 1895 a host of Maysville and Mason Co. Nomads have been reading, sharing ideas about what they read, and enjoying the resulting mental stimulation. Unfortunately, the lifestyle of today's woman has changed—many have both families and careers and find that little time remains for a good book. The goal of the organization, however, is still "to promote intellectual growth," which hopefully will propel it through a second century.

Nomads archives, Museum Center, Maysville, Ky.

Sue Ellen Grannis

NORFOLK SOUTHERN RAILWAY. In 1982 the Norfolk Southern Corporation, a newly formed holding corporation, acquired both the **Southern Railway** (SR) and the Norfolk and Western Railroad (N&W), and the two railroads became the Norfolk Southern Railway (NS). The SR controlled the Cincinnati, New Orleans and Texas Pacific Railroad, operator of the **Cincinnati Southern Railroad**. The N&W served the Cincinnati area by a line from Huntington, W.Va., through Portsmouth, Ohio, and westward across southern Ohio. That N&W rail bed was abandoned in 2003. In 1997, after a bitter fight with **CSX** over control of **Conrail**, the NS acquired 60 percent of Conrail and CSX purchased the remaining 40 percent. Conrail operated the former New York Central Railroad and the Pennsylvania Railroad lines through Cincinnati. Both of these lines became part of the NS. The NS major rail yard in Cincinnati is the Gest Street Yard. Both NS yards in Northern Kentucky, at Erlanger and at Ludlow, are subordinate to the Gest Street Yard. The NS is based in Norfolk, Va.

Day, Michele. "Riding the Rails," *KP*, March 23, 1985, 6K–7K.
Drury, George H. *The Train Watcher's Guide to North American Railroads.* Waukesha, Wis.: Kalmbach Books, 1992.
The Historical Guide to North American Railroads. 2nd ed. Waukesha, Wis.: Kalmbach Books, 2000.
NS Corporation. Norfolk Southern Corporation Annual Reports, 1990 to 2004, NS Corp., Norfolk, Va.

Charles H. Bogart

NORMANSVILLE. The small village of Normansville was just a few miles west of Beaverlick and north of Hamilton in western Boone Co. In the 1850s, John C. Miller's general store there stocked a wide range of items: farm implements, groceries and produce, hardware, and notions. The store shipped hogs and tobacco to Cincinnati via the Ohio River from the nearby Hamilton Landing. The Conner Carroll family later bought the store and used it for their trucking and hauling business. The building has since been converted into a private residence. In 1867 James W. Kennedy moved from Gallatin Co. to operate a general store and flourmill at Normansville. The flourmill was powered by a natural gas well (rare in Boone Co.) at the triangle of Ryle Rd. and Ky. Rt. 338. In 1921 the mill was dismantled. After moving to Union, Kennedy served as a Democratic state representative. Another store in Normansville sold patent medicines and tinware. From the early 1940s to the mid-1960s, Everett Jones operated this store, which included a barbershop. A blacksmith shop that once operated in the village is now a small barn at the corner of Big Bone Church Rd. and Ky. Rt. 338. The long-standing tollgate house on the Ryle Rd. side of the bridge burned down in the 1980s. Today, the village known as Normansville is gone; its most vivid lingering memories are from pictures in old photo albums.

An Atlas of Boone, Kenton, and Campbell Counties, Kentucky. Philadelphia: D. J. Lake, 1883.
Warner, Jennifer S. *Boone County: From Mastodons to the Millennium.* Burlington, Ky.: Boone Co. Bicentennial Book Committee, 1998.

Nancy J. Tretter

NORTHERN BANK OF KENTUCKY. In 1837 a building committee began receiving bids for construction of a bank building at Third and Scott Sts. in Covington to house the new Northern Bank of Kentucky. The bank originally had two floors, but during the 1890s a third floor was added. The impressive Greek Revival style building, which today is located in the same block as a new Kenton Co. courthouse and a parking garage, might have been torn down had not preservationists lobbied in 1999 for its adaptive reuse. The **Bank of Kentucky (modern)** (no relation to 19th-century banks of the same or similar name) paid the Kenton Co. Fiscal Court $550,000 for the old building—said to be the oldest commercial building in the city—and spent more than $3 million remodeling it. By April 2000 the Bank of Kentucky and another firm occupied the historic building.

After the War of 1812, economic panics and depressions stirred controversies concerning the nation's banking policies. People in the states west of the Allegheny Mountains, including a majority in Kentucky and Tennessee, generally supported politicians who wanted to decentralize the national banking system and institute more liberal monetary policies. After vetoing a bill renewing the charter of the Bank of the United States, President Andrew Jackson, a Tennessean who disliked the fiscal conservatism of the Bank of the United States and supported replacing it with state banks, was reelected president in 1832. Soon thereafter, in 1834, the Kentucky legislature chartered the Louisville Bank of Kentucky with six branches. In February 1835 the legislature chartered the Northern Bank of Kentucky with $3 million capital and located branches in Richmond, Paris, Louisville, and Covington. The Covington branch started with **Richard Southgate** as president, Philip S. Bush as cashier, and directors John B. Casey, James M. Clarkson, Carey Clemons, John T. Levis, George B. Marshall, **John W. Tibbatts**, Erastus Tousey, and William. W. Wade.

The Northern Bank of Kentucky played an integral role in the growth and development of Covington in the years leading up to the **Civil War**. A number of the city's most prominent businesses and their families were either customers or served on the bank's board of directors. In particular, two members of the prominent Ernst family of Covington, **William Ernst** and his son John P. Ernst, held a series of positions at the bank, including bank president. John Ernst's son **Richard Pretlow Ernst** later became a Republican U.S. senator (1921–1927). The Northern Bank of Kentucky began to fade with the relocation of Covington's commercial center toward Pike St. Several new banks, financed by some of Covington's wealthiest families, contributed to the Northern Bank of Kentucky's decline. The branch in Covington vacated its building in 1896 and the entire bank closed in 1897. Later, the bank's classic old building was used by a distillery; it also served over the years as a factory and as a warehouse. As time passed, the building assumed the name of a later occupant and became known as the Mosler Lock and Safe Company building.

Boh, John. "Northern Kentucky's Bush Family," *Bulletin of the Kenton County Historical Society*, November 2002, 1–3.

Kleber, John E., ed. *The Kentucky Encyclopedia*. Lexington: Univ. Press of Kentucky, 1992.

Kreimer, Peggy. "Saving the Mosler Building, Young Bank Resurrecting Oldest Bank," *KP*, June 26, 1999, 1K.

John Boh

NORTHERN KENTUCKY AFRICAN-AMERICAN HERITAGE TASK FORCE. On June 23, 1992, the Kentucky Heritage Commission started a campaign that included more than 60 individuals from across the state, to organize the Kentucky African-American Heritage Task Force (KAAHTF). Two years later, in 1994, Governor Brereton Jones (1991–1995) disbanded the task force but replaced it with the Kentucky African-American Heritage Commission (KAAHC), under the direction of the Education, Arts, and Humanities Cabinet. Based upon the pathbreaking work of KAAHTF, the commission subsequently established several regional groups to uncover, document, and preserve the history of African American Kentuckians. Established in 1995 by numerous individuals, such as Bennie Butler, Susan Cabot, Rhonda Culver, Theodore "Ted" Harris, Leslie Henderson, Robert Ingguls, Hensley Jemmott, Basil Lewis, Mary Northington, Jim Reis, Larry Wright, and Martha Wright, the Northern Kentucky African-American Heritage Task Force (NKAAHTF) is an outgrowth of this effort. The goals of NKAAHTF mirror those of the KAAHTF in its quest to educate, preserve, promote, and document the important role African American Kentuckians played in the inception and development of the 13 most northern counties of the state: Boone, Bracken, Campbell, Carroll, Fleming, Gallatin, Kenton, Lewis, Mason, Owen, Pendleton, and Robertson. At its inception, NKAAHTF had about 50 members. Over the years, the membership has fluctuated between 100 and 300.

The NKAAHTF has been involved with annual African American church celebrations, has participated in numerous local History Day events, has established connections to Northern Kentucky African American cemetery documentation projects, and has contributed to yearly historical conferences throughout Kentucky. At times, personnel changes, financial problems, irregular meeting schedules, and the lack of a comprehensive recruitment plan have plagued the organization, but despite these obstacles, the NKAAHTF continues to have a major impact on black American life in Northern Kentucky. For example, in 2003 the organization became involved in a successful campaign to preserve the **Rosella Porterfield** Park in Elsmere. In 2005 the NKAAHTF participated in the documentation and preservation of the Julius Rosenwald "Colored" School of Dry Ridge. Today, the NKAAHTF remains in the forefront in providing assistance to individuals, organizations, and communities in the region whose goal is to identify and promote the significant role black Kentuckians have played in the history and culture of Northern Kentucky.

Northern Kentucky African American Heritage Task Force Newsletters, Kenton Co. Public Library, Covington, Ky.

Whitehead, Shelly. "Black Graveyards at Risk," *KP*, February 13, 2001, 1K.

Eric R. Jackson

NORTHERN KENTUCKY AREA DEVELOPMENT DISTRICT. The Northern Kentucky Area Development District (NKADD) is one of 15 districts created by the Kentucky General Assembly and signed into law by Governor Wendell Ford (1971–1974). This network of regional development districts strives to bring community leaders together to solve common problems. The development district serves as a community and economic development tool and as a means for local officials to speak to the state and federal government in a unified manner. NKADD was organized and held its first board meeting in September 1971; its first executive director was Gordon Mullins. The annual budget was $60,000. As a result of its creation, local leaders from across Northern Kentucky came together for the first time in a spirit of cooperation that set the stage for many of the regional and cooperative approaches to problem-solving that have defined the region. The NKADD serves an area that takes in the counties of Boone, Campbell, Carroll, Gallatin, Grant, Kenton, Owen, and Pendleton.

NKADD services are varied. Its community development services include assistance in any effort to upgrade or expand community facilities and to create or retain jobs in the region's economic structure. NKADD may either support an economic development project entirely or assist a local government in implementing a project. Areas of activity include economic, industrial, and commercial development as well as programs in the areas of recreation, water and sewer, transportation, land use planning, and historic preservation. Assistance with grants administration and acquisition for local communities has brought millions of dollars into the region through various funding sources.

The district's public administration services involve management consulting to the district's clients in areas such as public administration, human resource management, risk management, finance, special studies, governance, and other areas necessary to improve the efficiency and effectiveness of the local governments and nonprofit organizations in the region. Specific examples of work include

—assistance in writing personnel policies;

—consulting on laws affecting the employer-employee relationship, personnel evaluation, pay issues, executive search, and hiring and firing;

—budget preparation assistance;

—tax rate assistance;

—revenue generation assistance;

—federal and state regulatory compliance; and

—special studies and feasibility analysis such as merger studies or service delivery.

The district also administers a revolving loan program for the establishment or expansion of small businesses and develops regional approaches to problems or issues such as the Northern Kentucky Regional Ethics Authority and the Northern Kentucky Drug and Alcohol Testing Consortium.

NKADD administers human service programs including those affecting senior citizens, caregivers, children, the disabled, and the homeless and furnishes oversight planning and implementation of such programs. Through its case management efforts, NKADD also provides services to individuals age 60 and over who require long-term care. NKADD serves as the Area Agency on Aging for Northern Kentucky. Federal food commodity programs, too, are handled by NKADD.

NKADD has the primary responsibility for planning and administration of job training and workforce development programs in Northern Kentucky. Many of these programs are funded through federal workforce development programs. The district has worked with a number of agencies in developing a stronger workforce in the region. NKADD has led efforts to help bring the One Stop Career Center System to Northern Kentucky. NKADD is the federally designated state workforce investment area for the region. Its offices are located in Boone Co., and the Board of Directors is composed of the county judges or executives, other elected officials, and citizen members.

Robert Schrage

NORTHERN KENTUCKY AREA PLANNING COMMISSION. In the 1960s the Kentucky legislature passed enabling legislation allowing for the creation of Area Planning Commissions. The legislation provided for creation of an Area Planning Commission and an Area Planning Council, where statutory conditions were met; it set up the council with oversight authority, including approval of the commission's annual budget; it provided the commission with a mandate to craft and adopt an Area-Wide Comprehensive Plan for its jurisdiction; it left the commission with final decision-making authority over all land-use changes (modified in the 1970s, to limit such decision-making authority to all items of "area-wide significance"); and it provided the commission with taxing authority. The Kenton and Campbell Co. fiscal courts and the city commission of Covington signed legal agreements creating the Northern Kentucky Area Planning Commission (NKAPC) and its Planning Council, which came into official existence in May 1961.

The Area Planning Commission comprised nine members, five from Kenton Co. and four from Campbell Co. The Planning Council comprised one representative from each fiscal court and each city. The commission contracted with legal counsel, hired an executive director and additional staff to provide professional planning-related services to all local governments, and began development of an areawide comprehensive plan as required by state law.

During the subsequent decade, 1960 through 1969, the Ohio-Kentucky-Indiana Regional Planning Authority (OKI) was created; it included the counties of Boone, Campbell, and Kenton in Northern Kentucky as members of this metropolitan countywide organization. The NKAPC performed all planning and transportation related services on behalf of Campbell and Kenton counties. Two NKAPC chairmen served lengthy terms as president of OKI, and the NKAPC staff has continuously served in many supportive and active leadership roles with OKI.

During the 1960s KRS Chapter 100 (Kentucky's basic local government planning law) was revised, allowing local governments to join together to create "joint planning units." The Kenton Co. and Municipal Planning and Zoning Commission (KC&MP&ZC) was created (automatically disallowing existence of any individual local planning units); but no similar organization was created in Campbell Co., thus allowing each local government in that county to retain its individual planning unit. The KC&MP&ZC contracted with the NKAPC to provide all professional planning and engineering services.

After many public meetings and hearings, the first areawide comprehensive plan for Kenton and Boone counties was adopted in September 1972. This plan has been updated and readopted every five years. A major finding has been that many of the long-range recommendations of this plan would be difficult, if not impossible, to realize owing to local government fragmentation (so many independent local governments and single-purpose special district decision-making entities). The Area Planning Commission authorized the NKAPC staff to undertake a study entitled "Northern Kentucky's Future—Plan for Government Restructure," which recommended many consolidating changes in the governmental structures within Northern Kentucky, with the intent to make wiser use of taxpayer's dollars and to provide more efficient service for citizens.

Also during the 1970s, the Campbell Co. Fiscal Court litigated against the NKAPC, arguing that such a nonelected body should not have final authority for land-use decisions. A subsequent court ruling found in favor of the fiscal court, thus automatically modifying some of the statutory authority originally provided to area planning commissions.

During the 1984 local government elections, Lloyd Rogers, a candidate for Campbell Co. judge-executive, included an "Axe-the-Tax" proposition in his platform. The NKAPC's minimal tax was his campaign target, and Rogers was elected. He initiated a petition drive and a referendum to eliminate the NKAPC's taxing authority in Campbell Co. The petition drive was successful and led to a follow-up referendum that passed by a small margin. Campbell Co. thus seceded as a member of the NKAPC. Campbell Co.'s local governments were no longer served by the NKAPC, so many of them (including even the fiscal court) contracted with the NKAPC for professional staff services.

During the 1980s, legislation was passed creating the Kentucky Office of Housing, Buildings, and Construction and requiring that all local governments would henceforth be bound by the newly created Kentucky State Building Code and would be responsible for ensuring that enforcement of this code was carried out by state-certified building inspectors. Most of the small cities in Northern Kentucky were without staff expertise to perform such inspections and administration. The NKAPC had been assisting some local governments with enforcement of their local codes and therefore maintained a qualified staff for this purpose. Nearly all the cities in Kenton and Campbell counties and both fiscal courts then contracted with the NKAPC for such services.

During 1984 NKAPC initiated installation of a cutting-edge Geographic Information System (GIS). This system, named PlaNet GIS (and later renamed Link * GIS) came fully on-line for use in 1988. It allowed for extremely accurate base mapping, using Global Positioning System (GPS) triangulation of data from multiple orbiting satellites. This accurate mapping of every structure, landform, roadway, waterway, and so forth allowed all such features to be tagged, by special computer technology, to related narrative information about the features. This major step put the NKAPC far ahead of the curve in this region and nationwide. Initially, the **Sanitation District No. 1**, the Kenton Co. Fiscal Court, the Kenton Co. property valuation administrator, and the Kenton Co. Water District joined with the NKAPC in this major GIS program. Soon, many school districts; fire, police, and emergency response agencies; and other entities joined the project and now benefit from this valuable program.

The decade of the 1990s witnessed the creation, with NKACP staff involvement, of the Commonwealth of Kentucky's first GIS program, which recently has gained national recognition. NKAPC staff leadership positions, both locally and nationally, in the American Planning Association have put the NKAPC in the forefront of planning and GIS-related efforts in both the Cincinnati–Northern Kentucky metropolitan region and nationally. NKAPC's efforts to provide professional planning-related services and its updating of the area plan for all local governments, the state, and OKI is ongoing and is assisted through cooperative programs with **Northern Kentucky University** and the University of Cincinnati.

Since 2000 the NKAPC has operated a One-Stop-Shop program that helps local governments consolidate and simplify the administration of local codes and ordinances. The Pendleton Co. property valuation administrator contracted with the NKAPC for GIS-related services and preparation and administration of county subdivision regulations. The Commonwealth of Kentucky gave the NKAPC authority to provide all state-level building-permit and plan-review services for Kenton Co. And the Kentucky Office of Housing, Buildings, and Construction leased space in the NKAPC offices, providing another benefit of the One-Stop-Shop objective (eliminating travel time to Frankfort for such services). NKAPC has also added a Long-Range Planning Department to help provide communities in Northern Kentucky with planning opportunities that involve long-range thinking. In October 2002 William W. Bowdy, executive director of NKAPC since 1970, retired. His successor was Dennis A. Gordon.

William W. Bowdy

NORTHERN KENTUCKY BAR ASSOCIATION. The Northern Kentucky Bar Association (NKBA) was incorporated on Law Day, May 1, 1984. Up to that time, there had been three separate county bar associations in Northern Kentucky: Boone, Campbell, and Kenton. The presidents of the three associations initiated the idea to form a unified Northern Kentucky association covering the 43 cities and many districts within the three counties. In the beginning, the association's annual dues were $50 and its roster included 375 attorneys.

By May 1985 a lawyer referral service was operational. NKBA hosted its first golf outing at the Kenton Co. Golf Course in September 1985, and the first Holiday Dance occurred in December of that year. Law school dean Henry Stephens originally agreed to house the NKBA offices on the campus of the Salmon P. **Chase College of Law**. Today, they are located in Crestview Hills.

Since 1984 the NKBA has grown in members, projects, and services and has become an integral part of the Northern Kentucky community. It is the only local provider of Continuing Legal Education courses. More than 90 percent of the attorneys in Northern Kentucky who have Kentucky licenses belong to the NKBA.

Fischer, John C. K. "Lawyers Unanimous in Establishing Northern Kentucky Bar Association," *KP*, May 2, 1984, 3K.

Northern Kentucky Bar Association. www.nkybar.com (accessed August 31, 2006).

Donna M. Bloemer

NORTHERN KENTUCKY BROTHERHOOD SINGERS. The late Robert "Butch" Gillespie was instrumental in the formation of this a cappella singing group in the early 1980s. It began as a male chorus called the Ninth St. Baptist Church Singers that sang African American gospel music. As members dropped out, a core group of singers was left, and the core group became the Brotherhood Singers. Some of the original members were Charles Fann, Richard Fowler, Robert Gillespie, Eric "Rick" Jennings, Robert Mullins, and Greg Page. As singers from other churches or elsewhere from Northern Kentucky came to be included, the group became known as the Northern Kentucky Brotherhood Singers. The Brotherhood Singers' a cappella style can be traced to the oral tradition of various groups in Covington and Newport during the 1950s and 1960s "doo-wop" era. The spiritual reference takes the form developed by older singing gospel groups, such as the Dixie Humming Birds, the Fairfield Four, and the Five Blind Boys.

The Brotherhood Singers were already well known in local church circles when they came to the attention of Bob Gates, director of the Kentucky Historical Society's folklife program. Gates invited the group to sing at various state programs, giving them more exposure and an opportunity to showcase their talents. At the time, the Brotherhood Singers were one of only three gospel groups in Kentucky who sang a cappella. For a number of years they were the mainstay of the Kentucky Folk Music tour sponsored by the Kentucky Arts Council and the National Endowment for the Arts.

In November 1995 the Brotherhood Singers sang in Frankfort at Governor Brereton C. Jones's Thanksgiving luncheon. By 1997 they had performed three times at the governor's mansion in Frankfort. Throughout the 1990s they performed at various folk festivals, at homeless shelters, and at the Northern Kentucky African American Heritage Festival.

Beginning in 2000, the singing group began to expand the reach of their sound by traveling to other cities in the United States, Canada, and Europe. While in Canada, they had the opportunity to open for Ray Charles in front of 10,000 people at the Ottawa Blues Festival. They have performed in Italy, Switzerland, Spain, and Portugal.

At home, the Brotherhood Singers work with neighborhood children at the **Duveneck House** in Covington. Today's Northern Kentucky Brotherhood Singers are Rick Jennings, Robert Mullins, Greg Page, Eric Riley, Luther Scruggs, and Shaka Tyehimba. Robert Mullins is the father of **Pamela Mullins**, a former member of both the Covington City Commission and the Covington Board of Education.

"A Brotherhood in Music," *KP*, November 15, 1995, 4KK.

Divita, Jonathan. "Singing in Perfect Harmony," *SC*, August 22, 2004, 1C.

Gutierrez, Karen. "Class Lets Kids Climb out of Chairs, Join in Song," *KE*, November 10, 2003, B1.

——. "Singers Take Act to Europe," *KE*, October 28, 2003, E10.

Herald, Donna. "Heritage Takes Center Stage," *KP*, August 7, 1996, 3KK.

Kriss, Amy Louise. "A Celebration of the Middle Ages," *KP*, September 10, 1997, 1KK–2KK.

"Minister 'Butch' Gillespie Had 'Big Heart,'" *KP*, January 19, 2001, 17A.

Samples, Karen. "Voices Raised on High—Brotherhood's Gospel Sounds Transport Masses," *KE*, September 21, 1997, B1–B2.

Theodore H. H. Harris

NORTHERN KENTUCKY CHAMBER OF COMMERCE. The Northern Kentucky Chamber of Commerce is a private, voluntary, not-for-profit business organization whose purpose is to develop strong businesses and a vibrant economy for Northern Kentucky through issue advocacy, leadership, and business development programs. On April 1, 1969, prominent leaders from the Covington-Kenton-Boone Chamber of Commerce and the Campbell Co. Chamber of Commerce voted to consolidate the two local chambers into a single regional organization. Walter Dunlevy was hired as the organization's first executive vice president, and Walter Pieschel was elected its first president. The Chamber's headquarters were first located in Newport. The organization was created to represent businesses in Boone, Campbell, and Kenton counties. Since then, the Chamber's membership has expanded into Gallatin, Grant, Owen, and Pendleton counties in Kentucky and into many Greater Cincinnati communities in Ohio.

The Chamber provides opportunities for large and small businesses to be involved in programs promoting international trade, workforce development, business networking, and special events that educate members about current issues and provide them with exposure to elected officials. The Chamber also sponsors Leadership Northern Kentucky, a program designed to use the community as a classroom in which to develop effective leaders to serve the region. The Chamber also sponsors similar programs for area educators and high school students.

The Northern Kentucky Chamber of Commerce has focused on projects and programs of regional significance. In its early days, the Chamber spent much of its energy on pushing the construction of two highways: I-275 as an interstate beltway across Kentucky's three northernmost counties and I-471 to connect this beltway directly to urban areas in Northern Kentucky and downtown Cincinnati. During this time, the Chamber was the primary driver in the region in lobbying state lawmakers to establish Northern Kentucky State College (now **Northern Kentucky University**), located in Highland Heights.

In subsequent years, the Chamber increased its lobbying efforts at Frankfort and in Washington, D.C. At the request of regional legislators, the Chamber created the Northern Kentucky Consensus Committee, which regularly brings together business, government, and community leaders to identify and prioritize the region's capital construction needs. This process allows the community to focus its attention on a list of priority projects in order to work more effectively to secure funding from state and federal officials. The work of the Consensus Committee has resulted in obtaining funds for a regional convention center, a regional juvenile detention center, the Natural Science Center at Northern Kentucky University (NKU), and the Special Events Center at NKU, as well as hundreds of millions of dollars in road projects built throughout the region.

The Chamber has achieved many significant accomplishments since its creation, including convincing Kentucky governor Julian Carroll (1974–1979) of the need for a grant to continue operation of the **Transit Authority of Northern Kentucky** (TANK); the Chamber then conducted an area-wide campaign to pass a local referendum to create a permanent funding source for TANK. The Chamber was also instrumental in the formation of the Northern Kentucky Convention & Visitor's Bureau and Northern Kentucky's business and industry recruiter, the Tri-County Economic Development Corporation (now **Northern Kentucky Tri-ED**).

Fuerst, Joseph A. "An Historical Overview of the Northern KY Chamber of Commerce: The Building of a Community," 1980, Northern Kentucky Chamber of Commerce, Covington, Ky.

Reis, Jim. "A Century of Boosting Business," *KP*, April 26, 2004, 4K.

——."Pair Promoted Industrial Club," *KP*, April 26, 2004, 4K.

Steve Stevens

NORTHERN KENTUCKY COMMUNITY ACTION COMMISSION. Founded in 1965 as part of the federal Economic Opportunity Act of 1964, the Northern Kentucky Community Action Commission (NKCAC) is an antipoverty agency serving Boone, Campbell, Carroll, Gallatin, Grant, Kenton, Owen, and Pendleton counties. Its main office is in Covington at 20 W. Pike St., but the agency operates from 17 centers around Northern Kentucky today. NKCAC's board of directors includes low-income individuals, other persons from the private sector, and public officials. Its Head Start program provides a child care and education service to low-income families at no cost in an attempt to break the cycle of poverty. Other services include home energy assistance, homelessness prevention, energy education, budget counseling, , transportation for children and for homeless persons, homeless case management, and medical prescription assistance. A unique service offered by NKCAC is its weatherization program, through which qualifying homes are insulated to conserve energy. NKCAC's Senior Community Service Employment Project (SCSEP) helps people 55 years and older to reenter the work force. NKCAC also operates 10 low-income apartment units in Crittenden, Grant Co., for qualifying residents. One program that is reserved for Covington residents is Youthbuild, which targets very-low-income residents between the ages of 16 and 24 who have dropped out of high school. This program provides supportive services while teaching educational and job skills. NKCAC publishes works such as the *White Paper on Poverty in Northern Ky.* and a monthly newsletter.

"Grant Awarded," *KE*, March 1, 1970, 6A.
"Lasting Impact," *KP*, December 1, 2005, 1K.
Northern Kentucky Community Action Commission. www.nkcac.org (accessed July 27, 2006).

Kareem A. Simpson

NORTHERN KENTUCKY CONVENTION AND VISITORS BUREAU. The mission of the Northern Kentucky Convention and Visitors Bureau (NKYCVB), which began in the 1970s and serves Boone, Campbell, and Kenton counties, is to bring money into the community through expenditures by visitors to the region, especially those who attend conventions and meetings. In 2007, for example, the direct economic impact of NKYCVB efforts in the three counties was $325 million.

The Bureau is funded by a tax on rooms at the more than 60 hotels and motels located in Boone, Campbell, and Kenton counties. Tom Kelly, owner of the Wildwood Inn Hotels in Florence and one of the founders of the NKYCVB, is persuaded that the creation of the tax transformed the landscape of the hospitality business in Northern Kentucky, helping to bring dollars into the region.

Over the years, the success of the NKYCVB in attracting functions created the need for a convention center. The Northern Kentucky Convention Center opened in 1998 as a vehicle for expanding the local convention market. Full-service major brand hotels then opened around the center, including the Cincinnati Marriott RiverCenter and the Embassy Suites RiverCenter.

The NKYCVB establishes contact with various groups, such as Kentucky state organizations and associations, corporate entities, military units holding reunions, religious organizations, planners of sports and hobby events, and many others, encouraging them to schedule their conventions in Northern Kentucky, either at the Convention Center or at one of the area's leading hotels. In addition to informing organizations about accommodations for their meetings, the NKYCVB makes them aware of public attractions in the region, including the **Newport Aquarium**, **Newport-on-the-Levee**, **BB Riverboats**, **Main Strasse** Village, the **Dinsmore Homestead**, and **Big Bone Lick** State Park, that may lead to a decision to come to Northern Kentucky. NKYCVB also assists state, regional, national, and international groups who visit the area by sending out direct-mail flyers announcing "things to do" in the region. In addition, representatives of the NKYCVB Services Department frequently provide ancillary service such as name-badge registration assistance, transportation, and media relations support. They may also distribute discount coupons for local attractions and restaurants.

Kentucky Department of Tourism. *Industry News*, October 28, 2005.
Travel Industry Association. www.tia.org (accessed March 10, 2006).

Pat Frew

NORTHERN KENTUCKY CONVENTION CENTER. Two separate organizations, the **Northern Kentucky Chamber of Commerce** and the **Northern Kentucky Convention and Visitors Bureau**, began independently to think about building a convention center somewhere in Northern Kentucky. Soon they joined forces, and many others became involved in the project; everyone hoped that a convention center would become a developmental catalyst for the region. The subsequent effort to obtain the needed state funds involved the entire Northern Kentucky community. In a 1995 special legislative session, the Kentucky legislature approved the group's funding request. Approval was also given later for additional moneys that covered the total $30.5 million cost of constructing the center.

Market studies that were done in conjunction with designing the convention center determined the size of groups likely to use the center and how they would want to use it. At the outset, the optimum size for a group using the center ranged between 900 and 1,000 people, and it was decided that the exhibit hall should accommodate about 200 booths. Designers also envisioned significant booking opportunities for corporate events.

The construction of the building, Madison Ave. and RiverCenter Blvd. in Covington, began in February 1997 and was completed in the fall of 1998. The finished product resulted from the cooperation of officials in three Northern Kentucky counties (Boone, Campbell, and Kenton), 39 area cities, the Kentucky legislature, and innumerable organizations, institutions, business leaders, and citizens. The convention center hosted its first event November 6, 1998. In its first seven years of operation, 1,392 events were held at the Northern Kentucky Convention Center. The center's economic impact, nearly $633 million, has been about 41 percent higher than original projections. The Northern Kentucky Convention Center Corporation is chartered by the Commonwealth of Kentucky, and the charter provides that all revenues generated by the center are to be used for the operation, upkeep, and improvement of the center.

The Northern Kentucky Convention and Visitors Bureau works with the convention center to market the center and book events. Events scheduled a year or more in advance are booked by the Convention and Visitors Bureau; arrangements for events scheduled less than a year ahead are handled by the convention center itself.

"Convention Center Names Chief," *KP*, July 8, 2006, 2A.
Pina, Phillip. "Northern Kentucky Shows Off Convention Center," *CE*, 8C.

Gretchen Landrum

NORTHERN KENTUCKY EMERGENCY MEDICAL SERVICES. The first organized ambulance corps in the nation was formed during the **Civil War**, and its vehicles were upgraded from two-wheel carts to four-wheel wagons by Gen. **Charles Stuart Tripler**, who served at the **Newport Barracks** in Newport. Over the following century, emergency medical services in Northern Kentucky, as in most nonmetropolitan areas throughout the United States, came to be provided by local funeral homes—if such services were available at all. The funeral home usually had a vehicle capable of transporting at least one person on a stretcher and in many cases was willing to put the vehicle into service as an ambulance. About 1960, however, the funeral industry quit providing ambulance services. Local civic-minded groups, often called first aid squads, rescue squads, or life squads, or the fire departments, which were mostly volunteer, then took on the task of emergency ambulance service. Fire department personnel were already trained in basic first aid skills to care for firemen who were injured during firefighting operations. As life squads became available in more communities, the training and equipment of such groups improved. Over time, women joined men as members of the squads, importantly adding volunteer hours in a period when there were no paid personnel and yet the number of calls kept increasing.

In the late 1960s and early 1970s, the federal government standardized the training and service provided by ambulance services. The Department of Transportation (DOT) established a national standard set of skills for advanced phases of emergency medical care. The emergency medical technician was thus born, as were new emergency centers; emergency rooms in local hospitals were expanded with new and better equipment; and larger hospitals were upgraded to trauma centers where the best and highest level of care, including surgery, was made available at all times. Emergency medicine became a specialty for doctors as emergency skills were introduced into the curricula of medical schools.

As advances in emergency care generally have progressed throughout the nation, Northern Kentucky has also experienced significant advances in its local care and training. It is now possible for a civilian injured in a traffic accident to be stabilized and transported to a trauma/surgical center within minutes while also receiving advanced medical care en route. The mobile and air ambulances used are referred to as emergency rooms on wheels (or wings). The goal is to have the injured person at a trauma center within a half hour, ready for surgery or other care.

The Northern Kentucky Emergency Medical Services Company (NKEMS) was formed in 1977, through a grant from the DOT, to assist the basic life support units in the counties of Boone, Bracken, Campbell, Gallatin, Grant, Kenton, and Pendleton. Many members of the local units have received the initial training of 120 hours for emergency medical technician (EMT) certification, which is issued and monitored by the State Medical Board. EMTs must continually update their training in order to maintain certification. The federal funds enabled NKEMS to expand the training programs throughout the region.

In 1979 paramedic services became available in Northern Kentucky. A certified paramedic, who must receive 1,200 hours of initial training, is able to provide more advanced medical treatment than an EMT can; for example, a paramedic can administer medications and conduct advanced heart monitoring. Like EMTs, paramedics undergo continual monitoring and receive updated training to maintain certification. Most of the Northern Kentucky region is served by volunteer life-squad departments. Although members of these volunteer departments are quite capable, they generally cannot spend the time required to become paramedics. Thus, a system has been developed whereby, in an emergency, NKEMS paramedics respond in a separate car to meet the local life squad, who generally arrive at the scene first. The EMTs determine whether paramedics are needed, and if so, they are advised to continue their response trip while the local unit completes the on-the-scene care. Once paramedics arrive or, to save precious response time, join the EMT squad en route to a hospital, they immediately begin more advanced care inside the ambulance. NKEMS also provides ambulances to handle the increasing volume of nonemergency transport services to and from medical facilities, freeing local units for emergencies.

The response system, called a two-tiered system, has proven quite effective and has enabled local counties to provide advanced levels of care. NKEMS provided the two-tiered paramedic services until 1999. Then TransCare, a joint nonprofit venture of St. Elizabeth and St. Luke hospitals, was incorporated and purchased these service operations from NKEMS. The two-tiered system continued until 2004, when operating expenses exceeded revenues. Several fire departments had begun providing their own paramedics, and insurance and government agencies had reduced their reimbursements for such services.

TransCare requested additional funding, without which its services would have to be cut. The counties, cities, and fire departments began studies to determine how they could assist with funding TransCare or provide tax-assisted transportation services of their own. Several of the larger cities started offering their own services. Other cities contracted to use transportation services provided by neighboring cities. These developments undercut TransCare's efforts to obtain tax-supported funding, and the initiative to secure it began to falter. The remaining contracts with TransCare were extended to give more time to find a satisfactory solution, which was found and in place by July 2005.

The history of ambulance services in the various cities within the region has varied greatly. The city of Maysville had no ambulance until 1957, and the one obtained then was an army surplus vehicle. In Covington, in 1903 a horse-drawn vehicle with gaping holes in its panels served as the ambulance; often patients were hauled in it to a hospital five miles away on the **Covington and Lexington Turnpike** Later, if the patient had died, the same vehicle was used to transport the body to the cemetery. By 1907 Covington officials believed they had solved their ambulance problems with a new vehicle they had acquired. They bragged, "No city anywhere has an ambulance for contagious diseases as fine as ours. . . . Not even Cincinnati or Louisville can boast its equal." By 1921, Jesse Sheets, superintendent of the Covington police department's patrol system, was demonstrating his new combination police patrol wagon–ambulance. It could be converted from one function to the other in 30 seconds.

Newport had the problem that ambulance operators on their way to Speers Hospital (see **Speers Memorial Hospital**) in Dayton were driving wildly through the city's West End, a lawless part of town where citizens were regularly injured in scrapes and drinking brawls. Newport wanted to take these victims of fights to the much closer hospitals in Covington, but officials in Covington refused. While cities such as Newport sometimes bragged about the success rates of their life-saving crews, the statistics told a different tale. On the ambulance runs made during the first half of the 1930s, Newport reported saving 14 lives while 10 people died either en route or after arriving at the hospital. In 1940 Newport obtained a modern ambulance for its Newport Life Saving Squad, and the police squad car they had been using as an ambulance, operated by policemen with little or no medical training, was at last retired .

"Can Transform Police Auto into Ambulance in 30 Seconds," *KTS*, December 23, 1921, 35.

"Dangerous Ambulances," *KP*, May 20, 1931, 4.

"Maysville May Get Ambulance," *KTS*, January 17, 1957, 8A.

"New Ambulance Accepted by City," *KP*, February 27, 1907, 2.

"Newport Life Squad Will Get Ambulance," *KP*, March 19, 1940, 1.

"Sketch of Ambulance Used to Take Patients to Covington Branch Hospital on Lexington Pike," *KP*, January 3, 1903, 1.

"Squad Save 14 Lives," *KP*, July 4, 1930, 8.

Robert Joseph Williams

NORTHERN KENTUCKY FUND. The Northern Kentucky Fund of the Greater Cincinnati Foundation (GCF) derived from **Forward Quest**, an organization formed to implement a community planning effort for Northern Kentucky. One of its goals was to establish a charitable fund for the community. The Northern Kentucky Fund was established in June 1998 with more than $1 million in challenge grants from 10 major donors, including a $100,000 grant from GCF. The fund provides resources to nonprofit organizations located in or primarily serving Northern Kentucky. An advisory board made up of 15 volunteers oversees its development and promotion, with support from GCF staff. The Northern Kentucky Fund and dozens of other named funds established to support the needs of the Northern Kentucky community make up the Northern Kentucky Family of Funds. "The Fund is important for the long-term viability of the region. We need access to funds to support the community's needs," said Mike Hammons, president of Forward Quest. "We came up with the goal of putting a permanent fund in place so resources would be available over the long-term."

Community pride for the region has driven the success of the fund's short history. **Judy Clabes**, its first chair, tapped this philanthropic spirit in 1999 with the Millennium Gift Campaign. Sponsored by the *Kentucky Post*, the campaign invited Northern Kentuckians to contribute their final hour of pay of the millennium. Gifts ranged from $5 to $10,000, bringing the total value of the Northern Kentucky Fund to $3,861,507 by December 2000. "It was a great way to tell ordinary people they count," Clabes remembered. "You don't need to be a millionaire to be a philanthropist."

In 2003 the fund reached its fifth anniversary; in the same year GCF marked its 40th year. In celebration, it was announced that GCF would match all unrestricted contributions (up to $40,000) to the Northern Kentucky Fund for one year. The fund's leadership raised the bar, and more than $200,000 was raised.

The Advisory Board has been creative with the fund's development. In 2004 an annual award for Northern Kentucky philanthropists was launched. The Devou Cup, named after William Devou, was first awarded to Ralph and Irmaleen Drees (see **Ralph Drees**). **R. C. Durr** was honored in 2005, and **Ralph Haile** and his late wife Carol Ann Haile were the 2006 recipients. The board announced the Haile Challenge in 2005. It challenges contributors to match Ralph Haile's annual $150,000 gift. The board has also reached out to future community leaders. Each year, the outgoing president of Legacy, an organization for young professionals, joins the board. Legacy has established its own fund in the Northern Kentucky Family of Funds.

Between 1998 and 2006, GCF awarded more than $3 million in grants to nonprofit organizations in Northern Kentucky, supported in part by contributions to the Northern Kentucky Family of Funds.

"Challenging Philanthropy," *Connect, the Newsletter of the Greater Cincinnati Foundation*, Spring–Summer 2005, 9.

Flischel, Sue, Judith Clabes, and Mike Hammons. Telephone interview by Julia Mace, June 23, 2006.

Gallagher, Janice. "Five Years of Philanthropy," *KP*, December 27, 2003, 4K.

"Judith Clabes: Northern Kentucky Fund Chair," *Connect, the Newsletter of the Greater Cincinnati Foundation*, Fall–Winter 1999, 4.

"Northern Kentucky Fund Celebrates Philanthropy," *Connect, the Newsletter of the Greater Cincinnati Foundation*, Spring–Summer 2004, 10.

Julia Mace

NORTHERN KENTUCKY HERITAGE LEAGUE. The Northern Kentucky Heritage League (NKHL), a fine arts organization for promoting the arts, heritage, and culture of Northern Kentucky, was formed in 1967. An initial task of the organization was to support a grassroots effort to establish a gallery for the works of world-renowned Covington artist **Frank Duveneck**. That goal was reached when the Frank Duveneck Memorial Gallery, Northern Kentucky's first public art gallery, opened in July 1967 within the Covington Library at Scott Blvd. and Robbins St. The son of Duveneck, Frank Boott Duveneck, and the son's daughter, Elizabeth Duveneck Davis, attended the dedication.

In late 1967 the NKHL found itself in a controversy over the **Mike Fink Floating Restaurant**, which wished to dock along Riverside Dr. in Covington and build a 200-car parking lot and a marina for private boats. The NKHL, concerned about the historic properties in the community, brought legal action (with Riverside Dr. residents John Kunkel and Richard Smith) to have the lease granted by the City of Covington declared void. Eventually the NKHL lost its battle to keep the restaurant out.

Also in the late 1960s, an urban renewal project was proposed in Covington to raze all of the historic homes along Riverside Dr. and the north side of Second St. from the **John A. Roebling Bridge** to the Licking River (See also **Licking-Riverside and Ohio Riverside National Historic Districts**). A hotel, apartments, and other commercial projects would replace the homes. Riverside Dr. residents, the NKHL, and other preservation groups opposed the project. After almost two years of struggle, the City of Covington lost but gained some concessions along Greenup St. This was a tremendous victory for the fledgling NKHL.

Around the same time, the NKHL was given approval to make improvements to the **George Rogers Clark** Park in Covington, which had fallen into disrepair. The park was once the site of the **Thomas Kennedy** house. The organization was able to reconstruct and beautify the area with a fountain, authentic gas lamps, and benches, completing the work by spring 1969. Plans were also made for a summer arts and crafts show that turned out to be the first Annual Duveneck Memorial Art Show. The event, which still continues each year, became the largest yearly project of the NKHL. This art show was created with the goals of stimulating interest in the arts, giving regional artists a place to display and sell their wares, and promoting local history through the Duveneck Purchase Award. Eligible paintings must depict a regional historic landmark more than 50 years old; award-winning works are displayed in Covington in the **Kenton Co. Public Library**.

Each year any moneys left over in the NKHL treasury are given out in the form of small grants, usually less than $1,000, to local organizations for the benefit of civic projects. Since 1980, grants have been given to more than 50 different state and local organizations. The NKHL sponsors programs that feature historic trips and speakers, preservation projects, and other activities to carry out its mission.

"Heritage League Marks 25 Years," *KP*, December 19, 1992, 2KK.

"They're Stubborn!—Riverside Residents Firmly Resist Bulldozers," *KE*, November 24, 1968, 6A.

"3 Projects Get Grants from League," *KP*, November 17, 1992, 3K.

Jane D. Purdon

NORTHERN KENTUCKY HOMEBUILDERS ASSOCIATION. See **Building, Residential**.

NORTHERN KENTUCKY INDEPENDENT DISTRICT HEALTH DEPARTMENT. Since 1981 the Northern Kentucky Independent District Health Department (usually called just the Northern Kentucky Health Department) has served Boone, Campbell, Grant, and Kenton counties. Before the consolidated district health department was established, each of these counties operated individual health departments. Newport and Covington and some of the other local cities had health departments that later merged with health departments in their respective counties to establish countywide health departments. In compliance with Kentucky Revised Statue (KRS) 212.120, the first of the four county health departments that were later grouped together began in Kenton Co. in January 1929. The Grant Co. Health Department followed in April 1931, the Campbell Co. Health Department in June 1946, and the Boone Co. Health Department in June 1950.

A push at the state level for county health departments to form district health departments began in the 1970s. In 1972 the Covington–Kenton Co. Health Department and the Campbell Co. Health Department merged, and William V. Banks, MD, became the consolidated health department's first health officer. Almost a decade later, in 1981, the four-county health department came into being when the Boone Co. Health Department and the Grant Co. Health Department joined. The move to a multicounty health department decreased administrative costs, lessened duplication of staff for mandated programs, increased specialized services, and created more collaboration among the communities. The present district administrative office is located in Edgewood, at 610 Medical Village Dr.

In 1991 Kentucky legislation enabled the Northern Kentucky Health Department to become an "independent district" health department, the only one in the state. Because it is independent, the Northern Kentucky Health Department does not need to follow the state merit system in hirings, job classifications, and salary levels, but it is required to follow state and federal funded program standards for its employees.

Kentucky legislation passed in 1982 allowed the establishment of local boards of health to deal with disease outbreaks such as typhoid fever, yellow fever, and other such communicable diseases. A district board and four local boards of health oversee the Northern Kentucky Health Department's mission. The District Board of Health is empowered by KRS 212 to pass regulations and adopt codes concerning issues of public health. It meets a minimum of four times a year and sets policy for the whole district; program plans, pay raises, and the total departmental budget are subject to its approval.

By Kentucky law, there are four local county boards of health that meet at least once each year. These boards set the rate for the county health tax, not to exceed four cents per $100 of assessment valuation. They oversee any construction or maintenance of the county's health center as well. In addition to the local tax moneys, the Northern Kentucky Health Department receives revenue from state and federal funding, grants, Medicaid/Medicare reimbursement, and service fees. Its total revenue for fiscal year 2005 was a little more than $13 million.

The Northern Kentucky Health Department is the principal government agency that exists in the region for the protection of the public's health. It manages the health status of the population through community assessment, public health policy development, and assurance of services and a healthy environment. The Northern Kentucky Health Department provides essential public health services and districtwide health services based on community assessment processes that result in action plans such as the most recent Master Health Plan for Northern Kentucky (January 2005).

Approximately 155 staff members work at the four county health centers and two administrative/education sites to provide more than 80 programs. Services include state and federal mandated inspections of restaurants, hotels, schools, public swimming pools, and private on-site sewage systems; communicable disease tracking; childhood immunizations; the WIC supplemental food program; HIV/AIDS case management; family planning; home visiting programs for young families; nutrition education; smoking cessation campaigns; school health education; and strategic collaboration toward community health system changes.

Life expectancy in Northern Kentucky has increased since the early 1900s primarily owing to the department's public health efforts in environmental sanitation, communicable disease control, and immunizations. In the 21st century, new challenges arise daily in the form of natural and man-made disasters, emerging infections such as West Nile encephalitis and SARS, drug-resistant strains of tuberculosis, bioterrorism threats, obesity, and sedentary lifestyles. Sometimes, challenges take the form of diverse opinions and decision-making to meet the needs of a community. Amid great achievements, new threats, and controversial decisions, the health boards, the district director, the staff, and the state are continually challenged in finding solutions satisfactory to all stakeholders.

Institute of Medicine. *The Future of Public Health.* Washington, D.C.: Academy Press, 1988.

——. *Who Will Keep the Public Healthy?* Washington, D.C.: Academy Press, 2003.

Kentucky Department for Public Health. *Administrative Reference for Local Health Departments.* Vol. 1, January 2005. Frankfort, Ky.: Kentucky Department for Public Health, 2005.

Leach, Rice. "A General History of Public Health," presentation for the Governor's Conference "The Future of Public Health in Kentucky: Partners for Progress," Louisville, Ky., March 11–13, 1997.

Northern Kentucky Independent District Health Department. www.nkyhealth.org (accessed March 24, 2006).

Peggy L. Kiser

NORTHERN KENTUCKY INDUSTRIAL FOUNDATION. The foundation, more popularly known as the Florence Industrial Park, can be traced to the mid-1950s, when the idea of a properly zoned concentrated geographic area of manufacturing and warehousing operations arose among the leaders of the Covington-Kenton-Boone Chamber of Commerce (see **Northern Kentucky Chamber of Commerce**). One leader was Andrew W. Clark, a former member of the **Committee for Covington–Kenton Co.**, who served as the group's attorney; others included Joseph Cuni of Peoples Liberty Bank and Trust Company and J. Wayne "Doc" Rusk of Montgomery Heating & Air Conditioning. It was Cuni's able assistant **Ralph Haile** who did much of the early legwork on this project; he subsequently went on to involve himself in many other civic and community endeavors that have benefited Northern Kentucky.

In 1958 the foundation hired Frankfort consultant E. Bruce Kennedy. Farmland extending over roughly 930 acres (expanded later to 990) just south of Florence in Boone Co. was identified, and about 14 local building and loans raised $1 million in seed money (see **Savings and Loan Associations**). The site, served by the **Southern Railway** (today the **Norfolk Southern Railway**), was near the Greater Cincinnati Airport (now the **Cincinnati/Northern Kentucky International Airport**), along the eastern edge of I-75, and relatively flat, with utilities. It offered most of the amenities any manufacturing or warehouse plant would require. Lots were sold for a relatively low cost per acre ($6,000), and the City of Florence annexed the park and issued tax-free industrial revenue bonds to finance construction. The first two occupants were the Great Lakes Carbon Corporation and the Crescent Paper Tube Company. Great Lakes (later known as Grefco) purchased 30 acres and began in April 1962 building a $3.5 million factory, where it made perlite insulation, employing 125 at first. The Crescent manufacturing firm followed in the fall of 1962 and occupied 11 acres; it made paper tubes for all kinds of applications, including incendiary uses during the **Vietnam War**. By summer 1979 some 45 manufacturers in and around the park employed approximately 7,600 workers.

The Florence Industrial Park has been a resounding success. It was the first of its size in Northern Kentucky and one of the first in the nation. The population growth of Boone Co., the **Florence Mall**, and subdivisions in southern Kenton and Boone counties can all be attributed in part to the Industrial Park's development.

Haile, Ralph. Interview by Paul Tenkotte, April 13, 2006, Cincinnati.

"Industrial Park Is in Business," *KP*, July 12, 1961, 6K.

Remlinger, Connie. "From Barnyard to Industrial Hub," *KP*, May 22, 1979, 1.

NORTHERN KENTUCKY INTERFAITH COMMISSION. An association of Christian denominations, the Interfaith Commission (IFC) was founded in 1969, after a merger of the Northern Kentucky Association of Protestant Churches and the Catholic Information Center. Today its delegates include representatives from the African Methodist Episcopal, Anglican Catholic, Baptist, Christian Church (Disciples), Episcopal, Lutheran, Presbyterian, Roman Catholic, United Church of Christ, and United Methodist churches. As well as encouraging Christian unity, the IFC works to encourage dialogue with members of other faith traditions. The organization's purpose was summed up by Rev. William Neuroth, its executive director from 1987 to 2002: through Interfaith, the churches "do together what we cannot do alone."

Under the leadership of its founding members—Harley Fisk, the IFC's first president, and Rev. Don Hellman, its first vice president, as well as Alvin Aldermeyer, Ron Brock, Joseph Kuchle, Clarence Lassetter, O. Worth May, Mary Middleton, Otwell Rankin, Karl Vercouteren, and William White—the IFC emphasized unity activities such as interracial and interreligious dialogue and recreational and Bible school events. Members of suburban churches joined members of inner-city churches in Newport and Covington to work on youth activities, interchurch worship services, concerts, and retreats. Mary Pons was the commission's first secretary and later its first executive director. Under her successor, Sister Martha Walther, a Benedictine sister (see **Sisters of St. Benedict**) from St. Walburg Convent, Villa Hills, the IFC's range of activities broadened to include an emergency assistance program, Good Friday and Thanksgiving community services, interfaith prayer groups, and welcome breakfasts for new clergy.

In 1983 the IFC established the Exodus Jail Ministry program. Trained volunteers provide a "listening ministry" for the spiritual needs of inmates at Northern Kentucky county jails and juvenile facilities. The program eventually became a joint venture of Interfaith and the Northern Kentucky Mental Health Association. As well as continuing to promote understanding between Christian denominations, the commission sponsors the area's annual Yom HaShoah Holocaust memorial service.

During the tenure of Rev. Carolyn Tyler as director, the IFC initiated a disaster-response program after the calamitous tornado of March 1985 devastated parts of the region. The program inspired an overwhelming response from individuals, churches, and organizations and led to the hiring of a part-time staff person to provide on-site assistance to individuals and families, primarily in Newport and Covington.

Under Neuroth's leadership, the commission was reorganized. Three sections replaced previous committees to encourage greater participation from denominational delegates: the Faith and Order Section to promote ecumenical and interfaith experiences, with an emphasis on educational opportunities, worship, and dialogue; the Work and Life Section to focus on community and social needs, including interracial issues; and the Operations Section to address financial matters and new denominational recruitment.

The IFC continued to be a lead agency in the 1990s. It either established or supported the following programs and organizations in response to social services and community needs.

The Cincinnati/Northern Kentucky International Airport Chaplaincy Program

This idea was envisioned by two ministers, Dr. Michael Watts and Rev. Larry Leslie. The IFC provided initial organizing support and called an organizational meeting in November 1989 to create a ministry of "presence" and prayer for both travelers and employees, and a chapel in the airport's Terminal 3 was dedicated in February 1997. Cliff Wartman is the program's current director.

The Interfaith Organization (ECHO)

In February 1991 Sister Mary Dorgan, a **Sister of Divine Providence**, called together clergy and laity to discuss the need for a "soup kitchen" for the homeless and hungry in Campbell Co. The IFC initially served as the contact agency for promotion, information, and contributions. On April 18, 1991, the program's first weekly meal was served at the First Church of the Nazarene, Newport. Later that year a permanent facility at Ninth and York Sts. in Newport was purchased, renovated, and given to ECHO by David Hosea, a Northern Kentucky businessman. Under its present director, Karen Yates, ECHO serves more than 200 meals each evening.

The Interfaith Hospitality Network (IHN)

In June 1993 the IFC became the prime mover in establishing the Interfaith Hospitality Network of Northern Kentucky. IHN is a national program providing shelter, meals, and support for homeless families, primarily through local churches, volunteers, and social service agencies. "Host congregations" provide meals and temporary shelter for homeless families on a weekly rotating basis. "Support congregations" provide volunteers to assist in meal preparation, dinner, overnight hosting, and other activities. Currently the program is located at Ninth and Patterson Sts. in Newport, and the director is Jawanna Spencer.

The Interfaith Commission Flood Relief Program

The massive flooding of the Ohio and Licking Rivers in March 1997 led to the IFC's Flood Relief Program. In collaboration with the **Salvation Army** and the **American Red Cross**, the commission coordinated the work of volunteers from churches throughout the Midwest who assisted survivors as they moved from crisis to recovery.

The Interfaith Commission's offices moved to the Henry Hosea House at Ninth and York Sts., Newport, in October 1996. At the same time, the commission adopted a new mission statement that continues to guide its members: The Northern Kentucky Interfaith Commission is an association of Christian denominations and congregations interested in encouraging ecumenical and interfaith dialogue. It is committed to fostering unity among all Christian churches in Northern Kentucky through dialogue, cooperative ministry, and occasions for joint worship. It also encourages and participates in dialogue with members of other faith traditions.

"Churches Unite for Worship," *KE*, January 12, 1993, B3.
"Interfaith Commission Seeks Homeless Shelters for Families," *KP*, June 12, 1993, 1K.
"Interfaith Links Churches to Meet Society's Need," *KP*, February 8, 1989, 1KK.

William C. Neuroth

NORTHERN KENTUCKY PORT AUTHORITY. The Northern Kentucky Port Authority (NKPA) was formed in 1968 by a joint effort of the fiscal courts of Boone, Campbell, and Kenton counties, with the goal of promoting river navigation, river transportation, and river port facilities. The intent is to attract industrial or commercial operations in connection with these activities to Northern Kentucky. The NKPA plays an important role in the economic development of the region.

The NKPA board of directors is made up of nine members appointed by those same three county fiscal courts. Members serve as business representatives for the NKPA and are residents of the three counties. The NKPA has the ability to issue multicounty industrial revenue bonds (tax-free) for state and local purposes. The current activity of the NKPA is to market the former Newport landfill, a current Environmental Protection Agency Superfund site. This former Newport dump, consisting of approximately 44 acres, is located in Wilder in Campbell Co., along Ky. Rt. 9, and has access to and frontage on the Licking River.

"Port Authority to Aid Newport with Landfill," *KP*, December 27, 1978, 5K.
"Port Authority Tours Licking by Tug," *KP*, October 29, 1977, 2K.
"Port Baits Hook for Industry," *KP*, May 13, 1976, 1K.

Dan Tobergte

NORTHERN KENTUCKY RIGHT TO LIFE. Northern Kentucky Right to Life (NKRTL) is an IRS 501(C3) not-for-profit, nondenominational organization founded in 1971. The oldest and largest prolife organization in Kentucky, NKRTL is dedicated to the sanctity and defense of all human life and to propagating the views that human life begins at fertilization, that the significance of individuals is that they were created by God, and that human worth is not dependent upon the person's functional capacity or determined by any other person. NKRTL believes that all direct assaults upon innocent human life (abortion, assisted suicide, cloning, euthanasia, and human experimentation) are always morally wrong and unacceptable and destructive of the foundations of a free society.

NKRTL's activities include publishing a newsletter, distributing prolife literature, sponsoring speakers and films, providing voter and legislative information, holding regular prayer services, and advertising in the media. NKRTL's history (and the history nationally of the prolife movement) is chronicled in a recent book, *That Reminds Me of a Story . . . Reflections of a Pro-Life Warrior.* There are two affiliated organizations, Northern Kentucky Right to Life Educational Fund Inc., also nonprofit, and Northern Kentucky Right to Life Political Action Committee, which endorses political candidates.

Cetrulo, Robert C. *That Reminds Me of a Story . . . Reflections of a Pro-Life Warrior.* Covington, Ky.: Northern Kentucky Right to Life Educational Foundation, 2003.

Robert C. Cetrulo

NORTHERN KENTUCKY SERVICES FOR THE DEAF. The Northern Kentucky Services for the Deaf (NKSD), on Cavalier Rd. in Florence, was founded in 1999 by Hunter H. Bryant and Teresa R. Moon Flaherty, both certified and qualified interpreters. The NKSD provides sign-language interpreting services to its deaf and hearing-impaired clientele in courtrooms, law offices, classrooms, government services offices, and medical facilities; at conferences and meetings; and for social services. Interpreting services are also provided at special community events throughout Northern Kentucky.

Deaf or hearing-impaired individuals who communicate solely in sign language are the main focus of the NKSD. The NKSD will, however, provide other means of communication in order to meet the deaf client's specific needs. The organization also acts as an advocate for issues concerning deaf culture and deafness and maintains an information resource center. On-site workshops on deafness and classes on sign language can be arranged by NKSD for any group desiring better interaction or communication with the deaf or hearing-impaired.

The NKSD is committed to the mission of connecting the two worlds, those of the deaf and the hearing. For persons with normal hearing, it can offer a better understanding of the diverse deaf–hearing-impaired community. For example, commonly unknown facts among the hearing are that not all deaf persons can lip-read and that deaf persons who are not fluent in the English language may not be able to understand written messages.

Kentucky Commission for the Deaf and Hearing Impaired. *Interpreter Directory.* Frankfort, Ky.: KCDH, 2004. Also available at www.kcdhh.org.
Kentucky Commission on the Deaf and Hard of Hearing. www.kcdhh.org.

Margaret Prentice Hecker

NORTHERN KENTUCKY TRANSIT INC. Northern Kentucky Transit (NKT), which is based in Burlington, was chartered in 1978 as a private nonprofit transportation brokerage. Its mission is "to help meet the special transportation needs primarily of elderly persons and persons with handicaps in the counties of Boone, Campbell, Carroll, Gallatin, Grant, Kenton, Owen and Pendleton by coordinating the provision of transportation services to meet the needs of various agencies and organizations." Founded by psychotherapist Dr. Clarence R. Lassetter, an employee of the Comprehensive Care Center of Northern Kentucky (**NorthKey Community Care**), the corporation began operations in 1979. Lassetter led the organization for some 22 years, retiring in 2001; his broad-based service included driving, coordinating, and even maintaining the fleet of vans and buses.

In May 1992 NKT occupied its new building at 1452 Production Dr. in Burlington. NKT operates within two modes: providing rural public transportation and providing a charter service, funded mostly by federal and state moneys. The rural transportation serves Boone, Carroll, Gallatin, Grant, Owen, and Pendleton counties via a contract with either an individual transportation provider or an agency. The NKT charter service has been available to business or industry, churches, clubs, the elderly, the general public, the handicapped, hospitals, nursing homes, schools, social service agencies, and the United Appeal. NKT now has a fleet of vehicles numbering more than 30.

"Helping Others Brings a Dividend," *KP*, February 28, 1992, 1K.
"Van Charter Company Receives Federal Funds," *KP*, May 28, 2001, 2K.

NORTHERN KENTUCKY TRI-ED. Northern Kentucky's emergence as a desirable business incubator is largely a result of the efforts of Northern Kentucky Tri-ED. Today, an impressive array of world-class companies call Northern Kentucky home. Many have located or expanded in the area in recent years as a direct result of the aggressive efforts that began with the creation of the Tri-County Economic Development Corporation, or Northern Kentucky Tri-ED, in 1987. Notable achievements for Northern Kentucky Tri-ED include attracting firms such as **Fidelity Investments**, **Toyota**, **Lafarge**, Xanodyne, and Sachs Automotive.

The story of Tri-ED actually begins in 1981, when then Kentucky governor John Y. Brown Jr. (1979–1983) brought together a group of Northern Kentucky business leaders to determine how the region could pool its efforts to attract new businesses. Under the chairmanship of Corporex president William P. Butler, the group envisioned an economic development agency that would serve the three counties of Boone, Campbell and Kenton. The agency would be the focal point of cooperative efforts to recruit businesses and promote economic growth that would ultimately benefit all Northern Kentuckians.

The group's vision came to life a few years later, when attorney William T. "Bill" Robinson III, then chairman of the **Northern Kentucky Chamber of Commerce**, saw an opportunity to create a unique public-private partnership that would become the economic development agency for Northern Kentucky. In 1986 Robinson presented the Tri-County Economic Development Corporation to area officials, and Northern Kentucky Tri-ED was born. Initially funded by local governments and the private sector, Northern Kentucky Tri-ED, the Northern Kentucky Chamber, and the Northern Kentucky Legislative Caucus obtained passage of state legislation in 1995 that provided the agency with a permanent funding source from rental car license fees. These revenues are shared by the three counties through Northern Kentucky Tri-ED's regional efforts. Private-sector contributions to the Northern Kentucky Tri-County Economic Development Foundation (Tri-EF) continue to support Northern Kentucky Tri-ED's mission.

Northern Kentucky Tri-ED's efforts are governed by a 17-member board of directors led by the three judges-executive of the member counties, plus private-sector appointments from each county, **Forward Quest**, and the Northern Kentucky Chamber of Commerce. Northern Kentucky Tri-ED's staff of nine professionals now focus not only on the attraction but also on the expansion and retention of primary industries. Primary industries are those that export products or services from an area and import money into an area from the sale of such products or services. Further, primary industries are not dependent upon the local economy for growth and survival and thus can be located anywhere, making the competition for such industries quite fierce across the United States.

Since the creation of Northern Kentucky Tri-ED more than 20 years ago, its success has been astounding. The organization has directly facilitated the attraction or expansion of 428 primary-industry companies, the creation of 41,000 primary jobs, and new capital investment of $4.1 billion in Northern Kentucky. This success has garnered national attention for the agency, as witnessed by *Site Selection* magazine's naming Tri-ED as one of the top 10 economic development organizations in the United States in 1995, 1997, 1998, 1999, and 2005. While the statistics related to Northern Kentucky Tri-ED's accomplishments are impressive, the agency's impact on Northern Kentucky goes far beyond the numbers. Perhaps Northern Kentucky Tri-ED's most enduring legacy will be how its creation ushered in an age of unprecedented community-wide cooperation.

Northern Kentucky Tri-ED. "Tri-County Economic Development Corporation of Northern Kentucky Tenth Anniversary Report," 1997, Northern Ky. Tri-ED, Fort Mitchell, Ky.

"Tri-Ed Office Trying to Bag the Big Ones," *KP*, February 27, 1990, 8K.

Dan Tobergte

NORTHERN KENTUCKY UNIVERSITY. Northern Kentucky University (NKU) has its roots in a small community college, Northern Community College of the University of Kentucky (NCC), but has evolved into a dynamic university. In 1966 consultant M. M. Chambers, as a result of a study he conducted for the Kentucky Council on Public Higher Education (KCPHE), recommended that one more senior college be established for the state and that it be set in Northern Kentucky. He reasoned that because Northern Kentucky was the second-largest metropolitan region in the state, with a population then at a quarter of a million, it needed a public institution. At that time, the proportion of Northern Kentucky high school graduates going on to college was lower than the percentage doing so statewide. In 1946 the University of Kentucky began a series of extension courses at the Trailways Bus Station in Covington. In 1948 they rented space at First District School in Covington and began a limited two-year college program, thereby establishing the first community college of the University of Kentucky. In 1961 NCC moved into a newly constructed building in Park Hills, on land once part of Devou Park. It became the largest community college of the University of Kentucky, and the tuition from its enrollment was used to bond other community colleges statewide. A sign erected on the hilltop above the roadway that became interstate I-75 was lit up at night with the letters "UK" for all to see. NCC had a center director, a finance officer, a registrar, and a full- and part-time teaching staff composed mainly of instructors with MA and MS degrees. Often, local high school teachers supplemented their incomes as part-time instructors at NCC, and sometimes local lawyers, accountants, and other businessmen taught a class or two. The two-year nursing program was the most popular one offered at NCC, experiencing intense competition for admission.

Generally, students at NCC had one of three goals: they were seeking to better themselves in their jobs, or they just wanted to take some courses, or they were completing a two-year program before transferring to a campus where four-year college degrees were offered. Both the students and the staff at NCC thrived in its highly personal atmosphere; enrollment surged to well over 1,000 by the mid-1960s. It was this climate of growth and educational success that converged with need to produce a new four-year state college in Northern Kentucky.

The merger of the new Northern Kentucky State College (NKSC) with NCC was approved by UK and the KCPHE but also needed approval by Kentucky's legislators. The legislators approved, and on July 31, 1969, the land and buildings at NCC (today the site of NKU's Covington campus) were deeded to NKSC. The site selection committee was still rushed for time because building space was tight in Covington. Several sites were under consideration, one each in Boone, Campbell, and Kenton counties. Each of the counties argued why its site should be selected, but on March 29, 1969,

Northern Kentucky University, Highland Heights; the heart of the main campus around Lake Norse.

the site in Campbell Co., 328 acres of farms and houses located in Highland Heights, was chosen. The reason given was that the site was centrally located, with easy access from all areas of Northern Kentucky, and that there was plenty of space for a new college and future growth. Three other unspoken and unpublicized factors in the choice were, first, the Boone Co. site was remote and not closely connected to an existing or proposed interstate highway; second, the site in Kenton Co. was close to **Thomas More College** and might create financial problems by pitting higher private tuition against the lower tuition of a public institution; and, third, several influential people, including Art Schmidt, a powerful Republican state representative from Campbell Co. and a close friend of Governor Nunn, had lobbied successfully to have the college built in Campbell Co.

The most important unfinished task was choosing the college's first president. The Board of Regents agreed to offer a long-time UK administrator, Dr. A. D. Albright, the position, but he declined and instead accepted a Fulbright Fellowship in Belgium. The Board of Regents then offered the position to Ronald Carrier of Memphis State University, but he also turned down the offer. Finally, the offer was extended to Dr. W. Frank Steely, a native of Murray, Ky., who as dean at Clinch Valley Community College in Virginia had helped convert that school into a four-year institution. Steely accepted the offer, and on December 11, 1969, he was named the first president of NKSC.

After meeting with the board of regents in December 1969 at Butler State Park, outside Carrollton, to begin formulating a plan of action, Steely returned to Murray during the Christmas holidays and began hiring the college's first employees. On December 27, he persuaded Dr. James C. Claypool, whom Steely had hired earlier while heading the history department of Murray State College (now a university), to become dean of admissions and professor of history and left him with the following instruction: "We need somebody up there to represent us right away, so get up there, and get to work." Claypool, who was from Northern Kentucky, arrived and began work at the new college on February 1, 1970. Steely, meanwhile, was busy assembling more staff. Dr. Ralph Tesseneer, the graduate dean at Murray State College, was hired as the vice president for academic affairs and agreed to move to Northern Kentucky in time to help NKSC conduct its first academic offering, the summer session in July 1970. A few weeks later John Kilkenny, who was knowledgeable about the state's budget procedures, was hired, and by July he too was at work. Steely had arrived in Northern Kentucky in April, having already been hard at work for months. One of his first official acts as president was to go to Frankfort to lobby for money for the college's new budget. While he was there, on February 6, 1970, NCC was officially transferred to NKSC. Republican governor Nunn, who had been elected partly because of the significant numbers of votes he had received in Northern Kentucky, felt close to the new college and tried to do everything he could to help it. One of his administrative aides, John DeMarcus, who was the son of an influential Republican legislator, was told by Nunn to oversee the college's birth. DeMarcus and Steely worked closely together at this time; and later, after Nunn was replaced as governor by Democrat Julian Carroll (1971–1975), DeMarcus was hired by Steely and in 1971 became the college's first administrative vice president.

The leaders and employees of the new college were immediately confronted with many issues and challenges. Critics frequently raised questions about accreditation, about the quality of instruction, and about crowded facilities. The absorption and transference of NCC's faculty and staff into the new college at times also proved difficult. Each issue was addressed and resolved. The response about accreditation was that NKSC was a state school and would have the budget, faculty, facilities, and programs necessary for accreditation. The quality of instruction was established when, because there was a glut of qualified people (some experienced and some not) seeking to become college teachers, NKSC got "the pick of the litter." Many of those hired during the college's initial years, sensing the excitement of this new enterprise, decided to stay on for many years. In a short time, the quality of the programs and the growth of the college's facilities spoke for themselves as well. The concerns voiced by members of NCC's former staff (who as part of the overall agreement were to be retained) worked out in two ways. A few left on their own accord and went to other positions. The larger number, who stayed, were treated just as all other employees were, except that instructors from the former NCC were given the added security of immediate tenure.

The original 328 acres in Highland Heights was purchased in April 1970, about one month after Steely and his family had moved to Northern Kentucky. Plans for the first building at the Highland Heights campus were taking shape. Meanwhile, classes in Covington opened for the fall semester of 1970 with 1,644 students and 37 faculty members. From its beginnings, NKSC offered bachelor's degrees.

Classes continued at the overcrowded Covington campus for two years while construction progressed in Highland Heights. The ever-rising enrollments at the campus in Covington filled all the existing classroom facilities to capacity and necessitated buying metal trailerlike outbuildings that were made into additional classrooms. The teachers who taught in these makeshift facilities, however, took the adventure in good spirits, as did the students. In fact, many from those times remember all of these trials and challenges nostalgically.

Groundbreaking for the first building on the Highland Heights campus was held March 31, 1971, on a sunny day, before a large crowd; music was provided by the Campbell Co. High School band. This building was named for Governor Louie B. Nunn (1967–1971), who had been so instrumental in getting the college started. Construction on a second multipurpose arena and auditorium, named Regents Hall, started just six months later, thanks to Nunn, who had "somehow found" just the right amount of money needed to build it.

As the college's first two buildings and roadways were being built, upon lands that for generations had been family farms, the new college was offered a unique proposal. The Salmon P. Chase College of Law, long one of Ohio's and the nation's most productive nighttime law schools, was being forced out of its building in Cincinnati and needed to affiliate with a college to retain its accreditation. NKSC's progressive-minded regents and the college president, Steely, jumped at the chance to have a law school affiliated with NKSC, and Nunn and the KCPHE did not disapprove. However, there were many who did disapprove and a real political donnybrook ensued. The local press vacillated, sometimes seeming to like the idea of this merger while at other times seeming to disapprove. UK and the University of Louisville, the only two schools in the state with law schools, did not relish gaining more competition, and many of their alumni agreed, especially those holding law degrees. Making matters more difficult was the fact that most of the legislators in Kentucky had law degrees from one of these two law schools, and the idea of supporting what had always been an Ohio-based school, albeit one that often served students from the Northern Kentucky region, did not sit well with these lawmakers. Two crucial decisions won the day for the proposed merger. After Nunn had been persuaded by John DeMarcus to support the plan, the college asked the Kentucky attorney general to rule on whether "a college that was not a university" could operate a law school. His opinion, as the attorney general and a lawyer, was that a lawyer's JD (Juris Doctorate) degree was a student's first postgraduation degree and could be offered at schools that were colleges. Next, during a heated debate at a KCPHE meeting held on NKSC's Covington campus, a vote was called on the merger issue and it passed 5 to 4. In June 1972, the Chase College of Law moved to and occupied most of the Covington campus, just as NKSC moved onto the new Highland Heights campus.

The year 1972 was a good facilities growth year for NKSC, because Nunn Hall and Regents Hall were both completed. With only one classroom building and one office building, however, space at the new campus was limited. So a new science building was authorized by the state, and ground was broken for its construction that summer. Meanwhile, several houses located on John's Hill Rd., next to campus, were purchased and used for offices; but with 4,100 students attending NKSC, classroom and parking space was still at a premium.

The first commencement ceremonies at NKSC were held in spring 1973 with 611 graduates. That summer, the administration formulated plans to start a graduate program in education. Groundbreaking for the library, named the W. Frank Steely Library, was held in October 1973. In December 1973, NKSC received conditional accreditation from the Southern Association of Colleges and Schools (SACS). Not until December 1978 did the school earn full accreditation.

As fast as the buildings could be opened, they were filled to capacity, as the enrollment climbed to 5,000 in fall 1974. That semester the science building opened. In spring 1975, construction started on the Fine Arts Center. Construction on the Charles O. Landrum Academic Center was begun three months later.

Even with all of the progress and successes at NKSC, there were problems. Not only was space a major issue, but there were also disagreements within the administration. Citing no specific cause other than problems with the faculty, Steely resigned on September 15, 1975. He stayed on to teach history, and the board of regents appointed Academic Vice President Ralph Tesseneer as interim president.

Finding a president and creating unity within the faculty were among Tesseneer's goals. The most notable accomplishment of his term as interim president included a status change for the college. The governor of Kentucky, Julian Carroll (1975–1979), in his campaign for governor, promised to make NKSC a university. This was necessary because NKSC had a master's program in education and a law school, pushing it away from the undergraduate category. On June 19, 1976, Northern Kentucky State College became Northern Kentucky University (NKU).

The search for a new permanent president was progressing, with more than 200 applicants for the position. Tesseneer made it to the final five, but the faculty and the board of regents could not agree on a candidate. Finally, they returned to their original choice, A. D. Albright, who had become the executive director of the Kentucky Commission on Higher Education. In July 1976, Albright agreed to serve as president for a four-year term, which was later extended to seven years. At the time, NKU had more than 6,000 students and employed about 150 faculty members. Albright was inaugurated at the spring commencement ceremonies in 1977.

NKU was continuing to grow. Ground had been broken for the University Center (UC) in January 1976. Albright was so busy that the administration began looking for a provost to help "reorganize the academic structure." Dr. Leon Boothe was one of the applicants, but the person chosen for the position, in December 1976, was Dr. Janet Travis. With this appointment, she became the highest-ranking female academic administrator in the state at the time. In November of that year, the Landrum Academic Center opened; in spring 1977, the Fine Arts building opened; and the UC opened in the fall. NKU's growth was causing problems once again, this time with traffic. The interstates to NKU were not yet completed, and the smaller streets leading to the institution were congested. This, and crowded parking lots, added to everyone's frustration.

In 1977 the Chase Law School, still housed on the Covington campus, was also experiencing space problems. To get full accreditation from the American Bar Association, Chase needed more room, so a plan was developed to move the law school into Nunn Hall on the Highland Heights campus. One of the stipulations of the law creating NKU, however, was that the college should retain a presence in Kenton Co. So even after Chase College of Law had departed from the Covington campus, NKU would, because of this mandate, continue offering a schedule of lower-level and noncredit courses at its Covington facilities.

Construction began in 1978 on the Business, Education, and Psychology building (BEP), into which all undergraduate classes from Nunn Hall would eventually move, thus helping to fulfill the law school's space needs for accreditation. Most of the university's administrative offices were still housed in Nunn Hall at this time, so one more building would be needed before Chase could move to Highland Heights. The Lucas Administrative Center was delayed because of funding problems, but construction finally began in October 1979; the building was completed in June 1981. Just as Chase was about to solve the space problem, another controversy arose. A citizens' advisory committee for the state had decided that there were too many law schools in Kentucky and that one of the law schools had to close. Being the newest law school in the state, Chase College of Law was the one they chose. After much deliberation, it was decided that all three law schools would remain open, but their enrollments would be limited. This issue surfaced a few more times, but Chase College of Law responded by expanding its numbers of in-state students and limiting out-of-state enrollment, thereby removing one of the major criticisms that had been raised concerning the former Ohio law school. The Chase Law School moved into Nunn Hall on the Highland Heights campus in early 1982.

As NKU's enrollment grew to 5,900 in fall 1978, the administration realized that on-campus housing would soon be needed to serve students from outside of the region. In October 1978, a federal loan was obtained that would help to build dorms; construction was postponed for two years, however. In September 1980 construction began for dorms that would hold 400 students. The university's new housing facilities were opened in spring 1982.

Throughout NKU's initial growth years, during the 1970s and 1980s, the university continued to add to its curriculum and to expand services. Several academic departments were aided by the fact that there was a glut of doctoral degrees in several teaching fields during these years; thus NKU was able hire an amazing number of highly qualified instructors with degrees from some of the most prestigious institutions both in the United States and in other countries. Many of the persons hired in this period have remained at the university, contributing to its growth and helping to define its quality array of academic offerings. Moreover, several have held leadership positions within the university and have, through publications and other services, achieved prominence in their fields.

As NKU continued to expand, President Albright realized that Regent's Hall was too small a facility for a university. A new health center, later named the A. D. Albright Health Center, was the answer to this problem, and construction on the building began in July 1982. This new $9.3 million health-recreational center, located adjacent to Regents Hall, opened in 1984. It offered a swimming pool, racquetball courts, fitness rooms, classrooms, and offices.

The health-recreational center was a huge boost for the athletic department, which was already successful. The sports program had been started in 1970 by President Steely and James C. Claypool. Martin "Mote" Hils, a highly successful local high school basketball coach, and Bill Aker, a student attending NKU who had been a top prospect of the Cincinnati Reds, were hired as the basketball and baseball coaches, respectively. Both men compiled remarkable records at NKU in careers that, combined, totaled more than 30 years of service.

NKU also was a pacesetter in Kentucky in establishing women's athletic programs on an equal footing with men's programs. Among Kentucky's eight public universities, it was the first to offer women full athletic scholarships. The women's program, like the men's, has had multiple NCAA Division II Tournament appearances and has made several significant accomplishments. Both Hils's and Aker's teams achieved high national rankings, had victories over ranked NCAA Division I and II schools, and won regional and national championship games.

Nancy Winstel, who played basketball at NKU for two years, became the women's basketball coach in 1983 and took the team to the NCAA Division II Final Four in 1987 and 1999. In 2000 the women's basketball team won NKU's first-ever national title. They reached the Elite Eight in 2002 and the final game in 2003, but did not win that year. The 2005 women's softball team holds the longest intercollegiate win record in NCAA history, with 55 victories; it was ranked number one in the nation in NCAA Division II and finished in the final four in the national tournament. In 2008 NKU's women's basketball team again won the NCAA Division II National Championship, becoming the first women's team in Kentucky to win two national championships. In women's volleyball and soccer, men's golf, soccer, and tennis, NKU teams have also excelled, been ranked nationally, and advanced in several rounds of regional and national tournaments.

Dr. Albright announced his retirement in October 1982, and once again the board of regents had to find a new president. After a six-month search and more than 200 applicants, the board chose Dr. Leon E. Boothe as NKU's third president. He came to the university from Illinois State University, where he had served as the vice president and provost. Boothe was inaugurated in December 1983. One of his priorities as president was to diversify the university by adding more international programs.

Just one month before Dr. Boothe's inauguration, Chase Law School was given full accreditation from the Association of American Law Schools.

In 1987 a baseball field was built on campus, and there was talk about the team's going to the NCAA Division I sports level. The school's officials also began asking for a sports convocation center, but the issue was forced to the background by other pressing budget issues. In 1990 it resurfaced; however, because of political fighting in the legislature, the arena was dropped from the budget. In 2004 the administration of Governor Ernie Fletcher (2003–2007) included in its budget $42 million to build a regional special-events center at NKU. Subsequently, the **Bank of Kentucky** made a large donation in return for naming rights. In 2008 the Bank of Kentucky Arena opened on campus, seating 10,000 for concerts and other shows and 9,400 for basketball, having cost $64.2 million The architects were GBBN of Cincinnati and Three Sixty Architecture of Kansas City, Mo.

As usual, space was a problem for NKU. In spring 1990, enrollment had surpassed 11,000 and more classrooms were needed. The Applied Science and Technology Center was opened that semester and provided a large computer lab along with more classrooms and office space. The Fine Arts building gained some much-needed additional space when an addition was constructed in 1991 to house the Greaves Concert Hall, and more student housing was built in 1992. Dr. Boothe saw NKU through many expansions along with the addition of many new degrees. When he announced his resignation early in 1997, NKU again had to search for a president. Boothe stayed and began teaching history, retiring in 2007.

James C. Votruba, who had been teaching at Michigan State University, became the next president and was inaugurated on August 1, 1997. He has helped NKU become an economic factor in Northern Kentucky. NKU currently offers more than 70 baccalaureate degrees and 17 master's programs. Votruba's term as president so far has seen the addition of a new $38 million Science Center, designed by Omni of Lexington, which opened in the fall of 2002. A new housing unit called University Suites opened in fall 2003, bringing the total housing capacity to 1,400. In March 2007 the university purchased the closed Lakeside Manor Nursing Home and converted it into housing for 460 students, at a total cost of $19 million; it opened in fall 2008 and was named for longtime Campbell Co. Democratic legislator James Callahan.

Desiring to expand the university into the community, Votruba opened the NKU Grant Co. Center in 1998 and the NKU Metropolitan Education and Training Services (METS) Center, which cost $12 million, in September 2003. The METS Center is a training and learning center for local businesses that also provides a connection to NKU.

A new $40 million student center opened in August 2008, designed by Omni of Lexington. In the same year, the City of Highland Heights annexed the main campus of the university. The Carol Ann and **Ralph V. Haile** Jr./**US Bank** Foundation donated $15 million to NKU's College of Business in August 2008; it was the largest single private donation in the university's history.

Carter, D. J. "METS Attract Business to Region," *Northerner,* August 27, 2003.

Mackenzie, Stuart. "New $1.2 Million Planetarium in Works," *Northerner,* October 6, 2004.

Neltner, Susan. "Student's First Assignment: The Dorm," *Northerner,* August 27, 2003.

Stallings, Frank L., Jr. *Groundbreakings: Northern Kentucky University's First Twenty-Five Years.* Highland Heights, Ky.: NKU Publications, 1992.

Steely, Will Frank. *Northern: Birth of a University.* Cincinnati: Gateway, 1993.

Van Benschoten, Amanda. "Northern Kentucky's Most Influential People: #1 Jim Votruba," *SC,* May 31, 2005, 2K.

Wartman, Scott. "Bank of Ky. Arena Era Set to Commence," *KE,* May 9, 2008, A1.

———. "New Facility to Aid Student and Faculty Research Education," *Northerner,* April 24, 2002.

James C. Claypool and Elizabeth Comer Williams

NORTHERN KENTUCKY UNIVERSITY, GRANT CO. The Northern Kentucky University (NKU) Grant Co. Center opened in 1998 on Paris St. in Williamstown. The goal was to provide better access to college classes for students in the Grant Co. area, reducing travel to NKU's main campus in Highland Heights, 40 miles north.

The idea was first discussed in the 1970s, when an area vocational school was planning to relocate. Grant Co. competed to be selected as the site for the vocational school but did not win the bid. In March 1997 the idea resurfaced at a meeting between NKU interim president Jack Moreland and the community, where options for improving NKU's community outreach services were discussed. Another conference was held in September 1997 with Dr. **James Votruba**, incoming president of NKU. About 30 Grant Co. residents attended, showing their support. They wanted improved local access to higher education and wanted a school in which to train the county's growing workforce. This meeting went well, and some 30 more gatherings were held that year.

After these initial talks, things began to move quickly. NKU performed impact studies to see whether there was a need and whether there was enough interest to develop the concept. The residents of Grant Co. created the Grant Co. Higher Education Foundation and raised more than $40,000 for operational costs for the project, and they leased a building with three classrooms. NKU agreed to cover the additional $100,000 needed for instructional and administrative costs.

The Grant Co. community worked together to bring NKU to the county. Scholarships were donated by area businesses and registration for courses offered at the new center was held at the Chamber of Commerce in Williamstown. The first semester's enrollment was anticipated to be 20 full-time and up to 60 part-time students. Classes began on August 26, 1998, with 11 different classes. Those first classes were not held in the designated building, because it was still being renovated. Again, the community stepped in and classes were held next door at the **Williamstown United Methodist Church** until the center's building was ready. The NKU Grant Co. Center was officially dedicated on October 7, 1998, just over a year after that initial meeting held with President Votruba.

The curriculum consisted of the standard first-year college classes as well as continuing education classes. All earned credits could be transferred to other institutions or other NKU sites. Many students, expecting to transfer their credits, felt that the NKU Grant Co. Center would give them an easy transition into college. Students who might not have attempted college otherwise gained a chance to at least try out college work, and the center serves as a recruiting satellite for the NKU main campus.

The new center has been a success, but with the larger class sizes, the building quickly became too small. The former Williamstown City Building, which was about to be partially demolished and used for storage, was selected to provide more space. The renovation of this building was estimated to cost $200,000. Construction began and the dedication was held in September 2004. By then there were almost 400 students enrolled in 26 classes. The new building doubled the amount of space available. It has four classrooms, wireless Internet access, and a technology resource room with 13 computers. Currently, the NKU Grant Co. Center offers classes that lead to certificates, associate degrees, and bachelor degrees.

Baker-Nantz, Jamie. "NKU Finds New Home: City Hall Saved from Demolition," *Grant County News,* August 7, 2003.

"Northern Is on the Grow: Grant County Unit Expands," *KP,* September 9, 2004, 1K.

Pressley, Darrell S. "NKU Leaders Studying Branch in Grant County," *KE,* September 14, 1997, B1.

Tortora, Andrea. "New NKU Campus to Be Dedicated," *KE,* October 1, 1998, B2.

———. "NKU Courses Come to Grant," *KE,* June 22, 1998, A1.

Wilson, Brenda. "Long-time Dream of Local College Center Finally Comes True in Grant County," *Grant County News,* February 18, 1999, 11.

Yeager, Wayne. "Higher Education: NKU–Grant Co. Center Gets New Home," *Grant County News,* September 16, 2004, 1K.

Elizabeth Comer Williams

NORTHERN KENTUCKY WATER DISTRICT. The first public water systems in Northern Kentucky were formed by the City of Covington in 1871 and the City of Newport in 1873. In 1926 the Kenton Co. Water District No. 1 (KCWD) was formed with the purchase of the Dixie Water Company, which was serving areas along **Dixie Highway** (U.S. 25); the KCWD included one water-treatment plant at the time. In 1977 the KCWD purchased Covington's water system and thereby acquired one more water-treatment plant, located in Fort Thomas. The Campbell Co. Kentucky Water District (CCKYWD), formed in 1955, purchased water from both the KCWD and the Newport Water Works, also located in Fort Thomas. Legal suits ensued between the two districts over the amount and purchase price of the water. Both CCKYWD and KCWD acquired many smaller systems after being established.

On the initiative of the judge-executives of Campbell and Kenton counties and the boards of commissioners of CCKYWD and KCWD, and with the approval of the Kentucky Public Service Commission (KPSC), the two water districts were merged effective January 1, 1997, to form the Northern Kentucky Water Service District. In approving this step, the KPSC noted that combining the districts would improve customer service, consolidate debt, eliminate duplication of costs, and permit efforts that would ultimately result in economies of scale, lower costs, and a higher level of service to the public. The new district operated with a 10-member board, consisting of all commissioners from the two former boards, for its first year, and later with four Kenton Co. commissioners and two Campbell Co. commissioners, based on the populations of the two counties. The name of the district was changed in 2000 to the Northern Kentucky Water District (NKWD), and its commissioners began to serve staggered four-year terms.

The NKWD is the primary source of treated water in Northern Kentucky today; the merger made the NKWD the largest water district in Kentucky and the third-largest water provider in the state. The district is regulated by the KPSC, which approves and regulates the district's capital projects, rates, fees, and service standards. The NKWD provides water to more than 81,000 service points, supplying approximately 350,000 people in Kenton and Campbell counties and portions of Boone, Grant, and Pendleton counties, including the **Cincinnati/Northern Kentucky International Airport**. In recent years, it also has acquired the water utilities of the cities of Newport and Taylor Mill. The NKWD is a special district of the Commonwealth of Kentucky in that it is independent of county government but was established to furnish a water supply to the citizens of Campbell and Kenton counties residing within the boundaries of the district.

The NKWD maintains approximately 1,170 miles of main, 3 raw-water pump stations, 3 water-treatment plants, 12 distribution pump stations, and 17 water-storage tanks and covers a service area of more than 208 square miles. The district draws raw water from the Ohio River and the Licking River. The total filter capacity is 64 million gallons per day, with an average daily consumption of 32 million gallons. The district employs 155 people to handle all customer service, engineering, water-quality, production, and distribution aspects of the system.

Throughout the years, the NKWD has acquired smaller water systems in the area. The acquisition of the Newport water system in 2002 added a 10-million-gallon-per-day (m.g.d.) treatment plant that had an expansion capacity of 20 m.g.d. and saved ratepayers more than $34 million in comparison to building a new plant. The purchase also maintained critical redundancy between systems, was already sited and in operation, and will help provide adequate supply for the region until 2030.

The NKWD has recently acquired a 24-acre complex at the northeast corner of the junction of I-275 and I-75 in Erlanger that formerly was home to the Cincinnati Steel Treating Co. The property gives the water district two things it had been looking for since the merger: a central location inside the I-275 beltway and additional space in which to grow.

In response to increasing water-system demands, water-quality regulatory requirements, aging and wear of equipment and facilities, the needs for attention to customer service and proper redundancy in system components, and various other factors, the NKWD developed its Asset Management Plan for implementation and scheduling of contemplated projects. The plan weighs the necessity of each improvement, its appropriate or required timing, and the associated costs. The projects are identified with a timeline based on their appropriate years for implementation. The key components of the improvement program include supply and delivery improvements, infrastructure renewal, regulatory compliance, treatment enhancements, and utility operations and management. Since the district is under the regulatory authority of the KPSC, all improvements and projects must have the approval of that body.

Reis, Jim. *Pieces of the Past*. Vol. 1. Covington, Ky.: Kentucky Post, 1988.

"Water District Oks Purchase—Taylor Mill Already Had Approved Deal," *KP*, November 12, 2003, 2K.

Connie Pangburn

NORTHKEY COMMUNITY CARE. NorthKey Community Care, formerly known as Northern Kentucky Comprehensive Care Center, provides mental health, substance abuse, and developmental disability services to clients in the eight Northern Kentucky counties of Boone, Campbell, Carroll, Gallatin, Grant, Kenton, Owen, and Pendleton. From its inception in 1966, the agency has been governed by a regional board made up of individuals from each of the counties served. NorthKey Community Care's mission is to work "in partnership with the community to improve the quality of life of all its members through service, education and prevention." The organization is very similar in its mission to its neighbor to the east, **Comprehend Inc.**

The opportunity to develop and provide these services in Northern Kentucky sprang from federal legislation, the Mental Retardation Facilities and Community Mental Health Centers Act, enacted in 1963, which provided matching funds for states that created community treatment centers for persons with mental health and related needs. Kentucky's plan called for the creation of regional boards throughout the state, made up of volunteers who would be responsible for developing and overseeing the needed services within their region. The plan was called Pattern for Change and was submitted to the governor in 1965. Its goal, in keeping with the federal act, was to develop community mental health care systems throughout the state.

One year later, in 1966, Northern Kentucky became the second region in the state to incorporate; its organization became known as the Northern Kentucky Mental Health–Mental Retardation (MH-MR) Regional Board. Wilbert Ziegler was elected to serve as the first chairman, and shortly thereafter, Dr. Joseph Emmanuel Willett was hired as executive director. He and one additional employee began outpatient services in a converted three-room apartment at 412 E. Fourth St. in Covington.

During Willett's 26-year tenure as director, the agency greatly expanded its services as well as its physical presence throughout the region in order to better serve the community. As early as 1967, the agency was providing educational, referral, and screening services in addition to outpatient treatment. Day treatment services began that same year in a building at Second and Greenup Sts. in Covington, owned by the Kentucky Highway Department, and continued there until the state sold the property in the 1980s to private enterprise. To meet the needs of more individuals, in 1968 a building was purchased at 718 Columbia St. in Newport, and traveling clinics began servicing Carroll and Grant counties. These clinics, made up of a psychiatrist and a nurse, were available twice monthly to residents of each county. Inpatient services were also beginning to be offered through various affiliates, including **Speers Memorial Hospital** in Dayton, Ky. The name Comprehensive Care Center came into use at about this time in order to parallel similar agencies serving other areas.

Numerous additions to the array of services occurred during the 1970s. At 1408 Greenup St. in Covington, the Droege House opened in 1970 to house and treat male alcoholics. Short Term–Long Term Residential was established in 1971 to provide housing and other services for developmentally disabled adults, and by 1976 several Adult Work Habilitation centers had become operational in Boone, Carroll, Grant, and Pendleton counties. As of 1972, individuals in the criminal justice system gained access to a forensic psychiatric evaluation and treatment team. Senior citizens and children both saw additional services open up for them in 1977, by way of the Life Center, a senior services center in Covington that also has a children's outpatient counseling center. MH-MR services were extended to Gallatin Co. during the following year.

In 1978 a separate governing board was created to manage a psychiatric hospital, and an inpatient mental health unit was opened on a single floor of the Covington–Kenton Co. Hospital at 502 Farrell Dr. in Covington. Previously, this hospital had served only **tuberculosis** patients. Amid some initial controversy over the mixing of patients with mental health problems and those with TB, the facility was gradually converted to one occupied solely by those in need of mental health services. This transition was completed in 1980. Dr. Edward G. Muntel was employed in 1981 as the director of inpatient services, and in 1983 the facility was expanded and renovated in order to meet the special mental health needs of children and adolescents. The name was then officially changed to Children's Psychiatric Hospital. Muntel succeeded Willet as president and CEO of Comprehensive Care in

1992, and the hospital's board was merged with that of the MH-MR Regional Board in 1998.

Both inpatient and outpatient services for children were a major focus of the agency's growth in the 1980s and 1990s, and inpatient services for adults were discontinued in 1981. Among the highlights of this focus on youth was the opening of a Children's Treatment Center in Fort Thomas, and several partnerships developed with area school districts to provide day treatment services.

The goal of having the board's programs licensed by an accrediting body in the field was achieved in 1984, when outpatient services received accreditation from the Joint Commission on Accreditation of Healthcare Organizations (JCAHO). One year later the hospital was accredited by the same group. To maintain its accreditation, staff and board members began a continuing cycle of long-range planning, implementation, and self-evaluation for all of its programs. In 1995 the agency achieved a high rating in every category, thus gaining JCAHO's Accreditation with Commendation status.

Further expansion of the outpatient services provided by Comprehensive Care and the Children's Psychiatric Hospital took place in the latter part of the 1980s and the 1990s. New offices in Covington and in Owen and Pendleton Counties were opened in 1985, 1989, and 1999, respectively. In 1991 the J. E. Willett Treatment Center began providing residential services for adults with developmental disabilities; various other services were provided to clients of all ages.

Along with the ever-expanding services provided by Northern Kentucky Comprehensive Care Center since its inception came the continual need for more space. During the early years, office space was rented, but gradually the organization purchased or built its own facilities throughout the area to house various programs. NorthKey Community Care currently has staff in 24 office sites throughout the region and owns 14 of the buildings that house programs. The Regional Board office itself moved from Second and Greenup Sts. to 430 Garrard St. in Covington in 1972. In 1980 this office was moved to 503 Farrell Dr., Covington.

Another issue that has faced the organization throughout its history is obtaining adequate funding. While the start-up funds came from the state, with federal matching dollars, additional sources have been sought to maintain current programs and to implement new services. In 1976 an MH-MR Services tax was first proposed to the fiscal courts in the eight counties NorthKey Community Care serves. The tax was placed on the ballots for voter approval and passed in several counties in 1980. Many of the programs provided by NorthKey Community Care continue to receive support through local, state, and federal dollars, but the board has at times encountered budget challenges related to funding changes. In order to maintain a highly qualified clinical staff for the delivery of services, the board has blended funding streams and melded support for services from a wide variety of sources. In addition, Medicaid, Medicare, private insurance, and fees for services (charged on a sliding scale, based on clients' ability to pay) round out the funding that sustains service delivery.

Following the merger of Comprehensive Care and the Children's Psychiatric Hospital, the agency's name was changed in 1999 from Northern Kentucky Comprehensive Care Center to NorthKey Community Care. This name is now used for all services offered by the Northern Kentucky MH-MR Regional Board. Muntel continues to serve as the president and CEO. A senior management staff of 15 supervises approximately 430 employees in the various service branches, including diagnosis, treatment, support, and education. NorthKey Community Care's outlook for the future includes the continuation and further expansion of these programs to meet the needs of the Northern Kentucky community.

Hicks, Jack. "TB Sanatorium Open to Mental Patients?" *KP*, January 18, 1975, 15.
"Muntel New CEO at Hospital," *KP*, August 21, 1992, 2K.
NorthKey Community Care. www.northkey.org/live/index.asp (accessed December 2, 2005).
Vance, Debra Ann. "Social Services Struggle to Keep Aid Going," *KP*, February 8, 1977, 2K.
Weathers, Rosemary. "Mental Health Pioneer Willett Retires," *KP*, August 21, 1992, 1K–2K.

Janet M. Lester

NOTRE DAME ACADEMY. Notre Dame Academy (NDA), in Park Hills, is owned and operated by the **Sisters of Notre Dame**, a Roman Catholic religious order. The academy began in 1875 as a school for children in kindergarten through eighth grade, with an added two-year commercial school. The enrollment in fall 1875 was seven. The sisters erected a four-story building on Fifth St. in Covington to serve as a convent, and the school there was dedicated on July 26, 1876. By the time a high school program had been added to the curriculum in 1906, Sister Mary Agnetis had put in 30 years of service as the school's principal. In 1937 it was necessary to close the elementary school in order to accommodate the rapidly growing secondary-level program. By the 1950s, the building on Fifth St. became inadequate as the school's enrollment grew to record numbers. It was impractical to renovate such an old facility, so a new Notre Dame Academy, costing nearly $1.5 million, was built on the grounds of the sisters' provincial house in Park Hills. Alumnae, friends, parents, and corporate sponsors such as Conrad Hilton (of the hotel chain family, who donated $500,000) contributed generously to the project. The new school, on Hilton Dr., opened in October 1963 with an enrollment of 562. In 1994 NDA launched a $2.9 million campaign to renovate the old building and to construct a new addition housing seven classrooms and a gymnasium. In 1996 the new addition was completed, and the U.S. Department of Education named the academy a Blue Ribbon School of Excellence. In 2007 the school launched a $12 million fundraising campaign to renovate its facility and to add athletic fields and a performing arts center.

As a Catholic school, NDA continues to offer its students an opportunity to grow in the knowledge and practice of faith. Notre Dame's educational program is founded on four cornerstones that are part of the educational heritage of the Sisters of Notre Dame: teacher dignity, individual worth, the centrality of religion, and thoroughness of instruction in all subjects. Today the school has an enrollment of about 600 students and more than 60 faculty and staff. It is governed by a four-member administrative team and supported by dedicated staff, parents, more than 9,000 alumnae, and community and business leaders.

Notre Dame Academy. *Alumnae Directory*. Bloomington, Ind.: University Publishing, 2004.
"Notre Dame Academy: Celebrating 100 Years of Women Making a Difference," *Messenger* (special supplement), September 22, 2006.
Ryan, Paul E. *History of the Diocese of Covington, Kentucky*. Covington, Ky.: Diocese of Covington, 1954.

Donna M. Bloemer

NOURSE, MARY M. (b. July 5, 1870, Mount Healthy, Ohio; d. June 23, 1959, Fort Thomas, Ky.). Artist Mary Madeline Nourse was the sixth of seven children born to Charles E. and Viola J. Seward Nourse. She attended the Cincinnati Art Academy, and in 1891 she became a decorator for the Rookwood Pottery on Mount Adams in Cincinnati. She remained there for 14 years. Nourse learned wood carving from Benn Pitman, an uncle by marriage. She taught basket-weaving and jewelry-making and taught art as a volunteer at a Catholic school in Cincinnati. Mary was the niece of Elizabeth Nourse, an internationally known artist. Mary's work is displayed at museums in France and Norway. For many years she resided along E. Fourth St. in Covington; she was a member of the **Covington Art Club** for at least 55 years, and in 1920 she designed the organization's insignia. Mary Nourse kept a scrapbook, which contains many photographs of the early artists at Rookwood Pottery. She died in 1959 at her home in Fort Thomas and was buried at Spring Grove Cemetery in Cincinnati.

Cummins, Virginia Raymond. *Rookwood Pottery Potpourri*. Silver Spring, Md.: Cliff R. Leonard and Duke Coleman, 1980.
"Death Takes Retired Artist," *KP*, June 23, 1959, 6K.
Spring Grove Cemetery Records, Cincinnati.

NURSING HOMES AND RETIREMENT HOUSING. The long-term-care industry (nursing homes licensed to provide skilled and intermediate care) and the retirement housing business are active in Northern Kentucky, as they are throughout the country. Facilities for care of the elderly proliferated nationwide after Medicaid and Medicare were created during the early 1960s. Before 1960 about 2,000 nursing homes operated in the United States; today, there are nearly 20,000, containing approximately 2 million beds, and some 70 percent of nursing home residents participate in Medicaid or Medicare, mainly Medicaid.

In recent years, some demographers have suggested that given current usage patterns, the United States needs to open one new 100-bed nursing home each day just to keep up with demand. The over-age-85 segment of the nation's population is the fastest-growing age group, and the average age of residents in nursing facilities today is around 82. Furthermore, a greater percentage of the elderly age cohort now needs nursing home care because of increases in the mobility of adult children, in two-wage-earner households, and in divorce rates. The once common three-generation household has become rare. Thus, the odds of a person's living alone in later life have risen dramatically, and this factor is the main predictor of one's need to enter a nursing or retirement home.

In former years, elderly care facilities in the Northern Kentucky region were government run. Each county, as required by early state legislation, was responsible for its indigent poor and elderly people, who were placed in the local county home, specifically the county farm, where the county fiscal court provided for elderly citizens as well as orphans and people who were physically or mentally ill. Often called the local "pest house," these facilities were actually farmlike settings where the residents grew their own produce and raised their own livestock. In the 1870s Mason Co. began referring to its "pest house" as the "county infirmary." Such facilities have been recorded in Maysville; in Bracken Co.; in Campbell Co., first in Alexandria and later in Highland Heights; in Kenton Co., at Latonia and along the **Covington and Lexington Turnpike**, just south of Covington's city limits; and in Owen Co., just southwest of downtown Owenton. At least two of these government-run care operations evolved into modern skilled-nursing facilities: in Latonia, the Kenton Co. Infirmary became Rosedale Manor, and in Highland Heights, the Campbell Co. Home (infirmary), renamed Lakeside Terrace, operated until it was closed in 2006.

For elderly military veterans, the U.S. Veterans Administration operates a 64-bed nursing facility in Fort Thomas, the **Veterans Administration Medical Center**. In the late 1940s it replaced the short-term convalescent hospital (nursing home) for U.S. Army Air Force personnel that operated for a short time at the **Fort Thomas Military Reservation**, just after **World War II**. A similar facility existed briefly in the former resort hotels of Fort Thomas just after **World War I** (see **Altamont Springs Hotel**; **Shelly Arms Hotel**). Other federal or state-run nursing homes that care for Northern Kentuckians are located in Dayton or Chillicothe, Ohio; Anderson, Ind.; and in Wilmore in Jessamine Co., Ky.

Modern skilled-care and intermediate-care nursing homes operate in all the counties of Northern Kentucky today. These homes, participants in the Medicaid and Medicare programs, had to obtain a certificate of need from the Kentucky State Health Department in order to build and operate. Health planning, an idea born of the 1960s, limits the beds available under the federal programs in a given county based upon the county's population of individuals over age 65. This measure represents an attempt by the federal government to contain costs. Gone are the many small 15-to-25-bed nursing homes operating out of former residential houses, structures not built to accord with modern construction or fire-prevention standards.

Along Highland Ave. in Covington is a large former skilled-nursing facility that offers only retirement housing today. Developed by former Campbell Co. judge **Andrew J. Jolly** in the 1970s as Geriatrics Inc., this multistory concrete structure, at 300 beds, was once the largest nursing facility in Kentucky. Its startup was marred with politics, lawsuits, and trouble, but it eventually became the St. John Nursing Home. In recent years, following another period of flux and name and ownership changes, this nursing home became a part of Baptist Life Communities, a group noted for its quality management; however, the facility no longer provides licensed skilled nursing home care.

Retirement housing denotes a lower level of care, provided to residents who on average are somewhat younger than nursing home residents. They live in apartments, rather than two to a room as is common in a nursing home. Retirement housing facilities may be operated by proprietary or nonprofit groups or by government entities. The federal government, in conjunction with local nonprofit sponsors, has constructed several HUD (Housing and Urban Development) independent-living housing projects for seniors in Northern Kentucky. Examples include the Golden Tower and the Panorama Apartments in Covington (both designed by architect **Carl Bankemper**), the Grand Tower and the Saratoga Apartments in Newport, Colonial Heights in Florence, and Parkview Manor in Williamstown. Residents' rent is subsidized so that they pay no more than 25 percent of their income in rent, which includes utilities. Only housing and a small number of activities are provided; residents do their own cooking. Baptist Life Communities operates independent-living units next to its Village Care Center in Erlanger.

Congregate and assisted-living housing are types of retirement housing that provide other levels of care. In congregate housing, at least one meal per day is included in the monthly charge; assisted-living arrangements usually offer three meals each day and general care, in contrast to the skilled or intermediate care of nursing homes. The federal government does not subsidize congregate or assisted-living housing. Examples in Northern Kentucky include Colonial Heights in Florence (a facility of the Retirement Housing Foundation of Long Beach, Calif.), which offers assisted living in addition to independent living; Griesser Farm in Burlington, a Baptist Life Communities facility offering independent living plus; Brighton Gardens, developed and first owned by Marriot Senior Living but now owned by Sunrise Senior Living, along Turkeyfoot Rd. in Edgewood; and the two facilities of Atria Senior Living of Louisville in Kenton Co.: Summit Heights in Crestview Hills and the Matt Toebben–built Highland Crossings in Fort Wright. The latter is near the St. Charles Care Center, which also offers a similar level of care. Many local nursing homes are beginning to offer a small number of independent-living units on their grounds.

A recent trend in Northern Kentucky has been the establishment of hospices, which provide care for the terminally ill either at home or in a separate facility. Within the past 10 years, the Hospice of Northern Kentucky, an affiliate of the Hospice of the Bluegrass, has opened in Fort Thomas at 1463 Alexandria Pk. Its patients are cared for at home, in other long-term-care facilities, and in hospitals such as the nine-bed unit it operates within St. Luke Hospital East. A similar facility has recently opened on the campus of the **St. Elizabeth Medical Center** in Edgewood as a result of a $2 million gift from the **Ralph Haile/US Bank** Foundation. It is Northern Kentucky's first freestanding hospice, with room for 16 patients.

Boone Co. Infirmary, 1918.

The Methodist retirement group of Cincinnati (now called Life Enriching Communities), the longtime operator of the Methodist Home at College Hill, Twin Towers, and other similar operations in Ohio, purchased a few years ago the land where the **Beverly Hills Supper Club** once stood in Southgate, Ky. The group's announced plan was to build on the site a multifaceted continuing-care retirement community consisting of independent living, congregate housing, and nursing home care. However, construction has not yet begun. Perhaps Life Enriching Communities judges that the potential occupants of a retirement community will be reluctant to live at the location of the Beverly Hills Supper Club fire in 1977, in which 165 adults and teens and two unborn children died. The event may be too fresh in their memories. If developed, the facility will be the first such full-service retirement housing operation in Northern Kentucky. Several retirement-housing development companies have considered that site since the fire but have passed it by, despite its excellent location from an operations point of view.

Northern Kentucky Nursing Homes

Boone Co.

Florence Park Care Center, Florence

Harborside Healthcare (formerly Woodspoint), Florence

St. Luke Hospital West, Florence (a few long-term-care beds)

Bracken Co.

Bracken Co. Nursing and Rehabilitation Center, Augusta

Campbell Co.

Baptist Convalescent Center, Newport

Carmel Manor, Fort Thomas

Highlands, Fort Thomas

St. Luke Hospital East, Fort Thomas (has a few long-term-care beds)

Carroll Co.

Green Valley Health and Rehabilitation Center, Carrollton.

Gallatin Co.

Gallatin Health Care Center, Warsaw

Grant Co.

Grant Manor HealthCare Center, Williamstown

Kenton Co.

Covington Ladies Home (an **Amos Shinkle** charity of a century ago)

Garrard Convalescent Home, Covington

Madonna Manor, Villa Hills

Rosedale Manor, Latonia

St. Charles Care Center, Fort Wright

St. Elizabeth Medical Center North, Covington

Village Care Center, Erlanger

Villaspring of Erlanger

Woodcrest Manor Care Center, Elsmere

Mason Co.

Maysville Nursing and Rehabilitation Facility

Owen Co.

Harborside Health Care Facility, Owenton

Pendleton Co.

River Valley Nursing Home, Butler

Robertson Co.

Robertson Co. Health Care Facility, Mount Olivet

Mendelson, Mary Adelaide. *Tender Loving Greed.* New York: Knopf, 1974.

Vladeck, Bruce. *Unloving Care.* New York: Basic Books, 1980.

Michael R. Sweeney

OAK ISLAND BAPTIST CHURCH. Oak Island Baptist Church began in a log schoolhouse on top of Bowman Hill in southern Kenton Co. The church, organized on July 31, 1858, as Bowman Baptist Church, drew its members from congregations of Baptist churches in Covington, Crittenden, DeCoursey Creek, Lee's Spring, and Wilmington. The first pastor of Bowman Baptist Church was N. H. Carlisle. The congregation met for more than 10 years in the schoolhouse on Bowman Hill. In 1869, when more space was needed, the church obtained a plot of land on Cruise Creek in Kenton Co. Because the creek ran around both sides of the plot, creating an island where more than one dozen oak trees grew, the church changed its name to Oak Island Baptist Church on August 21, 1869. However, when it rained, the creek would run high and the church's meetinghouse was in danger of being swept away. In November 1882, church trustees purchased an acre of ground known as Van Patten Corner, located on a hill near Morning View. The building on Oak Island was then torn down and moved to the present location of the church. It was used as both a school and a church until 1908, when a new building was constructed on the site and a separate one-room schoolhouse was built. The church continues weekly meetings today and is a member of the Northern Kentucky Baptist Association.

"Oak Island Hosts a Revival," *Erlanger Dixie News*, April 29, 1993, 19.

"Recording the '80s: A Decade in Review," *Kenton County Recorder*, December 26, 1989, 1.

Andrea Watkins

OAKLAND BAPTIST CHURCH. The Oakland Baptist Church, on Johnson Rd. in Gallatin Co., between Glencoe and Warsaw, was organized in 1859. Its first church building was erected in 1862 on land donated by Alfred Arrasmith in a deed dated August 6, 1862. Joseph Ambrose (1798–1881), from Estill Co., was the first minister and the organizer of the church; he was buried in the church's cemetery. The first members of the new church included U. C. Allphin, Joseph Arrasmith, Joseph Brett, E. N. Casey, T. J. Clements, Elkanah Crouch, Henry Crouch, John Crouch, Peter Dorman, Ben Duncan, Josiah Ellis, Thomas Ellis, Alfred Kemper, David Lilly, and Joseph Myers.

An earlier church, Providence Baptist Church, existed in the neighborhood as early as 1831 and was a forerunner of the Oakland Baptist Church. Both churches were members of the Ten Mile Baptist Association, which reorganized Providence Baptist Church as the Oakland Baptist Church. The new Oakland Baptist Church established a school in 1867 and maintained it until November 8, 1902, when it was sold to the Gallatin Co. School District for $10.

The first Sunday school at the Oakland Baptist Church began in 1904, and the church's first organ arrived in 1917. No church meetings were held during the winter of 1918–1919 because of the influenza epidemic in the nation. The church was remodeled in 1921, and a new entrance, a steeple, and a church bell were added. The front porch was added and electricity was installed in 1938. The parsonage was built in 1952, and the church has undergone numerous improvements since. In 2006 the Oakland Baptist Church was still meeting.

Unsigned typescript distributed by the Oakland Baptist Church, Kenton Co. Public Library, Covington, Ky.

Bernie Spencer

OAKLAND CHRISTIAN CHURCH. The Oakland Christian Church is located at 5161 Milford Rd. in Falmouth. Before there was a church, the residents of Browningsville, on Willow Creek, would meet in the general store to discuss everyday business, the weather, and the Bible. In 1860 the Browningsville Christian Church was organized after seven men formed a Bible study group. The Browningsville log schoolhouse was the church's first meeting-place, and the first pastor was William P. Houston. The initial few years were difficult for the church, with the **Civil War** causing division among members. But despite the hardships of war, and although there were members fighting on different sides, families continued to attend church together. Some brought their slaves to services. As the membership grew, the need for a more centrally located place of worship became apparent. Therefore, the church was moved into the Oakland school. In 1869 the Oakland Christian Church's first permanent sanctuary was erected in a grove of oak trees on land in Falmouth donated by Lorenzo Colvin. In 1916, under the leadership of David W. Nicholas, the first church structure was demolished and a new one built. The new church was erected on the old foundation stones and cost $3,000. Today, the church is still using the pews that were purchased when this building was erected. William M. Lenox served as pastor from 1918 through 1964. In 1929 the Oakland Christian Workers women's group was formed. In December 1964, the church began holding weekly, rather than monthly, services. The building was remodeled by addition of a choir loft, a baptistery, a library, a minister's office, and several classrooms. The size of the sanctuary was also increased. In 1984 John Lang, and later David Mason, were called as youth ministers. Today, the Oakland Church has an attendance of about 175 each Sunday, and John M. Byard is the minister.

Belew, Mildred Bowen. *The First 200 Years of Pendleton County.* Falmouth, Ky.: M. B. Belew, n.d. [ca. 1994].

"Oakland Christian Church Observes Centennial," *Falmouth Outlook*, July 18, 1869, 8.

Oakland Christian Workers. *Oakland's Centennial Cook Book, 1869–1969.* Chicago: Women's Club, 1969.

Melissa J. Wickelhaus

OAK RIDGE. Oak Ridge is a central Kenton Co. neighborhood located just south of Taylor Mill. The businesses and homes at the intersection of Hands Pk. (Ky. Rt. 1501) and Taylor Mill Rd. (Ky. Rt. 16) in Oak Ridge serve as a reminder of the small communities that dotted central Kenton Co., before the wave of annexation that began during the 1960s. Established during the early 1800s, Oak Ridge was a farming community. An Oak Ridge booster reported to a Covington newspaper in 1883 that "peace and friendship and plenty prevail at the Ridge." The names of early Oak Ridge families including Hand, Klette, Lipscomb, and Senour survive as street names. **Latonia Lakes**, originally a resort village, was carved out of Oak Ridge during the early 1930s. After **World War II**, Oak Ridge began the slow transition from a farming to a suburban community. Annexations over the past 30 years have almost removed Oak Ridge from the map, as Covington, Independence, and Latonia Lakes have partitioned the area. This process has not always been smooth. During the early 1980s, for instance, a staffing reduction at the Oak Ridge Fire Department, operated by Covington since annexing it in 1978, brought a backlash from Oak Ridge residents. The proposed widening of Taylor Mill Rd. (Ky. Rt. 16) may bring more disruptions to Oak Ridge. Landmarks remaining in Oak Ridge include the **Oak Ridge Baptist Church**, founded in 1844, and the Oak Ridge School building, which now houses the Bible Baptist Church.

An Atlas of Boone, Kenton, and Campbell Counties, Kentucky. Philadelphia: D. J. Lake, 1883.

"Cuts at Oak Ridge Still Issue for Residents," *KP*, March 3, 1983, 5K.

"Kenton County," *DC*, March 20, 1883, 4.

"900 Cottage Sites Established at Latonia Lakes," *KP*, June 14, 1931, 9.

Greg Perkins

OAK RIDGE BAPTIST CHURCH. The Oak Ridge Baptist Church, at 6056 Taylor Mill (Ky. Rt. 16) in southern Kenton Co., is part of the Southern Baptist denomination and a member of the Northern Kentucky Baptist Association. It celebrated its 160th anniversary in October 2004.

The church was organized October 4, 1844, by 37 families belonging to the Banklick Baptist Church (known today as the Hickory Grove Baptist Church), who wanted a church closer to their homes in the Decoursey Pk. (Ky. Rt. 177) area. The new church's name at first was the DeCoursey Creek Baptist Church, and meetings were held in a store on Klette Rd. until the following year, when a church building was constructed on the east side of Decoursey Pk. about one-half mile south of the top of Pye's Hill and five miles south of Latonia. Local physician George White donated the 1.5-acre lot. This first structure, which is used today as a private residence, was a two-story white frame building. It served as both a school and a church until 1872. In that year the DeCoursey Creek Baptist Church moved into the Richardson Schoolhouse, on Taylor Mill Rd. opposite Klette Rd.; the church's name was changed to the Oak Ridge Baptist Church. That building is now used by the Brucewood Presbyterian Church. In June 1879, a new one-room frame church was built on the site of the present church grounds on Taylor Mill Rd., property donated by the Richardson family. The old building on Decoursey Pk. was deeded over to the Kenton Co. Board of Education and served as a school until 1929.

In 1942 the frame church built in 1879 was moved to the present church property and placed on a new basement. In 1954 construction was begun on the basement of the present structure, in 1957 construction of the main sanctuary started, and on October 15, 1958, the first services were held in the present brick structure during the church's 114th anniversary. In 1955, 42 members left the Oak Ridge Baptist Church to form the Amity Baptist Mission at Plantation Heights in Taylor Mill. The old frame building on the present grounds was torn down in 1960 to make way for additional parking space. An educational building was completed on the north side of the sanctuary that same year.

Oak Ridge Baptist Church 100th Anniversary Booklet. Latonia Lakes, Ky.: Oak Ridge Baptist Church, 1944.

"Special Services Mark Anniversaries at Two Churches," *KP,* September 26, 1987, 6K.

"Taught Sunday School 62 Years," *KP,* October 15, 2003, A15.

Pat Workman

O'HARA, JAMES J. (b. May 6, 1825, New Liberty, Ky.; d. August 21, 1900, Covington, Ky.). Judge James J. O'Hara, a Democrat and a prominent lawyer, was the son of lawyer James O'Hara Sr., a native of Ireland, who settled at New Liberty in Owen Co. James J. O'Hara was educated at St. Mary's College, near Lebanon, Ky. After graduation, he moved to Crittenden in Grant Co., where he began the practice of law. During the **Civil War**, his activities in support of the South led to his being imprisoned by the Union for several years at Camp Chase, in Columbus, Ohio. O'Hara was a first cousin of Col. Theodore O'Hara, author of *The Bivouac of the Dead.* James O'Hara married Oberia Conn of Bourbon Co., and the couple had one daughter. In 1859 they moved to Covington, where O'Hara spent the rest of his life. About 1863 he created a law partnership with **John G. Carlisle**. In 1868 he was elected a judge of Kentucky's 12th District, a position he held until 1874, when he became a law partner of former Kentucky governor **John W. Stevenson** (1867–1871). Stevenson retired from the firm in 1881, and O'Hara formed a new partnership with his associate **James W. Bryan**, who served as Kentucky's lieutenant governor from 1887 until 1891, and also with future Kentucky governor William Goebel (1900). That firm lasted until 1893, when another law partnership was formed with **Shelley D. Rouse**. After a long and distinguished career, O'Hara died of Bright's disease at age 75 in 1900, at his home at 27 W. 11th St. in Covington. Funeral services were held at St. Mary Cathedral and burial was in the Linden Grove Cemetery in Covington.

"Bar of Kenton County Took Suitable Action," *KP,* August 23, 1900, 3.

"Judge James J. O'Hara Died Tuesday Night," *KP,* August 22, 1900, 5.

"Judge James J. O'Hara Funeral," *KP,* August 23, 1900, 3.

Levin, H., ed. *The Lawyers and Lawmakers of Kentucky.* Chicago: Lewis Publishing, 1897.

"Mrs. Judge O'Hara," *KP,* March 22, 1893, 4.

O'HARA, JOHN "JAY" (b. October 1, 1922, Covington, Ky.; d. December 7, 1997, Edgewood, Ky.). Kenton Co. attorney John "Jay" O'Hara was the son of J. Earl O'Hara, who worked in the tobacco business and later owned a Ford automotive dealership in Ludlow. Jay O'Hara said that as far back as he could remember, he always wanted to become an attorney. However, **World War II** interrupted his schooling, and he spent several years in the U.S. Army. During the war he was injured and sent to a hospital in Louisville for treatment. There he met a nurse from Idaho, named Dorothy Arnold, and a romance soon developed. In 1946, after the end of the war, the couple married and made their home on 17th St. in Covington. Jay O'Hara entered Xavier University in Cincinnati and graduated in 1947. He then attended the University of Kentucky Law School at Lexington, graduating in 1949. By that time, the first two of the couple's seven children had arrived, and the family moved into a larger house, located on Old State Rd. in Park Hills. They later moved to a home on Park Dr. in Edgewood. O'Hara worked as a partner in the law firm of O'Hara, Ruberg, Cetrulo, and Osborne. In 1958 O'Hara was elected Kenton Co. commonwealth attorney, a position he held for the next 18 years. During the 1960s he saw the need for a drug-education program and began speaking to high school, college, and civic groups throughout Kentucky, Indiana, and Ohio about this growing problem. He served as president of the Kentucky Bar Association in 1973 and as president of the National Association of District Attorneys in 1974. O'Hara was appointed a Kentucky Supreme Court justice in 1982 but was defeated when he ran for election the following year. In 1990 he was diagnosed with prostate cancer but continued to work in his law practice. He went public with his illness and campaigned tirelessly about the need for regular prostate examinations. After their children were grown, O'Hara and his wife enjoyed spending time at the **Summit Hills Golf and Country Club** in Edgewood, golfing, dancing, playing bridge, and just socializing. They also became world travelers, visiting Ireland a number of times and also Belgium, France, Germany, Italy, and Switzerland. John Jay and Dorothy O'Hara had been married for 51 years when he died in his Edgewood home at age 75. Funeral services were held at the St. Agnes Catholic Church in Fort Wright, and burial was in St. Mary Cemetery, Fort Mitchell.

"John J. O'Hara," *KP,* December 10, 1997, 4K.

"Judges Mourn Death of John 'Jay' O'Hara," *KP,* December 9, 1997, 1K.

"Justice John J. O'Hara," *KP,* December 9, 1997, 16A.

Local History Files, Kenton Co. Public Library, Covington, Ky.

OHIO RIVER. The Ohio River, which begins at Pittsburgh with the confluence of the Allegheny and Monongahela rivers, flows 981 miles generally southwest to its confluence with the Mississippi River near Cairo, Ill. Its halfway point is at mile 490.5, in Boone Co., near where Garrison Creek flows into it. The Ohio River forms the northern boundaries of Mason, Bracken, Pendleton (a small section), Campbell, Kenton, Boone, Gallatin, and Carroll counties in Northern Kentucky. Kentucky, using the claims of old Virginia to the low-water mark of the northern shore, long claimed ownership of the Ohio River through Northern Kentucky. Through the years, as the river changed and high-lift dams raised its level, a series of lawsuits concerning the boundary line worked their way to the U.S. Supreme Court, until *Kentucky v. Indiana* (decree entered 1985) and *Ohio v. Kentucky* (decided 1980; decree entered 1985) finally established the existing boundary. Today the river remains an important conduit for the shipment of industrial goods and natural resources. It also serves recreational purposes, including boating, fishing, and water skiing.

The present course of the Ohio River in Northern Kentucky was established during the Pleistocene epoch of the Quaternary period (see **Geology**), during the time of the Illinoian **Glacier**, about 200,000–250,000 years ago. The glacier formed an ice dam, forcing the pre-Illinoian Deep Stage Ohio River (which flowed as far north as present-day Hamilton, Ohio) to be deflected southward and causing the modern Ohio River to assume its present course from the area of Lunken Airport in Cincinnati to Lawrenceburg, Ind. The Deep Stage Licking River (which had emptied into the Deep Stage Ohio River near present-day St. Bernard, Ohio) was also forced south by the glacier, and the confluence of the Licking River with the Ohio River shifted to its present-day location (**the Point**) between Covington and Newport and across from Cincinnati.

After the retreat of the Wisconsin glacier about 10,000 years ago, Paleo-Indians began to live in the Greater Cincinnati region (see **American Indians**). Evidence of habitation exists in Northern Kentucky from the Paleo, Archaic, Woodland and Late Prehistoric–**Fort Ancient** periods. The Adena, Hopewell and Newtown cultures of the Woodland period (ca. 1000 B.C.–A.D. 1000) largely centered on rivers and streams and included burial mounds. The Late Prehistoric–Fort Ancient period (A.D. 1000 until after 1600) was marked by villages along the Ohio River and its tributaries, where American Indians collected mussel shells, eating the mussels and using the shells for tools. They also cultivated corn, beans, and squash. By the 1600s some sites of habitation, such as that at Petersburg in Boone Co., include archaeological evidence of a trading network with European explorers, trappers, and missionaries.

For early transportation along the Ohio River, dugout canoes were used by both American Indians and early explorers. Sometimes as large as 60 feet long and 5 feet wide, dugout canoes took much time to make. Before the advent of steamboats, early settlers used keelboats and flatboats. Keelboats, with a keel running along the center of the hull, ranged from 40 to 100 feet long and from 7 to 20 feet wide. The keel, along with a pointed bow and stern, contributed to stability and maneuverability. Oars, poles, and sometimes sails were used to move keelboats both downstream and upstream. Flatboats, in contrast, were downstream vessels. Commonly, they were 25 feet wide and 50 feet long. Often built by German immigrants living in Redstone, Pa., on the Monongahela River, they were sold to settlers. A flatboat generally contained a cabin for the passengers and the crew, a fireplace, and a pen or stable for livestock. Long stern oars, as well as two to four side oars, were used for steering. Many of the settlers disembarked at Maysville or at other places in Northern Kentucky. The flatboats would be disassembled and their materials used to build cabins and small outbuildings.

The French made early claims to the Ohio River Valley and what became Northern Kentucky, based upon the 1682 exploration of René-Robert Cavelier La Salle, who specifically claimed the entire watershed of the Mississippi River (which includes that of the Ohio River Valley) for King Louis XIV. In 1749 French explorer Pierre-Joseph Céloron de Bienville designated it as French territory. Early French explorers, traders, and trappers who passed through the area were under the administration of Quebec. The Treaty of Paris (1763), ending the **French and Indian War**, resulted in the loss of all of this French territory east of the Mississippi River to Great Britain. The British, in turn, issued the Proclamation of 1763, forbidding settlement west of the Appalachian Mountains until the area could be stabilized. In 1774, the Treaty of Camp Charlotte, ending **Lord Dunmore's War**, set the Ohio River as the boundary between American Indians and settlers, with the Shawnee Indians agreeing to stay north of the Ohio River and the settlers south of it. In 1783, by the Treaty of Paris, which ended the **Revolutionary War**, the United States gained title to the Ohio River Valley and the area of Northern Kentucky. During the Revolutionary War, several battles were fought along the Ohio River, including Lochry's Defeat and **Rogers' Defeat**. The Point was the gathering site of two major, 1,000-man expeditions against the Ohio Indians, allies of the British. In 1784 the Spanish, who had regained old New Orleans by the Treaty of Paris in 1783, closed the Mississippi River and the port of New Orleans to U.S. citizens, upsetting Kentuckians. By the Treaty of San Lorenzo (Pinckney's Treaty) in 1795, Spain granted the United States navigation of the Mississippi River and also opened its port of New Orleans.

The land that became Northern Kentucky was claimed by the State of Virginia until Kentucky became a state, in 1792. Settlement followed the haphazard, shingled-over pattern of Virginia, with early land grants awarded to veterans of the Virginia lines in wars ranging from the French and Indian to the Revolutionary. Kentucky retained the slaveholding of old Virginia. North of the Ohio River, with the exception of the Virginia Military District, lying east of the Little Miami River, settlement proceeded according to the regular grid pattern outlined by the Northwest Ordinance, which also forbade slavery. Hence, the Ohio River was traditionally considered a part of the historic **Mason-Dixon Line**, separating slave territory in Northern Kentucky from free territory in Ohio and Indiana.

Although debate continues concerning who actually invented the steamboat, it is agreed that the *New Orleans* (owned by Robert Fulton, Robert Livingston, and Nicholas Roosevelt) was the first steamboat on the Ohio River, making its voyage downstream from Pittsburgh to New Orleans in 1811. In 1815 Henry M. Shreve's *Enterprise* made the first upstream steamboat trip, from New Orleans to Louisville. Steamboats could travel upstream, against the current, more quickly than keelboats. At the Falls of the Ohio at Louisville, however, it continued to be necessary to off-load cargo, transship it by land to below the falls, and then reload it, at least until the completion of the Louisville and Portland Canal in 1830.

In 1816 Henry Shreve launched his packet boat *Washington* on the Ohio River. With its boilers placed horizontally on the main deck, rather than in the hold, it was the first packet boat with a truly shallow draft, an important innovation for the then-shallow waters of the Ohio and Mississippi rivers. Three years later, in 1819, the U.S. Congress passed an act permitting the Federal Post Office Department to contract with steamboats for the transport of mail, and Shreve built his *Postboy* the same year to carry the U.S. mail. In 1824 in Cincinnati, Shreve launched the *George Washington,* whose innovations included a third deck, private staterooms, and two wheels that were independently operated by two separate engines. Before this time, sidewheel steamboats were powered by a single engine with a common shaft. These innovations gave the *George Washington* greater power and maneuverability and made it more comfortable for passengers.

Northern Kentucky was the home of **boatyards** (see **Paris Brown**) that constructed steamboats, and one of the first of these steamboats was the *Missouri,* launched in Newport in 1819. Steam ferryboats, which eventually replaced horse ferries, also plied the Ohio River (see **Ferries**; **Anderson Ferry**; **Augusta Ferry**), carrying passengers and freight between the shores.

Steamboats and ferries contributed to vast changes in commercial trading patterns. For instance, hogs raised in the bluegrass area of Lexington, transported to Covington by drovers and later by railroad, were slaughtered at Covington's massive Milward and Oldershaw packinghouse (see **Meatpacking**). Prepared especially for the British market, they were transported by steamboats down the Licking, Ohio, and Mississippi rivers for shipment to Europe. Northern Kentucky's antebellum ties to the South were strengthened by steamboat trade and travel. Major port cities included Maysville, Augusta, Newport, Covington, Petersburg, Warsaw, and Carrollton. Also, by merely waving a handkerchief or lighting a lantern, a farmer along the Ohio River could hail a steamboat for shipment of agricultural goods or livestock from the farm landing.

Northern Kentucky also had its share of steamboat owners, captains, and pilots, such as **Frederick Laidley** and the **Fearn family**. Northern Kentuckian Captain **Edward Maurer** had a distinguished career, setting a Louisville-to-Cincinnati record of nine hours and 42 minutes aboard the *City of Louisville* in 1894. Captain **Richard M. Wade**, a resident of Covington, was a longtime riverboat captain. In 1868 he was master of the ***United States*** when it collided near Warsaw with the ***America*** (see **Steamboat Disasters**).

In antebellum times, the Ohio River marked the dividing point between freedom and **slavery**. **Abolitionists** in the Ohio River counties of Northern Kentucky worked along with their counterparts in Ohio and Indiana as part of the **Underground Railroad**, secreting slaves who were moving toward freedom. During the **Civil War**, President Abraham Lincoln (1861–1865) closed the Ohio River to trade with the Confederate States of America and placed gunboats along the river. A pontoon bridge (see **Pontoon Bridges, Civil War**) connected Cincinnati to Covington.

The **John A. Roebling Bridge** was the first bridge across the Ohio River in Northern Kentucky, opening between Covington and Cincinnati in 1866–1867. It was followed by numerous other bridges, including the **L&N Bridge (Purple People Bridge)**; the **Cincinnati Southern Railroad Bridge**; the **Chesapeake and Ohio Railroad Bridge**; the **Simon Kenton Memorial Bridge**, Maysville; the **Markland Dam** Bridge; the **Carroll C. Cropper Bridge**; the **Combs-Hehl Bridge**; the **Daniel Carter Beard Bridge**; the **Taylor-Southgate Bridge**; and the **William H. Harsha Bridge**.

The Ohio River has been subject to flooding throughout historical times. Before the use of gauges to measure the river's depth, only educated estimates can be given of major floods, including that of 1774, when its depth was about 76 feet. Official records of floods on the Ohio River in the Cincinnati–Northern Kentucky area date from 1858. The **flood of 1884** reached 71.1 feet on the Cincinnati gauge; the **floods of 1907** crested at 65.2 feet; the **flood of 1913** at 69.9 feet; and the worst in history, the **flood of 1937**, at 79.9 feet. After the flood of 1937, the U.S. Army Corps of Engineers oversaw construction of a massive series of concrete and earthen floodwalls in Northern Kentucky (see **Flood Control**).

The Ohio River was also subject to periods of extremely low water in dry seasons, halting all navigation. For instance, the Ohio River stage at Cincinnati fell to the lowest level on record, 1.9 feet, in 1881. Sandbars along the Dayton and Bellevue shoreline impaired navigation but enabled recreational opportunities like swimming (see **Ohio River Beaches**). A rockbar was situated in front of the mouth of the Licking River inferior to the deeper natural channel and port on the Cincinnati side. Beginning in 1887, the U.S. Army Corps of Engineers began underwater blasting of the Licking rockbar, and by 1895 it had removed 29,862 cubic yards of material, much of which was subsequently used to build dikes along the Ohio River locally to channel the water for navigational purposes. Also, each year the U.S. Army Corps of Engineers used snagboats, such as the *E. A. Woodruff*, whose iron hull was built in Covington in 1874, to clear the river of dangerous snags.

While the removal of sandbars, rockbars, and snags aided navigation, they were not enough to provide a deep channel for year-round commerce (see **Ohio River Navigation**; **Ohio River Locks and Dams**). In 1875 the U.S. Congress appropriated the initial funds for construction of the Davis Island lock and dam below Pittsburgh, completed in 1885. Work on locks and dams along the Ohio River continued throughout the late 19th and early 20th centuries. In 1895 the Ohio Valley Improvement Association, based in Cincinnati, began lobbying the U.S. Congress to fund further improvements of the Ohio River. In 1910 Congress passed the Rivers and Harbors Act, providing for construction of more than 50 locks and dams along the river, which were needed to maintain a nine-foot slackwater channel. The canalization of the river between Maysville and Carrollton included seven completed locks and dams: No. 33 (Maysville); No. 34 (Chilo); No. 35 (New Richmond) (see **Center for Ohio River Research and Education**); No. 36 (Coney Island); No. 37 (Fernbank); No. 38 (Belleview); and No. 39 (Markland). These dams were of chanoine wicket movable construction. That is, during higher water, the movable wicket dams could be lowered to the river bottom, allowing for unimpeded navigation over the dam; vessels could bypass the locks. In times of lower water, the wickets were raised to maintain a guaranteed nine-foot pool of water, and boats passed through the concrete locks. The wicket dams were replaced by the modern locks and dams, **Meldahl Dam** (completed in 1962) and Markland Dam (completed in 1963).

In addition to commerce, the Ohio River has long functioned as an avenue of culture. The latest trends in art, architecture, fashion, entertainment, and music traveled its course up and down. **Showboats** brought entertainment to isolated communities. Cincinnati and Northern Kentucky, as Ohio River ports, were centers of **ragtime**, **blues**, and **jazz** music. The river even provided people with a way of life. Shantyboats lined the riverbanks in some areas and provided a bohemian lifestyle that appealed to Northern Kentucky artist **Harlan Hubbard** and his wife, **Anna Hubbard**, for example. Northern Kentucky residents sought relief from the summer heat at beaches, rode steamboats to Boone Co.'s Parlor Grove for picnics, and boarded the steamer Island Queen for Cincinnati's Coney Island Amusement Park. Ludlow's **Lagoon Amusement Park** and Dayton's **Tacoma Park** also lay along the Ohio River. In more recent times, **BB Riverboats** has provided river excursions, and customers have flocked to eat at the **Mike Fink Floating Restaurant** (see **John Beatty**; **Ben Bernstein**; **Betty Blake**) in Covington, at **Caproni's Restaurant** in Maysville, and at **Newport-on-the-Levee**.

After decades of neglecting their riverfronts, river cities like Covington rediscovered their roots and began massive restoration and redevelopment projects such as the **Licking-Riverside, Riverside Drive, and Ohio Riverside National Historic Districts**. The redevelopment of Covington's riverfront includes the **Roebling Murals** on the Covington floodwall and Riverwalk statues of **John James Audubon**, **James Bradley**, **Little Turtle**, **Mary B. Greene**, and **John Roebling**. Maysville has also sponsored a series of floodwall murals. Cincinnati's Tall Stacks celebration (see **Virginia Bennett**), a weeklong event recapturing the steamboat era, includes river exhibits on the Northern Kentucky shoreline.

Gillespie, Michael. *Come Hell or High Water: A Lively History of Steamboating on the Mississippi and Ohio Rivers.* Stoddard, Wis.: Heritage Press, 2001.

Hedeen, Stanley. *Natural History of the Cincinnati Region.* Cincinnati: Cincinnati Museum Center, 2006.

Hunter, Louis C. *Steamboats on the Western Rivers: An Economic and Technological History.* New York: Octagon Books, 1969.

Johnson, Leland R. *The Falls City Engineers: A History of the Louisville District, Corps of Engineers, United States Army.* Louisville, Ky.: U.S. Army Corps of Engineers, 1974.

Klein, Benjamin F. *The Ohio River Handbook and Picture Album.* Cincinnati: Young and Klein, 1969.

Lytle, William M., and Forrest R. Holdcamper, comps. *Merchant Steam Vessels of the United States, 1790–1868, "The Lytle-Holdcamper List."* Rev. and ed. Kenneth R. Hall. Staten Island, N.Y.: Steamship Historical Society of America, 1975.

McCall, Edith. *Conquering the Rivers: Henry Miler Shreve and the Navigation of America's Inland Waterways.* Baton Rouge: Louisiana State Univ. Press, 1984.

Robinson, Michael C. *History of Navigation in the Ohio River Basin.* Washington, D.C.: Government Printing Office, 1983.

Way, Frederick, Jr., comp. *Way's Packet Directory, 1848–1983.* Athens: Ohio Univ. Press, 1983.

Vic Canfield and Frank X. Prudent

OHIO RIVER BEACHES. Before the construction of dams in the 20th century, the Ohio River's bend along the northern boundary of Campbell Co. tended to erode its northern shore and to deposit sand and silt along its southern one. After possibly thousands of years of such action, sandbars and large beaches were created along the Bellevue and Dayton riverfronts. The sandbar at Dayton (originally called Sandy Hook because of its shape) was the site of the 1779 **Revolutionary War** battle known as **Rogers' Defeat**.

In 1889 the first of many boat races was held along the Bellevue-Dayton waterfront, then known as Long Beach. An 1894 advertisement by the City of Bellevue called Long Beach "one of the finest and pleasantest bathing places in this section of the country." The beach soon became nationally known and was one of the reasons Cincinnati was chosen as the site of the 1898 Grand Army of the Republic (GAR) convention. One of the first developments along the waterfront was Bellevue's Riviera or Queen City Beach, which opened in 1902 at the foot of Ward Ave. William E. Kroger of Newport and Nat C. Coulter of

Queen City Beach, Bellevue.

Queen City Beach, Bellevue, 1909, with the steamer *Island Queen.*

Bellevue were two of the major promoters of the project. Supposedly, three barges were beached there and were used in the construction of dressing rooms. Later improvements included a two-story pavilion, a restaurant, and a dance hall. In 1928 Bellevue native Ed Rohrer leased the site from owner Perry Tucker and changed the name of the development to **Horseshoe Gardens**. He built a floating party room and dining hall with lights arranged in the shape of a horseshoe, the source of the beach's new name.

The next beach to the east was the Palace or Primrose Beach, at the foot of O'Fallon St. in Dayton. There canoes could be rented, and the beach had storage space for about 300 boats. Just upriver, also in Dayton, was Club Dorney's. Continuing eastward, one would come to the Manhattan Beach, located at Walnut St. in Dayton. Above that was Berlin Beach, built in 1904 at Clay St. in Dayton. It had facilities for aquatic sports, lockers, a pavilion, and a large covered metal building that was used for both dancing and roller-skating. The last beach to the east in Dayton was Gem Beach, which operated for only a short time at Clark St. In July 1905, when it was known as Clark's Grove, it was the site of a speech by future five-time Socialist Party presidential candidate Eugene Victor Debs. Gem Beach was reopened in 1921 as part of the new **Tacoma Park**.

Ohio River water levels fluctuated greatly before the construction of dams. In extremely dry periods, it was even possible to walk across to the Ohio shore. For example, the Ohio River measured a record low of one foot nine inches in 1881 and two feet nine inches, its second-lowest level, on September 27, 1908. In the 1920s the beaches began to experience problems as the slow-moving river water became polluted. Furthermore, beach accidents led to the filing of many lawsuits. The final death knell to the beaches was the construction of a series of dams along the Ohio River in the 1920s, designed to raise the river level for navigational purposes. The higher pool stage that resulted flooded most of the beaches. Tacoma Park managed to survive by building a 130-by-150-foot in-ground pool (filled with water from an artesian well), as well as amusement park rides and a dance floor–skating rink, which was moved from Berlin Beach. The Ohio River **flood of 1937** destroyed much of the Tacoma Park complex, and it never fully recovered. In subsequent years the park was alternately used for greyhound and midget car racing, boxing and wrestling matches, a drive-in movie theater, and a mobile home park; currently it is the site of the Watertown Marina. While the river is used primarily for commercial shipping today, pleasure boating abounds, and the shores along Bellevue and Dayton are popular once again as gathering places for family picnics and fishing, but not for swimming.

Bellevue and Dayton Beaches. Charlie Tharp Collection, Dayton, Ky.

Reis, Jim. "Beach a Popular Draw," *KP,* July 18, 2005, 4K.

———. "They Once Packed Kentucky's Shoreline," *KP,* June 6, 1983, 4K.

Souvenir, Dayton, Ky., G.A.R. Encampment, September, 1898.

Tacoma Park, Dayton Ky. Charlie Tharp Collection, Dayton, Ky.

Jack Wessling

OHIO RIVER LOCKS AND DAMS. The two locks and dams on the Ohio River in the Northern Kentucky region, operated by the U.S. Army Corps of Engineers, provide safe and efficient navigation. These projects serve navigation only; they do not provide flood protection to communities along the river. The locks and dams, referred to as "high-lift" structures, were built to replace old moveable wicket dams, built in the early 1900s. They are nonnavigable dams, which means that all river traffic must pass through the locks.

Markland Locks and Dam, located at mile 531.5 below Pittsburgh, 3.5 miles below Warsaw in Gallatin Co., takes its name from the nearby community of Markland, Ind. The pool above the dam extends upstream 95 miles to the **Meldahl** Locks and Dam and for a short distance up three navigable tributaries, the Miami, the Licking, and the Little Miami rivers. The concrete, gated dam is 1,395 feet in length, with 12 gates, each 100 feet wide and 42 feet high. Two locks are located on the Kentucky side of the river, one 110 feet wide and 600 feet long, and the other, the main lock, 110 feet wide and 1,200 feet long. The locks can raise or lower a vessel 35 feet. A vehicular bridge connects U.S. 42 on the Kentucky side of the river with Ind. 156 on the north side. Synergy Inc. operates a hydroelectric plant on the Indiana side of the dam. The locks were built between 1956 and 1959. The dam was completed in 1963 and replaced old wicket dams numbered 35, 36, 37, 38, and 39. The cost of the locks and dam was $63.1 million. The Markland project is operated by the Louisville District of the Corps.

Captain Anthony Meldahl Locks and Dam is located at mile 436.2 below Pittsburgh, near the community of Chilo, Ohio. It is named for a well-known steamboat pilot on the Ohio River. The pool above the dam extends upstream 95 miles to the Greenup Locks and Dam. The concrete, gated dam is 1,756 feet in length and has 12 gates the same size as those at Markland. Two locks are located on the Ohio side of the river, one 110 feet wide and 600 feet long, and the other 110 feet wide and 1,200 feet long. The locks, built between 1959 and 1962. can raise or lower a vessel 30 feet. Construction of the dam began in 1961 and was completed in 1964, replacing old wicket dams 31, 32, 33, and 34. The cost of the locks and dam was $74 million. The Meldahl project is operated by the Huntington (W.Va.) District of the Corps.

Johnson, Leland R. *The Falls City Engineers: A History of the Louisville District Corps of Engineers United States Army.* Louisville, Ky.: Louisville District of the U.S. Army Corps of Engineers, 1974, 1984.

———. *Men, Mountains, and Rivers: An Illustrated History of the Huntington District U.S. Army Corps of Engineers, 1754–1974.* Huntington, W.Va.: Huntington District of the U.S. Army Corps of Engineers, 1977.

———. *The Ohio River Division U.S. Army Corps of Engineers: The History of a Central Command.* Cincinnati: Ohio River Division of the U.S. Army Corps of Engineers, 1992.

Charles E. Parrish

OHIO RIVER NAVIGATION. The Ohio River basin is a vast region of 204,000 square miles reaching northeast into New York, west to the flat land of Illinois, and south through the drainage area of the Tennessee River, extending into Georgia, Alabama, and Mississippi. Through the heart of this huge portion of the United States, the 981-mile-long Ohio River carries a larger volume of water than any other tributary of the Mississippi River. Formed by the juncture of the Allegheny and Monongahela rivers at Pittsburgh, Pa., the Ohio River borders Kentucky for 665 miles, from Catlettsburg to its mouth, where it empties into the Mississippi River; the Ohio River is the northern boundary of the Northern Kentucky region. This river was one of the two principal routes of transport during the great migration to the trans-Appalachian West in the 18th and 19th centuries. Goods were carried first by canoe, then by flatboat and keelboat, and after 1811 by steamboat. In its natural, unimproved state, the Ohio River was littered by snags and strewn with boulders. Its flow was broken by sandbars, rocks, rapids, and, at Louisville, by the Falls of the Ohio, where in a distance of 2.5 miles, the level of the river drops 26 feet. The unaltered river fluctuated widely from a series of shallow, stagnant pools in drought season to raging torrents rising 80 to 100 feet in flood times. As cities along the river grew and as riverine vessels evolved, authorities sought ways to overcome these impediments to safe, dependable navigation. Two surveys of the Ohio River, in 1819 and in 1821, identified the worst obstructions to navigation; they recommended the removal of rocks, snags, and other obstacles and proposed a canal around the Falls at Louisville. The reports from these surveys formed the foundation of the eventual federal program of navigation improvements on the river.

The Rivers and Harbors Act of 1824 appropriated $75,000 for improving the Ohio and Mississippi rivers, assigning this responsibility to the U.S. Army Corps of Engineers, its first official assignment on the Ohio River. Under the command of Maj. Stephen H. Long, the engineers set about building a wing dam at Henderson, Ky., to improve channel conditions at low-water stages. They removed the worst snags and rocks at many river locations. The act also provided a cash prize for the design of a snagboat, later improved by Capt. Henry M. Shreve, who headed the work into the 1840s, until it was halted on constitutional grounds. Further work did not resume until the Act of 1852 was passed. During the **Civil War**, the federal role in navigation improvements was minimal, and as a result many steamboats were lost to obstructions, as the wing dams built earlier deteriorated. The major barrier to navigation was the Falls at Louisville, 600 miles downstream from Pittsburgh. The Falls were navigable only during seasons of high water, and even then it was a perilous adventure to "shoot the rapids" over rock outcroppings and narrow channels between sandbars and riffles. To overcome this hazard, and in response to years of debating, petitioning, and politicking, the Kentucky legislature in 1825 chartered the Louisville and Portland Canal Company, a stock venture, to construct a canal with a lock system to provide navigation around the Falls. The project was completed in 1830. The U.S. government later became the largest stockholder in the company, and in the 1860s army engineers aided in a major project at the canal in which the noted hydraulics engineer Theodore Scowden had designed improvements that were not completed until 1872. This work widened the canal and built a two-flight lock, the largest in the world at that time. Following years of urging by navigation and political interests, the federal government assumed jurisdiction at the Falls in 1874, placing the project under the management of the U.S. Army Corps of Engineers.

After the Civil War, army engineers sought long-term improvements that would achieve the ultimate goal on the Ohio River: a year-round dependable navigation depth adequate for the barges and towboats used by the growing coal and shipping trade. After investigating navigation projects on rivers in Europe, engineer officers concluded that the Ohio River could best be improved by constructing a series of locks and dams along the length of the river. The first project was completed at Davis Island, a few miles below Pittsburgh, in 1885, and after proving its worth, Congress passed the Rivers and Harbors Act of 1910, authorizing construction of the slack-water pool system with a depth of nine feet. At its completion in 1929, the canalization project consisted of 51 movable dams with wooden wickets and a lock chamber 600 feet long and 110 feet wide. At low-water stage, the dams were raised to pool water requiring lockage, and at high-water stage, the wickets were lowered to the river bottom, allowing open river navigation.

Further improvements at Louisville during this period consisted of widening the canal to 200 feet and building a new movable dam; the lock size was the typical 600 feet by 110 feet. The project at the Falls was designated Lock and Dam No. 41. Twenty-five of the 51 dams bordered Kentucky, some with locks located on the commonwealth's boundary and others with locks on the north side of the river.

During **World War II**, and in the years immediately following, diesel-powered towboats began replacing steam-powered boats, allowing longer tows of larger barges, which carried ever-increasing tonnage. At the 600-foot locks, this required "double lockage": longer tows had to be locked through in two maneuvers.

In the 1950s, army engineers undertook the Ohio River Navigation Modernization Program to replace the obsolete system. Each of the new high-lift concrete-and-steel dams completed by 1980 replaced at least two of the old structures. Each comprises two locks, one 1,200 feet long and 110 feet wide and another 600 feet long and 110 feet wide. At Smithland Locks and Dam there are two 1,200-foot locks. All of the new high dams are nonnavigable, meaning all river traffic must transit the locks. Eight of the new high dams border the commonwealth; two, **Meldahl** and **Markland**, are in the Northern Kentucky region. Two of the old movable dams, Locks and Dams Nos. 52 and 53, remain in operation on the lower Ohio. These will be replaced by the Olmsted Locks and Dam, slated for completion in 2012. All the lock and dam structures on the Ohio River serve navigation purposes only; they do not furnish flood control; contrary to popular misconception, they were never intended for that purpose.

Nearly two-thirds of the freight traffic on the Ohio River now consists of energy-related commodities such as coal and petroleum products, along with aggregates, iron and steel, chemicals, and grain. More commerce moves along the Ohio River navigation system annually than through the Panama Canal. In addition, the Ohio River supplies water and provides recreational boating and harbor facilities for the nation's heartland.

Johnson, Leland R. *The Falls City Engineers: A History of the Louisville District Corps of Engineers United States Army.* Louisville, Ky.: Louisville District, 1984.

Ohio River Navigation: Past, Present, Future. Cincinnati: Ohio River Division Corps of Engineers, United States Army, 1979.

Charles E. Parrish

OHIO RIVER WAY. The Ohio River Way Inc. (ORW) is a nonprofit 501(c)3 corporate organization, founded in 1999. It consists of four action teams: River Arts and Heritage, River Commerce, River Recreation and Ecology, and Greenways and Trails. The ORW focuses on regional planning and implementation activities. These range from creating a continuous 150-mile hike and bike trail along both sides of the Ohio River from Maysville, Ky., to Madison, Ind., to the creation of art, cultural, and historical venues in communities along this stretch of the river. The largest ORW event is its annual Paddlefest, which includes the Educational Expo for grade school children, the Ohio River Music Festival, the Equipment Auction, and a six-mile canoe and kayak trip along the Ohio River. The ORW's trail from Madison to Maysville began to be built in 2006, with the first section of the trail from downtown Cincinnati to the Lunken Airport on that city's East Side.

"Group Promoting Ohio River Changes Name," *KP,* February 26, 2003, 3K.

"Ohio River Way Makes Debut," *CE,* February 26, 2003, 1D.

"Paddlefest Making Pitch for Boating Lovers," *KP,* June 18, 2003, 2K.

"Taking Me to the River," *SC,* July 4, 2004, 1D.

Chris Lorentz

OKI. The Ohio-Kentucky-Indiana Regional Council of Governments (OKI), the regional planning body for the Greater Cincinnati area, is made up of representatives of all of the tri-state's major city and county governments as well as state transportation officials. OKI was a result of the Federal Aid Highway Act of 1962, which required any metropolitan area of more than 50,000 people to have a coordinated, comprehensive planning organization to serve the entire region. OKI's mandate was to "conduct a continuing, comprehensive, and coordinated process for the development of transportation improvement projects." The council is primarily funded by federal tax dollars through the U.S. Department of Transportation.

After spending four years collecting data and creating a plan, OKI in 1971 published the OKI Regional Transportation and Development Plan. It called for a rapid expansion of the region's highway system, including an outer loop through central Boone, Kenton, and Campbell counties and a freeway along the Covington and Newport riverfronts. Mass-transit options are seldom discussed in the 1971 plan beyond increasing some bus routes, and it does not allow for rail-based commuting. In terms of the urban core, the OKI favored clear-cutting "dilapidated" neighborhoods and constructing new office, commercial, and residential space in the International architectural style.

In successive plans since its initial offering, OKI, and planners in general during this period, have slowly distanced themselves from recommending the use of the automobile and the highway as the primary means of solving problems. A 1979 survey conducted by OKI demonstrated that many citizens did not favor spending tax dollars on more highways that divided neighborhoods and displaced people. In its 1981 plan, Transportation 2000, OKI said that it had been wrong in its initial approach. The energy crisis of the 1970s is credited with changing the anti-urban tone of OKI's plans. Modest mass-transit plans based on existing railways were proposed in the 1981 plan, along with setting up a few transit centers around the area.

By 1993, with new federal regulations in place, OKI was forced to incorporate alternative transportation methods. In the OKI publication *Managing Mobility: Year 2010 Regional Transportation Plan*, the organization recommends "improving bus service and developing rail transit." Protecting air quality, respecting financial concerns, and the management of congestion in existing roadways are all given strong and serious thought. Some of the methods offered are an extensive light- and passenger-rail system, mass transit, HOV (high-occupancy vehicle) lanes on interstates, and increased bus routes and time schedules to connect to regional transit centers.

Ohio-Kentucky-Indiana Regional Council of Governments. *Managing Mobility: Year 2010 Regional Transportation Plan*. Cincinnati: OKI, 1993.

———. *OKI Regional Transportation and Development Plan*. Cincinnati: OKI, 1973.

———. *OKI Regional Transportation Plan: A Transportation Plan for the OKI Region to Guide Transportation Investment and Service Decisions Now and in the Future*. Cincinnati: OKI, 1981.

———. *2000 Transportation Questionnaire*. Cincinnati: OKI, 1979.

Chris Meiman

OLD BAPTIST CHURCH ON THE DRY RIDGE. The first church to be organized in the area that later became Grant Co. was known as the Old Baptist Church on the Dry Ridge. It was organized on the fourth Sunday of August 1791, near **Campbell's Blockhouse**, with nine founding members: Robert Childers Sr., William Conrad, Jesse Conyers, Rachel Conyers, Elizabeth Franks, Jacob Franks, John Lawless, Absolam Skirvin, and John Skirvin Sr. Two ministers were involved in starting the Dry Ridge Old Baptist Church. One was Elder John Conner, who made yearly trips to the frontier, preaching to scattered congregations. In 1811 he settled in Harrison Co. Like many ministers of the time, he had extensive landholdings and did not accept any compensation for his ministry. The other minister involved in the church's founding was Elder Lewis Corban, who had paid little attention to either education or religion until he was age 30. After a long struggle with religious matters, he was baptized in 1786. Corban was so effective in his preaching that he was ordained in 1790, once he had moved to Kentucky.

The newly established church on the Dry Ridge met on the fourth Sunday of each month and the Saturday preceding, which was set aside for church business. Male members were appointed to take turns serving as sentries to guard against Indian attacks. The peace of the church was maintained; any member who had a complaint against another brought it before the church for settlement. Meetings were held in the open near the blockhouse when the weather was good and there was no immediate threat of an Indian attack. The few surviving minutes detail an attack by 12 Shawnee warriors on the fourth Saturday in September 1793, while the church was meeting in the blockhouse. The Shawnees attempted to set fire to the building but were driven off with rifle fire, which wounded two or three of them. By 1799 the church occupied its first true church building. A description by Elder Corban explains that the "struxure [was] of good yeller poplar logges well hewed, duff tailed and chinked 20 foot long, 15 foot wide and about 15 foot to the rigepol."

The congregation, numbering about 40 members, withstood Indian attacks, cholera, and privation, but in 1817, it faced a new religious doctrine that threatened its existence. Elder Christian Tomlin came into the area preaching the free-will Baptist doctrine. The adherents to the free-will doctrine were also known at various times as separate Baptists, free-will Baptists, new school Baptists, and later as missionary Baptists. Eleven members of the Dry Ridge Old Baptist Church congregation accepted the new doctrine and on July 12, 1817, organized a church based on the new teachings. Elder Tomlin was the 12th member. The new church was initially known as the Baptist Church at the Dry Ridge, Free-Will, and is today the Dry Ridge Baptist Church.

The congregation of the Old Baptist Church on the Dry Ridge (also called predestinarian, particular, and primitive) and the free-will congregation at Dry Ridge reached an agreement in 1818 to share their Bibles and hymnbooks. The free-will congregation met on the second Saturday and Sunday of each month; and the predestinarian congregation continued to meet the fourth Saturday and Sunday of each month.

The congregation of the Old Baptist Church suffered a second severe loss in 1818 when 16 members moved their membership by letter to organize the Old Baptist Church at Fork Lick. Without a minister in attendance, with their membership in a state of decline, and with their identity being overshadowed by the growth of the free-will congregation, the Old Baptist Church on the Dry Ridge decided to "organize anew" at Williamstown. Jacob and Elizabeth Franks were dismissed to assist David Lillard in organizing an Old Baptist Church at Mount Zion, Ky., and Asa Tungate and wife were granted letters to join the Salem Old Baptist Church in Salem, Ill. The seven remaining members of the Old Baptist Church on the Dry Ridge reorganized in 1826 into the Williamstown Church of Christ, Particular Baptist.

In February 1827 William Conrad was ordained as minister. By 1829 the church was prospering, with 33 members. After meeting for a time in the old Williamstown Seminary, the church constructed its own meetinghouse, which was replaced with a new building during the 1880s that served the congregation until 1919. The site of this old church (including its cemetery) is now within the Williamstown Cemetery.

Conrad, John B., ed. *History of Grant County*. Williamstown, Ky.: Grant Co. Historical Society, 1992.

Franks, Lloyd W., ed. *The Journal of Elder William Conrad, Pioneer Preacher*. Williamstown, Ky.: RF, 1976.

John B. Conrad

OLD CEDAR BAPTIST CHURCH. The Old Cedar Baptist Church, founded sometime before 1816, is now located at the intersection of U.S. 127 and Ky. Rt. 607 in southern Owen Co. The church's first log cabin structure, located on Cedar Creek about two miles north of the current church building, was known as the Mouth of Cedar Creek Meeting House. The congregation belonged to the Franklin Co. Baptist Association from before 1816 through 1899 and then joined the **Owen Co. Baptist Association**. In 1839 the church moved into a frame building located in front of the current building on land that is now partly covered by U.S. 127. That building had a pot-bellied stove on each side and a partition, the same height as the benches, down the center. Women and men entered through separate doors and sat on separate sides of the church. James Duvall was the first pastor in this second structure, and he served about 26 years. The frame structure was converted into a parsonage and was torn down about 1954. Members constructed the current stone structure in two phases. The second phase, a top floor, was built and paid for while W. M. Wilson was pastor, 1949 through 1955, and was dedicated October 1, 1950.

The church is a member of the Southern Baptist Association. James Robert Bondurant, the current pastor, has been ministering since 1989. He is one of 12 men who have been called or ordained into the ministry from the church. The Old Cedar Baptist Church was entered into the National Register of Historic Places on September 5, 1997.

Murphy, Margaret Alice, and Lela Maude Hawkins. *The History of Historic Old Cedar Baptist Church and Community, 1816—2004*. Frankfort, Ky.: Lynn, 2004.

Margaret A. Murphy

OMNICARE INC. Omnicare Inc., the nation's largest provider of pharmaceutical care to seniors, has its headquarters in the RiverCenter office towers along the Ohio River in Covington. Omnicare Inc. serves 1.4 million persons each day in thousands of skilled-nursing, assisted-living, and other health care facilities in 47 states with its unit-dosage method of patient drug delivery. The company prepares each individual dose off-site, and up to three times each day it brings a drug cart through the health care facility, dispensing the medication at the patient's bedside. The drugs are not stored at the facility. Omnicare Inc. also has become a worldwide leader in the field of clinical research services for the pharmaceutical and biotechnology industries.

Omnicare Inc. began as a 1981 spin-off from two Cincinnati-based corporations, W. R. Grace and Company and the Chemed Corporation. Since its inception, the new corporation has been led by one man, CEO Joel F. Gemunder. In 1997, as a result of receiving $8 million in tax abatements, the company moved to Covington with 50 employees; the number of workers increased to 322 in 2004, as additional tax breaks were granted.

Over the years, Omnicare Inc. has purchased more than 80 similar companies, in both friendly and hostile takeovers. Two of its major acquisitions include NeighborCare and NCS Health Care. It competes in a very aggressive and competitive industry, one that is highly regulated. Along with success have come negative circumstances, for example being accused of Medicaid fraud in several states and subsequently having to pay large settlements.

Listed as "OCR" on the New York Stock Exchange, the company ranked 94th on the Fortune list in 2002. Its annual revenues in recent years have totaled as much as $6.5 billion.

Feldman, Jason. "Omnicare Looks to Future," *SC*, August 1, 2004, 7B.

"1997 Top 10 Stories," *CP*, December 31, 1997, 6C.

Omnicare. www.omnicare.com (accessed on June 19, 2007).

ONEONTA. The small town of Oneonta in southeastern Campbell Co., where Twelve Mile Creek empties into the Ohio River, was founded in the 1850s. The town was named for the New York state birthplace of Henry Edwards Huntington, the nephew of railroad magnate Collis P. Huntington, who developed the **Chesapeake and Ohio Railroad** (C&O) through the area. The name Oneonta comes from the Iroquois Indian word *Onnontee,* which can be translated as "between the hills or mountains." The Campbell Co. town's use of the Indian name proved to be quite appropriate because it has been learned that a **Fort Ancient** Indian village and burial ground once existed there. A *Kentucky State Journal* article of 1889 said Indian artifacts had been discovered around the Oneonta site; however, no archaeological examination of the area was made at that time. In 1938, however, during excavation for the new **Mary Ingles Highway**, the skeletal remains of seven individuals were uncovered at Oneonta. Archaeologists from the Northern Kentucky Chapter of the Kentucky Archaeological Society received permission from the owners of that property to cut a ditch through the site. Archaeological excavations in the 1940s revealed two villages, one along the shore of the Ohio River and the other about 220 yards to the west. Thousands of artifacts came to light, including 856 bones and bone fragments, animal teeth, pottery vessels, stone tools, projectile points, ceramic bowls, and various effigies. Many of those items are housed in the collections of the **Behringer-Crawford Museum** in **Devou Park**, in Covington. Archaeologists named the area the Bintz Site, after the owners of the property.

The 1889 *Kentucky State Journal* article also predicted that Oneonta would develop into a major railroad and steamboat facility; however, that never happened. At the time, the town consisted of about 30 buildings, including a church, a general store, a hotel, a post office, and a number of small residences. The Oneonta Inn became a popular stop for steamboat travelers along the Ohio River and for passengers of the Chesapeake and Ohio Railroad, which came through town. Over the years, many tales have been told about the Oneonta Inn. Some people have claimed that it was haunted, others have asserted that Davy Crockett stayed there, and still others have said that the notorious bank robber John Dillinger used it as a hideout. The Oneonta Inn and other town structures were severely damaged in the **flood of 1937**, but the inn was later completely restored and is now used as a private residence.

"Campbell County," *KSJ*, January 17, 1889, 7.

MacCord, Howard. *The Bintz Site.* Covington, Ky.: Behringer-Crawford Museum, 1984 (reprint from *American Antiquity* 18, no. 3 (January 1953).

Reis, Jim. "Southern Campbell Has Own Rich Heritage," *KP*, April 14, 1986, 4K.

Jack Wessling

OPTIMIST INTERNATIONAL. See **Civic Associations**.

ORANGEBURG. Orangeburg is a community in the eastern part of Mason Co. on Stone Lick Creek, a tributary of the Licking River. In 1775 Col. Robert Patterson explored the area, one of the first parts of the county explored. When John Williams and Henry Parker drew up the town in 1796, they named it Williamsburg. Williams's grandfather Francis McDermid owned the original 1,400 acres where the town was established. The town grew quickly, and in 1836 the Kentucky legislature renamed it for Providence Orange Pickering, a leading citizen and a tailor.

Schools were established in Orangeburg in the mid-19th century, and in 1890 a school for blacks was opened. The schools in the local area (Bernard, Dickson, Mount Gilead, Stonelick, and eventually Plumville and Rectorville) were consolidated into the Orangeburg School in 1912, in 1922, and later. Orangeburg High School opened in 1922 and closed in 1960. The lower grades were consolidated into other schools in the 1970s.

At the turn of the 20th century, Orangeburg was the home of the Orangeburg Rolling Mills, the Red Man's Lodge, dry goods stores, and several churches. The community continues to have places of worship, houses, and some businesses, including a large furniture store and a bakery.

Calvert, Jean, and John Klee. *The Towns of Mason County: Their Past in Pictures.* Maysville, Ky.: Maysville and Mason Co. Library Historical and Scientific Association, 1986.

Rennick, Robert M. *Kentucky Place Names.* Lexington: Univ. Press of Kentucky, 1984.

John Klee

ORR, ALEXANDER D. (b. November 6, 1761, Alexandria, Va.; d. June 21, 1835, Paris, Ky.). Alexander Dalrymple Orr moved to Bourbon Co., Ky. (then part of Virginia), around 1782 and later settled on a plantation along the Ohio River west of Maysville. He was elected to the Virginia House of Delegates in 1790 and to the Virginia Senate in 1792. Kentucky was admitted to the Union that same year, and Orr was elected as one of the first representatives of the new state to the 2nd U.S. Congress. He served three terms altogether, from 1792 to 1797, the final term aligned politically with the emergence of the Jeffersonian Republicans. After leaving politics, Orr returned to farming in Mason Co. He died in 1835 and was buried in the Paris Cemetery at Paris, Ky.

Biographical Directory of the United States Congress, 1774–1989. Washington, D.C.: Government Printing Office, 1989.

Biographical Encyclopedia of Kentucky. Cincinnati: J. M. Armstrong, 1878.

Collins, Richard H. *History of Kentucky.* Vol. 1. Covington, Ky.: Collins, 1882.

Thomas S. Ward

ORR, GERTRUDE (b. January 17, 1891, Covington, Ky.; d. August 1971, Washington, D.C.). Screenwriter Gertrude Orr was the youngest daughter of John E. and Luella Roberts Orr. She was the niece of **Richard P. Ernst**. In Covington, her father was a U.S. gauger; by 1900 the family was living in Denver, Colo., where her father worked in tanneries and paper mills.

Gertrude Orr became involved with the **American Red Cross** while attending Vassar College in upstate New York and found herself working in battlefield military hospitals of the Serbian Campaign during **World War I**. In 1919 she was decorated by Prince Alexander of Serbia for her efforts there. Shortly before the war and for a time afterward, Orr was a feature writer and reporter for the *Denver Post.* In 1921 she visited China.

Orr moved to California, where between 1925 and 1938, she wrote more than 30 scripts for Hollywood films, including *Marriage* (1927), *Mother Machree* (1928), *Waterfront* (1928), *Little Men* (1935), *Country Gentlemen* (1936), and *Call of the Yukon* (1938). *Marriage* was cowritten with Maysville, Ky.'s **Elizabeth Pickett Chevalier**.

In 1943 Orr published *Here Come the Elephants*, a book about the history and psychology of elephants. She died during the month of August 1971 in the nation's capital; her burial location is not known.

"Covington Girl Decorated," *KP*, August 29, 1919, 1.
Orr, Gertrude. *Here Come the Elephants*. Caldwell, Idaho: Caxton, 1943.

ORR ACADEMY/RUGBY SCHOOL. The histories of the Orr Academy and the Rugby School, two schools that operated in Covington, are often confused. In fact, the only thing they have in common is that for a few short years, beginning at the end of the 19th century, the Rugby School occupied the same building that the Orr Academy had used about 40 years earlier.

The Orr Academy, whose official name was Covington Female Seminary, opened in the city in 1843, in the 600 block of Sanford St., on the east side of the street. The academy was very popular with young women. Tuition cost $65 per 20-week session, and there were two sessions each year. The Orr family, who operated the academy, were from Bracken Co. About two years after the family's patriarch, Rev. William Orr, died in 1857, the school was moved by other family members to Cincinnati. Usually, while in Covington, the school was advertised as Orr's Female Academy, rather than as the Covington Female Seminary.

A Professor Lord organized the Rugby Military Academy, a coeducational prep school, in 1885, and it began in a one-story frame building in Covington along Fourth St., near Russell St. The school soon was moved to 12th St. east of Madison Ave., once the home of Roman Catholic priests of the Diocese of Covington. It was at this location that the school flourished, with its annual enrollment rising into the hundreds. By then, the school was under the direction of Professor K. J. Morris and three assistants. The boys enrolled at Rugby Academy wore natty blue uniforms and were easily recognized throughout the city. Students of ages 7 through 18 were admitted, and many of them were from out of town. Rugby was where the social elite of Covington sent their children: prominent Covington family names like Shinkle and Hill were common at the school. The Rugby School was the largest private school in Northern Kentucky. It moved from 12th St. to its new Sanford St. address in 1898. Soon, enrollment began to drop. In 1903, 42 students were enrolled; in 1904, 35 were enrolled. After losing almost $1,000 annually, Morris decided, in early 1906, that the school would not reopen that September. He felt that there were no longer enough people in Covington who could afford the Rugby School. The emergence of a public school system had also lessened the need for such institutions. In 1907 Morris's wife, Sallie, who owned the Sanford St. property, sold the building. For many years the building was rental property, but recently Everett Dameron rehabilitated the structure and converted it to exclusive condominiums.

Mills, Howard H. "A History of Education of Covington, Kentucky," master's thesis, Univ. of Kentucky, 1929.
"Rugby School Sold," *KP*, September 19, 1907, 2.
"Rugby School Will Not Reopen," *KP*, September 13, 1906, 2.

ORTNER FREIGHT CAR COMPANY. This firm once manufactured and rebuilt railroad freight cars at a sprawling property at 21st and Augustine Sts. in Covington. Its location was an industrial area surrounded by railroad yards. The business was established in June 1948 by Joseph L. Ortner (1893–1969), who had started his career in 1911 in an Erie Railroad car shop in Meadville, Pa. Ortner was promoted over the years to higher positions within Erie's car department. In 1933 he was hired by the David J. Joseph Company of Cincinnati to manage the salvage and recycling of parts from obsolete freight cars. Fifteen years later, Ortner bought the business from the Joseph Company and brought his two sons into the business as partners. In 1953 they began to rebuild old cars for the secondhand market. Two years later, Ortner was building new cars. By then the era of the 40-ton freight car was nearly over, so the firm began to specialize in oversize cars with 70-ton to 100-ton capacities. In 1960 one of the company's draftsmen, Norman S. Adams, developed an ingenious scheme for the fast unloading of hopper cars. The new method solved a long-standing problem in car design and won the Ortner Company orders for new cars. Soon they were building 2,000 rapid-discharge cars a year.

Joseph Ortner retired in 1961, and his son Robert took over as president, with Joseph Jr. as vice president. They merged with the Ogden Corporation of New York in 1968. A new plant opened in Milford, Ohio. Before long they were building lightweight hopper cars with aluminum bodies and double-deck stock cars, large enough to carry 120 animals. In 1976 another car plant was built in Mount Orab, Ohio, about 25 miles east of Cincinnati.

The car-building business suffers greatly during economic slowdowns. By May 1983, bad times had led to an almost complete shutdown of the production lines. New contracts would mean the employees would be rehired and then another slump would develop. This was the nature of the railroad car business. All such builders faced the same boom-or-bust order cycles. Investors wanted not just steady profits but expanding profits. They and the firm's management team were not pleased by the car-building trade. Ogden Corporation transferred Ortner to Avondale Industries in 1985. About one year later, Trinity Industries of Dallas, Tex., took over the plants. In 1988 the Covington plant was closed, and not long afterward, Mount Orab shut down as well. This firm that had prospered so well under local management was soon just another forgotten part of smokestack America.

Combes, C. L., ed. *Car and Locomotive Cyclopedia of American Practice, 1966*. New York: Simmons-Boardman, 1966.
Ellsworth, Kenneth G., ed. *Car and Locomotive Encyclopedia of American Practice, 1984*. Omaha, Neb.: Simmons-Boardman, 1984.
Hurley, Daniel. *Cincinnati: The Queen City*. Cincinnati: Cincinnati Historical Society, 1982.
"Joseph L. Ortner, 75, Company Founder," *CE*, May 2, 1969, 40.
"New Company Formed by Local Executive," *CE*, June 2, 1948, 18.

John H. White

O'SHAUGHNESSY, PETER (b. January 18, 1843, Tullamore, King's Co., Ireland; d. August 1, 1926, Newport, Ky.). Irish-born Peter O'Shaughnessy, a real estate investor, a distiller, and a philanthropist, was the son of Hugh and Bridgett McDermott O'Shaughnessy. Just before 1865 he immigrated to the United States and settled in Newport. O'Shaughnessy taught at the Immaculate Conception Grade School in the city's **West End** and began investing in real estate. He wisely anticipated the future value of land on the city's east side and eventually built many homes there. For example, in July 1899 alone, he obtained building permits for 13 two-and-a-half-story dwellings along Maple Ave., between Eighth and Ninth Sts.

A devoted member of the **Immaculate Conception Catholic Church** in Newport, O'Shaughnessy married Emma Daly (1856–1923) there on July 30, 1874, in a ceremony performed by Rev. Patrick Guilfoyle. Emma was the daughter of former Newport mayor Michael V. Daly. The O'Shaughnessys and the Dalys were major supporters of **Immaculata Academy**, the school across the street from the church.

O'Shaughnessy became involved in the distilling business by working for his friend James N. Walsh (see **Walsh Distillery**). He began as a foreman at the distillery at the southeast corner of Front and Scott Sts. in Covington and finished as a partner in the enterprise. His relationship with the Walsh family lasted from the early 1870s until O'Shaughnessy retired from distilling in 1915. O'Shaughnessy and the Walsh family were major benefactors in the building of the **Cathedral Basilica of the Assumption** in Covington. Their Roman Catholic religion was a most important part of their lives. In November 1908 O'Shaughnessy served as an undisclosed agent for the **Sisters of Divine Providence** in acquiring the land in Melbourne, eastern Campbell Co., on which they built their U.S. motherhouse, St. Anne Convent, which opened in 1919. From the early 1890s until his death, O'Shaughnessy resided at 835 York St. in Newport, in an 1876 three-story brick Italianate mansion with 14 rooms. After his death, the home became the Muehlenkamp, Cositgan, and Roll Funeral Home, and it remains a Muehlenkamp-Erschell facility (see **Funeral Homes**).

When O'Shaughnessy died, he was one of Newport's wealthiest citizens. Seven children survived him. His wife, Emma, who was an organist at Immaculate Conception Church for some 30 years, had died three years earlier. His three sons, Eugene, Victor, and William, continued in the distilling business at Lawrenceburg, Ind., long after **Prohibition**. One daughter became Sister Celeste Marie (1883–1971) of the Sisters of Divine Providence and the provincial of the order from 1937 until 1965. After a funeral mass at Immaculate Conception Church celebrated by Bishop Francis W. Howard, O'Shaughnessy was buried at the St. Anne Convent Cemetery; he was one of the few men buried there. Some 19 priests were present at his graveside ceremony, along with more than 200 nuns from various orders. His estate was valued at $1 million and was distributed equally among his children.

"Building Boom," *CE*, July 1, 1899, 2.
Kentucky Death Certificate No. 19453, for the year 1926.
"Mother Celeste, Headed St. Ann," *KP*, August 16, 1971, 15.
"Peter O'Shaughnessy," *Catholic Telegraph*, August 5, 1926, 4.
Ryan, Paul E. *History of the Diocese of Covington, Kentucky*. Covington, Ky.: Diocese of Covington, 1954.

Michael R. Sweeney

OUR LADY OF PROVIDENCE ACADEMY. The Roman Catholic congregation of the **Sisters of Divine Providence** came to Northern Kentucky during the late 1880s from France's Alsace-Lorraine region. Shortly after the first three sisters arrived on August 23, 1889, the Jones Mansion (see **Thomas Laurens Jones**), located on a six-acre tract of land at the head of Monmouth St. in Newport, was purchased for their use. Here the sisters established the **Mount St. Martin** Convent.

That fall, the sisters promptly opened a day school, Mount St. Martin Academy, with an enrollment of three pupils, at the convent. Because course offerings included French, needlework, music, art, and classical subjects with a decidedly European flavor, the school soon became known as the French Academy. By 1901, as the sisters marked their 12th anniversary in the United States, they had outgrown their hillside home because of expanding enrollment and the growing novitiate (training school for young sisters). That same year, a tract on E. Sixth St. in Newport was purchased from Aloysius Schabell for $20,000; an adjacent parcel was purchased on August 23 of the following year from **Robert Nelson**, then mayor of Newport, for $10,000. Louis Goldkamp won the bid for construction and formally signed the contract on May 7, 1902. along with Mother Maria Houlné, provincial superior; William A. Byrne, attorney; and Charles Hannaford, architect (see **Hannaford, Samuel, and Sons**). Construction began on June 9, 1902.

Upon completion, the grand, five-story structure, containing approximately 60,000 square feet of space, boasted an elaborate array of decorative embellishments typical of the Beaux-Arts style: decorative masonry adorned many openings, coupled columns framed the main entryway, dormer windows jutted from the mansard-style roof, and symmetrical, advancing wings flanked the structure's receding central section, which was crowned with a distinctive, copper-topped bell tower. The building's interior was equally lavish, featuring black slate stairwells, oak handrails, and terrazzo floors; the front entrance, with its grey Knoxville marble stairway and Venetian mosaic floor, was reserved for guests and visiting dignitaries. Carved above the entryway was the new name of the school, "Académie de Notre Dame de la Providence," reflecting the French origin of the order (though the institution became known as the Academy Notre Dame of Providence, or ANDP). Just above the inscribed entablature, carved within a round pediment, was a bas-relief cartouche featuring the newly constructed academy's saintly patroness, Mary, Our Lady of Providence, along with a crown and a cross; the edifice also bore an inscription of the academy's motto, "Religioni et Artibus" ("Religion and Arts"), carved just below a second, triangular pediment upon which the distinctive bell tower appeared to rest.

Dedicated by Bishop Maes on August 23, 1903, the ANDP had an enrollment of 108 pupils when classes began that September; this large number reflected the growth of the Diocese of Covington's Catholic population, which had increased to nearly 50,000. Although the academy initially offered elementary, secondary, and some postsecondary educational programs, for the first eight years, only the grade school was coeducational; upon reaching eighth grade, boys were no longer enrolled at the school. Providence's high school department included classical, English, and commercial courses. Highly qualified instructors taught the academy's exemplary music, art, and language classes and also offered more advanced courses and private lessons for gifted students. In addition to their normal curriculum, the sisters sought to serve the surrounding populace by offering special classes in subjects such as needlework, art, and music to girls and women not formally enrolled as students at the academy.

During the early years, the ANDP's highly regarded and classically based academic program drew young women from many Northern Kentucky and Greater Cincinnati cities, including Newport, Fort Thomas, Ludlow, Bellevue, Dayton, Mount Adams, and Hyde Park. The academy's later affiliations with the University of Kentucky at Lexington in October 1905, and with the Catholic University of America at Washington, D.C., in 1914 further enhanced the school's ranking and reputation. In 1929 Bishop **Francis W. Howard**, hoping to increase accessibility by defraying tuition charges, designated the ANDP as Campbell Co.'s central Catholic high school for girls; students' individual parishes assisted them if they could not afford to pay the full tuition amount. That same year, Howard established the school that evolved into Newport Catholic High School as the central Catholic high school for Campbell Co.'s male student population.

Despite the onset of the **Great Depression**, the academy's enrollment had increased so significantly that in June 1934 the grade school department was discontinued, allowing the institution to focus solely on secondary education. Operating under the auspices of the Covington diocese, the ANDP had operating expenses of $10,145 in 1935. It was staffed by 3 diocesan priests and 13 sisters and charged tuition of $40 per year.

With the academy's financial constraints eased by designation as the central Catholic high school for girls of Campbell Co., the student body soon reflected a broader spectrum of the local population; accordingly, the curriculum was altered to better reflect the school's expansive and dynamic cultural and educational traditions. In 1965, decades after the first three sisters had arrived in Northern Kentucky from France, the "French Academy" became known by its American title, Our Lady of Providence Academy, or OLP, its more commonly known acronym. The name change not only reflected the academy's embrace of its adopted American homeland but also, on a practical note, prevented confusion between it and Covington's **Notre Dame Academy**.

In 1968 OLP enrollment peaked at 464 students, making it the fourth-largest of Northern Kentucky's 12 Catholic high schools. By 1978, as the school prepared to celebrate its 75th anniversary, declines in Northern Kentucky's Roman Catholic population had led to decreases in enrollment. Population shifts, increasing operating expenses, and shrinking student enrollment further exacerbated mounting financial woes even as OLP attempted to address remodeling needs and ongoing maintenance and building upkeep issues. That year, OLP faced an $88,000 deficit. Covington's **La Salette Academy** had closed the previous year as it faced many of the same issues.

A newly formed booster club assisted Sister Margaret Anne Kraemer, principal of OLP, in raising funds to correct the structure's fire code violations by installing smoke alarms and enclosing stairwells. The booster club's efforts were supplemented by an increase in the school's tuition; for 1978–1979, tuition was increased by $90, to $390. Although OLP had valiantly upheld the exemplary educational traditions established by the Sisters of Divine Providence for decades, in 1980 the results of a study conducted by the Diocese of Covington concluded that the only way to preserve an institution for secondary Catholic education in Newport would be to merge OLP with Newport Catholic High School.

The OLP Beaux-Arts building had remained a stunning architectural feast for the eyes, but the costs of necessary upgrades and remodeling exceeded the $500,000 required to expand Newport Catholic High School's hillside structure. Completed in 1955, the more modern boys' high school facility was located very near the site where the sisters had first established Mount St. Martin's Academy; after 80 years, the school returned to its hilltop home. Having graduated nearly 4,000 young women, OLP had its final day of classes on June 1, 1983; that fall, classes were held at the coeducational **Newport Central Catholic High School**.

Since the 1983 closure of the academy, the 103-year-old building has gone through several incarnations and multiple conversions. First functioning as residential units known as the Hannaford Apartments in 1997, the building was later converted into extended-stay corporate suites known as the Hannaford Suites. Currently, the grand old structure and the smaller, similarly styled companion building at the rear of the grounds are being touted by a local real estate agent as the Hannaford, a forty-unit condominium community. In addition, 12 similarly designed townhouses facing Nelson Pl. are planned for the northern edge of the historic grounds.

Archives of the Congregation of Divine Providence, Melbourne, Ky.
Archives of the Diocese of Covington, Erlanger, Ky.

"Our Lady of Providence," Local History files, Kenton Co. Public Library, Covington, Ky.
Paeth, Greg. "The Old Gal Looks Good for Her Age," *KP*, January 22, 1983, 6K.
Plattner, Elissa May. "How Beautiful upon the Mountains: The Sisters of Divine Providence and Their Mission to Kentucky Appalachia," PhD diss., Univ. of Cincinnati, 1987.
Ryan, Paul E. *History of the Diocese of Covington, Kentucky*. Covington, Ky.: Diocese of Covington, 1954.

Janice Mueller

OUR LADY OF THE HIGHLANDS SCHOOL. This school was an aspect of the ministry begun by the Roman Catholic order of the Sisters of Our Lady of Charity of the Good Shepherd in Fort Thomas in 1873. The first foundation of the Sisters of the Good Shepherd in the United States had opened in 1842 at Louisville. By 1857, a group of Louisville sisters had established a convent in southwestern Ohio, which was centered eventually at Carthage, Ohio. In 1873 the sisters at Carthage acquired the Robert Beaton property at 938 Highland Ave. in Fort Thomas, Ky., and over the next century, the sisters operated an orphanage, a protective home for troubled girls, Our Lady of the Highlands School, and a retirement community for aged sisters there. The Fort Thomas property was eventually expanded to include more than 75 acres.

The orphanage for girls was the first ministry conducted by the sisters in Fort Thomas, using the original Beaton home. Over time, many additions were constructed, including a limestone chapel in the shape of a Greek cross, dedicated on October 19, 1884. In 1885 the sisters began a residential program for troubled girls, and a wing for this purpose was built in 1890. Many of the girls in this program were sent to the sisters by the local court systems. In 1908 the sisters financed the construction of a school wing on the campus. In time, this school became known as Our Lady of the Highlands and educated both elementary and secondary students.

The school program at Our Lady of the Highlands was open to both Catholic and non-Catholic children. Non-Catholic children were given instruction in Christian doctrine, while Catholic children received religious instruction typical of that given in most parochial schools of the day. In 1946 a new school building with 27 classrooms was constructed on the grounds. A gymnasium was added to the school's facilities six years later. The growth of the school and changing societal patterns resulted in the closing of the orphanage in the late 1950s.

Beginning in the 1970s, the Sisters of the Good Shepherd renovated one of the wings of the building into a retirement home for their community of sisters. A new structure, named Pelletier Hall, was constructed on the convent grounds for this purpose in 1982.

In 1981 Sister Mary Janice Rushman, R.G.S., was appointed superior of the Our Lady of Highlands School. At that time, 17 nuns were in residence, and the school enrollment stood at 25. It soon became apparent to the sisters that the cost of maintaining such large buildings, coupled with declining enrollment, made the program unsustainable. Following the 1982–1983 academic year, Our Lady of the Highlands School closed. Much of the Fort Thomas property was sold for use as the right-of-way of I-471 and a small shopping center. However, the sisters continue to own Pelletier Hall, which has remained the retirement residence for the Sisters of the Good Shepherd of the Carthage Province.

Reis, Jim. "Bells of Good Shepherd Still Echo in Fort Thomas," *KP*, October 11, 1999, 4K.
Remlinger, Connie. "Lady to Bid Farewell to Her Flock on the Hill," *KP*, March 31, 1983, 4K.
Ryan, Paul E. *History of the Diocese of Covington, Kentucky*. Covington, Ky.: Diocese of Covington, 1954.
Tenkotte, Paul A., David E. Schroeder, and Thomas S. Ward. *To Be Catholic and American in Northern, Central, and Appalachian Kentucky: The Diocese of Covington, 1853–2003*. Forthcoming.
Tucker, Alan. "Time for Change," *KP*, February 14, 1981, 11K.

David E. Schroeder

OUR SAVIOR CATHOLIC CHURCH. The Our Savior Catholic Church, located on E. 10th St. in Covington, was the only Roman Catholic parish for African Americans within the Diocese of Covington. For a number of years, the parish also operated a grade and high school. The parishioners are primarily from Northern Kentucky.

Before 1943, a few African Americans attended the **Cathedral Basilica of the Assumption** in Covington. That year it was decided, at the encouragement of Bishop **Francis W. Howard**, to form a separate African American church and school in Northern Kentucky as a mission of the cathedral. The site selected was on E. 10th St. in Covington. The plans were to convert a two-family home into classrooms and a convent for the **Sisters of Divine Providence**, who were going to teach at the school. The school opened in September 1943, after the renovations for the school and convent were completed. Because of illness, Bishop Howard was unable personally to dedicate the Our Savior Church, so Rev. Msgr. Walter Freiberg, pastor of the parish of the cathedral, officiated at the dedication.

In 1946 the pastor of the Our Savior Church was Rev. Henry Haacke, and Rev. Anthony Deye directed the school's athletic program. Deye set up baseball, football, and basketball teams. The church was part of the Northern Kentucky Catholic High School League and the Northern Kentucky Holy Name Basketball League. In 1945 William Lane, an associate at the cathedral and the only African American priest in the diocese, was assigned to work at the parish. On September 19, 1948, a new school building was finished and blessed by Bishop **William T. Mulloy**. The building had four spacious, well-lighted classrooms and a cafeteria, and there was a large recreation room in the building next door.

The high school closed in 1956 because of the movement toward integration. One of the more famous students impacted by its closing was **Thomas Thacker**, a basketball player who attended William Grant High School and later played on the University of Cincinnati's national championship teams. The grade school closed on May 31, 1963. In 1981 the Our Savior Church became an independent parish with its own pastor, Daniel Saner. Today, the parish is overseen by Sr. Janet Bucher, C.D.P.

"Catholic Schools Merged and Split over the Years," *KP*, April 17, 1987, 2K.
Reis, Jim. "Our Savior Fills Unique Niche," *KP*, January 17, 1994, 4K.

Theodore H. H. Harris

OWEN, ABRAHAM, COLONEL (b. 1769, Prince Edward Co., Va.; d. November 7, 1811, Tippecanoe Battlefield, Indiana Territory). Abraham Owen, an **American Indian** fighter and the namesake of Owen Co. (as well as Owensboro), was the son of Brackett Owen, who in 1782 moved to Jefferson Co., Ky., about four miles from what is now Shelbyville, and established Owen's Station, a small frontier fort used during the latter part of the **Revolutionary War** for protection from Indian attacks. In 1785, at age 16, Abraham Owen joined his father in the Virginia territory that seven years later (in 1792) became the Commonwealth of Kentucky. Abraham Owen accompanied Col. John Hardin and Col. James Wilkerson in their campaigns against the Northwest Indians in northern Ohio and Indiana. Later, he served under Gen. Arthur St. Clair and joined the contingent of 1,400 men that marched against the Indians led by Chief **Little Turtle**. This force was surprised by a sudden Indian attack (known historically as St. Clair's Defeat) led by Little Turtle, and the majority of the force was killed or wounded. Owen was wounded and returned to Fort Washington (Cincinnati).

Eventually promoted to colonel, Owen returned to his home in Shelby Co., where his wounds slowly healed. After Kentucky attained statehood, Owen helped lay out the new town of Shelbyville. There, he was a town trustee and magistrate as well as county surveyor. Elected to the legislature and chosen as a member of the Kentucky constitutional convention in 1799, Owen began a life of public service.

In 1811 another Indian war was brewing on America's western frontier. William Henry Harrison, a general in the U.S. Army and governor of the Indiana Territory, called for volunteers to deal with the Indian threat. Owen responded to Harrison's call and left Kentucky with Capt. Frederick Geiger's company. About 60 Kentuckians linked up with Harrison at the mouth of the Vermillion River in Indiana, to join the main army of volunteers from Ohio and Indiana.

Owen became commander of the 18th Kentucky Regiment. They marched up the Wabash River to within a few miles of the junction of that stream with the Tippecanoe River. Owen was killed during the Battle of Tippecanoe.

Kleber, John E., ed. *The Kentucky Encyclopedia*. Lexington: Univ. Press of Kentucky, 1992.
Vertical files, Owen Co. Public Library, Owenton, Ky.

Doris Riley

OWEN CO. Within the state of Kentucky, Owen Co. is regarded as being in the north central section; within the Northern Kentucky region, it is in the southwestern corner. It is bordered by Carroll, Franklin, Gallatin, Grant, and Henry counties and has an area of 354 square miles. Owen Co. was created in 1819, the 63rd in order of formation in the state, and like its county seat, Owenton, Owen Co. was named for **Revolutionary War** soldier and Indian fighter Col. **Abraham Owen**. Rolling hills and farmlands characterize the terrain of the county's 354 square miles. The county was formed from parts of Franklin, Gallatin, and Scott counties. It has been referred to as **Sweet Owen**, a term of endearment first proffered by Democratic congressional candidate John C. Breckinridge, when the votes he received in Owen Co. helped elect him to the U.S. House of Representatives during the early 1850s.

The county was and remains an agricultural area, once heavily dependent on **tobacco** production. In the 19th century its western boundary, the Kentucky River, allowed for the delivery of goods through steamboat stops at Moxley, Gratz, Monterey, and other smaller places. For a short period around 1900, **lead** mines around Gratz exported their product via the boats. In recent years some industry has operated just outside of Owenton (see **Owen Co. Industry**), but with no railroad connection, with the boats gone from the Kentucky River, with three interstate highways surrounding the county (but not close by), and with the county's meager aviation facilities, it has been difficult to attract manufacturing into Owen Co.

During the **Civil War**, the county was a Confederate stronghold (see **Confederate Recruiting in Owen Co.**), and during **World War II** the county produced several successful and important military leaders: Vice Adm. **Willis Augustus Lee**, Rear Adm. **Arnold Ellsworth True**, Rear Adm. **Evan White Yancey**, and Gen. **Gerald Walter Johnson**.

Owen Co. Courthouse, Owenton, completed in 1858.

Perhaps the most famous person from Owen Co. is **Ben Holladay**, who grew up in the 1820s at New Liberty in the northern part of the county. Holladay owned and operated the famed Pony Express as well as several other stagecoach lines, railroads, and steamship companies in the West. With his wealth, it was said that he literally "owned" the U.S. senators from the state of Oregon, where Holladay's business operations were based. A suburb in Portland, Ore., is named for him. Another person from Owen Co., Dr. **Richard C. Arnold**, a native of Squiresville, also achieved significant fame. Arnold was a member of the U.S. Public Health Service during the late 1930s, and he revolutionized the treatment of syphilis by demonstrating the effectiveness of using penicillin. Before that discovery, people commonly died of the dreaded disease.

In literature, the county was home to **Alfred Cobb**, a native of Lusby's Mill, who in his *Liffy Leman; or, Thirty Years in the Wilderness* (1890) described life in the county before the Civil War in a semifictional style, and to **Ed Porter Thompson**, the founder of the **Harrisburgh Academy** (later known as **Owen College**) and author of several works, including his epic 1,104-page Civil War chronicle *The History of the Orphan Brigade* (1898).

In recent times two talented African Americans from the county have attained regional attention. **William "Bill" Livers** of Long Ridge, known for his fiddle playing, produced several recordings. Livers performed in the Capitol Building in Washington, D.C., and at the World Fair in Knoxville, Tenn. **Theodore "Teddy" Vinegar** became an expert on both saddle horses and farming techniques (hillside planting without erosion) while residing at his **Mountain Island** farm in Owen Co.

In 1900 Owen Co. had a population of 17,533, but by 2000 the population had decreased to 10,547.

Houchens, Mariam Sidebottom. *History of Owen County: "Sweet Owen."* Louisville, Ky.: Standard, 1976.

Kleber, John E., ed. *The Kentucky Encyclopedia.* Lexington: Univ. Press of Kentucky, 1992.

U.S. Census Bureau. "American Fact Finder. Data Set. Census 2000 Summary File 1 (SF1) 100-Percent Data. Custom Table." www.census.gov (accessed June 3, 2006).

OWEN CO. BAPTIST ASSOCIATION. The present Owen Co. Baptist Association was created by merging two previous associations in 1925. One of these, the Concord Association, dated from 1821 and the other, the Owen Association of Baptists, was formed in 1880. Beginning in 1925, they were joined together to become the Owen Co. Baptist Association. Never meant to become a central authority in matters of scripture and theology, the Owen Co. Baptist Association instead organizes and sponsors multiday annual meetings and revivals where speakers are brought to Owen Co. to preach the Gospel. The site for these annual events changes from year to year within the county. At the association meetings the members of the Baptist churches in Owen Co. hear about the results of their missionary support and receive reports on the Baptist hospitals and children's homes to which they contribute money. The annual meeting is also where statistics for Baptist churches in the county are totaled and collated for the past year: baptisms, marriages, births, and deaths. In 2005 the Owen Co. Baptist Association held its 80th annual session.

Arnold, Ruth. *A History of Owen County Baptist Association and It's* [sic] *Churches.* Owenton, Ky.: Privately published, 1965.

Houchens, Mariam Sidebottom. *History of Owen County: "Sweet Owen."* Louisville, Ky.: Standard, 1976.

OWEN CO. INDUSTRY. The first industrial jobs in Owen Co. came with the construction of the Kraft Cheese plant near downtown Owenton. The Kraft plant, built in 1936 and enlarged in 1944, supplied the only industrial jobs in the county until the 1970s. The Kraft Cheese facility provided a convenient outlet for local dairy farmers to sell their milk, but by 1980 it had closed. In 1973 the Scholl Industry built a sandal-manufacturing plant in Owenton on Sparta Rd. (**U.S. 127**) north of the Independent Order of Odd Fellows Cemetery; the plant was dedicated in 1974. During the mid-1980s that factory was sold to Schlumberger, a diversified technology company, and then in the mid-1990s it was resold to Actaris Metering Systems, a maker of gas metering equipment, fittings, and regulators. In 2000 Actaris employed 223 workers. The state of industry in Owen Co. can be best appreciated by looking at the Owenton Industrial Park: of its 63.8 acres, all remain available. There is no rail service, no adequate airport, and no barge transportation. Accordingly, it is easy to understand why Owen Co. has not been successful in attracting much-needed industrial jobs for its employment base. Perhaps the proposed rebuilding of Ky. Rt. 22 east to I-75 will help alleviate the problem by making access to Owen Co. easier for industry.

Houchens, Mariam Sidebottom. *History of Owen County: "Sweet Owen."* Louisville, Ky.: Standard, 1976.

Vertical files, Owen Co. Public Library, Owenton, Ky.

OWEN CO. PUBLIC LIBRARY. The Owen Co. Public Library got its start in 1946, with Elizabeth Thomas's desire to provide books for students at the Owenton School (grades 1–12). Thomas lived at the corner of W. Perry and N. Main Sts. in Owenton, across Perry St. from the school. Soon the Owen Co. Woman's Club began a library with the goal of fulfilling Thomas's wish. At the beginning, individuals donated books from their personal libraries; these were placed in the front parlor of the Thomas home. Checkout of books was based on the honor system: a person would bring one book to trade in for another. A library committee was appointed, and it met in a small room in back of the **Kroger** grocery, located at the corner of E. Seminary and S. Main Sts.

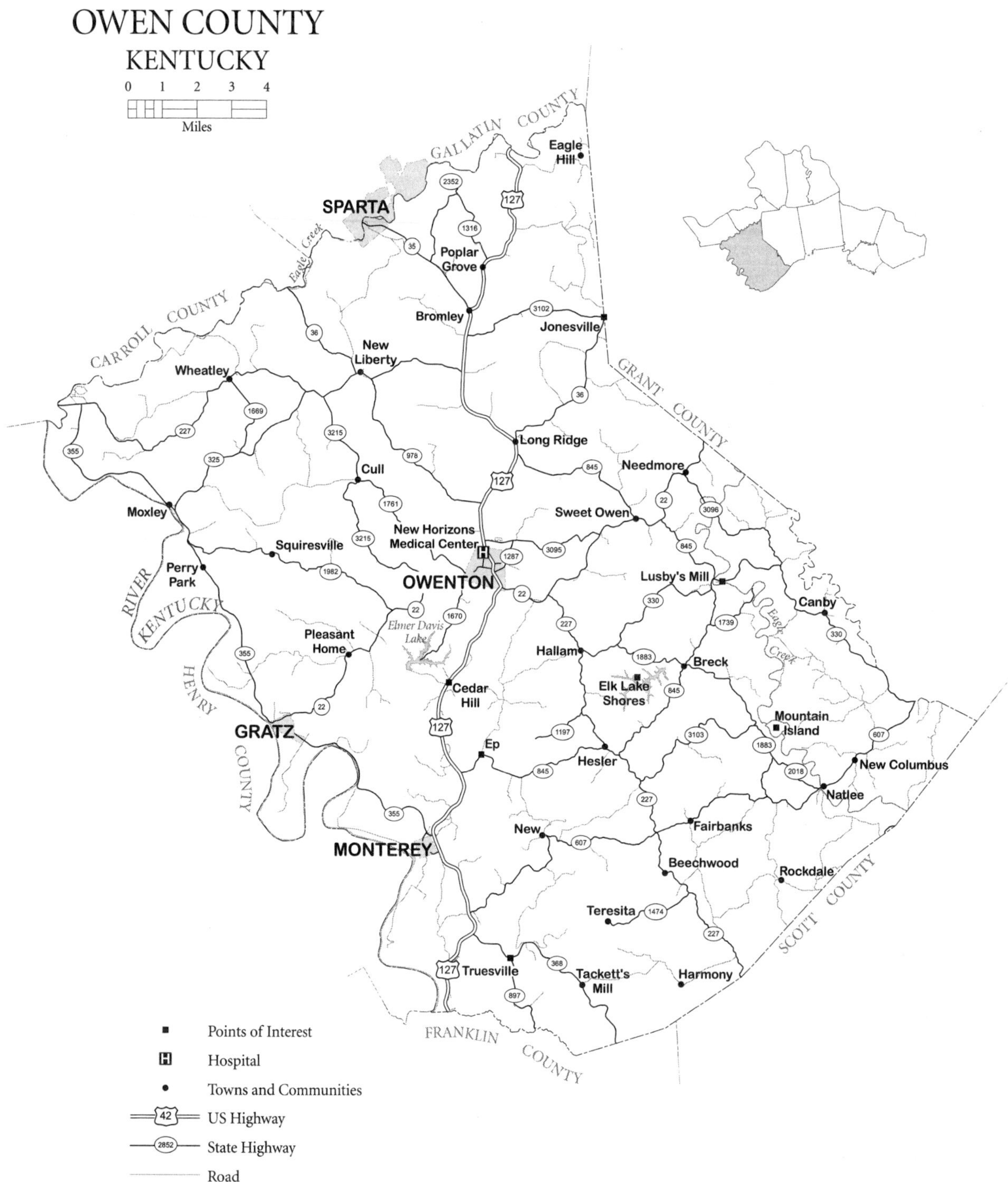
OWEN COUNTY
KENTUCKY
0 1 2 3 4
Miles
GALLATIN COUNTY
CARROLL COUNTY
GRANT COUNTY
HENRY COUNTY
SCOTT COUNTY
FRANKLIN COUNTY
KENTUCKY RIVER
Eagle Creek
SPARTA
OWENTON
GRATZ
MONTEREY
Eagle Hill
Poplar Grove
Bromley
Jonesville
New Liberty
Wheatley
Long Ridge
Needmore
Cull
Moxley
Sweet Owen
New Horizons Medical Center
Squiresville
Perry Park
Lusby's Mill
Canby
Elmer Davis Lake
Pleasant Home
Hallam
Breck
Elk Lake Shores
Cedar Hill
Mountain Island
Ep
Hesler
New Columbus
Natlee
Fairbanks
New
Beechwood
Rockdale
Teresita
Truesville
Tackett's Mill
Harmony
Points of Interest
Hospital
Towns and Communities
US Highway
State Highway
Road

As the library began to grow, it moved in October 1952 to four rooms above the First National Bank on W. Seminary St. There, the library shared space with the **American Red Cross**, the Homemakers, and the hospital auxiliary, which used the location as a meeting place. The library's 1952 annual report showed that 5,500 books were circulated and that a children's story hour was begun in the preceding year. The library had also received a state grant of $1,528. The first bookmobile arrived in October 1954, one of 84 that were purchased by the Philip Morris Company as part of a statewide program established by Kentucky governor Lawrence Wetherby (1950–1955). The library continued its growth and, in 1961, moved to the upper floor of city hall at 102 N. Main St., remaining at that spot until the opening of the present facility, a building authorized by the passage of a countywide tax levy. In July 1970, the library board purchased a home at the corner of W. Perry and S. Main Sts., the very same home in which the library was first organized, and construction began on a completely new building that opened in 1973.

In 2001 the library underwent a complete face-lift and reopened its doors in December. With a total of 4,650 square feet, at present it houses books, audio books, CD's, videos, magazines, newspapers, and historical records. The library offers story-hour programs, summer reading programs, and a bookmobile service. Meeting rooms and computers are available in the facility for the public's use.

Historical Society files, Owen Co. Public Library, Owenton, Ky.

Doris Riley

OWEN CO. PUBLIC SCHOOLS. When Owen Co. was established in 1819, public officials and residents demonstrated little interest in public education. Education was provided mainly through private schools, where tuition had to be paid. Because these schools were mostly in New Liberty and Owenton, the county's largest towns, the majority of school-age children had little opportunity to attend school.

By the early 1820s, public (common) schools had opened in New Liberty (1817) and Pleasant Grove (1820) near New Columbus. By 1845, Owen Co. reported one district with an enrollment of 55 students; it is known that other schools existed, but these apparently did not report. With the outbreak of the **Civil War**, the school system could not obtain qualified teachers, because many male teachers went to war. In addition, enrollment in the county's schools declined as children were needed at home to help with crops. Following the war, social and political problems and limited funds left the county unable to provide public schools.

From 1861 to 1867, funds for public education came from various fines and a dog tax, and this money was designated for white schools only. The common school system allowed districts to have schools if residents were willing to pay a personal tax for support of the schools. It is unclear whether the Owen Co. court system decided not to enact this tax, or whether there was no need for the tax since there were some private schools in operation in the county. In 1878–1879 the first Owen Co. school for African Americans was opened in Owenton by J. W. Womack. In 1879 the county created a three-trustee system for each of its districts. By 1881 there were 75 white schools in the county and 1 black school. Most of the schools were one-room schools operating for a term of five months; average attendance per school per month was 15. By 1910, the school term changed to 6 months, and there were 63 white schools and 7 black schools; 4,678 students attended schools in Owen Co., including the four independent school districts of Owenton, Gratz, New Liberty, and Sparta. Owenton High School was established in 1902; Wheatley High School was founded in 1912. By the 1920s, county high schools were operating at Gratz, Lusby's Mill, Monterey, New Columbus, and Hesler (a two-year high school), and there were also high schools in the independent districts of New Liberty, Owenton, Sparta, and Wheatley.

Throughout the early 20th century, the need to save funds, a shortage of teachers, the improvement in the county's roads, and the use of buses to transport students all contributed to the closing of several of Owen Co.'s small public community schools through consolidation. In 1936, with the entrance of the school at Sparta into the county school system, the only remaining independent system in the county was at Owenton. In 1951, with the building of a high school just outside Owenton to serve the entire county, the consolidation of the county's high schools began, and the Owenton independent system was dissolved.

Currently Owen Co. Public Schools operates four schools, all located on Ky. Rt. 22 East in Owenton: Owen Co. Primary, established in 1985; Owen Co. Elementary, opened in 1970; Bowling Middle School, opened in 1985; and the original Owen Co. High School, built in 1951 and now operating in a new building built in 2002.

Forsee, John. "Education, Owen County," Owen Co. Public Library, Owenton, Ky.

Houchens, Mariam Sidebottom. *History of Owen County: "Sweet Owen."* Louisville, Ky.: Standard, 1976.

Vertical files, Owen Co. Public Library, Owenton, Ky.

Doris Riley

OWEN ELECTRIC COOPERATIVE. This nonprofit electric cooperative in north central Kentucky provides electricity to many businesses and residents in Boone, Campbell, Carroll, Gallatin, Grant, Kenton, Owen, Pendleton, and Scott counties. Owen Electric, formerly known as Owen Co. RECC (Rural Electric Cooperative Corporation), was formed in 1937. Five farmers from Owen Co. met to discuss bringing electricity to the rural parts of the county with the help of the Rural Electrification Administration. In January 1938, Kentucky governor A. B. "Happy" Chandler (1935–1939, 1955–1959) attended a special dedication ceremony during which he flipped a switch at the New Liberty substation, providing power to the first 100 homes across 45 miles of line in Owen Co. RECC's service area. In the years following, Owen Co. RECC expanded its service area to include eight other counties in the region. By 1940 Owen Co. RECC had approximately 700 miles of line and 1,965 members. In 1978 there were 20,000 members, 3,782 miles of line, and 82 employees, with four offices and three service facilities.

In 1988 Owen Co. RECC celebrated its 50th anniversary. In 1990 the cooperative shortened its name to Owen Electric Cooperative. During the 1990s, Owen Electric saw the addition of many commercial and industrial consumers, such as Toyota Motor Manufacturing North America, Gallatin Steel, and the Kentucky Speedway. In addition, residential development companies were buying land quickly in Owen Electric's service area to develop subdivisions like Triple Crown and Derby Estates in Boone Co. By 1998 Owen Electric had over 40,000 members, 4,300 miles of line, and 116 employees. In 2000 Owen Electric joined Touchstone Energy, a national network of electric cooperatives established to provide better resources to cooperatives and their members. In 2002 Owen Electric became one of the first electric utilities in the state to offer green-power energy generated from renewable sources to its customers. In 2003 Owen Electric and East Kentucky Power Cooperative started local production of EnviroWatts (Owen Electric's name for green power produced from biomass) from methane gas collected off the Bavarian Landfill at Walton, Boone Co.; also in 2003, Owen Electric moved into its new state-of-the art headquarters facility, which includes a community room, a storm-hardened dispatch center, a call center, and a museum (open to the public). The cooperative started purchasing EnviroWatts for the new facility in 2004. Also that year, Owen Electric made another environmental commitment by installing biodiesel pumps on-site at its two service facilities and using biodiesel fuel in its entire diesel-powered fleet. In 2005 Owen Electric had more than 52,000 members, 4,800 miles of line, and 120 employees reporting out of four customer service offices and two service centers.

Houchens, Mariam Sidebottom, *History of Owen County: "Sweet Owen."* Louisville, Ky.: Standard, 1976.

Deloris Foxworthy

OWENS, THURMAN "JESSE," BRIGADIER GENERAL (b. March 15, 1925, Livingston, Ky.; d. February 22, 2004, Edgewood, Ky.). Thurman Owens, a veteran of three U.S. wars, was born in Rockcastle Co., the son of Walter and Flossie Mullins Owens. By 1930 the family lived in Covington and Walter Owens worked for the railroad. Thurman graduated from **Holmes High School** in 1943, where he was a star football player, and immediately joined the Marine Corps Reserves. In 1945 he was commissioned a 2nd lieutenant, just as **World War II** was nearing its end. He participated in the Allied occupation of China and then was discharged from the military in 1947. In 1949 Owens captained the University of Cincinnati football team, where he was a 176-pound defensive end under coach Sid Gillman. Owens earned his BS from that school in 1950. He taught and coached at the Elkhart, Ind., high school before being recalled to active military duty during the **Korean War**. With the exception of a brief period during 1954, he spent the next 23 years as a Marine officer, rising to the rank of brigadier general. He served in Vietnam and earned a Bronze Star and two Legion of Merit awards. He also was the deputy chief of staff for programs at the Marine Corps headquarters. After retiring from the military in 1978, he became the assistant director of the University of Cincinnati Foundation, advanced to director of the foundation in 1980, and retired in 1991. Even after leaving his job at the University of Cincinnati, he helped countless college students to obtain financial aid. Owens was a member of the Boone Co. Planning Commission and the Kenton Co. Airport Board. He was selected for the sports halls of fame of Holmes High School, Northern Kentucky, and the University of Cincinnati. Owens died in 2004 at the St. Elizabeth Medical Center South, in Edgewood, and was buried at Highland Cemetery in Fort Mitchell.

BioMilitaryStyleold. "Gen. Thurman Owens." www.usmc.mil/genbios2.nsf (accessed June 20, 2007).

Meiman, Karen. "Distinguished Grads Recognized," *KP*, May 18, 2004, 3.

"Thurman Owens, 78, Marine Corps General," *KP*, February 24, 2004, 4A.

OWENTON. The county seat of Owen Co., Ky., is the centrally located fifth-class city of Owenton, which is situated where **U.S. 127** and Ky. Rt. 22 meet. It lies in the middle of Kentucky's "Golden Triangle," an area of economic prosperity bounded by Northern Kentucky on the north, Lexington on the south, and Louisville on the west. Unfortunately, Owen Co. and Owenton have yet to benefit from being surrounded by the three thriving areas of commerce. The town, like the county, was named for **Revolutionary War** soldier and Indian fighter Col. **Abraham Owen**.

Owenton was not Owen Co.'s first county seat, but in 1822, after the county's formation in 1819, the center of government was moved to Owenton from Hesler (Heslerville). Incorporated in 1828, Owenton became the center of religion, education, health care, and commerce for Owen Co. Many of the major denominations are represented in the city; churches in town include the Assembly of God, the First Baptist, the Second Baptist, the First Christian, the St. Edward Catholic, and the First Methodist. Owenton was the home of the first secondary school in the county, **Caldwell Academy**, and now the Owen Co. High School is located in Owenton (see **Owen Co. Public Schools**). Owenton has the hospital that serves the county, **New Horizons Medical Center**, and Owenton is where area residents go for services and shopping. It is also home to the **Owen Co. Public Library** and the *Owenton News-Herald* newspaper. During the **Civil War**, city residents tended to favor the South, with two Confederate recruiting stations nearby (see **Confederate Recruiting in Owen Co.**). During **World War II**, several successful and important military leaders had ties with Owenton: Gen. **Gerald Walter Johnson**, Vice Adm. **Willis Augustus Lee**, Rear Adm. **Arnold Ellsworth True**, and Rear Adm. **Evan White Yancey**. The town has also produced jurists of statewide influence: Judge **James Cammack Sr.** and Judge **James Cammack Jr.**

What little industry has existed in the county has been and is located on the outskirts of town (see **Owen Co. Industry**). Many workers travel daily to cities outside the county, especially Frankfort, located to the south along U.S. 127. The major factor hindering Owenton economically is its location with respect to transportation routes. Flanked by I-71 on the north, I-75 on the east, and I-64 on the south, Owenton is bypassed by people and commerce crossing Kentucky, and its citizens are drawn to one of the three points of the "Golden Triangle" for some of their needs. The town is not easily accessed from the major arteries of travel and commerce. The town, and most of the county, has no railroad connection.

Owenton serves as the center of the county's agricultural community, which has relied heavily on the production of tobacco in the past. The Owen Co. courthouse dominates the center of town, within the town square. Over time, whereas the county has lost population, Owenton's population has remained stable or increased slightly. The city's population in 1990 was 1,306, and in 2000, 1,387.

Houchens, Mariam Sidebottom, *History of Owen County: "Sweet Owen."* Louisville, Ky.: Standard, 1976.

Kleber, John E., ed. *The Kentucky Encyclopedia.* Lexington: Univ. Press of Kentucky, 1992.

U.S. Census Bureau. "American Fact Finder. Data Set. Census 2000 Summary File 1 (SF1) 100-Percent Data. Custom Table." www.census.gov (accessed June 3, 2006).

OWENTON NEWS-HERALD. Newspapers in Owen Co. have started, stopped, experienced rivalries, and merged, but through the years they have had a major role in the development of the county's communities by providing a place for the expression of ideas. Three early newspapers published in Owen Co., the *Owen News,* the *Owenton Herald,* and the *Owen County Democrat,* helped to form the *News-Herald*, which serves the county today.

The *Owen News* was first published in 1868 in New Liberty by J. M. Clark, who soon moved the *Owen News* to Owenton. Afterward, the newspaper was published continuously for several years under various owners. By 1883 George S. Lee was editor and proprietor of the *Owen News.* Then in April 1895, George S. Lee and Emmett Off were listed as the publishers of the *Owen News.* Frank C. Greene became editor of the *Owen News* in January 1900. During his short term of ownership, the newspaper's circulation increased from 1,200 to 1,500.

Sometime after 1874, Jerry D. Lillard became editor and owner of a second paper in the county, the *Owen County Democrat.* By 1884 Col. R. C. "Bob" Ford Sr. was this newspaper's publisher. Then Ford left Owenton, and the paper was not printed between 1888 and 1902. In about 1902, **Evan Settle** and Frank Greene resurrected the *Owen County Democrat.*

In 1893 a new newspaper, the third one in the county, appeared as the *Owenton Herald,* established by Col. William Lindsay and Evan Settle. They were followed as owners by B. J. Newton. It is believed that about 1902 the *Owenton Herald* purchased the *Owen News* and they merged to become the *News-Herald.*

Around 1903, local attorney M. H. Bourne purchased the *News-Herald.* In 1907 the *Owen County Democrat* and the *News-Herald* submitted competing bids for a contract to print the Owen Co. Fiscal Court's list of delinquent taxpayers (580 names). The lowest bidder was the *Owen County Democrat* at a cost of 2.5 cents per line. Keen competition existed in July 1907 between the *Owen County Democrat* and the *News-Herald* concerning circulation. The *News-Herald* claimed it mailed 500 more copies of its issues than the *Owen County Democrat.* However, the rivalry was friendly, for in September 1907, when the *Owen County Democrat* had printing press motor trouble, the *News-Herald* helped out one week by printing the *Democrat.*

In late 1903, John H. Westover, nearby publisher and editor of the *Williamstown Courier,* became the publisher of the *Owen County Democrat.* He sold the paper to Kentucky state senator L. C. Littrell in 1907 and then left the county to establish a newspaper in Arizona. L. C. Littrell & Son published the *Owen County Democrat* until Littrell's death in 1942; it was sold by the Littrell estate on January 1, 1943, to Joe T. Slocum.

In November 1943, Bourne sold the *News-Herald* to John H. Perry. Perry then bought the *Owen County Democrat* from Slocum in March 1944 and merged the two papers into the *News-Herald and Owen County Democrat.* In 1953 Perry; C. H. Bourne, son of M. H. Bourne; and Clayton Roland formed a partnership that became known as the News-Herald Publishing Company. Bourne and Roland subsequently purchased Perry's interest in the paper.

The *News-Herald* is now owned and published by Landmark Community Newspapers Inc.

Vertical files, Owen Co. Public Library, Owenton, Ky.

Doris Riley

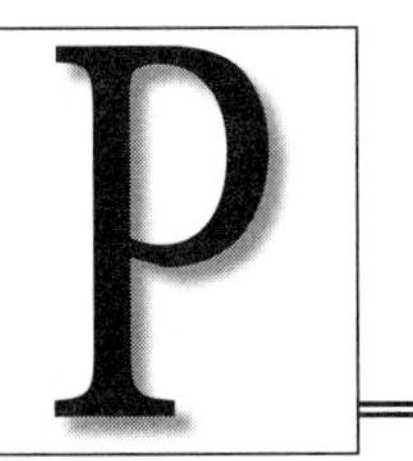

PAINT LICK. The old Louisville Rd. heading west from Boone Co., now U.S. 42, traverses a small piece of higher ground between Paint Lick Creek, Little Sugar Creek, and the Ohio River in eastern Gallatin Co. In fall 1861 this narrow neck of land was the scene of a **Civil War** skirmish; also, the Paint Lick Baptist Church was established nearby.

Just before the war, James Alexander, Ralph Bright, Conrad Denzler, John Hudson, James H. Jackson, Charles Rider, Elsberry Seaver, and the L. B. and Henry Sisson families inhabited the land around Paint Lick Creek. As the events of the Civil War unfolded, these families established a Baptist congregation that apparently met during the war. In February 1866 this congregation purchased two acres of land on the Ohio River from Levi and Elizabeth Jackson for $200, using funds donated by Ralph Bright. According to the deed, half of the land was to be used as a cemetery. Henry Sisson donated the timber for the building. That same year, the Paint Lick Baptist Church was admitted to the Ten Mile Baptist Association. In 1886 the Paint Lick Baptist congregation built a church building on the knoll that was used for over 100 years. In 1957 it purchased an additional tract of land from Willie B. Norton for $1,500 to expand the church cemetery. In 2000 a modern church and Sunday school building was erected on the old church site. This is an active congregation today.

Jonathan Howe, whose son Silas was a captain in the 18th Kentucky Union Infantry, maintained a general store at the hamlet of Sugar Creek near the Ohio River. Jonathan Howe was born in Auburn, N.Y., to a family who migrated to Patriot, Ind., and became leaders in the antislavery Universalist Church there. Several of his nephews were steamboat pilots and were believed to be useful in giving information to the Union during the Civil War. Completely dedicated to the Union cause, Howe organized a company of Home Guards numbering 18 to 20 men. Their training camp, called Camp Boyle, was on Paint Lick Creek.

On October 30, 1861, two soldiers from Captain Jonathan Howe's Home Guards were captured by a party of Confederates said to be 30 to 40 in number, led by Luther Green, a local recruit to the CSA. News came to Captain Howe that these two men were about to be hanged, so he immediately began pursuit and caught up with the Confederates. In the ensuing skirmish, Confederates Robert Herndon and T. J. Hughes were killed, and Luther Green was taken prisoner and sent to Cincinnati via steamboat to be incarcerated at Camp Chase in Columbus, Ohio. The two captured Home Guards were freed unharmed, and small arms and personal equipment were confiscated in the Battle of Paint Lick.

Several of the families in the Warsaw, Paint Lick, and Sugar Creek area sent sons into the Union Army. Officers in the 18th Kentucky Infantry included Lt. Col. John J. Landrum; captains D. R. Pugsley, Henry P. Richey, and James C. Bacon; and 1st Lt. Weedon C. Sleet. Officers in the 55th Kentucky Infantry were Capt. John C. Richards (mustered in as a 2nd lieutenant in the 18th Kentucky Infantry), Capt. Silas Howe (mustered in as 1st lieutenant in the Kentucky 18th), and 2nd Lt. George W. Story. The Union 7th Cavalry officers included Capt. George M. Sisson, 1st Lt. John S. Stoghill, 1st Lt. John Thomas Hopkins, and 2nd Lt. Robert E. Carlton. William M. Simpson served as quartermaster sergeant in the 11th Kentucky Cavalry.

Bogardus, Carl R., Sr. *The Story of Gallatin County.* Ed. James C. Claypool. Cincinnati: John S. Swift, 2003.

Howe, Daniel, as reported in *A Tour through Indiana in 1840: The Diary of John Parsons of Petersburg, Virginia,* ed. Kate Milner Rabb. New York: Robert M. McBride, 1920.

Diane Perrine Coon

PALM, EUGENE JIMMY "GENE" (b. November 8, 1930, Newport, Ky.; d. February 20, 1987, Huntsville, Ala.). Gene Palm, who worked in missile development with the U.S. Army, was the only son of railroad mechanic Walter James "Jimmy" and Mayme Elizabeth Phirman Palm. Gene grew up along the west side of Saratoga St., near 10th St., in Newport, and he and his father were heavily involved in knothole baseball. Gene graduated from Newport High School in 1949. He attended the University of Cincinnati and earned a BS (1954) and an MA (1956) in chemical engineering. He finished school while the Hungarian uprising during the cold war was taking place in 1956, was drafted into the military, and went to Fort Knox for U.S. Army basic training. At the end of basic training, when most soldiers were assigned to train at specialized military schools, Palm was pulled aside and handed special orders. After two weeks of leave, he was to report to the Redstone Missile Base in Huntsville, Ala. There he was to report to Dr. Wernher von Braun, the former Nazi missile scientist, who was then heading up the U.S. missile development program. For the duration of his two years in the army, Palm was paid as a private while serving as one of von Braun's assistants. Afterward, he was formally hired as a civilian by the U.S. Army Missile Command, where he worked for the next 30 years. Because of national security regulations, he was not allowed to discuss what he did, other than to explain that he worked with rocket fuels. He had a top-secret clearance and traveled the world. Early one February morning in 1987, at his Huntsville home, Palm had a diabetic attack from which he did not recover. He was buried in a Huntsville cemetery. The work Palm did in Huntsville as one of von Braun's assistants in missile research remains classified.

Phirman Family File, vertical file, Kenton Co. Public Library, Covington, Ky.

Michael R. Sweeney

PARISH KITCHEN. When Rev. William Mertes was appointed pastor of **Mother of God Catholic Church** in Covington in 1971, he initiated many changes in the parish. One of them was inspired by his discovery that homeless and low-income individuals were often coming to the rectory looking for something to eat (see **Homelessness and Homeless Shelters**). He started a food kitchen in the parish hall, serving soup and sandwiches to those in need. In 1974, because of the need for more room to cook and serve, Mertes moved the soup kitchen to a former bar in Covington, located at the corner of Pike and Russell Sts., and called it the Parish Kitchen. Mary and James LaVelle helped to run the soup kitchen, along with many other parishioners, until Molly Navin became director in 1987. The building that houses the Parish Kitchen was remodeled from a front-room bar to a full room in the back of the building, with a commercial kitchen and tables and chairs. The Parish Kitchen serves a full hot meal from 11:30 a.m. to 1:30 p.m., seven days a week. More than 300 guests are served each day, and there are more than 300 active volunteers who cook and serve at the kitchen or prepare desserts and entrées at home to be served at the Parish Kitchen. Others pick up donations from local restaurants such as Panera Bread, which offers the Parish Kitchen its overstocked goods each Sunday. To brighten holidays such as Thanksgiving, eager volunteers cook and serve turkey, dressing, and other traditional fare and offer fellowship to the homeless, low-income families, and anyone else who comes through the door.

The **Kenton Co. Public Library** sponsors a reading program for children at the Parish Kitchen. On two Wednesdays each month, Erin Seitz, a children's programmer with the library, comes in during the lunch hour and, moving from table to table, reads to the children. Thanks to donations from the community, Seitz also distributes books that the children may take with them. Used paperback books are also available for adults to borrow or keep.

Bogenschutz, Pat, Joan Burkhart, Mary Clare Duhme, Jodi Keller, and Molly Navin. Interviews by Nancy J. Tretter, 2006, Covington, Ky.

Hicks, Jack. "At Parish Kitchen, Kindness Takes No Holiday," *KP*, December 25, 1998, 1K.

Kreimer, Peggy. "Nourishing Body and Mind," *KP*, January 29, 2005, 1K.

Nancy J. Tretter

PARKER, ANNA VIRGINIA (b. March 28, 1889, Ghent, Ky.; d. March 23, 1979, Ghent, Ky.). Anna V. Parker, the daughter of Belvierd D. and Susan Ferguson Sanders Parker, was a family historian. Her father was a native of North Carolina; her mother was the daughter of Joseph and Mary Eliza Lathrop Sanders. Never married, Anna Parker became educated and was a grade school teacher in Carroll Co. for many years. She lived with her brother, Will Parker, in Ghent.

Anna Parker collected original letters, diaries, manuscripts, and documents relating to her great-grandfather Lewis Sanders and his family estate,

Grass Hills, located near Sanders. In 1966 the Coleman Publishers of Madison, Ind., published Parker's book, *The Sanders Family of Grass Hills.* From its release, this book has been acknowledged as a superior example of family history and genealogy. Kentucky's premier historian, Thomas D. Clark, extolled Parker's use of original letters and family documents to tell the stories of Lewis Sanders and George Nicholas Sanders in their own words. Clark also called attention to the detailing of the history of early Kentucky agriculture through these characters and applauded Parker's attempt to draw more rounded portraits by describing their participation in the local political scene as it related to national events.

When Parker gave a voice to the individual slaves who were owned by Lewis Sanders at Grass Hills, she was among the first of the state's local historians to include slaves' own words in such an account. She also provided a relatively unvarnished view of the personalities of the Sanders family members. At the end of the book, Parker detailed collateral family genealogies and traced the interweaving of the Craig and Sanders cousins in the antebellum and Victorian periods.

Through her will, probated in May 1979, the major portions of Parker's collection of Sanders family materials went to the Filson Club in Louisville (now the Filson Historical Society) and are kept in the special collections archives of the Filson Historical Society. Included are the correspondence, the journals, and the diaries; meticulous records of pedigreed short-horned cattle and sheep and thoroughbred horses; and clippings of articles and letters submitted by Lewis Sanders to various agricultural journals and magazines.

Parker was a member of the Ghent Methodist Episcopal South Church, the Daughters of the American Revolution, the United Daughters of the Confederacy, and the Port William Historical Society. She was a longtime member and past president of the Caby Froman Club and the Carroll Co. Homemakers Club. She died in 1979 and was buried in the Ghent Cemetery.

Accession Records, Filson Historical Society, Louisville, Ky.

"Obituary of Anna V. Parker," *Carrollton Democrat,* March 28, 1979.

Parker, Anna V. *The Sanders Family of Grass Hills.* Madison, Ind.: Coleman, 1966.

Sanders Family Papers, Filson Historical Society, Louisville, Ky.

Diane Perrine Coon

PARKER, ELIZABETH F. (b. January 27, 1916, Cincinnati, Ohio). Entrepreneur Elizabeth Frances Parker is the daughter of Garrett and Mollie Howard Jett of Brooksville. She attended Florida State College for Women in Tallahassee, Fla., and the University of Kentucky in Lexington, where she was a student of aviation. After her marriage to undertaker John S. Parker, the couple operated the Moore and Parker Funeral Homes in Augusta and Brooksville from 1937 until John's death in 1994. Currently, Elizabeth and her son John G. Parker direct the two businesses, and she continues to live at the funeral home location on Elizabeth St. in Augusta. An avid historian, Elizabeth was a board member of the Kentucky Historical Society and is a recipient of the Bracken Co. Historical Society Living History Award. She actively contributes to educational and historical functions and to the local DAR and is the principal organist at the Augusta Christian Church.

"Elizabeth Jett Joins Flying Club," *Bracken Chronicle,* October 17, 1935.

Caroline R. Miller

PARKER, LINDA (b. Genevieve Muenich, January 18, 1912, Covington, Ind.; d. August 12, 1935, Mishawaka, Ind.). Although often promoted as having been born in Covington, Ky., to mask her illegitimacy, country singing star Linda Parker (her stage name) was actually born in Covington, Ind. She had no known ties to Northern Kentucky.

Indiana Death Certificate No. 176, St. Joseph Co., Ind., for the year 1935.

Samuelson, Dave. "Linda Parker: WLS's Sunbonnet Girl." *Journal of the American Academy for the Preservation of Old-Time Country Music* 30 (1995): 16–17.

PARK HILLS. Park Hills is located on the hilltops just west of the city of Covington and is adjacent to **Devou Park**. Served by both the **Dixie Highway** and Amsterdam Pk., the city is bordered by Fort Wright to the south, Covington to the east, and Devou Park to the north and west. The land on which Park Hills sits is known for its considerable natural beauty. Coram, Spencer and Corry Development Company first acquired a portion of the property, situated along Old State Rd., in the 1840s. The company subdivided the tract and laid out streets, but they were never graded. Robert C. Simmons, a prominent Northern Kentucky attorney, and Ed Renz acquired Spencer and Corry's tract in 1907. The two laid out Audubon Rd., hoping to develop the property, but they failed to grade it.

The true development of Park Hills began when D. Collins Lee purchased a tract of land at the end of what is now Emerson Rd. in 1922. To acquire city conveniences, such as gas, sewer, and water, Lee decided to purchase more land and subdivide it to make those city conveniences possible. The resulting partnership between Simmons and Lee proved advantageous to both (Renz was deceased when Lee bought the land). They formed the Lee & Simmons Development Company and recorded numerous plats for the subdivision of Park Hills in 1924.

The company encountered a property dispute that slowed the development of Park Hills. The Light estate, which made up the north portion of Park Hills, including part of Emerson St., Morgan Ct., and Breckenridge and Upper Jackson Sts., was an essential piece of property. An elderly, eccentric man named Rufus Light claimed to own the property. He maintained a small refreshment stand near what is now Montague Rd. Light lived in a small shack near his stand until he was evicted on March 25, 1924, and moved into a tent. Light claimed to own the land, but the Covington Savings Bank and Trust Co. and the Covington Park Board disagreed. Light's father had presumably presented the land to county authorities before his death. Ultimately, the Covington Savings Bank and Trust Co. dispossessed Light of his land for the payment of a debt against the estate. The Lee & Simmons Development Company acquired the property from the bank.

Before building any homes, Lee and Simmons paid for city water, sewer, and gas to be supplied to each lot. The direct access to the Fort Mitchell **streetcar** line also added to the city's convenience. The Park Hills trolley station has since been converted into a playground and public garden called Trolley Park. Simmons and Lee visualized a subdivision featuring beauty combined with convenience. All of their decisions seem to support this directive. Architects Deglow and Henthrone and C. F. Cellarius and the homeowners themselves designed many of the first homes built in Park

White Horse Tavern, Dixie Highway, Park Hills. The tavern was destroyed by fire in 1972.

Hills. Lee's home at the end of Emerson, built in an English Manorial style with slate imported from England, is still standing today. Park Hills features many diverse architectural styles in the homes constructed in the early years of the development.

To ensure further the picturesque quality of Park Hills, Lee and Simmons limited the business district to a small tract of land opposite the city's entrance to Dixie Highway. The developers intended for the area to house a grocery, a drug store, and a restaurant. Today, the area is occupied by a green grocer, a dentist, a beautician, an auto repair shop, several restaurants, and various offices.

Park Hills proved to be a popular place to live. Many Covington residents moved to the developing subdivision to escape city pollution and congestion. Park Hills also offered a riding club, a tennis club, and an archery club to entice buyers. These features were made possible by arrangements with Devou Park. By 1927, 100 homes had been built, with more planned. In addition, a 1927 Lee & Simmons Development Company brochure indicates that the company had already invested $1.5 million in the development, with another $1 million planned. This rapid growth prompted citizens to hold a mass meeting to decide whether or not the city should join with Covington or incorporate as an independent city. The group voted in favor of incorporation, and the City of Park Hills was officially incorporated on June 28, 1927. A board of trustees was named to govern the city until an election could be held. The first members of the board were Stanley G. Disque, Joseph Hermes, William Middendorf, R. M. Rankin, and William Ruef. At the time of incorporation, Park Hills had 500 inhabitants and property valued at nearly $4 million.

Park Hills became a fifth-class city in 1937. This status meant the city would administer its own affairs with a board of equalization, a city assessor, a tax collector, and a six-person council, presided over by an elected mayor. The first mayor was Lawrence Taylor. A mayor and a six-member council currently govern Park Hills. The first police chief of Park Hills was Melvin Crump, who received the meager salary of $75 a month. Crump did an excellent job, but it became apparent to city leadership that a second patrolman was needed, so Fred Hiltz was added to lighten the load. On the eve of **World War II**, an auxiliary police department was employed. These people received no salary and had to provide their own uniforms. The police department currently employs seven people, six of them full-time. Not until 1942 did Park Hills officially establish its own volunteer fire department. Previously, the city depended upon Covington's fire services. Local newspaper columnist Jim Reis once noted that these services may have cost Park Hills $50 per run. Park Hills also built a city building in 1942 at 1006 Amsterdam Rd. The first chief of the new fire department was Norbert Brahm. A volunteer rescue squad was added to the fire department.

The first public school in Park Hills was built for $35,000 in 1928—one year after incorporation. Two prominent Catholic high schools, **Covington Catholic High School** and **Notre Dame Academy**, were later moved from Covington to Park Hills. Covington Catholic was built on the site of the Kremer farm; Notre Dame was built on part of the St. Joseph Heights Convent's property. Both schools are still active and growing. The former Park Hills Elementary School is now owned and occupied by the **Gateway Community and Technical College**.

There are two churches within the city of Park Hills. The first, the Faith Christian Center (formerly **Gloria Dei Lutheran**), is located on Amsterdam Rd. directly across from the city building. The other, the Church of the Nazarene (see **Nazarenes**), is on Dixie Highway near Covington Catholic High School.

The 1930s saw an economic boom along the Park Hills section of **Dixie Highway**. It became known as the **Gourmet Strip**, largely because of the excellent eateries inside Park Hills, which included the Blue Star Tavern and the White Horse. In 1933 Covington passed a resolution permitting a suit to be brought against Park Hills for using Covington sewers without authority from the city of Covington. The suit was designed to force Park Hills to pay for the construction and maintenance of the Amsterdam Pk. and Willow Run trunk sewers. Ultimately, in 1935, as part of a Works Progress Administration project, Park Hills built a sewer at the end of Audubon Rd. and on the west side of Altavia Rd. that was designed to empty into a sewage disposal plant. The project cost $25,912, of which the government paid $21,418. In 1937 the St. James sewer was constructed, and the city paid the entire costs of $4,014.03. In that same year, Park Hills annexed Mocking Bird Valley, located along Old State Rd. In 1938 a sewage disposal plant was built, at a cost of $20,000.

The Park Hills Civic Association, responsible for many of the Park Hills signature events and city-beautification projects, was founded in 1934. Funds from the annual Civic Association fund drive are allocated, in part, to the Park Hills Police Department, the Park Hills Volunteer Fire Department, and the Park Hills Rescue Squad.

The present boundaries of Park Hills were established largely by acquisitions in the 1940s of Cecilia Ave. (developed by William Dickman), Scenic Dr. (developed by the Newport Finance Company), the St. Joseph Ln. section, and the Mount Allen section, which included all of the Dickman properties, such as the sizable Dickman apartment complex. There has been little development of Park Hills in recent years, since nearly every usable lot was taken long ago.

According to the U.S. Census Bureau report, the Park Hills population in 2000 was 2,997. By 2005 that figure had dropped to 2,803. In 2008, 600 houses in the city were added to the National Register of Historic Places.

"Aged Recluse Is Evicted," *KP*, March 25, 1924, 1.
"City Fight with Park Hills on Sewers Pushed," *KP*, November 16, 1933, 2.
The City of Park Hills: Kentucky's Most Beautiful City. Brochure. Covington, Ky.: Lee and Simmons Development Company, 1927.
Clark, Russell. "Development of Park Hills," tape recording, 1985, files of the City of Park Hills.
"Gift Wrap the China; This Is Park Hills' 20th Anniversary," *Pride of Park Hills*, 1947. Newsletter of the Park Hills Civic Association.
Kenton Co. Deed Book 203, p. 521; Book 206, pp. 642–50; Book 209, pp. 519–20, Covington, Ky.
"Light to Leave Covington," *KP*, April 1, 1924, 4.
"Park Hills Becomes City in Less than Five Years," *KP*, December 30, 1928, 7.
Park Hills Board of Trustees Minutes, June 30, 1927, Park Hills, Ky.
Park Hills: The New City on the Hilltops. Brochure. Covington, Ky.: Lee and Simmons Development Company, 1927.
"Park Hills to Begin Career as Fifth Class City at Meeting of Trustees on Monday," *KP*, December 30, 1937, 1.
Reis, Jim. "Park Hills was Model for Suburbia," *KP*, October 1, 1984, 4K.
"Sewage Plant for Park Hills," *KP*, October 10, 1939, 1.
Udry, Mrs. Richard J. "History of Park Hills Is Traced," *KP*, August 8, 1940, 2.
U.S. Census Bureau. "American Fact Finder. Data Set. Census 2000 Summary File 1 (SF1) 100-Percent Data. Custom Table." www.census.gov (accessed May 25, 2007).

Iris Spoor

PARKS, ELIZABETH (b. May 1888, New York; d. May 7, 1925, Washington, D.C). Singer Elizabeth Parks was the daughter of Dr. Robert and Elizabeth Parks, both of whom were English. Her father was a well-known veterinary surgeon in Covington, and her mother was active in the **Covington Art Club**. The family lived at 1444 Madison Ave. and later at 1113 Scott St. Elizabeth attended the Covington public schools. Well recognized for her fine voice, she was prominent in the musical circles of Covington and for a time the soloist at **Trinity Episcopal Church** in Covington. Around 1910 she moved to Canada, and later during **World War I**, she traveled overseas to sing for the Allied troops as part of an entertainment tour sponsored by the **YMCA.** It was during this time that she met and married her husband, Herbert Hutchinson. In 1921 she gave birth to a daughter, Elizabeth. She and her husband, who was a district secretary for the YMCA, resided in Ottawa, Canada. During a visit to Washington, D.C., in 1925 Elizabeth died; her husband and her young daughter survived her. She was buried at Highland Cemetery in Fort Mitchell, Ky.

"Deaths," *KP*, May 8, 1925, 12.
Highland Cemetery Records, Fort Mitchell, Ky.
"Singer Dies at Washington," *KTS*, May 8, 1925, 1.

PASSIONIST NUNS. Shortly after his arrival in Covington in 1945, Bishop **William T. Mulloy** invited the Nuns of the Congregation of the Passion of Jesus Christ (Passionists) to come to the Diocese of Covington (see **Roman Catholics**). The Passionist Nuns are a contemplative congregation of women religious who devote their lives to prayer and penance. As such, they live in an enclosed community (a cloister) and speak to guests only through a grille. In response to the bishop's request, five sisters from the Passionist Congregation in Pittsburgh, Pa., headed by Mary Matilda Hartman, arrived in Covington in 1947. Mulloy reserved a place for them on the **Marydale** property that the diocese had just recently purchased in Erlanger. In 1949 the congregation of nuns acquired a site along Donaldson Rd. in Erlanger from the diocese and lived temporarily in a farmhouse while their convent was under construction. Mulloy dedicated the new Passionist Convent on January 24, 1951. Before becoming enclosed, the sisters held a two-week-long open house so the public could view their new convent's facilities.

Today, the convent, home to eight nuns, is open on Sunday and weekday mornings for visitors to join in their celebration of the Eucharistic liturgy or Mass, though the nuns are still separated by a screen. The congregation of nuns makes altar breads that they sell, providing income and supplying the Eucharistic bread or hosts for many parishes of the diocese. The Passionist Nuns also have a special ministry of prayer for the needs of the Diocese of Covington and the larger Catholic Church, as well as for the needs of the entire world.

"Bishop to Dedicate Passionist Convent at Marydale," *Messenger*, January 14, 1951, 1A.
"Diocese Fund Aids Retirees," *KE*, December 10, 2005, B3.
"Passionist Nuns Arrive," *Messenger*, May 4, 1947, 12.

Thomas S. Ward

PATRICK, IRENE (b. August 7, 1929, Kenton Co., Ky.; d. December 23, 2007, Hebron, Ky.). Irene M. Patrick, a Boone Co. commissioner, was the daughter of Dalton and Nora Colston Martin. She married Charles Patrick in 1949, and the couple had two daughters. In 1977 Patrick ran against incumbent Galen McGlasson for county commissioner and became the first woman in the entire state to be elected to that position. Patrick was also a Girl Scout leader, a Homemakers officer, a PTA president, and the chair of the Junior Red Cross, as well as working at the family business, Patrick Auto Parts. After serving as commissioner for 17 years, she lost one election but later returned for 9 more years; throughout her career, she served with four judge executives. Patrick was always interested in helping Boone grow and prosper. When property owners living in Rabbit Hash wanted to put in a dock for boats that would bring tourists to their town, they approached the county commissioners for assistance. Patrick not only endorsed the plan but recruited volunteers to help build the dock. In appreciation for her assistance, the dock was named in her honor. In 1999 Patrick was honored with the Outstanding Woman of Northern Kentucky award for her notable achievements, outstanding service, and personal qualities of integrity, perseverance, and leadership. She died in 2007 and was buried in Hebron Lutheran Church Cemetery.

Crowley, Patrick. "Patrick Served Passionately," *KE*, December 25, 2007, B1.
"Five Lives of Service and Achievement," *KP*, April 20, 1999, 6K.

Irene Patrick, 1978.

Warner, Jennifer S. *Boone County: From Mastodons to the Millennium*. Burlington, Ky.: Boone Co. Bicentennial Book Committee, 1998.

Nancy J. Tretter

PATTERSON, ANNE LEE (b. October 20, 1912, Ludlow, Ky.; d. December 13, 2003, Camarillo, Calif.). Anne Lee Patterson was the daughter of John W. and Anna L. Burns Patterson. Her father worked for the **Southern Railway**, and the family lived in Ludlow at 29 Kenner St. She attended St. James School in Ludlow and **La Salette Academy** in Covington. Patterson appeared in beauty contests at the Coney Island Amusement Park in Cincinnati and worked as a model and a clerk for the **Coppin's Department Store** in Covington. In 1931, at age 18, she was crowned Miss United States at Galveston, Tex. Later that year, she was named runner-up in the Miss Universe Contest, finishing ahead of future movie glamour queen Dorothy Lamour. On June 25, 1931, the city of Ludlow put on a parade in Patterson's honor, and it was attended by thousands of Northern Kentuckians. Beauty contests in those days were totally based on beauty, and not on the talents of the contestants. Patterson was five feet and five inches tall, with a 26-inch waist, and weighed 118 pounds. From 1931 through 1933, she performed with the famous Ziegfield Follies and in the musical *Showboat,* on the Broadway stage. She married a shirt-manufacturing executive, Joseph Bandler, and they moved to Los Angeles, where they raised two sons. Her husband, who was 14 years her senior, died in 1993, and Anne died in 2003. Her burial location is not known at this time.

Hicks, Jack. "In 1931, Ludlow Teen Was Crowned Miss U.S." *KP*, September 27, 1999, 1K.
"'Miss America' Wins Home Town Plaudits," *KP*, June 26, 1931, 1.
Reis, Jim. "A Summer of Contests: Paper, Theaters Have Gimmick," *KP*, June 3, 1991, 4K.

PATTIE, JAMES OHIO (b. 1803, Augusta, Ky.; d. ca. 1833, place of death unknown). James Ohio Pattie is the author of one of the most important early travel narratives in U.S. literature, *The Personal Narrative of James O. Pattie*. He and his father, **Sylvester Pattie**, were among the first pioneers in the U.S. Southwest and California and are widely acknowledged to have led the first party of explorers to thread the South Rim of the Grand Canyon and record that journey. Born in Augusta, Ky., James Pattie was the oldest of the eight children born to Sylvester and Polly Pattie. In 1812 his family moved from Kentucky to Missouri.

As noted by historian and Pattie scholar Richard Batman in his book *American Ecclesiastes: An Epic Journey through the American West*, Pattie's family prized education. Into his late teens, Pattie attended a school his grandfather had helped found, Bracken Academy at Augusta, which later became **Augusta College**. While not completely prepared for life as a fur trapper and explorer, this young frontiersman was uniquely positioned to record his adventures.

The first published narrative recording an overland journey to California, Pattie's story covers his sojourn of five years and several thousand miles. From 1825 to 1830, his trapping and exploring led him, his father, and his companions through the Southwest, as they crossed the arid peninsula of Lower California and eventually reached Mission Santa Catalina on the Pacific coast. Trespassing onto Mexican territory without passports, they were placed in custody and taken to San Diego, a Spanish settlement. Sylvester Pattie died in jail and became the first U.S. citizen buried in California, but eventually James Pattie was paroled. He traveled up and down the coast of California for another year before sailing to Mexico in an attempt to secure reparations for furs lost before and during his and his father's imprisonment in San Diego. After a half decade of exploration and fortune hunting, in 1830 Pattie arrived by ship in New Orleans, La. By the time he finally returned to the place of his birth on the Ohio River, he was physically and emotionally exhausted, not to mention penniless. He had only the stories recorded in his journal.

Before long, word of Pattie's western narrative reached Timothy Flint, a well-known preacher, author, publisher, and propagandist of American Protestant expansion who lived in Cincinnati. He was fascinated by Pattie's journey and set about making arrangements for publication of the account. Ever since Pattie's narrative first appeared in print in 1831, it has been in continuous publication. Some have argued that much of it was invented and written by Flint himself—a viewpoint discredited by Pattie expert Batman. Based on a variety of compelling reasons, the narrative is credited to the frontiersman rather than Flint's imagination.

After his book was published, James Pattie vanished without a trace. The last record was his appearance on the Bracken Co. tax list in 1833.

There have been an abundance of theories and reported sightings over the ensuing years, but the most likely scenario is that he was a victim of the wide-spread cholera epidemics that struck Kentucky in 1833 and was buried anonymously in a mass grave.

Batman, Richard. *American Ecclesiastes: An Epic Journey through the Early American West.* New York: Harcourt Brace Jovanovich, 1984.

Cleland, Robert Glass, and Glenn S. Dumke, ed. *From Wilderness to Empire: A History of California.* New York: Alfred A. Knopf, 1962.

Coblentz, Stanton A. *The Swallowing Wilderness: The Life of a Frontiersman—James Ohio Pattie.* New York: Thomas Yoseloff, 1961.

"Kentuckians Early California Pioneers—Father and Son, Bracken Co. Natives, Helped Open Up," *KP*, June 21, 1931, 8.

Pattie, James O. *The Personal Narrative of James O. Pattie.* Cincinnati: E. H. Flint, 1831.

Steven Pattie

PATTIE, SYLVESTER (b. August 25, 1782, Craig's Station, Ky.; d. May 24, 1828, San Diego, Calif.). Sylvester Pattie, the son of John and Ann Pattie, led the first party of U.S. citizens into Lower California. His parents had traveled overland from Virginia to Kentucky in about 1781. They entered the state as part of Lewis Craig's Traveling Church, a large Baptist fellowship from Spotsylvania Co., Va., traveling west to escape religious persecution by the Anglican Church. Although the Patties were part of this caravan, they may or may not have subscribed to the church's religious views, since Craig welcomed all. The migrating congregation established Craig's Station in Kentucky (sometimes referred to as Burnt Station) in 1780–1781.

Sylvester Pattie grew up in Bracken Co., where his father, a veteran of the **Revolutionary War**, helped establish the town of Augusta. He married Polly Hubbard and they had eight children. After serving in the **War of 1812**, Sylvester Pattie moved from Kentucky to the Ozark Mountains of southern Missouri. There he founded and ran a lumber mill, served on county commissions, and became relatively prosperous. However, his good fortune ended when his wife died suddenly. His son James later reported that his father had been left "silent, dejected, and inattentive to business." Aware of the western migration of others, the 42-year-old Pattie decided to pack up and head west in 1825. He took with him his first-born child, 22-year-old **James Ohio Pattie** and dispersed the remaining children among his family. Other adventuresome individuals joined the Pattie Party, their primary purpose being to trap and explore the West.

Pattie, his son, and the rest of their party were among the first to explore the U.S. Southwest. Pattie led what was likely the first party of explorers to see and to traverse the South Rim of the Grand Canyon (hence the naming of Pattie Butte). After four years of trapping and, at one point, working a copper mine in what became New Mexico, they crossed the arid peninsula of Lower California and reached Mission Santa Catalina on the Pacific coast. Because they had trespassed onto Mexican territory, Mexican governor Jose Maria Echeandia took the party into custody on March 27, 1828. While confined at the San Diego Presidio, Sylvester Pattie became seriously ill and died in May 1828. He was interred on the grounds of the Presidio and is believed to be the first U.S citizen buried on California soil. A plaque mounted on the stone jailhouse immortalizes his contributions by referencing the key role he played in the development of the American West: he was a "pathfinder, leader of the first party of Americans into Alta California over southern trails."

Batman, Richard. *American Ecclesiastes: An Epic Journey through the Early American West.* New York: Harcourt Brace Jovanovich, 1984.

"Kentuckians Early California Pioneers—Father and Son, Bracken Co. Natives, Helped Open Up," *KP*, June 21, 1931, 8.

Pattie, James O. *The Personal Narrative of James O. Pattie.* Cincinnati: E. H. Flint, 1831.

Steven Pattie

PAUL, BARBARA (b. June 5, 1931, Maysville, Ky.). Author Barbara Paul attended Bowling Green State University in Bowling Green, Ohio (BA, 1953), the University of the Redlands in Redlands, Calif. (MA, 1957), and the University of Pittsburgh at Pittsburgh, Pa. (PhD in theater, 1969). She has taught at Berry College in Mount Berry, Ga., Erskine College in Due West, S.C., and the University of Pittsburgh. She also served as drama director at Erskine College. She has produced at least 24 novels; the first was *An Exercise for Madmen,* a science fiction piece, in 1978. With *The Fourth Wall* (1979), she began writing mysteries with theatrical settings. Paul then shifted to historical mysteries and homicide detective thrillers such as *Jack Be Quick and Other Crime Stories* (1999), which comprises stories about the infamous Jack the Ripper murders of London prostitutes during the 1880s. For several years, Paul lived and wrote in Pittsburgh. Along with **Ben Lucien Burman**, she is one of the more prolific authors born in Northern Kentucky.

Barbara Paul. www.barbarapaul.com (accessed December 6, 2005).

Contemporary Authors. New Revision Series. Vol. 62. Detroit: Gale Research, 1998.

The Writers Directory. 11th ed. Detroit: St. James Press, 1994.

PAUL, GABRIEL RENE, BRIGADIER GENERAL (b. March 22, 1813, St. Louis, Mo.; d. May 5, 1886, Washington, D.C.). Gabriel Rene Paul was the son of Rene and Eulalie Chouteau Paul. Before immigrating to the United States, his father had served as a colonel of engineers under Napoleon Bonaparte and on the French flagship at the naval battle of Trafalgar in 1805, where he was severely wounded. Gabriel Rene Paul began his U.S. military career by obtaining an appointment to the U.S. Military Academy at West Point, N.Y., from which he graduated in July 1834. He was assigned to frontier duty in the 7th Infantry and stationed at Fort Gibson in present-day Oklahoma. On March 24, 1835, he married Mary Ann Whistler, daughter of Col. William Whistler. Mary's father and grandfather were both military men previously stationed at the **Newport Barracks**, and Mary Whistler was probably born in Newport about 1815.

Paul served several years of recruiting duty and in 1842 fought the Seminole Indians in Florida. He then served in the **Mexican War**, taking part in the defense of Fort Brown, the battle of Monterey, the siege of Vera Cruz, and several other battles, including the Cerro Gordo battle, where he was wounded. He led a storming party at Chapultepec, capturing the enemy flag, and for that act he was brevetted a major. The citizens of St. Louis, Mo., presented a sword to him for his service in the Mexican campaign. During the 1850s he was involved in tours in Texas, and in the 1852 Rio Grande expedition, he captured Carvajal and his gang of desperadoes.

In 1854 William Whistler moved his family back to Newport, possibly bringing the Paul family with him. The marriage of Mary Whistler and Gabriel Rene Paul broke up at some point, and Paul married Louise Rodgers in Campbell Co. on April 13, 1858.

From 1858 to 1860, Paul served in the Utah expeditions, in the course of which he was engaged in the surprise and capture of a camp of hostile Indians. He was promoted to major and transferred to the 8th Infantry in April 1861. Then from July to December 1861 he served as acting inspector general of the Department of New Mexico. He was appointed a colonel and commanded Fort Union and the southern military district of New Mexico. In April 1862 he was made a lieutenant colonel. Paul was elevated to the rank of brigadier general of volunteers on September 5, 1862. Transferred to the Army of the Potomac in March 1863, he took part in the battles of Fredericksburg and Chancellorsville.

It appears that about the time Paul transferred east, his wife Louise returned to Newport, where she appears in the 1863 tax list with a town lot. On July 1, 1863, at about 2:00 p.m., at the Battle of Gettysburg, Paul's brigade was attacked from three directions by elements of four Confederate brigades and, after a stiff fight, was overwhelmed. A musket ball struck Paul's right temple an inch and a half behind his eye, severed the right optic nerve, passed through his head, and exited through the left eye socket, removing the eye. Paul fell unconscious and was left for dead on the field; a dispatch from Gen. George Meade to Gen. Henry Halleck reported him killed. However, he was found alive by Union prisoners working as stretcher-bearers, carried to a local residence, and placed under the care of the surgeon of the 11th Pennsylvania. Paul apparently returned to Newport to recover from his Gettysburg wounds, because the 1864 and 1865 tax lists include both Louise and G. R. Paul. The 1866 tax list shows only Louise Paul.

In February 1865, Paul was retired from active military service "for disability resulting from wounds received in the line of duty." Despite being totally blind, suffering violent attacks of head pain, and having epilepsy, he was at that time made deputy governor of the Soldiers' Home near Washington, D.C. In June 1865 he was placed in charge of the military asylum at Harrodsburg, Ky., where he served until December 1866. A resolution of Congress granted him full pay and allowances of brigadier general on April 12, 1870. Records show that his seizures increased, occurring several times per day in the later years. Paul died at his residence in Washington, D.C., on May 5, 1886. He was given a hero's burial in Arlington National Cemetery, and a monument was erected over his grave by his comrades of the Grand Army of the Republic (GAR).

Abraham Lincoln Papers, Library of Congress, Washington, D.C.

Arlington National Cemetery Web site. "Gabriel Rene Paul." www.arlingtoncemetery.net/grpaul.htm (accessed June 8, 2006).

"G. R. Paul Pension Record," National Archives, Washington, D.C.

Polley, Daryl. "Gabriel Paul," *Campbell County Historical and Genealogical Society Newsletter*, January 1999.

Daryl Polley

PAVY, JOHN (b. March 17, 1791, Sussex Co., Del.; d. November 9, 1869, Decatur Co., Ind.). Like many Baptist preachers in Kentucky before the Civil War, John Pavy took a bold public stance against institutional slavery. In 1823 Pavy, who was preaching at Fredericksburg (Warsaw) in Gallatin Co., was run out of town for his views opposing slavery. It is unclear how John Pavy became an abolitionist or whether his relatives in Harrison and Campbell counties also held antislavery views, but three Harrison Co. Paveys moved into Switzerland and Decatur counties on the Indiana side of the Ohio River.

Sometime before 1761, John Pavy's grandfather, Samuel Pavey (Pavy), brought the family south from New Hampshire into Accomack Co., Va. The Pavy family migrated through Maryland and Delaware before coming to Northern Kentucky about 1808. John Pavy married Jane S. Winn, September 5, 1811, in Harrison Co. Their family of 11 children included seven sons, three of whom became Baptist ministers. Five of the oldest children were born between 1812 and 1822 in Gallatin Co. Following an 1823 incident at Warsaw, John Pavy crossed the Ohio River into Indiana. He purchased a farm that straddled what is now Ind. Rt. 56 at the top of a hill above Vevay, Ind. (Switzerland Co.), on the Mount Sterling Rd. Pavy preached at several local Baptist churches before moving to the Sand Creek Baptist Church in Decatur Co., Ind., during the mid-1840s. He also preached at the Adams, Liberty, and Salem Baptist Churches nearby.

The first documented safe house for runaway slaves in Switzerland Co., Ind., was established by John Pavy along with his eldest son, Samuel Husk Pavy, and fellow Kentuckian Stephen R. Gerard (also spelled Girard, Garrard, and Jerrard by various census takers). These three men operated the Vevay and Craig Township Underground Railroad station for many years. Samuel H. Pavy continued his father's antislavery activities after John Pavy moved to Decatur Co.

Girard, Mary, and Roy Girard. *The Pavy Family History*. Privately published, 1999.

History of Switzerland County, Indiana. Chicago: Weakley, Harraman, 1885.

Switzerland Co., Indiana, Photo Album. http://myindianahome.net/gen/switz/photos/index.html (accessed March 24, 2007).

Switzerland Co. Complete Civil Order Book F, September Term, 1832, Vevay, Ind.

Diane Perrine Coon

PAXTON INN. One of the earliest public inns in Kentucky is still standing in the town of Washington. The inn, built between 1810 and 1819, was owned by James Paxton, who lived in a house next door. Records indicate that the inn was being operated by James Artus in 1819. Paxton was a lawyer, and customers for the successful inn included persons working in the nearby courthouse and other lawyers, as well as travelers to the area. Paxton moved to Ohio in 1823 because he was an **abolitionist**, not a popular stance in slaveholding Kentucky. He died in a fall from a buggy while on a visit back to Kentucky in 1824. The inn was sold by Paxton's heirs, and Willis Lee was still using it as a tavern as late as 1838. A two-story, plainly styled brick Federal row house with a basement, the structure eventually became the headquarters of the Mason Co. Telephone Company and then was purchased by succeeding telephone businesses. The Continental Telephone Company was the last of those companies; when the building no longer met their needs, the firm decided in the mid-1960s to tear the structure down. Led by Mrs. Andrew Duke, an effort was started to save Paxton Inn. Continental Telephone was supportive, and the building was turned over to the Limestone Chapter of the **Daughters of the American Revolution** (DAR) in 1967. As restoration efforts continue, the house is used by the local DAR chapter for its functions and is open to the public, who can observe its early-19th-century fireplaces, mantels, and woodwork. A portrait of William Beatty, a local lawyer and jurist in the 1830s and a relative of James Artus, is one of the artifacts placed in the house during restoration. Each floor features a room 18 feet wide by 36 feet long. These rooms were occupied by inn patrons, and the one on the second floor was sometimes used for dancing. A concealed staircase, speculation by locals, and the history of Paxton's abolitionist leanings point to the inn as perhaps having been used as a station on the **Underground Railroad**.

Collection of the Kentucky Gateway Museum, Maysville, Ky.

"Maysville Preserver of the Past," *KP*, July 6, 1983, 8K.

"Walk into 158 Years of Paxton Inn History," *KP*, August 17, 1968, 1K.

"Washington Rings in Christmas," *KP*, December 1, 1983, 12K.

John Klee

PAYNE, WILLIAM HERMAN (b. December 28, 1943, Covington, Ky.; d. March 9, 1970, Bel Air, Md.). William Payne, the son of Emmett Payne Jr. and Emma F. Robinson Payne, became the first African American from Covington killed during the modern **civil rights movement**. Payne was raised in Covington and attended **Lincoln-Grant School**, then graduated in 1963 from the William Grant High School, where he was the basketball team manager. After graduation, he served with the U.S. Naval Reserves for two years of active duty during the **Vietnam War**. He attended Xavier University in Cincinnati, and while in college he became active in the Student Non-Violent Coordinating Committee (SNCC), the youth organization of the Southern Christian Leadership Conference, which was formed by Martin Luther King Jr. Payne has been described as highly intelligent and an organizer.

In 1967 he moved to Atlanta, Ga., and traveled throughout Alabama, Georgia, and Mississippi on civil rights and voter-registration drives. He became a friend of SNCC's national chairman, Herbert "H. Rap" Brown, and its former leader Stokely Carmichael. It was while Payne was in Atlanta that he became known as Ché, a name also used by the well-known revolutionary leader from Cuba. In 1970 Brown went to Bel Air, Md., where SNCC had established a presence because of civil rights issues; he was to face charges stemming from various protest marches and rallies. While traveling in Maryland to support Brown, Payne and a companion, Ralph Featherstone, were killed on March 9, 1970, when their car exploded. The incident was publicized nationally as part of the civil rights movement. Payne was buried in Mary E. Smith Cemetery in Elsmere, Ky.

Harris, John. "Black Leaders Eulogize Payne," *KP*, March 17, 1970, 1K–2K.

———. "Black Struggle Leader Buried," *KP*, March 16, 1970, 4K.

———. "Nobody Can Say He Was a Militant," *KP*, March 13, 1970, 1K–2K.

"Services Held for Bomb Blast Victim," *KP*, March 17, 1970, 5K.

Theodore H. H. Harris

PEACH GROVE INN. The original Peach Grove Inn was located on a lane that was part of **Washington Trace Rd.**, about a mile off Ky. Rt. 10, near the **Wesley Chapel Methodist Church**, in northeastern Pendleton Co. In 1858 Lacky and Sarah Lancaster conveyed the property to George Daniel, who transferred it to Garrett Daniel. The inn was a two-story log cabin (one room and a loft), and it had sections of the logs cut out to serve as gun ports. It may be that the occupants wanted to protect themselves against American Indians, or perhaps the building was used as a Confederate military post and stronghold. Two local Confederate operatives, **William Francis Corbin** and **Thomas Jefferson McGraw**, were captured at this inn in 1863 during the **Civil War**. They were arrested for recruiting soldiers into the Confederate Army and later were shot to death by the Union Army at Johnson's Island, Ohio.

The 1884 Lake atlas shows the structure, identified as a home, located just northwest of the Peach Grove post office, which in turn was located at the cemetery and next to the old Second Mile Baptist Church. The former inn was owned by F. M. Ellis at this time. Dean Richards Maxddon restored the inn in the 1970s.

Lathrop, J. M. *An Atlas of Bracken and Pendleton Counties, Kentucky*. Philadelphia: D. J. Lake, 1884.

Mildred Belew

PEASELBURG. This quaint little village, now within Covington, was founded in the mid-1800s and originally was known as Silkyville. The neighborhood boundaries were 19th St. on the north, 26th St. on the south, Madison Ave. on the east, and Benton Rd. on the west. Most of the residents were German Catholics, but a few Irish families lived there, helping to make life in the neighborhood varied and interesting. Many of the men of the town worked for the nearby **Kentucky Central Railroad** or at the car barn at Madison Ave. and State St.

The **Monte Cassino Chapel** and monastery were located on the hills above Peaselburg. Each morning, noon, and evening the monastery bells rang, to remind residents to bow their heads for a time of prayer and meditation. The monks tended their vineyards and made wine on the monastery property for sacramental purposes and for commercial sale. They regularly made home deliveries of their wine in Peaselburg, as milkmen of their day delivered milk.

Hundreds of geese roamed freely in the city, most of them owned by the Drees, Niehaus, and Uhlmann families, who were called by some people goose ranchers. How anyone knew who owned which geese was a mystery to everyone. The aggressive geese ruled almost every sidewalk, street, and yard in the community and would attack anyone or anything that challenged them. Eggs could be found behind many bushes, and quills and feathers were everywhere. The goose population supplied goose grease, which people used to tame their unruly hair, goose feathers to fill mattresses and pillows, and the goose liver and goose eggs that were used to make sandwiches for children's school lunches. Geese were as symbolic of Peaselburg as horses are of the state of Kentucky.

A favorite playground for many of the Peaselburg children was the nearby, enchanting, **Willow Run** Creek valley. The frequent fistfights and stone-throwing battles between the Irish and the German youth turned into a popular spectator sport. The biggest event of the year was the annual Easter fire, set on the vacant lot bounded by 18th, 19th, Russell, and Holman Sts. Peaselburg residents also loved to watch the Covington Blues baseball team perform on their field at 19th and Euclid Sts. Life for most Peaselburg families centered on activities at the **St. Augustine Catholic Church**, which originally was located on Russell St. just south of Willow St. In 1912, much to the chagrin of baseball fans, the Blues' playing field was razed for construction of a new St. Augustine Church. Some of the better-known families living in early Peaselburg were named Drees, Heidel, Holtsman, Kruse, Niehaus, Shoemaker, Trenkamp, and Uhlmann.

A Covington *Ticket* newspaper article of September 1876 addressed the puzzling name of Peaselburg with the question "Who or what is peasel?" Townspeople had often wondered also. It turned out that early German residents had named the town Peaselburg (also spelled Peasleburg), based on a Low German term that can be translated as "the city of goose droppings." Once the secret was out, the name became an embarrassment to the community and attempts were made to change it. A *Ticket* article also ridiculed the name by referring to Peaselburg as Goose Town. In 1876 there was an attempt to rename the city Wolfsburg, but nothing came of the idea. Central Covington, which included Peaselburg, was incorporated by the state in 1880. In 1906 the voters of Central Covington approved annexation to Covington.

Geaslen, Chester F. *Strolling along Memory Lane*. Vol. 1. Newport, Ky.: Otto, 1971.
"The Kentucky Legislature," *Covington Ticket*, May 4, 1880, 2.
Reis, Jim. "Goats, Geese, and Goons Colored Life in Suburbs," *KP*, July 9, 1984, 9K.
——. *Pieces of the Past*. Vol. 1. Covington: Kentucky Post, 1988.
"Who or What Was Peasel?" *Covington Ticket*, September 28, 1876, 3.

Jack Wessling

PECK, JOHN MASON (b. October 31, 1789, South-Farms, Litchfield Co., Conn.; d. March 15, 1858, O'Fallon Station, Ill.). John Mason Peck, the son of Asa and Hannah Farnun Peck, humble family farmers, became a noted Baptist preacher and educator. By 1813 he was a minister at Catskill, N.Y., and by 1817 he was assigned to the western missionary frontier at St. Louis, Mo. He traveled thousands of miles through Illinois, preaching, publishing, and founding Baptist colleges and seminaries, and it was said that perhaps no man had done more to guide the thoughts, mold the manners, and form the institutions of the West than John Peck.

On November 10, 1834, Peck formed the Western Baptist Educational Society, which evolved into Covington's **Western Baptist Theological Institute**. He took part in the doctrinal and political compromises that enabled the institution to open in fall 1844. Although he leaned toward the Southern position on the slavery issue, he did everything in his power to keep this issue from destroying the new school.

Peck published several books and newspapers and wrote histories. He also produced a sketch of **Daniel Boone**. Peck recognized early in his career the importance of educational training for ministers and the populace. He established some 900 churches and saw 600 ministers ordained and 32,000 persons become Baptists. He received a DD degree from Harvard at Cambridge, Mass., in 1852. While president of the Western Baptist Theological Institute in 1854, he caught a fever from which he never fully recovered. He also served as the pastor of the **First Baptist Church** in Covington. Peck died in 1858 and was first buried in Rock Springs, Ill. His remains were later moved to the Bellfontaine Cemetery in St. Louis, Mo.

"Death Notice," *CJ*, March 27, 1858, 2.
Wilson, James Grant, and John Fiske, eds. *Appleton's Cyclopedia of American Biography*. New York: D. Appleton, 1894.

PELHAM, WILLIAM (b. 1803, Maysville, Ky.; d. 1879, Manchaca, Tex.). William Pelham, who became the only Confederate governor in the New Mexico Territory, was the son of Charles Pelham and Isabella Atkinson. He moved westward during the 1820s. He was appointed as a U.S. auditor and then as U.S. surveyor general of the Arkansas Territory. He married Mary Ann Conway, and they had three children. In 1849 Pelham and his family, with their slaves, moved to Texas, where he established a ranch. In 1854 he was appointed the U.S. surveyor general of the Territory of New Mexico, where he was active in promoting the opening of the territory to slavery.

When Texas seceded from the Union in 1861, all residents in the Territory of New Mexico were ordered by its governor, Henry Connelly, to take an oath of allegiance to the United States. Pelham refused and was arrested and jailed at Santa Fe. On July 23, 1861, Confederate forces invaded New Mexico, but it was not until 1862 that they advanced to Santa Fe. On March 10, 1862, Santa Fe fell to the Confederate Army. Pelham was released from jail and appointed the Confederate governor of the territory. Confederate forces were defeated at Glorieta Pass on March 28, 1862, and forced to retreat to Texas. Santa Fe was evacuated by the Confederates on April 8 of that year, and Pelham retreated with the Confederate Army, but he and his escort were captured by Union troops before reaching Texas. Pelham spent the remainder of the war in confinement. During the war, his only surviving son, Charles, was killed while serving as a Confederate soldier in 1864 in the fighting around Atlanta, Ga.

In 1865 Pelham was released and allowed to leave New Mexico. He returned to Manchaca, Tex., where he established another ranch and was active in Democratic politics. He died at his ranch in 1879.

Kerby, Robert L. *The Confederate Invasion of New Mexico and Arizona, 1861–1862*. Los Angeles: Westernlore Press, 1958.
Museum of New Mexico. *The Civil War in New Mexico*. Santa Fe, N.Mex., 1961.

Charles H. Bogart

PENDLETON, EDMUND (b. September 9, 1721, Caroline Co., Va.; d. October 23, 1803, Richmond, Va.). Edmund Pendleton has as his namesake Pendleton Co., Ky., which was created on December 13, 1798, from portions of Campbell and Bracken counties. He was a well-known Virginia politician, lawyer, and judge. Pendleton was admitted to the Virginia bar in 1745 and became the justice of the peace for Caroline Co., Va., in 1751. He was a member of the Virginia House of Burgesses from 1752 to 1776 and represented Virginia in the Continental Congress from 1774 to 1775. He was the first Speaker of the Virginia House of Delegates and became the first judge of the High Court of Chancery in 1777. Pendleton was president of both the Virginia Supreme Court of Appeals from 1778 to 1803 and the Virginia Ratification Convention in 1788. Eventually, he refused appointment to the federal judiciary in 1788 because of advancing age. Pendleton died in Richmond, Va., in 1803. He was buried first in Edmundsbury, near Bowling Green, Va., but his remains later were moved to Bruton Parish Church Cemetery in Williamsburg, Va., in 1907.

Biographical Directory of the United States Congress. "Pendleton, Edmund (1721–1803)." http://bioguide.congress.gov (accessed April 5, 2006).

Mays, David J. *Edmund Pendleton, 1721–1803: A Biography.* Cambridge: Harvard Univ. Press, 1952.

——, ed. *The Letters and Papers of Edmund Pendleton.* 2 vols. Charlottesville: Univ. Press of Virginia, 1967.

Jenny Plemen

PENDLETON ACADEMY. The Pendleton Academy in Falmouth began in 1814 under the direction of Professor R. C. Robinson of Moscow, Ohio, in a one-story building, 20 by 30 feet. The brick used in the building was available on-site. Constructed on land purchased from Reuben Turner for $30, the academy's building was at the corner of Broad and Fourth Sts. For many years, this private school was simply called the seminary. In 1848 a new one-story building, 20 by 56 feet, was erected where the present Falmouth Middle School now stands. It was later known as Pendleton Academy.

Belew, Mildred Bowen. *The First 200 Years of Pendleton County.* Falmouth, Ky.: Mildred Bowen Belew, n.d. [ca. 1994].

Mildred Belew

PENDLETON CO. This 281-square-mile county is bordered by Grant, Kenton, Campbell, Bracken, and Harrison counties. The Ohio River borders Pendleton Co. for five miles along its northeastern border, and Falmouth is the confluence of major forks of the Licking River. The terrain consists of fertile river valleys surrounded by undulating hills. Most of the farm production is burley tobacco and beef and dairy cattle. The county was created on December 13, 1798, from portions of Campbell and Bracken counties and was named after **Edmund Pendleton** (1721–1803), a longtime member of the Virginia House of Burgesses (1752–1774) and the Continental Congress. Falmouth is the county seat. The other incorporated city in the county is Butler, located on the Licking River seven miles north of Falmouth. In 1820, 250 square miles of the county were taken to establish Grant Co.

The Licking River was an important avenue for the early exploration of Kentucky. Along with an overland route through the county, the English captain Henry Bird (see **Bird's [Byrd's] War Road**) took the river in leading 600 Indians and Canadians in the June 1780 attack on Ruddell's and Martin's stations in Central Kentucky. The first settlement in the county is believed to have been the one at the fork of the Licking at some time around 1780. The settlement, which became Falmouth, was established by James Cordy, Peter DeMoss, Samuel Jones, Gabriel Mullins, and James Tilton.

With the exception of the county seat, Pendleton Co. remained rural during the 19th century. The farm economy was based on tobacco, and legend has it that the first crop was raised in the southwestern part of the county with seed brought from Virginia. In the 1830s Oliver Browning floated 100-pound hoop-pole packages of the crop from McKinneysburg on flatboats down the Licking River to Cincinnati and points beyond. The coming of the **Covington and Lexington Railroad** through the county in 1853 gave sellers a connection to markets at Cincinnati and Louisville.

By the 1890s, intensive tobacco production had depleted much of the soil in Pendleton Co. Sweet clover brought from Alabama in 1895 was planted in worn-out tobacco fields, restoring profitability to tobacco cultivation, as well as to apiary and dairy industries. Pendleton, "the county that came back," nevertheless lost one-third of its residents at the height of the economic crisis. Another forage crop that succeeded in the county was alfalfa, probably introduced between 1900 and 1910 by traveling Mormon preachers. By 1925 local tanners produced hundreds of tons and were exporting alfalfa to other areas.

In the late 1850s, a company of Pendleton Co. soldiers was organized to perform peacekeeping duties among the Mormons in Utah. During the **Civil War**, the county sent men to both armies. A Union recruiting camp was established in Falmouth in September 1861. Two Confederate recruiters were captured and executed in the Peach Grove area of northern Pendleton Co. In July 1862 a number of county citizens were rounded up by Union troops during a crackdown against suspected Confederate sympathizers. In June 1863 a number of women were arrested at DeMossville because they were believed to be potential spies "dangerous to the federal government." Falmouth was the site of a small skirmish on September 18, 1862, between 28 Confederates and 11 Home Guardsmen (see **Falmouth, Battle of**).

The city of Butler was established in the 1850s when the Covington and Lexington Railroad was built through the area. Originally called Clayton, for reasons unknown, the city was named for **William O. Butler**, a U.S. congressman, when it was incorporated on February 1, 1868. Like Falmouth, Butler in the 1870s and 1880s was a major tobacco market and its other businesses included lumber and sawmills, flour- and gristmills, churches, schools, a railroad depot, a blacksmith shop, and various stores. In 1871 a covered bridge was built across the Licking River at Butler (see **Butler Covered Bridge**). The bridge was used until the 1937 flood weakened its supports. The structure was later torn down and replaced with a steel bridge.

Major floods of the Licking River in 1937, 1948, 1964, and 1997 made flood control a major concern of residents (see **Flood of 1937**; **Flood of 1964, Licking River**; **Flood of 1997, Licking River**). The creation of Falmouth Lake (now Kincaid Lake) State Park near Falmouth, a 200-acre impoundment, failed to prevent the 1964 flood (see **Kincaid Lake State Park**). Initial planning for a 12,000-acre impoundment of the Licking River nine miles south of Falmouth got under way in the mid-1970s, but because of the magnitude of the project, it was abandoned.

The completion of the **AA Highway** in 1990 has made Pendleton Co. more accessible to the urban areas of Northern Kentucky and Cincinnati. Many county residents not engaged in farming are employed outside of the county, commuting to jobs within the metropolitan area. The population in 2000 was 14,390.

Belew, Mildred Boden. *The First 200 Years of Pendleton County.* Falmouth, Ky.: M. B. Belew, n.d. [ca. 1994].

Kleber, John E., ed. *The Kentucky Encyclopedia.* Lexington: Univ. Press of Kentucky, 1992.

U.S. Census Bureau. www.census.gov/ (accessed January 2, 2008).

Warren J. Shonert and Staff

PENDLETON CO. MEMORIAL HIGH SCHOOL. Pendleton Co. Memorial High School opened its doors on September 8, 1959, in its present single-story brick structure, situated on a bluff outside Falmouth on **U.S. 27** North. In its first year, the school enrolled 360 students from the former Morgan and Butler high schools. In fall 1968, the **Falmouth High School** was merged into Pendleton Co. Memorial High School. In fall 1971, many students from the St. Xavier High School in Falmouth also joined the school's rolls.

In May 1960, the high school's first graduating class consisted of 70 students. Adopting the traditions of its predecessor high schools, Pendleton Co. Memorial High School observes unique, multi-event graduation ceremonies. On Class Night, students are introduced to the audience, noting their parents' names and their home community within the county. Scholarships and awards are presented, and members of the graduating class perform vocal and instrumental selections, skits, and dances. The following Sunday evening, baccalaureate is held at a local church. On the third evening, commencement itself takes place.

Pendleton Co. Memorial High School's mascot is the Wildcat, and the school's colors are red, white, and black. The school has published its yearbook, *The Pendleton Echo*, each year since it opened. A school newspaper, known originally as *The Pendletonian* and later as *The Cats' Paws*, has been published intermittently.

The high school's facilities have undergone several renovations over the years, with a major one during the late 1980s. In spring 2007, the school began a major expansion (designed by architects Sherman, Carter, and Barnhart of Lexington) that included eight new classrooms, a 450-seat auditorium, an auxiliary gym, a new library–multimedia

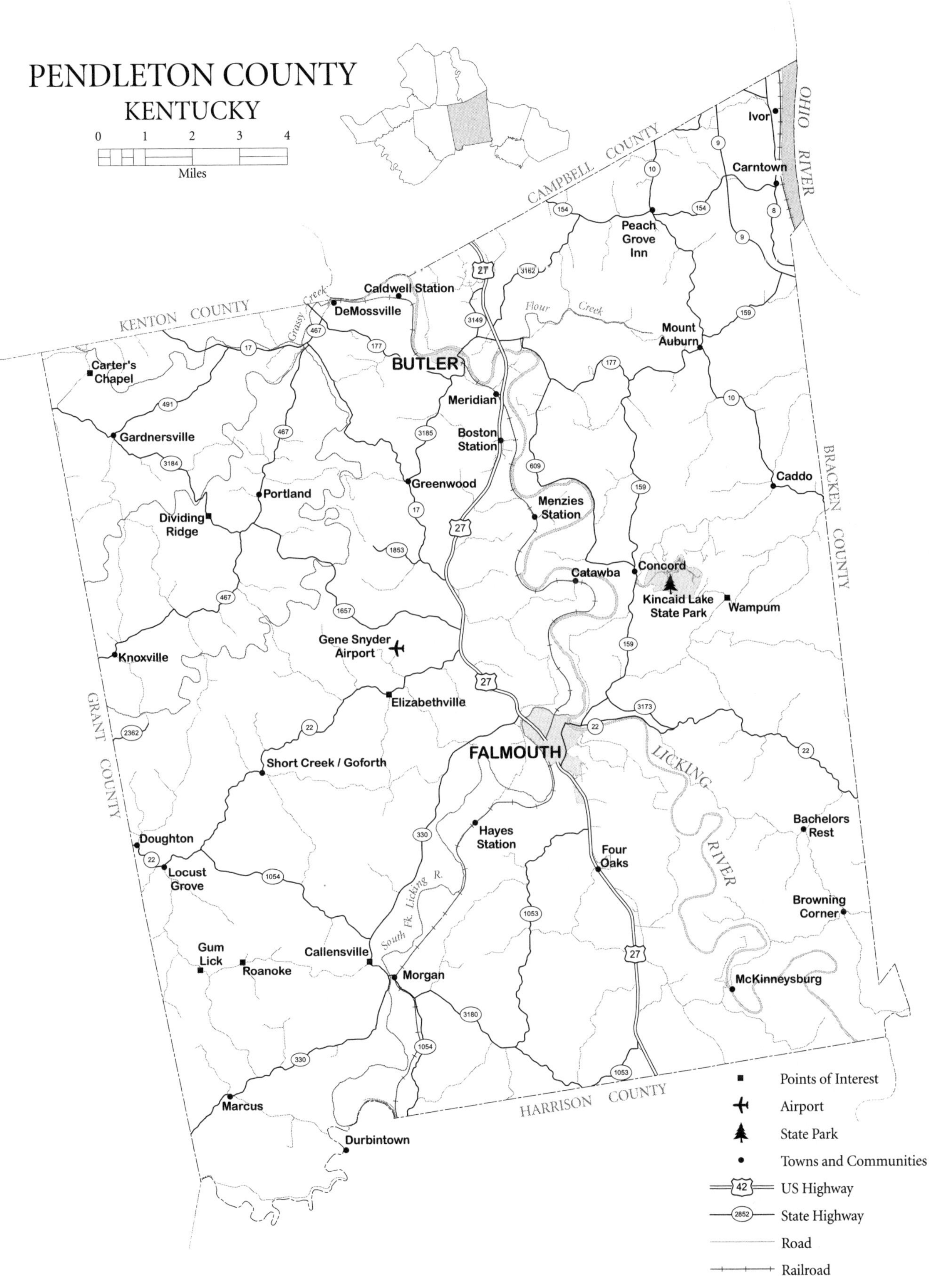

PENDLETON COUNTY
KENTUCKY
0 1 2 3 4
Miles
CAMPBELL COUNTY
KENTON COUNTY
BRACKEN COUNTY
GRANT COUNTY
HARRISON COUNTY
OHIO RIVER
LICKING RIVER
South Fk. Licking R.
Grassy Creek
Flour Creek
Ivor
Carntown
Peach Grove Inn
Caldwell Station
DeMossville
Mount Auburn
BUTLER
Carter's Chapel
Meridian
Boston Station
Gardnersville
Greenwood
Portland
Dividing Ridge
Menzies Station
Caddo
Concord
Catawba
Kincaid Lake State Park
Wampum
Gene Snyder Airport
Knoxville
Elizabethville
FALMOUTH
Short Creek / Goforth
Hayes Station
Bachelors Rest
Doughton
Four Oaks
Locust Grove
Browning Corner
Gum Lick
Roanoke
Callensville
Morgan
McKinneysburg
Marcus
Durbintown
Points of Interest
Airport
State Park
Towns and Communities
US Highway
State Highway
Road
Railroad

center, and renovation of all of the former classrooms; it was scheduled for completion in fall 2008. In 2008 the enrollment was 850. The high school offers a varied curriculum, including many dual-credit and advanced placement courses, and a very competitive sports program. The school also has a functioning greenhouse. Pendleton Co. Memorial High School counts among its graduates a Nobel Prize winner, **Philip A. Sharp**.

Belew, Mildred Bowen. "History of Pendleton County Schools." www.rootsweb.com/~kypendle/schoolhistory.htm (accessed on September 29, 2006).

Dennie, Debbie, and Patty Jenkins, comps. *Forks of the Licking, Bicentennial Edition, 1798–1998.* Falmouth, Ky.: Falmouth Outlook, 1998.

Hornbeek, Carolyn, and Bobby Nordheim, eds. *The Farewell, 1959.* Butler, Ky.: Butler High School, 1959.

Morris, Linda S. Thornton, ed. *The Pendleton Echo, 1960.* Falmouth, Ky.: Pendleton High School, 1960.

Pendleton Co. Schools. www.pendleton.k12.ky.us (accessed October 2, 2006).

Michael D. Redden and Aprile Conrad Redden

PENDLETON CO. PUBLIC LIBRARY. The Pendleton Co. Public Library began in 1953 when Pendleton Co. received a grant from the Commonwealth of Kentucky and additional funds from the Falmouth City Council, the Falmouth City School, the Pendleton Co. Fiscal Court, and the Pendleton Co. Schools. The library opened in the Falmouth City Hall council chambers, and the first chairman of the library board was Ray Hogg. The library was able to obtain a bookmobile, which served the general population by making stops in subdivisions and community centers, nursing homes, senior citizens centers, and remote rural areas. Josephine Dougherty and Josephine McKenny were early librarians. On October 15, 1967, the library moved to the LLL Building on the corner of Shelby and Main Sts. in Falmouth, where it remained until 1976.

In August 1967 the board bought the former George B. Held property and cleared it to make way for a new building with adequate parking. In 1975 the board received a $135,000 building grant; that grant, combined with funds from the board's savings account and a $90,000 bank loan, made it possible to construct a new library, which ended up costing more than $200,000. The new Pendleton Co. Public Library, at 228 Main St. in Falmouth, was dedicated in an impressive ceremony on September 26, 1976. A large crowd visited the library to see the collection of some 10,000 books and view the Barton Papers collection housed there. Othelia Moore was the librarian at the time. She retired and was replaced by Janie Harter in 1985. When Harter retired in 2005, Cheri Figgins was appointed librarian.

The **flood of 1997** devastated the library's interior and its holdings. Because the water rose to four feet on the main floor, very few items were salvaged; but through help from both state and federal agencies and private individuals and groups, such as the Campbell Co. Historical Society, the building's interior was restored and its bookshelves filled again. Many people donated books and information about their families to restock the genealogical research room. Today there are about 38,000 items housed at the library.

Belew, Mildred Boden. *The First 200 Years of Pendleton County.* Falmouth, Ky.: M. B. Belew, n.d. [ca. 1994].

"Hundreds Turn Out to View Pendleton Library," *KP*, September 27, 1976, 8K.

Mildred Belew

PENDLETON CO. PUBLIC SCHOOLS. Public education in Pendleton Co. began in Butler with a school that included multiple grades and was located in three rented rooms on the upper story of the Armstrong Store. A one-room schoolhouse was built in the town around 1856 from what had been an old blacksmith's shop; all grades were taught there, including high school. By 1875, there were about 70 schools for whites and 3 for blacks in Pendleton Co. By 1895 or so, the Falmouth independent public school system was established.

In 1909, the county had three independent public high schools at Butler, Falmouth, and Morgan (see **Butler High School**; **Falmouth High School**; **Morgan High School**). Around this time, the Butler Graded and High School was relocated to Matilda St. in Butler and housed in a two-story frame building. In 1915 the county had 62 schools for whites and a single school for blacks. In 1927 the Butler Graded and High School moved into a larger, multistory brick building that was built to replace the former building on the same site; 12 rooms were added to the new school in 1940.

By the 1920s, the county had public schools for whites for grades one through eight in at least the following locations: Auburn, Butler, Falmouth, Goforth, McKinneysburg, Morgan, Mount Auburn, and Portland. In 1924 the elementary school at Goforth became Kentucky's first rural school to offer a hot lunch program; the lunches were free of charge, with local farmers donating goods and students supplying the volunteer labor. The school sponsored a box social to raise the seed money for the endeavor, and a school bookstore funded the ongoing operation of the program. The school at Goforth was also the first among Kentucky's rural schools to include home economics in the grade school curriculum.

In 1930 there was at least one school for African Americans operating in the county; it was known as the Pendleton Co. or Falmouth Colored School. At the December 1955 Falmouth Board of Education meeting, this building was sold to Bob Best, a local realtor, for $1,250. Oral tradition indicates that for some time after the school closed, its students were bused to neighboring Harrison Co., rather than being integrated into Pendleton Co.'s or Falmouth's school system.

The Morgan and Butler high schools ceased to exist at the close of the 1958–1959 school year, when the Pendleton Co. Board of Education consolidated its upper grades into the newly constructed **Pendleton Co. Memorial High School**. In the fall of 1968, Falmouth High School was merged into Pendleton Memorial High School.

In the early 1970s, the Pendleton Co. Board of Education began the countywide consolidation of its primary schools with the opening of Southern Elementary, located at U.S. 27 North and Woodson Ln. in Falmouth, and Northern Elementary, located at 925 Ky. Rt. 177 East in Butler; both schools serve grades one through six. At this time, the Falmouth High School building was converted into the countywide Pendleton Co. Middle School, for grades seven and eight. In January 1998 the middle school was relocated to a new facility at 35 Wright Rd. and U.S. 27 North in Butler and re named the Phillip A. Sharp Middle School. It began serving grades six through eight, to ease spacing concerns at the elementary schools, which today offer preschool and kindergarten classes.

Over time, the old school buildings have found new and varied uses. The school building at Butler was used as a low-income apartment complex until it was damaged by fire; it is now vacant. The Morgan High School building served as a recreation center with a roller skating rink until it was purchased by a private citizen. The high school building in Falmouth is maintained by the county school system and is the Falmouth School Center, offering GED, career placement, and other services. The Mount Auburn school is a senior citizen apartment complex; the McKinneysburg school is now a privately held apartment complex.

Belew, Mildred Bowen. "History of Pendleton County Schools." www.rootsweb.com/~kypendle/schoolhistory.htm (accessed September 30, 2006).

Bray, Nancy, transcriber. "Common School Directory of Pendleton County, Kentucky 1915–1916." www.rootsweb.com/~kypendle/comschool.htm (accessed September 30, 2006).

Butler Woman's Club, comp. *As I Remember Butler.* Butler, Ky.: Butler Women's Club, 1975.

Dennie, Debbie, and Patty Jenkins, comps. *Forks of the Licking, Bicentennial Edition, 1798–1998.* Falmouth, Ky.: Falmouth Outlook, 1998.

"Looking Back through the Years," *Falmouth Outlook*, December 27, 2005, 2.

Wolfe, Ronald Glenn, ed. *The Morganeer, 1958–1959.* Morgan, Ky.: Morgan High School, 1959.

Michael D. Redden and Aprile Conrad Redden

PENN GROVE CAMP MEETING. The land now occupied by the Penn Grove Campground, on the edge of Mount Olivet in Robertson Co., was first an informal gambling resort known as Long Branch. Cards and craps were the games of choice, and they were played at all hours of the day and night. In 1893, Rev. William A. Penn and his brother Lew desired to do something about the grounds, so they purchased the 30-acre tract and built the campground, which eventually included an auditorium, a dining room, and 36 cabins. Gambling ceased, and religious camp meetings replaced that unsavory activity. Various citizens from throughout the county bought shares of stock in the venture. For many years, Penn Grove was the major mass meeting place for wholesome events in Robertson Co., in addition to the typical southern-style church summer camp meetings, which were held by many different religious denominations.

Moore, T. Ross, ed. *Echoes from the Century, 1867–1967.* Mount Olivet, Ky.: Robertson Co. Historical Society, 2000.

PENTECOSTALS. Some of the earliest Pentecostal churches in Northern Kentucky included the First Church of God at 502 Johnson St. in Covington, the Church of God at 1044 Prospect St. in Covington, the First Church of God of Erlanger, and the Full Gospel Assembly of God in Newport. The First Church of God, Covington, moved to 524 Southern Ave. in Covington, where a basement church was built in 1949, and a new sanctuary above it in 1955. The Full Gospel Assembly of God in Newport was founded in 1948 by Rev. Orville A. Morgan, a native of Lee Co., Ky. Christ's Chapel Assembly of God in Erlanger was founded by Rev. Terry Crigger in 1986. One of the largest Pentecostal churches in the region is the Heritage Assembly of God in Florence, which also operates the **Heritage Academy**.

Currently, Church of God (Cleveland, Tenn.) congregations are located in Alexandria, Cold Spring, Covington, Crescent Springs, Dayton, Falmouth, Florence, Highland Heights, Newport, Walton, and Williamstown. There are Assembly of God churches in Alexandria, Bellevue, Boone Co., Brooksville (see **Brooksville Assembly of God**), Covington, Dry Ridge, Erlanger, Falmouth, Florence, Maysville, Mount Olivet, Newport, and Owenton. There are also many Pentecostal churches of other denominations, as well as unaffiliated congregations, in Northern Kentucky.

Pentecostals are Christians who derive their name from the Pentecost of the New Testament, the occasion at which Christians believe that the Apostles received the Holy Spirit. Worldwide today, Pentecostalism is the fastest-growing movement in Christianity and, measured by actual membership, the second-largest denomination of Christianity, next to that of **Roman Catholics**. Pentecostal Protestants trace their earliest roots to John Wesley (1703–1791), founder of the Methodist Church (see **Methodists**). Wesley emphasized a two-step religious experience for individuals, conversion or "justification," followed by Christian perfection or "sanctification." In conversion, individuals realized their sinfulness and were forgiven for their own personal sins. In the second phase, their "inbred sin" or "residue of sin," a consequence of the "original sin" of Adam and Eve, was removed as they received the Holy Spirit; they then grew in "holiness." The American camp meeting (see **Reeves' Campground**), featuring thousands of attendees in a highly emotional setting marked by trembling, trances, and other "gifts of the Spirit," had its origins at Cane Ridge in Bourbon Co. in 1801. "Holiness" revivals—the basic foundation of modern Pentecostalism—spread throughout the nation before the **Civil War**. In contrast to the Calvinism of some religious denominations of the time, which stressed predestination and the selectivity of salvation, the holiness revivals stemmed from Arminianism, which maintained that all could be saved. This democratic and dramatic individualistic element of the Holiness movement of Methodism proved especially appealing in frontier areas like Kentucky.

After the Civil War, the Holiness movement experienced resurgence. By the 1880s, however, for a variety of reasons, Methodists began to dissociate themselves from what they viewed as an increasingly radical movement that appeared to be taking on an antidenominational stance. Holiness churches began to be formed, beginning with Daniel S. Warner's organization of the Church of God in Anderson, Ind., in 1880 and continuing with the **Nazarenes** and the Pilgrim Holiness Church, founded in Cincinnati in 1897. By the 1890s the term *Pentecostals* came into wider usage, led by Henry C. Morrison of Asbury College in Wilmore, Ky., and others.

The modern Pentecostal movement is traced to Rev. Charles Fox Parham of Kansas, who stressed a "third experience," a baptism with the Holy Spirit, as subsequent to and wholly separate from the second experience, "sanctification," which Parham viewed as a cleansing from inbred sin. According to Parham, glossolalia, or speaking in tongues, was evidence of baptism in the Holy Spirit; before this time, glossolalia was a little-known phenomenon. Beginning in 1906 and lasting for three and a half years in a church on Azusa St. in Los Angeles, William Joseph Seymour, an African American follower of Parham, oversaw enthusiastic Pentecostal revivals marked by glossolalia on a massive scale. Azusa St. captured the attention of the media, as thousands flocked to Los Angeles, and modern Pentecostalism was born and spread quickly throughout the world. By 1910 Rev. William H. Durham of Chicago officially introduced the doctrine of the "finished work," denying the "residue of sin" and claiming that at the time of conversion an individual was sanctified and would grow progressively in grace thereafter. Some Pentecostals, namely the newly formed Assemblies of God (1914), adopted the "finished work" doctrine, departing from the three-step process of other Pentecostals. Those denominations believing in the three original steps of grace became known as "second work" or Wesleyan Pentecostals and included the Church of God of Cleveland, Tenn. A third division of Pentecostals, represented by the United Pentecostal Church, are called "Oneness" or "Jesus Only," meaning that they are Unitarians rather than Trinitarians; they regard the terminology of Father, Son, and Holy Spirit as different titles for Jesus. In the 1940s and after, Pentecostal revivalism concentrated on healing. Originally associated with the poor and minorities, Pentecostalism was largely scorned by older, mainline Christian denominations. Slowly, Pentecostals, especially preachers such as Oral Roberts (who became a Methodist in 1968), achieved acceptance. Also, by the 1960s and 1970s some members of mainline denominations began their own charismatic renewals, making Pentecostalism more understandable and palatable.

Anderson, Robert Mapes. "Pentecostal and Charismatic Christianity." In *Encyclopedia of Religion,* ed. Lindsay Jones. 2nd ed. Detroit: Thomson Gale, ca. 2005.
"Anniversary," *KTS*, March 18, 1955, 2A.
"Church of God to Break Ground," *KTS*, April 4, 1958, 8A.
"Evangelistic Services," *KP*, January 17, 1931, 2.
"First Service in New Church," *KTS*, January 28, 1955, 6A.
"Orville Morgan, 95, Founded Newport Church," *KE*, October 14, 2003, 4B.
"Pastor Heeds Call to Start New Church," *KP*, January 11, 1986, 9K.
"Revival to Be Continued," *KP*, November 18, 1930, 3.
Synan, Vinson. *The Holiness-Pentecostal Tradition: Charismatic Movements in the Twentieth Century.* 2nd ed. Grand Rapids, Mich.: Wm. B. Eerdmans, 1997.

Paul A. Tenkotte

PEOPLE'S-LIBERTY BANK AND TRUST COMPANY, COVINGTON. People's-Liberty Bank of Covington, once the largest bank in Northern Kentucky, was the result of a 1928 merger between People's Savings Bank and Trust Company and the Liberty National Bank (formerly German National Bank) of Covington.

The German National Bank of Covington was founded in 1871 and in January 1890 moved to a Richardsonian Romanesque–style building still standing at 609–611 Madison Ave. In 1913 it merged with the Merchants National Bank, retaining the name German National Bank. Because of the backlash against German culture during **World War I** (see **Anti-German Hysteria, 1917–1920**), in 1918 the bank changed its name to Liberty National Bank of Covington. In 1921 it purchased the Walsh Building at the southeast corner of Sixth St. and Madison Ave. (see **Covington, Downtown**) and in 1923 opened on the site a new bank, designed by architect Harry Hake of Cincinnati in the Neoclassical style. The **Carl Brothers** provided the cut stone, granite, and masonry for the building.

People's Savings Bank and Trust Company was organized in Covington in 1903 and soon opened offices on the ground floor of the newly completed (1904) Farmers and Traders National Bank (see **First National Bank and Trust Company of Covington**) at the northwest corner of Sixth St. and Madison Ave. It moved across the street, to the southwest corner of Sixth St. and Madison Ave. (originally called the Walker Dry Goods Building and later the Degginger Dry Goods Building) in 1912, after architect **Bernard T. Wisenall** oversaw remodeling of the structure into a bank. In 1926 U.S. Senator **Richard Pretlow Ernst** and businessman **L. B. Wilson** purchased controlling interest in the bank.

After its 1928 merger, People's-Liberty Bank and Trust Company was the second-largest bank in Kentucky and the largest in Northern Kentucky.

In 1933 People's-Liberty merged with the Central Savings Agency, located at 20th St. and Madison Ave. in Covington. In March 1933, during the **Great Depression**, President Franklin D. Roosevelt (1933–1945) declared a "bank holiday," to allow government officials time to examine the solvency of banks nationwide. People's-Liberty passed inspection and reopened immediately. In 1942 the bank named Joseph N. Cuni as president and Clifford E. Homan as executive vice president; in 1958 Homan became president and Cuni chairman of the board. In 1959 Kentucky state law first allowed banks to open branches outside of their city of incorporation but within the same county. People's-Liberty subsequently opened a branch in Elsmere. In 1969 the bank named **Ralph Haile** president and chief executive office; he served for 19 years. In 1970 the Bank of Independence merged with People's-Liberty. In 1983 the bank formed a holding company called Peoples Liberty Bancorporation, of which People's-Liberty Bank became a wholly owned subsidiary. First National Cincinnati Corporation, a holding company that owned 12 banks including First National Bank in Cincinnati and Newport National Bank, expressed its interest in People's-Liberty in 1987, and the purchase was approved by the stockholders of People's-Liberty in January 1988. In 1989 First National Cincinnati Corporation changed its name to Star Bank. In 1993 Star Bank, N.A., Kentucky, which had acquired **First National Bank and Trust Company of Covington** in 1991, moved its headquarters from RiverCenter to the old People's-Liberty Bank on the southeast corner of Sixth and Madison Aves. In 1999 Star Bank was renamed Firstar, and in 2000 **US Bank** purchased Firstar.

"Built the Bank: Men Whose Work Shows in New Structure," *KP*, September 5, 1923, 5.
"Ernst and Wilson Buy People's Bank," *KP*, February 6, 1926, 1.
"Merger of Two Banks Voted," *KP*, January 10, 1928, 1.
"New Bank: The People's Savings Society of Covington Will Organize within a Few Weeks," *KP*, February 18, 1903, 1.
"Peoples Bank Opens Its New Quarters," *KP*, March 9, 1912, 3.
"Peoples Liberty Bancorporation: 1983 Annual Report," vertical files, Kenton Co. Public Library, Covington.
"Trust Company Will Have New Bank Quarters," *KP*, January 11, 1911, 2.

Paul A. Tenkotte

PERKINS, CHRISTOPHER WALLACE, SR., "C.W.," SERGEANT (b. June 19, 1915, Florence, Ala.; d. May 6, 1998, Cincinnati, Ohio). Jazz musician C. W. Wallace was the son of Constantine and Willie Bertha McMillan Perkins (see **Constantine Perkins**). C.W. was named after his father's childhood friend William Christopher Handy, the "Father of the Blues," and after his father's favorite teacher, Professor Y. A. Wallace. C.W. moved with his parents and older brother Carranza to Covington, Ky., in 1921, when C.W. was six years old. He briefly attended Lincoln Grant School in Covington, but his father later enrolled him in a Catholic school in Cincinnati because it had a better arts program. C.W.'s father was his first music teacher; like his father, C.W. had a strong love for music and exhibited great talent at an early age. Even though he learned to play mainly religious and classical music at school, he was drawn to the sound of jazz music by his teens, and he turned to his father for help in improving his jazz-playing skills. When the Cincinnati Cotton Club opened in 1934 in the city's West End, Perkins became its first-chair trumpet player. From 1934 to the 1950s, Perkins was one of the best-known black musicians in Greater Cincinnati. He was nicknamed the "Granddaddy of the Cotton Club" by his protégé **Nelson Burton**. Perkins also performed as a backup musician for King Records in Cincinnati in 1947.

The only time Perkins was not playing for the Cotton Club during those years was when he was drafted and served in the U.S. Army. He became a member of the army band and achieved the rank of sergeant because of his advanced talents. During those years he also traveled for less than a year with a well-known entertainer, Maurice Morocco.

When Josephine Baker, an internationally known entertainer, performed at the Albee Theatre in Cincinnati in 1951, she refused to go on stage until the theater provided her with an integrated band. Perkins was one of four men that the Albee hired from the Cotton Club to play for Baker. The Albee planned to have the "colored" musicians just be on standby and not perform, but Baker insisted that they play. In retaliation, the Albee selected an extremely difficult part for Perkins to perform, hoping that he would fail and that they could dismiss all four African American musicians. Instead, Perkins hit every note, high or fast, with perfection. After his performance, the Albee kept its band integrated. In the *Cincinnati Times Star*, a writer who did not realize that Perkins was a local musician reported that Baker had a "very hot trumpet player." Perkins was asked by many famous entertainers (for example, Josephine Baker, Count Basie, and Nat King Cole) to go on the road after he performed with them during the famous musical jam sessions at the Cotton Club. Perkins would never leave, though, because he did not want to be away from his young sons. Even after the Cotton Club closed, he continued to perform with local bands such as the Frank Payne Quartet. He was a well-sought-after backup musician, performing with entertainers like Tony Bennett and Luther Vandross when they were in town.

In the 1980s Perkins began serving as a musician at Holy Name Church in Mount Auburn, Ohio. He performed every Sunday until he became ill in 1998. He died one month before his 83rd birthday and was buried at Gate of Heaven Cemetery, Montgomery, Ohio.

Burton, Nelson. *Nelson Burton: My Life in Jazz.* Cincinnati: Clifton Hills Press, 2000.
CTS, June 15, 1951, 8.
Perkins, Christopher W., Sr., to Jessica Knox-Perkins, April 1997.
Ruppli, Michel. *The King Labels: A Discography.* Westport, Conn.: Greenwood Press, 1985.

Jessica Knox-Perkins

PERKINS, CONSTANTINE, JR., "CONSTANT" (b. May 15, 1870, Florence, Ala.; d. October 31, 1942, Covington, Ky.). Constantine Perkins, a musician and the father of **Christopher Perkins**, was born to former slaves Constantine T. Perkins Sr. and Victoria Simpson Perkins. When he was only five, Constant was skilled as a pianist and quickly mastered several musical instruments, especially the cornet. He became known in Florence, Ala., as a musical prodigy. His father became a wealthy businessman after slavery and owned a barbershop at which young Perkins would play the piano. Musicians from traveling minstrel shows who frequented the shop during their travels were astounded at the young musician's talent. By the time he was 20, Perkins was known throughout Alabama for having one of the finest black bands in the state.

W. C. Handy, the "Father of the Blues," was a childhood friend of Perkins. In Handy's autobiography, he recognized Perkins as a strong musical influence on his life: he was responsible for teaching Handy how to play Ragtime and the Blues, the type of music that brought fame and notoriety to Handy. Perkins and Handy joined the Mahara Minstrel Show and performed widely in the United States, Canada, and Cuba. Both were very popular musicians with the show, and their unique style of music made a major impact on other musicians.

Perkins left the show and returned home when his young daughter became very ill, a twist of fate that removed Perkins from the music world while Handy continued to advance. Back in Alabama, Perkins joined his father's barber business and became even more prosperous than his father. However, his success was interrupted when he refused to comply with Alabama's expanding laws requiring segregation. He had to leave Alabama and everything that he had accomplished and acquired. In Alabama Perkins had worked with organizations like the **NAACP** to help put an end to segregation and the lynching of blacks, and when he moved to the Greater Cincinnati area, he continued his work for civil rights. He did not live to see the passing of the antilynching law (1947) or the Civil Rights Act (1964), though. Perkins died of a stroke in 1942 while residing at 1209 Russell St. in Covington. He was buried at St. Mary Cemetery, Fort Mitchell.

Florence (Ala.) Times, August 22, 1890, 3.
Handy, W. C. *W.C. Handy: Father of the Blues.* New York: Macmillan, 1941.
Kentucky Death Certificate No. 24816, for the year 1942.
"What's Happening," *Florence (Ala.) Herald*, August 5, 1897, 1.
Willie Bertha Perkins to Jessica Knox-Perkins, June 1980, Cincinnati.

Jessica Knox-Perkins

PERKINS, GEORGE G. (b. July 10, 1839, Burlington, Ky.; d. August 17, 1933, Lake Mohonk, N.Y.). George Gilpin Perkins, a lawyer, a longtime Kenton Co. Circuit Court judge, and a member of the **Democratic Party**, was the son of John Hilton and Mariah R. Stansifer Perkins. His father was a native of Bourbon Co. who had moved to Burlington in 1828. George's mother was a member of the prominent Boone Co. Stansifer family. George was the second of the 10 children born to the couple. The Perkins family moved to Covington in 1849 and several years later to land across from the Kruempelmann Farm, on what is now **Dixie Highway**. The former Perkins land today encompasses the entire city of old Fort Mitchell. They built their home where the **Fort Mitchell Country Club** now stands.

George Perkins's early education was mostly by private tutor. After the family moved to Covington, he attended the private school of Professor Tackett Read, which was located on the second floor, above a firehouse, on the southwest corner of Washington and Pike Sts. Perkins later was a student at Shelby College in Shelbyville, Ky. Just before the **Civil War**, he joined the reserves and underwent military training during the summers, between college terms. While in training with the Madeira Guards in Harrison Co. during the summer of 1859, he contracted typhoid fever and spent the next year at home, recuperating. He then entered Farmer's College (later known as Ohio Mechanics Institute and later still as Ohio College of Applied Science) in Cincinnati, where he graduated in 1861. Perkins apprenticed law under Judge James Pryor and was admitted to the bar in 1863.

In June 1864, Perkins married Lavinia Jane Smith of Madison, Ind., who was a cousin of Mary Todd Lincoln. The couple had a son, Gilbert and a daughter, Anna. The family lived on Garrard St. near Fifth, where they were neighbors of future governor **John White Stevenson**. Perkins also became a close personal friend of **John G. Carlisle**, who later served as treasury secretary under President Grover Cleveland. Perkins was a prominent figure in Kentucky horse racing circles and was one of the founders of the Latonia Jockey Club.

He entered politics in 1867 and was elected to the Kentucky legislature, where he served for two years. In 1869 he was elected judge of the Kenton Co. court and served there until he was appointed in 1874 as judge of the Kentucky 12th Judicial District's criminal court. In January 1893, a new state constitution went into effect and the state's courts were redesigned; thereafter he became judge of the new Kenton Co. Circuit Court. Eventually, he resigned to become a lawyer in New York City. He remained there for about five years and then retired to an estate called Greenacre, in Chevy Chase, Md., just outside of Washington, D.C.

Judge Perkins wrote a book about his life, entitled *A Kentucky Judge,* which was published in 1931. He died in his summer home on Lake Mohonk, N.Y., at age 94. Funeral services were held in Washington, D.C.

"Death Takes Former Judge," *KTS*, August 18, 1933, 1.

"G.G. Perkins Is Dead; Kentucky Patriarch," *NYT*, August 19, 1933, 11.

Levin, H., ed. *The Lawyers and Lawmakers of Kentucky.* Chicago: Lewis, 1897.

Perkins, George Gilpin. *A Kentucky Judge.* Washington, D.C.: W. F. Roberts, 1931.

PERRY PARK. Three large creeks, named the Mill, the Little Twin, and the Big Twin, drain most of northwestern Owen Co. and empty into the Kentucky River within a few hundred yards of each other. This is where the community known as Perry Park is located. According to legend, the area was first called Lick Skillet after a pioneer surveyor running short on rations was reputed to have remarked, "We would eat everything in sight, then lick the skillet"; later the community was referred to as Cleveland in honor of two-term U.S. president Grover Cleveland (1885–1889 and 1893–1897); next it was called Ball's Landing for some of its early settlers, the Ball family; and finally the name was changed to Perry Park to honor the Perry family, longtime residents of the community.

Being one of the major landings for large boats traveling the Kentucky River made the Perry Park area a site of continual activity. James Ball was the first local wharfmaster. A road ran to the water's edge, and freight could be loaded onto wagons for various inland destinations or stored in a nearby warehouse.

In the early days of the settlement, school was held at a home in town and in one located at nearby Zion Hill. The Methodist Church, originally located on Gratz Rd., was moved to town. At one time, the town of Perry Park had a picture gallery, a millinery store, three blacksmith shops, some general stores, the Star Hotel, and a doctor's office. The post office was located in the drug store. The **lead** mine on Big Twin Creek was operated by a Colorado syndicate from 1899 to 1901 and employed a number of miners. The ore was shipped away on riverboats. This mine was reopened during **World War I** but was closed shortly afterward.

Perry Park no longer exists as a town. It has become the Glenwood Hall Resort, a resort area with homes, condominiums, a restaurant, a golf course, and a landing strip (see **Airports**). The resort's clubhouse is the original home, with some modifications, of the Perry family. Today, it is used as a meeting area.

Friedberg, Mary. "Get-Aways Not Far Away," *KP*, August 1, 1995, 8K.

Vertical files, Owen Co. Public Library, Owenton, Ky.

Doris Riley

PERSIMMON GROVE. Persimmon Grove is a small farming community in Campbell Co. located at the intersection of Persimmon Grove Pk. and Race Track and Wagner Rds. The centerpiece of the community is its Baptist church. The community, the road, and the church derive their names from the same nearby grove of persimmon trees. The 1883 Lake atlas shows a post office, a tobacco warehouse, a store, and a Methodist church in the area. A cemetery dating far back in time is located beside the Persimmon Grove Baptist Church. Two public schools also carried the Persimmon Grove name: one was located directly behind the Baptist church's cemetery, and the other (a replacement of the first school) was a two-room building just down the road. Persimmon Grove is much as it always was, a farming community where most residents travel to town for nonagricultural work opportunities.

An Atlas of Boone, Kenton, and Campbell Counties, Kentucky. Philadelphia: D. J. Lake, 1883.

Campbell Co. Historical Society. *Campbell County, Kentucky, 200 Years, 1794–1994.* Alexandria, Ky.: Campbell Co. Historical Society, 1994.

Hartman, Margaret Strebel, and W. Rus Stevens. *Campbell County Kentucky History & Genealogy.* Campbell Co., Ky.: W. R. Stevens, 1984.

Kenneth A. Reis

PETERS, AMO LUCILLE POWELL (b. December 5, 1912, Cynthiana, Ky.). Amo Lucille Powell Peters, the leader of the **civil rights movement** in Maysville, as a child dreamed of serving as a missionary in Africa, but later she dedicated her life to the enrichment of the lives of African Americans in Mason Co. She married the late James Peters, and the couple had six children, three sons and three daughters. A longtime member of Maysville's **Bethel Baptist Church**, Amo Peters served as a Sunday school teacher, as president of the Senior Choir, and as president of the Women's Missionary Society; in 1985, at age 73, she received her church's Woman of the Year Service Award. She continues at age 94 to serve as a trustee on the Administrative Board.

Peters was the first African American hired at the former **Hayswood Hospital** in Maysville, where she worked for 30 years. At first a nurse's aide, Peters earned her Licensed Practical Nurse degree and eventually was promoted to night nurse in charge. Later she worked as coordinator for the hospital's information and referral services.

In the 1960s Peters organized local marches and peaceful demonstrations to end segregation and unfair conditions for African Americans. She became chairman of the Maysville–Mason Co. Human Rights Commission and helped plan the 1964 March on Frankfort in support of the Public Accommodations Act. More than 10,000 people attended the march, which featured singer Mahalia Jackson, Rev. Martin Luther King Jr., and former baseball player Jackie Robinson. Although the bill never made it out of committee, local organizers such as Peters worked for the next two years to persuade their state representatives to pass civil rights legislation in 1966. Her personal visits with the owners of local businesses and civic leaders led many to support her efforts to hasten integration. Under her leadership, Maysville saw the integration of its theater, its hospital, its restaurants, its local stores, and other facilities. Because of her persistent efforts for negotiation, the first black postal worker and the first black employee at the Social Security office in Maysville were hired. She also led the first local black troop of the **Girl Scouts** of America. The Black Caucus of Maysville arranged for Peters to receive a Kentucky Colonel Commission in 1985.

Continuing in her local activism long after her retirement, Peters has worked on behalf of disabled, elderly, and poor citizens. She has served on the Board of Commissioners for the Five County

Aging Council, the Buffalo Trace Aging Advisory Council, the Licking Valley Handicapped Board, the **American Red Cross** local chapter, the **Comprehend** Foster Grandparents Board, the Low Income Advocacy Committee, the Interagency Council, and the Buffalo Trace Senior Olympics Steering Committee. In 1982 Governor John Y. Brown (1979–1983) appointed Peters as a member of the Kentucky Institute for Aging. She was the first black to serve on the Planning and Aging Commission. Peters served as the physical fitness coordinator for the Buffalo Trace Adult Day Care and was coordinator of activities for senior centers. Maysville mayor **Harriett Cartmell** appointed Peters in 1988 to the local Housing Commission, where she served as commissioner, chairman, and vice chairman. Peters also served on the committee for the Revitalization of Downtown Maysville. As a member of the Mason Co. Homemakers Association, she served on the board for the Martin Luther King Jr. Scholarship. In her eighties, Peters continued to volunteer in local organizations, such as the Hospice of Hope and the Licking Valley Community Action Program. She remains active in the Retired Senior Volunteer Program, where in the past she organized physical education programs.

Peters has claimed a number of prestigious awards, including the Outstanding Black Women's Award in 1981, from the National Black Coalition, and the Community Service Award in 1985 for Outstanding Leadership and Devotion, from the Black Caucus at Morehead State University. In 1989 the National Black Caucus presented her with the National Community Service Award in Washington, D.C. Local honors include Maysville's Community Service Award in 1988 and recognition of outstanding community service in 1996 from the Students United for Minority Awareness at **Maysville Community and Technical College**; she was named Maysville's Lady of the Year in 1988 by the Alpha Nu Chapter, Beta Sigma Phi Sorority.

In 1998 the Maysville Housing Authority named its new building on Meadow Dr. the Amo Peters Community Center. In 2000 the Kentucky Gateway Museum's Curator, Sue Ellen Grannis, nominated Peters for the Kentucky Civil Rights Hall of Fame, and she was nominated two more times in subsequent years. In 2003 the Christian Women United of the Maysville–Mason Co. area (an organization she had formerly served as president) presented her with its first Valiant Woman's award. On January 15, 2004, the Kentucky state legislature passed resolutions honoring Peters and recognizing her as the recipient of the Martin Luther King Jr. Citizenship Award from the Martin Luther King Jr. State Commission. The Mason Co. Fiscal Court honored her the next month with the Frontiersman Award, and Maysville gave her a key to the city. Asked during an interview in 1996 to sum up her philosophy, Amo Peters said, "I am a firm believer that the good Lord does his part, and he expects you to do your part."

Kentucky House of Representatives Resolution No. 77 and Senate Resolution No. 28, January 15, 2004.

Long, Barbara Phillips. "Donating Their Time: R.S.V.P. Volunteers Provide a Wide Range of Services," *Maysville Independent-Ledger*, April 20, 1996, C1–C2.

"Maysville Community College Offers Computer Classes at Amo Peters Center," *Maysville Independent-Ledger*, December 8, 2000, A3.

Peters, Amo. "How Much Farther Do We Have to Go?" *Maysville Independent-Ledger*, 1994, clipping in the collection of Robert S. Peters.

Stahl, Matt. "Amo Peters Community Center to Be Dedicated in Friday Ceremony," *Maysville Independent-Ledger*, May 7, 1998, B1–B2.

Randolph Hollingsworth

PETERSBURG. Petersburg, the oldest town in Boone Co., was built on the ruins of even older settlements. A large prehistoric village had existed there, which was inhabited at various times between about A.D. 1250 and A.D. 1650. Petersburg is a well-known **Fort Ancient** Indian cultural archaeological site, which was first studied and recorded during the 1940s. Archaeologists have revisited the site periodically ever since. In 2004 archaeological salvage excavations documented a series of prehistoric burials that will almost certainly reshape archaeologists' understanding of the Fort Ancient culture in the Ohio River Valley.

The stage was set for developing the land at Petersburg when a 1,000-acre tract in the vicinity was surveyed for William Holliday of Stafford Co., Va. The property changed hands several times before Col. John Grant of North Carolina, who was a nephew of Daniel Boone, purchased 750 acres of it. In 1789 a Baptist preacher from North Carolina named John Tanner led a party to the site and built a stockade there. Known as Tanner's Station, this became the first permanent Euro-American settlement in the territory that in 1799 became Boone Co. Although the Tanners remained for only a few years, the Tanner Stone House can still be seen along the road below the sharp switchback on Ky. Rt. 20 as one descends into Petersburg.

By 1806 John Grant had established a ferry and a tavern and had laid out 100 acres of his land for a town to be called Caledonia. Short of funds, he transferred his holdings to his son-in-law John James Flournoy. The development of Petersburg between 1810 and 1830 was closely entwined with Flournoy's many business enterprises. He has been referred to as a Frenchman, but it is believed that he came to Petersburg from North Carolina. With the permission of the Boone Co. Court, Flournoy established a warehouse at Tanner's Station for the purpose of inspecting flour, tobacco, pork, and hemp. In September 1817, he platted a town on the site of Grant's Caledonia, and the Kentucky legislature recognized the settlement as Petersburg the following year. He soon began advertising "free lots for artisans and tradesmen" who were willing to become permanent settlers, a common practice in the settlement-era Ohio River Valley. Flournoy also established the Petersburg Steam Mill Company, which eventually became the largest distillery in Kentucky (see **Petersburg Distillery**), and the Petersburg Bank. He sold his interest in the mill in 1825 and left Petersburg before 1840.

The town's location on the Ohio River encouraged its growth throughout the 19th century, as did the mill complex, which incorporated a distillery in the 1830s. In large part because of the distillery, Petersburg soon became the most populous and prosperous town in Boone Co. In 1850 it had 250 residents, a flourmill, a tobacco factory, a tavern, schools, and churches. The town's population was diverse. In 1860 half were native Kentuckians; immigrants from Ireland, Britain, and Germany, as well as people who had come from elsewhere in the United States, made up the other half. African Americans were part of the town from its earliest days. In 1865 the *Kentucky State Gazetteer and Business Directory* described Petersburg as a "flourishing post village . . . [with] a good landing and an active trade . . . and about 600 inhabitants." By 1879 the *Gazetteer* reported: "This town . . . has more life than many Kentucky villages. It has 1 distillery, 1 stave factory, 2 churches, 1 public and 1 private school, and ships whisky, live stock, grain and willows. Two mails daily."

The layout of Petersburg reflects its preeminence, as well as the town founders' hopes for the future. The town plat consists of a formal grid of 24 square blocks perpendicular to the river, two central squares reserved for public use, and broad streets. Imposing, multistory brick buildings such as the Masonic Lodge, the 1892 opera house, and the 1913 Odd Fellows Hall also testify to the town's prosperity. Vintage postcard views of the town show wide, tree-lined streets with neat houses, churches, and shops. Contrary to legend, Petersburg was never planned as the capital of Kentucky; that distinction fell to a paper town of the same name on the Kentucky River, founded years earlier.

Steamboats shaped the fortunes of Petersburg. As many as three would dock at the wharf at one time to have their cargoes loaded or unloaded, while barges were being loaded with coal or corn for the distillery. The distillery had its own boat, the *Levi J. Workum*, named after one of the later owners. The boat, which featured a whiskey barrel mounted between the two stacks, made regular runs up and down the Ohio River. Steamboats brought mail, newspapers, and imported goods and carried passengers. Hundreds of sacks of corn and mountains of wood were brought to the distillery by steamboat, and thousands of barrels of whiskey were shipped away. Ferries also crossed the river to Aurora and Lawrenceburg, Ind. People traveled by ferry to shop, attend school, see doctors, and board trains to distant points. Contractors and artisans also crossed the river to find work.

During the 19th century, students seeking secondary education traveled to Aurora or Lawrenceburg to attend high school. A graded school was built in Petersburg in 1910, several years after Boone Co. schools were consolidated. The sturdy, cross-plan brick structure was a landmark on the eastern side of town until 2003. Petersburg also pioneered school busing in 1913, by transporting pupils from the local Berkshire and Terrill districts.

Another educational milestone was the establishment of the county's first public library in Petersburg in 1949. The Chapin Memorial Library, donated by Petersburg native Edward Young Chapin, was housed in an addition to the Petersburg Christian Church, where it remains today. Among the treasures of the library are the original diaries of resident Lewis A. Loder, which record in great detail daily life in Petersburg from 1857 to 1903. Loder's residence, the Loder House on Front St., built about 1840, is one of the best-known historic taverns in the county. It and the nearby Jonathan Carlton House (Schramm's Tavern), dating from about 1825, welcomed travelers with broad, river-oriented galleries.

A wide terrace, with rich farmland, surrounds Petersburg. Perhaps the most famous farm of Petersburg Precinct was Prospect Farm, the home of **Joseph Carter Jenkins**, who was born in Orange Co., Va., and came to Boone Co. in 1832. He eventually became part owner of the distillery. Always a gentleman farmer, Jenkins raised fine livestock, including Jersey cattle, Cotswold sheep, and Chester hogs, on his 1,200-acre estate. Jenkins's grand residence was built in 1860. Superbly sited on a lofty hilltop overlooking the town, the structure is an artful composition of Italianate, Gothic, Greek Revival, and Moorish elements. At the western edge of Petersburg, within view of the Jenkins house, is the Jenkins-Berkshire House. A frame Gothic Revival dwelling of the Downing Cottage type, it was built for Jenkins's son in about 1860. A local tradition maintains that the house was sited so the son could be seen but not heard.

By the end of the 19th century, the distillery at Petersburg had grown into one of the largest in the nation, surpassed in production only by the massive distilleries of Peoria, Ill. The Freiburg & Workum Company operated the facility for 30 years but finally sold out in 1899 to the Kentucky Distilleries and Warehouse Company. This New Jersey–based company acquired 59 Kentucky distilleries, most of which they eventually closed. Production at the Petersburg distillery was curtailed and ended in 1910. The October 10, 1910, edition of the *Kentucky Post* noted, "The removal will affect the revenue service of this district and deprives many Petersburg families of employment." Bottling continued until the warehouses were depleted and then demolished one by one for brick salvage. Distillery bricks were used to construct many buildings in Petersburg, including the 1916 Petersburg Jail and the Petersburg Baptist Church. The foundations of the distillery are still visible, and the former cooperage presently serves as a barn. Numerous ancillary buildings associated with the operation also survive, including the 1885 distillery superintendent's house, the scales office (ca. 1850), and many workers' cottages.

As the 19th century wore on, river traffic was supplanted by railroad transportation, negatively affecting Boone Co. river communities such as Taylorsport, Petersburg, and Hamilton. As its star fell, Petersburg's population declined and, like many other Boone Co. towns, it became a quiet rural trading center. The same loss of prosperity has, however, preserved the town's matchless stock of historic architecture.

Becher, Matthew E. "The Distillery at Petersburg, Kentucky: Part 1, Snyder's Old Rye Whiskey," *NKH* 9, no. 2 (Spring–Summer 2002): 49–55.

——. "The Distillery at Petersburg, Kentucky: Part 2, a Kentucky Giant," *NKH* 10, no. 1 (Fall–Winter 2003): 35–47.

Boone Co. Historic Preservation Review Board. *Historic Structures of Boone County, Kentucky.* Burlington, Ky.: Boone Co. Historic Preservation Review Board, 2002.

Warner, Jennifer S. *Boone County: From Mastodons to the Millennium.* Boone Co., Ky.: Boone Co. Bicentennial Book Committee, 1998.

Margaret Warminski and Matthew E. Becher

PETERSBURG DISTILLERY. For more than a century, the Petersburg Distillery, the leading industry of Boone Co., operated along the banks of the Ohio River in Petersburg. The business began about 1816 as a steam mill; the distillery was added in the mid-1830s. Throughout the rest of the 19th century, the mill and distilling complex was continually expanded by a succession of owners. In the last decades of the century, it was the largest distillery operating on Kentucky soil and one of the largest in the nation.

The early development of Petersburg was closely tied to a North Carolinian named John James Flournoy. In September 1817, Flournoy platted a town at Tanner's Station, and the Kentucky legislature recognized the settlement as Petersburg the following year. Flournoy also conveyed two and a half acres and $1 to the "president, directors, and company of the Petersburg Steam Mill Company," who agreed to build a steam mill on the property. Flournoy was an officer of that company, together with George Cornelius, Reuben Graves, and John Terrill.

William Snyder, who came from Virginia, was the one who transformed the mill into an industrial power. In 1833 John and William Snyder bought the steam mill and the adjacent dwellings. By 1836 Snyder had begun operating a distillery in conjunction with the mill, and in 1840 he had $34,000 invested in the complex. By 1850 Snyder's mill and distillery complex was a successful concern worth tens of thousands of dollars.

In 1860 the distillery produced a staggering 1.125 million gallons of whiskey. Snyder's whiskey was moving up and the down the Ohio River, as was his flour; 30 men were employed in his mill, distillery, and cooperage. But despite the apparent success of the distillery, Snyder was unable to repay the sum of more than $30,000 loaned to him by some of Petersburg's most influential men. In February 1862 William Snyder's personal property and real estate were liquidated to pay his creditors. His son-in-law William Appleton bought the mill and distillery lot, the cooperage, and Snyder's residence. Snyder quietly moved his family to Chattanooga, Tenn.

Col. William Appleton had begun operating the distillery complex before Snyder was gone. By 1862 Appleton was shipping flour and whiskey on the Ohio River to Lawrenceburg, Ind., to Cincinnati, and to points beyond. During much of the **Civil War**, Appleton weathered the exorbitant federal liquor taxes, but he was eventually forced to sell most of his interest in the firm to **Joseph C. Jenkins** and James Gaff of Aurora, Ind. Jenkins owned 50 percent of the Petersburg Distillery and Gaff and Appleton each owned 25 percent.

Under J. C. Jenkins & Company, the distillery closed for a short time, although whiskey was coming off the stills again by 1865. Jenkins was a well-to-do farmer and a leading Petersburg citizen. He was well acquainted with the distillery's operations, having partnered to some extent with its previous owner, William Snyder. Jenkins's partner James Gaff was the brother of Thomas Gaff, who,

Petersburg Distillery during the flood of 1907.

in 1855, built Hillforest, a notable home, in Aurora, Ind. James and Thomas Gaff also operated the T. & J. W. Gaff & Co. Distillery in Aurora. James Gaff's mansion, Linden Terrace, was located at Fourth and Main Sts., Aurora. In 1869 ownership of the distillery changed again when Jenkins sold his share to the Cincinnati firm of Freiburg & Workum, headed by Bavarian-born Julius Freiburg and his brother-in-law Levi J. Workum. Gaff sold his 25 percent share to Freiburg & Workum in 1872, and Appleton followed suit in 1874.

Cincinnati's whiskey industry of the late 19th century was marked by expansion and agglomeration, and the Freiburg & Workum firm was the biggest fish in a very large pond. Under Freiburg & Workum, the Petersburg Distillery experienced a period of progress and stability that continued through the end of the century. By 1880 the distillery in Petersburg was making more whiskey than any other distillery in the state. That year, the distillery was worth $250,000 and produced 975,820 gallons of whiskey. By comparison, the nine distilleries in famed Bourbon Co., Ky., produced only 433,263 gallons of whiskey in 1880. The only distillery in the state that came close to the Petersburg Distillery's 1880 production figures was the G. W. Robson & Company Distillery in Campbell Co., which produced nearly 790,000 gallons.

By 1897 the Petersburg Distillery complex had elements on the Indiana shore, and its products were available in national and international markets. The distillery's capacity of 4 million gallons of whiskey per year was more than four times the amount produced in 1880. The daily capacity of the stills (12,000 gallons) was more than 14 times that of the average 1890s Kentucky distillery and was comparable to the capacities of the 14 massive distilleries of Peoria, Ill.

In 1899 Freiburg & Workum sold the Petersburg Distillery to a firm known as the Kentucky Distilleries and Warehouse Company (KD&WHC). Between 1899 and 1916, the KD&WHC bought 59 distilleries in Kentucky, most of which they eventually shut down. In 1910 the KD&WHC announced plans to close the Petersburg Distillery. Over the next several years, the remaining bonded whiskey was withdrawn and the massive brick warehouses were dismantled one by one. Much of the brick was reused in construction projects outside Boone Co. However, a number of buildings in Petersburg were built from distillery brick, including the tiny 1916 Petersburg Jail. Along with several houses, the National Register lists the 1913 Odd Fellows Hall and the 1916 Petersburg Baptist Church, also built of distillery bricks.

Today, the Petersburg Distillery is an archaeological site with remnants of stone, brick foundations, and walls. The only distillery building on the parcel is the distillery cooperage (ca. 1870), located in a cow pasture at the end of First St. The distillery scales office (ca. 1850), at the corner of Mill and Front Streets, is now a small wood-frame residence. The finest surviving building is the 1885 distillery superintendent's house, across Front St. from the scales office. The brick building is an exceptional Queen Anne–style double house with an urban form, unique in Boone Co. This is all that remains of a distillery that was once the largest in Kentucky.

Becher, Matthew E. "The Distillery at Petersburg, Kentucky: Part 1, Snyder's Old Rye Whiskey," *NKH* 9, no. 2 (Spring–Summer 2002): 49–55.

——. "The Distillery at Petersburg, Kentucky: Part 2, A Kentucky Giant," *NKH* 10, no. 1 (Fall–Winter 2003): 35–47.

Boone Co. Historic Preservation Review Board. *Historic Structures of Boone County, Kentucky.* Burlington, Ky.: Boone Co. Historic Preservation Review Board, 2002.

Matthew E. Becher

PHARMACY. No clear records of the earliest pharmacies established in Northern Kentucky have been found. There were several drugstores in Covington as early as 1839, and there is a record of a drugstore in Newport at Fourth and York Sts. before the **Civil War**. However, through much of the first half of the 19th century, doctors prepared and dispensed many of their own medicines. Some even kept small doctors' shops, where medicines were compounded and dispensed. Such shops were usually connected with the office where the doctor practiced. In Northern Kentucky's early days, much of the commerce along the Ohio River took place on the Cincinnati side, and so when **John Uri Lloyd** and his father were searching for a pharmacy apprenticeship in 1864, there were no openings in Covington; a position was eventually found with the Gordon Brothers in Cincinnati.

Most pharmacists in the 19th century learned their trade through an apprenticeship. Not every established pharmacist accepted apprentices, however, even though apprentices were a source of relatively inexpensive labor. Joseph Feth and Louis Holzhauer were two pharmacists who trained apprentices in Newport. When the first colleges of pharmacy were established, students still had to work four years in a drugstore before receiving their degrees. In 1850 the first pharmacy school west of the Appalachians opened in Cincinnati, but not until after the end of the Civil War were significant numbers of students enrolled. The first college of pharmacy in Kentucky opened in Louisville in 1870; it became part of the University of Kentucky in 1947 and was moved to Lexington in 1957. In 1883 a short-lived pharmacy college for women opened in Louisville, but it operated only until 1893. Many of the young men and women from Northern Kentucky who wanted to become pharmacists went across the Ohio River to the closer Cincinnati College of Pharmacy (now the University of Cincinnati College of Pharmacy) for their professional education.

The first national association of pharmacists, the American Pharmaceutical Association (now the American Pharmacists Association), was formed in Philadelphia, Pa., in 1852. Pharmacists from the colleges of the period, including those in Cincinnati, agreed to work together to limit the importation of adulterated drugs and to establish standards of practice. The first pharmacists from Northern Kentucky to join the national association were Richard G. Mauss (1869), and Peter Nodler (1870), whose drugstore was located at the corner of Fifth St. and Madison Ave. in Covington.

In 1874 Kentucky passed legislation to regulate the sale of medicines and poisons; it was one of the first states to do so, but the law applied only to Louisville. In 1876 an amendment expanded coverage to all cities having a population of at least 5,000. In 1877 a preliminary meeting to form the Kentucky Pharmaceutical Association was held in Frankfort,

F. A. Pope Drug Store, Ritte's Corner, Latonia, before 1941.

and pharmacists from Covington, Maysville, and Newport were part of the organizing body. G. A. Zwick and M. Heermance, both of Covington, were elected second and third vice president, respectively, and Peter Nodler, also of Covington, was elected treasurer. One of the organization's first orders of business was to strengthen the poisons act and establish a state board of pharmacy.

By 1890, there were more than 100 pharmacies operating in Northern Kentucky. Scientific pharmacy was advanced in the United States when German-trained pharmacists immigrated. In both Cincinnati and Northern Kentucky, a number of German immigrants opened Apothekes, or pharmacies. G. A. Zwick, Covington; A. F. Goetze, Dayton; and G. Holzhauer and Otto Breck, Newport, were among the early German pharmacists working in Northern Kentucky.

Pharmacy was largely a male occupation during the 19th century. The few women who became pharmacists were typically apprenticed to relatives and only slowly gained admittance to the early colleges of pharmacy. Marcella Feth was one of the early women graduates of the Cincinnati College of Pharmacy in 1897. She joined her father, Joseph B. Feth, in his store at the northwest corner of Eighth and York Sts. in Newport (the location today of the York St. Café).

Traditionally, pharmacies were small businesses, owned by the pharmacist and frequently staffed by family or a hired clerk or two. The owner's spouse and children were handy, if sometimes unwilling, workers. Edward C. Farrell opened a drugstore in Ludlow in 1908; two of his sisters and his sons William and John became pharmacists, as did John's son. Henry Morwessel, an 1883 Cincinnati College of Pharmacy graduate, opened his pharmacy in Covington, and it was operated by three generations of the family, continuing into the late 1990s. Its final location was on the southeast corner of W. Sixth and Russell Sts. in Covington.

By the beginning of the 20th century, pharmacy store chains were forming. Cora Dow founded the Dow chain in Cincinnati (see **Dow Drug Stores**), and by 1916 the firm had opened stores in Newport and Covington. The Dow drugstore chain was one of the largest of its kind in the United States at the time, larger than the Walgreens chain, which started in 1901. Louis Liggett, who had the idea of forming a cooperative that would allow independent drugstores greater buying power, in 1903 launched the Rexall business concept. The Rexall cooperative-purchasing way of doing business quickly spread; at one time, at least 20 percent of the nation's pharmacies were members, including the Dow Drug Stores. The other major franchise program of the period appeared in 1929 with the introduction of Walgreen Agency stores. The Rexall and Walgreen Agency drugstores competed for business in the smaller communities; each had one-cent sales designed to entice consumers to stock up on store rather than national brands. In 1923 the Model chain of pharmacies in Cincinnati, owned by African Americans, had a store in Covington (see **Model-Evans Pharmacy**).

Relationships between pharmacists in Northern Kentucky and Cincinnati were excellent. Leaders from both sides of the Ohio River were involved with the Ohio Valley Druggists Association. The Widrig brothers, T. J., Louis, and Edward, had separate stores in Newport. Louis Widrig (see **Widrig Family**), a graduate of the Cincinnati College of Pharmacy, was for a number of years the treasurer and a stockholder in the Cincinnati Reds professional baseball team. He was also the president and principal stockholder of the Alexandria Turnpike (**U.S. 27**).

Modern pharmacy has changed from the days when it merely involved the dispensing of compounded prescriptions at the corner drugstore. Institutional pharmacy in hospitals and nursing homes has become an important part of the profession. In general, the one-owner store has given way to the large chain pharmacies such as Walgreens, CVS, and the pharmacies operated in Kroger grocery stores (see **Bernard H. "Barney" Kroger**). In 1998 **Omnicare** moved its headquarters to Covington. Originally formed in 1981 to provide pharmacy services to nursing homes, this company continues to expand its services to institutional health care providers. There are still independent drug and pharmacy stores in Northern Kentucky, however; for example, Blanks Pharmacy in Covington has been in operation for more than 100 years. Pharmacists continue to develop new ways to provide services to their patients. The Ruwe family, involved in pharmacy for multiple generations, has expanded its retail counter operation to include providing clinical pharmacy services in senior apartments located throughout Northern Kentucky. Beginning in 2002, persons in need have received help through the charitable pharmacy program of the **Society of St. Vincent de Paul**.

Flannery, M. A., and D. B. Worthen. *Pharmaceutical Education in the Queen City.* Binghamton, N.Y.: Pharmaceutical Press, 2001.

Poweleit, A. C., and J. A. Schroer. *A Medical History of Campbell and Kenton Counties.* Cincinnati: Campbell-Kenton Co. Medical Society, 1970.

Dennis B. Worthen

PHILIPPS, MIKE (b. June 30, 1946, Muncie, Ind.). *Cincinnati Post* editor John Michael Philipps is the son of John Albert and Jean Philipps. He grew up in Lima, Ohio, and at age 16 he became a freelance photographer for the *Lima News.* In 1968 he graduated from the Virginia Military Institute at Lexington, Va., with a degree in English literature and a regular U.S. Army commission. He immediately was sent to active military duty in Vietnam, where he worked in military intelligence under future CIA head William Colby. Philipps then returned to the *Lima News,* where his boss was his future wife, Carole Simeon. In 1977 they both joined the staff of the *Cincinnati Post.* Over the years, Philipps held various positions at the *Post* and became the editor of both the *Cincinnati Post* and the *Kentucky Post* in 2001. He is a boater, an airplane pilot, a ham radio operator, and a photographer and has also been a member of several important civic boards and organizations in the Greater Cincinnati and Northern Kentucky area.

PHISTER, ELIJAH C. (b. October 8, 1822, Maysville, Ky.; d. May 16, 1887, Maysville, Ky.). Elijah Conner Phister, a legislator and a mayor, was the son of Conrad Phister, from Germany, and Mary W. Conner, of Maryland. Elijah Phister attended the Seminary of Rand and Richardson in Maysville and graduated from **Augusta College** in Augusta in 1840. He undertook the study of law with John Sargent in Philadelphia, Pa., and was admitted to the bar in 1844. As a lawyer, Phister practiced in Mason Co. with the firm Payne & Waller. He was elected mayor of Maysville in 1847 and 1848. From 1856 to 1862, Phister served as a judge on the circuit court. He was affiliated with the **Whig Party** and a supporter of Henry Clay but later became a Democrat. After the **Civil War**, he was elected a state representative in Kentucky, serving from 1867 to 1871 and holding the chairmanship of the Judiciary Committee in his second term. Kentucky governor Preston H. Leslie (1871–1875) wanted to appoint him to a commission to revise the Kentucky statutes in 1872, but Phister turned down the offer. He was elected as a Democrat to the 46th and 47th U.S. Congresses, holding office for two terms from 1879 to 1883. He died in Maysville in 1887 and was buried in the Maysville-Mason Co. Cemetery.

Biographical Cyclopedia of the Commonwealth of Kentucky. Chicago: John M. Gresham, 1896.

Biographical Directory of the United States Congress, 1774–1989. Washington, D.C.: Government Printing Office, 1985.

Biographical Encyclopedia of Kentucky. Cincinnati: J. M. Armstrong, 1878.

Thomas S. Ward

PIATT'S LANDING. Piatt's Landing was a ferry landing established by Robert Piatt (1769–1857) in the East Bend Bottoms of Boone Co., about three miles below Rabbit Hash, along the Ohio River. In the early 1800s, several ferries were operated by members of the Piatt family, including ferries between Touseytown, Ky., and Lawrenceburg, Ind.; between Rabbit Hash, Ky., and Rising Sun, Ind.; and between East Bend, Ky., and North Landing, Ind. The Piatts came to the Ohio River Valley from New Jersey about 1800. Robert Piatt acquired 200 acres in East Bend Bottoms in 1810 and moved to the site about 1812. That year he requested permission from the Boone Co. Court to establish a ferry at East Bend and to build a road from the landing. He commenced building a house at East Bend about the same time. His home, renamed Winnfield Cottage by its second owners, was one of the finest vernacular Greek Revival residences in the county.

As a ferry landing, Piatt's Landing was typical of Ohio River transportation of the day. Piatt's Landing will always be remembered as the birthplace of **Edward Richard Sprigg Canby**, who rose to the rank of general in the Union Army and accepted the final surrender in 1865 of Confederate forces commanded by generals Richard Taylor and Edmund Kirby Smith. Today, the East Bend Power Plant occupies the site.

Shaffer, James F. *Piatt's Landing East Bend.* Cincinnati: Cincinnati Gas and Electric Company, General Engineering Department, 1978.

Warner, Jennifer S. *Boone County: From Mastodons to the Millennium.* Boone Co., Ky.: Boone Co. Bicentennial Book Committee, 1998.

Matthew E. Becher

PICKETT, JAMES C., COLONEL (b. February 6, 1793, Faquier Co., Va.; d. July 10, 1872, Washington, D.C.). Col. James Chamberlayne Pickett, a lawyer, a legislator, and a diplomat, was the eldest son of Col. John and Elizabeth Chamberlayne Pickett. When James was three years old, his family moved to Mason Co., Ky. His early education was at the best schools, and he attended the U.S. Military Academy at West Point, N.Y. Pickett was an excellent student, proficient in several languages. After graduation, he served as an officer in the U.S. Army during the **War of 1812.** He left the army after the war to become a lawyer. In 1816 he served as editor of the *Maysville Eagle* newspaper. He returned to the army in 1818 with the rank of captain and was later promoted to colonel. In 1821 he resigned his commission and entered the practice of law in Mason Co. He was elected to the Kentucky House of Representatives in 1822 for one term and then served as Kentucky secretary of state from 1824 to 1828. Appointed by President Andrew Jackson (1829–1837), he served with the U.S. legation to Colombia from 1829 until 1833. Pickett was appointed superintendent of the U.S. Patent Office in 1835 and then served as an auditor of the U.S. Treasury from 1836 to 1838. Afterward he headed U.S. diplomatic relations with Ecuador and the Peru-Bolivia Confederation. Returning to Washington, D.C., he retired to private life and became the editor of the *Congressional Globe* (an insert to the *Washington Globe* newspaper) from 1848 until 1853. In addition to his other accomplishments, Pickett was a prolific writer, especially on scientific subjects; he also wrote extensively about diplomatic history. In his 75th year, he published a book of poems. His writings were marked by notable clarity, power, and intellectual vigor. Pickett was well liked and established numerous friendships throughout his life. A close friend for 58 years was Judge **Lewis Collins**, the author of the extremely popular work *Historical Sketches of Kentucky* (1847). Pickett died in Washington, D.C., at age 79 and was buried at the Congressional Cemetery. In October 1818, he married Ellen Desha, daughter of Kentucky governor Joseph Desha (1824–1828). They had two sons, Joseph Desha Pickett, a college professor at Bethany College in West Virginia and at the University of Kentucky in Lexington, and Col. John T. Pickett, who served as consul to Mexico.

Kleber, John E., ed. *The Kentucky Encyclopedia.* Lexington: Univ. Press of Kentucky, 1992.

Padgett, James A., ed. "Letters of James Chamberlayne Pickett," *RKHS* 37, no. 119 (April 1939): 151–70.

PIERCE, JEANNETTE RIGG (b. October 12, 1922, Pendleton Co., Ky.; d. August 27, 1998, Falmouth, Ky.). Jeannette Rigg Wyatt Pierce of Falmouth, a pioneering special education teacher, began her teaching career at the Goforth and Morgan elementary schools in Pendleton Co. and subsequently took an interest in the nascent field of special education. She earned certification as a special education teacher at the University of Kentucky at Lexington and then helped start Northern Kentucky's first state-supported special education program in Pendleton Co. She was selected by her school's superintendent, Richard Gulick, as the program's first teacher. Pierce not only taught the children; she looked after their welfare, even making a good breakfast for them each morning.

After the Pendleton schools were consolidated, Pierce taught at Southern Elementary School; later she taught more severely challenged students at the county's Middle School. She helped organize the Pendleton Co. Mental Health Association, out of which came the George Gedge workshop and other opportunities for the county's special-needs children. In 1972 she was honored as the Outstanding Elementary Teacher in America for her work with mentally handicapped children.

Her husband, Samuel E. Pierce, also taught school. He died in 1998, just two months before Jeannette died. The Pierces were members of the Morgan Christian Church in Morgan, and they were both buried in the Morgan Cemetery.

"Falmouth's Jeannette Pierce, Pioneering Special-Ed Teacher," *KP*, August 28, 1998, 16A.

Kentucky Death Certificate No. 26725, for the year 1998.

Diane Perrine Coon

PIKE, ZEBULON MONTGOMERY (b. January 5, 1779, Lamington, N.J.; d. April 27, 1813, Lake Ontario, N.Y.). Military officer and explorer Zebulon M. Pike was the son of Zebulon and Isabella Brown Pike. His father was a military officer who served in the **Revolutionary War** and, afterward, along the western frontier. His mother was a sister of John Brown, a Revolutionary War officer from New Jersey, who settled as a planter in Boone Co., Ky. Pike followed his father into the regular army, where he too served on the frontier. After delivering supplies to the forts in the Ohio wilderness and protecting shipments of supplies on the Mississippi and Ohio rivers, the younger Zebulon Pike led his famous explorations into Minnesota and the central Rockies, where he first saw the peak near Colorado Springs, Colo., later named for him, and up the Arkansas, Red, and Missouri rivers.

The Boone Co. home of his uncle, the Brown plantation near the Ohio River, was one of the places Pike regularly visited. Pike and his cousin Clarissa "Clara" Harlowe Brown wanted to marry, but her father refused to sanction the marriage. Nevertheless, Pike and Clara Brown married on March 4, 1801, in Boone Co., after eloping (see **Sugar Grove Plantation**). Five children were born to the couple, but only one, Clarissa Brown Pike, reached adulthood.

Throughout his military career, Pike rose rapidly through the ranks, and he kept daily records of his experiences. During the **War of 1812**, he was sent to the Canadian theater, where he was mortally wounded in the battle fought at York. While a captured British flag lay under his head, Pike died on the deck of the gunboat *Madison* on Lake Ontario and was buried with full military honors at Sackett's Harbor, N.Y.

Carver, Harvey L. *Zebulon Montgomery Pike: Pathfinder and Patriot.* Colorado Springs, Colo.: Denton, 1956.

Castel, Albert. "Zebulon Pike, Explorer," *American History Illustrated* 7, no. 2 (1972): 45–48.

Hollon, W. Eugene. *The Lost Pathfinder: Zebulon Montgomery Pike.* Norman: Univ. of Oklahoma Press, 1949.

Hyslop, Stephen G. "An Explorer or Spy?" *American History* 37, no. 3 (August 2002): 58–65.

Peterson, William J. "The Zebulon M. Pike Expedition," *Palimpsest* 49, no. 2, (February 1968): 41–80.

Margaret Prentice Hecker

PIKET, LOUIS A. (b. December 12, 1839, Utrecht, Holland; d. January 25, 1910, Cincinnati, Ohio). Noted architect Louis A. Piket was born and raised in Holland, where he received a solid education in both construction and music. By age 15 he was an accomplished musician and singer and was employed as an organist in his hometown. In 1857 he and his father, Anton (Anthony) Piket (1805–1888), immigrated to the United States and settled in Cincinnati, where Anthony Piket worked as a carpenter. Louis took a position as an organist. By 1858, both Louis and his father were listed as practicing architects. They apparently formed a partnership, which according to the 1860 Cincinnati city directory was named Anthony Piket and Son. By 1866 Anthony Piket had moved to Newport, and two years later to Covington, while Louis remained in Cincinnati. A similar pattern was seen in other architectural firms, such as **Dittoe and Wisenall** and **Walter and Stewart**; the purpose, apparently, was to attract business from both sides of the Ohio River.

The Pikets designed and built Anthony's home at 715 Bakewell St. in Covington. They also designed the **St. Joseph**, **St. Aloysius**, and **St. Patrick Catholic** churches in Covington and the **Immaculate Conception Catholic Church** in Newport. The Pikets seemed to prefer Gothic Revival design for churches and Renaissance or Italianate design for other structures. Both Anthony and Louis Piket became teachers of architecture and mechanical drawing at St. Xavier College in Cincinnati. Anthony Piket retired in 1884, moved to Cincinnati, and died in August 1888. Louis Piket later designed the **Sacred Heart Catholic Church** in Bellevue and designed improvements to the **Trinity Episcopal Church** in Covington. He also drew the architectural plans for numerous other churches, schools, stores, and factories throughout the Greater Cincinnati area. After a long and colorful career, he died in 1910 at age 70. Funeral services were held at St. George Catholic Church in the Clifton section of Cincinnati, and he was buried in St. Mary Cemetery, St. Bernard, Ohio. His wife was Mary Koehler Piket, who died in 1916.

Goss, Charles F. *Cincinnati: The Queen City, 1788–1912.* Chicago: S. J. Clarke, 1912.
"New Church Edifice," *CDE*, May 23, 1867, 3.
St. Mary Cemetery Records, St. Bernard, Ohio.
"Suburban News, Covington," *CDG*, September 11, 1871, 3.
Tenkotte, Paul A. *A Heritage of Art and Faith: Downtown Covington Churches.* Covington, Ky.: Kenton Co. Historical Society, 1986.

PINER. Piner is a small, unincorporated town located in southern Kenton Co. at the intersection of Ky. Rt. 17 (Madison Pk. or the **Three-L Highway**), Ky. Rt. 14 (Bracht-Piner Rd.), and Rich Rd. It is about 20 miles south of Covington and 7 miles south of Independence. Piner and its close neighbor Fiskburg, located two miles farther south along Madison Pk., are collectively known as the Piner-Fiskburg Fire District. The Piner-Fiskburg Volunteer Fire Department, organized in 1961, is located in Piner. The population of the Piner-Fiskburg area, which numbers about 1,450, is served by the Morning View post office.

Piner was originally called Piner Crossroads, for Brack Piner, who owned and operated the first grocery store there in 1849. A market at the southwest corner of the intersection and the Piner Elementary School on Rich Rd. still exist. The original school was a one-room log structure built in 1849 on the current site of the Goshen Christian Church on Bracht-Piner Rd., a half mile from the intersection. Called Goshen Grammar School, it included grades one through eight and also served as a church on Sundays. Around 1870 a four-room frame building was built at the site of the present school on Rich Rd., and in 1914 a new four-room frame building was constructed to accommodate grades 1 through 12. The first graduating class of **Piner High School** was in 1917. This 12-grade school consolidated six one-room schools from the area. When **Simon Kenton High School** in Independence was finished in early 1937, the school at Piner reverted to being a 6-grade elementary school.

In 1881 Piner had a tobacco-drying warehouse, a grocery, and a combination blacksmith shop and livery stable. The combined enterprise was converted into an automobile garage in 1909 and into a milk-hauling business in 1945.

Piner Baptist Church is located on the west side of Ky. Rt. 17 about a half mile from the intersection of Ky. Rts. 17 and 14. It was organized in 1952 by a group of 110 members of the Wilmington Baptist Church. The congregation built a larger sanctuary in 2001 to accommodate its current membership of 400.

The Piner-Fiskburg area contains many large family farms, which have begun to be sold for residential development. Since the area is served with city water and is located only seven miles from the Walton exit off I-75, it is expected to grow quickly. So far, large developers have not attempted to build in this area, however, owing to the lack of sanitary sewers. The farms being subdivided are in 5- and 10-acre tracts, with sufficient land area for septic tanks.

The Piner-Fiskburg area remains a very close-knit community, even though most of its citizens work and shop in Florence, Covington, and Cincinnati. There are only three full-time working farms remaining in the area, all dairy farms. Other farmers are bivocational in order to supplement their incomes.

"Development Slowly Creeping South with Water, New Homes," *Kenton County Recorder*, September 14, 1994, 3.
"Piner," *KP*, June 20, 1928, 2.
"Piner High School Dedicated," *KP*, September 28, 1914, 1.
Reis, Jim. "Tiny Towns," *KP*, July 30, 1986, 4K.
"2 County Schools to Open in Kenton," *KP*, September 3, 1937, 9.

Pat Workman

PINER HIGH SCHOOL. Piner High School was the second of four Sullivan Law–inspired public high schools that opened in Kentucky within the Kenton Co. school district. Passed by the Kentucky legislature in 1908, the Sullivan Law overhauled public school funding in Kentucky and required that each county have at least one public high school. In May 1912 the Kenton Co. School Board authorized construction of a high school in Piner to serve the southern portion of the county. Completed in October 1914, at a cost of $6,083, the two-story brick Piner High School eventually housed both primary and secondary students. Later campus additions included a gymnasium, a cafeteria, and an auditorium. Elma Taylor served as Piner High School's principal through much of its existence. In 1937 the Kenton Co. School Board closed Piner High School and merged it into the new Simon Kenton High School in Independence. The Piner High School building continued as an elementary school until its replacement by a new facility during the early 1960s. Perhaps the most famous graduate of Piner High School was Brig. Gen. **Jesse Auton**, a **World War II** Army Air Force pilot who died in an aviation accident at Omaha, Neb., in the early 1950s.

Caywood, James A. "A Brief Sketch of the Development of the Kenton County School System," an address delivered to the Filson Society, January 14, 1958, Louisville, Ky.
Klotter, James C. *Kentucky: Portrait in Paradox, 1900–1950.* Lexington: Univ. Press of Kentucky, 1996.

Greg Perkins

PIPE ORGANS. Found in many churches in Northern Kentucky, pipe organs differ from electronic organs in the fundamental way sound is produced. Pipe organs have various sets of pipes (ranks) made of metal or wood, in varying shapes, which produce different sounds, or timbres, when air moves through them. The size of the pipe is related to its pitch, that is, whether it produces high or low notes. Electronic organs, in contrast, produce sounds electronically through speakers. Before electricity was available, of course, the pipe organ was the only type of organ; a person (often a choirboy or a parish son) would pump a bellows lever that generated the flow of air to the pipes. The organist plays a pipe organ using manuals (keyboards; the instruments usually have two or more manuals) and pedals, which amount to keyboards for the feet. Older organs most often have a straight pedal board, in which the pedals are arranged in a straight line. Modern organs have a curved pedal board; the pedals radiate outward from the organ bench to the pedal tips and are set also in a curve from the middle upward toward the sides, allowing more comfort and ergonomic effectiveness for the performer. A rank is a set of pipes tuned to match the keys on the keyboard; each rank has its own distinctive timbre. Scale in pipe-organ construction refers to the length (height) and circumference (width) of a pipe. A stop is the knob or button that activates a rank. A division is a set of ranks, usually called Great, Swell, Choir, Pedal, and sometimes Positiv. Stoplike knobs or buttons that can be set to combine several manuals or divisions activate a combination, or coupler. Trackers, the original link systems between the keys or pedals and the ranks of pipes, are thin strips of (predominantly) wood.

In recent years, little distinction has been made between pipe organs and electronic organs. Both seem to be taken as viable alternatives in modern art culture; for example, the current installation at the Cincinnati Music Hall replaced a historic pipe instrument with an electronic one. The acoustic pipes produce timbre and pitch by air moving past an aperture, tempered by the shape, material, and fine-tuning of a physical pipe, much as any wind instrument, such as a trumpet, flute, or oboe, functions. The electronic organ imitates the actual acoustic reality of timbre and pitch by electronic means, relying on a speaker as resonator and an electronic generation of the same sound-wave size and shape for timbre and pitch. Overtones (the elements of sound that are usually not evident to an untrained ear) are produced in very different ways in the two instruments. Pipe organs do not require much more than regular tuning and infrequent repairs, but for a pipe organ that has not been maintained, the repair bill can be quite high.

The three most important names in Northern Kentucky organ building before the 20th century are Matthias Schwab (d. 1864), Johann Heinrich Köhnken (d. 1897), and Gallus Grimm (1827–1897). Of these crucial figures, Schwab was the eldest and could be called the founding member of the organ-building culture in Northern Kentucky. He opened his organ factory in Cincinnati about 1831, and Köhnken joined the company in 1839. Schwab retired in 1860 from the arduous business of organ building, and Köhnken took over the business. After Grimm joined Köhnken in 1875, the company took on major contracts. Köhnken retired in 1896, and afterward Grimm went on to build a few more organs. Both Köhnken and Grimm died in 1897, and the business was sold to Alfred Mathers in 1908. Between 1865 and 1892, every organ in the Catholic churches of Covington was built by the firm of Köhnken and Grimm. In the 1850s, Schwab built and installed the organ at the St. Mary's Cathedral along E. Eighth St. in Covington.

Schwab built what was perhaps his masterpiece for the German-speaking parish of **St. Joseph Catholic Church**, located until 1970 at the corner of Greenup and 11th Sts. in Covington. That instrument, built in 1859–1860, has been described by visiting recital organists as a direct American link to one of the most influential German organ builders, Gottfied Silbermann. The St. Joseph Schwab organ is unusual among Northern Kentucky Roman Catholic historic organs. It was saved from destruction by **Robert Schaffer** of the **Cathedral Basilica of the Assumption**, who organized the careful removal of the instrument from St. Joseph Catholic Church before the building was demolished in 1970. The German parish had been one block from the Irish Cathedral of St. Mary of the Assumption (now the Cathedral Basilica of the Assumption); in the 19th century, parishioners from the two parishes rarely interacted; they spoke their different languages and celebrated the Roman liturgy in their own culturally distinct ways. It is either irony or beauty, therefore, that the originally Irish parish of the cathedral now is a loving home for the German instrument from the German parish. The estimated cost to restore the Schwab organ to its original state was more than $300,000; however, it has been tended to regularly and is in basically good condition. The Cathedral Concert Series accepts donations regularly, which assist in the maintenance of the instrument. During his meticulous restoration of the later (1866) Schwab organ at the historic Isaac Wise (Plum St.) Temple in Cincinnati, German organ builder and restoration specialist Fritz Noack consulted this instrument to gain a full understanding of Schwab's tonal concept and technical construction.

Another instrument built by Schwab survives in Falmouth at **St. Francis Xavier Catholic Church**. Originally at St. Walberg Convent in Covington (next to St. Joseph Catholic Church), it is a small instrument with one manual and a small pedal division, but it is well suited to the size and acoustics of the church. It is still used as the primary service music accompaniment.

After Schwab retired from the company, **Mother of God Catholic Church** in Covington commissioned the firm of Köhnken and Grimm to build its organ. Köhnken seems to have voiced his ranks more in keeping with the popular American tastes of the day, a broader scale of sound. The broader-scale pipes allow for a more diffuse, perhaps more comfortable sound from the instrument. Schwab, in comparison, created instruments based on the traditional German idea of brilliant clarity of sound.

St. John Catholic Church in Covington houses the first installation by Walter Holtkamp's own company of Cleveland, Ohio.

In the same manner as J. S. Bach's friend and organ builder, Gottfried Silbermann in Baroque Germany, Ferris Steiner had the business sense to offer a free installation to the Diocese of Covington (see **Roman Catholics**) as a model of his work for demonstration. When it turned out that finances were prohibitive, Bishop **William Mulloy** allowed the diocese to pay for the installation in the chapel of the **Covington Latin School**. The first Steiner pipe organ installation remains in the third-floor chapel; it is functional and used for school liturgies. It is, however, like many other pipe organs in the area, in need of funding for repair and maintenance.

Another Steiner instrument was installed in the **Seminary of St. Pius X**, in Erlanger, which closed in 1986. Most recently the beautiful seminary buildings housed the Catholic Center, which was home to many offices of the Diocese of Covington; the Catholic Center has been moved into downtown Covington in the interest of fiscal management, and the future of the old seminary building and its organ remain uncertain at this time.

The most recent full-tracker-action installation in Northern Kentucky is the 2003 instrument built by the Noack Organ Company of Lawrence, Mass., for the **Lakeside Presbyterian Church**. Organist Tom Miles oversaw the project.

Hart, Kenneth Wayne. "Cincinnati Organ Builders of the Nineteenth Century," *BCHS* 31, no. 2 (Summer 1973): 79–103.

Listerman, Mary Lu. "Church Pipe-Organ Season Begins," *KE*, October 15, 2006, B3.

Ochse, Orpha. *The History of the Organ in the United States*. Bloomington: Indiana Univ. Press, 1975.

Rebecca Schaffer Wells

PLEASANT HOME. The community of Pleasant Home, located in the northeast corner of Owen Co., near Eagle Creek and the Eagle Tunnel, had two of the county's original one-room schools: one was for white students, the other for African American students. The church, the schools, and the stores at Pleasant Home have been the traditional focal points of life in the community. The church is known as the Mount Pleasant Church (not to be confused with the Pleasant Home Baptist Church in neighboring Eagle Hill), and it dates back to the 1840s. One of the common surnames in the local area is Lowdenback, the name of the family that ran many of the area's businesses. For many years, a member of the Lowdenback family operated the local store. During the **Civil War**, patrols from both sides of the conflict roamed Owen Co., and the Lowdenback store at Pleasant Hill was a favorite spot to raid. The raids took place so often that the family finally abandoned the store for the duration of the war. Another family member ran the barbershop and had a photography studio. During the first half of the 20th century, people countywide would travel to Pleasant Hill to have pictures made. A member of the Lowdenback family also had a jewelry store at Pleasant Hill. Only one store, no longer operated by a Lowdenback, remains today.

An Atlas of Owen County, Kentucky. Philadelphia: Lake, 1883.

Houchens, Mariam Sidebottom. *History of Owen County: "Sweet Owen."* Louisville, Ky.: Standard, 1976.

PLEASANT RIDGE BAPTIST CHURCH. The Pleasant Ridge Baptist Church, believed to have been organized on August 14, 1855, is located in west-central Pendleton Co., between Dividing Ridge and Portland, along what is today Ky. Rt. 467. The first surviving record of the church's business activities dates to September 8, 1865, when Kennedy Blackburn transferred to the trustees of the church one and one-half acres of property for $10. The earliest surviving minutes are dated December 1867. No church records exist for the period 1855–1867, except for two pages, believed to be from the 1855 minute book. The first pastors at the Pleasant Ridge Baptist Church were Elder Thomas Stephens and William Lancaster. Some of the charter members were Benjamin Blackburn and his wife, Kennedy and Angeline (?) Blackburn, Simeon and Martha Bush, J. N. Colcord Sr., Samuel Colcord, William Lancaster, Jesse and Susan Stith, and Elrod and Frances Tewell. The committee for construction of a new building consisted of Elder Thomas Stephens, Newton Belew, Jackson H. Gardner, J. J. Plunkett, T. F. Sanders, Jesse Stith, and James Elrod Tewell. When the church was five years old, it became a charter member of the Crittenden Baptist Association and continues today to send delegates to the association's convention. Sunday School, then called Sabbath School, at the Pleasant Ridge Baptist Church was begun in 1870. The first prayer meetings were held in 1873; in 1946 it was decided to start holding them weekly, and this practice continues today. In 1885 the congregation sold its log building to the school district and constructed a new church.

The church has helped support orphanages from its beginnings. In the earlier years, each fall a barrel of jars was received from the Children's Home, and the jars were filled with fruit, vegetables, jellies, and jams to be returned to the Children's Home at Thanksgiving, along with crates of eggs and coops of chickens. Today, members donated one day's worth of their pay for this cause. In 1939 the Women's Missionary Society was started at the church and in 1945 the first Vacation Bible School was held. In 1949 a parsonage was built on the Straight Shoot Pk. about a half mile from the church. When the Pleasant Ridge Baptist Church held its centennial celebration on August 14, 1955, the church's official register showed an attendance of 447 that day. On August 16, 2005, this church celebrated its 150th anniversary.

Belew, Mildred Boden. *The First 200 Years of Pendleton County*. Falmouth, Ky.: M. B. Belew, n.d. [ca. 1994].

Mildred Belew

PLEASURE ISLE SWIM CLUB. Pleasure Isle was a popular swimming pool located near the intersection of the **Three-L Highway** and Hands Pk. just north of Independence in central Kenton Co. The pool was a state-of-the-art facility when it opened in the years before **World War II**; it reached its zenith in popularity in the postwar boom years as residential development expanded in the area.

Banklick Creek (see **Banklick Creek and Watershed**), which runs near the property, was already a popular swimming hole and picnic destination before George Winholtz bought the property in 1933. He made improvements to the grounds, calling the area Island Lodge. Talk of constructing a sportsman's club to go along with the swimming hole and the fishing lake began around 1937. Irvin J. Klein headed a group of sportsmen's organizations that sponsored a park there, called Pleasure Isle, that offered tennis courts, an archery range, horseshoe pits, table tennis, badminton, shuffleboard, trapshooting, and even a nine-hole mini-golf course. The ambitious project was completed and opened to the public on May 25, 1940. A group of Hopi Indians visited the park that year.

In the 1940s a sand-bottomed pit was constructed that eventually became the Pleasure Isle Pool. The pit was replaced in 1951 by a concrete pool, which remained until the park's closure. The park was successful from the start. Pleasure Isle also became a popular destination for outings for employees of the **Coppin's Department Store** in Covington, for the Covington **Rotary Club**, and for other groups.

Klein, who became the first manager of the complex, led an effort to build a subdivision near the park. He and a group of local investors in July 1946 created the Pleasure Isle Real Estate Company, which completed a $1 million, 120-house subdivision near the pool along a road that became known as Pleasure Isle Drive. The housing area was created with Federal Housing Authority money and was intended for use by returning World War II veterans. The subdivision successfully repelled an annexation attempt by the City of Covington in 1968, before becoming a part of Erlanger.

A fire in February 1976 disrupted the operation of Pleasure Isle. On the morning of February 4, Charlie Robinson, owner of the complex, awoke in his office to the sound of breaking glass, which turned out to be caused by a raging fire. The blaze destroyed Robinson's on-site barbershop and bar, which doubled as a clubhouse for the pool. Robinson had just purchased the pool in August 1975 from Fred "Bud" Winholtz, who had operated Pleasure Isle for 26 years.

The fire was only the beginning of the end for the park. The 1980s and 1990s saw declining attendance as the pool competed with larger, regional swimming pool amusement parks that were opening in Ohio. Pleasure Isle's fate was sealed with the planned widening of the 3L Highway in the late 1990s. The final season was in 1997, and the park was demolished in 1999, though its famous entryway remained standing for several years. The widening of 3L Highway was completed in 2001, opening this already fast-growing area to further commercial and residential development. By 2006 a new family-activity center was built near the Pleasure Isle site. Called the Fun Center at Pleasure Isle, it did not include a swimming pool but did offer other social and recreational activities.

"Pools Out for Summer—Forever—Pleasure Isle Is Road Kill," *KE*, June 3, 1998, B1.
"Owner Flees as Fire Guts Pleasure Isle," *KP*, February 4, 1976, 6.
"Million Dollar Project Set in Kenton County," *KP*, July 27, 1946, 1.

Chris Meiman

POGUE, CHUCK (b. January 18, 1950, Cincinnati, Ohio). Charles Edward Pogue, the son of Charles and Betty Hick Pogue, is a Hollywood screenwriter, an author, and an actor in regional Kentucky theater. He grew up in Fort Thomas and graduated in 1968 from **Highlands High School**, where he was active in theater productions. He is also a cofounder of the Mercury II Theatre in Fort Thomas. Pogue earned a degree in theater arts from the University of Kentucky at Lexington, and his stage work took him to places like Odessa, Tex., and introduced him to stars as diverse as Cyd Charisse and Bob "Gilligan" Denver. Pogue began writing plays and screenplays after moving to Los Angeles.

He has written screenplays for major motion pictures, such as *The Fly*, starring Jeff Goldblum and Geena Davis; *Psycho III*, starring Tony Perkins; *Dragonheart*, starring Dennis Quaid; *D.O.A.*, starring Dennis Quaid; and *Kull the Conqueror*, starring Kevin Sorbo. *The Fly* and *Dragonheart* were nominated for a number of Academy Awards. Pogue has also written novels based on his screenplays. In 1990 he wrote and coproduced the television miniseries *Hand of a Murderer* for CBS, and in 2005 he wrote the screenplay for *Hercules*, another television miniseries.

Pogue is married to Julieanne Beasley and resides in Georgetown, Ky. He and his wife are active in theater productions in Lexington.

Schroeder, Cindy. "Actor Speaks at Alum Luncheon," *CE*, November 5, 2006, 1B.
"Script Changes Irk Writer," *CE*, June 9, 1996, D6.

Bill Thomas

POGUE, HENRY E. "BUD," IV (b. September 18, 1920, Maysville, Ky.; d. December 4, 2006, Fort Thomas, Ky.). Henry "Bud" Pogue, a developer, a real estate agent, and a member of the Kentucky Board of Education, was the son of Henry E. and Mary Parker Pogue, a Mason Co. distillery family. The Pogues moved to Fort Thomas in 1925. A 1938 graduate of Highlands High School, Bud Pogue attended Dartmouth College, in Hanover, N.H., where he played basketball in the 1942 NCAA championship game that Dartmouth lost to Stanford. During **World War II**, Pogue served in the navy. Following the war, he became a general contractor, developer, and real estate agent and helped to build many of the houses in Fort Thomas, including several in the areas around Rossford and Winston Hill Aves. He also constructed and renovated schools and public buildings in Cincinnati and St. Bernard, Ohio, as well as in Campbell and Kenton counties. Included among these projects were building projects at the Piner and Park Hills elementary schools in Kenton Co. and renovations at the **Veterans Administration Medical Center** in Fort Thomas.

Kentucky governor A. B. "Happy" Chandler (1935–1939 and 1955–59) appointed Pogue a member of the Kentucky Board of Education in 1956, and seven successive governors, extending through the administration of Martha Layne Collins (1983–1987), reappointed him to this post. He was one of the longest-serving chairmen of the board. Pogue helped steer education in Kentucky toward modernity during the 1960s, 1970s, and 1980s. For example, there were more than 1,500 one-room schoolhouses in the state in 1956, when Pogue was appointed to the state's education board; only about 50 of them remained when he left his post 35 years later. Two of his achievements while serving on that board were the reconciling of Kentucky's Administrative Regulations for Education with the Kentucky Education Reform Act (KERA) of 1990 and bringing board attention to the need for improvements to some school districts in Eastern Kentucky. A longtime member of the Northern Kentucky University Board of Regents, he received the university's prestigious Lincoln Award in 1995. Pogue was a Northern Kentucky civic leader for more than 60 years.

"Envision a New Urban Community, Then Cooperate to Make It a Reality," *KP*, January 4, 1983, 4K.
"N. Ky. Counts Its Successes—Group Looks Back on 35 Years Working with Chamber," *KE*, September 17, 2004, C1–C2.

Paul L. Whalen

THE POINT (LICKING RIVER). To early explorers and settlers of the Ohio River Valley, the southwestern juncture of the Ohio and the Licking Rivers, now part of Covington, was known as the Point. It was the place where migrating buffalo crossed the Ohio River for possibly thousands of years before the coming of the Europeans. Numerous **American Indians** of various tribes used it as a lookout post and as a meeting place during hunting and warring expeditions.

One of the first white men known to visit the Point was **Christopher Gist** in 1751, with his band of men exploring for the Ohio Company. Several friendly Indians took the group to **Big Bone Lick** in modern Boone Co., to view the huge prehistoric animal bones found on that site. Two women, **Mary Ingles** and her companion the "mad" Dutch woman (possibly Frau Stumpf), visited the Point in 1755 while attempting to return home after escaping from Indian captivity at Big Bone Lick. In 1765 Col. John Croghan came to the Point during his exploration of the western territory. **Simon Kenton** stopped at the site numerous times, the first time with John Strader and George Yeager in 1771, on their way back from a trip to the Falls of the Ohio (Louisville). About that same time, two explorers named Hinkson and Miller, with 14 other men, also visited while exploring the Licking River valley.

In the late 1700s and the early 1800s, the Point was a favored gathering place for military personnel, especially when assembling for attacks against the

Shawnee Indians living in central Ohio. In spring 1779, 300 Kentuckians gathered there in preparation for an attack against the Indian town of Chillicothe. After the battle they reassembled at the Point to divide the plunder and then returned to their Kentucky homes. That attack led, several months later, to reprisal attacks by Capt. Henry Bird against Ruddle's and Martin's stations, along what was called **Bird's War Road** in Kentucky.

In 1780 Col. **George Muse** was awarded a patent for 200 acres at the Point as part of his payment for service in the **French and Indian War**. Several months later, he transferred ownership to his friend Col. James Taylor Sr., who shortly thereafter sold the property to Col. Stephen Trigg of the Kentucky Court of Land Commissions.

In August 1780 an army of 1,000 men led by Gen. **George Rogers Clark** assembled at the Point before attacking the Ohio Indian towns of Piqua and Miami. In February 1781 ownership of the land known as the Point was transferred to John Todd Jr., and several months later to James Welch. In 1789 Francis Kennedy came to Cincinnati and began operation of a ferry between that city and Covington. Shortly thereafter his brother, Thomas Kennedy Sr., moved to the Kentucky side of the river and operated the southern shore's ferry landing (which became known as Kennedy's Ferry), perhaps initially renting the land owned by Welch. In 1801 Thomas Kennedy Sr. officially completed the purchase of the 200 acres at the Point.

The Kennedy family sold 150 acres of the farm in 1814 to a partnership of Thomas D. Carneal, **John S. Gano**, and Richard Gano for $50,000. That group of men established the City of Covington in 1815 and began the sale of building lots. They named the city in honor of Brig. Gen. Leonard Covington, a U.S. Army officer who had been mortally wounded on November 11, 1813, at the Battle of Chrysler's Field in Canada during the **War of 1812**.

"Early Incidents at the Point," *Colonel Covington's Chronicle*, June 1, 1979, 11.

"Gano Got the Point in 1814," *CE*, December 11, 1994, D4.

"Point of View," *CE*, June 18, 1995, H1.

Smith, Allen Webb. *Beginning at "the Point," a Documented History of Northern Kentucky and Environs, the Town of Covington in Particular, 1751–1834*. Park Hills, Ky., Self-published, 1977.

Tenkotte, Paul A. "Rival Cities to Suburbs: Covington and Newport, Kentucky, 1790–1890," PhD diss., Univ. of Cincinnati, 1989.

Jack Wessling

THE POINT/ARC OF NORTHERN KENTUCKY. The Point/Arc (formerly the Association for Retarded Citizens of the United States; now The Arc of the United States) of Northern Kentucky (The Point/Arc) is a nonprofit agency that provides educational, residential, social, and vocational opportunities to adults with mental and developmental disabilities. It also offers special educational services to assist parents and caregivers of children with mental and developmental disabilities while these children are receiving appropriate public education. The Point/Arc is the only local organization that offers a comprehensive and diverse group of programs in these areas. Furthermore, the programs are provided in an integrated setting as opposed to a segregated one. Located in Covington, The Point/Arc serves Boone, Campbell, and Kenton counties.

The organization was founded in 1972 as Northern Kentucky Association for Retarded Citizens (NKARC), by parents of children with mental or developmental disabilities; the name was changed to The Point/Arc of Northern Kentucky in 1998. Before 1972, the group that became NKARC existed under the name Helpers of All Retarded Children (HARC). It was a loose coalition of supportive parents whose children attended various private schools for children with special needs in Campbell and Kenton counties. These dedicated parents generated financial support through an annual holiday fundraiser called Joy to the World, held at the **Beverly Hills Supper Club** in Southgate. The fundraiser, which was continued by NKARC and The Point/Arc, has been ongoing and is now held at the Drawbridge Inn in Fort Mitchell. The current executive director of The Point/Arc is Judi Gerding, who has been with the organization since its early days and was one of the moving forces behind the formation of both HARC and NKARC.

NKARC's initial goal was to provide support for the students at the **Riverside–Good Counsel School**, which was dedicated exclusively to the education of kindergarten through high school–aged children with special needs. When the U.S. Congress passed the Rehabilitation Act of 1973, it required school districts to provide "free appropriate public education" to all individuals with disabilities and mandated that children with disabilities be transitioned into the public school system. Subsequently, NKARC, still primarily a parents' advocacy group, began focusing solely on services for mentally and developmentally disabled adults in the community. The group organized fundraisers and supported a variety of programs in Boone, Campbell, and Kenton counties. One of NKARC's services was to help make buildings more handicap accessible and provide transportation for people with mental and physical disabilities.

In 1978, when Gerding became president of NKARC, she recognized the organization's need to be housed in its own building. NKARC's first office opened at Ninth and Willow Sts. in Covington, but the agency remained there only a few years, until the city razed the building, clearing the land for a park. In 1981 NKARC established a permanent office by purchasing the Roeding Insurance Building at the "point" of Pike and Washington Sts. in Covington. The following year, the Point Restaurant, now called the Point Deli and Catering, opened at 45 W. Pike St., the site of an earlier restaurant known as the Clock Hamburgers. The restaurant established by NKARC serves as a real work environment in which to train individuals affected by mental retardation or developmental disabilities and teach them interpersonal and customer-service skills. In 1985, when NKARC's Employment Services Program was established to provide clients with new and varied job training and work experiences, the Point Deli and Catering became part of the new program.

Typically, clients are referred to the Employment Services Program by other agencies, school programs, or the Department of Vocational Rehabilitation. Trained counselors assist clients by assessing existing employment skills and potential future skills, providing realistic job training, and helping with work expectations, grooming, and punctuality. The purpose is to enable the clients to hold employment outside that offered by The Point/Arc Trainees usually remain at The Point/Arc for three to six months before advancing to a job in the private sector. Counselors work with employers in the community to match individuals with suitable jobs. After outside employment is secured, The Point/Arc counselors provide personal training according to the employer's specifications; they also provide lifelong follow-up coaching to clients to ensure their success.

Besides the restaurant, the Employment Services Program includes three other businesses: the Point Laundry Company, the Point Commercial Cleaning Company, and the Point Distribution Company. The Point Laundry Company began in 1996, with an exclusive contract to provide laundry services to the Netherland OMNI Hotel in Cincinnati (now the Hilton). Currently located in Dayton, Ky., the laundry employs 35 trainees and cleans 3.5 million pounds of linens per year. The Point Commercial Cleaning Company started in 1985 and currently employs two full-time and eight part-time custodians who service commercial buildings in Northern Kentucky and Cincinnati. The newest business venture, the Point Distribution Company, sells brand-name batteries and safety equipment to individuals and businesses. Trainees sort, count, bag, and package products; prepare packages for shipment; and take inventory.

The Point/Arc's residential program began in response to the growing number of cases in which mentally disabled clients' aging parents or families were no longer able to care for them. In each of 10 homes that The Point/Arc owns in Boone, Campbell, and Kenton counties, between three and five clients reside along with one or two live-in caretakers. The clients are carefully placed based upon their individual preferences and personalities, and the caretakers and the clients in each home operate as a family in an atmosphere of consistency. The success of a recent capital fund drive has made it possible to expand the residential program to include additional homes.

The agency's extensive Activities Program, begun in 1999, serves more than 300 clients annually through an array of events. The full-time activities director plans opportunities for clients to socialize in the community among their peers. Weekly events, such as dinners at a restaurant, movies, and trips to the museum, zoo, aquarium, or sporting events are chaperoned by adult volunteers and are open to any mentally or developmentally disabled adult. There is also a seasonal sports program, six annual dinner dances held at the Point Pavilion, and four out-of-state vacations scheduled each year. These events enable clients to make the connections necessary for forming friendships.

The Educational Services Program reaches thousands of elementary school students annually. The Everybody Counts program is a volunteer-run weeklong lesson for students in kindergarten through eighth grade. It makes students aware of the physical and emotional realities that people with disabilities face. Helpful training tools and specially designed lessons for students with disabilities are offered to schools at no charge.

In 2004 the Citizen Advocacy Program of Northern Kentucky merged with The Point/Arc, becoming Point One by One Special Education Advocacy Services. This program assists parents and caregivers of children with mental and developmental disabilities to obtain most efficiently "the free appropriate public education" that was mandated by federal law. Special educational advocates meet with concerned parents and caregivers to discuss the child's needs and educational rights under the law; they may intervene on the child's behalf at the parent's request. The advocates also provide information about resources and referral to other services if necessary.

For more than 30 years The Point/Arc (formerly NKARC) has helped persons with mental and developmental challenges by emphasizing ability rather than disability. Annually, The Point/Arc organization assists more than 600 clients with educational, residential, social, or vocational needs so that they may live, play, or work independently and improve their quality of life. It obtains 90 percent of its funding from its own programs and charitable donations and is supported by more than 1,000 volunteers annually. In 2008 the Point restaurant moved its operations from Pike and Washington Sts. to the Panorama Apartments on Fourth St. in Covington.

ARC of Northern Kentucky. www.thepointarc.org/ (accessed December 26, 2007).

Gannon, Tammy, activities director, The Point/Arc of Northern Kentucky. Interview by Sarah A. Barlage, January 26, 2006, Covington, Ky.

Gerding, Judi, executive director, The Point/Arc of Northern Kentucky. Interview by Sarah A. Barlage, January 26, 2006, Covington, Ky.

Kreimer, Peggy. "Point to Expand Training Programs," *KP*, December 21, 2007, 2A.

Schroeder, Cindy. "Point Changes Name to Emphasize Its Deli-Style Foods and Catering," *KE*, January 20, 2006, B4.

Sarah A. Barlage

POLICE DEPARTMENTS. With the arrival of European settlers in Northern Kentucky came the need for an ordered society, and thus the need for law enforcement. At first, county sheriffs had the responsibility of enforcing the law. For example, when Owen Co. was formed in 1819, **Cyrus Wingate** was elected the first sheriff of the county; gradually, as the population increased, a staff of deputy sheriffs was assembled. In the more urban areas, formal city police departments developed.

In Covington, Jacob Hardin was the captain of the patrol as early as January 1817. His territory was the city of Covington and eight miles out, and he soon was assisted by others, including Bartlett Graves Jr. At incorporation, in 1834, the city's first mayor, **Mortimer M. Benton**, appointed Isaac Martin as the first marshal. Eight months later, Edward G. Bladen replaced Martin, to serve a two-year term. It was said that Bladen patrolled the city by day, and when night came he sought his home and family; the door of his residence would be "rapped" whenever there was trouble. He delivered arrested individuals to police court, or to the mayor's court, an institution that persisted until the early 1980s (see **Court Systems**). From the time of Bladen until 1883, the top law enforcer in Covington was elected by voters. As the city grew in population and wealth, so did its police force. In May 1856, Marshal Clinton Butts lost an arm in the Turner riots. Butts served two complete terms, and during his third term, in 1874, he died and was replaced by his brother John. By 1870 an important aspect of modern law enforcement, keeping crime statistics, had begun. By 1873 patrolmen were wearing a recognizable dress uniform. On January 1, 1883, the first department under a chief of police was sworn in, under chief John A. Goodman. Goodman was both the last town marshal and the first police chief. As police chief, he reported to the mayor rather than being elected every two years; the system was altered in an attempt to remove politics from the head law-enforcement position. In 1894 the new city charter called for the chief of police to be appointed by a board of police and fire commissioners, which included men such as Judge **George G. Perkins**. In 1906, under chief Henry B. Schuler, the Covington police force consisted of 5 officers, 4 detectives, and 38 patrolmen. When the city-manager form of government was instituted, the Covington police department came under the direction of the city manager. Today, Covington has a 100-member modern police department.

The development of Newport's police force parallels that of Covington's. Before 1875, the city had a town marshal. The first Newport chief of police was David R. Lock, who served from 1873 to 1879. After 1933, the Newport police chief answered to the city manager, rather than the mayor. Today, Newport has a 50-member department. In the mid-20th century, in both Newport and Covington, the presence of criminal elements controlled from outside the region often put the police in the spotlight.

The role of the sheriff varies in Kentucky. In areas where there are local police departments as part of city government, the sheriff's role is relegated to that of tax collector, protector of the local county courthouse, and server of important legal documents. In areas with lower population, the sheriff carries out those tasks and has police powers as well.

Both Kenton and Campbell counties today have county police forces, which exist to provide law enforcement in the unincorporated areas of each county. For many years, the Kenton Co. Police were headquartered in a small building at 1825 **Dixie Highway** in old Lookout Heights. Today they are located at 11777 Madison Pk. in Independence. The Campbell Co. Police have an administration building along U.S. 27 south of Ky. Rt. 10 in Alexandria, along Constable Dr. In recent years several cities have merged their police forces, realizing dramatic savings in the cost of administration. One such example in Kenton Co. was the Dixie Police Authority, a combination police agency for the cities of Crescent Park, Crescent Springs, and later Bromley. That authority was dissolved in 1997. Another example, dating from 1968, is the merger of the Lakeside Park and Crestview Hills police departments into the Lakeside Park–Crestview Hills Police Authority, which continues today.

Since 1948 the Kentucky State Police have served the entire state. Formerly called the Kentucky Highway Patrol, which was founded in 1936, the State Police operate in Northern Kentucky from three command posts: Post 8, in Morehead, covers Mason Co.; Post 5, in Campbellsburg, covers Carroll, Gallatin, and Owen counties; and Post 6, in Dry Ridge, covers the remainder of the region. Statewide, there are around 1,000 troopers, whose purpose is to supplement county sheriffs and local police departments. Generally speaking, they have been involved in the cities of Covington and Newport only when their assistance has been requested. The State Police have full police powers; they do more than just patrol highways, which is where citizens are most aware of them.

There are several specialized police departments in Northern Kentucky today. The **Cincinnati/Northern Kentucky International Airport** has its own police force, which carries out the police functions needed at a major airport. **Northern Kentucky University**, in Highland Heights, has its own force, as does the **Veterans Administration Medical Center** in Fort Thomas; the latter force is made up of federal police. The U.S. marshals operate out of the U.S. Federal Courthouse in Covington and protect the facilities there. There are waterway police on the Ohio and Licking rivers, and there are various wildlife law-enforcement officials in the region. The railroads have their own police officers with full police powers related to railroad activities.

Flinker, Paul Joseph. "Development of Policing in Covington, Kentucky: The Nineteenth Century, 1815–1900," unpublished thesis, 1994, Union Institute, Cincinnati.

History of the Covington Police Department. Covington, Ky.: Policemen's Benevolent Association, 1906.

Reis, Jim. "Evolution of Law Enforcement," *KP*, January 10. 1994, 4K.

POLUSMIAK, SERGEI (b. March 5, 1951, Kharkiv, Ukraine). Sergei Polusmiak is an internationally prominent concert pianist and the Tom and Christine Neyer Professor of Music at **Northern Kentucky University** (NKU), where he has taught since 1998. Born in Kharkiv, Ukraine, to Sergei Ivanovich and Lyubov Ivanovna Polusmiak,

Sergei was less than one year old when his parents moved the family to Vorkuta, Russia, in the tundra near the Arctic Ocean. At age 11 he learned to play the piano on a paper keyboard, since the family had no piano. The following year he attended a newly opened music school in Vorkuta; passionate about music, he completed the school's seven-year program in three years. At age 15 he returned to his birthplace to attend Kharkiv Music College, a college preparatory school. After he graduated at the head of his class, he was accepted at the Kharkiv Institute of Arts, where he studied with Regina Horowitz, sister of Vladimir Horowitz. He earned a Post Graduate Diploma from the Kiev Conservatory. Between 1975 and 1998, Polusmiak served as professor at the Kharkiv Institute of Arts and the Kharkiv Special School for Gifted Children, Ukraine. He earned the title Honored Artist of Ukraine from the Ukrainian president. In 1998 Polusmiak immigrated to the United States.

A dedicated and tireless teacher, Polusmiak has coached pianists entering international competitions. He is also a jury member for major international piano competitions, such as the first international Competition for Young Pianists in Memory of Vladimir Horowitz, Kiev, Ukraine. He is the founder and director of the Ukrainian Children's Music Theatre of Kharkiv, which performed with Cincinnati's May Festival Chorus in 1992 and 1994. His piano students at NKU include international scholars from Europe and South America.

Among Polusmiak's numerous recordings are *Sergei Plays Sergei (and Alexander)* (piano works by Rachmaninoff and Scriabin), *Hommage à Shostakovich* (music for two pianos, with French pianist Thérèse Dussaut), *Music for Clarinet and Piano* (with Ukrainian prodigy Alexander Bedenko), *Beautiful Music for Friends* (music by Bach, Mozart, Chopin, Liszt, Brahms, and Rachmaninoff), and *Thérèse Dussaut, Sergei Polusmiak, Piano 4 Hands* (music by Tchaikovsky and Dvorak).

Polusmiak has performed concerts in Argentina, Belgium, Canada, France, Germany, Mexico, Russia, and the United States. He has appeared with the Cincinnati Chamber Orchestra, the **Kentucky Symphony Orchestra**, and the Russian Chamber Orchestra of San Francisco. He has also served as featured artist and adjudicator for the Ohio and Kentucky chapters of the Music Teachers National Association, highlighted artist at the NKU Summer Piano Institute, and visiting artist at the Pedagogical University of Luhans'k, Ukraine.

His daughter Anna Polusmiak (born 1983 in Kharkiv, Ukraine) has flourished as a concert pianist under her father's tutelage and has performed in numerous European and North American venues.

Gwynne, Bill. *Sergei Polusmiak: Sergei Plays Sergei (and Alexander)*. Cincinnati: Cricket Records, 1995. Recording annotations.

Hutton, Mary Ellyn. "Pianist and Teacher Building a Legacy at NKU," *CP*, December 2, 2005, 1B.

——. "Young Piano 'Lioness' Is Guest at CSO," *CP*, April 25, 2006, 1B.

Northern Kentucky Univ. Music Department. "Sergei Polusmiak." http://music.nku.edu/polusmiak.htm (accessed June 5, 2007).

Polusmiak, Sergei, to John Schlipp, e-mail, July 20, 2007.

John Schlipp

POMPILIO'S RESTAURANT. Since 1902 the building at the southwest corner of Sixth and Washington in Newport has housed a bar and a restaurant. In April 1933, at the end of **Prohibition**, Pompilio's came into existence there. Founded by Italian immigrants who had tried several previous enterprises, including moonshining, the restaurant quickly became a local favorite and eventually a famous Northern Kentucky tradition. Tasty Italian food, inexpensive drinks, and general good cheer lasted throughout the years (1933–1982) when Col. John Pompilio and his family owned the business and have continued under the Mazzei family more recently.

Pompilio's is where the famous toothpick scene, involving actors Dustin Hoffman and Tom Cruise, took place in the 1988 Oscar-winning movie *Rain Man.* Visitors often look for the yellow table where Rain Man (Hoffman) ordered pancakes in the movie. "If it is Tuesday, I want pancakes," he mumbled. Later, Rain Man spilled a box of toothpicks and immediately called out the number of picks on the floor to the amazed Cruise. Another Hollywood production, the 1993 skateboard movie *Airborne,* also filmed a scene at Pompilio's. For *Airborne,* the outside of the building was decorated beyond recognition.

Over the years additions have been made (dining rooms, boccie ball courts, parking spots), but Pompilio's remains what it has been for more than 75 years, a neighborhood establishment with regional appeal and a new national interest.

"For Pompilio's and Newport It Has Been 63 Years of Amore," *KE*, October 2, 1996, B1A.

Sweeney, Michael R. "Pompilio's Restaurant, a Centennial History: 70 Years of Spaghetti and More," *NKH* 11, no. 2 (Spring–Summer 2004): 2–20.

Michael R. Sweeney

PONTOON BRIDGES, CIVIL WAR. In late summer 1862, Cincinnati and Northern Kentucky were targeted for invasion by the Confederate armies of generals Braxton Bragg, Kirby Smith, and Henry Heth (see **Civil War**). After a Confederate victory at Richmond, Ky., the South hoped to gain control of Cincinnati, then the seventh-largest city in the nation and a major manufacturing center with strong commercial ties to the South. By September 1862, Gen. Lew Wallace, later author of *Ben Hur,* had assumed command of Union forces at Cincinnati and called for volunteers to protect the city. Thousands of citizen-soldier farmers, known as Squirrel Hunters, responded. They crossed the Ohio River on a hastily constructed pontoon bridge made of coal barges.

It was assembled within a 30-hour period, from roughly noon September 2 to sunset September 3. Architect Wesley M. Cameron (1813–1895) had said to Wallace, "Give me a steamboat and 48 hours, and I'll build you a bridge." Taking coal barges from the mouth of the Licking River, probably barges belonging to **Amos Shinkle**, Cameron lashed them together and topped them with wooden planks, creating a deck 24 feet wide. The pontoon bridge was protected by the USS *Izetta,* a Union ironclad lurking in the shadows of the half-completed piers of the **John A. Roebling Bridge** and effectively preventing navigation on the Ohio at Cincinnati. The engineer of the pontoon bridge was George A. Smith (1820–1888), who already had worked on the piers of the Suspension Bridge and later built the Cincinnati Street Railway and inclines.

During the latter part of the first week of September, thousands of troops crossed the rapidly constructed bridge, which stretched from the foot of Walnut St. in Cincinnati to the foot of Greenup St. in Covington. They quickly went to their entrenchments along the Northern Kentucky hilltops from Ludlow on the west to the District of the Highlands (Fort Thomas) on the east. The Confederates, under Gen. Henry Heth, tested the Union lines at Fort Mitchell, but they were repelled and had to retreat southward. As quickly as they had come, the Squirrel Hunters went home, back across the pontoon bridge. General Wallace publicly thanked the people of the region and the volunteers for their help.

The bridge proved especially handy later when the Louisville telegraph line at the bottom of the river broke: a replacement line was quickly laid across the bridge's planks. The pontoon bridge lasted until mid-November 1862; most importantly, it was this pontoon bridge that convinced leaders that it was vital for the incomplete Suspension Bridge to be finished. In September 2004 a Kentucky State Highway Marker was dedicated near the foot of Greenup St., designating the spot where the pontoon bridge had joined the Kentucky shore. Nearby, a floodwall mural depicts the historic pontoon bridge crossing (see **Roebling Murals**).

There was another pontoon bridge in the vicinity. It was a few miles up the Licking River, linking what was then Camp King (Meinken Field) in Kenton Co. to the Moock Rd. area in Wilder, Campbell Co., in order to solidify the line of defense across Northern Kentucky. A pontoon bridge was also built at Paducah during the Civil War, by U.S. Army engineers; it took them about three months to construct it.

Adams, Roger C. "Panic on the Ohio," *Journal of Kentucky Studies* 9 (September 1992): 80–98.

CDE archives, August–November 1862.

Cornell, Si. "Cameron Bridge—Why Not?" *CP*, January 10, 1963, 11.

Frank Leslie's Weekly, September 27, October 4, 1862. Excellent contemporary lithographs of the pontoon bridge.

Ramage, James A. "Panic in Cincinnati," *Blue & Gray Magazine* 3, no. 5 (April–May 1986): 12–15.

Roth, David E. "'Squirrel Hunters' to the Rescue," *Blue & Gray Magazine* 3, no. 5 (April–May 1986): 16–18.

A pontoon bridge over the Licking River near Covington.

Walden, Geoffrey R. "The Defenses of Cincinnati," *Blue & Gray Magazine* 3, no. 5 (April–May 1986): 19–33.
Workum, Bert. "A Confederate Threat Roused Support for Suspension Bridge," *KP*, July 12, 1982, 4K.

Patrick M. Flannery

POOCK, KATHERINE HALL (b. January 28, 1886, Covington, Ky.; d. April 12, 1948, Cincinnati, Ohio). Singer Katherine Hall was the daughter of John and Ida Herndon Hall. The family lived at various locations in Covington but mostly at 644 Sanford St. Katherine's mother, who was widowed, taught in the Covington Public Schools (see **Covington Independent Schools**). In 1911 Katherine played the role of Kathyrn Nordyk in Covington playwright Will Smith's *Thanks to Bettina*. In that production she sang "Childhood Dreams" before an appreciative audience on the stage at Covington's **Trinity Episcopal Church**. Katherine graduated from the Cincinnati College of Music in Cincinnati, where she was the recipient of the prestigious Springer Gold Medal for outstanding work as a student in music education. She went on to appear as a soloist in the Cincinnati May Festival and with the Cincinnati Symphony Orchestra. A member of Trinity Episcopal Church, she also sang there. She became the president of several musical clubs and societies throughout Greater Cincinnati. In April 1948 she died of cerebral hemorrhage at the Verona Apartments on Park Ave. in the Walnut Hills section of Cincinnati and was survived by no children. Her husband, Louis Poock, had died in 1923. She was buried in Highland Cemetery in Fort Mitchell.

Covington City Directories, 1890–1910.
"Covington Enjoys 'First Night' of a Local Author's Comedy," *KP*, December 16, 1911, 3.
Highland Cemetery Records, Fort Mitchell, Ky.
"Katherine Hall Poock Dies; Symphony Orchestra Soloist and Active in Several Clubs," *CE*, April 13, 1948, 6C.

POORE, FLOYD G. (b. August 25, 1937, near Flingsville, Grant Co., Ky.). This prominent Grant Co. physician, politician, and entrepreneur is the son of G. J. and Pearl Harris Poore. In 1948 the Poores moved to Barnes Rd. in Williamstown, where Floyd graduated from the Williamstown High School in 1955 (see **Williamstown Independent Schools**). He earned a BA from Georgetown (Ky.) College in 1958 and in 1962 graduated from the University of Louisville Medical School; he was the second-youngest graduate in the medical school's history. He was first married in 1957 to Shirley Thomas of Louisville; he married Margaret Mayo in 1972. He has six children.

Beginning in 1963, Poore practiced medicine in Florence, Ky., where he was a leader in developing the Florence Medical Arts facilities. From 1992 through 2006, he practiced jointly with Michael Goodman, with whom he developed the Family Medical Center on Barnes Rd. in Williamstown.

A longtime friend of Dr. Bill Collins and his wife, Poore served as secretary of transportation from 1983 to 1985 in the cabinet of Kentucky governor Martha Layne Collins (1983–1987), Bill Collins's wife. Poore later ran for governor and from 1987 to 1990 was a public liaison officer for Kentucky governor Wallace Wilkinson (1987–1991). During this period, Poore was credited with bringing into Northern Kentucky $750 million in state and federal moneys; he sometimes flew to Washington, D.C., to lobby for roads, bridges, and interchanges, along with Williamstown mayor Herbert Caldwell. Projects Poore was involved with included the **AA Highway** through Campbell Co., a new bridge on Ky. Rt. 36 near Cordova, a new Ky. Rt. 22 running west from Falmouth to Williamstown to I-75, and Williamstown's Barnes Rd. I-75 interchange. Poore turned the first shovelful of dirt in July 2002 for the interchange, which provides faster emergency medical connections with St. Elizabeth–Grant Co. Hospital (see **St. Elizabeth Medical Center**) on Barnes Rd. He also helped obtain federal funds for development of the Dry Ridge Industrial Park, where Dana Corporation currently provides many manufacturing jobs for Grant Co. citizens.

In 1998 Poore was cited as an excellent role model for students and became one of the "stars" on the Williamstown Independent Schools Board of Education Wall of Fame. He and members of his family have purchased their ancestral farm along Barnes Rd., where they plan to build an upscale residential development centered on the family's preserved and restored farmhouse. Currently, Poore lives in Florence and practices medicine half-time at Warsaw.

"Dr. Poore Moves to Warsaw," *Grant County News*, June 15, 2006, 3.
Feldman, Jason. "Big Changes Expected at Barnes Road Interchange," *Grant County News*, July 17, 2002, 1.
Kinman, Marlene. "Grant County, a County Whose Time Has Come," *Back Home in Kentucky*, January–February 1992, 14.

POPLAR GROVE. Poplar Grove is a community in northern Owen Co. along U.S. 127, just south of where Ky. Rt. 1316 intersects from the north. It is within the Poplar Grove Precinct. Life there centers on the Poplar Grove Baptist Church, located eight miles north of Owenton. Both the church (established in 1827) and the post office (operated from 1838 to 1903) derived their names from the area's grove of yellow poplar trees. Poplar Grove had a one-room schoolhouse for many years. The community was best known as the home of Rev. John Allie Lee, a hymn writer and a dedicated patriot. He made sure that each boy from Owen Co. who went off to **World War I** had a dollar in his pocket, and he was the impetus behind the erection of the Soldier's Monument at the Owenton Cemetery. There have been several businesses at Poplar Grove: grocery stores, a drugstore, a blacksmith, a pool hall, and a bowling alley; and various doctors have practiced medicine there. Poplar Grove was also the longtime home of **Rena Lusby Yancey**, a local historian and poet, author of *Kentucky Trails*, a book of poems.

Houchens, Mariam Sidebottom. *History of Owen County: "Sweet Owen."* Louisville, Ky.: Standard, 1976.

POPULIST PARTY. The Populist Party, also known as the People's Party, was a short-lived U.S. political organization established during the late 19th century. Never strongly supported in Northern Kentucky, it flourished mainly among farmers in the western and the Great Plains states. The movement grew out of economic discontent over the collapse in farm product prices during the economic Panic of 1873. In the late 1880s, the Farmers Alliance was formed, which had as its goal that collective action would be taken by farmers against commodity brokers, railroads, and eastern banking interests, which were blamed by farmers for their falling income. A Kentucky branch of the Farmers Alliance opened in 1890 and backed independent candidates for office that year. In 1891, the Populist Party was founded in Cincinnati, and its first official political ticket was nominated at Covington that year. In the 1892 state election campaign, the organization supported the Populist Party, which ran a full slate of candidates in Kentucky. The Populist Party collected 25,631 votes and elected one state senator and 12 state representatives.

In Northern Kentucky, the Populist Party ran many relatively unknown candidates and had limited success. Its local ticket was led by one Professor Crawley, J. J. McDermott, and John Oster. The Populist Party in Kentucky had its greatest support among farmers residing in the tobacco belt. The national Populist Party adopted a political agenda opposing many capitalist ideologies: it called for abandonment of the gold standard, unlimited coinage of silver, the abolishment of national banks, graduated income tax rates, the direct election of senators, and an eight-hour workday. In the 1892 presidential election, the Populist Party's candidate, James B. Weaver, received more than 1 million votes and carried four states, Colorado, Idaho, Kansas, and Nevada. During the 1896 campaign, U.S. treasury secretary **John G. Carlisle**, a Democrat, came back to his native Covington, Ky., to make a speech at the Odd Fellows Hall (see **Independent Order of Odd Fellows**), at Fifth St. and Madison Ave. During his speech, Carlisle was driven from the stage by an angry mob of Populist Party supporters, railing against his support of the gold standard. By the time of the 1896 election, economic conditions had begun to improve, and the Democratic Party sought to strengthen its base by supporting many Populist ideas.

Those two developments caused serious erosion of Populist support and the ultimate demise of the party. However, the debate over the gold standard and "free silver" continued to rage and was one of the factors leading to the assassination in 1900 of Kentucky governor **William Goebel** (1900). In later years, many of the Populist Party's ideas were adopted into law. The country began electing senators directly, instituted a graduated income tax, abandoned the gold standard, and eventually arrived at an eight-hour workday. Some economists, but certainly not all, agree with the Populist Party's position that remaining on the gold standard often created problems associated with tight money and exacerbated the banking crisis that occurred during the **Great Depression**.

Clark, Thomas D. *A History of Kentucky.* New York: Prentice Hall, 1937.

"People's Party—An Organization Being Perfected in Kenton," *KP*, September 3, 1894.

"The People's Ticket (J. J. McDermott and Professor Crawley Nominated for the Legislature)," *KJ*, July 14, 1891, 3.

PORK-PACKING. See **Meatpacking**.

PORTER, WILLIAM S. (b. 1824, Newport, Ky.; d. September 10, 1889, Newport, Ky.). Pioneering American photographer William Southgate Porter was the son of Walter and Mary Stewart Porter. William S. Porter and his Newport business partner, Charles Fontayne (1814–1901), made a major contribution to the history of American photography with *The Cincinnati Panorama of 1848*, which was published in September 1848. They climbed onto a roof in Newport, about where **Newport-on-the-Levee** is located today, and set up a camera to photograph a panoramic view of Cincinnati's riverfront. In eight whole-plate daguerreotype images, each 6 1/2 by 8 1/2 inches, they produced the earliest photo of Cincinnati. It covers a two-mile stretch of the Ohio River riverfront, from the public landing on the west (left) to what was then the village of Fulton, Ohio, on the east (right). Because there were no bridges or floodwalls at the time, and because the level of the river was much lower than it is today, many of the long-lost and forgotten buildings and streets of Cincinnati appear in that photographic panorama. The photograph shows more than 60 steamboats, many of which have been identified as research into the contents of this daguerreotype continues. The picture clearly demonstrates how, because of its river trade, Cincinnati became the sixth-largest city in the United States by 1850 and the nation's largest inland port; and it suggests how neighboring Newport and Covington also benefited from Cincinnati's economic fortunes. For some, this panorama depicted the promise and opportunities of an area that during the 1860s was still being viewed as part of the American West. The piece was shown at several exhibitions worldwide during the 19th century, but then it was lost for many years, until Porter's son sold the plates to the Cincinnati library in 1948. Today, the images from this daguerreotype can be seen as a printed mural on a wall in the library's circulation department; the original plates are preserved in the library's files. William Porter also crafted another outstanding panoramic view, that of Philadelphia's Fairmont Waterworks, in May 1848.

Porter's relationship with Fontayne ended in 1856, when Fontayne moved to Cleveland, Ohio; he returned to the Cincinnati area for a short time again, before leaving for New Jersey. Advertisements for photographic galleries that Porter operated appeared in newspapers in both Cincinnati and Northern Kentucky until his death. He had photographic shops on Fourth St. in Cincinnati, on Madison Ave. in Covington, and on York St. in Newport. At his death in 1889, his gallery was located on Beech St. in the Walnut Hills section of Cincinnati; this gallery was inherited by his photographer son, Edward P. Porter (b. 1856). William S. Porter was buried at Spring Grove Cemetery in Cincinnati; his wife, Francis P. Porter, survived him. Today, William Porter's photographs are collector's items. He produced countless individual and family portraits and became a well-known scene painter for Cincinnati theatrical performances, but unlike many artists, Porter produced his grandest achievement, *The Cincinnati Panorama of 1848*, near the beginning of his career; he was 24 at the time.

William S. Porter resided in a stately house that is still standing at 1850 **Dixie Highway** in Fort Wright.

"Another Nonagenarian Gone," *DC*, May 22, 1880, 1.

Cincinnati City Directory, 1890–1892.

"The City," *KSJ*, September 24, 1889, 3.

Covington Ticket, September 16, 1876, 4. Advertisement.

"Daguerreotype Studio Opens on Madison St." *CJ*, January 29, 1855, 3.

Kesterman, M'Lisa, and Keith Kuhn. "The Cincinnati Panorama," *Timeline* 18, no. 1 (January–February 2001): 14–25.

"Man First Appears before the Camera's Eye," *Life*, April 26, 1954, 146–53.

"National Magazines Take Note of Cincinnati," *CP*, April 23, 1954, 16.

Paschke, Margaret, "If Woods Had Tongues and Walls Had Ears," *KP*, January 5, 1970, 6K.

Spring Grove Cemetery Records, Cincinnati.

Williams, Caroline. "A Spot in Kentucky," *CE*, September 21, 1969, 2H.

Michael R. Sweeney

PORTER-FALLIS-LOVELL HOUSE. One of Northern Kentucky's largest single-family homes, the historic Porter-Fallis-Lovell House, at 412 E. Second St. in Covington, was built by Thomas Porter in the early 1850s, originally in the Tuscan Villa style. Porter was a Cincinnati merchant who had been born in Flemingsburg and had moved to Covington in 1849. In 1861 he sold the house to Daniel James Fallis, a native of Fredericksburg, Va., who had moved in 1853 to Cincinnati and had become a prosperous banker. Fallis and his wife, Ann Poage, had two children, John, who died in 1893, and Harriet. After Daniel Fallis's death of a heart attack on June 9, 1893, he was buried in the Highland Cemetery in Fort Mitchell, Ky. When Daniel Fallis's wife, Ann, died on January 8, 1897, she left the house to her daughter, Harriet, who was married to Charles G. Rodgers.

In about 1900 Harriett Fallis Rodgers hired the Cincinnati architectural firm of Elzner and Anderson to enlarge and remodel the house. At that time, it acquired its present Colonial details, including a massive two-story portico on the Second St. side and a new classical frieze that united the third-floor addition and the new two-story east and west wings. The family lived in the house until Harriet's death on June 13, 1922.

May F. Rodgers Lovell, the daughter of Howard and Harriet, continued to live in the house until her death on March 6, 1950. She was married to Howell Lewis Lovell Jr., an heir of the Lovell-Buffington Tobacco Company fortune of Covington. After the death of May Lovell, the house became the property of a niece, Annie Pierce Kershaw, the wife of Judge Jacob Kershaw. In 1950 it was purchased by Mrs. Julius P. Giancola, and later by Dean Howe Jr., who eventually became curator of a nonprofit organization, Mimosa Restoration Inc., that operated the house as a museum until 1998. The house was purchased by private owners in 1999 and has been completely restored.

Biographical Cyclopedia of the Commonwealth of Kentucky. Chicago: John M. Gresham, 1896.

Driehaus, Bob. "Mimosa Curators Leave," *KP*, September 1, 1998, 1.

Greve, Charles Theodore. *Centennial History of Cincinnati and Representative Citizens.* Vol. 2. Chicago: Biographical, 1904.

Langsam, Walter E. *Great Houses of the Queen City.* Cincinnati: Cincinnati Historical Society, 1997.

Jack Wessling

PORTERFIELD, ROSELLA FRENCH (b. December 28, 1918, near Owensboro, Ky.; d. November 6, 2004, Florence, Ky.). Teacher, librarian, and **civil rights** pioneer Rosella French Porterfield was one of eight children born to a poor farming couple. The family lived about 12 miles south of Owensboro, Ky., on a 40-acre farm that her father had inherited, in a community known as Crane Pond Frog's Ankle Station. Rosella's early education was in an all-black one-room schoolhouse about three miles from her home. After she finished there, she attended the all-black Western High School in Owensboro, where she was valedictorian of her graduating class. She then entered Kentucky State College at Frankfort and earned a BA in English in 1940. Rosella married Vernon Porterfield in 1944 and they had one son, David. The family moved into a home on Chambers Rd. in Walton, where Rosella lived for the remainder of her life.

Porterfield's first teaching position was at the all-black Dunbar School in Elsmere. She had no automobile, so she traveled to school each morning on a Greyhound bus that operated between Lexington and Cincinnati. One morning, she started to sit near the front of the bus and was told by the driver that blacks had to sit in the back. She sternly informed the driver that she had three brothers in U.S. military service, fighting for their country, and that fact entitled her to sit anywhere she chose. The other passengers all applauded her action, and a white serviceman, home on furlough, stood up and offered her his seat. Porterfield said that she never considered herself an activist, or even a role model, but she did not appreciate being treated like a second-class citizen. She taught the first three grades at Dunbar School for seven years and then became head teacher at the all-black new Wilkins Heights School, part of the Erlanger-Elsmere Schools. When she arrived at her new position, she found no books or supplies, not even an encyclopedia. She immediately told the Erlanger-Elsmere school superintendent, Edgar Arnett, that she needed materials to properly teach, and he saw that they were provided. When the U.S. Supreme Court ruling in 1954 made segregated schools illegal, the Erlanger-Elsmere School District, at the urging of Porterfield, became one of the first districts in Kentucky to desegregate peaceably. Porterfield retired from teaching in 1980, and the community honored her by naming an Elsmere playground and a school library for her. For many years she was a member of the **Zion Baptist Church** in Walton, where she served as Sunday School superintendent, organist, teacher, and choir director. She died at age 85 in the St. Luke Hospital West, in Florence, Ky. Funeral services were held at the First Baptist Church in Elsmere, and she was buried in the Richwood Cemetery in Walton.

"Before Rosa, There was Rosella," *CP*, December 18, 2003, 1C.

"Civil-Rights Pioneer Porterfield Honored," *KE*, July 25, 2002, C1.

"Rosella French Porterfield," *KP*, November 8, 2004, 8A.

"Rosella French Porterfield, 85, Helped Integrate Schools," *CE*, November 10, 2004, C4.

PORT WILLIAM. Port William, located at the mouth of the Kentucky River where it meets the Ohio River, was originally the county seat of Gallatin Co. The community was established as a town on December 13, 1794. Several Europeans had visited the area much earlier. In March 1751, pioneer explorer **Christopher Gist** and a companion came down the Ohio River, to the site where Port William was later built, on their way to the Falls of the Ohio (later Louisville). Explorer **James McBride** came to the area in 1754, while on an expedition on the Ohio River. Port William was named for Col. William Peachey, who received a 2,000-acre tract from the British government for his services in the **French and Indian War** in 1760. Records indicate that in 1771, explorer **Simon Kenton** camped on Peachey's land, and James Harrod camped there with his group of settlers while making his way to establish the first permanent settlement in Kentucky at Harrodsburg in 1774.

The earliest attempts to settle at Port William were not successful. The Ohio River Valley was the home and hunting ground of American Indian tribes, who were not always friendly to settlers. For example, a log house built at Port William by a family named Elliott was burned by Indians in 1785. A Captain Ellison, who built a blockhouse there, also left the area within two years after arriving in 1786–1787. In 1790 Peachey sold land parcels to **Benjamin Craig** and James Hawkins. In 1791, Gen. Charles Scott, who was later a Kentucky governor, built at the confluence of the rivers a larger blockhouse that was elevated and fortified with picket palisades. The location allowed Scott's command, the Kentucky Volunteers, to have a view up and down the riverbanks. Although there was still danger, the protection that Scott's men provided encouraged settlers to move in. Some 613 acres of Peachey's land grant was used to plat out the town of Port William in 1792. The new landowners advertised lots for sale on Saturday September 20, 1794, in the *Lexington Gazette*, citing Benjamin Craig and James Hawkins as among the town's sellers. Another ad in the paper on October 11, 1794, declared: "A new town, mouth of the Kentucky, to be sold."

The trustees of Port William met at the home of Richard Masterson, naming **Percival Butler** (Kentucky's first adjutant general) as town clerk, and John Vanpelt took the oath of sheriff. The court, the church, and the jail were housed in the homes of citizens until proper buildings could be erected. The first courthouse of Port William was made of logs and located along Water St., near the Ohio River. The first tavern was built also along Water St. in 1805; it was the Point House, an establishment visited by Gen. **George Rogers Clark**. Port William was already known as a center for trappers and traders, but by 1800, it also had a produce market and merchants selling wares. The confluence of the Kentucky and Ohio Rivers proved ideal for importing and exporting goods, and these activities led to the growth and prosperity of the town. Homes and buildings of old Port William are visible today within the historic district of Carrollton. In 1838 the town of Port William was renamed Carrollton and that portion of Gallatin Co. became a part of a newly created county named Carroll Co.

Carroll Co. Deed Book A, 1–13; Book B, 1–3.

Collins, Richard H. *History of Kentucky.* Vol. 1. Covington, Ky.: Collins, 1882.

Kentucky Gazette, January 10, 1789; September 20, 1794.

Evelyn Welch

POST & COMPANY. Post & Company was a manufacturer of railway supplies, such as passenger-car hardware, lamps, luggage racks, locomotive headlights, and switch locks. Lamps appear to have been a specialty; they were very ornamental and beautifully finished in bright brass or bronze in the Queen Anne and Eastlake styles. The firm also made student lamps for household use. For at least the decade of the 1880s, Post & Company operated in Northern Kentucky.

The founding dates of 1854 and 1863 have been offered for the business, but it is believed the latter date is correct based on biographical details available for the principal partner, Henry Albertson Van Zo Post (1832–1914). Post was a member of an early New York City family. His father was an ironmaster, and Henry worked as a draftsman as a young man. He joined the U.S. Army and was seriously wounded at the **Civil War** Battle of Antietam, September 1862. Leaving the army as a colonel, he settled in Cincinnati during the following year. He formed a partnership with Charles C. Perkins and Edward Livingston to establish a railway supply company on W. Front St., and the business was incorporated in 1869 with Post as the president. He returned to New York City about two years later to become a banker and remained there until his death.

Post was succeeded by an up-and-coming business leader, Joseph Kinsey (1828–1889), who began his career in the hardware trade as a clerk but advanced quickly to become a partner in Tyler, Davidson & Company. In the early 1860s, he joined the Globe Rolling Mill, located near the present-day I-75 bridge. By 1866 he was president of that firm.

Post & Company had its factory on E. Front St. in Cincinnati. A large office, showroom, and warehouse stood at the corner of Pearl and Elm Sts. In June 1879, the Front St. factory burned. Afterward a large number of employees were sent into the ruined building to salvage whatever could be saved. Suddenly, the top floor collapsed and fell, taking several other floors with it. Seven people were killed and many were injured. Kinsey was present during this ill-advised search.

Rather than rebuild the old plant, it was decided to begin anew in Ludlow, Ky. A handsome brick factory measuring 60 by 160 feet was built near the river's edge just east of the Cincinnati **Southern Railway** bridge. By 1890 a sizable wing built of corrugated iron and an L-shaped brass foundry with 25 furnaces had been added. There were 50 metal lathes in the lock department alone, and three to six pattern-makers were kept busy turning out wooden patterns for the casting department. In all, 240 workers were employed in this large and crowded factory. In July 1881, the company had abundant orders and shipped to customers around the globe. Post & Company was introducing a new line of lamps, baggage racks, and sash locks. A new 100-horsepower Corliss engine was being readied to boost production.

Meanwhile, a five-story warehouse of the company on Pearl St. in Cincinnati was stocking the wares of other manufacturers, such as Babcox and Wilcox boilers, Krupp tires, **Roebling** wire rope, Tredegar spikes, and Hicks and Smith double-burner center lamps. The Pullman sleeping-car company had adopted the latter style of car lamp. An entirely new product line, telegraph keys, sounders, and relays, had been added in the late 1870s. Telephones were also made, because Cincinnati was a pioneer in adopting this new means of communications.

Yet, Post & Company was hardly the lone railway supplier in the nation; the competition between the rival firms was intense. Price-cutting reduced the profit on many items to a thin margin, and seemingly every large city had its own wholesale railway supplier. Chicago, for example, had two such large businesses, John Crerar and Adams and Westlake. Overshadowing all suppliers was the giant New York firm of Manning, Maxwell, and Moore, established in 1880. This jobber and distributor came to dominate the trade by employing super salesmen, such as Diamond Jim Brady. Post & Company began to break down in the 1880s. In 1886 E. A. Kinsey, the secretary of the company, took over the retail sales part of the business in a new location on W. Fourth St. in Cincinnati. Four years later, George Puchta and F. X. Pund, as part of their Queen City Supply Company, absorbed the wholesale branch of Post & Company. Joseph Kinsey's death in 1889 hardly helped the fortunes of the business. In April 1892 the Dayton Manufacturing Company took over the manufacturing end of the business and the factory in Ludlow and abandoned the making of railroad car hardware.

Oliver Kinsey, the secretary of Post & Company, organized a new company, the Post-Glover Electric Company, which made electrical apparatus for steel mills and mines. How much longer the Northern Kentucky shop remained in operation is uncertain.

One relic that exists from this long-forgotten business is a locomotive headlight dating from about 1876 that is on display in the National Museum of American History in Washington, D.C.

Barrett, Richard C. *Illustrated Encyclopedia of Railroad Lighting*. Vol. 1. Rochester, N.Y.: Railroad Research Publications, 1994.

"Col. Henry A. V. Post," *NYT*, January 27, 1914, 9.

Kenny, David J. *Illustrated Cincinnati*. Cincinnati: Geo. E. Stevens, 1875.

National Car Builder 12 (July 1881): 77; 23 (April 1892): 66.

"Works of Post & Co. Located at Ludlow, Ky., near Cincinnati," *Street Railway Journal* 6 (February 1890): 70.

"Yesterday's Horror," *CC*, June 6, 1879, 1.

John H. White

POST OFFICES. Within the 11 counties of Northern Kentucky, there were fewer than four dozen post offices in operation by the turn of the millennium, out of the 354 that have existed at some time over the years. Most of the active post offices were the center of villages with concentrated populations, and nearly all served at least a store or two, a church, a school, a landing, or a rail station. Not every town has a post office, however. Many of the currently incorporated towns, as well as other communities and rural portions of the Ohio River Valley, are served by branches of active post offices, such as the Covington post office.

The names given to post offices have been richly varied, and although the origins of some names are obvious or have been recorded, other name origins have been lost. Furthermore, post office names have changed for various reasons: Names derived from persons or places known to or admired by their name-givers but having little to do with the place itself or of no significance to later residents, were often changed. So were names associated with abandoned establishments such as stagecoach stops, landings, mills, or rail stations. Names were also changed in response to alterations in the appearance or character of the place or to commemorate some important event that occurred there after the original naming. Some changes were made to improve the community's public image.

Of the post offices that have existed in the region, 143 (40%) were named for local persons or families, and 21 (6%) honored prominent nonlocals; 29 offices (8%) were named for distant places, while 59 (17%) had the names of nearby features (mostly streams); 20 (6%) were given geographically descriptive names; 7 were named after local or area activities (usually economic) or the businesses that engaged in them; another 4 referred to the counties themselves; and 9 had other derivations. For the remaining 62 post offices (18%), no name derivation has been determined. A post office does not always bear the same name as the place it serves; in Northern Kentucky, 66 offices (19%) served communities, neighborhoods, rail stations, or landings with other names. And 70 post offices (20%) experienced name changes.

Following is a list of all the post offices that have operated in the 11 counties of Northern Kentucky. Currently active post offices are designated by italics.

Boone Co.

Banes, 1830–1831

Beaver Lick, 1853–1944

Belleview, 1826–1828; reestablished. as Grant, 1826–1974

Big Bone Lick, 1820–? and 1829–1831

Bigbone, 1890–1941

Boon Court House, 1807; name changed to Burlington, 1820–present

Bullittsburg, 1813–1814

Bush's Cross Roads, 1829; name changed to New Lancaster, 1832–1839, reestablished as Grubb, 1877–1879

Carlton, 1879; name changed to Rabbit Hash, 1879–1912

U.S. Post Office and Federal Building, Third and Scott Sts., Covington; designed by William Appleton Potter, supervising architect of the U.S. Treasury, with M. P. Smith as the local superintendent; dedicated in 1876 and demolished in 1968.

Connersville, 1828; name changed to Florence, 1830–present

Constance, 1853–present

Corneliusville, 1827; name changed to Mitchellsville, 1848; to Bullittsville, 1853–1918

Crescent, 1888; name changed to Devon, 1907–1909

East Bend, 1856–1856; reestablished, 1876–1877

Elijahs Creek, 1846–1859; reestablished as Taylorsport, 1909–1959; continued as a rural branch of Hebron until 1968

Francisville, 1830–1845; reestablished as Sandrun, 1903–1908

Gaines, 1815; name changed to Gaines Cross Roads, 1823; to Walton, 1840–present

Gunpowder, 1883–1907

Hamilton, 1817; closed before 1834, when it was reestablished as Big Bone Landing; it became Hamilton again, 1834; name changed to Landing, 1836; back to Hamilton, 1846–1944

Handysburg, 1828–1829; may never have existed in Boone Co.

Hathaway, 1886–1907

Hebron, 1858–present

Hume Store, 1891; name changed to Humestore, 1895–1897; reestablished as Hume, 1899–1916

Kite, 1884–1886

Landing, 1882, 1901–1918

Limaburgh, 1885; name changed to Limaburg, 1894–1907

Middle Creek Mills, 1846; name changed to Boone, 1858–1869

Northcutt's Store, 1858–1870

Petersburg, 1819–present

Piatt's Landing, 1833–1848

Richwood, 1859–1918

Slusher, 1853–1854; reestablished as Berkshire, 1881–1882; reestablished, 1888–1919

Touseytown, 1811

Union, 1830–present

Utzinger, 1886; name changed to Idlewild, 1890–1910

Verona, 1834–present

Walnut Ridge, 1842–1846

Waneeda, 1901–1908

Bracken Co.

Augusta (or Bracken Court House), 1800–present

Belcourt, 1890–1891; reestablished as Waelder, 1901–1903

Bladeston, 1884–1886; reestablished, 1891; name changed to Cumminsville, 1901–1933

Bracken Cross Roads, 1829

Bridgeville, 1857–1861; reestablished, 1875–1877

Browningsville, 1854–1879; reestablished as Rama, 1881–1884

Chatham, 1871–1904

Coleman's, 1828–1830

Dix's, 1840–1842

Elmgrove, 1890–1940

Foster's Landing, 1847; name changed to Foster, 1850–present

Germantown, 1817–present

Gertrude, 1891–1906

Harmon, 1866–1870

Hillsdale, 1872–1874; reestablished, 1891; name changed to Bethesda, 1892–1894

Holt's Creek, 1843–1847

Johnsville, 1879–1906

Lenoxburg, 1874–1906

Locust Grove, 1830–1831

Locust Mills, 1839–1873

Metcalfe's Landing, 1863; name changed to Bradford, 1866–1956

Milford, 1832–present

Morris, 1893–1904

Mount Hor, 1871–1904

Neave, 1879–1906

Parina, 1880–1906

Pearl, 1880–1882; reestablished, 1887–1904

Petra, 1864–1904

Pleasant Ridge, 1837; name changed to Berlin, 1859; to Hagensville, 1859; to Berlin, 1859; to Hagensville, 1860; to Berlin 1865; to Hagensville, 1865; to Berlin, 1868–1913

Powersville, 1832–1904

Santa Fe, 1848–1861; reestablished as Santafe 1886–1905

Stanton, 1851; name changed to Hedges, 1853; to Hansonville, 1853–1855

Tietzville, 1870; name changed to Rockspring, 1884–1910

Walcott, 1901–1922

Willowgrove, 1891–1910

Woodwards Crossroads, 1825–1828; reestablished as Brookville (Court House) 1839–1901; name changed to Brooksville, 1901–present

Campbell Co.

Alexandria, 1819–present

Bird Woods, 1852–1854

Brayville, 1886–1903

Brent, 1890–1914

Brooklyn, 1849–1856; reestablished as Dayton, 1867; in 1896 it became a Newport branch

California, 1852–present

Camp Springs, 1871–1907

Campbell (or Newport) Court House, 1800; name changed to Newport, 1800–present

Carthage, 1828–1907

Cold Spring, 1832; in 1958 it merged with Highland Heights to form the Newport branch of Cold Spring–Highland Heights

Dale, 1856–1899; replaced by Station A, Newport, later renamed Fort Thomas

Flagg Spring, 1870; name changed to Flaggspring, 1895–1907

Grant's Lick, 1806–1950

Grant's Mill, 1817

Guber's Mill, 1870–1872; reestablished as Gubser, 1881–1906

Hawthorne, 1880–1914

Hayfield, 1845–1847

Indian Spring, 1858–1880; reestablished as Ross, 1880–1918

Johns Hill, 1890–1913

Kennedy's Ferry, 1813; name changed to Flagg Spring, 1817; moved to California in 1863

Kohler, 1900–1909

Licking River, 1879–1882

Marr, 1881–1882

Melbourne, 1891–present

Mentor, 1882–1976

Oneonta, 1890–1926

Persimmon Grove, 1856–1857; reestablished as Kane, 1860; name changed to Schoolfield, 1903–1909

Pond Creek, 1868; name changed to Clayville, 1876–1919

Pools Creek, 1890–1915

Rouse, 1900–1907

Silver Grove, 1913–present

Southgate, 1822–1824

Ten Mile, 1867–1910

Tibbatts Cross Roads, 1840–1875

Trace, 1891–1913

Carroll Co.

Adcock, 1894–1903

Carson, 1894–1903

Eagle Creek, 1832–1835; reestablished as Big Lick, 1836–1837

Eagle Station, 1870–1964

Easterday, 1890–1903

English, 1876–1975

Ghent, 1816–1876; a contract post office, 1976–?

Glass Hills, 1837–1858

Lock Number One, 1845–1846

Locust, 1879–1903

Mill Creek, 1847–1851

Port William, 1806; name changed to Carrollton, 1838–present

Prestonville, 1844–1876; reestablished as Wide-Awake, 1880; name changed to Prestonville, 1893–1957

Sandefer's Store, 1851–1873

Sanders Mill, 1816–?

Tandy, 1882–1903

Worthville, 1847–1861; reestablished, 1867–present

Gallatin Co.

Beech Park, 1825–1844

Brasher, 1881–1887; reestablished as Brashear, 1895–1931

Castleman's, 1831–1838

Conners, 1824; name changed to Napoleon, 1841–1912

Drury, 1900–1903

Ethridge, 1886–1911

Fredericksburg, 1816; name changed to Warsaw, 1831–present

Gex, 1898–1906

Glencoe, 1848–present

Munk, 1900–1939

South Fork Big Bone, 1831–1842

Sparta Station, 1870; name changed to Sparta, 1882–present

Sparta, 1853–1870

Sugar Creek, 1858; name changed to Sugar, 1894–1906

Walnut Lick, 1866; name changed to Ryle, 1885–1931

Grant Co.

Arnold's, 1809–1813(?); reestablished, 1820; closed 1820; reestablished in 1822 as Williamstown Court House; soon became Williamstown

Blanchett, 1891–1907

Cherokee Creek, 1830–1831(?)

Clarks Creek, 1868–1898

Cordova, 1849–1906

Corinth, 1868–present

Delia, 1890–1903

Downingsville, 1844–1846; reestablished 1847 as Johnson's; name changed to Downingsville, 1848–1909

Dry Ridge, 1815; name changed to Collins Store, 1855; back to Dry Ridge, 1855–present

Elliston, 1870–1976

Flingsville, 1876–1907

Folsom, 1893–1916

Foot of the Ridge, 1840–1841

Goldvalley, 1903–1912

Gouge's, 1855; name changed to Mason, 1877; closed

Hanks, 1898–1916

Hard Scrabble, 1860–1861; reestablished as Cherry Grove, 1891–1906

Heekin, 1887–1903

Holbrook, 1876–1906

Keefer, 1889–1903

Lawrenceville, 1876–1906

Leniton, 1884–1888

Macedonia, 1858–1866; reestablished 1877 as Jonesville

Mount Zion, 1869–1871; reestablished, 1889–1913

New Eagle Mills, 1870–1905

Sanders, 1820; name changed to Crittenden, 1834–present

Sherman, 1865–1969

Stateley's Run, 1854–1871

Stewartsville, 1817; reestablished, 1867–1906

Zion Station, 1871–1952

Kenton Co.

Atwood, 1890–1908

Bank Lick, 1848; name changed to Latonia Springs, 1858–1874; reestablished as White House, 1876–1879

Bank Lick, 1870–1905

Barry, 1832–1850; reestablished as Grants Bend, 1879; name changed to Springlake, 1898–1968

Brown's, 1863–1864

Buffington, 1893–1910

Cloyds Cross Roads, 1830–1835

Covington, 1815–present

Crescent Springs, 1891–1918

Cruiser Creek, 1868

Dry Creek, 1825–1866

Everetts Creek, 1837; name changed to Crews Creek, 1837; to Bagby, 1838; to Independence, 1840–present

Fiskburg, 1834–1858; reestablished as Fiskburgh, 1877; name changed to Fiskburg, 1894–1903

Fowler's Creek, 1855; name changed to Scott, 1866–1917

Greenwood Station, 1877; name changed to Greenwood Lake, 1878; to Erlanger, 1882; became a Covington branch in 1920

Honesty, 1886; name changed to Sanfordtown, 1893–1912

Kenton, 1858–present

Key West, 1877–1910

Latonia, 1878–1880

Licking Valley, 1842–1844

Ludlow, 1864–1906; now served by a Covington branch

McGill, 1892–1893

McVean, 1911–1913

Morgansville, 1891–1905

Morning View, 1855–present

Mullinsville, 1899–1907

New Canton, 1855; name changed to Visalia, 1859–1934

Nicholson, 1888–1907

Piner's Cross Roads, 1847–1858; reestablished as Piner, 1891–1903

Pruett, 1887–1907

Ryland, 1873–1879

Sayers, 1832–1835

South Covington, 1872; name changed to Milldale, 1880; to Latonia 1900; became part of Covington in 1909 and post office became a Covington branch

St. Johns Asylum, 1876–1894

Staffordsburg, 1850; name changed to Beauford, 1851; name changed to Staffordsburg, 1852–1855

Staffordsburg, 1890–1902

Timberlake, 1829–1835

Towers, 1900–1907

Visalia, 1826–1835

Weaver's Mill, 1850–1851

Mason Co.

Bernard, 1889–1906

Bramel, 1896; name changed to Needmore, 1899–1907

Chester, 1880–1892; soon incorporated into Maysville

Dickey Tanyard, 1830

Dover, 1823–present

Ebersole's Warehouse, 1852–1855

Farrows Mill, 1865–1867

Fern Leaf, 1854–1907

Hamer, 1848–1851

Helena, 1837; name changed to Millwood, 1858–1861; Helena, 1861–1924

Helena Station, 1878–1937

Howard, 1889; name changed to Sharon, 1905–1934; reestablished as South Ripley, 1935–1944

Kennard, 1891–1904

Limestone, 1794–1795; reestablished as Maysville, 1799–present

Mayslick, 1800–present

Mill Creek, 1830–1835; 1886; name changed to Millcreek, 1894–1907

Minerva, 1812–present

Moranburgh, 1886; name changed to Moranburg, 1892–1907

Mount Gilead, 1837–1906

Murphysville, 1830–1906

North Fork, 1828–1832

Peed, 1886–1906

Plumbville, 1886–1906

Rectorville, 1873–1915

Shannon, 1830; name changed to Sardis, 1846; became a contract post office and rural branch of Maysville, 1957

Shannon, 1873–1907

Slack, 1850–1884

Springdale, 1865; name changed to Jenkins, 1883; to Springdale, 1883–1964

Tangletown, 1891–1909

Tuckahoe, 1880–1909

Washington Court House, 1794; shortly became Washington, until 1990

Wedonia, 1892–1924

Williamsburg, 1813; name changed to Orangeburg, 1850–1906

Owen Co.

Arnold's, 1854–1857

Avery, 1890–1902

Balls Landing, 1887; name changed to Perry Park, 1932–1941

Beechwood, 1888–1963; existed as an Owenton branch until 1975

Bethany, 1876–1915

Breck, 1881–1904

Bromley, 1881–1906

Canby, 1873–1903

Clay Lick, 1844; name changed to Gratz, 1851–1993
Clegg, 1901–1904
Cull, 1900–1903
Dallasburg, 1850–1863; reestablished as Wheatley, 1886–present
Danish, 1900–1906
Eagle Hill, 1859–1913
Eastland, 1900–1901
Elk Ridge, 1879–1881
Ep, 1881–1903
Fairbanks, 1904–1935
Fawnburgh, 1884–1887; reestablished as Teresita, 1903–1938
Greenup Fork, 1876–1878
Hallam, 1883–1904
Harrisburg Academy, 1873; name changed to Harrisburgh, 1875; to Harrisburg, 1892; to Long Ridge, 1909–1966
Hartsough, 1881–1883; reestablished as Moxley, 1886; name changed to Perry Park, 1941–present
Haydon's, 1837–1851
Hermitage, 1862–1865
Hesler, 1880–1904
Heslersville, 1820–1821
Hills, 1869–1875; reestablished as East Eagle, 1875–1912
Jameson's, 1850; name changed to Harmony, 1852–1904
Lee's Mills, 1849; name changed to New Columbus, 1852–1908
Lemon, 1882–1884
Lone Oak, 1873–1875
Lusby's Mill, 1852; name changed to Lusby, 1894–1903
Macedonia, 1858; name changed to West Union, 1866–1888
Mallorys, 1888–1903
Margaret, 1892–1898
Marion, 1819–1820; reestablished, 1832–1834
Morgadore, 1901–1909
Mountain Island, 1816(?)–1827
Mouth of Cedar, 1816; name changed to Cedar Creek, 1825; to Monterey, 1847–1965
Natlee, 1898–1905
New, 1895–1938
North Savern, 1871–1876
Owenton, 1822–present
Pleasant Home, 1860–1907
Poplar Grove, 1838–1903
Proverb, 1916–1919
Rock Dale, 1852–1864; reestablished 1868; name changed to Rockdale, 1895–1952
Savern, 1849–1863
Scott's Mill, 1848–1849; reestablished as Stamper's Mills, 1849–1851
Severn Creek, 1827–1839
Slayton, 1895–1905
Squiresville, 1871–1903
Stamperton, 1860–1863
Sweet Owen, 1873–1902
Swope, 1902–1909
Tackitts Mill, 1891; name changed to Tacketts Mill, 1909–1951
Truesville, 1876–1945
Twin Meeting House, 1816; name changed to New Liberty, 1823–present

Pendleton Co.

Aspen, 1872
Aspen Grove, 1856–1862; reestablished, 1871–1873
Batchelors Rest, 1870; name changed to Mains, 1887–1903
Brass Bell, 1837–1842
Caddo, 1887–1903
Callensville, 1846–1860
Catawba, 1858–1933
Clayton, 1857; name changed to Butler, 1860–present
Dividing Ridge, 1862–1896
Doudsville, 1851–1880; reestablished as Doudton, 1883–1903
Elizabeth, 1862–1903
Emery, 1894–1903
Ezra, 1901–1905
Flower Creek, 1832–1874
Flynnville (or Flinnville), 1867–1869
Four Oaks, 1891–1903
Gardnersville, 1858–1908
Goforth, 1881–1907
Grassy Creek, 1820; name changed to DeMossville, 1854–present
Greenwood Hill, 1878–1879
Hightower, 1890–1903
Ivor, 1893
Johnson, 1830–1835
Knoxville, 1848–1849; reestablished, 1860–1906
Levingood, 1866–1909
Licking Grove, 1840–1843; reestablished as Ash Run, 1844–1857
Magoburgh, 1885; name changed to Aulick, 1885–1893; reestablished as Ernst, 1897–1898
Marcus, 1891–1903
McKinneysburg, 1890–1929
Meridian, 1855; name changed to Boston Station, 1860–1922
Morgan, 1856–1957
Motier, 1839–1872; reestablished 1873; name changed to Carntown, 1891–1920
Mount Auburn, 1879–1902
Ossipee, 1890; name changed to Pindell, 1902–1905
Peach Grove, 1875–1907
Pendleton Court House, 1800; name changed to Falmouth, 1807–present
Penshurst, 1887–1903
Portland, 1884–1904; reestablished as Schuler, 1891–1905
Travellers Rest, 1833–1842
Tur, 1895–1905
Wampum, 1891–1903
Wright's Station, 1855–1860

Robertson Co.

Abigail, 1883–1913
Alhambra, 1900–1933
Bratton's Mill, 1865–1875; reestablished as Bratton, 1882–1941
Bridgeville, 1890–1915
Burika, 1890–1916
Hitt, 1897–1910
Kentontown, 1830–1918
Mount Olivet, 1850–present
Piqua, 1889–1937

Rennick, Robert M. *Kentucky Place Names*. Lexington: Univ. Press of Kentucky, 1984.
——. *The Post Offices of Northern Kentucky*. Lake Grove, Ore.: Depot, 2004.
U.S. Post Office Department. "Site Location Reports, 1866 to 1950," Record Group M1126, National Archives, Washington, D.C.

Robert M. Rennick

POVERTY. Perhaps the starkest demonstrations of poverty in Northern Kentucky occurred during the **Great Depression**. Local political entities were overwhelmed by the need for assistance. By 1935 the situation was so dire that in Newport authorities stopped a mob from stealing food from a local supermarket. In Covington things were not much better: people blocked traffic to draw attention to their desperation. Families were living on only $2 a week. Some were literally starving. Cities and counties had relief committees and commissions but few resources to satisfy the needs of their citizens. Northern Kentucky in these years, and in the years before and after, shared the views of poverty prevalent in the state and the nation.

Poverty existed in America as early as colonial times. In 1720 the New Jersey colony, for instance, passed a law that permitted ships to be searched for old persons, especially aged widows; they were to be sent away so as to avoid the spread of pauperism. A century later, Liwwat Boke, a pioneer woman, wrote her observations of how the poor, the infirm, and the aged were treated at the end of their voyage from Germany to the United States. Passengers who had not paid for their travel were kept on the ship until someone purchased them, and people who were not young and strong (thus able to work) sometimes lay on the ship for weeks, until they died. Selling the labor of the poor was practiced openly as late as the 1930s.

Throughout U.S. history, public policy has danced between two opposing views: the poor themselves are responsible for their poverty, or the system is responsible. The "blame the poor" premise suggests that the poor must be prodded to change their ways. The "blame the system" argument suggests that one of the purposes of government is to provide for the most vulnerable citizens, as well as to create a system that provides equal opportunity to obtain society's scarce resources. As a nation, the United States embraces the ideology of individualism. Embedded within individualism is the blame-the-victim stance—the belief that one's success in life is dependent upon individual choices. Individualism means that societal factors matter little in one's life and that one's present or past economic status has no bearing on future outcomes. Individualism, then, is compatible with "blame the poor" thinking; according to this view, individuals are poor because they lack ambition and motivation.

Initially, the lands that became the commonwealth of Kentucky were part of Virginia, and thus settlers in Kentucky followed English Poor Laws, albeit through the political and legal filter of Virginia. In fact, many of the **Revolutionary War** veterans of Virginia were given land in Kentucky, often substantial tracts, as payment for their military service. Thus land ownership in Kentucky became concentrated, and wealth was concentrated as a result. After Kentucky attained statehood, the Kentucky legislature decreed that county courts were responsible for the territory's poor. To discourage pauperism, the county could issue a warrant to anyone importing poor people from other states or nations. A number of statutes and legal remedies aimed at the undeserving poor were instituted. For example, in the early 1800s, workhouses were established for persons declared vagrants as well as for those who broke the law and were too poor to pay their fine. Then in 1821, poorhouses were put in place for those who were unable or unwilling to pay their debts.

There were also attempts to ameliorate the suffering of the deserving poor. For example, Kentucky's Indigent Widows Act of 1820 allowed widows with less than $100 in assets to be given vacant and nonappropriated state land. Other deserving poor, the "lunatics and idiots," were given an allowance from the county. A little more than 100 years later, the Mother's Allowance Act was passed by the state legislature and the Kentucky Child Welfare Commission was established for the care of dependent children who were found to be neglected in some manner.

In the early 1900s, the state acknowledged that the elderly should be cared for but at the same time maintained that the fiscal burden should fall to the state or county only as a last resort. The law held adult children responsible for a parent who could not care for himself or herself owing to old age or illness. Thus, children's legal obligation for parents superseded that of the county. Yet the elderly and children who were deemed to need and deserve protection were, as late as 1914, housed with the insane and the "feeble minded," often in intolerable conditions—chained, even caged in pens. Activists and writers implored the Kentucky legislature to provide better care, and eventually children were moved to orphanages. In the 1800s, laws had been enacted that permitted nonprofit organizations to develop institutions to house children and the elderly; however, it was not until 1928 that the Kentucky Children's Bureau was established to replace the Kentucky Child Welfare Commission and charged with overseeing the care of children who were considered neglected, delinquent, or disabled in some form.

Other groups of the deserving poor arose as a result of war: widows and orphans as well as badly wounded soldiers who returned home from battle unable to participate fully in society. Even before the Soldier's Assistance Act of 1912 was enacted to address the needs of persons returning from military service, the legislature was providing material aid. For example, veterans of the Mexican War received artificial limbs paid for by an appropriation from the state legislature.

The Kentucky Old Age Assistance Act of 1926 acknowledged again that care for the elderly was a public duty; however, access to assistance was limited. A successful applicant needed to be at least 70, to have been a resident of the United States for 15 years and a resident of the county for at least 10 years, and to have no other means of support, such as children. Furthermore, any county that was in fiscal crisis was permitted to relinquish support after a year. By 1934, when the state was in the throes of the **Great Depression**, only 14 counties had a provision for the elderly.

By 1929, in the midst of the Depression, millions of Americans were on their way to financial destitution. Because of the magnitude of human need, most Kentucky counties could not provide adequately for all who were suffering. The federal government had to step in to help and was joined by the **American Red Cross** and various private groups, such as the American Friends Service Committee, which assisted in the relief efforts.

If there was a bright spot to emerge from the Great Depression, some would argue that it was the passage of the legislation that created Social Security. Because the elderly were hit hardest and had the least time to recover, passage of the Social Security Act, initially vehemently opposed as too socialistic, was assured. Over the years, Social Security, Medicare, and the indexing of Social Security to inflation have been key factors in the declining rates of poverty among the elderly. However, even with those programs in place, 15 percent of Kentucky's elderly still live in poverty.

After **World War II**, the nation's and the state's economies flourished. Poverty became generally invisible to most people, until Michael Harrington's best seller *The Other America* called attention to the continued existence of millions of poor Americans. Harrington's book helped to inspire President Lyndon Johnson (1963–1969) to begin the War on Poverty; however, the idea of "handouts" was anathema to the U.S. Congress's notion of individualism. Instead, programs that offered a helping hand were established (including improving education, health care, and urban renewal) for those who had been systematically denied access to societal resources. By the 1970s, President Richard Nixon (1969–1974) viewed the War on Poverty as a huge mistake. Even at that, the U.S. Congress passed legislation to provide supplemental security income for people unable to work. The Earned Income Tax Credit (EITC) was enacted during the same period. EITC is now the largest federal antipoverty program, considered palatable by policymakers because it purportedly rewards low-income workers. In order to take advantage of EITC, workers have to file a specific claim form with their tax return.

The recession of the 1980s had President Ronald Reagan (1981–1989) cutting food stamp programs, welfare, child nutrition, and the job corps. Then in the 1990s, when President Bill Clinton (1993–2001) declared war on welfare, he promised the poor that if they "played by the rules . . . [they] shouldn't be poor." Clinton signed the Personal Responsibility and Work Opportunity Reconciliation Act in 1996. Jeffrey T. Grogger, an economist at the University of Chicago, argues that the nation has made the welfare poor the working poor. At least 10 percent of former recipients of welfare are worse off than before welfare reform. In industries adding the most jobs in the United States, the pay is about 20 percent lower than for jobs being replaced. In the next 10 years, the 20 fastest-growing jobs will pay less than $20,000 a year.

As people are moved into low-income jobs, their housing options decrease. Coincidental with the demise of welfare, more than 1.3 million affordable rental units have disappeared, and less than half of them have been replaced. For every 100 low-income renters, there are only 39 affordable, available housing units. One in 50 of available housing units are substandard. A confluence of factors—gentrification, increased land costs, aging housing stock that continues to deteriorate, and the expiration of federal housing programs—have had a negative impact on housing for the working poor and those in extreme poverty. Of new construction, 80 percent has focused on the middle- and top-income groups, while only 20 percent has been constructed to meet the housing needs of those who are at the bottom economic level of the market.

Households with one full-time worker earning twice the minimum wage (about $19,776 per year) spent 50 percent or more of their income on housing. The Economic Policy Institute (EPI) estimates that an adequate monthly budget in Kentucky would require $2,319 a month—at least $14.50 an hour, or $27,828 a year. EPI's estimates for Kentucky—a relatively inexpensive state in which to reside, help to explain why the U.S. Department of Health and Human Services reported that about 25 percent of persons who have been removed from welfare are unable to pay their rent. Yet, 75 percent of those eligible for assistance do not receive any.

The Kentucky Housing Corporation (KHC), a nonprofit housing assistance agency, closed access to its waiting list in July 2004. KHC serves four counties in Northern Kentucky: Carroll, Gallatin, Grant, and Owen. Section 8 Vouchers (rental assistance) provide recipients the latitude to rent a house, an apartment, or even a trailer. However, in Kentucky there can be a two- to five-year wait for a voucher. It is no wonder, then, that a survey conducted in January 2005 found almost 20,000 Kentuckians without a home (see **Home-**

lessness and Homeless Shelters). The poverty rate for children in Kentucky is 1 in 5, and rural areas have higher rates. The most significant concentrations of poverty are in Covington and Newport, two Northern Kentucky cities that have experienced tremendous economic growth and development.

The modern long-term-care industry, which is reimbursed nationwide by Medicaid and Medicare at roughly 72 percent, evolved out of the 19th-century poorhouses. In Northern Kentucky these were run by county government until the arrival of the modern welfare system and Medicaid and Medicare in the early 1960s (see **Nursing Homes and Retirement Housing**). In 2000 a community assessment of the needs of the poor in Northern Kentucky was completed, titled "White Paper on Poverty in Northern Kentucky." Some of its recommendations were these:

—Health services, especially for the rural poor, could be improved with the use of mobile units.

—Public assistance for those whose wages are $7.00 per hour or less could boost their income to the level recommended by EPI ($14.50 per hour).

—A War on Illiteracy could be declared and reframed so that people who need instruction would not feel ashamed to come forward.

—Because most of the services for homeless people are concentrated in Kenton and Campbell counties, more services could be instituted in rural areas.

—Head Start could become an all-day program, with after-school instruction opportunities in the arts as well as in sports. Some of the costs could be a trade-off for the funding now used for child care. (The thinking is that less would be needed for child care if children are staying at school.)

—Because transportation is a major issue for those who work at low-wage jobs, multiple solutions are needed: corporations could provide vans to pick up employees without reliable transportation; church vans could be used to assist with transportation needs; and a volunteer bank could be established to provide volunteer drivers to transport people to work or to doctor's appointments.

—More churches could be used for day care centers.

Economic Policy Institute. "Basic Family Budget Calculator." www.epinet.org (accessed October 3, 2006).

Fischer, David Hackett. *Growing Old in America*. New York: Oxford Univ. Press, 1978.

Harrington, Michael. *The Other America: Poverty in the United States*. New York: Macmillan, 1962.

Henry J. Kaiser Foundation. The Kaiser Commission on Medicaid and the Uninsured (Kentucky and the United States), 2006, Henry J. Kaiser Foundation, Washington, D.C.

Kentucky Housing Corporation. www.kyhousing.org (accessed September 30, 2006).

Knapke, Luke B. *Liwwat Boke: 1807–1882, Pioneer*. Minster, Ohio: Minster Historical Society, 1987.

Northern Kentucky Community Action Commission. "White Paper on Poverty in Northern Kentucky," 2002, Northern Kentucky Community Action Commission, Covington, Ky.

PBS. "Frontline: Country Boys: Readings: A Short History of Kentucky/Central Appalachia," 2005. www.pbs.org (accessed October 3, 2006).

Pear, Robert, and Erik Eckholm. "A Decade after Welfare Overhaul, a Fundamental Shift in Policy and Perception," *NYT*, August 21, 2006, A12.

Reis, Jim. "Hard Times in 1935: Food Riots, Mobs Symbolized Severity of Great Depression," *KP*, April 21, 1997, 4K.

Sunley, Emil McKee. *The Kentucky Poor Law, 1792–1936*. Chicago: Univ. of Chicago Press, 1942.

Swartz, Rebecca, and Brian Miller. *Welfare Reform and Housing*. Washington, D.C.: Brookings Institution, 2002.

Barbara Arrighi

POWELEIT, ALVIN C. (b. June 8, 1908, Newport, Ky.; d. July 13, 1997, Covington, Ky.). War hero and medical pioneer Alvin Charles Poweleit was the second of four children of Charles A. and Aurellia Bambock Poweleit. Alvin and his brother were placed in the Campbell Co. Orphanage after their mother died suddenly in May 1917, and life in the orphanage taught Poweleit the self-reliance and resourcefulness that characterized his entire life. Five years later his father, a traveling salesman, remarried and the family was reunited. Poweleit was a star athlete and honor student at Newport High School, graduating in 1926. He attended the University of Kentucky for one year and then transferred to the University of Cincinnati to be near his future wife, Loretta Thesing. After graduating in 1932, he studied surgical medicine at the University of Louisville and received his MD degree in 1936.

Poweleit was a resident physician at Covington's St. Elizabeth Hospital and in need of money when he joined the U.S. Army Reserves as a captain in 1937. On December 4, 1940, he was called to active duty as the medical officer of Kentucky's newly formed 192nd Tank Battalion and was sent to the Philippines a year later. In the fighting that ensued, Poweleit became the first U.S. Army medical officer decorated for combat valor: he dived into a river to rescue two soldiers trapped in a burning vehicle. As the only doctor in one column of the Bataan Death March, Poweleit saved several lives during the ordeal and later, while a prisoner from 1942 to 1945, applied his vast knowledge of indigenous plants to keep fellow prisoners alive. Liberated in 1945, Poweleit returned home weighing a mere 99 pounds and with a guard-inflicted back injury that forced him to give up the work of a surgeon. He entered Harvard Medical School in 1946, retrained as an eye, ear, nose, and throat specialist, and in September 1949 set up his practice in Northern Kentucky. He was the first board certified physician for the eye, ear, nose, and throat specialty in the state. Thus began 39 years of service locally, a period during which Poweleit won acclaim as the nation's foremost innovator and pioneer in treating cancers related to his specialties. Over the years Poweleit, sporting a trademark bow tie and eyes twinkling, treated many thousands of people, often at no cost to patients. He kept the vow he had made for surviving his imprisonment: treatment was always free to veterans. He also authored two books about his war experiences, an autobiography, and several publications concerning the medical history of Northern Kentucky. Poweleit ended his practice in 1987 but remained active in local and national civic causes, especially those concerning the rights of ex-POWs. Ironically, after surviving so many wartime ordeals, Poweleit died in 1997 of complications from injuries received in a taxi accident just one block from his home. He was buried in St. Stephen Cemetery, Fort Thomas.

"Alvin C. Poweleit, 89, Pioneered Cancer Surgery—N. Ky. Doctor Bataan Death March," *KE*, July 15, 1997, B4.

"Alvin Poweleit, Noted Doctor Dies," *KP*, July 14, 1997, 1.

Poweleit, Alvin C. *Kentucky's Fighting 192nd G.H.Q. Tank Battalion*. Lakeside Park, Ky.: Privately published, 1981.

Poweleit, Alvin C., and James C. Claypool. *Kentucky's Patriot Doctor: The Life and Times of Alvin C. Poweleit*. Fort Mitchell, Ky.: T. I. Hayes, 1996.

Poweleit, Alvin C., and James A. Schroer. *A Medical History of Northern Kentucky to Date*. Lakeside Park, Ky.: Privately published, 1989.

James C. Claypool

POWER, PATIA (b. Helen Emma Reaume, March 1882, Indianapolis, Ind.; d. September 29, 1959, Canterbury, N.H.). Helen Emma Reaume was the daughter of Charles W. and Adelaide Schuster Reaume. From the early 1890s until the 1930s, her family lived in Covington, where they operated schools for the dramatic arts. One of these was the Reaume School of Elocution and Physical Culture. Helen appeared in local theatrical productions; she performed at the Covington Auditorium (in the former Carnegie Library) and at the Colonial Theater, 425 Madison Ave., in Covington. In 1910 she appeared in a play with the famed actor Frederick Tyrone Edmund Power in Cincinnati. In 1912 she married Power in Canada, and the wedding was closely followed in the Northern Kentucky newspapers. She began appearing in Shakespearean plays with her husband, assuming the stage name of Patia Power. On May 5, 1914, Patia gave birth to a son, Tyrone Edmund Power, in Cincinnati. A daughter, Anne Power, was born on August 26, 1915. Because of their son's poor health, the family moved to San Diego, Calif. After divorcing in 1920, and after a failed second marriage, Helen moved her family back to Cincinnati in 1923. She became the assistant dean at the Schuster-Martin School of Drama at Peebles Corner in Walnut Hills. She taught acting, elocution, diction, breathing, and articulation; and later Madame Patia, as her students addressed her, taught at the Villa Madonna Academy in Park Hills, Ky. Her daughter, Anne, attended Villa Madonna Academy. Her son, Tyrone, who became a Hollywood heartthrob during the 1930s, 1940s, and 1950s, attributed much of his acting success to Patia. He won the 1946 International Sound Research Institute's Award for diction and always thanked his mother for her influence. After he became a noted Hollywood actor, Patia Power moved to California, where she lived for several years. She died in 1959 in New Hampshire at the home of her daughter, Anne Power Hardenbergh. Tyrone Power, the movie industry's "Mr. Debonair," had died while filming the movie *Solomon and Sheba* in Spain the year before, but because of Patia's declining health, she never learned of her son's death.

Obituary, *CE*, September 30, 1959, C6.

Power, Patia, "My Son Tyrone Power," *Hollywood Magazine*, March, 1940.

Michael R. Sweeney

POWER PLANTS. Of the nine electric power generating stations along the Ohio River between Mason and Carroll counties, four are in Ohio, two are in Indiana, and three are within the Northern Kentucky region. Most are coal-fired, although the W. H. Zimmer plant at Moscow, Ohio, opposite the Campbell Co.–Pendleton Co. line in Kentucky, was originally planned as a nuclear operation; it was switched to a coal-burning facility during construction. The Ohio River is important to these operations because fuel to operate them is delivered by coal barges, and water from the river is used for cooling purposes. Locally, the area where these nine power plants are located is often referred to as the Little Ruhr Valley of the United States. The six plants just across the Ohio River from Northern Kentucky are important to the Northern Kentucky region because they dominate the riverscape in their vicinity and because most of them contribute to the electric needs of the region as well.

These facilities are owned and operated by regional electric utilities. Most are joint ventures: their owners share the tremendous costs and risks and maintain interconnection on a regional power grid that can provide backup power when needed. From the east, moving downriver, the three power plants in Northern Kentucky are

—East Kentucky Power's H. L. Spurlock Power Station, just west of Maysville at Charleston Bottoms, a facility that has been supplying power to Eastern Kentucky since the early 1980s;

—the former Cincinnati Gas and Electric (CG&E)/Cinergy, now Duke Energy's East Bend plant, at Rabbit Hash in Boone Co., supplying power to Northern Kentucky and Cincinnati; and

—the former Kentucky Utilities' Ghent Generating Station in Carroll Co., now part of the holding company that owns Louisville Gas & Electric and provides electricity for Central Kentucky.

In Ohio the power plants are

—the J. M. Stuart Plant, at Manchester, Ohio, opposite Mason Co., Ky., a joint venture of CG&E/Cinergy (Duke), Dayton Power & Light, and Columbus & Southern Electric;

—the William H. Zimmer facility at Moscow, Ohio, opposite the Campbell Co./Pendleton Co. line in Ky., group-owned by the former CG&E/Cinergy (Duke), Dayton Power & Light, and Columbus & Southern Electric, starting in the 1980s;

—the former CG&E/Cinergy (Duke) Walter C. Beckjord plant at New Richmond, Ohio, opposite Melbourne in Campbell Co., Ky., operating since 1952; and

—Miami Fort, at North Bend, Ohio, where the Great Miami River flows into the Ohio River in western Hamilton Co., a joint venture of the former CG&E/Cinergy (Duke), Dayton Power & Light, and Columbus & Southern Electric, opposite Boone Co., Ky., beginning in 1925.

In Indiana there are two power-generating facilities opposite the Northern Kentucky region:

—the Tanner's Creek facility near Lawrenceburg, an American Electric Power property; and

—the former CG&E/Cinergy (Duke) Markland Dam hydroelectric plant at Switzerland, Ind.

Just outside the region are several other plants both upriver and downriver, such as the Clifty Creek facility and the failed nuclear operation Marble Hill, both near Madison, Ind. A third plant, at Patriot, Ind., for the Indianapolis Power & Light Company, was planned to open during the early 1980s but was not built.

These operations produce enormous amounts of electric power. For example, the Ghent plant, which began in 1973, at one time generated 75 percent of Kentucky Utilities' power—more than the company's four other coal-burning stations combined. That station alone consumes, on average, some 14,000 tons of coal each operating day.

At the Beckjord plant, the ash by-product is barged across the Ohio River, to be off-loaded at the new **Lafarge** plant in Silver Grove, Ky., where it is used in the making of drywall. The new Gilbert Unit in operation at Spurlock has the ability to burn, in addition to coal, more than 1 million car tires and 150,000 tons of sawdust and other wood products annually. In recent years these plants have made improvements with regard to their emissions under new EPA compliance requirements.

These power plants represent the results of consolidation. At the beginning of the electric age, in the 1880s, there were several small power-generating stations throughout Northern Kentucky cities, such as the one at the **Dueber Watch Case Company** in Newport, which sold power in its neighborhood, ancillary to its main line of business. Later, the **Wadsworth Watch Case Company** in Dayton, Ky., did the same. The first street lights in Newport were powered by electricity generated in a Covington station along Madison Ave. and delivered by wires strung across Covington's Fourth Street Bridge to Newport. In 1901, when the new street lamps in Newport, Bellevue, and Dayton were installed, power for them was switched to the electric generating powerhouse at the foot of 11th St. in Newport, the same building that supplied the **Green Line** streetcars. Gradually, as the utilities added generating capacity, these smaller plants closed, because it was easier, less expensive, and cleaner to buy power from the line in the street.

Today these power plants, recognized by their smokestacks that seem to reach to the heavens, are attended by contradictions. Consumers have come to expect convenient, clean, and instantaneous electricity at the flick of a switch; yet environmentalists and health officials warn of the environmental dangers inherent in power plants because of the tons of emissions. In the past 30 years, stack scrubbers and other means have been used to reduce the amount of sulfuric and nitrous oxides released, but the northeastern states, as recipients of what blows upwind and out of the Little Ruhr Valley, continue to file suits in federal court for acid rain damage.

"Clear the Air." www.cleartheair.org (accessed May 10, 2006).

"'Little Ruhr Valley' Gets Big Power Plan," *KP*, October 16, 1970, 1.

"Power Plant OK'D," *KP*, September 14, 2005, A10.

"Pulling the Plug," *KP*, May 3, 1977, 4.

POWERSVILLE. Powersville, established in the center of Bracken Co. on the main road between Augusta and Georgetown, may have been named for John F. Power, who in 1833 became the town's first postmaster. Several of the first settlers were named Blade, Hamilton, Morford, Nesbitt, Power, and Wood. The location of the town was well positioned for an overnight stay on the journey from Augusta to Cynthiana, and perhaps this is why Capt. **Phillip Buckner** moved to this area when he sought a more remote dwelling than the town of Augusta offered. His lodge and sporting activities involving his fox-hunting hounds became the focus of the remainder of his life. Buckner is buried near the center of town on Goose Ridge, and his Kentucky State Historical Marker is located along Ky. Rt. 19. Since 1884, the Downard family has operated a general store or a hardware store in Powersville. Before the advent of the automobile, Ben Croswell was a prominent blacksmith and wagon maker in town.

Bracken Co. Extension Homemakers. *History of Bracken County.* Bicentennial ed. Brooksville, Ky.: Bracken Co. Extension Homemakers, 2002.

Caroline R. Miller

PRESBYTERIANS. Presbyterians have been influential in Northern Kentucky's history from the earliest years of its settlement. Rev. David Rice (1733–1816), who came to the Kentucky frontier in 1783, is considered the father of the Presbyterian church in Kentucky; he chaired a conference in 1785 to organize Presbyterianism in Kentucky. As a member of the 1792 constitutional convention, which wrote the first constitution for the State of Kentucky, Rice led an attempt to ban slavery from the state but lost by a vote of 26-16. The first **antislavery** publication west of the Appalachians was written by Rice in 1792.

Early Kentucky Presbyterians included slaves, freed slaves, slave owners, and non-slave-owners. The Presbyterian Church in Kentucky reflected the population of the state at that time in having a divided stand on slavery and regional differences. The proximity of Kentucky, a border state, to free states mitigated the effects of slavery as an institution and kept the question of the abolition of slavery in debate. In 1794 the Kentucky Presbytery passed a resolution regarding the treatment of slaves: they should be taught to read, provided religious instruction, and given vocational training to prepare them for freedom. In 1796 the General Assembly of the Presbyterian Church voted that slavery was a moral evil but recognized that slave owners were not all alike. Some freed their slaves due to their religious convictions and others obtained and kept slaves out of ethical concerns for them. The practice of some Presbyterian churches of excluding slave owners from membership was not upheld.

When Kentuckians gathered in 1849 to write a new state constitution, Presbyterians again led the antislavery movement. Presbyterian William Breckinridge gave an emancipation address and Presbyterian Robert Breckinridge wrote the motion. Of the 21 ministers who served as delegates, 13 were Presbyterians, as were many of the lay delegates. The proslavery forces won once again, and Kentucky remained a slave state. When Kentucky failed to abolish slavery, the Presbyterian Church endorsed gradual emancipation. Presbyterians decided their primary mission was evangelism, not social reform. Their efforts were redirected toward conversion of members of both races to Christianity, with the hope that the men in power would, with conversion, have a change of heart and then work to change the law. The thrust of religion became inward rather than outward, individual rather than societal.

Presbyterianism in Northern Kentucky has historical ties to Cincinnati and especially to the Beecher family. Rev. Lyman Beecher and his seven sons were early Presbyterian ministers and leaders in the denomination as well as noted scholars, educators, and reformers. Lyman Beecher was the first president of Lane Seminary in Cincinnati. One of his three daughters was Harriet Beecher Stowe, who married a Presbyterian minister and later became the well-known author of *Uncle Tom's Cabin,* a book that had a profound impact on the antislavery movement in the decade before the **Civil War**. Her sister Isabella was a national leader in the women's suffrage movement.

Presbyterian Rev. **John G. Fee**, a native of Bracken Co., was an outspoken abolitionist and a founder of Berea College. Presbyterian Rev. John Rankin (1793–1886), who moved from Kentucky to Ripley, Ohio, opposite Mason Co., after his life was threatened, was active there in the antislavery movement and the **Underground Railroad**. He founded the American Reform Tract and Book Society and published more than 200 books and tracts, as well as a newspaper. He founded Iberia College in Ohio in 1854 and was a friend of the Beechers.

The **Washington Presbyterian Church** in Washington (now Maysville), Ky., established in 1792, is the oldest Presbyterian church in Northern Kentucky. The **Sharon Presbyterian Church** and the **Augusta Presbyterian Church** both trace their roots to a Bracken Co. congregation of 1803; the **First Presbyterian Church** in Maysville dates to 1817; and the **Richwood Presbyterian Church** in Boone Co. was founded in 1834. The Augusta, Maysville, Sharon, and Washington churches, as well as the Mayslick Presbyterian Church, currently belong to the Transylvania Presbytery of Kentucky. The **Community of Faith Presbyterian Church** in Covington, the **Lakeside Presbyterian Church** in Lakeside Park, and the Richwood Presbyterian Church are members of the Presbytery of Cincinnati, as are congregations in Dayton (Ky.), Dry Ridge, Fort Thomas, and Union. The historic **First Presbyterian Church** of Newport and **Lebanon Presbyterian Church** are now closed.

Presbyterians derive their name from the Greek word *presbyteros,* which means "elder." They have a democratic form of government, with leaders, or elders, elected by the members; ruling elders are members of the congregation, and teaching elders are ordained ministers. The ruling elders and the minister convene as a Session and are responsible for the governance and mission of the church. At congregational meetings, each member has a vote. A minister moderates the meetings, and decisions are documented in the Session Books, which are the official church record. The minister is elected by the congregation and approved by the Presbytery, the governing body of several churches in the same geographic area.

Presbyterianism emphasizes the sovereignty of God, the authority of the Bible, and salvation by the grace of God through faith in Jesus Christ. Presbyterians believe in the forgiveness of sin. Their five primary tenets can be stated as the love of God, the word of God, faith in God, belief in Christ, and glory to God. The roots of Presbyterianism can be traced back to Martin Luther and the Protestant Reformation in 1517. Luther influenced the French-Swiss theologian John Calvin (1509–1564), who several decades later developed Reformed Theology. Calvin, in turn, taught those principles to Scotsman John Knox (1505–1572) in Switzerland, and Knox returned to Scotland to join the Reformation in 1560. The Presbyterian Church then arose in Scotland and spread from there to other countries. Rev. Francis MacKemie arrived in Philadelphia from Ireland in 1683 and organized the first Presbyterian church in the United States in 1706. The first General Assembly was convened in Philadelphia in 1789 by Rev. John Witherspoon, the only minister to sign the Declaration of Independence.

The Presbyterian Church has a long history of separations, based on doctrinal differences, and reunifications. The largest Presbyterian denomination is the Presbyterian Church (U.S.A.), created when the "southern" and "northern" branches reunited in 1983; the denomination's national headquarters are in Louisville. In 2006 the total membership was over 2 million, and there were more than 11,000 churches in all 50 states.

Boles, John B. *Religion in Antebellum Kentucky.* Lexington: Univ. of Kentucky Press, 1976.

Davidson, Robert. *History of the Presbyterian Church in the State of Kentucky.* Lexington, Ky.: Charles Marshall, 1847.

Weeks, Louis B. *Kentucky Presbyterians.* Atlanta, Ga.: John Knox Press, 1983.

Ruth Wade Cox Brunings

PRESCOTT, MARIE (b. Marie Victor, 1850, Lexington, Ky.; d. July 28, 1893, New York City). Actress Marie Prescott was the daughter of William B. and Mary Jane Hawkins Davis Victor. Marie attended schools in Lexington, Paris, and Carrollton, Ky. In 1869 her father was committed to the Eastern State Lunatic Asylum at Lexington. The same year, she married Edward James Burke of Ohio, who built a dry goods and grocery store in Carrollton; the building still exists. They had three sons, Victor, Norbourne, and Edward. The family moved to Cincinnati in 1871, remaining until October 1875; while they were there Norbourne died as a baby. They then moved to Covington, and two months later, Marie's husband left the family.

Marie transformed herself into an actress, vowing to become a star. She took her brother-in-law's middle name, Prescott, and studied acting. Her first appearance was in 1877 at Cincinnati's Grand Opera House as Lady Macbeth. Roles as Lady Teazle in *The School for Scandal* and as Nancy Sykes in *Oliver Twist* followed. Her manager, R. E. J. Miles, next contracted her for a tour, on which she appeared in Chicago with Robert McWade in *Rip Van Winkle* and in Philadelphia playing roles in *Heroine in Rags* and *How Women Love.* She returned to Kentucky, where she appeared in *Travels in Germany* at Cynthiana, received a testimonial benefit in Covington, and also performed in Lexington.

In fall 1877, she went to New York City, engaged that season by Col. William E. Sinn to perform in Brooklyn. The next season Maggie Mitchell engaged her. She made her New York City debut in April 1878, as John McCullough's leading lady. The *Brooklyn Eagle* newspaper described her as a "rising and talented young actress." Prescott next spent two seasons in San Francisco. Hailed as "one of the most deserving young actresses on the stage," she returned to New York City to join Dion Boucicault's company in 1879. After Boucicault closed, she joined Daniel Edward Bandmann's company, then John Stetson's. From March through May 1880, she toured New England playing roles in *Galley Slave* and *Mother and Daughter.*

By late August 1880, she organized her own company, with Ernest Harvier, her lover, as manager. They traveled south along the Ohio River, stopping in Louisville late in September. The cast expected more touring, but Prescott and Harvier left town, stranding the company. Harvier testified in a sensational libel trial two years later that Prescott had needed an abortion.

In December 1880, Tomasso Salvini, the famed Italian actor, invited Prescott to join him in a collaboration that lasted through the 1883 season. As Salvini's leading lady, she toured from Boston to Atlanta, acting in *The Gladiator, Othello, Macbeth,* and *Ingomar.* Recently divorced from Burke, she swore in New York City Superior Court that she had married William Perzel in New York City. Advertisements announcing her performances proliferated as a result of this relationship. In the fall season of 1881, she embarked on a two-month tour in the Northwest.

In 1882, despite her heavy schedule, Prescott initiated one of the earliest libel trials in the country when she sued the president of the American News Company, charging that a paper it distributed had reported she "had become a certain man's mistress." The trial held New York City spellbound for a week; even the *New York Times* ran lengthy articles about Prescott's testimony. In the courtroom, she spoke arrogantly, dishonestly, and blithely; in the process, she received a great deal of free publicity, earned the jury's sympathy, and won the case. The judgment was reversed on appeal, but, as a result of her suit, the American News Company changed its distribution practices for decades, and journalists reported more respectfully about actors.

Through a mutual friend, Steele Mackaye, actor, playwright, and theatrical inventor, she met Oscar Wilde and arranged in 1883 to star in and produce his first play, *Vera,* in New York City. After finishing the season with Salvini, she put on *Vera* beginning August 20. Lampooned by critics, it closed after one week. Wilde waited nearly seven years before writing another play, but Prescott, with customary aplomb, moved without delay to a different play, appearing next in *Belmont's Bride.*

The years 1884 through half of 1886 were slow, although she did some acting. Her new company disbanded in Cincinnati in January 1884 amid rumors of numerous difficulties. Advertisements appeared in New York City's drama newspapers announcing that she was "resting," and "disengaged." Early in 1886, she advertised that she was "at liberty" for the season.

Prescott's life took a dramatic turn in May 1886 when she acted in *Pygmalion and Galatea* in New Orleans, opposite a handsome young amateur actor, Rezin D. Shepherd (1859–1948). He became successful, taking the stage name R. D. MacLean (also spelled McLean). Reviewers referred to his "physique" and "magnetism." Listings for "Marie Prescott & Co." or "Prescott & Co." became "Prescott & MacLean," then in 1889, "MacLean & Prescott."

In February 1887, William Perzel advertised that he had given up managing Prescott "and no longer holds any relations, business or otherwise, with her." In March 1887, he asserted that he had never married her. Undaunted, in the Bourbon, Ky., Court of Common Pleas, she filed for divorce in 1889, charging abandonment. When the court decided in Perzel's favor, she appealed. The Court of Appeals reversed the lower court's judgment in 1891, granting her an annulment. No marriage was ever proven; at the trial Prescott had testified that she had no marriage certificate, explaining, "I did not get any."

From fall 1887 until mid-April 1893, Prescott and MacLean traveled the country to popular acclaim; theirs was one of about 286 touring companies. They traveled to grand opera houses as far north as Canada, as far west as Montana, through the South to Florida, and all through the Northeast. They toured about twenty states each month, stopping to perform plays at twenty-five to seventy-five towns. They stayed only a night or two, usually giving evening performances as well as a matinee. Their repertoire consisted primarily of twenty plays, half by Shakespeare; in *Othello,* Prescott played Iago wearing tights and a mustache. In February 1888, their performances in Galveston, Tex., introduced audiences to *Pygmalion and Galatea, As You Like It,* and *The Merchant of Venice.* Spectators, accustomed to a lower class of plays, minstrel shows, or troupes of trained dogs, appreciated the fare.

In 1891 MacLean's father died, leaving him more than $1 million and a 1,200-acre farm in West Virginia. Prescott and MacLean married in June 1892, planning to retire soon to MacLean's Wild Goose Farm. Instead, Prescott died in July 1893 in New York City, after abdominal surgery. She was buried in Elmwood Cemetery in Shepherdstown, W.Va., and her tombstone was engraved "Marie Shepherd," a name she fleetingly bore.

"An Actress's Libel Suit," *NYT,* October 14, 1882, 8.

Davis, William A. Interview by Lydia Cushman Schurman, August 23, 2003, Carrollton, Ky.

Davis, William A., to Lydia Cushman Schurman, e-mail messages, 2002–2007, available in author's files.

"Events in the Metropolis; Marie Prescott on the Stand," *NYT,* October 13, 1882, 8.

Johnson, Oscar. Records from the family Bible of Oscar Johnson, Millersburg, Ky.

"Marie Prescott," unidentified news clipping dated November 22, 1879, New York Public Library, Performing Arts, Billy Rose Theatre Collection, Locke Collection Folder 1796.

"Marie Prescott in Court," *NYT,* October 17, 1882, 8.

"Miss Prescott Indignant," *NYT,* October 18, 1882, 8.

"Miss Prescott's Success," *NYT,* October 20, 1882, 8.

O'Dell, George. *Annals of the New York Stage.* New York: AMS Edition, 1970.

Payrouse, Jack. "Rezin Davis Shepherd, III (R.D. MacLean): He Loved His Shakespeare as His Life," *Magazine of the Jefferson County Historical Society* 57 (December 1991): 16–59.

Salyers, Kathryn. Interview by Lydia Cushman Schurman, August 23, 2003, Carrollton, Ky.

Victor Family file, Kentucky Historical Society, Frankfort, Ky.

Lydia Cushman Schurman

PRESTON, WILLIAM, MAJOR GENERAL (b. October 16, 1816, near Louisville, Ky.; d. September 21, 1887, Lexington, Ky.). William Preston, a politician and a **Mexican War** and **Civil War** veteran, graduated from Yale University, New Haven, Conn., in 1835 and the Harvard Law School, Cambridge, Mass., in 1838. In preparation for entry into Yale, Preston attended **Augusta College** in Bracken Co. In 1840 he married Margaret Wickliffe of Lexington, daughter of Robert Wickliffe, the state's largest slaveholder. They had five daughters. Preston served with the 4th Kentucky Volunteers in the Mexican War, where he rose to the rank of lieutenant colonel. After the war he established a successful law practice in Louisville and later entered politics. In 1851 he won a seat in the Kentucky House of Representatives, and a year later he became a state senator. He took a proslavery position in the election of 1855, which contributed to his defeat by Humphrey Marshall. In 1858 he was appointed U.S. minister to Spain, a position he held until 1861. With the start of the Civil War, he joined the Confederate Army and attained the rank of major general. He saw action in the battles of Fort Donelson, Nashville, Shiloh, Vicksburg, and Chickamauga. At Shiloh his brother-in-law Gen. **Albert Sidney Johnston**, from Mason Co., died in his arms. At the war's end, fearing retribution by the North, he fled in exile to England and Canada, before receiving a pardon and returning to Lexington. He again won a seat in the Kentucky House of Representatives in 1868, representing Fayette Co., and served for two years. Preston spent the remainder of his life managing the large estate that his wife had inherited. He died in 1887 at Lexington and was buried at Louisville's Cave Hill Cemetery.

Dorman, J. Frederick. *The Prestons of Smithfield and Greenfield in Virginia.* Louisville, Ky.: Filson Club, 1982.

Kleber, John E., ed. *The Kentucky Encyclopedia.* Lexington: Univ. Press of Kentucky, 1992.

Sehlinger, Peter J. *Kentucky's Last Cavalier: General William Preston, 1816–1887.* Lexington: Univ. Press of Kentucky, 2004.

PRESTONVILLE. Prestonville in Carroll Co. is located at the confluence of the Kentucky River and the Ohio River directly west of old **Port William**. Prestonville was named for William Preston, an early Virginia surveyor and land speculator who received a land grant for several thousand acres on the west side of the Kentucky River. Although Preston never settled at this location, during the early settlement period, Elijah Craig Jr. built a warehouse and used a fleet of flatboats to export merchandise from Central Kentucky up the Kentucky River to Prestonville. As early as February 1, 1795, Craig advertised his capability of exporting and warehousing goods from as far away as the town of Frankfort and the Dix River.

The Kentucky River was an important early route for commerce and settlement, and the ferrymen at Prestonville provided the most important of several ferries across it. Smith's Ferry was one of the earliest approved for use by the Gallatin Co. Court. In 1799 two major roads were authorized, one along the west bank of the Kentucky River from Prestonville to New Castle and Frankfort, the other along the Ohio River bank west to the Corn Creek Settlement, in modern-day Trimble Co.

During the 1820s and 1830s, the town of Prestonville began to grow, but at no time did it ever rival the mercantile prowess of the nearby larger Gallatin Co. city of Port William (Carrollton). The entire hamlet of Prestonville was wedged into two blocks. Darling Distillery and Bonded Warehouse, Wise's General Store, two hotels, a cooperage, and a gristmill jostled for space in town along the river.

The A. W. Darling Company of Prestonville was selected as the contractor for Lock No. 1 on the Kentucky River just upstream from Prestonville. Construction based on U.S. Army Corps of Engineers designs began in 1836; huge slabs of limestone formed the face of the dam, and great timber logs formed the sides of the locks. On February 14, 1840, the *Argo,* the first steamboat through Locks No. 1 through No. 4, arrived at Frankfort.

After the War of 1812, Kentucky welcomed back its heroes of battle at the Raisin River in Michigan and the Battle of New Orleans. The euphoria from the victory at the Battle of New Orleans in 1815 translated into wholesale renaming of many of the local place names in what was then Gallatin Co.: McCool's Creek became Ghent when Kentucky statesman Henry Clay suggested honoring the site of the peace treaty of the **War of 1812**, Ghent, Belgium. Prestonville named itself Wide Awake, a phrase from the very popular contemporary song "The Hunters of Kentucky," which was used by Andrew Jackson in his presidential campaign of 1828. "But Jackson he was wide awake, and wasn't scar'd at trifles, for well he knew what aim we take, with our Kentucky rifles." The postal maps, however, continued to refer to the hamlet as Prestonville. The 1883 *Atlas of Carroll and Gallatin County* used both names, Prestonville and Wide Awake.

For nearly 100 years, the ferry at Prestonville carried the overland road traffic from Louisville, New Castle, and Bedford across the Kentucky River into Carrollton. The first bridge over the Kentucky River between Carrollton and Prestonville was built in 1898. At that time an interurban line from Covington to Louisville was in the preliminary planning stage, and this bridge was built with sufficient strength to carry the load when it was completed. The interurban was never constructed, but U.S. 42 as the main route from Cincinnati to Louisville changed the dynamics of the village of Prestonville. Slowly over time, U.S. 42 became the main commercial artery, bypassing the hamlet under the bridge. The modern bridge was opened to traffic in 1952 and has been repaired and renovated several times since.

Floods of the Ohio and Kentucky rivers submerged Prestonville numerous times; the greatest damage was the back-to-back punch to Prestonville of 1883–1884 and the great **flood of 1913**, when all the tributaries backed up. But it was the 1937 flood that impacted the entire town so badly it has never really recovered. All of Prestonville was flooded to its rooftops; the Ohio River was 30 feet above flood stage at Cincinnati, reaching 80 feet. The **Great Depression** left most people with little cash to rebuild their homes and businesses.

In 1867, under the plan developed by W. B. Gullion and L. B. Wilson, Carroll Co. was divided into common school districts. Prestonville was designated District 10, and the first deed noted for a public school was in 1866, when Henry Lindsay granted to the town of Prestonville land on the road to the Little Kentucky River. The school trustees were B. R. Elston, Samuel Hisle, and H. Wetherall. In 1874 Prestonville held the first election in Carroll Co. to vote on an ad valorem tax of 25 cents per $100 assessed valuation to build a school building. The vote was approved by a vote of 21 to 1. In 1878 Henry Westerill and Fannie, his wife, sold a lot along the Carrollton–New Castle Rd. at the southwest corner of A. W. Darling's line for construction of a common school. In the 1870s other one-room common schools were built in the Prestonville Precinct: District 14, Hisle's on the New Castle–Prestonville Turnpike; District 23, Malin's Branch; Shiloh School, to the west past Carrico's Landing on the Little Kentucky; District 30, on Kings Ridge; and District 27, Gullions on the New Castle Turnpike. In 1881 the Prestonville Common School District reported having a total of 100 possible students.

In 1891 Rachael Block granted land in Prestonville for a large brick building that would house the grade school. The **flood of 1907** damaged the school but did not destroy it. Pressure from the state Board of Instruction to improve the quality and cost-effectiveness of rural schools caused a series of consolidations. In 1900 the county school board decided to send high school students to the three Independent Districts, Carrollton, Ghent, and Worthville; the Sanders District was added later. Two-year high schools were established at Locust and English. By 1910 elementary students and high school students in Carroll Co. were attending consolidated schools at Sanders, Worthville, English, Locust, Ghent, and Carrollton. The effects of the **Great Depression** and low enrollments caused county school superintendent Curtis Shirley in September 1938 to send high school students from Prestonville, Locust, Ghent, and English to the new **Carrollton High School**. The Prestonville elementary students were consolidated into the new U.S. 42 County Elementary School in 1965.

Bevarly, R. W. "History of Education in Carroll County," master's thesis, Univ. of Kentucky, 1936.
Campbell, Justine Tandy. "History of the Carroll County Schools," 1976, Carroll Co. Public Library, Carrollton, Ky.
Carroll Co. Deed Book 9, p. 468, Carrollton, Ky.
Gentry, Mary Ann. *A History of Carroll County.* Madison, Ind.: Coleman, 1984.
Parker, Anna V. "A Short History of Carroll County," 1958, Carroll Co. Public Library, Carrollton, Ky.

Diane Perrine Coon

PRETLOW, RICHARD (b. November 27, 1811, Southampton Co., Va.; d. February 20, 1894, Covington, Ky.). Physician and banker Richard Pretlow was the son of Samuel and Edna Bailey Pretlow. Richard was educated in the best schools of the day. When he was 17, his family moved from Virginia to Springboro, Ohio. At age 21 he came to Cincinnati to attend the Ohio Medical College, from which he graduated in 1837. In the same year, he married Elizabeth A. Lynch of Lynchburg, Va., and they had a son and a daughter. He set up his first medical practice in Richmond, Ind. In March 1843 the family moved to Covington, where he continued to practice medicine. Pretlow was named president of the Covington Branch of Farmers National Bank in 1867 and held the post for many years. His wife Elizabeth Ann died in 1867, and Pretlow married his second wife, Cassie Prague, on June 1, 1869. Richard Pretlow died at his Covington home at Fourth and Greenup Sts., where he had lived for more than 50 years, and was buried at the Highland Cemetery in Fort Mitchell. Later, his wife, Cassie, had a beautiful stained-glass window installed in his honor at the Presbyterian Church they attended in Covington. The window pictured "Christ as the Great Physician."

Biographical Cyclopedia of the Commonwealth of Kentucky. Chicago: John M. Gresham, 1896.
Biographical Encyclopedia of Kentucky. Cincinnati: J. M. Armstrong, 1878.
"Last Honors," *KP,* February 20, 1894, 1.

PRICE, JACOB (b. April 1839, Woodford Co., Ky.; d. March 1, 1923, Covington, Ky.). Born in Central Kentucky, clergyman Jacob Price spent most of his life in Covington, where for more than 60 years he was one of the city's leading African Americans. Price, a freeman before the end of slavery, was listed in the 1860 census as a laborer and a minister of the Gospel. He lived on Bremen St., which was renamed Pershing Ave. during **World War I**, and it was rumored that he was a conductor on the **Underground Railroad** from that location. Price formed the **First Baptist Church, Covington [African American]**, and, at the church, the first private school for African American children in the city. He was a businessman and was involved in civil, political, and education rights.

Price was the first pastor of First Baptist Church, and after a dispute split the church's membership, he became the pastor of Ninth St. Baptist Church. While at the First Baptist Church, Price was instrumental in the founding of the Ninth St. Methodist Episcopal Church.

In 1869 Price, **Isaac Black**, and Rev. William Blackburn served as members of a delegation representing Covington at the Freedmen's Bureau for Education convention in Louisville. After they returned, Price and the other Covington delegates organized a board of trustees for the city's proposed first two public schools for blacks, one housed in a Baptist church and the other in a Methodist church.

On February 25, 1870, the first statewide African American political convention was scheduled for Frankfort. Some of the newly enfranchised African Americans wanted to vote the straight Republican ticket. However, Jacob Price, Isaac Black, and William Blackburn preferred to vote for anyone

Headquarters for Lumber!

JACOB PRICE,

DEALER IN ALL KINDS OF

ROUGH and DRESSED LUMBER,

Shingles, Lath, Locust and Cedar Posts,

No. 412 Madison St.,

Bet. Fourth and Fifth, COVINGTON, KY.

8nov-3m

Advertisement for Jacob Price's lumber yard.

who favored policies in the best interests of the African American community. This political position later benefited Covington's African American community when **William L. Grant**, a white politician, asked Price and other African American community leaders for their support. Grant was an influential businessman and Covington city council member seeking the Democratic nomination for the office of Kenton Co. representative in the Kentucky legislature. Grant proposed that if the African American voters supported him for office, he would have the city charter of Covington amended to provide for a public school for black children. William Grant received the nomination, and a new Covington city charter soon provided for an African American school. Price's political acumen had been demonstrated.

In 1882 Price owned and operated a lumberyard and sheds in the area of Fourth St. and Madison Ave. The sheds occupied an area 60 by 90 feet and had a storage capacity of a half million board feet of lumber. He continued in the lumber business until 1894. In 1899 Price was named president of the Colored Laborers' Union.

Price died in 1923 at age 84 in Covington and was buried in Evergreen Cemetery in Southgate. On January 26, 1939, the Covington Municipal Housing Commission named the new housing complex for blacks in honor of Price, stating that "no Negro citizen is better known than the late Jacob Price."

"Colored Labor Union," *KE,* March 5, 1899, 3.
"Headquarters for Lumber," *DC,* November 28, 1882, 2.
"Housing Project to Be Named Latonia Terrace: Negro Settlement to Be Known as 'Jacob Price Homes' in Honor of Leader, Board Reports," *KP,* January 26, 1939, 1.
"Negro Pastor Dies," *KP,* March 2, 1923, 1.
"Organized First Negro Church," *KTS,* March 2, 1923, 37.
"School Opened Oct 14 in Basement of Methodist Church on Madison St. between 2 & 3," *CJ,* October 19, 1872, 3.

Theodore H. H. Harris

PRICE, KENNY (b. Covington, Ky., May 27, 1931; d. Florence, Ky., August 4, 1987). Fondly nicknamed the "Round Mound of Sound" because of his six-foot-three, 300-pound frame, country musician James Kenny Price sang equally well in three registers—tenor, baritone, and bass. Although he made an impression with fans in the Greater Cincinnati region on the regionally televised program *Midwestern Hayride,* he gained his national fame from appearances on the popular *Hee Haw* television variety show.

Kenny was born at 1311 Holman Ave. in Covington in 1931, and his family moved in the mid-1930s to a farm near Florence, Ky., where he spent most of his youth. Country music became a part of his life at an early age. He received his first guitar for Christmas from his parents at age five—it was an auditorium-sized Sears & Roebuck Silverstone, and he played it with other family musicians on the farm. Both parents, William and Mary Clayton Nunnelley Price, sang in their church's choir. Kenny attended Florence Elementary School, where he performed in a jamboree-style school play in the first grade.

Price appeared in local musical talent shows, winning prizes with his commanding voice and guitar accompaniment. At age 14 he made his radio debut playing guitar on Northern Kentucky's **WZIP Radio**. During his teen years, his family moved frequently. Price played in the school band at his first high school, in the Boone Co. area. He graduated in 1949 from Morgan High School in Pendleton Co., where he also played basketball for the school team.

Price's professional music career started in the roadhouses and honky-tonks of Northern Kentucky during the late 1940s. He later frequently reminisced that this was a time when **country music** was socially out of favor. However, he played folk and country music at local clubs for square dances in Boone Co., where country music was popular. In 1949 he appeared on a WCPO-TV country music show, *Midday Merry-Go-Round,* in Cincinnati.

In 1952, while Price was serving in the U.S. Army, he performed with the Horace Heidt USO show in Korea. Upon military discharge, he married Donna G. Stewart in 1954. They met at the Kresge **five-and-dime store** in Covington, where she worked as a clerk. In addition to singing and playing guitar, Price also mastered the drums, the banjo, and the bass fiddle. In 1954 his long association with WLW television in Cincinnati began. He first appeared on the *Midwestern Hayride,* which became one of the longest-running country music programs on broadcast television. He also sang lead for a local band, the *Hometowners,* with Freddy Langdon, Jay Neas, and Buddy Ross. In 1957 the band won a television competition in New York City on the *Arthur Godfrey Show.* During the 1959–60 school year, Price studied music, theater, and broadcasting at the Cincinnati Conservatory of Music. After many years as a regular cast member, in 1970 he was appointed host of the *Midwestern Hayride* and continued through the end of its long run in 1972. After a few guest appearances in 1973, Price became a regular cast member of the syndicated Nashville television show *Hee Haw.*

Price composed more than 1,000 songs. Of his many recordings, 34 became chart single records.

Kenny Price, mid-1950s.

He recorded nearly two dozen long-play albums. His first hit was "Somebody Told Mary/White Silver Sands" in the early 1960s. His first song that made the top 10 on the country chart was "Walking on New Grass" in 1966, and later that same year he charted in the top 10 country with "Happy Tracks." From the late 1960s through the 1970s, additional hits by Price included "My Goal for Today," "California Women," "Turn on Your Light (and Let It Shine)," "Let's Truck Together," "Easy Look," "Too Big a Price to Pay," and "Biloxi." Price's top 10 country hit "The Sheriff of Boone County" crossed over to the pop charts with the famous lyric "You're in a heap of trouble now, boy." It was about this time when he gained national popularity as a regular cast member on *Hee Haw*. Price also made a few guest appearances on the *Grand Old Opry* and performed at hundreds of live concerts around the nation. "She's Leavin' (And I'm Almost Gone)" was his last chart single, recorded in 1980.

From his first public performance at Florence Elementary School through his comedic antics for *Hee Haw*, Kenny Price was a true musician first; he appreciated all kinds of music, from folk and classical to country and rock. He is generally remembered for his genuine warmth and smiling face. He never turned away from a handshake or an autograph request, and he always found time to spend a few minutes with his fans, treating them as if they were his neighbors or friends. During his days at WLW television in Cincinnati, fans frequently greeted him on the outdoor steps of Crosley Square, the studio of the *Midwestern Hayride*. Price died in Florence in 1987 at age 56 and was buried at Forest Lawn Memorial Park in Erlanger. He was survived by his wife Donna and their three children, Kenny Jr., Chris, and Jennifer.

Clarke, Donald, ed., *The Penguin Encyclopedia of Popular Music*. New York: Viking, 1989.

Feiertag, Joe. "Friend Saw Kenny Price as a Happy Family Man," *Boone County Recorder*, August 13, 1987, 1.

"Kenny Price: The 'Mound of Sound,'" *KP Weekend*, March 30, 1974, 1–4.

Kreimer, Peggy. "Kenny Price, a County Boy Who Never Wanted to Lose Country," *KP*, August 8, 1987, 1K–2K.

Sandhage, Doug. "Kenny Price Down Home," *CE Magazine*, November 27, 1983, 6–10.

——. "A Legendary Music Man with a Common Man's Touch," *KP*, March 29, 1982, 8K.

Williams, Joel. "Popular Star Just a Country Boy from Florence," *Boone County Recorder*, November 19, 1981, 6.

Workum, Bertram. "'Hee Haw' Star Kenny Price Dies," *KP*, August 5, 1987, 1K–2K.

John Schlipp

PRINCE OF PEACE LUTHERAN CHURCH. In January 1892, a small group of Bellevue residents persuaded Dr. E. K. Bell, pastor of the First Lutheran Church in Cincinnati, to begin holding church services in their city. The group met at the Calvary Methodist Episcopal Church building on Sunday afternoons. The Board of Missions of the Lutheran General Synod agreed to assist the new congregation financially. On April 1, 1892, the church hired its first pastor, Rev. George G. Clark. Trinity Lutheran Church was officially organized on April 19, 1892, with 51 charter members present. For the next year, the church held services in the Balke Opera House, at the corner of Berry and Fairfield Aves. in Bellevue. In July 1892, the church took an option to purchase property at the southeast corner of Taylor Ave. and Center St. The General Synod granted an interest-free loan to the church to purchase the site. The cornerstone for a new building was laid on November 13, 1892, and it was dedicated on May 14, 1893. Growth of the congregation was slow, but under the leadership of Rev. John M. Bramkamp, the church reached a membership of 100 by 1902. A parsonage was built on a lot behind the church in 1916.

Rev. C. Myron Danford became pastor of Trinity in 1936, and during his eight years there, church attendance nearly tripled. The church that had struggled financially for many years was now in an improved financial condition, which permitted them to remodel the facility, increase the pastor's salary, and become self-supporting. In 1950 Trinity added an educational wing and new art-glass windows and had the entire church rewired.

In 1957 Col. Harry T. Klein donated about $100,000 worth of Texas Oil Company stock to the church. The congregation used the gift to purchase a duplex next to the church, which was demolished to enlarge the educational wing. Improvements were also made to the parsonage and the pastor's study. The congregation held their 75th-anniversary celebration in November 1967; a former pastor, Rev. Charles Masheck, served as the featured speaker. Special services were held in July 1970, to celebrate the 100th anniversary of the founding of the City of Bellevue. On that occasion, the popular former pastor Rev. Danford delivered the sermon. By 1971 the church reached its peak membership of 258.

Trinity suffered the same plight as several other urban churches, with attendance falling dramatically as members moved to the suburbs. To help solve this problem, Trinity and **St. Mark Lutheran Church** of Newport (at Seventh and Monroe) merged their congregations in 1978 and adopted the name Prince of Peace Lutheran Church. The Newport location was to be vacated and combined services were to be held in Bellevue. Within a short time, however, friction developed between the two groups, especially over a decision to sell the Newport church building. As a result of this dispute, the merger was rescinded. Newport members reopened the St. Mark Church, and the Bellevue church continued using the new name, Prince of Peace Lutheran Church.

In August 2004, Dr. Timothy Hungler was hired as interim pastor of Prince of Peace. He had been raised Catholic but later embraced the Lutheran Church and became a Lutheran pastor. He was well educated and an excellent speaker and soon became immensely popular with the congregation. There was renewed enthusiasm within the church, and the future appeared bright, but tragedy soon struck. After returning from church on February 12, 2006, Rev. Hungler suffered a cerebral hemorrhage, from which he died several days later. The church was devastated but began the search for a new leader. A pastor from Lexington, Rev. Jerry Cantrell, served as interim pastor. Today, the church has 94 members, dedicated to continuing the work begun so many years ago as Trinity Lutheran Church. The congregation is a member of the Evangelical Lutheran Church in America (ELCA).

Davis, Alan Dawson. "A History of Trinity Lutheran Church," 1962, Trinity Lutheran Church, Bellevue, Ky.

Veatch, Norman, and Monika Veatch. Interview by Jack Wessling, Bellevue, Ky., August 6, 2006.

Waltmann, Henry, ed. *History of the Indiana-Kentucky Synod of the Lutheran Church of America: Its Development, Congregations, and Institutions*. Indianapolis, Ind.: Central, 1971.

Jack Wessling

PROGRESSIVE BUILDING AND LOAN ASSOCIATION. The Progressive Building and Loan Association, a creation of the African American community of Covington, was formed to provide otherwise scarce home financing and business loans for that community. The association submitted its articles of incorporation to the Kenton Co. clerk's office in June 1906. The new corporation's officers were F. L. Williams, principal of Covington's **Lincoln-Grant School**, president, and **Wallace A. Gaines**, a funeral director, secretary. The board of directors included **Charles E. Jones**, a funeral director, and Lawson Thompson, the owner of Steam Carpet Cleaners. The other incorporators were James C. Campbell, a laborer; Charles Carson, a janitor; Nathan A. Fleming, a teacher at Lincoln-Grant School; Ollie B. Havelow, pastor at Lane Chapel C.M.E. Church; and Robert P. Johnson, the principal of the Latonia Colored School. The corporation's capital stock of $50,000 was divided into four classes of shares: $400 shares required payments of 80 cents per week, $200 shares required payments of 40 cents per week, $100 shares required payments of 20 cents per week, and $50 shares required payments of 10 cents per week. Indebtedness of the firm was capped at $20,000. The office was located at the corner of Seventh and Scott Sts., adjacent to the W. A. Gaines Funeral Home.

The Progressive Building and Loan Association was a milestone for the African American community of Covington. The association drew its leaders from all walks of life, and many of them remained in business locally for three or four decades. The distinguished educators and religious leaders who served with the association were consistently chosen for both their abilities and their dedicated service within Covington's African

American community. Available records do not indicate what happened to the association after 1910.

"Building Association Will Be Organized," *KP*, May 31, 1906, 2.
"Estill Is President," *KP*, May 6, 1910, 3.
"Negroes File Papers," *KP*, June 12, 1906, 2.

Theodore H. H. Harris

PROHIBITION. Although Northern Kentucky had its share of reformers advocating prohibition, there were plenty of others who, after it was instituted, took advantage of its opportunities.

Strictly speaking, Prohibition began with the ratification of the 18th Amendment to the U.S. Constitution on January 16, 1919, which prohibited the importing, exporting, transporting, selling, and manufacturing of intoxicating liquor; however, enforcement of the amendment did not begin until the passage, on October 10, 1919, of the Volstead Act, a law named for a U.S. representative from Minnesota. For years, social reform groups such as the Women's Christian Temperance Union and the Anti-Saloon League had argued for passage of a law making it illegal to manufacture, sell, or dispense alcoholic beverages. They believed that many of the ills in society were the results of drinking alcoholic beverages and that the solution was simply to eliminate the alcohol. Reformers viewed the casual and routine consumption of alcohol by new immigrants as only exacerbating the problem.

The fact of the matter was that roughly one-third of the United States was already dry before Prohibition, and some entire states had been dry for a long time, such as Maine, which had gone dry as early as 1851, with seemingly little effect. On the national level, Prohibition clearly demonstrated the inability of government to legislate behavior. It seems that the larger the city and the more wealthy and politically influential its residents, the less likely it was that the decrees of the Volstead Act would be imposed. "Do as we say, not as we do" was what many members of the U.S. Congress in particular proclaimed by their actions. In Washington, D.C., "speakeasies" (nightclubs that served illegal alcoholic beverages to customers) thrived, offering illegal drinks to the nation's leaders openly, while hardworking employees of the Pittsburgh steel mills were expected to go home and drink tea. Elected officials at all levels of government commonly supplemented their incomes by accepting bribes, and cities such as New York City, Chicago, and Cincinnati were rampant with abuse and corruption.

On the local level, the king of corruption was clearly George Remus, who worked primarily out of Cincinnati. Many of the freight cars transporting his illegal liquor were loaded and unloaded along railroad sidings in Covington, however. Remus had moved to Covington after being acquitted in a well-publicized trial for the murder of his wife, Imogene. On a smaller scale, Newport's John M. Pompilio (see **Pompilio's Restaurant**), before his restaurant days, built and ran several illegal whiskey stills in Campbell Co. Whenever he was caught, he was given veritable slaps on the wrist, and it was the same for hundreds of others like him engaged in the illegal whiskey trade who appeared before Judge Oscar T. Roetken, the Covington-based special Prohibition federal administrative law judge. Eventually Roetken himself fell to the temptation of corruption and accepted bribes. Many fire-department runs of the day were linked to bootleggers and their overheated stills.

Speakeasies abounded in Covington and Newport. In the early 1920s, Carl Weber built his 219 Riverside Dr. bungalow along the riverfront in Covington to conform to contemporary speakeasy standards. The design included separate entrances to the basement and the upstairs, where betting action and drinking took place. Western Union telegraph wires that brought the horse-racing results for the book upstairs can still be found along the wall inside a first-floor closet. Weber was later caught and convicted for these illegal activities. Meanwhile, hundreds of restaurants simply shut down with the arrival of Prohibition, and those that remained open frequently served illegal alcoholic drinks on the side. Consumers had less reason to go out to eat, when they could not have an accompanying drink. Prohibition popularized the mixed drink, as a means to disguise alcohol by mixing it with colorful liquids such as orange or tomato juice. In the less urban areas of the Northern Kentucky region, many of which were dry to begin with, low levels of bootlegging continued as before, generally unnoticed. They continue, to some extent, to this day.

Several unintended consequences arose out of Prohibition. Organized crime seized the opportunity to fill in the gaps of alcoholic beverage supply lines. The profits were so great that other activities illegal in Kentucky, such as **prostitution**, the sale of drugs, and gambling, soon were added. The lurid histories of Newport and Covington attest to those developments. Government officials learned that the value of office-holding was not so much the amount of one's salary, but what could be derived from the take. Often, when officials made raids, little or no evidence of illegal activities was found. For example, in Maysville in January 1925, agents raided the St. James Hotel, a known moonshine joint, and found just a pint of fruit juice. Obviously, the proprietor had been tipped off about this raid in advance. Banal solutions such as near beer were dismal and laughable failures. The great comic W. C. Fields summed it up best when he said, "The man who called it 'near beer' was a bad judge of distance."

By the end of the 1920s, the handwriting was on the wall; even many of the original supporters of Prohibition were acknowledging its lack of success. Although not intrinsically an anti-Prohibitionist, President Franklin Delano Roosevelt (1933–1945) knew where the votes were, and once in office, he approved the passage of the Beer and Wine Revenue Act in March 1933, allowing the sale of 3.2 percent beer and light wines, even as the states were working on the ratification of the 21st Amendment to repeal Prohibition, sent to them by Congress in February of that year. On December 5, 1933, when Utah became the 36th state to ratify the 21st Amendment, Prohibition, the so-called noble experiment, died.

Behr, Edward. *Prohibition: The 13 Years That Changed America*. London: BBC Books, 1997.
"50 Years Ago Today, Beer Prohibition Ended," *Maysville Ledger Independent*, April 7, 1983.
"Prohibition Raids Saturday Night Are Fruitless," *Maysville Ledger*, January 26, 1925, 1.
Sweeney, Michael R. "Pompilio's Restaurant: A Centennial History, 70 Years of Spaghetti and More," *NKH* 11, no. 2 (Spring–Summer 2004): 2–20.

PROSTITUTION. Prostitution has been present in Northern Kentucky's history since early times. During most of the 19th century, U.S. Army soldiers were stationed at the Newport Arsenal (see **Newport Barracks**), and prostitution filtered into the area around the barracks and near the Licking River. During the **Civil War**, soldiers came from nearby cities to visit the many brothels located in the river town of Newport. In the 1890s the army moved to the nearby **Fort Thomas Military Reservation**, but soldiers stationed there continued to visit Newport's brothels. In 1916 Newport city commissioners fought to keep these "questionable houses" from opening. They tried to prevent Brighton St. property owners in the city's **West End** from renting housing to single women. When young women appeared in court and were convicted of prostitution, they were given the option of going to jail or paying a $15 fine and leaving town forever. During this same period, policemen from nearby Covington assisted in raiding rooming houses located on W. Fourth St. in Newport, arresting tenants and their guests, and charging them with disorderly conduct.

Prostitution did not become organized until the 1930s, with the arrival of the "syndicate boys" from Chicago and later from Cleveland, Ohio. In order to accommodate travelers to Northern Kentucky and locals working various shifts at industrial jobs in the area, soon there were "day houses" and "night houses" of prostitution operating in Newport. This quick and convenient service was not the only one available for brothel guests. There were also more upscale prostitution houses that came alive in the late afternoon and stayed open all night. During the 1930s there were about 15 known brothels in Newport. Some of them were houses but a brief walk away from York and Monmouth Sts. in what was known as the more disreputable side of Newport, not far from the police station and the city jail. Streetwalkers were also commonplace in town, overseen by their pimps, who trailed them close by.

Bar girls, or B-girls, were yet another source of prostitution. They were professional dancers, second-rate and often off-key singers, or waitresses, all working the strip clubs operating along Monmouth and York Sts. The girls received a percentage of the club's take, based on the dollar value of the drinks they sold. The more a patron drank, the more physical attention the B-girls provided. There were about 300 women working as prostitutes in Newport during the 1940s, all within an area of less than one square mile. The numbers of such "working girls" would increase when a convention came to Cincinnati. Visiting out-of-towners were assisted by taxi drivers in selecting a particular brothel. The driver would receive a kickback or a tip from the money taken in by the operators of the brothel. For years the joke circulated that the population of Newport was "30,000 by day, and 100,000 at night."

During the mid-1950s, police raids occurred, and arrests were made at Corky's Café in Newport and at the Haidi Club in Covington, as well as at Big Jim Harris's notorious Hy-Dee-Ho Club in Wilder. At Corky's Café on Saturday nights, cars would line up along Southgate Alley. Customers would drive to Newport from as far away as Indian Hill in eastern Hamilton Co., Ohio, for their weekly clandestine trysts with prostitutes. During the late 1950s, a group of local civic leaders and ministers formed the Committee of 500 (see **Newport Reform Groups**) with the goal of ridding Newport and Campbell Co. of vice, including prostitution.

By the 1960s there were several strip clubs operating openly instead of in back rooms. These places, which usually stayed open until 3:00 a.m., hired well-known dancers, such as "Baseball's Kissing Bandit," Morganna Roberts, who kept an establishment full of customers. A darkened booth in the corner was available for any physical activities. Business was brisk, especially after a Cincinnati Reds baseball game.

In 1982 Newport issued a ban on nude dancing as a response to a public outcry, and the town's image changed as the strip clubs gradually were forced out of business. Today only a couple of adult clubs still operate in Newport, and they no longer feature nudity or topless dancing.

In 1997 nearby Kenton Co. completed an investigation that led to the dismantling of a prostitution ring; charges were brought against the bar owner involved and three of his dancers. In 2004, as a warning to anyone looking for a prostitute in his city, the mayor of Covington sent "Dear John" letters to wives of the men convicted of soliciting prostitutes in Covington. A recent U.S. Supreme Court decision has prompted many Northern Kentucky cities to adopt a zoning ordinance for the "Regulation of Sexually Oriented Business," clearly delineating where the clubs may legally operate. Given prostitution's long-established and persistent history locally, only time will tell how effective such efforts as these will be.

Cathie John. "Gambler Shot Gangland Style in Newport." www.cathiejohn.com/jp2.html.

Commonwealth of Kentucky, Co. of Kenton Ordinance No. 451.9 as Amended, December 14, 2004.

DeMichele, Matthew, and Gary Potter. "Newport Gambling, Sin City Revisited: A Case Study of the Official Sanctioning of Organized Crime." In "Open City," Justice and Police Studies, Eastern Kentucky Univ., Richmond, Ky.

Driehaus, Bob. "Bar Owner, Dancers Indicted," *KP*, September 20, 1997, 2K.

"18 Girls Leave Newport by Tonight or Go to Jail," *KP*, August 17, 1916, 1.

Flynn, Terry. "Cincinnati's 'Sin City,'" *CE*, July 29, 2003, 16E.

Houck, Jeanne. "John's Letters Target Prostitution," *KP*, December 16, 2004, 2K.

"Lew Wallace Newport History Collection," Archives of the W. Frank Steely Library, Northern Kentucky Univ., Highland Heights, Ky., http://library.nku.edu/mnc/newport.html.

Martin, Chuck. "One Brassy Lady," *KE*, May 22, 2005, 1F.

"Newport Vice Raid Are Tipped Off—No Arrests Made by Raiders (Empty Beds Found)," *KTS*, November 30, 1956, 1A.

Ramos, Steve. "Everyone Was on the Payroll at That Time: The Police Were Directing Traffic for People Breaking the Law," *City Beat*, January 12, 2000. http://citybeat.com/gyrobase/Home.

"Vice Raids Net 4 Arrests," *KP*, October 8, 1919, 1.

"Woman, 22, Caught in Vice Raid," *KTS*, December 1, 1956, 1.

Jeanne Greiser

PROTECTION AND ADVOCACY. Protection and Advocacy (P&A) is the agency designated by the governor of Kentucky to provide legal advocacy to persons with disabilities. It is independent from the service-providing and funding agencies of the state. P&A has federal and state mandates to gain access to records, conduct investigations, pursue legal remedies, and educate policymakers concerning the rights of individuals with disabilities.

Kentucky P&A functions in three ways: it provides information, referral, and technical assistance to persons with disabilities, their families, and supporters about issues and concerns that are disability-related; it provides training for individuals to become more knowledgeable about their rights as a person with a disability, as well as training for families and the greater community about those rights; and it provides legal advocacy on behalf of individuals whose rights have been violated as a result of their disability. The emphasis on legal advocacy addresses systemic problems, so that the ripple effect from P&A's representation has influence for many other persons with disabilities. P&A is available to all residents of the Northern Kentucky region.

Kentucky Protection and Advocacy. www.kypa.net (accessed March 24, 2006).

Robin Rider Osborne

PURE PRAIRIE LEAGUE. This rock-influenced **country music** band was initially known as a bar band playing in and around Cincinnati and Northern Kentucky. Named after a woman's temperance movement depicted in the 1939 Errol Flynn movie *Dodge City*, Pure Prairie League (PPL) was founded by John David Call, Craig Fuller, George Powell, and drummer Tom McGail at Chillicothe, Ohio, in 1969.

PPL signed a recording contract with RCA following an appearance in Cleveland, Ohio. The band's self-titled debut album did not sell well, so several changes were made in the band's composition. Fort Thomas native William "Bill" Hinds joined Pure Prairie League as its third drummer. In need of a keyboardist, Hinds asked Michael Connor of Latonia also to join. With Hinds and Connor, PPL recorded its second RCA-labeled album, *Bustin' Out*, in 1972. The album contained what became PPL's most enduring hit, "Amie," which was composed by Fuller. In September 1972 Hinds recruited another friend, Fort Thomas native Michael "Mike" Reilly, as the group's bass guitarist. This trio from Northern Kentucky, along with Call and Powell, were the members of PPL after Fuller left the group in 1973; he had filed for conscientious objector status when he received his Vietnam draft notice. While Fuller performed alternative service at a Covington hospital, RCA dropped its contract with the band.

In 1975 the group's burgeoning popularity on college campuses, including significant radio airtime for "Amie," caused RCA to re-sign PPL and release "Amie" as a single, which crossed over to the *Billboard* top 40 pop charts. The band's third album, *Two Lane Highway*, followed and included Fort Thomas–born Larry Goshorn. It also climbed to the top 40, as did *If the Shoe Fits*, PPL's fourth album. In 1977 Goshorn's brother Tim, also from Fort Thomas, joined the group, replacing Call, the band's last founding member. Shortly thereafter PPL again fragmented, leaving only Northern Kentuckians Hinds, Connor, and Reilly as the band's members.

In 1979 Patrick Bolin and Norman, Okla., native Vince Gill joined with the Northern Kentucky trio. The quintet's disappointing sales of *Can't Hold Back* prompted RCA to drop PPL for a second time. The group subsequently signed with Casablanca Records and replaced Bolin with Kentuckian Jeff Wilson.

PPL's popularity catapulted as its traditional sounds melded with the influences of songwriter Dan Greer, lead singer Gill's bluegrass-country-rock sound, and the inspiration of prolific songwriter Troy Seals. The band's next two albums, *Firin' Up* and *Something in the Night*, became two of its most successful productions. Those albums resulted in five hit singles, including "Let Me Love You Tonight," which reached the top 10 on the *Billboard* pop charts in 1980. PPL's national prominence faded once again following the bankruptcy of Casablanca and the departure of Gill to pursue a solo career. The band's attempt to recruit former Orleans lead singer Larry Hoppen fizzled, and the group sustained itself through the mid-1980s without a record label. The band dissolved in 1987. In 1998 it resurfaced led by founding member Fuller,

Michael Connor, and Mike Reilly. Pure Prairie League continues performing today at places like the Fort Thomas Fall Festival, although it performs without Connor, who died September 2, 2004, at age 54.

"Country Music Television." www.cmt.com (accessed November 3, 2005).

"Fort Thomas Fall Festival," *SC,* October 3, 2004, 2C.

"Michael Connor, 'Amie' Pianist—Pure Prairie League Member Was 54," *KE,* September 9, 2004, B7.

Pure Prairie League. www.pureprairieleague.com (accessed November 3, 2005).

"Pure Prairie League Reunites, Will Do June 13 Show at Jillians's," *KE,* June 3, 1999, C1.

Ruhlmann, William. *All Music Guide to Rock.* Austin, Tex.: Frugal Media, 1995.

Whitburn, Joel. *The Billboard Book of Top 40 Hits.* New York: Billboard, 1985.

William Morris Agency. www.wma.com (accessed November 3, 2005).

Paul A. Carl Jr.

QUALLS, ROXANNE (b. March 3, 1953, Tacoma, Wash.). Former Cincinnati mayor Roxanne Qualls is the daughter of Eugene Van Lear and Kathryn Vetter Qualls. The family moved to Erlanger, Ky., in 1961. Roxanne began her education at **St. Henry** Elementary School in Erlanger and went on to **Notre Dame Academy** in Park Hills, graduating in 1971. She attended **Thomas More College** in Crestview Hills from 1971 to 1973 and the University of Cincinnati from 1973 to 1975.

Qualls served as director of the Northern Kentucky Rape Crisis Center and later as director of the Women Helping Women organization. She directed what is now known as the Cincinnati office of the Ohio Citizens Action group.

As an unknown contender for Cincinnati City Council in 1987, she came in 14th out of the 25 candidates vying for a seat. In 1991, on her third run for city council, she was elected and served for two years. In 1993 Qualls became the first popularly elected mayor of the city. She proved to be well liked by the citizens, had a good relationship with council members, and worked well with the city's business interests. She sought to improve the city by her Zero Tolerance Initiative, which targeted the city's slum landlords. She also founded the Cincinnati Homeownership Partnership, consisting of 32 organizations, which encouraged and assisted citizens who were buying homes. Mayor Qualls was also instrumental in the redevelopment of the Cincinnati riverfront, which is now anchored by two new sports stadiums. She served as mayor from 1993 to 1999 and left office at that time because of term limits.

Qualls then became a fellow at the Institute of Politics in the Kennedy School of Government (KSG) at Harvard University. In the fall of 2001, she was named a Loeb Fellow in the Graduate School of Design at Harvard. She earned an MPA (master's in public administration) degree from the KSG in 2002 and subsequently was a Malcolm Weiner Fellow at the KSG .

In January 2004 Qualls began serving as a visiting professor at **Northern Kentucky University**, where she teaches in public administration. She is also director of the university's Public Leadership Initiative. She presently resides in downtown Cincinnati. Qualls is one of three Northern Kentuckians to serve as mayor of Cincinnati, the other two being **Theodore M. Berry** and **David Mann**. In fall 2007 she was named to the Cincinnati City Council to replace Jim Tarbell, who had resigned. In November 2007 she was reelected to the Cincinnati City Council.

CNN.com. "Candidate Profile from Congressional Quarterly." www.cnn.com (accessed February 8, 2007).

"Ex-Mayor Qualls to Teach at NKU," *KP*, November 3, 2003, 7K.

Maloney, Sharon. "Even the GOP Sees Roxanne Qualls as a Formidable Candidate." www.cincypost.com (accessed February, 7, 1998).

Northern Kentucky University. "Former Mayor Was SOP Student." www.nku.edu (accessed February 8, 2007).

"Notice Well Deserved," *KP*, February 8, 1996, 4K.

Qualls, Roxanne. E-mail to Paul A. Tenkotte, February 13, 2007.

——. Telephone interview by Jack Wessling, February 8, 2007, Alexandria, Ky.

Trapp, Doug. "Roxanne Isn't Done," *City Beat*, January 3, 2002, www.citybeat.com (accessed February 7, 2007).

Jack Wessling

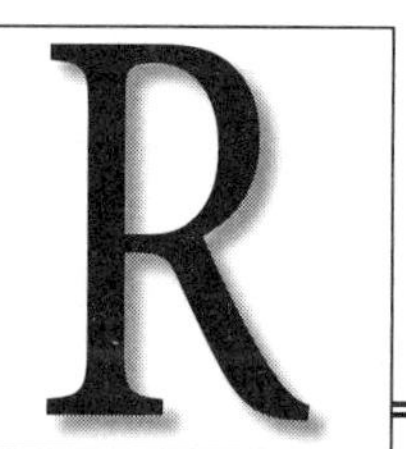

RABBIT HASH. On the southern bank of the Ohio River, at mile number 506.1 (from Pittsburgh, Pa.), is nestled an early-19th-century river hamlet, Rabbit Hash, in Boone Co. It remains much the same as in preceding generations. This area of Boone Co. can trace the settlement of its rural communities to around 1813, when the Boone Co. Court issued its first ferry covenant bond to Edward Meeks to establish a ferry boat service in the vicinity of Rabbit Hash. Since Kentucky's official boundary line was the low-water mark of the Ohio River on the opposite shore, all decisions, regulations, and permits concerning the river fell under Kentucky's jurisdiction. Meeks's Ferry was upstream from Rabbit Hash, near the mouth of Middle Creek. It was established to transport people, livestock, and farm products across the river to what became Rising Sun, Ind. The town of Rising Sun was established in 1814, before the Indiana territory became a state in 1816. At this time transportation on the Ohio River by steamboat was in its infancy. It became necessary to provide a mode of physical communication between the north and south shores of the river as the two settlements grew. The region's economy began to rely more on river transportation, and transporting farm products to and from steamboats was the early business in Rabbit Hash. An expansive sandbar on the Kentucky shore prohibited steamboats from tying up or landing on the community's shores. Instead, they put in at Rising Sun, where the channel was deeper and access was easier. These conditions made a ferry connecting the two cross-river communities an economic necessity. Goods for export were ferried across to the steamboats and imports were ferried back.

As the population increased, and river commerce and transportation progressed, more goods and products made their way down to the ferry landing. Eventually, when the need arose for a place to store these items until the steamboats arrived, a group of local farmers built a storehouse on the Rabbit Hash bank. The storage facility was managed, and then eventually owned and operated, by a single proprietor, James A. Wilson, who was only 17 years old when it opened in 1831. That business, which has been in continuous operation ever since, with very little change, came to be known as the Rabbit Hash General Store. The general store soon became the heart and soul of the community.

An early name of the community, derived from the name of its magisterial district, was Carlton. The magisterial district, encompassing much of western Boone Co., presumably was named for an early settler of the area, James Carlton. In winter 1847, the area where the general store is located began to be called Rabbit Hash. During a Christmastime freshet, a group of individuals were sitting outdoors, watching the water. One person remarked that he was going to have rabbit hash that evening, since the rising water was forcing the rabbits to leave their holes. This fellow quickly was given the nickname Rabbit Hash, and the town soon was being called Rabbit Hash as well.

From 1825 to 1875, most mail traveled up and down the rivers by steamboat. Because more and more mail intended for the Carlton district was mistakenly delivered to Carrollton, 39 miles downriver, the postal service decided to build a new post office in the Carlton district and asked locals to choose a new name for it. Their choice was Rabbit Hash, already the informal name of the town. Accordingly, Rabbit Hash became the official name of both the town and its post office, as postmarks soon attested.

Rabbit Hash has had to fight two natural enemies, floods and ice, in order to survive as a community. Half of the town of Rabbit Hash was severed from its Ohio River location by the **flood of 1937**. But the flood of 1937 was not Rabbit Hash's first encounter with natural disaster. Significant Ohio River floods had also occurred in 1849, 1883, **1884**, and **1913**. The people of Rabbit Hash took note. The local blacksmith in the 1880s devised a solution for the ever-threatening problem. He designed and installed a series of threaded rods bolted on all four corners of the general store between its bottom sill and top plate logs. Beneath the store, these rods have a hook. Another rod-and-hook system is anchored by concrete in the ground just below these rods. When floodwaters rise and begin to float the store, these hooks engage and secure the building in place until the water subsides. Mud from the 1937 flood can still be seen in the attic of the general store, proving the effectiveness of this protective system.

The ice that formed on the river in 1918 did little significant damage to the town, but it was a rare spectacle. There is photographic evidence that cars and trucks drove across the Ohio River on the ice that year, not to mention the scores of pedestrians taking advantage of nature's new bridge to Indiana. Rabbit Hash fared much better than Cincinnati and other river cities up and down the river that lost boats, landings, and warehouses to the destructive ice event. In 1945, however, ice crushed and buried the last ferryboat in Rabbit Hash, the *Mildred*.

As time passed, communications between Rabbit Hash and Rising Sun ceased and the towns grew further apart. In earlier times, people from Rabbit Hash had frequented Rising Sun on a regular basis. They worked there, worshipped at the town's churches, went to school in Rising Sun, shopped and doctored there, and were buried there. This close interaction and relationship ended when the river level was raised during the 1960s by the new **Markland Dam**. With the Ohio River's new system of navigational locks and dams, Rising Sun is cut off from its former neighbor.

From the 1960s to the late 1970s, Rabbit Hash's economy declined. The convenience of automobile transportation and the establishment of trendy shopping complexes and malls were sounding the death knell for Rabbit Hash. The winter of 1978–1979 was another time when stretches of the Ohio River froze over completely. Rabbit Hash suffered no losses or damage, but this was the ice event that totally obliterated Big Bone Island downstream. As before in 1918, people walked over the ice from Rabbit Hash to Rising Sun, mainly just to say they did it. This was also the winter when Lib and Cliff

Rabbit Hash General Store.

Stephens decided they would no longer own the Rabbit Hash General Store. The town was dead and their business was as well. Louie Scott had just purchased the old Ryle Brothers Store in town from his uncle Clayton Ryle, when Cliff offered to sell the general store to Scott. Scott bought it and then purchased other properties in town until he finally owned them all. He believed the town needed saving, and thanks to his efforts, Rabbit Hash was rescued and given new life. On December 13, 2002, Louie Scott sold his holdings in Rabbit Hash to the Rabbit Hash Historical Society (RHHS) for a nominal price to ensure the community's continued preservation. A very generous donation of $250,000 bequeathed to the RHHS in 2001 by Edna Flower, a local resident, made this transaction and a subsequent endowment fund possible. Locally, in Boone Co., Rabbit Hash is a landmark and has been granted the only Historic Overlay zoning in the county. The general store has been designated as a Kentucky Landmark since the late 1970s and has been on the National Register of Historic Places since the early 1980s. In December 2003, the entire town and 33 acres of contiguous properties were designated by the National Park Service and the Department of Interior as a National Register District; it was the second National Register District in Boone Co. In 2004 First Lady Laura Bush honored Rabbit Hash by recognizing it as a Preserve America Community. Preserve America is a White House initiative developed in cooperation with the Advisory Council on Historic Preservations, the U.S. Department of Interior, and the U.S. Department of Commerce to highlight worthy efforts to preserve America's national heritage.

Over the past 25 years, there have been five different proprietors of the store, and each has added a distinctive color to Rabbit Hash's history, keeping intact the store's claim of continuous operation since 1831. Rabbit Hash hats, shirts, and other souvenirs have been bought and carried by the store's customers to many parts of the world.

Nelson, William H. *The Buried Treasure: A Rabbit Hash Mystery.* Lawrenceburg, Ind.: Sam Chapman, ca. 1890. Reprint, Rabbit Hash, Ky.: Rabbit Hash Historical Society, 1997.

Don Clare

RADIO. Northern Kentucky was a center of early amateur radio and has been home to a number of important commercial radio stations. In 1923 J. G. Harbord, president of the Radio Corporation of America, delivered a speech before the Agricultural Society at Topeka, Kans. Harbord proclaimed the invention of radio to be a "miracle of the ages" and an invention that touched human interest and human welfare as closely as the wooden printing blocks invented by Gutenberg five centuries earlier.

Wireless communication actually began much earlier than 1923. The idea was entertained in the early 1800s when scientists Joseph Henry and Michael Faraday theorized that that electrical currents traveling over one wire could produce current in another wire. Heinrich Hertz experimented with the transmission of noise, but not until 1895 was a system produced, by Guglielmo Marconi, using Hertz's ideas. In March 1899 the first wireless messages were transmitted across the English Channel, and in December 1901 the first transatlantic message was sent. In December 1900, Reginald Fessenden, an employee of the U.S. Weather Bureau, transmitted speech, using a high-frequency spark; this appears to have been the first audio radio transmission. Just over one year later, on January 1, 1902, Nathan B. Stubblefield demonstrated a radio transmitter-receiver in Murray, Ky., by transmitting his son's voice about one mile to a receiver before an audience of about 1,000.

Radio began much as the computer did, owned and operated by amateurs who dabbled in scientific apparatus and generally communicated only among themselves. The strange collection of batteries and wires and tuning devices that they used, hooked up to a brass key and headphones, could create sound that could travel to remote areas that were not connected by the telegraph. In Northern Kentucky, as well as the rest of the world, these amateurs became the businessmen who began to produce the simple sets that became popular in people's homes.

The United States did not start licensing radio stations until December 1912. The nation was divided up into districts, and Kentucky was a part of the ninth district. The licensing authority was the U.S. Commerce Department. When the first list of stations was published on July 1, 1913, none of the 22 stations in the ninth district were in Kentucky. On October 1, 1913, the first supplement to the list included three licenses in Kentucky, one at Frankfort and two in Newport. The licensees in Newport were Ervin B. Mattenheimer and John H. Flynn Jr. In 1914 two more licenses were added from Newport, so four of the first five stations licensed in the state were in Newport. In effect, Newport had become "the radio capitol" of Kentucky. Flynn was featured in a *Kentucky Enquirer* article in 1914, when he and a few other amateurs formed the Ohio Valley Radio Association for the purpose of relaying messages.

Although the possibility of transmitting speech and music had been demonstrated, actual broadcasting to the public on a scheduled basis by designated stations did not begin before 1919. Station KDKA of Pittsburgh, Pa., claims to be the first station to hold a schedule of brief announcements and music; however, the Ohio River Valley had what has been also claimed as the first station, located at Peebles Corner in the Walnut Hills neighborhood of Cincinnati. Owned by the Precision Equipment Company, the station eventually known as 8XB held regular broadcasts of music in 1919. Former employee Lt. Harry Breckel claimed that Precision was selling wireless apparatuses in 1919. To stimulate sales, he and several other engineers built and operated a station playing music under the call letters PC in 1919. They received the call letters 8XB in 1920. The story was substantiated by one of the station's engineers, Thomas New.

With the advent of regular broadcasts, manufacturers quickly saw that there would be a market for radio receiving sets among the public. John Flynn became one of the men from Northern Kentucky to take advantage of this new business opportunity, and by 1922 he had formed the United Radio Labs in Cincinnati and was making and selling radio apparatuses. Numerous men pursued the same path between 1921 and 1925. The first receiving sets were of the crystal type, soon followed by battery-powered sets employing tubes. By 1930, most sets being sold were powered by electricity on alternating current. Radio shops and repair facilities sprang up in nearly every city, along with additional broadcasting stations.

By 1929 Kentucky had three commercial radio stations operating, WLAP, WHAS, and WFIW. A fourth station, **WCKY**, was constructed in Covington in 1929. To broaden his audience and revenues, that station's owner, **L. B. Wilson**, later moved WCKY's transmitter to Cincinnati but kept the station's broadcasting license in Kentucky. By 1932 it was estimated that 20 million Americans owned radios, or 64 percent of the population. By 1950, when television began taking some of the attention away from radio, 40 million Americans owned a radio, about 94 percent of all households (see also **WFBE**; **WFTM**; **WCVG**; **WNOP**; **WNKU**; **WZIP**).

Leming, John E., Jr. Personal collections of various papers and clippings on local area radio, Cold Spring, Ky.

"Ready to Give Wireless Warnings," *KE*, February 7, 1914, 1.

John E. Leming Jr.

RAGAN, GEORGE WARREN (b. April 19, 1865, near Independence, Ky.; d. September 27, 1937, Cold Spring, Ky.). George W. Ragan, a physician and a state senator, was the son of Eli and Sarah Carter Ragan. His grandfather was a true Kentucky pioneer, born in the state in 1797. George Ragan grew up on the family farm listening to the adventures of his mother's father, Warren Carter, whom **Daniel Carter Beard** colorfully described in his book *Hardly a Man Is Now Alive*.

Ragan began the study of medicine at the age of 18. Traveling to his employment by either steamboat or the Short Line (the **Louisville, Cincinnati, and Lexington Railroad**), he worked in his spare time to support himself and pay for his schooling. In March 1891 he graduated from the University of Louisville Medical School, and that same year he married Effie Morrison Riggs, a schoolteacher, also from the Independence area. They had two sons, Dr. David Yandell Ragan, who also graduated from the University of Louisville Medical School, and Allen Edgar Ragan, an Ohio State University history professor who graduated from Miami University, Oxford, Ohio.

George Ragan's strong desire to serve where he was most needed sent him on horseback over the countryside in Kentucky, talking with residents; after much consideration, he decided to practice medicine in Campbell Co. He built the family home in Cold Spring, along **U.S. 27**, on a site that is today the offices of **Griffin Industries**. Ragan became known as a friend to the common people. He served all the surrounding areas in the county where he practiced and also provided care to the children in the St. Joseph Orphanage (see **Diocesan Catholic Children's Home**). A true country doctor, he regularly helped the sick where he found them, even though it meant traveling by horse and buggy over the back roads in all kinds of weather. As he aged and his practice grew, and as the county changed with the times, he opened an office at his residence. His 1925 journal listed more than 550 patients, some living south of Alexandria and others north of the Ohio River.

Ragan was a member of the Cold Spring School Board for more than 27 years. This service, along with his desire to reduce taxes for the farmers in the area and build better roads, led to his nomination for the office of state senator in 1931, at age 66. Defeating Republican senator **Ellsworth Regenstein** by a large majority, he was elected, and then he was reelected in 1935. While in office Ragan introduced a bill dealing with revenue and taxation in 1934 and was present when the Whiskey Bill passed in 1936. He was a close personal friend of Kentucky governor A. B. "Happy" Chandler (1935–1939, 1955–1959), president of the Bank of Cold Spring, and a member of the Alexandria Lodge of **Masons**.

Ragan practiced medicine as a country doctor for 47 years. He was 72 when he died of a heart attack at his home in Cold Spring in 1937. He was buried at the Independence Cemetery in Kenton Co., and his widow Effie was buried next to him in 1952.

"Honor Ragan—Orphanage Pays Tribute to 40 Years Service," *KP*, November 30, 1931, 1.
"Senator Ragan Dies of Heart Attack in Home," *KP*, September 27, 1937, 1.
Special Collections and Archives, Univ. of Louisville Medical School, Louisville, Ky.

Deborah R. Neace

RAGTIME. Ragtime, America's first original music, flourished during the first two decades of the 20th century. Popular largely for its lively and syncopated style, it gained momentum in St. Louis and New York City, but Cincinnati and Northern Kentucky were also important ragtime hubs. The migration of **African Americans** from the southern states helped spread the ragtime style. Riverboats on the Ohio River, the *Island Queen* steamboat in particular, also served to expose audiences to the popular style of music.

Ragtime should not be confused with an earlier related style known as the Cakewalk. Ragtime is a musical form written in 2/4 or 4/4 time that has a syncopated melody and "ragged" rhythmic accents on the weak beats. Although band performances of ragtime were not uncommon, ragtime was initially and more often played on the piano.

The birth of ragtime is commonly credited to African American composer and pianist Scott Joplin in St. Louis, Mo., during the early 1890s. John Edward Hasse, a music historian from Cincinnati, has noted that there were four ragtime styles: instrumental rags, ragtime songs, ragtime waltzes, and the earlier style that involved "ragging" existing music. During its peak period (1897–1919), ragtime was credited with increasing the popularity of pianos and player pianos nationwide. Ragtime tunes were popularized through sheet music, available at music retailers and **five-and-dime stores**. In addition, solo piano performances at vaudeville shows throughout the nation assisted in introducing the style to mainstream America.

A notable ragtime artist was Artie "Mr. 814" Matthews, who founded the Cosmopolitan School of Music on W. Ninth St. in Cincinnati and operated it from the 1920s into the late 1950s. He trained countless artists and had many Northern Kentucky connections. Matthews was secretary-treasurer of the Cincinnati Musicians' Local 814 African American union. He had arranged and composed many rag tunes earlier in St. Louis at the Stark Music Company; his most famous piece, however, is an early jazz classic entitled "Weary Blues."

Covington native Louis H. Mentel was a ragtime composer; he published "A Daisy Girl" in Covington in 1905. In 1910 Covington's William M. Hickman wrote and published "Diplomat Rag," also in Covington. The **Gasdorf Music Publishing Company** of Newport, one of several ragtime music houses in the region, represented a rare melding of African American and German culture. Music historian Hasse says that Alfred Gasdorf, who was born into a musical family in Newport about 1883, performed in orchestras on the *Island Queen* steamboat. Northern Kentucky composer Floyd H. Willis (born in Falmouth) published many rags in Covington, including "Kentucky Rag" in 1908. He was also a Cincinnati movie theater accompanist. Two other Northern Kentucky artists dabbled with ragtime during careers known for other forms of music. Covington-born **Justin Huber**, a regional bandleader, as a young man in 1911 published a "catchy" Indian ragtime piece called "Fire Water"; and **Larry Vincent**, locally remembered for his years of piano playing at the **Beverly Hills Supper Club** and at the **Lookout House**, had a previous career of vaudeville, in which he was not above trying a rag or two.

Ragtime was virtually displaced by the introduction of **jazz** in the early 1920s. It gained a renewed following upon the release of the Oscar-winning motion picture *The Sting* (1973), which won an Academy Award for Marvin Hamlish's adaptation of Scott Joplin's classic piano ragtime tunes featured in the film.

Hasse, John Edward. *Cincinnati Ragtime: A List of Composers and Their Works*. Cincinnati: John Edward Hasse, 1983.
Jasen, David A., and Gene Jones. *That American Rag: The Story of Ragtime from Coast to Coast*. New York: Schirmer Books, 2000.
Sadie, Stanley, ed. *The New Grove Dictionary of Music and Musicians*. Vol. 5. New York: Grove, 2001.
Steib, Murray, ed. *Reader's Guide to Music: History, Theory, Criticism*. Chicago: Fitzroy Dearborn, 1999.

Kareem A. Simpson

RAILROAD DEPOTS. At the Northern Kentucky railroad depots, passenger tickets were sold or freight was deposited for shipment or after being shipped, or both functions were carried out. Not every train station had a depot. From the beginning of railroad service until the 1950s, the railroad depot was the heart and soul of a town. Therefore, the stationmaster at the depot was a man of importance in the town, and his coming and goings were reported in the local newspaper.

The railroad depot was the place to see who was arriving and who was departing, since it served as the portal through which most people arrived and left the community. Friends were welcomed and loved ones kissed goodbye. The depot was also a scene of bereavement, for the trains carried friends and relatives who had died while away from the community and were being returned home in their caskets for burial.

Because the Western Union telegraph office was at the depot, it was also the place to hear the latest news. Announcements of sporting events were often passed over Western Union wires to be posted by the telegraph operator on the depot bulletin board. Before radio became common, major league ball games came to life in a community through those bulletin-board postings; the telegraph operator chalked up inning-by-inning scores and sometimes even descriptions of important plays. The depot was also the site where the U.S. Post Office Railway Express received outgoing mail and unloaded incoming mail.

Most of the goods moving into and out of town came through the freight depot, loaded in a boxcar (lumber), on a flatcar (farm machinery), in a gondola car (pipes), or in a hopper car (coal); or they came via the Railway Express Agency (REA). The REA, which was the UPS and FedEx of its time, handled all less-than-carload shipments. If a town did not have a freight depot, it would have a railroad siding where cars to be loaded or unloaded could be staged. The shipper or receiver of the goods would back a wagon up to the rail car at the siding to load or unload merchandise. Because enough space had to be provided for a wagon with its team of horses to pull next to the rail car, these sidings were referred to as team sidings. The depot began to lose its place in the community in the 1920s; by the 1960s, depots had fallen into disuse. Freight moved by truck or was carried in containers on trains that stopped only at major terminals.

Until the 1960s, many railroads ran frequent passenger service over their lines, allowing a person to go to Cincinnati in the morning to shop or attend a Cincinnati Reds baseball game, and to return home that night. For a number of years at the start of the 20th century, the **Southern Railway** (SR) offered commuter service between Cincinnati and Williamstown and stations in between. Passenger service was dropped by most railroads in 1971. Today the only passenger train that travels through the Northern Kentucky region is Amtrak's Cardinal, which stops in Maysville and in Cincinnati on its way from New York City to Chicago via Washington, D.C.

As the railroads abandoned their depots, they usually demolished the structures, since state and local governments carried them as real property on the tax rolls. It made no sense for a railroad to pay property tax on buildings no longer in use. Only four Northern Kentucky depots still survive: The **Chesapeake and Ohio** (C&O) depot and the Louisville and Nashville (L&N) depot in Maysville are both owned by the City of Maysville, the C&O depot serving as a public transportation center and the L&N depot housing the police station. The SR depot at Erlanger is owned by the City of Erlanger and now is a museum. The Covington depot, formerly a C&O depot but also shared by the L&N, was sold to a private individual and turned into an office building. The Sparta depot (L&N) stood until 2003, when CSX tore it down after the City of Sparta failed to exercise its option to purchase the building.

Railroad Depots in Northern Kentucky

Boone Co.
Devon (SR)
Kensington (SR)
Richwood (SR)
Walton (L&N and SR)

Bracken Co.
Augusta (C&O)
Brooksville (**Brooksville and Ohio Railroad**)
Foster (C&O)
Wellsburg (Brooksville Railroad and C&O)

Campbell Co.
Bellevue (C&O)
Brent (C&O)
California (C&O)
Dayton (C&O)
Mentor (C&O)
Newport (near 11th and Saratoga) (C&O and L&N combined passenger station; C&O freight station)
Newport (Jefferson [Sixth St.] and Saratoga Sts.) (L&N, originally **Louisville, Cincinnati, and Lexington Railroad**, passenger station until 1888; L&N freight station thereafter)
New Richmond (C&O)
Ross (C&O)

Carroll Co.
Carrollton (Carrollton Railroad)
Eagle Station (L&N)
Sanders (L&N)
Worthville (Carrollton Railroad and L&N)

Gallatin Co.
Glenco (L&N)
Sparta (L&N)

Grant Co.
Blanchett (SR)
Corinth (SR)
Crittenden (SR)
Dry Ridge (SR)
Elliston (L&N)
Mason (SR)
Sherman (SR)
Williamstown (SR)
Zion (L&N)

Kenton Co.
Bank Lick (L&N)
Bracht (SR)
Buffington (SR)
Covington (C&O and L&N)
Erlanger (SR)
Highland (SR)
Independence (L&N)
Kenton (L&N)
Latonia (L&N)
Ludlow (SR)
Morning View (L&N)
Spring Lake (L&N)
Visalia (L&N)
Woodside (SR)

Mason Co.
Dover (C&O)
Helena (L&N)
Marshall (Lewisburg) (L&N)
Maysville (C&O and L&N)
Somo (L&N)
South Ripley (C&O)

Owen Co.: no rail service

Pendleton Co.
Butler (L&N)
Falmouth (L&N)

Robertson Co.: no rail service

Charles H. Bogart

RAILROADS. The history of railroads in the Northern Kentucky region is intimately tied to railroad developments in Cincinnati. Railroads, when they came to the region in the 19th century, brought a new mode of transporting goods. Large, heavy loads could be moved at considerable speed overland in a more-or-less straight path. Railroads did not need to worry about the depth of the water in a river channel. Trains began serving Cincinnati in the mid-1840s, and by the 1850s they also served Northern Kentucky.

In terms of the development of railroads, Cincinnati and Northern Kentucky initially found themselves at a disadvantage because of their topography. To the east and the south, the Allegheny and Appalachian mountains formed a barrier that was expensive to penetrate and demanded new engineering techniques. To the north and the west, major cities had already carved out their own markets for goods, supplanting Cincinnati's canals in those directions. The principal areas remaining for economic opportunities were those traditionally linked to the region—the east and the south—and it was in those directions that Cincinnati and Northern Kentucky concentrated their railroad building. Yet, railroads to the east and the south were not an end in themselves, because these same roads became mutually dependent upon rails reaching to the west and the north.

During most of the 19th century, there was no agreement as to the gauge of railroad tracks. Rail gauge refers to the space between a track's two iron rails. Most railroads in the United States today operate on standard gauge, which is 4 feet 8.5 inches—the same gauge as the wheels of a Roman chariot. Railroad tracks wider than this were referred to as "broad gauge," and tracks narrower than this were called "narrow gauge." Railroads of one gauge could not interchange their equipment with railroads of another gauge without special arrangements such as a third rail. Thus, at places where railroads of different gauges met (called a connection), goods had to be off-loaded tediously and expensively and reloaded onto other lines. Moreover, tracks within a central city did not always mesh with rail lines at the city's outskirts. Further complicating matters, early railroads often had to stop at major geographic barriers such as the Ohio River. Locally, that problem was resolved with the opening in 1872 of the first railroad bridge across the river in Northern Kentucky, at Newport, called the **L&N Bridge**. Gauge mismatches were fixed on May 30, 1886, when the **Cincinnati Southern** and **Kentucky Central** (KC) tracks were converted to standard. Thereafter, all major railroads serving Cincinnati were standard gauge, connecting with one another and having access into the Northern Kentucky region via bridges across the Ohio River by ownership, track rights, or interchange agreement. By 1890 Cincinnati was the third-busiest rail center in the United States.

In the 19th century, at least 14 major railroads operated within the city of Cincinnati, and 4 of them served Northern Kentucky. But before the region had railroad connections to the north, the **Covington and Lexington Railroad** (C&L), the first to begin business within Northern Kentucky, was completed to Covington in December 1854; via Ohio River ferries, its cargoes supplied Cincinnati with hogs, grain, and other agricultural products. Its direct connection to Cincinnati, under the name of a successor, the **Louisville and Nashville Railroad** (L&N), was made possible by the opening of the **Chesapeake and Ohio Railroad Bridge** in 1888. The second line to arrive in Northern Kentucky, and the first with tracks into Cincinnati, was the **Louisville, Cincinnati, and Lexington** (LC&L), the "short line" between Newport and Louisville, which a few years later extended into Cincinnati via the L&N Bridge. The third railroad to enter the region was the Cincinnati Southern, with the opening of its bridge at Ludlow in 1877. The fourth railroad, the **Chesapeake and Ohio Railroad** (C&O), arrived from the east and ran along the southern shore of the Ohio River from Maysville through Newport and Covington and across the C&O Bridge into Cincinnati. At the beginning of the 20th century, three class one railroads, as a result of mergers, operated within the Northern Kentucky region: the **Southern Railway** (SRR) as the leaseholder of the Cincinnati Southern, the Louisville and Nashville Railroad, and the Chesapeake and Ohio Railway.

Other railroads operated in Northern Kentucky but did not serve Cincinnati. These included the **Maysville and Lexington** (M&L), completed to Maysville from Paris in 1873; the **Carrollton and Worthville Railroad**, begun in 1906 and still serving as Carrollton's link to the L&N's short line at Worthville; and the **Brooksville and Ohio Railroad**, entirely within Bracken Co., built in 1906 to connect Brooksville to the C&O at Wellsburg and abandoned in 1931. Additional railroads were chartered for construction in the Northern Kentucky region, but for various reasons their promoters were not able to fund construction. The most successful of these proposals was the **Covington, Flemingsburg, and Pound Gap Railroad** (CF&PG). It progressed beyond the paper stage and did lay some track in 1876, first as narrow gauge. Although later converted to standard gauge, it became nothing more than a short line linking Flemingsburg to Flemingsburg Junction on the L&N (along the former M&L), which ceased operations in 1956. Neither Covington nor Pound Gap, Va., the endpoints of the railroad's proposed route system, ever saw a CF&PG engine.

Today conditions have changed. On the south bank of the Ohio River to the east is **CSX**, operating the old C&O track from Huntington, W.Va., via Maysville. This track served the Stevens' Yard at Silver Grove (named for a former C&O president), but the **Chessie System** closed that yard in 1981 with the opening of its Queensgate Yard in Cincinnati. Amtrak uses this route to carry its passenger train, the Cardinal, between New York and Chicago. Today the former Stevens' Yard is the location of the world's largest drywall manufacturing plant, **LaFarge**.

Crossing the Ohio River at Covington, over the C&O Bridge, and paralleling the Licking River south of the KC Junction (16th and Madison) is CSX's line (formerly the L&N) to Winchester and Corbin, Ky. At one time this line had two rail yards, one in Covington, developed early by the C&L, and the DeCoursey Yard, south of Latonia, which opened in 1918 for the L&N. The latter was a hump yard, where by means of a manmade hill, or hump, train cars were sorted downhill by gravity to the proper outbound trains. The Stevens, DeCoursey, and Covington yards have been closed since the opening of the Queensgate Yard in Cincinnati in 1981. The Latonia Yard is now home to the **Railway Museum of Greater Cincinnati**.

Currently CSX also operates the L&N's old "short line" to Louisville. Since the removal of its tracks northward along Saratoga St. in Newport and the conversion of the old L&N railroad bridge to pedestrian use only, this line begins and ends at 11th and Monmouth Sts., where the NX Cabin once stood. The NX Cabin, now demolished (the **Trauth Dairy** occupies this site today), was the joint passenger station of the L&N and C&O railroads as well as a freight station of the C&O. Adjacent to the station was a diamond, a junction of two tracks at grade (street level), where the C&O and L&N lines crossed.

Before CSX's Queensgate Yard in Cincinnati was developed, C&O trains were broken down and made up into new trains at Stevens' Yard in Silver Grove. L&N trains used the DeCoursey Yard for the same purpose. Both Stevens' and DeCoursey were hump yards. Each railroad had a roundhouse serving steam engines and, later, diesel engines. A vestige of one of these structures can be seen at the former C&O Yard in Covington, at W. 14th and Neave. It is now part of the Duro Paper Bag Manufacturing Company complex along Madison Ave. Northern Kentucky yards also ran interchange trains with other rail yards in the Cincinnati area, whereby they dropped off cars consigned to other railroads and returned with cars for their own system.

Crossing the Ohio River at Ludlow is the **Cincinnati Southern Railroad** (CSRR), now operated by the **Norfolk Southern Railway** (NS). Its Ludlow and Erlanger Yards continue to have some activity by local switchers and helper engines. NS uses helper engines not only to push departures southbound up Erlanger Hill but also to provide dynamic braking for arrivals descending the long hill northbound. NS's main train yard is across the bridge, the Gest Street Yard in Cincinnati, located near the Cincinnati Union Terminal. Southern Railway trains were made up and broken down at the Gest Street Yard.

Seven railroad bridges across rivers were built within Northern Kentucky. The first, about 1854, was the original C&L Bridge, now CSX, across the Licking River at Falmouth. The next bridges were the LC&L bridges over the Kentucky River near Worthville, in Carroll Co., and over the Licking River between Latonia and Wilder, both now CSX and both built in 1869. These were followed by the L&N Bridge between Newport and Cincinnati, which was erected by the Little Miami Railroad to give access into Cincinnati for the LC&L; it is now abandoned except for use as a pedestrian bridge (the Purple People Bridge). The next bridge was the CSRR Bridge between Ludlow and Cincinnati (1877), now used by NS. The final bridges were the C&O Bridge across the Licking River between Newport and Covington (1888) and the C&O Bridge across the Ohio River between Covington and Cincinnati (1888), the latter built by the Covington and Cincinnati Elevated Rail & Transfer & Bridge Company. In 1929 this bridge was converted to a vehicular traffic bridge, and a new railroad bridge was built adjacent to it. Most of the other railroad bridges have been modified or rebuilt since their original construction. The original LC&L Bridge over the Licking River (Latonia to Wilder) is one that has not; it remains adjacent to its replacement, carrying only water lines into Covington.

The Cincinnati and Northern Kentucky region remains a rail center. By 2004 roughly 100 trains originated, terminated, or passed through Cincinnati daily. Many of these traverse the Northern Kentucky region via the two surviving railroad bridges, the Cincinnati Southern and the C&O.

Condit, Carl W. *The Railroad and the City.* Columbus: Ohio State Univ. Press, 1977.

Federal Writers' Project. *They Built a City: 150 Years of Industrial Cincinnati.* Cincinnati: Cincinnati Post, 1938.

Tenkotte, Paul A. "The 'Chronic Want' of Cincinnati: A Southern Railroad," *NKH* 6, no. 1 (Fall–Winter 1998): 24–33.

——. "Rival Cities to Suburbs: Covington and Newport, Kentucky, 1790–1890," PhD diss., Univ. of Cincinnati, 1989.

White, John H. *On the Right Track—Some Historic Cincinnati Railroads.* Cincinnati: Cincinnati Railroad Club, 2003.

Charles H. Bogart

RAILWAY MUSEUM OF GREATER CINCINNATI. The Railway Museum of Greater Cincinnati is an outdoor museum devoted to the collection, preservation, and display of historic railroad equipment that once served the Greater Cincinnati metropolitan area. The museum's collection of rolling stock helped create a great deal of romance on the rails before coming to park at the museum's permanent home in the **Latonia** neighborhood of Covington. The museum was founded in 1975 by a group of six railroad buffs as a nonprofit educational organization under the name Railway Exposition Company. The organization's first undertaking was to establish a tourist excursion service on an abandoned line between Brookville, Ind., and Hooven, Ohio. The line operated for more than 10 years before the directors decided it was too similar to a tourist service operated by the nearby White Water Railroad. Through donations and direct purchase, the group had gathered quite a collection of rail cars and needed a place to keep them. It sold the Indiana site to the Indiana and Ohio Railroad, a for-profit freight short line, and leased track areas in Riverside, then Storrs, Ohio. The organization then began offering its six Pullman cars for Rail Cruises, weekend excursions on a rail car hitched to the back of Amtrak trains. The most popular of these departed from Cincinnati on a Friday night and took customers to Washington D.C., where their Pullman parked on a private track and served as a hotel room during the weekend, returning to Cincinnati by midday the following Monday. This venture, lasting about four years, allowed the group to generate capital to invest in further acquisitions and repair of rail cars in the collection.

The railway museum finally arrived at its permanent home in Latonia in 1988. The property at 315 W. Southern Ave. was a railroad site as early as 1869, when the **Louisville, Cincinnati, and Lexington Railroad** built a rail line connecting Newport with Louisville. Back in the 1850s, the **Covington and Lexington Railroad** had built a line through Latonia to connect Covington with Central Kentucky. This railroad intersection figured prominently in the development of Latonia as an independent town. The **Louisville and Nashville Railroad** system acquired both lines, and it eventually merged into the giant **CSX** Corporation, from which the Latonia site was acquired.

The museum collection features 20th-century freight and passenger railroad equipment of seven major railroad systems that served the Greater Cincinnati region, set on 16 outdoor rail tracks to provide an authentic working rail yard environment. Notable pieces in the collection include two kitchen-equipped dining cars, a 1910 Post Office car, Pullman sleeper cars with private compartments, an authentic caboose with windowed cupola and crew living quarters, an army sleeper car used to transport troops across the country during **World War II**, and a 1906 plush and polished private car of a railroad vice president, which served as a traveling office and living quarters. Visitors are invited to climb aboard selected rail cars.

Franzen, Gene. "Now and Then," *KE*, October 15, 2000, B1–B2.

Hyde, Tim, executive vice president for operations of the Railway Museum of Greater Cincinnati. Interview by Rebecca Mitchell Turney, June 29, 2005, Latonia, Ky.

The Railway Museum of Greater Cincinnati. Brochure. Latonia, Ky.: Railway Museum of Greater Cincinnati, 2004.

Rebecca Mitchell Turney

R.A. JONES & COMPANY INC. Lexington dentist and entrepreneur Dr. Ruel Anderson Jones founded this company in 1905. He was born around 1874 in the western part of the state at Columbia. The company's first product was a novelty "advertising soap," a bar of toilet soap with a pressed label encased in wax on one side, which would last as long as the soap. In 1910 Jones moved to Covington. Before 1912 each bar of soap that his company made had to be set by hand, but in that year Jones and his plant superintendent, Harry Struewing, fashioned the first automatic soap press, increasing productivity 10-fold. In 1913 Jones built a plant in Covington on E. 15th St. Realizing that the company's future was not in soap but in the manufacturing process, Jones sold the soap business and in 1919 introduced the first of his many automatic cartoning machines. In 1921 the Procter & Gamble Company of Cincinnati, the world's largest manufacturer of soap products, purchased the first Jones cartoner to package soap. By 1933 most of the world's mass-produced consumer products (for example, razor blades, toothpaste, and soaps) were being packaged by Jones-made machines, equipment such as the Constant Motion Cartoner Machine, which packaged and sealed both solid and semisolid articles.

In 1966 R.A. Jones & Company moved to a new 235,000-square-foot plant in Crescent Springs, Ky.; today it employs 500 workers. The company has become a world leader in the manufacturing of high-speed packaging machinery. Some of its equipment can package up to 2,500 items per minute. R.A. Jones & Company's industrial machines are known for their simplicity, long life, speed, and efficiency. The Jones client list includes Anheiser Busch, Kraft, Kellogg's, and P&G. Until 1987 the company had had only two presidents, R. A. Jones himself and his son, Wickliffe. R. A. Jones, who lived at 422 Wallace Ave. in Covington, died October 20, 1941, at Holmes Hospital in Cincinnati; Wickliffe Jones, who held some 21 patents, died at his Indian Hill home on the east side of Cincinnati February 18, 1989. Both are buried in the family lot at Highland Cemetery in Fort Mitchell.

In 1998 R.A. Jones & Company, a privately held venture, was sold to the British conglomerate BWI, which in turn has been sold to the German company IWKA. Marketing its goods and services to the food, beverage, electronics, communications, and pharmaceutical industries, the company has annual sales of close to $50 million and sees its future growth coming from international markets. Only twice did the company fail to show a profit, in 1945 and in 1946. It is proud that there have been no layoffs of employees since 1953. Today, R.A. Jones & Company is one of the largest exporters of goods in the Northern Kentucky region. For almost 100 years, the company has been a successful and innovative firm employing many Northern Kentuckians. Today, it is part of OYSTAR Jones (formerly IWKA).

"Dr. R.A. Jones Widely Known Inventor Dies," *CP*, October 21, 1941, 2.

Obituary, *CP*, February 20, 1989, 2C.

OYSTAR Jones. "R.A. Jones & Company Inc." www.rajones.com (accessed December 10, 2006).

"R.A. Jones Deal Protects Employees," *KP*, August 18, 1898, B18.

"R.A. Jones Manufacturing," *NKH* 13, no. 2 (Spring–Summer 2006): 2–12.

Slade, Adele. "Intricate Machines Made in Covington Package Large Part of World's Products," *KP*, September 25, 1933, 1.

RAMAGE, JAMES A., CIVIL WAR MUSEUM. See **James A. Ramage Civil War Museum**.

RANDOLPH, JAMES E. (b. January 17, 1888, Hannibal, Mo.; d. May 23, 1981, Newport, Ky.). James E. Randolph was an African American medical doctor who practiced in Covington for 59 years. He was the first African American permitted to practice in any Northern Kentucky hospital. Randolph graduated from the Meharry Medical School in Nashville, Tenn., in 1917. The grandson of a slave, he worked his way through medical school as a railroad Pullman porter. Randolph began his practice at Shelbyville, Tenn. He served in the U.S. Army Medical Reserve Corps in **World War I**. In 1922 Randolph moved to Covington. He lived first at 1039 Greenup St. and later, in 1950, moved across the street to 1002 Greenup.

Randolph was the staff physician at the Lincoln-Grant School in Covington for more than 40 years. In 1973, after the school's name was changed to 12th District School, he began treating children from the school at his nearby office.

A grove of trees on the campus of Northern Kentucky University in Highland Heights memorializes Randolph's achievements. In 1974 the City of Covington named an Eastside neighborhood park in his honor. In 1976 he received from the parochial **La Salette Academy** in Covington a Gold Medal for service to the community. He was an active member of the St. James A.M.E. Church in Covington. He died in 1981, at age 93, at the Baptist Convalescent Center in Newport, following cataract surgery, and was buried at the Mary E. Smith Cemetery in Elsmere.

On May 9, 1997, Randolph was inducted into the region's Leadership Hall of Fame during ceremonies held by the Northern Kentucky Chamber of Commerce. He was acknowledged as the first African American physician on staff at St. Elizabeth Hospital in Covington and as the first African American member of the Campbell-Kenton Medical Society. A Kentucky Historical Society Highway Marker along Greenup St. was dedicated to Randolph on September 10, 2004.

"Dr. Randolph Was 'There to Help Us,'" *KP*, May 25, 1981, 1K.

"He's 85 . . . Still One of the Busiest Doctors," *KP*, February 15, 1973, 11.

"Leaders Who Made Mark Inducted in Hall of Fame," *KP*, April 29, 1997, 3K.

"N. Ky. Hall Adds Three," *KE*, May 9, 1997, C1–C2.

"Pioneering Covington Physician Recognized," *KP*, September 11, 2004, B1.

"Portrait of an Epic Journey," *KP*, June 1, 1995, 1K.

"Students' Book Celebrates Covington's Black History," *KP*, February 26, 1997, 2K.

Theodore H. H. Harris

RATTERMAN, GEORGE (b. November 26, 1926, Cincinnati, Ohio; d. November 3, 2007, Centennial, Colo.). George William Ratterman, the son of Leander and Claribell Cahill Ratterman, made Northern Kentucky history in two areas: sports and politics. He grew up on Burch Ave. in the Hyde Park neighborhood of Cincinnati and graduated from St. Xavier High School in Cincinnati in 1944. Ratterman attended the University of Notre Dame in the summer of 1944 in the V-12 naval officer college program. After two years there, he was accepted by the Notre Dame law school (standard practice for medical and law schools during the war). He took law classes at Notre Dame, the University of Michigan, and a few other law schools before eventually graduating from Salmon P. Chase Law School (see **Chase College of Law**).

In 1947 quarterback Ratterman led the College Football All-Stars to victory over the Chicago Bears of the National Football League (NFL) in the annual College All-Star game in Chicago. He played 10 years of professional football: 3 with the Buffalo Bills of the old All-America Football Conference (1947–1949), 2 with the New York Yanks of the NFL (1950–1951), and 5 with the NFL's Cleveland Browns (1952–1956). He also played one season (1951) with the Montreal Alouettes in the Canadian Football League. Injuries cut short his football career in 1956. After retirement, he worked for ABC (1960–1964) and NBC (1965–1973) as a television commentator on AFL and NFL game broadcasts.

Ratterman worked as an investment adviser in Cincinnati while attending the Salmon P. Chase

The Glenn Hotel–Tropicana Club, 928 Monmouth St., Newport, where Ratterman was framed.

Law School at night, when that school was located in the Cincinnati **YMCA**; he graduated in 1956. In 1961 he became involved with the Committee of 500 in Campbell Co. (see **Newport Reform Groups**), a citizens' group formed to rid the county of gambling and **prostitution**. He was a resident of Fort Thomas, not Newport, the city most needing to be cleaned up. In addition, he was a Roman Catholic who was chosen as a sheriff candidate by the Protestant ministers behind the Committee of 500 because they wanted to broaden the group's base of support. In April of 1961 Ratterman agreed to run as a reform candidate for the office of Campbell Co. sheriff, and he soon became involved in a nationally publicized series of events that included an attempt by mob operative **Tito Carinci** to frame Ratterman and discredit him as a sheriff candidate. The ensuing courtroom trials were closely watched by Robert F. Kennedy, then U.S. attorney general, and Kentucky governor Bert T. Combs (1959–1963). The charges against Ratterman were dropped, and he went on to be elected county sheriff. Once Ratterman and his deputies began to enforce the laws against crime and vice, the operators of the casinos and nightclubs left town and law and order began to prevail. In 1965 Ratterman lost the election for Campbell Co. judge to **A. J. Jolly Jr.** In 1966 he lost to **Gene Snyder** in a bid for the area's U.S. congressional seat. In 1967 Ratterman, his wife, and 8 of his children moved to the Denver, Colo., area, where he lived and worked until retirement. He died in 2007 and was cremated; his remains were placed at Chapel Hill Cemetery in Centennial, Colo.

Davidson, Bill. "The Great Kentucky Scandal," *Look Magazine,* October 24, 1961, 88–96.

Kleber, John E., ed. *The Kentucky Encyclopedia.* Lexington: Univ. Press of Kentucky, 1992.

Latimer, Clay. "On Football and Strippers," *Rocky Mountain News*, reprinted in *KP*, January 8, 2005, 1K.

Ratterman, George. *Confessions of a Gypsy Quarterback.* New York: Cowan-McCann, 1962.

Shearer, Jason G. "Urban Reform in Sin City: The George Ratterman Trial and the Election of 1961 in Northern Kentucky," *RKHS* 98, no. 4 (Autumn 2000): 343–65.

Michael R. Sweeney

REAMS, LEE ROY (b. August 23, 1942, Covington, Ky.). Lee Roy Reams, an internationally acclaimed Broadway star, has danced and sung his way from a humble beginning in Covington to the brightest footlights of the entertainment world. He is the youngest of seven children of Robert and Flora Moore Reams. Recognizing early his interest and talent in the arts, his mother made sure that there was always money for his dance and music lessons. He graduated from **Holmes High School** in 1960 and received a BA from the University of Cincinnati in 1964. During his student days, he appeared in productions on the *Showboat Majestic,* at the Playhouse in the Park in Cincinnati, and at Memorial Hall in Dayton, Ohio. In 1982 he received an MA from the University of Cincinnati and was awarded an honorary doctorate in performing arts by his alma mater in 1998. He has toured the country coast to coast and appeared as an entertainer on numerous cruise ships around the world. His starring role for many years in Broadway's *42nd Street* won him Tony and Drama Desk nominations. He has appeared on Broadway with Carol Channing in *Hello Dolly* and with Lauren Bacall in *Applause.* His dancing partners have included Ann Miller, Juliet Prowse, Cyd Charisse, Mitzi Gaynor, Anne Bancroft, Jane Powell, Ethel Merman, Goldie Hahn, Chita Rivera, and Suzanne Farrell. He has performed before U.S. presidents Jimmy Carter, Ronald Reagan, Bill Clinton, and George H. W. Bush, and also before first lady Lady Bird Johnson. He was a guest star with both the Cincinnati and New York Pops orchestras. He has also appeared at New York's Carnegie Hall, London's Palladium, Istanbul's Hilton, Brazil's Manaus Opera House, Cairo's Opera House, the Rockefeller Center's Rainbow and Stars, and the Kennedy Center in Washington, D.C. One of his most endearing attributes is that he never forgets his family and his roots. When his beloved sister-in-law Pat Reams died in 2004, he interrupted an appearance at the Kennedy Center to come home to Covington for her funeral. He owns property in New York City and in Connecticut.

Holden, Stephen. "Singer-Dancer's Imperative: He's Gotta Get to Broadway," *NYT,* December 21, 1998, E3.

McElfresh, Tom. "For Covington's Reams, '42nd Street' Is Bittersweet," *CE,* November 23, 1980, F7.

Radcliffe, E. B. "Nothing but Applause for Lee Roy Reams," *CE,* December 12, 1971, 18.

Stein, Jerry. "Showboat Books Lee Roy Reams," *CP,* May 25, 1982, 8A.

Alice Kennelly Roberts

REBEL LANDING. Rebel Landing, a distinctive home situated on the Ohio River two miles east of Carrollton in Carroll Co., has been featured in magazine and newspaper articles and is often cited for its connection to pioneer **Benjamin Craig**. Craig built one of the earliest brick homes on the Ohio River, known to river pilots as Halfway House, at the halfway point between Cincinnati and Louisville. Heirs of his daughter Sally Craig Price later owned this tract of land.

Price's granddaughter Nancy Price "Nannie" Shaffer married Louisville distillery owner Nicholas L. Fitschen, and in 1883 they purchased the Ogburn tract east of the Craig-Price tract, building upon it a home dubbed Rebel Landing by later owners. Nancy Price Peak, Mrs. Fitschen's aunt, lived nearby on the old Craig tract. Craig's desolated home was torn down and its brick used to build a small guesthouse behind the Fitschen's new home, possibly as quarters for the elderly Mrs. Peak. Within a few years, the Fitschens returned to Louisville, where Mrs. Peak died in 1888, and the Fitschens sold the home in 1893. After her husband's death, Nannie Fitschen returned to Carroll Co. and lived in a cottage at the site of Craig's original house, cared for by her widowed daughter-in-law, Nell Wade Fitschen.

Nell Wade Fitschen inherited the property and built a motel nearby. Her murder in the hotel office in 1969 was the most shocking local crime of its generation, unsolved until one of the men involved confessed, 25 years later.

The Fitschen cottage was razed, and the site of Benjamin Craig's original house is now graced by the new home of a descendant, businessman Clarence "Duper" Craig. A Kentucky Historical Marker for Benjamin Craig's grave is nearby. Following the death of Mary Bruce Grobmyer, the longtime owner of the home called Rebel Landing, civic leader Nancy Jo Grobmyer, the current owner, restored the home.

Gentry, Mary Ann. *A History of Carroll County.* Madison, Ind.: Coleman, 1984.
Masterson, Mary. *Historic Carroll County.* Carrollton, Ky.: Carroll Co. Chamber of Commerce, n.d. [ca. 1970s].

Kathyrn Salyers

RECORDER NEWSPAPERS. Nine award-winning weekly newspapers serving various communities in Boone, Campbell, and Kenton counties and the specific cities of Erlanger, Florence, and Fort Thomas are currently owned by the Virginia-based Gannett Company, which operates more than 100 daily newspapers nationwide, including the *Cincinnati Enquirer.*

The nine local newspapers trace their roots to the *Boone County Recorder,* founded in September 1875 and edited by Bob Berkshire. From 1935 to 1979, the newspaper was owned by Pete and Margaret Stephens and based in Burlington. In 1979 Margaret Stephens, who owned and operated the newspaper in the years following the death of her husband, sold the 4,500-circulation newspaper to Gloria Bushelman of Florence, Ky. Bushelman also merged the Scripps-Howard-owned *Florence Leader* with the independent *Walton Advertiser* (founded in 1914) to create the *Kenton County Recorder.* And it was under Bushelman's leadership that the small chain bought the Scripps-Howard-owned *Campbell County Recorder.*

In 1986 Bushelman sold the three newspapers to the Gleaner-Journal Publishing Company of Henderson, which in turn sold them in 1991 to a group of businessmen led by Gene Clabes of Fort Mitchell, editor of the *Ludlow News Enterprise* and the husband of then *Kentucky Post* editor **Judy Clabes**. Gene Clabes developed the content and sold the papers to Community Newspapers in Cincinnati. He stayed on as editorial director and developed the three county newspapers, known as Recorder Newspapers of Northern Kentucky, with a circulation of 9,000, into nine community newspapers with a combined circulation of more than 50,000.

The Gannett Company purchased Community Newspapers' 26 suburban weekly newspapers in 2004. At the time of the sale, the roster of Northern Kentucky newspapers included the *Boone County Community Recorder,* the *Boone County Recorder,* the *Campbell Community Recorder,* the *Campbell County Recorder,* the *Community Recorder of Northern Kentucky,* the *Erlanger Recorder,* the *Florence Recorder,* the *Fort Thomas Recorder,* and the *Kenton County Community Recorder.*

In 2005 Gene Clabes was named to the Kentucky Journalism Hall of Fame.

Bushleman, Gloria. Interview by Stephen M. Vest, June 29, 2005, Florence, Ky.
Stephenson, Margaret. Interview by Stephen M. Vest, June 29, 2005, Florence, Ky.
Thomas, Wayne. *Boone County 175th Anniversary Book: 1798–1973.* Burlington Ky.: Boone Co. 175th Anniversary Committee.

Stephen M. Vest

RECOVERY NETWORK. This nonprofit, independently operated consumer resource center at 605 Madison Ave. in Covington functions in collaboration with **Mental Health America of Northern Kentucky**. It is a consumer-run agency that provides services to persons living with mental illnesses and the homeless; its activities are planned, directed, and staffed by persons with mental illness. The services offered include assistance with preparation of résumés, computer technology, typing, operating systems, Microsoft Office Suite desktop publishing, and Microsoft Certification Training. General Education Diploma (GED) classes, practice software, and computer literacy training are also available. In addition the Recovery Network offers employment services and training in job-interviewing techniques, including computer-simulated interviews. The network also provides basic needs for the homeless, and support groups.

Recovery Network of Northern Kentucky. www.rnnk.org (accessed March 24, 2006).

Robin Rider Osborne

REDWOOD REHABILITATION CENTER. The Redwood Rehabilitation Center in Fort Mitchell serves persons with physical or mental disabilities by providing programs that include occupational, physical, and speech therapy; specialized computer training; life skills training; vocational training; employment services; and the After Work/After Care Program. The center's program began in 1951; its first client was Bill and Sue Reder's son Ron, who was developmentally delayed. In that post–**World War II** period, there was no such service in Northern Kentucky for children with disabilities of this type. Parents had to travel to Louisville for help.

The Reders, along with Al and Dorothy Wood, the parents of a little girl with cerebral palsy, created United Cerebral Palsy of Northern Kentucky in May 1953. After receiving a $400 allotment from a 1954 national telethon, they began a journey that took them to a basement room at Covington's **St. Augustine Catholic Church**, then to larger quarters at **St. Benedict Catholic Church** in Latonia, and subsequently, in 1957, to a building in Latonia that they purchased with the help of the Community Chest, a local Women's Guild, and many volunteers. This new facility, named after the Reders and the Woods, was called Redwood. The center opened in 1958, with Dorothy Wood as its first full-time executive director and inspiration.

Redwood's goal from the beginning was to provide comprehensive services for all people with disabilities, regardless of age. Over the years, there were many challenges, particularly financial, but under Dorothy Wood's dedicated leadership, a building fund campaign was successful. A new facility opened in 1967, along Orphanage Rd. in Fort Mitchell, on land leased from the **Roman Catholic** Diocese of Covington for one dollar per year. The new facility allowed Redwood to serve a wider range of developmental disabilities. By 1974 Redwood had once again outgrown its building, and Dorothy Wood began to raise funds for an expansion. In that same year, the *Cincinnati Enquirer* honored her as one of Greater Cincinnati's Outstanding Women. Into the 1980s, Redwood was identified with many exciting and significant projects and an expansion of programs. For example, the center's Cotton Ball was for nearly 40 years considered by many a prime social event of Northern Kentucky. Under Barbara Howard's direction, the 1980s saw dramatic growth of Redwood's adult services with the addition of the adult activities, training in business computer skills, employment services, and technological services programs.

In 1991 Howard became Redwood's executive director. This was the same year as the advent of the Kentucky Education Reform Act (KERA), which required a full integration of Redwood's school children into the public schools. Thus Redwood began to focus on a new range of community needs. Redwood pioneered a therapeutic child care center, a before- and after-school program, and outreach services. These were followed by the establishment of adult day health care, an after-work program, an assistive technology resource center, and a partnership with Cincinnati Children's Hospital Medical Center to bring physical and occupation therapy services to Northern Kentucky through a satellite program at Redwood. The organization's leaders coined a new term, "Redwood-ability," for the long-standing determination to do things with "vision, commitment, compassion and hope."

With the new century approaching, the Redwood building reached its capacity and it was time to launch another expansion campaign. In November 2005, a ribbon-cutting ceremony followed a June 2004 groundbreaking to celebrate a 41,000-square-foot building addition. On the heels of the successful Promise & Potential expansion project, the *Cincinnati Enquirer* once again named a Redwood executive director one of Greater Cincinnati's Outstanding Women of the year—this time Barbara Howard.

Howard, Barbara. "The History of Redwood," 2005, Redwood, Fort Mitchell, Ky.
———, comp. "March of Presidents: Perspectives on Being President of Redwood's Board," 2005, Redwood, Fort Mitchell, Ky.
"Redwood." www.redwoodrehab.org/ (accessed May 27, 2008).

Raymond G. Hebert

REED, STANLEY FORMAN (b. December 31, 1884, Minerva, Mason Co., Ky.; d. April 2, 1980, Huntington, Long Island, N.Y.). Supreme Court justice Stanley Reed was the son of John Anderson Reed and the former Frances Forman. Stanley earned a BA from Kentucky Wesleyan University at Winchester in 1902 and a second undergraduate degree from Yale University, in New Haven, Conn., in 1906. He studied law at the University of Virginia at Charlottesville and later at Columbia University in New York City. On May 11, 1908, Reed married Winifred Elgin, who was from his hometown of Maysville, and they had two children, John A. and Stanley Jr. He studied law under Judge John Newell and was admitted to the Kentucky bar in 1910. That same year, he traveled to Paris, France, to study at the Sorbonne. He was elected to the Kentucky House of Representatives in 1912 and reelected in 1914. During **World War I**, Reed served as a 1st lieutenant in the U.S. Army. In 1920 he was a central figure in the restoration of the Burley Grower's Co-operative and served as its lawyer. During the administration of President Herbert Hoover (1929–1933), Stanley was appointed counsel for the Federal Farm Board in 1929, serving until 1932, when he accepted a similar position with the Reconstruction Finance Corporation, which he held until March 1935. Reed was appointed solicitor general of the United States in March 1935, and although a Republican, he was appointed an associate justice of the U.S. Supreme Court in 1938 by President Franklin D. Roosevelt (1933–1945), a Democrat. In 1957 Justice Reed retired and returned to Maysville. A day-long celebration was held in his honor, which included the placing of a bronze plaque on the courthouse and naming a street for him. Reed died in 1980 and was buried at the Maysville Cemetery.

Kleber, John, ed. *The Kentucky Encyclopedia*, Lexington: Univ. Press of Kentucky, 1992.

O'Brien, F. William. *Justice Reed and the First Amendment*. Washington, D.C.: Georgetown Univ. Press, 1958.

Tapp, Hambleton, ed. *Kentucky Lives*. Hopkinsville, Ky.: Historical Record Association, 1966.

REEVES' CAMPGROUND. Reeves' Campground was an early-19th-century Campbell Co. religious campground named for the owner of the land. Stacey Reeves, who was from Mason Co., married Sarah Lawrence, the daughter of Michael and Elizabeth Lawrence, on February 4, 1802. The couple moved to Cold Spring and were instrumental in the formation of the Asbury Methodist Church (see **Asbury United Methodist Church**). Reeves owned land along Three Mile Rd., not far from the Licking River and six miles south of Newport. The campground named for Reeves opened in May 1818. It is believed to have been the site of the first camp meeting held in Northern Kentucky. Religious meetinghouses (churches) had not become common yet, and the church buildings that existed would not accommodate large groups. Camp meetings typically occurred in the summer months. A large outside area was selected near a productive spring, where there was shade, and a wooden stand with a crude pulpit was constructed and placed in front of a defined semicircular area in which worshippers could sit. Men sat on one side, women on the other. At night, fires were built around the perimeter. As many as 2,000 people in family groups might attend, and they remained for up to five days of religious preaching and healing. Generally, these meetings were interdenominational.

It is not known how long the summer camp meetings at the Reeves' Campground continued. Stacey Reeves resided in the county until 1838 and then moved to Putnam Co., Ind. While living in Campbell Co., he served as a judge for elections and as the justice of the peace, and he was the sheriff in 1834–1835. Reeves also sold approximately 50 acres of land for use as Campbell Co.'s first poorhouse, along the west side of present-day **U.S. 27**, opposite Enzweiler Rd. in Alexandria.

Papers of Margaret Strebel Hartman, Campbell Co. Historical and Genealogical Society, Alexandria, Ky.

REGENSTEIN, ELLSWORTH (b. ca. 1875, Mason Co., Ky.; d. March 23, 1957, Louisville, Ky.). Ellsworth Regenstein, a lawyer, a politician, and a school administrator, attended local schools and in 1893 earned his BA from the University of Kentucky at Lexington. At age 18 he became a schoolteacher in Maysville. After several promotions, he was named superintendent of Maysville Schools. In 1904 he married Marian Newman Wormald, and they moved to Newport, where Ellsworth once again taught. Within two years, he was promoted to high school principal, and later he became superintendent of Newport schools. During that time, he earned his law degree from the Cincinnati YMCA Law School, a night program that has evolved into today's **Chase College of Law** in Highland Heights. In late 1907 he was named director of the State Board of Examiners under the Kentucky superintendent of public instruction J. B. Crabbe. When Crabbe resigned in 1910, Regenstein was named as his successor. After completing his term, Regenstein opened a law office in Newport. In 1929 he was elected a Kentucky state senator representing Campbell Co. While holding that office, he passionately fought alongside **Charles B. Truesdell** for the preservation of Cumberland Falls, in Whitley Co., and for the creation of a state park there. During the summer of 1931, he took an active part in the Beech Grove Reunion (see **Beech Grove Academy**), near Flagg Springs, which was attended by 2,000 people. In that same year, he was named a director of the Inter-Southern Insurance Company. Regenstein moved to Louisville in 1932, where he helped to organize the Kentucky Home Life Insurance Company and was made its president. He became a leading promoter of the Louisville Zoo, and the zoo honored him and his family by naming its gorilla exhibit after them. During the 1950s Regenstein developed a serious illness, from which he died at age 82 in 1957. He was buried at Cave Hill Cemetery in Louisville.

"Former Newport School Head Dies at Louisville," *KP*, March 25, 1957, 1.

Reis, Jim. "Beech Grove Reunion Dates to 1870," *KP*, June 16, 2003, 4K.

———. "He Fought to Preserve the Falls," *KP*, June 16, 2003, 4K.

Jack Wessling

REIS, JIM (b. September 10, 1951, Covington, Ky.). James "Jim" W. Reis, who reported for the ***Kentucky Post*** in Northern Kentucky for 36 years, is the son of Gilbert and Ruth Schalk Reis of Fort Thomas. He attended St. Thomas Elementary School and **St. Thomas High School**, graduating in 1969, and was hired that year at the *Kentucky Post* as a copy boy. By 1973 he was a writer-reporter covering county government in 12 counties across Northern Kentucky. It was during this time that he began writing a column on people and events. In 1974, Reis completed a BA in English at **Thomas More College** in Crestview Hills. That same year, he married Janet Rose, a high school classmate; the couple had two sons.

In the early 1980s, Reis was assigned the local Newport City Council beat. He often said that these meetings were the best show in town. Subsequent assignments included suburban government in Campbell Co., Covington government and higher education, **Northern Kentucky University**, Thomas More College, and suburban government in Boone, Kenton, and Campbell counties.

One of the most important days at the *Kentucky Post* for Reis was in 1982, when his editor asked him what kind of column he would like to write. Reis suggested a local-history column. The new feature column, titled *Pieces of the Past*, began May 30, 1982, with a story about the Ludlow Lagoon (see **Lagoon Amusement Park**). The column ran continuously until August 2005, and Reis chose the Ludlow Lagoon to be the topic of his last column as well. He celebrated a milestone of 1,000 columns on Dec. 31, 2001, and reached a total of 1,100 by 2005. Reis decided, along the way, that he wanted his history column to be based on firsthand research. He spent so many hours in research at the **Kenton Co. Public Library** in Covington that someone there took any mail that arrived marked "Occupant" and saved it for him. Reis was especially pleased when he could show how national events played out locally. After years of dedication to "getting the facts right," as he put it, he developed a reputation of respect throughout the region and has often been quoted during discussions about the events he explored in columns. He is also often quoted as a primary source in all kinds of local histories.

Among the significant events Reis covered in his years at the *Kentucky Post* were the **Beverly Hills Supper Club** fire (he was the temporary morgue reporter at the armory in Fort Thomas), the Air Canada airline fire at Northern Kentucky's CVG Airport, the mergers of cities in the area, and countless elections. His favorite *Pieces of the Past* columns were the ones about Ludlow Lagoon, **Pearl Bryan**'s murder, the construction of I-75, the **Civil War**, steamboats, and the Newport gambling era. The *Kentucky Post* had Reis put together four local history books based on his columns. Three of them were separate volumes titled *Pieces of the Past* and the fourth was a collaboration with Robert Flischel on a Scripps-Howard book titled *Then and Now*. The four books combined eventually sold more than 15,000 copies and were featured at the Kentucky Book Fair in Frankfort four times.

Since 1979, because of his vast knowledge of local history, Reis has been called upon to deliver more than 150 talks. He was a member of the board of Covington's **Behringer-Crawford Museum** and a founding member of the Campbell Co. Historical Society (see **Historical Societies**). He was one of the organizers of the first Northern Kentucky Local History Day, held at Northern Kentucky University in Highland Heights, and of the **Northern Kentucky African-American Heritage Task Force** committee. Reis served on the Campbell Co. and the Newport Bicentennial Committees. He has contributed to the *Kentucky Encyclopedia*, to *Campbell County, Kentucky, 200 Years, 1794–1994*, and to *The Encyclopedia of Northern Kentucky*. Reis has been a longtime member of the Kentucky Historical Society and the historical societies of Boone, Campbell, Grant, and Kenton counties.

"Country Loving City Girl Named Our KPC Regional News Editor," *KP*, November 26, 1975, 6.
"It's Time to Meet Jim Reis," *KP*, May 4, 1973, 4K.
Reis, Jim. *Pieces of the Past*. 3 vols. Covington, Ky.: Kentucky Post, 1988, 1991, 1994.
Reis, Jim, with Robert A. Flischel. *Then and Now: Cincinnati and Northern Kentucky*. New York: Scripps Howard, 1995.
"Staff Volunteers for Variety of Community Endeavors," *KP*, March 10, 1987, 4K.
"State Book Fair Draws 136 Authors," *KP*, November 15, 1995, 1KK.

Kenneth A. Reis

RELIGION. See names of specific denominations and churches.

REMKE MARKETS. In 1897 William Remke opened a meat market at the corner of 13th and Holman Sts. in Covington. Home delivery, by a huckster wagon, amounted to 75 percent of the meat market's sales. In 1922 the store moved to 19th and Holman Sts. in Covington. The store was passed on to William's three sons, Robert, William, and Lewis, who in 1935 opened one of the region's first self-serve grocery stores in Fort Mitchell. At the time, one could by a pound of fresh ground beef or a pound of coffee for 29 cents.

After two of the Remke brothers died, Robert's son Bill Remke took over store operations during the early 1970s. During his ownership, Remke Markets has expanded to additional locations in the region: Crescent Springs, Deer Park, Florence, Fort Mitchell, Hebron, Independence, Newport, and Taylor Mill; the company also has a warehouse in Erlanger and made a brief foray into the market at Amelia, Ohio. In 1980 the Fort Mitchell store was remodeled to include one of the Remke chain's first in-store banks. In 1991 the Covington store closed after 94 years of service. In 1996, in a significant move, Bill Remke, remaining as CEO, transferred the majority of stock ownership in the company to its employees. Beginning in 2002, Remke's Drugstores, full-service pharmacies, opened in two of the stores, and pharmacies were later added to three additional stores.

"Food Fight Heats Up: Wal-Mart Puts Area into a Market War," *CE*, April 16, 2005, J1–J2.
"Greater Cincinnati/Northern Kentucky 100—Region's Largest Private Companies," *CE*, November 14, 2004, E4–E5.
Reis, Jim. "An Intersection's Storied Past—Ft. Mitchell Corner Vibrant," *KP*, July 22, 1996, 4K.
———. "Remke Evolved from Butcher to Grocer," *KP*, July 22, 1996, 4K.
Remke Markets. "The Remke History." www.remkes.com (accessed March 23, 2006).
"Remke Prospers, Expands Untroubled by Big Chains," *KP*, May 27, 1997, 7D.

Nancy J. Tretter

RENTZ, WILLIAM E., BRIGADIER GENERAL (b. November 10, 1905, Newport, Ky.; d. February 22, 1985, Boca Raton, Fla.). Air Force officer William Edward Rentz was the son of William and Eva Mehan Rentz and grew up at 518 E. Sixth St. in Newport. He graduated from St. Xavier High School in Cincinnati in 1923 and the University of Kentucky at Lexington in 1928. At the university he participated in the Reserve Officers Training Corps and was commissioned an officer in the U.S. Army upon graduation. He worked for the Civilian Conservation Corps during the early 1930s before going on active military duty. With the creation of the U.S. Air Force during the late 1940s, he became an Air Force officer and spent much of his career working at the Pentagon in Washington, D.C. Rentz served as a deputy to Gen. Curtis LeMay, the former Air Force chief of staff. He was a military adviser to Chiang Kai-shek in China, to a commanding general in Wiesbaden, Germany, and to the commanding officer of the Air Force training school at Biloxi, Miss. He oversaw the construction of the U.S. Air Force Academy in Colorado Springs, Colo., and air force bases in the southern United States. Rentz retired to Boca Raton, Fla., where he died in 1985; he was buried at Arlington National Cemetery in Arlington, Va.

Florida Death Certificate No. 20276, for the year 1985.
"3 in Graduating Class," *KP*, June 16, 1928, 2.
"William E. Rentz, Retired General," *CE*, February 23, 1985, C2.

Michael R. Sweeney

REPUBLICAN PARTY. For most of the late 19th century and nearly all of the 20th, Northern Kentucky was a bastion of the **Democratic Party**; in the late 20th and early 21st centuries, Boone and Campbell counties became strongholds of the Republican Party.

The 1850s represented a dynamic time in U.S. politics as the **Whig** and **Democratic** parties began to fragment along sectional lines over the issues of slavery, nativism, temperance, and states' rights. These issues were highly charged and helped to create a political environment ripe for the development of new political parties, organized primarily at the expense of the Whigs. By 1854 the American Whig Party existed in name only and had been largely replaced on the national stage by the nativist **Know-Nothings**, irrevocably breaking the two-party system of Whigs versus Democrats.

In the North, the growing abolitionist movement gave impetus to disaffected Democrats, Free-Soilers, and many northern Whigs to join the newly formed Republican Party. In 1856 former Whig Abraham Lincoln, born in Kentucky, joined the Republican Party, supporting John C. Fremont as the party's first candidate for the presidency. Democrat James Buchanan won the election and Kentucky's electoral votes, but the Republicans won majorities in 11 of the 16 free states. With this electoral strength, and the eventual dissolution of the Know-Nothings along sectional lines over the slavery question, the Republicans established themselves as the more viable successor to the Whigs.

Four political parties vied for the presidency in 1860, three of which represented sectional divisions of the Democratic Party. Lincoln, representing abolitionist sentiment, received less than 1 percent of the state's vote, while John Bell of Tennessee, the Constitution Union candidate whose party sought to preserve the Union, received 45 percent and won the state. Favorite son John C. Breckinridge captured 36 percent of the vote for the Southern Democrat party, which favored states' rights, and a second Democrat, U.S. senator Stephen Douglas of Illinois, representing a segment of the Democrat Party that tried to appeal both to Northern and Southern voters, garnered only 18 percent. Campbell (314 votes for Lincoln, or 11.9%) and Kenton (267 votes for Lincoln, or 7.5%) were the only two counties in Kentucky where Lincoln received more than 200 votes. In the presidential election of 1864, Lincoln carried Kenton Co. (1,716 votes, or 55.5%), and Campbell Co. (1,504 votes, or 53.9%).

Before the **Civil War**, there were few Republicans in Kentucky; however, Northern Kentuckians **William S. Bailey** and James R. Whittemore of Newport represented the state at the Republican national convention in 1856. Charles Hendly, also of Newport, and Abner Williams and Hamilton Cummings of Covington joined Whittemore at the party's 1860 nominating convention. The first major politician to join the Republican Party from Northern Kentucky was **Samuel Swope** of Pendleton Co., who had served in the Kentucky legislature as a Whig yet became affiliated with the Republican Party in 1856.

During the Civil War, politics in Kentucky could be described as a shifting montage of party affiliations. Although the Democratic Party controlled state politics, Democrats were not all of one mind; they were divided over the issues of slavery and unionism. The Peace Democrats did not want the state to take action against secession, while the Union Democratic Party supported ending the secessionist movement but was opposed to what it considered to be the unconstitutional efforts of the Republicans to end slavery. Yet, even this group had dissident elements who believed that the institution of slavery should be sacrificed for the good of the Union. These Democrats, the "Unconditional Unionists," supported preserving the Union and the Republican administration of Lincoln at all costs.

In Northern Kentucky, "unconditionalists actually controlled the Democratic Party's Sixth

District Convention," which was charged with nominating a candidate for the U.S. Congress for the 1863 election. **Green Clay Smith** was selected over the incumbent Constitutional Union congressman, **John W. Menzies**. Smith was chosen primarily because he was the preferred candidate of **Mortimer Benton**, the leader of the Democratic Party in Northern Kentucky, former mayor of Covington, and president of the **Kentucky Central Railroad**. Although Smith had lived in Covington only since 1858, he was a nephew of Cassius Marcellus Clay (Kentucky's great abolitionist leader), had won election to the state legislature in 1860, had served in the Union Army, and had been made a brigadier general in 1863, commanding forces in the state. Smith won the 1863 U.S. congressional election, with almost half of his votes coming from Kenton and Campbell counties. One explanation is that many voters in Northern Kentucky were relatively new to the United States and politics and were not enamored with either slavery or the agricultural lifestyle. Since the 1840s, Covington and Newport in particular had experienced a large influx of immigrants and a growing industrial and commercial economy. These new voters saw the benefits of preserving Kentucky's ties to the Union.

In 1864 the Peace Democrats joined forces with the Union Democrats in opposition to Lincoln's reelection bid. Smith and two other Unionist congressmen did not join this new coalition, known as the Conservative Democrats. Working for Lincoln's reelection, they earned the spite of the *Louisville Daily Democrat,* which stated, "There is a Republican Party in Kentucky and they have representatives in Congress; and it is not to be disguised that they represent a considerable party at home."

The state and congressional elections that followed on the heels of Lincoln's death and the ending of the war were defined by the issue of support for the proposed 13th Amendment to the U.S. Constitution, ending slavery. In February 1865, the Kentucky legislature had rejected the amendment, but Smith had supported the amendment in Washington. Despite his break with the party leadership, the Conservative Democratic sweep of the state legislature, and the party's winning five of the state's seven congressional seats, Smith won his district nomination by acclamation and was returned to the U.S. Congress, winning in a tight election over a Conservative opponent. Smith's victory was made possible by the strong support he had in the more industrialized northern counties of Campbell and Kenton.

Although a growing number of Kentuckians were willing to vote Republican, thanks to the efforts of the Unconditional Union Democrats, the state remained firmly in the grasp of the Conservative Democratic Party following the Civil War. With the slavery issue resolved, the Democratic Party began to unite behind the banner of states' rights, bolstered by returning Confederate veterans who were renewing their political associations and by the effects of Reconstruction and the perceived abuses of the Republican Congress in Washington. In most of Kentucky, being a Republican became a political liability.

The Republican Party of Kentucky continued to be a minority within the state throughout the Reconstruction period, offering opportunities for aspiring politicians but holding little threat to the majority Democrats who controlled the state legislature and governorship for the next 30 years. One such prominent Northern Kentuckian, who benefited from the existence of a Democratic alternative, was **William Henry Wadsworth** of Maysville, who had previously served in the Kentucky Senate (1853–1856) and was elected to the U.S. Congress representing the Constitutional Union Party for two terms (1861–1865). In 1885 Wadsworth returned to the U.S. Congress as a Republican for a single term before retiring. Although Republicans were able to challenge for individual offices, the party's eventual ability to compete for state political supremacy was primarily due to the splintering of the Democratic Party. In 1895 the cause of "Populism" provided issues that led to another Democratic fragmentation and the first Republican statewide victories in Kentucky.

The fragmentation of the Kentucky Democratic Party occurred as a result of several events, among them the movement for municipal reform in Louisville, where the Democratic-controlled city government was seen as corrupt; the rise of Populist-leaning leaders in the party, such as **William Goebel** in Covington; and the resistance of the Democratic Party leadership, known as "Gold Democrats," to the idea of adopting a platform, including support for "free silver," which might induce state Populists to join the party.

Republican organizational developments enabled the Republican Party to make significant political gains at the county level. In the 1894 Kenton Co. elections, for example, Hayden Polk Stephens won the race for county judge, John O'Donnell was elected sheriff, and John McKnight became county jailer. Under the leadership of **Richard P. Ernst** of Covington, the Kenton Co. Republican Party was formally organized in 1895. Stephens served as Kenton Co. judge from 1894 through 1897 and then again from 1902 until 1910, and Ernst ran for the U.S. Congress unsuccessfully in 1897 but was later elected to the U.S. Senate.

A relative Republican stronghold since Reconstruction, Campbell Co. sent to Frankfort several legislative delegations containing a Republican between 1900 and 1930. Among Campbell Co.'s most successful Republican representatives early in the century was William A. Burkamp, who served in the state House of Representatives during the sessions of 1900 and 1902 and then returned in 1928 for a term as Kentucky senator. In 1908, 1920, 1922, and 1928, Campbell Co.'s entire delegation was Republican. Harry E. Weitkamp represented Campbell Co. in the state House of Representatives in 1906 and returned in 1908 to serve alongside the county's other Kentucky House member, Oliver P. Applegate, and Kentucky senator George Wilhelmi. In 1916 Jacob Metzger was Campbell Co.'s only Republican in the state House of Representatives, but he was elected Kentucky senator in 1920 and, with **Charles B. Truesdell** and Charles M. Ciarlo, composed an entirely Republican delegation. In 1922 Republican Herman Q. Thompson replaced Ciarlo, while in 1924 Truesdale took Metzger's state seat, serving until 1928. Truesdale served another term in the Kentucky House of Representatives in 1930. Also in 1930, Republican **Ellsworth Regenstein**, of Newport, who had earlier been the superintendent of public schools in Kentucky (1911–1912), took Burkamp's seat in the Kentucky Senate to complete his term.

During the first 30 years of the 20th century, Mason Co. also raised a crop of Republican representatives, including state senator **William H. Cox**, who served two terms from 1900 to 1908; he was elected lieutenant governor in 1907, serving until 1912. In the Kentucky Senate, Bert C. Grigsby, who also served until 1912, replaced him. In 1916 Kentucky senator Lewis N. Rayburn was elected to represent the county, and in 1918 he was joined by Republican Kentucky House member Addison L. Baldwin, who served one term before being replaced by William S. Yazell, part of the Republican House majority during the 1920 session. Pendleton Co. sent Republican state House member John L. Bradford to Frankfort in 1918 and, during the 1926 legislative session, was represented, along with Bracken Co., by Republican state House member Charles N. McCarty.

Despite its leading role in the early formation of the state Republican Party, Kenton Co. sent relatively few Republicans to Frankfort in the first half of the 1900s. Republican Edward J. Hickey was elected to the state House of Representatives in 1901, and Robert H. Fleming was elected to the Kentucky Senate in 1903. Another Republican, H. D. Gregory, who also served one term, replaced Hickey in 1904. In 1908 Kenton Co.'s state senator Edward E. Walker and House member Charles C. Chase added muscle to the Republican cause, and in the 1920 legislative session, Rodney G. Bryson added to the Republican majority in the Kentucky House of Representatives.

In 1925 Kenton Co. Republican Ray R. Rogers was elected to the state House of Representatives. Although it was not until 1964 that Kenton Co. sent another delegate to the state legislature, the county did have its share of deeply committed Republicans. **Maurice L. Galvin** of Covington, beginning in 1912, was a delegate to seven straight Republican national conventions and managed the successful 1919 Republican gubernatorial campaign of Edward Morrow. In that election, Covington's Republican mayor, John Craig, was elected state auditor. Soon after, in 1920, Richard P. Ernst, a member of the Covington city council from 1888 to 1892, was elected to the U.S. Senate. The county also contributed Republican **Judson Lincoln Newhall**, who was director of music in Covington public schools from 1913 to 1929 except for a short stint during **World War I**, to the U.S. House of Representatives for the 1929–1930 legislative session. Newhall served one term, was defeated for reelection in 1930, and again ran unsuccessfully in 1934.

Statewide, 27 governors were elected in Kentucky between 1900 and 2003, and only six of them were Republican. And in only two presidential elections in the first half of the 20th century was Republican voting strength sufficient to throw Kentucky's electoral votes to Republican candidates, helping to elect Calvin Coolidge (1923–1929) in 1922 and Herbert Hoover (1929–1933) in 1928.

The decades of the 1930s, 1940s, and 1950s were not bountiful years for the Northern Kentucky Republican Party. Stanley C. Moebus was elected to the Kentucky House of Representatives from Campbell Co. in 1938 and again in 1940. Four years later, Campbell Co. sent Republican J. Garvey Davis to the Kentucky Senate and George T. Smith to the state House of Representatives. Davis and Smith each served one term. In 1948 Charles W. Wirsch won the first of six elections to the Kentucky House of Representatives, serving until 1960. Wirsch was the only elected Republican from the region in either the state House of Representatives or the state Senate from the time of his election until 1964.

Despite limited state political victories, Republican political strength continued to develop. Since the middle of the 20th century, Kentucky voters have given the state's electoral votes to Republicans in the presidential elections of 1952, 1956, 1960, 1968, 1972, 1980, 1984, 1988, 2000, and 2004. This trend exhibited a growing willingness on the part of voters to support national Republicans.

Although the Republican candidate for president lost the 1964 election in a landslide, the year marked the beginning of a comeback for Northern Kentucky's Republicans. Elected to the Kentucky Senate that year from Campbell Co. was Donald L. Johnson, and to the state House of Representatives Carl A. Bamberger and Arthur L. "Art" Schmidt. From Kenton Co., Kenneth F. "Ken" Harper was elected to the Kentucky House of Representatives. This represented the largest number of Republicans elected to the legislature from Northern Kentucky since 1920 and signaled the beginning of an almost meteoric rise in Republican Party membership at the county level and in the number of state representatives from the region. In national politics, the Northern Kentucky region began increasingly to vote Republican, and by the 1990s Republicans dominated regional politics.

Ken Harper was elected three times to the state House of Representatives, serving from 1964 to 1968, when he resigned and was appointed by the governor as assistant commissioner of child welfare. In 1970 he was named the state's public information commissioner, and in 1971 he filled the remaining term of the Kentucky secretary of state. In 1986 Harper returned to political office, serving another five terms in the Kentucky House of Representatives and being named House minority chairman for the 1988 and 1990 legislative sessions. Campbell Co.'s Donald Johnson remained in the Kentucky Senate for four terms, serving from 1964 to 1980, while Art Schmidt was elected to the state House of Representative in 1963 and in 1970 became the first Northern Kentucky Republican House member to be named to a leadership post, serving as minority caucus chairman during the 1970 session and as minority whip during the 1972, 1974, 1978, and 1980 sessions. In 1982 Schmidt was named minority floor leader in the Kentucky House of Representatives. In 1984 he was elected to the Kentucky Senate and reelected in 1988 and 1992, serving as minority caucus chair in the state Senate during the 1992 session.

Another Republican from Kenton Co., Clyde W. Middleton, joined Harper in Frankfort in 1968, when he was elected to the Kentucky Senate. Middleton served five terms there, being named minority whip in 1978, 1980, and 1982 and minority caucus chairman in 1984 and 1986. Middleton was defeated for reelection in 1986 but returned to Kenton Co. and was elected judge-executive. He resigned from office in 1998, the same year that Republicans won the judge-executive offices in Northern Kentucky in Boone, Campbell, and Kenton counties.

Throughout the latter half of the 20th century, as Northern Kentucky's population grew, and as residential construction shifted farther from the urban core, political boundaries, which had often matched county lines in the past, began to experience rapid change and become more complicated. Through a series of legislative redistricting, representatives who had had their political districts centered in one county in one election found themselves running from a dramatically changed district in the next. Some representatives had districts that stretched across three or more counties, and it became more difficult to associate an elected official with one county. For example, while a member of the Kentucky House of Representatives in 1974, Schmidt, of Campbell Co., found himself representing portions of Pendleton Co. as well. In 1984 Jon David Reinhardt began a tenure of more than 22 years in the state House of Representatives, representing, at various times, portions of Boone, Campbell, Kenton, and Pendleton counties. As a state senator, from 1984 through 1994, Schmidt represented portions of Bracken, Boone, Campbell, Kenton, and Pendleton counties.

While redistricting was able to create a bastion of Democratic Party strength in the urban core of Northern Kentucky, the shifting boundaries often meant Republicans were representing areas of the region's rural counties, which had historically been strongly Democratic. The increasing Republican Party strength could also be seen in light of the growing shift in the region away from an industrial economy to one that emphasized services and the quickening pace of suburbanization, which often created dramatic swings in party alignment on the metropolitan fringe. Beginning in the early 1980s, Northern Kentucky's suburbs had a sizable Republican voting majority. Although it proved to be an anomaly in 1968 when Republican Leo Lawson was elected to represent Boone and Gallatin counties in Kentucky's 60th House District for one term, less than 20 years later Boone Co. was hailed as a core area for Republican votes in Northern Kentucky, and in 1992 the county's entire state delegation was Republican.

The Kenton Co. Republican Party ran three county commission candidates (**Ralph Drees**, Ron Turner, and Gordon Wade) in the 1981 elections. Although Democrats won all three seats, the Republican Party's strong showing further emboldened the local party to compete more vigorously, with Republican commissioner candidate Dick Combs winning election in 1984. Turner was later named mayor of Covington (1987) to fill an unexpired term, while a Republican governor appointed Drees Kenton Co. judge-executive in 2004.

The growing tide of Republicanism in Northern Kentucky in the years since 1990 contributed to the naming of more Northern Kentuckians to party leadership positions in Frankfort. Joining Harper, Middleton, and Schmidt in leadership positions was Charlie Borders, state senator from Bracken and Mason counties, who was named minority whip in 1994 and majority caucus chairman in 2000, when, for the first time, Republicans won the majority in the Kentucky Senate. Dick Roeding, from Kenton Co., was named senate minority whip in 1996, senate minority caucus chairman in 1998, and president pro tem of the state Senate in 2000. Other Northern Kentucky Republicans named to leadership positions in the state legislature included Charlie Walton from Boone and Kenton counties, named House minority whip in 1996, and Katie Kratz Stine, representing Campbell and Pendleton counties, who was named president pro tem of the state Senate in 2005.

Indicative of the growing impact of the Northern Kentucky wing of the Republican Party upon state politics was the election of **Trey Grayson**, originally from Kenton Co., as Kentucky secretary of state in 2003. Of national import was the election of **Jim Bunning**, former Fort Thomas city councilman (1977–1979), Kentucky senator (1979–1983), and five-time U.S. congressman (1987–1999) to the U.S. Senate in 1998 and again in 2004. Bunning successfully managed to ride the growing tide of Republican Party strength in Northern Kentucky to become only the second Republican U.S. senator from the region.

Currently, the relative political advantage of being a Republican in Northern Kentucky is significant and can be seen not only in the substantial increase in party voting strength and party leadership positions held by Northern Kentuckians but also by the number of elected officials who have switched party allegiances in order to take advantage of the party's new dominant political position. Two of the more high-profile examples were state representative Thomas Kerr's switch in 2003 after serving for 18 years as a Democrat in the state House from Kenton Co., and Kenton Co. and attorney Garry Edmondson's switch in 2001 to run against another former Democrat, Eric Deters, in the Republican primary election. Republicans in Northern Kentucky have played a leading role in the development of Kentucky's Republican Party.

Crowley, Patrick. "State Rep. Kerr Switches to GOP," *KE*, October 11, 2003, B1.

Holt, Gina. "GOP Primary Pits Two Ex-Democrats," *KE*, May 21, 2002, B1.

Hood, James Larry. "For the Union: Kentucky's Unconditional Unionist Congressmen and the

Development of the Republican Party in Kentucky, 1863–1865," *RKHS* 76 (July 1978): 197–215.
Jonas, E. A. *A History of the Republican Party in Kentucky.* Louisville, Ky.: J. P. Morton, 1929.
Terwort, William H. "History of the Kenton County Republican Party," paper presented to the Kenton Co. Republican Party Executive Committee, August 28, 2006.

J. T. Spence

REVOLUTIONARY WAR (1775–1783). The Revolutionary War (also called the American Revolution) in Kentucky—part of what was then considered the West—is understood most clearly in connection with its antecedents. The Treaty of Paris of 1763, which ended the **French and Indian War** (also called the Seven Years' War), gave the British all of the territory of North America east of the Mississippi River, including Canada and Florida, but not New Orleans. Concerned about the ability to defend this expanse, Britain issued the Proclamation of 1763, forbidding settlement west of the crest of the Appalachian Mountains until a western policy for the region was adopted. Explorers and settlers disregarded the proclamation. In 1774 Harrodsburg, the first permanent white settlement in Kentucky, was created. Upset by incursions into their land, American Indians responded. In 1774 **Lord Dunmore's War** (named after the Virginia governor) resulted in the Treaty of Camp Charlotte, whereby the Shawnee Indians agreed to stay north of the Ohio River and the white settlers south of it. By the time the Revolutionary War began in 1775, Kentucky was part of Fincastle Co., Va. Shortly thereafter, with the encouragement of **George Rogers Clark** (1752–1818) as a delegate from pioneer Kentucky, the Virginia legislature created the new county of Kentucky, effective December 31, 1776. Hence, the Commonwealth of Virginia was responsible for the security of frontier Kentucky during the course of the Revolutionary War.

Although sparsely settled, Kentucky was an important battleground between the Colonies, on the one hand, and the British and their American Indian allies on the other. In Kentucky, the war proceeded as a series of offensive and counteroffensive actions, largely between George Rogers Clark and British lieutenant governor Henry Hamilton of Detroit. Appointed a lieutenant colonel by Virginia governor Patrick Henry, Clark led a 1778–1779 offensive against Henry Hamilton north of the Ohio River, capturing the settlements of Kaskaskia, Cahokia, and Vincennes. In October 1779 the "Great Renegade" turncoat, **Simon Girty**, with British and American Indian forces, surprised Capt. David Rogers and about 65 colonial American soldiers above the mouth of the Licking River, at a sandbar near present Dayton, Ky. The battle was a massacre for the Americans (see **Rogers' Defeat**). In spring 1780 the British launched a counteroffensive against Clark. British captain Henry Bird (Byrd) led an army of nearly 1,000 British and American Indian soldiers south from Detroit to raid Kentucky settlements. Crossing the **Point** at the mouth of the Licking River, they proceeded to attack settlements in the interior of Kentucky on **Bird's War Road** (also called Clark's War Road). Clark, in turn, mounted a counteroffensive, assembling a 1,000-man army at the mouth of the Licking River (the Point) in July 1780. On August 1, Clark and his men moved against the Shawnee Indians at Chillicothe and Piqua.

In autumn 1780 Gen. George Washington gave Virginia governor Thomas Jefferson permission for Clark to borrow military supplies from Fort Pitt (Pittsburgh) for a planned attack against Detroit. Jefferson made Clark a brigadier general in the Virginia army, but Virginia's decision to give up its claims to most of the lands north of the Ohio River reduced enthusiasm for undertaking the expenses of the campaign. Clark left Fort Pitt with 400 men, hoping to raise more troops in Kentucky. He was followed by a group of Pennsylvania soldiers led by Col. Archibald Lochry. In August 1781 the Indian allies of the British ambushed Lochry's men near the mouth of the Great Miami River opposite present Boone Co., Ky., and 107 colonials died or were captured. As the Revolutionary War approached its end, Clark's proposed attack against Detroit never transpired.

In October 1781, British general Charles Cornwallis surrendered at Yorktown, Va. However, the British continued to occupy forts in the West and to encourage the Indians to raid settlements. As a result, the battle raged on in Kentucky, and 1782 earned the title of the Year of Blood. By July 1782, to deter Indian attacks, Clark built a 73-foot-long boat, manned by 100 men and armed with cannons, and placed it in operation near the mouth of the Licking River. Nevertheless, in August 1782, Simon Girty and more than 300 white and Indian troops met and defeated the Kentuckians at the Battle of Blue Licks in current Robertson Co., which some claim was the last major battle of the Revolutionary War but others maintain was part of the Indian Wars following (see **Blue Licks, Battle of**; **Blue Licks Battlefield State Resort**; **Blue Licks**). As a counteroffensive, Clark assembled another 1,000-man army at the mouth of the Licking River in November 1782 and led an expedition against the Indians.

Officially, the Treaty of Paris of 1783 brought an end to the Revolutionary War. By the treaty's terms, the United States gained all of the territory east of the Mississippi River except British Canada, Spanish Florida, Spanish West Florida, and Spanish New Orleans.

Hammon, Neal O., and Richard Taylor. *Virginia's Western War, 1775–1786.* Mechanicsburg, Pa.: Stackpole Books, 2002.
Harrison, Lowell H. *George Rogers Clark and the War in the West.* Lexington: Univ. of Kentucky Press, 1976.
Harrison, Lowell H., and James C. Klotter. *A New History of Kentucky.* Lexington: Univ. Press of Kentucky, 1997.

Paul A. Tenkotte

REYNOLDS, MATTIE BRUCE (b. 1854, Covington, Ky.; d. September 24, 1916, White Sulfur Springs, W.Va.). One of the best-known women in Northern Kentucky, Mattie Bruce Reynolds had a keen interest in charities and civic affairs, especially women's suffrage. She was the daughter of **Eli Metcalf Bruce**, a cotton merchant and a member of the Confederate Congress from Kentucky, and Elizabeth Sallie Withers, the daughter of Maj. Charles A. Withers (see **Withers Family**), for whom Withers Park (modern Park Pl.) in Covington was named. Mattie Bruce married noted physician Dudley Sharpe Reynolds in 1881. The wedding, at **Trinity Episcopal Church**, was called "the most brilliant society event that has probably ever taken place in Covington." Mattie Reynolds was active in the United Daughters of the Confederacy, the **Daughters of the American Revolution**, and the **Covington Art Club**. She campaigned for the establishment of a shelter house in Covington's **Devou Park**.

Women's suffrage was the area of Mattie's greatest activity. She hosted national suffragist organizers in her home, at 502 Greenup St. in Covington, and in 1913 marched with four other Kenton Co. women in a suffragist parade in Washington, D.C. Mattie Reynolds died in 1916, from injuries received in a runaway buggy accident at White Sulfur Springs, W.Va. After her death, a Kenton Co. Equal Franchise Association resolution proclaimed that she was one of the most prominent and valued members of the organization, having been an active worker and officeholder and having served that body in the state conventions. Reynolds was buried at Highland Cemetery in Fort Mitchell, Ky.

"Graves Will Be Decorated," *KTS*, June 2, 1914, 2.
"Memory of Arts Club Leader Is Honored," *KTS*, April 9, 1917, 10.
"Services Held Wednesday for Mrs. Reynolds," *KP*, September 27, 1916, 1.
"They Fought to Secure Equal Rights for Women," *KP*, August 4, 2004, 4K.

Ann Hicks

RHINOCK, JOSEPH L. (b. January 4, 1863, Owenton, Ky.; d. September 20, 1926, New Rochelle, N.Y.). Politician and businessman Joseph Lafayette Rhinock, the son of Joseph and Eliza Short Rhinock, moved from Owenton to Covington with his family at age seven. He attended public school in Covington but left after a few years, saying that he had all the education he needed. His first job locally was at the Diamond Tobacco Factory. At age 14 he went to work for Covington's **Hemingray Glass Company**. He left that job to become a messenger in Cincinnati. His next employment was with the Cincinnati Chamber of Commerce, where he remained for 11 years; his duties were to check the accuracy of business scales and gauges. Rhinock married Emma McKain in 1883, and they had two sons and two daughters. In his mid-20s, he entered politics and was elected a Covington city councilman. In 1893, at age 30, he became the youngest mayor in Covington's history. He ran for the Kentucky Senate in 1901 but lost to Robert H. Flemming, the mayor of Ludlow. Rhinock served in the U.S. House of Representatives from 1905 until 1911. After leaving office,

Rhinock moved to New York City, where, for the next 20 years, he was involved in theatrical enterprises. During that period he served as vice president and treasurer for the Shubert Theater chain. He also developed an interest in horse racing and made newspaper headlines several times for winning large sums of money at the races. Rhinock died at age 63 at his home called Bonnie Crest in New Rochelle, N.Y. He was buried in a mausoleum at Highland Cemetery in Fort Mitchell.

Biographical Directory of the United States Congress. "Rhinock, Joseph Lafayette." http://bioguide.congress.gov (accessed November 22, 2005).

"Biography of New Mayor," *KP,* December 19, 1893, 1.

"Brief Biography—Joseph L. Rhinock," *KP,* October 18, 1893, 1.

Claypool, James C. *The Tradition Continues: The Story of Old Latonia, Latonia, and Turfway Racecourses.* Fort Mitchell, Ky.: T. I. Hayes, 1997.

RHYTHM AND BLUES. See **Blues**; **Jazz**.

RICE, HOMER (b. February 20, 1927, Bellevue, Ky.). Homer Cranston Rice, a football coach and athletic director, is the son of Samuel C. and Grace Wilson Rice. He grew up in Fort Thomas and graduated in 1945 from **Highlands High School**, where he was an all-state quarterback, an all-conference basketball guard, and a track champion. He graduated in 1950 from Centre College in Danville, Ky., earning Little All-American honors as a quarterback there. He later earned an MS at Eastern Kentucky University in Richmond, an MED from the University of Kentucky in Lexington, and a PhD from Columbia Pacific University, a proprietary institution at Novata, Calif.

A versatile athlete, Rice also played professional baseball in the Brooklyn Dodgers' organization. He coached high school football in Tennessee before returning to lead the football team at Highlands High School. His teams at Highlands won 50 consecutive regular season games and Class AA state football championships in 1960 and 1961. He finished his high school coaching career with a win-loss record of 102-9-7. Rice, who is credited with the development of the triple-option offense at Highlands, wrote a book about his innovative offense while coaching there. The book featured photographs of many of his Highlands players. The triple-option offense became a mainstay in college football during the 1960s and 1970s.

Rice continued his coaching career as an assistant coach at the University of Kentucky and the University Oklahoma at Norman, and he served as head coach at the University of Cincinnati and at Rice University in Houston, Tex. He later became head coach of the professional football Cincinnati Bengals for a season. Rice has served as an athletic director at three major universities: North Carolina in Chapel Hill (1969–1975), Rice University (1976–1977), and Georgia Tech in Atlanta (1980–1997).

The National Association of Collegiate Directors of Athletics established the Homer Rice Award to honor the athletic director or conference commissioner who most contributes to exemplary service to college athletics. It is the highest national honor bestowed by the organization. Rice has served as president of the National Association of Collegiate Directors of Athletics, chairman of the NCAA Football Rules Committee, chairman of the NCAA Television Committee, and chairman of the Atlantic Coast Conference Rules Committee. Rice has written numerous books on motivation and leadership skills, and his "Total Person Concept" for student-athletes has served as the model for more than 170 colleges around the country. His books include *The Explosive Short T; Homer Rice on Triple Option Football; Winning Football with the Air Option Passing Game; Leadership Fitness: Developing and Reinforcing Successful, Positive Leaders; Lessons for Leaders: Building a Winning Team from the Ground Up*; and *Leadership for Leaders: The Attitude Technique Philosophy, a Total Person–Total Success Concept.*

Today, Homer Rice and his wife, Phyllis, reside in Atlanta, Ga.

Boemker, Terry. "Rice Molded Highland Winning Tradition," *KP,* August 19, 1999, 9K.

Moore, Terrence. "Rice's First Goal Will Be Reducing Bengal Miscues," *CE,* October 3, 1978, C1.

Bill Thomas

RICHARD P. ERNST HOME. The Richard P. Ernst Home, located at 405 Garrard St. within the **Licking-Riverside** and **Ohio Riverside National Historic Districts** in Covington, was built about 1890 for tobacco industry gentleman John S. Matson. The Queen Anne style house was designed by Cincinnati architect Samuel Hannaford (see **Samuel Hannaford and Sons**), who also designed the Cincinnati Music Hall and many other structures in the region. The Ernst Home has 26 rooms, including five fireplaces, and 12-foot ceilings.

In 1908 this mansion became the home for Richard P. Ernst, his wife, Sarah B. Ernst, and their two children, Sarah and William. Richard Ernst served as a U.S. senator from Kentucky from 1921 to 1927. The Ernst family lived in the mansion until Susan Brent Ernst's death in June 1935. Richard had died on April 13, 1934.

In 1937 the property was sold to Bracken Co. native Patrick Michael Flannery, an attorney, who converted it into the Flannery Hotel. It was used for that purpose until roughly 1975. University of Kentucky fraternity brothers Jerry Bressler, Dan Wolff, and Rob Martin, who owned Phoenix Properties, purchased the building from Patrick Maurice Flannery, the son of the hotel's founder, and restored it for office use in 1982. In the restoration of the elegant structure, the ornate woodwork and the grand open wooden staircase were maintained. The Miami Purchase Association recognized the Ernst Home as a historic preservation property in 1982. In April 2005 a Kentucky State Highway Marker was placed in front of the structure to recognize its historical significance.

"Covington Board OKs Rehab Project," *KP,* March 10, 1983, 6K.

Carolyn Zink

RICHARDSON, DARRELL C. (b. May 17, 1918, Baxter Springs, Kans.; d. September 19, 2006, Memphis, Tenn.). A clergyman and an author, Darrell Coleman Richardson was the son of Coleman D. and Edna Ellen Nipper Richardson. Darrell grew up in Missouri, where he received his early education. He entered Furman University at Greenville, S.C., in 1938 on an athletic scholarship and earned varsity letters in basketball, football, tennis, track, and swimming. Described as a very muscular individual, Richardson was six feet four inches tall and weighed about 250 pounds. He graduated in 1942 and soon after married Sarah Louise Sanders, a student at Furman. The couple had two children, Darrell Jr., born in 1945, and Donald, born in 1949. Richardson undertook postgraduate studies at Columbia University, in New York City; Yale University, in New Haven, Conn.; Western Kentucky University, in Bowling Green; the University of Cincinnati; and the University of Kentucky, in Lexington. He eventually earned a doctorate and five master's degrees. He was also a graduate of the Southern Baptist Theological Institute in Louisville. While attending college and seminary, he worked during the summers as director of Camp Ridgecrest, a home for boys in Ridgecrest, N.C. During that time he also served as scoutmaster of a Boy Scout troop that had a larger membership than any other in the United States.

In 1943 and 1944, he served as pastor at Ormsby Village, a home for delinquent and dependent children in Anchorage, Ky., and at the same time coached the school's football and basketball teams. In 1945 he was interim pastor of the Walnut Street Baptist Church in Louisville. Richardson came to Northern Kentucky in March 1947 to accept a position as pastor of the **Fort Mitchell Baptist Church**. He proved to be a very popular and charismatic leader, and the church membership doubled during his tenure. His sermons were described as outstanding and were often interlaced with stories of his life experiences, only slightly embellished. While in Northern Kentucky, he held many influential positions in church and civic organizations. He was a director of the **Booth Memorial Hospital** and of the Dan Beard Council of the **Boy Scouts of America**. He also served as president of the Kenton Co. Ministerial Association and the Northern Kentucky Pastor's Conference. During the 1950s he was one of the leaders of the crusade against gambling and crime syndicates operating in the area. He also served as the publicity director for the Billy Graham Crusade held in Cincinnati.

In January 1954, longing for a new challenge, he resigned as pastor of the Fort Mitchell Baptist Church and volunteered to become a U.S. Army chaplain. He was trained at the army's chaplain school in Fort Slocum, N.Y., and assigned to the 3rd Armored Division, located in Germany. Elvis Presley was also a member of that unit, and they met and became friends. While serving in the army, Richardson wrote numerous articles for military publications. After leaving active duty in the 1960s, he moved to Memphis, Tenn., to accept a position as editor for the Brotherhood

Commission of the Southern Baptists. In that post he wrote and edited much of the literature distributed by the Southern Baptist Convention. He was known to visit with Presley at Graceland Mansion in Memphis.

Throughout his life, Richardson retained his boyhood fascination with larger-than-life individuals, both real and fictional, including Billy Graham, Elvis Presley, and comic strip heroes like Tarzan. Richardson often told people that one of his lifelong role models was Tarzan. He eventually became a friend of Johnny Weissmueller, the first actor to play Tarzan in the movies.

Richardson's novels have been described as bold, brilliant, and bursting with adventure. A friend called him an extremely fascinating and charismatic individual who worked tirelessly at his crafts. He has also been described as a mentally and physically active individual with multiple talents and the zealous desire to use all of them. He authored 44 books and about 100 newspaper and magazine articles, many dealing with science fiction and often written under pseudonyms. Three of his most important books were *Max Brand: The Man and His Work, Counseling in Times of Crisis,* and *A Christian Facing a World of Change.* Richardson lived a life delightfully similar to those depicted in many of his novels. He traveled to more than 40 countries on archaeological digs and spent considerable time in the Middle East, where he visited the biblical sites he had often read about in his Bible.

While living in Memphis, Richardson founded the Memphis Science Fiction Association and was its first president. The organization now bestows an annual Darrell Award for the best science fiction, fantasy, or horror story submitted. During his long and distinguished career, Richardson won a number of awards, including the Phoenix Award, the E. E. Evans Big Heart Award, the Lamont Pulp Fiction Award, and the Southern Baptist Convention's Good Shepherd Award.

Richardson died in Memphis, at age 88. His wife, Sarah, preceded him in death. His sons were his only close surviving relatives.

Dowd, James. "Dr. Richardson 'Bigger Than Life,'' *Memphis Commercial Appeal,* September 21, 2006, www.freepagesmiscrootsweb.com (accessed December 30, 2006).

ERBzine. "Darrell C. Richardson." www.erbzine.com (accessed December 30, 2006).

Richardson, Darrell C. "Elvis Wanted to Be Just One of the GI's," January 14, 2005, www.elvis.com (accessed January 3, 2006).

Tapp, Hambleton. *Kentucky Lives: The Blue Grass State Who's Who.* Hopkinsville, Ky.: Historical Record Association, 1966.

Jack Wessling

RICHARDSON, MARY CABELL (b. ca. 1864, Covington, Ky.; d. April 10, 1925, Covington, Ky.). Although she made a point of not mentioning her age, Mary C. Richardson, a newspaper reporter and a poet, was apparently born around 1864 to Robert Carter and Marie Louise Harris Richardson. She spent her entire life in Covington. Her father was a **Mexican War** veteran, a Covington attorney, a state representative, and a remote cousin of President William Henry Harrison (1889–1893); her mother's father was Col. Henry C. Harris, a Kentucky state representative and senator. Lineage was very important to Richardson. In 1899 she first applied for the job of Covington librarian but then went to work in the clerk's office of the U.S. Circuit Court and District Court in Covington. Although she had been writing news for the local press for some time, in 1903 she formally became a reporter for the *Cincinnati Commercial Times,* covering the Northern Kentucky social scene. Her writing was often described as "breezy." She was also a poet and wrote a book of poems, one of which, "Be British," became a war slogan in England during **World War I**. She was active in **Trinity Episcopal Church** in Covington and was a founding member of an organization that collected scrap metal to be sold for war relief. She was heavily involved in the Daughters of the American Revolution and the Colonial Dames. Richardson resided on Garrard St. in Covington; she died in 1925, at approximately age 61, at the William Booth Memorial Hospital from an acute intestinal obstruction. She was buried at the family lot in Highland Cemetery in Fort Mitchell.

Kentucky Death Certificate No. 9887, for the year 1925.

"Writer Is Dead," *KP,* April 11, 1925, 1.

RICHARDSON, ROBERT, COLONEL (b. May 18, 1826, Louisville, Ky.; d. June 28, 1896, Covington, Ky.). Robert Carter Richardson, a military officer, a lawyer, and an author, was a son of Samuel Q. and Mary Harrison Richardson. Although Robert's parents died while he was quite young, he obtained an education with the help of family friends. After attending local schools, he entered Transylvania University in Lexington, where he earned a BA in 1846 and a JD in 1848. During the **Mexican War**, he served for one year in a company commanded by Cassius M. Clay. Afterward Richardson set up a law office in Lexington. He moved to Covington in 1850, where he became a distinguished lawyer and an author of some renown. He contributed to *Appleton's Encyclopedia* and wrote educational treatises and numerous other literary works. In Northern Kentucky he became active in Democratic politics; he was elected a state representative in 1855 and held that office until 1859. He served as a colonel during the **Civil War**, commanding two Union Home Guard companies. In 1859 he married Mariah Louise Harris of Prestonburg, a daughter of Col. Henry Harris, who served in both the House of Representatives and Senate in Kentucky. The couple had eight children. From 1859 to 1863, he served as the superintendent of public instruction for the Commonwealth of Kentucky. He died at age 70 at his home at 21 E. 12th St. in Covington and was buried at Linden Grove Cemetery in that city. He had been an attorney for 46 years.

Biographical Cyclopedia of the Commonwealth of Kentucky. Chicago: John M. Gresham, 1896.

Levin, H., ed. *The Lawyers and Lawmakers of Kentucky.* Chicago: Lewis, 1897.

Perrin, William Henry, J. H. Battle, and G. C. Kniffin. *Kentucky: A History of the State.* Louisville, Ky.: F.A. Battey, 1888.

Reis, Jim. "They Served as Legislators When War Clouds Billowed," *KP,* January 27, 2003, 4K.

RICH LADDER COMPANY. Founded in Carrollton as the Adkinson Brothers Lumber Mill in 1893, this business was purchased in 1945 by Howard B. Rich Sr. and Louis Bunning. Rich and Bunning expanded the mill's products to include wooden ladders that were shipped to distribution points in the eastern United States.

In 1966 the Huenefeld Company acquired the business and built a new mill in 1972 that covered more than an acre at Seventh and Polk Sts. in Carrollton, near the railroad. The new owner renamed the business the Kentucky Ladder Company. In 1978 it had more than 150 employees working three shifts. In addition to ladders, the company produced wood crates that were shipped to all parts of the United States. In the late 1980s, the Werner Company of Chicago, a longtime leader in aluminum and fiberglass ladders, scaffolds, and climbing equipment, expanded by acquiring three wooden ladder companies in the South, among them the Kentucky Ladder Company. In 1990 Werner built a modern wood factory and consolidated all of its wood products at Carrollton. At that time Werner was the largest producer of climbing products in the world.

Gentry, Mary Ann. *A History of Carroll County.* Madison, Ind.: Coleman, 1984.

Landoll. "Material Handling Success Stories—Boost Productivity with Bendi." www.landoll.com (accessed May 5, 2006).

Werner. "Werner Ladder—History." www.wernerladder.com (accessed May 5, 2006).

Diane Perrine Coon

RICHWOOD. The unincorporated community of Richwood in southeastern Boone Co. dates back to the late 1700s and early 1800s. It was originally called Richwood Station and denoted a fortified structure for residents seeking safety in the event of an Indian attack. When hostilities ceased, the community's name was shortened to Richwood. **American Indians** inhabited the Richwood area before the pioneers arrived; an archaeological survey by the University of Kentucky at Lexington has confirmed the location of a **Fort Ancient** Indian village there. Today, the town of Richwood is at the intersection of the former **Covington and Lexington Turnpike**, built in 1830 (U.S. 25), and Richwood Rd. (Ky. Rt. 338).

The rolling farmland of Richwood, drained by the Mud Lick Creek, contains the most fertile soil in eastern Boone Co. This fertility, along with the area's good transportation system, made a flourishing agriculture possible. The early cash crop was hogs, produced for the Cincinnati pork-packing industry (see **Meatpacking**). **Tobacco** later became the main crop, until hay for horses and cows took its place, as this industry gained prominence in Boone Co.

During the late 1700s large land grants were given to **Revolutionary War** soldiers by the federal government as payment for their military service. The tracts in the Richwood area were divided, sold, and then settled by some very prosperous men in the early 1800s. The Bedingers, the Clarksons, the Gaineses, the Hudsons, the Hugheses, the Menzieses, and the Southgates who settled Richwood were well-educated professional men—attorneys and physicians. In the 1850 Boone Co. census, the two wealthiest men in the county, **Benjamin Franklin Bedinger**, MD, and James Gaines, owned farms in Richwood. Beautiful brick houses were built in the area, two of which, the Hughes and Hudson residences, still stand and are listed on the National Register of Historic Places.

John P. Gaines bought 221 acres near Richwood in 1827, built a house, and raised his family on his Maplewood farm. He was a soldier in the War of 1812, a major in the **Mexican War**, a representative in the Kentucky legislature, a U.S. congressman, and governor of the Territory of Oregon. Archibald Kinkead Gaines, John's younger brother, bought Maplewood from his brother when John moved to Oregon in 1849. **Margaret Garner** was a slave owned by the **Gaines** family at Maplewood when in January 1856 she made a dramatic attempt to escape slavery.

During the **Civil War** there was a Union Army encampment along Richwood Rd. Rev. Everett Bedinger, minister of **Richwood Presbyterian Church**, after publishing his views on states' rights, fled to Canada to avoid arrest as a Confederate sympathizer. One of the only two Civil War military engagements in Boone Co. occurred at **Snow's Pond** along the Covington and Lexington Turnpike, near Richwood. During the late 1870s, the railroad that became the **Cincinnati Southern Railroad** was constructed parallel to the **Dry Ridge Trace**, with a station at Richwood. A depot and a section house for the railroad construction workers were also built. Passengers and shipments of goods were unloaded at the Richwood depot and then transported by wagon to nearby farms. A small town grew up around the railroad station, with a general store, mail service, a livery station, a barn for livestock, and a stock scale. A bank was founded in the Richwood community in 1909 but closed several years later. The brick bank building became a grocery store that later also operated a gas pump and an auto repair garage. A tavern was located across Richwood Rd. from the grocery store's properties in later years.

The center of community life in Richwood was the **Richwood Presbyterian Church**, the oldest Presbyterian church in Boone Co., which was founded in May 1834 by Rev. Joseph Cabell Harrison. The church leaders were also community leaders with progressive social views on issues like slavery, states' rights, and public education.

In the 1920s, sections of the Covington and Lexington Turnpike became part of the **Dixie Highway** (U.S. 25), a road that began in Covington and ended in Florida. The Dixie Highway came through Richwood on the way to Walton, bypassing the section of the turnpike that curved through Kensington. Traffic through Richwood increased as the community became a flag stop for Greyhound buses. In the 1960s, I-71-75 was constructed parallel to the Dixie Highway through Richwood, with an exit onto Richwood Rd. The eastern part of Old Richwood Rd., from the Dixie Highway, now ends at the interstate, and a new section was built under the interstate to connect with the Dixie Highway. Once again, traffic increased and Richwood became a major travel center for trucks and cars.

As a transportation center, Richwood attracted industrial development during the late 20th century. This growth accelerated in the 1990s as the industrial corridor extended from Florence south through Richwood and on to Walton. Richwood is rapidly changing as a result of housing developments that have replaced farms and brought urban sprawl in recent years.

An Atlas of Boone, Kenton, and Campbell Counties, Kentucky. Philadelphia: D. J. Lake, 1883.

Tenkotte, Paul A. "The 'Chronic' Want of Cincinnati—a Southern Railroad," *NKH* 6, no. 1 (Fall–Winter 1998): 24–33.

Warminski, Margo. *Historic Structures of Boone County.* Burlington, Ky.: Boone Co. Historic Preservation Board, 2002.

Ruth Wade Cox Brunings

RICHWOOD PRESBYTERIAN CHURCH. Richwood Presbyterian Church, the first Presbyterian church established in Boone Co., is one of the oldest Presbyterian churches in Northern Kentucky. It was founded in 1834 by Rev. Joseph Cabell Harrison and has maintained continuous worship services since that time. Harrison (1793–1860) had many influential connections in the region. He was a first cousin of President William Henry Harrison (1841); he and his cousin John Breckinridge established the first religious newspaper published in Kentucky, the *Western Luminary*, in 1824 in Lexington; and Harrison's wife was Sophia Rice, the granddaughter of Rev. David Rice, the founder of Presbyterianism in Kentucky.

The Richwood congregation met in a brick schoolhouse and in homes in the early years. On October 4, 1842, the trustees of the church purchased for five dollars from William Mosley a one-half-acre lot on the Mud Lick branch of Big Bone Creek, where the Burlington and Big Bone roads intersected. In 1844 a church was built there. After that structure was struck by lightning and burned in 1869, the congregation built a new church building, completed by September 1870. The small white frame country church, situated in a beautiful rural setting—surrounded by a stone wall and maple trees opposite a creek—has been a subject for artists, including **Caroline Williams**, and photographers for many years.

As a small church, Richwood Church was not always able to support a full-time minister. Some early ministers were employed on a part-time basis and served other churches in the area as well. Some had other sources of income, such as farming, or other employment, such as teaching. Rev. Samuel Lynn had a school and boarded students during the week. Rev. William White also had a private school, White Haven, on U.S. 42, down the road from the current public school, New Haven. There were periods when the pulpit was filled with "stated supply" from the Presbytery, seminary students (licentiates), guest ministers, or elders of the church.

The culture of the 1850s and 1860s was reflected in records that were kept in the Session Books. For example, the elders took stern disciplinary action when members failed to obey the Ten Commandments or to fulfill their obligations as members. Documented transgressions included absence from worship, intemperate drinking, frequenting places of public resort, adultery, insubordinate conduct as a servant, the use of profane language, and leading dissolute and worldly lives. Offenders were suspended from church membership until they repented. The names and sins of those suspended were announced from the pulpit.

Richwood Presbyterian Church had an early commitment to foreign missions, formed missionary societies, and sponsored missionaries, including Rev. Charles Foreman. Two of the early ministers of Richwood Church, Rev. William White and Rev. Everett Wade Bedinger, had children who became foreign missionaries. Bedinger, the longest-serving minister in the history of the church, had not only children but also sons-in law, a grandson, and a niece who were missionaries. At the onset of the **Civil War**, Bedinger published a "Plea for Peace" in the *Covington Journal* in defense of states' rights. Even though he was against slavery, the Union Army sent soldiers to arrest him as a Southern sympathizer. He escaped to Canada, returned through enemy lines to Kentucky, and took his family on a dangerous journey to Virginia, where he ministered to soldiers on both sides of the conflict. He returned to the Richwood Church after the war.

Revivals, called protracted meetings, produced new converts who were subsequently brought into church membership. Among the converts were slaves in the Richwood community. The first slave to join Richwood Presbyterian Church was Moses Carter on January 5, 1843; he was followed by Rachel, Drusylla, Plato, Hannah Patterson, Hannah Hughes, and **Margaret Garner**. In 1855 there were 26 white members and 7 slave members of the church. Plato was hired as the church sexton in 1844, on completion of the church building, and continued in this employment until December 1856, when he moved to Covington with his owner, William Menzies. Margaret Garner fled slavery with her family in January 1856, less than a year after she joined the church. Surrounded by a posse in Cincinnati, Garner killed her daughter rather than see her return to slavery. The impact of this event on the Richwood Church and community was profound. Everett Wade Bedinger, who was an elder, the clerk of Session, and an opponent of slavery, recorded in the church's Session Book II on June 1, 1856, that the Session had met and ordered a day of fasting. Members were instructed to "repair to the house of God for solemn worship, confession of sin and deep humiliation before God on account of our sins and departures from Him as a congregation and as individual members" and for the return of God's spirit to enable the conversions of others.

The congregation built a community house, with a kitchen, in the in the 1940s. Church activities such as wedding receptions, youth group meetings, and potluck dinners took place in this building as well as Thanksgiving dinners for the neighborhood. In 1946 the current stone manse was built by Stanley Ranson with help from other men of the church. The Sunday School Annex was built onto the back of the church in 1960. A fellowship hall with offices and additional classrooms was added onto the church to replace the community house and dedicated in 1991. Major celebrations with dinners and festivities occurred every 50 years as Richwood Church had its 50th, 100th and 150th anniversaries. On January 17, 1971, a historical marker, awarded to Richwood Presbyterian Church by the Kentucky Historical Society, was dedicated during a ceremony that included speeches, music, and a reception.

In 1935 Richwood Presbyterian Church was transferred from Ebenezer Presbytery (which originally included all of Kentucky) to the Presbytery of Louisville of the Presbyterian Church of the United States. In 1985 it was transferred again to the Presbytery of Cincinnati of the Presbyterian Church (U.S.A.). In 1967 the Board of Deacons was disbanded, their duties assumed by the elders; the board was reinstated in 2000. The first woman minister was Rev. Jean Hyde Frable, 1998–2007.

From the beginning, Richwood Church had a church cemetery for members and their relatives. The first burial was George Michael Bedinger Jr., who died of cholera at Big Bone in 1833. In 1880 the cemetery acquired an additional acre and was extended to the east by a section now designated Division C. In 1930 Richwood Cemetery separated from the church and became a community cemetery. The first burial of an African American, Mary Sleet Sechrest, was in Division C in 1933.

Ferguson, Calvin Gordon. "History of Richwood Presbyterian Church, May 1834 to May 1984," Richwood Presbyterian Church, Richwood, Ky.

Richwood Church Session Books, Richwood Presbyterian Church, Richwood, Ky.

Ruth Wade Cox Brunings

RICKETT, FRANCES (b. February 16, 1921, Covington, Ky.). Author Merle Frances Rickett is the daughter of Merle Lowe and Mary Kerrigan Rickett. Her father was a salesman and her mother was a news journalist and politician. The family lived at 13 E. 31st St. in Latonia. Frances graduated from high school in Crawfordsville, Ind., and her undergraduate degree (1943) is from DePauw University, Greencastle, Ind. She has an MFA degree (1947) from the Catholic University of America in Washington, D.C. She began writing at age six and, except for occasional moments when she thought about being an actress, always wanted to be an author. During **World War II**, Rickett was a civilian cryptanalyst for the U.S. Army Signal Corps at Arlington, Va. She went on to work as a staff writer for RCA, NBC, and *Woman's Day* in New York City. In 1957 she began devoting herself to freelance writing. Her first novel was *The Prowler*, published in 1963. It was followed by *Tread Softly* (1964), her most popular work, and then *A Certain Slant of Light* (1968), *An Affair of Doctors* (1975), *Totaled* (in collaboration with Steven McGraw; 1981), and *Stalked* (1983). Under the pseudonym Martha Winslow, she wrote *The Abortionist* (1970), and she produced two novelizations of soap operas under the pseudonym Kate Lowe Kerrigan: *Another World I* and *Another World II* (both in 1978). She has written extensively for both television and radio. She often recounts the difficulty she had finding a publisher for her first novel, *The Prowler*. Rickett readily admits that writing catalog copy for merchandisers like the JCPenney Company prompted her to write concisely and thus helped her to become published. Today, Rickett lives in New York City.

Contemporary Authors. Vol. 107. Detroit: Gale Research, 1983.

Rickett, Francis, to Michael R. Sweeney, November 2004.

RIDDELL, FOUNTAIN (b. January 9, 1833, Boone Co., Ky.; d. May 30, 1903, Burlington, Ky.). A lawyer and a politician, Fountain Riddell was the son of John and Florenda McKay Riddell. His father was a farmer of Scottish descent. Fountain was educated at the Morgan Academy in Burlington and after graduation taught there for one year. He then entered Indiana Asbury University (later named DePauw University) at Greencastle, Ind., where he studied law. After returning to Burlington, he apprenticed under lawyer **James W. Calvert**. In 1858 Riddell began his own law practice in Burlington. He entered politics in 1859 and was elected to the Kentucky House of Representatives, where he served for two years. Riddell married Louisa Hawes in March 1870, and they had four children, two of whom lived to adulthood. In October 1870 Fountain Riddell purchased the Boone House, on Jefferson St. in Burlington, behind the courthouse; the Boone House was formerly a tavern/inn. He renovated the building to serve as his residence and law offices. Riddell was named president of the Boone Co. Deposit Bank in 1885 and served until 1903. He died in 1903 at age 70 and was buried in the Burlington Cemetery. After his death, the Boone House passed to his wife, and at her death in 1922, to their daughter Henrietta, who was married to Alvin Boyers Renaker. It then became known as the Renaker House. Boone Co. purchased the building in 1967 and had it remodeled into office space for the Human Services Department.

Boone County Recorder, historical edition, September 4, 1930.

Reis, Jim. "Historic Renaker House Began as Tavern in 1830," *KP*, April 14, 1997, 4K.

RIDDELL, NATHANIEL E. (b. July 17, 1872, Burlington, Ky.; d. September 1, 1942, Burlington, Ky.). Lawyer, judge, and banker Nathaniel Edson Riddell was the son of **Fountain Riddell** and Louisa Hawes Riddell. Nathaniel grew up in Burlington, where his early education was at the Morgan Academy. He then attended the Cincinnati Law School and graduated in 1895. After leaving school, he entered into a legal partnership with Boone Co. judge **John M. Lassing**. On June 6, 1900, he married Katie L. Huey; the couple had no children. In 1903, when his father, Fountain Riddell, died, Nathaniel replaced him as president of the Boone Co. Deposit Bank. He served in that position until 1930, when the bank was merged with the Peoples Deposit Bank of Burlington.

In 1906 Riddell was elected Boone Co. attorney, and he held that office until 1920. He resigned when he was appointed Boone Co. judge by Kentucky governor Augustus O. Stanley (1915–1919). Riddell served in that position for the remainder of his life. He was also one of the organizers and president of the Consolidated Telephone Company in Boone Co. He bought and operated, for several years, the *Boone County Recorder* newspaper, which his uncle W. L. Riddell had started in 1875. For many years, Nathaniel Riddell was an active member of the Burlington Masonic Lodge and also the Knights of Pythias. In 1942 he died in his Burlington home at the age 70. Funeral services were held in the Renaker House, then owned by his sister, Henrietta Riddell Renaker. Riddell was buried in the Highland Cemetery in Fort Mitchell.

Boone County Recorder, historical edition, September 4, 1930.

Reis, Jim. "Big Man in Boone County," *KP*, December 12, 2002, 4K.

——. "Historic Renaker House Began as Tavern in 1830," *KP*, April 14, 1997, 4K.

——. "Riddell Served 6 Terms as Judge," *KP*, April 14, 1997, 4K.

Warner, Jennifer S. *Boone County: From Mastodons to the Millennium*. Burlington, Ky.: Boone Co. Bicentennial Book Committee, 1998.

RIDGEVIEW HEIGHTS. Ridgeview Heights was a sixth-class city located in central Kenton Co. across from the Kenton Co. Golf Course, near the intersection of Richardson Rd. (Ky. Rt. 1829) and Turkeyfoot Rd. (Ky. Rt. 1303). The subdividing of the 100-acre Perry farm during the late 1940s led to the founding of the town. Attracted by the lure of "country living," throngs of Northern Kentucky urbanites flocked to the new development and others like it during the 1950s. The neighborhood incorporated as a city in 1962 to finance road improvements. The name Ridgeview Heights reflected the area's topography. For several years, the city's residents enjoyed some of the county's lowest tax rates. By the late 1970s, however, operating this small residential community had become expensive. Increased road maintenance and federally mandated sewer construction placed an enormous tax burden on Ridgeview Heights residents. Hemmed in by Erlanger and Independence, Ridgeview Heights could not raise additional tax revenue through annexation. When key leaders died or moved away, the city's fiscal problems were compounded. Left with few options, the Ridgeview

Heights city council sought budget relief by exploring a merger with one of the neighboring cities. The merger talks led to the annexation of Ridgeview Heights by the City of Independence on January 1, 1984. The Ridgeview Heights population at the time was approximately 760.

"Death of a City—Lack of Interest Was Main Factor in Ridgeview Heights' Demise," *KP*, January 2, 1984, 9K.
Ridgeview Heights vertical file, Kenton Co. Public Library, Covington, Ky.
"Who Runs Ridgeview Heights?" *KE*, May 28, 1979, A2.

Greg Perkins

RIEVESCHL, GEORGE, JR. (b. January 9, 1916, Cincinnati, Ohio; d. September 27, 2007, Cincinnati, Ohio). Scientist and philanthropist George Rieveschl Jr. was the only son of George and Alma Hofling Rieveschl. He grew up along Arlington Ave. in the Arlington Heights section of Cincinnati; his father worked in a paper mill. A gifted student, Rieveschl graduated from the Ohio Mechanics Institute in Cincinnati with a commercial art major and an interest in chemistry. His educational path turned to chemistry when he enrolled at the University of Cincinnati (UC), where he earned a BA in 1937, an MS in 1939, and a PhD in 1940. After graduation he accepted a position at UC teaching chemical engineering. His PhD research on local anesthetics and antispasmodics led to the discovery of a novel antihistamine that became Benadryl.

In 1943 Rieveschl joined the research department at Parke, Davis & Company in Detroit, Mich. The company began marketing Benadryl, the first commercially available antihistamine, in 1946. After 23 years, during which he held management positions ranging from scientific assistant to vice president of commercial development, Rieveschl left Parke, Davis & Company and spent four years as a consultant to the pharmaceutical industry. In 1970 he returned to UC as the acting vice president of research for university president Walter Langsam.

Rieveschl was involved in a number of innovative programs within the university system, including the partnership arrangement with the Environmental Protection Agency and the first campus computer initiative. His skills became especially evident, however, when Warren Bennis, then the president of the university, appointed Rieveschl as the first president of the UC Foundation in 1972. It was under his leadership that the Charles McMicken Society was formed to solicit support of alumni and other friends of the university for the mission of the growing university. In 1973 Rieveschl established the annual Dr. George Rieveschl Award to recognize significant scholarly or creative achievements of full-time faculty, with an emphasis on work carried out at UC. He retired from the university in 1982, and in 1987 UC named the main science building, containing the chemistry department and laboratories, after him.

Rieveschl won his first award, the Hochstetler Prize, for excellence as a teaching assistant at the University of Cincinnati in 1937. His subsequent awards from the university included the William Howard Taft Medal and the Award for Excellence. Rieveschl was also an active leader in the community. He served on the boards of the Cincinnati Zoo and Botanical Garden, the Lloyd Library and Museum in Cincinnati, and the Cincinnati Museum of Natural History. His greatest affection, however, was for art; he served in a number of leadership and fundraising roles for the Contemporary Arts Center in Cincinnati and the Cincinnati Art Museum. For a number of years he served on the board of the Contemporary Arts Center. He also served the Cincinnati Art Museum in various roles, including chair of the board of trustees, founder of its Founder's Society, and chair of the Treasures for the Queen: A Millennium Gift to Cincinnati. In 1999 the Cincinnati Art Museum established the George Rieveschl Medal for distinguished leadership and philanthropic service.

George Rieveschl Jr. in his lab, 1947.

Rieveschl received many honors for his work in the Greater Cincinnati area. In 1989 the Juvenile Diabetes Association named him Cincinnatian of the year, and in 1990 the Greater Cincinnati Chamber of Commerce added the title of a Great Living Cincinnatian. In 1995 he was inducted into the International Science and Engineering Hall of Fame.

Rieveschl, who resided in Covington for a number of years, was also very active in supporting arts and education initiatives in Northern Kentucky, such as the Carnegie Visual and Performing Arts Center. In December 2002 **Northern Kentucky University** awarded him an honorary doctorate (DSc). In 2003 Rieveschl gave $1 million toward the new science building at Northern Kentucky University. Carnegie Visual and Performing Arts Center in Covington has a gallery named for him, and his foundation funded many other philanthropic activities in the region.

Cincinnati USA Regional Chamber. "George Rieveschl." www.gccc.com (accessed April 17, 2006).
Horstman, Barry M. "George Rieveschl: Sneezers Can Thank Him for Relief," *CP*, November 1, 1999, 1B.
O'Farrell, Peggy. "Thank Him for Benadryl," *CE*, May 17, 2006, C1.
"Salute," *KP*, June 29, 1988, 1KK–2KK.

Dennis B. Worthen

RINGO, DAVID L. (b. January 5, 1912, Hamilton, Ohio). David Leer Ringo was both a pioneering and a nationally recognized transit industry executive. In the summer after David had completed the sixth grade, his father, a pharmacist, accepted a position with a store in Covington. Thereafter, David was educated in the Covington Public Schools (see **Covington Independent Schools**). He attended John W. Hall Junior High School and then graduated with honors from **Holmes High School** in February 1930 (as a member of the class of 1929).

Needing funds to enter the University of Kentucky in Lexington, Ringo accepted a job in March 1930 as a track laborer for the Cincinnati, Newport, and Covington Railway (CN&C) (the **Green Line Company**). He attended the University of Kentucky for two years, again working in summer 1931 for the CN&C. The financial pressures of the Great Depression prompted Ringo to begin full-time work for the Green Line the next year. He was hired as an assistant to the chief traffic engineer. By the time of the **flood of 1937**, he had become a traffic engineer. He worked up to 16 hours a day, seven days a week, for the next few months to help supervise the restoration of transit service to the flood-ravaged cities of Bellevue, Covington, Dayton, Ludlow, and Newport. In early 1939 Ringo was named assistant superintendent of transportation by the Green Line management. On July 8, 1939, he married Ruth Jean McDonell; the couple had three sons.

Ringo is credited with settling the December 1940–January 1941 strike of the Green Line Company by Local No. 628 of the Amalgamated Association of Street and Electric Railway Employees. He made use of some innovative ideas centering on future job protection. By this time, Ringo was a member of the Kentucky Society of Professional Engineers and had become the first registered transportation engineer in the state.

In 1945 the new owners of the Green Line, Allen and Company, appointed him as assistant general manager of both the Green Line and its suburban transit subsidiary, the **Dixie Traction Company**. Ringo and his boss, Philip G. Vondersmith, helped their company reach an agreement with the Kenton Co. Airport board to provide exclusive bus service from downtown Cincinnati to the soon-to-be-opened Greater Cincinnati Airport (later the **Cincinnati/Northern Kentucky International Airport**) in Boone Co. and to be the sole provider of outbound taxi service at the airport. Both services were profitable enterprises for the Green Line over the next 25 years.

In April 1947 Ringo was named general manager of both the CN&C and the Dixie Traction

Company and assumed day-to-day operational control. On May 18, 1950, he was named president of both companies, becoming the youngest chief executive of a major transit system in the nation. Over the next eight years, the Green Line remained the most profitable of the many transit properties owned by Allen and Company. From 1947 to 1957, the Green Line won about a dozen first-place awards for service, safety, and maintenance (in the 300-to-1,000-employee category) from the American Transit Association.

During the early 1950s, Allen and Company, the owners of the Green Line, purchased 16 additional transit companies and formed a new conglomerate, American Transportation Enterprises (ATE). The Green Line was the senior member of the group, and under Ringo's direction it remained ATE's most profitable company. In 1957 the Allen family selected Ringo to run the entire operation. As executive vice president, he was responsible for the management of the 16 component companies, which owned more than 1,600 buses and employed more than 5,000 people.

By 1963, however, it had become clear that privately owned transit companies had no future. Although perceived as public utilities by the average citizen, they had no governmental standby guarantees if revenues failed to match expenses. Although the federal and state mania for building new expressways encouraged many Americans to forsake public transportation, many people, for various reasons, still needed public transit to go places. In 1963 members of the American Transit Association, led by ATE chief executive Ringo, met with representatives of city governments, labor, and other interested parties to form the Urban Passenger Transportation Association, which lobbied for federal transit aid. Their efforts brought almost immediate results. As part of his Great Society program, President Lyndon B. Johnson (1963–1969) signed the Urban Mass Transportation Act into law on July 9, 1964, providing a firm base for the future granting of transit subsidies.

The Urban Mass Transportation Administration (UMTA) took control of all federal transit programs on July 1, 1968. Thereafter, federal funds became available through UMTA to assist communities in the purchase and operation of privately held transit companies. UMTA required the formation of a public transit authority and local public financial participation before any federal subsidies could be provided for a takeover of a private system. In June 1971, by the action of the fiscal courts in Boone, Campbell, and Kenton counties, the **Transit Authority of Northern Kentucky** (TANK) was created.

Ringo realized early that transit companies would be publicly owned in the future. As a result, he and his associates formed a new company to manage the new public transit agencies. On January 1, 1970, ATE Management and Service Company Inc. (ATEMS), based in Cincinnati, was opened for business. Ironically, it started with a five-year contract to manage all of ATE's remaining transit companies. By 1980 Ringo's group had contracts with about 50 public transit agencies in the United States, including the Green Line Transit successor, TANK.

David's son Philip J. Ringo succeeded him as ATEMS president, serving from 1981 until 1999. In 1986 ATEMS was sold to Ryder Systems Inc. of Miami, Fla. At that time, ATEMS was involved with managing some 52 transit properties. In July 1999 First Group, a British company, purchased Ryder's transit management business.

David Ringo was elected to the American Transit Association's Hall of Fame in 1984; he was further honored during the 1999 convention of the American Public Transit Association in Orlando, Fla., by First Transit senior vice president Rich Clair, who spoke of Ringo's "vision and outstanding leadership of ATE." In 1970 the University of Kentucky named Ringo to its Hall of Distinguished Alumni. Ringo's wife of 60 years, Ruth, died in October 1999, and today Ringo lives in Florida.

Lehmann, Terry W., and Earl W. Clark, *The Green Line.* Chicago: Central Electric Railfans' Association, 2000.

Terry W. Lehmann

RIPPLETON, WASHINGTON (b. April 16, 1842, Danville, Ky.; d. May 12, 1911, Newport, Ky.). Although born in Danville, Washington Rippleton spent most of his life in Newport, and for more than 50 years he was one of Newport's leading African American figures. Rippleton married a local woman named Lucy, and they resided in Newport on Rickey St., raising four children. From 1867 through 1876, Rippleton's occupation was listed in the local city directory as either a hostler or a coachman. He was involved in other aspects of the community as well.

In 1866 Washington Rippleton, Beverly Lumpkin, and others formed a board of trustees for the newly established African American school, which opened under the direction of the Missionary Aid Association and the Freedmen's Bureau. In April 1870 Rippleton led a delegation of Newport's residents during a parade celebrating the passage of the 15th Amendment to the U.S. Constitution. That parade wound from Newport to Covington. In November 1872 Rippleton helped to organize the **Corinthian Baptist Church** on Roberts St. in Newport. In February 1873, continuing his activities with social and educational issues, Rippleton, Rev. Dennis Lightfoot, **Robert Littleton**, and a delegation from Newport attended the Colored Education Convention in Louisville. The convention informed the attendees of the proposed new state law that would allow for public schools for African American children. In August, when the **Southgate St. School** was authorized, Rippleton was active in the planning that took place for it.

In February 1883 the African-American Literary Circle was organized in Newport, with Washington Rippleton as president. He remained involved in Campbell Co. Republican politics throughout the 1890s, as did his close friend Robert Littleton. In July 1891 the Campbell Co. Republican executive committee named Rippleton a delegate to their county convention. In August, Rippleton, Littleton, and other African American Republicans formed the first Republican League Club. Rippleton was one of five men to serve on the executive committee. In March 1892 the league elected Rippleton as president for the ensuing year. At the July meeting, held at the African Methodist Episcopal Church on Southgate St. in Newport, the club announced that the membership was 80 strong and increasing daily. In May 1894, the African-American Republican League Club was renamed the Crispus Attucks Club; Rippleton remained as president.

From 1878 through 1892, Rippleton worked at the **Newport Barracks** and lived nearby at 249 Liberty St. Throughout the 1890s, he served as a storekeeper in government service under a Republican administration. Afterward, Rippleton operated a shoeshine parlor at 405 York St. in Newport until his death in 1911. He was buried in Evergreen Cemetery in Southgate.

Annual Report of Board of Education of Newport, Kentucky. Newport, Ky.: Newport Printing, 1873.
"A Card to the Colored Citizens," *KJ*, May 13, 1892, 4.
CDG, April 15, 1870; November 29, 1872; February 11, 1873.
"The City," *KSJ*, February 10, 1883, 1.
"Colored Club," *KJ*, May 25, 1894, 6.
"The Colored League," *KJ*, March 4, 1892, 4.
"Colored Schools," *CDE*, August 1, 1866, 2.
Covington Ticket, August 14, 1875.
"Deaths in Newport," *KP*, May 13, 1911, 5.
"Delegates Selected," *KJ*, July 7, 1891, 3.
"First in the State," *KJ*, August 13, 1891, 5.
"The Outs Knock Out the Bloody In," *KJ*, March 8, 1892, 4.

Theodore H. H. Harris

RISEN, ARNIE DENNY "STILTS" (b. October 9, 1924, Lexington, Ky.). Basketball player Arnold "Arnie" Risen is the son of John Denny and Elvira Scroggins Risen. He grew up in Grant Co. and graduated from Williamstown High School (see **Williamstown Independent Schools**) in 1942. After attending Eastern Kentucky University for one year on a basketball scholarship, this six-foot-nine center transferred to Ohio State University, where he was an All Big 10 Conference player in 1943 and 1944 and a Converse All-American in 1945. He led the Buckeyes to the NCAA Tournament in 1944 and 1945. After college Risen played with the Indianapolis Kautskys of the old National Basketball League before joining the Rochester (N.Y.) Royals of the National Basketball Association (NBA), with whom he played from 1948 until 1955. He finished his career with the Boston Celtics in 1958. He completed 13 professional seasons, and although not large or burly (he weighed only 200 pounds), he was known as a reliable scorer, a rugged rebounder, and a strong competitor. He was a member of Rochester's 1951 NBA championship team. In 1998 Risen became the second person from the Northern Kentucky region, after **Dave Cowens**, to enter the Naismith Memorial Basketball Hall of Fame in Springfield, Mass. Risen has retired and lives in the Cleveland, Ohio, area.

Basketball Hall of Fame. "Hall of Famers: Arnold D. 'Arnie' Risen." www.hoophall.com/halloffamers/bhof-arnie-risen.html (accessed May 24, 2007).
"Risen," *Grant County News,* January 27, 1983, 12.

Michael R. Sweeney

RITCHIE FAMILY. The Ritchie family moved to Ludlow from Cincinnati in 1860. In that year, Casper Ritchie Jr. (1827–1890) built a large, two-story brick house at the northwest corner of Elm and Locust Sts., for the then huge sum of $20,000. Casper and his brother Jacques had begun to prosper from the dry goods wholesale store that they had started in Cincinnati in May 1851. In 1853 the two brothers married sisters from the wealthy Moore family of Mount Adams, the hill just east of downtown Cincinnati, and according to family lore, Moore family money helped pay for the Ludlow home.

Casper Ritchie Sr. (1800–1873) had immigrated from Switzerland in 1834, settling in Cincinnati the next year. Because he was unable to find work during the bank crises and economic hardship of the early 1840s, he returned with his family to Switzerland in 1842. On their return to Cincinnati in 1847, the Ritchie family identified with the Germans of Cincinnati and grew alarmed at the growth of the anti-immigrant Order of the Star-Spangled Banner, or **Know-Nothing**s. After the Know-Nothing riots of 1855, Casper Ritchie Jr., a son of Casper Ritchie Sr., resolved to leave Cincinnati. He already owned property in Ludlow, which he considered a place of "Arcadian simplicity," and began building a home there in 1858. During the **Civil War**, Ritchie Jr. served in a Home Guard unit to protect the area from Confederate attack and prevent the sale of contraband.

Casper Ritchie Jr. was one of a number of prosperous businessmen who lived in the suburban quiet of Northern Kentucky and commuted by ferry into the noisy, crowded industrial city across the river. His Ludlow home had a slate roof and a widow's walk. A two-story porch at the rear, from which friends and family observed the fireworks on the Fourth of July, caught the breezes of the Ohio River and provided a view of Cincinnati. In 1864 Ritchie added a one-story library, fitted out in solid black walnut, and in 1865 he built an extensive glass greenhouse, where he grew exotic species. In addition to two maids and a hired hand who lived at the Ludlow estate, Ritchie employed a gardener for many years. The bucolic setting of the Ritchie home declined after the opening of the **Cincinnati Southern Railroad Bridge** (1877), which turned Ludlow into a rail center and introduced the very same industrial conditions Ritchie had sought to escape—noise, smoke, and vandalism that destroyed the greenhouse. Ritchie's Cincinnati business declined as well, until it became, in the words of his son Walter, "a junk shop." Still, the home continued to be enjoyed by four generations of the family. The Ritchie property was sold in 1958, the house was demolished, and a **Kroger** grocery store was constructed on the site.

Casper Jacques Ritchie (1862–1902), another son of Casper Ritchie Sr., married Glenna Jolly (1866–1937), whose father, Oscar B. Jolly, piloted the ironclad Union gunboat USS *Cairo* in preparation for the siege of Vicksburg. The son of Glenna and Casper Jacques, Edgar Barrick Ritchie (1892–1918), a 1st lieutenant in the 355th U.S. Army Infantry, was the first Ludlow native to die in **World War I**. The **American Legion** Post of Ludlow, established in August 1919 and dissolved in 1967, was named for Edgar Ritchie.

Highland Cemetery Records, Fort Mitchell, Ky.
National Park Service. "Vicksburg National Military Park." www.nps.gov/vick (accessed September 20, 2006).
Ritchie Family Papers, Cincinnati Historical Society, Cincinnati.
Tenkotte, Paul A. "Rival Cities to Suburbs: Covington and Newport, Kentucky, 1790–1890," PhD diss., Univ. of Cincinnati, 1989.

Daniel Edgar Ritchie

RIVERSIDE–GOOD COUNSEL SCHOOL. As late as the early 1950s, the schools in Northern Kentucky had no special education classes. In 1952 a group of parents concerned about the need for teaching and training children with mental disabilities founded the Riverside School in the basement of the First Presbyterian Church on W. Fourth St. in Covington. The school moved to 430 Garrard St. in Covington the next year. The Roman Catholic Diocese of Covington initiated similar programs at two locations in 1955: Benedictine Sister Wendeline Burkhard gathered 10 "special needs" children in a classroom at the **St. Aloysius** School in Covington; and a **Sister of Divine Providence**, Sister Isabella, did the same at **Corpus Christi** School in Newport. Admission to these schools was not restricted to Catholics, nor to children whose families could pay full tuition. Eventually, the region's Catholic schools joined together to form the Good Counsel School, which operated out of the **Mother of God** School building along W. Sixth St. in Covington. At the same school, Sister Mary Leopolda, a Sister of Charity of Nazareth, held classes for the visually handicapped. In the late 1960s, the Good Counsel School merged with the Riverside School, to create the Riverside–Good Counsel School. In 1972 the new school occupied a new school building in Fort Wright, where instruction was provided from kindergarten through high school. With mainstreaming of special needs students into the public schools, Riverside-Good Counsel School redirected its efforts. The organization changed its name to New Perceptions Inc. in 1985 to reflect the broader array of services offered. New Perceptions Inc. moved to Sperti Dr. in Edgewood in 1990 and brought all of its components together in one location. In 2002 the organization celebrated its 50th year of helping persons with "special needs."

"Good Counsel, Riverside Merge," *Messenger,* March 5, 1967, 14A.
"Kenton Board Votes to Buy Riverside," *KP,* December 17, 1981, 19K.
Main, Anita. "New Perceptions Offers Aid to Disabled," *Messenger,* December 22, 1985, 22.
"New Perceptions," *KP,* January 2, 1985, 8K.
"New Perceptions, Inc." www.newperceptions.org (accessed May 2, 2007).
Tenkotte, Paul A., David E. Schroeder, and Thomas S. Ward. *To Be Catholic and American in Northern, Central, and Appalachian Kentucky: The Diocese of Covington, 1853–2003.* Forthcoming.

RIVER TRADE. For Northern Kentucky the importance of river trade has ebbed and flowed in different periods of the region's history, but such trade has always been significant. At the end of the 18th century, shipment of goods by river offered lower-cost and faster travel than the transportation of goods over the Appalachian Mountains by wagon or packhorse. The average distance goods could be moved per day using horsepower was 12 miles, and for each 100 miles the goods were moved, the cost doubled. Thus, the cost of transportation could far exceed the value of the goods. Transportation by river did require following the course of the river, which often meant that a greater distance was covered, but the cost was much lower, even so. Goods could be shipped by river 1,000 miles or more and still cost less than moving them 100 miles overland.

During the 1790s, river shipment quickly developed along the Mississippi River and its tributaries. Finished goods would be transported by horsepower west across the mountains to Pittsburgh, Pa., or Wheeling, W.Va., and then would be loaded onto rafts or keelboats and floated down the Ohio River. Human labor, using push poles, was needed, however, to move such craft upstream against the current. The average keelboat could carry up to 10 tons of goods as quickly as six miles an hour downstream and up to one mile per hour upstream.

Although the river transportation was cheap, it did have negative features. The river could be used only during part of the year. The Ohio and Kentucky rivers during the 18th and 19th centuries fluctuated from having very little water to raging floods. Generally, the river was not usable from January through March owing to ice, and from July through September owing to low water. Thus, there were two shipping seasons, April through June and October through December. The length of the seasons varied depending on when the spring and fall rains occurred and how much water they brought. Too much rain meant a swift-running river, unsafe to navigate. If shipping was not possible in one of the seasons, goods had to be warehoused until they could be shipped; merchants were required to stock shelves with two to three months' worth of supplies or face depleted inventories. Another impediment to river travel was the Falls of the Ohio at Louisville. This stretch of rapids during low water often prevented boats from proceeding past the falls. Goods in this instance had to be off-loaded and transported by wagon to another boat above or below the falls.

In 1811 the steamboat *New Orleans* was built at Pittsburgh, ushering in the era of mechanically powered boats on the western rivers. Steamboats were not yet viable on the rivers, however. The first steamboats had ship hulls, and their machinery was below the waterline; they could operate only during high water. It was not until the 1840s that the shallow-draft packet boat, with its machinery above the waterline and a paddle wheel for propulsion, became the mover of goods. These boats could move as much as 500 tons of goods up to 10 miles an hour.

Steamboats were soon being built in the Northern Kentucky region. In 1816 the *Calhoun* was built on the Kentucky River. In 1819 the *Henry Clay* was built on the Licking River, and the *General Robinson* and the *Missouri* were launched at Newport. Between 1817 and 1880, 1,374 vessels were built in the Cincinnati area. Northern Kentucky owed much of its prosperity to its ability to receive raw material, convert it into finished products, and ship the products away by river.

With the development of the western river steamboat, interest arose within the business community to canalize the Ohio, Licking, and Kentucky rivers. In 1836 the Commonwealth of Kentucky began building locks and dams on the Kentucky River. Lock No. 1 was constructed at Carrollton; the last Kentucky River lock was built in 1917. These locks were closed to commercial traffic in the year 2000.

The canalization of the Ohio River started in 1830 with the opening of the Portland Canal at Louisville, which circumvented the Falls of the Ohio, and was completed in 1929. The canalization provided a year-round navigational channel of nine feet with its 51 locks and dams between Pittsburgh, Pa., and Cairo, Ill. In Northern Kentucky, the Ohio River locks and dams were No. 33 in Mason Co., No. 34 in Bracken Co., Nos. 35 and 36 in Campbell Co., Nos. 37 and 38 in Boone Co., and No. 39 in Gallatin Co. In the last half of the 20th century, 17 new dams with larger locks replaced the older locks and dams. Two of the new dams are located within Northern Kentucky region, the **Markland Dam** in Gallatin Co. and the Captain Anthony **Meldahl Dam** in Bracken Co. Although locks were proposed for the Licking River, and construction was even started, no locks were ever completed.

During the 19th century, a packet-boat trade based in Cincinnati developed on the Ohio River between Pittsburgh and Louisville, serving all landings in between as well. Because of competition from the railroads, however, packet service on the Ohio River and its tributaries slowly diminished. It ended on the Kentucky River in the 1930s and on the Ohio in the 1940s. Northern Kentucky was able to maintain its transportation edge as packet-boat service ended by developing railroad, highway, airline, and towboat services.

The towboat industry moved barges on the rivers. The barges were originally towed alongside or behind packet boats, but soon they were being pushed up and down the river by towboats. During the 1930s these towboats began to use diesel power; they had screw propellers for propulsion. Before long, steam and paddle wheels became historical curiosities. Whereas a packet could carry 500 tons of goods, a modern tow pushing 12 barges can move 12,000 tons of goods, including grain, coal, petroleum products, chemicals, scrap metal, and finished metal. Barge companies generally own their towboats.

In 2002 Cincinnati–Northern Kentucky, served by 32 barge companies, was the fourth- or fifth-largest port in the United States. In that same year, the port generated or received 13 million tons of goods, and an additional 52 million tons passed through it.

Ambler, Charles H. *A History of Transportation in the Ohio Valley.* Glendale, Calif.: Arthur Clark, 1932.

Hunter, Louis C. *Steamboats on the Western Rivers: An Economic and Technological History.* Reprint, New York: Dover, 1993.

Kane, Adam I. *The Western River Steamboat.* College Station: Texas A&M Press, 2004.

Klein, Benjamin F. *The Ohio River Handbook.* Cincinnati: Young and Klein, 1958.

Charles H. Bogart

RIVERVIEW. This two-story brick house sits on a knoll overlooking the Ohio River between Ghent and Carrollton in Carroll Co. Built by Benjamin Craig Jr. in 1809, it remained his home until New Year's Day 1847, when Craig and five others perished after high winds toppled their skiff into the icy Ohio River. Family legend says a servant found two doves on Craig's bed that day and that his wife Elizabeth Morris Craig, a niece of a signer of the Declaration of Independence, thereafter marked the anniversary of her husband's death secluded in her bedroom.

In 1886 the home was owned by Confederate military veteran Thomas M. Barrett and was the site of a notable tragedy. Barrett's erratic young relative William Fuqua Whitehead shot and killed Barrett's governess, Laura Harwood, before killing himself. A diagram of the upstairs bedroom where the bodies were found appeared in the local paper. There was considerable melodramatic speculation about "the Carrollton Tragedy." The current owner believes the house to be haunted.

In 1914 Perry J. Gaines, who had grown up at nearby **Scott's Landing**, purchased the home and remodeled it extensively into a showpiece for his Riverview Farms. Gaines was prominent in state and national agricultural and cattle organizations and served in the Kentucky state senate. After Gaines's death in 1947, his son Logan Gaines built and operated the Riverview Drive-In Theater east of the house. The Dow Corning Corporation bought the properties and in 1966 opened a chemical plant on the theater site, later selling the house to Owen Harris, son of Kentucky's agricultural commissioner, Thomas Oscar Harris. First Lady Rosalyn Carter attended a political rally there during her husband's 1976 presidential campaign. Owen Harris died in 2005 while still residing at Riverview, and his wife Linda Harris survives him there. Further development of the surrounding Dow Corning property could render the home uninhabitable.

Crawford, Byron. "Haunted Feeling Comes with House for Carroll Couple," *LCJ*, October 31, 2003, B1.

Bill Davis

ROANOKE CHRISTIAN CHURCH. The first place of worship in the Roanoke community in Pendleton Co. was the schoolhouse, which was located in the cemetery. The structure also served as a place of worship for the Gum Lick Baptist Church until 1882. In 1881 the Roanoke Christian Church was built on land across the road from the cemetery, donated by George W. Shipp Sr. A member of the community built the pews. Among regular attenders, women sat on one side of the church and men on the other; visitors sat in the middle.

During this period, many people walked, came in horse-driven buggies, arrived on horseback, or drove wagons to church. Marriages performed in the church were a rarity; home weddings were more common. In 1929 the second church was built, and while it was under construction, services were again held in the Roanoke schoolhouse. The seating custom soon changed so that families sat together in the services. In 1973 Roanoke built its third church, where it currently holds services.

"New Roanoke Christian Church," *Cooperative News*, January 1974, 5. Available in the vertical files, Pendleton Co. Public Library, Falmouth, Ky.

"Roanoke Christian Church History 100 Years Old August 2, 1981," *Falmouth Outlook*, July 10, 1981, 5.

Melissa J. Wickelhaus

ROBERT CHAMBERS HOUSE. The Robert Chambers House on East Bend Rd. just south of Burlington is one of the most spectacular Greek Revival residences in Boone Co. The house was built for Robert Chambers between 1832 and 1836 by mason Jessie Kelly and master woodworker Thomas Zane Roberts Sr. Although seldom used, the elaborate north doorway represents one of the most academically correct uses of the relatively sophisticated Greek Doric order in the county. It contains engaged columns and original leaded stained-glass sidelights. The doorway columns and those flanking the mantels in the main parlors are fluted, and a spiral staircase is set against a curving wall. The rear ell contains a recessed porch with square columns. The property was in the Caldwell family, and maintained by them, from 1944 to 2005.

Boone Co. Historic Preservation Review Board. *Historic Structures of Boone County, Kentucky.* Burlington, Ky.: Boone Co. Historic Preservation Review Board, 2002.

Kentucky Heritage Commission. *Survey of Historic Sites in Boone County.* Frankfort: Kentucky Heritage Commission, 1979.

Gail Chastang

ROBERTS, ALICE KENNELLY (b. April 27, 1920, Covington, Ky.). Author, newspaper columnist, and educator Alice Roberts is the daughter of Bruce and Elizabeth B. Payne Kennelly. She completed high school in the Covington Public Schools (see **Covington Independent Schools**) and has a BS from Eastern Kentucky University in Richmond and an MA from Cornell University in Ithaca, N.Y.; she has completed additional graduate studies at the University of Colorado at Boulder, the University of Cincinnati, the University of

Kentucky in Lexington, and Harvard University in Cambridge, Mass. She spent a half century in teaching and educational administrative positions, first at **Holmes High School** in Covington and later at Oak Hills High School in Cincinnati. In 1954 she married her high school sweetheart, Edward Roberts, and they shared a happy married life, including travels to all parts of the world, until his death in 1990. The couple had no children. Alice Roberts has been active in many local civic and social organizations and has published three books of poetry and one of prose. Her poetry books include *Bluegrass* (1949), *Bluegrass Junior* (1952), and *Bluegrass Seasons* (1959); her prose work, the story of her Irish ancestors, is titled *Shamrocks and Bluegrass* (1998). Both she and her husband were elected to key offices in the local **Christopher Gist Historical Society**, an organization in which Alice remains "the driving force." Roberts's annual Christmas cards, which feature original verse, have become treasured and valuable collectors' items. A features columnist for many years, variously with the ***Kentucky Times-Star***, the ***Kentucky Enquirer***, and the ***Kentucky Post***, she still writes a weekly column for the *Cincinnati Post*. She has often incorporated into her columns verses she deftly composed in just a few minutes. A long-time resident of Covington, Roberts now lives in a Covington retirement community.

Minutes and Proceedings of the Christopher Gist Historical Society, Archives, Northern Kentucky Univ., Highland Heights, Ky.

Roberts, Alice Kennelly. *Shamrocks and Bluegrass*. Covington, Ky.: Padgett Press, 1998.

James C. Claypool

ROBERTS, ELIZABETH MADOX (b. October 30, 1881, Perryville, Ky.; d. March 13, 1941, Orlando, Fla.). A novelist and a poet, Elizabeth Madox Roberts was the daughter of Simpson and Mary Elizabeth Brent Roberts. As a child she moved to Springfield, Ky., which she thereafter considered her home. Illness, including tuberculosis and other respiratory ailments, plagued her throughout her life. Elizabeth's parents decided to send their talented daughter to finish high school in a facility that offered more than the high school in Springfield, so she attended high school in Covington. Some relatives of her mother's family, the Brents, had moved to Covington during the late 1800s and operated a boardinghouse. Like many others from rural areas, Roberts must have gained an urban—if not a cosmopolitan—sense from living in Northern Kentucky. She began in 1897 and completed her high school education in May 1899. Covington is the archetype for the fantastic city Mome in the prologue to Roberts's novel *My Heart and My Flesh*.

At age 36 Roberts enrolled at the University of Chicago. Chicago was one of the most exciting literary places in the United States at the time, and Roberts became part of a literary group that included Yvor Winters and Glenway Westcott. Roberts was elected president of the University of Chicago's Poetry Club and won the McLaughlin Prize for Essay Writing and the Fiske Prize for Poetry. She graduated from the University of Chicago in 1921, with a degree in English.

Roberts's literary career began with the publication of *In the Great Steep's Garden* (1915), a collection of poems written to accompany Kenneth Hartley's photographs of mountain flowers. Shortly after her graduation, she published her second work, *Under the Tree* (1922). Having begun as a poet, Roberts found her voice and highest acclaim as a fiction writer. Her most significant and well-received books were novels: *The Time of Man* (1926), *My Heart and My Flesh* (1927), *Jingling in the Wind* (1928), *The Great Meadow* (1930), *A Buried Treasure* (1931), *The Haunted Mirror* (1932), *He Sent Forth a Raven* (1935), and *Black Is My True Love's Hair* (1938). Her short stories are collected in *The Haunted Mirror* (1932) and *Not by Strange Gods* (1941), and her poetry books are *Under the Tree* (1922) and *Song in the Meadow* (1940). Perhaps her best-known work is *The Great Meadow,* which tells the story of Kentucky's settlement and early days. She had a great love for her state, its history, and its significance in her life. During this prolific time as a writer, Roberts continued to be ill. She was suffering from tuberculosis and died in 1941 at the Orange Hospital in Orlando, Fla., of Hodgkin's disease. She was buried on Cemetery Hill in the Springfield City Cemetery, Springfield, Ky.

Roberts is often considered a lesser southern regionalist and is not often read today, although scholars sometimes mention *The Time of Man* and *The Great Meadow.* She is regarded by many as a forerunner of William Faulkner, Thomas Wolfe, Robert Penn Warren, and others of the Southern Renascence.

Campbell, Harry Modean. *Elizabeth Madox Roberts: American Novelist.* Norman: Univ. of Oklahoma Press, 1956.

Ward, William S. *A Literary History of Kentucky.* Knoxville: Univ. of Tennessee Press, 1988.

Danny Miller

ROBERTS, THOMAS ZANE (b. October 4, 1851, Boone Co., Ky.; d. January 15, 1925, Boone Co., Ky.). Described as a "rural genius," Thomas Zane Roberts was a teacher, a farmer, an astronomer, a carpenter, and an inventor. He is best known for building the monumental celestial Clock of Middle Creek in Boone Co. Roberts was the son of Thomas and Roxanne Odell Roberts, who in the 1830s came from New Jersey to Boone Co., via Cincinnati, where they spent a couple of years. The Robertses acquired a 257-acre "steam mill" tract on Middle Creek in 1846. T. Z., as Roberts was known, spent most of his life on the farm, where his father taught him farming, carpentry, and milling grain. He attended common school at Locust Grove and Willoughby in Boone Co. and enrolled at the Morgan Academy in Burlington in 1873.

By 1875 Roberts had graduated from school and had been elected president of the local Farmers' Grange, where his skill as an orator was well received. For a time, he submitted poems and short narratives to the new *Boone County Recorder*, using the pen name of Zane. After his father's death in 1876, T. Z. Roberts returned to farming and milling, although he still set aside time for academic and spiritual pursuits. He obtained a teaching certificate from Boone Co. in 1878 and taught frequently in local schools and churches until 1902. Roberts then became more involved in the pursuits that led him to design the monumental clock that is his legacy. While continuing to farm and run the mill, he worked as a carpenter and took up astronomy. He also built his magnificent home on Middle Creek, which incorporated household inventions ranging from a hand-cast fireplace blower and a swinging bed to foldaway walls and suspended ceilings.

In 1909 Roberts discontinued most of his other pursuits to devote himself to the Clock of Middle Creek. Local folklore holds that he built an observatory, studied the planets for a year, and secretly built the clock so that he would never again miss Sunday services. In fact, he had begun working with clocks in 1882; the only time he ever forgot about Sunday church was in 1883. Roberts had made a smaller calendar clock in the 1880s and probably built the celestial clock as an improvement on that one. The Clock of Middle Creek, seven feet high, includes a standard clock dial, a calendar, a moon-phase disc, and a planetarium. The planetarium is a miniature solar system comprising the Sun, Venus, Earth, Mars, and Jupiter. The orbit of each planet is precisely geared: while Venus gains one degree of arc in 1,656 days, Jupiter loses one degree of arc over 250 years. The clock has never been opened, so the true nature of Roberts's invention remains somewhat of a mystery.

Roberts died on the family farm in 1925, at age 73, and was buried in the Burlington IOOF Cemetery. Today, his clock is located at Burlington in the lobby of the Heritage Bank on Burlington Pk. It is still running and keeping time.

Becher, Matthew E., Michael A. Rouse, Robert Schrage, and Laurie Wilcox. *Images of America: Burlington.* Charleston, S.C.: Arcadia, 2004.

Frohlich, Anthony W. "Thomas Zane Roberts and the Clock of Middle Creek," *Boone County Recorder*, April 20, 27; May 4, 1977.

——. *Timekeeper: Thomas Zane Roberts, A Kentucky Renaissance Man.* Union, Ky.: Enchanted Valley, 2008.

Theoret, Nancy. "Timepiece Burlington Man's 'Claim to Fame,'" *Dixie News*, April 4, 1991, 13.

Matthew E. Becher and Anthony W. Frohlich

ROBERTSON, GEORGE (b. November 18, 1790, Mercer Co., Ky.; d. May 16, 1874, Lexington, Ky.). Judge and legislator George Robertson was the son of Alexander and Margaret Robinson Robertson, who moved from Virginia to Kentucky in 1779 and settled in modern-day Mercer Co. near Fort Harrod. Robertson attended some of the finer private schools in Central Kentucky. He read law under the tutelage of his brother-in-law Samuel McKee, a U.S. congressman, and became licensed to practice law at age 19.

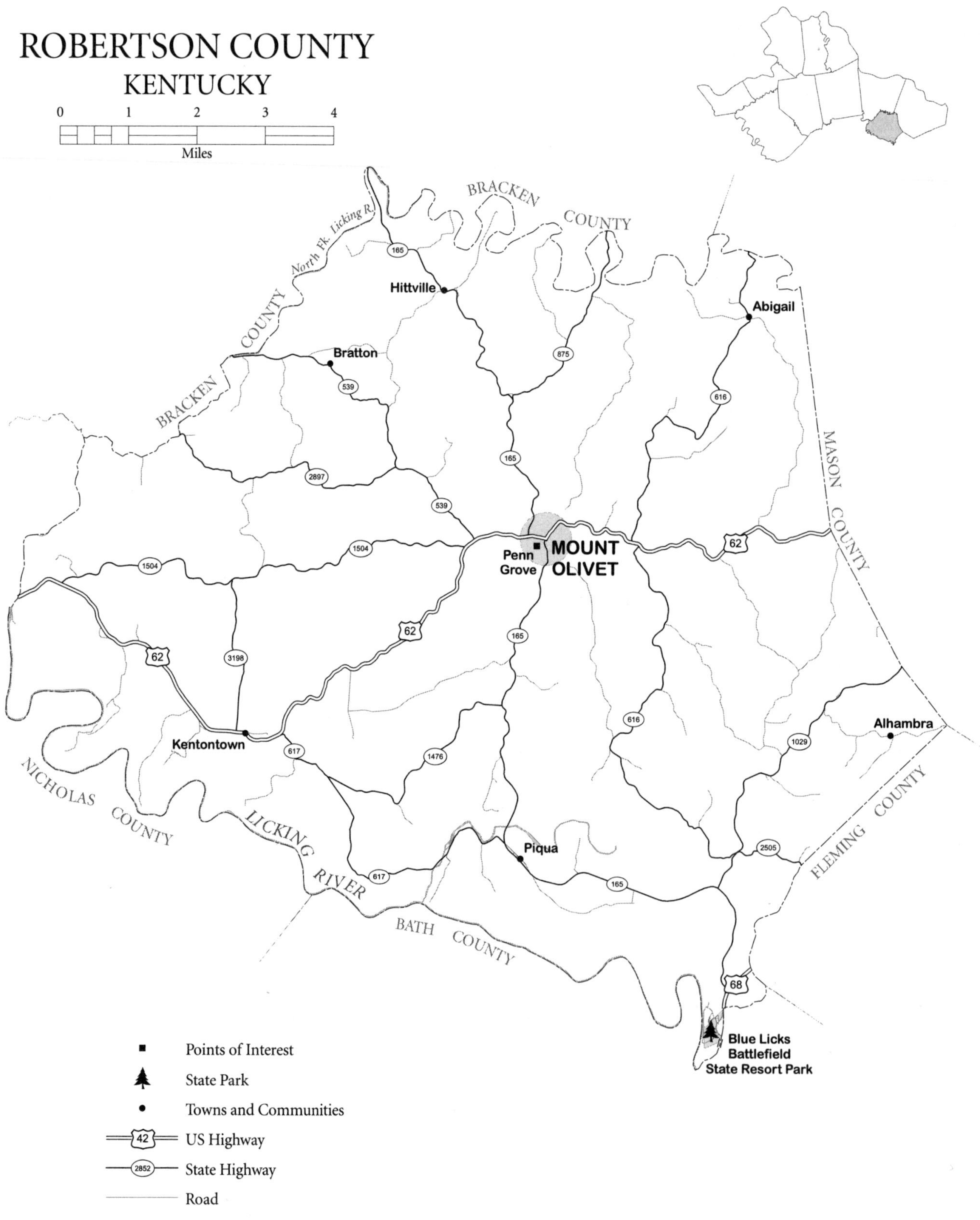

ROBERTSON COUNTY
KENTUCKY
0 1 2 3 4
Miles
BRACKEN COUNTY
North Fk. Licking R.
MASON COUNTY
FLEMING COUNTY
BATH COUNTY
NICHOLAS COUNTY
LICKING RIVER
Hittville
Bratton
Abigail
Penn Grove
MOUNT OLIVET
Kentontown
Alhambra
Piqua
Blue Licks Battlefield State Resort Park
165
875
539
616
2897
1504
62
3198
617
1476
1029
2505
68
Points of Interest
State Park
Towns and Communities
42
US Highway
2852
State Highway
Road

At age 26 he was elected to the U.S. Congress and served two terms before resigning in 1821 to attend to family obligations at home. Back in the commonwealth of Kentucky, Robertson moved his family to Lexington and turned his professional attention to state government. He was a member of the Kentucky legislature from 1822 to 1827 and served briefly as the Kentucky secretary of state in 1828.

Robertson's distinguished judicial career began in 1828, when he was appointed to the Kentucky Court of Appeals, the highest court in the state at the time. He served on that court until he resigned in 1843, and he was chief justice for most of those years. After his resignation from the bench, he practiced law in Lexington and won election to the Kentucky legislature two more times in 1848 and 1851. Robertson enjoyed a long and productive relationship with Transylvania University in Lexington, a school he attended briefly before leaving to read law. He was a professor of law at Transylvania University from 1834 to 1857 and wrote in his autobiography that he had "helped to make more than 1200 lawyers."

In 1847 Robertson met future president Abraham Lincoln (1861–1865), who was visiting his wife's family, the Todds, in Lexington. From then on, Robertson and Lincoln enjoyed a cordial friendship, corresponding occasionally about issues of the day. Robertson represented Lincoln, along with his wife Mary Todd Lincoln and other Todd heirs, in a lawsuit brought in Fayette Circuit Court in 1855.

During the **Civil War**, Robertson strongly supported the Union cause. Despite his pro-Union stance, however, he remained a slave owner until the conflict's bitter end. He successfully sued a Union Army colonel in federal court for refusing to surrender a Robertson family slave. The slave had sought refuge in one of the Union troop encampments located near Lexington during the war. Robertson was ultimately compensated $900 for the loss of this runaway, money that had to be appropriated by a special act of the U.S. Congress in 1873.

In 1864 Kentucky voters returned Robertson to a seat on the Kentucky Court of Appeals. His second period of judicial service produced some controversial criminal law holdings. For instance, an 1870 opinion authored by Robertson held that shooting someone in the back constituted self-defense. An earlier opinion rendered by Roberston, one that contravened all existing law of the period, recognized drunkenness as a legitimate defense against murder charges. Despite such legal aberrations, Robertson remained popular with most Kentuckians. During the 1867 Kentucky legislative session, the legislature moved to name a county "in honor of the distinguished son, statesman, and jurist of Kentucky, George Robertson." On August 1, 1867, the boundaries of Bracken, Harrison, Mason, and Nicholas counties were officially redrawn, and Robertson Co. became the 111th Kentucky county.

Toward the end of his life, Robertson, who had grown large not only in reputation but also in physical stature, acquired the nickname "Old Buster." In 1871 he suffered a debilitating stroke and a few months later resigned from the Kentucky Court of Appeals when his condition failed to improve. He died in 1874 and was buried in the Lexington Cemetery after a large public funeral procession. His home, Rokeby Hall, still stands in Lexington, where it is part of the city's South Hill Historic District.

Robertson Co. Courthouse, Mt. Olivet.

Biographical Directory of the United States Congress, 1774–1989. Washington, D.C.: Government Printing Office, 1985.

Biographical Encyclopedia of Kentucky. Cincinnati: J. M. Armstrong, 1878.

Coleman, J. Winston, Jr. "Lincoln and 'Old Buster,'" *Lincoln Herald* 46, no. 1 (February 1944).

Kleber, John E., ed. *The Kentucky Encyclopedia.* Lexington: Univ. Press of Kentucky, 1992.

Deborah Diersen Crocker

ROBERTSON CO. On August 1, 1867, Robertson Co. became the 111th county to be created within the Commonwealth of Kentucky. It was named for Judge **George Robertson** and was formed by carving out portions of Bracken, Harrison, Mason, and Nicholas counties. Mount Olivet is the county seat. Robertson is the county that contains the **Blue Licks Battlefield State Resort Park** and the **Johnson Creek Covered Bridge**. In 1880 the county had a population of 5,800; today, with roughly 2,100 residents, it is the least-populated county in the state. At approximately 100 square miles, Robertson Co. ranks as the second-smallest county in land area within Kentucky.

Robertson Co. is located in the northeastern region of Kentucky known as the Outer Bluegrass. The terrain is hilly, the roads are winding, and hardwood forests cover 25 percent of the county. Its northern boundary mainly consists of the North Fork of the Licking River; to the south, its boundary with Harrison and Nicholas counties is the main fork of the Licking. Robertson Co. is drained by those rivers and several major creeks, including Cedar, Clay's, Drift Run, Fire Lick, Helm, Johnson's, Painter, Shannon, and West creeks. The elevation of the county varies between 550 and 1,000 feet above sea level.

The enabling legislation to form the county was proposed by Harrison Co. state representative **Duncan Harding** of Kentontown. At that time, Kentontown was part of Harrison Co., as well as Harding's home, and he owned most of the town. Harding therefore had the most to gain if this hamlet became the county seat. He won legislative approval for his new county, but not for the name he proposed, Cass Co. (after Lewis Cass, the **War of 1812** hero and 1848 Democratic presidential candidate who had just died). Moreover, Harding was not able to convince his colleagues that Kentontown should be the county seat; instead, the more centrally located Mount Olivet became the county's seat. Mount Olivet formerly had been within Nicholas Co., the southeastern adjacent county and the one that had surrendered the most land area for the new county. The portion of land that had been surrendered was the Nicholas Co. land north of the Licking River, which was often difficult to cross.

The major industry in Robertson Co. is farming, in particular tobacco. The county has continued to lose population since its formation. More than half of the people employed work outside the county, and those people tend to give up their long commutes eventually and move closer to their jobs. High school graduates who do not take up farming or tobacco have very few career options near home.

Robertson Co. has no hospital, no airport and no major shopping area. Railroads pass through adjacent counties, but not through Robertson. In

1898 subscriptions were being sold for a railroad, to be built by the Dover, Kentucky, and South Atlantic Railway Company, the successor to the Ohio River, Frankfort, and Western Railway Company. The new railroad was proposed to run from Dover in Bracken Co. along the Ohio River, connecting with the C&O (Chesapeake and Ohio) there, then pass through Germantown, Mount Olivet, and Kentontown on the way to Cynthiana in Harrison Co. The railroad was never built. The completion of the **AA Highway** in the past 20 years, which does not enter the county, has made it easier for travelers to go elsewhere, much to the chagrin of local providers of goods and services. In recent years, a new **nursing home**, the Robertson Co. Health Care Facility, was built in Mount Olivet for the long-term care of the county's elderly population. The need for such care may be even greater in Robertson Co. than in most areas, because longevity (length of life) is much greater in Robertson Co. than in most places in the world. The average age at death in the county is 84, versus a worldwide average of 77. There are only four places in the world with such high longevity, and for reasons that demographers have yet to discover, Robertson Co. is one.

For several years, planners have proposed a highway linking Lexington, Ky., and Columbus, Ohio. If built through Robertson Co., this roadway would help reduce the county's relative isolation. Also, if the on-again, off-again talks of building a flood-control dam on the Licking River just south of Falmouth in Pendleton Co. ever come to fruition, Robertson Co., which includes many Licking River tributaries, could quickly become a fishing and recreation mecca. In recent years the State of Kentucky has funded the continued development of the Blue Licks Battlefield State Park. Some new jobs for area residents have been created thereby, and a small lodge with outlying cabins is a new addition to the park.

Gifford, Anjanette. "The Formation of Robertson County," *NKH* 9, no. 1 (Spring–Summer 2001): 65–74.

Moore, T. Ross, ed. *Echoes from the Century, 1867–1967.* Mount Olivet, Ky.: Robertson Co. Historical Society, 2000.

ROBERTSON CO. PUBLIC LIBRARY. The Robertson Co. Public Library was founded in 1952 in the basement of the Robertson Co. Extension Office on Court St. in Mount Olivet. Because the state library wanted to have a public library available for each county, the state provided funding and books for demonstration libraries throughout the state. The first Robertson Co. public librarian was Donnie Lane Morford King, who served as director of the library from 1952 to 1957. The county purchased a Dewey decimal classification manual and provided homemade furniture for the one-room library. The county judge executive appointed the first library board members, who were Etta Buckner, Guy Craig, Earl Mac Linville, and Mary Allen Wilson.

A few years later, the library moved to a larger facility along N. Main St., the former Mount Olivet Natural Gas Office building. Counties that had these demonstration libraries were encouraged to form their own tax districts to support their public libraries. After Robertson Co. failed in a second attempt to pass a tax levy, representatives of the state came and collected the books that had been provided, and the library was closed.

Concerned citizens of the community banded together in 1979 to form a new library board of trustees. On November 6, 1979, Robertson Co. finally passed a library tax levy. In 1979–1980 this board received two state grants to establish the new library. In 1981 paperwork was signed between the Robertson Co. Fiscal Court, the City of Mount Olivet, and the Library Board to lease a 1,220-square-foot, one-story city-county building at 407 E. Walnut St. to house the new library. The library rapidly grew and needed to expand. City and county officials therefore agreed to deed the leased building over to the Robertson Co. Library Board of Trustees. This deed allowed the board to apply for a 1990 State Construction Grant, which was received and provided funds to purchase the 900-square-foot fire station next door to the library. The fire hall was renovated to accommodate a new children's area and a community meeting room.

In 1999 the library was outgrowing its quarters. In 2001 Kentucky state senator Charlie Borders and Kentucky state representative Tom McKee presented to the library a $175,000 "seed money" grant from Kentucky legislative funds for a new library facility. In 2002 the library received a construction grant of $635,000 from the Kentucky Department for Libraries and Archives. On March 10, 2003, a new 5,053-square-foot library opened its doors at 148 N. Main St. The library has 22 computers with high-speed Internet access, book and media collections, and numerous programs for children and adults.

In August 2003 the library facility at 407 E. Walnut St. was renamed the Robertson Co. Public Library Annex. This facility serves as a branch library that currently houses the county's adult education program, the 21st Century Community Learning Center, and the City Hall.

"Library Wants to Lower Tax," *KP*, November 7, 1983, 2K.

"Mt. Olivet Opens Library Project," *KP*, April 12, 1979, 5K.

"Robertson, Mt. Olivet Seek New Library," *KP*, July 15, 1977, 15K.

Carol Mitchell

ROBERTSON CO. PUBLIC SCHOOLS. In 1867, when Robertson Co. was created, there were 26 one- or two-room elementary schools within the county: 24 were for white students and two were for African Americans. With the dramatic decrease in the county's total population, from 5,800 in 1880 to approximately 2,200 in 2000, the student-aged population has dwindled proportionally. For this reason and because of the general consolidation of small schools, which has taken place statewide, only two schools remain in the county. Both of these are centrally located, in Mount Olivet, at the site of the Deming High School on N. Main St: Deming School, an elementary school and a combined junior-senior high school. Before the 1890s, no secondary education was available to children in Robertson Co. Students desiring instruction at the high school level had to go elsewhere. The first attempts to provide secondary education in Robertson Co. were private in nature and began in the 1890s: the **Mount Olivet Male and Female Academy** and Colyer's Special School. Not until 1910 did a tuition-free high school begin; that school was first known as the Robertson Co. High School. **Kate Zoller** was instrumental in establishing it. The county was mostly agricultural at that time, so farming responsibilities prevented many students from attending classes. Students would walk to the closest school "for their learning," when time permitted. George Washington "Wash" Bratton, one of the founders of Bratton's Mill (Pinhook) in the northern part of the county, recognized the need to train teachers. During the 1860s, he attempted to operate a normal school for that purpose in a three-story building at Pinhook. Although he had great hopes that his school would one day become a great instructional academy, the venture did not last long; he could not find people to train as teachers. Today, Robertson Co. students are transported to the Deming School for all their education, both elementary and secondary.

Moore, T. Ross, ed. *Echoes from the Century, 1867–1967.* Mount Olivet, Ky.: Robertson Co. Historical Society, 2000.

ROBSION, JOHN MARSHALL (b. January 2, 1873, Bracken Co., Ky.; d. February 17, 1948, Barbourville, Ky.). Lawyer, educator, and politician John Marshall Robsion was the son of John A. and Mary Hyland Robsion. Both of John's parents died while he was a young boy. He put himself through school, attending National Northern University in Ada, Ohio; Holbrook College in Knoxville, Tenn.; and National Normal University in Lebanon, Ohio. He graduated from the latter institution and then entered law school at Centre College, Danville, Ky., where he received his degree in 1900. Robsion married Lida Stansbury on January 25, 1902, and they had three children. He taught in the Barbourville public schools and at Union College in the same city. In 1911 he became president of the First National Bank of Barbourville. Robsion entered politics in 1919 as a Republican and was elected to the U.S. House of Representatives, where he served until 1930. In that year Kentucky governor Flem Sampson (1927–1931) appointed Robsion to the U.S. Senate to fill the unexpired term of Frederick M. Sackett. At the end of this term, Robsion lost his bid for election to M. M. Logan. Robsion was again elected to the U.S. House of Representatives in 1934, where he served from 1935 until his death on February 17, 1948. He was buried in the Barbourville Cemetery.

Biographical Directory of the United States Congress, 1774–1989. Washington, D.C.: Government Printing Office, 1985.

Kleber, John, ed. *The Kentucky Encyclopedia*. Lexington: Univ. Press of Kentucky, 1992.
Southward, Mary Young. *Who's Who in Kentucky*. Louisville: Standard, 1936.

ROCKDALE. Rockdale is a community in southern Owen Co. near the Scott Co. border. It is within the Caney Precinct. The 1883 Lake atlas suggests that at that time there were a post office and a store at Rockdale.

Houchens, Mariam Sidebottom. *History of Owen County: "Sweet Owen."* Louisville, Ky.: Standard, 1976.
Rennick, Robert M. *Kentucky Place Names*. Lexington: Univ. Press of Kentucky, 1984.

RODGERS, HOWARD S. (b. 1867, Covington, Ky.; d. June 14, 1936, Franconia, N.H.). Howard S. Rodgers, born at 412 E. Second St. in Covington, was the son of Charles and Harriet Fallis Rodgers. He attended local schools and then became one of the first persons in the country to earn an electrical engineering degree. However, he never worked in the electrical field, preferring rather to engage in the brokerage business. He later became a vice president of Merchants National Bank, the forerunner of the First National Bank of Cincinnati. Rodgers was an avid boatman. Some have claimed that Rodgers invented the hand grenade; however, it is more likely that he only developed the modern version of the weapon. The hand grenade is believed to have originated in the ancient Middle East; its name was derived from the Latin word for pomegranate. Rodgers married Henrietta Orr, and the couple was childless. He died at age 68, at his summer home in Franconia, N.H. His body was returned to Covington for burial in the Highland Cemetery, Fort Mitchell.

"Heavy Assessments of the Rodgers," *KTS*, September 29, 1902, 3.
Highland Cemetery Records, Fort Mitchell, Ky.
"Rites for Inventor of Grenade Today," *KP*, June 17, 1936, 1.

ROEBLING, JOHN AUGUSTUS AND WASHINGTON AUGUSTUS (John: b. June 12, 1806, Mühlhausen, Prussia; d. July 22, 1869, Brooklyn Heights, N.Y.; Washington: b. May 26, 1837, Saxonburg, Pa.; d. July 21, 1926, Trenton, N.J.). These two, father and son, were world-renowned engineers and bridge builders (see **John A. Roebling Bridge**). John Roebling was the youngest son of Christoph Polycarpus and Christine Frederike Dorothea Mueller Roebling. John's father operated a tobacco store in their Prussian home. His mother was very ambitious, instilling in each of her five children the value of education and of the rewards of hard work. She was frugal and saved for John's future education. His early training was in the local public school, and then he entered the city's *Gymnasium* (comparable to high school). He excelled in mathematics, science, and drawing but was not so successful in Latin and religion. Therefore he transferred to a school more suited to his talents, the private school of the famous teacher Dr. Ephraim Solomon Unger, at Erfurt.

Unger taught mathematics, surveying, and the sciences, while encouraging his students to think clearly, analytically, and logically. After graduation, Roebling was able to enroll at a prestigious engineering school, Berlin's Royal Polytechnic Institute, where he studied engineering, architecture, foundation construction, and bridge building. One of his instructors was the world-famous philosopher Georg Wilhelm Friedrich Hegel. During his senior year, Roebling visited a suspension bridge under construction at Bamberg, Bavaria, an experience that helped to crystallize his desire to become a bridge builder. In 1826 he received a civil engineering degree from the Royal Polytechnic Institute, graduating with honors. Roebling worked for the Prussian government as an assistant engineer, building roads and small bridges, but because he felt restricted by the governmental bureaucracy, which seemed to stifle his creativity, Roebling decided to immigrate to the United States. The move was against his parents' wishes. On May 11, 1831, John boarded the steamship *August Eduard*, on his way to America. His mother was so grieved at seeing him depart that she suffered a heart attack as the ship left the dock. She lived for several more weeks, until receiving word that her son had arrived safely in Philadelphia.

Roebling moved from Philadelphia to a farm that he purchased at Saxonburg, about 20 miles north of Pittsburgh. In 1836 he married Johanna Herting, and they had nine children. In 1837, he became a naturalized citizen of the United States. For the next few years, he farmed and attempted to improve a steam engine for the operation of farm equipment. Discontented with farming, he returned to engineering and took a job with the State of Pennsylvania, surveying and building canals and railroads. His next venture was to establish a factory at Saxonburg for the manufacture of iron wire rope. In 1844 Roebling was awarded a contract to build a wooden aqueduct, suspended by cables, along the Pennsylvania Canal. He also built a suspension bridge across the Monongahela River at Pittsburgh. In 1848 he undertook construction of a series of four suspension aqueducts in Pennsylvania and New York, completing them in two years. He started his next project in 1851, building a double-deck suspension bridge across the Niagara River, just downstream from the falls, connecting the New York Central Railroad with Canada's Great Western Railway. Four years later, the first train crossed that new span.

John A. Roebling.

In fall 1856 Roebling laid the foundations for the towers of the Covington and Cincinnati Suspension Bridge (later renamed the John A. Roebling Suspension Bridge) across the Ohio River, but the project was delayed because of a national economic panic, the subsequent lack of funding, and the start of the **Civil War**. During the delay he began work on a new suspension bridge over the Allegheny River at Pittsburgh, which was completed in 1861. In 1863 he resumed work on the bridge at Covington, finishing it in 1867. Later that year, he began drawing plans for the Brooklyn Bridge over the East River, connecting Brooklyn to Manhattan; however, in July 1869 he was injured while surveying for the location of one of the bridge towers. Several days later, a surgeon amputated the toes of his injured foot, infection set in, and Roebling died of lockjaw. He was buried in Riverview Cemetery in Trenton, N.J. After John Roebling's death, his son Washington A. Roebling took over management of the project.

Washington Roebling earned an engineering degree from the Rensselaer Polytechnic Institute at Troy, N.Y., and had assisted his father in building the Pittsburgh and Covington bridges. He had also been trained in Europe in the use of caissons for the construction of deepwater piers. Essentially a huge diving bell, a caisson contained compressed air, making underwater construction possible. Unfortunately, little was understood at the time about the condition known as caisson disease or the bends, caused by nitrogen bubbles forming in the blood, a consequence of decompression during a rapid return to the surface. As the work on the Brooklyn Bridge progressed, many workers fell ill from it, including Washington Roebling. In summer 1872 he was carried from the caisson nearly unconscious and was confined to bed. At age 35 he was partially paralyzed, his vocal cords severely damaged, and his hearing and sight almost gone. For the remainder of the construction, he supervised the project from his bed, as his wife carried instructions back and forth. The Brooklyn Bridge was formally opened on May 24, 1883, and Washington Roebling viewed the ceremonies through binoculars from his apartment window. In 1888 he assumed management of the Roebling Steel plant at Trenton, N.J., but he lived in constant pain for the remainder of his life. In 1926 he died at his home in Brooklyn Heights, N.Y., at the age of 89.

He was buried at the Cold Spring Cemetery in Cold Spring, N.Y.

Schuyler, Hamilton. *The Roeblings: A Century of Engineers, Bridge-Builders, and Industrialists.* Princeton, N.J.: Princeton Univ. Press, 1931.

Stevens, Harry R. *The Ohio Bridge.* Cincinnati: Ruter Press, 1939.

Tolzmann, Don Heinrich. *The John A. Roebling Suspension Bridge on the Ohio River.* Max Kade Occasional Papers in German-American Studies, no. 1. Cincinnati: Max Kade German Center, Dept. of Germanic Languages and Literature, Univ. of Cincinnati: 1998.

Jack Wessling

ROEBLING BRIDGE. See **John A. Roebling Bridge**.

ROEBLING MURALS. The Roebling Murals are located along the Covington riverfront on the floodwall at the foot of the **John A. Roebling Bridge**. The largest display of public art in the area, the murals span the riverfront from Greenup St. to Madison Ave., creating a memorable landmark and an attractive entryway for Northern Kentucky. The series consists of a title panel and 17 mural scenes, each of which is 25 feet tall by either 20 or 40 feet wide. Each panel depicts a significant occurrence in Northern Kentucky's history, with a special emphasis on the importance of the suspension bridge and its creator, **John A. Roebling**.

Subjects of the various murals include Covington's 1914 centennial celebration; **Daniel Carter Beard**, founder of the Boy Scouts of America; the Ohio River **flood of 1937**; **Jacob Price**, an African American community leader; local artists **Henry Farny** and **Frank Duveneck**; religious centers of Covington; the **Latonia Racecourse**; the **Covington Blue Sox** and the old Covington Ball Park; Kennedy's Ferry; Union troops crossing the pontoon bridge; John A. Roebling and **Amos Shinkle** with the construction of the Roebling Bridge; the flight of the Garner family (see **Margaret Garner**); The Great Buffalo Rd. (see **Buffalo Traces**); the meeting of **George Rogers Clark**, **Simon Kenton**, **Daniel Boone**, and Benjamin Logan; the Tall Stacks Festival; **Devou Park**; and German heritage.

Robert Dafford, from Lafayette, La., was commissioned exclusively to complete the project. Dafford is known as the nation's foremost experienced floodwall muralist, having completed more than 350 large-scale public works in the United States, Canada, Belgium, England, and France. Sites of other Dafford projects in the United States include Maysville, Catlettsburg, and Paducah, Ky., as well as Portsmouth, Ohio; Camden, N.J.; and Vicksburg, Miss. While designing the images, he received direction from a local historical committee and advisory board. Dafford worked with a crew of five other artists to complete the project, which was commissioned in 2002 and completed in 2008. Owing to inclement weather conditions, painting was done only during the summer months.

The Roebling Murals project was initiated by Legacy, a young professional group in Northern Kentucky that is committed to fostering leadership skills and personal relationships through training, direct community involvement, and public initiatives. Legacy was given project approval by the U.S. Army Corps of Engineers and exclusive rights by the City of Covington for the floodwall murals and the surrounding area. The monies raised by Legacy were the only funds that were used for the Roebling Murals project. In 2005 Legacy was recognized for the Roebling Mural project by receiving the Editor's Award at the Post Corbett Awards Ceremony.

"Murals along the Ohio," *KP*, October 24, 2003, 1C, 7C.

Lou Settle

ROEBUCK, MARY WILTON "MINNIE" (b. 1863, Canada; d. June 16, 1931, Brooklyn, N.Y.). Singer Minnie Roebuck, the daughter of John S. and Emily Bowles Roebuck, moved to Newport with her family when she was two years old. Her father was a farmer and superintendent of the Cincinnati Gymnasium, and her mother taught piano and organ at the family's residence, 178 Columbia St. Later the family lived in Cold Spring, along Licking Pk., four miles south of Newport. Minnie's brother John became a well-known Newport attorney and bicycle and hydroplane racer; her sister Katherine, a graduate of Cincinnati's Laura Medical College, was one of Newport's first female physicians and a suffragist. Mary studied voice at the Cincinnati College of Music, the National Academy of Music in New York City, and the Royal Academy in London, England. While in England in 1892, she appeared in at least two productions: *Il Trovatore* and *The Flying Dutchman.* Sometime before 1909, she married physician Dr. O. L. Mulot, moved with him to Brooklyn, N.Y., and gave up her singing career. Minnie died in 1931 at her home in Brooklyn and was buried in Brooklyn.

Advertisement for Mrs. J. S. Roebuck, *Newport Local,* October 20, 1877, 2.

"Hear of Death," *KP,* June 17, 1931, 1.

"Newport's Wealth," *KJ,* April 16, 1892, 4.

"Sketch," *KP,* October 15, 1898, 1.

Michael R. Sweeney

ROFF, IDA MITCHELL (b. June 24, 1859, Mason Co., Ky.; d. April 23, 1939, Mayslick, Ky.). Women's suffrage activist Ida Mitchell Roff, the daughter of Nathaniel and Elizabeth Mitchell Roff, grew up in the Mason Co. community of Mayslick. In the 1880s she taught elocution at 11th and Scott Sts. in Covington, and in the 1890s she and **Jennie Rugg**, a fellow suffragist, organized and arranged meetings for the Kentucky Equal Rights Association (see **Women's Suffrage**). Later in life, Ida lived in Cincinnati and wrote articles on astronomy and other subjects for the *Cincinnati Enquirer.* She resided in the Walnut Hills neighborhood of Cincinnati, along Melrose Ave., and in Clifton along Senator Pl., where she rented rooms. She became a staunch Christian Scientist and for many years was in charge of the reading room at the First Church of Christ Scientist on Park Ave. in Walnut Hills. She was widely read and appreciated for her knowledge and intellectual pursuits. Roff, who never married, lived the last year of her life in Mayslick. She died of an apparent heart attack at the home of her brother, Maysville banker Sandford M. Roff, and was cremated at the Cincinnati Crematory.

"End Is Unexpected for Miss Ida Roff at Brother's Home," article dated April 23, 1939, from a Maysville, Ky., newspaper (no name indicated), Kentucky Gateway Museum Center, Maysville, Ky.

"Equal Right Association," *KJ,* September 28, 1892, 8.

Kentucky Death Certificate No. 11006, for the year 1939.

"Local News," *DC,* November 28, 1884, 4.

ROGERS' DEFEAT. In August 1779, Capt. David Rogers (a cousin of Gen. **George Rogers Clark**) and a contingent of colonial American soldiers were sent from Fort Pitt in Pennsylvania to New Orleans to purchase gunpowder and other military supplies from the Spanish. On their return, they stopped at Louisville, where they met another group of soldiers, commanded by Col. **John Campbell** (namesake of Campbell Co.), who were also headed to Fort Pitt. The latter group had delivered a message to Gen. George Rogers Clark at Fort Kaskaskia, along the Mississippi River in the Illinois Territory. The combined group of about 65 men in five keelboats decided to return together. By October 4, 1779, they had reached the sandbar at what later became Dayton, Ky., where they decided to stop and prepare breakfast. Shortly after arriving, they noticed several Indians, who had come out of the Little Miami River, approaching. Captain Rogers ordered his men to surround the Indians when they landed. Without warning, 200 Indians and British soldiers, led by the white renegade Simon Girty, sprang from the willow trees that covered the sandbar and overwhelmed the colonials. Only a few of the soldiers were able to avoid death or capture. Five men who had been guarding the keelboats managed to escape downriver in one of the boats and returned to Louisville. The next morning Capt. **Robert Benham** crawled out from underneath a tree, where he had remained undetected. He met another soldier, John Watson, who had also managed to hide during the massacre. Both men were wounded, but at the confluence of the Ohio and Licking rivers, some six weeks later, they were able to hail a boat that was traveling downriver, and the two soldiers were safely returned to Louisville. Both men fully recovered and subsequently were able to rejoin their military units. Robert Benham later owned property in Newport. Benham St. in Dayton, Ky., is named for this fortunate soldier. Capt. David Rogers was killed in the battle at Dayton, and Col. John Campbell was captured. Campbell was held prisoner until November 1782, when a large cash ransom was paid for his release.

Collins, Richard H. *History of Kentucky.* Vol. 2. Covington, Ky.: Collins, 1882.

Cooley, Elizabeth M. "The Benham Brothers—Robert, Peter, and Richard," *BCHS* 10, no. 1 (January 1952): 69–78.

Greve, Charles Theodore. *Centennial History of Cincinnati and Representative Citizens.* Vol. 1. Chicago: Biographical Publishing, 1904.
Wessling, Jack. *Early History of Campbell County, Kentucky.* Alexandria, Ky.: Privately published, 1997.

Jack Wessling

ROMAN CATHOLICS. The eastern portion of Kentucky was part of the Diocese of Louisville in the middle of the 19th century. For a brief time, an area of Northern Kentucky extending three miles south of the Ohio River was placed under the jurisdiction of the Archdiocese of Cincinnati. Disputes between the bishops of the two dioceses resulted in a petition to the Vatican in Rome asking for the formation of a new diocese in Kentucky. As a result, on July 29, 1853, Pope Pius IX issued a papal bull creating the Diocese of Covington. George A. Carrell, S.J., was named the first bishop of the new diocese.

Carrell began his tenure in the new diocese with little money, six parishes with numerous attendant missions, and only six priests for an area that extended to the Tennessee border and included the Appalachian area of Eastern Kentucky. Many new churches and schools were soon established. According to the custom during much of the 19th century, many of the parishes in Northern Kentucky were created for either German or Irish congregations. St. Mary Catholic Church, the diocese's first cathedral, was built on Eighth St. in Covington in 1854 (see **Cathedral Basilica of the Assumption**). Several religious orders of women came to teach in the schools. They joined the Sisters of Charity of Nazareth, who were already present and who started **La Salette Academy** in Covington in 1856. The **Sisters of St. Benedict** came in 1859 and made Covington a foundation of their order. They started St. Walburg Academy in 1863. St. Elizabeth Hospital (see **St. Elizabeth Medical Center**) began in Covington in 1861, staffed by the Sisters of the Poor of St. Francis.

Augustus Toebbe became the second bishop of Covington in 1870, two years after Carrell's death. He brought the **Sisters of Notre Dame** to the diocese in 1874. They taught in many parish schools and opened the **Notre Dame Academy** in 1875. Toebbe established two diocesan orphanages, St. John for girls and St. Joseph for boys (see **Diocesan Catholic Children's Home**). During Toebbe's tenure, the diocese faced a major financial crisis: three parishes went bankrupt after their business ventures failed. The bishop helped solve the problem and made new rules for parish operations.

The third bishop, **Camillus P. Maes**, who began in 1885, remained in office for 30 years. He was responsible for the construction of the current Gothic-style cathedral at the corner of Madison Ave. and 12th St., which opened in 1901. Maes also welcomed the **Sisters of Divine Providence** to the diocese in 1889. They started the **Our Lady of Providence Academy** in Newport in 1903. Maes oversaw the creation of many new churches and schools, including some in the mountain region of the diocese.

Ferdinand Brossart, a priest of the Diocese of Covington, became its fourth bishop in 1916. The German-born bishop had to deal with anti-German prejudice during **World War I**. He established regular geographical parish boundaries in 1920 so that parishes would not be based on nationality. Brossart retired for health reasons in 1923.

His successor, **Francis W. Howard**, made education his specialty. Arriving in 1923, he established the **Covington Latin School** that year (the present building next to the cathedral opened in 1949), the Lexington Latin School in 1924, and **Covington Catholic High School** in 1925. In 1928 he made Villa Madonna College in Covington a diocesan institution. It moved to Crestview Hills and became **Thomas More College** in 1968. During the **Great Depression**, the diocese founded Catholic Social Services (see **Catholic Charities**) to help people through the financial crisis.

Covington's sixth bishop, **William T. Mulloy**, came to the diocese in 1945. He expanded the number of parishes and schools, especially in the growing suburbs of Northern Kentucky. He also started many rural-life programs. Mulloy was responsible for purchasing the **Marydale** property in Erlanger in 1946, on which he found a summer camp (closed in 1988) and a retreat house. On the same property, in 1955, he started a diocesan seminary, St. Pius X, which closed in 1987.

Richard H. Ackerman was made the seventh bishop in 1960 and led the diocese through the challenging period following the Second Vatican Council of the early 1960s. Catholics had to adapt to many changes, including having the Mass said in English. The diocese had to adjust to the loss of priests and teaching sisters who left their ministries. Ackerman's tenure also saw a decline in the number of inner-city Catholics, and as a result, several urban parishes and schools were closed. The St. Elizabeth Medical Center South was built in 1973. Ackerman retired in 1978.

In 1979 William A. Hughes was installed as the eighth bishop of Covington. He greatly increased the number of diocesan offices, to fill many new functions of service to the people of the diocese, and opened more ministries to the laity. A major change occurred in 1988 when the Vatican created the new Diocese of Lexington, reducing the 57-county Diocese of Covington to the 14 northernmost counties. Hughes continued the process of closing or merging parishes and schools that could no longer function as they were and moved the diocesan offices to the Catholic Center, the former seminary building in Erlanger. He also initiated the Diocesan Annual Appeal in 1983 to raise money for the needs of the diocese. Hughes retired in 1995.

Bishop Robert W. Muench, installed in the diocese in 1996, sold a large part of the Marydale property, which was cut off from the rest by the new Houston Rd. extension, and started a large capital campaign to fund an extensive renovation of the cathedral that was completed in 2001. The following year, Muench was transferred to the Diocese of Baton Rouge, La.

The current bishop, Roger J. Foys, came in 2002. He had to respond to the clergy sexual-abuse crisis and the large class-action lawsuit that resulted from it. Foys met personally with many persons who had been abused. As a result of the settlement, most of the rest of the Marydale property was sold. He decided to move the diocesan offices from the Catholic Center to the third floor of St. Elizabeth Hospital North in Covington. To meet the needs of the growing Latino population (see **Latinos**) in Northern Kentucky, Foys in 2003 created the **Cristo Rey Parish**, and it utilized part of the former Catholic Center.

In 2007 the 14-county Diocese of Covington was home to 92,250 Roman Catholics with 47 parishes and 6 missions.

Ryan, Paul E. *History of the Diocese of Covington, Kentucky.* Covington, Ky.: Diocese of Covington, 1954.
Tenkotte, Paul A., David E. Schroeder, and Thomas S. Ward. *To Be Catholic and American in Northern, Central, and Appalachian Kentucky: The Diocese of Covington, 1853–2003.* Forthcoming.
Ward, Thomas. "The Bishops of Covington—Meeting the Challenges of Their Time," *Messenger,* July 19, 2002, 33A.

Thomas S. Ward

ROOT, IRA (b. May 4, 1806, Piermont, Grafton Co., N.H.; d. February 12, 1868, Newport, Ky.). Ira Root, one of seven children of Ephraim and Vashti Birge Root, was one of Campbell Co.'s most influential citizens. He was a lawyer, a state representative, a delegate to the 1849 Kentucky Constitutional Convention, an antislavery advocate, an educator, an orator, and a veteran of the Newport Home Guard at the first battle of Cynthiana. Root attended Miami University of Ohio and studied law in Newport. After being admitted to the Kentucky bar, he practiced law until his death. He married Sarah Ann Perry in Newport on December 25, 1834. They had four children who survived childhood, and their three sons (Oliver W., Albert, and James) all became distinguished attorneys. At the 1849 Kentucky Constitutional Convention, Ira Root was one of the main advocates for making a state school system part of the new constitution. He was not successful in his attempt to insert an antislavery clause into the same proposed constitution. He remained an antislavery advocate for the rest of his life. Root served under Capt. John Arthur in the pro-Union Home Guard at the battle of Cynthiana, and his son **Oliver W. Root** was in that same **Civil War** unit. Ira Root, a much-sought-after orator, spoke at a meeting of the Friends of Emancipation at the Newport Courthouse on February 18, 1864. Four years later he died. He was a member of the fifth generation of the Root family in America. Ira Root's wife, Sarah, died on January 12, 1909, in Newport. At the time of Sarah's death, she was reported to be the oldest native-born resident of Newport. The Root family members are buried at Evergreen Cemetery in Southgate.

"Death Notice," *CE,* February 13, 1868, 3.
Evergreen Cemetery Records, Southgate, Ky.
"Obituary," *CTS,* January 12, 1909, 7.

Reis, Jim. "The Root Family of Campbell County Earned a Reputation for a Very Independent Spirit," *KP,* March 8, 1993, 4K.
Root, James Pierce. *The Root Family.* New York: R. C. Anthony, 1870.
Tenkotte, Paul A. "Rival Cities to Suburbs: Covington and Newport, Kentucky, 1790–1890," PhD diss., Univ. of Cincinnati, 1989.

Paul John Schewene

ROOT, OLIVER WYATT (b. October 23, 1835, Newport, Ky.; d. August 3, 1904, Newport, Ky.). Oliver Root, a lawyer and a **Civil War** soldier, was the son of **Ira Root** and Sarah Perry Root. He graduated from Miami University of Ohio in 1858 and then taught literature in the Newport public schools and at Brook's Academy and the Chickering Institute in Cincinnati before beginning the practice of law. He served in the Campbell Co. Home Guard during the Civil War, in the same unit as his father. They were at the first battle of Cynthiana, under Capt. John S. Arthur, where the entire outfit was captured and paroled by **John Hunt Morgan**'s men. On January 15, 1861, the Southern-leaning postmaster of Newport tried to disrupt the attempt of the Washington Artillery, a Kentucky state guard unit, to raise the U.S. flag. In response, Root, George Webster, and George Fearon arrested the postmaster. The postmaster was later acquitted of the charge of inciting a breach of the peace, because of the Southern allegiance of many Newport residents. Root was elected several times as city and county attorney, and he was a great campaigner for the Republican Party. He attended several national conventions as a delegate or presidential elector. In 1868 he seconded the nomination of Gen. Ulysses S. Grant for the presidency. He was praised for his eloquent speech by none other than Roscoe Conkling, one of the founders of the Republican Party. Root was widely known for his lectures on Shakespeare.

Oliver Root never married. He and his brother, Albert Tell Root, took over the legal practice of their father upon their father's death. Oliver ran for U.S. Congress twice, losing both times; one of those times he lost to John G. Carlisle. He died in 1904, and his funeral service was conducted by the pastor of St. Paul's Episcopal Church of Newport. His will distributed money to various churches and orphanages and to Christ Hospital in Cincinnati. He directed in his will that a stained-glass window be placed in memory of his mother at St. Paul's Church. Another stained-glass window was placed in his memory at Grace Methodist Church in Newport. He was buried in Evergreen Cemetery, Southgate, in the Root family plot.

"Death," *CTS,* August 4, 1904, 1.
Evergreen Cemetery Records, Southgate, Ky.
"Home Guard," *CDC,* July 14, 1862, 3; July 17, 1862, 3; July 24, 1862, 1.
"Last Will of Oliver Root," Will Book No. 7, 132–34, Campbell Co., Ky.
Purvis, Thomas L., ed. *Newport, Kentucky: A Bicentennial History.* Newport, Ky.: Otto Zimmerman, 1996.
Reis, Jim. "The Root Family of Campbell County Earned a Reputation for a Very Independent Spirit," *KP,* March 8, 1993, 4K.

Paul John Schewene

ROPEWALKS. The words *cordage* and *ropewalk,* which mean very little to people today, played an important role in the lives of many Northern Kentuckians in the 19th century. A ropewalk was a long, narrow building in which rope or cordage was manufactured. Some ropewalks were more than 1,000 feet long, because industry standards required that the rope be 120 fathoms, or 720 feet, in length.

In the early and mid 1800s, hemp, more commonly known today as marijuana, was grown extensively in Northern Kentucky, especially on the hills above Dayton. During the 1800s hemp was freely grown and used to make many useful products, including rope, twine, cable, and string. In the 19th century, hemp was one of Kentucky's leading cash crops. At the pinnacle of their success, ropewalk manufacturers employed hundreds of Northern Kentuckians.

Early manufacture of rope was done by hand, but in later years the operation was carried out mostly by machinery. In the manual process, workers broke the stalks into fibers, which were combed and carried around a worker's waist while he spun the hemp into yarn. It was next twisted into strands, and other strands were added, to make rope of various diameters. All this occurred while the worker walked backward the length of the building.

Workers in ropewalks often developed lung problems after prolonged breathing of the hemp fiber's fine particles. The malady, which doctors called hemp pneumonia, frequently proved fatal. Another safety problem was that the dry hemp fiber was extremely flammable; it was involved in numerous fires that were difficult to extinguish. Slaves or prisoners were occasionally used in the industry, especially for the more dangerous jobs.

The primary customers for the manufactured rope were the owners of riverboats and ocean vessels. Some of the largest local customers were the boatyards at Fulton, Ohio, across the Ohio River from Dayton. In addition to the Dayton residents employed in the manufacture of rope, many others worked in the construction and maintenance of boats at Fulton. For the convenience of workers, a ferry was operated from Dayton to the shipyards.

In 1840 there were 111 ropewalks operating in Kentucky, 11 of them in Dayton, which was locally known as the "king of cordage." The Dayton firms manufactured rope, cable, twine, string, and thread. The local ropewalks produced hundreds of tons of rope and bagging each year. The largest of the firms was the Victoria Cordage Company, located at Fourth and Clay Sts., which had several hundred employees. The impact of the industry on the local economy was immense, because of the buying power of its workers. In 1832 the Newport Manufacturing Company began processing hemp into cloth for making work clothes, called Kentucky Jeans. The ropewalk industry gradually faded from importance, owing to decreased activity at the boatyards, increased competition, and the use of new technology. The Victoria Cordage Company sold its complex in 1893 to National Cordage of New Jersey, which continued to operate under the Victoria name until 1899. At that time the plant was closed. Some of the buildings were sold to the **Harvard Piano Company** and others to the **Wadsworth Watchcase Company**.

Centennial Program of Dayton, Kentucky, 1849–1949. Newport, Ky.: Michaels, 1949.
Hopkins, James F. *A History of the Hemp Industry in Kentucky.* Lexington: Univ. of Kentucky Press, 1951.
Reis, Jim. "Dayton: King of Cordage—Riverboats Built City's Key Industry," *KP,* April 7, 2003, 4K.
Souvenir Dayton, Kentucky G.A.R. Encampment. Dayton, Ky., 1898.

ROSEMARY CLOONEY HOUSE. The **Rosemary Clooney** House, located along the scenic southern bank of the Ohio River, at 106 E. Riverside Dr., Augusta, in Bracken Co., opened on June 1, 2005. It is a project of a nonprofit remodeling and preservation foundation set up by former Kentucky lieutenant governor Steve Henry (1995–2003) and his wife, **Heather French** Henry, who was Miss America 2000. The museum's dedication on October 1, 2005, was attended by a crowd that included family and friends of Rosemary Clooney (1928–2002) from both Kentucky and Hollywood. The foundation's purpose is to preserve Clooney's house (built in 1835) and to house the memorabilia of one of Northern Kentucky's most famous Hollywood personae. Maysville-born Clooney used the home for the last 20 years of her life as a retreat from Hollywood. Her brass bed, the costumes she wore in the 1954 classic hit movie *White Christmas,* rare photographs of the actress, and clothing that belonged to her and to actors such as Jack Benny, Cary Grant, Bob Hope, Vivien Leigh, and Barbara Stanwyck are among the many items displayed at the museum. It was 1951 when Clooney sang her hit song "Come-on-a My House," but visitors today can "Come-on-a Rosie's House" to see where Kentucky's favorite "Girl Singer" lived.

"Henrys Restore Clooney House," *KE,* April 20, 2005, C1.
Kiesewetter, John. "Bless This House: Rosemary Clooney Fans Feel the Love in Museum," *KE,* October 2, 2005, A1.
The Rosemary Clooney House, Augusta, Ky. www.rosemaryclooney.com/house (accessed October 27, 2006).

ROSE V. COUNCIL FOR BETTER EDUCATION. *Rose v. Council for Better Education* is the Kentucky Supreme Court Case that resulted in the 1990 Kentucky legislature's enactment of the Kentucky Education Reform Act (KERA), which produced a historic reorganization of the financing and governance of the state's public schools. Plaintiffs in the case included the Independent Board of Education of Dayton, Ky., along with 66 other school districts, and the Council for Better Education (headed by Jack Moreland, superintendent at the time of the **Dayton Public Schools**), as well as parents of students from various school districts throughout Kentucky, including the Dayton Independent Schools.

The case originally filed in the Franklin Co. Circuit Court found Kentucky's common school finance system to be unconstitutional and discriminatory and held that the legislature had not provided the state with an efficient system of common (public) schools. This was a state action, since there are no provisions under the U.S. Constitution concerning education. Moreover, most public schools receive more than 50 percent of their funding from the state and less than 5 percent from federal sources, with the balance of funding coming from the local communities. The Kentucky court also ruled that under Section 183 of the constitution of Kentucky, public education is a fundamental right of all Kentuckians. The Kentucky Supreme Court ruled that the Kentucky legislature had "failed in its responsibility to establish an efficient system of common schools throughout the Commonwealth." The court ordered the legislature to provide adequate funding and look at improving the "whole gamut of the common school system in Kentucky."

In June 1990, the Kentucky legislature passed the most sweeping educational reform act in the history of the United States, KERA. Responding to the state Supreme Court's ruling that the schools were inequitable and inefficient, the legislature totally revamped Kentucky's public education system in the areas of finance, governance, and curriculum in an attempt to provide equal educational opportunities for all Kentucky children regardless of the property wealth of the district in which they live. Legislative leaders from Northern Kentucky who supported KERA legislation included Senator Joseph Meyer from Kenton Co. and Representative Jim Callihan from Campbell Co. A number of legislators from Northern Kentucky, however, did not vote in favor of this legislation.

KERA was unique. Unlike the reforms in many other states, it was not limited to setting higher educational standards and creating new organizational structures, although it introduced a new statewide assessment accompanied by rewards and sanctions. One of the assessments, called CATS, (Commonwealth Accountability Testing System) was considered innovative in that it included open-ended essay questions that stimulated thoughtful analysis. In addition, KERA created additional support systems for teachers, families, and students in the form of increased funding for staff development to help teachers learn to implement the new mandates, a preschool program for economically at-risk four-year-olds and children with disabilities, an extended school services program for students who need more time to learn before or after school or in the summer, and family resource youth service centers to put students and their families in touch with needed health and social services.

In response to the state Supreme Court's mandate for financial equity, the legislature authorized an extra $1 billion for education to be appropriated over a two-year period, in addition to changing the state funding formula. This appropriation constituted a 35 percent increase in funding between 1990 and 1992, increasing per-pupil spending by nearly $1,000 to $4,600.

The legislature did not stop there. In addition to this huge increase to correct inequities, the school reform act also called for sweeping changes in the way the state operated its educational system. These reforms eventually included the establishment of cash awards for teachers whose schools show improvement over a two-year period; these awards were abandoned because of budget cuts in 2004. There was also the assembly of a statewide technology network designed to put a computer-ready telephone line in every classroom, providing linkups with libraries, research databases, governmental agencies, and even other schools and classrooms. By 2004 most classrooms in Kentucky had a ratio of one computer for every five students, and there was a telephone in more than 95 percent of the classrooms in the state.

New institutions were created, such as the Education Professional Standards Board, to set and enforce teaching standards. In 1991 an appointed education commissioner, who was given a mandate to reorganize the Department of Education, replaced the elected superintendent of public instruction as the head of the state school system. With the enactment of KERA, the members of the State Board of Education were replaced by 11 new members appointed by the governor.

KERA aided school districts such as Covington, Dayton, and Newport; school districts such as Beechwood, Boone Co., and Fort Thomas were not scheduled to receive significant increases under the new formula. As a result, they were covered by the "hold harmless" provision, which provided that they would not receive any less support from the state.

Because of the increased costs of mandates from the federal No Child Left Behind Act and the decrease in the percentage of the state budget devoted to primary and secondary education during the first decade of the 21st century, there is discussion among many school districts in Northern Kentucky, as well as within the Council for Better Education, of reopening the case of *Rose v. Council for Better Education* in order to revisit how the Commonwealth of Kentucky funds its public schools.

Kentucky Department of Education. www.kde.state.ky.us/KDE/ (accessed April 10, 2008).

Rose v. Council for Better Education, 790 S.W. 2d 186 (1989).

Paul L. Whalen

ROSS. Ross, formerly known as Indian Springs, is an unincorporated area in southeastern Campbell Co. along the Ohio River, the **CSX** Railroad, and the **Mary Ingles Highway** (Ky. Rt. 8) east of Melbourne. The name was changed to Ross before the coming of the railroad in 1888, so the railroad station there was called Ross. With the construction of the Mary Ingles Highway in the 1920s and 1930s, the hope for Ross was that it would become a resort area. A hotel was built there, and the Boyer family of Alexandria developed Campbell Co.'s first airport at Martz's Grove (Martz's Playground, Ross Resort). Martz's Grove was the brainchild of contactor Jacob Martz, a longtime Campbell Co. commissioner. Martz's Grove eventually had a two-story wooden grandstand, swimming pools fed by artesian wells, a concessions area, baseball fields, horseshoe and tennis courts, and, near the entrance along the railroad tracks, summer cottages. Beauty pageants were often staged there. On April 30, 1946, a U.S. Army Air Force bomber en route from Memphis, Tenn., to Cleveland, Ohio, made a successful emergency landing at the Ross airfield. In the 1960s, several former Cincinnati Redleg baseball players (pitcher Jim O'Toole in particular) played at Ross in a semipro baseball beer league on Sunday afternoons. The railroad crossing into the resort was always somewhat dangerous; several automobile-train collisions occurred at that crossing. Ross also had two popular roadhouses, Huck's Tavern and Coy's Riverdale Restaurant, which were well known for their good food, particularly for fried chicken and fish. Situated in the flood plain of the Ohio River, the area has survived several floods. In recent years, the opening of the AA Highway has lessened traffic along Ky. Rt. 8 through Ross, but the development push into southeastern Campbell Co. has resulted in the addition of new homes, and thus more population, to the Ross community.

"Oneonta," *KSJ*, January 24, 1889, 7.

"Park Drew Crowds," *KP*, December 12, 1999, B1.

ROTARY CLUBS. The first Rotary clubs in Northern Kentucky were chartered in Newport and Covington on November 1 and December 1, 1920, respectively. The Rotary Club of Cincinnati sponsored both clubs, and it was said that the "daddy" of these two clubs was Robert Chapman, president of the Rotary Club of Cincinnati.

The Covington Rotary Club began a major effort on behalf of crippled children in 1923, and the first summer camp in Kentucky for crippled children was sponsored in 1928; in 1930 the club, with help from the Newport Rotary Club, was instrumental in forming the Kenton-Boone Chapter of Crippled Children. With their support, an orthopedic unit was formed in 1944 at Covington's St. Elizabeth Hospital (see **St. Elizabeth Medical Center**). In 1950 a crippled children's opportunity school was completed and put into operation as a result of a collaborative effort by Rotary, the local chapter of Crippled Children, and the **Covington Independent Schools**. It was the first one in Kentucky. The Northern Kentucky Crippled Children Treatment Center was opened in 1957 and expanded in 1974. Another special project of the Covington Rotary Club was the establishment of the Rotary Grove in Covington's **Devou Park**. These are examples from a long list of projects sponsored by two of the most active Rotary Clubs in Northern Kentucky. Each of the clubs in the region is involved in service projects. Most of the

Northern Kentucky Rotary clubs are part of Rotary International's District 6740, which includes 43 clubs with about 2,000 members throughout Northern and Eastern Kentucky, including Lexington.

The organization known today as Rotary International was initiated by Paul Harris, an attorney, who met with three friends, Gustavus Loehr, a mining engineer; Silvester Schiele, a coal dealer; and Hiram Shorey, a merchant tailor, on the evening of February 23, 1905, in Chicago. As this group continued to meet weekly for fellowship and to enlarge their circle of business acquaintances and activities, their membership grew and meetings rotated among members' offices. Soon they adopted the name Rotary for their group. Other groups, called clubs, were started, and the organization became international in 1910 when the first club outside the United States was formed. A few years later the motto "Service Above Self" was adopted to signify Rotary International's identity as the world's first service organization. The organization's 4-Way Test, adopted in 1943, asks "Of the things we think, say or do: 1) Is it the truth? 2) Is it fair to all concerned? 3) Will it build goodwill and better friendships? and 4) Will it be beneficial to all concerned?" Primarily designed to bring together business leaders committed to these principles and to their communities, the Rotary Club concept grew rapidly. By the beginning of the 21st century, there were well over 1 million members in 650–700 clubs worldwide.

Rotary Clubs in Northern Kentucky

Newport, November 1, 1920; changed to Rotary Club of Fort Thomas–Southgate in 1989; changed back to Newport in 1991; became Rotary Club of Campbell Co. in 2003

Covington, December 1, 1920

Maysville, November 6, 1923

Falmouth, November 20, 1924

Owenton, 1925

Carrollton, June 1, 1926

Augusta, 1920s

Erlanger, January 6, 1938; became Rotary Club of Erlanger–Fort Mitchell, 1993; now Rotary Club of Kenton Co.

Ludlow, March 28, 1938; changed to Rotary Club of Fort Mitchell in 1984 and expanded territory; canceled its charter and joined Rotary Club of Erlanger–Fort Mitchell, 1993

Bellevue, 1938–1991; merged with Newport club, 1991

Florence, November 3, 1944

Walton, 1945 (the club lasted only a short time)

Boone Co., 1976–mid-1980s

"Club Charters to Be Received by Kentucky Rotarians in Newport and Covington," *KP*, December 16, 1920, 1.

"Crippled Kiddies Entertained by Rotary Club," *KP*, December 24, 1927, 1.

"Falmouth Rotary Club Leads District in Attendance," *KP*, October 31, 1929, 7.

"Quota Raised by Rotary Club: $5000 Added to State Fund for Crippled Children," *KP*, November 8, 1928, 1.

"Rotary Club Told of Camp," *KP*, August 19, 1931, 2.

"Rotary Grove Dedicated in Devou Park," *KP*, June 8, 1932, 1.

Rotary International: The Rotary Foundation. www.rotary.org (accessed December 20, 2006).

Raymond G. Hebert

ROTH, GEORGE F., JR. (b. January 18, 1905, Covington, Ky.; d. October 22, 1989, Covington, Ky.). Noted architect, author, and historian George Frederick Roth Jr. was born and grew up in Covington. He earned a degree in architecture from the University of Cincinnati in 1927 and an MA degree there in 1929. He then became a partner in the architectural firm of Potter, Tyler, Martin, and Roth, later known as Roth Partnerships. Roth designed many of the hospitals (and hospital additions) in the Greater Cincinnati area, including **St. Luke** in Fort Thomas; **St. Elizabeth** in Covington; and Bethesda Hospital, University Hospital, Jewish Hospital, Children's Hospital, and the Shriners Burns Institute in Cincinnati. He also designed hospitals in Florida, Maryland, New Jersey, Ohio, and Jamaica. He was the architect of several churches, including Grace Episcopal in Florence, Ky. Roth taught architecture for more than 37 years at the University of Cincinnati. He was a president of the American Institute of Architects (AIA), from which he won several awards for professional excellence; he was named an AIA Fellow in 1983. Roth served for 11 years on the Cincinnati Board of Education and 27 years on the board of the **Baker-Hunt Foundation**. He was also a historian; he helped preserve Cincinnati's Union Terminal, an act that earned him the U.S. Department of the Interior's Historic Preservation Award. Roth was a member of the Cincinnati Historical Society and the Filson Club in Louisville. Later in life, he wrote a book about the history of his church, **Trinity Episcopal Church**, in Covington. Roth died of cancer at age 84, in Covington's St. Elizabeth Hospital. Funeral services were held at Trinity Episcopal Church and he was buried at Highland Cemetery in Fort Mitchell. His wife of 52 years, Ruth Marley Roth, and a son, George Frederick Roth III, survived him.

"George Frederick Roth, Jr." *KP*, October 24, 1989, 4A.

"George Frederick Roth Jr., 84," *CE*, October 25, 1989, 5E.

"George Roth Left His Mark as Architect," *KP*, October 23, 1989, 1K–2K.

Roth, George F., Jr. *The Story of the Trinity Episcopal Church in Covington*. Covington, Ky.: Trinity Episcopal Church, 1991.

Tenkotte, Paul A. *A Heritage of Art and Faith: Downtown Covington Churches*. Covington, Ky.: Kenton Co. Historical Society, 1986.

ROUSE, ARTHUR B. (b. June 20, 1874, Burlington, Ky.; d. January 25, 1956, Lexington, Ky.). Arthur Blythe Rouse, a lawyer, a legislator, and a businessman, was the son of Dudley and Elizabeth Blythe Rouse; Dudley was president of the Boone County Deposit Bank. He was born in Burlington, but at an early age he moved with his family to a house on Commonwealth Ave. in Erlanger. Rouse's early education was in Erlanger Public Schools (see **Erlanger-Elsmere Schools**), and he attended Hanover College in Madison, Ind., where he graduated in 1896. He continued his education at the Louisville Law School, receiving his JD degree in 1900. He set up a legal practice in Burlington. Rouse entered Democratic politics by serving as a congressional secretary to **Daniel Lynn Gooch** and later to **Joseph L. Rhinock**. In 1910 Rouse became the Democratic candidate for the U.S. House of Representatives, running against Bellevue's mayor, Charles W. Nage. Rouse won the race easily and held the seat for the next 16 years. He married Minnie Elizabeth Kelly on December 14, 1910, and they had two sons, Arthur Jr. and Robert.

Rouse retired in 1926, saying that he wanted to spend more time with his family, and **Orie S. Ware** succeeded him in the U.S. House of Representatives. Rouse returned to Northern Kentucky and resumed his legal practice. In 1927 he was made a vice president of the Liberty National Bank. He also joined a group of builders who began constructing homes near Kyles Ln., in Fort Wright. Rouse and his cousin F. Walton Dempsey entered the public transportation business and started five bus companies. One was the **Dixie Traction Company**, which later became part of the **Green Line Company**; another was the Blue Line Transit, which was incorporated into the Greyhound Bus System. Kentucky governor Ruby Laffoon (1931–1935) appointed Rouse State Revenue Commissioner in 1931, a position he held for the next eight years. In 1953 Rouse was appointed Federal Court Clerk for the Eastern Kentucky District, with offices in Lexington. Rouse moved his family there but retained his Northern Kentucky business connections. He died in his Lexington home at age 81 in 1956 and was buried in the Lexington Cemetery.

"A. B. Rouse Sr. Dies at Age of 81," *KP*, January 26, 1956, 1K.

"A Man of Achievements," *KP*, January 27, 1956, 2.

Boone County Recorder, Historical ed., September 4, 1930.

The Political Graveyard. "Rouse, Arthur Blythe (1874–1956)." www.politicalgraveyard.com (accessed December 31, 2005).

Reis, Jim. "Arthur B. Rouse Was Influential in Congress," *KP*, April 19, 1993, 4K.

ROUSE, SHELLEY D. (b. February 19, 1867, Crittenden, Ky.; d. March 2, 1944, Covington, Ky.). The well-known Covington attorney Shelley D. Rouse was the son of a Grant Co. farmer, Thomas Rouse, and his wife, the former Nancy Henderson. Shelley's early education was in public schools in Grant Co. He earned his BA degree from Centre College, Danville, Ky., and acquired his law degree from the University of Cincinnati. On November 20, 1895, he married Alice Read of Covington, and they became the parents of one daughter. Rouse was a brother-in-law of **John Uri Lloyd**, a renowned scientist and author of several books, including ***Stringtown on the Pike***. Rouse's first job was as an associate with the law firm of O'Hara and Bryan in Covington. After **James W. Bryan** retired, Shelley entered into a partnership with Judge **James O'Hara**, which continued until O'Hara's death in 1900. Later in life, Shelley was a partner in the Covington law firm of Rouse, Price, and Adams. He served one term as president of the Kentucky State Bar Association and several terms as president of the Kenton Co. Bar Association. He was also a member of the Kenton Co. Board of Education. Rouse belonged to the Filson Club in Louisville, the Kentucky Historical Society in Frankfort, and the University and Literary clubs in Cincinnati. He died of a heart attack on March 2, 1944, at age 77. Funeral services were held in the family home at 427 Wallace Ave. in Covington, and the body was cremated.

"Noted Attorney Succumbs at His Home in Covington," *KE*, March 3, 1944, 1.
Reis, Jim. "Call Up the Infantry," *KP*, August 31, 1998, 4K.
"Rouse and Hemingray," *KP*, August 31, 1905, 2.
"Shelley D. Rouse Dies," *KP*, March 2, 1944, 1.
Southard, Mary Young, and Ernest C. Miller, eds. *Who's Who in Kentucky: A Biographical Assembly of Notable Kentuckians.* Louisville, Ky.: Standard, 1936.

RUGG, JENNIE (b. June 13, 1836, Newport, Ky.; d. March 27, 1923, Ashland, Ky.). Women's suffrage activist Virginia Adeline Rugg, known as Jennie Rugg, was the daughter of Samuel A. and Emeline (Amelia) Beaumont Rugg. She grew up amid relative wealth and privilege. By the 1880s she had become one of Northern Kentucky's leading suffragists, pleading the cause of the franchise for women—a radical political thought in those days. In 1884, along with two other **women's suffrage** activists from Newport, Mrs. John A. Williamson and Mrs. Thomas Laurens Jones, Rugg served as a delegate to the Kentucky Equal Rights Association convention in Lexington. At that meeting she delivered an address entitled "Mrs. Americana Samantiawa Gloriana Smith, on Women's Suffrage." In 1909 she distributed a petition throughout Campbell Co., with the goal of persuading the U.S. Congress to grant women the right to vote. This petition was part of an effort to secure a million signatures nationwide.

Rugg, who never married, spent her entire life in Newport, with the exception of the last few months. For many years her address was 523 York St. Failing health forced her to give up her political activism around 1915. Finally she moved to Ashland, Ky., and lived with the family of her former minister at Newport's **Grace United Methodist Church**, Rev. E. R Overby. In 1923, at age 87, Jennie Rugg died at the King's Daughter Hospital in Ashland, knowing that her efforts of 40 years had helped to enact the 1920 constitutional amendment enfranchising women. Many contemporary suffragists did not live to see that day. Rugg was cremated in a ceremony officiated by Rev. Overby in Cincinnati at the Cincinnati Crematory, and her ashes were buried at Evergreen Cemetery in Southgate.

"Equal Rights Association," *KSJ*, September 28, 1894, 8.
Kentucky Death Certificate No. 6773, for the year 1923.
"Miss Rugg Is Dead," *KP*, March 28, 1923, 6.
"Personals," *KSJ*, October 19, 1894, 8.
"Suffragettes Will Petition Congress," *KP*, March 20, 1909, 9.

RUSSELL THEATER. Col. (Kentucky Colonel) James Barbour "J. B." Russell, who planned and built the Russell Theater, was born at Maysville in 1866. He was one of the three sons of Milton C. and Elexene Porter Russell and was educated in the local public school system. Russell worked in the family wholesale grocery business until his father's death in 1902. He then purchased his mother's interest in the business and became the sole owner. He also succeeded his father as president of the Mason Co. Building and Loan Association.

James's brother Thomas owned the **Washington Opera House**, and as a result James also became interested in theaters. James Russell sold most of his investments in the stock market shortly before the 1929 market crash. With the money received from those sales, he decided to build a marvelous new Spanish Colonial Revival style movie theater at 9 E. Third St. He commissioned the Lexington architectural firm of Frankel and Curtis to design the building. The theater cost $125,000 to build (a staggering sum at the time) and opened for business in 1930. The exterior of the building had two Moorish columns and a tile roof; the sculptured faces of Comedy and Tragedy and two lion heads were mounted on the front wall. The ticket window was completely tiled, and the tiles were said to be Rookwood Pottery. Inside the theater, there was a replica of a Mediterranean garden, complete with Lombardy trees and ivy-covered colonnades. There were also busts of literary figures in niches along the walls. The ceiling featured twinkling stars, billowing clouds, a moving moon, and a large rainbow that appeared above the stage at the end of each show. The theater seated 700 on the main floor and two balconies, one of which was reserved for African Americans and could be entered only from outside the building.

The theater's grand opening occurred on December 4, 1930, with the showing of the movie *Whoopee,* starring Eddie Cantor. Numerous plays and vaudevillian acts were later performed on the theater's curved, foot-lighted stage, which had a lowered orchestra pit in front. As a child, singer and movie star **Rosemary Clooney** appeared on the Russell stage. Colonel Russell operated the theater until 1935, when he leased it to the Shine Group. Russell suffered a stroke on October 12, 1937, and was confined to his home, where he died on April 10, 1939. After his death, the Russell Theater passed through a succession of owners. In 1953 Rosemary Clooney held the world premiere of her first movie, *The Stars Are Singing,* at the Russell Theater. The theater ceased operations in 1983 and was later used as a restaurant, a furniture store, and a storeroom for a local newspaper. The Russell Theater suffered a final devastating blow when a storm tore off part of the roof. The building was not repaired and over the next several years sustained severe damage to the interior. In 1996 a Maysville businesswoman, Sandra A. Marshall, formed a nonprofit organization called Rescue the Russell, which purchased the theater with the hope of restoring it. Experts called in to assess the damage concluded that restoration would cost between 2.5 and 3.5 million dollars. The Clooney family, including Rosemary, began holding annual fundraisers to obtain the money needed for restoration. With the funds collected so far, the front facade has been restored and the damaged roof replaced. More money is needed to complete the project, but it is hoped that someday the Russell Theater can be brought back to its former splendor.

Cinema Treasures. "Russell Theater, Maysville, Kentucky." www.cinematreasures.org (accessed January 21, 2006).
The Rosemary Clooney Palladium. "Russell Theater." www.rosemaryclooney.com (accessed January 21, 2006).
Russell, Marion, Mary R. Anderson, and Donald Buckley. "The Russell Family Legacy in Maysville, Kentucky," *NKH* 7, no. 2 (Spring–Summer 2000): 9–19.

Jack Wessling

RUTER, MARTIN (b. April 3, 1785, Charlton, Mass.; d. May 6, 1838, Washington-on-the-Brazos, Tex.). Martin Ruter, Methodist minister and educator, was the son of Job Ruter. Self-educated in the classics, Martin became a Methodist in 1801 and then a minister. He helped to found three Methodist colleges: New Market Academy in New Market, N.H.; **Augusta College** in Augusta, Ky.; and Allegheny College in Meadville, Pa. He was the first president of Augusta College and helped to attract the dynamic faculty who served the college during its few years of existence. In 1822 Transylvania College in Lexington awarded Ruter a DD degree. In 1837 he resigned the presidency of Allegheny College to volunteer for Methodist missionary service in the new Republic of Texas. His intention was to establish a college there, but that was not accomplished until after Ruter's death. He died of pneumonia in 1838. His vision to found a Methodist college in the Texas territory was realized in 1840 with the formation of his namesake Rutersville College, today's Southwestern University at Georgetown, Texas.

The Handbook of Texas Online. www.tsha.utexas.edu (accessed April 5, 2007).

RYAN, TOMMY (b. Thomas J. Lidington, November 16, 1913, Newport, Ky.; d. April 15, 1989, Jackson Heights, N.Y.). Singer Thomas J. Lidington was the son of Thomas B. and Lydia Schorry Lidington. The family lived at 420 Lindsey St. in Newport's **West End**. His father worked for more than 50 years at the nearby **Andrews Steel Mill**, where Tommy also began his work career. During the 1930s Lidington became nationally known as a singer and dance bandleader. He changed his name to Tommy Ryan and sang with the Sammy Kaye Orchestra. Ryan was participating in the broadcast of Sammy Kaye's Sunday Serenade on NBC's Red Radio Network on December 7, 1941, when it was interrupted to announce the attack on Pearl Harbor. During **World War II** Ryan managed the

Blue Barron Orchestra while the orchestra's leader went off to war. Afterward, Ryan had his own band, which played in prominent clubs along the East Coast. Songs that he recorded include "My Buddy" (1937), "Rosalie" (1937), "Love Walks In" (1938), "I Understand" (1941), "This Is No Laughing Matter" (1941), "Mexicali Rose," "Until Tomorrow," "When You Wish upon a Star," and "You Stepped out of a Dream." He retired from the entertainment world before 1950, and he died in 1989.

"T.B. Lidington Dies Suddenly of Heart Attack," *KP*, April 18, 1952, 1.

Michael R. Sweeney

RYLAND HEIGHTS. The small Kenton Co. community of Ryland Heights is located along Decoursey Pk. (Ky. Rt. 177), just south of Fairview. Ryland Heights grew up around a **Kentucky Central Railroad** Depot (predecessor of the **Louisville and Nashville**), which was built in the mid-1850s. The city's name is taken from a prosperous farmer and early settler of the area, James W. Ryland. The surrounding countryside is quite scenic, with a panoramic view of both the Licking River and several nearby beautiful lakes. Ryland Heights was granted a post office in 1873, but it was closed six years later. A group of businessmen from Cincinnati and from Northern Kentucky opened the Crystal Lake Country Club nearby in 1892. The club's name was changed to the Kentucky Fishing and Shooting Club in 1904 and to the Ryland Country Club in 1918.

Ryland Heights was incorporated as a sixth-class city in 1972, primarily to make it more difficult for neighboring communities, such as Covington, to annex the area. The **Northern Kentucky Area Planning Commission** has designated Ryland Heights as an agricultural and rural residential area, a classification that requires larger-than-average home building lots. Residents hope that such restrictions will discourage rapid development, especially the construction of large subdivisions, and help preserve their quiet way of life. Since originally founded, the city itself has made several annexations and now contains an area of about five square miles. The 2000 U.S. Census listed Ryland Heights as having a population of 799 people. A publicly elected mayor and city council govern the city. Ryland Heights has a volunteer fire department and an ambulance service, but its police protection is provided by the Kenton Co. Police Department.

Reis, Jim. "Tiny Towns," *KP*, June 30, 1986. 4K.

"Ryland Heights: A Rural Community and Residents Like It That Way," *KP*, March 28, 1991, 4K.

U.S. Census Bureau. "American Fact Finder. Data Set. Census 2000 Summary File 1 (SF1) 100-Percent Data. Custom Table." www.census.gov (accessed January 21, 2006).

Voorhees, Elaine G. *Ryland: The First 100 Years*. Cincinnati: Graphic Information Systems, ca. 1992.

RYLAND LAKES COUNTRY CLUB. The residential country club Ryland Lakes was established along the Licking River in a scenic valley served by the **Kentucky Central Railroad**. The club's history goes back to 1892, when 18 businessmen leased 55 acres of land from a Kenton Co. farmer, John Mendenhall, to establish the Crystal Lake Fishing Club. In 1904 that club reorganized as the Kentucky Fishing and Shooting Club, incorporated, expanded its membership, and purchased a total of 163 acres (including its originally leased 55 acres). Some of the land was divided into sites for the building of member cottages; 38 cottages had been built by 1907. While some residents lived there year-round, many made it a summer home. Because the club was conveniently located along the railroad, businessmen could commute daily to and from their jobs in Covington or Cincinnati and spend the evenings with their families in this "summer resort." In 1905 a large clubhouse was constructed, and a chef was hired shortly thereafter. Swimming, fishing, canoeing, and shooting were activities available to members in the early years. In 1919 the Kentucky Fishing and Shooting Club changed its name to Ryland Lakes Country Club. Ryland was the name of the railroad station serving the area, as well as of a local family who had intermarried with the Mendenhalls and had built, in 1872, a large hilltop home (still standing) that overlooks the club. By the 1920s, a nine-hole golf course and two clay tennis courts were built; a saddle club and a baseball field followed by the 1940s. Over the years the club purchased additional acreage. In April 1979 the clubhouse was destroyed by fire and a new one was subsequently built. The club acquired the nickname of Little Switzerland, given to it by well-known member and artist **Frank Duveneck**. Other prominent members included **Clement Barnhorn**, **Richard Pretlow Ernst**, **Maurice L. Galvin**, and the Jergens, Herschede, and Whiting families of Cincinnati.

McLean, M. H. *Little Switzerland*. Covington, Ky.: Wolff's Standard, 1943.

Paeth, Greg. "Life Is Ever So Easy at Ryland Lakes," *KP*, July 9, 1983, 1K.

Voorhees, Elaine, and Steven Schwierjohann. *Ryland: The First 100 Years*. Cincinnati: Graphic Information Systems, 1992.

Paul A. Tenkotte

SACRED HEART CATHOLIC CHURCH. Before 1873 the small Catholic population of Bellevue attended St. Stephen Catholic Church (see **Holy Spirit Catholic Church**) in neighboring Newport. At that time, the mixed German and Irish Catholic laymen of Bellevue organized a society to raise funds for the erection of a church in their town. In March 1873, they obtained the permission of Covington bishop Augustus Maria Toebbe to proceed with plans for a church. The society bought two lots on Division St., and a one-story brick building that would serve temporarily as both church and school was quickly constructed. It was dedicated to the Sacred Heart of Jesus by Toebbe on November 22, 1874. A year later, the bishop assigned Sacred Heart Parish its first resident pastor, Bernard H. Hillebrand. Another story was added to the building in 1876 as enrollment in the school increased. The **Sisters of Notre Dame** taught in the school.

The parish grew, and the original building proved inadequate by the end of the 1880s. When Pastor William Cassander approached Bishop **Camillus Paul Maes** about the needs of the parish, the bishop approved plans for a new larger church. The stone Gothic-style church that stands today at the corner of Division St. and Taylor Ave., a design of architect **Louis Piket**, was begun in 1892 and dedicated on October 1, 1893. The old building was used exclusively as a school until a new school, designed by architect J. F. Sheblessey, was completed in 1915. The present exterior of the church was stuccoed in imitation rough-surfaced Indiana limestone in 1923. In the 1930s the parish ran a commercial high school for girls, as did many Catholic parishes.

At a time when national parishes were important to immigrant Catholics, Sacred Heart served as the German parish in Bellevue, and the newer **St. Anthony** Parish (1889) was the Irish parish. These two churches stood only a block apart. The need for separate parishes receded as the 20th century progressed. As more Catholics moved out of the inner cities to the suburbs, enrollments in most urban parish schools declined accordingly, and the long-standing goal of a school in every parish became a financial burden hard to justify. To meet this new reality, the schools of the two Bellevue parishes were merged into St. Michael School in 1987. In the early 21st century, the shortage of priests within the Diocese of Covington made it impractical to maintain two separate parishes in Bellevue within a block of each other. The parishes were merged in 2003 to form the new Divine Mercy Parish, utilizing the Sacred Heart structure. In 2002 Bellevue's Catholic students became part of Holy Trinity School, which serves students of Newport and Dayton, Ky., as well.

"Bellevue Churches Share Faith a Block Apart," *KP*, February 24, 1992, 1K–2K.

"Cornerstone of the New Bellevue Catholic Church Will Be Laid Tomorrow Afternoon," *KP*, September 24, 1892, 8.

Golden Jubilee Sacred Heart Parish: 1874–1924. Bellevue, Ky., 1924.

Ryan, Paul E. *History of the Diocese of Covington, Kentucky*. Covington, Ky.: Diocese of Covington, 1954.

"Sacred Heart Commercial School Graduates," *KTS*, June 24, 1931, 3.

Tenkotte, Paul A. *A Heritage of Art and Faith: Downtown Covington Churches*. Covington, Ky.: Kenton Co. Historical Society, 1986.

"2 Bellevue Parishes Will Merge," *KP*, June 11, 2001, 2K.

Thomas S. Ward

ST. AGNES CATHOLIC CHURCH. In 1930 Bishop **Francis W. Howard** established St. Agnes Chapel as a chapel annex to Covington's St. Mary Cathedral (see **Cathedral Basilica of the Assumption**) for parish Catholics living in Park Hills and its vicinity. From September 1930 until October 1931, Rev. Gerhard H. Geisen, chancellor of the diocese, oversaw and organized this new congregation. On September 8, 1930, St. Agnes School was opened under the care of the **Sisters of Notre Dame**, with an enrollment of 26. By October 3, 1930, a temporary frame chapel off Old State Rd. in Lookout Heights (now Fort Wright) had been built, and on October 5, 1930, the first mass was offered in the new chapel, which was dedicated to St. Agnes. In spring 1931, since St. Agnes Chapel had an 11-acre tract of land available for athletic purposes, Geisen formed a Catholic athletic association at the chapel. On August 28, 1931, a bell formerly located at the 12th St. Fire House was donated to St. Agnes Chapel by the City of Covington and was blessed for use at the chapel by the Very Reverend Joseph A. Flynn, V.G. In October 1931 a resident cathedral assistant pastor was appointed to St. Agnes Chapel to minister under the direction of the pastor of St. Mary Cathedral.

In May 1938, because the St. Agnes congregation of about 200 families had outgrown the temporary chapel, construction of a larger one was begun at a site on the Dixie Highway near its intersection with Old State Rd. in Lookout Heights (now Fort Wright). The project was overseen by Walter A. Freiberg, pastor of St. Mary Cathedral. On Sunday, May 22, 1938, Howard laid the cornerstone for the new St. Agnes Chapel. The new chapel, built of brick and stone in the Italian Lombard style, was completed in less than a year and formally dedicated by Howard on Sunday, February 5, 1939.

In 1941 a new St. Agnes Chapel school, consisting of four classrooms and a large basement for recreational purposes, was built. At that time, it was predicted that this new structure, in conjunction with classrooms in the chapel building, would meet the parish's educational space needs for a number of years. Howard officiated at the dedication of the new school on Sunday, August 24, 1941. As the suburbs surrounding it continued to grow, the school was replaced by a new 16-classroom, three-story school, completed in 1957; 4 more classrooms were added in 1962; and in 1990 a third addition featuring classrooms, science labs, and a gymnasium was completed. By 1968, with an enrollment of 936 students, some of them taught in classrooms in the church basement, St. Agnes School was the second-largest Catholic elementary school in the state.

On August 9, 1954, a decree was signed, by authority of the bishop of Covington, establishing St. Agnes as a separate parish, severing its ties to the cathedral and its parish. The St. Agnes parish was served long and well by the Sisters of Notre Dame, who continued to teach in the school until 1995. Currently, St. Agnes Catholic Church has about 1,600 households and a total of 4,600 people registered in the parish. Five hundred students are enrolled in its grade school, as the inner ring of suburbs has experienced an aging population.

The Church of St. Agnes. "History." www.saintagnes.com.

Ryan, Paul E. *History of the Diocese of Covington, Kentucky*. Covington, Ky.: Diocese of Covington, 1954.

"St. Agnes Chapel Becomes Parish, Pastor Assigned," *Messenger*, August 22, 1954, 1.

Donna M. Bloemer

ST. ALOYSIUS CATHOLIC CHURCH. Formerly one of the largest German American Catholic congregations in Northern Kentucky, the architecturally significant St. Aloysius Church stood on the southeast corner of W. Seventh and Bakewell Sts. in Covington's **West Side**, only blocks from the Irish American congregation of **St. Patrick Catholic Church**. The St. Aloysius congregation was founded in 1865, when a three-story combination church, school, and convent was constructed. In 1867 the parishioners completed a grandiose Romanesque Revival style church, with a pointed Gothic spire. Designed by noted architect **Louis Piket**, the church was later embellished with elaborate stained-glass windows by the Royal Institute of Bavarian Glass Painting in Munich, Germany, under the supervision of F. X. Zettler. In 1889 the parish built a facsimile of the famous Grotto of Lourdes of France in its basement, featuring exquisite hand-carved statues imported from Germany that depicted the first miracle at Lourdes. Bishop **Camillus Paul Maes**, who had been architecturally trained, encouraged the congregation to rebuild the Gothic spire in 1911–1912 in Romanesque style to match the predominant features of the church. In 1914–1915 the church underwent an interior redecoration that included new plaster arabesque ornamentation. By the early 20th century, the church building was one of the most beautiful ecclesiastical edifices in the city.

St. Aloysius Parish built several school buildings throughout its history. The most recent, still standing on W. Eighth St. and renovated into apartments in 1982–1983, was completed in 1933. Its construction provided needed work for the unemployed during the **Great Depression**. At its height in the early 20th century, the parish school had the largest enrollment of all of the Catholic elementary schools in the city of Covington. Suburban migration, though, quickly took its toll. In 1923 St. Aloysius School enrolled 707 students; by 1953 the enrollment had dropped to 313. When nearby **Mother of God** School suspended operations at the end of the 1961–1962 academic year and neighboring St. Patrick Church and School closed in 1967, St. Aloysius School enrolled their students. The mergers and a baby boom following **World War II** were not enough to stem the tide, however, and enrollment fell to 99 students during St. Aloysius School's last academic year of operation, 1978–1979. The parish itself did not long outlast the school. On May 16, 1985, lightning struck the church, and a resultant fire destroyed the building. The parish was subsequently closed and merged with Mother of God Church.

"Covington Pastor Announces Parish School Will Close," *Messenger*, February 25, 1979, 1.

"St. Aloysius Apartments: Deal Took Time but Finally Closed," *Messenger*, April 24, 1983, 7.

Tenkotte, Paul A. *A Heritage of Art and Faith: Downtown Covington Churches.* Covington, Ky.: Kenton Co. Historical Society, 1986.

Tenkotte, Paul A., David E. Schroeder, and Thomas S. Ward. *To Be Catholic and American in Northern, Central, and Appalachian Kentucky: The Diocese of Covington, 1853–2003.* Forthcoming.

Paul A. Tenkotte

ST. ANDREW'S EPISCOPAL CHURCH. Founded in 1905, St. Andrew's Episcopal Church is located at Chalfonte and S. Fort Thomas Aves. in Fort Thomas. It is part of the Episcopal Diocese of Lexington. In 2005 the church had a congregation of approximately 625 members. The church's name, St. Andrew's, is thought to be Scottish in origin. The present church was built in 1909, a parish house was constructed in 1928, and an addition to the main church was constructed in 1995.

The clergy who have served St. Andrew's Episcopal Church over the years are Rev. Custis Fletcher (1907–1912), Rev. Arthur Seiter (1912–1915), Rev. Arthur Marshall (1915–1918), Rev. William B. Dern (1919–1929), Rev. J. Wilson Hunter (1930–1938), Rev. Allen Person (1938–1968); Rev. David D. Heil (1968–1983); and Rev. Dr. Ronald W. Summers (1984–present). Dern was a popular local speaker, a broadcaster on the Cincinnati radio station WLW, and the author of *A Parson Takes a Gander.* He went on to serve 19 years at St. Paul's Episcopal Church in Newport.

"Death Takes Rev. Will Dern," *KP*, June 2, 1959, 1.

Dern, William B. *A Parson Takes a Gander.* Newport, Ky.: Beek, 1949.

Swinford, Francis Keller, and Rebecca Smith Lee. *Great Elm Tree: Heritage of the Episcopal Diocese of Lexington.* Lexington, Ky.: Faith House Press, 1969.

John West

ST. ANTHONY CATHOLIC CHURCH. The early history of St. Anthony Catholic Church was tied to the fortunes of the railroad line through DeCoursey in Kenton Co. With the opening of the **Kentucky Central Railroad** in the 1850s, many Roman Catholics moved into the Licking River valley to work on constructing the new route between Covington and Lexington. Irish Catholics were fortunate to have Rev. James Smith, pastor of **St. Patrick Catholic Church** in Covington, come and offer Mass for them in a home they purchased near Spring Lake. Because there was no German-speaking Catholic church in the vicinity, German Catholics had to travel five or six miles to **St. Augustine Catholic Church** in the Peaselburg neighborhood of Covington to hear sermons in their own language. In 1877 Rev. William Robbers, pastor of St. Augustine Church, received a donation of three acres of land in DeCoursey for a church and school. In 1878 the church was completed and dedicated to St. Anthony the Hermit. A mission of St. Augustine Catholic Church for its first three years, it then was a mission of Holy Guardian Angels Catholic Church in Sandfordtown until 1902, when Bishop **Camillus Maes** established it as a parish, with Rev. Henry Looschelders as its first pastor.

The **Sisters of Notre Dame** from **Mother of God Catholic Church** in Covington conducted a school in the basement at St. Anthony Catholic Church. The sisters rode the train from Covington but terminated their services after four years owing to the lack of adequate funding. During the pastorate of Rev. Bernard Baumeister (1907–1911), a small frame school was erected. When a house was bequeathed for a convent, the Sisters of Notre Dame lived on-site and again staffed the school for about five years. The parish then turned to the **Sisters of St. Benedict** to teach at its school.

The railroad continued to affect the growth of the parish. In 1918 the **Louisville and Nashville Railroad** (L&N) built a new railroad yard at DeCoursey and used eminent domain to take part of the parish property, for which the parish was later reimbursed $10,000, following litigation. The smoke and noise produced by the railroad yard made the church's location undesirable. Furthermore, the parish's population decreased after the DeCoursey Station rail stop closed in 1917. Therefore it was decided to try to relocate St. Anthony's Church to a more favorable site. In 1927, when the L&N Railroad acquired the rest of the church property through a condemnation proceeding, Pastor Bernard Nurre chose a new location, in the growing subdivision of Forest Hills (now Taylor Mill), two and a half miles closer to Covington, and a new church and parish plant were built, including a rectory and convent fashioned entirely from white stone. Bishop Francis W. Howard dedicated the new St. Anthony Church on April 14, 1929. The small school built at the time was intended to be temporary. As enrollment increased, a new school building was constructed in 1952.

St. Anthony Parish grew through the 1950s and 1960s. In 1963 Covington bishop Richard H. Ackerman split off part of the parish to create the new St. Patrick Parish. St. Anthony Church underwent a significant remodeling during the early 1970s. The parish continues to maintain its own school.

The Centennial Celebration of Saint Anthony Church, Taylor Mills, Kentucky, 1878–1978. Taylor Mill, Ky.: St. Anthony Catholic Church, 1978.

Ryan, Paul E. *History of the Diocese of Covington, Kentucky.* Covington, Ky.: Diocese of Covington, 1954.

Tenkotte, Paul A., David E. Schroeder, and Thomas S. Ward. *To Be Catholic and American in Northern, Central, and Appalachian Kentucky: The Diocese of Covington, 1853–2003.* Forthcoming.

Thomas S. Ward

ST. AUGUSTINE CATHOLIC CHURCH, AUGUSTA. Because early Catholic residents of Augusta in Bracken Co. did not have a church or the services of a priest, they requested that the Catholic pastor of the church in New Richmond, Ohio, attend to their needs. Rev. Augustus M. Toebbe obliged them and said Mass at Augusta in the home of a layman. Toebbe later became the second bishop of the Diocese of Covington (see **Roman Catholics**). Soon, Benedictine priests from Covington took over the care of the small congregation in Augusta. They encouraged their parishioners to raise funds to build a new church, and soon a building lot had been purchased on Fourth St. Bishop George A. Carrell, the first bishop of Covington, laid the cornerstone for the new church on May 29, 1859. The event was advertised in the Cincinnati and Northern Kentucky area; three steamboats carried passengers on the excursion upriver to Augusta for the celebration. Four months later, on October 7, 1860, Rev. Thomas Butler, vicar general of the Diocese of Covington, dedicated the completed St. Augustine Catholic Church at Augusta.

The Benedictine Fathers continued to minister to the church in Augusta. The first resident pastor, Rev. Alto Hoermann, O.S.B., was appointed in 1866. Rev. Caspar Ostlangenberg, O.S.B., became pastor in 1875. At his request, the **Sisters of Notre Dame** in Covington started a parish school for St. Augustine Catholic Church that same year.

A shortage of priests in the Diocese of Covington during the 1990s forced a number of local parishes to make adjustments. In 1997 a two-parish, one-priest arrangement was decided for the **St. James Catholic Church** in Brooksville and the St. Augustine Catholic Church in Augusta. Both retained their status as parishes (rather than one church becoming a mission of the other, the more common arrangement), but one pastor began to oversee both. Rev. Daniel Saner became the first pastor to serve both parishes, with the assistance of Deacon Ernie Hillenmeyer.

"Augusta, Brooksville to Share Pastor," *Messenger*, May 8, 1998, 1.

"Corner-Stone Excursion for St. Augustine's Church, Augusta, Bracken County, Kentucky on Sunday, May 29, 1859," *Cincinnati Telegraph*, May, 28, 1859, 8. Advertisement.

Ryan, Paul E. *History of the Diocese of Covington, Kentucky.* Covington, Ky.: Diocese of Covington, 1954.

St. Augustine Centennial, 1859–1959. Augusta, Ky.: St. Augustine Catholic Church, 1959.

Thomas S. Ward

ST. AUGUSTINE CATHOLIC CHURCH, COVINGTON. With the German Catholic population of Covington continually growing because of an influx of immigrants, a new German congregation was established in the **Peaselburg** area of the city in 1870. The parish was established during the tenure of Covington's second bishop, Augustus Maria Toebbe, and named St. Augustine after his patron saint. A two-story building was constructed to house both a church and a school that was staffed by the **Sisters of Notre Dame**. The bishop dedicated it on October 16, 1870, and the church's first pastor was Rev. L. Neumeier.

While Rev. Joseph Goebbels was pastor (1871–1877), he cooperated with the lay trustees of the parish to form two business ventures that they hoped would be a financial boon to St. Augustine Catholic Church, bringing the parish to self-sufficiency and helping to pay its debts. In the early 1870s, the church started a brick-manufacturing operation with two brickyards in the Peaselburg neighborhood near the railroad tracks. Shortly afterward, Goebbels purchased a nail-making machine from Germany and started a wire nail factory, thought to be the first of its kind in the United States. However, Goebbels proved not to be an astute businessman. He did not supervise record-keeping for the accounts of the two businesses, and some of the proceeds were diverted from the parish. Matters became further complicated because the trustees made the parish liable for payment of most loan obligations. When the national depression that began in 1873 caused a business decline throughout the country, the St. Augustine Catholic Church business enterprises failed, leaving the parish saddled with an enormous debt. The parish was bankrupt and many parishioners lost the savings they had invested in the parish's businesses. After lengthy litigation, the Covington Court ordered the entire property of the parish put up for sale to satisfy creditors.

William Robbers was appointed pastor in 1877. With new trustees, he formed a corporation called the Roman Catholic German Church of Central Covington, Kentucky, which repurchased the church edifice and property that had been lost. The situation improved enough that by the early 20th century, Pastor Paul Abeln was able to start raising funds for a new church. During the pastorate of Rev. Richard Kathman, the current red-brick Italian Renaissance–style church, designed by architect **David Davis**, was built on 19th St. between Jefferson and Euclid Aves. Bishop **Camillus Paul Maes** dedicated the structure on December 29, 1914. A new parish school was constructed in 1916; in 1953–1954, a gymnasium and two additional classrooms were built St. Augustine Catholic Church is one of the few parishes in the urban Northern Kentucky area that has its own school, rather than being part of a clustered school system.

Ryan, Paul E. *History of the Diocese of Covington, Kentucky.* Covington, Ky.: Diocese of Covington, 1954.
St. Augustine Centennial Booklet. Covington, Ky.: St. Augustine Catholic Church, 1970.
Tenkotte, Paul A., David E. Schroeder, and Thomas S. Ward. *To Be Catholic and American in Northern, Central, and Appalachian Kentucky: The Diocese of Covington, 1853–2003.* Forthcoming.
Trauth, Mary Philip, S.N.D. Unpublished paper, 1988, Archives of the Diocese of Covington, Erlanger, Ky.

Thomas S. Ward

ST. BENEDICT CATHOLIC CHURCH. The area of Covington known as **Austinburg** had been part of the **St. Joseph Catholic Church** parish since the mid-1850s. Catholics in this predominantly German area wanted to have a church in their immediate vicinity and received permission from Augustus Toebbe, bishop of Covington, to build one. A site was obtained in the early 1880s. The combination church and school building was dedicated by Bishop **Camillus Maes** on July 5, 1885, and named St. Benedict Catholic Church. The new parish was carved out of St. Joseph Parish and was made a mission of it. Rev. Aegidius Christoph, O.S.B. (Order of St. Benedict), the pastor of St. Joseph Church who had overseen construction, was given charge of St. Benedict Catholic Church. **Sisters of St. Benedict** from St. Walburg Convent near St. Joseph Church taught in the school. When a rectory was completed in 1889, the church was made into a parish. Maes put it in the care of the Benedictines of St. Vincent Archabbey in Latrobe, Pa., with Rev. Theodore Schmitt, O.S.B., as its first pastor. The parish had long been collecting funds for a new church. In the early 20th century, it acquired property in Covington between 16th and 17th Sts. for a church, and Cincinnati architect **Samuel Hannaford** designed the large brick building. On December 20, 1908, Maes dedicated the St. Benedict Church that stands today along 17th St. A rectory was soon added. In 1922 a new school with a large auditorium was constructed on 16th St. north of the church. The old combination church and school building was torn down to make room for a new school. Besides providing the usual first through eighth grades, the school also housed the two-year St. Benedict Commercial School, which offered business courses to students of any parish. The parish built a new convent for the Benedictine Sisters in 1926.

Like most urban parishes, St. Benedict began a steady decline in membership by the 1960s. The church underwent a significant renovation of its sanctuary in 1970, but the number of parishioners continued to decrease. In 1988 the parish school was merged into the new Holy Family School, which included the **Cathedral** and **Our Savior** schools in Covington. St. Benedict's school building was used as Holy Family's facility. Rev. Emeric Phiester was the last Benedictine pastor of St. Benedict, ending nearly a century of the order's service to its namesake parish. In 1987 Rev. Robert Henderson became the first diocesan priest to serve as pastor.

Reder, Dianne. "Jubilee Cross Visits St. Benedict Church, Covington," *Messenger,* June 16, 2000, 6.
Ryan, Paul E. *History of the Diocese of Covington, Kentucky.* Covington, Ky.: Diocese of Covington, 1954.
St. Benedict Church Golden Jubilee, 1885–1935. Booklet. Covington, Ky.: St. Benedict Catholic Church, 1935.
Tenkotte, Paul A., David E. Schroeder, and Thomas S. Ward. *To Be Catholic and American in Northern, Central, and Appalachian Kentucky: The Diocese of Covington, 1853–2003.* Forthcoming.

Thomas S. Ward

ST. BERNARD CATHOLIC CHURCH. The Catholic population of Jamestown (today a part of Dayton, Ky.), a town on the Ohio River in Campbell Co., attended **Corpus Christi Catholic Church** in Newport during the 1840s. These families, numbering about 40, decided to work toward building their own church. To that end, they formed two societies, one for men and one for women—the St. Joseph Society and the St. Mary Society—to plan and raise money for a church. In 1853 Bishop Martin John Spalding of Louisville (in the Diocese of Louisville, of which Northern Kentucky was a part before the creation of the Diocese of Covington) led the cornerstone-laying ceremony, and the church in Jamestown was completed and dedicated to St. Francis of Assisi the following year.

When George A. Carrell became the first bishop of Covington in 1853, he had only six diocesan priests in his service and could not appoint the first pastor, Rev. Michael Herzog, to St. Francis of Assisi Catholic Church until several months after its dedication. Herzog suffered from poor health and was replaced in 1857 by Rev. Charles Schaffroth. In 1866 Pastor Francis Grome started a new church, designed by architect Ludwig Riedinger, which was dedicated by Carrell on September 23 of that year.

The St. Francis of Assisi Catholic Church was rocked by a financial crisis in the 1870s. Because Grome made some unsound business speculations late in his pastorate, which ended in 1877, payments on notes issued in the name of the parish could not be made when they were due. A court ordered the church closed in 1880, though the judge eventually transferred the deed to the bishop of Covington, Augustus Toebbe. The next pastor, Rev. William Cassander, faced an enormous task to put the parish's finances back in order. He was successful enough that by 1888 Pastor Stephan Schmid was able to build a new school for the parish.

The state of parish finances, however, delayed plans to build a new church. The current church was initiated by Rev. Bernard Greifenkamp, who bought an entire city block in Dayton for the project in 1909. Extensive damage to the old church caused by the **flood of 1913** accelerated the process. The new church, designed by **Samuel Hannaford and Sons**, was dedicated on August 23, 1914, and renamed St. Bernard Catholic Church. But the church was not fully completed until the construction of its Romanesque facade in 1929. A school at the new site was erected in 1925.

Dayton, like most of urban Northern Kentucky, experienced extensive flight to the suburbs after **World War I**. In spite of a dramatic dwindling of its membership, the St. Bernard Church has remained viable. The parish managed to keep its own parochial school until 2002, when it was merged into the new Holy Trinity School, formed for Catholic students of Dayton, Bellevue, and Newport. St. Bernard Parish now shares a pastor with Divine Mercy Parish in Bellevue.

Caulfield, Patricia. "St. Bernard Church Traces History to 1852: Flood, Fire among Highlights in Background of Dayton Parish," *Messenger*, May 10, 1953, 9A–10A.

Gallagher, Janice. "Still 'God's Acre': Event Celebrates 150 Years as a Catholic Community," *KP*, July 15, 2004, 1.

Ryan, Paul E. *History of the Diocese of Covington, Kentucky*. Covington, Ky.: Diocese of Covington, 1954.

Tenkotte, Paul A., David E. Schroeder, and Thomas S. Ward. *To Be Catholic and American in Northern, Central, and Appalachian Kentucky: The Diocese of Covington, 1853–2003*. Forthcoming.

Thomas S. Ward

ST. CATHERINE OF SIENA CATHOLIC CHURCH. The suburban city of Fort Thomas did not have a Catholic parish until 1902, when **St. Thomas Catholic Church** was established. A mere 28 years later, Bishop **Francis W. Howard** established a second parish for the growing population and appointed Rev. John J. McCrystal as its pastor. Howard purchased for the new parish four acres and a small house, which was to serve as a temporary church. After a few months, a small frame church, named for St. Catherine of Siena, was built in 1930 on N. Fort Thomas Ave. In 1949 the parish built its first school, and the Sisters of Charity of Nazareth, Ky., supplied the teachers. To accommodate the growing enrollment, the parish added a second floor to the school in 1957.

In 1962 the parish broke ground for a new church, and by the following year, parishioners celebrated Mass in the basement of the rising structure. On May 3, 1964, the church was completed and dedicated by Bishop Richard H. Ackerman. The modern structure features a quarter-round front as the base of a triangular shape leading to a point at the sanctuary. At the front stands a bell tower with a relief of the church's patron saint, St. Catherine, made from stone quarried near her home city in Italy. The parish purchased a new rectory and convent in the 1970s. The parish still has its own school, though without the Sisters of Charity of Nazareth.

Commemoration Booklet for the Dedication of Saint Catherine of Siena Church. Fort Thomas, Ky.: St. Catherine of Siena Catholic Church, 1964.

Ryan, Paul E. *History of the Diocese of Covington, Kentucky*. Covington, Ky.: Diocese of Covington, 1954.

St. Catherine of Siena Parish, 1930–2005. Fort Thomas, Ky.: St. Catherine of Siena, 2005.

Welch, Bettie. "St. Catherine, Ft. Thomas: Parish Celebrates 50 Years of Spirit," *Messenger*, May 11, 1980, 2.

Thomas S. Ward

ST. CECILIA CATHOLIC CHURCH. The town of Independence in southern Kenton Co. had a small Catholic congregation long before it had a Catholic church. Priests from **St. Paul Catholic Church** in Florence attended to the spiritual needs of Catholics in Independence as early as 1860, by saying Mass for the people there in private homes. It was not until 1880 that a church dedicated to St. Cecilia was built for the congregation by Rev. Edward Burke, pastor of St. Paul Catholic Church. The community at Independence bought a parcel of land for a new church, hoping that soon it would be granted the status of a parish. This finally happened in April 1919, when Bishop **Ferdinand Brossart** named Rev. Henry Heringhaus, an associate pastor from St. Paul Catholic Church, to be the St. Cecilia Catholic Church's first resident pastor. His pastorate began just a month after a fire had destroyed the old church. On a previously purchased site near the old church, the parish built a brick church that could hold 250 people. The official dedication occurred on November 30, 1919. A rectory was constructed in 1921, and a school staffed by the **Sisters of Divine Providence** in 1923.

The town of Independence grew rapidly after **World War II** as people moved out of the inner cities to the suburbs. In spite of regular enlargements of the instructional space, the old school was proving inadequate by the 1950s, so a larger school was built in 1958. Under the direction of Rev. George Bamberger, the church building was doubled in size in 1965. The back wall was removed and a new section built on from there, so that the altar was midway between the two halves.

Even though two new parishes (St. Patrick in Taylor Mill and St. Barbara in Erlanger) were created within the boundaries of the St. Cecilia parish during the 1960s, the St Cecilia parish continued to grow. The need for a new church became obvious by the late 1980s. Several fund drives were initiated under the leadership of pastors Robert J. Urlage and David Shockey. Ground was broken in 1990, but the church was built only gradually as funds were raised. Finally, Rev. Paul Bershied saw the plans through to completion, and Bishop Robert Muench dedicated the new St. Cecilia Catholic Church, designed by Robert Ehmet Hayes & Associates, Architects, on December 14, 1997. In 2007 a painting of Christ by artist **Leon Lippert**, which originally adorned Corpus Christi Church in Newport and was thought to have been destroyed, was found at St. Cecilia Catholic Church in Independence. It was restored and now hangs in the sanctuary.

Cherishing Our Past . . . Planning for Our Future. Dedication booklet. Independence, Ky.: St. Cecilia Catholic Church, 1997.

One Hundred Years of Serving God and His People. Centennial booklet. Independence, Ky.: St. Cecilia Catholic Church, 1980.

Ryan, Paul E. *History of the Diocese of Covington, Kentucky*. Covington, Ky.: Diocese of Covington, 1954.

Tenkotte, Paul A., David E. Schroeder, and Thomas S. Ward. *To Be Catholic and American in Northern, Central, and Appalachian Kentucky: The Diocese of Covington, 1853–2003*. Forthcoming.

Thomas S. Ward

ST. CHARLES CARE CENTER. The Sisters of Notre Dame (S.N.D.) founded the St. Charles Care Center in 1961, as a nursing facility for the care of the frail and elderly. Sister Mary Edwin Paetzold, S.N.D., was the center's first administrator. Notre Dame sisters Mary Dolorita Broering, Mary Jeanette Wess, and Mary Luann Bender served as the center's administrators in subsequent years. The St. Charles Care Center is located along St. Charles Dr. in Fort Wright.

In 1985 ground was broken for St. Charles Village, a neighborhood of 44 cottages where seniors live independently, with the option of sharing in the services and amenities of the larger campus. In 1986 the St. Charles Care Center initiated its Adult Day Health Program, in which aging members of the Northern Kentucky community are cared for during the day while family members are working or when family caregivers need a respite. The Lodge at St. Charles, consisting of 72 senior living apartments, was built in 1991. There residents live independently in an atmosphere of community, warmth, and wellness. Its presence on the St. Charles Care Center's campus adds to the center's continuum of care. St. Charles Care Center has also responded to the needs of the broader community by offering private-duty nursing and case management in the home; inpatient and outpatient physical, speech and occupational therapies; and a wellness program.

"Housing for Elderly in Demand—St. Charles Expands with Expansion Plan," *KP*, September 29, 1998, 1K.

Ryan, Paul E. *History of the Diocese of Covington, Kentucky*. Covington, Ky.: Diocese of Covington, 1954.

St. Charles Care Center and Village. www.stcharlescare.org (accessed September 1, 2006).

Tenkotte, Paul A., David E. Schroeder, and Thomas S. Ward. *To Be Catholic and American in Northern, Central, and Appalachian Kentucky: The Diocese of Covington, 1853–2003*. Forthcoming.

Donna M. Bloemer

ST. ELIZABETH MEDICAL CENTER. Today's St. Elizabeth Medical Center has its origins with the first hospital in Northern Kentucky, the St. Elizabeth Hospital ("the Sisters' Hospital") located along Seventh St. in Covington between Madison Ave. and Scott St. It began in 1861 as a result of the combined efforts of **Henrietta Cleveland** of Cincinnati, benefactor Sarah Peter, the Sisters of the Poor of St. Francis, and Bishop George Carrell, the first bishop of the Roman Catholic Diocese of Covington (see **Roman Catholics**). From its inception, St. Elizabeth has been available to people of all races and creeds.

The first home for the hospital was a former grocery store. The diocese purchased the three-story structure and necessary equipment for $2,272.

St. Elizabeth Hospital, W. 11th St., Covington, late 19th century.

Funds were raised for the acquisition at a Hospital Fair held at the Odd Fellows Hall in Covington during the Christmas holidays of 1860 (December 17, 1860–January 2, 1861). The hospital opened on January 6, 1861, and the sisters assigned to the facility received their first patient around January 22. Before moving into the building, the sisters stayed at their order's first hospital in the United States, St. Mary Hospital in the West End of Cincinnati, which they had founded in 1859. St. Elizabeth was truly a charitable hospital in the beginning, for most of the first patients could not pay for their care, and the sisters went out into the Covington community and begged for food. Bread, soup, and coffee were the staples of their diet. Soon the **Civil War** erupted, and wounded soldiers from both sides found treatment at the hospital. The sisters also began a tradition that lasted into the early 20th century, the care of orphans and foundlings (babies left abandoned). The children of men killed in the war, and foundlings from the immediate area and from Cincinnati and Columbus, Ohio, where the sisters also had a hospital, were taken in and raised at the Covington hospital. Upwards of 50 children at one time lived at the hospital.

In 1867 a building was purchased that dated from the 1840s and had been part of the **Western Baptist Theological Institute,** along the north side of 11th St. in Covington. The St. Elizabeth Hospital moved there, opening the facility in spring 1868. The structure, which cost $50,000, plus $12,000 for new equipment, had 50 rooms and space for 110 beds on its four floors; the 11th St. hospital began with 40 patients and 50 orphans (who had been foundlings). It was just east of the railroad, whose constant noise and dirt annoyed both patients and staff, particularly after the **Chesapeake and Ohio Railroad Bridge** opened in 1888 and rail traffic increased. At various times between 1870 and 1900, the City of Covington asked the sisters to help with the care of the people living at the Covington pest house (poorhouse), and the sisters kindly did so. Occasionally, the dilapidated pest house had to be closed for remodeling, and at those times the sisters provided a place for the residents. The hospital received its first X-ray equipment as early as 1895 because the manufacturer, the **Kelley-Koett Company,** was also in Covington. In 1905 Nicholas Walsh (see **Walsh Distillery**), a longtime benefactor of the Diocese of Covington, contributed funds to build the first real laboratory at the hospital.

In May 1909 the diocese purchased land at 21st St. and Eastern Ave. in south Covington for a future St. Elizabeth Hospital. A new four-story modern building designed by **Samuel Hannaford and Sons** was opened on that site in 1914; at the time it was one of the finest medical facilities in the state. In December 1915 the St. Elizabeth School of Nursing began, as a means to supply properly trained nurses for the hospital. It became the first nursing school in Kentucky to earn national recognition. Dr. William Gerding, who practiced medicine in Newport for more than 60 years and was a member of the staff of the hospital, taught at the school of nursing from its inception. The nursing school opened in 1915, closed in 1922, reopened in 1929, closed again in 1950 to reorganize, and graduated its last class in April 1968.

After 1918 children no longer lived in St. Elizabeth Hospital; they were moved to the St. John Orphanage (see **Diocesan Catholic Children's Home**) in Fort Mitchell and the Good Shepherd Home in Fort Thomas. Separate departments within the hospital began to form: a maternity department in 1919, an anesthetics department in 1921, and a pediatrics department in 1925.

The hospital was accessible only by rowboat during the **flood of 1937**, and special steam engines were brought to the building to keep the heating system intact during that crisis. In 1947 Tarsicia Hall was constructed as a home for 200 nurses. A neurological department and a two-floor contagious disease unit were created within the northwest wing of the building in 1953.

In April 1968 the hospital hired its first lay administrator, Earl Gilrath. In February 1973 St. Elizabeth merged with Speers Hospital (see **Speers Memorial Hospital**) in Dayton, Ky., and by September 1 of that year, Speers Hospital had closed. In December 1973 ownership of the hospital was transferred from the Sisters of St. Francis of the Poor to the Diocese of Covington. A parking garage was constructed in 1976, after a long fight with the residents of the neighborhood. In 1978, in anticipation of the opening of St. Elizabeth Hospital South in Edgewood, the name of the organization became the St. Elizabeth Medical Center.

Suburbanization took its toll on the St. Elizabeth Hospital in Covington, and in response a 260-acre parcel of land was purchased in 1969 in Edgewood, near the campus of **Thomas More College,** where Dudley Rd. meets Thomas More Pkwy. Ground was broken in 1975 and a 182-bed hospital, the St. Elizabeth Medical Center South, opened and accepted its first patient on October 10, 1978. Thus far, several hundred millions of dollars have been expended at the medical village for health-care-related facilities: the general hospital, patient towers, a cancer center, outpatient-care areas, surgery suites, laundries, medical offices, an adjacent rehabilitation hospital, and a hospice. There is no end in sight, as this general area has clearly become the center of medical care in Northern Kentucky. The **Gateway Community and Technical College** has begun to teach nursing at its medical village campus, with close ties to both the hospital and Thomas More College. Construction has become almost constant at the Edgewood campus.

Regional expansion has also taken place. In Grant Co., planning began in 1960 for a small 30-bed hospital in Williamstown. Dr. **Doris Vest Clark**, county judge R. Lester Mullins, and Dr. **Fred Scroggin** were integral parts of the group that opened the Grant Co. Hospital in July 1964, along Barnes Rd. However, as many county governments across the nation have found, it is difficult to operate such a small hospital because of the spiraling costs of modern health care. In 1990 Grant Community Health Services Inc., which leased the Grant Co. Hospital, signed a management agreement with the St. Elizabeth Medical Center for operation of its facility; and in 1993 the Grant Co. Hospital became St. Elizabeth Medical Center–Grant Co. as the St. Elizabeth Medical Center took ownership of the Williamstown facility. With the increasing population of Grant Co., the St. Elizabeth Medical Center has tripled the size of its hospital there while bringing several medical specialists into the county for weekly office hours. In turn,

St. Elizabeth in Edgewood gains those referrals that cannot be attended to in Grant Co. Both the Edgewood and the Williamstown facilities have heliports for critical patient transport.

The St. Elizabeth Medical Center has not forgotten its historical hometown as it enters the 21st century. While occupancy rates and the number of hospital beds decreased at the North Unit in Covington, St. Elizabeth made plans to build a new Covington facility on an 11-acre site, south of 12th St. and just east of I-75, where the former Jefferson Ave. northbound exit of the interstate led into Covington. The three-story facility will include an emergency room to replace the one at St. Elizabeth North, along with diagnostic, outpatient, and medical offices. Groundbreaking was in April 2008, and completion is scheduled for 2009.

In 2006 **St. Luke Hospitals** expressed its intent to withdraw from the Health Alliance of Greater Cincinnati. Thereafter, in October 2008, St. Elizabeth Medical Center and St. Luke Hospitals completed a merger agreement, under the sponsorship of the Roman Catholic Diocese of Covington. The merger will include five major facilities in Covington, Edgewood, Fort Thomas, Florence, and Williamstown, with a total of 1,068 beds, 31 primary care offices, and 4,638 full-time employees.

A Century in Covington. Brochure. Covington, Ky.: Sisters of the Poor of St. Francis, 1961.

Diamond Jubilee, St. Elizabeth's Hospital. Brochure. Covington, Ky.: Sisters of the Poor of St. Francis, 1935.

One Hundred Twenty-Five. Brochure. Covington, Ky.: St. Elizabeth Medical Center, 1987.

Peale, Cliff. "St. E, St. Luke Finish Merger," *KE*, October 29, 2008, B1.

Reis, Jim. "St. Elizabeth: Old Grocery to New Center," *KP*, August 13, 1984, 10K.

Ryan, Paul E. *History of the Diocese of Covington, Kentucky*. Covington, Ky.: Diocese of Covington, 1954.

"The Sisters' Hospital," *CDG*, October 30, 1867, 9.

Steitzer, Stephenie. "Medical Center on the Horizon," *KP*, September 13, 2005, 2K.

"St. Elizabeth Has Served Sick since 1861," *Messenger*, August 1945, 3.

"St. Elizabeth Purchases Land for New Covington Facility," *Messenger*, January 26, 2007, 23.

"St. E Moving North's Beds," *KP*, January 31, 2004, 1K.

Tenkotte, Paul A., David E. Schroeder, and Thomas S. Ward. *To Be Catholic and American in Northern, Central, and Appalachian Kentucky: The Diocese of Covington, 1853–2003*. Forthcoming.

"A Visit to the New St. Elizabeth Hospital, of Covington," *Christian Year*, March 7, 1914, 7.

Weathers, Rosemary. "St. Elizabeth Goes Regional with Hospital," *KP*, April 10, 1993, 1K.

Michael R. Sweeney

ST. FRANCIS DE SALES ACADEMY. Operated by the Roman Catholic Visitation order of nuns, this Maysville educational institution provided day classes and boarding for women from 1865 to 1899. In 1864 Rev. Peter McMahon asked Bishop George Carrell to invite the Visitation Order into the Diocese of Covington (see **Roman Catholics**). That same year, McMahon purchased property on Third St., not far from St. Patrick Church, for a school, and on June 6, 1865, Carrell canonically established the order at Maysville. Photos of the academy show a five-story building that was home to the convent and school. The prospectus used to attract students from 1890 describes "a commodious range of buildings . . . advantages of ample grounds," and "a beautiful view of the Ohio." The "good rail and river communication" were important for pupils coming to the academy from other states. Practical instruction was emphasized, but the "ornamental" branches of instruction were not ignored. Such instruction included, for example, elocution, embroidery and chenille work, guitar, harp, and painting on china and slate. In photos from the academy, groups such as the Mandolin Club can be seen; the students are shown in high-necked, long-sleeved, floor-length dresses, the sisters are pictured in black habits that reveal only their faces and hands. Practical instruction at the school included common subjects such as botany, history, and mathematics. Students also were taught Christian doctrine, object lessons, orthography, and rhetoric.

St. Francis de Sales Academy.

Boarding students were not encouraged to go home during the year, and visits by parents were limited. Students were given a list of items to bring with them, such as a napkin ring, a shawl, and six table napkins. Fees varied depending on the extra courses taken. Board and tuition for a session of five months was $75, according to the prospectus. Students of other religions were welcomed to the school, and it was stated that "daughters of the best families of the State" were among the pupils. Sister Mary Gonzaga Carragher was noted for her leadership as the first superior of the Visitation Order in Maysville. The academy building no longer stands, and the Visitation Order left its Georgetown convent in Kentucky in 1987.

"Prospectus of the Young Ladies, Academy of the Visitation," Museum Center, Maysville, Ky.

Ryan, Paul E. *History of the Diocese of Covington, Kentucky*. Covington, Ky.: Diocese of Covington, 1954.

"St. Francis de Sales Academy," Computer File and Collections, Museum Center, Maysville, Ky.

St. Patrick's Church: 150 Years of Faith. Maysville, Ky.: St. Patrick Church, 1998.

John Klee

ST. FRANCIS DE SALES CATHOLIC CHURCH. Founded in 1912 as a mission of St. Stephen Roman Catholic Church in Newport, this church and school are now closed. Rev. Stephen Schmid recognized the need for a church in the part of Newport known as **Cote Brilliante**. Peter Ridder, who lived nearby on Chesapeake Ave., donated three lots at the corner of Chesapeake and Grand Aves. toward the church's establishment. The St. Francis de Sales Church, designed by Cincinnati architect Anton Rieg, was dedicated on October 13, 1912, and construction of a grade school building was begun. The first pastor was Rev. Edward Klosterman. In the mid-1920s, for a brief period, the parish operated a commercial high school that met at night in its school building. In 1949 a replacement school was completed by Rev. John Bankemper, and in 1976 an addition to it was finished. For several years during the 1960s and 1970s, because classroom space was limited, some grade school classes of the St. Frances de Sales School were held in an old, rundown two-story brick building that was once the Cote Brilliante School of the Newport City School System (and before that, a part of the **Campbell Co. Public Schools**). This school building at the corner of Park and Grand Aves. was torn down in 1978.

The 1960s and 1970s saw the peak enrollment for the school and membership for the parish. Soon thereafter, the ravages of suburban development turned on St. Francis. In 1982 the completion of I-471 removed households from the parish and somewhat isolated it from nearby Woodlawn. For years, the pastors of St. Francis de Sales Parish had recognized how important it was for them to keep the people of Woodlawn in the parish fold. Now, families began to move away to the southern parts of Campbell and Kenton counties. New residents of the area were generally not owners, but renters, and most of them were not Catholics. The last full-time pastor was Rev. James P. Gerrety. Declining numbers at the church eventually led to its closing in July 1999, but the school building continued to be used until 2005 as part of the combined Holy Spirit School. In 2003 the City of Newport purchased and tore down some 90 homes in the area as part of its Pavilion development project. With the closing of St. Francis de Sales Church and its school, a memorable chapter of Newport's history ended. The church and the school were torn down during the last week of February 2007.

Ryan, Paul R. *History of the Diocese of Covington*. Covington, Ky.: Diocese of Covington, 1954.

Tenkotte, Paul A., David E. Schroeder, and Thomas S. Ward. *To Be Catholic and American in Northern,*

Central, and Appalachian Kentucky: The Diocese of Covington, 1853–2003. Forthcoming.

Michael R. Sweeney

ST. FRANCIS XAVIER CATHOLIC CHURCH. The first Roman Catholic Church in Pendleton Co. was founded in Falmouth as a mission in 1857. Missionary priests visited Falmouth from Frankfort and Lexington as early as 1851, and tombstones in the St. Francis Xavier Cemetery on Woodson Rd. in Falmouth date as far back as 1849, indicating that there were Catholic families in the county earlier. The cornerstone for the first Catholic church in town, along Main St., was laid in 1857, under the direction of Rev. H. G. Allen. On October 4, 1860, the first bishop of Covington, George A. Carrell, dedicated the brick structure as St. Francis Xavier Church. Rev. James McNerney became its pastor in 1873.

By that time, the number of Catholics in the community had grown, and the parish, under the guidance of Rev. August Gadker, began construction of a new and larger church and rectory. The new cornerstone was set at the intersection of Second and Chapel Sts. in Falmouth in 1877, and dedication services were held on September 12, 1880. Every other Sunday, Gadker delivered his sermon in German, a practice that displeased many of the Irish members. The early congregation was mostly Irish immigrants who had come to Pendleton Co. to work for the railroad. Gadker was also in charge of three missions: one at Butler, **St. John** on the Dividing Ridge, and St. Patrick at Double Beach (along Kincaid Creek). The 1884 Lake atlas includes all three of these churches.

About 1888, Gadker had bells from the Catholic churches at Butler and Double Beach placed in the tower of the church in Falmouth. Rev. Joseph M. Lelen, a respected author and literary figure, widely published in newspapers and magazines, came to the St. Francis Xavier Catholic Church in 1918 and was pastor there for 35 years. The **flood of 1997** did severe damage to the St. Francis Xavier Catholic Church building, but it has since been restored.

Belew, Mildred Boden. *The First 200 Years of Pendleton County.* Falmouth, Ky.: M. B. Belew, n.d. [ca. 1994].

Falmouth Outlook, September 26, 1980, 20.

Ott, James. *Seekers of the Everlasting Kingdom: A Brief History of the Diocese of Covington.* Strasbourg, France: Éditions du Signe, 2002.

Ryan, Paul E. *History of the Diocese of Covington, Kentucky.* Covington, Ky.: Diocese of Covington, 1954.

Tenkotte, Paul A., David E. Schroeder, and Thomas S. Ward. *To Be Catholic and American in Northern, Central, and Appalachian Kentucky: The Diocese of Covington, 1853–2003.* Forthcoming.

Mildred Belew

ST. HENRY CATHOLIC CHURCH. St. Henry Catholic Church in Elsmere was begun as a mission of St. Paul Church in Florence, Ky., by about 10 families. In the late 1800s, lots in Elsmere were being sold for homebuilding, and several of these new homeowners were Catholics who needed a church. A small brick church was built for them at the corner of Garvey and Shaw Aves. in South Erlanger, now Elsmere, at the direction of a Rev. Gorey. The parish was named after Henry II, emperor of Germany from 1003 to 1024, who was made a saint in 1152; the name reflected the predominance of German families in the area. In 1893 the parish erected a small school opposite the church, where 60 children were to be taught by lay teachers. However, one month before the beginning of the school term, the church burned to the ground. It was decided to move the church and school to a more central location, at Garvey Ave. and the Covington-Lexington Turnpike, now known as **Dixie Highway**, a dirt path at the time. Having received only $1,000 of insurance money from the burned church, parishioners hauled rock for the foundation of the new church. The parish rented a nearby cottage for a schoolhouse, which opened in 1899, when the **Sisters of St. Benedict** were invited to take charge of the children's education. From 1899 through 1988, 147 Benedictine nuns served as teachers in the St. Henry parish. The new church building, opened in 1901, included living space for the sisters and classrooms for the children. Over the next 20 years, additional lots nearby were purchased for a school playground.

In 1929, with the congregation growing and the numbers of children increasing, a two-room frame schoolhouse was built between the church and the rectory. Another two rooms were added in 1933 to accommodate increased enrollment. This building was used until 1967, when it was razed to make room for a new high school. Also in 1933, the pastor and the congregation saw the need for a new church and began making construction plans. Bishop Francis W. Howard dedicated the new St. Henry Church in May 1936.

A high school was begun with one grade in 1933 and had increased to four by 1936. The first high school graduation (12 students) was held June 8, 1937. In 1949 a building was constructed that included a gymnasium and kindergarten classrooms; at the same time a separate playground was provided for older students. In 1950 St. Henry was the only parish in the Covington Diocese offering K–12 Catholic education. In 1965, its peak year, the school had 1,426 students, 1,099 in grades K–8 and 327 in high school.

The years 1960–1964 saw more improvements, including a school expansion and a new rectory. A new high school was built in 1967; because it was outgrowing its space by 1998, the school was relocated to a larger facility on Donaldson Rd. in Boone Co. The old high school building became a grade school building. In 2004 parishioners financed a major renovation of the church interior.

The hallmark of St. Henry Parish has always been its support for Catholic education, which continues today. The parish supports the grade school annually in the amount of $400,000, keeping tuition as affordable as possible.

By 2005 St. Henry Catholic Church had 1,454 registered parishioners and nearly 450 school children in grades K–8. From 1890 to 2005, the parish had witnessed 8,153 baptisms, 2,342 weddings, and 2,225 funerals.

"Saint Henry Church Centennial Celebration, 1890–1990," 1990, St. Henry Catholic Church, Elsmere, Ky.

Saint Henry Church Golden Jubilee Celebration, 1890–1940. Elsmere, Ky.: St. Henry Catholic Church, 1940.

St. Henry Parish Records, 2005, St. Henry Catholic Church, Elsmere, Ky.

Larry Klein

ST. HENRY DISTRICT HIGH SCHOOL. This school, with extensive modern educational facilities and sporting venues and an enrollment of 520, sits on 33 acres of land across from the Marydale Retreat Center on Donaldson Rd., in Boone Co.

The school began in 1933 as a one-grade high school. Rev. Edmund Corby took on the task of beginning a high school to serve the children of the St. Henry parish in Elsmere. In each succeeding year, a grade was added, requiring more space, so that by the time the first class of 12 students graduated in 1937, the high school had expanded into the former church building. Despite early struggles, by 1939 the State of Kentucky awarded the St. Henry High School a Class A school rating.

By 1966 enrollment had reached 327 students. This continuing expansion placed a strain on the older school buildings of the parish. Over the years, the high school operated out of a variety of structures on the St. Henry campus, at one point utilizing four different buildings. A new $700,000 high school building was completed in 1968, featuring 13 classrooms, a library, laboratories, offices, and a cafeteria.

In 1984 St. Henry became a district high school, serving seven parishes: All Saints, Immaculate Heart of Mary, Mary Queen of Heaven, St. Barbara, St. Henry, St. Paul, and St. Timothy. At that time a plan was suggested to the Diocese of Covington for a gradual move of the school to a parcel of diocesan land, opposite the entrance to the Marydale Retreat Center in Boone Co. This was considered advisable because Boone Co. had no Catholic high school of its own, and the majority of the parishes served were in that county. However, Bishop William Hughes and his advisers rejected the plan owing to the costs involved.

After a dip in enrollment to 238 students for the 1989–1990 year, enrollment climbed, straining the school building's resources and requiring creative space management; even the cafeteria was used as a classroom. Coupled to the student body increase were the inadequacies of the sporting venues at the high school. Indeed, to provide adequate seating, many home basketball games were scheduled at **Thomas More College** in Crestview Hills.

In 1991 a recommendation was made again to move the high school to Boone Co., preferably to the Marydale site. After a brief start and stop because of funding issues, in 1994 a fund drive was begun with the intent of raising $4.5 million to relocate the high school to the Donaldson Rd. site, on land donated by the diocese. Construction on the new campus began in late 1997 and was completed in time for classes to begin in September 1998. The $5.27 million school features a 600-student capacity, a 1,100-seat gymnasium, more than 30 classrooms and laboratories, and on-site athletic facilities.

Ryan, Paul E. *History of the Diocese of Covington, Kentucky.* Covington, Ky.: Diocese of Covington, 1954.

St. Henry District High School Archives, Boone Co., Ky.

Tim Herrmann

ST. JAMES A.M.E. CHURCH. The St. James African Methodist Episcopal (A.M.E.) Church of Covington began in 1869, only a few years after the **Civil War** ended. The church was started by Martha Ann Taylor, a devoted local Christian woman, who for years conducted numerous church services, taught weekly Sunday school classes, and organized nightly prayer meetings from her home in Covington. With the growth of church membership, Taylor moved the congregation to a newly built schoolhouse located in the Austinburg area of Covington. Several years later the congregation moved to a building in Covington on Maryland Ave., near Oliver St., and later to a structure on Ninth St., between Greenup and Prospect Sts. Two subsequent moves took the congregation to downtown Covington (see **Covington, Downtown**), at the corner of Seventh St. and Madison Ave., and to the Domestic Science Department at the Lincoln Grant School. Finally, in 1922, under the leadership of Rev. J. A. G. Grant, the congregation developed a plan to construct a permanent structure on several acres of land, located in Covington at 120 Lynn St., which the church had purchased in 1918. Under the direction of Grant, donations and pledges were collected from hundreds of local African Americans for the construction of a new church. Grant also gained the support of Bishop A. J. Carey, who appealed to A.M.E. church members throughout Kentucky and Tennessee to invest in this venture. The first phase of the building program, which included a large sanctuary and several meeting rooms, was completed in late 1922.

After the departure of Grant, each subsequent pastor contributed substantially toward guiding the continuous construction at St. James A.M.E. Church. For instance, Rev. S. R. Reid, who served as the church's pastor for only one year (1925–1926), created a church building fund, which later was used to acquire furniture and a new furnace for the church. By the late 1950s, most of the building was completed with the use of these funds. Today, St. James A.M.E. Church continues to serve the spiritual and community needs of hundreds of African American Northern Kentuckians.

"Diamond Jubilee Celebration and Mortgage Burning of St. James A.M.E. Church—September 10th to 16th, 1945," Northern Kentucky African American Heritage Task Force Collection, W. Frank Steely Library, Northern Kentucky Univ.

Reis, James. "Black Churches Offered Stability in Troubled Times," *KP*, January 20, 1997, 4K.

"St. James A.M.E. Church—118th Anniversary 1987—Covington, KY," Northern Kentucky African American Heritage Task Force Collection, W. Frank Steely Library, Northern Kentucky Univ.

Eric R. Jackson

ST. JAMES CATHOLIC CHURCH. Catholics in Bracken Co. had only intermittent visits from priests during the first half of the 19th century. In the 1840s, priests from St. Mary Parish in Covington visited Catholics in Bracken Co. and at the mission at Maysville in Mason Co. After St. Patrick Catholic Church in Maysville was established with a resident pastor, Rev. John McSweeney began to attend a small station (a congregation without a church) at Milford in southern Bracken Co. Catholics at Brooksville were served occasionally by missionary priests who celebrated Mass in private homes. Some Catholics traveled from Brooksville to Augusta, which since 1860 had its own church attended by Benedictine fathers. Finally in 1866, Rev. Alto Hoermann, O.S.B., of **St. Augustine Catholic Church** in Augusta, organized the congregation in Brooksville and oversaw construction of a church there. In 1868 a priest of the Diocese of Covington (see **Roman Catholics**), Rev. James McNerney, was appointed as the first pastor. The following year the church was expanded and named for St. James. The parish included a mission church in nearby Minerva in Mason Co., also named St. James.

While Rev. James Redmond was pastor, St. James Parish started a school. Redmond also hoped to build a new church, but the plan was discarded after Rev. Thomas Kehoe took over as his successor. It was not until Rev. Thomas Coleman arrived as pastor that the parish decided to build the new church. Bishop **Camillus Maes** dedicated it on December 16, 1914. Rev. Edmund Corby initiated a small four-year parish high school. In spite of its small size (in 1956 it was noted for having the smallest enrollment—16 students—of any high school in the county), St. James High School managed to remain open until 1962. The grade school closed in 1968 owing to the low enrollment. A new St. James Catholic Church in Minerva was constructed in 1941, a year after the prior church building burned. The pastors of St. James continued to have Mass in both the parish and mission St. James churches. Because of the shortage of priests in the Diocese of Covington beginning in the 1990s, new arrangements were made for many parishes. A two-parish, one-priest arrangement was settled upon for St. James in Brooksville and St. Augustine in Augusta. Both retained their status as parishes (rather than the more usual situation of one church being made a mission of the other), but one pastor oversaw the two parishes. St. James in Minerva remained a mission of St. James in Brooksville but without weekly Sunday Mass. Rev. Daniel Saner served as the first pastor in the two-parish arrangement, with the assistance of Deacon Ernie Hillenmeyer.

"Augusta, Brooksville to Share Pastor," *Messenger*, May 8, 1998, 1.

"Bracken County Parish Has Rich 125-Year History," *Messenger*, August 6, 1993, 10–11.

Ryan, Paul E. *History of the Diocese of Covington, Kentucky.* Covington, Ky.: Diocese of Covington, 1954.

Tenkotte, Paul A., David E. Schroeder, and Thomas S. Ward. *To Be Catholic and American in Northern, Central, and Appalachian Kentucky: The Diocese of Covington, 1853–2003.* Forthcoming.

Thomas S. Ward

ST. JOHN, VINCENT (b. July 6, 1876, Newport, Ky.; d. June 21, 1929, San Francisco, Calif.). Vincent St. John, a socialist and a labor leader, was the only surviving son of New York native Silas St. John and Irish immigrant Marian "Mary" Cecilia Magee. By 1888 the family had moved to the West, where Silas abandoned his wife and children, forcing 13-year-old Vincent to work to help his mother and sisters survive. When he was 17, he started a career in the mining industry, becoming deeply involved in the labor movement as a member of the Western Federation of Miners (WFM). In 1900, at age 24, he was elected president of the WFM's Telluride, Colo., Local 63. A year later he led a successful strike against the Smuggler-Union Mining Company for its recently implemented wage system that reduced miners' wages to starvation levels. However, before the strike had come to a conclusion, hired strikebreakers shot at union pickets, causing a riot at the mine. St. John was instrumental in quelling the riot. His friends called him "Saint" or "the Saint." A man of integrity who inspired hundreds to join the union, St. John was persecuted the rest of his life by the mining corporations. He endured several attempts on his life, numerous arrests, and illegal incarcerations in Colorado, Idaho, and Nevada.

Because of persecution, St. John quietly went to Idaho and worked under an alias in 1905–1906; he was unable to attend the founding meeting of the Industrial Workers of the World (IWW) in Chicago in 1905. He joined the IWW, or "Wobblies" (as the members were later called), for the first convention and soon became an organizer. In 1907 he was instrumental in the successful organization of Goldfield, Nev.: the entire town was unionized, from the paperboys on up. Nevada industrialists were alarmed at St. John's ability to attract large numbers of workers to the radical IWW. They threatened to lynch him, vilified him in the press, and publicly suggested that someone should shoot him. In 1907 an assassination attempt resulted in permanent serious damage to his right arm. He recovered and, at the end of that year, was elected general secretary of the IWW, its highest position. The Wobblies, whose motto is "An injury to one is an injury to all," were steered away from political action during St. John's tenure (1908–1914). Advocating "direct action" and "industrial democracy," he led the union during the height of its most successful strikes. The IWW waged campaigns for free speech, living wages, the rights of workers, and the end of child labor.

Owing to its antiwar views, the union was targeted by the U.S. Government in 1917. Although St. John had retired in 1915 from the "one Big Union," as it was called, and was mining in New Mexico, he was arrested during the sweeping government raids on IWW offices across the country. With hundreds of others, he was convicted under the Espionage Act, despite the lack of evidence. Imprisoned at Leavenworth in 1918, he served only a portion of his 10-year sentence but contracted tuberculosis while in prison. In 1923 President Warren G. Harding freed him and many other political prisoners, which included hundreds of Wobblies, Socialists, and military conscientious objectors. Upon his release, St. John attempted mining in the hills of Arizona, yet his health was shattered. In 1928 he moved to California, where his sisters lived. He died of a cerebral hemorrhage June 21, 1929, at St. Francis Hospital in San Francisco, having spent his last years in relative anonymity. He was buried in Mountain View Cemetery in Oakland, Calif., without a marker; but in 1992 a group of Bay Area labor activists gained permission to place a memorial at "the Saint's" final resting place. The simple red-granite stone honored his lifelong commitment to the cause of labor.

"Attacks Labor Leaders: Western Federation Officer Calls Mitchell and Gompers Traitors," *NYT,* August 4, 1907, C5.

California Death Certificate No. 34491, for the year 1929.

"Inner Circle Man Tells of Arrests," *KP,* July 30, 1907, 3.

Martin, MaryJoy. *The Corpse on Boomerang Road: Telluride's War on Labor, 1899–1908.* Montrose, Colo.: Western Reflections, 2004.

Reis, Jim. "Union Trailblazer Once Called Newport Home," *KP,* September 1, 2003, 3K.

St. John, Vincent. *The I.W.W.—Its History, Structure, and Methods.* Chicago, 1911.

"Vincent St. John: Associate of 'Big Bill' Haywood Dies in San Francisco," *NYT,* June 24, 1929, 16.

"Vincent St. John, I.W.W. Aide, Dies," *San Francisco Examiner,* June 23, 1929, 16.

Patrick M. Flannery and MaryJoy Martin

ST. JOHN CATHOLIC CHURCH. The original Roman Catholic St. John Church was at the corner of Leonard and Worth Sts. in the Lewisburg neighborhood of Covington. The cornerstone for the church, an offspring of the **Mother of God** parish, was laid on Palm Sunday, April 8, 1854. The solemn dedication took place December 27, 1854, at the feast of St. John the Evangelist. The establishment of St. John Church predated the founding of the Diocese of Covington (see **Roman Catholics**). It was the third Catholic church in Covington, the other two being Mother of God and the St. Mary Cathedral Parish (now the **Cathedral Basilica of the Assumption**). The first pastor of the St. John Catholic Church was Rev. Joseph Gezowsky, who had been an assistant pastor at Mother of God. The first school building, a frame structure, was begun on the site of the church in 1849; the second school building, a brick structure, was built in 1861.

In 1909 Rev. Anthony Goebel became the pastor of St. John Catholic Church. By this time, the school and church on Leonard and Worth Sts. needed repair so badly that they were in jeopardy of being condemned as unsafe. On Labor Day 1913, ground was broken for the new church at the present-day site of the school, in Covington along Pike St. Construction moved quickly, and the new combination church-school, designed by architect J. F. Sheblessey, was dedicated on December 27, 1914, 60 years to the day after the first dedication. This new church building became the present school building. It contained the church, the rectory, the convent, and a school accommodating 400 students. Mass was celebrated in the auditorium, which seated 600 people.

In 1922 ground was broken for a new church adjacent to the combination church and school. Designed by Frank Ludewig and Henry Dreisoerner of St. Louis, Mo., it was dedicated on Thanksgiving Day, November 27, 1924, and remains in use today. Goebel remained pastor of St. John Catholic Church until his death on January 6, 1954. His nephew, Rev. Henry Hanses, whom he had helped to raise, was named the next pastor of St. John on January 18, 1954. Hanses remained pastor until 1971, when he retired to **Carmel Manor**, Fort Thomas. Hanses died on January 19, 1982.

In 1945 St. John Catholic Church had more than 2,500 registered parishioners. By 2000 that number had fallen to fewer than 300. The biggest impact on the parish was the building of I-75, which eliminated many nearby homes. Yet the parish has survived. St. John School, which became known as Prince of Peace School in 1986, serves the parishes of St. John, St. Ann, **Saints Boniface and James**, and Mother of God.

Hartman, Ralph C. *Fr. Henry Hanses—How Handsome before the Lord: A Brief Diary of a Kentucky Mountain Missioner.* Covington, Ky.: Katherine Landwehr, 2000.

Ryan, Paul E. *History of the Diocese of Covington, Kentucky.* Covington, Ky.: Diocese of Covington, 1954.

Schmitz, Raymond A. *St. John's Catholic Church, Covington, Kentucky, 1854–2004: 150 Years.* Covington, Ky.: T and W, 2006.

Tenkotte, Paul A., David E. Schroeder, and Thomas S. Ward. *To Be Catholic and American in Northern, Central, and Appalachian Kentucky: The Diocese of Covington, 1853–2003.* Forthcoming.

Nancy Due Bloemer

ST. JOHN CEMETERY, FORT MITCHELL. The St. John Cemetery is a Roman Catholic Cemetery in Fort Mitchell that was opened by the **St. John Catholic Church** of Covington in 1867. The St. John Catholic Church, the third Catholic congregation established in Covington, is now located on Pike St. in Covington, although it was first located at the corner of Leonard and Worth Sts. Andreas Michel, the pastor at the church, arranged to purchase a tract of land to the west of the **Covington and Lexington Turnpike** (**Dixie Highway**) in early 1867, recognizing the need for a cemetery for the parish. The parish held a consecration ceremony on May 19, 1867, but burials had already begun before that date. An older man, name unknown, was buried sometime that spring, and his grave was marked only by a large wooden cross. On April 19, 1867, Anna Borgelt was buried. These first two interments were later moved. According to Diocese of Covington records (see **Roman Catholics**), the church did not take title to the land until 1869. Use of the cemetery began slowly, with few burials before 1870.

During the last several decades of the 19th century, the St. John Catholic Church made improvements and landscaping changes at the cemetery. For example, William Tappert (1873–1879) oversaw the construction of a permanent road system and significant landscape improvements. The cemetery is designed with winding, narrow lanes and natural landscaping in the rural style. Sometime during this period, A. M. Meyer, pastor of the St. Boniface Church (see **Saints Boniface and James Catholic Church**) in Ludlow, built a frame chapel dedicated to the "Comforter of the Afflicted" (the Virgin Mary). In the late 19th century, additional changes were made near the entrance to the cemetery.

The ownership of the St. John Cemetery was transferred in the 1960s to the Diocese of Covington Cemetery System. In 1968 the diocese dedicated a new chapel to replace the original frame building. A small mausoleum for aboveground interments has been added since. The cemetery retains its rural landscape character although it is surrounded by residential development today.

"Consecration of a Cemetery," *CE,* May 20, 1867, 3.

"Memorial Day Stirs Interest in Civil War," *KP,* May 26, 1986, 4K.

Reis, Jim. "Cemeteries," *KP,* April 21, 1986, 4K.

Tenkotte, Paul A., David E. Schroeder, and Thomas S. Ward. *To Be Catholic and American in Northern, Central, and Appalachian Kentucky: The Diocese of Covington, 1853–2003.* Forthcoming.

Jeannine Kreinbrink

ST. JOHN LUTHERAN CHURCH. Early in the 19th century, many German immigrants came down the Ohio River by flatboat from Pittsburgh, Pa., and a number of them settled along the river near what are now Melbourne and Camp Springs in Campbell Co. To serve their spiritual needs, a Lutheran missionary, Rev. Christian Dingeldey, came to the area in 1860. He began holding church services in a schoolhouse on the John Weidinger farm. In 1861, Dingledey organized St. John's Church as a German Evangelical Protestant Church. The congregation built a stone house of worship in 1866, similar to the many other stone buildings that they were constructing at Camp Springs. The land for the church was donated by Peter and Catherine Schreier and was located next to a cemetery that dated back to 1847. After the church was completed, the cemetery became known as the St. John Cemetery. In 1879 the church acquired additional land adjoining its property and built a parsonage and a school that the congregation operated for about 11 years. In 1903 the parsonage was torn down and a new frame one built on the site. The stone church was renovated in 1917 by installing new furniture and stained-glass windows. For the first 53 years of its existence, St. John Church's services were held in German, but in 1914, worship in English was begun. Between 1860 and 1912, the church had 21 pastors, all supplied by the German Evangelical Protestant Church organization.

In 1922 the members of St. John Church decided to leave the German Evangelical fellowship and unite with the Evangelical Lutheran Church; the name subsequently became St. John Lutheran Church. That move permitted them to hire their own pastors and therefore to choose pastors more compatible with their beliefs. The first pastor hired under the new affiliation was Rev. Clemens Schirmer, who remained for eight years. From 1922 to 1992, the church had six pastors, with Rev. Otto Emmelhainz serving for about 35 of those years. Emmelhainz also spent many years teaching at **Campbell Co. High School**. When he died in 1991, he was buried in St. John Cemetery.

Extensive remodeling and repairs were done to the church in 1933. Before the church's centennial in 1961, further improvements were made to the facilities. The following year, a Sunday school addition was attached to the side of the church. After serving the needs of the congregation for more than 95 years, the old stone church was torn down in 1962 and was replaced by a beautiful modern brick and glass sanctuary with a seating capacity of 250. Today, the church has many outreach programs, including summer camp, a vacation Bible school, quilting classes, a visitation program for the sick and elderly, and a food pantry. In a recent year, the congregation sent 25,000 pounds of food to the needy in McCreary Co., Ky. The present pastor is Rev. Phillip Garber, who is a 1994 divinity graduate of Trinity Lutheran Seminary in Columbus, Ohio. The congregation is a member of the Evangelical Lutheran Church in America (ELCA).

100th Anniversary, 1861–1961: St. John Evangelical Lutheran Church, Melbourne, Kentucky. Melbourne, Ky.: St. John Evangelical Lutheran Church, 1961.

Waltmann, Henry G. *History of the Indiana-Kentucky Synod of the Lutheran Church in America*. Indianapolis, Ind.: Central, 1971.

ST. JOHN MISSION. Since the 1850s, Roman Catholics have worshipped at St. John Mission, Dividing Ridge, in northwestern Pendleton Co. The mission is located along Ky. Rt. 457 within the Portland community, an area first settled by Irish Catholic immigrants. The present church building was completed in 1882. The congregation is small, and since 1912 it has been a mission of St. William parish in Williamstown. It was in that year that Rev. James J. Taaffee, a popular priest who had served at St. John Mission for 18 years, was transferred to Williamstown. After he died, Taaffee was buried in the St. John Mission Cemetery. In recent years, there has been a slow growth in attendance at the mission of St. John.

Meiman, Karen. "Church's Community Spirit," *KP*, August 12, 2000, 6K.

Ryan, Paul E. *History of the Diocese of Covington, Kentucky*. Covington, Ky.: Diocese of Covington, 1954.

Tenkotte, Paul A., David E. Schroeder, and Thomas S. Ward. *To Be Catholic and American in Northern, Central, and Appalachian Kentucky: The Diocese of Covington, 1853–2003*. Forthcoming.

Mildred Belew

ST. JOHN'S COMMUNITY CHURCH. This architecturally significant church, built of stone, is located at 1411 St. John's Ln., formerly the Licking Pk., in Wilder. Founded in about 1876 by 24 German families in the Poole's Creek area of Campbell Co. near the Licking River, the church was originally known as St. John's German Protestant Church. The stone church building, dedicated in June 1877, included a room that was originally used for a public school. The church's first minister was Rev. August Mueller. In about 1925 the congregation became known as St. John's Evangelical Congregational Church, and in 1957, when the Evangelical and Reformed Church and the Congregational Christian Church merged to form the United Church of Christ, it adopted the name St. John's United Church of Christ. During the pastorate of Rev. Edward C. Sinning (1951–1969), an educational building containing six classrooms and an assembly room was added to the rear of the church, as well as a new covered entrance to the front of the church. In May 1975 the church officially terminated its ties with the United Church of Christ and became St. John's Community Church. Beginning in 1990, Bonny and George Kees operated a private religious school called Churchill Academy in the educational wing of the building; the academy moved and was renamed in the early 21st century. In 2008 the small congregation was still holding a Sunday worship service.

Reis, Jim. "St. John's Homecoming: Church Marks 120 Years, Faces Uncertain Future," *KP*, September 25, 1995, 4K.

Paul A. Tenkotte

ST. JOHN'S UNITED CHURCH OF CHRIST. On April 26, 1847, a group of 31 German families met to organize a church in Newport. They wanted to worship in their own language and according to their religious traditions, but they did not wish to continue traveling to the Over-the-Rhine section of Cincinnati to do so. This group organized the First German Protestant Evangelical Church in Newport. On May 20, 1847, they purchased a lot at 139 Rickey St. (now Dayton St.) in Newport from Gen. **James Taylor**. Taylor donated another parcel to the church. Construction was completed and the new church was dedicated in December 1847. The congregation's first regular pastor was Fredrich Boettcher, who served from June 1848 until June 1849, when he died of cholera. On June 7, 1857, the members of the congregation purchased property at Seventh and Mayo (now Columbia) Sts. in Newport and built a church there that they dedicated on January 30, 1859. In 1860 a pipe organ was installed in the balcony, and in 1861 a Sunday school program was initiated. Children of the congregation learned German at a daily school conducted by the church. At this time, there were no public schools in Newport. In 1863 the church's school had 200 pupils; it operated until 1873. In 1874 the congregation decided to change its name to First Evangelical Protestant St. John's Church of Newport, removing *German* from the name of the church. At the same time they began to hold bilingual (English and German) worship services.

On December 21, 1892, a number of members left the church to form St. Paul's Evangelical Church (see **St. Paul United Church of Christ, Fort Thomas**). Around 1924, another group of the congregation departed and formed a church known as St. Mark's German Lutheran Church. In 1957 the worldwide United Church of Christ was formed in Cleveland, a merger of evangelical and reformed congregations, and St. John's changed its name.

St. John's United Church of Christ has had a strong commitment to social issues; for a long time it has supported the **Campbell Co. Protestant Orphans Home**, which now is located in rural Campbell Co. along **Washington Trace Rd.** Harold Barkhau was installed as the 21st pastor of St. John's on April 2, 1933. During his pastorate, the congregation grew from 300 to 1,454 members. Barkhau was also the chairman of the Committee of 500 (see **Newport Reform Groups**) during the reform movement that cleaned up vice in Newport during late 1950s and early 1960s. On January 10, 1939, a fire of undetermined origin destroyed the church building. The only item salvaged was one stained-glass window, which was reinstalled in the current church. Having decided to move away from the city's flood area, the congregation obtained a lot in the eastern part of the city at Park Ave. and Nelson Pl., which was known as the Col. Henry Nelson homestead. Until their new church building was completed, the church met at the **Newport High School**, on Eighth St., for almost two years. On Sunday, April 21, 1940, the new structure was dedicated. Ten years later, a Christian education building was added. William Schraer was elected to serve as a full-time director of Christian Education, and he faithfully served in that capacity for 33 years.

"90th Anniversary Celebration of Evangelical Church Planned as Tribute to Pioneer Germans," *KP*, April 23, 1937, 1.

Reis, Jim. "Church Owes Much to Rev. Barkau," *KP*, April 7, 1997, 4K.

———. "Through Fire, Name Changes, St. John's Survived," *KP*, April 7, 1997, 4K.

Souvenir of Ninetieth Anniversary Celebration, 1847–1937: St. John's Evangelical Protestant Church (Congregational), Newport, Kentucky. Newport, Ky.: H. Otto, 1937.

Donald E. Grosenbach

ST. JOHN THE BAPTIST CATHOLIC CHURCH. The St. John the Baptist Catholic Church had an early beginning as one of several churches created to serve the needs of German Catholics in rural Campbell Co. The German Catholic settlers of the John's Hill vicinity sought to have a priest in their community. In 1847 they built a small log church at the top of John's Hill (a small, gated St. John's Cemetery still remains) that was then attended as a station by the priests of **Corpus Christi Catholic Church** in Newport. Rev. John Voll celebrated Mass there every fourth Sunday of the month. The log church burned down in 1857 after being struck by lightning, so the congregation began to plan for a new church. The Diocese of Covington (see **Roman Catholics**) offered land next to St. Joseph Cemetery on John's Hill Rd. in Wilder. The modest stone two-story structure was completed the following year and dedicated under the patronage of St. John the Baptist by bishop of Covington George A. Carrell on November 25, 1858. The first floor was used as a school and the second as the church.

The rather remote location of the new site allowed St. John Parish to avoid being swallowed up by the development in southern Campbell Co. during the latter 20th century. But the parish did grow. The first resident pastor, Rev. Anthony Athmann, arrived in 1877. In 1891 the church was forced to revert briefly to its former mission status, again attached to the Corpus Christi Catholic Church, owing apparently to a shortage of priests. St. John the Baptist Catholic Church had Mass only twice a month during this mission period. A new pastor for the church was appointed in 1894.

The education of children in the parish was at first provided by the parish itself, but in 1909 the **Sisters of Notre Dame** were engaged to teach in the parish school, which remained in the 1858 building until the mid-1960s. At that time the parish bought a bar and dancehall near the church property and converted it into a school. In 1980 the school was closed because there were too few students in attendance. Afterward, the school was used as a home for four young women of the Children of God community who provided music for St. John's Sunday liturgies.

The 1858 St. John the Baptist Catholic Church on John's Hill Rd. remains to this day the oldest church building standing in the Diocese of Covington. The rectory next to it was built in 1907. The church building survived in part because the **Great Depression** scuttled plans to build a new one. Today, the church retains the atmosphere of a rural church, even though it is encircled by a rapidly expanding suburban area that is just barely out of view behind woods and hills.

125th Anniversary of Dedication of the Present Church Building, 1983. Wilder, Ky.: St. John the Baptist Catholic Church, 1983.

Reis, Jim. "Rural Church Untouched by Nearby City," *KP*, November 22, 1982, 4K.

Ryan, Paul E. ***History of the Diocese of Covington, Kentucky.*** Covington, Ky.: Diocese of Covington, 1954.

St. John Centennial booklet, 1858–1958, St. John the Baptist Catholic Church, Wilder, Ky.

Tenkotte, Paul A., David E. Schroeder, and Thomas S. Ward. *To Be Catholic and American in Northern, Central, and Appalachian Kentucky: The Diocese of Covington, 1853–2003.* Forthcoming.

Thomas S. Ward

ST. JOHN THE EVANGELIST ANGLICAN CATHOLIC CHURCH. Established during the early 1870s by Episcopalians living in Bellevue and Dayton, Ky., this church has, since 1978, served as the parish church of Anglican Catholics from southwestern Ohio and southeastern Indiana, as well as Northern Kentucky. The church was founded as a mission of **St. Paul's Episcopal Church** in Newport. After being granted full parish status by the Episcopal Diocese of Lexington in 1873, its members built two churches. One of them, consecrated in 1899, was erected at Eighth and O'Fallon Aves. Because this location is the dividing line between Bellevue and Dayton, and since the growing congregation was composed of residents of both communities, the church became known as St. John Episcopal Church, Bellevue-Dayton. A parish hall was added to the original building in 1924, and the church's first rectory, on nearby Ward Ave. in Bellevue, was purchased during the 1940s.

During the 1950s, Rev. Eugene Lefebvre introduced an Anglo-Catholic influence that has been a hallmark of the church ever since. Among the traditional, or high-church, practices that were adopted were the celebration of the Holy Eucharist every Sunday, the creation of a Tabernacle on the main altar, and the use of holy water fonts.

Like many inner-city churches, this church was confronted by the challenge of suburbanization in the post–**World War II** years, as longtime members moved to new communities in Campbell and Kenton counties. Despite the distances involved, many of these families continued to attend the St. John church, especially during the rectorship of Rev. John Philip Storck, from 1963 to 1976. The church maintained a thriving Sunday school, directed by Wesley Branch, a teenage youth group, and an adult fellowship organization called Manawi.

A critical phase in the church's history began with the tenure of Rev. James Bjorkman, who was the rector from 1976 until 1982. During this period, the national Episcopal Church underwent dramatic changes that, in the view of church traditionalists, constituted a fundamental departure from the Anglican Communion's Catholic heritage. In the mid-1970s a crisis in the Episcopal Church erupted over two issues: the ordination of women to the priesthood and a radical revision of the Book of Common Prayer. In a nearly unanimous vote held early in 1978, the St. John church's congregation severed its ties with the Episcopal Church and was officially received into the Anglican Catholic Church. There ensued a 10-year court battle with the Episcopal Diocese of Lexington for control of the parish's property and assets. Although this upheaval led to the departure of a few members, most of the local church's parishioners remained. In the midst of this situation, Rev. William Neuroth was named rector in June 1983. A Northern Kentucky native, he had been previously ordained as a **Roman Catholic** priest in the Diocese of Covington.

The church's protracted court battle with the Episcopal Diocese of Lexington was finally settled in October 1988, when the Supreme Court of Kentucky unanimously decided to grant all properties and assets to the present members of the church. Following that victory, the church undertook a series of projects that had been delayed, pending the court's decision. A complete renovation and creation of four Sunday school rooms took place in the parish hall in 1990; a new front porch and handicap ramp were constructed later in the decade; and a state-of-the-art electronic organ was purchased in 1996. The following year, the church purchased and demolished the structure on the adjoining property and created a church garden, where members of the community as well as members of the church may find a place for reflection.

In the early 21st century, the congregation at St. John the Evangelist Anglican Catholic Church was thriving with approximately 125 members. The 1928 Book of Common Prayer and the 1940 Hymnal continue to guide the church in its worship, and it is a leading parish in the Anglican Catholic Diocese of the Midwest. Its members also are involved in a variety of activities that benefit the wider community, including a Thanksgiving and Christmas meals program for low-income families in Dayton and the making of handcrafted quilts for drug-addicted infants born at **St. Luke Hospital** in Fort Thomas and Children's Hospital in Cincinnati.

Reis, Jim. "'Spirited' and 'Spiritual' Define St. John's in Dayton," *KP*, May 25, 1998, 4K.

William C. Neuroth

ST. JOHN THE EVANGELIST CATHOLIC CHURCH. Before the Diocese of Covington (see **Roman Catholics**) was established in 1853, the town of Carrollton, on the Ohio River, was part of the Diocese of Louisville. Catholics in Carrollton asked the diocese to provide the services of a priest. In 1850 Franciscan Rev. Leander Streber came from Louisville to offer Mass once a month in the home of Catholic layman Henry Grobmeyer. Streber helped the people prepare to build a church. Bishop Martin John Spalding of Louisville presided at the laying of the cornerstone for the new church in Carrollton on July 30, 1853, the day after the creation of the new Diocese of Covington was decreed in Rome. Carroll Co., where Carrollton is located, was the western limit of the diocese. When the church was finished, it was dedicated to St. John the Evangelist. Bishop George A. Carrell, Covington's first bishop, appointed Rev. Charles Schaffroth as St. John's first pastor in 1855. Because Schaffroth celebrated Mass only once a month, the bishop approved a layman, Anthony Rudolphy, to read the Gospel in German for the mostly German congregation and to lead the saying of the Rosary on the other Sundays.

The Sisters of St. Francis of Oldenburg, Ind., arrived in 1863 to staff the small brick parish school. When these sisters were recalled by their congregation, Bishop Augustus M. Toebbe replaced them with **Sisters of Notre Dame** who had left Germany during the anti-Catholic Kulturkampf of the 1870s.

The parish grew significantly during its first half century. By the early 20th century, the congregation planned to build a large red-brick Gothic-style church, designed by Leon Coquard, who also was the architect of Covington's **Cathedral Basilica of the Assumption**. The parish trustees promptly began to raise funds, and the cornerstone was laid on October 5, 1902, while Rev. Ignatius Ahmann was pastor. He continued construction of the church, as funds were made available, until the exterior was complete in 1907. But construction had to be suspended at that point until more funding could be secured. The parishioners and pastors did all they could to reduce expenses for the parish as work resumed at a slow pace. Bishop Ferdinand Brossart dedicated the new St. John Church on June 25, 1916.

By the late 1950s, the old school had deteriorated and a new one was clearly needed. Bishop William Mulloy wanted Pastor John T. Walsh to build a large enough school to accommodate future growth, and a $100,000 school and convent were built. However, by the late 1960s school enrollment was dropping as young adults were leaving the community for urban areas. This factor, coupled with a decreased number of sisters available to teach in Catholic schools, prompted the closing of St. John School in 1973.

Ahmann, Ignatius Mary. *Forget-Me-Nots of Past and Present.* Carrollton, Ky.: Ignatius Ahmann 1902.

Bishop William Mulloy to Fr. John Walsh, September 14, 1957, Archives of the Diocese of Covington, Covington, Ky.

Grant, Frederick Stanhope. "Golden Jubilee Celebration of St. John," *CC*, September 28, 1902, 21.

"Pastor Plans New Buildings at Carrollton," *Messenger*, January 18, 1959, 16A.

Ryan, Paul E. *History of the Diocese of Covington, Kentucky.* Covington Ky.: Diocese of Covington, 1954.

Tenkotte, Paul A., David E. Schroeder, and Thomas S. Ward. *To Be Catholic and American in Northern, Central, and Appalachian Kentucky: The Diocese of Covington, 1853–2003.* Forthcoming.

Thomas S. Ward

ST. JOHN UNITED CHURCH OF CHRIST. On September 12, 1887, a small group of local residents held a meeting in a tailor shop at 77 Ross Ave. to organize what became the St. John Evangelical Protestant Church of Bellevue. The group began holding German-language services in a rented room at the Balke Opera House at Fairfield and Berry Aves. Early in 1888, representatives of the church met with members of the St. Paul Evangelical Church in Dayton, Ky., at which time it was decided to hire one pastor to serve both congregations. The churches selected a man named Gerber to serve in that capacity. Several months later, the Bellevue church purchased two lots on Foote Ave., where the congregation planned to build their first house of worship. Construction began in 1890, and the building was completed and dedicated on February 8, 1891. During the next 30 years, 11 different pastors served the congregation. St. John purchased a parsonage at 234 Foote Ave. in 1915. The church had grown to a membership of 327 by 1921.

Property was acquired on the southwest corner of Fairfield and Ward Aves. in 1932, where a new, larger church was built at a cost of $63,500. In 1934 the Evangelical Synod of North America and the Reformed Church of the United States merged, so the church name was changed to the Evangelical and Reformed Church of Bellevue. It retained that name until 1957, when the Congregational Christian Church and the Evangelical and Reformed Church merged, resulting in yet another name change, this time to the St. John United Church of Christ of Bellevue.

Until mid-1964 the church thrived. It held two Sunday morning services and had a vibrant music program, a Women's Guild, a Quilting Group, adult and youth fellowship meetings, and a women's evening circle. The church also sponsored several bowling teams. However, about that time, church membership began to decline, as the "flight to the suburbs" began. In 1964 the church started holding a Lenten Quiet Hour and, shortly thereafter, an annual Easter Breakfast, both of which became quite popular. In 1997 Pastor Eriksen began a computer training class called "GHN—Geeks, Helping Nerds," where interested individuals could learn to operate a computer. When Eriksen resigned as pastor in 1999, a party was given in his honor on Super Bowl Sunday, which later developed into an annual event known as the Souper Bowl. Funds raised at that affair were used to help support local soup kitchens. St. John also formed a partnership with the **Prince of Peace Lutheran Church** in helping to collect grocery items for the Bellevue Food Pantry. Rev. Keith Haithcock, from Dayton, Ohio, became the interim pastor of St. John United Church of Christ in 1999 and was installed as its 18th permanent pastor on February 25, 2001. Under his leadership, the church encouraged diversity in the congregation and opened its doors to a broader spectrum of society. Haithcock continues as pastor of the church.

"Church of the Week," *KP*, July 29, 2004, 8K.

St. John United Church of Christ. "History." www.stjohnchurch.net (accessed June 6, 2007).

ST. JOSEPH CATHOLIC CHURCH, CAMP SPRINGS. The early 1840s witnessed the first influx of German Roman Catholic settlers into a region of Campbell Co. known as Four Mile Creek (later called Camp Springs), about 12 miles south of Newport. The settlers' closest Catholic church was Holy Trinity Church, across the Ohio River in Cincinnati; attending there involved making a difficult journey mostly on foot or by horse. Priests from Holy Trinity Church occasionally visited the small community at Four Mile Creek. By 1844, Rev. Charles Boeswald, stationed first in Covington and later in Newport, was ministering to the community. At the instigation of Boeswald, the Camp Springs community began to plan for a church, and in 1846 they built a small log church in Camp Springs dedicated to St. Joseph. At first, St. Joseph Catholic Church was a mission of **Corpus Christi Catholic Church** in Newport, visited monthly or semimonthly by priests of that parish.

In 1851 members of the community petitioned Bishop Martin John Spalding of the Diocese of Louisville, of which most of Northern Kentucky was then a part, to provide the St. Joseph Church with a resident pastor. The bishop appointed Rev. John Voll, who soon started a small parish school in another log cabin built for that purpose. But in 1853, Voll was transferred to Corpus Christi Catholic Church, and St. Joseph Catholic Church reverted to mission status.

The Diocese of Covington (see **Roman Catholics**) was established in 1853. By then, the congregation at St. Joseph Catholic Church had grown from a few parishioners to 65 families. In 1855 Covington's first bishop, George A. Carrell, deemed St. Joseph Parish to be ready for a resident pastor again, and he appointed Rev. Andrew Schweiger. By the end of the 1850s, St. Joseph Parish was serving an extensive area of Campbell Co. St. Joseph proved to be the mother parish of many other Campbell Co. parishes, most of which became larger than it. In 1863 Pastor Lawrence Spitzelberger determined that a larger church building was warranted. The task of building it was left to his successor, Rev. Eberhard Schulte, who oversaw the completion of a Roman-style structure and its dedication by Bishop Carrell on June 15, 1865. A new school was added in 1868 and an addition to the church in 1888. In 1890 the **Sisters of Divine Providence**, who had just arrived in the diocese the year before, took charge of the school. Rev. Joseph Haustermann faced strong opposition from parishioners in the 1890s when he wanted to move the church to a new location; instead, a separate parish, St. Philip, in Melbourne, was split off in 1910. Rev. Charles Woeste became the St. Joseph Church pastor in 1909. During his tenure, the church acquired three large oil paintings by artist **Leon Lippert**, which remain in the sanctuary of the church.

In the 21st century, St. Joseph continues as a parish, one of the oldest in the Diocese of Covington, though it no longer has a resident priest as pastor. The parish continues to operate its school, though the Sisters of Divine Providence left in 1978. The school is the longest-operating Catholic school in the Diocese of Covington.

Bach, Jean. "Through 150 years, Some Things about St. Joseph, Camp Springs, Haven't Changed," *Messenger*, July 7, 1995, 12–13.

Doyle, Patrick A. "Catholicism in Campbell County," *Messenger*, December 16, 1973, 12A (*Our Sunday Visitor* supplement).

Ryan, Paul E. *History of the Diocese of Covington, Kentucky.* Covington, Ky.: Diocese of Covington, 1954.

Tenkotte, Paul A., David E. Schroeder, and Thomas S. Ward. *To Be Catholic and American in Northern,*

Central, and Appalachian Kentucky: The Diocese of Covington, 1853–2003. Forthcoming.

Thomas S. Ward

ST. JOSEPH CATHOLIC CHURCH, COLD SPRING. The St. Joseph Orphanage (currently the site of the **Disabled American Veterans**; see **Diocesan Catholic Children's Home**), was founded in 1869 on Alexandria Pike and predates the Catholic parish established in Cold Spring in Campbell Co., by one year; it seems likely that the parish itself developed out of the orphanage. On land adjacent to the orphanage, a small frame church was built in 1870 and dedicated by Covington bishop Augustus M. Toebbe. The parish soon started a school, which was staffed by the Brothers of Mary from Dayton, Ohio. The Sisters of Notre Dame replaced the brothers in 1877. By the 1880s, St. Joseph Parish was ready to build a more substantial church. Rev. Herman Kramer, appointed pastor in 1881, oversaw the construction of a brick church; a site near the church provided clay for the bricks, which were baked in a kiln on the church premises. Toebbe came to dedicate the new church on October 8, 1881.

The St. Joseph Parish built new schools as it outgrew its previous ones. The original frame school building was replaced in 1892 with a two-story one. This school served the needs of the parish's children until a more modern brick building was constructed in 1929 on land purchased a quarter mile south of the church itself, not far from St. Joseph Orphanage. After **World War II**, a new subdivision called Vets Village was created to offer housing to returning veterans. This signaled the beginning of an era of uninterrupted growth for Cold Spring, with a corresponding need for more classroom space for the increasing number of Catholic children. Under Pastor Lawrence Leinhauser, the parish built a new, larger school near the spot where the 1929 school stood. Bishop **William T. Mulloy** dedicated this structure on May 14, 1951. Before long, extra classrooms had to be added.

The same demographic exigencies that demanded more classroom space also figured into Leinhauser's decision to build a new church. He wanted to build the church on the same location as the school so that children would not need to hike down busy **U.S. 27** to go from school to the church. Mulloy approved a new contemporary church, which was not completed until after his death in 1959. Bishop Richard H. Ackerman dedicated the new St. Joseph Catholic Church on April 9, 1961. A new parish hall was built at the back of the church in the early 1980s. St. Joseph continues to grow along with suburban development, so that at the beginning of the 21st century, it is one of the largest parishes in the Diocese of Covington (see **Roman Catholics**).

Dedication Booklet of St. Joseph Church, April 9, 1961. Cold Spring, Ky.: St. Joseph Catholic Church, 1961.

Dedication Booklet of St. Joseph School, May 14, 1951. Cold Spring, Ky.: St. Joseph Catholic Church, 1951.

Rev. Lawrence Leinhauser to Bishop William T. Mulloy, December 29, 1957, Archives of the Diocese of Covington, Covington, Ky.

Ryan, Paul E. *History of the Diocese of Covington, Kentucky.* Covington, Ky.: Diocese of Covington, 1954.

"Vision Crowd Small but Fervent," *KP*, August 31, 1992, 1K–2K.

Thomas S. Ward

ST. JOSEPH CATHOLIC CHURCH, COVINGTON. The parish of St. Joseph in Covington was established in 1853, the same year the Diocese of Covington was founded (see **Roman Catholics**). The southeastern section of Covington was largely German, and the 80 families who showed interest in the church were all recent immigrants who had moved into an area of Covington known as Helentown. In 1854 ground was broken for a new church at the northwest corner of 12th and Greenup Sts., designed by Anthony Piket and Son (see **Louis Piket**). Construction was halted, however, for lack of funds. Eventually a much smaller combination church and school were dedicated. In 1855 Bishop George Carrell was so short of German-speaking priests that he was unable to supply the parish with a full-time pastor. He approached the Very Reverend Boniface Wimmer, abbot of St. Vincent Monastery, in Latrobe, Pa., to take charge of the new St. Joseph parish, and the Benedictine order agreed to staff the congregation. The Romanesque St. Joseph Church building, surmounted by a 128-foot tower, was blessed by Bishop Carrell in 1859. The church's massive reredos altars, dedicated in 1865, were the work of the **Covington Altar Stock Building Company**, and murals in the church were painted by **Johann Schmitt**. Benedictine Sisters from Erie, Pa., were invited to take over the parish grade school. Men lay teachers were hired to teach the older boys. A three-story building was constructed on 12th St. for use as a boys' school.

The parish council decided to invest in some moneymaking ventures, with mixed results. The real estate investments turned out to be a mistake, and the subsequent financial panic of 1880 saddled the church with a heavy debt. The pastor at the time, Aegidius Christoph, managed to save the parish by tight budgeting. He replaced the lay teachers with the Brothers of Mary, a Catholic religious order from Dayton, Ohio. In 1915 a devastating tornado struck the church and dropped the church tower into the middle of Greenup St. It was rebuilt with the design of **Samuel Hannaford and Sons**, with a giant clock added, by Christmas Day 1915.

The parish purchased lots along Scott St. from 12th St. to Bush St. for construction of a new school, which opened in September 1927. The church was renovated in 1952, and its new Permastone outside coating gave it a distinguished appearance. But by then the number of families in the parish had dropped to 325. The membership continued to decline during the next decade, and by the mid-1960s the parish was merged with the **St. Benedict Catholic Church**. The newly decorated St. Joseph Church was demolished in 1970.

"Growth of Covington," *CJ*, September 10, 1959, 2.

Reis, Jim. "Saint Joseph Church," *KP*, December 11, 1995, 4K.

Ryan, Paul E. *History of the Diocese of Covington, Kentucky.* Covington, Ky.: Diocese of Covington, 1954.

Tenkotte, Paul A., David E. Schroeder, and Thomas S. Ward. *To Be Catholic and American in Northern, Central, and Appalachian Kentucky: The Diocese of Covington, 1853–2003.* Forthcoming.

Joseph F. Gastright

ST. JOSEPH CATHOLIC CHURCH, CRESCENT SPRINGS. One of the largest suburban Roman Catholic churches in Northern Kentucky, St. Joseph was established in 1916 in Crescent Springs, then a "railroad" suburb along the **Cincinnati Southern**. After **World War II**, the parish grew substantially, especially following the opening of I-75 in 1963, bringing new suburban development to Crescent Springs, as well as to the neighboring suburb of Villa Hills (incorporated in 1962). Architect Charles Hildreth designed a new brick school, completed in 1952, for the parish and also a contemporary church and rectory, dedicated in 1962. Growing school enrollment led the congregation to remodel parts of the old church and school for its elementary classes, to construct a second floor for the new school building in 1976, to build a 10-classroom addition to the school in 1986, and to add 10,000 square feet to the school and 4,000 square feet to the church in 1995.

Tenkotte, Paul A., David E. Schroeder, and Thomas S. Ward. *To Be Catholic and American in Northern, Central, and Appalachian Kentucky: The Diocese of Covington, 1853–2003.* Forthcoming.

Paul A. Tenkotte

ST. JOSEPH CATHOLIC CHURCH, WARSAW. In the early 19th century, Catholics in Warsaw in Gallatin Co. could attend the infrequent masses offered in private homes by priests from St. Francis Mission in White Sulphur, the oldest church (1794) in what later became the Diocese of Covington (see **Roman Catholics**), or from St. Mary Cathedral Parish in Covington (see **Cathedral Basilica of the Assumption**). Not long after the establishment of the Covington diocese in 1853, Bishop George A. Carrell started the St. John the Evangelist Catholic Church in Carrollton, down the Ohio River from Warsaw, and Warsaw became one of its stations (a station was a congregation without a church or a pastor). Although services in Warsaw became more frequent, local Catholics still wanted their own church. In 1868 they built a small brick church that they dedicated to St. Joseph. It became a mission of St. John the Evangelist Church in Carrollton at that time, though later it was transferred to the care of the St. Patrick Parish, which was created in Verona in 1878.

The population of Warsaw grew slowly in the post–**Civil War** 19th century. Yet by the turn of the century, the parish priests in the surrounding areas supported St. Joseph Church's claim that Warsaw should have parish status. The Catholics in Warsaw took the optimistic step of purchasing a house near the church in the hope that it would serve as a rectory. Rev. Edward Donnelly, pastor of St. Patrick Church, asked Bishop **Camillus P. Maes** to make St. Joseph Church a parish and St. Patrick Church its mission, reversing their current status. On March 11, 1904, Maes appointed Donnelly as the first resident pastor of St. Joseph Church. The church underwent some remodeling in the 1920s during the pastorate of Hubert Schmitz, especially after the structure was damaged in a fire. Because of its relatively small population, the parish at Warsaw did not build a school.

In 1962 St. Edward Mission was created in Owenton and attached to St. Joseph Parish. The parish population in Warsaw and Gallatin Co. grew during the 1980s and 1990s. Because of recreational amenities for boating and fishing in the region, St. Joseph Church experienced fairly large gatherings for Sunday masses that strained its seating capacity. It was time for a new church, and Pastor George Schumacher started a fund drive in 2000. The plan utilized part of the old structure, including a bell tower built in 1920. Bishop Roger J. Foys dedicated the new structure on November 10, 2002.

Ruschman, Albert. *The Church in the Smallest County: History of Gallatin County and the Catholic Church*, Warsaw, Ky.: Self-published, 1967.

Ryan, Paul E. *History of the Diocese of Covington, Kentucky*. Covington, Ky.: Diocese of Covington, 1954.

"St. Joseph, Warsaw—Celebrating New Church Symbolizing New Growth," *Messenger*, November 15, 2002, 11.

Tenkotte, Paul A., David E. Schroeder, and Thomas S. Ward. *To Be Catholic and American in Northern, Central, and Appalachian Kentucky: The Diocese of Covington, 1853–2003*. Forthcoming.

"Towering above Warsaw," *Messenger*, February 15, 2002, 3.

Thomas S. Ward

ST. LUKE EVANGELICAL LUTHERAN CHURCH. Several Northern Kentucky Lutheran churches sent members to canvass the Cold Spring area in November 1950, in anticipation of starting a new Lutheran work in central Campbell Co. Because of that outreach, some of the persons contacted began holding services in the Cold Spring School gymnasium. St. Luke Evangelical Lutheran Church was officially organized as a United Lutheran Church in America (ULCA) Synod congregation on November 8, 1953, with 63 adults and 36 children listed as charter members. The organizational meeting was officiated by synod president Dr. Gerard D. Busch and Dr. A. M. Knudsen of the Board of American Missions. During that early period, Rev. George Derrick, Rev. Charles Masheck, and Rev. Day B. Werts assisted in directing the activities of the new congregation. The church also received some financial program support from the synod in its early years. St. Luke continued to hold services in the Cold Spring School gymnasium for about 10 years.

The first pastor was Rev. Frank L. Barcus, who stayed for two years. During his tenure a parsonage was purchased at 24 Terrace Ave., in nearby Crestview. The second pastor was Rev. Bernard W. Crocker, who served for about 15 months. During his term, the church purchased 1.33 acres of land at 3917 Alexandria Pk. (**U.S. 27**), on which they planned to build their first house of worship. After Crocker resigned, St. Luke was without a regular pastor for about a year. At such times, a succession of seminary students often filled the pulpit. The next pastor was Rev. John W. Kerrick, who led the congregation for about seven years. During his tenure, the church purchased an additional .66 acre of land adjoining their property. He also instituted a building program and had plans drawn for the proposed church. Ground was broken for the new edifice on May 15, 1960, and it was completed and dedicated on February 12, 1961. The facility had a sanctuary with a seating capacity of 130, a kitchen, an office, and several meeting rooms and was built at a cost of $96,500.

St. Luke joined the Indiana-Kentucky Synod of the Lutheran Church of America in 1963 and soon became a self-supporting congregation. Membership as of December 31, 1970, was 192 baptized, 119 confirmed, and 115 communing.

In 1996 the church purchased a 12-acre tract on U.S. 27, about a mile and a half south of their building, at a cost of $167,000, and opened a new, larger edifice on that site in 2008. The present pastor is Rev. Anne R. Benson, who is a graduate of the University of Kentucky and Trinity Lutheran Seminary. The congregation is a member of the Evangelical Lutheran Church in America (ELCA).

"Church Anniversary," *KP*, November 8, 2003, B6.

"Churches Welcome Pastors," *KP*, June 24, 1995, 9K.

Waltmann, Henry G., ed. *History of the Indiana-Kentucky Synod*. Indianapolis, Ind.: Central, 1971.

ST. LUKE HOSPITALS INC. The St. Luke Hospital of Campbell Co., at 85 N. Grand Ave. in Fort Thomas, began with a $1 million bond issue passed by the citizens of the county on November 2, 1948. Under the leadership of board chairman Daniel D. Schwartz, board member Dr. Ervin G. Heiselman, and hospital administrator R. Arthur Carvolth, the building was dedicated on a warm Sunday afternoon in July 1954. The new structure, built on a portion of the former Gaddis family's estate, had 128 beds on three floors and featured state-of-the-art equipment, including oxygen piped into each room. When additional space was needed, citizens again passed a bond issue, so that in 1963 two more floors were added to the structure and the number of hospital beds was increased to 201. The location, on the boundary line between Newport and Fort Thomas, was a compromise between what were the two most populated cities in the county; the present site of the **Newport Shopping Center** had been previously considered as a site for the hospital.

John Hoyle became assistant administrator in 1968. Hoyle later replaced Carvolth and served as the hospital's administrator until he retired in 1997. A well-conceived and practiced disaster plan was already in place at St. Luke Hospital when the nearby **Beverly Hills Supper Club** in Southgate caught fire on May 28, 1977. The hospital and its staff went into action immediately, working around the clock to treat the 75 injured persons admitted to the hospital. Off-duty personnel responded to aid families of the injured and to help at the temporary morgue set up in the Fort Thomas armory gymnasium. The situation received worldwide attention, and the hospital was praised for its efficient response.

In 1980 the Pendleton Co. Hospital (28 beds) at 512 Maple Ave., in Falmouth was purchased by St. Luke Hospital, which, with this transaction, became St. Luke Hospitals. The Falmouth facility was converted into an inpatient alcohol and drug treatment center. St. Luke Hospitals next purchased the **Booth Memorial Hospital** (177 beds) at 7380 Turfway Rd. in Florence, Ky., from the **Salvation Army** in 1989. The purchase price of $23.9 million was financed through the sale of revenue bonds. The newly acquired hospital was named St. Luke Hospital West, making it part of St. Luke Hospitals Inc., under one management. Over the years, St. Luke Hospitals Inc. has continued to add other facilities: the Pediatrics Center, at 103 Landmark Dr. in Bellevue; the Sports Health and Wellness Center, at 5874 Veterans Way in Burlington; a hospital laundry; an ambulance service; three other medical facilities; and a partnership in three MRI centers. In 1995 St. Luke Hospitals Inc. became part of the Health Alliance of Greater Cincinnati, which also includes the Christ Hospital, the University Hospital, the Jewish Hospital, the Fort Hamilton Hospital, and Alliance Primary Care.

The St. Luke Community Foundation, a nonprofit support organization, began with a resolution from the Hospital Board of Directors in December 1983. The first meeting of the St. Luke Community Board of Directors was held in February 1984. The foundation raises funds to help provide equipment and supplies for many hospital departments so that St. Luke Hospitals Inc. will remain on the cutting edge of technology and to serve Northern Kentucky communities with information for healthy living. Caring and concerned individuals and businesses support these efforts through donations, sponsorships, and special events.

Both the St. Luke East Hospital in Fort Thomas and St. Luke West in Florence have introduced a number of medical firsts. In 1958 Northern Kentucky's first Regional Poison Information Center was opened by the St. Luke system and the first myocardial pacemaker was implanted. Fiber-optic instrument use in surgery, the single-channel blood analyzer, and the Coronary Care Unit were in place in St. Luke hospitals by 1970. St. Luke hospitals also introduced the region's first birthing suites, along with Kid Kare, a sick-child day care service; started the formal outpatient Cardiac Rehabilitation Program–Phase II and the Children's Advocacy Center; added the YAG Laser to the Argon and Cot Laser; and opened a joint-venture MRI technology site. Elderlife, the hospital system's senior membership program, was introduced with the advent of the Gerontology Unit and a Sleep Disorders Clinic in 1988. St. Luke hospitals sponsored a Disaster Medical Service Team for the U.S. Public Health Service in 1989 and now have a specially equipped Medvan on call for use in disasters. Moreover, the area's first Souter Strathcycle Elbow Replacement was introduced in 1990 by a St. Luke hospital. In 1991 the hospital system's first Hyperbaric Oxygen Center was opened and the first Diabetes Center was accredited. OccNet, the corporation's first hospital-based Industrial and Corporate Health Service, was opened in 1994. Pediatric Urgent Care for treatment after doctors' hours began in 1997. The tri-state area's first hospital-based Medical House Call program for seniors began in 2002. In 2003 St. Luke Hospitals Inc. began a procedure with Patients First Physicians Group to use the M2A Capsule Endoscope for certain small intestinal disorders. In 2004 its west facility opened the Vascular Institute of Northern Kentucky, the Outpatient Adolescent Chemical Dependency Program, and the Tristate Surgical Weight Loss Center.

The full spectrum of hospital care now available for women throughout the region at St. Luke hospitals includes the Center for Breast Health, Birthing Centers, the Perinatal Center, the Center for Diabetes and High-Risk Pregnancy, the Center for Reproductive Health, the Physicians for Women OB/Gyn care, and the nationally recognized Women's Heart Advantage program. Because 90 percent of the women in Northern Kentucky are at risk for a heart attack, this vital program at St. Luke hospitals offers education, screenings, and prevention opportunities.

In 2004 the St. Luke Hospitals Inc. had 515 licensed beds, 659 physicians treating 275,000 patients annually, and more than 1,100 full-time staff members as it celebrated 50 years of quality medical care. The emergency rooms of St. Luke Hospital East, which is close to I-471 and I-275, and St. Luke Hospital West, near I-71–I-75, treat some 70,000 patients annually. Among the specialized departments administered by St. Luke Hospitals Inc. are the Anticoagulation Clinic, the Burlington Pharmacy Health Care, the Cardinal Hill Long Term Acute Care Facility, the Health Ministries, the Hospital-Based House Call Program, the Mental Health Program, the Midwife Program, the Northern Kentucky Cancer Treatment Center, the Nutrimed Weight Loss Center, Orthopedic Programs, Radiology Treatment, Reproductive Health Treatment, the Skilled Nursing Center, the Adolescent OB/Gyn Center, and the Wound Treatment Center. As of 2008, St. Luke Hospitals was negotiating a withdrawal from the Health Alliance of Greater Cincinnati and a merger with **St. Elizabeth Medical Center.**

"Booth Price—$23.9 Million," *KP*, June 14, 1989, 1K.
"Hospital 'Defend in Place' Disaster Strategy Self-Contained," *SC*, October 23, 2005, 2A.
Kingsbury, Gilbert, Sr. "Booth Hospital—From War Camp to Hospital," *Boone County Recorder*, June 7, 1979, 18.
"St. Luke Celebrating 50th Anniversary," *KP*, May 27, 2004, 5K.
The St. Luke Hospitals: The History, 1954–2004, Celebrating 50 Years of Serving Northern Kentucky. Fort Thomas, Ky.: St. Luke Hospitals, 2004.
"St. Luke—The Hospital Is Where It Is Today Because So Many People Helped," *KP*, October 21, 1985, 4K.
"St. Luke Tower Is Complete," *KP*, July 6, 1984, 1K.

Betty Maddox Daniels

ST. MARK LUTHERAN CHURCH. In 1894, 28 people who had been members of St. John's United Church of Christ in Newport relocated to a building at Seventh and Orchard Sts. and adopted the name Independent Martini Evangelical Protestant Church. When the Vesper Printing Company purchased the property where the church was located, the congregation moved temporarily to Seventh and York Sts. on property owned by Charles Wiedemann, president of the George **Wiedemann Brewing Company**. Later, the members purchased property at Eighth and Monroe Sts. in Newport, where the church now stands. On October 20, 1897, the St. Mark Evangelical Lutheran Church of Newport was officially organized.

Architect John Banderman was hired to design and oversee construction of a Victorian Gothic edifice at a cost of $15,000. It was built 30 feet by 60 feet, two stories high, with an attic. The south tower has a pyramidal roof, an east tower has a conical roof, and the southeast bell tower is over a double-door main entrance with a stained-glass transom. Because of economic hardships experienced by the church, no bell was ever purchased for the tower. The original sanctuary had curved pews with two aisles, and a manually powered pump organ.

Falling into unmanageable debt, the church sought help as a Lutheran congregation and was admitted to the Miami Synod of the General Synod in 1898. Rev. Frank C. Longaker was the first called pastor. By 1905, there were 189 communicant members and the church was self-supporting. Rev. H. W. Hanshue succeeded Longaker at that time. In 1907, 12 women of the congregation founded the Women's Missionary Society. Pastor Lewis J. Motschman served for seven years beginning in 1912 and helped the church reduce its debt despite the disruption of **World War I**. Rev. Cornelius J. Kiefer assumed pastoral duties in 1919 and served until his death in 1927. During his tenure the church eliminated its original debt, built a parsonage at 730 Park Ave. for $8,500, and also completed renovations for $25,000; the construction projects were dedicated on May 27, 1927.

Rev. David M. Funk guided St. Mark's during the **Great Depression** and the early months of **World War II**, until 1942. In 1934, Funk was elected as the first secretary of the newly formed Kentucky-Tennessee Synod, while also conducting an aggressive evangelism program, which brought many new members to St. Mark's. From late 1942 until early 1963, there was a succession of six pastors, including Rev. Day B. Werts, a former military chaplain, who served for six years. For many years during the 1950s and 1960s, St. Mark's Church was home to a very popular weekly teenage dance, or "canteen." In 1963 St. Mark's was assigned to the new Indiana-Kentucky Synod and became involved in the Board of American Missions urban church program in 1969.

As many members moved to the suburbs in the 1960s and after, attendance fell. To help solve this problem, St. Mark and Trinity Lutheran in Bellevue merged their congregations in 1978 and changed their name to **Prince of Peace Lutheran Church**. The Newport location was to be vacated and combined services were to be held in Bellevue. Within a short time, friction developed between the two groups, especially over a decision to sell the Newport church building. As a result of this dispute, the merger was rescinded. Newport members reopened St. Mark Church, and the Bellevue church continued using the new name, Prince of Peace Lutheran Church.

In 1981 the Commonwealth of Kentucky designated the St. Mark Church building a historic landmark. St. Mark Evangelical Lutheran Church celebrated its 100th anniversary in 1997.

St. Mark Lutheran Church Records, Newport, Ky.
Waltmann, Henry G., ed. *History of the Indiana-Kentucky Synod*. Indianapolis, Ind.: Central, 1971.

Melinda G. Motley

ST. MARY CEMETERY. St. Mary Parish in Covington, established in 1837 as an English-speaking parish, later became the cathedral parish of the Diocese of Covington. In 1850 the parish bought 10 acres of land outside the city limits for a cemetery. St. Mary Cemetery was originally located near what is now the **Behringer-Crawford Museum** in **Devou Park**. Because of the poor roads accessing the cemetery and the inability of poorer parishioners to purchase plots, few persons were interred in the cemetery; the last burial took place in 1864. Bishop **Camillus P. Maes** sold this cemetery to the Devou family in 1900 and moved the graves to the newer St. Mary Cemetery. In addition to the 10 acres in what became Devou Park, the diocese in 1857 filed a plat for a new cemetery of 168 lots, called "St. Mary's Burying Ground" and located on Prospect St. in Covington; it is not known whether any interments were made there.

The current St. Mary Cemetery on **Dixie Highway** began in 1870 with the purchase of 41 acres adjacent to **Highland Cemetery**. Maes did what he could to improve the new cemetery, having a fence erected between it and Highland Cemetery and building a sexton's house on the grounds. But the cemetery was not self-sustaining. Its plots sold for considerably less than those in Highland Cemetery.

In 1968 Bishop Richard H. Ackerman established the Cemetery Office for the Diocese of Covington. St. Mary Cemetery was the first cemetery to be placed under the new office as a diocesan cemetery rather than a parish cemetery. When the old cathedral along Eighth St. in Covington was torn down in 1904, the bodies of former bishops George Carrell and Augustus Toebbe, which had been buried beneath the floor, were removed and re-interred at St. Mary Cemetery. Since then, all of the deceased bishops of Covington have been buried at St. Mary Cemetery, with the exception of Bishop Ferdinand Brossart, who was buried at St. Anne Convent in Melbourne, where he spent his final years in retirement.

Gorey, James L. "Letter to Patrons of St. Mary's Cemetery," June 11, 1907. Archives, Diocese of Covington, Covington, Ky.

Ryan, Paul E. *History of the Diocese of Covington, Kentucky.* Covington, Ky.: Diocese of Covington, 1954.

Tenkotte, Paul A., David E. Schroeder, and Thomas S. Ward. *To Be Catholic and American in Northern, Central, and Appalachian Kentucky: The Diocese of Covington, 1853–2003.* Forthcoming.

Trauth, Mary Philip. Unpublished sketch of the History of the Cemetery Office, 1985, Archives, Diocese of Covington, Covington, Ky.

Thomas S. Ward

ST. MARY OF THE ASSUMPTION CATHOLIC CHURCH. The first Catholic church in southern Campbell Co. was **St. Joseph Catholic Church** at Camp Springs (Four Mile). Priests of this small parish served the congregation of Catholics in Alexandria, who gathered there to form a station (a congregation without a church) of the St. Joseph Church. In 1860 the congregation of about 30 families bought four acres of land fronting Jefferson St. after Rev. Lawrence Spitzelberger, pastor of the St. Joseph Church, convinced Bishop George A. Carrell that Alexandria should have a church of its own. Members of the congregation at Alexandria subscribed $700 and quickly built a church. Spitzelberger dedicated the church on November 25, 1860, in honor of the Assumption of the Blessed Virgin Mary. The St. Mary of the Assumption Church was now elevated to the status of a mission of the St. Joseph Church. Then the St. Mary Church became an independent parish after the congregation bought a house to serve as a rectory and Carrell appointed Rev. D. Beck as its first pastor in 1865. The new parish built its first school in 1867 and began building a second school in 1875, and the **Sisters of Notre Dame** came to staff it the following year.

By the time the parish celebrated its silver jubilee, parishioners were ready to build another church. Under Rev. Herbert Thien, a new brick church was erected. Rev. Ferdinand Brossart, vicar general of the Diocese of Covington and future bishop, dedicated it on October 25, 1891. A new rectory was built in 1928 and a parish hall in 1935. During the long pastorate of Rev. Francis DeJaco (1932–1966), the parish in 1949 purchased a nearby public school. The renovated building became home to a parish high school that opened in 1950. The St. Mary parish high school was converted into a diocesan program in 1961 and renamed **Bishop Brossart High School**. A new parish grade school opened in 1963.

Suburban growth brought great changes to Alexandria and the St. Mary of the Assumption Parish in the second half of the 20th century. Near the end of Msgr. Otto Hering's term (1968–1981) as pastor, the means for building a larger church became available when in 1978 a $220,000 estate was given to St. Mary of the Assumption Parish. The parish raised additional money through a fund drive and bought property west of the school for the new church; it also had a new road, St. Mary Dr., built to provide access from Main St. A modern design by the local firm of Robert Ehmet Hayes and Associates was chosen, and groundbreaking occurred in 1982, soon after Rev. Joseph Boschert became pastor. The modern church structure was dedicated on December 11, 1983.

Church of St. Mary of the Assumption, Alexandria, Kentucky: A Story of Faith, booklet printed for centenary of the church, 1960.

Dedication Booklet of St. Mary Church of the Assumption, December 11, 1983.

Historical Sketch of St. Mary Church, Alexandria, Kentucky, booklet printed for Diamond Jubilee Celebration, 1935.

Ryan, Paul E. *History of the Diocese of Covington, Kentucky.* Covington, Ky.: Diocese of Covington, 1954.

Tenkotte, Paul A., David E. Schroeder, and Thomas S. Ward. *To Be Catholic and American in Northern, Central, and Appalachian Kentucky: The Diocese of Covington, 1853–2003,* Forthcoming.

Thomas S. Ward

ST. PATRICK CATHOLIC CHURCH, COVINGTON. Formerly one of the largest Irish American Catholic churches in Northern Kentucky, the architecturally significant St. Patrick Church stood at the northwest corner of Philadelphia and Elm Sts. in Covington's **West Side**, only blocks from the German-speaking **St. Aloysius Catholic Church**. Founded in 1870, the congregation completed an impressive church building in 1872, designed by noted local architect **Louis Piket**. The church opened an elementary school in 1876, which was housed at first in the rectory and later in a two-story frame building constructed in 1891. In 1913 the parish completed a large brick school building, designed by architect **David Davis**, at the southwest corner of Fourth and Philadelphia Sts. In 1917 the exterior of the brick church was covered with an imitation stone finish, and in 1921 the interior was embellished with murals above the main altar by Charles Svendson and frescoing by Nino Passalaqua. In 1928 the congregation built a brick convent for the teaching sisters of the school (the Sisters of Charity).

Damaged extensively by the Ohio River **flood of 1937** and suffering from the financial exigencies of the **Great Depression**, the parish incurred indebtedness that finally was erased by 1946, under the direction of longtime pastor Rev. Thomas J. McCaffrey (pastor 1913–1957). However, the congregation could not overcome the effects of the 1963 opening of I-75 and its Fifth St. exit-entrance ramp, cutting a swath through the city's West End. More of the neighborhood disappeared in the city's unsuccessful urban renewal efforts. St. Patrick School closed at the end of the 1966–1967 academic year, as many West End residents were migrating to the suburbs, and the church itself held its solemn closing on Sunday, August 27, 1967. The congregation was merged with that of St. Aloysius Church. In October 1968 the church was demolished, making way for a gasoline station.

St. Patrick Catholic Church, Covington.

"Six North Kentucky Schools in Merger," *Messenger,* March 5, 1967, 1A.

Tenkotte, Paul A. *A Heritage of Art and Faith: Downtown Covington Churches.* Covington, Ky.: Kenton Co. Historical Society, 1986.

Tenkotte, Paul A., David E. Schroeder, and Thomas S. Ward. *To Be Catholic and American in Northern, Central, and Appalachian Kentucky: The Diocese of Covington, 1853–2003.* Forthcoming.

"Then There Will Be None," *KE,* October 4, 1968, 22.

Paul A. Tenkotte

ST. PATRICK CATHOLIC CHURCH, MAYSVILLE. St. Patrick Catholic Church in Maysville is located downtown on the corner of Limestone and Third Sts. The church marks its beginning as 1847, when the first permanent Catholic church building opened in Maysville. It was dedicated to St. Patrick, recognizing the Irish descent of most of its early members. Catholic worship in the community had begun much earlier, when the community was still called Limestone. Rev. Stephen Badin passed through Limestone (Maysville) in 1793, and he and others held services for Roman Catholics in Maysville and the nearby county seat of Washington over the next few decades. St. Francis Catholic Church in White Sulphur, west of Georgetown, was charged with the care of Catholics residing in the Maysville area.

In the 1840s several Catholic families, including the Browns, the McCarthys, the McLains, and the O'Neils, asked to have a resident priest appointed and a parish established in Maysville. The land for the first St. Patrick Church building, on Limestone St., was purchased by Rev. Edward McMahon, who had traveled from Lexington to minister to the Catholics of the area. That church, which faced Limestone St., was a sturdy structure in the Romanesque style with some pointed-arch features and a sanctuary on the second floor. John Joyce was the church's first pastor, serving from 1847 to 1852. In the 1880s, the German members of the parish petitioned for their own church and pastor. No separate German church was built, but some services continued to be conducted in German.

An important mission of St. Patrick Catholic Church is education. The parish's first parochial school held classes in the rectory of the church during the early 1860s. In 1864 the Visitation nuns accepted an invitation from Bishop George Carrell to come to Maysville to teach, and the **St. Francis de Sales Academy** was established for that purpose in an imposing structure located on Third St. The Visitation nuns ran this combination day and boarding school and the St. Patrick Girls School and also taught classes for boys in the church basement until 1899. The boarding school closed in that year. The Sisters of Loretto taught at the school operated by St. Patrick Catholic Church briefly, and then the Sisters of St. Francis of Clinton, Iowa, provided much of the instruction at the school from 1910 into the 1980s. From 1989 to 1995, the Sisters of St. Joseph the Worker provided the personnel that ran the school. From the 1970s onward, lay teachers carried out most of the instruction, and after 1995 there have been no sisters teaching at the school. The St. Patrick School is the only one in the Diocese of Covington supported by a single church that has a complete school system from preschool through high school. St. Patrick Catholic Church also provides religious instruction for those schoolchildren not enrolled in the parochial system.

The present St. Patrick Catholic Church, facing Third St. and running along Limestone St., is an impressive Gothic-style building in a cruciform shape with large stained-glass windows. It was built on the site of the previous church building during the pastorate of Rev. P. M. Jones. The initial architect was Leon Coquard, architect of Covington's **Cathedral Basilica of the Assumption**, but as in the case of the cathedral, Coquard became disenchanted with the diocese, and architect **David Davis** completed the plans for St. Patrick. The church was dedicated on June 26, 1910. The two large stained-glass windows feature St. Patrick along Limestone St. and St. Boniface on the other side of the building. The main altar, constructed in Austria, was a special feature of the sanctuary.

Rev. Leo B. Casey, who was pastor from 1941 to 1965, oversaw the construction of the church's new school building, designed by Howard McClorey of Cincinnati and completed in 1949. In 1956 the parish finished an addition to the school building, which was used by **St. Patrick High School**. Rev. Casey also decorated the church with Gothic motifs and oil paintings of the Evangelists and of St. Patrick. These paintings were the work of Leo Mirabile of Louisville in celebration of the centennial of the church in 1947. Mirabile's oil paintings were eliminated in fall 1972, and in spring 1973 remodeling removed the ornamentation and the original altars and communion rails. St. Patrick Catholic Church did not escape the scandal that began in the 1990s regarding abuse by priests. Some former associate pastors of the church were accused and, in the case of Earl Bierman, convicted of abuse that occurred while serving at the Maysville church.

During the pastorate of Rev. William Hinds (1996–2008), needed maintenance at the church provided the opportunity to remodel the sanctuary once again, and a recreated main altar based on the original one was installed. In addition to the work inside and outside St. Patrick Catholic Church, a new school addition nearly doubling the size of the St. Patrick School was built in 1999. Hinds oversaw the raising of the millions of dollars necessary for these projects.

St. Patrick Catholic Church is currently home to more than 600 Catholic families. Special ministries to Latino families (see **Latinos**) grew under Hinds, who conducted a Spanish-language mass weekly. The church's support of the school provides an educational alternative to the community. The St. Patrick Catholic Church Cemetery is located three miles south of the church, in the community of Washington.

Archives of the Diocese of Covington, Covington, Ky.

Ryan, Paul E. *History of the Diocese of Covington, Kentucky.* Covington, Ky.: Diocese of Covington, 1954.

St. Patrick's Church: 150 Years of Faith. Maysville, Ky.: St. Patrick Church, 1998.

John Klee

ST. PATRICK HIGH SCHOOL, MAYSVILLE. St. Patrick High School, located on the corner of Limestone and Fourth Sts. in downtown Maysville, has operated there since 1926. St. Patrick Catholic Church had supported education in Maysville since the 1860s, and a day and boarding school, **St. Francis de Sales Academy**, also in Maysville, served Catholic girls from 1864 until 1899. St. Patrick High School was an extension of a parochial school system established by the St. Patrick Catholic Church in 1902. Rev. P. M. Jones was the pastor who oversaw the expansion of the school's offerings into high school, and the Sisters of St. Francis of Clinton, Iowa, operated the school until 1988. From 1926 to 1995, the principal at the school was a religious or a priest.

The first high school class enrolled in 1926, and four years later three boys and six girls graduated. Since that time the high school has enrolled between 60 and 100 students annually. The high school shares a building with the other grades offered by the school. That school building was first constructed in 1948, and sizable additions were completed in 1956 and 1999. St. Patrick High School offers a complete program of study, although it is best known for its ability to prepare students for college. From its beginning in 1926 until the 1970s, the Sisters of St. Francis provided art, piano, voice, and other specialized training for students. Since fewer and fewer sisters have been available to teach at the school from the 1970s on, the high school has faced recurring financial challenges. On several occasions, particularly in the early 1980s, during the pastorate of Rev. Cyril Eviston, serious discussions were held about closing the high school. The school has attempted to maintain a balance of student accessibility, quality, and expenses. This challenge is somewhat unusual because St. Patrick High School is the only high school in the Diocese of Covington (see **Roman Catholics**) completely supported by a single parish. In the 1990s the high school began to enroll Latino students whose parents are migrants to the area (see **Latinos**). Nearly all students participate in extracurricular events, either academic or athletic.

Ryan, Paul E. *History of the Diocese of Covington, Kentucky.* Covington, Ky.: Diocese of Covington, 1954.

St. Patrick's Church—150 Years of Faith. Maysville, Ky.: St. Patrick Church, 1998.

John Klee

ST. PAUL A.M.E. CHURCH. The St. Paul African Methodist Episcopal (A.M.E.) Church of Newport was formed in 1901 and changed its name in 1914. An A.M.E. Church had existed in Newport since 1880, and on several occasions it was confused with the Colored Methodist Episcopal (C.M.E.) denomination, of which there was at least one congregation in Newport; however, there is a difference between the two denominations. In February 1880 the A.M.E. congregation, under the leadership of Rev. Henry Harris, dedicated the recently leased and repaired church previously pastored by Peter H. Jeffries, a Lutheran minister. The building was in Newport at the corner of Mayo St. and Central Ave. In April 1884, at the Kentucky Methodist conference held in Covington, Rev. H. G. Jenkins was appointed pastor of the A.M.E. Church in Newport.

In June 1901 a new A.M.E. church was dedicated in Newport along Saratoga St. The following year, the famous singing group African Missionary Singers was engaged by Rev. J. H. Clark, formerly of the Payne Theological Seminary, Wilberforce, Ohio, pastor at the A.M.E. church. The singers performed at the camp meeting held at Nelson Place in East Newport. In July Tanner's Chapel was the name first given to the A.M.E. church at 714 Saratoga St. In August Rev. J. W. Frazier, presiding elder of the Lexington district A.M.E. church, preached and served Communion at the Saratoga St. church. In September the church's annual festival was held at Memorial Hall next to the church.

In December 1905 the A.M.E. church negotiated to purchase the former **Corpus Christi Catholic Church** on Chestnut St. in Newport. The church had been abandoned for several years after the Catholics opened a new church in town at

Ninth and Isabella Sts. The A.M.E. congregation purchased the property for $2,000. Rev. J. R. Rooks, who had served as pastor of Tanner's Chapel for less than a year, was instrumental in this purchase, completed in January 1906; afterward the church building on Saratoga St. was abandoned. In April a large celebration and formal opening of the newly acquired church building was held, with Rev. J. W. Frazier in town again to deliver the sermon.

From 1908 to 1917, church services continued to be held at the A.M.E. church on Chestnut St. By 1914 the congregation's name had changed from Tanner's Chapel to St. Paul A.M.E. Church. By 1923 St. Paul A.M.E. Church had moved to 210 W. Seventh St. in Newport, and Rev. Elmer Reid was pastor. On October 4, 1925, at the Kentucky Conference of A.M.E. Churches held in Danville, Ky., Rev. D. C. Carter was made pastor of St. Paul A.M.E. Church. Carter died in 1926, and Rev. Edward J. McCoo was appointed his successor. In 1942 W. M. Mitchell served as pastor and from 1944 through 1946, Rev. J. L. Madison served. In the eight years between 1948 and 1954, various ministers attended to the spiritual needs of the congregation.

On Sunday evening, March 28, 1954, the Wright Gold musical ensemble from Cincinnati was brought by the St. Paul A.M.E. Church's current pastor, Eugene Russell, to perform. On October 14, 1959, the Kentucky Annual Conference of A.M.E. Churches held in Lexington appointed Rev. F. L. Durden as pastor at St. Paul A.M.E. Church. The following year, on October 16, at the same conference held again in Lexington, Rev. M. H. Johnson was appointed pastor at St. Paul and served until replaced in late 1963 by Rev. **Edgar L. Mack**.

Mack was one of the most active pastors within the local African American community. He helped organize and led the Northern Kentucky delegation from Boone, Campbell, and Kenton counties in the 1964 Civil Rights March on Frankfort. Rev. Martin Luther King Jr. and the legendary baseball player Jackie Robinson led an estimated 10,000 persons in the march. In 1971 Mack led a delegation of Northern Kentucky clergy to attend the funeral of Whitney M. Young Jr., a Kentucky native who had been executive director of the National Urban League. In 1983 Rev. R. Mitchell arrived at St. Paul A.M.E. Church as its last pastor. In the late 1980s, the church was dissolved owing to a lack of members. A vacant lot now occupies the space where the church once stood.

"Church Notes," *KSJ*, February 28, 1880, 1.
Covington and Newport City Directories, 1894.
"Freedom! Freedom! Freedom!" *KE*, March 6, 1964, 2.
"Kentucky Rites Set for Young," *KE*, March 16, 1971, 16.
"King Marched in Frankfort in 1964," *KP*, January 20, 2003, 4K.
"Newport News," *KTS*, August 25, 1902, 3.
"Sale Is Under Way; Old Corpus Christi Church Is to Become Africa M.E. Church," *KP*, December 6, 1905, 5.

Theodore H. H. Harris

ST. PAUL CATHOLIC CHURCH. During 2004 the St. Paul Catholic Church in Florence, Ky., celebrated its 130th anniversary. However, the first Catholic presence in Florence actually dates from nearly a quarter of a century before St. Paul Catholic Church was founded. A Catholic stonemason, Cornelius Ahern, volunteered his house in 1851 as a place where local Catholics could meet. Thomas Butler, the pastor at St. Mary Church in Covington, traveled to the Ahern house once every three weeks to celebrate Mass. In September 1855, construction began on a church building at Shelby and Center Sts. in Florence, with Ahern as the primary builder. Members of the **Know-Nothing** Party, a virulently anti-Catholic political group, tried to stop construction of the church, but various parishioners guarded the construction site during evenings. The church was dedicated in June 1856, and a Catholic mass was held once per month. The church was a mission church until Rev. Joseph Bent became its first resident priest in 1874. Bent also started a parish school and taught all of the classes.

St. Paul Catholic Church served a wide geographical area, including Elsmere, Independence, Verona, and Warsaw as well as Florence. In the early 1900s, the church had 47 families, 33 of them English-speaking and 14 German-speaking, for a total of 185 parishioners. A brick Gothic Revival church was completed in 1911 on the **Dixie Highway**, and the old frame church building was converted into a parish meeting hall. In 1921 a parish festival was held for the first time; the festival proved to be a popular annual event.

The parish school closed in 1913, but reopened in September 1923 with 25 students. Sister Mary Irene Schwartz, OSB, a member of St. Paul Catholic Church and the first parishioner to enter religious life, was the school's first principal. Sr. Irene, an excellent teacher, was so forceful a presence that she made the Ku Klux Klan back down from threats they had been making to other teachers. She served as the principal until 1935 and returned to serve the school again from 1964 to 1972. The Benedictine order provided the entire faculty for the new school in its early years, and 72 sisters worked for St. Paul's parish school over the years. Thirteen other nuns from the order succeeded Sr. Irene as school principals. By 1929 the school had 43 students, a number that remained constant over the next decade.

St. Paul Catholic Church's parish experienced a period of growth during the post–World War II period. For 30 years Msgr. Edward Carlin served as pastor, from 1940 until 1970. School enrollment increased, and a modern new school building was added to the original building in 1951. The church community and Carlin saw the need for the church to expand. Carlin was also a good, tightly focused financial manager. When money was needed for the new church, he was able to put down half of the cost before construction started by selling land that the church owned. The new church, dedicated on May 5, 1963, featured an assembly hall, five classrooms, and a hand-carved Italian crucifix, as well as a wooden ceiling and terrazzo floors. The old church building was demolished, and a plaza area was created in its place.

The St. Paul School also went through changes. The first lay teachers hired by the school were Helen Kiffmeyer, in 1958, and Rita Zint, in 1959. Additional lay teachers joined the faculty as the decade of the 1960s progressed. A school board was set up for the school during the mid-1960s.

St. Paul Catholic Church continued to grow in the 1970s, and so did the areas it served, as the new Florence Mall opened. The facilities of the parish grew also: a new addition was added to the school, which included a gymnasium, a cafeteria, and a kitchen. The school also doubled as a parish center, named for Msgr. Carlin, and was dedicated as such on November 2, 1980. The school continues to grow and flourish.

In 1987 Angie Adams was hired as St. Paul Catholic Church's first youth minister. The youth ministry grew steadily, and in 1991 it joined with **St. Henry Catholic Church** in Erlanger to form a combined prayer-centered youth group known as the Youth Knights. In 1992 the Youth Knights reached its peak membership, attracting close to 100 teenagers per week. For many years following, it was not uncommon to see 50 teenage youths inside the Carlin Center in Florence on Thursday nights. In 1989 a number of St. Paul Catholic Church parishioners joined the newly formed St. Timothy Catholic Church in Union but continued to send their children to St. Paul's School. St. Paul's parish, at that time, had 1,700 families.

Thomas Sacksteder became pastor of St. Paul's in January 2000. In August of that year, a new addition to the school was dedicated that added three classrooms and three meeting rooms.

Archives of the Diocese of Covington, Catholic Center, Erlanger, Ky.
Diamond Jubilee Celebration, St. Paul Church, Florence, Kentucky, 1856–1931. Covington, Ky.: Matt. J. Crolley, 1931.
St. Paul Parish Records, St. Paul Catholic Church, Florence, Ky., boxes 1, 2, 3, 5.

Rob Langenderfer

ST. PAUL CHRISTIAN CHURCH. On May 1, 1847, a small group of German Protestants met in Covington to form the St. Paul German Evangelical Church. Several weeks later, the group purchased a lot at 11th and Banklick Sts. in town for $150. A small frame house of worship was soon constructed on the lot, and their first service was held there on August 29, 1847. The church's first pastor was a local resident, Rev. Henry Christian Dolle; he conducted services in German. The new church was quite successful and within a few years outgrew its building. A large, impressive brick edifice was then built on the same site and was dedicated on April 26, 1868. Over the years, several additions were made to the building, and it served the needs of the congregation well for the next 100 years.

In 1923 the church purchased a parsonage in Covington at 1521 Holman St. for their pastor at the time, Rev. Philip Wiggerman. He served faithfully

St. Paul German Evangelical Church, 11th and Banklick Sts., Covington.

at the church for the next 35 years. When he resigned as pastor in December 1958, the parsonage was sold to him for a nominal sum. St. Paul joined the Evangelical Synod of North America in 1934 and changed its name to St. Paul Evangelical and Reformed Church. In 1957 the church affiliated itself with United Church of Christ. In 1959 a new parsonage was purchased at 23 Buttermilk Pk. in Lakeside Park, for $18,500.

By the 1960s, the neighborhood around the Covington church building had begun to decline and many of the members had moved away to the suburbs. In 1962 the congregation purchased a 7.2-acre site on Fort Henry Dr. in Lookout Heights (now Fort Wright), where they intended to build a new, modern church. In 1966 architects from William F. Brown and Associates of Newport drew plans for a new structure. Ground was broken on May 21, 1967, and the completed building was dedicated on October 28, 1968. The sanctuary, which has exposed-brick walls, can seat 350, and there is also a large fellowship hall. Plenty of parking space is available. By 1977 the active membership of the church was about 275. In December 1964 the parsonage on Buttermilk Pk. was sold, and the church began providing the pastor with a housing allowance, which permitted him to live anywhere he chose.

In 1998 the congregation withdrew from the United Church of Christ. It subsequently joined the Disciples of Christ and changed its name to St. Paul Christian Church.

Hundredth Anniversary, 1847–1947: St. Paul Evangelical Church, Covington, Kentucky. Covington, Ky.: St. Paul Evangelical Church, 1947.

Reis, Jim. "Northern Kentucky Protestant Churches," *KP*, August 11, 1986, 4K.

"St. Paul Burns Mortgage," *KP*, November 21, 1978, 8K.

"St. Paul Has Survived Plenty in 130 Years," *KP*, May 21, 1977, 6K.

ST. PAUL LUTHERAN CHURCH. The St. Paul Lutheran Church at Chatham in Bracken Co. traces its roots back to the last quarter of the 19th century when an itinerant minister, a Rev. Andes, traveled to one-room schoolhouses throughout the county. The people he served called a permanent minister, William Roper, and constructed a church near Locust Creek where Ky. Rt. 9 (the **AA Highway**), and the Augusta-Berlin Rd. intersect today. Twenty-seven families, primarily of German heritage, dedicated the building in 1884 as the First German Protestant Church. In about 1900, the church joined the Lutheran Joint Synod of Ohio with the name Trinity Evangelical Lutheran Church.

Under the pastorate of H. W. Foster, a new church building was built in the Chatham area near the parsonage. It was dedicated, along with a new name for the church, St. Paul Evangelical Lutheran Church, on December 23, 1928. By 1930, the "old" church building on the Augusta-Berlin Rd. had been sold and the congregation had joined the American Lutheran Church Synod.

Over the next 40 years, the St. Paul Lutheran Church's members not only made numerous changes and improvements to the building; they also altered the church's customs. One striking addition to the new church building was the stained-glass window at the front, depicting the Good Shepherd. Donations from the profits of the women members' egg sales helped to purchase it. Over the past 75 years, the women of the congregation have played important roles in the small church community. During preparations for the first service at the new St. Paul Lutheran Church, members broke with custom and agreed that men and women should no longer sit separately on opposite sides of the church, but should sit together during services. In 1999 the first woman member of the church council was named.

By the 1970s, St. Paul Lutheran Church was finding it difficult to keep a full-time pastor. It joined into an agreement with Trinity Lutheran Church in Maysville, whereby they share one pastor between the two parishes, an arrangement that has been successful in rural Mason and Bracken counties. St. Paul became a part of the Evangelical Lutheran Church in America in January 1988. The church celebrated its 125th anniversary in September, 2000. Many descendants of the families that established the church in 1875 continue as members today.

Bracken Co. Extension Homemakers. *History of Bracken County.* Bicentennial ed. Brooksville, Ky.: Bracken Co. Extension Homemakers, 2002.

Millie Bush

ST. PAUL'S EPISCOPAL CHURCH. Founded on Easter Sunday in 1844, St. Paul's Episcopal Church is located at the corner of Court and York Sts. in Newport. It is part of the Episcopal Diocese of Lexington. The present Gothic Revival church building, of stone construction with a soaring bell tower, was designed by J. R. Neff. Its cornerstone was laid in June 1871; the church was completed in August 1873, and a parish house was added in 1929. In 2005 St. Paul's Episcopal Church had about 90 members.

St. Paul's Episcopal Church was the place of worship for Newport's founding family, the Taylors. Col. **James Taylor Jr.** donated the land on which it was built. This is also where members of the prominent Wiedemann family attended church, and George Wiedemann Jr. was deeply involved there until his death at the young age of 35 in 1901. From this church many of Newport's leaders were buried, such as the lawyer Col. George Washington, in 1905; a son-in-law of Taylor, Col. **James Abert**; and Taylor's wife, Lucy Taylor. It was the first Episcopal church in the United States to have a vested choir, and when the Episcopal diocese of Lexington was formed in 1896, St. Paul's Episcopal Church in Newport was its largest congregation. For the past 35 years, it has been home to the St. Paul's Episcopal Church Child Care Center. The church also has provided a meeting place for Alcoholics Anonymous.

Over the years, St. Paul's Episcopal Church has been an important part of the vibrant Episcopal community in Northern Kentucky, consisting of St. Paul's, **Trinity Episcopal Church** in Covington, **St. Andrew's Episcopal Church** in Fort Thomas, and Grace Episcopal Church in Florence.

Barr, Frances Keller. *Ripe to the Harvest: History of the Episcopal Diocese of Lexington, 1895–1995.* Lexington, Ky.: Diocese of Lexington, 1995.

Kreimer, Peggy. "St. Paul's to Get Facelift," *KP*, May 21, 2001, 1K.

Swinford, Francis Keller, and Rebecca Smith Lee. *Great Elm Tree: Heritage of the Episcopal Diocese of Lexington.* Lexington, Ky.: Faith House Press, 1969.

John West

ST. PAUL'S UNITED CHURCH OF CHRIST. Opened in 1850, this church was originally located about 500 feet from the southeast corner of Jefferson and Main Sts. in Alexandria. The German Protestants who constructed the log meetinghouse also built a school and a parsonage on Greenup St. The first pastor was Rev. Sinnig, who helped the congregation petition the neighboring residents for money to build the church. The membership grew quickly, and in 1899 the Lydia Verein, or Ladies Guild, was established. The name was in German, as were all records and services held at the time. The transition into using English for the guild's name did not begin until 1909.

The church's membership increased to exceed the facility's capacity, so in 1900 a new building was constructed on the northwest corner of Main and Jefferson Sts. In 1906 a new parsonage and school building were constructed behind the church, and the old buildings were sold.

An argument between the pastor and the congregation over funds exploded in 1922 into a legal battle. The court fight was top local news for the months that it lasted, and a suspicious fire in 1923 destroyed all of the church's documents. Rev. Paul

Roediger, who was the pastor under scrutiny, eventually resigned, and after a time the church resumed normal activities.

St. Paul's Church had been an independent church, but in 1931 it joined the Evangelical Synod of North America. It was because of a subsequent series of mergers undergone by that body that the name of the church became St. Paul's United Church of Christ.

The church building of 1900 was remodeled during the early 1970s, and St. Paul's United Church of Christ still holds its services there. As of 2000 the church had approximately 375 members. The congregation continues to participate in various philanthropic activities; it works with the **Boy Scouts** and the **Girl Scouts**, and members volunteer to work at a local soup kitchen.

"Answer Filed in Church Litigation," *KTS*, March 22, 1923, 33.

Campbell Co. Historical Society. *Campbell County, Kentucky, 200 Years, 1794–1994*. Alexandria, Ky.: Campbell Co. Historical Society, 1994.

"Church of the Week," *KP*, September 16, 2004, 8K.

"17-Year Mission Seeks Volunteers—Church Members Hand Out Food," *KE*, June 13, 2005, 3B.

Elizabeth Comer Williams

ST. PAUL UNITED CHURCH OF CHRIST, DAYTON. The St. Paul United Church of Christ opened in 1863 so that Dayton, Ky., residents could attend services closer to home than Newport. The first church meetings were held at the home of Frank Tinneman, one of the three men who helped bring the church into being. Later, the meetings were moved to the public school, then to the Presbyterian Church on Third St. in Dayton. This site, rented for $25 a year, was used from 1863 to 1869.

In 1864 the congregation elected its first pastor, Carl Clausen, who served until 1880. That same year, the Ladies' Aid Society, also known as the Frauenverein, was organized. Construction began on a new church building along Third St. in 1868. This building was used until 1915, when a new church, needed to accommodate church growth, was built on nearby Fourth Ave.

The St. Paul Church joined the Evangelical Synod of North America in 1885, which merged with the Reformed Church in 1938, causing the local church's name to be changed to the St. Paul Evangelical and Reformed Church Dayton. In 1961 a denominational merger with the Congregational Christian Churches changed the church's name again to the current one, St. Paul United Church of Christ Dayton.

In 1993 the St. Paul United Church of Christ Dayton celebrated its 130th anniversary with many activities and church services. The current pastor, James Hill, who has served the church since 1990, reports that although the St. Paul Church continues with its services each week, the membership is struggling as people move away from Dayton.

DeVroomen, Sacha. "St. Paul's Marks 130th Anniversary," *KP*, October 30, 1993, 9K.

St. Paul United Church of Christ. *One-Hundredth Anniversary: October 6–13, 1963*. Dayton, Ky.: St. Paul United Church of Christ.

Elizabeth Comer Williams

ST. PAUL UNITED CHURCH OF CHRIST, FORT THOMAS. In 1862, 31 members of the St. John's Evangelical Protestant Church at Seventh and Columbia Sts. in Newport (see **St. John United Church of Christ**) left to form a new church. On December 27, 1862, they organized the St. Paul's German United Evangelical Protestant Church. The congregation acquired a vacant frame Methodist church in Newport at 24 E. Eighth St. as their new home and held their first service on February 3, 1863. A new pipe organ was purchased a few months later for $550. Later, they erected a parochial school building to instruct their children about their faith and to teach them the German language. This school was continued until public school education became available in Newport. By 1882 the congregation had built and dedicated a new church building at the same site. In 1884 a new pipe organ replaced the original organ, and in 1892, the church purchased a residence at 805 Monroe St. in Newport to be used as a parsonage.

The church celebrated its 50th anniversary on April 6, 1913. The church and parsonage were repainted, the organ was rebuilt and enlarged, and new art-glass windows were installed in the sanctuary. At that time the congregation numbered 550 families. The Bible school had an enrollment of 938 students, the choir had 30 members, the Ladies' Aid Society had 203 members, and the Young People Society had 80. In 1918 the word *German* was removed from the church's name, and German services were discontinued. One year later, after a peace between the United States and Germany had been signed, ending World War I, the German-language service was reintroduced on a monthly basis; beginning in 1942, it was held only once a year, on Good Friday, and then two years later it was eliminated entirely. The church became affiliated with the Evangelical Synod of North America in 1923. The church's steeple, which had been weakened during a storm in 1891, was removed in 1925. A new parsonage was purchased nearby at 801 Overton St. in Newport. On June 14, 1931, the church's present three-manual Kilgen organ, costing $9,000, was acquired. Along with other churches in Newport, St. Paul's assisted in aiding the homeless during the **flood of 1937**. Later that year, the church became an active partner in the development of Camp Sunshine for the underprivileged, located near Mentor in eastern Campbell Co. In 1943 St. Paul's Church merged with the Evangelical and Reformed Church. That was when St. Paul's joined with other Newport Protestant churches in organizing the **Week Day School of Religion**. In 1957 the congregation laid the cornerstone for a new building on 13 acres of property located half in Newport and half in Fort Thomas. Today, the church is positioned between Grand and Newman Aves., at 1 Churchill Dr. The property in Newport at 24 E. Eighth St. was sold and currently is used as a parking lot. In 1957, at the national level, the Evangelical and Reformed Church merged with the Congregational Christian Church to form the United Church of Christ. Thus, the name of the local church became St. Paul United Church of Christ.

United Church of Christ. "St. Paul United Church of Christ." www.uccwebsites.net/stpauluccftthomasky.html (accessed May, 2005).

Donald E. Grosenbach

ST. PETER LUTHERAN CHURCH. Located in the rural area known as Hunter's Bottom on Ky. Rt. 36 in Carroll Co., four miles from Milton (in Trimble Co.), this church can be traced to 1848, when the Detmer family moved down the Ohio River from Rising Sun, Ind., to Hunter's Bottom, Ky., and found John Obertate and other recent German immigrants living nearby in Carroll Co. The Hopewell Methodist Church gave permission for a Lutheran congregation to use their meetinghouse at Hunter's Bottom for Sunday afternoon services, and the congregation hired Rev. Mueller, pastor of the German Evangelical and Reform congregation that dated back to 1841 at Madison, Ind. When Hopewell Methodist moved its building to high ground at Locust in 1895, the German American community worshipped at the Hopewell School at Hunter's Bottom, and within a year the group purchased land and built a church adjacent to the Hopewell School. The building committee included Johann Obertödler (Obertate), C. Fred Thiemann, and Frank Thiemann.

The 1896 church constitution written under supervision of the committee—Friedrich Detmer, Heinrich Hotfil, and Karl Walkenhorst—declared the congregation at Hunter's Bottom to be an independent German Evangelical Protestant Church; it required that pastors preach in German and that the school teach children the German language. The church was completely congregational in structure; the pastor did not have voting privileges, and only males were official members. A three-person executive committee ran the church, with a new person elected to the committee each year. All decisions were made by congregational vote, usually after church on Sundays. In June 1928 a new constitution required church minutes to be written in English and church services to be held in English. It also extended the right to vote in congregational matters to women.

The original church building, constructed on a grassy knoll by members of the congregation, was funded by a $400 loan from Ernst Thiemann at 5 percent interest. Each month there was a slight surplus used for debt repayment. During the 1990 renovations, which required resetting the doors, it was discovered that there was no true square in the original building; all measurements in 1896 were apparently eyeballed. The church has a bell tower equipped with the original 1896 brass bell from Germany; the constitution required the sexton to toll the bell one hour before and again just before Sunday services; on the feast days of Christmas, Easter, Pentecost, and Whitsunday; and for funerals. The roof is slate, and the 33-foot-high interior ceiling has 12-inch decorative tin squares; the Gothic windows along both sides of the church had late Victorian tinted glass, which in the 1950s was changed to clear glass. One stained-glass window, still intact, was placed high above the altar, and a smaller round window was mounted above the entrance door. A deep balcony was constructed above the narthex. The original carved church pews were painted white with black trim in the 1990 renovation. Ornately carved 36-inch altar candlesticks came from Germany. The pulpit originally was deeply carved and raised high above and behind the altar. The high pulpit was lowered and the altar moved against the back wall in 1928. The original sanctuary had intricate Victorian sets of gaslight globe chandeliers suspended from the center rafter down the center aisle. A drawing from 1946 shows two rows of neo-Gothic electric cathedral lights suspended over the pews rather than the center aisle.

The church was built perpendicular to the Ohio River and now lies close to Ky. Rt. 36; however, the original Hunter's Bottom turnpike hugged the Ohio River bank several hundred yards away. During the **flood of 1937**, the water rose to the eaves of the church and did extensive damage to the building; the congregation restored the building and furnishings by 1940. The **flood of 1997** reached the top of the steps leading into the sanctuary. The basement of the education building also flooded that year. Through a grant from the Evangelical Lutheran Church in America, St. Peter Lutheran Church underwent a major restoration in 1990.

The original church cemetery was located on the farm of August Raker. In 1931 a cemetery association was established, with grounds on the hill above the church. Graves were moved from the Raker farm to the new site, and in the 1940s the cemetery association became an independent community group.

Although the congregation received most of its pastors from the Indiana Synod of the United Lutheran Church in America (ULCA), St. Peter maintained its independence until June 1956, when it joined the Kentucky-Tennessee Synod of the ULCA as the St. Peter Evangelical Lutheran Church of Hunter's Bottom. In April of that year, the new education building was dedicated. And in 1958 the congregation adopted the Lutheran Service Book and Hymnal. St. Peter joined the Indiana-Kentucky LCA (Lutheran Church in America) Synod when that synod was formed in 1962 and from 1976 to 1990 formed a two-church parish arrangement with Resurrection Lutheran at Madison, Ind. In recent years, St. Peter has used the 1978 Lutheran Book of Worship Service but has received its pastors from Lutheran, United Church of Christ, and Episcopal traditions. At least seven current members of the church are descendants of the original charter members.

Buhlig, Dorothy. "History Notes of St. Peter Lutheran Church," August 1977, St. Peter Lutheran Church, Hunter's Bottom, Ky.

Daubendis, Frederick. *50th Anniversary Bulletin of Hunters Bottom Lutheran Church,* June 30, 1946, St. Peter Lutheran Church, Hunter's Bottom, Ky.

"The 1896 Constitution of the German Evangelical Protestant St. Peter Lutheran Church, Hunters Bottom, Ky.," translated from original German, St. Peter Lutheran Church, Hunter's Bottom, Ky.

St. Peter Lutheran Church Minutes, March 8, 1896, to June 1901, St. Peter Lutheran Church, Hunter's Bottom, Ky.

Thiemann, Mrs. Martin. "History of St. Peter Lutheran Church," ca. 1986, St. Peter Lutheran Church, Hunter's Bottom, Ky.

Vedell, Robert. *75th Anniversary Bulletin of St. Peter Lutheran Church,* June 27, 1971, St. Peter Lutheran Church, Hunter's Bottom, Ky.

Diane Perrine Coon

ST. PHILIP CATHOLIC CHURCH. For many years, the Catholics of Melbourne were part of **St. Joseph** Parish in Camp Springs. With the permission of Covington bishop **Camillus P. Maes**, Rev. Joseph Haustermann, pastor of St. Joseph, began building a small church in Melbourne to meet the needs of the people there. The cornerstone was laid on November 8, 1908, but construction was halted when Maes decided that costs had become too high for the already-indebted parish to bear. A year later, under the new pastor of St. Joseph, Rev. Charles Woeste, the congregation again took up the work. The church was completed in 1910, and the dedication occurred on May 16 of that year. The church was named St. Philip and was made a separate parish with Rev. Charles Rolfes as its first pastor. A rectory for the pastor was completed in 1912. The **Sisters of Divine Providence** from nearby St. Anne Convent staffed a small school that was conducted in a room partitioned off in the back of the church. A separate school building, including living quarters for the teaching sisters, was built in 1925. Parishioners built a wooden parish hall in 1923, and the students began a tradition of staging school plays there. St. Philip remains a small parish today and maintains its own school.

Ryan, Paul E. *History of the Diocese of Covington, Kentucky.* Covington, Ky.: Diocese of Covington, 1954.

St. Philip Church Diamond Jubilee. Melbourne, Ky.: St. Philip Catholic Church, 1985.

Tenkotte, Paul A., David E. Schroeder, and Thomas S. Ward. *To Be Catholic and American in Northern, Central, and Appalachian Kentucky: The Diocese of Covington, 1853–2003.* Forthcoming.

Thomas S. Ward

ST. PIUS X CATHOLIC CHURCH. The predecessor of this modern-day church in Edgewood was the Holy Guardian Angels Parish. In 1856, early settlers built a log cabin for a Catholic school near Horse Branch Creek in Sanfordtown, near what is currently the intersection of Dudley Rd. and Madison Pk. Because there was no church building, Mass was offered in homes of the parishioners by priests from other churches. A cemetery was attached to this site, which remains in use today. A former sisters' convent remains on the site also. In 1869 a rectory was built, and the first resident priest, Rev. John Beck, came to the parish. In 1877 he helped begin construction of a new church foundation, which was completed three years later. Under the leadership of Bishop Augustus Toebbe, the **Sisters of St. Benedict** came to staff the parish school in 1882, and a convent was erected. Under Rev. Joseph Schaefer, renovations and new constructions continued during the late 1800s and early 1900s. A new and larger school replaced the previous school building. Additions and renovations occurred at the church and at the pastor's house. More land, about 2.5 acres, was added to the cemetery property.

During the early 1950s, a new church was needed to accommodate the growing membership. However, the Holy Guardian Angels Parish experienced frequent flooding, so a new site was desired. In 1954 the brothers Lawrence and Bernard Gripsover donated to the parish 23 acres on the upper rise of Dudley Rd. in Edgewood, for a new church site. This is the current location of the church. Bishop **William T. Mulloy** issued a decree of establishment, allowing the parish to move from the former Holy Guardian Angels parish in Sanfordtown to a new location. Bishop Mulloy requested that the parish change its name to St. Pius X, in recognition of the newly canonized saint, a famous pope who lived at the turn of the 20th century. A groundbreaking was held May 29, 1955, for the combination church-school now named St. Pius X. Bishop Mulloy appointed Rev. Hugh Milligan as the pastor of the new St. Pius X parish when the pastor of the Sanfordtown Guardian Angels parish, Father Jobst, retired. The new church-school construction began on March 15, 1956, and was completed in 1958. On May 31, 1958, the last mass was offered at the Holy Guardian Angels church. The next day the first mass was said in the new church. The new school opened September 3, 1958, with an enrollment of 355 students. The new parish plant, which consisted of the church, 14 classrooms, a convent area, and a rectory, was blessed and dedicated on November 2, 1958, to St. Pius X.

Father Milligan retired in 1981, and Father Paul Tenhundfeld was appointed the new pastor. He implemented the idea of "shared responsibility," whereby the parishioners assumed leadership roles in the parish community through formation of various committees. In 1982, when Vatican II called for spiritual renewal, Father Tenhundfeld started the Renew program, and more than 1,000 parishioners participated. In 1983 the Parish Council was formed and began to integrate all parish activities. The council planned for a new church and for renovations and additions to the parish. On March 1, 1987, ground was broken for the present freestanding church, which was completed in 1988.

Rev. Douglas Fortner was appointed the new pastor in 1990, following Father Tenhundfeld's retirement. In 1999 Rev. Robert Wehage was appointed pastor. Under his guidance, the church membership grew rapidly. A large addition to the school and parish facilities, along with other repairs and renovations, was completed on June 6, 2004, more than doubling the parish school, administration, and recreational space. Today St. Pius X Catholic Church is a community of about 7,700 persons.

Ott, James. *Seekers of the Everlasting Kingdom: A Brief History of the Diocese of Covington.* Strasbourg, France: Éditions du Signe, 2002.

Ryan, Paul E. ***History of the Diocese of Covington, Kentucky.*** Covington, Ky.: Diocese of Covington, 1954.

St. Pius X. www.stpiusx.com (accessed April 3, 2006).

St. Pius X Church, 1955–2005. Chattanooga, Tenn., 2006.

Tenkotte, Paul A., David E. Schroeder, and Thomas S. Ward. *To Be Catholic and American in Northern, Central, and Appalachian Kentucky: The Diocese of Covington, 1853–2003.* Forthcoming.

Steven D. Jaeger

SAINTS BONIFACE AND JAMES CATHOLIC CHURCH. The Saints Boniface and James Catholic Church resulted from the 1980 merger of two Ludlow parishes, one with a German heritage and the other with an Irish heritage.

Catholics of German and Irish descent began establishing homes in the city of Ludlow in Kenton Co. during the 1850s. German Catholics were also farming along the Pleasant Run Turnpike (presently Bromley-Crescent Springs Rd.) south of the city. In 1870 the German-Catholic population of the area petitioned Bishop Augustus Maria Toebbe of the Diocese of Covington to establish a new parish, and in spring 1872, ground was broken on Adela Ave. in Ludlow for the new St. Boniface Church. The building, housing a school and a priest's residence on the first floor and a church on the second, was dedicated on November 3, 1872.

Herman J. Kramer became pastor of St. Boniface Parish in 1884. Under his guidance, the parish flourished. Lay teachers staffed the parish school from 1872 to 1890; then in 1890 Kramer arranged for the **Sisters of Divine Providence** to teach in the parish school. Classes were conducted in both English and German for many years, and the use of the German language was not entirely discontinued until 1920. Kramer also guided the construction of a new Romanesque Revival St. Boniface Church. Bishop **Camillus P. Maes** dedicated the new edifice, designed by architect John Boll, a Ludlow resident, on August 13, 1893. The building was extensively damaged by a tornado in 1915, but parishioners raised the necessary funds and repaired the structure, which was rededicated by Bishop Ferdinand Brossart in 1916. In 1928 the parish purchased a home in Ludlow on Church St. for use as a residence for the pastor. Other developments during this era included the complete renovation of the parish school, the establishment of a parish drama society, and the creation of a St. Vincent de Paul society. Enrollment in the parish school reached a peak during the 1930s with nearly 200 students.

The English-speaking Catholics of Ludlow initially attended either St. Ann Parish in nearby West Covington or St. Boniface Church. In 1886 James Kehoe, pastor of St. Ann Parish, began organizing these people into a second Ludlow Catholic congregation, made up primarily of people of Irish ancestry. The parish purchased the Armory Hall on Carneal St. in 1887 and renovated the building for use as a church. Bishop Maes dedicated the new St. James Church on May 1, 1887. St. James School was established in 1893 in the old Odd Fellows Hall on Oak St., and the Sisters of Charity of Nazareth agreed to staff the school. During its first year of operation, it enrolled 125 students.

Thomas D. Kehoe was appointed pastor of St. James Parish in 1894 and remained in that position until his death in 1921. Under his guidance, a new Gothic Revival–style church was built on Oak St. in 1903–1904 and dedicated by Bishop Maes on October 9, 1904. A new St. James School was constructed in 1911 and dedicated on March 18, 1912. Both the church and the school were designed by local architect Walter Sheblessy. A new parish rectory followed in 1922. Between 1928 and 1948, St. James Parish operated the coeducational St. James High School, which was housed in a small addition to the church, a nearby cottage, and on the first floor of the parish rectory. During its early years of operation, lay teachers and diocesan clergy staffed the school. For many years, Ruth Kelley held the position of principal. In 1942 the Sisters of Charity of Nazareth took over the staffing of the high school. Leo Egbring, who served as pastor of St. James Parish from 1947 until his retirement in 1977, renovated the church, the school, and the rectory and purchased additional nearby property for the parish.

During the post–**World War II** era, as the population of Ludlow declined, enrollments at both St. Boniface and St. James Schools also declined. In 1967 the diocese merged the city's two Catholic educational facilities to form St. James–St. Boniface Elementary School. Because of low enrollment, the combined elementary school closed its doors in 1984. The two Ludlow parishes were merged in 1980 under the guidance of copastors Robert J. Reinke and John Wordeman. The new parish of Saints Boniface and James was housed in the former St. James facility. This church was completely remodeled in 1981–1982.

Ryan, Paul E. ***History of the Diocese of Covington, Kentucky.*** Covington, Ky.: Diocese of Covington, 1954.

Schroeder, David E. ***United in Faith: A History of the Catholic Church in Ludlow, Kentucky.*** Ludlow, Ky.: Saints Boniface and James parish, 1997.

David E. Schroeder

ST. STEPHEN CEMETERY. In 1854, the same year that St. Stephen Parish in Newport began, the St. Stephen Benevolent Graveyard Society was incorporated. In 1855 the parish bought a plot of land for a cemetery on Alexandria Pk. about four miles south of the city. St. Stephen Cemetery remained in parish hands and remained financially dependent on the parish, although in 1941, bishop of Covington **Francis W. Howard** ruled that the cemetery account had to be kept separate from the regular parish account. St. Stephen Parish tried to maintain "perpetual care" of the cemetery. By the 1950s, the cemetery was virtually operated as a diocesan cemetery. In 1968 Bishop Richard H. Ackerman established the Cemetery Office for the Diocese of Covington, and St. Stephen Cemetery was placed under its care as a diocesan cemetery. In the 1970s, the diocese constructed, in stages, a large garden mausoleum. The new Communion of Saints Chapel at the cemetery was dedicated by Bishop Robert W. Muench on September 24, 2000.

Rules and Regulations of the Roman Catholic St. Stephen's Cemetery of Newport, Kentucky, 1903. Available at the Archives of the Diocese of Covington, Erlanger, Ky.

Ryan, Paul E. ***History of the Diocese of Covington, Kentucky.*** Covington, Ky.: Diocese of Covington, 1954.

Tenkotte, Paul A., David E. Schroeder, and Thomas S. Ward. *To Be Catholic and American in Northern, Central, and Appalachian Kentucky: The Diocese of Covington, 1853–2003.* Forthcoming.

Trauth, Mary Philip. Unpublished sketch of the history of the cemetery office, 1985, Archives, Diocese of Covington, Covington, Ky.

Thomas S. Ward

ST. THERESE CATHOLIC CHURCH. Soon after Southgate in Campbell Co., between Newport and Fort Thomas, was established as a city in 1907, Catholic residents in Southgate desired to have their own parish. Bishop of Covington **Francis W. Howard** acceded to their wishes and in 1927 created a new parish out of portions of **St. Thomas Catholic Church** in Fort Thomas and **St. Francis de Sales** and **St. Vincent de Paul** parishes in Newport. For the first pastor, he appointed Msgr. Borgias Lehr, who continued in the position until his death in 1957. Property on Alexandria Pk. (**U.S. 27**) that had belonged to the **Wiedemann Brewing Company** was purchased. A large resort known as Old Heidelberg on the property was converted into a church, a school, and a rectory. On August 21, 1927, the parish celebrated its first mass in its new worship space. Howard dedicated the church, officially named St. Therese of the Infant Jesus, and the school on October 2, 1927. The following day, St. Therese's Feast Day, the bishop declared the new church to be a diocesan shrine to the 19th-century saint popularly known as "The Little Flower." The school began classes that fall under the direction of the **Sisters of St. Benedict**. Howard visited Lisieux, France (hometown of the saint), in 1929 and obtained relics of St. Therese from a blood sister who was still alive.

The Old Heidelberg was not intended to be a permanent facility for the St. Therese church. Lehr planned to develop a full parish plant incrementally. Architect Edward J. Schulte's design for one large interconnected structure was chosen, and the first stage was the construction of the school-convent section, which was dedicated on January 4, 1953. Lehr did not live to see the completion of the new parish plant. He died on February 5, 1957, and his successor, Rev. Paul Brinker, saw the project through to completion. The spacious, modern church with attached rectory was completed in 1964 and dedicated by Bishop Richard H. Ackerman on June 7, 1964. The old parish building was demolished. The **Sisters of Notre Dame** took over the school in 1967. The parish has grown to around 1,000 families under Rev. Clarence Heitzman, the current pastor.

Reder, Diane. "Jubilee Cross Visits St. Therese in Southgate," *Messenger*, April 14, 2000, 6.

Ryan, Paul E. *History of the Diocese of Covington, Kentucky*. Covington, Ky.: Diocese of Covington, 1954.

St. Therese Church dedication booklet, June 7, 1964, St. Therese Catholic Church. Southgate, Ky.

Tenkotte, Paul A., David E. Schroeder, and Thomas S. Ward. *To Be Catholic and American in Northern, Central, and Appalachian Kentucky: The Diocese of Covington, 1853–2003*. Forthcoming.

Thomas S. Ward

ST. THOMAS CATHOLIC CHURCH. Today St. Thomas Parish, named for St. Thomas the Apostle, is located at E. Villa Pl. and S. Fort Thomas Ave. in Fort Thomas. The parish was founded in 1902 to serve the Catholic population at and around the **Fort Thomas Military Reservation**. Previously, Catholic services had been provided at various locations nearby, including at the Convent of the Good Shepherd along Highland Ave. in Fort Thomas.

In 1901 the Catholics in southern Fort Thomas, under the leadership of Rev. Mathias Leick, took the first steps to form a church. They chose four lots at Grand and Tremont Aves., and the lots, owned by Newport attorney Leonard J. Crawford and the members of the Fitch family, were donated to the parish. Here, on December 21, 1902, Bishop **Camillus Maes** dedicated St. Thomas's first parish church, built at a cost of $6,500, and blessed the elementary school located within the church. In 1921 the parish moved to its present location along S. Fort Thomas Ave. From 1921 until 2005, the former church building was used for apartments; then in 2005 the first church was razed as construction began on the existing multiunit condominium project at that site.

The first church at E. Villa Pl. and S. Fort Thomas Ave. was a combination church and school structure, much like the previous one. This building served St. Thomas Parish until 1939, when the present church was opened. The 1939 parish church was built under the direction of Rev. Herbert Hillenmeyer at a cost of $250,000 and was dedicated by Bishop **Francis W. Howard** on March 23, 1939. The new church was built in the Romanesque style: massive, lofty, and cruciform, with round arches, recessed portals, and a wooden roof. In 1952 the church's glass windows were replaced with stained-glass windows; in 1969 the altar area was remodeled; and in 2002 the grounds were newly landscaped.

St. Thomas Parish has prospered over the years, and in 2004 it served 900 families. Many of these present parishioners trace their family's Catholic heritage to the former Catholic parishes of Newport and Bellevue. As the social and economic well-being of these second- and third-generation Catholics improved during the 1950s and 1960s, many of them moved from Newport and Bellevue to the hills overlooking the Ohio River.

St. Thomas Elementary School was founded by the **Sisters of Divine Providence** in 1902 and provided instruction in grades 1–8. Kindergarten instruction was added in 1985. Starting in the 1960s, with the decline in religious vocations among the teaching order of nuns, more teaching duties at St. Thomas School were turned over to lay instructors. In 2004 St. Thomas School was totally staffed by lay instructors and served 240 K–8 pupils and 44 preschool children. In 1961, when St. Thomas School reached a high of 1,105 students, all teachers were nuns. In 1945 the parish founded the St. Thomas High School. In 1956 a new high school building was built to house a projected 400 students. High school enrollment, however, never reached that level, and in 1976, with enrollment down to 180 students, the high school was closed.

In 1978 the original St. Thomas church and school building, on E. Villa Pl., were renovated. The building continued to house classrooms, but it also became a multipurpose social and activity center for the parish.

St. Thomas has had 10 pastors during its first 102 years: Mathias Leick, 1902–1906; Aloysius J. Roell, 1906–1917; Martin R. Delaney, 1917–1918; Thomas Coleman, 1918–1919; Otto Hafen, 1920–1925; Herbert F. Hillenmeyer, 1925–1968; Thomas B. Finn, 1968–1981; Charles J. Hoffer, 1981–1989; John J. Riesenberg, 1989–1999; and William B. Neuhaus, beginning in 1999.

A History of St. Thomas Parish, 1902 to 1977. Fort Thomas, Ky.: St. Thomas Church, 1977.

Knapp, Paul T. *Ft. Thomas Kentucky—Its History*. Fort Thomas, Ky.: Fort Thomas Centennial Committee, 1967.

St. Thomas Church, 1902 to 2002. Fort Thomas, Ky.: St. Thomas Church, 2002.

Tenkotte, Paul A., David E. Schroeder, and Thomas S. Ward. *To Be Catholic and American in Northern, Central, and Appalachian Kentucky: The Diocese of Covington, 1853–2003*. Forthcoming.

Charles H. Bogart

ST. THOMAS HIGH SCHOOL. The St. Thomas High School, which opened just as **World War II** ended, was the vision of Msgr. Herbert F. Hillenmeyer, pastor of **St. Thomas Catholic Church** in Fort Thomas. Hillenmeyer wanted to reverse the flow of parish students who were opting to attend **Highlands High School** in Fort Thomas. He secured Bishop William Mulloy's permission to initiate only the first year of the high school, with another class to be added each year until the program extended to four years. It officially opened on September 10, 1945, with an enrollment of 20. By 1949 the student body consisted of 59 with a staff of 10 teachers. A new high school facility was dedicated on September 9, 1956, and served the parish for 20 years. St. Thomas High School continued to prosper in the 1960s, reaching its peak enrollment of 297 students in 1964. Its largest graduating class was 81 students in 1968. Enrollment began to decline during the early 1970s, mostly due to changing demographics. With the decreasing number of religious sisters to draw from as instructors, more lay teachers had to be hired. The increase of costs, along with a declining study body, forced the school to close in 1976. The last class of 40 seniors graduated in St. Thomas Church on June 1, 1976, and St. Thomas High School concluded 31 years of operation. The St. Thomas grade school has utilized the high school facility since. Although small by most standards, the St. Thomas High School was known for academic excellence and accomplishments in athletics. Most notable was the boys' basketball program under future multiple Hall of Fame coach **Ken Shields**, who began his storied career at St. Thomas and whose teams won 199 games over his 10 seasons (1965–1974) as coach.

"Cornerstone Laid at St. Thomas Site," *KTS*, February 20, 1956, 1A.

Reis, Jim. "Changing Times Bypassed Schools," *KP*, July 15, 1992, 4K.

Ryan, Paul E. *History of the Diocese of Covington, Kentucky*. Covington, Ky.: Diocese of Covington, 1954.

Tenkotte, Paul A., David E. Schroeder, and Thomas S. Ward. *To Be Catholic and American in Northern, Central, and Appalachian Kentucky: The Diocese of Covington, 1853–2003*. Forthcoming.

Rick Meyers

ST. TIMOTHY CATHOLIC CHURCH. St. Timothy Catholic Church is located in thriving western Boone Co. along U.S. 42 at Union, near **Larry A. Ryle High School**, on 15 acres belonging to the Diocese of Covington (see **Roman Catholics**). In 1989 the diocese established this parish, which included the former western and southern areas of **St. Paul Catholic Church** in Florence. In March of that year, Bishop William Hughes appointed Edward Brodnick as the first pastor. At first, since there was no church building, the parish used the **YMCA** facility on Camp Ernst Rd. and later accepted the Union Presbyterian Church's offer of space. Ground was broken on August 27, 1989, for the parish's new multipurpose building, and on Pentecost Sunday, June 3, 1990, 300 people dedicated the new structure. Immediately, the parish began to reduce its indebtedness as a prelude to funding construction of a new church. The St. Timothy parish had begun with 375 families; by 1999 more than 700 families were parish members. As the growth continued, the multipurpose center soon became overcrowded. By May 1997, $1 million had been pledged to a church building fund and the parish had also retired its recent debt.

In 1996 the parish began a capital campaign, which resulted in a new church building, dedicated in September 1998. Bill Hub was the architect and Hanson Millay Inc. was the construction manager.

"Boone County Parishes Experience Growing Pains," *Messenger*, November 1, 1996, 1.
"New Union Parish Holds First Mass at Camp Ernst," *Messenger*, July 16, 1989, 1.
"New Union Parish to Be 'St. Timothy,'" *Messenger*, April 23, 1989, 1.
"Parish Center Dedicated at St. Timothy," *Messenger*, June 17, 1990, 1.
St. Timothy: The Dedication of St. Timothy Church Program Booklet, September 27, 1998. Union, Ky.: St. Timothy Catholic Church, 1998.

John Boh

ST. VINCENT DE PAUL CATHOLIC CHURCH, NEWPORT. In 1913 Catholic residents of **Clifton** (now part of Newport) asked to have their own parish. Bishop **Camillus P. Maes** gave his permission for a church and school, but he died in 1915, before it was built. Although the people of Clifton had begun raising funds and had purchased property, it was not until 1916 that Rev. Herman Wetzel, associate pastor at St. Stephen Catholic Church, was given charge of the building project. St. Stephen was the parish that had previously included Clifton in its purview. Wetzel then became St. Vincent de Paul's first pastor. Construction of a small brick combination church and school began with a cornerstone-laying ceremony on June 11, 1916, and was ready for dedication by Bishop Ferdinand Brossart on September 17 of that year. The school opened that same fall under the care of the **Sisters of Divine Providence**. During the 1920s, an addition was built onto the school and a separate rectory and convent were constructed. A new church was dedicated on September 25, 1960.

In the early 1980s, as the number of Catholic school children in Newport began to decline, the Diocese of Covington's Board of Education decided to merge the four Newport parish schools into a new interparish school named Holy Spirit. The new plan went into effect for the 1984–1985 school year, with elementary classes to be conducted at the St. Stephen School and junior high classes at St. Francis de Sales in **Cote Brilliante**; the St. Vincent de Paul and **Corpus Christi** schools were closed.

The four Newport parishes merged in the next decade. With the pastors of three of the parishes retiring, and not enough priests available to take their places, Bishop Robert W. Muench decided to close the individual parishes and combine them into one new Holy Spirit Parish in 1997; the four churches continued to be used, but as missions to the one parish. In just a few years, however, the bishop closed all but St. Stephen Church, which became the one church for the consolidated parish. The other three were relegated to "profane, but not sordid use." This meant that St. Vincent de Paul Church was closed. For several years, Sr. Judith Niewahner, S.N.D., used the church for a preschool and day care program until the program was moved to the renovated Holy Trinity Junior High School. Afterward, the old St. Vincent de Paul School was sold and converted into apartments.

"Decree of Bishop Robert W. Muench," *Messenger*, April 25, 1997, 1.
Minutes of the Diocesan Board of Education meeting, March 8, 1984, Archives of the Diocese of Covington, Covington, Ky.
Ryan, Paul E. *History of the Diocese of Covington, Kentucky*. Covington, Ky.: Diocese of Covington, 1954.
Tenkotte, Paul A., David E. Schroeder, and Thomas S. Ward. *To Be Catholic and American in Northern, Central, and Appalachian Kentucky: The Diocese of Covington, 1853–2003*. Forthcoming.

Thomas S. Ward

ST. WILLIAM CATHOLIC CHURCH. Catholicism grew slowly at Williamstown in Grant Co. Priests of the Diocese of Covington (see **Roman Catholics**) from St. Stanislaus Seminary in White Sulphur ministered at Williamstown for a time. Bishop Augustus M. Toebbe himself sometimes attended to the small station at Williamstown, administering the sacraments in the homes of area Catholics, though the town also allowed the courthouse to be used for services. In 1893 Bishop **Camillus P. Maes** made Williamstown a mission of St. Luke Parish in Nicholasville. St. Luke's pastor, Rev. George Bealer, decided that his parish should build a church in Williamstown, so St. Luke Parish purchased property in Williamstown on Main St. in 1900. There, a small church dedicated to St. William was built. It was not until 1912, however, that St. William Catholic Church became a parish with the appointment of Rev. James Taaffe as its first resident pastor. At that same time, **St. John Mission**, at Dividing Ridge, became a mission of St. William Parish.

During his tenure as pastor, Taafe did his best to enhance the interior of the church with the small amounts of money available. One highlight of the interior was a painting of St. Joseph by artist **Johann Schmitt**. The church building deteriorated over the years, but the lack of financial resources delayed the building of a new church with a school until the 1950s. Rev. George Donnelly at that time received permission from Bishop **William T. Mulloy** to buy property for a parish complex that would include a school for the growing population of children, a convent, a rectory, and a new church. The construction was done in stages, beginning with the school. The new St. William Catholic Church, a 300-seat-capacity Bedford stone structure, was built last. Bishop Richard H. Ackerman dedicated the new church on November 26, 1961. This church served well until the population increased in the Williamstown area as a result of the opening of I-75 between Cincinnati and Lexington. A dramatic change came to St. William Church and Parish in 1995. St. William retained its status as a parish, but because there was a shortage of priests to staff all the parishes of the diocese, Bishop William A. Hughes appointed Sister Carol Leveque, S.C., to serve as administrator, a position that can be filled by a noncleric. A priest, Rev. Roger Kriege, was appointed as sacramental administrator to preside at weekend masses. During Sr. Carol's time, the parish began a capital campaign to build a larger church to fit its growing needs. The old church and some of the other buildings of the old complex were incorporated into the new one. Bishop Roger J. Foys dedicated the new church on October 6, 2002.

"History of St. William Parish, Williamstown," *Messenger*, October 25, 2002, 7A–8A.
Ryan, Paul E. *History of the Diocese of Covington, Kentucky*. Covington, Ky.: Diocese of Covington, 1954.
Tenkotte, Paul A., David E. Schroeder, and Thomas S. Ward. *To Be Catholic and American in Northern, Central, and Appalachian Kentucky: The Diocese of Covington, 1853–2003*. Forthcoming.

Thomas S. Ward

SALEM UNITED METHODIST CHURCH. The building at 810 York St. in Newport, now the **Stained Glass Theatre**, was once the home of Salem United Methodist Church. This church was one of Northern Kentucky's German Methodist Churches. It belonged to the Central German Conference of the Methodist Church, a conference of churches made up primarily of German immigrant families and their descendants; their services were often conducted in the German language in the years before the United States entered **World War I**.

Members of the Race St. Methodist Church in Cincinnati moved to Newport and began to meet in homes in the area as early as 1842. As the group increased in number, it began meeting in the old Campbell Co. Courthouse at Newport. At first, class leaders William Borcherding, Peter Margue, and Frank Nuelson, originally from the Race St. Methodist Church, ministered to the assembly. In November 1842, the church was organized as the Newport and Covington Mission with 22 charter members.

The first home of what became the Salem Methodist Church was on Todd St. (now Sixth St.), between Columbia and Central Sts. in Newport. It was started as a congregation of German immigrants in 1847 under the direction of Rev. Peter B. Becker and with help from members of the Race St. Methodist Church in Cincinnati. The frame building on Todd St. was constructed at a cost of $700. The second location was the corner of Mayo (now Seventh) and Orchard Sts. in Newport, where a lot was purchased in 1854 for $1,500. The following year, under the leadership of the Rev. H. Henke, a new brick structure was constructed at a cost of about $5,000, and Rev. Peter Moelling dedicated the new church building. During 1861–1862, the church gave up using the services of a full-time pastor in order to save money. Instead, the church relied on local preachers John Hueneke and Henry Roettinger.

After the Civil War, the Salem Methodist Episcopal Church had many revivals and was marked by a spirit of thankfulness, perhaps gratitude for the termination of that bloody conflict. Because of growth in membership, plans were made for construction of a new church building. A Queen Anne Gothic–style church building, which is listed on the National Historic Register, was designed by **Samuel Hannaford and Sons** and built at York and Ringgold Sts. (now Eighth St.). The building was dedicated on June 22, 1883, and accounts of the time said that it was "one of the finest buildings in the city." Rev. D. D. Bayless and Rev. C. G. Fritsche spoke at the dedication. At that time, the church membership comprised 247 members in full standing and 27 probationary members; there were 192 members of the Sunday School. The church had a Ladies Society, Merry Workers, Earnest Workers, an Achrenleset, and a Choral Society.

During fall 1884, the congregation of the Salem Methodist Church hosted the Central German Methodist Conference, which included all the German Methodist Churches in Indiana, Kentucky, Ohio, Michigan, Pennsylvania, and West Virginia, as well as parts of Tennessee and Illinois. The four-day conference or convention in the new church building featured meetings conducted in both German and English.

During the ministry of Rev. J. J. Baechtold, a revival in 1896 resulted in adding 335 members to the church. It was also during this period that the church building was completely remodeled at a cost of $3,600. In early 1905, the church installed a new pipe organ and made other improvements at a cost of $7,700. Rev. Richard Plueddemann was the minister from 1905 until 1907; during his term the English language was used in the Sunday evening services. Salem Methodist Church celebrated its 60th anniversary as a congregation in June 1908. A **Kentucky Post** article stated that the interior of the church was covered with flowers. The church's pastor then was Rev. J. P. Whitehead.

As a church with German roots, Salem Methodist Church was under pressure to give up the use of the German language in its services during World War I. In response, the church board in September 1918 voted to remove the sign in front of the church, "Salem Kirche." It was replaced with a sign in English, "Salem Methodist Episcopal Church." At the same time all signs and symbols inside the church written in German were removed. By then, all services were being conducted in English rather than German.

Salem Methodist Church's centennial was celebrated in May 1947. In July 1978 the church celebrated its 130th anniversary with a Homecoming Celebration attended by many former members. The church had been damaged by storms in September 1930 when lightning struck. On March 11, 1986, the church building was hit by another storm, which damaged the steeple, the roof, and the foundation of the church so severely that estimates for repairs were $215,000. The congregation, which had dwindled to 45 and had insurance coverage for only $150,000, voted to merge with the **Grace United Methodist Church** and sold the church building to the Footlighter Theatre Group, which operates the **Stained Glass Theatre** in the structure.

Campbell Co. Historical Society. *Campbell County, Kentucky, 200 Years, 1794–1994*. Alexandria, Ky.: Campbell Co. Historical Society, 1994.

Reis, Jim. "Historic Salem Church Now Used as Theater," *KP*, August 13, 2001, 4K.

"Salem M.E. Church a Bower of Beauty," *KP*, June 11, 1908, 5.

United Methodist Archives, Asbury Theological Seminary Library, Wilmore, Ky.

Paul L. Whalen

SALIN, LEWIS HENRY (b. July 2, 1829, Bavaria, Germany; d. May 12, 1897, Owen Co., Ky.). Lewis Henry Salin, who became a Baptist pastor, was born to Jewish parents (see **Jews**). His father was Rabbi Henry B. Salin, a Levite, and his mother was a descendant of the Aaronic priesthood. Lewis attended school for 12 years in Bavaria, Germany. In his youth, a rebellion broke out in Bavaria, and he joined the rebels. Supporters of the uprising drilled daily in preparation for battle. Salin was selected as a standard-bearer, but the movement quickly collapsed and the revolutionaries disarmed. Many of the rebels were severely punished after the rebellion ended; Salin, being a minor, was sentenced to only 12 hours of imprisonment.

On September 7, 1849, Salin, at age 20, sailed on a vessel for the United States, where his brother S. H. Salin had already emigrated. Lewis Salin landed at New Orleans, La., on November 4, 1849. He then took passage on the steamer *Ohio* headed for Cincinnati. However, someone advised him to go to Owen Co., Ky., suggesting that he might find hospitable ethnic Germans there. The Benjamin Kemper family, who lived near New Liberty, Ky., accepted him into their home. When Salin soon became critically ill with typhoid fever, the Kemper family sent for his brother, who was living in New Castle in Henry Co.; S. H. Salin nursed his brother back to health, with the help of neighboring families.

Lewis Salin subsequently became a merchant in Owenton and began to study beliefs held by the various Christian denominations. Influenced by Baptist elder Lewis D. Alexander of New Liberty, Salin was eventually drawn to that denomination's religious beliefs. He was ordained a Baptist minister on the third Saturday of March in 1857. At age 30, he married the former Mrs. Warren Foster (Barbara Ann Bourn) on November 15, 1859. The Salins were parents of three sons. Lewis Salin served as pastor of Mount Pleasant Baptist Church in Owen Co. for about 22 years. At the same time, he pastored nearby at Greenup Fork Baptist Church, dividing his time between the two churches. He was a half-time pastor at Monterey Baptist Church in Owen Co. from 1885 to 1886, and again from 1892 to 1895. His autobiographical book *The Converted Jew* chronicles his conversion and personal struggles. He died in 1897 at his home near Ep (Greenup) in Owen Co and was buried at the Monterey Cemetery in Owen Co.

Israel in Prophecy. "A Brief List of Most Famous Messianic Jews." www.israelinprophecy.org.

Murphy, Margaret A. *History of the Monterey Baptist Church and Community*. Frankfort, Ky.: Roberts, 1976.

Salin, Lewis Henry. *A Condensed History of the Experience and Church Relations of Eld. Lewis Henry Salin: A Converted Jew*. Louisville, Ky.: Caperton and Cates, 1877.

Waldrop, J. W. *History of Concord Association*. Owenton, Ky.: News-Herald Print, 1907.

Margaret A. Murphy

SALVATION ARMY. The Salvation Army (SA) has functioned in Northern Kentucky for more than 100 years. Its foremost presence was clearly the **Booth Memorial Hospital**, which it owned and operated along E. Second St. in Covington from 1914 to 1979; the hospital moved to Florence, Ky., and was sold to the **St. Luke Hospital** in 1989. The Booth facility was the first general hospital in the United States for the SA. Northern Kentuckian Maj. Glenn Sieler's parents worked at the Booth Hospital during his youth; later in life, he returned to help administer the same facility.

The SA was formed by William Booth in England in 1865. He took religion out into the streets of London, ministering to prostitutes, derelicts, the homeless, and the destitute. With food, housing, and concern, he converted the bottom of society. The organization was called an army because of the dress uniforms worn by his staff, in the pattern of the British Army. In the United States, the SA was present in Philadelphia by 1883, in Louisville and Cincinnati by 1885, and in Newport, operating out of the former Red Men's Hall, by 1888.

Although the SA is best known for fundraising with red kettles and ringing bells during the Christmas season (first used in San Francisco in 1891), other means of raising funds were implemented before the modern United Way (United Appeal) was established. In 1921 Harry H. Gardiner, the "human fly," was climbing bank buildings and courthouses in front of crowds of 15,000 in Covington and Newport as a means of encouraging donations for the SA. Society ladies' groups often held teas, bridal shows, and luncheons for the benefit of the SA.

In Newport, the SA operated over the years in several locations. In the 1940s and 1950s, the SA had a store where it sold restored furniture and appliances and other used items at 500 W. Sixth St. That store was part of the Adult Rehabilitation Program, in which clients being helped by the SA went around picking up used furniture and the like and restoring it before it was sold in such outlets. In 1978 the SA dedicated a new 15,000-square-foot community center at W. 10th and Patterson Sts. in Newport. Costing $650,000, the facility featured a gymnasium, meeting rooms, a chapel, offices, and an apartment for an SA staff member family. Later, an adult day care program for seniors was added. When the new facility opened, the SA family services group at 202 Garrard St. in Covington, where juveniles were counseled, moved to 10th and Patterson. The 10th and Patterson operation continues to this day, and in order to appeal to the neighborhood youth, a game room has been added recently. This SA facility works closely with the **Brighton Center** in helping the people of Newport's **West End**.

For many years, beginning in 1929, the SA had a building at 14 E. Eighth St. in Covington. Before that time, the SA was housed in several other locations in the city, such as 129 Pike in 1904 and 513–515 Madison Ave. in 1911. Today, its Covington headquarters is at 1806 Scott St., the former St. John Episcopal Church, where it moved in 1980 from the Eighth St. facility.

The SA has gone to war with U.S. troops, making doughnuts near the battlefields, comforting soldiers and sailors, and entertaining them as much as possible. It was a cofounder of the United Services Organization (USO). Stateside, the SA provided grief counseling to the survivors of the **Beverly Hills Supper Club** fire in Southgate in 1977, and in 1940 the SA was on the scene of the Latonia Theater fire, where many Covington firemen were injured. The organization has also been on hand during disasters such as the hurricanes Hugo in 1987 and Katrina in 2005.

The SA has sponsored summer camps for inner-city children, and it has arranged for Santa Claus to hand out Christmas gifts to children who otherwise may not have received any. At one time, itinerant SA bands crossed the nation providing free concerts, as music has always been an important medium for the SA. Each Sunday, the Covington location conducts Sunday school and a worship service.

"Army Celebrates Booth Victory," *KP*, June 7, 1979, 1K.

Farrell, Mike. "Reveille," *KP*, September 23, 1978, 5K.

"Harry H. Gardiner—Human Fly," *KP*, April 16, 1921, 1.

Murdoch, Norman H. "A Protestant Hospital for Covington: Booth Memorial Hospital," *JKS* 3 (October 1986): 107–49.

———. *The Salvation Army in Cincinnati: 1885–1985.* Cincinnati: Salvation Army, 1985.

"Salvation Army Bldg. Is Cleared of Debt," *KP*, July 14, 1939, 14.

SALYERS, KATHRYN (b. September 12, 1914, near Dry Ridge, Ky.). Born in Grant Co., Carroll Co. historian and genealogist Sara Kathryn Salyers is the youngest daughter of William Tandy and Emma Price Dunlap Salyers. In 1929 the family moved into the Carrollton home of Kathryn's grandmother, Sarah Spoonmore Salyers Haggard; this brick house on Seventh St. in Carrollton has remained Salyers's home for more than 77 years. Salyers became a bookkeeper in Gex Diuguid's tobacco warehouses and held the position until her retirement.

Following Kathryn's 1943 marriage to Paul Godman, her mother-in-law, Mayme Bowie Godman, awakened in her an interest in genealogy and local history, and she turned her meticulous attention for detail into compiling filing cabinets full of historical and genealogical information, which is frequently sought out by genealogists, reporters, and historians. In 2004 the **Church of Jesus Christ of Latter-day Saints** (Mormons) microfilmed her genealogical collection. The Kathryn Salyers History Room at the **Carroll Co. Public Library** will house her records upon her death.

Bill Davis

SANDERS. This sixth-class city is in the southeastern corner of Carroll Co., 10 miles east-southeast of Carrollton, where Ky. Rts. 36 and 47 meet. The site now known as Sanders was once a salt lick along the buffalo trace that ran from the mouth of the Licking River at Covington to Drennon Springs in Henry Co. First called Rislerville, after a local storekeeper, the town was renamed Sanders for the Sanders family who operated a gristmill there on Eagle Creek; Sanders has also been called Sanders Mill. For a time it was called Liberty Station, because the community was an important shipping point along the **Louisville, Cincinnati, and Lexington Railroad**. The town of Sanders was incorporated in 1871, and at that time it was located within Gallatin Co. A year later, when the county boundaries were redrawn, it became part of Carroll Co. The 1883 regional Lake atlas shows that the town once included a hotel (the Northcutt), doctors' offices, livestock corrals, a large railroad depot, clothing stores, a sawmill, a tobacco warehouse, and a post office, all located near the railroad. Frank Jacobs and his wife Ella Cannon Jacobs ran the Blue Lick Springs Hotel during the 1880s. Sanders was once the second-largest city in Carroll Co. In 1891 the railroad through town became part of the **Louisville and Nashville Railroad**. Late on Wednesday evening, October 18, 1899, Democratic presidential candidate William Jennings Bryan's train stopped at Sanders, and Bryan, renowned as perhaps the nation's greatest orator, delivered one of his famed speeches to a crowd estimated at between 2,500 and 3,000. The well-remembered Sanders Covered Bridge remained standing until it burned in 1948. At one time there was a high school in Sanders, before county schools were consolidated; and for many years the Sanders Fair was a favorite summer event. Today, freight trains on the routes between Cincinnati and Louisville rumble through town, stopping now far more seldom than in the past. A Christian church and a Baptist church continue to hold regular services in town. In 1980 Sanders's population was 332; by 2000 it had declined to 240. The shifting of automobile traffic from the two state highways that converge at Sanders to I-71, to the north, has significantly contributed to the town's decline.

An Atlas of Carroll and Gallatin Counties, Kentucky. Philadelphia: D. J. Lake, 1883.

"Liberty Sta. or Sanders Was Sizeable Town Back in 1883," *Carrollton News-Democrat*, May 16, 1963.

Rennick, Robert M. *Kentucky Place Names.* Lexington: Univ. of Kentucky Press, 1984.

SANDERS, GEORGE N. (b. February 21, 1812, Lexington, Ky.; d. August 12, 1873, New York City). George Nicholas Sanders, an entrepreneur, a political organizer, and a Confederate agent, was the son of Lewis and Ann Nicholas Sanders. In 1823 Lewis Sanders moved his family to their new **Grass Hills** estate near Ghent, in what is today Carroll Co. George Nicholas Sanders lived there until 1845. His early education was in private schools, including Dr. Joseph Buchanon's Select School, and later he attended Georgetown College in Georgetown. Until he was in his early thirties, Sanders worked on the Grass Hills estate, primarily involved in horse racing and animal breeding. Reading was also a popular pastime at Grass Hills, and it was through the family's subscription to the magazine *Passion Flower*, published in New York City by Samuel C. Reid and his daughter Anna Johnson Reid, that Sanders became acquainted with his future wife. When he wrote to Anna Reid to express how much he enjoyed reading the publication, a correspondence ensued. Then, without ever having met her, he asked Anna to marry him, and she accepted. They had four children together: Reid, Virginia, Lewis, and George Jr.

Sanders emerged on the national political scene in 1843 when he organized a nonpartisan meeting at a tailor shop in Ghent, in order to promote the annexation of Texas to the United States. Because these proceedings were never published, the group became known as the Mystic Thirteen. After a second meeting in 1844, the Mystic Thirteen requested the opinions of notable politicians on the Texas issue. Several persons responded, including Tennessee politician James K. Polk. Polk published his response, which was strongly in favor of annexation, and subsequently won the 1844 U.S. presidential election.

In 1845 the Sanders family moved to New York City, where George could engage in the larger world of politics and business. He served as an agent for the Hudson's Bay Company, attempting to negotiate the sale of the Oregon Territory to the U.S. government, but his contract lapsed before the sale was completed. He became better known as the leader of Young America, a progressive faction within the Democratic Party. Symbolizing youthful nationalism, Young Americans advocated capitalistic development, intervention in foreign affairs, and manifest destiny, and they supported the 1852 presidential bid of Illinois senator Stephen A. Douglas. In 1851 Sanders bought the *United States Magazine and Democratic Review* and made it a Douglas and Young America political organ. Although Sanders was known to possess a certain charm, he was not always reliable, and the articles in the *Democratic Review* during the campaign demonstrated his propensity for extreme behavior. When he called the Democratic Party regulars "old fogies," "nincompoops," and "vile toads," he alienated potential Douglas supporters as well as opponents, much to the consternation of Douglas. Ultimately, Gen. Franklin Pierce won the Democratic nomination. Sanders switched his support to Pierce, and in 1854 President Pierce (1853–1857) appointed Sanders as the consul to London, England. The Senate, however, refused to confirm Sanders, primarily because of his highly visible and controversial relationship with notable European revolutionaries. Sanders was later made navy agent of New York after promoting the successful 1856 presidential campaign of James Buchanan (1857–1861).

When the American **Civil War** erupted, Sanders became a Confederate agent; he attempted to procure various army supplies, from shoes to ironclad warships. He and his sons Reid and Lewis also ran a courier service between the South and Europe. In 1864 he joined a secret service operation in Canada on behalf of the Confederate government. Sanders was instrumental in organizing the St. Albans raid into Vermont and the abortive Niagara peace conference, two seemingly contradictory projects, though both were designed to achieve a favorable end to the war for the Confederacy. Then, on May 2, 1865, President Andrew Johnson (1865–1869) announced a $25,000 reward for Sanders's arrest in connection with President Abraham Lincoln's assassination. Sanders's numerous activities in Canada, including a possible meeting with John Wilkes Booth, were shrouded in secrecy. Although the charges were eventually dropped, Sanders spent seven years of self-imposed exile in Europe following the war. In 1872 he rejoined his family in New York City but lived only a year more. He died in 1873 and was buried in Greenwood Cemetery in New York City.

Curti, Merle E. "George N. Sanders—American Patriot of the Fifties," *South Atlantic Quarterly* 27 (January 1928): 79–87.

The Papers of George Nicholas Sanders, Library of Congress, Washington, D.C.

Parker, Anna Virginia. *The Sanders Family of Grass Hills*. Madison, Ind.: Coleman, 1966.

Melinda Senters

SANDERS, LEWIS (b. 1781, Virginia; d. 1861, Carroll Co., Ky.). Lewis Sanders, the originator of the agricultural county fair in Kentucky, was the son of John and Jane Craig Sanders, members of the Traveling Church of Baptists, who before 1782 migrated from Spotsylvania Co., Va., to Fayette Co., near Lexington, Ky. Lewis Sanders was related to the large Craig family that pioneered the settling of much of north central Kentucky. In 1795 his father, John Sanders, sold his farm in Fayette Co. and moved north to a farm on McCool's Creek, near Ghent, in what was then Gallatin Co. His mother, Jane Craig Sanders, died when Lewis was five years old, and apparently he was raised by his married sisters, who resided in Fayette Co.

So that Lewis could learn a trade, John Sanders placed his young son with Patrick McCullough, a leading early merchant in Lexington. Lewis acquired mathematical and accounting skills at the store. In about 1800, John Sanders gave Lewis his inheritance, the equivalent in cash of 200 acres, two horses, two cows, two slaves, and starter furniture, the same value of inheritance that he gave his other children. From those funds, in 1805, Lewis and A. B. Burton purchased the Lexington store where Lewis worked. Lewis also built three or four large three-story stores and a dwelling on his property between Mill and Broadway Sts. in Lexington and started a cotton spinning mill in one of the new buildings.

In 1806 the young entrepreneur, along with other Lexingtonians, became caught up in the Aaron Burr–Blennerhassett scandal, a scheme to populate huge tract of lands in the far west. Lewis, chiefly because Burr used Gen. James Wilkinson's name as an associate in the project, bought $16,000 of Burr's financial notes, most of them unsecured. His investment was a total loss, since Burr used the funds to purchase flatboats and supplies for a project that never developed.

In 1807 Lewis Sanders married quite advantageously. His wife was Ann Nicholas, daughter of George Nicholas, a politically powerful attorney with significant landholdings in Kentucky and an early supporter of Lexington's Transylvania College.

Sanders became infatuated with manufacturing. He opened a cotton thread mill in Lexington and then purchased a 500-acre estate just outside of Lexington on the Georgetown Rd. A half mile from his home, Lewis constructed a nine-story steam mill just off the Frankfort Rd. that produced woolen and cotton products. He built 4 large brick multifamily structures and 20 frame single-family homes to house up to 300 workers, a church, a school, and two brick homes for supervisory employees, thus starting an early company town, which he named Sandersville.

On May 31, 1816, Sanders advertised a "Cattle Shew," the first agricultural fair in Kentucky history, at his homestead farm two and a half miles outside Lexington. He recruited five well-known landed gentlemen as judges, representing five counties from the Bluegrass region of the state. Offering silver cups as prizes, the first fair featured cattle and sheep. One of the top prizes went to Buzzard, a bull owned by Capt. William Smith of Fayette Co. A single category, almost an afterthought, was opened for linen. A hand-woven, bleached cloth won the prize over a manufactured cloth. Shortly after the Sanders fair, the first Kentucky Society for Promoting Agriculture was formed July 25, 1816, with retired Kentucky governor Isaac Shelby (1792–1796 and 1812–1816) as the first president. The call for a fair in 1817 included categories for cheese, domestic woolen cloth, homemade linen, and distilled whiskey and added more classes for cattle and horses to the list of exhibits. Sheep were to be shown with a sample of their fleece. A saddle show was added in the 1818 event. By 1819 the Kentucky fair had been moved to September to permit more farmers to attend and show, and the number of classes of domestic products and livestock had tripled. Six women were exhibitors. Horses moved into a premier position, and soon a horse trotting track was added to the fair. The concept that Lewis Sanders pioneered soon expanded into counties around the Bluegrass region. Sanders recalled in a letter in 1856 that Bourbon, Franklin, Mercer, Jefferson, and other counties had begun to hold annual fairs.

Shortly after the first agricultural fair, in 1817, Lewis Sanders imported a herd of 12 blooded cattle from England, thus infusing Kentucky's cattle stock of the 19th century with Durham and Teesdale shorthorn and English Longhorn stock. That same year Henry Clay imported two British cattle. The Sanders and Clay stock were called the Seventeens.

At that very moment of success in 1817, Lewis Sanders lost his merchant and manufacturing businesses, his land, his home, and all of the imported cattle herd plus 100 of his Merino sheep to private and public auction in a major financial loss. The loss was due partly to his loss of funds in 1806 in the Burr speculation fiasco and partly to an economic bank panic that swept the western states. Sanders was far too overextended, and his creditors demanded payment. Sandersville went bankrupt, and Sanders's partially constructed home, with two oval and two octagonal rooms, was purchased by his father-in-law. George Nicholas also aided the young Sanders family, which had six children at the time, by giving his daughter, Ann Nicholas Sanders, 900 acres of upland in Gallatin Co. from the 17,000 acres he had purchased there between McCool's and Eagle Creeks.

In 1819 Lewis Sanders, a nephew, and the Sanders slaves, Georgi, Black John, Black Jim (Jem), old Christian, and Lewis, headed for the lands along McCool's and Eagle Creeks and began the long process of building a showcase agricultural farm out of the wilderness. Sanders believed the uplands were ideal for orchards and for pastureland for his Merino sheep, cattle, and horses. Large pear and apple orchards were planted at the site, and later a horse trotting track was built. The large house on the plantation was not finished until 1823, because Sanders insisted on soaking the timber in the farm pond for several months to cure it before constructing the homestead (see **Grass Hills**). Sanders built a long, rambling house with very large rooms. Anne Sanders finally moved the family to Grass Hills in 1823 and in 1827 gave birth to Jane Craig Sanders. Sanders leased other slaves, Zilla, Lottie, Manerva, Mr. Smith, and Mr. Emmey, the gardener, to help make continuous improvements to the farm.

Once again Sanders, having invested heavily in the farm, was in financial trouble. And once again the Nicholas family came to his aid. Judge Samuel Smith Nicholas of Louisville; Ann Nicholas Sanders's brother, Richard Hawes, of Winchester; her brother-in-law, Dr. William D. Richardson; and Robert Scott of Lexington purchased one-third of Sanders's original imported herd of cattle from the estate of William Smith and gave it to Lewis Sanders at Grass Hills, easing the financial strain.

Ann Nicholas Sanders died in 1830, and she and her young daughter Jane Craig Sanders, who died in 1831, were the first of the family buried at Grass Hills. During the early 1830s, George N. Sanders, a son of Lewis and Ann, took over as farm manager and purchased the cattle portion of the business. Lewis Sanders began to write extensive diaries; develop written pedigrees of Grass Hills cattle, horses, and sheep; and encourage other Kentucky breeders also to keep meticulous records. He wrote learned and somewhat opinionated articles for publication in several agricultural journals and newspapers throughout the Midwest.

Both Lewis Sanders and George Nicholas took a lively interest in politics. In 1843 they were instrumental in starting the first national rump caucus in favor of the Texas Annexation, at a meeting held at Ghent. Afterward, a firm resolution in support of annexation was sent to all presidential candidates. James K. Polk was the only presidential candidate to respond favorably. Much of the population residing in Carroll Co. was supportive of a war with Mexico, and Sam Sanders, the family's third son, enlisted along with several of his cousins. He was massacred by Santa Ana's Mexican troops on March 27, 1836, as were all the others under U.S. Colonel Fannin's command. Also serving in the **Mexican War** was the family's second son, John Sanders, who had made the army his career. He married a Pittsburgh, Pa., socialite and rose from the rank of captain to major during the Mexican War.

Lewis Sanders became an expert in hemp production and in 1843 was appointed as the agent for the U.S. Hemp Agency in Louisville at a salary of $1,000 a year. In the days of sailing ships, hemp was important to the state's economy. But the secretary of the navy had been advised that Russian hemp was superior to the hemp subjected to the water-soaking process used in Kentucky. In 1849 Sanders conducted a series of experiments proving that the Kentucky process for making hemp produced stronger, more durable rope and that this hemp was cheaper to manufacture into rope.

In 1847 George N. Sanders moved to New York City with his young family and left the active farm management of Grass Hills in the capable hands of his youngest brother, Joseph Hawkins Sanders, who lived there with his family until 1862. In that year Grass Hills passed out of the control of the Sanders family. Lewis Sanders died in 1861. As his inheritance, his son John Sanders took the 2,580 raw acres in Texas that had been given to the family by the U.S. government because of Sam Sanders's death in the Mexican War. The Sanders daughters had already received their inheritance when they married. That left Grass Hills to George N. and Joseph H. Sanders. However, George N., a former consul to London, England, was serving the Confederacy in high-profile negotiations with European countries and had to stay in Europe for years until it was safe to return home to New York City after the **Civil War**. The Sanderses were afraid the government would confiscate their property, so they sold the entire estate in 1862 to James Frank of Ghent, who in turn sold it to John Montgomery, whose son Curtis Montgomery lived there well into the 20th century.

The Kentucky State heritage historical marker that was placed at Grass Hills in 1965 calls attention to Lewis Sanders's founding the state's agricultural fairs. Grass Hills was placed on the National Register in 1975, and when I-71 was constructed, 91 acres of the original estate were taken for highway rights of way.

Green, Karen Mauer. *The Kentucky Gazette, 1787–1800.* Baltimore: Gateway Press, 1983.

——. *The Kentucky Gazette, 1801–1820.* Baltimore: Gateway Press, 1985.

Henlein, Paul C. *Cattle Kingdom in the Ohio Valley, 1783–1860.* Lexington: Univ. of Kentucky Press, 1959.

Parker, Anna V. *The Sanders Family of Grass Hills.* Madison, Ind.: Coleman, 1966.

Sanders Family Papers, Filson Historical Society, Louisville, Ky.

Diane Perrine Coon

SANDERS, SAMUEL (b. April 16, 1813, Franklin Co., Ky.; d. March 15, 1902, Franklin Co., Ky.). The son of Peter and Sarah "Sally" Byrns Sanders, Samuel Sanders was the owner of a large amount of land in Owen Co. and a well-known riverboat pilot. He married Penelope Duvall on January 26, 1852.

Sanders was mate and pilot on the *Blue Wing*, a vessel constructed in Louisville in 1845 that ran the local Louisville-Frankfort trade. During the Civil War, he was master of the *Blue Wing #2* (built in 1850), the only steamer then in regular service on the Kentucky River. The vessel was commandeered during the Confederate occupation of Frankfort in October 1862. Union forces confiscated the *Blue Wing #2* in December 1862, because it had been trading with the Confederates, and converted it into a military transport on the Lower Mississippi River. There, Confederates captured and burned the boat later that same month. Next, Sanders piloted the *Wren*, constructed in 1862 for the Louisville-Frankfort trade, amid periodic Confederate sniper fire. The *City of Frankfort,* built in 1881, was the last steamboat commanded by Sanders. In July 1882, a newspaper named the *Yeoman* reported that "Capt. Sanders, age 69, landed the boat at Frankfort, with the Madison Indiana Brass Band aboard, drawing 1,000 spectators to the Kentucky River Landing."

Sanders's wife, Penelope, died November 6, 1887. Sanders then began selling his Owen Co. land and moved to Frankfort on September 14, 1891. At age 78, he sold land to the W. G. Simpson Masonic Lodge 472 for a cemetery in Monterey that is still in use. He also sold land in Monterey for a new brick school on June 17, 1901. Sanders died in 1902 at his home on Ann St. in Frankfort at age 89, after only a few days of illness caused by a fall. He was buried in the Frankfort Cemetery.

Coleman, J. Winston, Jr. *Steamboats on the Kentucky River.* Lexington, Ky.: Winburn Press, 1960.

"Frankfort's Oldest Citizen Passes Away," *Frankfort Newspaper Roundabout,* March 22, 1902, 4.

Murphy, Margaret Alice, and Lela Maude Hawkins. *The History of Historic Old Cedar Baptist Church and Community.* Frankfort, Ky.: Lynn, 2004.

Way, Frederick Jr., comp. *Way's Packet Directory, 1848–1983.* Athens: Ohio Univ., 1983.

Margaret A. Murphy

SANDERS HIGH SCHOOL. The combined Sanders grade school and four-year high school in Sanders was organized in 1909, and Everett Gregg, a graduate of Eastern State Normal School (Eastern Kentucky University) at Richmond, was hired as the first principal of Sanders High School. Emma O. Sanders and Rudy D. Smartt were teaching assistants.

By 1911 there were high schools operating in Carroll Co. at Carrollton, English, Ghent, Sanders, and Worthville. From 1912 to 1914, R. W. Haskins of the Western Kentucky Normal School (Western Kentucky University) at Bowling Green was the principal at Sanders High School. In 1912 J. Elmer Weldon took gold medals in English, history, medieval history, and physical geography at the Northern Kentucky Academic Tournament held at the **Dry Ridge High School**. Weldon, along with Minor Hunter, Katy Ransdall, and Amanda Tandy, graduated from Sanders High School in 1914.

A succession of principals and high school teachers were hired to serve the school between 1914 and 1926, and the enrollment in the high school ranged from 12 to 23 during those years. In 1925 a large brick school was built to house both the grade and the high schools. A year later, Sanders High School, now housed in a brand new brick building with classrooms and a gymnasium, became part of the Carroll Co. School System. In 1926 A. M. Setzer was hired as principal, and Sanders High School obtained a Class B accreditation from the state in 1927. William Harris was hired as principal in 1928 and organized the upper levels on a 6-6 plan (six months of school, six months off), with three teachers assigned full-time to the junior high and senior high school students.

In 1938 R. B. Cartmell served as principal of the Sanders Consolidated School, which had 228 students enrolled. Cartmell was superintendent of Carroll Co. Schools from 1940 to 1965. The consolidated elementary school, first known as U.S. 42 School, was renamed Cartmell Elementary School in his honor.

With the construction by the Works Progress Administration in 1938 of the large addition to the **Carrollton High School** and its new 1,000-seat gymnasium, there was now room for all the county high school students. Sanders High School was the last of the county high schools to be consolidated into Carrollton High School. By **World War II**, all the county high school students were being bused into Carrollton.

Bevarly, R. W. "History of Education in Carroll County," master's thesis, Univ. of Kentucky, 1936.

Campbell, Justine Tandy. "History of the Carroll County Schools," 1976, Carroll Co. Public Library, Carrollton, Ky.

Carrollton News Democrat, December 1, 1938, 1.

Gentry, Mary Ann. *A History of Carroll County.* Madison, Ind.: Coleman, 1984.

Parker, Anna V. "A Short History of Carroll County," 1958, Carroll Co. Public Library, Carrollton, Ky.

Diane Perrine Coon

SANDFORD, THOMAS, GENERAL (b. 1762, Westmoreland Co., Va.; d. December 10, 1808, Cincinnati, Ohio). Thomas Sandford, a Revolutionary War general, a politician, and a farmer, was described as a man six feet three inches tall who was bold and muscular and stood as straight as an arrow. General Sandford married Peggy Bell on November 10, 1805, and they had one son. The general also had two sons by a previous marriage. He came to Kentucky in 1792 and settled on the highlands south of Covington. He was a Kentucky state senator (1800–1802) and a state representative (1802). He served in the U.S. House of Representatives for two terms (1803 to 1807). Sandford appeared to have a bright future in politics, but those dreams were dashed on Saturday,

December 8, 1808. Sandford and two of his servants had gone to Cincinnati to sell some wheat they had grown on Sandford's farm, which was about three miles below the mouth of the Licking River. Sandford considered the price he was offered for the wheat too low, so he decided to take it to a mill up the Little Miami River and have it ground into meal. The weather was very stormy and both the Ohio and the Little Miami rivers were running high and swift. Sandford and his two servants battled against the current on the Ohio River and somehow managed to start the trip up the Little Miami River. The wheat was very heavy, and with the weight of the three men, the boat was barely afloat. Seeing that it was impossible to continue, Sandford turned around and returned to the Cincinnati landing on the Ohio River. When the boat struck the shore, Sandford was thrown into the river and drowned. He was 46 years old at the time of his death. Because the river was covered by ice near the shores, his body was not recovered until six weeks later. Sandford was well respected by his colleagues; at his death a resolution was passed asking members of the Kentucky General Assembly and their officers to wear black armbands for 30 days in mourning. Sandford was buried at Highland Cemetery in Fort Mitchell.

Biographical Directory of the United States Congress, 1774–1989. Washington, D.C.: Government Printing Office, 1985.

Biographical Encyclopedia of Kentucky. Cincinnati: J. M. Armstrong, 1878.

SAND RUN BAPTIST CHURCH. The Sand Run Baptist Church, located in the Hebron area of Boone Co., was constituted on March 20, 1819, with 78 members: 55 whites and 23 African Americans. Among the prominent founding members were Chichester Matthews, who became the church's first pastor; William Montague, an ordained minister; Landen Robinson, a licensed preacher; and Lewis Webb, the former clerk of the **Bullittsburg Baptist Church**. Cave Johnson (see **Cave Johnson House**) and Jeremiah Kirtley, along with their families, also joined in founding the Sand Run Baptist Church.

The Sand Run Baptist Church was a strong church from its inception and increased in strength as a number of influential local Baptists transferred their memberships to join the congregation. By the end of 1819, the Sand Run congregation had decided to build a suitable building for worship, which was going to cost $2,100. Of this amount, $1,000 was raised by subscription, and the remainder was apportioned among the free male members of the church. This was done by dividing the church's members into classes ranked according to their ability to pay. The first class was to pay $76 each, the second class $56, the third class $35, the fourth class $18, and the fifth class $11. One man was appointed to collect from those who could pay in cash, and another man was to collect from those who paid in tobacco. On Sunday, February 20, 1820, the Sand Run congregation worshipped in their new meetinghouse, although it was unfinished and without stoves. Until then, they had worshipped in private homes.

During the 19th century, three ministers at the Sand Run Baptist Church served for long periods: the church's first pastor, Chichester Matthews, served for nearly 10 years; William Whitaker, the second pastor, served for 41 years; and Robert E. Kirtley, the eldest son of Rev. Robert Kirtley and a brother of Rev. James A. Kirtley, pastored at the Sand Run church for 26 years. Robert E. Kirtley wrote the first history of the church in 1876. The church met one Saturday a month for business and one Sunday a month for worship during most of the 19th century. In 1870 the church purchased ground for a cemetery.

Barnabas, an enslaved African American who was member of the church, was recognized for his preaching ability and was encouraged to preach among the church's other slave members. He was one of only two slave preachers in the Baptist churches then operating in Boone Co.

During the 1830s, the Sand Run Baptist Church's pastor, William Montague, became influenced by the teachings of Alexander Campbell, who taught that baptism was necessary for salvation. The congregation at the Sand Run Baptist Church believed that salvation was "by grace through faith in Jesus Christ." They held a hearing, and shortly afterward Montague left the Sand Run church and joined a group that followed Campbell's teachings.

The Sand Run Baptist Church's building was damaged by fire in 1941 and subsequently repaired. In 1961 the Hebron Baptist Church was established by members who had previously belonged to the Sand Run Baptist Church; 97 members were granted letters of recommendation to the new Baptist church in Hebron. A new Sunday School building was dedicated by the Sand Run Baptist church in 1976.

Pastors during the 20th century who served for long periods at the Sand Run Baptist Church included C. J. Avery, Roy A. Johnson, Everett C. Walters, and J. R. Armstrong. Presently, the Sand Run church's pastor is Rev. Steve Cable.

Sand Run Baptist Church directories, Sand Run Baptist Church, Hebron, Ky.

James R. Duvall

SANFORDTOWN. Sanfordtown (Sandfortown) was a small community located on the **Three-L Highway** (Ky. Rt. 17) near its intersection with Dudley Pk. in Kenton Co. The eastern portions of Horsebranch and Orphanage Rds. were also considered part of this community. Early references to Sanfordtown, which was a few miles south of Latonia and Covington, were appearing in local newspapers by the 1850s. The settlers in the vicinity of Sanfordtown included English, German, and Irish immigrants as well as local residents moving from Covington. Many were Catholic, and they soon organized what became the Holy Guardian Angels parish, which began as a mission of the **St. Benedict Catholic Church** in Covington in 1856. As they outgrew their original quarters, the parishioners built a series of church and school buildings during the later 19th century.

The community was named for one of its most prominent citizens, B. F. Sanford, who lived along Ky. Rt. 17 in the early 1850s and served a variety of roles in local and national commerce and in politics. He apparently was a clerk in the U.S. State Department during the **Civil War** and by 1864 became a commercial agent in Haiti. Sanford was also a bank president and a newspaper editor. He resided in Sanfordtown until his death in 1883.

It was reported that local residents were involved in a Civil War visit by Confederate general **John Hunt Morgan** during August 1862. Confederate cavalry moved into the Sanfordtown area, said to be led by Morgan himself. John Dinser saw the Confederate troops remove a Union flag from the home of John Weisenberger and destroy it. He also reported a skirmish between the Union Home Guard and the Confederates, although no one was injured. As the Confederates retreated, they apparently captured several local Home Guardsmen, including Dinser's uncle Marcus Beach, who lived in Sanfordtown. Beach was released farther south in Crittenden.

Sanfordtown had its own post office from 1893 to 1912, and John Weisenberger was its first postmaster. The community also included at least one hotel, a grocery store, and other small, family-owned commercial enterprises through the mid-20th century. Other local family names associated with the community include Argo, Arlinghaus, Berkemier, Bilz, Boemker, Breiner, Carney, Dobblehoff, Duncan, Elam, Eubank, Farmer, Fernandes, Fey, Franxman, Goedde, Goodhew, Gripshover, Harmeling, Hellman, Hillman, Hunter, Jump, Kahmann, Krebs, Kunkel, List, Luke, Mattingly, Meiman, Merkle, Moormann, Mueller, Nageleisen, Reed, Rousch, Speaks, Wendling, and Works.

Both the 1897 flood and the **flood of 1937** caused damage to homes and to the Holy Guardian Angels Church. The church remained part of the community until it was closed in 1958, upon the completion of **St. Pius X Catholic Church** on Dudley Pk. at the top of the hill. That church served as the successor to the Holy Guardian Angels Church. At this time the Sanfordtown community was becoming less residential and more commercial and industrial.

Sanfordtown had its own fire department in the mid-20th century, until the department's merger with Edgewood's during the late 1990s. Many families had already moved away by then; the flood of 1937 and the **Great Depression** seemed to mark the beginning of the end for this small farming community. After **World War II**, most residents sold their farms. By the 1970s, much of the original farmland had become industrial or commercial property. The construction of I-275 in the 1970s finished the demise of the area as a residential and farming community. Part of Sanfordtown is now in Fort Wright and part in Edgewood.

"Postmaster Now," *KP*, September 11, 1893, 1.
Reis, Jim. "Golden Time for Edgewood: Upscale Suburb to Celebrate 50 Years as Incorporated Area," *KP*, January 12, 1998, 4K.
Ryan, Paul E. *History of the Diocese of Covington, Kentucky*. Covington, Ky.: Diocese of Covington, 1954.

Jeannine Kreinbrink

SANITATION. In towns throughout Northern Kentucky, as late as the mid-20th century, it was assumed that waste of all kinds could safely be discharged into the Ohio River, via the nearest stream or creek. Today residents of the region understand that appropriate wastewater facilities and infrastructure are essential to help prevent widespread epidemics and to protect the natural environment.

Acknowledgment of the need for formalized sewage disposal dates back to 4000 B.C. in the Mesopotamian Empire. The need for proper disposal of human waste was associated then with benefits such as odor reduction and other practical conveniences; the public health risk arising from exposed, untreated waste was not yet fully understood. From this time period until the collapse of the Roman Empire early in the first millennium, public storm-water drainage and aqueduct systems were already in place throughout many of the civilized societies, such as those in Greece, Egypt, and Rome. Some homes were directly connected to the storm-water system as a means to carry waste away from their property; however, the use of cesspools was more common.

Cesspools were covered pits underneath an opening in the floor of a home or a public latrine; the cesspool had a perforated lining into which raw sewage was filtered and discharged into the soil. Aside from direct connections to the storm-water system and the utilization of cesspools, public streets served as disposal sites for most garbage and excrement. It was common practice to dump jars of human waste out of windows and into the street. Extensive street-washing programs periodically cleaned the waste from the streets and moved it into the storm-sewer system. Communities throughout the United States, including the municipalities established in Northern Kentucky in the late 1800s and early 1900s, used these procedures as forms of sewage disposal. Privies, or outhouses, were also quite common in Northern Kentucky.

It was not until midway through the 19th century that efficient sewage systems developed in the United States. After the onset of cholera and typhoid epidemics, citizens began to establish the link between sewage disposal and public health, and this new association prompted the development of improved sewage disposal systems. The primary motivation at the time was to divert sewage away from sources of water, such as private wells; the environmental implications of dumping raw sewage onto land and into waterways had not yet become a major concern.

Two options were considered when communities wished to construct a sewage collection and disposal system—a combined system and a separate system. A combined sewer system carries sewage and storm water in the same pipe. A separate sewer system carries only wastewater; storm water is conveyed in a completely separate system. The sewer systems constructed in the early 1900s along the river cities of Northern Kentucky, including Bellevue, Covington, Dayton, Newport, and Southgate, were combined sewers. Storm water and sewage from these communities was collected in the already existing storm-water system and discharged into local waterways, which all eventually drained into the Ohio River. It was not until the 1960s that separate sanitary sewer systems were constructed in the region.

During the time when combined sewer systems were an acceptable means of sewage disposal, "dilution as the solution to pollution" was a common practice within many communities and was endorsed by many engineers and sanitarians. The concept was to dispose of sanitary sewage through dilution by discharging wastes into rivers, streams, lakes, and oceans. Engineers of the time concluded that it was less expensive to obtain good drinking water by filtering river water filled with sewage than to treat sewage before discharging it into the rivers. Communities did not want to face the fiscal burden of funding both sewage treatment facilities and water filtration facilities, and they did not believe both were necessary.

It was not until the development of more stringent environmental regulations in the mid-1900s that communities in Northern Kentucky were required to implement a method of sewage treatment. The Federal Water Pollution Control Act of 1948, which preceded the Clean Water Act of 1977, established the basic structure for regulating the discharge of pollutants into the waters of the United States. Because of the growing amount of residential, commercial, and industrial waste that accompanied the development of the Northern Kentucky region, it was no longer an acceptable practice to dump raw sewage into the environment.

After recognizing the ever-increasing role that municipalities must play in the design and construction of sewers, most cities, by this time, had acquired ownership of the sewer systems within their communities. Although each municipality owned and maintained its own system, the need to establish a regional sanitary district to treat the sewage collected from each municipality was recognized, and in 1946 **Sanitation District No. 1** was formed. In 1954 Northern Kentucky's first wastewater treatment plant began operation in the city of Bromley. Over the ensuing years, Sanitation District No. 1 has grown into a regional storm-water and wastewater utility that owns and maintains more than 1,500 miles of sanitary sewer line and serves 33 communities within Boone, Campbell, and Kenton counties.

Smaller package treatment plants throughout Northern Kentucky serve counties outside of Boone, Campbell, and Kenton. The areas of Northern Kentucky that are not served by a public sewer system utilize on-site disposal systems, or septic systems. Septic systems are self-contained sewage treatment systems that distribute wastewater to an underground storage area and rely on bacterial action to decompose solid waste. Failing septic systems can lead to surface water contamination and groundwater pollution, causing a potential health hazard. As a result, assessment projects continue to take place throughout the region in order to extend public sewer service into the rural communities of Northern Kentucky.

"District Flush with Upgrades," *SC*, September 25, 2005, 3A.
Dunn, Megan. "After the Flush," *KP*, June 20, 1994, 4K.
"$880M Sewer Solution," *SC*, October 9, 2005, 1A.
"Sewer Merger Closer," *KP*, September 10, 1991, 1K–2K.
Tracking Down the Roots of Our Sanitary Sewers. www.sewerhistory.org (accessed July 19, 2006).
Wolfe, Pamila. "History of Wastewater." In *World of Water 2000—The Past, Present, and Future*. Tulsa, Okla.: Pennwell Magazine, 1999.

Maggie Mulshine

SANITATION DISTRICT NO. 1. Sanitation District No. 1 was established in 1946 by the Division of Sanitary Engineering of the Kentucky Department of Health, pursuant to an amendment of Chapter 220.00 of the Kentucky Revised Statutes (KRS 220.00). Before 1946, a small system of sewer lines already existed in Northern Kentucky; however, the region was still in need of proper wastewater treatment. KRS 220.00 provides the Sanitation District with the authority to prevent and correct the pollution of streams, regulate the flow of streams for sanitary purposes, clean and improve stream channels for sanitary purposes, and collect and dispose of sewage and other liquid wastes produced throughout the established service area. It also granted the Sanitation District authority to construct sewers, trunk sewers, laterals, intercepting sewers, siphons, pump stations, treatment and disposal works, and other appropriate facilities. The Sanitation District's authority under KRS 220.00 also includes responsibility for the maintenance and operation of these structures and facilities.

The original area served by the Sanitation District included 17 municipalities and covered 25 square miles. It was the Sanitation District's responsibility to construct a sewage-treatment plant and a large interceptor sewer system that would collect and convey sewage from the various municipalities to a treatment facility. At that time, each community maintained ownership of its own sewage collection system. In 1954, after many years of planning, the Sanitation District completed construction of Northern Kentucky's first wastewater treatment plant in Bromley, along the Ohio River in northern Kenton Co. Serving Campbell and Kenton counties, the Bromley Wastewater Treatment Plant provided primary treatment of wastewater before discharging it into the Ohio River.

The Bromley Wastewater Treatment Plant eventually became outdated due to increasingly stringent water-quality regulations, advancements in wastewater technology, and the area's growing population. In 1970 the Ohio River Valley Water Sanitation Commission adopted requirements for secondary treatment of sewage for all waters that feed into the Ohio River. In 1977 the U.S. Congress passed the Clean Water Act, granting the Environmental Protection Agency (EPA) authority further to regulate the discharge of pollutants into the waters of the United States. The original Bromley plant provided minimal treatment and could not comply with these new regulatory standards. Therefore, the Sanitation District constructed the Dry Creek Wastewater Treatment Plant, which began service in 1979. This project also included the construction of new interceptor sewers and pump stations. Located in Villa Hills, the treatment plant was designed to treat 30 million gallons a day (mgd). In 1993, because of the continued population growth of Northern Kentucky, the plant was upgraded to a design capacity of 46.5 mgd.

In 1994, because of pending changes in environmental regulations and increased public interest in consolidation of services, KRS 220.00 was amended, allowing the Sanitation District to assume ownership of the cities' sewage and drainage systems located within its jurisdictional boundaries. On July 1, 1995, 28 cities in Northern Kentucky turned over ownership of their sanitary sewer systems to the Sanitation District. On December 31, 1995, Boone Co. officially merged its sanitary sewer system with the Sanitation District, and subsequently the cities of Independence and Alexandria transferred ownership of their sewer lines to the District. As a result of these consolidations, the Sanitation District assumed ownership and operational responsibility for approximately 900 additional miles of sanitary sewer lines and related pump stations.

Legislation adopted in 1998 by the Kentucky legislature granted the Sanitation District authority to regulate and finance storm-water facilities within its designated service area. In response to requests from 35 Northern Kentucky communities, the Sanitation District accepted the responsibility to develop and implement a regional storm-water management program to comply with U.S. EPA's 1999 Federal Stormwater Phase II Regulations. This role was formalized in 2003, through the development and adoption of interlocal agreements to provide Kentucky Pollutant Discharge Elimination System storm-water discharge permit services and other storm-water-related services in Boone, Campbell, and Kenton counties. The cities and counties agreed to maintain ownership of the storm-water collection systems, with the understanding that the Sanitation District would assume responsibility for the operation and maintenance of the public storm-water systems.

Today, the Sanitation District is the second-largest public sewer utility in Kentucky, with ownership and maintenance responsibilities for all of the sanitary sewer systems in Northern Kentucky, with the exception of Florence and Walton. The Sanitation District maintains more than 1,600 miles of sewer line, 127 pump stations, 15 flood pump stations, 8 package treatment plants, and one major wastewater treatment plant. It employs more than 200 persons and serves approximately 90,000 customer accounts. The three judge executives of Boone, Kenton, and Campbell counties provide governance of the Sanitation District. The judge executives appoint a total of eight directors to serve staggered four-year terms on the Sanitation District's board.

In 2004 the Sanitation District opened Public Service Park at its administrative office site in Fort Wright. Featuring environmental best-management practices and formalized educational programming, the park provides an interactive means to learn about the impacts of polluted storm-water runoff. The Sanitation District has also created a water-quality curriculum that is taught in nearly every elementary school in Northern Kentucky and in addition offers classroom presentations and tours of its treatment facility.

In April 2007 the Sanitation District entered into a consent decree with the U.S. Environmental Protection Agency, the Commonwealth of Kentucky, and the U.S. Department of Justice, requiring an estimated $1.1 billion investment over the next 20 years to address sewage overflows in Northern Kentucky. Included in the consent decree is the requirement to construct two new regional wastewater treatment plants, a 4 mgd plant in Campbell Co. and a 20 mgd plant in Boone Co. The Campbell Co. facility began operation in September 2007 and the Boone Co. facility is scheduled to be completed in 2013. In making future improvement plans, the Sanitation District will take a watershed approach, holistically evaluating the cumulative impacts of pollution sources on receiving waters. Adopting a watershed approach will lead to more rapid improvements in water quality in critical areas and more efficient and cost-effective solutions for the region.

Kentucky Revised Statutes, Chapter 220.00.
Sanitation District No. 1. www.sd1.org (accessed April 1, 2006).
"State Approves New Treatment Plant in Boone," *KP*, December 21, 2005, 2K.

Peggy Casey

SARDIS. Sardis is a town of about 150 people in the southwest corner of Mason Co., along the Robertson Co. line. It was incorporated on February 14, 1850. The town's first trustees were Luke Dye, John Murphy, Isaac Reid, James Vanderburg, and Peyton White. During the **Civil War**, the community was ransacked by Confederate general **John Hunt Morgan**'s men on June 12, 1864. The Bank of Sardis opened in 1904, with Louden Grover as its president, but the enterprise failed in 1912. J. M. Wheatley's opera house was built in 1907 and had seating for 500. Elementary grade schools were established in the community from its beginning, and a high school began in the years between 1910 and 1920. The girls' basketball team at the high school was the state tournament runner-up in 1922. A fine brick school was dedicated in 1931. The high school remained until 1936, and earlier grades were taught there until 1967. Sardis had both proslavery and antislavery Methodist churches, which united after the Civil War. The United Methodist Church in town has worshipped in its present building since 1941. A small picturesque post office serves the community.

Calvert, Jean, and John Klee. *The Towns of Mason County: Their Past in Pictures.* Maysville, Ky.: Maysville and Mason Co. Library Historical and Scientific Association, 1986.
Clift, G. Glenn. *History of Maysville and Mason County.* Lexington, Ky.: Transylvania, 1936.

John Klee

SAVINGS AND LOAN ASSOCIATIONS. Savings and Loan Associations, which were referred to as Building and Loan Associations until about 1930, enabled many Americans, including Northern Kentuckians, to own their homes. The first building and loan association (B&L) in the United States was opened in Philadelphia in 1816. Other B&Ls soon followed, and there was modest growth in the industry before the **Civil War**. Those early associations were primarily small local lenders, to whom working-class people could entrust their savings and from whom they could borrow funds for the purchase of a home. The number of B&Ls grew from just a few hundred, many located in the eastern and midwestern states in 1850, to many thousands spread across the nation by 1900. There were two types of institutions. One was a nonprofit mutual company, in which depositors became part owners, with voting rights; in the other type, stock was issued, and the company operated as most other for-profit businesses did. There were both advantages and disadvantages in operating a B&L. The federal government granted preferential treatment, by allowing B&Ls to offer higher savings interest rates than commercial banks. This enabled B&Ls to attract more deposits and thereby provided them with the ability to grant more home loans. The disadvantages were that they were not permitted to offer checking accounts and other bank services; as a result, many of their customers also had to deal with a commercial bank. The B&Ls became a strong economic force during the 20th century, and offices were found in most Northern Kentucky cities. In 1900 there were about 5,300 associations nationwide, and by 1925 the number had grown to 12,000. Many B&Ls had their origins in local ethnic neighborhoods. The Austinburg district of Covington had the Burnett Perpetual Building and Loan Association at 1607 Eastern Ave., with strong German ties to its nearby patrons; the city's African Americans organized the **Progressive Building and Loan Association** as a means to bring home ownership to a population not readily served; since 1880 Ludlow has had the Home Savings Bank at 216 Elm St., an organization that has helped to bring roots to the many railroad workers of that Kenton Co. river city; and in Campbell Co., firms such as the Clifton-Southgate Federal Savings and Loan Association, at 10th and Monmouth St. in Newport, financed numerous homes in the area.

After 1930 most of these institutions were called savings and loans (S&Ls). In 1932 the Federal Home Bank System was created to oversee the operation of S&Ls and to provide their customers with FSLIC (Federal Savings and Loan Insurance Corporation) insurance on deposits. The number of S&Ls decreased during the **Great Depression**, primarily because of poor economic conditions and widespread unemployment. During **World War II**, the S&Ls continued to suffer, and by war's end their number had decreased to about 6,100. The post–World War II housing boom was the most financially successful period ever for S&Ls. By 1965 they controlled more than one-fourth of all personal savings accounts and nearly half of all single-family mortgages. Real estate developers owned a controlling interest in many S&Ls, as they made loans to themselves and their affiliated companies. As a result, many S&Ls became insolvent, and their numbers had dropped to 4,000 by 1980. The federal government, in an attempt to allow the institutions to "grow out of their problems," gave them the right to make both secured and unsecured loans and to grant commercial credit. The government also relaxed accounting rules, which permitted the associations to begin listing intangible assets, such as goodwill, on their balance sheets, making their financial condition appear better than it actually was. As a result of those changes, many loan officers who lacked the lending experience, knowledge, and integrity to properly evaluate loan risks made numerous bad loans.

For many years, the state with the most S&Ls was Ohio, and more than half of Ohio's S&Ls were in Hamilton Co., Ohio. In Cincinnati, **German Americans** sponsored many S&Ls, and that tradition spilled over the Ohio River into Northern Kentucky. Known as *bauvereins*, meaning "building societies" in German, they were an important means of home ownership in the metropolitan area. In the early 1980s, when it merged with another institution, Covington's General Savings and Loan was the longest-operating S&L in Kentucky, having remained in business just over 110 years.

During the 1980s, more than 500 S&Ls failed, and the FSLIC insurance fund was depleted. To protect depositors, the federal government intervened and financially bailed out many of the insolvent companies. The Federal Home Loan Bank Board, which oversaw the Federal Home Bank System, was abolished and replaced with the Office of Thrift Supervision, and the FSLIC was replaced with the FDIC (Federal Deposit Insurance Corporation) deposit insurance. Laws were changed to allow S&Ls to offer checking accounts and other banking services. As was typical of what was happening across the country, many Northern Kentucky S&Ls ceased operating, merged with other financial institutions, or became virtually indistinguishable from commercial banks. Some inserted the word *bank* in their company's name. Because of those factors, only about 1,100 savings and loan institutions survived to the year 2000. However, many of the survivors had grown very large, and the industry still controlled nearly $900 billion in assets. At the present time, the Kentucky Federal Savings and Loan, Citizens Federal, and the Guardian Savings Bank are among the few that remain in the Northern Kentucky counties of Boone, Campbell, and Kenton.

"Cincinnati's Thrifts Seem About to Lose Old German Flavor," *Wall Street Journal*, March 26, 1985, 1.

Eckberg, John. "Neighborhood Tradition Started Savings Industry," *KE*, March 24, 1985, A1.

EH.net. "Savings and Loan Industry (U.S.)." www.eh.net/encyclopedia (accessed December 21, 2005).

"Grand Opening Saturday for Home Building," *Ludlow News Enterprise*, September 17, 1959, 1.

Infoplease. "Savings and Loan Association." www.infoplease.com (accessed December 21, 2005).

Wikipedia. "Savings and Loan Association." www.wikipedia.org (accessed December 21, 2005).

SAWMILLS. Sawmills were established in Northern Kentucky during the 19th century as settlers began to build frame structures rather than hand-hewed log buildings. The lumber turned out by sawmills was needed to build not only houses but also outbuildings, public buildings, factories and businesses, boats, wagons, and bridges; additional needs for lumber included the making of furniture and other items.

The early sawmills were water powered and located along streams with adequate water flow. Permission had to be secured from the county court system, since millponds could flood the properties of adjacent landowners. It was not uncommon for gristmills and sawmills to be operated at the same location. Dams built of logs or stone provided the water supply to power these mills. A millrace or flume (an elevated wooden trough) was constructed to convey the water from the dam to the mill, where the water was converted into power by using water wheels or turbines that turned a main shaft. Steam engines later permitted the construction of mills in small communities far from streams and in urban contexts. By the early 20th century, water-powered sawmills had nearly disappeared from Northern Kentucky, replaced by sawmills powered by steam engines. Most sawmills were simple buildings equipped with saws and a carriage for pushing the logs to the saw blade. Later sawmills had more complex equipment and performed other tasks beyond rough sawing.

The technology for producing lumber changed through the years. The earliest method utilized a whipsaw that two men operated by pushing up and down to cut one board at a time. Early machine-powered saws were sash saws that moved up and down to saw boards. Muley saws (with heavy iron blades and no wooden frames) followed these and were faster than the sash saws. The subsequent circular saws were 10 times faster than the muley saws but were much more wasteful.

Northern Kentucky once had numerous sawmills. Little information is available regarding the earliest ones. By the mid-19th century, statewide gazetteers and city directories became available that listed these businesses. These sources, along with city directories, permit a partial listing of mills that were active in Northern Kentucky.

Boone Co.

At Petersburg, a 19th-century manufacturing center, were the sawmills of J. C. Jenkins & Company (1865–1866), Grant & Riggs (1876–1877), J. Frank Grant (1879–1884), and Merit Lening (1887–1888). In Walton, Rouse Brothers (1879–1888) and Walton Lumber (1930–1949) were important producers of lumber.

Bracken Co.

Most of the county lumber producers were located in Augusta. They included G. W. Moneyhon and Brother (1876–1877), G. W. and H. Moneyhon (1879–1880), W. B. Allen's saw and planing mill (1884), George T. Kearns's saw and planing mill (1884), G. W. Moneyhon's saw and planing mill (1884), the G. W. Moneyhon Company (1896–1906), and Moneyhon, Kearns & Company (1881–1883).

Campbell Co.

Among Campbell Co. lumber producers were John Gubser's steam sawmill (see **Gubser's Mill**). At Bellevue, lumberyards were operated by Phillip Lewis on Fairfield Ave. at the corner of Patchen Ave. (1878–1880); McHenry & McGuire, at the southeast corner of Popular St. and Lafayette Ave. (1892); the Bellevue Planing Mill Company, at the foot of Van Voast Ave. (1894–1900); the Bellevue & Dayton Planing Mill Company, at the foot of Van Voast Ave. (1897); the J. A. Brownfield Company, at the foot of Van Voast Ave. (1898); the Kentucky Manufacturing Company, at 52 Fairfield Ave. (1898–1900); and the G & F Hardware & Builders Supply Company, at 155 Fairfield Ave. (1923).

Newport was the largest center of the lumber industry in Campbell Co. and the second-largest producer of lumber in Northern Kentucky. Only Covington had a larger lumber industry. The numerous companies and individuals sawing and selling lumber in Newport included many with locations on Monmouth St.: John Taylor & Sons, at the northeast corner of Monmouth and Ringold Sts. (1861–1869); J. C. Gaddis & Company (1869–1874); James K. Stone (later Stone & Miller) (1878–1905); Joseph Weingartner, whose firm became Weingartner Lumber Company Inc. and later moved to John St. (1880–1924); Eagle Planing Mill & Star Lumber Company (1888–1891); Philip J. Veith (1892–1894); Veith & Rashe (1895); Fred Miller (1906–1917); and the Cincinnati Poplar Company (1910–1911).

The community of Dayton was the second-largest lumber center in Campbell Co., after Newport. The many sawmills and lumberyards in Dayton included Meade & Cibber (1873–1874); George Maxey, at the southwest corner of Sixth and Main Aves. (1884–1885); Maxey & Harris, at the southeast corner of Third and Berry Aves. (1884–1885); Willison & Wilmer, at the northwest corner of Fairfield Ave. and McKinney St. (1886–1887) and then at 67 Fairfield Ave. (1888–1891); Wilmer Bros., at 67 Fairfield Ave. (1892); the Dayton Lumber Company, at the northwest corner of Fairfield Ave. and McKinney St. (1894); Kennedy & Bevland, at the northwest corner of Walnut and Popular Sts. (1894); Hugh Kennedy, at the corner of Walnut St. and the **Chesapeake and Ohio Railroad** (1895–1897); the Newport and Dayton Lumber Company, at 212 Lindsey St. (1904–1905) and at

214 Lindsey St. (1906–1907); the W. J. Wilmer Lumber Company, at 120 Sixth Ave. (1908–1911); the G & F Hardware & Lumber Company, at 214 Lindsey St. (1928–1929); and the G & F Lumber Company (1945).

Carroll Co.

Carrollton had the greatest concentration of lumberyards in Carroll Co. They included P. Hunley (1859–1860), Samuel Johnston (1859–1860), T. F. Landers (1859–1860), John Meier (1873–1877), F. J. Miller & Company (1873–1874), Ebenezer Hafford (1876–1887), Baker & Gin (1879–1880), Baker, Ginn & Company (1881–1883), G. F. Bannock (1883), J. G. Ginn (1883), Adkinson Brothers (1896), Ginn & Stanton (1896), the Grobmeyer Coal and Lumber Yard (?–1948), Howard B. Rich Inc., on Sixth St. (1949), and the East End Lumber Company (1955–1958).

Gallatin Co.

Sawmills and lumber mills at Warsaw were D. B. Dailey (1873–1874), James A. Howard (1876–1888), the Sparta Lumber & Manufacturing Company (1949), and the Wilson Manufacturing Company (1949).

Grant Co.

John Collins (1883–1884) sold lumber in New Eagles Mills, while John R. Shigger (1879–1882), Benjamin Burkley (1887–1888), and Thomas Carter (1887–1888) sawed lumber in Stewartsville. At Williamstown, lumber was produced and sold by Frank Carder (1879–1884), Hudson (1887–1888), R. H. Elliston & Company (1906), and James Lummis & Company, located four miles east of Williamstown.

Kenton Co.

Covington, which supported more sawmills, lumberyards, and related businesses than any other area of Northern Kentucky, had a major lumber industry during much of its history. Over the years, some of the companies changed their names and underwent changes in ownership. There were companies with long histories and others that existed only briefly. A couple of businesses appear to have sold recycled lumber; one group of businesses sold lumber but did no sawing. Among the companies involved in lumber production and sales were these: the Licking Valley Saw Mill, on the Licking River between 12th and 13th Sts. (1851–1855); E. T. Rusk & Company (1855); Rusk & Carithers's steam sawmill, on the bank of the Ohio River just below Willow Run (1855–1897); Ezra Baily & Son, on the river between Main and Johnston Sts. (1861), at the northeast corner of Second and Main Sts. (1866–1867), at the corner of Seventh and Main Sts. (1868), at the foot of Main St. (1871–1872); C. A. and W. C. Culbertson, south side of the Seventh St. Market (1861); W. C. Culbertson, on the north side of Pike St. opposite the depot (1861), on Seventh St. between Washington St. and Madison Ave. (1866), on Eighth St. between Madison Ave. and Washington St. (1871–1872); the Covington Saw Mills, on the south side of Second St. between Main and Johnston Sts. (1866–1867); John Harremeier, on the north side of Pike St. between Craig and Greer Sts. (1866); **J. D. Shutt** and Company, on the west side of Scott St. between Second and Third Sts. (1866–1867), 225 Scott St. (1868–1877); Culbertson & Alexander, 23 Seventh St. near Depot (1868–1869); Creen, Culbertson & Company, at the corner of Second and Main Sts. (1876–1877); D. C. Culbertson & Brother, Main St. at northwest corner of Second St. (1878–1897), at the northeast corner of Second and Main Sts. (1880–1894); J. A. Culbertson & Company, 16–32 W. Eighth St. (1878–1881), 22 W. Eighth St. (1888–1889); C. C. Hagemeyer & Company (1881–1882), **Jacob Price**, 412 Madison Ave. (1884–1885), 428 Madison Ave. (1886–1889), 426 Madison Ave. (1890–1896), 425 Madison Ave. (1897–1903); **J. T. Hatfield**, 111 Powell St. (1886–1887); Clemens Hellmann, 165 W. 12th St. (1886–1905); the Ohio Scroll & Lumber Company, at the northwest corner of 12th and Washington Sts. (1886–1895), at the northeast corner of Russell Ave. and Stewart St. (1900–1901), on the north side of Stewart east of Russell Ave. (1918–1921, 1951–1954); the Covington Lumber Company, on the west side of Madison Ave. near the Kentucky Central Shops (1892–1902), Madison Ave. near the **Louisville and Nashville Railroad** Shops (1902–1906), at the southwest corner of Madison Ave. and Hicks St. (1908–1911); the Covington Saw Mill Company, at the northeast corner of Second and Main Sts. (1895–1897), at the foot of Main St. (1898–1903); W. Jas. Salter, 225 Scott St. (1897); George Lubrecht, at the northwest corner of Pike and York Sts. (1904–1905); Heilmann Lumber Company (1906); Hellmann Lumber & Manufacturing Company, 165 W. 12th St. (1906–1919), 321 W. 12th St. (1920–1932), 321 W. 12th St. (1936–1958); Veith & Zweigart, 22 W. Eighth St. (1908–1915), at the southwest corner of 16th St. and Madison Ave. (1916–1919), at the southwest corner of Madison Ave. and 24th St. (1920–1921); the Beets Lumber Company, at 32nd St. and DeCoursey Ave. and Union St. (1916–1932); the A. M. Lewin Lumber Company, at the southwest corner of Madison Ave. and 24th St. (1923–1954); the Yates-Lahner Company Inc., Southern Ave. and the Louisville and Nashville Railroad (1923–1937); Ray Price, 103 W. 10th St. (1926–1927); the Advance Millwork Company, on Garrard at the southeast corner of Eighth St. (1929–1958); the Yates Lumber Company Inc., Southern Ave. and the Louisville and Nashville Railroad (1929–1939), 34th St. and DeCoursey Ave. (1940–1956); and Kelly Brothers Lumber Company, Latonia Ave. at the southeast corner of 35th St. (1948–1995).

The three lumber producers at Erlanger included the Boone-Kenton Lumber Company Inc., at 219 Crescent Ave. (1931–1966); the Erlanger Lumber Company, at **Dixie Highway** and the **Southern Railway** (1931–1941), at Dixie Highway near corner of Crescent Ave. (1943–1956); and Bass & Company, Kenton Lands Rd. (1957–1958). Still operating is the Independence Lumber and Supply Company in Independence.

Lumber producers operating in Ludlow were H. Barr and Company, on Ash at the northeast corner of Carneal (1878–1879); James H. Barr, on the northeast corner of Ash and Carneal Sts. (1879–1887); R. H. Fleming, at 83 Elmond St. and the foot of Carneal St. (1888–1889), on the northeast corner of George and Elm Sts. (1890–1893), at the foot of Kenner St. (1894–1896), 92 Elm St. (1897–1899); Ludlow Lumber Company, at the foot of Carneal St. (1902–1903); and the Ideal Supply Company Inc. (J. J. Weaver, president; Williams S. Ludlow, vice president; **Ulie J. Howard**, secretary), at 312 Adela Ave. (1928–1929), 512 Adela Ave. (1931–1948).

Mason Co.

Maysville was the center of the lumber business in Mason Co. Sawmills and lumberyards included R. W. Thompson, lumberyard on Second St. below Fish St. (1829); Morris A. Hutchins (1831); Rueben Case (1833); F. McLanahan (1859–1860); W. B. Mathews (1876–1880); Charles Phister (1876–1877); Collins, Rudy & Company (1881–1884); W. B. Mathews & Company, at 341 E. Second St. (1881–1914); J. L. Manker (1881–1882); Collins & Rudy Lumber Company (1887–1896); Ohio River Lumber Company (1902–1914); H. H. Collins Lumber Company (1906); Mason Lumber Company Inc., at E. Second St., northeast corner of Limestone St. (A. A. McLaughlin and L. N. Behan) (1913–1918); Limestone Lumber Company, 329 E. Second St. (1916–1921), Second St. and the northwest corner of Commerce St. (1922–1935); and Maysville Lumber Company, at 139–143 E. Second St. (1922–1934).

Owen Co.

Bart Mason (1886) had a lumber business at Lusby's Mill. Sawmills in Owenton included the Roland Brothers (1876–1884), C. G. Kenney (1883–1888), I. F. Mundy (1883–1884), the Kenney Brothers (1896), James Johnson (1906), and C. W. Kenney (1929).

Pendleton Co.

Many small communities participated in the lumber industry in Pendleton Co. B. F. Hume placed an ad in the May 10, 1851, issue of the *Covington Journal* offering for sale a steam sawmill about eight miles from Falmouth. The mill was warranted to saw 4,000 feet of lumber in 12 hours. The county seat of Falmouth had the following saw and lumber mills: J. E. and J. W. Thompson, at Main and Cross Sts. near the Licking River (1874–1880); J. E. Thompson (1881–1884); J. W. Ashbrook (1883–1884); Bidge Bishop (1883–1888); William Fardo (1883–1884); G. W. Galloway (1883–1884); George Myers (1896); and T. M. Shoemaker & Company (1887–1906). At Gardnersville, R. McNay (1879–1888) sawed lumber.

Clark, Victor S. "Manufactures of Wood." In *History of Manufactures in the United States,* vol. 3. New York: Peter Smith, 1949.

Clift, G. Glenn. *History of Maysville and Mason County.* Lexington, Ky.: Transylvania, 1936.

Collins, Richard H. *History of Kentucky.* Vol. 1. Covington, Ky.: Collins, 1882.

Hawes, George W. *George Hawes' Kentucky State Gazetteer and Business Directory for 1859 and 1860.* Louisville, Ky.: George W. Hawes, 1859.

Hodgman, George H. *Hodgman & Co.'s Kentucky State Gazetteer, Shippers' Guide, and Business Directory, for 1865 and 1866.* Louisville, Ky.: Hodgman, 1865.

——. *Kentucky State Directory, Travelers and Shippers' Guide, for 1870–1871.* Louisville, Ky.: John P. Morton, 1870.

Ohio Valley Publishing Company. *Kentucky State Directory and Shipper's Guide for 1873–1874.* Louisville, Ky.: Ohio Valley, 1873.

Purvis, Thomas L., ed. *Newport, Kentucky: A Bicentennial History.* Newport, Ky.: Otto Zimmerman, 1996.

Seiller, Edward F. *Kentucky Natural Resources, Industrial Statistics, Industrial Directory, Descriptions by Counties.* Kentucky Bureau of Agriculture, Labor, and Statistics, Bulletin 34. Frankfort, Ky.: State Journal, 1929.

Tenkotte, Paul A. "Rival Cities to Suburbs: Covington and Newport, Kentucky, 1790–1890," PhD diss., Univ. of Cincinnati, 1989.

T. J. Smith and Company. *Covington City Directory.* Cincinnati: T. J. Smith, 1868, 1871.

Williams and Company. Williams' Covington and Newport city directories, 1861–1948.

Worrel, Stephen W., and Anne W. Fitzgerald. *Boone County, Kentucky County Court Orders, 1799–1815.* Falls Creek, Va.: Privately published, 1994.

Young and Company. *Business Professional Directory of the Cities and Towns of Kentucky.* Atlanta, Ga.: Young, 1906.

Charles D. Hockensmith

SCHAFFER, ROBERT J. (b. December 12, 1921, St. Bernard, Ohio). Robert Joseph Schaffer, the son of John Jacob and Mary Ann Gerwin Schaffer, has contributed much to the musical life of Northern Kentucky and Cincinnati in his roles as music director at Covington's **Cathedral Basilica of the Assumption**, series director and founder of the Cathedral Concert Series, and music professor at **Thomas More College** and at the former **Seminary of St. Pius X**. In addition, he helped to establish the transition in Roman Catholic music for the liturgy after the vast changes of the Second Vatican Council (1963–1967).

Robert was educated in Cincinnati at St. Clement Elementary and Roger Bacon High School. During **World War II**, he served in a U.S. Army band in Coventry, England; after several years the band moved to London, to fill the place of the Glenn Miller U.S. Army Air force band, which had been transferred to Paris, France. After the war, Robert returned to Cincinnati to work as an organist and as a freelance trombonist-pianist. He studied Gregorian chant at the Atheneum of Ohio in Cincinnati and earned a BA in music (organ performance) with Parvin Titus at the Cincinnati Conservatory of Music.

It was at the organ department of the conservatory that Schaffer met Rita Avram, a fellow organ student, whom he eventually married. Both completed graduate degrees in New York City. Robert Schaffer entered the Graduate School of Arts and Sciences at New York University in New York City and studied musicology. Among his professors were noted scholars Curt Sachs and Gustav Reese; Schaffer's focus was the polyphonic masses of the Renaissance masters. Rita earned an MA in sacred music at Union Theological Seminary School of Sacred Music in Cincinnati, studying organ with Vernon de Tar. The couple's three children have worked solely in music: Mark (d. 1993) earned a PhD in musicology from the Cincinnati College–Conservatory of Music; as a Fulbright Scholar in organ at Hamburg (Germany), he studied with Heinz Wunderlich. At the time of his death, he was director of music at the Hyde Park (Ohio) Community Methodist Church. Gregory (b. 1956), associate organist–choral assistant at the Covington Cathedral Basilica of the Assumption, is an improviser and a freelance keyboardist. Rebecca Schaffer Wells (b. 1960) earned her BA from Thomas More College and studied music as a graduate student at Miami University, Oxford, Ohio. During the first years of marriage and children, Robert Schaffer continued his education at Columbia University in New York City, in doctoral composition.

Schaffer's longest professional association has been as music director for the Covington Cathedral Basilica of the Assumption. He was hired as organist in 1949, left to complete his graduate work, and returned in 1952. His role was expanded to music director under Bishop **William Mulloy** in 1958 (see **Cathedral Basilica of the Assumption Choral Music; Pipe Organs**).

When the Second Vatican Council opened the way for liturgy in the vernacular, that is, the local language of each country, Schaffer composed numerous masses, including *For American Martyrs, Chorale, American Wedding Program,* and choral works. His former Cathedral colleague, Omer Westendorf, of the World Library of Sacred Music, published these works. *For American Martyrs* and *Chorale* are used currently in many dioceses in North America.

Schaffer taught in Covington at the Cathedral Lyceum (the Cathedral Basilica of the Assumption's parish elementary school) and at **La Salette Academy**. Eventually, he was asked to assist Sr. Marcella Fedders, O.S.B., in her teaching duties at Covington's Villa Madonna College (now Thomas More College), and upon her retirement Schaffer assumed the faculty position, teaching music history and chorus. Schaffer still relishes teaching music history there. Several of his Thomas More students, as well as students from the other institutions where he has taught, have participated in the Bishop's Choir at the Cathedral Basilica of the Assumption. In 1998 Thomas More College awarded him the honorary degree LittD. Schaffer was concurrently professor of music at the diocesan seminary, St. Pius X Seminary, where he taught many priests of the Diocese of Covington and other dioceses (see **Roman Catholics**).

Schaffer is a member and former dean of the American Society of Composers, Authors, and Publishers and a member of the American Guild of Organists and the Conference of Roman Catholic Cathedral Musicians. He has been a faculty member at sacred music workshops throughout the United States and Canada and is a former member of the Board of Directors of the Composer's Forum for Catholic Worship. He was an organist for the Cincinnati Symphony Orchestra under music director Max Rudolf (1958–1970) and has worked with conductors of world stature, such as Leonard Bernstein, James Levine, and Robert Shaw, and with the Cincinnati Symphony Orchestra, the Cincinnati Opera, and the Cincinnati May Festival.

"Blessed by Music—Covington Cathedral Has Been the Concert Home for the Schaffers," *KP,* January 13, 2005, 4K.

Business letters of Msgr. Francis Mielech and Bishop William Mulloy, June 1955–September 1958, Archives of the Diocese of Covington, Erlanger, Ky.

"Cathedral 'Maestro' Has Heavenly Touch," *KP,* March 22, 1994, 1K–2K.

"Organists Conduct Special Concerts," *KP,* July 17, 1990, 8K.

Rebecca Schaffer Wells

SCHMITT, JOHANN (b. 1825, Heinstadt, Baden, Germany; d. June 10, 1898, Covington, Ky.). One of Covington's most illustrious residents of the second half of the 19th century was the German immigrant painter Johann Schmitt. As a young man, Schmitt lived in Munich, the capital of Bavaria, where he absorbed the lessons of contemporary German religious art without having to attend an art school. In 1848 he came to the United States and settled in Melrose, Westchester Co., N.Y. He called himself "a painter of real Catholic art" in his 1861 advertisement in the weekly Catholic newspaper *Der Wahrheitsfreund.* Johann Schmitt's first commission in the United States was to paint murals for the church of St. Alphonsus in New York City. Other commissions for murals in churches along the eastern seaboard followed.

In 1862 Schmitt joined the **Covington Altar Stock Building Company**, where he became a painter of altarpieces as well as murals. With his first wife, Margaret Reichert, he settled in a house along Covington's Greenup St., near the company's workshop. Devout Catholics, Schmitt and his wife worshipped at **St. Joseph Catholic Church, Covington**, and Schmitt became a member of the Cincinnati-based Society of Christian Art. The couple adopted a daughter, Mary, who was her father's model for the Virgin Mary in many of his paintings. The daughter died in 1885, at age 23. After Schmitt's first wife died in 1891, he married again. His new wife, Elizabeth Scheper Meyer Racke (twice a widow), had six children. One of them, Frank Meyer Jr., assisted Schmitt in his later years with mural paintings.

Schmitt quickly became the leading painter of the Altar Building Stock Company. Examples of his work may be found in several Northern Kentucky churches and in chapels, monasteries, convents, and cathedrals across the Midwest and the East. The first commission Schmitt fulfilled after his arrival in Northern Kentucky, in 1862, was a decoration of St. Francis Seraph Church, at Liberty and Vine Sts. in Cincinnati. He painted the four theological doctors of the Western, or Roman

Johann Schmitt, ca. 1892–1893

Catholic, Church: St. Ambrose, St. Augustine, St. Gregory, and St. Jerome, on a gold-leaf background. In the same year, Schmitt began creating seven paintings over the main and side altars at the Immaculata Church (today's Holy Cross–Immaculata Church) on Cincinnati's Mount Adams. They depict scenes from the life of the Virgin Mary and occupied the artist until 1870.

Church decorations by Schmitt can be found in rural Northern Kentucky in many places where German Catholic immigrants had erected small churches. Seventeen miles south of Covington, on a hillside above Morning View, Schmitt painted *Mary's Assumption* in a church by the same name. In nearby Alexandria an identical composition is displayed in the local Catholic church, and at **St. Joseph Catholic Church, Camp Springs**, Schmitt painted *St. Joseph with the Christ Child*, a favorite image among local German Catholic settlers.

The painter charged from $500 to $800 for his massive murals and $100 to $200 for the smaller ones. For his altar paintings, the number of faces determined the price. But when he painted for poor mission churches, he frequently donated his artworks.

Schmitt specialized in certain religious topics, including the Holy Family and St. Joseph, but occasionally he dealt with less-well-known images. In 1868 he began an ambitious project of decorating the Chapel of the Ursuline Sisters in Louisville with the legend of the martyred St. Ursula, who was killed by Attila the Hun outside the walls of the city of Cologne in Germany. Three other Louisville churches also received paintings by Schmitt: St. Martin of Tours, St. Peter Claver, and St. Boniface.

At the St. Joseph Church in Covington, the artist created two large murals between 1875 and 1879, *The Death of St. Joseph* and *St. Joseph, Protector of the Universal Church*. The latter has been called Schmitt's artistic masterpiece. It recalled the triumph of the Roman Catholic Church over the German Chancellor Otto von Bismarck, who had instigated the so-called *Kulturkampf*, intended to curtail the power of the Catholic Church in Germany. In Schmitt's composition St. Joseph hovers above St. Peter's Cathedral in Rome, blessing Pope Leo XIII and numerous cardinals, archbishops, bishops, and abbots, who kneel in adoration. Each of the men portrayed in the gathering was an accurate portrait of a contemporary church dignitary. Schmitt created a silver-point drawing of the painting for the pope, which remains in the collection of the Vatican Museum. Unfortunately, when the St. Joseph Church was razed in 1970, Schmitt's murals were destroyed.

At Covington's **Mother of God Catholic Church**, Schmitt painted five large murals titled *Joyful Mysteries of the Rosary* in 1890, late in his life. The first Mother of God Church in Covington had been dedicated in 1842. The second, larger building, was erected in 1870–1871, and in 1890, its interior received entirely new decorations.

In addition to murals and altar paintings, Schmitt created easel paintings with religious themes. The **Sisters of St. Benedict** in Covington received several such artworks. The largest shows St. Walburga, the founder of the sisters' order, blessing Covington's St. Joseph Church, St. Joseph School, and the St. Walburg Monastery (see **Sisters of St. Benedict**).

The painter left works in Illinois, Indiana, Kansas, Minnesota, Pennsylvania, and Wisconsin, in addition to his paintings in New York and along the East Coast. His largest mural is a 35-by-50-foot depiction of the Crucifixion above the high altar in St. Xavier Cathedral at Green Bay, Wis.

Johann Schmitt has been called "the first Christian artist of America." He died in 1898 at his Covington house along Greenup St. and was buried in the Mother of God Cemetery in Latonia.

During his early years with the Covington Altar Company, Schmitt became the first teacher of a young boy, **Frank Duveneck**, who was born in Covington to German immigrant parents. After years of study at the Munich Royal Academy of Art, Duveneck became one of the most famous American impressionist painters of the late 19th and early 20th centuries.

Pohlkamp, Diomede, O.F.M. "A Franciscan Artist of Kentucky, Johann Schmitt, 1825–1898," *Franciscan Studies* 7 (June 1947): 147–170.

Scheessele, Mary Kenneth, O.S.B., and Annemarie Springer. "German-American Religious Art in Southern Indiana," *Indiana German Heritage Society* 2 (1998): 54–57.

Springer, Annemarie. *Nineteenth Century German-American Church Artists*. www.ulib.iupui.edu/kade/springer/index.html (accessed November 17, 2005).

Ven, Sister Hilary, C.S.B. "Johann Schmitt's Masterpiece." In *Souvenir of the Golden Jubilee Celebration in Commemoration of the Fiftieth Anniversary of the St. Joseph Boys' School, 1870–1920*. Covington, Ky.: Alban Wolff, 1920.

Annemarie Springer

SCHOOLFIELD, FRANK E. (b. October 28, 1861, Foster, Ky.; d. January 2, 1939, Covington, Ky.). Poet Frank Schoolfield was the son of Benjamin and Lora Boss Schoolfield. His father died when Frank was two years old, and he was sent to live in Newport with his maternal grandfather, Alexander Boss. Frank received only an eighth-grade education, yet he became known as the poet laureate of Northern Kentucky, composing more than 100 poems. Most of the poems are about his life experiences, such as the horrors of the **Civil War**, the joy of riding in a mule-drawn cart, and the thrill of walking across the **John A. Roebling Bridge** for the first time. He wrote extensively about Kentucky's natural beauty and its abundant wildlife. When Schoolfield was about 50, he wrote a poem titled, "Dedicated to Governor James B. McCreary," which spoke about his great love for Kentucky and about its fantastic scenery. Schoolfield sent the poem to the governor and was thrilled to receive a letter back, encouraging him to keep writing and to make a book of his poems. However, he never attempted to capitalize on his talent but instead earned his living as a foreman with the **Houston, Stanwood & Gamble Company**, manufacturers of steam engines and boilers in Covington. He married a girl whose name was Missouri, and they had two sons and two daughters. Schoolfield died of stomach cancer at age 77 at his home at 123 W. Fourth St. in Covington. He was buried in the Highland Cemetery in Fort Mitchell. His wife preceded him in death, but his four children survived him.

"Covington Poet Shuns Acclaim," *KP*, April 15, 1938, 9.

"F. E. Scoolfield Succumbs at Age 78," *KP*, January 3, 1939, 1.

Kentucky Death Certificate No. 1802, for the year 1939.

SCHRODER, WILFRID ALBERT "WIL" (b. April 19, 1946, Cincinnati, Ohio). Wilfrid Albert Schroder, who became a Kentucky Supreme Court judge, is a resident of Fort Mitchell, Ky., the son of Wilfrid R. and Mary Magdalen Arlinghaus Schroder. He received both his BA (1968) and his JD (1970) from the University of Kentucky and also holds an advanced law degree, the LLM, from the University of Missouri in 1971. He was admitted to practice law in Kentucky in 1970 and in Missouri in 1972. He married Susan Marie Wahlbrink in 1993.

In 1971, while completing his LLM, Schroder worked as an attorney for the Kansas City Legal Aid Society, and then as a corporate attorney for the St. Paul Insurance Company (1971–1972), before returning home to Kentucky. He was an assistant law professor at the Salmon P. **Chase College of Law** for its first three years in Kentucky, 1972–1975. From 1975 to 1983, he was in private practice in Covington with his brother Robert. Wil Schroder was appointed Newport city attorney when the reform commission was elected and served at the onset of Newport's early riverfront development (1982–1983). He spent 22 years as a judge before his election to the Kentucky Supreme Court, including a term as trial court judge (Kenton District Court) for nearly eight years (1983–1991) and service on the Kentucky Court of Appeals for more than 15 years (1991–2006). In November 2006 Schroder was elected a justice of the Kentucky Supreme Court. He was the fourth person elected to serve there for the Sixth Judicial District since it was created by a 1975 Amendment to the Constitution of Kentucky. He succeeded Justice Donald Wintershiemer as Northern Kentucky's representative on the court.

Kentucky Court of Justice. "Justice Wil Schroder." http://courts.ky.gov/courts/supreme/justices/schroder.htm (accessed July 10, 2008).

Paul L. Whalen

SCHUELER, ROGER (b. July 16, 1921, Buffalo, N.Y.; d. March 5, 1994, Decatur, Ill.). **Jazz** artist, composer, trumpeter, and band leader Roger Edward Schueler received a BA from Indiana Central University in Indianapolis, Ind., in 1943 and an MM from the Cincinnati College Conservatory of Music in 1949. He did further graduate work at the Berkeley School of Music and the University of Illinois in Urbana. He also studied for six summers with Pierre Montreux, the French-born internationally renowned conductor, and was the recipient of a Ford Foundation grant to study with Cincinnati Symphony Orchestra conductor Thor Johnson.

Schueler taught at **Dixie Heights High School** in Edgewood for 10 years, ending in 1964. In 1963 he lived at 25 Beechwood Rd. in Fort Mitchell. He married Northern Kentucky native Alma Welsh, whom he met while teaching at Dixie Heights. While at Dixie Heights, Schueler created a dance band–jazz ensemble that he named the Cool Colonels. This group produced four albums, and the third, *Cool Colonels on Tour* (1963), contained all original compositions by Dick Fenno, a Californian. The *On Tour* album, recorded at King Records in the Cincinnati neighborhood of Evanston, which was then the home of James Brown, is listed as a jazz classic and a collector's item. Shueler created the Cool Colonels as a regularly scheduled hour-long daily course, unusual even now in a public school. In addition, the group rehearsed every Wednesday evening, and section leaders were expected to conduct after-school sectional practices weekly. Schueler's intense and uncompromising rehearsals produced a stream of talented musicians, including Ted Piercefield, who played trumpet with Bill Chase, and Barry Campbell, an alto saxophonist who performed with Stan Kenton.

After his departure from Northern Kentucky, Schueler taught at the University of Wisconsin–Green Bay for one year and then became the director of jazz and commercial music at Milliken University in Decatur, Ill., where he remained for some 23 years, leading that school's award-winning jazz band. The group toured internationally. During the Milliken years, Schueler's reputation grew as an influential jazz educator, rehearsal technician, director, and author. Jazz educator Jim Culbertson, in the April 2005 *International Association of Jazz Educators Journal,* wrote 11 years after Schuler's death, "He was a strong taskmaster, but so full of music. He approached music in such a cool way in that it was a very attractive way to learn about life. I learned a lot about how to rehearse. It was about not settling for anything less than possible."

One of Schueler's students at Milliken was Thomas Rotondi, the leader of the U.S. Military Academy's band, who also described Schueler as a major influence in his musical life. Schueler died of a brain tumor in 1994. During his career, he produced several records and wrote one book. A number of music awards have been named in his honor. As recently as 2003, the Illinois unit of the International Association for Jazz Education presented its prestigious Outstanding Jazz Educator Award to Roger Schueler, nine years postmortem.

The Cool Colonels. *The Cool Colonels: Dance Time.* Directed by Roger Schueler. LP-U., n.d. Musical Americana Collection, 1930–1960, Record Series 12/9/50, Univ. of Illinois Library (MAC).

——. *The Cool Colonels: On Tour.* Directed by Roger Schueler. LP-U., 1963. MAC.

Dixie Heights Concert Band. *Dixie Heights Spring Concert.* Directed by Roger Schueler. LP-U., 1963. MAC.

Schueler, Roger. *So You Want to Lead a Jazz Band.* Winona, Minn.: Hal Leonard, n.d.

The Sousa Archives, Center for American Music, Univ. of Illinois, Urbana, Ill.

Gary Lynwood Johnston

SCHUETZEN CLUBS. Northern Kentucky had several *schuetzen* clubs, target shooting clubs modeled after early European, especially German, groups of shooters. In Covington there were the Deutsche Schuetzen Gesellschaft of Covington, Kentucky, organized in 1882, and the Lewisburg Schuetzens, organized about 1883. At least one other club existed in the region, based in Bellevue in Campbell Co. The Covington group maintained shooting grounds at Highland Pk. and the **Three-L Highway**. The Lewisburg group met at Turner Hall on Pike St. and did their shooting at the Alpenrose Schuetzen Park on Amsterdam Rd. near Montague Rd., just outside the Covington city limits, now within Park Hills. Heidel Hall, on the northeast corner of 21st and Russell Sts., where many of the Covington *schuetzen* balls were held, stands today; the building is now in the Peaselburg neighborhood of Covington and is used for apartments. Just across the Ohio River in Cincinnati, a *schuetzen* ground was located in what is today the English Woods section, just south of Westwood-Northern Blvd., on the first hill west of the Mill Creek Valley.

The German word *schuetzen* has no exact literal English translation, but in this context the word means shooting, as in target shooting. The practice of *schuetzen* brought with it from Europe many colorful ethnic social customs. During the last half of the 19th century, most cities and towns of any size in the United States that had a significant Germanic population hosted one or more *schuetzen* clubs. In the larger cities, the clubs often had indoor shooting galleries. However, where possible, the competitions were held outdoors at shooting grounds. *Schuetzen* clubs were copies of similar clubs in Germany. They celebrated shooting prowess, good fellowship, good citizenship, and camaraderie. The membership included Catholics and Protestants, Republicans and Democrats, common laborers, entrepreneurs, and corporate officers. A good lager beer was seldom far from the *schuetzen* club's social activities and may have helped knock the sharp edges off of any social, religious, or political differences among members. Discussion of religion or politics, as well as quarreling with peers at meetings, was strictly forbidden, on pain of immediate expulsion.

The whole movement was oriented toward defensive shooting and harked back to mostly Germanic origins. The emphasis was on defense of the home against wild animals and human intruders. Targets used by the groups often featured an *Adler* (eagle), which, it was supposed, might carry off one of their small children. There were annual competitions at which an eagle figure made of wood was placed on a tall pole and shot at with rifles until no vestige of the eagle remained. The shooter knocking the last piece down was declared the *Koenig* (king). He would select a *Koenigin* (queen) and a court and would reign at an elaborate ball. Shooting at conventional targets occurred at other meetings. Such shooting can be dated back as far as the 10th century in Europe, when bows and arrows were employed. It came to a sudden halt in Germany with the 1934 *Schuetzenfest* in Germany, which was taken over by Hitler, who disbanded the peaceful *schuetzen* clubs.

The Old World customs made their way to Northern Kentucky with German immigrants. In addition to monthly shooting occasions, the pageantry of king, queen, court, uniforms, parades, and balls was continued in the United States. Photographic evidence reveals that *schuetzen* clubs' paramilitary uniforms had sashes, medals, and walking sticks or swords. About every four years, national shoots were held in the United States, and prizes up to $5,000 in gold were awarded.

The demise of the *schuetzen* movement in the United States was due to the anti-German sentiments that arose after the United States entered **World War I** (see **Anti-German Hysteria**). Citizens with Germanic names who owned guns were not to be trusted or allowed to exercise their right of assembly. Alien women were required to register with the police. The Covington *schuetzen* clubs were disbanded and their remaining assets turned over to the **American Red Cross**. Based upon pro-Germany statements they had allegedly made, some of the Covington *schuetzen* clubs' prominent members, who were also prominent members of the community, were tried for sedition and sent off to prison for five to seven years at the Atlanta Federal Penitentiary in Georgia. The local prosecutor publicly stated that free speech was not an issue in these cases.

Today there are scattered fragments of *schuetzen* organizations surviving in the United States. One club operates in Texas, and a few revival clubs exist elsewhere, but none survive in Northern Kentucky.

Locally, the *schuetzen* clubs were swept away by the wave of patriotism accompanying World War I and never reconstituted.

"Only 3 Dress Part but Thousands Look Good at Keg," *KE*, September 25, 1977, B2.

Schiffer, T. D. *Muzzle Blasts: The Deutsche Schuetzen Gesellschaft of Covington, Kentucky.* National Muzzle Loading Rifle Association, 1984.

Souvenir Program of the Deutsche Schuetzen Gesellschaft of Covington Kentucky. Covington, Ky., 1910.

"Spectacular Incidents Mark Summoning of Latonia Men in an Alleged Sedition Inquiry," *CTS*, July 4, 1918, 1.

Thompson, Jesse, and Tom Rowe. *Alte Scheibenwaffen* (Old target arms). Vol. 1. Maynardville, Tenn.: Tom Rowe, 1999. In English.

Thomas D. Schiffer

SCHULKERS, ROBERT F. (b. July 21, 1890, Covington, Ky.; d. April 6, 1972, Cincinnati, Ohio). Author Robert Franc Schulkers, son of Covington policeman Henry Herman Schulkers and Maria Elizabeth Wueller, was born at 120 E. 13th St. in a section of Covington known as Helentown. His mother was born in Germany, and his father was of German parentage. Robert attended **St. Joseph** parochial grade school in Covington and was an altar boy at St. Joseph Catholic Church. After graduating from St. Joseph High School (today's **Covington Catholic High School**) in 1906, he studied architectural draftsmanship. In 1915 he married Julia Buckley Darnell, a distant relative of President Thomas Jefferson (1801–1809); they lived at 1012 Park Ave., Latonia. Schulkers loved horses and betting on horse races and for a time worked at the **Latonia Racecourse**. He and his family lived in Cuba for a time. In 1934 they moved to the Hyde Park neighborhood of Cincinnati, later to Ault Park in Cincinnati, and in 1936 to Tremont Rd. in Upper Arlington, Ohio, a Columbus suburb. During that time Schulkers was secretary to Ohio governor John Bricker, in charge of publicity and development for the state of Ohio. In 1942 The Schulkerses returned to Cincinnati. Schulkers died in 1972 and was entombed in a mausoleum at Spring Grove Cemetery in Cincinnati.

Schulkers is best known as the author of the Seckatary Hawkins series of children's books. In 1911 he became the secretary to the publisher of the *Cincinnati Enquier,* W. F. Wiley. He began to write stories for children in the paper. In 1918 he was asked to contribute a weekly story, and on February 3, 1918, the first Seck Hawkins story, "The Snow Fort," appeared. His father's songs and stories were the stimulus for these mysteries for young boys, which were set primarily in the Covington area. The author hoped to promote, through his stories, tolerance and fair play for all, including people often branded as different because they were, for example, overweight. The character Seckatary Hawkins himself was portly.

In addition to the books that resulted from the newspaper column, Schulkers wrote the text for a newspaper comic strip series from the 1920s. Until 1928 it was illustrated by Carll B. Williams (father of **Caroline Williams**), long-time director of the *Cincinnati Enquirer's* art department. The Seckatary Hawkins book series also led to the establishment of the Seckatary Hawkins Fair and Square clubs. Anyone who promised to live up to the club rules of morality, decency, and honesty could join. Among the rules were "Always be fair and square," "Tell the truth," "Never give up," and "Try to learn one new thing each day." The club colors, blue and white, may relate to Catholic vestments, Schulkers's German ancestry, or the U.S. flag. At the height of its popularity, the club had several million members. Seck Hawkins Days were popular at the Cincinnati amusement park Coney Island; there were parades, picnics, and other entertainments associated with the clubs. The Seckatary Hawkins books had an influence on Harper Lee, who used a quotation from one of them,*The Gray Ghost*, at the end of *To Kill a Mockingbird* to reinforce the moral ending of the novel. Hawkins's grandson states, "To everyone he ever met, he was a righteous champion of justice for any that might be slighted, maligned or misunderstood." The club is still in existence.

"Artist's Brush Is Laid Aside; Carll Williams Called by Death," *CE,* February 11, 1928, 12.

"Robert Schulkers," *CE,* April 9, 1972, 6B.

Seckatary Hawkins. www.seckatary.com/ (accessed April 3, 2006).

Spring Grove Cemetery Records, Cincinnati, Ohio.

Danny Miller

SCHWARBERG, WILLIAM "BILL" (b. August 25, 1912, Newport, Ky.; d. September 13, 2001, Covington, Ky.). Athletics coach and administrator William "Bill" D. Schwarberg was the son of William F. and Mary Cunningham Schwarberg. He played on Covington's undefeated 1931 **Holmes High School** football team and graduated in 1932. He entered the University of Cincinnati (UC) in Cincinnati, where he played halfback and quarterback in football and shortstop on the baseball team. He graduated from UC in 1936 and became the quarterback of the first Cincinnati Bengals professional football team in 1937. That team played at Crosley Field in Cincinnati, in the original American Football League, which folded in 1941. Schwarberg coached and taught at **Dixie Heights High School** in Edgewood and later at Holmes High School; his undefeated 1942 football team won the Kentucky state championship. Meanwhile, he completed an MA and then spent two years in the U.S. Navy, beginning in 1944. After the war Bill became an assistant football coach at UC and also was in charge of intramural athletics. In 1952 he became UC's golf coach; no less than 15 of his golfers entered the professional ranks during Schwarberg's 29 years in that position. He became "Dr. Bill" in 1956 when he received a PhD from Columbia University in New York City. Over the years he held various positions within the administration of UC's athletics program. Schwarberg later often talked about how, as UC's assistant athletic director, he had to arrange special segregated hotel arrangements in the South for one of the greatest collegiate basketball players in history, the Big "O," Oscar Robertson. For a few years, Schwarberg also served as head baseball coach at UC. He retired from UC in 1985. He was the recipient of many awards during his career and was inducted into several sports halls of fame. He was a member of the Covington School Board. Schwarberg always thought of himself not as a successful athlete, not as a great coach, which he was, but first and foremost as a teacher. Schwarberg died in 2001 at his home in Kenton Hills, overlooking his beloved Covington. He was married to Ruby Lovell, a long-time teacher in the Cincinnati and Kenton Co. public school systems, who had died in 1992.

Billman, Rebecca. "UC Legend Bill Schwarberg Dies," *CE*, September 15, 2001, B14.

"Bill Schwarberg, 1st Bengals' Quarterback, UC Coach, Teacher," *KP*, September 14, 2001, 17A.

"Northern Ky. Hall of Fame Will Induct Four Members," *KP*, December 10, 1996, 6K.

SCIENCE AND SCIENTISTS. See **Archaeology**; **Geology**; **Glaciers**; **Pharmacy**; **Weather and Climate**; names of specific scientists.

SCOTT, JOHN (b. May 8, 1767, Londonderry Co., Ireland; d. November 12, 1846, Carroll Co., Ky.). In 1788 John Scott, who became a Baptist minister and a surveyor, immigrated to the United States, carrying a letter of recommendation that stated he was a member of the Presbyterian Church, entitled to all its privileges. He arrived in Lexington in November 1789, where he converted to the Baptist faith and united with the Town Fork Baptist Church in September 1790. He later moved to Franklin Co. and became a member of the Forks of Elkhorn Church. Scott was ordained a minister on the second Sunday of March 1802. He served as pastor of the Twins Church (now the **New Liberty Baptist Church**) in Owen Co. from 1802 to 1833; his was the longest pastorate in the history of that church. He is also generally regarded as the first minister to arrive in what is today Owen Co. In 1803 Scott was also called to the Ghent Baptist Church, where he served as its second pastor and donated the land on which the present church building now stands at Ghent in Carroll Co. Kentucky governor Christopher Greenup (1804–1808) appointed Scott the Gallatin Co. surveyor, and while he served in this capacity (from 1808 to 1813), he surveyed the original boundaries for the town of Ghent. He moved to a site within present Carroll Co. in 1825 and helped to establish the Sharon Baptist Church. He remained a member there from its establishment in 1825 until his death in 1846.

In 1795 Scott married Jane Sneed. After she died in 1832, he married Mrs. Mary Adams Whitehead Bailey. His second wife died in 1840, and in 1842 he married Maria Alexander. He had 13 children in all.

Darnell, Ermina. *Forks of Elkhorn Church.* Baltimore: Genealogical, 1980.

"The History of the New Liberty Baptist Church, New Liberty, Kentucky," 1951, New Liberty Baptist Church, New Liberty, Ky.

Sandra Thomas

SCOTT, PATRICIA A. "PAT" (b. July 14, 1928, Covington, Ky.). Pat Scott is the daughter of Wilfred and Irene Patrick Scott of Burlington and one of only about 600 women to play baseball professionally in the All-American Girls Professional Baseball League (AAGPBL).

A natural athlete, Scott began playing baseball when she was age eight. The family farm included a baseball field where semipro teams played and held practice sessions, and the ballplayers playing at this field took Scott under their wings. During her high school years, she became known as a particularly fine fast-pitch softball player in the Cincinnati area.

Scott graduated from **St. Henry District High School** in Elsmere, Ky., in 1948. During her senior year, her father called her attention to a newspaper notice about tryouts for the AAGPBL to be held at Wrigley Field in Chicago. The AAGPBL was a professional baseball league for women that operated from 1943 to 1954. In 1942 the owner of the Chicago Cubs, Philip K. Wrigley of the Wrigley chewing gum empire, became concerned that a loss of ballplayers (due to the draft of men for **World War II**) would mean no baseball would be played in Wrigley Field during the war. He set out to devise a plan to prevent that from happening. With the help of Ken Sells, the general manager of the Cubs, the idea of a baseball league for women was born. The AAGPBL debuted in 1943 with four teams and quickly grew in popularity; by 1948 the league had 10 teams, and 1 million fans were paying to attend its games in parks around the upper Midwest.

When Scott traveled to Wrigley Field in 1947, she was 1 of 90 women to try out that day and 1 of 35 players selected for the league. She began the 1948 season with the Springfield (Ill.) Sallies but returned home early in the season when her mother became sick. While helping out at home, Scott returned to pitching for local softball teams, even playing a stint for the Covington Belles, a professional softball team that existed briefly in 1950. In 1951 Scott was asked to return to the AAGPBL, and she pitched for the Fort Wayne Daises from 1951 to 1953. In 1952, under manager Jimmie Foxx, a member of the National Baseball Hall of Fame, Scott was the pitcher when Fort Wayne defeated the Rockford Peaches to win the season championship.

In 1954 Scott was offered a chance to go to Austria as a 4-H agricultural exchange student. Unable to turn down the opportunity, she finished her pitching career with 48 wins against 26 losses, a 2.46 ERA (Earned Run Average), 187 strikeouts, and an outstanding .977 fielding percentage. When she returned to the United States, she enrolled at the University of Kentucky (UK) at Lexington, graduating in 1959 with a major in zoology. At UK she played on the basketball, volleyball, and field hockey teams and was president of the women's athletic association for a year.

Following college, Scott became a medical technologist and research assistant and worked for Hamagami Labs in Cincinnati for 32 years before she retired in 1993. In 1988 the National Baseball Hall of Fame in Cooperstown, N.Y., honored the AAGPBL, unveiling a permanent exhibit called "Women in Baseball," which includes a photo of Scott pitching for the Fort Wayne Daisies. The exhibit spawned the idea for the 1992 hit movie *A League of Their Own,* starring Geena Davis, Tom Hanks, and Madonna, among others, and brought the AAGPBL to increased modern-day attention and fame. Scott and some of her former teammates were present on the set when the movie filmed in Evansville, Ind.

Since 1965 Scott has lived in Walton, Ky. Before she retired, she trained and showed registered Appaloosa horses. Today, she walks up to two miles per day, bowls, plays golf, and enjoys oil painting and other hobbies. In 1997 Scott was selected as the torchbearer for the 12th Annual Northern Kentucky Senior Games. She has participated in these games many times—including the softball toss, discus, shot put, golf, and bowling—and is a frequent medal-winner in her events (in 1993 she took home five gold medals, three silver medals, and a bronze medal). In 2002 the baseball diamond at Walton Community Park was named Pat Scott Field in her honor, and in 2006 Scott became the first woman to be inducted into the Northern Kentucky Sports Hall of Fame. She had broken new ground previously at her high school alma mater, when she became the first woman to be inducted into St. Henry High School's Sports Hall of Fame. Growing up in Boone Co., she was a babysitter for the famous Northern Kentucky international jockey champion **Steve Cauthen**, who was her neighbor.

Flynn, Terry. "Field Named for Pro Pitcher," *CE,* March 9, 2002, 1B.
Friedberg, Mary. "Pitching the Senior Games: Walton Woman, 67, Played Pro Baseball," *KP,* April 2, 1997, 1.
Madden, W. C. *The Women of the All-American Girls Professional Baseball League: A Biographical Dictionary.* Jefferson, N.C.: McFarland, 1997.
Scott, Pat. Telephone interview by Verna L. Bond-Broderick, December 18, 2005.
"Scott Heads Hall of Fame Inductees," *KP,* January 16, 2006, 7K.

Verna L. Bond-Broderick

SCOTT, RAY (b. January 17, 1917, Junction City, Ky.; d. July 3, 2001, Florence, Ky.). Longtime **WNOP** disk jockey Ray L. Scott grew up in western Pendleton Co. listening to his father strum the banjo. He was the son of Raymond H. and Catherine Crabtree Scott. He learned to love music of all types and easily made the transition to **jazz** from **country music** when the Newport station changed its format in 1961. For 40 years Scott worked there. He served in the U.S. Army Air Corps during **World War II**, and upon returning in 1948, he began his radio career at **WZIP** in Covington. On the radio at WNOP, he became known as "the grey wolf," because his hair had grayed prematurely. He died in 2001 from complications of Alzheimer's and was buried at Highland Cemetery in Fort Mitchell. He was survived by his wife of 55 years, Jean.

Highland Cemetery Records, Fort Mitchell, Ky.
"Ray Scott, 84, Retired Radio Announcer," *KP,* July 5, 2001, 9A.
"'Ray' Scott, 84, Was Veteran Jazz Announcer with WNOP," *KE,* July 5, 2001, B4.

SCOTT HIGH SCHOOL. Scott High School, at 5400 Old Taylor Mill Rd. in Taylor Mill, is the newest of the three high schools in Kenton Co. It received accolades for its many design innovations when it opened in 1978. The school's name honors Robert Riggs Scott, who was a strong supporter of education in Kenton Co. When illness compelled Scott to sell the farm his family had operated in Crescent Springs, he used $1 million of the proceeds to fund college scholarships for graduates of Kenton Co. schools and for members of his church. Scott also served on the Kenton Co. Board of Education from 1952 to 1976, including 16 years as chairman.

Local architect Robert Ehmet Hayes's stunning design for the new school, a 150,000-square-foot brick structure, contained several modern amenities. Completed at a cost of $13 million, Scott High School featured interior brick walls and staircases, carpeting, tile kitchen and restroom floors, an auditorium with coliseum seating, an indoor swimming pool, and central heating and air conditioning. Budget-minded critics questioned the choice of interior brick walls and tile floors over less expensive building materials; however, Hayes insisted that their lower maintenance costs made them a wise investment. The two-story library and cafeteria are central, communal spaces, designed in accord with the school's open-classroom concept. Scott High School's 78-acre campus, which it now shares with Woodland Middle School, features an impressive athletic complex with lighted baseball, football, and soccer fields; tennis courts; and a cross-country course. Robert Konerman served as the high school's first principal, retiring in 1993. Students voted to name their athletic teams the Eagles. Scott High School's colors, blue and gray, come from the school colors of its "parent" schools in the county—blue from **Simon Kenton High School** and gray from **Dixie Heights High School**.

On two occasions Scott High School students shared facilities with another Kenton Co. high school. Scott High School did not open until the middle of the 1978–1979 academic year, so its students attended evening classes at Dixie Heights High School in Edgewood while construction continued on the new building; two years later, Simon Kenton High School students attended Scott High School in the evening while their own physical plant underwent repairs after a gas-leak explosion (see **Simon Kenton High School Explosion**).

Scott High School's students, athletes, and marching bands have won several honors. In 1992 Scott High School merited recognition as a Tier One Model School by the National Alliance for Restructuring Education, an honor bestowed that year on only three schools nationwide. The high school's alumni include Doug Pelfrey, a former kicker for the NFL Cincinnati Bengals. Pelfrey founded Kicks for Kids, a charitable organization that strives to provide area at-risk children with opportunities to pursue their dreams. Scott High School's current principal is Clay Dawson, and its enrollment is approximately 1,160.

"Kicks for Kids Scoring Big," *KP*, November 24, 2005, 1B.
"Robert Riggs Scott, Provided Scholarships," *KP*, April 19, 2004, A4.
"'Turn Over' New Scott High," *KP*, December 1, 1978, 2K.

Greg Perkins

SCOTT'S LANDING/*REDSTONE*/GAINES HOUSE. One of Carroll Co.'s few remaining antebellum Ohio River homes marks the site of the county's worst steamboat disaster. This elegant two-story brick home was built by Boone Co. natives Squire G. and Harriet Huey Scott, who had purchased the land three miles east of Carrollton in 1847. On the afternoon of April 2, 1852, the steamboat *Redstone* pulled over to Scott's Landing to pick up the Scotts' son Rev. Periander "Perry" Scott, a popular young Baptist minister and educator from Boone Co. As the steamboat was backing away from the landing, its boilers exploded, "tearing the boat to atoms, and causing her to sink in less than three minutes in 20 feet of water." The upper part of Scott's body was reportedly found more than a half mile away from where the explosion took place. At least 14 persons, and perhaps as many as 35, were killed. Some believed the *Redstone* was in an informal race against another steamboat and that irresponsible behavior by the crew caused the explosion.

Squire G. Scott died in 1867, and in 1870 his heirs sold the home to another native of Boone Co., Benjamin Logan Gaines. Gaines died in 1917, and his wife Eugenia Brady Gaines remained there until her death in 1947, at the age of 101. In 2006 the home continued to be owned by Gaines heirs.

Reis, Jim. "Blown into Eternity: Popular Minister among Several to Die on Fateful Day in 1852," *KP*, August 17, 1998, 4K.

Bill Davis

SCOTT UNITED METHODIST CHURCH. Rev. Henson Talbert organized this Mason Co. church as the Scott Methodist Episcopal Church in 1864 in downtown Maysville. In 1869 the church joined the Lexington (Methodist) Conference; Rev. Adam Nunn was the Maysville church's pastor in 1869–1870. The present site of the church was purchased for $800 in 1881, when Rev. John Moreland Sr. was pastor. Construction on the building continued from 1884 until it was completed and dedicated in 1890. In 1884 the church became known as Scott Chapel Methodist Episcopal (M.E.) Church. Construction oversight passed on to Rev. John Moreland Jr. The *Maysville City Directory* in 1884–1885 lists Scott's Chapel M.E. Church under the heading "Colored Churches." At the time, there were three major African American Methodist Church denominations in the South: the African Methodist Episcopal Church, the Christian Methodist Episcopal (C.M.E.) Church, and the A.M.E. Zion Church. The Scott United Methodist Church was one of many local churches that closed during the influenza scare from October 1918 until January 1919. In 1974, all the Methodist black conferences were united with the white conferences.

Emerson, Chas. *Maysville City Directory, 1884–1885.*
Fields, John D. *Scott United Methodist Church 100th Anniversary, 1884–1984.* Maysville, Ky.: Scott United Methodist Church, 1984.

Alex Hyrcza

SCROGGIN, FREDERICK R. (b. January 24, 1916, Grant Co., Ky.; d. December 11, 2000, Edgewood, Ky.). Physician Fred R. Scroggin graduated from Mason High School at Maysville, the University of Kentucky at Lexington (1940), and the University of Cincinnati Medical School. He married Jane Wiegman in 1942. Scroggin served in **World War II** as a flight surgeon in the 339th Fighter Group, U.S. 8th Air Force, in Europe. Returning home in late 1945, he opened a physician's office in Dry Ridge. He was noted for his willingness to make house calls. Sroggin was active in the League of Kentucky Sportsmen, serving on its board, and was instrumental in the founding of the Grant Co. Hospital in Williamstown (see **St. Elizabeth Medical Center**). Later, he served for three years as president of the National Wildlife Federation, which had 3.5 million members. He also owned the local Ponderosa Stock Farm, where he bred prize cattle. Scroggin died in 2000 at the St. Elizabeth Medical Center South in Edgewood and was entombed at the Williamstown Mausoleum.

"Dr. Fred R. Scroggin, 84, Doctor with Many Talents," *KP*, December 13, 2000, 14A.
"North Kentucky U.K. Graduates," *KP*, August 24, 1940, 1.

John B. Conrad

SEABOARD COAST LINE. The Seaboard Coast Line operates rail lines in Northern Kentucky. At the beginning of the 20th century, the Atlantic Coast Line (ACL) owned 35 percent of the **Louisville and Nashville Railroad** (L&N). The ACL allowed the L&N to operate as an independent company. However, when the ACL fell under the ownership of Seaboard Coast Lines (SCL) in 1967, the situation changed. The SCL began to acquire additional L&N stock, and by 1971 it controlled 99 percent of the L&N. The 1970s saw L&N cars and locomotives being painted with the SCL "The Family Lines" logo, operational authority having been transferred from Louisville to the SCL headquarters in Jacksonville, Fla. In 1982 the L&N ceased to exist as a separate corporate entity. Later, the SCL was folded into the **CSX**.

Drury, George H. *The Train Watcher's Guide to North American Railroads.* Waukesha, Wis.: Kalmbach Books, 1992.
The Historical Guide to North American Railroads. 2nd ed. Waukesha, Wis.: Kalmbach Books, 2000.
Hoffman, Glenn. *A History of the Atlantic Coast Line Railroad.* Jacksonville, Fla.: CSX Corporation, 1998.

Charles H. Bogart

SEBASTIAN, ALEXANDER (b. 1795, Garrard Co., Ky.; d. 1856, Indiana). Alexander Sebastian, an antislavery preacher, was the son of William and Sarah "Sally" Embry Sebastian. The Sebastian family came from Wake Co., N.C. They were associated with Shubal Stearns's Separate Baptists of the old Sand Creek Association, who joined the traveling church migration from Spotsylvania, Va., into frontier Kentucky. As a young boy, Alexander certainly knew that in 1804 the proslavery leaders of the Elkhorn Baptist Association expelled antislavery leader Rev. David Barrow from the unified Baptist Association. As a result, Barrow formed the Baptized Licking-Locust Association, Friends of Humanity, with member churches from Barren, Bracken, Fleming, Garrard, Harrison, and Lewis counties. In 1808 Barrow and Carter Tarrant formed a statewide Abolitionist Society comprising 15 preachers and 19 laymen, an organization dedicated to the immediate emancipation of Kentucky's slaves. A Presbyterian, John Finley Crowe, who later became president of Hanover College in Madison, Ind., edited the society's antislavery newspaper, *Abolition Intelligencer and Missionary Magazine,* out of Lexington and later Shelbyville, Ky.

As a young man, Alexander Sebastian preached against slavery both in Northern Kentucky and in southern Indiana. At that time the southern Indiana Separate Baptists were part of the Kentucky associations. In about 1820 Alexander married an Indiana native, Malinda, and accepted a call to be pastor of a Freewill Baptist congregation of about 70 people that met in a log church at Bryant's Creek, near Florence, Ind., across the Ohio River from Warsaw, Ky. On the surface, it appeared that Freewill Baptists and Separate Baptists shared a common emphasis on immersion, an Arminian tradition opposed to Calvinistic predestination. They tended toward an antislavery position, and both Baptist denominations had grown out of the First Great Awakening in New England.

However, the northern Freewill Baptists demanded very strong antislavery planks in local church constitutions and insisted on strong association covenants; they believed intrinsically in an educated, ordained clergy and adhered to relatively standard associational bonds. Separate Baptists, and particularly Alexander Sebastian, welcomed local lay ministry; they were less concerned about education and resisted association control. But of most concern, the Separate Baptists practiced distinctive revival fervor in their Sunday services. The differences led to an eruption and eventually a split in the Bryant's Creek Church.

At first Alexander Sebastian was welcomed warmly. The Bryant's Creek congregation was noted for the outspoken antislavery position written into its charter. Kentuckians crossed the river to heckle Sebastian's preaching. Sebastian and an older man, Rev. Benjamin Leavitt, from New York, who lived in Madison, Ind., served as Freewill Baptist evangelists in the river counties for three years. Although Sebastian was ordained as a Freewill Baptist minister in 1823, at the 1826 Freewill Baptist yearly meeting in Maineville, Ohio (northeast of

Cincinnati), he was excluded. He refused to surrender his Freewill Baptist credentials, though. For the next 30 years, Sebastian continued to preach and found new churches in southeastern Indiana, the most notable ones being Separate Baptist congregations at Centre Grove, East Enterprise, and Cross Plains. All of those congregations had leaders active in aiding runaway slaves. Sebastian's congregation at East Enterprise merged with the Freewill Baptists and formed New Liberty Baptist at Quercus Grove, a strong station on the Underground Railroad.

The Regular Baptists in the region objected to Sebastian's performing marriages, claiming that his ordination was not proper. A district court sided with Sebastian, who claimed that if a church called him and he was ordained by them, then he could legally perform marriages. Although they agreed with his antislavery and Arminian stance, the Freewill Baptists from Ohio and New England were always uncomfortable with Sebastian's extreme independence from associational oversight and with his emphasis on revival-type preaching.

Sebastian moved inland and purchased a farm between Bryant's Creek and Quercus Grove; he founded a Separate Baptist church between East Enterprise and Quercus Grove in Cotton Twp. At Cross Plains, Ind., in Ripley Co., Sebastian founded a second Separate Baptist church about 1832. He is also believed to have been associated with congregations at nearby New Marion and Olean and in the Indian-Kentuck Creek Valley. In 1834 he ran for the Indiana Third District state senate seat as an unaffiliated antislavery candidate, losing by a wide margin; he ran again in 1844 as an antislavery candidate for the Indiana legislature and lost again. In October 1841 Sebastian preached strongly against slavery in Warsaw in Gallatin Co., Ky. Forced by angry townsmen to leave, Sebastian once again fled north across the Ohio River. After Sebastian died in 1856, some of his churches, now without his leadership, began to follow Barton Stone and became Church of Christ or Christian Churches. The Cross Plains congregation later became the Salem Christian Church (Disciples of Christ).

Barrow, David. *Slavery Examined, on the Principles of Nature, Reason, Justice, Policy, and Scripture.* Lexington, Ky.: D. and E. Bradford, 1808.

January 27, 1825, Hugh Buntain, sec. 27, 160 acres, Ripley Co. Tract Book, Versailles, Ind.

Marriage Record Book 5: 160, Ripley Co., Versailles, Ind.

McDonald, Larry S. "Frontier Thunder: Principles of Evangelism and Church Growth from the Life of Shubal Stearns," PhD diss., Southeastern Baptist Theological Seminary, 2000.

November 25, 1835, 39.52 acres, NEQ sec. 19, York Twp., Switzerland Co., Ohio Land Records, Cincinnati.

Powell, Josh. "Shubal Stearns and the Separate Baptist Tradition," *Founders Journal,* Spring 2001, 16–31.

Sparks, John. *The Roots of Appalachian Christianity: The Life and Legacy of Elder Shubal Stearns.* Lexington: Univ. Press of Kentucky, 2001.

Diane Perrine Coon

SECOND BAPTIST CHURCH, CARROLLTON. The Second Baptist Church at Carrollton was constituted in April 1872 in the basement of the town's white First Baptist Church. The names of early members of the Second Baptist Church can be found on the membership roles of the white First Baptist Church in the antebellum period, as slaves and as free people of color. On August 10, 1875, Smith and Lavinia Reed gave part of in-lot 285 in town to the trustees of Second Baptist Church, which was at the time under the leadership of Rev. S. P. Lewis. The brick church at 611 Sycamore St. was built on that site and continues in use. At the time the church was erected in 1875, the deacons were Oscar Bradford, Alley Clay, James W. Harris, and Smith Reed. The Harris family has been active in this congregation for more than 100 years. Although the early church records are gone, Maggie Stone and other parishioners recalled that early officers included Oscar Bradford, Jim Harris, Henry Jones, Elic Myers, and Washington Stone. In 1898 Oscar Wood gave an additional part of lot 285 to the Second Baptist Church. A structure on that property served as a parsonage and later as a pastor's study and fellowship hall.

During the 1980s a number of renovations were accomplished: a new floor and carpet were installed, the exteriors of the church and the parsonage were painted, and new furnishings in the Fellowship Hall and new commodes were acquired. In addition, new songbooks and new Bibles were purchased and a ceiling fan was installed. In March 1993 a new roof was placed on the church building and the pastor's study. The church is active today, although most of the original families have moved away from the area or have died. Several African American families who have moved into Carroll Co. and are Baptists have replaced them. In 2006 the pastor was Rev. Howard Potter and the deacon was Tim Brightwell.

Carroll Co. Deed Book, book 12, p. 448; book 24, p. 415, Carrollton, Ky.

Gentry, Mary Ann. *A History of Carroll County.* Madison, Ind.: Coleman, 1984.

Todd, Deacon Clifford. "Second Baptist Church," typed manuscript in author's file.

Diane Perrine Coon

SECOND BAPTIST CHURCH, MAYSLICK. Mayslick in Mason Co. is home to an African American church congregation that dates back to 1789. Records exist indicating that in that year slaves were holding worship services and that the white Baptist church ministered to the black population. **Elisha Green**, a Mayslick slave who became a founder of African American churches and a Republican leader, was a member of the church. According to oral tradition, black worshippers at the town's Baptist church sat along the walls and in the back of the church during services. This segregated but united system of worship continued until June 17, 1855, when permission was granted by the white congregation for the 175 black members to form their own church, the Second Baptist Church of Mayslick. For more than a decade this congregation met in homes, barns, and whatever other places could be found. After William Mitchell donated land to the **Maysville and Lexington Turnpike** Company for a school and a church for the African American Baptists of Mayslick, Andrew M. January, as the authority of the turnpike company, deeded the property on August 27, 1868, to the trustees of what was termed the "Colored" Baptist Church and their successors. Those first trustees were Stephen Breckinridge, Henry Jackson, and John Middleton. A church and a school were built on the property. A Rev. Natis, the first pastor in 1855, was there for the building of the first church. The original deed stated that other black congregations should be allowed to use the church for services when it was not being used by the local black Baptists.

The first church burned, and the structure built to replace it in 1913 continues to serve the congregation. The first black school in the town was replaced by a larger structure next door, and the original school building is used by the church. In 1889 the Second Christian Church opened in Mayslick, giving the community two predominately African American churches. The Second Christian Church closed in the 1990s, and the Second Baptist Church congregation has declined to around 30 members. Approximately 30 pastors have served the Mayslick Second Baptist Church since its beginning.

American Association of University Women (Maysville Branch). *From Cabin to College: A History of the Schools of Mason County.* Maysville, Ky.: G. F. McClanahan, 1976.

Ramsey, William, elder of the Second Baptist Church. Interview by John Klee, October 2, 2006, Mayslick, Ky.

Vertical files of the Kentucky Gateway Museum Center, Maysville, Ky.

John Klee

SECOND BAPTIST CHURCH, NEWPORT. On December 28, 1945, the Second Baptist Church of Newport was formed as a mission of the Ninth St. Baptist Church in Covington. Albert Lowe served as pastor of this mission, and the congregation purchased a lot at 315 Isabella St. for the sum of $250. In 1947 the mission became the Second Baptist Church, with Rev. Edward Smith serving as moderator. After Pastor Lowe died, on April 16, 1950, Robert J. Brown became pastor; at the time, the church had only six members and $6 in the treasury. In 1951 the Housing Authority of Newport purchased the church's property on Isabella St., and the congregation decided to relocate to 112 Central Ave in Newport, where Brown constructed a church building himself. In 1957 the Housing Authority of Newport took the church's property on Central Ave., and the church was forced to look for yet another home. Land was purchased at the church's current location, 713 Brighton St. in Newport, and another building was built, again without needing to obtain a loan. Rev. Brown again, along with friends, did the work. The name of the church was changed to Mount Zion Baptist Church with this move. Brown remained pastor until 1976. From 1976 to 1979, several ministers served at the church: James Streeter, James Crawford, Elmore Morris, and Herman L. Harris. In 1979 the church's name was changed back to Second Baptist Church. In March 1980 Rev. Paul D. McMillan was called to lead the Second Baptist Church. Under his leadership, the church became involved in many community and civic activities, such as the Martin Luther King Jr. celebration held at the Northern Kentucky Convention Center on January 16, 2001.

Historical notes on file at Second Baptist Church, Newport, Ky.

Installation Service for Rev. H. L. Harris, Sunday, May 20, thru Sunday, May 27, 1979, Mount Zion Baptist Church, Newport, Kentucky. Newport, Ky.: Mount Zion Baptist Church, 1979. Pamphlet.

"Simpson Recalls Rights Struggle," *KP*, January 16, 2001, 3K.

Theodore H. H. Harris

SECOND METHODIST CHURCH. There were two locations of this congregation at Carrollton, the Sycamore Chapel on Sycamore St. and the Wilkerson Chapel on Eighth St. African Americans who were Methodists in Carrollton can be traced back to 1824, when the George Boorom Class for Methodists had four slave members. Membership lists of the Methodist Episcopal (M.E.) Church and the Methodist Episcopal Church–South provide slave names along with the names of their white masters.

In 1850 Christian Gangelback deeded part of lot 288 on Sycamore St. to be used as the Second Methodist Church, a congregation comprising slaves and free people of color. The building, owned by the white M.E. Church, was completed in 1852 and used by the African American Methodists until 1890, when a new church building was built in town on Eighth St. The deed for the Sycamore St. property was turned over to the trustees of the Colored Methodist Church in 1872.

Two deeds, one from Mary Harris in 1899 and another from J. A. Donaldson in 1906, refer to the Colored Methodist Episcopal Church of Carrollton. This church's last deed for the Eighth St. location was dated 1923, and it named Kitty Keene, an African American member of the church. This new brick church was named Wilkerson Chapel in honor of Rev. Prentice Wilkerson, who copastored a church in Bowling Green, Ky., and at Carrollton for many years. Eventually the congregation became too small to sustain itself and the church closed. The building was sold as a residence but later was destroyed.

The Carrollton Women's Club purchased the old church building on Sycamore St. and used it as a meeting place and public library until 1950, when a new library was built in the downtown area. The Sycamore St. building was then sold as a residence.

Gentry, Mary Ann. *A History of Carroll County.* Madison, Ind.: Coleman, 1984.

Diane Perrine Coon

SECOND TWELVE MILE BAPTIST CHURCH. The Second Twelve Mile Baptist Church, located in the northeastern Pendleton Co. community of Peach Grove, along Ky. Rt. 159, near the intersection of Ky. Rt. 10, was established on May 8, 1841, when 33 former members of the **Flagg Springs Baptist Church**, with favorable letters of dismissal from that church, met at the home of John Ellis to form a new church. The congregation began as the Fellowship Baptist Church but soon changed its name to Second Twelve Mile Baptist Church, for the Twelve Mile Creek that flows into the Ohio River nearby. Services initially were held in a local school and neighboring homes. At the first business meeting, which took place on June 5, 1841, at Ellis's home, Fergus German and John Cutter were elected as the first deacons. Five trustees were elected and instructed to purchase land for a church. John Ellis offered 14 acres, which included the Ellis Graveyard, now called the Old Cemetery, located across the road from the church. At the August 14, 1841, business meeting, William Morin was called as the church's first pastor. The congregation joined the Campbell Co. Association, today's Northern Kentucky Baptist Association. Services were to be held twice a month, and an annual revival was to be held each year on the second Saturday in November, after the harvest. A brick building, 34 by 44 feet in size, was built to serve as the congregation's first house of worship. The church first met on December 13, 1845, in their new meetinghouse. In 1860, owing to increasing attendance, the first church was torn down and its material was used in building a larger church, which was 35 by 55 feet and cost $1,500. The second church building was completed in summer 1861. The Second Twelve Mile Baptist Church worships today in its third building.

Belew, Mildred Boden. *The First 200 Years of Pendleton County.* Falmouth, Ky.: M. B. Belew, n.d. [ca. 1994].

Mildred Belew

SEGER, DANIEL (b. ca. 1856, Iowa; d. 1927, Sigourney, Iowa). Daniel T. Seger, "Covington's popular architect," lived and worked in Covington during the late 19th century. He secured numerous commissions from the local German American community and from the Diocese of Covington (see **Roman Catholics**); he was commissioned for projects in Cincinnati as well. The buildings he designed have been described as having "a somewhat distinctive, if provincial late Queen Anne–Richardsonian Romanesque character."

A laudatory 1893 account labeled Seger Covington's "leading architect and superintendent of building construction." During his six years of work in Covington, he drew plans for some of the finest buildings that were built in that period, including several in what is now Covington's **West Side–Main Strasse** Historic District. He also designed numerous small dwellings and storerooms in Covington and some fine houses in Cincinnati and its suburbs.

Seger began his architectural practice in Covington in 1886 and is listed in local city directories from 1890 to 1900. For several years German American architect William A. Rabe, later a member of the firm of Schofield & Rabe, worked in his office. Seger was married and lived with his wife and child in a house he designed and had built in 1893 at 1553 Holman St. in Covington's Peaselburg neighborhood. It is a two-story, gable-fronted edifice with an encircling spindle-work porch.

Among Seger's leading works was the former Fire Station No. 1 at Sixth and Washington Sts. in Covington, which is a Richardsonian Romanesque edifice in rock-faced sandstone and pressed brick. An innovative "iron truss," capable of bearing 154 tons, supported the roof and the second floor. The firehouse has been adaptively reused as a bar and restaurant (Tickets Restaurant). Seger also designed two imposing commercial Queen Anne–style edifices, both of pressed brick, at the prominent corner of Pike St. and Madison Ave., for many years the center of downtown Covington. One was the Eilerman Building (1896), which housed the clothing store of the same name (see **Eilerman & Sons, Men's Clothiers**). The building's canted corner, with an arched stained-glass window, addressed the intersection. The other was the Pieper Block, with a circular corner turret, which was home to Covington's Citizens National Bank and several storefronts. When the Pieper Block was "modernized" in the 1960s, the turret was removed and the walls wrapped with metal screening, which has since been removed.

In 1920 Seger, his wife Ellen, and his son Charles J. were living in Sigourney, Keokuk Co., Iowa, where the federal census indicates that he was employed as an architect building schools and residences. Seger died there in 1927 and was buried in the West Cemetery in Sigourney.

Other buildings in Covington identified as Seger's work include the Catholic Orphans' Home, **Dixie Highway**, 1889 (demolished); **John R. Coppin**'s residence, Madison Pike, the Latonia-Lakeview (demolished); the Henry Grisan Building, 18 W. Seventh St., 1896; the **Holy Cross Catholic Church** rectory, 1892 (demolished); the Phoenix Furniture Factory, Fourth and Russell Sts., ca. 1890 (demolished); the **St. Aloysius Catholic Church** parsonage, 716 Bakewell St., 1890; Fred Schmitz's "Swiss Cottage," Rosedale section of Covington, 1896; the Frank Wegman house, W. Covington, 1896; and the J. B. Worsham house addition, 84 Martin St., 1896. In addition, the following buildings have been attributed to Seger: Covington Fire Station No. 2, on the west side of the 400 block of Greenup St., 1890s (Richardsonian brick with stone trim); an unknown house, 611 W. Seventh St., 1890s; and the Wood Property Remodeling building, Madison Ave, probably on the west side in the 500 block.

Burns, Christopher. "Northern Kentucky Architects Provided Unique Character," *Ludlow News Enterprise*, July 12, 1989, 1–2.

Covington and Newport city directories, various years.

"Daniel Seger," *KP*, March 18, 1893, 6.

Langsam, Walter E. "Biographical Dictionary of Architects Who Worked in the Greater Cincinnati Area prior to World War II," 1986, Cincinnati Preservation Association, Cincinnati, Ohio.

"Outlook Good, for a Lively Building Season in Covington," *KP*, February 26, 1896, 5.

Ryan, Paul E. *History of the Diocese of Covington, Kentucky.* Covington, Ky.: Diocese of Covington, 1954.

Margaret Warminski

SEGOE, LADISLAS (b. August 17, 1894, Debrecen, Hungary; d. April 4, 1983, Cincinnati, Ohio). Ladislas Segoe was a Hungarian immigrant who helped to make professional planning an indispensable part of city government. As the son of Adolph and Leana Segoe, he grew up in a well-to-do Jewish family, attending the Royal Catholic Gymnasium and later the Royal Technical University (now the Technical University of Budapest). **World War I** interrupted his education, as he fought in the horse artillery for the Hungarian Army. Returning to his studies at the Royal Technical University after the war, he graduated in 1919 with a degree in civil engineering and architecture. Segoe immigrated to New York City in 1922 and accepted a position with the Technical Advisory Corporation (TAC), a cutting-edge engineering firm that was interested in expanding into the uncharted field of city planning. In 1923, on behalf of TAC, which had just contracted with Alfred Bettman's United City Planning Committee for a plan of the city of Cincinnati, Segoe came to Cincinnati. The resulting 1925 Cincinnati plan was the first comprehensive document of its kind for a major American city. It reflected a late-Progressive-movement effort to reform city government by including as many experts as possible in the city's governance. The comprehensive plan combined land-use projects, like zoning, with long-range planning for roads and mass transit. Segoe believed that professional planners should develop plans and present them to the city manager for approval.

In 1926 Segoe's fiancée, Vilma Czittler, also of Debrecen, Hungary, came to the United States and the two were married. In 1928 he founded his own planning consulting firm, Ladislas Segoe and Associates, in Cincinnati. Segoe's pioneering efforts in the field of city planning were increasingly marked by extensive consulting, teaching, research, and publishing.

After working for a time as the Covington zoning coordinator, Segoe wrote a comprehensive plan for Covington, which was approved in 1932. The plan was remarkable for its complete vision for the city and its environs. Industry, recreation, and education were among the areas Segoe meticulously covered. He made himself available to explain the planning process, frequently answering questions posed to him in newspapers and in live forums sponsored by organizations such as the local Chamber of Commerce (see **Northern Kentucky Chamber of Commerce**). Segoe worked with the Covington City Planning Commission on a plan that called for the development of infrastructure such as roadways, railroads, and even an airport near the city. Reprinted in 1974 by Arno Press as a volume in Richard C. Wade's "Metropolitan America" series, the *Comprehensive Plan for Covington, Kentucky and Environs* has become a textbook example of model city plans for its period. Segoe also served as consultant for Newport's Planning and Zoning Ordinance of 1949.

Segoe continued a successful private planning practice in Cincinnati and completed planning documents for several regional and national cities. He was involved with plans for Madison, Wis.; Dayton, Ohio; Charleston, W.Va.; and Detroit, Mich., among others. In addition, his firm did work for the cities of San Francisco, Calif.; Toronto, Canada; Louisville, Ky.; Richmond, Va.; Tucson, Ariz.; and Tulsa, Okla. A well-respected author, Segoe wrote two of the most important early texts on city planning. In 1937 he headed the research for a landmark report, *Our Cities: Their Role in the National Economy,* by the Urbanism Committee of the National Resources Committee. By 1941 Segoe had composed another work, *Local Planning Administration.* The International City Management Association named the latter as its first "Green Book" selection as a manual for city planning.

Segoe worked in his private practice until 1968. Scholarships in his name are given at the University of Cincinnati's school of planning. Professor David J. Edelman of that school says that Segoe's successful career "was due to the strength of his personality, the coherence of his vision of planning as an encompassing process, consistent and conscientious follow through, and an insistence that planners be responsible, reasonable, and honest professionals." A foundation was set up in honor of Segoe and his wife, Vilma, and funds from it have been used for support of planning projects as well as arts and parks development. Ladislas Segoe died in 1983, and Vilma died in 1990; both were cremated, and their ashes are buried at the United Jewish Cemetery in Walnut Hills, Cincinnati.

Cornell, Si. "You Drive? Lad's Your Friend," *CP*, March 8, 1968, 11.

Covington Planning and Zoning Commission. *Comprehensive Plan for the City of Covington, Kentucky and Environs.* Cincinnati: L. Segoe, 1932. Reprinted as a volume of the Metropolitan America Series, ed. Richard C. Wade (New York: Arno Press, 1974).

Edelman, David J., and David J. Allor. "Ladislas Segoe and the Emergence of the Professional Planning Consultant," *Journal of Planning History* 2, no. 1 (2003): 47–78.

Harper, Brett. *Ladislas and Vilma Segoe: A Visionary Couple and Their Love for Life.* Cincinnati: Ladislas and Vilma Segoe Family Foundation, 2001.

"Ladislas Segoe, City Architect," *CP*, April 5, 1983, 9B.

"Ladislas Segoe, 'Visionary' Planner, Riverfront Advocate," *CE*, April 5, 1983, C2.

Planning and Zoning Ordinance of the City of Newport, Kentucky. Newport, Ky.: Michaels, 1949.

Chris Meiman

SEGREGATION. The Union's victory in the **Civil War**, the passage of the 13th, 14th, and 15th amendments to the U.S. Constitution (abolishing slavery, granting African Americans citizenship, and giving them the right to vote), and the gains made during Reconstruction (1865–1877) were seen by African Americans in Kentucky as steps toward the fulfillment of the promises of freedom, full citizenship rights, and human dignity. But these promises were broken and betrayed a few years after emancipation, when new laws were passed that, along with continuing social customs, maintained white supremacy, racial oppression, and a segregated society.

The Hayes-Tilden Compromise of 1877, which sanctioned the removal of federal troops from the South, and the various U.S. Supreme Court rulings that essentially gutted the 14th and 15th amendments brought Reconstruction to an end and laid the foundation for the American version of racial apartheid, or segregation. Encouraged by the U.S. Supreme Court's *Plessy v. Ferguson* decision (1896), legalizing "separate but equal," the Kentucky legislature, step by step, year after year, passed "Jim Crow" laws that both disenfranchised blacks and separated them from whites in most aspects of life. These state segregation laws, founded upon the principle of states' rights, along with a rigid social code that developed, were meant to ensure that African Americans would never forget "their place" in Kentucky's social, economic, and political hierarchy.

In Northern Kentucky separate facilities were always unequal, and in many cases they were nonexistent. Segregation meant that African Americans were denied access to public parks, such as **Devou Park** and Goebel Park; movie theaters; bowling alleys; restaurant lunch counters; bathrooms; and recreation facilities such as the **YMCA**. Blacks were also denied equal employment (generally other than service or labor jobs), hotel accommodations, fair trials, open housing, and adequate health care facilities, while being constantly humiliated and denied social forms of respect.

When whites could not gain African American obedience and submission to these laws and social codes of white supremacy, they sometimes resorted to lynching, mob violence, and other forms of racial terrorism. While the Ku Klux Klan did not become a strong force within Northern Kentucky, Klan groups were present, especially in rural areas, and used "white-sheet" tactics and cross-burnings to intimidate blacks. African Americans throughout Northern Kentucky during the years of segregation (1865–1964) continually resisted, individually and collectively, the various forms of disenfranchisement, segregation, and racial violence.

Some African Americans resisted by escaping across the Ohio River into Cincinnati; others joined the Exodusters, who moved west into Kansas, Oklahoma, and Montana in 1879–1881; still others went farther north with the Great Migration (1890–1940) to such cities as Chicago, Ill.; Detroit, Mich.; and New York City, hoping to find a better life. This constant migration out of Northern Kentucky depleted the number of talented and ambitious individuals in the community.

Those who remained to struggle against segregation and racial oppression organized and participated in such diverse groups as the Anti–Separate Coach Movement, the Council on Interracial Cooperation, the Kentucky Negro Education Association, the Kentucky Association of Women for the Prevention of Lynching, the **NAACP** (National Association of Colored People), the National Association of Colored Women, the National Negro Business League, the **Congress of Racial Equality**, the Kentucky State Colored Chautauqua, the Kentucky Commission to Study Negro Affairs, and many other groups.

Education was very important to blacks recently freed from slavery. After the Civil War, one of the first schools for African Americans, a Freedman School (see **Freedmen's Bureau Schools**), was organized in 1866 in Covington under the direction of **Jacob Price**. Even before the Kentucky legislature passed the 1904 Day Law, legally requiring the segregation of public and private schools, the vast majority of schools, other than Berea College in Berea, were already segregated. In 1874 the Kentucky legislature passed laws creating a comprehensive public school system that included segregated schools for African Americans. The revenue for the maintenance of these schools was derived from the taxes on property. For African American schools, this means of support automatically reduced the school term to 2 or 3 months a year, while the term for white schools was 5 to 10 months a year. The African American schools in Northern Kentucky, which according to state law had to be located at least one mile from a white school, were separate and unequal. The William Grant School and the **Our Savior** School in Covington, the **Southgate St. School** in Newport, the Paul Lawrence Dunbar and Wilkens schools in Elsmere, and the **John G. Fee Industrial High School** in Maysville were schools for blacks built in Northern Kentucky. Although far inferior to white schools in physical, material, and financial aspects, these schools provided their students with an outstanding education that rivaled the one offered in white schools, thanks to dedicated teachers and principals. African American schools were closed during the era of desegregation following the U.S. Supreme Court decision of *Brown v. the Board of Education of Topeka, Kans.* in 1954.

In 1892 the Kentucky legislature passed a law requiring separate railway cars for African American and white passengers on interstate railroads. Minnie Myers, while traveling from Cincinnati to Lexington, Ky., in 1895, arrived in Covington and was required to move out of her first-class railway car seat in an integrated car into a segregated car designated "for colored only." As part of the Anti–Separate Coach movement, she protested her physical removal and later sued the **Louisville and Nashville Railroad**. Such courageous and defiant acts of resistance were commonplace during the "Jim Crow" era.

Segregation was the norm in Kentucky, just as it was in most other states, but there were areas in Northern Kentucky where segregation did not take root. When the Covington Public Library (see **Kenton Co. Public Library**) opened in 1900, its open-door policy, allowing blacks full access to its books and services, made it the first desegregated main library in the South and one of the few in the United States. Since there were no state laws requiring segregated facilities at public libraries, the Covington public library was never legally confronted about this policy, thanks to cooperative community leaders and forward thinking library staff who avoided public scrutiny.

Since 1893 the **Green Line** carried streetcar passengers with integrated seating between Cincinnati and Northern Kentucky. In 1916 the company was indicted by a Kenton Co. grand jury and found guilty of not providing separate facilities as required by Kentucky's separate coach bill. Appealed to the U.S. Supreme Court, this conviction was upheld in 1920, but the Green Line Streetcar Company found ways to evade the state laws by amending its charter and never instituted segregated streetcars.

Many Christians fought against the evils of segregation. For example, when the Diocese of Covington (see **Roman Catholics**) built Camp **Marydale** in Boone Co. during the 1940s, Rev. **Anthony Deye**, a teacher and coach at the all-black Catholic Our Savior School, made certain that the camp was open to all children, regardless of race.

Despite some advances, however, racism reigned supreme. "Legal lynching" was condoned under the public hanging law in effect at the time. African Americans accused of crimes, especially if the alleged crime was raping a white woman, were tried under hostile circumstances, with no real opportunity to prove their guilt or innocence, and customarily given a death sentence. In other cases, the victims of lynching were not even accused of a specific crime, except, perhaps, violating some unwritten social convention. During the 30-year period 1899–1930, Northern Kentucky residents were partners in and witnesses to three rape trials that gained national attention. In 1899, 18-year-old Richard Coleman was charged with the rape and murder of a white woman in Maysville. To avoid a possible lynching, the local sheriff transported Coleman to Covington for safekeeping. After being ordered by a grand jury to return him to Mason Co., the sheriff turned Coleman over to a mob of hundreds of white men, women, and children who proceeded after a quick "trial" to burn Coleman alive and cut off his body parts as souvenirs. No persons were ever charged in this sensational act of mob frenzy and extreme brutality. In March 1930, a white woman from Crescent Springs in Kenton Co. charged an African American youth, Anderson McPerkins, with rape. After a quick trial he was found guilty and sentenced to death by hanging. He was saved from being lynched by a white mob through the combined efforts of the Cincinnati branches of the International Labor Defense and the NAACP, the Kentucky Commission on Interracial Cooperation, the Cincinnati chapter of the ACLU (American Civil Liberties Union), and the **Ninth St. Methodist Episcopal Church** of Covington. In 1932 his verdict was overturned, and he was released from prison. In 1935 John Pete Montjoy was accused of robbing and raping a white woman and given a quick trial. He was found guilty and sentenced to death by hanging. Again, individuals and groups from Covington and Cincinnati joined together in an attempt to have Montjoy's verdict overturned. This time they were not successful. On December 17, 1937, Montjoy was hanged in front of the Covington city-county building.

In 1954 the U.S. Supreme Court, in *Brown v. Board of Education of Topeka, Kans.*, after 80 years of ruling in favor of segregation, finally declared state-sponsored segregation unconstitutional. But it took 10 more years and a growing **civil rights movement**, which made use of boycotts, sit-ins, and marches, together with the 1964 Civil Rights Act, to bring the era of "Jim Crow" to a close.

Kentucky Commission of Human Rights. *Kentucky's Black Heritage*. Frankfort, Ky.: Kentucky Commission of Human Rights, 1971.

Wright, George C. *A History of Blacks in Kentucky*. Vol. 2, *In Pursuit of Equality, 1890–1980*. Frankfort: Kentucky Historical Society, 1992.

Jim Embry

SEIGEL, GREG AND REBEKKA (Greg: b. 1947, Cincinnati, Ohio; Rebekka: b. 1948, Columbus, Ohio). Greg Seigel, a traditional potter, and Rebekka Seigel, a contemporary quilt-maker, both inherited from their grandparents a passion for hand-making items. Greg Seigel was always interested in art, but it was not until he moved into a house that was set up for pottery-making that he got his hands into working with clay. Largely self-taught and strongly influenced by the inventiveness of his machine-making grandfather, Greg began creating functional pieces with touches of whimsy. Moving to rural Owen Co., Ky., allowed him to incorporate local materials into his clays and glazes and to build his own brick kilns, where he creates stoneware art and utility pieces using traditional hand-firing techniques. Greg's legacy is embedded in the hallways of the Owen Co. Elementary School, where he has worked beside students in grades 4–12 to design, create, and glaze tiles and then install them into murals on the school's walls.

Rebekka Beer Seigel grew up in Cincinnati, where she met and married Greg Seigel in July 1973. While expecting the birth of the first of the couple's two children, she learned basic quilting skills from her grandmother; but she found traditional patterns uninspiring. She preferred to tell stories in quilts and sought to express herself in fabric. The subjects of her intricate hand-sewn, pictorial appliqué quilts frequently honor female pioneers in all fields. Some of her quilts are in the permanent collections of the Kentucky History Museum in Frankfort and the Evansville (Ind.)

Art and Science Museum. Others are in private collections. Her most acclaimed quilt was chosen to represent Kentucky in the 1986 Statue of Liberty contest at the Museum of American Folk Art in New York City. In 2004 Rebekka was awarded the Al Smith Fellowship of the Kentucky Arts Council for excellence in visual arts.

George, Phyllis. *Kentucky Crafts: Handmade and Heartfelt*. New York: Crown, 1989.

Hicks, Jack. "Couple Crafts Works of Art in Their Home," *KP*, January 20, 1993, 1K.

Rebecca Mitchell Turney

SELDEN, DIXIE (b. February 28, 1868, Cincinnati, Ohio; d. November 14, 1935, Cincinnati, Ohio). Renowned local artist Dixie Selden was the first and only surviving child of John Roger and Martha McMillen Peyton Selden. In 1870 when Dixie was two years old, the family moved to 101 W. Fourth St., Covington, the first of several residences in Covington. Even though John Selden served in the Union Army during the **Civil War**, both he and his wife later developed unequivocal sympathies with the South. They named their first child Dixie, so that there would never be any doubt concerning their pro-Southern feelings.

Dixie and her parents were proud of their ancestry, which extended back to New England and the American Revolution, and accordingly they joined the recently founded Sons and **Daughters of the American Revolution** (SAR and DAR). In 1894 Dixie commemorated her acceptance into the DAR by painting her own portrait, *Daughter of the Revolution*, which was exhibited at the Woman's Art Club that fall. For unspecified reasons, the Seldens dropped out of the SAR and the DAR in 1899.

Dixie Selden's interest in the arts was cultivated by her parents through travels abroad. Their travels were undertaken for other reasons, but the Seldens later said the trips served as crucial groundwork for Dixie's artistic career. Newspaper accounts described Martha Selden as a prominent member of the Culture Club, a local literary society, and an associate member of the **Covington Art Club**. Dixie's parents also participated in the Shakespeare Society. While most of the family's activities centered on Covington, the family moved freely in elite social circles on both sides of the Ohio River. Later, when Dixie became a working artist, her parents' social connections provided easy access to a society that required a steady flow of portraits and paintings. After Dixie's mother and father died in 1907 and 1908, respectively, Dixie continued to live in her parents' home in Covington on W. Fourth St.; she later moved to two other residences in Covington. In about 1910, she moved to 1106 Cross Ln. in the East Walnut Hills neighborhood of Cincinnati.

Selden was educated at Miss Virginia Simpson Private School in Covington, Miss Clara E. Nourse Select Girls School in Cincinnati, and Miss Bartholomew's English and Classical School for Girls in Cincinnati. She was determined early in life to be a painter, initially concentrating on portrait painting. Selden's parents set up an art studio for her in their home while she was attending these schools. In 1884 her love of art led her to enroll in the McMicken School of Design in Cincinnati (later the Cincinnati Art Academy, CAM). Six years later, on November 1, 1890, the internationally famous Covington artist **Frank Duveneck** taught his first class at this school, and Selden was enrolled in the class. She responded well to Duveneck's teaching and continued her education at the academy off and on until 1912. She was one of Duveneck's favorite students, and she made excellent progress under his teaching. He called her "the little one" because of her short stature. After six years of drawing and watercolor classes and nearly two years of painting with Duveneck, Selden began publicly exhibiting her work. Her first art exhibition was at the Covington Art Club in 1890. She received prizes for best portrait and painting in oil.

In 1891 Selden entered her second art exhibition, with four paintings at the more prestigious Cincinnati Art Club. In June 1892 she received the distinction of being invited to show three of her paintings with Frank Duveneck, **Henry Farny**, Frank H. Lungren, Edward Potthast, and Charles Henry Sharp at Barton's Gallery. This was the moment when she shed her amateur status. In the same year, she became a founding member and twice served as president of the Cincinnati Woman's Art Club. She gained further experience and recognition through her exhibitions with the Woman's Art Club. The 1893 spring exhibit was held at Closson's Art Gallery, where she received further praise. Additional semiannual exhibitions with the Woman's Art Club provided venues for the quick sale of her works.

Selden was best known for fine portraits and lively landscapes. Many of her later works were displayed in the Cincinnati Art Museum, the Chicago Art Museum, the New York Art Academy, the Pennsylvania Academy of the Fine Arts, and other places. Some of her more celebrated portraits are those titled *Mary M. Emery, Frederick Hicks, The Dana Boys, Spanish Gypsy, Eleanor Simpson Orr, Frank Duveneck, Little Parker Girl, Arab Bride, Aunt Patsy, Fishermen's Wives,* and *Wife of Martinez*. Selden received many awards throughout her life.

In the 1890s Selden completed approximately 10 major works per year. In addition to portraits of family, her subjects initially were pets, domestic life, and flowers. By 1894 she was advertising her career as a portrait painter in Covington, and her portraits soon gained more fame. One of her most notable portraits, from 1896, was *Soudanese Woman*. Some of her portraits were similar to those called Etudes, small exercises of partially unfinished works of society's disadvantaged. As Selden perfected her painting skills, her artistic talents and horizons broadened. By 1909 she had become a painter in the impressionistic style of portraits, genre, and landscapes as well as an illustrator. She is still considered to be one of the premier impressionists from the Greater Cincinnati area.

Further distinction came to Selden when Frank Duveneck received the honorary Doctor of Laws in 1917 from the University of Cincinnati. She painted his portrait from brief sittings owing to his poor health. The portrait was exhibited both at the New York National Academy of Design and at the Pennsylvania Academy of the Fine Arts in 1918. Duveneck's portrait brought her considerable recognition when it was exhibited at the Pennsylvania Academy. This was one of the few times Selden exhibited in the eastern United States. In May of the same year, Duveneck's portrait was exhibited at the 25th Annual Exhibition of American Art at the Cincinnati Art Museum. Duveneck died on January 30, 1919.

After **World War I**, Selden's living quarters were damaged by a fire, and she visited friends in Lexington while repairs were being made. One of her best portraits, *Madeline McDowell Breckenridge,* was painted while she was in Lexington. She also participated in the Southern States Artists Association, the McDowell Society, the National Association of Women Artists and Sculptors, the National Art Club (New York City), and the Louisville Art Association.

Selden's portrait of Henry Feltman, the founder of the **Citizens National Bank** of Covington, was touted as a fine example of her power and fine imagination. In the last 25 years of her life, she traveled the world, recording scenes of streets and markets and producing portraits of newfound friends in Belgium, Brittany, China, Cuba, Denmark, England, Germany, Ireland, Italy, Japan, Morocco, Mexico, Normandy, Spain, Switzerland, the Middle East, and Yugoslavia. Her traveling companions at various times were a Miss Coit, Mary Ives Duhme, Jeanie D. McKee, and Emma Mendenhall, a watercolorist.

Selden died of a heart attack at age 65 in her apartment on Cross Ln. in Cincinnati. Funeral services were conducted in her home by Rector Frank Nelson of Christ Cathedral, and she was buried at Highland Cemetery in Fort Mitchell, near her parents. She never married or even had a beau of enough importance to be mentioned in accounts of her life. From March 4 to April 8, 1936, the Cincinnati Art Museum held a memorial exhibit of 60 of her works, which dated from 1903 to 1935. Most came from private collections.

Alexander, Mary L. "Cincinnati Artist Completes Portrait of Covington Banker," *KTS*, March 5, 1923, 16.

———. "Is True Art: Cincinnati Artist Depicts Charm of Venice Atmosphere," *KTS*, October 15, 1923, 12.

Bauer, Marilyn. "Strong Impressionist: Cincinnati Art Galleries Celebrates Dixie Selden Biography with Exhibit of Native Daughter's Paintings," *CE*, July 25, 2002, 3E.

"Cincinnati's Most Collectible Artists," *CE*, April 19, 1998, 6H.

"Gallery Will Show State Art," *KP*, April 20, 1983, 10K.

"Honor Carlisle," *KP*, June 11, 1925, 2.

McLean, Genetta. *Dixie Selden: An American Impressionist from Cincinnati, 1868–1935*. Cincinnati: Cincinnati Art Galleries, 2001.

Reis, Jim. "Dixie Selden, Artist," *KP*, October 31, 2005, 4K.

——. "Dixie Selden Studied with Duveneck and Farny, Later Earned National Recognition for Landscapes," *KP*, September 6, 1993, 4K.

Williams, Hal. "Kenton, Campbell Exhibits Displayed in Kentucky's Historical Museum," *KTS*, March 12, 1958, 2A.

Richard M. Sacksteder

SEMINARY OF ST. PIUS X. Bishop William T. Mulloy decided in the early 1950s to build a diocesan seminary to educate priests for the Diocese of Covington (see **Roman Catholics**). The **Marydale** property in Erlanger provided a convenient location. The seminary program was initiated in the fall of 1955 in the old horse barn at Marydale, which also served as a retreat house. The high-school- and college-level seminarians lived in the barn and received their spiritual formation there. They were bused to **Covington Latin School** for their general education; on weekends they were allowed to go home. Msgr. Elmer Grosser was the first rector of the seminary, which was named St. Pius X in honor of the early-20th-century pope of that name.

By 1958 the architectural firm Betz and Bankemper (see **Carl A. Bankemper**) had been hired to design a permanent seminary building. It was constructed across the small lake from the recently built Marydale retreat house, which had been designed by the same architects. Students took up residence in the new building in January 1960. The new bishop of Covington, Richard H. Ackerman, dedicated the residence on September 4, 1960. A separate gymnasium, with racquetball courts and a bowling alley, was constructed in 1963 and dedicated to the memory of Mulloy, who died in 1959. The seminary discontinued its high school program in 1965. The Southern Association of Colleges accredited the college liberal arts academic program, centered on philosophy, in 1968.

In the period following the Second Vatican Council (1962–1965), several changes were introduced into seminary programs around the country. Many Catholic priests and educators questioned the wisdom of continuing the rigidly structured model of seminary formation, which mandated a self-contained environment in which seminarians had little contact with others outside of the seminary. A more open program was being promoted, one that allowed students more individual freedom in assuming responsibility for their education and formation. But there were other Catholics, including Ackerman, who disagreed with the new approach. Ackerman was very concerned about the growing number of priests and sisters nationwide who were leaving their ministries in the late 1960s and early 1970s and about the concomitant drop in seminary enrollments. He believed that part of the problem was that the new seminary model did not offer the proper formation for seminary students. He intended to keep the Seminary of St. Pius X in line with the more traditional model. To boost enrollment, he made the Seminary of St. Pius X accessible to students from other dioceses. Some like-minded bishops from around the country were glad to have the seminary in the Diocese of Covington available as an alternative to what they considered the overly liberal seminaries that seemed to dominate the field. Throughout the 1970s, under the rectorship of Rev. William G. Brown, Ackerman retained the traditional model of formation at the Seminary of St. Pius X.

Ackerman's successor, however, did not support that model. Soon after his arrival as bishop of Covington in 1979, William A. Hughes initiated a study of the seminary by a committee appointed by the National Council of Catholic Bishops (NCCB). The study was conducted in the spring of 1981 and headed by Bishop Walter Sullivan of Richmond, Va. The committee used the criteria established in the NCCB's "Program of Priestly Formation" as the basis for its evaluation of the program at St. Pius X. Following the committee's recommendations, Hughes announced in 1982 that the Seminary of St. Pius X would introduce major changes. The seminarians would no longer attend classes at the seminary but would now travel to **Thomas More College** in nearby Crestview Hills for their education. Nor would their lives be as regimented by routine. In addition they would discard the traditional garb worn by students at St. Pius. He appointed Rev. Raymond Holtz as the new rector.

These changes meant the loss of many students from other dioceses whose bishops had favored the previous program. The resulting smaller enrollment (it still included students from other dioceses in Kentucky and Tennessee) made it difficult to sustain the seminary. After closing the seminary building and sending seminarians to live in a separate dorm facility on the Thomas More Campus for the 1986–1987 academic year, Hughes and the Seminary Board determined that it was no longer economically feasible to continue the seminary program, so the Seminary of St. Pius X's program ended in 1987. The following year, the diocesan offices were moved from downtown Covington into the old seminary building, which was renamed the Catholic Center. The Diocese of Covington then began sending its seminarians to seminaries in other parts of the country.

"Bishop Announces Sept. Opening for Jr. Seminary," *Messenger*, February 6, 1955, 1A.

"Bishop Hughes Announces Decision: St. Pius X Seminary Program to Be Phased Out," *Messenger*, November 15, 1987, 1.

"Bishop to Dedicate St. Pius X Seminary," *Messenger*, September 4, 1960, 1A.

"Building Set for New Seminary: Construction Features Classical-Colonial Design," *Messenger*, March 30, 1958, 1A.

"Cardinal Ritter Dedicates Memorial Gymnasium," *Messenger*, May 19, 1963, 1A.

Fagan, Sean. "The New Approach to Seminary Training," *Furrow* 16, no. 5 (May 1965): 269–70.

"New Look Seminary Opens Doors, Collars," *Messenger*, August 29, 1982, 2.

O'Donoghue, Joseph. "Reforming the Seminaries," *Commonweal* 81, November 6, 1964, 195.

Seminary of St. Pius X Student Catalogues, 1962–1963, 1963–1964, 1969–1970, Archives of the Diocese of Covington, Erlanger, Ky.

"St. Pius X Board Decides: Seminarians to Go to Thomas More," *Messenger*, 18 April 18, 1982, 1–2.

"St. Pius X Seminary Trains First Priest-Aspirants," *Messenger*, October 23, 1955, 16A–17A.

Thomas S. Ward

SEMINARY SQUARE. See **Western Baptist Theological Institute**.

SENIOR SERVICES OF NORTHERN KENTUCKY. Senior Services of Northern Kentucky (SSNK), under various names, has been serving the region since 1962. In December of that year, a group of concerned citizens and community leaders from **Trinity Episcopal Church**, the Diocese of Covington (see **Roman Catholics**), and **Mother of God Catholic Church** established the first senior center in the state in the American Legion Hall at 115 E. Fourth St. in Covington. The center soon moved to the community rooms at Trinity Episcopal Church. The organization, which began under the name of Senior Center Inc. as a recreational center funded by the Community Chest, later expanded as a Title III project of the Older Americans Act, while adding more centers and conducting limited outreach. In 1971 service and senior centers were established throughout the eight-county **Northern Kentucky Area Development District** with an array of offerings: congregate meals/senior centers, home-delivered meals, transportation, outreach, protective services, a nursing home ombudsman, information and referral, lifeline, homemaker services, the retired senior volunteer program, the Northern Kentucky senior games, the *Sentinel Newspaper*, and one church–one elder. In 1974, free hot meals were made available at the senior centers.

In 1989 the Covington senior center and the regional administration moved into the former Elks Hall at 34 W. Fifth St.; in April 1993, the organization moved into the former **Knights of Columbus** building at 1032 Madison Ave. in Covington, consolidating its offices and its commissary. In January 1994, its name became Senior Services of Northern Kentucky Inc. Today, SSNK is the only agency in the eight counties responsible for meals-on-wheels. For many elderly people, the delivery of these daily meals is the only contact they have with the outside world. Today, after 40 years, SSNK continues to support the independence and dignity of persons over age 60 in the following eight Northern Kentucky counties: Boone, Campbell, Carroll, Gallatin, Grant, Kenton, Owen, and Pendleton. SSNK and some 300 volunteers are prepared to meet the needs of the aging baby boomer population of Northern Kentucky.

Senior Services Northern Kentucky. www.seniorservicesnky.org (accessed October 30, 2006).

Senior Services of Northern Kentucky. *Older Adults: The Resource Guide.* Covington: Senior Services of Northern Kentucky, 2005.

"Start New Agency: Senior Citizens Not Just Rockin'," *KP*, January 24, 1969, 1K.

Donna Oehler

SETTLE, EVAN E. (b. December 1, 1848, Frankfort, Ky.; d. November 16, 1899, Owenton, Ky.) Evan Evans Settle, an Owen Co. lawyer and politician, was the son of William H. and Harriet Evans Settle. Evan's early education was at the prestigious B. B. Sayre Academy in Frankfort. The family moved to Louisville, where Settle attended Louisville Male High School, graduating in 1864. He worked for a year in Louisville in the U.S. Provost Marshall's office during the **Civil War** and then moved to Frankfort and worked for the state auditor. Settle studied law and was admitted to the bar in 1870. He set up his first legal practice at Owenton. He married Lizzie Herndon on October 20, 1875, and they had six children. Settle served as Owen Co. attorney from 1878 until 1887 and was then elected to the Kentucky legislature. In 1897 he won a seat in the U.S. House of Representatives, where he served until his death at age 50. Settle was buried in the Odd Fellows Cemetery at Owenton.

Biographical Directory of the United States Congress. "Settle, Evan Evans." http://bioguide.congress.gov (accessed November 22, 2005).

Houchens, Mariam Sidebottom. *History of Owen County: "Sweet Owen."* Louisville, Ky.: Standard, 1976.

SHALER, NATHANIEL BURGER (b. July 21, 1805, Massachusetts; d. January 17, 1882, Newport, Ky.). Dr. Nathaniel Burger Shaler, a physician, attended schools in the city of Lancaster, Mass., before graduating from medical school at Harvard University in Cambridge, Mass. He had a somewhat combative personality, which occasionally got him into trouble. Shaler went to Havana, Cuba, to practice medicine because he had a connection with the U.S. consul there. After that did not work out, he moved to the frontier town of Newport, Ky., in 1832, at the height of the worst cholera epidemic the state of Kentucky had ever experienced. As Shaler cared for those victims, he quickly gained the respect of the community. He was one of the first physicians to abandon the medical practice of bloodletting. In October 1835 Shaler married Ann Southgate, the daughter of **Richard Southgate** and Nancy Hinde Southgate. The newlyweds built a home in what is now **Evergreen Cemetery** in Southgate. Shaler was known for treating difficult cases with some degree of success. In 1847 he became the surgeon at the local **Newport Barracks** and later served as a Union Army medical officer during the **Civil War**. His hospital at the barracks had a higher rate of success in achieving cures than other military hospitals. Shaler was a member of the Covington and Newport Medical and Surgical Society and the Newport city school board. Often his name would appear in the newspapers of the day in the lists of individuals owing back taxes. He was the father of **Nathaniel Southgate Shaler**, a noted geologist, teacher, and historian who went on to become one of the great teachers of the 19th century at Harvard University. Late in life, Dr. Nathaniel B. Shaler moved into a mansion on Taylor St. in Newport (E. Third St. today), where he died in 1882. He was buried in Evergreen Cemetery in Southgate, near his former home.

Poweleit, Alvin C., and James A. Schroer, eds. *A Medical History of Campbell and Kenton Counties.* Cincinnati: Campbell-Kenton Medical Society, 1970.

SHALER, NATHANIEL SOUTHGATE (b. February 20, 1841, Newport, Ky.; d. April 10, 1906, Cambridge, Mass.). Nathaniel Southgate Shaler was an educator, a geologist, and one of Northern Kentucky's most prolific authors. He was the eldest surviving son of **Nathaniel Burger Shaler**, an eminent physician and surgeon, and Ann Hinde Southgate, the daughter of a prosperous attorney and landowner, **Richard Southgate**. Because he was born soon after his parents had lost their first-born son in an accident, and because of his own frail health, his early boyhood was exceedingly sheltered. His lifelong love of nature, domestic and wild animals, and earth sciences was no doubt fostered during these early years, when he often accompanied his father on horseback rides down to the Ohio River and throughout the rustic Northern Kentucky countryside. As a youngster, Nathaniel also spent a great deal of time with his maternal grandfather, Richard Southgate, at his grandfather's residence in Newport.

During the first decade of Nathaniel's life, the significant early influences of his father and his maternal grandfather, open access to their well-stocked home libraries, and free rein to explore the natural world around him supplied ample fodder for his insatiable curiosity and precocious mind. Between the ages of 11 and 12, Nathaniel attended the school at the nearby **Newport Barracks**. There he studied Latin, Greek, and mathematics, although ill health (in the form of "sick headaches," which continued to plague him throughout his life), as well as his dislike of the school, often interfered with his attendance. When he reached age 15, his father hired a private tutor to supplement Nathaniel's somewhat unorthodox education. Johannes Escher, a clergyman of Swiss and German heritage, not only furthered Nathaniel's education but also provided him with a sterling example of scholarly discipline. Under Escher's expert tutelage, Nathaniel built a sound, classically based foundation that included German, Greek, and Latin literature, as well as the philosophy of Hegel, Kant, and Schelling.

When Nathaniel reached age 17, his parents determined that their eldest son should enroll in an institution of higher learning. Dr. Shaler, a Harvard graduate from the class of 1827, deemed his son to be a fitting candidate for his prestigious alma mater. Despite Nathaniel's somewhat jumbled early education, he was enrolled as a sophomore at Harvard in 1859. While there, he studied earth sciences under the noted naturalist Louis Agassiz.

Nathaniel Southgate Shaler's years of undergraduate study were also spent preparing for whatever role he might be called upon to play for his native Kentucky in the escalating conflict between the Northern and Southern states. The militaristic influence of his boyhood experiences at the Newport Barracks, where his father served as army surgeon, along with his father's resolve that Nathaniel, from a very early age, should become proficient in the use of the rifle and the sword, certainly prepared him for soldierly duty, but they did little to blunt his sensibilities to the harsh realities of war. As the specter of war loomed, Shaler supplemented his Harvard curriculum with martial activities: he participated in a drill club, studied various works on military tactics, and performed soldierly duties and clerked at the nearby military base Fort Independence in Boston Harbor.

The outbreak of the **Civil War** occurred during Shaler's last year as a student at Harvard. Wrestling with his conflicting desires—to take his final examinations or to delay his degree conferment to enlist in the army Shaler returned to Kentucky and sought the counsel of trusted friends and family members. Following the advice of his grandfather, Richard Southgate, placed him on the Union side. But family and friends urged him to postpone his enlistment in the Union Army until after he had obtained his degree, so Shaler went back to Cambridge and prepared for his final examinations. On July 8, 1862, he graduated summa cum laude with a BS in geology from Harvard's Lawrence Scientific School.

Almost immediately, he traveled to Frankfort, Ky., where he received a commission as captain of the Union Army's 5th Kentucky Battery. He and his unit fortified one of the hillside battlements that had been hastily constructed earlier in 1862 when Confederate troops threatened Cincinnati and Northern Kentucky. Because his father owned the land upon which the structure was built and graciously opened his vineyards to allow for the battlement's construction, it was later named Shaler Battery in his honor. (Now a part of the **Evergreen Cemetery** grounds, Shaler Battery's earthen ramparts remain visible atop the highest hill of the cemetery's rolling acreage.) Although severe bronchitis forced Captain Shaler to resign his post, he was deeply affected by his wartime experiences and later wrote of his poignant military reminiscences in a posthumously published book, *From Old Fields: Poems of the Civil War.* In that same year, 1862, he married Sophia Penn Page. The couple had two daughters, Gabriella and Ann Penn.

In 1864, prompted by pressing reasons of health and employment, he returned to the cooler climate of Cambridge and the welcoming environs of Harvard Yard. His beloved teacher and mentor, Agassiz, appointed him assistant lecturer in paleontology at the Museum of Comparative Zoology. One year later, Agassiz's declining health prompted increased teaching responsibilities for Shaler, as he took over instruction in both zoology and geology. From 1866 to 1868, he traveled extensively throughout Europe, collecting fossils and other specimens for the museum and conducting fieldwork in the Alps, France, and Italy. His travels also included a trip to Kentucky in 1868, when he participated in a paleontological dig at **Big Bone Lick** in Boone Co. Upon his return to Harvard in 1869, the 28-year-old Shaler was granted a full professorship in paleontology (his title was changed to professor of geology in 1888).

Shaler's ties to his native state were reaffirmed in 1873, when Kentucky governor Preston H. Leslie (1871–1875) appointed him director of the newly revived Kentucky Geological Survey. Shaler served the Commonwealth of Kentucky in this capacity until 1880, and during those years he undertook the first comprehensive survey of the state's natural resources, publishing the findings in an 1876 monograph entitled *A General Account of the Commonwealth of Kentucky*. His work led to the state's later emergence as a leader in the coal industry. In addition to revitalizing the Kentucky Geological Survey, in 1875 he initiated Harvard's first summer school for geology and conducted its opening installment at Cumberland Gap in Kentucky. Shaler was also instrumental in revitalizing Harvard's Lawrence Scientific School in 1886 and was appointed dean in 1891, a position he retained for the rest of his life.

Shaler vibrant classroom lectures, delivered extemporaneously, conveyed his passion for earth sciences to a nearly 40-year procession of Harvard students. He instructed every undergraduate who entered the university between 1884 and 1891, largely because of the popularity of Geology 4, his introductory geology class. His reputation was mythical among Harvard's student body, not only because of his teaching abilities but also because of his caring and compassionate demeanor toward his students, especially those who were challenged financially, intellectually, or physically. His students called him "Uncle Nat."

Shaler published a large number of scholarly writings over the course of his long academic career. Yet he wrote on many nonacademic subjects as well. The bibliography of his published works, which lists 29 books and 234 articles, includes an acclaimed introductory textbook, *The First Book of Geology* (1884); a history of his native state, *Kentucky: A Pioneer Commonwealth* (1884); and a late-life social trilogy, *The Individual* (1900), *The Citizen* (1904), and *The Neighbor* (1904). His hundreds of articles and essays covered highly diverse topics: a few titles are "On the Formation of Mountain Chains" (1866, natural science), "Race Prejudices" (1886, social philosophy), "The Summer Schools" (1893, education), and "The Dog" (1894, domestic animals).

Throughout his life, Shaler's substantial mental energy was equaled by his physical vigor. Despite his boyhood frailty and lifelong battles with chronic headaches and vertigo, he maintained an ambitious exercise regimen. He often walked up to six miles a day, heedless of adverse weather, and regularly visited the campus gymnasium. In early spring 1906, Shaler set out on foot to visit an ill friend; the ground was still covered with hard-packed snow, which made the return trek very strenuous. Shaler fell ill soon afterward and underwent surgery for appendicitis. He then contracted pneumonia and died April 10, 1906, at his home in Cambridge. He was buried at Mount Auburn Cemetery in Cambridge.

So highly had the Kentucky-born Harvard professor and dean been regarded by the people of Cambridge, his Harvard colleagues, and the student body that on the afternoon of his funeral, all flags in the city and on campus hung at half-mast, shops were closed, classes were suspended, and the entire undergraduate student population of both the college and the Scientific School lined both sides of the street from Shaler's home on Quincy St. to Appleton Chapel on the campus.

"Dean Shaler Died Yesterday," *Harvard Crimson*, April 11, 1906.

Livingstone, David N. *Nathaniel Southgate Shaler and the Culture of American Science*. Tuscaloosa: Univ. of Alabama Press, 1987.

Purvis, Thomas L., ed. *Newport, Kentucky: A Bicentennial History*. Newport, Ky.: Otto Zimmerman, 1996.

Shaler, Nathaniel Southgate, and Sophia Penn Page Shaler. *The Autobiography of Nathaniel Southgate Shaler with a Supplementary Memoir by His Wife*. Boston: Houghton Mifflin, 1909.

Shaler, N. S. Papers, Harvard Univ. Archives, Pusey Library, Harvard Univ., Cambridge, Mass.

Janice Mueller

SHANTYBOATS. The shantyboats and shantyboat communities that used to be scattered along the Ohio, Licking, and Kentucky rivers within the Northern Kentucky region are perhaps best known from literature and film. Ideally, shantyboats were tucked away in protected inlets and backwaters. Families resided within these makeshift floating houses (shanties) on the fringes of the larger river towns, from Maysville to Carrollton and up the Kentucky River to Frankfort. The boats were of all types: oil-drum pontoons, houseboats, and log rafts, tied to the shore wherever they were allowed. They were built of whatever scrap materials could be scavenged. One-story shacks, seldom longer than 30 feet and not much wider than Conestoga wagons, they were mainly homes of low-income persons. Many believe that the shantyboat design was a direct descendant of early Ohio River flatboats. Some shantyboats evolved into somewhat comfortable living quarters, but most did not. Shantyboaters anchored to the shore, paying no property taxes, and sent their children to local schools. They bartered whatever they could collect, often fish, for what they needed from shore. Smoked river-bottom carp was one of their dietary delicacies and trade commodities. The fathers of shantyboat families often were temporary day laborers, but unlike **Gypsies**, shantyboaters were not transient.

Some shantyboat colonies numbered as many as 8 or 10 boats, roped to each other and to the bank. They were visited by floating grocery stores (hucksters) that docked next to them and supplied their needs. These communities once existed at Brent in Campbell Co., at Dayton, at Sandy Hook, on the Newport waterfront between the bridges, in West Covington, and in other more remote spots. Perhaps the most famous Kentucky shantytown was in front of downtown Frankfort along the Kentucky River, where the families of prisoners in the old state penitentiary tied up and remained, an easy walk from the jail for visits. Shantyboaters cooked with grills on the boats, raised chickens, and had small gardens on board. For local officials, they were legal nightmares: jurisdiction over them, services, and so forth were constantly at issue. The shantyboat population seems to have peaked with the **Great Depression**, when they represented a rent-free housing option. The farther south one traveled, the more shantyboats one saw, since the climate more easily allowed the lifestyle; in contrast, locally, the December 1917 Ohio River ice gorge destroyed much of the local fleet of shantyboats.

Beginning with the **flood of 1937**, which caused unbelievable damage, the shantyboats gradually have almost disappeared. The raising of the Ohio River pool stage in the early 1960s also contributed to their demise, because the higher water level made anchorage more difficult to find. One Brent shantyboat family, on encountering this dilemma, simply moved up the bank and into the attic of the Brent train station of the **Chesapeake and Ohio Railroad** (C&O); they managed and cared for the station until the depot closed. Later, housing codes further prompted the wane of shantyboats.

As late as the 1970s, Boone Co. area resident Robert Cannon lived on the Ohio River near Rabbit Hash. Cannon, 75 years old in 1976, was a former steamboat captain who once tried living in a city apartment but, unable to sleep, gave it up. He spent his retirement combing the Ohio River from his cypress skiff, seeking aluminum he could sell as junk and other salable flotsam. Cannon was also a hunter and trapper; possum skins brought him $3 each.

In the 1980s, Walter Harding, in his sixties, and his live-in friend, 30-something Helen Beck, lived in a shantyboat along the Newport bank of the Licking River, just south of the C&O Bridge. The D. Krischner and Sons scrap yard nearby allowed them to remain there. Harding's dogs were tied up outside on the bank, to warn of visitors and to ward off the rats coming out of the junkyard's scrap piles. Harding paid the government $10 annually for the license on his boat.

In literature, the shantyboater population appears often in the works of Covington's **Ben Lucien Burman**. His many books about river life are peppered with savory and unsavory characters from the shantyboat era. Other local literary figures who popularized the shantyboat were the independent-minded **Harlan and Anna Hubbard** and Gallatin Co.'s Dr. **Carl Bogardus**. The motion picture *Tammy and the Bachelor*, which was the 1957 movie of the year, and its theme song etched the shantyboat lifestyle into the minds of viewers. The heroine, Tammy, played by Debbie Reynolds, was the beautiful poor girl from the wrong side of the tracks, the local shantyboat community, who fell for a young man from another social class. "Tammy, Tammy, Tammy's in love," goes the song. Dickey Lee referred to the social stigma that came with a shanty address in his 1962 popular hit song "Patches": "Down by the river . . . there lives a girl everybody calls Patches, Patches my darling of old shanty town." Much like Tammy, she fell in love with a boy from the other end of town, but the relationship ended tragically.

Today few shantyboats remain, and most are recreational fishing or hunting shacks. Changing times, regulations, and riverside development have flooded out this part of Northern Kentucky history.

Bogardus, Carl R. *Shantyboat.* Indianapolis, Ind.: Jobber, 1959.

Ellis, William E. *The Kentucky River.* Lexington: Univ. Press of Kentucky, 2000.

Hubbard, Harlan. *Shantyboat: A River Way of Life.* Lexington: Univ. of Kentucky Press, 1977.

"A Life on the River," *KP*, June 14, 1976, 1.

Wecker, David. "Shanty Boat Floats Away Their Worldly Cares," *KP*, March 15, 1982, 2K.

Michael R. Sweeney

SHARON, MARY BRUCE (b. September 6, 1878, Kansas City, Mo.; d. October 1, 1961, New York City). As a young child, Mary Bruce Green, who became a noted painter, moved to Covington with her mother, Henrietta Bruce Green, after the death of her father, Richard, in 1880. Mary lived a privileged childhood with her wealthy grandfather, Col. **Henry Bruce Jr.**, a Confederate sympathizer and businessman who helped hire **John Roebling** to design and build the **John A. Roebling Bridge** in Covington. Mary's playroom in the Bruce home on Sanford St. in Covington was equipped with working appliances. She met famous people, including Sitting Bull, Tom Thumb, and Buffalo Bill, and for part of each year, she traveled with her family to New York City, where she first visited the Metropolitan Museum of Art at age seven. Both her mother and her grandfather were interested in art and collected artwork.

As a young adult, Mary continued traveling with her mother. They lived in Boston, where for a time Mary took singing lessons for an opera career. She stopped when her mother told her that "nice girls didn't go on the stage." They eventually returned to Kansas City, Mo., and Mary wed Fredrick Christy Sharon, who was in the real estate business and active in the community. They lived there until 1939, when they moved east and lived in New York City and Connecticut. After her husband died in 1944, Mary went to live with her only daughter, Henrietta Bruce Sharon Aument.

When her son-in-law, abstract painter Carroll Aument, saw the illustrations that accompanied the stories she had written as a child, he encouraged her to paint. So at age 71 Mary Bruce Sharon, known as Mouse to her friends, began painting. She continued until her death in 1961, completing 150 paintings in 13 years.

Mary's childhood in Kentucky influenced her artwork. The clothing, architecture, furnishings, and family traditions depicted in her paintings offer a glimpse into the world of a wealthy child in the 1880s. She portrayed barbecues and dinners, in works such as *Christmas Dinner in Covington,* painted in 1886. Pony rides, torchlight political parades, fishing with Grandpa Bruce, and horse racing are seen in other paintings, for example *My First Visit to the Kentucky Derby.* She often included herself in the paintings as a small, happy, blond-haired girl. Mary remembered her mother's story of asking Grandpa Bruce to build a bridge. "Pa, won't you please build us a bridge over the Ohio River? We've got to cross on the ferryboat every day to go to school in Cincinnati, and a bridge would be so much better." The Suspension Bridge is shown in Mary's painting *Over the Rhine on Grandpa's Bridge,* now housed in the collection of the Cincinnati Art Museum. Roebling stayed with the family for six months as he designed the John Roebling Bridge connecting Covington to Cincinnati.

As the works of a primitive artist, her paintings are full of detail, especially in the clothing and furniture patterns and the use of an array of bright colors. The flat, two-dimensional quilt-pattern look is representative of the primitive style. Mary worked mostly with a dense watercolor pigment known as gouache. Her works were acclaimed almost immediately in the New York City art world. *Life* magazine gave her a three-page spread, and art magazines and critics were enthusiastic. When she exhibited in France, she was labeled "the American Matisse." *ARTS Magazine* wrote after her death, "Though Mrs. Sharon was born in 1878, there is a scented but fading antebellum flavor to her nostalgic primitive painting. . . . unlike Grandma Moses, her style is not only primitive, but Early American primitive, as if Mrs. Sharon painted during the period she so charmingly documented. Her work rightly belongs in that category known as Americana."

Mary Bruce Sharon's first public showings were in her hometowns: Cincinnati (the Taft Museum), Kansas City, and New York City (the Metropolitan Museum of Art). Her works have been included in a Smithsonian traveling exhibit and are published in her book *Scenes from Childhood.* They are represented in the collections of the Dwight D. Eisenhower family, the Hubert H. Humphrey family, the national board of the **YMCA**, and many family members and friends. The **Behringer-Crawford Museum** in **Devou Park**, Covington, holds 12 Mary Bruce Sharon paintings in its permanent collection, owing to the generous donation of Covington residents Eva G. and Oakley Farris in 2004.

In 1961, at age 83, Mary died at her home on W. 22nd St. in New York City.

"Cincinnati's 'Grandma Moses'—The Late . . . ," *CE*, April 5, 1964, Pictorial Sec., 46–47.

Findsen, Owen. "Covington's Native Daughter," *CE*, November 1, 1981, H7.

Foreman, B. J. "Painting Show Comes Home to Covington," *CP*, October 21, 1981, 10B.

"Mary Bruce Sharon," *CP*, October 3, 1961, 4.

"Mrs. Mary Bruce Sharon Dies; Gained Attention as Artist at 70," *NYT*, October 3, 1961, 39.

Reis, Jim. "Art Career Blossomed Late in Life," *KP*, December 22, 1986, 4K.

Sharon, Mary Bruce. *Scenes from Childhood.* New York: E. P. Dutton, 1978.

Laurie Risch

SHARON PRESBYTERIAN CHURCH. In 1803 Rev. Robert Wilson organized the first Presbyterian Church in Bracken Co. at Sharon, near Germantown. However, by 1812 the meeting place had been moved to Augusta, where the church met in the courthouse in the city park. The first permanent meetinghouse of the Sharon Presbyterian Church was built in 1818, on the northeast side of Main and Third Sts. in Sharon. Arthur Thome, father of **James Thome** and a leading local citizen, built the brick church, which lasted into the 20th century. In 1836 a second church was built near the original Sharon Presbyterian Church's location, and in 1893 the current church building was constructed. The Best, Fee, Taliaferro, and Taylor families were among the members attending services at the church after 1836.

Bracken Co. Extension Homemakers. *History of Bracken County.* Bicentennial ed. Brooksville, Ky.: Bracken Co. Extension Homemakers, 2002.

Caroline R. Miller

SHARP, PHILLIP ALLEN (b. June 6, 1944, Cynthiana, Ky.). Biochemical research scientist and Nobel Prize–winner Phillip Sharp, the son of Joseph and Katherine Colvin Sharp, was raised along a Licking River bend near McKinneysburg in Pendleton Co. He attended McKinneysburg Elementary School and Butler Elementary and **Butler High School** and graduated from **Pendleton Co. Memorial High School** (1962). Sharp earned his undergraduate degree in chemistry and mathematics from Union College in Barbourville (1966) and his doctorate in chemistry from the University of Illinois (1969). He was a staff member at Cold Spring Harbor Laboratory in New York from 1971 to 1974, the year he assumed a faculty position at Massachusetts Institute of Technology (MIT) in the Center for Cancer Research.

In 1977, while working at MIT, Sharp discovered that genes could be discontinuous, that is, a gene could be present in several well-separated DNA segments. This fundamental discovery changed the way scientists looked at how higher organisms develop during evolution. The implications as they relate to cancer research are highly significant. For this work, Sharp and another scientist, Richard Roberts, shared the 1993 Nobel Prize in Physiology or Medicine. Roberts, while working at Cold Spring Harbor Laboratory, had independently made a discovery similar to Sharp's. Later in 1993, Sharp was honored by Kentucky governor Brereton Jones (1991–1995) and by both bodies of the state legislature. In 1985 he became director of the MIT Center for Cancer Research, in 1991 head of the MIT Department of Biology, and in 2000 founder of MIT's McGovern Institute. He currently holds MIT's highest academic rank, institute professor. He cofounded Biogen Inc. (now Biogen Idec), one of the first biotech companies, in 1978 and Alnylam Pharmaceuticals in 2002, both of Cambridge, Mass., and he currently serves on the boards of both companies. Sharp has been a member of the editorial board of the journal *Cell.* He once turned down the MIT presidency. When it was announced that Sharp had won his Nobel Prize, he said that he "had done pretty good for a Kentucky farm boy." Sharp is the paramount scientist of the Northern Kentucky region. Today, he lives in Newton, Mass., with his wife, Ann Holcomb Sharp. They have three daughters.

Nobelprize.org. "Phillip A. Sharp." www.Nobelprize.org (accessed May 31, 2005).

"Scientist's Work Helped Map New Frontier in Gene Research," *KP*, October 16, 1993, 1–3.

"Two from Mass. Win Nobel for Medicine," *Boston Globe*, October 12, 1993, 1.

Michael R. Sweeney

SHAW, THOMAS, 1ST SERGEANT (b. August 23, 1846, Covington, Ky.; d. June 23, 1895, Rosslyn, Va.). Thomas Shaw was born into slavery to an African American mother and a white father. Thomas spent his youth in the Mississippi River town of Louisiana, Mo. In January 1864, after gaining his freedom at age 18, he joined the Union Army and served with the 67th Infantry Regiment of the U.S. Colored Troops. Despite the hardship of being garrisoned and bivouacked in the swamps of Port Hudson, La., Shaw remained with the regiment until the newly formed 9th U.S. Cavalry Regiment was organized in Louisiana in 1866. His 28-year army career stretched over both the **Civil War** and the Indian Wars. Shaw saw firsthand the expansion and settlement of the West, where he served as a guardian of settlers and travelers at some very remote outposts. His regiment moved to Texas, and within 10 years Shaw rose to the rank of 1st sergeant. There he trained a fellow Kentuckian, African American trooper and future **Medal of Honor** winner Brent Woods. While in the New Mexico Territory, Shaw participated in the pursuit of renegade warriors from the Southern Ute and Apache tribes. He helped to enforce the law and patrol the area during the Colfax and Lincoln Co. wars. As a result of his troop's pursuit of the Apache subchief Nana in 1881, following the death of Chief Victorio, Shaw earned a Medal of Honor. However, he did not receive his medal until December 7, 1890, while he was serving with K Troop, 9th Cavalry, at Fort Robinson, Neb. While serving in Nebraska, Shaw fought in the last major Indian war against the Sioux Indians of South Dakota. Shaw and the K Troop were then reassigned in April 1892 to Fort Myer, Va., where they performed ceremonial garrison duty. Shaw retired from the Army in January 1895. Later that year, he died at his home in Rosslyn, Va., and was buried with full military honors at Arlington National Cemetery, Arlington, Va.

"Battle of Carrigo Canyon." In *The Black Military Experience in the American West*, ed. John M. Carroll. Fort Collins, Colo.: Old Army Press, 1970.

"Monument to Honor War Heroes," *KP*, August 10, 2001, 16A.

Register of Enlistments, United States Army, 26 September 1871. Washington, D.C.: National Archives and Record Service (NARS), Government Printing Office, 1871.

Reis, Jim. "Acts of Heroism Won Local Men Nation's Highest Military Award," *KP*, November 29, 1982, 4K.

———. "A Slave Who Earned Honors as a War Hero." In *Pieces of the Past*, by Jim Reis, vol. 2. Covington: Kentucky Post, 1991.

Theodore H. H. Harris

SHEEHAN, AUGUST F., JR., "GUS" (b. April 30, 1917, Covington, Ky.; d. October 30, 2000, Fort Thomas, Ky.). Kentucky legislator and journalist Gus F. Sheehan was the son of August F. and Louise Barkau Sheehan. At age 18, he started a weekly newspaper, the Ludlow *News Enterprise*. He wrote most of the articles for the paper and also acted as sales and circulation manager. During **World War II**, Sheehan served in the South Pacific combat zone but continued to write his newspaper articles. He sent them back to his father, who handled their publication in Gus's absence. Sheehan was educated in Ohio at the University of Cincinnati, Xavier University, and later the **Chase College of Law**. He entered politics in 1950, serving two terms in the Kentucky House of Representatives. After passing the bar examination, he practiced law in Covington. Sheehan ran for the Kentucky Senate and won a seat that he held for the next 16 years. During his long tenure in the state Senate, he backed legislation that created the Northern Kentucky Transit Authority (see **Northern Kentucky Transit Inc.**) and was also a proponent of the Kentucky State Lottery. In local politics he was known as Mr. Democrat. Gus Sheehan had a lifelong compassion for the less fortunate and was always eager to help.

Sheehan and his wife, the former Mary Catherine Welp, had four children, Martin, Joyce, Janet, and Patricia. Their son, Martin, became a lawyer, served in the Kentucky House of Representatives, and is now a Kenton Co. Circuit Court judge. Gus Sheehan owned the *News Enterprise* for 52 years and then sold it in 1988 to Gene Clabes, who merged it into the *Kenton County Recorder* (see **Recorder Newspapers**). Sheehan's wife, Mary Catherine, died in 1985. After a long illness, Gus Sheehan died at age 83 at the Highlands Nursing Home in Fort Thomas. Funeral services were held at St. Ann Church in Covington and burial was at St. Mary Cemetery, Fort Mitchell.

"Legend Gus Sheehan Dies," *KE*, October 31, 2000, B1B.

Kenton Co. Library. "Sheehan, August 'Gus.'" www.kentonlibrary.org/genealogy/bios/.

"Suburban Recorders Bought by Gene Clabes," *KP*, January 9, 1991, 8K.

SHELLY ARMS HOTEL. The Shelly Arms Hotel, in the area of Bivouac Pl. (now Crown Ave.) in Fort Thomas, was built in 1907 by **Samuel Bigstaff** to provide a less expensive hotel than the nearby **Altamont Springs Hotel**. The Shelly Arms was smaller and more affordable for families taking vacations and did not have the prominent location and the wide verandas found at the Altamont. The Shelly Arms was a short distance away from the electric streetcar line connecting Fort Thomas to Cincinnati, Covington, and Newport. The hotel was well patronized in the summer by visitors coming either for a few days or for a prolonged vacation.

During **World War I**, when the hospital at the **Fort Thomas Military Reservation** became full, the Army Medical Corps established convalescent wards in the entire Shelly Arms Hotel and in a section of the Altamont Springs Hotel. Nurses attending the patients were housed in the **Avenel Hotel**, only a few blocks away. Just as some soldiers who had been stationed at the Fort Thomas military post came back to live in Fort Thomas after discharge from military service, so did some of these convalescents. A number of these men met and married local women after the war ended in 1918.

The success of the Shelly Arms Hotel was tied to the fortunes of the Altamont Springs Hotel and Mineral Baths, which featured health treatments whose popularity had begun to wane by 1920. The resort atmosphere and vacation spots in Fort Thomas were ruined further as growing numbers of privately owned automobiles transported potential customers to new vacation spots farther away from the city. By July 1928 the hotel had been unoccupied for a year and a half following closure of the federal government's hospital for disabled veterans there. Adam Haas, a Newport-based real estate developer, purchased the property, and the building was razed; the area was developed into Crown Ave., Altamont Ct., and the development known as Crown Point.

"Hotels Bought: Altamont and Shelly Arms Sold to Haas for $101,000," *KP*, June 29, 1928, 1.

Stegeman, A. Vinton. "The Legend of the Highlands' Mineral Springs," *Fort Thomas Living*, February 1987, 21.

Betty Maddox Daniels

SHEPHERD, JEAN (b. July 21, 1921, Hammond, Ind.; d. October 16, 1999, Sanibel Island, Fla.). Movie script writer and radio and television personality Jean Shepherd grew up in Hammond, Ind. After a stint in the Army Signal Corps during **World War II**, he arrived in the Cincinnati area, doing late-night talk shows on radio stations **WCKY**, WKRC, WSAI, and WLW from 1948 until the mid-1950s. He was fired from many of these jobs for not playing enough songs each given hour. He ad-libbed and became a favorite of truck drivers traveling on the roadways east of the Mississippi River.

Shepherd lived in an apartment along Madison Ave. in Covington and frequently talked about walking across the **John A. Roebling Bridge** on his way to work. He broke into television on WLWT with a comedy show called *Rear Bumper*. In 1955 he moved to Philadelphia and soon to New York City, where on WOR radio he gained a large following of late-night listeners along the East Coast. Jack Paar later recommended that Shepherd should be the one to replace him on *The Tonight Show*. In 1983 Shepherd wrote the screen play *A Christmas Story*, the story of nine-year-old Ralphie Parker's attempt to persuade his parents to buy him a Red Ryder BB gun. Although this semi-autobiographical movie did not win an Academy Award, it has become a seasonal television classic and the inspiration for the television show *The Wonder Years*. Shepherd died of natural causes in southwest Florida in 1999 at age 78.

Miller, Mark K. "Humorist Jean Shepherd Dies at 78," *NYT*, October 27, 1999, 9.

"Radio Wit Jean Shepherd Dies," *CE*, October 17, 1999, A4.
Wallace, Charlton. "'Old Shep' Bounced from Job to Job," *CTS*, August 31, 1956, 18.

SHERMAN. The town of Sherman in northern Grant Co., along U.S. 25 and four miles north of Dry Ridge, developed around a tavern built in 1812 by Louis Myers, who held a large land grant from Virginia. The tavern property was sold in 1832 to Louis Cason, whose descendants owned the property until 1975. The origin of the community's name, Sherman, is unknown, although there is a local story that Union general George Sherman rode through the community during the **Civil War**.

As population in the area increased, the Sherman School District No. 6 was opened in 1858. A post office was established in 1865, discontinued in 1869, reestablished in 1870, discontinued again in 1871, and reestablished in 1873. It operated continuously until 1969, when postal service was again discontinued. George Robert Atkins, the last Sherman postmaster, also operated a general store. Ed Singleton had a general store and a bus depot; Robert Snow ran an automobile and a farm machinery garage.

Today, Sherman consists of a residential area and farmland. The school was consolidated years ago with the Dry Ridge School. The businesses closed as owners retired or died during the 1980s. Four churches continue to be active and well supported by their members.

Conrad, John B., ed. *History of Grant County*. Williamstown, Ky.: Grant Co. Historical Society, 1992.
"Your Town," *KTS*, March 5, 1957, 15.

John B. Conrad

SHERMAN, SIDNEY, MAJOR GENERAL (b. July 23, 1804, Marlborough, Mass.; d. August 1, 1873, Galveston, Tex.). Sidney Sherman was the son of Micha and Suzanna Dennison Sherman. At age 16, Sherman worked for a merchant in Massachusetts. He moved to New York City, aspiring to become a store owner, then in 1826 began to move westward. Eventually he arrived in Cincinnati, where he settled in 1831. Shortly afterward, he moved to Newport, where he became involved in establishing factories in the area. He operated a sheet lead plant in Covington and was the first person to manufacture sheet lead in the region. He also operated a successful cotton bagging plant in Newport. In April 1835, Sherman married Isabella Catherine Cox at Frankfort, and they resided in a house adjacent to their factory at Third and Monmouth Sts. in Newport. Kentucky governor James T. Morehead (1834–1836) commissioned Sherman to command a volunteer militia company. It was at this time that Texas had begun its effort to achieve independence from Mexico. Sympathizing with the Texans in their struggles, Sherman organized a company of 50 men from Cincinnati, Covington, and Newport. The group, billeted at the **Newport Barracks**, became known as the Newport Rifles. On December 18, 1835, Sherman's company officially became enlisted in the Army of Texas. The women of Newport, led by Sherman's wife, made and presented a flag to this company of volunteers. On December 31, 1835, Sherman and his men boarded a steamboat, the *Augusta*, at Newport and departed to aid Texas in its fight. On March 12, 1836, Sherman was elected lieutenant colonel of the 1st Regiment of Texas Volunteers. After a second regiment was organized, Sherman was made a colonel. Following the defeat of the Texans stationed at the Alamo, Sherman was in command of a small cavalry unit on April 20, 1836, at the battle of San Jacinto, the decisive victory for the Texas Volunteers in their war for independence. He gallantly led a squadron of 68 soldiers in a skirmish that day, attacking a detachment of the enemy. The next day, the full-scale battle of San Jacinto began. Sherman led the left wing and initiated one of the major onslaughts of the battle. He was the first to sound that now famous battle cry "Remember the Alamo!" The flag made by the women of Newport was the only flag carried that day by the Texas troops.

After the victory, Texas was declared a free and independent republic. Sherman tendered his resignation as a colonel of the Texas Volunteers. However, David G. Burnet, president of the newly founded Republic of Texas, and the son of Cincinnati's Jacob Burnet, would not accept it and instead gave him a commission as a colonel in the new Army of Texas. Burnet ordered Sherman to return to Newport and raise more troops for the army. Sherman came home and afterward took his family to Texas. In 1839 he was made a major general of the Republic of Texas. In 1842 he was elected a representative in that republic's Congress and appointed chairman of the Military Committee. In 1845 the Lone Star Republic, as Texas was affectionately known at that time, entered the Union, adding one more star to the nation's flag. In 1850 Sherman acquired a charter and built the first railroad in Texas; its first locomotive was named the *General Sherman* in his honor. From 1852 to 1853 he served in the Texas legislature. Sherman died in 1873 and was buried at Lakeview Cemetery in Galveston, Tex.

Reis, Jim. "Newport Unit Battled Santa Anna," *KP*, July 25, 1998, 4K.
———. "Proud Soldiers in the Battle for Texas," *KP*, March 9, 1992, 4K.
Truesdell, Charles B. "Newport's Great Hero—General Sidney Sherman," *Papers of the Christopher Gist Historical Society*, March 25, 1952, 47–76.

Robin Caraway

SHERMAN BROTHERS (Chester Sherman: b. August 10, 1895, Cincinnati, Ohio; d. November 4, 1976, Fort Thomas, Ky.; Joseph Vani: b. June 12, 1913, Chicago, Ill.; d. March 21, 2008, Montgomery, Ohio). The Sherman Brothers were a two-man clown act that appeared in hundreds of circus performances around the United States, Canada, and Mexico. The members of the team were Chester Sherman, who grew up in Bellevue, and his "brother," Joseph Vani, who was from Illinois. Sherman was the creative artist and designer of roles, skits, and costumes; Vani played the straight man. As a team they performed for more than 43 years (1932–1975), until Chester's death. When they were not on the road, they called 418 Van Voast Ave. in Bellevue their home. In 1995 the team was voted into the International Clown Hall of Fame at Delevan, Wis. Chester Sherman was buried at Spring Grove Cemetery in Cincinnati. Joe Vani was buried at St. Alphonsus Church Cemetery in New Munster, Wis.

"Clown Gets Extra Bow—in the Hall of Fame," *CP*, September 6, 1995, 1A.
Spring Grove Cemetery Records, Cincinnati, Ohio.

Michael R. Sweeney

SHIELDS, KEN (b. December 23, 1941, Covington, Ky.). Basketball coach Robert Kenneth Shields is the son of Jack and Blanche Kenney Shields. In 1960 he was named most outstanding athlete as a senior at **Covington Catholic High School**, where he played four years of basketball and baseball. He graduated from the University of Dayton in 1964 with an education degree. He also earned an MA in 1970 in educational administration and a Rank I degree in 1972, both from Xavier University in Cincinnati. Shields's first coaching position was at Covington Catholic High School. He began there in 1964–1965 as an assistant coach in men's basketball. He became men's head basketball coach at the now-defunct **St. Thomas High School** the following season, winning 199 games in 10 years there; he coached men's basketball for the next 13 years at **Highlands High School**, winning 261 games. In 1979 the Highland High School Bluebirds claimed their first Ninth Region title in 45 years. Shields won a total of five regional championships while coaching basketball at Highlands High School. His cumulative 460-257 record at St. Thomas and Highlands high schools still ranks him as the winningest Northern Kentucky men's high school basketball coach ever.

In August 1988, Shields was hired as men's head basketball coach at **Northern Kentucky University** (NKU). He made that school's program into one of the finest in NCAA Division II. Shields achieved a record of 306-170 in 16 seasons at NKU, becoming the school's winningest men's basketball coach, and guided the NKU Norse to national championship game appearances in 1996 and 1997. The school had not won the Great Lakes Valley Conference championship or made the NCAA Tournament since 1978, when Shields's team did both in the 1994–1995 season. As a result, Shields was named national coach of the year by the *Division II Bulletin*. The Norse qualified for the NCAA Tournament in seven of Shields's final 10 seasons.

Shields retired from coaching after the 2003–2004 season yet remains at NKU as a part-time teacher. He was inducted into the Covington Catholic Hall of Fame in 1994, the Greater Cincinnati Basketball Hall of Fame in 1998, and the Kentucky Association of Basketball Coaches Hall of Fame in 2005.

Ernst, Ryan. "Shields' Pupils Await His Next Move," *CE*, October 12, 2003, 15C.
———. "Shields Will Retire after This Season," *CE*, October 8, 2003, 2B.
Schmidt, Neil. "Shields Says Retirement Seems Likely," *CE*, May 15, 2003, 1B.

Neil Schmidt

SHILOH. The history of Shiloh, a community located in Grant Co., began long before it was named. Most of the area in present-day Grant Co. south of Williamstown was originally covered with dense forests and sparsely populated. Absentee owners with large land grants held title to much of the area. One of these owners was the Frenchman Francis Simon (1806–1892), who settled between modern Corinth and Keefer and built a road known as Simon's Passway, the currently usable part of which is now known as Ragtown Rd. Here Simon and his wife, Eliza Musselman Simon, built a "manor house." The house is long gone, but a family cemetery and a slave cemetery remain nearby.

The first semipublic building constructed in the community of Shiloh was the Shiloh Baptist Church, erected in 1875. It was a log building with two stories, and the second floor was used for community recreation. When the building became unsafe, it was replaced by the church's present one-story frame structure.

The second public building, a one-room school called Oakland, was built on donated land in 1881. Officially known as Grant Co. School District 8, the Oakland School was closed in 1903. The pupils then walked to Keefer to attend school. The section of Simon's Passway from the foot of Ragtown Hill to the Shiloh Rd., once traveled by buggies, carriages, horses, and wagons, is impassable now and is so marked on county road maps. In 1998 there was a suspicious fire at the Shiloh Community Baptist Church, after which the church was rebuilt.

Conrad, John B., ed. *History of Grant County*. Williamstown, Ky.: Grant Co. Historical Society, 1992.
"Motives for Fires Sought," *KP*, November 9, 1998, 2K.

John B. Conrad

SHIMFESSEL, ALICE THORNTON (b. June 27, 1901, Xenia, Ohio; d. December 5, 1983, Cincinnati, Ohio). Alice Thornton was the daughter of Rev. Isaac and Laura Thornton. Alice married Elmer T. Shimfessel. In 1941 she became the first secretary of the newly opened Jacob Price Homes housing project in Covington. During the early 1950s, she was at the forefront of the **civil rights movement** and accepted a challenge from the city of Covington and neighborhood residents to find a place for African American youth to play. She stated in a local newspaper:

Alice Shimfessel, 1970.

> Now that the sun is about to shine on both sides of the street the kids in this end of town are looking for a place to go. They do not have a YMCA, Boys' Club, canteen, Community Center, picture show or any place where they might find recreation. Not even a ball field where they can play a game of ball. Friends, this is really serious to me. We talk about juvenile delinquency but are we doing anything about it? I still say any old building or even a prefab building would solve the problem. I am anxious to get started on a drive for just such a place. I wonder if anyone is willing to help?

She appeared before the Covington Board of City Commissioners to request aid. Shimfessel also encouraged the African American community to support the Covington–Kenton Co. **Tuberculosis** Sanatorium.

Several attempts were made to establish a **YMCA** in Peaselburg (central Covington), on a site owned by the **L. B. Fouse** Civil League. This civic activity evolved into the effort to start the community center on E. Bush St. that became the L. B. Fouse Civic League building. Shimfessel served as its president for many years. Many civil rights activities, including **Congress of Racial Equality** freedom riders protest demonstrations, **NAACP** meetings, and teen dances, were launched out of the L. B. Fouse Civic League.

During the late 1950s and early 1960s, Shimfessel was involved in protest activities against segregated restaurants, movie theaters, and department stores in Covington. She led the protestors who were carrying signs in front of the Madison and Liberty **movie theaters**. In 1958 she found herself in federal district court supporting the enrollment of an African American student, Jesse Moore, at **Holmes High School**. Shimfessel's efforts were successful; Jesse Moore was permitted to enter the high school, thereby breaking the color barrier that had existed there. In later years, Shimfessel was instrumental in getting the Civic League to participate in serving senior citizens locally through the Meals on Wheels program. She also taught preschool at the Civic League.

Shimfessel was a member of **First Baptist Church** for more than 50 years and served as church clerk and financial secretary for most of that time. Shimfessel received a plaque from the local chapter of the NAACP for outstanding community service and also was named an outstanding senior citizen by the Junior Chamber of Commerce. She was a charter member of the Charles Henderson American Legion Post Ladies Auxiliary. Shimfessel died in 1983 at age 82 and was buried at Mary E. Smith Cemetery in Elsmere.

"Alice T. Shimfessel: A Clear Voice Who Espoused Concern, Involvement," *CP*, December 6, 1983, 10A.
"A Check for $525," *KTS*, April 22, 1952, 5.
"Early Start Planned for Negro Center," *KTS*, February 9, 1955, 2A.
Fisher, John C. K., "Blacks Join Together on a Positive Note; Program Teaches Children about Heritage," *KP*, February 29, 1988, 1K–2K.
"Fouse League Is Getting Results," *KP*, August 1, 1957, 1.
"Negro Building in Dispute," *KTS*, September 21, 1956, 1A.
"White Only Sign in Store Is Hit," *KP*, July 19, 1960, 1K.

Theodore H. H. Harris

SHINE, MICHAEL T. (b. June 15, 1850, Ireland; d. June 20, 1930, Covington, Ky.). Michael Thomas Shine, a lawyer, judge, and politician, was born in Ireland. His family immigrated to the United States when Michael was a young boy and settled in Northern Kentucky, where Michael was educated in local schools. His first job was working at the Covington railroad terminal. He apprenticed law under Judge **Walter W. Cleary** and, after passing the bar exam, set up his legal practice in Covington's **Boone Block**, at Fourth and Scott Sts. His office adjoined those of **John G. Carlisle**, **William Goebel**, and Judge **James P. Tarvin**. Shine's legal practice grew quickly, and he became one of Northern Kentucky's most successful attorneys. He

Michael Shine.

married Rose Jennings in 1881; the couple had three daughters and two sons.

In 1884 Shine entered Democratic politics and was elected a judge of Kenton Co. He held that position for the next 16 years. In 1900, when he ran for reelection, he was defeated by a coalition of Republicans and Democrats aligned with William Goebel. Shine served as president of numerous fraternal organizations, including the Cathedral Holy Name Society, the Catholic Knights of America, and the Ancient Order of Hibernians. He was also a member of the **Knights of Columbus** and the Knights of St. John and an exalted ruler of the Covington Elks Club (see **Civic Associations**). In 1923 Shine's former residence at 12th St. and Madison Ave. became the first home of the **Covington Latin School**. For many years, he lived at 804 Scott St. in Covington. Shine underwent an operation in early 1930 and developed complications from it. After a long and successful career, he died later that year at age 80 in Covington's St. Elizabeth Hospital (see **St. Elizabeth Medical Center**). Funeral services were held at the Cathedral Basilica of the Assumption and burial was in St. Mary Cemetery in Fort Mitchell. Michael Shine was part of a group of successful Irish immigrants (others were **Peter O'Shaughnessy** and James Walsh [see **Walsh Distillery**]) who were members of the Covington Cathedral parish and who became both religious and social leaders of the community.

"Body of Jurist Will Lie in State," *KP*, June 21, 1930, 1.
"Former Judge Is Taken in Death," *KTS*, June 21, 1930, 1.
Kentucky Death Certificate No. 4668, for the year 1930.
"Michael Thomas Shine," *KP*, June 22, 1930, 2.
"School Begun in Former Home of Judge," *KP*, September 21, 1998, 4K.

SHINKLE, AMOS (b. August 11, 1818, Brown Co., Ohio; d. November 13, 1892, Covington, Ky.). Amos Shinkle, the son of Peter and Sarah Day Shinkle, was Northern Kentucky's foremost philanthropist and business leader for most of the second half of the 19th century. At age 18 he began working as a cook on a flatboat. In 1846 or 1847 he arrived in Covington, where he established a coal business that supplied fuel to steamboats on the Ohio River. Then starting in the 1850s, he built and sold steamboats. During the **Civil War**, he held the rank of colonel of the Kentucky Home Guards during the 1862 siege of Cincinnati. He also helped to organize the "Shotgun Company," which later became the Union's 41st Kentucky Volunteer Infantry. The United States purchased at least two of his steamboats for conversion into ironclads during the war. Shinkle was involved in numerous businesses, including the Champion Coal and Tow-boat Company (founded in Covington 1865) and the First National Bank of Covington (see **First National Bank and Trust Company of Covington**). In 1856 he became the major stockholder in the Covington and Cincinnati Bridge Company and was the major force behind the construction of the **John A. Roebling Bridge**. It was due in part to the efforts of Shinkle that engineer John Roebling came to Northern Kentucky to build the first bridge to span the Ohio River in this area. For that reason many people have lobbied to have Shinkle's name added along with Roebling's to the name of the bridge. Shinkle was also president of the Covington Gaslight Company in 1863 (see **Gas Lighting and Gasworks**).

Shinkle founded an orphanage, which was located first on Madison Ave. in Covington. It later relocated to **Devou Park** and today operates as the **Children's Home of Northern Kentucky**. As a civic leader, Shinkle served on the Covington City Council from 1853 to 1866. He also was a member of the Covington Board of Education and served on the board of trustees of the Freedmen's Aid Society, which aided freed slaves in the area. In Ohio, he was on the board of Cincinnati's Wesleyan Female College, whose most famous graduate became first lady Lucy Hayes, the wife of President Rutherford B. Hayes (1887–1891).

A prominent Methodist, Shinkle was a member of Covington's Union Methodist Episcopal Church at Fifth and Greenup Sts., which became First Methodist Church and later, in 2005, a downtown campus of Immanuel United Methodist Church. Shinkle served as superintendent of his church's Sunday School from 1867 until his death in 1892. His financial support assisted Epworth Methodist Church (West Covington), Main St. Methodist Church (Covington), and the Shinkle Methodist Church (Covington), the latter named in his honor in 1892. The Shinkle Methodist Church has since moved to Independence.

Shinkle married Sarah Jane Hughes on November 10, 1842, and they had one son, Bradford. The family owned several residences in Covington and a summer home in what is now Crestview Hills, a property known locally for many years as the Lookout Stud Farm. Amos Shinkle died on November 13, 1892, just after he and his wife had celebrated their golden wedding anniversary. During his time, Amos Shinkle was thought to have been one of the richest persons in Covington. At his death, he left an estate valued at more than $2.5 million, even after making significant contributions to his church and his community. Shinkle was buried in Highland Cemetery in Fort Mitchell.

"Amos Shinkle—The Philanthropist and Financier," *KP*, November 14, 1892, 1.
Biographical Encyclopedia of Kentucky. Cincinnati: J. M. Armstrong, 1878.
Covington City Death Certificate No. 708, for the year 1892.
Highland Cemetery Records, Fort Mitchell, Ky.
Johnson, E. Polk. *History of Kentucky and Kentuckians*. Chicago: Lewis, 1912.
Kenton Co. Public Library. "Amos Shinkle." www.kenton.lib.ky.us (accessed February 15, 2006).
Reis, Jim. "Amos Shinkle: Rags to Riches Story," *KP*, March 4, 2002, 4K.

Paul L. Whalen

SHINKLE, BRADFORD (b. September 29, 1845, Higginsport, Ohio; d. May 7, 1909, Covington, Ky.). Bradford Shinkle was the son of wealthy Covington businessman **Amos Shinkle** and his wife, Sarah Hughes Shinkle. The family moved to Covington when Bradford was one year old. He was educated in Covington public schools and then attended Miami University, Oxford, Ohio. During the **Civil War**, Bradford left college to serve with the Union Home Guard, in which his father held the rank of colonel. Bradford later returned to Miami University and graduated in 1864. Amos Shinkle gave Bradford his first job, serving as a clerk on a steamboat the elder Shinkle owned, the *Magnolia*. On March 21, 1868, while headed to Cincinnati from Maysville, the boat's boilers exploded, killing about 50 persons. Bradford was blown into the river but managed to swim to safety. Although one of his eyes was injured and he suffered some burns, he recovered fully. In October 1868, Bradford married Ann Hemingray, daughter of **Robert Hemingray** and Mary Carroll Hemingray, owners of the **Hemingray Glass Company** in Covington. Bradford and his wife lived in the Hemingray family mansion at 165 E. Second St.; they also had a summer home in Rhode Island. Bradford and Anna Shinkle had two children, Camilla and Amos Clifford. Ann Shinkle died on October 1, 1884, and Bradford married her sister, Mary Ann Hemingray, on January 6, 1887. He and his second wife had one child, Bradford Shinkle Jr.

Amos Shinkle was president of the Covington and Cincinnati Bridge Company and was the driving force behind the building of the **John A. Roebling Bridge**. At his father's death in 1892, Bradford succeeded him as president of the bridge company. Bradford also served as president of the Champion Ice Company and was the largest shareholder in the Fifth-Third Bank of Cincinnati and the First National Bank of Covington (see **First National Bank and Trust Company of Covington**). He served on the boards of directors of many local organizations. However, much of his time was spent with the Shinkle, Wilson & Kreis Wholesale Grocery Company, in which he was a partner. Bradford Shinkle prided himself on living a very normal life, preferring to spend his leisure time at home rather than at parties and other social functions. He neither smoked nor drank alcohol and attempted to keep himself physically fit. He was a founding member of the **Fort Mitchell Country Club** in Fort Mitchell. He developed heart problems, which brought about his death at age 63. Because Shinkle had a morbid fear of being buried alive, he left specific instructions that his body should be observed for a reasonable time after death before being buried. For 11 days, guards opened his casket every hour, to make sure that he was not alive. He was buried in the Highland Cemetery, Fort Mitchell, which he had helped establish. In 1914 the Gothic three-story, 33-room Shinkle mansion was given to the **Salvation Army**, which operated the **Booth Memorial Hospital** in Shinkle's opulent former home.

"Bradford Shinkle Claimed by Death," *KP*, May 8, 1909, 1.

"Feared Burial Alive: Casket Is Guarded," *KP*, June 10, 1909, 2.

"Funeral Rites over Remains of Capitalist," *KP*, May 10, 1909, 2.

Johnson, E. Polk. *History of Kentucky and Kentuckians*. Vol. 2. Chicago: Lewis, 1912.

Reis, Jim. "Bradford Shinkle Made Own Name in Business," *KP*, March 4, 2002, 4.

SHONERT, WARREN J., JR. (b. September 26, 1922, Falmouth, Ky.; d. April 29, 2002, Falmouth, Ky.). Newspaper publisher Warren Jeffrey Shonert Jr. was the son of Warren J. and Grace Ridgway Shonert. He was also a grandson of a Union Army veteran, a nephew of a Confederate Army officer, and a great-grandnephew of Capt. **John Waller**, an early Pendleton Co. pioneer. Shonert Jr. loved history and spent most of his adult life chronicling historical events. From 1941 to 1985, he served as the owner, publisher, and editor of the *Falmouth Outlook*, carrying on the tradition of journalism begun by his father, W. J. Shonert Sr., who founded the newspaper in 1907. Shonert Jr. sold the newspaper in 1985 to Delphos Herald Inc., which continues publishing it.

Warren Shonert Jr. also was a director and an employee of the former First National Bank of Falmouth and Butler and an active community leader in Pendleton Co. He was a president of the Falmouth Rotary Club. He and his wife, Genevieve Hancock Shonert, traveled across the state of Kentucky while Warren was district Rotary governor. Shonert was a Republican Party leader, and his wife was a leader within the Democratic Party. He was a member of the Chamber of Commerce, the Pendleton Co. Industrial group, and the Riverside Cemetery board. He was vice chairman of the Pendleton Bicentennial Commission and a regent of **Northern Kentucky University** (NKU) and held membership in a number of Masonic lodges and orders, as well as the Sons of the American Revolution, and the Confederate Veterans Camp No. 1342. He was a Paul Harris Fellow of Rotary International and a Kentucky Colonel. As a member of the NKU board, Shonert was deeply involved in the turbulence that beset the college in the mid to late 1970s.

In 1985 he and his wife donated a valuable book collection of more than 1,500 titles to the NKU archives. The collection deals with the **Civil War**, Kentucky history, the life of Abraham Lincoln, and other topics and includes more than eight years of *Falmouth Outlook* issues. In the early 1990s, Shonert was a contributor to *The Kentucky Encyclopedia,* published by the University Press of Kentucky. Survivors include a daughter and a son. Shonert was buried in the Riverside Cemetery in Falmouth.

"*Falmouth Outlook* Sold after 78 Years," *KP*, December 30, 1985, 1K.

"NKU Gets Valuable Collection," *KP*, January 18, 1985, 1K.

"Warren Shonert, 79, *Falmouth Outlook* Owner and Publisher Dies," *Falmouth Outlook*, May 7, 2002, 1.

"Warren Shonert, 79, *Falmouth Outlook* Owner and Publisher Dies," *KP*, May 2, 2002, 17A.

Mildred Belew

SHORT CREEK/GOFORTH. Located in west-central Pendleton Co., along Ky. Rt. 467, Short Creek was a thriving community during the mid-1800s. The town had a blacksmith shop; a general store; a tobacco warehouse; an ice storage house, where in the winter ice was cut from ponds and stored in sawdust for use in the coming summer; a school; and a thriving Baptist church, which was the center of social as well as religious life. There were two practicing physicians, Dr. Bethel and Dr. N. B. Chipman. Chipman, who moved to Falmouth in 1890, also dealt extensively in tobacco and operated the Old Tub Fowler Distillery at Falmouth. After Chipman left Short Creek, Dr. George W. McMillian and Dr. N. H. Ellis practiced medicine there. McMillian later moved to Covington, and Ellis relocated to Williamstown.

In 1880 a post office was established at Short Creek. Until about 1920, it was common for couriers on horseback to carry the mail between community post offices. The post offices were usually located in a general store, since rural free delivery was not established until the turn of the 20th century. The Post Office Department in Washington, D.C., discovered there was another Short Creek, Ky., so, at the suggestion of Chipman, the name of the town's post office was changed to Goforth; thus the community had two names. Early settlers had initially referred to it by a third name, Cold Springs, which described the cold spring water they found in the area.

One of the outstanding houses at Short Creek was a huge log house that was built before 1859, when some of the area around Short Creek was almost a wilderness. It was the home of John R. Wadsworth. James Mitchell Ballinger owned this home in 1924, when the logs were sold and moved to Kenton Co. The log home Wadsworth had built was reconstructed and is still standing near Pleasure Isle on Ky. Rt. 17, south of Covington; it now houses the Log Cabin Restaurant.

The Baptist Church of Christ at Short Creek was constituted in 1833, with six members. Rev. Christian Tomlin was the first pastor and served in that capacity until 1837. The church met to worship in a log schoolhouse near the waters of Short Creek until 1840, when a house of hewed logs was built for worship. This church building, which had a large stone fireplace at one end, was near a spring on one of the tributaries of Short Creek, on the land of Amos Eggleston. The cost of building the church was about $15, aside from material and labor furnished by the church people. In 1852 the congregation completed a new house of worship, a hewed-log house about 50 by 60 feet in size, costing about $75. On the morning of May 5, 1908, that church building was struck by lightning and burned; it was a total loss, and there was no insurance carried on the building. The congregation quickly rebuilt their church building and dedicated it on May 23, 1909. Services are still being held in it.

Belew, Mildred Boden. *The First 200 Years of Pendleton County.* Falmouth, Ky.: M. B. Belew, n.d. [ca. 1994].

Monroe, John. "Historical Sketch," *Falmouth Outlook*, April 28, 1916, 3.

Mildred Belew

SHORTWAY BRIDGE. The former Shortway Bridge, which linked E. 12th St. in Covington to W. 11th St. in Newport, was marked by tragedy even before it was completed. On June 15, 1892, while still under construction, it collapsed into the Licking River, killing at least 22 workers and injuring others, several of whom died later. This was not the first Licking River bridge to fail. On January 16, 1854, the **Newport and Covington Suspension Bridge** (at the location of the current Fourth St. Bridge) dropped into the water below. Work on the 1892 bridge resumed right away, and it opened in December of that same year with a single lane running in each direction. The Bridge Company of Cleveland completed the structure at a cost of roughly $200,000. The span was closed on May 10, 1914, because of structural safety issues. A new, sturdier bridge was erected, capable of carrying the heavy electric **streetcars** of the **Green Line** company; the bridge, opened on April 7, 1915, was known by various names: the Green Line Bridge, the 11th St. Bridge, and the 12th St. Bridge. It had a 358-foot main truss and approaches at each end totaling another 1,200 feet. For years it was owned by a sister corporation of the region's bus company but operated by the Green Line. The bridge provided quick access to Covington for Green Line streetcars and buses from the company's bus barn located in Newport. In 1970 some 10,620 vehicles crossed the bridge daily. In 1978 the toll for passenger cars was raised to 10 cents, the first increase since 1932. In 1983 about 5,800 cars were crossing daily, and in March of that year the toll went to 20 cents for passenger cars.

In later years, the bridge became known as the Shortway Bridge. It generated roughly $250,000 in annual revenue during the early 1970s. On July 26, 1976, a fire caused by children playing with fire under the Newport approach stopped bridge traffic until August 10 of that year. Until February 1977, when the I-275 Poweleit Bridge at Wilder opened, Kenton and Boone Co. **Northern Kentucky University** students crossed the Licking River on the Shortway Bridge, winding their way to the school's Highland Heights campus.

Tolls on the bridge stopped being charged on September 9, 1986, the day the Commonwealth of Kentucky purchased the bridge for $1.25 million. It was the last privately owned toll bridge in the state. The bridge closed forever on April 2, 2001. An adjacent downstream state-funded replacement bridge across the Licking River opened in September 2001, which since has been named the Licking River Girl Scout Bridge. The Girl Scout Bridge is a welcome roadway with two lanes in each direction. It greatly improves traffic flow between the two cities of Covington and Newport and across Northern Kentucky as part of Ky. Rt. 1020. Kentucky tried to give away the old Shortway Bridge but could not find a taker. On August 25, 2003, it was imploded and cut up for scrap.

"Fire Closes Short-Way Bridge," *KP*, July 26, 1976, 1K.
Lehmann, Terry W., and Earl W. Clark. *The Green Line*. Chicago: Central Electric Railfan's Association, 2000.
Reis, Jim. "A Link with Death: Collapse of Shortway Bridge's Predecessor Claimed 31 Lives," *KP*, May 2, 1983, 4K.
Reiter, John. "Tolls Will Rise on Short Way," *CP*, July 11, 1978, 11.
Remlinger, Connie. "One Last Toll," *KP*, September 10, 1986, 1K.
"Shortway Bridge Toll Removed," *KP*, September 10, 1986, 1.

SHOWBOATS. In early August 1945, the Menke brothers' showboat *Hollywood* (formerly the *Columbia)* tied up at the foot of Greenup St. in Covington for 10 nights of *Clouds and Sunshine,* with the curtain rising at 8:30 p.m. It was one of the last times for such a stop at Covington. Beginning in the 1830s, similar boats had plied the navigable rivers of the region—the Ohio and the Kentucky—bringing smiles and fun. The previous showboat to dock in Covington had been the behemoth 1,400-seat *Golden Rod,* in 1939. River records suggest that at least 100 showboats were built for the inland waterways. Big and small, these migratory vaudevillian emporiums, gingerbread constructions set atop mostly unpropelled barges, were towed to venues at Maysville, Augusta, Dayton, Bellevue, Newport, Covington, Ludlow, Warsaw, and Carrollton on the Ohio, at Gratz and Monterey on the Kentucky, and sometimes all the way to Frankfort and beyond. Calliopes would announce their arrival; then the evening bill was typically a melodrama full of villains and tear-jerking plots, with multiple roles performed by members of the boat's crew. Popcorn and penny candy were available for purchase. These annual summer visits were greatly anticipated by people of all ages. The larger cities, being the first to open movie theaters, were the first to lose their showboats; but gradually, throughout the region, the floating palaces of a bygone era ceased coming round the bend.

Many rivermen and showboaters retired to Newport and Covington. In 1931 Captain Edwin A. Price died at his home at 324 Park Ave. in Newport. He and his son, Steven E. Price, had operated several showboats (the *Grand Floating Palace,* the *Water Queen,* and the *New Era)* on the Ohio and Mississippi rivers, from Pittsburgh and St. Paul to New Orleans. They did so until 1928, when Steven Price died. The Prices' large floating theaters were welcome sights for the people of the region for many years. The popular *Bryant's Show Boat* was retired in 1942, after 24 seasons on the water. The few boats that survive are novelties. The *Showboat Majestic,* for example, is permanently moored at the public landing at Cincinnati; it does not leave its berth.

The lore of showboating has captured the literature and arts of America. Based upon an Edna Ferber novel of the same name, the Jerome Kern and Oscar Hammerstein epic musical *Show Boat* opened at the Ziegfeld Theater in New York City in December 1927. It had a run of one and a half years and has been redone many times, professionally on Broadway (and even recently in London's West End) and nonprofessionally by schools and local groups. Some critics have called it perhaps the greatest American musical. The production's continued success demonstrates the degree of nostalgia for this now-missing part of the American landscape, which the Northern Kentucky region once so thoroughly enjoyed firsthand.

Bryant, Betty. *Here Comes the Showboat.* Lexington: Univ. Press of Kentucky, 1994.
"Here Comes the Showboat," *KP*, August 6, 1945, 2.
Reis, Jim. "We Build on Their Efforts: Unsung Stalwarts Created Community," *KP*, June 19, 2000, 4K.
"Services for Proprietor of Show Boats," *KTS*, March 15, 1928, 3.
Way, Frederick, Jr. *Way's Packet Directory, 1848–1994.* Athens: Ohio Univ. Press, 1994.

Michael R. Sweeney

SHUTT, JACOB D. (b. 1830, Warren Co., Pa.; d. February 24, 1895, Covington, Ky.). Jacob D. Shutt became a very wealthy banker in Northern Kentucky after the **Civil War**. Although his background is somewhat obscure, Shutt moved from Pennsylvania to Covington around 1850. He started working in the lumber business, married an employer's daughter (Sarah A. "Nannie" Richardson), and found political success. In 1863 he won a seat on the Covington city council and later was chosen council president. In 1864, as a Republican, Shutt won election to the Kentucky legislature and served from 1865 to 1867. In 1881 he lost a bid to become a state senator. In 1868 he purchased four city lots in Covington. At 26 W. Fifth St. in Covington still stands the elegant Shutt mansion, now housing professional offices. After the Civil War, Shutt's career paralleled that of many Republican businessmen and bankers. Following passage of the national banking act of 1864, Shutt built his career in the new banking system as one of local businessman **Amos Shinkle**'s associates. In 1877 Shutt was elected a director of Shinkle's First National Bank in Covington. In 1880 Shutt was one of the bank's seven directors, along with Vincent and Amos Shinkle. In 1885 Shutt was president of the City National Bank of Covington. At the time of his death, he was vice president of the First National Bank. Shutt joined the Washington Lodge and the **Independent Order of Odd Fellows**, served on the board of the Covington Protestant Children's Home (see **Children's Home of Northern Kentucky**), gave time and money to the new Union Methodist Episcopal Church (see **First United Methodist Church**), and was a director of **Highland Cemetery** in Fort Mitchell (1879–1895). A Highland Cemetery brochure lists Shutt with 25 other men and 1 woman (**Una Merkel**) as distinguished persons interred there. Shutt was entombed alone in 1895 in a $40,000 mausoleum, with his own life-size statue on top.

Bricking, Chuck. *Covington's Heritage: A Compilation of the City's Historical Houses and a Short Biography of the Inhabitants.* Covington, Ky.: Privately published, 1980.
Covington Death Record No. 119, for the year 1895.
Kenton Co. Deed Book 17, May 29, 1868, 610–11.
"Mr. Shutt's Death—Positions Held in County," *KP*, February 25, 1895, 1.

John Boh

SIEWERS, SARAH M. (b. March 1, 1855, Cincinnati, Ohio; d. April 22, 1926, Massillon, Ohio). Medical doctor and suffragist Sarah M. Siewers was the daughter of Charles G. and Rebecca Carpenter Siewers. The family moved to Newport when Sarah was a young child. She attended public school in Newport and graduated from **Newport High School**. Shortly thereafter, she became a grade school teacher and later taught at Newport High School. Siewers attended a series of lectures on chemistry and physiology during the time she was teaching high school, and she decided to pursue a medical career. She left teaching and enrolled in the Eclectic Medical College of Cincinnati in Ohio, the only area medical school that would accept female students. Another well-known doctor who attended that school was **Louise Southgate**, who set up her medical practice in Covington. Siewers graduated with a medical degree in 1891. She did postgraduate work at the Cincinnati City Hospital and at the Ohio Hospital for Women and Children. After her postgraduate work was completed, she opened her medical practice at 209 E. Sixth St. in Newport. She also became involved in social issues and joined the **women's suffrage** movement, eventually serving as president of the Susan B. Anthony Club of Cincinnati. Siewers also worked tirelessly for educational reform and became the first woman elected to the Cincinnati Board of Education. She was an active member of the Women's Christian Temperance League, which promoted abstinence from alcohol and tobacco. She continued her medical practice in Newport until 1916, when she moved to Massillon, Ohio. She died there of Bright's Disease (a kidney disorder), at age 71. After she was cremated, her ashes were buried in a family plot at Spring Grove Cemetery in Cincinnati.

Goss, Charles Frederick, ed. *Cincinnati: The Queen City, 1788–1912.* 4 vols. Chicago: S. J. Clarke, 1912.
Reis, Jim. "Doctor Didn't Limit Crusades to Women," *KP*, June 11, 1984, 8K.
Rootsweb. "Sarah M. Siewers." www.rootsweb.com (accessed April 25, 2006).

SILVER GROVE. Silver Grove in eastern Campbell Co. lies along the Ohio River where Ky. Rt. 8 (**Mary Ingles Highway**) and Ky. Rt. 547 (Four Mile Pk.) intersect. Melbourne is to the east along the river, and Alexandria is located seven miles to the south. Silver Grove, incorporated as a sixth-class city in 1948, was an active community early in the 20th century. The Four Mile Creek, a major watershed of central Campbell Co., lies to the west of Silver Grove and empties into the Ohio River.

The first owner of the land that comprises the city was Hugh Mercer, who was born in 1720 in Aberdeen, Scotland. For his service as an officer in the **French and Indian War**, he was granted 5,000 acres along the Ohio River; he later served also in the **Revolutionary War**. Mercer died in New Jersey in 1776, and no one from his family is known to have set foot in the Silver Grove area. In 1817 the Mercer heirs sold the land in Silver Grove to Gen. **James Taylor Jr.** On the 1883 *Lake County Atlas* for Campbell Co., the area is shown as being in the Hayfield Precinct, with 35 structures stretching from Four Mile Creek to Ten Mile Creek.

Silver Grove takes its name from the second of two parks in the area. The first, Phoenix Grove Resort, was developed during the late 19th century to provide a destination for train and steamboat day excursions from Cincinnati and Newport. The location was along the Ohio River across from today's intersection of Ky. Rts. 1998 and 8. Popular for only a few years, the park was closed and became the site of the U.S. Army Corps of Engineers Dam No. 36 in 1920. Silver Grove Park opened in June 1890, on a site that is now a baseball field (bounded by Ash, Second, and Oak Sts. and the backs of houses facing Ky. Rt. 8). The silver maple trees there gave rise to its name. More than just a public picnic ground, the park included beer stands, a lunch house, a clubhouse, a dance hall, an electric light plant, a boiler, and a engine house, surrounded by a fence. The Silver Grove Park existed for only one year before the county sheriff closed it for a debt of $12,000 that was owed.

In the 1880s, the C&O Railroad purchased land in Silver Grove; it was along the Ohio River, 13 miles upstream from Cincinnati. Tracks were laid in the late 1880s, and by 1912 the railroad had built a new million-dollar facility on the site. The rail yard was named for George W. Stevens, president of the C&O Railroad from 1899 to 1920. The yard expedited freight (fruits, vegetables, and phosphates), eastbound passenger services, and coal cars returning to the coalfields. During Stevens's tenure as president of the railroad, a rail hump was built to sort cars for eastbound trains onto the proper tracks. An arc-shaped row of thirteen repair and maintenance shops was arranged around an electrically driven turntable 85 feet in diameter. A 100-room hotel operated by the **YMCA** served trainmen and other employees. Taylor Park, named for a C&O railroad superintendent, was completed in 1912; across from the fire station that had been built was another park that remained open until 1940.

After its rail yard was established in 1912, the company established the Silver Grove Land and Building Company. Because there were only a few houses in the area, the C&O Railroad Company purchased land along Ky. Rt. 8 to provide 400 lots for the building of employee housing. Employees purchased their land and either built homes or bought them from local builders. This was the first town in Kentucky in which every home had running water, electricity, and a furnace. Water and electricity were subsidized by the C&O Railroad Company and cost only one dollar a month. Fireplugs were installed and a volunteer fire company was established. Although heavily influenced by the railroad, Silver Grove became an independent entity in 1951. The railroad, however, was instrumental in the formation of the **Silver Grove Public Schools**, and the high school maintains its nickname of "the big trains."

Semipro baseball was a popular Sunday afternoon activity in many localities after **World War I**, and Silver Grove had a fine field for playing it. With grandstands under a roof and surrounded by an eight-foot-high wooden fence faced with large advertising signs, this was considered one of the best fields in the region. All of the semipro baseball facility was lost in the 1937 flood. Thereafter, the field was converted into a baseball field for the high school. Horse and mule races were once held at the Newport Fairgrounds and Driving Association Racetrack along Ky. Rt. 8. Later these grounds were used as an airfield for flying lessons. After the grounds were donated to the Campbell Co. Fiscal Court by Ed Morscher in 1974 and designated for recreational use, this site became Morscher Field, a well-used public playground.

Over the years, there have been several churches in Silver Grove; like almost everything in town, they have suffered devastation from occasional floods. Not one structure in Silver Grove was spared when floodwaters of the Ohio River rose and spilled over into the town in January 1937. Reaching a crest of 80 feet, well above flood stage, the murky, swift-flowing water filled basements and first floors, turning some of the homes over on their sides. A few houses on higher foundations could accommodate the people who escaped in rowboats. It was necessary to boil all the water; and the Red Cross immunized everyone in town with typhoid shots. Most residents joined in the cleanup and only a few families left or sold their houses. The foul-smelling ruins were cleaned up and, by Easter, things had basically returned to normal. Another serious flood in town occurred in March 1997, when heavy rains raised the level of nearby Four Mile Creek. The city was cut off on all sides and its 700 residents had to seek refuge elsewhere while National Guardsmen protected the area.

The town firehouse on Four Mile Pk. was erected in 1964 and has two fire engines, an EMS crew, an ambulance, and a fire-and-rescue boat for use on the Ohio River. The city also has a full-time police chief. The city building is located at W. Third and Oak Sts. Mail deliveries were first made by boat from Newport to the Hayfield District (Silver Grove area) in 1845. The present-day service is by truck to the post office building (built in 1969) on Four Mile Pk., where residents go to pick up their mail.

After the C&O Railroad left the Stevens yard in 1981, the city annexed 504 unincorporated acres along three miles of the riverfront to the east. The greatest change came to this small city in 1999 when the French-owned **Lafarge** Gypsum Company began to construct its $90 million plant on the site of the former Stevens Rail Yard. The half-mile-long green-and-white building uses calcium sulfate from the nearby Cinergy Zimmer electric plant in Moscow, Ohio, to make drywall materials. It is the largest single-assembly-line facility in the United States. The plant produces 900 million square feet of drywall annually. In 2000, the U.S. Census reported the population of Silver Grove as 1,215.

Campbell Co. Historical Society. *Campbell County, Kentucky, 200 Years, 1794–1994*. Alexandria, Ky.: Campbell Co. Historical Society, 1994.

Betty Maddox Daniels

SILVER GROVE PUBLIC SCHOOLS. The Silver Grove school system began in about 1911, when the **Chesapeake and Ohio Railroad** founded the city of Silver Grove and built the Stevens Rail Yard along its tracks there, adjacent to the Ohio River in southeastern Campbell Co. At first, classes were held in a house donated by the railroad, since this fifth-class city began as a company-owned town. Later, classes were moved into a two-and-a-half-story brick building near the intersection of River Rd. (Ky. Rt. 8) and Four Mile Rd. Some 125 students attended that original school. On January 24, 1924, the school building was damaged by fire on the same day a schoolhouse in nearby Dayton also burned. In 1927 plans were drawn for a new 10-room school building, costing $65,000, that could house both high school and elementary students. The new school was dedicated on September 21, 1929. Just as the town of Silver Grove has been inconvenienced by Ohio River floods, so has the school district. In the **flood of 1937**, the records of the school system were lost. In 1959 an elementary school addition was completed; a middle school addition was finished in 1969, and a high school addition in 1979. The 1929 building was torn down in 1986. Today the school district has preschool through grade 12 in the same building, which is located along Four Mile Rd. For many years the railroad contributed extensively toward the expenses of the school, but the railroad has been gone now for more than 20 years. Silver Grove currently has a population of 1,000; in 2003 the school district, the second-smallest independent school system in Campbell Co. and one of the smallest in the state, had 262 students. The system has changed to an all-year schedule, with three school breaks during the academic year. It has started an innovative recreation program and an on-site student health clinic. It competes on the junior high school and high school levels in men's and women's basketball; men's baseball, golf, and cross country; and women's softball, volleyball, and cross country. There have never been enough students to field a football team. The school's teams are called the Big Trains, reflecting the era when the town was owned and run by the railroad. The Silver Grove school system struggles for funding, as most of the public school districts in the state do, but the diseconomies of scale inherent in Sliver Grove's small numbers make its future survival questionable. The town has a major employer, **Lafarge North America**, whose dry-wall-production facility in Silver Grove is the world's largest, but the French-owned firm, unlike the C&O Railroad, has never been involved in the operation of the town's public school system.

Reis, Jim, "Two Cities, Two Fires on the Same Frozen Day in 1924," *KP*, November 6, 2000, 4K.

SIMMONS, ROBERT C. "BERT" (b. August 7, 1867, Covington, Ky.; d. June 4, 1953, Park Hills, Ky.). Lawyer and politician Robert C. Simmons was the son of Robert and Delia Schofield Simmons. He grew up in Covington and became a lawyer, with offices in the First National Bank building in Covington at Sixth St. and Madison Ave. (see **First National Bank and Trust Company of Covington**). He served as a president of both the Kentucky and the Kenton Co. bar associations. He also held the office of Kenton Co. attorney from 1894 to 1902. He then served in the Kentucky legislature, four years in the House of Representatives and eight in the Senate. Simmons played a prominent role in the development of Park Hills, where he lived for many years. He married Alma Lawton in December 1926; there were no children from the marriage. Simmons was a charter member of the Covington Elks Club (see **Civic Associations**) and the University Club in Cincinnati. He was also board chairman of the **Baker-Hunt Foundation** in Covington for the first 16 years of its existence. Simmons was a lifelong member of Covington's **Trinity Episcopal Church**, where he sang in the choir for 30 years. After a long illness, he died of anemia at age 85, in his home at 1300 Amsterdam Rd., Park Hills. Memorial services were held at the Trinity Episcopal Church, and burial was in Highland Cemetery in Fort Mitchell.

Kentucky Death Certificate No. 12823, for the year 1953.
"Robert C. Simmons Dies at Age of 85," *KP*, June 5, 1953, 1.
"Robert C. Simmons Dies; Dean of Kenton Lawyers," *KTS*, June 5, 1953, 1.

SIMON KENTON HIGH SCHOOL. The fall 1937 opening of Simon Kenton High School, located at 11132 Madison Pike (Ky. Rt. 17) in Independence, represented progress in the development of public secondary education in Kenton Co. Before the establishment of Simon Kenton High School and **Dixie Heights High School**, in Edgewood (also in 1937), the high schools of Kenton Co. had drawn unfavorable comparisons with more modern high school facilities in Covington and with the independent-district Beechwood High School in S. Fort Mitchell (Fort Mitchell). Indeed, in those years dissatisfied Kenton Co. residents often sent their children out-of-district to attend high school. A 1935 state review of Kenton Co. schools produced a plan to replace the county system's inadequate **Independence High School**, **Piner High School**, and **Crescent Springs High School** buildings with two new high schools, one for each of the northern and southern portions of Kenton Co. Partial funding for the schools came from the Works Progress Administration, a New Deal federal agency. For the proposed southern high school, the Kenton Co. School Board acquired 28.5 acres along the west side of Madison Pike about one mile south of Independence. The name for the new school came from frontiersman **Simon Kenton**. Architect Howard McClorey's design for Simon Kenton High School, constructed at a cost of about $176,000, included 18 classrooms, a cafeteria, a gymnasium, and an Art Deco facade. Reuben C. Hinsdale served as the school's first principal, continuing until he was appointed Kenton Co. schools superintendent in 1960. Students chose Pioneers for the name of their athletic teams. The opening of Simon Kenton and Dixie Heights High Schools contributed to a nearly 50 percent increase in secondary enrollment within the Kenton Co. school system.

Simon Kenton High School's campus has undergone many changes over the years. Additional classrooms, a new library, and a new cafeteria were constructed during the 1950s and 1960s. A 1980 renovation resulted in expanded classroom, gymnasium, music, and industrial arts facilities. A four-phase $21 million renovation and expansion that began in 2001 produced a substantially new, state-of-the-art building but preserved the facade of the original 1937 structure. The first three phases of the renovation, , which were completed by 2005, gave Simon Kenton High School a new media center, expanded science and computer labs, an auditorium with stadium seating, an expansive library, a modern climate-control system, and expanded athletic and dining facilities. Phase four construction, including a new softball field, began in 2007.

The 1980–1981 academic year may be Simon Kenton High School's most memorable. On October 9, 1980, an explosion (see **Simon Kenton High School Explosion**) caused by a boiler-room gas leak ripped through the high school's newly constructed north wing, claiming the life of junior Robert Williams II and injuring several other students. The blast resulted in damages totaling $1.5 million and closed the school for a year, forcing Simon Kenton students to attend classes in the evening at Scott High School in Taylor Mill. Nevertheless, the men's basketball team won the state championship in 1981; it was the 9th Region's only state tournament title up to that date.

The current principal at Simon Kenton High School is Rick Culross. Enrollment is approximately 1,430.

Caywood, James A. "A Brief Sketch of the Development of the Kenton County School System," an address delivered to the Filson Society, January 14, 1958, Louisville, Ky.
"Simon Kenton's Sweet Memory," *KP*, November 29, 2005, 7K.
"Tight Deadlines to Meet—As Summer of Construction Winds Down, Schools Rush to Opening Day," *KP*, July 24, 2003, 1K.

Greg Perkins

SIMON KENTON HIGH SCHOOL EXPLOSION. On October 9, 1980, two explosions ripped apart the **Simon Kenton High School** in Independence, Ky. Aside from the **Beverly Hills Supper Club** fire of 1977, no event drew greater emergency response in Northern Kentucky's history. Every Kenton Co. fire and police department, and nearly all the Boone Co. fire and police departments, hurried to the scene of the disaster. The first explosion, in the boiler room adjacent to an art room, blew out a concrete wall and fatally injured a talented 16-year-old art student, Robert Williams. Because personnel were unable to locate the valve to turn off the natural gas, a spark ignited the built-up gas in the school, resulting in a more extensive and violent second blast that ruined more than half of the school building and injured 36 others, mostly firemen. While repairs were being made, the Kenton Co. School Board sent the entire student body of Simon Kenton High School to night school at the nearby Scott High School. After three months, the students returned to their repaired building. In a remarkable irony, the Simon Kenton Pioneer varsity boys' basketball team, despite not having a home gym for three months, later that season won the 1981 state championship. Led by head coach Larry Miller and assistant coaches Dave Schadler and Bill Pelfrey Jr., players Dave Dixon, Sean Dougherty, Troy McKinley, Dave Medley, Billy Meier, Alan Mullins, and Greg Ponzer accomplished what no Northern Kentucky team in 93 years of the state tournament had achieved. In 2006 Eric Deters, married to Mary Zimmerer, a cheerleader from the team, published a book called *Pioneer Spirit* about the explosion and the championship team.

Deters, Eric. *Pioneer Sprit: One High School's Rise from Tragedy to Glory.* Morley, Mo.: Acclaim Press, 2006.
"Simon Kenton Closed," *KE*, October 11, 1980, A2.
"Student Killed, 33 Injured in Blast—Explosions Rock Simon Kenton," *KE*, October 10, 1980, A1.

Eric Deters

SIMON KENTON MEMORIAL BRIDGE. For 138 years, ferries plied the waters of the Ohio River between Maysville, Ky., and Aberdeen, Ohio. Then, on the day before Thanksgiving, November 25, 1931, the two cities were linked by the Simon Kenton Memorial Bridge, commonly called the Maysville-Aberdeen Bridge. On that cold day, local school classes were dismissed for the event, and the bands of four high schools and the University of Kentucky gathered at the newly completed silver-painted suspension bridge. The ceremony attracted a crowd of more than 15,000. Maysville had competed with Augusta as the site for the bridge. Even though the new span was a toll bridge, no tolls were collected for the first three days after opening. The new bridge was reported to be a prototype of San Francisco's Golden Gate Bridge. The Dravo Company of Pittsburgh poured the bridge's substructure, and the J. A. Roebling Bridge Company completed the superstructure (see **John A. Roebling**; **John A. Roebling Bridge**). The world-renowned bridge-building company of Modjeski & Masters of Harrisburg, Pa., was retained as the design-engineering firm and construction supervisor for the project. The Modjeski firm later built another bridge in Northern Kentucky, the I-75 **Brent Spence** Bridge at Covington, completed in the early 1960s. Including its approaches, the bridge between Maysville and Aberdeen spans 3,163 feet, and its deck is about 100 feet above the river at pool stage. The total cost for the bridge was $1.6 million, which included a one-time $50,000 buy-out of the former Maysville Ferry. The new bridge connected the **Mary Ingles Highway** with the old Atlantic and Pacific Highway, U.S. 52, in Ohio.

The economic environment in Maysville changed for the better after the opening of the bridge. The much easier access to Maysville's downtown district brought more shoppers from Brown and Adams counties in Ohio. The **Hayswood Hospital** gained patients from those same areas, and Ohio tobacco farmers, hauling truckloads of their crops, used Maysville markets more often. Travelers en route from Lexington, Ky., to Columbus, Ohio, had a new route, no longer needing to divert west to Newport or east to Portsmouth, Ohio, for a quick crossing of the Ohio. Often those people stopped, shopped, dined, and sometimes stayed in Maysville. The Simon Kenton Bridge, named for **Simon Kenton**, the pioneer frontiersman so instrumental in the settlement of the Maysville area, was an overnight shot in the arm for Maysville's economy.

Although the bridge began as a toll bridge, no tolls were charged after October 1, 1945. The original tolls were $0.05–$0.60 for cars, $0.85–$1.50 for buses, $0.55–$2.00 for trucks, $0.50–$0.80 for animal-drawn vehicles, and $0.05 for pedestrians.

As traffic increased over the years, the relatively narrow lanes became dangerous at times. During the **cold war**, the bridge was painted green to blend in with the vegetation and water below, making it less visible to a possible bombing attack. During the early 1990s, the bridge structure was lighted with four 1,000-watt floodlights and 140 other strategically placed hanging lights, presenting a dramatic scene at night along Maysville's riverfront. In January 2001 the Simon Kenton Bridge was bypassed somewhat with the opening of the **William H. Harsha Bridge** a few miles downstream. That allowed for the Simon Kenton Bridge to close for a few months twice, once in 2002 and once in 2003, for much-needed repairs; the reduced traffic into Maysville and the resulting decline in business during those closings demonstrated how important the bridge remains in the economic life of the city's downtown. The Harsha Bridge, in the meantime, has taken much of the heavy truck traffic out of downtown. Now on the National Register of Historic Places, the bridge is open again, having been in place for more than 75 years. It is one of only about 10 Roebling-type suspension bridges remaining in the United States.

Comer, Martha. "Bridge's Birthday Is Nov. 25," *Maysville Ledger Independent*, October 30, 1991, n.p.

Dunbar, Lisa. "Repair Time for Bridge Shortened," *Maysville Ledger Independent*, October 9, 2002, A1–A2.

"Maysville Schools Closed," *Maysville Daily Independent*, November 25, 1931, 1.

Pheifer, Julie. "Bridge Opened 60 Years Ago," *Maysville Ledger Independent*, November 25, 1991, n.p.

Reis, Jim. "Maysville's Bridge to Ohio Twice Cause for Celebration," *KP*, July 28, 1997, 4K.

Simon Kenton Bridge Vertical File, Mason Co. Museum, Maysville, Ky.

SIMPSON, ARNOLD R. (b. April 26, 1952, Somerset, Ky.). Arnold Ray Simpson is the first African American to serve as Covington's city manager and the first of his race to be elected a state representative in Kentucky's 65th district. The son of funeral directors James and Zona Pennington Simpson, he was educated in the public schools of Covington and attended Kentucky State University in Frankfort and the University of Kentucky College of Law in Lexington. On October 10, 1981, he married Jo Ann Hill of Cincinnati.

In October 1986, Simpson was appointed city manager of Covington, after serving as the assistant city manager since 1980. He was picked for the top job following city manager Donald Eppley's resignation. In November 1989 Simpson resigned from the city manager position. In November 1993 Marty Sheehan, having been elected a Kenton Co. district court judge, resigned as the Kentucky 65th District state representative, and the Kenton Co. Democratic Party selected Simpson as its candidate to compete in a special election. Simpson defeated Republican Jerry Hatfield in that January 1994 election. The following May, Simpson ran in the Democratic primary against James Redwine and won both the May primary and the November election, in which his opponent was Republican Eileen Wendt; he continues to serve in the Kentucky legislature. Simpson lives in Covington with his family.

Collins, Michael. "City Manager Leaving," *KP*, October 30, 1989, 1K–2K.

——. "Covington Picks Simpson to Be Manager," *KP*, October 15, 1986, 1K–2K.

Fischer, John C. K. "Simpson Victory Decisive," *KP*, November 9, 1994, 7K.

Hicks, Jack. "Simpson Elected in 65th," *KP*, January 12, 1994, 1K–2K.

——."Simpson Likely Candidate to Fill Vacated Seat in General Assembly," *KP*, November 25, 1993, 1K.

——. "Simpson to Run for State House," *KP*, December 13, 1993, 1K–2K.

——. "Simpson Wins Right to Try and Keep Seat," *KP*, May 25, 1994, 5K.

"Redwine Challenges Simpson Again for Party's Nod," *KP*, May 20, 1994, 5K.

"Stage Set for Fall," *KP*, May 25, 1994, 1K.

Theodore H. H. Harris

SIMPSON, JAMES, JR., "JIM" (b. July 24, 1928, Somerset, Ky.; d. February 18, 1999, Covington, Ky.). Jim Simpson, the first African American to be elected and serve on the Covington city commission, was the son of James and Zetta West Simpson. He was educated in public schools in Covington and then joined the U.S. Army in 1947. Following his tour of duty in the army, he entered the Cincinnati College of Mortuary Science, graduating in 1951. In 1952 Simpson began working for Anna Jones, the owner of the C. E. Jones Funeral Home in Covington (see **Funeral Homes**). In 1961, following the retirement of Jones, Simpson took over the operation of the funeral home and became part owner of the business, the firm's name changed to Jones & Simpson Funeral Home. In 1972 the City of Covington acquired the funeral home's property at 633–635 Scott St., and the business moved to its current location at 1129 Garrard St.

In 1971 Simpson ran successfully for the Covington city commission. He served the full two-year term and later completed an unexpired term of Nyoka Johnston on the commission in 1991. Simpson served on the Kenton Co. Airport Board for eight years and in 1978 was elected its chairman; he also served on the boards of the People's Liberty Bank; the **Booth Memorial Hospital**, Covington; the St. Elizabeth Hospital, Covington (see **St. Elizabeth Medical Center**); and the Kenton Co. **Tuberculosis** Sanatorium. Simpson was the father of **Arnold R. Simpson**, a Covington city manager and a Kentucky state representative. James Simpson Jr. died February 18, 1999, and was buried in Highland Cemetery, Fort Mitchell. In June 2001 Simpson was nominated for the Kentucky Civil Rights Hall of Fame.

Fisher, John C. K. "Dignified Leader Laid to Rest; James Simpson, Jr. Called a 'True Friend,'" *KP*, February 23, 1999, 2K.

——. "Simpson Is Nominated for Rights Hall of Fame," *KP*, June 28, 2001, 3K.

"Kentucky Deaths," *KP*, February 20, 1999, 13A.

Reis, Jim. "Funeral Directors Assumed Civic Roles," *KP*, February 2, 1987, 4K.

"Simpson Wins at Wire; Covington Vote Close," *KE*, November 3, 1971, 1A.

Theodore H. H. Harris

SIMRALL, CHARLES B. (b. 1843, Madison, Ind.; d. September 22, 1901, Crittenden, Ky.). Attorney Charles Barrington Simrall was the son of John W. G. Simrall and the former Mary Bartow. Charles's early education was in the public schools of Covington, and later he studied in Württemberg, Germany, and at Miami University in Oxford, Ohio. He studied law under Covington attorney William Pryor and earned his law degree in 1865 from the Cincinnati Law School. He married Belle Pierce, and the couple had six daughters. Charles Simrall and his family lived on Wallace Ave. in Covington, but Simrall kept his law office in Cincinnati. He served for 15 years as the general counsel for the **Cincinnati Southern Railroad** and the **Chesapeake and Ohio Railroad**. He also served as counsel for the local **Green Line**

(Transit) **Company**. He was a member of the First Presbyterian Church of Covington (see **Community of Faith Presbyterian Church**). After a lengthy bout with cancer, Simrall died of pneumonia at age 58 at his summer home in Crittenden and was buried in the Highland Cemetery in Fort Mitchell.

"C. B. Simrall Laid to Rest," *KP*, September 25, 1901, 8.
"C. B. Simrall Passes Away," *KP*, September 23, 1901, 1.
"Funeral of Charles B. Simrall," *KP*, September 24, 1901, 3.

SISTERS OF DIVINE PROVIDENCE. The Sisters of Divine Providence in Covington have their origin in 16th-century France. In 1792 Jean Martin Moye founded the Roman Catholic order (sisters) of the Congregation of Divine Providence (CDP) in France. The sisters under his direction had a special concern for teaching poor children in the Alsace-Lorraine region, where their order began. When this area came under the control of Germany in 1871, following the Franco-Prussian War, the Sisters of Divine Providence of St. Jean-de-Bassel found it difficult to carry on their teaching ministry. In 1889 the Superior General of the congregation, Mother Anna, contacted Covington bishop **Camillus P. Maes**, himself a native of Belgium, about the possibility of establishing a branch of the Sisters of Divine Providence in the United States. Bishop Maes was happy to invite the sisters to come to the Diocese of Covington (see **Roman Catholics**).

A small number of sisters came to Northern Kentucky in August 1889 and stayed briefly with the Sisters of the Poor of St. Francis at St. Elizabeth Hospital in Covington (see **St. Elizabeth Medical Center**). In October Bishop Maes offered them the Jones mansion (see **Thomas Laurens Jones**), located on a hill in Newport. That house, which they called Mount St. Martin, was the motherhouse of the Sisters of Divine Providence for many years. The sisters opened their first school, **Mount St. Martin** Academy, in the same building. This location became the center of the first American province of the congregation, who were incorporated in the state of Kentucky as the Sisters of Divine Providence of Kentucky. The sisters also served as teachers in many parish schools in the diocese as well as in other states that were included in their province.

By 1900 Mount St. Martin Academy was too small for its enrollment, so in 1903 the congregation built a new school on Sixth St. in the east end of Newport. The Academy Notre Dame of Providence, which later became **Our Lady of Providence Academy**, opened in 1908 as a secondary school for girls. The sisters also opened St. Camillus Academy in Corbin, Ky., in 1915. A Catholic institution in the mountains of Eastern Kentucky was unusual, since the area was largely Protestant. But by their manner and success as teachers, the sisters overcame the prejudice many of the local population felt toward Catholics. The sisters went on to open more schools and hospitals in the mountains.

In 1909 **Peter O'Shaughnessy**, a wealthy resident of Newport, assisted the sisters in the acquisition of a large piece of property near Melbourne, in Campbell Co. On this site the sisters built their current motherhouse, St. Anne Convent, which they occupied in 1919. It also became the headquarters of the American province of the CDP. The picturesque setting at St. Anne Convent was depicted in some of the scenes in the 1988 movie *Rainman*. Sr. Celeste Marie O'Shaughnessy, daughter of Peter, was elected provincial superior in 1937. On the same property in 1957 the sisters built the Holy Family Home for use as a residential care facility for their elderly sisters and opened the Moye Spiritual Life Center (a retreat house) in 1980. In December 2004 **Thomas More College** named as its 13th president a member of the Sisters of Divine Providence, Sr. **Margaret Stallmeyer**.

After the Second Vatican Council of the early 1960s, the sisters underwent a process of change, which they called "Corporate Renewal," that allowed them to maintain their traditional identity while meeting the new exigencies of the times. They continued their focus of education, though with an added emphasis on serving the poor. Some sisters entered forms of ministry in which the congregation had not been engaged in the past. Today the Sisters of Divine Providence face the same difficulties that many religious orders do: a shortage of professed novices to carry out all the obligations the sisters once had, and an aging congregation. But the sisters remain active in many ministries in their American province and even participate in ministry in other countries that are missions of their international congregation based in France, known as the Sisters of Divine Providence of St. Jean-de-Bassel.

Congregation of Divine Providence. *1889–1989: One Hundred Years.* Melbourne, Ky.: Congregation of Divine Providence, 1989.
Ryan, Paul E. *History of the Diocese of Covington, Kentucky.* Covington, Ky.: Diocese of Covington, 1954.
Tenkotte, Paul A., David E. Schroeder, and Thomas S. Ward. *To Be Catholic and American in Northern, Central, and Appalachian Kentucky: The Diocese of Covington, 1853–2003.* Forthcoming.

Thomas S. Ward

SISTERS OF NOTRE DAME. The Sisters of Notre Dame serve the **Roman Catholics** of the Diocese of Covington, primarily in teaching and medical roles. The order was founded in Namur, Belgium, by St. Julie Billiart during the early 19th century. Sisters M. Aloysia Wolbring and Ignatia Kuhling joined the community of sisters in Amersfoort, Holland, in 1850, though they actually took up the religious habit in Coesfeld, Germany, a city in which they had been teaching poor children. In 1855 they started at Coesfeld an offshoot of the congregation as they separated from their motherhouse in Amersfoort. While the anti-Catholic Kulturkampf was raging in Germany, Sr. Aloysia joined a group of seven sisters who immigrated to the United States in 1874. At the request of Richard Gilmour, the bishop of Cleveland, Ohio, the sisters established in that city the motherhouse of what became the first American province of the Sisters of Notre Dame. Bishop Augustus Maria Toebbe of Covington had a sister in that congregation. Although he did not know whether his sister was among them, Toebbe invited some of the sisters in Cleveland to come to Covington in 1874. The bishop's sister, Mary Modesta, did not arrive in Covington until a year later.

The Sisters of Notre Dame constructed the first wing of their academy and convent on Fifth St. in Covington in 1876. They also took charge of the **Mother of God** School in Covington. Over the next several years, the sisters expanded their teaching ministry to parochial schools in Alexandria, Augusta, Bellevue, Carrollton, and Newport. They took over operation of St. Joseph Orphans Asylum in Cold Spring from the Franciscan Brothers of Cincinnati in 1877. The congregation in the Covington Diocese continued to grow into the 20th century until it had 17 houses and about 700 sisters.

The Sisters of Notre Dame in Covington achieved a milestone in 1924 when Covington became the seat of a separate province of the congregation. It was established as the Immaculate Heart of Mary Province, with Mother Mary Angela Meiners as its first provincial superior. In 1926 the sisters began work on a new provincial motherhouse and convent, on property they had acquired earlier, located on Dixie Highway in Park Hills. Bishop Francis W. Howard dedicated the order's new property, known as St. Joseph Heights, on November 13, 1927. In 1963 the sisters built the new **Notre Dame Academy** for girls on the same property behind St. Joseph Heights. In 1961 the sisters took charge of the new **Diocesan Catholic Children's Home**, created from the merger of the St. Joseph and St. John orphanages. The Sisters of Notre Dame engaged in health care as well as teaching. They opened **St. Charles Care Center** in 1960, as well as two hospital facilities in the mountains of Kentucky (Notre Dame Hospital in Lynch and St. Claire Medical Center in Morehead). In 1986 the Covington province was given a singular honor when its provincial superior, Sr. Mary Joell Overman, was elected superior general of the congregation worldwide, a position she held until 1998.

Ryan, Paul E. *History of the Diocese of Covington, Kentucky.* Covington, Ky.: Diocese of Covington, 1954.
Sisters of Notre Dame. "Legacy: Mission for Life and Love: 75th Anniversary of the Immaculate Heart of Mary Province," *Messenger*, March 24, 2000, supplement.
——. *The Sisters of Notre Dame: A Celebration of Life.* Strasbourg, France: Éditions du Signe, n.d.
Tenkotte, Paul A., David E. Schroeder, and Thomas S. Ward. *To Be Catholic and American in Northern, Central, and Appalachian Kentucky: The Diocese of Covington, 1853–2003.* Forthcoming.

Thomas S. Ward

SISTERS OF ST. BENEDICT. On June 3, 1859, three sisters at the Benedictine convent in Erie, Pa., answered the call of the first American Benedictine abbot, Boniface Wimmer, O.S.B., to staff the St. Joseph Girls' School in Covington. On August 2, 1859, Mother Alexia Lechner, O.S.B., founding prioress, arrived in Covington to establish St. Walburg Monastery. For monastic women, prayer is primary; ministry follows. Nevertheless, the community of sisters taught, built the four-story St. Walburg Monastery and a boarding school (St. Walburg Academy, 1863–1931), and carried out the work of a small farm. Over time, as they gained in numbers, the bishop asked them to assume care of the St. John Orphanage in present-day Fort Mitchell (see **Diocesan Catholic Children's Home**) and other schools in addition. From the Covington monastery, which was on 12th St. in Covington, three other monasteries were established, in Ferdinand, Ind. (1867), Covington, La. (1873–1987), and Cullman, Ala. (1902).

Mother Walburga Saelinger was the second prioress (1889–1928) in Covington. She purchased the **Villa Madonna Academy** (VMA) site in 1903 from the DeWitt Collin estate and established a boarding school for girls in Villa Hills. An adjacent 32 acres, purchased from E. S. Lee in 1932, became home to the Benedictine novitiate in 1916 and to Villa Madonna College (1921–1929). The college became diocesan, moved to Covington, and in 1968 occupied a new campus in Crestview Hills, becoming **Thomas More College**. Villa Madonna remained a boarding academy through 1979. Coeducation followed.

The convent's third prioress, artist Mother Margaret Hugenberg (1928–1931), beautified the site of the Villa Madonna Academy and laid out a sisters' cemetery. Before that, sisters had been buried at **Mother of God Cemetery**, Covington. German-born Mother Lioba Holz, the fourth prioress (1931–1943), erected a monastery on the site, reintroduced the Divine Office, and answered the plea of Covington's bishop to begin hospital work in Appalachia. The fifth prioress, Mother Domitilla Thuener (1943–1955), insisted that every teaching sister have a degree and that the community join the Federation of St. Scholastica. The convent's sixth prioress, Mother Hilda Obermeier (1955–1961), recognized the need for a new Villa Madonna High School building (1958) and published a centennial pictorial, *The Challenge*. The community was at its highest membership, 266 sisters, at that time. The seventh prioress, Mother Benedict Bunning (1961–1970), began the local Madonna Manor Nursing Home and Senior Citizen Village, razed the original convent on 12th St. in Covington, and conducted a renewal program in 1969 to follow the teachings of the Second Vatican Council.

Sisters Ruth Yost (1971–1978), Justina Franxman (1978–1986), Mary Catherine Wenstrup (1986–1998), and Rita Brink (1998–present) have served as prioresses since Sister Benedict. These four prioresses implemented several changes: they opened a Montessori school; withdrew the order from its hospital work; established a Benedictine associate program; helped VMA become coeducational; added lay persons to the boards of VMA and Madonna Manor; renovated the monastery building, including the chapel and the infirmary; and established the Social Needs Fund to help organizations serving in the areas of health, hunger, housing, and education. The community of sisters has supported the VMA Capital Campaign to renovate the school and to build a new sports complex. A new ministry called the Center of Spirituality offers programs for those who seek to strengthen their relationship with God.

Today, St. Walburg has 77 finally professed members, one member in first vows, and 51 covenanted associate members. Monastery sisters serve in four dioceses: the Archdiocese of Cincinnati and the dioceses of Covington and Lexington, Ky., and Pueblo, Colo.

"New Convent for Benedictines at Villa Madonna Being Built," *KP*, November 13, 1936, 6.

Ryan, Paul E. *History of the Diocese of Covington, Kentucky*. Covington, Ky.: Diocese of Covington, 1954.

Schwartz, Joann R. "St. Walburg Monastery, Covington, Kentucky, 1859–1899," master's thesis, Xavier Univ., 2005.

Wolking, Teresa, O.S.B., and Joann Schwartz. "The Story of Villa Madonna Academy and the Benedictines," *NKH* 11, no. 1 (Fall–Winter 2003): 2–16.

Teresa Wolking

SISTERS OF ST. JOSEPH THE WORKER. The Sisters of St. Joseph the Worker were founded in the Diocese of Covington. The Second Vatican Council of the Roman Catholic Church, held at the Vatican in four autumn sessions, 1962–1965, brought many dramatic changes to the practices and traditions of Catholicism. Although the most noticeable ones were changes to the liturgy, most aspects of Catholic life were affected, including the vowed religious life of nuns and sisters. Religious orders of women went through a process of renewal called for by the Second Vatican Council and accordingly altered their traditions in numerous ways. Interior renewal and a return to the spirit of the founders of their orders were the main emphases. Yet, most other Catholics were more aware of external changes, such as modifying or discontinuing the special clothing that distinguished them as sisters and pursuing ministries other than teaching and nursing. But the communities of women religious who went through this process were far from unanimous in their opinions about the changes that were adopted.

The Sisters of Charity of Nazareth were a community founded in Kentucky in 1812 with a special emphasis on teaching in Catholic schools. They staffed many parish schools in the Diocese of Covington (see **Roman Catholics**). When their process of renewal was completed in the late 1960s and new rules for the community were composed (which had to be approved later by Rome), some sisters, including Sister Ellen Curran, were concerned that too many of the traditions of the past had been abandoned, things that were essential to the nature of religious life. She first petitioned the leadership of the Sisters of Charity of Nazareth to allow her and a group of like-minded sisters to continue the traditional practices in a separate house, though they would still belong to the community. When no mutually satisfactory arrangement could be found, Bishop Richard H. Ackerman of Covington, who agreed with Sr. Ellen's assessment of the changes to religious life, offered to assist her in founding a new community of sisters that would no longer be part of the Sisters of Charity of Nazareth. With Ackerman's assistance, permission was finally obtained from the Sacred Congregation for Religious and Secular Institutes at the Vatican in 1974 to establish a new order of sisters that would be a diocesan congregation under the direction of the bishop of Covington.

At the suggestion of Ackerman, the group of sisters took the name Sisters of St. Joseph the Worker and elected Sr. Ellen as their first superior in 1974. They adopted a more traditional way of life, including religious garb. After living in temporary quarters, the sisters found a permanent home in Walton, where they built St. William Convent. In 1976 the sisters took over the closed school of **All Saints Catholic Church** in Walton and reopened it as St. Joseph Academy. They also took control of Taylor Manor in Versailles, a nursing home that the sisters now operate. The Sisters of St. Joseph the Worker remain a relatively small congregation today.

Curran, Mother Ellen, S.J.W. *History of the Sisters of St. Joseph the Worker*, 1997. Available at the Archives of the Diocese of Covington, Erlanger, Ky.

Tenkotte, Paul A., David E. Schroeder, and Thomas S. Ward. *To Be Catholic and American in Northern, Central, and Appalachian Kentucky: The Diocese of Covington, 1853–2003*. Forthcoming.

Thomas S. Ward

SKATING RINKS. Northern Kentuckians ice-skated indoors from the mid-20th century on; they had a roller-skating rink at least as early as 1886.

Ice-skating can be traced back to the Stone Age, when early humans tied animal bones to their feet and skated across frozen lakes and rivers. Scandinavian tales from about A.D. 1200 tell of the skating ability of their national heroes and their gods. Many early Dutch people became expert skaters and were even known to engage in military battles on ice skates. During the Middle Ages, residents in London, England, attached bones to their feet and propelled themselves across the ice with pointed sticks. The people of the Netherlands later found that they could use iron blades as runners and thereby greatly improve their skating ability. During the late 1800s, ice-skating became quite popular in both Europe and North America. When the first indoor ice rink was built in 1912, it led to the growth of figure skating, ice hockey, and speed skating. Northern Kentucky's first indoor ice rink was the Dixie Gardens Ice Bowl in Fort Wright, which opened in the early 1960s and closed in the late 1980s and was located next to the Dixie Gardens Drive-In Theater (see **Drive-Ins**). The Northern Kentucky Ice Center opened in 1990 at the former home of the Northern Kentucky Racket Club, in Crescent Springs. However, much of the ice-skating in the region continues to be done on lakes and ponds and on parking lots that have been flooded for the purpose. In Fort Thomas, before the recent renovation of the mess hall at the old fort, the tile floor was flooded during the winter, the windows opened, and the heat turned off, allowing indoor ice-skating.

Ice hockey was added to the Summer Olympic Games at Antwerp, Belgium, in 1920, and figure skating was moved to the winter games in 1924. During the 20th century, choreographed ice-skating shows became a popular form of entertainment throughout the world.

The first recorded use of roller skates was in a play on the London Stage in 1743. John Joseph Merlin invented a three-wheel in-line roller skate in 1760, primarily to allow ice-skaters to skate during warm weather. The first patent for roller skates was issued to a Frenchman, Monsieur Petitbled, in 1819. However, those early roller skates proved to be difficult to control. To correct the problem, in 1863 James L. Plimpton invented a four-wheel roller skate, which he called the quad. His skates had rubber cushions between the plate and the front wheels, which permitted skaters to maneuver easily, by shifting their weight from side to side. His innovation made it possible for roller skaters to perform moves previously made only by ice-skaters. In 1866 the first public roller-skating rink opened in the United States, in the ballroom of the Atlantic House Resort Hotel in Newport, N.J. Within a short time, improvised roller-skating rinks began appearing in ballrooms, town halls, and similar buildings across the country. In later years, many portable skating floors were also set up at events like carnivals and county fairs.

One of the first Northern Kentucky roller skating rinks was opened in 1886, at the old Masonic Hall (see **Masons**) on York St., in Newport. Shortly thereafter, another opened in the ballroom of the **Independent Order of Odd Fellows** Hall, at Fifth St. and Madison Ave. in Covington. In the late 1800s, there was also a combination skating rink and dance hall operated at Berlin Beach in Dayton, Ky. That building was later sold and moved to **Tacoma Park**, where it continued to operate into the 1950s. A large combination roller-skating rink and bowling alley, called the Roll and Bowl, opened in Florence, Ky., during the early 1970s but closed about two years later, when the entire building was made into a bowling alley, the Super Bowl. Currently the largest roller rink in Northern Kentucky is the Fundome, located off I-75 (see **Expressways**) and Ky. Rt. 18 in Florence. Jimmie's Rollerdome has been operating in Elsmere since 1948, and Reca Roller Rink in Alexandria has been serving Campbell Co. skaters since 1960.

In Maysville, the Princess Skatorium on E. Second St. opened to much fanfare in 1907; later the Americana Rink operated for many years in the mid-1900s. In Maysville today is the Maysville Roller Rink, at the corner of Lexington St. and the **Chesapeake and Ohio Railroad**; it is open on weekends. South of town, Rudy's Roller Rink has operated since 2001 near Lewisburg along Ky. Rt. 3071. In 1959 the Coasters skating club was formed in Maysville at the Maysville Roller Rink; several of its Maysville members participated that same year in the less-than-12-hour skate run from nearby Aberdeen to Portsmouth, Ohio, eastward along U.S. 52.

Over the years, family-run roller-skating rinks have appeared in most Northern Kentucky cities; however, few survive today. Roller Derby in the 1950s and 1960s, skateboarding in the 1980s, and the in-line skating craze of the 1990s have hurt attendance at most indoor rinks. Large nationally or regionally owned conglomerates have taken over much of the industry. Those corporations often operate huge, glitzy rinks that offer restaurants, game and party rooms, exercise classes, and child care; and small family-owned rinks cannot compete. Also, high admission prices, caused partly by soaring liability insurance costs and other operating expenses, have contributed to the demise of many rinks.

The first U.S. Speed Roller Skating Championships were held in 1937, at the Arena Gardens in Detroit, Mich. Dance and figure skating championships were added in 1939. Roller-skating competition was included in the Pan American Games in 1979 and in the Summer Olympics at Barcelona, Spain, in 1992. Speed Roller Skating is scheduled to appear for the first time in the Summer Olympic Games in 2012.

The Diagram Group. *Enjoy Skating*. Edinburg, Scotland: Morrison and Gibb, 1978.
"Healy Building in Newport Has New Owner Now," *KTS,* August 11, 1921, 25.
"Kids on Wheels," *KP,* March 20, 2001, 8K.
National Museum of Roller Skating. "John Joseph Merlin-Monsieur Petitbled." www.rollerskating museum.com (accessed July 2, 2006).
"Skating," local history files, Kentucky Gateway Museum, Maysville, Ky.

Jack Wessling

SLAVERY. The American form of slavery had already been codified by constitutional provisions, legislative acts, and municipal ordinances in Virginia and other English colonies when Dr. Thomas Walker in 1750, **Christopher Gist** in 1751, and **James McBride** in 1751 began to map the eastern and northern regions of Kentucky. As prescribed by these laws in the colonies, slaves were, for the first time in history, defined as chattel, as property; slavery was perpetual, that is, slave status was inherited; and legal racism was embedded in slavery, because slaves were defined as being black and of African descent. The economic benefits to white slave owners in the United States through chattel slavery developed over the next 100 years through the transatlantic slave market and the domestic buying and selling of slaves. As the **Civil War** neared, in 1860 nearly 4.5 million people of African descent were working for white landowners for free or for a pittance and millions more had died in servitude.

There were counterforces. By the time Kentucky became a state in 1792, Vermont, Rhode Island, Pennsylvania, Connecticut, New York, New Jersey, and Massachusetts had already abolished slavery in various forms. The Northwest Territories had also been declared free of institutional slavery, making Ohio and Indiana free states as they entered the Union in 1803 and 1816, respectively. And earlier, in 1795, France had declared all slaves free both on its native soil and throughout its colonies.

At the Kentucky Constitutional Convention at Danville in 1792, Rev. David Rice and other ministers fought against Article 9, which would legalize slavery. Their efforts met with defeat, however, and slavery was permitted within the new commonwealth of Kentucky's boundaries. Sixteen men voted against Article 9, including Northern Kentuckians **Miles Withers Conway** and George Lewis of Mason Co. and John Wilson of Woodford Co. (which then covered all of Boone, Campbell, Grant, Kenton, and Owen counties). Later, by virtue of a provision in the 1799 Kentucky Constitution, slaves became perpetual chattel, and the importation of slaves subsequently began in earnest; 165,213 slaves had entered the commonwealth of Kentucky or had been born into slavery in the state by 1830. By 1860 there were 225,483 slaves, 11,483 of them living in Northern Kentucky.

Put into perspective, Northern Kentucky had 0.2 percent of the nation's slaves and the state of Kentucky about 5 percent. The human misery of those enslaved is recorded in hundreds of slave interviews, now accessible in collections and books. Historians, sociologists, novelists, and poets have published the stories of individual slaves and slave families, creating fully dimensional people from the myths, stereotypes, and cartoon figures of recent memory. And several of Northern Kentucky's slaves have been immortalized in books, music, poems, and even, in the case of **Margaret Garner** of Boone Co., recently in an opera.

Active slave trading occurred in Northern Kentucky at slave markets in Maysville and Washington. Slaves in the region built houses and fences, cleared fields, planted, harvested, took produce to market, and worked the steamboats and river craft, all through forced slave labor. Even though the counties of Northern Kentucky had just 6 percent of the state's slaves, institutional slavery played its part in this region's history.

In 1833 the Kentucky General Assembly banned importation of slaves into Kentucky except by emigration, inheritance, or marriage. This new law was generally ignored. In 1849 the advocates of slavery in Kentucky, flush with their victory at that year's State Constitutional Convention, gained yet another victory when the Kentucky legislature repealed the Non-Importation Act of 1833 and passed the third-strictest set of restrictions on free people of color and slaves in the nation, rivaling the codes of the Deep South. Furthermore, in 1865, 1868, and 1870, Kentucky failed to ratify the three U.S. constitutional amendments that made former slaves citizens of the nation. Dismayed, Union general Clinton B. Fisk characterized members of the Kentucky legislature as "the meanest, unsubjugated, and unreconstructed rascally rebellious revolutionists" he had ever had the displeasure of encountering.

Local municipal ordinances, particularly in the northern counties of Kentucky bordering the Ohio River, frequently prohibited a slave owner from hiring out his or her slaves, yet that became a common practice during the 1830s and 1840s. Grand juries in Gallatin and Carroll counties indicted several slaveholders for violating this law; however, hiring out slaves for a season or for the year was lucrative, and the fines were too modest to prevent this practice.

Slave trading in Northern Kentucky was basically unregulated and, except for the regular slave market held in Mason Co., small in scale. Buying and selling of human chattel took place in the large slave markets at Lexington and Louisville on a regular schedule. By comparison, the slave market conducted at Washington in Mason Co. was not large. Often it involved small numbers of slaves in coffles brought by traders passing through the area or sales conducted by local slave owners themselves.

In Northern Kentucky the density of the slave population was highly dependent on the type of underlying farmland. The planter culture, mimicking Virginia's patricians, took root immediately in the rich river bottoms and upland grasslands of Mason, Boone, and northern Owen counties. Mason and Boone counties, with more than 6,400 slaves in 1840, accounted for 55 percent of all slaves held in Northern Kentucky. In 1840 Campbell and Grant counties had only 289 and 348 slaves, respectively.

Rural areas within Boone and Mason counties rivaled the Bluegrass region of Kentucky, with more than 40 percent slave populations. Mason Co., in particular, jumped from 1,747 slaves in 1800 to 4,309 by 1840. Boone Co., in the same period, climbed from 325 slaves in 1800 to 2,183 in 1840. Numbers in Gallatin Co., part of which went to form Carroll Co. in 1838, rose from 329 slaves in 1800 to 604 slaves in Gallatin Co. plus 731 slaves in Carroll Co. in 1840. Among Northern Kentucky counties, Owen Co. had the third-largest slave population in 1840, 1,281; that number increased in 1860 to a peak of 1,660 slaves, almost all of whom resided in the upland pastureland between Owenton and New Liberty. The urban areas that developed along the Ohio River, Maysville, Augusta, Newport, Covington, Fredericksburg (Warsaw), and Port William (Carrollton), had less than 20 percent slave populations before the Civil War.

There were many slave owners in Boone Co., about 36 percent of all families, but the number of slaves per plantation was generally fewer than 10 per household. In the villages, only 1 or 2 slaves were owned by about 20 percent of the families. The total number of slaves in Boone Co. grew rapidly from 629 in 1810 to 2,183 in 1840 and then declined as the impact of the **Underground Railroad** and the selling of excess slaves to the Deep South began to reduce slave numbers in this county. By 1860 there were 1,745 slaves and 11,118 whites in Boone Co. However, the value of these slaves as property had increased substantially. Slaves were only 15 percent of the tax base in 1850 but had climbed to 24 percent by 1860.

Boone Co. never had many free people of color; there were only 27 free blacks in 1840, 37 in 1850, and 48 in 1860. After the Civil War, the black population of Boone Co. declined severely. In 1840 blacks made up 21.8 percent of the population; in 1870 they were only 9.5 percent, representing a loss of more than 1,170 black citizens from the county.

By 1840 the slaves in Mason, Boone, and Owen counties accounted for 28 percent, 22 percent, and 16 percent, respectively, of the total population, compared to 50 percent in Fayette Co., in the heart of the Bluegrass region. Counties in the northern portions of Kentucky such as Lewis, Grant, and later Robertson, where the more rugged hill country dominated, counties that were settled chiefly by yeomen with small landholdings, had slave populations of less than 10 percent. The urbanized counties Campbell and Kenton had few slaves. In Bracken Co. slave density approximated 30 percent in certain upland districts, while in other areas the population was less than 10 percent slaves.

Kentucky remained a part of the international slave trade until 1808, when federal law banned the importation of slaves. However, by 1833, when the Kentucky legislature forbade any further importation of slaves, more than 150,000 slaves had entered Kentucky with landowners or through inheritance. After the 1808 federal ban on the importation of slaves into the United States, a domestic slave trade sprang up and thrived in Kentucky. Mason Co., with its tobacco-based economy, established the earliest recorded domestic slave-trading market in Kentucky at Washington, which is located on a hill above Maysville. In about 1826, Capt. John W. Anderson, who lived near Washington in Mason Co., took over the northern region's major slave-trading operations from Edward Stone of adjoining Harrison Co. Stone had been killed in a slave revolt. The domestic slave market at Washington later became famous as the inspiration for Harriet Beecher Stowe's *Uncle Tom's Cabin*. She had observed the selling of human beings in the center of Washington during her visit to the **Marshall Key** house in Mason Co. The height of Anderson's domestic slave sales operation was reached about 1830; slaves from Mason Co. were shipped through the Dover landing in Kentucky to Natchez, Miss. Anderson was taking in $50,000 in revenues each year, nearly $1 million in terms of today's monetary values. When he died, legend has it that he was chasing a runaway slave. James McMillen then took over Anderson's domestic slave trade business and also served as an agent for Bolton, Dickson & Co., large-scale slave traders at Lexington; Memphis; Charleston, S.C.; Natchez, Miss.; St. Louis; and New Orleans.

From 1830 to 1863, slave trading in Kentucky constituted a major component of the U.S. domestic slave trade; thousands of Kentucky-born slaves were sold south through Vicksburg and Natchez, Miss., and New Orleans markets. It was common for local slavers to go to Washington or to Lexington and pick up a small coffle of slaves to sell in the rural areas. By the 1840s, slavers were taking excess slaves from these same rural areas to sell into the Southern markets at prices reaching $800 to $1,000 per male slave. By the mid-1840s, selling slaves south became one of the largest sources of cash in Northern Kentucky.

Locally, slave owners did their own trading quietly among themselves and frequently hired slaves out for cash to support increasingly expensive private schools, household furnishings, and especially horse racing. The *Kentucky Gazette*, the *Maysville Eagle*, the *Licking Valley Register*, and the *Bracken Sentinel* all carried numerous advertisements to buy or sell individual slaves, announcements of estate sales of slaves, and notices of rewards for runaway slaves.

Slaves designated as prime field hands brought $300 to $400 in 1820, but with the opening of the Vicksburg and New Orleans slave markets, prices rose substantially. It was not uncommon by 1860 for a male slave to fetch $800 to $1,000 or sometimes even more in the Lexington market. And Northern Kentucky's slave owners tended to pay the highest prices for mulatto, or mixed-race, slaves, a preference established originally by landed Virginia owners. Obviously, these mulatto men, women, and children sold at auction were sons and daughters of white slave owners, a fact the Northern abolitionists found abhorrent, immoral, and unacceptable.

The patrollers searching for runaway slaves were known to the slaves as paddywhackers, or padrolers. The patroller system was instituted in the Ohio River counties of Kentucky quite early in the history of these counties' administrative courts as a form of control to keep slaves from running away. In the June 1799 Gallatin Co. Court Order Book 1, it was ordered that Benjamin Craig, Simeon Crosby, and Martin Hawkins be appointed patrollers for three months from that date, along with George Burton and Nicholas Lindsay. Among the earliest court orders in Boone Co. was the 1808 authorization for slave patrollers to receive one dollar per 10 hours worked. The court collected a special poll tax on slave owners to pay for these patrols. Patrollers were generally slave owners, and working as patrollers often served as a rite of passage for older sons; the patrollers were assigned 10- to 12-mile circuits along the Ohio River that they were to guard at night. Because of the distances involved, most patrollers along the Ohio River used horses. Patrollers were also authorized to whip any slave caught, with the prescribed numbers of lashes codified in Kentucky law.

By the early 1840s, as the numbers of runaway slaves became politically sensitive, legislators in Kentucky acted to expand patroller controls; counties farther removed from the Ohio River created patroller systems aligned with constable jurisdictions. Thus, in practice, the controlling of runaway slaves became a matter supported by all taxpayers, not just owners.

Many of the Underground Railroad's stories from Indiana about small Kentucky posses trying to recapture runaway slaves actually described patrollers on duty at night who had access to a skiff or a ferry. As the slave losses mounted in Boone Co. and the surrounding region, patrollers used scent dogs to aid them in their attempts to recapture runaway slaves. A brutal bloodhound named Nero figured in the following runaway-slave story that took place in Boone Co. at Cooper's Bottom. Lindsay Cooper of Cooper's Bottom owned between 8 and 10 slaves before 1850. Ike, one of Cooper's slaves, purchased his freedom and that of his wife and settled just across the river in Indiana. When they tried to purchase their four children, Cooper refused. He bought or borrowed John G. Moore's savage dog Nero to prevent runaways, but the four children of Ike poisoned the dog and escaped across the Ohio River. By 1860 Cooper owned only one slave; the rest had gone.

Slave codes and local municipal ordinances established a vehicle for violence against slaves. Because of the economic value of slaves, punishment of slaves was most often provided by whipping, rather than penal offenses. For example, for a particular crime, whites would be incarcerated in the penitentiary, but slaves would be punished at the whipping post or killed. White offenders during slavery times were executed only for murder and certain kinds of rape. Slaves were put to death for murder; manslaughter; rape of a white woman; attempting to commit crimes of robbery, arson, or burglary; conspiring to rebel; administering poison with intent to cause death; shooting and wounding a white person; and shooting without wounding. Although slave patrollers were limited in the number of whiplashes they could administer if a runaway slave was caught, slave owners and slave traders had no such restrictions.

Long before the Ku Klux Klan marauded through Central Kentucky, a long, sordid history of violence, lynchings, false accusations, rape of slave women, and brutal whippings of slaves and freedmen had become part of Kentucky's history. The various historical collections of slave eyewitness reports refer to the occurrence of such outrages before 1865, while George C. Wright's *Racial Violence in Kentucky, 1865–1940* catalogs the hundreds of lynchings and brutal violence against slaves and free people of color occurring after the Civil War.

Slaves' quest for escape from bondage was continuous. Slaves escaped from and through Northern Kentucky before 1787, when the *Kentucky Gazette* first began posting runaway want ads. Only a strong motivation to achieve freedom or to find their separated family members would cause a slave on the frontier to run into forests controlled by Indian tribes. Slaves in Northern Kentucky counties along the Ohio River had the most opportunity to flee, but as the slave density in the Bluegrass region approached 40 percent, slave escapes increased in spite of patrollers and the increasing use of slave-catchers, detectives, and other forms of control. For the first 30 years of the 19th century, runaway slaves made it to the Ohio River on their own, found some kind of raft or conveyance, and trekked through the Northwest Territories, sometimes finding a friendly person, sometimes melting into the populations of free black agricultural communities or into friendly Indian tribes. Once the antislavery societies were organized in Ohio and Indiana during the late 1830s, aid to runaway slaves improved from the haphazard fits and starts of earlier times.

In Northern Kentucky, Patrick Doyle's abortive attempt to bring a group (somewhere between 40 and 75) of slaves from Lexington through Bracken Co. occurred in 1848. Rev. Calvin Fairbank and Delia Webster helped Lewis, Harriet, and Jo Hayden successfully escape through Maysville in 1844, but both Fairbank and Webster were imprisoned upon their return to Kentucky. John Fairfield successfully led 15 slaves in crossing from Boone Co. into Indiana during the early 1850s. Robert and Margaret Garner's tragic attempt to escape from Boone Co. in 1856 has been immortalized in books and an opera. When **Elijah Anderson** moved his base of operations from Madison to Lawrenceburg, Ind., in 1846, Boone Co. slave owners began to experience the loss of slaves almost immediately. By 1853 Boone Co. was losing 50 slaves a month. Anderson himself claimed to have helped 1,000 slaves escape Kentucky between 1850 and 1856; in 1856 he was arrested and sent to prison at Frankfort, Ky.

Some of the most famous stories in Northern Kentucky of slaves reaching freedom involve these individuals:

—Eliza Harris, Mason Co., whose escape across the icy Ohio River was codified for all time in Harriet Beecher Stowe's *Uncle Tom's Cabin*.

—Henry Bibb, who escaped from Bedford, Trimble Co., Ky., was jailed at Covington in Kenton Co., and became the first black editor of a newspaper in Windsor, Canada. He and his wife Mary were designated persons of distinction by the Canadian legislature.

—Andrew Gagnon of Bracken Co., who, trying to impress a young woman, learned how to conduct runaway slaves to Ripley, Ohio, and maintained a regular passage to freedom during the 1850s.

—John White, who escaped from Rabbit Hash, Boone Co., and with the aid of Michigan abolitionist Laura Haviland, returned to Kentucky in an abortive attempt to rescue his wife. He eventually made it back to Michigan.

—Richard Daly of Hunter's Bottom, Carroll Co., who aided 30 runaway slaves in their escapes before taking his own family of five in 1856 to freedom in Canada.

—**Adam Crosswhite**, who took his family of five to Marshall, Mich., with the aid of the Madison, Ind., Underground Railroad. When pursued by a Kentucky posse, the Crosswhites were helped by local black and white citizens of Marshall and taken to Windsor, Canada. After the Civil War, the Crosswhite family returned to Marshall, and a bronze tablet was later placed at the site of their cabin by the Michigan Historical Society.

—**Wheeling Gaunt**, a Carroll Co. slave, who purchased his own and his family's freedom, moved to Yellow Springs, Ohio, after the Civil War, amassed a fortune of more than $30,000, and became a leading Ohio philanthropist, aiding Wilberforce College.

—Rev. **Elisha W. Green**, a Baptist preacher at Maysville and Paris and founder of the Consolidated Baptist movement after the Civil War.

—**Jacob Price**, a businessman and community leader in Covington, who organized the William Grant School.

—**James Bradley**, born in Africa and enslaved in South Carolina, who purchased his freedom, gained an education, and participated in the Lane Seminary debates with Theodore Weld in 1833; his statue is in Covington today.

—John P. Parker, enslaved in Virginia and Alabama, a trained foundry worker, who gained his freedom in 1845 and migrated to Jeffersonville, Ind., to New Albany, Ind., to Cincinnati, and eventually to Ripley, Ohio. He was chiefly responsible for transporting hundreds of runaway slaves across the Ohio River from Mason Co. to the Ohio Underground Railroad activists.

Blassingame, John W. *Slave Testimony: Two Centuries of Letters, Speeches, Interviews, and Autobiographies.* Baton Rouge: Louisiana State Univ. Press, 1977.

Coleman, J. Winston. *Slavery Times in Kentucky.* Chapel Hill: Univ. of North Carolina Press, 1940.

Collins, Richard H. *History of Kentucky.* Vol. 1. Covington, Ky.: Collins, 1882.

Fisk, Gen. Clinton B., to Maj. Gen. Oliver O. Howard, House Executive Document No. 70, 39th Cong., 1st sess., 1865–1866, p. 230.

Hudson, J. Blaine. *Encyclopedia of the Underground Railroad.* Jefferson, N.C.: McFarland, 2006.

——. *Fugitive Slaves and the Underground Railroad in the Kentucky Borderland.* Jefferson, N.C.: McFarland, 2002.

Lewin, H., ed. *The Lawyers and Lawmakers of Kentucky.* Chicago: Lewis, 1897.

Lucas, Marion B. *A History of Blacks in Kentucky.* Vol. 1, *From Slavery to Segregation, 1760–1891.* Frankfort: Kentucky Historical Society, 1992.

Miller, Carolyn R., comp. *African-American Records: Bracken County, Kentucky, 1997–1999.* Brooksville, Ky.: Bracken Co. Historical Society, 1999.

Works Projects Administration. *Slave Narratives: A Folk History of Slavery in the United States from Interviews with Former Slaves.* Vol. 7, *Kentucky Narratives.* Washington, D.C.: Federal Writer's Project of the WPA, 1941.

Wright, George C. *Racial Violence in Kentucky, 1865–1940.* Baton Rouge: Louisiana State Univ. Press, 1996.

Diane Perrine Coon

SLAVES IN NORTHERN KENTUCKY, 1840 TO 1860, AND FREEDMEN IN NORTHERN KENTUCKY, 1870

County	*1840*	*1850*	*1860*	*1870*
Boone	2,183	2,104	1,745	1,012
Bracken	819	840	750	636
Campbell	289	177	116	282
Carroll	731	949	1,045	540
Gallatin	604	704	708	690
Grant	348	532	696	509
Kenton	751	830	567	1,656
Mason	4,309	4,281	3,772	3,582
Owen	1,281	1,514	1,660	1,176
Pendleton	437	509	424	641
Robertson*				257
	11,752	12,443	11,483	10,981

*Robertson Co. was not established until 1867.

SLAVERY IN BOONE CO. Most Boone Co. farms in the 19th century had a handful of enslaved persons, who worked the fields in good weather and performed household tasks or honed their skills as coopers, wheel-makers, and blacksmiths after the growing season.

"Slavery," according to Jane Smiley, a present-day commentator on Harriet Beecher Stowe's book *Uncle Tom's Cabin*, "was an economic system dependent upon bankers" as well as on farmers and plantation owners. The rationale for enslavement ranged from biblical quotes to claims of white intellectual superiority to "simple economic interest and convenience." In Boone Co., the demand for slaves was sufficiently low that at times slaves were sold out of the county, often to markets that supplied the Deep South. But the economic system of slavery was a lively enterprise for many Boone Countians from the time of the county's formation in 1799 until the end of the **Civil War**. The assessed value of most adult slaves was between 10 and 20 times the value of an acre of land. Surnames of Boone Co. slaveholders include Brashear, Coleman, Dinsmore, Gaines, Johnson, Parker, and Riddell. Enslaved blacks comprised one-fifth to one-quarter of the county's population from 1799 to 1860. Free blacks represented a tiny minority. After the end of the Civil War, African Americans exited Boone Co. en masse.

Remote areas of Boone Co. such as Rabbit Hash and the North Bend Bottoms were prime areas for escape from bondage. Active **Underground Railroad** connections in Indiana and Ohio beckoned enslaved persons in Boone Co. The best-known fugitive slave story in Boone Co. is that of **Margaret Garner**, who was enslaved by Archibald Gaines of the Maplewood Farm, Richwood. She was the central character in the 20th-century novel and movie *Beloved*, and the *Margaret Garner Opera* played at Music Hall in Cincinnati during summer 2005. All three art forms have drawn attention to the tragic story of this pregnant enslaved mother of four who fled with her family on a frigid January night in 1856. The Garners tasted a few sweet hours of freedom in Cincinnati before the family was captured. Margaret slit the throat of her young daughter Mary and attempted to kill her other three children, declaring that she would rather see them dead than enslaved. Margaret did not hang for the murder of her child. Instead, she was remanded to the custody of Gaines, who sent Margaret and her husband to a plantation in the Deep South. Margaret died there in 1858.

On March 21, 2005, students from St. Joseph Academy in Walton dedicated a memorial to the Underground Railroad in Boone Co. The inscription remembers and honors "all the slaves in Boone Co., those who helped them, and the slaves' descendants." The memorial is the first of its kind in the county.

Boone Co. Heritage Education Curriculum. *River Born, Kentucky Bred*. Burlington, Ky.: Boone Co. Historic Preservation Review Board, 2001.

McNutt, Randy. "Boone Grows Big, Stays Small," *CE*, April 29, 2003, 2E.

Stowe, Harriet Beecher. *Uncle Tom's Cabin*. Ed. Jane Smiley. New York: Random House, 2001.

Tanner, Paul. *Slavery in Boone County (And Its Aftermath)*. Frankfort, Ky.: P. Tanner, 1986.

Yanuck, Julius. "The Garner Fugitive Slave Case," *Mississippi Valley Historical Review* 15, no. 1 (June 1953): 47–66.

Jannes W. Garbett

SLAVERY—THE KENTUCKY RAID (also known as the Cassopolis Outrage). Two large groups of enslaved people, altogether numbering at least 35, escaped from Kenton and Boone counties during spring 1847. The first party of 22 departed Saturday night, April 24; the second group followed a couple of weeks later. Aided by "conductors" of the **Underground Railroad,** both groups traveled north through Ohio and Indiana and on into Michigan. There, in the southwestern part of the state, they found refuge in rural Cass Co.

The fugitives from slavery spent the summer in Cass Co., living and working on farms owned by Quakers. They joined a growing black pioneer population that included free African Americans who had migrated to this Northern refuge site. Cass Co.'s abolitionist reputation also caught the attention of white Kentuckians, including several aggrieved slave owners in Boone and Kenton counties.

The slaveholders hired a spy to pursue their missing human "property." Around June 1847, the spy arrived in Michigan, posing as an abolitionist from Massachusetts seeking subscribers for antislavery periodicals. Using this guise, he traveled from farm to farm, talking with the locals and secretly creating a map detailing the fugitives' whereabouts. He then returned to Kentucky and issued his report. A posse was gathered, comprised of 22 slave owners and their agents. Fully armed, and with wagons equipped to transport captives back to Kentucky, the slave-catchers arrived in Cass Co. on August 20, 1847. In the early hours of that Friday morning, the posse split into smaller raiding parties and set out to capture fugitives simultaneously at four different farms. As dawn broke, the slave-catchers pounded on cabin doors and began their roundup. At some farms they captured entire families; at others, either a wife or a daughter escaped and sounded the alarm. As the alarm spread, the raiding parties attempted to rendezvous at the local mill with their 10 captives. The Kentuckians soon found themselves surrounded by a growing number of locals, both black and white, who were armed with guns, axes, hoes, straw-cutters, and even fence posts that they had hastily pulled out of the ground. The Kentuckians, in turn, brandished their guns and bowie knives. Violence was averted when the Kentuckians agreed to take their captives to the county courthouse and submit proof of their ownership claims to a judge.

The entourage of slave-hunters, captured fugitives, and determined locals marched off together to the courthouse in Cassopolis, the county seat. Word of the raid continued to spread over the course of their five-mile trek, and the number of Michiganders in the crowd swelled to 200 or 300. When they all arrived in town, 14 of the Kentuckians were arrested for attempted kidnapping, trespassing, and assault and battery. They also were served with a writ of habeas corpus, requiring that they produce the people they had abducted before the court. The Kentuckians posted bail and awaited trial.

The county's judge was unavailable, so the neighboring Berry Co. commissioner presided over the habeas corpus trial. Unbeknownst to the white Southerners, the commissioner was an abolitionist and a covert member of the Underground Railroad. When the Kentuckians appeared before him to prove their ownership claims, the commissioner refused each type of evidence they presented, such as bills of sale and power-of-attorney documents. Instead, he insisted that they produce Kentucky's statutes proving that slavery was legal in the state. Although the statutes clearly existed, the Kentuckians did not have them in their possession and the commissioner denied them time to obtain them. Consequently, he ruled that the captives should go free.

As soon as the captives and their families had left the county, all charges against the Kentuckians were dropped, in what Michiganders called "the Kentucky Raid." The Kentuckians, however, returned home, infuriated. They described their experience in the local newspapers as the "Cassopolis Outrage"—in which Northern abolitionists defied the nation's laws to help slaves escape. The slave owners and their allies pressured the U.S. Congress to pass a new fugitive slave law that would increase the penalties for helping slaves attain freedom. They also filed six lawsuits against the white abolitionists in Michigan, charging them with violating the Fugitive Slave Law of 1793. One lawsuit eventually went to trial in Detroit, in December 1850. Although the case ended with a hung jury, the defendants settled rather than face a second trial subjecting them to the new 1850 Fugitive Slave Act that had just been passed by Congress.

"The Cassopolis Outrage—the Rights of Slavery, Parts I–IV," *LVR*, October 15, 1847, 3; November 5, 1847, 1.

"Kidnapping by the Wholesale," *National Antislavery Standard,* November 4, 1847.

Rogers, Howard S. *History of Cass County, from 1825 to 1875.* Cassopolis, Mich.: Vigilant Book and Job Print, 1875.

Sanford, Joseph, and John Hatfield. Interviews in *The Refugee; or, The Narratives of Fugitive Slaves in Canada,* by Benjamin Drew. Boston: J. P. Jewett, 1856; reprint, Toronto: Prospero, 2000.

Sanford, Perry. "Out of Bondage: How Perry Sanford Escaped from Slavery: Thrilling Experience on His Way to Michigan," *Heritage Creek: A Journal of Local History* 9 (Winter 1999): 78–81.

Debian Marty

SLIP UP. This crossroads community is located along U.S. 62 in southwestern Mason Co., near Shannon and not far from the Robertson Co. boundary. It is within the Murphysville Precinct. At one time, Slip Up had a school, but it was consolidated into the Sardis School. The community also was once home to a mill. During the 1960s and 1970s, a popular news feature in the Maysville newspaper was entitled the *Slip Up News.* Only a store remains at the once busy crossroads. Local people used to say that they were going to "slip up" to the store, and thus the name Slip Up became attached to the community.

Calvert, Jean, and John Klee. *The Towns of Mason County: Their Past in Pictures.* Maysville, Ky.: Maysville and Mason Co. Library Historical and Scientific Association, ca. 1986.

SMITH, ALBERT CLARENCE, LIEUTENANT COLONEL (b. January 7, 1904, Monterey, Ky.; d. March 9, 1973, Fort Knox, Ky.). Albert C. Smith, a Kentucky representative and a veteran of World War II and the Korean War, was the only child of Evan Forest and Maude Karsner Smith. He enlisted in the U.S. Army in 1924 and served three years in Panama. He married Mary Etta Power on October 3, 1929, and they became the parents of one child, Etta Maud. Smith was employed by the Kentucky Highway Patrol. In 1935 he joined the Kentucky Army National Guard and served on active duty during the **flood of 1937** and during the Harlan coal strikes in 1939. On February 29, 1941, Smith's unit was federalized and designated Battery A, 103rd Separate Battalion Coast Artillery (anti-aircraft).

He served in the continental United States until June 1945, when he was ordered to the Far East, entering Japan with the Occupation Army as an assistant provost marshal in Tokyo. In 1948 he was reassigned as provost marshal to Fort Gordon, Ga. In November 1951, he was sent to Korea. From April 1953 to April 1954, Smith served as the provost marshal in Sasebo, Japan. When he retired in 1957 as a lieutenant colonel, he was serving as senior adviser to the Lexington, Ky., area U.S. Army Reserve. His decorations included the Bronze Star with Valor and the Army Commendation Medal. Upon retirement, he moved back to his family home on Cedar Creek in Owen Co., Ky., where he lived the rest of his life.

Smith served one term as a representative to the Kentucky legislature for Owen and Grant counties in 1960. He spearheaded the Korean Bonus Bill passed that year by the legislature. He was a service officer and commander at VFW Post 3119 in Owenton and also served as chairman of the Owen Co. American Red Cross Chapter. Smith died in 1973 and was buried in the Monterey Cemetery with full military honors.

Murphy, Margaret A. *"Looking Back": Our Smith Family History.* Frankfort, Ky.: Lynn, 1998.

Margaret A. Murphy

SMITH, GREEN CLAY, GENERAL (b. July 4, 1826, Richmond, Ky.; d. June 29, 1895, Washington, D.C.). A general, congressman, governor, and preacher, Green Clay Smith was a son of John Speed and Elizabeth Louis Clay Smith. At age 15 he enlisted in the army, where he served for a year as a 2nd lieutenant in the 1st Kentucky Cavalry during the **Mexican War**. On his return, he attended a preparatory school in Danville, Ky.; Transylvania University in Lexington, where he graduated in 1849; and the Lexington Law School in Lexington. He gained admittance to the bar in 1852.

In 1858 Smith moved to Covington, where he practiced law until the political unrest of 1860 occurred. At that time he ran for a seat in the Kentucky legislature and won election to the House of Representatives. After the **Civil War** broke out, Smith enlisted as a private in the Union Army, but once his previous service record was discovered, he was promoted to the rank of major. The following year he was promoted to colonel and sent into the field with the 4th Kentucky Cavalry. He pursued Confederate raider and fellow Kentuckian Gen. **John Hunt Morgan** through Kentucky and into Tennessee, where he helped to defeat Morgan at the Battle of Lebanon (Tenn.) on May 5, 1862. This action contributed to Smith's promotion to brigadier general the following month. He resigned his seat in the Kentucky legislature that August and ran for a seat in the U.S. Congress. A strict Unionist, he was elected by a small margin in a district sharply divided by Civil War politics. He won reelection in 1864.

After being soundly defeated when he next met Morgan in battle in 1863, Smith resigned his commission and focused on his work as a congressman. The army refused his resignation, instead promoting him to the rank of major general. In the U.S. Congress, Smith united with the other two strict Unionist congressmen from Kentucky, refusing to entertain a compromise with the South. This position eventually brought about a split in the Kentucky Democratic Party; it broke into factions based on loyalties to the North or the South. While in office, Smith also voted for controversial bills including the establishment of the **Freedmen's Bureau**.

In 1865 Smith resigned from his congressional seat in order to accept an appointment as territorial governor of Montana. He found the territory hopelessly in debt and harassed by the local American Indian tribes, but he went to work lobbying his former colleagues in the U.S. Congress for soldiers, weapons, and most importantly, money. During his short time as governor, he led the militia on the battlefield, put the territory firmly on the road to financial recovery, and introduced the first signs of eastern "civilization" in a rough-and-tumble western land.

On Smith's return to Kentucky, his life took an entirely different turn when he was ordained a Baptist minister. Smith pastored churches throughout Kentucky and is credited with starting many more. He was a popular preacher at revivals, where the oratorical skills he had sharpened in the U.S. Congress helped to enlist innumerable founding church members.

Smith made one more try at politics in 1876: he ran for president on the National Prohibition Party ticket. Receiving fewer than 10,000 votes, Smith gave up politics and returned to the quieter ministerial life. In 1890 he accepted a position at the Metropolitan Baptist Church in Washington, D.C., where he remained until his death on June 29, 1895. He was buried in Arlington National Cemetery.

Biographical Encyclopedia of Kentucky. Cincinnati: J. M. Armstrong, 1878.

Collins, Richard H. *History of Kentucky.* Vol. 1. Covington, Ky.: Collins, 1882.

Hood, James Larry. "For the Union: Kentucky's Unconditionalist Unionist Congressmen and the Development of the Republican Party in Kentucky, 1863–1865," *RKHS* 76 (July 1978): 197–215.

Hubbell, John T., and James W. Geary, ed. *Biographical Dictionary of the Union: Northern Leaders of the Civil War.* Westport, Conn.: Greenwood, 1995.

Kleber, John E., ed. *The Kentucky Encyclopedia.* Lexington: Univ. Press of Kentucky, 1992.

Reis, Jim. "Green Smith: A Man of Many Talents," *KP*, April 13, 1987, 4K.

Jennifer Gregory

SMITH, HERBERT LEE "HUB" (b. June 18, 1912, Claxon Ridge, Owen Co., Ky.; d. May 26, 1986, Owenton, Ky.). Herbert Lee Smith, a county sheriff and a hospital administrator, was the son of Elza and Susan Ora Smith. He married J. Ward Marston on June 4, 1932, and they had one child, Johnny Marston Smith. Hub Smith was a farmer in Owen Co. In 1942 he began his political career as deputy sheriff of Owen Co. and in 1948 became the high sheriff. He was appointed county Democratic chairman and accepted the position of administrative assistant to the Kentucky commissioner of finance in 1954. In February 1955, Smith was appointed state director of personnel. He was named the administrator of the Owen Co. Memorial Hospital (see **New Horizons Medical Center**) in 1956 and continued in that position for 15 years. Smith was also a director of the Peoples Bank and Trust Company in Owenton for 30 years and, for four years, director of the Burley Tobacco Association. When his health failed, he retired on December 30, 1971, and lived in Owen Co. until his death at age 74. He was buried at the Monterey Cemetery in Monterey.

"Herbert 'Hub' Smith Remembered," *Owenton (Ky.) News-Herald*, June 5, 1986, 1.

Murphy, Margaret Alice, and Lela Maude Hawkins. *The History of Historic Old Cedar Baptist Church and Community, 1816–2004*. Frankfort, Ky.: Lynn, 2004.

Margaret A. Murphy

SMITH, MORGAN LEWIS, BRIGADIER GENERAL (b. 1822, New York; d. December 28, 1874, Jersey City, N.J.). **Civil War** veteran Morgan Smith left home at age 21 and taught school in Indiana. He then joined the U.S. Army and from 1845 through 1850 served as a sergeant and drill instructor at the **Newport Barracks** in Newport, Ky., using the alias of Mortimer L. Sanford. From 1850 until after the Civil War began, he lived on Saratoga St. in Newport while working as an Ohio River steamboat agent. During the war Smith led the 8th Missouri Volunteers in combat at Shiloh, at Vicksburg, and in several other engagements and was severely wounded. Gen. William T. Sherman said of him: "He was one of the bravest men in action I ever knew." In 1866 U.S. President Andrew Johnson (1865–1869) appointed Smith U.S. consul in Honolulu, Hawaii. Returning in 1868, Smith was employed in Washington, D.C., dealing with claims against the government and contracting for mail routes. He also worked for a building association. Smith died while visiting in Jersey City, N.J., in 1874 and was buried with full military honors at Arlington National Cemetery in Arlington, Va. He was the older brother of U.S. General Giles A. Smith. Morgan Smith was one of the many nationally famous people who passed through Newport Barracks and resided in Northern Kentucky.

Donnelly, Joseph L. *Newport Barracks: Kentucky's Forgotten Military Installation*. Covington, Ky.: Kenton Co. Historical Society, 1999.

Virtualology.com. "Morgan Smith." www.famousamericans.net (accessed June 25, 2007).

SMITH, SAWYER A. (b. April 9, 1883, Barbourville, Ky.; d. November 3, 1969, Park Hills, Ky.). Lawyer and politician Sawyer A. Smith was the son of George W. and Sarah McKinney Smith. Sawyer's early education was at the Barbourville Baptist Institute in Barbourville. He earned his BA from Cumberland College at Williamsburg. On December 29, 1913, he married a classmate, Effie Barton. Smith taught in the Knox Co. schools for five years, then left teaching, returned to school, and earned a law degree from Valparaiso University, Valparaiso, Ind. He began his legal career by forming a partnership with attorney Flem D. Sampson, who later became governor of Kentucky (1927–1931).

Smith moved to Northern Kentucky, where he soon earned a reputation as one of the region's best defense attorneys. He entered politics in 1908 and was elected as a Republican to the Kentucky legislature, where he served for two years. President Warren G. Harding (1921–1923) appointed Smith Assistant U.S. Attorney for the eastern district of Kentucky, a continuing under the administrations of presidents Calvin Coolidge (1923–1929) and Herbert Hoover (1929–1933). On August 31, 1933, Smith resigned and returned to his law practice. His most publicized case was his defense of 16-year-old Joan Kiger, who had been charged with the murders of her father, Carl Kiger (Covington's vice mayor), and her six-year-old brother, Jerry. Smith won an acquittal by arguing that Joan was having a nightmare at the time of the killings and therefore could not be held responsible for the deaths. Smith died in 1969 at age 86 in the St. Charles Care Center, Fort Wright, and was buried in the Forest Lawn Cemetery in Erlanger.

"Honored," *KP*, April 5, 1930, 4.

"Post Editorial Read," *KP*, February 10, 1930, 4.

Reis, Jim. "A Distinguished Legal Career," *KP*, October 3, 1994, 4K.

"Schoolday Romance Ends in Marriage," *KP*, December 30, 1913, 10.

Tapp, Hamilton. *Kentucky Lives*. Hopkinsville, Ky.: Historical Record Association, 1966.

SNOW'S POND. During the September 1862 invasion of Northern Kentucky by the Confederate Army, one of the two **Civil War** skirmishes to take place in Boone Co. occurred at Snow's Pond. The site is located roughly along the Old Lexington Pk. (see **Covington and Lexington Turnpike**) between Richwood and Walton, seven miles south of Florence, Ky. The pike is parallel to modern U.S. 25 (see **Dixie Highway**). There, on September 17, 1862, about 100 Confederate troops under the command of Col. Basil Duke of the 2nd Kentucky Cavalry were encamped at Snow's Pond and were attacked by a Union cavalry force. One Union and five Confederate soldiers were killed, and one Union and seven Confederate soldiers were wounded. Civilian Larkin Vaughn, a local farmer, was killed by a stray bullet. Duke's men captured 49 Union soldiers, who were marched off to Falmouth and later were exchanged.

The Union Army camped at Snow's Pond for three weeks afterward. The Confederates had left the carcasses of 13 dead mules in the water. The Union Army eventually discovered these remains, which explained why some of the federals camped at the pond had become sick. In recent years the Snow's Pond site has been a hub of metal-detecting and artifact-hunting. Several items have been found, mainly lead bullets. On May 14, 1999, a Kentucky Historical Marker was placed at the site of Snow's Pond, on land held by the Dixon family since the 1870s.

Dixon, Daniel F. *Snow's Pond: The Forgotten Civil War Skirmish in Boone County, Kentucky's Past*. Mount Vernon, Ind.: Windmill, 1999.

Goetz, Kristina. "Civil War Field Marked," *KE*, August 9, 1999, C1.

Rouse, Jack. *The Civil War in Boone County*. Mount Vernon, Ind.: Windmill, 1996.

SNYDER, MARION GENE (b. January 26, 1928, Louisville, Ky.; d. February 16, 2007, Naples, Fla.). Marion Gene Snyder was a real estate broker, a homebuilder, and, for many years, a Republican member of the U.S. House of Representatives. His parents were Marion Gustavus and Lois E. Snyder. Gene attended Louisville public schools and graduated from Louisville's duPont Manual High. He earned both his LLB and JD degrees from the Jefferson School of Law (now part of the University of Louisville) in 1950 and set up his law practice in Louisville. In 1961 Snyder married Mary Louise Hodges, and they had one son, Mark. The couple divorced in 1973.

Snyder entered politics in 1954 and served as Jeffersontown city attorney for four years and as Jefferson Co. magistrate for the next four. He served in the U.S. House of Representatives from 1963 to 1965 (January–January) but was defeated when he ran for reelection in 1964. In 1966 he won the seat back and held it from January 1967 until January 1987. During his tenure in the U.S. Congress, he was instrumental in gaining approval for many projects in his home state, including the construction of Northern Kentucky University in Campbell Co. and the Snyder Freeway in Louisville. He worked tirelessly for a Licking River dam at Falmouth but was unsuccessful in obtaining funds for it. He retired from politics in 1986 and returned to his Oldham Co. farm.

He married his second wife, Patricia Creighton Robertson, on April 10, 1973, and they became the parents of two children, Chris and Ginger. Snyder died in Naples, Fla., at age 79 and was buried in the Floydsburg Cemetery in Oldham Co., Ky.

Biographical Directory of the United States Congress. "Snyder, Marion Gene." http://bioguide.congress.gov (accessed February 24, 2007).

"Former Congressman Gene Snyder Dies," *CJ*, February 17, 2007, 1.

Kleber, John E., ed. *The Kentucky Encyclopedia*. Lexington: Univ. Press of Kentucky, 1992.

SOCIALIST PARTY. The Socialist Party was fairly strong in Northern Kentucky in the late 19th and early 20th centuries. Branches existed in Covington, Latonia, Ludlow, Newport, and other urban areas; the party drew its largest support from such places. Immigrants working in factories in Cincinnati and Northern Kentucky tended to accept Socialist views, and many of them joined the party.

The Socialist Party made inroads in politics, although in Northern Kentucky, unlike other regions of the country, no party member was elected to any major political office. The socially progressive views of the party struck a chord with many Northern Kentuckians, and as a result many political races were affected by these views. In the 1904 elections in Kenton Co., the Socialist Party received a significant portion of votes for a minority party. Although it never came close to defeating candidates from the two major parties, it received more votes than any of the other small parties, such as the People's Party or the Prohibition Party.

In 1904–1905, Eugene Victor Debs, the perennial Socialist presidential candidate, spoke to a following at the Ludlow Lagoon (see **Lagoon Amusement Park**), to a gathering at Clark's Grove in Dayton, Ky., and before a crowd of 500 in Covington's Congress Hall Auditorium. The Socialist Party in Northern Kentucky had many leaders of its own. Rev. **Thomas McGrady** (1863–1907) was a Roman Catholic priest serving for years at St. Anthony Church in Bellevue, Ky. A nationally known Socialist author and speaker, he was in conflict with the political views of the Roman Catholic Church. In 1902 he resigned from the priesthood, refusing to comply with an ultimatum issued by Bishop **Camillus Paul Maes** (1846–1915) ordering him to retract his views and statements. It was reported that many of his parishioners wept at his departure. He remained in Bellevue for a short while before moving to San Francisco, where he practiced law. Because of his speaking abilities, McGrady was a conspicuous figure at Socialist conventions. Despite his disagreement with the church, he received the last rites and died as a member of the Roman Catholic Church.

Another local Socialist figure was **Walter Lanfersiek** (1873–1962), a Newport attorney who ran unsuccessfully for governor of Kentucky in 1911. Lanfersiek was active in the Socialist Party and in 1913 was elected executive secretary of the national party. Lanfersiek's wife, Pearl A. Blanchard Lanfersiek, was also active in the party; in 1912 she was one of three Socialist candidates for seats on the Newport school commission. Pearl Lanfersiek and fellow Socialists Gussie Balser and Jacob Raphaelson pledged themselves to accomplish progressive measures, some of them unheard of at the time, such as these: free textbooks, playgrounds and physical education instructors, night schools for working children and adults, a "penny lunch," better pay for teachers, equal pay for equal work regardless of gender, the right to present grievances, and free kindergartens.

The Bolshevik Revolution in Russia and the resulting "Red Scare" in the United States did a great deal of damage to the Socialist Party in Northern Kentucky and throughout the nation. Although the party continued to put forth candidates for many elections, the candidates often fell victim to mob violence and assault. One Socialist Party member who suffered in the backlash against socialism was Northern Kentuckian John Thobe. Thobe was a candidate for Kentucky lieutenant governor when antisocialist groups began to intimidate him. At a Socialist meeting in Covington in November 1919, a group of soldiers, reportedly just returned from **World War I**, forced Thobe to stop speaking by threats of violence. Later another group of soldiers made a bonfire of Socialist literature and also burned the box upon which Thobe was speaking. In addition, Socialist documents belonging to Thobe were stolen, possibly by the same group that had forced him to stop speaking. In September 1924, after making a political speech, Thobe was ambushed and beaten while walking along 16th St. in Covington. He was struck three times on the head with an iron pipe. His assailant, according to witnesses, leaped into a waiting automobile and fled. By then the Socialist Party was in decline and never again rose to the level of influence it had held during the first two decades of the 20th century.

"Father M'Grady Dies in Frisco," *KP*, November 27, 1907, 2.
"Lanfersiek Lands Socialist Office," *KP*, May 16, 1913, 5.
"Newport Socialists Have Progressive School Ticket," *KP*, August 14, 1912, 3.
"Socialist Was Compelled to Stop Speaking," *KTS*, November 14, 1919, 30.
"They Got a Big Vote," *KP*, November 10, 1904, 1.
"Thobe Is Beaten," *KP*, September 15, 1924, 1.
"Two Packages of Socialist Papers Gone," *KTS*, November 19, 1919, 27.

Rob Farrell

SOCIETY OF ST. VINCENT DE PAUL. The Society of St. Vincent de Paul operates thrift stores and a free pharmacy, as well as other services, for the poor of Northern Kentucky. The society is named for a 17th-century French saint of the Roman Catholic Church. As a priest, Vincent de Paul devoted himself to helping the poor and founded the Confraternity of Charity for women. He founded several Vincentian organizations, but the one he founded for men did not last. A young college student in Paris, France, Frederick Ozanam, started the current Society of St. Vincent de Paul for men in 1833, to assist the poor in Christian charity and for the spiritual good of its members. This new Catholic lay society was approved by the Vatican and soon spread throughout Europe. The Society of St. Vincent de Paul was first accepted in St. Louis, Mo., in 1845 and, with the blessing of America's Catholic bishops, rapidly spread across the nation. George A. Carrell, the first bishop of the Diocese of Covington (see **Roman Catholics**), welcomed it to his diocese in the 1860s.

In the structure of the society, local parish conferences are the primary division. Over these is the Diocese of Covington Council, which in turn is part of the Mideast regional conference. All of the regional councils are part of the National Council of the United States, Society of St. Vincent de Paul Inc. All of the conferences worldwide are united under the Council-General. Many parishes within the Diocese of Covington formed their own conferences. The various Northern Kentucky Society of St. Vincent de Paul conferences were linked together under the Particular Council of Covington, which was established on October 29, 1923. Part of the mission of the society is to serve anyone in need without regard to color, race, creed, or origin. Parish conferences work on the local level, accepting monetary donations placed in offering boxes at church doors and donations of food and clothing. Members of the society then allocate items to those

St. Vincent de Paul store, Greenup St., Covington, in 1946. *Front row:* Margaret Grumbie and Alma Schwede; *back row:* Paul Ison, Andy Lonneman, Charlie Burman, and Ed Miller.

who call for assistance after members make a home visit to assess needs. Members also visit the sick and elderly in nursing homes and hospitals.

One popular feature of the Society of St. Vincent de Paul's charitable outreach is its stores, or salvage bureaus as they were designated originally, which accept donations from anyone and sell salvageable items at low prices. At the instigation of **William T. Mulloy**, bishop of the Diocese of Covington, the first two St. Vincent de Paul stores in Northern Kentucky were opened in Covington and in Newport in 1946. Both stores were under the direction of Andrew Lonneman. Stores were opened later in Dayton and Crescent Springs. The Crescent Springs location houses the warehouse that serves Northern Kentucky. The society's trucks travel to homes locally to pick up donations of larger items, such as furniture and appliances. The society even sponsors a used-car program for donated automobiles still in working condition. The society also conducts a coat giveaway for students and others in need of a warm coat. In 2002 the diocesan council began a pharmacy program. The pharmacy, located at the Crescent Springs office, dispenses donated sample medicines from doctors or pharmacies to fill prescriptions for persons in need. In 2008 the charitable pharmacy operation was officially renamed Faith Community Pharmacy.

"Free Pharmacy Plan: Grow," *KP*, September 17, 2002, 1K.
Laukonis, Kathryn. "St. Vincent De Paul Society: Followers of Charity-Saint Active for Diocesan Needy," *Messenger*, July 17, 1955, 1A.
Rules of the Society of St. Vincent de Paul, and Indulgences Granted by the Sovereign Pontiffs. New York: Superior Council, 1909.
Stapleton, Joe. "St. Vincent de Paul Expands Activity," *Messenger*, December 1946, 2.
"Society of St. Vincent de Paul, Covington." www.svdpcovington.org (accessed June 24, 2008).
"St. Vincent de Paul Society Celebrates 160 Years," *Messenger*, April 30, 1993, 8.

Thomas S. Ward

SOMERSET HALL. William Butler Kenner, the builder of Somerset Hall, and his brother George Kenner were two of the four sons of Louisiana plantation owners William and Mary Minor Kenner (see **Kenner Family**). The family lived in luxury, as did most other families of the southern antebellum elite. Their 2,200-acre Louisiana plantation, called Ashland, was often the scene of private balls, dinner parties, and horse races for their aristocratic friends. This Ashland was named after Henry Clay's estate in Lexington, Ky. Much of the Kenner land in Louisiana later became part of the city of Kenner, La., where the New Orleans International Airport is now located. William Butler and George Kenner were privately tutored, receiving the typical southern classical education. Afterward they traveled extensively. While visiting Cincinnati, they met many members of the city's social elite, including two sisters, Ruhamah and Charlotte Riske, who were half sisters of Israel Ludlow Jr. George married Charlotte and William Butler married Rumalah. In 1840 George and Charlotte Kenner bought **Elmwood Hall** and some surrounding acreage from Israel Ludlow Jr. The family lived most of the year in Louisiana but used the Ludlow home as a summer retreat from the oppressive heat and diseases of the Deep South.

William Butler Kenner purchased nine acres of land near Elmwood Hall from his brother George in 1845, and he and his wife built Somerset Hall there, shortly after the purchase. Their home was constructed as an elaborate lodge, with the best materials and architectural designing available at the time. Somerset Hall has a 120-foot-long porch, which is said to have been the longest in Kentucky. Despite the cost and elaborate planning for his home, William Kenner did not retain ownership long. He became discouraged after many of his slaves escaped to freedom across the Ohio River. Some have said that Somerset Hall later served as an important stop on the **Underground Railroad**. William Butler Kenner died of yellow fever in 1853, in New Orleans. In 1852 Somerset Hall was sold to Thomas Keevan, who sold it in 1854 to Cincinnati balloonist **Richard Clayton**. Henry Jenkins, a wealthy Cincinnati jeweler, purchased the house in in 1862. In 1875 **A. B. Closson Jr.**, a partner in Closson's Art and Home Furnishings Store in Cincinnati, purchased Somerset Hall for his residence. Several generations of the Closson family lived in the house until 1925, when it was sold for use as a Masonic Lodge (see **Masons**).

In December 1996, Stephen and Paula Chapman purchased Somerset Hall from the Masons. They have completely remodeled the house, attempting to return it to its original splendor. However, in order to make the home a comfortable dwelling, the Chapmans have installed two furnaces, added air conditioning, installed modern wiring, and added modern kitchens and bathrooms. The Chapmans have indicated that they may eventually use the house as it was originally intended, by spending their winters in the South (Florida) and their summers at Somerset Hall.

"How the City of Ludlow Just Missed," *KP*, September 6, 1925, 8.
"Ludlow," *KP*, February 22, 1995, 1KK–2KK.
Marsh, Betsa. "A Legend in Ludlow," *Cincinnati Magazine*, January 2003, 93–96.
"Summer Home, Closson House, now Masonic Lodge," *Ludlow News Enterprise*, January 25, 1973, 1.

SOUTHBANK PARTNERS. Founded as a Kentucky nonprofit organization in 1997, Southbank Partners serves as a coordinating body for the redevelopment of the core areas of Campbell and Kenton counties. The desire for a convention center in Covington was the original impetus for this organization. The Covington Business Council, along with Jim Huff, Chris Mehling, and Wally Pagan, promoted the idea. It was a contentious issue because the Drawbridge Inn supported an alternate plan for a convention center in the Fort Mitchell area. During a 1995 special session of the Kentucky legislature, the State of Kentucky awarded $40 million for the construction of a convention center in Covington. It was funded in 1996 and opened in November 1998.

The question arose, What would the conventioneers do after they arrived? While the existing RiverCenter and the restaurants were nice, there were not enough area attractions to support the convention industry. Consequently, Southbank organizers felt a need to expand their vision.

The original Southbank founders were Ray Beil, president of EGC Construction; Paul Knue, editor of the ***Kentucky Post;*** Roger Peterman from the law firm of Peck, Shaffer & Williams L.L.P.; and Stephen C. Schatteman, president of PNC Bank of Northern Kentucky. Ray Beil, who had just returned from Paris with its famous Left Bank, suggested the name Southbank. About a year later, Wally Pagan became president of the organization.

The cities of Newport and Covington were attracted to the idea and joined, and then the City of Bellevue petitioned to become a member of Southbank Partners. A great deal of time was spent preparing development strategies such as the renovation of the **L&N Bridge** as a pedestrian link named Riverwalk, between Newport and Cincinnati, and the revitalization of historic Main Street areas. Many of the ideas were the consequences of the vision of **Forward Quest/Vision 2015**.

The Southbank goal of developing partnerships within Northern Kentucky began to be reached when the **Transit Authority of Northern Kentucky** (TANK) helped create the Southbank Shuttle in 1999. The Southbank Shuttle, subsidized by TANK, is the first real inner-city connector between Cincinnati, Covington, Newport, and Bellevue. Although there was initial resistance from Cincinnati, eventually it became apparent that the traffic went both ways and benefited all.

Southbank Partners was also involved in the creation of the **Millennium Monument World Peace Bell**, the world's largest swinging bell. It was cast in Nantes, France, in 1998, installed in Newport, and rung in 2000. This was part of the Millennium Monument project, which was to include the Millennium Tower and a park between **Newport-on-the-Levee** and the bell. Neither of those projects was completed, although two-thirds of the $120 million needed was obtained.

The next project was modeled after a project in Chattanooga, Tenn., that was centered on an aquarium and the 107-year-old Walnut St. Bridge over the Tennessee River. There the organization known as RiverValley Partners worked to convert the bridge into a pedestrian bridge linking sections of Chattanooga. About that time the **L&N Bridge** in Newport was scheduled for demolition and the Kentucky Department of Transportation was ready to let demolition bids. In 2000, Representative Jim Callahan led the effort to save the bridge on the House side of the Kentucky legislature. As majority caucus leader, he was close to the governor; with the support of the Northern Kentucky delegation, he was able to obtain $4 million to rejuvenate the bridge. The money budgeted for demolition was used instead to save it.

A significant portion of the funds was used for a structural study, because a pedestrian bridge actually has a larger load factor than a vehicular bridge. There is more weight per square foot with people. Planning, including a paint analysis, took more than two years. Lead paint was removed by pressure washing, and a coat of purple epoxy paint was applied. At first, it was thought the bridge might be called the Barney Bridge because of its color, but after Wally Pagan developed the alliterative name Purple People Bridge, that became the preferred name. The operation of the bridge was formalized in 2003 in the incorporation of the Newport Southbank Bridge Company, a partnership between the City of Newport and Southbank Partners. The bridge has now become a pedestrian link used by thousands of people. During Tall Stacks 2006, more than 150,000 people crossed the bridge.

In 2004 a creative use for the bridge was proposed. Dennis Spiegel developed a feasibility study for Thom Jackson that was presented to the Newport Southbank Bridge Company: the idea was to build a bridge climb. The company leased the climbing rights to help cover the constant bridge operating expenses, and eventually Dennis Spiegel bought the rights to the project. When the Purple People Bridge Climb was opened in 2006, it was first climbing bridge in the Northern Hemisphere; at that time Auckland, New Zealand, and Sydney and Brisbane in Australia were the only other places in the world that had climbing bridges; however, the Purple People Bridge Climb closed in 2007 due to lack of patronage.

Southbank Partners has had a role in the creation of **Newport-on-the-Levee**, assisting with the tax credit for Hofbrauhaus Newport and with condo developments in both Bellevue and Newport. It obtains its own funding from city and county funds and through a contract with **Northern Kentucky Tri-ED**, whereby it promotes development in the inner-city areas.

Cities do not always have the development staff they need, and the continuity, expertise, and collaborative spirit that Southbank Partners provides enables projects to move forward. Southbank Partners is concerned with economic development in Covington, Newport, and Bellevue and assists with matters of public policy in Ludlow, Dayton, and Fort Thomas. Since there are many areas of common ground among those cities, the city managers of Newport and Covington regularly meet with the city administrators of Bellevue, Dayton, Fort Thomas, and Ludlow under the aegis of Southbank Partners to discuss new projects, such as a river walk along Bellevue, Newport, and Covington and the $800 million Ovation development in Newport. Bill Scheyer succeeded Wally Pagan as president in 2008.

McNair, James. "Bridge-Climb Sale Lawsuit Tossed Out," *KE*, February 27, 2007, 10A.

Pagan, Wally. Interview by Bob Stevie, November 26, 2006, Newport, Ky.

Robert W. Stevie

SOUTHERN RAILWAY. The Southern Railway (SR) is a predecessor of the **Norfolk Southern Railway**, one of the two major railroad systems operating in the Northern Kentucky region today. In 1894 the SR was founded by combining the assets of the bankrupt Richmond and Danville Railroad and the East Tennessee, Virginia and Georgia Railroad (ETV&G) to form a new viable railroad. The SR ran its locomotives over the **Cincinnati Southern** rail lines through its control of the Cincinnati, New Orleans, and Texas Pacific Railroad. The SR, in acquiring the ETV&G, came into possession of the successor of the **Cincinnati and Charleston Railroad**. Thus, with the formation of the SR, the connecting railroad between Cincinnati and Charleston, S.C., finally became a reality. The SR was merged with Norfolk and Western (N&W) in 1982 to form the Norfolk Southern Railroad.

Davis, Burke. *The Southern Railway.* Chapel Hill: Univ. of North Carolina Press, 1985.

Drury, George H. *The Train Watcher's Guide to North American Railroads.* Waukesha, Wis.: Kalmbach Books, 1992.

The Historical Guide to North American Railroads. 2nd ed. Waukesha, Wis.: Kalmbach Books, 2000.

Charles H. Bogart

SOUTHGATE. Southgate, named for the prominent Southgate family who owned much of the town's land, is a city of nearly 3,500 residents. Located in the northeastern section of Campbell Co., it is one mile south of Newport. **Richard Southgate** settled in the Southgate area in 1795. The town was laid out in 1896 and incorporated in 1907. The police department was started in 1907, and the fire department followed in 1909.

The 1883 Lake atlas shows slaughterhouses, greenhouses, a saloon, and the Kentucky House as businesses in operation in Southgate at that time. The city is home to **Evergreen Cemetery**. Begun in 1847, this is the largest cemetery in Campbell Co. Most of an early Newport "burying ground" was transferred to the cemetery, because Newport needed more land for businesses and housing during the 1840s. The **Civil War** came to Southgate in the form of earthwork fortifications, and a fortification known Battery Shaler was built in Evergreen Cemetery (see **Civil War Fortifications**).

The Southgate School system, which began in 1901, is one of the smallest in Kentucky (see **Southgate Independent Schools**). The city once was home to the famous Two-Mile House and the Heidelberg Inn. Where the latter once stood is now the site of the **St. Therese Catholic Church** and school. Moock Rd., which borders the south side of the cemetery running west to Wilder, is named for George Moock, a longtime local dairy operator who resided and operated his business on properties adjoining the road.

By far the most famous place in Southgate was the **Beverly Hills Supper Club**. Opened in 1936, it was billed as the "showplace of the nation." Members of an organized crime family reportedly took the club over during the 1940s, and the nation's most famous performers and performance acts of the 1940s, 1950s, and 1960s came there to entertain. Things changed on the night of May 28, 1977. A fire broke out, and before it ended 165 people had died.

Southgate today boasts new homes, apartments, and condominiums. A new city building and community center opened in 1994. I-275 and I-471 (see **Expressways**) are located nearby. In 2000 the city had a population of 3,472.

An Atlas of Boone, Kenton, and Campbell Counties, Kentucky. Philadelphia: D. J. Lake, 1883.

Campbell Co. Historical Society. *Campbell County, Kentucky, 200 Years, 1794–1994.* Alexandria, Ky.: Campbell Co. Historical Society, 1994.

Kleber, John E., ed. *The Kentucky Encyclopedia.* Lexington: Univ. Press of Kentucky, 1992.

U.S. Census Bureau. www.census.gov/ (accessed April 28, 2007).

Kenneth A. Reis

SOUTHGATE, LOUISE (b. February 20, 1857, Walton; Ky.; d. August 15, 1941, Bracht Station, Ky.). Louise Southgate, a physician, was born to parents from prominent families of Campbell and Kenton counties. Her great-grandfather, **Thomas Kennedy**, owned much of the land in early Covington, and her grandfather was George Maris Southgate. Louise was the daughter of Dr. Bernard H. and Eleanor Fleming Southgate. In 1871 both of her parents died in a cholera epidemic, and Louise and her siblings moved to their Aunt Nancy Kennedy's home at 124 Garrard St., Covington.

Southgate attended the Western Female Seminary in Oxford, Ohio, and the Women's Medical College of Cincinnati, where she graduated in 1893. She continued her education by attending lectures in Vienna, Austria, and at the Pasteur Institute in Paris, France. There she became a firm believer in the germ theory of disease. Returning to Covington, she opened a medical practice and became known to family, friends, and patients as Dr. Louise; in 1902 her office was located at 107 W. Fourth St. Southgate traveled to the Hindman Settlement School in rural Knott Co., Ky., in summer 1905, to volunteer her services there. Back in Covington, she and the Women's Emergency Club of Covington assisted the school in its fundraising efforts.

Southgate purchased, in 1909, the old stone home of Thomas Kennedy on Riverside Dr. in Covington, as well as her deceased Aunt Nancy's house on Garrard St. She lived in the latter stately Greek Revival home with her sister Virginia, a teacher in the Cincinnati Public Schools. She also moved her medical practice to the Garrard St. house. She offered the old stone Kennedy home to the City of Covington; when the city declined, she had the house demolished. The **George Rogers Clark** Park on Riverside Dr. now occupies the site of the former Kennedy homestead.

Southgate was actively involved with the Cincinnati Women's Club, the Equal Suffrage Club (see **Women's Suffrage**), and the Kentucky Federation of Women's Clubs. She was also cofounder of the Central Suffrage Committee of Hamilton Co., Ohio, and president of the Pioneer Woman's Suffrage Association. In 1910 she spoke at the Kentucky Equal Rights Association state convention in Covington on the topic "The Sisterhood of Women." She helped rid the city of its unsavory and notorious poolrooms and also initiated the practice of conducting physical examinations for schoolchildren in Covington. Southgate was an active member of the former **Booth Memorial Hospital** and its auxiliary and a member of the American Medical Association.

In 1930, a year after the death of her sister Virginia, Southgate retired from medical practice. Following a long illness, she died in 1941 at age 84 at the home of her sister Eleanor Green. Services were held at the Madison Ave. Presbyterian Church, and her cremated remains were buried in Linden Grove Cemetery in Covington. In recognition of Southgate's medical services to Northern Kentucky, the **St. Luke Hospitals** named one of their service facilities the Louise Southgate Women's Center in 1990.

"The Club a School for Suffrage," *KP,* August 16, 1941.

Kentucky Death Certificate No. 20333, for the year 1941.

Mueller, Jan. "Dr. Louise Southgate," *JKS* 21 (September 2004): 144–54.

Russell, Steven. "Area's First Woman Doctor Believed in Women's Rights," *Dixie News,* January 28, 1993, 8.

Betty Maddox Daniels

SOUTHGATE, RICHARD (b. January 23, 1774, New York City; d. July 24, 1857, Newport, Ky.). Richard Southgate was the son of Capt. Wright and Mary Lush Southgate. He received his bachelor's degree from William and Mary College in Virginia and his law degree in Albany, N.Y. He arrived in Newport about 1795 and soon became a distinguished attorney. On July 10, 1799, he married Ann Winston Hinde (known as Nancy), daughter of Dr. **Thomas Hinde**, the renowned physician.

Richard and Ann Southgate had eight children. He was a very generous father and gave a house to each of his children when they married. His daughter Ann married Dr. **Nathaniel Burger Shaler**, and they had a famous son named **Nathaniel Southgate Shaler**, who was said to be the favorite grandson of Richard Southgate. Richard wanted his grandson to have a superior education, so he hired a private tutor for the boy's early training and then sent him to study at Harvard University in Cambridge, Mass. After graduating, Nathaniel Southgate Shaler became a professor of geology and paleontology at Harvard University, a position he held for life, and also the author of many books. One of them, his autobiography, is a source of much information about the Southgate family.

In 1814 Richard Southgate used labor provided by British **War of 1812** prisoners from the **Newport Barracks** to build his magnificent home, which still stands at 24 E. Third St. in Newport (the **Southgate House**). Many of the socially elite of that era, including Henry Clay, James Polk, and Zachary Taylor, were known to have visited the home. In 1803 Richard Southgate was elected to the Kentucky House of Representatives, and in 1817 he was elected a state senator, an office he held until 1833. In addition to being a very successful lawyer and politician, Richard Southgate also owned vast amounts of real estate and was one of the wealthiest men in the state. For many years his family operated a well-known health resort called Southgate's Mineral Wells, which historians believe was located between Evergreen Ave. and the Alexandria Pk. in Southgate. Richard Southgate died in 1857 and was buried in Evergreen Cemetery in the city of Southgate. The name Southgate was given to the family in earlier generations because they were the keepers of the south gate into London, England, when it was a walled city.

Biographical Encyclopedia of Kentucky. Cincinnati: J. M. Armstrong, 1878.

Collins, Richard H. *History of Kentucky.* Vol. 1. Covington, Ky.: Collins, 1882.

Shaler, Nathaniel Southgate. *Autobiography of Nathaniel Southgate Shaler.* Boston: Houghlin Mifflin, 1908.

Wessling, Jack. *Early History of Campbell County, Kentucky.* Alexandria, Ky.: Privately published, 1997.

Jack Wessling

SOUTHGATE, WILLIAM WRIGHT (b. November 22, 1800, Newport, Ky.; d. December 26, 1844, Covington, Ky.). William Wright Southgate, a distinguished lawyer and politician, was the son of lawyer and businessman **Richard Southgate** and Ann Winston Hinde Southgate. William's early education was by tutors and in private schools. He received his degree from Transylvania College in Lexington and then moved to Covington, where he studied law and was admitted to the bar in 1821. Southgate set up his first law practice in Lexington. He married Adliza Keene in 1823, and they had thirteen children. William Southgate purchased the **Gano-Southgate House** in Covington in 1825, adding a Greek Revival wing in 1835. He served as a prosecuting attorney from 1825 to 1827 and as a state representative from 1828 to 1840. After leaving politics, he returned to Covington and resumed the practice of law. In 1844 he served as a presidential elector for the Whig candidate Henry Clay. He died a young man and was buried in the Linden Grove Cemetery in Covington.

Johnson, E. Polk. *History of Kentucky and Kentuckians.* Vol. 2. Chicago: Lewis, 1912.

Langsam, Walter E. *Great Houses of the Queen City.* Cincinnati: Cincinnati Historical Society, 1997.

Wessling, Jack. *Early History of Campbell County.* Alexandria, Ky.: Self-published, 1997.

William Wright Southgate.

SOUTHGATE HOUSE. Located at 24 E. Third St., Newport, the Southgate House (also known as the Southgate-Parker-Maddux House and the Knights of Columbus Hall) is one of the city's oldest and most historically significant antebellum structures. Sometime between 1814 and 1821, the two-story house was erected for **Richard Southgate**. According to local tradition, the mansion was at least partially constructed by British prisoners from the **War of 1812** who were being held at the nearby **Newport Barracks**.

For Southgate, who was wealthy, influential, and socially prominent, both locally and nationally, the Newport mansion provided an elegant backdrop for lavish entertaining and also served as an island of civility that drew affluent visitors from all parts of the state and the nation. Tradition has placed many distinguished persons within its walls, including Henry Clay, Abraham Lincoln, James K. Polk, and Gen. Zachary Taylor. Not all of these visits, however, have been officially substantiated.

An 1840 visit by the soon-to-be married Abraham Lincoln and Mary Todd to attend a gala ball, though unconfirmed, is plausible based on the friendship between Southgate and Mary Todd's father, Col. Robert Smith Todd; the two men had similar social and political beliefs and were related by marriage through the Parker family. A second visit by Lincoln, in 1856, was noted by Southgate's grandson **Nathaniel Southgate Shaler**, the eminent Harvard professor, dean, and renowned geologist, in his autobiography. This visit has also been disputed, though not completely discounted; recent scholarship fails to confirm an 1856 visit to the state but instead places Lincoln in the area during an 1855 trip to Cincinnati, at which time he may have visited the Southgate House. Tradition and fact again mingle in regard to the Southgate House's association with the Texas Revolution. Legend has it that the house was the site of an extravagant send-off party on December 30, 1835, for 50 men under the leadership of Newport resident **Sidney Sherman**. The Kentucky unit later fought for Gen. Sam Houston, assisting the Texans in their defeat of Santa Anna at the 1836 Battle of San Jacinto.

Richard Southgate's long life came to an end at age 83 at his Newport mansion in 1857, and he was buried at Evergreen Cemetery in Southgate. He had generously provided for each of his living children within his will. His vast estate, then valued at $1.5 million, included extensive landholdings in Ohio and Kentucky, securities, real estate, and the family's Newport homestead, the Southgate House, which he left to his eldest daughter, Frances Mary Taliaferro Parker.

Frances owned the house from 1857 to 1869 and then deeded it to her daughter, Julia Maria Taliaferro Thompson, who was married to James Thompson, a lieutenant colonel in the army, a West Point graduate, and a military science professor at Indiana University at Bloomington, Ind. Frances continued to reside at the mansion until she died there in 1883; her funeral was held at the house as well.

Julia's son **John Taliaferro Thompson**, born at the Southgate House in 1860, had a long and distinguished military career, but he is perhaps best remembered for the invention he and his son Marcellus engineered in 1919: the Thompson machine gun, or "Tommy Gun." This groundbreaking automatic weapon soon became standard issue for the military and was utilized by law-enforcement organizations, owing to its exceptional design. To Thompson's dismay, the weapon also gained extreme popularity among the ranks of organized crime syndicates.

For nearly the entire first century of its existence, the Southgate House was owned by a member of the Southgate family. Julia Thompson's sale of the house on March 31, 1888, to its fourth owner, Fannie F. Maddux, the wife of Louis Oliver Maddux, passed it to a new family. The structure continued to serve a long-established purpose, though; according to newspaper accounts of the time, the Maddux family entertained frequently in their Newport mansion, just as the Southgate family had done. L. O. Maddux died there on October 22, 1909.

Given the Southgate family's prominent position as one of Northern Kentucky's founding pioneer families, the Southgate House was an appropriate setting for another event that occurred there during Fannie Maddux's ownership. On May 18, 1894, the Keturah Moss Taylor Chapter of the Daughters of the American Revolution was founded at the house. According to several sources, this new organization had the distinction of being the first chapter in Kentucky.

Sometime during the Maddux family's ownership, or perhaps while Frances Mary Taliaferro Parker or her daughter, Julia Thompson, owned the home, extensive renovations and additions were undertaken, significantly altering the structure. It is believed that only the walls of the two-story main block and the basement remain from the original antebellum structure. Yet, the grand old residence's intact Georgian-style features include the front facade's symmetrical composition, five bays, and Flemish-bond brickwork. At the end of the 19th century, Second Empire–style features were added, including a concave mansard roof, punctuated by altered dormers replete with decorative fanlights; cast-iron hoodmolds over the front windows; and a four-story entrance tower with a mosaic-floored vestibule on the first floor. Other 19th-century renovations included the addition of a third-story ballroom and a late Victorian porch; its delicately rendered posts, spandrels, and openwork railing complemented the newly added tower and decorative slate-tiled roof.

Fannie Maddux continued to reside at the house until May 9, 1914, when she sold it to attorney John William Heuver. Before the year was up, on November 13, 1914, the house again changed hands when Heuver sold it to the Newport Knights of Columbus for $10,000. For more than six decades, this organization made good use of its mansion meeting place, which became known as the Knights of Columbus Hall. The Knights of Columbus held bimonthly meetings there and hosted bingo games, dances, wedding receptions, and fundraisers. During this period, ceiling beams and wainscoting were added in several interior rooms. Exterior alterations included the replacement of the delicate wooden porch with the current square-tiered brick porch, the addition of a corbelled brick balustrade on the front and the east side (which has since been enclosed), and the addition of a large auditorium wing at the rear of the structure.

Twice during the Knights of Columbus's ownership, the Southgate House was damaged by fire. In July 1925, flames from a fire at the Abe Colker Chewing Gum Factory, located at the intersection of Southgate and York Sts., just behind the mansion, spread to the house. The structure sustained more than $6,000 in damage. In 1948 the auditorium addition was destroyed by fire on Thanksgiving Day. Damage from the blaze was estimated at $50,000. The resilient fraternal organization repaired the structure and rebuilt the auditorium not long after the end of **World War II**.

On September 15, 1976, The Knights of Columbus sold the aging mansion to Morrell Ross and Bess Raleigh for $65,000. Raleigh, a lifelong resident of Newport and an inspector for the Campbell Co. Health Department, had heard rumors that the stately old mansion would be slated for demolition once the Knights of Columbus had moved. So he bought the historic house to save it from the wrecking ball. A year later, the Southgate House was placed on the National Register of Historic Places. From 1978 to 1980, the mansion stood vacant as Raleigh scrambled to make costly, desperately needed repairs while devising a plan that would keep his historic-preservation venture financially solvent.

In 1981 Raleigh opened the Southgate House as a short-lived country music and entertainment venue called Mom's Opry. By 1982 the house again was vacant, though Raleigh was far from giving up on his plans for the historic old homestead. In 1983 he reopened it as an entertainment venue with its original name, the Southgate House. Raleigh, his daughter Morella, and her longtime friend Chris Schadler have successfully positioned one of Newport's most important antebellum structures as a revitalized center for arts and music. Now, more than a century and a half after its construction, the elegant and expansive ancestral home of the Southgate family continues to be the site of social gatherings, vibrant entertaining, and cultural events. Included are local, regional, and national musical performances, art exhibits, poetry readings, and other attractions.

"K.C. Fire Loss $50,000; 10 Overcome," *KP*, November 26, 1948, 1.

"Newport K. of C. Buy Building," *KP*, March, 12, 1914, 12.

Purvis, Thomas L., ed. *Newport, Kentucky: A Bicentennial History.* Newport, Ky.: Otto Zimmerman, 1996.

Ramos, Steve. "Owners of Newport's Historic Southgate House Have High Hopes for a Rich Future, but Local Development Plans Might Stop Them in Their Tracks," *City Beat,* April 2–8, 1998, 12–15.

Reis, Jim. "Newport's Southgate House Dates Back to the Early 1800s," *KP,* May 16, 1994, 4k.

——. "Soldiers and Gangsters Used the 'Tommy' Gun." In *Pieces of the Past,* by Jim Reis, vol. 2. Covington: Kentucky Post, 1991.

Richard Southgate Will, Campbell Co. Will Book C, 200.

Shaler, Nathaniel Southgate. *The Autobiography of Nathaniel Southgate Shaler: With a Supplementary Memoir by His Wife.* Boston: Houghton Mifflin, 1909.

Southgate Family file. Local History files, Kenton Co. Public Library, Covington, Ky.

Southgate House file. Local History files, Kenton Co. Public Library, Covington, Ky.

"Still Blamed in $250,000 Fire—Newport Chewing Gum Factory Destroyed by Flames; Owner Cited on Liquor Charge, Which He Denies; Garages and Autos Burned," *KP,* July 18, 1925, 1.

Janice Mueller

SOUTHGATE INDEPENDENT SCHOOLS. Southgate Independent Schools refers to a single school, the Southgate School, located at the northwest corner of William Blatt and Evergreen Aves. in Southgate, Campbell Co. Before the city of Southgate was incorporated in 1907, a Campbell Co. school was in operation at the site of the current school. It opened in October 1901 as a one-room frame structure on land donated by the Shaler estate. A brick building was erected to replace the frame schoolhouse in 1903, and additions were made to the school in 1930 and in 1995. The school has operated only as a grade school through the eighth grade; for Southgate high school students, the City of Southgate makes tuition payments to various nearby high schools, including **Highlands High School** in Fort Thomas, **Newport High School**, Bellevue High School (see **Bellevue Public Schools**), Dayton High School (see **Dayton Public Schools**), and **Campbell Co. High School**.

One of the graduates of the Southgate School is Harold H. Smith, the 16th president of Pikeville College in Pikeville, Ky. The Southgate School has always been noted for the individualized attention it provides students and for the school's low student-teacher ratio. Southgate is the smallest independent school district in Kentucky, and over the years there have been discussions of merging the city with adjacent cities and school districts or closing the school for reasons of diseconomies of scale. Today, the Southgate School has approximately 200 students in nine classrooms. With recent plans made for new construction in Southgate, the school is anticipating increases in its student population in the near future.

Harden, Crystal. "Southgate Ends Tuition Subsidy," *KP*, March 10, 2003, 2K.

Schafer, Ray. "Always Small, Always Beloved," *KE*, May 15, 2001, B1.

SOUTHGATE ST. SCHOOL. Newport's Southgate St. School, organized in 1873 for the African American citizens of Campbell Co., was located on the north side of Southgate St. between Saratoga and Washington Sts. The school would not have been finished without the help of Dennis Lightfoot, **Robert Littleton**, and **Washington Rippleton**, who were involved from the very beginning, along with educators such as Dennis Anderson, Lavina Ellis, **Charles D. Horner**, and Elizabeth Hudson. But the commitment of two important local governmental bodies, the Newport City Council and the city board of education, was also essential. Each of these bodies used state legislation and the Freedmen's Bureau to establish the school.

Early teachers at the Southgate St. School were Elizabeth Hudson, who taught from 1873 to 1878; Mr. F. Mackoy, 1878–1879; and Dennis R. Anderson, 1879–1890. The 1880s witnessed an increase of more than 50 percent in the African American population in both Newport and Campbell Co. The Southgate St. School served the entire county, and even some children from nearby Bracken Co. On June 26, 1893, the school held its first graduation exercise at the Park Avenue School hall; the first two graduates were Louisa Smith and Lavina Ellis. In attendance were the president of the board of education, E. G. Lohmeyer, and a representative from the school, C. W. H. Johnson. Johnson was one of the committee members who had originally petitioned the Newport City Council for free public education for African American children in the city. Lohmeyer addressed the audience, urging parents to persevere in keeping their children in school; he said education, and not legislation, would prove the best solution to the race question. The second graduating class consisted of only one person, Beatrice Genevieve Johnson. The commencement exercise took place on June 19, 1896, again at the Park Avenue School hall.

In 1901 the city school board determined the curriculum for the high school, based on a three-year school program. The Southgate school's principal, Charles D. Horner, asked to have the course requirements extended to cover four years, so that the students would have the same educational advantages as students at the white Newport High School; however, a four-year program was never implemented. With the addition of a second floor, two more classrooms were added to the building and another teacher was hired. Each teacher had to teach three grades, and the principal taught the three high school grades. On June 5, 1921, Superintendent E. F. Sporing recommended to the Newport educational board that the Southgate high school be discontinued for the coming school year, because of unsatisfactory conditions, and that the high school students be sent to William Grant High School in Covington. He believed that there they would receive an "all grade high school education, and upon graduation, the students would be eligible for admission to the leading Universities and Colleges which are open to African-American students." Given the small number of graduates from the Southgate high school, and the cost of only $50 in tuition per student to send them to the Covington high school, it was an easy decision for Newport's educational board to send students to Covington. African American students did not again attend high school in Newport until fall 1955.

From 1916 through 1940, the Southgate St. School principals were chosen from within the school. In August 1921 W. S. Blanton, who had been principal at the Southgate St. School since 1909, resigned and was replaced by Nora H. Ward, who had been a teacher of domestic science in the sixth and seventh grades at the school. The teachers' dedication to the school and the community was a source of pride for all African Americans in Newport. Lavina Ellis, who was in the first graduating class of 1893, returned to teach at the school about 1900 and stayed until she retired in 1936. She saw a need and opened a day nursery for African American children nearby. Ellis lived on Covert Run Pk. in Bellevue. She had the longest tenure of any teacher, serving under three principals: Charles D. Horner, W. S. Blanton, and Nora H. Ward. Elise Gooch, who began teaching at the school in 1910, was the sister of Elizabeth Gooch, a teacher at Covington's Lincoln-Grant School from 1912 until 1953. Elise had direct contact with all the new students from Newport. Most faculty members at the Southgate St. School were lifelong residents of Covington with connections throughout Northern Kentucky. Ruth Bond taught at Southgate from 1936 to 1957. She was from Louisville, where her family had strong educational ties. When the Southgate St. School was closed because of integration, she was transferred to another Newport school and retired in 1957.

In 1926 Anderson D. Owens was appointed superintendent of the Newport schools. Under his direction, the Southgate St. School received considerable attention. For example, Owens wanted to replace the old Southgate St. School building with a larger, modern school. In 1938 he proposed to the city's school board that a new school for African Americans be built. The board proposed building the new school under the federal Public Works Administration (PWA). The application to the PWA for funding was supplemented with a local bond issue and sent to the Newport City Council, which approved both applications and placed the issue on the ballot for voters. The law required that all bond issues be approved by voters with a two-thirds majority. Owens, the board, and the council had done their part. But in the general election on November 8, 1938, the voters defeated the new school bond issue; a majority, but not the required two-thirds majority, voted in favor of the bond issue.

In 1940 Charles Harris replaced Nora Ward as principal at the Southgate St. School. Harris had been a teacher there since November 1932. Harris's staff of teachers included Ruth Bond, Melissia Bruce, and Leila Patton. This staff remained at the school until after the 1954 U.S. Supreme Court rendered its decision mandating school desegregation.

On June 27, 1955, Superintendent Owens submitted to the city board of education a program for the desegregation of Newport Public Schools. He asked the board to adopt a policy requiring that all African American children through the 11th grade attend Newport schools during the 1955–1956 school year, thereby closing the segregated Southgate St. School. All African American students in the 12th grade who were attending William Grant High School in Covington were given the choice of either finishing their senior year there or attending Newport High School. The superintendent also placed African American teachers in desegregated schools. Thereby, the Newport school system became the first public school system in Northern Kentucky to integrate. The closing of the Southgate St. School was much like its beginning, accomplished without the hostility, lawsuits, and study groups that many communities experienced during the period of school desegregation. But Superintendent Owens's concern for the equitable placement of the now-defunct school's former teachers was equally important. Charles Harris retired in 1956; Ruth Bond, Melissa Bruce, and Leila Patton continued teaching at their new schools, and all three of them retired after the 1957–1958 school year.

The old Southgate St. School building has remained very much a part of Newport's African American heritage. In 1959 the Newport Masonic Lodge No. 120 purchased the building. The Southgate St. School Alumni Association is leading the restoration project for the school building as part of the neighborhood's historic district. A Kentucky State Historical Society Highway Marker was dedicated in front of the former Southgate St. School on October 6, 2001.

Annual Report of the Board of Education, Newport, Kentucky. Newport, Ky.: Newport Printing, 1873.

City Council Records, 1874, Newport, Ky.

"Colored School Graduation Exercises," *KSJ*, June 6, 1893, 4.

"First Day School Figures Go Up," *KP*, September 7, 1955, 1.

Harris, Theodore H. H. "Southgate School Newport, Kentucky (1866–1955)," *NKH* 4, no. 2 (Spring–Summer 1997): 34–42.

"Integration Delay May Bring Suit," *KP*, September 1, 1955, 1.
"Integration Will Begin in Newport," *KP*, August 15, 1955, 1.
"Local Schools Openings to See Changes," *KP*, September 5, 1955, 1.
"Negro Educational Convention," *CC*, February 19, 1873, 3.
"Newport," *CDG*, August 28, 1873, 2; August 30, 1873, 3; September 8, 1873, 3.
"Newport School Appointments," *Newport Local*, June 11, 1878, 3.
"Newport School Committee on Salaries," *Newport Local*, June 3, 1879, 1.
"Newport Voters Defeat Bond Issues," *KP*, November 9, 1938, 1.
Reis, Jim. "Superintendents Notable for Longevity, Leadership," *KP*, March 6, 1995, 7.

Theodore H. H. Harris

SOUTHGATE UNITED METHODIST CHURCH. The Southgate Methodist Church was founded 1906 as an outreach in the village of Southgate by the **Grace United Methodist Church** of Newport. Starting a Sunday school in Southgate was the vision of Louis Wilson of the Grace Church. Between 1900 and 1906, the Grace Church held Sunday school on Sunday afternoons in the old two-room school that was located on Elm St. in Southgate. Later, church services were held at the same location two Sundays each month. Eventually, a Ladies Aide Society was organized and money was raised to build a church in Southgate. Shaler Berry donated a lot across from the Southgate School, and Catherine Wright and her husband donated another lot for a church building. The building itself was financed by picnics, lawn fetes, bazaars, and other fundraising activities. The 36-by-40-foot church, designed by architect L. H. Wilson of Newport and costing $8,000, was dedicated in 1908. The original building had a sanctuary and two small rooms in the back. Rev. George Bunton was the first pastor, and William Theis was the first Sunday school superintendent. Between 1908 and 1939, three additions to the church were built. By 1939 church membership was about 300 and Sunday school membership was 189.

A parsonage was built and dedicated on May 14, 1950, nearby in town at 226 Evergreen Ave. Rev. T. O. Harrison was the first pastor who occupied it. In May 1952, "the Little Church by the Side of the Road," as the church was known, was torn down in order to build a new structure on the property. The church furnishings were taken across the street to the Southgate School, where the congregation met during the construction of its new building. The first service in the new sanctuary was held April 19, 1953, with Pastor H. K. Carl presiding. **Orie S. Ware**, a Masonic Past Grand Master (see **Masons**), presided at the cornerstone-laying ceremony, which was conducted by the Newport Masonic Lodge No. 358 on May 17, 1953. When the final payment on the $120,000 mortgage had been made, in January 1966, the building was formally dedicated as part of the 60th anniversary of the founding of the Southgate United Methodist Church in 1906. During the 1970s and 1980s, the church was known for its promotion of scouting in the Southgate community.

By the 1990s, the Southgate United Methodist Church had become an urban church, and it began to experience a decline in attendance and membership. As a result, it was reorganized as the New Hope Church. Finally in 2004 it became the New Hope Campus of the **Immanuel United Methodist Church** in Lakeside Park, in order to continue to serve the communities of Southgate and south Newport.

"Corner-Stone of Edifice Laid," *KP*, September 9, 1907, 5.
Dedication Program, 1966. Southgate, Ky.: Southgate Methodist Church, 1966.
"Site Is Deeded for M.E. Church," *KP*, March 28, 1907, 5.
"Southgate Methodists to Dedicate," *KP*, June 20, 1908, 5.
"Throngs of People Attend Dedication," *KP*, June 22, 1908, 5.

Paul L. Whalen

SOUTH HILLS. Perched on a hill above the southwestern border of Covington, the area now known as South Hills was once home to **Battery Hooper**, one of the **Civil War** fortifications built to defend Cincinnati. South Hills began in the late 1920s as a 121-acre subdivision of more than 400 lots, its name derived from the company that developed the first streets. Fred W. Staengle, a Covington realtor, led much of the original housing development.

South Hills was widely known in its early years as one of the largest and most attractive developments in Northern Kentucky; it touted amenities such as electricity and gas, as well as the "Heart's Desire" model home on Crittenden Ave., which was visited by thousands of people in the late 1920s, according to newspaper reports. In 1927, lot prices in the subdivision ranged from $25 to $50, and a nice house could be had for $5,000. In addition to Crittenden Ave., original streets included St. Anthony, Cumberland, and Henry Clay, which was the only road open from Covington to the south during the Ohio River **flood of 1937**.

In 1949 the South Hills subdivision incorporated as a sixth-class city to block potential annexation by Covington and to create the taxing authority to provide basic government services such as infrastructure maintenance and police. Council meetings were held in the basements of various residences until the South Hills Civic Club was built in 1957. The Civic Club also served as the city building. South Hills mayors included A. J. Jung, Royal Clark, George Schulte, and M. A. Groening.

Nearly all residential, South Hills was a close-knit community that had a community club as early as 1941 and for many years sponsored an annual festival and other events at the Civic Club. Rumors of annexation and consolidation with neighboring cities swirled many times between the early 1940s and the late 1950s, and finally in 1960 South Hills was annexed by neighboring Fort Wright. South Hills continues, however, to maintain a typical neighborhood atmosphere.

City of Fort Wright. *City of Fort Wright 50th Anniversary Booklet*. Fort Wright, Ky.: City of Fort Wright, 1991.
"Henry Clay Avenue Maintenance Asked," *KP*, May 8, 1941, 1.
"Historic Spot Converted into Subdivision," *KP*, March 27, 1927, 6.
"Park Hills, Ft. Wright, Lookout Heights Talk More on Merger," *KE*, March 21, 1967, 19.
Reis, Jim. "The City They All Seem to Want," *KP*, November 11, 1985, 4K.
"South Hills One of Northern Kentucky's Largest Developments," *KP*, December 30, 1928, 7.

Dave Hatter

SPARKS, HENRY, CORPORAL (b. June 16, 1753, Culpeper Co., Va.; d. August 14, 1836, Owen Co., Ky.). Henry Sparks was one of the family members of Capt. James Clark's sons and daughters, who arrived in Owen Co. as early pioneers: the Clarks, the Marstons, the Smoots, the Sparkses, the Towles, and the Hancocks. Each of these families had received large land grants, and Henry Sparks owned 1,000 acres along the Kentucky River north of Monterey. He had earned his land by serving in the **Revolutionary War** as a bodyguard of Gen. George Washington, whose military unit was said to be the "flower and pick of the American army." Sparks fought at the battles of Brandywine Creek (September 11, 1777) and Germantown (October 3–4, 1777) in Pennsylvania and was discharged from military service on February 2, 1778, at Valley Forge, Pa. In 1795 he came to Kentucky and settled in what is today Owen Co. He died there in 1836. Sparks was buried at Sparks Bottom Cemetery near Monterey, his grave site marked with a military stone. He is one of several Revolutionary War soldiers who chose to settle in Owen Co., which was at the time part of the new American West.

Owen Co., Kentucky. "Henry Sparks." www.rootsweb.com/~kyowen (accessed June 25, 2007).

SPARTA. The town of Sparta straddles Owen and Gallatin counties, where Ky. Rts. 467 and 35 intersect. In 1779 Jacob and John Carlock migrated to Kentucky from the Holsten Valley of Virginia and arrived in the valley on the north side of Eagle Creek in early summer. They set up camp at the mouth of the Two-Mile branch of the creek and began to establish the town that later became known as Sparta. Accompanying the Carlock brothers were Dave and John Alcor, William Swango, and Jacob Walters. Soon there were families of settlers living on both sides of the creek. By 1804 a gristmill, a tanning business, a distillery, a mechanic's shop, and shoemakers were operating in town. By 1806 Enoch Winkfield had opened a storehouse there as well. Those who chose to be farmers grew cotton and hemp as cash crops.

When Owen Co. was established in 1819, Eagle Creek was the dividing line between Gallatin and

Owen counties. The Sparta homes and businesses established earliest were in Owen Co., in what was later referred to as Old Sparta. These original settlers were dismayed to learn that they had no legal claim to their land. Several large syndicates (May, Bannister & Company, the Crosley Company, and J. Fellows & Company) had purchased the land in 25,000-acre plots and sold sections to other farmers, thus preempting the founding settlers' land claims. Some of the displaced original settlers moved to Missouri or the Northwest, but others stayed and bought property from the land syndicates.

The first bridge, built across Eagle Creek in 1851, soon fell because it could not withstand the amount of traffic that crossed it, and in 1873 George Wagel constructed a second bridge there. The first church and school at Sparta was that of Little Hope on Two-Mile Branch. During the early 1870s, a school district was formed in town to serve students of the area from both Owen and Gallatin counties. A. D. Mason donated a large lot for the school building, which came to be called "The Old Red Schoolhouse." The building also served as a community center. The Samuel brothers planted trees, making a portion of the school grounds into a playground area. In 1875 John T. Hawkins, pastor of the Christian Church at New Liberty, led in the formation of a church at Sparta, in Gallatin Co. In 1881 the Sparta Baptist Church was built on property within Owen Co.

The exciting news of a railroad coming through Sparta meant that the residents could have a connection to larger cities. Since the old part of town was surrounded by hills and most of the valley had been used for businesses and homes, the intended railroad could not come through Owen Co.; its path was moved across Eagle Creek into Gallatin Co. After surveys had been taken and legalities cleared by the Kentucky legislature, the construction of the **Louisville, Cincinnati, and Lexington Railroad** began in spring 1867. African American, German, Irish, and Swedish workers built the twisting, rollercoaster-like rail pathway through the valleys and hills adjacent to Sparta. Florian and **Atilla Cox** had charge of the railroad depot, which also housed the post office, a store, the freight department, a waiting room, and offices for the railway agent and the telegraph operator.

With the building of the depot and its associated businesses came the expansion on the other side of Eagle Creek in Gallatin Co. that became known as New Sparta. The Sparta Deposit Bank opened its doors at New Sparta in 1900, the Sparta Lumber and manufacturing Company in 1908, the Standard Oil Company in 1921, and the Stock Yards in 1928.

The Sparta Transfer Company, begun in 1800, took horses and mules on treks to Owenton and Warsaw. Its owners, Cox & Company, referred to their enterprise as the Stage Coach. It was later run by **June Gayle**, P. O. Minor, John Thomas, and F. P. Jacobs. The first silent movies, which were free and were shown outdoors, began in 1918. Other businesses opened later in Sparta were the hotel, a used-car dealership, service stations, taverns, general merchandise stores, groceries, a fertilizer and coal company, and a restaurant.

Like many other small communities, both parts of Sparta have declined. Today, in Old Sparta there are only homes. The first church building stands abandoned, but the community uses the church's outside wall to mark water levels of floods. It is believed that the decline of the pioneer side of Sparta (Old Sparta) was due mostly to the lack of space to build and to the devastating Eagle Creek floods. With no dam for flood control, this area remains at the mercy of the weather. The Gallatin Co. section of Sparta now consists of a service station, a tavern, a general store (known for its old country hams), and the families who still call it home. The completion of I-71, just to the north, during the 1960s, diverted much automobile traffic away from Sparta. Not far away in Gallatin Co. is the new **Kentucky Speedway**, which has a Sparta address. Sparta is one of four cities in Northern Kentucky that overlap two counties; the others are Jonesville (Owen and Grant), Germantown (Mason and Bracken), and Walton (Boone and Kenton).

Historical Society Files, Owen Co. Public Library, Owenton, Ky.

Houchens, Mariam Sidebottom. *History of Owen County: "Sweet Owen."* Louisville, Ky.: Standard, 1976.

Doris Riley

SPEERS MEMORIAL HOSPITAL. When a wealthy Dayton, Ky., resident, Elizabeth L. Speers, died in August 1894, she bequeathed $100,000 to construct a hospital in her hometown of Dayton to be named in memory of her deceased husband. Charles Speers had made his fortune selling cotton during the **Civil War**. Elizabeth Speer's will directed the Campbell Co. Circuit Court judge to appoint three trustees, who would be authorized to build the hospital and hire the required personnel. In accordance with those instructions, Judge Charles Helm appointed as trustees John Trapp, Charles Nagel, and Dr. C. B. Schoolfield. The trustees first met on July 6, 1895, and John Trapp was chosen president, Dr. Schoolfield vice president, and Charles Nagel secretary-treasurer. The hospital was built on the block bounded by Main and Boone Sts. and Fourth and Fifth Aves., at a cost of $75,000. Anna Sutton was hired as hospital superintendent to oversee the operation of the facility. The trust fund provided money for construction of the building and purchase of equipment but no operating capital. Construction took two years, and the facility opened for business on October 10, 1897, with the admission of its first patient, Carolyn Meyer. The building contained four hospital wards and 15 private rooms and was designed by the architectural firm of Crapsey and Brown (see **Charles Crapsey**). The hospital staff was made up of 31 prominent doctors; among them were J. L. Pythian, C. B. Schoolfield, Frank H. Southgate, R. W. Thornton, William M. Truesdell, and Lee C. Wadsworth from Northern Kentucky and S. G. Ayres, C. H. Good, Charles M. Paul, Ed Walker, and W. S. Weaver from Cincinnati. In 1901 the hospital started a nurses' training program, one of the first in Kentucky. Three years later, the first class of seven young ladies received their nursing diplomas, in ceremonies held at the Dayton High School auditorium (see **Dayton Public Schools**).

In 1911 an east wing was added to the hospital, which provided a children's ward and seven private rooms. In 1912 the hospital arranged with the **Chesapeake and Ohio Railroad** to care for its workers, making it a so-called railroad hospital. In 1924 a residence for student nurses was constructed at the east end of the property. By 1937 several other additions had been made, which brought the hospital's capacity to 100 beds, in five wards and 38 patient rooms. Disaster struck Speers Memorial Hospital that year, when floodwaters of the **flood of 1937** entered the basement and the

Speers Memorial Hospital, Dayton, Ky., ca. 1923.

first floor. All patients had to be moved to other sites, including Dayton High School, the Poplar Street School in Bellevue, and the Cote Brilliante School in Newport. The flood ruined some of the hospital's equipment and caused considerable damage to the building, forcing a complete renovation. Funds for the work came from a campaign launched by the Campbell Co. Chamber of Commerce (see **Northern Kentucky Chamber of Commerce**). In 1938 a number of prominent physicians lectured at the hospital. The speakers included the world-renowned brain surgeon Dr. Frank Mayfield and the developer of the first live polio vaccine, Dr. Albert Sabin.

As the Speers Memorial Hospital and its equipment aged, the finances were not available to upgrade properly and maintain the facility. A number of fundraisers were held in an attempt to save the hospital, but to no avail. In the late 1940s, seven area doctors sought voter approval of a $1 million bond issue to build a new, larger, more modern hospital in Campbell Co. Voters approved the request, and in 1954 **St. Luke Hospital** was built in Fort Thomas. The new hospital facility was out of the flood district, was more centrally located, and had room for expansion. Speers Memorial Hospital ceased operations in 1973, when St. Elizabeth Hospital of Covington acquired it. The Speers hospital building remained vacant until 1979, when the King Wrecking Company tore the structure down. A senior citizens' housing development was built on the site in 1983. The Speers Memorial Hospital was the second hospital in Campbell Co. (the medical facility at the **Newport Barracks** was the first) and the third in Northern Kentucky. Some instruments and items of equipment from Speers were saved and placed on display in a medical museum at St. Luke Hospital in Fort Thomas. In 2006 the museum was moved to the Campbell Co. Historical and Genealogical Society's office in Alexandria.

"Demolition Begins at Speers," *KP*, October 18, 1978, 7K.

"Like an Old Friend, Speers Hospital Is Dying," *KP*, July 26, 1973, 8K.

Poweleit, Alvin C. *A Medical History of Campbell and Kenton Counties.* Cincinnati: Campbell-Kenton Co. Medical Society, 1970.

Reis, Jim. "Wealthy Widow's Gift Led to Campbell's First Hospital," *KP*, December 21, 1998, 4K.

SPENCE, BRENT (b. December 24, 1874, Newport, Ky.; d. September 18, 1967, Fort Thomas, Ky.). Brent Spence, a lawyer and a long-term legislator, was the son of Col. Philip Brent Spence, a Confederate cavalry officer, and Virginia Berry Spence. He was also a nephew of **Albert Seaton Berry**, founder of Bellevue, Ky.; a grandson of **James Berry**, founder of Jamestown, Ky.; and a great-grandson of **Washington Berry** and Alice Thornton Taylor, sister of **James Taylor Jr.**, founder of Newport. Spence's education was in local public schools and at the University of Cincinnati Law School, where he graduated in 1895. He was admitted to the bar that same year and joined the law firm of his uncle Albert S. Berry. Spence was a Kentucky state senator from 1904 until 1908 and city solicitor of Newport from 1916 until 1924.

Brent Spence, ca. 1940.

In 1920 he married Ida Billerman, and the couple had no children. Spence, a Democrat, ran for the U.S. House of Representatives in the Sixth District in 1928 but lost. In 1930 he was elected to the first of 16 consecutive terms in the U.S. House, serving from March 4, 1931, until January 3, 1963. In Congress he earned a reputation as a strong, liberal leader. He became a staunch supporter of President Franklin D. Roosevelt (1933–1945) and his policies during the **Great Depression**. As a longtime chairman of the powerful Committee on Banking and Currency of the U.S House, Spence was a delegate to the Bretton Woods conference in 1944. He guided the House passage of the Bretton Woods Agreement, which allowed U.S. participation in the International Monetary Fund and the International Bank. Spence also used his influence to get the federal government to finance construction of the Greater Cincinnati Airport (now the **Cincinnati/Northern Kentucky International Airport**) in Boone Co., which contributed greatly to the economic growth of the Northern Kentucky region. Other projects he championed were bonuses for **World War I** veterans, public housing for low-income families, the **Internal Revenue Service Center** in Covington, and the construction of floodwalls in Covington, Newport, and Maysville. Spence retired from the U.S. House of Representatives in 1962, at age 88. When the new I-75 bridge between Covington and Cincinnati was opened in 1963, it was named in his honor (see **Brent Spence Bridge**). He died at age 92 and was buried in Evergreen Cemetery in Southgate.

Biographical Directory of the United States Congress. "Spence, Brent." http://bioguide.congress.gov (accessed November 22, 2005).

Hedlund, Richard. "Brent Spence and the Bretton Woods Legislation," *RKHS* 79 (Winter 1981): 40–56.

The Honorable Brent Spence. Newport, Ky.: Otto Printing, 1996.

Purvis, Thomas, L., ed. *Newport, Kentucky, a Bicentennial History.* Newport, Ky.: Otto Zimmerman, 1996.

Reis, Jim. "Brent Spence, the Man," *KP*, August 5, 2005, 4K.

Jack Wessling

SPERTI, GEORGE SPERI (b. January 17, 1900, Covington, Ky.; d. April 29, 1991, Covington, Ky.). Inventor and scientist George Speri Sperti was the son of George A. and Caroline Speri Sperti, Italian immigrants. He was educated in the Covington public schools, including the old Covington High School, and he graduated from the University of Cincinnati College of Engineering in 1923. While still a college student, Sperti invented a utility meter for which General Electric paid him $30,000, making the young inventor a celebrity in the field of invention. Sperti held the first patent for fluorescent lights and developed the Sperti Sunlamp. In 1925 he became the director of the University of Cincinnati's Basic Science Research Laboratory.

During the **Great Depression**, Sperti left the University of Cincinnati, and in 1935 he co-founded the Institutum Divi Thomae (the St. Thomas Institute) in Cincinnati with Archbishop John T. McNicolas. The St. Thomas Institute, a small doctorate-granting research institute, was organized as an old-fashioned institute of higher learning, with students and teachers living and working on campus. However, Sperti himself never lived on campus, preferring to remain on his farm near Burlington, Ky. In 1936 Pope Paul XI appointed Sperti to the Pontifical Academy of Sciences.

Sperti's research at the St. Thomas Institute helped develop such world-famous products as Sperti Ointment burn salve and Preparation H hemorrhoid cream. As a researcher and inventor, he developed products and processes used in the food and drug industry, in electronic and radiation devices, and in cosmetics. He searched for a cure for cancer much of his life and pioneered cancer research at the St. Thomas Institute. For financial reasons, the institute stopped granting degrees in 1987, but research there continued.

Sperti died in 1991 and was buried in St. Mary Cemetery in Fort Mitchell. He had never married. Following his death, the St. Thomas Institute campus was sold and the proceeds designated for scholarships at **Thomas More College** and the College of Mount St. Joseph in Cincinnati. Sperti's farm in Boone Co. became a nature preserve.

DeVroomen, Sasha. "Thomas More Gets Gift from Sperti," *KP*, May 31, 1991, 2K.

Harden, Crystal. "George Sperti, Scientist and Inventor, Dead at 91," *KP*, April 30, 1991, 1K.

Kleber, John E., ed. *The Kentucky Encyclopedia.* Lexington: Univ. Press of Kentucky, 1992.

William S. Bryant

SPHAR BRICK COMPANY. The Sphar Brick Company, located about two miles from Maysville, near the Ohio River in Mason Co., was established by A. C. Sphar, who also started the **Maysville Brick Company**. The *Maysville Daily Independent* reported in 1935 that the company was organized in 1904. However, according to other sources, it may have begun as early as 1878. At least during 1906–1908, the Sphar Brick Company and the Maysville Brick Company were operating at the same time.

The Sphar Brick Company was incorporated in July 1912 by A. S. Clark, H. T. Miles, E. A. Robinson, A. C. Sphar, E. S. Sphar, and W. N. Stockton. Sphar and his wife, who together owned 387 of the 500 shares, controlled the company. The capital stock of the corporation was $50,000, divided into shares valued at $100 each. A. C. Sphar was president and H. T. Miles was secretary and treasurer. After Sphar died in 1920, A. S. Clark and H. T. Miles assumed ownership of the company.

In 1908 the company had five rectangular brick kilns, a drying shed, two sorting sheds, a structure for storing bricks and hay, a corn crib, an oil house, a polishing house, an office, a brick machine with an 85-horsepower engine, and a water tank. The **Chesapeake and Ohio Railroad** provided transportation for the brickyard. By 1914, additions to the property included two large brick kilns and a second drying shed, and by 1926 a small hot-air drying shed and a new brick machine had been added.

By 1922 the Sphar Brick Company had a large and well-equipped modern brickyard. Heinrich Ries described Sphar's operation as follows: "Clay was excavated with a steam shovel, loaded into dump cars, and hauled to sheds. A brick machine was used to produce 30,000 to 45,000 pressed bricks per day. Tunnel dryers were employed to dry the bricks prior to firing. Seven rectangular kilns, including five downdraft and two up-draft kilns, were used to fire the bricks." The company later produced a wire-cut "Face Building Brick" in smooth and rough textures. Ries noted that the bricks were a good red color, usually a deep or dark red; textured bricks were fired to different shades of red. Sphar bricks were sold in Kentucky and other states, almost exclusively through dealers. The company used the Sphar brand name on its bricks.

The Sphar Brick Company's corporate status expired on July 15, 1937. In December 1955, a new corporation with the same name was incorporated by F. H. Peters and Mrs. M. R. Peters of Dayton, Ohio, with 15,000 shares of stock without par value. F. H. Peters was president; the company employed 35 men in 1955–1956, had 40 employees in 1957–1958, and had 35 employees in 1959–1960. The company closed sometime between 1959 and 1961.

Kentucky Death Certificate No. 23181, for the year 1920.

Ries, Heinrich. *The Clay Deposits of Kentucky: An Economic Consideration of the Pottery, Brick, and Tile Clays, Fire Clays, and Shales of Kentucky, with Notes on their Industrial Development.* Series 6, vol. 2. Frankfort: Kentucky Geological Survey, 1922.

The Spirit of Greater Maysville & Mason County. Maysville, Ky.: Daily Independent, 1935.

Charles D. Hockensmith

SPILMAN, FRANCIS "FRANK" (b. 1756, King George Co., Va.; d. September 22, 1828, Alexandria, Ky.). Frank Spilman, a **Revolutionary War** veteran, a civic leader, a humanitarian, and the founder of the city of Alexandria, Ky., came to the highlands of central Campbell Co. in 1796. He named the town he founded after the one he had left in Virginia. During the Revolutionary War, Spilman served as a sergeant in the Virginia Cavalry and later served with Gen. **George Rogers Clark**. According to Spilman family tradition, Spilman met his wife Rebecca by honoring the request of a dying soldier. While he was serving in the army, a buddy named Mumford, when near death from a battle wound, asked Spilman to take care of his wife Rebecca. Spilman married her in 1786, and the couple had eight children. Spilman was a shoe and boot maker by trade; but in his new town of Alexandria, he became a civic leader, serving as justice of the peace, county commissioner, and road surveyor. In 1819 he donated 12 acres of land on which to construct public buildings and had the town lots platted. After his close friends Benjamin and Jeannette Beall died, Spilman raised their two infant sons. He was a strong advocate of education and each day took children to the **Walnut Hills Academy** in Cold Spring, which was the finest school in the area. The original Spilman log cabin was located just north of where the First Baptist Church now sits. Spilman died in 1803 and was buried in the Spilman Family Cemetery, next to the church.

Wessling, Jack. *Early History of Campbell County.* Alexandria, Ky.: Self-published, 1997.

Jack Wessling

SPLIT ROCK CONSERVATION PARK. Split Rock Conservation Park at Petersburg in Boone Co., more commonly known as Split Rock, is a unique outdoor conservation education facility. It was opened to the public, on a limited basis, in spring 2002 by Wildlife Conservation Kentucky Inc., whose mission is to address the conservation issues in the Northern Kentucky area. Split Rock is a 165-acre park located at the confluence of the Ohio River and Woolper Creek. The highlight of the park is the geologically significant formation known as Split Rock, a conglomerate formed by an Illinoian glacier some 132,000 to 300,000 years ago. The park offers educational programs on the archaeology, the ecology, the geology, and the history of the area, including evidence of early human habitation at Split Rock. All education programs stress the need for visitors to conserve these valuable local resources for the community while exploring the park's two miles of trails. Included in the park are scenic overlooks, ponds, 40 acres of native grasses, more than 10 different species of native trees, a four-acre wetland, and wildlife watering holes. By 2005 more than 4,500 visitors had experienced this unique outdoor center for educational and scientific research. Split Rock works with local cultural, historical, and scientific organizations to enhance and expand its conservation mission.

"Conservation Field Day," *KP,* September 7, 2005, 2K.

Jacobs, Mark. Interview by Gabrielle Summe, March 26, 2006, Petersburg, Ky. Jacobs is executive director of Split Rock Conservation Park.

Uhde, Andrea. "Rock Solid Treasure," *KP,* May 24, 2002, 1K.

Wildlife Conservation Kentucky. "Split Rock." www.splitrockpark.org (accessed April 1, 2006).

Gabrielle Summe

SQUIRESVILLE. Squiresville in Owen Co. is five and a half miles west of Owenton along Ky. Rt. 1982. The village of Squiresville reportedly derived its name from the number of squires and magistrates who once lived there. Within the commonwealth of Kentucky, anyone who becomes a squire or a magistrate can use the title for life. Local surnames such as Montgomery, Nuttall, Burke, Long, and Bibb were common in the village. A post office existed there from 1871 to 1903. For many years, there was a school at Squiresville. The town was the boyhood home of Gen. **Gerald "Jerry" Walter Johnson**, an ace fighter pilot of **World War II** who rose in his military service career to become the U.S. Air Force inspector general. It was also the home of **Richard C. Arnold**, MD. Arnold, a career U.S. Public Health Service employee, revolutionized the treatment of syphilis by demonstrating the effectiveness of penicillin as a therapeutic agent. At the Squiresville Cemetery are the graves of **Rena Lusby Yancey**, an Owen Co. poet and historian, and members of her family. Rena Yancey was the author of *Kentucky Trails* (1957), a book of poems.

Houchens, Mariam Sidebottom. *History of Owen County: "Sweet Owen."* Louisville. Ky.: Standard, 1976.

Rennick, Robert M. *Kentucky Place Names.* Lexington: Univ. Press of Kentucky, 1984.

STAFFORDSBURG. Staffordsburg is a small Kenton Co. community located southeast of Independence. It is flanked by White's Tower to the west and Visalia to the east. Like many communities with their roots in the early 1800s, this small town developed around the need for a place for local residents to worship. In 1877 Rev. J. W. Hughes, later instrumental in the forming of Asbury College at Wilmore, held services at Staffordsburg in a small school building. A year later, a one-fourth-acre piece of land owned by W. W. Coleman was conveyed to be the building site for the new Ebenezer Methodist Church. Although two general stores, a school, and a blacksmith's shop were already present, it was only after the church's arrival that a true sense of community was formed. The church has been renovated many times over the years, most extensively in 1959. At that time a full basement was added, as well as brick veneer on the exterior, a choir loft, a new organ, and new pews from the dismantled Holy Guardian Angels Catholic Church located at the bottom of the Dudley Turnpike in Sanfordtown. Today, the general stores and the blacksmith's shop are long gone, but the church thrives as the center of the small rural community.

"Kenton County—Staffordsburg," *DC*, August 17, 1983, 2.

"Staffordsburg Church Celebrates Centennial," *Advertiser*, August 17, 1983, 4.

Staffordsburg United Methodist Church. *Centennial Directory, 1878–1978*. Staffordsburg, Ky.: Staffordsburg United Methodist Church, 1978.

Robert D. Webster

STAINED GLASS THEATRE. The Stained Glass Theatre began in 1987, when a community theater group moved into the building at 802 York St. in Newport that for more than a century had been home to the **Salem United Methodist Church**. The 19th-century church was designed by **Samuel Hannaford and Sons**. The Salem United Methodist Church was dedicated in 1883, when the congregation was made up of German Methodists. After a 1986 **tornado** left major steeple and roof damage, repair of the badly damaged building was financially unrealistic for the church's active membership of fewer than 50. Therefore, the Salem United Methodist Church merged with **Grace United Methodist Church** in Newport and put the grand building up for sale.

Footlighters Inc., a nonprofit community theater organization established in 1963, purchased the building for $65,000. The group had previously performed at local high school auditoriums and at Westwood Town Hall in Cincinnati. After purchasing the marred yet extraordinary building, Footlighters proceeded to convert the historic structure from a church into a theater. The first floor was made into a 75-seat theater, and a second-floor theater with 162 seats opened in 1991. The continuing renovation efforts at the Stained Glass Theatre have been supported by other community organizations: the Edgecliff College Theatre in Ohio donated lighting and seating, and Cincinnati's WCPO-TV donated additional lighting equipment in 2004. Opening season for the Stained Glass Theatre in 1988 featured a performance of *A Funny Thing Happened on the Way to the Forum*. Performances since then have included *The Secret Garden*, *South Pacific*, *Gypsy*, and *West Side Story*. The building is listed on the National Register of Historic Places.

Franzen, Gene. "Tornado Ended Church Function," *CE*, November 5, 2000, B1.

Reis, Jim. "Historic Salem Church Now Used as Theater," *KP*, August 13, 2001, 4K.

Stein, Jerry, and T. C. Brown, "Church to Become 'Stained-Glassed Theatre,'" *KP*, June 2, 1987, 1B.

Judy L. Neff

STALLMEYER, SISTER MARGARET (b. August 18, 1946, Dayton, Ky.). Sister Margaret Stallmeyer, C.D.P., became the 13th president of **Thomas More College** on December 15, 2004. She came to Thomas More from the convent of the **Sisters of Divine Providence** in Melbourne, Ky. Sister Margaret was born in Dayton, Ky., to Robert T. and Ruth Newman Stallmeyer. She joined the Congregation of Divine Providence in 1962 and took her vows in 1970. She received a BA in mathematics and secondary education from Thomas More College in 1968, an MEd from Xavier University in Cincinnati in 1972, and a degree in canon law from the Catholic University of America, Washington, D.C., in 1987. Sister Margaret worked as an educator and administrator in two high schools in the Diocese of Covington for two decades. She served from 1988 to 1994 as tribunal director and judge for the Diocese of Lexington. From 2001 through 2003 she was a member of the Board of Governors of the Canon Law Society of America. Sister Margaret also has considerable financial knowledge. She served as treasurer for the Sisters of Divine Providence for 10 years, from 1994 to 2004, and was on the Thomas More College Board of Trustees from 1998 to 2004 and on the **St. Elizabeth Medical Center** board from 1996 to 2005, the last four as chairperson.

She is an active member of numerous professional organizations, including the American Association of Colleges and Universities, the Council of Independent Colleges, the Association of Independent Kentucky Colleges and Universities, the Greater Cincinnati Consortium of Colleges and Universities, and the Canon Law Society of America. Her involvement in the Greater Cincinnati and Northern Kentucky area includes board membership on the **Northern Kentucky Chamber of Commerce** and membership on the leadership team for Vision 2015, a contemporary planning effort for Northern Kentucky.

"Thomas More Adds Five Trustees," *KE*, October 4, 1998, C1D.

"Thomas More Announces 13th President," *SC*, December 19, 2004, 2A.

"Stallmeyer Inaugurated—'68 Graduate Is 2nd Woman President," *KE*, April 30, 2005, 1A.

Kelly Marsh

STANBERY, HENRY (b. February 20, 1803, New York City; d. June 26, 1881, New York City). U.S. attorney general Henry Stanbery, the son of physician Dr. Jonas Stanbery, moved with his family to Zanesville, Ohio, at age 11. He entered Washington College (later named Washington and Jefferson College) in Washington, Pa., at age 12 and graduated four years later. He began the study of law in Zanesville and was admitted to the bar in 1821. At that time he attempted to open his own office but soon learned that Ohio law did not permit persons under age 21 to practice law. So he worked under another attorney until 1824, before establishing his own law practice. About 1825 he married Frances Beecher, and they had three children. His wife died when the children were quite young, and he married his second wife, Cecelia Bond. Stanbery soon distinguished himself as an attorney; in 1846 he was appointed Ohio's first attorney general. He spent the next five years in Columbus, where in 1850 he helped draft Ohio's constitution. When his term in office ended, he returned to Zanesville. In 1856 he arrived in Cincinnati and the next year moved across the Ohio River to the District of the Highlands (now Fort Thomas) in Campbell Co. In 1866 he drafted the paperwork to incorporate that town, which was approved by the state in 1867. President Andrew Johnson (1865–1869) appointed Stanbery as the U.S. attorney general in 1866. When the U.S. House of Representatives voted to impeach Johnson on February 24, 1868, Stanbery resigned as attorney general to serve as the lead attorney for the president's defense. The trial caused him so much anguish that he soon became ill and had to relinquish his duties. When the impeachment vote failed, President Johnson attempted to return Stanbery to his former position as attorney general; however, the U.S. Senate would not approve his reappointment. Stanbery returned to his home in Kentucky and invested in local real estate. His eyesight slowly began to fail, and in 1880 he went to New York City for an operation, in an attempt to regain his sight. He died there in 1881. His body was returned to Cincinnati for burial at that city's Spring Grove Cemetery. Today's Stanbery Ridge Rd. in Fort Thomas is on the site of Stanbery's farm.

Biographical Encyclopedia of Kentucky. Cincinnati: J. M. Armstrong, 1878.

Greve, Charles Theodore. *Centennial History of Cincinnati and Representative Citizens*. Vol. 2. Chicago: Biographical Publishing, 1904.

Rim, Jim. *Pieces of the Past*. Vol. 2. Covington: Kentucky Post, 1991.

STANLEY, BEUFORD E. (b. February 13, 1914, near Williamstown, Ky.; d. March 21, 1995, Cincinnati, Ohio). Funeral director Beuford Elwood Stanley was the youngest of three children born to William Saul and Elizabeth Ellen Lawrence Stanley. His father, a farmer and a building contractor, moved his family to Independence, Ky., and later to Covington, where Beuford graduated from **Holmes High School** in 1932. He chose his lifelong profession of funeral directing and embalming with the encouragement of his sister. After graduating from the Melton School of Embalming in Louisville and passing his examinations, he became a state-licensed embalmer and funeral director at the youngest eligible age of 21.

Stanley's 60-year career as a funeral director and embalmer began when he was employed by O. P. Elliston in Williamstown; he purchased the funeral business from Elliston at the age of 23, in 1937. In 1939 Stanley married Frances Rae Clinkscales, and together they served Northern Kentucky as owners of the Elliston-Stanley Funeral Home.

Stanley's life was characterized as one of compassionate service to others, not only in his chosen profession, but also as a charter member and president of the Williamstown **Rotary Club** and the Williamstown Kiwanis and as a 16-year member of the Williamstown Board of Education, which he chaired from 1970 to 1972. He was a longtime member of the **Williamstown Baptist Church**, where he served on the church's building committee. He was a member of the first board of directors of Parkview Manor Apartments, a public housing project for senior citizens sponsored by his church, a 50-year member of the Masonic Lodge (see **Masons**) and Order of the Eastern Star, and a longtime member of the Shrine and Scottish Rite.

Stanley's legacy of service remains as his wife and two sons, Michael and Dennis Stanley, along with grandsons Patrick and Douglas Stanley, continue to operate Stanley Funeral Homes in Williamstown, Crittenden, and Verona, Ky. In 2006 they observed the 125th anniversary of the founding of the business.

Baker-Nantz, Jamie. "Friends Recall Stanley's Life," *Grant County News,* March 30, 1995, 1.
"Beuford E. Stanley," *CP,* March 22, 1995, 9A.
Conrad, John B., ed. *History of Grant County.* Williamstown, Ky.: Grant Co. Historical Society, 1992.
Stanley, Frances Clinkscales. Interview by William Michael Stanley, March 18, 2006, Williamstown, Ky.

William Michael Stanley

STANTON, HENRY T. (b. June 30, 1834, Alexandria, Va.; d. May 9, 1898, Frankfort, Ky.). Poet Henry T. Stanton, the son of Richard Henry Stanton, a U.S. congressman from Kentucky, and Asenath Throop, moved to Maysville, Ky., with his family at age two. As a young person he developed an interest in poetry. He attended the Maysville Seminary (**Maysville Academy**) and later was admitted to the U.S. Military Academy at West Point, N.Y., but did not graduate. He married Martha R. Lindsey on June 4, 1856. Shortly after the **Civil War** began, Stanton enlisted in the 5th Kentucky Confederate Regiment and served as captain in Company B. During the war he held the position of assistant adjutant-general on the staffs of three different commanders: Gen. John S. Williams, Col. Henry L. Giltner, and Gen. John Echols, under whom he was promoted to major. He also served under fellow Kentuckians Gen. John C. Breckinridge and Gen. **John Hunt Morgan**. At the war's conclusion, Stanton returned to Maysville and became editor of the *Maysville Bulletin,* continuing until 1870. He moved to Frankfort in that year to become chief assistant in the office of the state commissioner of insurance. He continued to write poetry, and some of his poems appeared in newspapers and periodicals. Several volumes of his poetry were published, two of them posthumously: *Poems of the Confederacy* and *The Poetical Works of Henry T. Stanton.* His most famous poem was "The Moneyless Man." He had one novel to his credit, the 1889 work *A Graduate of Paris.* Stanton died in Frankfort in 1898 and was buried at the Frankfort Cemetery.

Biographical Encyclopedia of Kentucky. Cincinnati: J. M. Armstrong, 1878.
Browning, M. Carmel. *Kentucky Authors: A History of Kentucky Literature.* Evansville, Ind.: Keller-Crescent, 1968.

Thomas S. Ward

STANTON, RICHARD (b. September 9, 1812, Alexandria, Va.; d. March 20, 1891, Maysville, Ky.). Richard H. Stanton, a lawyer, a judge, a newspaperman, and a U.S. congressman, was the son of Richard and Harriet Perry Stanton. He arrived in Maysville, Ky., in 1835 and served as the editor of the *Maysville Monitor* until 1841. In 1839 he was admitted to the Kentucky bar, in 1845 he became the postmaster of Maysville, and in 1849 he was elected to the U.S. Congress, serving three terms. During the **Civil War**, he was arrested by Gen. **William "Bull" Nelson** for his pro-Southern stance, reportedly for his advocacy of Kentucky's secession from the Union. This action encouraged many of his Maysville friends to join the Confederate side. Stanton signed an oath of allegiance to the Union cause and was released.

In Maysville, Stanton resided at the northwest corner of Walnut and Front Sts., in a home that burned down in 1897. He retired from the practice of law in 1885 after serving as a district judge in Mason Co. He married a Miss Throop in Alexandria, Va., in 1833 and was the father of **Henry T. Stanton**, the poet laureate of Kentucky. He died in 1891 in Maysville and was buried at the Maysville Cemetery.

Biographical Encyclopedia of Kentucky. Cincinnati: J. M. Armstrong, 1878.
Calvert, Jean, and John Klee. *Maysville, Kentucky: From Past to Present in Pictures.* Maysville, Ky.: Mason Co. Museum, 1983.
Clift, G. Glenn. *History of Maysville and Mason County.* Lexington, Ky.: Transylvania, 1936.

Michael R. Sweeney

STAVERMAN, LARRY (b. October 11, 1936, Cincinnati, Ohio; d. July 12, 2007, Edgewood, Ky.). Larry Joseph Staverman was the first basketball player to come out of Newport Catholic High School (see **Newport Central Catholic High School**) and play in the National Basketball Association (NBA). He was the son of Matthew and Loretta Siemer Staverman. He grew up in Covington but attended high school in Newport. Although best known as a basketball player, he was also an accomplished baseball pitcher, playing both sports for legendary coach **Jim Connor** at Newport Catholic High School. Staverman was a member of the class of 1954. He went on to graduate from Villa Madonna College (see **Thomas More College**) in 1958 and was drafted in the NBA's ninth round that year by the Cincinnati Royals. He was a six-foot-seven forward who played professionally for five years with the Royals, the Chicago Zephyrs/Baltimore Bullets, and the Detroit Pistons.

Larry Staverman.

While an assistant at Notre Dame University in South Bend, Ind., Staverman was selected as the first coach of the American Basketball Association's Indiana Pacers in 1967 and served in the same capacity with the NBA's Kansas City Kings in 1978. For 15 years he was the superintendent of the old Cleveland Stadium in Cleveland, Ohio, and later helped to build the new multipurpose stadium downtown in Nashville, Tenn. He died in 2007 and is buried in Mother of God Cemetery in Covington.

"Larry Staverman." www.wikipedia.org (accessed January 5, 2007).
"Our Larry Leader of Kings," *KP,* January 10, 1978, 9K.
Staverman, Larry. Telephone interview by Michael R. Sweeney, January 9, 2007.
"Staverman New King's Assistant," *KP,* December 15, 1977, 27K.

Michael R. Sweeney

STEAMBOAT DISASTERS. The first steamboat appeared on the Ohio River in 1811, when the *New Orleans* came through on its way to New Orleans. Although the new invention represented a huge advance in transportation, it carried serious risks. The elements were unpredictable; the equipment used, such as the boilers and the gauges, was relatively primitive; and the operators of early steam vessels often lacked necessary knowledge or caution. The average life of a steamboat in the 19th century was approximately four years. While nature provided hazards in the form of snags, ice, fog, and high and low river levels, manmade disasters such as explosions, collisions, and fire (which often occurred during racing) were among the reasons vessels—and many lives—were lost.

Steam packets carrying cargo and passengers grew in popularity. As business developed, pressures such as cargo and passenger deadlines grew as well and could encourage risk-taking. Voyages were undertaken even when the water level was low, exposing the packet and its contents to special hazards. During the late 1840s, bulk cargo carriers in the form of steam towboats made their appearance, and after the **Civil War** they began to supplant the packet trade. Far fewer towboats were lost, for many reasons. Business was much less pressing for bulk cargo than for passenger and miscellaneous cargo transport. Steam towboats, like their modern propeller-driven diesel descendants, were generally under contractual obligation to one or more parties simply to deliver their cargoes intact, and thus did not fall victim to accidents caused by speed or racing. The towboats' heavier machinery called for stronger hulls and adequate bracing, which in turn required a greater depth of hold. Before channel improvements were made in the early 20th century (See **Ohio River Navigation**), the river was shallower, and towboats frequently were laid up during low-water season. As a result the life of their hulls and machinery was prolonged.

The Northern Kentucky shore between Maysville and Carrollton was the scene of many disasters. In the lists below, the boats are packets unless identified otherwise, and all the vessels were lost except the few noted otherwise.

Boiler Explosions

Union, below Big Bone Island, December 2, 1826

Tally-ho, Dover Landing above Augusta, May 1, 1830

Redstone, Carrollton wharf while racing with *Wild Wagoner,* April 2, 1852

Raven (towboat), Covington, April 5, 1870, raised and returned to service

Phantom, Brooks Bar above Maysville, while racing with *Handy,* June 28, 1881

Collisions

Polander and *Hornet,* opposite Cincinnati, Ohio, April 19, 1832

Brooklyn and *Confidence,* Big Bone Island, November 6, 1849

Brooklyn (towboat) and *Scioto,* Augusta, 1853

John C. Fremont and *Switzerland,* near Ghent, January 1855, both returned to service

Kentucky Home and *Telegraph No. 3,* Sugar Creek Bend, July 30, 1855, returned to service

Lady Walton and *Norman,* one mile above Warsaw, August 2, 1864

Highland Chief rammed by *Major Anderson,* two miles above Ghent, August 18, 1864

C.T. Dumont and *Tom Rees* (towboat), Big Bone Island, December 14, 1865, both returned to service

America and ***United States,*** Rayls Landing near Warsaw, December 4, 1868

Henry M. Stanley and *Joseph Walton* (towboat), Rabbit Hash, sinking the latter, April 4, 1900

Cincinnati and *Belfont* (diesel sternwheeler towboat), below Carrollton, May 24, 1928

Weather-Related Incidents

Helen Mar, ice, Maysville, February 24, 1855, raised and returned to service

Albertine, Flag, Madonna, and *Salem,* ice, Covington, February 24, 1856

Washington, ice, Covington, February 1867

C.T. Dumont, **tornado**, Warsaw (Ky.) wharf boat, August 19, 1867

Champion No. 6 (towboat), below Cincinnati, December 12, 1869; later returned to service

Swallow, snowstorm, two miles below Covington, December 1869

Etna, ice, opposite Ripley, Ohio, January 12, 1879, raised and returned to service

Al Martin (towboat), ice, Carrollton, December 1903

Big Kanawha, ice, Maysville, 1906

Hattie Brown, windstorm, Carrollton, March 1915

Princess, ice, mouth of Kentucky River, Carrollton, January 1918

Fire

Circassian and *Trenton,* Maysville, February 27, 1848

Belle Quigley and *Vermont,* Carrollton, February 5, 1856

Henry A. Jones, one mile below Augusta, February 27, 1858

Andy Fulton, Carrollton, July 29, 1861

Bostona No. 3, Maysville (Ky.) wharf boat, October 8, 1866

D.M. Sechler, Carrollton, December 4, 1868

Uncle Sam (towboat), Carrollton, October 17, 1914

Laurance, Maysville, 1930, rebuilt and returned to service

Ohio (ferryboat), Carrollton, May 15, 1936, rebuilt and returned to service

A.C. Ingersoll Jr. (towboat), one mile above the Tietzville Light, August 23, 1940

John J. Kelly (towboat), near Rabbit Hash, August 29, 1958

Captain Hook's (floating restaurant, originally the towboat *Destrehan*), Covington, October 14, 1971

Miscellaneous Disasters

Metropolis, sank at Sugar Creek near Warsaw, December 26, 1858

Tiger (towboat), struck Kirby's Rock on Kentucky shore at Mile 500, June 7, 1864, raised and returned to service

Arrow (towboat), capsized opposite Aurora, Ind., December 14, 1865, raised and returned to service

National, retired and wrecked by high water at Covington wharf, October 1873

Wildwood, sank at Augusta, ca. 1880

Bengal Tiger (towboat), wrecked against bridges near Covington, April 1883, returned to service

Minnie Bay, sank on Kentucky shore opposite Moscow, Ohio, October 15, 1889

W.F. Nisbet, sank at Wellsburg, in Bracken Co., January 1, 1900

Fulton (towboat), capsized beneath Central Bridge, Newport, July 7, 1915

Jim Wood No. 2 (towboat), sank after striking pier at Lock and Dam No. 33 above Maysville, November 9, 1917

Margaret (towboat), capsized near Maysville, December 18, 1920, raised and rebuilt

Helper (towboat), capsized in Cincinnati harbor, March 16, 1922, raised and returned to service

W.H. Warwick (towboat), sank above Dam 36, November 1923, and burned while sunk, November 27, 1923

Sallie Marmet (towboat), sank above Lock No. 36, August 1925, raised and returned to service

Calvin B. Beach (towboat), sank on bar opposite Higginsport, Ohio, January 8, 1938, raised and returned to service

G.W. McBride (towboat), struck the **L&N Bridge** at Newport and capsized, February 22, 1942

Omar (towboat), sank at mouth of Licking River, May 22, 1948, raised and returned to service

Chief of Engineers, U.S. Army, comp. *The Ohio River, 1934.* Washington, D.C.: Government Printing Office, 1935.

Lloyd, James T. *Lloyd's Steamboat Directory, and Disasters on the Western Waters.* Cincinnati: James T. Lloyd, 1856. Lithographed (Cincinnati: Young and Klein, 1979).

Lytle, William M., and Forrest R. Holdcamper, comp. *Merchant Steam Vessels of the United States, 1790–1868, Supplement No. 1.* Ed. C. Bradford Mitchell. Staten Island, N.Y.: Steamship Historical Society of America, 1978.

Way, Frederick, Jr., comp. *Way's Packet Directory, 1848–1994.* Athens: Ohio Univ. Press, 1994.

Way, Frederick, Jr., and Joseph W. Rutter, comps. *Way's Steam Towboat Directory.* Athens: Ohio Univ. Press, 1990.

Barbara Huffman

STEINFELDT, HARRY A. (b. September 29, 1877, St. Louis, Mo.; d. August 17, 1914, Bellevue, Ky.). Major league baseball player Harry Albert Steinfeldt was the son of Henry and Charlottte Todde Steinfeldt. The family moved to Bellevue, Ky., when Harry was a young boy. There, he met and married a local girl, Myrtle Lockwood, and they took up residence at 220 Ward Ave. in Bellevue. The couple had one child, a daughter. Steinfeldt began his big league career as a right-handed batting and throwing infielder/outfielder with the 1898 Cincinnati Reds. His best season with Cincinnati was in 1903, when he batted .312 and batted in 83 runs. He played with the Reds for seven seasons before being traded to the National League's Chicago Cubs in 1906. Steinfeldt played third base for the Cubs, on the team that had the famous double-play combination of Tinkers, Evers, and Chance. That Chicago team played in the World Series in 1906, 1907, 1908, and 1910 and won the World Championship in 1907 and 1908.

They were considered one of the greatest baseball teams ever assembled. In 1909, when the Cubs failed to win the National League pennant, it was primarily due to the brilliant pitching of Covington, Ky., native **Howie Camnitz**, who led his Pittsburgh Pirates to the league championship. When Frank Chance, first baseman for the Cubs, retired as a player in 1908 to become manager of the team, he moved Steinfeldt from third base to first. The move was not popular with Cubs fans, who later blamed Steinfeldt for the team's not being World Champions in 1909 and 1910. Steinfeldt was traded to the National League's Boston Braves in 1911 and retired from baseball at the end of that season. During his 14-year major league career, Steinfeldt appeared in 1,646 games, batted .267, hit 27 home runs, and batted in 762 runs.

After retiring he remained popular in his hometown, where he was expected to become the next mayor of Bellevue; however, he decided not to run. He was just 36 years old when he died unexpectedly of a cerebral hemorrhage in his Bellevue home. He was a member of the Christian Science faith, and his pastor, Rev. Otterman of Cincinnati, conducted the funeral services. Floral tributes and letters of condolence were received from all major league teams and nearly every prominent baseball player in the United States. Steinfeldt's body was placed in a vault at Evergreen Cemetery, Southgate, but in 1921 it was moved to the Spring Grove Cemetery in Cincinnati.

The Baseball Page. "Harry Steinfeldt." www.thebaseballpage.com (accessed January 7, 2007).
Kentucky Death Certificate No. 20419, for the year 1914.
Reference.com. "Harry Steinfeldt." www.reference.com (accessed January 7, 2007).
Reis, Jim. "Famous Infield Also Included Bellevue's Steinfeldt," *KP*, March 30, 1998, 4K.
——. "The Wonder of Wonderville," *KP*, March 8, 2004, 4K.
Spring Grove Cemetery Records, Cincinnati.
"Steinfeldt Funeral Set for Thursday," *KP*, August 19, 1914, 1.

STEINFORD, GEORGE AND ROSE (George Steinford, b. February 22, 1900, Covington, Ky.; d. July 9, 1980, Covington, Ky.; Rosalyn Barnett Steinford, b. February 8, 1899, Paris, Ky.; d. December 22, 1973, Covington, Ky.). George Steinford was the son of stonecutter Charles G. and Anna Casselman Steinford; his wife, Rosalyn Steinford, was the daughter of James and Mary A. Salmons Barnett. George and Rosalyn married in May 1923. During the **Great Depression**, the couple recognized that poor children in their neighborhood in Covington were not happy at Christmastime. The Steinfords, who had no children of their own, began to purchase and repair used toys for the neighborhood's needy children. Thus began a lifelong project for Rose and George, who was a Kenton Co. commissioner and a Kentucky state representative.

During the next 50 years, the Steinfords quietly developed a network to secure the names of needy children and anonymously delivered the toys to the children's families during the Christmas season. What started as a neighborhood project soon expanded to include children in Kenton, Boone, and Campbell counties. The Steinfords' home, at 513 W. Sixth St. in Covington, grew to resemble Santa's workshop. Throughout the year, as toys were repaired and refurbished, the Steinfords developed their list of needy families and packed the gifts for those families. Friends of the Steinfords pitched in to handle the distribution of the toys.

When Rose Steinford died in 1973, it appeared that a tradition and much-needed service had ceased. George Steinford's health was failing, but several Covington–Kenton Co. **Jaycees** who had been involved in the project persuaded Steinford to continue to organize the Christmas project at least one more year. He did, and with the success of the project that year and the growing support of his friends, in 1974 he formed the Rose and George Steinford Toy Foundation Inc. to perpetuate the service and continue to fulfill the couple's stated wish, "that the Christmas spirit will fill a child's heart in time of need."

George died in 1980, but the Rose and George Steinford Toy Foundation continues the tradition of generosity that the Steinfords established. George Steinford was buried next to his wife of 50 years at the Mother of God Cemetery in Latonia. Since the formation of the foundation, volunteers have provided Christmas presents for nearly 2,000 children in Northern Kentucky each year.

"Ex-Kenton Commissioner George Steinford Dies," *KP*, July 10, 1980, 8K.
Kreimer, Peggy. "Mrs. Santa Claus Won't Deliver Toys This Year," *KP*, December 24, 1973, 3K.
Reis, Jim. "Single Vote Launched Career, Ended Another," *KP*, January 22, 2001, 4K.
The Steinford Toy Foundation. "History of the Foundation." www.steinford.org (accessed August 30, 2006).

Donna M. Bloemer

STEPHENS, LEONARD, GENERAL (b. March 10, 1791, Orange Co., Va.; d. March 8, 1873, Florence, Ky.). Legislator and sheriff Leonard Stephens was one of 11 children born to Benjamin and Dorothy Waller Stephens. The family left Orange Co., Va., in 1806 and came, by way of Bryants Station, to their new home along the Banklick Creek in Kenton Co. Stephens served as a brigadier general in the **War of 1812**, where he fought in campaigns against the Indians. He married Catherine Sanford on August 14, 1813. Stephens was elected to the Kentucky House of Representatives in 1824 and served until 1828. In 1828 Stephens was elected to the state Senate, where he served until 1832. When Kenton Co. was split off from Campbell Co. in 1840, he was appointed the first sheriff of Kenton Co. and held that office for two years. Stephens continued to work his large farm until he was 75 years old. He distributed most of the land to his children while he was still living. The 1,500-acre Stephens farm, known as Locust Grove, originally extended from today's Stevenson Rd. to Richardson Rd. In 1855 Stephens helped to organize in Florence, Ky., the **Florence Baptist Church**, where he remained a member for the rest of his life. He moved to Florence shortly before his death. He died on March 8, 1873, at age 81 and was buried in the family graveyard, near Richardson Rd. in Independence.

Ellison, Carol. "A Dusty Reminder of Past," *KP*, September 2, 1975, 5.
"Obituary of General Leonard Stephens," *CJ*, March 15, 1873, 2.

STEPHENS, ROBERT F. (b. August 16, 1927, Covington, Ky.; d. April 13, 2002, Lexington, Ky.). Robert Francis Stephens, a lawyer and a Kentucky Supreme Court justice, attended Beechwood High School in Fort Mitchell (see **Beechwood Public Schools**), where he was valedictorian of his graduating class in 1945. He served in the U.S. Navy from 1945 to 1946. He enrolled in a prelaw program at Indiana University at Bloomington, Ind., in 1948 and graduated from the University of Kentucky Law School at Lexington in 1951. Stephens served as a law clerk for the Kentucky Court of Appeals through 1952. He worked for a year as an attorney for the Kentucky Department of Insurance. From 1953 through 1958 he served as legal counsel and executive officer for the Salvage Lumber and Manufacturing Company. He was assistant county attorney for Fayette Co. during 1964–1969. He was elected Fayette Co. judge (the position now known as judge executive) and held that office from 1970 to 1975. In this position, he was instrumental in implementing the historic merger of the governments of the City of Lexington and Fayette Co. into the state's first urban-county government.

Stephens served as attorney general of Kentucky from 1975 to 1979 and was then appointed a Kentucky Supreme Court justice by Governor Julian Carroll (1974–1979). In 1980 Stephens was elected to fill an unexpired term on this court and was subsequently reelected for eight-year terms in 1984 and 1992. During his tenure, he was part of a progressive court, which handed down a number of opinions that had a dramatic effect on all citizens of Kentucky. Their highest-profile decision was in the 1989 case ***Rose vs. Council for Better Education, Inc.***, in which the court declared the funding of the state's public school system to be unconstitutional. That ruling resulted in the 1990 enactment of the Kentucky Education Reform Act (KERA), which balanced the funding of schools across the state. Explaining the importance of the educational reform, Stephens said, "the children who live in poor districts and those who live in rich districts, must be given the same opportunity and access to an adequate education." The court also mandated continuing education for judges and other court employees. Justice Stephens lobbied the General Assembly to have video cameras installed in courtrooms, making it possible to review tapes of trials, rather than sort through stacks of paperwork. Stephens resigned as chief justice in 1998 but continued to serve as a justice. The following year he resigned completely from the court to accept an appointment as secretary of the Justice Cabinet. He had served on the court for almost 20 years, 16 of them as chief justice. Stephens died of lung cancer at age 74 at his Lexington home and was buried in the Lexington Cemetery.

Houck, Jeanne. "Robert F. Stephens: 1927–2002," *KP*, April 15, 2002, 1K.

STEVENSON, JOHN WHITE (b. May 4, 1812, Richmond, Va.; d. August 10, 1886, Covington, Ky.). Prominent attorney and Democratic politician John White Stevenson was the son of Andrew and Mary White Stevenson. His early education was by private tutor, and he earned BA and JD degrees at the University of Virginia at Charlottesville. Afterward, he lived for a short time at Vicksburg, Miss., before coming to Covington in 1841. He married Sibella Winston in 1843, and they had five children. Stevenson was elected to the Kentucky House of Representatives in 1845, where he served for four years. He next served in the U.S. House of Representatives from 1857 to 1861. In 1867 Stevenson was elected Kentucky lieutenant governor on the Democratic ticket to serve with Governor John L. Helm (1867). When Governor Helm died after five days in office, Stevenson became governor. During his term in office, Stevenson had to call out the state militia several times, to quell violence against African Americans who were attempting to assert their right to vote. He resigned as governor in 1871 upon being appointed to the U.S. Senate, where he served for six years. Stevenson died at age 73 and was first buried at Highland Cemetery in Fort Mitchell, then reinterred at the Spring Grove Cemetery in Cincinnati.

Biographical Directory of the United States Congress. www.senate.gov (accessed May 20, 2008).
Kleber, John E., ed. *The Kentucky Encyclopedia*. Lexington: Univ. Press of Kentucky, 1992.

STEWART IRON WORKS. The Stewart family, who came from the Glens of Scotland, arrived in Louisville during the early 1800s. Thomas Stewart was a contractor in Louisville who died young; two of his sons became steamboat captains. A third son, Richard C. Stewart (1829–1906), learned the blacksmith trade. By 1850 R. C., as he was known, was managing his own blacksmith business in Louisville. He resided for a time in Cleveland, Ohio, where his sons Richard C. and Wallace A. Stewart were born, and in Newport, but by 1862 R. C. Stewart Sr. had set up a business in Covington. Under the company name Architectural Iron Works, R. C. Stewart manufactured verandas, balconies, stairways, doors, shutters, cellar gratings, awnings, stirrups, anchors, hog chains, bolts, hinges, railings, bridge iron, and sheet iron at 813–815 Madison Ave.

Richard C. Jr. (1857–1937) and Wallace A. (1858–1910) followed their father into the iron industry, working from several locations within Covington. In 1886 the brothers ventured west to Wichita, Kans., where for a few years they successfully engaged in the iron business. For unknown reasons, they had moved back east to Cincinnati

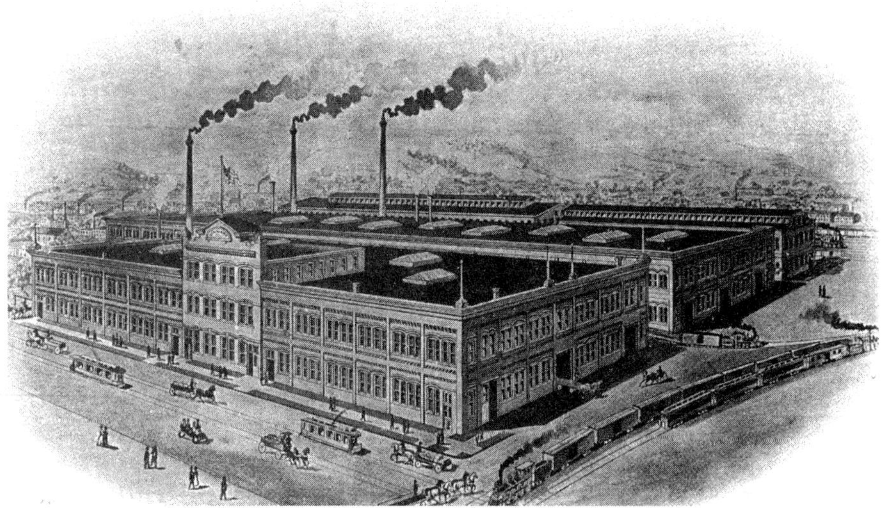

Stewart Iron Works, Covington.

by 1895 and eventually became involved in enterprises such as jail-cell construction and decorative iron work. In 1903 their Stewart Iron Works (SIW) moved to a new modern plant at 17th St. and Madison Ave. in Covington. The facility was located at what was known as the KC Junction, the intersection of the **Louisville and Nashville** and the **Chesapeake and Ohio Railroads**, a major railhead connection that facilitated making shipments nationwide. Ultimately, the local ironworking firm used four buildings at the Madison Ave. site for a wrought iron furniture and fence division, a truck division, the jail cell division, and, much later, a chain-link fence division. The company supplied iron fencing to the Sears and Roebuck Company of Chicago, under a 23-year contract.

Stewart Iron Works built railroad entrance gates for the Panama Canal and an iron fence around the British Embassy in Washington, D.C. Recently the company as it is now configured restored the entrance gates to the White House that were in place during the term of President Rutherford B. Hayes, for the President Hayes Memorial Museum in Fremont, Ohio. During the Victorian era, Stewart Iron Works products were shipped internationally and graced the fronts of French châteaus, of London townhouses, of houses on San Francisco's Nob Hill, of brownstones in New York City, of homes in New Orleans, and of countless cemeteries. At the 1904 World Fair in St. Louis, the SIW was awarded the Grand Prize and the gold medal of merit in construction for its numerous designs of iron fencing and lawn furniture.

During **World War I**, Stewart Iron Works manufactured one-, two-, and three-ton trucks, under the name of the United States Motor Truck Company (incorporated 1914). Some of the trucks made by the firm were sold to local individuals; the first one off the assembly line went to John Craig, a contractor and former mayor of Covington. Some were delivered as far away as Australia. Over the years, customers for SIW's motor truck division included **Dow Drug Stores**, the *Cincinnati Enquirer*, the *Cincinnati Post*, Firestone Tire & Rubber, and Cincinnati's Hoffmann Meats and French Bauer Dairy. The motor truck division's high point was reached in 1918, when it delivered 100 trucks to the U.S. Army. The company also made heli exhaust manifolds for use in the diesel engines of submarines. The SIW truck division ceased in 1928.

The jail cell division delivered products to prisons such as the federal penitentiaries at Atlanta, Ga.; Alcatraz; and Marion, Ill., and to state penitentiary facilities at Sing Sing and Attica, N.Y., and New York City's Rikers Island. According to a story told in the history of the Stewart Iron Works Company, during the early 1930s, a load of jail cells en route from the dock at San Francisco to Alcatraz Island slipped off the barge and rests still today at the bottom of the bay. The last jail cells were produced in 1985, when prisons began using electronic locking mechanisms. An extant example of a local Stewart jail product is the no-longer-used lockup at Brooksville, in Bracken Co. The old jail at Latonia (before Latonia became part of Covington) was Stewart-made. All told, the company built cells for at least 92 prisons and 85 smaller city station houses and lockups nationwide. The SIW also produced bank vaults.

During **World War II**, the SIW fashioned portable Bailey bridges for the U.S. Army. By folding and extending, these quickly laid iron bridges allowed military troop movements to cross waterways. The company also made folding landing-strip mats, tank parts, and machine gun mountings. The SIW and its employees held at least 27 U.S. patents, covering such products as racehorse track starting gates; jail-cell locking systems, including remote-control mechanisms; joist hangers; wedge-shaped hoof pads for horseshoes; self-closing gates; radiator protectors; dumping devices for trucks; and fence rail connectors. The company has retained many of the century-old drawings, patterns, and molds of its products from its heyday, and some of them are still used today.

An outstanding employee of the SIW—one among many—was Robert C. "Cap" Bunge, a prison expert. In the early 1930s, the Federal Bureau of Prisons consulted with him in the planning stage before constructing Alcatraz, the strongest prison in the world, which was to be escape-proof and to house the nation's most hardened criminals. He also served on a U.S. commission to develop the federal prison system. In 1949 Bunge retired from the firm's prison division after 19 years as its chief engineer. His nickname Cap was from his rank of captain in the U.S. Army during **World War I**.

Over the years, the Stewart family was heavily involved in the Northern Kentucky community. R. C. Stewart Jr. was one of the founders of the Covington Industrial Club, the predecessor of the modern **Northern Kentucky Chamber of Commerce**. He was also a baseball team owner and was instrumental in bringing to Covington its 1914 Federal League baseball franchise, the short-lived **Covington Blue Sox**. The family converted the old Star baseball park in Covington at 17th St. and Madison Ave., across from the firm's factories, into Stewart Park, beautiful grounds available to both company employees and the public; it also served as a showroom for the SIW's outdoor products. The Stewarts were benefactors of the **Linden Grove Cemetery** in Covington, lending time, workers, and funds toward its upkeep. They were members of Covington's **First Christian Church**.

R. C. Stewart Sr. died in 1906, and Wallace A. Stewart died in 1910. The last Stewart family member to lead the company was Stanley M. Stewart, R. C. Stewart Jr.'s grandson, who headed the firm from 1944 until 1955. In 1966 the company was taken over by Pott Industries of St. Louis, which merged the SIW with Decatur Iron and Steel. In 1974 Pott Industries ordered Stewart-Decatur to sell off all its divisions except the jail works. One former division of Stewart Iron Works went to Erlanger, where it continued to make chain-link fence and ornamental iron gates, railings, and fences. In 1987 the Erlanger division of the new Stewart Iron Works returned to Covington to Building 3 at its former Madison Ave. site.

The company has since changed ownership several times but continues in a reduced state, specializing in ornamental gates, fencing, and furniture. Much of today's production is for historic restoration and architectural accents. Privately held, the firm is a mere shadow of itself in its heyday, the early 20th century, when there were at least 300 employees and Stewart Iron Works was Covington's largest employer. Today's book of business has included projects such as at the Flagler Mansion in Palm Beach, Fla., two miles of fencing for a cemetery in Toledo, Ohio, and a city fountain (an elaborate dog, horse, and human drinking fountain) in Ligionier, Pa. During the early 1900s, the SIW was the world's largest manufacturer of iron fencing and lawn furniture and is still remembered for once having been Covington's industrial giant.

"Covington Is to Secure Big Motor Plant," *KP,* June 6, 1914, 1.

"Famed Prison Expert Retiring to Have Fun," *KP,* March 26, 1949, 1.

Franzen, Gene. "Ironworks Spans 3 Centuries," *KE,* December 30, 2001, B1.

Guido, Anna. "Iron Works Profits in Past," *CE,* May 25, 2006, A10.

Hunnicutt, John M. "Profile of the Stewart Iron Works Company, Inc., Covington, Kentucky," paper delivered to the Christopher Gist Historical Society, May 28, 1963, Northern Kentucky Univ. Archives, Highland Heights, Ky.

Kreimer, Peggy. "Artisans Ply Ancient Trade," *KP,* May 27, 2000, 1K.

Lietzenmayer, Karl J. "Stewart Iron Works, a Kentucky Centenary Company," *NKH* 5, no.1 (Autumn–Winter 1997): 1–14.

"Motor Truck Company Has Its Election," *KP,* July 17, 1914, 1.

"Stewart Iron Works." www.stewartironworks.com (accessed June 10, 2006).

"The Stewart Iron Works: A Credit to Covington and to the State," *KP,* April 8, 1905, 8.

Stewart Iron Works Archives, Covington, Ky.

Sharon Jobert

STEWARTSVILLE. Stewartsville is located on Ky. Rt. 36, eight miles west of Williamstown, in Grant Co. During the 19th century, Stewartsville was a vital town: on Saturdays, its general stores were busy with grocery shopping, political rallies, and socializing. There also was plenty of work for the town's blacksmith. The area's rural economy was based on corn, tobacco, cattle, sheep, poultry, and horses. Transportation was improved when in 1891 the Stewartsville and Owen Co. Turnpike was incorporated locally, with Robert Clay Blain as president. By 1900 the use of tollgates on this turnpike was terminated because its users revolted. Three churches anchored the community, the Stewartsville Baptist Church (still active), the Hopewell Methodist Church, and the Old Salem Methodist Church.

The schools of Hopewell/Sheriff, Smoky Row, as well as the Stewartsville School (still standing) were social centers, where pie suppers were held or pupils from the school gave recitations. Stables were provided at school for students arriving on horseback or in buggies. The yearly school census named each child between the ages of 6 and 20 as well as the head of each child's household. Eight grades could be completed at the school under the instruction of qualified teachers who were supervised by the trustees. The Gaugh, Salem, Mitts Rd., and Sheriff cemetaries are nearby. A post office operated at Stewartsville from 1868 until the arrival of rural free delivery in 1906.

Chapman, Virgil, Sr., comp. *Grant County Cemeteries.* Vol. 1. Williamstown, Ky.: Grant Co. Historical Society, 1988.

Conrad, John B., ed. *History of Grant County.* Williamstown, Ky.: Grant Co. Historical Society, 1992.

Pease, Janet, comp. *Abstracted County Court Records.* Vol. 9. Williamstown, Ky.: Grant Co. Historical Society, 1992.

Mary Louis Evans

STOBER, HENRY BERNARD (b. August 25, 1901, Cincinnati, Ohio; d. early January 1945, aboard the Japanese prisoner-of-war ship *Enoura Maru*, Takao Harbor, Formosa). Rev. Henry Stober, a Catholic priest and a **World War II** chaplain and hero, was the son of Martin and Philomena Luhn Stober. Raised in Cincinnati, he attended minor seminary (studying philosophy) at St. John's Seminary in Little Rock, Ark., and major seminary (studying theology) at Mount St. Mary Seminary in Cincinnati. After his ordination in 1931, Stober served at **St. John Catholic Church**, Covington; St. Elizabeth Hospital, Covington (later **St. Elizabeth Medical Center**); **Mount St. Martin**, Newport; **St. Agnes Catholic Church**, Fort Wright, the **Sisters of Notre Dame** at St. Joseph Heights, Park Hills; and the **Cathedral Basilica of the Assumption**, Covington. In 1932–1933, he served as secretary to Bishop **Francis W. Howard**. Suffering from chronic sinusitis, for which he underwent surgeries, Stober followed the advice of his surgeon and spent time during the mid-1930s in the drier climates of Arizona and California, where he served as a priest. His health restored, he returned to Covington and in 1939 was appointed pastor of **St. William Catholic Church**, Williamstown. In 1940 he volunteered for service as a chaplain in the U.S. Army, spending some time at Kelly Field and Brook Field, both in Texas. His rank was 1st lieutenant. The following year, he was deployed to the Philippine Islands as chaplain of the 14th Engineer and the 57th Infantry regiments and promoted to the rank of captain. On April 9, 1942, after U.S. forces on the mainland of the Philippines surrendered to the Japanese, Stober became a prisoner of war (POW) and was subjected to the horrible inhumanities of the Bataan Death March. On April 17, 1942, he arrived at the Japanese-controlled Camp O'Donnell in the Philippines. There Dr. **Alvin C. Poweleit** of Newport recognized Stober, who was emaciated and suffering from dysentery, malaria, and beriberi. Poweleit nursed Stober back to health, and in September 1942 Stober was sent for work detail on the island of Mindanao, at the Davao Penal Colony, where he ministered to Christians and Jews alike. In June 1944 he was sent aboard a prison ship to Manila and then to a POW camp at Cabanatuan. In December 1944 he and 1,600 other POWs boarded the *Oryoku Maru*, a "hell ship" bound for slave labor in Japan. Bombed by American airplanes, the ship sank, but Stober and others avoided drowning and were transferred to the Japanese ship *Enoura Maru,* where Stober died while the ship was anchored in the harbor of Takao, Formosa (Taiwan). Varying accounts place his death as sometime between January 1 and January 9, although the most plausible is the latter, when the *Enoura Maru* was bombed by U.S. planes. Deceased POWs were either buried or cremated at

Takao. Stober was posthumously awarded the Bronze Star (for valor), the Purple Heart, the Prisoners of War Medal, and the Asiatic and Pacific Campaign Medal. His name was included on the Chaplains' Hill Monument in Arlington National Cemetery in Washington, D.C.

Mahoney, A. Joseph. *The Chaplain: Henry Bernard Stober Story, Captain United States Army, 1901–1945.* Lake San Marcos, Calif.: Privately published, ca. 2001.

Tenkotte, Paul A., David E. Schroeder, and Thomas S. Ward. *To Be Catholic and American in Northern, Central, and Appalachian Kentucky: The Diocese of Covington, 1853–2003.* Forthcoming.

Paul A. Tenkotte

STOWE, HARRIET BEECHER, SLAVERY TO FREEDOM MUSEUM. See **Harriet Beecher Stowe Slavery to Freedom Museum**.

STREETCARS. Originally horse-drawn and later electrified, streetcars were the first major form of public transportation in American cities. The Covington Street Railway began operating the first horsecars in Covington along its Madison Ave. route in August 1867. In the same month it inaugurated service across the **John A. Roebling Bridge** to Cincinnati; by July 1868 the Covington streetcars were carrying 2,600 passengers per day across the bridge. In 1867 the Newport Street Railway Company established horsecar service in Newport, extending it across the Newport and Covington Bridge at Fourth St. A third franchise, the Newport and Dayton Street Railway, completed construction of a line to Dayton, Ky., in 1870. A fourth corporation, the Covington and Cincinnati Street Railway Company, built north-south horsecar lines along Main and Scott Sts. in Covington in 1875, connecting them in a continuous loop along east-west streets Fourth and Pike. The following year, the Newport Street Railway Company completed tracks across the Newport and Cincinnati Bridge (the L&N Bridge). Expansion of the horsecar lines continued, and in the 1880s the four main streetcar companies of Covington and Newport were consolidated into one, which became known as the **Green Line**. The Green Line began conversion of its horsecars to electric streetcars in 1890 in Covington and in 1892 in Newport. The Maysville Street Railroad and Transfer Company began the operation of horsecars in Maysville in August 1883 and gained permission to convert to electricity in 1890.

The electric streetcar was the dominant form of urban passenger transportation in Northern Kentucky between 1890 and 1930. Running on two steel rails and propelled by electricity accessed from an overhead wire by means of a trolley wheel or shoe, the streetcar represented a quantum leap in speed and comfort compared to the horse and buggy or even the early automobiles when they had to traverse largely unpaved, and sometimes almost impassable, streets and roads.

A streetcar right-of-way in urban areas was usually shared with horse-drawn (and later automobile) traffic. When a street railway built extensions to newly developing suburbs where a private right-of-way was the norm, the streetcars could double their average urban speed from 7 to 15 miles per hour. As a consequence, the streetcar was a primary factor in the development of business districts and residential subdivisions at ever-increasing distances from traditional inner-city areas. The streetcar enabled individuals to reside outside the inner city, with its congestion and its often foul air, yet be within easy commuting distance of their downtown job site.

Although streetcar motors were typically powered by 550- to 600-volt direct current (DC), cheaper alternating current (AC) was either produced or purchased by transit companies for conversion to DC. By means of substations located at various points on a street railway, the AC current was fed through rotary converters that transformed it to safer DC for use by streetcars.

Direct current of 550 volts was supplied to the Northern Kentucky streetcars of the Green Line; it flowed from the trolley wire down the trolley pole to the motorman's controller box on the front platform. The controller was a device for regulating the amount of current to be sent to the car's motors. A slight turn or "notch" of the controller completed an electric circuit between the trolley wire, the motors, and the rail, allowing current to flow to the motors through a labyrinth of thin, cast-iron "grids" that offered considerable resistance and thereby limited the current to the right amount to produce a smooth start. As the motorman pulled the controller handle farther around, a drum switch inside the controller box gradually reduced the resistant grids until full line voltage was sent to the motors, causing the streetcar to run at top speed.

Each streetcar motor was contained in a watertight housing. The car axle passed through bearings at one end of the housing, and the other end rested on springs attached to the truck frame. A large gear on the axle meshed with a pinion on the armature shaft, and the motor revolved around the axle at about four times the speed of the car wheels. To retard the speed of a streetcar, a motorman "notched down" his controller.

A streetcar built around 1900 was a marvel of the woodworker's art. The car bodies were made almost completely of wood; the car floors under the seats were made of standard yellow pine, but the more durable maple was used for aisle floors. Interior trim, sashes, and doors were made from cherry and mahogany. Side and end panels were constructed of five-eighths-inch yellow pine covered with a heavy-gauge steel.

The Green Line in Northern Kentucky employed two primary types of streetcars. Some 200 single-trucked streetcars (two-axle cars) made up the bulk of the Green Line fleet as late as 1929. These 30-foot-long cars, seating about 35 passengers, had a crew of two: a motorman (the "driver") and a conductor who stood by the backdoor entrance and collected fares, called out designated stops, and looked after the general well-being of the passengers. In 1917 the Green Line purchased 25 double-trucked (four-axle) cars measuring more than 45 feet long and capable of seating more than 50 passengers. These new cars were fitted with four 25-hp motors as compared to the two 35-hp motors in the single-truck cars. As an economy measure, the large cars were rebuilt in 1937 with larger front doors for passenger entry and with a fare box installed near the motorman's seat, eliminating the need for a conductor.

The double-trucked cars were equipped with air brakes. Air pressure was supplied by an air pump driven by a small electric motor. As the pressure dropped, the motor driving a compressor would start up, to manufacture compressed air that was stored in a reservoir tank suspended from the car body. A small valve allowed the motorman to admit air under pressure from the reservoir to the brake cylinder and stop the car in a smooth and safe manner. The same compressed air was also used to apply sand to the car rails for an emergency stop or when the rails were slippery. A downward pressure on the brake valve actuated the rail sanders.

In addition to carrying passengers (some 14 million in 1900 and more than 25 million by 1929), Green Line streetcars also hauled the U.S. Mail. Early cars were proudly lettered "U.S. Mail." In 1894 the Green Line started a closed-pouch mail service to and from the General Post Office (GPO) at Fifth and Walnut Sts. in Cincinnati, connecting to Northern Kentucky points. The mail was generally loaded among the passengers, but where the conductor could keep an eye on it. By 1900 there were mail routes from Cincinnati to Milldale (Latonia), to Dayton, Ky., and to Fort Thomas. In addition, the Green Line carried the mail from the Covington Post Office to Ludlow. Mail service to Dayton, Fort Thomas, and Ludlow was discontinued in 1901, but the Green Line continued closed-pouch mail service from Cincinnati to Newport (six trips per day), to Covington (nine trips), and to Latonia (two trips) for almost two more decades. The Green Line's involvement with the U.S. Mail ended in 1919. With the ever-increasing automobile traffic in downtown Cincinnati, the use of Green Line streetcars for on-street loading and unloading of mail in front of the GPO caused delays to both Green Line passengers and vehicular traffic. By then the motor truck was coming into its own, and the Post Office found that off-street dock loading onto the more flexible trucks afforded better protection of the mail from both the weather and potential thieves. The last Green Line car to carry mail left for Covington on July 26, 1919.

The Green Line also possessed two parlor cars, so named because they were equipped with curtains, carpeting, wicker tables and chairs, cut-glass dome lights, and even an ice-cooled refrigerator. Although the parlor cars were designed primarily for the use of company officials during inspection trips and for entertaining important business clients, the public could also rent these cars. The two cars, the *Bluegrass* and the *Kentucky,* could be chartered for local excursions to the **Lagoon Amusement Park**, the **Latonia Racecourse**,

Tacoma Park, or just a summer night out with a group of friends. Birthday parties in the parlor cars were especially popular, and until the 1930s, the *Bluegrass* and the *Kentucky* carried the well-dressed partygoers to the new suburbs while they sipped pink lemonade, enjoyed cake and ice cream kept cool by the newfangled "dry ice," and sang along with an accordionist or a violinist. The *Kentucky* remained available for use until 1950, when it was donated to the **Behringer-Crawford Museum**, where it survives today as one of the museum's centerpieces. Built in 1892 and converted to its parlor-car configuration in 1912, it is one of the two oldest extant streetcars in the United States. The car was restored by the volunteer efforts of **Transit Authority of Northern Kentucky** employees in the late 1990s.

In spite of their quiet operation and nonpolluting nature, streetcars fell out of favor with transit operators in the 1930s. Since roads were being paved at an ever-increasing rate by municipalities and other governmental authorities, motor buses were soon substituted whenever possible. With their use, the expense of maintaining streetcar tracks was avoided. Motor buses, not confined to a narrowly fixed rail path, could also more easily detour around traffic wrecks and flooded areas, and they could easily reach new subdivisions and industrial parks not accessible via the existing streetcar trackage.

Streetcars suspended operation in Maysville on December 31, 1936, being replaced by buses. The last streetcar line in Campbell Co., No. 11–Fort Thomas, was discontinued on August 23, 1947. All streetcar service in Northern Kentucky ended on July 2, 1950, when the No. 1–Fort Mitchell line was converted to motor buses.

Calvert, Jean, and John Klee. *Maysville, Kentucky: From Past to Present in Pictures.* Maysville, Ky.: Mason Co. Museum, 1983.
Clift, G. Glenn. *History of Maysville and Mason County.* Lexington, Ky.: Transylvania, 1936.
Lehmann, Terry W., and Earl W. Clark. *The Green Line.* Chicago: Central Electric Railfans' Association, 2000.
Tenkotte, Paul A. "Rival Cities to Suburbs: Covington and Newport, Kentucky, 1790–1890," PhD diss., Univ. of Cincinnati, 1989.

Terry W. Lehman

STRINGTOWN (BOONE CO.). The name Stringtown is not unique to Boone Co. As a matter of fact, throughout this country's history there have been hundreds of Stringtowns. It was a very common name given to the lineal towns and villages that sprang up along major roads, rivers, and ridges. A debate among locals concerns which geographical and topographical identifiers describe the "real" Stringtown in Boone Co. When **John Uri Lloyd** wrote his first novel, *Stringtown on the Pike*, set in his boyhood neighborhood of Florence, Ky., during the immediate post–**Civil War** era of the 1860s, he chose the name Stringtown instead of Florence, just as he chose the name Judge Elford in his text instead of Judge Herman Ashley, or Professor Drake instead of his father's real name. Lloyd readily admitted that all his characters were based on real people he knew who lived in the town. The people of Florence knew that Stringtown was really their town. Some even went so far as to lobby for the name to be officially changed to Stringtown. That did not occur, but Stringtown remained Florence's affectionate nickname over the years. The Stringtown that achieved official recognition was a little community also in Boone Co., just downriver from Anderson Ferry and Constance, on Ky. Rt. 8 along the Ohio River.

Reis, Jim. "Tiny Unincorporated Towns Abound in Boone," *KP*, December 9, 1985, 4K.
"Stringtown Goes a Bit Uptown," *CE*, December 31, 2001, Weekend section, 14.
Warner, Jennifer S. *Boone County: From Mastodons to the Millennium.* Burlington, Ky.: Boone Co. Bicentennial Book Committee, 1998.

Don Clare

STRINGTOWN (GRANT CO.). Stringtown in southeastern Grant Co. is strung out along three roads: Ky. Rt. 36, the Williamstown-Cynthiana Rd.; the Corinth-Stringtown Rd.; and the Stringtown-Webber Rd. It may be said that the center of Stringtown is the junction of Ky. Rt. 36 and the Corinth-Stringtown Rd. This is not the Stringtown made famous by Northern Kentucky author **John Uri Lloyd**.

The first settlers at Stringtown, arriving in 1818, were Francis and Mary Terrell Robinson, their 14 children, some of whom were married with children, and their 25 slaves. Francis Robinson built a large log cabin for his family and other cabins for his slaves. As each of his children married, the couple was given a tract of land and had a cabin built for them. Thomas T. Thompson, who married Frances Robinson, appears to have assisted in providing for the housing needs of each of the children as they married.

The first school was a log structure, replaced by a white frame building in 1910. This school was consolidated in 1926 with the school at Corinth. The Stringtown Christian Church was established in 1848 and rebuilt in 1877 on land donated by Benjamin Robinson, who specified that the church was to be named the Elizabeth Christian Church in honor of his daughter. This church is the only vestige remaining of the original town.

Conrad, John B., ed. *History of Grant County.* Williamstown, Ky.: Grant Co. Historical Society, 1992.

John B. Conrad

STRINGTOWN ON THE PIKE. In 1900 a novel by an obscure and unknown avocational author (but a famous and well-respected chemist and eclectic pharmacology genius) from Cincinnati named **John Uri Lloyd** (1849–1936) was serialized on the pages of the *Bookman* magazine. *Stringtown on the Pike* was presented in the magazine's serial sections over 10 issues. Later that same year, Dodd, Mead, and Company acquired the rights to publish the book by offering Lloyd more money than had ever been offered to any author, including Mark Twain. The book's first run of 50,000 copies sold within three months. The setting for the novel was Florence, Ky., where Lloyd grew up after coming to Northern Kentucky from New York with his family. His father was a civil engineer who relocated to help design and lay out a new railroad that never materialized. Instead of moving back, the Lloyds remained in Florence.

The characters and events of the book were all based on real people and true occurrences in Lloyd's boyhood, as he often confirmed to the media. He portrayed himself as Sammy Drew; Judge Elford was actually Judge Herman Ashley, a man of the highest principles and morals, who presided for many years over Boone Co. courts; Professor Drake, a very learned and analytical man who instructed the youth of the county, was Lloyd's own father. All the other characters were equally identified, recognized, and verified by the real residents of Florence, even 40 years later. Featuring the mixed sentiments and emotions of the **Civil War** and the Reconstruction era, coupled with an unprecedented treatment and presentation of local dialect and folklore, beliefs, and superstitions, *Stringtown on the Pike* quickly became an American favorite and classic, establishing Lloyd as one of America's new and aspiring young authors and initiating a series of Stringtown novels.

Grayson, Frank X. "Historic Spots in Greater Cincinnati," *KTS*, August 23, 1933, 7.
Kleber, John E., ed. *The Kentucky Encyclopedia.* Lexington: Univ. Press of Kentucky, 1992.
Lloyd, John Uri. *Stringtown on the Pike: A Tale of Northernmost Kentucky.* New York: Dodd, Mead, 1900.
Ward, William S. *A Literary History of Kentucky.* Knoxville: Univ. of Tennessee Press, 1988.

Don Clare

STRUBEL, EDWARD (b. April 4, 1875, Bavaria, Germany; d. January 10, 1964, Covington, Ky.). Edward Strubel, who became a church organist, attended a teachers' seminary in Arnstein and a music conservatory in Speyer, both in Germany. Trained as an organist, he left Germany at age 19 for the United States, arriving at Ellis Island on June 19, 1894. He had an aunt, Gertrude Strubel, in New Albany, Ind., where he found a home and was able to set up a studio to teach music.

During a visit to Cincinnati in August 1895, Strubel learned of an opening for an organist at **Mother of God Catholic Church**, Covington. He went to see musician-priest Henry Tappert (see **William and Henry Tappert**), then assistant pastor, and applied for the position. Tappert gave Strubel one of his compositions, and Strubel promptly played several variations on the organ. The young virtuoso was hired on the spot. His training had been as a church musician in the Catholic Caecilian tradition, which was popular at that time. Strubel's subsequent 55 years of service at Mother of God Church was interrupted only once when he left in 1905 for a position at St. Anthony Church in Brooklyn, N.Y. Tappert coaxed him back to Mother of God after only four months. Strubel had a measure of regret when he later discovered that the Brooklyn position was more lucrative as well as more prestigious.

Perhaps the main reason for Strubel's return to Covington was Rose Schmeing, a member of the St. Gregorius Society, for which he was organist. Tappert was the director of this 50–70-voice mixed adult choir. Rose and Strubel met during choir practices and fell in love. They married in 1906, both at age 31, and rented an apartment at 501 Russell St. in Covington. Edward could conduct private music lessons there as well as walk to work. By 1908 the family purchased a small house at 1040 Scott St., where they raised a son and a daughter.

In 1909 Professor Strubel (as he and other organists were known by students) and several prominent Northern Kentucky musicians, including Professor Sylvester Eifert (organist at **St. Aloysius Catholic Church**, Covington) formed the Mendelssohn Singing Society. After only three years of guiding the Mendelssohn group, Strubel had also become director of at least four male singing societies in Cincinnati and one as far away as Hamilton, Ohio. Most of them rehearsed with him at Grammer's Café on Liberty and Walnut Sts., in the Over-the-Rhine neighborhood of Cincinnati. Strubel directed the regional Bayerisch Männerchor (Bavarian Men's Choir) through its 50th anniversary in 1937.

The highlight of Strubel's career, as it concerned directing German singing societies, occurred in 1924. To celebrate a diamond jubilee, the Nordamerikanischen Sängerbundes (North American Singing Society) conducted a national contest for new compositions of American folk songs. Both music and lyrics had to have been composed by Americans. After much searching, Strubel came upon James Whitcomb Riley's poem "When Evening Shadows Fall." He set the poem to music and arranged the work for a four-voice male chorus; the piece won first prize. Strubel later attended the national festival of 1924 and directed his prizewinning song with 152 societies in attendance and almost 4,000 singers.

By 1938 the Strubels had moved into their final home at 2014 Greenup St. In 1946 Strubel received the papal medal Pro Pontifice et Ecclesia in recognition of 50 years of service at the parish. Strubel had many compositions for church use published by McLaughlin & Reilly, J. Fischer & Brothers, and the Theodore Presser Company. In 1958 he collaborated with local poet-columnist **Alice Kennelly Roberts** on a song dedicated to Covington's **Garden of Hope**. He died in 1964, as did his wife Rose, and both were buried at Mother of God Cemetery, Covington.

Litzenmayer, Karl J. "Professor Edward Strubel, Composer, Church Musician, Teacher (1875–1964)," *NKH* 1, no. 1 (Autumn–Winter 1993): 27–37.

Karl Lietzenmayer

SUBSTANCE ABUSE TREATMENT. In Northern Kentucky, Alcoholics Anonymous (AA), at least two hospitals, and other organizations, offer assistance to substance abusers. AA, which began in 1935, came to Northern Kentucky about 1945, when a man remembered as Mr. Meyerson held one of the first group Alcoholics Anonymous meetings in the region, according to Tony D., an AA historian. (Because of AA's principle of anonymity, full names of individuals involved are rarely available.) An AA group is a gathering of two or more people who share their stories, their pains, and their hope for a better life.

A booklet titled *The History of the Fellowship of Alcoholics Anonymous in Cincinnati: 1941 through 1964* describes the establishment of a large home at 405 Oak St., in Cincinnati's Mount Auburn neighborhood, as the central location for anyone sharing the desire to stop drinking. A prominent Cincinnati lawyer, whose son suffered from alcohol abuse, knew the homeowner, whose father and brother were active alcoholics. Through those chance acquaintances, 405 Oak St. developed into what it is today, the most well-known alcohol recovery center in Greater Cincinnati. Today, 405 Oak St. remains AA's unofficial headquarters in Greater Cincinnati, offering meetings, information, and fellowship every day of the week, 365 days per year.

Northern Kentucky's first official AA group was formed and chartered in New York City on July 11, 1947; founding members were Vertna C., Lawrence D., Farrell H., Hetty H., Albert K., Jack McG., and John T. That group met at St. Mary's School on Madison Ave. (see **Cathedral Basilica of the Assumption**) in Covington, between 11th and 12th Sts.

By 1964 there were six groups in Northern Kentucky. Meetings were held several times each week in Newport, Covington, and Erlanger. One of them, called the Covington Group, met in Covington at the **Madison Ave. Christian Church**, 1530 Madison Ave., at 8:30 p.m. on the third Sunday of the month. As of summer 2006, that group, now named the Madison Group, was meeting every Sunday night.

During the late 1960s, an AA group met in a restaurant at 237 Court St., Covington, a facility now buried under the southbound ramp of the **John A. Roebling Bridge**. By July 1980 that group had outgrown the Court St. space. A brief history, with no author listed, says, "A committee consisting of Fred Read, Cy Dilhunt, Larry Droege and Ted 'Jelly Roll' Vale searched for [a] new building for drunks to call home." Rev. William Mertes, of **Mother of God Catholic Church**, guided the group to a rundown building in Covington at 531 Russell St. A lifeboat for those in need of help, Father Mertes, now deceased, was an unwavering supporter of anyone down on his luck or trying to improve his life. The first official meeting of a group at 531 Russell was on February 14, 1981, and the last was on November 27, 1999. Roughly 2,000 people per month had been attending meetings there. A shotgun-style building at 722 Washington St., once used for food storage, became the new Covington AA clubhouse in late 1999. A coffee shop and meeting area comprising a front room and a large back room, about the size of a small gym, remained in operation there as of summer 2006.

According to a March 2006 AA listing, approximately 25 meetings were being held in Northern Kentucky; there were one or more meetings every day of the week, each day of the year, and special meetings were scheduled on major holidays such as Christmas. AA's central Northern Kentucky office, located in Covington at 1729 Madison Ave., offers staffed services Monday through Saturday, and an emergency phone operates around the clock. Clubhouses include one at 722 Washington St., Covington; the Promises Club (formerly the **Ninth St. United Methodist Church**) at Ninth and Anne, Newport; and the Alano Club, 249 Main, Florence.

The **St. Elizabeth Medical Center** and the **St. Luke Hospitals** offer a variety of inpatient, outpatient, and residential treatment plans. At the end of treatment, or as part of treatment, each medical facility sends patients to AA. **Transitions Inc.**, formerly known as the Comprehensive Care Center (see **NorthKey Community Care**), an offshoot of the Northern Kentucky Regional Mental Health–Mental Retardation Board, offered substance abuse treatment and education in the late 1960s and early 1970s. In spring 2006 Transitions gained approval to build a substance abuse rehabilitation facility in Erlanger, in the **Pleasure Isle Swim Club** area off Madison Pk. in Kenton Co., using approximately $3.5 million in federal and state funds. The new facility will be modeled after The Healing Place in Louisville, which carries out cutting-edge substance abuse treatment. Homeless alcoholics are taken by the police to The Healing Place's detox center as an alternative to drying out in a drunk tank. After a week, individuals are offered a choice to enter The Healing Place's program or return to their former way of life. About 50 percent choose the program. Another source of assistance is Droege House, named for longtime substance treatment advocates Larry Droege and his sisters, Virginia and Margaret, which is currently located in the former Speers Hospital nurse quarters, 925 Fifth Ave., Dayton, Ky. (see **Speers Memorial Hospital**).

Even though help is available from various organizations, the region's substance abuse rate continues to grow. More and more, mental health associations, hospitals, insurance companies, and treatment centers see alcohol and drug abuse as a national health crisis. Costs of substance abuse show up, for example, in spouse or child abuse, burglaries, job loss, divorces, homelessness, medical malpractice, and negligent homicide while driving under the influence. The road to recovery recommended by AA is to follow a 12-step program on a daily basis. Key ingredients in the program are helping others, spirituality, and removing harmful thinking from one's mind. All detox programs are temporary solutions; individuals are generally referred to AA for long-term or permanent recovery from alcoholism or drug addiction.

"Combating Drugs, Alcoholism," *KP*, April 7, 2000, 3K.
Eigelbach, Kevin. "Rehab Center OK'd: Erlanger Board Approves Project," *KP*, April 25, 2006, 1A.

"Help for the Most Helpless," *KP*, October 21, 1908, 4.
"Transitions Offers Addicts a Way Out," *KP*, November 11, 1989, 8K.

Roger Auge II

SUDDUTH, HORACE (b. August 8, 1888, Covington, Ky.; d. March 19, 1957, Washington, D.C.). Businessman Horace Sudduth was the son of Charles Sudduth and Mattie Lee Howard Sudduth. In 1906 Horace graduated from Covington's African American high school, William Grant High School, while also working as a messenger for the U.S. Post Office. One of Sudduth's teachers stated, "Horace was a dedicated pupil and his high school education was all the formal training he received. But he obtained the skill and confidence needed to pursue a career in business." It was during his high school graduation commencement that Sudduth first acknowledged in public his personal admiration for business. His oration was "The Growth of Industrial Pursuits."

By marrying Melvina Jones, the sister of **Charles E. Jones**, a funeral director in Covington, Sudduth established the family bonds necessary to proceed with the new business development he had planned for Covington. But it was across the Ohio River in Cincinnati where Sudduth became a business and civic leader. He soon proved to be astute both in developing modern business practices and in establishing organizations to promote such endeavors. He founded the Horace Sudduth and Associates Real Estate Agency and was owner of the Manse Hotel, the place where influential African American visitors such as Sammy Davis Jr. stayed while in the area.

Sudduth served as president of two national organizations, the National Negro Business League, whose sole purpose was to promote black-owned businesses, and the Industrial Federal Savings & Loan Association. He was also president of the Crawford Old Men's Home and the New Orphan Asylum for Colored Children of Cincinnati. Sudduth's greatest impact, however, was in helping to promote progressive business thinking among fellow African Americans both in Cincinnati and in his hometown, Covington. Along with Charles Jones, his father-in-law, Sudduth helped establish and lead Covington's **African-American Businessmen's Association**. For many years he and his wife were members of the **Ninth St. Methodist Episcopal Church**. Sudduth died at age 68 in 1957 in Washington, D.C., where he had traveled on business. He was buried in the United American Cemetery in the Madisonville, Ohio, suburb of Cincinnati.

Garretson, Joseph. "A Tribute to a Negro Hotel Operator," *CE*, April 16, 1950, sec. 2, p. 3.
"Long Illness Fatal to Horace Sudduth," *CP*, March 20, 1957, 6.
Middleton, Stephen. "We Must Not Fail!!! Horace Sudduth: Queen City Entrepreneur," *QCH* 49, no. 2 (Summer 1991): 3–20.
"Open House at New Manse Hotel," *CE*, April 1, 1950, 12.
"Wm. Grant High School Commencement," *KTS*, June 8, 1908, 1.

Theodore H. H. Harris

SUGAR GROVE PLANTATION. Reportedly named for the sugar maple trees on the property, the Sugar Grove Plantation was located at river light number 247 along the Ohio River, in North Bend in Boone Co. The original 650-acre plantation was included in land granted to Christopher Clark and surveyed in his name. Over the years, Sugar Grove has been touched by fame and the roots of American history. John Brown (1752–1824), a New Jersey native and a **Revolutionary War** veteran, settled the land he later named Sugar Grove Plantation sometime in the 1790s. Brown, along with neighbors Cave Johnson and Jacob Piatt, was prominently involved in the establishment of Boone Co. in 1799 (see **Cave Johnson House**). Brown was known for his close association with John Cleves Symmes, a fellow veteran and a neighbor across the Ohio River. Brown lived on the Sugar Grove Plantation with his only surviving child, Clara Harlow Brown (1783–1847).

Clara Brown married her young first cousin **Zebulon Montgomery Pike** (1779–1813) on March 4, 1801. She resided at Sugar Grove while her husband, the famed explorer and general for whom Pike's Peak was named, was engaged in adventures for the military. In April 1813, Pike died from wounds received in the Battle of York. Clara and their surviving daughter Clarissa remained at Sugar Grove. Clarissa Pike (1803–1837) eventually married John Cleves Symmes Harrison (1798–1830), the eldest son of President William Henry Harrison; John and Clarissa Harrison had six children.

When John Brown died in the fall of 1824, his will stated that the Sugar Grove Plantation (642 acres at the time), including all its contents, was to go to his infant son John Brown, born on August 11, 1824. Clara Pike was to be given other properties, but she would receive Sugar Grove only if her half brother did not reach maturity. Clara assumed responsibility for the property taxes in 1825. After Clara's death, an 1847 amendment to John Brown's will stated that John Brown's "infant son and devisee John Brown departed this life in his tender infancy and without issue." In June 1847 the then 667.5-acre estate was divided among Clara Pike's six grandchildren, who had been raised by her after being orphaned 10 years earlier.

According to Marjorie Byrnside Burress, in the mid-1840s the original Sugar Grove mansion burned, taking most of the Brown-Pike history with it. Oral tradition holds that a new residence was built farther away from the river, using the bricks from the original house. The property passed into the hands of the Southgate family after 1915. The Southgates did not reside on the property, and the second residence fell into disrepair and eventually burned in the late 1980s. The Brown-Pike-Harrison Family Cemetery remains on the property.

Bond, Beverly W. *The Intimate letters of John Cleves Symmes and His Family.* Cincinnati: Historical and Philosophical Society of Ohio, 1956.
Boone Co. Tax List, 1799, Boone Co. Courthouse, Burlington, Ky.
Boone Co. Tax List, 1825, Boone Co. Courthouse, Burlington, Ky.
Boone Co. Will Book B, pp. 156–61, Boone Co. Courthouse, Burlington, Ky.
Boone Co. Will Book E, pp. 58–59, 79–84, Boone Co. Courthouse, Burlington, Ky.
Cist, L. J. *Cincinnati Gazette*, April 5, 1881.
Worrel, Stephen, and Anne W. Fitzgerald. *Boone Co., Kentucky, Marriages, 1798–1850.* Falls Church, Va.: S. Worrel, 1991.

Bridget B. Striker

SUMME, GREGORY LOUIS (b. November 25, 1956, Covington, Ky.). Gregory L. Summe, a business executive, is the 5th of 12 children of James and Mary McQueen Summe. He graduated from **Covington Catholic High School** and entered **Thomas More College**, then transferred to the University of Kentucky, where he received a BS in electrical engineering. His postgraduate degrees include an MS from the University of Cincinnati in electrical engineering and a MBA from the Wharton School at the University of Pennsylvania.

In 1983 Summe joined the international consulting firm McKinsey & Company Inc. and became a partner in 1990. From his home in Atlanta and later, for a time, Hong Kong, he traveled the globe in service of his clients. In 1992 he became the general manager of Commercial Motors for General Electric. From 1993 to 1998, he was president, successively, of the General Aviation Avionics, Aerospace Engines, and Automotive Products Group divisions of AlliedSignal, now Honeywell Corporation.

Summe became the president and operating officer of EG&G (originally Edgerton, Germeshausen and Grier Inc.) in 1998. In 1999 he became the chief executive officer and also the chairman of the board. He directed the transformation of a company that was primarily a diversified government contractor into to a focused high-tech corporation. In October 1999 the corporate name was changed to PerkinElmer Inc. He streamlined the company's focus from a broad base of defense and industrial markets to two emphases—life and analytical sciences and photonics. PerkinElmer is a leader in the field of neonatal genetic testing and scientific instruments for discovering new drugs. PerkinElmer Inc. has 8,000 employees serving customers in more than 125 countries and is a component of the S&P Index.

Summe is a director of the State Street Corporation. He also serves on the Board of Advisors for Boston College and on the University of Kentucky Electrical Engineering Advisory Board. He is a former director of the TRW Corporation and a former member of the Singapore-U.S. Business Council. He has been active in many civic endeavors, including the United Way, **Boy Scouts**, and the March of Dimes. In 2004 he was the Massachusetts recipient of the Franklin Delano Roosevelt Humanitarian Award. He is married to Susan Louise Stevie and has three children. They reside in Weston, Mass.

Heimbouch, Hollis. "Racing for Growth: An Interview with PerkinElmer's Greg Summe," *Harvard Business Review*, November–December 2000.

PerkinElmer. "Summe Biography," in e-mail to author, October 2, 2006.
Univ. of Kentucky College of Engineering Hall of Distinction. "Gregory L. Summe." www.engr.uky.edu/alumni/hod/summe (accessed September 25, 2006).

Robert W. Stevie

SUMME, PATRICIA M. (b. May 20, 1953, Covington, Ky.). Patricia Mary Summe, the first woman Kenton Co. Circuit Court judge, is the daughter of prominent attorney Joseph L. Summe and Kathleen "Kit" Maguire Summe. The third of six children, Patricia lived in Covington until 1957, when the family moved to Fort Wright. She attended **St. Agnes Catholic Church** grade school and graduated from **Notre Dame Academy**, in Park Hills, in 1971 and Xavier University, in Cincinnati, in 1975. She received a JD degree from **Chase College of Law**, in Highland Heights, in 1979. Following the death of her father in 1980, she became a partner in Summe & Summe attorneys at law. Summe served as city attorney of Fort Wright from 1982 to 1994 and as city attorney of Ludlow from 1990 to 1994. After practicing in the areas of family law, municipal law, personal injury, and real estate, Summe successfully ran for the Kenton Co. Circuit Court in 1994. She serves on the Kentucky Bar Association's committee for judicial concerns. She was board president of the Chase College of Law Alumni Association from 1983 to 1985, was president of the Redwood School (see **Redwood Rehabilitation Center**) from 1988 to 1995, and served on the board for the First Bank of Northern Kentucky. Summe's commitment to the community earned her the ***Kentucky Post***'s "Outstanding Woman of the Year" award in 1998, and in 2003 she received the Martin Luther King award from the local chapter of the **NAACP**. She is active in her parish and in various charities and nonprofit organizations.

"Notre Dame Recognizing 3 Alumnae," *KP*, February 25, 2004, 3K.
Summe, Patricia. Interview by Gabrielle Summe, January 1, 2006, Fort Wright, Ky.
"Woman Breaches Male Bastion," *KE*, November 15, 1994, B3.

Gabrielle Summe

SUMMERS, HOLLIS S. (b. June 21, 1916, Eminence, Ky.; d. November 14, 1987, Athens, Ohio). Novelist and poet Hollis Spurgeon Summers Jr. was the son of a Baptist minister, Rev. Hollis Spurgeon Summers Sr., and Hazel Holmes Summers. During his youth, Hollis Jr. and his family lived in parsonages at Campbellsville (Taylor Co.), Louisville, and Madisonville, Ky. He earned his BA from Georgetown College in Georgetown, Ky., in 1937, his MA from the Bread Loaf School of English at Middlebury College in Middlebury, Vt., in 1943, and his PhD from the University of Iowa at Iowa City in 1949. His first employment was as an English teacher at **Holmes High School** in Covington. His next teaching position was at his alma mater, Georgetown College. In 1949 he was appointed chair of the English department at the University of Kentucky (UK) in Lexington, where he taught for the next 10 years. While at UK, he and his colleague Robert Hazel played major roles in the nurturing and development of five "world-class" writers: Wendell Berry, Ed McClanahan, James Baker Hall, Gurney Norman, and Bobbie Ann Mason. After leaving UK, Summers taught at Ohio University in Athens from 1959 to 1986. He married Laura Vimont Clarke on June 13, 1981, and they had two sons, David Clarke Summers and Hollis S. Summers III. Colleagues of Hollis Summers described him as a cultivated, sophisticated individual, "punctilious" and a good, sharp critic, who expected his students to dot every *i* and cross every *t*. Between 1948 and 1984, five novels, seven books of poetry, and numerous short stories written by Summers were published. He used his home state of Kentucky as the setting for many of his writings, and the underlying theme often dealt with the lifelong conflict between religious teachings and human love affairs. His brother Joseph H. Summers Sr. was also a writer and an English professor, at the University of Rochester in New York. Hollis Summers Jr. died at his home in Athens, Ohio, at age 71 and was buried at the Millersburg Cemetery in Millersburg, Ky. After his death, Ohio University began awarding, in his honor, the Hollis Summers Poetry Prize for the best unpublished poem submitted each year, a practice that continues today.

Department of English & Theatre. "Hollis Summers." www.english.eku.edu (accessed May 8, 2006).
Kentucky Educational Television. "The U.K. connection." www.ket.org (accessed May 8, 2006).
Summers, Hollis Spurgeon. *Brighten the Corner.* New York: Doubleday, 1952.
Ward, William S. *A Literary History of Kentucky.* Knoxville: Univ. of Tennessee Press, 1988.

SUMMERS, JANE ROBERTA WHATLEY (b. May 5, 1895, Selma, Ala.; d. June 29, 1992, Covington, Ky.). Community activist Jane Roberta Whatley Summers was the daughter of Calvin and Minerva Kendall Whatley. In 1934, at age 16, Jane Summers moved with her family to Covington. She soon developed a community-service mindset. She joined the **St. James A.M.E. Church** and became one of the denomination's most active members, both locally and nationally. As both a wife and a mother, it seemed that daily Summers was helping someone in need. For example, if she encountered a person who required medical attention, she would contact a local physician and stay at the person's side until medical help arrived. Throughout the years, because of such generosity, most local African American Kentuckians described Summers as an angel of mercy.

At age 50 Summers became the first African American manager of Covington's Jacob Price Homes housing community, which was built in 1939. As manager, she helped numerous residents by conducting yearly fundraising events, by offering individual counseling sessions on health-care topics, and by sponsoring workshops on how to gain access to local governmental agencies. During these years, many local residents referred to Summers as "Mama Janie."

Even after leaving her Jacob Price Homes position at age 75, Summers continued to serve her community. She was a member of the **Northern Kentucky Community Action Commission**, the **Northern Kentucky Interfaith Commission**, the local Meals on Wheels program, and the Kentucky Human Rights Commission. She also was active in the local **NAACP** chapter and helped to organize a regional Poor People's Campaign.

In 1992, as a testament to her various humanitarian activities and extraordinary community service, Summers was inducted into to the Northern Kentucky Leadership Hall of Fame. After her death that year, Summers continued to receive posthumously notable awards, celebrity plaques, and recognition decrees, such as a key to the City of Covington, a proclamation from the Kenton Co. Fiscal Court, an honorary and recognition letter from U.S. senator and former Kentucky governor Wendell Ford (1971–1974), a Community Service Award from the Covington–Kenton Co. Jaycees, and election into the Gallery of Great Black Kentuckians by the Kentucky Commission on Human Rights. Throughout her 97 years, Summers was an essential and preeminent community activist, who waged a lifetime battle against racism, homelessness, illiteracy, and hunger.

African American National Biography, s.v. "Jane Roberta Summers," by Lois Schultz. Oxford Univ. Press, forthcoming.
Fisher, John C. K. "African American History Has a Devoted Caretaker," *KP*, October 18, 1997, 1K.
"Happy Birthday—Our Role Model—This Is Your Life—Jane Summers: 96 Years Young—May 5, 1991," Northern Kentucky African American Heritage Task Force Collection, W. Frank Steely Library, Northern Kentucky Univ.
"Jane Summers," *KP*, July 2, 1992, 10A.
"Jane Summers, 97, Mentor to Many in Covington," *KP*, July 1, 1992, 10A.
"Local Activist Added to Gallery," *KP*, November 14, 2001, 21A.
Northington, Mary. Interview by Eric R. Jackson, September 2004, Covington, Ky.

Eric R. Jackson

SUMMERS, SCOTT (b. March 25, 1967, Warren Co., Ky.). Scott Patrick Summers, a champion cross-country motorcycle racer, is the son of Wade and Fran P. Garrison Summers. He grew up in Petersburg in Boone Co. Scott began riding motorcycles at age five and began racing them at age seven. He attended Ockerman Junior High School and graduated from **Conner High School**. By age 21, Summers had become a competitor within the American Motorcyclist Association race circuit. He won at least 10 national motorcycling titles. On the circuit, he traveled upwards of 60,000 miles annually. He has three practice tracks on his farm off Synder Ln. in Boone Co., where he spends several hours riding motorcycles each day.

Success in motorcycling competitions brought Summers more than 18 corporate sponsors, including makers such as the American Honda Manufacturing Company. He has written columns for *Dirt Bike* magazine and has hosted a television show called *OHV* [off-highway vehicle] *Video Magazine.* Summers retired from competitive racing in 1991 but continues to develop racing-related equipment for various companies at his Boone Co. farm.

Boehmker, Terry. "Motorcycle Racer Going for 10th National Title," *KP*, July 14, 1998, 5K.

Fields, Jerry. "Summers Rides to Top of His Profession: Connor Grad Tops in Off-Road Cycling," *KP*, August 5, 1991, 6K.

Warner, Jennifer S. *Boone County: From Mastodons to the Millennium.* Burlington, Ky.: Boone Co. Bicentennial Book Committee, 1998.

SUMMIT HILLS GOLF AND COUNTRY CLUB. A young Covington businessman and an avid golfer, Joseph Macke, leased the Summit Dairy Farm in Kenton Co., at the corner of Turkeyfoot Rd. and Dudley Pk. in Crestview Hills, from his father-in-law and during the late 1920s began what came to be known as Summit Hills Golf and Country Club. Today, the Summit Hills Golf and Country Club boasts a rolling and challenging 18-hole par 70 course.

The original course was designed by Bill Jackson, the golf professional at Camargo Country Club in Cincinnati, and featured a popular design considered a classic in the United States. Jackson used a topographical map, and all the work was done by hand, with the exception of the leveling and other ground preparation, which were accomplished by several horse-drawn scrapers. Although this was Jackson's only course design, he laid out a course recognized for its premium on shot-making skills and tactics, strength, and accuracy.

The new country club opened in 1930 with 150 members and a clubhouse converted from a large cattle barn; it featured a mansard shake roof and two silos. The club suffered through a fire in late November 1931, which caused $20,000 worth of damage. During the **Great Depression** of the 1930s, Macke was forced to sell his interest to a group headed by the original landowner, Harry Hartke.

In the 1940s the membership initiation fee was $5.00 and full family membership dues were $75.00. For members with transportation problems, the club provided a shuttle service from a **Dixie Highway** bus stop. In 1944 the membership purchased the club from Hartke for $150,000 and gave it its present name of Summit Hills Golf and Country Club.

The first clubhouse was struck by lightning on Labor Day 1952 and burned to the ground. One of the original farm silos survived, and a new clubhouse, built around it, opened in May 1953. Summit Hills Golf and Country Club has several old photos of the club, and an aerial photo of the original golf course and clubhouse is displayed on the old surviving silo in the club's entrance foyer.

Golf course remodeling projects in 1980 and 1985 by the architectural team of Jack Kidwell and Michael Hurdzen paved the way for the 2003 facelift by Brian Hundley, a protégé of noted golf course designer Arthur Hills. Nearly every hole at the golf course was remodeled in some manner, and the course was lengthened to 6,471 yards. There is a new irrigation system, the course's fairways and bunkers were reconfigured, and seven new greens were built. The course rating rose to 71.2, a stroke tougher, and the slope is now 131, up from 125 as determined by the Greater Cincinnati Golf Association. Women's par is 71. The head golf professional since 1978 has been John Steinbrunner. Summit Hills Golf and Country Club is a full-service private club with dining facilities, a full-size swimming pool, and tennis courts. In 2006 the golf membership was 380 and the total club membership almost 550.

"Loss $20,000 as Fire Sweeps Summit Hills Country Club," *KP*, December 1, 1931, 1.

"New Golf Course and Country Club Planned in Kenton County," *KTS*, September 26, 1929, 8.

Dennis W. Van Houten

SURTEES, ROBERT L. (b. August 9, 1906, Covington, Ky.; d. January 5, 1985, Monterey, Calif.). A legendary cinematographer known for his beautiful Hollywood golden-age camera work, Robert Lee Surtees won three Academy Awards for the MGM classic films *King Solomon's Mines* (1950), *The Bad and the Beautiful* (1952), and *Ben-Hur* (1959). Surtees was one of the few cinematographers from the studio system to adapt successfully to the contemporary, more independent era of motion pictures in the 1960s. He was the son of James D. and Elizabeth R. Sayers Surtees, and public records indicate that the family moved across the river to Cincinnati before Surtees attended school. While a student at Withrow High School in Cincinnati, he became interested in photography. Before long he became a serious photographer and was retouching photographs in a Cincinnati portrait studio.

In the late 1920s, Surtees moved to Hollywood and lived next door to the head cameraman for Universal Studios, who gave Surtees an entry-level position as a camera assistant to famous cinematographers such as Gregg Toland and Joseph Ruttenberg. During his early technician years, Surtees was sent to Universal Studios in Berlin, Germany, to develop his craft further. Subsequently, he worked as a camera assistant at various Hollywood studios during the 1930s before settling at work with MGM, where he officially became director of photography in the early 1940s. In 1944 he received his first Oscar nomination, for *Thirty Seconds over Tokyo.*

Surtees's popularity grew from his lush location images captured in color films such as *King Solomon's Mines* (1950), for which he won his first Oscar. Surtees helped establish the realistic look in Technicolor with innovative camera filtering and lighting techniques. Film historians have suggested that post-Renaissance impressionist artists inspired his work. His photography for *The Bad and the Beautiful* (1952) helped place that film among the best black-and-white works of the legendary film director Vincente Minnelli. Minnelli acknowledged in his autobiography that without Surtees the film would not have captured the contrasting affectionate and cynical moods for which it is remembered. Surtees achieved these effects by the use of lush, velvety black and intensely white images. Years later he successfully revived his black-and-white film noir style for Peter Bogdanovich's *The Last Picture Show* (1971), during a largely color era of modern films.

Robert Surtees was a leading pioneer during the introduction of wide-screen motion pictures. Most notable was his artistry in the Broadway-to-Hollywood adaptation of Rodgers and Hammerstein's legendary musical *Oklahoma* (1955), released by 20th Century Fox. In 1955 *American Cinematographer* reported that for *Oklahoma* Surtees capitalized on the wide-screen format by creating visual images that seemed to wrap around the viewer, staging the characters to move within a more stationary wide-screen frame, and engaging his illumination skills to focus attention on subjects with distinctive key lighting. Surtees also introduced a modern, clean treatment of the vast Western and rural themes in the backdrops of *Oklahoma,* inspired by the paintings of Peter Hurd. The continued success of his many wide-screen works peaked with two MGM movie remakes: one of the memorable spectacle *Ben-Hur* (1959), for which he won his third and final Oscar, and the other of *Mutiny on the Bounty* (1962), in which he demonstrated his skillful lighting of seascapes.

Surtees's other notable film highlights include *Quo Vadis* (1951), *Mogambo* (1953), *Raintree County* (1957), *The Graduate* (1967), *Sweet Charity* (1968), *Summer of '42* (1971), and *The Sting* (1973). *Variety* described Surtees as "a prolific filmmaker and persistent competitor." With 16 Oscar nominations, some twice in the same year, Surtees's successes ultimately were the reason for the change in Academy Award rules, limiting cinematographers to one nomination yearly. When Surtees retired in 1979, he held the highest number of Oscars in his category. In a career spanning more than 50 years, 35 of them as a director of photography, his name was credited to nearly 100 feature films.

Surtees and his wife Maydell had four children, including cinematographer Bruce Surtees. Robert Surtees died in 1985 and was cremated; his ashes were scattered over Point Lobos, Monterey Co., Calif. A Kentucky Historical Marker in his honor is displayed at Covington's Goebel Park, Fifth and Philadelphia Sts.

"Covington-Born Oscar-Winner Dies," *KP*, January 8, 1985, 2B.

Digital Content Producer.com. "ASC Hands Out Student Heritage Awards." http://millimeter.com/news/video_asc_hands_student/index.html (accessed January 25, 2006).

Katz, Ephraim. *The Film Encyclopedia.* New York: Harper Perennial, 1998.

"Lenser Robert Surtees, 78, Dies: Won Oscar for '*Ben-Hur,*'" *Variety*, January 16, 1985, 8.

Lightman, Herb. "Shooting *Oklahoma!* in Todd-AO," *American Cinematographer* 36, no. 4 (April 1955): 210.

Maltin, Leonard, ed. *Leonard Maltin's Movie Encyclopedia*. New York: Dutton, 1994.

Minnelli, Vincente, and Hector Arce. *I Remember It Well*. Garden City, N.Y.: Doubleday, 1974.

Nicholas, Thomas, ed. *International Dictionary of Films and Filmmakers*. Vol. 4, *Writers and Production Artists*. Chicago: St. James Press, 1996.

John Schlipp

SUTHERLAND, LOIS OGDEN (b. April 3, 1921, Campbell Co., Ky.; d. April 26, 2002, Fort Thomas, Ky.). Lois Ogden Sutherland, an educator and a journalist, was the daughter of dentist Dr. Max Ogden and Nell Young Ogden. She graduated from **Holmes High School** in Covington in 1939. When she went to the University of Kentucky (UK) at Lexington, her experience writing for the school's student newspaper, the *Kentucky Kernel*, prompted her to major in journalism. After earning her BA in 1943, she began reporting for the *Cincinnati Times-Star* and became one of the first American women to cover major sporting events and to do locker-room interviews.

As **World War II** was winding down, Lois met and married William "Bill" Sutherland of Fort Thomas, who became a well-known local photographer. They had three children. For most of their 56-year marriage, they lived on a California, Ky., farmstead that had passed down through Lois's family. It was part of a land grant given to the Young brothers by George Washington in payment for surveying work they did in Northern Kentucky.

During the late 1940s, Lois Sutherland's career began evolving when she went to work for *Fox and Hound Magazine* in Lexington. She later did public relations work for Procter and Gamble in Cincinnati and, a few years later, began substitute teaching in Bellevue. She taught English at **Campbell Co. High School** from 1958 to 1966 and, after earning an ME from Xavier University, Cincinnati, in 1967, taught English and journalism at UK's Northern Community College in Covington. That institution was replaced by Northern Kentucky University (NKU), and Sutherland became a charter member of the NKU faculty, serving as its first journalism instructor and as the founding adviser of its student newspaper. In 1977, when NKU was large enough to establish a Communication Department, she was named interim department chair and guided its first year of operation.

Even after retiring in 1987, Sutherland remained engaged in work at NKU and in journalism. She supervised NKU journalism interns into the 1990s, wrote a regular column for the *Campbell County Recorder* through 2000, and did occasional freelance writing for the *Cincinnati Enquirer*. Her name lives on at NKU in an annual award presented to the outstanding member of the student newspaper staff. She died in 2002 and was cremated.

"Lois Sutherland, 81, Post Sportswriter, Professor," *KP*, April 27, 2002, 8A.

Mayhew, Chris. "Lois Ogden Sutherland, 81, Had Passion for Journalism," *CE*, April 27, 2002, 12B.

Steely, Will Frank. *Northern: Birth of a University*. Cincinnati: Gateway, 1993.

Turney, Michael L. "Evolution of the Northern Kentucky University Communications Department," November 1991, Northern Kentucky Univ. Communication Department, Highland Heights, Ky.

Michael L. Turney

SWEENEY, BILL (b. March 6, 1886, Covington, Ky.; d. May 26, 1948, Cambridge, Mass.). William John Sweeney was the son of John M. and Mary Knagge Sweeney. His father was an Irish-born salesman. Bill graduated from St. Xavier High School in Cincinnati in 1904 and began playing baseball in a Saturday league in Norwood, Ohio. When he was 18, he started his baseball season with Toledo, Ohio, in the American Association. He finished the 1904 season with Rock Island, Ill., of the Three-I League that operated throughout the Midwest. At the end of the 1906 season, the Chicago Cubs drafted Sweeney. He was 21 years old when he made his major league debut on June 14, 1907. On June 20, 1907, after a slow start, he was traded to the Boston Doves. There he started as a third baseman and moved to shortstop. In 1910 he found his position as he became an outstanding second baseman.

In 1911 he married Katherine Leonard; they had five children. The year 1911 was also marked by a 26-game hitting streak for Sweeney. In 1913 he tried to use his baseball fame as an actor during the off-season, when he appeared at the Orpheum Theater in Cincinnati; he received high praise for his acting performances. At the time, he was living at 324 Overton St. in Newport. He also raised money for the victims of the Ohio River **flood of 1913** in Newport, by accepting a bit acting part at the Temple Theater in Newport. Eventually, the Sweeneys moved to Cambridge, Mass., and Sweeney built a successful insurance business and became a public speaker. In 1914 the Chicago Cubs offered him a 50 percent raise, a signing bonus, and a three-year contract. While he was playing in Chicago, however, his baseball career declined. He played his last game on October 5, 1914, and soon was released. He retired with a lifetime batting average of .272 and focused his attention on his insurance business and his family. He had played eight seasons in the major leagues, appearing in 1,031 games, mainly at second base for the Boston Doves of the National League, beginning in 1907. Sweeney, remembered as a player who loved baseball, died of a heart attack in 1948 in Cambridge and was buried in the St. Joseph Cemetery at W. Roxbury, Mass.

The Baseball Biography Project. "Bill Sweeney." www.bioproj.sabr.org (accessed September 25, 2006).

James, Bill, et al., eds., *Stats All-Time Major League Handbook*. Skokie, Ill.: Stats, 1998.

"Old-time Player Taken by Death," *CTS*, May 27, 1948, 27.

Reis, Jim. "Bluegrass Players Left Mark," *KP*, December 20, 1993, 4K.

Steven D. Jaeger

SWEET, KATIE (b. August 31, 1957, Covington, Ky.). Hollywood child star Katherine Marie "Katie" Sweet was discovered in 1959 by Ozzie and Harriet Nelson, who needed a precocious two-year-old for a part in one of their upcoming television shows. From there, Sweet's career blossomed. She appeared on television in *Ben Casey*, *The Danny Thomas Show*, *The Lucy Show*, *Wagon Train*, *The Joey Bishop Show*, *Lassie*, *The Farmer's Daughter*, *My Favorite Martian*, *Hank*, and *Bonanza*. Her movie roles included appearances in Alfred Hitchcock's *The Birds*, in *Crimson Kimono*, and in *Fine Young Cannibals*. By 1970, however, Sweet's acting career (once likened to that of Shirley Temple) had ended at age 13. She did not make it to the Broadway stage, even though she recorded a few songs such as "I Love to Rock" in 1960. In 1967 she attended Turkeyfoot Junior High School in Kenton Co., while living with her grandparents. Later, Sweet and her family moved to Hollywood, Calif., where they lived near the corner of Hollywood and Vine Sts. Today, Sweet lives in California with her two daughters.

Bird, Rick. "Queen City Star Power," *KP*, August 25, 2007, A1.

Reis, Jim. "1967 a Banner Year for Education," *KP*, August 24, 1992, 4K.

SWEET OWEN. Sweet Owen has three designations. First, it was the nickname applied by Democratic candidate John C. Breckinridge after his overwhelming 1853 victory in Owen Co. earned him reelection to the U.S House of representative from Kentucky Eighth District, a district traditionally dominated by the **Whig Party**. After the 1853 election, Breckinridge always referred to the county as "Sweet Owen" and friends and family began to call his young son John Witherspoon "Owen County." Following the election, the unnamed town around the current intersection of Ky. Rts. 22 and 845, four miles east of Owenton, near the modern **Eden Shale Farm**, also became known as Sweet Owen, the second designation. When a post office was established there in 1873, Sweet Owen became the town's name, and the name remained after the post office closed in 1902.

The third meaning of "Sweet Owen" generally refers to the county of Owen. It is a term of affection or endearment for the entire county, suggesting that it is a wonderful place in which to live. The idea has stuck, as evidenced by one of the histories of Owen Co., which is subtitled "Sweet Owen."

An Atlas of Owen County, Kentucky. Philadelphia: Lake, 1883.

Houchens, Mariam Sidebottom. *History of Owen County: "Sweet Owen."* Louisville, Ky.: Standard, 1976.

Rennick, Robert M. *Kentucky Place Names*. Lexington: Univ. of Kentucky Press, 1984.

SWOPE, SAMUEL F. (b. March 1, 1809, Bourbon Co., Ky.; d. April 19, 1865, Falmouth, Ky.). Lawyer and politician Samuel Franklin Swope attended Bourbon Co. public schools and later attended Georgetown College at Georgetown, Ky.

He studied law and was admitted to the bar in 1830, setting up his practice in Falmouth in 1832. Swope was elected to the Kentucky House of Representatives in 1837, where he served for two years. He then served in the Kentucky Senate from 1844 to 1848. He was elected to the U.S. House of Representatives in 1855 and served until 1857. At the end of that term, he resumed his legal practice in Falmouth, where he lived until his death at age 56. He was interred in the Riverside Cemetery in Falmouth.

Infoplease. "Swope, Samuel Franklin." http://infoplease .com (accessed November 26, 2005).
"Samuel F. Swope Is the American Party Candidate for Congress," *CJ*, May 26, 1855, 2.
"Swope Elected to Congress from Tenth District," *CJ*, August 11, 1855, 2.

SYNAGOGUES. Throughout most of the 19th century, there were too few **Jews** living in Northern Kentucky to warrant the establishment of synagogues. By the turn of the 20th century, however, more Jews had settled in Newport and Covington, and in 1897 the Jews of Newport founded the United Hebrew Congregation with an initial membership of 31. This assembly met in temporary quarters for several years, but by January 1905 it had purchased the building of the Fifth Street Christian Church at 117 E. Fifth St. and converted it into a synagogue. The United Hebrew Congregation was Orthodox, meaning that it retained traditional practices such as allowing only men to conduct services and providing separate seating for men and women in its sanctuary. Over the years, one or more smaller prayer groups broke away from the United Hebrew Congregation, most likely because of personality conflicts rather than philosophical disagreements, but none of these groups survived long. From about 1918 until about 1925, for example, a congregation called Ohave Sholom (lovers of peace) worshipped in a house at 430 W. Sixth St. in Newport.

The Jews of Covington established a congregation in 1906. It was usually called the Temple of Israel, but its name sometimes appeared as Temple Israel or even as Heichal Israel, in Hebrew. Like its Newport counterpart, this congregation was Orthodox, and in its early years it met in temporary quarters, including the ***Kentucky Post*** building on Madison Ave. In November 1915, however, the Temple of Israel moved into a Neoclassical synagogue that it had erected at 107 E. Seventh St., between Greenup and Scott. Designed by local architect George W. Schofield, this building was square and had a two-columned portico and a small cupola. Its main-floor sanctuary had a seating capacity of about 200, and in the basement were a small kitchen, a classroom, and living quarters for a caretaker. The campaign to construct Covington's first synagogue was spearheaded by the Russian-born insurance agent Maurice A. Chase; the money for the building came from a variety of sources, including fundraising activities organized by the ladies' auxiliary of the Temple of Israel and donations from both inside and outside the city.

Temple of Israel. Built in 1915, it was demolished in 1937.

The Temple of Israel remained in its original building until 1937, when the federal government acquired the block where it stood to build a new post office and a courthouse. The congregation again had to meet in temporary facilities as it awaited construction of a new synagogue, but because its Seventh St. building had not yet been demolished, members of the congregation decided to use it for the High Holidays of Rosh Hashanah and Yom Kippur (the New Year and the Day of Atonement) in the fall of 1937. They broke the seal on the building and held services there. Taken to court for trespassing, they won acquittal by arguing that because the government had not yet paid for the appropriated building, it still belonged to the congregation.

With the proceeds from the sale of its old synagogue, the Temple of Israel congregation constructed a new building in Covington at 1040 Scott St., at the corner of Lynn. Designed by Cincinnati architect Leslie Moss and dedicated in March 1939, it was a functional structure with little character. It had a sanctuary with gender-segregated seating on the main floor and a social hall and small stage in the basement, together with a kitchen, a coatroom, and a three-room apartment. It is believed that money donated by Jewish gamblers from out of town helped support the synagogues of both Covington and Newport.

Lay leaders were extremely important to the functioning of Northern Kentucky's synagogues, for they had rabbinic leadership only sporadically. It appears that the first rabbi to serve in Newport was the Lithuanian-born Samuel V. Levinson, who had immigrated to the United States around 1885 and arrived in Kentucky in 1901. By 1906 Levinson had been replaced by M. Partnoff. He was followed in 1908 by Joel Salaman, who also stayed for only a few years. Rabbi Levinson remained in Northern Kentucky, however, for it is reported that he served as rabbi at the Temple of Israel in Covington in 1911 and stayed with that congregation until around 1930, when he was succeeded by Rabbi Jacob Jacobs. The first rabbi to serve the Temple of Israel in its Scott St. synagogue was Alfred Seelig, a refugee from Nazi Germany who arrived in 1939 and remained until 1942, when he was succeeded by Rabbi Gerson Frankel and then by Rabbi David Gurewitz, both of whom served short terms. In the meantime, Newport's United Hebrew Congregation seems to have gone for long periods without regular rabbinic leadership; only occasionally do city directories indicate that the congregation had a rabbi: Harry Finkenstein in 1926, for example, Abraham Lobel in 1928, and Morris Harris in 1938. The clergymen serving Northern Kentucky's Jewish congregations often were accorded the title *reverend* rather than *rabbi*, suggesting that they had not been formally ordained. Moreover, some of Northern Kentucky's rabbinic leaders held additional jobs and served their congregations only part-time. For instance, Rabbi Levinson ran a variety store on Scott St. in Covington while he was the Temple of Israel rabbi in the mid-1920s, and Rabbi Frankel of Newport worked also as a kosher slaughterer in a Cincinnati meatpacking plant.

By the middle of the 20th century, a great many Jews had left Northern Kentucky (many moving to Cincinnati) and few new Jewish families had moved into the region, so activities in the local synagogues were considerably reduced after the 1940s. During the 1950s, services were held at the Temple of Israel only on the High Holidays, and the congregation ceased functioning around 1960. Its synagogue building, falling into disrepair, was sold to the Church of God congregation in 1973 on the initiative of Abraham Wander, one of the few remaining stalwarts of the congregation. Proceeds from the sale were donated to charity. Similarly, the United Hebrew Congregation closed down permanently around 1966, and its building was sold to the Apostolic Temple of Newport in 1969. An attempt by a small group of Jewish residents to revive congregational life in Northern Kentucky in the late 1960s had failed by the early 1970s, and no other attempts have been made. With no synagogues remaining in the region, Jewish residents of Northern Kentucky seeking congregational affiliation have joined synagogues in Cincinnati.

Lapides, Leslie. "Judaism Then and Now," *KP,* March 19, 1983, 1K.

Lassetter, Leslie A. "Covington's Schule, the Temple of Israel," 1976, Kenton Co. Public Library, Covington, Ky.

Reis, James. "Remnant of Jewish Community Remains," *KP,* August 17, 1987, 4K.

Weissbach, Lee Shai. *The Synagogues of Kentucky: Architecture and History.* Lexington: Univ. Press of Kentucky, 1995.

Lee Shai Weissbach

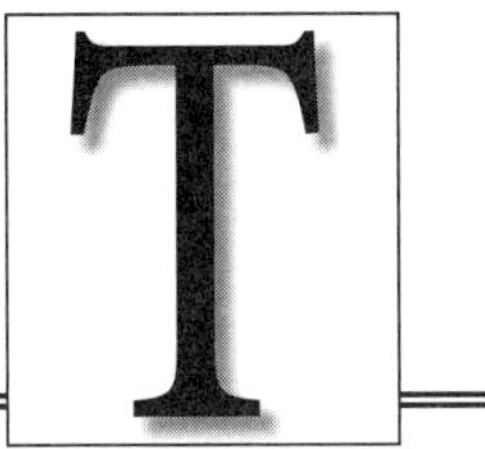

TACKETT'S MILL. Tackett's Mill, a small community in southern Owen Co., is located along Ky. Rt. 368, just north of the Kleber Wildlife Area (see **Wildlife Areas in Owen Co.**) and not far from the Scott Co. boundary. It is within the Harmony Precinct, about 10 miles south of Owenton. The 1883 Lake atlas shows two stores in the area. There was also a one-room school at Tackett's Mill.

Griffing, B. N. *An Atlas of Owen County, Kentucky.* Philadelphia: D. W. Lake, 1883.

TACOMA PARK. The site of the Tacoma Park amusement center in Dayton, Ky., was once owned and operated as a farm by Peter Werne. In 1880 Werne sold the farm to Louis Oliver Maddux, who was a partner in the Maddux-Hobart Distillery of Cincinnati. Maddux developed a distillery on the farm and named the business the Winchester Distilling Co. He had a stable, a barn, a millhouse, an office, and a warehouse built on the property and operated the business until 1894, when he became seriously ill with Brights Disease, a kidney disorder. He sold the complex to the Thorne Distilling Company, which ran it until 1906, and then it was sold to the Hazel Gap Distillery, which operated until 1911.

About that time, the Dayton sandbar (site of the **Revolutionary War** battle **Rogers' Defeat**) began to be used as a public bathing beach. Several other beaches were already established nearby along the Ohio River, in Bellevue and Dayton, Ky. (see **Ohio River Beaches**). At the height of their popularity, there were six beaches along the riverfront: the Queen City in Bellevue, and the Princess, Manhattan, Berlin, and Tacoma beaches in Dayton. It was reported that Tacoma Park was named after Tacoma, Wash. In those days the river water was relatively clean, and most beaches had 1,000 feet of white sand extending into the river. The beaches soon became very popular, and the area was often referred to as the Atlantic City of the West. The Queen City Beach (later known as **Horseshoe Gardens**) at the foot of Ward St. in Bellevue was the largest and most spectacular one. It had a two-story pavilion that included a large bathhouse, a dining room, and an elaborate dance hall.

After many years of successful operation, problems began to develop along the beaches. River water pollution; lawsuits against owners; and the construction of dams along the river, which flooded many of the beaches, caused most of the difficulties. Tacoma Park fared better than the other beaches, because its owner, Tony Gesser, had anticipated the changing conditions and had begun to make adjustments. He had built a 130-by-150-foot in-ground swimming pool filled with clean water from an artesian well. The pool was accompanied by a modern, 1,000-locker bathhouse. Gesser also added to the site a roller coaster, a whip ride, a merry-go-round, and a penny arcade. He bought the combination dance floor and **skating rink** that had previously been an attraction at Berlin Beach and moved it to Tacoma. The park gained popularity as an amusement park and picnic grounds. Gesser held marathon dance contests, which created quite a sensation until police later stopped them, claiming that they endangered the health of participants. During the late 1920s, wrestling and boxing matches were staged at Tacoma. In 1927 the park hosted a World Lightweight title fight between Frank "Midge" Guerrea and Sammy Mandell. Well known local pugilist **Joe Anderson** fought there also. In 1936 a greyhound racetrack, with a 5,000-seat grandstand, was built at Tacoma, and it operated successfully for one season. Early in its second season, the state police closed the track, after a court ruled that gambling on dog races violated state law.

The Ohio River **flood of 1937** destroyed much of Tacoma Park and its attractions, and it was not able to completely recover. In 1940 an attempt was made to introduce midget car racing at the park, but the operation was closed after just one season when police discovered slot machines on the premises. The track did not reopen, and the grandstands were later razed. Thereafter, the park was used primarily as a picnic ground, swimming pool, dance pavilion, and skating rink. For many years the park was owned by Robert J. Lunsford and Stephen R. Rutherford. In 1948 Woodrow and Ruth Bressler built the Riverview Drive-in movie theater at Tacoma (see **Drive-Ins**), which they successfully operated until about 1960, about which time the pool closed. At that time they sold Riverview to Redstone Theaters, the firm that later also owned the Dixie Gardens and Pike 27 drive-in theaters in Northern Kentucky. The Riverview Drive-in ceased operations in 1982. Tacoma swimming pool's new owner, Bill Daley, sold the site in 1988 to Riverport Enterprises, which built a $9 million marina called the Watertown Yacht Club, one of the finest marinas in Greater Cincinnati.

Tacoma Park was the second amusement center in Northern Kentucky to be built at the end of a **streetcar** line: it was at the eastern terminus of the No. 12 Dayton **Green Line** streetcar in Campbell Co., and the **Lagoon Amusement** Park in Ludlow was at the western end of the No. 3 Ludlow Lagoon streetcar in Kenton Co.

Croyle, William. "100 Years Ago, River Was Clear, Sand White," *KE,* July 29, 2003, 12E.
Reis, Jim. "Tacoma Park Packed in Fight Fans in Late 20s," *KP,* April 22, 2002, 4K.
"Summer Fun Spot," *KP,* March 11, 1985, 8K.
"Tacoma Park Drew Crowds," *KE,* February 20, 2000, 1B.

TANNEHILL BROTHERS (Jesse Niles "Tanny" Tannehill, b. July 14, 1874, Dayton, Ky.; d. September

Sax section of the orchestra at the Tacoma Park Dance Pavilion, Dayton, Ky., 1942. *Left to right:* Paul Bauer, Charles Tharp, Robert Thoney, and William Bunge.

22, 1956, Dayton, Ky.; Lee Ford Tannehill, b. October 26, 1880, Dayton, Ky.; d. February 16, 1938, Live Oak, Fla.). The older of these two major league baseball players, Jesse, was a 5-foot-8-inch 150-pound pitcher whose big league debut was with the Cincinnati Red Stockings in 1894. He was a switch hitter until 1903, but after that he batted only from the left side. He went on to play for the Pittsburgh Pirates, the Washington Senators, the Boston Americans, and the New York Americans. In 1904, while with Boston, he threw a no-hitter against the Chicago White Sox. His lifetime pitching record, for 15 years in the majors, was 195 wins and 118 losses, with a .261 earned run average. Jesse was proud of his hitting ability as a pitcher. He finished his career back in Cincinnati and afterward continued to play some semipro baseball. Later he worked in a machine shop, and during those years he was often seen at Crosley Field rooting for the Cincinnati Reds. He died from a stroke in 1956 at Speers Hospital in Dayton, the city where he lived for his entire life, and was buried at Evergreen Cemetery in Southgate. He was survived by his wife, the former Beulah Anderson.

Lee Ford Tannehill made his debut with the Chicago team in the American League in 1903. He was a 5-foot-11-inch 170-pound infielder who mainly played third base and shortstop. He batted and threw right-handed. Lee played for only one major league team, Chicago, for 10 years, and saw action in the 1906 World Series. He played in a total of 1,089 games, with a lifetime batting average of .220. Lee Tannehill died in 1938 at Live Oak, Fla., and was buried nearby at the Antioch Baptist Church Cemetery.

The Baseball Encyclopedia. 9th ed. New York: Macmillan, 1983.

"Former Major Leaguer Dies," *KTS*, September 22, 1956, 1.

Michael R. Sweeney

TANNER, MARY ELLEN (b. Covington, Ky., November 9, 1946). Daughter of Robert and Lauretta Baker Tanner, Mary Ellen was raised in Covington and Fort Mitchell. She is a singer of popular music and **jazz** and a Cincinnati television personality best known as a cast member of **Bob Braun**'s *50-50 Club* on WLWT and the former AVCO regional television chain.

Tanner made her public singing debut as a child in the choir of the Main Street Methodist Church in Covington. Her father always encouraged her to sing professionally. At age 12 she appeared at park concerts with the Deke Moffitt Big Band. She sang locally at dances at the Castle Farm on Reading Rd. in Cincinnati, at the Newport Stadium, at county fairs, and in other local settings. After graduating from Beechwood High School in Fort Mitchell (see **Beechwood Public Schools**), Tanner appeared as a singer contestant on the national CBS television *Ted Mack Amateur Hour* in 1964.

She attended classes at Northern Kentucky State College (now **Northern Kentucky University**) and worked as a secretary for a few years before beginning to sing professionally. She sang with groups such as Dee Felice and his Mixed Feelings Band at regional nightclubs. Later she performed with the Frank Vincent Trio. After a long engagement, Frank Vincent and Tanner were married for a short period.

Tanner studied voice while she performed as a regular on **Nick Clooney**'s WCPO variety television show in the early 1970s. After guest appearances on Bob Braun's *50-50 Club*, she joined his midday live television program as a regular cast member in 1978 and stayed until it ended in the early 1980s. In addition to her role as a cast singer, Tanner interviewed guests and supported Bob Braun with many program duties.

Following her tenure with Bob Braun, she sang at numerous local venues and served as house vocalist at the Celestial Incline Lounge in Mount Adams in Cincinnati for more than 15 years and later at Michael G's Restaurant, located on Kellogg Ave. in Cincinnati. Recently she has been a regular singer at Chez Nora's Restaurant in Covington. She has become one of the Midwest's most respected vocalists, performing with the Illinois Philharmonic, the Dayton Philharmonic, the Les Brown Orchestra, and others. She has received the local Cammy award for Best Jazz Vocalist multiple times. Tanner taught as an adjunct professor for 11 years in the jazz department at the University of Cincinnati College–Conservatory of Music and recorded numerous jazz albums. She lives in Covington with musician **John Von Ohlen**, her life partner for more than 20 years.

Jacobs, Gabriella. "A Star Is Born: Ft. Mitchell's Tanner Is Learning to Wow 'em on Daily Television, Nightclubs," *KP*, June 16, 1979, 5K.

Kennelly Roberts, Alice. "Vocalist's Personality Sparkles with Holiday Season," *KP*, December 6, 1995, 2K.

Pulfer, Laura. "Mary Ellen Tanner's Song of Her Youth," *CE*, May 5, 1998, 1B.

"TV Network Films N. Kentucky Girl," *KE*, June 29, 1964, 2.

Wood, Mary. "Ft. Mitchell Singer Joins 'Bob Braun Show,'" *CP*, October 18, 1978, 14.

John Schlipp

TANNERIES. By 1810 at least six Northern Kentucky counties had tanneries to convert leather, as a raw material, into useful items. In those days the hides of cows, calves, horses, deer, pigs, and sheep were tanned and fashioned into footwear, clothing, gloves, saddles, articles used on ships or as parts of carriages, and so forth. Tanning was a time-consuming task that took up to two years. Initially, the hides were soaked in wooden or masonry vats containing lime. Next, the hides were placed on a beam and the hair and remaining tissue was removed. They were often soaked in a vat to restore pliability and then washed in pure water. The hides were then placed in tan pits containing oak bark and water, where they were allowed to soak to complete the tanning process.

The importance of tanneries in Northern Kentucky is illustrated by Coxe's listing of manufacturers for the year 1810. Figures were provided for the number of tanneries by county, the value of the tanneries, and sometimes the number of hides and skins. Six of the Northern Kentucky counties were included in Coxe's publication. Nine tanneries operated in Boone Co. with a value of $2,510, while two tanneries, valued at $600, were located in Bracken Co. In Campbell Co., two tanneries processed 1,100 skins and hides with a value of $6,050. Eleven tanneries operated in Gallatin Co. with a value of $1,078. The eight tanneries in Mason Co. processed 3,695 hides and skins with a value of $10,900. In Pendleton Co., two tanneries processed 370 hides and skins with a value of $1,150.

Kentucky historian Lewis Collins reported an extensive tannery in Bracken Co. in 1847. Three men were listed as tanners in the 1850 census for the county: George Donissham, Richard H. King, and Thomas Muller. James Donovan of Brooksville was listed as a tanner in the *Kentucky State Gazetteer, Shippers' Guide, and Business Directory* for 1865 and 1866 and for 1873–1874. And George Doniphan operated a tannery west of his home in Augusta.

Two tanners were listed in Campbell Co. during the late 19th century. They were Jacob Daut & Company of Newport during 1883–1884 and Peter Youmans in 1896.

In Kenton Co., many of the 19th-century tanneries, including that of the Burger family in the 1860s and 1870s, operated in the heavily German neighborhood of Lewisburg in Covington. Other Lewisburg tanneries included R. Kessler & Company, Barney Mueller, the Ohio & Kentucky Kid Leather Manufacturing Company, the Renz family, and the Steinharter family.

In Mason Co. George Doniphan, a lawyer and a professor at **Augusta College**, owned and operated a tannery west of his home in Maysville. Three other tanners in Maysville included P. R. McCordle & Company during 1865–1866, Jacob Outten during 1879–1880, and Poyntz & McAedie during 1873–1874.

Nancy O'Malley, in her publication *A Village Called Washington,* cites early Mason Co. Court records that mentioned Enoch Barr's tanyard at the north end of Washington in Mason Co. The January 6, 1829, issue of the *Maysville Eagle* carried an ad for the sale of Enoch Barr's tanyard by virtue of a decree from Mason Co. Circuit Court. The public auction was forced by Thomas Black's victory over Barr's heirs in court. The ad noted that the property had formerly been known as Barr & Walton's Tan Yard.

Collins, Richard H. *History of Kentucky*. Vol. 1. Covington, Ky.: Collins, 1882.

Coxe, Tench. *A Statement of the Arts and Manufacturers of the United States of America, for the Year 1810*. Philadelphia: A. Comman, 1814.

Hodgman, George H. *Kentucky State Gazetteer, Shippers' Guide, and Business Directory, for 1865 and 1866*. Louisville, Ky.: Hodgman, 1865.

O'Malley, Nancy. *A New Village Called Washington*. Maysville, Ky.: McClanahan, 1987.

R. L. Polk Company. *Kentucky State Gazetteer and Business Directory*. Detroit: R. L. Polk, 1873–1895.

Charles D. Hockensmith

TANNER'S STATION. In 1789 a Baptist preacher from Virginia, John Tanner, led a settlement party to the area now known as Petersburg, Ky. Tanner built a stockade that became known as Tanner's Station. He had owned a partial interest in another tract of land in the area but sold it to acquire the stockade parcel from James Garrard. Garrard, the future Kentucky governor (1796–1804), was a politician and fellow Baptist minister who lived near Paris, Ky. Tanner stayed only a few years at the station that bore his name; the Tanners moved west after Tanner's sons Edward and John Jr. were kidnapped by Indians. The details of the abductions have been recounted in various forms, but it is clear that Tanner moved to track down his children. In 1806 Col. John Grant, a North Carolinian, laid out the 100-acre town of Caledonia at Tanner's Station. The town did not become Petersburg until 1818, after the Kentucky legislature approved a formal plat drawn up by Grant's son-in-law, John James Flournoy.

Boone Co. Historic Preservation Review Board. *Historic Structures of Boone County, Kentucky.* Burlington, Ky.: Boone Co. Historic Preservation Review Board, 2002.

Warner, Jennifer S. *Boone County: From Mastodons to the Millennium.* Boone Co., Ky.: Boone Co. Bicentennial Book Committee, 1998.

Matthew E. Becher

TAPPERT, WILLIAM AND HENRY (William Hubert Tappert, b. January 18, 1848, Düren, Rhineland, Germany; d. March 18, 1907, Covington, Ky.; Henry M. Tappert, b. April 9, 1855, Düren, Rhineland, Germany; d. November 17, 1929, Covington, Ky.). The nationally prominent Catholic priests and siblings William and Henry Tappert were leaders of the local German American community (see **German Americans**). William Tappert, who was studying for the priesthood in Germany, immigrated to the United States in June 1870, completed his studies at Mount St. Mary Seminary in Cincinnati, and was ordained a priest in September 1872 for the Diocese of Covington (see **Roman Catholics**). After serving as pastor at the Catholic churches **St. Joseph** in Cold Spring, **St. Mary** in Alexandria, and **St. John** in Covington, Rev. William Tappert became the longtime pastor (1879–1907) of the German American **Mother of God Catholic Church** in Covington. There he oversaw the impressive ornamentation of the church in 1890–1891.

Henry Tappert immigrated to the United States in June 1875, studied at Mount St. Mary Seminary in Cincinnati, and was ordained a priest for the Diocese of Covington in May 1879. He served as an assistant pastor at St. Mary Catholic Church, Alexandria, and at St. John Catholic Church, Covington, as well as at his brother's parish, Mother of God Church. In 1907, after the death of William, Henry became pastor (1907–1929) of Mother of God Church.

William Tappert had been one of the organizers of the Deutsch-Amerikaner Priester-Verein (the German-American Priests' Society), which, at its first conference in Chicago in February 1887, appointed him president. At the same meeting, Tappert proposed that the society work for the establishment of a house of refuge for newly arrived German immigrants in New York City. The Priester-Verein also organized a *Katholikentag*, a conference of both priests and laymen modeled after those offered in Germany, for Chicago in September 1887. The Chicago Katholikentag (also called the First American German Catholic General Assembly) attracted 2,500–3,000 attendees, who elected William Tappert as vice president. Tappert addressed the assembly on the need for an immigrant house of refuge. He and others began to raise funds for the establishment of that institution near Castle Garden in New York City. It was called Leo-Haus (Leo House; named for then Pope Leo XIII). In October 1888 William Tappert became one of the 14 original members of the newly incorporated Leo House. In 1889 Tappert continued his involvement with the second American *Katholikentag*, held in Cincinnati. Bishop **Camillus Paul Maes** of Covington, an Americanist who desired to downplay the ethnic differences of Catholics in the United States, did not personally attend the conference. In summer 1889 Tappert was the official American delegate to the German Katholikentag in Bochum, Westphalia. He returned to Cincinnati to be met by a grand procession through its streets and those of Covington, accompanied by fireworks. William Tappert died in March 1907 and was buried in Mother of God Church, at the base of the church's Our Lady of Perpetual Help altar.

Rev. Henry Tappert was a German-trained musician, who supported the newer Cecilian reform music of the Catholic church of the period, stressing polyphony and chant, rather than the old German Singmesse (Sing Mass) of Covington's **Bernard H. F. Hellebusch**. Henry Tappert's compositions were published in the popular *St. Cecilia Hymnal*, and his 1929 obituary in the *New York Times* referred to him as a "noted composer." He was buried next to his brother in Mother of God Church.

Ryan, Paul E. *History of The Diocese of Covington, Kentucky.* Covington, Ky.: Diocese of Covington, 1954.

Tenkotte, Paul A., David E. Schroeder, and Thomas S. Ward. *To Be Catholic and American in Northern, Central, and Appalachian Kentucky: The Diocese of Covington, 1853–2003.* Forthcoming.

Paul A. Tenkotte

TARVIN, JAMES P. (b. November 13, 1859, Covington, Ky.; d. August 19, 1907, Cleveland, Ohio). Judge James P. Tarvin was the son of Henry Tarvin. His mother was the former Eliza Pryor, daughter of Circuit Court judge James Pryor of Covington. James P. Tarvin was educated in public schools and then entered the Cincinnati Law School, from which he graduated in 1881. He apprenticed under lawyers Pryor and Chambers. In 1890 he formed a partnership with another lawyer, Walker C. Hall. In politics he was a Democrat and was chairman of the Kenton Co. executive committee of that party. In 1898 Tarvin was elected to the office of circuit judge, taking office January 1, 1898. He died of asthma at age 47, while he and his wife were staying at the Hollenden Hotel in Cleveland. They had just left the home of a friend, Mrs. Eugene Shinkle of Waukegan, Ill. His body was returned to Covington for burial in the Highland Cemetery at Fort Mitchell. His wife, Louella Belt Tarvin, and a stepson, J. W. Belt, survived him.

Highland Cemetery Records, Fort Mitchell.

"Judge James Tarvin Dies in Cleveland," *KP,* August 20, 1907, 2.

Kerr, Charles. *History of Kentucky.* 5 vols. Chicago: American Historical Society, 1922.

US Gen Web Archives. "Kenton County, Kentucky." www.rootsweb.com (accessed April 5, 2007).

TAYLOR, ASA (b. before 1800, Virginia; d. after 1839, Kentucky). Asa Taylor, an enslaved African American who was living in Kentucky, has been called the first African American preacher in Boone Co. He and his siblings, all enslaved, came to Kentucky with Rev. **John Taylor**, a Baptist evangelist who had many slaves, from Virginia. Asa Taylor was one of 31 African Americans who were accepted into the fellowship of the **Bullittsburg Baptist Church** in August 1800. That summer, John Taylor baptized by immersion a few young people, including Asa, whom Taylor had raised and taught to read. Another man, a slaveholder named Christopher Wilson, was baptized at the same time. Wilson was later called as the first moderator or pastor of the Baptist Church at Middle Creek (present-day **Belleview Baptist Church**). Asa Taylor and Wilson often traveled throughout Boone Co. together, teaching and preaching. John Taylor said of Asa, "May he be useful among his fellow Blacks as there is the greatest sphere of his action."

Asa Taylor's sister Letty, also raised by John Taylor, did not share her brother's religious fervor. Letty had so great an aversion to religion that it took stern measures by John Taylor to force her to join the Taylor family prayers and worship. John Taylor described Letty as having "masculine strength" and an unflagging determination. After Asa Taylor's conversion, Letty was apparently stricken by her own "consciousness of guilt," and she called upon Asa for his counsel. Asa responded that Letty was "of the Devil" and was not ready for baptism or acceptance into any Baptist church. Despite Asa's assessment of her, Letty made a confession of faith three weeks after Asa's conversion and was baptized and accepted as a member of the Bullittsburg Baptist Church.

Unlike Wilson, who was ordained May 2, 1807, Asa Taylor was never officially ordained as a Baptist preacher. For the first 18 years of his ministry, the Baptist elders held Asa in tight rein. The church finally relaxed its hold and allowed him to share freely his "gift of exhortation."

Boone Co. slave schedules indicate that Asa was a slave of several Boone Co. men. When John Taylor left Boone Co. for Gallatin Co. in 1802, Asa Taylor was listed with John Graves. From 1819 to 1835, two other slaveholders claimed ownership of Asa. In 1839 the Bullittsburg Baptist Church minutes recorded the request of a "Brother Ezra Ferris, who asked that Asa [Taylor] and his wife, Rachel, be granted dismissal from the Bullittsburg congregation." It is possible that Ferris, who lived in Dearborn Co., Ind., had manumitted Asa and Rachel. It is believed that Asa Taylor lived at least until 1839; there is no record of his death or his burial.

Jackson, Eric R. *Black America Series: Northern Kentucky.* Charleston, S.C.: Arcadia, 2005.

Taylor, John. *Baptists on the American Frontier: A History of Ten Baptist Churches of Which the Author Has Been Alternately a Member.* Ed. Chester Raymond Young. 3rd ed. Macon, Ga.: Mercer Univ. Press, 1995.

Jannes W. Garbett

TAYLOR, HUBBARD, SR. (b. August 2, 1760, Midway, Va.; d. October 7, 1840, Pine Grove, Ky.). Legislator and judge Hubbard Taylor was the first son of James and Ann Hubbard Taylor Sr. He was the older brother of Gen. **James Taylor Jr.**, founder of Newport. James Taylor Sr. was the deputy surveyor for Caroline Co., Va., and when he resigned the post in 1778, his son Hubbard was appointed to be his successor. Hubbard was a militia volunteer during the **Revolutionary War**, serving in the area surrounding Williamsburg, Va. In February 1780 he came to Northern Kentucky to survey land for **George Muse**, for Hubbard's father, and for others. Hubbard returned to his Virginia home in spring 1782 and in that year married Clarissa Minor; they had 10 children.

In 1790 the family moved to a farm named Spring Hill along Boone's Creek in Kentucky, 12 miles east of Lexington. In 1791 Hubbard came to Northern Kentucky and platted some lots for a town, which he named New Port; his brother James Jr., however, settled in Newport and is credited for the town's founding and development. Hubbard served as a delegate to Kentucky's first constitutional convention at Danville in 1784. He represented Fayette Co. in the state's first legislature, and he was instrumental in the creation of Clark Co. in 1792. He served as a quarter session judge in Clark Co., and from 1796 to 1800 he was a state senator from Clark Co. When his senate term ended, he retired to his home. Hubbard Taylor Sr. died in 1840 on his farm at Pine Grove, Ky., and was buried there in the Taylor Graveyard.

"Interesting Historical Facts," *CJ*, April 12, 1873, 1.

"The James Taylor Narrative," 1840, Kenton Co. Public Library, Covington, Ky.; Campbell Co. Historical and Genealogical Society, Alexandria, Ky.

Reis, Jim. *Pieces of the Past.* Vol. 2. Covington: Kentucky Post, 1991.

Jack Wessling

TAYLOR, JAMES, JR., GENERAL (b. April 19, 1769, Midway, Va.; d. November 7, 1848, Newport, Ky.). Investor and city founder James Taylor Jr. was the fifth child born to James Taylor Sr. and Anne Hubbard Taylor. His early education was by private tutor, and later he attended the Rappahannock Academy. His father bought from his friend George Muse 2,700 acres of land in Northern Kentucky that included most of modern-day Covington, Newport, Bellevue, and Dayton, Ky. It was land Muse had been awarded for his military service in the **French and Indian War**; Muse requested, in this transaction, that a 1,000-acre tract, now part of Dayton, be deeded back to two of his daughters, Katy and Caroline Muse. A 200-acre tract on the west side of the Licking River was sold to Col. Stephen Trigg of the Kentucky Court of Land Commissions. James Sr. gave his son James Jr. 500 acres and retained ownership of the remainder. In May 1792 James Jr. arrived in Northern Kentucky to help develop and sell his father's land. He brought with him three slaves, Moses, Humphrey, and Adam, along with an English army deserter, Robert Christy, and Christy's wife and their three children. James Jr. stated that when they arrived in the area, there were about 150 people living at present-day Cincinnati, plus about 50 army personnel. On the south side of the Ohio River, there were just a few squatters living in crude log cabins. The party of settlers who arrived with James Taylor Jr. built several small log cabins and planted about 15 acres of corn, near the Licking River. Taylor walked the land and found a beautiful ridge overlooking the Ohio River, where he planned to build his home. He raised a log cabin there and later replaced it with a frame dwelling, which was destroyed in 1837 by a fire set by a disgruntled slave. Afterward Taylor built the brick mansion now standing in Newport at 335 E. Third St.

Gen. James Taylor Jr.

In 1791–1792, James Taylor Jr. laid out the town of Newport, and in 1793 he marked out the basic route that has become **U.S. 27** to Lexington. When his friend **David Leitch** died in November 1794, Taylor was named executor of his estate and a year later married Leitch's widow, Keturah Moss Leitch. James and Keturah Taylor had 11 children, but only 4 survived to maturity. In 1798 Taylor donated land for the establishment of the **Newport Academy**, the first public school in the Cincinnati area. He also donated another two-acre tract in Newport on Fourth St., between York and Columbia Sts., for construction of a courthouse and jail.

The Taylor family had two cousins, James Madison and Zachary Taylor, who later became presidents of the United States. In 1803 James Taylor Jr. solicited the help of James Madison, who was then U.S. secretary of state, to persuade the federal government to move the Fort Washington military post from Cincinnati to Newport. As an inducement, Taylor donated five acres of land at the confluence of the Ohio and Licking rivers on which to build the facility. The federal government, in turn, awarded Taylor the construction contract for what became the **Newport Barracks**. During the **War of 1812**, he held the rank of brigadier general in the Kentucky Militia. Taylor served under Gen. William Hull in the ill-fated Detroit Campaign, in which Taylor was captured by the British but soon paroled. Afterward, Taylor was made quartermaster and paymaster general of the Northwestern Army. Since the federal government lacked the necessary funds to pay for supplies and equipment for the army, Taylor often helped finance it with his own money and credit. Later, when Taylor attempted to obtain reimbursement from the federal government, he was refused on the basis that his records were insufficient. Many years of intense litigation followed, but Taylor was never fully compensated.

During a storied lifetime, James Taylor Jr. operated ferries across both the Ohio and the Licking rivers, helped to found banks such as the Newport Bank, invested in the mammoth Newport Manufacturing Company, operated saw- and gristmills along the Licking River, was part owner of a saltworks at Grants Lick, Ky., ran a tanning business, and in his spare time was known to collect fossils and hunt buffalo at Big Bone Lick in Boone Co. During Zachary Taylor's run for the presidency in 1848, election officials came to the bedside of the dying James Taylor Jr. to record his vote. After casting his ballot for his cousin, Taylor reportedly said, "I have fired my last shot for my country." He died several hours later, at age 79, and was survived by his wife, Keturah, and four children, James III, Keturah Taylor Harris, Ann Taylor Tibbatts, and Jane Taylor Williamson. He was laid to rest in the Taylor family plot at Evergreen Cemetery, in Southgate. James III served as executor of his father's estate, which included land in 26 Ohio counties and about 60,000 acres in Kentucky. At his death, James Taylor Jr. was said to be one of the wealthiest men in the state of Kentucky, with an estate valued at more than $4 million. Much of his land had been acquired from veterans of the French and Indian and Revolutionary Wars. Several roads in Northern Kentucky carry the Taylor family name. The community of Taylor Mill is named for the gristmill Taylor once owned on Banklick Creek, at the intersection of Grand Ave. and Reidlin Rd. Likewise, Taylorsport, along the Ohio River in Boone Co., was founded by him. Although the three James Taylors who were prominent in Northern Kentucky's history are usually known as James Taylor Sr., James Taylor Jr., and **James Taylor III**, according to *The James Taylor Narrative* they were actually the fourth, fifth, and sixth males named James in the family line.

Biographical Encyclopedia of Kentucky. Cincinnati: J. M. Armstrong, 1878.
"The James Taylor Narrative," 1840, Kenton Co. Public Library, Covington, Ky.; Campbell Co. Historical and Genealogical Society, Alexandria, Ky.
Kleber, John E., ed. *The Kentucky Encyclopedia.* Lexington: Univ. Press of Kentucky, 1992.
Purvis, Thomas L., ed. *Newport, Kentucky, a Bicentennial History.* Newport, Ky.: Otto Zimmerman, 1996.
"Sketch of General Taylor's Life," *CJ*, July 28, 1848, 2.
Tenkotte, Paul A. "Rival Cities to Suburbs: Covington and Newport, Kentucky, 1790–1890," PhD diss., Univ. of Cincinnati, 1989.
Wessling, Jack. *Early History of Campbell County, Kentucky.* Alexandria, Ky.: Privately published, 1997.

Jack Wessling

TAYLOR, JAMES, MANSION. See **James Taylor Mansion**.

TAYLOR, JAMES, NARRATIVE. See **James Taylor Narrative**.

TAYLOR, JAMES, III (b. August 9, 1802, Newport, Ky.; d. March 29, 1883, Newport, Ky.). James Taylor III was a lawyer, businessman, and actor. He and his twin sister, Keturah, were children of **James Taylor Jr.**, founder of Newport, and his wife, **Keturah Moss Leitch Taylor**, widow of Maj. **David Leitch**. James III's early education was at the private school of Rev. Robert Stubbs, near Newport. He then studied at the Pestalozzian School of Dr. Joseph Buchanan, near Lexington, and in 1818 entered Transylvania University at Lexington, where he received his undergraduate degree in 1822. He returned to Newport, joined an acting society, and opened a theater at the Newport Barracks. Soon James was considered the equal of any actor of his day; he performed at theaters in both Cincinnati and Newport. He committed to memory many of the works of William Shakespeare and of Lord Byron, which he often recited to family and friends.

In 1823 James III entered the Transylvania Law School, from which he graduated in 1825, and was admitted to the Kentucky Bar. Although he became an accomplished lawyer, he never entered into public practice; instead, he spent his time managing the legal affairs of his father's vast holdings. At Frankfort on May 20, 1824, he married Susan Lucy Barry, daughter of William T. Barry, Kentucky's secretary of state. They had three daughters and two sons. When his father died on November 7, 1848, James III was named executor of the estate. Like his father, James III played a prominent role in area business and civic affairs. He was one of the founders of Covington's **Northern Bank of Kentucky** and served as its president for 25 years. In politics, he was a Democrat but cast his presidential vote for two Whig candidates, his cousin Zachary Taylor in 1848 and Henry Clay in 1824. James Taylor III died at age 80 and was buried in the Taylor family plot at Evergreen Cemetery in Southgate.

Biographical Encyclopedia of Kentucky. Cincinnati: J. M. Armstrong, 1878.
"The James Taylor Narrative," 1840, Kenton Co. Public Library, Covington, Ky.; Campbell Co. Historical and Genealogical Society, Alexandria, Ky.
Wessling, Jack. *Early History of Campbell County, Kentucky.* Alexandria, Ky.: Privately published, 1997.

Jack Wessling

TAYLOR, JOHN (b. October 7, 1752, Virginia; d. April 12, 1835, Forks of the Elkhorn, Ky.). John Taylor, a farmer, a preacher, and a frontiersman, was associated with 10 separate early Baptist Churches in Kentucky. The son of Lazarus and Hannah Bradford Calvert Taylor, he was born in the Virginia Piedmont region, matured in the Great Valley of the Virginia frontier, pushed farther out into the wilderness as a youthful missionary, and farmed in early settlements in Kentucky. Taylor was raised in an Anglican home that in matters of religion used the Book of Common Prayer. His education was sparse. He was exposed at an early age to the economic basis of slavery, the "peculiar institution" that greatly benefited him as a Kentucky landowner. Evangelical Calvinism, "the gospel of salvation," swept Virginia's Great Valley, and after youthful escapades with gambling and fist-fighting, Taylor accepted the Baptist view of salvation that he was taught there. With Joseph Redding as his traveling companion, Taylor began preaching with missionary zeal and powerful oratory.

Taylor married Elizabeth "Betsy" Kavanaugh in Orange Co., Va., in September 1782. One year later, John sold the family's Northumberland plantation there and sought to improve his economic status in the fertile Bluegrass region, remaining in the Elkhorn Creek area of Kentucky until April 1795. He then purchased from John David Woolper a large tract of land along the North Bend of the Ohio River. He and fellow Baptist preacher John Tanner (of Tanner's Station, present-day Petersburg in western Boone Co.) joined forces in selling off parcels of the Woolper land, a venture that continued until Tanner's death in 1812.

In Boone Co., Taylor counted among his assets 400 acres, horses, household goods, and 15 slaves. Taylor and Redding were two of the seven charter members of the Great Bend of the Ohio Baptist Church, renamed the **Bullittsburg Baptist Church**. Sixteen preachers, most of whom were ordained as the result of Taylor's ministry, emerged from that church. Taylor baptized two men who were important to the Baptist movement in Boone Co., Christopher Wilson and **Asa Taylor**, one of Taylor's slaves.

John Taylor planted Baptist congregations with the same energy and devotion with which he planted his crops. His book *A History of Ten Baptist Churches* is considered a theological treasure. John and Betsy Taylor were dismissed by letter from Bullittsburg Baptist and moved to Mount Byrd along the Ohio River in Kentucky, near Trimble Co. He spent his last years at the Forks of the Elkhorn, Franklin Co., and died April 12, 1835. He was buried in a newly created cemetery on a bluff overlooking South Elkhorn Creek.

Taylor, John. *Baptists on the American Frontier: A History of Ten Baptist Churches of Which the Author Has Been Alternately a Member.* Ed. Chester Raymond Young. 3rd ed. Macon, Ga.: Mercer Univ. Press, 1995.

Jannes W. Garbett

TAYLOR, KETURAH MOSS LEITCH (b. September 11, 1773, Richmond, Va.; d. January 18, 1866, Newport, Ky.). Keturah Moss, who eventually became the wife of **James Taylor Jr.**, was the daughter of Capt. Hugh and Jane Ford Moss. In December 1790 she married Maj. **David Leitch**, who owned a farm at Bryan's (Bryant's) Station, near Lexington. They settled at Leitch's Station along the Licking River in Campbell Co., where he built a log cabin. While surveying one of his properties, Leitch slept outdoors in a cold rain and apparently developed pneumonia. A physician from Fort Washington (Cincinnati) was called to treat him, but to no avail; David Leitch died in November 1794, at age 38. He left his estate to Keturah Leitch and named Gen. James Taylor Jr., founder of Newport, as his executor. A romance arose between Taylor and Keturah, and they were married on November 15, 1795, at Tuckahoe, near Bryan's (Bryant's) Station, Ky. They took up residence in Newport. Keturah had no children by David Leitch but bore 11 to James Taylor Jr. Only four of the children survived infancy: James Taylor III and Keturah Taylor Harris (twins), Ann Taylor Tibatts, and Jane Maria Taylor Williamson. James Taylor Jr. died in 1848 and was buried in the Taylor family plot at Evergreen Cemetery in Southgate. When Keturah Taylor died in 1866, at age 92, she was buried next to David Leitch, rather than James Taylor Jr., but not far from the Taylor family lot.

"The James Taylor Narrative," 1840, Kenton Co. Public Library, Covington, Ky.; Campbell Co. Historical and Genealogical Society, Alexandria, Ky.
Jones, Mary Keturah. *History of Campbell County, Kentucky as Read at the Centennial Celebration of 4th of July, 1876.* Reprint ed., Fort Thomas, Ky.: Rebecca Bryan Boone Chapter, Daughters of the American Revolution, 1974.
Wessling, Jack. *Early History of Campbell County, Kentucky.* Alexandria, Ky.: Privately published, 1997.

Jack Wessling

TAYLOR MILL. The city of Taylor Mill in Kenton Co. derives its name from a sawmill and gristmill once owned by **James Taylor Jr.** on Banklick Creek (see **Banklick Creek and Watershed**). The site of the mill is now at the end of Reidlin Rd., where it intersects with Grand Ave. The mill was built on land that was part of a 5,000-acre patent awarded to Raleigh Colston (see **Colston Family**) in 1790 for his service during the **Revolutionary War**. A man named William Wilson leased the mill from Colston and operated it until the land was purchased in 1810 by wealthy landowner James Taylor Jr., founder of Newport. Taylor soon learned that John Crittenden also claimed ownership of the mill site, as part of a 5,000-acre tract he owned in the area. Lengthy litigation followed, and in

1825 Crittenden descendants sold their interest in the property to Taylor. With that concession, Taylor owned most of the land along the west side of the Licking River from north of today's Latonia to the top of the Taylor Mill hill. From that time on, the community, the mill, and the road carried the Taylor name. Court records indicate that Taylor leased the mill and 300 acres surrounding it to George Perry in 1819. When that lease expired, he leased it to James Foley, who managed the mill and the adjoining farm until about 1842. In Taylor's will, signed in 1844, he bequeathed the 1,200 acres around the mill equally to his four children, **James Taylor III**, Keturah Taylor Harris, Ann Taylor Tibbatts, and Jane Taylor Williamson. Because of sporadic and insufficient water flow to the mill, it ceased operation in the late 1850s.

Taylor Mill, located south of Covington, was incorporated as a sixth-class city in 1956 but today is listed as a fourth-class city. It now includes communities previously known as Forest Hills, Sunny Acres, and Winston Park. Since the 1960s a number of subdivisions have been built in the city, making it one of the fastest-growing communities in Kenton Co. In 1988 Taylor Mill annexed land along Decoursey Pk., significantly increasing the city's size. Good leadership and wise planning have made Taylor Mill a model community, with city water, sanitary sewers, and good streets. Much of the city's progress can be attributed to Cincinnati businessman Afton Kordenbrock, who moved to Taylor Mill in the 1950s. He had been a three-sport star athlete at both **Holmes High School** and Eastern Kentucky University, and in 1997 he was inducted into the Northern Kentucky Sports Hall of Fame. He served on the **Northern Kentucky Area Planning Commission** and the Ohio-Kentucky-Indiana Regional Council of Governments (see **OKI**), in addition to being a councilman and the mayor of Taylor Mill for more than 21 years.

A mayor and four city councilmen presently govern Taylor Mill, and the city operates its own police and fire departments. The 2000 U.S. Census listed the population of Taylor Mill as 6,913. In recent years, Taylor Mill has felt the impact of the arrival of **Fidelity Investments**'s new campus of buildings nearby in south Covington.

Hammons, Michael J. *History of Taylor Mill, Kentucky*. Covington, Ky.: Sandy Cohen, 1988.

Kleber, John E., ed. *The Kentucky Encyclopedia*. Lexington: Univ. Press of Kentucky, 1992.

"New City Formed on Taylor Mill," *KTS*, June 1, 1956, 1A.

Reis, Jim. "Suburban Kenton County Slowly Making Its Mark," *KP*, February 10, 1986, 4K.

U.S. Census Bureau. "American Fact Finder. Data Set. Census 2000 Summary File 1 (SF1) 100-Percent Data. Custom Table." www.census.gov (accessed December 8, 2006).

Jack Wessling

TAYLOR'S BOTTOMS. Taylor's Bottoms, or Taylor's Mill Bottoms, or simply "the fill," is the land area situated along Taylor's Creek between Newport and Bellevue. The area is at a low elevation and easily floods when the waters of the Ohio River rise. When Gen. **James Taylor Jr.** owned this land, he used it as a horse racing track. In 1895 a Cree Indian tribe from Montana, in Kentucky as part of a traveling cultural exhibition, once spent a month camping in the bottoms. The area was annexed by Newport in 1911. Both Bellevue and Newport had their waste incinerators and original dumps (land fills) in Taylor's Bottoms, and hence the nickname "the fill" began to be used. For many years, athletic fields have been situated in the bottoms: the Bellevue Vets field; another athletic field on land once owned by the underworld's Sammy Schrader, where the Bellevue Kroger is today along Donnermeyer Dr.; and two baseball fields, known as Newport Recreation Fields No. 3 and No. 4, where the **Newport High School** is located now. Newport Recreation had two other fields in Taylor's Bottoms also: Field No. 1 remains as part of the revamped Ralph Mussman Sports Complex; Field No. 2 was covered over as those changes were made. Newport High's football stadium opened in the bottoms in 1939. On the Bellevue side of the creek, there are similar athletic fields. All of these fields have been laid out on top of the garbage dumps of earlier years.

Today, an elevated interstate highway, I-471, runs along the Newport-Bellevue boundary. At the south end of the bottoms' west side is the Newport city garage, home to the town's fleet of vehicles. From east to west, at this point of the bottoms, are the tracks of the **CSX** Railroad. A culvert beneath the rails allows storm waters to flow from Duck Creek to the Ohio River, meeting Covert Run (a creek running from the east) to form Taylor's Creek. At the far north end of Taylor's Creek, just before it flows into the Ohio River, and under the parking lot of the Party Source store, is a large, now covered, concrete bowl, which funnels the creek water under Fairfield Ave. (Ky. Rt. 8) into the river. When this land depression was open, it was known as "the horseshoe," a dangerous place for local children, some of whom failed to heed their parents' warnings and drowned in its slimy water. In 1901 a streetcar coming out of Dayton, Ky., careened over the embankment into the horseshoe. There was a dance club near this site for a while during the 1930s, fittingly called the Horseshoe Club. The **Bellevue Vets** Club, located along Fairfield Ave. in the northern end of the bottoms, appeared after **World War II**. During the 1960s, local traffic helicopters would land occasionally at the fill. Sixth St. crosses the fill east to west, so the area is sometimes referred to as the Sixth St. fill. At the corner of Sixth St. and Maple Ave. in Newport, a tollbooth once stood, for travelers leaving Newport on the Covert Run Turnpike. In 2004 the new Newport branch of the **Campbell Co. Public Library** opened on the site where an A&P grocery once stood, just to the north of the tollbooth's former location.

"Bellevue Fireman Burned at Dump," *KP*, August 26, 1940, 3.

"Newport Annexes Sixth St. Tract," *KP*, April 20, 1940, 1.

"New Street Is Opened to Public," *KP*, November 8, 1929, 1.

TAYLOR-SOUTHGATE BRIDGE. This bridge across the Ohio River was named for three Northern Kentuckians: Dr. **Louise Southgate**, Covington's pioneer woman doctor; **Richard Southgate**, an early local landowner; and **James Taylor Jr.**, founder of Newport. The bridge opened in November 1995, at the site of the demolished **Central Bridge**, which once connected Newport and Cincinnati. The present bridge has four automobile lanes, an 850-foot span, two approach spans, and two river piers. There is a pedestrian walkway on each side of the traffic lanes. The bridge itself is 1,849 feet long; including its approach ramps, it totals 3,000 feet in length. It links the U.S. Bank Arena (formerly the Riverfront Coliseum) and the other sports and museum venues nearby on the Cincinnati side of the river with the **Newport-on-the-Levee** entertainment complex and the downtown area of Newport.

The Taylor-Southgate Bridge was built at a total cost of just under $34 million by the John Beasley Construction Company of Dallas, Tex. Once the two river piers were in place and ready, the bridge's trusses were cantilevered from each side of the river toward the center. Where the two trusses met, the variance was within one inch, which was easily fixed by jacking up one end before connecting the sections. The new bridge's daily volume of traffic has increased as the driving public has become accustomed to once again having a bridge at that location.

"Bridge's Name Official; Taylor-Southgate Replaces Central," *KP*, December 1, 1995, 2K.

"Cincinnati to Newport: Missed by an Inch," *KP*, July 29, 1994, 1K.

Cincinnati-Transit.net. "Taylor-Southgate Bridge." www.cincinnati-transit.net (accessed October 31, 2006).

TAYLORSPORT. The community of Taylorsport in Boone Co. was known as Taylorsville until the Kentucky legislature changed its name to Taylorsport in 1849. Named for Newport's Taylor family, whose members were involved in its development, the settlement is located along the Ohio River and Ky. Rt. 8, five miles northeast of Burlington. Elijah Creek flows into the Ohio there. Lots went on sale in the village in 1846. In 1882 the U.S. Census Bureau determined that the geographical center of the nation's population was located less than two miles southeast of Taylorsport. An 1883 atlas shows a few streets platted in town, and there was at one time a post office, which closed in 1909. On April 3, 1974, when hundreds of tornadoes struck the region, one destroyed Morehead's Marine Service at the town's Ohio River dock and damaged more than 100 boats tied up there. In 2000 the U.S. Census Bureau reported that there were about 100 people living in the now-unincorporated town of Taylorsport and its immediate environs.

The 1883 Atlas of Boone, Kenton, and Campbell Counties. Philadelphia: D. J. Lake, 1883.

"Lots for Sale," *LVR*, November 21, 1846, 3.

Reis, Jim. "Taylorsport Is Truly Survivor among Towns," *KP*, July 10, 2000, 4K.

——. "Tornado Destroys Businesses, Homes," *KP*, July 10, 2000, 4K.

U.S. Census Bureau, "American Fact Finder. Data Set. Census 2000 Summary File 1 (SF1) 100-Percent Data. Custom Table." www.census.gov (accessed April 7, 2005, for Blocks 3002 and 3003, Block Group 3, Census Tract 704.01, Hebron CCD).

Warner, Jennifer S. *Boone County: From Mastodons to the Millennium.* Burlington, Ky.: Boone Co. Bicentennial Book Committee, 1998.

TELEGRAPH. The telegraph came to Cincinnati in August 1847 and to Lexington, via Northern Kentucky, in 1851. Samuel F. B. Morse had perfected the long-distance telegraph line only a few years earlier, in 1843. By the end of the 1850s, Maysville had been connected to Nashville, Tenn., via the telegraph (through Lexington), and a line also had been laid northward beneath the Ohio River at Maysville. During the **Civil War**, the telegraph was in wide use. Confederate raider Gen. **John Hunt Morgan** had a telegrapher with him in his ranks, who often frustrated his Union counterparts by tapping into lines with bold and cryptic false transmissions concerning Morgan's location and his intentions. It is also known that the telegraph line to Louisville was operating by September 1862, when the transmission line under the Ohio River at Covington broke. The **pontoon bridge**, set up in 1862 across the Ohio River to help thwart a threatened Confederate invasion, saved the day as a newly spliced Louisville telegraph connection simply was routed over the pontoon bridge for the short term, serving as a vital link for the Union's defense of the area.

Telegraph wires were often strung along railroad rights-of-way, and they became the means of dispatch and communication for the trains. The telegraph permitted outlying cities of the Northern Kentucky region, such as Falmouth, to notify Covington that an inbound scheduled **Covington and Lexington Railroad** train was running on time, for example. Soon important messages were being sent regularly, as commercial telegraph companies were developed. Rail beds today are littered with the remains of a once vigorous telegraph wire network: tilted poles, hollow copper wires, and glass insulators. The **Hemingray Glass Company** of Covington became the nation's leader in the production of those glass insulators, which kept telegraph wires taut, parallel, separated, and ungrounded. The namesake of the southern Kenton Co. town of Nicholson, Dr. **Henry C. Nicholson**, invented an improved system of transmitting messages, increasing the message-sending capability of the wires, and as a result he was sued by inventor Thomas A. Edison for patent infringement. By the 1890s towns along the rails were reporting all sorts of happenings through the telegraph wires. For the new **Chesapeake and Ohio Railroad** river city of California in eastern Campbell Co., the telegraph assisted its growth and prosperity. Town businesses could order goods and materials via telegraph, and they could be quickly sent from Newport on the train. Being remote no longer meant being isolated for the outlying parts of Northern Kentucky.

In the 1880s Alexander Graham Bell elevated communications to a new level when he successfully transmitted the human voice over wires, in a vast improvement over telegraphy's fast series of electronic clicks of code. However, the telegraph lingered well into the 20th century, because it was well suited to certain applications of data transfer. Ultimately, microwave transmission rendered telegraphy's long-distance hard wiring obsolete.

In 1900 two competing telegraph companies were open for business in both Covington and Newport: in Covington, Western Union was at 636 Madison Ave., while the Postal Telegraph-Cable Company operated from 29 W. Sixth St.; in Newport, Western Union was at 607 York St., and Postal Telegraph was down the street at 326 York. Telegraph keys were set up for special occasions at such places as the **YMCA**, churches, and poolrooms. Poolrooms installed them for the purpose of receiving distant horse-racing results, critical to their illegal betting activities. Several individuals became well-known telegraphers, such as young Walter Grimm, who in 1917, at the age of 16, was a station manager in Newport. Telegraph offices moved frequently because neighbors did not like the all-night foot traffic of the strangers who frequented the offices. In 1943, as the telephone appeared in more households in the United States, declining business led the Postal Telegraph-Cable Company to merge with Western Union.

The telegraph offices that once dotted the Northern Kentucky region, bringing early major league baseball game scores, national election results, and other important announcements, have disappeared, along with the square-hatted, bicycle-riding telegraph delivery boys. They have yielded to modern technology, just as telegraphy itself had earlier retired the commercial carrier pigeon to his roost (see **Homing Pigeons**).

"Church to Have an Electric Wire," *KP*, November 3, 1916, 4.

City Directories, Covington and Newport, Ky., for 1880–1950.

Coleman, J. Winston, Jr. *Stage-Coach Days in the Bluegrass.* Louisville, Ky.: Standard Press, 1935.

"He's Smallest and Also Youngest Manager at Key," *KP*, October 22, 1917, 4.

"Nicholson vs. Edison—Quadruplex Telegraphing," *Chicago Daily Tribune*, May 5, 1879, 3.

"Wager by Wire," *KP*, July 29, 1897, 4.

"YMCA to Have Wire Vote Night," *KP*, October 31, 1916, 1.

Michael R. Sweeney

TELEPHONE. The telephone came to Northern Kentucky soon after Alexander Graham Bell invented it in 1876. The first phones in Northern Kentucky were owned by businesses, and they had very short ranges: they reached just to the other end of their individual phone lines. Three examples from the late 1870s in Covington include the **Hemingray Glass Company**, which had a wire running from its Second St. factory to a product showroom in downtown Cincinnati; the **Walsh Distillery**, also along Second St., which had a telephone connection to its other facility on the north side of downtown Cincinnati; and the Thomas Reed & Son firm, furniture dealers and undertakers, which also had a link to Cincinnati. These companies were near the Ohio River in Covington; from there it was relatively easy to reach the **John A. Roebling Bridge** and string phone cables across it. From central Covington it was necessary to pay the cost of installing telephone poles. These were private ventures, since no telephone companies existed yet. In Covington one of the first household telephones, called Edison Telephones, belonged to the well-connected Dr. **Richard Pretlow**, whose wife proceeded to buzz Covington society with her pioneering telephonic chitchat beginning in 1879. In 1899 one of the first long distance telephones in the area was installed at the Highlands Garden, a drinking establishment along Alexandria Pike in Southgate. It was placed in the beer garden owned by William Kettenacker, who used it as a draw to his business and as a means to reach his customers' homes in Newport, three miles distant.

The telephone exchange, the very heart and soul of any phone company, came later, allowing users to call many different locations from one phone. Exchanges, staffed by operators, were necessary in an era when phones did not have dialing devices. A primitive exchange, and perhaps the first in Northern Kentucky, was installed on the third floor of a building at the southwest corner of Fifth St. and Madison Ave. in Covington, in 1879. By 1910 Covington's "South" exchange had opened at 57 E. 4th St. It lasted until 1940. The first modern telephone exchange for Covington and Newport remains in use at 11th and Scott Sts. in Covington. Replacing the "South" exchange, this "Covington" exchange "cut in" (consolidated) 6,000 telephones at 10:00 p.m. Saturday, January 20, 1923. About 80 women operators, known as Hello Girls, were hired to work shifts on the second floor of the new building. Their work facility included a high-quality cafeteria and even an emergency hospital. The $600,000 building, designed by Cincinnati architect Harry Hake, later had its windows filled in with granite panels to protect the electronic switching equipment eventually installed inside. Today, although the Hello Girls are long gone and new exchange names and numbers have been added with increased phone use over the years, land line telephone calls continue to be routed through that subdued and secure structure. Land line (noncellular) telephone bills today still show "Covington, Ky." as the place of origin or the destination of long distance calls, the exchange through which those calls pass.

The exchange was the property of the Citizens Telephone Company. That organization was founded in Newport in 1895, and because of its innovative practices, such as the exchange, it won out over the multitude of smaller telephone companies throughout Northern Kentucky. It seemed at first that each little town had its own local operator, party line, exchange, and phone company, but the necessity for connections across the state, the nation, and the world led to consolidation into Citizens. In 1901 the Citizens Telephone Company became a subsidiary of the Cincinnati Bell Telephone Company, but for regulatory reasons, it continued to exist as a separate Kentucky corporation, regulated from Frankfort, Ky. Meanwhile, the many smaller telephone companies, confronted with increasing regulation and the high cost of telephone switching equipment, ceased operation. The Citizens Telephone Company eventually added exchanges with suburban growth in Erlanger (the Dixie exchange, in 1936) and Fort Thomas (the Highland exchange, in 1949). On January 31, 1969, Citizens Telephone had 108,251 phones in service in its system. One of the last phone systems acquired by Citizens was the Consolidated Telephone Company of Boone Co., which it absorbed on May 22, 1967, taking in an additional 12,087 phones. Boone Co. phones had not all been converted to phones with dialing devices until 1960. In Maysville the city government in 1895 granted the first telephone franchise to Thomas Davis, for the operation of local service for a period of 20 years.

One Northern Kentuckian has the honor of having developed the 1960s telephone marketing sensation the vintage Princess Phone. **Bartlett T. Miller** from Jonesville in Bracken Co., who rose to a vice-president position within AT&T, envisioned and designed the Princess. Satellites, the computer, the deregulation of the industry, and the invention of cellular technology have brought wholesale changes to the world of the telephone. As the cellular revolution continues, massive hard-wired telephone exchange buildings will soon be obsolete.

"Boone-Co Phone All 'Dial' Now," *KP,* May 2, 1960, 1K.

"Give One Name to Phone Co." *KP,* March 5, 1969, 4K.

"Local Matters," *DC,* February 15, 1879, 1.

"New Telephone Building to House Dixie Exchange," May 22, 1936, 3.

"6,000 Telephones Answer 'Covington,'" *KP,* January 20, 1923, 1–3.

Michael R. Sweeney

TEN-EYCK, SIDNEY DeFOREST (b. Sidney Eick, July 22, 1905, Mechanicsburg, Pa.; d. December 22, 1990, Edgewood, Ky.). Sidney Ten-Eyck, a major player in Cincinnati's rich broadcasting history, was born Sidney Eick but changed his name for professional reasons. At age 17, he served with the U.S. Marines (1922–1925). Through a friend, he met his wife, Dorothy "Dolly" Tretter, and they moved to Covington.

Ten-Eyck began his career in early radio in 1929 at Northern Kentucky's **WCKY**, when the station first went on the air. He returned briefly to that same station in the late 1960s before final retirement in 1970. In the 1930s he worked for Cincinnati's WLW radio, where he was well known for his syndicated *Doodlesockers* Saturday night comedy program, which included stories of his great-grandfather Tarbaby Ten-Eyck. Among his other characters were a pianist and a violinist, neither of whom could play their instruments. But real musicians would line up to join in the parody. The famous Mills Brothers performed on his shows, as well as the Clooney sisters (**Rosemary Clooney** and **Betty Clooney**) and many other well-known entertainers. He directed, produced, and ran his own shows. For his "man on the street" program, he dangled a microphone by its cord from a window down to the street. He also conducted live interviews and hosted live music on his shows. During those years, Ten-Eyck's radio career included a stint as a Cincinnati Reds baseball announcer (1931–1933). He returned to the military in **World War II**, serving in the U.S. Navy, and received several medals for bravery.

After his World War II service, Ten-Eyck moved to San Francisco and worked for a while in radio before becoming a corrections officer at the San Quentin prison. He worked 17 years in that tough penitentiary. In 1964 Ten Eyck and his wife returned to Northern Kentucky; they lived in Dayton and then in Covington.

Ten-Eyck was a prolific "letters to the editor" writer; he spoke at various high schools in the region, painting a true portrayal of the dire results of a life of crime; he was interviewed by WCET about his early radio days. Four months before his death, his 86th birthday was celebrated by such notable media personalities as **Nick Clooney**, Len Goorian, Bill Nimmo, Tony Sands, Elsa Sule, and **Mary Wood**.

In a 1990 *Cincinnati Post* round-up of "deaths felt around the globe," Ten-Eyck was included at the end of a list of such notables as a Supreme Court justice, generals, authors, celebrities, and composers: "Sidney Ten-Eyck, 86, of Covington, former broadcaster who worked in Greater Cincinnati radio since the 1920s." Ten-Eyck was cremated.

Clooney, Nick. "Readers Distill Sayings to Ease Vagaries of Life," *CP,* July 11, 1990, 1B.

"Deaths Felt around the Globe," *CP,* December 31, 1990, 2B.

Hicks, Jack. "This Man's Always Worth Listening To," *KP,* November 21, 1990, 1K.

Kieswetter, John. "Public Can Add to WVXU's Audio History of Cincinnati Radio," *CE,* March 27, 2000, C1.

"Sidney Ten-Eyck, Radio Pioneer," *KP,* December 24, 1990. 4A.

Nancy J. Tretter

TEN MILE BAPTIST CHURCH. The Ten Mile Baptist Church, the fifth-oldest Baptist church in Kentucky, is located north of Eagle Creek at Napoleon in Gallatin Co. It was organized in April 1804 by original members Elder William Bledsoe, who was the first preacher, and his wife; Mr. and Mrs. Preston Hampton; Mr. and Mrs. James Richardson; Solomon and his wife; Mr. and Mrs. Barnet Spencer; Mr. and Mrs. Edward Spencer; John Spencer; and Col. and Mrs. Joseph Spencer. Solomon and his wife are identified in church histories as "colored." The original location of the church was in Grant Co. about two miles north of Elliston Station. In 1840 the congregation began meeting a short distance away, across the new county line into Gallatin Co., where a new church was built on the site of the present-day church.

David Lillard became pastor of the church in 1806 and continued as pastor for the next 42 years. The church's history notes, regarding Lillard, "When he commenced the church it did not exceed 50 members; before he closed it numbered nearly 400." At Ten Mile Baptist Church and at other churches for which he was a circuit-riding preacher, Lillard baptized more than 4,000 people. Moreover, he was a successful farmer and at one time owned nearly 100 slaves.

Additional churches were also started by the circuit-riding Lillard. Ten Mile Baptist Church originally belonged to the North Bend Association of Baptist Churches, but in 1831, at the instigation of Lillard, the Ten Mile Association of Baptists was organized. The following Baptist churches belonged to the new association: Dry Ridge, Grassy Creek, Lick Creek, Mount Zion, New Bethel, New Salem, Poplar Grove, Providence, and Ten Mile. These nine churches had a total of 383 members. Since the Ten Mile Baptist Church existed before these other churches were founded, virtually all of the members of the new churches were former members of the Ten Mile Baptist Church. Many Kentucky Baptist churches during the 1830s and 1840s lost members to **Alexander Campbell**'s Reform Church (today's Christian Church, or Disciples of Christ), but the churches of the Ten Mile Association reportedly lost very few members. The creation of new Baptist churches whose members had originally attended the Ten Mile Baptist Church continued: Glencoe, Oakland, Pleasant Home, Verona, Vine Run, and Warsaw all established new churches. After widespread religious revivals in 1842, the memberships of both the Ten Mile Baptist Church and the Ten Mile Association of Baptists grew substantially. In response to its growth, the Ten Mile Baptist Church erected a new church building in 1862, replacing the 1840 structure.

At the Ten Mile Baptist Church's centennial celebration in 1904, it was estimated that more than 1,000 persons had joined the church during the previous century, under the leadership of 16 different preachers and 25 different deacons. The church did not enjoy the same growth in the beginning years of the new century, but the membership stayed loyal, although preaching dropped to one Sunday per month. Then in spring 1942, the brick church building dating from 1862, which was the Ten Mile Baptist Church's third home, burned. Skeptics thought the fire would be the end of the Ten Mile Baptist Church, but the church's membership responded quickly to this loss, and by 1943 a new frame church building had been built. The new building was the catalyst the church had needed, as full-time preaching resumed, the membership grew, and the church's finances improved. Rev. Will Smith, the pastor from 1937 to 1954, served longer than any other pastor in the church's history except for Lillard, and was responsible for the church's revitalization. As the church prospered, the congregation erected a new brick church in 1963, which is in use today; it was made possible by a gift from Walter "Jeff" Hendrix. The Ten Mile Baptist Church, the mother church for so many other Baptist churches in Kentucky, celebrated its 200th anniversary in 2004.

Johnson, Lafayette. *History of the Ten Mile Baptist Church of Christ, Gallatin County, Kentucky.* Louisville, Ky.: Baptist Book Concern, 1904.

Kirkpatrick, Edwin. "History of the Ten Mile Baptist Church of Christ, Gallatin County, Kentucky," 1976, Gallatin Co. Free Public Library, Warsaw, Ky.

Bernie Spencer

TERESITA (WALNUT GROVE). Teresita was the post office's official name for the southern Owen Co. community of Walnut Grove. The town is located along the Teresita-Shirley Rd., Highway 1476, west of Beechwood and about nine miles south of Owenton. Teresita is within the Harmony Precinct. There is no record of a school ever operating at Walnut Grove, only a post office. Presumably, the area derives its name from a grove of walnut trees. The source of the name Teresita has not been determined. The town sits just north of the Kleber Wildlife Area (see **Wildlife Areas in Owen Co.**) and only a few miles from the Scott Co. boundary.

TEVIS, WALTER STONE, JR. (b. February 28, 1928, San Francisco, Calif.; d. August 9, 1984, New York City). Writer Walter Stone Tevis Jr. was the son of Walter Stone and Anna Elizabeth Bacon Tevis. In 1938 Walter moved along with his family to Richmond, Ky., where he graduated from Model High School. After high school he served a stint in the Pacific Theater (1945–1946) with the U.S. Naval Reserves. Tevis received a BA in English from the University of Kentucky (UK) at Lexington in 1949, taught high school at various schools in Kentucky, and was a part-time instructor at UK in 1955–1956. He completed an MA in English at UK in 1957 and in 1958 briefly taught English at UK's Northern Community Center (now **Northern Kentucky University**) in Covington. While a graduate student, Tevis spent many hours at a popular Lexington pool hall, gathering materials for his first novel, *The Hustler* (1959). He eventually gave up teaching to write full-time, producing six additional novels that center on pool or chess: *The Man Who Fell to Earth* (1963); *Mockingbird* (1980); *Far from Home* (1981); *The Queen's Gambit* (1983); *The Steps of the Sun* (1983); and *The Color of Money* (1984). Three of his novels were made into movies: *The Hustler,* starring Paul Newman and Jackie Gleason; *The Man Who Fell to Earth,* starring David Bowie; and *The Color of Money,* starring Paul Newman and Tom Cruise. Tevis was married twice and had two children by his first wife. He died in New York City in 1984 and was buried in the Richmond Cemetery, Richmond, Ky.

Kleber, John E., ed. *The Kentucky Encyclopedia.* Lexington: Univ. Press of Kentucky, 1992.

Maltin, Leonard, ed. *Leonard Maltin's 2007 Movie Guide.* New York: Signet Books, 2006.

James C. Claypool

TEWES POULTRY. This small Northern Kentucky poultry dynasty was founded in 1911 by John Henry Tewes Sr. He started the family business in the old Fort Perry neighborhood of Fort Wright. In the early years, the business was known as the Safe and Sane Hatchery, and the incubators were located in the basement of the Tewes's house. Tewes soon moved to a 30-acre farm in what is today Edgewood. He patented a process for coloring the feathers of baby chicks with vegetable dye, thereby enhancing the hatchery's profitability. In the 1920s a dozen eggs sold for 10 to 12 cents; the colored baby chicks, which came to be known as Easter chicks, were sold at the incredible price of 25 cents each.

In 1944 Tewes's son John H. Tewes Jr. moved the poultry business to a 115-acre farm in Erlanger and changed the focus of the business from hatching to raising chickens, both as layers and for frying or roasting. Initially, chicks were obtained from local hatcheries. As local suppliers went out of business, Tewes Poultry had to acquire most of its chicks from out of state. In the 1950s the firm expanded by adding tan turkeys to its product line. From 1960 to 1995, Tewes Poultry trucks covered the entire Northern Kentucky region, delivering fresh eggs, fryers or roasters, and, during the winter, turkeys. Later, Tewes Poultry limited delivery service to individuals who were housebound and to local grocers. One of the largest producers in Northern Kentucky, Tewes Poultry sells approximately 3,000 turkeys, 6,500 chickens, and 3,500 dozen eggs annually. In 2001, to accommodate nutrition-conscious customers, Tewes Poultry switched from tan turkeys, which have large amounts of dark meat, to white turkeys because they have more white meat.

In 1958 the farm was physically divided into two sections when the government purchased right-of-way to build I-75 (see **Expressways**). The family house and the poultry buildings are contained on 37.5 acres. The 56 acres on the other side of the highway lay dormant until 2001, when the Tewes family and Pilot Contracting Corporation entered into a joint venture to create a business park. John Henry Tewes Jr. brought formal organizational structure to the family business when he created three business entities: Tewes Farm Corporation, the parent company, responsible for the Tewes Business Park; Tewes Poultry Property, which secures the farm's property; and Tewes Poultry Products, which protects the business products.

John Henry Tewes Jr. and Mary Ratterman Tewes married in 1935 and had 18 children. John died in 1988 and Mary in 2002; they were survived by 17 children. At the death of John Henry Tewes Jr., Daniel N. Tewes became president of Tewes Poultry and Tewes Poultry Products, and Robert A. Tewes was named president of Tewes Farm Corporation.

Account No. 6372900, Kenton Co. Property Valuation Department.

Deed Books 312, p. 14, and C-747, p. 121, Kenton Co. Clerk's Office.

"Feeding the Thousands," *KP,* November 19, 2003, 2K.

"Mary Tewes, Tewes Poultry Matriarch, Mother to 18," *KP,* March 28, 2002, B5.

May, Lucy. "Northern Kentucky to Get Business Park," *Business Courier,* February 23, 2001.

Tewes, Daniel N. Interview by Blanche Gaynor, March 12, 2005, Erlanger, Ky.

Tewes, Daniel N., and Darlene Tewes. Interview by Blanche Gaynor, October 11, 2004, Erlanger, Ky.

Tewes, Robert A. Interview by Blanche Gaynor and Paul A. Tenkotte, August 24, 2004, Fort Mitchell, Ky.; telephone interview by Blanche Gaynor, March 12, 2005.

"Trimming of Prices Bad News for Turkeys," *KE,* November 1, 2003, A1–A10.

"Turkey Time for Tewes," *KP,* November 19, 1999, 1K.

Blanche Gaynor

TEXTILES. The textile trade, originally conducted in colonial homes, had arrived in Northern Kentucky in the form of a business before the 19th century. By 1799 Daniel Mayo and Eli Williams had built a ropewalk manufacturing plant along Columbia St. in Newport. By 1817 the pioneer Indian fighter **Jacob Fowler** was operating a bagging factory. **Sidney Sherman** began with a bagging factory in Newport in this same era and also ran a "bullet manufacturing factory" in Covington, supplying the military before he departed, amid much fanfare, to fight in the **Mexican War**. In 1828 Newport lost out to its neighboring city Covington when Charles MacAllister chose to open his cotton factory on Covington's riverfront instead of in Newport. Nevertheless, by the 1840s Newport had become the acknowledged local center for fabric production. The Newport Manufacturing Company (see **John Wooleston Tibbatts**), incorporated in 1831, purchased 27 acres along the Ohio River and built 36 workers' dwellings, a cotton and a woolen factory, a ropewalk, and a hemp-bagging mill in town. The Cincinnati *Daily Gazette* recalled that in October 1835 this Newport manufacturing company, employing 329, had manufactured "4,056 batting, yards of Kentucky jeans, 3,716 yards of linseys, 5,299 yards of cotton plains, 200 lbs. of cotton, 2,500 lbs of cotton yarns, 18,284 lbs. of bale rope, and 36,568 yards of bagging." An expansion plan soon contributed to an increase in annual production of bale rope and bagging. The short supplies of American-grown hemp and high prices for this product necessitated purchases by the Newport Manufacturing Company of "354,201 pounds of Russia Hemp." But ordinarily Newport manufacturers enjoyed access to Mason Co. hemp crops, Ohio sheep farms, and Memphis, Tenn., cotton merchants.

By the early 1840s, William B. Jackson and his brother had opened a business called the **Newport Silk Manufacturing Company**, and in 1854 the company won an award at a prominent industrial exposition in New York City. By 1843 another new textile firm had opened a steam mill and ropewalk, "the most extensive" in the West. Newport's Licking Valley Steam Cordage and the Oakum Manufacturing Company made hemp into thread by machine before laying three or four strands into rope, "from ½ inch to 12 inch cable." Strong industrial leadership later built for Newport a reputation as a major steel center that lasted well into the 20th century, but as late as 1900, 21 percent of the city's industrial workers were still engaged in the manufacture of clothing.

The Covington Cotton factory opened in 1828, in a four-story building 120 by 40 feet in size that cost $66,000 to build. It operated 2,288 spindles, employed 60 workers, and produced 4,000 pounds of cotton yarn and 2,000 yards of cloth daily. In 1836 it produced yarn and "wick" worth $75,000 and "cotton gins" worth $35,000. The cotton factory expanded to add the manufacture of jeans and linseys. In 1840 it employed 90 workers, who produced 30,000 pounds of yarns. In 1844 it consumed 850 bales of cotton, made 32,500 lbs of yarn, employed 70 to 100 employees (three-fourths of whom were women), and paid wages of from $1.50 to $3.25 weekly. A 40-horsepower steam engine at the factory used 22,000 bushels of coal. Covington also had three ropewalks. In 1864 a Cincinnati company purchased the Covington cotton factory for conversion to a woolen factory. In 1866 the Glaser brothers were manufacturing wool at Scott and Front Sts in Covington. By 1869, however, the two woolen mills located in Covington were situated at Eighth St. and Madison Ave. and on Pike St. and the Glasers' operation at Scott and Front Sts. apparently had been closed.

Another Covington merchant, Thomas Bakewell, opened the Covington Bagging Factory at Second and Philadelphia Sts. in town. In the early 1830s, it produced $25,000 worth of finished "hemp goods" per year. In 1836 Covington and Newport produced nearly one-half million yards of bagging for wrapping Southern cotton bales. In 1849 Pepper and Blair operated Bakewell's former plant, known also as the Globe Mills and Bagging Factory; it was one of the largest processors of hemp in Kentucky. That was just a little more than one decade before the 1860s Union blockade during the Civil War cut off Southern cotton trade; afterward Kentucky's hemp economy faded.

In 1860 the Cincinnati city directory listed 4 cotton factories, 2 cotton dealers, 12 rope and cordage firms, 2 wool dealers, and 1 woolen manufacturer. After the **Civil War**, commerce to the east and west of the Greater Cincinnati region accelerated. Cincinnati remained both a "jobber," or commercial center, and a manufacturing center. Following a wool and woolen fabrics exposition in Chicago, Cincinnati boosters arranged an Exposition of Textile Fabrics in August 1869, inviting manufacturers of cotton, flax, hemp, silk, and wool, and also growers, to attend. This exposition inaugurated a series of general industrial expositions.

In 1866 the Covington city directory listed 2 woolen mills, 1 rope manufacturer, 2 carpet weavers, and 20 tailors and clothiers. Newport had 1 rope manufacturer, 1 cotton-batting factory near the **Newport Barracks**, and 3 tailor shops. In 1876 Covington listed 4 carpet weavers, 22 dressmakers, 26 tailors, and 8 sewing machine companies, including a branch of the Singer Manufacturing Company at 540 Madison Ave.

After the Civil War, new partners set up a national business, the Putnam-Hooker Company, which specialized in Southern cotton goods. In Covington, the Putnam-Hooker Company oversaw the Argonaut Cotton Mill (1892–1915) and the Reliance Textile and Dye Works, which operated into the mid-1980s, when the market for such processing had declined. The last owner-manager of the firm, by then known as the Reliance Dyeing and Finishing Corporation, was Harold J. Krantz Jr. He recalled that, while employing up to 25 workers, the highly mechanized firm dyed and finished fabric and components for carpet, vacuum cleaner, furniture, and car manufacturers nationwide. It imported cotton and modern synthetics from the South and overseas and dyes from Cincinnati, Germany, and elsewhere. Back in 1891, the Putnam Hooker Company claimed to represent about 30 of the largest cotton and woolen mills in the southern and western parts of the United States.

Established in 1880 with an office in Cincinnati, the Overman and Schrader Cordage Company operated the Eagle Twin Mills on W. Sixth St., Covington. In 1901 it was processing cords and ropes, cotton, flax, hemp, and sisal. In 1888 Covington had three rope and cordage firms in the vicinity of the city's railroad terminal and commission offices. Newport listed no rope and cordage manufacturing; Bellevue had one such firm; and located across from Cincinnati's Fulton shipyards, Dayton, Ky., had eight. In 1910 Covington had the Argonaut Cotton Mill, a carpet weaver, 87 dressmakers, and more than 40 tailor shops. Newport had 64 dressmakers, 7 men's finishing shops, and more than 50 tailor shops. In 1910 Cincinnati listed cotton brokerage offices, mills, and other cotton firms, including the Putnam Hooker Company. In 1926 Covington had the Reliance Company, 36 dressmaking shops, and 15 tailor shops. Newport had 14 dressmakers and 16 tailor shops.

In 1952 Newport shoppers could purchase ready-to-wear clothing, drapes, window shades, blankets, linens, hosiery, and underwear at the Brandt Dry Goods Store, operated by Albert, August, and Charles Brandt at 906 Monmouth St. David, Oscar, and Nathan Levine operated Hyde Park Clothes, a "clothing manufacturer," at 603 Washington St. in Newport. In 1962 Newport listed two manufacturers, the Palm Beach Company at the southeast corner of Washington and Fifth Sts., and Hyde Park Clothes, one block away at Washington and Sixth Sts., which operated into the 1970s. In the 1960s, 1970s, and 1980s, the Palm Beach Company, on Kenton Lands Rd. in Erlanger, manufactured men's and boys clothing. In 1991 the Palm Beach Mill Outlet ("retail") occupied the southeast corner of Washington and Fifth Sts. in Newport.

The textile industry changed rapidly from natural and synthetic fabrics and dyes to handicraft and manufactured ready-to-wear goods. It also changed drastically with new industrially engineered processes, new household technologies, new patterns of advertising and marketing, and shifting lifestyles.

Hopkins, James F. *A History of the Hemp Industry in Kentucky.* Lexington: Univ. of Kentucky Press, 1951.

Krantz, Harold J., Jr. Interview by John Boh, July 11, 1990, Covington, Ky.

Purvis, Thomas L., ed. *Newport, Kentucky: A Bicentennial History.* Newport, Ky.: Otto Zimmerman, 1996.

John Boh

THACKER, THOMAS (b. November 2, 1939, Covington, Ky.). Thomas Porter Thacker, the son of William T. and Velma M. Arvin Thacker, played basketball on three national championship teams: the NCAA (at the University of Cincinnati, 1960–1961 and 1961–1962), the NBA (for the Boston Celtics, 1967–1968), and the ABA (for the Indiana Pacers, 1970–1971).

Thacker's success in basketball began in grade school at the Roman Catholic African American school in Covington, **Our Savior**. His team played in the Northern Kentucky Holy Name Basketball League, winning the league's championship in 1955. In 1956, when integration closed Our Savior's High School, Thacker enrolled at William Grant High School. In 1956 African American schools were admitted to the Kentucky High School Athletic Association. That year his basketball team won the district tournament but lost in the regional tournament. William Grant had a season record of 23-4. In 1957–1958, Thacker's second year, William Grant High School won the district and regional basketball tournaments but lost in the first round of the state tournament. The school's basketball season ended with a record of 26-5. In 1958–1959, Thacker's final year, his high school won the district and regional tournaments but lost in the quarter finals of the state tournament. The school's season ended with a record of 31-7.

Thacker, still needing a few high school credits to graduate, attended the Holmes High School during summer 1959, then in the fall entered the University of Cincinnati. He earned a BA and an MA there. As a six-foot-two forward, he had a distinguished college playing career that included twice being named a basketball All-American. Following college, Thacker played basketball professionally for a time with the Cincinnati Royals alongside Oscar Robertson. After his NBA-ABA career, Thacker played and coached some minor league professional basketball teams. He also coached the University of Cincinnati's Lady Bearcats basketball team for a short period.

Thacker was named to the Northern Kentucky Sports Hall of Fame in 1986 and the Northern Kentucky Black Hall of Fame in 1989. He currently lives in Cincinnati, where during his retirement he does occasional substitute teaching for the Cincinnati Public School System.

Fisher, John C. K. "Black Hall of Fame Inductees Transcend Sports," *KP*, February 25, 1989, 1K.

"Our Savior Wins," *KTS*, January 5, 1955, 7A.

Reis, Jim. "Many Tried, Few Defeated William Grant in '50s, '60s," *KP*, February 23, 1998, 4K.

——. "Our Savior Fills Unique Niche," *KP*, January 17, 1994, 4K.

Straub, Bill. "Brain Busters: Quick Quiz of Forgettable Facts," *KP*, August 13, 1982, 5K.

Weber, Dan. "Thacker, Hils, Grant Top All-Time Hoop Picks," *KP*, December 25, 1984, 10K.

Theodore H. H. Harris

THEISSEN, HELEN MCNEEVE (b. May 28, 1906, Covington, Ky.; d. April 11, 2005, Covington, Ky.). Catholic charities activist Helen Theissen was the oldest of four children of Frank and Ellen "Nellie" Grossman McNeeve. She attended **La Salette Academy** in Covington, earned her first bachelor's degree from Sacred Heart College in Cincinnati's Clifton neighborhood (1928), and received an additional BS in education from the University of Cincinnati (1929). Thereafter, she taught for four years in public schools in Cincinnati's poorer West End district. Helen married Mark A. Theissen, an aeronautical engineer, in December 1935. He died in 1966, and she subsequently donated the hand-carved Sacred Heart Altar in Covington's **Cathedral Basilica of the Assumption** to his memory and that of her parents.

Active in Catholic charitable causes for the Archdiocese of Cincinnati, Helen served as treasurer of the Cincinnati Catholic Women's Association in 1958–1959. Under Bishop **William T. Mulloy** of the Diocese of Covington (bishop 1945–1959), she became involved in the Diocesan Council of Catholic Women (DCCW), an affiliate of the National Council of Catholic Women (NCCW) (see **Roman Catholics**). From 1958 until 1960, she served as president of the NCCW, then composed of 13,000 chapters and 9 million members. Under Theissen's leadership and through the influence of Miss Eileen Egan of Catholic Relief Services, the NCCW brought Mother Teresa of Calcutta (1910–1997) to its 1960 national convention in Las Vegas entitled "Women in the Sixties." The visit was a historic occasion, as it marked the very first time that Mother Teresa had left India since her arrival there in 1929. Still relatively unknown to the outside world at the time, Mother Teresa and her Missionaries of Charity later became famous worldwide for their avocation on behalf of the poor. Mother Teresa received the Nobel Peace Prize in 1979. Theissen and her sister Rosemary McNeeve became friends of Mother Teresa and sponsored one of the many babies that Mother Teresa rescued from the streets. Theissen also advised Mother Teresa before she opened a facility in New York City.

Theissen and McNeeve dedicated many years to the Diocese of Covington's annual DCCW Seminary Ball, providing funds for the construction and operation of the **Seminary of St. Pius X**. The two sisters were also members of the Equestrian Order of the Knights and Ladies of the Holy Sepulchre of Jerusalem, a society dedicated to supporting hospitals, schools, and orphanages for Middle Eastern children. Theissen received the prestigious Pro Ecclesia medal for her charitable work from Pope John XXIII. She died in Covington in April 2005. Her funeral mass was at the Cathedral Basilica of the Assumption, and she was buried at St. Mary Cemetery in Fort Mitchell.

Egan, Eileen. *Catholic Relief Services: The Beginning Years: For the Life of the World.* New York: Catholic Relief Services, 1988.

"Highest Office Goes to Mrs. Theissen," *KP*, September 25, 1958, 1.

Tenkotte, Paul A. "Helen Theissen Introduced Mother Teresa to the United States," *Cathedral Chimes* 15, no. 4 (Summer 2005): 1–2.

Tenkotte, Paul A., David E. Schroeder, and Thomas S. Ward. *To Be Catholic and American in Northern, Central, and Appalachian Kentucky: The Diocese of Covington, 1853–2003.* Forthcoming.

Paul A. Tenkotte

THIEN, WENCESLAUS (b. May 17, 1838, Bokel, Germany; d. November 13, 1912, Cincinnati, Ohio). Artist Wenceslaus Thien (his first name was also given as Wenzeslaus and Wenzel) was the son of Gerhard Thien, a master blacksmith, and Gesina Gerdes Thien. Wenceslaus, born in Bokel, was baptized in the nearby Catholic parish at Aschendorf. He was the third of five children, and with his younger brother Heribert (Herbert) (1844–1919), he immigrated to the United States. Wenceslaus and Herbert boarded the ship *New York* at the port of Bremen in Germany and arrived in New York City on August 14, 1866. Twenty-eight years old at the time of his immigration, Wenceslaus was a respected artist in Germany and had earned the recommendation of the bishop of Münster, Johann Georg Müller. In addition, in the winter of 1869 he traveled throughout Europe, further studying Christian art and decoration. Herbert, who had studied at the Gymnasium Carolinum (secondary school) in Osnabrück, was a rector at a rural parish in Germany. The brothers chose Cincinnati as their destination. Herbert completed his studies for the priesthood at Mount St. Mary Seminary in Cincinnati and was ordained a priest for the Archdiocese of Cincinnati in May 1867.

Wenceslaus Thien was peripatetic, like many artists of his day, first appearing in the Cincinnati City Directory in 1870. He was associated with the **Covington Altar Stock Building Company** in Covington, which employed fellow artists **Wilhelm Lamprecht** and **Johann Schmitt.** By the time that the Covington Altar Stock Building Company moved to St. Vincent's Abbey in Latrobe, Pa., in the early 1870s, Wenceslaus Thien had set out on his own as a fresco artist; his office was located for many years in the Johnston Building, on the southwest corner of Fifth and Walnut Sts. in Cincinnati. In 1874 Thien offered Covington artist **Frank Duveneck** a position in his firm, but the latter declined. By 1892, at the height of its success, the W. Thien Decorating Company had headquarters in Cincinnati's prestigious Carew Building, on the southwest corner of Fifth and Vine Sts., and included artists L. Emrich and Paul Hein. Thien's artistic creations, like those of Lamprecht and Schmitt, are still found at Covington's **Mother of God Catholic Church**, where he painted exquisite *a secco* paintings on the ceiling and walls in 1890–1891.

The exact number and location of Thien's artistic works may never be known, because ecclesiastical artists often did not sign their creations. Overpainting has destroyed some Thien works, while the demolition of many fine old churches has destroyed others. Nevertheless, Dr. Beate Stock of the National Gallery of Canada in Ottawa has identified a long list of Thien's works before 1872 through articles appearing in Cincinnati's German-Catholic newspaper the *Wahrheits-Freund.* Still intact are artworks by him and Wilhelm Lamprecht for St. Romuald (L'Église de Saint-Romuald-d'Etchemin) in New-Liverpool, Quebec, dating from 1868–1869. Also remaining are creations that he painted for St. Anthony of Padua Catholic Church in St. Louis, Mo., operated by the Franciscans. That same province of Franciscan priests and brothers, based in St. Louis, employed him as an artist at St. Joseph Catholic Church in Cleveland, Ohio, the size and magnificence of which earned it the title the Cathedral of the East Side; it closed in 1986 and was destroyed by fire in February 1993. Thien's 1867 artwork for St. Lawrence Catholic Church in Lawrenceburg, Ind., has been overpainted, as well as his three-month-long decoration of Isaac M. Wise Temple (Jewish) on Plum St. in Cincinnati in fall 1874. Lost are his 1869 works for St. Philomena Catholic Church in Cincinnati (demolished), his 1871 commissions for St. Elizabeth Hospital's Chapel on W. 11th St. in Covington (demolished) (see **St. Elizabeth Medical Center**), and his masterpieces for St. Stephen Catholic Church in Hamilton, Ohio. The St. Stephen church was formerly operated by the Franciscans, Cincinnati Province; Thien's works there were overpainted, and later the building was rebuilt after a fire in 1990. In 1877 Thien painted the walls and ceiling of the old St. Boniface Catholic Church (formerly operated by the Franciscans, Cincinnati Province) in Louisville, Ky., which was replaced by the present structure in 1900. In 1885 he executed frescoes for the old St. John Catholic Church on Worth St. in Covington (demolished).

Wenceslaus Thien remained single throughout his life, devoted to his painting and to his brother Herbert. Rev. Herbert Thien transferred to service in the Diocese of Covington in 1872 and was a longtime pastor of **Corpus Christi Catholic Church** in Newport. He returned to Germany and the Diocese of Osnabrück in 1895. Wenceslaus Thien died in Cincinnati in November 1912. His funeral mass was held at Cincinnati's first German American Catholic parish, Holy Trinity on W. Fifth St., and he was buried at Old St. Joseph Cemetery in Cincinnati.

Central Catholic Church Archive (Diozösanarchiv), Osnabrück, Germany, to Beate Stock, National Gallery of Canada, Ottawa, Ontario, October 16, 2006. In Paul A. Tenkotte's personal files.

"Deaths," *Cincinnati Commercial Tribune*, November 15, 1912, 5.

Heller, James G. *As Yesterday When It Is Past: A History of the Isaac M. Wise Temple—K. K. B'nai Yeshurun—of Cincinnati in Commemoration of the Centenary of Its Founding.* Cincinnati, 1942.

Müller-Koppe, Jens, Historical Research Services, Bremen, Germany, to Paul A. Tenkotte, October 31, 2006. In Tenkotte's personal files.

Ryan, Paul E. *History of the Diocese of Covington, Kentucky.* Covington, Ky.: Diocese of Covington, 1954.

State of Ohio, Bureau of Vital Statistics, Certificate of Death for Wenzel Thien, vol. 924, no. 59,944, for the year 1912.

Stock, Beate, National Gallery of Canada, Ottawa, Ontario, to Paul A. Tenkotte. E-mail messages and letters. In Tenkotte's personal files.

Tenkotte, Paul A., David E. Schroeder, and Thomas S. Ward. *To Be Catholic and American in Northern, Central, and Appalachian Kentucky: The Diocese of Covington, 1853–2003*. Forthcoming.

"Unser Decorationsmaler," *Cincinnati Wahrheits-Freund*, February 12, 1873, 221.

Paul A. Tenkotte

THOMAS, GEORGE H., GENERAL (b. July 13, 1816, Newsoms Depot, Va.; d. March 28, 1870, San Francisco, Calif.). The city of Fort Thomas is named in honor of **Civil War** general George Henry Thomas. A West Point graduate and a veteran of the **Mexican War**, Thomas chose to cast his lot with the Union during the Civil War. Following his defeat of the Confederates at Mill Springs, Ky., in 1862, his troops joined Gen. Don Carlos Buell's forces and fought at Nashville and Pittsburgh Landing, Tenn. Later, Thomas distinguished himself at Murfreesboro and Chickamauga, Tenn. His gallant stand in the second of these battles against twice his numbers won him his nickname, "the Rock of Chickamauga." Thomas fought with Gen. William T. Sherman in the 1864 Atlanta campaign. In December of that year, he crushed the Confederate Army at Nashville in the most decisive Union victory of the war. Thomas was promoted to major general in the regular army and received a special vote of thanks from the U.S. Congress. He died in 1870 and was buried at the Oakwood Cemetery in Troy, N.Y.

"Ft. Thomas Gives Old General a New Sheen," *KP*, June 19, 1984, 1K.

Reis, Jim. "Civil War Legacy," *KP*, February 20. 1983, 4K.

——. "Fort Thomas Named to Honor Union General," *KP*, October 14, 2002, 4K.

Bill Thomas

President Lyndon Baines Johnson (in academic garb, on left) at the Thomas More College dedication ceremonies, September 28, 1968.

THOMAS MORE COLLEGE. Thomas More College is a Roman Catholic liberal arts college in Crestview Hills, Kenton Co. The **Sisters of St. Benedict** of Covington established the institution in 1921, under the name Villa Madonna College. The school was originally located on the Villa Madonna Academy property in Villa Hills. On August 14, 1923, Villa Madonna College received a charter from the Commonwealth of Kentucky. It was the first four-year, degree-granting college in Northern Kentucky. The first dean of the college was Benedictine sister M. Domitilla Thuener. Villa Madonna College was established primarily to educate the members of the Benedictine Order who were teaching in the Catholic schools of the region. From the very beginning, however, laywomen were also accepted as students. New teaching certification standards in Kentucky required college-level training for all teachers. This left the **Sisters of Notre Dame** and the **Sisters of Divine Providence**, whose members were also teaching in area Catholic schools, without a local college program. During the early 1920s, both orders began plans for college programs of their own. When Bishop **Francis W. Howard**, an eminent educator, was appointed to the Diocese of Covington (see **Roman Catholics**) in 1923, he quickly saw that it was inadvisable to sponsor three Catholic colleges in Northern Kentucky. In 1928 he placed Villa Madonna College under the sponsorship of the Diocese of Covington. By the spring of 1929, the Sisters of St. Benedict had determined that they could no longer afford to support both Villa Madonna College and the Diocesan Normal School. The sisters decided to close Villa Madonna College and to concentrate their energy in the normal school. On June 4, 1929, the Benedictines' Villa Madonna College graduated its first and last class. Several weeks later, on June 20, the Diocesan Normal School graduated its first class of scholars. Bishop Howard decided to operate the Diocesan Normal School under the original charter and name of Villa Madonna College. The choice to use the charter and name of Villa Madonna College was primarily based on Bishop Howard's fear of state intervention. An application for a new state charter would require the college to conform more closely to the state's view of higher education—a conformity that Bishop Howard found unacceptable. The college was staffed by diocesan clergy and by the Sisters of St. Benedict, the Sisters of Divine Providence, and the Sisters of Notre Dame. The college was moved in 1928 to St. Walburg Academy (see **Sisters of St. Benedict**) on E. 12th St. in Covington.

The first dean (chief operating officer) under diocesan sponsorship was Rev. Michael Leick (1928–1943). Other early deans of the college included Rev. Edmund Corby (1943–1944), the Very Reverend Thomas McCarty (1945–1949), and Rev. Joseph Z. Aud (1949–1951). Beginning in 1929, an official board of trustees was established. Members of the board included the bishop of the Diocese of Covington, the dean of the college, and the mothers superior of the Sisters of St. Benedict, the Congregation of Divine Providence, and the Sisters of Notre Dame. Lay members were added to the board in 1967. A student representative was added in 1970, and two faculty representatives were added in 1971.

Villa Madonna College steadily increased in stature and enrollment under diocesan sponsorship. In order to furnish well-qualified faculty and staff members, the three orders of women religious agreed to divide the departments on an equal basis. In this way, each order could prepare members in specific disciplines. Sisters were sent to various Catholic and secular universities to earn doctoral degrees. Diocesan clergy staffed the theology and philosophy departments. Despite these efforts, the clergy and religious orders of the region could not fully staff the college. Dedicated laymen and laywomen have served as staff members and on the faculty for many decades.

Rev. Leo Streck, headmaster of the Covington Latin School, began offering college-level courses to the graduates of that all-male school in 1934, and he named this new endeavor St. Thomas More College. These classes eventually became accredited through the all-female Villa Madonna College. In 1945 Bishop William T. Mulloy announced that Villa Madonna College would become coeducational. When a flood of male students, especially those receiving the GI Bill, enrolled, classroom space soon became insufficient. In order to solve this problem permanently, the college purchased a large tract of land known as the Klaene Estate in Fort Thomas, Campbell Co., in 1948. Plans called for the construction of a new campus on the property, and ground was broken for the new campus on April 23, 1950, by the Most Reverend Amleto Giovanni Cicognani, the Vatican's apostolic delegate to the United States. But the new campus was never built on this site. The property was sold when college officials purchased a new site along Turkeyfoot Rd. in Crestview Hills in 1954.

Financial difficulties delayed the construction of a new campus on the Crestview Hills property. In the meantime, buildings were rented or purchased near the main building on E. 12th St. in Covington to house the growing enrollment. In 1945 classrooms at St. Joseph School along Scott St. in Covington were acquired by the college. Other buildings used for classrooms in Covington included the **Mother of God** School on W. Sixth St., the Cathedral Lyceum and Columbus Hall on Madison Ave., Aquinas Hall and Bernard Hall North and South along Scott St., Cabrini Hall on 12th St., and Thomas More Hall (an old firehouse) on 12th St.

In 1951 Rev. John F. Murphy was appointed dean of Villa Madonna College (he received the title of president in 1953) and remained in that post until 1971. It was under Murphy's guidance that the college was accredited by the Southern Association of Colleges and Secondary Schools in 1959 and that the new campus was built. In 1966 plans for the new Crestview Hills campus were completed. Ground was broken on May 9, 1966, and construction on the multimillion-dollar project began. The campus was ready for occupancy in January 1968. During the following month, Bishop Richard H. Ackerman announced that the name of the institution was to be changed to Thomas More College, after the lord chancellor of England who was martyred for his faith by King Henry VIII. The college was officially dedicated on September 28, 1968. A surprise guest at the dedication was President Lyndon B. Johnson (1963–1969).

The Thomas More College campus in Crestview Hills has been a work in progress. Marian and Howard Residence Halls were ready for use during the 1968–1969 school year. Ackerman Hall, also a dormitory, was ready during the following year. In 1972 the Science Building was completed, and in 1989 the Connor Convocation Center was ready for athletic competition. More recent additions have included the Holbrook Student Center (1999) and Rev. John F. Murphy Residence Hall (2003). In 1967 the college acquired the U.S. Lock and Dam on the Ohio River in rural Campbell Co. This facility has been utilized as a biological field station ever since (see **Center for Ohio River Research**).

Presidents of Thomas More College since Murphy have included Dr. Richard DeGraff (1971–1978), Dr. Robert Giroux (1978–1982), Dr. Thomas Coffey (1982–1985), Dr. Charles Bensman (1986–1992), Father William F. Cleves (1993–2001), Dr. E. Joseph Lee (2001–2004), and **Sister Margaret Stallmeyer**, C.D.P., who was officially inaugurated the 13th president of Thomas More College on April 28, 2005. Today there are approximately 1,500 students enrolled at the college, both full- and part-time, and two graduate programs are offered (business administration and a masters of arts in teaching).

Kleber, John E., ed. *The Kentucky Encyclopedia.* Lexington: Univ. Press of Kentucky, 1992.

Reis, Jim. "Thomas More: College of Many Sites, Missions," *KP*, November 25, 1985, 4K.

Saelinger, Sister M. Irminia. *Retrospect and Vista: The First Fifty Years of Thomas More College.* Newport, Ky.: Wendling, 1971.

Schroeder, David E. "Thomas More College Archives Inventory," 2000, Thomas More College Library, Crestview Hills, Ky.

David E. Schroeder

THOME, JAMES A. (b. January 20, 1813, Augusta, Ky.; d. March 4, 1873, Chattanooga, Tenn.). Antislavery activist James Armstrong Thome was the son of Arthur Thome, an emancipator accused of being a conductor of fugitive slaves in Augusta in Bracken Co. James A. Thome, who was also involved in helping slaves escape (see **Abolitionists**), was threatened with arrest and imprisonment if he returned to his home at Augusta from Oberlin College, where he was working on a theology degree. The threat had been issued because James had successfully removed a slave, Judah, from Augusta across the Ohio River to Ripley, Ohio, and then on to Canada. Perhaps Thome's zeal concerning the **antislavery** movement is best expressed in his own words: "Oh! The slave kitchens of the South are the graveyards of the mind. Every countenance of their miserable inmates is the tombstone of a buried intellect, and the soulless eye is its dreadful epitaph!"

Arthur Thome (1769–1855) was one of Augusta's first settlers, quickly becoming wealthy in the flourmill business and other enterprises. His three-story mansion was later the home of the Marshall family, ancestors of Gen. George C. Marshall. At the insistence of his son James, Arthur Thome freed his men and women slaves between 1832 and 1836 and also became one of the area's most successful conductors of the **Underground Railroad**, the escape network helping to take fugitive slaves to freedom. One former slave from Maysville reported in the June 1, 1839, issue of the *Colored American,* published in New York, that the Thomes were highly instrumental in the work of the Underground Railroad. According to slave Robert, "[Arthur] Thome would get out of his bed in the middle of the night to help runaway slaves out of the reach of their masters. He would give them clothes and money and send them across the Ohio River. He was very rich, he said, or he could not live there, meaning, it was understood, that his great wealth made his slave-holding neighbors afraid to injure him."

Arthur's son James was educated at **Augusta College**, where debates on slavery were held as early as 1826. **Martin Ruter**, the first president of the college, was one of the founding members of the Kentucky Colonization Society, an organization that endorsed sending emancipated slaves to the colony established in the newly formed West African country of Liberia. After graduation from college, James Thome entered the prestigious Lane Seminary in Cincinnati. In 1833 and 1834 he participated in the noted Lane Debates on slavery that caused Theodore Weld, Thome, and 50 other students to leave the Lane Seminary, eventually becoming members of the first theology class at Oberlin College. Thirty of Thome's letters to Weld, some of which were written in Augusta, were published in *Letters of Theodore Dwight Weld, Angelina Grimke Weld, and Sarah Grimke.*

Thome delivered a speech in May 1834 to the Annual Meeting of the American Anti-Slavery Society, of which he became a vice president. In 1836 this group commissioned Thome to examine the results of immediate emancipation in the West Indies, in order to advance the cause in the United States. In winter 1837, Thome penned from his home in Augusta the manuscript for his *Emancipation in the West Indies,* which was published in 1838.

Not all of Thome's influential writings were devoted to the cause of the enslaved; he also wrote a lesser-known pamphlet, *Address of the Females of Ohio.* Thome's views in the pamphlet were delivered by him at the Ohio Anti-Slavery Anniversary in April 1836 and then later published by the Ohio Anti-Slavery Society in Cincinnati.

Both Arthur and James Thome suffered consequences for their acts of conscience. Family letters on file at Oberlin College refer to their plight while they lived in Augusta, where they endured difficulties ranging from harassment to outright threats against their personal safety. As these actions became more severe, the elder Thome and his family sold the Thome mansion and businesses in Augusta at a financial loss and moved to Athens, Mo., where he is credited with establishing another Underground Railroad pathway to freedom.

James A. Thome became an influential minister in Cleveland and Mount Vernon, Ohio. After the **Civil War**, he traveled to Europe, raising money for the education of former slaves; his Augusta College friend **John G. Fee** had been similarly engaged at Berea College. Thome's later years were spent as a successful minister. In 1871 he became pastor of the First Congregation Church in Chattanooga, Tenn., the town where he died of pneumonia two years later.

Miller, Caroline R. "Abolitionists of Augusta's 'White Hall': Arthur and James Thome," *NKH* 11, no. 1 (Fall–Winter 2003): 46–55.

Caroline R. Miller

THOMPSON, EDWIN PORTER (b. May 6, 1834, Center, Metcalfe Co., Ky.; d. March 4, 1903, Frankfort, Ky.) Educator and author Edwin Porter Thompson was the eldest son of Lewis M. and Mary R. Thompson. He was 12 years old when his father died, and he soon learned to become a survivor. Before the **Civil War** he was studying for the bar, but the war dashed his plans for a law career. During the war, he was a captain and fought with the 6th Kentucky Infantry (CSA). Wounded twice, he carried several bullets in his body to his death. After the war, he went to Owen Co. and established the **Harrisburgh Academy** in 1869, which in 1876 became **Owen College**. The school flourished into the late 1880s. As an academic, Thompson was a mathematician and a linguist. During the course of his lifetime, he wrote six books. Before the war, he published a mathematical textbook, *Academic Arithmetic,* that was used statewide.

Later, in 1868, appeared his *History of the First Kentucky Brigade,* a 931-page volume. He also authored *Young People's History of Kentucky* in 1897, and the same year *The Priest's Temptation* was published. Thompson's most important and lasting work is his 1,104-page *The History of the Orphan Brigade* (1898). In 1888 Kentucky governor Simon Bolivar Buckner (1887–1891) appointed Thompson as the state librarian; in 1890 Buckner made Thompson his private secretary; and in 1891 Thompson was elected state superintendent of public instruction and served for four years. Afterward, he began to compile Kentucky's Confederate War records, a project still in process when he died in 1903 at Frankfort. He was survived by his wife of 45 years, Marcella.

Biographical Cyclopedia of the Commonwealth of Kentucky. Chicago: John M. Gresham, 1896.
"Captain Ed Porter Thompson Dead," *Lexington Leader,* March 5, 1903, 6.
Frankfort Cemetery . . . in Kentucky. Frankfort: Kentucky Historical Society, 1988.
Jillson, William R. *Literary Haunts and Personalities of Old Frankfort: 1791–1941.* Frankfort: Kentucky Historical Society, 1941.

THOMPSON, JOHN TALIAFERRO "TOMMY GUN," BRIGADIER GENERAL (b. December 1, 1860, Newport, Ky.; d. June 21, 1940, Great Neck, N.Y.). Inventor John Thompson was born in the historic Southgate House along Taylor St. (24 E. Third St. today). He was the son of U.S. Army lieutenant colonel James Thompson; his mother was Julia Maria Taliaferro, from a prominent early Campbell Co. family. Among his ancestors were Gen. **James Taylor**; Dr. **Thomas Hinde**, Newport's first medical doctor; and the Taliaferro and Southgate families. **Nathaniel Southgate Shaler** and Dr. **Louise Southgate** were cousins of his. John T. Thompson's parents met while his father was stationed at the **Newport Barracks**. Thompson's father planned the artillery batteries across Northern Kentucky in 1862 as part of the defense of Cincinnati during the **Civil War**.

John Thompson had a long and productive military career, but he is best known as the inventor of the Thompson submachine gun. He grew up on various military installations around the United States. In 1877, while living in Indiana, where his father was a professor of military science, he enrolled at Indiana University in Bloomington. One year later, he was awarded an appointment to the U.S. Military Academy at West Point, N.Y., where he graduated 11th in the class of 1882. Lt. "Talie" Thompson, as he was then known, served his first duty assignment at Fort Leavenworth, Kans.

Thompson resigned from the U.S. Army in 1914. His career had been distinguished in the areas of ordnance and logistics: he was skilled at moving men and equipment around. He also recognized the need for the army to develop a better gun for the foot soldier, whose weapon had not been substantially improved in 40 years. He went to work for the Remington Arms Company, as their chief engineer in charge of small arms development, and in that capacity he oversaw the construction of two new small arms factories. With the outbreak of **World War I**, he was called into service again as director of arsenals, with the rank of brigadier general. In a gutsy move, he halted production of the older guns for a few months while retooling for an improved weapon. He believed that he could manufacture the newer guns twice as fast. He was successful, and soon American soldiers in Europe were carrying improved rifles, while production at home quickly overcame the shortage.

After World War I, Thompson founded the Auto-Ordnance Corporation. In 1919 he earned his nickname of "Tommy Gun Thompson" when he developed the Thompson submachine gun, and warfare was never the same again. Now a mobile soldier could create a fusillade of bullets that was possible previously only with a Gatling gun. Much to Thompson's chagrin, his new weapon became the favorite of the underworld. The image of mobsters standing on running boards of speeding black getaway cars holding their blazing tommy guns, however exaggerated, is engrained in the folklore of the roaring 1920s.

Thompson's son, Marcellus Hagens Thompson, also a West Point graduate, who was a vice president of Auto-Ordnance, was indicted in the early 1920s for sending illegal machine guns to Ireland. A shipment of some 500 guns was uncovered en route, but it turned out that Thomas Ryan, another vice president of the Auto-Ordnance Corporation and a longtime supporter of Irish independence, was the culprit. John Thompson's wife, Juliet Robinson Thompson, died in 1930. Marcellus Thompson died in 1939, before his famous father's death in 1940. "Tommy Gun" Thompson was buried on the grounds of the U.S. Military Academy in New York; his funeral service was at the Old Cadet Chapel there. He had spent 38 years in service to his country. Inasmuch as war and warfare influence world events, few others from Northern Kentucky have impacted the course of human history more than John T. "Tommy Gun" Thompson.

"Gen. Thompson, 79, Dies," *NYT,* June 22, 1940, 15.
Reis, Jim. "Tommy Gun: Newport Native Made Gangster's Weapon," *KP,* October 29, 1984, 8K.
Southard, Mary Young. *Who's Who in Kentucky.* Louisville, Ky.: Standard, 1936.

THORN HILL DRAG STRIP. Long before the appearance of the **Kentucky Speedway** at Sparta, there were two other places in Northern Kentucky to race motorized vehicles legally. One was the **Florence Speedway** along U.S. 42 near Union, and the other was Thorn Hill Drag Strip along Ky. Rt. 177 at Kenton in southern Kenton Co. In the early 1950s, Ralph E. Payne bought more than 80 acres along the Licking River south of Visalia and began clearing the land of its heavy thicket of thornbushes and cleaning up the 40-acre lake on the property. People started coming there to fish. As the idea of legal competitive drag racing began to sweep the country, the Thorn Hill Drag Strip on Payne's acreage was born. First it was just dirt and only one-eighth mile in length; gradually the racing surface was paved and the track lengthened to a quarter mile. This was not only one of the first drag strips in the state, but also one of the first in the nation. Thorn Hill had the first clock-faced starting system in the Midwest. The winner of the first race in 1953 won a case of Wiedemann beer. Prizes have improved, as stock cars, rail dragsters, and motorcycles have raced at the strip over the years. Families who did not compete came to picnic and watch. It was not uncommon to have a crowd of 1,000. However, newly arrived neighbors nearby often complained about the noise of the high-performance motors. Since 1969 a court order by a judge has restricted racing to Saturdays between 6:00 p.m. and midnight, mainly during the summer months. Many of the nation's more famous drivers have raced at Thorn Hill. Payne died in 1994; Al Childers, the owner since 1997, attempted to continue the tradition, but the drag strip has not operated in the past few years.

Meiman, Karen. "Speed Seekers: Racing Fever Benefits Small Northern Kentucky Tracks," *KP,* August 4, 2001, 6K.
"Ralph E. Payne, 88, Brought Joy to Other People with Fishing Lake," *KP,* March 2, 1994, 7A.

THREE-L HIGHWAY (LLL). The three L's of this highway's name stand for Louisville, Lexington, and Latonia but the initials were never intended to indicate that the highway connected those cities. There was a consortium of horse-racing tracks, called the 3-L Association, in the three cities; that is apparently the first use of the term. The racing circuit consisted of Churchill Downs in Louisville, the Association Track at Lexington, and the **Latonia Racecourse** near Covington. The Three-L name was not assigned by the Commonwealth of Kentucky and never appeared on any official state map. The name was shown on a privately published Kentucky Motor Club map, printed in 1921, and also the same year on a Rand McNally Highway Map of Kentucky.

The Three-L Highway in Northern Kentucky ran between Covington and Lexington. and then on to Louisville. The road roughly followed what is known today as Ky. Rt. 17 to **U.S. 27** between Butler and Falmouth, and then went south through Cynthiana to Lexington. Few people today are even aware that this once-popular highway existed.

Claypool, James C. *The Tradition Continues: The Story of Old Latonia, Latonia, and Turfway Racecourse.* Fort Mitchell, Ky.: T. I. Hayes, 1997.
"Highway Open Road One of Best in Country," *KP,* November 26, 1925, 1.
Slade, Harold. "LLL Highway Again," *Harrison County Historical Society Newsletter,* January 2004.
"Three L Needs to be Finished," *KP,* March 17, 1925, 1.
Winn, Matt J. *Down the Stretch: The Story of Colonel Matt J. Winn.* New York: Smith and Murrell, 1945.

Jack Wessling

TIBBATTS, JOHN WOOLESTON (b. June 12, 1802, Lexington, Ky.; d. July 4, 1852, Newport, Ky.). John Wooleston Tibbatts, a lawyer, a **Mexican War** veteran, and a politician, received his BA and JD degrees from Transylvania University at Lexington and was admitted to the bar in 1826. He opened a law office in Newport. He married Ann Taylor, a daughter of **Gen. James Taylor Jr.**, founder of Newport, and their first home was a magnificent mansion in Newport, at the corner of Third and Washington Sts. Tibbatts held several local offices and became the first resident of Newport to be elected to the U.S. House of Representatives. He served in that capacity from 1843 to 1847. During the Mexican War, President James Polk (1845–1849) commissioned Tibbatts a colonel in the army and called on him to organize the reactivated 16th U.S. Infantry Regiment. During the war he was sent to the Rio Grande River area in the Texas Territory to serve with his father-in-law's relative Gen. Zachary Taylor. After the war, Tibbatts returned to his law practice in Newport. By 1850 he and his wife had a combined estate worth of $2.5 million, making them one of the wealthiest couples in the state. Tibbatts's career was on the ascent and he was projected to be the next Democratic nominee for Kentucky governor or senator. However, he fell ill from a disease that he likely contracted during military service in Mexico, his health gradually deteriorated, and he died on July 4, 1852, at age 50. He was buried in Evergreen Cemetery in Southgate.

Biographical Directory of the United States Congress. http://bioguide.congress.gov (accessed August 31, 2007).

Purvis, Thomas L., ed. *Newport, Kentucky: A Bicentennial History.* Newport, Ky.: Otto Zimmerman, 1996.

TIMBERLAKE HOUSE. Maj. William Thornton Timberlake, a native of Caroline Co., Va., who served in the War of 1812, moved to Northern Kentucky at the end of the war, settling in what is now the town of Dayton, Ky. He married Sophie Berry, the daughter of a respected local family, and then began to acquire land in what is now Erlanger. His thousands of acres stretched from the present-day Hallam Ave. in Erlanger to Garvey Ave. in Elsmere.

In 1826 the Timberlakes built their home next to the George Town Rd., a rough dirt trail that served as the only direct connection between Georgetown and Covington. It was later transformed into a macadamized thoroughfare, the **Covington and Lexington Turnpike**, and eventually replaced by the **Dixie Highway** (U.S. 25). Timberlake named his two-story colonial brick house Sugar Grove, but it is now known as the Timberlake House. Timberlake and his wife raised three children in the home. The oldest, a daughter named Alice Elizabeth, married a local doctor, John H. Stevenson. When Major Timberlake's health began to decline in 1855, the Stevensons moved into Sugar Grove.

The town of Erlanger, which developed around Sugar Grove, was first named Timberlake, in honor of the influential family. When the **Cincinnati Southern Railroad** began to look for a right-of-way for its trains, Dr. Stevenson added his voice to those lobbying for a route through the town. In order to ensure that the trains and the vital economic growth they represented would come through the town, Dr. Stevenson granted the company land through his front yard for the rail line.

Timberlake House, Erlanger, ca. 1888–1889.

Stevenson also helped to establish what is believed to have been the first school in Erlanger. He donated a former slave cabin behind his home for the first classes in the late 1860s, though the students had to bring their own tables and chairs. The one small window in the cabin admitted just enough light for the children to see their books. School was held in the Sugar Grove backyard for some years, until the log structure was no longer large enough to accommodate the growing enrollment.

Sugar Grove received extensive decoration in the form of carved wood, paintings, and intricate ironwork during the next generation. It was carried out by Katherine Elizabeth, the wife of Thomas, one of John and Alice Stevenson's children. After Katherine's death, the house passed to a new generation of the family, Thomas and Katherine's daughter Mary Alice and her husband Mayo Taylor. The Taylor family lived in the home until the death of Mayo Taylor in 1980. At that time the property was sold outside the family.

The home was remodeled after the **tornado** of 1915 ripped through Northern Kentucky, damaging more than 1,000 buildings across the region. The Timberlake House lost most of its upper story and was remodeled into a one-story structure. To this day, bits of brick can be dug out of the backyard.

The historic home is located at 108 Stevenson Rd. in Erlanger and is listed on the National Register of Historic Places. In 1978 a state historical marker was placed in front of the house, detailing the importance of the family and the home in local history.

Onkst, Wayne, ed. *From Buffalo Trails to the Twenty-First Century: A Centennial History of Erlanger, Kentucky.* Erlanger, Ky.: Erlanger Historical Society, 1996.

Reis, Jim. "Tornado—Take Cover! Whether Winter, Spring, or Summer, Twisters Frightful," *KP,* February 1, 1999, 4K.

Jennifer Gregory

TOBACCO. Tobacco has been grown in every Northern Kentucky county from pioneer days to the present. It was the single most important agricultural product (see **Agriculture**) from the mid-19th century through the end of the 20th century, and the manufacturing of tobacco products served as an economic engine for the region up through the first few decades of the 20th century. Politics and the culture of the region have been significantly linked to tobacco until recent years.

The use of tobacco precedes the European pioneer, since from the earliest times **American Indians** had used tobacco. American Indian tobacco pipes are a common artifact in Northern Kentucky and date back to prehistoric periods. Many pipes have been discovered at **Fort Ancient** Indian sites. Tobacco was the economic salvation of the colony of Virginia and was also important in Maryland and Pennsylvania. As migrants from those areas came to Kentucky, they brought their primary crop with them. To preserve the integrity of the crop, the Virginia legislature sanctioned tobacco inspection warehouses, and such a sanction was given to Limestone (Maysville) in 1797.

Tobacco was important, but it was only part of the Northern Kentucky agricultural mix in the early 1800s. Corn, wheat, hemp, livestock, and a variety of other products that were grown in different regions rivaled tobacco for importance. That scenario changed in the 1830s and tobacco became the cash crop for most farmers in Northern Kentucky for the next 100 years. Tobacco was packed or "prized" in large barrels called hogsheads that weighed upwards of 1,000 pounds. Transport of such large containers favored the counties situated on waterways with access to Louisville, which was

Home Tobacco Warehouse, Maysville.

the most important market for Kentucky growers during the early 19th century. When the Louisville and Portland Canal overcame the difficulty of navigating the Falls of the Ohio River in 1830, and steamboats opened up the Ohio River for traffic in both directions, the tobacco business exploded in the subsequent decade. The two great tobacco-growing regions of the state were in Western Kentucky and in the Northern Kentucky counties from Trimble on the west to Mason on the east. One of the popular types of tobacco at this time was called Mason County tobacco, and some of the best of that type was grown in Bracken Co. When the first leaf tobacco fair was held in Cincinnati on May 21, 1858, growers from Bracken and Mason counties won all the major prizes.

By the time of the **Civil War**, railroads were developed, and Cincinnati became a major tobacco market, as the tobacco could now travel east by rail. Thus the growing of tobacco and its manufacture in Northern Kentucky were stimulated again. Kentucky historian Richard Collins's *History of Kentucky* describes some of the tobacco manufacturing in Northern Kentucky counties around 1870. In Covington, there were 8 tobacco factories and 21 cigar factories. In Maysville, 1 large cigar factory is mentioned and several small ones. Augusta is described as an important shipping port for tobacco. In Owenton, there was a tobacco drying house that processed a half million pounds of tobacco yearly. Mount Olivet had four tobacco prizing houses. It is likely that most of the larger towns had small tobacco manufacturers and tobacco warehouses, places where tobacco was packed for market in hogsheads. Auction warehouses came later. Tobacco products at this time were primarily cigars and plug tobacco.

An important event was the accidental development of a new type of tobacco. It has been called white burley, golden burley, and, for most of the state in the 20th century, just burley (see **White Burley Tobacco**; **Laban J. Bradford**). Except for some dark and other tobacco varieties in Western Kentucky, air-cured light burley, the type that started with the Bracken Co. seed, has been grown in most of the state to the present time. This type of burley is bitter and can hold the sweeteners added to plug; in addition, it eventually proved to be the tobacco that was important for flavor in cigarette blends. By the 1890s, Covington trailed only Louisville in the manufacture of tobacco products.

Changes came quickly in the first decades of the 20th century and affected tobacco in diverse ways. In 1904 the first loose-leaf tobacco auction warehouse opened in Lexington. This innovation provided markets closer to farmers. The second and third auction warehouses opened in Maysville in 1909 and 1910, and soon warehouses operated throughout the state. Maysville and Carrollton were among the leading auction markets in the state until 2001–2004, when contracting replaced most auctions. At the same time as auction warehouses began to develop, the tobacco "wars" in Kentucky started. They had to do with the low tobacco prices offered by the monopoly of the American Tobacco Company. Although less publicized than the violence in the black-patch areas of Western Kentucky, **Night Riders** burned barns and warehouses and were involved in intimidation throughout Northern Kentucky. The purpose was to make farmers reduce the supply of tobacco so that prices would rise. The various farmers' associations wanted members to sell their crops together, to get the highest price. On March 26, 1908, Night Riders set fire to the T. S. Hamilton & Company's tobacco warehouse at 4th and Bakewell Sts. in Covington, destroying it, a blacksmith shop, and five adjoining houses, as well as damaging another home and three adjoining businesses. In the same year, the tobacco crop was reduced, and it was reported that no tobacco was grown in Bracken Co. that season. Court cases against the Night Riders, the use of the state militias to keep the peace, and the breakup of the American Tobacco Company in 1911 ended the tobacco wars. A final early-20th-century development was the manufacture of cigarettes, which became the most popular way of using tobacco.

An economic downturn for farmers started soon after **World War I** and did not end until the late 1930s. Tobacco manufacturing faded from Northern Kentucky. However, the tobacco business—farming, warehouses, processing factories, and support businesses—remained important in terms of employment and economic impact. The number of farms, tenants, and black farmers began a decline that continues to the present. In Northern Kentucky, only Mason Co. had more than 10 African American farmers as of 2002. The Burley Tobacco Cooperative Association was formed in the 1920s, and most area farmers participated. That group began the administration of the tobacco program established by the U.S. Agricultural Adjustment Acts of 1933 and 1938. This was a program that balanced supply and demand by controls on production and price supports. It gave tobacco farmers some guaranteed income from the 1930s through the 1990s.

Many tobacco-related problems came to a head from the 1980s to the turn of the century. They include anti-tobacco feeling, foreign competition, labor shortages, and the lure of "town" jobs. International trade agreements meant that tobacco use in U.S. cigarettes could not be legislated. As companies bought cheaper foreign tobacco, poundage allotments fell and the price was adjusted downward. The result was that tobacco became less profitable. Employment in nearby communities and good roads to get to them pulled many off the farms or made them part-time farmers. The labor shortage was somewhat abated by the use of workers from Mexico. It was the tobacco farmers who provided the first work in the region for **Latino** immigrants, who quickly sponsored other immigrants and moved into other work. The last tobacco redryer, Parker Tobacco in Maysville, closed in the 1980s. In 2000 tobacco companies began contracting directly with area burley farmers, and by 2005 auction warehouses in Northern Kentucky, which at one time numbered in the dozens, had diminished to one, in Maysville. A tobacco buyout in 2004 ended the program that had started during the **Great Depression**; therefore, in most counties in Northern Kentucky, the largest portion of farm income for the following year came from government payments. After the 10-year payout period ends, the future of farms in the region, whose number has declined by more than two-thirds in the past century, is uncertain. As of 2002, Northern Kentucky farms continue to produce tobacco. In that year the number of farms in the region growing the crop ranged from a low of 122 in Gallatin Co. to a high of 423 in Mason Co. Public smoking bans have been discussed in some counties but have been relatively unsuccessful to this point.

Axton, William F. *Tobacco and Kentucky,* Lexington: Univ. of Kentucky Press, 1975.

Collins, Richard H. *History of Kentucky.* Vol. 1. Covington, Ky.: Collins, 1882.

"Night Riders Burn Covington Warehouse, Homes Destroyed," *KP*, March 26, 1908, 1.
"Tobacco Manufacturing in Covington," *CJ*, June 28, 1862, 3.

John Klee

TOBACCO, WHITE BURLEY. See **White Burley Tobacco**.

TONEY, JOHN E. (b. September 19, 1889, Covington, Ky.; d. December 21, 1974, Cincinnati, Ohio). John Edward Toney, the son of Samuel and Mattie Wells Toney, was a Cincinnati policeman whose reputation as a tough and rugged law enforcement officer earned him the nickname of "Black Chief." Toney was born and raised in Covington and attended the **Lincoln-Grant School**. Joining the Cincinnati Police Department on August 3, 1925, he was assigned to the detective bureau and worked in the West End of Cincinnati. In 1930 Toney received a letter of commendation from the Cincinnati city manager, C. O. Sherrill, for solving numerous murders and other major crimes. On June 1, 1948, Toney retired after 22 years of service on the Cincinnati police force. He had worked the last few years in District 7 in Walnut Hills, where he also resided. Following his retirement, "Pop Toney," as he was known, was a private investigator until shortly before his death. He was buried in Spring Grove Cemetery in Cincinnati.

Dabney, Wendell P. *Cincinnati's Colored Citizens*. Cincinnati: Dabney, 1926.
"John Toney," *CE*, December 25, 1974, 2B.
"John Toney, 85, the Black Chief," *CP*, December 26, 1974, 18.
"West End Sleuth to Retire," *CP*, April 16, 1948, 26.

Theodore H. H. Harris

TORNADOES. Although the famed "tornado alley" of the United States is located hundreds of miles west of the Bluegrass State, Northern Kentucky has an extensive and well-documented history of violent weather, and records of tornadoes date back to pre–**Civil War** days.

The earliest record of tornado activity for the region is from February 20, 1857. No deaths were reported, but according to damage estimates, the tornado's path covered nearly five miles across Bracken Co. and included the town of Augusta. Buildings, barns, and homes were either destroyed or shifted from their foundations during this storm.

The first account of fatalities from tornado-like storms followed three years later, May 21–22, 1860. What was termed a "massive storm," or by some eyewitnesses a "hurricane," blew through Northern Kentucky and killed almost 100 people. Most of them drowned in the Ohio River while working on coal boats and skiffs. This series of storms, which is believed to have been spawned near Louisville, quickly traveled northeast. Storm reports ranged from Louisville to Lexington and points north through Northern Kentucky and into southwestern Ohio. Three counties in Northern Kentucky were greatly impacted during these two days of stormy weather; Grant, Kenton, and Boone counties reported severe damage, mostly to homes, barns, and fences. Larger structures were not altogether spared, as a brick storehouse and the courthouse at Independence suffered moderate damage. Aside from the deaths on the Ohio River, three men died locally as a result of falling trees.

St. Boniface Catholic Church, Ludlow, showing damage from the tornado of July 1915.

There were no fatalities from the 1867 tornado that went through Bellevue and Newport. It arrived between 1:00 and 2:00 p.m. on August 26, and its touchdown destroyed six houses under construction. Workers scrambled from rafters to open fields to escape flying debris. A large animal stable was completely lifted up and dispersed in several pieces; some of its timbers were found one-fourth mile away. The *Allegheny Belle,* moving along the Ohio River with several barges in tow near the Bellevue bank, lost two barges during the height of the storm. There were many reports of buildings and boats damaged significantly in and around Newport and Bellevue, but no human injuries were reported. After the storm five or six cows that were recovered were missing their horns; it is believed that wind-blown debris had knocked them loose.

A tornado of March 25, 1884, did its greatest damage in Harrison Co., practically wiping out the town of Colemansville. This storm eventually raced north to the Ohio River, but damage there was difficult to assess because the area was still cleaning up after the massive flood of one month earlier, rivaled only by the **flood of 1937**. Reports from residents near the river said most of the flood-damaged homes and buildings were blown over in the high winds spawned during the storm, and coal barges were scattered. One report stated that any damage that happened on March 25, 1884, from the tornado was considered minimal, compared to the damage received a month before, during the immense flood.

The next significant storm with a possible tornado arrived six years later in Newport, on August 2, 1890. The storm whipped down shortly before 1:00 p.m., causing heavy damage in town, mostly east of Washington Ave. Numerous homes were destroyed, and there were accounts of roofs being completely lifted off and two-story brick buildings receiving substantial damage. Total storm damage was estimated at around $3,000, with no injuries.

The 1800s had only one more documented tornado account in Northern Kentucky. It occurred in Boone Co. in April 1895. No deaths were reported, but damage and injuries occurred in the town of Union when the storm developed, around midday. The force of the storm is believed to have carried a wagon two miles.

The turn of the century brought greater commercial and residential development in Northern Kentucky along the banks of the Ohio River and in surrounding counties. As population increased and people gathered into communities, building additional homes and other buildings, there were more eyewitness accounts of weather incidents and at the same time more opportunities for widespread damage and injuries. On May 20, 1907, the first documented tornado of the century smashed into Covington, downing wires and trees and leaving minor damage. A more impressive storm struck eight years later.

It was termed the "the Big Blow," and it ravaged parts of Northern Kentucky on July 7, 1915, just after dark. The tornado dropped down on the town of Bromley a little after 9:00 p.m. Damage was considerable, especially in the area of Pike (Ky. Rt. 8) and Main Sts. In minutes, the rotating storm pushed east into Ludlow, where the **Lagoon Amusement Park** received storm damage estimated at $50,000. Its roller coasters, merry-go-rounds, dance pavilion, and famed motor-dome were completely flattened. Two hundred visitors that evening were sent scrambling, but fortunately no deaths, only some injuries, were reported. The tornado did substantial damage to St. Boniface Church (see **Saints Boniface and James Catholic Church**). Continuing on its easterly path, at approximately 9:26 p.m., the tornado unleashed its largest fury in Covington. Eyewitness accounts recall the tornado staying on the ground for six minutes. The weather bureau reported winds exceeding 60 miles per hour. As the tornado carved through the streets of Covington, substantial damage occurred at 14th St. and Madison Ave., where the entire front of the three-story brick office building of the **Chesapeake and Ohio Railroad** was exposed. Two blocks northeast, at 12th and Greenup Sts., the steeple of the **St. Joseph Catholic Church** was toppled over and spread across streetcar tracks, along with portions of the J. Donavan Café. In all, the cities of Covington, Bellevue, Southgate, Elsmere, Ludlow, Newport, Dayton, Fort Thomas, Erlanger, and Carrollton were affected by this massive storm, with more than 1,000 buildings and homes damaged or destroyed, with countless injuries, and with costs exceeding $3 million. Three deaths were recorded in Northern Kentucky as a result of the storm, 16 for the entire state of Kentucky, and a total of 36 including Ohio and Indiana. To date, it remains the one of the deadliest tornadoes on record for the tri-state area.

Tornado reports continued to become more frequent with population growth, urban sprawl, and the addition of storm spotters throughout Kentucky. During the period 1950–2003, tornado damage was reported in each of the 11 counties in Northern Kentucky. The National Weather Service (NWS) office located in Wilmington, Ohio, which oversees all storm damage for Northern Kentucky, southeastern Indiana, and southwestern Ohio, maintains these records.

The 20th-century tornadoes causing the most loss of life in Northern Kentucky occurred on April 23, 1968. A "family" of tornadoes hit in the early afternoon, killing five, injuring at least 150, and leaving an estimated $3–4 million in damage from Falmouth to Maysville. One tornado touched down shortly after 1:30 p.m., moving toward Falmouth, and continued in its eastern movement for nearly 20 minutes. One-third of the city of Falmouth was completely flattened before the storm moved out of Pendleton Co. A total of 506 persons were left homeless. In the town of Dover, in Mason Co., 93 percent of the homes were reported severely damaged. Four were killed in Falmouth, and some severely injured. The other fatality was in Minerva, in Mason Co. Other locations struck by these tornadoes included Berlin, in Bracken Co., and Maysville. The series of storms also reached beyond the Ohio River, killing 11 in Ohio. The NWS later ranked one of the tornadoes as a possible F4 to F5 in intensity, with winds ranging from 207 to 318 miles per hour. The path was estimated at 79 miles long with a width reaching 550 yards.

The 1974 "Super Outbreak" of April 3 and 4 spared most of Northern Kentucky. Damage assessments and tornadoes were spotted and recorded in Owen, Boone, Robertson, and Mason counties, and there was heavy damage—but nothing like what happened in the eastern states, where many people were killed. This horrific two-day event involved an estimated 148 tornadoes and killed about 330 people in all. In Boone Co. on April 3 around 4:10 p.m., there appeared an F1 to F2 tornado, which grew into an F5 tornado with a width that was estimated near 533 yards at the height of the storm, once it moved over into Hamilton Co., Ohio. No fatalities took place in Boone Co., but 20 persons were injured. All the fatalities from this tornado were recorded in Ohio. It crossed the Ohio River near Rising Sun, Ind., and entered Kentucky at Bellview, moving northeast just west of Burlington, Ky., before crossing back across the river into Sayler Park, Ohio. In Boone Co., three square miles of damage occurred near Bullittsville, where mobile homes were overturned. In Robertson Co. on the same day, around 6:55 p.m. an F3 tornado with a width of 10 yards traveled on the ground for 19 miles, injuring 27. In adjoining Mason Co., around 8:25 p.m., an F1 tornado with a width of 10 yards was on the ground for .10 of a mile but injured no one. The tornado touched down four miles west of Maysville. Also, in Owen Co., around 5:15 p.m., an F1 tornado with width of 10 yards was on the ground for 31.7 miles, injuring 18. This tornado ended near Bromley in Owen Co.

The volatile storm of November 19, 1981, that hit Northern Kentucky was termed the "untimely tornado" or "freak mini-tornado." This late-season tornado struck around 7:30 p.m. on a Thursday night, leaving extensive damage in a very localized area. Fort Mitchell received the heaviest blow, with a half million dollars in damage. The tornado's path was very narrow, a maximum of 60 yards wide, and it traveled for a half mile just east of the **Dixie Highway**, damaging 37 homes or other buildings, along with numerous cars and trees. Two injuries were reported from this storm. The NWS classified it as a F1 tornado, meaning winds were estimated from 73 to 112 miles per hour.

On March 10, 1986, a "cloud-veiled tornado" combined with intense straight-line winds blew through Northern Kentucky. Uncertainty remains about exactly what this storm was or what it should be called, since it has never been classified by the NWS and is not found on the agency's historical records for 1950–2003. Regardless of its classification, Boone, Kenton, and Campbell counties received an enormous blow economically that day: $18 million in damage. Some 1,039 homes, plus 24 businesses, had been damaged, some heavily, by the time the "downburst" of wind exhausted itself from the storm and began moving northeast. The storm started just east of Burlington and shot northeast, lasting around 10 minutes and ending in Newport. The path of damage indicated that strong winds had blown in one direction for up to 15 miles; a tornado, in contrast, would have left debris spread out in all directions. Several historic structures in Covington, including the **Mother of God Catholic Church**, the First Methodist Church (see **First United Methodist Church**), and the **Covington Art Club**, were damaged, as well as the **Salem United Methodist Church** in Newport. To this day, the March 1986 event remains the costliest storm on record; remarkably, no deaths were reported.

"Cloud-Veiled Tornado Skipped across Rooftops," *KP,* March 12, 1986, 1.
"Double Tragedy," *KP,* March 12, 1986, 3.
"Famous Storms Date Back to 1857," *KP,* May 19, 2003, 4K.
"Furious Tornado—Houses Blown Down in Bellevue," *CE,* August 26, 1867, 3.
Geaslen, Chester F. *Strolling along Memory Lane.* Vol. 2. Newport, Ky.: Otto, 1986.
The Kentucky Climate Center. http://kyclim.wku.edu/ (accessed July 7, 2006).
National Weather Service Forecast Office, Wilmington, OH. www.erh.noaa.gov/iln/ (accessed July 7, 2006).
"Newport Not Outdone 1890," *KSJ,* August 2, 1890, 3.
"People Died, Boat Sank in '15 Tornado," *KP,* August 21, 1965, supplement, 6K.
"Small Towns in 1884 Faced Trial by Wind, Fire," *KP,* June 4, 2001, 4K.
"Storm's Fury Strikes Covington," *KP,* May 20, 1907, 2.
"Take Cover, Twister Coming—May in Kentucky: Keep Eye on Sky," *KP,* May 19, 2003, 4K.
"Thursday Storm Listed Officially as Tornado," *KP,* November 21, 1981, 2K.
"Weathermen Left in the Dark," *CE,* April 4, 1974, 8.

Jim O'Brien

TOSSO, JOSEPH (b. August 3, 1802, Mexico City, Mexico; d. January 6, 1887, Covington, Ky.). Joseph Anguel Augustin Tosso, a musician, was the son of Don Carlos and Dona Maria Grat Tosso. His father was of Italian descent and was a dealer in fine jewels. Joseph grew up among wealth and refinement and was exposed to the arts and music early in life. At age six he was considered a child prodigy, and by age eight he was attending the Paris Conservatory in Paris, France, studying vocal music, violin, and other instruments under the world-renowned teachers of his day. In 1817 he came to the United States, and in 1825 he was in Cincinnati to play at a reception for the famed French general the Marquis de LaFayette. In 1827 Tosso moved his family to the area and became a professor of music in Cincinnati and a favorite of the daunting Mrs. Trollope, playing concerts and theater music in her legendary bazaar along E. Fourth St. in Cincinnati. For almost 60 years the Cincinnati and Northern Kentucky area had the benefit of his fine music and musical productions. He played classical music, but he could also pick up a fiddle and play the most common of tunes. He wrote and often played his most famous piece, ***The Arkansas Traveler,*** which became one of the campaign songs later used by the Democratic Party in the 1928 U.S. presidential election. In the 1870s the Tosso family moved to a home named Rose Cottage in Latonia Springs (today Latonia). Later they lived at 25 Powell St. (now 15th St.) in Covington. Tosso often performed in Covington and Newport. He was clearly one of the greatest musicians ever to live in the Northern Kentucky region. Tosso died in 1887 and was buried at Spring Grove Cemetery in Cincinnati.

"Composer of Famous Song was Covingtonian," *KP,* June 30, 1928, 1.
Smith, Ophia D. "Joseph Tosso, the Arkansaw Traveler," *Ohio History* 56 (1947): 16–45.

TOUSEY HOUSE. In about 1817, wealthy businessman Erastus Tousey bought a plot of land on N. Jefferson St. in Burlington and built the Tousey House, which became a Boone Co. landmark, completing it in 1822. The Touseys were among the first settlers in Boone Co., and Erastus Tousey, with his wife Catherine and family, lived in the house until his death in 1863. After Catherine Tousey died in

1895, the house was sold several times before being purchased in 1917 by the Gulley and Pettit families. They used the house for more than 60 years as a residence and operated a general store in two of the first-floor rooms. Over the years, the building was converted into an inn for visiting judges and other government officials and was later used as office space and a dress shop. Former Boone Co. judge-executive Bruce Ferguson purchased the building around 1980 and extensively renovated it. It was sold in 1998 to Dan and Kristy Schalck, who opened the Tousey House Restaurant there in 2001; the restaurant closed in 2006. The owner of the **Greyhound Tavern** subsequently purchased the home, made restorations, and opened a restaurant there in 2008. Located just north of the courthouse square, the Tousey House is on the National Register of Historic Places. It is one of the best-preserved residences of early Burlington and was described in the National Register nomination as Federal-style, with a five-bay facade of Flemish bond brickwork. A semicircular fanlight is over the front door.

Becher, Matthew E., Michael D. Rouse, Robert Schrage, and Laurie Wilcox. *Images of America: Burlington.* Charleston, S.C.: Arcadia, 2004.

Boone Co. Historic Preservation Review Board. *Historic Structures of Boone County, Kentucky.* Burlington, Ky.: Boone Co. Historic Preservation Review Board, 2002.

Gabrielle Summe

TOWER UNITED METHODIST CHURCH. In about 1852, Joseph Link and his family moved from Cincinnati to Jamestown (now Dayton, Ky.), and made their home there at the corner of Front and Main Sts. The Links were Methodists, and finding no church of that denomination in town, they began holding church services in their home. In 1853 the Methodist bishop of Cincinnati sent Rev. Joseph Blackburn to Jamestown to start a new church. For a short time, services continued in the Link home, but then they were moved to a small schoolhouse nearby on Seventh Ave. In 1855 a man named Carr gave the church a 75-foot-wide lot in town at 522 Fifth Ave., on which to construct a permanent building. At that time the church membership consisted of only about a half dozen families, including the Links, the Peaks, the Van Sants, and the Wrights. Men of the church brought lumber from a mill in Cincinnati and built a small one-room structure. The pastor of the church at that time was Rev. P. F. Tower, for whom the church was named. By 1900 the church had about 250 members and had outgrown its building. In 1914 the pastor, H. D. Cooper, encouraged the congregation to build a new church. The old building was razed and a new one constructed on the same lot. In 1997, with inner-city demographics changing, the Tower United Methodist congregation merged with the Bellevue Methodist and sold their church building in Dayton to the Healing Church of God.

Northern Kentucky Views. "Tower Methodist Church." www.nkyviews.com (accessed March 31, 2006).

"Tower Methodist Episcopal Church," *Tower Church Herald* 3, no. 12 (February 2, 1901).

Tower United Methodist Church, 125th Anniversary Booklet, 1853–1978. Dayton, Ky.: Tower United Methodist Church, 1978.

TOWNBALL. Townball was originally a child's bat-and-ball game played in parts of America, including the Ohio River Valley, during the early 19th century. The game had no formal rules until the 1830s, when a group of young businessmen in Philadelphia adopted the game for recreation and exercise. They codified the sport and created townball clubs with officers and bylaws much like the literary clubs, political clubs, and other civic organizations that thrived in pre–**Civil War** America.

In May 1858, several members of the Young Men's Gymnastic Association in Cincinnati, including many Northern Kentuckians, took their fitness training outdoors by playing townball on a field near Newport. The *Cincinnati Daily Commercial* held that while the majority of participants "had not handled a bat in ten or twelve years," persistence and practice would soon have them playing with the "skill of schoolboys." The group named itself the Gymnasts' Town Ball Club and created a formal organization. Within weeks, the Gymnasts' club had spawned two other townball teams, the Excelsior Town Ball Club of Cincinnati and the Kentucky Town Ball Club of Newport. The Kentucky Town Ball Club, led by rising attorneys John P. Jackson and Frederick C. Jones, mostly consisted of Northern Kentuckians from the other two clubs. By September 1858, the Gymnasts' club had merged into the Excelsior club, and the first official match between Cincinnati area townball clubs occurred on September 18, 1858, at the Newport Race Course. Competing were the Kentucky club and the Excelsiors.

By late 1860 townball clubs had spread to other Northern Kentucky river cities. Covington reportedly had 10 townball clubs, prompting the *Covington Journal* to declare townball "the rage among the boys of this city." Townball matches in Covington often occurred at College Square near the intersection of 10th and Madison Sts. Maysville had two townball clubs, the Maysville Town Ball Club and the Union Town Ball Club. Compared to the English game cricket, which was also a regional pastime, townball took far less time to play. A townball game lasted a few hours, whereas a cricket match could take two days to complete.

The Kentucky club version of townball was fast-paced and high-scoring. Inside an 8-foot square, the batsman (batter) and the catcher faced the giver (pitcher), who stood 35 feet away. The first corner (base) was pitched 60 feet from the batsman's goal, with four other corners spaced 54 feet apart. Upon either striking the ball, swinging at and missing three pitches, or taking six pitches without swinging, the batsman ran to the first corner. A batsman could be put out only if the ball was caught on the fly or the batsman was struck by a thrown ball. Fielders wore no gloves for protection. The batsman had to touch every corner and could not pass another runner, and no two runners could occupy the same corner. Each team, made up of 15 players, brought its own umpire to matches, and the teams mutually selected a referee to settle any disputes. Townball games lasted four innings with scores sometimes reaching 100 runs per side.

Townball meshed well with urban Northern Kentucky's growing interest in organized physical fitness. Throughout the 1850s, new gymnasiums in Cincinnati and Covington attracted young Northern Kentucky gentlemen who wanted to build character and muscles. Moreover, military companies like the Covington Fencibles, the Kenton Cadets, and the Kentucky Grays offered physical activity, camaraderie, and competition through parades and drill contests with other military companies. Townball clubs offered similar benefits.

The growth of journalism in urban America also bolstered townball's popularity in the Ohio River Valley. Newspapers in Cincinnati, Covington, Newport, and Maysville often reported townball matches. Northern Kentucky townball devotees could also connect with sports enthusiasts in other cities through nationally circulating sporting periodicals like the *New York Clipper* and the *Spirit of the Times,* whose correspondents described cricket, townball, and baseball games played throughout the country.

As measured by newspaper coverage, the Kentucky Town Ball Club was Northern Kentucky's preeminent team. Box scores from Kentucky Town Ball Club matches reveal an economically cohesive membership made up of young professionals, proprietors of small businesses, clerks, and the sons of Covington's and Newport's social elite. The Kentucky Town Ball Club even had its own uniform: blue shirts, blue caps, white pants, and black belts with the club's name embossed in gilded letters. Its apparent class cohesion did not, however, insulate the Kentucky Town Ball Club from the tension between slavery and freedom that permeated life in antebellum Northern Kentucky. The Kentucky club's members included young men from both abolitionist and slaveholding families.

Townball, as an organized pastime in Northern Kentucky, did not survive the double onslaught of the Civil War and the postwar national baseball boom. The Kentucky Town Ball Club played a sporadic match schedule during the Civil War. Confederate threats to Northern Kentucky and Cincinnati, prolonged martial law in Covington, and the absence of young men called to military duty curtailed many social activities in metropolitan Cincinnati, including sporting events. Several members of the Kentucky Town Ball Club served in the Union Army. Col. Fred C. Jones, the club's president, was killed at the Battle of Stones River. In the months following the war, Northern Kentucky townball clubs disintegrated; their members dispersed among the baseball clubs that were forming throughout the Ohio River Valley.

Block, David. *Baseball before We Knew It: A Search for the Roots of the Game.* Lincoln: Univ. of Nebraska Press, 2005.

"A Game of Town Ball," *CDC,* May 14, 1858, 2.

"Sporting Matters," *CDC,* July 2, 1860, 1.

Greg Perkins

TOYOTA NORTH AMERICA. Toyota Motor Manufacturing (TMMNA), headquartered in Erlanger, was established in 1996 as the U.S. home for Toyota's rapidly expanding North American manufacturing operations. Ten years earlier Toyota had opened a plant in Georgetown, which is the company's largest plant in North America; 7,000 employees there produce more than 500,000 Avalons, Camrys, and Solaras annually. In his first address at the new headquarters, Teruyuki Minoura, president and CEO of TMMNA, stated, "I want to establish a sense of community here. I sincerely look forward to building something special." With 10 manufacturing facilities in North America, Toyota's manufacturing process had grown too large to be managed from Japan. Having a parent company in the United States allows Toyota to streamline operations and control purchasing, production engineering, quality control, and production planning. Considering that TMMNA buys more than $8 billion worth of goods and services from more than 500 North American suppliers, consolidation of these key manufacturing functions has helped reduce costs and improve efficiency. In 1998 Toyota began construction on an 843,000-square-foot auto parts distribution center on North Bend Rd. in Boone Co., at a cost of approximately $85 million. This facility became operational in 2001 and holds about 2.5 million auto parts with a total inventory valued at $54 million. By establishing headquarters and an auto parts distribution center in Northern Kentucky, Toyota has created jobs and has stimulated growth in other companies in the region, including Sachs Automotive in Florence, a supplier of shocks and struts to Toyota. Toyota is also a generous and involved community partner. As the largest U.S. automaker, the firm believes its growth and continued success in the marketplace depend on its ability to understand and respect the unique qualities and different needs of people and their local communities.

Peale, Cliff. "N. Ky. Becomes Toyota's Parts Hub," *CP*, December 18, 1998, 7B.

Toyota. www.toyota.com (accessed April 5, 2006).

Gabrielle Summe

TOYS. Northern Kentucky has been home to two notable toy stores and, in earlier years, a manufacturer of baseballs and dolls.

Until the rise of the toy-manufacturing industry in the first half of the 20th century, which brought on the scene companies such as A. C. Gilbert, Lionel, Hasbro, Mattel, Wham-O, and Kenner Products (in Cincinnati), toys for boys were often smaller versions of the tools or implements their fathers used, while the standard toys for girls were dolls and doll accessories. There were some dangerous toys, or at least some toys were perceived to be dangerous. For example, the City of Covington passed an ordinance during the 1880s outlawing toy pistols, with fines of between $10 and $50 plus confiscation.

Toys were sold out of general stores or hardware stores, and for the most part they were seasonal items, available near Christmas. The newspapers advertised the prices and availability of toys. Sleds generally could be bought at the local hardware store as cold weather approached. In the last quarter of the 19th century, the Covington-born Beard sisters (see **Lina and Adelia Beard**) wrote books for girls, which included instructions for making and playing with dolls and toys. The Beard sisters' most famous publication was *The American Girls Hand Book,* in 1887; it has gone through at least 12 printings.

Between the late 1870s and 1895, dolls and baseballs, both requiring hand sewing, were manufactured in Covington by at least two firms: Wolf Fletcher, at 714 Madison Ave., and Phillip Goldsmith, at Pike and Harvey Streets. Goldsmith merged with Fletcher, and their four-story plant employed as many as 150 people, six days per week, making upwards of 75 dozen balls daily. After an 1891 fire, the company moved into the former **Hemingray Glass Company**'s quarters along Second St. In 1895 Goldsmith drowned while on vacation in Wisconsin, and his sons moved the operation to Cincinnati. That company evolved into the sporting-goods giant the McGregor Company, which made baseballs in Williamstown, Ky., for many years under the Goldsmith name.

With mass production came the toy store. In Campbell Co., the closest thing to a real toy store was Federle's general store in Newport, along the east side of Monmouth St., between 10th and 11th Sts., run by the Federle family from the 1920s until almost 1980. It was known to have almost anything one could possibly want or need. Merchandise hung in buckets or sometimes was stored in a corner in the basement, to be found only by Nicholas O. Federle. Federle's seemed to sell everything—candy, racing forms, cigars, horse bridles, hunting and fishing licenses, lunchmeat. It was known even to sell a few illegal fireworks in the summer; and in the winter, Christmas trees and toys.

Toys sold so well at Federle's that around 1959 the two brothers, Nicholas O. and William A. Federle, opened a freestanding toy store in a separate nearby building, which featured the various items of the season, all year long. Children and parents from throughout Newport and the rest of Campbell Co. came to Federle's for the latest fad. Children's eyes grew big as they came into the store. Federle's toy store operated until 1977 or so, when it burned. The general store remained in business until late December 1987, when William A. Federle was found murdered in the side lot of the store. His death remains one of Newport's few unsolved crimes. Nicholas, who had retired before his brother's death, died in 1994 at age 85. The Federles are remembered fondly as friendly proprietors along Monmouth St.

The **Newport Shopping Center**, which opened in 1956, did not include a toy store; Hart's Hardware and Woolworth's Five and Ten Cent Store sold some toys, though. The Klingenberg chain of hardware stores and other smaller stores along Monmouth St. sold toy items, but Federle's was the place to begin shopping, for reasons of price and selection. Only the large department stores in downtown Cincinnati, of which there were at least 10 by the mid-1950s, and Johnny's Toys in Latonia had a larger variety of toys.

In Kenton Co., the Johnny's Toys store began in 1939, when Bill Martin took over Miss Mary's, a candy and school supply store along Decoursey Ave. in Latonia. Since that time Johnny's has developed into a small chain of toy stores, not only in Northern Kentucky but also in Greater Cincinnati. Now in its fourth different location in Latonia along Howard Litzler Rd., in a 44,000-square-foot building, Johnny's has proved itself the marketing leader in the field. The family-run operation has been able to do things that the large chains could not possibly accomplish. During the 1960s the store ran specific ads in the ***Kentucky Post*** that included details of what model electric train engines and cars were on sale that week and the quantity of each available. Johnny's also advertised on the popular *Uncle Al Show* for children on Cincinnati television. Because that broadcast reached regional markets such as Dayton, Ohio, the Latonia store became a destination for the families of children outside of Northern Kentucky.

Longtime employees have certainly been a key aspect of success for Johnny's Toys. Some staff members worked at Johnny's for more than 40 years, and several have passed the 30-year mark. Helen Warren retired after 50 years as the store's original birthday elf; one year later, because she missed the children who came into the store as well as the feeling of joy she received from working there, she returned, staying until age 79. Warren was in charge of the birthday club; each year she sent birthday cards to as many as 160,000 children throughout Northern Kentucky and Cincinnati. Charles "Ed" Wendt was the specialist who worked in the model railroad section for some 35 years. Other staff greeted youngsters in front of the store's Birthday Castle, a special area where only the children could go, and where they would receive a free gift. They gained entrance using a key that had been sent with their birthday card.

Today, in the parking lot of the Latonia store, a half-scale trolley, the Otterville Trolley, takes children for a ride to visit the Easter Bunny in spring or, in the fall, to attend a marshmallow roast with ghost stories. A trip to Johnny's Toys around Christmas always includes visiting with Santa Claus for a few moments. Often, over the years, Santa was played by the husband of Mary Elizabeth Johnson, a 35-year employee who oversaw the important layaway department—he wanted to share in the fun his wife brought home. For many years Johnny's has rented extra warehouse space as Christmas approached, to store layaway items until just before Santa's arrival.

Johnny's Toys is known for its annual train show, which has been held each January for more than 30 years. The store's bicycle repair shop is akin to an automobile repair operation for the family car. Johnny's is where girls have gone for the latest dolls, and boys for model ships, airplanes, and rockets. The new Latonia store has a children's amphitheater for special performances. Other events include the annual Shop with a Cop, a program sponsored by the Covington Fraternal Order of Police. Founder Bill Martin, the marketing genius of Johnny's, died in 1999.

Kenton Co. **department stores** such as **Coppin's**, JCPenney, Sears, Kmart, and Wal-Mart have also sold toys, offering an expanded selection around Christmas. Some of the smaller hardware stores, such as Landwehr's in Covington, do the same. In the mid-1920s, Covington's Landwehr family, who had owned grocery stores near 11th and Greenup Sts., opened their first hardware store on Madison Ave. Bernard Landwehr managed the new store. They had stores at various locations, but by 1951 the Landwehrs had settled into a hardware, gift, and toy store at 826 Madison Ave. Under Bernard's grandson, Tom Landwehr, the store today sells mainly hardware; various toy lines remain, however.

As the toy industry expanded, Northern Kentuckians became involved in the industry; many work for Cincinnati's Kenner Products, known as the home of the 1956 classic children's item Play-Doh. **Mary Ann Kelly** of Ludlow, a well-known television scriptwriter and author, designed toys in her spare time.

"An Ordinance," *DC*, July 25, 1882, 4.
"Charles Wendt 'Train Man' at Johnny's Toys in Latonia," *KP*, May 10, 2003, A11.
Cross, Gary. ***Kids' Stuff: Toys and the Changing World of American Childhood.*** Cambridge: Harvard Univ. Press, 1997.
Duennes, Terry. "Ghost Stories Told by the Campfire at Totter's Otterville at Johnny's Toys," *KP*, October 24, 2006, A2.
Duke, Kerry. "Time for Trains," *KP*, January 29, 2005, 5K.
"Helen Warren, Toy Store's Birthday Elf," *KP*, February 7, 2006, A11.
"Lessons at Johnny's Toys," *KP*, May 20, 2006, N5.
"Taylor Mill's Mary Elizabeth Johnson, 'Ultimate Grandmother,' Sold Toys," *KP*, May 8, 2000, 12A.
"Time for Trains," *KP*, January 29, 2005, K5.

TRACY, FRANK M. (b. May 5, 1872, Covington, Ky.; d. March 6, 1947, Covington, Ky.). Frank M. Tracy, a legislator and a judge, was the son of Patrick and Julia Aylward Tracy, local grocery owners who were born in Ireland. Frank received his elementary and high school education in Covington, attended St. Xavier College in Cincinnati, graduating in 1892, and then studied law at the Cincinnati Law School, where he graduated in 1894 with an LLB. He also studied at the Georgetown University Law School in Washington, D.C. Tracy was admitted to the Kentucky bar and became active in Democratic politics. He was a member of the Kentucky House of Representatives in 1898, served as Kenton Co. attorney from 1902 to 1910, and was a Kenton circuit judge from 1910 to 1924. In 1924 Tracy formed a law partnership with **Maurice L. Galvin** under the name of Galvin & Tracy, and the firm represented many large business interests, among them some of the local utilities. Tracy engaged in several civic and charitable interests. He chaired the campaign to build St. Elizabeth Hospital (see **St. Elizabeth Medical Center**) in Covington and was an exalted ruler of the Covington Elks (see **Civic Associations**), a charter member of the **Fort Mitchell Country Club**, a member of the Fraternal Order of Eagles, a member of the Latonia Jockey Club, and a founder of **WCKY** radio. He married Margaret C. Brown on April 27, 1904. Tracy died in 1947 at the Arthur Apartments along Greenup St. in Covington and was buried at St. Mary Cemetery in Fort Mitchell.

"His Character Shone in Good Works," *KP*, March 7, 1947, 2.
"Judge Frank M. Tracy Dies at Age 74," *KP*, March 6, 1947, 1.
Kentucky Death Certificate No. 6598, for the year 1947.

William Terwort

TRAFFIC. The increase of traffic on streets and highways is a serious concern in Northern Kentucky and nationally. The situation is worsened by the public's choice of the flexibility and convenience of auto travel over mass transit. An Ohio-Kentucky-Indiana Regional Council of Governments (**OKI**) report states that in 2000, among those in Boone, Campbell, and Kenton counties using roads to commute to work, more than 85 percent drove alone, while only 3 percent used the bus system. Over the years, numerous strategies have been utilized to relieve traffic congestion. Removal of parking, one-way operations, and designated turning lanes have improved traffic flow. The first traffic signal in a Northern Kentucky town was installed in Erlanger at the intersection of the **Dixie Highway** and Commonwealth Ave. in June 1928.

A comprehensive plan prepared for the City of Covington by **Ladislas Segoe** in 1932 emphasized adapting the community to the automobile. Relying heavily on traffic counts and population projections, the plan noted specific locations where widening, paving, improving curves, and eliminating railroad crossings would enhance safety and mobility. Owing to the cost involved, many of the plan's major features were never undertaken. These included a proposed regional highway system with three radial boulevards emanating from the downtown Covington area.

By the end of **World War II**, rush-hour traffic in Northern Kentucky was a serious problem; traffic would back up from downtown Cincinnati across all four Ohio River bridges, through Covington and Newport, to the routes leading to the steadily developing suburban communities. In the 1950s one-way traffic was instituted on the **L&N Bridge** during the morning and afternoon peak periods. **U.S 27** through Newport was made one-way north on Monmouth and one-way south on York St., and a similar plan was put into effect in Covington on Greenup and Scott Sts. Because of the hilly terrain of Northern Kentucky, a street grid system had developed only in the more level river communities. Suburban growth relied on major existing arterials that allowed few alternate routes to bypass blockages or heavy congestion. The opening of the **Brent Spence** (I-71/I-75) Bridge in late 1963 initially provided major relief to the rush-hour congestion in Kenton Co. However, it was 1976 before the **Daniel Carter Beard Bridge** (I-471) opening alleviated congestion in Campbell Co. It was obvious, even before construction started, that the I-471 link would attract a heavy volume of traffic from the growing areas of eastern Hamilton and Clermont counties in Ohio. However, an OKI study decided against recommending designated higher-occupancy-vehicle lanes on I-471. The Kentucky Department of Highways began a more systematic collection of traffic-count data in the early 1960s, and the Kentucky legislature adopted the 1961 Manual for Uniform Traffic Control Devices (MUTCD) for all roads and streets in the commonwealth. The federal Traffic Operations Program to Improve Capacity and Safety (TOPICS) program in the early 1970s was an attempt to address problems at key intersections. Several of these projects were completed, either as designed or with modifications. A major improvement under this program was the alignment of Stevenson Rd. with Commonwealth Ave. in Erlanger.

By the mid-1980s, the region was exploring "Intelligent Transportation" systems. The Kentucky Transportation Cabinet (KYTC) was the leading agency for the ADVANTAGE 75 system to monitor trucking on I-75 from Canada to south Florida. One of the first monitoring stations was installed in Kentucky on southbound I-75 between Walton and Crittenden. Traffic signals had advanced from pretimed to partially traffic-activated. Later, the signals had been interconnected along the major arterial routes, and the system along the Dixie Highway could be adjusted from the District Highway office in Crescent Park. This system extended along U.S. 42 to Hopeful Rd. and later included Mall Rd. and the segment of Ky. Rt. 18 in Florence, Ky. Urban signal systems were installed in Covington and Newport.

The development of the Advanced Regional Traffic Interactive Management and Information System (ARTIMIS) was coordinated by OKI and financed largely with federal clean-air funding. An electronic network of fiber-optic cable carries data to a control center in Cincinnati just north of the Brent Spence Bridge. The system includes cameras, changeable message signs, roadway sensors, highway advisory radio, and service patrol vans on Cincinnati and Northern Kentucky freeways. The system, fully operational by late 1996, included several national innovations, among them the 511 highway information hotline.

A Federal Highway Administration report in 1996 compared national travel factors since 1970. It indicated that the total miles driven had grown 4 times as fast as the population, twice as fast as the number of licensed drivers, and 18 times as fast as additional road mileage. The number of vehicles had increased by 90 percent since 1970. The traffic count in both directions on I-71/I-75 between Buttermilk Pk. and the Dixie Highway at Fort Mitchell was 39,600 vehicles per day in 1965. In 1975 it was 80,800; in 1995, 131,000; and in 2005, 159,000.

As traffic increased, the river crossings again became bottlenecks. The emergency shoulders on both the Brent Spence and the Daniel Carter Beard bridges have been converted to provide additional traffic lanes. The planning under way in 2007 to replace the Spence Bridge structure anticipates as many as seven lanes in each direction. The heavy traffic seeking to reach new attractions on the Newport and Bellevue riverfronts will require a major redesign of the exit ramp at the south end of the I-471 Beard Bridge. A corridor study of the Dixie Highway segment between Florence and I-75 in Covington was completed in 2005. The goals are to improve traffic flow and reduce delay without constructing additional lanes. The volume of truck traffic is steadily increasing. This will worsen congestion, which, in turn, will threaten the long-term viability of some businesses. Residential and commercial development throughout Northern Kentucky continues to outpace the resources allocated to provide adequate roadway access.

America's Rolling Warehouses. Washington, D.C.: The Road Information Program (TRIP), 2004.

Comprehensive Plan for Covington, Kentucky and Environs, Covington Planning and Zoning Commission. 1932. Reprint, New York: Arno Press, 1974.

"Erlanger First," *KP*, June 28, 1928, 1.

"Eyes on the Roads: ARTIMIS Cameras and Technicians," *CP*, October 12, 2002, 1K.

Federal Highway Administration. *America's Roads: 1776–1976.* Washington, D.C.: U.S. Department of Transportation, 1976.

Tenkotte, Paul A. "Adaptation to the Automobile and Imitation of the Suburb, Covington, Kentucky's 1932 Plan as a Test Case of City Planning," *JKS* 1, no. 1 (July 1984): 151–70.

Traffic Congestion and Reliability: Linking Solutions to Problems. Washington, D.C.: Federal Highway Administration, 2004.

Ralph Wolff

TRANSIT AUTHORITY OF NORTHERN KENTUCKY. The Transit Authority of Northern Kentucky (TANK) was created by the fiscal courts of Boone, Campbell, and Kenton counties in July 1971. TANK was formed in response to an announcement by the Cincinnati, Newport, and Covington Transportation Company (CN&C) (the **Green Line Company**), a private transit company, that it would cease to serve Northern Kentucky by the end of 1972. In June 1972 a bond issue to fund TANK was authorized by the governing bodies of Boone, Campbell, and Kenton counties, for placement on the November 7, 1972, election ballot. The move was timely, since the CN&C Transportation Company halted all operations on November 4, 1972. In that election the voters approved a $5.4 million public transit operating bond issue, with Kenton Co. residents contributing $3.1 million, Campbell Co. residents $1.9 million, and the citizens of Florence in Boone Co. $400,000. The issue passed, in all three counties, by more than 70 percent of votes. Thus TANK was funded and the populace again had an alternative to the automobile.

Preparations were made to get the buses rolling the next morning after the bond issue passed. The newly appointed TANK board arranged during the night for liability and workman's compensation insurance and made credit agreements for fuel and tires. Arrangements with owners of the now defunct Green Line allowed TANK to lease 58 buses, along with the Newport storage and maintenance facilities. Also during the night, former Green Line drivers and mechanics were notified that their services would be needed as early as the next morning.

The most immediate problem facing TANK was that it did not have enough operable buses to put on the road. The buses obtained from the Green Line, except for eight purchased in 1967, were 18 years old, on average, and suffered from deferred maintenance. To ensure availability of a large enough fleet of operable buses to meet basic schedules, TANK immediately purchased 20 used buses from the Kansas City Area Transit Authority.

In the next 24 months, TANK launched some major initiatives. The basic fare was reduced to 25 cents, and service headways on many routes were improved to achieve a phased increase of 44 percent more service mileage. In addition, passenger shelters were placed at many boarding locations, and an information center was established to provide the public with continuous schedule and route information.

In 1973 TANK developed new branches of its most patronized route, No. 1–Erlanger-Florence, to serve the rapidly developing areas of southern Kenton and Boone counties, and it established a new route to reach another growing area around Taylor Mill and Independence in southeastern Kenton Co. In Campbell Co., TANK increased service along both Highland and Grand Aves. to Fort Thomas. Rush-hour express runs were reinstituted from Fort Thomas, Dayton, and the Cold Spring–Alexandria area to Cincinnati.

In 1975, having received a capital grant from the federal government, TANK purchased 74 AM General 41-passenger air-conditioned transit buses and was able to retire most of the worn-out Green Line buses. The delivery of the new buses gave TANK a distinctive new look; they were painted white overall with diagonal red, yellow, and blue stripes amidships, representing the unity of Campbell, Kenton, and Boone counties.

As a result of the 1975–1976 OPEC oil crisis, which led to localized gasoline shortages and much higher fuel prices, TANK carried a record 5,731,517 passengers in 1976, almost double the number of persons who rode the Green Line in 1971. This increase encouraged TANK to seek additional public funding; but the voters proved to be fickle. In November 1976 they rejected the proposed one-quarter-percent sales tax increase for additional transit operating funds. Faced with a doubling of the price of diesel fuel, TANK was forced to raise its basic fare to 40 cents in 1977 and to curtail much of its late evening and weekend service. Predictably, ridership declined noticeably in 1977.

In 1978 TANK proposed to the voters of Kenton and Campbell counties a permanent fund base centered on a payroll and net-profit tax. TANK employees and their families, along with many other northern Kentuckians, went door-to-door to gain support for the upcoming ballot initiative. The voters passed the issue in November 1978, and TANK was endowed with its first permanent funding base. During the early 1980s, as gasoline prices stabilized, more people returned to their automobiles for commuting to work and visiting the doctor or stores, and TANK saw its ridership gradually decline. From a high of almost 6 million passengers in 1976, TANK carried fewer than 5 million passengers in 1982. However, in 1981 TANK secured a federal Urban Mass Transit Act grant to replace its old, cramped, inefficient maintenance and storage facility (a former Green Line **streetcar** barn) at 11th and Brighton Sts. in Newport. A new TANK office and maintenance facility was constructed on Madison Pike in Fort Wright and dedicated on November 20, 1982 by general manager Stephen L. Morris. Further purchases of 20 new buses between 1980 and 1983 meant that for the first time the entire TANK fleet of 95 buses was air-conditioned.

Public transportation took a backseat in the mid-1980s as the federal government gradually reduced its aid to mass transit. Caught in a financial squeeze, TANK had to raise its basic fare, first to 60 cents and eventually to 75 cents. Therefore, despite a combination of clean, well-kept equipment, convenient schedules, and the establishment of numerous park-and-ride locations, ridership slipped to near the 4 million level by 1989. There was some modest route expansion during the 1980s. A new service was launched to the newly opened **St. Elizabeth Medical Center** South in Edgewood. Seven trips a day were scheduled, primarily at shift change times, to transport hospital workers.

The 1990s saw a flurry of progress and innovation at TANK. Spearheaded by Mark Donaghy, general manager (1990–2003), the authority began expanding its routes to serve the needs of the developing southern ends of the three-county region. Service to Northern Kentucky University and the Cold Spring–Alexandria area was expanded, and new service was added to various areas of Boone Co. (centered on Empire Dr.) and to Walton and Hebron. A new No. 2–Airport Express route was instituted between downtown Cincinnati and the **Cincinnati/Northern Kentucky International Airport**, with the schedule primarily aimed at shift change times at the airport.

Not to be left out of TANK expansion plans were the newly developing business districts and the new condominiums along the Northern Kentucky riverfront. On May 6, 1998, TANK launched the Southbank Shuttle, a new bus route linking the downtown business districts of Cincinnati, Covington, Newport, and Bellevue. The Shuttle was designed to join the downtown Cincinnati's sports stadiums and its retail and restaurant district with both the Covington and the Newport shopping and entertainment districts along the Ohio River and Covington's **Main Strasse** Village. The Southbank Shuttle was conceived by TANK, and **Southbank Partners**, a public-private group, provided marketing support. The shuttle was a complete success, so much so that TANK found it necessary to order new, larger buses in 2001.

One negative development occurred in September 1996, when the Transit Authority of Northern Kentucky was notified that its tenancy in the **Dixie Terminal** in Cincinnati would be terminated on October 18. TANK and its predecessor, the Green Line, had used the off-street structure as its primary Cincinnati terminus since 1921. However, that development gave impetus to implement TANK's long-range plan to operate a primary transfer facility in downtown Covington. A new indoor facility, located on the ground floor of the Kenton Co. parking garage on Madison Ave. between Second and Third Sts., was opened on July 25, 1998. Named the Riverfront Transit Center, the facility, designed to serve as TANK's major transfer point, replaced the former main transfer locations in congested downtown Cincinnati as well as the nonsheltered Third and Madison transfer point in Covington. Almost immediately the new facility was nicknamed the Covington Transit Center by the press and by TANK itself.

Further initiatives by TANK from 1995 to 2005 included assisting employers and social service agencies by instituting reverse commuting service. For example, people are transported from urban areas to their work in outlying parts of the three counties, where new and more abundant employment opportunities such as the airport have developed. Another TANK innovation to lure people back to public transit was the Guaranteed Ride Home Program. TANK guaranteed its customers a ride home (up to four times per year) if unplanned overtime or a family emergency arose during the workday. During the same time period, TANK also added more park-and-ride lots in the suburbs to enable citizens to avoid the hassle of driving in congested areas.

Another community outreach program instituted by the authority was its Transit Subsidy Program, whereby companies could provide up to $65 per month in tax-free benefits to employees if they used TANK to commute to work. To assist the mobility-impaired, TANK instituted in 1978 its Regional Area Mobility Program, known as RAMP. From a modest beginning using four buses to provide door-to-door service for 80 monthly riders, RAMP had grown by 2004 to serve more than 4,000 people monthly. Also by 2004, TANK had put into service on regular routes 51 low-floor buses, fully accessible to many people with limited mobility. The employees of TANK's maintenance department, under the direction of Donald Neltner, volunteered their free time to restore the *Kentucky,* one of the oldest existing streetcars in the United States, for eventual display at the **Behringer-Crawford Museum** at **Devou Park** in Park Hills. They also restored a number of historic buses for use in local events and parades.

In late 2003 David Braun succeeded Mark Donaghy as TANK's general manager. In 2004 the Transit Authority of Northern Kentucky operated more than 130 vehicles throughout the three counties of Boone, Campbell, and Kenton (and to downtown Cincinnati) on more than 30 regular and express routes. TANK employed 200 full-time and 56 part-time individuals and carried more than 3,700,000 passengers in 2004.

Lehmann, Terry W., and Earl W. Clark, *The Green Line.* Chicago: Central Electric Railfans' Association, 2000.

Terry W. Lehmann

TRANSITIONS INC. In 1969 the Northern Kentucky Regional Mental Health–Mental Retardation Board (known then as the Comprehensive Care Center but now as **NorthKey Community Care**) encouraged the formation of a "substance abuse task force." Executive Director Dr. J. E. Willett initiated the effort and oversaw the project administratively. The staff person who took up the challenge to help in treating substance abuse was Dr. Clarence Lassetter, a therapist at the center. He was joined by a few citizens who were very concerned about the lack of substance abuse treatment programs for the uninsured and indigent in Northern Kentucky. Three of the most committed members of the group were from the same family—Virginia, Margaret, and Larry Droege.

During 1969 the group gained a few more supporters and raised a small amount of money but was stymied by having neither a building in which to provide services nor the funds to buy one. The group often met in the living room of Virginia and Margaret Droege at 1408 Greenup St. in Covington. During one meeting in late 1969, Virginia reportedly looked at Margaret and said, "You know, we could start doing treatment services right here." The two women proceeded to move in with relatives and donated their home to the cause. The new agency was named Droege House Inc. and was registered as a nonprofit charity. The first board chair was Tony Wirtz, also a board member of Northern Kentucky Regional Mental Health–Mental Retardation Board.

In 1971 the program grew to include outreach services and a drop-in center on 11th St. in Covington, as a result of collaborations with the Community Alcoholism Services of the federal Office of Economic Opportunities. Locally, the Northern Kentucky Community Action Commission (NKCAC) had sponsored these services. NKCAC's Alcoholism Services were officially delegated to Droege House Inc. in October 1974. In addition, the Mental Health–Mental Retardation Board and Droege House Inc. signed an affiliation agreement; as a result of the agreement, a nonmedical detoxification unit was established and added to the services at Droege House Inc.

In July 1975 Droege House Inc. changed its name to the Northern Kentucky Alcohol Abuse Program Inc. (NKAAP). In the following month, the agency was awarded state formula grant funds to establish a detoxification unit. In October of the same year, the treatment program (a halfway house) moved into what had been the nurses' quarters at Speers Hospital (see **Speers Memorial Hospital**) in Dayton, Ky., and that building was renamed the Droege House.

During the three decades since then, the agency, renamed Transitions Inc. in 1984, has focused on providing substance-abuse-related services to assist the indigent, the uninsured, the incarcerated, the homeless, and the working poor of Northern Kentucky. It provides services in three major areas: **substance abuse treatment**, community corrections, and assistance for the homeless and others with housing problems.

Transitions Inc. has become known for its innovative programming. Among its many firsts are the nonhospital residential substance abuse program in Greater Cincinnati (1969); the nonmedical detoxification unit in Northern Kentucky (1975); the substance abuse program for offenders (1978); the halfway-house services in Eastern Kentucky (1987); a women's and children's substance abuse program (1992); the Oxford House Recovery Group Home (1993); the Community Corrections Advisory Board in Northern Kentucky (the latter became the catalyst to establish the Kenton Co. Community Corrections Advisory Board Inc.) (1996); the Intensive-Out-Patient program for offenders in Northern Kentucky (1997); the first drug court in Northern Kentucky (Kenton Co. Adult Drug Court), of which Transitions Inc. is a cofounder (1998); and a HUD housing grant for the formerly homeless (1999).

From 2000 to 2005, Transitions Inc. was an integral part of the community effort that founded the Life Learning Center Inc., and in 2006 Transitions Inc. was approved to establish a new 100-bed treatment facility in Erlanger, as part of the Recovery Kentucky initiative sponsored by Kentucky governor Ernie Fletcher (2003–2007). The new facility was under construction in 2008.

On its 35th anniversary, in 2004, the agency owned 16 buildings, including five residential care facilities in Boyd, Campbell, and Kenton counties, and was serving an average of 270 residents per day and an additional 260 outpatient clients per week. In 2005 the agency's revenues were $5.5 million. Transitions Inc. receives clients from across the state of Kentucky but primarily serves Boone, Campbell, Carroll, Gallatin, Grant, Kenton, Owen, and Pendleton counties in Northern Kentucky.

Derks, Rose Marie, O.S.F. "Alcohol Abuse Program of Northern Kentucky: A Look at Financial Resources," 1978, Xavier Univ., Cincinnati.

Eigelbach, Kevin. "Rehab Center OK'd: Erlanger Board Approves Project," *KP,* April 25, 2006, 1A.

Transitions Inc. *Birth of an Agency.* 2005. 35th anniversary brochure.

Mac McArthur

TRANSKENTUCKY TRANSPORTATION RAILROAD INC. The TransKentucky Transportation Railroad, better known as the TTI, operates the former **Louisville and Nashville Railroad** (L&N) track in Kentucky between Paris and Maysville. Originally, it was the **Maysville and Lexington Railroad** that finished the track between Maysville and Paris, and the first trip was made from Maysville to Paris on March 4, 1872. The connecting section between Paris and Lexington was part of the **Covington and Lexington Railroad**, built in the mid-1850s. The road became part of the **Kentucky Central Railroad** (KC) in 1876. Collis P. Huntington acquired the KC in 1881 to provide linkage for his **Chesapeake and Ohio Railroad** to reach Louisville via Lexington. In 1891, after Huntington's railroad empire was thrown into financial difficulties, the L&N gained ownership of the line. Although the L&N viewed the line as having profit potential, demonstrated by the substantial depot (see **Railroad Depots**) it constructed at Maysville (today the police station), the line became relegated to local traffic, unable to generate through traffic. In 1979 the L&N sold this section to the TTI, which uses it mainly for coal hauling, moving Eastern Kentucky coal dropped off at Paris by the L&N and the **CSX** to a barge terminal on the Ohio River at Maysville. The TTI remains an independent railroad, but the CSX is a major stockholder in the company.

"First Railroad Trip to Paris," *Maysville Bulletin,* March 7, 1872, 3.

Herr, Kenneth A. *The Louisville & Nashville Railroad.* Lexington: Univ. Press of Kentucky, 2000.

Lewis, Edward A. *American Shortline Railway Guide.* 4th ed. Waukesha, Wis.: Kalmbach Books, 1991.

Charles H. Bogart

TRANSPARENT PIE. Transparent pie is a delicious dessert, usually prepared as a tart or a pie, which seems to have originated in Maysville and environs. Its origin is unknown, but it dates back at least several generations. Maysville's oldest residents remember transparent pie as always being part of local life. **Rosemary Clooney** purchased transparent pie on her visits home, and her nephew **George Clooney** has been known to transport it to movie sets in Hollywood. The tarts are a featured item of McGee's Bakery and are even baked at chain store bakeries in the community. Hula Duke, a prominent local preservationist, always served transparent pie tarts to visitors to the community. On a return visit, one of those guests asked to have, once more, some of that wonderful dessert, whose name she could not remember; she asked for "invisible" pie. Recipes for transparent pie vary, but they include eggs, sugar, butter, milk, and small amounts of flour and vanilla, mixed and placed in pie shells. The result is a sweet, rich confection, golden brown on the surface with a light yellow body that is almost clear—giving the pie its name.

Meiman, Karen. "Taste of Tradition from Farms to Kitchens," *KP,* January 10, 2004, 3.

John Klee

TRAUTH DAIRY. Louis Trauth Dairy was established in May 1920, when Louis J. Trauth and his wife Clara Stephany Trauth bought a milk route from the Fred Schuerman Dairy, which was at the present site of the Newport Shopping Center. At first the Trauth Dairy operated from a 600-square-foot plant behind the Trauths' home at 11th and John Sts. in Newport; by 1926 it had been expanded to 1,500 square feet. Despite competition from more than 50 Northern Kentucky dairies, and the impact of the **Great Depression** and **World War II**, Trauth Dairy grew from a partnership between Louis Trauth and his two sons into a corporation in 1956. The new corporation acquired the Niser Ice Cream Company in 1968 but did not create its own line of ice cream products (see **Candy and Ice Cream**) until July 1990; by November 1990 the dairy had introduced more than 43 new ice cream products. Plant improvements by 1985 included three multimillion-dollar expansions that increased production and distribution. A new ice cream production plant was added in 1993. One of the first dairies in the region to vacuum-pasteurize milk, Trauth Dairy has consistently introduced innovative packaging and products, including tamper-evident packaging, sweet acidophilus milk, and 1 percent plus A/B milk. It is also the exclusive manufacturer of fat-free plus A/B milk, which tastes like 2 percent but is actually skim fortified with calcium and with acidophilus and bifidum cultures—the cultures in yogurt. Twelve varieties of milk, three kinds of cream, eggnog, chip dips, cottage cheese, fruit drinks, and more than 20 flavors of ice cream are manufactured at the Newport plant. Two other distribution facilities operate in Louisville and in Osgood, Ind.

In 1997 the dairy was purchased by Suiza Foods Corporation of Dallas, Tex., one of the largest dairy firms in the United States. The Trauth Dairy thereby became involved in a national market, manufacturing ice cream under the Pet and Carnation labels in addition to its own brand and private labels. Today its ultramodern facility covers five city blocks. The dairy has received gold medals and blue ribbons each year for numerous products at the Kentucky State Fair, and *Cincinnati Magazine* has named its eggnog and sour cream Cincinnati's best. In addition Louis Trauth Dairy was named the Dairy of the Year in 2003 and the best fluid milk plant in 2004, by the All Star Dairy Association.

"As Other Dairies Vanish, Trauth Company Expands," *CP,* July 31, 1984, 11B.

"Ice Cream Venture Could Help Trauth Frost Local Competition," *Cincinnati Business Courier,* November 29, 1993, 27.

Louis Trauth Dairy. www.trauthdairy.com (accessed April 5, 2006).

Gabrielle Summe

TRIMBLE, MARY BARLOW (b. 1831, Paris, Ky.; d. September 20, 1912, New York City). Mary Trimble was an ardent supporter of **women's suffrage** and a close friend of Susan B. Anthony and other suffragists, such as **Anna Shaler Berry**, Lillian Blauvelt, Laura Clay, **Jessie Firth**, Clara Loring, Nancy McLaughlin, Mary Light Ogle, **Mattie Bruce Reynolds**, and Dr. **Louise Southgate**.

Mary Barlow Trimble's parents were Martin and Frances Cantrell Barlow; both parents died when Mary was young, and she went to live with her uncle Col. Joseph Cantrell. She married **William Wallace Trimble**, a wealthy attorney and legal scholar who lived at Cynthiana. William was the author of *Trimble's Kentucky Digest,* which was used as a textbook by the Cincinnati Law School. The couple moved to Covington in 1873, where they lived in a mansion at 1026 Madison Ave. Mary and William had five children.

Like many other women of wealth and position of her day, Mary was involved in numerous social issues, especially women's property rights and the right to vote. She was one of the founders of the Covington Equal Rights Club. In 1894 Susan B. Anthony came to Cincinnati to attend the Ohio Women's Suffrage convention at the Sinton Hall in the **YMCA**. While in the area, she and the treasurer of the organization, Helen Taylor Upton, stayed with the Trimble family in their Covington home. On other visits to Cincinnati and Northern Kentucky, Anthony often was hosted by other local members of the women's movement, including Anna Shaler Berry. The suffrage organizations fought tirelessly for a woman's right to vote; however, many of their leaders passed from the scene before the voting rights amendment to the U.S. Constitution was ratified in 1920.

Mary Barlow Trimble died of a stroke at age 81, at the Gregorian Hotel in New York City, while visiting with her granddaughter, Grace Ludlow. Mary's body was returned to Covington, where funeral services were held in the family home on the southeast corner of Madison Ave. and Robbins St. Rev. Macgruder of Covington's Trinity Episcopal Church and Rev. Plemmons of the Madison Avenue Baptist Church in Covington conducted her funeral services. Members of the Covington Equal Rights Club attended the services as a body. A special train carried the body and the funeral party to Cynthiana, where Mary was buried next to her husband, William, in the Battle Grove Cemetery. Her five children, William Trimble, Robert Trimble, Helen Trimble Highton, Grace Trimble Fackler, and **Kate Trimble Woolsey** survived her.

Each of Mary's daughters followed in her mother's footsteps by becoming involved in the women's rights movement. Grace Trimble Fackler was the most active, although daughter Kate Trimble Woolsey wrote a book in 1903 called *Republics versus Woman,* in which she criticized governments for not giving women the same legal rights as men. Both of Mary's sons became successful financiers.

"Death Notice," *KP,* September 21, 1912, 7.

"Mrs. Trimble Dies in N.Y. Hotel—Brief Biography," *KP,* September 20, 1912, 1.

Reis, Jim. "They Fought to Secure Equal Rights for Women," *KP,* August 4, 2003, 4K.

———. "Winning the Right to Vote," *KP,* November 8, 2004, 4K.

TRIMBLE, ROBERT (b. November 17, 1776, Augusta Co., Va.; d. August 25, 1828, Paris, Ky.). Robert Trimble was the second person to serve as a federal judge for Northern Kentucky and the first federal trial judge appointed to the U.S. Supreme Court. Trimble attended Transylvania College in Lexington and was admitted to the bar in 1802. Before his federal judicial appointments, he served as a member of the Kentucky General Assembly (1802) and as a justice of the Kentucky Court of Appeals. In 1817 President James Madison appointed Trimble to the District Court of Kentucky, where he served eight years. In 1826 President John Quincy Adams elevated him to the U.S. Supreme Court. It was believed that Secretary of State Henry Clay, a Kentuckian, was influential in Trimble's appointment to the Court. While Trimble's tenure on the Court was brief, due to his sudden and unexpected death, he wrote 16 opinions on a Court that was dominated by Chief Justice John Marshall. He wrote the only opinion in which Chief Justice Marshall was in the minority during Marshall's 34-year tenure (1801–1835). Trimble died at his home in Paris, Ky., in 1828 of a "malignant bilious fever," just 27 months into his tenure as a justice. His close friend on the Court, Justice Joseph Story, said of Trimble, "We are persuaded that if he had lived 10 years longer, in the discharge of the same high duties, from the expendability of his talents, and his steady devotion to jurisdiction, he would have gained still higher rank." During the 1829 term of the Court, the justices wore black armbands on their left arms honoring Trimble's memory. Trimble Co., Ky., was named in his honor.

Kleber, John E., ed. *The Kentucky Encyclopedia.* Lexington: University Press of Kentucky, 1992.
The Supreme Court Historical Society. www.supremecourthistory.org/ (accessed February 5, 2007).

Paul L. Whalen

TRIMBLE, VANCE H. (b. July 6, 1913, Harrison, Ark.). Vance Henry Trimble, a journalist and an author, is the son of attorney Guy Lee Trimble and Josephine Crump Trimble. Vance grew up in Wewoka, Okla., where he attended public school. When he was 14 years old, he acquired an after-school job as a cub reporter for the *Okemah (Okla.) Daily Leader,* and he later worked part-time as a courthouse reporter, a sports editor, and a city editor for the *Wewoka (Okla.) Times-Democrat.* Trimble graduated from Wewoka High School, where he was editor of the high school newspaper, in 1930. Because jobs were so difficult to find and keep during the **Great Depression**, Trimble worked part-time for various Oklahoma newspapers. In 1932 he married his high school sweetheart, Elzene Miller, and they became the parents of one child, Carol Ann. Elzene Trimble was described as having steel will sheathed in southern charm; she was Vance's closest friend, his greatest supporter, and at times his most astute critic.

During the depression Vance Trimble resorted to repairing typewriters as a means of helping to support his family. In 1939 he was hired as a copy editor for the Scripps-Howard–owned *Houston Press* and within six months was promoted to city editor. During **World War II**, Trimble served for two years with the U.S. Army. Afterward he rejoined the *Houston Press,* where he held the title of managing editor. In 1955 he was transferred to the Scripps-Howard Bureau in Washington, D.C., and served as news director. While there, he wrote a series of articles exposing nepotism and corruption within the U.S. Congress. That series led to his receiving the triple crown of journalism in 1960. He was awarded the Pulitzer Prize for national reporting, the Sigma Delta Chi Award for distinguished Washington correspondence, and the Raymond Clapper Award for the year's best Washington reporting. In 1963 he left Washington to become editor of the ***Kentucky Post,*** in Covington. For Vance, that was like a homecoming, since his father and both of his grandfathers had been born and raised in Kentucky.

Kentucky Post employees described Trimble as a very demanding boss, nearly impossible to please, who almost daily threatened to fire everyone. However, Trimble also had a compassionate side and was very sympathetic to the personal problems of his employees. While at the *Kentucky Post,* he designed and built a new home at 1013 Sunset Dr. in Kenton Hills (Covington), with a commanding view of the Ohio River and downtown Cincinnati. In 1974 Trimble was inducted into the Oklahoma Journalism Hall of Fame. He retired from the *Kentucky Post* in 1979 but remained in Covington.

After 67 years of happy marriage, Elzene died on July 5, 1999, and was buried in Wewoka, Okla. Vance moved back to Wewoka after his wife's death, so he could be near her grave. In retirement Trimble has written biographies about Wal-Mart founder Sam Walton, Kentucky governor Albert B. "Happy" Chandler (1935–1939, 1955–1959), Federal Express founder Fred Smith, and communications magnate Chris Whittle. When Trimble informed his publisher that he was going to write the Walton biography, the publisher told him not to write it because someone was already writing one. Vance became angry and wrote the biography anyway; another company published it. The book was an instant success, selling more than a half million copies. In recent years Vance placed his manuscripts, working files, and correspondence in the Ohio University library at Athens. He also donated more than 3,000 books to the public library in Wewoka. Now in his nineties, Vance Trimble continues to enjoy retirement in the town where he grew up, Wewoka, Okla.

The Cincinnati Post. "Lifetime of Love Goes On." www.cincypost.com (accessed February 5, 2006).
"Editor in Hall of Fame," *KP,* November 1, 1974, 1.
"Editor-Turned-Author," *KP,* November 26, 1990, 1B.
Hicks, Jack. "The Astonishing Mr. Trimble Never at Loss for Words," *KP,* August 6, 1993, 1K–2K.
NNDB. "Pulitzer Prize for National Reporting." www.nndb.com (accessed February 5, 2006).
Ohio University Libraries. "Vance H. Trimble Collection." www.library.ohiou.edu/find/ (accessed February 5, 2006).
"Pulitzer Prize Winner Named Ky. Post Editor," *KP,* January 14, 1963, 1K.

Jack Wessling

TRIMBLE, WILLIAM W. (b. December 31, 1821, Cynthiana, Ky.; d. August 31, 1886, Covington, Ky.). Lawyer, judge, and author William W. Trimble was the son of John and Eliza Porter Trimble. William's father took great interest in the education of all his sons; he and an uncle of William, Robert Macmillan, a former college professor in Edinburgh, Scotland, homeschooled all the Trimble boys. William Trimble received additional training at a private school in Danville, Ky. He became a lawyer in 1853 and practiced law in Cynthiana for 20 years. He was married twice, first to a granddaughter of Kentucky governor James Garrard (1796–1804), and later to Mary Barlow (see **Mary Barlow Trimble**), daughter of Martin and Frances Cantrell Barlow. From his first marriage he had no children, but by his second wife, Mary, he had five who lived to maturity, Kate, Fannie, Helen, William Jr., and Robert. In 1856 William Trimble was elected Circuit Court judge of the Ninth District of Kentucky, comprising the counties of Bracken, Campbell, Harrison, Kenton, and Pendleton. He served in that position until 1864, when he was elected Circuit Court judge of the Second District. In 1873 Trimble moved to Covington, where he continued his legal practice and earned the reputation of having one of the finest legal minds in the region. A voracious reader, he spent much time studying fine literature. He wrote extensively; one of his books was *Trimble's Kentucky Digest,* which was used for many years as a textbook at the Cincinnati Law School. William's daughter Kate married Edward J. Woolsey and gained fame as an ardent feminist and women's rights activist and as the author of the 1903 book *Republics versus Woman* (see **Kate Trimble Woolsey**). Judge William W. Trimble was 64 years old when he died in his Covington home, at the southeast corner of Madison Ave. and Robbins St. Funeral services were held at the Cynthiana Episcopal Church, and Trimble was buried in the Battle Grove Cemetery in Cynthiana.

"August Election," *CJ,* July 4, 1856, 3.
"Covington Nominations," *CDC,* May 23, 1864, 2.
"Obituaries," *KSJ,* September 2, 1886, 4.
"R. J. Trimble to Make His Home in California," *KTS,* May 25, 1920, 19.
Woolsey, Kate Trimble. *Republics versus Woman.* London: Gay and Bird, 1903.

TRINITY EPISCOPAL CHURCH. Founded in 1842, Trinity Episcopal Church is located at Fourth St. and Madison Ave. in Covington. Its present building was built in stages over the period 1859–1888 to replace a smaller frame building at the same location, built in 1843. Additions and improvements over the years were made by noted architects Herbert Tinsley of Cincinnati, and William

Trinity Episcopal Church.

Stewart (see **Walter and Stewart**) and others. **George Roth Jr.**, a prominent architect and a member of Trinity Episcopal Church, described the architecture of the present church building as an "American Victorian Gothic parish church design." The most noticeable feature of the church is a magnificent bell tower, which, along with the church's west facade and its baptistery, was designed by **Louis Piket** in 1888; the tower houses chimes given to the church in 1888 by John W. and Henrietta A. Baker, prominent Covington residents and longtime members of Trinity Episcopal Church. Howell Louis Lovell Sr. donated the funds for the baptistery. In 1886 Piket also designed the church's Parish House, called the Guild Hall, which still remains. The architectural firm of Porter, Tyler, Martin, and Roth (George Roth) designed a new Parish House for the congregation, completed in 1959.

Added to the National Register of Historic Places in 1982, Trinity Episcopal Church contains priceless stained-glass windows, including work of the John Riordan Studio of Cincinnati. The St. Michael Archangel window in the north transept, a gift of the Lovell family, was made by the famous studio of Louis Comfort Tiffany of New York. Hand-carved furnishings and wall panels were created by female students of renowned artists Henry and William Fry, as well as those of Benn Pitman. **Kate E. P. Mosher**, a student of Pitman, carved three exquisite wood panels in the altar as well as many of the wall panels.

The Trinity Episcopal Church has been the site of many important Covington events. In 1901 it hosted the 13th Annual State Convention of the **women's suffrage** movement. Successful community organizations that received their start at Trinity Episcopal Church include **Senior Services of Northern Kentucky** (which occupied the lower level of the Parish House for ten years), the **Family Nurturing Center**, and the Covington Community Center, which was the forerunner of the **Center for Great Neighborhoods of Covington**. Groups such as the Kiwanis Club (see **Civic Associations**) and the Kenton Co. Historical Society (see **Historical Societies**) have found meeting space at the church sanctuary. The membership rolls of the church over the years read like a who's who of Northern Kentucky: politician **John White Stevenson**, columnists Mary T. Hall (see **Hall Family**) and **Annette Cornell**, singers **Elizabeth Parks** and **Katherine Hall Poock**, architects **Otto Dan Wolff** and Roth, the Baker family of the **Baker-Hunt Foundation**, the Confederate **Withers family**, and horseman **Polk Laffoon**.

Many clergy have served Trinity Episcopal Church since its founding in 1842. Those in recent times include Rev. Joseph Pennington (1989 to present); Rev. Robin P. Smith (1983–1988); Rev. David Rich (1980–1982); Rev. O. Worth May (1959–1979); Rev. Bruce A. Weatherly (1952–1959); Rev. Paul D. Wilbur (1946–1952); and Rev. C. D. Snowden (1943–1946).

Over the years, Trinity Episcopal Church has been an important part of the Northern Kentucky community and of the Episcopal community, consisting of Trinity, **St. Andrew's Episcopal Church** in Fort Thomas, **St. Paul's Episcopal Church** in Newport, and Grace Episcopal Church in Florence. Trinity Episcopal Church, part of the Episcopal Diocese of Lexington, in 2005 had a congregation of approximately 600 members, drawn from both Northern Kentucky and Cincinnati.

Barr, Frances Keller. *Ripe to the Harvest: History of the Episcopal Diocese of Lexington, 1895–1995.* Lexington, Ky.: Diocese of Lexington, 1995.

Roth, George F., Jr. *The Story of Trinity Episcopal Church in Covington.* Covington, Ky.: Trinity Episcopal Church, 1991.

Swinford, Francis Keller, and Rebecca Smith Lee. *Great Elm Tree: Heritage of the Episcopal Diocese of Lexington.* Lexington, Ky.: Faith House Press, 1969.

Tenkotte, Paul A. *A Heritage of Art and Faith: Downtown Covington Churches.* Covington, Ky.: The Kenton Co. Historical Society, 1986.

John West

TRINITY LUTHERAN CHURCH. The earliest record of Lutherans in Maysville was found in the German Evangelical Protestant Church, formed in 1869; this congregation worshipped in a building on Second St. and closed about the time of **World War I**. In 1923, brothers Ewald and Herman Pawset, owners of Wald Manufacturing Company in Sheboygan, Wis., were searching for a new location for their bicycle-parts plant. After they moved to Maysville, their Wisconsin pastor notified Pastor Walter Littmann in Madisonville, Ind., of their change in residence and their need to find a new spiritual home. Littmann visited the Pawset brothers and then moved to Maysville to become a resident Lutheran minister to a new Lutheran congregation. The first service was held in the home of Ewald Pawset on Forest Ave. in spring 1924, with six adults and seven children attending. An early worship service was held once a month, and biweekly services were instituted as the attendance grew.

In 1929, the Wisconsin-based Carnation Milk Company established a manufacturing facility in Maysville and brought a few more Lutheran employees to the area. The growing church needed more room than the Pawset home provided, so space was located in the Mason Co. Women's Club, where weekly services were conducted. In the same year, Gustav Reschke, a student at Concordia Seminary in St. Louis, Mo., was sent to Maysville to serve the small church of 15 people as an intern. The vacant German Evangelical Protestant Church on Second St. was given to Trinity, and the first service was held there on September 29, 1929. Trinity Lutheran Church was officially organized in the Missouri Synod by an assembly of six members on October 18, 1929, with four elected officers; Herman Pawset, president; Francis Lindert, vice president; Paul Hillmann, treasurer; and John Bratz, secretary. Five members of the former German Evangelical Protestant Church joined the Trinity congregation, and a Sunday School was also begun.

Alvin Stark, another Concordia student, was sent to serve the small church in 1930. The congregation grew as the area was canvassed for worshippers. The church wanted to have a full-time, ordained minister, so Pastor Reschke was officially called to serve Trinity, and on August 9, 1931, more than 100 people attended his installation service.

The German Evangelical Protestant Church building was purchased in 1954, and a parsonage was built in Deerfield Village. In 1966 the church building was sold to cotton manufacturer January & Wood Company, and the congregation again rented space for worship services. During 1969 property was purchased along Parker Rd., and a new building was dedicated in 1975. The cornerstone from the demolished German Evangelical Protestant Church building is now an artifact at the modern Trinity Lutheran Church. Today, worship services are held in a contemporary-design building with about 40 members.

"A Child Is Born—100 Creches on Display," *KP*, December 9, 2004, 4K.

"It Happened in Kentucky—Maysville," *KTS*, August 6, 1957, 1A.

"Minister for Forty Years," *KTS*, September 2, 1957, 3A.

Pawset, Ken. Telephone interview by Melinda G. Motley, September 26, 2006.

Melinda G. Motley

TRIPLE CROWN COUNTRY CLUB. The Triple Crown Country Club is located in Boone Co. just west of I-75 and the Richwood exit, at 1 Triple Crown Blvd. in Union. This country club was established in 1989, and its challenging 18-hole golf course was ready for use in 1991. The par 72 championship course was designed by Gene Bates, a highly respected designer who was once a golf course architect in the Jack Nicklaus design group.

The Triple Crown Country Club is private and has a membership of more than 350, of which 125 are social members. The general manager since the club's inception has been Patrick Green, and its only golf professional has been Wayne Oien. The Triple Crown Country Club's membership includes PGA Tour participant **Steve Flesch**, who holds the course record of 63, and **Steve Cauthen**, thoroughbred horse racing's 1978 Triple Crown winning jockey.

Green, Patrick. Interview by Dennis Van Houten, May 2, 2006, Villa Hills, Ky.

"Triple Crown Country Club," *CE*, July 20, 2003, H1–H2.

Triple Crown Country Club. www.triplecrowngolfclub.com/ (accessed June 23, 2006).

Dennis W. Van Houten

TRIPLER, CHARLES STUART, GENERAL (b. January 19, 1806, New York City; d. October 20, 1866, Cincinnati, Ohio). Gen. Charles Stuart Tripler, after whom Tripler Army Medical Center in Honolulu, Hawaii, is named, made many contributions to military medicine. One of these, providing standard guidelines for military inductees undergoing physical exams, was conceived while Tripler was assigned to the **Newport Barracks** in Newport. In 1830, after graduating from the College of Physicians and Surgeons in New York City, he was commissioned as an assistant surgeon in the U.S. Army. His military career spanned six decades (1818–1865), from the Seminole Wars in Florida through the **Mexican War** and the **Civil War**. In 1858, while stationed at the barracks in Newport, he published his famous *Manual of the Medical Officer of the Army of the United States*, which became the bible for other medical officers by standardizing the physical requirements of U.S. Army recruits. It was the definitive guide on the subject as late as the mid-1920s. Tripler also redesigned the army's ambulance from two-wheel carts to four-wheel wagons, making for much smoother rides. Tripler died in 1866 in Cincinnati and was buried with full military honors in Detroit, Mich., the hometown of his wife's family.

Donnelly, Joseph. *Newport Barracks—Kentucky's Forgotten Military Installation*. Covington, Ky.: Kenton Co. Historical Society, 1999.

Pacific Regional Medical Command. "Brigadier General Charles Stuart Tripler." www.tamc.amedd.army.mil/history/gentrip.htm (accessed April 5, 2007).

Purvis, Thomas L., ed. *Newport, Kentucky: A Bicentennial History*. Newport, Ky.: Otto Zimmerman, 1996.

Michael R. Sweeney

TRUCK FARMING. Truck farming was a popular profession in Northern Kentucky from the turn of the 20th century until the 1960s. Farmers would bring their crops to the urban areas of Newport and Covington to sell. At least as long ago as 1900, according to existing records, Northern Kentucky farmers met to discuss crop-growing and marketing issues in organizations such as the Campbell Co. Farmers' Club, the Kenton Co. Vegetable Growers Association, the Pickle Growers of Kenton Co., and the Tri-County Fruit Growers. An attraction in these meetings was often an extension agent from the University of Kentucky, who would explain the latest developments in farming, such as fertilizing and seed care.

In the 19th century, city markets featuring farmers' goods had been founded in major cities like Covington, Newport, and Cincinnati. In the 1920s there were farmers' stands along Philadelphia St. and along Scott St. in Covington, where farmers parked their horses and buggies (in later years their trucks) and sold their produce from the backs of their vehicles. This impromptu market continued on Saturday mornings for years. For daily trade, farmers would take their farm products to the Cincinnati Growers Market located along the Ohio River in Cincinnati. It was not uncommon for farmers to arrive at 3:00 a.m., their trucks loaded with the current crop. This location, known as the Bottoms, was just west of the Suspension Bridge. Commission produce houses such as Castellini's, which was founded in 1896, Caruso Inc., DeGaro, Flatow, Fries Brothers, Gentile Brothers, and Riley would buy large quantities of produce from the farmers and sell it directly to grocery stores and restaurant owners. These Ohio-based businesses, in which Northern Kentucky was much involved, thrived in this location for almost 100 years.

Kruempelmann Farm, Fort Mitchell, ca. 1970.

As subdivisions started popping up in suburbs, occasionally farmers would take their trucks to the suburbs or peddle produce from house to house. Newport had peddlers named Sanzenbacker and Torline. With the completion of I-75 in the early 1960s, customers drove to the country to buy produce directly from farmers. Truck farmers sometimes built market sheds to serve the customers who came to their farms. Ky. Rt. 8 in Boone Co. remains a popular weekend destination for many Northern Kentuckians and Cincinnatians, who purchase fresh fruits and vegetables from farming families such as the McGlassons and the Dolwicks. Kenton Co. truck farmers included the Kruempelmann and Kremer families.

The commission houses in Cincinnati were torn down in the 1990s to make room for Paul Brown Football Stadium and the reconfiguration of Fort Washington Way. The businesses either closed up completely at that time or moved outside the Cincinnati city limits. Robert Castellini moved his produce house to Wilder, along the Licking River in Campbell Co.

Today truck farmers are dwindling in numbers, although growers can find seasonal farmers' markets in each county to sell their produce. There is a farmers' market in Covington, for which officials are actively planning a more permanent facility. In nearby Cincinnati, historic Findlay Market in the Over-the-Rhine neighborhood has operated since 1852.

"Farmers' Schools—Growing of Truck Crops to Be Discussed before Kenton Countians," *KP*, March 3, 1931, 6.

"Fruit Growers Meeting in Kenton," *KTS*, August 2, 1957, 2A.

Kremer, Julie. Interview by Deborah Kremer, January 31, 2005, Villa Hills, Ky.

Maegley, Earl. Interview by Deborah Kremer, November 15, 2004, Villa Hills, Ky.

"Truck Growers Elect Officers," *KP*, March 9, 1931, 1.

Deborah Kohl Kremer

TRUE, ARNOLD ELLSWORTH, REAR ADMIRAL (b. January 23, 1901, Hallam, Owen Co., Ky.; d. December 11, 1979, Santa Clara, Calif.). Naval officer Arnold Ellsworth True, the son of L. D. and Nannie True, graduated from Owenton High School as class valedictorian in June 1917. True had hoped to attend law school, but his family's finances could not cover the costs of tuition, so he pursued an alternate path. He sat for a competitive entrance exam for the U.S. Naval Academy at Annapolis, Md., and scored well. He obtained an appointment to the academy as soon as he graduated from high school and left Kentucky for Maryland that fall.

True graduated from the Naval Academy in June 1920. Before **World War II**, he completed two tours of duty with the Asiatic Fleet and trained in aviation at Pensacola, Fla. He also worked as an officer for the *Shenandoah* and the *Los Angeles,* two zeppelins in service during the navy's short-lived experimentation with airships. In 1929 True completed postgraduate work at the Naval Academy in Aerology and went on to receive a MA in Meteorology from the Massachusetts Institute of Technology, Cambridge, Mass., in 1931. He then served as a meteorological officer at sea and at the Naval Operations Base in Hampton Roads, Va. He worked with the U.S. Weather Bureau to coordinate Pacific weather reporting, a joint project that paid dividends when the war erupted.

In 1939 True was given command of a newly built destroyer, the USS *Hammann.* Launched from the Brooklyn Navy Yard in August, the ship and its crew trained with the Pacific fleet at Pearl Harbor in 1940 and part of 1941. In May 1941, however, the *Hammann* was ordered to the Atlantic to aid in the transfer of lend-lease supplies to Great Britain. This move saved it from almost certain destruction in the Japanese attack on Pearl Harbor that December.

After the Pearl Harbor attack, the *Hammann* returned to the Pacific and quickly became indispensable, because few destroyers remained at that time. Its crew was instrumental in rescuing survivors from the USS *Lexington* at the Battle of the Coral Sea. On June 6, 1942, the *Hammann* itself was torpedoed and sunk while assisting the USS *Yorktown,* which had been disabled during the Battle of Midway. True refused to leave the sinking destroyer until all his surviving crew members were off the vessel. Because of his delay in abandoning ship, he was still nearby when depth charges exploded, causing him serious internal injury. When True was finally pulled from the sea, he was struggling to hold the heads of two enlisted men out of the water despite his own extensive injuries.

In December 1946, True left the navy on disability retirement. His promotion to rear admiral became effective that same month. After retirement he embarked on a second successful career as a professor of meteorology at San Jose State University at San Jose, Calif. He remained on the San Jose State faculty for the rest of his life and eventually attained the title of professor emeritus.

During the 1960s, True began to offend the navy hierarchy, some of his former academy classmates, and many fellow American citizens as well, when he spoke out against the **Vietnam War**. He was placed under government surveillance and threatened with court-martial, but he stood firm to his stated belief that U.S. policy in Vietnam ran counter to everything he had fought for during World War II. True's carefully researched writings and speeches led U.S. senator J. William Fulbright, chairman of the Senate Foreign Relations Committee, to achieve a change in military regulations so that retired navy personnel would be guaranteed freedom of speech on political matters.

In 1971 True was diagnosed with cancer. He declined chemotherapy and radiation in favor of alternative treatment involving the controversial drug laetrile. Despite doctors' dire predictions, he lived for seven years after his diagnosis in excellent health, continuing to write, travel, accept speaking engagements, and oversee the 1,000-acre cattle ranch he and his wife owned in California. His eventual death in 1979 was primarily attributed to complications from his earlier injuries on the *Hammann.* True was cremated, and his remains were interred with full military honors in Arlington National Cemetery at Arlington, Va. His numerous awards included the Purple Heart, the Navy Cross, the Distinguished Service Medal, the Victory Medal, and the Bronze Star. His papers are now housed in the Hoover Institute at Stanford University, Stanford, Calif.

Buzzanco, Robert. *Masters of War: Military Dissent and Politics in the Vietnam Era.* New York: Cambridge Univ. Press, 1997.

Houchens, Mariam Sidebottom. *History of Owen County: "Sweet Owen."* Louisville, Ky.: Standard, 1976.

Shaw, Norman W. *Arnold Ellsworth True: Destroyer Captain, Maverick Admiral.* Catskill, N.Y.: E and G Press, 1980.

Deborah Diersen Crocker

TRUESDELL, CHARLES B. (b. April 26, 1890, Fort Thomas, Ky.; d. January 3, 1966, Covington, Ky.). Charles Benjamin Truesdell, a Kentucky legislator, was born on his parents' farm near the **Fort Thomas Military Reservation** in what at the time was called the District of the Highlands. He was the son of William H. and Cynthia Anna Eplin Truesdell. Known as "C. B." or "Truesy" to his friends, he was from a long-established and prominent family in the Northern Kentucky region. Charles was educated in the Fort Thomas public schools and afterward attended the Campbell Commercial School in Cincinnati, where he studied banking and business law. He also attended Georgetown College in Georgetown, Ky. He became a lawyer and the Newport correspondent for the *Cincinnati Enquirer.* He was employed with the legal department of the Union Gas and Electric Company in Cincinnati. Politically, Truesdell was a Republican. He was elected a member of the Kentucky House of Representatives in 1919 and was reelected in 1921 and 1923. In 1921 he was appointed by Governor William J. Fields (1923–1927) as a delegate to attend the unveiling of a Henry Clay statue in Venezuela, celebrating the Panama Congress Sesquicentennial; he graciously declined the honor in favor of Clay's great-granddaughter. From 1924 to 1926, he served as a state senator and secured the passage of much important legislation: the bill creating the Kentucky State Parks Commission, the blind pension bill, the bill that eliminated railroad grade crossings, the bill empowering county clerks to issue automobile licenses at more than one place in a county, and the bill that brought about the building of the **Mary Ingles Highway**. Other legislation that he wrote included a bill that dealt with the registering of nurses in Kentucky, the original Police and Fireman Pension Fund Act, and a bill prohibiting companies from dumping waste into the Ohio River. Truesdell also assisted in drafting the bill creating the Kentucky State Highway Commission. He sponsored the bill that made Alexandria Pk. a state and federal highway, **U.S. 27**. In 1932 he was an alternate delegate to the Republican National Convention in Chicago. Truesdell was very interested in improving education in the state, and he served on the Committee for Education while in the Kentucky legislature. In 1920 he secured the passage of a bill raising Fort Thomas from a sixth-class to a fourth-class city, thereby paving the way for the city of Fort Thomas to take the lead in education. As a result, **Highlands High School** remains a top-ranked school in the state. An avid historian, Truesdell was a founding member of the **Christopher Gist Historical Society** and the Northern Kentucky Historical Society. He was instrumental in obtaining historical markers for various historical landmarks throughout the state. He used his political influence to advocate for the expansion of the new airport in Boone Co., which is today's **Cincinnati/Northern Kentucky International Airport**. Truesdell stands as one of Northern Kentucky's most influential and leading statesmen. In his later years, he switched to membership in the Democratic Party, because it was becoming difficult to win elected office as a Republican in Campbell Co. at the time. His wife of 40 years, Estella Josephine Ulmer Truesdell, died in May 1965, and Charles B. Truesdell died the next year at William Booth Memorial Hospital in Covington. He was laid to rest at the Alexandria Cemetery in Alexandria.

Bodley, Temple. *History of Kentucky: The Blue Grass State.* Vol. 4. Chicago: S. J. Clarke, 1928.

"Lawmaker Truesdell Dies," *KP,* January 3, 1966, 1.

Southard, Mary Young, and Ernest C. Miller, eds. *Who's Who in Kentucky: A Biographical Assembly of Notable Kentuckians.* Louisville, Ky.: Standard, 1936.

Robin Caraway

TRUESDELL, HELEN (b. December 6, 1820, Fayette Co., Ohio; d. July 23, 1911, Brodhead, Wis.). Poet Helen Truesdell was the daughter of Judge Wade Hampton and Mary Pancoast Loofbourrow. She was a direct descendant of Anne Bradstreet, who was considered to be the first Anglo-American poet of merit in the early American colonies. At an early age, Helen showed a remarkable talent for poetry. She regularly contributed poems to *Parlor Magazine,* the *Ladies' Repository,* and other periodicals. In 1838 she married prominent Virginian Edmund Le Wright, in Fayette Co., Ohio. He drowned several months after their marriage, and Helen poured her heartbreak into verse, composing many poems during this period. In 1839 she married John E. Truesdell, a prestigious newspaper editor from nearby Wilmington, Ohio. Truesdell died in 1852. Helen was a friend of the Smalley family of Newport; she wrote and dedicated a poem to Mrs. Smalley. In 1853 Helen's poems were assembled and published in a book, *Poems by Mrs. Helen Truesdell.* Praised for its high poetic merit, it sold successfully. She continued to work on another book, *Tales for My Pets.* In 1854 she wrote the lyrics to "Away with the Past," a song whose music was composed by the renowned musician George Washbourne Morgan. Helen lived in Newport in 1856 when her book of poetry was being published in its fifth edition. Her literary attainments brought her much recognition.

In 1859 Helen married Peter Harris in Nashville, Tenn., and they moved to Brodhead, Wis., to be close to relatives. Helen was highly regarded as a writer. During the **Civil War**, she devoted her literary energies to promoting the Union cause. Peter Harris died in 1883, leaving her widowed a third time. Her remaining years were spent advocating for church and humanitarian causes. Helen Loofbourrow Le Wright Truesdell Harris died in 1911 at age 90, at the home of her sister in Brodhead, and was buried at Greenwood Cemetery in Monroe, Wis.

Collins, Richard H. *History of Kentucky.* Vol. 1. Covington, Ky.: Collins, 1882.

"Death of Mrs. Helen Harris," *Green Co. (Wis.) Independent-Register*, July 26, 1911, 1.

"Mrs. Helen Harris," *Green Co. (Wis.) Independent-Register*, August 2, 1911, 1.

Truesdell, Helen. *Poems by Mrs. Helen Truesdell.* 12th ed. Cincinnati: E. Morgan, 1859.

Robin Caraway

TRUESVILLE. In the mid-19th century, three brothers, George William True, John White True, and Silas W. True, moved from Spotsylvania, Va., into a sparsely settled area along Cedar Creek in southern Owen Co. In 1850 the brothers began to clear the land and till the soil to earn their livelihood. As in most of Kentucky, tobacco was the cash crop, but corn, grains, fruit trees, and vegetables were grown for personal use and barter. The families were semi-isolated by the local topography of hills, hollows, and streams and by the traditionally poor quality of the 19th-century roads.

As the population increased, a small farming community came into existence, which came to be known as Truesville because of the many members of the True family living there. The growing local demand for manufactured goods spurred Silas True to open and operate a general store. By November 16, 1876, the federal government appointed Silas as postmaster and his store served as the post office. The Truesville post office operated until June 30, 1951.

In the 1850s, a one-room school was built to educate residents' children. The Poe School served the community until 1938, when it was closed because there were too few school-age children. Truesville's remaining five school-age students were transported to Peaks Mill in Franklin Co. for their education.

Over time, several trades sprang up in the community. Andrew "Andy" Hodson owned and operated a gristmill on Cedar Creek from 1871 until his death in 1901. He ground corn into meal and grains into feed for human and livestock consumption. John Rodgers was working as a wheelwright in 1870, and Ronald Henry operated a blacksmith shop in 1880. These trades and others were short-lived, because the community was not large enough to support full-time tradesmen. However, there was a need for part-time tradesmen; for example, Vernon "Scratch" True was both a farmer and a part-time blacksmith who shod horses and mules between 1910 and 1950.

The Old Cedar Baptist Church, also in southern Owen Co., met the hamlet's early spiritual needs. Then in 1865 the Trues and several other families began to hold church services in the Poe School House. In August 1872, they appealed for help in establishing a church, and the Old Cedar Church pastor, John Alfred Head, led a church committee to help organize a church. By September 1872, the Mount Vernon Baptist Church was constituted and had adopted the Philadelphia confession of faith of the Baptist belief. The first pastor was Thomas Burton, and the first church clerk was James White True, who served until James Luther True replaced him in 1883. The church became a member of the Franklin Co. Baptist Association in 1873. Between 1873 and 1886, the Mount Vernon church sent representatives to the annual meetings of the association. During this period a church was built on a ridge near the Owen-Franklin Co. line. After a fire in about 1935 destroyed the church and its records, the meetinghouse was rebuilt in 1936. From 1936 to the present, the church and the adjoining cemetery continue to serve the area. The Mount Vernon Baptist Church was the only church organized in Truesville's history.

The growing adult population of the community could not be supported by agribusiness, and no other large business existed to employ the expanding workforce. Thus, Truesville's population began to decline after 1910. High-paying jobs in Ohio and Indiana drew many residents away. Asphalt roads, affordable automotive transportation, out-migration, declining farm prices, and other social and economic issues led to Truesville's demise. Today, only a few farm families live there.

Murphy, Margaret Alice, and Lela Maude Hawkins. *The History of Historic Old Cedar Baptist Church and Community, 1816–2004.* Frankfort, Ky.: Lynn, 2004.

Margaret A. Murphy

TUBERCULOSIS. This disease, commonly known as TB, was a public health problem in early Northern Kentucky especially for persons who lived in protected settlements or one-room homes, where family members were easily exposed to one another's cough. Tuberculosis has, in fact, plagued humankind for all of recorded time. Some ancient Egyptian mummies have shown evidence of tuberculosis infection. There are several forms of TB, but the public health nemesis is *Mycobacterium tuberculosis*, a bacterium that grows slowly. It also lingers in a dormant fashion, able to awaken when the body's defenses are down.

TB almost always invades the body through the lungs, in the form of infectious balls called granulomas. These can progress to destroy surrounding lung tissue and cause cavities. From there, the infection can spread in the bloodstream to many other organs, including the bones and the brain. The lung disease results in a chronic cough, which constitutes a public health nightmare, since the airborne droplets contain TB and can easily be inhaled by others within close range. Thus the disease spreads.

Once considered a leading cause of death, TB became an important public health issue as cities grew in population and density. The tuberculosis organism cannot live outside the body for long; in order for it to spread, the cough droplets must be inhaled into other lungs before they become dry. The infectious etiology was not understood until the 1800s. The disease had many names; one was "consumption." Probably not everyone diagnosed with this malady actually had TB. The nonspecific manifestations were usually chronic fatigue and weight loss, accompanied by a cough. TB often caused a bloody cough and a fever, along with night sweats.

As Northern Kentucky became urbanized, TB grew into a constant public health issue. Soldiers or workers were vulnerable in long-term camps and in close-quarter hospitals. No age group was safe. Children often contracted the illness from staying close to their parents or from sleeping in the same room as an infected parent. It was not until the 1850s that isolation of patients in sanatoriums was first proposed, and the first U.S. sanatorium opened in the 1880s. In Northern Kentucky, patients were isolated only by the command of their doctors, often in their homes. Strict bed rest was enforced, not only to prevent the organism from spreading but also to limit deep breathing and thus prevent the bacterium from obtaining oxygen. Physicians performed surgery to collapse the lung so that the TB would be contained, buying time for the immune system to fight the bacterium while it was starved for oxygen.

The public health efforts to eradicate TB in Northern Kentucky were originally aimed at community education, spearheaded by the Anti-Tuberculosis League, which was founded by the efforts of Dr. Robert Carlton in the early 1900s. That organization opened a free chest X-ray/TB screening clinic in 1933. In spite of a crusade starting in 1916, Northern Kentucky's original isolation structure was not opened until 1937. This sanatorium was located in Fort Wright, in the facility formerly known as the "pest house." Various diseases were isolated there, and it was commonly thought that when a patient went into the pest house, he or she would never come out. In 1945 Kentucky was experiencing the third-highest death rate from tuberculosis in the nation.

The era of the modern tuberculosis sanatorium was ushered in by Dr. Charles J. Farrell (1901–1977), a TB specialist who staffed an X-ray TB clinic in his medical office, at 10th St. and Madison Ave. in Covington. Farrell was a graduate of St. Xavier High School in Cincinnati, and he received his MD from the University of Cincinnati in 1929. He relentlessly lobbied for the 1947 county levy that funded the Covington–Kenton Co. TB Sanatorium, at the site of the pest house off Kyles Ln. in Fort Wright. Previously, there had been talk of the state's building one of six proposed tuberculosis hospitals in Northern Kentucky, but the nearest facility was awarded to the Paris, Ky., area. The Kyles Ln. facility provided state-of-the-art isolation and on-site laboratory procedures, surgical treatment, and nursing care. Patients would often stay for months until their TB was dormant or cured. The new $600,000 four-level brick hospital received its first 17 patients on April 15, 1951, with Farrell as superintendent. The patients were residents of the old pest house at that site. The new hospital was a project of architect Howard McClorey.

In the middle of the 20th century, effective drug treatment emerged for TB. Active cases required multiple drugs to eradicate the organism and prevent the emergence of resistant strains. The long-term infectious threat diminished, the need for TB sanatoriums vanished, and the Covington–Kenton Co. TB hospital closed in 1979, two years following the death of Farrell. He had retired in 1976. The former TB facility is now a psychiatric hospital operated by **NorthKey**. The access road, formerly Sanitarium Dr., has been renamed Farrell Dr. after the sanatorium's founder.

TB remains a public health issue, but not on the scale of a century ago. The AIDS epidemic has caused a reemergence of several types of TB. All health care workers and others exposed to an active case of TB receive a skin test to see whether they have been infected, and if the test is positive, they are treated or monitored to avoid the emergence of active disease.

Bell, Mary Kathryn. "History of Tuberculosis, Called T.B. in Northern Ky.," Kenton Co. Public Library, Covington, Ky.

"The Case for Saving Our TB Hospital," *KP*, January 14, 1966, 8K.

"Dr. Farrell, Retired Founder of TB Hospital, Dies at 76," *KP*, June 8, 1977, 1.

"New Hospital to Be Erected for $600,000," *KP*, March 26, 1949, 1.

"State Is Third in Tuberculosis Deaths in U.S." *KP*, November 19, 1945, 1.

"State to Put Hospital on Site at Paris," *KP*, February 16, 1945, 1.

"TB Hospital Here Wins State Praise," *KP*, November 31, 1955, 1.

James Farrell

Opening day at the new Latonia Racecourse, Florence, August 27, 1959. Governor "Happy" Chandler is second from the left.

TURFWAY PARK RACECOURSE. From fall 1959 until spring 1986, the horse-racing track in Northern Kentucky located in Florence was named Latonia. It was the second racecourse in Northern Kentucky known as the **Latonia Racecourse** (the first, which was open from 1883 to 1939, was in Covington). The Florence track properties were sold on April 9, 1986, to Jerry Carroll and James Thornton and renamed Turfway Park. Thornton was a successful Central Kentucky businessman involved in several enterprises, the foremost being Thornton Oil, a chain of filling stations–convenience stores scattered throughout Kentucky. Carroll, who had grown up outside Aurora, Ind., had founded a realty company in 1972, a firm that became the most successful developer of commercial properties in Nashville, Tenn. Carroll bought 363 acres in Florence during the 1980s that he intended to develop for commercial uses. The proximity of these properties to the Latonia Racecourse, coupled with Carroll's interest in horse racing, led him to form a partnership with Thornton to purchase Latonia from its owners, the Delaware North Corporation. Once the sale had been completed, it was agreed that Delaware North would operate the track through the Spring Meet of 1986, after which it would be turned over to the new owners and become Turfway Park. In the time between the track's spring and fall meets, the new owners spent $2 million on improvements. Turfway ran its first race on September 3, 1986, the Fall Meet's opening day. It soon became clear, however, that Thornton and Carroll had opposing views on how to operate the business. Carroll, who had a larger stake in Turfway's success because it was tied to his plans to develop commercial properties nearby, put together a new partnership in August 1987 and he and his partners purchased all of Turfway for $18.2 million. This left Carroll, now the majority interest holder, in charge.

Carroll moved quickly to convert Turfway Park into a modern-day state-of-the-art racing facility. One of his first moves was to hire a capable local banker, Mark Simendinger, as the track's chief financial officer. Carroll could then focus on shedding his track's image of being an outmoded small-time race plant. Earlier, he had converted the track's biggest race, the Jim Beam Stakes, from a Grade III $350,000 race into a Grade II $500,000 event. In 1993, when the purse was raised to $600,000, the Jim Beam Stakes was on its way to becoming momentarily the top-money prep race leading up to the Kentucky Derby. Also by 1993 Carroll had wrested control of the Spring Spiral Festival, which was tied to the race, from a local committee and had begun to stamp his own mark on the festivities associated with the race. There followed a remarkable run during the 1990s that saw Jim Beam champions win each of the Triple Crown races (Summer Squall, the 1990 Preakness; Hansel, the 1991 Preakness and Belmont; Lil E. Tee, the 1992 Kentucky Derby; and Prairie Bayou, the 1993 Preakness). In addition, three Beam Champions (Summer Squall, 1990; Prairie Bayou, 1993; and filly-champ Serena's Song, 1995) won Champion Horse Eclipse awards. In 1998 the Jim Beam Distillers dropped sponsorship of the Turfway race, a new one-year sponsor signed up for 1999, and the race became the Gallery Furniture.com Stakes. For the next two years, the race had no outside sponsor and was run as the Turfway Spiral Stakes in 2000 and 2001 and the Spiral/Lane's End Stakes in 2002. Stability returned to Turfway's top race in 2003 when Lane's End Farm of Versailles, Ky., became the full sponsor of what has become the Lane's End Stakes. The success story of Turfway's top race had an impact industry-wide as older Derby-prep races like the prestigious Bluegrass Stakes (now the Toyota Bluegrass Stakes) at Keeneland Racecourse in Lexington, and even the Kentucky Derby in Louisville, found corporate sponsors and competitively raised their purses.

Under Carroll, Turfway made a mark throughout the industry when on December 28, 1994, the Race Book, a first of its kind (and soon copied) simulcasting wagering operation, was opened. Simulcasting and betting on races from as far away as Australia is now a common way for racetracks and other betting venues to increase revenues. The success of Turfway's Race Book and the rise of its top race came under the stress of nationwide competition by the year 1999, and Carroll sold the track on January 15, 1999, to a partnership made up of the Keeneland Association, Dreamport (a division of the GTECH Corporation), and Harrah's Entertainment. Together with a new group of investors, Carroll built the **Kentucky Speedway** LLC near Sparta, an ultramodern auto- and truck-racing facility designed to attract a NASCAR Racing Circuit event. In 2006 GTECH sold its interest in Turfway Park to the other two investors. Although the Lane's End Stakes draws crowds exceeding 20,000 and is televised on ESPN, since the new owners took over, Turfway has struggled to make a profit and to keep and expand its fan base. Mindful of the need to attract new people to the track who might become fans, Turfway has made its facilities available to local groups for special events and meetings. The track has also tried several special promotions, including live-music performances, radio-sponsored promotions, and giving away such things as track calendars, hats, and souvenir drinking glasses. The most successful promotion, and one that has been expanding exponentially, is to cater to younger patrons on Friday nights by offering them a gathering place on one of the track's upper floors where they can listen to bands, participate in contests and games, purchase dollar beers and hot dogs, and make affordable bets on races, including the popular new 10-cent superfecta wager, which involves picking the horses to finish in exact one-two-three-four order. Another successful promotion at Turfway is called Fast Track. Bettors present a personalized numbered plastic card whenever they bet and build up point credits that can be cashed in for such things as free programs, food, souvenirs, or even wagering vouchers. These cards also allow the track to contact bettors who have failed to cash winning tickets, which are sometimes lost or overlooked, and issue cash vouchers to replace the tickets; this unique service at Turfway has drawn national attention, interest, and publicity. Recently Turfway has completed a multimillion-dollar facilities makeover that features such things as a totally revamped paddock and saddling area, a new gift shop, and modernized track food facilities. And true to its traditions, the track once again was on the industry's cutting edge when in 2005 Turfway became the first track in North America to convert its racing surface to Polytrack, a synthetic material that allows racing to be conducted even in extreme weather. Other North American tracks, including parent-owner Keeneland, have followed Turfway's lead and converted to Polytrack racing surfaces. Several states now allow racetracks to have slot machines, video poker, and live poker games on their premises. Tracks in these states have therefore become entertainment destinations featuring hotels, live performances, restaurants, and shopping. Currently, such gaming is prohibited at Kentucky racetracks, but since Harrah Entertainment is a half owner at Turfway, and since the track is located in populous Greater Cincinnati, the passage of gaming legislation in Kentucky would most certainly lead to similar developmental capital expenditures by Harrah's at Turfway Park. Finally, in recent years Turfway has become a proving ground for several talented young riders: female jockey Chris Prather, Rafael Bejarano, and Julian Leparoux have set meet records for wins. However, these achievements have been tempered by a career-ending injury to Prather and Michael Rowland's death on February 9, 2004, from injuries sustained while riding at Turfway.

Claypool, James C. *The Tradition Continues: The Story of Old Latonia, Latonia, and Turfway Racecourses.* Fort Mitchell, Ky.: T. I. Hayes, 1997.

James C. Claypool

TURNER, JOHN W. (b. June 5, 1939, Houston, Breathitt Co., Ky.). Basketball-player John W. Turner is the son of John W. Langley and Ellen McIntosh Turner. In 1943 the Turner family moved to Northern Kentucky and John grew up in the **West End** of Newport, attending Newport public schools. He became one of the greatest athletes ever to graduate from **Newport High School** (1957). While there, John earned All-State honors in both football (as an end) and basketball (as a center and a forward). He received several college offers in both sports. Upon graduation the six-foot-five Turner chose the University of Louisville, where he played from 1958 to 1961 under coach Peck Hickman. In his senior year at the University of Louisville, he received All-American honors. Turner went on to play for the Chicago Packers in the National Basketball Association after college. Following his professional basketball career, he played for a basketball team sponsored by baseball's Cincinnati Reds, while working locally for Frisch's restaurants and the Alco Door Company. He is a member of the Northern Kentucky Sports Hall of Fame and the University of Louisville's Athletic Hall of Fame. Turner is retired and lives in Newport.

Louisville. http://uoflsports.cstv.com/ (accessed April 5, 2007).
"Newport's Turner Chosen All-State," *KTS,* March 26, 1956, 3A.
Schmidt, Neil. "Kentucky Sports—Turner Honored," *KE,* January 26, 1957, C6.

Michael R. Sweeney

TURNER, ULYS R. "RED" (b. March 17, 1916, Middlesboro, Ky.; d. September 6, 1995, Covington, Ky.). Red Turner, a **country music** performer and a Baptist minister, was the son of James Franklin and Sofa Jane Rose Turner of Bell Co., Ky. Friends said that Turner seemed to be born with musical talent, and he always dreamed of becoming a professional musician. He mastered the banjo, the fiddle, the piano, and the rhythm guitar, in spite of never having taken a music lesson. Turner married Emma Munday on August 25, 1936, and they had two children. He began his musical career singing over Cincinnati radio station WLW, shortly after **World War II**. In 1948 he began performing with the *Renfro Valley Barn Dance* show, which aired on WLW from Cincinnati's Music Hall during its first year and from Memorial Auditorium in Dayton, Ohio, its second year. The show then moved to its permanent home in a large barn at Renfro Valley, Ky. Also in 1948, Turner joined the cast of WLW's *Midwestern Hayride,* which was a popular local show during the late 1940s and early 1950s. He and his brother Lige became local television celebrities, singing and playing country music while performing comedy routines. Red also made some country gospel recordings at King Records in Cincinnati, with Grandpa Jones and the Delmore Brothers, as part of the group *Brown's Ferry Four.* Turner was later inducted into the Renfro Valley Hall of Fame, and his favorite guitar was placed on permanent display there. After retiring from show business, Turner became an evangelist. He spoke at numerous churches in the Greater Cincinnati area and founded the Covington Baptist Temple, at 1813 Holman St. in Covington, where he served as pastor for 17 years. He was an avid golfer, often playing with fellow preachers. He spent his later years as a member of the Northern Kentucky Baptist Church in Lakeside Park. Turner died at age 79 in the Garrard Street Convalescent Home, Covington, and was buried in the Forest Lawn Cemetery in Erlanger.

"Red Turner, TV Musician, Founded Church," *KP,* September 7, 1995, 14A.
"Rev. Turner," *KTS,* July 20, 1956, 2A.
Turner, James Franklin, son of Red Turner. Interview by Jack Wessling, May 5, 2006, Cold Spring, Ky.
Wolfe, Charles K. *Classic Country: Legends of Country Music.* New York, N.Y.: Routledge, 2001.

TURNER RIDGE BAPTIST CHURCH. Delegates from several different area churches met to establish the Turner Ridge Baptist Church of Christ in the Pendleton Co. community of Turner Ridge on December 11, 1875. Many people in the community were members of churches located as far away as 10 miles, and they wanted to have a local church in order to avoid traveling under the difficult conditions of the time. Surviving minutes indicate the charter members as Samuel E., Annie Elizabeth, and Missouri DeCoursey from the Short Creek Baptist Church (see **Short Creek/Goforth**). During the first year there were 23 people added to the church roll. The church met for its first 18 years at the old Turner Ridge School House that once stood at the site of the present Turner Ridge Cemetery. In the early years, meetings were held once a month on Saturday morning and evening and Sunday morning. Subsequently, the church has occupied three separate buildings.

The first building was a small frame church built in 1893, located on a tract of land previously owned by Abraham Turner. A portion of the present cemetery occupies this site today. During this time, the Sunday School was under the direction of James Mockabee. By about 1899 the church minutes started using the name Turner Ridge Baptist Church. There was no church cemetery in those early days; people were buried on farms in family plots. In 1894 the church obtained a tract of land for a cemetery from a man named Sargent, and some of the church's first members were buried there.

In 1913 Elisa Sharp entered into a contract to build the second new building for the church. The 1893 church building was rolled to the back of the lot, to be used while the new church was being built. After the new church was completed, the old one was sold to Bob Adams, who used the lumber and the windows of the church to build two of the downstairs rooms in a house located on Turner Ridge Rd. The house remains today on the property of Ruth Miller.

In 1925 the old pulpit stand was replaced by one donated by the Falmouth Lutheran Church, which had dissolved its membership. The third Turner Ridge Baptist Church building was built in 1950 on a five-acre tract about a quarter mile from the cemetery, at the corner of Ky. Rt. 22 and Fooks Rd. The property was purchased from the heirs of William Fookes.

Belew, Mildred Boden. *The First 200 Years of Pendleton County.* Falmouth, Ky.: M. B. Belew, n.d. [ca. 1994].

Mildred Belew

TURNPIKES, CAMPBELL CO. During the 19th century, the Kentucky legislature chartered private companies to build turnpikes linking the farm communities of the rural southern two-thirds of Campbell Co. with Newport and its surrounding population centers in the north part of the county. The turnpikes opened markets for farm products and provided access to government offices at both of the county's seats, Newport and Alexandria. Thus, most roads outside the cities became privately owned. Ideally, the turnpikes would have had a right-of-way 60 feet wide, a macadamized roadway (that is, paved with stones and covered with crushed stone for a smooth surface) about 15 feet wide, and drainage ditches on each side. In reality, the turnpikes were often unpaved dirt, which became a quagmire in wet weather, and so narrow that it was difficult for two wagons to pass each other. Turnpike owners could charge tolls for the use of their roads, but the state legislature regulated the toll amounts. Generally, a tollhouse and tollgate could be erected every five miles. An extra tollgate could be added at a bridge whose construction and upkeep were more expensive. Because the turnpike construction business was at times a perilous economic venture, many of the chartered roads were never built. Successor companies were chartered, and many turnpikes bore several names through the years.

The Campbell Turnpike Road Company was chartered on February 17, 1846, to build a 12-mile turnpike from Newport to Alexandria to replace that section of the old state road authorized in 1818 to run from Newport to Cynthiana in Harrison Co. and extended to Winchester in Clark Co. in 1837. The Campbell Turnpike (now **U.S. 27**) became the backbone of the county's road grid.

Along the Ohio River border on the east side of the county, the **Twelve Mile Turnpike**, chartered on March 1, 1854, traversed 12 miles from the Campbell Turnpike in the Highlands (Fort Thomas) to Twelve Mile, where the New Richmond, Ohio, ferry docked at Oneonta, Ky. The Dayton and Four Mile Road Company turnpike connected Dayton, Ky., with the Twelve Mile Turnpike, where the latter left the river and turned west to reach the Highlands. Completing the eastern border was the Newport and Dayton Turnpike Road Company's gravel turnpike and its bridge over Taylor's Creek, connecting Newport and Dayton.

On the western border along the Licking River, the Newport, Licking, and Alexandria Turnpike Company eventually linked Finchtown (just north of Wilder) with Alexandria, a distance of 12 miles. Several turnpikes were chartered to join southern Campbell Co.'s rural communities with Alexandria. The Alexandria and Persimmon Grove Turnpike covered the 5 miles between those two towns in 1865–1866; the Alexandria and Flagg Spring Turnpike, 11 miles, was completed in 1884; the Alexandria and Melbourne Turnpike in 1891; and the Old State Road and the Ripple Creek Turnpike as well as the Alexandria and Licking Turnpike joined Alexandria with separate points on the Ripple Creek Turnpike.

Smaller turnpikes connected communities in southern Campbell Co.: the California, Gubser Mill, and Old State Road Turnpike; the California and Twelve Mile Turnpike; the Grants Lick and Old State Road Turnpike; the Grants Lick Turnpike; and the Claryville, Grants Lick, and Butler Turnpike from Claryville to Alexandria, with connections to the Old State Road Turnpike and to Braysville on the Grant's Lick Turnpike. Two turnpikes, the Twelve Mile and Persimmon Grove and the Belmont and Flagg Springs, ran from the Ohio River inland. Several planned turnpikes, such as the Campbell and Pendleton County, the Alexandria and Pendleton County, and the Alexandria and Tibbatts Cross Roads, were never completed.

The population centers in the middle of the county were also connected. For example, the Four Mile Turnpike (later the Four and Twelve Mile Turnpike) covered the 8 miles from the Twelve Mile Turnpike at Brent to the Alexandria and Flagg Spring Turnpike at Brush Creek near Carthage. Cold Spring and Claryville were joined by the Ripple Creek Turnpike.

Connector turnpikes were also prevalent in the northern end of Campbell Co. The Jamestown (Dayton) Pike, chartered on March 1, 1854, ran 5.25 miles from that town through the Highlands to meet the Campbell Turnpike where the Samuel Woodfill School now stands. The Covert Run Turnpike, 1.5 miles long, began at a tollhouse gate at Taylor Ave. in Bellevue and terminated at the Jamestown Pike (today's N. Fort Thomas Ave.). Access to Newport from the Bellevue end of the pike was by a pontoon bridge over Duck Creek to Sixth St., or over Taylor Ave. to today's Cowens Dr. (previously Riverside Dr.). The Campbell Turnpike, at the current **St. Therese Catholic Church** in Southgate, was connected to the Jamestown Pike in the Highland's central business district by the Highland Turnpike in 1878. Finally, in 1888, the legislature chartered **Samuel Bigstaff**'s Grand Avenue Turnpike to run from Waterworks Rd. (previously Reservoir Rd.) and E. 10th St. in Newport, through the Highlands, to intersect with the Jamestown Pike where Grand now meets S. Fort Thomas Ave. One of the purposes of this road was to give the newly established **Fort Thomas Military Reservation** in the Highlands direct and quick access to Newport. It also opened the Highlands to development, as the incorporators of the turnpike owned much of the land through which the road ran. The Grand Avenue Turnpike was meant to be an extension of the **Cote Brilliante** and Ingalls Park (Park, Chesapeake, and Ohio Aves.) developments adjacent to Newport. A 100-foot-wide right-of-way was designated for the turnpike in the Highlands, still evident today where homes in Fort Thomas sit far back from the street, namely on Grand Ave; through Newport the right-of-way was just 60 feet wide.

By the late 19th century, farmers were demanding free access to the population centers, and as automobile use began and increased, drivers called for elimination of the tollgates. Judge **Albert Seaton Berry** vowed to make the roads free; the Newport Business Men's Club also backed the free road movement. In response, the Kentucky legislature eventually authorized counties to purchase the turnpikes and eliminate the tolls, but county budgets often prevented doing so. Reactions ranged from fund-raising drives to help the county buy the toll roads to destruction of tollgates by masked men and threats against tollgate keepers. By 1916 there were only 60 miles of road on which tolls were still being collected in Campbell Co. Many of the turnpike companies had previously lost their charters for failure to maintain the roads, and the roads themselves were forfeited. Other turnpike owners merely abandoned their roads to the county. The remaining 60 miles were appraised, and on August 16, 1916, four turnpikes were purchased by the county for their estimated values: Licking Turnpike plus Ripple Creek Turnpike, $17,000; Old State Road Turnpike, $7,750; and Twelve Mile Turnpike, $19,300. Some turnpike owners held out and received higher sale prices. For example, Four and Twelve Mile Turnpike brought $14,000, and Grants Lick Turnpike, $5,000; both were purchased in August 1919. When a group named the Campbell County Good Roads Association was formed on December 16, 1921, additional pressure was applied to free the last turnpikes. June 7, 1922, saw the county's purchase of the Campbell Turnpike for $80,000 and the Grand Avenue Turnpike for $10,000. Finally, on December 18, 1923, the Covert Run Turnpike, the last toll road in the county, was purchased for $2,500, only $900 more than the 1916 estimated value. Thus ended the 100-year turnpike era in Campbell Co. In contrast to other sections of the commonwealth of Kentucky, Northern Kentucky received no modern state-built turnpike toll roads during the mid-20th-century years of interstate road building.

An Atlas of Boone, Kenton, and Campbell Counties, Kentucky. Philadelphia: D. J. Lake, 1883.

Campbell Co. Historical Society. *Campbell County, Kentucky, 200 Years, 1794–1994.* Alexandria, Ky.: Campbell Co. Historical Society, 1994.

Reis, Jim. "Down with the Toll Gates!" *KP,* July 13, 1998, 4K.

——. *Pieces of the Past.* Vol. 2. Covington: Kentucky Post, 1991.

Truesdell, C. B. "Early Turnpikes Which Led to and from the Newport-Covington Area," *Papers of the Christopher Gist Historical Society* 4 (1952–1953): 23–38.

Venable, Robert Michael. *Will and Gus.* Fort Thomas, Ky.: Privately published, 2002.

Robert Michael Venable

TWELVE MILE TURNPIKE. On March 1, 1854, the Kentucky legislature passed "An Act to Incorporate the Twelve Mile Turnpike Co.," authorizing the company to build a toll road from the mouth of Twelve Mile Creek at the Ohio River in eastern Campbell Co. to Metcalfe's Hotel on the Campbell Turnpike, a distance of about 12 miles. The main purpose for the turnpike was to enable farmers to visit the rural county seat of Alexandria, as well as to transport their crops to urban centers in the county, including the urban county seat of Newport. Using modern-day names, the turnpike began at Oneonta, on Ky. Rt. 8, the **Mary Ingles Highway**, where the New Richmond, Ohio, ferry docked. The road ran west to where I-275 currently crosses the Ohio River to California, Ohio (Coney Island). There it snaked up the hill to Fort Thomas, Ky., then known as The Highlands. Crossing S. Fort Thomas Ave., the turnpike dropped down a hill to intersect with the Campbell Turnpike at the place where Grandview Ave. now meets Alexandria Pk.

The original directors of the road-building corporation were J. W. Albert, **George B. Hodge**, William Clark. F. Dickey, H. T. Harris, George W. Jones, **Thomas L. Jones**, John Thomas, and George Ward. The company leased the Twelve Mile Turnpike to others to pave and manage. The building of the road did not begin until about 1858, and progress was extremely slow. It was going to be both difficult and expensive to bridge the Four Mile Creek at Brent, so the state legislature, on January 22, 1867, amended the corporate charter to make the bridge a toll bridge. Tolls paid for crossing the bridge were to be in addition to the tolls for use of the turnpike itself. It was not until April 27, 1867, that completion of the Twelve Mile Turnpike was actually assured. On that date the company contracted with partners William Wilmer and Cornelius Willison of Brent to finish construction of the road, to build a new bridge over Four Mile Creek, and to maintain and operate the turnpike. In return, Wilmer and Willison became major stockholders in the company and were entitled to all tolls for the term of the contract. Wilmer, age 41, was a farmer who had immigrated in 1848 from Prussia. He became the actual manager of the turnpike. The road and the new Four Mile Creek Bridge were completed in a timely fashion, with the road shortened by two miles and ending at Ten Mile Creek instead of Twelve Mile Creek. The roadbed was macadamized, that is, covered with compressed crushed stone. Tollhouses and gates were located at the intersection of present-day River Rd. and S. Fort Thomas Ave., at the Four Mile Creek Bridge, and at the five-mile mark within Melbourne.

The Wilmer/Willison partnership was dissolved on May 20, 1881, and Wilmer became sole operator of the turnpike. Throughout the existence of the Twelve Mile Turnpike, the company and its leaseholders were involved in numerous suits over rights-of-way, mortgage debt, and disputes with railroads—notably one suit against the Maysville & Big Sandy Railroad Company for diverting the waters of Four Mile Creek in such a way as to endanger the integrity of the turnpike's bridge at that location. In addition, residents along the turnpike often complained of road conditions and the "high" tolls, which were actually set by the state legislature. Moreover, the Four Mile Creek Bridge was subject to periodic flooding and had to be repaired or replaced several times. Nevertheless, it appears that William Wilmer's 28 years of operating the Twelve Mile Turnpike were a financial success for him and provided a quality roadway for his customers until his death on March 18, 1895. In the ensuing years, the turnpike fell into disrepair, and residents and automobile enthusiasts called for the elimination of the tollgates. That did not occur until the county purchased the road for $19,300 on August 22, 1916. Collection of tolls ended on September 16, 1916. By March 1925, the Ky. Rt. 8 section of the turnpike had been rebuilt by the state and was later dedicated as the **Mary Ingles Highway**.

Original corporate records of the Twelve Mile Turnpike Company, archival collection of Robert Michael Venable, Fort Thomas, Ky.

Papers and correspondence of Wilhelm (a.k.a. William) Wilmer, archival collection of Robert Michael Venable, Fort Thomas, Ky.

Venable, Robert Michael, *Will and Gus.* Fort Thomas, Ky.: Privately published, 2002.

Robert Michael Venable

TWIN OAKS GOLF COURSE. This championship golf course owes its existence to the creative vision of a group of prominent local businessmen led by **Harvey Myers Jr.** It was designed by Arthur G. Lockwood, one of the most prominent golf course architects in the United States. The course began as a 140-acre site, 6,600 yards in length; it extends almost a mile along the Licking River in the Rosedale section of Covington, at 43rd St. and Michigan Ave. Numerous old oak and elm trees grow on the beautiful property, which offers an unobstructed view of the river. A nonprofit corporation was established for administering the course, and about 65 charter members purchased stock. The initial list included **Stephens Blakely**, William Chatfield, **Richard Pretlow Ernst**, **James T. Hatfield**, **Polk Laffoon**, **John M. Lassing**, **John Menzies**, Clifford Shinkle, and **L. B. Wilson**. The stated goal of the organization was "to establish and maintain a golf course and other outdoor sports and recreation facilities, including tennis, boating, swimming and fishing." Construction began in 1922 and was completed in about two years. When finished, Twin Oaks was only the third 18-hole golf course in Kentucky, the first two being in Louisville. In its early years, this was the site of major golf tournaments. The **flood of 1937** wreaked havoc on the course and the clubhouse, making major renovation necessary before the opening of the 1938 golf season. In 1956 there was an unsuccessful attempt by a business group to buy Twin Oaks and build a horse-racing track on the site.

Today the well-designed and attractive clubhouse provides an excellent place for area businessmen to entertain clients, have parties, or just relax with family and friends. Reasonable usage rates were set, so that people of modest means could enjoy the facility. Rates for young people were set exceptionally low, to encourage them to become members. The country club continues today, owned by the Swingos family, who in recent years built a new clubhouse to replace the old, higher in the floodplain; the clubhouse is often rented for parties and social gatherings, and the grounds have been known to host other events over the years, such as an occasional circus.

"18-Hole Golf Course Open," *KP*, October 31, 1923, 1.

"Race Track Plea Is Made for Twin Oaks," *KP*, March 22, 1956, 1.

"Twin Oaks Being Restored for 1938 Golf Season," *KP*, 14.

"Twin Oaks to Be Name of New 18-Hole Golf Course," *KP*, December 5, 1922, 1.

TWIN VALLEY. Located in Owen Co., this valley hugs the Kentucky River near the Carroll Co. community of Worthville. Included in this basin are the communities of Ball's Landing, Carter's Landing, Cull, Danish, Moxley, and Webster Springs. Settlers arrived, established homes, and began to farm, operate stores, and run freight-wagon routes. Soon, the neighborhoods the settlers established grew and developed into these communities.

Ball's Landing had a general store, a pharmacy, a grocery, and a saloon. At one time, this town had three doctors: Attie Lusby, Avery Adams, and J. W. Gully.

Carter's Landing, on the north side of Twin Creek, consisted of a store owned by William Carter. Up the creek were the farms of Bill Abbott, John Doan, J. W. Tomlinson, and "Aunt Mary Woods," who also ran a small grocery store in her home. West of the Doan farm was the John Doan **Lead** Mine. To the east was the home of John Barnett, who was famous for growing fine sweet potato plants; folks from miles around came for the plants.

Farther up the creek was the Webster farm (Webster Springs), noted for its mineral water. The neighboring farm belonged to Benjamin J. Roberts.

Cull was named for David Cull, who owned and operated the community's general store; Sam Crawford operated its blacksmith shop. Since Cull was an inland community, dry goods and groceries were shipped by boat to Moxley and hauled to Cull by freight wagons.

In about 1901 or 1902, Harvey B. Ogden and his wife, Mary Ellen, built a small store across the road from the Roberts's farm. This was the beginning of the community of Danish. On September

2, 1908, a letter signed by the residents of this area was sent to the Fourth Assistant Postmaster General, Washington, D.C., requesting that a post office be established at Danish and that Mary Ogden be appointed postmaster. The request was made because the Rural Route 2 mail from Sanders had been discontinued, leaving the community of Danish without mail deliveries. The request was approved, and the Ogden family operated the post office until just before **World War I**. The Old Roberts Mill was located across the road from B. Roberts's farm. This was a water-powered mill that served the community for many years; the Roberts family also ran the local general store. Next to the Roberts farm was a lead mine owned by a Cincinnati firm. Ore from the mine was put in small sacks and hauled by a wagon about five miles to Moxley, where it was shipped away on boats. Farther down the road were the White Chapel School and the Salem Baptist Church (still in operation).

Moxley was settled by the family of Ed and Edith Miller. There were nine family residences, a general store, and two saloons there. Wilson Ball operated the store, Harry Riggs owned one of the saloons, and "Ole Dad" Stout ran the other. About 1902 the Moxley Baptist Church was erected by Ben Spaulding.

Vertical files, Owen Co. Public Library, Owenton, Ky.

Doris Riley

UNDERGROUND RAILROAD, BOONE, CARROLL, AND GALLATIN COUNTIES. What is known about slave escapes and Underground Railroad (UGRR) operations between Cincinnati, Ohio, and Madison, Ind., or, conversely, in Boone, Carroll, and Gallatin counties in Kentucky, comes chiefly from records in Indiana and Ohio, from anecdotes preserved, and from testimonies given by slave witnesses. The oral traditions concerning the activities of the UGRR that are so prevalent in parts of southern Indiana and Ohio are extremely rare in Kentucky. Successive generations of Confederate descendants have weaved a myth that often emphasizes how kind their slaveholding ancestors were and how happy the slaves were to work for the family.

In these Kentucky counties, criminal records from the pre–**Civil War** era that might be of use in researching UGRR activities are spotty at best. Also, antebellum Kentucky newspaper accounts frequently referred to UGRR activists as northern agitators, rather than as Kentuckians. For decades, Kentucky historians searched for white Kentuckians who might have led UGRR operations and found only a few, causing some writers to conclude that no sizable organized UGRR activities took place in Kentucky.

The truth is that most of Kentucky's UGRR was managed by small cells of free people of color and by individual slaves living on plantations. Kentucky's African American history and heritage was suppressed or ignored by most public and private histories until the latter 20th century. Only in fragments of oral tradition (often maintained within church histories), or in arrest and trial records, do hints of the aid given to fugitive slaves in Kentucky appear. During the past 20 years, historians have begun to build the public records beneath these oral stories. The people, both black and white, involved in the UGRR in Boone, Carroll, and Gallatin counties frequently moved north or west after the Civil War or just became silent as Confederate veterans took over political power in these counties.

The UGRR annals retained from Indiana clearly specify crossing points along the Ohio River where hundreds of fugitive slaves gained freedom. But they describe an Ohio River quite foreign to modern eyes: it lacked today's series of large dams and canals, it was up to 15 feet shallower, it had a considerably narrower channel, and it was subject to icing over in winter months and drying up during the summer. This riverfront of the past, in spite of patrollers, moreover, proved to be very porous.

Major Fugitive Crossing Points

Carroll Co.

—1838–1861, Hunter's Bottom, Ky., to Eagle Hollow, Ind.; key persons: John Carr, **Adam Crosswhite**, **Richard Daly**, Chapman Harris, Ike Johnson.

—1850s, Prestonville, Ky., to Brooksburg, Ind.; key person: unnamed fisherman at Prestonville.

—1840–1861, Carrollton, Ky., and Kentucky River to Lamb, Ind.; key persons: **Elijah Anderson**, William Anderson, Chapman Harris.

—1840–1861, Ghent, Ky., to Vevay, Ind., and to Craig Township in Switzerland Co., Ind.; key persons: George Ash, Stephen R. Gerard, William Lamb, Moses McKay, **John Pavy**, Samuel H. Pavy, Rev. **Alexander Sebastian**, Wright or Hildreth, John Shaw.

Gallatin Co.

—1840–1861, Warsaw, Ky., and Sugar Creek to Markland and Florence, Ky., and Patriot, Ind.; key persons: John Brookings, Alexander and Duncan Fuller (see **Fuller Brothers**), Lewis Hamilton, Daniel and Jonathan Howe.

Boone Co.

—1845–1861, Rabbit Hash, Ky., to Rising Sun, Ind.; key persons: Samuel Barkshire, Laura Haviland, Benoi Dixon, Joseph Edington, Col. A. C. Pepper, Orthaniel H. Reed, Nathan R. Steadman, William Thompson, Edmund Toliver, John White.

—1845–1861, Burlington, Ky., to Aurora, Ind., and the Manchester Landing; key persons: Elijah Anderson, Daniel Bartholomew, Rev. John Clark, Ralph Collier, Martin C. Eubank, John Fairfield, Joseph Hall, Thomas and John Hansell, John Hope, Seth Platt, William Wyman.

—1845–1861, Taylorsport, Ky., to Lawrenceburg, Ind., and Ohio River shore and Great Miami River; key persons: Elijah Anderson, Rev. John Clark, Martin C. Eubank, John Fairfield.

Carroll Co.

There is little evidence that any form of organized assistance to runaway slaves was available in Carroll Co. before 1835. After 1838, when Elijah Anderson and George De Baptiste, free blacks from Virginia, arrived at Madison, Ind., the town of Carrollton in Carroll Co. became the locus of an important junction for the UGRR routes that followed the Kentucky River north to the Ohio River from the Bluegrass region of Kentucky. Before both men were driven out of Madison, Ind., in the race riot of 1845–1846, the two traveled into Trimble and Carroll counties in Kentucky, and as far south as Frankfort, Ky., to establish UGRR links with free people of color and plantation slaves as well.

—In August and September 1820, Samuel Todd announced a $400 reward for the recapture of Patrick and a woman with a wound on her head, and Will French offered $100 for the return of Spencer; China, age 15; and Bob, age 50; the trio escaped from Kentucky near the Gallatin Steam Mill.

—In August 1843, Adam Crosswhite and his wife and children escaped from Francis Giltner in Hunter's Bottom, Ky., and made their way through the Madison, Ind., UGRR to Marshall, Mich.

—About 1845, 17 enslaved men and women, valued at more than $20,000, contracted with a poor white man with a skiff, making their own way through the wilderness to the Hicklin Settlement in Jennings Co., Ind.

—Slaves escaped via Prestonville, Ky., to the Brooksburg, Bee Camp, and Indian-Kentuck Creek area of Indiana. One group of young men, more than a dozen, was ferried across the Ohio River by a fisherman at Prestonville when they offered him money. James Stewart, a member of the Rykers Ridge abolitionists, aided these youngsters.

—Escaping slaves came down the hills above Canip Creek, where Peter Scott, the only free black head of a family at Milton, Ky., who headed the UGRR operations on the Kentucky side during the late 1840s and early 1850s, helped them escape. Family history claims that Christopher Pecar's (Pecard's) house near the river in Milton also was used to hide runaway slaves.

—Runaway slaves crossed over the Ohio River at Hunter's Bottom to the Eagle Creek area east of Madison, Ind. Richard Daly, a slave owned by Samuel Fearn Sr., took 30 fugitive slaves across the Ohio River before taking his own family of five to Canada in 1856.

—Slaves were aided at Lamb, Ind., directly across the Ohio River from Carrollton. Both the McClain and the Ash homes were said to have harbored fugitive slaves on occasion. Members of the Brushy Fork Baptist Church and the Caledonia Presbyterian Church, inland from Lamb, aided runaways as well.

—Near Vevay, Ind., Rev. John Pavy and his sons ran an active UGRR operation from Ghent to Carrollton, Ky., during the 1840s and 1850s.

—Rev. Alexander Sebastian and members of the Freewill Baptist congregation at Bryant Creek, near Florence, Ind., aided runaways in Kentucky chiefly from Ghent and the Warsaw area.

—During the 1850s, Rev. Chapman Harris, his wife Patsy, who was a former slave in Shelby Co., Ky., and their teenage sons ran the Eagle Hollow UGRR operation that was linked to 20 Kentucky slaves on plantations in Carroll and Trimble counties as well as free people of color in Madison, Ind. Harris lived up Eagle Creek about a half mile from the Ohio River. He was surrounded by white abolitionists Charlie Lutz, John Taylor, and William Woolen, a free black named Ike Johnson, and, at the top of the ridge, Charles Almond, the first of the several Rykers Ridge abolitionists. When slave owners from Kentucky tried to place a spy named Caleb McQuithy in Eagle Hollow, Henry, the oldest Harris boy, gave the man such a beating that he disappeared from the scene.

—Sandy Dean, a former slave emancipated by Gen. **William O. Butler**, lived in the Georgetown section of Madison, Ind., a gathering point for leaders of the UGRR during the 1840s and 1850s, and likely formed a liaison to free blacks and plantation slaves in Carroll Co., Ky.

—Some evidence suggests that Elijah Anderson, a strong leader within the African Methodist Episcopal (A.M.E.) church, and De Baptiste, an equally strong leader of the Black Baptist denomination, used the emerging slave churches in Carroll, Henry, and Shelby counties, Ky., and the separate African American churches at Frankfort, Ky., as major communications conduits in establishing UGRR links. De Baptiste, in particular, was known to favor the use of Prince Hall Masonic lodges as sites to establish trustworthy UGRR cells.

During the 1840s the American Anti-Slavery Society placed two white abolitionists, William Phelps and George Whitfield from Wheeling, Va. (today W.Va.), in Madison, Ind., to develop organized assistance and to encourage escaping slaves. They reportedly spent most of their time organizing UGRR cells south of the Ohio River. The effects of such organization showed up in the increased traffic of runaway slaves passing through the Madison UGRR during the 1850s.

The abolitionist leadership at Carrollton in Carroll Co., Ky., was apparently so feeble that after 1846, when Elijah Anderson moved his base of operations from Madison to Lawrenceburg, Ind., Alex Fuller was moved to Carrollton from Warsaw, Ky., where he had apparently been active in the UGRR operations. Fuller is a shadowy figure, likely one of the 100 field agents placed along the Ohio River by the American Anti-Slavery Society. Many of these agents were disguised as peddlers, fishermen, ferrymen, and boatmen, both black and white.

Gallatin Co.

What is known about aid to fugitive slaves in Gallatin Co. comes mainly from records of UGRR activities in Indiana or from family histories there. The public records in Gallatin Co. include one grand jury indictment in 1838 against Lewis Hamilton, a free black living near Sparta, Ky.; other criminal records or accusations have been either destroyed or quashed. Many of the Union sympathizers in Gallatin Co., who may have been involved with helping fugitive slaves, moved to Missouri, Kansas, and other western states after the Civil War, therefore causing the record of any such aid to be lost.

Warsaw in Gallatin Co. developed as a small Ohio River port in spite of large sandbars impeding all but the keelboat and packet steamboat traffic. Across the river, the hamlets of Florence, Lamb, Markland, Patriot, and Vevay, Ind., hosted a number of antislavery activists. By 1850 Switzerland Co. on the Indiana side and Warsaw on the Kentucky side had a substantial number of settlers—chiefly merchants, manufacturers, and craftsmen—who came from New York, New England, and Pennsylvania; these families tended to be pro-Union, and some of them were quite actively opposed to slavery. Pockets of settlers from New England and New York began giving aid to runaway slaves on an ad hoc basis. But there were also transplanted Kentuckians living in Indiana who favored slavery and had relatives in both Gallatin and Carroll counties.

In 1821 the first newspaper notice of a runaway slave from Gallatin Co. appeared in the Lawrenceburg, Ind., *Oracle*. Benjamin Waller offered a $200 reward for the recovery of Peter Shelley, a 44-year-old slave, who escaped by using a pass that was 10 years out of date.

The earliest recorded antislavery activist in Gallatin Co. was Rev. John Pavy, a Regular Baptist minister, who was chased out of Fredericksburg (Warsaw) in 1823 for preaching against slavery. Pavy moved across the Ohio River and established a farm on the Mount Sterling Rd. above Vevay, Ind. The move was timely, since in 1824 Vevay hosted visits from both Judge Stephen C. Stevens, a Presbyterian and a radical abolitionist at Vevay and Madison, Ind., and also Rev. James Duncan, a Presbyterian minister who authored *A Treatise on Slavery: In Which Is Shewn Forth the Evil of Slave Holding both from the Light of Nature and Divine Revelation.* In 1840 Stevens and Duncan were associated with the formation of the antislavery Liberty Party in Indiana. Stevens, in 1848, was a convener of the Free Soil antislavery party in Buffalo, N.Y.

For more than 20 years, John Pavy, his seven sons, and his son-in-law Stephen R. Gerard ran a major route of the UGRR at Vevay and later in Craig Township, Switzerland Co., Ind. At first such aid to runaway slaves was sporadic. During the late 1840s and early 1850s, a more organized approach to helping fugitive slaves developed, including signaling systems to reach activists in Ripley and Decatur counties farther north in Indiana. The Pavy family history claims that four sons became Baptist ministers and that one of them, Absalom, went west to serve as a missionary to American Indians. After Samuel H. Pavy established his farm in Craig Township, slaves were said to swim across the Ohio River there and hide in Pavy's barn, later being transported away in Gerard's flax wagon. The Gerards, the Lambs, and the Pavys had intermarried, reinforcing the oral tradition that George Ash, the ferryman from Carrollton, Ky., to Lamb, Ind., aided runaway slaves.

In March 1838 David Lilliard brought charges in the Gallatin Circuit Court against Lewis Hamilton, a free person of color, for enticing Lilliard's slave Billy to escape to Ohio. Because of the interstate aspects, the Kentucky commonwealth attorney brought the case to the March court term of 1838. The charges apparently were not sustained, because Lewis Hamilton was later listed in the Gallatin Co. 1850 census as a free black, a blacksmith, living near Sparta, Ky., with $400 property and a family of seven.

In October 1841 Rev. Alexander Sebastian, a Separate Baptist minister, was chased from Warsaw for his radical preaching against slavery and apparently for preaching against the Regular Baptists' dogma. He had been called to an antislavery Free Will Baptist congregation at Bryant Creek near Florence, Ind., and purchased a farm northwest of Patriot, Ind. Kentuckians were said to have crossed the Ohio River in order to heckle his preaching. For a short time, Sebastian was ordained in the Free Will Baptist denomination, but his teachings were too radical, and he was soon denounced at the Free Will Baptist Quarterly Meeting. He then went to an area near East Enterprise and Quercus Grove in Indiana to found Separate Baptist churches there and at Cross Plains, Ind., both of which had members active in the UGRR of Indiana's Switzerland and Ripley counties. The Sebastian congregation merged with the Liberty Free Will Baptist congregation, forming the New Liberty congregation, which continues today and prides itself on its abolitionist roots.

In 1847 a debate was held in Warsaw between Rev. J. L. Waller of the Baptist Church and Rev. E. M. Pingree of the Universalist Church. The Universalist Church, founded in the Boston, Mass., and the Concord, N.H., area, had developed a strong antislavery plank, and many of the nation's leading antislavery activists were members. Two of the most active Universalist congregations were at Patriot (1840) and Vevay (1852), Ind. The Silas and Jonathan Howe families, very strong Unionists, lived on both sides of the Ohio River, at Patriot and in the Sugar Creek area near Warsaw, Ky. Silas Howe became a captain in the 18th Kentucky Infantry and later a major in the 55th Kentucky Infantry, and his father, Jonathan Howe, was a captain in the Gallatin Co. Home Guards, a group of about 20 Union supporters.

Before the passage of the 1850 Fugitive Slave Act, nearly all Universalist preachers and lay leaders supported the abolition of institutional slavery by any means. Afterward, a few Universalist preachers claimed that the law of the land superseded acts that would entice slaves to run away or prevent authorities from reclaiming fugitive slaves.

By 1840 Alexander and Duncan Fuller were living in Warsaw. Sarah Fuller, a daughter of Alexander, writing shortly after the Civil War, claimed that Alexander was active in the UGGR and had moved from Warsaw to Carrollton, Ky., before 1860. There were several Fullers active in the UGRR in southeastern Indiana and southern Ohio.

Boone Co.

With 40 miles of shoreline, myriad creeks and forests, and several large plantations dotting the Ohio River, Boone Co. proved nearly impossible to patrol against runaway slaves. In Indiana, across from Boone Co., there were no free black agricultural communities and no sizable "Yankee" settlements close to the Ohio River. The UGRR operations in nearby Dearborn Co., Ind., came about almost entirely through organization of antislavery societies and through efforts of antislavery congregations among the Free Will Baptists, the Methodist Protestants (MPs), and the Universalists.

The most celebrated runaway slave from Boone Co. was **Margaret Garner**. Yet her tragic slave-escape story is not a story of the UGRR. Garner and her family escaped independently from Richwood, Ky., and took refuge with family members at Cincinnati. Apparently the escaping Garners attempted to reach activists in the local UGRR only after a posse from Kentucky had found them, and by then it was far too late for rescue.

Written histories of Boone Co. contain little evidence of an active UGRR. Records from Indiana, Ohio, and Michigan, however, reveal a substantial amount of UGRR activity in Boone Co. from 1838 to 1861. In fact, so many runaway slaves were handled in and through Boone Co. that agents of the American Anti-Slavery League were placed as ferrymen, fishermen, peddlers, and couriers. Two of the most famous conductors of the UGRR, Elijah Anderson and John Fairfield, completed major exploits while aiding escaping slaves in Boone Co. Many of the slave escapes were local to Boone Co., and the names of Boone Co. slave owners and slaves have been recorded in court proceedings in Indiana and Michigan. At one point in the early 1850s, when Elijah Anderson was operating out of Lawrenceburg, Ind., 40 slaves were lost in one month, and the newspapers speculated that monetary losses to slave owners in Boone and Kenton counties in Kentucky were reaching $50,000 per month.

William Wyman, the station master of the UGRR at Aurora, Ind., operated three main routes northward from the Manchester Landing crossing just east of Aurora's Public Landing. Wyman, although living on a farm just outside of Aurora, was a member of the Universalist Church at Manchester, Ind., and also a charter member of the East Fork Chapel of the Tanner's Creek MP Church. The Manchester Landing site probably was linked to American Anti-Slavery Society (or League) operatives working as ferrymen, since this crossing was used extensively for many years.

Wyman's first route was the Yorkshire route, which went north in Indiana to Collier Ridge Rd., then to Guilford, up to Harrison, and to the Quaker outpost in southern Franklin Co., Ind. This route was manned by recent immigrants from York Co., England, who spoke a dialect and were associated chiefly with the MP congregations of the Tanners Creek, Ind., Circuit (the West Bank Chapel of Tanners Creek, the East Bank Chapel of Tanners Creek, the Mount Pleasant Methodist Class, and the Bonnell MP Class) founded by Rev. John Clarke, cofounder and first corresponding secretary of the Indiana Anti-Slavery Society.

The radical antislavery activists in the Guilford area in Indiana date back to before 1834, when a split in the East Bank Chapel Methodists caused a number of families to withdraw to Joseph Hall's barn and become the West Bank Chapel MP Church. Years of cordial relationships and shared pastors between the two organizations using Union Church developed, so that the first formal meeting of the Anti-Slavery Society was called at the East Bank Chapel, which was hosting the association meeting of the Tanners Creek Circuit of the MP Church just outside Guilford in July 1838. Initially harassed by Kentucky and Lawrenceburg, Ind., proslavery elements, the abolitionists persevered. They elected Benjamin Metcalf president and John Hansell secretary. They also passed two major resolutions, to publicize the evils of slavery and to aid slaves attempting to escape bondage. Leaders of this Yorkshire route identified in the Siebert Family Papers included Ralph Collier, John Hall, John Hansell, and Thomas Hansell, the station manager. A strong link existed between William Wyman and Rev. John Clarke, both of whom served as directors and officers of the Indiana Anti-Slavery Society representing Decatur Co. William Wyman was a member of the West Bank of Tanners Creek MP Church and also a member of the Manchester Universalist Church. Thomas Hansell was one of the 50 abolitionist families from Dearborn, Ripley, and Jennings counties in Indiana who moved with the Hicklin brothers of Jennings Co. in Indiana to Oregon in 1850. The Yorkshire route was then managed by Ralph Collier, whose homestead remains on Collier Ridge Rd.

The second route was called the Universalist route. It led north from Aurora, Ind., to Manchester, to the James Angevin safe house at Yorkville, and to Cedar Grove and Brookville in Franklin Co., Ind. The leaders of this route included William Wyman of Aurora and Seth Platt of Manchester, identified by Siebert and James Angevin, of Yorkville, in the Siebert Family Papers.

If there was an active group in Kentucky aiding the Indiana UGRR, it probably was associated with the Universalist Church at Burlington, Boone Co. This congregation was linked to members of the Aurora and Manchester Universalist churches through a series of association meetings continuing into the 1890s. Although the Kentucky congregation was not constituted formally until 1878, its charter members were all residents of Burlington before 1860, and none were slaveholders.

The description of this central UGRR route as Universalist came from the James Angevin family history. This source also verified that there was a Universalist congregation at Wilmington, Ind. For some time an isolated UGRR conductor named Orthaniel H. Reed at Wilmington had planning meetings with the Donnells, the Hamiltons, and the McCoys, Presbyterians who managed the Kingston route of Decatur Co.'s UGRR. Reed brought fugitive slaves to Decatur Co. from Rising Sun, Ind.

William Thompson, one of the free blacks at the Clarksburg "Little Africa" settlement in Decatur Co., Ind., was known to have come down to Rising Sun to pick up runaway slaves as well. Sabra Matthews, who apparently served as spiritual leader of the "Little Africa" settlement, formed an A.M.E. church east of Clarksburg, Ind., on the Decatur-Franklin county line.

The third route that William Wyman operated was called the North Polar Star route; it led from Aurora, Ind., through Manchester to Moores Hill and Old Milan, where Stephen S. Harding's homestead was the number 7 station on that route. From Old Milan the North Polar Star route continued to Napoleon, Ind., through the Yankee Settlement of eastern Ripley Co. (Pierceville and Prattsburg and the Mud Pike Rd.). This route was operated chiefly by Freewill Baptists living east of Napoleon. It has been determined that there were UGRR activists in the Freewill Baptist Churches at Delaware (now Lookout), Franklin (now Old Pilgrim), Milan, Pierceville, and Prattsburg. It is believed that there were members of the Freewill Baptist Church at Aurora or Wrights Corner, Ind., who were also involved. The Shattucks, the Shockleys, and Dr. Myron Harding, who were active in the UGRR, were likely Freewill Baptists rather than Universalists. William Wyman and the Aurora crossing linked together the three denominations most prominent in the antislavery and UGRR activities in southeastern Indiana.

When Elijah Anderson moved his UGRR operations from Madison to Lawrenceburg, Ind., in 1846, it took only a few weeks for Boone Co. slave owners to feel the impact. This very experienced conductor was skilled in establishing safe routes and in selecting trustworthy slaves in place on plantations and free people of color on the Kentucky side of the river. His experiences at Madison convinced him that taking runaway slaves across one and two at a time was bound to run afoul of the patrollers. He determined to collect larger groups of slaves in Kentucky and, using experienced conductors, to take the groups all the way to Sandusky or Cleveland, Ohio. The likelihood was better by far that an entire group of 10, 12, or even (at one time) 50 runaways would get through without recapture. Anderson claimed to have brought out more than 800 runaway slaves, following passage of the 1850 Fugitive Slave Act.

In addition to cordial relations with William Wyman at Aurora, Anderson also had excellent working ties to Cincinnati's free black population and to the white leadership of the Ohio UGRR. He had established a cadre of free blacks at Lawrenceburg and Brookville, Ind., who were associated chiefly with the A.M.E. denomination. One declared member of this group was Gabriel Smith, an elderly free black from Brookville, who claimed to have helped conduct 50 slaves from Boone Co. up to Sandusky, Ohio, on Lake Erie.

Elijah Anderson was captured in Kentucky in 1856 and sent to the Kentucky State Penitentiary. The UGRR continued to operate in the Aurora and east-of-Lawrenceburg area, and it is likely that both white and black conductors continued the task that had placed Anderson in prison.

Annotated Plat C, 1848–1850, Madison, Ind.

Bordewich, Fergus M. *Bound for Canaan: The Underground Railroad and the War for the Soul of America.* New York: Amistad, 2005.

Coffin, Levi. *Reminiscences of Levi Coffin, The Reputed President of the Underground Railroad.* Cincinnati: The Robert Clarke Company, 1898.

Commonwealth of Kentucky vs. Elijah Anderson, Trimble Co. Circuit Court, Governors Papers, Kentucky Libraries and Archives, Frankfort, Ky.

Coon, Diane Perrine. "Southeastern Indiana's Underground Railroad Routes and Operations," 1999, U.S. Park Service and Indiana DNR, unpublished technical report available at Indiana Department of Historic Preservation and Archaeology, Indianapolis, Ind.

Deed Book 6: 320, Jefferson Co., Madison, Ind.

Documenting the American South. "Life and Narrative of William J. Anderson," UNC Univ. Library. http://docsouth.unc.edu (accessed April 6, 2007).

Griffler, Keith P. *Front Line of Freedom: African Americans and the Forging of the Underground Railroad in the Ohio Valley.* Lexington: Univ. Press of Kentucky, 2004.

Haviland, Laura S. *A Woman's Life-Work: Labors and Experiences of Laura S. Haviland.* Cincinnati: Walden and Stowe, 1881.

Hudson, J. Blaine. *Fugitive Slaves and the Underground Railroad in the Kentucky Borderland.* Jefferson, N.C.: McFarland, 2002.

Lawrenceburg Register, May 11, 1848; November 17, 1852; November 14, 1853.

Rogers, N. T. "Decatur County's Role in the Historic Underground Railroad of Slavery Days," and "Orthaniel Reed to Editor McClasky," *Greensburg (Ind.) Daily News,* February 3–17, 1914.

Siebert, Wilbur H. *The Underground Railroad from Slavery to Freedom.* New York: Macmillan, 1898.

Smith, George Henry. "Reminiscences of Tanner's Creek," 1898, and "Reminiscences of John Clark." In *History of East Fork Stone Chapel.* Guilford, Ind., 1921.

Tax Assessment Book 2, 1838–1847, Madison, Ind.

Thompson, Orville. "Fugit Township Pioneers," *Greensburg (Ind.) Daily News,* August 30, 1906.

Diane Perrine Coon

UNDERGROUND RAILROAD, BRACKEN CO. Antislavery feelings, including the colonization movement, were quite evident in Bracken Co. during the 19th century. **Abolitionists** and the Underground Railroad conductors helping slaves gain freedom in this Ohio River borderland often led perilous lives—risking injury, imprisonment, and occasionally death. Their names and the names of slaves living near the Ohio River (for the enslaved "the River Jordan") emerge from accounts of their activities. The term *Underground Railroad* refers to the network of people who helped fugitive slaves from south of the Ohio River reach freedom in the North. Abolitionists quietly organized this system of stations and conductors to move freedom-seekers along the route, while other sympathizers sought less dangerous methods of opposing slavery.

A young and impressionable visitor to his uncle's home in Augusta in Bracken Co. was **Stephen Collins Foster**, who during the 1840s and 1850s composed songs about life in the South. According to local historical accounts, Foster was often found sitting below the "Negro Church on the Hill," listening to the voices float softly down. Foster objected to the blackface performance style sometimes used by performers singing his songs. He instructed white performers not to mock slaves but instead to get their audiences to feel compassion for them.

Also living in the county during this time was **John G. Fee**, a leading abolitionist. Fee founded the Free Church and School on Hillsdale Rd. in Bracken Co. near Germantown. However, in 1850 Fee was described by the local Circuit Court as an intruder into this quiet community and ordered to leave the county. Many enraged citizens helped to enforce the circuit court's declaration. Again in 1860 the Bracken Co. Circuit Court demanded that Fee and his associates, who had already been driven from Berea College ("the Berean exiles"), depart the county immediately. They moved to Ohio.

Fee's wife, Matilda, and his mother-in-law, Betsy Hamilton, of Fegan Ridge, Ky., were also vocal and dynamic abolitionists. Matilda traveled with her husband and supported the schools and churches he founded by teaching the younger students, white or black. The Fees lost one of their own children to an illness that resulted from their constant travels. Adding to their mental anguish was the loss of Fee's nanny, **Juliet Miles**. Miles had attempted to return from Ohio and lead her enslaved family to freedom, only to be captured and sentenced to the state penitentiary in Kentucky, where she soon died. Betsy Hamilton placed herself in danger when she concealed a fugitive slave, Ed Mofford, from the local sheriff. Mofford was to be sold at a courthouse auction, but he was able to break loose and run five miles to the Hamilton home. Working with a young colporteur, William Lincoln, Matilda successfully concealed Mofford until his escape to Canada was arranged.

One of the leading abolitionists in Ohio was Bracken Co. native **James Armstrong Thome** (1813–1873). Thome was born in Augusta, graduated from local **Augusta College**, and was a participant in the famed Lane Seminary Debates held on slavery in Cincinnati in 1834. He later graduated from Oberlin School of Theology in Ohio. Thome was the son of a prominent citizen of Augusta, Arthur Thome, who emancipated his 15 slaves between 1832 and 1836. James Thome became vice president of the American Anti-Slavery Society and, as such, frequently spoke out with fervor against slavery in the United States. While living in Augusta in 1837 and writing his book *Emancipation in the West Indies,* James Thome was beseeched to help a fugitive slave woman cross the Ohio River to reach freedom in Ripley, Ohio. After completing this exploit, Thome realized that he was no longer safe in either Kentucky or Ohio. He immediately left his teaching position at Oberlin College in Ohio and went to the East, remaining there for a year to avoid arrest and extradition.

Arthur Thome, according to a slave narrative published in the *Colored American,* was reported to be the leading conductor for the Underground Railroad in Augusta. He supposedly supplied freedom-seekers with the necessary food and clothing and conducted them to Ripley, Ohio. As threats to him and his family increased, they moved to Athens, Mo.; there he built a new home, which became a station on the Missouri Underground Railroad.

Both Arthur Thome and Fee had close connections with Augusta College (founded December 7, 1822), the first Methodist college in Kentucky and only the third in the world. Several of the professors were abolitionists, and they allowed debates on the topic of slavery in Kentucky as early as 1826. An early president of the college, Rev. **Martin Ruter** of Ohio, was one of the founders of the Kentucky Colonization Society and an outspoken opponent of slavery. Because of the antislavery sentiments of the faculty and the lack of financial sponsorship of the supporting Methodist conferences, the Commonwealth of Kentucky finally revoked the college's charter in 1849.

Underground Railroad operative E. Patrick Doyle was considered the most courageous conductor in Kentucky. The largest slave uprising in Kentucky was masterminded by Doyle, who was at the time a student at Centre College in Danville, Ky. An estimated 40–75 slaves, assisted by Doyle, fled in the summer of 1848 from Central Kentucky into the hemp fields near Milford in southern Bracken Co. With 100 local men in pursuit, Doyle and his party were captured and jailed. Seven of the slaves Doyle was trying to rescue stood trial in Bracken Co., and three were convicted and sentenced to be hanged. Doyle was found guilty in an emotion-charged trial held in Lexington and sentenced to the state penitentiary, where he died of typhoid in 1863.

In addition to Doyle, Juliet Miles, and the seven runaway slaves who were tried as a part of the 1848 slave mutiny, there were eight men from Bracken Co. who were charged during the period leading up to the Civil War with enticing slaves to escape. Most were free persons of color, like David Alexander, who was arrested in 1853. Alexander allegedly assisted Alfred, a slave of John Fee Jr., in getting to the Ohio River shore, where both men were captured. Fortunately for Alexander, his case was filed away for the Bracken Co. Circuit Court's May term of 1855.

One of the most appalling cases in the county was that of Dr. Perkins, another free person of color, who was accused of trying to aid in the escape of Sanford, a slave who belonged to Blackstone Rankins of Augusta. The 70-year-old Perkins was found guilty of the crime and sentenced to the state penitentiary for three years. Even though a petition had been initiated among Augusta citizens to free Perkins, he died in the prison two years later.

Another conductor who operated in Bracken Co., but avoided the penitentiary, was John Fairfield. Considered an extremist by many, especially by noted Quaker and Cincinnati abolitionist Levi Coffin, he was able to arrange strikes into Kentucky to rescue slaves. However, Fairfield was betrayed while in Bracken Co. and jailed in the stone prison at Brooksville, where he became quite ill. After a winter of incarceration, local citizens were able to secure Fairfield's escape, and he fled to Ripley and to safety with Rev. John Rankin. Fairfield used many aliases. The only named person jailed at that time for enticing slaves to escape was James Cooper, a laborer; this perhaps was an alias Fairfield used. The man known as James Cooper spent the winter of 1853–1854 in the jail, which is the time most researchers believe that Fairfield was imprisoned.

Just before the **Civil War** ended, James Medley was ordered to appear in Bracken Co. Circuit Court to answer charges of enticing a slave named Henry away from B. C. Clayton. Medley stood trial in Bracken Co. in February 1865 and was found innocent. Also arrested at this time was J. P. McClanahan, who was charged with attempting to entice away slaves, in particular Bob, belonging to Henry Anderson. He was ordered to appear at the county's February 1865 circuit court hearing, but records do not reveal the result of this action. One accused conductor, Robert Mains, arrested in 1864 for ferrying unidentified slaves across the Ohio River, was released on bail; he failed to report to the February 1865 circuit court in Bracken Co. and forfeited his bail.

Although not arrested for enticing slaves to escape servitude, J. M. Mallett, a local colporteur, received a punishment almost as intolerable as imprisonment. Mallet, a teacher at the Free Church on Hillsdale Rd., was mobbed at Germantown in Bracken Co. by men attempting to "tar and feather" him for his abolitionist teachings. Dr. **Joshua T. Bradford** of Augusta led the mob, but their plan was thwarted when a Dr. Keith intervened in Mallet's behalf in the midst of the beating.

Abolitionism also took other forms in Bracken Co., as seen in records kept by locals Rev. James Savage and Thurston Thomas. According to Savage's Memorandum Book, dated 1827, he planned to emancipate his Negro slaves upon his death; their emancipations were to occur in various years, as stipulated in the book. Savage provided in his will for the local free people of color to have a place of worship, as long as they did not erect a place of sepulture. He also supplied money to be sent in support of the Kentucky Colonization Society and gave his emancipated slaves the option of going to live in the newly created nation of Liberia in Africa.

Thurston Thomas also took an unusual stance against slavery from 1831 to 1855; he made provisions in his will to emancipate his slaves during those years. Thomas also kept a family Bible, which gave a detailed accounting of births, marriages, and deaths of his enslaved Africans. Today that Bible is held at the National Underground Railroad Museum in Maysville.

The work of creating an antislavery atmosphere throughout Northern Kentucky was a tiresome yet worthy endeavor. With the active abolitionists and conductors spreading the word and leading freedom-seekers to a life of opportunity, generations of enslaved Africans could hope for a better life. The ministers and colporteurs created antislavery congregations and delivered a message to their Northern abolitionist partners that there were persons of like mind in Northern Kentucky.

The threats of violence and related consequences were constantly on the minds of men and women like Dr. Perkins and Juliet Miles, but that did not keep them from trying to free themselves. The Thomes, Fees, and Doyles also suffered great retribution for their acts of conscience, but they led others to rethink their attitudes concerning supporting that "peculiar institution"—slavery—south of the Ohio River.

Algier, Keith. *Antebellum Kentucky.* Maysville, Ky.: Standard Quick Print, 2002.

Bracken Co. Circuit Court Archives, Brooksville, Ky.

Sears, Richard D. *The Day of Small Things.* Lanham, Md.: Univ. Press of America, 1986.

Caroline R. Miller

UNDERGROUND RAILROAD, CAMPBELL AND KENTON COUNTIES. Underground Railroad stations were located throughout Campbell and Kenton counties, which are two of the three northernmost counties in Kentucky. These counties also have two of the state's largest cities, Newport and Covington, but the African American population in both counties was small. The total Campbell Co. African American population in 1860 was 204 (88 free, 116 enslaved); 95 of these (56 free, 39 enslaved) were Newport residents. Kenton Co., had 652 blacks (85 free, 567 enslaved; 273 of them (76 free, and 197 enslaved) lived in Covington.

African Americans from throughout the region visited Covington and Newport while on business, thus establishing contacts with residents. It is a common belief that, perhaps because of this possibility, only the most trusted enslaved blacks were allowed to travel to the area from surrounding counties. However, escaping slaves sometimes purposely avoided large population centers.

Numerous houses along both the Licking and Ohio rivers had tunnels, which had been dug to supply the dwellings with coal and other products from riverboats. In Covington, one of the supposed stations along the Underground Railroad was the **Gano-Southgate House**, which had such a tunnel. In 1967 a photograph booklet on the city of Covington, published by the Cincinnati Bell Telephone Company, included a picture of Mrs. Annie Hargraves and her daughter Betty Ann Jones, both African Americans, and Covington mayor Claude Hensley, taken at the exit from the house's tunnel on the western shore of the Licking River. Hargraves is shown holding the book *Reminiscences of Levi Coffin,* which contains "The Story of Jane," about Hargraves's grandmother's escape from slavery. Some viewers of the photo see in it an implied relationship between the Gano-Southgate House and the successful escape, although this is questionable since the history of this mansion has been misrepresented over the years.

Abolitionist **Henry Hathaway Jr.** used his Hathaway Hall residence as a station. It was located on Highway Ave. in West Covington, overlooking the Ohio River. Of Hathaway it was said, "He had the express purpose of helping fleeing slaves on their road to freedom." Bushrod W. Foley, mayor of Covington during this period, lost his slaves in an escape to Canada. In 1850 Foley had three slaves and lived on the southeast corner of Russell and Front Sts., less than 200 yards from the river. In 1853 he had five slaves. According to the *Covington Journal,* "On Sunday night last five slaves belonging to B. Foley, Esq., made their escape from this city, and are now probably in Canada. If they fare as well there as they did in Covington they will be truly fortunate." Perhaps Mayor Foley's home had a supply tunnel leading to the Ohio River. John W. Stevenson, future governor and U.S. senator from Kentucky, who resided at 320 Garrard St., had a tunnel leading to the Licking River. He was also a slave owner whose slave escaped to Ohio with **Margaret Garner** in 1856. In 1954 the former Stevenson residence on Garrard St. became state property when Kentucky decided to construct a state office building there.

Awaiting or assisting the escapees in Cincinnati were people like William Fuller, who housed runaways. There were also unscrupulous individuals such as Robert Russel, who played both sides, first helping the runaways and then turning them in to the slave catchers. After reaching Cincinnati, one important stop for escaping slaves was the city's Zion Baptist Church. This African American church was located in the area called the black bottom near the Mill Creek.

Besides houses with tunnels leading out to the banks of the Ohio River, there were several other documented Underground Railroad locations in Kenton Co. One was **Elmwood Hall** in Ludlow, at the corner of Forrest Ave. and Closson Ct. Away from the river's shoreline in Covington, there were the Weisnal House on Highland Ave., a house on the corner of 18th St. and Maryland Ave., a house at 310 Garrard St., and Homesdale, located at the site of **Holmes High School**. In Fort Wright, there was a station in the home at the corner of Kyles Ln. and **Dixie Highway**. Other Underground Railroad stations were located in Independence, Key West, Morning View, and Sanfordtown.

In Campbell Co. one of the Underground Railroad stations was the York St. Congregational Church. In the basement of the church's parsonage were accommodations for living, and it was reported that church members who were involved as conductors used honey carts with false bottoms to hide runaways. The **James Taylor Mansion** in Newport was another possible location. Stations were located in Alexandria, Bellevue, Cold Spring, and Grants Lick as well.

Whether assisted or not, the escaping slaves required food, water, and places to hide. The topography of Campbell and Kenton counties supplied the numerous creeks, streams, and rivers leading to the Ohio River that aided those escaping bondage. Once the slaves reached Ohio, fugitive slave laws made it necessary for them either to meld into a local African American setting or continue on to Canada.

Coffin, Levi. *Reminiscences.* Reprint, New York: Arno Press, 1968.

"Covington's Sesquicentennial Year," *KP,* August 21, 1965, 29K.

"The Era of the Golden Shovel: Covington, Kentucky," *Cincinnati Telephone Bulletin* 59, no. 10 (November 1968).

"Escape of Slaves," *CJ,* December 10, 1853, 2.

"Escape of Slaves—Arrest of Part of Them: Murder of a Slave Child by Its Mother," *CJ,* February 27, 1856, 2.

Gollar, C. Walker. "Possible Underground Railroad Stations and Conductors in Southern Ohio and Northern Kentucky," January 28, 1998. Unpublished paper, Kenton Co. Public Library, Covington, Ky.

Harris, Theodore H. H. "The Carneal House and the Underground Railroad," *NKH* 6, no. 2 (Spring–Summer 1999): 35–38.

Haviland, Laura S. *A Woman's Life-Work: Labors and Experiences.* Reprint, Salem, N.H.: Ayer, 1984.

"N. Ky. Facing Role in Underground Railroad: Stopovers on Freedom Path Documented," *CE,* May 25, 1997, B8.

Reis, Jim. "A Fiery-Spirited Governor from Covington," *KP,* July 11, 1983, 4K.

Tenkotte, Paul A. "Rival Cities to Suburbs: Covington and Newport, Kentucky, 1790–1890," PhD diss., Univ. of Cincinnati, 1989.

"The Underground Railroad and the Man Who Made It Obsolete," *Papers of Kenton County Historical Society* 3 (1990): 70.

Theodore H. H. Harris

UNDERGROUND RAILROAD, MASON CO. Sympathetic citizens north and south of the Ohio River who treasured the ideals of a free society began to organize a movement that became known as the Underground Railroad. Mason Co. was one of the earlier supporters of public antislavery societies and the Underground Railroad. As early as July 1818, the *Maysville Eagle* advertised a meeting of the supporters of the Maysville Abolition Society in Mason Co.

Church congregations in Mason Co. also assisted fugitive slaves with either food or clothing. The congregation of the Minerva Baptist Church, built by Lewis Craig in 1793, was one of these. The Minerva Baptists split over the slavery issue in the early 1800s, because some members supported the gradual emancipation of slaves, while others, as **abolitionists**, called for the immediate end to slavery.

Many church associations in the area approved of the African Colonization movement founded in 1816 in Washington, D.C. Residents Rev. John T. Edgar, Adam Beatty, James Morris, and other well-educated men were early members of the movement in Maysville. Although the original African Colonization Society founded in Maysville did not survive very long, there was later a resurgence of colonization activities, as indicated in the *Western Colonizationist* on May 27, 1839. This advertisement called for a colonization meeting to be held on that date in Maysville at the Methodist Church.

According to Mason Co. oral tradition, there were abolitionists and conductors whose records cannot be found among the archives at the Maysville courthouse. The earliest conductors mentioned in the writings of Levi Coffin of Cincinnati were members of the Lightfoot family and an unnamed barber living in Maysville. In nearby Washington, the **Paxton Inn** was often reported to have been a temporary refuge for freedom-seekers. In downtown Maysville, the Phillip's Folly mansion on Sutton St. also contains concealed areas in which slaves might have been secreted. The mansion had several owners before 1865, and oral tradition suggests that an owner of this house was providing a safe area. On Fourth St., near an area where free persons of color lived, is the Bierbower house, which was owned by carriage-makers Frederick and Jonathan Bierbower. Compelling accounts from Bierbower family members and from former resident Chris Maher suggest that slaves were secreted in the lower level of the house.

Abolitionists sometimes perpetuated their beliefs even after death, as seen in the 150 or so emancipation records found in the Mason Co. will books. In most accounts, money and livestock were the assets granted, and at times the wills stipulated that the slaves were to receive their freedom in later years, particularly on the date December 25.

Neighboring Ohio was home to a number of conductors on the Underground Railroad. John B. Mahan, a tavern owner from Sardinia, Ohio, in Brown Co., was accused at his trial on November 13, 1838, of enticing slaves from Mason Co. who were owned by William Greathouse. While awaiting trial, Mahan had to spend several months in the deplorable Maysville jail and over time became weak in body and mind. Fearing his death, Judge Walter Reid finally held his trial, announcing a lengthy verdict of guilty. Mahan was fined nearly $2,000, which he borrowed from William Dunlap of Ripley in order to pay the fine. With his health in dire condition and his spirit broken, the freed Mahan returned to Ohio, where he soon died.

John P. Parker, a freed slave living in Ripley, Ohio, was perhaps the most active conductor of enslaved Africans in Mason Co. from the decade of the 1850s through the **Civil War**. According to his interview with newspaperman Frank Gregg, Parker's working area was "a strip of land along the southern boundary of the free states, which prior to the Civil War could be truthfully called the borderland.... It broadened out to a breadth of fifty miles or more.... Every night of the year saw fugitives singly or in groups, making their way to the northern country." During Parker's daring forays, he was supplied with information from his "Grapevine Dispatch" network of allies regarding a large party of runaway slaves from Central Kentucky who were lost and without a guide. By word of mouth, Parker relayed the circumstances of the party to an unidentified white man in Kentucky who agreed to row Parker across the Ohio River and take him to another conductor. When the white man reached a predetermined location, Parker was startled at the hooting of owls, which he came to find out was another unnamed conductor hiding in an old cabin about eight miles south of the river. Parker described this man as an "Indian" in the woods, "Indian-like" in his manner in traversing the land quickly and silently. According to Gregg's transcript, the last encounter that Parker had with slave owners was his rescue of a young couple and their infant child from the house of James Shroufe (a worker at his foundry) at South Ripley, Ky., across from Parker's Ohio home on Ripley's riverbank. Again, Parker was successful in bringing the family out of slavery, even though the pursuing owner shot at him.

Working with Rev. John Rankin of Ripley, and perhaps with John Parker, was a young slave conductor from western Mason Co. Arnold Gragston (1840–1938) was owned by John "Jack" Tabb, whose farm was in Mason Co. on Walton Pk. An account by Gragston provides a strong image of the dangers he faced: "I don't know how I ever rowed the boat across that river. The current was so strong, and I was trembling. I couldn't see a thing in the dark, but Ripley, Ohio, always meant freedom for slaves, if I could get to that light." Gragston stated that after his escape he resided in Ohio and would often hide freedom-seekers in barns before crossing the fields east of Dover, Ohio, to a skiff hidden at the Ohio River's edge. He estimated that he might have rescued as many as 300 slaves in a period of four years. The October 6, 1938, *Bracken Chronicle in Ky.* commemorated Gragston's contribution to his fellow man with these words: "Conscious of the oppression of his people and shackled down with the fetters of slavery, Mr. Gragston ... became a vital cog in that renowned means of flight from the lash of the slave owners' whips—the Underground Railroad."

Sometimes information about the early conductors was mentioned only in a single court entry, and their stories were not published in national abolitionist journals. One such case occurred in 1834 when Benjamin Gooch (or Googe) was brought before the Mason Co. Court and charged with enticing a female slave, Susan, the property of Mary Morrison. He was indicted for aiding slave Mary in her escape from her owner and spiriting her into Ohio. In 1849 James Blackburn, a free man of color living in Mason Co., enticed a girl slave, Frances, the property of William Bradford, to leave for Ohio. Blackburn was found guilty in a trial in August 1850, and the jury recommended that he be confined in the Kentucky State Penitentiary in Frankfort for a term of nine years. The court set aside his sentence. However, this new verdict was overruled, the prisoner was again judged guilty, and he was remanded to serve nine years in the penitentiary.

Shortly after the Fugitive Slave Act of 1850 was enacted, John Davis, a free man of color who was living in Maysville, persuaded a slave woman, Tabby, to leave her lawful owner, John Gabby. In 1853 Charles, a free Negro, was indicted on a charge of enticing slaves away from their owner. The case was continued to the April court term of 1856, and bond was supplied for Charles by Thomas C. Newcomb. In the April 1856 trial, Charles did not appear and forfeited the bond paid by Newcomb. Another case in 1856 involved George Williams, a free man of color, who was charged in Mason Co. with enticing slaves to escape and assisting them in their escape. These slaves were the property of Dr. James E. McDowell. Williams was found guilty and sentenced to 15 years in the Kentucky State Penitentiary. A new trial was granted, but the record of its outcome is not available. The next year, in 1857, Charles, a free Negro, was charged with feloniously attempting to persuade and entice a Negro woman slave named Cordelia, the property of James Patton. Again, records do not reveal the outcome of the case. Benjamin Stokes, a free man of color, was prosecuted in 1858 for enticing the slaves of J. B. Pepper to leave his property. Two Negro boys escaped from Pepper on October 10, 1858, and John Sutherland witnessed the scene. Stokes was spotted in a skiff on the Ohio River near Beasley's eddy with two or three other Negro men, matching the descriptions of Pepper's fugitive slaves. Their skiff was found pulled up on Ripley's bank with footprints leading north. Stokes was brought to trial with the evidence overwhelmingly pointing to a guilty verdict, but information about the final outcome or sentence has not come to light.

One of the most unusual enticing trials in Mason Co. involved **John G. Fee**'s colporteur, William Haines, who was sponsored by the American Missionary Association. Officially, Haines was accused of enticing a slave woman, Hannah, and her children, belonging to Hezekiah Jenkins. Haines admitted under oath that he had encountered and spoken with a black man and asked the man questions as to how a person could obtain a skiff and where to obtain a likely route across the river.

While awaiting trial, Haines succumbed to a serious case of diarrhea and was under great mental and physical stress. When Fee visited Haines, Fee was attacked by one of his neighbors with a club so brutally that one of the blows to Fee's head broke the club. Fee was temporarily almost blinded and enveloped with blood, and shortly afterward his home was burned. The jury voted in Haines's favor and found him not guilty.

Abolitionist Rev. **Elisha Green** of Maysville was a minister to the enslaved and free people of color in north central Kentucky and had established Baptist churches in several towns, including Maysville and Paris, Ky. He was able to travel to his congregations because his owner had issued him a "pass" allowing him to travel on the train. The Dobyns and Warder families in Mason Co. owned Green, but when he was enslaved as a child in Paris, he had witnessed slave coffles walking to the infamous auction sales in Lexington. Green's only son was kidnapped into a coffle at **Blue Lick** Springs in Kentucky at age nine. Although Green quickly arranged in Maysville to secure the money necessary to meet the slave trader's demands, the coffle had moved on before Green could return, and Green never saw his son again. Several months after the **Civil War** ended in 1865, Green was indicted in Mason Co. Circuit Court for "harboring a fugitive." In fact, the fugitive he was hiding was his daughter, who was in danger of being sold. Since the war's ending did not prohibit the sale of slaves in Kentucky, the owner was within his legal rights. Green was found not guilty, however, and was able to secure a home for his third daughter. He had previously purchased his two other daughters and his wife and had provided the bond to emancipate them.

Strict slave laws, enforced by inhumane slave-catchers and bounty hunters, once made it necessary for persons seeking freedom to avoid arrest by temporarily fleeing to Ohio and Canada. For instance, several freed females in Mason Co. were kidnapped and placed on the slave market in nearby Lexington. James McMillen was the slave agent in Mason Co. for Louis Robard and was suspected of these outrageous deeds. In the August 30, 1851, edition of the *Maysville Eagle*, an article described the kidnapping of Negroes from Aberdeen, Ohio, and their transportation across the Ohio River to the Maysville jail. Although Aberdeen citizens tried to intervene, the individuals kidnapped were quickly sent to Lexington and the slave market.

Thousands of enslaved Africans in Mason Co. and the surrounding Kentucky counties were not able to escape to freedom and were thereby sentenced to a life of bare subsistence or constant threats that they would be sold "down South." Nevertheless, men and women of strong courage continued to press toward the North, and some of them eventually found liberty.

Green, Elisha. *Life of the Rev. Elisha W. Green.* 1888. http://docsouth.unc.edu/neh/greenew/greenew.html (accessed April 2, 2006). Part of the Documenting the American South series.

Hagedorn, Ann. *Beyond the River: The Untold Story of the Heroes of the Underground Railroad.* New York: Simon and Schuster, 2002.

Mason Co. Circuit Court Judgments and Order Books, Maysville, Ky.

Mason Co. Clerk Will Book, Maysville, Ky.

Sprague, Stuart Seely, ed. *His Promised Land: The Autobiography of John P. Parker, Former Slave and Conductor on the Underground Railroad.* New York: W. W. Norton, 1996.

Caroline R. Miller

UNIDENTIFIED FLYING OBJECTS. Sightings in Northern Kentucky of Unidentified Flying Objects (UFOs) have been reported over the years and continue in the present. A UFO, according to U.S. Air Force Regulation 80-17, is "any aerial phenomenon or object which is unknown or appears to be out of the ordinary to the observer." Though a manual at the U.S. Air Force Academy several decades ago stated that reports concerning UFOs may extend back 47,000 years, giving credence to the topic, the subject exploded publicly after two events. Kenneth Arnold saw nine "flying saucers" while piloting a small plane near Mount Rainer, Wash., on June 24, 1947. And on July 8, 1947, Lt. Walter Haut stated in a press release that the 509th Bomb Group at the Roswell Army Air Base in New Mexico had recovered a crashed "flying disc." The press release was initially rescinded by an official announcement that the "disc" was actually a weather balloon, but years later, many former military personnel at Roswell protested that an alien-piloted UFO had in fact crashed. Since then, tens of thousands of sightings have been reported annually all over the world. Many Northern Kentuckians have been especially interested in UFOs because they live only about 50 miles from Wright-Patterson Air Force Base in Fairborn, Ohio, where the debris of the alleged Roswell UFO was purportedly sent. Moreover, Kentucky Air National Guard captain Thomas Mantell died on January 7, 1948, when his P-51 Mustang crashed near Franklin after he reported closing in on a "metallic object" of "tremendous size" traveling at approximately 180 miles per hour.

The UFOs reported in Northern Kentucky range from a cylindrical craft with light formations on its sides, observed in Owenton on November 16, 1999; to a formation of diamond-shaped craft witnessed in Alexandria on December 11, 2000; to a more detailed description in another incident. A man stated that on August 29, 2004, he and his girlfriend were driving near Corinth when they saw a bright light traverse the horizon in about 10 seconds. The object stopped, mysteriously dropped a "dark bundle," and moved quickly toward them. Suddenly, the lighted object appeared in front of their car. They drove forward, and as it hovered over them they noticed that it had a triangular shape with lights on the corners. Looking through the sunroof of their vehicle, the couple saw the lights change into different patterns of red, blue, and yellow. They drove on and lost sight of it. Although these reports are often ridiculed, Stanford University physicist Peter Sturrock notes that scientists who investigate UFOs invariably become more interested, a fact suggesting that UFOs merit serious study. Indeed, although UFOs may be anomalous phenomena from Earth, the philosophy of science indicates that science cannot exclude visits of alien-piloted UFOs. Since the history of science reveals that scientific theories change over time, the current theories discounting travel through many light years of space-time may well be superseded by future theories that are more friendly to the possibility.

National UFO Reporting Center: State Report Index for KY. www.nuforc.org/webreports/ndxlKY.html (accessed November 23, 2005).

Sturrock, Peter. *The UFO Enigma: A New Review of the Physical Evidence.* New York: Aspect, 2000.

Trundle, Robert. *Is ET Here? No Politically but Yes Scientifically and Theologically.* Victoria, B.C., Canada: EcceNova Editions, 2005.

Wickramasinghe, Chandra, and Fred Hoyle, "The Unity of Cosmic Life and the Inevitability of Evolved Life Forms." In *The Search for Extraterrestrial Intelligence in the Optical Spectrum III*, SPIE Proceedings of the 2nd International Conference on Optical SETI, Vol. 4273-01, 2001.

Robert Trundle

UNION. Located near the geographic center of Boone Co., along U.S. 42, the city of Union is 3 miles from the **Florence Mall**, 18 miles from Cincinnati, and 10 miles from the **Cincinnati/Northern Kentucky International Airport**. It is a predominantly residential community of single-family homes and small agricultural estates today. In 1969 the area of the city was one square mile, and it has grown to approximately three square miles.

One of the earliest settlements in the county, Union may have existed as early as the late 1700s. Early settlers moved up from the Ohio River, or came via the Cumberland Gap from Culpepper Co., Va. They traveled the old buffalo trace that went from Northern Kentucky, through Union, into Central Kentucky. This was the first road that brought people to Union. Those coming from Virginia were predominantly of German descent. Many of these settlers acquired their land either from a land speculator named Humphrey Marshall or as a result of **Revolutionary War** grants. Building materials for the early homes were stone, logs, or home-fired brick.

The first recorded landowners were **Jacob Fowler** and a Revolutionary War soldier named Hugh Steers. Steers was an Irish immigrant who used Revolutionary War money to buy his land from Fowler, then later married Fowler's daughter. Steers and his wife were buried at what is today the

18th green of the Lassing Pointe Golf Course. He donated land for the Bethel Baptist Church on Frogtown Rd.

By the early 1800s, much of the land that now lies in Union was owned by the Fowler family. Fowler's son was Benjamin Piatt Fowler, who built a Federal style stone house on his land around 1817. The Fowler house, in later years sometimes called the Smith house, has walls that are 22 inches or more thick. It was built of limestone quarried from a nearby creek. In 1863 Gen. **John Hunt Morgan** spent some time at the Fowler home, after escaping from the penitentiary at Columbus, Ohio, with the assistance of W. P. Corbin. Morgan spent the night at Corbin's home, accompanied by Capt. Thomas H. Hines, during his escape through **Big Bone Lick** back to Confederate forces in Tennessee.

It has been recorded that Union was established as early as 1833, but existing documentation shows that Union was officially incorporated as a city in 1838. One source claims that Union was incorporated in 1871 but that the charter lapsed and was reactivated around 1976. The Kentucky secretary of state has 1854 as the date of incorporation. The community may have been named Union because it was a connection point between the city of Florence and Big Bone Lick. Or perhaps the name Union was chosen because of the junction of Old Louisville Rd. with Visalia–Big Bone Rd. Various sources disagree on the origin of the name. Salt was manufactured at Big Bone Lick during the early 1800s and brought to Union for distribution to other area settlements. Union was designated as a U.S. post office in 1830, and as early as 1850, Union had one store, two churches, a doctor, and a population of 50.

The local Lake atlas of 1883, which was published from actual surveys under the direction of B. N. Griffing, lists these business references: one attorney, a blacksmith, a magistrate, three school teachers, one painter, one dealer in general merchandise, one dealer in dry goods, groceries, and a livestock dealer. A bank was built at Union in 1905, and a large, two-story general store was located on the corner of Mount Zion Rd. and what later became U.S. 42. Across the street from the general store was a drugstore; the village blacksmith was around the corner from the bank, and nearby was a flourishing creamery.

One of the oldest organizations in Union is Boone Union Lodge No. 304, which was organized on September 1, 1854. According to the lodge's charter, the first master was W. H. Riley. However, according to the records of the lodge, William Wilkie was its first master. It is believed that Riley helped organize the lodge and served as master for a time, and Wilkie finished out the year. V. Dickerson was the first senior warden, while A. Stansifer served as junior warden that first year. The lodge suffered much from the effects of the **Civil War**, since at the time it was still trying to become established. There were three years during the war when no report was listed with the Grand Lodge and no master was elected in 1861, 1862, or 1864. In the late 1930s, the Boone Lodge consolidated with the Hamilton Lodge No. 354. The Hamilton Lodge was struggling to survive, and its only chance was the consolidation. Active today, the Boone Lodge has a membership of around 170.

One of the few arboretums in the commonwealth of Kentucky is located at Central Park in Union. The Boone Co. Arboretum has the distinction of being the nation's first arboretum within an active recreational park setting. It is open daily from dawn to dusk year round and contains more than 2,700 trees and shrubs. One can see specialized arrangements of plant families and observe selections rarely seen by the public. To ensure that the plants thrive in even the worst of droughts, there is a 41,000-linear-foot computerized irrigation system. The arboretum encompasses 121 acres and has more than two miles of paved walking trails, winding through the various plant collections, woodland settings, and athletic fields. Three informational kiosks containing horticultural information are located at the main trail entrances. Special attractions at the arboretum include the children's garden, a wildlife viewing area in the Native Kentucky Prairie, and a woodland walking trail. Throughout the year, various classes and programs are offered for all age groups, and many of the county extension horticulture classes are taught at the arboretum. Union is also home to Big Bone Lick State Park, a 547-acre park.

During the early 1900s, Union was unable to field a slate of officers to serve as a legislative body, and the official corporation lapsed. In 1969 a group of citizens felt that the time was right to reincorporate, and the modern City of Union was born. In 2005 Union moved up from a fifth- to a fourth-class city. In 1970 the official population figure for the city was 233; a 1990 census showed a population of 1,001; and by 2000 it had increased to 2,893, making Union the second-largest incorporated city in Boone Co. The current population is predominantly between the ages of 18 and 64 and almost equally divided between male and female.

An Atlas of Boone, Kenton, and Campbell Counties, Kentucky. Philadelphia: D. J. Lake, 1883.

U.S. Census Bureau. "American Fact Finder. Data Set. Census 2000 Summary File 1 (SF1) 100-Percent Data. Custom Table." www.census.gov (accessed July 28, 2006).

Warner, Jennifer S. *Boone County: From Mastodons to the Millennium.* Burlington, Ky.: Boone Co. Bicentennial Book Committee, 1998.

Bruce Ferguson and Gail Chastang

UNITED CHURCH OF CHRIST. The United Church of Christ is a popular Christian denomination in the urban areas of Covington and Newport, primarily owing to the large number of German immigrants who settled there. Nationwide, the United Church of Christ resulted from the 1957 merger of two denominations, the Evangelical and Reformed Church and the Congregational Christian Church. The Evangelical and Reformed Church, which was well represented in Northern Kentucky before 1957, was itself the outcome of a 1934 merger of the Reformed Church in the United States and the Evangelical Synod of North America.

German Protestant immigrants to Northern Kentucky were typically **Lutherans** or Reformed. This was a consequence of some important historical events in what is present-day Germany. In 1648 the Peace of Westphalia, ending the Thirty Years War, recognized three religious groups: **Roman Catholics**, Lutherans (Evangelical), and Reformed (Calvinists). In 1817 the northern German kingdom of Prussia, home to many German Protestants, forced the union of the Lutheran and Reformed churches. German Protestant immigrants to Northern Kentucky were therefore accustomed to a mixture of Evangelical and Reformed traditions and often formed congregations together. This is evidenced by the history of a number of German immigrant congregations in Northern Kentucky that eventually aligned themselves with the United Church of Christ: **St. John United Church of Christ** in Newport, founded in 1847 as the First German Protestant Evangelical Church; **St. Paul Christian Church**, Fort Wright (withdrew from the UCC in 1998; now Disciples of Christ), organized in 1847 as St. Paul German Evangelical Church; **St. Paul's United Church of Christ**, Alexandria, opened in 1850 as an evangelical congregation; **Grace United Church of Christ**, Covington, established in 1862 as the Evangelical Reformed Church of Covington, Kentucky; **St. Paul United Church of Christ, Dayton**, conceived in 1863 as an evangelical congregation; **St. John's Community Church**, Wilder, begun in 1876 as St. John's Evangelical Protestant Church (withdrew from the UCC in May 1975); **St. John United Church of Christ**, Bellevue, founded in 1887 as the St. John Evangelical Protestant Church of Bellevue; and **Immanuel United Church of Christ**, Bromley, established in 1894 as the German Reformed Church of Bromley, Ky. Many of these churches are still operating, as well as other United Church of Christ congregations such as St. Mark in the Latonia neighborhood of Covington, Christ Church in Fort Thomas, and St. Paul in Fort Thomas.

Gunnemann, Louis H. *The Shaping of the United Church of Christ: An Essay in the History of American Christianity.* New York: United Church Press, 1977.

United Church of Christ. www.ucc.org (accessed June 3, 2007).

Paul A. Tenkotte

UNITED MINISTRIES OF NORTHERN KENTUCKY. The United Ministries of Northern Kentucky, formerly Erlanger-Elsmere United Ministries, is a nonprofit social service agency staffed by nearly 70 volunteers that provides emergency aid to local residents in need. The agency currently serves up to 300 families each month. A local ministerial association opened the agency in 1983 as a food pantry, and its services have expanded over time to include help with rent and utilities. During the holidays, many families count on United Ministries for Thanksgiving dinners, Christmas dinners, and Christmas gifts for children. On-site literacy and family support programs, along with GED classes and budgeting/mortgage workshops, encourage clients to develop their independence. Originally operating exclusively in the Erlanger-Elsmere area, the agency has expanded its operations and now serves all of southern Kenton and Boone counties. In 1996, after years of borrowing and renting space from local churches, United Ministries built a new facility at 525 Graves Ave. in Erlanger. A rift between the founding volunteers and the board of directors prompted the board to close the doors of the agency in December 1998. It reopened in April 1999, minus the founding volunteers, who formed a separate local group, the United Christian Volunteers. Grants, donations, and fundraisers help to keep the United Ministries of Northern Kentucky going. A thrift shop operates out of the basement of the agency's building three mornings per week. Selling donated items at reasonable prices, the thrift shop serves a dual purpose: it is the agency's biggest fundraiser, and it provides an affordable place for low-income families to shop.

Croyle, William. "Help to Needy Expands with Thrift Shop Shopping with Dignity—and More Often," *KE*, May 12, 2004, C2.

Kreimer, Peggy. "Split Agencies Share Mission: The Poor," *KP*, July 17, 1999, 1K.

Laura Schaefer

UNITED STATES. The steamboat *United States*, owned by the U.S. Mail Line, was built in 1865 by Johnson, Morton & Company, Cincinnati. It was 294 feet long and had a 40-foot beam and a 6.5-foot-deep hold; it operated on the Ohio River between Louisville and Cincinnati, along with its sister boat the ***America,*** with which the *United States* collided on December 4, 1868, in one of the most fiery steamboat disasters on record. Capt. David Whitten, original master of the *United States,* had left the boat and was replaced by veteran captain **Richard M. Wade** on September 17, 1868, less than three months before the accident. Owen Co., Ky., native author **Alfred Cobb** was on board the *United States* that fateful night; he survived and wrote about it in his 1890 work *Liffy Leman or Thirty Years in the Wilderness.*

Certificate of Enrollment, Str. *United States,* April 10, 1868, Life on the Ohio River History Museum, Vevay, Ind.

Change of Master certificate, Port of Cincinnati, District of Mississippi, George W. Neff, Surveyor of Customs, September 17, 1868, Life on the Ohio River History Museum, Vevay, Ind.

Barbara Huffman

UNITED STATES PLAYING CARD COMPANY. The world largest manufacturer of playing cards and supplier to casinos worldwide, the United States Playing Card Company began in Cincinnati in 1867 as Russell, Morgan & Company, primarily a printer of circus and theatrical posters. In 1881 the company began to manufacture playing cards; in 1891 it was renamed the United States Printing Company; in 1894 the playing-card division became the United States Playing Card Company (USPC). USPC subsequently acquired other card firms, including New York Consolidated Cards, makers of Bee Playing Cards, which are still manufactured by USPC. USPC has been making its famous Bicycle playing cards since 1885. It also produces Aviator and Hoyle playing cards.

In 1900 USPC moved to a new facility on 30 acres of land in Norwood, Ohio, a plant that eventually comprised more than 600,000 square feet. The Norwood headquarters also housed radio station WSAI. Owned by USPC from 1922 until 1930, WSAI with its strong signal broadcast bridge lessons nationwide. During **World War II**, the company made parachutes for bombs, as well as playing-card decks that were sent to Americans in German prisoner-of-war camps; the prisoners could moisten and peel apart the cards to find maps of escape routes. From the 1960s until the 1980s, USPC was itself acquired by other owners. In 1994 USPC managers and local investors purchased the firm. In July 2008 USPC announced that it was moving its headquarters and 500 jobs to a 570,000-square-foot facility, formerly occupied by the Gap Inc., in the Mineola Industrial Park in Boone Co.

The United States Playing Card Company. "United States Playing Card Company History." www.usplayingcard.com/history.html (accessed August 10, 2008).

Van Benschoten, Amanda. "U.S. Playing Card Moving to N.Ky," *KE*, July 9, 2008, A1.

Paul A. Tenkotte

UNITY BAPTIST CHURCH. The Unity Baptist Church in Pendleton Co. was organized in spring 1817 by Rev. Christian Tomlin, who was also a physician. It was located on Haw Lick Branch, a tributary of the Middle Fork of Grassy Creek. The first building was a hewed-log structure. In 1844 that building was disassembled and moved about 300 or 400 yards from its first location. The second church building was next to the Unity graveyard on the main Middle Fork of Grassy Creek. In August 1860, when the Crittenden Baptist Association was organized, it was reported that the Unity Baptist Church had 33 members and that the church was represented in the association by J. Tomlin, W. Tomlin, and T. Morris. Asa Tomlin was one of the church's earlier preachers. The church was moved again about 1888. The original logs were used to construct the church's third building on land donated by Mary Agnes Detmus, widow of William McMillian. The site was on the ridge of Jagg Rd., later called Unity. In 1914 the log church was demolished and the present frame church building was built. In 1975 this church closed. It reopened on October 18, 1981, when a contingent of 77 worshipers from the Pleasant Ridge Baptist Church met there in search of a new church home. There were 121 interested persons gathered for the first Sunday service, with 4 former members present. At the April 1984 business meeting, the church voted to erect a new building next to the old church. It was dedicated on August 10, 1986. Today the old building is used for Sunday school and meetings.

Belew, Mildred Boden. *The First 200 Years of Pendleton County.* Falmouth, Ky.: M. B. Belew, n.d. [ca. 1994].

Mildred Belew

URBAN LEARNING CENTER. Northern Kentucky's Urban Learning Center (ULC) is a unique program developed to bring the campuses of the three local postsecondary educational institutions into the urban core. In the mid-1990s, through the **Forward Quest** visioning process, a group of civic leaders studied Northern Kentucky's urban communities and found that although a more educated population was going to be needed in modern times, none of the postsecondary institutions offered classes that urban residents could easily attend. Thus, the ULC was established to make postsecondary education accessible for this underserved population in Northern Kentucky.

The ULC is an educational partnership among Forward Quest, the **Center for Great Neighborhoods of Covington**, **Northern Kentucky University**, **Thomas More College**, **Gateway Community and Technical College**, **Covington Independent Schools**, Newport and Dayton Independent Public Schools, and the Scripps Howard Foundation. Through the cooperation of these partners, the program has overcome traditional bureaucratic barriers to deliver flexible, responsive educational programming for the "hard-to-serve" and "high risk" urban population. The partners are committed to using their resources in whatever ways necessary to meet student needs.

The ULC's innovative program eliminates the four most significant barriers that adult students experience in pursuing postsecondary education: lacks in the areas of finances, child care, transportation, and self-confidence. To overcome the financial barrier, the most common one, courses are offered at the low cost of $10 each. Furthermore, in some cases students may borrow textbooks for their courses at no charge through the **Kenton Co. Public Library**. Because many students have young children and do not have access to consistent child care that they can afford, the ULC provides on-site child care at no cost, utilizing the services and expertise of the Chapman Child Development Center. The care is both nurturing and developmental, thus extending the impact of the program beyond the parents. The ULC classes are offered in locations that have good access to public transportation: the familiar settings of public schools and the newly opened Urban Learning Center buildings, owned by the Covington Independent Schools and adjacent to **Holmes High School**. To bolster ULC students' self-confidence, the instructors and staff endeavor to make every student successful, offering support, encouragement, advice, and knowledge in every encounter with students.

ULC students regularly make the transition to the campuses of the center's partner institutions, earning degrees or certificates. Some have earned certificates at ULC urban locations and have obtained training that has helped them secure better jobs, thus providing Northern Kentucky with a more educated and skilled workforce.

"Adults Find New Option for College," *KE*, May 1, 2001, B1.
"Learning Center Celebrating Successes," *KP*, May 6, 2002, 1K.
"Quest Plan Puts College within Reach," *KP*, December 26, 1997, 1K.
Samples, Karen. "Older College Students Learn from Instructors," *KE*, December 10, 1998, B1.

Meg Winchell

URBAN PLANNING. The science of city planning dates back to the Progressive era of U.S. history. Northern Kentucky has played an important role in urban planning, particularly in **Ladislas Segoe**'s 1932 city plan for Covington, long considered a national model. While planning has occurred in various forms for as long as cities have existed, modern, comprehensive urban planning was the brainchild of reform-minded citizens in the early 20th century. Early pioneers in this field included Frederick Law Olmsted, planner of New York City's Central Park and the famous "White City" of the 1893 World Fair in Chicago. Olmsted's view was of a neat and orderly city, full of green space and classical architecture.

Until the 1920s, city planning was left to elected officials. As the "Gilded Age" of political corruption led to grassroots reform movements during the Progressive era, the notion of professional urban planners became reality. Before these professionals arrived, some very interesting possibilities were discussed. The years 1872 and 1873 saw the debate over a proposal to merge Kenton and Campbell counties and merge all of the cities in these counties into one large government. One reason cited for the proposal's failure was that it would cause individual local politicians to lose their influence.

Locally, two types of organizations were at the forefront of urban planning. Temporary groups were often set up in the cities in Northern Kentucky to face a specific problem or need. In 1922, fed up with the ever-increasing number of billboards, the citizens of Campbell Co. formed the County Planning Association and were lauded for their achievements by 1923. However, the group did not stay together, and by 1931 there was a clamor for a zoning board in the county. Decisions were often made either by elected officials or by local real estate associations who could persuade their members to adhere to decisions made.

The other type of organization was a permanent group, made up of professionals with expertise in fields related to city expansion, who made recommendations to elected officials. The best example of this type was the Covington Planning and Zoning Commission, a citizens' group born out of the Covington Betterment League. Formed in 1924, the commission was charged with making recommendations on the merits and pitfalls of proposed developments in Covington as well as initiating proposals for large-scale development in the city. **Harvey Myers Jr.**, president of the Northern Kentucky Good Roads Association, was chosen to head the commission. The member with the most lasting impact on Covington's Planning and Zoning Commission was Ladislas Segoe, an engineer and planner from Cincinnati. Segoe had worked on the 1925 Comprehensive Plan for Cincinnati, the first such plan for a major city in the United States. Duly impressed, Covington's city leaders hired Segoe in 1929 to coordinate zoning and later gave him the title of city planner. The City of Covington commissioned Segoe to create a master plan for the city, which he completed by 1932 and which has been a model for planning in middle-sized cities throughout Kenton Co. He and his Cincinnati firm were subsequently hired by dozens of Kenton Co. cities and towns to create similar plans. Segoe planned an integrated city, one in which transportation worked in concert with business, recreation, and educational opportunities.

Comprehensive urban planning took a backseat to the **Great Depression** and **World War II** during most of the 1930s and 1940s. Partly because so much destruction had been wrought on European cities and partly because the Progressive era's steam was running out for city planning, new ideas sprang up in urban planning. On one end of the spectrum was Mary Emery, who built her own dream village just north of the Lunken Municipal Airport, east of Cincinnati, and named it Mariemont. Convinced that urban planners had led the citizenry down the wrong path by trying to save the inner cities, Emery built her town based on a small New England community, complete with a town crier. The village was incorporated in 1941. On the other end was Franklin Roosevelt's concept of Greenbelt Communities, which called for creating a village that would be completely surrounded by parks and other green spaces. Only three Greenbelt Communities were built, including Greenhills, just north of Cincinnati. Although this type of planning was not evident in Northern Kentucky, its remnants were felt when planning resumed in Northern Kentucky.

Comprehensive urban planning in Northern Kentucky started again in full force in the 1960s, with government mandates replacing citizen initiatives. The Commonwealth of Kentucky authorized the creation of the **Northern Kentucky Area Planning Commission** (NKAPC) in 1961, "to prepare and assist in the implementation of a comprehensive plan for all incorporated and unincorporated areas." The NKAPC and the Northern Kentucky Area Development District, which focused on economic development, were the two state agencies in the Northern Kentucky region. The passage of the Federal Aid Highway Act of 1962 required any metropolitan area of more than 50,000 people to have a coordinated, comprehensive planning organization that would serve the entire region. Out of that act came **OKI**, the Ohio-Kentucky-Indiana Regional Council of Governments. OKI's mandate was to "conduct a continuing, comprehensive and coordinated process for the development of transportation improvement projects."

The first attempt at planning in this new environment came in 1967 with the publication of the NKAPC's Comprehensive Plan for the City of Covington. The plan was a fine example of mid-20th-century "anti-urban" planning. During the late 1960s and 1970s, there was a profound belief that there was something inherently wrong with cities. High crime, race riots, dilapidated buildings, and out-of-control abuse of drugs were too much for even the most optimistic urban booster. The best way to save cities, it was believed by urban planners, was to make them more automobile-friendly by adding parking and streets. The NKAPC plan suggested clearing out dozens of city blocks in the Central Business District of Covington, from Western Ave. to Greenup St. and south to Eighth St. NKAPC cited the success of the Internal Revenue Service building in Covington as a means of saving the city. Other areas were to be cleared as well, including a large section of the city's Eastside neighborhood. A similar plan came out in 1971, with the publication of the OKI Regional Transportation and Development Plan. The 1971 plan called for a rapid expansion of the region's highway system, including an outer loop through central Boone, Kenton, and Campbell counties and a freeway along the Covington and Newport riverfronts. Mass-transit options were barely discussed in the report except for increasing some bus routes, and there was no provision for rail-based commuting.

Both NKAPC and OKI learned many lessons from their initial foray into urban planning. In its 1981 plan, Transportation 2000, OKI goes so far as to say that its initial approach was wrong: "Developed in an era of major highway construction and declining mass transit usage, the plan was based on the assumption that automobiles would continue to be the predominant form of travel and that gasoline would be inexpensive and plentiful." Both organizations have labored in recent years to find more options for mass transit, pedestrians, bicycles, and mixed-use development. Light-rail and passenger-rail systems became the darlings of both organizations for some time.

By 1993, with new federal regulations in place, OKI and the NKAPC were forced to incorporate alternative transportation methods even more than before. In the OKI publication *Managing Mobility: Year 2010 Regional Transportation Plan*, the organization recommends not only improving highways but also "improving bus service and developing rail transit." The NKAPC, under state mandate to issue a comprehensive plan every five years, expanded its focus in its 2006 plan. Among the categories for which major goals have been set are, along with traditional planning categories such as transportation, housing, utilities, and public space, more recent concerns like public health and safety, cultural opportunities, education, and the environment.

Other similar planning organizations in Ohio have been instrumental in developing long-range plans that affect Northern Kentucky. The Port Authority of Cincinnati, the Cincinnati Center Development Corporation, and Downtown Cincinnati Inc. have kept Northern Kentucky in mind when developing large-scale projects like the redevelopment of Fountain Square, the Banks project, and so forth.

Recently the trend in cutting-edge urban planning has reverted to citizen-based organizations.

In Northern Kentucky, Forward Quest, founded in 1996 (see **Forward Quest Inc./Vision 2015**), published a 44-point strategy to strengthen the area by solidifying the urban core. Of the 44 proposals, the most interesting and controversial was the SkyLoop, a public rapid-transit system that was rejected by OKI in 2001. In 2005 Forward Quest updated its initial strategy to reflect some of its successes and overestimations. Called Vision 2015, the initiative seeks to reinvent the nature and economy of Northern Kentucky.

Covington Planning and Zoning Commission. *Comprehensive Plan for the City of Covington and Environs.* Cincinnati: L. Segoe, 1932.

Edelman, David J., and David J. Allor. "Ladislas Segoe and the Emergence of the Professional Planning Consultant," *Journal of Planning History* 2, no. 1 (2003): 47–78.

Northern Kentucky Area Planning Commission. *Comprehensive Plan, City of Covington, Commonwealth of Kentucky.* Newport, Ky.: Northern Kentucky Area Planning Commission, 1967.

Ohio-Kentucky-Indiana Regional Council of Governments. *Managing Mobility: Year 2010 Regional Transportation Plan.* Cincinnati: OKI, 1993.

Tenkotte, Paul A. "Adaptation to the Automobile and Imitation of the Suburb: Covington, Kentucky's 1932 Plan as a Test Case of City Planning," *Journal of Kentucky Studies* 1 (July 1984): 155–70.

Chris Meiman

US BANK. The U.S. Bancorp of Minneapolis, Minn., is the sixth-largest commercial bank holding company in the nation today. It operates about 2,500 banking offices and has approximately 5,000 ATMs in 35 states and Canada. In Northern Kentucky, the company has 25 banking offices, from Maysville on the east to Carrollton on the west. The bank began in 1853 as the Farmers and Millers Bank of Milwaukee, Wis. It later took the name of First National Bank of Milwaukee. In 1919 the bank merged with the Wisconsin National Bank and changed its name to the First Wisconsin National Bank, which at the time was the largest bank in Wisconsin. The bank became Firstar in 1988, as it began expanding into other states. In 2000 Firstar merged with the US Bank in Minneapolis and assumed the name US Bank. Corporate offices were moved from Milwaukee to Minneapolis.

In 1987 the First National Bank of Cincinnati changed its name to Star Bank and began expanding into Northern Kentucky. The president of First National at the time was Oliver W. Waddell, who had grown up in Falmouth, where his family had owned the Falmouth Deposit Bank. In 1999 Star Bank changed its name to Firstar. In the 1990s the US Bank, after acquiring a number of banks in several states during the 1990s, purchased Firstar Bank in Cincinnati and Northern Kentucky in 2000.

One of the Firstar branches acquired was the old Peoples Liberty Bank and Trust of Covington, at the corner of Sixth St. and Madison Ave. **Ralph Haile** had served as president of that bank for 19 years. Haile lived on the East Side of Cincinnati but had always been concerned about the health and growth of Northern Kentucky. He was deeply involved in many local projects, including urban renewal, the Covington Business Council, the Old Town Plaza, the Riverside Condominiums, and the **Behringer-Crawford Museum**. Haile also donated $2 million toward construction of a hospice addition to the **St. Elizabeth Medical Center** in Edgewood, Ky.

AllExperts. "U.S. Bank Center." http://en.allexperts.com (accessed April 11, 2007).

FindArticles. "New Bank Reviving First Wisconsin Name." www.findarticles.com (accessed April 11, 2007).

Jack Wessling

U.S. 25/42. See **Dixie Highway**.

U.S. 27. U.S. 27 (Alexandria Pk.) was chartered in 1818 as the Newport and Cynthiana Turnpike, a toll road designed, built, and owned by Gen. **James Taylor Jr.** The oldest turnpike in Northern Kentucky, it quickly became the transportation spine of both Campbell and Pendleton counties. Over the years, many different toll companies were formed to improve the highway. It ceased being a toll road in 1922, when **Brent Spence**, with the support of local automobile clubs and the Newport Chamber of Commerce, found state money ($90,000) with which Campbell Co. was able to purchase the turnpike. By 1928 the Alexandria Pk. had become U.S. 27, a designated federal highway eventually stretching from St. Ignace, Mich., to Miami, Fla. The road was built in sections; for example, the first leg in Campbell Co. was the 11.7-mile stretch between Youtsey's Hill near Alexandria and the Pendleton Co. boundary line. That work began in May 1946. Unfortunately for some towns, such as Alexandria in Campbell Co. and Butler in Pendleton Co., the road bypassed their central business districts. Out-of-state license plates became commonplace. Today U.S. 27's northern terminus is Fort Wayne, Ind.

For Northern Kentuckians, this was the road that took them to college at the University of Kentucky in Lexington and to fried chicken meals in Cynthiana. For central Kentuckians, this was the artery that led them to the nightlife of Newport and the commerce of Cincinnati. The highway has been graded, widened, straightened, and resurfaced. Cities sprang up along its path, and commuting time has been shortened. Monmouth St., the **Newport Shopping Center**, the **Evergreen Cemetery**, the **Beverly Hills Supper Club**, the Highland Country Club, **Northern Kentucky University**, Guys 'n Dolls Nite Club, the Pike 27 Auto Theater, the Spare Time Grill, A. J. Jolly Park, and the city of Falmouth all are or were located along its corridor. Less important today with the arrival of the interstates (I-75 and particularly I-471), U.S. 27 continues to handle increasing amounts of local traffic along certain segments.

"Breaking Ground for New Road," *KP*, May 25, 1946, 2.

"Transfer Pikes," *KP*, July 22, 1922, 1.

U.S. 127. Today, U.S. 127 extends through four states (Michigan, Ohio, Kentucky, and Tennessee), running from Grayling, Mich., to Chattanooga, Tenn. In years past, this federally designated route was somewhat longer. Generally speaking (except where it coincides with **U.S. 27** inside the city of Cincinnati), it runs west of the much longer U.S. 27. It crosses the Ohio River into Covington via the Clay Wade Bailey Bridge. In the Northern Kentucky region, U.S. 127 runs through Kenton, Boone, Gallatin, and Owen counties. South of the Ohio River, it follows the **Dixie Highway** to Florence and Union and on to Warsaw and Owenton, before leaving Owen Co. for Frankfort, remaining west of U.S. 27. The highway has been improved (straightened and widened) in recent years between Owenton and Frankfort. Its importance has not diminished in the interstate era, in that it lies between I-75 and I-65. U.S. 127 is best known for its annual 450-mile yard sale, which lasts 10 days each summer; people even come from foreign countries to attend. There have been 18 of the yard sales thus far, and the sale is being extended beyond U.S. 127 into Alabama. The sale is billed as the world's largest outdoor sale, and its promoters say it proves that back roads have something to offer.

127 Corridor. "World's Longest Yard Sale." www.127sale.com (accessed June 20, 2007).

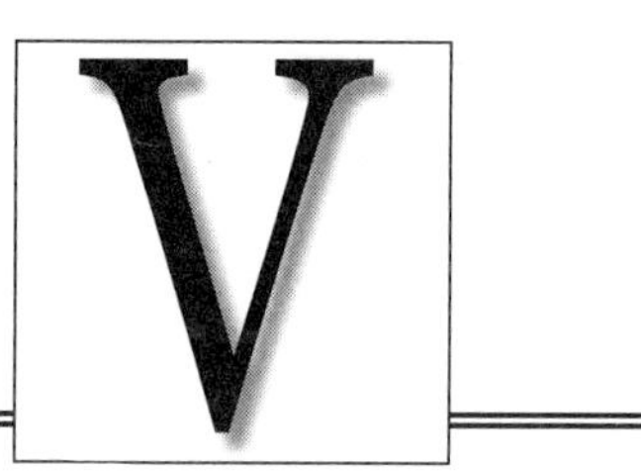

VAN VOAST, JAMES, GENERAL (b. September 19, 1827, Schenectady, N.Y.; d. July 16, 1915, Cincinnati, Ohio). James Van Voast, a commander of the Newport Barracks, was the son of John G. and Maria Teller Van Voast. His ancestors were some of the earliest settlers of New York. He acquired his early education at the Lyceum in Schenectady, N.Y., and received a BA from Union College in Schenectady in 1849. After college, he was admitted to the U.S. Military Academy at West Point, N.Y., graduated in 1852, and was made a 2nd lieutenant in the 3rd U.S. Artillery the next year.

On December 21, 1854, Van Voast was aboard the military steamship *San Francisco,* which was transporting troops from New York to California. The ship encountered a storm just out of New York Harbor, and the vessel was completely destroyed. Van Voast assisted the other officers in keeping the steamer afloat until rescue boats arrived and was praised for his gallant efforts. On December 5, 1855, Van Voast married Helen Francis Pierce in Massachusetts. That marriage produced two children. Later that year, Van Voast joined the 9th U.S. Infantry. In 1856, during the Yakima Indian Wars, he was stationed at Fort Dalles, Oregon Territory, along the Columbia River. He was also sent on an expedition to Fort Walla Walla in the Washington Territory, south of modern-day Spokane, Wash.

It was in the West that Van Voast spent the major portion of his military career—building and upgrading remote forts used to protect the settlers of the western migration and also to guard the workers constructing the transcontinental railroads from the plains Indians. His position toward the Indians was fairly lenient. In the mid-1860s, while in charge of Fort Laramie, then in Oregon Territory, he allowed local Indian children to attend the military post's school. He had opinions about how to deal with the **American Indians**, but his views held little influence in the chain of command above him. Occupied with military duties in San Francisco, he participated in the **Civil War** only at its conclusion, along the Florida panhandle.

Van Voast's first wife had died in childbirth, and on July 5, 1870, in St. Louis, Mo., he married Virginia Moss Harris, the daughter of a former mayor of Newport, Ky., and a granddaughter of Gen. **James Taylor**. Their daughter, Virginia Remsen Van Voast, born in 1873, became an acclaimed artist whose paintings were exhibited at the Cincinnati Art Museum. Van Voast and his second wife also had a son, Rufus Adrian Van Voast, who had a long and distinguished military career. In 1875 in a rare assignment in the Midwest, James Van Voast was the commander of the **Newport Barracks** and resided at 180 York St. in Newport. A local militia unit was formed in his honor at Newport. Known as the Van Voast Light Guard, its members assisted in the enforcement of the law and the preservation of order in the city.

Van Voast's career returned him to the West, and in April 1883 he was made a brigadier general of the 9th Regiment of the U.S. Infantry. He retired because of injuries sustained while in the line of duty in Texas. His wife, Virginia, inherited land in modern Bellevue, Ky., which she subdivided into town lots, and a street was named Van Voast in the family's honor. By 1900 the Van Voasts were living at 507 E. Third St., on the near east side of Cincinnati. James Van Voast died in 1915 of bronchial pneumonia at his home in Cincinnati and was buried at Evergreen Cemetery in Southgate.

Evergreen Cemetery Records, Southgate, Ky.
Ohio Death Certificate No. 38946, for the year 1915.
Robertson, E. B. "History of the Ninth Regiment of Infantry." www.army.mil (accessed June 1, 2006).
"Taps Sounded for Van Voast," *CE,* July 18, 1915, 12.
Who Was Who in American History—The Military. Chicago: Marquis Who's Who, 1975.

Robin Caraway

VAN ZANDT, JOHN (b. 1791, Mason Co., Ky.; d. May 25, 1847, Hamilton Co., Ohio). John Van Zandt, an abolitionist, a minister, and a plantation owner, was the son of a wealthy plantation owner. In the early 1800s, Van Zandt operated a large plantation in Boone Co. on which there were several slaves. As a result of his religious convictions, it became increasingly obvious to him that "slavery was a sin." He sold his plantation and moved to the "free state" of Ohio, freeing his slaves. Van Zandt became a Methodist minister in the Glendale, Ohio, area.

Van Zandt played a pivotal part in the **Underground Railroad**, harboring many runaway slaves. It has been suggested that the character John Van Trompe in Harriet Beecher Stowe's book *Uncle Tom's Cabin* is based on John Van Zandt. Stowe once took a female runaway slave to Van Zandt, who then delivered the slave to safety. On April 23, 1842, while driving his wagon just north of the Ohio River, Van Zandt spotted nine runaway slaves and gave them a ride. Slave-catchers eventually caught them with Van Zandt, and all but one, named Andrew, escaped. Salmon P. Chase, who later became chief justice of the U.S. Supreme Court, argued for Van Zandt that slavery was prohibited, based on a 1787 ordinance in the Northwest Territory, part of which later became the State of Ohio. The case reached the U.S. Supreme Court, and Chase lost. In 1841 Van Zandt was expelled from the Methodist Church for lying about his slave-related activities.

Once a prominent figure, Van Zandt sacrificed all for what he believed were injustices to humanity. Shunned by society, Van Zandt was also ruined financially by his efforts on behalf of runaway slaves. After the trial, his 11 children were sent to live with relatives throughout the United States. He died at age 56 and was buried at Wesleyan Cemetery in the Northside area of Cincinnati. His property was sold to pay the staggering debts incurred in the courts.

"Fugitive Slave Case Outlived Protagonists," *CE,* June 16, 2005, A12.
"Hero of Underground Railroad Honored," *CE,* June 16, 2005, A1.

VARBLE, RACHEL M. (b. February 3, 1893, Shelbyville, Ky.; d. August 14, 1976, Fort Wright, Ky.). Novelist Rachel McBrayer Varble was the daughter of James and Sophia Hardin McBrayer. She was a graduate of the Science Hill Female Academy in Shelbyville, Ky. Rachel married Pinkney Varble, and the couple had one child, Annabelle. Pinkney was an executive with the American Radiator Corp., which operated plants in several states. Because of periodic transfers by his company, the family lived in a number of different cities. In the late 1930s, they moved to Northern Kentucky, where they resided along Leathers Rd. in Fort Mitchell.

Early in her adult life, Rachel Varble was an active member of the **Daughters of the American Revolution** (DAR) and the Colonial Dames of America; later she devoted most of her time and energy to a writing career, authoring 14 novels, most of them for young readers. One, *Jane Clemens: The Story of Mark Twain's Mother,* was written especially for adults. Her novel *Three against London* was a 1962 Junior Literary Guild selection. Another of her works, *A Time Will Come,* written in 1940, had as its setting New York City in 1900. That novel recounted the lives of three women who suffered social and economic discrimination from a rich and tyrannical male relative. The problems of the women in the story symbolized the plight of most women, in that era's male-dominated society. Their predicament led them to become zealous supporters of the women's suffrage movement, led by Susan B. Anthony. The book was featured serially in a monthly women's magazine.

Later in life Rachel spent much of her free time working with a women's group at **Trinity Episcopal Church** in Covington. She died at age 83 in the **St. Charles Care Center** in Covington. Her husband and their daughter survived her. Funeral services were held at Trinity Episcopal Church, and she was buried in the Cave Hill Cemetery, Louisville.

"Author of Fourteen Novels, Dies," *KP,* August 16, 1976, 9.
"Varble, Rachel McBrayer," *KP,* August 16, 1976, 11.
"Women against Repression," *KE,* June 4, 1941, 5.

VENABLE, JOHN WESLEY (b. March 30, 1822, Washington, D.C.; d. January 29, 1908, Hopkinsville, Ky.). Rev. J. W. Venable, an Episcopal minister and an artist, was the grand chaplain of the Sovereign Grand Lodge of the **Independent Order of Odd Fellows** (I.O.O.F.) of the United States for 39 years. Venable was the son of Charles

Rev. John Wesley Venable, ca. 1872.

L. and Eliza W. Venable; his father was a tinsmith by trade and a common councilman for the city of Washington, D.C., and his mother was a member of the Shropshire family of Virginia. J. W. Venable attended the Capitol Hill Seminary in Washington, D.C., and later studied under the artist Charby, then resident in the capital. In 1840, at the age of 18, Venable set out for the plantations of Maryland, seeking portrait work. He met with success and made two additional journeys through Maryland that year and one into Virginia. In 1841 he made a second trip through Virginia and then sailed for Louisiana to be the company clerk in a logging-camp operation that secured live oak timber for the U.S. Navy.

In 1842 Venable moved to Covington, Ky., where he soon became involved in the community life of that fledgling river city. In November of 1842, Venable and 13 others signed the resolutions organizing **Trinity Episcopal Church**, and Venable served as the secretary of its first vestry. In 1843, in conjunction with his 21st birthday, he was admitted to Covington's Washington Lodge No. 3 of the IOOF, which membership was to become a life's work for him. He also joined the Kenton Riflemen, serving as an officer. In Covington, Venable painted portraits of the local gentry. On a grander scale, he painted parade banners for the Sons of Temperance, a pictorial flag for the Kenton Riflemen, and a portrait of George Washington for Washington Lodge No. 3. His work drew the favorable attention of the local press. The *Licking Valley Register* urged its readers to "visit the painting rooms of Mr. John W. Venable," claiming that "there they [could not] fail to admire the skill of the artist, and the accuracy of his portraits."

Periodically, Venable traveled to Danville, Ky., taking a room and advertising his availability for portrait work and art instruction. There in 1846 he married Sarah E. Farnsworth. Shortly after his marriage, Venable quit Covington for Central Kentucky to work in Danville, Shelbyville, and environs. It was probably in Shelbyville in 1848–1849 that Venable became the first drawing teacher to the very young Thomas S. Noble, whose depictions of slavery brought him early fame. Noble later, in 1887, led the newly opened Art Academy of Cincinnati, having directed its predecessors since 1869.

Venable was announced in 1849 as a candidate for Holy Orders in the Episcopal Church. After being made a deacon in 1851, he became an assistant to Rev. John N. Norton, rector of the Church of the Ascension in Frankfort, Ky. Norton tutored Venable in his religious studies. That year Venable also accepted his initial position of missionary at St. John's Church in Versailles, Ky. During these years of preparation for the priesthood, he taught drawing, painting, literature, and philosophy at Shelby College, an Episcopal institution in Shelbyville, Ky. In 1854 Venable was ordained by the Right Reverend Benjamin Bosworth Smith, bishop of Kentucky, at the Church of the Ascension in Frankfort.

Venable resigned his post in Frankfort in 1855 and moved to Versailles to focus on his work with St. John's Church. These first years in Versailles allowed him time for drawing and painting. However, in 1859 he began a 23-year period of ministering to two and three parishes concurrently. In his long career with the Episcopal Church, Venable was in charge of four Kentucky parishes: St. John's Church in Versailles, 1851–1882; St. Philip's Church in Harrodsburg, 1859–1862 and 1874–1878; the Church of the Holy Trinity in Georgetown, 1863–1882; and Grace Church in Hopkinsville, 1883–1894. For each parish Venable raised funds and built a new church. With the exception of the one at Versailles, the houses of worship he built stand and serve to this day. St. Philip's Church in Harrodsburg was found worthy of mention in Rexford Newcomb's *Architecture in Old Kentucky.*

Venable concluded his active ministry in 1894 owing to his age and increasing disability. In retirement, he was tended by his second wife, Fannie M. Venable, his first wife having died in 1873. Although retired, Venable continued in his role as the grand chaplain of the Sovereign Grand Lodge of the IOOF of the United States, a position he had held since 1868 and in which he continued for the rest of his life. He lived in Hopkinsville but maintained his membership in the McKee Lodge No. 35 of Versailles, where he was elected a member in 1854. With the duties of the parish behind him, Venable was able to prepare the conceptual layout of *The Official History and Literature of Odd Fellowship: The Three-Link Fraternity,* first copyrighted in 1897. The grand chaplain served as an associate editor of the 896-page tome. He also penned the closing chapters, which provide an overview of the order at a time when nearly 1 million members embraced the "Three-Links" of "Friendship, Love and Truth" and were committed to the order's primary mission of aiding the less fortunate, critically important in those years before government welfare and social services.

Venable died at his residence, Cottage Home, in Hopkinsville, and was buried on January 30, 1908, in Riverside Cemetery in Hopkinsville after services at his beloved Grace Church. Services at the cemetery were conducted by the Green River Lodge No. 54 of the IOOF. The news of his death was carried by the Associated Press and appeared in many of the nation's newspapers.

Averdick, Michael R. *J.W. Venable: Artist and Minister, 1822–1908.* Forthcoming.

"Portrait and Miniature Painting," *LVR*, November 11, 1843, 3.

Michael R. Averdick

VENT HAVEN MUSEUM. William S. Berger of Fort Mitchell, who was chairman of the Cambridge Tile Company from the mid-1930s through the 1940s, founded Vent Haven Museum as a charitable foundation in 1963. Over the previous 40 years, he had collected more than 500 ventriloquist figures ("dummies") and supporting memorabilia, and he contributed his entire collection to the museum. The Vent Haven Museum became, and continues to be, the largest of its type in the world and is a mecca for ventriloquists from all over the world. Its collection of figures has increased to 675 and grows each year from donations.

When William S. Berger died in 1972, museum president John R. S. Brooking constructed a building in Berger's honor to house the museum's best figures and to complement the other two buildings on the property at 33 W. Maple St., Fort Mitchell, which contain the balance of the collection.

The curator of the museum maintains the collection and gives tours from May 1 through September 30. The museum sponsors the Annual Ventriloquist Convention in July at the Drawbridge Convention Center in Fort Mitchell, where more than 400 ventriloquists, both amateurs and professionals, gather to promote the art of ventriloquism and support the museum.

More than 1,000 people visit the museum annually, and many professional ventriloquists bequeath their figures to the museum. The museum houses replicas of Edgar Bergen's Charlie McCarthy and Mortimer Snerd, originals of Jimmy Nelson's Danny O'Day and Farfel, Jeff Dunham's Walter and Peanut, Senior Wenses's Johnny, and many others.

"A Dummy's Guide to Dummies," *CE*, July 15, 1999, C1–C2.

"A Museum for Dummies," *KP*, July 22, 1998, 1KK–3KK.

"Talk about a Real Dummy," *KP*, July 16, 1994, 8A.

John R. S. Brooking

VERONA. Verona is a small rural community located in southern Boone Co. at the crossroads of Ky. Rts. 14, 16, and 491. The larger Verona area also encompasses portions of northern Gallatin and Grant counties. The exact circumstances leading to Verona's settlement, and its founders, are unknown. One of the earliest settlements in the Verona area was known as the Stephenson Settlement. It is mentioned in the "History of New Bethel Baptist Church," as Zadock and Delphia Stephenson deeded one acre of land to the church in 1845. Today, this property is part of the grounds of the New Bethel Cemetery. There are two theories as to the location of the Stephenson Settlement. According to one theory, Stephenson Mill, owned and operated by Arthur Stephenson, was located on McCoy's Fork Creek, and the Stephenson schoolhouse was nearby. The mill was located at the current I-71 overpass just north of the Verona interchange. Another possible location of Stephenson Settlement is along Eades Rd. near the Ky. Rt. 16 intersection.

Verona once was a thriving business community surrounded by farmland. A family could purchase the goods they needed in town. Businesses included a bank, a blacksmith shop, a building supply store, a creamery, a dry goods store, a funeral home, grocery stores, a jail, a post office, saloons, and tobacco shops. The local 1883 Lake atlas indicates that the H. Anderson family owned one of the early businesses in Verona; Anderson was a farmer and a wagon maker who settled in Verona in 1805. Names of other early families in Verona included Coyle, Hamilton, Johnson, Porter, Renaker, Richards, Ryan, Stephenson, Vest, Waller, and Whitson.

The Verona Post Office was established on March 24, 1834, and the first postmaster was Alexander McPherson. The post office was at the corner of Ky. Rts. 14 and 16 in a large building that also housed the local barbershop, the dry goods store, and the grocery store. Trains began delivering the mail to the Verona Depot soon after construction of the **Louisville, Cincinnati, and Lexington Railroad** (today the **CSX**) through Boone Co. in 1869. The old building now serves as a local gathering place called Verona City Hall. Currently, the post office is in the firehouse building. The train depot was at the current water station on Ky. Rt. 491. Trains provided an important mode of transportation for the citizens of Verona. For example, passenger trains transported students from other communities to Verona School. At one time, Verona was also a college town: Nancy E. Hamilton operated the prestigious League Institute at Verona in the 1880s. The local public school, Verona High School, was established in 1914.

The Verona Bank, one of the oldest banks in Boone Co., was established in 1904 by a group of concerned citizens and remained in operation throughout the **Great Depression**. William M. Whitson was the first president of the bank. It was the members of the Verona Bank Board of Directors who were responsible for the incorporation of the city of Verona in 1909. The new town's leadership became inactive, however, and the incorporation was eventually dissolved.

The Renaker family owned and operated Verona Garage. In the early days, when patrons purchased coal and feed at this garage, scales built in the ground were used to weigh each wagonload or truckload of goods. In later years, the owners of the garage sold gas products and provided towing and mechanic services. The Verona Garage and the Renaker home were destroyed by fire in January 2003.

Churches in the Verona vicinity have been important to the community as the sites of worship services, ice cream socials, and picnics. The New Bethel Baptist Church was established in 1840. There was a Methodist Church in Verona at the New Bethel Baptist Church site on Ky. Rt. 14. The **Concord Baptist Church** is located on Ky. Rt. 16 in nearby Gallatin Co. In the mid-1850s in Verona, Irish immigrants were attending a Roman Catholic mission, which became St. Patrick Church. In the early 1950s, St. Patrick Church merged with **All Saints Catholic Church** in Walton. The Verona Full Gospel Church was established in 1973, in the home of Nanny Gumm. During a small group prayer meeting, Gumm told Rev. David Hocker that he needed to start a church in Verona, and she gave him one dollar toward its establishment. Today, the church, with approximately 65 members, is active in the community.

The Verona Fire Department began in 1968, with an old army truck equipped with a water tank and a pump. The fire truck was housed in a garage along Ky. Rt. 491. The Life Squad dates back to 1978, after Dr. William M. Waller challenged the citizens of Verona to provide emergency services for the community. Nearly 35 dedicated volunteers today staff the Verona fire department and life squad.

An Atlas of Boone, Kenton, and Campbell Counties, Kentucky. Philadelphia: D. J. Lake, 1883.
Boone County Banner, March 1, 1897.
Boone County Recorder, historical ed., September 4, 1930.
Flynn, Terry. "Close to Home in Verona," *CE*, June 29, 1998, B1.
"History of New Bethel Baptist Church," 2001, New Bethel Baptist Church, Verona, Ky.
Reis, Jim. "St. Patrick in Verona Filled Spiritual Needs for 87 Years," *KP*, March 16, 1998, 4K.
"Schools and Teachers," *DC*, September 11, 1883, 1.
"Verona Fire Department Marks 25th Anniversary," *KP*, November 9, 1993, 9A.

Karen L. Leek

VEST, JOHN L. (b. November 13, 1875, Verona, Ky.; d. November 15, 1960, Walton, Ky.). Attorney John Lewis Vest was the eldest son of Carter Hamilton Vest and Miranda Jane Lewis Vest and a great-great-grandson of George Vest, a **Revolutionary War** soldier who had a land grant in Boone Co. on the north side of the Walton-Verona Rd. John Vest practiced law in Kenton, Campbell, and Boone counties for more than 60 years; at the time of his death, he was considered the dean of Boone Co. lawyers. For the most part a corporate lawyer, Vest served on the boards of numerous corporations and financial institutions, including the Formica Corporation, of which he was majority stockholder; Equitable Band & Trust Company of Walton, of which he was a founder; the Bank of Independence; the Income Life Insurance Company of Louisville; and Lexington's Angliana Loose Leaf Tobacco Warehouse.

Educated at National Normal University at Lebanon, Ohio, he first studied law under John G. Tomlin and passed the bar exam in August 1899; Vest opened his first law office in Independence. While practicing law there, he was also active in the formation of a fledgling telephone business. In the summer of 1904, Vest, serving as city attorney, found himself in need of a defense attorney, because he had shot and killed Tom Riley, the town marshal, in a dispute over a telephone exchange located in Riley's home and overseen by Riley's wife. The two men had had words on the morning of July 24, 1904, and had to be separated. That afternoon they met again, and witnesses said Vest walked away but Riley followed. After being restrained again, Riley came after Vest. Vest said he saw Riley reach for his pocket. Vest pulled out a revolver and shot three times, hitting Riley twice and killing him. A search of Riley's pockets turned up only a slingshot, but Vest was acquitted on a claim of self-defense.

In 1906 Vest married Edna May Loomis of Kenton Co., and they had one child, Walter Dudley Vest. In 1910 John Vest, in partnership with Tomlin, opened what became an extensive law practice in Walton, where he worked until his retirement in 1957. During his time in Walton, he was also active in various business interests, including a Chevrolet auto dealership that sold more than 500 cars annually in Boone and Gallatin counties. An attorney most of his career, Vest served as a special judge in the Campbell Co. Circuit Court in 1944, during a gambling abatement suit.

Vest's younger siblings were also active in the community: his sister, Lizzie Vest (1880–1967), was postmaster of Verona from 1920 to 1950; his brother, D. Hess Vest (1892–1979), was postmaster of Walton through the mid-1960s; and another sister, Sallie Vest (1877–1975), spent her career working with the U.S. State Department in Washington, D.C. John Vest was buried in Highland Cemetery in Fort Mitchell.

"John L. Vest," *Boone County Recorder,* historical ed., September 4, 1930.
"Noted Attorney Dies," *Walton Advertiser,* November 17, 1960, 1.
Reis, Jim. "Guns Brought Death to Three Who Wore Badge," *KP*, February 3, 1997, 4K.
"Rites Set Friday for John L. Vest," *KP*, November 16, 1960, 1.

Stephen M. Vest

VETERANS ADMINISTRATION MEDICAL CENTER. The Veterans Administration Medical Center in Fort Thomas is located at the intersection of S. Fort Thomas Ave. and River Rd. and is housed in an army barracks constructed in 1938.

From the 1890s until 1940, the military installation at Fort Thomas was home to various U.S. Army infantry regiments. Initially, the fort was able to house only part of a regiment in its barracks. In 1938 the Work Progress Administration (WPA) built a 375-man, multistory brick barracks, a facility that was used by the 10th Infantry Regiment from 1938 until 1940, when the unit shipped overseas. From 1940 until 1944, the barracks was used both as the post's headquarters and as a regional military induction center to process draftees into all branches of service. In 1944 the Army Air Force took over the barracks and used it as a rehabilitation center for its personnel until late in 1945.

In 1946 the barracks was turned over to the Veteran's Administration (VA), which spent $172,000 converting it into a hospital. This expenditure was announced as only the first step in locating a 750-bed VA hospital at the site in Fort Thomas. The first patients entered the hospital on September 2, 1947. The funds necessary to increase the size of the Fort Thomas facility to 750 beds, however, was never forthcoming from the U.S. Congress, in spite of the persistent efforts of local congressman **Brent Spence**. Instead, on January 23, 1957, the Fort Thomas VA Hospital was made a division of the newly built Cincinnati Veterans Hospital on Vine St. in the Cincinnati suburb of Corryville. In 1967 the Fort Thomas VA Hospital was converted into a 206-bed VA nursing home, and all other previously provided VA medical services were transferred to the Cincinnati facility.

The mission of the Fort Thomas facility has been changed, over the years, to supporting the needs of local veterans. In 2005 the Fort Thomas VA facility remained a division of the Cincinnati VA Medical Center, even though the two operations are situated in different federal regions. The Fort Thomas Veterans Administration Medical Center is now configured as a 131-bed Nursing Care Unit (presently using only about 60 beds), a 50-bed Homeless Veterans Domiciliary Unit, and a 10-bed Substance Abuse Domiciliary Care Unit.

Fogarty, Bob. "To Revamp Ft. Thomas VA as 'Model Nursing Home,'" *KP*, March 25, 1967, 1K.

"Ft. Thomas Post Passes to Air Force," *KP*, September 30, 1944, 1.

Fort Thomas VA Facility Historical File, Veterans Administration Medical Center, Cincinnati.

Charles H. Bogart

VETERANS' MEMORIALS AND MONUMENTS. Each of the 11 Northern Kentucky counties has a county veterans' memorial. The practice of constructing veterans' memorials and monuments in the United States began to expand in the late 19th and early 20th centuries. These early memorials and monuments were mostly dedicated to **Civil War** veterans; there were monuments to individual soldiers as well as to entire units that fought. Depending on the location, they honored soldiers from both the North and the South and were erected in towns and cemeteries and on battlefields. These memorials were constructed through the efforts and sometimes with the funding of veterans' organizations, including the Grand Army of the Republic (Union veterans) and the United Confederate Veterans Association, to honor their fallen comrades. As the United States became involved in other conflicts, especially **World War I** and **World War II**, individual states and counties as well as many cities and towns began to create memorials to their war dead. Today, veterans' me-

VETERANS' MEMORIALS AND MONUMENTS IN NORTHERN KENTUCKY

City	*Location*	*Focus*
Boone Co.		
Florence	Government Center	WWI, WWII, Korea, Vietnam
Walton	Center of town near railroad tracks	All veterans
Bracken Co.		
Augusta	Elizabeth St.	WWI, WWII, Korea, Vietnam
	Second and Bracken Sts.	WWI, WWII
Brooksville	Court House square, NE Corner	WWII
Campbell Co.		
Dayton	Veterans Park, Sixth Ave. and Berry St.	All veterans
Wilder	Behind city building	All veterans
Southgate	Park behind VFW Post	WWI, WWII
Newport	In front of city building	All veterans
Fort Thomas	Water Tower, Old Fort Thomas Post	Spanish-American War
Carroll Co.		
General Butler State Park	Hwy 227 at park entrance	All Kentucky veterans
Carrollton	County Courthouse Square	WWI, WWII, Iraqi freedom
Gallatin Co.		
Warsaw	100 Main St., Court House lawn	WWI, WWII, Korea, Vietnam
Grant Co.		
Williamstown	County Court House lawn	WWI, WWII, Korea, Vietnam
Dry Ridge	Beside Grant Co. Middle School, facing Dry Ridge Elementary School	WWI, WWII
Kenton Co.		
Villa Hills	Buttermilk Pk. and Collins Rd.	WWI, WWII, Korea, Vietnam
Erlanger	Commonwealth Ave. and Dixie Highway	Vietnam
Latonia	Rittie's Corner	Korea
	Inside entrance to American Legion Post 203	World War I
Covington	Linden Grove Cemetery	Civil War (Union and Confederate)
	Holmes High School Campus	WWII
Fort Wright	In front of city building	All veterans
Ludlow	City Park	Korea and Vietnam
Mason Co.		
Maysville	In front of County Court House	WWI, WWII, Korea, Vietnam
	Maysville Cemetery	Civil War (Union)
Owen Co.		
Owenton	In front of County Court House	WWI, WWII, Korea, Vietnam
	I.O.O.F. Cemetery	Civil War
Pendleton Co.		
Falmouth	In front of County Court House	WWI, WWII, Korea, Vietnam
	In front of VFW, Second and Park Sts.	All veterans
Robertson Co.		
Mount Olivet	In front of County Court House	All veterans
	City park, center of town	WWI, WWII, Korea

morials can be found in all 50 states. These tributes to veterans in many cases cover more than one conflict, and some honor all veterans regardless of when they served. The table is a sampling of veterans' memorials and monuments in Northern Kentucky, including their general location.

Carroll County Tourism. "Kentucky Veterans Memorial"; "General Butler State Resort Park and Conference Center." www.carrolltontourism.com/things_to_do.htm (accessed April 20, 2007).

War. www.waymarking.com/cat/details.aspx?f=1&guid=51c899fa-88c4-4eae-b8ff-c099130a6f62. A listing of Civil War veteran monuments with dates they were dedicated.

Robert B. Snow

VFW. The VFW (Veterans of Foreign Wars) is the oldest active military veterans organization in the United States, and it is strongly represented in Northern Kentucky. In 2004 the VFW included more than 2 million members organized into 9,781 posts worldwide. The VFW traces its origin to 1899 when demobilized Spanish-American War veterans formed a number of fraternal organizations. During the next few years, veterans of the Philippine Insurrection and the Boxer Rebellion in China also formed fraternal societies. These various separate fraternal groups slowly began to combine into one large organization modeled on the **Civil War**'s Grand Army of the Republic (GAR) veteran organization. In 1914 the 20th-century military fraternal veteran organizations merged to form the VFW.

Membership was open to any member of the U.S. armed service (Army, Navy, Marines, Coast Guard, and later, Air Force) who served in a military campaign outside the United States. As a result of this broadening of membership requirements to all veterans who had served outside the United States, participants in the Spanish-American War (see **National Guard, Spanish-American War**), the Cuban Pacification, and other U.S. overseas military actions were allowed to join.

Within a few years, the veterans of the Mexican Expedition Campaign of 1916–1917, **World War I**, and pacification missions in Central America and the Caribbean also began to join. In 1921 VFW membership was opened to women veterans. **World War II**, the **Korean War**, the Gulf and Iraq wars, and a host of other post–World War II overseas unilateral actions and United Nations–supported military missions have been added to the groups eligible.

Since its beginning, the VFW has promoted a strong defense establishment, veteran benefits (the GI Bill, the Veteran Bonus, veteran preference, and disability and survivor benefits), and patriotism. The VFW is headquartered in Kansas City, Mo. The Northern Kentucky region has 16 VFW posts: No. 3205 Alexandria, No. 9535 Augusta, No. 1484 Covington, No. 7099 Covington, No. 7453 Covington, No. 2899 Dayton, No. 6423 Erlanger, No. 1978 Falmouth, No. 6095 Latonia, No. 2734 Maysville, No. 1404 Newport, No. 5662 Newport, No. 3199 Owenton, No. 1095 Ryland Heights, No. 3186 Southgate, and No. 11140 Warsaw.

Mason, Herbert M. *VFW: Our First Century*. Lenexa, Kans.: Addax, 1999.

"VFW Elects Postal Carrier," *KTS*, June 17, 1958, 2A.

"VFW: More than Just a Bar," *KE*, July 3, 1995, A10.

"VFW Post Given Citation," *KE*, February 21, 1996, B3.

Charles H. Bogart

VIETNAM WAR (1959–April 30, 1975). Northern Kentuckians were among the courageous soldiers who served in the Vietnam War. The war in Vietnam is the longest military action by the United States in its history. The nation's role in Vietnam began in 1950 when U.S. equipment and advisers were sent to help French colonial forces fight an attempt by the Vietnamese to win their independence. By 1954 the French had lost this war and Vietnam was divided into two sections: the Communist North and the Democratic South. In 1956 the United States took over full responsibility of advising and building up the South Vietnamese military to prevent Vietnam from being unified under a Communist government. The first U.S. combat deaths in Vietnam occurred in 1959. By 1960 a new organization in the North, named the National Front for the Liberation of South Vietnam, was established with the goal of defeating the South through guerilla warfare and by insurgency operations. This group, called by Americans the Viet Cong (VC), began to step up operations in 1961, including incursions into neighboring Laos. By 1962, as a result of the worsening situation, the number of American advisers in Vietnam was increased from 700 to nearly 12,000, and American forces began providing air support for the South Vietnamese military. It was during this escalation that the first Northern Kentucky soldier was killed: on November 5, 1962, 1st Lt. William Tully of the U.S. Air Force (USAF), from Mason Co., was shot down while supporting South Vietnamese ground forces.

In August 1964 an incident was said to occur in the Gulf of Tonkin involving an attack on U.S. warships by North Vietnamese torpedo boats. Following this alleged incident, the United States attacked a North Vietnamese naval installation. Shortly afterward, the Gulf of Tonkin Resolution was signed by President Lyndon Johnson (1963–1969), increasing military involvement in Vietnam but not actually declaring war. In November 1965 the first major battle between North Vietnamese and U.S. forces took place when 450 soldiers of the 1st Cavalry Division (Air mobile) were airlifted by helicopter to the Ia Drang Valley in the central highlands of Vietnam. Their objective was to destroy a North Vietnamese force, but they were immediately surrounded by 2,000 North Vietnamese Army (NVA) troops. During the three-day battle, 234 Americans were killed, including Carroll Co.'s Sgt. Paris Dusch of the Army's 7th Cavalry Regiment, and more than 1,000 NVA soldiers were killed, making this the first major U.S. victory of the war.

From 1966 through 1969, the war escalated and the number of American troops in Vietnam steadily increased. The highest troop strength in Vietnam reached 543,582 on April 30, 1969. The only Kentucky National Guard unit to be called to active duty during the Vietnam war was Battery A, 2nd Battalion, 138th Field Artillery, from Carroll Co. It saw service in 1968 and 1969. This period was also among the costliest in terms of U.S. combat deaths, especially for Northern Kentucky, which lost 75 men during these years. One of the heaviest and costliest years of fighting was 1968. In January 1968 a combined force of NVA and VC units launched a surprise countrywide offensive known as the Tet Offensive. It was undertaken primarily because of the hope that it would incite an uprising against the South Vietnamese government. The offensive included attacks on 100 towns and cities, including 36 provincial capitals and the national capital, Saigon. Among the Northern Kentuckians killed during this offensive, which lasted from January to June 1968, were Army Cpl. Samuel G. Hurry of Kenton Co., who was killed on February 2, 1968, and Army Pfc. William Eldridge, also from Kenton Co., who was killed on April 4, 1968. During combat action that took place on May 27, 1969, Army Sgt. Charles C. "Chalkie" Fleek, of Boone Co., was serving with Charlie Company, 127th Wolfhounds, 25th Infantry Division, during an ambush operation in the Binh Doung Province. During this action a grenade landed near some of Fleek's men, and instead of taking cover he threw himself on the grenade and was killed, saving his men. For this act of heroism, Fleek was awarded the Congressional **Medal of Honor**; he was the most decorated Northern Kentucky soldier of the Vietnam War.

At various stages, the war involved clashes between small units patrolling mountain and jungle areas as well as amphibious operations and combat operations on the waterways of Vietnam. The war also saw guerrilla attacks on villages, towns, and even in the cities. A large-scale air war was also fought in Vietnam by both the USAF and the U.S. Navy (USN), which targeted North Vietnamese cities, industrial targets, and supply lines. Between 1966 and 1968, a major air campaign was fought over North Vietnam that included bombing raids, fighter support missions (which dealt with enemy fighters and surface-to-air missile sites), and flights to gather intelligence. It was during a mission over North Vietnam on October 21, 1968, that Kenton Co.'s Lt. Col. Alden O'Brien, USAF, was shot down and killed in action, making him the highest-ranking Northern Kentucky officer killed in action. The bombings of North Vietnam ceased on November 1, 1968, by order of President Johnson, as a gesture to bring the North to the peace talks in Paris, France. The air war shifted to Laos, and from there the North continued to stage attacks, until the North again became a target in 1972.

Aviation was also an important part of the war in South Vietnam. Helicopters played a vital role in troop movement, evacuation of casualties, command-and-control missions, ground troop support, and movement of supplies. They were used by all branches of the armed forces, but primarily by the Army and the Marine Corps (USMC). During a mission on August 28, 1968, a Marine UH-1E Huey gunship of Marine Squadron HML-167 was flying a night "Firefly" mission to spot and attack enemy positions. The helicopter was hit by enemy ground fire, crashed, and exploded, killing three members of its crew. Among those killed was Cpl. John B. Becker, USMC, of Campbell Co., who was the gunner on the mission. The USAF used light aircraft, such as the O-1E Birddog, for low-level reconnaissance and support missions. On September 8, 1967, during one such reconnaissance mission near Bien Hoa, Campbell Co.'s Air Force captains Albert Sayer and J. J. Cappel were shot down by automatic weapon fire. Both were trapped in the wreckage and survived the crash, but Sayer died from his wounds.

USN missions included attacking areas along the river that were used as supply and staging areas for the NVA and the VC, intercepting supplies being smuggled up and down the rivers, and supporting ground operations either by fire support or the transporting of assault troops to specific areas. On July 23, 1969, a 22-boat column transporting the 360th Infantry to designated landing beaches along the Rach Ben Tre River was ambushed. Two sailors on the lead boat were killed, and 15 were wounded during the assault; one of the two dead was BM1 John F. Bobb, USN, from Kenton Co. In an earlier river mission, called Operation Allen Brook, members of the 3rd battalion of the 5th Marines attacked Go Noi Island southwest of Danang, which was being used as a base by NVA and VC forces. During the assault on the island, four marines, including Kenton Co.'s Pfc. Bradley Bowling, USMC, were killed.

Following the election of President Richard Nixon (1969–1974), a gradual reduction in troops began. Throughout the war, especially after the Tet Offensive of 1968 and the Mai Lai massacre, antiwar protests heated up in the United States. Although many of these protests were peaceful, some did erupt into violence. In Northern Kentucky, war protests tended to be peaceful in nature. In 1970 President Nixon ordered operations against NVA and VC troops that were using Cambodia as a staging ground for attacks against U.S. forces. One of the few casualties of the fighting in Cambodia from Northern Kentucky was Kenton Co.'s 1st Lt. William J. Brewer, U.S. Army, who was killed in action on May 14, 1970. From 1970 to 1972, Nixon authorized reductions in troop strength seven times, and by May 1, 1972, troop levels had been reduced to 69,000. On March 30, 1972, the North launched the biggest offensive since Tet in 1968, and by April, Nixon renewed the bombing of the North. The operation, known as Linebacker II, included aircraft of the USN as well as units of the 7th and 8th Air Forces. The highest-ranking officer from Northern Kentucky to serve during the war was Owen Co.'s Lt. Gen. **Gerald Johnson**, USAF, commander of the U.S. 8th Air Force, based at Anderson Air Force Base, Guam. He held this command from 1971 to 1973 and was involved in the planning of Linebacker II.

Linebacker II forced the North back to the bargaining table, and by January 1973, peace was in sight. On January 27, 1973, the war officially ended and most U.S. troops were withdrawn. Even with the war officially at an end, some American troops remained to advise the South Vietnamese military. On March 9, 1975, the North launched their last major offensive in the South, taking control of the South in 55 days. They had gambled that the United States would not recommit its forces, and their gamble paid off. The last Americans left Vietnam with the evacuation of Saigon on April 29, 1975.

During the course of the war, Northern Kentuckians fought in every branch of the armed forces; some had joined voluntarily and some were drafted. Of the 1,103 Kentuckians that were killed in Vietnam, 109 were from Northern Kentucky counties. The losses by county were as follows: Boone, 11; Bracken, 1; Campbell, 35; Carroll, 2; Gallatin, 2; Grant, 4; Kenton, 44; Mason, 4; Owen, 4; Pendleton, 1; and Robertson, 1. By branch of service there were 5 in the Air Force, 66 in the Army, 35 in the Marine Corps, and 3 in the Navy. Two Northern Kentuckians are still listed as Missing in Action (see **Vietnam War, Missing in Action**); they are Campbell Co.'s Capt. John S. Ross, USAF, and Kenton Co.'s Pfc. Gary Lee Hall, USMC. Hall can also be considered the last Northern Kentuckian to lose his life, since he was listed as MIA on May 15, 1975.

Herring, George C. *America's Longest War: The United States and Vietnam, 1950–1975*. New York: Random House, 1988.

In Memory of Captain Albert Francis Jr Sayer. http://tanaya.net/cgi-bin/vmw.cgi?45697 (accessed May 10, 2007).

Kentucky Vietnam Veterans Memorial. www.kyvietnammemorial.net/data3.html (accessed May 14, 2007).

Kleber, John E., ed. *The Kentucky Encyclopedia*. Lexington: Univ. Press of Kentucky, 1992.

The National Archives. "State-Level Casualty Lists for the Vietnam War." www.archives.gov/research/vietnam-war/casualty-lists/state-level-by-town.html (accessed May 2, 2007).

No Quarter. "Vietnam Casualty Search Engine." www.no-quarter.org/gui/index.php (accessed May 4, 2007).

Rather, Julia D., ed. *Register of Vietnam War Casualties from Kentucky*. Frankfort, Ky.: Department of Libraries and Archives, 1988.

U.S. Naval Forces. "John F. Bobb." www.mrfa.org/navykia.htm (accessed May 10, 2007).

Vietnam War Statistics. http://capmarine.com/cap/statistics.htm (accessed May 15, 2007).

Vietnam War Timeline. www.landscaper.net/timelin.htm#time%20line (accessed May 5, 2007).

Robert B. Snow

VIETNAM WAR, MISSING IN ACTION. Two individuals from the Northern Kentucky region, Joseph Shaw Ross and Gary Lee Hall, went off to fight in the Vietnam War but never returned. They are still classified missing in action.

Capt. Joseph Shaw Ross is a descendant of a prominent Fort Thomas family. The Shaw family was present in Campbell Co. from the early days of its settlement. Ross, the son of Perry S. and Katherine Shaw Ross, grew up along Highland Ave. in Fort Thomas. In 1961 he graduated from **Highlands High School** in Fort Thomas, where he played football on the school's first state championship team of 1960. From there he went to the U.S. Air Force Academy, graduating with a commission in 1965. On August 1, 1968, while he was flying his F4D Phantom II out of Da Nang Air Force Base in South Vietnam with the 389th Tactical Fighter Squadron, his aircraft was shot down during a night reconnaissance mission. This took place near the Ban Karia Pass on the Laos-Vietnam border, in a mountainous area. There have been no reports indicating what happened to him, whether he is dead or alive, or whether he is living in captivity. A memorial service was held for Captain Ross at the Evergreen Cemetery Chapel in Southgate on March 17, 1975.

Gary Lee Hall was born in Covington on July 26, 1956, the son of Seldon and Norma Georgorie Hall. Gary graduated from **Holmes High School** in 1974. After high school, he enlisted in the U.S. Marine Corps, and in May 1975 was assigned to Company G, 2nd Battalion, 9th Marine, 3rd Marine Division. After the USS *Mayaguez* incident, when Cambodian naval forces captured the ship and its crew en route to resupply U.S. military bases in Thailand, President Gerald Ford (1974–1977) authorized military action to return the ship and its crew. Hall was a marine assigned to the Operation Mayaguez task force, and he took part in the combat that occurred; however, Hall was left behind in the confusion of battle. His memorial marker at Holmes High School reads, "Captured and executed by enemy forces after heroically defending the evacuation of his fellow Marines [at] Koh Tang Island, Cambodia May 15, 1975." If the account given on this marker is correct, though it has never been verified, Hall was the last or the second-to-last serviceman killed in a combat mission connected with the Vietnam War. Currently, however, the Defense Prisoner of War/Missing Personnel Office lists Hall as "unaccounted-for," just as it does Joseph Shaw Ross.

Holmes High School Alumni Records, Holmes High School, Covington, Ky.

"Tri-States Missing in Action," *CE*, April 2, 2000, A14.

VILLA HILLS. Villa Hills, a residential city in northern Kenton Co., is bordered by the Ohio River and Bromley on the north, by Erlanger and Boone Co. on the west, and by Crescent Springs on the south and east. It was incorporated as a sixth-class city in 1962.

The first known permanent settlers arrived in about 1785. Robert McKay, his wife, and seven children traveled from Frederick Co., Va., to settle on land that was deeded to him for service in the **Revolutionary War**. His land was bounded by the Ohio River, Dry Creek, and Pleasant Run Creek. It is believed that the McKays owned around 3,000 acres. In 1825, the granddaughter of Robert McKay married Charles W. Scott and was deeded about 300 acres. In 1843 the Scotts began construction of a two-story white brick house that stood until 2004 on Highwater Rd., overlooking the Ohio River. The Scott home place had been continuously occupied by family members from 1843 to 2004.

In 1903 the **Sisters of St. Benedict** purchased about 85 acres of the W. C. Collins Estate, on which were built the St. Walburg Convent and the **Villa Madonna Academy**, which was originally a boarding and day school for girls. The sisters continued to purchase adjacent property and currently own about 230 acres. This land is now home to Villa Daycare; Villa Montessori School; the modern Villa Madonna Academy, a private coeducational school for grades 1–12; the St. Walburg Convent and Motherhouse; several historic homes; a cemetery for the sisters; and the Madonna Manor Nursing Home, opened by the sisters in 1964. The full-care nursing home is surrounded by independent-living apartments.

Around 1900, what is now Villa Hills was unincorporated county farmland dubbed unofficially Madonna Acres and Ludlow. Some of the farm owners at that time were named Boh, Cleveland, Collins, Eubanks, Kremer, Krumpelman, Maegley, Schreck, Scott, Summe, and Thirs. The creation of I-75 in the early 1960s brought residents from the cities to the new suburbs. The streets existing then were Buttermilk Pk. and Collins and Amsterdam Rds. With the 1955 sale of the Boh and Schreck farms came the development of new streets: Ann, Frank, Kenridge, Mary, Rardin Ct., and Sunglow. In 1962 the population was 425.

Fearing annexation from Covington, a group of neighbors formed a board of trustees and borrowed $300 from the Villa Hills Civic Club to incorporate as a city. The original trustees of Villa Hills were George Parsons, chairman, William Krumpelman, Roger Nolting, Robert Springelmeyer, and Robert Stephenson. Harry Rigney was police judge; Gerhard Tebelman, marshal; Joseph Spille, treasurer; and Betty Stivers, secretary pro tem. The first order of business was to annex the property surrounding the original one-half square mile of Villa Hills. The property was obtained and Villa Hills grew to 3.5 square miles. The trustees realized that if they wanted growth, they must take on the huge project of replacing septic tanks with a sanitary sewer system. This was undertaken and accomplished, with the first families able to tap into the system in 1967.

The *Voice of Villa Hills,* a free monthly newsletter, was first published in June 1967 and delivered to 370 homes. Today, the newspaper continues to be published by an all-volunteer staff. By 1968 the state legislature passed a bill that raised Villa Hills to a fifth-class city. With this change, the city replaced the title of chairman of the board by that of mayor. So Tom Braun, who was the chairman at the time, became the first mayor of Villa Hills. In 1968 the **Vietnam War** claimed the life of one resident, Sgt. Ronald L. Niewahner. A street in the Amsterdam Village subdivision is named in his honor.

Recreation has always been important to Villa Hills residents. In the mid-1960s, teams were created for youth football, knothole baseball, and softball; in the mid-1970s, soccer was introduced to the area. The Villa Hills Civic Club purchased 28 acres of land, including a lake and a public building, from longtime residents Joe and Helen Franzen and created Franzen's Fields, used for baseball, softball, and soccer. The building is the home of the Civic Club and the site of social activities sponsored by the club, including the Easter Egg Hunt, the Christmas Party, and the Halloween Haunted Trail. The early 1970s found the city in need of more fields, so an agreement was signed with the Sisters of St. Benedict to lease acreage along Amsterdam Rd. for $1 per year. Originally, the baseball diamonds there were called Tom Braun Fields, in honor of the first mayor. A soccer field was added and named LeRoux "Bud" Cunningham Field in honor of the city's second mayor, who was instrumental in the creation of youth soccer teams in Northern Kentucky. Around 1980, the first Villa Hills City Building was built on Rogers Rd., providing a permanent home to the Villa Hills Police and Public Works departments. The year 1980 also brought the annexation of Prospect Point, a condominium and apartment community off Amsterdam Rd. overlooking the Ohio River. This community has 359 condominiums and 139 apartments.

In the late 1980s, Villa Hills was the first city in Northern Kentucky to institute a recycling program. It began with a voluntary program, in which residents brought recyclables to the City Building parking lot and volunteers separated the items. In 1990 the city began its curbside recycling program. River Ridge Elementary School, on Amsterdam Rd., opened in 1992, replacing the aged Crescent Springs School. At the time, River Ridge was the largest elementary school in the state, with a capacity of 1,200 children.

In 1994 Villa Hills was designated the Cincinnati area's most livable city by *Cincinnati Magazine.* During the late 1990s, sidewalks were expanded on three major roads, Amsterdam and Collins Rds. and Buttermilk Pk. The sidewalks for these busy streets were built and paid for through grants and donations, including citizens' donations of free labor. In 2003 the Villa Hills City Council instituted the No Knock Ordinance, the first of its kind in Northern Kentucky and now a model for other cities. Persons who sell door-to-door must get a restricted list at the city building or risk being fined for breaking the ordinance.

Villa Hills has developed from acres of farmland into now a residential fourth-class city. Almost all the farmland is gone, with only an acre or two tacked onto an old farmhouse. According to the 2000 census, Villa Hills is home to 7,984 residents.

Villa Hills Millennium/Historical Committee. *The Villa Hills Area: A Great Place to Live.* Villa Hills, Ky.: Villa Hills Millennium/Historical Committee, 1999.

Deborah Kohl Kremer

VILLA MADONNA ACADEMY. The Villa Madonna Academy (VMA) is Northern Kentucky's only private, coeducational Catholic school offering grades K–12. Since 1904 VMA has provided education to families from Northern Kentucky and Greater Cincinnati. Sponsored by the **Sisters of St. Benedict** of St. Walburg Monastery in Covington, VMA began on September 8, 1904, as the region's only boarding and day school for girls. There were 17 girls and 7 sisters living and studying in the former Collins homestead, in rural Kenton Co. (now Villa Hills), which was purchased by the Catholic Church in 1903. In 1906 the cornerstone for a new building, designed by Lyman Walker, was laid. In 1907 this new brick building opened, and in 1911 it graduated its first high

Villa Madonna Academy, ca. 1908.

school class, four females. The sisters added Villa Madonna College to the academy in 1921 and conferred the first college degrees and teaching certificates in 1929. During the 1920s, the college faculty included **Patia Power** (Helen Emma Reaume), the mother of noted actor Tyrone Power. Villa Madonna College became a diocesan college in 1929 and moved to 12th St. in Covington to allow for growth. In 1932, 32 acres adjacent to the high school in Villa Hills were purchased from **E. S. Lee**. The building VMA presently uses for its elementary and high school programs was built in 1957 next to the original 1907 building. In 2000 VMA erected a third building, a multipurpose sports complex. A fine arts center, complete with a state-of-the-art theater, was dedicated in February 2005.

Excellence in education for women was VMA's central feature until the parents of the students of Villa Madonna's Montessori school (which was established in 1971) encouraged the VMA board to welcome boys. Boys were enrolled in 1977 in the elementary grades and in 1985 in high school. In 1990 the first three males graduated from the high school.

VMA affiliated with the Catholic University of America in 1915 and renewed the affiliation in 1941. In 1923 the Kentucky Department of Education accredited the school as a Class A school. Since 1959 the entire school, grades K–12, has maintained full accreditation in the standard class. The high school has also been a member of the Southern Association of Secondary Schools and Colleges since 1925. VMA's test scores are in the top 10 percent in the nation, and the high school was named a Blue Ribbon school in both 2002 and 2003.

The school's small class sizes and low student-teacher ratios attract students. A student can enjoy full participation in the athletic program, high school advanced placement courses, a full array of fine arts, an integrated technology curriculum, progressive foreign language instruction, and choral and instrumental programs. VMA's economically, culturally, and religiously diverse student body currently numbers 500.

Reis, Jim. "Thomas More College Traces Its Roots to a Bluff above the River 70 Years Ago," *KP*, February 11, 1991, 4K.

Ryan, Paul E. *History of the Diocese of Covington, Kentucky*. Covington, Ky.: Diocese of Covington, 1954.

Schwartz, Joann R. "St. Walburg Monastery, Covington, Kentucky, 1859–1899," master's thesis, Xavier Univ., 2005.

Wolking, Teresa, O.S.B., and Joann Schwartz. "The Story of Villa Madonna Academy and the Benedictines," *NKH* 11, no. 1 (Fall–Winter 2003): 2–16.

Teresa Wolking

VINCENT, LARRY (b. Larry Vincent Allario, January 13, 1901, San Jose, Calif.; d. January 5, 1977, Fort Wright, Ky.). Patrons of the two famous dining and entertainment clubs in Northern Kentucky, Fort Wright's **Lookout House** and Southgate's **Beverly Hills Supper Club**, may not remember songwriter and performer Larry Vincent by name, but they certainly recall his piano talents and the songs he played. While waiting for a table, and perhaps while sipping drinks in the cocktail lounges, they were treated to the engaging and memorable sounds of Vincent's keyboard playing.

Vincent began his career in vaudeville by playing in most of the major cities of the United States. He came to the Lookout House in 1941 for a two-week booking and stayed to perform at the nightclub for five years. Later, he put in nine years performing at Beverly Hills. At this time he was residing in Park Hills, Ky., at 802 Arlington Rd. As a songwriter, he composed at least 50 songs, many of which, beginning in 1946, were produced by his own record company, Pearl Record. Vincent and the various music combo groups he headed, the Pearl Boys, the Pearl Trio, and the Lookout Boys, played in the side lounges of the large local entertainment clubs in the region. He referred to himself as the musical answer to W. C. Fields; 25 different recording artists recorded his million-and-a-half-selling 1949 composition "If I Had My Life to Live Over." It was also in the late 1940s that Vincent joined with **Haven Gillespie** to write the successful song "How's My Baby Tonight?" Together, they brought a little bit of Tin Pan Alley to Northern Kentucky for a short time. In the mid-1970s, Vincent wrote "The Whole Town's Batty about Cincinnati" to honor the World Champion Cincinnati Reds; area morning television viewers of that era may remember program host Ruth Lyon's zesty live rendition of it. Vincent died at the St. Charles Nursing Home in Fort Wright in early 1977 and was buried at St. Mary Cemetery in Fort Mitchell, a few months before his beloved Beverly Hills burned to the ground.

The Blue Pages. "The Encyclopedic Guide to 78 R.P.M. Party Records." www.hensteeth.com/ (accessed February 10, 2006).

"Songwriter Larry Vincent Dies at Age 76," *CE*, January 7, 1977, D2.

"Songwriters Strike Pay Tune," *CE*, September 11, 1949, sec. 3, p. 1.

"Songwriter Vincent Dies," *CP*, January 6, 1977, 16K.

Michael R. Sweeney

VINEGAR, THEODORE ROOSEVELT "TEDDY" (b. June 10, 1909, Owen Co., Ky.; d. August 7, 2001, Cincinnati, Ohio). Teddy Vinegar, an African American farmer who raised and trained horses in Owen Co., Ky., was the youngest son of a former slave whose family owned **Mountain Island** Farm in Kentucky. His parents were Cord and Charlotte Vinegar.

Vinegar was born on the 110-acre family property at Mountain Island, where he learned his farming skills from his father. Horses and farming were part of the family culture, and Vinegar worked with horses most of his life. In the 1930s he started to race horses at Mountain Island. He also used the roots of plants to make medicines to cure various horse ailments. The family moved away from Mountain Island in the 1940s but continued to own and maintain the farm. Vinegar bought a 40-acre farm on Ky. Rt. 330 in Owen Co., where he farmed and also raised horses. During **World War II**, Vinegar served in the U.S. Army with the 318th Engineering Combat Battalion.

In the 1950s Vinegar bred a black and white gaited pinto stallion named Hillrise, from a mostly thoroughbred mare with just a splotch of white on her and a gaited stallion named Rooster. For 50 years Vinegar bred for gait with the pinto stallion Hillrise and his offspring, and these horses were prized all around Owen, Grant, and neighboring counties. They undoubtedly represented a major contribution to the Spotted Saddle horse breed, first made official in the 1980s; hence a pool of compactly built, pinto-gaited horses was first bred in the Northern Kentucky region. Today many Spotted Saddle horses are part- or full-blooded Tennessee Walking breeds. Vinegar preferred a smoother and less "hip-jiggling" gait than that of many modern Tennessee Walkers, a gait more like that of the Plantation Walker.

Vinegar introduced an innovative farming technique, planting crops on hillsides in a way that would not cause erosion; he used only a horse and a plow in his farming. This technique was taught to agricultural students from the surrounding counties and at the University of Kentucky in Lexington.

Teddy Vinegar died in 2001 at the Veterans Administration Medical Center in Cincinnati and was buried in the Newby-Vinegar Family Cemetery, at New Columbus, in Owen Co., Ky.

Graham, Shelby. "Land Given to freed Slave Ties Grandson to His Past," *Lexington Herald-Leader*, March 1, 1992, 10–13.

"Kentucky Obituaries," *CE*, August 9, 2001, B2.

Williams, Geoff. "Volunteers Unearth Remnants of Civil War Community," *KP*, November 18, 1998, 1KK.

Theodore H. H. Harris

VINICULTURE. Northern Kentucky was a major producer of wine for a time in the 19th century. In 1798 Jean Jacques Dufour, a Swiss winegrower, established the oldest vineyard society in the United States when he started a commercial winery in Jessamine Co., Ky. Efforts to grow old-world *Vitus vinifera* grapes in the western regions of America proved quite difficult. In Cincinnati, Nicholas Longworth (1782–1863) experimented with 40 different varieties before he turned to native grapes. He offered a reward of $500 to anyone who could produce a variety well suited to the climate and soil of the Ohio Valley. The reward was claimed in 1826 when Major Adlum came up with a Catawba vine derived from the native *Vitus labrusca*. By 1840 Kentucky growers produced a mere 2,209 gallons of wine. Temperance societies had become prominent, prompting Methodists in Bracken Co. to produce an unfermented wine in 1842. At this same time, a large number of German immigrants from districts along the Rhine River arrived in the region, and Longworth made a standing offer to buy any and all the grapes brought to him, regardless of quality. Vineyards soon dotted the hillsides along the Ohio River, and Longworth began making a profit. In 1857 the *Cincinnati Commercial* called him "the founder of wine culture in America and author of sparkling Catawba."

In 1860 the federal census indicated that Kentucky had become the third-largest grape-producing state in the nation, with 136,000 gallons. Campbell Co. alone produced one-third of the national wine output. But soon downy mildew, black rot, and the **Civil War** exacted a serious toll on the Catawba vines in the region. In 1862 Kentucky's production dropped to 36,009 gallons, and the next year to 31,030 gallons. In 1865 Dr. **J. Taylor Bradford** (1818–1871) sold 10,000 gallons from his Bracken Co. vineyards to Longworth's Wine House in Cincinnati. At an average price of $2.43 per gallon, they yielded a hefty revenue of $24,300.

The death of Nicholas Longworth and the sale of his bottling operation in 1870 hurt growers. At the newly established Agricultural and Mechanical College of the University of Kentucky in Lexington, students like Thomas V. Munson (1843–1913) became fascinated with viniculture and wrote numerous papers and essays for the school journal. That interest helped grape growers in Bracken Co. to expand their production so that Bracken Co., with an annual production of 30,000 gallons, became one of the leading wine-producing counties in the United States. Along the Ohio River, Abraham Baker gained a widespread reputation for having one of the finest wine cellars in the nation. By July 19, 1899, an article title in the *Kentucky Post* announced, "More Money to Be Made in Cultivating Vineyards: Farmers Find Growing Tobacco Is Not Profitable." That situation changed with the Volstead Act, the federal legislation enacted to enforce the 19th Amendment (**Prohibition**) in 1920. The domestic wine industry ceased operation. Other crops replaced winegrowing, and it has only been in recent years that a resurgent interest in domestic wines has encouraged a few tobacco-growers to cultivate grapes and establish wineries.

By the 1950s and the 1960s, Campbell Co. experienced a resurgence in grape production. For example, the Schwerin family's Campbell Vineyard and Orchards harvested 36 tons of grapes annually, much of which was sold to the Meier's Winery in Ohio. In the early 21st century, the area of Camp Springs in Campbell Co. returned to its roots as a wine-producing center. Growers in the area initiated a Northern Kentucky Wine Festival at **St. Joseph Catholic Church** in Camp Springs in 2005. A major winery is Dennis Walter's Stone Brook Winery in Camp Springs. Currently, the Northern Kentucky Vintners and Grape Grower's Association, a group of 120 winemakers, grape growers, and related businesses, are attempting to turn the region into a weekend entertainment destination and tap into the commonwealth's agricultural tourism market.

"Bracken Winery Was Famous," *Bracken Co. Chronicle*, October 23, 1930.

Collins, Richard H. *History of Kentucky*. Vol. 1. Covington, Ky.: Collins, 1882.

De Bow, J. D. B., ed. "Progress of the Great West in Population, Agriculture, Arts, and Commerce," *Debow's Review* 4, no. 1 (September 1847): 64–65.

Lukacs, Paul. *American Vintage: The Rise of American Wine*. Boston: Houghton Mifflin, 2000.

U.S. Bureau of the Census. *Agriculture of the United States in 1860: From the Original Returns of the Eighth Census*. Under the Direction of the Secretary of the Interior, Joseph C. G. Kennedy. Washington, D.C.: Bureau of the Census, 1864.

Donald A. Clark

VINSON, FREDERICK M. (b. January 22, 1890, near Louisa, Ky.; d. September 8, 1953, Washington, D.C.). Frederick Moore Vinson, chief justice of the Supreme Court, was the son of James and Virginia Ferguson Vinson. He attended the Kentucky Normal School at Louisa and in 1911 graduated from the Centre College School of Law at Danville. Vinson served in the U.S. Congress from 1924 to 1929 as a representative from Kentucky's old Ninth Congressional District, which stretched along the Ohio River from Bracken Co. in Northern Kentucky to Lawrence Co. in Eastern Kentucky; he was elected again to serve from 1931 to 1938, representing Mason and Bracken counties in Northern Kentucky, in addition to counties in northeastern Kentucky (1931–1935, Ninth District; after 1935, Eighth District; see **Congressional Districts**). During his time in Congress, Vinson introduced legislation that would have funded a bridge across the Ohio River at Augusta in Bracken Co.

Vinson resigned from the Congress in 1938 to serve on the U.S. Court of Appeals for the District of Columbia Circuit. In 1943 President Franklin D. Roosevelt (1933–1945) appointed him director of economic stabilization, one of several posts in which he used his expertise in financial matters to help finance **World War II**. In 1945, President Harry S. Truman (1945–1953) appointed Vinson U.S. secretary of the treasury, and in 1946 Truman appointed him chief justice of the U.S. Supreme Court, a position that he held until his unexpected death from a heart attack in 1953. Vinson was buried in the Pinehill Cemetery at Louisa.

Frederick M. Vinson.

Hall, Kermit L. *The Oxford Companion to the Supreme Court of the United States*. New York: Oxford Univ. Press, 2005.

Kleber, John E., ed. *The Kentucky Encyclopedia*. Lexington: Univ. Press of Kentucky, 1992.

St. Clair, James E., and Linda Gugin. *Chief Justice Fred M. Vinson of Kentucky: A Political Biography*. Lexington: Univ. Press of Kentucky, 2002.

Paul L. Whalen

VISALIA. Visalia was a sixth-class city in eastern Kenton Co., wedged between Decoursey Pk. (Ky. Rt. 177) and the Licking River. First settled during the early 1800s, the city was founded in 1818 when the Campbell Co. Court authorized Nathaniel Vise to establish a town site. The name Visalia came from the founder's surname. The Vise family later moved to California, where they established another town, also named Visalia, in 1852. Because of its central location within Campbell Co., Visalia briefly served as the county seat in 1827. Visalia became part of Kenton Co. upon that county's formation in 1840.

The completion of the **Covington and Lexington Railroad** through Visalia in 1853 began a new chapter in the town's history. For several years, Visalia was also known as Canton Station, the name of its railroad depot. A post office opened in the town in 1855. The railroad brought enough prosperity to Visalia that the town formally incorporated as a city in 1869, and by the early 1880s, Visalia had a general store, a gristmill, a Methodist church, a sawmill, a school, and a large tobacco warehouse. The city honored American statesmen with such street names as Washington, Jefferson, and Clay. Besides providing Visalia farmers cheaper access to the Covington and Cincinnati markets, the railroad allowed affluent urban residents to establish country residences and still attend to their urban business interests. Gen. **John W. Finnell**, a leading Covington attorney, journalist, and politician, established an elegant home in Visalia called Sunny Side. On one occasion, Finnell had a special railroad car conduct guests to Sunny Side for an outdoor party at which they could admire the estate's abundant fruit trees.

Visalia's scenic beauty made it an outdoor recreation destination for Northern Kentuckians. Picnic grounds such as Finnell's Grove and Canton Grove in Visalia were popular during the 1870s. Visalia resident Thomas Mann owned and operated Canton Grove, which offered rental cabins, a dance floor, swings, and a ride called the Flying Dutchman. He also arranged for special railroad cars for Canton Grove excursionists. Patrons could also reach Canton Grove from Campbell Co. by ferry. By 1884 Canton Grove had passed from Mann's ownership and had been renamed Bethel Grove. The new proprietors further improved the grounds by constructing a dining hall and 16 additional two-room cottages available at a $15 summer rental fee. Bethel Grove's summer cottages and reduced railroad fares made it affordable for middle-class businessmen and their families to experience a taste of the bucolic life that Finnell enjoyed at Sunny Side. In 1901 Bethel Grove became primarily a religious camp and continued as such until the early 1970s.

The 1913 construction of a bridge at Visalia spanning the Licking River made Visalia part of a vital transportation route in rural Kenton and Campbell Counties. At the time, the decision to build the bridge stirred a controversy pitting rural and urban interests against each other. In Kenton Co., farmers favored the bridge's construction because of the potential markets it opened across the river. Covington merchants, however, feared a loss of business to Newport because the bridge would give Campbell Co. retailers access to rural Kenton Co. The new Al Schneider Bridge replaced the Visalia bridge in 1978.

As a functioning city, Visalia led a precarious existence beginning in the 1970s. It escaped the brunt of post–World War II suburbanization that transformed central Kenton Co. and reincorporated in 1976 but then began to be threatened with dissolution. In 1979 several residents tried to dissolve the city, claiming a lack of services received for their taxes. Garbage collection was the only city service provided. A decade later, Visalia's mayor also considered closing the city when city council vacancies went unfilled. In many instances, Visalia relied on write-in votes to elect city officials. The city survived the 1990s; however, the closing of Visalia Elementary School in 2003 dealt the community a severe blow. The Kenton Co. Board of Education cited budget cuts and declining enrollment as reasons for the school's closure. A Visalia resident filed a petition for the dissolution of the city's government in January 2006 after discovering that no one had the authority to issue a building permit (there had been no active city council since the early 1990s). In September 2006, Kenton circuit judge Gregory Bartlett ordered the dissolution of the city. Visalia's population was 198 in 1980, 190 in 1990, and 111 in 2000.

"City Fades from Lack of Interest," *KP*, March 12, 1988, 1K.
"Kenton County's Newest City Also Is Least Known," *KE*, May 21, 1979, 2A.
"Raspberry Festival," *DC*, June 21, 1880, 1.

Greg Perkins

VISION 2015. See **Forward Quest Inc./Vision 2015**.

VISITORS TO NORTHERN KENTUCKY. The first European visitors to the area that became Northern Kentucky were explorers. One of them was Robert de La Salle, a Frenchman who reportedly came down the Ohio River with his party during the mid-1700s. He camped on the beach at present-day Dayton, Ky. Later, **the Point** in Covington was well known to the English frontiersmen **Simon Kenton** and **Daniel Boone** and also served as a gathering place for the various pioneer military campaigns launched against the Indians under the command of Gen. **George Rogers Clark**. In 1751, while exploring the region, **Christopher Gist** stopped at **Big Bone Lick**. In 1803 Meriwether Lewis and William Clark, at the request of President Thomas Jefferson (1800–1808), also stopped at Big Bone to gather mastodon bones (see **Lewis and Clark in Northern Kentucky**). In 1824 the general Marquis de Lafayette, another Frenchman, who had helped the United States gain its independence from Great Britain, came through Northern Kentucky from Lexington en route to Cincinnati and upriver from there. Many notable Northern Kentuckians came out to greet the general, and some of them were privileged to have him stay at their homes: included among the latter were the Gaineses. The presence of the **Newport Barracks** in Newport brought significant military figures to Northern Kentucky: Robert E. Lee, George Custer, and **Charles Stuart Tripler**, to name just a few. As the region grew in population, there were more reasons for prominent politicians and entertainers to come and visit. Gen. Phillip Sheridan was in Newport during the late 1880s to select the site that became the **Fort Thomas Military Reservation**. Sent here by Gen. William T. Sherman, Sheridan rode his horse from Newport out the Grand Ave. Turnpike to the fort's site in the District of the Highlands (Fort Thomas). In 1893 Covington's Kate Trimble married Edward J. Woolsey of New York City (see **Kate Trimble Woolsey**). Kate's mother invited the king of Bulgaria, Princess Maria De Bourbon, and the dowager duchess of Wellington to the wedding ceremony.

Franklin D. Roosevelt speaking at the Latonia Racecourse, July 1938.

In the first years of the 20th century, socialists were plentiful in Covington and Newport, and future five-time presidential candidate Eugene Victor Debs spoke at Clark's Beach in Dayton in 1905. In November 1915, the Liberty Bell passed through along the **Louisville and Nashville Railroad** tracks, returning to Philadelphia from San Francisco's Panama-Pacific Exposition. The people of Covington were out in full force to catch a glimpse of this permanent piece of U.S. history. The **Beverly Hills Supper Club** in Southgate brought many big-time entertainers to the area, such as Jack Benny, Jimmy Durante, Ted Lewis, Marilyn Monroe, and Frank Sinatra. Famous strippers who have danced here include Gypsy Rose Lee, Morganna, and Sally Rand. Two of major league baseball's famous pitchers, Cy Young and Satchel Page, pitched in Newport at the old Rough Riders Park, at W. Fifth St. and the Licking River.

Sitting, former, and future U.S. presidents have also visited. Teddy Roosevelt (1901–1909) reportedly visited **Richard P. Ernst** in Covington for at least a few hours in the early years of the 20th century; Franklin D. Roosevelt (1933–1945) spoke at the **Latonia Racecourse** in July 1938; John Fitzgerald Kennedy (1961–1963) was here twice in October 1960, when he traveled to the Cote Brilliante neighborhood of Newport, campaigning; and Lyndon Baines Johnson (1963–1969) came to open the new campus of **Thomas More College** in Crestview Hills in 1968. Other presidents motorcaded through the area after the Greater Cincinnati Airport opened in 1947 in Northern Kentucky (see **Cincinnati/Northern Kentucky International Airport**). In April 1970, the funeral train for President Dwight D. Eisenhower (1953–1961) passed through Northern Kentucky along the C&O rail line, from east to west, on its way to Manhattan, Kans. There have also been suggestions that Abraham Lincoln (1861–1865) visited **Richard Southgate** at his Newport home during the mid-1850s. In more recent years, both Gerald Ford (1974–1977) and George W. Bush (2001–2009) visited the campus of **Northern Kentucky University**, in 1978 and 2006, respectively. William Jefferson Clinton (1993–2001) and former first lady and Democratic presidential candidate Hillary Clinton visited Northern Kentucky in May 2008, campaigning at **Main Strasse**'s Maifest in advance of the Kentucky primary.

Joseph Cardinal Mindzenty (1974) and Mother Teresa (1982) both came to Covington as a result of their Roman Catholic connections. Pope John Paul II came through the area on his way to Cincinnati in 1987.

The Beatles came through Northern Kentucky twice during the 1960s: first in 1964, from the airport to the Cincinnati Gardens to perform, and then in 1966 to sing at old Crosley Field. Similarly, Elvis Presley was here at least twice, once in 1971 and later in 1976. Several restaurants along the

Dixie Highway in Kenton Co. claim that, early in his career, Elvis ate there.

Because of its early strategic location as a transportation junction, many important people visited Maysville. Chief Justice John Marshall would visit his family members there, and both presidential candidate Henry Clay and President Andrew Jackson (1829–1837) stopped on their way to and from Washington, D.C., traveling along the **Maysville and Lexington Turnpike** and Zane's Trace heading to and from the National Rd. General Lafayette also passed through Maysville after a stopover in Cincinnati.

Reis, Jim. "Visitors," *KP*, February 17, 1986, 4K.

VON HOENE, RICHARD A. "DICK" (b. July 17, 1940, Cincinnati, Ohio; d. February 4, 2004, Cincinnati, Ohio). Comedian, actor, and newsman Dick Von Hoene, known professionally as the Cool Ghoul, was born in the Madisonville section of Cincinnati to Harry Frederick and Margaret Carolyn Fischer Von Hoene. Dick was educated in local schools and graduated from Purcell High School in Cincinnati in 1958. He entered the University of Cincinnati (UC), where he earned a BA in history and an MA in theater. While at UC, he performed in collegiate plays and also appeared in summer stock and community theater productions. In 1961, while a writer on the Bob Smith *Monster Mash* show, Von Hoene created the Cool Ghoul character for a Halloween production. He married and had two daughters. In 1962 he took a job as a copywriter for WCPO radio, remaining there for about five years, and then became an announcer on Cincinnati radio station WUBE. He revived his Cool Ghoul character in 1969, while hosting the weekly "scream-in" horror movie show on WXIX Channel 19 television in Cincinnati. The character became a phenomenal success, especially among school-age children. Von Hoene said that he created the cool ghoul from a number of different people, including the "poor soul" on the Jackie Gleason television show. Von Hoene even had an LP record cut on the Artists Label, called *The Cool Ghoul's Phantasma*. During the early 1980s, he entered a more serious period in his career when he took a position as news director for Storer Cable in Northern Kentucky. In the mid-1990s, he began hosting the *Northern Kentucky Magazine* show on Insight Cable (formerly Storer Cable) (see **Cable Television**). In that capacity, he interviewed many celebrities visiting the area, including singer Chubby Checker and Olympic gold medal gymnast Mary Lou Retton. In 1999 Von Hoene was inducted into the Greater Cincinnati Legends of Rock and Roll Hall of Fame. In his spare time, he was an avid golfer and a **Civil War** history buff.

While shopping on February 4, 2004, Von Hoene collapsed from an apparent heart attack and was rushed to Mercy Franciscan Hospital in Cincinnati, where he died. Funeral services were held at the Allison and Rose Funeral Home in Covington, and burial was in the Spring Grove Cemetery in Cincinnati. With the passing of this Greater Cincinnati legend, a memorable era of live television shows in the region came to an end.

"Appreciation," *CE*, February 8, 2004, 13D.
"Cool Ghoul Dick Von Hoene Dies," *KP*, February 5, 2004, 2K.
"'Cool Ghoul' Was Icon of Queen City," *CE*, February, 5, 2004, 1C.
"Kentucky Senate Resolution in Honor of Richard A. (Dick) Von Hoene," 2004 Regular Session.

Jack Wessling

VON OHLEN, JOHN (b. May 13, 1941, Indianapolis, Ind.). A jazz and big band drummer of national renown, John Von Ohlen is the son of Raymond and Alma Von Ohlen. He began classical piano lessons at age 4 and started playing the trombone at age 10. He was 14 when, while observing drummer Mel Lewis performing at a Stan Kenton concert, he decided that drumming would be his profession. He taught himself the drums at home and played them in his high school's jazz band. After graduating from North Central High School in Indianapolis, Von Ohlen began classes in Jazz Studies, a prestigious lab band program at North Texas State University, in 1960. He developed his drumming craft during a year and a half of performing with Ralph Marterie and two years in the army touring stateside with Showmobile.

In the mid-1960s, Von Ohlen returned to Indianapolis to perform as a nightclub drummer. Soon he started traveling the national circuit, joining the bands of Billy Maxted in 1966 and of the well-known Woody Herman between 1967 and 1968. In 1970 he received a call from his favorite legendary band leader, Stan Kenton, inviting him to play the drums; Von Ohlen toured the United States and Europe with the Kenton band for two years. His skills and confidence matured under Kenton's guidance. Kenton also conceived Von Ohlen's stage name, the "Baron," by which fans still know him today. Von Ohlen has played for the Tommy Dorsey Orchestra and has backed noted vocalists such as Tony Bennett, **Rosemary Clooney**, and Perry Como. He toured and recorded with jazz vocalists Carmen McRae and Mel Tormé.

After 12 years as a traveling musician, Von Ohlen settled back in the region to form the Blue Wisp Big Band in 1980. The band performed at the Cincinnati area club from which its name was derived, the Blue Wisp, one of the few remaining clubs devoted to jazz in the area. It has recorded seven commercial albums purchased by fans worldwide. Oscar Treadwell, the late Cincinnati radio jazz historian, stated that these world-class musicians have brought more jazz recognition to the community than any other band. Von Ohlen also plays weekly at the Dee Felice Café, as well as at Chez Nora Restaurant (with the Mary Ellen Tanner Quartet), both in Covington.

Von Ohlen has been an adjunct instructor of Jazz Drums at the College Conservatory of Music at the University of Cincinnati since 1985, mentoring students of percussion. His students call him the "Coach" because he prefers teaching by example and discussion rather than relying on textbooks.

Von Ohlen was honored with the Michael W. Bany Lifetime Achievement Award of the Cammy (Cincinnati Area Music) Awards and was inducted into its Cincinnati Entertainment Awards Hall of Fame, both in 2005. He resides in Covington with his life partner, jazz singer **Mary Ellen Tanner**.

Bird, Rick. "Blue Wisp Big Band Turns 25," *CP*, January 13, 2005, 5T.
——. "'Tribute:' Blue Wisp Big Band Honors Composers, Fans with New CD," *KP*, May 29, 2007, 1B.
CEA. "The Baron Gets His Due." http://citybeat.com/cea/05pages/halloffame.html (accessed October 1, 2007).
College-Conservatory of Music (CCM), Univ. of Cincinnati. "John Von Ohlen." www.ccm.uc.edu/faculty/facultyProfile.aspx?facultyid=54 (accessed October 1, 2007).
Knippenberg, Jim. "For the Love of Jazz: Drummer John Von Ohlen Could Play Anywhere in the World but His Heart Belongs to Downtown's Blue Wisp," *CE*, April 15, 2007, 1D.

John Schlipp

VOTRUBA, JAMES (b. March 26, 1945, East Lansing, Mich.). James Votruba, president of **Northern Kentucky University** (NKU), is the son of Jim and Betty Votruba. He earned his BA in political science (1968), his MA in political science and sociology (1970), and his PhD in higher education administration (1974) from Michigan State University at East Lansing. He began his career in higher education with faculty and administrative positions at Drake University in Des Moines, Iowa, and at the University of Illinois at Urbana-Champaign. He served as dean of the College of Education and Human Development at Binghamton University in Binghamton, N.Y., from 1983 to 1989 and as vice provost for university outreach and professor of higher education at Michigan State University from 1989 to 1997. He was named the fourth president of NKU on August, 1, 1997.

Votruba is a frequent lecturer, an author, and a consultant in the areas of higher education leadership, strategic planning, and public engagement. In 2002 he chaired the American Association of State Colleges and Universities (AASCU) National Task Force on public engagement and later served as a faculty member in the AASCU New President's Academy. In 2004 he delivered the annual AASCU President-to-Presidents Lecture, entitled "Leading the Engaged University." Votruba has served as president of the Coalition of Urban and Metropolitan Universities and on a variety of boards, including the National Campus Compact Board of Directors, the Association of Governing Boards Council of Presidents, and the Board of Directors of the Ohio National Mutual Holding Company.

Under Votruba's leadership, NKU became a national model for civic engagement in higher education by weaving its cross-discipline outreach programs into the university's undergraduate, graduate, and law classrooms. He helped the university to strengthen its position as a regional economic development engine through initiatives such as the Metropolitan Education and Training Services unit, the

Bank of Kentucky Center, and the creation of the College of Informatics. During Votruba's tenure, NKU's enrollment, its overall growth, and the state and private funding acquired by the university have reached new levels. The university's Dorothy Westerman Herrmann Natural Science Center, completed in 2002, was at the time Kentucky's largest academic facility. A new state-of-the-art student center was completed in August 2008. NKU also implemented comprehensive admission standards for the first time in the school's history in 2005.

Votruba's regional leadership extends far beyond NKU's Highland Heights campus. In 2005, as cochair of Vision 2015, the current planning initiative for Northern Kentucky, he guided a yearlong regional visioning process that set a 10-year agenda for Northern Kentucky's growth and development. He was named the "Most Influential Person in Northern Kentucky" by the *Sunday Challenger* newspaper in 2005.

Votruba lives in Lakeside Park with his wife, Rachel, who is actively involved in several community-based nonprofit organizations. The Votrubas have three children and five grandchildren.

May, Lucy. "NKU's Energizer," *Business Courier*, February 16, 2001, available at www.bizjournals.com/cincinnati/stories/2001/02/19/story2.html (accessed March 10, 2006).

"NKU Picks Michigan Educator," *KP*, April 4, 1997, 1K.

Pulfer, Laura. "At NKU, It's Really Not About Building at All," *KE*, October 9, 2003, B1.

Rick Meyers

WADE, RICHARD M. (b. May 11, 1816, Campbell Co., Va.; d. February 19, 1878, Covington, Ky.). Richard Marshall Wade, a steamboat captain in the commercial trade between Cincinnati and New Orleans, was the son of Edmund and Mildred Marshall Wade and a great-grandson of U.S. Supreme Court chief justice John Marshall of Virginia. Richard Wade's mother died when he was 5 years old. His father lost his fortune when Richard was 16 and moved his family to Kanawha, Va. (modern W.Va.). Richard then went to work to help support his family. He commanded a fleet of salt boats on the Kanawha River at age 17. In 1839 he married Sara Jane Reno, daughter of Lewis Reno, a prominent Cincinnati citizen. They moved to Pike St. in Covington in 1842.

Wade was the pilot of the sternwheeler *New Orleans* from 1834 until 1844. Between 1844 and 1861, he served sequentially as captain and master of the *Duchess*, the *Europa*, the *Swallow* (lost in a collision), the *Cincinnatus*, the *Queen of the West*, and the *Judge Torrence*. He was part owner of the *Queen of the West*, which became a ram boat during the **Civil War**, and the *Judge Torrence*. In 1862 Captain Wade joined the Union Army as a volunteer and served as executive officer on the gunboat *Carondelet*. He took part in the military campaigns at Fort Henry and Fort Donelson in Tennessee. His health declined while serving on the *Carondelet* and he was discharged in April 1862; he never returned to good health. From 1867 to 1870, he was captain of the *General Lytle*, the U.S. Mail Line (Cincinnati Mail Line) Cincinnati-to-Louisville service, and temporary captain or master of the ***United States*** in 1868. Wade's and another river pilot's confusion in signals on a foggy night resulted in the collision of the *United States* and the ***America*** on December 4, 1868, at Warsaw, causing the loss of 74 lives. As a result, both pilots had their licenses revoked. Wade's career continued as captain (but not as pilot) of the *Robert Mitchell*, the *St. James*, and the *Bostona*. He was made superintendent of the U.S. Mail Line in 1874, a position he held until his death from consumption in 1878 at age 62. He was buried at Linden Grove Cemetery in Covington. His wife, Sarah Jane, was a founder of the First Presbyterian Church in Covington. They had 12 children.

"Account of the Collision of the *America* and the *United States*," *S and D Reflector* 5, no. 4 (December 1968): 18–22.
"Death Notice," *CDE*, February 20, 1878, 5.
"Death Notice," *CE*, February 20, 1878, 5.
Linden Grove Cemetery Records, Covington, Ky.
"Pioneer Dying," *KP*, June 24, 1905, 2.

Marja Barrett

WADSWORTH, JOSEPH HENRY (b. June 18, 1903, Maysville, Ky.; d. December 5, 1974, New York City). Actor Joseph Henry Wadsworth was the son of John Gray and Ida Power Wadsworth. He grew up in the family's large ancestral home, Buffalo Trace, built by his grandfather, Adna Wadsworth. After graduating from **Maysville High School** in 1921, Joseph attended the University of Kentucky in Lexington. He studied acting at the Carnegie Institute of Technology's drama school in Pittsburgh, Pa. Using the stage name Henry Wadsworth, he appeared on the Broadway stage, in movies in Hollywood, and on television. He played several juvenile roles in films in the early 1930s, becoming known as "the perpetual juvenile." Wadsworth first appeared on Broadway in 1927 in the title role of Howard Lindsay's *Tommy.* Two years later, he made his movie debut in *Applause* as a sailor on leave in New York City. The two best-known films in which he appeared were *The Thin Man* and the Oscar-winning *It Happened One Night*, both released in 1934. His last film appearance was in the 1943 production of *Silver Skates*, and his last Broadway appearance was in Rodgers & Hammerstein's 1950 musical *The Happy Time.* After **World War II**, Wadsworth traveled to Japan to entertain American troops stationed there. During his acting career he also served as administrator of the Motion Picture Health and Welfare Plan and as president of the American Federation of Labor Film Council. Late in life, he turned to designing theater costumes while living in New York City. During summers he returned to his childhood home, Buffalo Trace. Wadsworth died in New York City in 1974 and was buried in the Maysville Cemetery in Maysville, Ky.

Calvert, Jean, and John Klee. *Maysville, Kentucky: From Past to Present in Pictures.* Maysville, Ky.: Mason Co. Museum, 1983.
——. *The Towns of Mason County: Their Past in Pictures.* Maysville, Ky.: Maysville and Mason Co. Library Historical and Scientific Association, 1986.
"Henry Wadsworth, Stage, Film Actor," *NYT*, December 7, 1974, 32.
Maysville Public Ledger, December 6, 1974, 1.

Thomas S. Ward

WADSWORTH, WILLIAM HENRY (b. July 4, 1821, Maysville, Ky.; d. April 2, 1893, Maysville, Ky.). Lawyer and legislator William Henry Wadsworth was the son of Adna A. and Mary Williams Ramsdell Wadsworth. He began his schooling at Tuckahoe Ridge in Virginia, then continued at the Maysville Seminary (**Maysville Academy**), and finally graduated with honors in 1842 from **Augusta College** in Augusta. He was admitted to the bar in 1844 after studying law in the office of Thomas Y. Payne and Henry Waller. He married Martha Morehead Wood. In 1853 Wadsworth was elected to the state Senate as a Whig. He lost his bid for reelection in 1856 to a candidate of the American Party who had the support of many Democrats. He ran as an elector for the Constitutional Union Party's candidates, John Bell and Edward Everett, in the momentous presidential election of 1860. During the campaign, Wadsworth worked vigorously and helped stir up Union sentiment in the state so that Kentucky's electoral votes went to Bell rather than to native-born John C. Breckinridge, standard-bearer of the Southern Democrats. With the **Civil War** approaching, supporters of the Union nominated Wadsworth to run for the 37th Congress in 1861 from the Maysville District, and he won handily. In Washington, D.C., he was a conservative Union man who supported the compromise proposals of fellow Kentuckian John J. Crittenden and opposed what he considered the coercive policies of Abraham Lincoln's administration and Congress toward the South. Yet he accepted the war, while wanting to ameliorate its destructiveness, and even served for a time in the Union Army. Bearing the rank of colonel, he was an aide to fellow Maysvillian Gen. **William "Bull" Nelson** at the Battle of Ivy Mountain and also served under generals **Green Clay Smith** and Lew Wallace. Wadsworth was reelected to the 38th Congress in 1863. After the war, he returned to the practice of law, though now supporting the Republican Party. In the presidential election of 1868, he campaigned for Gen. Ulysses S. Grant, who had been his schoolmate at the Maysville Seminary. As president, Grant appointed Wadsworth to an important commission that adjudicated millions of dollars worth of claims between the United States and Mexico. Wadsworth returned to politics when he was elected to the 49th Congress in 1884 but did not run again in 1886. He was serving as general attorney for the **Chesapeake and Ohio Railroad** Company in Kentucky upon his death in 1893. He was buried in the Maysville Cemetery.

Biographical Cyclopedia of the Commonwealth of Kentucky. Chicago: John M. Gresham, 1896.
Biographical Directory of the United States Congress, 1774–2005. Washington, D.C.: Government Printing Office, 2005.
Biographical Encyclopedia of Kentucky. Cincinnati: J. M. Armstrong, 1878.

Thomas S. Ward

WADSWORTH WATCH CASE COMPANY. In fall 1889 Harry A. Wadsworth, along with two partners, J. H. Stegeman and H. Remke, built the first Wadsworth Watch Case Company factory, a two-story structure at the southeast corner of Jefferson (modern Sixth St.) and Overton Sts. in Newport. In January 1892 the company incorporated, dissolving its former partnership structure. Within a few years it earned a national reputation for its gold-filled watch cases. During the 1890s the watch-case manufacturing operation moved to a nearby building, formerly the home of the **Dueber Watch Case Company**, Newport's first nationally recognized watch case company, at Fifth St. and Washington Ave. After it had operated in Newport for about a decade, rumors began to circulate that the company would be moving out of state; but instead, in November 1899, it moved to Dayton, Ky., and made watch cases in part of the former Victoria Cordage Company complex, a **ropewalk** business, at Fifth and Clay Sts. At first the Wadsworth firm shared space with the **Harvard Piano Company**. The building the companies shared was a block away from the new **Speers Memorial Hospital**. At the time, Dayton was a growing Northern Kentucky city.

Wadsworth employed 261 workers in 1900 and had an immediate impact on Dayton's economy and quality of life. The large steam engines originally installed by the rope-manufacturing plant produced more power than was needed to make watch cases, so the excess power was used to provide the city with electric lights for several years. Things did not always run completely smooth at the company; in 1913, for instance, the watch polishers union called for a strike. Nevertheless, Wadsworth's plant size and number of employees both increased over time, and 600 people were employed by 1920. The **flood of 1937** did some damage to the plant, but soon the machines were again humming as the factory turned out quality watch cases and ladies' compacts.

World War II brought changes: the firm answered the nation's call to duty by converting most of its facilities to the production of war materials, such as shell casings, machine guns, and radio parts. It was a time of high security, and early in the war Wadsworth erected a high fence on the property. Police were alerted to check on cars double-parked around the plant, out of concern that they could be used as bombs. A fire at the company in November 1943 initially raised some concerns, but it was found that instead of sabotage, it was a simple case of rubbish being ignited by a furnace. The fire created much smoke, and one employee was trapped in a basement room; he was eventually rescued by firefighters. The Wadsworth Watch Case Company proudly produced more than 100 million precision parts during the war and earned five separate "E" awards, which were given for excellence of effort in military production. Employment at the factory peaked at 1,350 workers in 1943. The firm dedicated a plaque at its plant on January 6, 1947, to honor its 246 men and women who had served in World War II.

At the end of the war, the company added 30,000 square feet of space and planned for its return to the production of watch cases and jewelry items. The postwar years included a 1947 strike for higher pay, but Wadsworth continued to operate until it was reported in the mid-1950s that the Wadsworth Watch Case Company was to be purchased by a competitor, the Elgin National Watch Case Company of Elgin, Ill., for $2.7 million. The Illinois watch case firm said that the plant would continue to function as the Wadsworth Watch Case Company under the direction of Arthur W. Wadsworth, the son of a cofounder. However, changes implemented after the sale did not work out well, and company officials announced on September 21, 1957, that the plant in Dayton would close on January 1, 1958. At the time, the Wadsworth Watch Case Company had some 200 employees and was Dayton's largest employer. It was often said around Dayton that almost everyone in town had worked at some time or another at "Waddy's."

"Articles of Incorporation," *KSJ*, January 7, 1892, 5.
Dayton Centennial Committee. *Centennial, Dayton, Kentucky, 1849–1949.* Dayton, Ky.: Dayton Centennial Committee, 1949.
"Dayton, KY., Boom," *KP*, November 23, 1899, 1.
"New Company to Open in City," *KP*, October 8, 1889, 2.
Reis, Jim. "Dayton: King of Cordage," *KP*, April 7, 4K.
———. "Smokestacks Once a Familiar Sight," *KP*, July 14, 1986, 4K.
"Strikers Form Union in Watch Factory Strike," *KP*, January 16, 1913, 5.
"To Move—Wadsworth Company to Locate Elsewhere," *KP*, August 4, 1899, 5.
"The Work Was Hard . . . the Friendship Sure," *KP*, September 21, 1990, 1K.

Daryl Polley

WAINSCOTT, GEORGE LEE (b. May 6, 1867, Owen Co., Ky.; d. May 15, 1944, Cincinnati, Ohio). George L. Wainscott, the creator of the Ale-8-One soft drink, was the son of G. W. and Elizabeth Hancock Wainscott. The first name Wainscott's parents gave him was Lee, but he added "George" because he wanted to be referred to as G. L. Wainscott. However, close friends, family, and associates still called him Lee. In 1896 he moved to Winchester in Clark Co. to operate the Rees House, a hotel. In 1902 he opened his first bottling plant, Wainscott Bottling Works, on Main St. in Winchester. He marketed various fruit-flavored drinks and soda water. In 1906 he began to sell Roxa-Kola, a drink named after his first wife, Roxanne. Roxa-Kola was a popular rival of the cola drinks, but it never became as successful as Coke, so it was discontinued about 25 years after Wainscott's death.

In 1926 Wainscott was inspired to create the Ale-8-One soft drink after acquiring several ginger-blended recipes during a visit to northern Europe. He created a unique and difficult-to-describe flavor in Ale-8-One. Some described it as a ginger and citrus flavor; others said it was like ginger ale with a hint of fruit. The beverage was named by a local girl in a naming contest that Wainscott held. Her explanation for the name Ale-8-One was that it meant "A Late One," the latest craze in soft drinks.

Wainscott was also involved in various other business endeavors. He was engaged in the coal and lumber business with his cousin Judge Joe Lindsay. For many years, he served as director and treasurer of the Clark Co. Health and Welfare League. He also operated a large farm near Becknerville and owned several buildings in Winchester. He was a member of the Board of Trustees of the First Baptist Church and served as director of the Kentucky Baptist Children's home at Glendale (near Louisville). He was also a delegate to the Democratic National Convention at Chicago in 1936. Wainscott was a president of the board of directors of the Clark Co. Hospital and one of the hospital's founders. Wainscott Hall, a nursing-home section of the hospital, was established with funds contributed by Wainscott. It was dedicated in 1933.

After a long illness, Wainscott died at a Cincinnati hospital in 1944 at age 77, leaving behind a wife and no children. His funeral was held at the Scobee Funeral Home in Winchester, and he was buried at the Lexington Cemetery in Lexington. He left half of his company to his wife, Jane Rogers Wainscott, and the remainder to company employees. A decade later, Jane died, and her brother, Frank A. Rogers, inherited her half of the company. In 1962 Rogers bought out his partners and incorporated into the firm now known as the Ale-8-One Bottling Company. Roger's son, Frank A. Rogers Jr., then became the manager and was later named president, and the company began to grow phenomenally. In 1974 the company ceased to produce the other Wainscott drinks, concentrating on Ale-8-One, and Frank A. Rogers III, Wainscott's grand-nephew, joined the company's management.

In Winchester, Ale-8-One is as well known as the cola giants Pepsi and Coca Cola. Some simply call it "Ale-8." Today, Frank Rogers III and his three children own the company. Wainscott's family has maintained his secret formula and the unique bottle and logo. The availability of Ale-8-One has expanded outside of the Winchester-Lexington area, and it is now available in Greater Cincinnati, Dayton, Louisville, and throughout much of Kentucky.

Ale-8-One: Company History. Ale-8-One Bottling Company Inc. www.ale8one.com/companyhistory.html.
"Death Takes G.L. Wainscott," *Lexington Leader*, May 15, 1944, 1.
Elmore, Deanna, public relations administrator for Ale-8-One Bottling Company. Telephone interview by Sharon McGee, August 11, 2004, Winchester, Ky.
"Funeral Rites for G. Lee Wainscott Planned Wednesday," *Winchester Sun*, May 15, 1944.
Lomax, Rebecca. "The Latest Thing: Popular Soft Drink Is Now Available in Cincinnati," *City Beat* 8, no. 36, July 18–24, 2002, available at www.citybeat.com/2002-07-18/diner.shtml.
"Long Illness Proves Fatal to G. L. Wainscott: City Soft Drink Manufacturer Dies at Cincinnati," *Winchester Sun*, May 15, 1944.

Sharon McGee

WALCOTT COVERED BRIDGE. The extant Walcott Covered Bridge across Locust Creek in Bracken Co. is located adjacent to Ky. Rt. 1159, about four miles north of Brookville. That location has had one bridge or another since 1824. The Walcott Covered Bridge is a 74-foot-long truss bridge made of sawed timbers. It was built in about 1880, using a combination of king and queen posts. The bridge, which is listed on the National Register of Historic Places, was closed to automobile traffic in 1954 and was repaired in 1984. The Bracken Co. Historical Society oversees its preservation.

Covered bridges were built to prolong the useful life of the wooden floors and the trusses of bridges. The sloped roof of the covered bridge protected the deck and main trusses of the bridge from rain and snow and the heat of the sun. Covered bridges once numbered in the hundreds within Kentucky, but many of them have been destroyed by bridge-burning during the **Civil War**, heavy vehicles, floods, storms, neglect, and arson.

Brandenburg, Phyllis, and David Brandenburg. *Kentucky's Covered Bridges.* Cincinnati: Kentucky's Writer Guild, 1968.

Powell, Robert A. *Kentucky's Covered Wooden Bridges.* Lexington: Kentucky Images, 1984.
White, Vernon. *Covered Bridges.* Berea: Kentucky Imprints, 1985.

Charles H. Bogart

WALKER, LYMAN R. (b. April, 22, 1880, Zanesville, Ohio; d. Feb. 23, 1933, Cleveland, Ohio). Architect Lyman Walker was the son of Richard B. and Lucretia Morgan Walker. When Lyman was 10 years old, his family moved to Covington, and his father, Richard Walker, became one of the city's prominent businessmen; he was in the real estate and brokerage businesses. Lyman received his early education in Zanesville Public Schools and later attended Covington Common Schools. In 1894, at age 14, he left school to work in an architect's office. He learned the profession quickly and was soon hired by **Samuel Hannaford and Sons**, in Cincinnati. He remained with that firm for three years. In 1900 he took a position with the U.S. Army Signal Corps as an assistant supervising architect in Cuba, where he remained until the military occupation ended in 1902. For the next two years, he did architectural work in Omaha, Neb. Walker was married twice, first to Helen Bondeson and later to Gayle Towson. He returned to Covington in 1904 and continued to work as an architect. Walker designed the **Villa Madonna Academy** in Villa Hills (1907); St. Stephen's Episcopal Church in Latonia; the Dan Cohen Building (see **Cohen Shoe Stores**) on Pike St. in Covington; Covington's Seventh District School, 21st and Center Sts.; and, in conjunction with architects Harry Hake and George W. Schofield, the old Farmers' and Traders' Bank (later, **First National Bank**), on the northwest corner of Sixth and Madison in Covington. In conjunction with George W. Schofield, Walker designed the **YMCA** building in Covington at Madison Ave and Pike St. in 1913. During **World War I**, Walker served as a lieutenant in the U.S. Army Signal Corps; he once captured 78 German soldiers by himself. After the war he moved to Cleveland, Ohio, where he specialized in the design of apartment buildings. He died at age 52 of nephritis at the Huron Road Hospital near Cleveland in 1933 and was buried at Highland Park Cemetery in Cleveland.

Highland Park Cemetery Records, Cleveland, Ohio.
"How One American Soldier Captured Seventy-eight German Troops," *KTS*, August 7, 1918, 2.
"Looters Caught at Work at Walker Fire," *KP*, June 5, 1913, 3.
Rootsweb. "Lyman Walker." www.rootsweb.com.

WALKER, MELVIN WADDELL, MAJOR (b. April 13, 1909, Covington, Ky.; d. January 19, 1995, Cleveland, Ohio). War hero and educator Melvin W. Walker was the only child of John and Helen Walker. He was a graduate of William Grant High School (1929) and the classmate of Covington attorney **John W. Delaney Jr.** Walker graduated from Wilberforce College in Ohio with a BA in 1933. While at Wilberforce, he took ROTC training. He later received a BS and an MA from the Ohio State University in Columbus. Walker entered the U.S. Army as a lieutenant in March 1941, trained at Camp Benning, Ga., and arrived in Italy as a member of the 366th Infantry Regiment, 92nd Infantry Division, in July 1944. In January 1945 Maj. Gen. Edward M. Almond, commanding officer of the 92nd Infantry Division, presented to Walker the Silver Star for meritorious service. The award reads, "Lieutenant Walker took a raiding party across a canal, penetrating enemy lines, smashing installations, returning with German prisoners." Walker was wounded in action in Italy and received numerous other medals, including the Purple Heart. After **World War II**, he moved to Cleveland, Ohio, where he worked for the U.S. Veterans Administration and later taught in the Cleveland Public School System. His teaching career as a mathematics teacher spanned 43 years, and he also did postgraduate work at Case Western Reserve University in Cleveland. Remaining in the Army Reserve, he obtained the rank of major. He often returned to Covington to visit his mother at the family residence on W. 15th St. At the age of 86 Walker died in 1995 in Cleveland and was buried there.

"Citations, Awards for Servicemen," *KTS*, January 19, 1945, 2.
Cohen, Haskell. "Decorate 17 in 92nd Division," *Pittsburgh Courier*, January 13, 1945, 5.
Harris, Ted. "Stories of African-Americans in WWII Went Untold," *KP*, February 28, 2002, 4K.
"Military Notes, Maj. Melvin W. Walker," *KTS*, July 23, 1956, 4A.
Perkins, Olivera. "Melvin Walker, Cleveland Teacher," *Cleveland Plain Dealer*, December 29, 1995, 6.

Theodore H. H. Harris

WALKER, STUART H. (b. March 4, 1880, Augusta, Ky.; d. March 13, 1941, Beverly Hills, Calif.). Stuart Walker, an actor and movie producer, was the son of Clifford S. and Matilda Taliaferro Armstrong Walker. By 1900 his family had moved to 63 Front St. in Covington, the town that claimed him. Walker's mechanical inclination foreshadowed his future early in his youth. He would build small theater sets and put on plays for his family. They begged him to produce new plays, so at age 12 he began to write his own stage productions. He studied engineering, graduating from the University of Cincinnati, and he also studied at the American Academy of Dramatic Arts in New York City. By 1912 he was in charge of two New York City theaters owned by the famed director David Belasco. Belasco was also the mentor of Covington actress **Dorothy Abbott**. Walker worked his way up from stage manager, playing minor parts, and was beginning to show great ability as an actor. He began performing in touring road shows. In the 1920s he returned to the Cincinnati–Northern Kentucky region and formed the Cincinnati Stuart Walker Company to promote, direct, and produce theatrical entertainment. He managed repertory seasons in Cincinnati; Indianapolis, Ind.; New York City; Dayton, Ohio; Chicago; Louisville; and Baltimore. He was the first producer to bring Booth Tarkington's *Seventeen* to the stage. Walker is also credited with founding the portmanteau theater movement, also called the little theater movement. He designed portable stages and sets for small productions that could be transported easily and set up quickly in small venues. His portmanteau productions were mainly a series of short one-act plays, vignettes. During the 1920s Walker sponsored high school dramatic competitions among the high schools of Northern Kentucky, and the prize was one of his portable sets. In 1930 his career changed as he went to Hollywood, Calif., where he wrote, produced, or directed several classic movies: *Tonight Is Ours, Great Expectations, The Mystery of Edwin Drood,* and *The Werewolf of London.* But his stellar Hollywood career was cut short at age 60 when he died of a cerebral hemorrhage in Beverly Hills, Calif. He was buried in Cincinnati at Spring Grove Cemetery in his family's lot.

"Death Takes Stuart Walker, Veteran Theatrical Producer," *CE*, March 14, 1941, 1.
Spring Grove Cemetery Records, Cincinnati.
Ward, William S. *A Literary History of Kentucky,* Knoxville: Univ. of Tennessee Press, 1988.

WALKER, WILLIAM ERNEST (b. November 19, 1869, Covington, Ky.; d. December 25, 1918, Chicago, Ill.). William E. Walker, a Chicago architect, was born and raised in Covington, where he attended both public and private schools. He entered Yale University at New Haven, Conn., and received a BA in architecture in 1891. His first job was as a draftsman with the Henry Ives Cobb architectural firm in Chicago. He was employed there until 1897, when he took a position as supervisor of construction for the Chicago Board of Education. In 1902 Walker left that job and opened his own architectural firm. Most of his work was in the design and planning of large commercial buildings and fireproof apartment houses. One of those was a nine-story apartment building at 136 Lake Shore Dr., believed to be the first in Chicago featuring a penthouse. He died of a heart attack in his home at 67 E. Division St. in Chicago, on Christmas Day 1918. Funeral services were held at St. Chrysostom Catholic Church, and burial was in Graceland Cemetery. Walker was survived by his wife, Mildred Rogers Walker, and their 12-year-old daughter, Edith.

Grossman, James R., Ann Durkin Keating, and Janice L. Reiff, eds. *The Encyclopedia of Chicago.* Chicago: Univ. of Chicago Press, 2004.
"William Ernest Walker Dies of Heart Ailment," *Chicago Daily Tribune*, December 27, 1918, 10.
Withey, Henry F., and Elsie Rathburn Withey. *Biographical Dictionary of American Architects (Deceased).* Los Angeles: Hennessey and Ingalls, 1970.

WALLACE WOODS. Wallace Woods is a neighborhood in Covington, named for the farm of Robert Wallace Jr. (1789–1863), who purchased these lands from Oneras Powell in 1828. The 80 or so acres were bounded on the east by the Licking River and on the west by the old Banklick road to Lexington. On the south side of the farm, several owners held the land later acquired by **Eugene Levassor** and **Daniel Holmes**. The farm's northern boundary became the southern city limit of Covington in

1850. The old road to Lexington was part of the ancient Great Buffalo Path, which crossed the Ohio River at the mouth of the Licking River. This pathway continued south to the Dry Ridge Trace at Walton, which connected Lexington and **Big Bone Lick** in Boone Co. In 1819, twice-daily stage runs carried the mail and passengers from Lexington to Covington.

The Wallace family, who were from Delaware, began their trip to Cincinnati in 1801, when Robert Wallace Sr., an artillery officer who had served under Gen. George Washington, moved west to Marietta, Ohio. In 1809 the Wallaces settled in Cincinnati, where they were counted among the city's pioneers in 1840. Robert Wallace Jr. became an aide de camp to Gen. William Hull as he marched in the **War of 1812** to capture Detroit, Mich., from the British. Wallace was captured with the rest of the garrison when Hull surrendered in August 1812.

After he was paroled, Wallace returned to Chillicothe, Ohio, in 1816, where he married Jane Eliza Sterrett and became a partner in the Miami Exporting Company with his brother-in-law Jacob Baum. Wallace built a steamboat, the *Hercules*, which he piloted from Louisville to New Orleans for the company. While in Louisville, Wallace acquired a family of slaves and from then on was a slaveholding Southern sympathizer. When he returned to the Cincinnati area in 1826, he moved from Cincinnati to Longwood, Ky., so that he could keep his slaves. He first built a log cabin in his woods along the **Banklick Turnpike**, in which he held a financial and an administrative interest. The new **Latonia Springs** outside Covington and three miles farther out the turnpike were drawing visitors from Cincinnati and from the South.

About 1840 Robert Wallace built a large house with a portico on the ridge overlooking the turnpike. He furnished it with fancy rugs and furniture purchased at his son-in-law's business, the John Shillito department store in Cincinnati. Wallace borrowed $12,000, using his estate, which was called Longwood, as collateral. In 1841 he found himself bankrupted by the financial crash that had occurred, but his brothers and his son-in-law were able to buy the Wallace farm and the Longwood mansion, and disaster was averted. In 1850 the City of Covington annexed all of the land up to the Wallace farm, which became the southern city limit. Wallace laid out a subdivision on the new Wallace Ave., which ran east of Greenup St. Only a few lots were sold before the **Civil War**, and the subdivision was closed. The large beech grove from Greenup St. east on Wallace Ave. became a community picnic ground, which by 1880 was known as Wallace Woods. From 1851 to 1854 the **Covington and Lexington Railroad** was completed west of the turnpike, and Covington began slowly to fill in the undeveloped land north of the farm.

With the rumblings of war in 1861, Union artillery batteries were developed on the hills south of Covington and Newport, the cannons targeting the roads to the South. In August 1862, the U.S. Army Corps of Engineers expanded the batteries into a defensive line that stretched along the Ohio River from Fort Thomas to above Ludlow. A wagon road, covered by rifle pits, connected periodic batteries. A **pontoon bridge** crossed the Licking River about where 26th St. in Covington now runs up to the Larz Anderson Battery on tunnel hill. Union general Lew Wallace's headquarters were located in the Thompson house in the winery that looked out over the Banklick Creek valley toward the Latonia Springs. Martial law was declared in the Wallace Woods area and southward and farms in the area were ordered vacated. A young soldier from Illinois described sleeping in a vineyard with hundreds of other Union troops behind vacated mansions. By mid-October it became obvious that Confederate general Henry Heth was not going to attack Covington or Newport, and within weeks the Union trenches were empty.

Col. Robert Wallace died of dysentery in August 1863, and his obituary recounted his military adventures in the War of 1812. It also listed his activities as a leader of the Democratic Party and as the head of grand juries in Covington dealing with slavery issues. After Jane Sterrett Wallace died in 1883, the Longwood mansion and grounds rested in the hands of C. G. Wallace, her younger son, and her orphaned granddaughter Jennie. The land north and west of the Longwood estate was incorporated as Central Covington in 1880. About 10 years later, the residents of the Wallace, Holmes, and Levassor farms petitioned Central Covington to annex them so that the residents could avoid the higher taxes in Covington, which was known to be interested in annexing these farms. C. G. Wallace died in 1893, and Jennie Holmes sued his heirs living in Ohio to force a subdivision of the Wallace farm, permitting settlement of Robert Wallace's estate. The first lots in the new subdivision were sold in 1894, but construction was slow because of the poor economy. More than half of the lots were built on by 1910 and the remainder were built on by 1920. When Central Covington was annexed by Covington in 1906, the Wallace farms became a neighborhood within Covington.

"Covington's First Suburb—Turning 100," *KE*, May 7, 1995, B3.

Gastright, Joseph F. *Gentlemen Farmers to City Folks: A Study of Wallace Woods, Covington, Kentucky.* Cincinnati: Cincinnati Historical Society, 1980.

"A Place for Pride to Endure; Wallace Woods Lives as Symbol of City's Spirit," *KP*, November 2, 1995, 1K.

Joseph F. Gastright

WALLER, JOHN, CAPTAIN (b. 1758, Stafford Co.,Virginia; d. February 1823, Bunker Hill, Pendleton Co., Ky.). John Waller, a **Revolutionary War** veteran and an early settler, who named the town of Falmouth, was one of the eight children of John and Mary Mathews Waller. He enlisted in the American Army on January 7, 1777, and was sworn in by Capt. John Mountjoy. After serving for three years in the 10th Regiment, he was honorably discharged in January 1780 at Philadelphia, having attained the rank of captain. He received a Land Office Military Warrant (no. 1567) for 2,300 acres in Kentucky. An 800-acre portion was located in Mason Co. and the remaining 1,500 acres in modern-day Falmouth.

John Waller and his brother Edward came west to Kentucky in spring 1784 and helped **Simon Kenton** establish Kenton Station. The Waller brothers then left the Maysville area and traveled to Blue Licks in modern Robertson Co. There they parted company: Edward went south to the Paris, Ky., area and John moved west down the Licking River to the territory that became Falmouth. John married Garner Routt, the daughter of William Routt of later Bourbon Co., on August 16, 1784, and they had 10 children; the records do not reveal why she left him, taking all their children with her to Western Kentucky, and never returned. Much of Waller's land was sold and resold several times to settle title disputes. Attempts to resolve the matters in Waller's favor through the Kentucky state legislature and the U.S. Supreme Court failed. Many of the Waller family's records that might have shed light on Falmouth's early history have been lost. A fire destroyed the original Waller cabin near Falmouth during the late 1800s, leaving many questions unanswered.

Waller was elected in 1791 as a representative to the general assembly of Virginia. On December 7, 1791, he received a certificate for being a Past Master in the Masonic Lodge. When the trustees of Falmouth held their first meeting in 1794, Waller was appointed clerk pro tem. The selling of lots in the town of Falmouth began on Monday, July 22, 1794, on order of the trustees, and Waller, as clerk, was instructed to advertise the sale.

Waller died in 1823 in the two-story log house that he erected on Bunker Hill in Pendleton Co. He was buried, as was the custom at the time, in the garden graveyard on that property.

Hartman, Margaret Strebel. *Life History of Captain John Waller, 1758–1823.* Falmouth, Ky.: Warren J. Shonert, 1985.

Kleber, John E. ed. *The Kentucky Encyclopedia.* Lexington: Univ. Press of Kentucky, 1992.

Mildred Belew

WALLING, ALONZO, AND SCOTT JACKSON (Walling: b. October 20, 1876, Mount Carmel, Ind.; d. March 20, 1897, Newport, Ky.; Jackson: b. March 1, 1869, Wiscasset, Maine; d. March 20, 1897, Newport, Ky.). Walling and Jackson gained notoriety through their convictions as murderers.

Early on the morning of February 1, 1896, young Jack Hewling trudged along an abandoned lane paralleling the Alexandria Pike (**U.S. 27**) in Northern Kentucky, south of Newport. In the dim light, seeing a bundle of dark clothing lying between two bushes, he stopped to investigate and then retched in horror as he recognized a woman's body lacking a head. Lurid details of this sensational case appeared in the press nationwide for the next 13 months.

Authorities discovered that the victim was four or five months pregnant and that she was wearing tiny, size 3B, shoes from a store in Greencastle, Ind. Ultimately, police found that she was **Pearl Bryan**, the 23-year-old daughter of a wealthy Greencastle farmer. Bryan's family thought she was visiting a friend in Indianapolis, Ind. Her parents had no knowledge of the pregnancy and were devastated when they were able to identify her clothing. After a week of investigation, Scott Jackson, a 26-year-old resident of Greencastle, and 21-year-old Alonzo Walling, of Mount Carmel, Ind. (just east of Brookville in the southeastern part of the state), were arrested and charged with Bryan's murder. Jackson and Walling were roommates and students at the Ohio Dental College in Cincinnati.

Alonzo Walling was born in Indiana, the son of Samuel A. Walling, who died when Alonzo was three years old. The family moved to Hamilton, Ohio, and in subsequent years lived in College Corners, Woodsdale, and Ripley, Ohio, and finally Greencastle, Ind.

Scott Jackson was born in New England, the son of Ebenezer Jackson, a well-known naval commodore. Scott's mother, Sarah, was a leading literary and social figure in their coastal Maine community of Wiscasset, north of Portland. During his turbulent youthful years, Scott was largely left to his own devices and had numerous close friends with poor reputations. He developed a taste for alcohol, fast living, horse racing, and women. Later, in New Jersey, Scott was charged with embezzling money from customers of the Pennsylvania Railroad and was granted immunity from prosecution by testifying against his codefendant, who subsequently went to prison. Humiliated, Sarah and Scott moved to Greencastle, Ind., to join his stepsister who lived there with her husband, a noted scholar at local DePauw University. Scott's shameful secret was safe there.

In fall 1894 Jackson enrolled at the Indiana Dental College in Indianapolis, but on New Year's Eve he was arrested for "consorting with a woman of ill-repute." He was expelled from school, his mother paid his fine, and they returned to Greencastle, where these demeaning events remained secret. In spring 1895 Scott promised his mother that he would reform and become the kind of son to make her proud. He entered the Ohio Dental College at Cincinnati that fall. Scott's best friend in Greencastle was Will Wood, son of a prominent local clergyman. Wood had introduced Jackson to Miss Pearl Bryan, the youngest daughter of Alex and Jane Bryan and a second cousin of Wood. Soon the naive Bryan became infatuated with the smooth-talking Jackson, and during the latter part of that summer, their relationship became a physical one.

In November Bryan was stunned to discover that she was pregnant, and she notified Jackson by mail of her condition. She hoped that he would agree to marry her. His response was not encouraging. In her anguish, she turned to Will Wood, imploring him to help convince Jackson that they should get married. Jackson informed Wood that he had no intention of marrying Bryan and that some way must be found to abort the baby. By mid-January, Bryan was four months pregnant and desperate. Jackson persuaded her to meet him in Cincinnati, where they could discuss their options. She departed by rail on Tuesday, January 28, 1896.

During the month of February, investigators pieced together the following likely sequence of events. Upon Bryan's arrival in Cincinnati, Jackson tried to convince her that there would be no wedding and that an abortion was the only escape from their dilemma. Jackson had previously asked Walling to help him in performing the abortion; they arrogantly assumed that their knowledge from anatomy and surgery courses would be sufficient to successfully carry it out.

Bryan strongly resisted the plan, but Jackson administered cocaine to her, suggesting that the drug could induce an abortion. When it failed to do so, late on the night of January 31, 1896, Jackson and Walling rented a buggy, crossed the Ohio River with the drugged and dazed Bryan, and drove to a secluded spot near the **Fort Thomas Military Reservation** in the Highlands. On a nearby hillside, it is likely that Jackson used surgical instruments to remove Bryan's head. Assuming that the body could never be identified without a head, they transported the head in Bryan's valise from the murder site back to Cincinnati, where they probably disposed of it in the dental school's furnace.

When arrested, Jackson and Walling blamed each other for the murder, perhaps thinking that a jury could not convict them without a confession. Feelings ran so high against the two that threats of public lynching were ever present in Newport. Jackson's trial began April 21, 1896, before Judge **Charles Helm** in Campbell Co.'s Newport courthouse. On May 14, after less than two hours of deliberation, the jury returned a unanimous verdict of guilty. Walling's trial ran between June 2 and June 18, with the same outcome. Both men were sentenced to death. Kentucky governor W. O. Bradley (1895–1899) refused to commute the sentences to life imprisonment. At 11:40 a.m., on March 20, 1897, in the jail yard in Newport, the two men were hanged. It was a beautiful spring morning, and until the last moment, Walling held out hope that Jackson would exonerate him in the actual killing, but Jackson did not. Walling's last words were "You are taking the life of an innocent man and I will call upon God to witness the truth of what I say."

Pearl Bryan's body was buried at Forest Hill Cemetery in Greencastle on March 27, 1896, without its head. H. A. Gobin, president of DePauw University, officiated at the ceremonies. Over the years, souvenir hunters have chipped away at the headstone until only the base remains to mark the grave. One can still find Lincoln-head pennies glued to the base by well-wishers who did not want Bryan to face Resurrection Day without a head. Alonzo Walling was buried in a private cemetery in Mount Carmel, Ind., next to his father; Scott Jackson was cremated.

"Alonzo Walling and Scott Jackson Were Hanged for the Murder of Pearl Bryan," *Kentucky Explorer*, June 1996, 14–17.

"Convincing Evidence That Pearl Bryan of This City Was the Ft. Thomas Victim," *Greencastle Banner Times*, February 6, 1896, 2.

"It's Out! Scott Jackson Accused of Murdering Pearl Bryan," *Indianapolis Sun*, February 6, 1896, 1.

"Jackson and Walling Die," *NYT*, March 21, 1897, 1.

"Stern and Quick to Speak Were the Jurors in the Jackson Case," *CE*, May 15, 1896, 8.

James L. McDonald and Arden G. Christen

WALNUT HILLS ACADEMY. In 1857 Rev. Nicholas C. Pettit, at age 30, founded the Cold Spring Academy, later named the Walnut Hills Academy. Several of the early settlers in the Cold Spring area, among them Robert Dodsworth, John Youtsey, Joseph Horner, Charles Horner, William Winters, and George Winters, donated money to finance the project. A well-known local Baptist preacher and bricklayer, Rev. **James Monroe Jolly**, constructed the building. It had four classrooms and an auditorium on the first floor and an apartment for the principal on the second. This was, at the time, one of the few all-brick schoolhouses in the state. Pettit served as the first principal, and three instructors were hired to teach mathematics, music, and English. The teachers boarded with a family named North, who lived next door. The school developed an excellent reputation and was recognized as one of the best in Campbell Co. Many famous men, including presidents Abraham Lincoln, Ulysses S. Grant, and William Howard Taft, are said to have made speeches from a large second-floor porch at the school. It was just before the **Civil War** that the name of the school was changed to the Walnut Hills Academy, for two large walnut trees that stood in front of the building. During the Civil War, the building was used as a Union Army provost headquarters, and Union Homeguard Troops camped on the grounds. The Walnut Hills Academy was sold in 1875 to the Cold Spring School District for use as a public school. It became both a grade and high school. When the original building was destroyed by fire on December 6, 1921, construction on a new school building began at once. During construction, classes were held at the Licking Pike Baptist Church. Several other modern buildings have been added on the site of the original Walnut Hills Academy.

Turner, Gary R. "N.K.U. Oral History Interview of a Jolly Descendant, 1996," Archives, Northern Kentucky Univ., Highland Heights, Ky.

Jack Wessling

WALSH, KATHY (b. April 11, 1947, Covington, Ky.; d. October 8, 1970, London, England). Actress Katherine Victoria Walsh was the oldest of five children born to Thomas A. and Martha "Marty" Weiss Walsh. She grew up at 55 Paul Hesser Dr. in Lakeside Place, Ky., and attended **Villa Madonna Academy**. At age 17 she was discovered by a talent scout and, a year later, signed a seven-year contract with Columbia Pictures. While she was attending the Royal Academy of Dramatic Arts in London, her insurance-executive father was killed when American Airlines Flight 727 crashed on November 8, 1965, on its final approach to the **Cincinnati/Northern Kentucky International Airport** (see also **Aviation Accidents**). In July 1969 in London, Kathy Walsh wedded an English baron, Piers Patrick Francis von Westenholz, who was a young horseman and a member of the city's trendy café society set. The marriage was soon annulled. Walsh starred in the movies *The Chase* (1967) with Marlin Brando, where she gave a memorable performance as a wild and sexy teenager, and *The Trip* (1967) with Peter Fonda. She appeared on U.S. television in *The Virginian,* in *Daniel Boone,* and with *The Monkees.* She also acted on the London stage and spent some time studying acting at the University of London. In 1970 Walsh's brief but ascending acting career was cut tragically short. During a party at her London apartment, she choked amid mysterious circumstances and quickly suffocated. Her body was returned to Mount Werner, Colo., home of her widowed mother, for burial. Later, it was reported that she was murdered.

Ancestry Library Edition. "Kentucky Birth Index." http://search.ancestrylibrary.com (accessed October 18, 2005).

"Bluegrass Starlets and Their Tragedies," *KP,* October 9, 1970, 1.

"Kathy Walsh Dead, Her Family Is Told," *CE,* October 9, 1970, 13.

"Kathy Walsh Dies in London," *KP,* October 8, 1970, 1.

"Wedding to Baron Happy Ending for Actress-Starlet," *KP,* July 10, 1969, 23K.

WALSH DISTILLERY. The Walsh Distillery, located along the south side of Front St. in Covington, between Scott St. and the **John A. Roebling Bridge**, was established during the early 1870s by liquor merchant James N. Walsh, an Irish immigrant. Early partners of Walsh were Charles Henry Kellogg and **Peter O'Shaughnessy**; Walsh's sons Nicholas and Dennis also joined him in the business. When James Walsh constructed the building, he promised the city that there would be no hog pens at his distillery. It was common to keep hogs near distilleries at the time; the hogs were fattened with the leftover mash, a by-product of distillation. Nearby was the **Hemingray Glass Company**, makers of many types of glassware including liquor bottles, but it is unknown whether its bottles were supplied to the Walsh Distillery.

In 1873 there were five distilleries in Covington; by 1913, 15 distillers, including the **New England Distillery**, and 14 liquor wholesalers operated in the city. Walsh's physical plant was state-of-the-art. In 1877 he connected the telephones at his distillery in Covington to those at his son Nicholas's distillery in Cincinnati, with a five-mile long telephone line. At the time when a half-million-dollar fire occurred in the building in 1893, Walsh's Covington facility was regarded as the largest of its kind in the world. It was quickly rebuilt. The Walsh building was well known for the several fires it endured during its years in the city.

The company was both a distiller and a redistiller (rectifier), meaning that the firm bought strong distilled products from other distillers and redistilled them into weaker blends. Walsh also served as a wholesale liquor distributor. The company enjoyed vertical integration; that is, it controlled the means to distribute its own products; it

James Walsh of Walsh Distillery.

bought other distillers' products and labels. Before 1905 Walsh also owned the Rossville Distillery in Lawrenceburg, Ind. Between 1905 and 1911, operations were shifted to Lawrenceburg, which came to be known as "the distillery city." In 1907 the James Walsh Distillery bought the "Old Hickory" brand and label from a distillery in Louisville. By 1911, after being rebuilt several times following fires, the Covington distillery was no longer in use.

"Another Fire: As Disastrous as the First," *KP,* March 20, 1893, 4.

Covington City Directories, 1870–1920.

"Dennis Walsh Died while Coughing," *KP,* June 14, 1905, 2.

Geaslen, Chester. "There Ran a Distillery or Two in Covington," *KE,* December 15, 1966, 2.

Goss, Charles Frederick, ed. *Cincinnati: The Queen City, 1788–1912.* 4 vols. Chicago: S. J. Clarke, 1912.

Kentucky Death Certificate No. 300, for the year 1890.

LaBree, Ben, ed. *Notable Men of Cincinnati at the Beginning of the 20th Century.* Louisville, Ky.: George G. Fetter, 1903.

"Local Matter," *DC,* November 12, 1877, 1.

"Sudden Summons," *CE,* June 2, 1915, 8.

Michael R. Sweeney

WALTER AND STEWART. The distinguished architectural firm of Walter and Stewart was one of the finest and most prolific in Greater Cincinnati during the 10 years before 1872. William Walter was born in Hammond, Pa., in 1815, the son of Henry Walter. Although little is known about the early life of either the father or the son, it is known that the family moved from York, Pa., to Cincinnati when William was a young man. Henry Walter lived in Cincinnati for the rest of his life and became the city's most significant Greek Revival architect, playing an important role in the design of the Ohio State capitol in Columbus. His finest work was possibly the design of the St. Peter in Chains Catholic Cathedral, on Plum St. between Seventh and Eighth Sts. in Cincinnati.

William Walter was educated in local schools and trained in his father's firm to be an architect. Whether these Walters were related to Thomas Ustick Walter, who designed the U.S. Capitol, is not known. After his father's death in 1851, William Walter entered into a partnership with James Keyes Wilson, a prominent Cincinnati architect. Wilson also was involved in the training of such notable local architects as **Samuel Hannaford**, James K. McLaughlin, and **Charles Crapsey**. While associated with Wilson, William Walter designed several churches and commercial buildings in Cincinnati.

William Stewart, the son of a builder and cabinetmaker, was born in 1832 and raised in Canada. His father apprenticed him to a local architect. After Stewart immigrated to the United States in 1857, he worked in Chicago and in St. Paul, Minn., for a short time and then moved to Covington. He and William Walter soon formed an architectural partnership called Walter and Stewart. Between 1857 and the time Stewart returned to Canada in 1872, the partners designed a number of Northern Kentucky churches. Among them were the **Mother of God Catholic Church**, the **First Baptist Church**, the First Methodist Church (see **First United Methodist Church**), the old First Presbyterian Church (see **Community of Faith Presbyterian Church**), and the Madison Ave. Baptist Church (built 1869; demolished ca. 1912), all in Covington. Few architectural firms designed so many high-quality church buildings for so many different religious denominations as did Walter and Stewart. They also designed the old Covington High School at 12th and Russell Sts., the Holly City Waterworks at the foot of Madison Ave. in Covington, and the palatial home of **Amos Shinkle** on East Second St. in Covington (demolished for the construction of **Booth Memorial Hospital**). Walter and Stewart made significant contributions to building designs on both sides of the Ohio River. After Stewart left the firm, he lived in Toronto and later in Hamilton, Ontario, where he practiced with his son Walter Stewart.

William Walter formed a new partnership with George Humphries of Ludlow, and their company, known as Walter and Humphries, lasted for about three years. Walter then worked as a solo architect, but none of his later work has been positively identified. William Walter died September 29, 1886, in Cincinnati and was buried at Spring Grove Cemetery in that city; William Stewart died in Canada in 1907.

Schottelkotte, Al. "Talk of the Town," *CE,* September 10, 1959, 5A.

Tenkotte, Paul A. *A Heritage of Art and Faith: Downtown Covington Churches.* Covington, Ky.: Kenton Co. Historical Society, 1986.

Withey, Henry F., and Elsie Withey. *Biographical Dictionary of American Architects (Deceased).* Los Angeles: New Age, 1956.

WALTON. Running along a ridge in southern Boone Co., Walton is a community that was settled, developed, and continues to grow because of its location at a crossroads. On early-19th-century maps of Kentucky (such as H. S. Tanner's 1839 *A*

New Map of Kentucky), it is referred to as Gaines Crossing, where the road from Covington divided into a route to Lexington (see **Covington and Lexington Turnpike**) and a road to Warsaw. There, Archibald Reid, a distiller and a major landowner, opened the first tavern in Boone Co. in about 1795–1803. In 1808 Abner Gaines, a prominent local citizen who later served as a Boone Co. justice of the peace and sheriff, became operator of the tavern (see **Gaines Tavern**). The community that grew up around the tavern and inn was called Gaines Fork Roads, then Gaines Crossroads. A post office, run by Gaines's son James, was established there in 1815. The Kentucky legislature renamed the community Walton in 1840.

Walton lies atop a topographical feature called the **Dry Ridge Trace**, a north-south spur of the Great Cumberland Mountains, which marks the dividing point for Northern Kentucky streams. The ridge road has been an important transportation route since ancient times, and Walton became an entrepot for various modes of land transportation. During the early 19th century, the ridge road became part of the **Covington and Lexington Turnpike**, a major toll road connecting Cincinnati with the central Bluegrass region of Kentucky. Beginning in the second decade of the 1800s, a web of stagecoach lines connected Walton with towns and cities of Northern and Central Kentucky. The turnpike was improved and macadamized in the 1840s, easing travel between distant towns. These early transportation improvements set the stage for the town of Walton's later growth.

In the mid-19th century, the small but lively community of Walton had 50 residents, as well as tobacco factories, livery stables, and carriage manufacturers. In the years following the **Civil War**, the town became the railroad center of the county and began to grow rapidly. During the late 1860s, the **Louisville, Cincinnati, and Lexington Railroad**, the Short Line later acquired by the **Louisville and Nashville Railroad**, laid tracks through Walton and adjoining Verona. In the mid-1870s, the **Cincinnati Southern Railroad** was built through Richwood and Walton.

Although Walton was not the only railroad town in Boone Co., it was the only community that prospered because of its rail facilities. It became the most important shipping point in the county for farm produce, as well as a local drop-off point for mail-order items. Soon passenger service was introduced, and daily commuter trains linked Walton with Cincinnati, Covington, and Ludlow. Traveling by train to shop in Covington and Cincinnati became popular in Walton during the late 19th century; additional runs were made on Saturdays to accommodate the standing-room-only crowds. As late as the 1920s, Walton residents commuted to work or school by train.

In the years after the Civil War, a small African American community formed in northern Walton. Several generations of the Steele and Ingram families, descendants of freed slaves, made their homes in the modest hall-parlor and saddlebag dwellings along Church St. The center of this community was the **Zion Baptist Church**, founded in 1872.

Walton was incorporated in 1870. It developed as a classic linear railroad town, bounded by the ridge and the rail lines. A business district flourished along Main St., with residential neighborhoods to the north and south. A small industrial and warehouse district grew up beside the Cincinnati Southern Railroad's tracks. By 1876, eight years after construction of its first rail line, Walton had a population of 300, along with a hotel, two general stores, a blacksmith shop, a boot and shoe store, a millinery shop, and a saloon. The local 1883 Lake atlas shows residential, commercial, and industrial buildings densely clustered along the turnpike, between Church and Depot Sts., and along High St. to the east. To the north and the south was open land, with scattered houses on large parcels of land.

Beginning in the 1880s, the town expanded south along the turnpike to the vicinity of the present-day Mary Grubbs Highway. New brick-and-frame residences of a variety of fashionable types and styles were built on large lots for business owners and professionals. S. Main St. residents of the late 1800s and early 1900s included mill owner A. Mott Rouse, banker David B. Wallace, clothing store owner Walsh Ridenour, and druggist Robert W. Jones. One of Boone Co.'s master builders, George Nicholson, the son of Dr. **Henry Clay Nicholson**, constructed many of Walton's new buildings. A resident of S. Main St., George Nicholson built schools, churches, bridges, residences, and commercial buildings in Boone and Kenton counties during the first half of the 20th century.

An 1889 account depicts Walton as a prosperous and progressive community with a hopeful future, because of its two rail lines and its location in a rich agricultural district. It had three tobacco warehouses with a capacity of more than 4 million pounds, a "large flouring mill," and three stores "doing a business from $30,000 to $90,000 annually." In 1879 the Walton Deposit Bank opened its doors; it was the only banking house on the turnpike between Covington and Williamstown. Walton had Boone Co.'s first fire department bucket brigade (1880) and its first streetlights (1890s). By 1900 Walton was the largest city in Boone Co., with a population of 583.

In 1900 the local school district, seeking a higher quality of education for its students, merged with the Verona schools, forming one of the county's first consolidated districts. The county's first high school opened at Walton in 1901. The building remains today on N. Main St., now used as apartments. Students from outlying areas boarded with town families during the week, returning home by train on weekends.

For the first half of the 20th century, Walton, with its business district and diverse manufacturing enterprises, remained the largest town in Boone Co. In 1914 the *Walton Advertiser* boasted: "Walton . . . is a 'regular' town, with a miniature Broadway, electric lights . . . a beautiful pike . . . two railroads. . . . [T]he metropolis of Boone County, [it] bids fair to become a great city, on account of the transportation facilities which it possesses." During the 1920s, the turnpike was rebuilt as the **Dixie Highway** (U.S. 25), the first highway in Kentucky to link the rural South of the United States with the urban North. The eastern division of the road was built through Boone Co., passing through Florence, Devon, Richwood, and Walton. The alignment was chosen by 1913, raising the value of undeveloped land along its future route. The new road, the widespread availability of automobiles, and the removal of tolls also helped to transform the lives of middle-class Boone Co. families. It opened up new mobility choices and employment opportunities but also initiated suburban sprawl.

Like many other cities along the Dixie Highway's path, Walton expanded and prospered, with new neighborhoods platted to the north and the south. By 1927 there were 50 buildings along S. Main St., between Depot St. and Richland Ct. The county's most ambitious residential development was the Alta Vista Subdivision, just north of the railroad junction. Platted in 1929, it featured a boulevard lined with a double row of trees. Due to the disruptions of the **Great Depression** and **World War II**, however, only one house, the Edward Blau residence, was built until the mid-1940s.

During the depression, a Civilian Conservation Corps camp was established in northern Walton, near today's Alta Vista Dr. The camp, in operation from 1935 to 1942, housed hundreds of youths employed in conservation and reclamation projects across Kentucky.

In 1950 Walton had a population of 750. Longtime residents recall mid-20th-century Walton as a "comfortable, self-sustaining community of just a few hundred people," with a hardware store and a half dozen groceries. Walton lost its preeminent position in the 1950s suburban boom. The town's local businesses began to decline as people drove to regional shopping centers with chain stores and large merchandise inventories.

A **tornado** swept through Walton in 1956. Although property damage was estimated at $500,000, not a single life was lost. Fire devastated the business district in 1971. The town also suffered a disappointment when plans to build a theme park (Fess Parker's Frontier World) north of town were scrapped. Walton met these challenges by joining the Kentucky Main Street program, which has brought new life to the town along with a deeper recognition of its distinctive heritage. In 2006 the town's S. Main St. Historic District was added to the National Register of Historic Places, becoming the county's third National Register historic district. In 2006 the city of Walton's successes were honored with a Preservation Award from the Boone Co. Historic Preservation Review Board. Walton entered its third century as a prosperous community, with new residential, commercial, and industrial development steadily building its population and tax base.

An Atlas of Boone, Kenton, and Campbell Counties, Kentucky. Philadelphia: D. J. Lake, 1883.

Boone Co. Historic Preservation Review Board. *Historic Structures of Boone County, Kentucky*. Burlington, Ky.: Boone Co. Historic Preservation Review Board, 2002.

Boone County Recorder, November 20, 1889; April 10, 1907, 6.
Flynn, Terry. "City Working to Keep Connected to Its Past," *KE*, September 2, 1996, B1.
Kentucky State Gazetteer and Business Directory. Detroit: R. L. Polk, 1876.
150th Anniversary, City of Walton, 1840–1990. Walton, Ky.: City of Walton, 1990.
Reis, Jim. "200 and Holding: Walton Was Once the Heart of Boone County," *KP*, November 19, 1984, 10K.
Sanborn Map Company. *Sanborn Fire Insurance Map of Walton, Kentucky*. New York: Sanborn Map, 1921, 1927.
Tenkotte, Paul A. "Rival Cities to Suburbs: Covington and Newport, Kentucky, 1790–1890," PhD diss., Univ. of Cincinnati, 1989.
"Walton, Boone County," *CJ*, April 23, 1870, 3.
Warner, Jennifer S. *Boone County: From Mastodons to the Millennium*. Burlington, Ky.: Boone Co. Bicentennial Book Committee, 1998.
"Your Town: Walton, Ky.—Just Plain American," *CTS*, April 25, 1956, 9.

Margaret Warminski

WALTON CHRISTIAN CHURCH. The Christian Church of Walton in Boone Co. was founded in 1876, and the first pastor was Rev. J. W. Beasley. The church is affiliated with the Christian Church (Disciples of Christ), a Protestant denomination with members mostly in the United States and Canada. The Walton Christian Church's history can be traced back to 1873, when Beasley conducted a revival meeting in Walton in the local Baptist Church. He had been called to conduct this revival by a group of Walton citizens. Three years later, and seventy-two years after Barton W. Stone, minister at Cane Ridge, first publicly set forth the principles that led to the birth of the Christian Church movement, a revival at Walton in 1876 led to the founding of the local church. During the first few years, other revivals were held; and the Walton Christian Church met in several locations, including the Masonic Hall (see **Masons**) and the local school. Money was raised, land purchased, and the first church structure was built in 1879. In 1905 the Walton Christian Church expanded to two services a month, and by 1911 individual communion service was started. In 1916 Rev. E. C. Lacy became the Walton Christian Church's first full-time pastor.

A new church building was constructed and dedicated on May 5, 1918. It was built in town along Main St. and cost approximately $20,000. Over the next 20 years membership and attendance at the church doubled, and the building was expanded in 1937. Ten years later, tragedy struck. On November 27, 1947, Thanksgiving Day, the building was destroyed by fire. Lost in the fire were the church's records, irreplaceable books, and a newly purchased organ. A new church structure, built on the foundation of the previous building, was dedicated on August 14, 1949, and it remains today. The new building's cost was approximately $75,000.

In the early 1950s, the church sponsored a large tent revival on the Walton school grounds for all denominations, reminiscent of the revival services held in the past. It included singing and preaching by a variety of local and national religious speakers. The Walton Christian Church remains an important part of the community.

Ervin, J. M. *Walton Christian Church*. Walton, Ky.: Walton Christian Church, 1938.
Rouse, Jack. *Walton Christian Church: A History*. Walton, Ky.: Walton Christian Church, 1973.

Robert Schrage

WALTON-VERONA INDEPENDENT SCHOOLS. The Walton-Verona Independent School District lies in the extreme southern part of Boone Co. The largest independent school district in the commonwealth, it includes the city of Walton, the community of Verona, and the surrounding area of approximately 26 square miles. As of October 2006, the district had 1,269 students enrolled in kindergarten through 12th grade.

The first public grade school in Walton was established in 1839 at the forks of Old Stephenson Mill Rd. and Old Beaver Lick Rd. It was operated by the county and at first had a three-month term; in 1869 the school term was expanded to five months. The first school in Walton to offer high school education was a private school started by Mrs. Cara Myers, who came to Kentucky from Vermont and had attended Georgetown College at Georgetown, Ky. A teacher at the school, Henry Newton, was recognized in a local atlas published in 1883 as a "teacher of the select school offering all branches of mathematics and a regular course of thorough instruction." This school operated until 1902, when it became a part of the new public school. It was located two doors north of the Christian Church in town, a site now covered by the church's parking lot.

William Ransler seems to have helped start the Walton Public School, the first public high school in the county, which included grades 1 through 12. It met in a new brick building built in 1900 on N. Main St. The building remains today and is used for apartments. Some of the subjects taught in the high school were four years of English, four years of Latin, German, geometry, trigonometry, ancient history, astronomy, botany, composition, and penmanship. A Mr. Hickey was the first principal-superintendent, but he remained at Walton only three years before moving on to teach at Harvard University in Cambridge, Mass. Hickey set a standard by which many capable successors over the years have been judged. The high school became widely known, and people moved into the district from other areas so that their children could attend; other families boarded their children with friends or relatives within the district for the same reason.

As early as 1880, there were two schools in Verona: one was the public grade school operated by the county, and the other was a private grade and high school known as the League Institute, which was begun by Miss Nannie Hamilton. More is known of the League Institute than of the public school in Verona. Tuition at the institute was $50 per year. A boarding house and cottages were maintained for the many boarding boys and girls. Two courses of study were offered: a scientific course, which included algebra, the physical sciences, history, English, and so forth, and a classical course, which stressed foreign languages (Latin and German), music, art, and public speaking. The private school continued until around 1910, when it consolidated with the public school. In 1914 a brick building was erected for grades 1 through 12, which remains standing today.

In fall 1935 the Walton and Verona schools were consolidated into one school district, with a grade school maintained at Verona and a grade and high school at Walton. Thus the district became known as the Walton-Verona School District. For several years, only students in grades 9–12 were transported from Verona to Walton. Later, students in grades 7 and 8 were also sent to Walton.

The Walton-Verona Schools have never been a part of the county system, nor do the communities of Walton and Verona desire them to be. In 1955 the present high school building was opened in Walton at the end of Alta-Vista Dr.; as the student body grew, additions to the building were made in 1962, 1973, 1989, and 1993. Currently, the Walton-Verona Board of Education is building a new high school wing that will accommodate further population growth of the community. In 1955 the first three grades in the entire district attended classes in the new building and only grades four through six attended classes in Verona. This arrangement continued until the present elementary school for grades kindergarten through sixth was constructed along Porter Rd. in Verona in 1971. This building has had several additions to accommodate the growth as well.

The hallmarks of the Walton-Verona schools have always been a very high scholastic standard, achieving recognition athletically, and producing well-rounded, productive citizens who excel in varied fields of endeavor. The district is unique in the willingness of parents and citizens to take an active part in maintaining an independent school district by paying higher taxes, volunteering to help with school programs, and having a direct voice in educating the children of the community. On December 15, 2007, the new Walton-Verona High School was dedicated. Built at a cost of $14 million and designed by architects Robert Ehmet Hayes and Associates, Fort Mitchell, it accommodates 700 students. According to Boone Co. planning officials, this new facility should adequately service growth for 10 years. A half-million-dollar renovation of the middle school was completed in 2008.

"Plan New Elementary School for Walton," *KP*, May 14, 1967, 2K.
"Walton Buying 117 Acres for 2 New Schools," *KP*, June 22, 2001, 2K.
"What Is Walton-Verona's Future?" *KP*, November 2, 1968, 2K.

Kelly Fulmer

WAMPUM. Wampum was a town located along the Falmouth and Lenoxburg Rds., about seven miles southeast of Falmouth in Pendleton Co.

Wampum was situated on Kincaid Creek, and much of it today is part of the **Kincaid Lake State Park**. Among the businesses once operating in Wampum were a sawmill, a gristmill, a blacksmith shop, and a flourmill; a gentleman named Kennedy operated the last blacksmith shop. Later, C. L. Myers opened a flourmill, but he eventually moved eastward to Caddo, located on Ky. Rt. 10. Myers's mill was powered by a 60-foot-long steam boiler that had once been used on a ferry that crossed the Ohio River while the **John A. Roebling Bridge** was under construction during the 1850s and 1860s. The boiler was transported to Falmouth via the railroad. From there, a former slave, Kirk Hitch, used a team of eight yoked oxen to bring it overland so it could be installed for use at the Myers's mill in Wampum. Three men, B. B. Thornberry, John Smith, and Grant Wills, operated the Wampum post office at various times. Today no businesses remain open at Wampum, and 15 feet of water cover the site of the old mill. The salt well that once served the people of the town has also long since been filled.

Belew, Mildred Boden. *The First 200 Years of Pendleton County*. Falmouth, Ky.: M. B. Belew, n.d. [ca. 1994].

Mildred Belew

WARD, ANNA BELL (b. December 28, 1897, Covington, Ky.; d. May 18, 1986, Lexington, Ky.). Theater manager Anna Bell Ward Olson was the daughter of Edward and Annetta Ferguson Ward. She was educated in the public schools of Chicago and Covington and at age 14 won a scholarship to the College of Music in Cincinnati, where she graduated. She was a child vocal soloist at Christ Cathedral (Cincinnati), the Cincinnati Zoological Gardens, and the Lyric Theater, and with John Philip Sousa's Band and the Cincinnati Symphony Orchestra. She performed in various local theatrical productions around Covington. At the age of 17, Ward began her business career as the owner-manager of the Pastime Theatre in Maysville. Her family eventually owned a chain of 35 theaters called Phoenix Amusements. She became an early expert in motion picture theater management and was recognized nationally for her ability to publicize movies. Ward produced a few westerns and starred in several as a young adult. She was also an author of short stories, including "Night Winds," "Big Business Girl," and "Uncle Andy's Secret." She helped to organize the Kentucky Colonels in the 1930s and, as the organization's first secretary, was the keeper of its seal. In her youth she held several long-distance swimming records. Politically she was an independent; religiously, she was a Methodist. For many years, Lexington was Ward's home; her office was in the Strand Theatre Building on Main St. In retirement, she lived in Somerset for many years before returning to Lexington for her last years. She died at Country Place in Lexington at age 90. She was buried at the Lexington Cemetery next to her husband, David A. Adolphus Olson of Somerset, who died in 1964.

"Kentucky Colonels Promoter Dies at 90," *Lexington Herald-Leader,* May 20, 1986, B-8.
"Show Worlds a Showing Bill at Colonial," *KP,* May 5, 1913, 5.
Southard, Mary Young. *Who's Who in Kentucky.* Louisville, Ky.: Standard, 1936.

Michael R. Sweeney

WARE, JAMES C. (b. February 3, 1913, Covington, Ky.; d. November 6, 1991, Edgewood, Ky.). Banker, lawyer, and politician James C. Ware was born and raised in Covington. He attended Kenton Co. Public Schools (see **Kenton Co. School District**) and later graduated from Centre College in Danville, Ky. After leaving school, he returned to Covington and for the next eight years worked for the Central Trust Banking Company in Cincinnati. He attended Cincinnati's **Chase College of Law** for two years while he worked for the bank, and after passing a law examination in 1940, he was admitted to the Kentucky bar. During **World War II**, Ware attempted to join the U.S. Army as an officer but was instead made a special agent for the Federal Bureau of Investigation. He left that position in 1946 and returned to Covington, where he joined his brother William O. Ware at the law firm of his father, **Orie S. Ware**. James Ware married Polly Dawson, and the couple had two children, James C. Ware Jr. and Mary Ware. The family lived at 83 Greenbrier Rd. in South Fort Mitchell (now Fort Mitchell). James Ware Sr. entered politics in 1957 and was elected to the Kentucky Senate, where he served for eight years. He held the office of Senate leader pro tem in 1964–1965. While in that position, he served as acting governor nine times, on occasions when both the governor and the lieutenant governor were out of state. As acting governor, he made about 50 people Kentucky Colonels.

During a long and colorful career, Ware served as a vice president of the First National Bank of Covington (see **First National Bank and Trust Company of Covington**), as chairman of the board of the **Baptist Convalescent Center**, as trustee of the Covington Children's Home (see **Children's Home of Northern Kentucky**), and as a member of the advisory council of **Booth Memorial Hospital**. He was an active member of the **Fort Mitchell Baptist Church** for more than 40 years, where he served as deacon, trustee, and Sunday school teacher. He was also a member of the Optimist Club and a president of the Kentucky Historical Society. His wife Polly Dawson Ware died in 1990, and in October of the following year, he married Jo Kummer, the mother of John Kummer, an associate in his law firm. After being married for less than one month, Ware died of an apparent heart attack, while a patient at the **St. Elizabeth Medical Center**, South, in Edgewood. Funeral services were held at the Fort Mitchell Baptist Church, and he was buried in Highland Cemetery in Fort Mitchell.

"Ex-Senator Ware, Acted as Governor," *KP,* November 8, 1991, 1.
Reis, Jim. "He Was Governor for Nine Days," *KP,* May 22, 1989, 4K.
"Ware Elected," *KTS,* May 29, 1958, 1A.
"Ware to Leave FBI Post," *KP,* January 2, 1946, 1.

WARE, ORIE S. (b. May 11, 1882, Peach Grove, Pendleton Co., Ky.; d. December 16, 1974, Fort Mitchell, Ky.). Attorney and congressman Orie Solomon Ware was the son of Solomon Grizzel and Ida Petty Ware. He received his education in the elementary schools of Covington and attended the academy of Professor George W. Dunlap at Independence. In September 1900, Ware entered the University of Cincinnati College of Law, graduating in 1903 with an LLB. He was admitted to the Kentucky and Ohio bars that year. Ware was a member of the Kentucky Bar Association and the American Bar Association and was a former president of the Kenton Co. Bar. At the time of his death, Ware was the longest-practicing attorney in Covington, having practiced law there a total 71 years.

Ware was active in politics. He was appointed postmaster of Covington by President Woodrow Wilson (1913–1921) and served from 1914 to 1921, when he resigned to become a candidate for the position of Kenton Co. commonwealth attorney; he was elected for a six-year term in November 1921 and served from 1922 to 1927. While in that position, Ware forbade dog racing in Kenton Co. and successfully argued the appeal of his decision against dog racing before the U.S. Supreme Court. In 1926 Ware became a candidate for the U.S. House of Representatives. In the 1926 Democratic primary, he defeated **Brent Spence**; in the general election that year, he defeated Republican Emmett Daugherty. In 1927 Ware took his seat in the 70th Congress. Later he served as a U.S. federal magistrate from 1942 to 1947 and as a Kenton Co. circuit judge in 1957 and 1958.

Ware was involved in countless civic activities, including building campaigns of St. Elizabeth Hospital in 1915 (see **St. Elizabeth Medical Center**), the **YMCA** in 1916, the **Booth Memorial Hospital** in 1923, and the Covington Protestant Children's Home (see **Children's Home of Northern Kentucky**) in 1925. During **World War I**, he was executive secretary of the Kenton Council of Defense and was the general chairman of the War Savings Stamp Drive. He was a member of the Chamber of Commerce (see **Northern Kentucky Chamber of Commerce**) for more than 50 years. In 1968 he was the first recipient of the Chamber of Commerce's Frontiersman Award. He was a director of the First National Bank of Covington (see **First National Bank and Trust Company of Covington**) from 1933 to 1970. Ware belonged to the **First Baptist Church** of Covington, where he served on the board of deacons for 52 years and as a church trustee for more than 30 years. He was an active member of the Masonic Order for 71 years and was Grand Master of the Grand Lodge of Kentucky in 1913; for more than 45 years he was a member of the jurisprudence committee of the Grand Lodge. Ware was a vice president of the local **Christopher Gist Historical Society**. He married Louise Culbertson on September 19, 1906. Ware died in Fort Mitchell in 1974 and was buried at Highland Cemetery there.

Bodley, Temple. *History of Kentucky: The Blue Grass State.* Vol. 4. Chicago: S. J. Clarke, 1928.
Murphy, John. "89 Years of Good Old Days," *KP*, June 28, 1971, 1K–2K.
Pashchke, Margaret. "'Give and Take' Wares Mark 65th Wedding Anniversary," *KP*, September 18, 1971, 1K–2K.
Reis, Jim. "A New Home for Orphans," *KP*, July 28, 1903, 4K.
———. "1925 Caravan Pitches Covington as 'Big City' to the Region," *KP*, March 25, 1996, 4K.
Southard, Mary Young, and Ernest C. Miller, eds. *Who's Who in Kentucky: A Biographical Assembly of Notable Kentuckians.* Louisville, Ky.: Standard, 1936.
Ware, Orie S., and Alpheus E. Orton. *Book of Constitutions of the Grand Lodge of Kentucky, Free and Accepted Masons.* Masonic Home, Ky.: Press of Masonic Home Journal, 1940.

William Terwort

WAR OF 1812. When the United States declared war on Great Britain in June 1812, the military installation at Newport, Ky., became a focal point for the war effort in the American West. **Newport Barracks**, located at the confluence of the Ohio and Licking rivers, acted as a supply depot and training center. Several militia and regular army units formed in Kentucky were bivouacked at "the Point," just across the Licking River on the current site of Covington, where they gathered, organized, and equipped themselves for campaigns throughout the Northwest Territory and later at New Orleans. The Newport Barracks also served as a way station for captured British officers who were being taken to the state penitentiary in Frankfort and as a longer-term prison for 439 captured British privates and noncommissioned officers. That number of prisoners nearly doubled Newport's population in November 1813. The men were held in confinement until July 1814, when they were moved to Canada. Tradition has it that these prisoners of war assisted in the construction of numerous buildings in Newport, including the **Richard Southgate** house.

Large numbers of Northern Kentuckians turned out to fight the British and the American Indians on the frontier, primarily in an effort to conquer Canada and wrest it from the British Crown. Kentuckians could be found on nearly all the battlefields of both the Northwest and the Southwest campaigns, serving in both state militia units and in regular U.S. Army regiments. Many of these men were prominent individuals, and some became prominent through their military service.

One of the earliest to tender his services to the cause was Newport's **James Taylor Jr.**, who received an appointment as military agent and district paymaster of the army, with the nominal rank of major. He gathered supplies and organized transportation for them and then joined Gen. William Hull's army at Detroit, Mich., whereupon Hull appointed Taylor his quartermaster general. Taylor was taken prisoner when Hull surrendered his entire force to the British on August 16, 1812. Paroled by the British, Taylor returned to Newport to find that his position had been supplanted by the federal government's creation of the U.S. Army's Quartermaster Department.

William Orlando Butler of Carroll Co. joined the army at the outbreak of war. Serving with Brig. Gen. James Winchester, Butler escaped the massacre in Michigan at the River Raisin in January 1813 because he was wounded and captured earlier at the Battle of Frenchtown. After his exchange, Butler returned to Kentucky and raised a company of volunteers to serve with Andrew Jackson in the New Orleans campaign, where Butler earned General Jackson's praise.

Another significant service performed by Northern Kentuckians occurred in August 1813. To combat the British on Lake Erie, Com. Oliver Hazard Perry hurriedly constructed a fleet of small warships. When he was unable to obtain a sufficient crew for the vessels, Perry appealed to Gen. William Henry Harrison for men. Harrison in turn requested volunteers from his army. More than 100 of the 120 men who responded were from Kentucky, and a significant number of them were from Northern Kentucky. Pvt. John Norris, of Petersburg in Boone Co., played a decisive role in Commodore Perry's crushing victory over a British fleet on Lake Erie. Norris was among the Kentucky militiamen who had also volunteered to fill out Perry's crew and was generally credited with firing the last shot of the battle and capturing the British vessel HMS *Hunter*, for which he received $300 in prize money. Each of the Kentuckians present received $214 in prize money, and many later received commemorative gold medals from the grateful Kentucky legislature.

Also in August 1813, Newport was the site of a rendezvous of 3,500 volunteers and militiamen answering the call of Kentucky governor Isaac Shelby (1792–1796, 1812–1816) for men. They were organized in Newport and dispatched to General Harrison's army in the Northwest. Among the regiments thus organized was Col. Richard M. Johnson's regiment of mounted riflemen, which included large numbers of Northern Kentuckians. Their participation proved decisive at the Battle of Thames in Upper Canada on October 5, 1813. The mounted riflemen were credited with breaking the British lines and with the death of noted Indian leader Tecumseh. This battle proved to be the final major battle in the Northwestern Theater. Maj. Richard Montgomery Gano was second-in-command of a regiment of Kentucky Volunteers at the Battle of the Thames. Gano served with distinction and later became one of the founders of Covington. (Covington was named for Brig. Gen. Leonard W. Covington, who was killed in the War of 1812 at the battle of Chrysler's Farm [Ontario, Canada] in 1813 while leading his men in an attack on British positions.)

Northern Kentuckians were also present for the final battle of the war at New Orleans, lending their services to Gen. Andrew Jackson's efforts to defend the city from British assault. More than 2,700 Kentuckians stood with Jackson at New Orleans, and more than two-thirds of that number stood in the lines of battle. The remaining men from Kentucky, who had not been furnished with arms by their state, performed other services to help repel the British assault and keep that valuable city out of British hands.

While it is impossible to say with certainty how many Northern Kentuckians served in the War of 1812, since military rosters did not list the places of origin for companies and regiments, it is certain that at least hundreds, if not more, of local men became involved in this conflict. Northern Kentuckians were present for the campaigns in Ohio, Michigan, Upper Canada, and Louisiana. They fought at the Raisin River, at the Thames, at Lake Erie, and at New Orleans. It is known that 4.6 percent of the troops who fought for the United States were from Kentucky and that 64 percent of the men who were killed in action were Kentuckians.

Donnelly, Joseph. *Newport Barracks—Kentucky's Forgotten Military Installation.* Covington, Ky.: Kenton Co. Historical Society, 1999.
Hammack, James Wallace, Jr. *Kentucky and the Second American Revolution: The War of 1812.* Lexington: Univ. of Kentucky Press, 1976.
Heidler, David S., and Jeanne T. Heidler, eds. *Encyclopedia of the War of 1812.* Santa Barbara, Calif.: ABC-Clio, 1997.

Tim Herrmann

WARREN, FRED, SR., MAJOR GENERAL (b. August 23, 1903, Newport, Ky.; d. December 16, 1986, Fort Thomas, Ky.). Frederick M. Warren Sr., a distinguished Campbell Co. judge and a **World War II** veteran, was born and raised in Newport. He was educated in public schools, graduating from **Newport High School**, and received both his bachelor's degree and his law degree from the University of Cincinnati. Shortly after leaving school, he served as police judge and city solicitor for the City of Southgate. Warren married Peggy Beaton, and they had one son, Frederick Warren Jr. In 1924 Judge Warren enlisted in the Ohio National Guard, where he served for five years and was discharged as a 2nd lieutenant. After he was admitted to the Kentucky bar in 1935, he set up his law practice in Newport. In the 1930s he took part in many of the organizational meetings for construction of the **Mary Ingles Highway**.

At the beginning of World War II, Warren was inducted into the U.S. Army, with the rank of major. He participated in many battles throughout Europe, including the Battle of the Bulge, and served for a short time under Gen. George S. Patton Jr. During his army service, he was awarded the Distinguished Service Medal, the Silver Star, and four Bronze Stars. He was released from active duty in 1946 but continued to work with reserve and guard units. He was promoted to brigadier general in 1949 and to major general in 1954. Warren was recalled to active duty in 1959 and made commander of the U.S. Army Reserves and the Reserve Officers' Training Corps (ROTC). He retired from the Army in August 1963. Warren was elected a Campbell Co. circuit court judge in 1964 and held that position for ten years. He retired as a full-time judge in 1974 but continued to work as a substitute. Warren died at St. Luke Hospital at age 83.

Funeral services were held at St. Thomas Church, and he was buried in a mausoleum at St. Stephen Cemetery, Fort Thomas.

"Fred Warren, Campbell Judge," *KP*, December 17, 1986, 2K.

"Fred Warren Advances to Major General Post," *KTS*, February 14, 1955, 1A.

"Jurist, Army General Frederick Warren Dies," *KP*, December 17, 1986, 1K.

WARRIOR TRAIL (ALANANT-O-WAMIOWEE). Many parts of the eastern United States have trails known as the "Warrior Trail." These trails, based on game trails or manmade paths, were used by the **American Indians** as trade routes, access to hunting grounds, and warpaths to attack neighboring tribes. Alanant-O-Wamiowee (Path of the Armed Ones) was the principal warrior trail through Kentucky. It is generally agreed that the trail ran from the Shawnee villages around Sandusky, Ohio, to the Cherokee settlements in the Great Smoky Mountains of North Carolina. Many consider the Alanant-O-Wamiowee Trail to be part of a system that extended from Sault Sainte Marie, Mich., to Charleston, S.C. Since it was used solely for foot traffic, the trail was only two to three feet wide. Its path was marked by blazes cut into trees, stone markers, carvings in rocks, and trees purposely deformed to serve as directional arrows.

The Alanant-O-Wamiowee Trail, with numerous branches, crossed the Ohio River several times between the Scioto and the Miami rivers. In other places, the Scioto, Miami, and Licking rivers served as waterway branches of the trail. The trail's main crossing of the Ohio River is thought to have been at Maysville. From Maysville the trail ran southward to Eskippakithiki (the last Shawnee town in Kentucky), in Clark Co., and on to Flat Lick in Knox Co. At Flat Lick the trail turned southeast toward the Cumberland Gap and the Smoky Mountains. From 1780 to 1820, the Alanant-O-Wamiowee Trail was used as the right-of-way for the portion of the Wilderness Road that ran from the Cumberland Gap to Flat Lick.

The **Battle of Blue Licks**, fought on August 19, 1782, on the banks of the North Fork of the Licking River in modern Robertson Co., took place along this trail.

Charles H. Bogart

WARSAW. Warsaw is the county seat and major city of Gallatin Co. Located along the southern bank of the Ohio River between Covington and Louisville, for many years it was an important stop and refueling place for the steamboat trade. It was first settled in the beginning years of the 19th century, and first called Great Landing. Early on there was a dockyard there, and the first boat was built in 1809. On December 7, 1831, the town was incorporated as Fredericksburg, but because there was already a town of that name in Washington Co., the name was changed to Warsaw. After the Short Line Railroad (the **Louisville, Cincinnati, and Lexington Railroad**) was completed through the inland part of the county (Sparta and Glencoe) in 1869, Warsaw's importance as a center of river commerce began to decline.

The town has a significant surviving historic district of some 60 Greek Revival structures, including that of **Lucy Dupuy Montz**, Kentucky's first woman dentist (see **Warsaw Historic Homes**). U.S. 42 was completed through town in the 1930s, connecting Cleveland, Ohio, via Cincinnati with Louisville. That road was largely bypassed in the late 1960s by I-71, a route that, like the railroad, ran through a more inland part of the county than Warsaw. A major fire did heavy damage to the Warsaw business district in 1932; in the early 1960s, the **Markland Dam** was completed on the river near Warsaw; in the late 1970s a bridge to Indiana was constructed across the top of that dam; and in 1987 the Sugar Creek firm, a maker of precast concrete products, was established. Warsaw became home to the late riverboat personalities Captain **John** and **Clare Beatty**, and the early-20th-century Cincinnati boxer Tony LaRosa, father of Cincinnati pizza king Buddy LaRosa, lived his final days in Warsaw. Dr. **Carl R. Bogardus** practiced medicine in Warsaw for many years, while becoming one of the Ohio River Valley's leading riverboat historians. Much of his collection was given to the archives at **Northern Kentucky University**. In recent years, Warsaw has been blessed with the newly constructed **Gallatin Co. Free Public Library**, where other Bogardus materials reside in the library's Kentucky Room.

In 2000 the fifth-class city of Warsaw had a population of 1,811, up from 1,202 in 1990. Its future is highlighted by the appearance of casino gambling across the Ohio River in Indiana at the Belterra Resort, the impact of the **Kentucky Speedway** nearby at Sparta, and new industry that has found a home in Warsaw, such as Warsaw Steel.

Bogardus, Carl R., Sr. *The Story of Gallatin County.* Ed. James C. Claypool. Cincinnati: John S. Swift, 2003.

Gray, Gypsy M. *History of Gallatin County, Kentucky.* Covington, Ky.: Self-published, 1968.

Kleber, John E., ed. *The Kentucky Encyclopedia.* Lexington: Univ. Press of Kentucky, 1992.

U.S. Census Bureau, "American Fact Finder. Data Set. Census 2000 Summary File 1 (SF1) 100-Percent Data. Custom Table." www.census.gov (accessed September 18, 2007).

WARSAW BAPTIST CHURCH. On July 29, 1843, Baptists living in Warsaw assembled at the Gallatin Co. Courthouse to form a new Baptist church. At this session the members, consisting of 12 whites and 8 **African Americans**, voted unanimously to adopt the articles of faith and the church covenant. Elder John Scott was called as the first pastor of the new Warsaw Baptist Church. Each member was charged 50 cents a month to meet expenses. In 1844 the church was received into the Concord Baptist Association. In July 1845, the present corner lot at 106 W. High St. was purchased for $100, and a brick building was constructed at a cost of $800. The building was completed in 1846. The Methodists rented the meetinghouse in 1857 for $1.00 a month for quarter-time services. The church apparently was inactive between 1862 and 1867. However, a reorganization took place in 1867. In May 1882 the old church was torn down, and a new one was built and dedicated the same year. In October 1900, the church was one of 13 that withdrew from the Concord Baptist Association to form the White's Run Baptist Association. In 1945 the Warsaw Baptist Church withdrew from the White's Run Association to join the Ten Mile Association. A building-remodeling program was started in late 1948. The dedication was not held, however, until April 1950.

An educational building was added in 1957 at a cost of $12,000. This building was severely damaged and the sanctuary completely destroyed by fire on November 20, 1973. The construction of the present auditorium and the repair of the educational building began a year later and were completed in time for evening services on January 18, 1976. During the interim period of planning and building, November 1973 through January 1976, the Warsaw Baptist Church held regular services in the Gallatin Co. Courthouse.

Ghent Baptist Church Minutes, Ghent Baptist Church, Ghent, Ky.

Warsaw Baptist Church History, Warsaw Baptist Church, Warsaw, Ky.

Ken Massey

WARSAW CHRISTIAN CHURCH. The Warsaw Christian Church in Gallatin Co. was organized on the first Sunday in April 1836, as the Congregation of Jesus Christ at Warsaw. Lyman Craig and 14 other citizens asked traveling evangelists David S. Burnett and John T. Johnson to come to Warsaw and preach. They did so, and before the end of the month, 114 members joined the new church. Johnson was the son of Col. Robert Johnson, founder of the city of Warsaw.

The church's first location was a small brick building at the corner of Main and First Sts. in Warsaw. The church purchased this building lot on December 28, 1843, for $60. Rev. Benjamin Tiller, the church's first pastor, served as elder, pastor, and business manager off and on for 42 years. He was unpaid for the first 20 years of his service. Early baptisms were done in the Ohio River. The church became inactive for a time during the **Civil War**. Tiller fled to Indiana for his safety, and the 20th Ohio Cavalry used the church as its headquarters. But on February 22, 1866, members met at the **Warsaw Baptist Church** to reorganize the church. All previous members were invited to return, and shortly thereafter the church increased its membership and constructed a new and larger building. The current church building on High St. was built in 1868 by Aaron M. Winters. A taller steeple was blown off during the 1930s. The house next to the church on the east corner of High and Fourth Sts. was built in the 1860s and has served as the church parsonage since April 21, 1959. An earlier parsonage (1905–1932) was at 204 Main St. Rev. T. Herbert Tinsley served Warsaw Christian Church for 31 years (December 1, 1935–June 8,

1966) and was also a six-term member of the Kentucky legislature. When the Ohio River **flood of 1937** washed away most of the riverfront housing, Tinsley was a driving force in the establishment of Warsaw's Red Cross Ave. On September 19, 2004, the church celebrated the modernization of its historic building.

Bogardus, Carl R., Sr. *The Story of Gallatin County.* Ed. James C. Claypool. Cincinnati: John S. Swift, 2003.

Spencer, Mrs. Earl, and Mrs. E. C. Threlkeld. Manuscripts and notes from original church records, Warsaw Christian Church, Warsaw, Ky.

Bernie Spencer

WARSAW FURNITURE FACTORY. The Warsaw Furniture Factory was the pride of Warsaw, employing almost 200 persons at its peak of production. Trained craftsmen manufactured its handsome furniture in a collection of styles out of beautiful, highly polished woods. These pieces were sought after not only throughout the South, but also at furniture markets in Chicago, Grand Rapids, and New York City. The factory was established by Owen Arthur Bogardus Sr., who arrived in Warsaw with his wife Nancy Ballard Bogardus on a riverboat from Cincinnati in 1902. Under his guidance the company became one of the leaders in the manufacture of fine furniture, and Warsaw became known as a furniture center.

At the beginning, designs were purchased. To these were added Bogardus's own designs and those of his eldest son, Claude Bogardus. Other sons, O. A. Jr., Carl, and Jim, all took their turns working on the factory floor, although as adults they moved on to other professions. The making of complete dining suites was divided between two factories. One plant made buffets, china closets, and serving tables; the other made dining tables and chairs. The most frequently used woods were butternut and mahogany. Catalogs compiled in the 1930s show the furniture to be of high quality and sophisticated design. The factory's noon whistle was the signal marker of the day in Warsaw.

At the time of his death in 1947, the factory's founder had become a man of means, and the name of Bogardus continues to be revered in Gallatin Co. In 1969 the factory was sold to Barry Brown, who became its manager. He later sold the factory and its grounds, and a BP gasoline station was built there. The factory was torn down in March 1995.

Bogardus, Carl R., Sr. "Family Memoir," Gallatin Co. Free Public Library, Warsaw, Ky.

——. *The Story of Gallatin County.* Ed. James C. Claypool. Cincinnati: John S. Swift, 2003.

Denny Kelley-Warnick

WARSAW HIGH SCHOOL. Warsaw High School was established in 1913, under the tutelage of Professor C. S. Joseph. The curriculum included four years of mathematics and Latin and two years of German. Warsaw High School was consolidated into **Gallatin Co. High School** for the beginning of the 1935–1936 school year.

Bogardus, Carl R., Sr. *The Story of Gallatin County.* Ed. James C. Claypool. Cincinnati: John S. Swift, 2003.

Steve Huddleston

WARSAW HISTORIC HOMES. When the town of Warsaw was nominated as a National Register Historic District in 1982, it was described as one of the best-preserved 19th-century Ohio River towns in Kentucky. It was compared to Petersburg and Augusta, river towns bypassed by newer modes of transportation that have, as a result, retained a small-town charm that resides to a great extent in original historic buildings.

The first settlement in the Warsaw area, called Great Landing, consisted of log buildings situated near the river. The one that remains, the Yates House, constructed in 1809, was the home of one of the men who subdivided and platted the streets of the community by then named Fredericksburg. The structure stands at the axis of the historic district, covered in wood siding, its interior walls revealing the original logs.

The town was laid out on a grid plan, and the first street built up from the fall line of the valley was High St., where 16 of the 60 historic buildings remain. Standing as sentinels on either end of the street are the John Payne House, an 1822 Virginia Tidewater with a Greek Revival portico, and the Captain William Payne House, known as Seven Pines, built in 1840 with an added Victorian veranda; both are sited to face the river. The **Lucy Dupuy Montz** House, home of Kentucky's first woman dentist, is an example of a Greek Revival I-house. Several painted-brick Federal houses still stand on High St. and one block south on Main. These houses, built in the 1830s, were the homes of the first residents who prospered as the town grew up from the busy river highway. Many of them were built by Willis Peak, whose name is retained in the names of several old homes in Warsaw. The second, and most often used, part of the houses' names refers to either the original or the longest-term owner. One of these Peak-built homes is the Peak Corkran House, mentioned below.

In 1831 Fredericksburg became Warsaw; in 1838 Warsaw was named county seat of Gallatin Co., and a courthouse was built on the public square at the junction of High and Main Cross. One of the oldest in continuous use in the state, the Greek Revival courthouse first faced the river but was remodeled in 1933 with a portico opening onto Main St. when Main St. was rebuilt as U.S. 42. With its painted white brick and two-story square columns, the courthouse is the county's landmark building. Another Greek Revival building, outside the district but a landmark to those entering the town from the east, is Heritage Hall, a private home built in 1869 on the river side of the road, part of the Hill's Nursery property (see **Gallatin Co. Plant Nurseries**).

Warsaw was built largely between 1840 and 1900. The earliest commercial buildings still standing, a post office and a grocery, now jointly house Maines Hardware, which retains the look of an old-time store. These buildings east of the courthouse and those south of it have ironwork facades and decorative tie rods and are built flush with the street. The south buildings were the first on Main Cross as it was built up, turning into the Sparta Turnpike. The only other original government building stands at the curve in the Sparta Turnpike. It is the county jail, built in 1880 and is, like most other county buildings in the district, a two-story brick painted white. The Yager Gutting House, next to Maines Hardware, had its second story removed by a former owner and now houses two county offices.

The five churches in the district span this time period, from the 1851 Presbyterian Church, which is now the Second Consolidated Baptist and once housed a private school on its second floor, to the Warsaw Methodist, built in 1901, with its Gothic Revival accents. Included are the Italianate Christian Church and the St. Joseph Church, both built in 1868–1869 and with historically sensitive recent additions. The Sunday school building is all that

Hawkins Kirby House.

remains of the earlier Warsaw Baptist Church after it burned, but a modern facade attractively juts out onto its grounds on High St.

On the same block are the Clark Warnick House, its rear addition home of the ***Gallatin Co. News,*** and One West High, which was built as the Warsaw Deposit Bank. The defining architecture of this era is Gothic Revival. The Hawkins Kirby House, built in 1843 and termed "a little jewel of a house" when it was restored by the Gallatin Co. Historical Society, is now the depository of much of the town's history. The former detached kitchen and dog trot, which have been enclosed as a single apartment along the side-facing porch, and the cabin of Miss Charity Keene, who served the Kirby family for many years, share the grounds of the house on the corner of Second and Market St. Back on High St. are Carpenter Gothic homes, the Bradley House, built for the daughter of Captain Kirby, and the Dailey House, which serves as the parsonage of the Christian Church. The only other house besides the Montz House that has a separate listing on the National Register is the Peak Corkran House on Main Cross, built in 1869 with the steep gables and decorative pointed arches that define this style (see **Warsaw Woman's Club**).

Several homes were built in the later Gothic Revival, such as the Queen Anne–style Allen House on Main St.; most of them are located out the Sparta Turnpike on larger lots, for example, the beautifully landscaped Mountjoy House and the two Payne Houses, one with its intact carriage house and the larger one at the city limits. All of these homes retain at least a few of their original outbuildings. Most of the architectural styles seen in Warsaw are represented on this road, including Federal, Tudor, four-square, and midcentury ranch. Other singular styles are interspersed throughout the district, including the Colonial Revival Blackmore House built on one-half of a city block, one duplex, a mansard-roofed former funeral home, several antebellum frame cottages, and former school buildings. Warsaw contains buildings of every style and period from 1820 to 1930, with good examples of every major 19th-century style that contribute to the historic district.

Bogardus, Carl R., Sr. *The Story of Gallatin County.* Ed. James C. Claypool. Cincinnati: John S. Swift, 2003.

Historic Walking Tour of Warsaw. Brochure available at Warsaw City Hall and the Gallatin Co. judge-executive's office, Warsaw, Ky.

National Register of Historic Places Inventory—Nomination Form, U.S. Department of the Interior, National Park Service, 1982, prepared from site survey by Kentucky Heritage Council, Frankfort, Ky.

Jacquelene P. Mylor

WARSAW METHODIST CHURCH. Methodism first came to Gallatin Co. in the form of a circuit-riding minister named Josiah Whitaker around 1824. Meetings were held in various homes during the winter months, and camp meetings were held in the spring. The Warsaw Methodist Episcopal Church was formed in 1844 and one year later became the Warsaw Methodist Episcopal Church South (proslavery). The founding members were Enoch Kirby and his wife Delilah, Capt. James McDannell and his wife Arena, Dr. John T. Robinson and his wife Eliza, and Dr. Robinson's mother, Mrs. Lydia Craig. The first minister was Larkin F. Price. The church held meetings in the homes of its members for several years. It was permitted to meet in the **Warsaw Baptist Church** during the 1850s. In 1867 the Methodist congregation in Warsaw rented the Missionary Baptist Church for one Sunday a month. This church building was the former Presbyterian Church, the first church building built in Warsaw. It stands across the street from the present Warsaw Methodist Church and now serves as the Second Consolidated Baptist Church. While the Methodists were holding meetings in the Missionary Baptist Church, a great revival took place, and services led by Rev. T. B. Cook continued the entire winter. Rev. S. X. Hall and Rev. B. F. Bristow assisted Cook. The congregation grew to more than 200 members during the 1860s. In the 1870s, the congregation purchased from the City of Warsaw the church building that had been the first Warsaw Christian Church and was later used as a school. Remodeled and dedicated as the Warsaw Methodist Episcopal Church South in 1878, it was used until 1901, when it was razed so that a new structure could be built. The 1901 building committee consisted of S. P. Griffin, J. H. McDannell, Hugh Montgomery, Rod Perry, and Dr. S. B. Robinson, and the pastor was Willard G. Cram. The building contract was awarded to two local brothers, Joseph and William Wilson. The new church was furnished with beautiful stained-glass windows and finished with oak walls and arched ceilings. The beautiful altar was crafted by Carl Hensen. The building, which cost around $7,000, was completely paid for by the time of its dedication on April 20, 1902.

During **World War I**, the church continued to prosper even though many of its members left to participate in the war. In the late 1920s, the church saw strong growth; it had a large men's Sunday school class and a Women's Missionary Society. During the late 1940s, when a modern parsonage was needed, the land next to the church was purchased for that purpose. The 50th anniversary of the new church building was held on July 15, 1951, and the parsonage was dedicated. In the 1950s, during the construction of the **Markland Dam**, the church grew again. Seven new Sunday school rooms were added at this time. However, during the construction the south wall of the church collapsed, causing $10,000 in damage. A large stained-glass window was lost, and the piano suffered damage. While the church was being repaired, services were held in the courthouse and the school gymnasium.

Today, this congregation remains in Warsaw at the corner of First and Main Sts., where it has been since 1878, in the present building, in use since 1901.

Bogardus, Carl R., Sr. *The Story of Gallatin County.* Ed. James C. Claypool. Cincinnati: John S. Swift, 2003.

Darrell Maines

WARSAW NEWSPAPERS. The first newspaper known to be published in Gallatin Co. was the *Warsaw Patriot,* printed by George Child and Asaph Kent. The first issue appeared on May 26, 1837. Exactly how long this paper was in print is unknown; however, there is mention of it in the minutes of the Warsaw town trustees in 1839. The *Patriot* was followed by the *Warsaw Herald,* which first appeared in October 1844. John Field was listed as proprietor and R. S. Yerkes as editor. The **Mexican War** (1847–1848) was the news of note at that time. Joseph B. Ricker published the first issue of his *Warsaw Weekly News* on December 7, 1869; it lasted only three years. The *Warsaw Record,* with James M. Vanice as editor and publisher, followed in 1872. The second and third pages were printed using preset metal sheets of type, known as "boiler plate." This is the first time the boiler-plate printing technique is known to have been used in Warsaw newspapers. During the later part of the 19th century, other newspapers were printed briefly in Gallatin Co.: the *Sign of the Times,* the *Gallatin Times,* and the *Gallatin County Democrat.*

The *Warsaw Independent* began publishing in May 1880, with David B. Wallace as editor, and it became a county institution; Wallace remained at the helm for 27 years. For the three years ending in 1912, the *Warsaw Leader,* put out by brothers Samuel and Roy Clore, was a competitor of the *Warsaw Independent.* William Downtain, who was from West Virginia, and later Will S. Griffin became owner-editors of the *Warsaw Independent* in turn. After the death of Griffin, the newspaper was purchased by J. Barker Holcomb, a Warsaw native. It was published by the Pendery Brothers of Vevay, Ind., but they soon discontinued publication. Soon afterward, a new owner named Berkshire, of Burlington, began publication of the newspaper. E. M. Mansfield, the editor of the *Carrollton Democrat,* followed him as publisher. The date of the last issue of the *Warsaw Independent* is not known; the ***Gallatin Co. News,*** established in 1926, edited in Warsaw and still in operation, superseded it.

Bickers, Russell. Interview by Denny Kelley-Warnick, March 17, 2006, Warsaw, Ky.

Bogardus, Carl R., Sr. *The Story of Gallatin County.* Ed. James C. Claypool. Cincinnati: John S. Swift, 2003.

Gray, Gypsy M. *History of Gallatin County, Kentucky.* Covington, Ky.: Self-published, 1968.

Denny Kelley-Warnick

WARSAW WOMAN'S CLUB. The initial meeting of Warsaw's Literary Society was held on Friday evening, October 27, 1899, at the residence of R. B. Brown and his wife Beall Summons Brown. There were 18 ladies and 4 men in attendance. The officers they elected were Miss Ona Brock, president; Mrs. H. T. Chambers, vice president; Dr. **Lucy Montz**, treasurer; Mrs. R. B. Brown, secretary; and Miss Temple North, librarian. The group was later renamed the Warsaw Classical Club. They met in members' homes as a study club on Monday evenings, "striving toward instruction as well as amusement." A constitution was adopted, along with the motto "More Light." As the club evolved into the Warsaw Woman's Club, the programs expanded from literature to include gardening, parliamentary law, and history. The women sponsored luncheons, teas, dinners, flower shows, and art exhibits. From the start, there was a great sense of civic duty, as members paid for school lunches for needy children, purchased a piano for the school, paid for a sidewalk built there, and conducted a book drive for the school library. The club also donated to the Kentucky Children's Home and to state and veterans' hospitals, aided homeless women, and fought for the preservation of Cumberland Falls. The Warsaw Woman's Club affiliated for several years with the Kentucky Federation of Women's Clubs but has been an independent club during most of its history.

In 1961 Louise Chambers Corkran deeded to the trustees of the Woman's Club her childhood home in Warsaw at 502 Sparta Pk. (now Main Cross) and its surrounding acre of land. The members deliberated accepting the gift, but a spirited appeal by trustee Sallie M. Brown persuaded the ladies to take over the house and to embark on the club's first renovation project, restoring the house as its meeting place. To help raise funds for their many projects, club members operated a thrift store downtown. They also continued their civic involvement by leading the effort to have Warsaw designated a historic district on the National Register of Historic Places in 1980 and by spearheading the "Trees for Warsaw" initiative; they had previously beautified the U.S. 42 right-of-way and supplied public trash containers for the city. The club's longest-continuing project has been the four-year college scholarship presented to a local high school graduate.

In 1997 the club's members formed the WWC Peak Corkran House Inc., a nonprofit corporation to ensure that the clubhouse could continue to be used for community purposes. And after generous contributions from families of past and current members provided matching funds for a restoration grant from the Kentucky Heritage Council, the house went through a second renovation and was prepared to serve as the site of the club's centennial celebration on June 13, 1999. In 2005 the City of Warsaw leased the house to be used as a meeting place and a visitor's center. The City plans to upgrade the house further, making it accessible to all of the community; the Woman's Club continues to meet there. The Warsaw Woman's Club is the second-longest-continuing organization in Warsaw, after the Masons.

Bogardus, Carl R., Sr. *The Story of Gallatin County.* Ed. James C. Claypool. Cincinnati: John S. Swift, 2003.

Bogardus, Sue M. "History of the Warsaw Woman's Club," 1999, Gallatin Co. Free Public Library, Warsaw, Ky.

Warsaw Independent, November 4, 1899.

Jacquelene P. Mylor

WASHINGTON. Washington, a prominent town in frontier Kentucky, was the county seat of Mason Co. from 1788 until 1847. It was established on the buffalo trace near Lawrence Creek that came to be called the **Maysville and Lexington Turnpike**. The town was chartered by the Virginia legislature in 1786 and laid out by Arthur Fox Sr. and the Baptist minister William Wood, on part of 1,000 acres purchased from **Simon Kenton**. It is the first town west of the Appalachian Mountains named for George Washington. The original trustees were **Daniel Boone**, Edmund Byne, **Miles Withers Conway**, Arthur Fox, John Gutridge, William Lamb, Henry Lee, Robert Rankin, and Edward Waller.

Three miles south of Limestone Landing on the Ohio River, Washington grew quickly on the cane lands that Kenton had found so desirable. The cane, often more than 10 feet tall, was easily cleared for farming and housing. Based on the first U.S. census, only Lexington was a larger city when Kentucky became a state. In 1790 Washington's 462 residents, including only 21 slaves, lived in 119 houses. Most of the houses were made of large logs, and some of them still remain. A handful of the dwellings were built of brick and stone. In the last decade of the 18th and the first decades of the 19th century, Washington was the center of trade, education, and government for a large region. In 1797 there were 17 stores in town. Schools were started and attracted students and professors. Mann Butler, who later wrote a well-known history of Kentucky, was a teacher in Washington. From 1807 to 1812, the school started by Louisa Keats, the Ladies Domestic Academy, was the most respected in the area. Newspaper testimonials attracted students. The daughters of leading families attended the academy and became the wives of prominent men such as U.S. senator John J. Crittenden, secretary of state Peter Porter, and Ohio governor Duncan McArthur. A later school, the Pillsbury School for Boys, closed when the headmaster, Josiah Pillsbury, joined the Confederacy.

Mason Co. Courthouse, Washington, Ky.

Washington was the hub of the mail distribution system for the Northwest Territory. Lewis Craig, the Baptist preacher and architect of Traveling Church fame, who led his Baptist congregation to Kentucky to escape religious persecution, was the builder of a grand two-story courthouse with a 25-foot tower. That building was destroyed by fire, but the keystone is preserved with the initials "L.C." and the date, 1794. Row houses, the oldest standing in the county, were constructed in 1795. In 1798 a $1,000 lottery raised the funds to build a system of wells, the first public waterworks system in the West. In 1788 Dr. **William Goforth** established a medical practice at Washington that lasted for a decade. Goforth mentored Dr. **Daniel Drake**, who wrote a book on pioneer life and became a leading citizen of Cincinnati. In 1809 future president Zachary Taylor (1849–1850) was stationed in the town as a military recruiter. Capt. **Thomas Marshall**, brother of John Marshall, the chief justice of the U.S. Supreme Court, was an Indian fighter and the first clerk of the Mason Co. Court. In the late 1700s, he built a large home named Federal Hill within sight of the courthouse on a hill near Washington. His famous brother was a visitor, and their parents lived in the house for the last years of their lives and were buried in a family plot near the home. Washington's population grew to more than 800 by 1810. The first part of the 19th century was the high point for the town's political and social prominence in the county. Limestone, by that time called Maysville, was increasingly the center of the area's development. The importance of the Ohio River and the end of the Indian threat brought about Maysville's growth in influence, population, and commercial importance. The Kentucky legislature debated for days in January 1847 whether Maysville should be named the county seat. Two votes had been held in the county, with slim majorities favoring such a move. The legislature actually voted against the move, but after Mason Co. representative Henry Waller worked to get another vote, the resolution making Maysville the county seat passed and was made official the next year by the legislature.

However, Washington retained both local and national prominence after losing the county seat. In November 1830 the first macadamized, or paved, road in Kentucky and west of the Alleghenies was completed between Maysville and Washington. That same year President Andrew Jackson (1829–1837) vetoed the **Maysville Road Bill**, which would have provided federal support for completing the highway between Washington and Lexington. This legislation was embroiled in the national debate between the philosophy of Henry Clay's American System and Jackson's philosophy of limited federal government in favor of states' rights. The veto stymied the growth of the region. Another national event connected to Washington that occurred in 1833 did not manifest itself until the 1850s. That year, Harriet Beecher visited her student Elizabeth Marshall Key at the **Marshall**

Key home in Washington. The home was just a few doors away from the courthouse lawn, where slave auctions were held. Tradition holds that the sights Beecher witnessed on this visit, perhaps along with others, inspired some of the characters and scenes in *Uncle Tom's Cabin* (1852). The slave auction portrayed in Beecher's chapter "Select Incident of Lawful Trade" mentions Washington and a slave auction before the "Court-house door."

On the local level, many fine homes were erected and large farms became prosperous in the community and its environs in the early 19th century. Along with the hundreds of log houses, such as that of founder Arthur Fox, which were the norm during the settlement period, brick and stone structures were built. In town they included the Marshall and the Marshall Key houses; the stone house of Dr. William Goforth; a brick building that housed one of the first banks in the state; the Taylor Brothers general merchandise store; the attorney James Paxton's house; the Pillsbury and McMurdy schools; a hotel called Washington Hall, built to try to keep the county seat; a proslavery Methodist church built in 1848; and many others. Near town were the George Wood house, whose entire upper floor was an open area for entertaining; the home of the Revolutionary War general **Henry Lee**, called Clover Hill, which was built of oak with ash floors and cherry woodwork; and the Richard Durrett house, which was used as a location for the 1986 PBS (Public Broadcasting Service) movie *Huckleberry Finn*. **John Chambers**, who became the territorial governor of Iowa in 1841, entertained future presidents William Henry Harrison (1841) and Ulysses S. Grant (1869–1877) and other dignitaries at his home called Cedar Hill, built in 1807. Woodburn, another stately home, completed in 1860, was one of the last built by slave labor in the county. These and many more fine old buildings are extant, but many other fine homes and buildings in Washington have been destroyed.

Another Washington connection to the nation's history was centered on a more modest clapboard house, the birthplace of Gen. **Albert Sidney Johnston**. A West Point graduate, secretary of war in the Republic of Texas, and a shining star in the Confederate army, he was killed early in the Civil War at Shiloh. Gen. **William "Bull" Nelson** used the same clapboard house during the Civil War. Camp Nelson, just south of Lexington, a wartime refuge for African Americans, is named for Nelson and is the site of a national cemetery.

Mary Ward Holton, born in 1887 at Washington, became the most noteworthy press agent for the Broadway stage, representing such performers as Lynn Fontaine, Julie Harris, Leslie Howard, and Alfred Lunt between the 1930s and 1970.

After the county seat moved, Washington remained an incorporated city until 1990, when it was annexed by its old rival Maysville. At the time of annexation, the fifth-class city of Washington had a population of 795, about the same as in 1810. The community built a substantial school in 1916 that was destroyed by fire in 1974. Over the years, Washington has been the site of a number of active churches, a post office, and businesses. A sewing factory and the **Maysville Community and Technical College**, which opened in the late 1960s, were both large employers before the annexation. It was in the 1950s that historic preservation efforts at Washington began, when the county government made arrangements to take possession of the Johnston house. Several nonprofit organizations followed, and today the community has a number of buildings open to the public, including an original log cabin that serves as the visitor's center, a museum dedicated to Simon Kenton, a church museum, the Johnston house, a log cabin that belonged to early settler George Mefford, and the Paxton House. There are numerous shops as well, and special festivals are held throughout the year, such as Frontier Christmas, one of the oldest and premier festivals in the state.

Calvert, Jean, and John Klee. *The Towns of Mason County: Their Past in Pictures*. Maysville, Ky.: Maysville and Mason Co. Library Historical and Scientific Association, 1986.

Clift, G. Glenn. *History of Maysville and Mason County*. Lexington, Ky.: Transylvania, 1936.

"Historical Past—Present Still," *KP*, January 1, 1973, 4K.

Kleber, John E., ed. *The Kentucky Encyclopedia*. Lexington: Univ. Press of Kentucky, 1992.

John Klee

WASHINGTON, GEORGE, JR. (b. December 25, 1844, Newport, Ky.; d. August 23, 1905, Newport, Ky.). George Washington Jr., a lawyer and a politician, was the son of George and Martha Doxon Washington. His father was a native of Jefferson Co., Va., and a steamboat captain whose base of operation was Newport, Ky. George Washington Jr.'s great-great-grandfather was Samuel Washington, brother of President George Washington (1789–1797). George Jr. received his early education in Newport and Cincinnati. His father died when he was 12 years old, and at age 16 George Jr. joined the Confederate Army. He served for one year, before receiving a medical discharge for battle wounds. When he returned to Newport, he was not well received because of his Confederate affiliation. Discouraged, he moved to Memphis, Tenn., where he roomed with Thomas Hines, another former Confederate soldier. Hines later became a Kentucky Supreme Court justice. Washington studied law under Gen. Albert Pike and was admitted to the Tennessee bar in 1866. He moved to Knoxville, Tenn., to begin a law practice and served as city attorney. In 1867 he married Jennie Ramsey, and they had seven children. Their daughter Bettie married John B. Taylor, son of **James Taylor III** and grandson of Gen. **James Taylor Jr.**, founder of Newport. In 1881 Washington returned to Newport, where he entered into a law partnership with **Robert W. Nelson**. Washington was an excellent orator and was active in Democratic politics. In his only run for office, he narrowly lost the race for appellate court judge in 1894. Kentucky governor William O. Bradley (1895–1899) honored Washington by naming him a Kentucky Colonel in 1898. George Washington Jr. died in 1905 at age 60. His funeral service was held at the Grace Methodist Episcopal Church in Newport and was attended by hundreds. He was buried at the Evergreen Cemetery in Southgate.

Perrin, W. H. *Biographical Sketches from Kentucky Genealogy and Biography*. Vol. 7. 1887. Reprint, Indianapolis: Researchers, 1993.

Perrin, W. H., J. H. Battle, and G. C. Kniffin. *Kentucky: A History of the State*. 7th ed. Louisville, Ky.: F. A. Battery, 1888.

Purvis, Thomas L., ed. *Newport, Kentucky: A Bicentennial History*. Newport, Ky.: Otto Zimmerman, 1996.

Jack Wessling

WASHINGTON ARCHAEOLOGY. In 2005–2006, an interdisciplinary archaeological investigation accompanied the City of Maysville's use of a backhoe to lay PVC pipe in trenches that connected more than 70 properties currently listed on the National Register of Historic Places. The excavations were carried out to bury public utilities for the historic district of old Washington in Mason Co. Archaeologists monitored these machine excavations on behalf of the city, while studying the archival, architectural, and archaeological evidence for several generations of this important 18th–19th-century town. From each of the 70-some properties investigated, the project recovered soil formation data, artifacts, and in many cases intact built features such as relict buildings, backfilled shafts, and buried pavements.

Previous archaeological investigations at Washington include the Stallings & Ross-Stallings excavations in the backyard of the Albert Sidney Johnston House and preliminary survey excavations at 15 properties, conducted by Nancy O'Malley. Both previous investigations established that the soils of Washington retain evidence of buried architectural ruins and the midden (trash) deposits of early settlers and latter-day occupants, a conclusion confirmed by the 2005–2006 excavations.

As expected, recovered artifacts include a huge sample of 18th- and 19th-century ceramics, glass, and iron; the ceramics and glass indicate that the frontier generation of settlers had fewer possessions than modern people and that most of their possessions were handmade. In contrast, the sheer volume of materials owned increases with industrialization and market access in the early 19th century. The surprise came in the high quality of the 18th-century "frontier" ceramics: creamware, tin-glazed earthenware, and Chinese export porcelain found next to long-stemmed clay tobacco pipe fragments.

What made the investigations unique was the rare opportunity to examine both the private properties and the public infrastructure of an entire town. Washington retains deeply buried, well-crafted urban public landscapes that are remarkable in their extent. Most of the town was built in what we would now call a wetland (the settlers called it a pasture). Already in the 1790s, the town required its citizens to assist in building flagstone sidewalks above the quagmire. The town today still has flagstone sidewalks, but the originals survive under the current surface, on the same alignments. When Washington was at the height of its power in the first quarter of the 19th century, every street intersection was graced with pedestrian crosswalks composed of end-laid limestone, set across the slope, in a technique stonemasons call "surface drains." The entire town was once laced with dry-laid stone drainage culverts, built in several styles, including box drains with huge limestone flags as lids, big enough for an excavator to crawl through. Taken together with the dry-laid stone fences typical of the Bluegrass, these findings indicate that Washington at its height must have presented a manicured air of prosperity and civil order. But all those civic improvements were buried and forgotten, leaving only the buildings to tell the story.

Washington has been subject to repeated Historic American Buildings Survey documentation ever since the 1930s and includes more than 90 properties recorded in the Kentucky Heritage Council's historic resource inventory. Washington is one of the only towns left in trans-Appalachian America where the architecture of the frontier survives side-by-side with high-style textbook urban townhouse architecture of the Federal period. The cabins themselves are steeple-notched or half-dovetailed, often with a Tidewater chimney and solid-panel shutters, built on stone footers rising out of the wetland muck. For the Federal period, there are fanlights, Flemish bond brick masonry with corbelled cornices, multipane windows, and basement windows with wooden pegs instead of glass. Paneled rooms with clever cupboards and elaborate fireplaces also are intact.

Conventional wisdom evokes an American frontier in which poor people wrested private property from the remote wilderness by the sweat of their brows. What the archival investigators found defies that conventional story of the frontier, while confirming the settlement models proposed by Richard C. Wade in his *The Urban Frontier,* as well as the burgeoning aristocracy on Kentucky's frontier, as suggested by Craig T. Friend in *Along the Maysville Road.* In 1959 Wade suggested that the trans-Appalachian frontier was populated from new urban cores growing out into pacified hinterlands, reversing the mythic order of isolated homesteads growing into cities. Washington was built as such an urban core and could proudly claim that it was never subject to **American Indian** attack. Frontier settlers foolish or desperate enough to settle on land removed from Washington often fell victim to the attacks that feature so heavily in the Draper Manuscripts and other frontier accounts. In 2005 Friend proposed that yeomen were socially eclipsed by an aristocracy early in Mason Co.'s history. Most of the first settlers were either young male entrepreneurs with capital to invest or indigent families with nothing to lose. Already by 1779, improvement claims, then called "preemptions," were illegal. Most of the pioneers on this frontier were tenants. By 1796, Washington had passed suffrage ordinances making the ownership of land prerequisite to voting privileges, at a time when most town residents were renters.

Eyewitness Harry Toulmin noted that in Mason Co. in 1793, the value of an estate of 100 acres could be doubled with one year's labor in improvements. A tenant farmer in a single year could double the value of his landlord's investment; hence, most tenants chose to continue moving West rather than settle here permanently. If their arrival and departure from the county fell in the interval between censuses, we will never know their names. However, we now have ample evidence for their landlord's refined porcelain and a remarkable urban infrastructure supporting refined early Federal surroundings.

Friend, Craig Thompson. *Along the Maysville Road: The Early American Republic in the Trans-Appalachian West.* Knoxville: Univ. of Tennessee Press, 2005.

Miller, Orloff. "Archaeological Investigations at Washington, for the City of Maysville's Utility Burial Project, Mason County, Kentucky," Orloff Miller Consulting, forthcoming.

——. "Archaeology of Washington, Mason County, Kentucky," a lecture presented to the Central Ohio Valley Archaeological Society, April 19, 2007.

O'Malley, Nancy. *A New Village Called Washington.* Maysville, Ky.: Old Washington Inc./McClanahan, 1987.

Toulmin, Harry. *The Western Country in 1793: Reports on Kentucky and Virginia.* Ed. Marion Tinling and Godfrey Davies. Reprint, San Marino, Calif.: Henry E. Huntington Library, 1948.

Wade, Richard C. *The Urban Frontier: Pioneer Life in Early Pittsburgh, Cincinnati, Lexington, Louisville, and St. Louis.* Chicago: Univ. of Chicago Press, 1959.

Orloff G. Miller

WASHINGTON BAPTIST CHURCH. This Washington, Ky., church, founded by Rev. William Wood, dates to 1785 and was one of the first churches in Northern Kentucky. Wood was a founder of Washington in addition to serving as the first preacher for the church; he also donated the land for the church building and the graveyard, which is still in use. In the cemetery are buried some of the pioneers of the area: family members of **Albert Sidney Johnston**, including his mother, Abigail; the early Presbyterian ministers Robert Wilson and Paradise Lost McAboy; and Arthur Fox Sr., the other primary founder of Washington. Also buried there are **American Indians** including a chief and his wives. Part of the graveyard was set aside for "strangers."

The Washington Baptist Church, which began as the Limestone Baptist Church, met in Limestone in 1785. Near there in 1788 Wood conducted some of the first baptisms in this part of the state. Baptized in the Ohio River at this time were Mary Rose, Ann Turner, Elizabeth Washburne, John Wilcox, and Elizabeth Wood. It was reported that Indians watched from the north side of the river, along with a large crowd from Limestone. A log structure was built in Washington in 1788 on the grounds donated by Wood, and the name of the church was changed to Washington Baptist Church in 1792. Wood continued as pastor until 1798, when his land purchases caused conflict with some members. It was in this first church and on its grounds that a series of debates was held in October 1823 between **Alexander Campbell**, representing the Baptists, and Rev. William McCalla, representing the Presbyterians. Thousands attended and both sides claimed to have won the debates. The Baptists hailed Campbell's performance, but in 1830 he led a split of the Baptists by launching his Disciples of Christ movement. Rev. Gilbert Mason was the pastor at the Washington Baptist Church from the 1840s until 1856 and was at the center of a controversy that briefly separated the Washington Baptist Church from the Bracken Baptist Association, a group that the Washington church had been affiliated with since 1799. Although the first church building was a sound structure, it was torn down in early 1871. The replacement church was destroyed by fire in 1889 and was not rebuilt; the Washington Baptist Church ceased to exist. In 1980 an effort led by Rev. Ken Forman and the Bracken Association of Baptists resulted in rebuilding the church of logs, which stands today on the original site. It serves the community on special occasions.

Collins, Richard H. *History of Kentucky.* Vol. 1. Covington, Ky.: Collins, 1882.

Masters, Frank M. *A History of Baptists in Kentucky.* Louisville, Ky.: Kentucky Baptist Historical Society, 1953.

Reis, Jim. "Cemeteries," *KP,* April 21, 1986, 4K.

John Klee

WASHINGTON OPERA HOUSE. This elegant theater at 116 W. Second St. in Maysville was constructed in 1851, on the site of the former Old Blue Church (Presbyterian). It is the fifth-oldest theater of this sort in the United States. In 1898 the Opera House was gutted by fire, and the local Washington Fire Company rebuilt it, at a cost of $24,000. It was renamed the Washington Opera House in honor of the fire company. Over the years, many of the nation's great performers graced the opera house's stage: Tom Mix, John Phillips Sousa and his band, and John L. Sullivan. With convenient steamboat and, later, railroad connections, the Washington Opera House was an easy one-night-stand for acts traveling to and from Cincinnati. The building later became a movie house, owned by Falmouth mayor **Max Goldberg**. By the mid-1950s, the legend was well established that the house was haunted by a young girl named Mary, who supposedly had fallen through a trapdoor while performing in the building, broken her neck, and died.

In 1962 the theater became home to the newly formed Maysville Players, a local theatrical group that opened its first season with the Thornton Wilder classic *Our Town.* Eventually, the Players acquired ownership of the building, and hundreds of plays have been staged there since. Today, the Maysville Players is the oldest group of its kind in the state. The Maysville Players raised $2.9 million for restoration of the theater, which included new heating and air-conditioning, restrooms, an elevator, new seats, floors, and sundry other improvements. The restored theater reopened with a black-tie gala celebration on November 25, 2006.

The Historic Washington Opera House. "Washington Opera House History." www.maysvilleplayers.com (accessed August 18, 2007).

WASHINGTON PRESBYTERIAN CHURCH. This church's congregation held its first meeting in the home of Isaiah Keith on April 24, 1792, in Washington in Mason Co. Its first officers were Isaac Cannon, Edward Harris, Andrew Henderson, Isaiah Keith, and Dr. John P. Campbell, who as one of the eight early Presbyterian missionaries to the area helped organized the church. In 1790 Washington was the second-largest city in Kentucky (which was not a state until 1792). The minutes of Kentucky's Transylvania Presbytery first mention the Presbyterian church at Washington in 1793. The church's first regular pastor was another of the early missionaries, Rev. Robert Wilson, who was installed in 1799; he also helped establish churches in Augusta and Maysville. Also in 1799 the church was transferred to the Washington Presbytery.

The Washington Presbyterian Church's first building was built in 1806 of brick and had a high ceiling; it was furnished with high-backed pews. A cemetery near the church was later destroyed by road construction. In 1815 the church was transferred to the West Lexington Presbytery. The 1806 building was torn down in 1844, and a second building was erected at a cost of $2,500 that same year on the site just opposite the present Washington Presbyterian Church. It was of similar construction but had a gallery for black servants. After this structure was deemed unsafe and torn down in 1868, the third (present) building, a framed one-room building, was built in 1870–1871 for $4,000.

In 1936 the Washington Presbyterian Church celebrated its 144th anniversary. Rev. William S. Smythe was its pastor, and the elders were David Rannells, who had conducted a classical school in the city for approximately 40 years, William Richey, and Isaiah Thompson.

The church has a vibrant history of missionary work. Mary Wilson (daughter of Robert Wilson) married Rev. **Lorin Andrews**, and the couple served as missionaries in the Sandwich Islands (Hawaii) in late 1827. The church also had several sewing societies and ladies aid societies. The Ladies Missionary Society was organized as early as 1886. The First Mission Study Class distributed pigs to collect money for the Leper Fund and also sent boxes of bedclothes and clothing to mountain schools.

Allen, James S., and Ruth R. "The Church with Its Cherished Memories since 1792 Organized in 1796," 1972, Washington Presbyterian Church, Washington, Ky.

Green, Thomas M. ed., *Weekly Maysville Eagle*, December 27, 1871.

Alex Hyrcza

WASHINGTON TRACE RD. A trace is a path or trail, usually of trampled vegetation, inadvertently left by animals or human beings as they travel from one place to another. In early historic times, numerous traces were made by animals such as bears or migrating bison (see **Buffalo Traces**). Many of our modern highways follow early bison traces. There were also trails or traces left intentionally by pioneers and explorers such as **Daniel Boone**, who marked his Wilderness Road by notching trees along the way. Washington Trace in Campbell, Bracken, and Mason counties is a road that roughly follows a trail left by early settlers traveling from Northern Kentucky toward the town of Washington in Mason Co., just outside Maysville. In the early days, the trace evidently began where today's Four Mile Rd. and Fender Rd. intersect in Campbell Co. From there it went out Fender Rd. to Four and Twelve Mile Rd., then to Twelve Mile Rd., and then to today's Washington Trace. The trace then meandered southeast through the towns of Carthage and Flagg Springs, where it began to follow present-day Ky. Rt. 10. It went through the towns of Peach Grove, Brooksville, Powersville, and Germantown, and when it neared Maysville, it followed for several miles present-day U.S. 68, going toward Blue Licks. The trace ended at **Simon Kenton**'s blockhouse in Washington.

Many noted Northern Kentucky people lived along the trace. **William Kennedy** and his son James built a log cabin at Flagg Springs in 1789, from which they surveyed much of northern and eastern Campbell Co. They were also buried near the trace. Elijah Herndon built a home for his family there in 1818, and the structure still stands today. His daughter Demarius Herndon White and her husband, Joseph Jasper White, raised their family at Carthage, on the trace. Demarius wrote an interesting diary from 1879 to 1883 about her everyday life there. Early preacher and builder **James Monroe Jolly** built at least two churches along the trace and was the pastor of the one at Flagg Springs. **Absolom Columbus Dicken** lived most of his life near the trace and referred to it in his **Civil War** diary. The executed Confederate Civil War veteran **William Francis Corbin** lived along the trace and was buried on his farm beside this historic road. The land along Washington Trace today remains relatively undeveloped.

Wessling, Jack. *Early History of Campbell County, Kentucky*. Alexandria, Ky.: Privately published, 1997.

Jack Wessling

WASHINGTON UNITED METHODIST CHURCH. The church currently known as the Washington United Methodist Church was the second Methodist church established in Kentucky and has been a constant religious presence in Mason Co. since its organization in 1786. Thomas and Sarah Stevenson, settlers from Maryland, sponsored the Methodist church at Washington. **Lewis Collin**'s *History of Kentucky* notes that the Stevensons were on the second flatboat down the Ohio River, landing at Limestone Landing in present-day Mason Co.; the earlier settlers of the area had come by canoe. While living at nearby Kenton's Station in 1786, the Stevensons entertained Rev. Benjamin Ogden, a Methodist preacher. In that same year they built a cabin near Washington, Ky.; Ogden returned with his church elder, James Haw, and the church now named the Washington United Methodist Church was established. From this beginning until 1818, circuit-riding preachers ministered to local Methodists in the courthouse, in homes, and even in the local jail. The first log church, built in 1818, was replaced in 1826 by a stone church located in town on the corner of Main and York Sts. The Methodist Episcopal Church, as this church was known at the time, prospered until the issue of slavery split the Methodists nationally in 1845. The Washington Church reorganized as the Washington Methodist Episcopal Church South, and a new church building was built in 1848. That building served the congregation for more than a century. It was sold in 1969 and now houses an interdenominational church museum that is open to the public.

By 1939 the local church had shortened its name to the Washington Methodist Church. Several pastors of note served the church around the turn of the century. Rev. Urban Valentine William Darlington served from 1896 to 1900 and later became bishop of the Kentucky Methodist Conference. Rev. J. J. Dickey was pastor at the Washington Methodist Church in 1902, 20 years after he had gone to Jackson, Ky., while a Presbyterian and organized Jackson Academy (later Lees College, and now part of the Hazard Community and Technical College) there. In 1899 a parsonage was purchased in Washington on Main St., but a new parsonage was built behind the church in 1955. During the pastorate of R. C. Mynear, in 1966, a decision was made to build a new church building. Land was purchased from an estate known as Cedar Hill, and the new church was dedicated on October 19, 1969, with Bishop Roy Short and the church's new pastor, Jackson Brewer, on hand. The year before, several groups had united nationally to form the United Methodist Church, so the church in Washington became the Washington United Methodist Church. The church building sustained heavy damage in January 1975 as a result of arson, but the damage was repaired and the church reopened that August.

"Arson Destroys Church," *KP*, January 22, 1975, 1K.

Collection of the Kentucky Gateway Museum Center, Maysville, Ky.

Collins, Richard H. *History of Kentucky*. Vol. 1. Covington, Ky.: Collins, 1882.

"To Rebuild Gutted Church," *KP*, January 24, 1975, 4K.

John Klee

WASTE DISPOSAL. Northern Kentucky was no more advanced in its early methods of waste disposal than the rest of the nation. Depending upon where people lived in Northern Kentucky, their trash was dumped in privies or local sinkholes, thrown in nearby rivers and streams, burned, or put in open dumps. Many in rural areas relied on the barrel and the match or disposed of trash on their own farm, while most city residents had someone dump it for them. In some cases, waste was thrown to hogs for forage. Some dumps burned the trash in favorable winds to minimize litter, odor, and vermin. For many years, each Northern Kentucky city had its own landfill, within its boundaries. **Taylor's Bottoms**, along each side of Taylor's Creek between Bellevue and Newport, served that purpose for those two cities; in Covington there were dumps along Crescent Ave. at Second St., farther south where present-day Meinken Field is, and along Banklick Creek (see **Banklick Creek and Watershed**). Fort Thomas had a similar facility along River Rd. behind the **Fort Thomas Military Reservation**. At many of these sites, large incinerators with tall smokestacks eventually were built. Such locations were eyesores for neighbors and smelled bad; today many of them are beneath public athletic fields.

The centralization of the waste industry began when people started relying on haulers to collect their waste and dump it at an open dump. Although the smaller dumps went unrecorded, the Kentucky Environmental and Public Protection Cabinet documented the larger dumps during the promulgation of Kentucky House Bill 174 and inventoried the unpermitted, inactive, and uncapped landfills throughout the state. According to the list, Northern Kentucky has 36 uncapped, inactive landfills: 2 are in Boone Co., 10 in Campbell, 1 in Gallatin, 7 in Grant, and 16 in Kenton.

Nearly all solid wastes in Northern Kentucky are collected and taken to one of these four landfill facilities: a landfill run by **Bavarian Trucking Company** Inc., in Boone Co.; CSI (owned by Republic Services Inc.), in Grant Co.; or one of the landfills owned by Rumpke Consolidated Companies Inc. in Colerain Township, Ohio, and Pendleton Co., Ky.

The Bavarian Trucking Company Inc. began operating its landfill west of Walton in Boone Co. in 1974. In 1995 Bavarian became the third waste-disposal firm in Kentucky to meet the new composite liner design standards, and in 2003 its landfill was the first in the state that used landfill gas to generate electricity. Bavarian now operates or controls approximately 600 acres at this site and employs approximately 100 people in Northern Kentucky.

Contiguous with the Bavarian Trucking Company Inc. landfill is a closed site that was originally operated by K&O Sanitation and later purchased by Northern Kentucky Sanitation. In 1967 access to the facility was cut off by the construction of I-71 through Stephenson Mill Rd., and the facility was closed. Northern Kentucky Sanitation later reopened the landfill at the end of McCoy Fork Rd., directly across I-71. In 1973 Browning Ferris Industries (BFI) bought Northern Kentucky Sanitation's landfill and operated the facility. From 1974 to approximately 1980, Bavarian and BFI operated the two landfills adjacent to each other. In a rare occurrence in the annals of the waste industry, Bavarian purchased BFI's property when it ceased all operations at the site. BFI's landfill was sold to Vienna Woods Inc., which capped and closed the facility.

The Epperson Landfill, owned by Republic Services Inc., is located off Cynthiana St., just outside the city limits of Williamstown in Grant Co. The landfill was started in 1968 by Hade Epperson, a Grant Co. resident who had been collecting garbage in the county since the 1950s. When he died in 1978, his son Freddie, then age 36, took over the operation. In 1991 Kentucky adopted stringent environmental regulations, dramatically increasing the cost of landfill operation. That year, Freddie Epperson sold the landfill to Addington Environmental, based in Lexington. The following year, the Epperson Landfill became the first facility in Kentucky to be permitted under the state's new composite liner design standards. In 1996 Addington was merged into Republic Services Inc., the third-largest waste company in the nation. Republic continued to operate the landfill, which accepts waste from Northern Kentucky and southwestern Ohio.

Rumpke's Pendleton Co. Landfill, six miles north of Falmouth, began operations in 1972. Rumpke purchased the site in 1980. The facility consists of approximately 650 acres, and all of the area except for the 148 permitted acres serves as buffer. Todd Rumpke, regional vice president, manages the facility, which has approximately 120 employees. The landfill is permitted to receive municipal solid waste and construction demolition debris. The Pendleton Co. Landfill is part of Rumpke Consolidated Companies Inc., which is headquartered in Colerain Township, Ohio, just outside of Cincinnati. Rumpke's operation was founded in 1932 by brothers William F. Rumpke and Bernard Rumpke. Their sons, cousins William J. Rumpke Sr. and Thomas B. Rumpke, expanded the business and extended Rumpke's service area into Northern Kentucky. Currently, Rumpke employs 2,300 people throughout Kentucky, Ohio, and Indiana.

Bavarian Waste Service. www.bavarianwaste.com (accessed December 20, 2006).

Rumpke. www.rumpke.com (accessed December 20, 2006).

Rick Brueggemann

WATERS, ROBERT L., JR., "BOB" (b. November 9, 1922, Covington, Ky.; d. January 6, 2006, Independence, Ky.). Guitarist Bob Waters and the Paradise Islanders hosted the renowned Hawaiian Luau and dinner show at the Howard Johnson's Hotel at the Sharonville, Ohio, exit off I-75 every Saturday night for more than 20 years during the 1960s, 1970s, and 1980s, performing two shows each night.

Robert L. Waters Jr. was the son of a **Chesapeake and Ohio Railroad** engineer, Robert L. Waters Sr., who in turn, was the son of a steamboat pilot. Robert Jr.'s mother was Jessie C. Duval. Young Robert relinquished the family transportation career tradition in favor of his first love, music, Hawaiian music in particular. Growing up along Scott St. in Covington, he, like so many other Covington boys, became heavily involved with **Daniel Beard**'s Sons of **Daniel Boone**, better known as the **Boy Scouts** of America, and achieved the rank of Life Scout. Bob began playing the guitar as a young teen, being mostly self-taught. The Troop 17 Hot Shots was the name of his Boy Scout band. He graduated from **Holmes High School** in Covington in 1942 and studied voice for a time. His instructors encouraged him to pursue an opera career, but after weighing the time and effort required to be a successful opera singer, he opted to dedicate all that energy to what he truly loved, playing guitar in a band.

Waters had a keen interest in Hawaiian music early on, in his preteen years. While on a visit to Los Angeles in 1941, he met Mamo Clark, the Hawaiian-born actress who graduated from the University of Southern California and starred opposite Clark Gable in *Mutiny on the Bounty*. That experience only sharpened his interest in Hawaiian culture and music. Then, while serving in the U.S. Marines during **World War II**, Bob was stationed in Samoa in the South Pacific during 1942–1943. The Samoans and the Hawaiians, who share common ancestors, have similar dialects and musical traditions. It was there that he put together a band with some locals and entertained the Marines on the base. Through his music he developed friendships with members of a native Samoan tribe, studied their customs and language, and perfected his music. The tribe's chief became very fond of Waters. He adopted him as a son and gave him the name Pulevai, which Waters carried and used for the rest of his life. *Pule* meant "great speaker or talker" and *vai*, Samoan for "water," was Waters's Samoan surname. He eventually learned to speak the Samoan language fluently, along with several other South Pacific dialects.

Bob "Pulevai" Waters had his own Hawaiian band from that time forth. He played with and studied under many of the Hawaiian music greats after the war, both in the Islands and stateside. He was well known and respected in Hawaiian music circles and became a very close friend of Jerry Byrd of Lima, Ohio, said to be the most recognized Hawaiian steel guitar player of all times. Byrd played country steel guitar and was featured on Cincinnati television station WLW's *Midwestern Hayride* for many years. Waters accompanied Byrd to the Hawaiian Steel Guitar Association (HGSA) conventions in Joliet, Ill., every October, to play backup for Byrd's clinics, demonstrations, and competition. Each May they traveled to Hawaii to play with the best bands performing there, and each July they attended the week-long Aloha International meetings in Winchester, Ind. Together, they amassed an impressive collection of HSGA awards to augment their professional reputations.

Julia K. Puou Waters, Bob's wife of 45 years, played the ukulele and performed as a dancer and singer in the Paradise Islanders alongside him for their entire careers. A native of the Big Island of Hawaii, Julia had served as a lady U.S. Marine from 1954 to 1957. When she was discharged, she came to Cincinnati with a Marine girlfriend for a visit. There, at a local Hawaiian Club get-together, she met Waters. She sat in with the Hawaiian music band that night, eventually replaced one of the two female dancers in the group, played the ukulele, and later married Waters.

Bob and Julia Waters both retired from the Paradise Islanders in 1986. Bob died in early 2006 at **St. Elizabeth Medical Center** South and was buried at Floral Hills Cemetery in Taylor Mill. Julia continues to live in their home in Independence. The musical legacy Bob Waters left was unique. He established, nurtured, and propagated the Hawaiian entertainment tradition and venue in the Greater Cincinnati area. Even after he retired, his band continued to perform, helping to seal his musical legacy.

Hicks, Jack. "He Brought Hawaiian Music Home," *KP*, July 15, 1994, 1K.

"Robert L. Waters," *KP*, January 9, 2006, A8.

Don Clare

WATKINS, SIMON J. (b. February 1868, Courtland, Ala.; d. November 6, 1948, Covington, Ky.). Simon J. Watkins, the son of Anderson and Mary Watkins, was the first African American physician in Covington. He was a physician, a surgeon, and a dentist. Watkins attended Tennessee A&I State College and the Meharry Medical School, both in Nashville, Tenn., receiving his degree in dentistry in 1888 and a degree in medicine in 1889. He served on the Meharry Medical School faculty until 1891. Later that year, he moved to Covington to begin his medical practice. He married a woman from Covington, Rosa A. Moore, on January 12, 1893. In 1894 Watkins's office was located at 429 Scott St. in Covington. Four years later he moved his office to 113 E. Ninth St. in Covington, where he maintained his practice until retiring in 1946. Watkins was appointed to the state Interracial Committee and was named a sanitary officer in Covington by the state Medical Board. In May 1912 he organized the state Medical Society of Colored Physicians, Surgeons, Dentists, and Pharmacists at a meeting in Covington.

Watkins was a member of Lane Chapel C.M.E. Church. In March 1895, he gave the welcome talk to the Mount Sterling District Conference of Colored Methodists meeting in Covington. He also served as a delegate to the Christian (Colored) Methodist Episcopal conference for three consecutive years. He was actively involved in the local Republican Party. Watkins died at his home in 1948 and was buried at Linden Grove Cemetery in Covington. His daughter Anna Mae Jones operated the C. E. Jones funeral home after the death of her husband, **Charles E. Jones**.

"Colored Conference," *KP*, March 4, 1895, 5.

"Colored Medical Men Meeting in Covington," *KP*, May 10, 1912, 11.

Dabney, W. P. *Cincinnati's Colored Citizens*. Cincinnati: Dabney, 1926.

Reis, Jim. "Historic Lane Chapel," *KP*, March 4, 1996, 4K.

Theodore H. H. Harris

WCKY. As radio became increasingly popular during the late 1920s, Kentucky had only three radio stations, WHAS and WLAP at Louisville and WFIW at Hopkinsville. Two businessmen in Covington, **Maurice L. Galvin** and **L. B. Wilson**, realized that a local station would be a valuable asset not only for entertainment but also, and more importantly, to promote the business and growth of the city.

In 1929 the Federal Radio Commission made an allotment for two additional stations in Kentucky, the first a 1,000-watt transmitter that would be shared with other stations, and the second a 5,000-watt transmitter located at 1480 KHz. U.S. senator Frederic Sackett was contacted, and he immediately went to work to investigate whether a station could be added in Northern Kentucky. After preliminary negotiations between the Federal Radio Commission and Senator Sackett, L. B. Wilson completed and filed an application on February 5. The application required that some preliminary plans for the station be made; one item was the location of the transmitting plant. At the time, because Cincinnati radio station WLW had built a new transmitter at Mason, Ohio, its old broadcasting plant at Harrison, Ohio, was available for purchase. So the original application included the plan to purchase the plant at Harrison. On February 6 the Federal Radio Commission granted the permit for the station. The permit was later amended to place construction of the transmitter in Kentucky, specifying that totally new equipment would be used.

In April 1929 the new corporation purchased RCA Victor equipment that duplicated the latest used by station WHAS in Louisville. Radio station engineers were asked to begin locating a site for the transmitter, and later in the year, a farm belonging to the Walton family, in Villa Hills, overlooking the Ohio Valley, was chosen. Engineers began testing and found that a very strong signal could be transmitted as far away as Louisville. The new station's offices and studio were located in the Peoples Bank (now **US Bank**) building at Sixth St. and Madison Ave. in Covington.

By September the dream to begin broadcasting had been realized and ground testing began. On September 16, 1929, at 7:45 p.m., the station opened with a 15-minute dedication ceremony from the Crystal Room at the Music Hall in Cincinnati, coordinated with the fifth annual radio dealers' show also being held there. The National Broadcasting Company, the *Kentucky Post*, and the *Cincinnati Post* presented several programs that day, which were followed by an announcement by Kentucky governor Flem D. Sampson (1927–1931).

In 1937 WCKY increased its power to 10,000 watts; in August 1939 the station switched its affiliation from the National Broadcasting System to the Columbia Broadcasting System (CBS) and at the same time increased transmitting power to 50,000 watts. At the same time, L. B. Wilson moved the studios from Covington to the Gibson Hotel in Cincinnati. The North American Radio Broadcasting Agreement Treaty of 1941 caused considerable shuffling of stations and expanded the AM dial to 1600 KHz. WCKY was subsequently moved up the dial to 1530 KHz. In 1945 the station dropped its CBS affiliation to become independent. Between 1946 and 1964, WCKY featured an all-night **country music** disk-jockey program that had a nationwide following. L. B. Wilson died in 1954, but WCKY continued as an L. B. Wilson station for another 15 years. In 1961 the station adopted the Mutual Broadcasting System network, and in 1963 the station's affiliation was changed to the American Broadcasting Company. The station thus is the only one in the region that has been affiliated with all four major radio networks.

In 1969 the estate of L. B. Wilson sold WCKY to Post Newsweek Broadcasting, and a country music format was retained for several years before changing to a news/talk format, competing with stations WKRC and WLW locally. WCKY was later sold to Jacor Communications; changing its call letters, it became WSAI "Real Oldies" at AM 1530 and featured the top 40 hits of the 1950s and 1960s. Although that programming was very popular, the owners switched back to a talk format and resumed using call sign WCKY in 2005. On July 7, 2006, WCKY again modified programming, now to a sports talk format, and became "WCKY 1530 Homer the Sports Animal." The studios are now located, along with other Clear Channel stations, in the Towers of Kenwood building in Sycamore Township in Ohio. At night the station can normally be heard as far away as Chicago, Miami, Detroit, and Wichita. The call letters WCKY signify, by the *W*, a radio station east of the Mississippi River; *CKY* stands for Covington, Ky.

Brinkmoeller, Tom. "WCKY Radio Breezes Past Half-Century Mark," *CE*, October 21, 1979, F6.

Hannaford, R. Clarke. "Merchandising Important Factor in Radio," *Broadcasting Magazine*, August 15, 1933, 21.

"Inaugural Edition Radio Broadcasting Station WCKY," *KP*, September 15, 1929, special sec., 1–15.

"One Station Is Due Kentucky," *KP*, February 6, 1929, 1.

John E. Leming Jr.

WCVG. Covington-based AM radio station WCVG dates to 1965, when Irving Swartz, manager and president of the Kenton Broadcasters (WCLU Broadcasting), served as the new station's general manager. The station went on the air under the call name of WCLU, with a daytime power of 500 watts; it was located at 1320 kHz on the broadcast band. WCLU began as a **country music** provider, featuring "Modern Country" music. The station soon moved its broadcasting studio to Milford, Ohio, but the transmitter remained behind the Latonia Plaza Shopping Center in Covington. In 1981 WCLU changed to a rock-and-roll music format and then in the mid-1980s to a contemporary-hit-music style. Swartz was one of the first to utilize a computerized method of selecting songs for airplay. In 1987 Swartz sold the station to Richard Plessinger, and the call letters changed to WCVG.

In 1987 WCVG switched to a contemporary country format, which did not last long; the station became the nation's first "All Elvis" station late in that same year. In 1988 it became an affiliate of the Business Radio Network, going to 24 hours of business news and talk. In 1992 the station moved its broadcast studio back to its transmitter site in Latonia and returned to country music and sports talk as a format. WCVG served the Northern Kentucky sports community with heavy coverage of high school sports and also aired **Northern Kentucky University** and **Thomas More College** sports. Former Mr. Kentucky Basketball (1978), **Holmes High School** standout Doug Schloemer, has served as a sports announcer for the station.

On July 16, 2006, WCVG was purchased for $1.9 million by the Davidson Media Group and became a Spanish-language station. Over the years, the station has struggled to find its market niche, as reflected by its many formatting changes.

Nash, Francis M. *Towers over Kentucky: A History of Radio and TV in the Bluegrass State*. Lexington, Ky.: Host Communications, 1995.

Wikipedia. "WCVG." www.wikipedia.org (accessed February 14, 2007).

Williams, Tom. "Radio Station Alters Format again as Country Music Replaces Business News," *KP*, January 23, 1992, 12A.

WCVN/KET. WCVN television, Channel 54 on the UHF band, is Northern Kentucky's link to the statewide KET (Kentucky Educational Television). WCVN began broadcasting from its 300-foot tower in Taylor Mill on September 17, 1969, after several months of delays. This local outlet for public television, PBS (Public Broadcasting Service), brings to Northern Kentucky programs from the PBS national network and local programming from KET production facilities in Lexington and Louisville. During the early part of the academic day, instruction in various subjects is supplied to classrooms in schools across the state; in the evening, national broadcasts are sent over the airwaves. This programming would not be available if not for the existence of sponsor-free, public educational television. Locally, WCVN has one of about 15 transmitters in the KET network, spread across the state and fed by a microwave system that emanates from the KET headquarters on the campus of the University of Kentucky in Lexington. There is no studio for local production of broadcasts at the tower site.

During spring 2007, KET aired its own production of *Where the River Bends*, narrated by **Nick Clooney**. An almost three-hour-long presentation on the history of the Northern Kentucky region, it was well-received and resulted in KET's most successful one-night fundraising effort in the network's history.

"Blame Bad Weather for ETV Station Delays," *KP*, May 12, 1969, 6K.

"Covington's ETV Is Near Start," *KP*, March 4, 1969, 6K.

"Getting Ready for 'Higher Education,'" *KP*, May 12, 1969, 1K.

"Our Educational TV Is On—'People Know We're Here?'" *KP*, September 17, 1969, 1K.

Reis, Jim. "Northern Kentucky's Quest for TV," *KP*, May 8, 1989, 4K.

WEATHER AND CLIMATE. Northern Kentucky is centrally located within the Ohio River Valley, at an elevation range of 425 to 1,000 feet above sea level. Geographically, this region is referred to as the Outer Bluegrass Region of Kentucky. Northern Kentucky experiences a vast array of weather conditions over the course of a year. Globally, nationally, and regionally, its location within the midlatitudes of the United States plays an integral part in the various storm tracks that move in and out on a daily, monthly, and yearly basis. Northern Kentucky is located in a transition zone between two climates, Humid Continental to its north and Humid Subtropical to its south.

Climatologically, Northern Kentucky is on the southern rim of a continental polar air mass (colder, drier, and more stable air) while hugging the northern fringe of a maritime tropical air mass (warm, moist, and more unstable air). This air-mass battleground can create some wicked weather extremes: large snowfall totals locally or very little snow in the winter months, flooding rains or widespread droughts, large heat spells or vast cold spells. The area can also receive decaying tropical storms in late autumn. It is where these extreme weather events collide and shift seasonally or annually, defining an eventual long-term climate for this territory.

Northern Kentucky's position within the midlatitudes, its distance from major bodies of water (the Gulf of Mexico, the Atlantic Ocean, and the Great Lakes), and its topography have created a certain annual "climate control" specified for this region. The "climate control" has helped to shape the "averages" or "normals," values that are used daily by local forecasters, farmers, and the general public as a guide to what the weather should be, dependent upon the time of the year or for a certain growing season. The numerical averages of precipitation and temperatures are the largest factors observed and have been roughly recorded for close to two centuries, beginning in the 1830s. These daily logbooks have helped to establish a better understanding of the region's weather annually.

Evolutionary factors such as urban sprawl, decreasing farmland, natural growth, manmade products, and congestion all have had some direct impact on today's climate status. However, average temperatures and precipitation referred to now are based only on the most recent span of 30 years. The frame of reference is the environment that surrounds Northern Kentucky currently, rather than the setting of the region 180 years ago. The following is a sampling of the most current 30-year averages, documented from one data-point setting in Boone Co. (the **Cincinnati/Northern Kentucky International Airport**, 1971–2000):

Annual average precipitation: 42.60 inches

Annual average snowfall: 23.7 inches

Annual average high temperature: 64.0 degrees

Annual average low temperature: 44.3 degrees

Annual average mean temperature: 54.2 degrees

This kind of data is a yearly representation for the entire Northern Kentucky region and is used as the basis for all counties within the Northern Kentucky region. The 30-year averages would likely vary from county to county due to their proximity and topography, but the averages listed serve as the standard for all counties within this localized area.

Spring: Meteorological Season March 1 to May 31

Spring begins the growing season for most local farmers, but this season is also known for its severe thunderstorms and massive floods. The transitional period from early March to late May can be a volatile one locally, with huge temperature swings from clashing and retreating air masses. The slow creep from winters's past can still unleash late-season snows and early spring tornadoes. Of all seasonal variations, spring in Northern Kentucky appears to be the most violent historically. Some of the greatest documented **tornadoes** in the region have occurred within this three-month time frame. Late-season snows, copious rains, and massive snowmelt rank March through May high for significant flooding along the Ohio River and its tributaries (see **Flood of 1884**; **Flood of 1907**; **Floods of 1913**; **Flood of 1937**; **Flood of 1964, Licking River**; **Flood of 1997, Licking River**). Historical data shows that 6 of the 10 greatest floods for this area occurred in the early spring months of March and April. As the days get longer with increased sunlight and milder with higher temperatures, spring flooding becomes less likely

SPRING METEOROLOGICAL SEASON

	March	*April*	*May*
Average mean temperature	43.9 degrees	53.7 degrees	63.7 degrees
Warmest monthly temperature	88.0 degrees	90.0 degrees	95.0 degrees
Coldest monthly temperature	−11.0 degrees	15.0 degrees	27.0 degrees
Average rainfall	3.90 inches	3.96 inches	4.59 inches
Heaviest monthly rainfall	12.18 inches	9.77 inches	9.48 inches
Heaviest one-day rainfall	5.22 inches	2.41 inches	3.02 inches
Average snowfall	3.80 inches	0.60 inch	0.00 inch
Heaviest monthly snowfall	13.0 inches	3.70 inches	0.20 inch
Heaviest one-day snow total	9.80 inches	3.30 inches	0.20 inch

along the Ohio River. It is around this time of the year that the melted snows have finally pushed downstream and that the average last spring freeze occurs (on April 21), a true sign that the growing season has begun.

Summer: Meteorological Season June 1 to August 31

Typically, the progression from spring into summer is a gradual one in this region. The month of June averages a robust rainfall total at 4.42 inches, placing it second only to May for annual precipitation totals, while the average daily high temperatures rise by 14 degrees from May 1 to June 30. Eventually, the summer's heat is felt by the last week of June and continues through late August. As the prevailing summertime winds turn southwesterly, moist air from the Gulf of Mexico becomes more prevalent. This regime of air not only makes for hotter days but also more humid ones. Daily storms become less common during this period as cooler air retreats north and upper-level winds relax, keeping most frontal boundaries with more organized thunderstorms concentrated across the Great Lakes region. The typical storm activity during this six-to-eight-week period is more limited and localized, but collectively July and August deliver an average rainfall total of 7.54 inches.

Excessively hot periods are documented for this region, especially in July. Most recent is the record heat occurring in 1988, which set eight new record high temperatures during the weeks of late June through August. Locally and nationally, the summer of 1988 was devastating in relation to heat and drought. Some 7,500 heat-related deaths occurred, mainly across the eastern United States, along with an estimated $61.6 billion in drought damage and aid. In 1944 an additional eight days of record heat were observed locally from late June through August. In the intensely hot summer of 1953, 51 days of 90-degree temperatures or greater were experienced, the most in more than 60 years; on average, Northern Kentucky's summer months produce only 18 90-degree days.

Historically, the years 1934 and 1936 stand out in terms of record heat and drought. The all-time record high temperature fell in the year of 1934, with a blistering 109 degrees on July 21. Seven record highs were recorded in 1934, five of them at or exceeding 100 degrees. The summer of 1934 may have held the hottest day in historical data, but 1936 was also extremely harsh. Eleven new record highs were set in the summer of 1936, all exceeding 100 degrees. Within the week of July 10, six days topped 100 degrees, and all were set as new records, which remain today. These two years represent extreme heat locally and drought conditions that also affected the "breadbasket" of the nation to the west. The Dust Bowl Years, which included 1934 and 1936, lasted for close to a decade in some parts of the country.

SUMMER METEOROLOGICAL SEASON

	June	*July*	*August*
Average mean temperature	72.0 degrees	76.3 degrees	74.5 degrees
Warmest monthly temperature	102.0 degrees	109.0 degrees	103.0 degrees
Coldest monthly temperature	39.0 degrees	47.0 degrees	43.0 degrees
Average rainfall	4.42 inches	3.75 inches	3.79 inches
Heaviest monthly rainfall	9.61 inches	8.70 inches	7.71 inches
Heaviest one-day rainfall	3.35 inches	3.93 inches	3.52 inches
Average snowfall	0.00 inches	0.00 inches	0.00 inches
Heaviest monthly snowfall	0.00 inches	0.00 inches	0.00 inches
Heaviest one-day snow total	0.00 inches	0.00 inches	0.00 inches

Autumn: Meteorological Season September 1 to November 30

Autumn in the Ohio River Valley is a rather tranquil season. Dry, warm days followed by clear, cool nights are the common theme from late September through early November. Although cold winter air begins building in southern Canada around this time, it is usually trapped across the northern United States and pushed east by the polar jet stream. Also in the autumn, tropical air begins to retreat slowly to the Gulf of Mexico. This places Northern Kentucky between two very active storm tracks, the polar jet stream and the subtropical jet stream. Meteorologically, it is termed a *split-flow,* and it keeps the weather somewhat quiet in this region for a span of about six weeks. With the exception of a dying tropical system that may be pulled north, rainfall is quite limited, making these three months the driest of the year. It is also around this time that autumn foliage brings a brilliant spread of colors, with peak colors arriving by mid-to-late October. This timing coincides properly with the average first frost of the season, expected around October 13.

A second severe-weather season is possible during the late autumn. Although storms are not as frequent as in the spring months, isolated severe outbreaks are somewhat common. Periodically, colder blocks of air will begin their surge southward and create some rough and dangerous weather conditions locally. Large temperature swings and contrasts during this transitional period should be noted. Many local forecasters have not overlooked the tornado potential during this time of the year. Although less common in autumn, tornadoes have spawned in this region just before the first snows of the winter hit the ground. November brings with it the first true signs of winter and its snow potential.

Average first trace of snowfall: November 7

Average first .10 inch of snowfall: November 21

Average first 1 inch of snowfall: November 28

Winter: Meteorological Season December 1 to February 28

When compared nationally, the winter months in Northern Kentucky are considered mild. Historically, there have been some exceptions, but big snowy periods and extreme cold spells are truly rare during these months and usually last only for a week to 10 days. For the most part, the winter season is the cloudiest of the year, and frequent passing snow showers or wintry mixes of rain, snow, sleet, and freezing rain eventually mount to an average snow total of 23.7 inches. January is the snowiest month on average at 7.9 inches.

Prevailing winds during this period are from the northwest, with cold-spell intervals followed by brief periods of sunny and milder days. Data indicates record high temperatures for these months ranging from the mid-60s to the mid-70s. This illustrates just how mild winters can be locally. Ironically, the month of January, which may be considered the "dead of winter," posted one of the warmest temperatures of the season in 1950: 74 degrees on January 25. However, the month of January also posted the coldest temperature of all time: –25

FALL METEOROLOGICAL SEASON

	September	*October*	*November*
Average mean temperature	67.4 degrees	55.7 degrees	44.7 degrees
Warmest monthly temperature	102.0 degrees	92.0 degrees	83.0 degrees
Coldest monthly temperature	31.0 degrees	16.0 degrees	0.0 degrees
Average rainfall	2.82 inches	2.96 inches	3.46 inches
Heaviest monthly rainfall	8.61 inches	8.60 inches	7.51 inches
Heaviest one-day rainfall	3.19 inches	4.30 inches	2.47 inches
Average snowfall	0.00 inches	0.40 inch	1.30 inches
Heaviest monthly snowfall	0.00 inches	6.20 inches	12.10 inches
Heaviest one-day snow total	0.00 inches	5.90 inches	8.70 inches

degrees on January 18, 1977 (see **Blizzards and Severe Winter Weather**).

Storm tracks are critical to how much snow falls during an event within this area. Clippers screaming out of southern Canada can provide brief but intense snows ranging from 2 to 4 inches followed by breezy, colder days as winds rush in from a northwesterly direction. Bigger snows actually come from the southwest, predominantly spawned in the state of Texas. Deep low-pressure systems dig south out of the Rocky Mountains, then eject northeasterly. Gulf of Mexico moisture surging out ahead of the approaching storms creates a great setup for larger snowfall totals. Lake Michigan and Lake Erie provide enhanced lake-effect snows in northern parts of Indiana and Ohio, but in most cases that moisture is limited and those winds are not strong enough to push heavy totals as far south as Northern Kentucky.

Some of the most memorable severe-weather events for an entire year have occurred during this three-month cycle. Two that stand out the most are the blizzard of 1978 and the flood of 1937. The blizzard of 1978, which occurred during January, is a memorable one for most people. Its impact was felt not only locally but regionally, affecting several states during a two-day span and beyond. An estimated 7 inches of snow was recorded in Northern Kentucky within a 48-hour period, but this total did not come near to the heaviest snowfalls for the area during a 24-hour period: 12.8 inches January 6–7, 1996; 12.6 inches February 4–5, 1998; 11.0 inches December 8, 1917;10.0 inches December 22, 1883; and 9.8 inches March 22, 1968.

The difficulties that occurred with the monumental 1978 storm and the days that followed were twofold. The early days of 1978 had already been a very cold and snowy period. Snow depths were at around 14 inches by January 21, just four days before the official blizzard arrived. Area roads were still recuperating from what had been a tough few weeks. The blizzard brought the cities of the region to a dangerous standstill. The two key elements that combined to make this storm so historic were heavy pockets of snow and incredible winds. Other names used for this blizzard were "Storm of the Century," "White Hurricane," and the like. Although Northern Kentucky did not experience the full wrath of wind and heavy snows, the brutal cold air that followed and the large snowdrifts caused several weeks of delays for incoming store supplies and required school closures. The Ohio River iced up in many locations locally, thereby delaying shipments by water until the cold air receded.

Another memorable weather phenomenon occurred in the late winter months of 1937. It had little to do with snow and much more to do with incredible rains in quick succession. The setup of a nearly stationary front, several storm systems, and heavy training (rain movement west to east) inundated the Northern Kentucky region. Although flooding is a common occurrence in and around river cities during the late winter season, to this day nothing rivals the Ohio River flood of 1937. It remains the largest mass of water to gather along the banks of the Ohio River; water levels crested from 20 to 28 feet above flood stage, beating the previous flood record set in February 1884 by nearly nine feet.

From January 13 through 25, 1937, rain poured across the region, with some 6 to 12 inches recorded. The semifirm to frozen wintertime ground facilitated extensive fast-moving runoff, which inevitably pushed down to the rivers. Excessive rainfall totals were unheard of for this time of the year, and January 1937 remains as the wettest month ever recorded for the Northern Kentucky–Cincinnati area, with 13.68 inches. The end result was dramatic, as thousands were left homeless locally.

Ahrens, C. Donald. *Essentials of Meteorology: An Invitation to the Atmosphere*. St. Paul, Minn.: West, 1993.

Bonnifield, Paul. *The Dust Bowl: Men, Dirt, and Depression*. Albuquerque: Univ. of New Mexico Press, 1979.

Clark's Kentucky Almanac and Book of Facts. Lexington, Ky.: Clark Group, 2006.

D'Aleo, Joe. "25th Anniversary of the 1978 Blizzards," *Intellicast*, February 3, 2003. www.intellicast.com (accessed August 18, 2006).

Dorman, Karla J. "No Ordinary Blizzard," *StormSpinner*, December 11, 2002. www.authorsden.com (accessed August 18, 2006).

Gibian, Jay. "Blizzard of '78, What Happened in Ohio: A Meteorologist Review," *UPI Broadcast Special*, February 17, 1978. www.bceo.org (accessed August 18, 2006).

Kentucky Atlas and Gazetteer. www.uky.edu/KentuckyAtlas (accessed August 16, 2006).

NASA. "NASA Explains 'Dust Bowl' Drought," *NASA*, March 18, 2004. www.nasa.gov (accessed August 18, 2006).

National Weather Service. www.nws.noaa.gov (accessed August 18, 2006).

National Weather Service Historical Records, 1971–2000, National Weather Service, Wilmington, Ohio.

Ritter, Michael E. *The Physical Environment: An Introduction to Physical Geography*. 2006. http: www.uwsp.edu/geo/faculty/ritter (accessed August 18, 2006).

The Weather Channel. "Normal Peak Times for Fall Color." www.weather.com (accessed on August 16, 2006).

Jim O'Brien

WINTER METEOROLOGICAL SEASON

	December	*January*	*February*
Average mean temperature	34.6 degrees	29.7 degrees	34.1 degrees
Warmest monthly temperature	75.0 degrees	77.0 degrees	75.0 degrees
Coldest monthly temperature	−20.0 degrees	−25.0 degrees	−17.0 degrees
Average rainfall	3.28 inches	2.92 inches	2.75 inches
Heaviest monthly rainfall	7.90 inches	9.43 inches	6.72 inches
Heaviest one-day rainfall	2.47 inches	3.97 inches	3.97 inches
Average snowfall	3.70 inches	7.90 inches	6.00 inches
Heaviest monthly snowfall	15.00 inches	31.50 inches	19.90 inches
Heaviest one-day snow total	7.50 inches	11.60 inches	11.80. inches

WEATHERBY, DENNIS W. (b. December 4, 1959, Brighton, Ala.; d. September 15, 2007, Fort Thomas, Ky.). Dennis Weatherby, an inventor, scientist, and educator, developed a stain-resistant lemon-scented composition used in Cascade liquid detergent while employed as an engineer at Procter and Gamble (P&G) in Cincinnati. His invention was granted a patent in 1987 and is used in most commercial lemon-scented cleaning products that contain bleach.

Weatherby is the son of Willie James Weatherby Sr. and Flossie Mary Dickinson Weatherby. His interest in consumer products goes back to his childhood curiosity over the identically shaped Pringles potato crisps stacked in canister packages. Part of a household of nine older siblings, he was encouraged to pursue his dreams, one of which was to become a professional football player. He was awarded a football scholarship to Central State University, a historically black institution, in Wilberforce, Ohio. Three chemistry department faculty members mentored and inspired him, and he graduated from Central State University with a BS in chemistry in 1982. He completed an MS in chemical engineering from the University of Dayton in 1984 and then joined the P&G engineering team.

In 1989 Weatherby returned to Central State University to teach, advise, and recruit students in its new International Center for Water Resources Management. His efforts contributed to the water program's 400 percent increase in student enrollment and its more than 80 percent rate of retention. He became an assistant professor of water quality at Central State University in 1994.

Weatherby completed his PhD in educational psychology at Auburn University in Alabama, focusing on student retention. He continued his success with retention and recruitment for minority engineering students as the school's first director of the minority engineering program, where he was appointed assistant dean for minority affairs at Auburn University in 1996. Subsequently, he headed retention and recruitment initiatives for PhD students as associate dean of the graduate school at the University of Notre Dame, South Bend, Ind., during 2004 and 2005. In autumn 2005, Dennis Weatherby and his family moved to Northern Kentucky, where he became the associate provost for student success at **Northern Kentucky University** in Highland Heights. He died on September 15, 2007, and was buried in Alexandria Cemetery.

"Dennis Weatherby, Associate Provost at NKU," *KP*, September 19, 2007, 6A.

Institute of Black Invention and Technology. "Dennis Weatherby: Cascade Lemon Formula Liquid Dishwashing Detergent." www.tibit.biz/inventor-2006-2.htm (accessed December 25, 2006).

Lemelson-MIT Program. "Inventor of the Week." http://mit.edu/invent/iow/weatherby.html (accessed December 22, 2006).

Nesbitt, Karen. "AU Engineering Minority Program Focuses on Communications Skills." Auburn Univ.News. www.ocm.auburn.edu/news_releases/communications.html (accessed December 25, 2006).

"Northern Kentucky University: Dr. Dennis Weatherby Is Appointed," *Diverse Issues in Higher Education*, June 1, 2006, 90.

Univ. of Notre Dame. "Corporate Win Opens Door to Life in Higher Education," *ND Works*, October 11, 2004, 4.

John Schlipp

WEBB, GARY S. (b. August 31, 1955, Corona, Calif.; d. December 10, 2004, Sacramento, Calif.). Gary Webb, the son of a military family, dropped out of journalism school in order to become an investigative reporter with the *Kentucky Post* during the late 1970s and early 1980s. Among his top stories was a series he did on crime in the coal industry in Kentucky, which involved a murder along Monmouth St. in Newport.

Webb always sought out the roots of corruption and was known in the trade as a street reporter. He lived along W. 11th St. in Covington, where in 1983 he shot a person in the leg who was breaking into his car to steal a tape player. He later worked for the Cleveland *Plain Dealer*, before moving west to the San Jose *Mercury News*. In 1990 Webb was part of a reporting team that shared a Pulitzer Prize for coverage of the Loma Prieta earthquake in California. In 1996 in the *Mercury News*, he alleged that drug traffickers in the 1980s had sold tons of crack cocaine in Los Angeles while funneling millions of dollars in profit to the CIA-supported Nicaraguan Contras. Later, much of what he reported was discredited.

In December 1997 he quit his job as a reporter and began to write the book *Dark Alliance: The CIA, the Contras, and the Crack Cocaine Explosion* (1999). He also went to work in California in state government in the late 1990s and was a member of an audit committee investigating former California governor Gray Davis's award of a $95 million no-bid contract to the Oracle Corporation. In 2004 he was found dead of a gunshot wound to the head in his Sacramento home. His death was ruled an apparent suicide.

"Gary Webb, 49, Former Reporter for Post," *KP*, December 13, 2004, A10.

Straub, Bill. "Wounded Suspect Convicted of Theft," *KP*, July 21, 1983, 9K.

WEBER BROTHERS ARCHITECTS. Edward Addison (1876–1929) and Christian Clay (1879–1954) were the sons of Christian and Elizabeth Meyers Weber. In the 1870s the family moved to Newport, where they operated a family grocery store at Fifth and Isabella Sts. Edward, Christian, and their younger brother, Morrison, attended public schools, graduating from **Newport High School**. It is believed that none of the three attended college. Though Edward and Christian Weber had no formal architectural training, they started a company called E.A. & C.C. Weber, Architects. Their brother, Morrison, was not a partner but worked for the company in some capacity. Edward and Christian served more as administrators than designers in their firm. They offered a wide range of services, including real estate acquisition, site development, architectural design, and construction. At the height of its success, the Weber brothers' company employed a large staff of architects, designers, draftsmen, and builders and also subcontracted some of their work to outside specialists. Their company drew the plans for numerous buildings in Kentucky, including the Governor's Mansion in Frankfort, the State National Bank in Frankfort, the Lafayette Hotel in Lexington, Eastern State College in Richmond, the Covington Trust Bank at Sixth St. and Madison Ave. in Covington (see **Huntington Bank**), the residence of Kentucky governor Ruby Laffoon (1931–1935), the Briarcliff Subdivision in Fort Thomas, the Fourth District School in Newport, and three local high schools: **Highlands High School**, **Holmes High School**, and **Newport High School**. The firm also designed several churches in Kentucky, including the **First Baptist Church, Fort Thomas**. In Maysville, they were the architects of many of the city's school buildings, as well as the Montgomery Ward store (see **Department Stores**), the **Bank of Maysville**, the Security Bank, the Kirk Apartment Building, the O'Keefe Building, and the Odd Fellows Temple Building.

The firm's most notable project was the Governor's Mansion in Frankfort, which was actually designed by one of the Webers' associates, John Scudder Adkins. Edward Weber had a long and successful career as a politician. He served as chairman of the Campbell Co. **Republican Party**, successfully directing the Northern Kentucky campaigns of Senator Frederick A. Sackett and Kentucky governor Flem D. Sampson (1927–1931). Edward Weber also served in the Kentucky legislature, from 1908 to 1910. Some believe that his political connections may have played a part in his firm's being chosen to design the Governor's Mansion. Edward Weber was a longtime member of the Newport Elks Club and was a Past Master of the Masonic Order. He died on November 16, 1929, at age 54, in his home at 21 Carolina Ave. in Fort Thomas. After Edward's death, Christian's son Stuart K. Weber was brought into the firm, and the company name was changed to C.C. and S.K. Weber, Architects. Christian Weber retired from the firm in 1950; ownership of it then passed from the Weber family. Christian died on February 2, 1954, at age 75, in his home at 40 Chalfonte Pl. in Fort Thomas. Both Edward and Christian Weber were interred in Evergreen Cemetery in Southgate.

"C. C. Weber, Architect Dies at Age 75," *KP*, February 2, 1954, 1K.

"E. A. Weber, Architect, Dies," *KP*, November 16, 1929, 1K.

"E. A. Weber, Architect and GOP Leader Dies at Ft. Thomas," *KTS*, November 16, 1929, 1.

Kentucky Death Certificate No. 3147, for the year 1954.

"Prominent Architect's Rites Set for Thursday," *KTS*, February 3, 1954, 2.

Seale, William. *The Kentucky Governor's Mansion: A Restoration*. Louisville, Ky.: Harmony House, 1984.

The Spirit of a Greater Maysville and Mason County. Maysville, Ky.: Daily Independent, 1930.

WEEK DAY SCHOOL OF RELIGION. The Week Day School of Religion is a released-time religious education program offered to elementary school children in Covington and Ludlow. The curriculum includes nondenominational moral instruction based on Judeo-Christian principles. William Wert, a Gary, Ind., school superintendent, started the movement in 1914. He believed in educating the whole child and was convinced that the public schools were not giving enough moral and religious training, so he invited local ministers to teach courses for those students who desired to be "released," for one hour each week. Today, about 250,000 students across the United States are leaving their school buildings each week to attend released-time Bible courses. More than 1,000 of these courses are in operation in 32 states. It is believed that the school in Northern Kentucky is one of the oldest.

In March 1922, with the support of H. S. Cox, superintendent of Covington Public Schools (see **Covington Independent Schools**), ministers and laymen from 20 churches met to discuss the formation of the Community Council of Religious Education. During a meeting at the Madison Ave. Presbyterian Church on June 6, 1922, the council was organized; the articles of incorporation were signed on June 19. On June 29 the council met and appointed a committee to work with the Covington Board of Education to formulate plans to release children for attendance at the Week Day School of Religion. The first classes met on February 23, 1923, with 250 students enrolled. Through the years, students in the Kentucky cities of Bromley, Covington, Crescent Springs, Erlanger, Fort Mitchell, and Ludlow have attended the school. During the 2005–2006 school year, courses were held only in Covington and Ludlow. Willard L. Wade, who was an executive of the Covington **YMCA** and active in that organization for more than 40 years, was also involved with the Week Day School for a long time. Principals have included Lila Pearl Attig, Debby Audry, Bernice Bowen, Helen Budd, Violet Detwiler, Catherine Lantz, Lula Jane Lee, Esther Lomb, Genevieve Morgan, Rita New, Martha Reed, Wrenda Taylor, and Gloria Wedding. The school is supported entirely by donations from local churches and individuals.

New, Rita. Interview by Sandy Banta, July 6, 2005, Covington, Ky.

"Willard Wade, Kentucky Y Leader for over 40 Years," *KE*, October 18, 1883, C2.

Sandy Banta

WEHRMAN, WILLIAM E., SR. (b. July 12, 1904, Ludlow, Ky.; d. February 5, 1997, Fort Mitchell, Ky.). Judge William E. Wehrman Sr. was born and raised in Ludlow. He studied law and was admitted to the Kentucky bar in 1931. He married Genevieve Reynolds in October 1932, and they had six children, Barry, Gregory, Mark, Mary Agnes, Paul, and William E. Jr. William Wehrman Sr. served as Kenton Co. attorney from 1938 to 1945 and as Kenton Co. judge (now judge-executive) from 1946 to 1962. Along with his sons Barry, Gregory, and William Jr., he operated a law firm called Wehrman and Wehrman. Judge Wehrman was a practicing lawyer in Northern Kentucky for more than 66 years. He also served on the board of directors of the Kentucky Federal Savings and Loan Company. Judge Wehrman became a close friend of U.S. Senator Alben W. Barkley, a Kentuckian, and that friendship led to the acquisition of federal funding for construction of the **Cincinnati/Northern Kentucky International Airport**. After a long illness, William Wehrman Sr. died in his Fort Mitchell home at age 92. Funeral services were held at the Blessed Sacrament Church, and burial was in St. Mary Cemetery in Fort Mitchell.

"Editor's Corner," *Ludlow News Enterprise*, November 6, 1958, 2.

"Former Judge Helped Land Airport for N. Kentucky," *KE*, February 8, 1997, 1C.

"Judge William Wehrman, Helped Create Airport," *KP*, February 6, 1997, 14A.

"Silver Anniversary," *KTS*, October 21, 1957, 3A.

WEINTRAUB, MORRIS (b. May 14, 1909, Newport, Ky.; d. January 19, 1996, Cincinnati, Ohio). Morris Weintraub, a prominent lawyer and a Speaker of the Kentucky House of Representatives, was one of the six children born to Hyman and Mollie Dolnickoff Weintraub. The Weintraubs were part of a massive migration of eastern European Jews to the United States around 1900. Hyman Weintraub lived for several years in New York City and then moved to Newport in 1906. He entered Campbell Co. politics and served both as a constable and as a jury commissioner.

Morris Weintraub was educated in local schools and then became an attorney in Newport. He represented a wide variety of clients, including community leaders and gambling figures. Like his father before him, Morris Weintraub was involved in Democratic politics; he served in the Kentucky Senate from 1940 to 1942 and in the Kentucky House of Representatives from 1946 to 1960, leading that body as Speaker of the House from 1958 until 1960. He married Justine Anness in 1945, and they had two children. Weintraub and his wife owned property in Newport and his law office was there, but some of his critics claimed that he actually lived in Cincinnati, making him ineligible to hold political office in Kentucky. However, his residency was never challenged in court and he continued to serve. Weintraub was the last president of the United Hebrew Congregation of Newport and also the founder of the Yavneh Day School in Cincinnati.

After his wife died in 1994, Weintraub lived in Florida for a while but later returned to Cincinnati, where he died at age 86 in 1996. He was buried in the Menorah Cemetery, Fort Lauderdale, Fla.

Hicks, Jack. "Secrets Died along with Colorful Lawyer," *KP*, January 24, 1996, 1–2K.

Legislative Research Commission. *Kentucky General Assembly Membership, 1900–2005*. Vol. 2. Frankfort, Ky.: Legislative Research Commission, 2005.

"Morris Weintraub," *KP*, January 23, 1996, 8A.

Reis, Jim. "Synagogue Once Stood on 5th Street in Newport," *KP*, December 10, 2001, 4K.

WELCOME HOUSE OF NORTHERN KENTUCKY. Founded in 1982 by a coalition of churches and Rev. William Mertes, Welcome House Inc. of Northern Kentucky is a Covington-based service organization that works together with the community to provide services to individuals and families who are either homeless or at risk of becoming homeless (see **Homelessness and Homeless Shelters**). In the early 1980s, there was a growing need in Northern Kentucky to provide assistance to the economically disadvantaged. In 1980 Mertes, then director of Catholic Social Services (see **Catholic Charities**), and others began to develop a comprehensive plan for churches in the area to manage the constantly increasing needs for food, clothing, and shelter. Welcome House was the result.

The first two programs developed by Welcome House were Emergency Assistance, designed to take care of food, rent, utilities, medical needs, clothing, and personal hygiene, and the Emergency Shelter. Michelle Budzek and Sister Mary Beth Schwing (now Mary Beth Gregg) were codirectors overseeing the operations of the organization. Welcome House hopes to eradicate homelessness by serving both those without homes and those who lack the means to obtain food and basic necessities.

In 1982 the Emergency Assistance Center opened. It provides meals, cleaning and household supplies, and personal care items to individuals and families with low, limited, or fixed incomes who often do not have the funds to pay rent each month. These clients could be referred to as the "working poor." If potential clients appear to need further assessment, they are interviewed by an intake counselor to determine the need for assistance and plan for a solution. The intake counselors receive an average of 15 calls and 2 or 3 walk-ins per day.

The Welcome House [Emergency] Shelter opened in 1983 at 141 Pike St. in Covington in response to the increasing numbers of homeless women and children. The clients' average stay at the shelter is four weeks. While at the shelter, families are provided with other services to help foster their independence, such as transportation, necessary medications, mental health assistance, and referrals to other resources. Welcome House remains the only shelter exclusively for women and children in the region. Previously, the Benedictine Sisters housed homeless women at 519 Russell St., Covington, and Welcome House worked in cooperation with that group. In 1988 an additional building at 205 Pike St. was renovated to provide more space for the shelter at Welcome House.

Since 1983 Welcome House has continued evolving to meet its goal of eradicating homelessness and breaking the cycle of poverty. In 1986 the Protective Payee Program, led by Sister Cathy Bauer, was implemented to address the problems of persons with chronic mental illness or physical disability. This program is a comprehensive system of financial and budgetary case management services for these individuals. The service helps individuals to manage their own resources better and to live independently, thus eliminating the need for emergency assistance and emergency shelter. In 1991 the Stabilization Program began, and its name was changed to Family Case Management in 1995. Welcome House recognized that providing clients with economic support was not always adequate. Without emotional support, many individuals would be unable to become self-sufficient. Family Case Management provides individual counseling, mentoring, and support, with a goal of leading families toward independence. Often, the case manager advises about housing options and assists in the application process or may suggest alternative housing or referral to other agencies.

Welcome House began employment services in 1997 with a pilot employment program for Social Security recipients. In 1998 the program expanded to include former welfare recipients. Today it serves 300 people each year. Clients often have minimal or inconsistent work histories due to physical and mental disabilities, inexperience, or lack of transportation. This program seeks to break down barriers to employment by providing individualized assessment and coaching, as well as outreach to employers for placement and retention.

Linda Young came to Welcome House as a program coordinator in 1988 and became executive director in 1995. In 1996, in partnership with HUD and the Kentucky Housing Corporation, Welcome House renovated two abandoned apartment buildings at 1116 Greenup St. in Covington; the Gardens at Greenup provides affordable housing and on-site support services for families to assist them with their goal of self-sufficiency. It includes a 20-unit apartment complex in which families may stay for up to six years while progressing toward the goal of financial independence. Eligible clients are families who commit to regular meetings with their case manager, career planning, and a specific plan for self-sufficiency. In 2000 Gardens Center was opened. Located directly across the street from the apartments, it features a licensed day care center, a community meeting room, and a computer lab.

The Homeless Services Project, begun in 2000, serves the needs of homeless men in the Northern Kentucky community by helping clients secure mental health treatment, substance abuse recovery, other benefits such as Social Security, and employment assistance.

Welcome House has grown enormously in the number and quality of services it offers. It now receives United Way funding and government grants, and it stages many fundraising events sponsored by Welcome House volunteers and community friends. Its goal continues to be moving those at risk from a "crisis" lifestyle to stability and, ultimately, economic empowerment. Welcome House retains its connections to its founding churches.

Welcome House of Northern Kentucky. www.welcomehouseky.org (accessed June 1, 2005).

Sarah A. Barlage

WELDON, NETTIE (b. March 3, 1881, Warsaw, Ky.; d. January 18, 1958, Warsaw, Ky.). Nettie Weldon was a practicing registered pharmacist in Warsaw for 26 years during the time when pharmacy was a profession dominated by men. She was the daughter of Richard and Margaret Turpin Weldon and a lifelong resident of Warsaw. In 1928 Benjamin Kirby Bailey employed her in his business, the B. K. Bailey Drug Store. She obtained her pharmaceutical education from Bailey under the "apprentice system" then in place in rural Kentucky. In the minutes of the January 21, 1932, meeting of the Kentucky Board of Pharmacy, it was reported that there were 11 applicants for the licensure exam. Nine of them passed, including Nettie Weldon. At that time Nettie was age 26. Never married, she worked for Bailey as his relief pharmacist until her death in 1958.

Warsaw Independent Newspaper, January 23, 1958, 1.

Judith Butler Jones

WERNWAG, LEWIS (b. December 4, 1769, Alteburg, Württemberg, Germany; d. August 12, 1843, Harper's Ferry, Va. [now W.Va.]). Lewis Wernwag arrived in Philadelphia from his native Germany in 1786. Once in the United States, he turned his talents to building machines and designing bridges. Early in his career, he invented a machine to make whetstones, and in 1809 he laid the keel for the first frigate constructed at the Philadelphia Navy yard. After building two lesser bridges, Wernwag created his masterpiece across the Schuylkill River near Philadelphia in 1812. This wooden structure was a single arch with a span of 340 feet, thought to be at the time the longest in the world. The behemoth became known as the Colossus of Fairmount and made Wernwag famous. He went on to build 29 other bridges; two attributed to him were built in Mason Co., Ky., while he resided briefly in Mayslick. Both of these bridges—one over Lee's Creek and one over the Licking River—were destroyed during the **Civil War**. In about 1826 Wernwag moved to Harper's Ferry, Va., where in 1833 he built his last bridge, a span over the Potomac River for the Baltimore and Ohio Railroad. In 1835, while living in Maysville in a home that he had built, he began construction on the **Mayslick Christian Church**. During that project, he moved to Mayslick again, next door to the church, and today that home is known as the Wernwag House. Wernwag died in 1843 in Harper's Ferry, Va.

Benson, John Lossing. *Harper's Encyclopedia of United States History from 458 A.D. to 1912*. Vol. 10. New York: Harper, 1912.

Laughlin, Walter. "Northern Kentucky Had Covered Bridges, Too!" *NKH* 2, no. 1 (Fall–Winter 1994): 1–18.

Wilson, James Grant, and John Fiske. *Appleton's Cyclopedia of American Biography*. Vol. 6. New York: D. Appleton, 1889.

Who Was Who in America Historical Volume, 1607–1896. Chicago: Marquis, 1963.

Thomas S. Ward

WESLEY CHAPEL METHODIST CHURCH. Wesley Chapel Methodist Episcopal Church is located in southern Campbell Co. along Ky. Rt. 10, a few feet from the Pendleton Co. border. Three roads intersect here, Shaw-Goetz Rd., Wesley Chapel Rd., and the Flagg Springs Turnpike (Ky. Rt. 10). The first church building was a log cabin, built in about 1830, when the congregation was first organized. This log building was covered with clapboards and sat near today's brick church building. The brick church standing today was built in 1856. Its dimensions are 30 by 40 feet, and there are four approximately nine-foot-high windows on each of the long walls, allowing for maximum sunlight inside. The two doors at the front of the church were used, one by men and one by women, according to the custom when the church was new. The inside ceiling is 14 feet high and is covered with pressed tin. The "theater type" wooden seats probably were added after 1900. The exterior walls, 18 inches thick, were built of bricks handmade and fired on-site. Rev. **James M. Jolly**, a Baptist minister and a brick mason, oversaw the construction of the building. The bricks were not fired as hard as today's bricks, a fact that led to a major structural failure many years later. The outside roof is steeply pitched and covered with tin. At the front is a small bell tower, which was originally open to the weather except for its small roof. The bell was installed around 1892. By 1880, there were 198 church members, and Sunday school was conducted regularly. There is a cemetery on three sides of the church that appears to be as old as the building.

Electricity was added sometime in the 1920s or 1930s. During a funeral in the 1950s, the wood floor collapsed under the weight of the casket, and the floor was then replaced with concrete. At the same time, a metal fence and a metal arch in front of the building were added. In this period, there were also many large locust trees growing in front of the building, where picnics were occasionally held.

The congregation declined in number, but the building continued in service until November 1993, when it was damaged by a heavy rain. The rain soaked the soft bricks at the rear of the church (a place where the stucco had broken and partially fallen off) and caused two-thirds of the structure's wall to collapse. This event occurred shortly after church services had ended one day. Because the wall was not a load-bearing wall, the building did not totally collapse. Cora Sabie, a member of the church, asked the Campbell Co. Historical Society for help. A subsequent examination of the damage revealed that the wall could be repaired but that the repairs would be costly and time-consuming. By that time, the United Methodist Church headquarters had already closed the building and wanted it demolished. A group of former church members and the historical society launched a campaign to save it and initiated discussions with leaders of the Methodist Church, who eventually agreed to sell the damaged building for one dollar to the independent board that oversaw the cemetery. Through newspaper appeals, money was raised, and a local brick mason, Ray Seiter, agreed to fix the damaged church wall.

In spring 1994, the repair work on the building was begun. Volunteers did much of the work. A roofer was hired to fix the roof and to build weatherproofing louvers for the bell tower. Donated paint was used to finish the paint job on the outside of the building. The inside was still in disrepair, but the building had been saved. From 1994 until 2003, the building remained in this condition. In 2004 a local couple planned to marry. The bride had attended Wesley Chapel Methodist Church and wanted to be married in the church building. Permission was granted for the couple to use the church for their wedding ceremony, if money could be raised and the inside of the building restored. Another appeal to the public for monetary donations went out, this time to finish the work left undone in 1994.

Money did come in, and work to refurbish the interior of the church was begun. Then it was learned that the bell tower was in such bad shape that the bell had collapsed onto the ceiling beneath the tower. A roofer again was hired to rebuild the bell tower, through the efforts of Marvin Record and Ken Barbian. Two months of volunteer work followed that brought the old church into a new chapter of its existence. Cleaning, painting, and repairs renovated the interior. The couple was married in the newly remodeled church on July 31, 2004, before a capacity crowd. Wesley Chapel now quietly awaits its next service.

Campbell Co. Historical Society. *Campbell County, Kentucky, 200 Years, 1794–1994*. Alexandria, Ky.: The Campbell Co. Historical Society, 1994.

Kenneth A. Reis

WESLEY UNITED METHODIST CHURCH. In preparation for starting a Methodist church in Ludlow, a group of 7 concerned citizens began holding weekly prayer meetings in private homes in September 1853. One month later, Sunday night services were added, and the number of worshippers increased to 12. In his will, Israel Ludlow, the city's founder and namesake, bequeathed lots on which to build both a Methodist and a Christian Church. In 1857 the small Methodist group began construction of a church on their lot, which was on the north side of Oak St. However, work was soon halted owing to lack of funds and fear of the looming **Civil War**. Several years later, the Ludlow Odd Fellows Club completed the building. Exactly how they acquired the title is unclear. However, the club permitted both the Methodist and the First Presbyterian churches to hold services there. The City of Ludlow also used the building as a city hall.

In 1889, after worshipping for 36 years without a church building, the congregation purchased a lot at 319 Oak St., across from the Odd Fellows Hall. There they built the present-day Gothic Revival church. By the mid-1920s, church and Sunday school attendance had increased enough that additional space was needed. In 1927 a two-story addition was constructed to the rear of the church, where two classrooms, a kitchen, an office, and a pastor's study were located. A street-level addition was made to the church in 1952, which contained several Sunday school classrooms, a nursery, and a fellowship hall. Wesley United Methodist Church's centennial celebration was held in the new addition the following year. Members refurbished the sanctuary in early 1979, in preparation for a homecoming celebration held on August 12 of that year. Since the founding of the Ludlow Wesley United Methodist Church, more than 50 pastors have served the congregation. Several of the recent ones have been women.

"Wesley Church Celebrates since 1853," *News Enterprise*, May 31, 1989, 3.
"Wesley United Methodist Church." www.wesleyumc.info (accessed December 14, 2006).
Wesley United Methodist Church Celebrating 150 Years, 1853–2003. Ludlow, Ky.: Wesley United Methodist Church, 2003.

WEST, CARL (b. January 14, 1942, Cincinnati, Ohio). Carleton Lewis West, an accomplished journalist, is the son of John Albert and Dorothy Lewis West. While a student at **Campbell Co. High School**, Carl West was the school's outstanding football player in 1960. As a college student, he had varied short-term work experiences. One of them was working on his family's 300-acre farm in rural Campbell Co., near Grants Lick along the Licking River; he also participated in management of the farm. He earned a BA in journalism from the University of Kentucky in Lexington in 1966.

West became an award-winning journalist in Covington with the *Kentucky Post* under demanding editor **Vance Trimble**, but he is probably best known as the founder of the popular Kentucky Book Fair. Held in Frankfort each fall, the fair draws writers and book enthusiasts from far and wide and raises money for libraries in Kentucky.

Football and farm work cemented the trait of tenacity in West. He was a persistent reporter, unearthing information on pollution in the Licking River and corruption in a federal housing agency and extracting truth from elected officials. During summer 1966 West became a general-assignment reporter for the *Kentucky Post*. He covered Boone Co. politics in 1967 and Newport's changing era in 1968 and became the paper's Frankfort bureau chief in 1969. Moving up again, West became an investigative reporter for the Scripps-Howard News Service, the owner of his newspaper, and was nominated for a Pulitzer Prize for stories on Medicaid-Medicare Fraud; he was nominated a second time for a series on congressional travel abuses. In 1979 he became editor of the *State Journal* in Frankfort. His news-writing peers elected him to the Kentucky Journalism Hall of Fame in April 2003.

"Carl West's FHA Expose: Nominated for Pulitzer Prize," *KP*, January 30, 1969, 1K.
"Honor Reporter and School Man," *KP*, March 4, 1970, 1K.
"Journalism Honor," *KP*, March 5, 2003, A8.

Roger Auge II

WEST, JUDY M. (b. June 9, 1941, Madison Co., Ky.; d. February 19, 1991, Chicago, Ill.) The distinguished Kenton Co. judge Judith Moberly West was one of four children born to Harold and Joyce Clouse Moberly. She was educated in local schools and graduated from Madison Co. High School in Richmond. She then attended the University of Kentucky at Lexington, where she earned her BA in 1962. Later that year, she married attorney Larry C. West, who became a partner in the Kenton Co. law firm of Ware, Bryson, West, and Kummer. The couple had three children. In 1977 Judy received her JD from the **Chase College of Law**, at **Northern Kentucky University**, Highland Heights, graduating in the top 10 percent of her class. In 1980 Kentucky governor John Y. Brown Jr. (1979–1983) appointed Judy West a Kenton Co. district court judge; she was the first woman in Kentucky to hold a district court post, and she was reelected to that position three times. In February 1987, Kentucky governor Martha Layne Collins (1983–1987) appointed West to the Kentucky Court of Appeals, where she became the highest-ranking woman judge in Kentucky history at the time. During her tenure as a judge, she was also a very caring mother and became a child advocate. She helped organize the Hope Cottage Guild and served as its first president. That group was responsible for the establishment of a permanent shelter for abused, neglected, and dependent children.

During Judge West's many years of public service, she was an active member of the Prichard Committee for Academic Excellence in Kentucky and the Kentucky Tomorrow Commission. In 1987 West was named one of Northern Kentucky's Most Outstanding Women. She also won the Prichard Committee award for Academic Excellence and in 1989 was named the Outstanding Alumnus of Northern Kentucky University. In 2002 the Kentucky Women Remembered organization honored West with a watercolor exhibit, which was placed on permanent display in the state capital building at Frankfort.

West died of breast cancer at age 49, in the Bernard Mitchell Hospital at the University of Chicago. A memorial service was held at the Fort Mitchell Baptist Church, Fort Mitchell, and burial was in Forest Lawn Memorial Park in Erlanger.

"Judge Named NKU Outstanding Alumnus," *KP*, January 27, 1989, 3K.
"Judge West Loses Cancer Fight," *KP*, February 20, 1991, 1K.
"Mourners Laud Warmth, Courage of Judge West," *KP*, February 23, 1991, 13K.

David Sorrell

WEST COVINGTON (Economy, Ky.). This West Covington neighborhood has been a part of the City of Covington since 1916. Before that time, West Covington was an independent city. The neighborhood lies along the Ohio River and is bordered by Ludlow to the west, Ridge St. to the east, and **Devou Park** to the south.

In the 1840s the land that is now West Covington was owned by Israel Ludlow, who decided to commission a plat for a small village on the property in 1846. The little community soon came to be known as Economy because of the frugality and industriousness of its residents. In 1858 the commonwealth of Kentucky incorporated the little town under the name West Covington. That same year, the first public school in the area was established (after West Covington was annexed to Covington, this school became known as Eleventh District School). By 1875 the population of West Covington had surpassed 1,000. The community was diverse, having among its residents immigrants from England, Scotland, Ireland, Germany, France, and Italy. This growth of the town resulted in an attempt by Covington to annex it, but the residents of West Covington resisted the efforts of their larger urban neighbor.

Churches played an important role in the lives of the West Covington people. The first congregation organized in the community was St. Ann Catholic Church, which completed a church building on Main St. (now Parkway Ave.) in 1864 and later replaced it by a Gothic Revival structure, dedicated in 1932. For many years the parish sponsored a parochial school, where initially students were taught by the Sisters of St. Francis; the **Sisters of Divine Providence** replaced them in 1891. The St. Ann School closed in 1981. Protestant residents of the community established two congregations. Epworth Methodist, organized in 1877, has a church building on Highway Ave. that was completed in 1953. In 1892 the German Protestants of the town established St. John German Evangelical Protestant Church (later St. John Congregational Church) and in the same year built a frame church in the Gothic style on Highway Ave.

The issue of annexation to Covington became serious in 1916. Many prominent West Covington residents supported the measure, seeing that there were many advantages of annexation: professional fire protection, access to the excellent Covington Public Schools (see **Covington Independent Schools**), lower taxes, and increased property values. In November 1916, West Covington residents voted in favor of annexation, and West Covington ceased to exist as an independent city.

Kenton Co. Public Library. "West Covington." www.kenton.lib.ky.us/genealogy.html.
West Covington Local History File, Kenton Co. Public Library, Covington, Ky.

David E. Schroeder

WEST END (NEWPORT). The West End of Newport, a collection of urban neighborhoods, is bounded by Monmouth St. on the east, the Licking River on the west, the Ohio River on the north, and the **CSX** railroad tracks on the south. Located there were the two major institutions that first defined

Newport: at the confluence of the Licking and Ohio rivers, the **Newport Barracks**, and farther south along the eastern bank of the Licking, the rolling mill owned by several steel companies in succession.

Beginning in the early 19th century, the presence of the military post made Newport's image, like it or not, that of an army town. The U.S. Army's early expansion into the American West of that day (Iowa, Minnesota, and Missouri) was provisioned out of the stores of the barracks. The army relied on river transportation to move troops, equipment, and supplies.

Later, with the arrival of the steel industry to the West End during the mid-19th century, streets lined with the small homes of steelworkers appeared. The steel industry depended upon the railroad as well as the rivers to move raw materials and coal to the mill and to deliver its finished product. The West Side Hotel (the modern-day West Side Café) at 11th and Brighton Sts. was built to accommodate the transient housing needs of those associated with the steel business. The 1930s-era songwriter and bandleader **Tommy Ryan** once labored beside the mill's hot furnaces, as did his father, who put in a 50-year stint at the plant.

The West End was the home of Andrews Field (Wiedemann Park), where the **Wiedemann Brewing Company** baseball team played, where the first night high school football games in Northern Kentucky were staged, and where circus trains unloaded tents and red-nosed clowns for their short stays in town. These special trains borrowed the **Louisville and Nashville Railroad** siding that had been built in the middle of Lowell St. to serve the rolling mill.

In Rough Riders Park, at W. Fifth St. and the Licking River, long before any floodwall got in its way, baseball greats Cy Young and Satchel Page reportedly played in exhibition games. The West End is where the **Green Line** built a car barn for its fleet of **streetcars**, at 11th and Brighton Sts. across from the West Side Hotel. From there it was just a short hop across the adjacent **Shortway Bridge** to Covington.

The two rivers were not always kind to the West End. The **floods of 1884**, **1913**, and **1937** covered the area and motivated the suburbanization that eventually occurred. The floodwalls along the Licking and Ohio rivers are products of the early 1950s, too late to prevent the flight of residents. Simultaneously, **Appalachians** settling in Northern Kentucky found jobs at the mills and inexpensive housing in the West End, adding another brushstroke to the image of its landscape. Some rowdy bars and saloons developed: the Bridge Café, Corky's, Mabel and Q's, and the TC Café. Where the barracks once stood, a federal subsidized housing project, Peter G. Noll Homes, was built and remained for almost 53 years; it was razed in 2006 to be replaced by riverview high-rise condominiums. Father south, entire city blocks have been leveled for industrial uses. It was often said that blight had become common in the West End.

Until the 1980s, the **Newport High School** was located at Eighth and Columbia Sts. **Newport Central Catholic High School** opened at Fifth and Columbia Sts. and later moved to Ninth and Isabella Sts., operating there until the mid-1950s. All these streets lay within Newport's West End. The **Corpus Christi Catholic Church** served the area until roughly 2000, and the **Immaculate Conception Catholic Church** had closed earlier (1969). Several Protestant churches existed in the West End: the **Ninth St. Methodist Episcopal Church**, the **Ninth St. United Methodist Church**, the **Salem United Methodist Church**, the **St. Paul United Church of Christ**, and the York St. Congregational Church; and some are there today: the Church of the Nazarene, the **First Baptist Church**, and the **St. Paul's Episcopal Church**. The Campbell Co. Courthouse has been at Fourth and York Sts. in Newport's West End since the 1880s. The Wiedemann Brewery, Newport's largest employer for a long time, was at Sixth and Columbia Sts. until it closed in 1983. The **Trauth Dairy** survives and prospers at 11th and Monmouth Sts.

Today, the neighborhood association that represents the southern part of the West End as part of the **Newport Citizens Advisory Council** derives its name, Buena Vista, from Gen. **James Taylor Jr.**'s early surveys and subdivision names in this part of Newport. The Buena Vista Neighbor Association district is bounded by Monmouth St. on the east, the Licking River on the west, 12th St. on the south, and Ninth St. on the north. This association, like most of the nine similar neighborhood groups in Newport today, is slowly trying to restore its part of town to its former glory.

Neff, Judy L, and Peggy Wiedemann Harris. *Newport*. Charleston, S.C.: Arcadia, 2004.

"Newport West End May See Growth," *KE*, February 15, 2000, B1.

Purvis, Thomas L., ed. *Newport, Kentucky: A Bicentennial History*. Newport, Ky.: Otto Zimmerman, 1996.

WESTERN BAPTIST THEOLOGICAL INSTITUTE AND SEMINARY SQUARE NATIONAL HISTORIC DISTRICT. The officials and others associated with the Western Baptist Theological Institute played a major role in the early history of Kenton Co. and in the development of the city of Covington. Organizers of this, the "first Baptist seminary west of the Alleghenies," purchased around 350 acres south of the original town of Covington. Afterward, they subdivided and sold lots. Sales of most of the acreage funded development and construction of a special 12-acre seminary campus in Covington, at the highest elevation between Madison Ave. and Russell St. and Robbins and 11th Sts. The campus was elegantly landscaped as a public gathering place and thus helped to encourage surrounding new home construction. However, the seminary held sessions only from 1845 to 1853. Meanwhile, in 1841 Covington annexed into the city all the seminary's properties to 12th St. and, later, the remainder of the theological institute's three subdivisions.

The origins of the Western Baptist Theological Institute in Covington were linked to a meeting of Baptists in Cincinnati in November 1833. There, they formed the Western Baptist Educational Society, which chose a site for a new Baptist seminary "immediately back of the city of Covington." In 1835 this society purchased more than 28 acres from Alfred Sandford, 193 acres that were known as the Fowler farm, and 120 acres of the adjacent Kyle farm. The acreage purchased started at the Licking River and Saratoga St. south of Eighth St., ran west to Banklick St., south to 11th St., west to present-day Holman Ave., south with Holman Ave. to around 15th St., then to approximately 16th St. and Madison Ave., north to Madison Ave., east to Byrd and Garrard Sts., north with Garrard St. to 11th St., and then east to and north along the Licking River.

The seminary project from its inception was subject to an atmosphere of distrust and suspicion. Organizing trustees from the Western Baptist Educational Society included 74 Baptists from Ohio, 18 from Kentucky, 8 from Indiana, 1 from Illinois, and 7 from "the east." The new seminary was founded to serve the needs of students from all the trans-Appalachian states in what was considered the nation's West; the majority of the organizers, moreover, were unfriendly to slavery. So to mitigate and blunt criticism concerning their stance on slavery, the Northerners who were founders had agreed to locate the seminary "on southern soil" in Kentucky.

In 1840 the Kentucky legislature "by special act" incorporated the Western Baptist Theological Institute "exactly one week" after creating a new county, named Kenton, west of the Licking River. The seven trustees appointed at the new seminary were Thatcher Lewis, Samuel W. Lynd, Ephraim Robins, and John Stevens from Ohio; J. L. Holman from Indiana; and Cave Johnson and Henry Wingate from Kentucky.

After renting some of the seminary's lands to farmers, the trustees, under the leadership of Ephraim Robins (1784–1845), decided to sell off excess property. Between 1839 and 1841, they raised $29,000 from these sales, retaining 198 acres plus the 12 acres for the seminary campus. Eventually, the seminary's original property encompassed more than 1,100 lots. The seminary's lots extended on both sides of the old Banklick Rd., leading into a narrow block at 15th St., and were centered at 10th and 11th Sts. from a line west of the Licking River to a line just short of **Willow Run** Creek. The 1851 city map of Covington shows subdivisions located on land sold off by the seminary filling out virtually all the space north of 14th St. as well as the space north of 15th St., except for a large block on the southeast corner belonging to O. R. Powell and a southwest corner marked "Cemetery," where Linden Grove Cemetery had been dedicated and opened in 1843. At the Licking River this map shows the Milward and Oldershaw Slaughter House between Robbins and 11th Sts., the Licking Rolling Mill between 11th and 12th Sts., and a sawmill and another slaughterhouse south of 12th St.

Philip S. Bush (ca. 1795–1871), a speculator in commercial and residential lots, and his partner, Humphrey Watkins, had sold the land used for the

Milward and Oldershaw Slaughter House and with his son John S. Bush had helped finance the Licking Rolling Mill. Bush St., named for the Bush family, was dedicated through the middle of seminary subdivision lands, running from the Licking Rolling Mill almost to Willow Run Creek. Bush's brother-in-law Cave Johnson was a seminary trustee.

Subdivisions from the Licking River to Willow Run Creek bearing the name of Humphrey C. Watkins (1797–1849) appear on maps. A Virginia native, Watkins moved from Cincinnati to Covington in 1839 to help with the seminary projects. A brick maker and supplier, he became an agent for the new Linden Grove Cemetery; Watkins St. was dedicated nearby. Both Watkins and Philip S. Bush were prominent members of Baptist churches in Covington.

Other seminary officials for whom Covington streets were named include J. L. Holman (Holman St.), Samuel W. Lynd (Lynn St.), and Robins (Robbins St.). Robins, an insurance company agent from Suffield, Conn., had proposed the fund-raising strategy to finance the seminary. Superintendent Robins oversaw development of the Linden Grove Cemetery and the 12-acre landscaped square on which the seminary complex was built. By 1843 about 150 other buildings already stood near the seminary's new campus.

Alfred Sandford, son of an early Kentucky congressman, earlier had built the Sandford House on the campus grounds. Sitting back prominently from the east-side curb of Russell St., it was the palatial mansion that became the seminary president's house. That structure and the "Professor's" house, on the southwest side of the campus along 11th St., are still standing. The Western Baptist Theological Institute constructed a large main building at east 11th St. and Madison Ave. that had classrooms on the first floor and dormitories above.

Seeking to create both a department of theology and a good classical school, the seminary in 1844 chose three highly qualified men for its beginning faculty: Rev. R. E. Pattison, DD, from Massachusetts, as president and professor of Christian theology; Rev. Asa Drury as professor of Greek; and Ebenezer Dodge as professor of Hebrew and of ecclesiastical history. Soon, however, resentment to Pattison festered, because he was friendly to abolitionism, as were the majority of the institution's trustees. This group represented the views of many of the Northerners who had primarily organized and funded the seminary project. In 1844, at a state convention of Baptists in Alabama, delegates passed resolutions stating that Baptist slaveholders should have equal privileges with other Baptists. In response, the Baptist Foreign Mission Society, of which Pattison was a member, considered a resolution to ban unreformed slaveholders from missionary work. Pattison was also suspected of authoring articles for the Baptist Publication and Sunday School Society arguing that church officials should not tolerate slavery.

In 1845 proslavery Baptist delegates from Southern states rallied at Augusta, Ga., where they split from Baptists in Northern states to form the Southern Baptist Convention. When the general (Northern) Baptist board met in Providence, R.I., they also recommended separate Northern and Southern associations. Soon thereafter, at a meeting in Georgetown, Ky., an association of Kentucky Baptists passed a resolution recommending against further support of the seminary in Covington, given the current conditions there. In response, Dr. Pattison was discharged and replaced by Dr. Samuel W. Lynd. Some of their concerns, at least for the moment, satisfied by Pattison's dismissal, the Association of Kentucky Baptists in 1848 voted approval of Lynd, who took office January 1, 1849.

Ultimately, what determined the seminary's fate was a resolution introduced more than a year earlier by a seminary trustee, proclaiming that slavery was "divinely instituted." The resolution received only four votes from the board, whose members now numbered at least 14. Apparently without the knowledge of the antislavery Northerners, advocates who supported slavery then persuaded the Kentucky legislature again to expand the seminary's board of trustees effective January 28, 1848, and to name the 16 new members. All of the new appointees had to be Kentucky citizens. In March, however, the old board of trustees refused to recognize the new one and refused to turn over the seminary's record books. A Kentucky lower-court judgment favored the newly appointed trustees. In 1854 the Kentucky Circuit Court reversed this ruling in favor of the old board. As this bickering continued, financial support for the seminary decreased. In 1855 the decision was made to divide and dispose of the Western Baptist Theological Institute's assets.

In 1853 the 12-acre campus was already changing dramatically as the **Covington and Lexington Railroad** laid tracks through its middle. In 1868 the Diocese of Covington (see **Roman Catholics**), which had purchased the old classroom-dormitory building, remodeled the building and dedicated it for use by the St. Elizabeth Hospital (see **St. Elizabeth Medical Center**). The hospital moved in 1914, and the old classroom-dormitory building on the seminary's campus was torn down in 1916.

Lynd, after serving at the seminary in Covington, joined the Baptists in Georgetown, Ky. The seminary divided and then sold its remaining assets to the Baptist Educational Society at Georgetown, Ky., and to Northern Baptists at the Fairmont Theological Seminary of Ohio. By 1856 Rev. Asa M. Drury was serving as president of the board of examiners and superintendent of schools in Covington (**Covington Independent Schools**). By 1860 he had become principal of the Covington High School. The moral issue of slavery at the Western Baptist Theological Institute tolerated no compromise. It previewed Kentucky's divided status in the **Civil War** as a border state. Kentucky supported the Union, but afterward some of its most influential citizens and leaders aligned themselves with the South.

In 1980 part of the area once owned by the Western Baptist Theological Institute was listed on the National Register of Historic Places as the Seminary Square Historic District. The district covers about 18 acres and is bounded on the north by Ninth St., on the south by 12th St., on the west by the rear property lines along Banklick St., and on the east by railroad tracks.

Map of the City of Covington. Covington, Ky.: Rickey, Kennedy, and Clark, 1851. From actual survey, ca. 1842.

Ware, Orie S. "The Western Baptist Theological Institute." *Papers of the Christopher Gist Historical Society*, vol. 1, presented November 22, 1949.

Weldon, Alexandra. "Historical Connections and Ideological Divisions," *Bulletin, Kenton County Historical Society*, October 2001.

John Boh

WEST SIDE (COVINGTON). An estate owned by James Riddle in 1810 first defined the boundaries of the West Side of Covington. His property extended from Craig St. to Willow Run Creek and from the Ohio River beyond Riddle St. (now Ninth St.) to the **Covington and Lexington Turnpike** (now Pike St.). Riddle also operated a licensed ferry (see **Ferries**) on the Ohio River at the foot of Ferry St. (now Main St.) that competed with the older ferry in Covington in the business of transporting hogs and other farm products to Cincinnati markets. By 1827, however, the Bank of the United States had foreclosed on a mortgage it held on Riddle's 580 acres in Covington. The bank subdivided the lands and began naming streets in Covington; it called one Philadelphia St., after the location of the bank's headquarters. Cincinnati civil engineer A. W. Gilbert recalled that in about 1830 his father had rented 25 acres and Riddle's mansion on the West Side of Covington, possibly the antebellum residence still standing on Emma St.

Thomas W. Bakewell (see **Bakewell Family**) and William S. Johnston acquired riverfront lots and the ferry's license from the Bank of the United States. Bakewell, a brother-in-law of famed naturalist John J. Audubon and an inventor of industrial equipment, during the 1830s built a mechanized hemp bagging factory that made wrappings for shipping cotton bales. After the national depression of 1837, Bakewell had to sell or assign his ownership in his property on Covington's West Side and in the bagging factory.

In the early 1840s, James G. Arnold, a wealthy businessman, owned a mansion at the western end of Seventh St. (demolished in the 1970s). An early schoolteacher and county and city official, Arnold built the Park Hotel at Sixth and Philadelphia Sts. in West Side Covington (now restored as a law firm's offices). After his death, his homestead was subdivided into what became Dalton St. The Englishman **William Bullock**, owner of **Elmwood Hall** in Ludlow, held acreage in the West Side extending across Willow Run Creek. At the time, many gentlemen of means liked to retreat to residences in Kentucky to escape what was termed "the grime of Cincinnati." They could also invest in their own pristine West Side projects. The wave of German and Irish immigrants that settled in Covington's West Side during the 1840s also helped stimulate growth.

In 1849 Covington industrialist Alexander L. Greer recorded a plat that marked new lots in the West Side along Willard, Main, Eighth, and Seventh Sts. Greer, who was a central figure with the **Covington and Lexington Railroad**, and his partners also built the **Covington Locomotive and Manufacturing Works**, a huge complex at Third and Philadelphia Sts. After Greer's death, his homestead addition was subdivided in 1888 into lots on Greer, Craig, Willard, Eighth, Pike, and W. Ninth Sts.

In 1873 John Mitchell, James Tranter, and associates purchased the old bagging-mill property near the mouth of Willow Run Creek and transformed it into the Mitchell and Tranter Rolling Mill. Around 1900, Republic Iron and Steel, a national trust, acquired the mill. Complaining of inadequate facilities, in 1907 the trust sold the property, ending production in what had come to be known as the mill neighborhood. In 1914 the **Houston, Stanwood & Gamble Company** purchased property at the Mitchell and Tranter Rolling Mill site, where they manufactured steam engines and boilers for heating buildings and commercial laundries and for powering southern and Caribbean mills.

In 1876 a sawmill at Second and Main Sts. in Covington's West Side sold lumber, "farm and well" pumps, and tubing regionally. In the same year Creen, Culbertson, and Company, a sawmill located in the West Side at the foot of Main St., sold dressed lumber, flooring, laths, and shingles. It ceased operations by 1910, but the newer Vogg Planing Mill nearby was in business until about 1920. Throughout the 1800s, supply and repair services for steamboats and other needs in the river trade provided business opportunities and jobs for the residents of the West Side. Some of the businesses that prospered during the steamboat era were machine shops, foundries, and several other small specialty shops catering to the needs of the steamboat business.

By the 1870s, an old burial ground at Craig and Sixth Sts. in Covington's West Side memorializing the city's pioneer days was overrun and obsolete. Covington decided that removing the remains would allow space for a new railroad right-of-way to Cincinnati and enable Sixth St. to be made into a through street. The railroad track was routed diagonally across Johnston, Sixth, Bakewell, and Main Sts., at street level, so that crowded trains would not impede street and sidewalk traffic. Also, some of the local mills in town sought to add spurs and railroad switches for direct access to rail services. In 1888 the **Chesapeake and Ohio Railroad** and its associates committed to constructing a railroad toll bridge that, for a nominal fee, would be open to pedestrian use. Longtime complaints about the monopolistic toll rates on the **John A. Roebling Bridge** had resulted in lobbying for a "free bridge." The railroad bridge, which because of its nominal toll was virtually a free bridge, later also provided commuters from Covington's West Side with a direct route to their jobs in Cincinnati. The bridge, and the elevated approaches leading to it, further separated the West Side from Covington's main commercial district, fortifying the identity of the West Side.

In 1892 Willow Run Creek, a tributary of the Ohio River, flowed through a western valley of the neighborhood. Until the completion of **flood control** projects following the **flood of 1937**, the creek valley was subject to backwaters during flooding. It was therefore not suited for housing and instead was utilized for ballparks and as a junkyard. The construction of I-75 (see **Expressways**) replaced the Willow Run, leaving only a small section as a ballpark.

Second only to Madison Ave. in commerce, Main St. in Covington's West Side has always seen intense business activity. Immigration during the 19th century filled up the city's West Side, bringing European architecture, shops, and crafts. Houses sat on narrow lots, and high population density made walking a convenience. The neighborhood was also served by inexpensive **streetcar** service. Workers on the West Side commuted to manufacturing jobs in Northern Kentucky and Cincinnati. Children walked to school, returned home for lunch, then walked back to school. Housewives walked to butcher shops and bakeries around the corner. Iceboxes provided limited shelf life, but the ice wagon came daily to fill orders specified on a card placed in a window. Conveniences included chilled milk and the morning newspaper at the doorstep before dawn; meat wagons; men on routes to sharpen knives and scissors; and a junkman to take away old rags and other discarded items. There was a market house located on Sixth St. in the West Side until its property was converted into a city park after 1907. Local vendors, on what remained of Sixth St., continued thereafter to host weekly sales of seasonal fruits and vegetables, which women from the neighborhood bought in large quantities to can. Since the late 1950s, the John R. Green Company has sold school supplies in its mammoth headquarters on W. Sixth St., opposite the park.

The German and Irish immigrants of the West Side supported a host of saloons, stores, and institutions. In 1876 the Covington City Directory listed some 120 saloons in the area. Until Prohibition, they were popular hangouts for men, with entrances for women located at the rear of the buildings. As an enticement to customers, local saloons frequently offered free food along with purchases of beer. Citizens also gathered in the saloons to play cards and to place illegal bets on horse races. At Prohibition, some of the saloons shifted to become soda fountain operations selling soft drinks and candy. Seven confectionaries operated on Main St. in 1920–1921, extending from the 200 to the 800 block. After Prohibition, the saloons that reopened were referred to as bars, restaurants, or cafés. Eleven restaurants, lunchrooms, and cafés operated in 1956 in the 100 through the 900 blocks of Main St. Saloons, and later cafés in the area, hosted informal social clubs where members could gather to pass the time. Trade unions and insurance and building and loan associations (see **Savings and Loan Associations**) met on the second floors of commercial buildings. The West End Odd Fellows Hall (see **Independent Order of Odd Fellows**) still stands at 731 Main St. Two other prominent social organizations, the West End Mutual Aid and the West End Welfare Association, occupied buildings in the West Side in 1923. West Side German culture became a victim of the **anti-German hysteria** of **World War I**. For instance, Bremen St. in the West Side, a quaint narrow street with buildings crowding the sidewalks, was renamed Pershing St. The Turners Club, which before World War I had the German name Turnverein, on Pike St. in the West Side remains open as an athletic and social facility, a product of the German culture's emphasis on intellectual and physical health.

The West Side of Covington was substantially Catholic and once included the German **St. Aloysius Catholic Church**, which burned in 1985, and the Irish **St. Patrick Catholic Church**, which was demolished for urban renewal. The German Reformed Church, changed to "Grace" in 1918 (see **Grace United Church of Christ**), was a major Protestant congregation. The Main St. Methodist Church, almost equal in architectural scale to the Catholic churches in Covington's West Side, is also closed.

In the 1960s, urban renewal took its toll on the West Side. Motels, gasoline stations, and other similar commercial ventures replaced residences and the former Heidelberg Brewery plant at Fourth and Philadelphia Sts. North of Sixth St. everything became commercial. In the 1970s, **Main Strasse** was created to revitalize the historical West Side. Goebel Park's **Carroll Chimes** Tower in Main Strasse is now a Covington West Side landmark.

Boh, John H., and Howard W. Boehmker. *Westside Covington*. Cincinnati: Cincinnati Historical Society, 1980.

Geaslen, Chester F. *Strolling along Memory Lane*. Newport, Ky.: Otto, 1971–1974.

Reis, Jim. "Tracing the Roots of Willow Run," *KP*, March 11, 1991, 4K.

Smith, Allen Webb. *Beginning at "the Point": A Documented History of Northern Kentucky and Environs, the Town of Covington in Particular, 1751–1834*. Park Hills, Ky.: Self-published, 1977.

Tenkotte, Paul A. "Rival Cities to Suburbs: Covington and Newport, Kentucky, 1790–1890," PhD diss., Univ. of Cincinnati, 1989.

John Boh

WFBE-AM. Radio station WFBE began operations at Seymour, Ind., but in October 1926 was sold and a radio broadcasting license was issued to the Park View Hotel in Cincinnati. Although located in Cincinnati, the station was important to Northern Kentuckians because of the remote broadcasting conducted from Covington in 1928.

Northern Kentucky was without a radio station at this time; in 1928 there were only three radio stations in Kentucky, WHAS and WLAP at Louisville and WFIW at Hopkinsville. Radio was becoming extremely popular and had been proven to encourage growth and revenue in areas supported by a station. It was also well known that local stations promoted sales of radio apparatuses. Through the efforts of the owners of the Edward P.

Cooper radio and electric shop in Covington and the management of station WFBE, the first remote-control radio studio in Northern Kentucky was designed and constructed with the latest equipment. The first broadcast was scheduled for Thursday, March 29, 1928, at 8:30 p.m. The mayor of Covington, **Thomas F. Donnelly**, delivered the opening address, announcing that "Covington should be proud of the fact that it has its own radio station and that all events of interest in the city and Northern Kentucky would be broadcast." Edward Cooper announced the upcoming schedule for the station, and then the station presented musical selections by a local band, the Latonia Night Hawks, and an hour of popular dance music by the Earl Fuller orchestra of New York. In the months that followed, many entertainers visiting the nightspots of Northern Kentucky were heard during daytime and evening broadcasts over the station. Cooper later reported that he had received hundreds of letters from the entire Northern Kentucky area in support of the station and its broadcasts. WFBE's remote broadcasts were heard for well over a year, until Covington finally became the hometown of a new radio station, **L. B. Wilson**'s WCKY, in September 1929. During the 1930s WFBE was sold to Scripps Howard, and it became station WCPO.

"Mayor Heard over Mike at New Studio," *KTS*, March 30, 1928, 2.

Nash, Francis M. *Towers over Kentucky*. Lexington, Ky.: Host Communications, 1995.

"Radio Studio to Be Opened in Covington," *KTS*, March 28, 1928, 2.

John E. Leming Jr.

WFTM. Shortly before **World War II**, two enterprising tobacco warehousemen, Charles P. Clarke and James M. Finch, began building a radio station at Maysville. Before the station could be completed, the war broke out, and construction was put on hold. After the war, Clarke and Finch applied for a broadcasting license; with help from friends in Washington, D.C., a license was granted on September 10, 1947. The original call letters assigned to the radio station were WKYO, and it operated at 1240 on the AM radio dial.

The broadcasting studios were planned for construction in front of the Standard Tobacco Warehouse in Maysville, and the equipment and towers were purchased. The first station manager, William Betts, who had been selected during the war years, brought several years of personal broadcasting experience to the station. The station was to be placed on the air at 12:01 a.m., January 1, 1948. Shortly before the station's debut, Finch discovered that a broadcasting license had been granted to a police station at Buffalo, N.Y., using the call letters WFTM. He thought those call letters would best fit his and Clarke's station because they would stand for "Worlds Finest Tobacco Market," so he struck a deal with the station owner in New York for a switch of call letters, which was approved by the FCC (Federal Communications Commission), and the new station in Maysville officially became WFTM.

At 12:01 a.m. on January 1, 1948, WFTM came on the air. One of the first musical selections played was "Smoke, Smoke, Smoke that Cigarette," written by Kentuckian Merle Travis. Program director Gene Waters, formerly of radio station WSAU in Bloomington, Ind., and chief announcer Hal Sargraves, formerly from station WPAY in Portsmouth, Ohio, kicked off programming, staying on the air for the first 24 hours.

WFTM was an immediate hit with local and more distant listeners, and its first successful program, *True to the Farm*, dedicated information and agricultural reports to a heavily populated farming community. Col. J. Scott True, who created the program, received national recognition for it. After his death, the show was taken over by Bill Stewart; Stewart won the Kentucky Farm Bureau's award of top broadcaster in 1977. Broadcast regularly from its inception, *True to the Farm* was aired for the 10,000th time in 1980.

Over the years, many well-known local broadcasters have been heard over the airwaves of WFTM, including Bud Boyd, **Nick Clooney**, and Walt Maher. In 1965 WFTM added WFTM-FM, located at 95.9 on the radio dial. Today, WFTM-AM and WFTM-FM broadcast to more than 369,000 homes in the Ohio River Valley, with north-south coverage ranging from Hillsboro, Ohio, to Morehead, Ky., and east-west coverage from Williamstown, Ky., to Portsmouth, Ohio.

"To Have Broadcasting Station Here," *Maysville (Ky.) Public Ledger*, September 10, 1947, 1.

"WFTM Will Go on Air Officially at 12:01 AM.," *Maysville (Ky.) Public Ledger*, December 31, 1947, 1.

John E. Leming Jr.

WHALLEN, JOHN H. (b. May 1850, New Orleans, La.; d. December 3, 1913, Louisville, Ky.). John Henry Whallen, an Irish Catholic entrepreneur and a Democratic Party boss, was the son of immigrants Patrick and Bridget Burke Whallen. When John was a young boy, the family moved from New Orleans to Maysville, Ky., and later to Newport. By the time Whallen was 11 years old, the family was living at Grants Lick, where he came into contact with some Confederate Army recruiters. He persuaded the recruiters to allow him to enlist even though he was so young, and he thus became one of the youngest soldiers ever to serve in the Confederate Army. He was assigned to the Kentucky 4th Cavalry, the same unit in which **Absolom Columbus Dicken**, **William Francis Corbin**, and Squire Grant (see **Grant Family**), also from southern Campbell Co., served. Whallen was a gunpowder carrier and later a courier for Gen. **John Hunt Morgan**. Gen. Basil Duke and Capt. Bart Jenkins described Whallen as one of their best soldiers. Whallen served for about three years, mostly in Virginia. For his military service, the Daughters of the Confederacy presented him with their highest award, the Cross of Honor. State officials in Kentucky also honored him by making him a Kentucky Colonel, and thereafter he was affectionately known as Colonel Johnny. At the end of the **Civil War**, Whallen moved to Saratoga and Williamson (now 11th) Sts. in Newport, where he worked as a horsecar driver and as a lieutenant with the Newport Police Department. He also began operating a bar on what later became Liberty St.

In 1880 John Whallen and his younger brother James opened a vaudeville showplace, the Buckingham Theater, in Louisville. The brothers soon learned that family-type businesses did not return sufficient profit, so they switched to the bigger and bawdier type of burlesque shows. As their business grew, they expanded their holdings by purchasing the Empire and Casino Theaters in Brooklyn, N.Y., and began operating a chain of burlesque theaters.

To protect his somewhat unsavory businesses, Whallen resorted to boss rule. He contributed to the emerging labor unions, paid off key officials, gave police free admission to his clubs, and set up assistance programs to help needy families. Many accused him of subverting the election process by paying people to vote and engaging in other ballot-box irregularities. In addition, he is said to have handpicked most of the Democratic candidates running for public office in Louisville. He also controlled the awarding of more than 1,200 city patronage jobs. Whallen felt that these moves would help protect his businesses from governmental controls and periodic protests by citizens groups. Although never elected to public office, Whallen virtually ran the City of Louisville from his Green Room at the Buckingham Theater. He became immensely popular, especially among Irish and German Catholics, blue-collar workers, and immigrants. In 1905, confronted with considerable evidence of wrongdoing, the Kentucky Court of Appeals removed from office all recently elected officials and appointed newspaper publisher Robert Bingham the temporary mayor. Thus ended more than 30 years of Whallen's boss rule, and Louisville politics eventually returned to some semblance of normalcy.

Whallen was married three times. His first wife was Marian Hickey, by whom he had three children, Ella, Nora, and Orrie. His second wife, Sarah Jane Whallen, was childless. His third wife, Grace Edwards Goodrich, had a daughter, Grace, whom Whallen adopted. Whallen died at age 63 in his Spring Bank Park home in Louisville. His funeral service was attended by numerous friends and politicians, including Kentucky governor James B. McCreary (1875–1879, 1911–1915). Whallen was buried in a mausoleum at the St. Louis Catholic Cemetery in Louisville. After John Whallen's death, his brother James attempted to continue running their empire but lacked his brother's charisma and political acumen. The land on which John Whallen's home and estate were located later became the site of Chickasaw Park.

EarthSciences.com. "Colonel Johnny, the Duke of Buckingham." www.earthsciences.com (accessed March 3, 2007).

Gray, Karen R., and Sarah R. Yates. "Boss John Whallen: The Early Louisville Years (1876–1883)," *JKS* 1 (July 1984): 171–86.

Kentucky Death Certificate No. 6570 (James P. Whallen), for the year 1930.

Kentucky Death Certificate No. 32298 (John H. Whallen), for the year 1913.
Military Shoulder Patches of the U.S. "John H. Whallen." http://ranger95.com (accessed March 3, 2007).

Jack Wessling

WHEATLEY (DALLASBURG). This Owen Co. hamlet along Ky. Rt. 227, 8.5 miles north of Owenton, is located within what is known as the Dallasburg Precinct. Dallasburg (the town's name at first) emerged in 1825, shortly after the county was formed. The church there, the Dallasburg Baptist Church, derived its name from the town's original name, not the reverse as has long been thought. The town was incorporated in 1850–1851. The name of the town's post office was Dallasburg from 1850 to 1863; then in 1886 the post office was reestablished as Wheatley, honoring Rev. Wesley Wheatley, the postmaster and a highly respected citizen of the community. The center of community life is the Dallasburg Baptist Church, which has long supported Baptist missionary work both in the state and abroad. Since its establishment in 1851, this church has been home to several multiday series of revival meetings. The village has had several grocery stores over the years, along with a bank, formed in 1899. From 1912 to 1951, it had a high school. Perhaps the most famous person who came from Wheatley was Rev. W. B. Riley, later of Minneapolis, Minn., a Baptist minister who was nationally known during the first third of the 20th century. Wheatley has often been called the garden spot of the county.

Houchens, Miriam Sidebottom. *History of Owen County, Kentucky: "Sweet Owen."* Louisville, Ky.: Standard, 1976.
"Kentucky-Owenton," *CE*, March 22, 1899, 8.
Rennick, Robert M. *Kentucky Place Names*. Lexington: Univ. Press of Kentucky, 1984.

WHIG PARTY. The Whig Party had considerable support in Northern Kentucky since Henry Clay, its principal leader, was a Kentuckian. The 1824 presidential election and the agenda of John Quincy Adams (1825–1829), the new president, created new lines of demarcation in American politics. The Whig Party that Adams headed had grown out of a factious conflict between "radical," or "Old," Republicans and the party's "Madisonian nationalists," represented by politicians such as Henry Clay and President Adams. The former group held disdain for the aggressive economic programs sponsored by the latter. The tariffs implemented by the nationalists to protect American industrial development hurt many southern states' economies; internal investments contributed to the expansion of the federal government, to the dismay of state's-rights advocates. Many southerners also saw the Adams administration as antislavery.

Adams and Clay, joined by former Federalist Daniel Webster of Massachusetts, represented the National Republican opposition party to the victorious Jackson Democrats after 1828. Henry Clay, titular head of the National Republican Party, developed the American System platform, highlighted by federally sponsored economic development programs, as a response to Jackson and the Democrats' laissez-faire economic approach. These ideas later became the philosophical basis for the Whigs.

Clay ran against Jackson for president in 1832 but did poorly in slave states, receiving only 37 percent of the national popular vote. The National Republicans disbanded as Clay and other anti-Jacksonians formed the new Whig Party in 1833. The formation of the Whig Party signaled the arrival of the second American party system: the Whigs and the Democrats.

Henry Clay was the Whigs' most powerful leader. Known as a great orator, Clay was also labeled "The Great Compromiser." The Whigs' two main southern strongholds were Kentucky and North Carolina. Because of the impact of Clay's leadership, the Kentucky branch of the party enjoyed particular success, causing the state to be termed the "Cradle of Whiggery."

By the late 1830s, Kentucky Whigs controlled their state's legislature and governorship. Part of this party strength had been built upon victories beginning in 1832 when **James T. Morehead** (1797–1854) was elected lieutenant governor and **Lewis Sanders** (1781–1861) was elected secretary of state. Morehead, who later practiced law in Covington, had a distinguished political career, becoming Kentucky's governor in 1834 and representing the state in the U.S. Senate as a Whig from 1841 to 1847. Sanders, of Carroll Co., served as U.S. district attorney from 1834 to 1838, following his term as secretary of state.

The Whig legislative agenda included organizing the **Bank of Kentucky** and the **Northern Bank of Kentucky** to stimulate economic development, investing in turnpikes and navigation projects on the state's rivers to improve transportation and communication, and increasing taxes to fund these projects. These efforts were appreciated so much by Kentucky voters that Whigs received a greater legislative majority in 1840 than in 1837.

The Whig Party had a mass appeal in Kentucky that was stoked by many of the state's newspapers. Local voices such as Covington's *Licking Valley Register*, the Covington *Journal*, and the *Maysville Eagle* informed the public of every minutia of party life. Thomas B. Stevenson, a Northern Kentucky native, edited the primary Whig organ in Cincinnati. These papers were an important aspect of politics for both Whigs and Democrats.

Although the Whig Party was known nationally as the party of the elite, in Kentucky it found its strength among wealthy slaveholders in the Bluegrass region, in cities such as Louisville and Covington, and among nonslaveholders in the "poor farming communities along the Ohio River." This alliance was held together by Whigs' successes in delivering their platform of internal improvements in the state, by the stature of several Whig leaders such as Clay and Stevenson, and by the perception of many people that the Whig Party was the party of opportunity. Whigs supported an active, interventionist approach, especially toward economic development. As long as these differences were highlighted, the Whigs did well, winning state elections from the mid-1830s into the late 1840s. Beginning in the mid-1840s, however, Whig electoral victories became more challenging; and the party found itself facing more internal divisions and being outflanked by the Democrats and political splinter groups with more extreme views.

Whig problems in Kentucky became evident in the state's 1849 party and constitutional conventions. The failure of the Whigs to take a firm position on the issue of slavery, instead calling for "popular sovereignty," motivated many emancipationists to leave the party. As the slavery issue grew more intense, more Kentucky Whigs began to leave the party, many joining the Democrats, who were seen not only as being more supportive of southern issues, but also more likely to find compromise on the national level and preserve the Union. Nevertheless, Whigs in Northern Kentucky still did well at the polls. In 1849 Whig state senator J. Russell Hawkins represented the 25th District (Boone, Carroll, and Gallatin counties), William K. Wall the 29th District (Bracken Co.), and John F. McMillan the 36th (Mason Co.). In the House, however, Northern Kentucky representation was split. The counties of Boone and Bracken were represented by Whigs Gabriel J. Gaines and **Joseph Doniphan**, but Mason Co. was split, with one representative being Whig J. McCarthey. Campbell, Carroll, Gallatin, Grant, Kenton, Owen, and Pendleton counties each had one Democratic representative.

Whigs were forewarned regarding their popularity in the state in 1850 when the new constitution was placed before voters and was approved overwhelmingly. The new constitution called for almost all of the state's elected offices to be on the ballot in the election of 1851: the governor and the cabinet, all seats in the House and the Senate, one U.S. Senate seat, and the entire congressional delegation (10 in all). The turnout in the 1851 election (71%) was lower than that of 1848 (87%), owing both to the new constitution's reduction in the number of days to vote (from three to one) and to a residency requirement. In addition, with the constitution adopted, little difference appeared to remain between Democrats and Whigs. Although nativist sentiment had begun to be felt in Kentucky, Whigs at first distanced themselves from this element of the electorate. Democrats won the governorship by less than 1,000 votes, while Whigs won all other statewide offices, kept majorities in the State House and the Senate, and gained half of the congressional delegation.

With the inability of the Whigs to elect Gen. Winfield Scott to the presidency in 1852, and the deaths of both Clay and Webster, the party's national standing ended. Although Whig candidates continued to be elected to the U.S. Congress until 1856, Kentucky was one of the few states where Whigs remained a viable political force.

In the 1853 election, Kentucky Whigs retained a majority in the state legislature and again split the congressional delegation. Kentucky Whigs and Democrats remained at a virtual political stalemate, but events were soon to overcome both. On the horizon was a growing nativist movement, and underlying all other political issues was the question of slavery.

Antiforeign sentiment had been seen in Kentucky politics as early as 1847. By summer 1854, however, secret fraternal lodges associated with the growing nativist movement in America were forming in the state's larger cities. To the political confusion were added temperance supporters, who were speaking of running a candidate for governor (among those mentioned was Norvin Green of Carrollton). Defectors from their parties to the temperance ranks hurt both Democrats and Whigs, but in particular Whigs seemed to provide the majority memberships of both the nativists and the temperance movement.

After the local election successes of the nativist Know-Nothing movement nationally and throughout Kentucky in late 1854 and early 1855, Whig leaders reluctantly acknowledged the death of the Whig Party and attempted to maintain a political presence by taking over the **Know-Nothing Party** machinery. Some benefit was gained by this strategy, as 26 former Whigs were elected in slave states to the national legislature in 1855.

Switching party allegiance to survive politically was common in the 1850s. **John W. Menzies**'s political history illustrates the phenomenon. Named as clerk to the Council in Covington in 1848, Menzies was a Whig; however, by 1855 he had become a member of the Know-Nothings and was elected that year to the Kentucky legislature representing Kenton Co.

Cole, Arthur Charles. *The Whig Party in the South.* Reprint. Gloucester, Mass.: Peter Smith, 1962.
"Complete List of Senators," *CJ*, September 29, 1849, 1.
Holt, Michael F. *The Rise and Fall of the American Whig Party: Jacksonian Politics and the Onset of the Civil War.* New York: Oxford Univ. Press, 1999.
Howe, Daniel Walker, ed. *The American Whigs: An Anthology.* New York: John Wiley, 1973.
Poage, George Rawlings. *Henry Clay and the Whig Party.* Reprint. Gloucester, Mass.: Peter Smith, 1965.
"The Popular Vote," *CJ*, August 11, 1855, 2.
"Representatives Elected," *CJ*, September 28, 1849, 1.
Volz, Harry August. "Party, State, and Nation: Kentucky and the Coming of the American Civil War," PhD diss., Univ. of Virginia, 1982.

J. T. Spence

WHITE, CLARENCE CAMERON (b. August 10, 1880, Clarksville, Tenn.; d. June 30, 1960, New York City). Clarence White, the son of James W. and Jennie Scott White, was a world-renowned African American opera composer and director. White studied at Howard University in Washington, D.C., and at the Oberlin Conservatory of Music (Oberlin, Ohio) and later spent the years 1908–1911 in London, England, with the black British composer and conductor Samuel Coleridge-Taylor. White also traveled to Paris, France. He began his teaching career in the public schools of Washington, D.C., and then served as director of music at West Virginia State College at Institute, W.Va. In 1937 he was named a music specialist for the National Recreation Association, established by President Franklin Roosevelt (1933–1945) under the Works Progress Administration. The association offered aid in organizing community arts programs.

In November 1938 White visited Covington to head a music institute for African Americans in Northern Kentucky. During the mornings, he conducted several institutes on music at Covington's **Lincoln-Grant School**. The purpose of the institute was to advance the musical interests of the community and to develop choral and instrumental group participation. Mrs. Sadye L. Dunham, director of the Negro Youth Recreation Association of Northern Kentucky, was instrumental in bringing White to the community. To keep the community involved, training sessions were held nightly at the **First Baptist Church** and the Ninth St. Baptist Church. The training period resulted in a public concert in which African American spirituals were featured. In 1960, after a long and successful career in the opera composition, White died at the Sydenham Hospital in New York City. His most acclaimed composition was his 1932 opera *Ouanga*, which was first performed that year by the American Opera Society of Chicago.

"Clarence White, Composer, Was 79," *NYT*, July 2, 1960, 17.
"Famed Negro Composer Heads Music Institute," *KP*, November 30, 1938, 2.
Notable Black American Men. Farmington Hills, Mich.: Gale Research, 1999.

Theodore H. H. Harris

WHITE BURLEY TOBACCO. The first boatloads of Kentucky tobacco went to New Orleans in the 1780s. By 1839 Kentucky ranked second only to Virginia in the quantities of locally stemmed and packed tobacco shipped to England. Sometime during 1858–1859, Bracken Co. grower **Laban J. Bradford** found a mutated plant that appeared much lighter in color and texture than the original dark leathery leaf known as red burley. He saved the seeds and the following year sowed them in a separate patch. Over the next four years, Bradford selected only the sturdiest plants in that patch for new seeds. He called the distinct variety white burley and gave some of the seeds to a neighbor, George W. Barkley. While Bradford was serving as president of the Kentucky State Agricultural Society from 1862 until 1863, he noted that Kentucky had become the largest tobacco-producing state in the nation.

In spring 1864, Joseph Fore and George Webb came across the Ohio river from Brown Co., Ohio, to Augusta, Ky., to obtain tobacco seeds. Barkley gave the men some white burley seeds, which they planted on land rented from Capt. Fred Kautz. Months later, Fore and Webb noticed that their new tobacco plants had a dirty yellow hue and light texture. This normally was a sign that plants were diseased, and so they burned that crop. The next year, however, when Webb saw the tobacco growing from the Kentucky white burley seeds he had brought back from Kentucky, he recognized that instead of being caused by a disease, the color and texture represented a definite new variety of tobacco. Webb also found that the new crop developed neither mold nor rot as red burley tobacco plants did. Better yet, he could cut down the entire plant, rather than picking each leaf as it ripened. Webb produced a crop of 20,000 pounds that commanded top dollar at the Cincinnati tobacco market in 1866. The following year, he went to the St. Louis Fair and won a first prize and a second prize in tobacco-crop competitions. When Webb tried to patent what he believed was a new tobacco strain, he failed because Bracken Co. White burley had already become common in the Ohio and Kentucky region. This adaptable tobacco leaf revolutionized the industry, and for a brief time, Augusta became a clearing port for Central Kentucky's production of white burley tobacco and the biggest market in the district. Steamboats lined the levee at Augusta for a mile and a half, and Cincinnati soon replaced Louisville as the region's foremost distributor for Central Kentucky's tobacco crops.

"Bracken County Cradle of the White Burley," *Bracken County Chronicle,* October 23, 1930.
Clowes, Jack. "'My Lady Nicotine' Becomes Cash Crop with Aid of Frankfort's Founder," *Lexington Herald-Leader,* August 10, 1969. An article based on an 1873 article in the *Frankfort Commonwealth* in which Bradford described his role.
Collins, Lewis, and Richard Collins. *History of Kentucky.* 2 vols. Reprint, Berea: Kentucky Imprints, 1976.
Heimann, Robert K. *Tobacco and Americans.* New York: McGraw-Hill, 1960.
Van Willigen, John, and Susan C. Eastwood. *Tobacco Culture: Farming Kentucky's Burley Belt.* Lexington: Univ. Press of Kentucky, 1998.

Donald A. Clark

WHITE'S RUN BAPTIST CHURCH. In March and April 1810, the Ghent Baptist Church sent John M. Price and Mordicah Jackson as helpers to constitute a new church at White's Run, along Ky. Rt. 36 in Carroll Co. At least six of the new church's charter members came from the church at Ghent. The White's Run Baptist Church held its first worship service on April 12, 1810. Meetings for worship and church business were held in the homes of members at first. A log structure was then built on an acre of land donated by the Easterday family out of the Whitehead land grant, in the community now known as Easterday.

Members brought their slaves to church, and the first baptism of a slave, named Nicy, was in July 1812. Baptisms in the early years were conducted either in the Ohio River or in White's Run Creek. It appears that during this period the church obtained money to pay expenses not through the practice of tithing but by levying a tax on members; male members usually paid a higher rate than females did. The early church believed in disciplining any member whose behavior was considered to be contrary to Christian beliefs. One of the early controversies occurred at the end of 1822, when charges were brought against two men for joining a Masonic Lodge. The church declared that the teachings of Jesus Christ were not compatible with the teachings of the Masons.

At first, the Baptist Church of Jesus Christ at White's Run was a member of the Long Run Association. It later joined the Franklin Association, and in 1818 it met with other churches to form the Concord Association.

On May 28, 1842, the congregation moved into a brick building that had been constructed alongside the old log house at Easterday. In 1900 the White's Run Baptist Church and other churches withdrew from the Concord Association to form the White's Run Baptist Association.

In March 1941 electric lights were installed in the church building, long before many homes in the area had them. Other improvements include a new Sunday school annex, added in June 1954; stained-glass windows, installed in July 1959; a parsonage, built in 1969; an education-fellowship building, completed and dedicated in 1984; and a new lighted sign, erected on the church grounds in 1995.

White's Run Baptist Church Minutes, White's Run Baptist Church, White's Run, Ky.

Ken Massey

WHITE'S TOWER. White's Tower is located at the intersection of Taylor Mill Rd. (Ky. Rt. 16), Marshall Rd. (formerly Old Decoursey Rd.), and Ky. Rt. 536 (the Visalia-Staffordsburg Rd.). White's Tower is an unincorporated area named for a white wooden tower built on what is today the McClure property, just opposite the intersection of Maverick Rd. and the Visalia-Staffordsburg Rd. The tower was built during the mid-1800s to observe and record topographic features of Kenton Co. at the location that was considered to be the highest point in the county. At that time, there were no airplanes to aid in the development of maps. The foundation for the tower still exists, and persons living in the area today who were born before the end of **World War I** remember seeing the tower. It was torn down during the mid-1920s, when airplanes became routinely used in cartography and as the tower became a liability. Locals referred to the white tower for a directional landmark, and the name mutated to "White's Tower" after its demise. A grocery, a garage, two saloons, and a restaurant were located at White's Tower until the early 1950s. There was also one-room school until the consolidation of Kenton Co. schools in 1929 closed the school and transferred students to the Independence School, four miles to the west. The current White's Tower Elementary School was built in 1965 at the intersection of Taylor Mill Rd. and Harris Rd. (Ky. Rt. 536). Also located at White's Tower are the Durr Extension Office and the YMCA swimming pool and soccer fields, all at the intersection of Marshall and Taylor Mill Rds.

"Kenton Co.—Voting Place and Officer," *KP*, November 1, 1929, 2.

Reis, Jim. "White Tower Inn Destroyed by Fire," *KP*, March 10, 2003, 4K.

Rennick, Robert M. *Kentucky Place Names*. Lexington: Univ. Press of Kentucky, 1984.

Pat Workman

WHITE VILLA. White Villa, an unincorporated community located in rural southeastern Kenton Co. along Decoursey Pk. (Ky. Rt. 177), takes its name from the White Villa Country Club. Developed in 1905 from the former Metz farm, the White Villa Country Club comprises about 150 acres wedged between the **Louisville and Nashville Railroad** tracks and the Licking River, with a one-mile-long frontage along the river. The club saw itself as a Catholic counterpart to the largely Protestant Ryland Lakes Country Club located nearby. Several prominent Northern Kentucky business leaders founded the White Villa Country Club, including department store proprietors **John R. Coppin**, Joseph Luhn, and John A. Stevie. Stevie served as the club's president for several years until his death in 1930. Initially, the club's grounds featured a clubhouse, an icehouse, and a spacious barn. Affiliated families built summer cottages on the grounds and fished in its lakes. To serve the spiritual needs of the club's summer dwellers, the Diocese of Covington established the St. Matthew Parish at White Villa in 1909. For several years, the church held Mass only during the summer months. Since its inception, the White Villa Country Club has hosted several gatherings including political rallies and Fourth of July celebrations.

"Another New Fishing Club," *KP*, January 24, 1905, 1.

"John A. Stevie Is Called by Death," *KP*, June 13, 1930, 1.

"To Dedicate a New Church at White Villa," *KP*, May 27, 1909, 2.

"White Villa Club Is a Reality," *KP*, May 3, 1905, 2.

Greg Perkins

WHITTLESEY, CHARLES W., COLONEL (b. October 4, 1808, Southington, Conn.; d. October 17, 1886, Cleveland, Ohio). Charles W. Whittlesey, the son of Asaph and Vesta Hart Whittlesey, designed the defenses of Cincinnati and Northern Kentucky during the **Civil War**. His family moved to Tallmadge, Ohio, in 1813, where he attended school while living on a farm. Whittlesey graduated from the U.S. Military Academy at West Pont, N.Y., in 1831. During his life in northeastern Ohio, he was a geologist, an archaeologist, a newspaperman, a lawyer, a soldier, an author, and a historian. His experience with geology certainly proved helpful in the role he played in the Northern Kentucky region. That is, during the Civil War, as a colonel in the 20th Ohio Volunteer Infantry, he designed and built in Northern Kentucky a line of fortifications extending from Ludlow on the west to the District of the Highlands (today Fort Thomas) on the east. The fortifications served as the successful line of defense for the city of Cincinnati. In September 1862, it was to Whittlesey that the Union Army looked when it came time to dig in against the Confederate troops commanded by Gen. Henry Heth that were threatening the Greater Cincinnati region. One of the defensive embankments erected in Kentucky was named for him: Fort Whittlesey (see **Civil War Fortifications**), located between the present-day Covington Reservoir and S. Fort Thomas Ave. in Fort Thomas. Anyone familiar with the path of the fortification line can recognize Whittlesey's knowledge of earth science at work. After the war, he returned to Cleveland and continued writing. He composed some 200 articles, tracts, essays, and reports in many fields, and several of his writings continue to be of value. Whittlesey was buried at Lake View Cemetery on the east side of Cleveland.

Burial Record from the Lake View Cemetery, Cleveland, Ohio.

Charles Whittlesey Papers, Western Reserve Historical Society, Cleveland, Ohio.

Van Tassel, David D., ed. *The Encyclopedia of Cleveland History*. Bloomington: Indiana Univ. Press, 1987.

WIDRIG FAMILY. Louis C. Widrig (1869–1932) was one of eight children of Thomas A. "Tobias" and Margaret Feth Widrig. Born in Newport, he completed his early education in that city and graduated in 1889 from the Cincinnati College of Pharmacy. He was licensed as a pharmacist in Ohio but returned to Kentucky to open his own pharmacy at Fifth and Columbia Sts. in Newport. He later had a number of other business interests. In 1909 he led a group that purchased the **Altamont Hotel** and the **Shelley Arms** in Fort Thomas. The Altamont was once a resort known for its mineral water, and both properties were acquired as part of bankruptcy proceedings. The plan was to operate them as a summer resort. Widrig was also a principal stockholder in the Alexandria Turnpike (see **Turnpikes, Campbell Co.**), which connected Newport and Alexandria, he became a part owner of the Cincinnati Reds baseball team, and in 1918 he was elected treasurer of the Cincinnati Exhibition Company. In spite of leadership changes, he maintained his share in the company and served as treasurer until his death. Widrig was a charter member of the Newport Elks Lodge. When Widrig was in New York City for a meeting of major league baseball executives, he was severely burned during a fire in his suite at the Commodore Hotel on January 31, 1932. He died on March 29, 1932, as a consequence of the burns and was buried at St. Stephen Cemetery in Fort Thomas. At the time of his death, his shares in the Cincinnati Reds were appraised at $13,000. He never married.

Two of Louis Widrig's brothers were also Newport pharmacists. Tobias J. "Tobe" Widrig (1865–1922) owned a drug store at Sixth and Washington Sts. in Newport. He was active in pharmacy and medical associations and served as a director of the Newport Mutual Fire Insurance Company. He died after a long illness and was also buried in St. Stephen Cemetery; he and his wife had no children. Edwin (also known as Edward) C. Widrig (1877–1941) graduated from the Cincinnati College of Pharmacy in 1898. He owned a store at Third and Saratoga Sts. in Newport for many years. His daughter married John T. Rawlings, Newport city manager during the Ohio River **flood of 1937**.

"Louis C. Widrig Dead," *O.V.D.A. Review*, April 1932, 2.

"Lou Widrig Dies after Long Fight," *KP*, March 29, 1932, 1.

"Shelly Arms Bought in by Louis Widrig," *KP*, March 30, 1909, 5.

Dennis B. Worthen

WIEDEMANN, CARL F. (b. May 18, 1892, Newport, Ky.; d. February 9, 1961, Cincinnati, Ohio). Carl Wiedemann, the son of Charles F. and Elizabeth Wagner Wiedemann and a grandson of the founder of the **Wiedemann Brewing Company**, assisted in the management of the firm. The brewery for many years was the largest employer in Newport. In 1890 George Wiedemann Sr. died, leaving control of the brewing empire to Carl's father, Charles.

In 1895 a 17-room three-story chateau, designed by **Samuel Hannaford and Sons** for Carl Wiedemann's grandmother Alice, widow of George Wiedemann Sr., was completed. It was located at the top of Park Ave. (house no. 1102) in **Cote Brilliante**, an up-and-coming city south of and not yet annexed by Newport. Later, Charles Wiedemann and his family moved into this home, which sat on an eight-acre estate. Carl's mother died when he was six, and his father remarried in 1908. In accordance with the Wiedemann family's manner of living, Austrian craftsmen were brought to Newport to install and carve the mansion's interior woodwork. Carl became accustomed to the finer things in life, such as his family's having Northern Kentucky's first private in-ground concrete swimming pool in the backyard and employing servants of Chinese origin. Gatsbyesque parties were common at the mansion, as the upper levels of society from Northern Kentucky and Cincinnati hobnobbed amid the lush, manicured grounds, nibbling on specially prepared foods, sipping champagne and other party beverages, or perhaps playing shuffleboard.

Carl also had an excellent education; he attended Yale University, where, from 1914 to 1916, he played left tackle and lettered in football. Somewhat older than most of the other students, Carl was often seen on dates with a gorgeous Broadway actress at his side. His every movement seemed to be tracked by local newspaper society columnists. He could not even change trains in Washington, D.C., en route to college, without newspapers back in Northern Kentucky reporting it.

Carl loved racehorses and racing and owned a small stable of thoroughbreds. He housed them at his horse farm in Lexington and soon became a regular figure on the Kentucky racing circuit. During a trip he made to Keeneland Racecourse in fall 1921, accompanied by the lovely Dorothy M. Rainey, daughter of one of Newport's first female medical doctors, Dr. Louise G. Rainey, a tragic incident took place. Shortly before midnight on October 25, while in Lexington, Dorothy Rainey, clothed only in a negligee, somehow tumbled from a window of the Lafayette Hotel to the sidewalk below. The next day, local authorities ruled it a suicide and released the body for transfer back to Newport, so as to not inconvenience the Wiedemann family; there was no mention or apparent concern for the interests of the Rainey family. Moreover, Rainey's fall instantly elevated her status from girlfriend to fiancée of Carl. His story concerning what happened was lame, but his family's influential Lexington-area relatives intervened on his behalf. Meanwhile, Dorothy Rainey, who had once held the title of "The Prettiest Girl in Newport," was sent back home and buried.

Carl Wiedemann's racing stable consistently competed in the best races on the prestigious Kentucky race circuit. In 1922, for example, he had horses that were nominated to run in both the Kentucky Derby at Churchill Downs in Louisville and the Latonia Derby at Latonia Racecourse in Covington. In 1923, in the Fall Championship at the **Latonia Racecourse**, Carl's horse In Memorium upset Kentucky Derby winner Zev, only to lose to Zev a few weeks later in a match race at Churchill Downs that was so close that its controversial result was long disputed. Both races had been followed by race fans with much anticipation, causing Carl Wiedemann's name to be catapulted into national prominence by the dramatic races taking place in Kentucky.

Also in 1923, with some help from the *New York Times,* Carl formally broke up with another girlfriend. During his days at Yale, he had met Allyn King, a Broadway comedy star and a member of the noted Ziegfeld Follies. When the relationship was over, Carl was quoted in the New York paper as saying that he and King were not engaged and that he "was still a member of the bachelors' club." Strangely, in March 1930 King fell to her death from a fifth-floor window at her New York City apartment. Carl was nowhere in the vicinity, but the Rainey incident was mentioned in the news media's coverage of King's death.

On October 25, 1925, Carl Wiedemann married Celia Dooin. By spring 1930 their strained marital relationship was being detailed by newspapers in Northern Kentucky. However, there is no record that a divorce took place. Thirty years later, Carl's obituary listed Celia as his surviving wife.

In 1928 the Wiedemann Brewery was prosecuted by the federal government for making alcoholic products stronger than the law allowed. The officers of the corporation were summoned to appear before the Federal Court in Covington just as Charles Wiedemann's health was deteriorating. Carl did perhaps the noblest thing of his life—he "took the rap" for his father and the others, paying a $10,000 fine and completing eight months of a two-year sentence in the federal penitentiary at Atlanta, Ga., before returning home for Thanksgiving that year, in what may be one of the first "shock probation" cases on record. Unfortunately, Carl did not make it home before his father died of cirrhosis of the liver on November 3, 1928.

Carl's annual trips to the Kentucky Derby in Louisville were legendary. In the 1920s, during Derby week, Carl seemed always to be trying to restore the social good times that had taken place before **Prohibition**. Louisville's society blue-bloods and the ladies of the evening were enthralled as Carl arrived in Louisville with a cold, fully loaded beer truck, whose contents they consumed before Carl left town.

While Carl was helping to manage the Wiedemann Brewing Company, there were many lawsuits. In 1927, for example, just as the federal government was about to charge him and the corporation, Carl was sued by the Frank Herschede Company of Cincinnati (jewelers) for the recovery of $996 due for merchandise. In November of that year, even though Carl was no longer racing any of his horses, the Early-Daniel Company of Cincinnati sued him for $165 for unpaid horse feed bills.

By 1940 Carl was gone from the brewing company's management team. He spent his time in various drinking establishments in and around Newport. Yet he retained his all- important ownership position at the brewery. The company kept him satisfied by sending him cash when needed, and when the bar tab became large, it was not uncommon to see a Wiedemann beer truck making a special delivery to settle Carl's bill.

In 1951 Carl's boyhood home on Park Ave. was sold to the Diocese of Covington for use as the residence of its bishop. Locally owned beer companies were rapidly becoming a thing of the past, and the Wiedemann Brewing Company was no exception. In 1967 the company was sold to the G. Heileman Brewery of La Crosse, Wis. Carl Wiedemann, the last of the family's owners, collapsed in February 1961 while living in Cincinnati and died later the same day at Cincinnati's General Hospital. He was 68 years old. After a sedate funeral service at the home of his sister Irma (Mrs. Charles T. Wagner), in Cincinnati's fashionable Hyde Park neighborhood, he was buried in the family plot at Evergreen Cemetery in Southgate.

"Brewery Head, Wiedemann, Is Dead," *KP,* November 4, 1928, 1.
"Carl Wiedemann Not to Wed," *NYT,* December 27, 1923, 13.
"Carl Wiedemann of Newport Nominated First Two Horses for Kentucky and Latonia Derbies," *KTS,* February 10, 1922, 27.
"C.F. Wiedemann Succumbs at 68," *KP,* February 10, 1961, 1.
"Kentucky Beauty Dies in 5-Story Fall," *NYT,* October 26, 1921, 12.
"Newport Man Who Met with Injury That Will Keep Him out of the Yale Line-up Saturday," *KTS,* October 24, 1914, 12.
"Personals," *KJ,* May 19, 1892, 8.
"Wiedemann Heir Seeks Divorce from Mate," *KP,* March 27, 1930, 1.

Michael R. Sweeney

WIEDEMANN, CHARLES (b. June 16, 1858, Cincinnati, Ohio; d. November 3, 1928, Cincinnati, Ohio). Charles Frank Wiedemann served as president of the George **Wiedemann Brewing Company** of Newport from 1890 to 1928. Son of the company's founder, George Wiedemann, Charles was an effective businessman trained specifically for this post in the family-controlled firm. He was educated in Cincinnati and received his early training in his father's brewery. From 1876 to 1877 he studied the technical and scientific aspects of brewing in Munich, Germany. On his return to the United States, he spent a year in Milwaukee before rejoining his father in Newport. Charles served as superintendent of the firm, then vice president, and finally president after the death of his father. Under Charles's leadership, the brewery continued to expand and to adopt the latest technological, distributive, and commercial advances. According to an 1894 source, "The high standing of the company in the financial world is due in the main to the business capacity of Charles Wiedemann."

In 1884 Charles married Elizabeth Wagner of Newport. A daughter, Lena, was born to the couple in 1888, and a son, Carl, in 1892. Elizabeth died in 1896. In 1908 Charles married Alice Mellinger of Covington.

During the 1880s Wiedemann resided in Newport on Jefferson St. (now W. Sixth St.), next to the brewery. By the 1890s he had relocated to a Second Empire–style brick house at 709 Overton St. in East Newport. Before June 1900 he had moved into a stately suburban residence commissioned by his widowed mother, Agnes Rohmanns Wiedemann, who had died in January 1899. He lived there, at 1102 Park Ave. in the **Cote Brilliante** section of Newport, until his death. He was a good neighbor; in 1912, when the Roman Catholic church of **St. Francis de Sales** was built at Chesapeake and Grand Aves. in Cote Brilliante, down the hill from his home, Wiedemann donated to the parish a Verdin Company–made bell, which hung in the church belfry until recent times.

In 1908 Wiedemann built a baseball park in Newport's **West End**, home to a professional ball team called the Brewers. The following year he was elected president of the Kentucky Brewers Association and also became a director of the Kentucky Manufacturers Association. He was a director of the First National Bank of Newport and of the **Evergreen Cemetery** Association. He was a member of St. Paul's Episcopal Church in Newport.

Wiedemann was no stranger to controversy. In 1908 he threatened to call in a $3,000 debt owed to the brewery by **St. Mark Lutheran Church** in East Newport, despite claims that that the payment would bankrupt the congregation. In 1910 a Mrs. Murphy fell to her death in an elevator shaft in the **Altamont Springs Hotel** in Fort Thomas, of which he was a co-owner. Her death resulted in a $31,000 lawsuit. Wiedemann sold his interest in the hotel to his partner in 1916. In 1928 the federal government prosecuted the Wiedemann Brewery for making illegal alcohol. Charles, confined to his home by a two-year illness, never appeared in court. His son, **Carl Wiedemann**, took the blame for the crimes of his father and others. In 1928 Charles Wiedemann died of cirrhosis of the liver at Jewish Hospital in Cincinnati, just as his trial was about to start. His widow, Alice, was his sole beneficiary, inheriting the Cote Brilliant mansion and $250,000. Charles Wiedemann was buried in the family plot in Evergreen Cemetery in Southgate.

History of Cincinnati and Hamilton County. Cincinnati: S. B. Nelson, 1894.

Holian, Timothy. *Over the Barrel: The Brewing and Beer Culture of Cincinnati. Vol. 1, 1800–Prohibition.* St. Joseph, Mo.: Sudhaus Press, 2000.

Langsam, Walter E. "Charles Wiedemann House," National Register of Historic Places Nomination, 1984, Kentucky Heritage Council, Frankfort, Ky.

"Newport, Kentucky Brewers Meet," *CE,* November 10, 1909, 11.

Ohio Death Certificate No. 66931, for the year 1928.

Purvis, Thomas L., ed. *Newport, Kentucky: A Bicentennial History.* Newport, Ky.: Otto Zimmerman, 1996.

Reis, Jim. "The Beer Baron: Local Man Founded Wiedemann Brewery," *KP,* October 20, 2003, 5K.

Margaret Warminski

WIEDEMANN BREWING COMPANY. During the late 19th and early 20th centuries, the George Wiedemann Brewing Company of Newport became one of the nation's largest and most progressive breweries. Its history and that of the chief officers of the firm—nearly all members of or related by marriage to the Wiedemann family—provides a microcosm of more than a century of the beer industry in the United States, particularly in the Midwest.

The company was founded by George Wiedemann Sr. (ca. 1834–1890), whose sons Charles Frank (1857–1928) and George Jr. (1866–1901) carried on the business after their father's death. George Wiedemann Sr. was born and educated in Saxony, Germany, and trained in the brewing business there. After immigrating to the United States in 1853, he spent a few years in New York State and in Louisville before moving to Cincinnati. There, he entered the business with George Frank Eichenlaub in Walnut Hills, a Cincinnati suburb. In 1860 Wiedemann began work as the foreman of Cincinnati's Kauffman Brewery.

In 1870 he became a partner of John Butcher, proprietor of the small Jefferson Street Brewery in Newport. Wiedemann's lager attracted many customers, who appreciated his use of the finest ingredients and the traditional German preparation of the brew. By the late 1870s, the brewery was the largest in Northern Kentucky. In 1878 Wiedemann acquired the entire firm, which continued to expand under his leadership. The firm marketed its products under the name of Butcher and Wiedemann.

In 1882 he added the former Constans Brewery at Monmouth and Liberty Sts. in Newport, near where the **CSX** Railroad crosses over **U.S. 27** today. Ironically, the Constans operation had been purchased by Wiedemann's former partner Butcher in 1878 but went bankrupt two years later. The scale of the Wiedemann Brewery's future growth is suggested by Wiedemann's improvements at the Constans site: he built a large malt house with a capacity of 200,000 bushels and a grain elevator that stored 160,000 bushels. The malt house survived a near-catastrophic fire in 1890 and remained until it was torn down in the early 1980s.

In the late 1880s, Wiedemann began a major expansion and modernization of the brewery facilities, which came to occupy five acres in Newport at Sixth and Columbia Sts. Capitalizing on his quarter century of experience, he built one of the world's largest and most efficient breweries, designed by Newport architect Charles Vogel. The brew-house was five stories tall, and the stable housed up to 150 horses. In 1893 master architects **Samuel Hannaford and Sons** of Cincinnati, who also designed George Wiedemann's widow's residence at 1102 Park Ave. in Newport's **Cote Brilliante** district, designed the company's ornate offices. The new plant brewed controversy, however, when it resulted in the displacement of the **Corinthian Baptist Church**, an African American congregation. Temperance and prohibition advocates denounced the move as an assault on religion in Newport.

By 1889 three of Wiedemann's brands—Standard Lager, Extra Pale Lager, and Muenchener—were sold widely in Kentucky, Ohio, and Tennessee.

Wiedemann Brewing Company.

In 1890, after the death of George Sr., his two sons, Charles and George Jr., took over operations of the brewery, incorporating it as the George Wiedemann Brewing Company. By the 1900s the brewery was the largest south of the Ohio River and east of the Mississippi River.

During **Prohibition**, Newport became a center for bootlegging, and the smell of mash hung heavily over the city's West End. Like Cincinnati breweries, Wiedemann's tried to survive the dry years by producing nonalcoholic brews. Throughout the 1920s, they also distilled millions of gallons of alcohol for "industrial purposes." At least half was the specially denatured variety used by the area's bootlegging kingpin George Remus. Wiedemann's became one of Remus's biggest suppliers but was able to evade close scrutiny because of Remus's political connections with prominent Republicans. In 1927 the company was charged by the federal government with producing more than 1.5 million gallons of illegal brew in violation of the Volstead Act, and the brewery was padlocked and closed. **Carl Wiedemann**, the grandson of George Sr. and the son of Charles Wiedemann, took the blame and served eight months of a two-year sentence in a federal penitentiary.

The Wiedemann Brewery reopened in 1933, following the repeal of Prohibition. It was reorganized in 1937 under the leadership of H. Tracy Balcom Jr., a grandson of the founder. Members of the family, who owned all the stock, continued to serve as its chief officers and spent a million dollars modernizing the plant. In the postwar era, Wiedemann's remained one of the most viable Cincinnati-area independent beer producers. Production grew from 150,000 barrels in 1938 to 850,000 barrels by 1955. New programs, such as year-round newspaper advertising, and new brands, such as the premium Royal Amber, contributed to its success.

Beginning in the 1950s, massive consolidation transformed the brewing industry. Heavily advertised national brands took over local breweries that had allowed their production facilities to become outdated. Wiedemann's kept itself competitive by investing in new technology, but it faced an uncertain future because national producers could afford to undersell its price and weaken customer loyalty.

In 1967 the Wiedemann Brewery was absorbed as an independent division by the Heileman Brewing Company of La Crosse, Wis. The Wiedemann brand proved profitable, but its production facilities were no longer cost-effective. In 1983 Heileman closed the Newport plant and shuttered the buildings. Because the Wiedemann Brewing Company had been the largest employer in Newport, the closure cost 400 regular jobs, reduced municipal payroll taxes by one-eighth, and slashed the Newport water department's annual revenues.

During the 1980s a commercial developer, National Redevelopment Inc., proposed reusing the Wiedemann Brewery buildings as an office and retail center called Wiedemann Square. The project won a federal Urban Development Action Grant but was never built. By the 1990s the entire brewery complex had been demolished. Part of the land was later redeveloped as the Campbell Co. Justice Center. A Thriftway supermarket, built on part of the acreage, closed in 2004.

Giglierano, Geoffrey J., and Deborah A. Overmyer. *The Bicentennial Guide to Greater Cincinnati: A Portrait of Two Hundred Years.* Cincinnati: Cincinnati Historical Society, 1988.

Holian, Timothy. *Over the Barrel: The Brewing and Beer Culture of Cincinnati. Vol. 1, 1800–Prohibition.* St. Joseph, Mo.: Sudhaus Press, 2000.

Langsam, Walter E. "Charles Wiedemann House," National Register of Historic Places Nomination, 1984, Kentucky Heritage Council, Frankfort, Ky.

Purvis, Thomas L., ed. *Newport, Kentucky: A Bicentennial History.* Newport, Ky.: Otto Zimmerman, 1996.

"Wiedemann Plant Delivers First Beer since Prohibition," *KP*, December 15, 1933, 1.

Margaret Warminski

WILDER. Wilder, situated along the Licking River and the AA Highway (Ky. Rt. 9 or Licking Pk.) in northwestern Campbell Co., was incorporated in 1935. Settlement in the area dates back to 1789, when Maj. **David Leitch** founded Leitch's Station nearby. The city and its environs have long had an industrial focus. The local 1883 Lake atlas describes the area as including Wilders Station, Finchtown, and Summerhill. The atlas shows a distillery, an icehouse, railroad yards, and the Licking Turnpike (a toll road). The Licking Turnpike (now Licking Pk.) was originally built by the Trapp Family and later sold to the Commonwealth of Kentucky. The name Wilder comes from Wilder Station, a railroad depot that operated during the early days of the city. Either named for a Covington eye doctor or a member of the **Louisville and Nashville Railroad** (L&N) Board of Directors, Wilder has always had an association with the Licking River and the railroad.

On the hills of Wilder during the **Civil War**, fortifications were built in 1862 to fend off a Confederate invasion of the region. Remnants of Wilder's Battery Holt remain on the tall hill overlooking the Licking River valley just above and behind today's United Dairy Farmers Store at Licking Pk. and Moock Rd (see **Civil War Fortifications**). A racetrack named the Queen City Track operated from the 1890s until 1905 in the river valley area where **Newport Steel** is located. A street at the site of the defunct racetrack is named Queen City Ave.

Wilder's riverfront and hills today are occupied by Newport Steel, the Frederick's Landing recreation area, and **Bobby Mackey's Music World** (formerly the Latin Quarter). Carlisle Construction (now Maxim), the Castellini Produce Warehouse, Queen City Ice, and Sun Rock Farm are other businesses in the area. Wilder built a new city building in 2000. The reconstructed Ky. Rt. 9, or AA Highway, and I-275 provide easy access to the city, where many new homes, condominiums, and apartments have been built. A movie theater, a sports complex, restaurants, and other businesses are located at the intersection of I-275 and the AA Highway. In 2000 Wilder had a population of 2,624.

An Atlas of Boone, Kenton, and Campbell Counties, Kentucky. Philadelphia: D. J. Lake, 1883.

Campbell Co. Historical Society. *Campbell County, Kentucky, 200 Years, 1794–1994.* Alexandria, Ky.: The Campbell Co. Historical Society, 1994.

U.S. Census Bureau, "American Fact Finder. Data Set. Census 2000 Summary File 1 (SF1) 100-Percent Data. Custom Table." www.census.gov. (accessed June 4, 2008).

Kenneth A. Reis

WILDLIFE AREAS IN OWEN CO. In Owen Co., two wildlife management refuges help to maintain the natural habitat for this part of the Northern Kentucky region, while providing noncommercial recreational opportunities to those who visit. In the northwestern area of the county, just north of Moxley, along Ky. Rt. 355 and the Kentucky River, is the Twin Eagle Wildlife Area. Established in 1962, this 166-acre tract is owned and managed by the Kentucky Department of Fish and Wildlife Resources. It runs along the steep Kentucky River terrace, consisting of woods, croplands, grasslands, and sloughs. Doves, rabbits, quail, deer, turkeys, and sometimes ducks can be seen there. Hiking, climbing, and fishing are permitted, but no camping. Included within its boundaries are 70 acres of river-bottom cropland.

The second wildlife refuge in Owen Co., also owned and managed by the Department of Fish and Wildlife Resources, is the Kleber Wildlife Area. It is in the southern part of the county, west of Harmony, along Ky. Rt. 368 (Cedar Rd.), near the Franklin Co. line. It lies between U.S. 127 and Ky. Rt. 227. In April 1953 the State of Kentucky purchased 750 acres of land to establish this wildlife refuge. Approximately 75 percent of the initial cost was funded by the will of John A. Kleber, a longtime Frankfort businessman. Today, the refuge has expanded to 2,556 acres and extends into Franklin Co. Hiking is available over terrains of steep hillsides, narrow ridges, and floodplains full of woods, brush, grasslands, and wildlife food plots. Quail, deer, squirrels, rabbits, turkeys, groundhogs, and raccoons can be observed. Bluegill fishing is permitted at the refuge's small pond and in Cedar Creek. Hiking and primitive camping are also allowed. This is the site of the annual Christmas Bird Count conducted by the Frankfort Bird Club and the Frankfort Audubon Society.

Houchens, Mariam Sidebottom. *History of Owen County: "Sweet Owen."* Louisville, Ky.: Standard, 1976.

WILEMAN, ABRAM G., MAJOR (b. 1821, Stark Co., Ohio; d. October 5, 1863, Knoxville, Pendleton Co., Ky.). Abram Wileman, a physician and a **Civil War** major, was the son of Mahlon and Elizabeth Logue Wileman, Quakers who moved to Stark Co., Ohio, from Columbiana Co., Ohio. In 1858, after having lived in Pendleton Co. for three years, Abram Wileman divorced his wife Elizabeth and married Parthenia A. Race of Pendleton Co. They resided along the Falmouth-Knoxville Rd. (Ky. Rt. 467). During the Civil War, Abram enlisted in 1861 on the Union side and was commissioned a captain in the 18th Kentucky Infantry. He saw action in several battles as an infantryman and was promoted to major. During the battle of Chickamauga, Tenn., in September 1863, Wileman suffered a gunshot wound in his left forearm and returned home to recuperate. On the evening of October 5, 1863, while he sat in his parlor with his wife and some neighbors, Confederate guerrillas burst in, reportedly under Gen. John C. Breckenridge's command. They took $200 from Wileman's neighbors but got nothing from the doctor. The invaders took Wileman a mile and a half down the road and murdered him with a shot through the head.

Wileman's murder emphasizes how divided Pendleton Co. was by the Civil War. Generally speaking, the northern part of the county was pro-Union, and the southern area, around Morgan and McKinneysburg, favored the Confederacy. Although the incident was investigated by the Union deputy provost marshal of Pendleton Co., no legal action ensued. Dr. Wileman's widow and three children moved to Stark Co., Ohio, and Wileman was buried at the Marlboro Cemetery, near Marlboro, Ohio.

Belew, Mildred Boden. *The First 200 Years of Pendleton County.* Falmouth, Ky.: M. B. Belew, n.d. [ca. 1994].

Warner, W. A. *Paris (Ky.) Western Citizen*, October 23, 1863.

Wileman, A. G., Military Payroll and Service Records, National Archives, Washington, D.C.

Mildred Belew

WILLIAM H. HARSHA BRIDGE. The William H. Harsha Bridge across the Ohio River, located 2.8 miles downstream from the **Simon Kenton Memorial Bridge** at Maysville, was dedicated on October 9, 2000, and was opened to traffic in January 2001. It was named for William H. Harsha, the longtime southern Ohio U.S. congressman from Portsmouth, Ohio, who served what was then the Sixth District of Ohio for 20 years (1961–1981). Construction began in April 1997. It is Kentucky's first cable-stayed suspension bridge; located at Charleston Bottoms, the bridge has two 12-foot auto lanes and two 12-foot shoulders. The bridge's five spans total a length of 2,100 feet, and for much of that distance the bridge hangs from two 343-foot-tall dominating H-shaped towers. Simply put, the bridge's design allows for movement to take place without any noticeable effect on the structure itself. Built at a cost of $37 million, the bridge does not replace the nearby Simon Kenton Bridge but complements it by diverting the heavy transient truck traffic from downtown Maysville, while encouraging the overall economic development of the area. The William H. Harsha Bridge provides an easy link between the **AA Highway** in Kentucky and U.S. 52 in Ohio. Sometime in the future, the William H. Harsha Bridge may become part of the proposed highway between Lexington, Ky. and Columbus, Ohio.

A similar type of bridge was constructed along the Ohio River upstream from Maysville at Portsmouth, Ohio, leading into Lewis Co., Ky. Known as the U.S. Grant Bridge, it opened for moving traffic on October 16, 2006.

"$3m Bridge Opens," *CP*, January 13, 2001, 7A.

WILLIAMS, BRIAN P. (b. May 8, 1972, Covington, Ky.; d. September 11, 2001, New York City). Brian Patrick Williams, a victim of 9/11, was the third of four children born to Kenneth E. and Kathleen G. Burke Williams. The other children were Ken Jr., Andy, and Tara. Brian attended **St. Pius X** Grade School in Edgewood and **Covington Catholic High School** in Park Hills. He was an excellent student and also earned varsity letters in basketball, football, and track in high school. He then attended Columbia University in New York City, majoring in economics, and after graduation began working as an agency salesman for Cantor-Fitzgerald, investment bankers in New York City. His office was located on the 104th floor of the World Trade Center. On September 11, 2001, when the two hijacked airliners crashed into the Twin Towers, Brian's family feared the worst but prayed for the best. They watched the television news and anxiously sat by their telephone, hoping to hear from Brian, but the call never came. The family was able to make contact with Brian's girlfriend, Lisa Kraus, in New York City, but she indicated that she had also been trying in vain to reach him. Some of Brian's New York City friends made the rounds of area hospitals, but those trips yielded no information about him. The FBI hotline that was set up to provide the names of survivors, those injured, and the known dead also gave no clue to Brian's whereabouts. After days of searching, Brian was still listed as missing. Some of his remains later were recovered, however, and returned to his grieving family. Prayer services were held at Covington Catholic High School, and a memorial Mass was held in his honor. His remains were buried in the Mother of God Cemetery in Covington. This tragedy was the second endured by the Williams family. In 1994 their son Ken Jr. died from head injuries suffered in a fall outside Riverfront Stadium in Cincinnati.

Brian Patrick Williams, June 2001.

Ancestry.com. Kentucky Birth Index. www.ancestry.com (accessed March 27, 2006).

Boehmker, Terry. "CovCath Grad Worked on 104th Floor Office," *KP*, September 12, 2001, 1K.

Williams, Ken, father of Brian. Telephone interview by Jack Wessling, March 23, 2006.

WILLIAMS, CAROLINE "LINE" (b. November 10, 1908, Covington, Ky.; d. March 9, 1988, Burlington, Ky.). Caroline Williams, the daughter of nationally recognized *Cincinnati Enquirer* artist Carll B. Williams and Mary Teal Williams, was an artist, a historian, a printer, and a writer. She was best known for her pen and ink drawings but also known for the masterful etchings she used on her own press and for her charm, warmth, sense of humor, and rugged individualism. Caroline spent her first five years in Kentucky. The family lived at various residences in Northern Kentucky until 1913, when they bought a home in Cincinnati. At age five Caroline picked up a pen and found her calling in art. She received her education at Cincinnati's Hughes High School, the University of Cincinnati (attending for one year), the Art Academy of Cincinnati, and the Art Students League in New York City.

Early in her career, Williams was keenly interested in portraiture; however, during the **Great Depression** it was difficult to make a living as a freelance artist. Four years after her father's death in 1928, the blue-eyed, slender Williams followed in her father's footsteps and began working for the *Cincinnati Enquirer,* where he had been artistic director, in March 1932. She did miscellaneous tasks, including some illustrating, and ran errands. Cincinnati artist E. T. Hurley, a friend to both Caroline and her father, had a strong influence on her.

After seven months with the *Enquirer,* she showed a few incidental sketches of city scenes to a managing editor, and the idea of a regular weekly feature entitled *A Spot in Cincinnati* was born. Her first sketch for this column was a skyline view from Liberty Hill, in the Mount Auburn section of Cincinnati, which appeared in the *Enquirer* in November 1932. Her sketches were in charcoal, ink, or pen. Occasionally, she would photograph a scene and then complete the sketch at home. She spent long hours at the Public Library of Cincinnati and Hamilton Co. and at the Cincinnati Historical Society, researching old buildings and sites. Her drawings of spots around Cincinnati appeared in the *Enquirer's* Sunday editorial pages for 47 years. At first, staff writers were assigned to write captions for Williams's sketches, but when the caption was missing one week, she took on the task herself. Soon readers began to look forward to her personal comments about each scene. Later some of her sketches featured sites in Northern Kentucky and Indiana. Williams remained at the *Enquirer* until 1945, when she began a freelance career; however, she continued her *A Spot in Cincinnati* for the newspaper.

Caroline Williams.

In the late 1930s, when Williams became concerned about the rise of Nazi aggression, she joined the Committee to Defend America, where she met its secretary, Dorothy Caldwell. They became fast and lifelong friends. During **World War II**, both women volunteered for the **American Red Cross** Motor Corps, transporting blood donors at a time when gasoline was rationed. They also drove busloads of soldiers from their base at Cincinnati's Lunken Airport to the city.

In 1941 Williams designed a stylized map of Cincinnati, which was sold during the Christmas season at Closson's, downtown Cincinnati's famous art gallery and furniture store. Between 1943 and 1945, she also sold real estate for the Morton Bruce Company. At the same time, her sketches were in great demand at galleries across the city. In March 1942 Closson's Gallery exhibited her drawings and etchings of towns in Quebec, Canada, made during a tour there with her friend Dorothy Caldwell.

Near the end of World War II, Williams purchased 52 acres in Burlington, which included two log cabins that she converted into a single two-story log cabin home, doing much of the carpentry herself. Her mother resided with her. Williams set up her presses (she eventually had four) in a corncrib and a smokehouse on the property. One of her favorite pastimes was fishing in her pond.

The mix of past and present was an ever-present theme of Williams's work well into the 1960s. She expressed frustration over some people's urge to tear down mellow old buildings. She became, for many Cincinnati and Northern Kentucky residents, the artist of the region's immediate past. Kentucky author Jesse Stuart wrote, "Artist Caroline Williams has a passion for old architecture. She weeps when a building goes."

Williams made original drawings for many corporations, including Christmas cards for the Fifth Third Bank of Cincinnati. Her snow scenes, including *Methodist Church of Florence* (March 12, 1950); *The Residence of Dr. George C. Kolb* (on Belmont Ave. in Cincinnati) (February 26, 1939); and *Pershing Avenue, off Main Street in Covington* (December 23, 1956), were especially well received.

In 1962 Williams received the Cincinnati Institute of Fine Arts award. She was the first woman to receive the Rosa F. and Samuel B. Sachs Prize, awarded for her book *Cincinnati—Steeples, Streets, and Steps*, which included 96 of her sketches. Williams carried out every aspect of her sketches, from the drawing, to the handset type, to the printing. She also received a citation by the Ohioana Literary Association for distinguished service to Ohio in the cause of the arts. It was said that she had done more to publicize Greater Cincinnati's and Northern Kentucky's beauty than any other person. Until she received the Sachs prize, Williams had refused *Enquirer* readers a visit to her home. After that, however, she permitted publication of a pictorial tribute, a photograph of her seated in her home.

Williams published five books, *The City on Seven Hills* (1938), *Mirrored Landmarks of Cincinnati* (1939), *As Always—Cincinnati* (1951); *Cincinnati Scenes: Steeples, Streets, and Steps* (1962), and *Louisville Scenes* (1971). The *Enquirer* produced the first of her books, and some of the later works were published in her Penandhoe Print Shop. She also produced illustrations for the literary magazine *Talaria* between 1936 and 1953, including the Talaria book *Garland for a City* (1946).

Williams's sketches showed up on napkins, checks, and plastic placemats. In 1973 Cincinnati's Newstedt, Loring, Andrews Jewelers sent her to Europe to develop a series of her sketches of scenes for English Wedgewood collector plates. At the time of her death, the 1988 commemorative Caroline Williams plates of Winton Place Railroad Station awaited shipment from England.

Her last two sketches, Cincinnati's *Plum Street Temple* and *St. Peter in Chains Cathedral*, appeared in 1979, when Williams was 71 years old. She stopped making sketches for the newspaper in early December 1980 and spent her final years creating watercolors in the style she had studied at the Sorbonne in Paris. One of her last watercolors was *Mother of God Church, Covington, Ky.*, painted at the request of Gerald Bogenschutz, a United Parcel Service driver who delivered supplies to Williams for nearly 20 years. He was a member of **Mother of God Catholic Church**, and in late summer 1987, he asked her to donate a painting to an auction for the benefit of the church's restoration, following a $1.5 million fire. She responded generously with this watercolor painting.

Williams died in her sleep at her log cabin in 1988 and was buried with her family at the Forest Hill Cemetery in Shelbyville, Ind. Shortly after her death, the Chidlaw Gallery at the Art Academy of Cincinnati presented an exhibition in honor of the City of Cincinnati's Bicentennial that included her treasured drawings, etchings, and watercolors as well as illustrations and cartoons by her father, Carll Williams; there were 60 works in all. She had kept the originals of most of her weekly entries in the *Enquirer*. The funds derived from the exhibition were used for the Caroline Williams Scholarship Fund at the academy. The original drawings for the *Enquirer* series became the property of the Cincinnati Historical Society, and more than 1,200 of them were offered for sale in February 1994.

Much of old Cincinnati and Northern Kentucky would have been forgotten without the sketches and paintings of Caroline Williams, who preserved the images of the past during a time of destructive urban renewal.

Canfield, Victor, cochair of restoration, Mother of God Catholic Church. Interview by Rick Sacksteder, December 11, 2006, Covington, Ky.

"Caroline Williams, Artist: Works Appeared on Enquirer Editorial Page," *CE*, March 10, 1998, D2.

Conrad, Mary T. "Remembering Caroline," *QCH* 48, no. 3 (Fall 1990): 17–21.

Cox, Mary. "As Always . . . Caroline," *Art Academy News*, May–June 1988, 11.

Findsen, Owen. "An Artist's View of the City," *CE*, August 5, 1988, B1.

———. "Log Home Perfect for Artist's Press," *CE*, November 28, 1999, F4.

Green, Joe. "Have You Met? Caroline Knits No More!" *CE*, July 22, 1961, 11.

Kain, Allan. "Caroline Williams," *CE*, May 26, 1963, supplement, 20–21.

Redman-Rengstorf, Susan. "The Queen City through the Eyes of Caroline Williams," *QCH* 48, no. 3 (Fall 1990): 3–16.

Stein, Jerry. "Capturing City Spirit in Pen, Ink," *CP*, August 5, 1988, B7.

Williams, B. Y., and Annette Patton Cornell, poems; Caroline Williams, drawings. *Garland for a City*. Cincinnati: Talaria, 1946.

Williams, Caroline. "Pershing Avenue, off Main Street in Covington," *CE*, December 23, 1956, sec. 3, p. 2.

Richard M. Sacksteder

WILLIAMS, ELLISON E. (b. April 19, 1766, North Carolina; d. August 11, 1850, Kenton Co., Ky.) Ellison Williams, a Northern Kentucky pioneer and road-builder, arrived in Kentucky with his family in 1775. He was present at Bryants Station in August 1782 when it was attacked by **Simon Girty** and his band of pro-British Indians. Williams became a friend and favorite hunting companion of **Daniel Boone**. After Williams came to Kenton Co. in 1785, he and his brother built the first house in Covington, near the mouth of the Licking River. Ellison Williams settled on a farm along what became the Banklick Turnpike, eight miles south of Covington, and lived there for some 65 years. He built many roads in Northern Kentucky, as the early Campbell Co. court order books attest, and was often a guide and escort for travelers between Northern Kentucky and Lexington. During Mad Anthony Wayne's campaign against the Indians in northern Ohio (1793–1794), Williams had the contract to supply Wayne's army with venison and wild game, which, according to records, he did quite satisfactorily. When Daniel Boone's remains were re-interred in Kentucky at the Frankfort Cemetery in 1845, Williams was a pall bearer, and at that time he requested that his own remains eventually be placed near Boone's grave. Williams died at his farm in 1850. In May 1860, in response to an 1860 order of the Kentucky legislature, his remains were moved to Frankfort for reburial near Boone's. Williams was known as a good woodsman, a fearless man, and a true friend.

"Ellison Williams," *CJ*, May 26, 1860, 2.

WILLIAMS, GLENROSE (b. January 4, 1921, Bullittsville, Boone Co., Ky.; d. April 26, 2008, Burlington, Ky.). Edith Glenrose Williams, who was a Boone Co. sheriff, was the daughter of J. T. "Jake" and Edith Carpenter Williams. In 1944, while serving as sheriff of Boone Co., her father died suddenly, and Glenrose Williams was appointed the first female sheriff in Boone Co. Williams had served as a deputy sheriff for her father, doing bookkeeping work. After his death, many people felt a woman could not carry out the job of sheriff. However, Boone Co. judge **Carroll Cropper** disagreed and recommended her appointment, which was approved by Kentucky governor Simeon S. Willis (1943–1947). The news of Williams's appointment to the sheriff position was published in newspapers as far away as Hawaii.

During Williams's tenure, the gambling interests prevalent in Campbell and Kenton counties wanted to expand into Boone Co., setting up a confrontation between the female sheriff and a representative of the Chicago mob. The big test came when the mob brought gambling just over the Boone Co. border to a location along the **Dixie Highway** (U.S. 25). Accompanied by her deputy, Williams entered the building, and a member of the mob approached her, smiling. In plain sight, in the front room of the building, was a bank of slot machines, and in the back other forms of gambling were occurring. Sheriff Williams arrested the mobster for gambling with the slot machines and ordered him to appear in court in the morning. He was never seen in Boone Co. again, and gambling did not spread to Boone Co. The confiscated slot machines were smashed with a sledge hammer, which Williams wielded for the first blow. The all-iron machines were destroyed on the sidewalk in front of the old courthouse, in public, as demanded by state law.

Williams did not seek another term because she did not expect to win. Her term as sheriff ran from 1944 to 1946, filling out her father's elected term. In later years, one time when Williams was leaving Flick's Grocery in Burlington, a young woman asked if she could help the elderly Williams with her bags. The young woman was a Boone Co. deputy sheriff, and when Williams told her that she had once been sheriff, the deputy was not able to believe her. Williams's husband, Byron Kinman, was the first police chief of the **Cincinnati/Northern Kentucky International Airport** and at one time also served as the sheriff of Boone Co. He died in 2006. Glenrose Williams died in 2008 and was buried in Florence Cemetery.

Ancestry.com. "Kentucky Birth Index, 1911–1999." www.ancestry.com/search/db.aspx?dbid=8788 (accessed December 4, 2006).

Warner, Jennifer S. *Boone County: From Mastodons to the Millennium*. Burlington, Ky.: Boone Co. Bicentennial Book Committee, 1998.

Robert Schrage

WILLIAMS, SHEILA (b. December 13, 1954, Columbus, Ohio). Novelist Sheila Williams is the daughter of James W. Williams Jr. and Myrtle Jones Humphrey. Born and reared in Columbus, Ohio, she was educated in the Columbus public schools, attended Ohio Wesleyan College, and graduated from the University of Louisville with a degree in political science. She was employed in the corporate business world as a legal secretary, a paralegal, and a mutual fund product manager; she worked for law firms, two banks (including Cincinnati's **Fifth Third**), and a Fortune 500 corporation. She gave up her career in the corporate world to pursue her passion for writing and published her first book at age 48. She is currently the author of four novels: *Dancing on the Edge of the Roof* (2002), *The Shade of My Own Tree* (2003), *On the Right Side of a Dream* (2005) (a Kentucky Educational Television Book Club discussion selection), and *Girls Most Likely* (2006). Her novels often deal with women "finding themselves" by overcoming issues such as domestic violence and pursuing their personal dreams in the popular romance genre. Her novel *Dancing on the Edge of the Roof* was nominated for the Kentucky Literary Award in 2005. Sheila and her husband moved to Cincinnati in 1999 and three years later moved to Newport, where they currently reside.

Sheila Williams. www.sheilajwilliams.com/ (accessed June 2007).

Wecker, David. "Former Exec Finds Niche as Author." www.cincypost.com/2003/11/20/wecker112003.html (accessed June 2007).

Danny Miller

WILLIAMSON, JOHN A. (b. July 9, 1826, Portsmouth, Ohio; d. July 7, 1898, Newport, Ky.). Riverboat captain and bridge-builder John Allen Williamson was the son of Samuel and Mary Slack Williamson. The family arrived in Newport in 1833, and Samuel died of cholera soon afterward. Son John became a steamboat pilot by age 18 and soon owned part of a line of boats operating on the lower Ohio River. Williamson was a successful steamboat captain for many years. In 1866 he leased the Newport and Cincinnati Ferry. In 1867 he was president of the Newport City Council. In 1884 he began to formulate plans for a bridge across the Ohio at Newport. He organized the companies to build it, incorporating them as the Central Railway and Bridge Company in Kentucky and the Central Bridge Company in Ohio; he was the president of both companies. His bridge, known as the **Central Bridge**, opened on August 29, 1891. It was at the time the second-longest bridge in the United States. In addition, Williamson was a bank president, was involved with the water company, served as president of the Newport Light Company, and consolidated the horse streetcar lines in Northern Kentucky. He died in Newport in 1898 and was buried at Evergreen Cemetery in Southgate. His wife, Elizabeth Kirby Williamson, whom he had married in 1848, and a son, Lawrence, survived him. His estate was valued at one-half million dollars. Williamson was also the uncle of well-known Newport-born suffragette **Josephine Williamson Henry**.

Biographical Cyclopedia of the Commonwealth of Kentucky. Chicago: John M. Gresham, 1896.

"Passed Away," *KP*, July 8, 1898, 3.

Reis, Jim. "Central Bridge a Symbol of Pride," *KP*, January 9, 1995, 4K.

Tenkotte, Paul A. "Rival Cities to Suburbs: Covington and Newport, Kentucky, 1790–1890," PhD diss., Univ. of Cincinnati, 1989.

WILLIAMSTOWN. This city, which is the seat of Grant Co., is located at the junction of U.S. 25, Ky. Rt. 22, and Ky. Rt. 467, east of I-75. The city is near the site of Littell's Station, which was established above the North Branch of Fork Lick by James Littell (1754–1833) and his wife, Michah Standiford, in about 1792. Their son William Littell (1789–1823) was instrumental in the creation of Grant Co. in 1820. Williamstown was laid out on land owned by Capt. **William Arnold**, who served in the Virginia line in the **Revolutionary War**, moved to Kentucky in the 1780s, and also fought in the Indian Wars, including Harmar's 1790 campaign, during which he was wounded. By July 1809, the area had a post office called Arnold's. In 1820 Captain Arnold donated land on which to build public buildings for the newly established county of Grant. The county court met in June 1820 at the new town of "Philladelphia [*sic*]." However, the state soon informed the county leaders that there was already a city in Kentucky by that name and that they would have to choose another. The name was changed to William's Town, in honor of William Arnold and also, presumably, William Littell, the surveyor of the county court. In the early 1820s, a jail and a courthouse were completed and the Grant Seminary opened. By 1822 a post office was established with the name of Williamstown Court House. An official plat of the city showed 99 one-fourth-acre lots on a 25-acre site.

The first church located at Williamstown was the Mount Nebo Church of Christ, organized in 1822 and closed by 1824. Other denominations followed: the Williamstown Particular Baptist Church in 1826, the Williamstown Christian Church in about 1827, the Williamstown Methodist Church (see **Williamstown United Methodist Church**) in 1847, the **Williamstown Baptist Church** in 1878, and the **St. William Catholic Church** in 1893.

In the early nineteenth century, Abner Gaines (see **Gaines Tavern**) began operating a stagecoach line through the county. By the mid-1830s Robert Coleman had opened a blacksmith shop on the corner of Main and Mill Sts. From the 1820s through the 1840s, many taverns or inns were opened in Williamstown, to serve the growing needs of stagecoach travelers along the **Covington and Lexington Turnpike**.

Diseases such as cholera and typhoid fever often struck the city, killing many citizens. Fires were also a constant threat, and at least three times fire destroyed most of the frame buildings in town. In 1859 a group of Williamstown businessmen purchased six acres of land on which to establish the **Williamstown Municipal Cemetery**.

In the early years, the town grew slowly; by 1870 it had only 281 residents. The city's first news-

Grant Co. courthouse, Williamstown, ca. 1908.

paper, the *Williamstown News*, began publishing on October 10, 1872, but ceased operations after about six months. In 1874 another newspaper, the *Williamstown Sentinel,* was begun. In 1879 the *Williamstown Courier* was established, and it merged in 1909 with the ***Grant Co. News,*** which since that time has been the only newspaper serving the city.

The first medical doctors to live and practice in Williamstown were Dr. Wesley Tully and Dr. Samuel Tungate. In addition to being a physician, Dr. Tully owned a general store on Main St., was a trustee of the city and of the Seminary school, and also served as deputy sheriff. The town's namesake, William Arnold, died in 1836, and his wife died several years later. A two-story log house once owned by the Arnold family has been restored and recently relocated (see **Arnold, William, and the Arnold Log House**).

During the **Civil War**, although Kentucky attempted to remain neutral, several skirmishes occurred in and around Williamstown. Some of the citizens fought for the Union, while others fought for the Confederacy, and many prominent citizens were arrested and jailed for their allegiances. On November 1, 1864, 32 Confederate soldiers raided the town, attempting to find a large cache of government money that they believed was held in a vault at Tunis Hardware, but none was found. After the fruitless search, the soldiers plundered the store (see **Williamstown Raid**). After the end of hostilities, the conflict gradually faded from memory and life returned to normal.

Better access to the town was gained in 1877, when the Cincinnati–New Orleans and Texas Pacific Railroad (see **Southern Railway**) laid tracks through the town and built a depot there. The train provided residents with access to employment and markets in Cincinnati and in the Georgetown-Lexington area in Kentucky. The city built a lake and a water tower in 1929, to provide a safe water supply for its residents. Williamstown became quite self-sufficient when in the 1970s it also built a modern sewage-treatment plant. By the mid-1950s, the city had outgrown the existing lake, so a new, larger one was built. Lake Williamstown, completed in May 1957, not only provided additional water for city growth but also offered recreational opportunities. In recent years there have been plans to enlarge the lake and try to make it into a state park.

The greatest change in transportation to Williamstown came in the 1960s, when I-75 was built just west of the city. The expressway provided easy access to most major cities in Northern and Central Kentucky. The 2003 completion of the Barnes Rd. intersection off I-75 has further improved the city's accessibility and has also provided an area for new commercial development outside of the older part of town. Williamstown is a fifth-class city governed by a mayor and a six-member city council. The 2000 census indicated that the city had a population of 3,227.

Chandler, Virgil, Sr. "William Arnold, First Sheriff of Grant County and Founder of Williamstown, Grant County, Kentucky," *Grant County Historical Society Newsletter*, no. 59 (June–July 1998): 365–70.

City of Williamstown. www.wtownky.org (accessed September 25, 2006).

Conrad, John B., ed. *History of Grant County.* Williamstown, Ky.: Grant Co. Historical Society, 1992.

Kleber, John E., ed. *The Kentucky Encyclopedia.* Lexington: Univ. Press of Kentucky, 1992.

U.S. Census Bureau. "American Fact Finder. Data Set. Census 2000 Summary File 1 (SF1) 100-Percent Data. Custom Table." www.census.gov (accessed October 3, 2006).

WILLIAMSTOWN BAPTIST CHURCH. On June 1, 1878, eight charter members in Williamstown organized the Williamstown Baptist Church, which was sponsored by the Elkhorn Baptist Association. The church was the fifth Baptist church in Grant Co. Initially it met in the courthouse under the leadership of its first pastor, Rev. C. H. McDowell, who resigned three months later. S. H. Burgess (1878–1886) replaced him as the church's minister. Church services continued to be held in the courthouse until the church's first building, located on the east side of Mill St. in Williamstown, was completed at a cost of $3,000 and dedicated in July 1883. In August 1889, to provide increased opportunities for fellowship with neighboring churches, the church requested dismissal from the Elkhorn Baptist Association and accepted membership in the Crittenden Baptist Association in June 1890.

Between 1902 and 1910, the Williamstown Baptist Church suffered a series of problems, and as a result, its membership declined from 200 to 114. Finally, the church began to grow in service, strength, and vision as membership returned to 200 by 1918. During the pastorate of John S. Ransdell (1918–1922), the church made an important decision, to move its 41-year-old church building from Mill St. to a more visible location in town along Main St., at a cost of $8,000. The first service at the new site was conducted on October 4, 1919, and church services were begun there on a full-time basis in 1920. A later remodeling and expansion project, costing $20,000, was finished in time for a dedication service on October 2, 1938. A day-long service was held celebrating the church's first 60 years. By that time, church membership had grown to 363. The first parsonage, a five-room brick house adjacent to the church, was built in 1949 for a cost of $12,569. In October 1955, the church called R. T. Daugherty as pastor. Under his leadership, a new building program began in January 1959, with the purchase of 7.5 acres adjoining the church. The first worship service in the new sanctuary was held on January 24, 1971. The total cost of the building and furnishings was $375,000.

Parkview Manor, a 34-unit complex for the elderly, was built in 1980 under the sponsorship of the Williamstown Baptist Church. The new complex was part of the vision of Rev. Daugherty. He was named pastor emeritus upon his retirement after 24 years of service, 1955–1979, the longest pastorate in the church's history. Rev. James P. Craigmyle, a missionary, was the next pastor (1990–1999); he served the second-longest term of the church's 38 pastors. Between 1898 and 1994, the church licensed five ministers to preach and four were ordained to the ministry.

Through the years, the Williamstown Baptist Church has been renowned for its emphasis on music. Its music ministry legacy began in 1905, with F. M. Clinkscales and his wife, Ann Blanchett Clinkscales. Members of this family remain active in the music ministry of the church.

In fall 2005 the Williamstown Baptist Church began a campaign called "Challenge to Build." Its purpose is to assist in building a $3 million expansion that will double the church facility's educational space and provide a new multipurpose wing. Church membership has expanded to 740.

Church Records, Williamstown Baptist Church, Williamstown, Ky.

Caroline Ransdell

WILLIAMSTOWN INDEPENDENT SCHOOLS. There are two school districts within Grant Co., the Grant Co. School District, and the Williamstown Independent Schools, a district that consists of two schools. In 1884, Grant Co. legislator Judge C. C. Cram guided through the General Assembly an act creating a graded free school in Williamstown; in 1887, residents approved a tax for the school. The Williamstown Graded Free School opened its doors in 1891 in a red brick structure along Main St., containing four classrooms, a principal's office, and an impressive 400-seat chapel–lecture room. By 1892 the school had an enrollment of 256. The following year, the institution graduated its first high school class. By 1920 a boosters club and a PTA were in operation, and in that year the girls' basketball team won the championship in Northern Kentucky, despite having to practice outdoors.

In March 1923, the old school building affectionately known as "the castle" burned, and classes were held in various locations throughout Williamstown until a new three-story brick school building opened in 1924, which was used as a high school until 1968. A school band was first organized in 1938 and has flourished ever since.

In 1956 the school system was racially integrated. Shortly thereafter, a new building to house kindergarten through the fourth grade was added to the Main St. campus; in 1968 the last class graduated from the Main St. School; a new one-story school building at 300 Helton St., still in use, opened that September. An elementary school addition was completed in the 1990s.

The most famous graduate of the Williamstown Independent Schools is **Arnie Risen**, of the high school class of 1942, who played in the National Basketball League and became the second person from Northern Kentucky to be inducted into the National Basketball Hall of Fame. The City of Williamstown recently renamed Helton St., where the schools are located, Arnie Risen Blvd. In 2006 the total enrollment of the Williamstown Independent Schools was 877, including 432 high school students.

Conrad, John B., ed. *History of Grant County.* Williamstown, Ky.: Grant Co. Historical Society, 1992.

WILLIAMSTOWN MUNICIPAL CEMETERY. Located just east of downtown Williamstown on the north side of Ky. Rt. 22, Williamstown Municipal Cemetery traces its beginnings to 1859, when a group of town leaders purchased from Alfred Kendall six acres adjacent to the existing cemetery of the Williamstown Particular Baptist Church. The Williamstown Cemetery Company owned and administered the grounds until it encountered financial problems during the Great Depression. In the mid-1940s a new state law was passed, which allowed the cemetery to be owned and operated by the City of Williamstown; at that time the cemetery was named the Williamstown Municipal Cemetery. Several additions to the property have been made over the years. In 1947, for example, the cemetery took control of the old burial grounds of the Williamstown Particular Baptist Church. It is not known who was the first person buried in the cemetery, nor does it appear that the grounds contain any **Revolutionary War** veterans' graves. There is at least one **War of 1812** veteran buried in the cemetery. Famous people interred there include Ziegfeld Follies girl Bertha Opp, Caroline J. Marie Dupuy Blanchet (the first woman to climb Mount Blanc), and **Doris V. Clark**. In the early 1960s, the Odor family constructed a mausoleum on the grounds for its family members. Burials continue today at the cemetery at the rate of 50 per year.

Chandler, Virgil, Sr. *The Williamstown Cemetery.* Williamstown, Ky.: Grant Co. Historical Society, 1987.

Reis, Jim. "Cemeteries," *KP*, April 21, 1986, 4K.

WILLIAMSTOWN RAID. At 3:30 a.m., November 1, 1864, a Confederate Cavalry force of 32 men commanded by Col. Robert J. Breckinridge and Maj. Theophilus Steele (the son and son-in-law of Rev. Robert J. Breckinridge of Fayette Co.) conducted a raid on Williamstown, Ky. The raiders expected to capture a large sum of U.S. Government money that they had been informed was in the safe in N. C. Tunis's store in Williamstown. The money had been removed already, but the raiders found 30 U.S. muskets that they confiscated. The raid was made without incident, and there was no reprisal by the U.S. forces that were occupying the area.

Conrad, John B., ed. *History of Grant County.* Williamstown, Ky.: Grant Co. Historical Society, 1992.

John B. Conrad

WILLIAMSTOWN UNITED METHODIST CHURCH. Little is known of the early history of the Methodist Church in Grant Co. Francis Asbury, Peter Cartwrite, William McKendree, and Barnabas McHenry are early preachers who traveled over large circuits, establishing churches throughout the Kentucky Methodist District. More than 100 years ago, Cartwrite visited the southeastern section of Grant Co., preached, and spent the night at the old Ackman homestead, where L. A. Ackman lived near Layton's chapel. In 1847, William Tucker and his wife Elizabeth deeded a plot of land in Williamstown to trustees of the Methodist Episcopal Church, South. This is the present site of the Williamstown United Methodist Church. In the late 1840s, Joseph Rand, a resident of Lexington, was pastor of the Crittenden Methodist Preaching Circuit, which included all of Grant Co. and part of Boone and Pendleton counties. It was a three-week circuit and preaching was largely in private homes. The Williamstown Methodist Church was one of the two churches in the circuit. Its old frame church building was destroyed by fire in 1885, and for three years, the church held services in the courthouse. Under the leadership of Dr. S. W. Spear, a brick church building was built in 1888 and dedicated in 1891. It was part of the Williamstown Methodist Preaching Circuit, sharing time with the Dry Ridge and Salem churches. In 1892 the Williamstown Methodist Preaching Circuit also included Bethel Grove. In 1915 the Williamstown Methodist Church became a station church, with Rev. J. W. Carter as pastor.

During the pastorate of K. O. Potts (1937–1941), a kitchen and classrooms were added, and there was a service of dedication in 1941. Methodist Bishop Darlington delivered the dedicatory address. At this time the church had two missionary societies, the Women's Society of Christian Service, of which Mrs. L. M. Ackman was the first president, and the Wesleyan Service Guild, whose first president was Mrs. H. T. Matthews. During the pastorate of Rev. C. B. Hogg (1961–1964), an educational building was added to the church. The dedication of a new church building by Rev. Charles Perry, district superintendent of the Covington Methodist District, took place on August 23, 1970. In May 1971, a large portion of the church's indebtedness was paid off through a substantial gift from the estate of Rev. George Ammerman and his wife, Nellie.

In 1939, after consolidation of the Methodist Episcopal Church; the Methodist Episcopal Church, South; and the Methodist Protestant Church, the Williamstown church dropped the word *South* from its name. In 1968, when the Methodist Church and the Evangelical United Brethren Church merged, the name was changed once again. The church is now officially known as the Williamstown United Methodist Church.

In January 2004, under the leadership and pastorate of Christopher Morgan, the Williamstown United Methodist Church purchased the building and parking area on the west side of the church property in order to meet the immediate and long-term space needs of the church. Members and friends now have access to ample parking near the church. This space will be available for future classroom and activity uses as the church continues to grow.

Conrad, John B., ed. *History of Grant County, Kentucky.* Williamstown, Ky.: Grant Co. Historical Society, 1993.

"Footsteps of the Past," *Grant County News,* historical supplement, February 3, 1994, 2–5.

Williamstown United Methodist Church. www.williamstownumc.com/History.aspx.

Marie Ackman

WILLIAMSTOWN WOMEN'S CLUB. The Williamstown Women's Club began during the early 1920s when a group of women organized the Welfare Club in Grant Co. The ladies met monthly at the county courthouse and paid club dues of 10 cents per month. They visited the sick, donated food for Christmas baskets, and brought fabrics to their meetings to make clothing for the poor. In 1924 the Welfare Club was reorganized as the Williamstown Women's Club, with Mrs. Thomas W. Clark as its first president.

In 1926, when the club affiliated with the General Federation of Women's Clubs, it became a part of one of the world's largest and oldest nonpartisan, nondenominational women's volunteer service organizations. The club now gained an expanded role in the community, with an emphasis on civic and self improvement. In the early years the women's club began a beautification project that has resulted in the placement of many trees, shrubs, and flowers throughout Grant Co. In 1939 the members established a book club that later became the **Grant Co. Public Library**. During **World War II**, the members sold Defense Bonds and Stamps, worked with the **American Red Cross**, and served on several home front committees. They collected scrap, worked with the Ration Board, donated blood, took first aid courses, made kit bags for the armed forces, and baked cookies for the soldiers of Company C, at Fort Thomas. When the Grant Co. Hospital opened in the early 1960s, the club gave the $1,500 that it had been saving for a clubhouse, to help furnish a room at the newly built hospital. Each year the club awards scholarships to two local high school seniors.

In recent years the Williamstown Women's Club has sponsored the establishment of the Arts Federation, has been instrumental in bringing Hospice Care and the **Northern Kentucky University** branch into the county, and has supported the creation of a children's garden at the new Grant Co. Public Library. Currently, with a membership of approximately 50 women, the club continues its commitment to community improvement by encouraging its members to develop personal and leadership skills and to participate in constructive public service.

Barnes, Betty M. "Williamstown Women's Club History, 1921–1983," vertical file, Grant Co. Public Library, Williamstown, Ky.

Clarke, Mrs. Thomas W. "History of Williamstown's Women's Club, 1921–1942," vertical file, Grant Co. Public Library, Williamstown, Ky.

Barbara Loomis Brown

WILLIS, CHARLES H. (b. November 3, 1859, Cincinnati, Ohio; d. January 27, 1951, Cincinnati, Ohio). Charles Willis, the owner of a music store, was the son of Harry and Caroline Willis, who were born in England. He married Emma L. Wendt on May 1, 1879, at Wesley Chapel Methodist Church in Cincinnati; two of the family's children lived to adulthood. Charles Willis entered the sheet music business in 1873. In 1899 he and his son William began publishing materials specifically designed for music teachers: teaching methods, collections, and special sheet music. The Willis Music Company's first store, at 41 E. Fourth St. in downtown Cincinnati, was one of a cluster of music-related businesses along Fourth St. between Walnut and Elm Sts., including sheet music and instrument dealers.

During the 1880s, the Willis family resided at 715 Monmouth St. in downtown Newport. From the mid-1890s through at least the mid-1910s, they lived in one of the most elegant residences in Newport: a turreted Queen Anne house at 525 E. Fourth St., in the **Mansion Hill** district. The house was built around 1894 of hard-fired brick with a porch of smooth-dressed sandstone. Stained-glass windows (later removed) illuminated the front parlor and the stair landing.

The Willis Music Company grew steadily by absorbing established local music businesses, including the John Church Music Company and the George B. Jennings Company. In 1901 the Willis music store relocated to larger quarters in the William Hooper Building at Fourth and Elm Sts. in Cincinnati. In 1910 the firm was renamed for William Willis, becoming W. H. Willis & Company. Shortly afterward, however, William died, leaving his father as sole proprietor of the growing enterprise.

In 1919 Charles Willis sold his business to Gustave Schirmer of Boston, Mass. Willis maintained a financial interest in the business after the sale and kept a desk at the Fourth St. store. In addition to his business interests, Willis was an avid tennis player and a member of the prestigious Cincinnati Club and the United Commercial Travelers.

In the 1920s, the Willis family sold their Newport house and moved to 3421 Middleton Ave. in a part of Cincinnati known as Clifton. Charles died at age 91 at Christ Hospital in Cincinnati in 1951 and was buried with his family at Evergreen Cemetery in Southgate.

During the 1950s, the Willis House in Newport's Mansion Hill district was owned and occupied by Chef John Boyar and his wife, Margaret. Like many big old houses in Newport's East Row Historic District, it was later divided into low-rent apartments. As maintenance was deferred, the historic Willis mansion gradually deteriorated. In 1985 the house was sold to preservation-minded new owners who renovated it and reversed many of the unsympathetic alterations made by previous owners. It was restored as a single-family residence in 2006.

Eckberg, John. "Willis Music Celebrates 100 Years of Service," *CE*, May 2, 1999, 6G.

Evergreen Cemetery Records, Southgate, Ky.

Garretson, Joseph. "In the Pink at 88 Years of Age," *CE*, May 4, 1947, 30.

"Music Company Founder Dies at 91—Charles H. Willis," *CP*, January 29, 1951, 20.

Margaret Warminiski

WILLOW (CREEK) BAPTIST CHURCH. The Willow Creek Baptist Church in Bracken Co. was established in 1818 under the auspices of the Union Association of General Baptists, which in 1813 had started a church at North Fork in Bracken Co. At the height of the Willow Baptist Church's membership in 1871, the congregation totaled nearly 300 and was considered the "mother church" to the Baptist churches that followed throughout the county. Willow Baptist Church built a new meetinghouse in about 1853 at the forks of Bullskin Rd. and Ky. Rt. 22 in Bracken Co.; it lasted more than a century, until the modern brick facility in the village of Willow was dedicated in 1967. That church building remains in service today.

Bracken Co. Extension Homemakers. *History of Bracken County*. Bicentennial ed. Brooksville, Ky.: Bracken Co. Extension Homemakers, 2002.

Lathrop, J. M. *An Atlas of Bracken and Pendleton Counties, Kentucky*. Philadelphia: D. J. Lake, 1884.

Caroline R. Miller

WILLOW RUN. An 1830 map shows Willow Run Creek flowing northward along the western edge of Covington and emptying into the Ohio River. The creek was an important source of water for the early settlers and for the abundant wildlife drawn to it. The land area that came to be known as Willow Run derives its name from the Willow Run Creek. One of the first owners of Willow Run was **Jacob Fowler**, who later assigned the land to the Bank of the U.S., in Philadelphia, in lieu of a mortgage. **Thomas D. Carneal** purchased the land from the bank. In 1827 **William Bullock** purchased **Elmwood Hall** and 710 acres (including Willow Run Creek) from Carneal. Bullock hoped to build a dream city called **Hygeia** around Elmwood Hall. He attempted to obtain financing for the project from investors in London, England, but was not successful. He then reluctantly sold the land to Israel Ludlow, who later started the city of Ludlow. The new owner had Willow Run laid out into lots, to form a development he named the Ludlow Subdivision. Numerous houses were soon built along the creek, including many near present-day Crescent Ave. in Covington.

Father James W. Smith organized the **St. Patrick Catholic Church** in 1872, for English-speaking residents living near Willow Run. He had the church building designed by architect **Louis Piket** and built by John G. Martin, at Fourth and Philadelphia Sts. in Covington. St. Patrick Church served the congregation well, for a century, before closing when the land was sold for commercial use. The St. Patrick's congregation was then integrated into the **St. Aloysius Catholic Church** in Covington. During the 1880s, commercial development occurred along Willow Run, including construction of the Bavarian Brewery. Over the years, two viaducts were built across the creek, one at Third St. and the other at 12th St,, which provided better access to downtown Covington. For many years, parts of the creek were used as a garbage dump, and some areas became partially filled. In 1914, after a long legal battle, the City of Covington acquired rights to build a major sewer line through the valley. An attempt was made in 1917 to develop a business district at Willow Run, but the move was not successful. Several ballparks were then built on the landfills, including the Goebel Park at Sixth and Philadelphia Sts. and the Covington Ballpark at Ninth and Philadelphia Sts. Over the years, the parks were used for picnics, baseball and football games, and also performances by **circuses**.

The history of Willow Run somewhat parallels what happened along the Sixth St. Fill (see **Taylor's Bottoms**) in Newport. That area in Newport was also once used as a landfill, later for ball fields, and still later for commercial development and an interstate highway. In 1957 the federal government purchased the land along Willow Run for construction of I-75 (see **Expressways**). With the new highway came numerous commercial and industrial businesses to the area. However, the once beautiful Willow Run valley soon disappeared from view, and the creek began flowing through huge underground pipes. All that is now visible is an eight-lane expressway.

"The City—Willow Run," *DC*, February 18, 1880, 1.
"Cover for Dump; Blackburn to Give Relief to Citizens," *KP*, September 17, 1927, 1.
Reis, Jim. "Tracing the Roots of Willow Run," *KP*, March 11, 1991, 4K.
"Renaissance of Ruin," *KP*, August 24, 1994, 1K–2K.

WILLSON, AUGUSTUS E. (b. October 13, 1846, Maysville, Ky.; d. August 24, 1931, Louisville, Ky.). Augustus Everett Willson, who later became governor of Kentucky, was born in Maysville, the son of Hiram and Ann Colvin Ennis Willson. He was the younger brother of the poet **Forceythe Willson**. Augustus was orphaned at the age of 12 and lived for several years with relatives in New York and Massachusetts. He attended Harvard University at Cambridge, Mass., graduating with the class of 1869. He moved to Louisville in 1870 and studied law under John Marshall Harlan, who later became an associate justice of the U.S. Supreme Court. After his apprenticeship, Willson was made a partner in Harlan's law firm. In 1875 Willson was appointed chief clerk of the U.S. Treasury Department in Washington, D.C., a position he held for just one year. He married Mary Elizabeth Ekins in 1877, and they had only one child, who died as an infant. In a predominately Democratic state, Willson ran as the Republican candidate for the Kentucky Senate in 1879 and was defeated. He then ran for the U.S. House of Representatives in 1884, 1886, 1888, and 1892 and lost each time. In 1907 he entered the gubernatorial race against Democratic candidate Samuel Wilber Hager and was elected Kentucky's 36th governor; he served until 1911. As governor, Willson declared martial law during the Black Patch War (see **Tobacco**). His administration bogged down over fights concerning the temperance issue and tax reform. At the end of his four-year term, Willson returned to his large and lucrative legal practice in Louisville. He entered politics again in 1914 and was defeated by the Democratic former Kentucky governor John Crepps Wickliffe Beckham (1900–1907) in his race for the U.S. Senate. Willson died at age 84 and was buried in the Cave Hill Cemetery, Louisville.

Kleber, John E., ed. *The Kentucky Encyclopedia.* Lexington: Univ. Press of Kentucky, 1992.
The Political Graveyard. "Willson, August Everett." http://politicalgraveyard.com (accessed April 9, 2006).
Rootsweb. "Augustus E. Willson." www.rootsweb.com (accessed April 9, 2006).

WILLSON, FORCEYTHE (b. April 10, 1837, Little Genesee, N.Y.; d. February 2, 1867, Alfred, N.Y.). Poet Byron Forceythe Willson was born in a one-room log cabin, the eldest child of Hiram and Ann Colvin Ennis Willson. In 1846 Hiram Willson loaded his family and their possessions onto a raft and descended the Allegheny River and then the Ohio River, landing several days later at Maysville, Ky. The family lived there for about a year, and then moved downriver to Covington. In his new city, Hiram, who had been superintendent of the common schools of Allegheny Co., N.Y., was instrumental in establishing the common school system, and Forceythe's early education was in the Maysville and Covington common schools. In 1853 Hiram relocated his family to New Albany, Ind. Ann Willson died there in 1856 and Hiram died three years later. The parents left a sizable fortune to their children, making it possible for them to receive a good education. Forceythe attended Antioch College at Yellow Springs, Ohio, for one year and later Harvard University in Cambridge, Mass. He contracted tuberculosis and had to leave Harvard before graduating. In 1858 he became involved in spiritualism and claimed to have become clairvoyant; he said he could read the contents of sealed mail and even communicate with the dead. He took a job as an editorial writer with the *Louisville Journal,* where, as the conflict between North and South escalated, he wrote numerous articles in support of preserving the Union.

Forceythe Willson married Elizabeth Conwell Smith of New Albany, Ind., in 1863. They moved to Cambridge, Mass., in early 1864, so he could supervise the education of his younger brother **Augustus E. Willson**, a future Kentucky governor (1907–1911). Elizabeth Willson died there in fall 1864, at age 22. Forceythe did not grieve his wife's death, claiming that he continued to be in regular contact with her.

While in Cambridge, Willson spent much of his time writing poetry. His most famous poem, titled "The Old Sergeant," was first printed on the front page of the *Louisville Journal,* anonymously. A collection of his poetry was published in Boston in 1866. Most of his poems had wartime themes and did not become well known—exceptions were "The Old Sergeant" and "The Enemy"—though some were published in the *Atlantic Monthly.* Although his poetry was not a commercial success, it was his lifelong, consuming passion. His wife had also been a poet, and Willson privately published her work in 1865. Many of his later poems made references to his deceased wife. Willson's tuberculosis became progressively worse, and he suffered a severe hemorrhage of his lungs in fall 1866. He died several months later at the age of 29; both husband and wife were buried in a small, ill-kept graveyard in the Whitewater Valley, at Laurel, Ind.

Piatt, John James. "Forceythe Willson," *Atlantic Monthly* 35, no. 209 (March 1879): 332–44.
Townsend, John Wilson. *Kentucky in American Letters, 1784–1912.* Cedar Rapids, Iowa: Torch Press, 1913.
Virtualology. "Willson, Forceythe." www.famousamericans.net (accessed May 2, 2006).
Willson, Forceythe. *The Old Sergeant, and Other Poems.* Boston: Ticknor and Fields, 1867.

WILMINGTON. The little town of Wilmington, situated on the land of John Grant (see **Grant Family**), was established by the Kentucky General Assembly on December 7, 1793. Located on the west side of the Licking River, opposite modern Grant's Lick in modern Kenton Co., the town was laid out in 100 lots. Purchasers had to agree to build, within four years, a house measuring at least 18 by 20 feet with a brick or stone chimney. The first trustees chosen for the town were Matthias Corwine, Joseph Floyd, Squire Grant, John Hay, William Henry, John Sanders, and John Thrasher. When Campbell Co. was created in 1795, Wilmington was chosen as the county seat of Campbell Co., owing to its central location. Because no public buildings had been constructed yet, the first quarter session of the court was held at the home of John Grant, for whom Grant's Lick is named. At that meeting Capt. Nathan Kelly was chosen to be the first sheriff and **James Taylor Jr.** was chosen as the clerk of courts. The justices selected for the first quarter sessions of the court were **Washington Berry, John Craig,** Charles Daniel Sr., John Grant, and John's brother Squire Grant. Permits were issued to John Grant to build a sawmill on the Licking River and to operate a ferry at Wilmington.

James Taylor Jr., one of the wealthiest men in Kentucky, had numerous friends in the military and in the federal government, including his cousins Zachary Taylor and James Madison. Since Taylor lived in Newport, he used his influence to move the county seat there in 1796. When Kenton Co. was fashioned from land west of the Licking in 1840, the court decided to locate the county seat near the geographic center of what remained of Campbell Co. It was decided that Alexandria best met that criterion. However, it soon became apparent that since most of the county's population lived near Newport, it would be more convenient to handle much of the court business there. So, in effect, Campbell Co. had two county seats, with Alexandria handling the rural business and Newport the urban. Tiny Wilmington was soon abandoned, and with the help of Licking River floods, it ceased to exist.

Collins, Richard H. *History of Kentucky.* Vol. 1. Covington, Ky.: Collins, 1882.
Hartman, Margaret Strebel, and W. Rus Stevens. *Campbell County Kentucky History and Genealogy.* Campbell Co., Ky.: W. R. Stevens, 1984.
Reis, Jim. "Doorway to Kentucky Licking River Gave Rise to Settlement," *KP,* June 17, 1996, 4K.
Tenkotte, Paul A. "Rival Cities to Suburbs: Covington and Newport, Kentucky, 1790–1890," PhD diss., Univ. of Cincinnati, 1989.

WILMINGTON BAPTIST CHURCH. The Wilmington Baptist Church, located at 11111 Madison Pk. in Fiskburg in southern Kenton Co., was organized on June 2, 1804, with six members. The congregation met at first in a log structure in the Wilmington Bottoms at the confluence of Cruises Creek and the Licking River near Bryant's Ford. The building also served as a school, a post office, and the courthouse (of Campbell Co. at that time). In 1842 members of the church sold the land by the Licking River and bought property in Fiskburg, where the church, which kept the name Wilmington Baptist Church, is presently located. The present brick structure is the third one on the Fiskburg site. The first was a log building 30 by 60 feet, and the second was a one-room white frame meetinghouse that was completed in 1875. The second building was dismantled in 1952 to make way for the current brick structure, which was dedicated on August 30, 1953. Later, a two-story education wing was added to the building and a brick parsonage was built across from the church.

The extensive Wilmington Baptist cemetery contains graves from the early 1840s through the present. Many graves date from the winter of 1917–1918, when influenza struck the community. The proximity of the cemetery to the church has helped to keep it well maintained and protected from vandals.

The Wilmington Baptist Church congregation has started several other churches in the area. In 1850, 20 members left to form the Crittenden Baptist Church. In 1858 the Oak Island Baptist Church was constituted by members who had attended at Wilmington. Two more spin-off churches followed: the Gardnersville Baptist Church (1891) and the DeMossville Baptist Church (1915). The most recent church begun by Wilmington members was the Piner Baptist Church (1952). The Wilmington Baptist Church is part of the Northern Kentucky Baptist Association, which is affiliated with the Southern Baptist denomination. The current pastor is Bill Scott, who began serving the church in June 2003. Over the years, the church has been the site of several series of special meetings; at one of those, in 1996, the popular **Ball Family Singers** held their homecoming.

"Fiskburg Revival," *KP*, March 24, 1996, 12K.
"Gospel Music to Fill the Air at Ball Family Homecoming," *KP*, August 31, 1996, 6K.
"Historic Cemetery to Be Beautified," *Falmouth Outlook*, October 17, 1924, 4.

Pat Workman

WILSON, EARL D. (b. October 16, 1887, Independence, Ky.; d. April 16, 1910, Annapolis, Md.). Football player Earl Wilson was the son of Wesley Berry and Lydia Beall Miles Wilson. His mother died in 1891, shortly after giving birth to his brother **L. B. Wilson**. Earl was educated locally in Covington schools, graduating from the old Covington High School. In 1906 he entered the U.S. Naval Academy at Annapolis, Md., where he became a leader in athletic programs: he played third base for Navy's baseball team and quarterback on the Midshipmen football squad.

On his 22nd birthday, October 16, 1909, tragedy struck Wilson. During a football game in Philadelphia, Pa., against Villanova University, while attempting a flying tackle, he broke his neck and sustained severe spinal cord damage. In those days, players saw action on both sides (offense and defense) of the football game. For six months, Wilson lingered in the Annapolis Naval Hospital, alternately improving and declining, until his death in April 1910.

Despite the navy's desire to bury their football hero at Annapolis, his body was returned to Covington for a funeral at the home of his brother-in-law **Maurice L. Galvin**, at 422 Garrard St. Wilson was buried next to his mother in the Independence Cemetery in Independence. Massive funeral ceremonies were held at both Annapolis and Covington. His death, along with a few others in college football action at about the same time, led the football rules committee to make changes in what was permissible in games played on the gridiron. Other Northern Kentuckians, such as Latonia's **Ron Beagle**, Newport's Alex "Zeke" Zechella, and Bellevue's Pat Uebel, followed Wilson to Annapolis to play football for Navy's Midshipmen.

"A Clipping," *KP*, January 18, 1910, 2.
"Death Ends Long Fight of 'Middie,'" *CTS*, April 16, 1910, 2.
"Earl Wilson Is Buried," *NYT*, April 19, 1910, 6.
"Earl Wilson May Recover," *NYT*, November 19, 1909, 9.
"'Soccer' Football May Be New Game," *NYT*, November 2, 1909, 10.

WILSON, L. B. (b. May 20, 1891, Covington, Ky.; d. October 28, 1954, Cincinnati, Ohio). Lyda Beall Wilson, a banker, theater owner, and radio station operator, was the son of Wesley Berry and Lyda Beall Miles Wilson. His mother died 11 days after giving birth to him, so he was named Lyda Beall Wilson. He grew up in Covington, where his father was once the Kenton Co. clerk, and graduated from the Covington High School in 1910. After leaving school, he and his brother Hansford toured Europe with a theatrical group. He returned in 1912 and was hired as manager of the Colonial Theater in Covington. About a year later, he opened a tobacco store at Sixth St. and Madison Ave., in Covington and operated it for several years. The smoke shop featured a **Richard P. Ernst** cigar. In 1915 he was named secretary of the Covington Industrial Club, the forerunner of the Covington Chamber of Commerce (see **Northern Kentucky Chamber of Commerce**). He became president of the club in 1929. Wilson joined with Senator Richard Pretlow Ernst, George Hill, and **Polk Laffoon Jr.** in an investment group, which purchased a chain of local movie theaters, including the Hippodrome, the Liberty, the Lyric, the Rialto, and the Strand. In 1926 Wilson and Ernst bought the controlling interest in the People's Savings Bank and Trust Company. Two years later, the bank merged with Liberty National Bank to form the **People's-Liberty Bank and Trust Company**. In the new bank, Ernst served as president and Wilson as executive vice president. At that time, the bank was the second-largest in Kentucky. In September 1929 Wilson started radio station **WCKY** in Covington. The station initially operated at just 5,000 watts, but the power was later increased to 50,000 watts. In 1939 WCKY moved its headquarters to the Hotel Gibson in Cincinnati. Wilson married movie star Jean Oliver on October 7, 1929, and they moved into a home on Summit Ln., in Fort Mitchell. No children were born to the couple. They separated on June 28, 1948, but never divorced. Some of the organizations Wilson was affiliated with during his colorful career were Churchill Downs Racetrack in Louisville, the Cincinnati and Covington Bridge Company, the Doerman-Roher Company in Cincinnati, Lincoln-Fields Racetrack in Illinois, and the **Houston, Stanwood & Gamble Company** in Covington. He was also a longtime member of the Elks Club (see **Civic Associations**) and the Masonic Lodge (see **Masons**). In 1954 Wilson died at age 63 in Cincinnati and was buried in Miami, Fla.

"About This Guy," *KP*, March 9, 1929, 1.
"Banker Marries Actress," *KP*, October 8, 1920, 1.
Kenton Co. Public Library. "Covington Biographies: L. B. Wilson." www.kenton.lib.ky.us (accessed April 25, 2006).
Kleber, John E., ed. *The Kentucky Encyclopedia*. Lexington: Univ. Press of Kentucky, 1992.

Jack Wessling

WINGATE, CYRUS (b. ca. 1790, place of birth unknown; d. after 1840, Owen Co.) Cyrus Wingate was the first sheriff of Owen Co. The earliest record of him is his marriage to Emily Milly Spicer in May 1808 in Franklin Co. Wingate was present when Owen Co. was established in 1819 and was part of the committee that built the first jail and courthouse. He held several governmental positions over the years: sheriff from 1819 to 1821; county tax commissioner in 1820; state representative 1824 to 1827; and state senator from 1828 to 1841. He and his wife Emily (perhaps his second wife) had 14 children, one of whom was Penelope Wingate Sullivan. Penelope Sullivan is the person from whom the village of Ep in Owen Co. derives its name: local children called her "Aunt Ep" because they had difficulty pronouncing "Penelope"; and since "Aunt Ep" lived there, the area became known as Ep.

Houchens, Mariam Sidebottom. *History of Owen County: "Sweet Owen."* Louisville, Ky.: Standard, 1976.

WINTERSHEIMER, DONALD C. (b. April 21, 1931, Covington, Ky.). Former Kentucky Supreme Court Justice Donald C. Wintersheimer is the son of Carl E. and Marie Kohl Wintersheimer. He graduated from Newport Catholic High School in Newport in 1949 and received his BA from Villa Madonna College (now Thomas More College) in Covington, his MA from Xavier University in Cincinnati, and his JD from the University of Cincinnati Law School. He was in private practice and served for 14 years as city solicitor for the City of Covington. In 1976 he was elected to the Kentucky Court of Appeals and in 1982 to the Kentucky Supreme Court (formerly called the Kentucky Court of Appeals); he was reelected in 1990 and in 1998. He is known as the most prolific writer on the court, averaging more than 40 written opinions a year.

A member of the adjunct faculty of **Chase College of Law** at **Northern Kentucky University** (NKU), Wintersheimer teaches a seminar course in state constitutional law. His writings have appeared in the NKU Chase Law School's *Law Review* and in numerous other law journals. Wintersheimer has been recognized as a distinguished alumnus of the College of Law of the University of Cincinnati. He is a former president of the Kentucky Municipal Attorney's Association and a founding member of the Chase American Inn of Court. He has received numerous awards from Thomas More College and is a former president of its Alumni Association. He and his wife, Alice, reside in Covington and are the parents of five children, three of whom are lawyers.

"Covington Native Is Senior Ky. Supreme Court Justice," *Challenger*, July 18, 2004, 5A.
Kentucky Court of Justice. www.kycourts.net.
Wintersheimer, Donald. Interview by Donna M. Bloemer, December 9, 2004, Frankfort, Ky.

Donna M. Bloemer

WIREMAN, WALLY (b. June 19, 1919, Beaver Lick, Boone Co., Ky.). Wallace H. Wireman, an inventor, an engineer, an author, and a businessman, was born to John and Augusta Wireman. He earned a BA in engineering from the University of Wisconsin at Madison and an MA in business administration from Wittenberg University in Ohio. Since 1952 he has resided in Walton, where he quietly plies his problem-solving and engineering talents at his companies, WIRED Inc. and AQW Inc. The possessor of 14 patents and two registered U.S. trademarks, he designs and manufactures many replacement parts for the U.S. military and for industry. His creative genius has played a role in the development of hundreds of modern products, such as the electronic supermarket checkout scanner, the vacuum tubes at bank teller drive-through windows, the wheeled golf club caddy, the hand-operated roller for reading credit cards, and drinking faucet filters. He owns the Walton-based AQW (Always Quality Work) Inc. and serves as engineering consultant for the firm, which he founded in the 1970s with his wife, Frances Flynn Wireman. The company has approximately 15 employees and is a government defense contractor and supplier of military parts for use in submarines, tanks, and aircraft. Its customer base includes NATO-member foreign governments and the United Nations as well as the U.S. government.

Twice the federal government has honored Wireman. He received the Department of Defense Value Engineering award for development of superior cost-effective and efficient products, and he was given a Certificate of Appreciation from the Department of Defense for his contributions to the success of Operation Desert Storm and Operation Iraqi Freedom. He also served in the U.S. Air Force during **World War II**, attaining the rank of master sergeant.

Wireman probably is best known for his invention and design of desiccants, or dehydrators, which eliminate moisture from missiles, fighter planes, and military equipment. In 1972 he invented a molecular adsorber, which, operating on similar principles, removes moisture from molecules and also eliminates odors. AQW Inc. has made hundreds of thousands of these products and supplied them to the U.S. military, saving the government significant amounts of money. The molecular adsorber is made available commercially through Wireman's other company, WIRED (Wireman Industrial Research Engineering and Development) Inc. and is sold under the names Adzorbit and Adsorb Star. These products, which first entered the market in 1988, remove odors and gases; they can even remove cigarette smoke odors from large spaces. Using small pellets of sodium aluminosilicate, the products draw moisture and odor molecules into themselves, thereby eliminating odor from the environment rather than hiding it. Wireman holds trademarks for Adsorb Star as well as for a product called Toxic Out, which works similarly to remove toxic fumes and gases from the air. Toxic Out is currently used in the printing industry as well as in the X-ray, radiology, and pathology departments of health care facilities.

Wireman has been a consumer safety advocate for most of his adult life, testifying regarding electrical safety as an expert witness at trials and before U.S. congressional hearings and committees. In 2003 he published *The Call to Solve: What Every Fireman Should Know*, which details his thoughts on electrical safety.

Wireman showed a natural genius for engineering, electronics, and creativity, even as a child. One of his first inventions was a basic intercom system that allowed his mother to summon him by "buzzing" his attic bedroom with the touch of a button. During the days before indoor plumbing, he also laid electrical wiring to illuminate the family outhouse. He was an industrious youth, either figuring things out on his own or learning from library books about electronics and engineering. He created his own toys from unwanted parts found in junkyards, built a bicycle tire out of a broken piece of garden hose, and rebuilt a Ford Model T automobile with a friend. During his teens, he worked as a golf caddy, and this work inspired him to develop the first pull cart for golf clubs.

During his youth, Wireman's family moved from Kentucky to Cincinnati, so that his father could take a job as a laborer with the Frank Taylor Company. The move allowed Wireman to attend and graduate from Withrow High School in that city. Afterward, the young Wireman also began work as a laborer at the Frank Taylor Company and was quickly promoted to maintenance electrician, supervisor, and then chief industrial engineer. He is a self-proclaimed problem-solver, who enjoys inventing solutions and then seeking out the next challenge. The now 87-year-old inventor maintains a daily presence at AQW Inc. and often answers the phone there.

Fulmer, Kelly F., executive vice president and chief operations officer, AQW Inc. Interview by Sarah A. Barlage, February 12, 2006, Walton, Ky.
"Saving Money for Uncle Sam," *KP*, February 6, 1990, 1K–2K.
Toxic Out: Molecular Adzorber. www.adzorbit.com (accessed July 2, 2006).
Wireman, Wally, president of AQW Inc. and WIRED Inc. Interview by Sarah A. Barlage, June 28, 2006, Union, Ky.

Sarah A. Barlage

WISENALL, BERNARD T. (b. September 4, 1869, Maysville, Ky.; d. July 16, 1942, Covington, Ky.). Bernard T. Wisenall was the son of John Bernard and Jane Eckmann Campbell Wisenall. In April 1893 he formed a partnership with Louis E. Dittoe, to create the architectural firm of **Dittoe and Wisenall**. The firm's architects designed a number of buildings in Northern Kentucky, including the Covington City Hall (on E. Third St. between Court and Greenup Sts., demolished), the **Kentucky Post** Building, the **First Christian Church, Covington**, and an addition to the **Citizens National Bank** Building. They also designed the Pugh Building (later called the Polk Building) in Cincinnati. In 1900 Wisenall married Emma Rambo of Newport. The partnership of Dittoe and Wisenall was dissolved in 1910, when Dittoe took a teaching position at the Ohio Mechanics Institute in Cincinnati.

Wisenall continued to design buildings in Covington on his own, including an addition to the **Kelley-Koett Company**'s building. With architect Chester Disque, he drew the plans for the John G. Carlisle Junior High School and the Third District School and was the project architect for the 1917 **Dixie Highway** Beautification Project. In 1924 he designed the Ben Adams Insurance Building on the northwest corner of Fifth St. and Madison Ave. Three years later, he drew plans for the Girls Friendly Building at the **Trinity Episcopal Church**. He was a staunch supporter of the Covington **YMCA**. Wisenall died at age 72 at his home, Hathaway Hall, at 1210 Highway Ave. in Covington. Funeral services were held at the Trinity Episcopal Church, and he was buried at Highland Cemetery in Fort Mitchell.

"Covington Architect," *KP*, January 2, 1917, 1.
Kenton Co. Public Library. "Covington Biographies: Bernard T. Wisenall." www.kenton.lib.ky.us (accessed September 24, 2007).
"New Building on Way," *KP*, May 15, 1924, 1.
Tenkotte, Paul A. *A Heritage of Art and Faith: Downtown Covington Churches*. Covington, Ky.: Kenton Co. Historical Society, 1986.

WITHERS FAMILY. The Withers family, merchants residing in Covington in 1861, found themselves "caught in the middle" when hostilities broke out in the **Civil War**. Descended from a long-established line of colonial Virginians, the pro-South Withers family were tobacco merchants. Their company's suppliers certainly had Southern sympathies, and to a lesser extent the same was true of customers in the markets they served; but the Withers family operated their tobacco business in a region that was predominantly pro-Union.

The patriarch of the family was Charles A. Withers, who was born in Stafford Co., Va., on June 10, 1800. His wife, Matilda Lynch, was born in Lynchburg, Va., on September 6, 1811. They arrived in Northern Kentucky about 1836, and Charles became a partner in the Withers & Carpenter Company, tobacco manufacturers. The business was located in Cincinnati, but the family lived in Covington at Greenup and Market Sts. (Park Pl.). Charles A. Withers was a founder of **Trinity Episcopal Church**, a member of the

Covington City Council during the 1840s, the first superintendent of the **Kentucky Central Railroad**, and president of the local branch of Frankfort's Farmers Bank. As superintendent of the railroad, he built the first 18 miles of track south of Covington with his own money. His daughter Elizabeth Sally Withers married **Eli Metcalf Bruce**, who shared the Withers family's Southern sympathies and who was involved in helping to finance the Confederate Army. It was said that the Witherses' home might as well have been a hospital, because the family often took in people in need. Charles Withers died while visiting relatives in Waynesville, Ohio, on Saturday, August 10, 1863, at the height of the war, and was buried at Linden Grove Cemetery in Covington.

Charles and Matilda had several children, the most celebrated being their son Charles A. Withers, who preferred to be known as C. A. Withers. Born in 1843 at Covington, he joined the Southern cause during the Civil War and rode with the famed Southern Cavalry raider, Gen. **John Hunt Morgan**. Withers rose to the rank of major and was Morgan's adjutant. After Morgan's death, a wake was held for him at the Witherses' home in the 600 block of Sanford St. in Covington. C. A. Withers moved to Augusta, Ga., after the war. He married the well-connected Clara De Antignac, a French Huguenot belle, and soon became one of the largest cotton brokers in the South. Later, he returned to Northern Kentucky and became the associate editor and drama critic for the *Cincinnati Commercial* newspaper. After his wife Clara died in 1913, Withers resided either at the Kentucky Confederate Home at Pewee Valley outside of Louisville or at the Hotel Emery in Cincinnati. He died from Bright's disease at age 82 on March 23, 1923, at the Booth Hospital and was buried in the family plot at Linden Grove Cemetery in Covington.

In 1915 the City of Covington named a park for the elder Withers in recognition of his services on the city's park board. Today, this park, located between Greenup and Scott Sts., is covered with pavement and called Park Pl.

"Death of an Old Citizen," *CDE*, August 11, 1863, 3.
Kentucky Death Certificate No. 8547, for the year 1923.
"Major C. A. Withers Dies," *KE*, March 24, 1923, 3.
Reis, Jim. "Covington Park Bloomed Briefly, Then Disappeared under Concrete," *KP*, August 26, 1991, 4K.
"Remains of Gen. Morgan," *CJ*, April 18, 1868, 3.

WITHROW, ETTA M. SMITH (b. March 4, 1937, Owen Co., Ky.; d. June 14, 2000, Lexington, Ky.). Etta Maude Smith Withrow, a chief warrant officer, was the daughter of Lt. Col. Albert Clarence and Mary Etta Power Smith. Although Withrow traveled the world as the child of a military father and the wife of a naval officer, she considered Owen Co. her home and returned to live there with her mother in the family home on Cedar Creek for several years. Withrow had one child, John Clarence Withrow.

Gen. Billy Wellman, the state adjutant general, appointed Etta Withrow as the first female warrant officer of the Kentucky National Guard in 1974. She retired in 1990 as chief warrant officer. Withrow was also the first woman in Kentucky to serve on the Governor's Advisory Committee on Veterans Affairs. She researched and prepared the adjutant general's report to the Kentucky legislature on the Vietnam Veterans bonus program. She served as a volunteer Veterans Administration service officer for veterans in Anderson Co. and as field representative for the Women's Military Memorial Foundation.

Withrow's military awards included the Meritorious Service Medal, the Army Commendation Medal, the Army Achievement Medal, the Humanitarian Service Award, the Army Reserve Components Achievement Medal, the Kentucky Distinguished Service Medal, the Kentucky Commendation Medal, the Kentucky Merit Medal, and the Kentucky State Active Duty Medal. Withrow was regent and treasurer for the Susannah Hart Shelby Chapter of the National Society of the Daughters of the American Revolution; vice president of the River Raisin Chapter of the United Daughters of the War of 1812; president of the United Daughters of the Confederacy Chapter 7; a member of the National Guard Association of the United States and Kentucky, American Legion Post 7; and vice president of the Bluegrass Chapter of the Retired Officers Association. After a long illness, she died at Central Baptist Hospital in Lexington in 2000 and was buried at the Monterey Cemetery in Monterey.

"Etta Maude Smith Withrow, 63," *Owenton (Ky.) News-Herald*, June 21, 2000, 6.
"Etta Withrow," *State Journal*, June 15, 2000, 2.
"Etta Withrow Dies: Was Chief Warrant Officer," *Lexington Herald-Leader*, June 15, 2000, B2.
Murphy, Margaret Alice Karsner. *The Power Line and Connections: Nine Generations in America*. Frankfort, Ky.: Lynn, 2000.
State Journal, May 16–22, 1994.

Margaret A. Murphy

WNKU. At 5:30 a.m. on April 29, 1985, WNKU, the fledgling public radio station of **Northern Kentucky University** (NKU), aired its initial broadcast on the local FM band. News director Maryanne Zeleznik, who had been hired just two weeks before, was the first live voice broadcast on the 89.7 MHz frequency. NKU could at last leave behind its unwanted distinction as the only state-supported university in Kentucky without a radio station. That first broadcast was the culmination of a seven-year struggle advanced by Dr. N. Edd Miller, chair of the school's Communications Department. Miller and members of his staff were joined by various university administrators, officials, and personnel in their endeavor to secure a spot on the local radio dial for WNKU-FM.

Their exhaustive efforts had garnered the support of university president Dr. Leon Boothe as well as the long-awaited approval of the Federal Communications Commission. General manager Rick Pender painstakingly laid the groundwork for WNKU's early success by guiding the station through the complicated certification and programming-approval process necessary to secure public radio status. A location near the student dormitories was selected for the tower and the 12,000-watt transmitter. Construction and installation of both components—completed between January and April of 1985—provided the station with a broadcast range that reached audiences within a 30-mile radius of the school's Highland Heights campus. Several classrooms on the third floor of the Landrum Academic Center were converted into the station's offices and studio, which consisted of 1,800 square feet. The start-up costs, which totaled approximately $300,000, were raised by the university through donations from various foundations, corporations, and private donors.

WNKU, the third National Public Radio (NPR) station serving the Northern Kentucky and Greater Cincinnati area, honored its local roots with its folk music programming and south-of-the-river news reporting. Another reason behind WNKU's focus on Northern Kentucky was its directional broadcast signal, which afforded stronger reception to the south than to the north. Although the station's news and public affairs coverage did not extend beyond the borders of its home base during WNKU's early years, nationally syndicated features such as NPR's *All Things Considered* and *Morning Edition* served to widen its programming scope and broaden its audience appeal. The station's music programming was a bold departure from that of other public and commercial radio station formats up and down the crowded dial. Touting itself as "Kentucky Folk Radio," WNKU embodied its slogan within its expansive and eclectic mix of rustic Kentucky **bluegrass**, Appalachian music, and international folk-based selections as well as similar offerings from various regions across America.

The station's first fund drive in June 1985 raised $3,000. Within six months of its first broadcast, the station's second public appeal, a four-day fundraising and subscription-membership drive, easily met its $10,000 goal. In a tremendous show of local support, 250 of the station's 453 members signed up during the drive. In July 1985 the Corporation for Public Broadcasting approved WNKU for funding, thus qualifying the station to receive a $16,000 base grant along with the promise of future incentive grants.

NKU holds the station's license and supplies a percentage of its operating funds, but supplemental contributions from membership drives and support from the Corporation for Public Broadcasting make WNKU editorially independent of the university while also supporting its positive community presence and outreach goals. Additionally, the noncommercial programming offered on WNKU prohibits the airing of revenue-generating commercials, although businesses, corporations, or other organizations may underwrite programming costs with grants, for which they receive on-air acknowledgment. Currently, 60 percent of the station's funding is generated by membership and underwriting, 30 percent is supplied by NKU, and 10 percent is received from the Corporation for Public Broadcasting.

Decreasing the station's dependency on university funding was one of the two goals general manager David Arnold was presented with when he was hired in 1991; the second was attracting more listeners. When focus group studies identified that a large proportion of WNKU's audience lived in Ohio and Indiana, the station's news coverage was broadened to include areas within the I-275 loop (see **Expressways**). That same year, music director Dan Reed modified WNKU's former all-folk programming by adopting a more progressive "Triple A" format—musical selections with an adult, album, and alternative focus. In keeping with the station's new direction, WNKU touted itself as "The Natural Alternative" and as "A New Direction in Acoustic Music." As it made these changes, WNKU carefully preserved its tremendously popular niche programs, such as Katie Laur's bluegrass show *Music from the Hills of Home,* Kathy Costello's *A Celtic Afternoon,* and Bob Beemon's *Mr. Rhythm Man.*

In 1995 WNKU's 10-year anniversary celebration was buoyed by listeners' positive responses to the station's expanded news and music programming. The popular public radio station boasted a weekly audience of 25,000 to 30,000 listeners, a significant increase from its 1991 totals, which averaged between 15,000 and 20,000. General manager Ben Singleton, hired in 2003, cited an even more impressive figure: 38,200 listeners per week were tuning in to 89.7 FM. Singleton also noted that the percentage of Ohio listeners—over the years averaging 80 percent, to Kentucky's 20 percent—had evolved in recent years along with population shifts; Kentucky listeners accounted for approximately 40 percent of the station's audience. The station has also taken advantage of developing technology to expand its broadcasting schedule and enhance audience accessibility. In January 2003, after purchasing a digital audio delivery system, WNKU began 24-hour broadcasting; in February 2006 the station began offering on-demand features and podcasts via its Web site. Local publications have also affirmed the station's tremendous public appeal; *Cincinnati CityBeat, Cincinnati Magazine,* and *Everybody's News* have recognized WNKU as the "Best Station in Cincinnati."

Under the longtime leadership of news director Maryanne Zeleznik—who, just before her August 2005 departure, was the only original WNKU employee—the station's news department won numerous national, regional, and local awards and honors. The Public Radio News Directors Inc., Ohio's Society of Professional Journalists, and the Kentucky Associated Press and Radio-Television News Directors Association are among the prestigious organizations that have repeatedly honored the WNKU News Department in many areas, including broadcast and feature writing, newscasting, and investigative reporting.

When WGUC-FM purchased public radio station WVXU-FM, WNKU lost Zeleznik and fellow news veteran Jay Hanselman to WGUC. General manager Singleton seized the opportunity to make programming and personnel changes that enable WNKU to maintain its long-standing commitment to Northern Kentucky news and public affairs coverage while also reshuffling and reshaping its winning mix of music and nationally syndicated program offerings. In December 2007 Chuck Miller became station manager.

WNKU's current slogan "NPR and great music!" clearly identifies the programming pillars upon which the station's award-winning reputation has been built. The station has been under the banner of NKU's University Advancement Division since 1999. In addition to WNKU, the division includes the Office of University Development, the Office of Marketing and Communications, the Office of Alumni Programs, the Office of Special Events, and the NKU Foundation. These dynamic offices work collaboratively to advance NKU's mission of "becoming a preeminent learner-centered, metropolitan university recognized for its contributions to the intellectual, social, economic, cultural and civic vitality of its region and of the Commonwealth."

"FM Radio Station Approved for Northern," *KP,* January 24, 1983, 10K.

Hall, Gregory A. "Fine-Tuning Sound of Public Radio—WNKU General Manager Hopes to Find Format, News Focus in Station's Roots," *KP,* June 25, 1991, 10K.

Kiesewetter, John. "WNKU Celebrates a 20-Year Musical Mix," *KE,* April 28, 2005, E1.

Kreimer, Peggy. "WNKU's Pender Leaving Station," *KP,* August 8, 1985, 9K.

Miller, N. Edd. Letter to members regarding WNKU's one-year anniversary, *Kentucky Folk Radio* (WNKU newsletter/pamphlet), April 1986.

Pender, Rick. "All Grown Up: Over 20 Years, Bouncing Baby WNKU Matures into Popular Radio Station," *Cincinnati CityBeat,* 2005, www.best-of-cincinnati.com/ (accessed August 3, 2006).

University Advancement. "Welcome to University Advancement." Northern Kentucky Univ. http://advancement.nku.edu/page.asp?p=0110000 (accessed August 3, 2006).

"WNKU-FM: On the Air for 10 Years," *KP,* April 24, 1995, 1K.

Zeleznik, Maryanne. Telephone interview by Jan Mueller, February 22, 2005.

Janice Mueller

WNOP. Radio station WNOP-AM originated in 1946 in the minds of a handful of businessmen of the Tri-City Broadcasting Company of Newport. The group, headed by James Lang, former sheriff of Campbell Co., sought a radio station operating at 1110 kilocycles with one kilowatt of power for the daytime only, a so-called sunrise station. At the time of their application to the Federal Communications Commission (FCC), another station was being proposed at Dayton, Ohio, using the same frequency. In early November 1946, hearings were held in Washington, D.C., and on May 29, 1947, the FCC granted a license to Tri-City Broadcasting and denied the application for the Ohio station. The call letters for the new radio station in Newport were to be WWNL. It appeared that Tri-City Broadcasting would be able to proceed with plans, but they had to be put on hold when the Dayton, Ohio, group appealed the FCC decision. In the meantime, Tri-City's newly purchased transmitting equipment was destroyed in a warehouse fire in Fort Thomas. Finally, after months of renegotiating and reengineering, Tri-City Broadcasting applied for construction of a station operating on 740 kilocycles, which was approved May 14, 1948. The transmitter was constructed in a field at Cold Spring, off Johns Hill Rd., and the studio was located on the second floor of the building at 606 Monmouth St. in Newport, above the old Mustang Bar. At 12:10 p.m., August 21, 1948, WNOP signed on the air for the first time. The first announcer introduced A. B. "Happy" Chandler (Kentucky governor 1935–1939 and 1955–1959), who was on hand for the occasion.

WNOP was not affiliated with a radio network; the original format was a combination of radio shows and country music programming. In 1956 **Ray Scott**, who later became one of the top 25 country disc jockeys in the nation, joined the team at WNOP. In 1962, amid pressure to compete and gain a more stable and loyal audience, the station changed its the format to all **jazz**. Oscar Treadwell was one of the station's well-known jazz personalities. In 1972 the original owners sold the station to Cincinnatian Al Vontz, owner of a beer distributorship in Ohio. Immediately, the rent charged the studio in Newport was raised, and Vontz made a major change in the station. He teamed with designer David Ziegler and arranged to have a new studio built. The Jazz Ark, the new studio's nickname, was constructed out of three oil tanks welded together, each 12 feet in diameter and 20 feet long. Together they held five rooms on two floors with interconnecting doors and stairs. The ark was built at Tucker Marine. Each tank was equipped with 20,000 pounds of ballast, and the facility was placed in the Ohio River to become a floating studio. It was anchored at the Stadium Marina, just east of the mouth of the Licking River. Windows made to look like large portholes gave the studio a bird's-eye view of the Cincinnati skyline. Above the studio were the large red neon letters WNOP; they produced an amazing sight at night, glimmering on the river. From there, Carolyn Rose, wife of Cincinnati Reds player Pete Rose, broadcast her show on WNOP.

The Jazz Ark, also known as "Radio Free Newport," continued until 1989, when the station decided to move from its tiny offices to a larger space in Cincinnati. The ark was donated to the Contemporary Arts Center in Cincinnati. Then in 1992, to accommodate the growing interest in national news, the station dropped its jazz format and adopted Ted Turner's CNN Headline News format from 6:00 a.m. to dusk daily. In 1994 the jazz format returned, and it continued until Sacred Heart Radio purchased the station at the end of 2000. On January 1, 2001, the WNOP format became religious programming. In January 2006 the new station, with the same WNOP call letters, celebrated five years of success; its studio is at the Holy Spirit Center in Norwood, Ohio.

Federal Communications Commission Reports. Vols. 12, 13, pp. 998–1001, 1276–88. Washington, D.C.: Federal Communications Commission, 1946–1948.

Johnson, David. "Loyal Listeners Keep Jazz Ark Afloat," *Campbell County Recorder,* June 5, 1986, 5.

John E. Leming Jr.

WOLF, JOANNES "BROTHER COSMAS" (b. January 6, 1822, Grosskissendorf, Swabia; d. April 7, 1894, Latrobe, Pa.). The church artist Joannes Wolf came to America as a young man in 1852 to join the Benedictine monastic community of St. Vincent at Latrobe, Pa., as a lay brother. Lay brothers take the final monastic vows but are not ordained for priestly duties. As a rule, lay brothers do tasks that require some manual skill. Wolf received the religious name of Brother Cosmas.

Boniface Wimmer, the abbot of St. Vincent, soon discovered Brother Cosmas's artistic talents and sent him in 1857 to the Munich Royal Academy of Art, where he studied for five years with the well-known German sculptor Johann Petz. Shortly after his return to the St. Vincent Monastery, Brother Cosmas took on an important assignment at Covington, Ky., where Wimmer had founded the **Covington Altar Stock Building Company**. Brother Cosmas assumed the job of business manager and chief designer of the company. He took Brother Claude Hauesler from the St. Vincent Monastery with him as a laborer.

The Covington Altar Stock Building Company designed and built altars, pulpits, confessionals, and baptismal fonts. Brother Cosmas created preliminary drawings of these structures with pen, ink, and a delicate wash. Fortunately, 52 of his exquisite drawings survive at the St. Vincent Monastery. Besides altars and other interior church decorations, they include designs for buildings such as rectories and schools and demonstrate the great talent of this German-born Benedictine artist.

Brother Cosmas's most successful creations were wooden altars, which he modeled after German Gothic prototypes. They had pointed arches with delicate carvings and were fitted with altar paintings that depicted biblical scenes from the Old and New Testaments, images of saints, and devotional renditions of the Madonna and the Christ Child. Most of the altars were tripartite, with a large central panel and two narrow side panels. The altars were painted white, and the altar paintings in most cases were placed on a gold-leaf background. Judging from the drawings by Brother Cosmas, he designed each altar with the appropriate paintings, to be executed by the artists who worked for him at the Covington Altar Stock Building Company. Because of the large number of altar structures the company produced, skilled workers were hired to do the carpentry and assemblage of the altars.

Brother Cosmas worked on most of the altars himself, from the Covington studio except when he needed to travel to Baltimore; Chicago; Cincinnati; Erie, Pa.; Pittsburgh; or Newark, N.J., to install new altars. The name of Brother Cosmas is not often mentioned in church chronicles. His talent and accomplishments seem to have gone unnoticed for the most part by writers of religious histories in North America. There are exceptions, however. The 1863 altar at St. Mary's Cathedral in Newark, designed and built at the Covington Altar Stock Building Company, is described in great detail in the cathedral's commemorative booklet. The altars that Brother Cosmas built for several Northern Kentucky churches are of special interest to admirers of the talents of the Benedictines. The altars at **St. Joseph Catholic Church** in Covington were among the most impressive of Brother Cosmas's structures; the main altar rose to a height of 40 feet. Unfortunately, when St. Joseph Church was razed in 1970, these altars were lost. After 10 years in Covington, Brother Cosmas moved the Altar Stock Building Company to St. Vincent in Latrobe, Pa., where he remained active in designing and building decorative structures for new mission churches until his death in 1894. He was buried in Latrobe, Pa.

Cochran, Nathan M., O.S.B. *Ora et Labora: The Saint Vincent Lay Brothers, 1846–1946.* Latrobe, Pa.: St. Vincent Abbey Press, 1988.

Pohlkamp, Diomede, O.F.M. "A Franciscan Artist of Kentucky, Johann Schmitt, 1825–1898," *Franciscan Studies* 7 (June 1947): 148–49.

Springer, Annemarie. *Nineteenth Century German-American Church Artists.* Bloomington, Ind.: Annemarie Springer, 2001, www.ulib.iupui.edu/kade/springer/index.html (accessed November 23, 2005).

Annemarie Springer

WOLFF, OTTO DANIEL, JR. (b. May 16, 1911, Newport, Ky.; d. February 28, 1955, Fort Mitchell, Ky.). The prominent Northern Kentucky architect Otto Daniel Wolff Jr. was the son of **Otto Daniel Wolff** Sr., a well-known Campbell Co. Circuit Court judge, and the former Christine Roth. Otto Jr. was raised in Newport, where he graduated from Newport High School. He earned his BA degree from Georgia Tech University in Atlanta, Ga., and his architectural degree from the University of Cincinnati. He married Mary Cobb, and they had two children, Otto Daniel III and Cynthia. For several years Otto Wolff Jr. worked for the Federal Housing Administration in Louisville. He returned to Northern Kentucky, where he designed numerous residential and commercial buildings. Some of those were the **Summit Hills Golf and Country Club**, the Fort Mitchell branch of the First National Bank of Covington (see **First National Bank and Trust Company of Covington**), and the Kentucky state office building at Fourth and Garrard Sts. in Covington. He was a member of the **Trinity Episcopal Church**, where he served as a vestryman. In February 1955 he underwent an operation that revealed that he had pancreatic cancer. He died three weeks later at his home in Fort Mitchell. Funeral services were held at the Trinity Episcopal Church, and burial was in the Highland Cemetery, Fort Mitchell. His son Otto Daniel Wolff III became a well-known Covington attorney.

"Otto D. Wolff, Editorial on Death," *KTS,* March 1, 1955, 4A.

"Otto Wolff, Architect Dead, Rites Wednesday," *KTS,* February, 28, 1955, 1A.

"Otto Wolff Dies: Noted Architect," *KP,* February 28, 1955, 1.

"Plan Resolution on Wolff Death," *KTS,* March 1, 1955, 2A.

"Wolff Estate Goes to Widow," *KTS,* March 8, 1955, 2A.

WOLFF, OTTO DANIEL, SR. (b. May 4, 1868, Newport, Ky.; d. August 21, 1937, Newport, Ky.). Otto D. Wolff Sr., a lawyer, a judge, and a banker, was the son of Daniel and Elizabeth Limberg Wolff. Born and raised in Newport, he attended primary school there and graduated from **Newport High School**. He earned a law degree from the Cincinnati Law College (now the University of Cincinnati) and was admitted to the Kentucky bar. Wolff married Christine Roth and they had two children, architect **Otto Daniel Wolff Jr.** and novelist **Ruth Wolff**. Otto Wolff Sr. was an associate of Judge Edward J. Boltz, and they maintained offices on the sixth floor of the Finance Building, at Fourth and York Sts. in Newport. Wolff was appointed master commissioner of the Campbell Co. Circuit Court in 1898 and served in that post for six years. At various times, he also held the positions of Newport city solicitor and city councilman. In 1910 he and Phillip Veitz started the Citizens Bank and Trust Company in Newport. Wolff served as president of the bank until it was merged with the Central Savings Bank and Trust Co. In the new consolidated bank, he was made a vice president. In 1915 he was elected Campbell Co. Circuit Court judge, a position he held until 1921.

Wolff was a civic-minded person, deeply concerned about the problems of the less fortunate. He served as secretary of the **Campbell Co. Protestant Orphans Home** and was instrumental in starting the penny-a-meal program, to help feed people who were poor and unemployed. In 1921 Wolff took a bold first step for women's rights by permitting women to serve on juries. For many years he was a member of the St. John's Evangelical Church (now **St. John's United Church of Christ**), where he taught classes in religion and held various leadership positions. He remained active in business and charitable work until he succumbed to a heart attack at age 69 in 1937. His body was laid out in the family home at 624 E. Third St. and was buried in the Evergreen Cemetery in Southgate.

"Bar Pays Tribute to Judge Wolff," *KP,* August 23, 1937, 1.

"Heart Attack Ends Life of Former Judge," *KP,* August 21, 1937, 1.

Kentucky Death Certificate No. 20338, for the year 1937.

Reis, Jim. "Otto Wolff Blazed Trail for Women," *KP,* June 24, 1996, 4K.

WOLFF, RUTH (b. March 31, 1909, Newport, Ky.; d. June 13, 1972, Fort Thomas, Ky.). Novelist Ruth Wolff was one of two children born to Circuit Court judge **Otto Daniel Wolff Sr.** and his wife

Christine Roth Wolff. Ruth's brother, **Otto Daniel Wolff Jr.**, became a prominent Northern Kentucky architect. During her formative years, Ruth and her family lived at 624 E. Third St. in Newport; later they moved to 105 Carolina Ave. in Fort Thomas. Ruth graduated from Newport High School in 1927 and attended Sullins College, in Bristol, Tenn. She graduated from Western College for Women (now part of Miami University), at Oxford, Ohio. Ruth did postgraduate work at the University of Cincinnati. Her first job was as a public school teacher for the Tennessee Valley Authority. She later worked for Pacific Mutual Life Insurance Company and United Cork Company of Covington and was a church secretary for Rev. Harold Barkau at **St. John United Church of Christ** in Newport. In addition she did volunteer work for Children's Hospital in Cincinnati.

In the early 1960s, she gave up outside employment to concentrate on her writing career. Wolff wrote four books, *I, Keturah* (1963), *A Crack in the Sidewalk* (1965), *A Trace of Footprints* (1968), and *A Space Between* (1970). She said that she was intrigued by the name Keturah, which she had seen on a gravestone in a local cemetery. That marker could have been for **Keturah Moss Leitch Taylor** (the wife of **David Leitch** and later of **James Taylor Jr.**), who was buried in **Evergreen Cemetery** in Southgate. Ruth's father, Otto Daniel Wolff Sr., was also interred there. The setting for Wolff's second book, *A Crack in the Sidewalk*, was her hometown of Newport, although in the novel she called the city Brockton. She indicated that the unusual title came from the fact that almost everything around her seemed to be covered with concrete, so that the only place where plants grew was in the cracks of the sidewalk. Ruth's books deal with the experiences of **Appalachians** in their attempt to adapt to the urban lifestyle; Newport was a frequent destination for Appalachians. In addition to her four books, Ruth wrote articles for *Ladies Home Journal*, *Redbook*, and other similar publications. In later life, she married J. Robert Wiseman, and the couple lived in Batavia, Ohio. Ruth Wolff Wiseman died of cancer at age 63, at St. Luke Hospital in Fort Thomas. She was buried in the Batavia Cemetery in Batavia, Ohio.

"Deaths, Mrs. Ruth Wolff Wiseman," *KP*, June 15, 1972, 4.

"Mrs. Ruth Wolff Wiseman," *KE*, June 15, 1972, 24.

"Parted Sidewalk, Site for City Flower Border," *KP*, December 8, 1965, 18K.

Wolff, Otto Dan, Jr. Telephone interview by Jack Wessling. October 2005.

Jack Wessling

WOMEN. Women of Northern Kentucky have made significant and varied contributions to all aspects of the region's development. Most notably, many were activists, community leaders, and women's rights champions. **Anna Shaler Berry** became a dedicated women's rights activist and a close friend of **Mary Barlow Trimble** and Susan B. Anthony. The three women campaigned tirelessly for the legal rights of women, especially the right to vote in the 40 years before the 19th Amendment was passed. Trimble was an ardent supporter of **women's suffrage** during the last 20 years of the 19th century. She was involved in numerous social issues, including women's property rights and the right to vote, and was one of the founders of the Covington Equal Rights Club. Her daughter was the internationally known suffragist author **Kate Woolsey**, who wrote *Republics versus Women* (1903).

Josephine W. Henry was a writer, teacher, and women's rights activist. She joined the Kentucky Equal Rights Association but was expelled from the organization owing to her extreme views regarding religion and marriage. Subsequently, the National American Woman Suffrage Association gave her its Pioneer Distinguished Service award in 1920. She died in 1928.

In 1923 **Jesse Firth** was the first woman to run for public office in Kenton Co. A leader in the women's suffrage and temperance movements, she also served as an officer of the Kentucky Equal Rights Association and later with the League of Women Voters.

Alice Lloyd, a teacher most of her life, was also a member of the Women's Temperance Union and the Kentucky Equal Rights Association. Lloyd died in 1951. She is not to be confused with the Alice Lloyd who founded an Eastern Kentucky College. **Mattie Bruce Reynolds** had a keen interest in charities and social affairs, but her strongest affiliation was with women's suffrage. She hosted national suffragist organizers at her home in Covington and marched with four other Kenton Co. women in a suffragist parade in Washington, D.C., in 1913. **Ida Mitchell Roff** taught elocution in Covington in the 1880s and later wrote articles on astronomy and other subjects for the *Cincinnati Enquirer*. She also organized and arranged meetings for the Kentucky Equal Rights Association. She died in 1939 in Mason Co., having spent all but the last two years of her life in the Cincinnati area. **Virginia Adeline "Jennie" Rugg** was one of Northern Kentucky's leading suffragettes, pleading the case of the franchise for women. She lived in Newport most of her life and died in 1923 at Ashland.

In the area of social work, **Henrietta Esther Scott Cleveland** moved to Covington and became involved in a ladies' society that dedicated itself to works of charity among the poor. In 1861 she was a founder of the St. Elizabeth Hospital (see **St. Elizabeth Medical Center**). Cleveland died in 1907. **Kate E. Perry Mosher** was a Southern sympathizer during the Civil War. After the war, she assisted the homeless victims of war in Northern Kentucky. She was also a clubwoman and an artist. **Mary Moser** became one of the founders of the Catholic Social Services in Northern Kentucky and arranged for more than 300 children to be placed in adoptive homes during her long career as one of the region's first social workers. Moser died in 1987. **Helen McNeeve Theissen**, who was active in Catholic charitable causes for the Archdiocese of Cincinnati, brought Mother Teresa to Covington. Theissen died in 2005.

In the area of **civil rights**, **Alice Thornton Shimfessel** served as president of the community center that became known as the L. B. Fouse Civic League. Many civil rights activities were launched out of the L. B. Fouse Civic League, including **Congress of Racial Equality** freedom riders and **NAACP** meetings. **Amo Lucille Powell Peters** organized local marches and peaceful demonstrations to end segregation and unfair conditions for African Americans. She became chairperson of the Maysville–Mason Co. Human Rights Commission and helped plan the 1964 march on Frankfort in support of the upcoming Public Accommodations Act. Her personal visits with the owners of local businesses and civic leaders led many to support her efforts to hasten integration. **Pamela E. Mullins** organized a student demonstration at Covington's **Holmes High School** to protest the school's inability to hire an adequate number of African American teachers and a history curriculum that disregarded the experience of black Americans. In 1988 she became the first African American woman elected to the Covington Board of Education. She lives in Covington today.

In politics, **Rebekah Hechinger Hord** became the first woman to serve on the Maysville city commission and, after her election as Maysville mayor in 1951, was the first woman ever to hold the position of mayor of a city in Kentucky. She participated in many civic and professional organizations. Her daughter **Harriett Cartmell** also became Maysville's mayor, in 1986. **Dixie Lee**, in 1966, was the first woman in Kentucky to run for Congress in the Democratic primary. She also ran for the U.S. Senate and made her final bid for office in a run for the Kentucky Senate in 1969. Lee continued her interest in politics by working for the Democratic Party for many years. She died in 2001. **Hanna Baird**, who moved to Florence, Ky., in 1964 with her family, became involved in Democratic politics and in women's and children's issues. She also served as a board member for the **American Red Cross**, the Community Chest, **Northern Kentucky University**, and several other institutions.

Nancy Diuguid of Carroll Co. broke new ground with gay and feminist themes in her theater productions on the London (England) stage in the 1980s and 1990s. She also launched arts projects, working with prisoners, traumatized children, and victims of illness, rape, and abuse.

Many Northern Kentucky women made their impact in the entertainment and acting arenas, including **Dorothy Abbott**, **Betty Clooney**, **Rosemary Clooney**, **Blanche Coldiron**, Frances Denny Drake (see **Mrs. Drake**), **Lyda Florence Lewis**, **Una Merkel**, **Erica Newman**, **Mary Wilton "Minnie" Roebuck**, and **Patricia A. "Pat" Scott**.

Notable Northern Kentucky women in business and the professions include **Vera Angel**; **Clare Elsie Beatty**; **Virginia Bennett**; **Betty Blake**; Dr. **Tracey Butler Ross**; **Judy Clabes**; **Martha Purdon Comer**; **Elizabeth B. Delaney**; Cora Dow, owner of **Dow Drugs**; **Mary B. Greene**; Dr. **Lucy Ann Dupuy Montz**; **Roxanne Qualls**; **Mary Cabell Richardson**; Dr. **Sarah M. Siewers**; Dr. **Louise Southgate**; **Patricia M. Summe**; **Jane Summers**; and **Mary Wood**.

Northern Kentucky has produced numerous outstanding educators, among them **Elizabeth B.**

Cook Fouse, **Ninona Miller**, **Rosella French Porterfield**, **Jessie O. Yancey**, and **Kate Zoller**.

Women talented in the fields of literature and art have also had Northern Kentucky connections: **Harriette Simpson Arnow**, **Mary Wilson Betts**, **Mary L. Mitchell Cady**, **Elizabeth Pickett Chevalier**, **Annette Cornell**, **Julia Stockton Dinsmore**, **George Elliston**, **Berniece Hiser**, **Sue Hamilton Jewell**, **Dorothy Ladd**, **Mary C. McNamara**, **Anna Virginia Parker**, **Barbara Paul**, **Frances Rickett**, **Elizabeth Madox Roberts**, **Dixie Selden**, **Mary Bruce Sharon**, **Helen Truesdell**, **Caroline Williams**, **Ruth Wolff**, **Eleanor Duncan Wood**, and **Rena Lusby Yancey**. **Lina** and **Adelia Beard** in the early 1880s founded the nation's first girl scouting group, which came to be known as the Camp Fire Girls. Lina and Adelia wrote several books, the most famous being *The American Girls Handbook*. **Daniel Carter Beard** was their brother, and artist **James Beard** was their father.

Women have been a part of the history of Northern Kentucky, though neglected for the most part in the historical record, since the days of **Mary Ingles**'s escape from Indian captivity at **Big Bone Lick** in the mid-1750s.

Irvin, Helen Deiss. *Women in Kentucky*. Lexington: Univ. Press of Kentucky, 1979.

Potter, Eugenia K., ed. *Kentucky Women: Two Centuries of Indomitable Spirit and Vision*. Louisville, Ky.: Four Colour Imports, 1997.

Karen McDaniel

WOMEN POLICE OFFICERS AND FIREFIGHTERS. The first policewoman in Northern Kentucky began to serve in the early 20th century. In 1914 Mrs. Murray Hubbard urged the Covington Women's Civic Commission to investigate the hiring of a woman police officer, stating that larger cities had done so with success. In March 1915 Alice Voorhees was given police authority under the Covington Department of Public Safety as a humane matron and worked with women and juveniles. Two years later, when a new mayor took office, she lost her job. Voorhees returned to public service from 1937 to 1940 as assistant police matron.

Joan Penick made headlines in 1970, when the Covington Police Department appointed her a police officer in the juvenile division. She rose to the rank of captain before her retirement in 1996. Also during that time, Janet Radenheimer was hired; she retired as a police sergeant. In 1975 Micki White was the first woman to serve on the Florence Police Department. Later she had police duties in Fort Wright and after that was a patrolwoman for the Kenton Co. police. When she began in Florence in 1975, she was not allowed to ride in a patrol car with a married officer.

In 1978, Sandy Tretter Schonecker, of Covington, was hired as the first woman Kentucky state trooper (KSP). In 1980 she joined special investigations as a state police detective; in that role she was an undercover officer investigating the bombings of coal tipples in Harlan Co. Posing as the niece of a mafia kingpin, she bought dynamite and witnessed bombings. The information she turned up from an informant led police to the persons responsible for bombing a Harlan Co. detective's home. For that work she was given the KSP medal for meritorious service. In 1987 Schonecker returned to Dry Ridge as a detective, working auto theft and child abuse cases. She retired on November 30, 1993.

Although there can be no doubt that over the years women took up positions on bucket brigades and participated in fire watches and firefighting when a fire occurred in their community, they were not recognized as firefighters until much more recently. In the 1970s, Michele Westermeyer began by serving two years as a volunteer firefighter with the Erlanger Fire Department and then joined the Covington Fire Department (CFD) on June 18, 1979. She was Covington's first woman firefighter, the first woman to drive the fire engine, the first woman lieutenant, the first woman captain, and the first woman to run a firehouse (Hands Pk.). She retired as captain after 26 years of service. Soon afterward, the CFD hired Betty Schwartz, who retired after 20 years as an emergency medical technician (EMT) driver. Tara Lytle, Covington's third woman firefighter, was hired in 2000.

Newport had a woman firefighter during the 1970s; Tammy Webster joined the fire department in Fort Thomas in 1999; captains Joy McVey and Jill James both served with the Florence Fire Department. Other Northern Kentucky departments with women firefighters include the Central Campbell Co. Fire Department and the departments of Dayton, Hebron, Independence, and Wilder. In 2005 Kentucky had 30 women serving with 14 fire departments.

"Micki N. White," *CE*, June 7, 2002, 4B.

"Sandy Schonecker," *KP*, December 27, 1978, 1K.

Nancy J. Tretter

WOMEN'S CRISIS CENTER. The Northern Kentucky Rape Crisis Center was started with 20 volunteers in 1975. In March 1979 its name changed to the Women's Crisis Center because the organization was extending its services to battered women. Some people then, and even today, do not know what constitutes a "battered woman"; this is true especially when the victims are young mothers or sexually abused women, or both. Often the victims do not know it is a crime to verbally, emotionally, or physically mistreat a person. Three individuals who were influential in the development and funding of women's crisis centers statewide and locally were former Kentucky governor Martha Layne Collins (1983–1987), local attorney Suzanne Cassidy, and well-known local businesswoman Marge Schott.

The mission of the Women's Crisis Center is to speak for and empower adults and children who have survived domestic violence, sexual abuse, or rape. Besides serving as an advocate for victims, the Women's Crisis Center provides crisis intervention, counseling, education, referrals to other kinds of social services agencies, and shelter for abuse survivors. There are two 24-hour crisis lines in operation within Northern Kentucky. The center's administrative office is at 835 Madison Ave., Covington, and other offices are located in Florence, Maysville, Williamstown, and Carrollton. In 2008 ground was broken for a new Regional Services Center in Hebron.

Currently, the Women's Crisis Center is the only shelter for battered women and their children in the eight-county **Northern Kentucky Area Development District** (NKADD). The agency works closely with NKADD to ensure that community services for its clients are coordinated with the efforts of other local social service agencies. The center maintains an updated resource manual so that it can mesh with other community services. When clients enter the shelter, they receive help in finding effective ways to facilitate the intervention, evaluation, and delivery of services; the purpose is to achieve an immediate resolution to the crisis at hand. First, the victim's most urgent needs are assessed. Then the delivery of needed items or services to alleviate the person's most pressing concerns follows.

For children, there are services offered that protect them from abuse and court-appointed legal advocates who try to help children to recognize that abuse is not their fault and is not an acceptable norm. Also, the center offers an array of nonresidential services that allow abused children to heal. Children learn that they have the right to say no, to get away from being abused, and to tell an adult what has happened when abuse has occurred. The center has found that the need for intervention through prevention and education is acute. Its team education program in the elementary schools works with an average of 500 disclosures of abuse of children annually.

A court advocate is available for the victim at any time in the process of filing for an emergency protection order, and this advocate also accompanies victims to court hearings. Court advocates explain to victims the nature and implications of legal procedures and facilitate child care and transportation services during court attendance while providing advocacy and emotional support. Hospital advocacy is also available from volunteers who offer rape crisis counseling in cases of domestic violence. Victims are made aware of resources and information during emergency room visits.

Kentucky Women's Crisis Center. http://mivictims.org/kentucky/mission.html (accessed June 7, 2006).

"Rape Crisis Center Gets Name Change," *Colonel Covington's Chronicle*, March 1979, 9.

Robin Rider Osborne

WOMEN'S SUFFRAGE. In Northern Kentucky as in the nation, the social activists dubbed "suffragettes" were women who generally came from families with at least some means. Most were educated, having attended schools other women could not afford; in addition, these woman had the leisure time to become involved in reform works. For the most part, they seem to have been mainline Protestants—Episcopalians, Methodists, and Presbyterians. Once slavery was abolished in 1863 with the Emancipation Proclamation, many of America's female social reformers turned their attention to the cause of women's voting rights. "Equal rights for men and women" was the clarion call of what soon came to be known as the women's suffrage movement.

Nationally, the best-known suffragette was Massachusetts-born Susan B. Anthony (1820–1906), the daughter of a Quaker abolitionist. She did not live to see the passage of the 19th Amendment to the U.S. Constitution, which allowed women to vote in the national elections of 1920. Anthony began her reform work in the temperance movement, then moved on to **antislavery**, before joining the battle for women's voting rights. She visited Northern Kentucky at least twice: in October 1879, she spoke at the Odd Fellows Hall in Newport and stayed at the home of **Anna Shaler Berry**, wife of **Albert Seaton Berry**; and in 1894 Anthony was a guest in the home of **Mary Barlow Trimble** of Covington.

In parts of Kentucky, some women (the few unmarried ones who owned taxable property) were permitted to vote in school-related elections as a result of a law passed in 1838, the first such school-suffrage bill in the nation. Their vote was restricted to school bonds and school trustee selection. In 1894 school suffrage was extended only to all women of second-class Kentucky cities—Lexington, Covington, and Newport—because the state legislature reasoned that only women from those areas had petitioned for the right. By 1902 even that limited privilege was reversed for racist reasons; it was feared that black women in Lexington might gain control of the city's school system. Thus, it could be argued that this short-lived taste of suffrage helped to propel the movement both statewide and in the nation.

Within Kentucky, the most famous suffragist was Laura Clay, daughter of abolitionist Cassius B. Clay. Within Northern Kentucky, there were several women, many of them friends of Laura Clay, who pushed, and pushed hard, for the right of women to vote. Perhaps the most famous Northern Kentucky women's rights activist was **Kate Trimble Woolsey**. She was the daughter of Mary Barlow Trimble, also a women's rights activist, and Judge **William Trimble**. Both Kate and her mother had the family wealth, time, and status to promote their cause. Kate Woolsey took her arguments to the streets of New York City and London, England, as well as those of her native Covington, where she lived in the Trimble mansion at the southeast corner of Robbins St. and Madison Ave., now the site of a Walgreen Drug Store. In 1903, while living in London, Woolsey published a book entitled *Republics versus Woman,* criticizing the inequities of modern democracies. In it she pleaded for passage of legislation on behalf of women's rights, which she claimed were being held back by slow-moving governments.

Kate's mother, Mary Trimble, was a prominent figure in national suffragette circles. A friend of Anthony, Trimble often was disparaged by Covington society for spending far too much time on her causes and neglecting her family. Trimble's rebuttal was that the hired help was able to care for her family. Other daughters involved in the movement included Grace "Fanny" Trimble Facklers, an international socialite who split her time between London and New York City, and Helen Trimble Highton, a delegate to the Kentucky Equal Rights Association (KERA) meeting in 1913, held in Louisville.

Newport-born **Josephine W. Henry**, the niece of **John A. Williamson**, was part of the wealthy Williamson family. In 1888 she was lobbying for women's voting rights in Frankfort before the legislature, and later she lobbied for women's property rights. She was an active member of KERA and a strong supporter of Laura Clay. At meetings she often spoke just before Clay on the program. In 1920 Henry was given a national award as "a pioneer of the women's rights movement." In 1890 she became the first woman to run for a state office in Kentucky, although at the time her fellow suffragettes could not cast their votes for her.

Another contemporary women's rights activist, **Jennie Rugg**, who came from a wealthy family, was also from Newport. In the early 1880s she demanded the franchise for women. She was a delegate to the 1884 KERA Convention along with fellow Newport residents Mrs. John A. Williamson and Mrs. **Thomas Laurens Jones** (Mary Keturah Taylor), a granddaughter of Gen. **James Taylor**.

A medical doctor who was part of this movement was Dr. **Louise Southgate**. Scion of the famous Southgate family, Southgate practiced in Covington and was on the staff of that city's **Booth Memorial Hospital**. She helped many young Covington ladies with issues of women's health and was a speaker at the KERA meeting held in Covington in 1909. Two other Covington suffragists were **Mattie Reynolds**, who hosted national suffragist organizers at her home at 502 Greenup St. and in 1913 marched with four other Kenton Co. women in a suffragist parade in Washington, D.C.; and Mrs. Eugenia B. Farmer, a Covington school board member.

From Germantown came **Alice Lloyd**, who became Mason Co.'s foremost women's rights leader. Another of Laura Clay's close friends, Lloyd did not support the proposed U.S. constitutional amendment as a solution to women's suffrage. Instead, she believed that each state individually should offer the vote to women—that it was not a federal issue.

KERA remained active from 1881 to 1920. Similar organizations in other states evolved into what became the League of Women Voters after the passage of the 19th Amendment. Since Covington and Newport provided many of KERA's initial members, several of the organization's annual meetings were held in Northern Kentucky, including those of 1897, 1901, and 1905. There was a Susan B. Anthony Club in Cincinnati, and many Northern Kentucky women were members, including the club's president in 1906, medical doctor **Sarah Siewers**. This club's legacy lives on through a Susan B. Anthony Day Dinner held annually in Cincinnati.

"Four Women Are Delegates," *KTS,* November 19, 1913, 14.
Fuller, Paul E. *Laura Clay and the Women's Rights Movement.* Lexington: Univ. of Kentucky Press, 1975.
Reis, Jim. "Winning the Right to Vote," *KP,* November 8, 2004, 4K.
Woolsey, Kate Trimble. *Republics versus Woman.* London: Gay and Bird, 1903.

WOOD, ELEANOR DUNCAN (b. January 10, 1869, Philadelphia, Pa.; d. June 13, 1936, Maysville, Ky.). Eleanor Wood's parents were Dr. Arthur F. Wood and Eleanor Duncan. Eleanor married Clarence L. Wood. A poet, she was one of 60 contestants who submitted poems in 1922 for the Memorial Building to honor those who died in **World War I**, which was being erected on the University of Kentucky campus in Lexington. Wood's poem, "In Memoriam," was chosen to adorn the side of the Memorial Building. Wood published a collection of her poetry titled *Largesse.* Some of her poems appeared in magazines; for example, "The Conqueror" was published in *Lippincott's Magazine* in 1913. Other poems of hers were "The Failure" and "In Nazareth." Eleanor Wood died of heart failure in 1936 at age 67 and was buried in Washington, Ky.

Calvert, Jean, and John Klee. *Maysville, Kentucky: From Past to Present in Pictures.* Maysville, Ky.: Mason Co. Museum, 1983.
Kentucky Death Certificate No. 17253, for the year 1936.
Noe, J. T. C. *A Brief Anthology of Kentucky Poetry.* Lexington: Univ. of Kentucky Extension Service, 1936.
Poets' Corner. www.theotherpages.org/poems.
"Prize Poem to Be Engraved on Memorial Building to Kentucky's World War Dead," *KTS,* April 18, 1922, 27.
"Prize-Winning Memorial Poem in Kentucky," *KTS,* October 2, 1922, 16.

Thomas S. Ward

WOOD, MARY (b. January 19, 1914, New Orleans, La.; d. May 6, 2002, Fort Wright, Ky.). Witty television and radio critic Mary Thompson Hawes Wood, a descendant of Confederate general **James Morrison Hawes**, was probably best known as a commentator and a humorist. She was the daughter of Lee and Ida May Thompson Hawes. In the 1930s her father was the business editor of the *Cincinnati Enquirer.* Mary attended **Holmes High School** and graduated from the Millersburg (Ky.) Female Institute. She later attended college both in Missouri and at Morehead State College in Kentucky. She married Charles P. "Chip" Wood in Newport on January 29, 1934. Mary Wood wrote soap operas for WLW radio, then worked for the *Cincinnati Post* for 36 years and enjoyed a loyal following as she covered the careers of **Bob Braun**, **Nick Clooney**, **Rosemary Clooney**, Paul Dixon, and Ruth Lyons. She became a good friend of the family of Larry Hagman, star of the successful television series *Dallas.* Her most popular columns probably were her animal stories, starring her beloved collie, Buster.

She lived in Covington and "led the effort to preserve Riverside Dr., fighting efforts to tear down these old homes and put up a highrise," according to Pat Flannery, an attorney friend and neighbor. In the announcement of her retirement, the *Post* said: "Every newspaper office needs a Mary, and few get them. Like the title of her first book, *Just Lucky I Guess,* we here at the *Post* most certainly have been." Mary Wood died in 2002, in a nursing home, and was buried at Highland Cemetery in Fort Mitchell.

Billman, Rebecca. "Witty and Fearless, She Was a Local Icon," *CE,* May 9, 2002, B9.

Bird, Rick. "She Covered Broadcasting with Style and Wit," *KP,* May 8, 2003, 2K.

Cornell, Si. "Mary Wood to Retire," *CP,* December 9, 1978, 2.

Wood, Mary. *In One Ear and Gone Tomorrow.* Cincinnati: Southgate Press, 1978.

———. *Just Lucky I Guess.* New York: Doubleday, 1967.

Ann Hicks

WOODEN, JOHN ROBERT (b. October 14, 1910, Centerton, Ind.). John R. Wooden is one of the premier collegiate basketball coaches of all time, the one whose teams have won the most NCAA championships (10). He was a three-time All-American guard at Purdue University in West Lafayette, Ind., and the college basketball player of the year for 1932. Wooden's first teaching-coaching job was at Dayton High School, Dayton, Ky. (see **Dayton Public Schools**). There he taught English and coached basketball for two seasons, 1932–1934, and his team's losing basketball record that first season was the only one Coach Wooden ever had. He was also the high school's football coach in 1932. From Dayton High School, he went to a coaching position in basketball at Central High School in South Bend, Ind. After serving in the U.S. Navy during **World War II**, he coached basketball at Indiana State University at Terre Haute. In 1948 he left to become head basketball coach at the University of California at Los Angeles (UCLA), where he became the legendary "Wizard of Westwood." He retired from coaching after the end of the 1974–1975 basketball season and today lives in Encino, Calif., not far from the UCLA campus.

Chapin, Dwight, and Jeff Prugh. *The Wizard of Westwood: Coach John Wooden and His UCLA Bruins.* Boston: Houghton Mifflin, 1973.

Wooden, John R., with Steve Jamison. *Wooden: A Lifetime of Observations and Reflections on and off the Court.* Lincolnwood, Ill.: Contemporary Books, 1997.

Michael R. Sweeney

WOODFILL, SAMUEL, MAJOR (b. January 6, 1883, Jefferson Co., Ind.; d. August 13, 1951, near Vevay, Ind.). Samuel Woodfill, a distinguished **World War I** veteran and **Medal of Honor** recipient , was the son of **Mexican War** and **Civil War** veteran John H. Woodfill. By age 10, after being taught by his father and gaining practice by hunting wild turkeys, the youth had become an expert rifleman. In March 1901 he entered the U.S. Army at Bryantsburg, Ind. His military career eventually led him from Louisville, Ky., to the Philippines and from a posting in Alaska to one in Kentucky at the **Fort Thomas Military Reservation**.

Woodfill received a Medal of Honor for his actions at Cunel, France, on October 12, 1918; a 1st lieutenant, he was serving there with the 60th Infantry, 5th Division. His citation relates how he led his company in battle when they were under German machine-gun fire. Through his skill and bravery, he overcame at least a dozen Germans armed with machine guns and inspired his men to successfully carry out their objective.

Woodfill married Lorena Blossom Wiltshire, a native of Covington, on December 26, 1917, in Fort Thomas. They lived in a home on the military post until he retired on December 23, 1923, after 22 years of active military service. Their next home was at the corner of Alexandria Pk. and Hawthorne Ave., in the southern part of the city of Fort Thomas. The couple had no children. The Samuel Woodfill Elementary School, named in Woodfill's honor, is now located within two blocks of their former home. Woodfill, a tall, quiet, retiring man, was recognized as a military hero throughout the community, but he never made a show of his accomplishments. When he was asked to run for a seat in the U.S. Congress, he declined.

While the ceremony of the burial of the nation's Unknown Soldier was being planned in 1921, some 3,000 names of outstanding soldiers of the Army Expeditionary Force (AEF) of World War I were reviewed. One hundred of these names were presented to Gen. John "Black Jack" Pershing; he was to select three of them to be among the U.S. Army's honor guard for the event. Upon seeing Woodfill's name, the general proclaimed, "I've already selected that man as the outstanding soldier of the A.E.F." The other two were the army's legendary Sgt. Alvin C. York and Col. Charles White Whittlesey, the wartime commander of the famed Lost Battalion. A whirlwind of activities preceded and followed the ceremony. Joined by his wife, Woodfill went to Washington, D.C., where Kentucky senator **Richard P. Ernst** of Covington took him to the White House to meet President Warren G. Harding (1921–1923). The U.S. Congress adjourned after recognizing Woodfill and held a banquet in his honor. Later in New York City, Woodfill was received and heralded by members of the New York Stock Exchange, which suspended business for three hours. Woodfill also met with Marshall Foch of France, was honored at a reception in the Hippodrome, and was given a banquet by the army's 5th Division.

After his retirement from the military, Woodfill attempted to operate an apple and peach farm between Silver Grove and Flagg Springs in Campbell Co., but the endeavor was not successful. He then worked as a watchman at the Andrews Steel Mill in Newport until **World War II** began. The famous radio commentator Lowell Thomas wrote a biography of him, *Woodfill of the Regulars.* During World War II, Woodfill was recalled to service and promoted to the rank of major; his duties during this period had to do with recruitment and with promotion of the sale of war bonds. Afterward, he moved back to a farm near Vevay, Ind., where he was found dead at age 68 on August 13, 1951. The date of his death was estimated to be August 10. He was buried first at the Jefferson Co. Cemetery near Madison, Ind., and later, on October 17, 1951, in Arlington National Cemetery in Arlington, Va., near the tomb of General Pershing. A marker was placed in the yard of the Jefferson Co., Ind., courthouse in memory of Woodfill. In Northern Kentucky a large bronze Kentucky State highway marker recounting Woodfill's exploits stands in front of the Samuel Woodfill School, and both the school and the Military Museum at the Fort Thomas Community Center have portraits of Woodfill.

Arlington National Cemetery Website. www.arlingtoncemetery.net/woodfil.htm (accessed May 14, 2008).

Committee on Veterans' Affairs. *Committees Print 15, Ninety-third Congress, First Session.* Washington, D.C.: Government Printing Office, 1973. Medal of Honor Recipients 1865–1973.

Daniels, Betty Maddox. "Fort Thomas Military Reservation Description and History," *NKH* 6, no. 2 (Spring–Summer 1999): 6–9.

Thomas, Lowell. *Woodfill of the Regulars.* Garden City, N.Y.: Doubleday, 1929.

"Woodfill Body to Be Taken to Arlington," *KP,* August 15, 1955, 1.

Betty Maddox Daniels

WOODLAWN. This sixth-class Campbell Co. city, incorporated on October 17, 1922, is located on a hill southeast of Newport. It is surrounded by the cities of Bellevue, Fort Thomas, and Newport. Earlier, the area was known as the Old Odd Fellows Grove. Around 1905, James E. McCracken and attorney Howard Benton subdivided the grove and formed the Woodlawn Home Company. The engineering firm of Glazier and Morlidge surveyed and laid out the initial five streets; the sewers and paving of roads came later. Newport's main water line underneath Waterworks Rd., Woodlawn's northern boundary, was tapped to supply the city with water. In 1912 the city was being considered as the home of a proposed Roman Catholic parish, which eventually became **St. Francis de Sales** in adjacent **Cote Brilliante**. In 1915 the Newport Women's Club opened its East End Park adjacent to Woodlawn along Waterworks Rd., next to the old Delicious Dairy. Although the park was not in Woodlawn, it quickly became the playground for Woodlawn children. For many years, the park was known as Maple Grove and was owned by Ed Bartlett, who operated a saloon at the site after **Prohibition**. Two sons of Bartlett were Thomas "Red" Bartlett, longtime Campbell Co. Boys Club and recreation director; and Lou Bartlett, the former Woodlawn fire chief. Maple Grove had tennis and horseshoe courts; a baseball field, which was home to the Woodlawn Volunteer Fire Department's summer baseball league; and, in the woods behind center field, a cave where local children played. In about

1917 the men of Woodlawn formed the Woodlawn Welfare Association for the purpose of road-building and other community improvements. Charles Pirman was its first president. During the 1920s, both Newport and Bellevue rejected Woodlawn's requests to be annexed. Wilson Rd. was constructed in 1926–1927, making access to Bellevue and the Fort Thomas streetcar line (see **Streetcars**) easier. The center of the community since about 1950 has been the Woodlawn Volunteer Fire Department firehouse. Other centers of community life included the gasoline station at the northwest corner of Waterworks and Wilson Rds., which for many years was Bernie Brinkman's Texaco Station, and the Woodlawn Inn at Waterworks and East Crescent, operated in the early 1960s by former Cincinnati Royals basketball coach Tom Marshall. There is no school in Woodlawn; public education is supplied by the **Campbell Co. Public Schools**. Woodlawn's predominantly Catholic population sends students to St. Francis de Sales in Cote Brilliante and to **Newport Central Catholic High School**. In the early 1960s, Carl Huber built the Woodlawn Terrace subdivision, adding 21 new homes to the city. In the early 1980s, the construction of I-471 (see **Expressways**) took many homes on the city's west side. The interstate also isolated Woodlawn from the east side of Newport and severed most of its previous connections with the Cote Brilliante neighborhood. Over the years there have been a few businesses in Woodlawn: Mary Wallace's fruitcake and candy company; Bartlett's Auto Body; and a number of builders, including Joe Becker, Barney Fehler, Adam Feinauer, Greg Ferring, and Carl Huber. Today the fire department continues, but the gas station and the Woodlawn Inn are gone. Newport provides police service. In 2000 the U.S. Census Bureau reported that Woodlawn had a population of 268.

Kentucky Land Office. "Kentucky Cities Database." http://apps.sos.ky.gov/land/cities/ (accessed March 29, 2005).

U.S. Census Bureau. "American Fact Finder. Data Set. Census 2000 Summary File 1 (SF1) 100-Percent Data. Custom Table." www.census.gov (accessed March 29, 2005).

Jerome L. Kendall

WOODS, GRANVILLE T. (b. April 23, 1846, Columbus, Ohio; d. January 30, 1910, New York City). Granville Woods, known as "the black Thomas Edison," was a pioneer African American inventor and businessman. After mastering the trades of a machinist and a blacksmith, and after working as a railroad fireman and engineer, Woods completed a series of college courses in electrical and mechanical engineering between 1876 and 1878. In 1880 he came to Cincinnati and founded the Woods Electric Company. In 1888 he moved to Covington and resided on Lynn St. In late 1888, while operating the Woods Electric Company in Cincinnati, he started a similar enterprise in Newport. He incorporated his manufacturing enterprise on January 21, 1889, as the G. T. Woods Manufacturing Company. The company manufactured electrical and mechanical devices such as switches, telegraph systems, and appliances. A short time later, Woods moved to New York City, where he sold a number of his patents to Thomas A. Edison and his General Electric Company, the American Bell Telephone Company, and the Westinghouse Air Brake Company. Woods obtained some 60 patents during his life. He never married. Woods died in 1910 at Harlem Hospital after suffering a stroke and was buried at St. Michael's Cemetery, Astoria, in Queens Co., N.Y.

KSJ, January 3, 1889, 4.

Low, W. Augustus, ed. *Encyclopedia of Black America*. New York: McGraw-Hill, 1981.

Theodore H. H. Harris

WOODYARD, WILLIAM (b. 1774, Virginia; d. 1858, Williamstown, Ky.). William Woodyard, an educated early settler of Grant. Co., arrived in 1808 and became a prosperous landowner. In 1820, with the formation of Grant Co. and its courts, he was appointed one of the first justices. Woodyard participated in granting tavern licenses, setting boundaries for precincts, and naming constables. In 1826 he became county sheriff and also served as tax collector, election judge, estate appraiser, and administrator. He and his wife Rebecca, a relative of Henry Clay, raised 10 children on a farm one mile north of the courthouse in Williamstown, on the west side of the Dry Ridge Trace (U.S. 25, **Dixie Highway**). Woodyard was buried near the Williamstown Particular Baptist Church.

Barnes, Betty M. "Woodyard Family," *Footsteps of the Past*, December 25, 1997, 19.

Conrad, John B., ed. *History of Grant County, Kentucky*. Williamstown, Ky.: Grant Co. Historical Society, 1992.

Pease, Janet K., comp. *Kentucky County Court Records, Grant, Harrison, Pendleton*. Williamstown, Ky.: Grant Co. Historical Society, 1985.

WOOLEN MILLS. The woolen industry was an important business in Northern Kentucky during the 19th century. By the beginning of the 20th century it was nearly gone, however, and today it has disappeared. Woolen mills were complex factories equipped with extensive equipment for processing raw wool into finished products. A glimpse of a woolen mill in Northern Kentucky appeared in an article in the June 29, 1867, *Maysville Republican,* describing how the Murphysville Manufacturing Company in Mason Co. operated. The article explained that after the wool was received at the factory, it was sorted into different grades on the basis of color and quality and then cleaned by machinery in a scouring room, dyed, rinsed, and dried. The wool still needed further cleaning at this stage, to remove dust, dirt, and other substances. In subsequent steps, it was oiled, weighed, and wound into rope, which was at first coarse and became smaller and stronger as processing continued. A machine called a condenser converted the rope into yarn, which could then be woven into cloth. After the cloth underwent several additional procedures, among them shrinking, having its nap raised and sheared, stretching, and pressing, it was ready for sale.

Little information is available concerning the woolen mills of Boone and Bracken counties. In his *History of Kentucky,* Richard Collins reported one wool factory at Burlington in Boone Co. and one wool-carding factory in Bracken Co. Will E. Walker was listed as a wool carder in the 1850 census for Bracken Co., but it is not known whether Walker was an employee of a factory or self employed. J. A. Lee ran a woolen mill or carding mill at Brooksville during 1876–1877.

The woolen industry was more established at Newport in Campbell Co., where Benjamin Clifford Jr., Darius B. Holbrook, S. R. M. Holbrook, William M. Walker, **James Taylor Jr.**, James Taylor Sr., Isaiah Thomas, **John W. Tibbatts**, and William M. Walker incorporated the Newport Manufacturing Company on November 26, 1831. By 1836 this company's extensive operations included a cotton factory, a woolen factory, a hemp mill, and other endeavors that employed 329 individuals. A story in the January 9, 1836, local *Daily Evening Post* reported that the company had "fifty power looms for the manufacture of Kentucky jeans, linseys, and cotton plains . . . and the necessary auxiliary machinery for the manufacture of cotton bagging, by steam power." Between 1892 and 1908, two other woolen mills were mentioned in Newport. The June 10, 1892, *Kentucky Post* indicated that the Forinshell Woolen Mills of Detroit, Mich., would consider a move to Newport if the city offered some inducements. The Ohio Valley Woolen Mills Company was located at the southwest corner of First St. and Park Ave. in Newport.

Historian Collins reported one wool-carding factory in Carroll Co. Three woolen mills in Carrollton were John Howe & Sons (1876–1880), John & W. F. Howe & Company (1881–1884), and Carrollton Woolen Mills (1887–1896).

Grant Co. had woolen mill operators in the community of New Eagle Mills, including G. W. Saylers (1876–1882), John A. Collins (1883–1884), and James F. Saylers (1883–1884). Two other woolen mills were in Williamstown: D. Cunningham & Company (1865–1866) and Daniel L. Cunningham (1883–1884).

In Kenton Co., four minor woolen mills operated in Covington: Glaser & Brother at the southeast corner of Scott and Front Sts. (1866), the Kentucky Woolen Mills at 738–740 Madison Ave. (1868), F. Gray on the northeast corner of Eighth St. and Madison Ave. (1869), and A & G. H. Montgomery at 258 Pike St. (1895). The Covington Woolen Mills (1876–1895), at 254 Pike St. during 1897–1902, appears to have been the primary woolen mill in Covington. It was owned by John Herold and his brother. The August 27, 1892, *Kentucky Post* indicated that Herold's Covington Woolen Mills had failed. However, subsequent city directories suggest that the mill continued until 1902. The varying company name and address were listed as J. & G. Herold, on the north side of Lexington Pk. between Main and Riddle Sts. (1861–1866); on the north side of Pike St, opposite

Kip St. (1866); at 252 Pike St. (1868); at 256–258 Pike St. (1869–1871, 1878); at 256 Pike St. (1872–1888); and John Herold & Sons at 256 Pike St. (1890 and 1896). John Herold was born in Bavaria, Germany, in 1819 and migrated to the United States in 1838. Initially, he worked five or six years in a woolen mill owned by a man named Geizendurf and subsequently began his own business.

In Mason Co., O. Hanna & Company operated a woolen mill in the community of Dover during 1883–1884. The Maysville Woolen Manufacturing Company was incorporated on January 16, 1866, by William W. Baldwin, David Clark, Robert A. Cochran, George L. Forman, Peter Lashbrooke, Elijah Loyd, Henry Smoot, and William E. Smoot. Murphysville, a small Mason Co. community about nine miles south of Maysville on the North Fork of the Licking River, had the Murphysville Manufacturing Company, which was incorporated on March 2, 1867. The dye house at the mill was under the supervision of Timothy D. Lutcliffe of Roxburg, Mass., who had previously worked at the Bay State mills and carpet factory in that state. The superintendent of the practical department was working under George S. Baker, formerly with Tilton and Baker, a cloth and woolen-goods manufacturer of Sanborndon Bridge, N.H. With equipment brought in from Massachusetts and Connecticut and experienced men with backgrounds in the woolen industry, the Murphysville Manufacturing Company was an impressive operation. It appears that successors to the Murphysville Manufacturing Company were Evans & Wright in 1876–1977 and Wright & Wood, who were listed in editions of the *Kentucky State Gazetteer and Business Directory* between 1879 and 1888.

The community of Washington in Mason Co. had an early wool factory owned by Enos Woodward. The December 19, 1827, *Maysville Eagle* carried an ad placed by Woodward seeking one or two weavers as employees for this factory. The following month, on January 23, 1828, the newspaper carried a long ad in which Woodward informed the public that he had purchased the wool factory formerly occupied by William Richey in Washington.

Woolen mills also operated in Owen and Pendleton counties. Miner & Parker ran a woolen mill at New Liberty in Owen Co. during 1865–1866. Collins reported in his history one wool factory in Pendleton Co. Later, two woolen mills existed in Falmouth: Joshua Woodhead's woolen mill near Zoder (1874–1884) and the Falmouth Woolen Mills (1887–1906). According to the local Lake atlas for Bracken and Pendleton counties, Woodhead was a woolen manufacturer from England who settled in Pendleton Co. in 1866. Two wool carders listed in the Pendleton census for 1850 included James P. Hopper and William J. Wheeler. To this day, the wool industry in Falmouth is celebrated with an annual wool festival.

Acts of Kentucky. Frankfort, Ky., 1832, 1866, 1867.
An Atlas of Bracken and Pendleton Counties, Kentucky. Philadelphia: D. J. Lake, 1884.
Clift, G. Glenn. *History of Maysville and Mason County.* Lexington, Ky.: Transylvania, 1936.
Collins, Richard H. *History of Kentucky.* Covington, Ky.: Collins, 1882.
Hodgman, George H. *Hodgman and Co.'s Kentucky State Gazetteer, Shippers' Guide, and Business Directory, for 1865 and 1866.* Louisville, Ky.: Hodgman, 1865.
Maysville Eagle, December 19, 1827; June 23, 1828.
Perrin, William Henry, J. H. Battle, and G. C. Kniffin. *Kentucky: A History of the State.* Louisville, Ky.: F. A. Battey, 1888.
R. L. Polk Company. *Kentucky State Gazetteer and Business Directory.* Detroit: R. L. Polk, 1876–1895.
R. L. Polk Company and A. C. Danser. *Kentucky State Gazetteer and Business Directory, for 1876–1877.* Detroit: R. L. Polk, 1876.
Tenkotte, Paul A. "Rival Cities to Suburbs: Covington and Newport, Kentucky, 1790–1890," PhD diss., Univ. of Cincinnati, 1989.

Charles D. Hockensmith

WOOLSEY, KATE TRIMBLE (b. ca. 1858, Cynthiana, Ky.; date and place of death unknown). Kate Trimble, an author and a suffragette, was the daughter of Judge **William W. Trimble** and Mary Barlow Trimble. Kate was exposed to some women's-rights influences from her birth family: In 1874, her father purchased a mansion at the southeast corner of Madison Ave. and Robbins St. in Covington, in the name of his wife. In 1894, when the Equal Rights Society of Covington attended the Ohio Woman State Suffrage Convention in Cincinnati, Ohio, Kate's mother entertained as her houseguests famous suffragettes Helen Taylor Upton and Susan B. Anthony.

In 1881 Kate Trimble married Eugene de Roode of Lexington. She subsequently spent four years as a widow in London, England. In 1893 she married Edward J. Woolsey of New York City, who was newly divorced and quite wealthy. For the couple's wedding, Kate's widowed mother invited many dignitaries to Covington, including the U.S. secretary of the treasury, **John G. Carlisle**, and foreign guests such as the king of Bulgaria, Princess Maria De Bourbon from the Bourbon royal family, and the English dowager duchess of Wellington. Kate Woolsey's book, a short volume entitled *Republics versus Woman,* was published in 1903. There she argued that the American republic was more oppressive for disenfranchised women than were the monarchies of Europe. She also claimed in her book that her great-aunt had urged her great-uncle Robert Trimble to draft a bill in support of married women's property rights and their guardianship rights. Also in 1903 Woolsey became a member of the Daughters of the American Revolution. Then in 1907, the newly organized Society of Colonial Daughters engaged her as a guest speaker. In her speech, "Women of the Colonial Period," she denounced the plight of females working in the southern textile factories. Women's status had fallen below that of male immigrants, ex-slaves, and the lower classes, she asserted. In November 1913, four prominent local suffragettes, including Woolsey's sister, Helen Highton, represented Covington at a convention of the Kentucky Equal Rights Association in Louisville. In 1915 the *Kentucky Post* reported that Kate Trimble Woolsey, "one of the leading writers in the suffrage cause" (see **Women's Suffrage**), was spending most of her time in New York City, Europe, and Covington, Ky. The story of Kate Woolsey's last years and death has yet to be uncovered.

Bronner, Milton. "Kentuckians Who Have Made Good in New York—Commonwealth Well Represented," *KP,* February 3, 1915, 1.
"Colonial Daughters Hold a Meeting," *KP,* December 2, 1907, 3.
"Four Women Are Delegates," *KTS,* November 11, 1913, 14.
"Ida S. Blick Letter," *KP,* October 16, 1905, 4.
"Judge Wm. W. Trimble Died," *KSJ,* September 2, 1886, 4.
"A Sharp Protest," *Lexington Leader,* April 12, 1903, 7.

John Boh

WORLD WAR I. Before the United States entered the war, a rally of Covington and Kenton Co. citizens was held at the **Covington Public Library** auditorium on May 1, 1916, to encourage political officials to stay out of the war in Europe. Many of the people in attendance were of German birth or ancestry. Their pleas were ultimately unsuccessful, and by April 1917, the United States was at war with the Central Powers.

Northern Kentuckians with German heritage soon found themselves in a precarious position. The overwhelming majority of them were loyal Americans, and many of the families had lived in the United States for generations. Some of their non-German fellow citizens, however, viewed them with distrust. This distrust was fueled by the creation of the Citizens Patriotic League in 1917 to rid the region of any pro-German activity (see **Anti-German Hysteria**). The league eventually claimed to have more than 1,000 members. The Citizens Patriotic League was successful in eliminating many aspects of German culture and language in the region. In summer 1917, the **Dayton Public Schools** in Dayton, Ky., stopped offering courses in the German language. During the next year, most other Northern Kentucky public school systems did the same. The Covington Public Library removed its sizable German-language collection, and the circulation of German-language newspapers was all but eliminated in Northern Kentucky. Many area businesses changed their names to remove any reference to Germany. The German National Bank in Covington was renamed Liberty National Bank, while the Newport German Bank became the American National Bank. Covington's Western German Savings Bank was renamed the Security Savings Bank. A number of streets were also renamed to get rid of any association with Germany. In Covington, Bremen St. became Pershing Ave., and in Newport, German St. became Liberty St.

The Citizens Patriotic League did not always use peaceful means to achieve its goals. On June 5, 1918, members of the league confronted Rev. Anton Goebel, pastor of **St. John Catholic Church** on Pike St. in Covington, on the porch of the parish rectory. Goebel was a German native who had come to the United States in 1890. The mob physically intimidated Goebel and several mob members struck him. Goebel was accused of refusing to allow the American flag to be brought into his church for a funeral. On June 24, 1918, a large group of league members confronted a farmer in rural Kenton Co. and accused him of supporting the German war aims. The man was tied to a tree and whipped.

The Citizens Patriotic League was also involved in one of the region's highest-profile court cases. In 1918 a private detective agency was hired by the league to place an electronic listening device in the shoe shop of Charles Schoberg in the Latonia neighborhood of Covington. League members had been informed that a group of men were gathering in the shop to discuss the war in terms that were sympathetic to the Germans. From the evidence collected, seven men were eventually charged under the Espionage Act of 1917 and the Sedition Act of 1918. The case focused on three men, Henry Feltman, J. Henry Kruse, and Charles Schoberg. All three were upstanding citizens who were active in the community. Feltman and Schoberg each had held public offices, and Feltman was a successful tobacco merchant. All three, however, were found guilty. Schoberg was given a sentence of 10 years, while Kruse received a 5-year term. Feltman was sentenced to a 7-year prison term and fined $40,000. On December 10, 1920, the three men were transported to Moundsville Penitentiary in West Virginia. A successful petition drive by their friends eventually led to their release in June 1921, when President Warren G. Harding (1921–1923) commuted their sentences.

Religious congregations with traditional German ties also distanced themselves from the German language and culture. Many German Evangelical Reformed congregations eliminated the use of the German language at all services and changed their names to reflect a more American perspective. The German Evangelical Reformed Church of Covington changed its name to Grace Reformed Church (see **Grace United Church of Christ**), and the Immanuel German Reformed Church in Bromley was rechristened Immanuel Reformed Church (see **Immanuel United Church of Christ**). For several generations, many Catholic parish schools had used the German language in instruction. In particular, the catechism was often learned in German. This practice came to an end during the war years in almost all the region's Catholic schools.

The center of war activities in Northern Kentucky was **Fort Thomas Military Reservation** in Campbell Co., which became a major induction center for the region. Local residents supported the soldiers at the fort with periodic entertainments. The **YMCA** provided religious services for the Protestants at the fort, and the **Knights of Columbus** did the same for Catholics in uniform.

Northern Kentuckians who remained on the home front supported the war through various activities. Liberty bonds sold very well in the region. Area churches opened their doors for **American Red Cross** activities, and many congregations purchased Liberty Bonds. Many congregations posted the names of their members who were in the service in prominent locations.

As the war drew to an end, area leaders began focusing their attention on the creation of suitable memorials. Bishop Ferdinand Brossart of the Diocese of Covington proposed a regional effort that would endow special wards at St. Elizabeth Hospital (see **St. Elizabeth Medical Center**) and **Booth Memorial Hospital** in Covington as a suitable memorial to those who lost their lives in service to their country. This regional approach did not prove popular. Instead, dozens of memorials were erected throughout Northern Kentucky. In the more rural areas, World War I veteran memorials can be found in many courthouse squares (see **Veterans' Memorials and Monuments**). In the more urban Campbell and Kenton counties, memorials were constructed in many of the cities.

Merriman, Scott A. "An Intensive School of Disloyalty: The C. B. Schoberg Case under the Espionage and Sedition Acts in Kentucky during World War I." *RKHS* 98, no. 1 (Winter 2000): 179–204.

——. "Ordinary People in Extraordinary Times? Defendants, Attorneys, and the Federal Government's Policy under the Espionage Acts during World War I in the Sixth Circuit Court of Appeals District," PhD diss., Univ. of Kentucky, 2003.

Reis, Jim. "Group Hoped to Keep America out of World War I," *KP*, February 14, 1983, 4.

Schmitz, Frederick W. *An Open Reply to John Richmond, President Blakely Club, Covington, Kentucky concerning Patriotic Activities.* Pamphlet published in Covington, Ky. July 14, 1921, available at Kenton Co. Public Library, Covington, Ky.

David E. Schroeder

WORLD WAR II (December 7, 1941–September 2, 1945). Northern Kentucky played a prominent role during World War II, especially in war production and military personnel (see also **African Americans in World War II**). Throughout the late 1930s, tensions had grown between the United States and Japan over Japan's war in China and apparent intentions to expand Japanese territories in the Pacific. At the same time, Adolph Hitler was rebuilding Germany and strengthening its armed forces. On September 1, 1939, World War II in Europe began: the German invasion of Poland started a conflict that by 1941 had engulfed Europe and North Africa in a bloody conflict. During this period the United States had remained neutral but had aided England, and eventually Russia, with war matériel through the Lend-Lease program. Most Americans wanted the United States to stay out of the war. Nevertheless, because of a recognized need to build up America's armed forces, a draft was instituted in 1940; and in early 1941, all National Guard units were federalized for possible war service.

The War in the Pacific Theater

For the United States, World War II began on Sunday, December 7, 1941, when aircraft from Japanese aircraft carriers attacked Pearl Harbor, Hawaii, in an attempt to cripple the U.S. Pacific Fleet. Although the main target of the attack was to be American aircraft carriers, none were in port, and the main damage was done to the battleship fleet moored along Ford Island. U.S. Navy Coxswain Warren Richardson, of Kenton Co., was aboard the battleship USS *Arizona* when it was hit by a bomb that detonated its powder magazine and sank it. Richardson was among the 1,177 men killed when the ship sank. Carroll Co.'s Pfc. Ellis O'Neal, of the U.S. Marine Corps (USMC), was also among the Northern Kentuckians present during the attack on Pearl Harbor. He survived the strafing and bombing attack at Ewa Marine Air Station near Pearl Harbor.

The United States had become suspicious of Japanese intensions before the attack on Pearl Harbor but had concluded that the Japanese would first strike U.S. military forces in the Philippine Islands. Based on this supposition, units including Covington's Company D of the 38th Tank Company, which became part of the 192nd Tank Battalion, were sent overseas to build up America's defenses in the Philippines. The Japanese attacked the Philippines on December 8, 1942, but it took nearly six months of fighting before they gained complete control of the islands. Capt. **Alvin C. Poweleit**, of Campbell Co., was in charge of the 192nd Tank Battalion's medical detachment during the defense of the islands, and Kenton Co.'s Rev. **Henry Stober**, a priest of the Roman Catholic Diocese of Covington, served as an army chaplain with the 12th Engineer Company. Both men survived the Bataan Death March, but only Poweleit returned home. Stober died while a prisoner of war in 1944. In early 1942, it was decided that it was necessary to attack Japan in some way, both to show the Japanese they could be struck militarily and to bolster U.S. moral. Bracken Co.'s Capt. Thomas Cline was chosen by the Army Air Corps to test the idea of launching land-based bombers from an aircraft carrier. His efforts, as well as those of many others, were behind the Doolittle Raid on Tokyo in April 1942.

Following the American naval victory at the Battle of Midway, the United States began a long series of island-hopping campaigns to cut Japanese supply lines and drive the Japanese back toward their mainland, a task that took until 1945. The Americans started their drive with an attack on the island of Guadalcanal. Campbell Co.'s Pfc. Edward H. Ahrens was among the marines that went ashore to capture the island. While fighting with the 1st Raider Battalion, he was killed in action, earning a Navy Cross for heroism. At sea, Owen Co.'s Rear Admiral **Willis Augustus Lee Jr.** commanded the battleship division that engaged and beat the Japanese navy force sent to help capture the island on November 14–15, 1942. As the United States captured Japanese-held islands, U.S. forces built airfields, naval facilities, and supply depots to help carry on the fight. On New Caledonia in 1943, Kenton Co.'s John Herndon, an African American, served with the Navy Seabees and helped build the island into a large air and supply base. Campbell Co.'s Charlie Tharp also served with the Seabees in the Marshall Islands during 1944.

As the island-hopping campaign came closer to Japan, the Japanese became more desperate, and fighting intensified. Bracken Co.'s Cpl. John Capito, USMC, earned a Silver Star and a Purple Heart for heroism during the capture of New Britain Island in January 1944, when he drove a bulldozer under fire across a creek bed to clear a path for advancing U.S. tanks and infantry. By late 1944, U.S. forces had begun operations to recapture the Philippines. Among the units taking part in the Philippine operation was the 38th Infantry Division, which included men of the 149th Infantry Regiment, Kentucky National Guard. Also among the invasion force was the 138th Field Artillery regiment of the Kentucky Guard, which provided artillery support for the 38th Division. As the island-hopping campaign progressed, Northern Kentuckians served elsewhere in the Pacific, including Alaska and the China-Burma-India area. Kenton Co.'s Sgt. Lawrence Keller served in the CBI (China-Burma-India Theater) as a cryptologist decoding Japanese messages for the 10th Air Force. Also from Kenton Co. was Leroy Waller, an African American serving with the engineers in the CBI to help build the Burma Rd.

Japanese commanders ordered their forces to fight to the death when they perceived that American forces were approaching Japan. In February 1945, Kenton Co. navy corpsman Noah Switzer landed on the island of Iwo Jima with the 28th Marines. He witnessed the raising of the flag on Mount Suribachi and served in combat for 37 days. Starting in March 1945, the final campaign of the war began as the largest amphibious invasion of the Pacific war was launched against the island of Okinawa. Among the ships of the invasion fleet was the USS *Kenton* APA-122 (named for Kenton Co., Ky.). In April 1945 the *Kenton* reached Okinawa and unloaded troops and supplies. On April 6, 1945, during a Kamikaze attack, the *Kenton* shot down two Japanese aircraft. After two atomic bombs were dropped on Japanese cities in early August 1945, the emperor of Japan announced the surrender of Japan on August 15. The formal surrender was signed on September 2, 1945.

The War in the European Theater

On December 11, 1941, Germany and Italy declared war on the United States, plunging the United States completely into the war. President Franklin Roosevelt (1933–1945) and many of his aides saw Germany as a greater and more immediate threat than Japan, and troops and equipment were sent to Europe first. In January 1942 the first American troops arrived in England. Among them was Col. Jesse Auton, from Kenton Co., who was sent by the Army Air Corps to evaluate sites for potential air bases for the newly formed 8th Air Force, which was to destroy German industry and military targets as well as the German air force. Auton returned to England in early 1943 as commander of the 65th Fighter Wing, the first operational American fighter wing in Europe. The job of the fighter wing was to defend bomber formations and to destroy the German air force in the air and on the ground. Owen Co.'s Maj. **Gerald Johnson** of the 56th Fighter Group flew under Auton's wing and is credited with being the second American fighter ace in the European Theater, chalking up 18 aerial victories by the war's end.

As the first Americans landed in England, war came to the shore of the United States in the form of German submarines. They preyed on merchant ships right off the U.S. East Coast throughout 1942 and early 1943 and also planted antiship mines. During the antisubmarine campaign, Owen Co.'s Capt. **Evan Yancey** (later an admiral) commanded the destroyer USS *Clemson* and modified its equipment to gauge better the depth of enemy subs, an improvement that enhanced the success of antisub operations. The first major action Americans were involved with in Europe was the invasion of North Africa in November 1942. Covington's 106th Coastal Artillery battalion (AA) landed on November 8 and fought in the battle of Kasserine Pass. The unit also participated in the invasion of Sicily in 1943, as did the 103rd Automatic Weapons Battalion, formally the 123rd Cavalry, Kentucky National Guard, from Covington.

Sicily was used as a jumping-off point for the invasion of southern Italy. Although most of southern Italy was occupied by late 1943, the fight for Italy was fought through April 1945. Kenton Co.'s Lt. Melvin Walker was an African American officer in the all-black 92nd Infantry Division. He was awarded the Silver Star for heroism in January 1945. On June 6, 1944, the Allies launched the invasion of France at Normandy, and Northern Kentuckians fought on land, at sea, and in the skies there. Boone Co.'s Sgt Robert L. Williams served with the 506th Infantry Regiment of the U.S. Army's 101st Airborne Division as part of the airborne force that dropped behind enemy lines before the invasion; Kenton Co.'s Sgt. Cassius Mullins jumped into Normandy with the 508th Infantry Regiment of the U.S. Army's 82nd Airborne Division. Mullins was later wounded during the invasion of Holland in September 1944. Kenton Co.'s naval Petty Officer 3rd Class Jack Story served aboard the USS *Corry,* a destroyer that was supporting the landings when it struck a mine. On June 8, 1944, the SS *Charles Morgan* was unloading troops and supplies off Utah Beach when a German plane dropped a bomb into its cargo hold. Kenton Co.'s Edward Brogan survived the attack and reached shore.

On shore the hedgerow country slowed the Allied advance, and Gen. George S. Patton's 3rd Army made a break out and drove across France. Campbell Co.'s army Pvt. Henry Lowe served in support of Patton with the 657th Ordnance Company, supplying ammunition for the advancing army. By late 1944, U.S. forces had engaged the German army in the Huertgen Forest in a costly winter battle fought along the border of Germany and Belgium. On December 9, 1944, Campbell Co.'s army SSgt. Vernon Napier of the 709th Tank Battalion was killed in action. He was posthumously awarded the Distinguished Service Cross for heroism. On December 16, 1944, the Germans launched their last major offensive of the war in the Ardennes Forest. In poor weather conditions that grounded most Allied aircraft, they attacked on an 80-mile front with complete surprise. Kenton Co.'s Maj. **John Hoefker** flew photo recon missions over the Ardennes and was twice shot down, but he was able to provide valuable information on the advancing Germans. As the Allies advanced into Germany, Owen Co.'s army Sgt. James Washington served with the African American 3760th Quartermaster Trucking Company. By April 1945, the Allies were closing in on the last remnants of the German Army. On April 24, 1945, less than a week before the end of hostilities, Kenton Co.'s army Pvt. Paul Horstman was killed in action while fighting as part of the 9th Army. On May 8, 1945, the war in Europe ended with Germany's surrender. Following the surrender, many American soldiers and airman were liberated from German prison camps; among them were Campbell Co.'s Pfc. Clifford Marz of the army engineers, who had been held at Stalag 4B, and Campbell Co.'s Air Corps SSgt. Lafon Wesley, who was shot down while serving as a gunner on B-17s in August 1944. By the war's end, 589 Northern Kentucky soldiers, sailors, and marines were listed as either killed or missing. The two counties with the highest causalities were Kenton (284) and Campbell (211).

On the home front, Northern Kentuckians experienced the rationing of such materials as gasoline, rubber, sugar, and meat. As both men and women went off to war and industries geared up for war production, many women left the home to work in war plants. Companies involved in war production in the region included **Newport Steel** and the **Wadsworth Watchcase Company** of Dayton,

Alma Wolfzorn Ciafardini working on war production at Wadsworth in Dayton, Ky., during World War II.

Ky., both of which began making shell casings and machine guns, and the Kentucky Shell plant that was located in Wilder. Northern Kentuckians also went across the Ohio River to work at the Curtis Wright aircraft plant, the Crosley Corporation, and other firms. Like the rest of the nation, Northern Kentucky held bond drives and collected scrap metal and grease for the war effort. Civil Defense workers held blackout and air-raid drills, and each community had a designated air-raid warden. As men enlisted or were drafted into the military, new military camps and bases were built or converted to particular special military needs across the nation. In Northern Kentucky, the **Fort Thomas Military Reservation** served as an induction center to process soldiers as they joined. Both men and women from the region served in all branches of the armed forces. The women were nurses, clerks, pilots, and carried out many other support roles. Grant Co.'s Capt. Doris Clark commanded the 151st Women's Army Corps Company stateside. Northern Kentuckians served in every theater of operations during the war, and many gave their lives.

Kleber, John E., ed. *The Kentucky Encyclopedia.* Lexington: Univ. Press of Kentucky, 1992.

KTS, May 9, 1945, 1.

"Liberated, War Contracts at Shell Plant Cancelled," *KTS,* May 8, 1945, 1.

The National Archives. "World War II Causalities." www.archives.gov/research/arc/ww2/ (accessed May 20, 2007).

Pranger, Arthur B. *Traveling through W.W.II: 2 Years, 2 Months, 29 Days.* Bloomington, Ind.: AuthorHouse, 2007.

Smith, Hope. "3 Former Sailors Relive Sinking of US Ship," *CE,* June 1, 1994, 1.

Snow, Robert. "Military Memories, Ph1 Noah Switzer," *Military Historian,* April 1995.

Williams, Robert L. *Return to Normandy.* Cincinnati: Sky Spec, 1997.

Robert B. Snow

WORTHVILLE. Worthville, located where Eagle Creek empties into the Kentucky River, was originally a tiny hamlet hugging the banks of these two waterways in Carroll Co. It was known in the town's early history as Coonskin, because the traders and merchants there bartered goods and services for skins. It was not until 1869, when the **Louisville, Cincinnati, and Lexington Railroad** was completed through town, that its name was changed to Worthville, in honor of Gen. William Jenkins Worth of **Mexican War** fame.

In 1802 an official governmental inspection station was in operation at the mouth of Eagle Creek, checking tobacco, hemp, flour, and goods shipped by flatboat from the interior Bluegrass region and the upper reaches of Kentucky. By 1820 seven steamboats made regular passage to Frankfort, Ky., and by 1836 coal barges were arriving at the Worthville area from Eastern Kentucky. During the 1850s Worthville witnessed a major growth spurt. Construction of the railroad brought many new people to town. In addition to sidings and loading docks, a popular "watering hole," Mac's Saloon, was a favorite among the construction crews. Wild hogs are said to have impeded work laying the track.

In April 1878 a Mrs. Sheehan began a private school about one mile above Worthville, and Miss Georgia Aiken taught nearby at Green Hill. In June of that year, the first common school trustees were elected, Asbury Ames, Jasper Lewis, and George Scott. The first public school for District 32 was completed at Worthville in time for the 1878 fall semester. The earliest church building at Worthville was Dean's Chapel, a Methodist affiliate, constructed on 1.5 acres along the Kentucky River on land donated by Samuel and Mary Goodwin to W. T. Dean, W. B. Winslow, and James McDaniel, trustees of the Methodist Episcopal Church–South. Later that building was removed and the Dean's Memorial Methodist Church was built on the land and dedicated in 1910. The Worthville Baptist Church was built as a log structure in 1880, but the facility was soon outgrown, and the congregation built another building just five years later. The old log church building was used afterward as Worthville's public schoolhouse. The community's second school was a two-story frame structure, and in 1912 a large brick school was constructed to house both the grade school and the high school. The **Worthville High School**, a four-year school, operated until 1939. The Worthville Consolidated School was one of the last of the county schools in Kentucky to close, serving the area until 1963. In 1890 the Old Mill Creek Christian Church was hauled from East Mill Creek to Worthville and set upon new foundations. The old church dated back to 1856, and its homemade benches also came to Worthville. The church was lost in a 1941 fire, and a new Christian Church building was constructed under the leadership of Pastor W. C. McCullum, one year later.

Two early African American churches, one Methodist and the other Baptist, and a school for African American students were up on the hill at Worthville. Miss Mary Henderson taught at that school, and her sister, Nannie Henderson, taught at a rural African American school in Owen Co., Ky. After the **Carrollton and Worthville Railroad** (C&W) was completed in 1905, the Worthville-area African American students were sent to Dunbar School in Carrollton, and later to the nearby Ghent Elementary School, the consolidated school for colored children in Carroll Co. Two residents of Worthville, Bessie Whitaker and her husband, Dudley Whitaker, taught at Dunbar and at the Ghent Colored School for many years during the 1920–1940 period. Area African American children of high school age were sent to boarding school at Lincoln Institute in Shelby Co., Ky.

By 1900 bridges had been built over Eagle Creek at Sanders, Eagle Station, and Worthville. All three of these were covered bridges, but in recent years they were replaced by concrete spans. Completion of the C&W Railroad in 1905 provided another major business for Worthville. Coal was shipped down the Kentucky River from coal mines in Kentucky and off-loaded at Worthville, then sent by the C&W to Carrollton and Ghent as fuel for the houses and businesses along the line. In its heyday, Worthville was a bustling railroad town centered on its rail depot. Passenger and freight service was handled every day. It is said that during the 1920s and 1930s, people would come to Worthville just to see the trains. The railroad water towers provided water to area farmers during the drought of 1929. Worthville boasted a literary society, plays, operettas, a local band, tent meetings, and every summer a **showboat** on the Kentucky River. For several years, a band of **Gypsies** with colorful horse-drawn wagons would come through town telling fortunes, selling handmade goods, and providing music and dancing. During the Ohio River **flood of 1937**, the **Louisville and Nashville Railroad** positioned a train at Worthville for people stranded by the high waters. Among the businesses at Worthville were Pollard's Confectionery, Schenck Bros. Hardware and Grocery, Gardner's Stockyard and Produce House, Worsham's Western Union, Bauer's Grocery, Goodwin's Hotel, Gentry's Grocery, Kemper's Restaurant and Boardinghouse, a telephone exchange, bakers, two barbershops, a tomato factory, a lumberyard, a shoe factory, two garages, a bank, and three doctors' offices.

Shock and dismay permeated Worthville on January 13, 1938, when J. P. Schenck, president of the Worthville Deposit Bank, announced that the bank was closed and the affairs turned over to the State Banking and Securities Administration. Originally founded in 1898, the Worthville Bank was capitalized at $15,000 with nearly $100,000 in deposits. Schenck stated that depositors were protected by the Federal Deposit Insurance Corporation up to $5,000 per account. Frozen loans and low earnings from effects of the **Great Depression** forced the closure. A. B. Suter was the cashier. The Ghent Bank in Carroll Co. had already gone into receivership at the time of the Worthville Bank collapse. By the end of the year, the depositors received 25 percent of their deposit value as an initial payment from the bank's assets.

In 1941 a major fire destroyed an entire block of businesses, the Christian Church, and two water towers. After **World War II**, the local railroad business declined gradually. Modern Worthville is but a shadow of its former commercial prowess. The long-haul trucks on I-71 (see **Expressways**) bypass Worthville; commercial traffic on the Kentucky River has been gone for more than 50 years; and even the once powerful L&N, now the **CSX**, carries freight right past the town. Coal goes by way of Ohio River barges direct to customer landings. The railroad connection of the old C&W, now also part of CSX, services some of the steel and chemical plants between Carrollton and Ghent.

Bogardus, Carl R., Sr. *The Story of Gallatin County.* Ed. James C. Claypool. Cincinnati: John S. Swift, 2003.

Carroll Co. Deed Book 10, p. 585, Carrollton, Ky.

Carrollton News-Democrat, July 1878; January 13, 1938.

Gentry, Mary Ann. *A History of Carroll County.* Madison, Ind.: Coleman, 1984.

Parker, Anna V. "A Short History of Carroll County," 1958, Carroll Co. Public Library, Carrollton, Ky.

U.S. Army Corps of Engineers. *Navigation Charts, Kentucky River, Louisville District.* Louisville, Ky.: Corps of Engineers, U.S. Army, Louisville District, 1993.

Diane Perrine Coon

WORTHVILLE BAPTIST CHURCH. In summer 1882 the Concord Association sent its missionary preacher, Thomas A. Spicer, to Worthville in Carroll Co. to conduct a revival, which resulted in conversions and transference of church membership by letter of 35 to 40 members. Spicer organized a Sunday School and came each month to preach at services held in the Worthville Schoolhouse. In July 31, 1883, when the Baptist membership in Worthville and the vicinity called for delegates, ministers, and laymen from nine adjacent churches to assist in organizing the Worthville Baptist Church. On this occasion, with eight ministers and an audience of 600 people present, the Worthville church members elected Spicer as their pastor. Land for a church building in Worthville was donated by Samuel Malin, and work on the building began in 1884. The completed church was dedicated in June 1889. In 1900 the Worthville Baptist Church and seven other churches withdrew from the Concord Association to form the White's Run Baptist Association. These eight churches were joined by three churches from the Sulphur Fork Association at an organizational meeting at the Carrollton Baptist Church.

The Worthville church parsonage was built in 1927 at the cost of $800. In 1930 the church had 228 members. The Worthville church held part-time services until 1943, when, under the ministry of W. G. Webster, a full-time schedule of services was begun. Over the years, improvements to the 1889 church building have included a basement dug in the 1940s to make two Sunday School rooms; more new Sunday School rooms in the back of the sanctuary, built in the 1950s; new rooms and a kitchen built in 1969; a baptistery installed in 1973; a handicap ramp built at the front entrance of the church in 1982; a new educational annex; and a new vestibule, added to the front of the church in 1999. Recently a Hispanic ministry has been started by the church to serve the needs of the increasing Hispanic population in Owen Co. (see **Latinos**).

Mefford, Phyllis. "Centennial History of the Worthville Baptist Church," 1983, Worthville Baptist Church, Worthville, Ky.
Worthville Baptist Church Minutes, Worthville Baptist Church, Worthville, Ky.

Ken Massey

WORTHVILLE HIGH SCHOOL. There were subscription schools at Worthville in Carroll Co. in 1906 and 1907, conducted by Professor Secretts in the upstairs of a residence that during the 1930s was owned by John Brock. In 1908 R. S. Tucker also taught by subscription in that same building. The Worthville community passed a bond issue and opened the town's first independent public high school in 1911, apparently on grounds shared with the subscription school. A new common grade school opened in 1912 on property purchased from J. R. Stout. Mr. Tucker, one of the new common school's first teachers, was musically inclined and started a tradition of presenting plays, entertainments, and musical recitals at the new school; he continued teaching there until 1916. That year, Worthville High School graduated its first student, Euclid Davis, and the trustees hired John Hunt Jackson, a distinguished expert in classical literature. Hunt had a large library that later was stolen while in storage in the high school's bell tower. A photograph from 1917 shows the Worthville High School being housed with the grade school in a substantial two-story brick building, with a full basement and front entrance portico. Under the leadership of Professor Franks, domestic science and manual training were added to the curriculum in 1917. A succession of one-year postings of school principals followed until Frank Hood, with a BA degree from Kentucky State University, was hired. His assistant was Ruth Bet Coghill, who had a BA from Oxford College at Oxford, Ga., and Worthville High School became accredited as a Class B school.

At the time, the Worthville High School PTA was very active, purchasing 12 books for the library, donating a drinking fountain, and providing an acetylene light system for the entire school. When the gym was added in 1924, only three feet of space was left for spectators around the rim of the floor, and each season the men and boys of the community had to erect a stage that took up one-third of the total gym floor for any public school performances. In 1923 Worthville High School, with 32 students, was second-largest in the county, but by 1929 the school had grown only to 37 students. Professor Curtis E. Shirley, who later became Carroll Co. superintendent of schools, had graduated from Transylvania University at Lexington; he was principal of the Worthville grade school and the high school from 1925 to 1930, when he was replaced by A. B. Clayton. The per capita cost to educate students was $80 a year in 1925. By 1929 the laboratory and machinery equipment was valued at $200, and $15 was spent that year on maps, globes, and charts. Even though so few students attended the high school, its Worthville Pirates basketball team, on November 17, 1938, under the direction of principal and coach Walter E. Cundiff, prevailed over the Bulldogs from Bethany High School, a larger school, by a score of 46 to 29.

Worthville High School's students came from the south-central portion of Carroll Co. The county ultimately built four-year high schools at Worthville, at Ghent, and at Sanders. Carrollton city schools also operated a four-year high school. There were two-year high schools in the county at English and Locust. During the 1930s, as the **Great Depression** impacted the available tax base, the county high schools began consolidating. Worthville was one of the last to retain its local high school, but in 1939 the school finally closed. The students went either to Carrollton High School or to Sanders High School.

Bevarly, R. W. "History of Education in Carroll County," master's thesis, Univ. of Kentucky, 1936.
Campbell, Justine Tandy. "History of the Carroll County Schools," 1976, Carroll Co. Public Library, Carrollton, Ky.
Carrollton News Democrat, July 1878.
Gentry, Mary Ann. *A History of Carroll County.* Madison, Ind.: Coleman, 1984.
Parker, Anna V. "A Short History of Carroll County," 1958, Carroll Co. Public Library, Carrollton, Ky.

Diane Perrine Coon

WRIGHT, HORATIO G., MAJOR GENERAL (b. March 6, 1820, Clinton, Conn.; d. July 2, 1899, Washington, D.C.). Engineer-soldier Horatio Gouverneur Wright is the namesake of both Fort Wright, the fort built in September 1862 to block a Confederate advance on Cincinnati, and the city of Fort Wright, which stands over that site. In 1841 Wright graduated second in his class from the U.S. Military Academy at West Point, N.Y., and was commissioned a 2nd lieutenant in the U.S. Army Corps of Engineers.

From 1846 to 1856, he supervised engineering and building projects across Florida, including the construction of Fort Jefferson. He served as assistant to the chief engineer of the U.S. Army from 1856 until the start of the **Civil War**. During the war, he auspiciously led combat troops, starting as chief engineer of a division at the first Battle of Bull Run (1861). He progressed through numerous commands, including the Army of Ohio and the 1st Division of the 6th Corps of the Army of the Potomac. Wright played a pivotal role in repulsing Confederate general Braxton Bragg's 1862 invasion of Kentucky while Wright was in command of the Army of Ohio.

General Wright was captured once and wounded twice. He attained the rank of major general of volunteers and advanced to command the famous 6th Army Corps, saving Washington, D.C., from capture in 1864 and subsequently spearheading the final assault on Petersburg, Va., and the pursuit of Gen. Robert E. Lee to Appomattox, Va., in 1865.

After his valiant service in the war, Wright held several commands and participated in many

Horatio Wright.

significant engineering projects across the nation. He was promoted to brigadier general in the regular army and appointed chief of engineers in 1879. Wright retired in 1884 and was involved in many prominent engineering projects, including New York City's Brooklyn Bridge. He also served as chief engineer for the completion of the Washington Monument in Washington, D.C. Wright died in 1899, survived by his wife, Louisa, and two daughters. He was buried in Arlington National Cemetery in Virginia under an obelisk erected by veterans of the 6th Corps.

U.S. Army Corps of Engineers. "Brigadier General Horatio Gouverneur Wright." www.hq.usace.army.mil/history/coc2.htm (accessed July 9, 2006).

Wikipedia. "Horatio Wright." www.wikipedia.com (accessed July 9, 2006).

Dave Hatter

WXIX. WXIX-TV, also identified as FOX19, is the FOX television network affiliate serving the Cincinnati–Northern Kentucky region. This UHF television station is licensed to the city of Newport, but its broadcast facility is in Cincinnati. WXIX was Cincinnati's first independent commercial TV station; it offered syndicated programs, classic movies, and children's shows long before the days of cable television superstations.

James Lang, owner of Newport's **WNOP** radio station, obtained the construction permit to build WXIX in 1955. The site originally planned for the station's studio and tower was cleared and graded in September 1954, on top of the hill where the residential development known as Wiedemann Hill is today, in the **Cote Brilliante** area of Newport. That facility was never built. The station ownership transferred twice before the station actually went on the air in 1968 as WSCO, channel 19. Metromedia purchased the station in 1972 and changed the call letters to WXIX, for the Roman numerals for 19 (XIX). Malrite Communications purchased WXIX in 1983. The station joined the new FOX commercial network, as a charter affiliate, in the late 1980s. Channel 19 launched Cincinnati's first local 10:00 p.m. evening news in 1993 and the area's first all-local morning newscasts in 1997.

During its first decade on the air, WXIX featured locally produced television shows, including the weekday children's favorite *Larry Smith's Puppets* and the weekend late-night science fiction movie program *Scream-In,* which featured host **Dick Von Hoene** as the campy "Cool Ghoul." WXIX is currently owned by Raycom Media.

Nash, Francis M. *Towers over Kentucky: A History of Radio and Television in the Bluegrass State.* Lexington, Ky.: Host Communications, 1995.

Raycom Media. "WXIX–Cincinnati, Ohio." www.raycommedia.com/stations/wxix.htm (accessed May 28, 2007).

Reis, Jim. "The TV Era Ushered in by Advertising," *KP,* June 21, 1993, 4K.

Wood, Mary. "Commercially Independent Ch. 19 Celebrates 10th," *CP,* August 16, 1978, 33.

John Schlipp

WYK (WICK), WALTER F. (b. December 4, 1889, Buffalo, N.Y.; d. February 28, 1969, Fort Thomas, Ky.). Walter Wyk learned to box at an early age and became a top performer in the boxing ring around Buffalo, N.Y., and in Northern Kentucky, where he was known as the "Covington Caveman." He is considered one of the greatest pugilists ever to box in the region. Boxing as a lightweight, Walter Wyk reached the pinnacle of his career just before **World War I**. Of his 182 bouts, he won 98 by knockouts. He defeated many opponents who later went on to become world champions. His record indicates that he fought at the International Athletic Club in Buffalo at least five times in 1911 and that as late as 1922 he fought in Indianapolis, Ind., and Covington, Ky. He knocked out Perry Nelson on July 26, 1922, in Covington at the former Riverside Park (the old Federal League Baseball Park) at Second and Scott Sts. Wyk lived at various locations in Covington: in a room on Court St., at 814 Scott St., and for many years at the **YMCA**. After his boxing career ended, he worked as a brakeman for the Pennsylvania Railroad, holding that job until he retired. For many years he continued to train boxers at a gymnasium in Morrow, Ohio.

After a long illness, Wyk died at St. Luke Hospital in Fort Thomas, survived by his wife, the former Mary Niedzielski, and four children. He was buried at Mother of God Cemetery in Latonia.

BoxRec. www.boxrec.com (accessed June 25, 2007).

"Brakeman Hurt," *KP,* September 13, 1927, 1.

"Death Notice," *KE,* March 2, 1969, 17E.

"Ohio River Is Richer by One $1200 Diamond," *KP,* July 16, 1927, 1.

Raver, Howard. "Walter K. Wyk, Former Boxer," *KP,* March 1, 1969, 3.

"Walter F. Wyk, 80, Railroader, Boxer," *KE,* March 2, 1969, 5D.

WZIP. WZIP, the "Voice of Northern Kentucky," went on the air October 5, 1947. This was the first Northern Kentucky broadcast station after WCKY moved to Cincinnati in 1939. ZIP, as it was called, had its offices and studios atop the building at the southwest corner of 6th and Madison in Covington. Its tower still stands along I-75, near Goebel Park.

The station began as a result of a year-long competition between two local groups to obtain a license that the Federal Communication Commission had made available in 1946. The winning group, Northern Kentucky Airwaves, was made up of Arthur Eilerman, Gregory Hughes, and Charles Topmiller. The station's frequency was set at 1050 kilocycles. It was a daytime station, with a 250-watt power base.

Arthur and Carmen Eilerman in WZIP studio.

WZIP supported the local community through innovative programming, including frequent interviews with community newsmakers, public officials, educators, business leaders, and religious figures. It featured local entertainers, sports teams, farm news, civic groups and events, and man-on-the-street interviews. Among its on-air personalities was Ernie Waites, Greater Cincinnati's first black disc jockey. Its local religious programming included a Saturday morning show with a rabbi from the Temple of Israel (see **Synagogues**) on Scott St. in Covington.

Station president Eilerman was elected president of the Kentucky Broadcasters Association in 1957; he was the only Northern Kentuckian ever to hold the post. His wife, Carmen, was a well-known personality who served as announcer, interviewer, and program director. Among her own shows, produced with studio audiences, were *Carmen's Corner, Bulletin Board,* and *Down Memory Lane.*

The station was sold in 1957 to Leonard Goorian and Alfred Kratz of Cincinnati. They sold it in 1959 to a group headed by Edward Skotch, who moved the offices to the Vernon Manor Hotel in Cincinnati. Skotch's group sold the station in 1960 to Carl, Robert, and Richard Lindner. After subsequent ownership changes, it operates today as WTSJ, a talk and Christian music station.

Files of documents, letters, and photographs relating to WZIP radio station, Covington, Ky., 1947–1956, Kenton Co. Public Library, Covington, Ky. Microfilm.

Nash, Francis M. *Towers over Kentucky: A History of Radio and TV in the Bluegrass State.* Lexington: Host Communications, 1995.

Reis, Jim. "The Voice of Northern Kentucky: WZIP Served Six-County Area," *KP,* October 21, 1996, 4K.

Chuck Eilerman

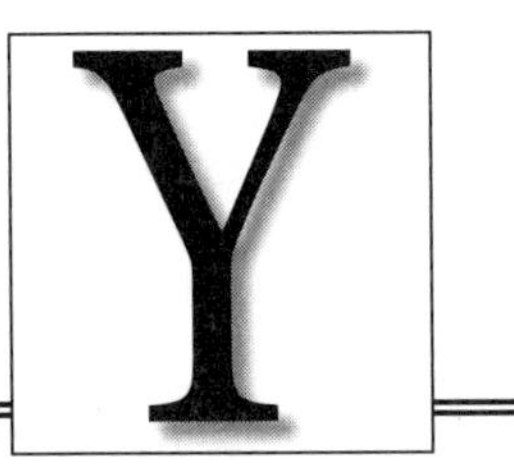

YAGER, WARD (b. July 2, 1891, Oldham Co., Ky.; d. February 24, 1967, Warsaw, Ky.). Judge Ward Yager, the son of J. B. and Elizabeth Alma Yager, became the judge of the former 15th Judicial District for the Commonwealth of Kentucky; his circuit was composed of Gallatin, Grant, Boone, Carroll, and Owen counties. He served for 28 years in that capacity, having previously been a commonwealth attorney in the circuit for 12 years. During his tenure as judge, he presided over the well-publicized Joan Kiger murder trial in 1943, and in 1949 he conducted the recount of the Boone Co. attorney election race between **William McEvoy** and John Crigler. After the recount, McEvoy won by 8 votes rather than the 13 votes shown by the original count.

In January 1956, Yager suffered a heart attack, but he was able to return to the bench October 1 of that year. He died in 1967 from another heart attack. His wife, the former Ruth Graham of Gallatin Co., had died in January 1967, and he was buried next to her at the Warsaw Cemetery.

Boone County Recorder, historical ed., September 4, 1930.

"Judge Yager, 75, Is Heart Victim," *KP*, February 25, 1967, 1K.

Reis, Jim. "Recounts Also Figure in Two Other Counts," *KP*, January 22, 2001, 4K.

"Return to Bench Planned by Yager," *KTS*, September 11, 1956, 4A.

YANCEY, EVAN WHITE, REAR ADMIRAL (b. August 21, 1907, Owen Co., Ky.; d. October 30, 1980, Pompano Beach, Fla.). Naval officer Evan W. Yancey was the son of W. Lindsay and Sherfy Bette Yancey of Owen Co., Ky. After graduating from Owenton High School, Yancey enrolled at Georgetown College in Scott Co., Ky., and studied there for three semesters. He secured an appointment to the U.S. Naval Academy at Annapolis, Md., where he graduated in 1931. In 1934 he married Marguerite Ziegler Davis.

Yancey began his naval career aboard the USS *Tattnall* and subsequently served at sea on four other ships. In 1939 he was promoted to lieutenant and briefly worked stateside as the assistant ordnance officer at the Brooklyn Navy shipyard in New York. In 1940 he began a tour of duty as the executive officer of the USS *Clemson*, an old **World War I** destroyer that was being used to transport gasoline to seaplanes in the Caribbean. When **World War II** broke out, the aging vessel was outfitted with antisubmarine gear and put to work. Yancey assumed command of the *Clemson*, escorting the USS *Bogue* throughout the Atlantic on antisubmarine missions for almost two years. Yancey developed a method for using the *Clemson*'s Fathometer (a sonic depth finder) to gauge the depth of the enemy subs below. This information enabled the *Bogue* to set its depth charges more precisely. As a result Yancey and his crew achieved more hits and ultimately received a Presidential Unit Citation "for extraordinary heroism in action against enemy submarines in the Atlantic area."

After the war Yancey's naval career took some interesting turns. He spent three years as chief of the U.S. Naval Mission in Ecuador, where he facilitated emergency airlifts of food supplies to civilians. He commanded the USS *Everglades* from July 1953 to June 1955, and that ship was awarded the navy's Battle Efficiency Plaque during his tenure. Following his successful stint on the *Everglades*, Yancey became inspector of naval material and attained the rank of rear admiral while serving in that capacity.

Yancey retired in July 1957, and he and his wife moved to Deerfield Beach, Fla. He died in 1980 at the Pinehurst Nursing Home and was cremated; his wife died in 1981. In addition to his Presidential Unit Citation, Yancey was awarded the Legion of Merit by President Roosevelt. He also received the American Defense, National Defense, and World War II Victory medals.

"Evan White Yancey '31," *Shipmate Magazine*, March 1981, obituary section, courtesy of the U.S. Naval Academy Archives, Annapolis, Md.

Florida Death Certificate No. 80993, for the year 1980.

Houchens, Marian Sidebottom. *History of Owen County: "Sweet Owen."* Louisville, Ky.: Standard, 1976.

Taul, Glen, Georgetown College archivist. Interview by Deborah Diersen Crocker, September 15, 2006, Georgetown, Ky.

Deborah Diersen Crocker

YANCEY, JESSIE O. (b. October 13, 1877, Maysville, Ky.; d. September 1, 1960, Lexington, Ky.). Jessie Yancey, the daughter of William Harrison and Rebecca Bell Oridge Yancey, was privately taught, yet she became a teacher in Mason Co. at many of the old one-room schools. Yancey was the first woman elected to public office in Mason Co., although at the time women could not vote: she became the first woman superintendent of schools in Mason Co., serving two terms (1910–1918). She was mostly associated with the Mayslick School, where she instituted a transportation system for the new consolidated Mayslick school in 1909. The provision of transportation precluded any excuses for students who used to say that they could not get to the more distant consolidated school. In 1918 Yancey moved to Lexington and worked for the Kentucky Health and Welfare League and later the Fayette Co. schools. She was interested in health issues, recognizing that students needed to be healthy to be able to learn. It was only in later life that she ever attended a college class, long after she had run the school system in Mason Co. Yancey knew that success in school was a function of being present to learn, and in 1940 in Lexington she headed a committee to address that issue. Yancey was a cousin of **Rebekah Hord**, mayor of Maysville, the first woman mayor in Kentucky. Yancey, an Episcopalian, died at Good Samaritan Hospital in Lexington in 1960 and was buried at the Maysville Cemetery.

"Juvenile Delinquency," *Lexington Leader*, March 4, 1940, 13.

Mason Co. Schools, Vertical File, Mason Co. Museum, Maysville, Ky.

"Miss Jessie O. Yancey Passes in Lexington," *Maysville Daily Independent*, September 8, 1960, 1.

YANCEY, RENA LUSBY (b. 1888, Owen Co., Ky.; d. July 12, 1964, Owenton, Ky.). Rena B. Lusby Yancey was an Owen Co. poet. In 1908 she married C. W. "Court" Yancey, an Owen Co. farmer. They lived near Poplar Grove, in the northeastern part of the county. She published a book of 69 poems entitled *Kentucky Trails*, in which she salutes all that God has created—nature and her family members. She was a member of the Poplar Grove Baptist Church, and she spent her entire life in Owen Co. Yancey was an associate of the Ten-Mile Baptist Association's Women's Missionary Society. She died at the Owen Co. Memorial Hospital (see **New Horizons Medical Center**) in 1964 after a long illness and was buried next to her husband at the Squiresville Cemetery along Ky. Rt. 1982.

"Mrs. Rena Yancey," *KP*, April 14, 1964, 7K.

USGenWeb Archives. "Squiresville Cemetery Records," Owen Co., Ky. Rootsweb.com. www.rootsweb.com.

Yancey, Rena Lusby. *Kentucky Trails*. Owenton, Ky.: Self-published, 1957.

YATES, RICHARD (b. January 18, 1815, Gallatin Co., Ky.; d. November 12, 1873, St. Louis, Mo.). Richard Yates, a legislator and a governor of Illinois, was the son of Henry and Millicent Yates, two of the earliest settlers of Gallatin Co. His father participated in the original laying out of the town of Warsaw (then called Fredericksburg). Richard Yates attended the common schools available in the county at the time. After his mother died in 1830, he and his father moved to Illinois, where Richard graduated from Illinois College at Jacksonville, Ill., in 1835. He returned to Kentucky to study law at Transylvania University in Lexington. Admitted to the bar in 1837, he set up his law practice in Jacksonville.

Yates served in the Illinois state house from 1842 to 1845 and 1848 to 1849. He was elected to the U.S. House of Representatives as a Whig and served from 1851 to 1855. He was elected governor of Illinois in 1860 and served until 1865. As Illinois's governor during the turbulent years of the **Civil War**, Yates was given considerable credit for stifling the pro-Confederate sentiment that was pervasive during the war, especially in the southern region of the state. While Governor, Yates took notice of a young army officer engaged in recruiting and training new troops in Galena, Ill., and appointed this young officer, Ulysses S. Grant, to the state adjutant general's office. In June 1861 Yates promoted Grant to colonel and put him in charge of an unruly regiment that was later named the 21st Illinois Volunteers.

Yates was defeated in a bid for a U.S. Senate seat in 1863. Toward the end of the war, however, he again ran for the U.S. Senate as a Republican and was successful. He served there from March 4, 1865, until March 3, 1871, and was actively involved in post–Civil War Reconstruction decisions. Upon leaving the U.S. Senate, Yates was appointed a U.S. Commissioner by President Ulysses S. Grant, who once had been Yates's aide. Yates was assigned to inspect a land subsidy railroad. He died suddenly of an unknown cause in St. Louis, Mo., in 1873 and was buried in Diamond Grove Cemetery in Jacksonville, Ill.

Biographical Directory of the United States Congress. http://bioguide.congress.gov/biosearch/biosearch.asp.

Bogardus, Carl R., Sr. "The History of Warsaw," Gallatin Co. Free Public Library, Warsaw, Ky.

——. *The Story of Gallatin County*. Ed. James C. Claypool. Cincinnati: John S. Swift, 2003.

Steve Huddleston

YMCA. The YMCA (Young Men's Christian Association) began in mid-19th-century England. George Williams founded the first "Y" in 1844, as a place where persons living on the streets of London could meet for Bible and prayer groups. The organization traditionally has been urban in location and Christian in spirit. The movement quickly spread throughout the industrialized Western world, arriving in Northern Kentucky before the **Civil War**. Later, YMCA's sprang up in places such as Ceylon and the Far East.

In the United States, the first Y's were started in the context of American Protestantism's evangelical reform attempts. The first Y in the country was established in Boston in 1851; by 1853 both Louisville and Lexington, Ky., had operating Y's. Before 1850, Cincinnati had an organization similar to the YMCA, and by 1850 it had become a Y; for a few years in the late 1850s, Cincinnati was the home of the YMCA national convention, as the headquarters was called, principally as a result of the role Cincinnatian William Neff had played at the national level. In downtown Cincinnati in 1893 there was a YMCA evening school that eventually evolved into the **Chase College of Law** of **Northern Kentucky University**. It became independent in governance in 1951 but not in location until its move to Covington in 1972.

Many of the first YMCA's provided temporary housing for men who were new to jobs in big cities, both freshly arrived immigrants and men who had come from the farm. The service was designed to keep them from drinking, gambling, smoking, and illicit sexual activity. In Northern Kentucky the connection with religion was clearly demonstrated early on, as the board members in Covington were required to be members of the local Protestant Ministerial Association.

In 1857 a YMCA was operating in Covington in a hall on the third floor of a building at Fifth St. and Madison Ave. that had a Christian reading room; in 1867 a Y was meeting at the Newport courthouse, and there were hopes of moving to the **Grace United Methodist Church**. Courthouses often provided the incubation space of such groups at that time. The Newport group lasted until 1898. Beginning in 1880, for a short time there was a Y at Sixth and Main Sts. on the west side of Covington, the West End YMCA. In 1888 a Covington Y operated at Sixth St. and Madison Ave.; a year later it occupied the second floor of a building at the northwest corner of Eighth St. and Madison Ave. It was led by banker **Jonathan David Hearne** and a young up-and-coming lawyer named **Richard P. Ernst**. Other cities in the area where early attempts were made at developing Y programs included Bellevue and Dayton in Campbell Co. and Latonia and Ludlow (which had a railroad Y) in Kenton Co.

Old YMCA building, opened in 1913 on Madison Ave., Covington.

In 1892 Ernst, the person most closely associated with the YMCA movement in Northern Kentucky, became the president of the Covington Y, a position he retained until his death in 1934. Ernst accomplished many other things, one of them serving as a U.S. senator, but he was most proud of his relationship with the Y. He was first and foremost a "Y boy." Covington's Y programs were so successful that additional space was needed; therefore in 1911, under Ernst's lead, construction was begun on a new facility at the southeast corner of Pike St. and Madison Ave. on the site of the landmark Magnolia House. The new Y was designed by architects George W. Schofield and **Lyman Walker**; it included a swimming pool, a gymnasium, meeting rooms, and a dormitory for short-term housing. That building opened in 1913. In 1918 Ernst proposed that the ladies and girls of Covington should also be served, and thus even today, one can see the separate boys' and girls' entrances to the building. It was the swimming pool that most interested the ladies, but women could not become formal members until 1929, when the Y added program emphasis on the family. Also in 1929, the Y expanded into the adjacent building, mainly for needed women's facilities. Ernst's early decision effectively precluded any appearance of a YWCA (Young Women's Christian Association) in Northern Kentucky. The Y sponsored football teams, basketball and baseball leagues, volleyball games, bicycle races, rifle teams, tennis tournaments, marathon races, and debating teams; provided an exercise area; and offered sewing classes for girls. Its facility was often the site of important civic meetings and banquets and religious gatherings. For many years, the Y employed an on-site masseur.

During the two world wars, the Covington Y was similar to a United Service Organization (USO) in welcoming active-duty armed service personnel. During **World War I**, the International YMCA recruited young women for service in the European theater as nurses and USO entertainers. One of these was singer **Elizabeth Parks**, a Covington native, who later married a top leader in the Canadian YMCA's involvement in the same effort.

The Covington branch was blessed with important and influential leadership, both in its hands-on management and on its board of directors. Willard L. Wade (1902–1983) served as a YMCA director for more than 50 years, including 40 years in Covington. The Y cooperated closely with the **Week Day School of Religion** and the Hi-y program at **Holmes High School**. The Y swimming pool was popular with people of all ages. The Y's cafeteria, opened in 1951, was a busy place where good meals could be had by anyone at a moderate price. Local businessmen and bankers in the immediate area crowded the cafeteria on weekdays at lunchtime. During the 1950s, local television star and heartthrob **Bob Braun** hosted teen dances in the building. The Covington Y, which came to be known as the Wade Branch, continued into the 1980s, providing athletic activities and other programs to all who came. It closed its door on May 1, 1987.

Before the 1920s, three specialized YMCA facilities arose in Northern Kentucky. Two were railroad Y's, more formally known as transportation YMCA's, established to help railroads deal with the saloon-attending problems of their overnight crews. In 1890 one of these facilities opened at 28 W. 15th St. in Covington; it moved in 1909 to 17th St. and Madison Ave., on the west side, at KC Junction, where the **Chesapeake and Ohio Railroad** (C&O) joined with the **Louisville and Nashville Railroad**. This was one of the busiest railroad intersections in the United States, and it was here that Ernst and others built the new Railroad YMCA Hotel, as a place where visiting train crews could stay overnight and eat, positioned near to their assigned trains for their trip home the next day. This Y attempted to create a community of out-of-towners by means of its monthly *News and Notes* newsletter. The building remains today but not as a hotel. The second railroad hotel appeared in late 1914 at Silver Grove in Campbell Co., along the C&O, near what became its Stevens Yard. This facility was open to the public, not just train crews. The third specialized Y in the region was on the grounds of the **Fort Thomas Military Reservation**, part of the Y's armed services division; it opened in July 1917 and remained for as long as the U.S. Army billeted soldiers there. Several photographs of the one-story Y building at the fort have survived in various collections. Since the **Civil War**, the YMCA has provided assistance and relief to the armed forces. It was this Y at the fort that created a YMCA tradition within the city of Fort Thomas, which continues to support the Campbell Co. YMCA just down the street. None of the three specialized YMCAs exist today.

During the 1920s, the Covington branch operated a camp in Rosedale, known as Ernst Lodge, south of town at the end of the streetcar line. This is where the Y tennis courts were located. At this time the Rosedale community was considered to be out in the country. During the late 1920s, Ernst bought the 80-acre former Underhill Farm near Burlington, the farm made famous in **John Uri Lloyd**'s novel *Warwick of the Knob*. In the mid-1930s he gave the farm to the Y to be used for summer outdoor recreation such as camping, fishing, hiking, and swimming. The intention was to bring urban children out to the fresh air of the country for a couple of weeks each summer. Today, expanded to more than 350 acres, it operates successfully as Camp Ernst and is occasionally used by other groups, such as the Cincinnati YWCA. Plans for a new lodge building at Camp Ernst were announced in 2005.

In recent years, the Y has gone suburban. Once families began leaving urban Covington in large numbers, the Pike St. and Madison Ave. YMCA, the Wade Branch, closed. It had been remodeled several times (in 1937, 1951, and 1967), only to be replaced in Covington with various satellite facilities offering social programs. The Wade building was sold in 1987.

In 1967 modern branch Y's opened in Fort Thomas and Florence. Florence, beginning in 1955, had operated as the Tri-City Y before its new building was completed in late 1967. It served the three cities of Erlanger, Elsmere, and Florence but recently moved west to Burlington and into a new facility named for benefactor **R. C. Durr**.

In 1983, nearly 50 years after Richard Ernst's death, his dedication to the YMCA mission made a surprising new impact. As a result of a previously undisclosed clause in Ernst's will, and after the death of all the relatives he named in his will, the trust fund's principal was divided; half of it, $350,000, went to the Covington YMCA.

Since the late 1980s, Northern Kentucky YMCA's have been under the umbrella of the YMCA's of Greater Cincinnati, which offers assorted programs at more than 20 sites on both sides of the Ohio River. In Campbell Co. there is the Campbell Co. YMCA in Fort Thomas and a teen center in Dayton; in Kenton Co. there are the Kenton Co. YMCA in Independence and programs offered in south Covington; in Boone Co. the Y has flourished, with Camp Ernst, the modern R.C. Durr facility at Boone Woods, and swimming pools at Union and Cherry Hill. There is one other YMCA within the Northern Kentucky region at Maysville along U.S. 68. During the 1980s, an attempt was made to start a Y program in Grant Co. Recently, these modern Y's have moved into the areas of child care, fitness, and wellness. In Boone Co. a new senior center is also in the works at the Durr facility.

"Covington Y Offers 4 New Dining Rooms," *KP*, September 28, 1951, 1.

"Ernst Gives History of Y at Banquet," *KP*, October 12, 1932, 1.

"New Home of Railroad Y.M.C.A. Will Be a Handsome Structure," *KP*, June 10, 1909, 2.

Phillips, Mike. "The Wade Y's Future," *KP*, January 18, 1984, 4K.

"R.C. Durr YMCA to Open in June," *KP*, May 1, 2004, 2K.

Reis, Jim. "YMCA's Kept Its Spunk Alive for 125 Years," *KP*, March 12, 1984, 8K.

"Willard Wade, Kentucky Y Leader for over 40 Years," *KE*, October 18, 1983, C2.

Young Men's Christian Association. *Northern Kentucky Young Men's Christian Association.* Frankfort: Kentucky Historical Society, 1989. Microfilm set available at the Kenton Co. Public Library, Covington, Ky.

Michael J. Poehner

YOUNG, CHARLES DENTON, COLONEL (b. March 12, 1864, Mayslick, Ky.; d. January 8, 1922, Lagos, Nigeria). Charles Young, who became a colonel in the U.S. Army, was an African American, the son of former slaves. During the **Civil War**, his father served as a private in the Colored Artillery Volunteers, at a time when the U.S. Army was segregated. Charles's family moved to Ripley, Ohio, when he was a young child. He attended the white Ripley High School, from which he graduated with honors at age 16. Afterward he taught at the black Ripley High School. Young was musically inclined and played the piano, the violin, and the guitar. While a teacher, he took a competitive exam for appointment to the U.S. Military Academy at West Point, N.Y., and placed second among the applicants. He graduated from West Point in the class of 1889, becoming only the third black ever to graduate, and was commissioned as a 2nd lieutenant. In 1903 he married Aida Barr, and they had two children. Also in 1903, he was named acting superintendent of the Sequoia and General Grant national parks, being the first black to hold that title. His duties as a military officer were to enforce park rules, supervise the activities of the rangers, and protect the park and its wildlife from harm. His greatest accomplishment during his tenure was the construction of more roads, and he encouraged the federal government to purchase additional park land. For his performance, he was promoted to the rank of captain. He served in the U.S. Army for 37 years, at assignments in the United States, Mexico, the Philippines, Haiti, and Liberia. At the start of **World War I**, he was diagnosed with Bright's disease (a kidney disorder) and was medically discharged. For the next two years, he served as a professor of military science at the all-black Wilberforce College in Ohio. In 1916 he was awarded the Springarn Medal, given annually by the **NAACP** for outstanding achievement by a black American. In fall 1918 Young rode a horse from Xenia, Ohio, to Washington, D.C., proving to government officials that he was physically fit, and he was subsequently allowed to rejoin the army. On November 6, 1918, he was promoted to the rank of colonel, becoming the first African American to reach that rank in the U.S. Army. In 1919 he was appointed military attaché to the Republic of Liberia. At the age of 58, while on a reconnaissance mission there, Young died from a kidney infection. He was buried in Lagos, Nigeria. In June 1923, at his wife's insistence, his remains were returned to the United States and he was reburied with full military honors at Arlington National Cemetery in Arlington, Va.

Arlington National Cemetery Website. "Charles Denton Young: Colonel United States Army." www.arlingtoncemetery.net.

Buffalo Soldiers and Indian Wars. "Colonel Charles Young." www.buffalosoldier.net.

NPS.gov. "Capt. Charles Young." www.nps.gov.

Wikipedia. "Charles Young." www.wikipedia.org.

Jack Wessling

YSAYE, EUGENE (b. July 16, 1858, Liege, Belgium; d. May 12, 1931, Liege, Belgium). Noted violinist and conductor Eugene Ysaye spent four years in Cincinnati. As a youth, he studied with his father, Nicolas Ysaye, before entering the Liege Conservatory in 1865. He made his first public appearance at age seven, attracting little attention. From 1876 he studied in Paris and had close contact with the French masters of the time—Camille Saint-Saens, César Franck, and Gabriel Fauré. He enjoyed success as a soloist and had many European engagements. From 1879 to 1882, he led the Bilse orchestra in Berlin. He was the first to perform some outstanding works, including Franck's *Violin Sonata* (1886), Ernest Chausson's *Concert*

(1889–1891) and *Poème* (1896), and Claude Debussy's *String Quartet* (1893). The celebrated pianist Ferdinand Hiller arranged to have Ysaye play for the great violinist Joseph Joachim, who remarked, "I have never heard the violin played like that before." Ysaye was instrumental in developing the modern style of violin playing; his influence spanned three generations. When he gave the first performance of Elgar's *Violin Concerto* in 1912, the greatest contemporary violinists were in the audience. Ysaye's career peaked with his first American tour in 1894 and continued unabated until the outbreak of **World War I** in 1914. He collaborated with notable pianists, including his brother Theophile. But it was his partnership with Raoul Pugno that was most exceptional, because they performed only sonatas; for the time it was a very unusual kind of program.

When poor health impaired Ysaye's playing, he turned to conducting. He was hired as music director of the Cincinnati May Festival in 1918 and shortly thereafter was offered the music directorship of the Cincinnati Symphony Orchestra. He lived in Fort Thomas. He was no stranger to Cincinnati audiences, as he had performed with the Cincinnati Orpheus Club in 1894 and had appeared with the symphony five times. Before his first May Festival concert, the *Cincinnati Times-Star* reported, "No singer is so famous that he or she does not feel a thrill of anticipation in knowing that the great Ysaye is to wield the baton." Ysaye's symphony concerts took on a patriotic theme and audiences warmly responded. At his first concert as conductor, he opened the program with the national anthems of the Allied countries, to commemorate the ending of the war 11 days earlier. Enthusiasm for the orchestra was never higher. During his tenure the orchestra toured extensively and was the first to have its music broadcast on **radio** throughout the country. In 1918 Ysaye's *Exile,* an elegy for string orchestra, premiered at the May Festival. The next year he gave a special concert at Music Hall for King Albert and Queen Elisabeth of Belgium. He resigned in 1922 and returned to his homeland. There he gave private lessons and occasionally performed, giving his last concert in 1930. Two months before he died on May 12, 1931, his opera *Peter the Miner* premiered in Liege, but Ysaye was too ill to conduct. It was possibly his greatest musical triumph, yet it remains unpublished.

Cincinnati Symphony Orchestra Centennial Portraits. Cincinnati: Cincinnati Symphony Orchestra, 1994.

"Famous May Festival Soloists Eager to Sing under Baton of Cincinnati's Renowned Leader," *CTS,* May 4, 1918, 7.

"Ysaye in Hospital Following Hunt for Burglar," *KP,* February 10, 1919, 1.

"Ysaye's Magic Bow Is Stilled," *CE,* May 13, 1931, 1.

Ann Hicks

ZEITZ, GRAY (b. August, 1949, Mobile, Ala.). A publisher of collectible books and an author, Gray Zeitz is one of two sons of Joseph and Kay Zeitz. He moved to Kentucky as a child, relocating several times in the early years because of his father's military career. He received an associate degree from the Elizabethtown Community College in Elizabethtown, Ky. In the late 1960s, he moved to Lexington, where he attended the University of Kentucky (UK), taking courses in English and history. His passion for printing emerged during his days at UK, where he apprenticed at the King Library Press. He learned fine handwork skills and typographic design working with Carolyn Hammer, who founded the press while also serving as curator of rare books.

In 1974 Zeitz moved to his current residence of 30 years, Monterey, in Owen Co. That same year, his love of print and of contemporary writers came together as he created Larkspur Press, one of the nation's model small presses. Zeitz began Larkspur on his land outside of Monterey, with a small supply of Emerson metal type and some used equipment. In 1975 Larkspur Press published its first work, *Bluegrass,* a collection of poems by Richard Taylor. With its appealing presentation in a beautifully finished style, *Bluegrass* set the standard for Larkspur publications. Zeitz prefers a handset type because it allows precise spacing and beautiful typefaces not found on computers. He also enjoys setting type by hand. He uses a process of printing that contains remnants of the methods invented by the German Johann Gutenberg, the 15th-century father of modern printing. The process involves printing by movable letters. Zeitz's process is not simple. He manually typesets the books by loading letters and other characters into viselike boxes called "sticks." The entire process takes a couple of years, so he can print only up to three books per year. In the process, Zeitz must choose the font and paper type for each book. If the paper is to be handmade, the time required can be multiplied by as much as a factor of 10. Paper or cloth must be chosen for each cover, and the covers are usually printed by hand. If color or illustrations are present, the sheets may have to be run through the press as many as six times. After printing, the regular editions are "jobbed out" to a small bindery. The special editions are hand sewn, hand bound, and decorated. The covers of the special editions are decorated with unique papers (marbled, pasted, or stamped).

Larkspur's publications include short fiction, collections of poems, short poems, and broadsides (single works printed on one side of a sheet of paper). Zeitz collaborates predominately with Kentuckians. Some of the authors whose books have been published by Larkspur are Wendell Berry, Guy Davenport, Jonathan Greene, James Baker Hall, J. Hill Hamon, Bobbie Ann Mason, Ed McClanahan, Gurney Norman, Steve Sanfield, Fred Smock, and Richard Taylor. Zeitz also has published his own poetry.

Gray Zeitz has played a major role in the lives of Kentucky writers. His work is a model of printing craftsmanship. In addition to his printing activities, he is a volunteer firefighter and Monterey city clerk. His wife, Jean, is a preschool teacher in Owen Co. They have a son and a daughter.

Grolier Club. "The Work of Victor and Carolyn Hammer." www.grolierclub.org/ExHammer.htm (accessed February 17, 2007).

Jones, Elizabeth. "Putting the Fine in Fine Press: UK Celebrates Twenty-Five Years of Gray Zeitz's Larkspur Press," *Ace Weekly,* www.aceweekly.com/acemag/backissues/981028/art_981028.html (accessed February 17, 2007).

King Library Press. "Larkspur Twenty-Five: Celebrating a Quarter Century of Gray Zeitz and Larkspur Press." www.uky.edu/Libraries/KLP/seminars/1998f.html (accessed February 17, 2007).

"Timeless Type of Work," *Lexington Herald Leader,* July 20, 1997, J1.

Young, Dianne, and Steve Millburg. "Printers in the Old Style," *Southern Living* 29, no. 12 (December 1994): 102–4.

Zeitz, Gray. Telephone interview by Sharon McGee, August 9, 2004.

Sharon McGee

ZIEGLER, RON (b. May 12, 1939, Covington, Ky.; d. February 10, 2003, Coronado, Calif.). Ronald Louis Ziegler was the son of Louis Daniel and Ruby Parsons Ziegler. He grew up at 1074 Altavia Ave. in Park Hills, a neighbor of longtime Cincinnati Reds public address announcer Paul Sommerkamp. Ziegler attended **Dixie Heights High School** in Edgewood, where he earned all-state honors in football. He began college at Xavier University in Cincinnati in fall 1957 with an athletic scholarship but gave up football and transferred to the University of Southern California (USC) in 1958. He graduated from USC in 1961. While an undergraduate student there, Ziegler became active in Republican politics; he was a member of the Young Republicans. In 1961 he served as a press officer of the California Republican State Committee, where he assisted in Richard Nixon's failed attempt to become governor of California in 1962. Public relations and marketing were Ziegler's real fortes, as evidenced by the successful work he did in these fields for the J. Walter Thompson advertising agency in California.

When Ziegler's friend H. R. "Bob" Haldeman became chief of staff for the newly elected President Nixon (1969–1974), Ziegler, at age 29, was appointed White House press secretary, the youngest ever. He coined two phrases that will live in American history: he is the person who called the Watergate incident the result of a "third-rate burglary," and he often responded to the White House news correspondences by calling things "inoperative." In 2003 Ziegler died at his California home and was cremated. His wife Nancy and two daughters survived him.

Hicks, Jack. "Former Nixon Press Aide Visits Home of His Youth," *KE,* July 11, 1983, C1.

"Ron Ziegler, Nixon Aide, Dies—He Was Born in Covington," *KP,* February 11, 2003, A6.

ZION BAPTIST CHURCH. Zion Baptist Church of Walton in Boone Co. was formed in 1872 to serve that area's African American community. Tradition has it that the church was organized by Timothy Smith, when he began to organize prayer meetings in his home. The earliest founders were George Chatman, Rev. and Mrs. John Greene, Courtney Watkins, Solomon Watkins, Daniel Williams, and John Williams. This first church was officially organized on September 20, 1872; Rev. Solomon Watkins was called as its pastor. The first house of worship was located on High St. and had a dual purpose: it served as a school as well as a church. In November 1877, Watkins held a baptism at Uncle Jack Arnold's pond; there were 10 converts in the procession, and many spectators lined the banks.

The church on High St. was abandoned and in 1884 a new building, which also functioned as a school and a church, was constructed on a hill overlooking the current church. It is believed that the Odd Fellows held their meetings there. After this building was demolished, its site became the burial place of Watkins.

Rev. J. S. Boles spearheaded the building of the present church. Male members of the congregation demolished the old building and built a new one at 35 Church St., which was dedicated on May 28, 1922. An all-day meeting and a basket dinner on the grounds accompanied the celebration.

On June 18, 1972, the Zion Baptist Church held its centennial celebration. Zion Baptist has gone through several phases of additions, rebuilding, and remodeling. In September 1994, Rev. O. B. Ford was called and continues to serve Zion Baptist Church.

"Church Notes," *DC,* November 7, 1877, 2.

Historical notes on file at Zion Baptist Church, Walton, Ky.

Paul, Smita Madan. "Neighborhood Contributed," *KE,* July 6, 1993, D1–D2.

Reis, Jim. "Black Churches Offered Stability in Troubled Times," *KP,* January 20, 1997, 4K.

Theodore H. H. Harris

ZION STATION. An unnamed settlement along Ten Mile Creek in northwestern Grant Co., part of a large land grant held by John H. Craig, was given the name Zion Station in 1869 when the **Louisville, Cincinnati, and Lexington Railroad**, the "Short Line" between Louisville and Cincinnati, was completed. Zion Station served as the railroad connection for the town of Mount Zion, just a few miles to the east.

A post office opened at Zion Station in 1871. The earliest schoolhouse was established about 1884 in a building that remained in use until 1914. A new frame structure then replaced the original one and served as the Zion School until 1933. Pleasant View Baptist Church was organized at Zion Station in 1867 in a log building that was replaced with a frame structure in 1907. In 1876 the *Kentucky State Gazetteer* indicated that Zion Station had two general stores, two physicians, two blacksmiths, a Baptist minister, and a flourmill.

On February 23, 1872, a fast train from Louisville collapsed the bridge near Zion Station, killing 2 people and injuring about 50. It was the third bridge collapse in the rail line's short history. In recent years, the county has had to repair the 100-year-old automobile bridge over the Ten Mile Creek connecting Zion Station with Napoleon. Without use of the bridge, important emergency vehicles in that part of Grant Co. can supply only limited service.

Conrad, John B., ed. *History of Grant County.* Williamstown, Ky.: Grant Co. Historical Society, 1992.

"Frightful Railroad Accident," *CJ*, February 24, 1882, 2.

Tortora, Andrea. "Grant Patching Wooden Bridge, Crossing Fingers on New Span," *KE*, August 22, 1996, B1A.

John B. Conrad

ZOLLER, KATE (b. July 12, 1853, Memphis, Tenn.; d. September 21, 1932, Mount Olivet, Ky.). Katherine Elinor Grace Farris, who became a school superintendent, was the daughter of William and Emmalene De Grasse Farris of Memphis, Tenn. She attended the Memphis schools and graduated from the Young Ladies Institute. She became a schoolteacher in the Cincinnati Public School system but later moved to Mount Olivet, Ky., at the advice of her physician, in order to improve her health. Soon she began teaching in private schools; she also taught music part-time in Robertson Co. On June 8, 1880, she married John W. Zoller, the owner and editor of the *Robertson County Tribune.* Kate was often seen helping out at the newspaper; she was a first-class writer who could produce copy quickly. Around 1910 she became the first woman superintendent of schools in Robertson Co. and always was known for her support of high educational standards. Kate Zoller died in 1932 at Mount Olivet and was buried at the Mount Olivet Cemetery.

Kentucky Death Certificate No. 22373, for the year 1932.

Moore, T. Ross, ed. *Echoes from the Century, 1867–1967.* Mount Olivet, Ky.: Robertson Co. Historical Society, 2000.

Select Bibliography

American Association of University Women (Maysville Branch). *From Cabin to College: A History of the Schools of Mason County.* Maysville, Ky.: G. F. McClanahan, 1976.

An Atlas of Boone, Kenton, and Campbell Counties, Kentucky. Philadelphia: D. J. Lake, 1883.

An Atlas of Bracken and Pendleton Counties, Kentucky. Philadelphia: D. J. Lake, 1884.

An Atlas of Carroll and Gallatin Counties, Kentucky. Philadelphia: D. J. Lake, 1883.

Averdick, Michael R. *A Directory of Silversmiths, Jewelers, Watch and Clock Makers, and Related Trades of Covington and Newport, Kentucky, and Vicinity, 1833–1900.* Covington, Ky.: Willard Street Press, 2002.

Barr, Frances Keller. *Ripe to the Harvest: History of the Episcopal Diocese of Lexington, 1895–1995.* Lexington, Ky.: Diocese of Lexington, 1995.

Belew, Mildred Boden. *The First 200 Years of Pendleton County.* Falmouth, Ky.: M. B. Belew, n.d. (ca. 1994).

Best, Edna Hunter. *Historic Washington Kentucky*. 1st ed., 1944. Reprint, Maysville, Ky.: Limestone Chapter of the DAR, 1971.

Bevarly, R. W. "History of Education in Carroll County," master's thesis, Univ. of Kentucky, 1936.

Biographical Cyclopedia of the Commonwealth of Kentucky. Chicago: John M. Gresham, 1896.

Biographical Directory of the United States Congress. www.senate.gov.

Biographical Encyclopedia of Kentucky. Cincinnati: J. M. Armstrong, 1878.

Bodley, Temple. *History of Kentucky: The Blue Grass State.* 4 vols. Chicago: S. J. Clarke, 1928.

Bogardus, Carl R., Sr. *The Story of Gallatin County.* Ed. James C. Claypool. Cincinnati: John S. Swift, 2003.

Boone Co. Historic Preservation Review Board. *Historic Structures of Boone County, Kentucky*. Burlington, Ky.: Boone Co. Historic Preservation Review Board, 2002.

Boone Co. Recorder. Historical ed., September 4, 1930.

Bracken Co. Extension Homemakers. *History of Bracken County*. Bicentennial ed. Brooksville, Ky., Bracken Co. Extension Homemakers, 2002.

Bricking, Chuck. *Covington's Heritage: A Compilation of the City's Historical Houses and a Short Biography of the Inhabitants.* Covington, Ky.: Privately published, 1980.

Browning, M. Carmel, Sr. *Kentucky Authors: A History of Kentucky Literature.* Evansville, Ind.: Keller-Crescent, 1968.

Butler, Tod Jordan. "The Cincinnati Southern Railway: A City's Response to Relative Commercial Decline," PhD diss., Ohio State Univ., 1971.

Cabot, Susan M., and Michael D. Rouse. *Boone County*. Charleston, S.C.: Arcadia, 1998.

Calvert, Jean, and John Klee. *Maysville, Kentucky: From Past to Present in Pictures.* Maysville, Ky.: Mason Co. Museum, 1983.

———. *The Towns of Mason County: Their Past in Pictures.* Maysville, Ky.: Maysville and Mason Co. Library Historical and Scientific Association, 1986.

Campbell, Justine Tandy. "History of the Carroll County Schools," 1976, available at the Carroll Co. Public Library, Carrollton, Ky.

Campbell Co. Historical Society. *Campbell County, Kentucky, 200 Years, 1794–1994.* Alexandria, Ky.: Campbell Co. Historical Society, 1994.

Campbell County Kentucky History and Genealogy. Falmouth, Ky.: Falmouth Outlook, 1978.

Caraway, Robin. *Images of America: Newport, the Sin City Years.* Charleston, S.C.: Arcadia, 2009.

Casebolt, Pamela Ciafardini, and Philip G. Ciafardini. *Images of America: Italians of Newport and Northern Kentucky*. Charleston, S.C.: Arcadia, 2007.

Cist, Charles. *Sketches and Statistics of Cincinnati in 1851*. Cincinnati: Wm. H. Moore, 1851.

Clark, Thomas D. *A History of Kentucky*. New York: Prentice-Hall, 1937.

Claypool, James C. *The Tradition Continues: The Story of Old Latonia, Latonia, and Turfway Racecourses*. Fort Mitchell, Ky.: T. I. Hayes, 1997.

Clift, G. Glenn. *History of Maysville and Mason County.* Lexington, Ky.: Transylvania, 1936.

Coffin, Levi. *Reminiscences of Levi Coffin, the Reputed President of the Underground Railroad*. Cincinnati: Robert Clarke, 1898.

Collins, Richard H. *History of Kentucky.* 2 vols. Covington, Ky.: Collins, 1882.

Condit, Carl W. *The Railroad and the City: A Technological and Urbanistic History of Cincinnati*. Columbus: Ohio State Univ. Press, 1977.

Conrad, John B., ed. *History of Grant County*. Williamstown, Ky.: Grant Co. Historical Society, 1992.

Conrad, William, comp. *The History of Boone County Schools*. Boone Co., Ky.: Boone Co. Community Educational Council, 1982.

———, ed. *Boone County: The Top of Kentucky, 1792–1992*. Fort Mitchell, Ky.: Picture This! Books, 1992.

Coon, Diane Perrine. "Southeastern Indiana's Underground Railroad Routes and Operations," U.S. Park Service and Indiana DNR, 1999, technical report available at Indiana Dept. of Historic Preservation and Archaeology, Indianapolis, Ind.

Costeloe, Michael P. *William Bullock, Connoisseur and Virtuoso of the Egyptian Hall: Piccadilly to Mexico (1773–1849)*. Bristol, U.K.: Univ. of Bristol, 2008.

———. "William Bullock and the Mexican Connection." *Mexican Studies/Estudios Mexicanos* 22 (Summer 2006): 275–309.

Cummins, Virginia Raymond. *Rookwood Pottery Potpourri*. Silver Spring, Md.: Cliff R. Leonard and Duke Coleman, 1980.

Davidson, Robert. *History of the Presbyterian Church in the State of Kentucky*. Reprint. Greenwood, S.C.: Attic Press, 1974.

Dayton Centennial Committee. *Centennial, Dayton, Kentucky, 1849–1949: Keepsake Program*. Newport, Ky.: Michaels, 1949.

Donnelly, Joseph. *Newport Barracks—Kentucky's Forgotten Military Installation*. Covington, Ky.: Kenton Co. Historical Society, 1999.

Donsback, Edna Tyson. *Our Church through 175 Years*. Covington, Ky.: First United Methodist Church, 2003.

Earnest, Ernest. *The Volunteer Fire Company: Past and Present*. New York: Stein and Day, 1983.

Ellis, William E. *The Kentucky River.* Lexington: Univ. Press of Kentucky, 2000.

Elsmere Centennial Committee. *City of Elsmere—Centennial Celebration Booklet, 1896–1996*. Elsmere, Ky.: City of Elsmere, 1996.

Federal Writers' Project. *They Built a City: 150 Years of Industrial Cincinnati*. Cincinnati: Cincinnati Post, 1938.

Friend, Craig Thompson. *Along the Maysville Road: The Early Republic in the Trans-Appalachian West*. Knoxville: Univ. of Tennessee Press, 2005.

Gastright, Joseph F. *Gentleman Farmers to City Folks: A Study of Wallace Woods, Covington, Kentucky.* Cincinnati: Cincinnati Historical Society, 1980.

Geaslen, Chester F. *Strolling along Memory Lane*. Newport, Ky.: Otto, 1971–1974.

Gentry, Mary Ann. *A History of Carroll County*. Madison, Ind.: Coleman, 1984.

Gifford, Anjanette. "The Formation of Robertson County." *Northern Kentucky Heritage* 8, no. 2 (Spring–Summer 2001): 65–72.

Gilham, Lisa Curtiss. *Images of America: Latonia.* Charleston, S.C.: Arcadia, 2009.

Goss, Charles Frederick, ed. *Cincinnati: The Queen City, 1788–1912.* 4 vols. Chicago: S. J. Clarke, 1912.

Gray, Gypsy M. *History of Gallatin County, Kentucky.* Covington, Ky.: Self-published, 1968.

Greve, Charles Theodore. *Centennial History of Cincinnati and Representative Citizens.* 2 vols. Chicago: Biographical, 1904.

Grossman, James R., Ann Durkin Keating, and Janice L. Reiff, eds. *The Encyclopedia of Chicago.* Chicago: Univ. of Chicago Press, 2004.

Hall, Charles G., ed. *The Cincinnati Southern Railway: A History.* Cincinnati: Ault and Wiborg, 1902.

Harrison, Lowell H., and James C. Klotter. *A New History of Kentucky.* Lexington: Univ. Press of Kentucky, 1997.

Hartman, Margaret Strebel. *The Early History of Falmouth, Pendleton County, December 10, 1793 thru February 20, 1837.* Falmouth, Ky.: Falmouth Outlook, 1983.

Hartman, Margaret Strebel, and W. Rus Stevens. *Campbell County Kentucky History and Genealogy.* Campbell Co., Ky.: W. R. Stevens, 1984.

Haviland, Laura S. *A Woman's Life-Work: Labors and Experiences of Laura S. Haviland.* Cincinnati: Walden and Stowe, 1881.

Hedeen, Stanley. *Big Bone Lick: The Cradle of American Paleontology.* Lexington: Univ. Press of Kentucky, 2008.

———. *Natural History of the Cincinnati Region.* Cincinnati: Cincinnati Museum Center, 2006.

Hopkins, C. Howard. *History of the Y.M.C.A. in North America.* New York: Association Press, 1951.

Hopkins, G. M. *City Atlas of Covington, Kentucky.* Philadelphia: G. M. Hopkins, 1877.

Houchens, Mariam Sidebottom. *History of Owen County: "Sweet Owen."* Louisville, Ky.: Standard, 1976.

Hubbard, Harlan. *Shantyboat: A River Way of Life.* Lexington: Univ. of Kentucky Press, 1977.

Irvin, Helen Deiss. *Women in Kentucky.* Lexington: Univ. Press of Kentucky, 1979.

Jackson, Eric. *Black America Series: Northern Kentucky.* Charleston, S.C.: Arcadia, 2005.

"The James Taylor Narrative," 1840, Kenton Co. Public Library, Covington, Ky.; Campbell Co. Historical and Genealogical Society, Alexandria, Ky.

Jewell, Simon, ed. *Campbell County Firefighters Educational Association.* Campbell Co., Ky.: Campbell Co. Firefighters Educational Association, ca. 2002–2003.

Johnson, E. Polk. *History of Kentucky and Kentuckians.* 3 vols. Chicago: Lewis, 1912.

Jones, Mary Keturah. *History of Campbell County, Kentucky as Read at the Centennial Celebration of 4th of July, 1876.* Reprint, Fort Thomas, Ky.: Rebecca Bryan Boone Chapter, Daughters of the American Revolution, 1974.

Kenny, D. J. *Illustrated Cincinnati.* Cincinnati: Geo. E. Stevens, 1875.

Kentucky Atlas and Gazetteer. Yarmouth, Maine: DeLorme, 1997.

Kentucky Secretary of State. "Kentucky Cities Database." http://apps.sos.ky.gov/land/cities/.

Kerr, Charles. *History of Kentucky.* 5 vols. Chicago: American Historical Society, 1922.

Kleber, John E., ed. *The Kentucky Encyclopedia.* Lexington: Univ. Press of Kentucky, 1992.

LaBree, Benjamin, ed. *Notable Men of Cincinnati at the Beginning of the 20th Century (1903).* Louisville, Ky.: Geo. G. Fetter, 1904.

Lake, Griffing, and Stevenson. *An Illustrated Atlas of Mason County, Kentucky.* Philadelphia: Lake, Griffing, and Stevenson, 1876.

Langsam, Walter E. *Great Houses of the Queen City.* Cincinnati: Cincinnati Historical Society, 1997.

Lathrop, J. M. *An Atlas of Bracken and Pendleton Counties, Kentucky.* Philadelphia: D. J. Lake, 1884.

Lehmann, Terry W., and Earl W. Clark Jr. *The Green Line: The Cincinnati, Newport, and Covington Railway.* Chicago: Central Electric Railfans' Association, 2000.

Leonard, Lewis Alexander, ed. *Greater Cincinnati and Its People: A History.* 4 vols. New York: Lewis Historical, 1927.

Levin, H., ed. *The Lawyers and Lawmakers of Kentucky.* Chicago: Lewis, 1897.

Ludlow Centennial Celebration Inc. *Ludlow Centennial Souvenir Program, 1864–1964.* Newport, Ky.: Acorn-OTTOmatic, 1964.

Lutes, Ann. *A Brief History of Boone County.* Florence, Ky.: Boone Co. Historical Society, 1954.

Masterson, Mary. *Historic Carroll County.* Carrollton, Ky.: Carroll Co. Chamber of Commerce, 1970s.

Maysville Centennial Exposition Commission. *As We Look Back: Maysville, 1833–1933.* Maysville, Ky.: Daily Independent, 1933.

Merriman, Scott Allen. "Ordinary People in Extraordinary Times? Defendants, Attorneys, and the Federal Government's Policy under the Espionage Acts during World War I in the Sixth Circuit Court of Appeals District," PhD diss., Univ. of Kentucky, 2003.

Messick, Hank. *Syndicate Wife: The Story of Ann Drahmann Coppola.* New York: Macmillan, 1968.

Moore, T. Ross, ed. *Echoes from the Century, 1867–1967.* Mount Olivet, Ky.: Robertson Co. Historical Society, 2000.

Murrell, Jesse L. *One Hundred and Sixty Years: First Methodist Church.* Covington, Ky.: First Methodist Church, 1965.

Nagle, Eric C., and Larry L. Ford. *Monument Inscriptions of Robertson County, Kentucky.* Dayton, Ohio: Ford and Nagle, 1995.

Nelson, William H. *The Buried Treasure: A Rabbit Hash Mystery.* Lawrenceburg, Ind.: Sam Chapman, ca. 1890. Reprint, Rabbit Hash, Ky.: Rabbit Hash Historical Society, 1997.

Noe, J. T. Cotton, ed. *A Brief Anthology of Kentucky Poetry: Selections of Poetry Written by Ninety-Three Persons Closely Identified with Kentucky, Most of Them Native Born.* Lexington: Univ. of Kentucky Department of Extension, 1936.

Onkst, Wayne, ed. *From Buffalo Trails to the Twenty-First Century: A Centennial History of Erlanger, Kentucky.* Erlanger, Ky.: Erlanger Historical Society, 1996.

Ott, James. *Seekers of the Everlasting Kingdom: A Brief History of the Diocese of Covington.* Strasbourg, France: Editions du Signe, 2002.

Parker, Anna V. "A Short History of Carroll County," 1958, available at Carroll Co. Public Library, Carrollton, Ky.

Perrin, William Henry, J. H. Battle, and G. C. Kniffin. *Kentucky: A History of the State.* Louisville, Ky.: F. A. Battey, 1888.

Pictorial and Industrial Review of Northern Kentucky. Newport, Ky.: Northern Kentucky Review, 1923.

Potter, Eugenia K., ed. *Kentucky Women: Two Centuries of Indomitable Spirit and Vision.* Louisville, Ky.: Four Colour Imports, 1997.

Poweleit, Alvin C., and James A. Schroer, eds. *A Medical History of Campbell and Kenton Counties.* Cincinnati: Campbell-Kenton Medical Society, 1970.

Powell, Robert A. *Kentucky Governors.* Lexington, Ky.: Kentucky Images, 1989.

Purvis, Thomas L., ed. *Newport, Kentucky: A Bicentennial History.* Newport, Ky.: Otto Zimmerman, 1996.

Ramage, James A. "Panic in Cincinnati." *Blue and Gray* 3 (April–May 1986): 12–15.

Rankins, Walter H. *Augusta College, Augusta, Kentucky: First Established Methodist College, 1822–1849.* Frankfort, Ky.: Roberts, 1957.

Rawe, Richard L. *Creating a World-Class Airport: Cincinnati/Northern Kentucky International, 1947–1997.* Encino, Calf.: Cherbo, 1997.

Reis, Jim. *Pieces of the Past.* Vols. 1–3. Covington, Ky.: Kentucky Post, 1988, 1991, 1994.

Rennick, Robert M. *Kentucky Place Names.* Lexington: Univ. of Kentucky Press, 1984.

———. *The Post Offices of Northern Kentucky.* Lake Grove, Ore.: Depot, 2004.

Report of the Adjutant General of the State of Kentucky. 2 vols. Frankfort, Ky.: Kentucky Yeoman Office, 1866.

Report of the Adjutant General of the State of Kentucky. Confederate Kentucky Volunteers, War of 1861–1865. Frankfort, Ky.: State Journal, 1915.

Roth, George F., Jr. *The Story of Trinity Episcopal Church in Covington.* Covington, Ky.: Trinity Episcopal Church, 1991.

Ryan, Paul E. *History of the Diocese of Covington, Kentucky.* Covington, Ky.: Diocese of Covington, 1954.

Schmitz, Raymond A. *St. John's Catholic Church, Covington, Kentucky, 1854–2004.* Covington, Ky.: St. John Catholic Church, 2006.

Schrage, Robert. *Boone County.* Charleston, S.C.: Arcadia, 2005.

Sesqui-centennial Souvenir Program: 150th Anniversary, 1815–1965, City of Covington, Kentucky. Covington, Ky.: T.&W., 1965.

Smith, Allen Webb. *Beginning at "the Point": A Documented History of Northern Kentucky and Environs, the Town of Covington in Particular, 1751–1834.* Park Hills, Ky.: Self-published, 1977.

Southard, Mary Young, and Ernest C. Miller, eds. *Who's Who in Kentucky: A Biographical Assembly of Notable Kentuckians.* Louisville, Ky.: Standard, 1936.

The Spirit of a Greater Maysville and Mason County. Maysville, Ky.: Daily Independent, 1930.

Spoor, P. Andrew. "Devou Park." *Northern Kentucky Heritage* 13, no. 1 (Fall–Winter 2005): 24–39.

St. Mary, Franklin J., and James W. Brown, comps. *Covington Centennial: Official Book and Program.* Covington, Ky.: Semple and Schram, 1914.

Tapp, Hamilton. *Kentucky Lives.* Hopkinsville, Ky.: Historical Record Association, 1966.

Taylor, John. *Baptists on the American Frontier: A History of Ten Baptist Churches of Which the Author Has Been Alternately a Member.* Ed. Chester Raymond Young. 3rd ed. Macon, Ga.: Mercer Univ. Press, 1995.

Tenkotte, Paul A. "Adaptation to the Automobile and Imitation of the Suburb: Covington, Kentucky's 1932 Plan as a Test Case of City Planning." *Journal of Kentucky Studies* 1 (July 1984): 155–70.

———. "The 'Chronic Want' of Cincinnati: A Southern Railroad." *Northern Kentucky Heritage* 6, no. 1 (Fall–Winter 1998): 24–33.

———. "A Note on Regional Allegiances during the Civil War: Kenton County, Kentucky, as a Test Case." *Register of the Kentucky Historical Society* 79, no. 3 (Summer 1981): 211–18.

———. "Rival Cities to Suburbs: Covington and Newport, Kentucky, 1790–1890," PhD diss., Univ. of Cincinnati, 1989.

Tenkotte, Paul A., with Walter E. Langsam. *A Heritage of Art and Faith: Downtown Covington Churches.* Covington, Ky.: Kenton Co. Historical Society, 1986.

Tenkotte, Paul A., David E. Schroeder, and Thomas S. Ward. *To Be Catholic and American in Northern, Central, and Appalachian Kentucky: The Diocese of Covington, 1853–2003.* Forthcoming.

Townsend, John Wilson. *Kentucky in American Letters, 1784–1912.* Cedar Rapids, Iowa: Torch Press, 1913.

Turner, Charles W. *Chessie's Road.* Clifton Forge, Va.: Chesapeake and Ohio Historical Society, 1986.

Ulack, Richard, Karl B. Raitz, and Gyula Pauer, eds. *Atlas of Kentucky.* Lexington: Univ. Press of Kentucky, 1998.

U.S. Census Bureau. www.census.gov/.

Vertical files, Owen Co. Public Library, Owenton, Ky.

Villa Hills Millennium/Historical Committee. *The Villa Hills Area: A Great Place to Live.* Villa Hills, Ky.: Villa Hills Millennium/Historical Committee, 1999.

Waltmann, Henry G. *History of the Indiana-Kentucky Synod of the Lutheran Church in America.* Indianapolis, Ind.: Central, 1971.

Ward, William S. *A Literary History of Kentucky.* Knoxville: Univ. of Tennessee Press, 1988.

Warminski, Margo. *Historic Structures of Boone County.* Burlington, Ky.: Boone Co. Historic Preservation Board, 2002.

Warner, Jennifer S. *Boone County: From Mastodons to the Millennium.* Burlington, Ky.: Boone Co. Bicentennial Book Committee, 1998.

The War of the Rebellion: A Compilation of the Official Records of the Union and Confederate Armies. Washington, D.C.: Government Printing Office, 1880.

Way, Frederick, Jr., comp. *Way's Packet Directory, 1848–1983.* Athens: Ohio Univ. Press, 1983.

Webster, Robert D. *Northern Kentucky Fires: A Summary of the Most Memorable Fires of the Region.* Covington, Ky.: Kenton Co. Historical Society, 2006.

Wessling, Jack. *Early History of Campbell County, Kentucky.* Alexandria, Ky.: Privately published, 1997.

White, John H. *On the Right Track—Some Historic Cincinnati Railroads.* Cincinnati: Cincinnati Railroad Club, 2003.

Williams, Michael L. "Sin City Kentucky: Newport, Kentucky's Vice Heritage, and Its Legal Extinction, 1920–1991," master's thesis, University of Louisville, 2008.

Withey, Henry F., and Elsie Rathburn Withey. *Biographical Dictionary of American Architects (Deceased).* Los Angeles: Hennessey and Ingalls, 1970.

Works Projects Administration. *Slave Narratives: A Folk History of Slavery in the United States from Interviews with Former Slaves.* Vol. 7, *Kentucky Narratives.* Washington, D.C.: Federal Writer's Project of the WPA, 1941.

Illustration Credits

Introduction: *Kentucky Progress Magazine*, October 1929; *Gateway to the Southland* (Maysville, Ky., 1929). **Allen, Robert S.**: LBJ Library, Austin, Texas. **Anderson Ferry**: Kenton Co. Public Library, Covington. **Andrews (Andriola), Frank J. "Screw"**: Kenton Co. Public Library, Covington. **Auton, Jesse**: Robert Snow. **Averdick, James Andrew**: Michael R. Averdick. **Bailey, Clay Wade**: Kenton Co. Public Library, Covington. **Barleycorn's Five Mile House, Lakeside Park**: Ken Heil. **Bavarian Brewing Company**: Kenton Co. Public Library, Covington. **Berry, Albert S.**: Kenton Co. Public Library, Covington. **Beverly Hills Supper Club**: Raymond E. Hadorn. **Bigstaff, Samuel**: Kenton Co. Public Library, Covington. **Braun, Bob**: Kenton Co. Public Library, Covington. **Burman, Ben Lucien**: Kenton Co. Public Library, Covington. **Butler, William Orlando**: *Biographical Encyclopedia of Kentucky* (Cincinnati: J. M. Armstrong, 1878). **Candy and Ice Cream**: Christine Einhaus (photo of the shop); the Papas family (hand-dipping candy). **Carlisle, John G.**: Kenton Co. Public Library, Covington. **Cincinnati/Northern Kentucky International Airport**: Cincinnati/Northern Kentucky International Airport. **Civil War Fortifications**: *Harper's Weekly*, September 27, 1862. **Clooney, Betty**: Nick and Nina Clooney. **Clooney, George**: Nick and Nina Clooney. **Clooney, Nick**: Nick and Nina Clooney. **Coal Companies**: Mary Jo Hardcorn. **Congress of Racial Equality, Northern Kentucky Chapter**: Kenton Co. Public Library, Covington. **Coppin's Department Store**: Kenton Co. Public Library, Covington. **Covington, Downtown**: Kenton Co. Public Library, Covington. **Crawford, Ellis C.**: Kenton Co. Public Library, Covington. **Crestview Hills**: Bob and Martha Hoppenjans Edwards. **Dairies**: Larry Hanneken. **Davis, "Skeeter"**: *Kentucky Post*. **Dixie Highway**: Boone Co. Public Library. **Duveneck, Frank**: Kenton Co. Public Library, Covington. **Erlanger**: Kenton Co. Public Library, Covington. **Ewing, Carroll Merlin "Hop"**: Boone Co. Public Library. **Expressways**: Raymond E. Hadorn. **Fairs**: Kenton Co. Public Library, Covington. **Fire Departments**: Larry Hanneken. **First National Bank and Trust Company of Covington**: Kenton Co. Public Library, Covington. **Fisk, John Flavel**: Kenton Co. Public Library, Covington. **Five-and-Dime Stores**: Kenton Co. Public Library, Covington. **Flood of 1937**: Jan D. Stanley. **Florence**: Boone Co. Public Library. **Football**: Kenton Co. Public Library. **Fort Mitchell**: Roy Moser. **Fort Wright**: City of Fort Wright. **Furniture and Home Furnishings**: Kenton Co. Public Library, Covington. **Galvin, Maurice L.**: Roger Auge II. **Gillespie, Haven**: Kenton Co. Public Library, Covington. **Goldberg, Max H.**: Kenton Co. Public Library, Covington. **Grant, Jesse Root**: Kenton Co. Public Library, Covington. **Hargraves, William Frederick "Billy"**: Kenton Co. Public Library, Covington. **Harrison, Henry Thomas "Harry"**: Sharon Jobert. **Helm, Charles John, Sr.**: *Biographical Encyclopedia of Kentucky* (Cincinnati: J. M. Armstrong, 1878). **Icehouses**: Mary Jo Hardcorn. **Jones, Frederick McKinley**: Minnesota Historical Society. **Kentucky Central Railroad**: D. J. Kenny, *Illustrated Cincinnati* (Cincinnati: Geo. E. Stevens, 1875). **Kluemper, Theodore**: Carol Rekow. **Lagoon Amusement Park**: Kenton Co. Public Library, Covington. **Lloyd, John Uri**: Lloyd Library and Museum, Cincinnati. **Martin, William Henry, Jr.**: Kenton Co. Public Library, Covington. **McCarthy, Aileen**: Kenton Co. Public Library, Covington. **Meanwell, Jack L.**: Kenton Co. Public Library, Covington. **Meatpacking**: Charles Cist, *Sketches and Statistics of Cincinnati in 1851* (Cincinnati: Wm. H. Moore, 1851). **Merkel, Una**: Kenton Co. Public Library, Covington. **Merritt, John Ayers**: Tennessee State University. **Milburn, Frank S.**: Boone Co. Historic Preservation Review Board. **Mitchel, Ormsby MacKnight**: Charles Cist, *Sketches and Statistics of Cincinnati in 1851* (Cincinnati: Wm. H. Moore, 1851). **Nelson, George Eaton**: Roger Auge II. **Newport and Covington Suspension Bridge**: *Ballou's Pictorial*, December 20, 1856. **Newport Barracks**: *Ballou's Pictorial*, December 20, 1856. **Newport Independent Schools**: *Ballou's Pictorial*, December 20, 1856. **Newport Shopping Center**: American Diversified Development Inc. **Newport Steel**: Kenton Co. Public Library, Covington. **Northern Kentucky University**: Northern Kentucky University. **Nursing Homes and Retirement Housing**: Boone Co. Historic Preservation Review Board. **Ohio River Beaches** (photo with the *Island Queen*): Kelly Sutkamp. **Patrick, Irene**: Kenton Co. Public Library, Covington. **Petersburg Distillery**: Boone Co. Historic Preservation Review Board. **Pharmacy**: Kenton Co. Public Library, Covington. **Pontoon Bridges, Civil War**: *Harper's Weekly*, September 27, 1862. **Price, Jacob**: *Daily Commonwealth*, November 9, 1882. **Ratterman, George W.**: Raymond E. Hadorn. **Rieveschl, George, Jr.**: Lloyd Library and Museum, Cincinnati. **Roebling, John Augustus and Washington Augustus**: Kenton Co. Public Library, Covington. **Schmitt, Johann**: Sharon Cahill. **Shimfessel, Alice Thornton**: Kenton Co. Public Library, Covington. **Shine, Michael T.**: *Kentucky Post*, May 26, 1894 **Society of St. Vincent de Paul**: Andrew Lonneman family. **Southgate, William Wright**: Kenton Co. Public Library, Covington. **Speers Memorial Hospital**: Kenton Co. Public Library, Covington. **Spence, Brent**: Kenton Co. Public Library, Covington. **St. Francis de Sales Academy**: Kentucky Gateway Museum. **Staverman, Larry**: Thomas More College Archives. **Stewart Iron Works**: Sharon Jobert. **Tacoma Park**: Charles R. Tharp. **Taylor, James, Jr.**: Kenton Co. Public Library, Covington. **Timberlake House**: Kenton Co. Public Library, Covington. **Truck Farming**: Kenton Co. Public Library, Covington. **Venable, John Wesley**: Michael R. Averdick. **Villa Madonna Academy**: Pete Rightmore. **Vinson, Frederick M.**: Kenton Co. Public Library, Covington. **Visitors to Northern Kentucky**: Kenton Co. Public Library, Covington. **Washington**: Kentucky Gateway Museum Center. **Williams, Brian P.**: Ken and Kate Williams. **Williams, Caroline "Line"**: Kenton Co. Public Library, Covington. **World War II**: Pam Ciafardini Casebolt. **Wright, Horatio G.**: *Harper's Weekly*, June 11, 1864. **WZIP**: Kenton Co. Public Library, Covington. **YMCA**: Raymond E. Hadorn.

All illustrations not attributed to some other source are from the collections of the editors in chief.

INDEX

Note: Page numbers in boldface refer to main encyclopedia entries. Page numbers in italics refer to illustrations.

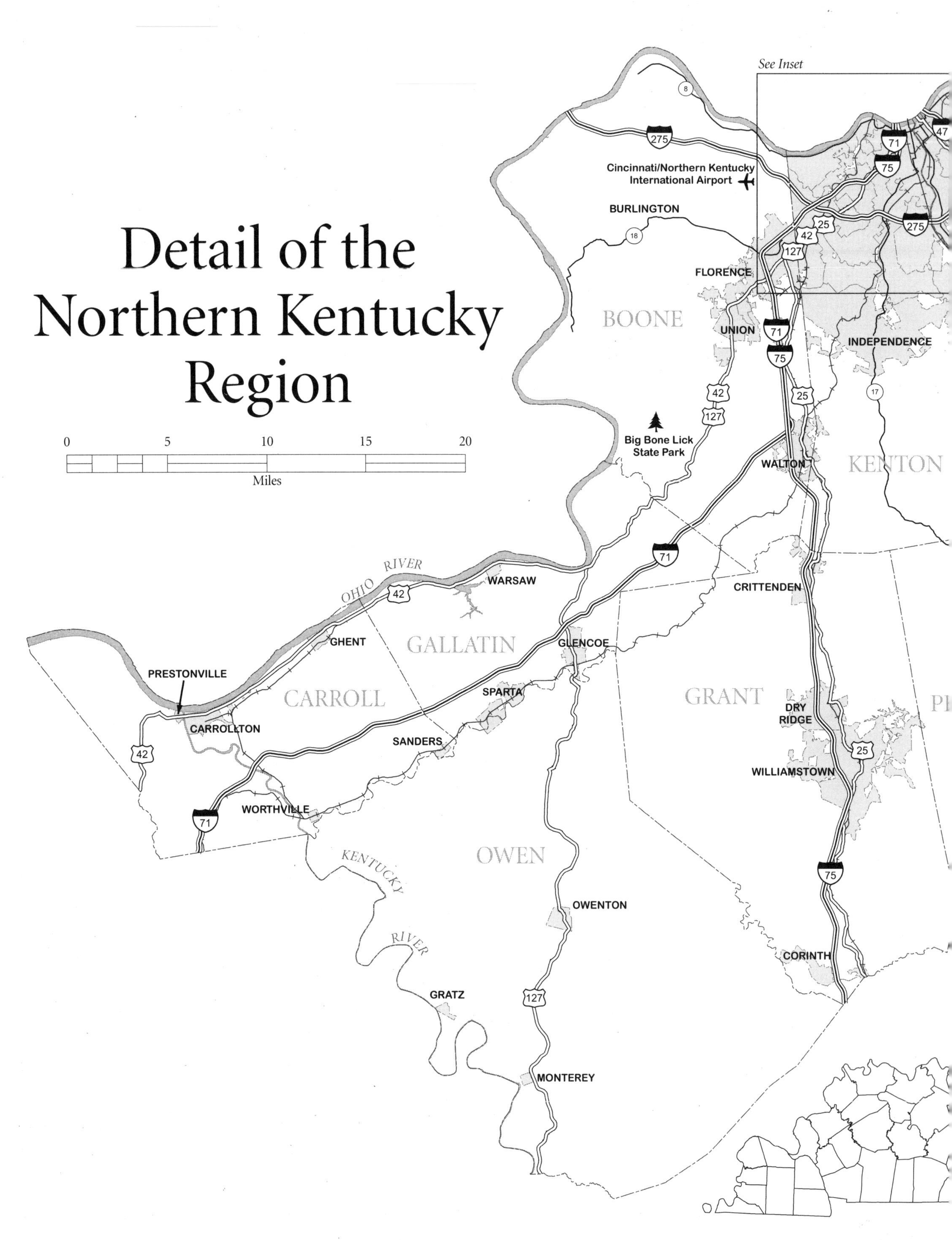
Detail of the Northern Kentucky Region
0
5
10
15
20
Miles
See Inset
Cincinnati/Northern Kentucky International Airport
BURLINGTON
FLORENCE
BOONE
UNION
INDEPENDENCE
Big Bone Lick State Park
WALTON
KENTON
OHIO RIVER
WARSAW
CRITTENDEN
GHENT
GALLATIN
GLENCOE
PRESTONVILLE
CARROLL
SPARTA
GRANT
DRY RIDGE
CARROLLTON
SANDERS
WILLIAMSTOWN
WORTHVILLE
KENTUCKY RIVER
OWEN
OWENTON
CORINTH
GRATZ
MONTEREY
8
275
71
75
47
18
25
42
127
17